Who Was Who in America ®

**Biographical Reference Works
Published by Marquis Who's Who**

Who's Who in America

Who Was Who in America

  Historical Volume (1607-1896)

  Volume I (1897-1942)

  Volume II (1943-1950)

  Volume III (1951-1960)

  Volume IV (1961-1968)

  Volume V (1969-1973)

Who's Who in the World

Who's Who in the East

Who's Who in the South and Southwest

Who's Who in the West

Who's Who in the Midwest

Who's Who of American Women

Who's Who in Finance and Industry

World Who's Who in Science

Who's Who in Government

Directory of Medical Specialists

Directory of Osteopathic Specialists

Who Was Who in America
with World Notables

Volume V
1969-1973
With Index to All Who Was Who Volumes

A Component of
Who's Who in American History

MARQUIS
Who'sWho

Marquis Who's Who, Inc.
200 East Ohio Street
Chicago, Illinois 60611 U.S.A.

Library of Congress Catalog Card Number 43-3789
ISBN 0-8379-0205-3

Printed and bound at St. Louis by The Von Hoffmann Press, Inc.

Table of Contents

This index lists all names which appear in the six Who Was Who volumes, keying each name to the volume in which the biographee is sketched.

Preface

The publication of Volume V of WHO WAS WHO IN AMERICA is an important step forward in the growth of a series of biographical reference books that seek to reflect both American history and the genealogical heritage of this country. *Who's Who in America,* the distinguished major component of the series, has advanced the highest standards of biographical compilation throughout its three-quarters of a century of continuous publication. Its more recent companion volumes, the four books comprising the Marquis Regional Library, emanate from and extend the scope and coverage of *Who's Who in America.* As a consequence, and for the first time, a WHO WAS WHO IN AMERICA volume will contain the names of deceased Marquis biographees whose careers had been of an essentially regional significance and whose listings were in publications other than *Who's Who in America.* Thus, the magnitude of American career achievement, particularly that of a regional nature, persuaded us to broaden the standards for inclusion in Volume V of WHO WAS WHO IN AMERICA.

In continuing improvements introduced with the immediate past volumes of WHO WAS WHO IN AMERICA, this new volume includes sketches of some Marquis biographees known to be 95 years of age or older. Lacking current information regarding these individuals, however, we make such inclusions in the hope that our apologies will be accepted should errors occur. Sketches of recently deceased world notables also are included, particularly of those international figures whose careers had a direct bearing on the course of recent American history.

Basically, however, the WAS books (to use the shortened form by which they are perhaps better known) inherited the unique characteristics that have made *Who's Who in America* both an internationally respected reference work and a household word here in the country of its origin.

Sketches, for example, have not only been prepared from information supplied by the biographees themselves, but have been approved personally—and frequently revised—before being printed in a Marquis publication during the subject's lifetime. As with all WAS volumes, many of these sketches have been scrutinized and revised by relatives or legal representatives of the deceased biographee. Except for the resulting changes and those ocasional variations interjected by the compilers, the WAS biographies are printed precisely as they last appeared during the subject's lifetime. As a result, many contain personal data unavailable elsewhere. The preface to the first volume of *Who's Who in America* selected this fact as one of that volume's outstanding characteristics, and stated: "The book is autobiographical, the data having been obtained from first hand." It follows that WHO WAS WHO IN AMERICA is autobiographical to a distinctive degree. In that respect, it is unique among American biographical directories. And although condensed to the concise style that Marquis Who's Who has made famous, the sketches contain all essential facts.

There results far more than a biographical directory of some 90,000 decreased American notables within the covers of these six volumes. WHO WAS WHO IN AMERICA is a vital portion of American history from the early days of the colonies to mid-1973. It is authentic history. It is the autobiography of America.

Table of Abbreviations

The following abbreviations are frequently used in this book:

*Following a sketch signifies that the published biography could not be verified.

††Non-current sketches of WHO'S WHO IN AMERICA biographees who were born 95 or more years ago (see Preface for explanation).

A.A., Associate in Arts.
A.A.A., Agricultural Adjustment Administration; Anti-Aircraft Artillery.
A.A.A.S., American Association for the Advancement of Science.
AAC, Army Air Corps.
a.a.g., asst. adjutant general.
AAF, Army Air Forces.
A. and M., Agricultural and Mechanical.
A.A.H.P.E.R., American Association for Health, Physical Education and Recreation.
A.A.O.N.M.S., Ancient Arabic Order of the Nobles of the Mystic Shrine.
A.A.S.R., Ancient Accepted Scottish Rite (Masonic).
A.B.C.F.M., American Board of Commissioners for Foreign Missions (Congregational).
A.B. (also B.A.), Bachelor of Arts.
A.,B.& C. R.R., Atlanta, Birmingham & Coast R.R.
ABC, American Broadcasting Company.
AC, Air Corps.
acad., academy; academic.
A.C.L. R.R., Atlantic Coast Line R.R.
A.C.P., American College of Physicians.
A.C.S., American College of Surgeons.
actg., acting.
a.d.c., aide-de-camp.
add., additional.
adj., adjutant; adjunct.
adj. gen., adjutant general.
adm., admiral.
adminstr., administrator.
adminstrn., administration.
adminstrv., administrative.
adv., advocate; advisory.
advt., advertising.
A.E., Agricultural Engineer.
AEC, Atomic Energy Commission.
A.E. and P., Ambassador Extraordinary and Plenipotentiary.
AEF, American Expeditionary Forces.
aero., aeronautics, aeronautical.
AFB, Air Force Base.
A.F.D., Doctor of Fine Arts.
A.F. and A.M., Ancient Free and Accepted Masons.
AFL (or A.F. of L.), American Federation of Labor.
A.F.T.R.A., American Federation TV and Radio Artists.
agr., agriculture.
agrl., agricultural.
agt., agent.
Agy., Agency.
a.i., ad interim.
A.I.A., American Institute of architects.
AID, Agency for International Development.
A.I.M., American Institute of Management.
AK—Alaska
AL—Alabama

Ala., Alabama
A.L.A., American Library Association.
Am., American, America.
A.M. (also M.A.), Master of Arts.
A.M.A., American Medical Association.
A.M.E., African Methodist Episcopal.
Am. Inst. E.E., American Institute of Electrical Engineers.
Am. Soc. C.E., American Society of Civil Engineers.
Am. Soc. M.E., American Society of Mechanical Emgineers.
A.N.A., Associate National Academician.
anat., anatomical.
ann., annual.
ANTA, American National theatre and Academy.
anthrop., anthropological.
antiq., antiquarian.
A.O.H., Ancient Order of Hibernians.
A.P., Associated Press.
appmnt., appointment.
apptd., appointed.
apt., apartment.
a.q.m., assistant quartermaster.
AR—Arkansas
A.R.C., American Red Cross.
archeol., archeological.
archtl., architectural.
Ark., Arkansas
Ariz.—Arizona.
Arts D., Doctor of Arts.
arty., artillery.
AS, Air Service.
A.S.C.A.P., American Society of Composers, Authors and Publishers.
ASF, Air Service Force.
assn., association.
asso., associate; associated.
asst., assistant.
astron., astronomical.
astrophys., astrophysical.
A.T.S.C., Air Technical Service Command.
A.,T.& S. F. Ry., Atchison, Topeka & Santa Fe Ry.
Atty., attorney.
AUS, Army of the United States.
Aux., Auxiliary.
Av., Avenue.
AZ—Arizona

b., born.
B., Bachelor.
B.A. (ALSO A.B.), Bachelor of Arts.
B.A.A.S., British Association for the Advancement of Science.
B.Agr., Bachelor of Agriculture.
Balt., Baltimore.
Bapt., Baptist.
B.Arch., Bachelor of Architecture.
B.& A.R.R., Boston & Albany R. R.
B.A.S. (or B.S.A.), Bachelor of Agricultural Science.
batn., batin., batt., battalion.
B.B.A., Bachelor of Business Administration.
BBC, British Broadcasting Company.
B.C., British Columbia.

B.C.E., Bachelor of Civil Engineering.
B.Chir., Bachelor of Surgery.
B.C.L., Bachelor of Civil Law.
B.C.S., Bachelor of Commercial Science.
bd., board.
B.D., Bachelor of Divinity.
B.DI., Bachelor of Didactics.
B.E. (or Ed.B.), Bachelor of Education.
B.E.E., Bachelor of Electrical Engineering.
BEF, British Expeditionary Force.
bet., between.
B.F.A., Bachelor of fine Arts.
bibl., bibilcal.
bibliog., bibliographical.
biog., biographical.
biol., biological.
B.J., Bachelor of Journalism.
Bklyn., Brooklyn.
B.L. (or Litt.B.), Bachelor of Letters.
Bldg., building.
blk., block.
B.L.S., Bachelor of Library Science.
Blvd., Boulevard.
B.& M. R.R., Boston & Marine R.R.
Bn. (or Batn.), Battalion.
B.O. (or O.B.), Bachelor of Oratory.
B.& O. R.R., Baltimore & Ohio R.R.
bot., botanical.
B.P., Bachelor of Painting.
B.P.E., Bachelor of Physical Education.
B.P.O.E., Benevolent and Protective Order of Elks.
B.Pd. (or Pd.B., or Py.B.), Bachelor of Pedagogy.
Br., branch.
B.R.E., Bachelor of Religious Education.
brig., brigadier, brigade.
brig. gen., brigadier general.
Brit., British; Britannica.
Bro., Brother.
B., R. & P. Ry., Buffalo, Rochester & Pittsburg Ry.
B.S. (also S.B. or ScB.), Bachelor of Science.
B.S. in Ry. M.E., Bachelor in Railway Mechanical Engineering.
B.S.A., Bachelor of Agricultural Science.
B.S.D., Bachelor of Didactic Science.
B.S.T., Bachelor of Sacred Theology.
B.Th., Bachelor of Theology.
bull., bulletin.
bur., bureau.
bus., business.
B.W.I., British West Indies.

CA—California
C.A., Central America.
CAA, Civil Aeronautics Adminstrn.
CAB, Civil Aeronautics Board.
CAC, Coast Artillery Corps.
Cal., California.
Can., Canada.
Cantab., of or pertaining to Cambridge University, Eng.
capt., captain.
C. & A. R.R., Chicago & Alton R.R., now Alton Ry. Co.
Cath., Catholic.

ABBREVIATIONS

cav., cavalry.

CBI, China - Burma - India theater of operations.

C.,B.& Q. R.R., Chicago, Burlington & Quincy R.R. Co.

CBS, Columbia Broadcasting System

CCC. Commodity Credit Corporation.

C.,C.,C.& St.L. Ry., Cleveland, Cincinnati. Chicago & St. Louis Ry.

C.E., Civil Engineer (degree), Corps of Engineers.

CEF, Canadian Expeditionary Forces.

C.& E.I. R.R., Chicago & Eastern Illinois R.R.

C.G.W. R.R., Chicago Great Western Railway.

ch., church.

Ch.D., Doctor of Chemistry.

chem., chemical.

Chem.E., Chemical Engineer.

Chgo., Chicago.

Chirurg., Chirurgical.

chmn., chairman.

chpt., chapter.

Cia, (Spanish), Company.

CIA, Central Intelligence Agency.

CIC, Counter Intelligence Corps.

C., I.&L. Ry., Chicago, indianapolis & Louisville Railway.

Cin., Cincinnati.

CIO, Congress of Industrial Organizations.

civ., civil.

Cleve., Cleveland.

climatol., climatological.

clin., clinical.

clk., clerk.

C.L.S.C., Chautauqua Literary and Scientific Circle.

C.L.U., Certified Life Underwriter.

C.M., Master in Surgery.

C. M., St.P.&P.R.R., Chicago, Milwaukee, St. Paul & Pacific R.R. Co.

C. N. Ry., Canadian Northern Ry.

C.& N.-W. Ry., Chicago & Northwestern Railway.

CO—Colorado

Co., Company;

C. of C.. Chamber of Commerce.

C.O.F., Catholic Order of Foresters.

C. of Ga. Ry., Central of Georgia Ry.

col., colonel.

coll., college

Colo., Colorado

com., committee.

comd., commanded.

comdg., commanding.

comdr., commander.

comdt., commandant.

commd., commissioned.

comml., commercial.

commn., commission.

commr., commissioner.

Com. Sub., Commissary of Subsistence.

condr., conductor.

conf., conference.

confed., confederate.

Congl., Congregational; Congressional.

Conglist., Congregationalist.

CONN—Connecticut.

cons., consulting, consultant.

consol., consolidated.

constl., constitutional.

constn., constitution.

constrn., construction.

contbd., contributed.

contbg., contributing.

contbn., contribution.

contbr., contributor.

conv., convention.

coop. (or co-op.), cooperative.

corp., corporation.

corr., correspondent; corresponding, correspondence.

C & O. Ry., Chesapeake & Ohio Ry. Co.

C.P.A., Certified Public Accountant.

C.P.C.U., Chartered Property and Casualty Underwriter.

C.P.H., Certificate of Public Health.

cpl. (or corpl.), corporal.

C.P. Ry., Canadian Pacific Ry. Co.

C. R.I.& P. Ry., Chicago, Rock Island & Pacific Ry. Co.

C.R.R. of N.J., Central Railroad Co. of New Jersey.

C.S., Christian Science.

C.S. Army, Confederate State Army.

C.S.B., Bachelor of Christian Science.

C.S.D., Doctor of Christian Science.

C.S.N., Confederate States Navy.

C.& S. Ry. Co., Colorado & Southern Ry. Co.

C.,St.P.,M.&O. Ry., Chicago, St. Paul, Minneapolis & Omaha Ry. Co.

Ct., Court.

C.T., Candidate in Theology.

CT—Connecticut.

c.Vt. Ry., Central Vermont Ry.

C.& W.I. R.R., Chicago & Western Indiana R.R. Co.

CWS, Chemical Warfare Service.

cycle., cyclopedia.

C.Z., Canal Zone.

d. (also dau.), daughter.

D., Doctor.

D. Agr., Doctor of Agriculture.

D.A.R., Daughters of the American Revolution.

D.A.V., Disabled American Veterans.

D.C., District of Columbia.-D.C.

D.C.L., Doctor of Civil Law.

D.C.S., Doctor of Commercial Science

D.D., Doctor of Divinity.

D.D.S., Doctor of Dental Surgery.

DE—Delaware.

dec., deceased.

Def., Defense.

deg., degree.

Del., Delaware.

del., delegate.

Dem., Democratic.

D.Eng. (also Dr. Engring., or e.d. Doctor of Engineering.

denom., denominational.

dep., deputy.

dept., department.

dermatol., determatological.

desc., descendant.

devel., development.

D.F.C., Distinguished Flying Cross.

D.H.L., Doctor of Hebrew Literature.

D.& H. R.R., Delaware & Hudson R.R. Co.

dir., director.

disch., discharged.

dist., district.

distbg., distributing.

distbn., distribution.

distbr., distributor.

div., division; divinity; divorce proceedings.

D.Litt., Doctor of Literature.

D.,L.& W.R.R., Delaware Lackawanna & Western R.R. co.

D.M.D., Doctor of Medical Dentistry.

D.M.S., Doctor of Medical Science.

D.O., Doctor of Osteopathy.

DPA. Defense Production Administration.

D.P.H. (also Dr.P.H.), Diploma in Public Health or Doctor of Public Health or Doctor of Public Hygiene.

Dr., Doctor, Drive.

D.R., Daughters of the Revolution.

D.R.E., Doctor of Religious Education.

D.& R.G.W. R.R. Co., Denver & Rio Grande Western R.R. co.

D.Sc. (or Sc. D.). Doctor of Science.

D.S.C., Distinguished Service Cross.

D.S.M., Distinguished Service Medal.

D.S.T., Doctor of Sacred Theology.

D.T.M., Doctor of Tropical Medicine.

D.V.M., Doctor of Veterinary Medicine.

D.V.S., Doctor of Veterinary Surgery.

E., East.

E. AND P., Extraordinary and Plenipotentiary.

ECA, Economic Cooperation Administration.

eccles., ecclesiastical.

ecol., ecological.

econ., economic.

ECOSOC, Economic and Social Council of UN.

ed., educated.

E.D. (also D.Eng., or Dr.Engring.), Doctor of Engineering.

Ed.B., Bachelor of Education.

Ed.D., Doctor of Education.

edit., edition.

Ed.M. (or M.Ed.), Master of Education.

edn., education.

ednl., educational.

E.E., Electrical Engineer.

E.E. and M. P., Envoy Extraordinary and Minister Plenipotentiary.

Egyptol., Egyptological.

elec., electrical.

electrochem., electrochemical.

electrophys., electrophysical.

E. M., Engineer of Mines.

ency., encyclopedia.

Eng., England.

engr., engineer.

engring., engineering.

entomol., entomological.

e.s., eldest son.

E.S.M.W.T.P., Engring. Science and Management War Training Program.

ethnol., ethnological.

ETO, European Theater of Operations.

Evang., Evangelical.

ABBREVIATIONS

exam., examination; examining.
exc., executive.
exhbn., exhibition.
expdn., expedition.
expn., exposition.
expt., experiment.
exptl., experimental.

F., Fellow.
F.A., Field Artillery.
FAA, Federal Aviation Agency.
F.A.C.P., Fellow American College of Physicians.
F.A.C.S., Fellow American College of Surgeons.
FAO, Food and Agriculture Organization.
FBI, Federal Bureau of Investigation.
FCA, Farm Credit Administration.
FCC, Federal Communications Commission.
FCDA, Federal Civil Defense Administration.
FDA, Food and Drug Administration.
FDIA, Federal Deposit Insurance Administration.
F.E., Forest Engineer.
Fed., Federal.
Fedn., Federation.
Fgn., Foreign.
FHA, Federal Housing Administration.
FL—Florida.
Fla., Florida.
FOA, Foreign Operations Administration.
Found., Foundation.
frat., fraternity.
F.R.C.P., Fellow Royal College of Physicians (England).
F.R.C.S., Fellow Royal College of Surgeons (England).
frt., Freight.
FSA, Federal Security Agency.
Ft., Fort.
FTC, Federal Trade Commission.

G.-1 (or other number), Division of General Staff.
gastroent., gastroenterological.
GA—Georgia.
Ga., Georgia.
G.A.R., Grand Army of the Republic.
GATT, General Agreement on Tariffs and Trade.
G.,C.& S.F. Ry., Gulf, Colorado & Santa Fe Ry. Co.
G.D., Graduate in Divinity.
g.d., granddaughter.
gen., general.
geneal., genealogical.
geod., geodetic.
geog., geographical; geographic.
geol., geological.
geophys., geophysical.
g.g.d., great granddaughter.
g.g.s., great grandson.
G.H.Q., General Headquarters.
G.,M.& N. R.R., Gulf, Mobile & Northern R.R. Co.
G., M.& O. R.R., Gulf, Mobile & Ohio R.R. Co.
G.N. Ry., Great Northern Ry. Co.
gov., governor.

govt., government.
govtl., governmental.
grad., graduated; graduate.
g.s., grandson.
Gt., Great.
G.T. Ry., Grand Trunk Ry. System.
GU—Guam.
G.W. Ry. of Can., Great Western Ry. of Canada.
gynecol., gynecological.

Hdqrs., Headquarters.
H.G., Home Guard.
H.H.D., Doctor of Humanities.
HHFA, Housing and Home Finance Agency.
H.I., Hawaiian Islands.
HI—Hawaii.
hist., historical.
H.M., Master of Humanics.
HOLC, Home Owners Loan Corporation.
homeo., homeopathic.
hon., honorary; honorable.
Ho. of Reps., House of Representatives.
hort., horticultural.
hosp., hospital.
Hts., Heights.
H.Ty. (or **H.T.**), Hawaiian Territory.
Hwy., Highway.
Hydrog., hydrographic.

IA— Iowa.
Ia., Iowa.
IAEA, International Atomic Energy Agency.
IBM, International Business Machines Corporation.
ICA, International Cooperation Administration.
ICC, Interstate Commerce Commission.
I.C.R.R., Illinois Central R.R. System.
ID—Idaho.
Ida., Idaho.
I.E.E.E., Institute of Electrical and Electronics Engineers.
IFC, International Finance Corp.
I.G.N. R.R., International - Great Northern R.R.
IGY, International Geophysical Year.
IL—Illinois.
Ill., Illinois.
ILO, International Labor Organization.
Illus., Illustrated.
IMF, International Monetary Fund.
IN— Indiana.
Inc., Incorporated.
Ind., Indiana, Independent.
Indpls., Indianapolis.
Indsl., Industrial.
inf., infantry.
ins., insurance.
insp., inspector.
inst., institute.
instl., institutional.
instn., institution.
instr., instructor.
instrn., instruction.
internat., international.
intro., introduction.
I.O.B.B., Independent Order of B'nai B'rith.

I.O.G.T., Independent Order of Good Templars.
I.O.O.F., Independent Order of Odd Fellows.
I.R.E., Institute of Radio Engineers.

J.B., Jurum Baccalaureus.
J.C.B., Juris Canonici Bachelor.
J.C.L., Juris Canonici Lector.
J.D., Doctor of Jurisprudence.
j.g., junior grade.
jour., journal.
jr., junior.
J.S.D., Doctor of Juristic Science.
Jud., Judicial.
J.U.D., Juris Utriusque Doctor: Doctor of Both (Canon and Civil) Laws.

Kan.—Kansas.
K.C., Knight of Columbus.
K.C.C.H., Knight Commander of Court of Honor.
K.P., Knight of Pythias.
K.N.S. Ry., Kansas City Southern Ry.
KS—Kansas.
KY—Kentucky.
Ky., Kentucky.

lab., laboratory.
lang., language.
laryngol., laryngological.
lectr., lecturer.
L.H.D., Doctor of Letters of Humanity.
L.I., Long Island.
lieut., lieutenant.
L.I. R.R., Long Island R.R. Co.
lit., literary; literature.
Lit. Hum., Literae Humanores (classics Oxford U., Eng.).
Litt.B. (or **B.L.**). Bachelor of Letters.
Litt.D., Doctor of Letters.
LL.B., Bachelor of Laws.
LL.D., Doctor of Laws.
LL.M. (or **ML.**). Master of Laws.
L& N. R.R., Louisville & Nashville R.R.
L.O.M., Loyal Order of Moose.
L.R.C.P., Licentiate Royal Coll. Physicians.
L.R.C.S., Licentiate Royal Coll. Surgeons.
L.S., Library Science.
L.S.A., Licentiate Society of Apothecaries.
L.S.& M. S. Ry., Lake Shore & Michigan Southern Ry.
lt. or **(lieut.)**, lieutenant.
Ltd., Limited.
Luth., Lutheran.
L.V. R.R., Lehigh Valley R.R. co.

m., marriage ceremony.
M.A. (OR **A.M.**), Master of Arts.
mag., magazine.
M.Agr., Master of Agriculture.
maj., major.
Man., Manitoba.
M.Arch., Master in Architecture.
Mass., Massachusetts.
Math., mathematical.
M.B., Bachelor of Medicine.
M.B.A., Master of Business Administration.

ABBREVIATIONS

MBS, Mutual Broadcasting System.
M.C., Medical Corps.
M.C.S., Master of Commercial Science.
mcht., merchant.
M.C. R.R., Michigan Central R.R.
Md., Maryland
MD—Maryland
M.D., Doctor of Medicine.
M.Di., Master of Didactics.
M.Dip., Master in Diplomacy.
mdse., merchandise.
M.D.V., Doctor of Veterinary Medicine.
Me., Maine.
ME—Maine.
M.E., Mechanical Engineer.
mech., mechanical.
M.E. Ch., Methodist Episcopal Church.
M.Ed., Master 'of Education.
med., medical.
Med. O.R.C., Medical Officers' Reserve Corps.
Med. R.C., Medical Reserve Corps.
M.E.E., Master of Electrical Engineering.
mem., member.
Meml. (or **Mem.**), Memorial.
merc., mercantile.
met., metropolitan.
metall., metallurgical.
Met.E., Metallurgical Engineer.
meteorol., meteorological.
Meth., Methodist.
metrol., metrological.
M.F., Master of Forestry.
M.F.A., Master of Fine Arts.
mfg., manufacturing.
mfr., manufacturer.
mgmt., management.
mgr., manager.
M.H.A., Master of Hospital Administration.
M.I., Military Intelligence.
MI—Michigan.
Mich., Michigan.
micros., microscopical.
mil., military.
Milw., Milwaukee.
Mineral., mineralogical.
Minn., Minnesota.
Miss., Mississippi.
M.-K.-I. R.R., Missouri - Kansas-Texas R.R. Co.
M.L. (or **LL. M.**), Master of Laws.
M.Litt., Master of Literature.
Mlle., Mademoiselle (Miss).
M.L.S., Master of Library Science.
Mme., Madame.
M.M.E., Master of Mechanical Engineering.
MN—Minnesota.
mng., managing.
Moblzn., Mobilization.
Mont., Montana.
M.P., Member of Parliament.
Mpls., Minneapolis.
M.P. R.R., Missouri Pacific R.R.
M.Pd., Master of Pedagogy.
M.P.E., Master of Physical Education.
M.P.L., Master of Patent Law.
M.R.C.P., Member Royal College of Physicians.
M.R.C.S., Member Royal College of Surgeons.

M.R.E., Master of Religious Education.
MS—Mississippi.
M.S. (or **M.Sc.**). Master of Science.
M.S.F., Master of Science of Forestry.
M.S.T., Master of Sacred Theology.
M.& St. L. R.R., Minneapolis & St. Louis R.R. Co.
M.,St.P.& S.S.M. Ry., Minneapolis, St. Paul & Sault Ste. Marie Ry.
M.S.W., Master of Social Work.
MT—Montana.
Mt., Mount.
mtn., mountain.
M.T.O.U.S.A., Mediterranean Theater of Operations, U.S. Army.
mus., museum; musical.
Mus.B., Bachelor of Music.
Mus.D. (or **Mus. Doc.**), Doctor of Music.
Mus. M., Master of Music.
Mut., Mutual.
M.V.M., Massachusetts Volunteer Militia.
M.W.A., Modern Woodmen of America.
mycol., mycological.

N., North.
N.A., National Academician; North America; National Army.
N.A.A.C.P., National·Association for the Advancement of Colored People.
NACA, National Advisory Committee for Aeronautics.
N.A.D., National Academy of Design.
N.A.M., National Association of Manufacturers.
NASA, National Aeronautics and Space Administration.
nat., national.
NATO, North Atlantic Treaty Organization.
N.A.T.O.U.S.A., North African Theater of Operations, U.S. Army.
nav., navigation.
NB—Nebraska.
N.B., New Brunswick.
NBC, National Broadcasting Co.
NC—North Carolina.
N.,C.& St.L. Ry., Nashville, Chattanooga & St. Louis Ry.
NDCR, National Defense Research Committee.
N.E., Northeast; New England.
N.E.A., National Education Association.
Neb., Nebraska.
neurol., neurological.
Nev., Nevada.
New Eng., New England.
N.G., National Guard.
N.G.S.N.Y., National Guard State of New York.
N.H., New Hanpshire.
NH—New Hampshire.
NIH, National Institutes of Health.
N.J., New Jersey
NJ—New Jersey
NLRB, National Labor Relations Board.
N.Ph.D., Doctor Natural Philosophy.
N.P. Ry., Northern Pacific Ry.
No., Northern.
NPA, National Production Authority.

nr., near.
NRA, National Recovery Administration.
NRC, National Research Council.
N.S., Nova Scotia.
NSC, National Security Council.
NSF, National Science Foundation.
NSRB, National Security Resources Board.
N.T., New Testament.
numis., numismatic.
N.W., Northwest
N.& W. Ry., Norfolk & Western Ry.
NV—Nevada.
N.Y., New York.
NY—New York.
N.Y.C., New York City.
N.Y. Central R.R. (or **N.Y.C. R.R.**), New York Central Railroad Company.
N.Y.,C.& St.L. R.R., New York, Chicago & St. Louis R.R. Co.
N.Y., N.H.& H. R.R., New York, New Haven & Hartford R.R. Co.
N.Y.,O.& W. Ry., New York, Ontario & Western Ry.

O—Ohio.
OAS, Organization of American States.
O.B., Bachelor of Oratory.
obs., observatory.
obstet., obstetrical.
OCDM, Office of Civil and Defense Mobilization.
ODM, Office of Defense Mobilization.
OECD, organization European Cooperation and Development.
OEEC, Organization European Economic Cooperation.
O.E.S., Order of the Eastern Star.
ofcl., Official.
OH—Ohio.
OK—Oklahoma.
Okla., Oklahoma.
Ont., Ontario.
OPA, Office of Price Administration.
opthal., ophthalmological.
OPM, Office of Production management.
OPS, Office of Price Stabilization.
O.Q.M.G., Office of Quartermaster General.
O.R.C., Officers' Reserve Corps.
orch., orchestra.
OR—Oregon.
Ore., Oregon.
orgn., organization.
ornithol., ornithological.
O.S.B., Order of Saint Benedict.
O.S.L. R.R., Oregon Short Line R.R.
OSRD, Office of Scientific Research and Development.
OSS, Office of Strategic Services.
osteo, osteopathic.
O.T., Old Testament.
O.T.C., Officers' Training Camp.
otol., otological.
O.T.S., Officers' Training School.
O.U.A.M., Order United American Mechanics.
OWI, Office of War Information.
O.-W.R.R.& N. Co., Oregon-Washington R.R. & Navigation Co.
Oxon., Of or pertaining to Oxford University, Eng.

ABBREVIATIONS

PA—Pennsylvania
Pa., Pennsylvania
Pa. R.R., Pennsylvania R.R.
paleontol., paleontological.
pass., passenger.
path., pathological.
Pd.B. (or B.Pd., or Py.B.), Bachelor of Pedagogy.
Pd.D., Doctor of Pedagogy.
Pd.M., master of Pedagogy.
P.E., Protestant Episcopal.
Pe.B., Bachelor of Pediatrics.
P.E.I., Prince Edward Island.
P.E.M., Poets, Playwrights, Editors, Essayists and Novelists (Internat. Assn.).
penol., penological.
pfc., private first class.
PHA, Public Housing Administration.
pharm., pharmaceutical.
Pharm.D., Doctor of Pharmacy.
Pharm.M., Master of Pharmacy.
Ph.B., Bachelor of Philosophy.
Ph.C., Pharmaceutical Chemist.
Ph.D., Doctor of Philosophy.
Ph.G., Graduate in Pharmacy.
Phila., Philadelphia.
philol., philological.
philes., philosophical.
photog., photographic.
phys., physical.
Phys. and Surg., Physicians and Surgeons (college at Columbia University).
Physiol., physiological.
P.I., Philippine Islands.
Pitts., Pittsburg.
Pkwy., Parkway.
Pl., Place.
P.& L.E. R.R., Pittsburgh & Lake Erie R.R.
P.M., Paymaster.
P.M. R.R., Pere Marquette R.R. Co.
polit., political.
poly., polytechnic.
pomol., pomological.
P.Q., Province of Quebec.
P.R., Puerto Rico.
prep., preparatory.
pres., president.
Presbyn., Presbyterian.
presdl., presidential.
prin., principal.
Proc., Proceedings.
prod., produced (play production).
prodn., production.
prof., professor.
profl. professional.
Prog., Progressive.
propr., proprietor.
pros. atty., prosecuting attorney.
pro tem, pro tempore (for the time being).
psychiat., psychiatrical; psychiatric,
psychol., psychological.
P.T.A., parent-Teacher Association.
PTO, Pacific Theatre of Operations.
pub., public; publisher; publishing; pub-lished.
publ., publication.
pvt., private.
PWA, Public Works Administration.
Py. B., Bachelor of Pedagogy.

q.m., quartermaster.
Q.M.C., Quartermaster Corps.
q.m. gen., quartermaster general.
Q.M.O.R.C., Quartermaster Officers' Reserve Corps.
quar., quarterly.
Que., Quebec (province).
q.v., quod vide (which see).

radiol., radiological.
R.A.F., Royal Air Force.
R.A.M., Royal Arch Mason.
R.C., Roman Catholic; Reserve Corps.
RCA, Radio Corporation of America.
RCAF, Royal Canadian Air Force.
R.C.S., Revenue Cutter Service.
Rd., Road.
R.D., Rural Delivery.
R.E., Reformed Episcopal.
rec., recording.
Ref., Reformed.
Regt., Regiment.
regtl., regimental.
rehab., rehabilitation.
Rep., Republican.
rep., representative.
Res., Reserve.
ret., retired.
Rev., Reverend, Review.
rev., revised.
RFC, Reconstruction Finance Corporation.
R.F.D., Rural Free Delivery.
rhinol., rhinological.
RI—Rhode Island
R.I., Rhode Island
R.N., Registered Nurse.
rontgenal., rontgenological.
R.O.S.C., Reserve Officers' Sanitary Corps.
R.O.T.C., Reserve Officers' Training Corps.
R.P., Reformed Presbyterian.
R.P.D., Rerum Politicarum Doctor (Doctor Political Science).
R.R., Railroad.
R.T.C., Reserve Training Corps.
Ry., Railway.

s., son.
S., South.
S.A., South Americe.
S.A. (Spanish) Sociedad Anonima, (French) Société Anonyme.
SAC, Strategic Air Command.
S.A.L. Ry., Seaboard Air Line Ry.
san., sanitary.
S.A.R., Sons of the Am. Revolution.
Sask., Saskatchewan.
S.A.T.C., Students' Army Training Corps.
Sat.Eve.Post, Saturday Evening Post.
Savs., Savings.
S.B. (also B.S. or Sc.B.), Bachelor of Science.
SC—South Carolina
S.C., South Carolina; San. Corps.
SCAP, Supreme Command Allies Pacific.
Sc.D. (or D.Sc.), Doctor of Science.
S.C.D., Doctor of Commercial Science.
sch., school.
sci., science; scientific.
S.C.V., Sons of Confederate Veterans.
SD— South Dakota.

S.D., South Dakota.
S.E., Southeast.
SEATO, Southeast Asia Treaty Organization.
SEC, Securities and Exchange Commission.
sec., secretary.
sect., section.
seismol., seismological.
Sem., Seminary.
sgt. (or sergt.), sergeant.
SHAEF, Supreme Headquarters, Allied Expeditionary Forces.
SHAPE, Supreme Headquarters Allied Powers in Europe.
S.I., Staten Island.
S.J., Society of Jesus (Jesuit).
S.J.D., Doctor Juristic Science.
S.M., Master of Science.
So., Southern.
soc., society.
social., sociological.
sos, Services of Supply.
S. of V., Sons of Veterans.
S.P. Co., Southern Pacific Co.
spl., special.
splty., specialty.
Sq., Square.
S.R.C., Signal Reserve Corps.
sr., senior.
S.R., Sons of the Revolution.
S.S., Steamship.
SSS, Selective Service System.
St., Saint; Street.
Sta., station.
statis., statistical.
Stblzn., Stabilization.
S.T.B., Bachelor of Sacred Theology.
S.T.D., Doctor of Sacred Theology.
S.T.L., Licentiate in Sacred Theology; Lector of Sacred Theology.
St.L.-S.F. R.R., St. Louis - San Francisco Ry. Co.
supr., supervisor.
supt., superintendent.
surg., surgical.
S.W., Southwest.

T.A.P.P.I., Technical Association Pulp and Paper Industry.
T. and S., Trust and Savings.
Tb (or TB), tuberculosis.
Tchrs., Teachers.
tech., technical; technology.
technol., technological.
Tel.&Tel., Telephone and Telegraph.
temp., temporary.
Tenn., Tennessee.
Tex., Texas.
T.H. (or H.T.), Territory of Hawaii.
Th.D., Doctor of Theology.
ThM., Master of Theology.
theol., theological.
TN—Tennessee.
Tng., Training.
topog., topographical.
T.P.A., Travelers Protective Assn.
T.&P. Ry., Texas & Pacific Ry. Co.
trans., transactions; transferred.
Transl., translation; translations.
transp., transportation.

xi

ABBREVIATIONS

treas., treasurer.
TV, television.
TX—Texas.
TVA, Tennessee Valley Authority.
Twp., Township.
Ty. (or Ter.), Territory.
Typog., typographical.

U. (or Univ.), University.
UAR, United Arab Republic.
UAW, United Automobile Workers.
U.B., United Brethren in Christ.
U.C.V., United Confederate Veterans.
U.D.C., United Daughters of the Confederacy.
U.K., United Kingdom.
UN, United Nations.
UNESCO, United Nations Educational Scientific and Cultural Organization.
UNICEF, United Nations International Childrens Emergency Fund.
UNRRA, United Nations Relief and Rehabilitation Administration.
U.P., United Presbyterian.
U.P. R.R., Union Pacific R.R.
urol., urological.
U.S., United States.
U.S.A., United States of America.
USAAF, United States Army Air Force.
USAC, United States Air Corps.
USAF, United States Air Force.
USCG, United States Coast Guard.
U.S.C.T., U.S. Colored Troops.
USES, United States Employment Service.

USIA, United States Information Agency.
USIS, United States Information Service.
USMC, United States Marine Corps.
USMHS, United States Marine Hospital Service.
USN, United States Navy.
USNA, United States National Army.
U.S.N.G., United States National Guard.
U.S.O., United Service Organizations.
USNG, United States National Guard.
USNRF, United States Naval Reserve Force.
USPHS, United States Public Health Service.
U.S.R., U.S. Reserve.
U.S.R.C.S., U.S. Revenue Cutter Service.
U.S.S., United States Ship.
USSR, Union of Soviet Socialist Republics.
U.S.V., United States Volunteers.
UT—Utah.

v., vice.
VA—Virginia.
Va., Virginia.
VA, Veterans Administration.
vet., veteran; veterinary.
V.F.W., Veterans of Foreign Wars.
V.I., Virgin Islands.
VI—Virgin Islands.
vice pres. (or v.p.,), vice president.
vis., visiting.
vol., volunteer; volume.
vs., versus (against).
VT—Vermont.
Vt., Vermont.

W., West.
WA—Washington (state).
WAC, Women's Army Corps.
Wash., Washington (state).
WAVES, Womens Reserve. U.S. Naval Reserve.
W.C.T.U., Women's Christian Temperance Union.
WHO, World Health Organization.
W.I., West Indies.
WI—Wisconsin.
Wis., Wisconsin.
W.& L.E. Ry., Wheeling & Lake Erie Ry. Co.
WPA, Works Progress Administration.
WPB, War Production Board.
W.P. R.R. Co., Western Pacific R.R. Co.
WSB, Wage Stabilization Board.
WV—West Virginia.
W. Va., West Virginia.

YMCA, Young Men's Christian Association.
YMHA, Young Men's Hebrew Association.
YM and YWHA, Young Men's and Young Women's Hebrew Association.
Y.& M.V. R.R., Yazoo & Mississippi Valley R.R.
yrs., years.
YWCA, Young Women's Christian Association.

zoöl., zoölogical.

ALPHABETICAL PRACTICES

Names are arranged alphabetically according to the surnames, and under identical surnames according to the first given name. If both surname and first given name are identical, names are arranged alphabetically according to the second given name. Where full names are identical, they are arranged in order of age—those of the elder being put first.

Surnames, beginning with De, Des, Du, etc., however capitalized or spaced, are recorded with the prefix preceding the surname and arranged alphabetically under the letter D.

Surnames beginning with Mac are arranged alphabetically under M. This likewise holds for names beginning with Mc; that is, all names beginning Mc will be found in alphabetical order after those beginning Mac.

Surnames beginning with Saint or St. all appear after names that would begin Sains, and such surnames are arranged according to the second part of the name, e.g., St. Clair would come before Saint Dennis.

Surnames beginning with prefix Van are arranged alphabetically under letter V.

Surnames containing the prefix Von or von are usually arranged alphabetically under letter V; any exceptions are noted by cross references (Von Kleinsmid, Rufus Bernhard; see Kleinsmid, Rufus Bernard von).

Compound hypenated surnames are arranged according to the first member of the compound.

Compound unhyphenated surnames common in Spanish are not rearranged but are treated as hyphenated names.

Since Chinese names have the family name first, they are so arranged, but without comma between family name and given name (as Lin Yutang).

Parentheses used in connection with a name indicate which part of the full name is usually deleted in common usage. Hence Abbott, W(illiam) Lewis indicates that the usual form of the given name is W. Lewis. In alphabetizing this type, the parentheses are not considered. However if the name is recorded Abbott, (William) Lewis, signifying that the entire name William is not commonly used, the alphabetizing would be arranged as though the name were Abbott, Lewis.

Who Was Who in America

AARON, CHARLES DETTIE, physician; b. Lockport, N.Y., May 8, 1866; s. Abraham Higham and Hanna (Barnett) A.; M.D., U. of Buffalo, N.Y., 1891; Sc.D., Heidelberg U., 1910; m. Winifred Comstock, June 23, 1902; 1 dau., Josephine Comstock. Began practice of medicine at Detroit, 1891; city physician, 1893-95; became prof. gastroenterology and dietetics, Wayne U. Coll. of Medicine, 1905, now emeritus; cons. gastroenterologist to Harper, Receiving, Tuberculosis, Shurly and Alexander Blaine hosps. Fellow West London Medico-Chirurg. Soc. (Eng.), Am. Coll. Physicians, Am. Therapeutic Soc.; mem. A.M.A., Mich. State Med. Soc., Wayne County Med. Soc., Detroit Acad. Medicine (ex-pres.), Am. Gastroenterol. Assn. (founder and sec. 14 yrs.), Northern Tri-State Med. Soc. (ex-pres.), Mich. Authors' Assn., Mich. Acad. Science, Arts and Letters, Am. Med. Editors' and Authors' Assn., Assn. for the Study of Internal Secretions, Am. Congress Internal Medicine; hon. mem. Jackson Co. Med. Soc., Kalamazoo Acad. Medicine, Eugene Field Soc.; mem. Phi Rho Sigma, Alpha Omega Alpha. Republican. Mason. Author: Diseases of the Stomach, 1911; Diseases of the Digestive Organs, 1915, 4th edit., 1927; also chapter on Dietetic Treatment of Disease (Oxford Index of Therapeutics), 1921, and many scientific papers in various foreign and American jours. Translator (from the German): Examination of the Feces by Means of the Test-Died, 1906, 2d edit., 1909. Home: 748 Seminole Av. Office: 76 Adams Av., W., Detroit MI‡

ABBOTT, FREELAND KNIGHT, educator, historian; b. Hartford, Conn., May 31, 1919; s. Frank Knight and Annabelle (Matthews) A.; A.B., Tufts Coll., 1942, A.M., 1949, Ph.D., 1952; m. Isabel Bradshaw Bennett, July 3, 1943; children—Freeland Knight, Deborah Ann, Ernest Bennett, John Bradshaw. Asst. prof. Miami U., Oxford O., 1947-49; mem. faculty Tufts U., 1949-71, prof. history, 1964-71, chmn. dept., 1965-71; Ford Found. research fellow, Pakistan, 1953-55; Fulbright research fellow, Pakistan, 1959-60. Served with USAAF, 1942-46. Mem. Assn. Asian Studies, Middle East Inst., Am. Hist. Assn., Am. Assn. U. Profs., Am Civil Liberties Union. Democrat. Author: Islam and Pakistan, 1968. Home: Medford MA Died Feb. 24, 1971; buried Pusan Public Tang-Gam Cemetery, Pusan Korea

ABBOTT, GEORGE ALONZO, prof. chemistry; b. Alma, Marion Co., Ill., July 7, 1874; s. John Baughman and Harriet (Stuart) A.; B.S., De Pauw U., 1895, M.A., 1896; Ph.D. in Chemistry, Mass. Inst. Tech., 1908; m. Ruth Ware, of Minneapolis, Minn., June 15, 1910; children—Marion Ware, Stuart Ware. Served as instr. in chemistry, high schs., Evansville (Ind.), Duluth (Minn.), Manual Tr. High Sch., Indianapolis; was Austin fellow and research asst., Mass. Inst. Tech., also fellow U. of Chicago; asst. prof. organic and industrial chemistry, N. Dak. State Coll., 1908-10; prof. chemistry and head of chemistry dept., U. of N. Dak., since 1910, also chmn. grad. dept.; exchange lecturer U. of Manitoba, 1912. Consulting chemist and court expert. Del. 8th Internat. Congress of Applied Chemistry, New York, 1922. Mem. Am. Chem. Soc., N. Dak. Acad. Science (sec.), Am. Assn. Univ. Profs., N.E.A., Delta Kappa Epsilon, Phi Beta Kappa, Sigma Xi; fellow Ind. Acad. Science. Republican. Methodist. Clubs: Fortnightly, Franklin, Commercial, Kiwanis Internat. (lt. gov.; dist. gov. Minn. and Dakotas). Contbr. to chem. jours.; contbg. editor Grand Forks ND‡

ABBOTT, PAUL, investment exec.; b. N.Y.C., 1898; s. Henry H. and Florence (Call) A.; Yale, 1920; m. Virginia Loney. Dir., mem. exec. and finance com. McGraw-Hill, Inc.; dir. Flintkote Co., Newton Falls Paper Mill, Inc. Bd. dirs. Madison Sq. Boys Club. Mem. bd. Am. Field Service. Capt. USNR ret. Decorated Legion of Merit, Bronze Star. Republican. Home: New York City NY Died 1971.

ABBOTT, WILLIAM LAMONT, engineer; b. Whiteside County, Illinois, February 14, 1861; s. Asa M. and Sarah (Sperry) A.; M.E., University of Illinois, 1884; m. Carrie Entwhistle, Sept. 14, 1887; children—Arthur William, Helen (Mrs. O.C.F. Randolph, dec.), Robert Edward, Josephine Ellenor. Dorothy Caroline (Mrs. Leonard Knopf). Machinist and draftsman in Chicago, 1884-87; president National Electric Construction Co., 1887-94; chief engineer, power house, Chicago Edison Co., 1894-99; chief operating engr. same, 1899-1935; retired; later with Otto Randolph, Inc., gen. contractors. Fellow Am. Inst. Elec. Engrs.; hon. mem. Am. Soc. Mech. Engrs. (pres. 1926), Western Soc. Engrs. (pres. 1907). Trustee U. of Ill., 1904-23 (pres. bd 14 yrs.), Republican. Clubs: Chicago Athletic, Engineers, University. Hon. LL.D. from U. of Ill., 1929. Recipient Washington Award from 4 nat. engring. socs. and Western Soc. Engrs., 1942. Home: 3500 Sheridan Rd. Office: 20 N. Wacker Dr., Chicago IL‡

ABEEL, ESSIE O., educator, resort owner; b. Neola, Pa., June 1, 1887; d. Samuel T. and Emma Agatha (Reinhart) Smith; B.S., East Stroudsburg State Tchrs. Coll., 1906; m. Howard Abeel, July 7, 1917; children—Paul Howard, Harriet (Mrs. Henry S. Bissex). Tchr. pub. schs. N.J., 1906-20; founded Essie Olive Abeel Pvt. Sch., 1920, owner, prin., 1920-65, prin.-emeritus, 1966; operator Shawnee (Pa.) Lake Camp, 1930-31, Abeel Camp, Minisink Hills, Pa., 1932-41; owner, operator Abeel Farm Summer Camp, Tannersville, 1942-62; co-owner Abeel's Hearthstone Cottages, Tannersville, 1962-68. Pres. Bergen County League Women Voters, 1932-38; bd. dirs. YWCA, 1946-50; leader formation Friendship, Hackensack-Passau 1952-68. Recipient citation for work in Am. Assn. U., 1950. Mem. Operation Town Affiliations, Inc., UN Assn. U.S.A. (chpt. pres. 1947-64, mem. bd. state br. 1952-68). Hackensack NJ Died Nov. 1968.

ABELES, JULIAN THEODORE, lawyer; b. Little Rock, Ark., Dec. 25, 1892; s. Samuel Milton and Sarah (Alexander) A.; prep. edn. U. Ark.; LL.B., N.Y.U., 1915; m. Rose Lieberman, Feb. 14, 1917. Admitted N.Y. bar, 1916, since practiced in N.Y.C.; specialist in motion picture, music, copyright and unfair competition law since 1918; counsel for motion picture, music pub. interests; chmn. bd., general counsel Nat. Assn. Orch. Dirs., 1927-36; gen. counsel Nat. Music Publishers' Assn., Inc., also for Harry Fox as agt. and trustee for music pubs. in licensing and enforcement of rights to their musical works. Mem. panel of cons. Librarian of Congress on gen. revision of Copyright Law. Mem. N.Y. State C. of C., Ark. Soc., Copyright Soc. U.S.A. (trustee). Club: Lotos. Contbr. of Ozark mountain stories to various publs. Home: New York City NY Died Mar. 7, 1973.

ABENDROTH, WILLIAM HENRY, army officer; b. Ft. Mead, S.D., Dec. 24, 1895; s. William Henry and Alice Amelia (Smith) A.; grad. Cav. Sch., 1930, Chem. Warfare Sch., 1940, Command and Gen. Staff Sch., 1946; m. Veda Mae Kirkman, May 5, 1934; children—William Henry, Wesley Wallace. Enlisted Ida. N.G., 1913, fed. service on Mexican Border, 1916-17; served Inf. and C.E., U.S. Army, World War I; commd. 2d lt. Cav., Ida. N.G., 1927, advanced through grades to maj. gen., 1952; insp. gen dept., 1941; provost marshal, hdqrs. comdt. IX Corps, Hawaii, P.I., Japan. U.S., World War II; detailed Office Chief of Staff, U.S. Army, apptd. resident N.G. mem., 1947-49; comdg. gen. D.C. Nat. Guard, 1949-68; chief army div., N.G. Bur., 1951-55; purchasing agt., budget dir., State of Ida., 1932-37; rural electrification mgr. Ida. Power Co., 1938-40; adj. gen., State of Ida., Apr. 1946, state dir. Selective Service Aug. 1946. Recipient Legion of Merit. Mem. exec. council Boy Scouts Am., Washington. Mem. Nat. Rifle Assn., N.G. Assn., Am. Legion, Vets. Fgn. Wars. Elk. Home: Falls Church VA Died Sept. 3, 1970; buried Arlington Nat. Cemetery, Arlington VA

ABERLY, JOHN, clergyman, educator; b. Albrightsville, Pa., Sept. 18, 1867; s. John and Catharine (Oberkercher) A.; grad. Fairview Acad., Brodheadsville, Pa., 1884; A.B., Gettysburg (Pa.) Coll., 1888, A.M., 1891, D.D., 1905, LL.D., 1936; m. Alice Strauss, 1889; children—Amy Strauss (Mrs. R.M. Duckelberger), Frederick Heyer. Ordained ministry Luth. Ch., 1890; missionary in India, 1890-1923; in charge Theol. Training Instn., Guntur, India; pres. Luth. Mission 8 yrs. and mem. Nat. Missionary Council of India, Burma and Ceylon 10 yrs.; prof. missions. Luth. Theol. Sem., Maywood, Ill., 1923-26; pres. Luth. Theol. Seminary, Gettysburg, 1926— also prof. systematic theology; elected prof. emeritus, 1940. Mem. Phi Beta Kappa. Author: Bible Biographies, 1910; Commentary on Romans, Madras, India, 1912; Commentaries on the Prophets, 1917; Life of Christ, 1921; Telugu Bible Dictionary, 1923— all in Telugu; Commentary on the Acts of the Apostles in the Luthern Commentary on the New Testament, 1936; An Outline of Mission History, 1945. Home: 308 Springs Av., Gettysburg PA‡

ABERNATHY, CHESS, JR., aerospace co. exec.; b. Gastonia, N.C., Mar. 2, 1912; s. Chess and Myra (Herman) A.; A.B., Emory U., 1934; postgrad. U. Mich., 1939, Pub. Relations Soc. Am. Inst., Cornell U., 1962; m. Martha Virginia McDonald, Sept. 24, 1937; children—Martha Virginia, Margaret Louise. Editor in chief Cobb County Times, Marietta, Ga., 1934-40; alumni sec., editor, then alumni dir. Emory U., Atlanta, 1940-50; pres. Brumby Inc., Times-Jour., Inc., Marietta, Ga., 1950-52; pub. relations coordinator Lockheed-Ga. Co., Marietta, 1953-58, pub. information mgr., 1958-69. Instr. journalism Emory U., 1940-43, Ga. State Coll., 1955-56. Mem. regional expansion council U.S. Dept. Commerce. Dir. Met. Atlanta Community Services, Cobb County Emergency Aid Assn.; bd. dirs. Cobb YMCA; alumni council Emory U. Served to capt. AUS, 1942-45; maj. Res. Decorated Legion of Merit. Recipient honor award Emory U., 1950; Rosenwald fellow, 1939-40. Mem. Pub. Relations Soc. Am. Cobb County C. of C., Assn. U.S. Army, Navy League, Army Aviation Assn. Am., Sigma Alpha Epsilon, Sigma Delta Chi. Methodist. Home: Marietta GA Died May 3, 1969.

ABERNATHY, HARRY THOMAS, banker; b. Leavenworth, Kan., May 23, 1865; s. James Logan and Elizabeth (Martin) A.; A.B., Hamilton Coll., Clinton, N.Y., 1887; m. Mary Stevenson, Jan. 1, 1890 (dec.); children—James Logan, Taylor Stevenson, Mary (Mrs. Paul Snyder); m. 2d, Bessie Cook Tinsman, July 2, 1921. With Abernathy Furniture Co., Kansas City, Mo., 1887-94; clk., 1st Nat. Bank, Kansas City, 1894-95, asst. cashier, 1895-1900, cashier, 1900-08, v.p., 1908-27, pres. since 1927; chmn. bd. Albernathy Furniture Co.; dir. Duff & Repp Furniture Co., Kansas City Title Ins. Co., Central Coal & Coke Co., Employers Reinsurance Co., Kansas City Fire & Marine Insurance Co. Mem. War Finance Com. and Capital Issues Com., 10th Dist., World War. Trustee and treas. U. of Kansas City (Mo.); Kansas City Clearing House (mem. exec. com.). Mem. S.R., Loyal Legion. Republican. Presbyn. Mason (Shriner). Clubs: Kansas City, University, Bankers, Kansas City Country, Horton Shooting. Home: 1228 W. 56th St. Office: 1st Nat. Bank, Kansas City MO*‡

ABERNETHY, ARTHUR TALMAGE, editor, educator; b. Rutherford Coll., Burke Co., N. C., Oct. 10, 1872; s. Rev. Robert L. (founder and pres. Rutherford Coll.), and Mary A. (Hayes) A.; grad. Rutherford Coll., A. M., 1890, A. M., Trinity Coll., 1890; post-grad. course JohnsHopkins Univ., 1890-1; m. Apr. 16, 1900, Effie M. Cable, Pittsburgh. Was associated in Phila. with editor of Latin Herald in reproduction of Latin classics with marginal notes in Latin on Delphinian principles; owned and published Woman's Home Mag. 1 year; prof. Latin and Greek, Rutherford Coll. several yrs.; contb'r. to a large number of newspapers, syndicate matter, mag. articles and serial stories. Licensed to preach by Bapt. Ch.; Republican. Author: Mechanics and Practice of The Electric Telegraph, 1890; Eva Schondorf, 1891; Bertie and Clara, 1895; Story of the State (3 vols. history of N.Y.), 1898; Did Washington Aspire to be King? 1904; The History of the Theatre, 1904. Address: 711 Spruce St., Philadelphia PA‡

ABERNETHY, WILLIAM SHATTUCK, clergyman; b. Cedar Rapids, Ia., Nov. 12, 1872; s. William J. and Mary Elizabeth (Jones) A.; B.A., U. of Minn., 1896; studied U. of Chicago; D.D., Shurtleff, 1912, Denison, 1925; m. Jane Reckard, Oct. 5, 1899; children—Robert W. (dec.), Theodore J., Bradford S. Ordained Bapt. ministry, 1899; pastor Berwyn, Ill., 1899-1912, First Church, Kansas City, Mo., 1912-21, Calvary Church, Washington, D.C., 1921-42; retired, 1942. Made Minister Emeritus, Calvary Bapt. Ch. on retirement. Served as war work sec. with Y.M.C.A. in occupied regions in France, Sept. 1918-Mar. 1919. Mem. bd. mgrs. Am. Bapt. Foreign Mission Soc. (pres. 1921-23); mem. exec. com. Bapt. World's Alliance; pres. Northern Bapt. Conv., 1933-34; convention preacher, 1926, Northern Bapt. Conv.; pres. Ministerial Union, Washington, D.C., 1939-40; chmn. Evangelistic Dept. Fed. Council of Chs., 1935-36. Mem. Am. Bapt. Home

Mission Soc. (pres. 1916-17), Delta Tau Delta, Theta Phi. Mason (32 deg.). Republican. Clubs: Theta Sigma, Theta Phi. Author: Left Handed Folks. Home: 101 Earlston Drive, Washington 16 DC‡

ABRAMS, CHARLES, lawyer, housing; b. Vilna, Poland, Feb. 16, 1902; s. Abraham and Freda (Rabinowitz) A; brought to U.S., 1904, naturalized, 1916; LL.B., St. Lawrence U., 1922; m. Ruth Davidson, Dec. 22, 1928; children—Judith, Abby. Admitted to N.Y. bar, 1923, practiced in N.Y.C.; specialist in city planning; co-author of municipal housing authorities law, 1934, author, 1935 law (successfully argued constitutionality); counsel N.Y.C. Housing Authority, 1934-37, Housing Shortage Investigation, 1936, Am. Fedn. Housing Authorities, 1937-39; lectr. econs. and housing, prof. grad. faculty New Sch. Soc. Research, 1936-60; chmn. city planning dept., prof. Columbia, 1965, chmn. div. urban planning, prof., 1965-67; Williams prof. dept. city planning Harvard, 1968-70; vis. prof. Mass. Inst. Tech., 1957-65, U. Pa., 1951-56; columnist N.Y. Post, 1947-49. Led UN missions to Ghana, 1954, Turkey, 1954. Pakistan, 1957, Philippines, 1958; advisor UN Missions Bolivia, 1959, Ireland, Japan, 1960, 62, Nigeria, 1962, Singapore, 1963, Kenya, 1964, ICA Mission Jamaica, Brit. W Indies, 1961. Cons. U.S. Housing Authority Alaska. State Housing Authority, Phila.; spl. counsel Joint Legislative Committee on Housing and Multiple Dwellings, 1946; N.Y. State rent adminstr. and commr. Temp. State Housing Rent Commn., 1955. Chmn. N.Y. State Commn. Against Discrimination and mem. of the Governor's Cabinet 1955-59; dir., mem. executive com. Nat. Housing Conf.; pres. Nat. Com. Against Discrimination in Housing; cons. Agy. for Internat. Devel.; chmn. N.Y.C. Task Force on Housing and Urban Renewal. Recipient Annual Award, League Indsl. Democracy, 1954; Catholic Interracial Council, Brotherhood award, 1959; award N.Y. chpt. Am. Inst. Architects, 1965; Medal award citation Am. Soc. Planning Ofcls., 1970; Distinguished Service award Am. Inst. Planners (posthumous), 1970. Mem. of the Am. Institute of Planners, Association Bar City of N.Y., N.Y. Co. Lawyers Assn. Author: Revolution in Land 1939; The Future of Housing, 1946; Race Bias in Housing, 1947; Urban Land Policies and Problems (United Nations), 1953; Forbidden Neighbors, 1955; Man's Struggle for Shelter, 1964; The City is the Frontier, 1965; Home Ownership for the Poor, 1970; The Language of Cities, pub. posthumously, 1971; also chpts. in books on housing and social trends. Contbr. nat. mags. All original papers in collection Regional History, Cornell U. Home: New York City NY Died Feb. 22, 1970; cremated.

ABRAMS, LEROY, botanist; b. Sheffield, Ia., Oct. 1, 1874; s. James DeWitt and Almina Barbara (Shoudy) A.; student U. of Southern Calif., 1895-96; Stanford, 1896-99, and 1900-04, A.B., 1899, A.M., 1902; studied Columbia, 1904-05, Ph.D., 1910; m. Letitia Patterson (A.B., Stanford, 1901), Mar. 29, 1909. Acting prof. botany, U. of Ida., 1899-1900; asst. in botany, Stanford, 1900-02, instr., 1902-04; fellow Columbia U., 1904-05; asst. curator of plants, Nat. Museum, 1905-06; asst. prof. botany, 1906-12, asso. prof., 1912-20, prof. Stanford U., 1920-40, emeritus, 1940-—; acting asso. prof. botany, U. of Calif., 1915. Fellow A.A.A.S., Calif. Acad. Sci., Am. Acad. Arts and Science; mem. Am. Bot. Soc., Calif. Bot. Soc., Sigma Xi. Author: Flora of Los Angeles and Vicinity, 1904, 11, 17; Illustrated Flora of the Pacific State, 1923, 41, 44, also bulletin, A Phytogeographical and Taxonomic Study of the Southern California Trees and Shrubs, 1910; etc. Home: Stanford University, CA‡

ABRUZZO, MATTHEW T., judge; b. Brooklyn, N.Y., Apr. 30, 1889; s. Leonard and Jennie Abruzzo; educated public schools until 1903, Commercial High School, 1903-06; LL.B., Brooklyn Law Sch., 1910; m. Jane Cecelia Miller, Sept. 21, 1926; 1 son, Matthew T. Admitted to N.Y. bar, 1910, and began practice in Brooklyn; judge U.S. Dist. Court, Eastern Dist. of N.Y., until 1971. Roman Catholic. Club: New York Athletic. Home: Brooklyn NY Died May 28, 1971.

ACHESON, DEAN GOODERHAM, sec. of State; born Middletown, Conn., April 11, 1893; s. Edward Campion and Eleanor (Gooderham) A.; A.B., Yale, 1915, M.A. (honorary), 1936; LL.B., Harvard U., 1918, LL.D. (hon.), 1950; LL.D., Wesleyan U., Conn., 1947, Yale, 1962, Johns Hopkins, 1963; D.C.L., Oxford U., 1952; L.H.D., Brandeis U., 1956, Cambridge U., 1958, U. Mich., 1967; m. Alice Stanley, May 5, 1917; children—Jane (Mrs. Dudley B. W. Brown), David Campion, Mary Eleanor (Mrs. William P. Bundy). Private sec. to Louis D. Brandeis, asso. justice U.S. Supreme Ct., 1919-21; with Covington, Burling and Rublee, 1921-33; apptd. undersec. of treasury, May 19, 1933, resigned Nov. 15, 1933; mem. Covington, Burling, Rublee, Acheson & Shorb, Jan. 1, 1934-Jan. 31, 1941; appointed assistant secretary of State, Feb. 1, 1941; under-sec. of State, 1945-47, sec. of State, 1949-53; pvt. practice law with Covington & Burling, Washington 1953-71. Chairman adv. com. on civil rules Judicial Conference. Vice chmn. Commn. on Orgn. Exec. Br. of the Govt. Ensign United States Navy, World War I. Awarded Order of Vasa (Swedish); Medal for Merit,; Order of Aztec Eagle (Mexico); Grand Master Nat. Order of So. Cross (Brazil); Grand Cross Order of Boyaca (Columbia); Grand Cordon, Order of Leopold (Belgium); Order of Rising Sun (Japan); Royal Order Cambodia; Presidential Medal of Freedom (U.S.), 1964. Fellow Yale Corporation, 1936-61. Mem. Am. Acad. Arts and Scis., Delta Kappa Epsilon, Scroll and Key. Democrat. Episcopalian. Clubs; Metropolitan (Washington); Century (New York). Author: A Citizen Looks at Congress, 1957; Publication; A Democrat Looks at His Party, 1955; Power and Diplomacy, 1958; Sketches from Life of Men I Have Known, 1961; Morning and Noon, 1965; Present at the Creation, 1969 (Pulitzer prize 1970); Fragments of My Fleece, 1971; Grapes from Thorns (posthumous), 1972. Died Oct. 12, 1971.

ACHESON, MARY VIRGINIA BERRY (MRS. JOHN C. ACHESON), b. Sedalia, Mo., Jan. 26, 1873; d. Dr. Thomas Franklin and Josephine (Dillon) Berry; grad. Girls' High Sch., Louisville, Ky., 1889, Bryant and Stratton Business Coll., Louisville, 1890; m. John Carey Acheson (now pres. Pa. Coll. for Women), of Pittsburgh, Pa., June 5, 1900. Sec. to pres. Western Coll. for Women, Oxford, O., 1894-7, to pres. Central U., Danville, Ky., 1897-9; teacher Harrodsburg (Ky.) Acad., 1900-2; dean Ky. Coll. for Women, Danville, 1902-15. Presbyterian. Home: Woodland Rd., Pittsburgh PA‡

ACIKALIN, CEVAT, Turkish govt ofcl.; b. 1898; ed. Galata Saray Coll., Istanbul, and U. Geneva. Sec., Turkish Consulate Gen., Geneva, 1920; sec., Financial Commn., Lausanne Conf., 1922; asst. legal adviser, Fgn. Office, 1923; sec. Turkish Legation, Warsaw, 1924; prin. asst. legal adviser, Fgn. Office, 1925; legal adviser, Afghan Govt., 1926; charge d'affaires, Prague, 1928; counsellor, Turkish embassy, Teheran, 1930, Moscow, 1931; dir.-gen. 2d sept. Fgn. Office, 1934; dir.-gen. 1st Polit. Dept., 1935; minister, 1937; envoy extraordinary, Hatay, 1938; dep. sec. gen., Fgn. Office, 1939; ambassador, Moscow, 1942; sec.-gen. fgn. Office, 1943; ambassador to U.S., 1945-52, to Italy, 1954-61; senator, Ankara, 1962-70. Address: Ankara Turkey Died 1970.

ACKEN, HENRY S., JR., obstetrician, gynecologist; b. Maplewood, N.J., Sept. 23, 1899; s. Henry S. and Edith (Bunnel) A.; M.D., Johns Hopkins U., 1924; m. Dorothy Niemeyer, Sept. 13, 1927; children—Janet (Mrs. Charles Havel, Jr.), Judith (Mrs. Paul L. Aylward, Jr.). Cons., Methodist Hosp; cons. obstetrics and gynecology Meth. Hosp., Bklyn., Grasslands Hosp., Valhalla, N.Y. Served to capt. M.C. USNR. Diplomate Am. Bd. Obstetrics and Gynecology. Fellow A.M.A., A.C.S., Am. Coll. Obstetrics and Gynecology. Home: Sherman CT Died Jan. 23, 1970.

ACKERMAN, CARL FREDERICK, journalist; b. Syracuse, N.Y., June 17, 1873; s. J. Daniel and Caroline F. A.; ed. Syracuse. Pvt. 101st N. Y. regt., Spanish-Am. war, 1898. In newspaper work since Jan. 1, 1891; corr. Leslie's Weekly in Philippines, 1899-1900, and in China, 1900-1, march to Peking and relief of legations. Now with New York Herald. Republican. Residence: 163 W. 91st St., New York‡

ACKERMAN, CARL WILLIAM, dean; b. Richmond, Indiana, Jan. 16, 1890; s. John F. and Mary Alice (Eggemeyer) A.; student U. of Chicago, 1910; A.B., Earlham Coll., Richmond, 1911, A.M., 1917; B.Litt., from Columbia U. Sch. of Journalism, 1913; LL.D., Univ. of Richmond, Northwestern University and Earlham College, 1935; Doctor Honoris Causa, University of San Marcos, Lima, Peru; University of Havana, 1944; m. Mabel Vander Hoof, May 24, 1914 (deceased August 22, 1954); 1 son, Robert Vander Hoof. Engaged as correspondent for United Press within central powers, 1915-17; spl. writer, New York Tribune, 1917; corr. Saturday Evening Post, in Mexico, Spain, France and Switzerland, 1917-18; corr. New York Times with allied armies in Siberia, 1918-19; dir. foreign news service, Phila. Pub. Ledger, 1919-21; pres. Carl W. Ackerman, Inc. (directing corporate pub. relations), 1921-27; asst. to pres. Gen. Motors Corp., 1930-31; dean Columbia U. Grad. Sch. of Journalism, 1931-56. Co-founder, with Dr. Hollington K. Tong, first Grad. Sch. of Journalism in Chungking, China. Lecturer on public opinion, Tokyo Imperial U., U. of Philippines and Sorbonne (Paris), 1935-36; elected hon. prof. Argentine Sch. of Journalism, U. of LaPlata, 1937. Investigated press, radio and cinema in Panama, Colombia, Ecuador, Peru, Chile, the Argentine, Brazil and Trinidad, 1937. Organized and directed Maria Moors Cabot prizes for Latin American journalists, 1937-56. Awarded gold medal by Inter-American University, Panama, 1944; Columbia University Alumni Federation medal, 1945; Commander Order of Southern Cross, Brazil, 1952; Chinese order of Brilliant Star 1948; Cabot gold medal, 1956. Elected mem. American Soc. of Newspaper Editors, 1934. Mem. social Service Mission to Venezuela, 1939; hon. mem. la Union Nacional de Periodistas de Ecuador, 1942. Mem. World Free Press Com., Am. Soc. Newspaper Editors, 1945; with Sevellon Brown, Providence Journal-Bulletin; established American Press Inst., 1946; mem. N.Y. State Soc. Newspaper Editors, Inter-Am. Press Assn. Clubs: Century, University. Author: Germany, The Next Republic?, 1917; Mexico's Dilemma, 1918; Trailing the Bolsheviki, 1919; Dawes, the Doer, 1924; Biography of George Eastman, 1930. Home: New York City NY Died Oct. 1970.

ACKERMAN, EDWARD AUGUSTUS, instn. exec.; b. Post Falls, Ida., Dec. 5, 1911; s. August and Augusta (Anderson) A.; A.B., Harvard, 1934, A.M., 1936, Ph.D., 1939; m. Adrienne Desjardins, Sept. 24, 1949; children—Helen, Francis, Julia, Justin, Elizabeth. Instr., Harvard, 1940-43, asst. prof., 1943-48; prof. geography U. Chgo., 1948-55; dir. water resources program Resources for Future, Inc., 1954-58; dep. exec. officer Carnegie Inst. Washington, 1958-60, exec. officer, 1960-73. Asst. chief Europe- Africa div., chief geog. reports sect. OSS, 1941-43; tech. adv. nat. resources sect. G.H.Q., SCAP, Tokyo, Japan, 1946-48; regional analyst Hoover Commn., 1948; mem. Pres.'s Water Resources Policy Commn., 1950-51; chief natural resources and pub. works br. U.S. Bur. Budget, 1951-52; asst. gen. mgr. TVA, 1952-54; chmn. ad hoc com. on geography Nat. Acad. Scis.-NRC, 1963-64; cons. to various depts. fed. govt., also Congl. coms. Trustee Washington Center Met. Studies, chmn. bd. trustees, 1964-69; bd. dirs. Analytic Services, Inc., Center for Environment and Man, Planning Found. Am., Geomet, Inc., Envirometrics, Inc. Member Assn. Am. Geographers, Phi Beta Kappa, Sigma Xi. Club: Cosmos (Wash.). Author: New England's Fishing Industry, 1941; (with J.R. Whitaker) American Resources, 1951; (with collaborators), Ten Rivers in America's Future, 1950; Japan's Natural Resources, 1953; (with G. O. G. Lof) Technology in American Water Development, 1959. Home: Washington DC Died Mar. 8, 1973.

ACKERMAN, FRED W., transp. exec.; b. San Francisco, Nov. 16, 1894; m. Helen J. Ackerman; children—Carol Jane Kilner, Frederick W. Chmn. bd., mem. exec. com. Greyhound Corporation; chairman of the board of Seaboard Finance Co., Lucky Lager Brewing Co.; dir., mem. exec. com., Crocker-Anglo Nat. Bank; dir. Boothe Leasing Corp., Capital Estates, Canadian Greyhound Corp., John Labatt Ltd., Can. Mem. Nat. Assn. Motor Bus Operators (dir.), U.S. C. of C. Clubs: Claremont Country, Stock Exchange, Rotary, Pinnacle, Family, Commonwealth; Links. Home: Piedmont CA Died Feb. 1972.

ACKERMAN, NATHAN WARD, psychiatrist, educator; b. Russia, Nov. 22, 1908; s. David and Bertha (Greenberg) A.; came to U.S., 1912, naturalized, 1920; B.A., Columbia, 1929, M.D., 1933; m. Gwendolyn Hill, Oct. 10, 1937; children—Jeanne (Mrs. Barry Curnan), Deborah. Intern Montefiore Hosp., N.Y.C., 1933-34; resident Menninger Clinic and Sanitorium, Topeka, 1935-36; mem. psychiat. staff Menninger Clinic, 1936-37; chief psychiatrist Jewish Bd. Guardians, N.Y.C., 1937-51; dir. Child Devel. Center, N.Y.C., 1946-51, Family Mental Health Clinic, Jewish Family Service, N.Y.C., 1957-66, profl. program Family Inst., N.Y.C., 1960-71; clin. prof. psychiatry Columbia Coll. Phys. and Surg. 1957-71; vis. prof. Tulane U., 1956, U. N.C., 1960; vis lectr. Albert Einstein Med Coll., 1962-71; lectr. Columbia Sch. Social Work, 1946-64. Recipient Adolph Meyer award Assn. Improvement Mental Health, 1959; Wilfred Hulse award Eastern Group Psychotherapy Psychotherapy Assn., 1965. Diplomate Am. Bd. Psychiatry and Neurology. Fellow N.Y. Acad. Medicine, Am. Psychiat. Assn., Am. Orthopsychiat. Assn., Acad. Psychoanalysis, Am. Acad. Child Psychiatry; mem. Assn. Psychoanalytic medicine (pres. 1957-59), Am. Psychopath. Assn., Group for Advancement Psychiatry, N.Y. Council Child Psychiatry, N.Y. Soc. Clin. Psychiatry, Am. Psychoanalytic Assn., Am. Group Therapy Assn., Mexican Psychoanalytic Assn. (hon.), Assn. Applied Psychoanalysis (hon.). Author: (with others) Personality and Arterial Hypertension, 1945; (with M. Jahoda) Antisemitism and Emotional Disorder, 1950; The Psychodynamics of Family Life, 1958; Treating the Troubled Family, 1966; also articles. Editor: Exploring the Base of Family Therapy, 1961; Expanding the Theory and Practice of Family Therapy, 1967; Family Process, 1970; also others. Editor: Family Therapy in Transition, 1970. Home: New York City NY Died June 12, 1971; buried Westchester Hills Cemetery, Hastings-on-Hudson NY

ACQUAVELLA, A. LAWRENCE, justice city court; b. Bklyn., Sept. 13, 1906; s. Patrick P. and Rose (Marchesiello) A.; LL.B., St. John's Coll., 1928; m. Constance T. Abbate, July 23, 1934; children—Lucille Lama (Mrs. Alfred Lama), John. Admitted to N.Y. bar, 1930; practiced in N.Y.C., 1930-39; sec. Supreme Ct. Justices Frank E. Johnson, Henry L. Ughetta, 1939-53; city magistrate, N.Y.C., 1953-58; justice Ct. Spl. Sessions, 1958-59, City Court of City of New York; judge of the Civil Court. Former district chairman Red Cross, March of Dimes, Boy Scouts Am.; founder, pres. Jefferson Boy's Club: state committeeman 5th Assembly Dist., Kings County, 1946-53; mem. bd. dirs. Bushwick Hosp., 1947-57. Mem. 28th Ward taxpayers Assn., Bklyn. Bar Assn., Catholic War Veterans (hon. life). Roman Catholic. K.C. Address: Brooklyn NY

ADAIR, FRED LYMAN, obstetrician, gynecologist; b. Anamosa, Ia., July 28, 1877; s. Lyman Joseph and Sarah Jennings (Porter) A.; B.S., U. of Minn., 1898; M.D., Rush Med. Coll. (U. of Chicago), 1901; M.A., U. of Minn.; m. Myrtle May Ingalls, Nov. 18, 1911; children—Agnes Jennings Kuhn, Robert Chamberlain, Richard Porter. Intern Michael Reese Hosp., Chicago, 1901-03; gen. practice, 1903-08; became connected with U. of Minn., 1905; studied in Berlin, 1908-09; specialized in obstetrics and gynecology since 1909; prof. obstetrics and gynecology, U. of Minn., 1926-29; chmn. dept. and emeritus prof. obstetrics and gynecology Univ. of Chicago since 1929; former chief of service Chicago Lying-in Hosp.; consultant Children's Bur., U.S. Dept. of Labor; chmn. Joint Maternal Welfare Comm. Cook County; former chief maternal and child division Ill. Department Public Health. Was maj. Minn. N.G.; physician with Red Cross in France, Belgium, World War I. Chmn. Com. on Prenatal Care, Hoover Conf. on Child Health and Protection; chmn. Am. Com. on Maternal Welfare, Inc.; chmn. 1st, 2d, 3d, 4th Am. Congress on Obstet. and Gynecology. Mem. Am. Medical Assn. (past pres. and sec. section on obstetrics and gynecology), Minn Academy Medicine, Central Assn. Obstetricians and Gynecologists, Am. Gynecological Soc. (past treas. and pres.), Chicago Gynecological Soc. (past pres.), Am. Board Obstetrics and Gynecology (past vice-pres.), American College of Surgeons, Illinois Medical Society, Sigma Xi, Delta Upsilon, Nu Sigma Nu. Past pres. Fedn. Obstetric & Gynecologic Soc. Awarded Croix Civique (Belgium). Club: Cosmos. Author: (with Stieglitz) Obstetric Medicine: (with Potter) Fetal and Neonatal Death, 1940; also textbooks on obstetrics and gynecology. Home: Box 340, Chesterton, Ind. Office: 24 W. Ohio St., Chicago 10 IL‡

ADAIR, HUGH ROGERS, jurist; b. Trego County Kan., Aug. 27, 1889; s. Asa Rogers and Emma May (Keyser) A.; student Spaulding Comml. Coll., Kansas City, Mo., 1908, Kan. State Normal Coll. (Western branch), 1909; LL.B. U. Kan., 1913; m. Jeanice Janes, Sept. 25, 1935 (died Feb. 1, 1944); 1 son, Hugh Rogers II. City atty., Helena, Mont., 1933 and 1934; rep., Lewis and Clark County, Mont. in legislative assembly, 1927-31; lieutenant governor Montana, 1937-41; president Montana Senate, 1937-39; asso. justice Supreme Court Montana, 1943-47, chief justice, later associate justice. Mem. Helena Earthquake Relief Com., 1935; Mont. State chmn. for Nat. Found. Infantile Paralysis, Inc., 1938-41; chmn, exec. bd. State Vocational Sch. for Girls, Helena, 1935-37. Served as pvt., U.S. Army, World War I, discharged, 1919. Mem. Helena Trail Riders Assn., Am., Mont., Lewis and Clark County bar assns., Am. Legion, Phi Alpha Delta. Elk, Eagle, Mason. (Shriner, past potentate). Club: Montana. Home: Helena MT Died Jan. 18, 1971; buried Helena MT

ADAM, PAUL JAMES, accountant; b. Dunlap, Kan., Aug. 17, 1909; s. Robert and Maude Jane (Dodderidge) A.; B.S. in Bus., U. Kan., 1933; m. Adrienne Zimmerman, Dec. 30, 1933; children—Paul James, Patricia Jane, Judith Zimmerman, Mary Sue. With PWA, 1933-36, Peat, Marwick, Mitchell & Co., C.P.A.'s, Kansas City, Mo., 1937-41; with Arthur Young & Co., C.P.A.'s, 1941-69, partner, Dallas, 1947-69. Chmn. Western div. U. Kan. Council for Progress, 1966. Trustee Child-Mercy Hosp., Kansas City, Mo., 1956-62, Kan. U. Endowment Assn., 1965-69; bd. dirs. Barstow Sch., Kansas City, Mo., 1959-62; hon. dir. Rockhurst Coll., Kansas City, Mo., 1960-69. C.P.A., Mo., Kan., Tex., Ill., Ia. Mem. Am. Inst. C.P.A.'s (council 1950-53), Mo. (pres. 1949-50), Tex., Ill., Kan., Ia. socs. C.P.A.'s. Mason (Shriner, Jester). Clubs: Dallas, Petroleum, Brook Hollow Golf, Preston Trail Golf (Dallas); Mission Hills Country, Kansas City (Kansas City, Mo.). Home: Dallas TX Died Dec. 6, 1969; buried Mt. Moriah, Kansas City MO

ADAMS, CHARLES ALBERTUS, college prof.; b. Arlington, Vt., Feb. 14, 1872; s. Orlando Ebenezer and Jennie (Kent) A.; B.S., Middlebury (Vt.) Coll., 1895, A.M., 1897; post-grad. work, Johns Hopkins, 1895-96; m. Bertha Brainerd, of Middlebury, Aug. 30, 1899; children—Frances Viola, Charles Orlando. Instr. St. Albans Acad., Knoxville, Ill., 1896-01; prof. English, U. of Wyo., 1901-02; prin. high sch., Adams, Mass., 1902-07; dean and prin. Md. Coll. for Women, Lutherville, 1907-08; supt. pub. schs., West Rutland and Castleton, Vt., 1908-12; prin. State Normal Sch., Castleton, 1912-20; head dept. of edn., R.I. Coll. of Edn., Providence, 1920-23; prof. edn., Middlebury Coll., since 1923. Mem. Phi Beta Kappa, Delta Kappa Epsilon. Episcopalian. Home: Middlebury VT‡

ADAMS, CHAUNCEY CORBIN, clergyman; b. Charlestown, N.H., Oct. 24, 1872; s. Aremas and Harriet E. (Davis) A.; grad. high sch., Bellows Falls, Vt., 1892; A.B., Dartmouth, 1896, D.D., 1923; grad. Chicago Theol. Sem., 1900; m. Donna G. Anderson, of Franklin, Vermont, October 24, 1900 (deceased); children—Bertha H. (Mrs. Earl C. Heap), Dorcas A. (Mrs. Edward G. Ludwig), Chauncey C. Ordained Congl. ministry, 1900; pastor Port Byron, Ill., 1900-01, Hinesburg, Vt., 1901-07, Essex Junction, 1907-15, Burlington, 1915-31, Middlebury since 1931; also prof. Middlebury Coll. Mem. bd. dirs. Vt. Congl. Conf.; mem. Winooski Assn. Congl. Ministers. Democrat. Mason, Odd Fellow, K.P. Club: Rotary. Home: 21 Redstone Terrace, Burlington VT‡

ADAMS, DOROTHY, advt. exec.; b. Dover, N.H., Feb. 6, 1908; d. James Birney and Minnie (Irish) Adams; B.S., U. Ill., 1928; grad. student, U. Chgo., 1930-32. Advt. mail order Montgomery Ward & Co., 1935-50; agy. v.p. Clyne-Maxon, N.Y.C., 1950-70, exec. v.p., 1965-70; dir. Cannon Point North, N.Y.C. Mem. Advt. Club N.Y., Advt. Women's Club N.Y. Home: New York City NY Died Feb. 16, 1970.

ADAMS, EDWARD RICHMOND, lawyer; b. Galesburg, Ill., July 7, 1892; s. Edward Quincy and Helen Louise (Gay) A.; student Knox Coll.; A.B., Harvard, 1914, LL.B., 1917; m. Frances Ruth Cummings, June 14, 1924; children—Edward Quincy, Frances Suzanne (Mrs. H. Charles Becker). Admitted to Ill. bar, 1918, also U.S. Dist. Ct. 7th Circuit, Ct. of Appeals, U.S. Supreme Ct.; practice of law, Chgo., 1919-72; mem. firm Miller, Gorham, Wescott & Adams. Dir. John B. Thompson Co., Drovers Nat. Bank, also director J. R. Short Milling Company. Served as 1st lt. U.S. Army, World War I. Fellow Am. Coll. Trial Lawyers; mem. Am., Ill., Chgo. bar assns., Bar Assn. 7th Fed. Circuit, Am. Judicature Soc., Soc. Trial Lawyers Chgo. Clubs: Law, Legal, University, Mid-Day (Chgo.); Indian Hill (Winnetka); Naples (Fla.) Yacht. Home: Winnetka IL Died June 1972.

ADAMS, ERNEST GERMAIN, investment banking; b. Honolulu, T.H., Sept. 15, 1874; s. Edward Payson and Ellen Germain (Fisher) A.; student Harvard, 1896-97; m. Mary Edith Russell, of Weston, Mass., Oct. 14, 1902; children—Margaret Germain (dec.), Elizabeth Fisher, Edward Payson, Mary Rogers. Began with E. Rollins Morse and Bro., Boston, 1897; mgr. Providence office Kidder Peabody & Co. since 1922; pres. Union Mills Co.; dir. Boston Consolidated Gas Co. Pvt. and 2d lt. 1st Corps Cadets, Mass. Vol. Militia, 10 yrs.; in U.S. Navy, World War, advancing to lt. comdr. Trustee and chmn. bd. Unitarian Foundation; head of campaign, 1920, which raised , 400,000 for the denomination; trustee Lincoln Sch. Mem. Unitarian Laymen's League. Republican. Clubs: Turks Head (Providence); Harvard (Boston); Army and Navy (Washington). Home: 57 Barnes St. Office: 100 Grosvenor Bldg., Providence RI‡

ADAMS, EUGENE TAYLOR, educator; b. Millersburg, Pennsylvania, Feb. 26, 1906; s. John Furman and Elizabeth (Taylor) A.; A.B., Susquehanna University, 1926, Litt.D. (honorary), 1952; Ph.D., Yale, 1934; married Esther Fowler, Apr. 30, 1943; children—Stephen F., James T., Ann Elizabeth. Instructor English and Am. lit. Sandy Twp. High Sch., DuBois, Pa., 1926-28; mem. faculty Colgate U. since 1931, prof. philosophy, 1945-71, dir. div. philosophy and religion, 1947-54, acting dean faculty, 1950-51, director university studies, dean faculty, 1954-61; vis. prof. Biarritz Am. U., France, 1945-46. Served as lt. USNR, 1942-46. Mem. Am. Philos. Assn., Phi Beta Kappa, Alpha Tau Omega. Author: Epistemology of John Dewey, 1934; Experience Reason and Faith (with others), 1939; The American Idea (with others), 1942. Contbr. to World Book Ency., 1958. Home: Hamilton NY Died Oct. 18, 1971; inurned Colgate University Cemetery, Hamilton NY

ADAMS, FRANCIS ALEXANDRE, editor; b. at New York, May 11, 1874; s. John Quincy and Marie Adele (Negrin) A.; student Coll. City of New York, 1893-96, New York U., 1897; m. Editor Gotham Monthly Magazine, 1890, Adams Magazine, 1891-95, Printer's Ink, 1896; asso. editor New York Commercial, 1904-18. Served in Spanish-American war, 1898. Captain 22d regt. corps engineers, N.Y.G., 1918; 1st lt., M.T.C., U.S.A., 1918-19. Republican. Author: Who Rules America? Truths About Trusts, 1900; The Philippine Question, 1900; The Transgressors (polit. novel), 1900; Roosevelt, 1909; American Minute Men of To-day, 1917. Office: 18 E. 41st St., New York NY‡

ADAMS, FRANK, irrigation economist; b. Chicago, Ill., Sept. 19, 1875; s. Edward Francis and Delia Ray (Cooper) A.; prep. edn., Cogswell Polytechnic Coll., San Francisco, and Belmont (Calif.) Prep. Sch.; A.B., Stanford, 1901; A.M., U. of Neb., 1906; LL.D., University of California, 1947; m. Amy Belle Hill, June 20, 1906; children—Helen (Mrs. Percy M. Barr), Francis Edward, David Hill, Thomas Cooper. Professor of irrigation, College of Agriculture, University of Calif., 1916-45, emeritus since Sept. 19, 1945; also irrigation economist in California Agricultural Experimental Station. Successively, 1900-06, and 1910-39, agt. and expert, irrigation asst., irrigation engr., irrigation mgr. and collaborator in irrigation investigations, U.S. Dept. Agr.; cons. engr. U.S. Bur. of Reclamation, 1926-40; consulting engineer, International Water Commission, United States and Mexico, 1928-30. Served with Army Ednl. Corps, in France, Apr.-June 1919. Mem. Advisory Commn. on Agrl. Colonization in Palestine, May-Nov. 1927; chmn. Calif. Econ. Research Council, 1930-32; consultant Nat. Resources Com. Rio Grande Joint Investigation, 1935-38. Fellow Am. Society of Agricultural Engrs.; mem. Western Farm Econ. Assn., Am. Geophysical Union, Tau Beta Pi. Awarded John Deere Gold Medal by Am. Society Agrl. Engrs., 1947. Decorated Officier du Merite Agricole. Republican. Conglist. Clubs: Faculty, Commonwealth. Author of numerous repts. and articles pertaining to irrigation, agriculture, etc. Home: 1831 San Juan Av., Berkeley 7 CA‡

ADAMS, GEORGE EDWARD, agronomist; b. North Kingstown, R.I., May 12, 1874; s. George L. and Annie (Gould) A.; B.S., R.I. State Coll., Kingston, R.I., 1894; grad. student, Cornell U., Ithaca, N.Y., 1899-1900; Master in Agr., Rhode Island State Coll., 1916; m. Oct. 20, 1903, Mary Gates Schermerhorn, of Malden, Mass. Asst. horticulturist, 1895-1901, asso. in agronomy, 1901-08, horticulturist, 1908-12, R.I. Expt. Sta.; chief agrl. dept., 1907-12, prof. of agronomy, 1907-38, R.I. State Coll., also dean sch. of agr. and home economics and dir. agrl. expt. sta. and extension service, emeritus since 1938. State statistical agt. R.I. for Bur. Statistics, U.S. Dept. Agr., 1901-14. Fellow A.A.A.S.; member American Breeders' Assn., Am. Soc. Agronomy, Mass. Hort. Soc., Phi Kappa Phi, Alpha Zeta. Mason, Grange. Home: Kingston RI‡

ADAMS, GEORGE SHELDON, M.D.; b. Lowell, Mich., Dec. 20, 1876; s. Francis David and Jane (Ashley) A.; S.D. Agrl. Coll., 1893-95; M.D., Rush Med. Coll., 1901; LL.D., U. of S.D., 1936; m. Valborg S. Smith, Dell Rapids, S.D., Nov. 10, 1910; children—Janet Sheldon (Mrs. Holden B. Bickford), Jean Michelet, (Mrs. John D. Thomas), Virginia Smith, Marjory Campbell, George Sheldon. Asst. phys., 1901; asst. supt., 1903; supt. Jan. 17, 1920—, Yankton State Hosp. Mem. A.M.A., S.D. State Med. Assn. (pres. 1921-22), Yankton Dist. Med. Soc., Am. Psychiatric Assn. (life mem.). Republican. Episcopalian. Mason (33 deg., Shriner), Elk, Rotarian. Address: State Hospital Yankton SD‡

ADAMS, HENRY FOSTER, psychologist; b. Oak Park, Ill., Nov. 11, 1882; s. Samuel Hawley (D.D.) and Mary H. (Dunbar; M.D.) A.; student Cazenovia (N.Y.) Sem., 1897-99, Erasmus Hall High Sch., Brooklyn, 1899-1901; Ph.B., Wesleyan U., 1905; Ph.D., U. of Chicago, 1910; m. Susan Hitch, Aug. 24, 1915; 1 son, Henry Hitch. Reporter, N.Y. Morning Sun, 1905-06; with Chicago Screw Co., 1906-07; asst. U. of Chicago, 1910-11; mem. faculty, U. of Mich., 1911-73, prof. of psychology, 1927-53, prof. emeritus, 1953-73. Fellow A.A.A.S.; mem. Am. Psychol. Assn. (life), Michigan Acad. Sci., Sigma Xi, Psi Upsilon. Club: Research (U. of Mich.). Author: Autokinetic Sensation, Psychol. Monographs, 1912; Advertising and Its Mental Laws, 1916; The Ways of the Mind, 1925; series of popular articles on aspects of psychology, Scribner's mag., 1920-21. Contbr. articles on Ann Arbor MI Died Feb. 16, 1973.

ADAMS, HERBERT H., railway official; b. at Detroit, Mich., 1876; s. Gen. Henry M. A.; B.A., Johns Hopkins, 1897; B.S. in Civ. Engring., Mass. Inst. Tech., 1899; asst. engr., 1899-1902, asst. chief engr., 1902-3, asst. div. supt., 1903-4, div. supt., 1904-9, M.C. R.R.; gen. supt., 1909-10, gen. mgr., 1910-12, Toronto, Hamilton & Buffalo R.R.; pres. Kansas City Terminal, 1912-17; lt.-col. 12th Regt. Engrs. (rys.) in France, 1917. Home: 3530 Walnut St., Kansas City MO‡

ADAMS, JOHN EMERY, geologist; b. Solon, Ia., June 5, 1899; s. Harry Delvie and Virginia (Bacon) A.; B.A., U. of Ia., 1922, M.S., 1923; grad. study, U. of Chicago, 1923-24, U. of Wis., 1925, U. of Tex., 1926-27; m. Margaret MacLaughlin, July 25, 1926; 1 dau., Mary Ann (Mrs. A.B. Plunkett). Began career as geologist at the Roxana Petroleum Corp., St. Louis, 1923; biology instr., Tex. A. and M. Coll., 1925-26; asso. Texas Bur. of Econ. Geology, Austin, Tex., 1926-27; geologist, later sr. geologist Cal. Co. and Standard Oil Co. of Tex., 1927-64; geological consultant, Midland, Texas, 1964-70. Mem. Am. Geophys. Union, Am. Assn. Petroleum Geologists (hon. mem.; pres. 1953), Geol. Soc. Am. (councilor, 1945-47), Soc. Econ. Paleontol. and Mineralogy, West Tex. Geol. Soc. (hon. life mem.; v.p. 1931, pres. 1940), Soc. Ind. Earth Scientists, Soc. Econ. Paleontologists and Mineralogists (hon. life), Sigma Xi. Unitarian. Interested in geology of Southwestern history. Home: Midland TX Died Sept. 29, 1970; buried Resthaven Meml. Park, Midland TX

ADAMS, LEVERETT ALLEN, prof. zoology; b. Lawrence, Kan., Sept. 23, 1877; s. James W. and Mary Jane (Pierson) A.; B.A., U. of Kan., 1903, M.A., 1906; PhD., Columbia U., 1914; m. Mary Louise Moss, Nov. 27, 1917; children—Leverett Allen, Virginia Louise, Mary Ladd. Mus. asst. U. of Kan., 1903-06; asst. prof. biology, State Teachers Coll., Greeley, Colo., 1906-14, head dept. biology, 1914-22; asst. prof. zool., U. of Ill., 1922-35, asso. prof., 1935-38; prof. zool. and curator Museum of Natural History, U. of Ill., 1938-48; now emeritus prof. Zool., emeritus curator, Museum Natural History. Fellow A.A.A.S.; mem. Soc. Ichthyologists and Herpetologists, Soc. of Zoologists, Asso. of Museums, Midwest Museums Asso., Acacia, Sigma Xi, Beta Theta Pi. Republican. Conglist. Author: Necturus, 1926; Introduction to Vertebrates, 1933; Adams and Eddy-Comparative Anatomy, 1949. Contbr. to jours. Home: 401 Vermont St., Urbana IL‡

ADAMS, LEWIS WHITAKER, economist, college adminstr.; b. Andrews, N.C., Apr. 8, 1904; s. Zala and Adaline (Whitaker) A.; B.S., U. N.C., 1925; Ph.D., Cornell, 1949; m. May Davidson, Dec. 31, 1929; children—Carol, Thomas, Hatcher. Instructor Cornell, 1925-26, 1930-31. Washington and Lee U., 1926-29, asst. prof., 1940-43, 1946-48, prof. econs., 1949-71, dean School of Commerce and Adminstrn., 1949-69; security analyst Holsapple & Co., N.Y. City, 1933-37, mgr. statistical dept., 1937-40. Served as adminstrv. officer Naval Tng. Schs., Harvard, 1943-44, Bur. Naval Personnel, Washington, 1944-45, exec. officer Field Adminstrn. Div., Bur. Naval Personnel, 1945-46. Mem. Am. Econ. Assn., Am. Finance Assn., Phi Kappa Sigma, Omicron Delta Kappa, Beta Gamma Sigma, Alpha Kappa Psi. Democrat. Presbyn. Home: Lexington VA Died Apr. 3, 1971; buried Lexington VA

ADAMS, LUTHER BENTLEY, educator; b. Angola, N.Y., Dec. 17, 1876; s. Charles W. and Laura A. (Bentley) A.; A.B., Brown U., 1900; spl. student Am. Sch. Classical Studies at Athens, Greece, 1906-7; m. M. Josephine Hall, of Waverly, N.Y., June 26, 1909. Instr. and vice-prin. Peddie Inst., Hightstown, N.J., 1901-4, 1905-6; instr. Dwight Sch., N.Y. City, 1904-5; instr., 1907-9, headmaster Jr. Sch., 1909-13, prin. since 1913, Shady Side Acad., Pittsburgh, Pa. Mem. Phi Beta Kappa, Kappa Sigma. Republican. Presbyn. Home: 5520 Avondale Pl., Pittsburgh PA‡

ADAMS, MALDON BROWNING, college pres.; b. Clarksburg, Harrison Co., W.Va., Sept. 29, 1869; s. John Browning and Martha Columbia (Holden); A.; student Broaddus Classical and Scientific Inst. Clarksburg, W.Va., 1888-90; Th.B., Southern Bapt. Theol. Sem., Louisville, Ky., 1893; D.D., Georgetown (Ky.) Coll., 1905, Bethel Coll., Russellville, Ky., 1911; LL.D., U. of Ky., 1916; m. Mae Marshall, of North Fork, Mason Co., Ky., June 4, 1895; children—Marshall Browning, Charles Dudley (dec.). Ordained Bapt. ministry, 1891; pastor Newcastle, Ky., 1891-93; Lewisburg Ch., North Fork, Mason Co., Ky., 1893-98, First Ch., Frankfort, Ky., 1898-1910; pres. Georgetown (Ky.) Coll. since June 15, 1913. Trustee Southern Bapt. Theol. Sem.; pres. Bapt. Young People's Union of Ky., 1899-1904; pres. Ky. Anti-Saloon League, 1900-07; corr. sec. Bapt. Edn. Soc. of Ky., 1910-13; asst. Moderator, Genl. Assn. of Baptists in Ky., 1909; pres. Ky. Bapt. Ministers' Meeting, 1910; pres. Ky. Assn. Colleges and Universities, 1914; chmn. Ky. Com. of Selection for Rhodes Scholars, 1913-28. Pres. Bapt. Edn. Soc. of Ky., 1918-22, v.p., 1922-27; pres. commn. on standardization and promotion of edn. bd. of Southern Bapt. Conv., 1923-28; pres. Southern Bapt. Edn. Assn., 1927-29. Mem. Ky. State Text Book Commn., 1923-24. Democrat. Home: Georgetown KY‡

ADAMS, NATHAN, banker; b. Pulaski, Tenn., Nov. 26, 1869; ed. Giles Coll.; m. Elizabeth Ardinger, Nov. 4, 1891 (dec.); 1 dau., Mrs. Frank N. Watson. Began as bank messenger boy, Pulaski; later in office Tex. & Pacific Ry., then clerk and cashier Exchange Bank; v.p. Am. Exchange Nat. Bank, later pres., until merged into First Nat. Bank in Dallas, of which is now honorary chmn. bd. Member bd. Nat. Credit Corp., 1931; pres. Tex. Bankers Assn., 1913-14; dir. of sales, Treasury Certificates, World War; mem. council Am. Bankers Assn., 1916-29; chmn. bd. Tex. Centennial Expn., 1936; same for Pan-American Expn., 1937; mem. Tex. World's Fair Com., 1938-39; v.p. and dir. Chamber of Commerce of U.S., 1931-36; mem. Home Owner's Loan Corp. Bd., 1932-33; dir. Southwestern Life Ins. Co., Republic Fire Ins. Co., Tex. Power and Light Co., Employer's Casualty Co., Murray Co., Tex. Short Line Ry. Co., Tex-O-Kan Flour Mills, Dallas Chamber of Commerce; dir. and pres. Dallas Clearing House Assn.; mem. Dallas Citizens Council; chairman of the board of trustees Texas Scottish Rite Hospital for Crippled Children; treasurer Texas Consistory and affiliated bodies, Scottish Rite; winner of Linz award for civic service, 1931. Episcopalian. Mason (33 deg., Shriner). Clubs: Brook Hollow, Ferndale. Home: 4604 Lakeside Drive. Office: 1401 Main St Dallas TX‡

ADAMS, NICHOLSON BARNEY, educator; b. 1895; A.B. (chemistry medal, English medal), Fredericksburg Coll., 1913; B.A. (Taylor scholar), Washington and Lee U., 1915, Litt. D., 1950; M.A., Columbia, 1920, Ph.D., 1922; student Universidad Central and Centro de Estudios Historicos, Madrid, Spain, 1922-23. Princ. Ottoman (Va.) High Sch., 1913-14; tchr. French and Spanish, Lynchburg (Va.) High Sch., 1915-17, 23-24; instr. French and Spanish, Columbia, 1920-22; prof. Spanish, U. N.C., from 1924; vis. prof. Spanish, U. Wis., 1940-41, summer 1945, U. Chgo., summer 1949, U. N.M., summer, 1950, Univ. of Ariz., 1966-67, Univ. of Texas, 1967-68, U. Ky., 1968-69. Served from sgt. to 2d lt. AEF, U.S. Army, 1917-19. Recipient prize Early English Text Soc. Mem. Modern Lang. Assn. Am., South Atlantic Modern Lang. Assn., Am. Assn. Tchrs. Spanish and Portuguese (president), Hispanic Society of America (corr. mem.), Royal Academy of Cordoba (corresponding). Author: The Romantic Dramas of Garcia Gutierrez, 1922; Brief Spanish Review Grammar, 1933; The Heritage of Spain, 1942; Espana, 1947. Editor: Don Juan Tenorio, 1931. Co-editor: Spanish Folktales, 1932; Popular Spanish Readings, 1932; El Abencerraje, 1942; Tales from Spanish America, 1944; Spanish for Today, 1964, others. Author articles, bibliographies, reviews. Address: Chapel Hill NC Died Oct. 2, 1970; buried Chapel Hill NC

ADAMS, OTTO VINCENT, engring. educator; b. Cadiz, O., Sept. 6, 1884; s. McNary Francis and Elizabeth (Cope) A.; B.S. in Civil and Irrigation Engring., Colo. State Coll. of Agr. and Mechanics, 1918; M.S.E., University of Mich., 1924; D.Sc., Colorado A. and M. Coll., 1945 m. Elsie M. Mathias, Dec. 22, 1909 (dec., 1945); m. 2d, Ada Vivian Johnson, Aug., 1947. Surveyor, Fort Collins, Colo., 1905-06; field asst., U.S. Reclamation Service, Mitchell, Neb., 1906-07, jr. engr., 1907-08; private practice of civil engring., Monte Vista, Colo., 1908-16; drainage engr. U.S. Dept. of Agr., Fort Collins, 1918; asst. commr. of works, Fort Collins., 1918; testing engr. and asso. prof. of civil engring., Colo. State Coll. of Agr. and Mechanics, 1919-27; asso. prof. of civil engring., Tex. Tech. Coll., Lubbock, Tex., 1927-32, prof. of civil engring., 1932-55, retired, dean engineering, 1932-49. Chmn. Northwest Texas Com. on Engineering, Science and Management War Training Asso. member Am. Soc. C.E. (v.p. Tex. sect.); mem. Soc. for Promotion Engring. Edn., South Plains Ret. Tchrs. Assn. (1st pres.), Lubbock Tech. Club, Tau, Beta Pi, Phi Kappa Phi. Presbyn. (elder emeritus). Mason (32 degree), Tex. Lodge Research (charter). Club: Kiwanis. Home: Lubbock TX Died Oct. 17, 1971; buried Lubbock TX

ADAMS, ROBERT MORTON, lawyer; b. N.Y.C., Jan. 16, 1900; s. Robert A. and Frances (Bennett) A.; M.E., Stevens Inst. Tech., 1921; LL.B., Fordham U., 1924; m. Mercedes M. Cullinan, June 19, 1937; children—Robert Morton, Richard Holbrook, Stephen Bennett, Mercedes Molyneux. Admitted to N.Y. bar, 1925; asso. firm Pennie, Edmonds, Morton, Taylor & Adams, and predecessor, 1921-30, partner, 1930-72. Trustee Norwalk (Conn.) Hosp., New Canaan (Conn.) Library. Served with USNRF, 1918-22. Mem. Am., N.Y. (bd. govs., officer 1938-41, 43-50, pres. 1946-47) patent law assns., Assn. Bar City N.Y. (exec. com. 1947-51), Pilgrims Soc., Alumni Assn. Stevens Inst. Tech. (pres. 1945-46), Beta Theta Pi, Delta Theta Chi. Roman Catholic. Clubs: University (N.Y.C.); New Canaan Country. Home: New Canaan CT Died Nov. 1972.

ADAMS, ROGER, educator; b. Boston, Jan. 2, 1889; s. Austin Winslow and Lydia (Curtis) A.; A.B., Harvard, 1909, A.M., 1910, Ph.D., 1912, D.Sc., 1945; D.Sc., Bklyn. Poly. Inst., 1935, Northwestern U., 1942, U. Rochester, 1943, U. Pa., 1947, Yale, 1948, Drexel Institute of Tech., 1955, University Ill., 1957. U. Bridgeport, 1960; LL.D., U. Mich., 1954; student U. Berlin. 1912-13, Kaiser Wilhelm Inst., 1913; m. Lucile Wheeler, Aug. 29, 1918; 1 dau., Lucile. Instr. organic chemistry Harvard U. and Radcliffe Coll., 1913-16: asst. prof. U. Ill., 1916-19, prof., 1919-57, head dept. chemistry and chemical engineering, 1926-54, research professor, 1954-57, emeritus prof., 1957-71. Dir. Champaign Nat. Bank. Mem. Ill. Bd. Natural Resources and Conservation, from 1942; mem. Nat. Inventors Council, 1945-63; dir. Council for Agrl. and Chemurgic Research, Nat. Sci. Found., 1954-60; mem. NDRC, 1941-46, scientific adviser to U.S. Deputy Military Governor Germany, 1945; chmn. sci. adv. com. U.S. Mil. Govt. Japan, 1947; mem. sci. adv. mission Japan, 1948. Trustee Battelle Meml. Inst., Sloan-Kettering Inst. Cancer Research; mem. bd. overseers Harvard, 1950-52. Commd. maj. CWS, 1918. Recipient (medals) Nichols, 1927, Gibbs, 1936. Cresson, 1944, Davy, 1945, Richards, 1946, Priestley, 1946, Hofmann, 1953, Midwest, 1953, Perkin, 1954, Parsons, 1958, Franklin, 1960, Am. Inst. Chemists, 1964, Nat. Medal of Sci., 1964; John R. Kuebler award, 1966; also the Northwestern University Centennial award, 1951. Decorated Medal for Merit (U.S.); hon. commander of civil div. Order Brit. Empire. Fellow A.A.A.S. (chmn. sect. C 1927, exec. com. 1941-45, 47-51, pres. 1950), Am. Inst. Chemists, Soc. Chem. Industry, Harvey Soc., German Chem. Soc.; mem. Internat. Union Pure and Applied Chemistry (v.p. 1951-55), Am. Chem. Soc. (dir. 1930-35, pres. 1935, chmn. bd. 1944-50), Am. Acad. Arts and Scis., Am. Philos. Soc., Nat. Acad. Scis. (council 1931-37, 59-62, chmn. chem. sect. 1938-41, fgn. sec. 1950-54); hon. mem. Chem. Soc. London, Societe Chimique de France, Polish, Swiss, Spanish, Japanese, Argentine chem. socs. Conglist. Author articles organic chemistry. Editor, Organic Reactions, 1941-68. Home: Urbana IL Died July 6, 1971; buried Mt. Hope Cemetery, Urbana IL

ADAMS, SUZANNE, operatic singer; b. Cambridge, Mass., 1873; d. John Gedney A.; musical edn., Paris; m. Leo Stern, violoncellist, Oct., 1898. Operatic debut as Juliet in Romeo and Juliet, in Paris, 1894, with the Maurice Grau Opera Co.; at Covent Garden, London, 1898 and 1901; Auditorium, Chicago, Nov., 1898; has appeared in leading operatic roles; was engaged for American season 1902; sang at state concerts, Buckingham Palace and Windsor Castle, and was presented by Queen Victoria with valuable brooches and bracelets as souvenirs; has sung at Covent Garden Opera and with the Maurice Grau Opera Co. for 5 successive seasons; at Covent Garden for the season of 1904; starred in concert tour in America. Address: Covent Garden Opera London*‡

ADAMS, WILLIAM II, c. of c. exec.; b. Birmingham, Ala., Aug. 6, 1922; s. Norwick Otho and Jocelyn Milner (Orr) A.; B.B.A., U. Tex., 1943; m. Betty Pollard, June 14, 1947; children—Lois Jocelyn, Nina Elizabeth, Kathryn Harriet, William Wright. Savs. and loan assn. exec., 1945-46; newspaper editor, Alice and Victoria, Tex., 1946-50; mgr. publicity dept. San Antonio C. of C., 1952-55; mgr. Pasadena (Cal.) C. of C., 1955-59; asst. gen. mgr. Los Angeles C. of C., 1959-61; exec. v.p. Seattle C. of C., 1961-70, Cleve. C. of C., 1970-73. Mem. faculty Western Inst. Orgn. Mgmt., U. Santa Clara. Chmn. editorial bd. Jour., pub. Am. C. of C. Execs., 1958-59; sec.-treas., 1963-64, pres., 1966-67; chmn. bd. regents Inst. Orgn. Mgmt., C. of C. U.S., 1965-66; v.p. Wash. State C. of C. Mgrs., 1963-68; pres. Greater Cleve. Growth Assn.; sec.-treas. Assn. Execs. Conf. Wash., 1963-70, Bd. dirs. Wash. State Internat. Trade Fair; mem. Seattle Traffic Assn., Gov. Wash. Com. Job Corps Commn. Served with USAAF, 1943-45, USAF, 1950-52. Fellow Acad. Orgn. Mgmt., U.S. C. of C.; mem. Pi Kappa, Alpha. Episcopalian (past vestryman, diocesan councilman). Clubs: Union, Country, Cleveland Racquet, Clevelander. Home: Pepper Pike OH Died Mar. 12, 1973.

ADANK, J. L., mfg. co. exec.; b. Chgo., June 24, 1907; s. John L. and Emma (Brangier) A.; student Loyola Acad., Loyola U.; m. Dorothy Wilbern. Formerly pres., chief exec. officer; later vice chmn., dir. Chemetron Corp., dir. Midwest Carbide Corp., Chemetron-Noury Corp., C.A. Gases Industriales de Venezuela, NCG Internat., C.A. Bd. dirs. Chemetron Found. Mem. Internat. Acetylene Assn. (dir., past pres.). Home: Chicago IL Died June 5, 1970.

ADERHOLD, OMER CLYDE, univ. pres.; b. Lavonia, Ga., Nov. 7, 1899; s. Joseph Peter and Mary Elizabeth (Farmer) A.; B.S.A., U. of Ga., 1923, M.S., 1930; Ph.D., Ohio State U., 1938; studied adult edn., Nova Scotia, 1939; LL.D., Mercer University, 1959; m. Bessie Parr, June 30, 1926; children—Elizabeth, Omer Clyde, Prin., Martin Inst., Jefferson, Ga., 1923-26; supt., Jefferson pub. schools, 1926-29; asso. prof. of edn. U. of Georgia, 1929-36, professor, 1936-46, dean of college of education, 1946-50, president, 1950-67 (part-time leave, 1942-44); director education panel Ga. Agrl. and Indsl. Development Bd., 1942-44; director state-wide survey of pub. edn. in Ga.; cons., state-wide survey in N.C., 1948-49; Mem. Southern Regional Conf. on Edn. for Grad. Study, Ga. Edn. Assn. (pres. 1949-50), Veterans Education Council of Georgia (vice chmn. 1946); mem. exec. com. National Commn. on Accrediting; mem. Southern regional edn. bd., Ga. Nuclear Adv. Commn.; mem. exec. com. Am. Council on Edn.; mem. Ga. Bapt. Edn. Com.; mem. Commn. on Instrn. and Evaluation, 1952-58; sr. participant Pres.'s Institute, Harvard; chairman plans and policies committee. Southern Regional Education Bd.; president Southern University Conference; mem. Ga. Sci. and Tech. Commn.; adv. council Ga. Dept. Edn.; planning and policy com. Ga. Dept. Vocational Rehab. Trustee Mercer U. Mem. Am. Assn. Land-Grant Colleges and State Univs. (exec. com.), Nat. Assn. State Univs. (exec. com.), So. Land-Grant Colls., Univs. (pres. 1954-55), Am. Council Edn. (dir.), Southeastern Conf. (pres. 1954-56), Gridiron, Blue Key, Sphinx, Beta Gamma Sigma, Alpha Kappa Phi, Alpha Zeta, Kappa Delta Pi, Phi Delta Kappa, Phi Kappa Phi. Democrat. Baptist (bd. deacons). Clubs: Capital City, Athens Country, Rotary. Editor of National Magazine for Teachers, 1939-40. Co-author: School Leaders Manual, 1946; Survey of Public Education of Less than College Grade in Georgia, 1947. Author bulletins on need for edn., pamphlets on pub. edn. in Ga.; contbr. articles to professional jours. Home: Athens GA Died July 4, 1969; buried Oconee Hills Cemetery, Athens GA

ADLER, CLARENCE, concert pianist; b. Cin., Mar. 10, 1886; s. Leopold and Rosa (Simon) A.; student Cin. Coll. Music, 1899-1905, Mus.D., 1938; student with Leopold Godowsky, Berlin, Germany, 1905; m. Elsa Richard, Apr. 25, 1916; 1 son, Richard. Founder, pianist N.Y. Trio, from 1919; soloist many leading orchestras U.S. and abroad. 1st Mozart Piano Concertos series in U.S., Town Hall, N.Y.C., 1942-43; pioneer broadcaster complete cycle chamber music works; mem. faculty Inst. Mus. Art (now Juilliard Sch.), from 1913; pvt. tchr. music, pupils include Aaron Copland, Walter Hendl, Doris Silbert, Paulina Ruvinska, Doris Pines, Jung Ho Kim, Amoram Rigai, Virginia LoFaro, Deanne Garcy, Suzanne Shades, Marcelita Kabayo, and others. Music editor G. Schirmer Co.; founder, dir Karinoke music camp, Lake Placid, N.Y.; pres., dir. Music Careers Inc. Mem. Beethoven Assn. Clubs: Lotos, The Bohemians. Contbr. Musical Courier, Musical America and others. Memorabilia at Library Congress, Washington. Home: New York City NY Died Dec. 24, 1969; buried Mt. Hope Cemetery, Hastings-on-Hudson NY

ADLER, FREYDA NACQUE, educator; b. N.Y.C.; d. Moritz and Rebecca (Margot) Pasternack; B.S., Columbia U., 1941; M.A., N.Y.U., 1968; 1 dau., Margot Susannah. Tchr. in charge of audio-visual edn., lit. and dramatics Bd. of Edn., N.Y.C., 1938-44; ednl. dir. Mutual Sta. KHBG, Okmulgee, Okla., 1944-45; dir. dramatics with U.S.O., Okmulgee, 1944-45; organizer, community Center for children on Martha's Vineyard, Mass., 1957; dist. film coordinator All Day Neighborhood Sch. P.S. 33 Manhattan, 1959-61, in charge of Operation Noon Canteen, P.S. 69 Manhattan, 1961-64, adminstr. paired schs. program, P.S. 191 and P.S. 199 Manhattan, 1964-70. Mem. exec. bd. Saturday Theatre for Children program of the All Day Neighborhood Schs. and Bur. Audio Visual Edn., N.Y.C. Bd. of Edn., 1963-70; bd. of adv. council for Children's Theatre of Am. Ednl. Theatre Assn.—children's theatre region 14. Author play, America's Heritage, 1941. Contbr. articles in field to profl. jours. Home: New York City NY Died Jan. 31, 1970.

ADLER, LEOPOLD, banker, merchant; b. Wolin, Czechoslovakia, June 10, 1861; s. Moses and Rosie (Fischl) A.; ed. common sch.; m. Hannah Guckenheimer, April 10, 1888; children—Rena Hannah (Mrs. Hugo I. Frank), Sam Guckenheimer, Melvin Leopold, Elsie H. (Mrs. M. Thomas Ackerland), Olga H. Pres. Chatham Bank & Trust Co. 25 yrs. until it consolidated with Savannah Bank & Trust Co., of which was chmn. bd., now dir.; pres. Pilot Navigation Co. for many yrs.; sr. mem. Leopold Adler (dept. store); dir. Ocean Steamship Co. and various corps. Chmn. Sinking Fund Commn., City of Savannah. Pres. Mickve Israel Congregation many yrs., now pres. emeritus; mem. exec. con. Am. Jewish Relief Com. Home: 1009 Whitaker St., Savannah GA*‡

ADRIAN, WILLIAM LAWRENCE, ret. bishop; b. Sigourney, Ia., Apr. 16, 1883; s. Nick and Mary (Paulus) A.; A.B., St. Ambrose Coll., Davenport, Ia., 1906, LL.D., 1939; S.T.L., North Am. Coll., Rome, Italy, 1911; student summer sessions, U. of Ia., 1914, 15. Mem. faculty St. Ambrose Coll., 1911-34, v.p. of coll. and prin. high. sch., 1935; pastor St. Bridget's Parish, Victor, Ia., 1935-36; bishop of Nashville, 1936-69; asst. at Pontifical Throne, 1961, ret., 1969. Address: Nashville TN Died Feb. 13, 1972; buried Calvary Cemetery, Nashville TN

AFFLECK, JAMES GELSTON, lawyer; b. Yonkers, N.Y., Dec. 15, 1892; s. James Gelston and Gertrude Louise (Burns) A.; Ph.B., A.M., Brown U., 1914; LL.B., Columbia, 1919; m. Francelia May Johnson, Sept. 11, 1918; children—James Gelston, May F. Admitted to N.Y. bar, 1919; asso. Masten & Nichols, 1919-31, Milbank, Tweed, Hope & Webb, 1931-33; became partner Milbank, Tweed, Hope & Hadley, 1934, now Milbank, Tweed, Hadley & McCloy. Dir. Milbank Meml. Fund, 1934-66. Served as 1st lt., inf., U.S. Army, 1917-18. Mem. Assn. Bar City N.Y., Am., N.Y. State bar assns. Home: Delray Beach FL Died Dec. 26, 1972.

AGAR, WILLIAM MACDONOUGH, geologist, author; b. N.Y. City, Feb. 14, 1894; s. John Giraud and Agnes Louise (Macdonough) A.; grad. The Newman Sch., Lakewood, N.J., 1912; B.S., Princeton, 1916; A.M., 1920, Ph.D., 1922; D.Sc. (honorary), Long Island Univ., 1967; m. Alida Stewart Carter, May 6, 1922 (dec. Mar. 1970); children—Alida Marie, Sylvia Carter, Catherine Macdonough, John Herbert Michael. Geologist Anaconda Copper Co., Butte, Mont., 1922-23; instr. in geology, Yale, 1923-26, asst. prof., 1926-28; asst. prof. of geology, Columbia, 1928-35; headmaster and trustee The Newman Sch., Lakewood, N.J., 1935-40; visiting lecturer in geology, Columbia U., 1940-41; sr. geol., U.S. Geol. Survey, 1942-45, gen. publicity (writing, radio) with Fight For Freedom, Inc., 1940-41; chmn. bd. Freedom House; with Dept. Public Information, United Nations, 1946-56; chmn. Met. region. American Assn. for the UN, 1956-59, chairman of the advisory committee, 1959, 60; chmn. Hampton chpt. A.R.C., 1960-63, treas. Southampton dist., from 1964; chmn. exec. council Southampton Coll.; chmn. Coll. Com. Eastern L.I., 1962-63. Author and lectr. Served as sous chef Service Sanitaire (Etats) Unis No. 16 (Am. Field Service), 1917; 1st lt. Air Service (pilot), U.S. Army, with A.E.F., 1917-18. Decorated Croix de Guerre (France). Mem. Geol. Soc. Am. Democrat. Roman Catholic. Club: Southampton (N.Y.). Contbr. articles on geology to tech. jours. Formerly mem. editorial advisor bd. and contributor articles and revs. to The Commonweal. Home: Southhampton NY Died June 10, 1972; buried Southampton NY

AGETON, ARTHUR AINSLIE, ret. naval officer, author, corp. exec.; b. Fromberg, Mont., Oct. 25, 1900; s. Peter Benjamin and Minnie Anna (Drummond) A.; student State Coll. Wash., 1918-19; B.S., U.S. Naval Acad., 1923; certificate, Naval Postgrad. Sch., 1931; M.A., Johns Hopkins, 1953; m. Jo Lucille Gallion, Nov. 24, 1933; children—Mary Jo, Arthur Ainslie. Commd. ensign USN, 1923, advanced through grades to rear adm., 1947, ret., 1947; ambassador to Paraguay, 1954-57; business rep. 1957-63. Decorated Legion of Merit, Bronze Star Medal (U.S.); Gran Cruz Orden Nacional del Merito (Paraguay). Mem. U.S. Naval Inst. Republican. Episcopalian. Clubs: Army and Navy, Army and Navy Country (Washington). Author: Dead Reckoning Altitude and Azimuth Table, 1932; Naval Officer's Guide, 1942; Naval Leadership and the American Bluejacket, 1944; Manual of Celestial Navigation, 1942; Mary Jo and Little Liu, 1945; The Jungle Seas, 1954; Admiral Ambassador to Russia (with Adm. William H. Standley), 1955; The Marine Officers Guide (with Gen. G. C. Thomas and Col. R. D. Heinl), 1955; Hit the Beach, 1961. Home: Annapolis MD Died May 1971.

AGNELLI, JOSEPH B., newspaper syndicate exec.; b. Brooklyn, Aug. 31, 1902; s. Bernard and Mary (Corno) A.; student Boys High Sch., 1916-18, Pace Inst., 1920-21; m. Muriel Nissen, June 1, 1929; children—Bernard F., Joseph B., Jr., Arthur C.; m. 2d, Robina Archibald. With Lehigh Valley Coal Sales Co., 1918-19, Frame Leaycraft & Co., 1919-21; joined Bell Syndicate, Inc., 1921, exec. v.p., gen. mgr., dir., until 1960; exec. v.p. gen. mgr., dir. Consol. News Features, Inc., McClure Newspaper Syndicate; exec. v.p., gen. mgr., dir. Asso. Newspapers, Inc., Women's News Service, North American Newspaper Alliance; secretary, member board directors Wheeler Development Corp. Author newspaper feature: Security Facts and Figures. Home: St Albans NY Died Apr. 1972.

AGNEW, GEORGE HARVEY, hosp. cons., physician; b. Toronto, Ont., July 26, 1895; s. John Henry and Mary (Law) A.; grad. Humberside Collegiate, Toronto, 1913; M.D., U. Toronto, 1918; post grad. student in N.Y., Vienna and London, Eng.; LL.D., Univ. Saskatchewan, 1955; m. Helen Moore Smith October 5, 1921 (died 1959); children—Phyllis Mary (Mrs. Russell Baldwin), Arnold Harvey Agnew; married 2d, Mary Ann Johnson, March 12, 1960. Intern Bellvue and Allied Hosps., N.Y.C., 1919-21; practice medicine, Toronto, 1921-27; dir. Dept. Hosp. Service and asso. sec. Canadian Med. Assn., 1928-45; exec. sec. Canadian Hosp. Council, now Canadian Hosp. Assn., 1931-50; editor The Canadian Hosp., 1938-50; partner Agnew, Peckham and Assos., hosp. cons., Toronto, 1950-71; prof. hosp. adminstrn. U. Toronto, 1947-71. Served with Canadian Army Med. Corps., World War I. Recipient George Findlay Stephens award for contbns. hosp. welfare Can. Hospital Association. Fellow A.C.P., Am. Coll. Hosp. Adminstrs.; mem. A.M.A., Am. (pres. 1938-39), Ontario (pres. 1954-55) hosp. assns., Am. Physicians Art Assn. (pres. 1946-47), Royal Canadian Inst. (pres. 1947-48), Assn. Univ. Programs in Hosp. Adminstrn. (pres. 1954), Am. Assn. Hosp. Cons. (pres. 1953-55), Alumni Fedn. U. Toronto (pres. 1931-32). Club: Granite. Home: Toronto Ontario Canada Died Sept. 1971.

AGNEW, PETER LAWRENCE, ednl. adminstr.; b. Lynn, Mass., May 17, 1901; s. Peter L. and Susan A. (Lydon) A.; B.B.A., Boston U., 1923; A.M., N.Y.U., 1928, Ph.D., 1940; Ed.M., Harvard, 1930. Adminstrv. asst. Merrill Bus. Sch., Stamford, Conn., 1924-26; head comml. dept. Orange (N.J.) High Sch., 1926-31; instr. N.Y.U., 1931, prof., 1948, asst. dean Sch. Edn., 1948-55, chmn. dept. bus. edn., 1955-60, budget coordinator, gen. asst. to chancellor, 1960-62, assistant executive vice president, 1962-64, v.p. bus. affairs, from 1964. Pres. bd. dirs. West Sq. Corp. Mem. Nat., Eastern (pres. 1940) bus. tchrs. assns., Nat. Assn. Bus. Tchr. Edn. Instns. (pres. 1948), Am. Assn. Sch. Adminstrs., Nat. Business Education Assn., Am. Bus. Edn. Assn., Internat. Soc. Bus. Edn. (internat. v.p., pres. American chapter), N.Y. Acad. Pub. Education (exec. bd. 1956-59), Nat. Office Mgmt. Assn. (dir. edn. activities N.Y. chpt. 1946-49, adv. council 1956-60), Phi Delta Kappa. Author: Business Filing, 1955; Office Machines Course, 1962; Clerical Office Practice, 1961; Key Driven Calculator Course—Advanced, 1962; Machine Office Practice, 1959; Secretarial Office Practice, 1960; Typewriting Office Practice, 1960; Key Driven Calculator Course, 1962; Rotary Calculator Course, 5th edit., 1963; Medical Office Practice, 1966. Home: New York City NY Died Sept. 1969.

AGNEW, WALTER D., college pres.; b. Littleton, Schuyler Co., Ill., Dec. 9, 1873; s. David and Margaret L. (Tucker) A.; A.B., Chaddock Coll., Quincy, Ill., 1897; A.B., Ill. Wesleyan U., 1901, D.D., 1906; S.T.B., Boston Univ., 1901; A.M., Columbia Univ., 1921, Ph.D., 1923; m. Mary J., d. Rev. B. W. Baker, late pres. Mo. Wesleyan Coll., Cameron, Mo., June 9, 1897. Ordained M.E. ministry, 1899; prof. 1902-05, pres. 1905-09, Mo. Wesleyan Coll.; dean Sch. of Theology, U. of Chattanooga, Tenn., 1909-11; pres. Hedding Coll., Abingdon, Ill., 1911-19; pres. Huntingdon Coll. (formerly Woman's Coll., of Ala.), 1922-38; retired June 1, 1938. Mem. Phi Delta Kappa. Methodist. Mason. Home: Montgomery AL‡

AGNON, SHMUEL YOSEF HALEVI, author; b. Buczacz, Poland, July 17, 1888; s. Shalom Mordecai and Esther (Farb-Hacohen) Czaczkes; ed. privately; m. Esther Marx, May 6, 1919; children—Emuna, Shalom Mordecai Hemdat. Lived in Galica, Poland, 1888-1907, in Palestine, 1907-13, in Germany, 1913-24, in Jerusalem, 1924-70. Recipient Israel prize (2), Bialik prize (2), Ussishkin prize, also Lit. prize N.Y.U.; fellow Bar-Ilan U.; D.Litt., Jewish Theol. Sem., A.; D.Phil. (hon.), Hebrew U.; named citizen of honour of Jerusalem; co-recipient Nobel prize for lit., 1966. Mem. Soc. Publn. Ancient Manuscripts (pres.). Author: Bridal Canopy; Both These and the Other Things; Upon the Handle of the Lock; A Wayfarer Staying the Night; In Times Past; Nigh and Visible; Thus Far; The Fire and The Wood; (anthology) Days of Awe; (collection writings divine revelation at Mt. Sinai) You Have Seen; Book, Author and Story; (posthumous) Shira, 1971; The City and All in it, 1973. Address: Jerusalem Israel Died Feb. 17, 1970; buried Mount of Olives, Jerusalem Israel

AHL, HENRY HAMMOND, painter; b. Hartford, Conn., Dec. 20, 1869; studied Royal Acad., Munich, Germany, under Alexander Wagner and Franz Stuck, landscape painting with Peter Paul Muller, and with Gerome, at Ecole des Beaux Arts, Paris (hon. mention twice); m. Eleanor I. Curtis, July 1902; 1 son, Henry Curtis. Exhibited at Nat. Acad. Design (New York); New York Water Color Club; Washington Art Club; Pa. Acad. Fine Arts; Boston Art Museum; Boston Art Club; Worcester Art Museum; Hartford Atheneum; Corcoran Gallery, Washington, D.C.; etc. Pictures on perm. exhbn. in Worcester (Mass.) Art Museum; Springfield Art Museum; Sweet Memorial, Portland, Me.; Whistler Memorial Home, Lowell, Mass.; Vanderpoel Art Assn. Collection, Chicago, Ill.; Wellesley (Mass.) Coll.; also represented in many private collections. Murals: 3 panels, Ch. of the Blessed Sacrament, Jamaica Plain, Boston; 14 panels, Ch. of the Blessed Sacrament, Providence, R.I.; 14 panels, Church of St. Michael, Providence. Portraits of the late Justice Moody of the Supreme Court of U.S.; the late Hon. David B. Henderson, speaker of Ho. of Rep. of U.S.; the late U.S. Senator Hoar. of Mass.; Pope Leo XIII; Monsignor Arthur T. Connolly; A.B. Wallace; etc. Mem. Conn. Acad. Fine Arts (Hartford), Artists Professional League, Am. Tree Assn., Mass. Hort. Soc., Am. Forestry Assn., Pi Gamma Mu.‡

AHLPORT, BRODIE E., judge; b. Kansas City, Mo., Apr. 1, 1898; s. August Frederick and Bessie (Olson) A.; A.B., U. Cal., 1922; postgrad. Harvard Law Sch., 1925-26; m. Margaret Boone Mennen, Feb., 1947; 1 son, Daniel. Admitted to Cal. bar, with firm O'Melveny, Tuller & Myers, 1928-39; practicing individually, Los Angeles, 1939-68; judge Superior Ct., 1957-68, ret., 1968. Mem., vice chmn. Cal. Code Commn., 1940-45. Regent, U. Cal., 1941-57; bd. dirs. Los Angeles Heart Assn., 1950-53. Served as pvt. U.S. Army, World War I. Mem. Cal. State Bar, Am., Los Angeles County bar assns., Phi Alpha Delta, Lambda Chi Alpha. Clubs: Lincoln, Los Angeles Athletic. Home: South Pasadena CA Died July 3, 1968; buried Forest Lawn Meml. Park Glendale CA

AHMANSON, HOWARD FIELDSTEAD, financial corp. exec.; b. Omaha, Neb., July 1, 1906; s. William H. and Florence (Hayden) A.; stu. U. Neb., 1923-25; B.S., U. So. Cal., 1927; LL.D., U. Neb., 1961; m. Caroline Leonetti, Jan. 14, 1965; 1 son, Howard F., Jr. Chmn. H. F. Ahmanson & Co., Inc., Los Angeles, 1927-68, Hollywood Savs. & Loan, 1940-45; vice pres., treas., dir. Victor Oil Co., 1930-40; pres. Nat. Am. Ins. Co., Omaha, 1943-52, chmn. bd., 1952-68; chmn. N.Am. Savs. & Loan, 1945-68, pres. Home Savings & Loan of Los Angeles, 1945-57, 64-68, chmn., 1946-68; pres., dir. Ahmanson Bank & Trust Co., Beverly Hills, 1957-58, chmn. bd., 1958-68; pres. chmn. So. Counties Title Ins. Co., 1958-68. Founder Ahmanson Found., 1952, pres., 1962-68. Vice chmn. Rep. state central com., 1954-56; nat. finance committeeman, Cal., 1955; chmn. host com. Cal., nat. conv., 1956. Pres. Otis Art Assos., 1956-60. Bd. directors Hollywood Boy's Club, 1941-50; member board govs. Otis Art Inst. Los Angeles County, Museum Assos.; trustee Kennedy Cultural Center for Performing Arts, 1963-68. U. So. Cal., Cal. Mus. Found., Los Angeles County Mus. Art; dir. All-Year Club So. Cal. Lt. USNR, 1943-45. Mem. U. Neb. Alumni, Am. Legion, Los Angeles World Affairs Council, Navy League U.S., Ocean Racing Fleet So. Cal., Phi Gamma Delta, Alpha Kappa Psi. Presbyn. Clubs: Stock Exchange, Jonathan, Economic Round Table, Los Angeles Yacht, Wilshire Country (Los Angeles); Newport Harbor Yacht, Newport Ocean Sailing Assn. (Newport Beach); Trojan, Santa Monica Yacht, Shadow Mountain, Shadow Mountain Golf; Eldorado Country (Palm Desert). Address: Los Angeles CA Died June 17, 1968; buried Forest Lawn Meml. Park, Glendale CA

AIKEN, EDNAH (MRS. CHARLES SEDGWICK AIKEN), writer; b. San Francisco, Calif., Sept. 7, 1872; d. Cornelius Preston and Ida Cornelia (Jarboe) Robinson; student Miss West's Sch., San Francisco, and U. of Calif.; m. Charles Sedgwick Aiken, Aug. 24, 1905 (now dec.); 1 son, Douglas Sedgwick. Education work U.S. Dept. of Labor, 1919-20; story and article writer for leading mags. and newspapers. Mem. P.E.N., League of Am. Penwomen. Clubs: Woman's City, Sequola, Women's Press (San Francisco). Author: The River, 1914; The Hate Breeders, 1916; The Hinges of Custom, 1923; If Today Be Sweet, 1923; Love and I, 1928; Snow, 1930. Home: 2335 Pacific Av., San Francisco CA‡

AIKEN, HOWARD HATHAWAY, educator, mathematician; b. 1900; B.S., Harvard; M.S., U. Wis.; Ph.D., U. Chgo.; Dr. Ing., Technische Hochschule, Darmstadt (Germany). Indsl. positions with Madison

Gas and Electric Co. (Wis.), also Westinghouse Electric Co.; faculty instr. physics and communication engineering Harvard, 1939-41, then asso. prof. and prof. applied math., 1941-61, dir. computation lab., from 1946, prof. emeritus, 1961-73; Distinguished Service prof. information tech. U. Miami (Fla.), 1961. Served to comdr. USNR, 1939-45. Decorated palmes de l'Acad. Francaise, chevalier Legion of Honor (France). Fellow Am. Acad. Arts and Scis.; mem. A.A.A.S., Econometric Soc. Address: Coral Gables FL Died Mar. 1973.

AIKEN, ROBERT LEON, accountant; b. Portland, Ore., Mar. 29, 1903; s. Jared Cyrus and Ella (Bach) A.; student Ore. Inst. Tech., 1929-30; U. Ore., 1930-31, U. Cal. at San Francisco, 1938-39. With Lybrand, Ross Bros. & Montgomery, Portland, 1929-37, San Francisco, 1937-48, Seattle, 1948-70, partner, 1954-70; cons. U. Wash. Sch. Bus. Administrn., 1950-55. C.P.A., Ore., Cal., Wash., Ill., La., Ga. Mem. Am. Inst. C.P.A.'s, Wash., Ore., Cal. socs. C.P.A.'s, Nat. Assn. Accountants, Inst. Internal Auditors. Conglist. (trustee). Mason (Shriner). Elk. Home: Seattle WA Died Mar. 19, 1970.

AIMES, HUBERT HILARY SUFFREN, sociologist; b. Martinstow, West Haven, Conn., Jan. 25, 1876; s. John Martin and Margaret Elizabeth (Thorton) A.; Ph.B., Sheffield Scientific Sch. (Yale), 1897; Ph.D., Yale, 1905; studied Columbia, 1906; sr. fellow, U. of Pa., 1907-09; m. Eloise Sorgen, of Kenton, O., Dec. 29, 1908; 1 son, Peter Martin. Asst. U.S. Naval Acad. Prep. Sch., 1899-1901; acting prof. history, Ursinus Coll., Collegville, Pa., 1905-06; tutor in history, Coll. City of N.Y., 1906-07; asso. prof. economics and sociology, 1914-16, prof. 1917-20, U. of South; prof. bus. administration, Syracuse U., 1920-22. Sec.-treas., 1917, pres., 1918, Sewanee Review. Mem. Alumni Advisory Council Yale Law Sch., Phi Gamma Delta, Sigma Xi. Author: History of Slavery in Cuba, 1907. Contbr. chapters to A. W. Knight's Lending a Hand in Cuba, 1915; articles on Negro Slavery in Spanish America and on anthropology. Mem. Am. Anthropol. Assn., Acad. Polit. Science; asso. mem. Ala. Anthropol. Soc. Home: West Haven CT‡

AINSWORTH, EDWARD MADDIN, newspaperman; b. Waco, Tex., June 7, 1902; s. Edward McCrea and Pearl (Maddin) A.; student Tex. A. & M. U., 1922-23; m. Katherine Lake, June 21, 1931; children—Sheila Beth, Cynthia Kate. Reporter, Waco (Tex.) News-Tribune, 1918-19; city editor San Pedro (Cal.) Pilot, 1920-21; telegraph editor Bakersfield (Cal.) Californian, 1921-22; state editor Atlanta Constitution, 1923-24; state editor, columnist Los Angeles Times, 1924-68, in charge editorial page 1941-46, feature writer, columnist, 1946-68. Bd. dirs. Kazanjian Found.; bd. govs. Los Angeles County Mus. Natural History. Asso. with So. Cal. hist. research groups. Fellow Am. Inst. Fine Arts; Mem. Death Valley '49ers (dir.), Zamorano Club, E Clampus Vitus. Republican. Author: Pot Luck, 1940; Eagles Fly West, 1946; California Jubilee, 1948; Western Barbecue Cook Book, 1949; Death Cues the Pageant, 1954; Painters of the Desert, 1960 (with Leo Carrillo) The California ILove, 1961; Beckoning Desert, 1962; Ernie Pyle's Southwest and Golden Checkerboard, 1964; Maverick Mayor, the Biography of Sam Yorty of Los Angeles, 1966; (documentary films) The Fallbrook Story, Freedom's Shores, 1952, The Man Who Shot the Devil, 1956; Cowboy in Art, 1968. Co-author: The California Story, 1950; In the Shade of the Juniper Tree; the life of Fray Junipero Serra, 1971. Contbr. to gen. mags. Home: Mecca CA Died June 15, 1968; interred El Camino Cemetery San Diego CA

AIRHART, JOHN C., former govt. ofcl.; b. Greencastle, Ind., July 4, 1916; s. Jesse Edgar and Bertha (Hovermale) A.; student Central Normal Coll., 1935-39; m. Dorotha A. Ford, Jan. 25, 1940. With Dept. Agr., 1940-42; with RFC, Washington, 1942-53, exec. asst. to gen. counsel, 1950-53; adminstrv. officer criminal div. Dept. Justice, 1953-58; asst. dir. Adminstrv. Office U.S. Cts., 1958-64; dep. asst. sec. def. Dept. Def., Washington, 1964-70; now ret. Home: Falls Church VA Died Sept. 1972.

AKERMAN, JOHN D., prof. of aeronautical engring.; b. Mitau, Courland, Latvia (then Russia), Apr. 24, 1897; s. David D. and Elizabeth J. (Ravovski) A.; grad. Aeronautical Sch., Imperial Tech. Inst., Moscow, 1917; student French aeronautical schs. at Avord, Pau, Cozeaux, 1917; B.S. in Aeronautics, U. of Mich., 1925, grad. student, 1927; m. Florence N. Simons, June 18, 1927. Came to U.S., 1918, naturalized, 1925. Engr. Stout-Ford All-Metal Aircraft, Detroit, Mich., 1925-27; designer Guggenheim Aeronautical Lab., U. of Mich., 1927-28; chief engr. in charge of design and construction all-metal transport sea and land planes, Hamilton Metalplane Co., Milwaukee, 1927-28, chief engr., developing New Pinto, low wing, monoplane and Mohawk-twin motored, low wing cabin plane capable of sustaining flight on one engine, Mohawk Aircraft Corp., Minneapolis, 1928-29; asso. prof. of aeronautical engring., U. of Minn., 1929-30, prof. and head of dept. 1931-59, in charge U. Minn. Supersonic Labs., Rosemont, Minn., from 1946; cons. Madaras Rotor Power Plant, charge design and supervision of constrn. of exptl. rotar, 1933; con. for Porterfield Aircraft & Engring. Corp., Kansas City, Missouri, Boeing Aircraft Corp., Seattle, Wash., 1940, Strato Equipment Co., Minneapolis, Minn., 1940-45; for Minneapolis Honeywell Regulator Co., 1942; official investigator Nat. Defense Research Council, 1942; commr. of Aeronautics for Minn., 1934-37; A.A.F. tech. representative in Europe, summer, 1945. Served as 2d lt. Engring. Corps (Aviation), Imperial Russian Army, 1916; pilote de chasse, French Army, 1917. Mem. Nat. Aeronautics Assn. (gov., Minn. 1939); Soc. for Promotion Engring. Edn., Am. Assn. Univ. Profs., Iota Alpha; Fellow Inst. of Aeronautical Sciences (mem. advisory board); fellow Royal Aero. Soc. (London), Sigma Xi, Tau Omega. Lutheran. Clubs: U. of Minn. Flying; Engineers (Minneapolis); University (St. Paul). Contbr. articles on aeronautical engineering, liquid oxygen use and the stratosphere to jours. Inventor Polio-traciatomy collar. Home: Minneapolis MN Died Jan. 8, 1972; buried Crystal Cemetery, Minneapolis MN

AKERS, MILBURN PETER, college pres.; b. Chicago, Ill., May 4, 1900; s. Edwin Wright (D.D.) and Anna May (Wilson) A.; A.B., McKendree Coll., 1925; hon. degrees Ill. Wesleyan U., 1952, Otterbein Coll., Fla. So. Coll., Ill. Coll., Lincoln Coll., Shimer Coll., St. Procopius Coll., So. Ill. U.; married Beulah M. McClure, Oct. 3, 1925; 1 dau., Judith Ann. Reporter St. Louis Post Dispatch, 1923-27, telegraph editor Ill. State Register, Springfield, 1927-30, Associated Press, Chicago, 1930-33, Springfield, 1933-34, Washington, D.C., 1934-37; supt. of reports, State of Illinois, 1937-39; exec. sec., Illinois Development Council, 1937-39; asst. to sec. of interior, 1939-41; with Chicago Sun and Chicago Sun-Times 1941-65, successively polit. and editorial writer, mng. editor, exec. editor, 1941-59, editor of Chicago Sun-Times, 1959-65; exec. dir. Fedn. Ind. Ill. Colls. and Univs., 1966-68; pres. Shimer Coll., Mt. Carroll, Ill., 1968-70. Trustee McKendree Coll., Lebanon, Ill., St. Xavier Coll,. Chgo. Mem. Sigma Delta Chi, Am. Soc. Newspaper Editors. Mason. Methodist. Clubs: Mid America (Chgo.). Home: Evanston IL Died May 27, 1970.

AKERS, OSCAR PERRY, prof. mathematics; b. Trenton, Mo., June 16, 1872; s. James and Eliza E. (Kackley) A.; A.B., U. of Colo., 1900, A.M., 1902; Ph.D., Cornell U., 1905; Gottingen U., 1913-14; m. Ella M. Tarr, July 16, 1896. Student Engring. Sch. U. of Colo., 1900-01; Oliver scholar, Cornell U., 1902-04; asst. in Dept. of Mathematics, same, 1904-05; asst. prof. mathematics, 1905-07, prof., 1907-1942, Allegheny Coll. (sec. of faculty 1918-1942), retired 1942; on leave of absence to study and travel in Europe, 1913-14. Mem. Am. Math. Soc., A.A.A.S., Circolo Matematico di Palermo, Sigma Xi, Omicron Delta Kappa, Delta Tau Delta. Contbr. to mags. and periodicals on math, topics. Home: R.D. 2, Meadville PA‡

ALBAUGH, GEORGE SYLVANUS, mfr.; b. Johnson Co., Mo., Aug. 30, 1871; s. Jacob Preston and Rebecca (Petry) A.; student Earlham Coll., (Richmond, Ind.), Ohio Northern U., Ada., O.; m. Mabel Harvey, of Jacksonville, Fla., Apr. 25, 1917. Teacher in pub. schs. 5 yrs.; sales mgr. for Powers, Higley & Co. 2 yrs.; associated with brother and O. T. Dover and founded the Albaugh-Dover Co., mfrs. cream separators, washing machines, etc.; founder Western Thread Co. (Elgin, Ill.), The Northfield Co. (Sheboygan, Wis.). Republican. Methodist. Clubs: Berwyn, Union League, Riverside Golf. Office: Chamber of Commerce Bldg., Los Angeles CA‡

ALBER, DAVID O., publicity, pub. relations; b. Brooklyn, Apr. 15, 1909; s. Samuel and Dora (Uhlber) A.; m. Doris Edelman, June 7, 1936; children—Michael, Emily. Pres. David O. Alber Assos., Inc.; dir. Spot News Syndicate, Radio-TV News Syndicate; writer column In the Spotlight, syndicated in 200 newspapers, since 1941; publicity and pub. relations for personalities, cos. products; writer radio, TV, movies, recordings, stage; pres. CFC Industries, Inc.; dir. CFC Funding, Incorporated. Director Camp Loyaltown; trustee Optometric Center of N.Y.; chairman of Safety Council, New Rochelle, N.Y. Mem. Am. Television Soc., American Pub. Relations Assn. (v.p.; chpt. dir.), Am. Soc. Travel Agents, Travel Writers Assn., T-Radio Executives Soc., Public Relations Society of America. Clubs: Publicity (dir.) (N.Y.C.); Friars; Mamaroneck Beach and Yacht. Author: Public Died Dec. 31, 1968; buried Sharon Gardens, Walhalla NY

ALBERS, GEORGE, b. Lingen, Prov. of Hanover, Germany, Mar. 12, 1872; s. Herman and Theresa (Voss) A.; ed. in Germany; m. Eva Manning, of Portland, Ore., 1907; 1 dau., Genevieve Gertrude. Came to U.S., 1892, naturalized citizen, 1897. In cereals, flour, grain and feed business since 1895; pres. Albers Bros. Milling Co., Albers Investment Co. Republican. Catholic. Clubs: Rainier, Arctic, Press, China. Address: Stuart Bldg., Seattle WA‡

ALBERT A(BRAHAM) ADRIAN, educator; b. Chicago, Ill., Nov. 9, 1905; s. Elias Albert and Fannie (Fradkin) A.; B.S., U. of Chicago, 1926, M.S., 1927, Ph.D., 1928; LL.D. (honorary), Notre Dame, 1965; Sc.D. (honorary), Yeshira University, 1968; L.H.D., U. Ill., Chgo., 1971; m. to Frieda Davis, December 18, 1927; children—Alan Davis, Roy M. (dec.), Nancy Elizabeth Fellow Nat. Research Council, Princeton, N.J., and Chicago, 1928-29; instr. in mathematics, Columbia U., 1929-31; asst. prof. mathematics, U. of Chicago, 1931-36; associate professor mathematics, 1936-41, prof. mathematics, 1941-72, chmn. dept., 1958-62, dean, division of physical sciences, 1962-71, Eliakim Hastings Moore Distinguished Service Prof., 1960; asso. dir. applied math. group Northwestern U., 1945-46; with Institute for Advanced Study, Princeton, 1933-34; visiting professor University of Brazil, Rio de Janeiro U. Buenos Aires, 1947, U. So. Cal., 1950; Yale, 1956-57, U. Cal. at Los Angeles, 1958; cons. Nat. Security Agy., Dept. Def., IBM Corp., U.S. Office Edn., 1963-66, Inst. for Defense Analyses. Member of the com. div. math., phys., engring. scis. Nat. Sci. Found., 1952-54; mem. gen. scis. panel Dept. of Def.; chmn. div. math. NRC, 1952-55; chairman sect. math. Nat. Acad. Scis., 1958-61; dir. communications research div. Inst. for Defense Analyses, 1961-62, trustee; until 1972; trustee Inst. for advanced Study. Recipient Cole prize for outstanding research in algebra, 1939. Fellow of American Academy Arts and Scis., member National Academy Science, Am. Math. Soc. (pres. 1965-66), Internat. Math. Union (v.p.), Math. Assn. Am., Acad. Scis. Buenos Aires, Brazilian Acad. of Sciences (corr. mem.), Phi Beta Kappa, Sigma Xi. Club: Quadrangle (Chicago). Author: Modern Higher Algebra, 1936; Structure of Algebras, 1939; Introduction to Algebraic Theories, 1940; College Algebra, 1941; Solid Analytic Geometry, 1947; Fundamental Concepts of Higher Algebra, 1957; (with R. Sandler) An Introduction to Finite Projective Planes, 1968; Tensor Products of Quaternion Algebras, 1972. Editor Bull. of Am. Math. Soc., 1939-43. Transactions of Am. Math. Soc., 1943-49. Colloguum Publs., 1951-57. Mathematical Surveys 1941-45. Home: Chicago IL Died June 6, 1972; buried Chicago IL

ALBERT, ALLEN DIEHL, sociologist; b. Williamsport, Pa., Oct. 3, 1874; s. Allen D. and Sarah Ann (Faber) A.; ed. pub. schs.; read law in offices of Heber J. May; attended lectures in law and polit. science, Columbian (now George Washington) U.; spl. lecturer depts. of English and polit. science, U. of Minnesota, 1912-14; Sc.D. in Sociology, Evansville Coll., Evansville, Ind., 1922; m. Janet Clark Jones, June 20, 1901; children—Maj. Allen D., Maj. Owen S.J. Reporter, Washington, D.C., and N.Y.; corr. in Spanish-Am. War; author critiques on graphic arts, music and theatre, various mags.; newspapers, Washington, D.C. and N.Y.C., 1898-1902. Chief editorial writer Washington (D.C.) Times, 1895-1910; pub. Columbus (Ohio) News, 1910-11; editor and associate pub. Minneapolis Tribune, 1912-16; vice-chairman Minn. State Art Commission, 1913-16; pres. Jacksonville (Fla.) Gas Co., 1923-25; assistant to president Century of Progress Exposition, Chicago, 1928-33, rep. to many European Capitals, 1929-30, commr. to Japan and China, 1932. Specializing since 1906 in causes of city growth and programs of city development; consultant to city development bodies, with commns. on training camp activities, 1917-18. Mem. National Committee on World Peace Organization, National Educational Planning Committee, etc.; pres. Minn. Acad. Political Science, 1914-15; pres. International Association Rotary Clubs, 1915-16; consultant to American delegation, United Nations Conference San Francisco, June 1945. Fellow American Geog. Society. Author many magazine articles on city planning, social change, etc. Episcopalian. Awarded silvercross for outstanding Christian Leadership, by Seabury-Western Episcopalian Sem., Evanston, Ill., 1938; lecturer many institutes on internat. affairs. Director Sheldon Swope Art Gallery, Terre Haute, Ind., 1941. Home: Blue Heron Farm, Paris IL‡

ALBERT, ALLEN DIEHL, JR., sociologist, historian; b. Washington, D.C., Apr. 27, 1902; s. Allen Diehl and Janet Clark (Jones) A.; student DePauw U., 1920-21; Ph.B., U. of Chicago, 1924, M.A., 1932, Ph.D., 1936; student Harvard Grad. Sch. Bus. Adminstrn., 1926-27; m. Emily Bartlett Davis, Sept. 6, 1934; 1 stepdaughter, Emily Carson (Mrs. Albert Hanahan). Employee, Jacksonville (Fla.) Gas Co., 1925, Evanston (Ill.) News-Index, 1927-28, Century of Progress Expdn., Chgo. 1928-29; prof. Old Testament and Semitic Langs., Seabury-Western Theol. Sem., Evanston, 1932-41; ordained deacon, Episcopalian Ch., 1938, priest, 1939; prof. sociology, Emory U., since 1946, chairman of division of social science, 1947-48, on leave as pub. relations mgr. Lockheed Aircraft Corp., Ga. div., since 1951. Hon. canon, Cathedral of St. Philips', Atlanta since 1948. Consultant to advisory committee of State Board of Health on Hospital Locations since 1950; chairman Local Govt. Commn., Atlanta and Fulton County. Captain to lt. col., Inf., U.S. Army, 1941-46; aide-de-camp to Gen. Omar N. Bradley, Maj. Gen. Leven C. Allen, 1941-42; asst. exec. officer to Maj. Gen. Fred L. Walker and Maj. Gen. John W. O'Daniel, all at Fort Benning Inf. Sch., Office Strategic Services, 1944; lt. col. Inf., U.S. Army Reserve. Mem. bd. Ga. Citizens Council, 1946-49, Atlanta Housing Authority (vice-chairman), Met. Planning Commission of Atlanta 1946-50, Community Planning Council, 1946-49, Commn. on Crime and Delinquency, Y.M.C.A. Commission on Boys' work. Greater Atlanta Area Greater Atlanta Chamber of Commerce, 1948-49, 52-53, Jr. League Sch. Speech Correction, 1946-52, Nat. Conference of Christians and Jews (Atlanta chpt.), Ga. Cooperative Services for the Blind. Mem. Army Adv. Com. of Greater Atlanta, Travelers' Aid Soc. Mem. Soc. of Planning Officials, Nat. Assn. of Housing ofcls., Pub. Relations Soc. Am. (pres. Atlanta chapt. 1952), Ga. Rose Soc., Am., So. social socs., Ga. Acad. Social Sciences, Ga. Ednl. Assn. Beta Theta Pi, Kappa Phi Kappa, Alpha Phi Omega. Democrat. Episcopalian. Clubs: Capital City, Rotary (award for contbn. to city, 1951). Author articles and papers on ancient Oriental cities; population studies of southeastern cities; delinquency and the family. Specializes in city studies. Author of law, Plan of Improvement, 1952. Elected life mem. for civic leadership, Atlanta Jr. C. of C., 1951. Home: Atlanta GA

ALBERT, CALVIN DODGE, mech. engr.; b. White Haven, Pa., Nov. 17, 1876; s. Frank Henry and Ella (Wood) A.; Poly. Inst., Brooklyn, 1896-97; Media (Pa.) Acad., 1897-98; M.E. Cornell U., 1902; m. Claudia Louise Agnew, July 5, 1905. In charge machinery design, Columbia Iron Works, St. Clair, Mich., 1902-03; designer Great Lakes Engring. Works, Detroit, 1903-04; with Cornell U. since 1904, prof. mach. design 1916-44, also head department of machine design, professor emeritus since July 1944. With U.S. Shipping Board Emergency Fleet Corporation, June 1917-Aug. 1919; chief supervising insp. Middle Atlantic Dist., later chief insp., sr. engr. and exec. asst., in charge tech. dept. steel ship constrn. Mem. Am. Soc. M.E., Am. Gear Mfrs. Assn., Sigma Xi. Co-Author: Kinematics of Machinery. Author: Machine Design Drawing Room Problems. Home: 205 Eddy St., Ithaca NY‡

ALBERTY, (BERNARD) HAROLD, educator; b. Lockport, N.Y., Oct. 6, 1890; s. Willard K. and Carrie L. (Post) A.; Ph.B., Baldwin U., 1912; LL.B., Cleveland Law Sch., 1913; A.M., Ohio State U., 1923, Ph.D., 1926; informal work with John Dewey, Columbia Tchrs. Coll., 1928; m. Anna Hower, Aug. 24, 1916 (dec.); 1 dau., Anna Elizabeth (Mrs. Allen Edwards) (dec.); m. 2d, Elsie June Stalzer, Dec. 11, 1954; 1 dau., Carole Lynn. Rural sch. tchr., Medina County, O., 1908-09; tchr. Berea, O., 1911-13, asst. high sch. prin., 1913-15, supt. schs., 1915-17; dist. supt. schs. Cuyahoga County, O., 1917-20, asst. county supt., 1920-24; mem. faculty Ohio State U. 1924-59, prof. edn. 1931-59, research asso., bur. ednl. research, 1936-37, dir. U. Sch., 1938-41, curriculum cons., 1941-45; vis. prof. U. Wash., summer 1932, U. Hawaii, 1 semester, 1935-36, U. So. Cal., summer 1949, 55, Emory U., winter 1945; instr. history edn., sch. law Baldwin-Wallace Coll., 2 summers. Supervisor tchr. tng. Ohio State Dept. Edn., 1927-28; curriculum cons. Commn. Tchr. Edn., 1940-41; State Dept. Mission to Berlin, Germany, 1953. Admitted to Ohio bar, 1913. Recipient Shatluck Sch. Centennial award for advancement secondary edn., 1958, merit award Baldwin-Wallace Coll., 1970, Centennial Achievement award Ohio State U., 1970. Mem. N.E.A., Am. Edn. Fellowship, Assn. Supervision and Curriculum Development (chmn. com. prep. core tchrs.), Am. Assn. U. Profs., Nat., Ohio assns. high sch. prins., John Dewey Soc. (bd. dirs., award for service to edn. 1971), Nat. Assn. Coll. Tchrs. Edn., Phi Delta Kappa. Author: Supervision in the Secondary School (with V. T. Thayer), 1931. Editor: (With B. H. Bode) Educational Freedom and Democracy, 1938. Reorganizing the High-School Curriculum, 1947. Contr.: Democracy in the Administration of Higher Education, 1950. Mem. bd. editors Ednl. Adminstrn. and Supervision since 1946. Contbr. articles ednl. jours. Ednl. recording: The Core Program in the High School, 1951. Home: Columbus OH Died Feb. 2, 1971.

ALBERY, BRONSON JAMES, theatre dir.; b. Greenhithe, Kent, Eng., Mar. 6, 1881; s. James and Mary (Moore) A.; B.A., Balliol Coll., Oxford; m. Una G. Rolleston, 1912; 2 sons 2 daus. Barrister-at-law; chmn. Theatres War Service Council, 1942-46; joint adminstr. Old Vic and Sadler's Wells, 1942-44; chmn. Old Vic Trust, 1951-59; mng. dir. Wyndham Theatres, Ltd., 1925-62, chmn., 1962-65. Pres. Soc. West End Theatre Mgrs., 1941-45, 52-53; gov. Old Vic; mem. Exec. Arts Council of Gt. Britain, chmn. Drama Panel, 1948-52. Served with Royal Navy Vol. Res., 1917-19. Created Knight; decorated chevalier Legion d'Honneur. Address: London England Died July 21, 1971.

ALBRIGHT, FULLER, physician; b. Buffalo, N.Y., Jan. 12, 1900; s. John Joseph and Susan (Fuller) A.; A.B., Harvard, 1921, M.D., 1924; Doctor of Science (honorary), Harvard, 1955; m. Claire Birge, May 20, 1932; children—Birge, Read Ellsworth. Asst. resident in medicine, Johns Hopkins Hosp., 1927-28; inst. medicine, Harvard Med. Sch., 1930-35, asso. instr., 1935-38, asst. prof., 1938-42, asso. prof., from 1942; physician at Mass. Gen. Hosp., from 1939. Commd. 2d lt. inf., World War I. Mem. Alpha Omega Alpha, Assn. Am. Physicians, Assn. Studies on Internal Secretions, Am. Soc. of Clin. Investigation, Nat. Acad. Sci., Am. Acad. Arts and Scis., Phi Beta Kappa. Clubs: Delphic, Aesculapian, Interurban, Peripatetic. Contbr. of articles in various med. jours. Home: Brookline MA Died Dec. 8, 1969.

ALBRIGHT, GUY HARRY, coll. prof.; b. Lamar, Mo., Dec. 17, 1876; s. John Albert and Abbie Carolyn (Bailey) A.; Ph.B., U. of Mich., 1899; B.A., Harvard, 1900, M.A., 1913; studied Brooklyn Poly. Inst., 1905-07; D.Sc., Colorado College, 1932; m. Aura Marguerite Smith, June 27, 1901; 1 son, Preston Bailey. With Colorado Coll. since 1907, prof. mathematics and astronomy since 1914; dir. Colorado Coll. Summer Sch.; exchange lecturer to Harvard, 1913. Mem. Math. Assn. America, Am. Assn. Univ. Profs., Phi Gamma Delta. Conglist. Club: Harvard. Writer of numerous articles on coll. adminstrn. Home: 1120 N. Tejon St., Colorado Springs CO‡

ALBRIGHT, JACOB DISSINGER, author; b. Lancaster Co., Pa., Jan. 29, 1870; s. Martin and Leah (Dissinger) A.; ed. Albright Coll., Pa., 2 yrs.; grad. Medico-Chirurg. Coll., Phila., M. D., 1893; m. Nov. 28, 1895, Florence Mae Kimes. Contb'r to med. mags. Author: The General Practitioner as a Specialist, 1900 A7. Editor of Albright's Office Practitioner, med. mag. Address: 900 N. 48th St., Philadelphia PA‡

ALBRIGHT, WILLIAM FOXWELL, orientalist; b. Coquimbo, Chile, May 24, 1891; s. Rev. Wilbur Finley and Zephine Viola (Foxwell) A.; A.B., Upper Ia. U., 1912, Ph.D., Johns Hopkins University, Baltimore, 1916, LL.D. (honorary), 1964; Litt.D. (hon.) Upper Ia., 1922, Yale, 1951, Georgetown U., 1952, U. Dublin, 1953, Loyola College, Balt., 1958; Loyola University, Chicago, 1960, Lake Erie College, 1966; D.H.L., Jewish Theol. Sem. in America, Jewish Inst. Religion, 1936, Hebrew Union Coll., 1948, Coll. Jewish Studies, Chgo., 1950; Th.D., U. Utrecht (Netherlands), 1936, U. Uppsala (Sweden), 1952; D. hon. caus., U. Oslo (Norway) 1946; LL.D., Boston Coll., 1947, U. St. Andrews, Scotland, 1949, Franklin and Marshall Coll., 1953; D.Phil., Hebrew U., Jerusalem, 1957; D.C.L., Pace Coll., 1957; Pd.D., La Salle Coll., 1958; Litt.D., Harvard U., 1962; L.H.D., Manhattan Coll., 1961, Colby Coll., 1966, Dropsie College, 1967, Yeshiva, Univ., 1969; H.H.D., Wayne State University, 1961, Brigham Young U., 1962; m. Ruth Norton, August 31, 1921; children—Paul N., Hugh N., Stephen Foxwell, David Foxwell. Acting dir. Am. Sch. Oriental Research, Jerusalem, 1920-21, dir. 1921-29, 33-36; W. W. Spence prof. Semitic langs. Johns Hopkins, 1929-58, emeritus, 1958-71; research prof. Jewish Theol. Sem. Am., 1957-59; dir. archeol. expdn., Palestine, 1922-34, mem. U. Cal. African Expdn., Sinai, 1947-48; chief archeologist S. Arabian Expdn., Am. Found. Study Man, 1950-51; pres. Palestine Oriental Soc., 1921-22, 34-35; Am. mem. consultative com., Internat. Congress Orientalists, 1931-48; pres. Am. Oriental Soc., 1935-36; 1st v.p. Am. Schs. of Oriental Research. from 1937. Mem. Am. Council of Learned Societies (vice chairman of the council 1939, recipient 10,000 prize 1961), Am. Philos. Soc. (v.p. 1956-59), Archeol. Inst. Am. (v.p., 1949) Soc. Bibl. Lit. (pres. 1939), Linguistic Soc. Am. (v.p. 1941), Internat. Orgn. Old Testament Scholars, (pres. 1956-59), Nat. Acad. Scis., Royal Danish, Flemish & Irish Acads.; corr. mem. Institut de France & Austrian Acad. Scis.; fellow Am. Acad. Arts & Scis., German Archeol. Inst.; hon. or corr. mem. many other tech. profl. socs. Author over 800 publs. on archeol., Bibl. and oriental subjects, including: The Excavation of Tell Beit Mirsim, 1932-43; From the Stone Age to Christianity, 1940; Archaeology of Palestine, 1949; History, Archaeology and Christian Humanism, 1964; Yahweh and The Gods of Canaan, 1968. Sr. editor: Anchor Bible, from 1956. Home: Baltimore MD Died Sept. 19, 1971.

ALBRIZIO, HUMBERT, sculptor; b. N.Y.C., Dec. 11, 1901; s. Alfonso and Angela (Rainmondi) A.; student Beaux Arts Inst. Design, 1918-27, New Sch. Social Research, 1930-31; m. Sonia Rösova, Mar. 29, 1930. Work rep. Walker Art Center, Mpls., U.S. Post Office, Hamilton, N.Y., State U. Ia., Joslyn Art Mus., Worcester Mus. Art, Ia. State Tchrs. Coll., U. Wis., Springfield (Mo.) Mus. Art, Montclair (N.J.) Coll., Colby Coll., Watertown, Me., Denver Art Mus., Ariz. State Coll., Des Moines Art Center, Cedar Rapids (Ia.) Art Gallery, Davenport (Ia.) Municipal Gallery, Huntington (W.Va.) Galleries, Art Mus., Iowa City; exhbns. include Mus. Modern Art, Whitney Mus. Am. Art, Nat. Acad. Design, Carnegie Inst., Pa. Acad. Fine Arts, Albany (N.Y.) Inst. History and Art, Art Inst. Chgo., Walker Art Center, Mpls., U. Neb.; prof. sculpture State U. Ia., 1942-67. Recipient award Walker Art Center, 1945, 46, 51, Des Moines Art Center, 1946-60, Denver Mus. Art, 1947, Audubon Artists, 1947, Joslyn Art Mus., 1949; recipient Arts and Humanities award Nat. Found. Arts and Humanities, 1967. Mem. Nat. Soc. Sculptors, Audubon Artists, Sculptors Guild. Home: San Diego CA Died May 1, 1970; cremated.

ALCIATORE, ROY LOUIS, restaurateur; b. New Orleans, Dec. 19, 1902; s. Jules Louis and Marie Althea (Roy) A.; student St. Aloysius Coll., New Orleans, 1913-17, Spring Hill Coll., Mobile, Ala., 1917-18, Chenet Inst., New Orleans, 1918-19, Tulane U., 1919; m. Mary Pearl Duggan, Apr. 9, 1932; 1 dau., Yvonne Elaine; m. 2d, Mrs. Fred N. Blount, Jr. Was an apprentice restaurant worker Pension Alciatore, New Orleans, 1920-23; continued studies in famous restaurants, France, 1923-30; mgr. Antoine's (founded by grandfather in 1840, formerly Pension Alciatore, 1930, proprietor); bd. commrs. New Orleans Pub. Belt R.R. Mem. Mardi Gras carnival orgns., also New Orleans Conv. and Visitors Bur. Bd. curators La. State Mus., 1937-41. Served as warrant machinist USCG. Decorated Grand Officer de la Confrerie du Tastevin (Nuits-Saint-Georges, France). Recipient Chevalier du Merite Touristique, France. Recipient Chevalier Du Merite Commercial, France. Mem. New Orleans Assn. Commerce (mem. council), La. Restaurant Assn. (pres. 1937), Wine and Food Soc. of London, Les Amis D'Escoffier Soc., New Orleans Sous Commanderie de Bordeaux, Gourmet Soc. of N.Y., Holy Name Soc., Internat. Mission Radio Assn., La Societe des Escargots Orleanais. Clubs: Young Men's Business, Southern Yacht, New Orleans Athletic, Bienville. Home: New Orleans LA Died Sept. 29, 1972; buried Metairie Cemetery.

ALCORN, DOUGLAS EARLE, neuropsychiatrist; b. Victoria, B.C., Can., Nov. 1, 1906; s. Duncan Rudolph and Addie L.B. (Olmstead) A.; student Victoria Coll., 1923-25; M.D., C.M., McGill U., 1931; postgrad. Harvard, U. Ia.; m. Doreen Evelyn Lougheed, Jan. 30, 1942. Intern, Royal Victoria Hosp., Montreal, Que., Can., 1931-32, Lenox Hill Hosp., 1935, Maudesley Hosp., London, 1937-38; practice medicine, specializing in neuropsychiatry, Victoria, 1938-41, 46-68; mem. staff Royal Jubilee, Veterans, Queen Alexandra Solarium hospitals (all Victoria), Hollywood Hosp., New Westminster, B.C. Served to maj., Royal Canadian Army Med. Corps, 1941-46. Fellow Am. Psychiat. Assn. (past pres. N. Pacific br.), A.A.A.S., Am. Geriatrics Soc., Am. Acad. Forensic Scis., N. Pacific Soc. Neurology and Psychiatry (past pres.). Home: Victoria BC Canada. Died Nov. 9, 1968; cremated.

ALDEN, CARROLL STORRS, college prof.; b. Medina, O., Mar. 15, 1876; s. Ezra Judson and Helen Frances (Storrs) A.; Beloit Coll., 1894-97; B.A., Yale, 1898, Ph.D., 1903; m. Meeta Campbell Graham, Oct. 1911 (died 1944); m. 2d, Mary Adair Skipworth, Apr. 1948. Asst. in English, Yale U., 1901-03; instr. in English, Grinnell Coll., 1903-04; instr. in English, 1904-19, U.S. Naval Acad., prof., 1919-41, head dept. English, history and govt., 1924-41, retired. Episcopalian. Editor: Jonson's Bartholomew Fair, 1904; Some Recent Essays and Poems, 1925. Author: A Guide to Annapolis and the Naval Academy (with W.O. Stevens), 1910; A Short History of the United States Navy (with others), 1911; Life and Letters of George Hamilton Perkins, 1914; Composition for Naval Officers (with W.O. Stevens), 1918; American Submarine Operations in the War, 1920; Makers of Naval Tradition (with Ralph Earle), 1925; Writing and Speaking— A Handbook for Naval Officers, 1927; Lawrence Kearney— Sailor Diplomat, 1936; The United States Navy: A History (with Allan Westcott), 1943. Home: 7 Wardour Dr., Annapolis, Md.; (summer) NH‡

ALDERMANN, LEWIS R., educator; b. Dayton, Ore., Oct. 29, 1872; s. A. L. and Charlotte (Odell) A.; ed. Linfield College; A.B., U. of Ore., 1898; Ph.D., American U., Washington, 1933; LL.D., Linfield Coll., McMinnville, Ore., 1938; m. Alice Barber, 1899 (dec.); children—Mrs. Fanny Ruth Tait, Robert Barber, John Clement; m. 2d, Lola E. Lake, 1924. Taught school; county supt. schs., Yamhill Co., Ore., 1904-07; city supt. schs., Eugene, 1907-08; asso. in dept. of edn., U. of Ore., 1908-10; state supt. pub. instrn., Ore., 1910-13; supt. of schs., Portland, 1913-19; with Army Ednl. Corps, in France and Germany, 1919; ednl. adviser U.S. Navy, 1919-24; mem. Survey Staff for survey New York pub. schs., 1924; senior specialist in adult edn., U.S. Office of Education, Washington, D.C., 1925-42; also instr. evening classes, George Washington U., 1929-32; director of edn. programs Fed. Emergency Relief Adminstrn. and Works Progress Adminstrn., 1933-1941. Mem. bd. of regents American Univ. since 1935. Mason, Odd Fellow. Author of ednl. bulls. Lecturer on ednl. subjects; contbr. on ednl. topics. Address: Dayton OR‡

ALDRICH, JOHN GLADDING, mfr.; b. Providence, R.I., Nov. 24, 1864; s. Elisha Smith and Anna (Gladding) A.; B.S. in M.E., Worcester Poly. Inst., 1885; m. Margaret Calder, Oct. 12, 1891; children—John Gladding, Putnam Calder, David. Supt. Foundry‡

ALDRICH, KILDROY PHILIP, former 1st asst. postmaster gen.; b. Alhambra, Ill., Feb. 16, 1877; s. Kildroy Philip and Annie Elizabeth (Avard) A.; ed. pub. schs., and Friends Acad., Washington, Kan., 1882-1893, U. of Chicago, 1893-94; m. Ruth Avarilla Pickard, June 14, 1903. With Post Office Dept. since 1897; ry. postal clerk, 1897-1902; asst. chief clk. Ry. Mail Service, 1903-13; post office insp., 1914-17; post office insp. and with A.E.F. Postal Service in France, 1918; insp. in charge St. Louis (Mo.) div., 1918-22, also in charge post office, Akron, O., 1919-21; insp. Chicago, Ill., div., 1922-27; in charge Chicago div., 1927-33; chief post office insp., 1933-43; first Assistant Postmaster Gen., Mar., 1943-July 1945. Democrat. Methodist. Mason (32 deg.). Lecturer on Post Office Dept. and postal service. Home: 1533 21st Av. N., St Petersburg FL‡

ALESSANDRI-PALMA, ARTURO, Chilean statesman; b. Linares, Chile, 1868; grad. in law, U. of Chile, 1893. Became associated with Liberal party, 1891; dep. from Curioco, 1897-1915; became minister of industry and public works, 1908, minister of finance, 1913; elected senator, 1915; prime minister, 1918-20; pres. of Chile, 1920-25, 1932-37. Address: Huerfanos Santiago Chile‡

ALEXANDER, CHARLES, author; b. S.Dak., Oct. 27, 1897; s. Thomas Samuel and Sarah Emily (Serry) A.; ed. pub. schs., Albany, Ore.; m. Margaret E. A. Smith, Jan. 14, 1917; children—Charles Douglas, Chloris Emily, Ardys Angela. Mem. Authors' League America Sigma Upsilon. Presbyterian. Elk. Author: The Fang in the Forest, 1923; The Splendid Summits, 1925; Bobbie, a Great Collie, 1926; North Smith, 1927; the Abel and Ailse" series, Northwest Historicals, 7 stories appearing in Collier's, 1939, 40, 41; also over 200 stories in Collier's, Sunset, Everybody's, Saturday Evening Post, etc.; winner of O. Henry Memorial award with story, As a Dog Should," 1922. Home: Albany, OR Died June 30, 1962; buried Willamette Meml. Park, Albany OR

ALEXANDER, FREDERICK, choral conductor; b. Fenton, Mich., Dec. 23, 1870; s. Samuel George and Martha Emma (Hanchet) A.; A.B., U. of Mich., 1894; musical edn. under masters in U.S.; organ under J.C. Batchelder, Detroit, and theory under Prof. A. A. Stanley, Ann Arbor, Mich.; unmarried. Head dept. of music, Mich. State Normal Coll., and dir. Normal Conservatory, Ypsilanti, 1909-41; retired June 1941; condr. Normal Choir and All Choral Ensemble; head of the dept. of music, U. of Calif., summers 1919-22; condr. of choral music, Calif. State Normal Sch., San Francisco, summer 1921; first production in Mich. of Bach St. Matthew Passion (Ypsilanti, Apr. 27, 1922); lecturer on history of music, Northwestern U., summer 1928; conductor Massed Chorus Festival, Washington, D.C., 1929-30; guest conductor National High Schools' Chorus, Chicago, 1930; conductor Bach Festival (combined choirs from Michigan high schools and Normal College), Ypsilanti, 1931-41; retired July 1, 1941. Inaugurated choral music in Folger Shakespeare Library, Washington, D.C., Apr. 23, 1934, under Elizabeth Sprague Coolidge Foundation. Republican. Clubs: University (Detroit and Chicago), Detroit Athletic, Detroit Boat, Washtenaw County Country. Address: P.O. Box 4, Santa Fe NM‡

ALEXANDER, GRACE, author; b. Indianapolis, Ind., June 14, 1872; d. George W. and Caroline (Nichols) A.; pub. sch. edn.; unmarried. Music critic and editorial writer Indianapolis News, 1891-1903; reader for Bobbs-Merrill Co., since 1905. Author: Judith, 1906. Home: 807 N. Pa. St., Indianapolis IN‡

ALEXANDER, HAROLD DAVID, dean law sch.; b. Albany, N.Y., Sept. 12, 1874; s. David M. and Rebecca (Hattersley) A.; LL.B., Albany Law Sch., 1895; M.A., Union Coll., 1925, LL.D., 1933; unmarried. Admitted to N.Y. bar, 1895, began practice at Albany; dist. atty. Albany Co., 1914-19; dean Albany Law Sch. (Union U.), 1924-45. Mem. Am., N.Y. State and Albany Co. bar assns. Republican. Protestant. Clubs: Ft. Orange, University, Burns, Albany Country. Home: 75 Willett St., Albany NY‡

ALEXANDER, HATTIE ELIZABETH, pediatrician; b. Balt., Apr. 5, 1901; d. William B. and Elsie M. (Townsend) Alexander; A.B., Goucher Coll., 1923; M.D., Johns Hopkins, 1930; hon. degree Wheaton Coll., Norton, Mass., 1967. Bacteriologist hygiene lab. USPHS, Washington, 1923-24; bacteriologist br. lab. Md. Pub. Health Service, Washington, 1924-26; intern Harriet Lane Home, Johns Hopkins Hosp., Balt., 1930-31; intern The Babies Hosp., N.Y.C., 1931-32, adj. asst. physician, 1933-38, asst. attending pediatrician, 1938-42, asso. attending pediatrician, 1942-51, attending pediatrician, 1951-68, Holt fellow diseases of children Columbia, 1932-34, asst. diseases of children, 1933-35, instr. diseases of children, 1935-36, asso. pediatrics, 1936-43, asst. prof., 1943-48, asso. prof., 1948-68, prof. pediatrics Coll. Phys. and Surg., 1958-68; asst. attending physician Vanderbilt Clinic, N.Y.C., 1933-39, asst. attending pediatrician, 1939-42, asso. attending pediatrician, 1942-51, attending pediatrician, 1951-68. Recipient E. Mead Johnson award for research pediatrics Am. Acad. Pediatrics, 1942; Stevens triennial prize Columbia, 1954, Distinguished Grad. citation for achievement in sci., 1954, Elizabeth Blackwell award, work on meningitis, 1956; 7th Oscar B. Hunter Memorial award in therapeutics Am. Therapeutic Soc., 1961; Babies Hosp. Distinguished Service award, 1963; Childrens Hosp. Phila. medal, 1965; Heart award Variety Club Phila., 1966; medal Columbia U. Coll. Physicians and Surgeons, 1967. Diplomate American Board of Pediatrics. Fellow A.A.A.S.; member of the Society Pediatric Research, Harvey Soc., Am. Pediatric Society (vice president 1959-60, pres. 1965), Soc. Exptl. Biology and Medicine, N.Y. Acad. Medicine, Am. Acad. Pediatrics, Goucher Coll. Alumnae Assn. (trustee). Contbr. profl. publs. Home: Port Washington NY Died June 24, 1968; buried Hopewell Presbyn. Ch. Yard, Huntsville NC

ALEXANDER, HENRY CLAY, lawyer, banker; b. Murfreesboro, Tenn., Aug. 1, 1902; s. Ellis De Witt and Nannie Eliza (Snell) A.; A.B., Vanderbilt U., Nashville, Tenn., 1923; student Law Sch., 1922-24; LL.B., Yale, 1925; m. Janet Hutchinson, Apr. 27, 1934; children—Henry Clay, Thomas Hunt, David Grant, Janet. Admitted to N.Y. bar, 1926; asso. with Davis, Polk, Wardwell, Gardiner & Reed, New York, 1925-39, partner, 1935-39; partner J. P. Morgan & Co., Feb. 1939 to incorporation, Mar. 1940; pres., dir. chief exec. officer, J. P. Morgan & Co. Inc., 1950-55, chmn. bd., chief exec. officer, 1955-59; chmn. bd., chief exec. officer Morgan Guaranty Trust Co. of N.Y., 1959-65, chmn. exec. com., 1965-67, dir., mem. exec. com., 1967-69; trustee Consolidated Edison Co. of N.Y., Inc.; dir. Gen. Motors Corp., Johns-Manville Corporation, A.V.C. Corporation, Standard Brands, Incorporated. Member of The Business Council. Vice-chmn. U.S. Strategic Bombing Survey, 1944-45. Recipient Presdl. Citation, Medal for Merit. Vice pres. trustee, Presbyn. Hosp. City of N.Y. Trustee Met. Mus. Art; v.p. bd. trust Vanderbilt U.; trustee Alfred P. Sloan Found., Walter and Lucie Rosen Found., U.S. Churchill Found. Mem. Am., N.Y. State bar assns., Bar Assn. City N.Y., N.Y. County Lawyers Assn., N.Y. Clearing House Assn. (pres. 1963), Kappa Alpha (Southern), Phi Delta Phi. Club: Links (N.Y.C.). Home: New York City NY Died Dec. 1969; buried Murfreesboro TN

ALEXANDER, JAMES WADDELL, II, mathematician; b. Sea Bright, N.J., Sept. 19, 1888; s. John White and Elizabeth A. Alexander; B.S., Princeton, 1910, M.A. (Gordon Macdonald fellow), 1911, Ph.D., 1915, D.Sc., 1947; student U. Paris, U. Bologna; m. Natalie Levitzkaja, Jan. 11, 1918; children—Irina, John. Instr., Princeton U., 1911-12, 15-16, asst. prof., 1920-26, asso. prof., 1926-28, prof., 1928-33, prof. Inst. for Advanced Study, 1933-51; Rouse Ball lectr. Cambridge (Eng.) U., 1936; a founder of modern topology. Served with tech. staff, ordnance dept. U.S. Army, overseas, 1917-18; ret. as capt.; mem. N.J. Nat. Guard. Recipient Bocher prize Am. Math Soc., 1928. Mem. Nat. Acad. Sciences, Am. Philos. Soc., Am. Math. Soc., Math. Assn. Am., A.A.A.S., Phi Beta Kappa. Clubs: American Alpine; Quadrangle; Nassau. Contbr. articles math. publs. Home: Princeton NJ Died Sept. 23, 1971.

ALEXANDER, MINNIE (REBECCA), missionary; b. Huntersville, N.C., Mar. 14, 1877; d. John Milton and Nancy Jane (Fulwood) A.; A.B., Claremont Coll., Hickory, N.C., 1898; U. of N.C. summer 1899, Harvard, summer 1900; spl. study in langs. Prof. English, Woman's Coll., Due West, S.C., 1900-6; missionary to India from Asso. Ref. Presbyn. Ch., 1906—. Punjab editor of The Temperance Record of India. Mem. nat. exec. com. Christian Endeavor Soc. of India; a founder Nancy Fulwood Hosp., Montgomery, India, 1912. Author: History of the Associate Reformed Presbyterians in India, 1912. Contbr. to church publs. Address: American Mission, Montgomery Punjab India‡

ALEXANDER, SAMUEL NATHAN, electronics engr.; b. Wharton, Tex., Feb. 22, 1910; s. Max and Minnie (Smith) A.; B.S., U. Okla., 1931, A.B., 1931; M.S., Mass. Inst. Tech., 1933; m. Eleanor Frances Magazine, Oct. 11, 1934; children—Harriet Phyllis (Mrs. Paul Lebowitz), Michael Norman, Diane Ellen (Mrs. Raul Zaritsky). Laboratory engr. with Simplex Wire & Cable Company, from 1935-40; research asst. Mass. Inst. Tech., 1939-40; physicist electronic instrumentation Navy Dept., 1940-43; sr. project engr. mil. telemetering equipment Bendix Aviation Corp., 1943-46; chief electronic computers lab. Nat. Bur. Standards, 1946-54, became chief data processing systems div., 1954, chief information tech., 1965-66, dep. and tech. dir. Center for Computer Scis. and Tech., sr. research fellow in engineering sciences until 1967. Committee dissemination of technol. information Materials Adv. Bd., Nat. Acad. Sci.-NRC; spl. tech. cons. automatic data processing applications and tech., U.S. govt. agencies, also govts. of Sweden, India. Recipient silver medal Royal Acad. Engring. Sci., Stockholm, Sweden, 1956, Harry Goode Meml. award Am. Fedn. Information Processing Socs., 1967. Fellow Inst. Radio Engrs.; mem. Am. Inst. Elec. Engrs., Assn. for Computing Machinery, Am. Phys. Soc., Am. Documentation Inst. (chmn. Washington 1959-60), Washington Acad. Scis., Phi Beta Kappa, Sigma Xi, Tau Beta Pi, Sigma Tau. Home: Chevy Chase MD Died Dec. 9, 1967.

ALEXANDER, (RICHARD) THOMAS, educator; born Smicksburg, Pa., July 3, 1887; s. William John and Mary Elizabeth (Wilhelm) A.; B.Ped. and M.Ped., Mo. State Normal Sch., Kirksville, Mo., 1905; A.B., Columbia, 1910, Ph.D., 1916; studied U. of Jena, Germany, 1909; Dr. of Literature, University of Louisville, 1948; LL.D. (hon.), Fairleigh-Dickinson Coll., 1951; m. Grace Elizabeth Andrews, Oct. 5, 1916; children—Richard Thomas, Mary Elizabeth. Prin. schs., Kirksville, Mo., 1905-06; teacher of science, Robert Coll., Constantinople, Turkey, 1907-09, Heathcote Prep. Sch., New York, 1910-12; foreign scholar, Columbia, 1912-14; exchange teacher, Realgymnasium, Stettin, Prussia, 1913-14; instr., philosophy of edn., Columbia Summer School, 1914; prof., elementary edn., George Peabody Coll for Teachers, 1914-23; prof. edn., Teachers College, Columbia, 1924-51, now prof. emeritus; chmn. New Coll. of Teachers Coll., Columbia, 1932-38; pres. Springdale Schools, Inc., since 1939; consulting, visiting prof. Adelphi Coll., 1950-53, in charge fgn. study 1952-71; vis. professor University of Indiana, summer, 1957; edn. cons. various colls. and indsl. firms. Chief Education Branch, Military Government for Germany, 1945-47; ednl. advisor to Mil. Govt. for Germany, 1948-49. Editor Johnson Edn. Series. Decorated Grand Merit Cross (West German Republic). Mem. N.E.A., Nat. Soc. Study Edn., Phi Delta Kappa, Phi Beta Kappa. Republican. Presbyn. Author: Schools of Western Europe, 1957-58; Teacher Education-U.S. and Europe, 58-59. Author or co-author several books, 1918-71. Home: Canton NC Died Oct. 16, 1971.1972.

ALEXANDER, WILLIAM HENRY, sr. meteorologist; b. Greenville, Tex., Jan. 10, 1867; s. Thomas Carroll and Martha Ann (Banta) A.; A.B., Sam Houston State Normal Coll., 1887, U. of Va., 1892; m. Mary P. Clonts, Aug. 29, 1894; children—Ralph Clonts (capt. U.S. Navy), Ryllis Clair (wife of Omar P. Goslin). Teacher high sch., Decatur, Tex., 1887-90; prof., Latin and Greek, N.W. Tex. Bapt. Coll., Decatur, 1892-94; prof. physics, Henry Coll., Campbell, Tex., 1894-98; observer and meteorologist U.S. Weather Bur., 1898-1937; now retired; climatologist for State of Md., 1913-16, for Ohio 1916-37. Fellow A.A.A.S., Am. Meteorol. Soc., Ohio Acad. Science (ex-pres., sec. 1923-1941). Mem. Columbus Geneal. Soc. (pres. 1930-35), Fed. Business Assn. of Columbus (ex-pres.), S.A.R. (state pres. 1937), Sigma Xi. Baptist. Mason (32 deg.). Club: Faculty (Ohio State U.). Author: Climatological History of Ohio; Fifty Stories About the Weather (manuscript form). Contbr. to scientific publs. Home: Normandie Hotel Columbus OH‡

ALEXANDER, WILLIAM VALENTINE, editor; b. Clinton, Mass.; s. Josiah and Lucy (Valentine) A.; in 9th generation of Alexanders in Mass.; pub. sch. edn.; m. Mary W. Aubin, of Boston, Apr. 24, 1894. Began active career on Boston Evening Transcript; reporter and city editor until resigned, 1898, to go to Phila.; on editorial staff Ladies' Home Journal, since 1898, most of time, and now mng. editor. Was pres. Boston Press Club, Boston Press Rifle Assn., Newspaper Chmn. of Boston (the founder); v.p. Internat. League of Press Clubs. Club: Franklin Inn. Collaborator on several books. Has traveled extensively in America. Home: Wayne, Pa. Office: Ladies Home Journal, Philadelphia PA‡

ALEXY, JANKO, painter, writer; b. Liptovsky Mikulas, Czecholsolvakia, Jan. 25, 1894; ed. Acad. Art, Prague, 1919-24. Tchr. drawing at grammar sch., Bratislava, 1924-27; ind. artist, from 1928; exhibited in numerous exhbns. in Czechoslovakia and abroad. Recipient Hon. diploma Paris, 1926, Provincial prize and prize City of Bratislava, 1937, Honoured Artist award, 1958, Nat. Artist award, 1964. Author: Jarmilka, 1923; Gretka, 1925; Easter, 1926; Freedom Unlimited, 1933; The Man Is on His Feet (Stefanik prize), 1937; Professor Klopacka, 1939. Home: Bratislava Czechoslovakia

ALFARO, RICARDO JOAQUIN, jurist; vice pres. Internat. Ct.; b. Panama, Republic of Panama, Aug. 20, 1882; s. Luis R. and Hortensia (Jovane) A.; ed. Balboa Coll., U. Cartagena, Colombia; LL.D., Nat. Faculty Law (Panama), U. So. Cal.; m. Amelia Lyons, Oct. 28, 1905; children—Victor, Ivan, Rogelio, Amelita, Yolanda. Under-sec. for fgn. affairs, Panama, 1905-08; legal counsellor Panamanian legation, Washington, 1912; mem. Codification Commn. for drafting Code of Procedure, 1913-16; sec. Dept. Interior and Justice, 1918-22; minister Panama to U.S., 1922-30, 33-36; v.p. Republic of Panama, 1928, pres., 1931-32; mem. Commn. to Draft Constn. of Panama, 1944; minister fgn. affairs, 1945-47; pres. Nat. Council Fgn. Affairs, 1956-57; judge Internat. Ct. of Justice, from 1959, v.p. ct., from 1961. Prof. civil law Nat. Sch. Law, 1917-22; prof. internat. law U. Panama, from 1948; del. Panama, Internat. Conf. on Radiotelegraphy, Washington, 1927, Internat. Confs. Am. States, Havana, 1928, Washington, 1928-29, Rio de Janeiro, 1947, Bogota, 1948, Caracas, 1954, UN Conf. at San Francisco, 1945, General Assembly sessions, 1946-49; mem. UN Internat. Law Commn., from 1948, chmn. Commn., 1952-53; mem. joint arbitration commn. Panama and U.S. for settlement expropriations claims for constrn. Panama Canal, 1915-18; mem. Permanent Ct. of Arbitration, from 1929, permanent conciliation commns. between Venzuela and Brazil, between Norway and Chile; pres. Arbitral Commn. U.K.-Greece in Ambatielos Case, 1956. Bd. dirs. Gorgas Meml. Inst., Washington. Recipient numerous decorations and honors from fgn. countries in Americas and Europe. Mem. Inst. Internat. Law, American Inst. Internat. Law (founder mem.; sec.-gen. 1938), other learned socs. Author: Dictionary of Anglicisms, 1950; The Question of an International Criminal Jurisdiction, 1950; The Question of Definition of Aggression, 1951, numerous others. Home: Panama Died Feb. 1971.

ALFREDSON, BERNARD V(ICTOR), educator; b. Chgo., Aug. 18, 1908; s. Victor Bernard and Kristina (Andersson) A.; D.V.M., Mich. State Univ., 1931, M.S., 1940; m. Pearline Roberta Haslip, Dec. 5, 1931; children—Carolyn Jane, James Bernard, Kenneth Bruce. With Mich. State Coll., 1935-68, successively instr. physiology and pharmacology, asst. and asso. prof., prof., 1945-66, professor of pharmacology, 1966-68, also head of dept., 1948-68. Mem. Am. Physiol. Soc., Am. Veterinary Med. Assn., Mich. Acad. Sci., Arts and Letters, A.A.A.S., Sigma Xi, Phi Zeta, Alpha Gamma Rho. Home: East Lansing MI Died Apr. 23, 1968; buried Deepdale Cemetery, Lansing MI

ALINSKY, SAUL DAVID, sociologist; b. Chgo., Jan. 30, 1909; s. Benjamin and Sarah (Tannenbaum) A.; Ph.B., U. Chgo., 1930, postgrad. Grad. Sch., 1930-32; LL.D., Saint Procopius Coll., 1958; m. Helene Simon, June 9, 1932 (dec.); children—Kathryn, David; m. 2d, Jean Graham, May 15, 1952 (div. 1969). Sociologist, Inst. for Juvenile Research, Chgo., 1931-36, 36-39; mem. state prison classification bd., div. criminology Ill. State Penitentiary System, Joliet, 1933-36; co-founder Back of Yards Neighborhood Council, Chgo.; exec. dir. Indsl. Areas Found. and Tng. Inst., 1969-72. Vis. prof. Vassar Coll., 1969, Antioch Coll., 1970. Will D. Wood fellow Amherst Coll., 1969. Recipient award for social justice Cath. Youth Orgn. Am., 1950. Mem. Authors League Am. Author: Reveille for Radicals, 1946, 70; John L. Lewis, a Biography, 1949, 70; (with Marion K. Sanders) The Professional Radical, 1970; Rules for Radicals, 1971. Contbr. numerous articles to sociol., psychol. and ednl. publs. Office: Chicago IL Died June 12, 1972.

ALINSKY, SAUL DAVID, sociologist; b. Chicago, Ill., Jan. 30, 1909; s. Benjamin and Sarah (Tannebaum) A.; Ph.B., U. of Chicago, 1930, student Grad. Sch., 1930-32; LL.D., Saint Procopius College, 1958; married Helene Simon, June 9, 1932 (dec.); children—Kathryn, David; m. 2d Jean Graham, May 15, 1952 (div. 1970); m. 3d, Irene Alinsky, May 1971. Sociologist with Institute for Juvenile research, Chicago, 1931-36, 1936-39; mem. state prison classification bd., div. criminology, Ill. State Penitentiary System, Joliet, 1933-36; co-founder Back of the Yards Neighborhood Council (Chicago); exec. director Industrial Areas Foundation, 1939-72. Mem. Authors League Am. Award for Social Justice, Catholic Youth Organization of America, 1950. Author: Reveille for Radicals, 1946; John L. Lewis, a Biography, 1949. Contbr. numerous articles to sociol., criminol. and psychol. publs. Lecturer on criminology, community orgn. and organized labor in various univs. Home: Chicago IL Died June 12, 1972

ALLEN, ALEXANDER JOHN, research physicist, educator; b. Glenwood Springs, Colo., Oct. 4, 1900; s. Alexander and Leah (Blotiaux) A.; A.B., U. Colo., 1923; Master Arts, New York University, 1926, Ph.D., 1928; m. Elinor Hale Waterhouse, Feb. 29, 1956. Engineer with the Mountain States Telephone Company, Denver, 1923-24; grad. fellow, N.Y. Univ., 1924-26, instr. in physics, 1926-28, research fellow, 1928-29, at Bartol Found., 1929-30; research physicist, U. Pa. Sch. Medicine, 1930-35, Biochem. Research Found., Franklin Inst., 1935-39; asso. prof. physics, U. Pittsburgh, 1939-41, Westinghouse prof. engring. and physics, and dir. Sarah Mellon Scaife Radiation Lab. 1944-68; staff mem. and research asso. Mass. Inst. Tech. Radiation Lab., 1941-44; asst. dir., Biochem. Research Found., Delaware, 1944; prof. physics, chmn. grad. study com. Centro Tecnico de Aeronautica, Departmento de Fisica, Sao Jose dos Campos, S. Paulo, Brazil, 1960-62. Consultant Atomic Energy Commn.; director of Navy Precision Scattering of Nuclear Particles" Contract; council rep. of U. of Pittsburgh for Argonne Nat. Labs. Fellow Am. Physical Soc.; mem. Am. Assn. U. Profs., Eta Kappa Nu, Sigma Xi. Club: University. Home: Pittsburgh PA Died June 7, 1968; buried Eagle CO

ALLEN, AUSTIN OSCAR, paint co. exec.; b. Gouverneur, N.Y., May 26, 1892; s. Oscar and Eliza (Steen) A.; B.S., St. Lawrence U., 1914; postgrad. Ohio State U., 1918; m. Mildred Briggs Stevenson, Aug. 10, 1916; children—Phyllis (Mrs. Don A. Brown), Sylvia (Mrs. Herb W. Watkins). Research chemist Gen. Chem. Co., Cleve., 1915-18; prodn. mgr. dry colors Glidden Co., Cleve., 1918-24; gen. mgr., dir. A. C. Horn Co., Long Island City, N.Y., 1924-39; v.p., dir. Vita-Var Co., div. Textron, New Brunswick, N.J., 1939-65, exec. con., 1965-70; guest lectr. Rutgers U. night sch., 1955-64. Recipient Pavac award, 1952, Roy Keenly award, 1961, Paint, Varnish & Lacquer Assn. award, 1961; outstanding contributions to industry award, St. Lawrence U. Alumni citation. Mem. Am. Chem. Soc., Am. Inst. Chemists, Soc. Corrosion Engrs., N.Y. Soc. paint Tech. (past pres.), Nat. Paint, Varnish and Lacquer Assn. (steering com. 1950-70), Sigma Alpha Epsilon. Methodist (pres. bd. trustees, ofcl. bd.). Mason. Clubs: St. Lawrence Golf & Country, (Canton, N.Y.). Trout Lake Rod and Gun (Edwards, N.Y.). Author: Practical and Theoretical Aspects of Pigment Wetting, 1942. Patentee in field. Home: De Kalb Junction NY Died Jan. 16, 1970.

ALLEN, BENJAMIN FRANKLIN, college pres.; b. Savannah, Ga., Sept. 8, 1872; s. of Albert Kelly and Elizabeth (Greene) A.; A.B., Atlanta U., Ga., 1894 (A.M., 1904; LL.D., Wilberforce U., 1904; Ph.D., Morris Brown Coll., Ga., 1905); m. Mayme Lee Williams, of Macon, Ga., June 25, 1907. Prof. Latin and Greek, Lincoln Inst., Jefferson City, Mo., 1894-1901; prof. English and pedagogy, Ga. State Coll. (colored), 1901-2; pres. Lincoln Inst., Mo. State Coll. for Negroes, 1902-18. Methodist. Mem. N.E.A., Am. Econ. Assn., Am. Acad. Polit. and Social Science, Nat. Assn. Colored Teachers, Am. Humane Soc., State Hist. Soc. (Mo.), Southern Sociol. Congress, Am. Sociol. Soc.; pres. Mo. State Assn. Colored Teachers; pres. Negro Farmers' Conv. of Mo.; mem. Am. Hist. Assn. Grad. student, U. of Wis., 1915. Mason, Odd Fellow, K.P. Address: Shelbyville TN‡

ALLEN, CLAY, judge; b. Erie, Kan., Aug. 23, 1875; s. James Montgomery and Eva (Foster) A.; A.B., Northwestern U., 1898; LL.B., Indiana Law Sch., Indianapolis, Ind., 1900; m. Lunella Coleman, of Louisville, Ky., Jan. 7, 1907. Admitted to Kan. bar, 1899; practiced at Muskogee, Okla., 1901-02; settled in Seattle, Wash., 1902; became U.S. atty., Western Dist. of Wash., 1913; then judge superior court. First lt. and adj. 22d Kan. Regtl. Vols., Spanish-Am. War. Democrat. Home: 911 Summit St., Seattle WA*‡

ALLEN, COURTNEY, sculptor; b. Norfolk, Va., Jan. 16, 1896; s. Joseph Bell and Elizabeth (Whitehurst) A.; student Corcoran Art Sch., Washington, 1915-16, Nat. Acad. Art Sch., N.Y.C., 1920-21, Charles W. Hawthorne, Provincetown, Mass., 1919-21, C.W.W. Bicknell, 1919; m. Erma Emmert Paul, Apr. 29, 1924; 1 dau., Charlotte E. (Mrs. Richmond Newton Long). Illustrator popular mags., 1922-57; exhibited in one man shows at New Rochelle Art Assn., 1946, Pelham Manor Club, N.Y., 1947, Norfolk Museum of Art, 1955; exhibited in group shows at New Rochelle Art Assn., 1925-50, Hudson Valley Art Assn., 1943-50, Allied Artists Am., 1936-53, Soc. Illustrators, 1943-45, Provincetown Art Assn., 1930-66, Chrysler Art Mus., Provincetown, Mass., 1961; principal works include Diorama of The Wharf, Diarama of 1810 Glass factory, Diorama Signing Mayflower Compact 1620, Provincetown Hist. Mus.; drawings and sculpture Norfolk (Va.) Art Mus. Partner, instr. Huguenot Sch. Art, New Rochelle, N.Y., 1946-50. Chmn., Conservation Commn., Truro, Mass., 1958-64; pres. Truro Hist. Soc., chmn. Hist. Commn. of Truro, 1967-69. Trustee, Chrysler Mus. Art. Mem. New Rochelle (past pres., award), Hudson Valley (award), Provincetown (trustee) art assns., Soc. Illustrators. Home and studio: North Truro MA Died Sept. 18, 1969; buried 1st Congregational Parish Cemetery Truro MA

ALLEN, DON CAMERON, author, educator; b. St. Louis, Dec. 5, 1903; s. Alvin James and Anna (Wienmann) A.; A.B., U. Ill., 1926, Ph.D., 1931, D.H.L., 1971; A.M., Washington U., 1927; L.H.D., U. Chgo., 1971; LL.D., Johns Hopkins, 1972; m. Mary Whitney Coble, Feb. 1, 1929; 1 dau., Mary Whitney. Asst. instr. English, U. Ill., 1927-28; instr. Purdue U., 1929-30; prof., head dept. Ill. Wesleyan U., 1931-32; instr. to asst. prof. State Coll. Wash., 1932-38; asst. to asso. prof. Duke, 1938-42; asso. prof. English, Johns Hopkins, 1942-45, prof., 1945-71, Sir William Osler prof., 1950. Vis. summer prof. Ohio U., N.C. Coll., 1939-42, Johns Hopkins, 1941, Northwestern U., 1947, U. Ill., 1949, N.Y. U., 1950; F.I. Carpenter prof. U. Chgo., 1948; Sesquicentennial lectr. U. N.C., 1946, Baskerville Brown U., 1947; Taft lectr. U. Cin., 1950; Scott lectr. Wash. U., 1956; lectr. U. Colo., 1957-61; Johnson prof. U. Wis., 1961-62. Am. Council fellow in Europe, 1935-36; Fulbright Research fellow, Oxford, 1950-51; NEH fellow, 1967-68. Mem. Modern Lang. Assn. (editorial com. 1946-61, v.p. 1966), Am. Assn. U. Profs., Malone Soc., Renaissance Soc. (council), Internat. Assn. U. Profs. English (exec. com.), Am. Philos. Soc., Am. Acad. Arts and Scis., Phi Beta Kappa, Sigma Delta Chi, Chi Psi. Club: Tudor and Stuart. Author: The Star-Crossed Renaissance, 1942; The Legend of Noah, 1950; Doubt's Boundless Sea, 1964. Editor: Treatise Poetrie (Francis Meres), 1933; Palladis Tamia (Francis Meres), 1939; The Owles Almanacke, 1943; The Essayes of Sir William Cornwallis, 1946 A Strange Metamorphosis, 1950; Recent Literature of the Renaissance, 1939-50; That Soveraine Light (with W. Mueller), 1952; The Harmonious Vision, 1954; Paradoxes, 1956; (with others) A Critical Bibliography of French Literature, 1956; (with others) Masters of British Literature, 2 vols., 1958; Four Poets on Poetry, 1959; Image and Meaning, 1960; Moment of Poetry, 1962; A Celebration of Poets, 1967; The Ph.D. in English and American Literature, 1967; (with H.T. Rowell) The Poetic Tradition, 1968; Mysteriously Meant, 1970. Editor: English Literary History; asso. editor Modern Language Notes, Revista di Litteratuer Moderne, Isis, Studies in English Literature, English Language Notes. Contbr. articles, revs., verse to Am., European philol., lit. jours. Home: Baltimore MD Died Aug. 4, 1972.

ALLEN, EDWARD NORMAND, department store executive; b. Hartford, Conn., Apr. 18, 1891; s. Normand F. and Carrie (Olmsted) A.; Ph.B., Sheffield Scientific Sch., Yale, 1914; m. Ruby Tuttle, Dec. 13, 1916; children—Jane, Caroline, Frances, Normand F. II, Mary; m. 2d, Mildred Pomeranz, Nov. 7, 1935. Clerk Sage-Allen & Co., Inc., 1915-20, v.p., 1920-36, pres., 1941-63, chmn. bd., 1963-72. Police commr., Hartford, 1920-24; mem. Conn. senate, 1927-29; mayor City of Hartford, 1947; lt. governor State Conn., 1951-55. Served as lt. Conn. Field Signal Corps, Mexican Border, 1916, 2d lt. F.A., World War I. Past pres., now dir., mem. exec. com. Nat. Retail Dry Goods Assn.; pres. Hartford Chamber Commerce, 1937-40; chmn. bd. dirs. Am. Retail Fedn., Washington, 1947; former mem. bd. dirs. C. of C., U.S., New England Council; chmn. Inter-racial Commission, State of Connecticut, 1948. Trustee Wadsworth Atheneum; bd. dirs. Hartford Pub. Library, Conn. C. of C., Hartford chpt. A.R.C. Republican. Conglist. Mason (32 deg.), Elk. Clubs: Hartford, University, Yale, Lambs. Home: Hartford CT Died Nov. 14, 1972.

ALLEN, ELIOT DINSMORE, coll. dean; b. Phila., Nov. 13, 1918; s. Harold Douglass and Mabel (Seeley) A.; grad. William Penn Charter Sch., 1936; B.A., Wesleyan U., Middletown, Conn., 1940; student U. Coll. South West (Eng.), 1938-39; A.M., Harvard, 1941; M.A., Princeton, 1947, Ph.D. in English, 1949; m. Dorothy Lois Douglass, Jan. 25, 1947; children—Lois, Harold, Douglass, Ethan. Instr. English, U. Va., 1947-49; asst. prof., then asso. prof. U. Mass., 1949-60; asso. prof. Stetson U., 1960-62, prof. English, 1962-68, dean humanities, 1968-70; dean humanities N.Y. State U. Coll., Plattsburgh, 1970-71. Served with USNR, 1942-46. Mem. Modern Lang. Assn., U.S. Naval Inst., Phi Betta Kappa, Phi Nu Theta, Sigma Phi Epsilon. Co-author: A Short Guide to Writing a Research Paper, MS Form and Documentation, 1963; A Short Guide to Writing a Critical Review, 1964; Effect of Practice and Evaluation on Improvement in Written Composition, 1964; The Student Writer's Guide, 1970. Editor: Challenges of Change to the Christian College, 1966. Home: Plattsburgh NY Died Dec. 8, 1971; buried DeLand FL

ALLEN, GEORGE EDWARD, lawyer; b. Bonneville, Miss., Feb. 29, 1896; s. Sam. P. and Mollie (Plaxico) A.; LL.B., Cumberland Univ., 1917, LL.D., 1938; Dr. Humane Letters (hon.) Temple Univ., Phila., 1949; m. Mary Keane, Sept. 10, 1930. Admitted to Miss. bar, 1917; in practice at Okolona, 1917-19; in hotel business, 1919-33; commr. of D.C., 1933-39; vice pres. Home Insurance Co. of N.Y., 1938-45; counsel Alvord & Alvord; p. chmn. bd. Duke Internat. Corp., N.Y., Victor Elec. Co., Cin.; mem. exec. com. and dir., AVCO Mfg. Corp., N.Y.; dir. Occidental Life Insurance Co.; trustee Penn. Mutual Life Insurance member board directors Air fleets, Inc., Borne Scrymser Co., City Products Co. Chgo., Duquesne Light Co., Pittsburgh, Pa., W. L. Maxon Corp., N.Y., Washington Mut. Investors Fund, Inc., District of Columbia, Republic Steel Corporation, Washington Properties, Inc., Central States Edison, Phila. Co., Standard Gas & Elec. Co., Steep Rock Iron Mines, Ltd., also S. Klein Department Stores, Sheraton-Astor and the Sheraton Closed-Circuit Television, Inc. Dir. R.F.C.; pres. R.F.C. Mortgage Co. Fed. Nat. Mortgage Assn., War Damage Corp.; treas. Dem. Nat. Congressional Com. since 1940; sec. Dem. Nat. Com., 1943. Trustee Ga. Warm Springs Foundn. Mem. Am. Red Cross (nat. adv. com.; pres. war. com., 1934-44), Boy Scouts of Am. (nat. exec. com.; awarded Silver Buffalo); mem. Nat. Foundation of Infantile Paralysis (v.p. and dir.), Kappa Sigma. Democrat. Methodist. Clubs: Metropolitan, Recess, Wings; Deepdale, Cloud (N.Y.); Burning Tree, Metropolitan (Washington). Author: Presidents Who Have Known Me, 1950. Home: Washington DC Died May 1973.

ALLEN, GEORGE VENABLE, govt. ofcl.; b. Durham, N.C., Nov. 3, 1903; s. Thomas Ellis and Harriet (Moore) A.; A.B., Duke U., 1924, LL.D., 1949, Harvard, 1929; m. Katharine Martin, Oct. 2, 1934; children—George, John, Richard. Teacher and prin. public schs., Buncombe County, near Asheville, N.C., 1924-28; reporter Asheville (N.C.) Times, Durham Herald-Sun at various times during 1925-29; entered U.S. Fgn. Service, 1930; vice consul, Kingston, Jamaica, 1930, Shanghai, China, 1931-34, Patras, Greece 1934-36; consul and diplomatic sec., Cairo, Egypt, 1936-38; with Middle Eastern div., dept. of State, Washington, 1938-46; U.S. ambassador to Iran, 1946-48; asst. sec. of state, Mar. 1948-Jan. 1950; ambassador to Yugoslavia, Jan. 1950-53; ambassador to India and Nepal, 1953; asst. sec. Bur. Near Eastern, South Asian and African Affairs, Department of State, Washington, 1955-56; United States Ambassador to Greece, 1956-57; dir. U.S. Information Agency, Washington, 1957-60; pres. Tobacco Institute, 1960-66; dir. of Fgn. Service Inst., Dept. of State, 1966-68; ambassador in residence George Washington U., from 1968; lectr. Am. U., 1941-43, Sch. Advanced Internat. Studies, 1944-46. Participated in Moscow Conf., 1943, Cairo Conf., 1943, U.N. Conf., San Francisco, 1945, Potsdam Conf., 1945; chmn. U.S. del. to UNESCO Conf., Beirut, 1948; chmn. People-to-People, Inc., Kansas City, Mo.; president Town Affiations, Inc.,

Washington. Recipient of the Chas. Sumner prize in Internat. Relations, Harvard, 1929. Mem. Diplomatic and Consular Officers Retired (pres.), Delta Sigma Phi, Phi Beta Kappa. Methodist. Clubs: Metropolitan, Chevy Chase (Washington). Home: Washington DC Died July 11, 1970; buried Dacor Meml. Park, Rock Creek Cemetery, Washington DC

ALLEN, GORDON, architect; b. Sherborn, Mass., Feb. 5, 1877; s. Edward Augustus Holyoke and Eugenia Sophia (Teulon) A.; student Friends Sem., 1890-94; A.B., Harvard, 1898; m. Harriott Magoun Kendall, Apr. 14, 1914; 1 son, Gordon. Architectural draftsman, 1898-1910; Carnegie Fellowship, American Sch., Athens, Greece, 1905-06; in private practice since 1910; principal works: Charokopeion (School of Domestic Science) Children's Hospital (both in Athens, Greece), Beaver Country Day School (Brookline, Mass.). Served as 1st lt., Air Service, U.S. Army, 1917-19. Fellow A.I.A. Home: 43 West Cedar St., Boston 14. Office: 126 Newbury St., Boston 16 MA*‡

ALLEN, GUY FLETCHER, b. Delhi, Mich., Feb. 19, 1877; s. George W. and Emily (Fletcher) A.; ed. high sch. and Valparaiso U.; m. M. Adaline Ramsey, Aug. 3, 1898 (dec.); children—Glenn Harold, Emily Mae (dec.), Bruce Ramsey, Earle Fletcher; m. 2d, Brownie H. Kerr, Dec. 27, 1947. Teacher and prin. pub. schs., 1897-1901; with U.S. Treasury Dept., 1901-21, as bookkeeper chief of division, asst. treas., and as acting treas. of U.S., Jan. 6-May 1, 1921; sent to France and Eng., 1918, to est. and install plan for providing funds and making payments for U.S. Army; apptd. exec. asst. to dir. Bureau of the Budget, Washington, D.C. 1922, became chief disbursing officer U.S. Treasury Dept.; retired. Col. U.S.A. Reserve Corps, Finance Dept., retired. Home: 1620 Fuller St., N.W. Washington DC‡

ALLEN, HARRIS CAMPBELL, architect; b. Rutland, Vt., Nov. 22, 1876; s. Charles Linnacus and Gertrude Margaret (Lyon) A.; B.A., Stanford U., 1897; student U. of Calif., 1897-98. Draftsman, 1898-1908; architect, 1908-17 and since 1919; editor Pacific Coast Architect, 1919-29, Calif. Arts and Architecture, 1929-34, Bulletin of State Assn. of Calif. Architects, 1934-42; zone architect Zone 5, Federal Housing Adminstrn., 1938-41; architectural examiner Federal Housing Adminstrn., War and Veterans Housing, 1941-45. Served as capt. U.S. Air Service, 1917-19. Fellow Am. Inst. Architects (v.p. No. Calif. Chapter 1925-27, pres. 1927-29, dir. 1922-25 and 1929-32); mem. State Assn. of Calif. Architects (pres. 1933, dir. 1930-32 and 1934-36), San Francisco Soc. Architects (pres. 1933-38), Am. Legion of Calif. (chmn. aviation com. 1921-25), Sons of the American Revolution, Nat. Aeronautic Assn., Phi Kappa Psi. Republican. Episcopalian. Mason (Shriner). Club: Bohemian (San Francisco). Contbr. to professional jours. Address: Bohemian Club San Francisco‡

ALLEN, HENRY CROSBY, congressman, lawyer; b. Paterson, N. J., May 13, 1872; s. Samuel Coit Morgan and Josephine Amelia (Crosby) A.; ed. Paterson pub. and pvt. schs.; grad. St. Paul's Sch., Garden City, L. I., 1889, Yale, B. A., 1893, New York Law Sch., LL.B., 1895; unmarried. Admitted to bar, 1895, and since then engaged in practice; mem. Congress, 6th N. J. dist., 1905-7; Republican. Mem. Phelps Guards. Baptist. Clubs: Hamilton, North Jersey, Lincoln (Paterson, N. J.); Army and Navy (Washington). Residence: Little Falls, N. J. Office: United Bank Bldg., Paterson NJ‡

ALLEN, HORACE EUGENE, lawyer; b. Swanton, Vt., July 19, 1890; s. Clarence Eugene and Minerva Saxe (Drury) A.; A.B., Dartmouth, 1912; LL.B., Harvard, 1915; m. Mary Frances Ballantine, July 13, 1918 (dec. Aug. 1961); children—Hortense Ballantine (Mrs. Warren F. Walker, Jr.), Richard Ballantine, Nancy Ballantine (Mrs. Paul D. Hubbe). Admitted to Mass. bar, 1915, practiced in Springfield, 1915-72; mem. firm Allen, Yerrall, Appleton & Thompson, 1923-72. Mem. Mass. Bd. Bar Examiners, 1947-63. Pres., trustee Horace Smith Fund. Served as 1st lt. Army Service Corps, 1918. Mem. Civilian Contracts Review Board Springfield Ordnance Dist., 1951. Chmn. Longmeadow Future Planning Com., 1959-63. Mem. Am. (ho. dels. 1946-50), Mass. (treas., 1931-47), Boston bar assns., Nat. Conf. Bar Examiners (council 1947-48). Republican. Conglist. Clubs: Kiwanis (pres. Longmeadow MA Died Nov. 5, 1972; buried Oak Grove Cemetery, Springfield MA

ALLEN, JAMES EDWARD, JR., government official; b. Elkins, W.Va., Apr. 25, 1911; s. James E. and Susan (Garrott) A.; B.A., Davis and Elkins Coll., 1932, LL.D., 1956; postgrad. econs. and pub. finance Princeton, 1939; M.Ed., Harvard, 1942, Ed.D., 1945; D.Ped., Niagara U., 1956; LL.D., Syracuse U., 1955, Union U., 1956; D.H.L., Hobart Coll., William Smith Coll., Alfred U., 1956; Litt.D., Hofstra Coll., 1957; Yeshiva Univ., 1957; Marshall College, 1958; LL.D., Harvard, U., Fordham Univ., 1960, N.Y.U., Yale, 1966, Manhattan Coll., 1968, Hamilton Coll., 1968; D.H.L., Columbia, 1964, Pace College, 1966; D.Hum., West Va. University, 1966; others; married Florence Pell Miller, April 23, 1938 (dec. 1971); children—James Edward III, Judith Pell (Mrs. John Dolven). Mem. of staff of West Virginia Education Dept., 1938-39; chief div. state aid and statistics W.Va., 1939; research asso. Princeton Surveys, 1939-41; research Center for Research in Ednl. Adminstrn., Harvard, 1941-43, sec. faculty, dir. placement Grad. Sch. Edn., 1943-44; operations analyst USAAF, 1944-45; asst. prof. edn., dir. Bur. Sch. Services, Syracuse U., 1945-47; exec. asst. to N.Y. Commr. Edn., 1947-50; dep. commr. edn. N.Y., 1950-55, commr. and pres. U. State N.Y., 1955-69; fed. edn. commr., asst. sec. for edn. U.S. Department Health, Education and Welfare, Washington, 1969-70; vis. lectr. Woodrow Wilson Sch. Pub. and Internat. Affairs, Princeton, 1970-71; trustee City and County Savs. Bank of Albany. Consultant to President's Commn. on Higher Edn., 1946-47; mem. Edn. Comm. of States Ednl. Devel. Center. Mem. N.Y. State Civil Def. Commn., State Recreation Council; mem. adv. council State Departments of Edn. Mem. adv. bd. Salvation Army, 1956-71; joint council Econ. Edn. Mem. Council Harvard Found. Advanced Study and Research, 1950-54; nat. adv. com. Nat. Ednl. TV and Radio Center, Inc.; trustee Dudley Obs., Danforth Found.; adv. com. Internat. Center: trustee Syracuse U., 1955-71, Cornell U., 1955-71, Hudson-Mohawk Council World Affairs; vis com. Harvard Grad. Sch. Edn.; adv. com. Harvard Program on Sci. and Tech.; dir. N.Y. State Sci. & Tech. Found., Saratoga Performing Arts Center. Recipient Charles Evans Hughes award Am. Soc. Pub. Administrn., 1954. Mem. Am. Assn. Sch. Adminstrs., N.Y. Council Sch. Supts., Am. Council Edn., Council Chief State School Officers, N.E. Commrs. Edn., N.Y. State Tchrs. Assn., N.Y. State Apprenticeship Council, Inst. Am. Strategy (bd. dirs.), Met. Area Council Internat. Recreation, Culture and Life-Long Edn. (trustee), Phi Delta Kappa. Presbyn. (elder). Clubs: Century; Rotary, University, Schuyler Meadows Country (Albany). Author: State School Fiscal Policy for New Jersey, 1944. Contbr. ednl. mags. Home: Loudonville NY Died Oct. 1971.

ALLEN, JOHN REX, lawyer; b. Phila., Aug. 15, 1900; s. John Rex. and Mary (Lowry) A.; B.A., Amherst Coll., 1922; LL.B., Chgo.-Kent Coll. Law, 1931; m. Evelyn Pardee, Jan 5, 1937; children—Mary Lowry (Mrs. Robert J. Olson), Barbara Jill (Mrs. Allan C. Bates), Ruth Elizabeth (Mrs. Jean-Claude Bleuze), Jennifer. Sec. Western Fed. Brokerage Co., Chgo., 1922-28; with Union Bank Chgo., 1928-32; admitted to Ill. bar, 1931; asso., then mem. firm Parkinson & Lane, Chgo., 1932-42; price atty. regional hearing com. OPA, 1942-45; mem. firm Hofgren, Wegner, Allen, Stellman & McCord and predecessor firms, Chgo., 1945-69, partner, 1947-69. Mem. bd. Highland Park (Ill.) High Sch., 1953-54; mem. bd. Vis. Nurse Assn. Deerfield Townships, Inc., 1952-64, pres., 1953-56. Mem. Am., Ill., Chgo. bar assns., Am. (pres. 1961-62), Chgo. patent law assns., Am. Judicature Soc. Lake Bluff IL Died Jan. 1969.

ALLEN, JOSEPH HOLMES, ex-mayor; b. Marshall Co., Ia., Nov. 12, 1870; s. Daniel Johnson and Elizabeth (Holmes) A.; Ph.B., LL.B., State U. of Iowa, 1895; m. Grace Gilchrist, of Laurens, Ia., June 29, 1899; children—Byron Gilchrist, Josephine. Began practice law at Laurens, Ia., 1895; moved to Pocahontas, Ia., 1900; in banking business Pocahontas and Ware, Ia., until 1918, when he moved to Des Moines; pres. First Mortgage Corpn. of Ia. since 1918; pres. Hawkeye Life Ins. Co., Fraternal Aid Assn. of Ia.; resumed law practice in Des Moines, 1928; mayor of Des Moines, 1936-38. Mem. Ia. Senate, 1906-16. Mem. bd. dirs. Y.M.C.A.; regent U. of Ia.; trustee Cornell Coll., Mt. Vernon, Ia. Served as pvt. 49th Ia. Regt. during Spanish-Am. War. Mem. Ia. State Bar Assn., Vets. of Fgn. Wars, Phi Delta Theta, Phi Delta Phi. Republican. Methodist. Mason (Consistory). Elk, Moose. Home: 2518 Forest Drive, Des Moines IA‡

ALLEN, LEO ELWOOD, congressman; b. Elizabeth, Ill., Oct. 5, 1898; s. Alphonso Arthur and Sarah Sadie (Steinberger) A.; A.B., U. of Mich., 1923; m. Gladys Dahl, May 31, 1924; children—Dawn Elizabeth, Richard Burns, David Warner, Eleanor Lee, Mary Carole. Taught sch., 1922-24; clk. Circuit Ct. of Jo Daviess County, Ill., 1924-32; in practice of law 1930-73; member 73d to 86th Congresses from the 16th Illinois District. Chmn. Rules Com., Ho. of Reps., 80th and 83d Congresses. Served as sergt. 123d Field Arty., World War. Republican. Presbyterian. Mason (33 deg.). Elk, I.O.O.F. Club: Galena Golf. Home: Galena IL Died Jan. 1973.

ALLEN, MRS. MARION BOYD, painter; b. Boston, Mass., October 23, 1862; d. Stillman and Harriet (Seaward) Boyd; ed. Gannett Inst., Boston; diploma, Sch. of Music of Fine Arts, Boston, 1909; m. William Augustus Allen, 1905 (died 1911). Exhibited at Nat. Acad. Design, New York; Pa. Acad. Fine Arts Phila.; Art Inst. Chicago; Corcoran Gallery, Washington, D.C.; Albright Gallery, Buffalo, N.Y.; Soc. Beaux Arts, Paris, France; etc. Awarded Hudson prize, Conn. Acad.; popular prize, Newport; fellowship prize, Buffalo; popular prize, Boston; New Haven Paint and Clay" prize; medal from French Soc. in N.Y., exhbn. of Nat. Assn. Women Painters and Sculptors. Works on permanent exhibition at Bowdoin Coll., Randolph Macon College (Va.), Harvard Club (Boston), Waltham (Mass.) Court House, Arlington Pub. Library, Ill. College, Seaman's Museum," Newport News, Virginia, etc. Member National Assn. Women Painters and Sculptors, Copley Soc. (Boston), Conn. Acad. Fine Arts. Club: Boston Art. Home: 60 Fenway. Studio: Fenway Studios, 30 Ipswich St., Boston MA‡

ALLEN, NELLIE BURNHAM, author; b. Danvers, Mass., June 10, 1864; d. James and Maria (Burnham) Allen; ed. Salem (Mass.) Normal Sch. and spl. courses at Harvard, Cornell U., Clark U. and U. of Chicago; unmarried. Teacher Hampton Inst., Va., and pub. schs., Mass., until 1895; with State Normal Sch., Fitchburg, Mass., 1895-1919, head of geographical department, 1900-19. Fellow National Council Geography Teachers. Conglist. Author: (series of geog. and industrial books) United States, 1910, 25, 37; Europe, 1913, 34, 38, 40; Asia, 1916, 35; S. America, 1918, 38; N. America, 1922, 35; Africa, Australia, Islands of the Pacific, 1923, 35, 38; Stories and Sketches, Vol. I, Children of Other Lands, Volume II, What People Are Doing, Volume III, Stories of Our Earth; How and Where We Live, An Open Door to Geography; Stories of Raw Materials (series)— Vol. I, Our Cereal Grains, Vol. II, Cotton and Other Useful Fibers. Co-Author: Jansen and Allen Geographies (for grades IV-VIII), 1939. Home: Lake Worth FL‡

ALLEN, RODERICK RANDOM, army officer; b. Marshall, Tex., Jan. 29, 1894; s. Jefferson Buffington and Emma (Albers) A.; B.S., Tex. A. and M. Coll., 1915, LL.B., 1946; Univ. of Toulouse, France, 1919; grad. Cav. Sch., 1923, Comd. and Gen. Staff Sch., 1929, Army War Coll., 1935, Naval War Coll., 1936; m. Maydelle Campbell, Apr. 25, 1917; children—Nancy Campbell, Gail Random. Commd. 2d lt., 16th U.S. Cav., Nov. 29, 1916, and advanced through the grades to major general, October 29, 1944; Captain 3d Cavalry A.E.F., France, October 1917-July 1919; comdr. combat Comd. A., 4th Armored Div., April 1942-Oct. 1943; comdg. gen. 20th Armored Div., Oct. 1943-Sept. 1944; comdg. gen. 12th Armored Div., Sept. 1944-Aug. 1945; comdg. gen. 1st Armored Div. (Germany), Aug. 1945-Feb. 1946; Dir. Operations, Plans and Training for U.S. Forces, European Command 1945-47; dir. Intelligence, Army Ground Forces, 1947-48; comdg. gen., 3d Armored Div., Ft. Knox, 1948-50; dep. chief of staff Gen. Hdqrs., Far Eastern Command and U.N. Command, Japan, and chief of staff Korean operations, Japan, 1950-51; comdg. gen. XVI Corps, Japan, 1951-52, 9th Inf. Div., Feb-July 1952, New Eng. Subarea and Boston Army Base and Ft. Devens, Massachusetts, July, 1952, till retirement, 1954. Honorary Kentucky Colonel. Decorations: Distinguished Service Medal, Silver Star Medal, Legion of Merit, Bronze Star Medal, Army Commd. Ribbon, Distinguished Marksman; Officer Legion of Honor, Croix de Guerre with Palm (French); Order of the White Lion and Victory, War Cross (Czechoslovakia). Clubs: Army-Navy, Army-Navy Country (Washington). Home: Washington DC Died Mar. 1970.

ALLEN, SAMUEL JAMES MCINTOSH, prof. physics; b. Maitland, N.S., Can., Oct. 5, 1877; s. Capt. James McIntyre and Elizabeth (Lawrence) A.; B.Sc., McGill U., Montreal, P.Q., 1900, M.Sc., 1901; Ph.D., Johns Hopkins, 1906; m. Eva Blanche Sircom, of Halifax, N.S., Aug., 1910; children—James Sircom, Samuel Stephen, George Churchill, John Edward, Florence Elizabeth. Demonstrator in physics, McGill U., 1900-03; fellow Johns Hopkins, 1903-04; with U. of Cincinnati since 1906, now prof. physics. Research asso. dept. terrestrial magnetism and electricity, Carnegie Instn., Washington, D.C., 1924. Naturalized citizen of U.S., 1917. Fellow Am. Physical Soc., Ohio Acad. Science; mem. Phi Beta Kappa. Episcopalian. Clubs: Faculty, Ohio River Launch. Mem., and ex-commodore, Chester (N.S.) Yacht Club. Contbr. numerous papers on researches in X-ray, radio-activity, and kindred subjects. Research physicist with Liebel Flarzeim Co.; developed Kuprox." Home: 2316 Auburn Crest Av., Cincinnati OH*‡

ALLEN, WYETH, educator; b. Milw., July 28, 1893; s. Stanton and Maria (McLaren) A.; B.Mech. Engring., U. Mich., 1915, D.Engring., 1953; m. Lillian Carnegie, Apr. 20, 1918; children—Stanton, Richard Crafts, Jean Carnegie. Foreman, Pfeiffer & Smith, 1915-16; works mgr. Allen-Bradley Co., 1916-21; resident engr. William Baum & Co., 1921-25; cons. management engr., 1925-48; exec. v.p. Globe-Union, Inc., 1948-49; pres., 1949-55; pres. Centralah Canada, Ltd., 1953-55; cons. mgmt. engring., 1955; prof. indsl. engring., chmn. depts. indsl. engring. and mech. engring. U. Mich., 1955-63; dir. Clinton Engines Corp. Prin. contract rep. ICA, Waseda U. (Tokyo, Japan) U. Mich., 1955-73. Vice pres. Am. Humanics Found.; trustee Found. Allergic Diseases. Mem. Acad. of Mgmt., 1956-73; panel mem. Am. Arbitration Assn., 1957-73. Pres. United Fund Ann Arbor, Barton Hills Assn.; dir. Ann Arbor Community Welfare Council; vice chmn. region 7, hon. life mem. exec. bd. Boy Scouts America. Mem. Am. Inst. Indsl. Engrs., Inst. Mgmt. Engrs., Am. Soc. M.E., A.A.A.S., Soc. Engring. Edn., Am. Soc. Advancement Mgmt., Am. Ordnance Assn., Navy League, U. Mich. Alumni Assn. (life dir.), Inst. Mgmt. Scis., Mil. Operations Research Society America, Sigma Xi, Delta

Phi, Tau Beta Pi, Alpha Tau Sigma, Pi Tau Theta. Clubs: University, Rotary; Raquet; Barton Hills Country. Home: Ann Arbor MI Died May 2, 1973.

ALLEY, CALVIN LANE, editorial cartoonist; b. Memphis, Oct. 10, 1915; s. James Pinckney and Nona (Lane) A.; student Memphis State U., 1933-34, Am. Acad. Arts, 1934-35, Chgo. Acad. Arts, 1935-36; m. Geraldine Jehl, Nov. 28, 1939; children—Jerrianne (Mrs. Harry W. Petrie), Carol Lee (Mrs. Harmon C. Williams), Calvin Lane, Irene Jehl (Mrs. Joseph M. Palvado), Richard Wesley. Cartoonist, Kansas City Jour., 1939-42, Nashville Banner, 1942-45, Memphis Comml. Appeal, 1945-70; creator The Ryatts daily comic strip Post-Hall Syndicate, 1954; Sigma Delta Chi distinguished service cartoon Over My Dead Body, Library of Congress Exhibit, 1955. Cons. Memphis Acad. Arts. Recipient Freedom Found. medals, 1960, 61, 63, 64, 66, 67, 69, Freedom Found. certificate, 1968, Cancer Soc. certificates, 1963, 65, 68, 69, Memphis and Shelby County Safety Council award, certificate of merit Am. Heart Assn., 1968, Mem. Assn. Am. Editorial Cartoonists (charter), Sigma Delta Chi. Methodist. Kiwanian (award Korean War Meml. services E. Memphis club 1953). Club: Colonial (Memphis). Home: Memphis TN Died Nov. 10, 1970.

ALLEY, CHARLES EDWIN (C. ED), news photographer; b. LaGrangeville, N.Y., June 13, 1912; s. J. Edward and Sophia (Thorne) A.; student public schools; married Carolyn Whitaker Brann; one son, Edward H. Sports editor Poughkeepsie Evening Star, 1929-41; then staff Newburgh (N.Y.) News; then asst. mgr. news dept. Harris & Ewing; with Acme Newspictures until 1948; with United Press Internat., Washington, 1948-66; managing editor Arlington (Va.) News, 1969-71; columnist, feature ed. Arone Publs., Arlington, Va., 1966-71; editor White House News Photographer, 1959-65. Recipient first prize, 1951, 52, 57 contests White House News Photographers, numerous others. Mem. White House News Photographers Assn. (exec. bd. 1959-66, sec. 1962-66), Nat. Press Club. Home: Fairfax VA Died May 22, 1971.

ALLGOOD, DWIGHT MAURICE, mgmt. cons., engr.; b. near Gastonia, N.C., Dec. 20, 1903; s. David Perea and Rose Hill (Baity) A.; student Werntz Prep. Acad., Annapolis Md., 1921; B.S., U.S. Naval Acad., 1925; post grad. work, Mass. Inst. Tech., 1925; m. Sophie Julia Wolf, Oct. 9, 1926; children—Judith Hill, Dwight Maurice. Commd. ensign, U.S. Navy, 1925; served at sea with Atlantic Fleet, 1925-27; factory supt., Ludlow Mfg. Associates, Boston, 1927-29; consulting management engr., Scovell Wellington C Co., Boston-N.Y. City, 1929-37; pres. U.S. Glass Co., Pittsburgh, 1937-38; sales mgr., Willard Storage Battery Co., Cleveland, 1938-47; vice pres., asst. to pres. Farnsworth Television & Radio Corp., Fort Wayne, 1947-49; management consultant 1949-67; asso. prof. N.Y.U., 1950-52. Exec. v.p. Drop Forging Assn., 1957-67. Mem. civilian Naval adv. com., Fort Wayne, 1948. Mem. Navy Alumni Assn. Club: The Country (Cleve.). Home: Cleveland OH Died Oct. 27, 1967; interred Knoelwood Mausoleum, Cleveland OH

ALLIN, BUSHROD WARREN, agrl. economist; b. Harrodsburg, Ky., Aug. 28, 1899; s. John Warren and Flora Bell (Gritton) A.; B.S., U. Wis., 1921, Ph.D., 1927; m. Thelma A. Otteson, Sept. 30, 1922; children—Thelma Jean (Mrs. Louis Dudrow), Bushrod Warren, John Otteson. Engaged as farm cost accountant U.S. Department of Agriculture, Elkhorn, Wis., 1921-23, economist Bur. Agrl. Economics, 1930-34, A.A.A., 1935-37, spl. rep. Office Land Use Coordination, 1937-39, head div. state and local planning Bur. Agrl. Econs., 1939-42, spl. asst. to chief, 1942-46, chmn. outlook and situation bd. Econ. Research Service, 1946-65, mem. Dept. Agr. Grad. Sch. Council, 1954-65; instr. U. Wis., 1926-28; taxation economist Forest Taxation Inquiry, U.S. Forest Service, 1928-30; research economist Wharton Sch. Finance, U. Pa., 1934-35. Recipient Distinguished Service award Dept. Agr., 1962. AID grantee, India, 1960. Mem. Am. Farm (pres. 1962), Am. econ. assns., Farm House, Alpha Zeta, Delta Sigma Rho. Author: (with Carter Goodrich) Migration and Economic Opportunity, 1936. Contbr. articles profl. publs. Home: Bethesda, MD Died Nov. 18, 1968; buried Ft. Lincoln Cemetery, Washington DC

ALLIN, GEORGE LITCHFIELD, lawyer; b. Brooklyn, N.Y., Aug. 29, 1875; s. George Albert and Heloise Marie (Litchfield) A.; A.B., Brooklyn Poly. Inst., 1894; LL.B., New York Law Sch., 1897; m. Edith Peverly Gaskell, Oct. 25, 1899; children—Marjorie Gaskell (Mrs. Laurence McGonigal), Ruth Purdy (Mrs. Henry H. John), Elinor Litchfield (Mrs. John F. Cannon). Admitted to the N.Y. bar, 1897; asso. in law dept. Title Guarantee & Trust Co., 1901-15, chief counsel, 1915-23, solicitor, 1923-27; sr. partner Stoddard & Mark, 1927-30; sr. partner Allin, Tucker & Allen, 1930-37, and Allin & Tucker 1937-41, and Allin, Riggs & Shaughnessy since 1941; Tucker 1937-41, and Allin, Riggs & Shaughnessy since 1941; pres., dir. Medical Chambers, Inc. Gov. and v.p. Real Estate Bd. of N.Y., Inc.; Trustee White Plains Y.M.C.A.; chmn. finance Com. Am. Bapt. Home Mission Soc. Mem. Westchester County Bar Assn., Assn. Bar City of N.Y., Soc. Colonial Wars. Republican. Presbyn. (elder). Mason (past dist. dep. grand master; K.T.). Clubs: Union League (N.Y.C.); University (White Plains). Home: 124 North Broadway, White Plains, New York; and New Preston, Conn. Office: 285 Madison Av., New York NY‡

ALLIS, OSWALD THOMPSON, theologian; b. Wallingford, Pa., Sept. 9, 1880; s. Oscar H. and Julia W. (Thompson) A.; A.B., U. of Pa., 1901; B.D., Princeton Theol. Sem., 1905; A.M., Princeton U., 1907; Ph.D., from U. of Berlin, 1913; D.D., Hampden Sydney College, 1927; m. Ruth Robinson, Sept. 21, 1927; children—Julia Thompson, Constance Ruth. Instr. Semitic philology, Princeton Theol. Sem., 1910-22, asst. prof., 1922-29; prof. O. T. history and exegesis, Westminster Theol. Sem., 1929-30, prof. of O. T., 1930-36. Editor Princeton Theol. Rev., 1918-29; editorial corr. Evangelical Quarterly (Edinburgh), 1930-73; contbg. editor Christianity Today (Phila.), 1938-48; Payton lectr. Fuller Theol. Sem., Pasadena, Cal., 1952; moderator of Presbytery of Phila. of Presbyn. Church in U.S.A., 1934. Commissioner to Synod, 1934; commissioner to General Assembly, 1935, 51. Versions com. Am. Bible Soc., 1915-61. Republican. Presbyn. Contbr. to Am. and Brit. blblical and theological jours. Author: The Five Books of Moses, 1943 (2d edit. 1949); Bible Numerics, 1944; Prophecy and the Church, 1945 (3d printing 1955); Revision or New Translation?, 1948; The Unity of Isaiah, 1950; God Spake by Moses, 1951; Revised Version or Revised Bible?, 1953. Contributing editor Christianity Today, Washington, 1957-73. Contbr. chpts. to A New Bible Commentary, 1953; Baker's Dictionary of Theology, 1960; The Biblical Expositor, 1960; Basic Christian Doctrines (ed. by C. F. H. Henry), 1962. Address: Wayne PA Died Jan. 12, 1973.

ALLISON, JAMES EDWARD, architect; b. Hookstown, Pa., Feb. 22, 1870; s. George A. and Sarah Christy (Nesbit) A.; ed. Oakdale (Pa.) Acad., under pvt. tutors and at night sch.; m. Stella Clark, 1897 (died 1906); 1 dau., Elizabeth Nesbit; m. 2d, Mary E. Holyland, 1911 (died June 1947). Began in architecture at Pittsburgh, 1893; moved to Calif., 1910; sr. mem. firm Allison & Allison. Fellow A.I.A. and ex-pres. Southern Calif. Chapter same Republican. Presbyterian. Mason (32 deg.) Retired. Home: 9547 Burnet Av., San Fernando CA‡

ALLISON, NOAH DWIGHT, editor; b. Spencer Ind., Feb. 9, 1899; son of Clayton Benbridge and Pearl (Coble) A.; A.B., DePauw U., 1921; grad. Command and Gen. Staff Sch.; grad. Brit. Sr. Staff Coll.; m. Tomi Charpentier, July 3, 1923 (dec.). Reporter, 1921; news editor Post-Enquirer, Oakland, Calif., 1922-24; Sunday editor The Record, Fort Worth, Tex., 1925; mng. editor The Light, San Antonio, 1928-67; Lozano prof. journalism Trinity University, 1968-71. Served as 2d lt. Royal Air Force, Gt. Britain, World War I; lt. col., Mil. Intelligence Res., U.S. Army, World War II; 36th Div. V Corps, Hdqrs. ETO, 12th Army Group; chief liaison officer, 12th to 21st Army Group (Brit.) in Continental operations; campaigns: Normandy, Northern France, Ardennes, Rhineland, Central Europe. brig. gen. AUS (ret.). Decorated Bronze Star, Bronze Service Arrowhead, Order of British Empire. Mem. Tex. Cavaliers, Beta Theta Pi, Sigma Delta Chi. Democrat. San Antonio TX Died Mar. 22, 1971.

ALLMAN, DAVID BACHARACH, surgeon; b. Phila., July 11, 1891; s. Millard Filmore and Ray (Bacharach) A.; M.D., Jefferson Med. Coll., 1914, also LL.D.; L.H.D. Hebrew Union Coll.; Sc.D. (honorary), Temple University; m. Ann J. Lorenzen, July 19, 1965. Internship with Atlantic City Hosp., 1914-15, later sr. cons. surg. chief; chief surgeon Betty Bachrach Home for Afflicted Children, also med. dir., chmn. bd. govs.; ofcl. physician, bd. dirs. Miss America Pageant. Vice pres. Guardian Savs. and Loan Assn. Trustee Jefferson Medical College and Hospital. Served as lt. comdr. USNRF, World War I; surgeon USPHS, World War II. Diplomate Am. Bd. Surgery (founders group). Fellow A.C.S., Phila. Coll. Medicine, Acad. Medicine N.J., Internat. Coll. Surgeons; mem. A.M.A. (past pres.), World Med. Assn., Assn. Mil. Surgeons (past pres. N.J. chpt.), Soc. Surgs. N.J. (past pres.), Mil. Order World Wars (past state comdr.), Med. Soc. N.J. Med. Soc. Atlantic County (past pres., also treas.), Phila. Coll. Physicians, N.Y. Acad. Scis., A.A.A.S., Am., N.J. hosp. assns., Am. Trudeau Soc., Am. Cancer Soc., Atlantic County Hist. Assn., Am. Legion, Surg. Acad. Peru (hon.), Naval Order U.S., Res. Officers Naval Services, Res. Officers Assn. U.S. Mason. Clubs: Atlantic City Lions (past pres.), Racquet, Tuna, Atlantic City Country, Sojourners (Atlantic City) Medical of Phila.; Army and Navy. Home: Brigantine NJ Died Mar. 30, 1971; interred Laurel Meml. Mausoleum, Atlantic County NJ

ALLMAN, JUSTIN PAUL, wholesale merchant; b. Phila., Pa., June 28, 1873; s. David and Pauline (Kayser) A.; ed. pub. schs.; m. Viola Hirsh of Phila., June 5, 1900 (died July 6, 1933); children—Henry Hirsh, Charles Kayser, Robert Justin; m. 2nd, Hortense Wolf, of Phila., June 30, 1936. Began in wall paper business, 1889; mem. of firm Kayser & Allman, Inc., wholesale wall papers, since 1894. Hon. pres. Fed. of Jewish Charities of Phila., Nat. Wall Paper Wholesaler's Assn.; pres. Decorative Trades Assn. Jewish religion. Mason; trustee Pa. Grand Lodge Endowment Fund for Masonic Homes, Freemasons Memorial Hosp. Clubs: Reciprocity (hon. pres. Nat., pres. Phila.), Philmont Country, 100 Club of Phila. (treas.). Home: 235 S. 15th St. Office: 1709 Walnut St., Philadelphia, PA‡

ALLPORT, GORDON WILLARD, psychologist; b. Montezuma, Ind., Nov. 11, 1897; s. John Edwards and Nellie Edith (Wise) A.; A.B., Harvard, 1919, A.M., 1921, Ph.D., 1922; grad. work U. of Berlin and U. of Hamburg, 1922-23, Cambridge U., 1923-24; L.H.D. (hon.), Boston U., 1958; Ohio Wesleyan U., 1962; D.Sc., Colby College, 1964; D.Litt. (hon.), Durham University (England), 1965; m. Ada Lufkin Gould, June 30, 1925; 1 son, Robert Bradlee. Instr. in English, Robert College, Istanbul, Turkey, 1919-20; instr. in social ethics, Harvard University, 1924-26; asst. prof. in psychology, Dartmouth College, 1926-30; asst. prof. psychology, Harvard Univ., 1930-36, asso. prof., 1937, prof. psychology since 1942. Mem. S.A.T.C. Past mem. nat. com. for UNESCO. Pres. Edn. Exchange Greater Boston; past dir. Nat. Opinion Research Center; past mem. Social Sci. Research and Nat. Research Councils. Recipient Gold Medal award Am. Psychol. Found., 1963. Hon. fellow Brit. Psychol. Soc.; hon. mem. Spanish, Italian psychological societies, Deutsche Gesellschaft fur Psychologie, Osterreichische Arztegesellschaft fur Psychotherapie; member Am. (mem. council 1936-38; pres. 1939), Eastern (pres. 1943) psychological associations, Phi Beta Kappa. Episcopalian. Clubs: Faculty, Harvard of N.Y. Author: Studies in Expressive Movement (with P. E. Vernon), 1933; The Psychology of Radio (with H. Cantril), 1935; Trait-Names; A Psycho-lexical study (with H. S. Odbert), 1936; Personality—a Psychological Interpretation, 1937; Psychology of Rumor (with L. Postman), 1947; The Individual and His Religion, 1950; The Nature of Personality, 1950; The Nature of Prejudice, 1954; Becoming: Basic Considerations for a Psychology of Personality, 1955; Personality and Social Encounter, 1960; Pattern and Growth of Personality, 1961; Letters From Jenny, 1965. Editor Jour. Abnormal and Social Psychology, 1937-49. Home: Watertown MA

ALLWORK, ELEANOR BLOOM (MRS. RONALD ALLWORK), interior designer; b. N.Y.C., Sept. 11, 1911; d. Edgar Selden and May (Wallace) Bloom; student Barnard Coll., 1929-33; spl. study Columbia Sch. Architecture, 1936-37; diploma interior architecture N.Y. Sch. Applied Design for Women, 1939; m. Ronald Allwork, Oct. 17, 1941; 1 dau., Winifred. Estimator, asst. designer H. F. Huber & Assos., 1933-37; owner, mgr. Bloomsbury House, 1939-41; sec.-treas. Allwork Co., N.Y.C., 1946-68. Mem. adv. com. on maintenance N.Y. Hosp., 1953-54. Recipient first award Gramercy Park Exhibit Nat. Arts Club, 1951. Mem. Am. Inst. Decorators, A.I.A. (pres. Women's Archtl. Aux. N.Y. chpt. 1964-65), N.Y. Jr. League. Republican. Presbyn. Home: New York City NY Died June 28, 1968.

ALLYN, STANLEY CHARLES, corp. official; b. Madison, Wis., July 20, 1891; s. Charles Herbert and Anna Louise (Cook) A.; A.B., U. Wis., 1913, LL.D., 1946; LL.D., Miami U., Oxford, Ohio, 1952; L.H.D. University Dayton, 1954, Univ. Cin., 1956; D.B.A. (honorary), Otterbein College, 1966; married Helen Probasco Compton, Sept. 29, 1917 (dec. 1967); children—Charles Stanley, Mary Louise, Compton; m. 2nd Patricia von Krell Turnbull, 1968. Accountant, asst. comptroller, comptroller, treas., exec. v.p., gen. mgr., Nat. Cash Register Co., Dayton, O., 1913-40, dir., 1918-61, pres., 1950-57, chmn. bd. chief executive officer, 1957-61, chmn. exec. com., 1962-64, dir. emeritus, 1964-70; dir. Dayco Corp., Mead Corporation (Dayton), Western Allegheny R.R. Co., Master Consolidated, Inc., Dayton, Ohio; trustee Northwestern Mutual Life Ins. Co. (Milw.). Bd. dirs. Nat. Conf. Christians and Jews; trustee Dayton Air Force Mus., Logistics Mgmt. Inst., Washington; vice president of the Grand Central Art Galleries; bd. trustees Com. for Econ. Development, N.Y., Thomas Alva Edison Found., N.Y.; mem. bus. adv. council Dept. of Commerce; trustee U.S. Council of Internat. C. of C., Nat. Aviation Hall Fame, Cox Coronary Heart Inst.; industries adv. com. The Adv. Council; pres., Community Chests and Councils of America, 1950-51; vice chmn. 1960, United Community Campaigns; Dir. U. Wis. Found.; hon. trustee Inst. Internat. Edn., N.Y.C.; trustee Asia Foundation, San Francisco; hon. mem. nat. council Boy Scouts Am. Head U.S. delegation Econ. Commn. Europe, 1956, 57, 9th gen. session Gen. Conf., UNESCO, 1956, chmn. com. on 6th nat. conf. of U.S. Nat. Commn. for UNESCO, 1957; mem. adv. council U.S. Com. for UN. Decorated Officer French Legion of Honor; recipient Presdl. Certificate of Merit; USN award Distinguished Pub. Service; named Industrialist of Year by Soc. Indsl. Realtors, 1961; recipient Good Citizenship medal S.A.R., 1962; named honorary citizen Athens, Greece. Mem. Psi Upsilon. Clubs: Blind Brook (Port Chester, New York), Lyford Cay, East Hill (Nassau, Bahamas), Buz Fuz, Moraine Country (Dayton); Greenwich CT Died Oct. 31, 1970; buried Greenwich CT

ALMERT, HAROLD, consulting engr.; b. Chicago, June 2, 1876; s. Andrew and Wilhelmina (Walhstrom) A.; ed. in engring., in Chicago, 8 yrs., law, 3 yrs., accounting, 2 yrs.; m. Anita C. Tiedeman, of Chicago, Dec. 28, 1907; children—John Gordon, Jane Louise. Consulting engring. practice in Chicago since 1909; tech. counsel to a number of the largest utilities and industrial companies, including Commonwealth Edison Co., Pub. Service Co. of Northern Ill. (Chicago), Washington Ry. & Electric Co., Potomac Electric Power Co. (Washington), etc.; with staff has constructed or appraised over $1,000,000,000 worth of public utility and industrial plants and approved the issue of over $500,000,000 par value of securities. Developed a chem. treatment for improvement of pig iron and gray foundry iron; invented device for converting hard coal burners to soft coal heaters, soot destroyer, etc. Patentee of the Almert Central Home Service plan. Dir. of conservation U.S. Fuel Administration for Ill., during the war. Mem. Am. Assn. Engrs. (ex-pres.), Am. Soc. C.E., Western Soc. Engrs., Am. Soc. M.E., Am. Inst. E.E., Nat. Elec. Light Assn., Am. Gas Assn. Republican. Clubs: Electric, Lincoln Park Gun, The Indians, South Shore Country, Midday (Chicago); Engineers' (New York). Home: 119 E. 84th St., New York NY‡

ALMSTEDT, HERMANN BENJAMIN, univ. prof.; b. St. Louis, Mo., Dec. 26, 1872; s. Hermann and Maria (Laging) A.; L.B. and Pe.B., U. of Mo., 1895; Ph.D., U. of Chicago, 1900; student univs. of Leipzig and Berlin; m. Elizabeth Wilde, Aug. 16, 1906; children—Ruth Elizabeth, Regina Esther, Margaret Florence, Elsa Hermina. With dept. Germanic langs., U. of Chicago, 1895-1901, dean, Univ. Coll., U. of Chicago, 1900-01; with U. of Mo. since 1901, prof. Germanic lang., chairman dept., 1907-42, in charge Sanskrit, 1935-42, prof. emeritus since 1942. Assistant ednl. dir. coll. sect. S.A.T.C. Fellow A.A.A.S.; mem. Modern Lang. Assn. America, Nat. Fed. Modern Lang. Teachers, Soc. Advancement of Scandinavian Studies, Am. Assn. Univ. Profs., Linguistic Soc. America, Verein fur Niederdeutsche Sprachforschung, Phi Mu Alpha, Phi Beta Kappa, Am. Guild of Organists, Am. Assn. of Teachers of German; Am. mem. Weimar Goethe Gsellschaft; mem. advisory council Living Age; collaborator and corr. mem. Schiller Akademie (Munchen); mem. advisory council Franklin Soc. (Zurich, Switzerland). Home: Columbia MO‡

ALMY, ROBERT FORBES, educator; b. New Bedford, Mass., Feb. 10, 1901; s. Edgar Maurice and Ethel Washburn (Denham) A.; A.B., Dartmouth Coll., 1922; A.M., Harvard, 1925, Ph.D., 1935; m. Eleanor Hale Bly, June 11, 1930; children—Natalie Hale, Judith Denham. Instr. in English, Northwestern U., 1925-27; asst. prof. English, Miami U., Oxford, O., 1929-39, asso. prof., 1939-47, prof. 1947-68, chmn. dept. English 1947-56. Mem. Modern Lang. Assn., Sigma Phi Epsilon. Unitarian. Editor: Approach to America (with Walter E. Havighurst and Joseph M. Bachelor), 1942; (with others) Selection: A Reader for College Writing, 1955. Contbr. articles to The Sat. Rev. of Lit., The Colophon. Home: Oxford OH Died Feb. 1, 1969.

ALSCHULER, BENJAMIN PHILIP;, b. Aurora, Ill., Nov. 8, 1876; s. Jacob and Caroline (Stiefel) A.; ed. pub. and high schs., Aurora; m. Lillian Reinheimer, Mar. 28, 1900; children—Jacob Edward, Corinne (Mrs. Milton E. Weil), Sam. Lawyer. Democrat. Mason. Elk. Home: 106 LeGrande Blvd. Office: 32 Water St., Aurora IL‡

ALT, HOWARD LANG, physician; b. Chicago, July 28, 1900; s. Frank Henry and Clara (Lang) A.; M.D., Northwestern U., 1924, Ph.D., 1934; m. Patricia Drew, June 19, 1935; children—Leslie (Mrs. John G. Mott), Abby Lynn (Mrs. L. Russell Cartwright), Robin Julie (Mrs. Crocker Snow, Jr.), Howard Lang. Winston Drew, Patricia Brooke (Mrs. Peter Kountz). House officer Wesley Memorial Hosp., Chicago, 1923-25; asst. resident and resident physician Peter Bent Brigham Hosp., Boston, 1925-29; teaching fellow in medicine Harvard Med. Sch., 1927-29; asst. to Prof. O. Warburg, Kaiser Wilhelm Inst. fur Biologie, Berlin-Dahlem. 1929-30; assistant at the Medizinische Klinik, Wuerzburg, Germany, 1930; asso. in medicine Northwestern Med. Sch., 1930-36, dir. hematology clinic, 1931-58, dir. labs. and in charge clin. pathology, 1935-39, instr. chemistry 1931-50, asst. prof. medicine, 1936-46, asso. prof. 1946-56, prof. from 1956; mem. staff Passavant, 1930, chief of medicine, 1958-63; consultant hematologist Children's Memorial Hosp., VA Research Hosp. Director, Hospital Service Corporation. Served as expert cons. in internal medicine, U.S. Army, 1946-47. Certified by Am. Bd. Internal Medicine Mem. Am. Coll. Physicians, Internat., Am. socs. hematology, Assn. of American Physicians, Central Society for Clinical Research. Inst. Medicine of Chicago, Chicago Soc. Internal Medicine, Sigma Xi, Delta Upsilon, Alpha Kappa Kappa Contbr. to med. jours. on hematology; made discoveries relating to pathologic physiology of anemia. Home: Evanston IL Died Feb. 12, 1972; buried Graceland Cemetery, Chicago IL

ALTER, DINSMORE, astronomer; b. Colfax, Wash., Mar. 28, 1888; s. Joseph and Jeannette (Copley) A.; B.S., Westminster Coll., New Wilmington, Pa., 1909; M.S., U. of Pittsburgh, 1910; Ph.D., U. of Calf., 1916; D.Sc., Monmouth Coll., 1941; m. Ada McClelland, Dec. 26, 1910; children—Helen Jeannette, Dinsmore (dec.). Instr. and adj. prof. physics and astronomy, U. of Ala., 1911-14; instr. astronomy, U. of Calif., 1914-17; asst. prof. of astronomy, U. of Kan., 1917-19, asso. prof., 1919-24, prof., 1924-36; dir. Griffith Observatory, Los Angeles, 1935-58, dir. emeritus, 1958. Served to maj. C.A., U.S. Army, World War I; col. T.C. Reserve; on active service, col. T.C., A.U.S., 1942-1947, World War II. Fellow, Royal Astron. Soc., Am. Meteorol. Soc. (v.p. 1926-27), American Geophysical Union, Institute of Math. Statistics, British Astron. Assn., Astron. Soc. of Pacific, A.A.A.S., American Astronomical Society American Legion, Forty and Eight, Sigma Xi. Democrat. United Presbyn. Contbr. to Lick Obs. bulls., Astron. Jour., numerous others. Known for original research in meteorol. periodicities and math. methods pertaining to same. John Simon Guggenheim memorial fellow in England for statistical research on rainfall, 1929-30. Home: Berkeley CA Died Sept. 1968.

ALTER, NICHOLAS M(ARK), pathologist, lab. dir.; b. Csanytclek, Hungary, Oct. 12, 1892; s. Joseph M. and Katherine (Csany) A.; M.D., U. Hungary, 1913, U. Vienna, 1914; grad. study U. Lelpzig, 1913, U. Heidelberg, 1914; m. Eleanor Cochran Reed, Apr. 11, 1931; children—Eleanor, Katherine, Nicholas Albert, Ernest Henry. Came to U.S., 1914, naturalized, 1923. Pathologist, lab. dir. H. A. Kelly Hosp., Baltimore, 1915-19, also asst. dept. pathology Johns Hopkins Hosp.; resident pathologist, instr. med. sch. Yale, 1919-20; pathologist W. Penn Hosp., Pittsburgh, 1920-22; asst. prof. internal medicine U. Mich., 1922-23; prof. pathology U. Colo., 1923-25, N.Y. Post Grad. Med. Sch., N.Y. City, 1925-30; later pathologist, lab. dir. Margaret Hague Hosp., Jersey City. Mem. bd. Mus. Assn. Jersey City, Internat. Inst., Jersey City Philharmonic Symphony. Served as lt. comdr., U.S. Navy, 1933-41. Diplomate Am. Bd. Pathology (anat. and clin. pathology). Fellow A.M.A.; mem. A.A.A.S., Am. Assn. Pathologists and Bacteriologists, N.Y. Path. Soc., N.J. Soc. Pathologists, China Inst. Study Oriental Art. Club: Hajji Baba. Slatersville RI Died Mar. 1970.

ALTHERR, ALFRED, architect, designer; b. Elberfield, Germany, Aug. 3, 1911; s. Alfred and Marta (Timmermann) A.; apprenticeship Zurich, studies at LeCorbusier, Paris, France, 1931-32; pupil Prof. Karl Moser, 1932-33, Prof. Alfred Roth, Zurich, Switzerland, 1933-34; m. Margaret Hofer, Dec. 14, 1935; children—Regula, George, Verena, Magdalena. Self-employed architect, Forch, Zurich, 1934-72; work includes family houses, homes for handicapped children, factories, schs.; tchr. constrn. design Switzerland mus. Applied Art, Zurich, 1939-54; dir. archtl. exhtns. and museum shows, Switzerland; del. World Design Congress, Tokyo, Japan, 1960. Mem. Internat. Congress Modern Architecture, Swiss Assn. Architects, Swiss Engring. and Architecture Soc. Author: New Swiss architecture, 1964; Three Japanese Architects, 1968. Designs include furniture, Forch Switzerland Died June 15, 1972.

ALTHOUSE, HOWELL HALBERSTADT, civil engineer; b. Pottsville, Pa., June 24, 1869; s. Daniel Seidel and Clara (Whitman) A.; ed. Pottsville High Sch.; m. Elizabeth C. McKenna, of Phila., Nov. 26, 1924; 1 dau., Harriet Marie. With Pa. Geol. Survey, hdqrs. Pottsville, 1888-89; engring. corps various rys., 1889-99; with Erie R.R., as asst. engr. at Galion, O., 1899-1902, Cleveland, 1902-08, New York, 1908-12, prin. asst. engr. lines west, July-Sept. 1912, chief engr., 1912-13; consulting practice, N.Y. City, 1913-19; cons. engr. for Chamber of Commerce, Reading, Pa., 1919-24, for elimination of grade crossings, Phila. & Reading Ry. main tracks through the City of Reading. Mem. Pa. N.G., 3 yrs. Mem. Am. Ry. Engring. Assn., Engrs.' Soc. of Pa. Republican. Episcopalian. Club: Harrisburg (Pa.). Home: 7242 Somers Rd., Philadelphia, PA Address: Chamber of Commerce Reading PA‡

ALTHOUSE, PAUL MARCKS, educator; b. Reading, Pa., Oct. 9, 1916; s. Solomon A. and Katie (Marcks) A.; B.S., Pa. State Coll., 1938, M.S., 1940, Ph.D., 1943; m. Virginia F. Feick, Aug. 16, 1941; children—Paul Richard, Nancy Jean. Mem. faculty Pa. State U., 1942-, prof. agrl. and biol. chemistry, from 1951, dir. gen. edn., 1962-65, asst. v.p. resident instrn., 1965-67, v.p. resident instrn., 1967-70, v.p. for academic affairs, 1970-71, acting pres., 1971, provost, 1971-72. Mem. A.A.A.S., Am. Chem. Soc., Am. Oil Chemists Soc., N.E.A., Assn. Gen. and Liberal Studies. Home: State College PA Died Feb. 4, 1972; buried Centre County Meml. Park, Centre County PA

ALTMAN, OSCAR LOUIS, govt. ofcl.; b. N.Y.C., Jan. 17, 1909; s. Benjamin and Rose (Sokoloff) A.; A.B., Cornell U., 1929, A.M., 1930; Ph.D., U. Chgo., 1936; m. Alberta Smith Neblett, 1942 (div. 1951);children—Peter A., Leslie V.; m. 2d, Adeline Furness Roberts, 1952 (div. 1965); 1 son, William H.F. Instr. econs. Ohio State U., 1936-38; sr. economist SEC, 1938-40; prin. economist Nat. Resources Planning Bd., 1940-42; with French Supply Council, 1945-46; with Internat. Monetary Fund, 1946-68, dep. dir. research, 1954-66, treas., 1966-68. Bd. dirs. D.C. Inst. Mental Hygiene, 1967-68, Washington Drama Soc., 1964-68. Served to lt. col. USAAF, 1942-45. Decorated Legion of Merit. Mem. Am. Econ. Assn., Phi Beta Kappa, Phi Kappa Phi Fraternity. Democrat. Jewish religion. Clubs: Army/Navy Country, also Cosmos (Washington); Army Navy Country (Arlington, Virginia). Author: Saving, Investment and National Income, 1942; also articles. Home: Washington DC Died Dec. 22, 1968.

ALTMEYER, ARTHUR JOSEPH, ex-govt. ofcl.; b. De Pere, Wis., May 8, 1891; s. John G. and Carrie (Smith) A.; B.A., U. Wis., 1914, M.A., 1921. Ph.D., 1931, Doctor of Laws (honorary), 1939; m. Ethel M. Thomas, July 3, 1916. Began as high sch. tchr., 1914-16, sch. prin., 1916-18; statistician Wis. Tax Commn., 1918-20; chief statistician Wis. Indsl. Commn., 1920-22, sec., 1922-33; chief compliance div. NRA, 1933-34; asst. sec. labor, chmn. tech. bd. Pres.' Com. on Econ. Security, 1934-35; mem. Social Security Bd. U.S., 1935-46, chmn., 1937-46; U.S. commr. for social security, 1946-53; vis. prof. U. Utah, U. Cal. at Los Angeles, U. N.C., U. Wis., U. Chgo., Salzburg, (Austria) Seminar in American Studies. Exec. dir. War Manpower Commn., 1942, mem., 1942-45; exec. com. Nat. Youth Adminstrn., 1935; chmn. U.S. del. Regional Conf. Am. States mem. ILO, Havana, Cuba, 1939; chmn. Am. delegation, 1st-5th Inter-Am. confs. on Social Security, chmn. Inter-Am. Com. on Social Security, 1942-52; U.S. rep. Social Commn. UN, 1946-53; exec. dir. Preparatory Commn. Internat. Refugee Orgn., 1947; pres. Nat. Conf. Social Work, 1954-55; social welfare advisor to govts. of Iran and Turkey, to nongovt. orgns., Peru, Columbia, to U.S. Mission, Pakistan, 1955-72. Chmn. social security com. Dem. Adv. Council, 1960. Chmn. bd. trustees Retirement Fund of Coat and Suit Industry, N.Y.C., 1943-65, Nat. Indsl. Group Pension Plan, Wash., 1966-72. chief appeals officer ILGWU Nat. Retirement Fund, N.Y.C., 1965-72. Decorated D.S.M. Mem. Phi Beta Kappa. Author: The Industrial Commission of Wisconsin, 1932; The Formative Years of Social Security, 1965. Co-author: Economic Study Peruvian Social Legislation, 1957. Home: Middleton WI Died Oct. 1972.

ALTON, ALFRED EDWARD, prof. Biblical lit.; b. Troy, N.Y., July 19, 1874; s. John and Jean (Robb) A.; A.B., Princeton, 1898; B.D., Colgate Theol. Sem., 1902; D.D., Hamilton College, Clinton, N.Y., 1926; m. Blanche Louise Warren, of Holden, Mass., April 3, 1906;children—Mrs. Jean A. Thayer, Henry Warren. Ordained Bapt. ministry, 1902; pastor First Ch., Holden, Mass., 1902-05, First Ch., Rome, N.Y., 1906-11; prof. Bibl. lit., Colgate U., 1911-34, and sec., 1921-30, prof. emeritus since 1934. Sec. Colgate Univ. Alumni Corpn., 1919-25; sec. bd. trustees Colgate U., 1923-34. Mem. Phi Beta Kappa, Delta Kappa Epsilon. Republican. Home: Holden MA‡

ALTSCHULER, MODEST, musician; b. Mogileff, Russia, Feb. 18, 1873; s. Isaak and Bertha (Sluzkin) A.; grad. Warsaw Conservatory, 1886; grad. Imperial Moscow Conservatory, 1895 (medals); m. Annie Altschuler, of Moscow, Russia, Mar. 5, 1896. Served in Russian Army; came to America, 1896; organized Russian Symphony Orchestra and toured U.S. as its leader, also playing at Chautauqua (N.Y.) Summer Assembly; conductor popular concerts in N.Y. City. Home: 645 W. 160th St., New York NY‡

ALVAREZ, ALEJANDRO, Chilean jurist; b. Santiago, Chile, Feb. 9, 1868; LL.B., U. Chile, 1892, J.D., 1895; student Liberal Sch. of Polit. Scis., Paris, 1898; LL.D., U. Paris, 1899. Sec. Chilean delegation to 2d Pan-Am. Conf. and cons. to Ministry of Fgn. Affairs, 1901; elected judge Internat. Court of Justice, for term of nine years, 1946. Home: Hotel Crillon, Santiago, Chile. Office: Peace Palace, The Hague The Netherlands‡

ALVES, HENRY F(RED), educator; b. New Braunfels, Tex., May 9, 1894; s. Emil and Mary (Pape) A.; A.B., S.W. Tex. State Tchrs. Coll., 1928; M.A., U. Tex., 1929; grad. study (Gen. Edn. Bd. fellowship) Tchrs. Coll. Columbia, 1929-30; m. Ruby I. Tracy, July 2, 1918;children—Anne Beth, Mary Virginia (Mrs. Horace W. Busby). Tchr. rural school, Tex., 1911-12; prin., rural school, 1913-14; tchr. math. high sch., 1914-16; prin. elementary and high schs., Tex., 1916-17; headmaster mil. acad., 1919-20; supt. Alamo Heights Pub. Schs., San Antonio, 1920-26; state high sch. supervisor Tex. State Dept. Edn., 1926-28, state coll. examiner, 1928-29, state dir. research and finance, 1930-35; specialist state sch. adminstrn. U.S. Office Edn., 1935-41, prtn. specialist state sch. adminstrn., 1941-44, chief div. sch. adminstrn., 1945, dir. div. surplus property utilization, 1945-46, asso. chief co. and rural sch. adminstrn., 1946-48, asst. dir., later dir. div. sch. adminstrn., 1948-50; instr. courses sch. adminstrn. U. Tex., 7 summers 1932-47, U. Mich., summer 1938, George Washington U., 1948-50; dir. southwestern coop. program ednl. adminstrn., prof. ednl. adminstrn. U. Tex. from 1950. Cons. on study of orgn. state depts. edn. Pres. Adv. Com. Edn., 1937. Served as sgt. M.C. and 2d lt. F.A., 1917-19. Mem. Am. Assn. Sch. Adminstrs., N.E.A., Nat. Conf. County and Area Supts., Nat. Council Schoolhouse Constrn., Assn. Sch.

Bus. Ofcls., Tex. Assn. Sch. Adminstrs., Tex. State Tchrs. Assn., Nat. Conf. Profs. Ednl. Adminstrn., Phi Delta Kappa. Author articles profl. jours. Home: Austin TX Died Aug. 1969.

ALVORD, IDRESS HEAD (MRS. CLARENCE W. ALVORD), writer; b. Roanoke, Missouri; d. John Calhoun and Susan (Wallace) Head; grad. as Mistress of English Literature, Howard Payne College, Fayette, Mo., 1897; Central Coll., Fayette, 1899; m. Clarence W. Alvord, of Urbana, Ill., Apr. 10, 1913. Teacher pub. schs., Fayette, 1901-02; hist. research sec. to Louis Houck while he was writing his History of Missouri, 1903-07; librarian and curator Mo. Hist. Soc., 1907-13; asst. in woolens sect. War Industries Bd., 1918; mem. advisory bd. Living Age; sec. Farm Dept. Adjustment in Missouri Resettlement Administration, 1934; assistant state director of historical records survey in New Mexico since 1937. Methodist. Member Mississippi Valley Historical Association (executive committee, 1912-13), Missouri Historical Society (associate), Pi Beta Phi Sorority, State Hist. Soc. of Mo., D.A.R. (hon.), U.D.C. (rec. sec. St. Louis Chapter, 1909-10; founder of Mo. State U.D.C. Library and Museum, 1908), Mo. Folk Lore Soc. (treas., 1909-13), Woman's Club (Minneapolis), Am. Assn. of Univ. Women; hon. mem. institute Historique et Heraldique de France, 1933; patroness Phi Beta Fraternity. Author: Historical and Intresting Places of St. Louis, 1909. Co-author: Inventory County Archives, Colfax County, N.M., 1937. Contbr. on hist. topics to newspapers and mags. Home: 56 Clarence Av., S.E., Minneapolis MN‡

ALVORD, KATHARINE SPRAGUE, educator; b. Sandusky, O., June 16, 1871; d. Frederick Wakeman and Caroline (Sprague) A.; A.B., U. of Mich., 1893; A.M., Columbia, 1908; studied U. of Wis., 1909-10, Cornell U., 1914-15. With dept. of history, Oshkosh (Wis.) State Normal Sch., 1897-1907; asst. prof. history, Miami U., Oxford, O., 1908-9; vocational adviser and head of Chadbourne Hall, U. of Wis., 1909-14; dean of women and asso. prof. history, DePauw U., since 1915. Mem. Am. Hist. Assn., Miss. Valley Hist. Assn., Assn. Collegiate Alumnae, Nat. Assn. Deans of Women (sec. 1920), Kappa Kappa Gamma. Democrat. Conglist. Address: Rector Hall, Greencastle IN‡

ALWAY, FREDERICK JAMES, chemist; b. Rockford, Ont., Can., May 28, 1874; s. Frederick and Rachel (Mason) A.; B.A., U. of Toronto, 1894 (D.Sc., 1927); Ph.D., Heidelberg U., 1897; m. Eva M. Cook, 1898; children—Mrs. Filomena Erica Robinson, Lazelle Martha and Leonore Katherine (twins), Mrs. Fredrica Jane Bull, Robert Hamilton. Prof. chemistry, Neb. Wesleyan U., 1898-1906; prof. agrl. chemistry, U. of Neb., 1906-13; prof. soil chemistry and chief div. of soils, U. of Minn., 1913-42; prof. emeritus since 1942. Fellow A.A.A.S.; mem. Am. Chem. Soc., Am. Soc. Agronomy, Soil Science Soc. America, Sigma Xi; corr. mem. Swedish Peat Soc. Baptist. Author numerous papers on organic and soil chemistry and soil physics. Home: 1386 Grantham Av., St Paul MN‡

AMBERG, SAMUEL, pediatrician; b. Cannstatt, Germany, Aug. 15, 1874; s. Jacob and Minna (Loewenbein) A.; prep. edn., Gymnasium, Cannstatt; student U. of Berlin; M.D., U. of Heidelberg, 1898; unmarried. Came to U.S., 1899. Asso. prof. pediatrics, Johns Hopkins, 1910-12; asso. prof. exptl. medicine, Rush Med. Coll., 1912-21; dir. Otho S.A. Sprague Memorial Institute Laboratory, Children's Memorial Hospital, Chicago, 1912-21; became associate professor pediatrics, Mayo Foundation Grad. Sch., U. of Minn., 1921, now emeritus; associate in pediatrics, Mayo Clinic, Rochester, Minnesota, since 1921. Served as pharmacologist, U.S. War Dept., 1917-18; ex-cons. Chem. Warfare Service; lt. col. Med. O.R.C. Mem. Am. Pediatric Soc., Am. Acad. Pediatrics, Am. Physiol. Soc., Am. Pharmacological Soc., Am. Biochem. Soc., Sigma Xi, Phi Beta Pi; corr. mem. Gesellschaft fur innere Medizin und Kinderheilkunde (Vienna). Author: (with H. F. Helmholz) Diseases of the Genito Urinary System in Infancy and Childhood, 1930. Home: 419 8th Av. S.W. Office: Mayo Clinic, Rochester MN‡

AMBROSE, PAUL, organist, composer; b. Hamilton, Ont., Oct. 11, 1868; s. Robert Steele (composer) and Elizabeth A.; ed. pub. schs. and Hamilton Collegiate Inst.; studied piano with father and A.R. Parsons, counterpoint with B.O. Klein, orchestration with Dudley Buck; m. Naomi Lambe, June 1905; children—Gwynneth, Robert Steele, Paul Hamilton. Organist, Madison Av. M.E. Ch., New York, 1886-90; organist and choirmaster, St. James' Ch., New York, 1890 to 1917; organist and choirmaster of First Presbyn. Ch., Trenton, N.J., 1917-1933. Prof. music, N.J. state schs., 1903-17; formerly for long period actively engaged as soloist and accompanist. V.p. Synthetic Guild of N.Y.; pres. for New Jersey of Nat. Assn. Organists, 1913, 14, 15, 1933-34, Canadian Coll. Organists, 1939-41. Composer numerous sacred and secular songs, vocal duets, part songs, piano solos, etc. Address: 155 Markland St., Hamilton Ontario Canada‡

AMDUR, ISADORE, univ. prof; b. Pittsburgh, Pa., Jan. 24, 1910; s. Benjamin and Mollie (Silberblatt) A.; B.S., U. of Pittsburgh, 1930, M.S., 1930, Ph.D., 1932; m. Alice Pauline Steiner, June 16, 1935; children—Stephen Benjamin, Nicholas John. Special lecturer U. of Pittsburgh, summer, 1932; nat. research fellow in chemistry, Mass. Inst. of Tech., 1932-34, instr., 1934-40, asst. prof., 1940-45, asso. prof., 1945-51, prof. phys. chemistry, 1951-70; vis. scientist U.S.-Japan Coop. Program sponsored by National Science Foundation, Kyoto University, 1965-66. Honorary president International Committee of High and Intermediate Energy Molecular Beams; chmn. local organizing com. VI Internat. Conf. on Physics Electronic and Atomic Collisions, 1969, mem. exec. com. for VII Conf. John Simon Guggenheim Meml. Fellow, 1955-56. Fellow Am. Phys. Soc.; mem. Am. Chem. Soc., A.A.A.S., Am. Acad. Arts and Scis. (recording sec., 1946-47, mem. council 1948-52). Sigma Xi, Phi Lambda Upsilon, Pi Lambda Phi, Phi Beta Kappa. Author: (with Gordon G. Hammes) Chemical Kinetics, 1966. Contbr. articles to sci. journals. Home: Belmont MA Died June 3, 1970.

AMES, LEWIS DARWIN, prof. mathematics; b. Keeseville, N.Y., July 11, 1869; s. Isaac Dow and Jane Lucy (Forbes) A.; student Doane Coll., Crete, Neb., Northern Ind. Normal Sch., U. of Chicago Summer Sch.; Litt. B., U. of Mo., 1899; A.B., Harvard, 1901, A.M., 1902, Ph.D., 1904; m. Linnie Edwards, Centralia, Mo., 1894; children—James Russell (dec.), Jane, Frances, Katherine, Afton, adopted (Mrs. Wilford M. Carpenter). Began as teacher, country schs.; teacher, Chillicothe (Mo.) Normal Sch., 1890-98, 1899-1900; instr., Harvard, 1901-02; instr., U. of Mo., 1903-06, asst. prof., 1906-12, asso. prof., 1912-20, also registrar, 1919-20; taught at Peabody Coll. for Teachers, Nashville, Tenn., summers 1916, 17; engaged in ranching, Calif., also high sch. teacher, 1920-25; asso. prof., Tex. Tech. Coll., Lubbock, Tex., 1925-26; teacher, U. of Calif., summer 1926; prof. mathematics, U. of Southern Calif., since 1926. Mem. Am. Math. Soc., Math. Assn. America, Am. Assn. Univ. Profs., Phi Beta Kappa, Sigma Xi, Phi Delta Kappa. Methodist. Mason. Home: 1328 W. 37th Drive, Los Angeles CA‡

AMES, SUSIE M(AY), educator; b. Pungoteague, Va., Jan. 10, 1888; d. Samuel William and Sarah Anne Edmonds (Mears) Ames; A.B., Randolph-Macon Woman's Coll., 1908; A.M., Columbia, 1926, Ph.D., 1940; summer sch. study U. Chgo., 1915, U. Cal., 1923. Tchr. high sch., Crewe, Va., 1908-09; high sch. prin., Harborton, Va., 1909-11, Pocomoke City, Md., 1911-13, Franktown, Va., 1915-17, Pungoteague, Va., 1917-20, Lynchburg, Va., 1920-23; instr. Eastern Ky. State Normal Sch., 1913-15; instr. history Randolph-Macon Woman's Coll., 1923-26, adj. prof., 1926-40, asso. prof. history, 1940-54, prof. history, 1954-55, prof. emeritus, 1955-69. Mem. Va. World War II History Commn., 1944-48. Mem. Am. Historical Assn., Va. Hist. Soc., Eastern Shore Va. Hist. Soc., Randolph-Macon Alumnae Assn., Assn. for Preservation of Va. Antiquities, Magna Charta Dames, Colonial Dames, Daus. Founders and Patriots Am., Daus. Am. Colonists, D.A.R., Phi Beta Kappa, Delta Kappa Gamma, Pi Gamma Mu, Kappa Alpha Theta. Methodist. Clubs: Eastern Shore of Virginia Garden, Woman's of Accomack County, Garden of Va. Author: Studies of the Virginia Eastern Shore in the Seventeenth Century, 1940; Some Colonial Foundations of the Virginia Eastern Shore, in the Eastern Shore of Maryland and Virginia, 1950; Reading, Writing and Arithmetic in Virginia, 1607-1699. Other Cultural Topics, 1957; Federal Policy Toward The Eastern Shore of Virginia in 1861, 1961; The Bear and the Cub: The Site of the First English Theatrical Performance in America, 1965. Editor: County Court Records of Accomack-Northampton, Virginia, 1954. Contbr. hist. publs. Home: Pungoteague VA Died July 30, 1969.

AMICK, ERWIN HAMER, JR., educator; b. Chgo., July 12, 1910; s. Erwin Hamer and Estella Anna (Murphy) A.; B.S., Mont. State Coll., 1932; M.S., U. N.D., 1933; Eng.D., Yale, 1938; m. Dorothy Evelyn Rose, Sept 16, 1939; children—Gail Elizabeth, Barbara Louise. Instr. Yale, 1937-38; research engr. Standard Oil Development Co., 1938-39, group supervisor process engring. dept., 1941-46; asst. prof. chem. engring U. Pa., 1939-41; asso. prof. chem. engring. Columbia, 1946-52, prof. since 1952, asso. dean sch. engring, 1950-57, chmn. department chem. engring., 1957-69; cons. Cons. to U.S. Mil. Govt. decartelization and deconcentration of I.G. Farben Industrie A.G., Germany, 1949, U.S. High Commn., 1950, 52; tech. dir. Fractionation Research, Inc., Bartlesville, Okla., 1953-54; vis. prof. Birla Inst. Tech. and Sci., Pilani, India, 1967-68. Licensed profl. engr., N.J. Mem. Am. Chem. Soc., Am. Inst. Chem. Engrs. Am. Soc. Engring. Edn., Sigma Xi, Alpha Chi Sigma, Phi Kappa Phi, Pi Kappa Alpha, Gamma Alpha, Phi Lambda Upsilon, Tau Beta Pi. Republican. Conglist. Author tech. articles. Holder patents. Home: Tenafly NJ Died July 9, 1970; cremated.

AMMONS, TELLER, ex-gov.; b. Denver, Colo., Dec. 3, 1895; s. Elias M. and Elizabeth (Fleming) A.; student U. of Denver, 1919-21; LL.B., Westminster Law Sch., 1929; m. Esther Davis, Sept. 9, 1933; 1 son, Davis. Admitted to Colo. bar. 1929; mem. State Senate, 1930-35; city atty. for City and Co. of Denver, 1935-36; gov. of Colo., 1936-38. Served with 154th Inf., A.E.F., World War I; commd. lt. col. A.U.S. 1942. On selection and assignment bd. all officers of mil. government under provost marshal gen. to 1944; served in provost court, chief justice, court of appeals, investigator and later trial judge advocate, Guam; separated Dec. 1945. Mem. Am. Legion, Vets. of Fgn. Wars, Sigma Alpha Epsilon, Phi Alpha Delta. Dem. Clubs: Denver Law, Denver Athletic. Address: Denver CO Died Jan. 1972.

AMORY, HARCOURT, bus. exec.; b. Beverly, Mass., July 7, 1894; s. Harcourt and Gertrude Lowndes (Chase) A.; A.B., Harvard, 1916; m. Susannah Stoddard Wood, Feb. 17, 1923; children—Harcourt, Susannah Lowndes. With Smith Barney & Company (previously Edward B. Smith & Co.), 1925-42, partner, 1931-42; dep. vice chmn. War Prodn. Bd., 1942-44; v.p. Hawaiian Pineapple Co., Ltd., 1945-47; v.p. Castle & Cooke, Ltd., 1945-47, Smith, Barney & Co., 1947-69; dir., mem. exec. and finance com. Ranco, Inc., Witco Co., Ranco, Ltd., Am. Motors. Vice pres. Lenox Hill Neighborhood Assn. Capt. U.S. Army, 1917-19. Treas. Mass. Rep. State Com., 1936-42; pres. Rep. Club of Mass., 1940-42. Mason, Clubs: Harvard, Racquet and Tennis, The Links, Recess (N.Y.C.); Southampton; The Detroit. Home: New York City NY Died Dec. 1969.

AMORY, ROBERT, textile mfg.; b. at Boston, Mass., Oct. 23, 1885; s. Robert and Katharine Leighton (Crehore) A.; A.B., Harvard, 1906; studied Mass. Inst. Tech.; m. Lenore Cobb, Sept. 20, 1910; children—Robert, Cleveland, Leonore (Mrs. T. M. Sawyers). Exec. v.p. Springs Mills, Inc.; director Springs Mills Inc., Allied Am. Liability Insurance Co., Arkwright Mutual Fire Ins. Co., Mut. Boiler Ins. Co., Boston Mfrs. Mutual Fire Ins. Company. Republican. Clubs: Somerset (Boston); Harvard, Merchants' (New York). Home: New York City NY Died July 1972.

AMOS, WILLIAM FREDERICK, M.D.; b. Cleveland, O., Sept. 3, 1869; grad. Willamette Univ., Portland, Ore., 1890; Coll. Phys. and Surgeons, New York, 1892; m. Lillian Catherine Mock, of Portland, Ore. July 11, 1903, ex-demonstrator anatomy and lecturer and lecturer materia medica, Willamette Univ.; has held numerous hospital apptmts.; surgeon for Preferred, Standard, Fidelity & Casualty, Md. Casualty, Travelers' Protective Assn., etc.; mem. staff North Pacific Sanitarium; sec. Portland Med. Soc., 1894-5; sec. Pacific Coast Assn. of Med. Examiners; councilor Ore. State Med. Soc. (sec. 1895-1901); Author of monographs on Anaesthesia; Urinalysis in Surgery; Treatment of Gonorrhoea in Women; State Restriction of Dangerous Communicable Diseases, etc. Address: Portland OR‡

AMRINE, WILLIAM FREDERICK, prison supt.; b. La Harpe, Ill., Dec. 20, 1875; s. Henry and Margaret (White) A.; student Ohio Wesleyan U., 1892-96; m. Bertha Yost, Dec. 20, 1899; children—Alice Catherine, Ruth, Mary Jane, Margaret Ellen, Robert Yost, Constance Ann. Began as teacher pub. schs., Perry Co., O., 1899; supt. industries, Ohio State Reformatory, 1902-10; asst. supt. Pa. Industrial Reformatory, 1910-14; parole officer, Ohio Penitentiary, Columbus, 1914-19; at London Prison Farm since 1919, supt. since 1925. Served as corpl. Co. G, 4th Ohio Vol. Inf., 1898-99, Spanish-Am. War. Mem. Sigma Chi. Republican. Methodist. Mason (K.T.). Rotarian. Home: London OH‡

AMYOT, LOUIS JOSEPH ADJUTOR, financier, industrialist; b. Quebec City, Que., Can., Feb. 20, 1884; s. George Elie and Marie Josephine (Tanguay) A.; student Comml. Acad., Que., also Upper Canada Coll., Toronto; m. Juliette Hamel, 1913; children—George, Alice, Pierre, France. Pvt. sec. to pres. Dominion Corset Co., Ltd., then mgr. Australia and New Zealand, 1907, v.p., 1912-29, mng. dir., Eng., 1914, pres., 1929-68, also dir.; v.p. Gen. Trust Can.; dir. Economy Bank Que., Donohue Bros. Bd. dirs. of Amyot Found. of chair in chemistry Laval U. Named hon. lt. col. Royal 22d Regt., La Citadelle, Que. Mem. St. John Ambulance Assn. (nat. dir.). Clubs: Quebec Garrison, Royal Quebec Golf, The National (Toronto); Canadian (N.Y.); Club Universitaire Laval (Que.). Home: Quebec City PQ Canada Died Apr. 10, 1968.*

ANASTASSY, Metropolitan and hon. pres. Synod of Council of Bishops, Russian Orthodox Ch. Outside Russia. Address: New York City NY Died May 21, 1966; buried Holy Trinity Monastery, Jordanville NY

ANDERSEN, BJORN, chem. engr.; b. Norway, June 29, 1897; s. Elling and Auguste Petrea (Lorensen) A.; B.S., Norway Inst. Tech., 1918, M.S., Chem.E., 1920, research fellow, 1920-23; m. Ingeborg Solberg, Mar. 27, 1924; children—Bjorn Andreas, Thor Bjorn, Erik Bjorn, Nils Olav, Lars Rolf. Came to U.S., 1924, naturalized, 1930. Asst. prof. Norway Inst. Tech., 1921-24, chief chemist Norway Inst. Testing Materials, 1920-22; research chemist Guggenheim Bros. Research Labs., N.Y.C., 1924-26, mgr. research, 1926-28; research asso. Celluloid Corp., 1928-30, technical dir., 1930-41; dir. research, tech. dir. plastic div. Celanese Corp. Am., 1941-47, dir. research Celanese Corp. Am., 1947-51, v.p., tech. dir. 1951-55, v.p., gen. mgr. Plastics div.,

Celanese Corp., 1955-59; vice president Celanese Devel. Company, 1959-62. Mem. Princeton adv. council Plastics Program, 1954-62, chmn., 1959-62; del. U.S. Dept. Commerce Trade Missions, Australia, 1961, Burma, 1962, Finland, 1964, Bulgaria-Hungary, 1966. Decorated Liberty Cross (Norway), 1947. Mem. Soc. Chem. Industry, Soc. Plastics Industry, Am. Soc. Testing Materials, Am. Inst. Chem. Engrs., Am. Chem. Soc., Am. Inst. Chemists, Am. Electrochem. Soc., N.Y. Acad. Scis., Plastic Pioneers Assn., A.A.A.S., Indsl. Research Inst. Clubs: Chemist (N.Y.), Appalachian, Maplewood Country. Author sci. articles. Holder 30 patents. Home: Maplewood NJ Died Sept. 27, 1971; buried Greenwood Cemetery, Brielle NJ

ANDERSEN, JOYCE MARILYN OFF (MRS. CHESTER W. ANDERSEN), assn. exec.; b. Watson, Sask., Can., Jan. 7, 1923; d. John Walker and Elizabeth Grace (Sanders) McIntyre; grad. high sch.; m. Clarence A. Hamm Off, May 24, 1944 (dec. 1945); 1 son Larry Jon Hamm; m. 2d, Chester W. Andersen, Feb. 13, 1954. With C., B.&Q. R.R., Chgo., 1941-43; mem. singing group McIntyre Sisters, Chgo., 1943-44; sec. U. Colo., 1947-49; with various state govt. agys., Denver, 1949-54; mng. sec. Colo. Soc. Engrs., Denver, 1960-69. Mem. Colo. Soc. Engrs. Aux. Republican. Presbyn. Home: Denver CO Died May 16, 1969.

ANDERSON, AMOS CAREY, educator; b. Centerville, Pa., June 25, 1897; s. Ernest H. and Kitty (Lamb) A.; A.B., U. Mich., 1922, M.A., 1924; Ph.D., Yale, 1931; m. Harriette Wright, Aug. 26, 1924; children—Laura J., Ernest W. Instr. psychology Central State Tchrs. Coll., Mt. Pleasant, Mich., 1922-23; prof. psychology Mayville (N.D.) State Tchrs. Coll., 1924-25; instr. to prof., Ohio U., 1925-67, prof., department psychology, prof. emeritus, 1967-72, chmn. dept., 10 years. Instr. Western Mich. Coll., Minot (N.D.) State Tchrs. Coll., Central State Tchrs. Coll., Mt. Pleasant, Mich., summer sessions; faculty Wilmington (O.) Coll., 1967-68, summer 1969, St. Lawrence U., Canton, N.Y., summer 1968. Mem. Am., Ohio, Midwest psychol. assns. (pres., Ohio, 1950), A.A.A.S., Phi Beta Kappa, Sigma Xi. Presbyn. Contbr. sci. jours. Home: Athens OH Died May 31, 1972; buried West Union Street Cemetery, Athens OH

ANDERSON, CARL MAGNUS, lawyer; b. Gary, S.D., Jan. 10, 1905; s. H.A. and Emma (Johnson) A.; A.B. cum laude, U. Minn., 1927; J.D., 1930, LL.D., Wagner Coll., 1966, Upsala Coll., 1970; m. Ida Johnson, Aug. 16, 1930; children—Eric Hall, John Anders, Mary Lisa. Bookkeeper, First Nat. Bank, Grantsburg, Wis., 1922-24; admitted to Minn. bar, 1930, N.Y. bar, 1932, U.S. Supreme Ct. bar, 1938; asso. Root, Clark, Buckner & Ballantine, N.Y.C., 1930-34; head legal dept. Merck & Co., Inc. Rahway, N.J., 1934-48, asst. sec., 1937-48, asst. to pres., 1942-50, dir. fgn. activities, 1950-52, sec., 1956-70, dir., 1969-70; v.p. Merck (N.A.), Inc., 1952-54, Merck-Sharp & Dohme Internat. Div., 1954-56. Pres., Merck Co. Found., 1964-70. Bd. dirs. United Negro Coll. Fund, nat. campaign chmn., 1964, 65; trustee Clara Maass Meml. Hosp.; bd. fellows Union Coll., chmn. bd. trustees Upsala Coll. Treas. Lutheran Ch. in Am., dir. Common Investing Fund. Recipient Outstanding Achievement award U. Minn., 1968. Mem. Assn. Bar City N.Y., Am. Bar. Assn., Am. Soc. Corporate Secs. (past v.p., dir.), Phi Beta Kappa Assos., Iron Wedge, Phi Beta Kappa, Theta Delta Chi, Phi Delta Phi, Phi Sigma Phi. Republican. Lutheran. Clubs: University (N.Y.C.); Beacon Hill (Summit, N.J.). Home: Summit NJ Died Aug. 26, 1972.

ANDERSON, CHARLES HARDIN, air force officer; b. Cape Girardeau, Mo., Nov. 3, 1907; s. Daniel Hardin and Marie (Boysen) A.; B.S., U.S. Mil. Acad., 1932; grad. Advanced Flying Sch., 1933, Air Command and Staff Sch., 1947, Air War Coll., 1948, Nat. War Coll., 1950; m. Mary Kathryn Glass, Feb. 20, 1936 (dec.); children—Kathryn Marie (Mrs. Waterbury), Patricia, Mary Sheridan. Commd. 2d lt., U.S. Army, 1932, advanced through grades to maj. gen. USAF, 1956; assigned 1st Pursuit Group, 1933-37; spl. duty Philippine A.C., 1938-39; comdg. officer Advanced Flying Sch., 1942-43; overseas duty, 1944-45; faculty Air War Coll., 1947-49; dir., office manpower requirements Office Sec. Def., Washington, 1953-55; asst. chief staff, Air and Spl. Operation, SHAPE 1955-58; asst. atomic energy, Hq. USAF, 1958-60; comdr. Lowry Tech. Tng. Center, 1960-67. Decorated Legion of Merit with oak-leaf cluster, D.F.C., D.S.M., Air Medal, Bronze Star Medal, Commendation Medal with 2 oak-leaf clusters (U.S.); Distinguished Service Star of Philippines. Address: Denver CO Died May 27, 1971; buried Arlington Nat. Cemetery, Arlington VA

ANDERSON, CHARLES LOFTUS GRANT, surgeon; b. near Hagerstown, Md., Mar. 8, 1863; s. George Washington and Anna Maria (Winter) A.; student Claverack (N.Y.) Coll., 1877-79; U. of Pa., 1881; M.D., Coll. Physicians and Surgeons (Columbia), 1884; m. Ruby Scruggs, July 7, 1910. House physician and surgeon, Jersey City Hosp., 1885; commd. 1st lt. and asst. surgeon, U.S. Army, 1886; resigned, 1888; acting asst. surgeon, U.S. Army, with 5th Army Corps, Santiago Campaign, Spanish-Am. War, 1898, then on duty at gen. hosps., Ft. Myer, Va., and Savannah, Ga.; maj. and surgeon, U.S. Vols. in Philippines, 1899-1901; asso. in surgery Emergency Hosp., Washington, D.C., 1905; physician, Isthmian Canal Commn., Canal Zone, Panama, 1905-07. Amateur swimmer of note. Major Med. R.C., active service with A.E.F., in France, with 2d Div. and in comd. of hosps.; promoted to lt. col. Med. Corps.; lt. col. Med. Res. Corps, retired, 1928. Med. specialist, U.S. Vets. Bur. Founder and v.p. Spanish-Am. Athenaeum. Fellow A.M.A., Am. Geog. Soc.; mem. Assn. Mil. Surgs. of U.S., Med. Soc. of D.C., Anthropol. Soc. Washington (pres.), Washington Acad. Sciences, United Spanish War Vets, Am. Legion, Institute de las Espanas. K.T. Clubs: University (Washington, D.C.); Army and Navy (New York). Author: Old Panama and Castilla del Oro, 1914; Life and Letters of Vasco Nunez de Balboa, 1941; also various articles on lit., med. and scientific topics. Home: 2407 15th St. N.W., Washington DC‡

ANDERSON, DAVID ALLEN, college pres.; b. Lamoni, Ia., Aug. 19, 1874; s. Andrew K. and Enger (Ormsdatter) A.; A.B., State U. of Ia., 1908, A.M., 1910, Ph.D., 1912; sr. fellow same, studying in Europe, 1910-11; m. Roxanna E. Gaylord, Lamoni, Ia., Apr. 4, 1900. Began teaching in Ia., 1893; prof. edn. and psychology, La Crosse (Wis.) State Normal Sch., 1912-13; asst. prof. edn., 1913-16, asso. prof., 1916-17, U. of Wash.; prof. edn. and head dept. of edn. and psychology, Pa. State Coll., 1917-26; pres. Kent (O.) State Normal Coll., 1926-28; pres. Northern State Teachers Coll., Aberdeen, S.D., 1928—. Instr. in edn. U. of Ia., summer 1911; prof. edn. State Normal Sch., Moorhead, Minn., summer 1912; State Normal Sch., La Crosse, Wis., summer 1913; asst. prof. edn. U. of Wash., summers 1914-15-16; asso. prof. edn. U. of Ill., summer 1917. Dir. of Pub. Edn. and Child Labor Assn., Pa.; fellow A.A.A.S.; mem. Am. Assn. Univ. Profs. N.E.A., Coll. Teachers of Edn., Nat. Soc. Study Edn., Phi Delta Kappa, Kappa Delta Pi. Republican. Mason. Club: Aberdeen Country. Author: The School System of Norway, 1913. Contbr. to Aberdeen SD‡

ANDERSON, EDGAR, botanist; b. Forestville, N.Y., Nov. 9, 1897; s. Anson Crosby and Inez (Shannon) A.; B.S., Mich. State Coll., 1918; M.S., Sc.D., Harvard, 1922; m. Dorothy Moore, June 21, 1923 (dec. 1971); 1 dau., Phoebe. Asst. in genetics Harvard, 1920-22; geneticist Mo. Botanical Garden, and asst. prof. botany, Washington Univ. (St. Louis), 1922-30, asso. prof., 1930-31, prof. from 1935; arborist Arnold Arboretum of Harvard Univ., 1931-35; Engelman prof. of botany Washington Univ., 1937-69; asst. dir. Mo. Bot. Garden, 1952-54, dir., 1954-56, curator useful plants, 1957-69; vis. prof. biology, Stanford U., 1952, vis. fellow mathematics, Princeton, 1957. Mem. U.S. Naval Res. Force, 1918-19. Fellow Nat. Research Council, 1929-30 (England); Guggenheim fellow (California and Mexico, 1943-44; Guggenheim Sr. fellow, 1957-69; fellow Center for Advanced Study in Behavorial Sciences, 1959-60. Decorated Order of the Yugoslavian Crown; Darwin Wallace silver medal, 1958; gold medal Men's Garden Clubs American, 1958, Federated Garden Clubs, 1959. Mem. Sigma Xi, Society American Naturalists, Herb Society America, Bot. Soc. Am. Author: Introgressive Hybridization Plants, Man and Life. Discoverer introgression; research on origin and evolution of maize. Home: St Louis MO Died June 18, 1969.

ANDERSON, EDWARD LEE, indsl. supply co. exec.; b. Moore, S.C., Nov. 28, 1913; s. David Buist and Teresa (Hollingsworth) A.; student Wofford Coll., 1933; diploma Internat. Accountants Soc., 1956; m. Elizabeth Jane Wyse, Dec. 26, 1935; children—Jeanne Buist (Mrs. Charles Caughman Derrick), David Frederick, Elizabeth Wyse (Mrs. John J. McKinney), James Mayson. Fiscal agt. Soil Conservation Service, U.S. Dept. Agr., Spartanburg, Newberry, Columbia, S.C., 1935-43; controller, sec., treas., dir. Columbia Supply Co., 1943-69, Augusta Mill Supply Co., Charleston Supply Co., Mathews-Morse Supply Co., Mill & Contractors Supply Co., Southeastern Steel Co.; sec., treas., dir. So. Mill Supply Co., Charleston, S.C. Mem. Conf. Am. Small Bus. Assn. (dir. finance, exec. com.), Soc. for Preservation and Encouragement Barber Shop Quartet Singing in Am. (past pres., dir. Columbia chpt.). Presbyn. (elder). Kiwanian (dir. Columbia). Club: Executives. Author: A History of the Anderson Family 1706-1955, 1955. Home: Columbia SC Died June 28, 1969; buried Elmwood Cemetery Columbia SC

ANDERSON, ELSIE GRACE, educator; d. Uriah and Catharine (Heatwole) A.; grad. high sch., Ann Arbor, Mich., 1890; student U. of Mich., 1891-93, 1895-96; grad. Montessori Sch., Rome, Italy, 1913. Established the Montessori Sch. in Toledo, O., in connection with the Smead Sch. for Girls; prin. (with sister), Smead Sch. since 1911, also trustee and sec. Mem. Head Mistresses' Assn. of Pvt. Schs. of Middle States (sec.), Gamma Phi Beta. Episcopalian. Address: The Smead School, Toledo OH‡

ANDERSON, ESTHER L., supt. of pub. instrn.; b. Farlington, Kan.; d. John and Augusta (Nelson) A.; student State Teachers Colls., Kan., Colo., Wash., summers 1917-23, and 1928; B.S., State Teachers Coll., Pittsburg, Kan., 1933. Grade sch. teacher, Loveland, Colo., 1920-25; teacher of science Casper, Wyo., jr. high sch., 1925-38; state supt. of pub. instrn., Wyo., since 1938. Mem. Nat. Women's League. Delta Kappa Gamma, Kappa Delta Pi, Phi Alpha Theta. Club: Casper Business and Professional Women's (past pres., past Wyo. state pres., hon. state pres.). Home: 301 E. 21st St. Address: Dept of Education, Capitol Bldg., Cheyenne WY*‡

ANDERSON, FREDERICK L., ret. Army officer; b. Kingston, N.Y., October 4, 1905; s. Frederick L. and Anna Elizabeth (Haulenbeck) A.; grad. U.S. Military Acad., 1928; m. Elizabeth Ann Travis, Aug. 30, 1928; children—Mary Winn, Travis. Commd. 2d lt., 1928, advanced through grades to major gen., 1943; graduate Kelly Field and Brooks Field, receiving his wings, 1929; served in Philippines, Hamilton Field, Lowry Field, and Washington; transferred to bombardment aviation in 1931; operations officer 7th Group; selected to start the first Bombardier's Instructor Sch., 1940; head of bombardment tactics bd. sent to England in 1941; deputy dir. bombardment, Washington, 1942; rep. of General Arnold on bombardment matters in Northern Africa and England, 1942; comdr. Fortress Wing in United Kingdom, 1943; comdg. gen., VIII Bomber Comd., Eng., 1943; dep. comdr. operations, Hdqrs. U.S. Strategic Air Forces in Europe, England, France, 1944-45; asst. chief, air Staff for Personnel, 1945-47, retired 1947; U.S. ambassador to NATO, 1952-53; dir. Lear Siegler, Inc., Am. Bakeries Co., Fed. Petroleum, Inc., Royal Industries, Inc., U.S. Leasing Corp.; trustee the Rand Corp. Trustee Menlo Sch. and Coll. Decorated Silver Star, D.F.C., D.S.M. with Oak Leaf Cluster, Air Medal, Legion of Merit, Order of Suvorov 3d Degree (Russian), Commander of the Bath (British), Legion of Honor, (French), Croix de Guerre with Palm (French). Mem. Nat. Aeronautical Soc. Club: Army-Navy (Washington, D.C.); The Links (N.Y.C.); Cypress Point (Pebble Beach, Cal.); Menlo Country (Woodside, Cal.), San Francisco Golf. Home: Woodside CA Died Mar. 2, 1969; buried Arlington Nat. Cemetery, Washington DC

ANDERSON, GEORGE, public relations co. exec.; m. Helen Anderson. With Pendleton Dudley & Assos., N.Y.C., 1937-45; partner Dudley-Anderson-Yutzy, N.Y.C., from 1945; v.p. Dudley-Anderson-Yutzy Pub. Relations, Inc., N.Y.C., until 1970. Former mem. adv. council N.Y. State Joint Legislative Com. on Consumer Protection. Mem. Pub. Relations Soc. Am. (charter). Home: Brick Town NJ Died Dec. 1970.

ANDERSON, GEORGE A., b. Chicago, 1885; chmn. bd. dirs. Charles Pfizer & Co., Inc., Brooklyn; dir. Brooklyn Union Gas Co., Surety Fire Ins. Co. Trustee Union Dime Savings Bank, Brooklyn Trust Co., Am. Surety Co. Home: Old Brookville NY Died Mar. 1970.

ANDERSON, GEORGE EDWARD, ret. physician; b. Bklyn., Aug. 29, 1897; s. Frederick William and Julia (Von Greiff) A.; A.B. magna cum laude, N.Y. U., 1919, M.D., 1922; m. Katherine Clifford Doherty, Sept. 27, 1924. Attending physician Bklyn. Hosp., 1933, dir. medicine, 1955-64, chief metabolic clinic, also acting dir. medicine Bklyn. Hosp-Cumberland Hosp. Center; cons. physician Bethany Deaconess Hosp., 1950-65; dir. out-patient services Bklyn. Cumberland Med. Center, 1964-68; cons. Lutheran and Methodist hosps.; clin. prof. emeritus medicine State U., N.Y. Coll. Medicine; curator and asso. directing librarian Library of Kings County Med. Soc. Fellow N.Y. Acad. Medicine, A.C.P.; mem. Am. Rheumatism Assn., Am. Diabetes Assn. (mem. council, sec. 1942-48), N.Y. Heart Assn., Endocrine Soc., N.Y. Diabetes Assn. (dir.; pres. 1944-45), Bklyn. Soc. Internal Medicine (pres. Brooklyn NY Died Aug. 26, 1972; buried St. Joseph's Cemetery, West Roxbury MA

ANDERSON, GEORGE WOOD, evangelist; b. Belle Center, O., Dec. 8, 1873; s. Calvary B. and Margaret Louise (Zupp) A.; A.B., A.M., Ohio Wesleyan U., 1899, D.D., 1912; m. Nelie Josephine Sharpe, Aug. 14, 1912; children—Robert Cushman, Jane Wickham. Ordained M.E. ministry, 1899; pastor Lima, O., 1899-1903, Troy, N.Y., 1903-09, Union Ch., St. Louis, Mo., 1909-12, Elm Park Ch., Scranton, Pa., 1912-15; evangelist since 1915, except Y.M.C.A. work with A.E.F., 1917-18, and Am. Army of Occupation, 1920. Began annual transcontinental trips, holding United Gospel Crusades in 8 important centers, 1921; nat. lecturer for Associated Ad Clubs of World; lecturer for Chautauqua and Lyceum on Bald Heads, Outside and In," The Wisdom of Foolishness," Michael Angelo," The Swordless Crusader"; became editor in chief of The Clergyman's Research Letter and pres. The Religious Research, Inc., 1940. Mason. Republican. Author: Chosen Words, 1916; Modern Misbeliefs, 1916; Problem—or Opportunity?, 1919; Serpent Eggs, 1921; Unfinished Rainbows, 1921; The White-Robed Christ, 1925; Picking Up Sticks, 1927. Home: Duquesne Lawn, New York NY*‡

ANDERSON, HAROLD, farmer services co. exec.; b. Webster Groves, Mo., June 9, 1894; s. David and Lilly (Hirsch) A.; student U. Wis., 1912, 14-16; D.Sc. in Bus. Adminstrn., Bowling Green State U., 1960; m. Margaret Meilink, Oct. 6, 1920; children—John David, Thomas

Harold, Robert James, Donald Edward, Richard Paul, Carol Jean (Mrs. Paul M. Kraus). Vice pres. Nat. Milling Co., Toledo, 1919-27, pres., 1927-37; partner D & H Anderson, Maumee, O., 1937-46; sr. partner The Andersons, Maumee, from 1946. Pres. YMCA, Toledo, 1949-52; v.p. Springfield Twp. Bd. Edn., Holland, O. Served to 2d lt. U.S. Army, 1918. Named Marketing Man of Year, Am. Marketing Assn., 1961; recipient Distinguished Service award Nat. Football Found. Hall of Fame, 1964. Mem. Toledo C. of C. (past v.p.), Alpha Kappa Psi, Alpha Zeta. Republican. Presbyn. (elder, deacon). Home: Maumee OH Died Dec. 25, 1968; buried St. Joseph's Cemetery, Maumee OH

ANDERSON, J(EFFERSON) RANDOLPH, lawyer; b. Savannah, Ga., Sept. 4, 1861; s. Edward Clifford, Jr., and Jane Margaret (Randolph) A.; prep. edn., Hanover Acad., Va., 1877-79; U. of Va., 1879-81; B.L., 1885; U. of Gottingen, Germany, 1881-83; U. of Va., 1883-85; D.C.L., U. of the South, Sewanee, Tenn., 1931; m. Anne Page Wilder, Nov. 27, 1895; children—Page Randolph (Mrs. Henry Norris Platt), Joseph Randolph. Began practice, Savannah, in offices of Chisholm & Erwin, gen. counsel Plant System of Rys., 1885; became mem. Anderson, Cann & Cann, 1911; now Anderson, Connerat, Dunn & Hunter; counsel Ga., & Ala. Ry., 1895-1900; div. counsel Seaboard Air Line Railway since 1900; pres. Georgia and Alabama Terminal Company; vice president Chatham Terminal Co.; dir. Savannah Bank & Trust Co., Savannah Electric &Power Co., Savannah Union Station Co. Member Georgia House of Representatives from Chatham County, 1905-06, 1909-10, 1911-12, Senate, 1913, 14 (pres.); mem. Dem. State Exec. Com., Ga., 1907, 1908; del.-at-large from Ga. to Dem. Nat. Conv., Baltimore, 1912. Chmn. bd. trustees 1st Dist. Agrl. and Indsl. Sch., Ga., 1906-22; chmn. Savannah Pub. Library Bd., 1915-21 and since 1931; was mem. State Bd. Vocational Edn. Chmn. Savannah Chapter Am. Red Cross., 1918-20. Episcopalian; sr. warden Christ Ch., Savannah; parliamentarian House of Deps. of Gen. Conv. P.E. Ch. in U.S. since 1919. Mem. Am., Ga. bar assns., Ga. Hist. Soc. (pres.), Soc. Colonial Wars, Soc. Descs. of Signers of Declaration of Independence, S.R., Alpha Tau Omega. Mason, Elk. Club: Oglethorpe. Home: 119 E. Charlton St. Office: Savannah Bank & Trust Bldg., Savannah GA‡

ANDERSON, JAMES CUYLER, news agy. exec.; b. Fargo, N.D., June 30, 1920; s. S. Cuyler and Birdie G. (Thorkelson) A.; student Phoenix Jr. Coll., 1938; m. Lore L. Dormeyer, Feb. 21, 1944; children—Carla Lore, Gail Elizabeth. Sports editor Santa Barbara (Cal.) News-Press, 1941-42; bur. mgr., polit. corr. U.P.I., Sacramento, 1951-63, news mgr. Pacific div., San Francisco, 1963-66; editor Sacramento Union, 1966-69. Served with inf., AUS, 1943-45. Mem. Baseball Writers Assn. Am., Cal. Golf Writers Assn., Profl. Golfers Assn., Sigma Delta Chi. Club: Press (San Francisco). Home: Carmichael CA Died Oct. 16, 1969.

ANDERSON, JAMES HOWARD, surgeon; b. Latrobe, Pa., June 15, 1875; s. Thomas Bigham and Lida (Brown) A.; Grove City (Pa.) Coll., 1890-91; B.A., M.A., Washington and Jefferson Coll., 1895; M.D., Jefferson Med. Coll., Phila., 1904; post-grad. work, Harvard and New York Post-Grad. Med. Sch.; m. Marguerite Emery, June 28, 1916 (died Aug. 6, 1917). Practiced at Hemphill, W.Va., since 1904; surgeon Kingston Pocahontas Coal Co.; asst. surgeon Norfolk & Western Ry. Co.; v.p. Atlantic Smokeless Coal Co.; dir. Crystal Black Coal & Coke Co., Welch Ins. Agency. Surgeon gen. on staff of Gov. Hatfield of W.Va., 1913-17; served as mem. Vol. Med. Corps and W.Va. State Council of Defense, World War. Mem. W.Va. State Med. Assn. (chancellor 8 yrs.; ex-sec. and ex-pres.), McDowell County Med. Soc. (sec. 5 yrs.; ex-pres.), Alpha Omega Alpha, Alpha Kappa Kappa. Ind. Republican. Presbyn. Clubs: Rotary, McDowell County Country. Home: Hemphill WV‡

ANDERSON, JOHN WILLIAM, lawyer; b. Buchanan County, Ia., July 21, 1871; s. Reese Babs and Emma Theresea (Davenport) A.; student Upper Ia. U., Fayette, Ia., 1887-91; m. Burdette Hopper, Sept. 24, 1895; children—Marjora Belle (Mrs. C. H. Schneider), Elma Irene (Mrs. H. W. Bails); m. 2d, Mary Agnes Peck, Apr. 15, 1933. Admitted to Ia. bar, 1893, bar of U.S. Supreme Court, 1933; practiced at Sioux City, 1893-96, Onawa, 1896-1915; county atty. Monona County, 1910-14; dist. judge, 4th Ia. Dist., 1915-21; again practiced in Sioux City, 1921-33; partner Jepson, Strubel & Anderson, 1921-33; justice Supreme Court of Ia., 1933-39; now in gen. practice of law, Sioux City, Ia. Mem. Am. and Iowa State bar assns., Am. Law Inst., Order of Coif, Izaak Walton League. Democrat. Mem. Christian (Disciples) Ch. Mason (32 deg.), K.T., Shriner, Odd Fellow, Elk. Club: Knife and Fork. Home: 32 McDonald Drive. Office: New Orpheum Bldg., Sioux City IA*‡

ANDERSON, KARL LEOPOLD, educator; b. Charlottetown, P.E.I., Can., June 26, 1905; s. Albert Hudson and Effie Elphinstone (Ross) A.; student Ottawa (Can.) Collegiate Inst., 1919-24; B.Sc., Mt. Allison U., Sackville, N.B., 1928; M.A., Harvard, 1930, Ph.D., 1932; m. Louise Laylander Fowler, Aug. 15, 1931; children—Jane Louise, Douglas Ross. Came to U.S., 1928, naturalized, 1942. Instr., tutor econs. Harvard, 1930-34; asst. prof., asso. prof. econs. Bryn Mawr (Pa.) Coll., 1934-46; price exec., econ advisor OPA, 1942-46; asst. chief, advisor internat. resources div. Dept. State, 1946-49; dir. Brit. Commonwealth div. office internat. trade Dept. Commerce, 1949-51, dep. dir. office internat. trade 1951-56; mem. faculty Nat. War Coll., 1956-57; George Adams Ellis prof. econs., chmn. social sci. div. Middlebury (Vt.) Middlebury VT Died July 14, 1968; buried Weybridge Cemetery, Weybridge VT

ANDERSON, LEE, author; b. Saxton, Pa., July 19, 1896; s. Samuel Andrew and Myra Agnes (Brode) A.; m. Helen Anderson White, Dec. 27, 1941; 1 dau., by previous marriage, Mary Jane. Self-employed as publisher, farmer, lectr. contemporary poetry, also reader of own poems on coll. campuses; research asso. Yale, 1959—; vis. lectr. U. Cal. at Berkeley, 1963-65; recordings of 155 Am. and Brit. poets reading own works, 1948—; coordinated Yale Series of Recorded Poets, 1959-61; distinguished vis. lectr. Frostburg (Md.) State Coll., 1966-67; poet in residence U. Wis., Eau Claire, 1967. Served with USNRF, World War I. Scholar, U. Pitts., 1916. Author: Prevailing Winds, 1944; The Floating World, 1953; The Floating World and Other Poems, 1956; Nags Head and Other Poems, 1960; Nags Head (recording), 1960; Eye Versus Ear, 1961; Bearstone Tetralogy, 1969. Address: Glen PA Died July 25, 1972.

ANDERSON, MARY MORTLOCK (MRS. WALTER ANDERSON), bus. exec., writer; b. Detroit, July 31, 1916; d. George Conan and Dorothy (Morley) Mortlock; student pub. schs.; m. Walter Anderson, Sept. 24, 1938; children—Alan Walter, Mary Ellen, Holly. Owner, New London Stenographic and Mailing Service (Conn.), 1961-69; pub. Stenographer New London Bd. Edn., 1967-68. Sec., Council of Chs. in Greater New London Area, 1965. Recipient 1st prize for non-fiction Nutmeg Writers' Conf., 1957. Mem. Nat. League Am. Pen Women, Bread Loaf Writers' Conf., Vt. 1965. Contbr. poems, articles Christian Sci. Monitor. Home: Waterford CT Died Nov. 10, 1969.

ANDERSON, MERLE HAMPTON, clergyman; b. New Bedford, Pa., Mar. 22, 1873; s. Rev. Thomas Bingham and Lida A. (Brown) A.; B.A., Washington & Jefferson Coll., 1893, M.A., 1897; grad. McCormick Theol. Sem., 1896; D.D., Miami U., 1904; m. Sallie Jeannette Nelson, June 30, 1904 (dec. Sept. 19, 1941); children—Thomas McDowell, Jean; m. 2d, Elizabeth Burgess MacLehose, Aug. 28, 1943. Ordained to ministry, Presbyn. Ch., 1896; pastor Ebenburg, Pa., 1896-1900, Mutchmore Meml. Ch., Phila., 1900-03, Third St. Ch., Dayton, O., 1903-09, Kingshighway Ch., St. Louis, 1909-11, South St. Ch., Morristown, N.J., 1911-19, North Ch., N.Y. City, 1933-41, First Ch., Eustis, Fla., 1941-51; sec. east dist. New Era Movement of Presbyn. Ch. of U.S.A., 1919-24, North Fla. rep., dept. ministerial relations, Columbus, O. since 1951; pastor First Ch., Ann Arbor, Mich., exec. sec. U. Mich. Presbyn. Corp., 1924-33. Mem. Phi Gamma Delta. Republican. Mason (32 deg.). Clubs: Rotary. University. Home: 151 Overlook Rd., Winter Park FL‡

ANDERSON, OSCAR V., clergyman; b. N.Y.C., Feb. 24, 1903; s. August and Augusta (Gustafson) A.; A.B., Upsala Coll., East Orange, N.J., 1929; B.D., Augustana Theol. Sem., 1932, Th.M., 1933, D.D., 1953; postgrad. Union Theol. Sem., Columbia U., U. Chgo.; m. Lilly V. Flodden, June 20, 1933; children—Sandra Ruth (Mrs. Robert C. Sanderson), Bruce Timothy. Prof. Christianity, Augustana Coll., 1932-35; pastor Calvary Luth. Ch., Chgo., 1935-39, Grace Luth. Ch., LaGrange, Ill., 1939-54, Bay Shore Luth. Ch., Milw., 1963-; pres. Central Conf. Augustana Luth. Ch., 1954-63. Mem. and officer numerous bds. and commns. Augustana Luth. Ch., Nat. Luth. Council, Luth. Council U.S. Am., Nat. Council Chs. of Christ U.S.A., study com. World Council of Chs.; bd. dirs. Luth. Sch. Theology, Chgo.; exec. council Luth. Ch. in Am. Mem. Am. Soc. Church History, Augustana Hist. Soc. Author pamphlets Milwaukee WI Died Sept. 30, 1972; buried Bronswood Cemetery, Oakbrook IL

ANDERSON, PAUL N(ATHANIEL), business exec.; b. Jamestown, N.Y., Sept. 10, 1898; s. Frank O. and Amelia S. (Norquist) A.; student Phillips Andover Acad., 1915-18; B.S., Mass. Inst. Tech., 1922; m. Cecille K. Ogren, June 21, 1922; children—Paul Nathaniel, Frank Olaus, Daniel Ogren, Raymond Quintus, John Timothy. Treas., asst. supt. Empire Case Goods Co., Jamestown, 1922-34; pres., gen. mgr. Dahlstrom Metallic Door Co. 1934-61; pres., gen. mgr. Dahlstrom Mfg. Corp., 1961-68, also dir.; Bank of Jamestown, Jamestown Furniture Mfg. Bldg. Commr. Bd. Pub. U, Jamestown, 1930-48. Dir. Jamestown Y.M.C.A.; trustee Chautauqua (N.Y.) Instn., Lakeview Cemetery Assn., Jamestown. Mem. Nat. Assn. Mfrs. (dir. 1948), Jamestown Mfg. Assn. (pres. 1945). Presbyn. Mason. Club: Union, Norden (pres. 1932), Sportsmans (Jamestown). Home: Bemus Point NY Died 1968.

ANDERSON, PAUL VERNON, M.D., neuropsychiatrist; b. Black Creek, N.C., Nov. 24, 1874; s. William Staton and Mary Virginia (Woodard) A.; A.B., Trinity Coll., Durham, N.C., 1897, A.M., 1901; M.D., U. of Va., 1904; m. Alice V. Boatwright, Aug. 23, 1924. Prin. Wilson (N.C.) graded schs., 1897-98; instr. English, Trinity Park High Sch., Durham, N.C., 1898-1901; interne Polyclinic Hosp., Phila., Pa., 1904-06; asst. phys. State Hosp., Morgantown, N.C., 1906-11; phys. in charge dept. for women, Westbrook Sanatorium, Richmond, since 1911, also sec., treas. and dir.; asso. in psychiatry, Med. Coll. of Va., since 1915. Capt. Med. Corps, U.S. Army, Base Hosp. No. 45, World War. Mem. Phi Beta Kappa, Kappa Sigma, Phi Chi, Alpha Omega Alpha. Democrat. Methodist. Home: Westbrook Sanatorium, Inc., Richmond VA*‡

ANDERSON, RICHARD JAMES, editor; b. Phila. Pa., Apr. 4, 1901; s. Richard R. and Jeannette (Waddell) A.; student Coll. of William and Mary, Williamsburg, Va., 1921-23; B.C.S., New York U., 1925; m. Louise De Voe Barnes, May 28, 1928. Began as newspaper reporter while still in college; editorial dept. Moody's Investors Service, 1925; investment dept. Farmers Loan & Trust Company (now First National City Bank), 1926; joined the editorial dept. Financial World 1926, asso. editor, 1928-30, mng. ed., 1939-48; chmn. Guenther Pub. Corp., pub., editor Financial World. Mem. Board 5 Selective Service System, N.Y. City. Mem. N.Y. Soc. of Security Analysts, N.Y. Financial Writers' Assn. Pi Kappa Alpha, Alpha Kappa Psi. Republican. Episcopalian. Clubs: Downtown Athletic, N.Y. Yacht (N.Y.C.). Home: Darien CT also New York City NY Died June 5, 1971; buried Cold Spring NJ

ANDERSON, ROBERT EDWARD, JR., business exec.; b. Richmond, Va., Jan. 17 1906; s. Robert Edward and Nellie Mildred (Wynne) A.; student McGuire's U. Sch., 1915-22; grad. U. Va., 1926; m. Vienna Amanda Cobb, Sept. 20, 1930; children—Robert Edward, Vienna Cobb. With Powers & Anderson, Inc., 1926-69, exec. v.p., 1950-69, pres.; Powers & Anderson of N.C., Inc., since 1940, Powers & Anderson Surg. Instrument Co., Inc., since 1945, Powers & Anderson Dental Co. of N.C., Inc., 1954-59. Surgical industry liaison representative to the Federal Government, 1945-47. Mem. Am. Surg. Trade Assn. (gen. chmn. distbrs. sect. 1948-50, v.p. 1952, pres. 1952). Mason (Shriner). Clubs: Kiwanis (dir.), Farmington Country, Princess Anne Country, Old Dominion Country (Va.). Home: Richmond VA Died Oct. 12, 1969.

ANDERSON, WILLIAM BEVERLY, business exec.; b. Portsmouth, O., Jan. 16, 1899; s. William B. and Ida (Russell) A.; A.B., Ohio Wesleyan U., 1921; m. Lucile Richards, Oct. 6, 1922. Vice pres., treas. Anderson-Newcomb Co., 1921-31, pres., from 1931; dir. First Huntington Nat. Bank, United Fuel Gas Co., Columbia Gas System, Inc., Central Ky. Natural Gas Co. Vice-mayor, Huntington, 1934-36, mem. bd. park commrs.; trustee Ohio Wesleyan U., Huntington (W.Va.) Public Library; bd. govs. Am. Nat. Red Cross. Served with infantry N.S. Army, World War I. Member National Retail Dry Goods Assn. (v.p.), W.Va. Retailers Assn. (pres. 1940-43), W.Va. State C. of C. (dir.), Huntginton C. of C., Phi Kappa Psi, Omicron Delta Kappa. Republican. Methodist (mem. bd. of trustees). Club: Guyan Golf and Country. Home: Huntington WV Died Mar. 1, 1970.

ANDERSON, WILLIAM DOWNS, v.p. Atlantic Refining Co.; b. Phila., Pa., Feb. 12, 1874; s. Robert and Elizabeth (Downs) A.; student Drexel Inst. and Wharton Sch. of Finance (U. of Pa.); m. Mary McBride, Oct. 1, 1904. With Atlantic Refining Co. since 1898, beginning as sec. to the sec. of co., became asst. sec., later sec., now v.p. and dir. in charge of exports. Home: 4948 Hazel Av. Office: 260 S. Broad St., Philadelphia PA‡

ANDERSON, WILLIAM DOZIER, judge; b. Pontotoc County, Miss., July 20, 1862; s. Charles W. and Mary (Dozier) A.; ed. Central U., Richmond, Ky., and law sch. U. of Miss; m. Lena B. Clayton, Jan. 27, 1886; children—Clayton, John R., Mary Agnes, Dilsie, Charles. Admitted to bar, 1883, and practiced at Tupelo. Was county atty., Lee County, Miss., and city atty., Tupelo; chmn. Dem. County Exec. Com. 10 yrs.; ex-mem. Bd. Aldermen, and mayor 10 yrs.; was mem. Miss. Ho. of Rep. and Senate; apptd. asso. justice Supreme Court of Miss., Apr. 1910, resigned Oct. 1911, and resumed practice; elected asso. justice Supreme Court, 3 terms, 1921-45. Trustee Miss. Hist. Soc. Mem. Am. and Miss. State bar assns. Democrat. Presbyterian. Home: Tupelo, Miss. Address: Jackson MS*‡

ANDERSON, WILLIAM HARRY, economist, educator; b. Marinette, Wis., June 9, 1905; s. John and Anna (Olsen) A.; B.A., U. Wis., 1928, LL.B., 1938, Ph.D., 1945; m. Ione E. Swanson, Sept. 2, 1936; 1 son, Harland. Security analyst Halsey Stuart, Chgo., 1928-29; chmn. social sci. dept. W. Chgo. Community High Sch., 1929-36; admitted to Wis. bar, 1938; practice in Madison, 1938-46; atty. Woodward & May, 1938-45; asst. prof. econs. U. Wis., 1945-46; asso. prof. econs. U. So. Cal., 1946-52, prof., 1952-66, chmn. dept. econs., 1957-61; John C. Lincoln prof. pub. finance Claremont (Cal.) Men's Coll. and Grad. Sch., 1966-72, chmn. dept. econs., 1968-71; finance cons. Inst. Adminstrv. Affairs,

Tehran, Iran, 1956-57; dir. Lincoln Sch. Pub. Finance, 1968-72. Mem. Am., Western econ. assns., Nat. Tax Assn., Western Finance Assn., Wis., Cal. bar assns., Artus. Author: Taxation and the American Claremont CA Died Oct. 6, 1972.

ANDRE, FLOYD, coll. dean; b. New Sharon, Ia., Sept. 13, 1909; s. Graham and Alice (Fox) A.; B.S. in Agronomy, Ia. State Coll., 1931; M.S. in Entomology, 1933, Ph.D., 1936; m. Hazel May Beck, June 22, 1935 (dec. Apr. 1956); children—Jacqueline, Alice, Richard Graham; m. 2d, Avis Lovell, Nov. 12, 1970. Asst. Ia. State Coll., 1932-34, instr. entomology and zoology, 1936-38, asst. entomologist, expt. sta., 1934-38, asso. entomologist Bur. Entomology and Plant Quarantine, U.S. Dept. Agr., 1938-40, entomologist and expt. sta. adminstr. Office Expt. Stations, 1940-43, sr. entomologist and expt. sta. adminstr., 1943-46; prof. econ. entomology U. Wis., also asst. dir. state agr. expt. sta., 1946-48, asst. dean Coll. of Agr., asst. dir. state agr. expt. sta. and agr. extension service, 1948-49; dean of agr. Ia. State U. and dir. Coll. Agr., 1949-72. Dir. Union Story Trust & Savs. Bank. Adviser on agrl. edn. to Argentina, 1960, 61 Paraguay, 1964, Brazil, 1964, 65, 67. Mem. Entomol. Soc. Am., Assn. Econ. Entomologists, Biol. Soc. Washington, Phi Kappa Phi, Alpha Zeta, Sigma Xi, Gamma Delta. Presbyn. Author of articles and bulls. on agrl. and entomol. subjects. One of the world's leading collectors of thrips. Home: Ames IA Died Jan. 18, 1972; buried Iowa State Univ. Cemetery.

ANDREASEN, MILIAN LAURITZ, coll. pres.; b. Copenhagen, Denmark, June 4, 1876; s. Lauritz and Caroline (Torgrensen) A.; prep. edn. in Denmark; student Battle Creek (Mich.) Coll., 1899-1900; B.A., U. of Neb., 1921, M.A., 1922; m. Annie Nelson, of Council Bluffs, Ia., Feb. 3, 1896; children—Vesta, Eunice (Mrs. Eugene Philips). Came to U.S., 1894, naturalized, 1909. Minister Seventh Day Adventist Ch., Chicago, 1901-05, N.Y. City, 1905-08; pres. Greater New York Conf., 1908-10; pres. Hutchinson (Minn.) Theol. Sem., 1910-18; dean Union Coll., Lincoln, Neb., 1918-22, Washington (D.C.) Coll., 1922-24; pres. Minn. Conf. Seventh Day Adventist Ch., 1924-31; pres. Union Coll. since 1931, also sec. bd. trustees; mem. bd. trustees Boulder Sanitarium, Porter Sanitarium, Christian Record. Mem. N.E.A., Soc. for Study Edn. Republican. Clubs: Quest, Research. Author: Isaiah, the Gospel Prophet, 1927. Regular contbr. to Signs of the Times." Home: 4734 Calvert St. Address: Union College, Lincoln NB‡

ANDREW, JOSEPH ATKINS, lawyer; b. West Point, Ind., July 13, 1885; s. Thomas M. and Lida M. (Atkins) A.; LL.B., U. Mich., 1909; m. Eulora J. Miller, Sept. 22, 1914; children—Dorothy (Mrs. Lewis E. Morrison), Sarah (Mrs. John C. Ohaver). Admitted to Ind. bar, 1909, U.S. Supreme Ct. bar, 1954; practiced in Lafayette, Ind.; dir. Purdue Bank. Mem. Ind. State Gen. Assembly, 1935-39. Mem. bd. govs. Nat. Red Cross; trustee Lafayette Home Hosp., Boy Scouts of America (Silver Beaver award); pres. Ind. State Board Public Welfare, 1945-48. Named Sagamore of Wabash, 1967. Mem. Am., Ind. State, Tippacanoe Co. bar assns., Am. Judicature Soc., Sigma Chi, Phi Delta Phi. Clubs: Country (Lafayette, Ind.); Columbia (Indpls). Home: Lafayette IN Died Aug. 10, 1967; interment West Point Cemetery, IN

ANDREWS, ALEXANDER SPEER, lawyer; b. Washington, Aug. 9, 1875; s. Chase and Maria Coyle (Speer) A.; A.B., Princeton, 1895; LL.B., Columbia, 1898; m. Sally M. Atterbury Crawley, Jan. 5, 1922; children—June H. (Mrs. R. C. Coleman Jr.), Alexander Speer, Susanne W. (Mrs. R. S. Foote). Admitted to N.Y. bar, 1899, since practiced in N.Y.C.; trustee testamentary trusts; dir. Harper & Bros. Home: 14138 33d Av., Flushing 54 N.Y. Office: 46 Cedar St., NYC 5‡

ANDREWS, CHARLES OSCAR, JR., lawyer, banker; b. Tallahassee, Oct. 11, 1910; s. Charles Oscar and Margaret (Spears) A.; LL.B., U. Fla., 1934; m. Mathilde Mizener, Mar. 12, 1938; children—Charles Oscar III, David W. Admitted to Fla. bar, 1934; practiced in Orlando, 1934-64; mem. Andrews & Smathers & predecessor firms, 1934-64, Andrews, Smathers, Tepper & Pleus, 1967-69; judge 2d Dist. Ct. of Appeal of Fla., Lakeland, later 4th Dist., Winter Park, 1964-67. Pres. dir. Colonial Bank of Orlando, 1951-55, chmn. bd., 1964-67; pres. 1st Nat. Bank of Cape Canaveral. 1963-64, chmn. bd., 1964-66; chmn. bd. Orlando Bank & Trust Co., 1967-69. Chmn., Fla. Welfare Bd., 1953-57, Fla. Milk Commn., 1961-64; former pres. Orlando Community Welfare Planning Council, Orlando Community Chest; chmn. Citizens Survey Com. on Health, Welfare and Recreation Services of Orange County, 1962; pres. Fla. Med. Research Assn.; charter mem. Central Fla. Devel. Com. Asst. city solicitor, Orlando, 1935-36; mem. Winter Park City Commn., 1946-47; mem. Fla. Ho. of Reps., 1949-52; del. Dem. Nat. Conv., 1960. Former chmn. bd. trustees, chmn. bd. dirs., chmn. exec. com. United Appeal of Orange County; nat. trustee United Community Funds and Councils Am.; chmn. Fla. adv. com. United Health Found.; pres. Fla. Technol. U. Found. Mem. Am., Orange County (pres. 1950) bar assns., Fla. Bar, Fla., Greater Orlando, Orlando Jr., chambers commerce, Fla. Conf. Social Work, Blue Key, Pi Kappa Alpha. Presbyn. Kiwanian (past pres. Winter Park). Clubs: University (Winter Park); Executive, Bay Hill Country, University, Orlando Country (pres. 1957-59) (Orlando); River (Jacksonville). Home: Winter Park FL Died Sept. 18, 1969.

ANDREWS, CLARENCE L., b. Ashtabula, O., Oct. 19, 1862; s. Harrison and Arminda Eliza (Whippie) A.; ed. rural schs.; grad. in acctg., Business College Philomath, Ore., 1883; m. Annie Anderson, 1885 (died 1886); m. 2d, Ida Swaggart, 1889 (died June 3, 1903); children—Mable Clare (dec.), Vashti (dec.), Anne Clare (dec.); m. 3d, Lillis G. Smith, 1913 (died 1932); m. 4th Eva L. Alvey, May 18, 1921. Stock rancher, Oregon, 1883; clerk of court, Morrow Co., Ore., 1886-90; dep. auditor King County, Wash., 1890-97; mountaineering with Abruzzi Expdn., 1897; dep. collector customs at Sitka, Skagway and Eagle, Alaska, 1897-1909; spl. agent U.S. Interior Dept. and lecturer, Alaska-Yukon Expn., Seattle, Wash., 1909; writer on Alaska-Yukon Mag., 1910-11; newspaper work in Alaska, 1914-16; with Red Cross Supply Div., 1917-19; statis. work Alaska bur., Seattle Chamber of Commerce, 1919-21; with Interior Dept. Sch. and Reindeer Service in Alaska, 1923-29; lit. work since 1930. Successful leader in publicity fight to secure protection of Eskimo-owned reindeer herds, 1929-45. Editor and pub. The Eskimo, a quarterly paper devoted to the cause of the Eskimo in Alaska. Mem. Odd Fellow, Pioneers of Washington, Pioneers of Alaska, Pioneers of the Yukon, Artic Brotherhood. Republican. Club: Mountaineers (Seattle, Wash.). Author: The Story of Sitka, 1922; The Story of Alaska, 1931; The Pioneer, and His Nuggets of Verse, etc., 1937; Wrangell and the Gold of the Cassiar, 1937; The Eskimo and His Reindeer in Alaska, 1939. Contbr. to various mags. Home: 1734 Villard St., Eugene OR‡

ANDREWS, GEORGE WILLIAM, congressman, b. Clayton, Ala., Dec. 12, 1906; s. George William, Sr., and Addie Bell (King) A.; LL.B., University of Alabama, 1928; married Elizabeth Bullock, Nov. 25, 1936;children—Jane M. (Mrs. Thomas M. Hinds), George William III. Practiced in Union Springs, Alabama, 1928-43; circuit solicitor 3d Judicial Circuit, State of Ala. (Bullock, Barbour, Dale and Russell counties, Ala.), 1931-43. Member of the 78th Congress (elected 1944 to fill vacancy), member 79th-87th, 89th-91st Congresses, 3d Ala. Dist., mem. 88th Congress Alabama at-large. On active duty as lt. (j.g.), U.S.N.R., World War II; released from active duty following election as member of Congress. Mem. Third Judicial Circuit and Ala. bar assns., Sigma Nu, Phi Delta Phi, Omicron Delta Kappa. Democrat. Baptist. Home: Union Springs AL Died Dec. 25, 1971.

ANDREWS, IRENE OSGOOD (MRS. JOHN B. ANDREWS), social worker; b. Big Rapids, Mich., Jan. 18, 1877; d. Lucius L. and Mary (Markley) Osgood; N.Y. Sch. Philanthropy, 1903; A.B., U. of Wis., 1905; U. of Wis. fellow at Univ. Settlement, Milwaukee; m. in N.Y. City, John Bertram Andrews, Aug. 8, 1910; 1 son, John Osgood. Agt. Asso. Charities, Minneapolis, Minn.; spl. agt. for relief work, Am. Red Cross, San Francisco, 1906; factory insp. Wis., 1906; head resident, Northwestern U. Settlement, Chicago, 1907; asso. sec. Am. Assn. for Labor Legislation since 1908. Mem. exec. com. N.Y. League of Women Voters; dir. Maternity Center Assn. (New York); mem. Am. Polit. Science Assn., Alpha Phi. Mem. Y.W.C.A. Nat. Industrial Commn. to Europe, 1919. Author of numerous articles and treatises, including: Minimum Wage Legislation; Working Women in Tanneries; Irregular Employment and the Living Wage for Women; The Economic Effects of the War Upon Women and Children in Great Britain. Home: 15 Gramercy Park. Office: 131 E. 23d St., New York NY‡

ANDREWS, LEILA EDNA, physician; b. North Manchester, Ind., Aug. 14, 1876; d. John Smith and Elizabeth (Strasbaugh) Andrews; M.D., Northwestern U., Chicago, 1900. Practiced at N. Manchester, 1900-07; practiced in Oklahoma City, Okla., since Jan. 1, 1908; mem. staff St. Anthony's Hosp. since 1912; asso. prof. medicine, U. of Okla., 1915-25. Served as mem. Med. Council of Defense and state chmn. Woman's Liberty Loan Com., 2d and 3d loans, World War. Fellow Am. Coll. Physicians (1st woman so selected), A.M.A.; mem. Okla. State and County med. assns., Assn. for Study of Internal Secretions, Southern Med. Assn., D.A.R. (since 1904), Alpha Epsilon Iota (pres. grand chapter 1923-25). Republican. Presbyn. Home: 515 N.W. 15th St. Office: Osler Bldg., Oklahoma City OK‡

ANDREWS, LELAND STANFORD, shipping co. exec.; b. Brentwood, Cal., Aug. 18, 1898; s. Walter Ferris and Charlotte Malisi (Gann) A.; student Los Angeles Poly-tech, 1913-16; m. Bernardine Anna Marenchick, Apr. 24, 1925; 1 dau., Maureen Elianore. Machinist, marine chief engr., 1916-21; chief engr. Munson S.S. Co., 1922-25; repair insp. U.S.S. Board, 1926-27; supt. engring. Am. Export Lines, 1928-34, operating mgr., 1934-49; v.p. operations Am. Export Lines, Inc., 1949-60, ret., 1960. Mem. Soc. Naval Architects and Marine Engrs. Mason (Shriner). Clubs: Propeller, Whitehall (N.Y.C.); Downtown Athletic. Home: Pompano Beach FL Died Feb. 27, 1969; buried Forest Lawn Cemetery, Pompano Beach FL

ANDREWS, ROBERT MACON, clergyman, educator; b. Orange Co., N.C., Aug. 18, 1870; s. Manley and Martha Jane (Cheek) A.; A.B., Yadkin Normal Sch., 1896; student Yale Div. Sch., 1905-06; D.D., Adrian (Mich.) Coll., 1919; m. Olive Pearle Harris, of Henderson, N.C., Oct. 15, 1909; children—Rosalie Martha, Alma Franklin, Dorothea Harris, Robert Macon. Ordained ministry M.P. Ch., 1897; pastor successively Whitakers, Henderson, Grace Ch., Greensboro and Mebane until 1911; editor Burlington (N.C.) News, 1912; again pastor Grace Ch., 1913-18; pres. N.C. Ann. Conf., 1919-24; 1st pres. High Point (N.C.) Coll., since 1924; organized and conducted campaign for building college. Trustee Children's Home, N.C. Bd. of Edn. Mason, Odd Fellow, K.P. Rotarian. Home: High Point NC‡

ANDREWS, SCHOFIELD, lawyer; b. N.Y.C., Aug. 7, 1889; s. Avery De Lano and Mary Campbell (Schofield) A.; grad. St. Paul's Sch., Concord, N.H., 1906; A.B., Harvard, 1910; LL.B., U. Pa., 1913; m. Lillian Forsyth Brown, Apr. 21,1921 (died May 1972); children—Schofield, Stuart Brown, Stockton Avery; m. 2d, Marie D. Grant, May 9, 1929. Admitted to Pa. bar, 1913, practiced in Phila.; mem. firm Ballard, Spahr. Andrews and Ingersoll, Phila., 1919-73. Served with U.S. Army, 1917-19; lt. col., asst. chief of staff, 90th Div., with A.E.F. Decorated D.S.M. Republican. Episcopalian. Club: Philadelphia. Home: Philadelphia PA Died May 1973.

ANDREWS, WILLIAM E., ex-congressman; b. Oskaloosa, Ia.; s. George R. and Sarah (Mendenhall) A.; A.B., Parsons Coll., Fairfield, Ia., 1885; m. Mira McCoy, of Fairfield, Sept. 1, 1885. Mem. faculty, Hastings (Neb.) Coll., 1885-93; pvt. sec. to Gov. Lorenzo Crouse, of Neb., 1893, 94; mem. 54th Congress (1895-97), 5th Neb. Dist.; auditor U.S. Treasury, 1897-1915; mem. 66th and 67th Congresses (1919-23), 5th Neb. Dist. Republican. Presbyn. Mason, Odd Fellow. Home: Hastings NB‡

ANDREWS, WILLIAM NOBLE, congressman; b. Hurlock, Dorchester Co., Md., Nov. 13, 1876; student Dixon Coll., 1 yr.; B.L., U. of Md.; m. Bessie Walworth, Oct. 18, 1903 (died Jan. 21, 1919); children—William N., Virginia Whittier, Elizabeth, Jane Walworth. State's atty., Dorchester Co., Md., 2 terms, 1904-11; mem. Md. Ho. of Rep., 1914, Senate, 1918 (resigned); mem. 66th Congress (1919-21), 1st Md. Dist. Republican. Home: Cambridge MD‡

ANDRUS, CLIFT, army officer; b. Fort Leavenworth, Kan., Oct. 12, 1800; s. Edwin Proctor and Marie Josephine (Birdwell) A.; Cornell Univ., 1912; F.A. Sch., 1927-28, Command and Gen. Staff Sch., 1928-30, Army War Coll., 1933-34, Naval War Coll., 1934-35, 1939-40; D.Sc (hon.), Drexel Inst. Technology, 1951; m. Marion Eleanor Lightfoot, Feb. 15, 1918; children—Margaret Josephine (dec.), Marion (Mrs. Seferlis). Commd. 2d lt., 4th F.A., 1912, advanced through grades to major gen., 1945, ret., 1952. Decorated Distinguished Service Cross, Distinguished Service Medal, Silver Star with oak leaf cluster, Legion of Merit with oak leaf cluster, Soldiers Medal, Bronze Star Medal with oak leaf cluster. Mem. Seal and Serpent, Scabbard and Blade, Semaphore (Cornell). Died Sept. 1968; buried Arlington Nat. Cemetery, Arlington VA

ANGELI, PIER (ANNA MARIE PIERANGELI), actress; b. Sardinia, June 19, 1933; d. Ernica Pierangeli; m. Vic Damone, 1954 (div.); 1 son, Perry Rocco Luigi. First motion picture role with Vittorio de Sica in Tomorrow is Too Late, 1950; appeared numerous films, latest being The Devil Makes Three, 1952, The Story of Three Loves, 1953. Flame and the Flesh, 1954, Somebody Up There Likes Me, 1956, Merry Andrew, 1958, Sodom and Gomorrah, 1962, The Vintage, SOS Pacific, The Angry Silence. Home: Rome Italy Died Sept. 1971.

ANGELL, ERNEST, lawyer; b. Cleve., June 1, 1889; s. Elgin Adelbert and Lily (Curtis) A.; A.B., Harvard, 1911, LL.B., 1913; LL.D., Bard Coll., 1954; m. 1915 (div. 1939); children—Nancy (Mrs. Stableford), Roger, Christopher C., Abigail B.; m. 2d, Elizabeth B. Chapin, 1939. Admitted to Ohio bar, 1914, N.Y. bar, 1920; practiced in Cleve., 1913-17, in N.Y.C., 1920-73; mem. firm Hardin, Hess & Eder, 1922-36; regional adminstr. for N.Y., SEC, 1936-38; mem. firm Spence, Hotchkiss, Parker & Duryee, 1938-54. Served to capt., inf. U.S. Army, 1917-19; A.E.F. Trustee Briarcliff Coll. Chmn. N.Y. area Loyalty Rev. Bd., 1948-50. Mem. Am., N.Y. State bar assns., N.Y. County Lawyers Assn., Assn. Bar City N.Y., Am. Civil Liberties Union (past chmn.), Am. Assn. for Free Jurists (chmn. bd.), Phi Beta Kappa. Clubs: Century Assn., Harvard, River (N.Y.C.). Author: Supreme Court Primer, 1937; Les Aspects Constitutionnels des Libertes Publiques aux Etats-Unis, 1964. Editor: The Rule of Law in the United States, 1958, 62. Contbr. articles to lit. jours. and law revs. Home: New York City NY Died Jan. 11, 1973.

ANGELL, L(ISBETH) GERTRUDE, educator; d. Byron Pomeroy and Gertrude (Bonham) A.; B.A., Wellesley Coll., 1894. Teacher mathematics and history, High Sch. Annex, 1896-98, West High Sch., 1898-99 (both Buffalo); teacher mathematics, 1899-1900, asst. prin., 1900-01, asso. prin., 1901-03, prin. since 1903, Buffalo Sem. Dir. Progressive Coll. for Women, Geneva, Switzerland. Mem. English-Am. Sch. Com. Mem. Headmistresses' Assn. of East and Middle West, Nat. Assn. Principals of Schs. for Girls, Assn. Colls. and Secondary Schs. of Middle States and Md. (mem. library commn.). Presbyn. Club: College of Buffalo (dir.). Address: The Buffalo Seminary, Buffalo NY*‡

ANGELL, NORMAN (RALPH NORMAN ANGELL LANE), author; b. in Eng., 1874; s. Thomas Angell and Mary (Brittain) Lane; ed. partly in Eng., Lycee de St. Omer, France, and Geneva, Switzerland; m. Beatrice, d. Pierre Cuvellier, of New Orleans, 1898. Came to U.S., 1890; newspaper work, 1896-8; Paris corr. various Am. newspapers, 1898-1900; editor Daily Messenger, Paris, 1900-4; gen. mgr. Paris Daily Mail, 1905-12. Author: Europe's Optical Illusion, 1909; The Great Illusion, 1911; The Foundation of International Polity, 1914; America and the World State, 1915; The World's Highway, 1915; Dangers of Half-Preparedness, 1916; Why Freedom Matters; The Need for a Parliament of the Allies; The British Revolution and the American Democracy. Home: Temple London England

ANGER, SISTER MARY ALACOQUE, educator; b. Laflin, Mo., Jan. 21, 1892; d. Alois and Louise (Buchner) Anger; B.S. magna cum laude, St. Louis U., 1937. Instr. radiologic tech. St. Louis U., 1937-51, asst. prof., 1951-57, asso. prof., 1957-63, prof., 1963-69, chmn. dept., 1937-69; asst. adminstr. St. Mary's Hosp., St. Louis, 1925-28. Mem. planning com. Forest Park Community Coll., St. Louis, 1967-69. Fellow Am. Soc. Radiologic Technologists; mem. St. Louis Soc. X-ray Technicians (life), Mo. Soc. Radiologic Technologists (life) (pres. 1947, 48), Nat. Assn. Parliamentarians, Am. Inst. Parliamentarians (mem. adv. council 1965-69). Asso. editor: Missouri Minutes, 1945-60. Contbr. articles in field to profl. jours. Author: A History of the Missouri Society of X-Ray Technicians, 1957. Address: St Louis MO Died June 30, 1969.

ANGEVINE, JAY B(ERNARD), lawyer; b. Highland, N.Y., May 21, 1890; s. Jay Ferris and Sarah Oliver (Bernard) A.; A.B., Williams Coll., 1911, Doctor of Laws, 1960; LL.B., Harvard University, 1915; married Hazel A. Mills, 1917 (died May 2, 1918); 1 daughter, Hazel Mills; married 2d Hallie Virginia Corbett, Oct. 20, 1926; children—Jay Bernard, James Hamilton, Hallie Virginia. Instr. Tome Inst., Port Deposit, Md., 1911-12; admitted to Mass. bar. 1915; asso. Hutchins & Wheeler, Boston, from 1915, partner from 1922; lectr. Northeastern U. Sch. Law, 1921-32; dir. Eastern Utilities Assos., Blackstone Valley Gas & Electric Co. Division chairman of Boston chapter A.R.C., 1945. Trustee emeritus Williams Coll. (chmn. development com.), trustee Rantoul Found., Sneath Found., Andover Theol. Sem., (mem. Adminstrn. Com.), Hyams Charitable Trust, Boston Legal Aid Soc., Belmont Hill Sch. Served as 2d lt. C.A., AUS, World War I. Mem. Am., Mass., Boston (chairman of federal tax committee) bar associations, Newcomen Soc., Phi Beta Kappa, Phi Gamma Delta. Rep. Conglist. Clubs: Williams (N.Y.), Harvard Faculty, Williams Faculty; Harvard (Boston). Home: Belmont MA Died 1969.

ANGLAND, EMMETT CYRIL, lawyer; b. Great Falls, Mont., July 6, 1909; s. Patrick and Elizabeth (Gallagher) A.; LL.B., U. Mont., 1937; m. Laura May Quaintance, Aug. 7, 1941. Admitted to Mont. bar, 1937; law clk. Mont. Ho. of Reps., 1939-41; sec.-counsel Mont. R.R. and Pub. Service Commn., 1940; Mont. dir. atty. Rent Control, 1942-45; successively asst. U.S. atty., acting U.S. atty., 1st asst. U.S. atty. Dist. of Mont., 1945-53; pvt. practice law, Great Falls, 1953-70. Mem. Montana State Board of Law Examiners, 1963-70. Mem. Am. (Montana state delegate 1960-70. member board of governors 1965-68), Montana (past president), Cascade County (past president), bar associations, C. of C. Elk, Moose. Club: Meadow Lark Country (Great Falls). Home: Great Falls MT Died Aug. 11, 1970; interred Hillcrest Lawn Meml. Mausoleum.

ANGLE, GLENN D(ALE), mech. engr.; b. Imlay City, Mich., Jan. 5, 1891; s. Vernon E. and Mary Edith (O'Neil) A.; student U. of Mich., 1911-13; hon. M.E., Lawrence Inst. of Tech., Highland Park, Mich; m. Eleanor B. Grantham, Sept. 6, 1916; 1 son, John Grantham. Chief draftsman Welch Motor Car Co., 1909-11, Dort Motor Car Co., 1916; designer Curtiss Aeroplane & Motor Corp., 1917; charge of engine design, U.S. Army Air Corps, 1918-24; vice-pres. and chief engr. LeBlond Aircraft Engine Corp., Cincinnati, O., 1928-31; prof. mech. engring., Lawrence Inst. of Tech., 1934-39; pres. Angle Engineering Sales Corp. Associate fellow Inst. Aeronautical Sciences; hon. mem. Eugene Field Soc.; mem. Alpha Tau Omega, Author: Airplane Engine Ency., 1921; Engine Dynamics and Crankshaft Design, 1925; Aerosphere, 1939, 41, 42, 43; Aircraft Engine Design. Contbr. Aero Digest (formerly tech. editor), Popular Aviation, Automotive Industries, Aviation, Sportsman Pilot. Address: Brooklyn MI Died Jan. 26, 1966;buried St. Michael and All Angels Cemetery, Cambridge Junction MI

ANGLEMAN, SYDNEY WINFIELD, univ. dean; b. Plainfield, N.J., May 20, 1902; s. Winfield Scott and Erence (Johnstone) A.; A.B., Amherst Coll., 1923; A.M., U. of Calif., 1925, Ph.D., 1937; Hum.D., U. Utah, 1968; m. Mildred Louise Bradford, Sept. 19, 1925, 1 son, Winfield Bradford. Teaching fellow, U. of Calif., 1924; asst. prof. of English U. Utah, 1927, asso., 1939. prof., 1943-71, dean of the Lower Div. 1942-48, asso. dean, U. Coll. and dir., gen. edn., 1948-71. Mem. of Utah State Merit Council, 1942-50, chmn., 1948-50; pres. Utah Conf. on Higher Edn., 1950, Northwest Conf. on Higher Edn. Mem. Am. Assn. of U. Profs., Phi Beta Kappa, Phi Kappa Phi, Theta Alpha Phi, Phi Gamma Delta. Clubs: Exchange; Aztec. Editor: (with Edwin R. Clapp) A Free Man's Forum, 1941; The College Quad, 1951. Home: Salt Lake City UT Died May 3, 1971; inurned Shrine of Memories Mausoleum, Salt Lake City UT

ANGLIN, MARGARET (MARY), actress; b. Ottawa, Can., Apr. 3, 1876; d. Timothy Warren and Ellen (McTavish) A.; ed. Loretto Abbey, Toronto, and Convent of the Sacred Heart, Montreal; grad. Empire Sch. of Dramatic Acting, New York, 1894; m. at New York Howard Hull, writer, May 8, 1911. Made professional debut in Shenandoah," New York, Sept. 1904; leading lady with James O'Neil, playing in The Courier of Lyons," Virginius," Hamlet," Monte Cristo," 1896-97; with E.H. Sothern, 1897-98, Richard Mansfield, 1898-99, and in Empire Theatre Stock Co.; starred in Zira," 1905-06; co-star with Henry Miller, in The Great Divide," 1906-07; produced The Awakening of Helena Richie," The Antigone" of Sophocles, Green Stockings," the Elektra" of Sophocles, etc.; toured extensively; prod. Elektra" at Metropolitan Opera House, New York, 1927; starring in Fresh Fields," 1935-36. Awarded Laetare medal by U. of Notre Dame, Ind, 1927. Catholic.*‡

ANGOOD, SIDNEY BERNARD, food mfg. exec.; b. Ontario, Can., Oct. 27, 1897; s. Arthur E. and Ellen M. (Tattersall); A.; m. Marguerite Stevens, Apr. 15, 1933; children—Arthur W., John B. Came to U.S., 1921, naturalized, 1940. With Kellogg Co., Battle Creek, Mich., 1929-67, mgr. standards dept., 1929-39, market research dir., 1939-45, asst. controller, 1945-48, comptroller, 1948-61, sr. v.p., 1961-67, dir., 1956-67. Mem. Am. Mgmt. Assn. Kiwanian. Home: Battle Creek MI Died Nov. 9, 1967.

ANJARIA, JASHWANTRAI JAYANTILAL, economist; b. Cutch-Bhuj, India, July 15, 1908; s. Jayantilal and Tuljakunwar (Hathi) A.; M.A., Bombay U., 1932; MSc. in Econs., London (Eng.) U., 1936; m. Harvidya Baxi, June 14, 1937; 1 son, Shailendra. Lectr., Fergusson Coll., Poona, 1933-34; prof. Sheth Lalbaai Dalpatbhai Arts Coll., Ahmedabad, 1937-38, Wilson Coll., Bombay, 1938-39; reader Univ. Sch. Econs., Bombay, 1939-44, 45-46; prof. U. Bombay, 1944-45; asst. div. chief research dept. Internat. Monetary Fund, 1946-48; dir. monetary research Res. Bank India, 1948-50; chief econ. div. Planning Commn. New Delhi, 1950-53, econ. adviser Ministry Finance, chief econ. div., 1953-56; chief econ. adv. Govt. India, also Ministry Finance, also econ. adviser Planning Commn., New Delhi, 1956-61; exec. dir. for India, Internat. Monetary Fund, 1961-67; dep. gov. Res. Bank of India, Hon. sec. Indian Soc. Agrl. Econs., 1942-46; pres. All India 1967-70. Hon. sec. Indian Soc. Agrl. Econs., Agrl. Econ. Conf., 1955, All-India Econ. Assn., 1959. Mem. Soc. for Internat. Devel. (council). Author: Grounds for Political Obligation in the Hindu State, 1934; Price Control and Food Supply, 1941; The Indian Rural Problem, 1943; Essays in Planning and Growth, pub. posthumously, 1972. Home: Bombay, India Died Apr. 10, 1970.

ANNADOWN, RUTH VIVIAN, physician; b. Chanute, Kan., Dec. 19, 1910; d. Paul Vivian and Leila Edna (Clark) Annadown; A.B., Tex. State Coll. for Women, 1937; M.D., U. Okla., 1946. Tchr. pub. schs., Sulphur, Okla., 1934-36, 37-39, Wichita, Kan., 1940-43; rotating intern U. Hosp., Oklahoma City, 1946-47, 49-50; resident psychiatry Wayne County Gen. Hosp., Eloise, Mich., 1958-61; dir. Hughes County Health Dept., Holdenville, Okla., 1947-49; practice medicine, Oklahoma City, 1950-56; now specializing in psychiatry, Vinita, Okla.; dir. research Western State Hosp., Ft. Supply, Okla., 1957-58; head female div. Eastern State Hosp., Vinita, 1962, clin. dir., 1963, 65, acting supt., 1963-64; team leader Ft. Logan Mental Health Center, Denver, 1965-67. Mem. Sulphur Camp Fire Girl Council, 1934-39. Mem. A.M.A., Okla. Med. Assn., Craig, Delaware, Ottawa Counties Med. Sulphur OK Died Nov. 28, 1967; buried Oaklawn Cemetery, Sulphur OK

ANSELL, SAMUEL TILDEN, lawyer; b. Coinjock, N.C., Jan. 1, 1875; s. Henry Beasley and Lydia (Simmons) A.; grad. U.S. Mil. Acad., 1899; LL.B., U. of N.C., 1904; m. Elmeda Tracy, Feb. 16, 1904 (dec. 1944); children—Elmeda (dec.), Burr Tracy, Samuel Tilden, Nancy Lydia; m. 2d, Anne Clay Clay, Nov. 8, 1948. Commd. 2d lt. 11th Inf., Feb. 15, 1899; promoted through grades to brig. gen., Oct. 5, 1917. Instr. law, U.S. Mil. Acad., 1902-04, 1906-09; duty with civil govt. in Philippines as pros. atty., Moro Province, 1909-11; atty. for Porto Rico and Philippine Islands before Federal Courts of U.S., by spl. assignment of War Dept.; acting judge advocate gen. U.S. Army, 1917-18; inaugurated movement resulting in reformation of army courtmartial system and adoption of liberalized articles of war; resigned from army to resume practice of law, July 21, 1919. Awarded D.S.M. for especially meritorious and conspicuous service" as acting judge advocate gen. Episcopalian. Home: 1957 Biltmore St., Washington, D.C.; (country) Rehoboth Beach, Del. Office: Tower Bldg., Washington DC‡

ANSERMET, ERNEST ALEXANDRE, condr.; b. Vevey, Switzerland; Nov. 11, 1883; s. Gabriel and Marie (Charoton) A.; ed. univs. Lausanne (Switzerland), Paris (France); hon. degrees U. Lausanne, U. Neuchatel. Tchr. mus. studies, Switzerland and France; m. Marguerite Jaccotet, 1940; Juliette Salvisberg, 1941. Math., Lausanne, 1906-10; condr. orch., Kursaal, Montreux, 1910-14; condr. symphony concerts, Geneva, 1915-69; founder, condr. Orchestre de la Suisse Romande de Geneve, 1918-67; chief condr. Orch. Radio Geneva; condr. Russian ballet of Serge Diaghilev, 1915-23; guest appearances in S.Am., Mexico, N.Am., Europe; Mayer lectr. Brit. Inst. Recorded Sound, 1963. Named officer Legion d'Honneur, Etoile Belge, citizen of honor State and City of Geneva, 1953. Author: Les fondements de la musique dans la conscience humaine, 2 vols., 1961. Address: Geneva Switzerland Died Feb. 20, 1969.*

ANSHEN, S. ROBERT, architect; b. Revere, Mass., Jan. 29, 1910; s. Louis J and Sarah (Jaffe) A.; B.Arch., U. Pa., 1935, M.Arch., 1963; divorced; children—Haven, John. Designer, Clarence Tantau, 1938-39; partner Anshen & Allen, architects, San Francisco, 1940-41, 45-64; draftsman Joslyn & Ryan, 1941-43; tech. dir. Housing Authority City of Vallejo, 1943-45; lectr. U. Cal. at Berkeley, 1952-53; projects include numerous devel. houses and pvt. residences, bldgs., also Coast Counties Gas & Electric Co., Taylor Instruments Co., Chapel of Holy Cross, Sedona, Ariz., Diamond House, Squaw Valley, home on Yankee Point, Carmel, Cal., Internat. Bldg., San Francisco, Chemistry Complex U. Cal. at Berkeley, Master plan U. Cal. at Santa Cruz, Natural Scis. Bldg. U. Cal. at Santa Cruz, Lawrence Meml. Hall Sci. U. Cal. at Berkeley, labs. for NASA, Bank of Cal. Office Bldg., San Francisco. Recipient numerous awards A.I.A., Sunset mag., Nat. Assn. Home Builders, Am. Inst. Steel Constrn., Church Archtl. Guild Am., House and Home, Life mag., Parents mag.; award U. Cal. Lawrence Meml. Hall of Sci. competition, 1962. Fellow A.I.A. Clubs: World Trade, Commonwealth (San Francisco). Home: Mill Valley CA Died May 26, 1964; buried Ferncliff Cemetery, Hartsdale NY

ANSLOW, GLADYS AMELIA, educator; b. Springfield, Mass., May 22, 1892; d. John and Ella (Leonard) Anslow; A.B., Smith Coll., 1914, A.M., 1917, Dr. of Sci. (honorary), 1950; postgrad. U. Chgo., 1921; Ph.D., Yale 1924; research fellow, University of Calif., 1938-39. Demonstrator in physics, Smith Coll., 1914-15, asst., 1915-18, instr., 1918-24, asst. prof., 1924-30, asso. prof., 1930-36, prof. physics 1936-60, research prof., 1960-—, Nat. Sci. Found. grantee, 1958-—, dir. grad. sch., 1940-58; special consultant, office of field service, Office of Scientific Research and Development, 1944-45. Vice president New England Conference on Graduate Edn., 1946-47; dir. of contract with Office of Naval Research, U.S. Navy, 1948-58. Awarded President's Certificate of merit, 1948. Fellow A.A.A.S., American Academy of Arts and Sciences, American Physical Soc. (vice chmn. New England section 1941-42, chmn. 1942-44); mem. Am. Physics Teachers Assn. (mem. exec. com. 1943-44; asso. editor Am. Jour. of Physics 1935-38), Am. Optical Society, Nat. Federation of Business and Profl. Women, American Assn. Univ. Profs., Am. Assn. Univ. Women (2d v.p. Mass. State Division, 1946-48), Phi Beta Kappa, Sigma Xi. Republican. Unitarian. Researches in nuclear physics, electron collisions, absorption spectra, biological effects of radiation. Contbr. of tech. articles to sci. jours. Home: Northampton MA Died Mar. 31, 1969.

ANSPACH, BROOKE MELANCTHON, gynecologist; b. Reading, Pa., Mar. 3, 1876; s. John Melancthon and Lydia Catharine (Bucher) A.; Lafayette Coll., class of 1896; M.D., U. of Pa., 1897; hon. Sc.D., Lafayette Coll., 1936, Jefferson Medical College, Philadelphia, Pa., 1946; m. Martha Brown McCormick, Nov. 1, 1906; children—Margaretta McCormick (Mrs. J. Kent Willing, Jr.), Catharine McCormick (Mrs. Geo. L. Pew). Asso. in gynecology, U. of Pa. to 1921; prof. gynecol., Jefferson Med. Coll., 1921-40, prof. emeritus since Aug. 1940; formerly cons. gynecol. Jefferson and Bryn Mawr hosps.; ret. Fellow Am. Coll. Surgs. Coll. Phys. of Phila., Am. Gynecol. Soc. (ex-pres.), Am. Gynecol. Club. Republican. Presbyn. Club: Union League (Phila.). Author: Gynecology, 1934. Home: 116 Mill Creek Rd., Ardmore PA‡

ANTHONY, EDWARD, writer; b. N.Y.C., Aug. 4, 1895; s. Robert and Rose (Friedman) A.; pub. edn.; m. Esther H. Howard, Dec. 17, 1928; 1 son, Richard W. Started newspaper work on Bridgeport (Conn.) Herald, 1917; stationed at Camp Merritt 1918-19 World War; with N.Y. Herald, 1920-23; associate editor Farm and Fireside, 1923-28; associate editor of Judge," 1923; staff American Magazine, 1929; press service director Crowell Group (American Magazine, Collier's, Woman's Home Companion), 1930-42; publisher Woman's Home Companion, 1942-52, Collier's mag., 1949-54; cons. to Am. Girl mag. 25 yrs.; now writer. Publicity dir. Hoover presidential campaign, 1928. Served as dir. pub. relations War Advt. Council, World War II. Trustee Herbert Hoover Birthplace Foundation. Clubs: Dutch Treat, Nat. Press, P.E.N., Players. Author: Merry-Go-Roundelays, 1921; The Pussycat Princess, 1922; The Fairies Up-to-Date, 1923; Razzberry, 1924; How to Get Rid of a Woman, 1928; Bring'Em Back Alive (with Frank Buck), 1930; Wild Cargo (with Frank Buck), 1932; The Big Cage (with Clyde Beatty), also screen version of same, 1933; Nowhere Else in the World (with G. B. Enders), 1935; I Live on Air (with A. A. Schechter), 1941; The Sex Refresher, 1943; Every Dog Has His Say, 1947; Oddity Land, 1957(with Clyde Beaty) Facing the Big Cats, 1965; (with Henry Trefflich) Jungle for Sale, 1967; (with Eric Sloane) Mr. Daniels and the Grange, 1968. Author book and lyrics of mus. comedy Good Luck Sam (while in Army); also numerous mag. articles. Home: New Milford CT Died Aug. 16, 1971; buried New Milford CT

ANTHONY, KATHARINE SUSAN, writer; b. Roseville, Ark., Nov. 27, 1877; d. Ernest Augustus and Susan Jane (Cathey) A.; student Peabody Coll. for Teachers, Nashville, Tenn., 1895-97; univs. of Heidelberg and Freiburg, Germany, 1901-02; Ph.B., U. of Chicago, 1905; unmarried. Instr., Wellesley Coll., 1907-08; research in economics with the Russell Sage Foundation, New York, 1909-13. Author: Mothers Who Must Earn, 1914; Feminism in Germany and Scandinavia, 1915; Labor Laws of New York, 1917; Margaret Fuller—A Psychological Biography, 1920; Catherine the Great, 1925; Queen Elizabeth, 1929; Marie Antoinette, 1932; Louisa May Alcott, 1938. Co-author: Civilization in the United States—An Inquiry by Thirty Americans, 1921. Translator of Memoirs of Catherine the Great, 1927. Contbr. to mags. Home: 23 Bank St., New York, N.Y., and Gaylordsville CT‡

ANTHONY, LOVICK PIERCE, editor; b. Conyers, Ga., Aug. 20, 1877; s. James and Martha (Ozier) A.; student Emory U., Oxford, Ga., 1896-97; D.D.S., Atlanta-Southern Dental Coll., 1901; m. Kittie Carroll, 1902; children—James C., Pierce Wilmot. Practiced dentistry, Atlanta, Ga., 1901-03; associated with Dental Cosmos (Dental Mag.) 1903, asso. editor, 1917, editor, 1929; asso. editor Journal Am. Dental Assn., 1936, editor, 1938, editor emeritus, 1945. Awarded Jarvie medal by New York Dental Society, Fones medal by the Connecticut Dental Society, Fauchard medal by International College of Dentists. Mem. Am. Dental Association, International Coll. of Dentists, Sigma Nu, Delta Sigma Delta, Omicron Kappa Upsilon. Democrat. Methodist. Author: Dental Dictionary (Lea & Febiger) 1922; Dental Terminology (Am. Dental) 1930; American Textbook Prosthetic Dentistry (Lea & Febiger) 1932. Home: 5950 Willow Springs Rd., La Grange IL‡

ANTHONY, NORMAN (HUME), editor, writer; b. Buffalo, N.Y., May 11 1889; s. Edward L. and Electa Perkins (Hume) A.; ed. Lafayette High Sch., Buffalo; Buffalo Art Students' League and New York Art Students' League; m. Margaret Eisele Hofheins, Aug. 25, 1910; children—Edith (Mrs. Taylor G. Belcher), Norman. Free-lance artist 10 yrs.; contbr. Judge, Life and other mags.; joined staff of Judge, 1920, editor Judge, 1922-28; editor Life, 1928-29; founder, editor Ballyhoo, from 1930. Author: How to Grow Old Disgracefully or Anthony's Adversities, 1946; What to Do Till the Psychiatrist Comes, 1947; (with O. Soglow) the Drunk's Blue Book, 1933. Home: Garrison NY Died Jan. 12, 1968.

ANTOINE, JOSEPHINE LOUISE, musician; b. Denver, Colo., Oct. 27, 1907; d. Arthur Hubert and Bertha Olive Antoine; B.A., U. of Colo., 1929; student Juilliard Grad. Sch. of Music, N.Y. City, 1930-35; hon. M.M., U. of Colo., 1935; married S. Edwin Hinkle, Nov. 20, 1948; dau. Myra Louise (Mrs. Buchanan). Recipient of Norlin award, Univ. of Colo., 1948. Winner 3d place, Atwater Kent Nat. Radio auditions, 1929; debut in Met. Opera Co., N.Y. city, 1936; mem. Chicago Opera Co., San Francisco Opera Co. Faculty American Operatic Lab., Los Angeles. Honorary mem. Am. Assn. Univ. Women, Daughters of Colorado, Business and Professional Women's Club, Sigma Alpha Iota, Phi Delta Gamma, Chi Omega; member P.E.O. Republican. Christian Scientist. Home: Greece NY Died Oct. 30, 1971.

ANTON, MARK, corp. exec.; b. Chgo., Dec. 3, 1892; s. Byron and Jane (Olwell) A.; ed. pub. schs., Newark, N.J.; m. Adele Buecke, Sept. 19, 1923 (dec. Feb. 6, 1961); children—Mark John, Jane. Asst. to works mgr. Hyatt Roller Bearings, 1916-20; formed Circle Stamping & Mfg. Co., later called Mark Anton Mfg. Co., 1920; established Suburban Gas Co., 1928, Inc., 1929; established Warren County Gas Co., 1931; organized Nat. Bottled Gas Assn. (now Liquefied Petroleum Gas Assn.), 1931, pres., 1931-34; bought Eastern Seaboard retail properties from Phillips Petroleum Co. and formed Suburban Propane Gas Corp., 1945, pres. and dir., 1945, chmn. bd., until 1972; treas. and dir. Warren County Gas Co.; dir. SBN Gas Co., Gas- Oil Exploration Co., Found. Life Ins. Co. Am., and Liquigas (Milan, Italy). Essex County freeholder, 1950-52; served as state senator from Essex County, 1953; mem. N.J. State Planning and Devel. Council, 1957; chmn. N.J. Navigation Com.; trustee Seton Hall U., N.J. Citizens Hwy. Com., N.J. Safety Council, Orange Meml. Hosp., Westminster Choir Coll.; vice pres., bd. trustees Kessler Inst. Rehab.; nat. trustee, exec. chmn. N.J. region Nat. Conf. Christians and Jews; bd. dirs. N.J. chpt. Arthritis and Rheumatism Found., Am. French Found., Essex County Service Chronically Ill.; county crusdae chmn. Am. Cancer Soc., 1965; drive chmn. United Cerebral Palsy of North Jersey, 1966, 1967. Served as lt. U.S. Army, World War I; nat. chmn. N.R.A. Code Authority for Liquefied Petroleum br. industry, 1933; chief fuel oil for Atlantic Coast, Petroleum Adminstrn. for War, 1942; N.J. mgr. Smaller War Plants Corp., 1943-44. Mem. Marymount Coll. Fathers' Council, N.J. C. of C. (dir.), Liquefied Petroleum Gas Assn. (dir.), Am. Legion, Clubs: Bankers, N.Y. Athletic, Circus Saints and Sinners (treas.), Economic (N.Y.C.) Lucullus Circle, Bayhead Yacht, Downtown, Rock Spring Country (N.J.); Capitol Hill; Manhasset Bay Yacht.; Great Oaks Yacht; Circumnavigators; Marco Polo; 744 Broad St. Short Hills NJ Died Dec. 1, 1972.

APPEL,GEORGE F(REDERICK) BAER, lawyer; b. Lancaster, Pa., Jan. 6, 1903; s. William Nevin and Marion Parker (Baer) A.; grad. Taft Sch., 1920; B.A., Yale, 1924; LL.B., U. Pa., 1927; m. Elizabeth Thomas, June 22, 1928; children—Elizabeth (Mrs. Lawrence A. Brown, Jr.), George, Rosalind (Mrs. Robert D. Ritchie), Beatrice (Mrs. Thomas A. Halsted), William, Marion (Mrs. Robert Gibbon, Junior). Admitted to the Pennsylvania bar, 1927, United States Supreme Court, 1958; sec. Chief Justice Robert Von Moschzisker, Supreme Ct. of Pa., 1927-28; with Townsend, Elliot & Munson, Phila., 1928-70, partner, 1938-70. Sec. Pa. Bd. Law Examiners, 1931-38, chmn., 1961-70; member Am. Bar Found.; Staff, Office Lend Lease Adminstrn., Washington, 1942-44, Fgn. Econ. Adminstrn., Washington, 1944-45, London, Eng., 1945. Chmn. Central br. YMCA, Phila., 1940-42. Mem. Am. Bar Assn. (chmn. sect. municipal law 1956-58, ho. of dels. 1958-62), Juristic Soc. of Phila. (past pres.). Episcopalian (vestryman, exec. council Diocese of Pa. 1954-56), Am. Judicature Soc. Clubs: Rittenhouse (solicitor) (Phila.); Merion Cricket (Haverford, Pa.); Yale (N.Y.C. and Phila.). Home: Wynnewood PA Died Mar. 12, 1970.

APPEL, MONTE, lawyer; b. Huron, S.D., Mar. 15, 1887; s. Samuel and Rose (Lyons) A.; A.B., U. of Wis., 1910; LL.B., Harvard, 1913; m. Gladys McGrew, June 16, 1926; children—Patricia, Jacquelin; m. 2d, Raimonda Bartol, January 16, 1965. Admitted to Minn. bar, 1913, D.C. bar, 1918; mem. firm Sanborn, Graves & Appel, St. Paul, 1917-18; practiced in Washington, 1920-33; later mem. Appel & Morton. Asst. counsel U.S. Shipping Board, 1917-18; spl. rep. of U.S. sec. of war, 1918-19; asst. atty. gen. of U.S., 1932-33; mem. Blair, Korner, Doyle & Appel, Washington, 1945-56. Cheavlier French Legion of Honor, 1918. Mem. Am., and District of Columbia bar assns., Delta Kappa Epsilon. Republican. Episcopalian. Club: Metropolitan (Washington, D.C.). Home: Washington DC Died May 23, 1970; buried Rockcreek Park DC

APPLEGATE, IRVAMAE VINCENT, coll. dean; b. Beulah, N.D., Sept. 18, 1920; d. Irving Joseph and Helen (Engberg) Vincent; B.S. N.D. State U., 1941, D.Sc. (hon.), 1963; M.A., U. Minn., 1951, Ph.D., 1957; m. Dwain William Applegate, Apr. 13, 1944. Tchr. pub. schs., Cass Lake, Minn., 1941-43; tchr., high sch. prin. pub. schs., Hazen, N.D., 1943-46; reporter-writer Independent Age, Aitkin, Minn., 1946-47; tchr., then high sch. prin. pub. schs., Princeton, Minn., 1947-56; mem. faculty St. Cloud (Minn.) State Coll., 1956-73, asso. dean tchr. edn., 1961-62, dean Sch. Edn., 1962-73. Mem. Minn. Adv. Com. Tchr. Edn., 1961-66, Minn. Mental Health Planning Council, 1963-65; mem. edn. com. Gov. Minn. Adv. Council Children and Youth, 1964; subcom. non- med. resources Minn. Mental Health Planning Council, 1964-65; employment com. Gov. Minn. Commn. Status Women, 1964-65; del. World Confedn. Orgns. Teaching Profession, 1967-73, exec., 1969-73; cons. U.S. Office Edn., 1969-73. Recipient Presdl. citation Audio-Visual Coordinators Assn. Minn., 1963; Hon. Awards certificate Minn. Elementary Prins. Assn., 1964; Outstanding Achievement award U. Minn., 1965. Mem. Minn. Assn. Supervision and Curriculum Devel. (bd. dirs., editor 1959-62), Zonta, Am. Assn. U. Women, Minn. (pres. 1963-65), Nat. (life mem., pres. 1966-67, chmn. compliance com. 1966-69, chmn. urban task force 1966-69) edn. assns., Minn. Press Woman, Nat. Council State Assn. Presidents (exec. com., 1963-64), Am. Legion Aux., St. Cloud C. of C., Kappa Delta, Pi Lambda Theta, Delta Kappa Gamma (pres. Eta chpt. 1960-62), Delta Psi Kappa. Author monthly column Assignment Education, 1963-66. Home: Sauk Rapids MN Died Mar. 1973.

APPLETON, WILLIAM CHANNING, ret. textile mfr.; b. March 15, 1897; s. William Channing and Edna Marion (Turner) A.; A.B., Harvard U., 1917; student New Bedford Textile Sch., 1919-20; m. Ellen Rockwood Sherman, May 8, 1920; children—Anna Turner, Sarah Sherman; m. 2d, Loraine Chadeayne Sinsabaugh, Mar. 24, 1934; children—Betsy Gale, Loraine C., William C., John G; m. 3d, Doryce Dane, Nov. 23, 1957. Cotton, wool and worsted mill hand, 1919-21; clk. and buyer Whitman Mills, 1922-23; cotton yarn salesman, Harding Tilton & Co. 1923-25; branch sales mgr. rayon yarn, Am. Viscose Corp., 1925-28, asst. gen. sales mgr., 1928-32, gen. sales mgr., 1932-35, dir., 1933-46, v.p., 1935-37, pres., 1937-46; pres. Selectronic Dispersions, Inc., Montclair, N.J., 1946-48, Empire Inc., N.Y. City; pres., dir. Delaware Mills, Inc., New Castle, Del. to 1958, ret. Mem. Am. Field Service, France, 1917; cadet U.S. AS, AEF, 1917-18; commd. 2d lt., 103d Sqdrn., 3d Pursuit Group, A.E.F., 1918. Former mem. Northern Textile Assn. Unitarian. Clubs: Seawanhaka Corinthian Yacht (Oyster Bay, N.Y.); Harvard (N.Y.C.); Wilmington Country, Brandywine Valley assn. (dir.) (Wilmington, Del.). Address: New Castle DE Died Mar. 29, 1972; buried Mt. Auburn Cemetery, Cambridge MA

ARAMBURU, PEDRO EUGENIO, Provisional President of Argentina; b. Rio Cuarto, Cordoba, Argentina, May 21, 1903; student Colegio de Militar de Nacional, 1918-22; married; children—1 dau., 1 son. Entered army service as sub-lt., 1922, and advanced to maj. gen., 1954; became gen. staff officer, 1936; mil. attache Argentine embassy, Rio de Janeiro, Brazil, 1951-53; dir. gen. Army Med. Corps, 1953; sub-dir., later dir., Escuela Superior de Guerra, 1954; following exile of deposed pres., Juan Peron, 1955, was named chief of staff by the succeeding pres., Eduardo Lonardi, whose adminstrn. fell, 1955; became provisional pres. of Argentina, Nov. 1955; major efforts of adminstrn. centered on reestablishment of more democratic principles in govt. and guidance to stable econ. and polic. recovery in the nation; has scheduled free nationwide elections for late in 1957, and has barred for candidacy in these elections all members of his provisional govt. Roman Catholic. Home: Buenos Aires Argentina Died July 1970.*

ARBUS, DIANE, photographer; b. N.Y.C., Mar. 14, 1923; d. David Irwin and Gertrude (Russek) Nemerov; grad. high sch.; m. Allan Arbus, Apr. 10, 1941; children—Doon, Amy. Exhibited in group shows at Mus. Modern Art, 1965, Guggenheim Group Show Phila. Coll. Art, 1966, Mus. Modern Art New Documents, 1967, Fogg Mus., 1967; represented in permanent collections Mus. Modern Art, George Eastman House, Rochester, N.Y.; tchr. Parsons Sch. Design, 1965-66, Cooper Union 1968-69. Guggenheim fellow, 1963, 66. Contbr. articles to mags. and newspapers. Home: New Died July 26, 1971.

ARBUTHNOT, CHARLES CRISWELL, economist; b. Pittsburgh, May 30, 1876; s. James Mackay and Rebecca McClure (Criswell) A.; grad. Prep. Dept., Geneva Coll.; B.S., Geneva Coll., 1899, LL.D., 1916; Ph.D., U. of Chicago, 1903; m. May Hill, Dec. 17, 1932. Began as asst. in history, Geneva Coll., 1899; fellow in economics, U. of Chicago, 1901-03; instr. in polit. economy, 1903-04, adj. prof., 1904, U. of Neb.; instr. in economics, 1904-06, asso. prof., 1906-08, prof. since 1908, Western Reserve Univ. Home: 2263 Demington Drive Cleveland OH‡

ARBUTHNOT, MAY HILL (MRS. CHARLES C. ARBUTHNOT), author; b. Mason City, Ia., Aug. 27, 1884; d. Frank and Mary Elizabeth (Seville) Hill; Ph.B., U. Chgo., 1922; M.A., Columbia U., 1924; m. Charles C. Arbuthnot, Dec. 17, 1932. Tchr. tng. Superior (Minn.) State Coll., 1912-17, Ethical Culture Sch., N.Y.C., 1918-22; became dir. Cleve. Kindergarten-Primary Tng. Sch. (merged with Western Res. U., 1927), 1922, asso. prof. edn., 1927-47; ret., 1947; rev. editor children's books Assn. Childhood Edn., Elementary English; lectr. Recipient Constance Lindsey Skinner medal, Bookwomen of Am., 1959, award in letters League Am. Pen Women, 1961, Regina medal Catholic Library Assn., 1964. Mem. Phi Beta Kappa, Pi Lambda Theta, Delta Kappa Gamma Author: Children and Books, rev. 1972; Time for Poetry, rev. 1968; The Arbuthnot Anthology, rev. 1971; Children's Reading in the Home, 1968; Time for Stories, 1968; Time for Biography, 1969; Time for Old Magic, 1970; Time for New Magic, 1971; Time for Discovery, 1971. Home: Cleveland OH Died Oct. 2, 1969.

ARBUTHNOT, THOMAS SHAW, physician; b. Allegheny, Pa., Feb. 18, 1871; s. Charles and Elizabeth (Shaw) A.; A.B., Yale, 1894; M.D., Coll. Phys. and Surg. (Columbia), 1898; M.R.C.S., Eng., 1900; L.R.C.P., London, 1900; LL.D., U. of Pittsburgh, 1919;

unmarried. Dean Med. Sch. of U. of Pittsburg, 1909-18. Pres. Carnegie Hero Fund; mem. bd. Carnegie Corp., N.Y., since 1933. Pres., Art Society of Pittsburgh since 1934; pres. Bd. of Children's Hosp. 1927-48. Mem. A.M.A. In service in France, 1917-19. Address: 6425 5th Av., Pittsburgh PA‡

ARCAYA, PEDRO MANUEL, diplomat; b. Coro, Falcon State, Venezuela, Jan. 8, 1874; s. Camilo and Ignacia (Madriz) A.; D. Polit. Sciences, U. of Caracas, Venezuela, 1895; m. Maria Teresa Urrutia, Mar. 22, 1913; children—Mariano, Isabel, Carlos, Ana, Maria, Ignacia, Pedro. In practice of law, Coro, 1895-1909; judge of Supreme Court of Venezuela, 1909-13; atty. gen. of Venezuela, 1913-14; minister of interior, Venezuela, 1914-17, 1925-29; spl. ambassador to Peru, 1924; E.E. and M.P. at Washington, D.C., 1922-24 and 1930-36; prof. law, U. of Caracas. Mem. Academia de la Historia, Academia de la Lengua, etc. Awarded Grand Cross Order Sol del Peru; Grand Cordon Order of the Liberator, Venezuela; Merito (Chile). Catholic. Author: Estudios sobre personages y hechos de la Historia Venezolana, 1911; Ensayos de Sociologia Venezolana, 1918; Estudio Critico de las Excepciones de Inadmisibilidad, 1909; La Propiedad Territorial, 1904; Memorias del Ministerio de Relaciones Interiores, 1915, 16, 17, 25, 26, 27, 28, 29. Contbr. to Boletin de la Academia de la Historia (Caracas), etc. Address: 2150 Wyoming Av. N.W., DC‡

ARCE, JOSE, Argentine diplomat, surgeon; b. Loberia, Province of Buenos Aires, Argentina, Oct. 15, 1881; s. Juvencio and Luisa A.; M.D., U. of Buenos Aires, 1903; Dr. honoris causa, U. of Madrid, 1924, U. of Rio de Janeiro, 1926; D.Sc., Temple U., Phila., Pa., 1937; M.D (hon.) U. of Johan Wolfgang Goethe, Frankfurth am Main, 1936; m. Amelia Bazan, Oct. 27, 1938. Asst. prof. clinical surgery U. of Buenos Aires, 1907-19, prof., 1919-23, became dir. Inst. of Clin. Surgery, 1923, rector of univ., 1922-26, vice rector, 1936-38; mem. Council Faculty of Med. Sciences, 1918-45, prof. of descriptive anatomy, 1907-10, of clin. surgery, 1919-41, of thoracic surgery, 1942-45; chief of emergency surgical services, Hospital Norte, 1904; chief of surg. service for mem. Hosp. Juan A. Fernandez, 1905; chief of surg. service for women Hosp. Teodoro Alvarez, 1905-10, of surg. service for men, 1910-11; chief of gen. surgical service Hosp. de Clinicas, Faculty of Medical Sciences of U. of Buenos Aires, 1923-41. Visiting prof. of exchange prof. to univs. in Paris, Rumania, Paraguay, Mexico and other foreign countries, 1907-45; also delegate to, and speaker before numerous internat. conferences and foreign learned societies. Deputy to legislature, Buenos Aires, 1909-13, pres. Chamber of Deputies, 1912-13; dep. of Province of Buenos Aires to Nat. Congress, 1913-20, 1923-28, 1934-38; v.p. Nat. Chamber of Deputies, 1926-27; ambassador for Argentina to China, 1945-46; pres. Argentine delegation to Gen. Assembly of United Nations, also permanent chief delegate to U.N., with rank of A.E. and P., since Sept. 1946. Decorated Gran Cruz de la Orden de Alfonso XII (Spain), Comdr. Legion of Honor (France), Comdr. Orden de la Corona (Italy), Comdr. Orden de la Estrella, Gran Cruz de la Orden de la Corona (Rumania), Cruz del Defensor (Paraguay), Grand Official of Orden al Merito (Chile), Official of Orden del Crucero del Sud (Brazil), Comdr. Orden del Libertador (Venesuela), Comdr. Orden de Vasco Nunez de Balboa (Panama). Recipient of gold medal of Faculty of Medical Sciences; gold medal of Medical Faculty of U. of Hamburg. Mem. and officer of numerous scientific and learned societies in Argentina and in foreign countries. Author: Neumatorax preoperatorio, Metodo Arce, 1941; also of a large number of sci. papers and contbns. Buenos Aires Argentina *

ARCHER, CLIFFORD PAUL, educator; b. Troy, Ia., Nov. 18, 1893; s. John Franklin and Martha Emiline (Hunt) A.; grad. So. Ia. Normal, 1911; A.B., Ia. State Tchrs. Coll., 1920; M.A., U. Ia. 1923, Ph.D., 1927; m. Myrtle Blair, July 5, 1918; children—Blair, Philip, Helen (wife of Dr. Wilfred Lundblad), Stephen. Rural sch. tchr., Davis Co., Ia., 1912-13; prin. Libertyville (Ia.) Schs., 1913-14; supervisor rural schs., Limecreek, Ia., 1916-17; supt. schs., Hudson, Ia., 1920-22; instr. summer sch. Ia. State Tchrs. Coll., 1921-23; head dept. edn. State Tchrs. Coll., Moorhead, Minn., 1923-26, 27-37; asst. prof. edn., dir. bur. recommendations U. Minn., 1938-42, asso. prof., 1942-50, prof., 1951-68, program coordinator Peace Corps project 1962-63; chief field party Inst. Inter-Am. Affairs, Bolivia, 1950-51; edn. program officer, Washington, 1952-53. Chmn. Minn. Commn. Study and Improvement Instrn., 1955-57. Chief boatswain's mate USNR, 1918-19; lt. col. U.S. army, comdt. Armed Forces Inst., Southwest Pacific, 1943-45. Mem. Nat. Instnl. Tchrs. Placement Assn. (pres. 1946-47), Minn. (pres. 1938-40), Western Minn. (past exec. sec.) edn. assns., N.E.A. (chmn. com. internat. edn. rural dept.; president department of rural edn. 1960-61), Am. Ednl. Research Assn., Nat. Elementary Sch. Prins. Assn., Nat. Dept. Rural Edn. (pres. 1960-68), Am. Assn., Suprs. and Curriculum Dirs., Nat. Council Tchrs. English, Nat. Council Research in English, W. Minn. Schoolmasters (pres., exec. sec. 1924-37), Minn. Soc. Study (pres. 1958-59), Minn. Elementary Prins. Assn. (life), Phi Delta Kappa, Psi Chi, Delta Sigma Rho, Kappa Delta Pi. Mason. Author: Elementary Education in Rural Areas, 1957. Contbr. profl. jours. Home: St Paul MN Died Nov. 18, 1968; buried Sunset Meml. Park, Minneapolis MN

ARCHIBALD, JAMES FRANCIS JEWELL, war corr.; b. New York, Sept. 22, 1871; s. Dr. F. A. and Martha Washington (Jewell) A.; grad. Ohio Wesleyan University. Served in Chinese-Japanese War; with Gen. Miles through labor riots, in the Sioux campaign, and the last Apache campaign; vol. a.-d.-c. 5th Army Corps through Spanish War; served in Santiago campaign; was on first scouting expdn. that landed in Cuba about a month before the Santiago expdn.; first man wounded in war with Spain; was in Chippewa campaign on Leach Lake; with army of occupation of Cuba with staff of Gen. Ludlow; with British forces in Soudan, 1899; with Boer Army in the South African War; with Castro's army during Barcelona campaign in Venezuela and later followed events of allied forces against Venezuela; with Philippine constabulary against Ladrones; with Russian Army from beginning Russo-Japanese War representing Collier's Weekly; with French Army in Morocco, 1910; with Turkish Army during the revolution in Albania, 1910; in Lisbon during Portuguese revolution, 1911; with Chinese troops during revolution, 1913; with Austrian and German armies for a time in 1915. While on way to Europe, from U.S., Aug., 1915, was detained by authorities of British Govt. and charged with carrying dispatches to representatives of govts. of Germany and Austria, at Berlin and Vienna; released, but dispatches confiscated, Sept., 1915; returned to U.S. Fellow Royal Geog. Soc. and Royal Soc. Arts, London, etc. Author: Blue Shirt and Khaki; Tales from the Trenches. Plays produced: The Outpost; The Field Hospital; The Last Bet; The Nick of Time. Address: 47 W. 34th St., New York NY‡

ARCTOWSKA, ADRIAN JANE, concert singer; b. Rochelle, Ill., Apr. 25, 1875; d. George and Caroline E. (Whitcomb) Addy; studied in Chicago, later in Paris, France, 1896-9; m. Henryk Arctowski (q.v.), Mar. 28, 1900. Began in Eng. as prima donna with D'oyly Carte Opera Co., 1899; sang in oratorios and symphony concerts in Belgium, Germany and England; also gave recitals in leading European cities, gaining established recognition as a lieder singer; returned to America, 1909. Since beginning of European war active in relief work by organizing and conducting the help extended to Polish intellectuals, refugees in France, Switzerland, Holland, Eng. and Italy; also has lectured extensively on Polish history, lit. and art. Mem. N.E. Soc., D.A.R. Home: 1 Livingston Av., Yonkers NY‡

AREF, ABDUL SALAM, prime minister of Iraq, from 1963. Address: Baghdad Iraq

ARENALES CATALAN, EMILIO, Guatemalan diplomat; b. Guatemala City, Guatemala, May 10, 1922; s. Alejandro Arenales and Anita Catalan; B.Sci. and Letters, Instituto Modelo, Guatemala City, 1939; B. Polit. and Social Scis., U. San Carlos, 1944, law student 1940-45, 50-51; m. Lucy Dorion Cabarrus, May 18, 1946; children—Rodrigo, Alvaro, Maria de la Luz, Maria de los Angeles. Participated in students' movement to overthrow Jorge Ubico, 1944; represented univ. students internat. confs., London, 1945, Prague, 1945; represented U. San Carolos, Oxford and Cambridge, Eng., 1945, Prague U., 1945; legal counsel Preparatory Commn. UNESCO, 1946, external relations counsellor, 1946-49; UNESCO observer 9th Pan-Am. Conf., 1948, and other internat. meetings; sec.-gen. Internat. Hylean Amazon conf., 1948; headed UNESCO mission Latin Am., 1948; Guatemalan del. 5th, 6th sessions com. on information from non-self governing tys., 9th session Gen. Assembly UN, 1954-55, pres. com., 1956; A.E. and P., permanent rep. Guatemala to UN, 1955-56; chmn. delegation 10th, 11th sessions Gen. Assembly, UN; chairman delegation Trusteeship Council, 1956-57, vice president, 1957, pres. Gen. Assembly, 1968-69; mem. law firm Oficina de Arenales, Guatemala City, 1943-45, 50-54. Home: Guatemala Died Apr. 17, 1969.

ARENBERG, ALBERT LEE, illumination engr.; b. Des Moines, Ia., Nov. 16, 1891; s. Max and Augusta (Kawin) A.; B.S., Ill. Inst. Tech., 1913, E.E., 1917; m. Claire Strauss, June 2, 1923; children—Ann (Mrs. Walter Fuld Gips, Jr.), Henry X., Jane (Mrs. David Eiseman III). Manager lighting division of the Central Electric Company, 1913-24; pres. New England Mills, jobber electric, automotive radio supplies, 1924-29; pres., dir. Harrison Wholesale Co., 1929-62, chmn. bd., 1962-69; pres., chief engr. Luminator Inc., Chgo., 1929-62, chmn. bd., 1962-69; pres. Luminator-Harrison, Inc., Chgo., 1950-62, chmn. bd. 1962-67, chairman of the exec. committee, 1967-69. Mem. Am. Inst. E.E., Western Soc. Engrs., Illuminating Engring. Soc., Am. Transit Assn. Clubs: The Arts, Lake Shore Country, Mid-Am. (Chgo.). Home: Highland Park IL Died Oct. 31, 1969; buried Chicago IL

ARENDT, MORTON, elec. engr.; b. Cincinnati, O., Mar. 24, 1877; s. Edward and Pauline (Fringant) A.; student Coll. City of of N.Y., 1890-94; E.E., Columbia, 1898; m. Marie F. Meyer, of N.Y. City, Oct. 11, 1917; children—Edward Theodore, Morton. With Columbia U. since 1902, asst. prof. elec. engring. since 1910; cons. elect. engr. to Dept. of Plant and Structures, City of N.Y.; consultant U.S. Navy Research Labs.; sec. Lovejoy Development Co. Inventor of ry. train lighting system, elec. arc welding apparatus, automotive power and lighting equipment, hydrogen detectors, etc. Lt. U.S.N.R., 1917-18; lt. comdr. 1918-19; comdr., 1919. Fellow Am. Inst. E.E., Sigma Xi, Zeta Sigma, Zeta Beta Tau, Epsilon Chi. Clubs: Thames (New London, Conn.); Amerita (Poughkeepsie, N.Y.). Author: Storage Batteries, 1905, 20; Machine Design, 1905, 19; Electric Motors, 1910, 15; Electricity on Submarines (U.S. Bur. of Engring.), 1918; Railway Train Lighting, 1919; The Storage Battery, 1927. Home: 3001 Spuyten Duyvil Parkway. Address: Columbia University, New York NY*‡

ARENS, HENRY, ex-congressman; b. Westphalia, Germany, Nov. 21, 1873; s. Joseph and Therese (Steinhoff) A.; pub. schs. of Germany, 1880-88, agrl. sch., 1888-90; m. Agnes Henkels, Feb. 7, 1899; 1 dau., Agnes J. Came to U.S., 1889, naturalized, 1894; has been farmer for many yrs.; v.p. Land O'Lakes Creamery. Mem. Minn. House of Reps., 1919-21, Senate, 1923-29; lt. gov. of Minn., 1930-32; mem. 73d Congress (1933-35), Minn. at large. Mem. Farm-Labor Party. Home: Jordan MN*‡

ARENS, RICHARD, commnr. U.S. Ct. Claims; b. Kansas City, Mo., Aug. 3, 1913; s. Ollie L. and Hazel (Payne) A.; A.B., Baker U., 1934; LL.B., Washington U., St. Louis, 1937; m. Margaret Marie Stark, Sept. 13, 1941 (dec. Jan. 1952); children—Margaret Ann, Janice Marie; m. 2d, Mary Jane, MacDevitt, June 29, 1955; children—Elizabeth Jane, Richard Thomas. Admitted to Mo. bar, 1937, also U.S. Supreme Ct.; gen. practice, Kansas City, Mo., 1937-41; legal sec. gov. Mo., 1941-45; mem. Mo. Pub. Service Commn., 1945-46; dir. reorgn. exec. depts. Mo., 1946-47; staff dir. immigration subcom. U.S. Senate, 1947-52, internal security subcom., 1952-56; staff dir. com. un-Am. activities Ho. of Reps., 1956-60; commr. U.S. Ct. Claims, 1960-69. Lectr. Communism; bd. mgrs. Council State Govts., 1941-45. Recipient Certificate of Merit, Patriotic Order Sons Am., 1953; Citation of Merit and Commendation, Am. Legion, 1954; citation Am. Coalition Patriotic Societies, 1958; Medal of Honor, Order Founders and Patriots Am., 1954; Citation of Merit and Distinction, Nat. Women's Patriotic Conf. Nat. Def.; Certificate of Merit, D.A.R., 1956; Vigilant Patriot award All-Am. Conf. Combat Communism, 1960; Freedom award Order Lafayette, 1961. Mem. Delta Theta Pi. Methodist. Home: Wheaton MD Died Oct. 25, 1969.

AREY, HAWTHORNE, lawyer, banker; b. Omaha, Neb., Oct. 31, 1905; s. Irving Hubert and Blanche Howe (Widmeyer) A.; student Grinnel (Ia.) Coll., 1924-26, Univ. of Neb., 1926-27; LL.B. cum laude, Creighton University, 1930, LL.D., Grinnell College, 1963; m. Ruth Gordon on August 21, 1929; children—Jane (Mrs. William E. Markham), Gordon Hawthorne. Admitted to Nebraska bar, 1930, and practiced law in Omaha as member law firm of Ritchie, Swenson and Arey, 1930-33; on legal staff, R.F.C., 1933-34, Home Owners Loan Corp., 1934-38; sec. and counsel, Export-Import Bank of Washington, 1938-43, v.p. and asst. gen. counsel, 1943-45, v.p. and gen. counsel, 1945-47, exec. v.p., 1947-49, dir., vice chmn., 1949-53, asst. dir., 1953-54, dir., 1954-61; comptroller, operations control Inter-American Devel. Bank, Washington, 1961-63, dir. div. operations control, 1963-66, director loan administration division, 1966-68; ret., 1968. Adv. U.S. del., U.N. Monetary and Financial Conf., Bretton Woods, 1944. Trustee Export-Import Bank, 1943-46. Decorated by Brazil, 1962; comdr. Order Merit (Italy), 1963; recipient alumni citation Grinnell College, 1957. Member Nebraska Bar Association, Delta Upsilon. Presbyterian. Clubs: The University, Congressional Country, The International (Washington); Farmington Country (Charlottesville, Va.). Home: Silver Spring MD Died Feb. 18, 1972.

ARKWRIGHT, GEORGE ALFRED, ret. jurist; b. Bklyn., Sept., 1888; s. George A. and Mary Augusta (McKeever) A.; A.B., Pa. U., 1911; LL.B., Fordham U., 1917; LL.D., St. John's U., 1951; m. Loretta Marie Cleary, Aug. 20, 1924; children—George Alfred, Harold Joseph, Evelyn A. Benson, Marjorie Marie, Richard Thomas. Taught pub. schs. N.Y. City, 1912-17; admitted to bar, 1917, clerked with Grout & Grout and Lewis & Kelsey; began gen. practice in Brooklyn, 1919; admitted to courts of N.Y. State, U.S. Dist., Circuit, and Supreme courts; mem. N.Y. Public Service Commn., 1943-50; justice Supreme Court of N.Y. State, 1950-58, 61-64, ofcl. referee, 1959-60; mem. Appellate Term, Supreme Ct., 2d Dept. N.Y., 1954-56; presiding judge Kings County Spl. Inquiry, 1956-58; trustee Kings Hwy. Savs. Bank (Bklyn.). Nat. council, exec. com. region 2, hon. mem. Greater N.Y. councils, mem. and past pres. Brooklyn council Boy Scouts of America. Am. Chmn., Law Library Bklyn.; former chmn. Del. Water Project Commn.; Prize Commr. for duration of war (apptd. by U.S. judges); former head Rep. Speaker's Bur. in city, state, nat. campaigns. Served With A.E.F. at Toule, St. Mihiel, Argonne. Recipient Silver Beaver and Antelope awards Boy Scouts Am. Mem. Am., Fed., N.Y. State, Bklyn. (3 times pres.; life trustee) bar assns., Bklyn-Manhattan Trial Lawyers' Assn., Catholic

Lawyers Guild, A.A.A.S., Am. Legion, Travelers Aid Soc. (bd. dirs.), St. Patrick's Soc., St. Edmund's Holy Name Soc., Emerald Soc., Supreme Ct. Judges Assn., Am. Ordnance Assn., Pa. Alumni Assn., National Geographic Society, Fordham Alumni Assn. Roman Catholic. K.C., Rotarian. Clubs: Automobile of New York, Lawyers of Bklyn., Cathedral, Breezy Point Surf, The Brooklyn. Home: Brooklyn NY Died Aug. 25, 1972; buried Greenwood Cemetery, Brooklyn NY

ARMITAGE, ALBERT T., investment banker; b. Danvers, Mass., Sept. 29, 1893; s. Joshua and Mary Gertrude (Tibbetts) A.; student Bryant & Stratton Comml. Sch., Boston; m. Marguerite Godfrey, Jan. 12, 1917 (now deceased); children—Hope, Godfrey Tibbetts; m. 2d, Helen Dodge Hood, Jan. 1, 1951. Clerk, then bond trader, later salesman in charge of Maine terr., Blodget & Co., Boston, 1912-18; salesman, later in charge wholesale distbn. in Boston, Nat. City Co., Boston, 1918-19; trader and sales mgr., then dir., treas. and v.p., Coffin & Burr, Inc. (name changed to Putnam, Coffin & Burr), 1919-40, pres., 1940-61, ltd. partner, 1961-68; v.p., dir. Keyes Devel. Corp.; dir. Canadian Keyes Fibre Co.; dir., chmn. exec. com. Keyes Fibre Co.; dir. Me. Central R.R., Penobscot Co., Portland (Me.) Terminal Co. Mem. exec. com., co-chmn. for Mass., U.S., Victory Fund Com. of First Fed. Res. Dist.; former v.p. and mem. exec. com. Investment Bankers Assn. Am., 1942-48, pres., 1949-50. Recipient citation for outstanding achievement in field business, Bryant and Stratton Sch., 1964. Republican. Mason (32 deg.). Clubs: Union, Down Town, Bond (pres. 1951) (Boston, Mass.); Dublin (N.H.) Lake; Cumberland (Portland, Me.). Home: Dublin NH Died Feb. 17, 1968; buried Danvers MA

ARMOUR, LESTER, banker; b. Chgo., Mar. 21, 1895; s. Philip Danforth and May Elizabeth (Lester) A.; prep. edn., St. Mark's Sch, Southboro, Mass.; B.A., Yale, 1918; m. Leola Stanton; m. 2d, Alexandra Galitzine. Chmn. bd., chief exec. officer Chicago Nat. Bank; ret. vice chmn. Harris Trust & Savs. Bank. Pure Oil Co. Chmn. bd. trustees Ill. Inst. Tech. Served as ensign U.S. Naval Aviation World War I; capt. USNR, World War II. Home: Lake Bluff IL Died Dec. 26, 1970.

ARMS, THOMAS SEELYE, army officer (ret.); b. Cleveland, O., Mar. 22, 1893; s. Charles Carrol and Sarah Elizabeth (Seelye) A.; B.S. Va. Mil. Inst., 1915; student basic course, Infantry Sch., 1923-24, advanced course, 1928-29; Command and Gen. Staff Sch., 1929-31; m. Gladys Josephine Schauweker, June 21, 1917; children—Thomas Seelye, Robert Joseph, William Henry. Commd. 2d lt., Inf., U.S. Army, Nov. 30, 1916; promoted through grades to brig. gen., April 27, 1942. Served on Mexican border, and during World War I, in U.S. and Siberia, later in P.I. and China; instr. R.O.T.C., Emory U., 1924-28; instr. tactics, Infantry Sch., Fort Benning, Ga., 1931-35; instr. Ohio Nat. Guard, 1935-40; comdg. officer 159th Inf., 1941-42; instr. with Chinese Army, 1942-46, ret., 1946; operator Armsley Farms, Easton, Md., 1946-70. Authors: Notes on Infantry Training for the Chinese Easton MD Died Nov. 1970.

ARMSTRONG, CHARLES WALLACE, physician and health officer; b. Montgomery County, N.C., Nov. 9, 1889; s. Charles Alfred and Florence (Moore) A.; student Trinity Park (prep.) Sch., Durham, N.C., 1904-07; grad. U. of N.C., 1912; M.D., U. of Md., 1914; m. Mabel Elise Harris, Nov. 9, 1915; children—Charles Wallace, William Harris, Rosa Lee, Florence Page. In general practice of medicine, 1914-17; health officer, City of Salisbury and Rowan County, N.C., from 1919. Served as capt., Med. Corps, U.S. Army, France, 1917-19. Pres. and dir. N.C. Tuberculosis Assn.; dir. Nat. Tuberculosis Assn.; trustee National Soc. Crippled Children and Adults; vice pres. Kiwanis International; past pres. N.C. Bd. of Med. Examiners; chmn. child welfare sect. Am. Legion; regional chmn. N.C. Good Health Assn. Past pres. N.C. Pub. Health Assn., Salisbury Kiwanis Club; past dist. gov. Carolinas District Kiwanis; pres. and mem. bd. trustees Kiwanis Internat., 1947-48. Mem. Am. Med. Assn., Rowan County and N.C. med. socs., Am. Pub. Health Assn. Mason. Methodist (trustee). Home: Salisbury NC Died July 21, 1968.

ARMSTRONG, CHARLOTTE (MRS. JACK LEWI), writer; b. Vulcan, Mich., May 2, 1905; d. Frank Hall and Clara (Pascoe) Armstrong; student Ferry Hall, Lake Forest, Ill., 1922, U. Wis., 1922-24; A.B., Barnard Coll., Columbia, 1925; m. Jack Lewi, Jan. 21, 1928; children—Jeremy Brett, Jacquelin, Peter Armstrong. Author: (plays) The Happiest Days, 1939, Ring Around Elizabeth, 1942; (books) Lay On, Mac Duff, 1942; The Case of the Weird Sisters, 1943; The Innocent Flower, 1945; The Unsuspected, 1946; The Chocolate Cobweb, 1948; Mischief, 1950; The Black-Eyed Stranger, 1951; Catch-as-Catch-Can, 1952; The Trouble in Thor, 1953 (Pseudonym Jo Valentine); The Better to Eat You, 1954; The Dream Walker, 1955; A Dram of Poison, 1956; The Albatross (collection short stories), 1957; Duo, 1959; The Seventeen Widows of Sans Souci, 1959; A Little Less Than Kind, 1963; The Witch's House, 1963; The Turret Room, 1965; Dream of Fair Woman, 1965; I See You (collected short stories), 1966; The Gift Shop, 1967; Lemon in the Basket, 1967; the Balloon Man, 1968; Seven Seats to the Moon, 1969; The Protege, pub. posthumously 1969; The Charlotte Armstrong Reader, 1970; The Charlotte Armstrong Treasury, 1972. Recipient Edgar Allen Poe award Mystery Writers Am., 1956. Home: Glendale CA Died July 18, 1969.

ARMSTRONG, CLARE HIBBS, army officer; b. Albert Lea, Minn., Jan. 23, 1894; s. DeWitt Clinton and Anna Caroline (Hibbs) A.; ed. Army and Navy Prep. Sch., Washington, D.C., 1913; B.S., U.S. Mil. Acad., 1917; grad. Coast Arty. Sch., 1930; Chem. Warfare Sch., 1930, Command and Gen. Staff Sch., 1936, Air Corps Tactical Sch., 1942, Ordnance Field Officer Motor Course, 1942; m. Mary Denard Coombs, May 1, 1917 (died 1938); children—Clare Hibbs, Elizabeth Anne (Mrs. Richard Louis Hennessy), DeWitt Clinton, Mrs. L. Bughman; 1 stepson, M. Nelson Taylor; m. 2d, Mary Weber Harter, June 5, 1939; m. 3d, Catherine Hays Taylor. Commd. 2d lt., U.S. Army, 1917, advanced through the grades to brig. gen., 1943, ret., 1953. Mason (Scottish Rite, Shriner). Club: Army and Navy Country (Washington, D.C.). Home: Albert Lea MN Died Aug. 1969.

ARMSTRONG, DALLAS WARREN;, b. Mercer Co., Pa., Apr. 20, 1872; s. Warren Esterbrook and Margaret (McCelland) A.; Ph.B., Grove City (Pa.) Coll., 1894, A.M., 1905, LL.D., 1926; m. Mary S. Griffin, of Worth Twp., Mercer Co., Pa.; children—Angus Griffin, Mary Elizabeth, Margaret, Frank Dallas, Katherine. Teacher and supervising prin. pub. schs., Venango, Mercer, Butler and Allegheny counties, Pa., 1890-1905; county supt., Venango Co., 1905-20; asst. state dir. rural edn., Pa., 1920-25; pres. Central State Teachers Coll., Lock Haven, Pa., since 1925. Mem. Pa. N.G., 1892-95; mem. Secret Service, World War. Mem. N.E.A., Pa. State Edn. Assn., Pa. Schoolmen's Club. Republican. Mason, Odd Fellow. Rotarian. Home: 410 North Fairview St., Lock Haven PA‡

ARMSTRONG, DONALD BUDD, physician; b. Bangor, Pa., Dec. 19, 1886; s. Elmer R. and Sarah (Budd) A.; Ph.B., Lafayette Coll., 1908, D.Sc., 1923; M.D., Columbia, 1912, M.A., 1912; M.S., Mass. Inst. Tech., 1913; m. Eunice Burton, Sept. 19, 1913; children—Donald, Stewart, Lincoln, Burton. Supt. Bur. Pub. Health and Hygiene and dir. Dept. of Social Welfare, N.Y. A.I.C.P., 1913-16, also chmn. sanitary com. Dept. of Health adv. Council, chmn. Dept. of Street Cleaning adv. Council, chmn. com. on block recreation of Recreation Alliance—all N.Y.C.; exec. officer Framingham (Mass.) Community Health and Tb Demonstration, Nat. Tb Assn., exec. officer Nat. Health Council (Washington, N.Y.); lectr. pub. health, N.Y. U., and Columbia; sec. tech. bd. and mem. adv. council Milbank Meml. Fund; 2d v.p. Met. Life Ins. Co., in charge of health and welfare work of policy holders; mem. Presidents Nat. Nutrition Conf. for Defense; mem. bd. cons. N.Y. State Dept. Health; mem. mng. com. Life Ins. Adjustment Bur.; dir. N.Y. Tb. and Health Assn.; former chmn. home safety com. and v.p. Nat. Safety Council; former mem. N.Y. State Com. on Prevention of Diphtheria, U.S.P.H.S., N.Y. State and N.Y.C. Pneumonia Control commns.; chmn. Med. Information Bur., mem. council N.Y. Acad. Medicine; mem. com. on cardivascular disease in industry, N.Y. Heart Assn.; dir. Am. Social Hygiene Assn.; mem. Tb and exec. coms. N.Y. State Charities Aid Assn.; vice chmn. Com. on N.Y. State Tb Control Project, from 1941; former bd. govs. Am. Pub. Health Assn.; bd. dirs. N.Y.C. Cancer Com.; vice chmn. gen. adv. com. Nat. Found. for Infantile Paralysis; bd. dirs. and v.p. Greater N.Y. Safety Council; bd. trustees Am. Mus. Safety; mem. exec. com., dir. and ex-pres. Nat. Health Council; mem. nat. adv. council, Cleve. Health Mus.; ex-pres. N.Y.C. Pub. Health Assn.; mem. hygiene reference bd. Life Extension Examiners; former mem. bd. dirs., War Community Service; mem. Nursing Procurement and Assignment Com., W.M.C.; adv. com. N.Y.C. Dept. of Health. Directed establishment of the first pub. laundry in N.Y.C.; investigated relation of flies to infant mortality; developed plans for Framingham Demonstration and program for Nat. Health Council, Diplomate Am. Bd. Preventive Medicine and Pub. Health, Fellow Am. Pub. Health Assn. (former chmn. com. on accident prevention), A.M.A.; mem. N.Y. State and N.Y. County med. socs., N.Y. Acad. Med., Nat. Tb Assn., Nat. Com. for Mental Hygiene, A.A.A.S., Chi Phi, Alpha Omega Alpha, Delta Omega, Omega Club. Author: Popular Encyclopedia of Health (with Lee K. Frankel and G. M. Fox), 1926; What to Do Till the Doctor Comes (with Grace T. Hallock), 1943; also numerous monographs and pamphlets on med. topics. Home: Scarborough NY Died Aug. 1968.

ARMSTRONG, FRANK ALTON, JR., air force officer; b. Hamilton, N.C., May 24, 1902; s. Frank Alton and Annie Elizabeth (Hobbs) A.; LL.B., A.B., Wake Forest Coll., 1925; m. Vernelle Hudson, Mar. 15, 1929; 1 son, Frank Alton III. Began as flying cadet, U.S. Army, 1928; commd. 2d lt. AC, 1929, and advanced through grades to lt. gen., 1956; served at airfields throughout U.S; as combat observer, Eng., 3 mos., 1940; and as asst. chief A-3 sect. AF staff, Washington; comd. 1st U.S. heavy bombing flights over France, Germany; comd. 101st Combat Wing, and 17th Training Wing, U.S., 315th Wing, Guam; leader B-29 bombing mission, Guam to Akita, Japan; comdr. in chief Alaskan Command, 1957-69. Decorated D.S.C., D.S.M., Silver Star, D.F.C. with oak leaf cluster, Air Medal; British Flying Cross (first air medal awarded U.S. airman, World War II). Mem. Kappa Alpha (Southern). Pioneered first polar flight from Alaska to Norway. Home: Nashville NC Died Aug. 20, 1969.

ARMSTRONG, H. C[illegible][illegible] exec.; b. Buffalo, 1904; grad. U. Mich[illegible] chief exec. dir. Williams & Co., Inc.[illegible] ondale Cemetery, dir. Pittsburgh F[illegible] at. Ben Franklin Ins. Co., William [illegible], Dormont-Mount Lebanon Savs. [illegible] ngstown Welding & Engring. Co. Bo[illegible] umni Assn. Home: Pittsburgh PA

ARMSTRONG, HA[illegible]ON FISH, editor, author; b. N.Y.C., Apr. 7, 189[illegible]; s. D. Maitland (artist; consul gen. to Italy) and Helen (Neilson) A.; A.B., Princeton, 1916, Litt.D., 1961; LL.D., Brown U., 1942, Columbia, 1963; Litt.D., Yale, 1957, Harvard, 1963; Dr. Hon. Causa, U. Basel, 1960; m. Helen Mac G. Byrne, Dec. 31, 1918; 1 dau., Gregor; m. 2d, Carman Barnes, Dec. 27, 1945; m. 3rd, Christa Von Tippelskirch, July 11, 1951. Commd. 2d lt. U.S. Army, Oct. 26, 1917, and assigned 22nd Inf.; 1st lt., 17, 1917; apptd. mil. attache to Serbian War Mission in U.S., 1917; apptd. acting mil. attache, Am. legation, Belgrad, Serbia, Dec. 1918; mem. editorial staff N.Y. Evening Post, 1919-21; spl. corr. in Eastern, Europe, 1921-22; mng. editor Fgn. Affairs (quar. rev.) 1922-28, editor 1928-72; mem. adv. com. on Post-War Fgn. Problems, State Dept., 1942-44; spl. asst. to U.S. ambassador in London, with personal rank of minister, 1944; spl. adviser to sec. of state, 1945; adviser U.S. delegation, San Francisco Conf., 1945; dir. Council Fgn. Relations, Inc. Trustee N.Y. Soc. Library (pres. 1944-58), Woodrow Wilson Found (v.p. 1928-30; pres. 1935-37); mem. President's Adv. Com. on Polit. Refugees. Decorated Order of St. Sava, 1918, Order of White Eagle (with swords), 1919, (both Serbian); Order of Crown (Rumania), 1924; Comdr. Legion of Honor (France), 1947; Order of White Lion (Czechoslovakia), 1947. Mem. Am. Philos. Soc. Club: Century. Editor: Book of New York Verse, 1918; (with W.L. Langer) Foreign Affairs Bibliography, 1933; The Foreign Policy of the Powers, 1935; The Foreign Affairs Reader, 1947. Author: New Balkans, 1926; Where the East Begins, 1929; Hitler's Reich-the First Phase, 1933; Europe Between Wars? 1934; (with A.W. Dulles) Can We Be Neutral? 1936, Can America Stay Neutral? 1939; We or They, 1937; Where There Is No Peace, 1939; Chronology of Failure, 1940; The Calculated Risk, 1947; Tito and Goliath, 1951; Those Days 1963; Peace and Counterpeace: From Wilson to Hitler, 1971. Contbr. to mags. Home: New York City NY Died May 1973.

ARMSTRONG, HOUSTON CHURCHWELL, banker; b. Selma, Ala., Oct. 9, 1875; s. William Park and Alice Isbell A.; prep. edn., Lawrenceville Sch.; B.S., Princeton, 1898; m. Mina Gary Lamar, of Selma, Ala., Dec. 30, 1909; children—Houston C., Alice Isbell, Mina Gary, Law Lamar. Identified with banking business at Selma since 1893; pres. City Nat. Bank since 1917; pres. City Savings Bank; dir. Central Ala. Dry Goods Co., Selma Times Jour., Dallas Compress, Isbell Nat. Bank (Talladega, Ala.), Southeastern Express Co. Trustee pub. schs., Selma. Presbyn. Club: Selma Country. Home: 604 Mabry St. Address: City National Bank, Selma AL‡

ARMSTRONG, JAMES EDWARD, newspaper pub.; b. Springfield, Ill., Jan. 10, 1915; s. John Edgar and Lucy (McCurdy) A.; student Springfield Coll., 1934; m. Violet Roberts, Aug. 25, 1940; children—John, Diane. With Ill. State Register, Springfield, 1937-64; pub. Ill. State Jour. and Register, 1964-68; v.p. The Copley Press, Inc., 1964-68, dir. Sec., mem. exec. bd. Regional Plan Commn. Springfield, 1957-59. Bd. dirs. Abraham Lincoln Assn., 1965-68. Mem. U.P.I. Ill. Editors Assn. (pres. 1961), Am. Soc. Newspaper Editors, Am. Newspaper Pubs. Assn., Inland Daily Press, TV, Radio and Newspaper Club Springfield (pres. 1958), Navy League. Mason (32 deg.). Clubs: Sangamo, Elks, Lake Shore Country (Springfield). Home: Springfield IL Died Mar. 24, 1968; buried Oakridge Cemetery, Springfield IL

ARMSTRONG, JAMES REVERDY, lawyer; b. near Scottsborough, Ala., Jan. 26, 1876; s. William Henry and Mary (Roberts) A.; ed. Ouachita Bapt. Coll., Arkadelphia, Ark.; LL.B., Southwest Baptist U. (now Union U.), Jackson, Tenn., 1901; m. Bertha F. Scott, June 1901. Admitted to Tenn. bar, 1900, Ark. bar, 1901; moved to Indian Ty., 1900, Boswell, I.T., 1902; established offices, Hugo, Okla., 1907; was dist. judge and justice Court of Appeals, Okla., 11 yrs.; now in private practice of law. Extensive land owner and interested in oil producing business and corps. operating in Mid-Continent, Gulf Coast and Pacific dists.; also interested in mining properties and corps. owning mines in Ariz., Calif. and Colo. Democrat. Baptist. Mason (32 deg.). Home: Boswell, Okla. Office: Hales Bldg, Oklahoma City OK*‡

ARMSTRONG, LILIAN HARDEN, pianist, composer; b. Memphis, 1903; m. Louis Armstrong, 1924 (div. 1942). Played with King Oliver, 1920; later worked with Red Allen, Zutty Singleton; toured Europe, played club outside Chgo. from late 1950s; active nightclub and recording work; tours of Can.; TV appearance Chicago and All That Jazz, 1961; recordings include Chicago, The Living Legends, Chicago and All That Jazz, Satchmo and Me. Address: Chicago IL Died Aug. 27, 1971; buried Lincoln Cemetery, Chicago IL

ARMSTRONG, LOUIS, musician; born New Orleans, July 4, 1900; s. Willie and Mary-Ann Armstrong; m. Daisy Parker, 1917 (div.); m. 2d, Lillian Hardin, Feb. 1924 (div.); m. 3d, Lucille, 1942. Musician, beginning with bugle, became clarinetist and trumpeter; singer, composer, orchestra leader, recording artist; professional career began with King Ory's band, 1917; cornettist with Joe (King) Oliver, Chicago, 1922; first N.Y. engagement, 1924; organized own band, Chicago, and abandoned clarinet for trumpet, 1925; his recording, You Rascal, You, scored a hit in Eng., and after touring U.S. with his band, he appeared in London at the Palladium, also toured Eng. and Scotland; toured Denmark, Sweden, Norway and Holland, 1933-34; appeared before King George VI of Eng., 1934; later appeared in concerts in Paris, France, Belgium and Italy; toured Australia and Europe, 1954-55, Gold Coast of Africa, 1956, Australia, New Zealand, Tokyo, P.I., Korea, 1963. Composer: (songs) Where Did You Stay Last Night; Satchel Mouth Swing; I've Got a Heart Full of Rhythm; Wild Man Blues; If We Never Meet Again; Sugar Foot Stomp; No Variety Blues; Back O'Town Blues. Appeared in motion pictures: Every Day's a Holiday, 1938; Going Places, 1938; Cabin in the Sky, 1943; Jam Session, 1944; Doctor Rhythm, Glory-Alley, The Strip, Glen Miller Story, 1953; High Society, 1956; The Five Pennies, 1959. Recordings number about 1500, many being valued as collector's items. Named Number 1 Male Singer, 16th Internat. Jazz Critics Poll, 1968, also Jazz and Pop 3rd Ann. Readers Poll. Mem. A.S.C.A.P. Home: New York City NY Died July 1971.

ARMSTRONG, MAURICE WHITMAN, educator; b. Bridgetown, N.S., May 29, 1905; s. Dr. Melbourne E. and Mary B. (Davis) A.; A.B., Dalhousie U., 1925, M.A., 1927, B.D., Pine Hill Div. Hall, 1930; S.T.M., Harvard, 1941, Ph.D., 1945; m. Irene Margaret MacDonald, May 23, 1928; children—Sheila (Mrs. R. W. Hallowell, Junior), Christina (Mrs. James E. Brouse), Ainslie (Mrs. John H. McLees, Jr.). Came to the United States in 1940, naturalized in 1946. Ordained to ministry, United Ch. of Can., 1928; pastor, Alberta, N.S., N.B., 1928-40; pastor Conglist. Chs., Scituate, also Belmont, Mass., 1940-45; teaching fellow history Harvard, 1942, lectr., instr. reformation history, div. sch., 1944; teaching fellow history Radcliffe Coll., 1942; prof. history Ursinus Coll., from 1945, head dept., 1947-67, faculty dean, 1952-54, acting head of the department of fine arts, 1967. chmn. social sci. staff, exptl. program in tchr. edn. Temple U., 1955-58; mem. Presbytery Phila.; interim pastor Walnut St. Presbyn. Ch., Phila., 1945-50. Chmn. bd. council Pa. Indsl. Home for Blind Women, Phila., 1950-67. Awarded Brewer prize ch. history, Am. Ch. History Soc., 1946, Distinguished Teaching award Lindbach Found., 1961. Mem. Presbyn. Hist. Soc. (dir. 1949, pres. 1960-64, distinguished service award 1957), Am. Hist. Assn. Am. Ch. History Soc. Author: The Great Awakening in Nova Scotia 1776-1809, 1948. Editor of The Presbyn. Enterprise, 1956. Contbr. hist jours. Home: Havertown PA Died Nov. 21, 1967; buried Valley Forge Gardens PA

ARMSTRONG, ROBERT HAYDEN, telegraph mgr.; b. New York, Aug. 31, 1869; s. Edward D. and Anne E. (MacNeill) A.; ed. pub. schs. and pvt. laboratory, New York; m. Cora Anne Dutcher, of Shandaken, N.Y., Oct. 29, 1893. Mgr. and supt. for Armour & Co., Chicago, at Washington, D.C., Charlotte, N.C., Nashville, Tenn., Birmingham, Ala., Houston, Tex., and various states and territories of Southwest, 1888-1906; gen. mgr. Pacific Coast and Western div., United Wireless Telegraph Co., since Mar., 1906. Republican. Methodist. Mason, Shriner. Clubs: Arctic, Press, Publicity. Office: 206 Grand Trunk Dock, Seattle WA‡

ARMSTRONG, WILLIAM GILBERT, mfg. exec.; b. Pitts., 1906; grad. U. Pa., 1928. 1928. Sr. v.p., dir., mem. exec. com. Arundel Corp., Balt.; dir. Maryland Slag Co., Arundel-Brooks Concrete Corp. Home: Baltimore MD Died Dec. 8, 1966; buried Baltimore MD

ARN, WILLIAM GODFREY, civil engr.; b. Terre Haute, Ind., Feb. 7, 1877; s. Godfrey and Elizabeth (Van Brunt) A.; B.S. in C.E., Rose Poly. Inst., Terre Haute, Ind., 1897; unmarried. With L. & N. R.R. Co., 1897-1906, as rodman, masonry insp., building insp., asst. engr. and roadmaster; engr. and supt. Southern Bitulithic Co., Nashville, Tenn., 1906; with I.C.R.R. Co., 1907-17, and since 1919 as asst. div. engr., asst. engr., roadmaster, asst. engr. maintenance of way and asst. chief engr., Chicago Terminal Improvement. Served in U.S. Army, May 8, 1917-June 1, 1919; capt., maj. and lt. col. 13th Engrs.; with A.E.F., in France; now lt. col. engrs., O.R.C. Mem. Am. Soc. C.E., Am. Ry. Engring. Assn., Western Soc. Engrs., Soc. Am. Mil. Engrs., A.A.A.S., Am. Legion, Mil. Order World War, Maintenance of Way Club of Chicago. Citation by Gen. Pershing. Republican. Methodist. Mason (32 deg., Shriner). Clubs: University, Engineers', Prairie, Sojourners, Adventurers', Cambridge, Lincolnshire Country. Home: 5202 Cornell Av. Office: I.C.R.R. Station, Chicago IL‡

ARNDT, ELMER JACOB FREDERICK, clergyman, educator; b. New Orleans, Nov. 10, 1908; s. William and Augusta (Scherer) A.; B.D., Eden. Sem., 1929; M.A., Washington U., 1930; S.T.M., Union Sem., N.Y.C., 1931; Ph.D., Yale University, 1944; Litt.D., Elmhurst College, 1964; D.D., United Theological Seminary, 1964; m. Irene Ruth Agricola, Aug. 23, 1935; children—Richard W., Jane D., David P., Samuel J. Faculty Eden Theol. Sem., 1931-—, asst. to asso. prof., 1931-41, prof. hist., theology and Christian ethics, 1941-69; chmn. bd. Church World Service Center, St. Louis, 1946-54, gen. mgr., 1954-64. Chmn. commn. on christian social action Evang. and Ref. Ch., 1941-57; chmn. commn. to prepare a statement of faith United Ch. of Christ, 1958-62, chmn. theol. commn.; mem. United Ch. of Christ delegation to consultation on church union; mem. commn. on faith and order World Council Chs. Mem. Am. Philos. Assn., Am. Theol. Assn. Author: The Heritage of the Reformation, 1952; The Faith We Proclaim, 1960; The Font and the Table, 1967; essays other volumes. Home: Webster Groves MO Died Dec. 30, 1969.

ARNOLD, ALMA CUSIAN, drugless phys.; b. at Hamburg, Germany, Dec. 9, 1871; d. Frederick and Mathilde (Juergens) Cusian; came to U.S., 1885; grad. Am. Coll. of Chiropractic, Cedar Rapids, Ia., 1903; grad. Maywood (Ill.) High Sch., 1907; grad. Piaten Inst., N.Y. City, 1907; M.D., Coll. Medicine and Surgery, Chiacgo, 1911; m. C. D. Arnold, of Cedar Rapids, 1888 (divorced 1903). Pioneer woman in America to practice drugless healing; orginator, 1903, and pres. The Healtharium, Washington, D.C., settled in N.Y. City, 1909. Mem. A.A.A.S. Club: Woman's Press (New York). Author: The Triangle of Health, 1918. Home: 2 W. 67th St., New York NY‡

ARNOLD, BENJAMIN WILLIAM, JR., prof. history; b. Charlotte Co., Va., Apr. 13, 1870; s. Rev. Joseph David and Elizabeth Jane (Moseley) A.; B.A., Randolph-Macon Coll., Ashland, Va., 1891, M.A., 1893; Ph.D., Johns Hopkins, 1896; m. Mary St. George Tucker Jackson, of Petersburg, Va., June 19, 1897; children—Benjamin William III, Douglas Anderson and Lilian Arnold (twins, latter dec.), St. George Tucker, Randolph McDonald (girl). Instr. Randolph-Macon Acad., Bedford City, Va., 1891-93; asst. master McCabe's Univ. Sch., Richmond, Va., 1897; instr. Randolph-Macon Acad., Front Royal, 1898; acting prof. history, Emory Coll., 1900; prof. history and English, State Female Normal Sch., Farmville, Va., 1900-02; prof. history and economics, Randolph-Macon Women's Coll., 1902-08, prof. history, 1908-39, head dept. of history, 1902-39, acting dean, 1920-21, prof. of history emeritus since June 1939. Mem. Am. Hist. Assn., Phi Beta Kappa (Randolph-Macon), Sigma Chi. Dem. Methodist. Club: Sphex. Author: (thesis) History of the Tobacco Industry in Virginia (1860-94), 1897; England's Progress (1793-1921), 1922; Queen Victoria and Her Chief Ministers, 1927; A Sketch of England's Empire, 1929; Religious Verities, 1931; also several hist. articles. Home: 2472 Rivermont Av., Lynchburg VA‡

ARNOLD, FELIX, author; b. N.Y., June 15, 1879; s. George and Eliza (Schick) A.; A.B., Coll. City of N.Y., 1898 (Phi Beta Kappa); Pd.M., N.Y.U., 1903, Pd.D., 1904; Ph.D., Columbia, 1905; m. Julia V. Resnick, 1924. Public sch. prin. N.Y., 1908-49; ret. Fellow A.A.A.S., N.Y., Acad. Sciences; member Am. Psychol. Assn., Am. Humane Soc., Am. Sociol. Soc., Am. Anthol. Assn., Royal Soc. Arts, London. Lectr. Dept. of Edn., Balt., 1906; lectr. philosophy U. Colo., 1907; lectr. on edn., N.Y.U., 1910; lectr. on edn., Coll. City of N.Y., 1915. Author: The Psychology of Association, 1906; Test-Book of School and Class Management, Vol. I, 1908, Vol. II, 1910; Attention and Interest, 1910; Outline History of Education, 1911; Special Methods of Instruction, 1913; Measurement of Teaching Efficiency, 1915. Contbr. on psychology, ethics and edn. Made statis. report for Dept. Edn. N.Y.C., 1913. Translator from French: Claparede—Psychology of Imitation. Mem. Plattsburg O.T.C., summer 1917. Home: Franklin Lakes NJ

ARNOLD, FRANCIS A(RTHUR), JR., USPHS officer; b. Orrville, O., Dec. 30, 1910; s. Francis A. and Bertha (Lacey) A.; student Arkansas U., 1928-30; B.S., Western Reserve University, 1930-34, D.D.S., 1934, D.Sc. (hon.), 1963; married Miriam Eyster, Mar. 28, 1937; children—Francis A. III, Richard C. Commd. officer USPHS, 1934-67, dental research Nat. Insts. Health, 1937-66, dir. Nat. Inst. Dental Research, 1953-66, chief dental officer USPHS, 1966-—. Fellow Am. Coll. Dentists, Am. Pub. Health Assn.; mem. Am. Dental Assn., Am. Epidemiological Soc., Washington Acad. Sci., Washington Acad. Medicine, Internat. Assn. Dental Research (councilor; pres. 1953-54). Club: Cosmos. Home: Bethesda MD Died Dec. 1, 1967; buried Gettysburg (Pa.) Nat. Cemetery.

ARNOLD, FRANK RUSSELL, writer; b. Braintree, Mass., Oct. 1, 1871; s. Franklin Edwards and Susan Ordway (Weeks) A.; A.B., Bowdoin, 1893, A.M., 1902; studied univs. of Paris, Bordeaux and Goettingen 3 yrs., also grad. work at Harvard and U. of Chicago; unmarried. Prof. French, Utah Agrl. Coll., since 1904. Mem. Modern Lang. Assn. America, Phi Beta Kappa, Phi Kappa Phi, Theta Delta Chi. Episcopalian. Contbr. to Scribner's, Collier's, Modern Lang. Jour., New York Sun, etc. Home: Logan UT‡

ARNOLD, JAMES E., naval officer, ret.; b. North Troy, Vt., May 5, 1895; s. Cyrus and Annie (Blenkhorn) A.; student Worcester Poly. Inst., 1915-17, U.S. Naval Acad., 1918, U.S. Navy Submarine Sch., 1918; m. Margaret Lewis, May 22, 1919; children—Barbara (Mrs. Vincent Thorpe), Hope (Mrs. Albert Barre), Margaret (Mrs. Henry Snelling), Ann (Mrs. Paul Driscoll), James E. Entered U.S. Navy, 1917; served with submarines and destroyers, 1918-27; sales engr., Leland-Gifford Co., 1927-40; on active duty with U.S.N., 1940-45; present rank, rear admiral, U.S.N.R.; became comdg. officer, Advanced Amphibious Base, Falmouth, Cornwall, 1943; comdg. officer (U.S. Navy) Normandy Beach during assault, France, June 6, 1944; comdg. officer U.S. Naval Base, Le Havre, France, 1944-45; pres. Gen. Court Martial, 1st Naval Dist., 1945, rear adm. U.S. N.R. (Ret.); pres. Arnold Realty Trust, Wilowood Corp.; mem. bd. Leland-Gifford Co. of Can.; Washington rep. Inland Constrn. Co., Omaha, Neb., 1951-71. Mem. Mass. Gen. Court, Ho. of Reps., 1932-34. Decorated Legion of Merit with one gold star (U.S.), Croix de Guerre (France). Mason. Club: Army and Navy (Washington). Home: Washington DC Died Nov. 1971.

ARNOLD, JULEAN (HERBERT), foreign service officer; b. Sacramento, Calif., July 19, 1876; s. Joseph Henry and Kate (Brissel) A.; B.S., U. of Calif., 1902; hon. LL.D., St. John's U., Shanghai, 1919, Pomono Coll., 1938, Calif. Coll. in China, 1940; m. Clara Gertrude Davis, Jan. 9, 1907; children—Millard Davis, Harrison Morton, Julean, Frances. Commd. by President Roosevelt, July 18, 1902, student interpreter to Am. Legation, Peking (1st student interpreter apptd. by U.S. Govt. to China); subsequently apptd. to various posts in Am. consular service in China and Japan, and consul gen., Hankow, 1914; Am. commercial attache, China-Japan, 1914-17; commercial attache, China, since 1914; commercial attache, Japan, Sept.-Nov. 1923. Retired, as Foreign Service Officer, Class 1, Dept. of State. Chmn. Am. del. to China Tariff Rev. Commn., Shanghai, 1918, 22, 26-27. Hon. high adviser Nat. Red Cross Soc. of China. Organized first party of non-Asiatics to ascend Mt. Morrison, Formosa (the highest mountain in the Japanese Empire), Nov. 1907. Field sec. Am. Red Cross in China, 1918-21; founder Am. Chamber of Commerce, Shanghai, 1915; founder China Club of Seattle, 1916; del. to Pan-Pacific Commercial Conf., Honolulu, 1915; charter mem. Amity Lodge, A.F. & A.M., Shanghai. Mem. Royal Asiatic Soc. (councillor 1935-37), China Soc. of America in N.Y. (hon.), Friends of China Soc. of Chicago (hon.). Clubs: Shanghai, American, Columbia Country (Shanghai); Rotary of Peiping (founder and hon. mem.). Decorated by Chinese Govt. with Order of the Double Dragon, 1907, Order of the Flourishing Grain, 1919, Chia Ho with sash, 1923. Episcopalian. Scottish Rite Mason. Author of numerous monographs on economic and commercial China, and the Commercial Handbook on China; also Some Bigger Issues in China's Problems and China Thru the American Window. Address: 262 Arlington Av., Berkeley CA‡

ARNOLD, LOIS J., banker; b. Fillmore, Ind., Nov. 3, 1904; s. Alonzo L. and Nannie E. (Herod) A.; student Central Bus. Coll., Indpls., 1923-24; m. Mae M. Mullins, Sept. 28, 1929; children—Jo Mae (dec.), Joyce A. (Mrs. Roy E. Noblitt), Judy E. (Mrs. Robert M. Calbert), Jerry M. From bookkeeper to v.p. 1st Citizens Bank and Trust Co., Greencastle, Ind., 1924-56; exec. v.p. 1st. Nat. Bank, Danville, Ind., 1956-59, pres., 1959-72; dir. Roberts Ford, Inc. Ind. envoy chmn. Christian Theol. Sem.; mem. budget and promotions com. Ind. Assn. Christian Churches 1963-69. Trustee, Greencastle Orphans Home, 1941-56. Mem. Ind. Bankers Assn. (president region 9, member of council of administration; state president 1968-69), A.I.M. (fellow president's council), Ind., Danville (dir. 1965-67) chambers commerce. Mem. Christian Ch. (elder). Mason (33 deg.), Rotarian (past pres. Danville, Danville IN Died Dec. 9, 1972.

ARNOLD, REMMIE LEROY, mfr., Masonic Lodge ofcl.; b. Petersburg, Va., Jan. 25, 1894; s. Andrew Alexander and Mary Virginia (Longworth) A.; student pub. schs.; m. Charlia Sears, Apr. 27, 1918; children—Remmie Le-Roy, Dorothy Lawrence (Mrs. Robert J. Waite). Founder Edison Pen Co., pres. 1915-35; Co., Inc., Petersburg, Va., from 1935; pres. Remmie Arnold Pen Co., Inc., from 1955; exec. dir. So. States Indsl. Council, 1941-44, pres., 1946-48; mem. industry com. Dept. Labor, 1941. Active all phases of Masonry, 33, Shriner; leader Shrine hosp. work; trustee Crippled Children Hosp. Bd. of the Shriners Hosp. of N. Am., since 1965; past imperial potentate, N.Y.C. Mem.

Nat. Register Prominent Ams., Va. Agrl. Extension Service, Wisdom Hall of Fame. Mem. Am. War Dads (nat. pres. 1943-44), Va., Petersburg (dir.) chambers commerce, Va. Mfrs. Assn. (dir. 1938-39), Va. Aviation Flying Corps, U.S.N. League, League Va. Municipalities, Newcomen Soc. Eng., Square and Compass, Sigma Alpha Chi, and others. Democrat. Baptist. Elk (exalted ruler, 1939-41, dist. dep. Grand exalted ruler, 1944), Eagle, Red Man, Kiwanian. Clubs: Circus Sinners and Saints (organizer, 1st pres. Will Rogers Tent, 1937, nat. pres. 1938-39, trustee), Ruritan (Prince George), Commonwealth (Richmond, Va.); Country, Indian Swamp Fishing (Petersburg) and others. Home: Petersburg VA Died June 23, 1971; buried Blandford Cemetery, Petersburg VA

ARNOLD, THURMAN WESLEY, lawyer; b. Laramie, Wyo., June 2, 1891; s. Constantine Peter and Annie (Brockway) A.; A.B., Princeton, 1911; LL.B., Harvard, 1914; M.A., Yale, 1931; LL.D., U. of Wyo., 1943; m. Frances Longan, Sept. 7, 1917; children—Thurman Wesley, George Longan. Admitted to Ill. bar, 1914, and began practice at Chicago; practiced at Laramie, Wyo., 1919-27; lecturer in law, U. of Wyo., 1921-26; dean Coll. of Law, W.Va. U., 1927-30; visiting prof. Yale, 1930-31, prof. law, 1931-38; assistant attorney general of U.S., in charge of antitrust, March 7, 1938-March 16, 1943; associate justice of United States Court of Appeals for District of Columbia, Mar. 1943-July 1945; member of law firm of Arnold & Porter. Member of the Temporary National Economy Committee representing the Department of Justice, 1938-41. Special asst. to gen. counsel of Agl. Adjustment Adminstrn. in suits involving constitutionality of Agrl. Adjustment Act, 1933; legal adviser to gov. gen. of Philippines by Sec. of Agr. in adminstrn. of sugar control under Jones Costigan Act, summer, 1934. Served as 1st lt. Field Artillery, United States Army, France, World War I; maj. and judge adv. gen., Wyo. Nat. Guard, 1924-27. Mem. Wyo. Ho. of Rep., 1921; mayor of Laramie, 1923-24. Mem. Am. Wyo. State and W.Va. State bar assns., Phi Beta Kappa. Democrat. Epicopalian. Author: The Symbols of Government, 1935; Cases on Trials, Judgments and Appeals, 1936; The Folklore of Capitalism, 1937; The Bottlenecks of Business, 1940; Democracy and Free Enterprise, 1942; Fair Fights and Foul A Dissenting Lawyer's Life, 1965; also articles in periodicals. Home: Alexandria VA Died Nov. 1969.

ARNOLD, WINIFRED, author; b. at Wyoming, N.Y., Oct. 26, 1874; d. Osman L. C. and Emma (Keith) A.; grad. Durfee High Sch., Fall River, Mass., 1891 (valedictorian); A.B., with honors, Vassar, 1896, grad. fellowship in modern langs., same, 1896-7. Presbyn. Mem. Woman's Ednl. and Industrial Union. Clubs: College Woman's, Vassar (Rochester, N.Y.). Author: Mis' Bassett's Matrimony Bureau, 1912; Little Merry Christmas, 1914; The Twins, Pro and Con, 1916; Miss Emeline's Kith and Kin, 1919; The Jitney Lady. Contbr. of short stories, articles and humorous verse to mags.; contbg. editor, Bapt. Pub. Co., Phila. Home: 6 Scio St., Rochester NY‡

ARNOLDSON, SIGRID (MME. FISCHOF), prima donna; b. Stockholm, Sweden; studied under Mme. Desiree Artot de Padilla and Maurice Strakosch; debut at Moscow, Russia, in Il Barbiere de Siviglia; sang several seasons at Opera Comique, Paris, and Covent Garden, London; appeared in grand opera in U.S. under Abbey & Grau; m. Albert Fischof; toured U.S., 1894.‡

ARNOTE, WALTER JAMES, lawyer; b. McAlester, Okla., Jan. 19, 1905; s. James Samuel and Stella (Rock) A.; A.B., LL.B., Okla. U., 1928; student Harvard Law Sch., 1929; m. Jean Black, Jan. 30, 1939; 1 dau., Christie (Mrs. Tony Ashmore). Admitted to Okla. bar, 1928, since practiced in McAlester; partner firm Arnote, Bratton & Allford, 1929-65; city atty., McAlester, 1949-65. Dir. atty. First Nat. Bank McAlester, Okla. Automatic Telephone Co.; sec. treas., dir., atty. Great Lake Oil & Gas Co.; dir. Mid-Continent Casualty Co. Mayor of McAlester, 1946-47. Served to lt. col. AUS, 1941-45; ETO. Decorated Legion of Merit; Croix de Guerre with gold star (France); Mil. Cross of Valor (Italy). Fellow Am. Coll. Trial Lawyers, American Bar Foundation; member of the American, Okla. (pres. 1961), Pittsburg County (pres. 1946) bar assns., U. Okla. Coll. Law Assn. (pres. 1959), Nat. Conf. Bar Presidents, McAlester C. of C., Am. Legion, Vets. Fgn. Wars, Harvard Law Sch. Assn., Okla. U. Alumni Assn., Phi Beta Kappa, Kappa Alpha. Mem. Christian Ch. Mason (33 deg.), Elk, Rotarian. Clubs: Country, Fin and Feather, Knife and Fork (McAlester). Home: McAlester OK Died Aug. 13, 1965.

ARNSTEIN, MARGARET G., nurse, coll. dean; b. N.Y.C., Oct. 27, 1904; d. Leo and Elsie (Nathan) Arnstein; A.B., Smith Coll., 1925, D.Sc. (hon.), 1950; R.N., Presbyn. Hosp. Sch. Nursing, N.Y.C., 1927; A.M., Columbia, 1929; M.P.H., Johns Hopkins, 1934; D.Sc. (hon.), Wayne State University, 1962, U. Mich., 1972. Staff nurse No. Westchester (N.Y.) Dist. Nursing Assn., 1929-20; county staff nurse and supr. Westchester County Dept. Health, 1930-33; cons. nurse, Communicable Disease Div., N.Y. State Dept. Health, 1934-37; asso. prof. and dir. course in pub. health nursing U. Minn., 1937-40; cons. nurse (dist. supervision), N.Y. State Dept. Health, 1940-46; chief nurse Balkan Mission in UNRRA, 1943-45; apptd. sr. nurse officer in USPHS, 1946, chief Div. Nursing Resources, 1949-57, chief div. pub. health nursing, 1958-60, chief div. nursing, 1960-64, assigned health manpower study conducted by Rockefeller Found. with AID, 1965, sr. nursing adviser internat. health Office Surgeon Gen., 1965; prof. pub. health nursing U. Mich., 1965-67; dean Sch. Nursing, Yale U., 1967-72. Recipient Rockefeller Pub. Service award, 1965. Mem. Nat. League Nursing, Am. Nurses Assn., Am. Pub. Health Assn. (Sedgwick medal 1971), Fgn. Policy Assn., Phi Beta Kappa. Club: Cosmopolitan (N.Y.C.). Author: (with Gaylord Anderson and Mary Lester) Communicable Disease Control, 1962. Contbr. numerous articles in profl. jours. Home: New Haven CT Died Oct. 8, 1972.

ARONOWITZ, LEON, lawyer; b. Albany, N.Y., 1893; s. Max and Dora (Ettleson) A.; A.B., Dartmouth, 1915; LL.B., Albany Law Sch., 1920; m. Mary Anker, Oct. 4, 1923; children—Lewis, Lee. Admitted to N.Y. bar, 1920; assisted orgn. State Income Bur., 1919-20; auditor revenue Comptroller's Office, 1920-21, 24-25, State Budget Bur., 1922-23; statistician Motor Vehicle Bur., 1925-36, dept. commr., 1938-42; dir. Traffic Commn., 1936-37; mem. O'Connell & Aronowitz. Mem. Albany Co., N.Y. State bar assns. Home: Albany NY Died Mar. 26, 1969.

ARONSON, MAURICE, pianist, writer, critic; b. Mitau, Kurland, Russia, June 24, 1869; s. Hermann and Annette A.; grad. Mitau Gymnasium, 1885; made splty. of chemistry but gave it up for music, which he had studied from 9th yr.; advanced musical ed'n in Riga, St. Petersburg, Berlin, 1885-8; unmarried. Came to U.S., 1888, settled in South as pianist and organist; pianist for Chicago Conservatory of Music, 1896-1900; founded, 1900, and directed until July 1, 1903, Maurice Aronson Studios for art of piano playing; went to Berlin July, 1903, to make additional studies in the theory and history of music and to become chief asst. to Leopold Godowsky. Made extensive studies in musical history, literature and theory. Contributed to Music," Chicago, Symphony and Symphonic Poem, 1897; Schumann's Song Cycles, 1897; Robert Franz In His Relation to Music and Its Masters, 1897; The Poles in Music, 1898; Franz Schubert (in memory of the 100th anniversary of his birth), 1897. Address: Care of Leopold Godowsky, 185 W. Kurfurstendamm Charlottenburg Berlin W. and 4916 Indiana Av. Chicago‡

ARONSON, ROBERT LOUIS, judge; b. Stafford Springs, Conn., May 8, 1907; s. Haskell and Minnie (Brilliant) A.; LL.B., Washington U., 1928; m. Ruth R. Cohen, June 26, 1935; 1 son, Gordon H. Admitted to Mo. bar, 1928; gen. practice law, St. Louis, 1928-69; judge circuit ct., St. Louis, 1939-69. Instr. trial practice Washington U. Recipient plaque Lawyers' Association St. Louis, 1951, award of honor, 1963. Member Judicial Conference Missouri (exec. com., v.p.), Acacia (hon.), Phi Delta Phi. Mason (33 degree); mem. B'nai B'rith, Order De Molay. Judge Robert L. Aronson Youth Fellowship of B'nai B'rith Found. of U.S. named in his honor. Home: St Louis MO Died June 18, 1969.

ARRINGTON, KENNETH BARTON, baking co. exec.; b. Milton, Wis., Apr. 28, 1908; s. Olen Ray and Nelle Lucille (Barton) A.; B.A., Beloit Coll., 1930; m. Edna Marion Olson, Dec. 30, 1933; 1 son, Kenneth Barton II. Newspaper pub., 1931-32; printing plant exec., 1932-34; radio writer, producer, 1934-35; advt. mgr., dir. marketing research Omar, Inc., Omaha, Neb., 1935-46; with Caples Co., Omaha, 1946-51, v.p. charge food div., 1950-51; with Colgate-Palmolive Co., N.Y.C., 1951-63, gen. product mgr. toilet articles div., 1959-63; with ITT-Continental Baking Co., Rye, N.Y., 1963-69, v.p. charge advt. and marketing, 1965-69; propr. Kenneth B. Arrington Assos., internat. trade consultants to govt. and industry, 1969-70. With AID, U.S. Dept. State, also Internat. Exec. Service Corps., 1969-70; speaker trade convs. Mem. honor roll United Community Funds Am., 1965-68. Mem. Assn. Nat. Advertisers (rep. 1963-70, chmn. newspaper com. 1966-70), Newcomen Soc. N.Am., Delta Sigma Rho, Sigma Chi. Home: Greenwich CT Died Nov. 22, 1970; buried Putnam Cemetery, Greenwich CT

ARROYO DEL RIO, CARLOS, President of Ecuador; b. Guayaquil, Ecuador; Dr. of Law, U. of Guayaquil, 1914. Formerly sec. bd. of edn. and dept. govt., Province of Guaya; sec. council Canton of Guayaquil, 1917-18, pres., 1921-22; dep. Province of Guayas to nat. legislature, 1922-23; then pres. Chamber of Depts., served as prof., U. of Guayaquil, then dean faculty of law; temporarily assumed exec. power, 1939; President Ecuador, 1940-44. Address: Quito Ecuador Died Nov. 1969.*

ARTER, CHARLES KINGSLEY, lawyer; b. Cleveland O., Apr. 24, 1875; s. Francis Asbury and Eliza (Kingsley) A.; A.B. Amherst, 1898; student Harvard Law Sch., 1898-1901; m. Grace Denison, Sept. 23, 1902; children—Elizabeth (dec.), Calvin Kingsley, Charles Kingsley. Admitted to Ohio bar, 1901; mem. Smith, Taft & Arter, Cleveland, 1901-18, now mem. McKeehan, Merrick, Arter & Stewart; pres. Frank A. Arter Co.; sec. The Ohio Rubber Co. dir. Addressograph-Multigraph Corp., Land Title Guarantee & Trust Co., Master Builders Co., Bettcher Mfg. Co., Hawthorn Construction Co., Willard Storage Battery Co., Leader Building Co. (also pres.). Alumni trustee Amhurst Coll., 1901-06; trustee Allegheny Coll. (Meadville), 1928-30, Baldwin-Wallace Coll. (Berea, O.), Welfare Fedn. of Cleveland, St. Luke's Hosp. (Cleveland), Cleveland Children's Aid Soc., Asso. Charities of Cleveland; fiscal trustee Phyllis Wheatley Home; pres. The Cleveland C. of C., 1936. Mem. Am., Ohio and Cleveland bar assns., Delta Kappa Epsilon. Republican. Methodist. Clubs: Union, Nisi Prius, Mayfield Country. Home: 4982 Clubside Drive, Cleveland 13‡

ARTHUR, HAROLD JOHN, gov. Vt.; b. Whitehall, N.Y. Feb. 9, 1904; s. Roma Sholes and Almina Calista (Wells) A.; grad. Albany (N.Y.) Bus. Coll., 1928; LL.B., LaSalle Extension U., 1932; LL.D. (hon.), Norwich U., Northfield, Vt., 1950; m. Mary Catherine Alafat, Nov. 11, 1939; 1 dau., Portia Mary. Bank clk. Brandon (Vt.) Nat. Bank, 1922-26; stenographer for Ambassador Warren R. Austin, Burlington, Vt., 1928-32, after admittance to Vt. State bar, 1932, practiced as asso. to 1940; mem. firm Arthur & Arthur, civil and criminal trial practice, 1940-71; justice of the peace, Chittenden Co., 1947-49. Clk. ho. of reps., State of Vt., 1939-43, 1947-49; lt. gov., 1949-50, gov. 1950-51. Enlisted as private, 172d inf., Vt. N.G., 1928; active service as lt. to maj., A.C., U.S. Army, 1941-46. Served as civic service chmn. Boy Scouts, 1935-39. Mem. Vt., Chittenden County bar assns., United Comml. Travelers (grand counselor N.E.), Am. Legion, Amvets, Farm Bur., S.A.R. Republican. Unitarian (trustee). Elk (pres. Vt. State assn., 1939-49), Vt. State Grange (master, 1946-58), Mason (K.T., 32 deg., Shriner), Eastern Star, Eagle, K.P., Odd Fellow. Compiler, pub., House Precedents, 1939. Home: Burlington VT Died July 19, 1971; interred Arthur Mausoleum, Lakeview Cemetery, Burlington, Vt

ARTHUR, JULIA, actress; b. Hamilton, Ont., 1869; real name, Ida Lewis, stage name taken from her mother's maiden name of Arthur; m. Benjamin P. Cheney, Jr. At 11 years of age played in amateur dramatic club, taking part of Gamora in The Honeymoon and of Portia in The Merchant of Venice; 3 yrs. later made professional debut as the Prince of Wales in Daniel Bandmann's presentation of Richard III; remained 3 seasons with that co.; first New York success was at Union Sq. Theatre in The Black Masque; later in A.M. Palmer's co. in several roles, notably in Mercedes, 1893; London debut, Feb. 1, 1895, in Henry Irving's co., playing roles next to Miss Terry; especially successful as Rosamond in a Becket, with Irving and Terry in U.S., 1896. In many roles since.*‡

ARTHUR, W(ILLIAM) C(ATHCART), bus. exec.; b. Bellevue, Pa., Dec. 23, 1885; s. Hugh Wilson and Anna Elizabeth (Watts) A.; A.B., Univ. of Pittsburgh, 1907, LL.B., 1913; m. Sara Margaret Warrick, Sept. 16, 1918 (dec. Aug. 4, 1934); children—William Cathcart, James Hartford; married 2d Carolyn Brownell Fahr, November 16, 1940; 1 dau., Margaret Fahr (Mrs. Margaret Kirkpatrick). Bank clk., Pittsburgh, Pa., 1907-09; high sch. instr., 1909-15; admitted to Pa. State Bar, 1913, and practiced in Pittsburgh, 1915-17; asst. counsel, asst. sec. and counsel, B. F. Goodrich Co., Akron, O., 1917-24, v.p. and dir., Internat. B. F. Goodrich Corp., 1924-27; sec., sec.-treas., v.p. and dir., Talon, Inc., Meadville, Pa., 1927-39, pres. and dir., 1939-44; dir., 4th Federal Reserve Bank, Pittsburgh br., 1943-44; dir. Anderson Corp.; pres., dir. Eberhard Faber Pencil Co., Eberhard Faber Rubber Co., resigned from both cos., 1949; mayor Meadville, Pa., 1961-65. Board directors Crawford County Unit Am. Cancer Society. Member U.S. Assay Commn., 1935, 36. Mem. Pa. State C. of C. (past pres. dir.). Former v.p., dir. Fathers Assn., Culver Mil. Acad., campaigner for Culver Memorial Chapel; mem., nat. nominating committee American Red Cross. Trustee, U. Pitts., 1941-45, Allegheny Coll.; Meadville City Hosp. Mem. Pa. Supreme Ct. Bar, Allegheny and Crawford Cos. (Pa.) Bars, Crawford Co. Bar Assn., Phi Gamma Delta. Republican. Protestant. Clubs: Duquesne (Pittsburgh); Country, Iroquois Boating and Fishing (Meadville). Home: Meadville PA Died Aug. 30, 1967; buried Greendale Cemetery, Meadville PA

ARTHURS, STANLEY M., artist; b. Kenton, Del., Nov. 27, 1877; s. Joshua M. and Nancy M. (Wright) A.; ed. Drexel Inst. Phila.; studied art under Howard Pyle, Wilmington, Del.; unmarried. Mural paintings: Occupation of Little Rock, Ark., by Federal Troops," in governor's room, State Capitol, St. Paul, Minn.; Landing of De Vries, at Swanendale, 1631," Univ. of Del., Newark, Del.; The Drum Beat of a Nation," The Crusaders," The First Day of Peace"—all in State Capitol, Dover, Del.; life size painting of George Washington, American Club, Shanghai, China; Arrival of Governor Printz at Fort Christina, 1642," in Gray School, Wilmington, Del. Mem. Architectural League of New York, Soc. Mural Painters, Salmagundi Club (New York), Wilmington Soc. Fine Arts (dir.), Franklin Inn Club (Phila.). Rotarian. Writer and illustrator hist.

articles in Scribner's Mag.; 54 paintings pub. in vol. The American Historial Scene." Home: 1305 Franklin St., Wilmington DE‡

ARTOM, CAMILIO, biochemist, educator; b. Asti, Italy, June 5, 1893; s. Vittorio and Gemma (Pugliese) A.; M.D., U. Padua, Italy, 1917, Ph.D. in Physiology, U. Messina, 1923; Ph.D. in Biochemistry, U. Palermo, 1926; m. Bianca M. Ara; July 28, 1928; 1 son, George Victor. Came to U.S., 1939, naturalized, 1946. Instr. physiology U. Messina, Italy, 1920-25; guest investigator dept. biochemistry U. Frankfurt, Germany, 1921, dept. physiology U. Amsterdam, 1924; asst. prof. physiology U. Palermo, Italy, 1925-27, asso. prof. biochemistry, 1927-30, prof., head dept. physiology, 1935-38; Rockefeller Found. fellow dept. physiology U. Naples, Italy, 1927; prof., head dept. physiology, U. Cagliari, Italy, 1930-35; prof. biochemistry Sch. Med. Scis., Wake Forest Coll., 1939-41, prof., head dept. biochemistry Bowman Gray Sch. Medicine, 1941-63, prof. emeritus, 1963-69; cons. Oak Ridge Nuclear Studies. Decorated Italian War Cross, Rumanian War Cross. Fellow A.A.A.S.; mem. Am. Soc. Biol. Chemists, Soc. Exptl. Biology and Medicine, Am. Chem. Soc., Societe de Chimie Biologique (Paris), Societa Italiana di Biologia Sperimentale (Italy). Club: Torch (Winston-Salem). Editor: Archives Intern Physiology (Belgium), Enzymologia (Netherlands). Home: Winston-Salem NC Died Feb. 3, 1970; buried Asti Italy

ARUNDELL, CHARLES ROGERS, judge Tax Court of U.S.; b. Washington, D.C., June 7, 1885; s. Charles Alexander and Lou (Rogers) A.; prep. edn., pub. schs., Washington; LL.B., George Washington U., 1908; m. Alice W. Robinson, nee Wright, Sept. 21, 1926; 1 dau., Elizabeth (Mrs. James H. Stallings, Jr.). Admitted to the Washington D.C. bar, 1908, Ore. bar, 1910, and began practice at Portland; chief of Alaska Field Div. of Gen. Land Office, in charge pub. lands of Alaska, 1916-19; spl. atty. and asst. solicitor Bur. Internal Revenue, 1921-25; apptd. mem. Bd. of Tax Appeals (The Tax Court of the U.S.), 1925-55, 55-68, chmn. 1937-41. Received Alumni Achievement award for notable achievement in public service from the George Washington U., 1939. Mem. Am. Bar Assn., Federal Bar Assn., Oregon Bar Assn. Clubs: Nat. Lawyers, Nat. Press. Home: Washington DC Died May 28, 1968; buried Rock Creek Cemetery, Washington DC

ASCHER, HANS ALBERT, investment banker; b. Springfield, Mass., Nov. 14, 1895; s. Moritz and Amalie (Boedlander) A.; B.A., Yale, 1916; m. Germaine Samuel, Aug. 23, 1945; 1 son, John Albert. With Hallgarten & Co., 1916-22; gen. partner R.W. Pressprich & Co., 1922-40; cofounder William E. Pollock Co., Inc., 1940, chmn. bd., 1965-70, now cons. Home: 415 E 52d St New York City NY Died Mar. 2, 1972.

ASDALE, WILLIAM JAMES, physician and surgeon; grad. Rush Med. Coll., Chicago, 1866; sec. Western Pa. Med. Coll.; prof. diseases of women, same; mem. Am. Med. Assn., Am. Assn. of Obstetricians and Gynecologists, A.A.A.S.; hon. mem. Calif. State Med. Soc.; mem. Pa. State and Allegheny Co. Med. Socs. Address: 5523 Ellsworth Av., Pittsburg PA‡

ASELTINE, WALTER MORLEY, canadian senator; b. Nappanee, Ont., Canada, Sept. 3, 1886; s. George S. and Harriet T. (Goldsmith) A.; B.A. Man. U., 1909; m. France A. Derby, July 20, 1911; 1 son, John M.; m. 2d, Laura I. King, Aug. 8, 1923; children—Morley G., Elaine (Mrs. Mervyn Johnson), Kenneth, Adele (Mrs. Fred Herbert). Called to Sask. bar, 1913: made King's Counsel, 1930; practiced in Rosetown, Sask., 1913-71; mem. firm Aseltine and Aseltine. Mayor of Rosetown, 1930-34; mem. Canadian Senate, 1933-77, leader govt. in Senate, 1958-62; mem. Privy Council, 1961-71. Sec. Rosetown Board Trade, 1920-34. Mem. Can., Sask. (sr. life) bar assns. Mem. United Ch. of Can. Mason. Home: Rosetown SK Canada. Died Nov. 14, 1971.

ASHBROOK, M(ILAN) FOREST, clergyman; b. Granville, O., May 20, 1896; s. Milan Pratt and Lucy Permelia (Shepardson) A.; grad. Doane Acad., 1917; Ph.B., Denison U., 1921, D.D., 1958; B.D., Colgate-Rochester Divinity Sch., 1924; D.D., Kalamazoo Coll., 1940; m. Elizabeth Barbour, Dec. 21, 1923 (dec. Jan. 1973); children—James Barbour, Byron Eugene. Ordained Baptist ministry, 1923; pastor First Ch., Adrian, Mich., 1924-27, First Ch., Kalamazoo, 1927-35; asst. exec. dir. Ministers and Missionaries Benefit Bd. of Am. Bapt. Conv., 1935-40, exec. dir., 1940-61, spl. writer, 1963-1968; trustee, v.p., chmn. operating com. Interchurch Center, 1957-61, mng. dir., 1961-62. First v.p., executive board Mich. Baptist Conv., 1927-30; past pres. Ministers' Assn., Kalamazoo; former mem. exec. bd. Better Citizenship Council, Kalamazoo; former mem. Bd. of Edn., Kalamazoo; trustee Kalamazoo Coll., 1930-38. Pres. Church Pensions Conference Am. 1943-44, 57-58; membeb Postwar Planning Commission Am. Baptist Convention, 1942-45 (member sec. council Christian education 1934-42); chairman council missionary coop. Am. Bapt. Conv., 1947-48, chmn. adminst. com., 1948-52, chairman commission on the ministry. Served as a private with United States Army, 1918. Alumni trustee Denison U., 1946-52. Trustee Colgate Rochester Div. Sch.; mem. Fund for Urban Improvement, N.Y.C.; dir., treas. Middle Income Housing Corp., N.Y.C. Mem. Phi Beta Kappa. Republican. Clubs: Rotary (Adrian); Kiwanis, Torch (Kalamazoo); Quill (New York). Contbr. to religious jours. Home: Phoenix AZ Died May 6, 1968.

ASHE, EDMUND MARION, art instr.; b. New York, N.Y., June 19, 1870; s. William Nathaniel and Katherine Anne (Long) A.; ed. pub. schs. and pvt. tutors; student Met. Mus. of Art, Sch. of Art, 1887-88, Art Students League, 1888-92; m. Estelle Egbert, of Port Richmond, Staten Island, Sept. 5, 1893; children—Dorothy Estelle (Mrs. Charles Lewis Thompson), Edmund Marion. Illustrator on staff of Harper's mag., 1893-94; free lance contbr. to mags., 1894-1910; also illustrator of books, head of dept. of painting and design, Carnegie Inst. of Technology since 1928; represented by paintings in Pa. State Coll., Carnegie Inst. and private galleries. Mem. Art Commn. for the City of Pittsburgh, Tau Sigma Delta. Democrat. Episcopalian. Home: 1241 Murdock Rd., Pittsburgh PA‡

ASHE, EDWARD JOSEPH, textile co. exec.; b. Knoxville, Tenn., July 28, 1889; s. Gregory Joseph and Mary Agnes (Brosnahan) A.; student Georgetown U., 1907-09, Phila. Textile Sch., 1909-11; m. Jennie Louise Brownlow, Oct. 21, 1915; children—Jane (Mrs. James E. Gettys), Isabel (Mrs. G. Gordon Bonnyman), Cathrine (Mrs. James G. Maloy). With Standard Knitting Mills, Inc., Knoxville, Tenn., 1911-68, v.p., gen. mgr., 1932-56, pres., gen. mgr., 1956-62, pres., 1962-63, co-chmn., 1963-64, chmn., 1964-68, also dir.; chmn. Home Fed. Savs. & Loan Assn., Inc.; dir. Hamilton National Bank, Knoxville, Fouche, Inc., Blue Diamond Coal Co. (Knoxville); mem. So. adv. bd. Am. Mut. Liability Ins. Co. Mem. Tenn. Smoky Mountain Park Commn. Bd. dirs. Knoxville Tourist Bur., Tenn. Tb Assn., Knoxville Boys' Club: honorary member of the advisory board of St. Mary's Memorial Hospital. Roman Catholic. Clubs: Civitan, Cherokee Country, City (Knoxville). Home: Knoxville TN Died Apr. 3, 1968; buried Highland Meml. Cemetery, Knoxville TN

ASHE, GEORGE B(AMFORD), naval officer (ret.); b. Raleigh, N.C., Jan. 19, 1891; s. Samuel A'Court and Hannah Emerson (Willard) A.; B.S., U.S. Naval Acad., 1911; m. Ellen Lane Jett Williams, June 10, 1916. Commd. ensign U.S. Navy, 1912, advanced through grades to rear adm., 1947; served at occupation of Vera Cruz, Mexico, 1914; with destroyer fiotilla, Queenstown, Ireland, 1917-18; stationed in China, destroyer squadrons, 1926-29; with amphibious forces, South Pacific, 1942-44; ret. from active duty, Jan. 1, 1947. Awarded Legion of Merit (World War II). Mem. Sons of Confed. Vets., Queenstown Assn., Soc. of the Cincinnati. Democrat. Episcopalian. Author: (with John I. Hale) Engineering Materials and Processes, 1926. Home: Berryville VA Died May 1971.

ASHTON, HENRY RUSLING, patent lawyer; b. Trenton, N.J., Nov. 12, 1898; s. John Hamilton and Ada (Larison) A.; LL.B., Cornell, 1921; grad. law student Harvard, 1921-22; m. Ruth Felton, Dec. 11, 1926; 1 son, John Felton. Admitted to Mass. bar, 1923, N.Y. bar, 1926, Supreme Ct. of U.S., 1934, Patent Office, 1925; asso. Fish & Neave, N.Y.C., 1925-36, mem. firm, 1936-70. Served as 2d lt., U.S. Army, 1918; dep. chief, operational research sect. hdqrs., 8th Air Force, Eng., 1944-45; chmn. Patent Law Coordinating Com. primarily responsible for codification patent laws, 1952. Fellow American College of Trial Lawyers; mem. Am., N.Y. State bar associations, American (pres. 1949-50), N.Y. (pres. 1957-58) patent law assns., Assn. Bar City N.Y. Clubs: Sky, Century Assn. (N.Y.C.); Am. Yacht (Rye, N.Y.); Siwonoy Country (Bronxville, N.Y.). Home: Bronxville NY Died May 2, 1970; buried Bronxville (N.Y.) Cemetery of Reformed Presbyterian Church.

ASHTON, JOHN WILLIAM, educator; b. Lewiston, Me., July 11, 1900; s. Albert William and Hattie Manetta (Flower) A.; A.B., Bates Coll., 1922, LL.D., 1952; Ph.D., U. Chicago, 1928; m. Florence Elizabeth Huber, Nov. 1, 1925; 1 dau., Elizabeth Mary Breatrice. Instr. English and speech Yankton (S.D.) Coll., 1922-23; instr. English State U. Ia., 1923-26, asst. and asso. prof. English, 1927-40; Internat. Research fellow Huntington Library, 1932-33; prof. English and chmn. dept. U. Kan., 1940-45; br. head English Shrivenham American U., County Berkshire, Eng., 1945; prof. English, dean Coll. Arts and Scis. Ind. U., 1946-52, v.p., 1952-58, v.p., dean grad. sch., 1958-65, prof. English and folklore, 1966-70, prof. emeritus, 1970-71. Mem. adv. com. on Nat. Def. Edn. Act fellowships under Office of Edn., 1962-66, dir. div. grad. programs, 1965-66, cons., 1966-71; mem. tng. grants com. Nat. Inst. Dental Research. Served C.O.T.S., Camp Lee, Va., 1918. Mem. Am. Folklore Soc., Modern Lang. Assn., Nat. Council Tchrs. of English, Religious Edn. Assn. (dir.), Council Grad. Schs. U.S. (chmn. 1964), Ch. Hist. Soc., N.E., Hoosier, Cal. folklore socs., Renaissance Soc. Am., N. Central Assn. Colls. and Secondary Schs., Phi Beta Kappa, Delta Sigma Rho. Episcopalian (mem. standing liturgical commn.). Editor: Trends in Graduate Work, 1931; Types of English Drama, 1940. Home: Bloomington IN Died Nov. 10, 1971.

ASHWORTH, HATTIE TILLER (MRS. EUGENE MARVIN ASHWORTH), librarian; b. Duty, Va., Aug. 15, 1904; d. Eivens and Frances (Calvert) Tiller; A.B., Emory and Henry Coll., 1928; postgrad. history U. Va., 1929-31, in library sci. U. W.Va., 1959-62; m. Eugene Marvin Ashworth, Dec. 22, 1928; children—Halbert Eugene, Don Wayne. Tchr. high sch. Raleigh County, W. Va., 1929-32; asst. librarian W. Va. Dept. Archives and History, Charleston, 1952-62, librarian, 1962-70. Mem. Emory and Henry Coll. Alumnae Assn., W. Va. Library Assn., W. Va. Hist. Soc. (exec. sec.), Pi Gamma Mu. Methodist. Home: Charleston WV Died Dec. 31, 1970.

ASPINWALL, GLENN WILLIAM, hardware co. exec.; b. Pearl City, Ill., Aug. 8, 1898; s. Marvin Luhman and Lydia (Kielsmeier) A.; B.A., Cornell Coll., Mt. Vernon, Ia., 1923; m. Mildred Irene Johnson, June 16, 1926; 1dau., Joanna. Tchr. pub. schs., Ia., 1923-32; supt. schs., Larchwood, Ia., 1927-32; owner Aspinwall Hardware & Furniture Co., Hawkeye, Ia., 1932-70. Mem. Nat. Retail Hardware Assn., 1932-70, bd. govs., 1952-70, pres., 1959-60. Methodist. Mason. Address: Hawkeye IA Died July 1, 1970.

ASQUITH, ANTHONY, film dir.; b. 1902; ed. Balliol Coll., Oxford (Eng.) U. Dir., Anthony Asquith Prodns. Ltd.; films include: Shooting Stars, Underground, Cottage on Dartmoor, Tell England, Dance Pretty Lady, The Lucky Number, Moscow Nights, Pygmalion, French Without Tears, Freedom Radio, We Dive at Dawn, Quiet Wedding, The Way to the Stars, While the Sun Shines, The Winslow Boy, The Woman in Question, The Browning Version, The Importance of Being Earnest, The Young Lovers, Carrington V.C., The Doctor's Dilemma, Libel, The Millionairess, Two Living One Dead, Act of Mercy, V.I.P.'S, The Yellow Rolls-Royce, Evening with the Royal Ballet. Address: London England Died Feb. 20, 1968.*

ASTON, RICHARD DOUGLAS, savs. and loan exec.; b. Bakersfield, Cal., July 8, 1901; s. Frank C. and Grace (Rigby) A.; student Cal. State Poly., 1920-21, U. Cal. at Berkeley, 1921-24; m. Ruth Elizabeth Hoffman, Jan. 1, 1924; 1 son, Robert D. Asst. mgr. Oak Knoll br. Security First Nat. Bank, Pasadena, Cal., 1924-28; sec.-treas. West Coast Bond & Mortgage Co., Pasadena, 1928-41, exec. v.p., 1945-49, pres., 1949-73; sec.-treas. Mut. Savs. & Loan Assn., Pasadena, 1930-41, cons., 1941-45, exec. v.p., 1945-49, pres., 1949-59, chmn. bd., pres., 1959-61, chmn. bd., 1961-73; pres. Wesco Financial Corp., 1959-61, chmn. bd., 1961-73. Served to maj. AUS, 1941-45. Rotarian. Clubs: University, Annandale Golf (Pasadena). Home: Arcadia CA Died Jan. 3, 1973.

ASTOR OF HEVER, BARON (JOHN JACOB ASTOR), newspaper pub.; b. N.Y.C., May 20, 1886; s. 1st Viscount Astor and Mary Dahlgren Paul; ed. Eton College; D.Lit. (honorary degree), University London; hon. degree, McGill U.; m. Lady Violet Mary Elliott, Aug. 26, 1916; children—Gavin, Hugh, John. Chmn. Times Pub. Co., London, Eng., 1922-59; chmn. Phoenix Assurance Co., 1952-56, dir. until 1962; chmn. London Guarantee and Accident Co. Ltd., 1952-56, dir. until 1962; dir. Hambros Bank Ltd. Mem. Parliament for Dover div. of Kent, 1922-45; ep. lt. County of Kent, 1936-62, justice of peace, 1929-62; Mem. council of St. Dunstans, 1922-62; v.p. Royal Coll. of Music, 1934-62; chmn. Middlesex Hosp., 1938-62. Pres. Newspaper Press Fund. Commonwealth Press Union; chmn. 4th through 7th Imperial press confs. Pres. Nat. Assn. for Employment Regular Sailors, Soldiers and Airmen, 1936-62; pres. Kent council, also Fleet St. br., Brit. Legion, 1934-62. Joined 1st Life Guards, 1906; a.d.c. Viceroy of India, 1911-14; served in World War I, 1914-18; lt. col. 5th Bn. City of London Home Guard, 1940-44. Chevalier Legion of Honor, 1918. Created 1st Baron Astor of Hever, 1956. Freeman Borough of Dover. Clubs: Press (pres.); Royal Yacht Squadron (Cowes). Address: Pegomas France Died July 19, 1971; buried Edenbridge, Kent England

ATHENAGORAS, HIS ALL HOLINESS, Archbishop of Constantinople, New Rome and Ecumenical Patriarch; b. 1896; grad. Orthodox Theol. Sem., Halki, Istanbul, 1910. Ordained deacon, 1910, later served as gen. sec. Athens Archdiocese; elected by Holy Synod as Metropolitan of Corfu and Paxos; apptd. archbishop of Greek Orthodox Ch. of N. and S. Am. with offices in N.Y.C., 1931; elected Patriarch of Constantinople by Holy Synod. 1948. Address: Istanbul Turkey Died July 1972.

ATKIELSKI, ROMAN R., clergyman; b. Milwaukee, Aug. 5, 1898; student Campton Acad., Marguette U., St. Francis Sem. (Wis.); LL.D. (hon.) Mt. Mary Coll.; ordained priest Roman Cath. Ch., 1931; served as curate, asst. chancellor and chancellor, 1937-47; consecrated auxiliary bishop and vicar gen. of Milw. Archdiocese titular bishop at Stobi, 1947. Home: Milwaukee WI Died June 30, 1969.

ATKINS, HARRY THOMAS, physician; b. Cin., Jan. 13, 1910; s. Frank Pearce and Louise (Isham) A.; M.D., U. Cin., 1937; m. Nina Augusta Anderson, Oct. 7, 1944; children—John Anderson, Thomas Pearce. Intern Cin.

Gen. Hosp., 1936-37, asst. resident obstetrics, 1937-38, resident obstetrics, 1938-39, later cons.; resident in surgery Christ Hosp., Cin., mem. staff, 1946-52; house surgeon Free Hosp. for Women, Brookline, Mass., 1940-41; mem. staffs Bethesda Hosp., Cin., 1946-52, Ft. Hamilton Hosp., Mercy Hosp., Hamilton, O., 1952-60. Instr. obstetrics, U. Cin. Served to comdr. M.C., USNR, 1941-46. Diplomate Am. Bd. Obstetrics and Gynecology. Fellow Am. Coll. Obstetrics and Gynecology; mem. A.M.A., Gyro Internat., Alpha Kappa Kappa. Republican. Presbyn. Home: Cincinnati OH Died Nov. 21, 1970; buried Spring Grove Cemetery, Cincinnati OH

ATKINS, HENRY HORNBY, mattress mfg. co. exec.; b. Duluth, Minn., May 25, 1939; s. Samuel F. and Barbara (Hornby) A.; B.A. in Bus. Adminstrn., Colo. Coll., 1961; m. Virginia D. Rea, June 12, 1959; children—Dale Rea, Allison Gwyn, Happy Hornby. Owner, mgr. Sanomade Mattress Co., Duluth, 1962-69; owner, mgr. Happy Sleeper Shops, Eau Claire, Wis., from 1966, Green Bay, Wis., from 1969, Madison, Wis., from 1967, Rochester, Minn., from 1969. Mem. Aircraft Owners and Pilots Assn., Nat. Assn. Bedding Mfrs., Civitan. Home: Duluth MN Deceased.

ATKINS, WILLARD EARL, prof. economics; b. Chicago, Ill., Mar. 28, 1892; s. Franklin Pierce and Catherine (Bursk) A.; student Mont. State Coll., 1910-11; Ph.B., U. of Chicago, 1916, A.M., 1917, J.D., 1918; m. Claire Culver, July 10, 1918; 1 dau., Nancy Claire. Instr. Albion (Mich.) Coll., 1914-16, U. of Chicago, 1919-23; asso. prof. economics, U. of N.C., 1923-25, prof., 1925-26; prof. economics, N.Y. Univ., from 1926; chmn. dept. economics, Washington Square Coll., from 1927; head div. of economics, Grad. Sch. of Banking, American Bankers Assn.; wages and hours disputes, Cotton Garment Industry, 1934-35; labor arbiter N.Y. Picture Arbitration Tribunal, also arbiter industrial disputes for Am. Arbitration Assn.; research The Brookings Instn., 1939. Served in 337th Inf., U.S. Army, A.E.F., 1918-19. Fellow Royal Econ. Soc., mem. Am. Econ. Soc., Am. Arbitration Assn. Democrat. Mason. Clubs: Andiron, Town Hall. Author: (with P. H. Douglas and C. N. Hitchcock) The Worker in Modern Economic Society, 1923; (with H. D. Lasswell) Labor Attitudes and Problems, 1924; (with others) Economic Behavior, 2 vols., 1931; (with A. Wubnig) Our Economic World, 1934; Gold and Your Money, 1934; A Problem Approach to Economics (with J. Magee), 1937; Economics, 1937; The Regulation of the Securities Market (with H. G. Moulton and G. W. Edwards), 1946. Home: New York City NY Died July 31, 1971.

ATKINSON, ALBERT ALGERNON, coll. prof.; b. Nelsonville, O., Mar. 7, 1867; s. Samuel Lawson and Sarah Ellen (Dean) A.; B.S., Ohio U., 1891, M.S., 1895; student physics and engring., U. of Mich., 1892-93; m. Julia A. McDaniel, Aug. 20, 1892; 1 dau., Mrs. Gertrude A. Stewart. Taught sch. part of time while acquiring edn.; supt. Township High Sch., E. Townsend, Huron County O., 1891-92; asso. prof. physics and elec. engring., 1893-95, prof., 1895-1936, dean Coll. of Applied Science, 1936-37, emeritus dean, same, since 1941, Ohio Univ. Presbyterian. Mem. or former mem. Ohio Acad. Science, American Inst. E.E., A.A.A.S., Am. Phys. Soc., Soc. for Promotion of Engring. Edn., Phi Delta Theta, Phi Beta Kappa. Mason. Author: Electrical and Magnetic Calculations, 1902-13; Laboratory Manual of Elementary Physics, 1909. Home: 26 Morris Av., Athens OH‡

ATKINSON, CHARLES R., economist; b. DeWitt, Ia.; s. Thomas (M.D.) and Anna M. (Holloway) A.; A.B., National Normal University, 1888; A.B., George Washington U., 1908; A.M., Columbia, 1910, Ph.D., 1911; m. Florence Cooper, of Fairbury, Neb.; 1 son, Carroll Holloway; m. 2d, Russella Scott, of Milwaukee, Wis., May 28, 1920. Began teaching in Dist. 5, nr. Endicott, Neb., at age of 16; since continuously engaged in study, teaching, research, lecturing and ednl. travel. Co. superintendent schools, Jefferson County, Nebraska, 1892-98; supt. schools, Table Rock, 1898-1899, Edgar, 1899-1900, York Nebr., 1900-03, Sheridan, Wyo., 1903-08; head of dept. history and politics, Ursinus Coll., Collegeville, Pa., 1911-12; head of dept. economics and politics, Lawrence Coll., Appleton, Wis., 1912-16; dean Coll. of Economics, Marquette U., Milwaukee, Wis., 1916-23; asso. prof. of bus. administration, U. of Wash., 1923-28; head dept. economics and business adminstrn., Hillsdale (Mich.) Coll., 1928-30; research in marketing, 1930-31; head dept. economics and business adminstrn., Ohio Northern University, 1931-32; head dept. of commerce and mem. commerce faculty Arizona State Teachers College, Tempe, since 1932. President and treasurer Wyo. State Teachers' Assn., 1906; pres. Bd. of Examiners, Wyo., 1907; treas. Neb. State Teachers' Assn., 1894-97; mem. Seattle Industrial Traffic Mgrs. Assn., N.E.A., state teachers assns. of Neb., Wis., Wyo. and Ariz., Am. Acad. Polit. and Social Sciences, Pan Xenia, Alpha Sigma Phi, Delta Sigma Pi, Mason, Eastern Star. Author numerous pamphlets, courses of study, etc. Considered an authority on parliamentary procedure, and current economic, political and social problems. Democrat since 1932. Home: 72 W. Moreland, Phoenix, Ariz. Office: Commerce Bldg., State Teachers College, Tempe AZ‡

ATKINSON, GUY F., constrn. co. exec.; b. Freeport, Pa., Jan. 16, 1875; m. Rachel Atkinson; children—George, Donald, Elizabeth (Mrs. Whitsett). Chmn. bd. Guy F. Atkinson Co., gen. mgr., until 1938, pres., until 1943. Mem. Am. Soc. C.E. (hon. life), Asso. Gen. Contractors Am. (pres. 1940). Prin. works include: Grand Coulee Dam, Hansen Dam, atomic energy plant Hanford, Wash., Mangla Dam, West Pakistan. Address: South San Francisco CA Died Sept. 12, 1968.

ATKINSON, HARRY HUNT, lawyer; b. Salt Lake City, Utah, May 22, 1881; s. Henry R. M. and Jessie (Erickson) A.; A.B. in Law, Stanford, 1903; postgrad. work same univ., 1905-06; m. Katherine Jackson, Nov. 28, 1908 (dec. 1954); children—Robert (dec.), Harry (dec.); m. 2d, Cecil Payn Chapman, Sept. 1, 1961. War corr. Salt Lake Tribune, 1898; admitted to Calif. and Nev. bar, 1906; and practiced at Tonopah until 1923; trial atty. Western Union Telegraph Co. for Southern Nev., 1913-23; dist. atty. Nye County, Nev., 1917-20; spl. asst. to U.S. atty. general on antitrust litigation, 1923-26; U.S. atty. for Nevada, 1926-34; counsellor to Rt. Rev. Wright, Episcopal Bishop Nev., 1948-65. Chairman of the Washoe County chapter American Nat. Red Cross, 1951. Served in 1st Troop Utah, U.S. Vol. Cav., as corp. and sergt., Spanish-Am. War, 1898. Mem. Am., Calif., Nev. and Washoe County bar assns., Stanford Alumni Assn. (life), United Spanish War Vets. (comdr. dept. Nev. 1950-51), Zeta Psi, Phi Delta Phi. Republican. Episopalian. Mason (33 deg. past grand master Nev. 1920-21); past potentate Kerak Temple Shrine, Reno NV Died Jan. 21, 1968.

ATKINSON, JOSEPH STORY, publisher; b. Toronto, Can., Apr. 8, 1904; s. Joseph E. and Elmina (Elliott) A.; B.A., U. Toronto, 1926; m. Catherine Cringan, Oct. 23, 1929 (dec. Apr. 1960); 1 dau., Catherine Elizabeth (Mrs. J. H. Crang Jr.); m. 2d, Elaine M. Barrett, Nov. 8, 1967. With Toronto Star, Ltd., 1926-68, sec.-treas., 1934-40, v.p., 1940-48, chmn., 1948-56, pres., 1957-66, chmn. bd., 1966-68. Chmn. Atkinson Charitable Found. Mem. Liberal Party. United Ch. of Can. Clubs: Granite, National (Toronto). Home: Toronto ON Canada Died Nov. 3, 1968.

ATTWOOD, FREDERIC, business exec.; b. East Haddam, Conn., Apr. 23, 1883; s. Frederic J. H. and Margaret (MacConnell) A.; grad. Bklyn. Latin Sch., 1900; M.E., E.E., Columbia, 1904; m. Gladys Hollingsworth, Oct. 27, 1917; 1 son, William Hollingsworth. Traffic engr. N.Y. Telephone Co., 1904-07; European rep. Air. Reduction Co., 1915-17; gen. European rep. Ohio Brass Co., elec. mfrs., 1919; v.p., dir. Canadian Ohio Brass Co., Ohio Brass Co. from 1927; dir. Melville Shoe Corp. Commd. maj. C.E., A.E.F., Nov. 1917; attached to Gen. Hdqrs. A.E.F., C.W.S., Gen. Tech. Bd. War Damages Bd. Am. Commn. to Negotiate Peace, U.S. Liquidation Commn.; hon. disch. Oct. 1919; col. O.R.C. Decorated Officer Legion of Honor (France). Pres. U.S. nat. com. Internat. Conferences Large Elec. Systems; World Power Conf., Internat. Electrotech. Commn. Mem. Inst. Elec. and Electronic Engineers, Phi Gamma Delta. Republican. Episcopalian. Clubs: Bankers, Engineers, Columbia University (New York City); St. Cloud Country; University; Interallied (Paris, France). Home: New Canaan CT Died Aug. 26, 1969; buried Lake-View Cemetery, New Canaan CT

ATWATER, EDWARD PERRIN, banker; b. Rochester, N.Y., July 5, 1902; s. Edward Congdon and Linda (Perrin) A.; grad. Choate Sch., Wallingford, Conn., 1920; student U. Rochester; student accounting, Rochester Bus. Inst., 1922; m. Rowena Marsh Washburn, Apr. 14, 1925; children—Edward Congdon, James Perrin, Julian Washburn. Engaged in constrn. work, Monte Cristi, Dominican Republic, 1923-24; with Wis.-Ala. Lumber Co., Sylacauga, Ala., 1924-26, Perrin-Curtin Lumber Co., Kosciusko, Miss., 1926-28, Southwestern, N.Y. Theatres, Inc., Jamestown, 1928-29, Pistell-Deans & Co., Inc., investments, Buffalo, 1929-31, George D. B. Bonbright & Co., brokers, Rochester, 1931-33; asst. cashier First Nat. Bank, Batavia, N.Y., 1934, pres., dir., 1934-63; v.p., dir. Batavia Broadcasting Corp., 1940-58; pres., dir. Bank of Elba (N.Y.), 1938-67; exec. v.p., dir. Liberty Nat. Bank & Trust Co., Buffalo, 1963-67. Home: Batavia NY Died June 6, 1967.

ATWOOD, EDWARD LELAND, clergyman, educator; b. Clinton, Ky., Oct. 30, 1872; s. Thomas Letcher and Hettie Frances (Bugg) A.; student Clinton Coll., 1892-96; A.B., A.M., Georgetown (Ky.) Coll., 1901; B.D., Crozer Theol. Sem., Chester, Pa., 1909; spl. study religious edn., Chautauqua, N.Y., 5 summers; D.D., Union U., Jackson, Tenn., 1916; m. Gertrude Lee, of Martin, Tenn., Sept. 12, 1905; children—Eva May, Lura Gertrude (dec.). Ordained Bapt. ministry, 1896; pastor Crum Lynne, Pa., 1908-10, Brownsville, Tenn., 1910-17, Dyersburg, Tenn., 1917-21; prof. Bible and religious edn., Tenn. Coll. for Women, Murfreesboro, Tenn., since 1921, pres. since 1923. Mem. Bapt. Home Mission Bd., Atlanta, Ga. Democrat. Mason, Woodman. Club: Kiwanis (pres. 1928). Home: 618 E. Main St., Murfreesboro TN‡

AUBERT, LLOYD LEES, oil producer; b. San Francisco, Apr. 25, 1898; s. Lucien J. and Catherine M. (Sheehan) A.; A.B., Stanford, 1922; m. Dorothy M. McNew, Aug. 12, 1924; children—Lloyd Lees, Virginia Catherine (Mrs. William C. Winterhalter). Superintendent General Petroleum Corporation, 1926; gen. mgr. Bankline Oil Co., San Francisco, 1927-41, pres. 1941-72. Served with ambulance service U.S. Army, 1917-19, with A.E.F., France, 18 mos. Mem. Phi Delta Theta. Clubs: California, Balboa Bay, Petroleum (Los Angeles, and Midland, Tex); The Family. Home: Corona del Mar CA Died 1972.

AUBREY, HENRY GEORGE, economist; b. Vienna, Austria, Apr. 6, 1906; s. Theodore P. and Selma (von Nassau) A.; Dr. rer. pol. (econ.), U. Vienna, 1928; m. Rachel Lowe Rustow; children—Stephen L., Janet S. Came to U.S., 1939, naturalized, 1944. Research asso. Inst. World Affairs 1950-52; econ. cons. Orgn. Am. States and Internat. Labour Office, 1952; cons. dept. econ. affairs UN, 1950, 52-53; cons. planning bd. Govt. Pakistan, 1955; economist research dept. Fed. Res. Bank of N.Y., 1954-56; dir. research Nat. Planning Assn., 1956-59; vis. prof. Grad. Faculty Polit. and Social Sci., New Sch. Social Research, 1950-68; vis. research fellow council Fgn. Relations, 1959-66; vis. prof. econs. Columbia, 1961-62, 65-66, univ. seminar asso., 1965-70, sr. fellow European Inst., 1967-70; prof. econs. Sarah Lawrence Coll., 1965-70. Served with USNR, 1943-45. Mem. Am. Econ. Assn., Royal Econ. Soc. Club: Cosmos (Washington). Author: United States Imports and World Trade, 1957; Coexistence: Economic Challenge and Response, 1961; The Dollar in World Affairs, 1964; Atlantic Economic Cooperation: The Case of the OECD, 1967; Behind the Veil of International Money, 1969. Contbr. articles profl. publs. Home: New York City NY Died Mar. 1, 1970.

AUBREY, JOHN EDMOND, lecturer; b. Clarksville, Tex., Nov. 27, 1870; s. Madison T. and Martha N. (Hinton) A.; A.B., Trinity U., Waxahachie, Tex., 1894; post-grad. work, U. of Chicago; studied theology at Trinity U. and U. of Chicago; m. Susan Marion Graham, of Bastrop Co., Tex., Sept. 6, 1894; children—Victor Kingsly, Velma Bernadine, Ruth Maurine. Ordained Presbyn. ministry, 1894; pastor Ardmore, Okla., 1894-96, Woodlawn mission, Chicago, 1896-97, LeRoy, Ill., 1897-1901, Gibson City, Ill., 1901-03, Sterling, Colo., 1903-09, Deport, Tex., 1909-11; pres. Presbyn. State Chautauqua, Waxahachie, Tex., 1911-13; pastor Denison, Tex., 1914-18; organizer and gen. lecturer, Redpath Bur. since 1918; sec. Chamber Commerce, Denison; later with W. L. Radcliffe enterprises, Washington, D.C., and with Associated Chautauquas. Made 177 speeches during World War; frequently called as expert in community affairs. Cited by President Wilson for war work. Mem. Internat. Lyceum and Chautauqua Assn. Clubs: Denison Rotary (awarded medal and life membership). Spl. lecturer to high schools and colleges of America. Address: Le Roy IL*‡

AUCOCK, ARTHUR MORGAN, clergyman; b. Dutchess County, N.Y., Oct. 11, 1861; s. Jonathan and Anne Elizabeth (Morgan) A.; B.A., Hobart Coll., 1887 (Phi Beta Kappa), M.A., 1890, D.D., 1911; B.D., Episcopal Theol. Sch., Cambridge, Mass., 1890; unmarried. Deacon, 1890, priest, 1891, P.E. Ch.; asst. minister, 1890-98, rector, 1898-1932, rector emeritus since 1932, All Saints' Memorial Ch., Providence, R.I. Mem. standing com. Diocese of R.I., 1901-32, and pres. same; del. from Diocese of R.I. to Gen. Conv., 1907-32 and dean of delegation; v.p. Diocesan Council, Diocese of R.I. Club: Sigma Phi (New York). Home: Route 2, Asheville NC‡

AUERBACH, BEATRICE FOX, dept. store exec.; b. Hartford, Conn., July 7, 1887; d. Moses and Theresa (Stern) Fox; ed. private schs. in Hartford, and travel abroad; M.A. (hon.), Wesleyan U., 1949; M.S. (hon.), Trinity Coll., 1951; D.H.L., U. Hartford, 1962; m. George S. Auerbach, Apr. 5, 1911 (died Nov. 13, 1927); children—Georgette A. Koopman, Dorothy A. Schiro. Asso. with father in mgmt. of G. Fox & Co., Hartford, 1928-38, pres., 1938-65, also treas., dir.; v.p., dir. May Department Stores Co.; dir. of Brown-Thomson, Inc. Established Auerbach Major at Conn. Coll. of New London, Conn.; also created and is now head of Beatrice Fox Auerbach Found. and Service Bur. for Women's Orgns. of Conn. Recipient Distinguished Pub. Service award State Bar Assn. Conn. Home: Hartford CT Died Nov. 29, 1968.

AUGENSTEIN, LEROY GEORGE, educator, biophysicist; b. Decatur, Ill., Mar. 6, 1928; s. Roy Henry and Minnie (Reifsteck) A.; student James Millikin U., 1944-46; B.S., U. Chgo., 1949; M.S., U. Ill., 1954, Ph.D., 1956; m. Elizabeth Schmalfuss, Sept. 23, 1950; children—David Leroy, Kimberly Beth. Began career as scientist at Brookhaven Nat. Lab., 1956-58, 60-62; research adminstr. AEC, 1958-60; sci. coordinator Seattle Worlds Fair, 1960-61; chmn. biophysics dept. Mich. State U., 1962-69, prof. biophysics, 1962-69. Mem. Mich. Bd. Edn., 1967-69; cons. NIH; lectr. for NATO, Internat. Atomic Energy Agy., Am. Inst. Biol. Scis. Mem. Ingham County Cancer Com., 1966-69. Precinct chmn., del. state Republican convs.; candidate for U.S. Senate, 1966. Bd. dirs. Univ. Internat. Served with AUS, 1946-48. Mem. Radiation Research Soc., Biophys. Soc., Sigma Xi, Sigma Alpha Epsilon. Author: Come Let Us Play God, 1969; also articles in field. Editor: Proceedings of Two International Symposia, 1960, 63; (rev. series) Advances in Radiation Biology, 1964-69. Home: Holt MI Died Nov. 9, 1969.

AUGSPURGER, OWEN BEAL, lawyer; b. Buffalo, June 19, 1913; s. Owen Beal and Mabel (Moulter) A.; B.A., Princeton, 1934; LL.B., U. Buffalo, 1937; m. Paula Norris, Mar. 13, 1945; children—John, Susan, Robert. Admitted to N.Y. bar, 1937, since practiced in Buffalo; partner firm Jaeckle, Fleischmann, Kelly, Swart & Augspurger, and predecessors, 1946-69. Sec., dir. Roblin Steel Corp., Jones Rich Milk Co., Backers Realty Corp., Lake Erie Rolling Mill, Inc., Erie Forge & Steel Corp.; secretary, director Rand Capital Corporation. Dir., sec. Greater Buffalo Development Found.; chmn. devel. campaign U. Buffalo, 1952; chmn. Buffalo chpt. A.R.C., 1953-55, vice chmn. nat. conv., Seattle, 1963, chmn. adv. com. Eastern Area, 1960-61; chmn. joint United Fund-A.R.C. com. Buffalo, 1956-59; mem. N.Y. State Commn. on War 1812, 1964-69; mem. council U. Buffalo, 1953-63. City councilman, Buffalo, 1950-51, vice chmn. University of Buffalo, 1950-51. Served to lt. col. AUS, 1941-46; PTO; brig. gen. N.Y. Guard. Fellow Company Mil. Historians; mem. Am., N.Y., Erie County (bd. dirs. 1954-56) bar assns., N.Y. State Jr. (pres. 1940), Buffalo Jr. (pres. 1938) chambers commerce, Buffalo Hist. Soc. (pres. 1964-69), Phi Delta Phi. Republican. Presbyn. Clubs: Buffalo Country, Buffalo Athletic. Author: World War II History of the 102d AAA Battalion, 1961; also articles. Home: Buffalo NY Died 1969.

AUGUST, HARRY WIRT, coll. adminstr.; b. Ashtabula, O., Apr. 17, 1899; s. John Wirt and Geortner May (Belknap) A.; student Ohio State U., 1918-20; m. Helen Bethel, May 16, 1953. Newspaper editorial staff Athens (O.) Messenger, Portsmouth (O.) Times, Akron (O.) Times-Press, Pitts. Press, 1921-42; faculty evening div. Duquesne U., 1936-42; fund-raising Ohio Republican Finance Com., Rep. Nat. Finance Com., Ketchum, Inc., 1946-56; v.p. for devel. Case Inst. Tech., 1956-61, dir. for bequests, 1961-68; dir. devel. Hawken Sch. for Boys, Cleve., 1968-70. Served as lt. comdr. USNR, 1942-46. Mem. Sigma Delta Chi, Alpha Sigma Phi. Home: South Euclid OH Died Mar. 11, 1970; interred North Lawn Cemetery, Canton OH

AULT, BROMWELL, chem. corp. exec.; b. Wyoming, O., June 28, 1899; s. George C. and Helene (Bromwell) A.; grad. Phillips Acad., 1918, Yale, 1922; m. Allie Burchenal, Oct. 18, 1923; children—J. Burchenal, Bromwell. Chem. engr. Ault & Wilborg Co., 1922-25 pres., gen. mgr. Ault & Wilborg Varnish Works, Inc., 1925-31 (both Cincinnati); v.p., dir. Internat. Printing Ink Corp., 1931-36, pres., dir., mem. exec. com. 1936-44; v.p., dir., mem. exec. com. Inmont Corp., 1944-64, ret., 1971; cons. chem. engring. and marketing, N.Y.C., 1971-73; trustee Bowery Savings Bank; former dir. Procter & Gamble (Cin.). Vice chmn. Episcopal Ch. Found., N.Y.C. Trustee Phillips Andover Acad. Recipient Yale medal for distinguished service, 1971. Mem. Mfg. Chemists assn., Nat. Indsl. Conf. Bd., Bus. Council Internat. Understanding, Advt. Council Bd. (past dir.). Clubs: Yale, Yacht (N.Y.C.); St. Elmo (New Haven); Piping Rock (Locust Valley, N.Y.); Edgartown (Mass.) Yacht. Home: New York City NY Died Jan. 1973.

AUMAN, RUSSELL FRANK, theologian; b. Rebersburg, Pa., Apr. 21, 1899; s. Thomas Aaron and Salome Jane (Bierly) A.; A.B., Susquehanna U., Selingsgrove, Pa., 1920, B.D., 1923, D.D., 1942; D.D., Wagner Coll., 1941; grad. student Bibl. Sem., Union Sem., N.Y.C.; m. Lillian Blanche Renick, Sept. 7, 1922 (dec. 1948); children—Naomia (Mrs. John Hutko), Ada Jane (Mrs. Wesley Walker); m. 2d, Helen Hazel Renick, Apr. 30, 1949. Oradined to ministry Luth. Ch., 1923, pastor. Thompsontown, Pa., 1923-25, Yeagertown, Pa., 1925-29, Scarsdale, N.Y., 1929-43, St. Peter's Luth. Ch., Manhattan, N.Y., 1943-53; prof. practical theology Hamma Div. Sch., Wittenberg U., 1953-67. Staff Luth. Leadership Tng. Sch., Ahrendtsville, Pa., 1936-50; radio preacher nat. network, 1943-51; Mem. Nat. Assn. Sem. Profs. in Practical Fields. Author: Youth's Faith in Action, 1940; The Way of the Witnesses, 1957; A Handbook of Table Prayers, 1972. Co-author: Uniform Lesson Commentary, 1960, 62. Home: Springfield OH Died Apr. 27, 1972; buried Glen Haven Meml. Park, New Carlisle OH

AURELL, GEORGE EMANUEL, fgn. service officer; b. Kobe, Japan, Jan. 8, 1905; s. Karl Emanuel and Hannah Antoinette (Christensen) A.; student Park Coll., 1922-23, Northwestern U., 1923-24; B.S., Okla. State U., 1927; m. Maxine Reagor, June 22, 1934; children—John Karl, Jane A. Croft. Vice consul Dept. of State, Yokohama, Japan, 1927-30; comml. manager Southwestern staff Gen. MacArthur, Dept. of Def., Tokyo, Japan, 1946-53; staff Far Eastern Affairs, Dept. State, Washington, 1953-56; spl. asst. ambassador, Manila, P.I., 1956-60; State Dept., Washington, 1960-62; spl. asst. to sec. gen. SEATO, Bangkok, Thailand, 1962-66, served to lt. col. AUS, 1942-46. Decorated Legion of Merit, Bronze Star with cluster. Mem. Phi Kappa Alpha, Alpha Kappa Psi. Episcopalian. Home: McLean VA Died Feb. 1970.

AUSTIN, HERBERT DOUGLAS, prof. Italian; b. Erie, Pennsylvania, July 24, 1876; s. Frank Augustin and Clara Ann (Mooney) A.; A.B., Princeton University, 1900, Page fellow in classics, 1900-01, A.M., 1901; grad. study U. of Florence (Italy), 1902-03; Ph.D., Johns Hopkins, 1911; Litt.D., U. of Southern Calif., 1946; m. Gladys May Hixson, June 14, 1920. Instr., in Latin and Italian, Princeton, 1901-02, in French and Italian, 1903-06; instr. in Italian and French, Amherst Coll., 1908-09; instr. in French, Johns Hopkins, 1901-11; instr. in Italian and French, U. of Mich., 1911-19, asst. prof. Romance langs., 1919-20; asso. prof. Italian and French, U. of Southern Calif., 1920-23, became prof., 1923, acting head of French dept., 1920-21, prof. of Italian and chmn. of Italian department 1923-47. Prof. Italian. Univ. of Chicago, summer 1930; special lecturer, University of Rome, summer 1931; research in Italy on American Council of Learned Socs. Grant, 1933-34. Awarded Gold Medal of Merit of Italy, 1938. Author of articles on Dante, etc., in Am. and foreign journals. Member Modern Language Assn. of America, Am. Assn. Univ. Profs., Am. Assn. Teachers of Italian (pres. 1933), Philol. Assn. of Pacific Coast (pres. 1934), Dante Soc. America, Mediaeval Acad. America, Phi Beta Kappa, Phi Kappa Phi. Presbyterian. Editor Italica, 1928-33. Home: 1040 W. 78th St., Los Angeles 44 CA‡

AUSTIN, HOWARD ALBERT, JR., ins. co. exec.; b. Kansas City, Mo., Oct. 31, 1915; s. Howard A. and Mamie (Corrigan) A.; B.S., Yale, 1937; m. Mary Virginia Snow, Apr. 27, 1946; children—Howard Albert III, Jeremy Winn. Spl. agt. Prudential Ins. Co. Am., 1938-46, dir. agencies, 1946-49, dir. field tng., 1949-56, 2d v.p., 1956, then v.p.; mgr. Knickerbocher Agy., N.Y.C., from 1962. Served from ensign to lt. USNR, 1940-45. Mem. C.L.U. Soc. Clubs: St. Elmo; Aurelian (Yale); Union, Badminton (N.Y.C.). Home: New York City NY Died Oct. 14, 1971; buried Kansas City MO

AUSTIN, JOHN CORNEBY WILSON, architect; b. Bodicote, Oxfordshire, Eng., Feb. 13, 1870; s. Richard Wilson and Jane Elizabeth A.; ed. pvt. schs.; apprentice course in architecture; m. Hilda Violet Myton, Aug. 16, 1902 (died Nov. 25, 1931); 8 children. m. 2d, Dorothy Kathleen Bell. Feb. 5, 1935. Practiced architecture since 1894 in Los Angeles, Calif.; asso. with Frederic M. Ashley, 1912-37; designed and supervised constrn. Shrine Auditorium, Los Angeles Chamber of Commerce, Calif. State Bldg., St. Vincent's Hosp., Griffith Observatory, Saint Pauls Church (all in Los Angeles); one of three firms to design and supervise building of Los Angeles City Hall; past chmn. for Southern Calif. of President Hoover's orgn. for unemployment relief; past pres. State Bd. of Archtl. Examiners and past mem. Southern Dist.; mem. Com. of Seven apptd. to adjust claims resulting from failure of San Francisquito Dam in 1928; chmn. Citizens Com. of Metropolitan Water Dist.; mem. President Roosevelt's Labor Mediation Bd. (Los Angeles Dist.); chmn. Legislative Advisory Com. on Defense and Employment (State of Calif. 1940). Past pres. Los Angeles Chamber of Commerce. Fellow Am. Inst. Architects (past pres. Southern Calif. Chapter), Royal Soc. Arts; mem. Am. Soc. C.E. Mason (32 deg.); mem. Al Malaikah Shrine. Clubs: Jonathan (past pres.), Lincoln. Home: 1275 Kenilworth Av., San Marion CA‡

AUSTIN, JOHN TURNELL, manufacturer; b. Poddington, Eng., May 16, 1869; s. Jonathan and Charlotte (Turnell) A.; ed. St. Michael's and All Angels' schs., London; m. Jane M. Rogers, Oct. 5, 1892. Came to U.S., 1889. In employ Farrand & Votey Organ Co., Detroit, Mich., 1889-93; with Clough & Warren Co., mfg. organs under his patents, 1893-98; pres. and gen. mgr. Austin Organ Co., Hartford, Conn., since 1898. Republican. Episcopalian. Home: 54 Beacon St. Office: 158 Woodland St., Hartford CT*‡

AUSTIN, LLOYD LEWIS, banker; b. Leadville, Colo., June 20, 1904; s. Fred P. and Mary E. (Henderson) A.; student U. So. Cal., 1922-23, U. Ariz., 1924-26; LL.D., U. Ariz., 1962, U. So. Cal.; m. Mary E. Berryman, Sept. 25, 1927; children—Elizabeth Ruth, Margaret Lewise (Mrs. Allen W. Mathies, Jr.). Began bus. career as accountant Lybrand, Ross Bros. & Montgomery, Los Angeles, 1926-33; credit man Security First National Bank, Los Angeles, 1933-35, asst. v.p., 1935-39, v.p., mem. exec. com., dir., 1953-55, pres., 1955-61, chmn. bd., chief exec. officer, 1961-67, chmn. bd., 1967-68; dir. Carnation Co., Northrop Corp., Kerr-McGee Corp., J. G. Boswell Co., So. Cal. Edison Co., Pacific Mut. Life Ins. Co.; v.p., dir. Music Center Operating Co.; chmn. bd. First Small Bus. Investment Corp. Cal. Trustee Occidental Coll., Com. Econ. Devel. (hon.), Cal. Inst. Tech.; bd. dirs., past pres. Automobile Club So. Cal., Children's Hosp. Los Angeles; bd. govs. Inter-Ins. Exchange; formerly chmn. Los Angeles chpt. A.R.C.; broad dirs. other civic orgns. Mem. Assn. Res. City Bankers, American, Cal. bankers assns., Cal. C. of C. (director), Beta Gamma Sigma, Sigma Alpha Epsilon, Alpha Kappa Psi. Mason. Clubs: California. University, Bond, Los Angeles Country, Los Angeles Stock Exchange, Lincoln, Petroleum, Athenaeum, Rotary, Sunset. Home: Los Angeles CA Died Dec. 30, 1968; buried Rose Hills Meml. Park, Whittier CA

AUSTIN, SAMUEL YATES, pres. Avondale Mills; b. Madison, Ga., July 21, 1877; s. John P. and Amanda (Wilson) A.; ed. common schools; m. Maude Jernigan, Mar. 28, 1907; children—Samuel Yates, Miriam (Mrs. E. C. Reuter), J. Paul. With Avondale Mills, textile mfg., Sylacauga, Ala., since 1940, pres. since 1940. Mem. Am. Cotton Mfrs. Assn., Ala. Cotton Mfrs. Assn. Democrat. Baptist. Mason (Shriner). Clubs: Westchester Country (Rye, N.Y.); Highland Country (La Grange, Ga.); Talladega (Ala.) Country, Rotary, Sylacauga, Ala.; National Democratic (N.Y. City). Home: Purefoy Apartments, Talladega, Ala. Office: Avondale Mills, Sylacauga AL*‡

AUSTIN-BALL, THOMAS, singer; b. Belfast, Ireland, Sept. 8, 1872; s. William and Agnes (Shilliday) B.; studied singing with Adolph Stussi, Belfast, T. A. Walworth and Winslow Hall, London, and Sbriglia, Paris; winner professional scholarship, Blackheath Conservatory of Music, London, diploma, 1904 (medal of highest award for singing); m. Alice Garland Steele, of N.Y. City, July 22, 1916. First sang in opera, London, 1898; debut as bass soloist, Hayden's Creation," at Hastings Festival, Eng., Dec. 12, 1903; was bass soloist St. James Ch., Piccadilly, and appeared with various musical socs. throughout British Isles; came to U.S., 1907; bass soloist Tompkins Av. Ch., Brooklyn, 1908-10; dir. vocal dept. Skidmore Sch. of Arts, Saratoga Springs, N.Y., 1911-14; head of vocal dept. All Saints Conservatory of Music, Sioux Falls, S.D., 1914-17; now teaching independently. Mem. N.Y. State Music Teachers' Assn. Republican. Conglist. Mason (32 deg., K.T., Shriner). Clubs: Musicians' (New York), Montclair (Montclair, N.J.). Home: 25 Melrose Pl., Montclair, N.J. Studio: Carnegie Hall, New York NY‡

AUSTRIAN, CARL JOSEPH, lawyer; b. Williamsport, Pa., Dec. 16, 1892; s. Joseph E. and Selma (Silverman) A.; A.B., Williams Coll., 1914; LL.B., Columbia, 1917; m. Beryl Siegbert, Mar. 7, 1923 (div. 1946); children—Carl J., Geoffrey David; m. 2d, Dorothy Steinam Feibleman, 1946. Admitted to N.Y. bar, 1917, and began practice N.Y. City, 1919; sr. partner firm Austrian, Lance & Stewart; attorney for superintendent of banks of New York State in liquidation of Bank of U.S., 1930-43; trustee Central State Electric Corp.; director Blue Ridge Mutual Fund, Incorporated. Special asst. to American ambassador to Turkey, Ankara, 1943-44. Trustee, counsel Mt. Sinai Hosp. Former v.p. Am. Jewish Com. Mem. Am., N.Y. bar assns., Assn. Bar City of N.Y., N.Y. County Lawyers Assn. Clubs: Harmonie (pres. 1935-37), Williams (past gov.), Bankers (N.Y.C.). Home: New York City Died June 25, 1970; buried Reading, PA

AUTHIER, GEORGE FRANCIS, newspaper corr.; b. Leicester Junction, Vt., Nov. 4, 1876; s. Edward and Mary (Cassavant) A.; A.B., Grinnell (Ia.) Coll., 1902; m. Nancy Russell Dunnigan, Dec. 24, 1914; 1 dau., Joy (Mrs. Robert W. Smeaton). Reporter Fort Dodge Messenger, 1902; reported Sioux City Journal, 1903-05; political writer Des Moines Register & Leader, 1905-07; city editor Helena (Mont.) Independent, 1907-08; same, Minneapolis (Minn.) Morning Tribune, 1908-09, polit. writer, 1909-12; sec. to Gov. A. O. Eberhart of Minn., 1912-14; Washington corr. Minneapolis Tribune, 1915-35; also with Washington burs. New York Herald, New York Sun-Herald, New York World, 1917-29; editor and pub. Foreign Affairs News Service, 1927-28; with Resettlement Adminstrn. (regional), hdqrs., Milwaukee, Wis., 1935-37, asst. regional dir.; with Farm Security Adminstrn. (regional), hdqrs., Milwaukee, Wis., 1937-42, asst. regional dir. Dir. publicity and chmn. speakers' bur., Roosevelt Agrl. Com., Presidental Campaign of 1936. Mem. Iowa Nat. Guard, 1893-95. Mason. Club: National Press of Washington (pres. 1924). Home: Milwaukee WI‡

AVANCENA, RAMON, jurist; b. Molo, Iloilo, P.I.; s. Lucas and Petra (Quiusay) A.; A.B., U. of Santo Tomas, 1898; m. Maria Flocerfina Abad, of Leyte, 1913; children—Jesus, Martin, Alberto, Emilio, Jovito, Miguel. Began as asst. atty. in office of atty. gen. P.I., 1902; successively judge Court of First Instance, 1905, atty. gen., 1914, asso. justice Supreme Court of P.I., 1917, chief justice since 1925. Catholic. Address: Supreme Court of Philippine Islands, Manila PI‡

AVERILL, JOHN H., dir.-gen. Charleston Exp'n. Connected with rys. many years; master transportation Charlotte, Columbia & Augusta R. R., during the war; div. supervisor B. & O. R. R., 1878-9; master transportation S. C. Ry., 1879-86; gen. supt. same, 1886-91; supt. Port Royal & Western R. R. of Ga., Jan. to March, 1891; gen. mgr. Charleston, Sumter & Northern R. R., 1891-5; also formerly gen. supt. Blackville, Alston & Newbury Ry., and supt. Charleston, Cincinnati & Chicago R. R.; receiver and gen. mgr. Port Royal & Augusta Ry. since 1893. Address: Charlston SC‡

AVERITT, GEORGE ALFRED, business exec.; b. Tallahassee, Fla., Oct. 28, 1895; s. George Hathaway and Susan Frances (Barco) A.; ed. pub. schs., of Tallahassee; m. Willie Lou Shepherd, May 27, 1926. Clerk Yeager Hardware Co., Tallahassee, 1913-17; dept. mgr. Ensley Motor Co., 1917-24, Ford-Ensley,

Ala., 1950; owner Dora (Ala.) Motor Co., Ford dealer, since Nov. 1925; partner Averitt & Sanders Coal Co., 1942-69; v.p. East Walker County Indsl. Development Assn. Dir., chmn. of board Doctor's Investment Corp., Mayor of Dora, Alabama. President East Walker District Gas Board, Conservationist of year, 1952; winner W.A.P.I. Handicap Trophy for State of Ala., 1948-49. Mem. Nat. Wildlife Fedn. (hon. pres.; mem. conservation edn. com.), Outdoor Writers Assn. Am., Ala. Wildlife Fedn. (mem. adv. bd.), Nat. Skeet Shooting Assn. Mason (Shriner). Clubs: Jasper Sportsmen's Dora AL Died May 2, 1969; buried Elmwood Cemetery, Birmingham AL

AVERY, CYRUS STEVENS, oil producer; b. Stevensville, Pa., Aug. 31, 1871; s. James Alexander and Ruie (Stevens) A.; A.B., William Jewell Coll., Liberty, Mo., 1897; m. Essie M. McClelland, of Liberty, Dec. 23, 1897; children—James Leighton, Gordon Steven, Helen Louise. Began in oil and investment business at Tulsa, Okla., 1907; pres. Avery Investment Co.; sec. and treas. Woodland Park Development Co.; dir. Tulsa Nat. Bank. County commr., Tulsa Co., 1913-16; mem. Tulsa dist. Exemption Bd., 1917-18; mem. Tulsa Water Bd., created to build Spavinaw Water Project, at cost of $7,500,000 and conducting water 60 miles, 1921-24; chmn. Okla. State Highway Commn., 1924-27; mem. Joint Bd. of Interstate Highways, U.S. Dept. Agr., 1925-27; appointed director of Works Progress Administration, 1st Oklahoma District (13 counties), 1935. Mem. Associated Highways of America (ex-pres.), Albert Pike Highway Assn. (pres. 1917-27), U.S. 66 Highway Assn. (v.p. 1927), Am. Assn. State Highway Officials (dir. 1925-26), Tulsa Chamber Commerce (pres. 1933-34), Phi Gamma Delta. Democrat. Baptist. Mason (32 deg.). Clubs: Rotary, Tulsa Country. Home: 2306 S. Cincinnati St. Office: Mayo Bldg., Tulsa OK‡

AVERY, JOHNSTON, mining exec.; b. Morganton, N.C., May 12, 1901; s. Alphonso C. and Mary (Johnston) A.; student State U.N.Y., 1918-19, U.N.C., 1919-22, Columbia, 1922; m. Virginia Davenport Hall, June 6, 1925; 1 dau., Virginia. Reporter Greensboro (N.C.) Daily News, 1923-24; editor Hickory (N.C.) Daily Record, 1924-28; editor, pub. Lenoir (N.C.) News-Topic, 1928-32; asst. to dir. U.S. Bur. Fgn. and Domestic Commerce, 1933-35; spl. asst. U.S. Atty. Gen., Washington, 1935-49; asst. adminstr. U.S. Tech. Coop. Adminstrn., Washington, 1949-52; pres. Liberian Am. Swedish Minerals Co., Monrovia, Liberia, 1952-70, dir., 1952-70; dir. Internat. African-Am. Corp., N.Y.C., 1952-55. Recipient Separk award editorial work, 1928, N.C. Press Assn. award, 1930; decorated knight Order Vassa (Sweden, grand comdr. Order African Star (Liberia), Grand Band Wilmington NC Died Oct. 1, 1970.

AVNET, LESTER FRANCIS, electronics co. exec.; b. N.Y.C., Nov. 12, 1912; s. Charles and Rose (Dorfman) A.; student bus. adminstrn. N.Y.U., 1929-30; M. Joan Grossman, Dec. 31, 1940; children—Rosalind, Carol, Jonathan. Mem. firm Charles Avnet, electronics part distbrs., N.Y.C., 1944-55; pres., founder Avnet Electronics Supply Co., N.Y.C., 1955-70 (name changed to Avnet, Inc., 1964), chmn. bd., 1964-70; dir. John Diebold, Inc., Continuing Ednl. Systems, Inc., Belding Heminway Co., Inc. Life mem. Air Force Hist. Found., Montgomery, Ala., 1963-70; patron Boy Scouts Am., UN Ball, Met. Opera, Mus. Modern Arts, Lincoln Center; bd. govs. Jewish Mus.; asso. mem. Guggenheim Mus.; life mem. Met. Mus. Art; mem., dir. Friends Whitney Mus. Bd. dirs. Nassau Heart Assn., Union Am. Hebrew Congregation; bd. dirs. United Jewish Appeal Greater N.Y., gen. chmn., 1968 fund raising campaign; bd. govs. Hebrew Union Coll.-Jewish Inst. Religion; trustee N. Shore Hosp., Am. Fedn. Arts; chmn. bd. trustees Great Neck Symphony Orch.; bd. overseers Albert Einstein Coll. Medicine; a founder Eleanor Roosevelt Meml. Found. Nat. commr. Anti-Defamation League, 1966. Trustee Brandeis U. Mem. Nassau County Council Indsl. Bus. Com., Arts Collectors Club Am., Mfg. Engring. Council (hon.), Air Force Hist. Found. (life). Jewish religion. Clubs: Glen Oaks Country (Glen Oaks); Palm Beach Country (Palm Beach Fla.); Hemisphere (N.Y.C.); Aspetuck Golf. Home: Kings Point NY Died Jan. 3, 1970.

AXELROD, HAIM IZCHAK, physician; b. Jerusalem, Palestine, Nov. 3, 1925; s. Louis and Sara Ethel Axelrod; B.A. in Physiology and Biochemistry, U. Toronto, 1947, M.D., 1951; m. Esther Gold, Dec. 20, 1952; children—Howard, David, Marsha, Caron. Jr. rotating intern Toronto (Ont., Can.) Western Hosp., 1951-52; postgrad. in anesthesiology U. Toronto, 1952-54; sr. anesthesiologist St. Michael's Hosp., Toronto, 1952, Toronto East Gen. Hosp., 1953, Toronto Gen. Hosp., 1954; asst. resident in anesthesiology Hosp. for Sick Children, Toronto, 1953; practice medicine specializing in anesthesiology, Toronto, 1954-71; attending physician dept. anesthesiology New Mt. Sinai Hosp., Toronto, until 1971. Diplomate Am. Bd. Anesthesiology, Nat. Bd. Med. Examiners. Fellow Am. Coll. Anesthesiology; mem. Canadian Med. Assn., Am. Soc. Anesthesists, Internat. Soc. Analgesia, Canadian Anesthesiologists Soc., Assn. Adminstrv. Assts. Home: Toronto Ontario Canada Died Jan. 4, 1971; buried Toronto Ontario Canada

AXELSON, CHARLES FREDERIC, chartered life underwriter; b. Princeton, Ill., Aug. 20, 1881; s. John F. and Anna (Pohlson) A.; prep. edn. S. Side Acad.; Ph.B., U. Chgo., 1907; C.L.U., Am. Coll. Life Underwriters, 1931; m. Katerine L. Strong, July 28, 1915; children—Charles F., Kenneth S. Agt. in Chgo., Northwestern Mutual Life Ins. Co., 1910-71, now agt. emeritus. Personnel supv. War Dept., World War I; commd. maj. Adj. Gen.'s Dept. O.R.C.; mem. War Finance Com., Ill., 1943-46. Trustee U. Chgo., 1923-51, hon., 1951-71; trustee Rush Med. Coll., 1925-41; trustee Inst. Current World Affairs, 1935-58, pres., 1939-57. Awarded U. Chgo. Alumni citation Useful Citizen, 1943. Mem. Nat. (exec. com. 1928-33), Ill. (pres. 1934-35), Chgo. (pres. 1926-27) assns. life underwriters, Ins. Fedn. Ill. (v.p. 1938-42), U. Chgo. Alumni Assn. (pres., chmn. alumni council 1922-24), Delta Tau Delta (pres. Chgo. alumni chpt. 1919-20), Chgo. Council Fgn. Relations, Am. Scandinavian Found., John Ericsson League. Republican. Baptist. Clubs: University, Quadrangle. Home: Chicago IL Died May 16, 1971.

AYARS, GEORGE W(ASHINGTON), state ofcl.; b. Wilmington, Del., May 29, 1897; s. John Joseph and Elma (Fisher) A.; B.S., West Chester State Tchrs. Coll., 1934; M.A., Columbia, 1941; m. Marion Pizer, Dec. 1, 1920; 1 son, H. Bruce. With Electric Hose and Rubber Co., 1912-16, Atlantic Steel Casting Co., 1916-19. Peoples Settlement, 1919-25, Wilmington Bd. Park Commrs., 1925-27, Wilmington High Sch., 1928-37; state dir. health and phys. edn. State Dept. Pub. Ins., Dover, Del., 1937-70. Dir. Del. Safety Council, Del. Anti Tb. Soc.; Welfare Council Del. Fellow Am. Assn. Health Phys. Edn. and Recreation (past pres. Eastern dist. assns.); mem. Nat. Soc. State Dirs. Health Phys. Edn. and Recreation (past pres.), Peoples Settlement Assn. (past pres.), Am. Legion (comdr.); Del. honor award 1947). Kiwanian (past Dover DE Died Jan. 19, 1970.

AYDELOTTE, DORA, novelist; b. Altamont, Ill., Jan. 10, 1878; d. John Patten and Carolina (Fox) Aydelotte; ed. Chicago Art Inst., 1896-97, Woman's Coll., Richmond, Va., 1902-04; unmarried. Fiction writer and novelist from 1931. Mem. Authors' Round Table (Chicago); hon. mem. Writer's Club (Oklahoma City); mem. Sigma Tau Delta (hon.). Democrat. Christian Scientist. Author: Long Furrows, 1935; Green Gravel, 1937; Trumpets Calling, 1938; Full Harvest, 1939; Run of the Stars, 1940; Across the Prairie, 1941; Measure Of A Man, 1942, Trumpets Calling and Full Harvest have been transcribed into Braille. Contbr. short stories, articles, to nat. mags. Home: Chicago IL Died Nov. 1968.

AYER, CHARLES FREDERICK, lawyer, mining exec.; b. Marysville, Cal., Dec. 11, 1863; s. Charles Alvin and Mary Kathryn (Norton) A.; m. Elizabeth Close, Aug. 25, 1897; 1 dau., Margaret Lucy (Mrs. Harold R. Colvin). Chmn. bd., dir. Newmont Mining Corp.; v.p., dir. Tex. Gulf Sulphur Co., Rio Blanco Ranch Co.; dir. Continental Oil Co. (Del.), Hudson Bay Mining & Smelting Co., Ltd. Chmn. Boyce Thompson Inst. for Plant Research; v.p., dir. Boyce Thompson Southwestern Arboretum. Home: 1 Slocum St., New Rochelle, N.Y. Office: 14 Wall St., NYC‡

AYER, FREDERIC EUGENE, dean; b. Sheshequin, Pa., Oct. 24, 1876; s. Oscar Francis and Anne (Morley) A.; student Susquehanna Collegiate Inst., Towanda, Pa., 1891-94; C.E., Lafayette Coll., 1900; m. Bessie Lyman Barnes, Sept. 6, 1906; children—Edward B. (dec.), Annetta Louise (Mrs. Clyde F. Falor, Jr.), Frederic Lyman. Draftsman and shop inspector, Pennsylvania Steel Company, 1900; draftsman American Bridge Co., East Berlin, Conn., 1901-02; chief draftsman, New Jersey Bridge Company, Manasquan, N.J., 1902-03; draftsman and timekeeper, Great Falls (Mont.) Iron Works, June-Oct. 1904; draftsman and office engineer U.S. Reclamation Service, Great Falls, 1904-06; successively instructor, asst. prof. and asso. prof. civil engineering., U. of Cincinnati, 1906-14; dean Engring. Coll., U. of Akron, 1914-46, prof. 1946-47, dean emeritus 1947. New engring. bldg. named Frederic E. Ayer Hall. Served as major, U.S. Infantry Reserve, 1925-40. Mgr. Community Fund Collection; president Family Service Soc.; dir. Boy Scouts of America; pres. Tallmadge School Bd. Mem. Soc. for Promotion Engring. Edn. (past dir.), Am. Soc. Civil Engrs., Sigma Tau, Sigma Chi. Republican. Universalist. Mason. Clubs: Nat. Sojourners, Akron City (Akron). Home: Tallmadge OH‡

AYERS, CLARENCE EDWIN, teacher, writer; b. Lowell, Mass., May 6, 1891; s. William S. and Emma (Young) A.; A.B., Brown U., 1912, A.M., 1914; studied Harvard; Ph.D., U. Chgo., 1917; m. Anna Bryan, 1915 (div.); children—Catharine, Muriel (Mrs. B. L. Towle), Kenneth R.; m. 2d, Gwendolen Jane, 1926. Fellow in philosophy, U. of Chicago, 1916-17, instr., 1917-20; asso. prof. philosophy, Amherst, 1920-23; prof. same, Reed Coll., Portland, Ore., 1923-24; asso. editor The New Republic, 1924-25; prof. principles of edn., Ohio State U., summer, 1927; lecturer in philosophy and adviser in Experimental Coll., U. of Wis., 1928-29; prof. economics U. of Tex., 1930-69; visiting prof., U. of Wash., autumn, 1940. Dir. San Antonio Br. Fed. Reserve Bank 1954-59. Dir. consumers div. U.S. Dept. of Labor, Washington, D.C. 1936; mem. Committee on the Southwest Economy 1950-53. Mem. Am. Philos. Assn., Am. Econ. Assn. Am. Assn. Univ. Profs., Southwestern Social Science Assn. (pres. 1939), Assn. Evolutionary Econs. (1st pres. 1966). Author: Science—The False Messiah, 1927; Holier Than Thou, 1929; Huxley, 1932; The Problem of Economic Order, 1938; The Theory of Economic Progress, 1944; The Divine Right of Capital, 1946; The Industrial Economy, 1952; Toward Reasonable Society, 1961. Contbr. articles and reviews. Address: Austin TX Died July 25, 1972.

AYLER, ALBERT, musician; b. Cleve., July 13, 1936; s. Edward and Myrtle (Hunter) A.; ed. pub. schs., Cleve.; m. Arlene Benton, Jan. 26, 1964; 1 dau., Desiree. Saxaphone player, 1943-70; appearances at music halls throughout U.S., also with numerous small groups, 1952-70; recording artists for Debut, ESP records; pvt. tchr. saxophone, 1959-70. Served with AUS, 1959-61. Composer: Spirits; Mothers; Ghosts; Variations; Holy Spirit; Holy Ghost; Wizard; Saints; Childrens, Angels and Bells; Holy People; albums include: The Grass, Albert Ayler in Greenwich Village at the Village Vanguard. Address: Cleveland OH Died Nov. 1970; buried Highland Park Cemetery, Cleveland OH

AYLING, CHARLES LINCOLN, banker; b. Centreville, Mass., Jan. 22, 1875; s. Augustua Davis and Elizabeth (Cornish) A.; m. Margaret Robertson, 1900; m. 2d, Alice Stephenson, 1928. Engaged in banking business, 35 yrs.; chmn. bd. Barnstable County Nat. Bank, Hyannis, Mass., from 1938; dir. and mem. financial com. John Hancock Mutual Life Ins. Co. since 1914. Chmn. bd. Cape Cod Hosp. Mem. Loyal Legion. Mason (K.T.) Clubs: Union, Algonquin (Boston). Home: Centreville MA Died June 1970.*

AYLSWORTH, LEON EMMONS, college prof.; b. New Berlin, N.Y., Oct. 26, 1869; s. Nelson Olin and Mary (Deming) A.; student S.D. Agrl. Coll., 1890-93; A.B., U. of Neb., 1900; A.M., U. of Wis., 1908; m. Bertha May Fraser, of Raymond, S.D., Sept. 21, 1895; children—Carol, Donald Fraser, Lloyd Deming. Asst. and fellow in Am. history and politics, U. of Neb., 1900-04; mem. faculty same univ. since 1904, prof. polit. science since 1915. Mem. Am. Polit. Science Assn., Nebraska Historical Society, American Assn. Univ. Profs., Nat. Municipal League, Neb. Public Efficiency Economy Association (sec.), Phi Beta Kappa. Republican. Unitarian. Clubs: Open Forum, Social Service. Contbr. Am. Polit. Science Rev., Nat. Municipal Rev. Home: 1840 S. 23d St., Lincoln NB‡

AYRES, ATLEE BERNARD, architect; b. Hillsboro, O., July 12, 1874; s. Nathan Tandy and Mary (Atlee) A.; ed. Art Students League and Metropolitan Sch. of Architecture, New York; m. Olive Moss Cox, Dec. 1896; children—Atlee Tandy, Robert Moss. Practiced at San Antonio, Tex., since 1899; mem. firm Atlee B. & Robert M. Ayres; firm architects of Smith-Young (35 stories), Plaza Hotel, Fed. Reserve Bank Bldg. etc. (all of San Antonio), also one of the architect for the Municipal Auditorium, San Antonio, Blind Inst., Austin, Tex., and Adminstrn., Bldg., Randolph Field, Tex. Pres. San Antonio Fiesta Assn., 7 yrs. originator of La Noche de Fiesta. Former chmn. State Asylum Bd. of Tex. Fellow Am. Inst. Architects. Mason (32 deg.). Club: Travis (ex-pres.). Author: Mexican Architecture, 1926. Home: 201 Belknap Pl. Office: Transit Tower. San Antonio TX‡

AYRES, BURT WILMOT, educator; b. Hartford City, Ind., Dec. 29, 1895; s. James Madison and Katharin (Shick) A.; student DePauw U., Ind., 1885-88; B.S. Taylor Univ., Upland, Ind., 1898, A.M., 1900, Ph.D. 1902 (LL.D., 1935); m. Mary Etta Huggins, Sept. 2, 1888; children—Arthur Hugo (dec.), Hubert Raymond (dec.), Beatrice Marie (dec.), Kenneth Dow, Wendell Willard, Gilbert Haven. Taught dist. sch. Ind., 1884-85, 1888-89; prin. Redkey (Ind.) pub. schs., 1889-90; supt. Montpelier (Ind.) schs., 1890-92, Warren (Ind.) schs., 1892-93; bookkeeper Dunkir Lumber Co., 1893-97; prin. normal dept. and prof. psychology and pedagogy, 1897-1902, dean and prof. philosophy, 1902-06, acting pres., 1904, Taylor U. Upland, Ind.; dean, 1906-10, acting pres. and pres. 1908-10, Central Holiness Univ. (now Kletzin Coll.); dean Taylor U., 1910-23, acting pres. and prof. philosophy, 1922, v.p. and prof. philosophy 1923-46, v.p. emeritus since 1946. Candidate for state supt. pub. instr., Ind., Prohibition ticket, 1900. Mem. Gen. Conf., M.E. Ch., 1916 and 1932. Home: Upland IN‡

AYRES, MILAN VALENTINE, electric ry. engr.; b. Hamlin, Brown Co., Kan., Feb. 14, 1875; s. Milan Church (q.v.) and Georgiana (Gall) A.; S.B., Mass. Inst. Tech., 1898; course in elec. engring., Gen. Electric Co., Schenectady, N.Y., 1899-1900; studied law with C. H. Innis, Boston, and admitted to Mass. bar, 1909; m. Emma Gertrude Stevens, of Newton Highlands, Mass., Sept. 14, 1910. With Gen. Electric Co., 1899-1902; elec. and mech. engr., Boston & Worcester St. Ry., S. Framingham, Mass., 1902-11; asst. gen. mgr., Rockland

Light & Power Co., Nyack, N.Y. (instituting methods of scientific management), July-Nov., 1911; chief engr. Mobile Light & R.R. Co., Nov., 1911-May, 1912; statistician with Ford, Bacon & Davis, consulting engrs., May, 1912-Apr., 1914; sr. elect. engr., Div. of Valuation, Interstate Commerce Commn., Washington, Apr. 1914-May 1918; maj. U.S.A. statistics branch, Gen. Staff, May 1918-Aug. 1920; chief statistical officer, Sept. 1919-Aug. 1920; chief statis. sect., adj. gens. office, Aug.-Dec. 1920; graphic statistician in private practice, Dec. 1920-Sept. 1921; editor of Index (weekly statis. pubn. Associated Gen. Contractors of America), 1921-2; statistician with Julian Armstrong, Inc., Chicago, since 1923. Conglist. Mem. Am. Statis. Assn., Progressive Ed. Assn. Maj. Signal Corps Reserve, U.S.A.; on gen. staff eligible list, U.S.A. Author of numerous technical papers and reports. Home: 5217 Dorchester Av. Office: 400 N. Michigan Av., Chicago IL‡

AYRES, PHILIP WHEELOCK, forester; b. Winterset, Ia., May 26, 1861; s. Elias J. and Ardelia (Wheelock) A.; Ph.B., Cornell U., 1884; Ph.D., Johns Hopkins, 1888; hon. D.Sc., U. of New Hampshire, 1926; Middlebury Coll., 1936; m. Alice Stanley Taylor, Aug. 8, 1899; children—Ruth Wheelock, Dwight Taylor. Gen. sec. Asso. Charities, Cincinnati, 1889-95; studied penal and charitable instns. in Europe, 1895; gen. sec. Bur. Asso. Charities, Chicago, 1895-97; asst. sec. Charity Orgn. Soc., New York, 1897-1900; forester, Soc. for Protection of N.H. Forests, 1901-35; cons. forester since 1935. Mem. N.H. Constl. Conv., 1919-21 and 1928; mem. N.H. Commn. on Arts and Crafts. Awarded medal of Am. Scenic and Historic Preservation Soc., 1935. Dir. Am. Forestry; fellow Soc. Am. Foresters; mem. Appalachian Mountain Club (pres. 1919-20). Clubs: Twentieth Century (Boston); Cosmos (Washington, D.C.). Contbr. articles forestry to mags. Address: Delafield Lane, Riverdale. New York NY‡

AZCARATE Y FLOREZ, PABLO DE, Spanish diplomat; b. Madrid, Spain, July 30, 1890; s. Cayo and Delfina Azcarate y. F.; ed. Institucion Libre de Ensenanza, Madrid, U. Madrid, U. Zaragoza, U. Paris; M.A., LL.D. Prof. adminstrv. law Santiago de Compostela U., 1913, Granada, 1915; mem. Spanish Parliament, 1918-19; mem. staff League of Nations, 1922; dir. adminstrv. and minorities sect. secretariat, 1929-33, dep. sec.-gen., 1933-36; ambassador to Gt. Britain, 1936-39; chmn. Servicio para la Emigracion de Republicanos Espanoles, 1939-40; hon. sec. Juan Luis Vives Scholarship Trust, 1942; dir., founder Instituto Espanol, 1942; chief UN Palestine Mission, 1948, UN Municipal Commn. for Jerusalem; sec. truce com. UN Palestine Commn.; prin. sec. UN Conciliation Commn. for Palestine, 1949-52. Recipient Carnegie Endowment for Internat. Peace, 1944. Author: El Regimen Parroquial en Inglaterra, 1912; La Intervencion Adminstrativa del Estado en los Ferrocarriles, 1917; La Guerra y los Servicios Publicos de Caracter Industrial, 1921; La Intervencion nazi-facista en la guerra de Espana, 1957; Memoria sobre las Vaughan Papers, 1957; La Guerra hispanoamericana de 1898, 1960; Wellington y Espana, 1960; Protection of Minorities, 1966; Mission to Palestine 1948-52, 1966; La guerra del 1898, 1968; Gumerrindo de Azcarate, 1969; Sanz del Rio, 1969. Address: Geneva Switzerland Died Dec. 12, 1971; buried Geneva Switzerland

AZUELA, MARIANO, Mexican physician and writer; b. Lagos, Jalisco, 1873; s. Evaristo Azuela and Paulina Gonzalez; ed. Faculty of Medicine and Pharmacy of Guadalajara, degree of doctor, 1898; m. Carmen Rivera; children—Salvador, Mariano, Carmen, Julia, Paulina, Maria de la Luz, Augustin, Eperanza, Antonio, Enrique. Author of many books since 1907, the most outstanding of which are: Mala Yerba, 1909; his most outstanding, Los de abajo (transl. by Anita Brenner under title of The Under Dogs); La malhora, 1923; El buho en la noche (theatre). Address: Alamo 242, Mexico DF‡

BABB, JAMES T(INKHAM), librarian; b. Lewiston, Ida., Aug. 23, 1899; s. James Elisha and Daisy (Tinkham) B.; grad. Phillips Exeter Acad., 1920; Ph.B., Yale, 1924, M.A., 1945; student Yale Law Sch., 1925-26; m. Margaret Bradley, Dec. 21, 1925; children—James Bradley, Barbara (Mrs. James L. Read, Jr.). With investment banking firm Edward M. Bradley & Co., New Haven, Conn., 1926-38; asst. librarian Yale U., 1938-43, acting librarian, 1943-45, librarian, 1945-65, librarian emeritus, 1965-68. Organized and selected titles for White House Library, 1962-67. Pres., Conn. Library Assn., 1945-46; mem. Am. Library Assn., Assn. of Research and Reference Librarians, Bibilog. Soc. Am. (council; pres. 1950-52), Bibliog. Soc. Eng., Salmon and Trout Assn. Eng., Hameronasset Fishing Assn. Fellow Davenport College, Yale. Clubs: Fence, Elihu, Elizabethan (Yale University); Grolier, Yale, Anglers (New York). Author: A Bibliography of the Writings of William McFee, 1930; The Library in the University, 1967; contbr. chpt. on Yale Library to Library Trends, vol. 15. Home: Hamden CT Died July 21, 1968.

BABCOCK, ALLEN, bishop of Grand Rapids, Mich. Address: Grand Rapids MI Died June 27, 1969; buried Resurrection Cemetery, Grand Rapids MI

BABCOCK, BERNIE, author; b. Unionville, O., Apr. 28, 1868; d. H. N. and Lottie B. Smade; removed to Ark. when 10 yrs. old; ed. Little Rock U.; m. William F. Babcock, Apr. 1886 (dec.); children—Mary Lucille (Mrs. S. G. Boyce), Charlotte Burnelle (Mrs. W. W. Shepherd), Frances M. (Mrs. J. E. Thornburgh, Jr.), William F., Mac Arthur. Was on staff of Ark. Democrat; later owner and editor The Arkansas Sketch Book (quarterly). Author: The Daughter of a Patriot, 1900; The Martyr, 1900; Justice to the Woman, 1901; At the Mercy of the State, 1901; An Uncrowned Queen, 1902; Santa Claus, the Stork and the Widow; Yesterday and Today in Arkansas; Manny; The Battalion of Death; The Bride of King Solomon; The Soul of Ann Rutledge, 1919; The Coming of the King, 1921; The Soul of Abe Lincoln, 1923; When Love Was Bold, 1924; Booth and the Spirit of Lincoln, 1925; Little Abe Lincoln, 1926; Lincoln's Mary and the Babies, 1928; Light Horse Harry's Boy, 1931; The Heart of George Washington, 1932; Little Dixie Devil, 1937; Hallerloogy's Trip with Santa Claus, 1939, 1942; Red Love, 1947. Pres. Ark. Museum of Natural History and Little Rock AR‡

BABCOCK, CHARLES HENRY, stock broker; b. Lafayette, Ind., Sept. 24, 1899; s. Charles Henry and Ella (Park) B.; B.S., U. Pa., 1920; m. Mary Reynolds, Dec. 16, 1929 (dec.); children—Mary Katharine (Mrs. Kenneth Mountcastle, Jr.), Charles Henry, Barbara Frances, (Mrs. Frederic H. Lassiter), Betsy Main; m. second, Winifred Penn Knies, September 8, 1954. With Guaranty Trust Co. of N.Y., N.Y.C., 1920-23; v.p. Mahjongg Corp. of Am., San Francisco, 1923-24; with Guaranty Co. of N.Y., Phila., 1924-31; sr. partner Reynolds & Co., N.Y., 1931-67; director Piedmont Publishing Co., Winston-Salem. Commr. pub. housing, Winston-Salem. Pres., treas. Mary Reynolds Babcock Found; vice pres., treas. Smith Reynolds Found. Served as pvt. U.S. Army, World War I, maj., World War II. Mem. Grolier Soc., Alpha Chi Rho. Clubs: Down Town Assn., University, Bankers (N.Y.C.); Twin Winston-Salem NC Died Dec. 13, 1967; buried Winston-Salem NC

BABCOCK, HAROLD DELOS, astronomer; b. Edgerton, Wis., Jan. 24, 1882; s. Emilus Welcome and Mary Eliza (Brown) B.; B.S., U. Cal., 1907; m. Mary G. Henderson, Mar. 9, 1907; 1 son, Horace Welcome. With scientific staff, Bur. of Standards, Washington, 1906-08; staff of Mount Wilson Observatory, 1909-48. Mem. Nat. Acad. Scis. (mem. commn. on Standards of Wave-Length, past pres.), Internat. Astron. Union, Am. Astron. Soc. (member council 1943), Astron Soc. of Pacific (president 1937; Bruce Gold Medal, 1953); Sigma Xi; asso. Royal Astron. Soc. (England). Has specialized in spectroscopy. Shared award of 1929 prize, Pacific Div., A.A.A.S. Author of more than 100 sci. papers. Address: Altadena CA Died Apr. 8, 1968; buried Mountain View Cemetery, Altadena CA

BABCOCK, LOUIS LOCKE, lawyer; b. Gowanda, N.Y., Dec. 14, 1868; s. Horace and Mary (Locke) B.; ed. Briggs Classical Sch., Buffalo, N.Y.; m. Georgia Woodin, June 18, 1896; children—Frances, John Carlton, Harriet, James Locke. Admitted to N.Y. bar, 1890, and began practice at Buffalo; formerly mem. firm Babcock, Hollister, Newbury & Russ, Buffalo; now counsel Hodgson, Russ, Andrews, Woods, & Goodyear. Enlisted as pvt. N.G. N.Y., 1890; served as capt. N.Y. Vol. Inf., Spanish-Am. War, May-Nov. 1898; brig. gen. N.Y.G., 1917-19. Mem. council and atty. for U. of Buffalo; dir. Buffalo Hist. Soc.; dir. Soc. of Natural Sciences. Mem. N.Y. State Bar Assn., Am. Bar Assn., Am. Law Inst., Soc. of Internat. Law, Newcomen Soc. Republican. Presbyn. Clubs: Buffalo, Saturn, Thursday. Author: The War of 1812 on the Niagara Frontier, 1927; The Tarpon, 4th edit., 1936; The Siege of Fort Erie; Manual of Riot Duty for N.Y. Guard, 1918. Home: 726 Delaware Av. Office: M. & T. Bldg. Buffalo NY‡

BABCOCK, WILLIAM WAYNE, surgeon; b. E. Worcester, Otsego County, N.Y., June 10, 1872; s. William Wayne and Sarah Jane (Butler) B.; grad. Binghamton (N.Y.) High Sch.; M.D., Coll. Physicians and Surgeons, Baltimore, 1893; studied summer sch., Harvard, 1893; M.D., Sch. of Medicine, U. of Pa., 1895; M.D., Medico-Chirurg. Coll., Phila., 1900; hon. A.M., Pa. Coll., Gettysburg, 1904; LL.D., Temple U., 1932; D.Sc., Ursinus Coll. 1944; L.H.D. Villenova, 1947; Med. Alumni Award, D.Sc., U. of Md., 1948; m. Marion C. Watters, May 14, 1918; children—Jane Butler, Catherine, Bonnie, William Wayne 3d (deceased). Resident physician St. Mark's Hosp., Salt Lake City, 1893-94, tng., Phila., 1895-1903; prof. gynecology Temple Coll., 1903, prof. surgery, clin. surgery, 1903-44, now emeritus; prof. oral surgery Phila. Dental Coll., 1907-08; surgeon to Temple U., cons. Phila. Gen. hosps., Phila. Has conducted researches leading to improved methods in surgery and invented a number of surg. instruments. Commd. capt., Med. Res. Corps, May 9, 1917; entered service Camp Greenleaf, Ga.; regtl. surgeon 318th F.A., Camp Jackson, August 1917; surg. chief, General Hospital No. 6, Fort McPherson, Georgia, September 1917-September 1919; commd. major, November 1917; lt. colonel, June 1918. Fellow Am. Coll. Surgeons, A.A.A.S; asso. mem. Academie de Chirurgie of France; hon. mem. Royal Soc. of Medicine (proctology), England; mem. A.M.A., Am. Therapeutic Soc. (pres. 1917-18), Pathol. Soc. Phila., Am. Assn. Obstetricians, Gynecologists and Abdominal Surgeons (pres. 1933-34), Internat. Coll. Surgeons, Am. Bd. Surgery, Societe des chirurgiens de Paris, Nat. Soc. Surgeons of Cuba, Phi Chi. Mason. Episcopalian. Clubs: Union League, Rotary. Home: 11 St. Asaph's Rd., Bala-Cynwyd, Pa. Office: 3401 N. Broad St., Philadelphia‡

BABER, GEORGE W., bishop; b. Cleve., Aug. 29, 1898; s. William B. and Effie (Griffen) B.; D.D. (hon.), Wilberforce U., also LL.D., and D.Humanities; B.D., Payne Sem.; m. E. Mayfield; children—June-Flora, Wilbur, Benjamin, Dawn. Ordained to ministry A.M.E. Ch.; bishop 2d Episcopal Dist. Del. World Council Chs., also mem. com. laity; bd. dirs. Nat. Council Chs. Dir. Home Fed. Sav. and Loan Assn., Detroit. Mem. Pres.'s Com. on Community Relations. Home: Philadelphia PA Died June 1970.

BABIN, VICTOR, pianist, composer; b. Moscow, Russia, Dec. 13, 1908; s. Heinrich and Rosalie (Wolk) B.; student State Conservatory, Riga, Latvia, 1921-27, Berliner Hochschule fur Musik, Berlin, Germany, 1928-31; A.F.D., U. N.M., 1961; m. Vitya Vronsky, Aug. 31, 1933. Came to U.S., 1937, naturalized, 1944. Appeared on concert stage, Europe, 1928-37; Am. debut as two-piano team with Vitya Vronsky, N.Y.C., 1937; transcontinental concert tour Am., 1937-73; soloist symphony orchs., appeared radio and TV; mem. Aspen (Colo.) Festival, 1949-73, dir. Aspen Inst. Music, 1952-54; mem. Festival Quartet (with Goldberg, Primrose, Graudan), 1956-62; dir. Cleve. Inst. Music, 1961-73; chmn. Tanglewood Inst. Berkshire Music Center, Lenox, Mass., 1965-67. Served with AUS, World War II. Recipient Cleve. Creative Arts award, 1966. Mem. Am. Guild Musical Artists, A.S.C.A.P., Pi Kappa Lambda. Composer: String Quartet, Piano Trio, Song Cycle Beloved Stranger" to lyrics by Witter Bynner; Sonata for Cello and piano; Konzertstuck for violin and orch.; Two Concerti for two pianos and orch.; Six Bach Sonatas and Stravinsky's Petrouchka Suite transcribed for 2 pianos; Three Concertos da Camera. Home: Shaker Heights OH Died Apr. 1973.

BABSON, PAUL TALBOT, corporation executive; born at Seward, Nebraska, November 22, 1894; s. Gustavus and Selma Glen (Talbot) B.; B.S. in Business Adminstrn., U. Neb., 1917; L.H.D., Boston U., 1956; LL.D., Springfield Coll., 1959; m. Edith Yungblut, Feb. 26, 1919; 1 son, Donald P. Prodn. engr., asst. mgr. John A. Colby & Sons, Chgo., 1919-23; v.p. Babson Park Co., 1923-24; pres. United Business Service, 1924-62; president of Gulf and Bay Corporation, Sarasota, Florida, 330 Beacon Street Corporation; chmn. Boston, Worcester & N.Y. St. Ry. Co.; chmn. bd. Standard & Poor's Corp.; dir. Wellesley Nat. Bank. Served in U.S. Army Aviation Service, June 1917-Dec. 1918. Dir. Newton-Wellesley Hosp.; mem. board directors. Boston Y.M.C.A.; chmn. International Committee Y.M.C.A. Received Distinguished Service Award from U. Neb., 1941; Lay-Churchman of the Year, 1956, by Washington Pilgrimage. Mem. Alpha Kappa Psi. Rep. Conglist. Clubs: Algonquin (Boston). Writer since 1931 of weekly editorials (under name of Paul Talbot) entitled, The Back Yard." Address: Boston MA Died Feb. 13, 1972; inurned Newton (Mass.) Columbarium.

BACCALONI, SALVATORE, basso; b. Rome, Italy, Apr. 14, 1900; s. Joaquin and Ferminia (Desideri) B.; grad. as architect, Inst. Belle Arti, Rome, Italy; L.H.D. (hon.), Wagner Coll.; Cross and Crescent Award Seton Hall U.; m. Elena Sviiarova, Nov. 17, 1928. Debut in Adriano Theatre. Rome, 1921; appeared in operas at Bologna, Palermo, Milan, Rome, London, Buenos Aires, San Francisco, Chicago, Berlin and Berne; sang 170 roles in 5 languages; sang at La Scala, Milan, 13 years, Colon, Buenos Aires, 11 years, 1st motion picture for Columbia, Full of Life. Decorated Knight, Crown of Italy, 1934. Clubs: New York Athletic, Lotos. Home: Sea Cliff LI NY Died Dec. 31, 1969.

BACH, RALPH EDWARD, publisher; b. Orange, N.J., Jan. 26, 1903; s. Edward John and Minnie (Clarke) B.; B.S., N.Y.U., 1925; m. Henrietta Steenman, July 3, 1926; children—Ralph E., Peter H. Analyst trust dept. Bankers Trust Co., N.Y.C., 1925-28; asst. mgr. trust dept. Bank of Am., 1928-29; financial writer Financial World, pub. by Guenther Pub. Corp., 1929-33, research editor, 1933-40, v.p., 1941-49, exec. v.p., 1949-55, pres., 1955-73, also pub. and dir. Mem. arbitration panel Am. Stock Exchange. Mem. N.Y. C. of C., Psi Upsilon. Clubs: Maplewood (N.J.) Country; Whitehall (N.Y.C.). Home: Short Hills NJ Died Jan. 26, 1973.

BACHARACH, ERIC WILLIAM, civil and sanitary engr., contractor; b. Cincinnati, O., June 14, 1883; s. Hugo and Hattie Louise (Karrmann) B.; student U. of Cincinnati, Engring. Coll., 1902-03 inclusive; U. of Mich., 1904-05, B.Sc. in Engineering (as of class of 1906), 1943; m. Lora Mary Hersey, July 15, 1911. With Pittsburgh Filter & Engring. Co., 1905-22, advancing to western mgr. and 1st v.p., in charge co.'s business west of Mississippi River; sole proprietor of E. W. Bacharach & Co., Kansas City, Mo., since 1922, pres. E. W. Bacharach, Inc. of Kansas City, Mo., 1948, chmn. bd., ret. 1960, now consultant, member board of directors; pioneer in introduction of modern methods of water purification; designed and installed plants for more than 800 towns, cities and indsl. concerns, and with others, for over 500 towns and cities, also has built many such plants for U.S. Govt. in connection with war projects. Inventor of chemical feeding machines and other devices used in connection with water purification plants used throughout the world. Received Modern Pioneer Award for achievements in sci., 1940; named hon. citizen Bacharach, Germany, 1956. Mem. bd. dirs., Juvenile Improvement Club; adv. bd. Salvation Army, Nat., Mo. socs. profl. engrs., Am. Soc. C.E., Am. Soc. Mil. Engrs., Starlight Theatre Assn. (dir.), Am. Water Works Assn., Kansas City Art Inst. Episcopalian. Clubs: Carriage, By-Line, Engineers (chmn. bd. dirs., 1925-26, 1928-29 and 1933-34), Kansas City, Rotary, Univ. of Mich. Home: Kansas City MO Died 1965.

BACHE, HAROLD L., corporation executive; b. N.Y.C., June 17, 1894; s. Leopold S. and Hattie (Stein) B.; student Ethical Culture Sch., N.Y.C., to 1910, Gunnery Sch., Washington, Conn., 1910-12, Cornell U., 1912-14; m. Alice Kay Bache. Asso. with J. S. Bache & Co., N.Y.C., excepting few assignments with affiliated cos., became partner, 1926, firm incorporated, 1945; pres., chmn. bd. Bache & Co., Inc., 1945-68; former officer several produce exchanges, firm mem. nat. and fgn. bds. of trade and produce exchanges. Dir. Far-East Am. Council, Japan Fund, Japan Soc., N.Y.C. Youth Bd., Queens Boys Club: trustee The Gunnery School, Museum of the American Indian, Jewish Federation, Cornell University. Served from pvt. to capt. U.S. Army, 1917-18; lt. col. Res. Mem. Commerce and Industry Assn. of N.Y. Inc. (dir.), N.Y. Bd. Trade, C. of C. N.Y. Clubs: Westchester Country; Cornell, Wall New York City NY Died Mar. 15, 1968; buried Salem Fields Cemetery, NY

BACHMAN, ALLAN EARNSHAW, assn. exec.; b. Pittsfield, Mass., Nov. 14, 1908; s. Eugene William and Annie (Earnshaw) B.; student Culver Mil. Acad., 1923-25; B.S., Princeton, 1929; m. Clarice Leslie Taylor, Nov. 26, 1929; children—Allan Earnshaw, Leigh (Mrs. Robert Read), Eugene William; married 2d, Florence Rhodes Drew, April 28, 1952; one daughter, Drewde Rhodes. With National Better Business Bureau, New York City, 1929-70, manager of financial dept., 1935-41, dir. div. solicitations, 1941-43, dir. bus. relations, 1943-46, editor, 1948-50, v.p., 1951, exec. v.p., 1952-70; exec. asst. to pres. Assn. Better Bus. Burs., 1947. Industry adv. com. Fed. Housing Adminstrn., 1957-61. Director North Conway Institute, 1964-70. Repulbican. Episcopalian (vestry). Club: Advt. (N.Y.); Cannon (Princeton, N.J.). Author: AGuide to National Advertising, 1939; Do's and Don'ts in Stamford CT Died Mar. 22, 1970; buried Woodland Cemetery, Stamford CT

BACHMAN, ROBERT ABRAHAM, engineer; b. Catasauqua, Pa., May 4, 1872; s. Edwin I. and Priscilla (Stewart) B.; pub. sch. education. Machinist and toolmaker; Bethlehem Iron Works, Pa., to 1891; engr. in charge constrn. of Allentown Consolidated Steel & Wire Works, 1891-8; elec. engr. and contractor, 1898-01; gen. supt. of labs. of Thomas A. Edison, 1901-11; v.p. and gen. mgr. Edison Storage Battery Co., Orange & Edison Chemical Works, Silver Lake, N.J., to date; also v.p., and gen. mgr. Lansden Co., Newark, N.J., 1912-14; mng. dir. Clark Process Corpn., E. Orange, N.J., and pres. Elec. Rectifier Co., E. Orange, Corpn. of Industrial Engrs., Steel Reenforcement Corpn. Mem. Am. Soc. Mech. Engrs., Soc. Automotive Engrs. Mason (32 deg.), and mem. various other orgns. Home: 145 N. Arlington Av., East Orange, N.J. Office: 51st floor Woolworth Bldg., New York NY‡

BACHMANN, RAPHAEL OTTO, univ. dean; b. Granville, Ia., Jan. 28, 1921; s. Joseph Franz and Eleanor Elizabeth (Bunkers) B.; B.S., Creighton U., 1942; Ph.D. (fellow Am. Found. Pharm. Edn. 1947-49), Purdue U., 1950; m. Mary Eleanor Mather, June 12, 1948; children—Linda Ann, Carolyn Sue, Richard Allen. Grad. asst. Purdue U., 1942-44, asst. prof. pharm. chemistry, 1949-51, asso. prof., 1951-54; prof. pharm. chemistry U. Ark., 1954-61; dean, prof. Sch. Pharmacy, W.Va. U., Morgantown, 1961-72. Mem. pharmacy rev. com. Bur. Health Manpower, Dept. Health, Edn. and Welfare. Bd. dirs. Am. Found. for Pharm. Edn. Served to lt. USNR, 1944-46. Recipient Lehn & Fink medal, 1942. Mem. Am. Pharm. Assn., Am. Assn. Colls. Pharmacy (chmn. chem. tchrs. sect. 1955-56, pres. 1969-70), Am. Chem. Soc., Am. Acad. Pharm. Sci., W.Va. Pharm. Assn. (dir.), Am. Inst. History Pharmacy (W.Va. rep.), A.A.A.S., Iowa, Monongalia County, Pulaski County (v.p.) Pharm. assns., Am. Coll. Apothecaries, Am. Soc. Pharmacognosy, U.S. Pharm. Conv., Am. Bd. Diplomates in Pharmacy (charter, regional dir.), Nat. Drug Trade Conf. (del.), Am. Acad. Social and Polit. Sci., W.Va. Acad. Sci., Morgantown C. of C., Sigma Xi, Rho Chi, Kappa Psi, Phi Sigma Kappa, Phi Lambda Upsilon, Alpha Chi Sigma, Alpha Sigma Nu. Rotarian. Home: Morgantown WV Died Dec. 18, 1972; buried East Oak Grove Cemetery, Morgantown WV

BACK, GEORGE IRVING, army officer; b. Sioux City, Ia., Feb. 25, 1894; s. Aaron and Carline (Dorum) B.; A.B., Morningside Coll., 1921; grad. work, Yale, 1920-21; m. Rosalie Henry Rives, Nov. 26, 1927. Commd. 2d lt., Signal Corps, U.S. Army, 1917, and advanced through the grades to brig. gen., 1945; student, communications engring., Yale, 1920-21; asst. dept. signal officer, Hawaiian Dept., 1922-24; chief, wire communications engring. section, Office Chief Signal Officer, Washington, 1924-29, Signal Corps Laboratories, 1929-33; student Signal Corps Sch., 1933-34; chief, Army Communications Service, 1934-38; student Command and Gen. Staff Sch., 1938-39; sec. Signal Corps Bd., 1939-41; chief communications div. signal section, G.H.Q., 1941-42; exec. officer, engring. and supply service, Office Chief Signal Officer, 1942-43, dir. distribution div., 1943-44; chief signal officer Mediterranean Theatre of Operations from 1944; chief Army Communications Service 1945-46; Signal Officer G.H.Q., F.E.C. and chief Civil Communications Sect., S.C.A.P. from 1947. Awarded Distinguished Service Medal, Legion of Merit (U.S.), Commander of British Empire (Gt. Britain), Grand Official and Order of Crown (Italy), Brazilian War Medal. Home: St Petersburg FL Died Sept. 1972.

BACKHAUS, WILHELM, pianist; b. Leipzig, Mar. 26, 1884; s. Guido and Clara (Schoenberg) B.; student Leipzig Conservatory under Alois Reckendorf, also Frankfort-am-Main under Eugen D'Albert; m. Alma Herzberg. Prof. piano Royal Coll. Music, Manchester, 1905; concert tours throughout Europe, U.S., Australia, New Zealand, Japan, South Am. Recipient Rubinstein prize in Paris, 1905. Address: Lugano Switzerland Died July 5, 1969.

BACKSTRAND, CLIFFORD J., business exec.; b. Los Angeles, Calif., July 21, 1897; s. John Ferdinand and Christine (Scott) B.; A.B., Pomona Coll., 1920, LL.D., 1954; B.S. in Econs., U. 1921; LL.D. (hon.), Elizabethtown (Pa.) Coll., 1952, Bucknell U., 1963; D.C.S. (hon.), Franklin and Marshall Coll., 1952; m. Virginia Parks Biggers, Sept. 8, 1939; 1 dau. by previous marriage, Barbara (Mrs. Paul Little); 1 stepdau., Virginia (Mrs. Richard H. Witmer). With Armstrong Cork Co., 1921-68, dir., 1935-68, v.p., 1938-50, pres., 1950-62, chmn. bd., 1962-68; dir. Bell Telephone Co., Pa. Trustee Lancaster YMCA, 1959-68; bd. govs. Am. Swedish Hist. Found., Phila., 1966-68; dir. Freedoms Found. at Valley Forge, 1961-68; trustee U. Pa., 1954-64, mem. bd. bus. edn., 1954-68; trustee Found. for Independent Colls. (Pa.), 1961-68; dir.-at-large Jr. Achievement, Inc., 1957-68; dir. Bus.-Industry Polit. Action Com., 1963-68. Served with O.T.C., Plattsburgh, N.Y., and Camp Pike, Ark., 1918. Head of linoleum unit, floor covering and upholstery sect., textile br. W.P.B., 1942. Dir. Lancaster (Pa.) Free Public Library Bd. Mem. Nat. Indsl. Conf. Bd. (sr. N.A.M. dir. 1959-66, div. v.p. 1963-66), Pa. Soc., Phi Gamma Delta, Phi Beta Kappa. Republican. Episcopalian. Mason. Clubs: Lancaster Country, Hamilton, University (Lancaster); Oysters Harbor (Cape Cod). Home: Lancaster PA Died Oct. 3, 1968; buried Greenwood Cemetery, Lancaster, PA

BACON, GEORGE MORGAN, civil engr.; b. Worcester, Mass., Mar. 28, 1872; s. George Andrew and Susan Lyman (Hillman) B.; grad. high sch., Syracuse, N.Y., 1889; B.S. in C.E., Cornell U., 1893; studied Hanover (Germany) Polytechnic, 1894; m. Isabel Gerry Dame, Feb. 5, 1898; children—Isabel Lyman (Mrs. Phillip Fox LaFollette), Dorothy York (Mrs. Lauchlin Bernard Currie), Lois Bigelow, Barbara Dame (Mrs. Philip Swain McConnell), Priscilla (Mrs. F. C. Gans). Constrn. of Boston Subway, 1894-98, Cripple Creek (Colo.) Short Line Ry., 1900; private practice, Salt Lake City, Utah, 1902-24, operating in 5 states; state engr. of Utah, 1925-33. Mem. Am. Soc. C.E., Utah Soc. Engr. (pres. 1916), Engring. Council of Utah (pres. 1925, 29), Soc. for Promotion Engring. Edn. Democrat. Episcopalian. Mason. Club: Alta (Salt Lake City). Author: Seven Poems, 1912; Seven Sonnets, 1913. Home: Salt Lake City UT‡

BACON, JOHN HARWOOD, author; b. Portland, Me., Nov. 6, 1875; s. H. E. and Jennie (George) B.; grad. La Crosse (Wis.) High Sch., 1893, Univ. of Wis., 1897; unmarried. Was pvt. Co. M, 3d Wis. Regt., during Spanish-Am. War, serving through Porto Rican campaign. Vice-consul-gen. of U.S. at Hong Kong, China, 1901-3. Mem. Wis. Soc. S.A.R., Wis. Alpha of Phi Delta Theta. Club: Milwaukee Press. Author: The Pursuit of Phyllis, 1904 H4. Contbr. short stories to mags. Residence: 304 W. 56th St. Office: 868 Carnegie Hall NY‡

BACON, JOSEPHINE DODGE DASKAM, author; b. Stamford, Conn., Feb. 17, 1876; d. H. Sawyer and Anne (Loring) Daskam; A.B., Smith Coll., 1898; m. Selden Bacon, July 25, 1903; children—Anne, Deborah, Selden Daskam. Mem. Nat. Speakers' and Writers' Bur., Civilian Defense Volunteer Offices; writer of War Loan Slogans and special articles for Writers' War Bd.; broadcasting for salvage campaigns and recruiting, 1941-44. Collect, curator, mus. of celebrities, Onteora Club. Member Girl Scout National Executive Board, 1914-24. Author: Smith College Stories, 1900; Sister's Vocation and Other Girls' Stories, 1900; The Imp and the Angel, 1901; Fables for the Fair, 1901; The Madness of Philip, 1902; Whom the Gods Destroyed, 1902; Middle Aged Love Stories, 1903; Poems, 1903; Memoirs of a Baby, 1904; Her Fiance, 1904; The Domestic Adventurers, 1907; Ten to Seventeen, 1908; An Idyll of All Fools' Day, 1908; In the Border Country, 1909; Biography of aBoy, 1910; While Caroline Was Growing, 1911; Margarita's Soul (pseudonym Ingraham Lovell"), 1909; The Inheritance, 1912; The Strange Cases of Dr. Stanchon, 1913; The Luck o' Lady Joan, 1913; To-Day's Daughter, 1914; Open Market, 1915. Compiled: Best Nonsense Verse, 1901; On Our Hill, 1918; Square Peggy, 1919; Blind Cupid, 1923; Truth O' Women, 1923; Medusa's Head, 1926; Counterpoint, 1927; Luck of Lowry, 1931; The Girl in the Window, 1932; Kathy, 1933; The Room on the Roof, 1934; Cassie-on-the-Job, 1936; The House by the Road, 1937; The Root and the Flower, 1939; The Door in the Closet, 1940; The World in His Heart, 1941. Winner of the League of Nations prize, with Hymn for the Nations." 1935. Compiler Girl Scout National Hand Book, 1920. Contbr. to mags. Home: 333 E 68th St.. New York NY‡

BACON, MARY SCHELL HOKE (DOLORES MARBOURG"), author; b. at Atchison, Kan., Nov. 20, 1870; d. Jacob Schell and Amma (Carter) Hoke; ed. under direction of maternal grandmother; studied music in New York and afterward in France; m. Charles E. Bacon, of Essex, N.Y., Oct. 1, 1898. Became mem. Frank Mayos theatrical co., 1886; left stage, 1887; spl. corr. New York Worlds in Europe, 1889, returned to France on professional missions, 1891-2, and 1897-8; spl. writer for Sunday Times, New York, 1901-2. Author: Ill Ne'er Consent, 1888; Juggernaut, (with George Gary Eggleston, q.v.), 1891; The Soul of a Woman, 1897; The Diary of a Musician, 1904; A King's Divinity; Crumbs and His Times; Old New England Churches; Songs Every Child Should Know; Hymns Every Child Should Know; Operas Every Child Should Know, 1906; Pictures Every Child Should Know, 1908. Plays (produced): Juggernaut; The End of the Century; Dead Heroes and Live Ones. Contbr. to mags.*‡

BACON, ROBERT STILLWELL, banker; b. Mobile, Ala., Apr. 8, 1907; s. Robert Stillwell and Venetia (Danner) B.; B.S., Washington & Lee U., 1929; m. Susanne Robinson, June 21, 1957; children—Perrin (Mrs. William E. Drew), Robert Stillwell, Richard Lee. Pres. First Nat. Bank, Mobile, 1967-73, also dir.; dir. Lerio Corp., Ala. D.D.&B. Co. Bd. dirs., chmn. drive Mobile Community Chest, 1943. Mem. Mobile C. of C. (dir.). Clubs: Mobile Country, Athelstan (Mobile); Lakewood Country (Point Clear, Ala.); Isle Dauphine (Dauphin Island, Ala.). Home: Mobile AL Died May 1973.

BADGER, PHILIP OWEN, coll. prof.; b. Augusta, Me., Sept. 16, 1891; s. Joseph Emery and Eliza Bradbury (Morrill) B.; student Phillips Exeter Academy, 1909-11; B.A., Yale University, 1915; LL.D., Temple Univ., 1947; married Herberta Torrey, Sept. 9, 1915; children—Philip Owen, Edward Torrey, Joseph Emery. Instr. business English, New York U., 1915-19, asst. prof., 1919-20, asso. prof. marketing, 1920-21, professor, 1922-53, professor emeritus, 1953-73, dir. day div. Sch. Commerce, Accounts and Finance, 1920-26, dir. Coll. Commerce Course, Univ. College of Arts and Pure Science, 1922-26, asst. to chancellor, 1926-52; chmn. Bd. of Athletic Control N.Y.U., 1930-48; bd. dirs. Gallatin House. Exec. dir. N.Y.U.-Bellevue Med. Center Fund, 1945-51. Mem. exec. com. Nat. Collegiate Athletic Assn., 1934-44; dist. v.p., 1937-39, pres., 1941-44. Assistant mgr. personnel div., subsequently asst. to gen. mgr. Gas Defense Plant, U.S. Army, Long Island City, N.Y., during World War I; co-chmn. Panel on Athletics of Joint Army and Navy Committee on Welfare and Recreation; mem. National Council on Physical Fitness of Federal Security Agency; mem. Civilian Advisory Committee of Physical Training Section of U.S. Navy, World War II. Member Am. Marketing Assn., Sportsmanship Brotherhood, Beta Theta Pi, Alpha Kappa Psi, Delta Sigma Rho, Beta Gamma Sigma, Alpha Delta Sigma, Alpha Phi Sigma, also the Sphinx Society. Congregationalist. Address: Denver CO Died Feb. 10, 1973.

BADGLEY, MAXWELL FORREST, lawyer; b. Jackson, Mich., Dec. 9, 1898; s. Forrest C. and Ann V. (Beers) B.; LL.B., U. Mich., 1923; student U. Chgo., 1919-20; J.D. (hon.), Detroit College of Law; m. Irene Reed, Feb. 4, 1924 (div. 1932); 1 son, Reed Maxwell; m. 2d, Helen Robson Haynes, Sept. 25, 1947. Admitted to Mich. bar, 1923, practiced in Jackson; partner firm McKone, Badgley, Domke & Kline, and predecessors, sr. partner Badgley, Domke, McVicker & Marcoux; lectr. insts. advocacy U. Mich., from 1952. Dir. City Bank & Trust Co. N.A., Nat. Casualty Company. Has served as secretary of Michigan Supreme Ct. Com. Jury Instructions, 1962-68; mem. nat. com. Law Sch. Fund, U. Mich., 1962-63. Hon. bd. dirs. Jackson Meml. Camp for Children. Served with USNR, World War I. Fellow Am. Bar Found., Am. Coll. Trial Lawyers, Internat. Acad. Trial Lawyers Internat. Soc. Barristers (gov. 1965-69); life mem. 6th Jud. Circuit Jud. Conf.; mem.

Am. (ho. dels. 1964-69), Jackson (pres. 1942) bar assns., State Bar Mich. (commr. 1956-62, pres. 1963), (co-chmn. com. revision criminal code), The American Judicature Society, also member Federation of Insurance Counsel, Nat. Assn. R.R. Trial Counsel, Am. Legion, 40 and 8 (grande advocat passe Mich. 1942), Beta Theta Pi, Phi Delta Phi. Clubs: Jackson Country (past dir.), Town (Jackson). Home: Jackson MI Died May 7, 1969; buried Woodland Cemetery, Jackson MI

BAEHR, WILLIAM FREDERICK OTTO, librarian; b. at Dorchester, Wisconsin on September 12, 1899; son of Otto and Louise (Theel) Baehr; student Concordia College, Milwaukee, 1913-19, Concordia Sem., St. Louis, 1919-24; B.L.S., U. Ill., 1927, M.A., 1930; fellow grad. library sch. U. Chgo., 1930-33; m. Edith Moecker, Aug. 24, 1927; children—William Frederick Moecker, David Jonathan Arthur, Nancy Miriam Edith, Sandra Elizabeth, Gratia Linnea. Acting librarian Concordia Sem., 1924-26; asst. library order dept. U. Ill., 1927-29, asst. loan dept., 1929-30; librarian Augustana Coll. and Theol. Sem., Rock Island, Ill., 1933-43; dir. Kan. State U. Library, 1943-59, gen. asst., 1960-64, reference librarian, 1956-70. Mem. Manhattan Bd. Edn., 1955-63; commr. Manhattan Housing Authority, 1970-72. Bd. dirs. Riley County Meml. Hosp., 1969-72. Mem. Concordia Hist. Inst., A.L.A., Ill. (pres. 1938), Kan. (pres. 1948), Mountain Plains library assns., Faculty Wranglers (pres. 1968-71), Pi Kappa Delta, Phi Kappa Phi, Beta Sigma Psi, Beta Phi Mu, Phi Alpha Theta. Republican. Lutheran. Kiwanian. Home: Manhattan KS Died Apr. 24, 1972; buried Sunset Cemetery, Manhattan KS

BAENSCH, WILLY E., physician; b. Magdeburg, Germany, 1893; M.D., Halle (Germany) U., 1910. Intern surg., med. and univ. clinics Halle U., 1914-19; clin. tng. Curie Inst., Paris, France, Radiumhemmed, Stockholm, Sweden, 1926, also Central Roentgen Inst., Vienna Austria, 1926; dir. radiology and cancer research, prof. radiology Leipzig U., 1926-45; dir. dept. roentgenology Georgetown U., Washington, also prof., 1947-72, chmn. dept. radiology; sr. cons. VA, Washington. Recipient Gold medal Georgetown U., 1967. Diplomate Am. Bd. Radiology. Hon. mem. German Roentgen Soc. (Rieder medal 1969). Address: Bethesda MD Died Nov. 1, 1972; buried Woodstock NY

BAER, JOHN M(ILLER), cartoonist; b. Blackcreek, Wis., Mar. 29, 1886; s. John Mason and Libbie Caroline (Riley) B.; A.B., Lawrence Univ., Appleton, Wis., 1909; student Federal Sch. of Art, Minneapolis, and Nat. Art Sch., Washington, D.C.; m. Estelle G. Kennedy, Dec. 28, 1910; children—John Mason, Alfred Sherman, Byron. Civil engring., 1904-10; engring. and cartooning, 1910-14; mem. 65th and 66th Congresses (1917-21), 1st N.D. Dist.; cartoonist for Labor (publ. ry. unions) from 1921; publicity dir. Union Label Trades Dept., Am. Fed. of Labor; mem. adv. bd. labor edn., Nutrition and Food Conservation Br., Food Distbn. Adminstrn., U.S. Dept. Agr. Recipient 1st award for best cartoon Internat. Labor Press Assn., 1963. Mem. Beta Sigma Phi. Democrat. Conglist. Club: National Press. Home: Chevy Chase MD Died Feb. 18, 1969; buried Washington DC

BAERWALD, PAUL, banker; b. Frankfort-on-the-Main, Germany, Sept. 27, 1871; s. Herman (Ph.D.) and Selma (Frenkel) B.; ed. real schule, Frankfort-on-the-Main; m. Edith Jacobi, June 2, 1909; children—Pauline Frances, Herman Frederick, Jane, Florence. Came to U.S., 1896, naturalized citizen, 1901. With Speyer banking firms, Frankfort-on-the-Main, London, N.Y. City, 1886-1906; resident gen. partner Lazard Freres, N.Y. City, 1907-28, spl. partner, 1928-30; dir. Gen. Am. Investors Corp., Fidelity-Phenix Fire Ins. Co. (chmn. exec. com.), Fohs Oil Co.; chairman American Joint Distribution Com.; dir. Loeb Convalescent Home. Mem. Presidents Advisory Com. on Polit. Refugees. Republican. Jewish religion. Club: Harmonie. Home: 25 E. 86th St. Office: 44 Wall St. New York NY‡

BAGDATOPOULOS, WILLIAM SPENCER, artist; b. Zante, Greece, July 23, 1888; s. Anastasius John and Amy Frederica (Sheath) B.; ed. Dulwich, Eng., Acad. van Beeldende Kunsten, Rotterdam, 1903-06, Athens Acad., 1906-07; m. Caralisa N. Nichols, 1938. Came to U.S., 1928, naturalized U.S. citizen. Chief artist Times of India publs., 1910-50; devel. advt. standards in India, affecting market for English and Am. goods; exhibited works Arlington Gallery, London, 1927, Kleeman Gallery, N.Y.C., 1928, Nat. Gallery, Washington, 1929, 30, 37, New Delhi, 1929, Los Angeles, 1931; rep. permanent collections Brit. Mus., London, Boyman's Mus., Rotterdam, Municipal Art Gallery, Amsterdam, Nat. Gallery Art, Washington, Nat. Pinakotec, Athens, Library Congress, Washington. Recipient bronze and silver medals South Kensington, London, 1913. Served with South African regt., British Army, World War I. Fellow Royal Soc. Arts, Imperial Art League (London); mem. Chgo. Soc. Etchers. Clubs: Column, London Sketch (London). Inventor folding boat puzzles. Home: San Francisco CA Died Dec. 22, 1965.

BAGG, RUFUS MATHER, college prof.; b. at W. Springfield, Mass., Apr. 19, 1869; s. Rufus Mather and Mary E. (Bartholomew) B.; A.B., Amherst, 1891; Ph.D., Johns Hopkins, 1895; m. Grace Raybold, of W. Springfield, Mass., Apr. 8, 1896. Prin. high sch., Lubec, Me., 1891-2; instr. geology and mineralogy, Worcester Summer Sch. for Boys, 1891-2; asst. in geology, Johns Hopkins, 1895-7; asst. N.Y. State Mus., winter of 1897; prof. geology, Colo. Coll., 1898-9; instr. in science, Colo. Springs High Sch., 1899-1900; sub-master Brockton High Sch., 1901-3; prof. mineralogy and petrography, N.M. Sch. of Mines, 1903-4; instr. geology, U. of Ill., 1907-11; prof. geology and mineralogy, Lawrence Coll., 1911-—. Hon. mineralogist to Paris Expn., 1900; lecturer on geology, Chautauqua of Mt. Lake Park, Md., Aug., 1900. Fellow A.A.A.S., Geol. Soc. of America; mem. Am. Inst. Mining Engrs., Geol. Soc. Washington, Nat. Geog. Soc., Ill. State Acad. Sciences, Paleontol. Soc. America, Sigma Xi (Ill. Chapter), Washington Acad. Sciences. Author of tech. articles and papers. Address: Appleton WI‡

BAGGS, WILLIAM CALHOUN, editor; b. Atlanta, Sept. 30, 1922; s. Crawford and Kate (Bush) B.; m. Joan Orr, July 7, 1945; children—Craig Calhoun, Robert Mahoney. Copy desk, Panama Star & Herald, Republic of Panama, 1941-42, Greensboro (N.C.) News, 1945-46; reporter Miami (Fla.) News, 1946-49, columnist, 1949-57, editor, 1957-69. U.S. observer at founding Caribbean Orgn., 1962. Dir., Fund for Republic. Served to lt. USAAF, 1942-45. Democrat. Episcopalian. Author: (with Harry S. Ashmore) Mission to Hanoi: AChronicle of Double-Dealing in High Places, 1968. Home: Coral Gables FL Died Jan. 7, 1969.

BAGLEY, CHARLES LELAND, lawyer; b. Tipton, Ia., Apr. 24, 1873; s. William H. and Mary (Leland) B.; LL.M., U. of Southern Calif., 1910; m. Gertrude Keller, Apr. 7, 1904. Admitted to Calif. bar, 1909, U.S. Supreme Court, 1933; practiced law, Los Angeles, Calif., since 1911; vice pres. Am. Federation of Musicians since 1931. Formerly a professional musician. Mason. Home: 2534 Seventh Av. Office: 408 S. Spring St., Los Angeles CA*‡

BAGSTAD, ANNA EMILIA, author; b. Yankton, S.D., Feb. 27, 1876; d. Matthias and Clara Zenobia (Lee) B.; student U. of Chicago, 1 yr.; A.B., Yankton (S.D.) Coll., 1905; studied at Emerson Coll. of Expression, Simmons Coll. and N.E. Conservatory, all of Boston; traveled abroad; hon. M.A. from Pacific University in 1924. Assistant in German and English, Yankton Coll., 1902-05; instr. Northland Coll., Ashland, Wis., 1905-10; teacher English and German, Northern Normal and Industrial Sch., Aberdeen, S.D., 1911-15; prof. French and Spanish, Pacific U., Forest Grove, Ore., 1915; teacher Spanish, State Normal Sch., Bellingham, Wash., 1919; prof. modern langs. and pub. speaking, Pacific U., 1919-27; instr. German and French, Pomona Coll., Claremont, Calif., 1927-—. Winner of state oratorical contest, Huron, S.D., 1903, and a week later of the interstate contest, at Fargo, N.D., with an oration on Goethe. Mem. Am. Assn. Univ. Women, hon. mem. Philomethean sorority. Republican. Protestant. Clubs: Woman's, Monday (Forest Grove); Women's (Claremont); Tourist (Aberdeen). Translator; The Romancers (from the French of Rostand, in verse), 1921; The Princess Far Away (from same, in verse), 1922; The Blockhead (from the German of Ludwig Fulda); Fanny's Consent (from the Spanish of Moratin). Contbr. to My Favorite Passage from Dante" (book), 1928, also to Text Book of South Dakota Poetry, 1928. Home: Claremont CA‡

BAGSTER-COLLINS, ELIJAH WILLIAM, college prof.; b. Pawtucket, R.I., Apr. 16, 1873; s. Henry and Elizabeth (Hollingworth) Collins; A.B., Brown, 1897; A.M., Columbia, 1898; studied Berlin, 1891-93, Leipzig, 1902-03; m. Edith Lilian Bagster, of London, Eng., 1897; children—Ashlyn H., Robert D., Jeremy F. Adj. prof. German, Teachers Coll. (Columbia), 1903, asso. prof., 1904-39; now retired. Mng. editor Modern Lang. Jour., 1916-19; mng. editor German Quarterly, 1927-37. Capt. U.S.A., Mil. Intelligence Div. Gen. Staff, 1918-19. Mem. Nat. Inst. Soc. Sciences, Modern Languages Assn. America, Am. Assn. Teachers of German (acting pres. 1927), Alpha Delta Phi, Phi Beta Kappa, Phi Delta Kappa. Author: Teaching of German in Secondary Schools, 1904; First Book in German, 1912; History of Modern Language Teaching in the United States, 1930. Editor: A First German Reader, 1925. Home: Montrose NY‡

BAILEY, ALBERT EDWARD, educator, author; b. N. Scituate, Mass., Mar. 11, 1871; s. Charles E. and Eudora (Turner) B.; A.B., magna cum laude, Harvard, 1894 (P.B.K.), A.M., 1916; m. Marion Breed Hall, of Cambridge, Mass., June 23, 1896; children—Lois (Mrs. F. Linden Naylor, Jr.), Morris Hall (dec.), Oriana (Mrs. Herbert H. Lank), Charles Edwd., Marion (Mrs. James E. Sparling, Jr.), Albert Edwd., Alden Herriott, Stephen Kemp. Instructor classics, 1894-96, master in English, 1896-1900, Worcester Acad.; owner and headmaster, Allen Sch., 1900-07; Oriental lecturer and sec. H. W. Dunning & Co., foreign tours, 1907-14; dir. religious edn., Worcester Acad., 1916-20; prof. interpretation of religious art, Boston U. Conglist. Author: On Nazareth Hill, 1916; Art Studies in the Life of Christ, 1917; Gospel in Art, 1917; History of the Hebrew Commonwealth, 1920; The Use of Art in Religious Education, 1921; Ednl. dir. with Temple Tours Co. Home: 21 Lake Av., Newton Center MA‡

BAILEY, ARTHUR SCOTT, author; b. St. Albans, Vt., Nov. 15, 1877; s. Winfield Scott and Harriet (Goodhue) B.; student U. of Vt., 1897-1900; A.B., Harvard, 1902; m. Estella Crampton Goodspeed, of St. Albans, Vt., Sept. 14, 1913. Lit. adviser, Duffield & Co., pubs., New York, 1904-09; book pub., New York, 1910-15. Mem. Sigma Phi. Republican. Unitarian. Author: Sleepy-Time Tales, 19 vols., 1916; Tuck-Me-In Tales, 15 vols., 1917; Slumber-Town Tales, 9 vols., 1921. Contbr. to mags. Home: 164 Watchung Av., Montclair NJ‡

BAILEY, CALVIN WESTON, ins. official; b. Newark, N.J., Jan. 20, 1861; s. George H. and Hannan M. (Ryder) B.; ed. Newark Acad.; m. Sara Armour, May 1, 1894; 1 son, Kenneth Armour (dec.). With Am. Ins. Co., of Newark (fire), 1876, becoming asst. sec., 1906, sec., 1909, v.p., 1914, pres., 1918-35, chmn. bd. since 1935; chmn. bd. Columbia Fire Ins. Co. (Dayton, O.), Bankers Indemnity Ins. Co., Dixie Ins. Co. (Greensboro, N.C.). Republican. Conglist. Club: Essex. Home: East Orange, N.J. Office: 15 Washington St., Newark NJ‡

BAILEY, CHARLES LANGDON, investment counselor; b. Fall River, Mass., Jan. 24, 1909; s. Joseph Wells and Edna (Stilson) B.; student New Bedford Inst. Tech.; m. Helene E. Pate, Nov. 28, 1935; 1 son, Charles Langdon. Statistician Hayden, Stone & Co., N.Y.C., 1929-30; asst. mgr. Booth Mfg. Co., New Bedford, Mass., 1931-34; rep. Babson's Reports, 1934-40, v.p., dir. 1940-53, v.p., dir. David L. Babson & Co., Inc., 1940-63; exec. v.p., dir. David L. Babson Mgmt. Corp., 1959-63 (all N.Y.C.); past pres. Aberdeen Mgmt. Corp., Aberdeen Fund, Income Estates of Am., Inc. (all N.Y.C.); later financial cons.; dir. Iiquois Industries, Inc., Precision Polymers, Inc. Mem. N.Y. Soc. Security Analysts. Conglist. Clubs: New Bedford Yacht; Long Ridge Tennis; Saint-Nom-La-Breteche. Home: Paris France also Stamford CT Died Jan. 1970.

BAILEY, JOHN HAYS, bacteriologist; b. Chicago, Ill., May 3, 1900; s. George Troy and Clara (Koch) B.; B.S., U. of Chicago, 1924; Ph.D., 1928; D.P.H., U. of Michigan, 1938; m. Gertrude Boyer, Apr. 20, 1939; children—Martha Deborah, John Hoyne. Research fellow, bacteriology, Nelson Morris Inst., Chicago, Ill., 1928-29; fellow, James Whitcomb Riley Hosp., Indianapolis, Ind., 1929-32; resident bacteriologist, Municipal Contagious Disease Hosp., Chicago, 1932-35; senior bacteriologist, Ill. Dept. Pub. Health, 1935-38, on leave Sept. 1937-June 1938; asst. prof. bacteriology, Sch. of Medicine, Loyola U., Chicago, 1938-41; research bacteriologist, Winthrop Chem Co., Rensselaer, N.Y., 1942-43, Chief, div. of bacteriology, 1943-45; chief division of bacteriology, Sterling-Winthrop Research Inst., from 1946. Mem. Am. Acad. Microbiology (gov. 1956-59, sec.-treas. 1956-58), Soc. Gen. Micro-biology (Eng.), N. Am. Lily Soc., Soc. Am. Bacteriologists (sec.-treas., 1953-57, treas., 1957-59), Chgo. Inst. Medicine, A.A.A.S., Am. Hort. Soc., Sigma Xi, Chi Psi. Club: Ferndale Rod and Gun (Chgo. and New Auburn, Wis.). Adv. editor: Jour. Bacteriology. Home: Castleton-on-Hudson NY Died May 1, 1968.

BAILEY, WILLIAM ARTHUR, newspaper pub., ret.; b. Baldwin, Kan., Mar. 6, 1884; s. Charles William and Mary Etta (Stark) B.; A.B., Baker U., 1905, LL.D., 1948; grad. work summers, U. of Kan., U. of Chicago; m. Myrtle Amela Thorne, Aug. 19, 1909; children—William Thorne, Elizabeth Jean. Principal high sch., Eureka, Kan., 1905-07; tchr. high sch., Wichita, Kan., 1907-09; prin. high. sch., Enid, Okla., 1909-13, Leavenworth, Kan, 1913-15; prin. Wyandotte High Sch., Kansas City, Kan., 1915-19; asst. cashier Exchange State Bank, Kansas City, Kan., 1919-20, dir.; editor, mgr. Kansas City Kansas, 1921-57, retired 1957. Dir. Bonds, Inc., Capper Publications, Inc., Topeka, Kan. Mem. bd. Bethany Hosp.; bd. trustees Baker U.; chmn. Kan. Com. Laymen and the Courts. Mem. Bd. of Publs. Meth. Information of Meth. Ch. Mem. Kan. Press. Assn. (past pres.), Inland Daily Press Assn., Kan., Kansas City (past pres.) chambers commerce, Delta Tau Delta, Phi Delta Kappa. Methodist. Mason (32 degree, Shriner). Clubs: Rotary (ex-pres.), Hi-Twelve, Milburn Golf and Country; Terrace. Home: Kansas City MO Died Aug. 23, 1968. Cremated.

BAILOR, EDWIN MAURICE, psychologist; b. Culbertson, Neb., May 13, 1890; s. John Martin and Harriet (Shellhammer) B.; student Simpson Coll. (Ia.), 1907-09; A.B., Washington State Coll., 1914, A.M., 1916; Ph.D., Teachers Coll. (Columbia), 1924; hon. A.M., Dartmouth, 1928; m. Jane Galt, Apr. 21, 1920. Teacher, prin. and supt. schs., Lewis County, Wash., 1909-13 and 1914-15; instr. Wash. State Coll., 1915-18; psychol. expert, civilian service, U.S. Army, 1919-21; training officer U.S. Vets Bur., 1921-23; asst. Teachers Coll. (Columbia), 1923-24, instr., 1924-25; asst. prof. psychology, Dartmouth, 1925-28, prof. 1928-58. Served as 2d lt. Psychol. Corps, U.S. Army, 1918-19. Mem.

A.A.A.S., Am. Psychol. Assn., Dartmouth Scientific Assn., Am. Assn. Univ. Profs., Howe Library Corp., Phi Delta Kappa, Kappa Delta Pi, Kappa Phi Kappa, Lambda Chi Alpha. Mason. Author: Developed Lessons in Psychology, 1929; also Content and Form in Tests of Intelligence, 1925, Contbr. to mags. Home: Hanover NH Died Feb. 16, 1970; buried Southview Cemetery, Canton GA

BAIN, EDGAR COLLINS, metallurgist; b. Marion County, O., Sept. 14, 1891; s. Milton H. and Alice Anne (Collins) B.; B.Sc., Ohio State U., 1912, M.Sc., 1916, Sc.D. (hon.), 1947; honorary Dr. Engring., Lehigh University 1936; married Helen Louise Cram, February 18, 1927; children—Alice Anne, David. Began as chemist United States Bureau Standards, 1914, instructor Univ. of Wis., 1916-17; chem. engr. B. F. Goodrich Co., 1917; physicist Nat. Lamp Co. (Gen. Electric Co.), 1918-23; research metallurgist Atlas Steel Co., 1923-24, Union Carbide & Carbon Research Lab., 1924-28; dir. phys. metall. research U.S. Steel Corp., 1928-35, asst. to v.p. research and tech., 1935-43, v.p., 1950-57, assistant exec. vice pres. of operations, 1956-57; vice-pres. in charge of research and technology, Carnegie Ill. Steel Corp., 1943-56; retired; consulting metallurgist, from 1957; Howe memorial lecturer, 1932; E. DeM. Campbell memorial lecturer, 1932. Schwab Meml. lectr., 1952, Andrew Carnegie lecturer, 1958. Served to first lieutenant U.S. Army, 1918. Awarded Robert W. Hunt medal for work on nonrusting steels, 1929; Henry Marion Howe medal, for work on hardening of steel, 1931; Am. Iron and Steel Inst. medal, 1934, for work on alloy steel; Benjamin Lamme medal, Ohio State U., for eminence in engring., 1937 Albert Sauveur Achievement Award, 1946; John Price Wetherill medal, Franklin Inst., 1949; Gold medal Am. Soc. Metals, 1949; Grande Medaille de la Societe Francaise de Metallurgie, 1952; Ambrose Monell medal, 1958; gold medal Japan Inst. Metals, 1964; Meiji Centennial award Order Sacred Treasure, Govt. of Japan, 1968. Fellow American Physics Society; member Iron and Steel Institute of Japan (hon.), Iron and Steel Institute Great Britain (honorary), National Academy Sci. (chmn. div. engring., industrial research), Am. Phys. Soc., Am. Inst. Mining and Metall. Engrs., Am. Soc. Metals (past nat. pres., dir., chmn. N.Y. sect.), Am. Soc. Testing Materials, Japan Inst. Metals (hon.). Clubs: Duquesne (Pitts.); Cosmos (Washington). Author: (with M. A. Grossmann) High Speed Steel, 1931; Functions of the Alloying Elements in Steel, 1939, rev. edit. (with H. W. Paxton), 1961; also numerous papers on steel metallurgy. Discovered steel constituent later named Bainite. Home: Sewickley PA Died Nov. 27, 1971; interred Marion OH

BAIN, FRED B., salt co. exec.; m. Florence Bain; children—Rudolph, Frederick. Hon. chmn. bd., Leslie Salt Co.; dir. Pacific Lighting Corp., Schilling Estate Co., James Dole Engring. Co.; mem. adv. com. Crocker Angio Nat. Bank. Home: San Francisco CA Died Nov. 19, 1968.

BAINES, EDWARD RICHARDS, business exec. b. Bklyn., Mar. 20, 1887; s. James Clarence and Lillian Mary (Rea) B.; student Comml. High Sch., Brooklyn, 1904; m. Ada Z. Vermilye, Mary 25, 1907 (dec.); 1 son, Robert Edward (dec.); m. 2d, Alice Horan Haley, Feb. 9, 1933. Asst. treas. Gen. Vehicle Co., Long Island City, N.Y., 1906-17; vice pres. and comptroller Underwood Corp., N.Y. City, 1919-47, v.p. finance and internat. operations, 1947-59. Served as maj., Motor Transport Corps, U.S. Army, 1917-19. Mem. Controllers Inst. America, Nat. Assn. Cost Accountants. Clubs: Wee Burn Country, National Republican. Home: Greenwich CT Died Jan. 24, 1969.

BAINES-MILLER, MINNIE WILLIS, author; b. Lebanon, N.H.; d. Horace F. and Minerva J. Willis; ed. common schools, Springfield, O.; (A.M., Wittenberg Coll.); m. Evan Franklin Baines, of Springfield, O., 1863; 2d, Leroy Edgar Miller, of Springfield, 1892. First sketch published in Waverly Magazine when 14 years old; writer of books, short and serial stories, poems, etc., for various papers and mags.; has lectured on temperance. Author: The Silent Land, 1890; His Cousin, the Doctor, 1891; The Pilgrim's Vision, 1891; Mrs. Cherry's Sister, 1909, etc. Address: Springfield OH‡

BAINTER, FAY OKELL, actress; b. Los Angeles, Dec. 7, 1893; d. Charles and Mary (Okell) Bainter; student Girls Collegiate Inst., 1904-07; m. Reginald S. H. Venable, June 8, 1921; 1 son, Reginald S. H. Actress, teacher, radio, TV, motion pictures; Broadway plays include Willow Tree, East is West, Jealousy, First Love, Admirable Crighton, Dream Girl, Dodsworth; motion pictures include White Banners, Maryland, Mrs. Wiggs, War Against Mrs. Hadley, Jezebel, (Acad. award for role Aunt Belle), The Children's Hour; TV appearances include Lux Video Theater, Studio One, U.S. Steel Hour, Robert Montgomery Presents; tour in play Long Days Journey Into Night. Served as entertainer hosp. tours. World War II. Address: Hollywood CA Died Apr. 17, 1968; buried Arlington Nat. Cemetery, Arlington WV

BAIRD, CORA, puppeteer; b. N.Y.C., Jan. 26, 1912; d. Morris and Anne (Burlar) Eisenberg; student Hunter Coll.; m. William Britton Baird, Jan. 13, 1937; children—Peter Britton, Laura Jenne. Appeared on stage with Eva Le Galleinne's Civic Repertory Theatre, Neighborhood Playhouse, Orson Welles prodns. for Dr. Faustus, 1937; full partner with husband in nightclubs, on TV, in films. Address: New York City NY Died Dec. 7, 1967; buried Abels Hill, Martha's Vineyard MA

BAIRD, LOUISE, aviation industry editor; b. Lebanon, Ky., Jan. 8, 1910; d. William Parcell and Ethel (Lewis) Baird; B.A., Ohio Wesleyan U., 1931. Reporter Daily Ind., Ashland, Ky., 1931-42, columnist 1936-42, soc. editor, 1931-42; pub. relations rep. Curtiss-Wright Corp., Columbus, O., 1942-50, editor plant weekly, 1943-50, pub. relations rep. N. Am. Aviation, Inc., 1950-68, editor plant weekly, 1950-68. Mem. Central Ohio Indsl. Editors Assn., Advt. Club (Woman of Year 1967), Columbus C. of C., Press Club, Theta Sigma Phi, Kappa Kappa Gamma. Episcopalian. Home: Columbus OH Died Aug. 10, 1968.

BAIRD, ROBERT W., investment banker; born Evanston, Ill., Apr. 1, 1883; s. Robert and Sarah (Heston) B.; A.B., Northwestern U., 1905; m. Ora Davenport, June 17, 1908. Partner Robert W. Baird & Co. (formerly) The Wisconsin Co., pres., 1922-60, ltd. partner, 1960-69; chmn. bd. Robert W. Baird & Co., Inc.; dir. Rex Chainbelt, Inc., Medford Corp., Roundy's, Inc. Mem. Phi Delta Theta, Phi Beta Kappa. Conglist. Clubs: Milwaukee, Wisconsin, University, Milwaukee Athletic, Rotary (Milwaukee); The Attic (Chicago). Home: Wauwatosa WI Died Mar. 12, 1969; buried Wisconsin Meml. Park.

BAITER, RICHARD ENGLIS, soap products mfr.; b. Short Hills, N.J., Dec. 11, 1913; s. Charles William Grevel and Madeleine (Englis) B.; A.B., Princeton, 1936; m. Barbara Dumont Baker, Sept. 12, 1936; children—Richard Englis, Peter B., David D., Barbara L. Vice pres. Standard Brands, 1953-56; merchandising mgr. Lever Bros. Co., 1956-60, marketing v.p. charge Pepsodent div., 1961-63, marketing v.p. Household Products division, 1963-66, trade development v.p., 1966-68, chmn., chief exec. officer subsidiary Glamorene Products Corp., 1968. Vice chmn. grad. inter club com. Princeton. Served to lt. col. USAAF, 1941-45. Clubs: Wee Burn Country (gov.) (Darien); Tiger Inn (gov., pres. Princeton, N.J.); Princeton of N.Y. Home: Darien CT

BAITY, JAMES L., auditor for War Dept.; b. La Plata, Mo., July 11, 1871; s. William D. and Frances E. (Ownbey) B.; pub. sch. edn.; m. Martha M. Sanders, of La Plata, Mo., Dec. 27, 1896. Was editor weekly newspaper, Mo.; asst. to James T. Lloyd, chmn. Dem. Nat. Congressional Com., 1908; was sec. to U.S. Senator James A. Reed and mgr. of his campaign for U.S. Senate; auditor for War Dept., May 9, 1913-—. Presbyn. Mason. Home: The Brighton. Office: Winder Bldg. Washington DC‡

BAKER, ALFRED ZANTZINGER, illustrator and writer; b. Baltimore, Jan. 4, 1870; s. William Sebastian Graff and Elizabeth Zantizinger (Cockey) B.; ed. pvt. schs., Baltimore; studied art, Charcoal Club, Baltimore; Julian Acad., and Ecole des Beaux Arts, Paris; m. Helen Louise Newell, On staff of Puck, 1898—, illustrated for Scriber's, Century. St. Nicholas, Harper's Life, etc. Exhbtd. Nat. Acad.; Design, 1893; Societe des Artistes Francais, 1907; Saion des Artistes Humoristes, 1907. Mem. Union Internationale des Beaux Arts et des Lettres, Paris. Progressive. Presbyn. Author: The Moving Picture Book, 1911; The Moving Picture Glue Book, 1912; The Torn Book, 1913.*‡

BAKER, BERTHA KUNZ, lecturer, dramatic reader; b. Erie, Pa.; d. Jacob and Caroline (Weiss) Kunz; grad. Erie High Sch., 1880, followed by pvt. study and foreign travel; m. Dr. L.B. Baker of Erie, Pa., Oct. 5, 1892 (died, Feb., 1907). Taught langs. and lit., Erie High Sch., 1883-92. Since 1890 engaged as lecturer and dramatic reader, at Chautauqua Assembly and in colls., univs. and lyceum courses throughout U.S.; especially interpretive recitals of masterpieces of classics and modern literature; lecturer and reader at Brooklyn Inst. of Arts and Sciences, U. of Chicago, Phila. Soc. for Univ. Extension, etc. Author: Art in Education of the Emotions; Practical Problems in Literary Interpretation; Studies in Emotional Expression. Home: 21 31st St., New York NY‡

BAKER, BRYANT, sculptor; b. London, England, July 8, 1881; s. John (sculptor) and Susan (Bryant) B.; student City and Guilds Tech. Inst., London; grad. Royal Acad. Arts, London, 1910; unmarried. Executed bust and heroic statue of King Edward VII; bust of King Olav of Norway; also busts of many notable persons of Eng. Came to U.S., 1916; made busts from life of Pres. Coolidge, Col. John Coolidge, Sens. H. C. Lodge, W. A. Clark and J. H. Bankhead. Gens. Pershing, March and Gorgas, Chief Justices White, Taft and Hughes, John Hays Hammond, Herbert Hoover, Newton Baker, Josephus Daniels, Percival Lowell, George Harvey, Cordell Hull; heroic statue of Chief Justice Edward D. White, New Orleans; heroic bronze statues of Grover Cleveland, Millard Fillmore and Young Lincoln, Buffalo, N.Y., Chief Justice John Marshall, Warrenton, Va., Elbert Gary, Gary, Ind.; John F. Kennedy heroic bronze statue, McKeesport, Pa.; 4 marble busts, U.S. Supreme Ct.; marble statues Caesar Rodney, John M. Clayton, patriots of Del., Statuary Hall, Washington, D.C.; Gov. Reuben Fenton statue, Jamestown, N.Y.; Bishop Freeman. Meml. Washington Nat. Cathedral; colossal bronze statue of George Washington, Masonic National Memorial Building, Alexandria, Va.; bronze bust of Sir Winston Churchill, in National Portrait Gallery, Washington, D.C. Works in bronze or marble throughout U.S., Europe. Ideal works in various private collections and in art galleries. Exhibitor at Royal Acad., from 1910, also Paris Salon, Corcoran Art Gallery, Etc. Served as sgt., M.C., U.S. Army, 1918-19. Winner of Marland competition for Pioneer Woman Statue, Ponca City, Okla.; D.A.R. medal for Americanism and achievement, also N.Y. State grand lodge medal for achievement, 1960. Fellow Nat. Sculpture Soc.; mem. N.A.D. Studio: New York City NY Died Mar. 29, 1970; buried Fordcombe England

BAKER, CORA WARMAN, clubwoman; b. Trenton, N.J., March 1, 1867; dau. of David and Rebecca Fair (Love) Warman; ed. Trenton Grammar and High Sch., Phila. Sch. of Design; m. Henry Fenimore Baker, Nov. 15, 1887; children—Marjorie (Mrs. Frank G. Breyer), Helen (Mrs. Charles S. Brawner), Albert Brewer, Edwin (dec.), Anne Love (Mrs. Herbert J. Leimbach), Henry Fenimore, Jr. Mem. Baltimore War Memorial Commn. since 1927, Am. Battle Monuments Commn. (commr.) since 1927; sent to Europe by Gen. Geo. C. Marshall on inspection trip to American cemeteries, May 1950. Pres. Baltimore Chapter Service Star Legion, since 1922, Nat. Service Star Legion, Inc., 1923-25. State chmn. Am. Merchant Marine Library Assn., 1933-36. Chmn. Home Dept. Federation Woman's Clubs, Blind Veterans' Club, 1924-27. V. pres. Women's Nat. Council of Women, 1932-37. Treas. Women's Joint Congressional Com., 1927-32. Proxy for pres. of Nat. Council of Women to London for Internat. Council, Apr. 1929. Has exhibited paintings at clubs and art institutes; drew and had published a map of Am. battle monuments abroad, which was sold for the benefit of Ednl. Loan Fund for Sons and Daughters of Ex-Service Men. Republican. Episcopalian. Mem. Federation of Woman's Clubs, Nat. Council of Women, D.A.R., Artists' Professional Leaque, Am. Red Cross. Home: Wyman Park Apts., Baltimore11, MD‡

BAKER, DAVID FLOYD, engring. educator; b. Blue Springs, Mo., Sept. 19, 1919; s. Floyd Allen and Eula (Ketteman) B.; B.Indsl. Engring., M.Sc., Ohio State U., 1952, ph.D., 1957; m. Martha Estella Heacock, Feb. 6, 1944; children—Janet Estella, Jeffrey David. With Unitcast Steel Corp., Toledo, 1949, Buckeye Steel Castings Co., 1950, 51, 52; mem. faculty Ohio State U., 1953-70, prof. indsl. engring., 1961-70, chmn. dept., 1964-70, mem. adminstrv. com. Engring. Expt. Sta., 1963-65, dir. systems research group, 1964-70; cons. in field, ad hoc arbitrator labor-mgmt. disputes. Mem. engring. edn. and accreditation com. Engineers Council for Profl. Devel., 1968-70. Served with U.S. Navy, 1940-47. Decorated Bronze Star with gold star. Mem. Am. Inst. Indsl. Engrs., Am. Soc. Engineering Education, Institute Management Science, Nat. Soc. Profl. Engrs., A.A.A.S., Nature Conservancy, Aircraft Owners and Pilots Assn., Sigma Xi, Alpha Pi Mu (nat. pres. 1966-68), Tau Beta Pi, Pi Mu Epsilon, Phi Eta Sigma. Clubs: Wheaton (Columbus); Brooks Bird (past pres.) (Wheeling, W.Va.). Home: Columbus OH Died Feb. 10, 1970.

BAKER, DOROTHY, writer; b. Missoula, Mont., Apr. 21, 1907; d. Raymond and Alice (Grady) Dodds; A.B., U. Cal. at Los Angeles, 1929; B.E., Occidental Coll., 1930; M.A., U. Cal. at Berkeley, 1933; m. Howard Baker, Sept. 2, 1930; children—Ellen, Joan. Recipient fellowship Nat. Inst. Arts and Letters, 1964. Author: Young Man With a Horn (1938 novel); Trio (novel), 1943 (God Medal, Commonwealth Club of Cal., for best novel pub. by a Californian in 1943); Trio (play in collaboration with Howard Baker), Belasco Theatre, New York 1944; Our Gifted Son (novel), 1948; The Ninth Day (TV Drama with Howard Baker); Cassandra at the Wedding (novel), 1962. Home: Terra Bella CA Died June 17, 1968; buried Porterfield CA

BAKER, EARL DEWEY, newspaperman; b. Spencer County Ind., Apr. 14, 1898; s. Samuel and Minnie (Haines) B.; student Central High Sch., Evansville, Ind., 1913-17, Evansville Coll., 1917-18; m. Grace Schellhase, June 27, 1918; 1 son, Jack Albert. Asso. with Scripps-Howard Newspapers since Aug. 1918, beginning as cub in advertising dept. Evansville Press, becoming asst. advertising mgr. of same, 1921; business mgr. Terre Haute Post, 1925-29, Washington (D.C.) Daily News, 1929-31, Indianapolis Times, 1931-37; asst. gen. Business mgr. Scripps-Howard newspapers since Jan. 1, 1937; also pres. and business mgr. Washington Daily News, 1938-47; v.p. and bus. mgr. The San Francisco News, from 1947. Mason (32 deg.). Clubs: San Francisco Press, San Francisco Advertising. Home: San Francisco CA Died Dec. 1970.

BAKER, EDGAR ROBEY, publisher; b. Washington, Oct. 16, 1920; s. Edgar Robey and Ida (Carroll) B.; A.B., George Washington U., 1941; m. Alice Newcomer, Sept. 6, 1944. Staff Lend-Lease Adminstrn., 1942-44; asst. to pub. Life mag., 1945; gen. mgr. Time-Life Internat., 1947-49; mng. dir., 1949-65, dir. corporate devel., 1965-69; v.p. Time, Inc., 1957-69; dir. Metro-Goldwyn-Mayer, Gen. Learning Corp., Inter-Am. Capital Corp., Chase (Manhattan Internat. Investment Corp. Co-dir. Internat. Indsl. Devel. Conf., San Francisco, Cal., 1957; co-chmn. Inter-Am. Investment Conf., New Orleans 1955. Co-chmn. N.Y. Citizens for Kennedy, 1960. Trustee Cordell Hull Found., U.S. Inter-Am. Council, George Washington U.; dir. Nat. Fgn. Trade Council, Far East America Council. Mem. Phi Beta Kappa, Omicron Delta Kappa. Home: Sharon CT also New York City NY Died June 11, 1969.

BAKER, ELIZABETH BRADFORD FAULKNER, economist; b. Abilene, Kan., 1886; d. Lothrop Hedge and Hattie (Bearce) Faulkner; B.L., U. of Calif. at Berkeley, 1914; A.M., Columbia, 1919 Ph.D., 1925. Mem. faculty Barnard Coll., Columbia, 1919-52, chmn. dept. econs., 1940-52, prof. econs., 1948-52, emeritus prof., 1952-73. Pub. mem., panel chmn. Region II, Nat. War Labor Bd., 1942-45; now panel mem. N.Y. State Mediation Bd. and Am. Arbitration Assn. Mem. Am. Econ. Assn., Nat. Planning Assn. Democrat. Author: Impact of Printing Technology, 1953; also articles. Home: New York City NY Died Feb. 1973.

BAKER, EMILIE (ADDOMS) KIP (MRS. FRANKLIN THOMAS BAKER), author; b. Brooklyn, N.Y., d. Henry and Emilie (Addoms) Kip; A.B., Teachers Coll. (Columbia), 1895; post-grad. work, Columbia, 1916-19; m. Prof. Franklin Thomas Baker, of Teachers Coll., Sept. 15, 1896; children—Richard (dec.), Lawrence Kip, Dorothy, Frances. Author: Out of the Northland, 1904; Stories of Old Greece and Rome, 1913; Stories of Northern Myths, 1914. Compiler: Children's Book of Poetry (3 books), 1915; Short Stories and Selections for Secondary Schools, 1916. Contbr. stories to mags. Home: Park Hill, Yonkers NY‡

BAKER, EZRA FLAVIUS, clergyman, educator, lecturer; b. Morgantown, Ky., Mar. 18, 1869; s. John and Mary Ann (Wood) B.; A.B., Mo. Valley Coll., Marshall, Mo., 1898; B.D., Cumberland U., Lebanon, Tenn., 1901; M.A., Columbia, 1904; B.D., Union Theol. Sem., 1905; grad. student Columbia and Union Theol. Sem., 1905-8; Ph.D., Trinity U., Waxahachie, Tex., 1910; post-grad. work, U. of Berlin, Germany, 1910-11; m. Katherine Elizabeth Swisher, of Marshall, Mo., Oct. 24, 1899. Ordained Presbyn. ministry, 1898; pastor Harrisonville, Mo., 1901-3; prof. philosophy and Bible, Trinity U., 1908-10; pastor 1st Ch., Waxahachie, 1908-9; pres. Waynesburg (Pa.) Coll., 1912-15. Fellow A.A.A.S. Home: 525 Eastwood St Marshall MO‡

BAKER, FRANK E., retired educator; b. Clymer, N.Y., Sept. 10, 1877; s. Horace and Amelia (Simmelink) B.; grad. Clarion (Pa.) State Normal Sch., 1895; A.B., Allegheny Coll., 1905, hon. A.M., 1915, L.H.D., 1929; A.M., Harvard, 1909; m. Florence Howard Fowler, June 14, 1911 (dec.); m. 2d, Ruth Mary Geiser, Nov. 1, 1926; children—Robert Fowler, F. Richard. Prin. Spring Creek (Pa.) Graded Sch., 1896-98, Clymer (N.Y.) Union Sch., 1898-1900, Randolph (N.Y.) Union Sch., 1900-02; v.p. Chamberlain Inst., Randolph, N.Y., 1903; prin. Greensburg (Pa.) High Sch., 1905-08; head science dept., Brooklyn Poly. Prep. Sch., 1909-11; prin. Northwestern State Normal Sch., Edinboro, Pa., 1911-21; prin. East Stroudsburg State Normal Sch., 1921-23; pres. Milwaukee State Teachers Coll. since 1923; lecturer, Northwestern U., summers, 1934, 37, 38, 39; visiting prof., U. of Ill., summer 1940. Mem. Eastern Montana Teachers Coll. Commn., 1926; trustee Allegheny Coll., 1926-29; pres. Am. Assn. Teachers Colleges, 1933-34; mem. exec. bd. Prog. Edn. Assn. of America since 1934, regional v.p., 1938-40; pres. Am. Assn. Teacher Educating Instns. in Met. Areas, 1941; mem. Nat. Council of Edn., 1941; adviser Inst. for Propaganda Analysis. Member Enemy Alien Hearing Board, Eastern Dist. of Wis., 1942. Mem. A.A.A.S., Kappa Phi Kappa, Phi Kappa Psi, Phi Beta Kappa, Kappa Delta Pi. Contbr. to various mags. Home: Sandy Loam Farm, R. 1, Hendersonville NC‡

BAKER, FRANKLIN, JR., mfr.; b. Phila., Pa., Nov. 16, 1872; s. Franklin, Sr., and Sarah J. (Hogue) B.; B.S., Lehigh U., 1895; m. Elizabeth M. Weaver, of Bethlehem, Pa., Nov. 19, 1897. Pres. The Franklin Baker Co., mfrs. coconut products, since 1900; chmn. bd. Colonial Trust Co.; dir. General Food Corpn. Clubs: Union League, Phila. Country, Phila. Cricket, Huntingdon Valley Hunt, Rose Tree Hunt, Radnor Hunt; New York, Bankers, University (New York). Home: 299 Park Av., New York, N.Y., and Bryn Mawr, PA. Office: Colonial Trust Bldg., Philadelphia PA‡

BAKER, FREDERICK VAN VLIET, artist; b. New York, N.Y., Nov. 6, 1876; s. Charles and Elizabeth Priscilla (Vanderpoel) B.; ed. Pratt Inst., Brooklyn, Ecole des Beaux Arts, Colorossi, Paris; m. Maud Lillian Forsbrey, Dec. 13, 1902. Pres. Colonial Studios (Inc.) since 1906; instr. in life drawing, painting and composition, Pratt Inst. Exhibited in salons, Paris, 1901, 02, 03, also at Ghent, Vienna, Chicago, New York, etc. Asso. Societe Nationale des Beaux Arts, 1901. Home: Mountain Lakes, N.J. Address: Pratt Institute, Brooklyn NY‡

BAKER, HAROLD BRUSS, ednl. adminstr.; b. Arcanum, O., Feb. 1, 1909; s. Roy and Mina (Bruss) B.; A.B., Heidelberg Coll., 1931; M.B.A., Northwestern U., 1932, Ph.D., 1940; m. Annabelle Powell, May 28, 1935; children—Gordon Powell, Joyce Ann. Prof. bus. adminstrn. Friends U., 1935-40; asso. prof. bus. Butler U., 1940-42; state rep. U.S. Bur. Labor Statistics, 1942; asst. to prodn. control supt. RCA Mfg. Div., Indpls., 1942-45; asst. prof. mgmt. Ind. U., 1945-46; chmn. bus. adminstrn. Gen. Motors Inst., Flint, Mich., 1946-50, dir. admissions and records, 1950-69; indsl. cons. Dist. chmn. Boy Scouts Am., 1964-67, mem. exec. bd., 1958-69. Mem. Flushing (Mich.) Bd. Edn., 1960-69, pres., 1967-69. Chmn. of Flushing (Mich.) Planning Commn., 1958-63. Named citizen of year, Flushing Jr. C. of C., 1964. Mem. Am. Econ. Assn., Coop. Edn. Assn., Am. Soc. Engring. Edn., Am., Mich. assns., collegiate registrars and admissions officers. Club: Flushing Lions (pres. 1952). Author: Mediation and Arbitration of Labor Disputes by State Agency in Indiana, 1942; Dealership Organization and Operation, 1950; Organization and Management, 1954. Home: Flushing MI Died May 26, 1969.

BAKER, HORACE, railway official; b. Missouri; s. Isaac Stroud and Napoleana (Mason) B.; pub. schs.; m. Anne Brydie Postal, 1885; children—Brydie (Mrs. S. T. W. Cull), William Postal, Margaret Louise (Mrs. Frank R. Dunbar), Robert Horace. Began ry. work, 1881; treas. and paymaster Havana, Rantoul & Eastern R.R., 1885-87; trainmaster Chicago dist., 1890-91, local freight agt., Chicago, Sept.-Dec. 1891, supt. Chicago div., 1891-1900, Amboy div., 1900-01, Freeport div., 1901-02, I.C. R.R.; supt. Charlotte div., 1902-04, asst. gen. supt. eastern dist., 1904-05, Southern Ry.; gen. supt. St. Louis, Iron Mountain & Southern Ry., 1905-06; gen. mgr. Cincinnati, New Orleans & Tex. Pacific Ry. and Ala. Great Southern R.R., 1906-Jan. 17, 1917; gen. mgr. Southern R.R. System, lines west, Jan. 17, 1917-Mar. 1, 1920; mem. Railroad Bd. of Adjustment, Mar.-Apr. 1920; mem. U.S. Railroad Labor Bd. Apr. 15, 1920-July 1926; gen. mgr. Exposition Car Co., Sept. 1926-June 1927; mem. R.R. Mgrs. Com. of Train Service Bd. of Adjustment, Dec. 1931-Aug. 1934. Spl. rep. Am. Shortline R.R. Assn. Home: 26 Lake Shore Drive, St MI‡

BAKER, MARY FRANCIS, botanist; b. Plainfield, Conn., Nov. 29, 1876; d. Rev. John Manning and Sarah Joanna (Kinne) Francis; ed. Plainfield and Norwich acads. and under pvt. tutelage; m. Thomas R. Baker, of Winter Park, Fla., Oct. 12, 1918 (died 1930). Congregationalist. Author: The Book of Grasses, 1912; Florida Wild Flowers, 1926, rev. edit., 1938. Contbr. to mags. Home: 225 Holt Av., Winter Park FL‡

BAKER, MURRAY M., ret. corp. exec.; b. Alton, Ill., May 4, 1872; s. Henry Southard and Mary Fall (Adams) B.; student Alton Pub. Schs.; LL.D., Bradley U., Peoria, Ill.; m. Mary Ellen Lyman, Apr. 20, 1904; children—Lyman, Mary Cossett (Mrs. Arthur T. Moulding), Emily (Mrs. Albert S. Weaver, Jr.). With John Deere & Co., St. Louis 1890; dist. rep. P.P. Mast & Co., Springfield, O., 1893-94; engaged in wholesale implement and warehouse business as M. M. Baker & Co., Peoria, Ill., 1904-09; purchased Colean Mfg. Co., Peoria, and inc. Holt Caterpillar Tractor Co., affiliated with Holt Mfg. Co., Stockton, Cal., 1909, which later became The Caterpillar Tractor Co., exec. v.p. and gen. mgr. until consol. with C. L. Best Gas Tractor Co. under name The Caterpillar Tractor Co., v.p. charge sales this orgn., 1926-30 now dir.; owner Baker Ranch; dir. of the Thomas Moulding Brick Co. General chairman of the Ill. Emergency Defense Council, later Ill. War Council. With Ordnance Dept., U.S. Army, as civilian in tank and mil. tractor prodn., 1917-40. Mem. Peoria Assn. Commerce, Ill. C. of C., Ill. State Hist. Soc., Isaac Walton League of Am. Republican. Episcopalian. Mason. Clubs: Peoria Country, Creve Coeur (Peoria); Union League (Chgo.). Home: 1222 W. Moss Av., Peoria IL‡

BAKER, ROY NEWSOM, coll. pres.; b. Whiteville, Tenn., July 25, 1906; s. William B. and Blanche (Newsom) B.; B.S., Memphis State Coll., 1934; A.M., Peabody Coll., 1944; D.Litt. (honorary), Bethel Coll., 1956; married Janie Nelson Mullen, Aug. 2, 1933; children—William Barry, Brenda Nelson, James Newsom. Tchr. Middleton (Tenn.) Elementary Sch., 1928-29, Adamsville, Tenn., 1929-30, Whiteville High Sch., 1931-41; prin., supt. schs., Martin, Tenn., 1941-45; pres. Bethel Coll. since 1945. Mem. N.E.A., Tenn. Edn. Assn., Tenn. C. of C., Phi Delta Kappa. Presbyn. (elder). Club: Rotary (McKenzie, Tenn.). Home: McKenzie TN Died Oct. 29, 1968; buried Melrose Cemetery, Whiteville TN

BAKER, W. BROWNE, cons.; b. Houston, Jan. 23, 1900; s. James A. and Alice (Graham) B.; grad. Hill Sch., Pottstown, Pa.; grad. Princeton, 1921; m. Adelaide Lovett, Dec. 23, 1922; children—W. Browne, Lovett, Graeme (Mrs. Clifford W. Vickery). With Tex. Nat. Bank (formerly S. Tex. Comml. Nat. Bank), Houston, 1917-66, clk. proof dept., 1921-23, asst. cashier, 1924-25, sr. v.p., dir., 1945-66 (now Tex. Nat. Bank of Commerce of Houston); asst. nat. bank examiner, 1923-24; v.p., trust officer, dir. Guardian Trust Co., 1925-45; later consultant in banking and real estate; dir. Tex. Nat. Bank of Commerce, Houston. Mem. bd. dirs., vice pres., life mem. Houston Met. YMCA. Served with USN, World War I; chief negotiation div. Office Sec. Navy, World War II. Recipient Distinguished Civilian Service award USN, 1945. Mem. Houston Com. Fgn. Relations, Philos. Soc. Tex., English Speaking Union, Friends of Rice. Episcopalian. Clubs: Ramada, River Oaks Country, Princeton (N.Y.C.); Cottage (Princeton). Home: Houston TX Died Nov. 17, 1968; buried Glenwood Cemetery.

BAKER, WALTER CUMMINGS, ret. banker; b. Oneida, N.Y., Mar. 29, 1893; s. William and Fannie E. (Wallace)B.; B.S., Union Coll., 1915, Doctor of Laws (honorary), 1955; married May Ida Case, September 15, 1921 (died 1946); married 2d Lois Dottie Wurtele, May 25, 1951. Salesman with Bond and Mortgage Guarantee Company, Brooklyn, 1915-18; with Guaranty Trust Co. of New York 1919-58, asst. trust officer, 1925-28, trust officer, 1928-45, vice pres., 1945-58. Served in U.S. Navy, rank of seaman, 1918-19. Dir. J.J. Newberry Co. Life trustee Union Coll., chmn. bd. trustees, 1941-63; gov., treas. Union U. Trustee, v.p., fellow in perpetuity. Met. Mus. Art; trustee, Archaeol. Inst. Am., treas., 1948-64, hon. life fellow, pres. N.Y. soc., 1951-54. Dir. Manhattan Eye, Ear and Throat Hosp., treas., 1942-47, pres., 1947-56; treas. Central Bur. of Research, Am. Otological Soc. since 1944; treas., dir. The Eye-Bank for Sight Restoration, Inc., 1945-47, president, director 1947-57; director Grand Jury Assn. N.Y. County from 1949; trustee Am. Acad. Rome, from 1949, treas, from 1957; mem. council of fellows Pierpont Morgan Library, 1957-60; trustee Youth Consultation Service, from 1958. Mem. board of trustees and treas. The William M. Sullivan Mus. Found.; trustee Cathedral of St. John the Divine, from 1953. Mem. adv. council dept. art, history and archaeology Columbia U. Mem. Master Drawings Assn. (pres.), Nat. Inst. Social Scis., Psi Upsilon. Republican. Episcopalian (vestryman). Clubs: The Links, University, Century, Grolier. Home: New York City NY Died Sept. 25, 1971.

BAKHSHI, CHULAM MOHAMMAD, prime minister Jammu and Kashmir; b. Srinagar, Kashmir, July 1907; s. Khwaja Abdul Guffar Bakhshi; student C.M.S. Schs., Kashmire. Tchr., Ladakh Dist., Jammu and Kashmire State; joined Muslim Conf., 1931, established student's and workers' unions; organized Bilcha Party in Khanyar, 1933-34; organizer, leader Youth Movement, 1936; active Quit Kasmir Movement, 1946-47; dep. prime minister, 1948-53, prime minister Jammu and Kashmir govt., 1953-72. Pres. All Jammu and Kashmir Nat. Conf., premier polit. orgn. of the state, 1954-72. Address: Jammu and Kashmir India Died Aug. 1972.

BAKKE, E. WIGHT, educator; b. Onawa, Ia., Nov. 18, 1903; s. Oscar C. and Harriet (Wight) B.; B.A., Northwestern U., 1926, LL.D., 1964; Ph.D., Yale, 1932; m. Mary Sterling, Sept. 1, 1926; children—Karl E., Carolyn S. (Mrs. Albert S. Bacdayan), William W. Instr. sociology Yale, 1932-34, asst. prof. econs., 1934-38, dir. unemployment studies, inst. Human Relations, 1932-39, dir. studies in trade unionism, from 1939, prof. econs., from 1938, Sterling prof., from 1940, dir. grad. studies in econs., 1940-50, dir. Labor and Mgmt. Center from 1944; Fulbright prof. to Denmark, 1953. Prin. cons. social economist Social Security Bd., 1936-39; dir. Nat. Bur. Econ. Research; chmn. appeals com. Nat. War Labor Board; cons. Dept. Labor, Navy Dept.; mem. several Presdl. emergency bds.; mem. adv. council Cornell Sch. Indsl. and Labor Relations; mem. Nat. Manpower Policy Task Force. Bd. overseers Amos Tuck Sch.; trustee Quinnipiac Coll., New Haven. Mem. Am. Econ. Assn., Indsl. Relations Research Assn. (pres. 1958), A.A.A.S., Internat. Indsl. Relations Assn., Am. Arbitration Assn., Conn. Acad. Arts and Scis., Corp. of Haverford, Delta Sigma Rho. Mem. Soc. of Friends. Author numerous publications on orgn., labor, unemployment, social security. Home: Woodbridge CT Died Nov. 23, 1971; buried Grove St. Cemetery, New Haven CT

BAKKEN, CLARENCE JOHN, ednl. adminstr.; b. Pequot, Minn., Sept. 28, 1902; s. John P. and Caroline (Brunes) B.; LL.B., YMCA Coll. of Law, Mpls., 1926; B.S., U. Minn., 1927; M.A., U. Denver, 1957, Ed.D., 1959; m. Cora Opland, June 30, 1931; children—Colette (Mrs. William Kerlin), Clarence Opland. Admitted to Minn. bar, 1926, commd. 2d lt. U.S. Army, Res. 1927, advanced through grades to col., 1956; with civilian conservation corps, 1933-42, inspector gen. Pacific, 1942-45, 5th Army, 1947-50; mil. post Heidelberg, Germany, 1950-53, Ft. Benning, 1953-56; ret., 1956; pvt. practice law, 1926-29; high sch. tchr. Mandan, N.D., 1929-32; counselor Parsons Coll., Fairfield, Ia., 1960-62; mem. student personnel faculty Cal. State Coll., Long Beach, 1962-67, dir. financial aids, 1963-67. Active in Boy Scouts Am., 1914-67, named Silver Beaver, 1952. Decorated Bronze Star.

Mem. N.D., (pres. 1938-39), S.D. (v.p., pres. 1941-46), res. officers assns., Am. Acad. Polit. and Social Sci., Am. Personnel and Guidance Assn., Am. Coll. Personnel Assn., Phi Delta Kappa, Kappa Delta Pi. Mason, Lion. Author monograph The Legal Basis for College Student Personnel Work, 1960. Home: Garden Grove CA Died Sept. 19, 1967; buried Ft. Logan Cemetery Denver CO

BAKKUM, GLENN A(LMER), sociologist, educator; b. Waukon, Ia., June 7; s. Gustav Adolph and Agnet Taernigen (Hanson) B.; B.S., Ia. State Coll., 1920; A.M., Columbia, 1925; Ph.D., Cornell, 1928; m. Florence Stahl, June 14, 1921. Supt. pub. schs. Ia., Minn., 1916, 18; prof. and head dept. sociology U. of Wichita, 1927-35, dir. Bur. Municipal Social Research, 1930-33; head dept. sociology Ore. State Coll., 1935-56, prof., from 1935; vis. prof. Ia. State Coll., Ia. and N.Y. State teachers colls., Province B.C. dept. edn., summer 1950, Cornell, 1950-51. Served as 2d lt., Inf., World War I. Recipient Fulbright award Am. University, Cairo, Egypt, 1951; Fulbright grant, lecturer in social psychology University Panjab, Lahore, Pakistan, 1961-62. Mem. American Association University Professors (national council), Rural Sociol. Soc., Alpha Chi Rho, Alpha Kappa Delta, Phi Delta Kappa, Delta Sigma Rho, Phi Kappa Phi, Am. Sociol. Soc.Lutheran. Home: Corvallis OR Died Apr. 6, 1972.

BAKST, HENRY JACOB, physician; b. Providence, May 19, 1906; s. Adolph and Sophie (Himowitz) B.; Ph.B., Brown U., 1927; M.D., Harvard, 1931; m. Ruth Elene Miller, June 23, 1933; 1 son, David Allan. Intern, resident physician Boston City Hosp., 1931-34, asst. vis. physician, 1935-72, teaching fellow histology and embryology Harvard, 1928-31; instr. medicine Boston U., 1935-45, asst. prof. medicine, 1946-48, asso. prof., preventive medicine, 1948-51, prof. preventive medicine, 1952-71, prof. emeritus, 1971-72, chmn. dept., 1952-66, asso. dean Sch. Medicine, 1965-69, dean, 1969-71, dir. med. scis. Boston U. Sch. Grad. Dentistry, 1971-72. dir. rehab. tng. Boston U., 1955-63; vis. physician Univ. Hosp., 1956-71, dir. ambulatory services, 1959-65, dir. div. health conservation, 1961-71, chief rehab. and phys. medicine. Chmn. health council United Community Services, Boston, 1953-57; mem. nat. adv. com. on pub. health tng. USPHS, 1965-69. Former trustee Univ. Hosp. Served as comdr. MC., USNR, World War II. Fellow A.C.P., Am. Pub. Health Assn.; mem. A.M.A., Mass. Assn. Mental Health (pres. 1956-57), Mass. Med. Soc., Assn. Tchrs. Preventive Medicine (sec.-treas. 1960-63, pres. 1963-64), Sigma Xi, Alpha Omega Alpha. Democrat. Jewish religion. Contbr. articles to med. jours. Home: Brookline MA Died Aug. 25, 1972.

BALABAN, BARNEY, motion picture exec.; b. Chicago, Ill., June 8, 1887; s. Israel Balaban and Goldie (Manderbursky) B.; ed. Chicago pub. schs.; m. Tillie Urkov, Feb. 22, 1929; children—Burton (dec.), Leonard, Judith R. Messenger boy for Western Union at age 12; later employed in cold storage plant; co-founder Balaban & Katz Corp., theater chain, Chgo.; hon. chmn. bd. Paramount Pictures Corp., N.Y.C.; hon. dir. Mfrs. Trust Co. Vice chairman of the American Heritage Foundation. One of first to introduce cooling systems into motion picture theaters. Home: Byram CT Died Mar. 7, 1971; buried Chicago IL

BALABAN, EMANUEL, condr., educator; b. Bklyn., Jan. 27, 1895; s. Joseph and Olga (Liebman) B.; student Inst. Mus. Art, N.Y.C., 1912-14, also pvt. study; m. Nina de Witt, Aug. 1923 (div. July 1942); m. 2d, Priscilla Sanford Brown, July 27, 1942. Accompanist for Zimbalist, Morini, Elman, others, 1915-22; asst. condr., Dresden (Germany) Opera, 1922-25; guest condr. Berlin Philharmonic, Nat. Symphony, Washington, N.Y. Philharmonic, others; dir. opera dept. Eastman Sch. Music, 1929-44; condr. Ballet Russe de Monte Carlo, 1944-45; condr. N.Y.C. Ballet, Eng., 1950; faculty Juilliard Sch. Music, 1947-73, condr., coach opera theatre and dept. vocal lit., 1963-73; faculty Tanglewood-Berkshire Music Center, 1953-56. Mem. Beethoven Assn., The Bohemians, AGMA. Home: New York City NY 10023 Died May 1973.

BALDANZI, GEORGE, trade union ofcl.; b. Black Diamond, Pa., Jan. 23, 1907; s. Natale and Clelia (Rutille) B.; m. Lena Parenti, Feb. 25, 1932; 1son, George M. An organizer, 1st pres. Dyers Fedn. Am., 1933; merged with Textile Works Union Am., CIO, 1939, exec. v.p., 1939-52; dir. orgn. United Textile Workers Am., AFL, 1952-53; on leave as regional dir. Eastern Conf. Teamsters, Internat. Brotherhood Teamsters, 1953-55; internat. pres. United Textile Works Am., AFL-CIO, 1958-72. Vice pres. United-Italian Am. Labor Council, 1958-72; mem. Sec. Commerce Textile Adv. Com., 1959-72. Chmn. Passaic County (N.J.) Area Redevel. Bd., 1963-72. Named Outstanding Citizen of Italian Descent in Passaic Area, Unity, Neighborliness, Integrity, Charity and Opportunity, 1956; recipient Star Solidarity, 1949, Order Merit, 1964 (Italy). Home: Hawthorne NJ Died May 1972.

BALDENSPERGER, FERNAND, literary historian, poet; b. Saint-Die (Vosges), France, May 4, 1871; s. Phillippe and Julie (Haas) B.; Cert. d'etudes, Ecole communale Saint-Die, 1880, B.L., College de la ville de Saint-Die, 1888, Lycee Louis-le Grand, Paris, 1889, Lic. Lettres, Univ. Nancy, 1890, Univ. Heidelberg Berlin, Bonn, 1890-91, Agreg, Univ. in Paris, 1892. Doct. Lettres, Univ. Paris, 1899, Univ. Zurich, London, Edinburgh, 1893; honorary degrees Columbia, Ann Arbor, Budapest; m. Marie-Marguerite Bonzon, Apr. 19, 1903; children—Pauline-Anne (deceased), Albert-Jean, Jules-Pierre, Marie-Claude (Mrs. Jean Caupenne). Asst prof. Univ. of Nancy, 1894; prof. Univ. of Lyon, 1900-10; asst. prof. and prof. Univ. of Paris, 1910-35; leave of absence spent at Harvard 1913-14, Columbia Univ. 1917-19, Univ. of Strasbourg 1919-23, Princeton 1932. Harvard 1935-40, University of California at Los Angeles, 1940-45. Private in Inf. Reg. 26 Nancy, 1892-93, intelligence officer, 1914-16. Croix de guerre, Instruction publique, Legion d'honneur, Ordres de Saint-Etienne (Hungary), Polonia Restituta, and Jugo-Slavia. Mem. Academie des Sciences morales et politiques, Academie polonaise, Am. Academy (Boston), Lincei (Italy). Clubs: Autour du Monde (Boulogne-sur-Seine), Harvard Faculty (Cambridge). Author: Vigny; Goethe en France; Gottfried Keller; Orientations etrangeres chez Balzac; La Litterature, Le Mouvement des Idees dans l'Emigration francaise, Etudes d'Histoire litteraire (4 Vols.). Les Sonnets de Shakespeare. Revue de Literature comparee; poems, Cassanedre, Tragedie, and others. Address: 13 rue d'Odessa Paris XIV France‡

BALDERSTON, LYDIA RAY, household economist; b. Cincinnati, O.; d. John Peck and Rachel Very (Stokes) B.; grad. Drexel Inst., Phila., 1896; B.S., Columbia, 1911, M.A., 1915. Formerly instr. household arts, Teachers Coll. (Columbia); now home economic consultant, at Home Making Center, 46th St. and Lexington Av., New York. Mem. Am. Home Economics Assn., Mem. Friends Ch. (Quaker). Club: New Century (Phila.). Author: Laundering, 1914, 23; Housewifery, 1919, 28. Home: 18 Gramercy Park, New York NY‡

BALDES, RAYMOND CHARLES, lawyer, univ. prof.; b. Newton, Mass., July 26, 1895; s. Frederick Louis and Nellie Agnes (Butler) B.; ed. Cambridge Latin School, Dartmouth College, Mass. Inst. Tech.; LL.B., magna cum laude, Boston U., 1920, LL.M., 1921, S.B., 1923; J.D. (hon.), Suffolk U., 1966; m. Elizabeth A. Fraser, Sept. 5, 1935. Admitted to Mass. bar, 1920. Federal bar, 1925; instr. Boston U. Sch. of Law, 1922-27, asso. prof., 1927-29, prof. 1929-68, chmn. faculty com. on intercollegiate athletics, 1934-40, Austin B. Fletcher prof. law, 1941-46; prof. law Suffolk U., 1946-68. Lectr. business law and securities, Am. Inst. Banking, 1928-32. Head legal liaison and planning Rent div. OPA, Washington, 1942; state rationing atty., Mass., 1943; hearing commr., 1944-46; exec. v.p. and dir. The Armstrong Co.; treas., dir. Internat. Inst. of Boston, Inc. Pres., trustee Hawes Fund of Boston. Mem. National Panel Arbitrators, Am. Arbitration Assn. Served in U.S. Navy, 1918-19, 1st lieut., U.S. Army, Judge Adv. Gen. Res., 1924-34. Mem. Am. Law Inst., Mass., Boston bar assns., Bostonian Soc. (life), Delta Theta Phi. Conglist. Mason. Clubs: Boston University, Varsity, Dartmouth. Author: Notes on the General Laws of Massachusetts, 1924; Perry on Trusts and Trustees, 7th edit., 1929; Massachusetts Annotations to the Restatement of the Law of Agency, 1936; Massachusetts Annotations to the Restatement of Property, 1941. Home: Boston MA Died Aug. 7, 1968.

BALDINGER, ALBERT HENRY, clergyman; b. Wetzel County, W.Va., Feb. 13, 1876; s. Henry and Sarah (Hook) B.; A.B., Westminster Coll., New Wilmington, Pa., 1900, D.D., 1923, B.D., Pittsburgh Theol. Sem., 1903; studied at Edinburgh and Glasgow univs., 1931; m. Mary Estelle Spencer, June 23, 1903; children—Wallace Spencer, Wilbur Henry, Rachel Duira, Ruth Alberta. Ordained ministry United Presbyn. Ch., 1903; pastor successively Springdale, Pa., Spokane, Wash., and Fowler, Calif., until 1915; asso. sec. Bd. of Home Missions, U.P. Ch., Pittsburgh, 1915-17; pastor Butler, Pa., 1917-30; prof. Old Testament lit. and exegesis, Pittsburgh-Xenia Theological Seminary, Pittsburgh, 1931-40, prof. practical theology 1940-47; pastor Mellwood, Pa., 1948-49, Fowler, Calif. since 1949. Associate editor United Presbyterian since 1925. Member Commission on Religion and Health, Federal Council of Churches. Republican. United Presbyterian (Moderator, Gen. Assembly, 1948-49). Club: Quiz. Author, Sermons on Revelation, 1924; also brochures, The Paramount Problem of Protestantism and Broken-Down Altars, The Ends of the Church, Infant Baptism in Theory and Practice. Editor: The Manual of Worship. Contbr. mag. articles. Address: 804 Fedora Fresno CA‡

BALDINGER, LAWRENCE H., educator; b. Galion, O., Jan. 12, 1907; s. Edward Nelson and Margaret (McCartney) B.; Ph.C., Western Reserve U., 1928, B.S., 1929; M.S., U. of Notre Dame, 1931, Ph.D., 1933; m. Helen Dwyer, Aug. 10, 1929; children—Lawrence H., Margaret Ann, James Edward, Charles Dwyer. Instr. dept. of pharmacy, U. of Notre Dame, 1929-33, instr. and head dept., 1933-39, asst. prof. chemistry, 1939-41, asst. prof. chemistry and asst. dean Coll. of Science, 1941-42, asst. prof. chemistry and acting dean, 1942-43, prof. of chemistry and dean, 1943-60, asso. dean, head dept. pre-profl. studies, 1960-70. Recipient of 1950 Notre Dame Lay Faculty award. Fellow A.A.A.S.; mem. Am. and Ind. chem. socs., Am. Pharm. Assn., Ind. Acad. Science (pres. 1961), Phi Delta Chi, Rho Chi, Sigma Xi. Contbr. to Jour. Am. Chem. Soc., Jour. Am. Pharm. Assn. Home: South Bend IN Died Nov. 28, 1970; buried South Bend IN

BALDRIDGE, KENNETH FERGUSON, newspaper pub.; b. Bloomfield, Ia., May 25, 1886; s. David Franklin and Margaret Jane (Ferguson) B.; student Southern Ia. Normal and Scientific Inst., 1903-04; LL.B., Drake U., 1909; m. Katharine McClure, May 17, 1910; children—John David, Josephine. Newspaper reporter, 1903-09; pub. and editor Bloomfield Democrat since 1909; organized Central Newspaper Co., consisting of 7 So. Ia. newspapers, pres., 1930-59, chmn. bd., 1959-71; postmaster, Bloomfield, 1916-24, and 1935-36, resigned to be Dem. candidate for Congress; reappointed postmaster, 1937; chmn. board. dirs. Nockonwood Industries, Inc., mfrs. Chmn. Dem. Central Comm. of Davis County; chmn. Nat. Code Authority for Non-Met. Printing and Pub. Industry, 1934-35; Davis County, Ia., relief adminstr., 1933-39. Received Ia. Master Editor-Publisher award from Ia. Press Assn., 1937; Amos Award, National Editorial Association, 1950. Mem. Nat. Editorial Assn. (pres. 1934-35), Ia. Press Assn. (pres. 1925-26), Southern Ia. Press Assn. (pres. 1914), Ia. Newspaper, Inc. (pres. 1928-32), Nat. Postmasters Assn. (pres. Ia. Chapter 1940-42), Sigma Delta Chi. Democrat. Mem. Disciples of Christ. Mason, K.T., Shriner, K.P., Rotarian. Author: Seven Months in Orbit. Address: Bloomfield IA Died Nov. 22, 1971.

BALDWIN, ARTHUR DOUGLAS, lawyer; b. Hawaiian Islands, Apr. 8, 1876; s. Henry P. and Emily (Alexander) B.; A.B., Yale, 1898; LL.B., Harvard, 1901; Dr. Humanities, Western Reserve U., 1939; m. Reba Williams, June 18, 1902; children—Henry P., Louise (Mrs. Woods King), Fred C., A. Alexander, Sarah (Mrs. Irwin C. Hanger), Lewis W. Admitted to Ohio bar, 1902; mem. firm Garfield, MacGregor & Baldwin (now Garfield, Baldwin, Jamison, Hope & Ulrich) since 1916; dir. and counsel North Electric Mfg. Co., Galion, O.; dir. and mem. exec. com. Sherwin-Williams Co., Cleve.; dir. Land Title Guarantee & Trust Co. Ex-chmn. bd. Western Reserve U. Chmn. bd. Cleve. Hosp. Service Assn., Legal Aid Society, Spies Com. for Clin. Research (affiliated with Northwestern U.). Awarded Cleveland C. of C. Medal for Distinguished Service to City of Cleveland, 1940; Cleveland Community Fund Distinguished Service Medal, 1941; hon. award, Am. Hosp. Assn., 1948. Served as lt., later capt., F.A., U.S. Army, World War I. Republican. Presbyterian (mem. bd. trustees Ch. of the Covenant). Clubs: Union, Kirtland Country, Tavern, Chagrin Valley Hunt. Author: Memoirs of Henry P. Baldwin, 1904. Home: 9534 Lake Shore Blvd.,Cleveland 8. Office: National City Bank Bldg., Cleveland 14‡

BALDWIN, EDWARD CHAUNCEY, college prof.; b. W. Cornwall, Conn., Nov. 30, 1870; s. Chauncey Edward and Julia Rebecca (Howard) B.; A.B., Yale, 1895, Ph.D., 1898; m. Mabel, d. Dr. C. G. G. Merrill, of New Haven, Conn., Sept. 7, 1898. Instr. English, Duluth (Minn.) High Sch., 1898-9. Adelbert Coll. (Western Reserve U.), 1899-1901; asst. prof. English, U. of Ill., 1901-—. Republican. Conglist. Mem. Modern Lang. Assn. America, National Inst. of Social Sciences, Alpha Sigma Phi. Clubs: Cosmopolitan, University. Editor: Dickens' A Tale of Two Cities, 1906; English Poems (with Dr. H.G. Paul), 1908; Dickens' David Copperfield, 1910; Bunyan's Grace Abounding, 1910; Lodge's Rosalynde, 1910; Biblical Narratives, 1910. Author: Our Modern Debt to Israel, 1913. Contbr. to philol. jours. Home: 1002 S. Lincoln Av., Urbana IL‡

BALDWIN, JAMES FOSDICK, prof. history; b. Chelsea, Mass., Apr. 29, 1871; s. Charles Jacobs and Adelaide (Fosdick) B.; A.B., Denison U., Granville, O., 1893; Ph.D., U. of Chicago, 1897; m. Ellen H. Adams, 1915; 1 son, Charles Adams. Instr., Denison U., 1893-94; fellow U. of Chicago, 1895-97; instr. in history, 1897-1902, asso. prof., 1902-07, prof., 1907-—, Vassar Coll. Fellow Royal Hist. Soc.; mem. Am. Hist. Assn., Delta Kappa Epsilon; hon. Mem. English Manorial Soc. Author: Scutage and Knight Service in England, 1897; The King's Council in England, 1913; Select Cases before the King's Council, Selden Society, vol. XXXV. Contbr. to hist. revs. and mags. Address: Vassar College Poughkeepsie NY‡

BALDWIN, JAMES H., judge; b. St. Joseph, Mo., Aug. 1, 1876; s. John T. and Emma Louise (Cockrell) B.; B.L., U. of Va., 1900; m. Myrtle White Meehan, July 25, 1907; children—Mary Louise (Mrs. Perry R. Gage), Emma Cockrell (Mrs. L. Randolph Jones). Admitted to Mont. bar, 1900, and has practised in Montana since 1900. Asst. co. atty., 1907-08; asst. U.S. dist. atty. of Mont., 1916-19; U.S. dist. atty. of Mont., Jan. 2, 1934-June 11, 1935; U.S. dist. judge, Dist. of Mont., since June 11, 1935. Trustee Sch. Dist. No. 1, Silver Bow Bounty, 1921-27. Democrat. Home: 1834 Lowell Av. Butte MT*‡

BALDWIN, JAMES HEWITT;, b. Pittsburgh, Pa., July 23, 1876; s. Johnson Hewitt and Henrietta (McAllister) B.; pvtly. ed.; m. Belle Frazer, of St. Joseph, Mo., Nov. 19, 1901; children—Eleanor Frazer, Anne Elizabeth. With engring. and textile interests, U.S. and Eng., 1902-22; pres. Crex Carpet Co., N.Y. City, 1922-29; dir. Societies Realty Co. Mem. N.Y.N.G., 1899-1911; served as capt. Am. Red Cross, dir. Southampton (Eng.) Area, 1918-19. Trustee League for Polit. Edn. Republican. Presbyn. Clubs: Union League, Town Hall (v.p.). Home: New Milford CT‡

BALDWIN, JANE NORTH, physician; b. Keeseville, N.Y., Feb. 10, 1876; d. George W. and Margaret Jane (Hargraves;) Baldwin; M.D., Cornell U., 1900; unmarried. Began as intern New York Infirmary for Women and Children, 1900; physician and prof. hygiene, Vassar Coll., since 1905, also chmn. dept. of health and hygiene; asst. in neuro-endocrine dept. Vanderbilt Clinic, N.Y. City; mem. courtesy staff Vassar Bros. and St. Francis hosps., Poughkeepsie. V.p. Am. Student Health Assn. (pres. N.Y. State sect.); mem. A.M.A., Soc. for Study of Internal Secretions. Presbyterian. Address: Vassar Coll., Poughkeepsie NY*‡

BALDWIN, LAVERNE, fgn. service officer; b. Cortland, N.Y., Aug. 2, 1899; s. Charles and Dora (Cox) B.; ed. Cortland High Sch., 1913-16. Cortland Normal Sch., 1916-18; A.B., M.A., Cornell, 1922-26; m. Isabella Hart, Jan. 9, 1943. Teacher, 1918-22; asst. Romance languages, Cornell U., 1925-26; clk., Am. Consulate Gen., Ottawa, Can., 1926, vice consul, 1927, diplomatic sec., 1928; vice consul, Santa Marta, Colombia, 1929-31; assigned to Dept. State, 1931; 3d sec., Ottawa, 1935, 2d sec. and consul, 1936; consul, Geneva, Switzerland, 1936, adviser, 21st and 22d sessions Internat. Labor Conf., 1936; consul and 2d sec., Managua, 1938; Dept. of State, 1941; 2d sec. and consul, Madrid, 1943; 1st sec. and consul, 1945; with U.S. Dept. of State 1946-47; adviser U.S. Del. to UN Assembly, 1947; 1st sec. Ankara, Turkey, 1947-49; consul gen., Istanbul, 1949-50, Bremen, Germany, 1950, Duesseldorf, 1950-54, Vancouver, 1955-56; counselor of embassy and supervising consul gen., Tokyo, 1956-59; mem. Free Europe Com., 1960-61; prof. history and polit. sci. Nathaniel Hawthorne Coll., 1964-65, N.W. Conn. Community Coll., 1965-66. Home: Taconic CT Died July 13, 1968; buried Sharon CT

BALDWIN, MAITLAND, neurosurgeon; b. N.Y.C., Sept. 29, 1918; s. Alvi Twing and Esther (McKean) B.; student Harvard, 1935-38; M.D., C.M., Queen's U., Kingston, Can., 1943; diploma neurol. surgery, M.Sc., McGill U., 1952. Asst. neurosurgeon Montreal Neurol Inst., 1950-52; lectr. in neurosurgery McGill U., 1950-52; asst. prof. neurosurgery U. Colorado, Denver, 1952-53; chief neurosurgeon, clin. dir. Nat. Inst. Neurol. Diseases and Blindness, Nat. Insts. Health, Bethesda, Md., from 1953, prof. clin. surgery Georgetown U. Hosps., from 1953; cons. NASA, Bethesda Naval Hosp. Served with USN, 1944-46. Diplomate Am. Bd. Neurol Surgery. Fellow A.C.S.; mem. Harvey Cushing Soc., Neurosurg. Soc. Am., Am. Acad. Neurology, A.A.A.S., N.Y. Acad. Scis., Soc. Neurol. Surgeons. Club: Cosmos (Washington). Home: Potomac MD Died Feb. 9, 1970; buried Gettysburg Nat. Cemetery.

BALDWIN, (LAWRENCE COUNSELL) MARTIN, art gallery dir.; b. Toronto, Can., Aug. 31, 1891; s. Lawrence Heyden and Ethel Mary B.; student Trinity Coll. Sch. Port Hope, Ont.; B.A.Sc. in Architecture, U. Toronto, 1913, LL.D., 1959; m. Evelyn May Wedd, Sept. 19, 1919; 1 dau., Diana Evelyn (Mrs. Gordon H. Madge). Architect, Sproatt & Rolph, Toronto, 1911-20; pvt. practice of architecture, 1921-26; sr. partner Baldwin & Greene, architects, 1926-33; executed commns. for several office bldgs., Toronto; councillor Ontario Coll. Art, 1933; curator Art Gallery of Toronto, 1932-47, dir., 1947-60, ret. as dir. emeritus. Served as trooper 2d King Edward's Horse, Brit. Army, 1914, from 2d lt. to capt. 9th Bn., South Lancashire Regt., 1915-18. Hon. mem. Art Museum Dirs. Assn. (dir. 1953-54); mem. Am. Assn. Museums (councillor 1951-60), Canadian Museums Assn. (pres. 1957-59),Internat. Assn. Art Critics, Phi Kappa Phi. Mem. Angelican Ch. Club: University. Home: Thornhill Ontario Canada Died May 11, 1968.

BALDWIN, OLIVER HAZARD PERRY, banker; b. Lansdowne, Pa., Feb. 26, 1904; s. Charles Edward and Marianne Moseley (Perry) B.; A.B., Harvard, 1927; grad. Rutgers U. Grad. Sch. Banking, 1943; m. Elizabeth S. Webb, Nov. 27, 1929; children—Oliver Hazard Perry, Roger Conant, Jean (Mrs. T.M. Ritchie, Jr.), Mgr., T. Hogan & Sons, Inc., port stevedores, N.Y.C., 1928-30; asst. cashier Nat. Shawmut Bank, Boston, 1930-44; v.p. First Nat. Bank of Akron, O., 1944-46; sr. v.p., Dir. Farmers Bank of State of Del., Wilmington, 1946-59, chmn. bd., pres., 1959-71, hon. chmn., 1971-72; pres. Mulco Products, Inc., 1953-55, dir., 1953-73; pres., dir. Kent Real Estate Corp., 1959-66; dir. Rollins Leasing Corp., Dover Builders, Inc., Newark Realestate & Ins. Co., Benjamin F. Shaw Co., Chesapeake Utilities Corp., Continental Am. Life Ins. Budd Chem Co., Del. News. Pres., Wilmington Clearing House Assn., 1950-52, 62-64, mem. exec. com., 1948-71; rep. Del. Savs. Bond div. U.S. Treasury, 1952-70. Bd. dirs., mem. exec. com. United Community Fund No. Del., 1948-66, chmn. campaign, 1951, pres., 1957-59; chmn. for Del. nat. U.S.O. campaign, 1955-63; bd. dirs., mem. exec. com. Wilmington Gen. Hosp., 1947-64, vice chmn., 1951, chmn. 1952-55, pres., 1955-58; mem. finance com., trustee Wesley Jr. Coll., 1959-72, vice chmn., 1964-68, chmn., 1968-72; trustee Bd. State Employees Pension Trustees, 1965-70, mem. fed. agy. relations com., 1965-67, fed. legislative com., 1967-70; bd. dirs. finance com. Wilmington Med. Center, 1965-72; chmn. trustees State Judiciary Retirement Fund, 1962-70. Mem. Am. (exec. council 1960-65. mem. fed. agy. relations com. 1965-67, fed. legislative com. 1967-70), Del. (exec. com. 1953-59, pres. 1958-59) bankers assn., Del. Econ. Devel. Bd., Del. C. of C. (exec. finance com. 1955-65, pres. 1962-64), Bank Pub. Relations and Marketing Assn., Robert Morris Assos., Assn. Mil. Banks (pres. 1963-64), Newcomen Soc. Rotarian. Clubs: Harvard (N.Y.C.); Wilmington, Wilmington Country; Thursday (Boston); Ponte Vedra (Fla.). Home: Wilmington DE Died Dec. 4, 1972.

BALDWIN, RALPH LYMAN, dir. public school music; b. Easthampton, Mass., Mar. 27, 1872; s. Lyman N. and Harriet (Miner) B.; grad. Williston Sem., Easthampton, 1890; music under George W. Chadwick, J. C. D. Parker, Stephen Emery, L. C. Elson, and Henry Heindl, Boston; Mus.B., Trinity Coll., 1925; m. Mary Pierce Hosford, May 27, 1896 (died Oct. 22, 1928); children—Mrs. Dorothy McCray, Robert Miner, Howard Hosford, Mrs. Barbara Pierce Mix, Mrs. Elizabeth Spencer Jackson, Mrs. Marion Lyman Cranson; m. 2d, Christine Reece, June 30, 1933. Organist, First Ch. Easthampton, 1894-96; organist, choirmaster, First Ch. of Christ, Northampton, 1897-1904; conductor, Vocal Club (male chorus), Northampton, 1896-1904; dir. pub. sch. music, Northampton, 1899-1904, Hartford, Conn., 1904-39 (retired); organist and choirmaster, Fourth Congl. Ch., Hartford, 1904-17, Immanuel Congl. Ch., Hartford, 1917-25. Conductor Hartford Choral Club (male chorus, 100 voices), 1907-37. Mendelssohn Glee Club (male chorus), New York, 1923-34; dir. Inst. Mus. Pedagogy, Northampton (summer sch.), 1900-29, and continues as dir. of the Institute, which affiliated with Skidmore Coll., 1929, and moved to Saratoga Springs; retired, 1931. Composer, Sonata, for organ, op. 10, 1902; Progressive Melodies, 1910; Progressive Songs, 1916; also many other pieces for organ, songs, church, etc. Compiler: (with Elbridge W. Newton) Standard Song Classics, 1913. Co-editor of Music Education (pub. school music course). Home: (summer) Canaan, N.H., (winter) 326 Edinburgh Dr., Winter Park FL‡

BALDWIN, RAYMOND PEACOCK, lawyer; b. Brookline, Mass., Nov. 3, 1894; s. Alvi Twing and Margaret Isabelle (Peacock) B.; A.B., Harvard, 1916; LL.B., 1921; m. Joan Waddy, July 28, 1920; children—Stephen Peacock, Rosemary Honor (Mrs. David Douglas Coffin). Admitted to Mass. bar, 1921, U.S. Supreme Ct., 1938, N.Y. bar, 1946, D.C. bar, 1947; asst. gen counsel Bd. Econ. Warfare, 1943, Fgn. Econ. Adminstrn., 1943-44; spl. asst. to U.S. Atty. Gen., 1944-45; mem. appeal bd. Office of Contract Settlement, 1945-53, chmn., 1951-53; regional counsel Renegotiation Bd., Boston, 1952-55. Cmdg. officer 140th Aero Squadron, 1918-19; chmn. N.E. Aviation Cadet Com., 1941-42. Clubs: Harvard (N.Y.C.); Cosmos (Washington). Author: (with Joan Baldwin) The Fun of Acting, 1951; (with David Dempsey) The Triumphs and Trials of Lotte Crabtree, 1968. Home: Concord MA Died June 1971.

BALDWIN, ROBERT JAMES, aircraft mfg. co. exec.; b. East Lansing, Mich., Aug. 11, 1917; s. Robert James and Bertha Lillian (Van Orden) B.; B.S. with honors in Chem. Engring., Mich. State U., 1940; m. Margaret Eloise Burlington, Oct. 19, 1941 (dec. July 1969); children—Bonnie Lee (Mrs. Jon MacDonald), Steven Robert; m. 2d, Ruth Feinstein, Oct. 24, 1970. With McDonnell Douglas Corp., St. Louis, 1940-73, chief systems engr., 1955-60, asst. chief engr., 1960-61, dir. aircraft engring., 1961-64, v.p. avionics engring., 1964-73. Mem. Am. Inst. Aero. and Astronautics, Navy League, Assn. U.S. Army, Phi Kappa Phi, Tau Beta Pi, Phi Delta Theta. Club: University (Washington). Home: St Louis MO Died Feb. 21, 1973.

BALDWIN, SHERMAN, lawyer; b. Bellport, L.I., N.Y., July 13, 1897; s. Henry de Forest and Jessie (Pinney) B.; A.B., Yale, 1919, LL.B., 1922; m. Harriet C. Rantoul, Sept. 13, 1930; children—Henry de Forest, Mrs. Lois B. Bishop. Admitted to N.Y. bar, 1923, Conn. bar, 1928; mem. Lord, Day & Lord, N.Y.C., 1929-69. Mem. Sch. Bd., Redding, 1940-47. Chmn. bd. finance Town of Redding, Conn., 1947-53. Sec., trustee Am. Acad. Rome; trustee Met. Mus. Art; bd. mgrs. N.Y. Bot. Garden; trustee Brearley Sch., N.Y.C., 1934-54, pres., 1944-54; trustee Pomfret School, Conn., 1930-48, Vassar Coll., 1951-65. Fellow Am. Bar Found.; mem. Bar Assn. City of N.Y. (v.p. 1955-56), Am., N.Y. State bar assns. Clubs: Century Association, Downtown Association (N.Y.C.). Home: Redding Ridge CT Died Jan. 21, 1969; buried Redding Ridge CT

BALDWIN, WILLIAM EDWARD, law editor, pub.; b. Cincinnati, O., Jan. 1, 1888; s. Thomas Francis and Katherine (Doyle) B.; ed. pub. schs., Cincinnati, O., and under pvt. tutors; studied law under Chas. B. Seymour, dean of law dept., U. Louisville; D.C.L., U. of South, 1933; LL.D., Cleveland-Marshall Law School, 1960; m. Roberta Luckett, Nov. 8, 1913 (dec. Oct. 1954). Admitted bar, Ky., 1910, O., 1920, Utah, 1912, Supreme Court of U.S., 1922; organizer, 1913, since pres. and editor-in-chief Baldwin Law Book Co., Louisville, Ky.; organizer, 1919, since pres. and editor-in-chief Baldwin Law Pub. Co., Cleveland; v.p. Banks Law Pub. Co., N.Y. City, 1924-26, editor-in-chief since 1924, pres. since 1926; editor-in-chief Banks-Baldwin Law Pub Co., 1933-67, chmn. bd., treas., 1960-67; spl. rep. (volunteer) Nat. War Labor Bd., 1942; chief labor relations, Cleveland Ordnance District, 1943-45; dir. publications dept. printing and graphic arts Harvard U., 1940-46; mem. bd. regents and finance com. U. of South, 1934-41. Mem. Am., Ky., Ohio, Cleve. bar assns., N.Y. County Lawyers Assn., Am. Inst. Graphic Arts, Sigma Alpha Epsilon, Pi Gamma Mu, Omicron Delta Kappa. Republican. Episcopalian. Clubs: Union, Rowfant, University (v.p., 1944-45; president, 1946-47) (Cleveland); Harvard, Lawyers, Grolier, Hundred Year (New York); Pendennis, Filson (Louisville); Faculty Club of Harvard University (Cambridge). Asst. editor, editor or editor-in-chief, law code books, digests, annotations, statute books, supplements to revised statutes codes and dictionaries, several of which have been adopted as ofcl.; ofcl. compilations of spl. statues and law cases; states covered included Ky., N.Y., Ohio, Tex., Ind., Mich. Home: Cleveland OH Died Dec. 5, 1967; buried Cleveland OH

BALENCIAGA, CRISTOBAL, couturier; b. Guetaria. Prov. of Guipuzcoa, Spain, 1895. Opened fashion house (his first). San Sebastian, Spain, 1916. Madrid, 1932, Barcelona, 1938; in Paris, 1937-72. Decorated Cross of Knight of Order of Isabella La Catolica (Spain). Home: Paris France Died Mar. 1972.

BALL, HERMAN FREDERICK, railroad exec.; b. Altoona, Pa., 1867. Vice chmn. Franklin Ry. Supply Co., Inc., N.Y. City; dir. Balmar Corp., Locomotive Booster Co., Superheater Co., Lima Locomotive Works, Inc., Am. Arch Co., Inc., G.M. Basford Co. Home: Westchester Country Club Grounds, Rye, N.Y. Office: 60 E. 42d St., New York 17 NY‡

BALL, NORMAN T(OWER), lawyer; b. Toledo, Ohio, February 14, 1905; son John Stanley and Nina Belle (Frary) B.; student U.S. Naval Acad., 1924-27, Universite de Poitiers, 1927; B.S., U. of Toledo, 1928; B.F.S., Georgetown U., 1929; J.D., George Washington U., 1934; student Harvard, 1943, Mass. Inst. Tech., 1943; m. Margaret Herrmann, Oct. 24, 1936. Aeronautics patent examiner, U.S. Patent office, 1928-37, classification examiner, 1937-47; exec. dir., com. on tech. information, Research and Development Bd., 1947-50; economic commissioner European Recovery Program, American Embassy, London, England, 1950-51; cons. electronics and microwave labs. Stanford U., 1952-53; program dir. Nat. Sci. Found., 1953-54, exec. sec. interdepartmental com. on sci. research and development, 1954-59, U.S. del. to com. cooperation and applied research Orgn. European Econ. Cooperation, Paris, 1956-59; counsel Nat. Council Patent Law Assns., 1960-61. Pres. Seacrest chpt. American Field Service, 1963-64, Fla. Atlantic Arts Inst. of Fla. Atlantic U., 1966-68. Served from lt. to comdr., 1940-46; U.S. Navy, Naval Intelligence, Western European sect., 1940-43; design of electronics aids to air navigation systems, 1944-46. Nat. Inventors' Council, 1940. Mem. A.A.A.S., I.E.E.E., Am. Patent Law Association. Mason. Author: sects. of books, also articles to profl. jours. Home: Delray Beach FL Died Nov. 22, 1971.

BALL, ROBERT LEE, lawyer, banker; b. Jackson County, Mo.; s. of Robert Austin and Elizabeth Constance (Rose) B.; civ. engring. course, U. of Kan. (non-grad.); m. Marion J. Cooke, Oct. 14, 1891; children—Elizabeth Constance (Mrs. Robert W. B. Terrell), Marion Ellen (Mrs. Walter R. Hensey, Jr.), Hallie Cooke (Mrs. H. H. Dewar). Asst. city engr., St. Joseph, Mo., 1879-80; admitted to Tex. bar, 1883, and began practice at Galveston; pres. Colorado (Tex.) Nat. Bank, 1889-94; moved to San Antonio, 1894; successively v.p., pres., and now chmn. bd. Nat. Bank of Commerce, San Antonio; engaged in ranching, cattle raising. Chmn. military com. State Council of Defense, Tex., World War; mem. Federal Advisory Council 11th Federal Reserve Bank Dist., 1920-23, inclusive. Pres. Tex. State Bar Assn., 1930-31; mem. Tex. Civil Judicial Council since its creation, 1927. Democrat. Methodist. Mason (33 deg., Shriner); life mem. all local Masonic bodies; Grand Comdr. K.T. of Tex., 1917-18. Home: 102 East Kings Highway. Office: Nat. Bank of Commerce Bldg., San Antonio TX*‡

BALL, WILLIAM DAVID, author, educator; b. Denver, Colo., Aug. 18, 1885; s. William and Jeanette Juliet (Sanguinette) B.; A.B., U. of Denver, 1907, A.M., 1908; special study U. of Southern Calif., 1918; m. Martha Jane Woosley, July 2, 1919; children—William

David, Martha Jane. Writer of short stories and articles on aviation, hunting and farming; editor Writers' Markets and Methods, 1927-46; pres. Palmer Inst. of Authorship, 1928-46. Roman Catholic. Author: Fundamentals of Creative Writing, 1924; also photoplays. Contbr. articles and fiction to nat. mags. Home: Wofford Heights CA Died Mar. 8, 1971; buried Midpines Cemetery, Midpines CA

BALL, WILLIAM SHERMAN, lawyer; b. nr. Hardinsburg, Breckinridge Co., Ky., Mar. 6, 1871; s. Thomas Jefferson and Judith Alice (De Jarnett) B.; studied Southern Normal Sch., Bowling Green, Ky., 1895-96; unmarried. Clk. Breckinridge Circuit Court, 1897-1903; postmaster Hardinsburg, 1903-07; admitted to Ky. bar, 1909; asst. sec. of state of Ky., 1909-11; county atty. Breckinridge Co., 1916-20; U.S. dist atty., Western Dist. of Ky., by apptmt. of President Harding, Aug. 1, 1922, resigned, Jan. 1, 1927; now engaged in gen. practice of law. Mem. Louisville Bar Assn. Republican. Baptist. Mason. Club: Lion's (Louisville). Home: 220 Weisenger Gualbert Apts. Office: 1603 Inter-Southern Bldg., Louisville KY‡

BALL, WILLIAM WATTS, editor; b. in Laurens County, S.C., Dec. 9, 1868; s. Beaufort Watts and Eliza (Watts) B.; A.B., S.C. Coll. (now Univ. of S.C.), 1887; post-grad. work, same 1888-89, LL.D., 1919; studied Law School U. of Va., summer, 1890; Litt.D., Oglethorpe U., 1937; m. Fay Witte, Apr. 21, 1897. Admitted to S.C. bar, 1890; editor and pub. Laurens Advertiser (weekly), 1890-93; editor Columbia (S.C.) Journal, 1894, Charleston Evening Post, 1895-97, Greenville (S.C.) Daily News, 1897; reporter Phila. Press, 1898; city editor Times-Union, Jacksonville, Fla., 1900-02; asst. editor Charleston News and Courier, 1904-09; mng. editor The State, Columbia, S.C., 1909-13, editor, 1913-23; dean Sch. of Journalism, Univ. of S.C., 1923-27; editor News and Courier, Charleston, 1927-50, retired, now an editorial writer and columnist. Del. Gold" Democratic Nat. Conv. that nominated John M. Palmer for president of U.S., 1896. Lay dep. Gen. Conv. of Episcopal Ch., Kansas City, Mo., 1940. Mem. Poetry Soc. of S.C. (ex-pres.), Alumni Assn. U. of S.C. (ex-pres.), Sigma Delta Chi, Phi Delta Theta, Phi Beta Kappa. Mem. bd. commrs. S.C. Instn. for Edn. of Deaf and Blind, Cedar Spring, S.C., by appt. of gov., 1921-34. Episcopalian. Mason. Author: The State that Forgot, 1932; also Essays in Reaction and other polit. and hist. monographs. Polit. editorial writer and active opponent of nat. prohibition. Independent Democrat. Editor of handbook for State of S.C., 1927. Club: Charleston. Home: 14 Water St. Office: News and Courier, Charleston SC‡

BALLANTINE, EDWARD, composer, teacher; b. Oberlin, O., Aug. 6, 1886; s. William Gay and Emma Frances (Atwood) B.; grad. high sch., Springfield, Mass., 1903; Harvard, 1903-07 (highest honors in music); studied piano with Mary Regal, Springfield, Edward Noyes and Helen Hopekirk, Boston; studied music, Berlin, 1907-09, composition with Rufer, piano with Schnabel and Ganz; Mus.D., Marietta Coll., 1940; hon. A.M., Harvard University, 1942; married Edith Perry, April 15, 1916 (divorced 1929); m. 2d, Florence Besse Brewster, June 25, 1932. Instr. music, Harvard, 1912, asst. prof. music, 1926, asso. prof., 1932-47; retired. Clubs: Harvard, St. Botolph, Composer: (orchestra) From the Garden of Hellas; (piano) Variations on Mary Had a Little Lamb in the styles of famous composers, 1st series, 1924, 2d series, 1943. Home: Vineyard Haven MA Died July 2, 1971; buried Oak Grove Cemetery, Springfield MA

BALLANTINE, JOSEPH WILLIAM, polit. scientist; b. of Am. parents, Ahmednagar, India, July 30, 1888; s. William Osborn and Josephine Louise (Perkins) B.; A.B., Amherst, 1909; LL.D., Roanoke, 1947; m. Emilia A. Christy, Oct. 30, 1917 (dec. 1952); children—Elizabeth Copley, Alice Field, Louise Adele; married 2d Lealey Frost, Aug. 23, 1952. With Am. Fgn. Service, 1909-47; sec. Am. del. London Naval Conf., 1930; consul gen., Canton, China. 1930-34, Mukden, 1934-37; assigned to Dept. of State, 1937-41; consul gen., Ottawa, Can., 1941; assigned Dept. State, 1942; dir. office Far Eastern Affairs, Dept. State, 1944; special assistant to the sec. of State, 1945-Feb. 1947; advisor Internat. Prosecution Sect., Allied Mil. Tribunal for the East, 1946; staff Brookings Instn., 1947-55; lectr. N.Y.U. Mem. Phi Gamma Delta. Conglist. Club: University (Washington). Author: Japanese as It Is New York City NY Died Jan. 29, 1973.

BALLENGER, EDGAR GARRISON, physician; b. Tryon, N.C., Nov. 20, 1877; s. Thomas Theodore and Anna (Garrison) B.; student, Furman U., 2 yrs., Harvard U. part of 1896 and U. of N.C.; M.D., U. of Md., 1901; m. Nora Gorman, of Baltimore, Apr. 20, 1904. Interne, U. of Md. Hosp., 1901-2; surgeon Md. Granite Co., 1902-4; removed to Atlanta, Ga., 1904, and since made splty. of genito-urinary diseases. Lecturer genito-urinary diseases, Atlanta Sch. of Medicine, since 1905; editor Atlanta Journal Record of Medicine since 1905; mem. staff Presbyn. Hosp. Mem. A.M.A., Southern Med. Assn., Ga. Med. Soc., Fulton County Med. Soc. (pres.), Sigma Alpha Epsilon, Chi Zeta Chi. Clubs: Atlanta Athletic, Piedmont Driving, University. Author: Genito-Urinary Diseases and Syphilis, 1908. Home: 128 Myrtle St. Office: Century Bldg., Atlanta GA‡

BALLENTINE, GEORGE ANDREW, educator; b. Jersey City, July 14, 1899; s. Robert and Elizabeth A. (Monypenny) B.; A.B., Colgate U., 1922; M.B.A., Harvard, 1924; Ph.D., Columbia, 1951; m. Frances L. Griswold, May 30, 1925; children—Patricia (Mrs. W. Weeden), Constance (Mrs. N. Merrill). Previously with Firestone Tire & Rubber Co., Nat. Cash Register Co.; instr. U. R.I., 1941-42, asst. prof., 1942-44, asso. prof., 1944-46, acting dean coll. bus. adminstrn., 1946-47, prof. econs., dean Coll. Bus. Adminstrn., 1947-66; prof. marketing, chmn. dept. bus. administration Coll. V.I., St. Thomas, 1966-68, temp. dir. extension studies, 1967. New Coll Bus. Adminstrn. bldg. U.R.I. named Ballentine Hall in his honor, 1967. Mem. Am. Marketing Assn., Alpha Tau Gamma, Beta Gamma Sigma, Phi Kappa Phi. Conglist. Author: Sales Quotas—Marketing Handbook, 1948. Address: Kingston RI Died Mar. 21, 1968; buried Kingston RI

BALLENTINE, JOHN JENNINGS, naval officer; b. Hillsboro, O., Oct. 4, 1896; s. George McClelland and Ora (Eakins) B.; B.S., U.S. Naval Acad., 1917; naval aviator, Pensacola, Fla., 1920; m. Catherine Howard Sheild, June 10, 1922; 1 son, John Jennings; Commd. ensign, U.S.N., 1917, advancing through the grades to vice adm., 1949; served with battleships during World War I; aviation assignments since, 1920, including command of torpedo and bombing squadrons in Orient and on U.S.S. Saratoga, later on duty in Navy Dept., Washington, D.C., testing and developing bombsights and allied equipment; exec. officer on carrier, Atlantic Command and in Pacific; comdg. officer U.S.S. Long Island, 1942 and U.S.S. Bunker Hill, 1942-44; dep. comdr. Air Force Pacific; comdr. Div. 7, Third Fleet; fleet liaison officer Supreme Commander Allied Powers, Tokyo, 1944; mem. U.N. Military Staff Com., 1946-47. Com. Car. Div. 1, 1947-49; comdr. Sixth Fleet in Mediterranean, 1949-51; comdr. Air Force, Atlantic Fleet, 1951-54, ret., 1954. Decorated Legion of Merit (twice, 2V), Bronze Star Medal, Commendation (V), Presidential Unit (Bunker Hill) Citation, Victory, Yangtse Campaign, Am., European, Pacific Areas (5 stars), World War II; Legion of Honor (comdr.); Grand Cordon Order Phoenix (Greece). Clubs: Chevy Chase (Washington); N.Y. Yacht. Home: Millbank Dogue VA Died May 21, 1970; interred Emmanuel Episcopal Ch., Port Conway VA

BALLY, LOUIS HENRY, coll. dean; b. Andover, Kan., Nov. 10, 1897; s. John Y. and Sylvia (Waggoner) B.; A.B., Fairmount Coll., Wichita, Kan., 1920; M.A., U. Kan., 1921, Ph.D., 1929; m. Mattie Edwards, June 9, 1923; children—John, Betty. Prof. biology faculty Northeastern State Coll., Tahlequah, Okla., from 1922, dean coll., from 1946. Vice pres., dir. Tahlequah Bldg. & Loan Assn. Served with inf. U.S. Army, 1918. Mem. Sigma Xi, Phi Sigma, Alpha Chi (nat. council). Methodist (bd.). Author articles anaphylaxis and hypersensitivity. Home: Tahlequah OK Died May 27, 1963.

BALTZLY, OLIVER DANIEL, clergyman; b. on farm near Ponca, Neb., Oct. 14, 1871; s. Simon Peter and Elizabeth (Stough) B.; A.B., Wittenberg Coll., Springfield, O., 1893, Ph.D., 1901; Mt. Airy (Phila.) Luth. Theol. Sem., 1893-94; A.M., B.D., Hamma Div. Sch., Springfield, O., 1896; D.D., Wittenberg, 1915; LL.D., Midland Coll., Fremont, Neb., 1920; married, June 11, 1896; 1 dau., Olive B. Ordained ministry Lutheran Ch., 1896; asst. pastor Fifth Luth. Ch., Springfield, 1895-96, pastor, 1896-99; pastor St. Luke's Ch., Mansfield, O., 1899-1911, Kountz Memorial Ch., Omaha, Neb., 1911-31, now emeritus. Trustee Wittenberg Coll., 1902-10; pres. Wittenberg Synod, 1906-08; pres. Luth. Synod Neb., 1920-22; del. to conv. organizing the United Luth. Ch. in America, New York, 1919; mem. Examining Com. for the Ministry for many years. Spl. lecturer Gen. All Luth. Conf., Seattle, 1929; spl. lecturer in Catechetical Evangelization," Luth. Chs., 1933-41; special Lenten preacher among Lutheran Churches, 1942-45. Mem. Library Bd., Omaha, 1922-30. Mem. Alpha Tau Omega. Republican. Clubs: Omaha Commercial, Omaha Athletic. Author: The Death Pot in Christian Science, 1920, 4th edit., 1935; Catechetical Evangelization, 1928, 2d edit., 1930; American Revision Volume of Prayers by William Jay, 1937; also author numerous brochures. Home: 2602 Farnam St., Omaha, Neb.; (summer) R.F.D. 1, Backus MN‡

BAMBERGER, RALPH, lawyer; b. Indianapolis, Ind., Dec. 24, 1871; s. Herman and Caroline (Daniels) B.; A.B., Indiana U., 1891; LL.B., Ind. Law Sch. (U. of Indianapolis), 1896; m. May Freiberg, of Cincinnati, O., Apr. 30, 1901. Admitted to Ind. bar, 1898, and since practiced in Indianapolis; mem. Bamberger & Feibleman; dir. Reliable Life Assurance Co.; mem. Ind. Ho. of Rep., 1893. Mem. Am., Ind., and Indianapolis bar assns., Indianapolis Chamber of Commerce. Mason. Republican. Hebrew religion. Clubs: Marion, Indianapolis, Turnverein, Deutsche Haus. Home: 2937 Washington Boul. Office: Merchants Bank Bldg., Indianapolis IN‡

BAMBOSCHEK, GIUSEPPE, opera condr.; b. Trieste, June 12, 1890; s. Benedetto and Giuseppina (Cumer) B.; studied in Europe; m. Carolina Ghidoni, Jan. 22, 1933. With Metropolitan Opera Co., 1913-29, mus. sec., 1916-29, condr., casting dir., 1930-32; mus. dir. St. Louis Municipal Opera, 1938-56; artistic and mus. dir. Phila. La Scala and Phila. Civic Grand Opera Co., 1938-56; dir. Charles Wagner Opera Co., 1939-45; dir. Chicago Opera Co., 1941-43; mus. dir. Opera Cameo TV, N.Y.C., 1952-56; gen. mgr., artistic dir. Phila. Grand Opera Co., 1957-67. Conducted at Opera Comique, Paris, Copenhagen, Berlin, Venice, Trieste, Alexandria, Havana, Balt., Cleve., Phila., Washington, Rochester, N.Y. Dir. Nat. Council of Met. Opera. Composer masses, Holy week choral services, many songs with orchestra or piano accompaniment, also arrangements of operas. Home: New NY Died June 23, 1969.

BAMFORD, MARY ELLEN, author; b. Healdsburg, Sonoma Co., Calif.; d. Dr. William and Cornelia (Rand) B.; grad. Oakland High Sch. Dist. sec. of literature for S. Pacific Dist. Woman's Am. Bapt. Home and Foreign Missionary Socs. Author: My Land and Water Friends, 1886; The Look About Club, 1887; Thoughts of My Dumb Neighbors, 1887; Father Lambert's Family, 1888; Marie's Story, 1888; The Second Year of the Look About Club, 1889; Up and Down the Brooks, 1889; A Piece of Kitty Hunter's Life, 1890; Elanor and I, 1891; Janet and Her Father, 1891; Number One or Number Two, 1891; Talks by Queer Folks, 1893; Three Roman Girls, 1893; Miss Millie's Trying, 1893; In Editha's Days, 1894; Jessie's Three Resolutions, 1894; Out of the Triangle (first published as $250 prize serial), 1898; Her Twenty Heathen, 1898; Ti, a Story of San Francisco's Chinatown, 1899; The Denby Children at the Fair, 1904; Angel Island, the Ellis Island of the West, 1917. Home: 1235 E. 15th St., East Oakland CA‡

BANAY, RALPH STEVEN, psychiatrist; b. Hungary, July 26, 1896; s. George and Helen (Vadas) B.; M.D., Royal Hungarian U., 1920; post grad. studies, Vienna, Munich, Amsterdam; m. Mary C. Allen; two daughters, Suzanne Eve and Mary Clare. Came to the United States of America, 1927; naturalized, 1937. Asst. prof. psychiatry and neurology, Royal Hungarian U., 1921-23; clinical practice Budapest, 1923-27; sr. asst. physician Manhattan State Hosp., N.Y., 1927-29; pvt. practice N.Y. City, 1929-39; dir. clin. psychiatry Boston State Hosp., 1939-40; chief dept. psychiatry Sing Sing Prison, Ossining, N.Y., 1940-43; lecturer on criminal psychopathology, N.Y. Univ. Sch. of Edn., 1942-43; research psychiatrist, Columbia U., 1943-49. Dir. research on social deviations, dept. neurology, Columbia, 1943-49; attending psychiatrist, New York Sch. for Edn. of Blind, N.Y., 1942-47; med. dir., Yale Plan Clinic, Yale, 1944, Greenmont-on-Hudson Sanatorium; Ossining, N.Y. Civic Center Clinic, Bklyn., from 1954; project dir. Cyclazacine Plus program N.Y. State Narcotic Control Commn., psychiatrist charge Youth Institute, Incorporated, Ossining; adj. prof. forensic psychiatry Manhattan Coll. Chairman Committee on Prisons, Am. Psychiatric Assn., 1942 (chmn. sect. on Legal Aspects of Psychiatry, 1951-52); member sci. bd. of Research Council on Problems of Alcohol, since 1942; chmn. com. on research and edn. Nat. Pvt. Psychiat. Hosps.; cons. psychiatrist Armed Forces Induction Center, N.Y. Diplomate Am. Bd. Psychiatry and Neurology. Fellow Am. Med. Assn., Am. Psychiatric Assn., N.Y. Acad. Scis; mem. N.Y. State and County med. assns., A.A.A.S., Soc. Med. History, Soc. Med. Jurisprudence, Med. Correctional Association, Academy Forensic Scis. (chairman section psychiatry, 1957), Am. Correctional Assn. (v.p. 1957), Internat. Assn. Correctional Medicine in Tokyo (sec.), Contbr. N.Y. Times, and mags. Author: Youth in Despair, 1948; We Call Them Criminals, 1957. Editor: Corrective Psychiatry and Jour. Social Therapy. Home: New York City and Ossining NY Died May 15, 1970; Buried Ferncliff, Hartsdale NY

BANCROFT, THOMAS MOORE, textile exec.; b. Sandy Spring, Md., Sept. 11, 1902; s. Milton H. and Margaret (Moore) B.; B.S., Princeton, 1924; m. Edith Woodward, June 12, 1929; children—Thomas Moore, William Woodward. With Mt. Vernon Mills, Inc. (formerly Mt. Vernon-Wood-Berry Mills, Inc.), Balt., 1925-70, pres., dir., 1946-70, chmn. board, 1967-70; treas. Turner Halsey Co. Inc., N.Y.C., 1932-45, exec. v.p., 1945-52, pres., 1952-53, chmn. exec. com., 1953-55, chmn. bd., 1955-66, also dir.; dir., mem. exec. com. Continental Ins. Co., Continental Corp., Mfrs. Hanover Trust Co., Mohasco Industries, Inc. (all N.Y.C.); dir., mem. banking com. Merc.-Safe Deposit & Trust Co., Balt.; dir., alternate mem. exec. com. Western Electric Co., N.Y.C. Trustee Inst. Textile Tech., Johns Hopkins Hosp., Middlesex Sch., Turner Halsey Charitable Found.; pres. Norwood Found., N.Y.C. Old Westbury LI NY Died Feb. 23, 1970.

BAND, CHARLES SHAW, banker; b. Dec. 14, 1885; s. Charles W. and Jessie (Shaw) B.; student Upper Can. Coll., 1900; married. Dir. Mfrs. Life Ins. Co., 1939-69; v.p. 1952-69; chmn. bd. Canadian Surety Co., Toronto, Ont., Can.; dir. Canada Permanent Trust. Vice pres. Toronto Red Cross, 1929-47; past pres. Art Gallery of Toronto; bd. dirs. Canadian National Inst. for Blind,

Canadian Cancer Soc., John Howard Soc.; past pres. Fedn. for Community Service. Decorated companion Order of Canada. Home: Toronto Canada Died May 27, 1969; buried Toronto Ontario Canada

BANKHEAD, HENRY MCAULEY, commercial attache; b. Moscow, Ala., Dec. 19, 1876; s. John Hollis and Tallulah (Brockman) B.; student U. of Ala., 1893-96; m. Alice B. Stickney, Nov. 3, 1903; children—John Long, Harriet, Katherine (Mrs. Flamen B. Adae). Capt. U.S. Vols., Spanish-Am. War; commd. 2d lt. U.S. Army, 1899; advanced through grades to lt. col.; retired, 1922; promoted to rank of col. retired by act of Congress. In real estate business, Miami, Fla., 1926-33; mem. City Council of Miami, 1928-30; commercial attache U.S. Legation, Ottawa, Can., since July 1, 1933. Address: 100 Wellington St., Ottawa Canada*‡

BANKHEAD, TALLULAH BROCKMAN, actress; b. Huntsville, Ala., Jan. 31, 1903; d. William Brockman and Eugenia (Sledge) Bankhead; ed. Convent of the Sacred Heart (N.Y.), Mary Baldwin Sem., Convent of the Visitation, Convent of the Holy Cross, Fairmont Sem. (Washington, D.C.); m. John Emery, Aug. 31, 1937 (divorced). Starred in Reflected Glory," Dark Victory," Forsaking All Others," The Little Foxes, Skin of Our Teeth, Tarnished Lady, The Cheat, My Sin, Thunder Below, Devil and the Deep; plays include Midge Purvis. Author: Tallulah, 1952. Appears on TV programs. Home: Bedford Village NY Died Dec. 12, 1968.

BANNER, JOHN, actor; b. Stanislaw, Poland, Jan. 28, 1910; s. David and Mina (Treiber) B.; came to U.S., 1938; m. Christine Gemenne, June 19, 1965. Actor plays Zurich, Switzerland, Vienna, Austria, N.Y.C., also films, TV; appeared as Sgt. Schultz in Hogan's Heroes, CBS-TV, 6 years. Home: Sherman Oaks CA Died Jan. 28, 1973.

BANTA, PARKE MONROE, lawyer; born in Berryman, Missouri, Nov. 21, 1891; s. Cyrus Newton and Susie (Learned) B.; student William Jewell Coll., Liberty, Mo., 1907-08; LL.B., Northwestern U., 1914; m. Gladys Nichols, Apr. 13, 1918; children—Doris Jean (Mrs. J. Roe Pree), Carol (Mrs. Scott R. Brewer), Mary Elizabeth (Mrs. James R. McHaney). Admitted to Missouri bar, practiced, Potosi, 1914-25; prosecuting attorney, Washington Co., Mo., 1917-18; mem. law firm Edgar and Banta, Ironton, Mo., 1925-41; adminstr. State Social Security Commn. of Mo., 1941-45; mem. 80th Congress, 8th Mo. Dist., 1947-49; law practice, Ironton, Mo., 1949-53; gen. counsel U.S. Dept. Health, Edn., and Welfare, 1953-61. Mem. first br. com. apptd. by Supreme Ct., 21st Jud Circuit, Mo., served many terms thereafter. Former v.p. Young Rep. Assn. Mo. Served from pvt. to 1st lt., U.S. Army, 1918-19. Mem. Am., Fed., D.C. bar assns., Mo. Bar, Holland Soc. N.Y., Am. Legion, Delta Theta Phi. Republican. Methodist. Mason. Rotarian. Home: Potosi MO Died May 12, 1970.

BANTEL, EDWARD CHRISTIAN HENRY, prof. civ. engring.; b. Troy, N.Y., Sept. 30, 1873; s. Christian and Frederika Sabilla (Lutz) B.; grad. Troy Acad., 1893; C.E., Rensselaer Poly. Inst., 1897; m. Mrs. Lillian M. Daniels, Oct. 27, 1904. Began as rodman, later topographer and insp. N.Y. and Ottawa R.R., during constrn. of the road; supervisor of track, Mexican Nat. R.R., 1898-1900, except 6 mos. in U.S. Army, Spanish-Am. War; asst. engr. mines and railroads, Cambria Steel Co., 1901; with U. of Tex. since 1901, prof. civ. engring. since 1913, also asst. dean of College of Engring. (now assistant dean emeritus). Fellow Texas Academy of Science; member Texas Philosophical Society, Am. Soc. C.E., Soc. for Promotion Engring. Edn., Am. Assn. Univ. Profs., Rensselaer Soc. of Engrs., Sigma Xi, Tau Beta Pi, Chi Epsilon. Democrat. Conglist. Mason (hon. 33 deg., K.T., Shriner). Club: University. Home: 2307 San Antonio St., Austin TX‡

BARACK, LOUIS BARRY, dept. store exec.; b. Pitts., June 7, 1910; s. Joseph and Martha (Katz) B.; B.S., U. Pitts., 1933; M.B.A., Harvard, 1935; m. Florence Schenberg, Feb. 16, 1941; children—Jane (Mrs. D. Paul Cohen), Peter, Marcy. Group sales mgr. Sears, Roebuck & Co., 1935-49; with Goldblatt Dept. Stores, Chgo., 1949-67, exec. v.p., gen. mgr., 1965-67. Mem. Ill. Retail Mchts. Assn. (bd. dirs.). Club: Briarwood Country (Deerfield, Ill.). Home: Highland Park IL Died June 19, 1967.

BARBA, CHARLES ELMER, mechanical engr.; b. Freemansburg, Pa., May 12, 1877; s. William Henry and Christiana (Smith) B.; student Bethlehem Prep. Sch., 1896-97; M.E., Lehigh U., 1901; m. Margarita E. Dunn, of Washington, D.C., June 22, 1904; children—Charles Elmer, Margarita Christiana, Dorothy Ann (Mrs. Dr. Bernard Wefers), Preston Albert, Francis William, William Henry, Elizabeth Dunn, Robert Eugene, John Edward. Draughtsman, Ordnance Dept., Washington, D.C., 1901-02; draughtsman, asst. chief draughtsman, asst. engr., Pa. R.R., Altoona, Pa., 1902-15; asst. engr., supt., Midvale Steel Co., Phila., 1915-17; supt. Mobile Carriage Shop, Watertown, Mass., 1917-19; supt. sea coast department, Watertown Arsenal, 1919-20, special duty, 1920-21; superintendent Osgood Bradley Car Co., Worcester, Mass., 1922-25; mechanical engineer, B.&M. R.R., N. Billerica, Mass., 1925-33; cons. practice, 1933-35; became chief engr., Junior Motors Corpn., Phila., and railroad consulting engr., 1936; now cons. engr. Ferrous Metals Corpn. Lecturer on railroads, State Coll. of Pa., 3 yrs.; on shop orgn. and management, foremanship and business administrations, Northeastern Univ., Boston, and mem. Mass. State Univ. Extension staff 3 yrs. Mem. Am. Soc. M.E. (chmn. r.r. div., 1935), Soc. for Promotion Engring. Edn., New England R.R. Club. Author of articles and tech. papers. Home: 11 Willard St., Newton, Mass. Office: 17 John St., New York NY‡

BARBEE, HUGH ARTHUR, physician; b. Point Pleasant, W.Va., Jan. 31, 1874; s. Andrew Russel and Margaret Ann Gillespie (Thompson) B.; M.D., U. of Pa., 1895; m. Mary Esther Byers of Pittsburgh, Dec. 18, 1901. Sec. and exec. officer, State Bd., of Health, W.Va., 1903; sec. U.S. Pension Examining Bd.; local surgeon B. & O. R.R. Mem. A.M.A., W.Va., State Med. Soc. Cabell Co. Med. Soc. Progressive. Mason (K.T.). Address: Point Pleasant WV‡

BARBER, H(ORATIO), aeronautical underwriter; b. Croydon, England, Sept. 11, 1875; s. Charles Worthington and Isabel (Loughborough) B.; student Bedford and Oxford U., 1888 to 1895; m. Bertha Louise Alexandra (von Hildenbrand), of Algiers, 1914; children—John Worthington, Marie Louise, Robert Cecil, Suzanne, James Christopher. Traveled extensively; began building and flying aircraft, 1908; designed, built and flew the first all-British airplane; presented 4 aircraft to British Govt., 1911; qualified as airplane and airship pilot; organized works of Aircraft Mfg. Co.; officer Royal Flying Corps during World War; organized Aviation Ins. Assn. of Lloyd's, etc.; came to U.S., 1922; pres. Aero Underwriters Corpn., Aero Ins. Co., Aero Indemnity Co., Barber & Baldwin, Inc., Aero Engineering & Advisory Service, Inc., Avbar, Inc., Aviation Syndicate, Inc.; dir. Globe Underwriters Exchange, Inc. Fellow Royal Aeronautical Soc., Royal Geog. Soc.; mem. Inst. of Aeronaut. Engrs. Clubs: Army and Navy (New York); American Yacht Club, Royal Societies (London), Royal Air Force, Royal Aero. Author: The Aeroplane Speaks, 1917; Aerobatics, 1918; Airy Nothings, 1919; also various text-books. Home: Hillcrest," East Portchester, Conn. Office: 122 E. 42d St., New York NY‡

BARBER, SIDMAN I(RA), lawyer; b. Stockton, Mo., June 9, 1898; s. Ira Everett and Martha Jane (Hawkins) B.; student pub. schs.; m. Bernadine H. Herring, May 1, 1937; 1 son, Wayne S. Admitted to Ida. bar, 1920; pvt. practice, Boise, 1920-37; admitted to N.Y. bar, 1938; pvt. practice N.Y.C. from 1938; mem. firm Reid & Priest from 1941. Asst. atty. gen. Ida., 1931-32. Served as sgt. U.S. Army, 1917-19. Mem. American Bar Association, American Judicature Society, Bar Association City New York. Methodist. Club: Lawyers (N.Y.C.) Home: Short Hills NJ Died Jan. 14, 1971.

BARBEY, DANIEL EDWARD, naval officer; b. Portland, Ore., Dec. 23, 1889; s. John and Julia Anna (Chlopeck) B.; B.S., U.S. Naval Acad., 1912; m. Katharine Graham, June 16, 1927. Commd. ensign USN, 1912, and advanced to vice adm., 1944; in charge War Plans sect. Bur. Nav., 1941-42; chief of staff, comdg. Service Force, also Amphibious Force, Atlantic Fleet, 1942; established and in charge Amphibious Warfare sect., staff comdr.-in-chief, Washington; as comdr. 7th Amphibious Force, conducted all amphibious operations S.W. Pacific area (eastern end New Guinea through Bismarck Archipeligo to Philippines); comdr. mopping-up amphibious landings, Philippines, N. Borneo, also landing Balikpapan, Borneo; participated at surrender Japanese comdr. of Korea, 1945; handled repatriation of over two million Japanese from Korea and China; served as comdt. Caribbean Sea Frontier; comd. 13th Naval Dist., 1950; ret., 1951. Dir. Civil Def., State of Wash., 1951-57. Decorated Navy Cross, D.S.M. with gold star, D.S.M. (Army), Legion of Merit (U.S.) Spl. Grand Order of Orange Nassau with Swords by Royal Decree (Netherlands), hon. Comdr. Mil. Div. Order Brit. Empire; Comdr. Order of Liberator (Venezuela); Grand Order of The Cloud and Banner (China); Order of Christopher Columbus, Degree of Great Cross, Silver Plaque; Order of Merit Juan Pablo Duarte, Degree of Great Cross, Silver Plaque (Dominican Rep.). Clubs: Army and Navy (Washington); New York Yacht; Seattle Yacht. Contbr. articles on nat. def. to well known mags. Currently writing a history of amphibious operations in S.W. Pacific in World War II. Home: Olympia WA Died Apr. 11, 1969; buried Portland (Ore.) Meml. Cemetery.

BARBIROLLI, SIR JOHN, symphony orchestra condr.; b. London, Dec. 2, 1899; son Lorenzo and Louise (Ribevrol) B.; ed. Trinity Coll. of Music, London, 1911-12, Scholar: Royal Acad. London, 1912-17. Asso. and Fellow; Fellow Trinity Coll., London; Mus. Doc. (hon.), Manchester U, 1950, Dublin, 1952, Sheffield U., 1957, London University, 1961; Mus. Doc. (hon.), Leicester University, 1964, Keele University, 1969; m. to Marjorie Parry (divorced); m. second, to Evelyn Rothwell, July, 1939. First public appearance as cellist, Queens Hall, London, 1911; cellist Internat. String Quartet, 1920-24; organized and condr. Barbirolli Chamber Orchestra, England, 1925; condr. Brit. Nat. Opera Co., 1926; guest condr. London Symphony Orchestra and Royal Philharmonic Soc. Concerts, 1927; condr. Internat. Opera, Covent Garden, London, 1927-33 and 1936 for Coronation season; condr. Scottish Orchestra and Leeds Symphony, 1933-36; guest comdr., Russia and Finland, Jan. 1935; condr. Philharmonic-Symphony Orchestra. New York, 1936-43; permanent condr. and musical dir. Halle Orchestra, England, 1943-58, conductor-in-chief and musical adviser, 1958-68, conductor laureate, from 1968-—; served as conductor in chief and musical adviser to Houston Symphony Society 1961-67, conductor emeritus, from 1967. Toured in Italy, Belgium, also toured in Holland, northern Germany, 1944-45; conducted at first postwar Salzburg festival; conducted for Vienna Philharmonic Society, Vienna, 1946; conducted in Florence, Rome, Turin, 1947, and various other European and Am. orchs., 1948-—. Served as lance corporal 1st Bn., Suffolk Regt., Brit. Army, during World War I. Received Knighthood, 1949. Freeman City of Manchester, 1958; Gold Medal Royal Philharmonic Soc., 1950; Bruckner Medal. Bruckner Soc. Am., 1959; Hon. Academician Nat. Acad. St. Cecilia, Rome; freeman City of Houston, 1964; comdr. Order White Rose of Finland 1st class; Order of Merit with rank of Knight Republic of Italy; officier l'Order des Arts et des Lettres, 1966; Mahler medal Bruckner Soc. Am., 1964; offcier L'Ordre National du Merite, 1968. Roman Catholic. Clubs: Lotos, Century Assn. (N.Y.C.); Lord's Traverners. Published serveral transcriptions of classical manuscripts. Address: Manchester England Died July 1970.

BARBORKA, CLIFFORD JOSEPH, diagnostician; b. Clinton, Ia., July 19, 1894; s. Joseph V. and Emma Marie (Schooley) B.; B.S., U. of Chicago, 1918; M.D., Rush Med. Coll., 1920; M.S., U. of Minn., 1923; D.Sc., Simpson Coll., 1932; m. Bessie Mae Long, July 28, 1919; children—Clifford Joseph, William Vincent. Interne, Presbyterian Hosp., Chicago, 1920-21; cons. physician Mayo Clinic, 1921-32; cons. gastroenterology, VA Research Hosp., Chgo.; professor medicine, chief gastrointestinal clinic, Northwestern U. Med. Sch. Attending phys., chief gastrointestinal service Passavant Memorial Hosp. Chairman international research committee World Orgn. Gastroenterology; member board directors of MEDICO, Incorporated; adv. panel gastroenterology U.S. Pharmacopea. Diplomate Am. Bd. Internal Medicine in gastroenterology. Fellow A.C.P.; mem. A.M.A., Ill. State Med. Soc., Inst. of Med. of Chicago, Soc. of Internal Medicine, Am. Gastroenterol. Assn. (pres. 1959), Central Soc. of Clinical Research, Assn. of Resident and Ex-Resident Physicians of Mayo Clinic, Am. Gastroscopic Soc. (pres. 1958), Beta Theta Pi, Nu Sigma Nu, Kappa Theta Psi, Sigma Xi, Alpha Omega Alpha. Author: Treatment by Diet, 1934, 5th Edition, 1948; also chpts. and sects. in books, articles, monographs. Co-author: Peptic Ulcer—Diagnosis and Treatment, 1955. Home: Chicago IL Died May 1971.

BARBOUR, ERWIN HINCKLY, geologist; b. Springfield, Ind.; s. Samuel Williamson and Adeline (Hinckly) B.; A.B., Yale, 1882, Ph.D., 1887; m. Margaret Roxanna Lamson, of New Haven, Conn., Dec. 7, 1887. Asst. palaeontologist U.S. Geol. Survey, 1882-88; Stone prof. natural history and geology, Ia. Coll., 1889-91; prof. geology, U. of Neb., state geologist, and curator Neb. State Mus., since 1891. Geologist Neb. State Bd. of Agr. since Feb., 1893. Supt. edn. for Neb., St. Louis Expn., 1904. Fellow Geol. Soc. America, A.A.A.S.; mem. Neb. Ornithologists' Union, Neb. Acad. Science, Palaeontol. Soc., Assn. of State Geologists, Seismol. Soc., Assn. Am. Museums. Contbr. on geol. and palaeontol. topics. Address: University of Neb., Lincoln NE‡

BARBOUR, JAMES JOSEPH, lawyer; b. Hartford, Conn., Dec. 28, 1869; s. Rev. H. H. and Frances E. B.; prep. edn., high sch., Newark, N.J.; studied law in office of Judge Frederick A. Smith, Chicago, 1888, and at Lake Forest U. Law Sch., 1889-92; m. Lillian Clayton of Chicago, Sept. 1, 1891. Atty. for Commercial Nat. Bank, until 1897; asst. state's atty. Cook County, 5 yrs. resigning Dec. 1, 1908; elected state senator 1916; spl. counsel to atty. gen. of Ill. in vice graft and murder prosecutions, Rock Island, 1923-27, and spl. asst. state's atty. Chicago graft cases, 1924; spl. asst. state's atty. in McHenry County prosecutions, 1928-29. Chmn. Local Advisory Bd., World War, and speaker for patriotic organizations. Mem. Am. Inst. Criminal Law and Criminology (ex-v.p.) and Ill. Soc. same (ex-pres.), New England Soc. of Chicago (pres. 1924-25). Baptist. Mason. News columnist and speaker on Am. history and biography. Compiler 3rd edit. Abbott's Brief for the Trial of Criminal Cases, 1925. Home: 2422 Hartzell Av., Evanston, Ill. Office: Chicago and 627 Grove St., Evanston IL‡

BARCLAY, MCKEE, journalist; b. Pewee Valley, Ky., Aug. 8, 1869; s. Rev. Thomas Philander and Louisa (Rhorer) B.; ed. Ky. Coll.; Louisville High Sch.;

Princeton Collegiate Inst.; m. Lena Rutledge Tyler, of Bowling Green, Ky., Feb. 18, 1893; m. 2d, Helen Church Yearley, July 2, 1928. Has worked on newspapers as Washington correspondent, editorial writer; cartoonist, St. Louis, New York and Baltimore; magazine writer; now asst. to pres. Davison Chem. Co. Presbyn. Co-Author: The Young Privateersman, 1911. Home: 425 Hawthorn Rd., Baltimore MD‡

BARCLAY, WADE CRAWFORD, church official; b. West Liberty, Ia., Aug. 8, 1874; s. Crawford S. and Emily H. (Wonsetler) B.; B.Ph., State U. of Ia., 1899; B.D., U. of Chicago, 1906; studied Teachers Coll. (Columbia); D.D., Simpson Coll., Indianola, Ia., 1911; m. May Hartley, Jan. 1, 1901; children—Lois M. (Mrs. Gardner Murphy), Hartley W., Gordon L., Margaret Eloise (Mrs. Philip H. DuBois), Gwendolyn. Ordained ministry M.E. Church, 1895; pastor chs. in Ia. and Ill. until 1909; ednl. dir. Bd. of Sunday schs., M.E. Ch., 1909-14; asso. editor Teachers' and Adult Publs., Meth. Bk. Concern, 1914-26; sec. Div. of Foreign Service, Bd. of Edn., M.E. Ch., 1926-27; exec. sec. Joint Commn. on Religious Edn. in Foreign Fields, 1927-44. Member educational commission and executive committee Internat. Council of Religious Education; chairman Commission on Christian Literature, Com. on Cooperation in Latin Am., 1941-46; hist. research, Div. Foreign Missions, Board of Missions and Church Extension, Meth. Church since 1946. Author: History of Methodist Missions, (6 vols.). Home: 54 Morningside Drive, N.Y.C. 25. Office: 150 Fifth Av., NY‡

BARCUS, JAMES SAMUEL, clergyman, educator; b. Tulip, Ark., Dec. 5, 1865; s. Rev. Edward Rosman and Mary Frances (Smith) B.; M.A., Southwestern U., 1890, D.D., 1923; student in theology, Vanderbilt, 1890-92; m. Minnie Florence Williams, June 6, 1893; children—Joseph Garland, Annie Edward (Mrs. T. H. Minga), Mary Frances (dec.), James Samuel. Ordained ministry M.E. Ch., S., 1892; pastor, successively Granbury, Clarendon and Ft. Worth, Tex., to 1901; pres. Clarendon Coll., 1901-04; dean Sch. of Theology and prof. Bible, Southwestern U., Georgetown, Tex., 1905-09; pres. Seth Ward Coll., Plainview, Tex., 1911; pastor Greenville and Bonham, Tex., 1912-14; presiding elder, Wichita Falls Dist., 1914-18; pastor McKinney and Denton, Tex., 1919-22; pres. Southwestern U., 1923-28; presiding elder Sulphur Springs Dist., 1928-32; pastor Sulphur Springs, Tex., 1932-35, McKenzie Memorial Ch., Clarksville, Tex., 1935-38. First Ch., Archer City, Tex., 1938-39; retired, 1941. Home: 409 E. 10th St., Georgetown TX‡

BARCUS, NORMAN, state ofcl.; b. Milw., Dec. 23, 1905; s. Jacob and Tillie (Finkelstein) B.; A.B., Wayne State U., 1930; m. Betty Lapinsky, Nov. 23, 1928; children—Ronald, Diane (Mrs. James F. Clarke). Tchr. Detroit high schs., 1928-37; statistician, labor market analyst, economist Mich. Employment Security Commn., Detroit, 1938-70, dir. research and statistics div., 1956-70. Mem. benefit financing com. Interstate Conf. Employment Security Agys., 1957-64, chmn., 1963, 67. Mem. Am. Statis. Assn., Am. Econ. Assn., Internat. Assn. Publs. include studies of benefits costs in unemployment ins., studies of labor market. Home: Oak Park MI Died Jan. 13, 1970.

BARD, ALBERT SPRAGUE, lawyer; b. Norwich, Conn., Dec. 19, 1866; s. Charles and Eliza Perkins (Daniels) B.; A.B., Amherst, 1888; LL.B. and A.M., Harvard, 1892; unmarried. Admitted to Conn. bar, 1890, began practice after admission to N.Y. bar, 1893; mem. Bard & Calkins, 1901-35; asst. sec. U.S. Finishing Co., 1899-1946. Vice chmn. and mem. exec. and other coms. of Citizens Union, N.Y.; ex-pres. Municipal Art Soc.; treas. Fine Arts Federation, New York; sec. The Mayor's Billboard Adv. Commn., 1913; charter mem. N.Y. Young Rep. Club, Honest Ballot Assn. (v.p.); vice chmn. and counsel Nat. Roadside Council; chmn. Nat. Interfraternity Conf., 1920, and received its gold medal for distinguished service to youth, 1940. Hon. mem. Art Commn. Associates (N.Y. City), 1948. Chmn. Local Draft Bd. 154, N.Y. City, 1917-18. Mem. Assn. Bar City of New York, Chi Psi (ex-pres.). Clubs: City (v.p.), Town Hall. Home: 64 Midland Av., East Orange, N.J. Office: 25 Broad St., New York NY‡

BARD, SARA FORESMAN, artist; b. Slippery Rock, Pa.; d. Jackson Eugene and Mary (Foresman) B.; studied at Pratt Inst., Art Inst. of Chicago, Grand Central Sch. of Art, N.Y. City. Awarded group prize, Baltimore Water Color Club, 1928; N.Y. Water Color Club prize, 1928; Lloyd Griscom prize, Am. Water Color Club, 1929; Clement Studebaker prize, Hoosier Salon, 1929; Terre Haute star prize for oils, 1931; Nat. Assn. Woman Painters and Sculptors medal, 1931; John McCutcheon water color prize, Hoosier Salon, 1934; Buckingham water color prize, Hoosier Salon, 1936; water color prize, Springfield Art League, 1939; numerous hon. mentions. Mem. Washington, Baltimore, Am. Water Color Club; Nat. Assn. of Women Artists, Springfield (Mass.) Art League (Phila.), Pa. Acad. Fine Arts, Woodmeere Gallery (Phila.), Presbyn. Home: Philadelphia PA Died July 25, 1971.

BARDGETT, EDWARD RUSSELL, ry. official; b. Fort Erie, Ont., Can., Aug. 17, 1875; s. George

Frederick and Jane Sartin (Daggert) B.; came to U.S., 1882, naturalized, 1900; ed. pub. schs. and business sch., Buffalo, N.Y., 1882-95; m. Emily Maude Jackson, Mar. 9, 1898 (died July 13, 1938); children—Emily Maude (Mrs. Donald H. Babbitt), Jane Jackson (Mrs. Roger H. Milne), Edward White; m. 2d, Mrs. Myrtle Sutherland Douglas. Successively with Northern Steamship Co., L.V. R.R., C.&A. R.R., 1894-1918; port agent, Ore & Coal Exchange, 1918-19; gen. freight agent, Cunard White Star, Ltd., 1919-30; gen. traffic mgr. Western Md. Ry. Co., 1930-33, v.p. 1933-45; retired. Pres. Pub. Library Assn., Glen Rock, N.J. Republican. Episcopalian. Mason. Clubs: Traffic (New York, Pittsburgh, Baltimore). Home: 51 Washington St., Westfield NY‡

BARING, MAURICE, author; b. London, Eng., Apr. 27, 1874; s. Edward Charles and Emily (Bulteel) B.; student Eton Coll., 1887-91, Trinity Coll., Cambridge, 1903-04; unmarried. In British diplomatic service, 1899-1904; war corr. to Morning Post, 1905; spl. corr. to Morning Post, 1905-07; spl. corr. in Turkey to Times, 1912. Served in Royal Flying Corps and Royal Air Force, 1914-18. Decorated Chevalier Legion d'Honneur, 1915, Officer, 1933; O.B.E., 1918. Roman Catholic. Clubs: Athenaem, White's, Beefsteak (London). Author: Outline of Russian Literature, 1914; Puppet Show of Memory, 1921; Collected Poems, 1921; Cat's Cradle, 1925; C, 1924; Daphne Adeane, 1927. Address: Half-Way House, Rottingean Sussex England‡

BARKER, ELLEN BLACKMAR (ELLEN BLACKMAR MAXWELL), author; b. at West Springfield, Pa.; d. John Simmons and Rebecca M. Blackmar; ed. Edinboro, Pa.; m. Rev. Allen J. Maxwell, 1879 (died Lucknow, India, 1890); 2d, Albert Smith Barker (q.v.), 1894. Author: The Bishop's Conversion; Three Old Maids in Hawaii; The Way of Fire. Address: Washington DC*

BARKER, ERNEST FRANKLIN, coll. prof.; b. Listowel, Ontario, Can., Mar. 16, 1886; s. Charles Hewlett and Minnie (Feetham) B.; B.S., U. of Rochester, 1908; M.A., U. of Mich., 1913, Ph.D.,1915; m. Emma Swigart, Dec. 27, 1916; children—Paul Raymond, Stephen Francis; came to U.S., 1888, naturalized citizen, 1898. Physics teacher, East High Sch., Rochester, N.Y., 1908-11; instr. mathematics, U. of Rochester, 1911-13; asst. in mathematics, U. of Mich., 1913-14; prof. physics, U. of Western Ontario, 1915-19; nat. research fellow, U. of Mich., 1919-22; asst. prof. physics, 1922-27, asso. prof., 1927-31, prof., 1931-56, chmn. dept. of physics, 1941-55; prof. physics Alma Coll., 1956-58; Consultant to Argonne National Lab., 1950-55. Fellow A.A.A.S., Am. Phys. Soc. Mem. Am. Assn. Univ. Profs., Am. Assn. Physics Teachers, Phi Beta Kappa, Phi Kappa Phi, Sigma Xi, Sigma Pi Sigma, Theta Delta Chi. Congregationalist. Club: University (Mich.). Home: Ann Arbor MI Died Jan. 24, 1970.

BARKER, JOHN, JR., lawyer and insurance company executive; born at Brookline, Massachusetts, Mar. 18, 1906; s. John and Miriam A. (Trowbridge) B.; A.B. cum laude, Williams Coll., 1927; LL.B., Harvard University, 1930; married Mary Cleave, January 15, 1944; one son, John Cleave. Admitted to Mass. bar, 1930; asso. Choate, Hall & Stewart, Boston, 1930-36; atty. New Eng. Mutual Life Ins. Co. Boston, 1936-42, counsel, 1942-48, gen. counsel, 1948-59, vice president, 1950-64, sr. v.p., 1964-66, sr. v.p., gen. counsel, 1966-70, chmn. agy. adminstrn. com., 1960-66, dir., 1960-70; dir. Boston Safe Deposit & Trust Co., Boston Co., Inc. Dir. Massachusetts Hosp. Service, Incorporated, 1953-56, Mass. Higher Edn. Assistance Corp., New Eng. Med. Center Hosps., Medic Alert Found., Internat., World Affairs Council; trustee Dexter School, Brookline. Served as comdr., U.S. Navy, 1942-46, comdr., USNRF. Mem. American Bar Assn. (mem. ho. dels., 1955-58, standing com. unemployment and social security) Nat. Conv. Lawyers and Life Ins. Cos. (co-chmn. 1950-55), Assn. Life Ins. Counsel (exec. com. 1951-59, pres. 1954-55), Life Ins. Assn. Am., Am. Life Conv. (chmn. legislative com. 1956-57), Res. Officers Assn., Phi Beta Kappa, Delta Kappa Epsilon. Epicopalian (sr. warden). Clubs: Country (Brookline); Somerset (Boston); Algonquin. Articles on ins. profl. jours. Contbg. author: Life and Health Insurance Handbook. Home: Chestnut Hill MA Died Dec. 11, 1970.

BARKER, LILLIAN MARION, author, biographer, reporter; b. Atlanta; d. Charles Louis and Katherine (Harman) Barker; student parochial schs., Atlanta. Author, biographer Dionne Quints, The Dionne Legend, 1951; spl. corr. for N.Y. News on quint case, 1935-64; writer syndicated serials for Street & Smith Publs., 1932-40; U.S.O. publicity dir. for S.E., 1942-46; conducted writers workshops in White Plains, N.Y., 1940-41, Am. Assn. U. Women, Jr. League creative writing groups, Atlanta, 1954-55; writer biographical sketch of Dionne Quints for Colliers Ency., 1966. Recipient Ann. prize for article Nat. League Am. Pen Women, 1960. Mem. Nat. League Am. Pen Women, Ga. Writers Assn. Home: Atlanta GA Died Oct. 6, 1968.

BARKER, NELSON W(AITE), physician; b. Evanston, Ill., Apr. 25, 1899; s. Earle Sherman and Ollive (Waite) B.; A.B., Dartmouth, 1921; M.D., U. Chgo., 1925; M.S., U. Minn., 1929; m. Florence Buswell, Apr. 6, 1926; children—Sylvia, David, Robert. Interne, Cook County Hosp., Chgo., 1924-26; fellow Mayo Found., 1926-29, 1st asst., path. anat. Mayo Clinic, 1927-28, 1st asst. medicine, 1928-30, asso. in med., staff, 1930-48, head sect. med. 1948-57; instr. med. Mayo Found. Grad. Sch., U. Minn., 1930-33, asst. prof. med., 1933-38, asso. prof., 1938-48, prof., 1948-64, emeritus prof., 1964-68; med. cons. Rochester State Hosp., 1957-68. Fellow Am. College Phys., circulation sect. Am. Heart Assn. Diplomate Am. Bd. Internal Medicine, 1937. Mem. A.M.A., Minn. State Med. Assn., Southern Minn. Med. Assn., Minn. Soc. Internal Medicine, Central Soc. for Clin. Research, Am. Soc. for Study of Arteriosclerosis (pres. 1953), Kappa Sigma, Alpha Kappa Kappa, Phi Beta Kapp, Sigma Xi (pres. Mayo Found. chpt. 1955-56). Independent. Author: Peripheral Vascular Diseases (with E. V. Allen and E. A. Hines), 1946, 2d edit. 1955, 3d edit., 1962; (with Florence B. Barker) Bird Songs of Southeastern Minnesota with birdsong recs.; many contbns. to med. lit. on diseases of the blood vessels and circulation, blood coagulation and anticoagulants. Home: Rochester MN Died Aug. 21, 1968.

BARKER, RALPH HOLLENBACK, pub. utility exec.; b. Hillsdale, Kan., Feb. 9, 1912; s. Edgar Russell and Edna (Morrison) B.; certificate proficiency in accounting U. Kan., 1944; m. Eunice Katherine Miller, May 27, 1931; 1 dau., Delores Marie (Mrs. Jess O. Ewing). With Gas Service Co., Kansas City, 1929-71, dir., 1962-71, sec., 1962-71, treas., 1964-71. Mem. Nat. Assn. Accountants (past dir.), Financial Execs. Inst. (past dir.), Inst. Internal Auditors (past treas., dir.). Presbyn. (ruling elder, treas.), Mason (Shriner); mem. Order Eastern Star. Club: Kansas City. Home: Hillsdale KS Died Sept. 24, 1969; buried Hillsdale Cemetery, Hillsdale KS

BARKER, SAMUEL HAYDOCK, financial consultant; b. Wyncote, Pa., Feb. 20, 1872; s. Wharton and Margaret Corlies (Baker) B.; prep. edn. at home; certificate of proficiency in biology, U. of Pa., 1889; m. Ada Mae Long, Apr. 9, 1902; children—Eleanor Wharton, Redwood, Robert White, Rowland. Began as clk. with banking firm, Philadelphia, Pa., 1890; financial editor The North American, Philadelphia, 1901-26; an organizer, 1927, and subsequently pres., Bankers Trust Co. Mem. Acad. Natural Sciences of Philadelphia, Am. Acad. Polit. and Social Science, Pa. Soc. Republican. Originator of plan followed in placing $500,000,000 loan to Great Britain in U.S. early in World War. Home: Wall Garden," Port Royal Av., Roxborough, Philadelphia PA*‡

BARKSDALE, ALFRED DICKINSON, judge; b. Halifax, Va., July 17, 1892; s. William Randolph (judge Sixth Judicial Circuit of Virginia) and Hallie Poindexter (Craddock) B.; ed. Cluster Springs Academy, 1907-08; B.S., Va. Mil. Inst., 1911; LL.B., U. Va., 1915; m. Louisa Estill Winfree, Dec. 15, 1934; children—Louisa Estill Winfree, Mary Owen. Admitted to Va. bar, Aug. 13, 1915, and began practice in Lynchburg; judge Sixth Judicial Circuit of Va., 1938-40; judge U.S. Dist. Court, Western Dist. of Va., 1940-72. Mem. Va. Senate, 1924, 26, 27. Served as capt. 116th Inf., U.S. Army, with A.E.F., World War. Decorated Distinguished Service Cross; Chevalier Legion of Honor, Croix de Guerre. Trustee Hollins Coll.; bd. visitors U. Va. Mem. Am., Va., Lynchburg bar associations, Kappa Alpha, Phi Delta Phi, Phi Beta Kappa. Democrat. Episcopalian. Clubs: Boonsboro Country (Lynchburg); Lynchburg VA Died Aug. 16, 1972; buried Spring Hill Cemetery Lynchburg VA

BARKSDALE, JOHN WOODSON, surgeon; b. Vaiden, Miss., Nov. 20, 1876; s. Charles Henry and Emily St. Albans (Woodson) B.; ed. pvt. schs. and under tutors until 1893; M.D. U. of Ala., 1899; m. Emily Meade Hawkins, Apr. 18, 1900; children—Elizabeth Vaiden (Mrs. Wm. D. Lawson, Jr.), Emily Woodson (Mrs. Wm. G. Humphrey), Charlotte Milstead (Mrs. Thomas A. Turner, Jr.), Theresa Hawkins (Mrs. Geo. Vinsonhaler), John Woodson, Henry Edward, Battle Malone. Began practice at Birmingham, Ala., 1899; instr. surgery Memphis (Tenn.) Hosp. Med. Coll., 1905-06; surgeon and pres. Winona (Miss.) Infirmary since 1910; surgeon and chief of staff, Jackson Infirmary, since 1923; visiting surgeon Miss. State Charity Hosp.; div. surgeon I.C. R.R., Miss. Sanatorium for the Tubercular; dir. Miss. Fire Ins. Co., Plaza Investment Co. Served as lt. col., sr. surgeon Hosp. Center, Rimaucourt, France, and comdg. officer Base Hosp. 58, World War; now col. Med. Sect. O.R.C. Fellow Am. Coll. Surgeons (gov.), Southern Surg. Soc.; mem. A.M.A., Southern Med. Assn., Miss. State Med. Soc. (ex-pres.), Tri-State Med. Soc. (ex-pres.), Miss. Reserve Officers' Assn. (ex-pres.); hon. mem. West Tennessee Medical and Surgical Soc., Newcomen Soc. of Engineers (chmn. Mississippi Committee). Mem. Founders Group American Bd. Surgery. Democrat. Episcopalian. Mason, Elk. Clubs: University (ex-pres.), Jackson County (ex-pres.), Rotary, Tennessee (Memphis). Home: 1440 N. State St. Address: Jackson Infirmary, 121 N. President St., Jackson MS*‡

BARLEY, REX, newspaper exec.; b. London, Eng., Nov. 10, 1913; s. Frank Ernest and Gertrude Mary (Miller) B.; grad. with honors, Poly. Sch., London, 1928; m. Topsy Steel, June 3, 1939; 1 son, Simon Rex. Came to U.S., 1948. Office boy, later asst. sales mgr. Kellner Partington Agy., London, 1928-39; purchasing agt. Norwegian Govt. in Exile, 1939-40; European bus. mgr. United Press Assns., 1945-48; exec. mgr. Times-Mirror Syndicate, Los Angeles, 1948-50; dir. Los Angeles Times Syndicate; dir. Los Angeles Times, Washington Post News Service; pres. Gen. Featurer, N.Y.C. Lit. critic. Served to acting wing comdr. R.A.F., 1941-45; ETO, MTO. Author: Cross To Bear Proudly. Home: Pasadena CA Died June 1, 1971.

BARLOW, CLAUDE HEMAN, physician; b. Lyons, Mich., Oct. 13, 1876; s. Nathan Pratt and Eliza Jane (Humphrey) B.; M.D., Northwestern U., 1906; certificate London Sch. of Tropical Medicine, 1914; D.Sc., Johns Hopkins U., 1929; m. Grace Eugenia Hawley, Dec. 31, 1907; (dec. 1967); children—Mary Ruth (Mrs. N. W. Abrahams), Harriet Hawley (Mrs. J. W. McConnell), Hester Hunt (Mrs. Donald Richon), Elizabeth Jean (Mrs. Steven Davids). Health officer, Engadine, Mich., 1906-07; med. missionary Am. Baptist Fgn. Missions Soc., Huchow, China, 1908-10; Shaohsing, 1911-25 (supt. of hosp., 1911, 1919), Ningpo, 1925-28 (supt. hosp. 1926); port physician, Ningpo, Chinese Maritime Customs, 1925-28; head Schistosom Studies, Rockefeller Foundation, Eqypt, from 1929; staff mem. Internat. Health Div., The Rockefeller Foundation; official examiner for British Red Cross. Discovered life cycle of Fasciolopsis buski; worked on Clonorchis sinesis; researches on Schistosomes in Eqypt. Director of Bilharzia Snail Destruction Section in the Ministry of Public Health, Cairo, Eqypt, resigned to contract with the South African Council for Scientific and Industrial Research for work on the control of Bilharzia Snail hosts. Awarded Cert. of Merit for medical research, February 8, 1948. Member of Soc. Tropical Medicine, Helminthological Soc., Soc. of Parasitologists (China branch), Ornithological Soc. of Mich., Royal Soc. of Tropical Medicine, China Med. Soc. Surgery, Delta Omega, Sigma Xi, Theta Kappa Psi. Author: Monograph on Fasciolopsis buski, 1925. Author articles on researches on control of Schistosomiasis in Eqypt. Amateur lapidist. Home: Trumansburg NY Died Oct. 9, 1969.

BARLOW, HOWARD, symphonic orchestra condr.; b. Plain City, O., May 1, 1892; s. Earl W. and Nettie (Dunham) B.; student U. of Colo., 1911-12; A.B., Reed Coll., Portland, Ore., 1915; post-grad. student Columbia, 1915-17; m. Jeannette Thomas, Dec. 12, 1926. Condr. choral socs., 1917-19; made debut as orchestral condr., at MacDowell Festivals, Peterborough, N.H., 1919; condr. Am. Nat. Orchestra, 1923-25; condr. and musical dir. Neighborhood Playhouse, N.Y. City, 1923-27; symphonic condr. Columbia Broadcasting System, 1927-43; conducting for Symphonic Hour, Philco Radio Hour, Everybody's Music, March of Time, and others; condr. Philharmonic Symphony, 1942-43 and 1943-44; condr. Baltimore Symphony Orchestra; guest condr. Met. Opera Co. and most of major symphonies in U.S.; condr. orchestra on N.B.C., Voice of Firestone; condr. Harvest of Stars on NBC. Served as sgt. U.S. Army with A.E.F. during World War I. Mem. Sigma Nu. Address: Bethel CT Died Jan. 31, 1972; buried Portland OR

BARLOW, WILLIAM HARVEY, oil co. exec.; b. Neosho, Mo., Oct. 11, 1910; s. John T. and Diva E. (Rudy) B.; B.S. in Petroleum Engring., U. Okla., 1931; grad. Advanced Mgmt. Program, Harvard, 1957; m. Edna M. Lough, Dec. 20, 1937; 1 son, Michael Harvey. With Phillips Petroleum Co., 1932-36; petroleum engr. U.S. Bur. Mines, 1942-52; with Ohio Oil Co. (name changed to Marathon Oil Co. 1962), 1942-69, mgr. research dept., 1954-59, mgr. research and planning, 1959-61, dir. 1959-69, v.p. chems., planning and research, 1961-66, v.p. research and chems., 1967-69, also mem. research, computer policy, finance coms. Mem. exec. bd. Put-Han-Sen Area council Boy Scouts Am. Mem. Am. Petroleum Inst., Am. Inst. Mining, Metall. and Petroleum Engrs., Findlay Area (trustee), Ohio (dir.) chambers of commerce, N.A.M., Phi Gamma Delta, Tau Beta Pi, Sigma Tau. Presbyn. (deacon, bd. Findlay OH Died Feb. 9, 1969; buried Bartlesville OK

BARNDS, WILLIAM PAUL, bishop; b. Sweet Springs, Mo., Aug. 5, 1904; s. William Tyson and Virginia (Larsen) B.; B.A., Mo. Valley Coll., 1925, D.D. (hon.), 1947; M.A., U. Mo., 1927; Ph.D., U. Neb., 1949; B.D., U. Chgo., 1940; S.T.M., Seabury-Western Sem., 1944, S.T.D. (hon.), 1967; D.D., U. of South, 1967; m. Ida Lou Sterrett, June 30, 1930; children—William Joseph, Mary Ida (Mrs. James W. Garrard), Virginia Lou (Mrs. Nicholas George Albanese, Jr.). Ordained deacon Episcopal Ch., 1932, priest, 1933, bishop, 1966; rector in Mo., Kan., Neb. and Ind., 1933-56; lectr. philosophy and lit. Ind. U. extension at South Bend, 1954-56; rector Trinity Ch., Ft. Worth, 1956-66; suffragan bishop Diocese Dallas, 1966-73; adj. prof. philosophy Tex. Christian U., 1956-73. Chmn. dept. Christian edn. Diocese Kan., 1939-44, dept. Christian social relations Diocese Neb., 1945-48, dep. promotion, also mem. bishop and council Diocese No. Ind., 1954-56; mem. exec. council depts. Christian edn., promotion and div. missions Diocese Dallas, 1956-66, mem. standing com., 1958-61; dep. to gen. convs., 1937, 43, 46, 49, 52, 55, 58, 61, 64. Club: Torch. Author articles. Home: Fort Worth TX Died Jan. 1973.

BARNES, CHARLES BENJAMIN, lawyer; b. Boston, Nov. 1, 1868; s. Charles Benjamin and Clara Louisa (Page) B.; A.B., Harvard, 1890, LL.B., 1893; m. Josephine Lea Low, Nov. 17, 1897; children—Bertha Lea (Mrs. Robert G. Stone), Charles R., Clara (Mrs. John Lee), John Pindar. Began practice in 1893 with Long and Hemenway, now Hemenway & Barnes; dir. Webster & Atlas Nat. Bank, Boston, New Eng. Mutual Life Ins. Co., Hingham Mut. Fire Ins. Co.; trustee Hingham Inst. for Savings. Referee in bankruptcy, 1898-1901; instr. suretyship, Harvard Law Sch., 1897-98; moderator Town of Hingham 25 yrs.; mem. Pilgrim Tercentenary Commn.; chmn. Mass. Sesquicentennial Commn. Mem. Am. Bar Assn., Mass. Bar Assn., Bar Assn. City of Boston, Mass. Society Mayflower Descendants (Governor). Clubs: Union, Somerset, Harvard (New York); Curtis, Lawyers', The Law Club, Cohasset Golf (pres.). Home: Hingham, Mass. Office: 334 Tremont Bldg. Boston MA‡

BARNES, CLARENCE ALFRED, lawyer; b. Brooklyn, N.Y., Aug. 28, 1882; s. William D. and Mabel F. (Harding) B.; grad. Yale Univ. and Yale Law Sch., 1904, 06; married Helen Long, March 13, 1906 (died Dec. 3, 1915); children—Clarence A., David H., Jane F. (Mrs. Carlisle Moore), John R.; m. 2d, Doreen Kane, Oct. 8, 1927; children—Thomas K., Samuel E., Rosalee I. (Mrs. David McCullough), Peter McC., Margot (Mrs. Alfred Street). Atty. gen. for the Commonwealth of Mass.; former mem. House of Reps., Mass.; mem. constitutional convention; exec. councillor, Mass.; town counsel and town moderator, Mansfield; del. Republican Nat. Convs. Mem. Bristol County (past pres.), Am., Boston, Mass. bar assns. Republican. Conglist. Mason Home: Mansfield MA Died May 25, 1970; buried Springbrook Cemetery, Mansfield MA

BARNES, FRANK HASLEHURST, neurologist, psychiatrist; b. Mohawk, Herkimer County, N.Y., June 1872; s. Charles Tappan and Flora Ann B.; grad. Utica (N.Y.) Free Acad., 1891; studied under pvt. tutor M.D., New York Med. Coll., 1896; m. Ella Betts Jerman, Sept. 22, 1897. Propr. Dr. Barnes Sanitarium, Stamford, since 1898. Formerly assistant prof. neurology, N.Y. Post-Grad. Hosp.; cons. neurologist Stamford Hospital; consultant psychiatrist Greenwich Hospital, St. Joseph's Hospital, Stamford, Conn. Ex-pres. Peoples Nat. Bank of Stamford. Ex-pres. Stamford Chamber of Commerce; ex-vice pres. Stamford Y.M.C.A.; ex-mem. Sch. Com. of Stamford. Mem. Med. Advisory Bd. during World War I. Diplomate Am. Bd. Psychiatry and Neurology. Mem. A.M.A., Am. Psychiatric Assn., Conn. State Med. Soc., Fairfield County Med. Assn. (ex-pres.). Republican. Presbyterian. Club: Woodway Country. Home: High Ridge Rd Stamford CT‡

BARNES, GEORGE EDWARD, physician, surgeon; b. Fairfield, N.Y., Apr. 26, 1871; s. Hiram Smith and Harriet Maria (Neely) B.; 8th generation from Thomas Barnes, Marlboro, Mass.; A.B., Cornell U., 1894; vice-principal High Sch. at South Orange, N.J., 1894-5; M.D., Coll. Phys. and Surg. (Columbia), 1899; studied insanity at the State Hosp., Binghamton, N.Y., summer of 1897; unmarried. Practiced in N.Y. City, 1899-08; phys. Vanderbilt Clinic, various depts., 1902-8; head of clinic for diseases of stomach and intestines, Univ. and Bellevue Hosp. Med. Coll. Dispensary, 1907-8; removed to Herkimer, N.Y., 1908. Fellow A.M.A.; mem. Med. Soc. State of N.Y., S.R., Delta Phi. Contbr. many articles setting forth results of original investigations, particularly relating to disturbances of arterial tension and neurasthenic diseases. Address: 125 Mary St., Herkimer NY‡

BARNES, HENRY A., traffic engr.; b. Newark, Dec. 16, 1906; s. Herman Myron and Maudie Louise (Henion) B.; student U. Mich., Mich. State Coll. Extension Sch., Gen. Motors Inst. Tech.; Sloan fellow, Yale, 1945; Ph.D. (honorary), Susquehanna Univ., 1965; married Hazel Mae Stone, Sept. 1, 1928; children—William Henry, Virginia Nancy. Elec. maintenance engr. Chevrolet Motor Co., 1933-37; traffic engr., capt. police, City of Flint, Mich., 1937-47; traffic dir., City and County of Denver, 1947-53; dir. traffic City of Balt., 1953-57, commr. of transit and traffic, 1957-62; commissioner of traffic for N.Y.C., 1962-68; cons. U.S. Congressional sub-com. on traffic safety for Interstate and Fgn. Commerce Com., 1957-58; research and devel. traffic control devices; cons. devices; cons. traffic Am., European, S.- and Central Am. cities; developed traffic signal improvements and automatic electronic correlation of signal timing to traffic vols. Mem. Nat. Hyw. Research Bd. Bd. dirs. Eno Found. Hwy. Traffic Control, Inc., Saugatuck, Conn. Recipient Presdl. award for activities war transp.; Theodore M. Matson Meml. award, 1968 Mem. Am. Inst. E.E., Inst. Traffic Engrs., Am. Pub. Works Assn., Bklyn. Engrs. Club (life), Balt. Advt. Club, Chi Epsilon. Methodist. Mason (32 deg.), Elk. Author; The Man with the Red and Green Eyes, 1966. Author articles on traffic control, transp. Home: Bayside NY Died Sept. 16, 1968.

BARNES, HOWARD, drama and motion picture critic; b. London, Eng., Nov. 26, 1904; s. Earl and Anna (Kohler) B.; brought to U.S., 1906; A.B., Yale, 1925; student Queens Coll., Oxford U., 1919-20, Sorbonne U., 1925-26; m. Katherine Vincent, Apr. 27, 1942; 1 dau. (by previous marriage), Virginia Thurston. With New York World, 1926-29, New York Herald Tribune, 1929-51, drama and motion picture critic, 1937-51; war corr., European and Pacific Theaters, World War II. Mem. Drama Critics Circle, New York Film Critics. Club: Elizabethan (New Haven). Contbr. articles to magazines. Home: New York City NY Died Mar. 12, 1968.*

BARNES, JOHN POTTS, govt. ofcl., lawyer; b. Montgomery, Ala., Aug. 13, 1902; s. Justus McDuffy and Ethel (Rawdon) B.; student U. Va., 1918, U. Ala., 1919-21; Ph.B., U. Chgo., 1923; J.D. cum laude, 1924; m. Thelma Jeannette Boyd, Oct. 18, 1926; children—Thelma (Mrs. Edward Keith Banker), Judith. Admitted to Ala. bar, 1925, Ill. bar, 1933, Cal. bar, 1944; asst. legislative counsel U.S. Senate, 1927-28; spl. atty. Bur. Internal Revenue, 1929-33; tax atty. Armour & Co., 1929-33, tax asst. gen. counsel, 1940-44; lectr. U. Chgo. Law Sch., 1930-35; master-in-chancery U.S. Dist. Ct. for No. Dist. Ill., 1934; counsel stock fire ins. cos., Middle West, 1952-55; chief counsel Internal Revenue Service, Washington, 1955-57; mem. MacLeish, Spray, Price & Underwood, Chgo., later mem. firm Reavis, Pogue, Neal & Rose, Washington. Trustee Roycemore School for Girls, Evanston, Ill., 1943-44, 46-47, Westridge Sch. for Girls, Pasadena, Cal., 1944-45. Mem. Am., Cal., Ill., Los Angeles, Chgo. bar assns., Chgo. Tax Forum, Order of Coif, Sigma Alpha Epsilon, Phi Alpha Delta. Baptist. Clubs: Law, Literary, University, Union League Keswick VA Died May 1970.

BARNES, JOSEPH FELS, newspaperman, editor; born Montclair, N.J., July 21, 1907; s. Earl and Anna (Kohler) B.; B.A., Harvard, 1927; m. Kathleen Middleton, 1928 (div. 1935); m. 2d, Elizabeth G. Brown, 1936; children—Ann (Mrs. Joseph Halper), Andrew, Nancy. With Equitable Trust Co., N.Y. City, 1928-31; on staff Inst. of Pacific Relations, in Russia, Manchuria, Japan, China, 1931-34; with N.Y. Herald Tribune, 1935-39, foreign news editor, 1940-41; dep. dir. overseas branch, Office of War Information, 1941-44; accompanied Wendell Willkie on trip to Russia and China, 1942; fgn. editor N.Y. Herald Tribune, 1944-48; editor N.Y. Star, 1948-49; editor for firm of Simon & Schuster, New York City. Recipient P.E.N. Translation Award for translation of The Story of Life, by Konstantin Paustovsky, 1964; Children's Book award Child Study Assn. Am. for transl. What It's All About by Vadim Frolov, 1969. Club: Century. Author: Willkie, 1952. Editor: Empire in the East, 1931. Translator many books from French and Russian. Home: New York City NY Died Feb. 28, 1970.

BARNES, MAYNARD BERTRAM, foreign service officer; b. Leroy, Minn., June 28, 1897; s. Bertram Thomas and Nellie (Spencer) B.; A.B., Grinnell Coll., 1919; m. Jean Cattell, Apr. 5, 1924; 1 dau., Julie Maynard. Vice-consul, Patras, Greece, 1919-21; consul, Smyrna, 1922-23; sec. of embassy, Istanbul, 1923-24; consul, St. Gall, Switzerland, 1924-25; Berlin, Germany, 1925-26; Dept. of State, 1926-30; sec. of legation, Sofia, 1930-34; Dept. of State, 1934-38; 1st sec. of embassy, Paris, 1938-41, in charge of embassy, 1940-41; sec. of legation, Reykjavik, Iceland, 1941-42; counselor and consul gen., Dakar, French W. Africa, 1942-44; U.S. representative in Bulgaria, with rank of minister, 1944-47. Mem. Sigma Delta Chi. Home: Washington DC Died Aug. 1970.*

BARNES, PARKER THAYER;, b. at Marshfield, Mass., Dec. 29, 1874; s. J. Fletcher and Anna Elizabeth (Baldwin) B.; student Bussey Inst. (Harvard) 1 yr.; practical work, N.Y. Agrl. Expt. Sta., 3 yrs., Ia. Agrl. Coll. and Expt. Sta., 1 yr., Mo. Bot. Garden, St. Louis, 3 yrs.; married. In Philippine Forestry Service 2 yrs., 1903, 1904; hort. editor Garden Magazine, 1905-7, Suburban Life, 1907-11; with Pa. Dept. Agr. since 1912, asst. zoologist, 1915-19, now exec. asst. Bur. of Plant Industry. Author: House Plants and How to Grow Them, 1909. Home: Harrisburg PA‡

BARNES, RAYMOND JOSEPH, business exec.; b. Phila., Pa., Oct. 13, 1897; s. Henry Francis and Martha Agnes (Cavanaugh) B.; ed. Phila. pub. schs.; m. Mary Leslie Love, June 8, 1923; children—Raymond Joseph, Maryellen. In grain trade, 1916-69; chmn. Erie Grain Elevator Corp., Tidewater Grain Co., R.J. Barnes & Son, Inc.; pres. Tidewater Grain Co. (Md.), Eastern Grain Co., Tidewater Mill & Elevator Company, Eastern Commodities Corporation, Commodities Management Corporation, also Barnes, Donegan and Company, Barnes, Murphy and Company, Inc., Phila.; dir. Nat. Grain Trade Council. Past pres. Comml. Exchange Philadelphia; president N.A. Export Grain Assns., New York; mem. Chicago Bd. of Trade, Winnipeg Grain Exchange, Minneapolis Grain Exchange, Chicago Mercantile Exchange, Commodity

Exchange, Inc., N.Y., N.Y. Produce Exchange. Mem. nat. laymen's com. Cath. Com. on Scouting. Mem. Soybean Council of Am. (dir.), Am., Pa. Angus assns., Balt. C. of C., also Chamber of Commerce of Greater Philadelphia. Republican. Roman Catholic. Clubs: Union League, (Philadelphia, Chicago), Seaview Country (Absecon, N.J.); Huntingdon Valley Country (Abington, Pa.). Owner Holly Tree Farms; farmer; cattle breeder. Home: Wrightstown Bucks County PA Died Mar. 20, 1969.

BARNES, STUART KNOWLTON, lawyer; b. Salt Lake City, Utah, Dec. 9, 1907; s. Claude Teancum and Annie (Knowlton) B.; A.B., U. of Utah, 1929; LL.B., George Washington U., 1933; m. Mary Louise Thatcher, Aug. 28, 1929; children—Maryanne, Nancy Thatcher, Susan Knowlton, Stuart Michael. Law clerk, U.S. Dist. Ct., Wash., D.C., 1930-32; atty., asst. counsel Reconstrn. Fin. Corp., 1932-36; sr., prin. atty. Securities and Exchange Commission, 1936-41; vice pres. Defense Supplies Corp., 1941-45; exec. dir. Office of Defense Supplies R.F.C., 1945-47; vice pres. U.S. Commercial Co. 1946-47 (all of Washington, D.C.); asst. res. atty. Guaranty Trust Co. of N.Y., 1947-50, asst. sec., 1949-50, sec., resident atty., 1950-58, v.p., sec., resident attorney, 1958-59; mem. Murray, Voorhees & Congdon, 1948-50; sr. partner Barnes, Voorhees & Congdon, 1950-59, Barnes, White & Congdon, 1960-65, Barnes & White, 1966-68; v.p. resident counsel Morgan Guaranty Trust Company of N.Y. (formerly Guaranty Trust Co. N.Y.), 1959-61, vice pres., sec., resident counsel, 1961-68. Mem. N.Y. County Lawyers Assn., Assn. Bar City of N.Y. Am., N.Y. State bar assns., Am. Soc. Corporate Secs., Inc., Order of the Coif, Phi Delta Theta, Delta Theta Phi. Club: West Side Tennis. Home: Forest Hills NY Died Feb. 21, 1968; buried Woodlawn Cemetery, Bronx NY

BARNET, HERBERT L., soft drink exec. Formerly v.p., dir. Pepsi-Cola Co., N.Y.C., exec. v.p. until 1955, became pres., 1955, chief exec. officer, 1959, chmn. bd. 1963; dir. Marine Midland Trust Co. of N.Y., Columbia Pictures Corp. Address: New York City NY Died Dec. 1970.

BARNETT, CLAUDE A., newspaper exec.; b. Sanford, Florida, Sept. 16, 1889; son of William and Celena (Anderson) B.; grad. Tuskegee Inst., 1906. Dr. Humanities, 1949; m. Etta Moten, June 24, 1934;children—Sue (Mrs. G. W. Stanley Ish, Jr.) Gladys, Etta (Mrs. Alvis Lee Tinnin). Founder Asso. Negro Press, Chicago, 1919, director, 1919-66; special assistant U.S. Secretary Agr., 1944-52. Trustee Tuskegee Inst. of Ala., Provident Hosp. (pres. bd. 1936-40). Mem. bd. govs. Nat. A.R.C. 1948-51, 1953-56. Director Phelps-Stokes Fund, N.Y. Colonization Society. Booker Washington Inst., Kakata, Liberia, 1945-55, Afro-Am. Fellowship. Life mem. Chgo. Art Inst.; asso. life mem. Chgo. Mus. Natural History. Member board Council Social Agencies, Chicago, 1937-40. Methodist. Clubs: Forty, Chicago Assembly. Appomattox. Decorated by Rep. of Haiti, Chevlier Order of Honor and Merit, 1951; Comdr. Star of Africa. Liberia, 1952. Home: Chicago IL Died Aug. 2, 1967.

BARNETT, EUGENE EPPERSON, ret. YMCA sec.; b. Leesburg, Fla., Feb. 21, 1888; s. Robert H. and Sarah (Epperson) B.; A.B., Emory University, 1907; post graduate, Vanderbilt University, 1907-08, U. of N.C., 1908-10, Teachers Coll., Columbia, 1923, 30; LL.D., Emory, 1944, U. of N.C., 1946; m. Bertha Mae Smith, July 20, 1910; children—Robert Warren, Eugenia Mae (Mrs. Fred Schultheis), Henry DeWitt, Arthur Doak. Student sec. Y.M.C.A. of U. of N.C., 1908-10; founder and gen. sec. Y.M.C.A., Hangchow, China, 1910-21; nat. student sec. Y.M.C.A. of China, 1921-23, nat. city sec. same, 1923-25; sr. sec. Internat. Com. of Y.M.C.A. for China, 1925-37; exec. sec. Internat. Com. of Y.M.C.A.'s of U.S. and Can., 1937-41, also gen. sec.; gen. sec. Nat. Council YMCA's in U.S., 1941-53; mem. World Council YMCA's, Geneva, Switzerland., from 1955. Member U.S. national commission for UNESCO. Mem. Phi Beta Kappa, Alpha Tau Omega, Tau Kappa Alpha. Methodist. Mason. Home: Arlington VA Died Aug. 7, 1970; buried Arlington Nat. Meml. Park Cemetery, Arlington VA

BARNETT, GEORGE ERNEST, economist; b. Cambridge, Md., Feb. 19, 1873; s. Edward D. and Elizabeth (Meredith) B.; A.B., Randolph-Macon Coll., 1891; Ph.D., Johns Hopkins, 1902; unmarried. Instr., asso. and asso. prof. polit. economy, 1901-11, prof. statistics, since 1911, Johns Hopkins University. Member American Economic Association (president, 1932). Am. Statis. Assn., Am. Assn. for Labor Legislation. Author: State Banking in the United States, 1902; The Printers, 1909; State Banks and Trust Companies, 1911; Mediation, Investigation and Arbitration in Industrial Disputes (with D. A. McCabe), 1916; Machinery and Labor, 1926. Editor: A Trial Bibliography of American Trade Union Publications, 1904. Co-editor of Studies in American Trade Unionism, 1906. Home: 827 Park Av., Baltimore MD‡

BARNETT, HERBERT PHILLIP, artist educator; b. Providence, July 8, 1910; s. Phillip Herbert and Elizabeth (Feldt) B.; grad. Sch. Mus. Fine Arts, Boston, 1931; European study and travel, 1931-33; m. Elizabeth Lewellyn Lettinger, Aug. 7, 1940; 1 son, Peter Herbert. Instr. painting U. Vt., 1943; instr. painting Norfolk Art Sch., Yale, 1948, dir. sch., 1949; head Sch. Worcester (Mass.) Art Mus., 1940-51; affiliate prof. art Clark U., 1946-51; dean Art Acad. Cin., 1951-72; adj. prof. art U. Cin., 1958-72; one man exhbns. include Robert Hall Fleming Mus., Manchester, Vt., Phila. Art Alliance, Fitchburg (Mass.) Art Center, Worcester Art Mus., Cin. Art Mus., Grace Horne Gallery, Boston, Marie Harriman Gallery, N.Y.C., Contemporary Arts, N.Y.C., Mortimer Levitt Gallery, N.Y.C., Wittenberg (O.) Coll., Miami (O.) U., Dayton (O.) Art Inst., rep. permanent collections Cin., Worcester art museums, Pa. Acad. Fine Arts, Amherst Coll. Mus. Art, Randolph-Macon Womans Coll. Art Gallery, U. Ariz. Gallery Art, Hallmark Co., Hallmark Internat. Gallery; works included in numerous invitational exhbns.; juror nat. and regional arts exhbns.; frequent lectr. Instl. rep. Nat. Assn. Schs. Art; mem. diocesan com. fine arts Episcopal Diocese So. Ohio. Recipient Lambert purchase prize Pa. Acad., 1938; Hallmark Internat. award, 1950. Mem. McDowell Soc., Art Dirs. Club, Print and Drawing Circle, Mens Art Club Cin., Profl. Artists Assn., Allied Artists Am. Home: Cincinnati OH Died June 26, 1972; buried Riverside Cemetery, Pawtucket RI

BARNETT, JAMES FOOTE, lawyer, financier; b. Grand Rapids, Mich., June 17, 1869; s. James Melanchthon and Lucy E. (Foote) B.; grad. Phillips Acad., Andover, Mass., 1887; B.A., Yale, 1891, M.A., 1902; LL.B., New York Law Sch., 1893; M.A., Columbia, 1901; m. Oct. 6, 1913, Katharine Waddell; 2 daughters. Admitted to bar, Kent Co., Mich., 1896; now devotes attention largely to financial interests; dir. Old-Kent Bank (Grand Rapids), Antrim Iron Co. (Marcelona, Mich.), and other corpns. Mem. State Constl. Conv., 1907-08. Republican. Conglist. Mem. Am. Soc. Internat. Law, Psi Upsilon (Yale). Club: Peninsular (Grand Rapids). Home: Grand Rapids Township R.R. 3, Grand Rapids MI*‡

BARNETT, R(OBERT) J(OHN), horticulturist; b. Denison, Kan., Jan. 16, 1874; s. James Hagah and Margaret (Linton) B.; B.S., Kan. State Agrl. Coll., 1895, M.S., 1911; grad. Kan. State Normal Sch., 1896; m. Mary Florella Day, May 31, 1899; 1 dau., Dahy Baskett. Teacher pub. schs., 1896-1901; in U.S. postal service, 1901-06; instr., Kan. State Coll., 1906-11; prof. pomology, State Coll. of Wash., 1911-20; prof. horticulture, Kansas State College of Agriculture and Applied Science since 1920, head dept. horticulture 1930-38; prof. horticulture emeritus since 1944. Dir. Mil. Red Cross Relief, Pullman, Wash., 1918; fellow A.A.A.S.; mem. Sigma Xi, Phi Kappa Phi, Alpha Zeta, Gamma Sigma Delta, Acacia. Mason. Contbr. tech. publs. Home: 1203 Thurston St., Manhattan KS‡

BARNETT, SAMUEL JACKSON, physicist; b. Woodson County, Kan., Dec. 14, 1873; s. Rev. James (D.D.) and Margaret Lees (Duff) B.; brother of James D. Barnett; A.B., U. of Denver, 1894; grad. Sch. of Astronomy, U. of Virginia, 1896; Ph.D., Cornell U., 1898; m. Lelia Jefferson Harvie, July 30, 1904. Instr. physics and biology, U. of Denver, 1894-95; asst. in Obs., U. of Va., 1895-96; univ. scholar, later Pres. White fellow Cornell U., 1896-98; instr., asst. prof., and prof. physics, Colo. Coll., 1898-1900, Stanford, 1900-05, Tulane, 1905-11, Ohio State U., 1911-18; physicist, Carnegie Inst. of Washington, 1918-26 (dept. of terrestrial magnetism, 1918-24; research associate, 1924-26); prof. of physics, U. of Calif. at Los Angeles since 1926, emeritus since 1944; research asso. Calif. Inst. of Technology since 1924. Magnetic observer U.S. Coast and Geod. Survey, 1902-04. Awarded Comstock prize for electricity, magnetism and radiation, Nat. Acad. Sciences, for discovery of magnetization by rotation, 1918. Faculty research lecturer, U. of Calif., Los Angeles, 1928. Mem. internat. Reunion d' Etudes sur le Magnetisme, Strasbourg, 1939. Mem. Nat. Research Council, 1922-24, (also mem. coms. on theories of magnetism and electromagnetic induction). Fellow Am. Assn. for Advancement of Science (mem. exec. com. Pacific Div., 1927-34), Am. Physical Soc., Am. Acad. Arts and Sciences; mem. Am. Geophys. Union, Philos. Soc. Washington, Sigma Xi (Cornell) (pres. Calif.-Los Angeles Chapter, 1933-34), Phi Beta Kappa (U. of Va.). Club: Athenaeum of Calif. Inst. Tech. Author: Elements of Electro-magnetic Theory, 1903; co-author: Theories of Magnetism, 1922; Le Magnetisme, 1940. Contbr. articles, especially on theoretical and exptl. electricity and magnetism. Home: 315 S. Hill Av., Pasadena CA ‡

BARNETT, STANLEY PUGH, mng. editor; b. Danville, Ind., July 28, 1892; s. Levi Allen and Florence (Pugh) B.; A.B., DePauw U., 1915; student U. of Wis., 1916; m. Roberta Lang, June 14, 1922; 1 son, Thomas Allen. Teacher, 1915-17; reporter Lorain (O.) Daily News, 1917-18, Richmond (Ind.) Item, 1918-19, Youngstown (O.) Telegram, 1919-20, Detroit News, 1922; with Cleveland Plain Dealer, 1920-57, beginning as reporter, asst. editor, 1956-57. Served in U.S. Army, 1918. Chmn. Associated Press Managing Editors Assn., 1948. Mem. Cleveland C. of C., Am. Soc. Newspaper Editors (dir. since 1951), Sigma Chi. Democrat. Mem. Disciples of Christ. Clubs: City (pres. 1955), Mid-day (Cleve.). Home: Columbus NC Died Nov. 1969.

BARNETT, STEPHEN TRENT, surgeon; b. Lynchburg, Va., Sept. 8, 1871; s. Edward Hammett and Caroline Louise (Trent) B.; A.B., Hampden-Sydney (Va.) College, 1891; M.D., U. of Virginia, 1896; m. Allen Watlington, June 11, 1903 (died Aug. 9, 1938); children—Stephen Trent, Frances Watlington (wife of Maj. George D. Crosby, U.S. Army). Interne, U.S. Marine Hosp. Corps 1 yr., N.Y. Polyclinic Hosp. 1 yr., N.Y. Lying-In Hosp. 4 mos.; surgeon Presbyn. Hosp., Atlanta, Ga., 1901-10; asst. gynecologist, 1904-10 and gynecologist, 1911-17, Grady Hosp.; asst. prof. gynecology, 1905-07, prof. obstetrics and gynecology, 1907-13, Atlanta Coll. Phys. and Surg.; surgeon McVicker Hosp., 1904-12; prof. obstetrics and gynecology, Atlanta Med. Coll., 1913-15; gynecologist St. Joseph's Infirmary, Davis-Fisher Sanitarium; cons. gynecologist Ga. Bapt. Hosp. Trustee Oglethorpe U. Fellow Am. Coll. Surgeons; mem. A.M.A., Med. Assn. of Ga., Beta Theta Pi, Pi Mu, etc. Presbyterian. Mason (Shriner). Home: 1746 Pineridge Road, N.E. Office: 26 Linden Av., N.E., Atlanta GA*‡

BARNEY, AUSTIN DUNHAM, bus. exec., lawyer; b. Hartford, Conn., Nov. 7, 1896; s. Danford Newton and Laura (Dunham) B.; A.B., Yale, 1918, LL.B., 1922; D.Eng. (hon.), Rensselaer Poly. Inst., 1950; LL.D., University of Hartford, 1962; m. Katharine Derr, June 1924; children—Harriet (Mrs. William Lidgerwood), Katharine (Mrs. Wyatt Garfield). Admitted to Conn. bar, 1922; counsel Hartford Electric Light Co., 1924, gen. counsel, 1928, v.p., 1936, pres., 1946, chmn. bd., 1951; pres. Conn. Power Co., 1950, later chmn. bd. merged co. Hartford Electric Light Co., ret.; dir. Hartford Steam Boiler & Inspection Company, Hartford Nat. Bank & Trust Co., Conn. Gen. Life Ins. Co., Veeder Root, Inc., Farmington Savs. Bank, Aetna Insurance Co., pres. Assn. Edison Illiminating Cos., 1955-57. Chmn. Conn. Council Crime and Delinquency; chmn. Farmington Village Green and Library Assn., Farmington Redevel. Agy.; chmn. bldg. and devel. program U. Hartford, 1958-68; mem. Conn. Council on Correction, 1967-71. Trustee Nat. Council on Crime and Delinquency; regent U. Hartford; dir. Hartford Hosp. Pres. Conn. Pub. Welfare Council, 1936-55; served Town of Farmington in various capacities, and as 1st selectman, judge, and chmn. town council, 1924-49; Conn. State senator, 1933-37. Served as 1st lt., 303d F.A., 76th Div., A.E.F., 1918. Mem. C. of C. of U.S. (dir. region 1, 1959-63). Home: Farmington CT Died May 8, 1971.

BARNHART, JOHN D(ONALD), historian; b. Decatur, Ill., Sept. 22, 1895; s. John D. and Effie Frances (Clothier) B.; A.B., Ill. Wesleyan Univ., 1916; A.M., Northwestern, 1919; student U. of Minn., 1920-21; Ph.D., Harvard, 1930; m. Zella Marie Petty, January 3, 1917; children—John Dale (deceased), Frank Alvin, Frances Mary (Mrs. Jens C. Zorn). Teaching assistant University of Minnesota, 1920-21, Harvard, 1924-25; head history dept. Neb. Wesleyan U., 1921-23; asso. prof. Ind. U., 1925-26; instr. to asso. prof. W.Va. U., 1926-33; head social sci. dept. West Liberty State Teachers Coll., 1934-36; asso. prof. history La. State U., 1936-41, Ind. U., 1941-46, prof., from 1948, acting head, 1947-48, chmn., 1948-53, Hoosier Author, 1953. Mem. adv. com. on history to Sec. of Navy, 1954-63. Mem. Ind. Ter. Sesquicentennial Commn., 1950. Mem. Indiana Historical Society (pres. 1957-60), Am., So. and Miss. Valley hist. assns. Author: Henry Hamilton and George Rogers Clark in the American Revolution, 1951; Valley of Democracy, The Frontier versus the Plantation in the Ohio Valley, 1953; Indiana, from Frontier to Industrial Commonwealth (with Donald F. Carmony) (2 vols.), 1953; (with Carmony) Indiana, the Hoosier State, 1959; (with Dorothy L. Riker) Indiana to 1816: the Colonial Period, pub. posthumously, 1971 (Ind. Author's Day award 1972). Editor: Ind. Mag. History, 1941-55; mem. editorial bd. Jour. So. History, 1936-39; Miss. Valley Hist. Rev., 1953. Home: Bloomington IN Died Dec. 25, 1967; buried Fairlawn Cemetery, Decatur IL

BARNOUW, ADRIAAN JACOB, educator; b. Amsterdam, Holland, Oct. 9, 1877; s. Pieter Jacob and Wilhelmina Cornelia (Matthes) B.; Municipal Gymnasium, Amsterdam; Ph.D., U. of Leyden, 1902; U. of Berlin, 1900-01; m. Anne Eliza Midgley, July 13, 1905; children—Willem Cornelis, Elsa, Erik, Victor. Prof. Dutch lang. and lit., Municipal Gymnasium, The Hague, 1902-19; lecturer in English, U. of Leyden, 1907-13; corr. at The Hague of New York Nation, 1913-19; Queen Wilhelmina prof. Dutch lang. and lit., Columbia, 1921-48. Associate editor Weekly Review, 1919-21. Carnegie Corp. visitor in South Africa, 1932. Mem. Maatschappij der Nederlandsche Letterkunde (Leyden), Modern Lang. Assn., Am. Council on Fgn. Relations, Philol. Soc.; pres. Netherlands U. League of N.A., Knight Order Netherlands Lion, Comdr. Order Orange-Nassau. Author: Text-kritische Untersuchungen nach dem Gebrauch des bestimmten Artikels und des schwachen Adjectivs in der altenglischen Poesie, 1902; Schriftuurlijke Poezie der Angelsaksen, 1907; Anglo-Saxon Christian Poetry (trans. by Louise Dudley), 1914; Beatrijs, A Middle Dutch Legend, 1914; De Tragedie van Johan van Oldenbarnevelt naar het Engelsch van John Fletcher en Ph. Massinger, 1923; Holland under Queen Wilhelmina, 1923; Vondel, 1925; A Trip Through the Dutch East Indies, 1927; A Middle Low German Alexander Legend, 1929; Language and Race Problems in South Africa, 1934; The Dutch, a Portrait Study of the People of Holland, 1940; The Land of William of Orange, 1944; The Making of Modern Holland, 1944; The Fantasy of Pieter Brueghel, 1947; Coming After (an anthology of poetry from the low countries), 1948. Translator: De Vertellingen Van de Pelgrims naar Kantelberg (metrical translation into Dutch of Chaucer's Canterbury Tales), 1930-33 (3 vols.). Clubs: Century, Authors, Netherland. Home: New York City NY Died Sept. 27, 1968.

BARNOWE, THEODORE JOSEPH, educator; b. Sioux City, Ia., Jan. 1, 1917; s. Anthony and Antionette (Tokarczyk) B.; B.A., Morningside Coll., 1939; M.A., U. Wash., 1940, Ph.D., 1946; postgrad. Harvard, 1946-47; m. Bonnie Jean Wallen, May 30, 1942; children—Barbara Jean, James Thaddeus, Kathryn Louise, Christine Anne, Rebecca Marie, Marilyn Frances. Indsl. psychologist Wash. State Dept. Vocational Edn., Bremerton, Wash., 1941-42; prof. human relations and adminstrn. Coll. Bus. Adminstrn., U. Wash., 1947-71; vis. prof. human relations and adminstrn. U. Turin, Turin, Italy, 1953-54; vis. prof. human relations Banff Sch. of Advanced Mgmt., U. Alberta, 1952-70; cons. organizational behavior and mgmt., 1947-71. Served with USNR, 1942-46, now capt. Res. NIH grant 1963-66. Mem. Am. Psychol. Assn., Am. Sociol. Assn., A.A.A.S., Pacific N.W. Personnel Mgmt. Assn. Seattle WA Died Feb. 25, 1971.

BARR, DAVID GOODWIN, army officer; b. Nanfalia, Ala., June 16, 1895; s. William Walter Barr; student Ala. Presbyn. Coll.; grad. Inf. Sch., 1921, Tank Sch., 1924, Army War Coll., 1939; commd. 2d lt., Inf. Reserve, 1917; 1st lt. Inf., U.S. Army, 1920, advanced through grades to maj. gen. (temp.) Feb. 1944; m. Vivian Louise Bell, Nov. 5, 1924; children—Virginia Lane, Patricia Bell. Became asst. G-4, Armoured Corps, 1940, asst. chief of staff G-4, Armored Force, 1941; chief of staff, Armored Force, 1942; dep. chief and chief of staff, European Theater of Operations, 1943; chief of staff North African Theater of Operations, and chief of staff 6th Army Group, 1944-45; G-1 Army Ground Forces, 1945-48; chief, Army Adv. Group, Nanking, 1948-49; comdg. gen. 7th Inf. Div., 1949-51; comdg. gen. Armored Center, 1951. Served with 1st U.S. Inf. Div., World War I. Decorated Silver Star with oak leaf cluster, D.S.C., D.F.C., D.S.M. with 2 oak leaf clusters, Legion of Merit, Air Medal with 3 oak leaf clusters, French Legion of Honor, Commander's Degree, Croix de Guerre with Palm, Brazilian Order of Military Merit; Gold Cross of Merit with Swords (Polish). Home: Arlington VA Died Sept. 26, 1970; buried Arlington Nat. Cemetery, Arlington VA

BARR, JOSEPH SEATON, orthopedic surgeon; b. Wellsville, O., Oct. 16, 1901; s. William Banks and Anna E. (Seaton) B.; B.S., Coll of Wooster (Ohio), 1922, D.Sc., 1952; M.D., Harvard, 1926; m. Dorrice Nash, Apr. 16, 1932; children—Joseph Seaton, Mary Bicknell. Interne Peter Bent Brigham Hosp., 1926-27; resident in orthopedic surgery, Children's Hosp., Mass. Gen. Hosp., 1928-29; practice of orthopedic surgery, Boston 1929-64; mem. faculty, Harvard Univ. Med. Sch., 1930-64, John B. and Buckminister Brown clinical prof. of orthopaedic surgery, 1948-63, John B. and Buckminster Brown prof., 1963-64; chief of orthopedic surgery, Mass. Gen. Hosp., 1948-64; surgeon in chief, New England Peabody Home for Crippled Children. Commd. lt. comdr., M.C., U.S. N.R., 1935, rear adm. Res. (ret.). Fellow Am. Acad. Orthopedic Surgery (pres. 1952) mem. A.M.A., Sandwich MA Died Dec. 6, 1964; buried Abington MA

BARR, LYMAN, investment banker; b. Edgewood, Pa., Oct. 22, 1896; s. F. X. and Catherine (Brennan) B.; ed. pub. schools of Highland Park, Ill.; m. Lucy McCarthy, Feb. 26, 1926; children—Jane, Courtney, Meredith. Clerk, Halsey, Stuart & Co., Chicago, 1916-17, 1919-20; with Paul H. Davis & Co., Chicago, 1920-53, salesman, 1920-30, gen. partner, 1930-53; founding partner Ralph W. Davis & Co., Chgo., 1953-68. Mem. Midwest Stock Exchange (mem. bd. govs. from Chicago), Chicago Stock Exchange. Clubs: Exmoor Country, Republican, Executive, Chicago Athletic Assn. Home: Highland Park IL Died July 10, 1968.

BARRETT, CHARLES RAYMOND, author; b. Saratoga Springs, N.Y., Jan. 17, 1874; s. Beebe Raymond and Laura Melissa (Allen) B.; grad. Univ. of Chicago, Ph.B., 1897; unmarried. In lit. work since 1898. Author: Short Story Writing, 1899 B1. Residence: 5254 Indiana Av. Office: Steinway Hall, Chicago IL‡

BARRETT, CLIFFORD LESLIE, educator; b. Connecticut, Dec. 3, 1894; s. Charles Leslie and Catherine Luella (Gibson) B.; A.B., Occidental Col., Los Angeles, Calif., 1917; A.M., Princeton, 1920; student U. of Calif., 1921-23; Ph.D., Syracuse U., 1926; research in Eng., France, 1939, Harvard, 1950; m. Nancy Whitton, May 17, 1923; 1 son, Norman Whitton. Instr., asst. prof., and chmn. philosophy dept. U. of Calif., at Los Angeles, 1923-25, 1926-31; asst. prof., deptl. rep. Princeton, 1931-40; honors examiner Swarthmore Coll., 1935, 37, 39; prof. of philosophy Scripps Coll. and Claremont Graduate College, 1940-66, professor emeritus, 1966-72; Alexander professor at Scripps Coll., 1961, acting dean, 1962-66; chmn. Intercollegiate Program Grad. Study; regional asso. Am. Council of Learned Socs., 1957-71; vis. prof. (summers) U. of Calif. at Los Angeles, 1932, College of William and Mary, 1946; Harvard, 1948. Mem. Am. Philos. Association, Mind Assn. (Gt. Brit.) Phi Beta Kappa. Republican. Clubs: Princeton (New York). Editor: (and contributor) Contemporary Idealism in America, 1932. Author: Ethics, 1933; Philosophy, 1935; What Makes Anything Important?, 1949; Norms of a Rule of Law, 1965. Contbr. Am. Philosophy, 1954; Insight and Vision. Contbr. articles to jours. Home: Pasadena CA Died Oct. 29, 1971; buried Forest Lawn Meml. Park, Glendale CA

BARRETT, FRED DENNETT, educator; b. Sheboygan, Wis., Sept. 19, 1906; s. Edward Jenner and Julia (Dennett) B.; B.A., U. Wis., 1928, M.A., 1931, Ph.D., 1953; m. Eileen Gertrude Meyer, Feb. 15, 1936; 1 dau., Cynthia Julia (Mrs. Bruce B. Wilson). Asst. psychology U. Wis., 1929-31; commd. 2d lt. U.S. Army, 1928, advanced through grades to col., 1960; retired, 1966; supt. schs., Grand View, Ida., 1948-50, Melba, Ida., 1950-52; dir. extension div. Ida. State Coll., 1953-55; prof. edn., chmn. dept. coll. Wooster (O.), 1955-70. Research comparative edn. U. London, 1960-61, Ministero della Pubblica Istruzione, Rome, 1966-67. Mem. Am. Assn. U. Profs., Nat., Ohio edn. assns., Phi Delta Kappa, Tau Kappa Epsilon. Rotarian, Kiwanian, Elk. Home: Madison WI Died Dec. 2, 1970; buried Roselawn Cemetery, Madison WI

BARRETT, LINTON LOMAS, educator; b. Lanett, Ala., Sept. 1, 1904; s. Linton Stephens and Carrie Elizabeth (Lomas) B.; B.A. magna cum laude, Mercer U., 1928; duPont fellow, U. Va., 1930-31; Ph.D., U. N.C., 1938; Catedratico Vitalicio (hon.), Universidad Central. Quito. Ecuador, 1953; m. Elizabeth Elliott, June 1929 (dec. 1932)); 1 son, Arthur Lomas; m. 2d, Marie Hamilton McDavid, May 26, 1937; 1 dau., Ellen Marie. From instr. to prof. Mercer U., U. Ala., Furman U., U. N.C., Princeton, U. Kan., 1928-48; prof. Romance langs., Washington and Lee U., head dept., 1960-70, prof., 1970-72; vis. prof. Spanish, U. N.C., summers; pub. affairs officer Am. embassy. Bogota, Colombia, 1951. Quito, Ecuador, 1951-53; fellow Southeastern Institute Medieval and Renaissance Studies, Duke University, summer 1966; lecturer Universidad Central, 1952; bd. examiners Coll. Entrance Exam. Bd., 1954-57; dir. NDEA Lang. Inst., 1965; research fellow cooperative program in the humanities Duke-N.C., 1965-66. Mem. Modern Lang. Assn. (sec., chmn. various groups), Am. Assn. Tchrs. Spanish and Portuguese (pres. Va. chpt.). Internat. Colloquium Luso-Brazilian Studies, Southeastern Conf. on Latin Am. Studies (past sec.-gen.), Modern Fgn. Lang. Assn. Va., Phi Beta Kappa. Episcopalian. Author: The Supernatural in the Spanish Non-Religious Comedia of the Golden Age. 1938. Editor: A Mediaeval Italian Anthology, 1938; Five Centuries of Spanish Mediaeval Italian Anthology, 1938; Five Centuries of Spanish Literature: From the Cid to the Golden Age, 1962. Translator 10 novels, other books from the Portuguese. Asso. editor: Hispania, 1950-64. Contbr. articles to profl. jours., U.S., Mexico, Ecuador, Spain. Address: Lexington VA Died Mar. 8, 1972; buried Lexington VA

BARRETT, RAYMOND F., lawyer; b. Boston, Mass., Jan. 27, 1904; s. Edward Tilton and Anne (Collins) B.; student Suffolk U.; LL.B., Boston U., 1925; m. Margery Finegan; children—Barbara, Edward T. Admitted to Mass. bar; spl. asst. atty. gen. U.S., 1959; mem. Mass. Jud. Survey Commn., 1955. Fellow Am. Coll. Trial Lawyers, Am. Bar Found.; mem. Am. (ho. of dels.), Mass. (pres. 1957-59, bd. dels., exec. com.), Norfolk County (past pres., mem. council), Boston, Quincy bar assns., Jud. Council Mass. Home: Milton MA Died Sept. 11, 1968.

BARRETTE, (JOSEPH MARIE) ANTONIO, premier of Que.; b. Joliette, Que., Can., May 26, 1899; s. Ernest and Robea (Cote) B.; D.S.Sc., Laval U., 1945, Montreal U., 1948; LL.D., Bishop's U. (Lennoxville, Que.), 1954; Dr. Juris Altruiusque, McGill University, 1960; m. Estelle Guilbault, July 2, 1924; children—Alain, Serge, Lise (Mrs. Gerard Notebaert), Nicole (Mrs. Gay Barrette). Night messenger Canadian Nat. Rys., 1913, apprentice machinist, 1915, ry. machinist, Que. and Ont., to 1930; Antonio Barrette & Son, insurance brokers, Joliette, 1935-68. Canadian Joliette County seat Que. Prov. Legislature, 1935, dep. for Joliette County, 1936-68; minister of labor, Que., 1944-51, chmn. Regional War Labor Bd., 1944-46, rep. Que. to ILO Conf., Paris, 1945, Montreal, 1946, Geneva, 1951; prime minister, Que., 1960; ambassador to Greece, 1963-66. Rep. P.Q. to Holy Year inauguration, Vatican, 1949, 51, 56. Decorated Grand officer Order St. Gregory. Mem. Internat. Assn. Machinists (past sec.). Mem. Union Nat. Party. Clubs: Reniassance, Seigniory (P.Q.). Home: Joliette PQ Canada Died Dec. 15, 1968.

BARRETTO, LAURENCE BREVOORT (LARRY), author; b. Larchmont, N.Y., May 30, 1890; s. Gerard Morris and Laura (Brevoort) B.; ed. Hoosac (N.Y.) Sch., 1902-08; m. Anna Appleton Flichtner, Oct. 20, 1923. Asst. editor Adventure Magazine, 1920-24; attached to Am. Field Service Hdqrs., 1942; war corr. Caribbean theatre, 1943, China-Burma India theatre, 1944. Enlisted Ambulance Service. United States Army, June 4, 1917; served in France and Belgium; honorably discharged April 20, 1919. Decorated Croix de Guerre (French), January 1919. Mem. bd. World Affairs Council, 1950's; mem. bd., sec. Monterey Inst. Fgn. Study, 1960's. Episcopalian. Clubs: Century (New York); Old Capital (Monterey, Cal.). Author: A Conqueror Passes. 1924; To Babylon, 1925; Walls of Glass, 1926; Old Enchantment, 1928; Horses in the Sky, 1929; The Indiscreet Years, 1931; Children of Pleasure, 1932; Three Roads from Paradise, 1933; Bright Mexico, 1935; Tomorrow Will be Different, 1936; Hawaiian Holiday (with Bryant Cooper), 1938; Journey Through Time, 1940; The Great Light, 1947, also articles on metaphysics. Home: Carmel CA Died Dec. 30, 1972.

BARRIENTOS, RENE ORTUNO, president of Bolivia, 1964-69. Home: La Paz Bolivia Died Apr. 27, 1969.*

BARRIER, JOSEPH HENRY, ins. exec.; b. Yazoo County, Miss., Sept. 30, 1890; s. Forester and Cady (Wood) B.; B.S., Miss. State Coll., 1910; m. Annie Milton Norman. Instrument man, draftsman Bogue Hasty Drainage Dist., Miss., 1910-12; field engr. drainage projects Capt. West, Greenville, Miss., 1912-14; resident engr. Miss. Levee Bd., 1914-17; mortgage loan insp. Guaranty Bank & Trust Co., Memphis, 1919-20; field engr. oil terminal Doullott & Williams, Tampico, Mexico, 1920-21; mortgage loan insp. Jefferson Standard Life Ins. Co., 1921-25, mgr. mortgage loan dept., 1925-46, v.p., 1945-55 dir., exec. and finance com., 1947-51. Served as capt., F.A., U.S. Army, 1917-19. Mem. S.A.R., George Rifles Club. Methodist Episcopal. Mason (Shriner), Elk. Clubs: Merchants and Manufacturers; Greensboro Country. Address: Greensboro NC Died July 21, 1970; buried Green Hill Cemetery, Greensboro NC

BARRINGER, PAUL BRANDON, JR., lawyer; b. Davidson, N.C., Aug. 28, 1887; s. Paul Brandon and Nannie (Hannah) B.; B.A., U. Va., 1907; LL.B. U. Mich., 1914; m. Lucy Landon Minor, Nov. 28, 1917; children—Charles Minor, Rufus. Engaged in bus., N.C., 1907-10, Tex., 1912-13; admitted to N.Y. bar, 1915, also U.S. Supreme Ct.; asst. counsel Nat. Biscuit Co., 1914-15, Am. Sugar Refining Co., 1916-17; asso., then partner firm Jackson, Nash, Brophy, Barringer & Brooks, and predecessors, N.Y.C., 1919-73. Trustee, mayor Village of Matinecock, L.I., N.Y., 1928-38. Trustee Soc. St. Johnland, 1940-63, Locust Valley Pub. Library, 1937-73. Served to capt. U.S. Army, 1917-19; AEF in France. Mem. Am., N.Y. State bar assns., Assn. Bar City N.Y., Am. Law Inst., Phi Beta Kappa, Order of Coif, Zeta Psi, Phi Delta Phi. Democrat. Episcopalian (vestry). Clubs: Century Assn., Pilgrims, Down Locust Valley NY Died Jan. 27, 1973.

BARRON, ELBERT MACBY, lawyer, business exec.; b. Van Alstyne, Tex., Feb. 13, 1903; s. John Macby and Rilla (McWilliams) B.; LL.M., Cath. U. Am., 1940; Sapientiae Mundane Dr., Boswell-Johnson Inst. Great Britain, 1960. Admitted to bar, 1924; member firm Hay, Finley, Wolfe & Barron, Sherman, Tex.; pres. Southern Gem Mining Co.; engaged in general civil practice and represented oil, r.r. and utility cos. until 1939, except 4 yrs. as counsel govt. agencies; assigned War Dept. Gen. Staff, Jan. 1940; following emergency served as chief legislative officer and chief of War Dept. litigation, later served PTO; ret. with rank of col.; formerly officer Tex. N.G. Mem. Tex. ligislature, 1932-35; exec. head and author report of legislative tax survey commn. which led to reorg. Tex. tax structure. Mem. bd. devel. U. Tex. Western Coll.; mem. devel. bd., founding mem. chancellor's council U. Tex. Bd. dirs. El Paso Mus. Fine Arts, Witte Meml. Mus. Mem. Tex., Oklahoma, D.C. and U.S. Supreme Ct. bars. British Gemmological Assn., Alumni Assn. Loyola U., Am. Gem. Soc., Heroes of '76, Disabled Officers of World Wars, El Paso Geol. Soc. (chmn.), Del. several Dem. nat. convs. Author: Current Reports on Mexican and Southwestern Minerals; Minerals of Mexio. Home: El Paso TX Died Jan. 5, 1969; buried Van Alstyne (Tex.) Cemetery.

BARROW, ELIZABETH N., author; b. Skaneateles, N.Y., Oct. 1, 1869; d. George and Caroline M. (Tyler) B.; grad. Skaneateles (N.Y.) High Sch., 1885. Favors woman suffrage. Author: The King's Rivals, 1898; The Fortune of War, 1900. Contbr. to mags. since 1895. Address: Skaneateles NY‡

BARROWS, DAVID PRESCOTT, univ. prof.; b. Chicago, Ill., June 27, 1873; s. Thomas and Ella Amelia (Cole) B.; B.A., Pomona Coll., 1894; M.A., U. of Calif.,

1895, Columbia, 1896; Ph.D., in anthropology, U. of Chicago, 1897; LL.D., Pomona, 1914, U. of Calif., 1919, Mills Coll., 1925; Dr. honoris causa, U. of Bolivia, 1928; Litt.D., Columbia U., 1933; m. Anna Spenser (Nichols), July 18, 1895; children—Anna Frances (wife of Brig. Gen. Floyd W. Stewart, Army of United States), Ella Cole (Mrs. Gerald Hagar), Thomas Nichols, Elizabeth Penfield (wife of Lieut. Col. F. G. Adams, United States Army); m. 2d, Mrs. Eva S. White, 1937. City supt. of schools, Manila, P.I., 1900; chief, Bureau Non-Christian Tribes of P.I., 1901; gen. supt. (afterwards styled director) of education for P.I., 1903-09; prof. edn. 1910, dean Grad. Sch., 1910, prof. polit. science, July 1, 1911, dean of faculties, 1913, and pres., 1919-23, prof. polit. science, emeritus, since 1943, Univ. of California. Pres. trustees Mills Coll., Calif., 1910-17; mem. bd. dirs. Calif. State Sch. for Deaf and Blind, 1912-17; mem. Calif. State Commmn. on Rural Credit and Colonization, 1915-17; dir. East Bay Pub. Utility Dist., 1924-27, 1932-34; trustee Carnegie Endowment for Internat. Peace. Mem. Belgian Relief Com., in charge food supply of Brussels, 1916, Commd. maj. of cav., N.A., 1917; lt. col. cav. U.S. Army, 1918; active duty in P.I. and Siberia, 1917-19; on original gen. staff list, U.S. Army 1919; col. 159th Inf., N.G., Calif., 1921; brig. gen. 79th Inf. Brigade, Calif. N.G., 1925; maj. gen. Army U.S., comdg. gen. 40th Div., Calif. N.G., 1926-37. First state comdr. for California, American Legion, 1920. Carnegie visiting prof. of Internat. Relations (Latin-America), 1928; Theodore Roosevelt prof., U. of Berlin, 1933-34; expert consultant to Secretary of War, 1941; representative Office Strategic Services, 1942; radio commentator, 1943-44; columnist International News Service, 1943-49. Decorated Chevalier Legion of Honor (French), promoted to officer, 1932; Order of the Crown (Belgian), Croix de Guerre (Czecho-Slovak); Order of the Sacred Treasure (Japanese); Order of the Crown (Italian); Comdr. Order of Polonia Restituta (Polish). Corr. mem. Royal Acad. of Polit. and Moral Science (Madrid), 1923. Republican. Conglist. Mem. Phi Beta Kappa. Clubs: Faculty (Berkeley); Bohemian (hon.), University (hon.), Commonwealth (San Francisco); Army and Navy (Los Angeles). Author: The Ethno-Botany of the Coahuilla Indians, 1900; A History of the Philippines, 1903, rev. 1924; A Decade of American Government in the Philippines, 1915; British Politics in Transition (with E. M. Sait), 1925; (with Thomas Barrows) Government in California, 1926; Berbers and Blacks (also transl. into French), 1927. Traveled in Asia, Malaysia, Central and South America and in Africa (Timbuktu, the French Sudan and British Nigeria). Home: 85 Parkside Dr., Berkeley 5 CA‡

BARRY, ETHELDRED BREEZE, author; b. at Portsmouth, N.H., Feb. 26, 1870. Illustrator children's books and designer The Church Kalendar, published yearly by Taber-Prang Co., from 1899 until 1904. Author: Little Tong's Mission, 1899; The Countess of the Tenements, 1900; Miss De Peyster's Boy, 1902; Little Dick's Christmas, 1903; What Paul Did, 1904. Contbr. children's stories to various mags. Formerly Mother St. John's House for Children (Order St. Anne). Apptd. Mother Superior, St. Anne's Convent, Duxhurst, Reigate, Eng., Apr. 1917. Address: St. Anne's Convent, Duxhurst Relgate England‡

BARRY, PETER, banker; b. Rochester, N.Y., Mar. 22, 1912; s. William C. and Grace (Goodloe) B.; student Mass. Inst. Tech., 1934. With Rochester Gas & Electric Corp., 1936-65; with Monroe Savs. Bank, 1965-73, exec. v.p., 1965-67, pres., 1968-73, also trustee; pres. Ellwanger & Barry Realty Co., 1964-66; dir. Lae Ont. Cement Co., Ltd., Livonia, Avon & Lakeville R.R., Instl. Securities Corp., Rochester & Genesee Valley R.R. Pres. Soc. Genesee and the Lakes, 1967-70; v.p. Otetiana council Boy Scouts Am., 1962-73, chmn. finance com., 1966-69; chmn. Rochester regional Red Cross Blood Program, 1951-56; exec. com. bd. advisers Salvation Army; mem. ad hoc com. Greater Rochester Transp. Authority, 1967; pres. Rochester Clearing House Assn., 1967-70; mem. Genesee Area Regional Planning Bd., 1967-73. Councilman, Rochester, 1950-65, mayor, 1955-62; commr. Rochester-Monroe Civic Center Commn., 1956-73. Trustee Rochester C. of C.; chmn. bd. regents Nazareth Coll., 1967-73; bd. dirs. Rochester Gen. Hosp., Genesee River Basin Regional Water Resources Planning Bd., Rochester Bus. Opportunity Corp., Vis. Nurse Service of Rochester and Monroe County. Better Rochester Living, Inc., Council Social Agys., Rochester Community Chest. Served with U.S. Merchant Marine, 1934-36; from ensign to comdr. USNR, 1941-46. Recipient Civic medal Rochester Mus. Arts and Scis., 1958; Lester P. Slade award Real Estate Bd. Rochester, 1961; named Man of Year, Rochester Rotary Club, 1964, Citizen of Year, Rochester Kiwwanis Club, 1965; recipient Civic award Rochester Fire Fighters Assn., 1965. Mem. Nat. Assn. Mut. Savs. Banks. Home: Rochester NY Died Jan. 23, 1973.

BARSANTI, OLINTO MARK, army officer; b. Tonopah, Nev., Nov. 11, 1917; s. Silvio and Agatha (Vangeliste) B.; B.A., U. Nev., 1940; M.A. in Internat. Affairs, George Washington U., 1962; grad. Nat. War Coll., 1958, Command and Gen. Staff Coll., 1946; m. Aletha Imogene Howell, Oct. 22, 1942; 1 dau., Bette (Mrs. Harvey Daniels). Commd. 2d lt. U.S. Army, 1940, advanced through grades to maj. gen., 1967; assigned Europe, 1943-45. Korea, 1950-52; chief staff, Berlin, Germany, 1955-57; assigned Army Staff, 1958-60, Joint Chiefs Staff, 1961-62; comptroller U.S. Army, Europe, 1963-65, Army Material Command, 1966; comdg. gen. 101st Airborne Div., Vietnam, 1967-68; chief staff 5th U.S. Army, 1968-71; mem. faculty Command Gen. Staff Coll., 1946-49; ret., 1971. Decorated D.S.C., D.S.M., Silver Star (5), Purple Heart (7), Legion of Merit (2), Bronze Star (8), D.F.C. Mem. Northbrook IL Died May 3, 1973; buried Arlington Nat. Cemetery, Washington DC

BARSS, JOHN EDMUND, teacher; b. Wolfville, Nova Scotia, June 21, 1871; s. Andrew de Wolf (M.D.) and Elisabeth Esther (Crawley) B.; B.A., Acadia Coll., Wolfville, 1891; B.A., Harvard, 1892, M.A., 1893; research student, Cambridge U., England, 1913; m. Emma Sedgwick Knight, of Sharon, Conn., June 24, 1899. Teacher, Roxbury Latin Sch., Boston, 1893, The Hotchkiss Sch., Lakeville, Conn., 1894-—. Baptist. Mem. Am. Philol. Assn., Harvard Club of Conn., Litchfield Co. University Club, New England Classical Assn. Author: Writing Latin (Books I and II), 1903; Beginning Latin, 1906. Editor: Cornelius Nepos (Selected Lives), 1896; Cornelius Nepos (20 Lives), 1900; Third Year Latin for Sight Reading, 1911. Address: Lakeville CT‡

BARSTOW, EDWIN ORMOND, chemist; b. Rockport, O., Nov. 13, 1879; s. Edwin F. and Emma J. (Blodgett) B.; grad. Case Sch. Applied Sci., 1900, D.E., 1941; m. Florence Katherine Schade, July 21, 1903; children—Ormond Edwin, John Carlton, Robert Osborn, Frederick, Ruth Gertrude, Richard. With Dow Chem. Co. from 1900. Dir. Chem. State Savs. Bank, Midland, Mich. Patentee of electrolytic cells and apparatus and methods for oil extraction; also processes for mfr. lead arsenate, magnesium chloride, and other salts, phenol. benzoic acid, etc. Trustee Midland Community Center. Mem. Am. Chem. Soc., Sigma Xi, Tau Beta Phi. Presbyn. Mason. Club: Rotary. Home: Midland MI Died Apr. 21, 1967; buried Midland (Mich.) Cemetery.

BARTH, GEORGE BITTMAN, army officer; b. Leavenworth, Kan., Dec. 19, 1897; s. Charles H. and Harriet (Bittmann) B.; B.S., U.S. Mil. Acad., 1918; grad. F.A. Sch., Ft. Sill, Okla., 1926, Command and Gen. Staff Sch., 1936; m. Mary S., June 21, 1935. Commd. 2d lt. U.S. Army, 1918, advanced through grades to maj. gen., Mar. 16, 1953; served with inf., also F.A., assigned R.O.T.C. duty, Auburn, Ala.; instr. arty. N.Y.N.G., 27th Div.; chief staff 9th Inf. Div., North Africa, Sicily, Normandy landing; regtl. comdr. 357th Inf., 90th Inf. Div., Normandy; with Gen. Patton's Third Army in breakthrough across France, 1944; prof. mil. sci. N.Y. Mil. Acad., 1946; dir. operations, tng. dept. Command and Gen. Staff Coll., Ft. Leavenworth, Kan., 1948, chief staff, 1949; arty. comdr. 25th. Inf. Div., Japan, 1949-50; assigned 24th Inf. Div., Korea, 1950, 25th Inf. Div., 1950-51; asst. div. comdr. 5th Inf. Div., Indiantown Gap, 1951; comdg. 5th Inf. Div., 1952-53; chief C.I.C., Sept.-Oct. 1953; chief Joint U.S. Mil. Aid Group, Greece, 1953-55; dep. comdg. gen. 1st Army, 1955-57. Decorated D.S.C., Silver star with 2 oak leaf clusters, Legion of Merit with 2 clusters, Bronze Star with cluster, Air Medal, Purple Heart. Mem. Alpha Tau Omega. Club: Rotary. Home: Leavenworth KS Died Aug. 1969.

BARTH, KARL, theologian; b. Switzerland, 1886; s. Fritz and Anna (Sartorius) B.; student univs. Berne, Berlin, Tubingen, Marburg, Prof. Gottingen U., 1921, Munster Univ., 1925; Bonn U., 1930-34, guest prof., 1946-47; leader German Church opposition to nazification, 1934; prof. Basle U., 1935-68. Author: Romerbrief, 1921; Credo, 1935; Christengemeinde und Burgergemende, 1946; Kirchliche Dogmatik, 1932-67, Die Protestantische Theologie im 19, Iahrhundert, Dogmatik in Grundriss, 1947; Evangelical Theology: An Introduction, 1962. Home: Basle Switzerland Died Dec. 11, 1968.

BARTHEL, OLIVER EDWARD, cons. engineer; b. Detroit, Mich., Oct. 3, 1877; s. Albert Edward and Elizabeth (Haerter) B.; ed. pub. schs., Detroit, and mechanical course at Detroit Business University; married Adele Gertrude Vargeson, May 18, 1906 (deceased, May 25, 1950); 1 son, Oliver Edward. Draftsman, Chas. B. King Co., Detroit, 1895-1901; designer, Henry Ford Co., 1901; chief engr. Cadillac Motor Car Co., 1902, Barthel Motor Co., 1903; expt. engr., Ford Motor Co., 1904, Oldsmobile Motor Works, 1905; hydraulic and ry. survey, Tenn., 1906; cons. engr., Detroit, since 1907; with Standard Steel Car Co., Pittsburgh, Pa., 1912-19. Became supervising engr. Federal Emergency Relief Adminstrn., in charge relief work at Detroit Police Dept. and Public Library, Apr. 1934; also area supervising engr. W.P.A., Aug. 1935-July 1937. Fellow A.S.M.E.; mem. Soc. American Military Engrs., Society Automotive Engrs., Nat. Aeronautic Assn. U.S.A. (at large), Acad. Polit. Science, Am. Geog. Soc. (fellow), Engring, Soc. of Detroit (charter mem.), Detroit Old Timers Assn. (past pres.), Detroit Mus. of Art. Founders Soc., Automobile Oldtimers, Inc., of N.Y. (life), Detroit Hist. Soc., Nat. Audubon Soc., Nat. Soc. Professional Engrs., Am. Polar Soc., Fgn. Policy Assn., Inc., Mich. Hort. Soc., Am. Acad. Polit. and Social Science, Am. Ordnance Assn.; charter mem. Mich. Soc. Profl. Engrs. Rep. Episcopalian. Mason. (K.T.). Clubs: Ingleside, Noontide, Detroit Yacht, Detroit Automobile, Holder of 35 patents for inventions and improvements. Home: Detroit MI Died Aug. 28, 1969; interred Evergreen Cemetery, Detroit MI

BARTHOLF, JOHN CHARLES PALMER, army officer; b. Plattsburg, N.Y., Oct. 26, 1891; s. John Henry and Isabella (Palmer) B.; student Phillips Exeter Acad., 1908-09, A.B., Harvard, 1913; m. Madeline Edith Tomlinson, Jan. 15, 1918; children—Edith Isabelle (Mrs. Charles Robert Clark), Anne Palmer Rawlings, John Copeland (brig. gen. USAF). Commd. 2d lt. inf., 1913, and advanced through grades to brig. gen., 1943; Aviation Section Signal Corps, 1916; junior military aviator, 1916; engaged primarily in training and test pilot duties during World War I. Club: Army-Navy (Washington, D.C.). Home: Great Barrington MA Died Sept. 22, 1969; buried Arlington Nat. Cemetery, Arlington VA

BARTHOLOMEW, RUDOLPH A., obstetrician; b. Des Moines, Apr. 19, 1886; s. William M. and Margarethe (Kori) B.; A.B., Univ. Mich., 1908, M.D., 1912; m. Eva A. Salstrom, Sept. 22, 1914 (died 1925); 1 d., Lucile; m. 2d, Rubye C. Dekle, June 12, 1926; children—Donald, Philip, Gale. Post grad. training in obstetrics and gynecology, under Dr. Reuben Peterson, Univ. Hosp., Ann Arbor, Mich., 1913-17; pvt. practice, obstetrics, Atlanta, Ga., since 1918; mem. faculty, sch. of medicine Emory Univ. since 1917; as instr. in gynecology and obstetrics, 1918-21, asso. prof. obstetrics and clinical gynecology, 1921-28, asso. prof. obstetrics, 1928-30, clin. prof. obstetrics, from 1930. Recipient Aven citizenship award Civil Def., 1956, Lamartine Griffin Hardman award for outstanding contbn. field of medicine Med. Assn. Ga., 1962. Fellow Am. Gynecol. Soc. (v.p. 1962-63), A.C.S.; mem. Fulton County Med. Soc., South Atlantic Assn. Gynecologists and Obstetricians (past pres.), Alpha Kappa Kappa, Alpha Omega Alpha. Prebyn. Contbr. Articles on splty. med. jours. Research on toxemia of pregnancy. Home: Atlanta GA Died Jan. 4, 1969; interred Westview Abbey, Atlanta GA

BARTLETT, ALDEN EUGENE, clergyman; b. Boston, Mass., Dec. 13, 1872; s. Alden Eustis and Sarah Elizabeth (Jacquith) B.; B.D., Tufts Div. Sch., 1897; spl. courses, Emerson Sch. of Oratory and Harvard; S.T.D., Lombard Coll., 1912; m. Josie S. Newman, Oct. 5, 1899. Ordained ministry, 1897; pastor Manchester, N.H., 1899-1905, Stamford, Conn., 1905-07, Chicago, 1907-14, All Souls Ch., Brooklyn, N.Y., 1914-22, First Congregational Church, Pontiac, Mich., 1922-27; pastor Grand View Heights Community Church, Lancaster, Pa. Republican. Mason (K.T.). Club: Tufts College. Author: The Joy Maker, 1918; Harbor Jim, 1923; Least Known America, 1925; Out-of-the-Way Places of Europe, 1928. Frequent lecturer at chautauquas and before clubs, extensive traveler in out-of-the-ordinary places. Home: 640 McGrann Blvd., Lancaster PA‡

BARTLETT, ALICE HUNT (MRS. WILLIAM ALLEN BARTLETT), b. Bennington, Vt., July 31, 1870; d. Seth B. (a founder of the Independent) and Lucy Bartlett (Thompson) Hunt; ed. Annie Brown Sch. for Girls, New York; m. William Allen Bartlett, M.D., Apr. 3, 1893. Actively interested in nat. defense from 1915; assisted in organizing and training aerial reserves; mem. exec. bd. and chmn. aviation com., 1915-19; organized woman's nat. defense rallies, Carnegie Hall (New York), Newport (R.I.), Nassau, etc.; founder and chmn. Treasure and Trinket Fund, 1917-18; report on airmen's needs, pub. as Senate Document. Diploma of Merit and hon. membership, Aerial League America. Organized and directed poetry and dramatic celebrations held at New York World's Fair, 1939-40. Founder, Am. editor Am. sect. Poetry Review (London, since 1923; chmn. con. for celebration of Virgil's 2000th anniversary; chmn. Nat. Arts Com. for Celebration of Washington's 200th Birthday; founder Barlett sea sonnet prize; Bartlett city sonnet prize. Organized Star Sonnet Contest, Music Contest, Poetry Contest, Ballad Contest, 1924-25, The Poe Poem Contest (with Mrs. Charles D. Dickey, John D. Rockefeller, Jr., Mrs. Percy Stewart), contests for best poems on illusion, best poems about science, best poems about animal pets, best poems on the ideal of service, best poems on civilization, best poems on leaders, best poems of flight, best poems on art, best poems packed with thought, best poems about cathedrals and the best poems about power. Awarded gold medal by Poetry Soc. of Great Britain, 1924. Mem. Poetry Soc. of London (v.p. and exec. com.), Poetry Soc. America, Am. Lit. Assn., Nat. League of Am. Pen Women (chmn. arts since 1939), Sulgrave Instn., English-Speaking Union; life mem. Shakespeare Memorial Theatre of Stratford-on-Avon; mem. Advisory Board of Allied Broadcasters; mem. Authors' League of America. Wrote: Memories; Life's Recessional; Patrollers of the Sky; The Trans-continental Mail; Amundsen; Radio; The Sea;

What America Is Doing for Poetry; The Internationalism of American Poetry; The Revival of the Sonnet; Survey of American Poetry (series in Poetry Rev.), 1923-24; Dynamics of American Poetry (Poetry Rev.), 1923-48; The Sea Anthology, 1925; The Anthology of Cities, 1926; Road Royal (verse), 1927; Caesar—the Undefeated (poetic drama), 1929; Mediterranean Ports (a poetic account of visits to Mediterranean cities), 1929; Two Thousand Years of Virgil, 1929; Washington Pre-Eminent (historic drama giving 35 key scenes); Masque of America; White Robed Choir; In Defense of the Founders of the United States; Freedom of the Mediterranean, 1938; The Pageant of the American Flag (produced at N.Y. World's Fair), 1939; Visitation (poems), 1939; Ode to Santos-Dumont—First to Navigate the Air, read on Santos-Dumont and Pan-Am. Aviation Day, N.Y. World's Fair, 1939, and Santos-Dumont Day, New York City, 1942; Six Historic and Romantic Leaders Who Visioned World Peace, 1947. Chmn. Nat. Poetry Council since 1937; chmn. Third, Fourth, Fifth Congresses of Am. Poets (N.Y. World's Fair), 1938-40; First Internat. Congress of American Poets (N.Y. World's Fair), 1939; member Nat. Arts Council, since 1936; Charles Dickens-Washington Irving Fellowship Centenary, 1938-40; 400th Anniversary of Sulgrave Manor, 250th Anniversary of the British Bill of Rights, Sesquicentennial of the Am. Bill of Rights, Mary Washington Sesquicentennial, Sesquicentennial of the Am. Theatre, Sesquicentennial of the Am. Industries, Sesquicentennial of the Founding of the Republican Form of Government. Proposed and originated Buy American" movement. Home: 299 Park Av., New York NY‡

BARTLETT, ALLAN CHARLES, editor; b. Faribault, Minn., Oct. 9, 1897; s. George William and Alice Regina (Conners) B.; student Morningside Coll., 1915-18, U. of Denver Law Sch., 1921-22; m. Madonna Morse Todd, Aug. 22, 1927; children—Todd Allan, Jeanne Alice. Began newspaper work as reporter for the Sioux City (Ia.) Tribune, 1915-17; reporter, state editor and sports editor, Rocky Mountain News, Denver, 1919-22; night cable editor Associated Press, San Francisco, 1923; reporter and city editor San Francisco News, 1924-25, mng. editor, 1926-32; editor San Diego (Calif.) Sun, 1932-35; editor Houston (Tex.) Press, 1936-46; owner, publisher Baywood Press, Pt. Reyes Station, Cal., 1951-56. Radio operator, U.S. Navy, 1918-19; member Colo. Nat. Guard, 1922. Mem. Sigma Delta Chi, Pi Kappa Delta, Phi Alpha Delta. Episcopalian. Mason (Shriner, Jester). Club: San Mill Valley CA Died Aug. 1970.

BARTLETT, EDWARD LEWIS, U.S. Senator (Alaska); b. Seattle, Wash., Apr. 20, 1904; s. Ed and Ida (Doverspike) B.; grad. Fairbanks (Alasak) High Sch., 1922; student U. Washington, 1922-24, U. Alaska, 1924-25; m. Vide Marie Gaustad, Aug. 14, 1930; children—Doris Ann (Mrs. Doris Ann Riley), Susan Bernice. Reporter, editor, 1925-33; in govt. service, 1933-36; gold miner in Alaska, 1936-39, apptd. sec. of Alaska, 1939, reapptd., 1943; resigned, 1944; delegate to Congress, 1945-59; mem. U.S. Senate for Alaska, 1959-68. Chmn. Unemployment Compensation Commn. of Alaska, 1937-39. Democrat. Mem. Pioneers of Alaska. Elk. Home: Juneau AK Died Dec. 11, 1968; buried Fairbanks AK

BARTLETT, FREDERIC PEARSON, foreign service officer; born in New York City, November 15, 1909; s. Frederic Huntington and Eleanor Brooks (Pearson) B.; student Philips Acad., Andover, 1924-27, U. Chgo., 1927-29, Oxford U., Eng., 1929-30; A.B., Columbia, 1933; grad. student Harvard, 1937-38; student Nat. War Coll., 1953-54; m. Gladys Irene Jones (dec.); children—David F., Stephen Pearson; m. 2d, Jessie Hendrick Hardie, May 29, 1963. Economist, Dept. Agr., 1933-37; adminstr. Dept. City Planning, N.Y.C., 1938-42; dir. Caribbean Office, Nat. Resources Planning Bd., 1942-44; fgn. service officer, London, 1947-50, Indo-china, 1950-53, New Delhi, 1954-57; dir. Office South Asian Affairs, Dept. State, 1957-60; ambassador to Malagasy Republic, 1960-62; dir. Office African and Malagasy Union Affairs, Dept. State, 1962-64. Served to lt. USNR, 1944-46. Decorated Bronze Star. Club: Washington DC Died Jan. 1970.

BARTLETT, FREDERICK ORIN, author; b. Haverhill, Mass., July 2, 1876; s. Daniel C. and Katherine Page (Wilder) B.; ed. Proctor Acad., 1891-96, Harvard, 1896-98; A.B., Harvard, 1926; m. Katherine Hall James, June 29, 1908; children—Brooks (dec.), Jane (dec.), Kent, Ann. In newspaper work on Boston Record, 1900-02, Boston Herald, 1902-06. Clubs: The Players (New York); Authors' (pres.), Harvard, St. Botolph, Oakley Country. Author: Mistress Dorothy, 1901; Joan of the Alley, 1905; The Web of the Golden Spider, 1909; The Seventh Noon, 1910; The Prodigal Pro Tem, 1911; The Forest Castaways, 1911; The Lady of the Lane, 1912; The Guardian, 1912; Whippen, 1913; The Wall Street Girl, 1916; The Triflers, 1917; Joan & Co., 1919; Big Laurel, 1922; Out of the Night, 1923; (under name of William Carleton) One Way Out, 1911; New Lives for Old, 1913; The Red Geranium, 1915; (anonymously) One Year of Pierrot, 1917. Also short stories. Articles signed The Old Dog" in Saturday Evening Post, 1925-26. Home: 8 Felton Hall, Cambridge MA‡

BARTLETT, GEORGE A., ex-congressman; b. San Francisco, Nov. 30, 1869; s. Mason B. and Barbara B.; removed with family to Nev. in infancy; pub. sch. edn.; LL.B., Georgetown U., Washington, 1894; m. Pearl Gates, of Eureka, Nev., Feb. 14, 1899. Admitted to bar, 1893, and since in practice in Nev.; dist. atty. Eureka Co., Nev., 1899-1900; mem. 60th and 61st Congresses (1907-11), Nev. at-large; Democrat. Address: Carson City NV‡

BARTLETT, GEORGE GRIFFITHS, clergyman; b. Sharon Springs, N.Y., June 3, 1872; s. Edward T. and Emily S. (Pile) B.; A.B., Harvard, 1895; grad. Div. Sch. P.E. Ch., Phila., 1898; m. Cecilia Helen Neall, May 9, 1905; children—Emily Neall, Edward Totterson, George Neall. Deacon, P.E. Ch., 1898, priest, 1900; asst., Grace Ch., New York, 1898-1902; rector Memorial Ch. of St. Paul, Overbrook, Phila., 1902-08; dean Cathedral of Our Merciful Savior, Faribault, Minn., 1908-11; rector Ch. of Our Savior, Jenkintown, Pa., 1911-15; dean and prof. Div. Sch. P.E. Ch., Philadelphia, 1915-37, retired. Home: 2021 Spruce St., Philadelphia 3 PA‡

BARTLETT, JOHN FRANK, educator; b. Flatwoods, W.Va., Aug. 25, 1902; s. William P. and Minnie I. (Goodwin) B.; A.B., W.Va. Univ., 1925, A.M., 1927, Ph.D., 1932; m. Constance Sharpless, May 28, 1928. Teacher of sci., Gassaway High Sch., 1925, 27, prin., 1928-30; instr. chemistry, Marshall Univ., Huntington, W.Va., 1932-33, asst. prof. chem., 1933-34, asso. prof., 1934-38, prof. of chemistry, 1938-45, dean Coll. Arts, Scis., from 1945. Fellow A.A.A.S.; mem. Am. Chem. Soc., Am. Assn. U. Profs., Phi Lambda Upsilon, Phi Eta Sigma, Omicron Delta Kappa, Chi Beta Phi, Sigma Alpha Epsilon. Mason. Kiwanian. Sigma Xi. Home: Huntington WV Died May 16, 1969; interred Huntington WV

BARTLETT, LOUIS, lawyer; b. San Francisco, Calif., Feb. 20, 1872; s. Columbus and Louise (Mel) B.; Ph.B., U. of Calif., 1893; LL.B., Hastings Coll. of Law, 1896; m. Mary Olney, June 13, 1903; children—Mary, Mrs. Muriel B. Petty, Mrs. Ruth B. Thomas. Practiced law at San Francisco from 1896 to 1938, served as mayor of Berkeley, California, 2 terms, 1919-23; organized East Bay Municipal Utility Dist., 1923, member board directors 1923-24; legal and economic consultant Central Valley Project of California, 1939-41; member Central Valley-Central Coast Drainage Basin Committee and Lahontan Drainage Basin Committee of the National Resources Planning Board 1940-41, Calif. State Planning Board, 1942-43, California Lands Classification Commission, 1942-43. President League of California Municipalities, 1921-22. Trustee John Randolph Haynes and Dora Haynes Foundation 1927-47, vice pres., 1938-44. Mem. Calif. bar. Mem. Phi Beta Kappa, Beta Theta Pi. Democrat. Conglist. Club: Commonwealth (San Francisco), Faculty Club (Berkeley, Calif.). Home: 2434 Warring St.; Berkeley 4 CA‡

BARTLETT, LYNN MAHLON, govt. official; b. Portland, N.Y., July 12, 1904; s. William and Ella Emma (Stine) B.; B.A., U. Mich., 1927, M.A., 1930, Ph.D., 1954; LL.D., Northern Michigan U., Marquette, 1960; m. Josephine Katherine Kriser, July 24, 1937; children—Lynn Michael, Sharon Anne. Tchr. rural sch., Cherry Creek, N.Y., 1921-23; asst. bur. ednl. ref. and research U. Mich., 1926-27, teaching asst., 1935-36; psychologist psychol. clinic Detroit Pub. Schs., 1927-29; dir. dept. pupil personnel, asst. supt. Grosse Pointe Pub. Schs., 1929-57; instr. ednl. psychology Eastern Mich U., summer, 1930; instr. Wayne State U., 1945-46, 55-56; supt. pub. instrn., Mich., 1957-65; dep. asst. sec. edn. and manpower resources Dept. Def., 1965-68; asst. sec. for edn. Dept. Health, Edn. and Welfare, 1968-69; ednl. cons., 1969-70. Past pres. Tri-State Conf. on Pupil Personnel. Bd. advisers Nat. War Coll., Indsl. Coll. Armed Forces; regent emeritus U. Mich.; trustee emeritus Mich. State U. Recipient Meritorious Civilian Service medal Sec. of Def., 1968. Mem. Am., Mich. (past pres.) psychol. assns., Internat. Council Exceptional Children, Mich. Edn. Assn., N.E.A., Am., Mich. assns. sch. adminstrs., Phi Delta Kappa, Phi Kappa Phi. Democrat. Clubs: Detroit Psychology (past pres.); Rotary (Grosse Pointe). Contbr. articles to profl. jours. Home: McLean VA Died Nov. 28, 1970; buried Mt. Olivet Cemetery, Detroit MI

BARTLETT, WALTER MANNY, prof. dentistry; b. New Orleans, La., Jan. 15, 1862; s. Frank Adams and Emma (Gagnet) B.; prep. edn. New Orleans Mil. Inst.; D.D.S. and M.S., Washington U., 1890; m. Edith Bartlett, Sept. 25, 1888. Practiced in St. Louis since 1890; now emeritus prof. prosthetic dentistry, Washington U. Sch. of Dentistry, St. Louis, and emeritus dean of faculty. Ex-pres., Mo. State Bd. Dental Examiners. Mem. Nat. Dental Assn., Mo. State Dental Soc., St. Louis Dental Soc. (ex-pres.), Xi Psi Phi, Omicron Kappa Upsilon; hon. mem. Tex. State Dental Soc. Democrat. Episcopalian. Club: Faculty. Home: 5000 Waterman Av., St Louis MO‡

BARTLEY, DONALD, shoe co. exec.; b. Fulton, Mo., 1897; ed. Westminster Coll., 1919. Pres., dir. Nunn-Bush Shoe Co., Milw., 1960-68. Home: Milwaukee WI Died Apr. 24, 1968.

BARTOL, JOHN WASHBURN, physician; b. Lancaster, Mass., Jan. 10, 1864; s. George Murillo and Elizabeth (Washburn) B.; grad. Phillips Exeter Acad., Exeter, N.Y., 1883; A.B., Harvard, 1887, M.D., 1891; m. Charlotte H. Cabot, Oct. 2, 1900; children—Janet, Dorothy, Ann, Priscilla, George M., Louis C. Began practice at Boston, 1893; asst. in clin. medicine, Harvard Med. Sch., 1905-10. Mem. Mass. State Bd. of Health, 1902-07. Served as lt., advancing to maj., Med. Corps, U.S. Army, 1917-19. Pres. Boston Med. Library, 1927-33; mem. corp. Simmons Coll., Boston, 1906-39. Mem. Am. Med. Assn., Mass. Med. Soc. (pres. 1921-23). Unitarian. Home: 1 Chestnut St., Boston MA‡

BARTON, FRANCIS BROWN, prof.; Romance langs.; b. Palmer, Mass., Mar. 15, 1886; s. Francis Dexter and Anna Elizabeth (Brown); A.B., Williams Coll., 1907; Docteur de l'Universite de Paris, Sorbonne, Paris, 1911; student Junta para Ampliacion de Estudios, Madrid, 1913; m. Bernice Hart, July 29, 1916. Instr. in French, The Concord (Mass.) Sch., 1907-09; Williams Coll., 1911-15; asst. prof. Romance langs., U. of Minn., 1915-23, asso. prof., 1923-29, prof. 1929-37, chmn. dept., from 1937. Mem. Modern Lang. Assn. Am., Am. Assn. Univ. Profs., Phi Beta Kappa. Editor Spanish Review (with J.A. Cuneo), 1944. Home: Minneapolis MN Died Apr. 20, 1971.

BARTON, LELA VIOLA, plant physiologist; b. Farmington, Ark., Nov. 14, 1901; d. Henry and Mary Frances (Miller) Barton; B.A., U. Ark., 1922; M.A., Columbia, 1927, Ph.D., 1939. Sci. tchr. Sr. High Sch., Van Buren, Ark., 1922-24; biology tchr. Sr. High Sch., Little Rock, Ark., 1924-26; plant-physiologist Boyce Thompson Inst. Plant Research, Yonkers, N.Y., 1928-66. Mem. Torrey Bot. Club (pres. 1956-57), A.A.A.S., Botanical Soc. Am., Sigma Xi, Sigma Delta Epsilon (nat. pres. 1947, nat. hon. mem.). Author: (with William Crocker) Twenty Years of Seed Research, 1948, Physiology of seeds, 1953; Seed Preservation and Longevity, 1961; Bibliography of Seeds, 1966. Home: Tucson AZ Died July 31, 1967; buried Fayetteville AR

BARTON, LEVI ELDER, clergyman; b. near Jonesboro, Ark., Apr. 25, 1870; s. William Henderson and Eliza Martha (Morgan) B.; A.M., Union U., Jackson, Tenn., 1898, D.D., 1911; student Southern Bapt. Theol. Sem., Louisville, Ky., 1898-99; m. Rosa Belle Hurt, 1899;children—Anne Alethia (wife of Chas. H. Chapman, M.D.), Jenny Dean, Lee Edward, Elizabeth Lumpkin. Ordained ministry Bapt. Ch., 1896; pastor Hope, Ark., 1899-1900, Suffolk, Va., 1900-04, Quitman, Ga., 1905-08, West Point, Miss., 1908-13, Jackson Hill Bapt. Ch., Atlanta, Ga., 1913-16, 1st Bapt. Ch., Fayetteville, Ark., 1916-19, gen. sec. exec. bd. Ark. Bapt. Conv., 1920-21; pastor Larchmont Bapt. Ch., Norfolk, Va., 1922-25, 1st Bapt. Ch., Andalusia, Ala., 1926-29; pastor 1st Bapt. Ch., Jasper, Ala., 1936-41; first vice-presdient Ala. Bapt. Conv., 1942-43; pres. Montgomery Ministerial Association, 1943. Member executive bd. Ala. Bapt. Conv., 1926-29, gen. sec. and treas., 1929-35, now chmn. social service com.; v.p. Southern Bapt. Conv., 1927; chmn. com. Constitution and By-laws, since 1942; mem. Promotion Com. Southern Bapts., 1931-33; mem. and gen. dir. State Promotion Com. of Ala. Mem. com. to invite Lloyd George, 1919. Mem. exec. com. Ala. Temperance Alliance since 1933, pres., 1934; state chmn. Com. Against Repeal of 18th Amendment, 1933; mem. exec. com. Ala. Anti-Saloon League. Presdl. elector Prohibition Party, 1940. Member coordination com. war activities, Montgomery; member Alabama State War Chest. Executive secretary Baptist Foundation of Alabama since 1941; member Am. Baptist Historical Soc. (hon.), Alabama Baptist Hist. Soc. (dir.), Southern Bapt. Hist. Soc. (1st charter mem.), Eugene Field Soc. Authors and Poets, Sigma Alpha Epsilon Fraternity. Democrat. Mason. Clubs: Rotary (del. to internat. conv., Ostend, Belgium, 1927, Minneapolis, Minn., 1928), Kiwanis (Jasper). Author: Three Dimensions of Love, 1929; Take Heed, 1942; also brochure, Four Pillars of the Baptist Temple. Author of resolutions opposed to compulsory Bible reading in pub. schs., Gen. Assn. of Va., 1925. Editor Walker County Tribune, 1937. Nominated for vice pres. of U.S. by Prohibition Party, 1944; declined. Home: 1607 S. Hull St., Montgomery AL‡

BARTON, WILLIAM EDWARD, judge; b. Pickens County, S.C., Apr. 11, 1868; s. William and Harriett (King) B.; student Steelville (Mo.) Normal and Business Inst.; LL.B., U. of Mo., 1894; m. Marietta Tweed, Dec. 19, 1900. Admitted to Mo. bar, 1894, and began practice at Houston; pros. atty. Texas County, Mo., 1901, 02; circuit judge, 19th Jud. Circuit, Mo., 1923-28; mem. Barton & Moberly. Mem. 72d Congress (1931-33), 16th Mo. Dist.; judge 19th Jud. Circuit of Mo., term 1934-40; reelected in Nov. 1940 for 6 yrs. Served as sergt. Mo. Inf., U.S. Vols., May-Nov. 1898. Democrat. Baptist. Mason (K.T., Shriner), Odd Fellow, Modern Woodman. Home: Houston MO‡

BARTOW, HARRY EDWARDS, educator, author; b. Delaware Co., Pa., Sept. 11, 1877; s. Isaac Farra and Elizabeth Margaret (Edwards) B.; grad. South Chester High Sch., 1895, Peirce Sch. (Phila.), 1898; m. Hannah

R. Carlon, of Chester, Pa., Aug. 26, 1901; 1 son, James Carlon. Sec. Peirce Sch. since 1916; lesson writer for Am. S.S. Union since 1914; local preacher M.E. Ch. Mem. Eastern Commercial Teachers' Assn., Am. S.S. Union (life). Republican. Odd Fellow. Club: City. Author: Our Boy, 1913; Sunday School Teaching and Management (with James L. McConaughy), 1916; The Superintendent's Guide, pub. yearly since 1917. Contbr. to mags. Home: Collingdale Pa Office: 1420 Pine St., Philadelphia PA‡

BARUS, ANNIE HOWES, writer; b. S. Yarmouth, Cape Cod, Mass.; d. Osbone and Abby (Crowell) Howes; grad. Vassar, 1874; m. Carl Barus (q.v.), Jan. 20, 1887. Pres. Associate Alumnae of Vassar, 1890-1, Assn. of Collegiate Alumnae, 1892-4; sec.-treas. latter, 1895-8. Contbr. to newspapers, mags., etc., especially on health of college women, child study and child-labor. Address: 30 Elmgrove Av., Providence RI‡

BARZINI, LUIGI, editor, author; b. Orvieto, Italy, Feb. 7, 1874; s. Ettore and Maria (Bartoccini) B.; grad. as expert in state and commercial adminstration, Tech. Sch. of Perugia, Rome, 1894; m. Mantica Pesavento, of Milan, Italy, Dec. 5, 1905; children—Emma, Luigi Giorgio, Ettore, Ugo. Began as spl. newspaper corr., London, Eng., 1899; has visited the principal countries of the world and witnessed most of the great events for a period of 25 yrs.; was corr. Boxers' War, 1900, Russo-Japanese War, 1904, Italo-Turkish War, 1911, Balkans War, 1913, World War, 1914-18; traveled in automobile from Peking, China, to Paris, France, in 60 days; settled in U.S., 1922; founder, 1922; editor and pub. the Corriere d'America (illustrated daily), New York. Decorated Grand Officer Crown of Italy and Knight of Italian Star; Knight of the British Empire; Knight Legion d'Honneur (French); Officer Royal Crown of Belgium, etc. Catholic. Author: From Peking to Paris in Automobile, 1908; The Little Match Man, 1921; also other books in European countries-22 vols. in all. Home: 158 State St Flushing NY New York NY

BARZYNSKI, JOSEPH E., army officer; b. St. Paul, Neb., Mar. 13, 1884; s. John and Virginia (Wilkosheski) B.; B.S., U.S. Mil. Acad., 1905; student Ecole de l'Intendence, Paris, 1924-26, Command and Gen. Staff Sch., 1931-33; m. Theresa M. New. Sept. 23, 1908; children—Joseph E. (col. A.C., U.S. Army), Eunice (2d lt. W.A.C., U.S. Army). Commissioned 2d lieutenant Inf., U.S. Army, 1905, and advanced through the grades to brig. gen., 1940; with Inf., Wyo., 1905-12, Philippine Islands, 1912-15; Mexican Punitive Expdn., 1916-17; Q.M., 86th Div., Camp Grant, and sailed with the 86th Div. to France; Q.M., 32d Div., France and Germany, 1918-19; duty with U.S. Liquidation Commn., Paris, 1919; Am. Legation, Warsaw, Poland, 1920; mem. War Dept. Gen. Staff. Washington, D.C., 1927-31; chief of motor transportation, 1940-41; comdg. gen. Chicago Q.M. Depot Oct. 1941-72. Received Mexican Punitive and World War I service decorations. Mem. Soc. Automotive Engrs. Clubs: Army and Navy, Army and Navy Country (Washington, D.C.); South Shore Country, Union League, Tavern (Chicago). Address: Chicago IL Died Aug. 1972; buried Arlington Nat. Cemetery.

BASALDELLA, MIRKO, sculptor; b. 1910; ed. Acads. Fine Arts, Venice, Florence, Monza. Works exhibited in Italy, France, Belgium, Spain, Austria, Hungary, U.S., 1935—; executed decoration and floral balustrade, F.A.O. Palace, Rome, mosiac fountain, La Spezia, meml. monument to Italian dead at Mauthausen, Austria, Initiation for Krannert Art Mus., U. Ill., Urbana, also others in private collections; one-man shows N.Y.C. World House Gallery, 1961, Krannert Art Museum, Urbana, 1962, Institute of Contemporary Art, Boston, 1964, Ward-Nasse Gallery, Boston, 1965; professor of fine arts, director of workshop courses Harvard, 1957-69; designed, executed the bronze memorial gates for Ardeatine Caves, Rome, Italy, 1951. Recipient 2nd prize for monument to Unknown Polit. Prisoner, London, 1953; 1st prize for sculpture, Sao Paulo Biennial, 1956. Carrara, Italy, 1957; Accad. dei Lincei prize, 1958. Address: Cambridge MA

BASCH, ANTONIN, economist; born Nemeckybrod, Czechoslovakia, June 5, 1896; s. Albert and Matilde (Basch) B.; J.D., Charles U., Prague, 1919; student U. of Vienna, 1917-18, U. of Berlin, 1920-21; m. Eleanor Mary Fuchs, June 19, 1923; children—Monica H. E., Jan. A. (dec.). Came to U.S., 1940. Official, Ministry of Commerce, Czechoslovakia, 1919; with Czechoslovak Economic Service, Berlin, 1920-23; sec. Czechoslovak Chamber of Commerce and Ministry, Prague, 1923-26; dir. research dept. Czechoslovak Nat. Bank, Prague, 1926-34; gen. mgr. United Chem. and Metall. Works, Prague, 1934-39; visiting prof. econ. Brown U., 1940-42; lecturer in economics, Columbia, since 1942 chief economist Internat. Bank for Reconstrn. and Development, Washington, 1942-57, resident rep. in India, 1957-59, head of the capital market unit, 1959-61; vis. prof. econs. U. Mich. Ann Arbor, 1961-65; consultant Inter-Am. Development Bank, 1966, Asian Institute for Development and Planning, 1967-68. Mem. Am. Economic Assn., Society for International Development. Author: A Price for Peace; New Europe and the World Markets, 1945; Internat. Bank, 1945-49 (a review), 1950; The Future of Foreign Lending for Development, 1962; Financing Economic Development, 1964; Capital Markets of the European Economic Community, 1965; APragmatic Approach to Economic Development, 1971. Home: Washington DC Died Mar. 18, 1971.

BASDEVANT, JULES, judge Internat. Court of Justice; born Anost, Saone and Loire, France, April 15, 1877; s. Louis and Maria (Gauchey) B.; Bachelor, Coll. of Autun, 1894; LL.D., faculty of law, Paris, 1901; m. Renee Mallarme, Aug. 5, 1905; children—Suzanne (Mrs. Paul Bastid), Andre, Jean, Pierre, Maurice (died for France, 1940), Marie Louise, Francois (assassinated by German Army, July 13, 1944). Lecturer at the faculty of Law, Rennes, 1903-06; fellow, faculty of law at Rennes, 1906-07; fellow, faculty of Grenoble, later prof., 1907-18; fellow of the faculty of law, Paris, later prof. of the law of nations, 1918; deputy legal advisor, later legal advisor Ministry of Fgn. Affairs, forced to resign following a letter to Marshal Petain, May 29, 1941; relieved of position as prof. at request of enemy, later sent into retirement, 1944; reinstated both as legal advisor and prof. at time of liberation; judge Internat. Ct. of Justice, from 1946, became v.p., 1946, pres., 1949; mem. Permanent Ct. Arbitration; mem. com. for unification private law, Inst. International Law. Representative French government San Francisco Conference also 1st Assembly United Nations at London. Mobilized as sergeant, later lt. World War I. Decorated comdr. of the Legion of Honor. Mem. Inst. of France, Royal Acad. of Belgium, fgn. asso. Mem. Inst. Internat. Law, Soc. Comparative Legislation, Soc. Legislative Studies, Eduenne Soc., Centre d'Etudes de Politique Estranger, American Soc. Internat. Law. Author: On the Reports of the Church and the State on Legislation of Marriage, 1900; The French Revolution and the Law of the Continental war, 1901; Hugo Grotius, 1904; Collection of International Treaties of the 19th Century, 1914; Deportation from Belgium and the North of France and International Law, 1917; Treaties in Force between France and Foreign Powers, 1918-20. Home: Paris France Died Jan. 5, 1968.

BASHEV, IVAN HRISTOV, Bulgarian diplomat; b. 1916. Mem. Workers Youth Union, 1934-72, also Gen. Union Students Bulgaria; mem. staff newspaper Akademik; editor Narodna Mladej (People's Youth) newspaper, 1944-46-51; mem. Bulgarian Communist Party, 1946-72, mem. central com.; mem. exec. com., sec. propaganda work World Fedn. Democratic Youth, Paris, France, 1946-51; sec. central com. Dimitrov Union of People's Youth, 1951; chief bd. Ministry Edn. and Culture, 1954-56; dep. minister edn. and culture, 1956; dep. minister fgn. affairs, 1962, minister fgn. affairs, 1962-72; also mem. Parliament. Office: Sofia Bulgaria Died Jan. 1972.

BASHORE, HARRY WILLIAM, cons. engr.; b. Marion County, Mo., July 3, 1880; s. Morgan Barnett and Sophia Maria (Heinze) B.; A.B., LaGrange (Mo.) Coll., 1899; B.S. in Civil Engring., U. of Missouri, 1906; LL.D. U. Wyo., 1949; m. Gladys Dorothy Hubbell, Dec. 14, 1918; children—Harry W., Audrey Elaine. Asst. on engring. corps, Baltimore & Ohio South Western R.R., 1906; with Bureau of Reclamation 1906-45, 52, jr. engr., sr. engr., construction engr. and project supt., North Platte Project, Neb.-Wyo., 1906-27, constrn. engr., Vale Project, 1927-30, sr. engr., Columbia Basin Project (Wash.), 1930-32, sr. engr. Central Valley Project (Calif.), 1932-33, constrn. engr. Kendrick Project (Wyo.), 1933-39, asst. commr., Washington, D.C., 1939-43, commr., 1944-45, retired Dec. 1945; appointed cons. Interior Dept.; presidential rep. and chmn., Upper Colorado River Basin Compact Commn., 1949; consultant Water Development for Israel, 1951, World Bank's comprehensive plan for utilization of waters in Indus Basin in India and Pakistan, 1952-73. Recipient Distinguished Service award, Dept. of Interior, 1950. Mem. Am. Soc. C.E.; hon. mem. Sigma Tau. Home: Mitchell NB Died Apr. 1, 1973.

BASKIN, ROBERT N., formerly asso. justice Supreme Ct., Utah; chief justice, 1903. Democrat. Address: Salt Lake City UT‡

BASS, CHARLES CASSEDY, M.D.; b. Carley, Miss., Jan. 28, 1875; s. Isaac Esau and Mary Eliza (Wilks) B.; M.D., Med. Dept., Tulane U., 1899; hon. D.Sc., U. of Cincinnati, 1921; LL.D., Duke U., 1937; m. Coraline Howell, Oct. 17, 1897; children—Cassie Juanita, Rachel Ernestine, Helen Corinne, Charles Cassedy. Practiced, Columbia, Miss., 1899-1904; began researches in hookworm disease, 1903; continued same in lab. of Dr. Charles E. Simon, Baltimore, and at Johns Hopkins Med. Sch., 1904; located in New Orleans, 1904, and conducted researches in intestinal parasites of man; pub. first successful cultivation of malaria plasmodia in vitro, 1911; made further research in cultivation of malaria plasmodia with Dr. F. M. Johns, in U.S. Govt. Hosp., Ancon, C.Z., 1912; successfully cultivated all 3 species of the malaria parasite; was scientific dir. malaria control demonstration of Internat. Health Bd., in Bolivar County, Miss.; prof. experimental medicine and director laboratories of clinical medicine, 1912-40, Sch. of Medicine, Tulane Univ., also dean Sch. of Medicine, same univ., 1922-40 (retired 1940). Mem. American Society Tropical Medicine (pres.), Southern Medical Association (pres.), Louisiana State Medical Society, Orleans Parish Medical Society, Soc. Am. Bacteriologists, Assn. Am. Physicians, American Coll. Physicians, Am. Soc. for Clin. Investigation (pres.), Am. Therapeutic Soc., Soc. for Exptl. Biology and Medicine, Stars and Bars Soc., Sigma Xi, Alpha Omega Alpha, Phi Chi. Awarded gold medal, Southern Med. Assn., 1912, for achievement in med. research; gold medal, A.M.A., 1913, for research exhibit in malaria; gold medal, Miss. State Med. Assn., 1913, for extraordinary scientific achievement; medal, Nat. Inst. Social Sciences, 1913, for contributions to welfare of mankind; spl. gold medal, Orleans Parish Med. Soc., 1914, for achievements in researches in malaria; given key to Stars and Bars Soc. of Tulane Med. Coll., 1915, for scholarship. Author: (with George Dock, M.D.) Hookworm Disease, 1909; (with F. M. Johns, M.D.) Alveolodental Pyorrhoea and Practical Clinical Laboratory Diagnosis, 1915; also more than 100 brochures and articles on hookworm disease, malaria, pellagra, test for typhoid fever, diphtheria, medical edn. prevention of the loss of teeth, etc. Home: 1445 Philip St., New Orleans 13 LA‡

BASS, GEORGE ARTHUR, pres. Hydraulic-Press Brick Co.; b. Kankakee Co., Ill., Aug. 16, 1864; s. Myron Hawley and Ann Elizabeth (Kelly) B.; Ph.B., Northwestern U., 1888; m. Zitella Ebert, Nov. 16, 1898; children—Ruth Ebert (Mrs. Robert Chancellor Saunders), George Ebert. Began as mfr. of brick, at Washington, D.C., 1895; settled in St. Louis, Mo., 1909; pres. Hydraulic-Press Brick Co., St. Louis, since 1909. Mem. Phi Kappa Psi. Republican. Clubs: Noonday, Bellerive Country. Home: 4651 Lindell Blvd. Office: 705 Olive St., St Louis MO*‡

BASSETT, HARRY WINFRED, b. Jonesville, Ind., Dec. 14, 1875; s. Hiram Harrison and Susan Caroline (Duncan) B.; educated public schools; m. Emma Hope Pearce, of Indianapolis, Ind.; children—Mary Elizabeth, Catherine W. Active in labor councils for many yrs.; mem. Indiana legislature, 1909-11; sec. to Mayor of Indianapolis, 1913-17; Dem. candidate for State Senate, Ind., 1922, 24; editor The Union (oldest labor paper in U.S.) since 1911; mem. U.S. Employees Compensation Commn. since June 23, 1925, as Democratic mem. Mem. 1st Army Corps, 27th Ind. Light Battery, Spanish-Am. War, 1898. Mem. United Spanish War Vets., Vets. of Foreign Wars; hon. mem. Pi Gamma Mu. Mason (K.T., 32 deg., Shriner, Jester), Eagle. Home: 3813 E. Washington St.,Indianapolis, Ind. and Fairfax Hotel, Washington. Address: Land Office Bldg., Washington DC‡

BASSETT, LEE EMERSON, coll. prof.; b. Salem, Wis., Nov. 26, 1872; s. Volney L. and Adeline (Foster) B.; Lawrence U., Appleton, Wis., 1891-94; Cummock Sch. of Expression, Los Angeles, 1896-98; Curry Sch. of Expression, Boston, 1900-01 (hon. Dr. Sc. of Oratory, 1939); A.B., Stanford Univ., 1901; Oxford Univ., Eng., 1907-08; m. Florence Jackson, June 10, 1903; children—William M. (died in service, December 18, 1944), David Lee. Instructor public speaking, University of Southern Calif., 1898-99; instructor English, 1900-05, assistant professor, 1905-13, Stanford University; associate professor public speaking, Univ. of Washington, 1912-13; asso. professor English, 1913-19, professor, 1919-38, professor emeritus since 1938, Stanford Univ., visiting prof. U. of Hawaii, 1934-35; dean Max Reinhardt Workshop, Hollywood, 1939-40. Pres. Western Assn. of Teachers of Speech, 1931, Nat. Assn. of Teachers of Speech, 1933. Mem. Nat. Assn. of University Professors, Phi Beta Kappa, Alpha Kappa Lambda (Beta Chapter). Author: A Handbook of Oral Reading; A Handbook of Extemporaneous Speaking, Contbr. ednl. CA‡

BASSETT, SARA WARE, author; b. Newton, Mass., Oct. 22, 1872; d. Charles Warren and Anna Augusta (Haley) Bassett; of Pilgrim descent; grad. Lowell Sch. of Design, 1894; grad. Symonds Kindergarten Tr. Sch., Boston, 1897; studied Boston U., Radcliffe Coll. Kindergarten teacher public schs., Newton, 1897-1917. Congregationalist. Clubs: Authors', Boston Manuscript (hon.), Woman's City Club (Boston). Author: Silver Moon Cottage, 1945; The Beacon, 1946; Head Winds, 1947; Within The Harbor, 1948; The White Sail, 1949; Echoes of The Tide, 1951; Beyond the Breakers, 1952; The Whispering Pine, 1953; Adrift, 1954; The Girl in the Blue Pinafore, 1957. Home: 56 West Cedar St., Boston MA‡

BASSI, AMADEO, operatic tenor; b. Florence, Italy, July 25, 1876; studied under Marchese Pavesi Negri; m. Reina Ceppi, of Ancona, Mar. 14, 1899. Made debut as the Duke in Rigoletto," at Arena Nazionale, Florence, 1898; later appeared in leading cities of Italy, and in Russia, Spain, England and S. America; first sang in U.S. with Manhattan Opera Co., 1906, and continued 2 seasons, first tenor parts, in Italian operas; with Chicago-Phila. Opera Co., 1909-10; appeared with Chicago Grand Opera Co., on inaugural night of the opera, as Radames, in Alda," Nov. 3, 1910. Other roles: Dick Johnson, in The Girl of the Golden West"; chief role in Mascagni's Le Maschere," etc.; repertoire includes nearly all Italian operas now being sung. Home: Villa Bassi, Florence Italy‡

BASTIAN, ROBERT OWEN, editorial cartoonist; b. Stockton, Cal., Apr. 2, 1917; s. Bertram Richard and Marian (Galli) B.; A.B., Coll. of Pacific, 1940; student Cal. Sch. Fine Art, 1946; m. Beverly C. Wright, Nov. 20, 1940; children—Ellen (Mrs. Michael McHenry), Ann, James. News photographer, 1940-41; engaged in various art activities, 1946-52; editorial cartoonist San Francisco Chronicle, 1953-68, KQED Endl. TV Sta., San Francisco, 1968-70. Served with USMCR, 1942-46. Home: Belvedere CA Died Sept. 22, 1970.

BATCHELDER, ERNEST ALLEN, teacher; b. Nashua, N.H., Jan. 22, 1876; s. Charles and Mary (Sleeper) B.; ed. Mass. Normal Art Sch., Boston; Sch. Arts and Crafts, Birmingham, Eng.; married. Dir. of art, Throop Poly. Inst., Pasadena, Cal., 1901-8; dir., Handicraft Guild, Minneapolis, 1903-8; mfr. interior furnishings in tile, metal and enamel, Pasadena, 1910—. Mem. Internat. Jury Awards, St. Louis Expn., 1904; mem. Am. com. Internat. Congress Art, Dresden, 1911. Mason. Author: Principles of Design, 1901; Design in Theory and Practice, 1910. Residence: 626 Arroyo Drive. Office: 769 S. Broadway, Pasadena CA‡

BATCHELOR, JAMES MADISON, surgeon; b. Pointe Coupe Parish, La., Oct. 5, 1870; s. Charles J. and Ella V. (Gayle) B.; B.Sc., La. State U., 1890; M.D., Tulane, 1895; m. Mrs. Bernice Bowling Fassman, May 2, 1937. Practiced at New Orleans since 1895; pres. and prof. surgery, Loyola Post-Grad. Sch. of Medicine, 1918-24; chief of 1st surg. div. Charity Hosp.; chief surgeon Presbyterian Hosp.; supt. pub. health City of New Orleans. Supt. Pub. Health City of N.O., 1935-40; consultant, City New Orleans Bd. Health. Mem. La. State Med. Soc., Orleans Parish Med. Soc. Democrat. Episcopalian. Home: 2329 Audubon St. Office: City Hall, New Orleans LA‡

BATEMAN, ALAN MARA, geologist; born Kingston, Ontario, Canada, January 6, 1889; son of George Arthur and Elizabeth J. (Mara) Bateman; graduated Kingston Collegiate Institute, 1905; B.S., Queens University, Canada, 1910, D.Sc., 1970; Ph.D., Yale, 1913; m. Grace Hotchkiss Street, June 3, 1916. Asst. geologist German Development Co. Can., 1906-09; asso. geologist Can. Geol. Survey, 1910-12; instr. Yale, 1913; field geologist, Secondary Enrichment Investigation, Harvard U., 1913-15; asst. prof. geology, 1916-21, asso. prof., 1922-25, prof. geology Yale, 1925-41, Silliman prof., 1941, former chmn. department of geology; cons. geologist to Kennecott Copper Corp. from 1916; head of special U.S. mission to Mexico, 1942, dir. Metals and Minerals, Foreign Econ. Adminstrn., Washington, 1942-46; expert cons. S.C.A.P., Tokyo, 1949; cons. Department Interior E.C.A., NSRD, ODM, National Science Foundation; editor in chief Jour. of Econ. Geology; former editor Am. Jour. Science. Trustee Sheffield Scientific Sch. Yale U. Penrose Gold medallist, Soc. Econ. Geologists, 1962. Member American Inst. M.E., Inst. Mining and Metallurgy (pres. 1954), Geol. Soc. America, Soc. Econ. Geologists (pres. 1941-42), Am. Assn. Petroleum Geologists, Washington Acad. Sciences, Am. Academy Arts and Sciences; hon. mem. Chile Soc. Mineralogy and Geology; hon. member Soc. Geologique de Belgique; mem. Sigma Xi, Theta Xi. Republican. Conglist. Clubs: Graduate, New Haven Country, Yale, Lawn (New Haven, Connecticut); Cosmos Club (Washington); Mining, Yale Club (New York City). Author: Economic Mineral Deposits; Formation of Mineral Deposits; also papers on origin of mineral deposits. Home: New Haven CT also Pleasant Valley CT Died May 11, 1971; buried East Lawn Cemetery, East Haven CT

BATEMAN, GEORGE MONROE, retired educator; b. Bloominton, Ida., Sept. 12, 1897; s. Alfred John and Clara (Hess) B.; B.S., Utah State U., 1921; M.S. in Chemistry, Cornell U., 1926, Ph.D., 1927; m. Florence Harris, May 24, 1922; children—Cornella (dec.), Flora Mae, Georgia Rose, Harold Harris. Instr. sci. and math. Grace (Ida.) High Sch., 1921-22; prin. sch., Arimo, Ida., 1922-24; instr. dairy chemistry Cornell U., 1925-27, prof. chemistry, head sci. dept., 1927-51; prof. chemistry Ariz. State Univ., Tempe, 1936-69, emeritus prof., 1969-72, head phys. sci. div., 1951-64. Bishop, Tempe Ward, Church of Jesus Christ of Latter-day Saints, 1944-48. Served as pvt. U.S. Army, 1918; O.R.C., 1932-42; capt., C.W.S., 1941-42. Recipient Silver Beaver award Boy Scouts Am. Fellow A.A.A.S., Am. Inst. Chemists, Ariz. Acad. Sci., Phi Kappa Phi, Sigma Xi. Author Tempe AZ Died Jan. 28, 1972; buried Double Butte Cemetery, Tempe AZ

BATES, ALBERT CARLOS, librarian; b. East Granby, Conn., Mar. 12, 1865; s. Carlos and Hannah S. (Powers) B.; grad. Conn. Lit. Instn., Suffield, 1885; hon. M.A., Trinity Coll., Hartford, 1920; m. Alice Morgan Crocker, Oct. 19, 1912. Entered employ Conn. Hist. Soc., 1892, and became its librarian, Jan. 1, 1893, recording sec., May 1896, mem. Pub. Com., May 1897 (chmn., May 1901); appt. librarian emeritus for life on resignation, May 1940. Mem. Conn. Ho. of Rep., 1905. Mem. Conn. Hist. Soc., Bibliog. Soc. America, New London County Hist. Soc., Am. Antiq. Soc., S.A.R. Author of Bibliography of Connecticut Laws, 1900, Early Conn. Engraver, Conn. Gore Land Co., Charter of Conn., and other hist. pamphlets. Editor Conn. Hist. Soc. Collections, Vols. VIII-XXIV, and other of its publs., also several publs. of Acorn Club, Simsbury Records, Turkey Hills Records, Vols. I-III, etc. Home: 24 Marshall St., Hartford CT‡

BATES, HARRY C., labor leader; b. Denton, Tex., Nov. 22, 1882; s. Jefferson Davis and Minnie (Smith) B.; stu. high sch., Denton, 1894-98; m. Susie Hines, 1904 (dec.); m. 2d, Marguerite Roddy, 1933. Began as bricklayer, Waco, Texas, 1900; pres. Bricklayers Local Union, Dallas, Tex., 1910-14; pres. Tex. State Conf. Bricklayers Unions of Tex., 1912-20; spl. rep. Bricklayers, Masons and Plasterers Internat. Union of America, 1914-22, vice-pres., 1920-24, treas., 1924-28, pres. 1936-67; emeritus v.p., mem. exec. com. AFL; mem. amalgamation com. AFL-CIO, 1954-55; v.p., mem. exec. com. AFL-CIO, 1955-67; mem. Wage Adjustment Bd., 1943-45, WSB, 1951-52. Del. to trade union confs., Eng., Italy, Sweden. U.S. rep. ILO, Geneva, 1958, 60, 61. Home: Washington DC Died Apr. 3, 1969.

BATES, JOSEPHINE WHITE (MRS. LINDON WALLACE BATES), author; b. near Ottawa, Can.; d. George E. and Mary White; student Lake Forest (Ill.) U. (now Lake Forest Coll.), 1876-80; m. Lindon W. Bates, of N.Y. City, Apr. 6, 1881. Chmn. women's sect. of Nat. Preparedness, 1916-17. Clubs: Colony (New York); Fortnightly, Friday (Chicago). Author: A Blind Lead, 1889; Bunch-Grass Stories, 1892; Mercury Poisoning in the Industries of New York City and Vicinity, 1912. Summer Address: Lebanon Park, Mt. Lebanon, NY Address: 615 Fifth Av., New York NY‡

BATES, PUTNAM ASBURY, consulting engr.; b. New York, Dec. 27, 1875; s. Alfred Willard and Cephise Catherine (Towar) B.; E.E., Columbia, 1897; m. Emeline Goold Vernam, of Morristown, N.J., June 21, 1906. Mfr. elec. machinery, 1897-04; executive officer Crocker-Wheeler Co., Ampere, N.J.; consulting engr., 1904-13. Trustee N.J. State Chamber of Commerce. Mem. Squadron A Cav., N.G.S.N.Y., 9 yrs., 1897-06. Mem. Am. Inst. Elec. Engrs., 1910, Illuminating Engring. Soc., Am. Soc. Heating and Ventilating Engrs., New York Elec. Soc., Alpha Delta Phi, Tau Beta Pi. Clubs: University, Engineers', Morris County Golf. Home: Madison Av., Convent, N.J. Office: 2 Rector St., NY‡

BATES, SANFORD, lawyer, penologist, educator; b. Boston, July 17, 1884; s. Samuel W. and Nellie G. (Sanford) B.; LL.B. cum laude, Northeastern U., 1906, LL.D., 1937; L.H.D. (hon.), Rutgers U., 1954; m. Helen S. Williams, Oct. 3, 1908; children—Mary Elizabeth, Sanford Loring. Admitted to Mass. bar, 1906, U.S. Supreme Ct. bar, 1933, N.Y. bar, 1940; mem. firm Achorn & Bates, Boston, 1906-21; commr. Mass. Dept. Correction, 1919-29; supt. fed. prisons, 1929-30; dir. U.S. Bur. Prisons, 1930, 33-37; exec. dir. Boys Clubs Am., 1939-40; faculty N.Y. Sch. Social Work, from 1937; instr. div. handicapped Columbia Tchrs. Coll., from 1938; parole commr. N.Y. State, 1940-45; commr. Instns. and Agys., N.J., 1945-54; cons. pub. adminstrn. to states, municipalities, also Fed. Prison Bur., from 1954; pres. Fed. Prison Industries, Inc., from 1940; hearing officer U.S. Dept. Justice. Ofcl. U.S. del. Internat. Prison Congress, London, 1925, Prague, 1930, v.p. congress, 1930-31; chmn. delegation Internat. Penal and Penitentiary Congress, Berlin, 1935, presided over congresses, 1950, 55; pres. Internat. Panel and Penitentiary Commn., 1946, 55; v.p. Inst. Criminal Law and Criminology; mem. Commn. Investigate Criminal Law; chmn. nat. adv. com. prisoners and parolees SSS, from 1944; cons. restoration mil. prisoners War Dept., from 1944, Am. Law Inst., 1955-62, Am. Bar Survey on Criminal Justice, 1957-59; mem. UN Commn. Crime Prevention, 1951; adv. council dept. econ. and social instns. Princeton; Parole Compact adminstr., 1945; chmn. council Compact Adminstrs., 1946; mem.-at-large Nat. Social Welfare Assembly; mem. N.J. Rehab. Com.; cons penology Am. Bar. Found.; cons. President's Committee on Crime, 1966, Com. on Correctional Manpower, 1966; U.S. corr. to UN; ofcl. del. UN Conf. Crime, London, 1960; spl. cons. N.J. Dept. Instns. and Agys., from 1969. Mem. George Washington council Boy Scouts Am. Bd. dirs. N.J. Welfare Council, Nat. Boys Tng. Sch., Citizenship Edn. Service, N.J. Tb League, Nat. Com. Mental Hygiene, Correctional Services Fedn.; trustee Vineland Tng. Sch. Mem. Mass. Ho. of Reps., 1912-14. Mass. Senate, 1915-16. Decorated Order Orange Nassau. Fellow Am. Assn. Mental Deficiency; mem. Nat. Probation Assn. (trustee), Assn. Pub. Welfare Ofcls. (dir.), Nat. Conf. Social Agys., Nat. Conf. Juvenile Agys., Nat. Probation and Parole Assn. (trustee), Am. Pub. Welfare Assn., Am. Hosp. Assn., Morrow Assn. Correction (v.p.), Royal Arcanum, Am. Bar Assn., Am. Prison Assn. (pres. 1926), Am. Parole Assn. (pres.), Am. Crime Study Commn. (exec. com. 1927), Nat. Acad. Arts and Sci., Am. Pub. Health Assn., Am. Sociol. Assn., Am. Assn. Parole Compact Adminstrs. (pres. 1949), Acad. Polit. Sci., Morrow Assn. on Correction (N.J.), Nat. Jail Assn., Nat. Council Crime and Delinquency, Inst. Criminology Republic Argentina (hon.). Unitarian (moderator 1938-39). Rotarian. Author: Prison and Beyond, 1938; also numerous articles. Home: Pennington NJ Died Sept. 8, 1972; buried Ewing Ch. Cemetery, Ewing Twp., Trenton NJ

BATES, THEODORE LEWIS, advt. exec.; b. New Haven, Sept. 11, 1901; s. Vernal Warner and Elizabeth B. (Hailes) B.; student Andover Acad., 1916-20; B.S., Yale, 1924; m. Evelyn Turull, Aug. 4, 1934; children—Evelyn B. Owen, Patricia B. Johnson (twins). Advt. mgr. Chase Nat. Bank, N.Y.C., 1924-25; with George Batten & Co. and Batten Barton Durstine & Osborn, Inc., N.Y. City, 1925-35, v.p., 1929-35; v.p. and dir. Benton & Bowles, Inc. 1935-40; president and treas. Ted Bates, Inc., now chmn. of bd. dirs., mem. exec. committee; honorary chmn. bd., past chairman exec. committee Ted Bates & Co.; director Advertising Council. Knight Malta (comdr.). Clubs: Moisie Salmon; Yale (N.Y.C.); Lawrence Beach, Cedarhurst Yacht, Rockaway Hunting (L.I.); The Country, Havana Yacht (Havana). Home: New York City NY Died June 1972.

BATES, VYRL RAYMOND, steel co. exec.; b. Youngstown, O., June 29, 1903; s. Charles W. and Edna (Card) B.; student high sch., Youngstown; m. June Ann Flynn, June 26, 1915; 1 dau., Trish Ann. With Detroit Steel Co., from 1944, v.p., 1955. Home: Dearborn MI Died May 9, 1971; interred Mausoleum, Woodlawn Cemetery, Detroit MI

BATES, WILLIAM H., former congressman; b. Salem, Mass., Apr. 26, 1917; s. Hon. George J. and Nora (Jennings) B.; student Worcester Acad.; Brown U., Harvard Sch. Bus. Adminstrn.; m. Jean Dreyer, Feb. 12, 1943; 1 dau., Susan. Served in USN, advanced through grades to capt. Res. Mem. 81st to 91st Congresses, 6th Mass. Dist. Republican. Home: Salem MA Died June 22, 1969; buried Salem MA

BATH, ALBERT ALCUS, cotton merchant; b. Memphis, Tenn., May 26, 1876; s. William and Hedvig (Alcus) B.; m. Adele Levy, Dec. 30, 1913; children—Harriet, Billie Adele. Organized Bath-Gans Co. and pres. since 1929; pres. Houston Cotton Mills Co., Wagner Realty Co., Houston Harbor Land Co.; v.p. Brays Bays Development Co.; dir. Union Nat. Bank. Dir. Houston Cotton Exchange and Board of Trade. Clubs: Houston, Houston Country, Westwood Country, Bankers (N.Y. City). Home: 609 Avondale Av. Office: Cotton Exchange Bldg., Houston TX‡

BATHON, WINGROVE, editor; b. Baltimore, Sept. 26, 1876; s. Joseph G. and Mary (Wingrove) B.; self-ed. since 13 yrs. of age, when he left Calvert Hall Coll., Baltimore. Writer of fiction in various mags., etc., short stories to Cosmopolitan since 1898; asst. editor Feb., 1902, mng. editor since Feb., 1903, Cosmopolitan Mag.; Nov., 1903, staff writer New York Sunday World; Apr., 1904, lit. critic Collier's Weekly; Mar., 1905, editorial staff Hearst's Boston American, and sp'l writer New York American and Journal. Unmarried. Residence: Tarrytown NY‡

BATISTA (Y ZALDIVAR), FULGENCIO, President of Cuba; b. Banes, Oriente, Cuba, Jan. 16, 1901; s. Belisario Batista Palermo and Carmela Zaldivar Gonzalez; chiefly ed, by pvt. study; grad. Escuela Nacional de Periodistas; m. Elisa Pilar Godinez Gomez (div. 1945);children—Marta, Ruben, Elisa Aleida; m. 2d, Martha Fernandez Miranda; children—Jorge, Roberto Francisco, Carlos Manuel, Fulgencio Jose. Entered Nat. Army, 1921, promoted col., 1933, gen., 1941; chief of staff of army, 1933-39; constitutional pres. of Cuba, 1940-44 (under constitution a pres. may not seek re-election until after 8 yr. interval); elected senator from Santa Clara Prov., 1948; leader of mil. coup which ousted Pres. Prio Socarras, Mar. 10, 1952; provisional president 1952-55; constitutional president, 1955-59. Decorated Legion of Honor, France, Grand Cross. Member of Asociacion Nacional de Periodistas, Asociacion de Reporters, Academia de Artes y Letras. Author: Sombras de America, 1946. Address: Havana Cuba Died Aug. 6, 1973.

BATJER, LAWRENCE PAUL, research horticulturist; b. Abilene, Tex., June 6, 1907; s. W.F.D. and Lois (Minter) b.; B.S., Tex. A. and M. Coll., 1928; M.S., Mich. State U., 1930; Ph.D., Cornell U., 1933; m. Ire Danner, July 2, 1936; children—William Dunbar, John Danner. Extension specialist pomology Cornell U., 1933-34; research and extension horticulturist W.Va. U., 1935-36; research plant physiologist Dept. Arg., Beltsville, Md., 1937-44, prin. physiologist regional lab., Wenatchee, Wash., 1945-67. Pres. Western region Am. Soc. Hort. Sci., 1950, nat. pres. elect, 1964; pres. N.W. Assn. Horticulturists, Entomologists and Plant Pathologists, 1961. Mem. Wenatchee Sch. Bd., 1954-67, pres., 1957, 61; chmn. jr. coll. com. Wash. State Sch. Dirs. Assn., 1964-65. Bd. dirs. N. Central Wash. Regional Library, 1948-51, Wenatchee YMCA, 1947-49. Recipient Norman J. Coleman award American Nurserymen's Association, 1966; Superior Service award U.S. Dept. of Agr., 1967. Fellow Am. Assn. Horticulture Scientists; mem. Am. Inst. Biol. Scis., Sigma Xi, Alpha Zeta. Lion (pres. Wenatchee 1949). Home: Wenatchee WA Died May 28, 1967.

BATMAN, LEVI GORDON, clergyman; b. Bedford, Ind., May 16, 1869; s. Henry Harrison and Catherine J. (Bailey) B.; A.B., Ind. U., 1895; postgrad. Columbia, 1895-98; grad. Union Theol. Sem., 1898; m. Cora L. Dodds, July 6, 1898. Ordained to ministry Christian

Disciples Ch., 1898; pastor First Ch., Mansfield, O., 1898-1903, First Ch., Phila., 1903-09, First Ch., Youngstown, O., from 1909. Mem. exec. com. Fed. Council Chs. of Christ in Am. Mem. Sigma Chi. Republican. Address: Youngstown OH

BATTLE, HENRY WILSON, clergyman; b. Tuskegee, Ala.; s. Gen. Cullen A. and Georgia (Williams) B.; nephew of Archibald J.B., D.D., LL.D.; ed. Pinckard's Acad. and Park's High Sch., Tuskegee, and Mercer U., Macon, Ga.; D.D., Wake Forest Coll.; by spl. act of Ala. Legislature was admitted to bar before age of 20; practiced law at Eufaula 3 yrs.; grad. in special studies, Southern Bapt. Theol. Seminary, 1880; m. Margaret, d. Rev. J.L. Stewart, of Clinton, N.C., June 11, 1889; children—John S., Henry W., Florence B., Mrs. Emily Wood, James M., Hawthorne. Ordained Bapt. ministry, 1880; pastor First Ch., Columbus, Miss., 3 yrs., where entertained Southern Bapt. Conv., health being impaired by malaria, occupied smaller fields until pastor First Ch., Petersburg, Va., 1892-1903, First Ch., Greensboro, N.C., 1903-07 (handsome church edifice erected during this period), First Ch., Kinston, N.C., 1907-09, High St. Ch., Charlottesville, 1909-25, later Leesburg, Fla., retired; now serves chs. during critical ad interim periods. Preacher Southern Baptist Conv., Hot Springs, Ark., 1908; pres. Bapt. S.S. and Bible Bd. of Va., etc. Has delivered many addresses, spl. sermons, etc., in leading cities of the North and South, and conducted evangelistic meetings with great success in Boston, Richmond, Charlotte, etc. Represented the South on program of Buffalo Conv., B.Y.P.U., and at 25th anniversary of Chautauqua Assembly, N.Y.; Founders' Day orator, Southern Bapt. Theol. Sem., Louisville, Ky.; commencement orator for many colleges and univs.; reunion orator" at reunion of United Confederate Vets., Richmond, Va., June 1915—the only other son" thus honored up to that time being Col. Robert E. Lee, grandson of Gen. R. E. Lee. Preached memorial service in honor of President McKinley, Brooklyn, 1901, President Harding, Baltimore, 1923. Delivered address, by invitation, before N.C. Senate which broke the opposition and inaugurated campaign of state-wide prohibition; has made many pub. appeals in behalf U. of Va. and local interests. Has published many sermons and lit. and religious articles. Many times chaplain-in-chief Sons Conf. Vets. Mason (K.T.). Mem. S.A.R.; presented badges of honor to heroes of World War for Va. Soc., S.A.R. Clubs: Redland, Kiwanis. Guest for life" of Monticello Nat. Shrine. Home: Charlottesville VA‡

BATTLE, HYMAN LLEWELLYN, textile mfr.; b. Rocky Mount, N.C., Aug. 11, 1896; s. Thomas Hall and Sallie Dorch (Hyman) B.; student U. N.C., 1915-16; m. Mamie Louise Braswell, June 22, 1921; children—Hyman Llewellyn, Thomas Braswell. With Rocky Mount (N.C.) Mills 1919, treas., mgr., dir. 1933, pres., 1954; v.p. Rocky Mount Cord Co., 1937; dir. Sterling Cotton Mills, Coastal Plain Life Ins. Co., Planters Nat. Bank & Trust Co., Rocky Mount Investment Co., A.C.L. R.R., Waltzinger, Inc. State, Bus. Found. Adviser to employer del. Internat. Labor Conf., Washington, 1937; expert yarn cons. O.Q.M.G., AUS, 1945; mem. carded yarn adv. com. OPA and Civilian Prodn. Adminstrn., Washington, 1942-51, Chmn. Housing Authority. Pres. bd. trustees Rectory Sch., Pomfret, Conn., 1937-41; trustee St. Marys Sch. and Jr. Coll., Raleigh, N.C., 1954-57. Served with U.S. Army, 1917-19. Recipient Distinguished Service award U. N.C. Sch. Medicine, 1957. Mem. Rocky Mount C. of C., S.A.R., Soc. Colonial Wars, N.Y. So. Soc., Newcomen Soc. Democrat. Episcopalian. Clubs: Princess Anne Country (Virginia Beach, Va.); Benvenue Country (Rocky Mount, N.C.). Home: Rocky Mount NC also Virginia Beach VA Died May 1973.

BATTLE, JOHN S(TEWART), lawyer; b. New Bern, N.C., July 11, 1890; s. Rev. Henry Wilson and Margaret (Stewart) B.; student Wake Forest Coll.; LL.B., U. Va., 1913; LL.D., Hampden-Sydney Coll. (Va.), U. Richmond, Wake Forest Coll., William and Mary Coll.; married Mary Jane Lipscomb, June 12, 1918; children—John Stewart, William Cullen. Admitted to Va. bar, 1913, and began practice, Charlottesville, Va.; became mem. Ho. of Dels., Va. Gen. Assembly, 1929; state senator, 1934-49; gov. of Va., 1950-54; mem. law firm Perkins, Battle & Minor, from 1954. Mem. Civil Rights Commn., 1959. Served with U.S. Army, World War I. Mem. Va. Bar Assn. (pres. 1940-41), Phi Beta Kappa, Alpha Tau Omega. Mason. Address: Charlottesville VA Died Apr. 9, 1972; buried Monticello Meml. Park, Charlottesville VA

BATTLEY, JOSEPH F., retired army officer; b. Norfolk, Va., Dec. 19, 1896; s. Joseph Franklin and Effie Ada (Sadler) B.; student Norfolk (Va.) Academy; M.B.A., Harvard University, 1926; graduate Army Indsl. Coll., 1933, Chem. Warfare Sch., 1938, Army War College, 1946; m. Joyce Russell Zannia. In Federal service with Va. Nat. Guard, 1917; commd. 2d lt., Engrs Reserve Corps, U.S. Army, 1918, and advanced through the ranks to brig. gen., 1944; served with Chem. Warfare Service, France, 1918; exec. officer Chem. Warfare Service Arsenal, Edgewood, Md., 1920-23; with Office of Under Sec. of War, 1932-36, on loan to NRA to serve as div. adminstr., chem. div., 1933-36, later asst. to adminstr. W.P.A. in New York, N.Y., to 1936; assigned to Edgewood Arsenal, 1936-39, chief, protective development div., developing and perfecting fully molded gas mask and plastic lenses, also chief, war plans div. to 1939; mem. joint Army and Navy Munitions Bd. for indsl. and manpower phases of plans for emergency, 1939-41; assistant construction, Q.M.C., 1940-41; chief manpower and liaison div., Office of Under Secretary of War, 1941-42, also consultant, labor div., O.P.M. (later W.P.B.), 1942; also nat. occupational adv. Selective Service System, 1940-42; chief, administrative mgt. br., control div., Army Service Forces, 1942; exec. for Service Comds. Office Chief of Administrative Services, Oct. 1942-May 1943; exec. officer dept. chief of staff for Service Comds., 1943-44, dep. chief of staff, 1944-46, asst., Office of Comdg. Gen. Army Service Forces, charge Army Service Forces pub. relations, 1946; spl. around world mission Aug.-Sept. 1945; exec. chief pub. information, Office Gen. Eisenhower, 1946, retired 1947. Exec. asst. pres. Sands, Las Vegas, Nev.; partner Labor-Mgmt. Sales Consultants. Pres. Nat. Clean-up Paint-up Bureau. Member of National Planning Council; sponsor Atlantic Council U.S. Awarded Army Commendation Ribbon with two clusters, D.S.M., Legion of Merit. Mem. Nat. Paint Varnish and Lacquer Assn. (pres. 1947-61). Clubs: Nat. Press; Harvard; Harvard Business School of S.C., SKAL. Internat.; Army Navy. Home: Riverside Died Dec. 18, 1970.

BAUCUM, A. W., petroleum co. exec.; b. 1910; B.S., Tex. A. & M. Coll., 1934; m.; children—Joanne, Jean, Jill, Julie, Jennifer. With Texaco, Inc., 1934-72, v.p., 1958-61, exec. v.p., 1961-64, chief exec. officer So. operations, Houston, 1964-72. Home: Houston TX Died Jan. 1972.

BAUER, GEORGE NEANDER, educator; b. Jordan, Minn. Jan. 8, 1872; B.S., U. of Minn. 1894; M.S., U. of Ia., 1898; Ph.D. Columbia, 1900; m. Bertha M. Blum, June 18, 1907 (died 1919); 1 dau. Elisabeth B.; m. 2d, Hildred Craig, Dec. 30, 1944. Instructor mathematics, University of Iowa, 1895-98; instr., 1900-02, asst. prof., 1902-07, prof. mathematics, 1907-18. U. of Minn. State chmn. War Savings Soc. for Minn. under the U.S. Treasury Dept. during 1918; asso. dir. War Savings Orgn. of 9th Fed. Reserve Dist., 1919; pres. East Hennepin State Bank, 1920-24; served as v.p. Exchange State Bank, Minneapolis; prof. of mathematics, University of New Hampshire, 1924-42, professor emeritus since 1942. Research worker in agrl. econ., during World War II. Member A.A.A.S., American Assn. Univeristy Profs., Am. Statistical Assn., Society for Quality Control. Author: The Parallax of Mu Cass, and the Positions of Fifty-six Neighboring Stars, 1900; Plane and Spherical Trigonometry (with William E. Brooke), 1907; Transcendental Curves and Numbers and Algebraic and Transcendental Numbers (with Dr. H. L. Slobin); Mathematics Preparatory to Statistics and Finance, 1929. Home: 574 Circuit Rd., Portsmouth NH‡

BAUER, H(ANS) G(USTAV), corp. exec., engr.; b. Stettin, Germany, Nov. 21, 1903; s. Gustav and Elsa (Kaesemacher) B.; student engring. Technische Hochschule Hannover, Germany, 1921-26; m. Erica M.E. Lagemann, Aprl 1, 1936; 1 son, Peter Gustav Hans. Came to U.S., 1931, naturalized, 1938. Mem. Merchant Marine, Germany, Eng., Scotland, 1926-31; engring., sales work Am. Bauer-Wach Corp., Hydraulic Coupling Corp., N.Y.C., 1931-37; intermittent position as chief engr. merchant marine dept. A. G. Weser, Bremen, Germany, 1936; sales, engring. DeLaval Steam Turbine Co., Trenton, N.J., 1937-45, mgr. marine div., 1945-48, exec. engr., 1948, dir., from 1948, v.p., exec. engr., 1949-51, v.p. engring., 1951-54, v.p., gen. sales mgr., 1954-58, exec. v.p., 1958-62; exec. v.p. De Laval Turbine, Inc., 1962-63, sr. v.p., 1964-69; bd. directors De Laval Turbine Can., Ltd., De Laval Turbine Internat., Inc., De Laval-Holroyd, Inc., Jens Risom Design, Inc., Mem. Soc. Naval Architects and Marine Engrs., Am. Soc. Naval Engrs., Inst. Marine Engrs. (London, Eng.). Clubs: The Trenton, Trenton Country; Engineers (Trenton); Nassau, Pretty Brook Tennis (Princeton). Contbr. articles tech. publs. Home: Pennington NJ Died Dec. 18, 1969; buried Trinity All-Saints Cemetery, Princeton NJ

BAUER, LELAND MASON, educator; b. Portersville, Ind., June 17, 1904; s. Jacob and Ella (Petry) B.; A.B., Oakland City Coll., 1929, LL.D., 1959; student U. Mich., 1930; M.A., U. New Mexico, 1933; m. Martha Ellen Price, Aug. 5, 1941; 1 dau., Marilyn Ruth. Tchr. DuBois County, Ind., 1923-27; high sch. prin., Gibson County, Ind., 1929-31; math. tchr. Menaul High Sch., Albuquerque, from 1931, prin., 1931-46, dean, 1946-55, dean, and bus. mgr., 1955-58, bus. mgr., from 1958, chmn. plant sub-com. Long Range Planning com.; chairman of the Irrigation Ditch Committee. Treas. Presbyn. Nat. Missions Credit Union; mem. Albuquerque Citizens Com. Registered profl. engr., N.M. Mem. N.M. Edn. Assn., N.M. Soc. Profl. Engrs., Math. Assn. Am., Nat. Assn. Secondary Sch. Prins., C. of C., Phi Delta Kappa, Kappa Mu Epsilon, Phi Kappa Phi, Mu Tau Kappa. Presbyn. Odd Fellow. Club: Optimist (pres. 1962-63, sec., dist. sec.-treas. 1963-64). Research in bi-lingual problem in high sch. field. Address: Albuquerque NM Died May 18, 1970; buried Lemon Cemetery Jasper IN

BAUER, WILLIAM CHARLES, elec. engr.; b. Cincinnati, Dec. 26, 1873; s. Ludwig and Wilhelmina (Buehler) B.; B.S. (in elec. engring.), U. of Cincinnati, 1896, post-grad. course and instr. civ. engring., 1896-97, student U. of Chicago, 1905; Sc.D., Baker U., Baldwin, Kan., 1908; m. Alice Jeannette Strahley, Aug. 24, 1896;children—Mary Virginia, William Malcolm. Prof. physics and chemistry, Baker U., 1897-1908; prof. physics and elec. engring., U. of Denver, 1908-09; prof. elec. engring., Northwestern U., 1909-39, acting dir. Coll. of Engring. many years, dean School of Engineering, 1927-38, retired, 1939; cons. engr., Northwestern U. in connection with a large group of buildings, 1925-33. Magnetic observer and dir. Baldwin Magnetic Obs., U.S. Coast and Geod. Survey, 1900-02; magnetic observer in Can. of eclipse for same, 1905; consulting elec. engr. since 1903; designed and built also supt. Baldwin (Kan.) Municipal Light Plant, 1906-08. Mem. Sigma Xi (pres. Northwestern Chapter, 1918-19); life mem. Tau Beta Pi. Home: 725 Milburn St., Evanston, Ill.; also 917 Alberca St., Coral FL‡

BAUGHER, NORMAN J., clergyman; b. York County, Pa., Aug. 4, 1917; s. Jacob I. and Lillian (Stermer) B.; A.B., Elizabethtown (Pa.) Coll., 1940, D.Lit., 1962; B.D., Bethany Theol. Sem., Chgo., 1943, D.D., 1958; m. Ruth Christ, June 1, 1940; children—Gregory W., Daryl B. Ordained to ministry Ch. of the Brethren, 1938; pastor in Md., Pa., N.Y., Ind., Cal., 1939-52; mem. gen. brotherhood bd. Ch. of the Brethren, 1948-52, gen. sec. gen. brotherhood bd., 1952-68. Rep. gen. assembly World Council Chs., Evanston, Ill., 1954; rep. gen. assembly Nat. Council Chs., Denver, 1952, St. Louis, 1957, Miami Beach, 1966, rec. sec., 1957-60; ofcl. ch. visits to Ecuador, Nigeria, Europe; chmn. div. Christian Life and Mission, 1960-63; v.p. Nat. Council Chs. U.S.A., 1963-66, chmn. general planning and program com., 1966-68; rep. 3d assembly World Council of Chs., New Delhi, 1961, mem. central com., 1961-68; co-chmn. Inter-religious Com. Against Poverty, 1965-68; chmn. team of ch. men vis. S.E. Asia for Priority Program on Peace, Nat. Council Chs., 1965, mem. peace program adv. panel, 1965-68. Home: Elgin IL Died Apr. 20, 1968.

BAUMANN, RUDOLF, Austrian diplomat; b. Christofen, Lower Austria, Dec. 9, 1910; s. Rudolf and (Juroszek) B.; LL.D., U. Vienna; m. Doris Przibram. Magistrate, Vienna, 1935-38; pvt. industry staff, 1938-45; Fed. Minister Property Control and Economy Planning, 1945-47; joined Fgn. Service, 1947; sec. Austrian legations, Ankara, Turkey, Athens, Greece, 1948-49; polit. rep., Bucharest, Rumania, 1951-53; charge d'affaires, Mexico, Central Am. Republics, Panama, 1955; A.E. and P., 1958-64; dept. head Fgn. Office, 1961-71; A. E. and P., Thailand, 1964-71, Malaysia, S. Vietnam, Singapore, Philippines, 1965-71, vice. gov. Asia Devel. Bank, Manila. Recipient grand cross 1st class Mexican Order Aztec Eagle; grand cross Thai Order White Elephant; grand officer Liberian Order African Redemption; comdr. cross Menelik II Order Ethiopia. Contbr. articles and Vienna Austria Died Apr. 26, 1971.

BAUMGARTNER, APOLLINARIS, bishop Roman Cath. Ch. Address: Agana Guam Died Dec. 1970.*

BAUMGARTNER, WILLIAM JACOB, zoologist; b. Excelsior, Morgan County, Mo., May 14, 1871; s. A. and Barbara (Garber) B.; student Bethel Coll., Newton, Kan.; A.B.; U. of Kan., 1900, A.M., 1901; studied U. of Chicago, 1901-04; Ph.D., U. of Munich, Germany, 1929; m. Olga Leisy, Dec. 19, 1900; 1 dau., Leona. Teacher pub. schs., Kan., 7 yrs.; instr. zoology, 1904, asst. prof., 1905, asso. prof., 1913, prof. since 1930, U. of Kan. Mem. staff Puget Sound Marine Sta., 1908-15; mem. scientific expdn. to Ore. fossil fields, 1905, to Ariz. for insects, 1906, to Puget Sound for sea animals, 1908; conducted expdn. to Gulf Goast, Tex., 1907. Mng. editor Science Bull., U. of Kan., 1914-20 (issuing 6 vols.). Fellow A.A.A.S.; mem. Soc. Am. Anatomists, Am. Zool. Soc., Kan. Acad. Science (life; also mng. editor), Phi Beta Kappa, Sigma Xi, Phi Chi. Republican. Presbyn. Club: University. Author: A Laboratory Manual of the Foetal Pig, 1925; also many articles in scientific and ednl. jours. Originator of campaign for million dollar Stadium-Union Fund for U. of Kan. and raised most of the subscriptions. Home: 1209 Lawrence KS‡

BAWDEN, WILLIAM THOMAS, educator; b. Oberlin, O., Nov. 6, 1875; s. Rev. Henry H. and Harriet Newell (Day) B.; A.B., Denison U., Granville, O., 1896; spl. diploma, Mechanics Inst., Rochester, N.Y., 1898; B.S., Teachers Coll. (Columbia), 1903, Ph.D., 1914; married Ora Richardson, August 17, 1898 (died March 25, 1945); 1 son, William Richardson; married 2d, Maude Mary Firth, April 16, 1949. Instructor, Cedar Valley Seminary, Osage, 1896-97; instructor, New York State Reformatory, Elmira, 1898; instr. in manual training, pub. schs., Buffalo, 1898-1902; dir. Manual Training Dept., Ill. State Normal U., 1903-10; asst. dean, Coll. of Engring., U. of Ill., 1910-12; specialist in indsl. edn., U.S. Bur. of Edn., 1914-19, asst. to commr., 1919-23; asso. supt. of schs., Tulsa, Okla., 1923-28; head dept. of indsl. and vocational edn. and dir. of grad. courses ii indsl. and vocational edn., Kan. State

Teachers Coll., 1935-45; dir. of publs. since 1945. Mem. N.E.A., Am. Vocational Assn., Phi Beta Kappa. Chmn. sub-sect. Indsl. Edn., 2d Pan-Am. Scientific Congress, Washington, D.C., Dec.-Jan. 1915-16. Baptist. Author: Leaders in Industrial Education, 1950; History of Kansas State Teachers College, 1952. Editor Indsl. Education Mag., Peoria, 1909-39, mng. editor, 1928-35. Address: Kansas State Teachers College, Pittsburg KS‡

BAXTER, EARL HAYES, peditrician; b. Mt. Vernon, O., Sept. 9, 1892; s. Charles Chase and Ethelyn Alice (Hayes) B.; M.D., Ohio State Univ., 1918, student U. of Mich., 1918, Rush Med. Coll., 1921, Vienna Clinics, 1936; m. Cora Helen Leech, Aug. 22, 1918 (dec. Sept. 7, 1950); 1 dau., Cora Jane; m. 2d Dorothy C. Conrad, Dec. 30, 1952. Instr. clin. microscopy, O. State U., 1918-19; resident physician Children's Hosp. of Phila., 1919-20; instr. pediatrics Coll. of Med., Ohio State U., 1920-26, asst. prof., 1926-38, asso. prof., 1938-41, prof. of pediatrics and chairman of the department of pediatrics, 1941-63, emeritus prof. pediatrics, 1963-71; chief of staff Children's Hosp., 1939-63; chief of pediatric service University Hosp., 1937-63; attending pediatrician Riverside Meth., Grant, Mt. Carmel, St. Anne's hosps. Mem. Ohio SSS, 1967-70. Trustee Center Sci. and Industry of Franklin County Hist. Soc., also v.p. soc., 1963-70. Recipient Alumni Achievement Award Ohio State U. Coll. Medicine, 1961, Honored Alumnus award, 1968, also Golden Circle certificate. Diplomate Am. Bd. Pediatrics. Mem. Am. Acad. Pediatrics, A.M.A., Midwest Pediatric Research Soc., Columbus Acad. Medicine (pres. 1955-56), Ohio Med. Assn., Central Ohio Pediatric Soc., S.A.R., Alpha Omega Alpha, Phi Rho Sigma. Mason, Rotarian. Clubs: Faculty (Columbus, O.). Contbr. articles to profl. jours. Home: Columbus OH Died July 16, 1971.

BAXTER, GEORGE EDWIN, M.D., b. Griggsville, Ill., Oct. 27, 1874; s. Edwin Walter and Helen Maria (Harvey) B.; Ph.B., Ill. Coll., Jacksonville, 1896, A.M., 1924; M.D., Northwestern U., 1899; post grad. student Vienna, 1909; m. Maude Hitchcock, of Chicago, June 7, 1905. Interne St. Luke's Hosp., Chicago, 1899-1901; practice in Chicago, 1901-36; instructor haemotology and pathology, Northwestern U., 1903-05; instr. medicine, 1905-09; instr. grad. pediatrics, U. of Chicago,, at Children's Memorial Hosp. and asso. attending physician, 1910-36; consulting pediatrician Grant Hosp., 1930-35; attending pediatrician Ravenswood Hosp., 1907-36. Trustee Ill. Coll., Jacksonville, since 1924 (chmn. bd. 1932-36); trustee Chicago Med. Soc., 1926-36; 1st sec. and pres. North Shore branch Chicago Med. Soc.; sec. and pres. former Physicians' Club, Chicago. Fellow Am. Coll. Physicians (life mem.); mem. A.M.A., Ill. Med. Soc., Chicago Pediatric Soc., Am. Acad. Pediatrics, Chicago Inst. of Medicine (mem. bd. govs. 1927-30), Soc. Colonial Wars, S.R., Nu Sigma Nu, Phi Beta Kappa. Clubs: University (Chicago); University (Claremont, Glendora CA‡

BAXTER, GREGORY PAUL, chemist; b. Somerville, Mass., Mar. 3, 1876; s. George Lewis and Ida Florence (Paul) B.; A.B., Harvard, 1896, A.M., 1897, Ph.D., 1899; hon. Sc.D. from U. of Mich., 1929; m. Amy Bailey Sylvester, June 2, 1906; 1 dau., Elizabeth Paul Boardman. Asst. chemistry, 1895-97, instr. 1897-99, Harvard; instr. chem., Haverford College, Pa., 1899-1900; asst. prof. chemistry, Swarthmore, 1900-02; instr. in chemistry, Harvard, 1902-05, asst. prof. 1905-15, prof. 1915-25, Theodore William Richards prof., 1925-44, Theodore William Richards prof. emeritus, 1944. Chmn. Internat. Com. on Atomic Weights, 1930-47. Rep. Unitarian. Theodore W. Richards medalist, 1934. Fellow Am. Acad. Arts and Scis.; mem. Nat. Acad. Sciences, Am. Chem. Soc., Phi Beta Kappa, Sigma Xi. Club: Harvard (Boston). Author: Researches upon the Atomic Weights, 1910, also papers in chemical periodicals. Home: 59 Francis Av., Cambridge MA‡

BAXTER, PERCIVAL PROCTOR, ex-gov. Me.; b. Portland, Me., Nov. 22, 1876; s. James Phinney and Mehetabel Cummings (Proctor) B.; A.B., Bowdoin, 1898; LL.B., Harvard, 1901; unmarried. Began law practice at Portland, 1901; mem. Me. Ho. of Rep., 1905-06, 1917-18, 1919-20, Senate, 1909-10, and 1921-22; del. Rep. Nat. Convention, 1920, 24 and 1928; gov. of Me., term ending Jan. 1923, reelected, term ending Jan. 8, 1925. Led in fight for conservation of water power of Maine; donated to State of Maine, Baxter State Park (201,018 acres) including Mount Katahdin (5,267 feet) for a public park and game sanctuary. Mem. Delta Kappa Epsilon, Phi Beta Kappa. Conglist. Clubs: Harvard (Boston and New York); Cumberland (Portland). Home: Portland ME Died June 12, 1969; cremated.‡

BAXTER, WILLIAM JOSEPH, economist, author; b. Worcester, Mass., Oct. 12, 1899; s. John J. and Mary (F.) B.; A.B., Clark U., 1920; M.B.A., Grad. Sch. Bus. Adminstrn., Harvard, 1922; m. Beatrice Premo, Aug. 1929; children—Jane Premo, William J. Cons. economist, 1922-70; pres. Baxter Bros., Inc., Roses & Myrrh, Incorporated; dir. Lancaster Process, Inc.,; mng. dir. Internat. Econ. Research Bureau. Clubs: Larchmont Yacht, North Fork Country. Author: Chain Store Distribution and Management, 1926; America Faces Its Greatest Business Depression, 1937; America Faces a Complete Breakdown in Government, 1938; How to Survive the Coming Breakdown, 1939; Japan and America Must Work Together, 1941; No Inflation Coming, 1944; Lower Prices Coming, 1950; Wages Are Going Lower, 1951; Today's Revolution in Weather, 1953; Warmer Weather—Boom in North, 1955; Gold Is Going Higher, Larchmont NY Died Apr. 1970.

BAYARD, FAIRFAX, b. Washington, D.C., Feb. 1, 1874; s. Albert F. and Marian J. (Craigen) B.; C.E., Lehigh U., 1896; LL.B., Nat. U., Washington, D.C., 1905; m. Mabel Hatch, of Keene, N.H., Oct. 27, 1909. With the Patent Office, Washington, D.C., 1896-1920; examiner of interferences, 1907-10; EXaminer in chief, 1910-20. With General Electric Co. since Dec. 1920. Mem. Tau Beta Pi (Alpha of Pa). Home: 815 Union St., Schenectady NY‡

BAYLES, EDWIN ATKINSON, lawyer; born N.Y. City, Dec. 1, 1875; s. Dr. George and Catharine Segvine (Johnson) B.; A.B., Columbia, 1896, M.A., 1897, LL.B., 1899; m. Eleanor Madeleine Gould, Oct. 20, 1903. Admitted to N.Y. bar, 1899, Dist. of Columbia bar, 1919; practiced law in N.Y. and Dist. of Columbia, 1899-34; ret., 1934; dir. Home Ins. Co., Home Indemnity Co., N.Y. City. Chief counsel, Housing Div., U.S. Shipping Bd., Emergency Fleet Corp., World War I. Member Phi Gamma Delta. Republican. Episcopalian. Clubs: Phi Gamma Delta, Columbia University (New York). Home: Main St., Dennis MA‡

BAYLEY, FRANCIS REED, clergyman; b. Millville, N.J., Oct. 25, 1877 s. William Henry and Mary Jacobs (Sheldon) B.; A.B., Dickinson Coll., 1900, D.D., 1920; LL.D., Western Maryland College, 1944; m. May S. Merryman, December 17, 1903; children—Francis C., Mary Anna (Mrs. Marshall H. Barnard), John S. Ordained Meth. ministry, 1904; admitted to Baltimore Annual Conf., M.E. Ch., 1902; served various pastorates, 1902-21; dist. supt. M.E. Ch., 1922-28; superintendent East Baltimore District, 1934-40; field representative Asbury Methodist Home for Aged 1945-50. Delegate to the General Conference since 1920 (chmn. judiciary com. 1932-36); del. to Uniting Conf. of Methodism, 1939. Pres. Judicial Council, 1939-48. Mason (past Grand Chaplain, Grand Lodge). Home: Avon Park FL‡

BAYLIS, CHARLES T., preacher, lecturer; b. Liverpool, Eng., Apr. 17, 1869; s. Thomas and Louise (Dudley) B.; brought to America in infancy; ed. in Can. and at Taylor U., Upland, Ind., A.M., and Ph.D., Taylor, 1894; post-grad. work Chicago Theol. Sem.; m. Elizabeth Dillingham Hovey, of Lowell, Mass., May 24, 1898; children—Marjorie Elizabeth, Gertrude Louise, Esther Victoria, Miriam Joy. Ordained Congl. ministry, 1897; pastor 1st Ch., Brecksville, O., 1898, 99, Bushwick Av. Ch., 1900-06, Ch. of the Open Door, Brooklyn, N.Y., 1906-10; travelogue and lyceum lecturer since 1910. Pres. Nat. Sesqui-Centennial Com. Sent to Europe on spl. missions by Herbert Hoover during World War, and was on three boats that were sunk on return trips; delivered war lecture, One Thousand Miles over the Battlefields of Europe," in many cities; other lectures: Under Tropical Skies; Making a Better America; The Kind of People We Meet; Rifts in the Clouds; etc.; lectured in 46 states, 1921-23, inclusive. Home: 170 Parkside Av., Brooklyn NY‡

BAYLOR, WILLIAM HENRY, clergyman; b. Princess Anne Co., Va., Oct. 25, 1865; s. Richard Henry and Annie Elizabeth (Holt) B.; student U. of Richmond, 1888, Rochester Theol. Sem., 1889, Southern Bapt. Theol. Sem., Louisville, Ky., 1897; D.D., U. of Richmond, 1917; m. Julia Phillips, Jan. 21, 1896; children—Mabel Louise (Mrs. Wallis P. Jester), Ralph Phillips, Selma Elzabeth (Mrs. Charles M. Knobloch), Mary Ellen (Mrs. Fred E. Brumble). Ordained ministry Southern Bapt. Ch., 1890; pastor Cavalry Bapt. Ch., Portsmouth, Va., 1890-94, First Baptist Church, New Albany, Ind., 1895-98; Grace Church, Baltimore, Md., 1898-15; sec. State Mission Bd. and supt. Missions, Md. Bapt. Union Assn., 1915-26; pastor Park View Ch., Portsmouth, Va., 1927-41. Trustee U. of Richmond, Southern Bapt. Theol. Sem. Mem. Virginians of Md. Mason. Author: Better Not, or 20 Don'ts for Preachers, 1948. Retired June 30, 1941. Address: Homewood Apts., Charles and 31st Sts., Baltimore MD‡

BAYNE-JONES, STANHOPE, bacteriologist; b. New Orleans, La., Nov. 6, 1888; s. Stanhope and Minna (Bayne) B.; A.B., Yale, 1910; M.D., Johns Hopkins, 1914, M.A., 1917, Sc.D., U. Rochester, 1943, Emory University, 1954; LL.D., Tulane University, 1956; married Nannie Moore Smith, June 25, 1921. Interne, Johns Hopkins Hosp., 1914-15; Rockefeller fellow in pathology, 1915-16, asso. prof. bacteriology, same, 1922-23; prof. bacteriology Sch. of Medicine, U. of Rochester, 1923-32; dir. Rochester Health Bur. Labs., 1926-32; prof. bacteriology, Yale Sch. of Medicine, 1932-47, and dean of the School of Medicine, 1935-40; also master of Trumbull Coll. (Yale), 1932-38. Served as capt. and maj., M.C., with British and Am. armies in France, Italy and Germany, 1917-19; sanitary insp. 3d Army, in Germany, 1919; brigadier gen. medical corps, U.S. Army, dept. chief preventive med. service, Office of the Surgeon Gen., 1942-46; adminstr. Army Epidermiological Board. Director, United States of America Typhus Commn., 1944-46; chmn. div. med. scis. National Research Council, 1932-33. Director Board of Scientific Advisers, Jane Coffin Childs Memorial Fund for Med. Research, 1937-47; scientific dir. Internat. Health Div., Rockefeller Foundation, 1939-41; director Josiah Macy, Jr. Foundation, 1939-41 and from 1948; president Joint Administration Board of New York Hospital-Cornell Medical Center, 1947-53; tech. dir. research Army Med. Research and Development Program, 1952-56; mem. Army Sci. Adv. Com., from 1954; chmn. sec.'s cons. on med. research and edn. U.S. Dept. Health, Edn. and Welfare, 1957-58; mem. Surgeon gen.'s com. on smoking and health USPHS from 1962. Mem. N.Y.C. Bd. Hosps., 1950-52, Nat. Manpower Council, 1951, Commn. on Financing Hosp. Care, 1951, Hosp. Council of Greater N.Y., 1948-51; mem. Yale Corp., 1956-57. Mem. A.A.A.S., A.M.A. (council on pharmacy and chemistry, 1930-34), Society Am. Bacteriologists (president 1929-30), Am. Assn. Immunologists (pres. 1930-31), Soc. Exptl. Biology and Medicine, Assn. Am. Physicians, Am. Assn. Pathologists and Bacteriologists (pres. 1940-41), Am. Pub. Health Assn., Am. Soc. Tropical Medicine, Assn. of Am. Med. Coll. (exec. council 1938-40), Am. Soc. for Control of Cancer (exec. com. 1938-1940), Am. Assn. for Cancer Research, Leonard Wood Memorial (med. advisory board 1937-41), Nat. Bd. Med. Examiner (1936-41), Zeta Psi, Nu Sigma Nu (hon. council), Phi Beta Kappa, Alpha Omega Alpha. Decorated Mil. Cross, Croix de Guerre, Distinguished Service Medal, U.S. of America Typhus Commn. Medal, Army Commendation Ribbon, Silver Star (with 2 oak leaf clusters), Order of British Empire (hon. comdr.). Episcopalian. Clubs: University, Metropolitan, Army and Navy, Cosmos. Contbr. on pathology and bacteriology. Home: Washington DC Died Feb. 20, 1970; buried Arlington Nat. Cemetery, Arlington VA

BAYOL, EDGAR SANSOM, pub. relations cons. newspaper assn. exec.; b. Greensboro, Ala., Aug. 29, 1907; s. Benjamin Matthew and Annie Lucile (Sansom) B.; grad. Fishburne Mil. Sch., Waynesboro, Va.; student U. Va.; LL.B., Wash. Coll. Law, 1939; m. Mary Lee Burgess, Aug. 13, 1927; m. 2d, Terry McGarrity, Nov. 29, 1950; m. 3d, Mary Walker, May 17, 1954; m. 4th, Bernice Morris, Aug. 24, 1969; children—Permelia Burgess, Sieglinde. Admitted to D.C. bar, 1939, Va. bar, 1942; v.p., gen. mgr. Alexandria (Va.) Gazette, 1940-41; gen. promotion mgr. Washington Star, 1942-45; editorial promotion mgr. N.Y. World-Telegram, 1946-48; press counsel Coca-Cola Co., 1948-58; exec. v.p., gen. mgr. Nat. Editorial Assn., 1958-60; pres. Edgar S. Bayol & Assos., 1960-70, Am. Newspapers Study Missions, Inc., 1961-70, Study Missions Internat., Inc., 1961-70. Mem. Am. Patent Law Assn. N.Y. Promotion mgrs. Assn. (past pres.), Nat. Newspaper Promption Assn. (past pres.), U.S. Trademark Assn. (past pres.), Internat. Patent and Trademark Assn. (past chmn. pub. relations com.), Am. Bar Assn., Pub. Relations Soc. Am. Mason (past master). Club: Lions of Alexandria (past pres.); N.Y. Athletic (N.Y.C.). Home: Falls Church VA Died Sept. 3, 1970; buried Warrenton Cemetery, Warrenton VA

BEA, AUGUSTIN CARDINAL, clergyman; b. Riedbohringen, Baden, Germany, May 28, 1881; ed. U. Fribourg, Jesuit Coll., Valkenburg U. Innsbruck, U. Berlin. Joined Soc. of Jesus; ordained priest Roman Catholic Ch., 1912; Jesuit provincial for Upper Germany, 1921-24; dir. higher studies Jesuit Coll., Rome, Italy, 1924-28; prof. Pontifical Bibl. Inst., 1924-59, rector, 1930-49; cardinal deacon, 1959-68. Decorated grand cross Sovereign Order of Malt. Mem. and hon. mem. various socs. Author: De Pentateucho, 1928; De Inspiratione S. Scripturae, 1935; Pontificii Instituti Biblci de Urbe Quinque Prima Lustra, 1935; Liber Psalmorum cum Canticis Breviarii Romani, 1944-45; Il Nuovo Salterio Latino, 1946 (translated into French, German, Spanish, Portuguese, Polish); Liber Ecclesiastae. . . nova interpretatio latina cum notis criticis et exegeticis, 1950; Il Trasformismo, 1950; Canticum Canticorum, 1953; Officium Parvum B.V.M., 1953; Unione dei cristiani, 1962; Unity in Freedom, 1964; The Church and The Jewish People, 1966; The Way to Unity after the Council, 1967; The Church and Mankind, 1967; The Word of God and Mankind, 1967; Ecumenism in Focus, 1969; We Who Serve, 1969. Contbr. numerous articles to revs. and profl. publs. Editor: Biblica. Home: Rome Italy Died Nov. 16, 1968; buried Riedbohringen, Baden Germany

BEACH, STANLEY YALE, aeronautic expert; b. Stratford, Conn., July 9, 1877; s. Frederick Converse and Margaret Allen (Gilbert) B.; Ph.B., Sheffield Scientific Sch. (Yale), 1898; m. Helen Birdseye Curtis, of Stratford, Conn., Sept. 15, 1897. Automobile editor Scientific American, 1898-1912, aeronautic editor, 1900-—; owner Beach Engring. Co., Scientific Aeroplane Co. Solicitor of patents and trade marks, especially relating to aeronautics. Sec. Aero Science Club of America; charter mem. Aero Soc. of America; mem. Aero Club of America. Home: 30 W. 53d St. Office: Beach Bldg., 125 E. 23d St., New York NY‡

BEACHLEY, RALPH GREGORY, educator; b. Hagerstown, Md., Aug. 12, 1895; s. Harry K. and Alice (Taylor) B.; grad. Mercersburg Acad., 1914; student Johns Hopkins, 1914-16; M.D., George Washington U., 1920; Dr. P.H. U. Ga., 1926; m. Carolyn Bates, Apr. 2, 1921; 1 dau., Eleanor Louise (Mrs. Roy Collins). Resident intern Children's and Emergency hosps., 1918-20; acting asst. surgeon USPHS, 1921; asst. dir., health officer Washington Co. Health Demonstration, 1922-23; dir. health dept. Dillon Co., 1923-25, Spartanburg Co., 1925-26; dep. state health officer Md. Health Dept., 1926-36; dir. student health service, instr. pub. health, hygiene Washington Coll., 1928-36; instr. pub. health nurses tng. sch. Southwest Hosp., Abingdon, Va., 1936-38; dir. dept. rural health Va. Health Dept., 1936-38; dir. pub. health and welfare Arlington Co., Va., from 1938; adj. prof. pub. health practice George Washington U., from 1938; asst. prof. pub. health and preventive medicine Med. Coll. Va., from 1938; guest lect., sch. pub. health Yale, 1953. Vice chmn. Council Social Agencies, Arlington Co., from 1939; chief med. officer Civil Def., No. Va. Orgn., 1950; dep. chief med. officer Civil Def., D.C., 1950. Served with U.S. Army, 1918. Diplomate Am. Bd. Preventive Medicine and Pub. Health, American Academy of Pediatrics. Fellow of the American Public Health Assn., Royal Soc. Health Eng.; mem. Am. Assn. Pub. Health Physicians, A.M.A., So. Med. Assn., Med. Soc. Va., Royal Soc. Med. Officers of Health Eng., Md. Hist. Assn. S.A.R., Am. Legion, (past comdr. 1924-25), Nat. Geog. Soc., Am. Sch. Health Assn., Arlington County Med. Soc., Met. Health Officers Assn. Washington (sec. treas. 1939, 1939-57, pres, 1957,), Washington Acad. Medicine (dir.), Alpha Omega Alpha, Phi Chi, Phi Sigma Kappa, Lambda Chi Alpha. Episcopalian. Clubs: Rotary, Cosmos (Washington). Editor of various publications on public health. Assistant editor Journal S.C. Medical Society, 1923-26. Home: Arlington VA Died Jan. 25, 1969; buried Columbia Gardens Cemetery, Arlington VA

BEAKE, HAROLD CARNES, lawyer; b. South Haven, Mich., Aug. 31, 1895; s. George W. and Katherine Anne (Cameron) B.; student Kalamazoo (Mich.) Coll., 1913-15; A.B., U. Mich., 1917; LL.B., Georgetown U., 1923; m. Ida May Jenkins, Nov. 28, 1931. Admitted to Mich. bar, 1923, since practiced in Detroit; mem. firm Cook, Beake, Miller, Wrock & Cross, 1949-59; counsel Cross, Wrock, Miller, Vieson & Kelley, from 1960. Dir. Leonard Refineries, Inc. Mem. Nat. Acad. Polit. Sci., Am. Judicature Soc., Am., Mich., Detroit bar assns. Presbyn. Clubs: Venice Yacht, Venice Golf and Country. Home: Venice FL Died Feb. 11, 1971.

BEAL, GEORGE DENTON, chemist; b. Scio, O., Aug. 12, 1887; s. James Hartley and Fannie Snyder (Young) B.; Ph.C., Scio Coll. Pharmacy, 1906, Pharm. D., 1907; Ph.B., Scio Coll., 1908; A.M., Columbia, 1910, Richard Butler scholar in chemistry, 1910-11, Ph.D., 1911; Pharm.M., Phila. Coll. Pharmacy, 1933; Sc.D., Mount Union College, 1933; Sc.D., Rutgers University, 1943; m. Edith Downs, July 3, 1912; children—George Denton, Marjorie Downs. Assistant in chemistry, Scio Coll. Pharmacy, 1906-08; instructor in chemistry, University of Illinois, 1911-14, asso., 1914-18, asst. prof., 1918-20, asso. prof. analytical and food chemistry, 1920-24, prof., 1924-26; asst. dir. of the Mellon Inst., Pitts., 1926-51, dir. research since 1951; professorial lectr. pharmacy U. Pitts., 1946-72; dir. Am. Druggists' Insurance Company. Collaborator with com. on revision U.S. Pharmacopoeia, 1920; mem. com. of revision U.S. Pharmacopoeia, 11th to 15th revisions (chmn. subcom. on organic chemicals); member U.S. Pharmacopoeial Conv., 1930, 40, 50; 1st vice chmn. Commn. Rev., 1940, trustee 1955-72; adv. bd. Q.M. research and development problems, N.R.C., 1946. Trustee Mt. Union Coll. (Alliance, O.), Phila. Coll. of Pharmacy and Sci.; com. on pharm. survey, Am. Council on Education 1946-51. Fellow A.A.A.S. (vice president, chemistry 1951), American Public Health Association; member American Chemical Soc. (chmn. medicinal division 1938; councilor-at-large 1939-44; Pittsburgh award 1955), Am. Leather Chemists Assn., American Pharm. Assn. (1st vice-pres. 1934-35; pres. 1936-37; member of council 1942-52, 54-72, chmn. council 1945-52), Pa. Pharm. Assn., American Council on Pharm. Education (pres. 1948-72, Pa. Chem. Soc. (pres., 1946-48), Am. Soc. Testing Materials, Industrial Hygiene Found., Pa. Chamber of Commerce (com. on pollution abatement), Lambda Chi Alpha, Sigma Xi, Alpha Chi Sigma, Phi Lambda Upsilon (national president 1917-19), Gamma Alpha, Psi Kappa Omega. Winner Ebert prize, American Pharmaceutical Association, 1920, Remington medal, 1941. Republican. Methodist. Clubs: University, Univ. of Pittsburgh Faculty (Pittsburgh); Chemists' (New York); Contbr. to Jour. Am. Pharm. Assn., Jour. Am. Chem. Soc. Home: Pittsburgh PA Died 1972

BEAL, GERALD F., chmn. J. Henry Schroder Banking Corp.; b. Hanover, Mass., July 14, 1895; s. John W. and Mary W. (Howes) B.; student Thayer Acad. and Harvard Coll.; m. Dorothy McHugh, June 9, 1923; 1 dau., Virginia. With Discount Corp., 1919-23; with J. Henry Schroder Banking Corp., from 1923, becoming chmn. and dir. Schroder Trust Co.; dir. Schroder-Rockefeller & Co., Am. Home Asssurance Co., Francisco Sugar Co., Grange Trust, Ltd., Manati Sugar Co. Treas., dir. Greater N.Y. Councils, Boy Scouts Am., Philharmonic-Symphony Soc. N.Y., Fgn. Policy Assn. Clubs: Links, Recess; River. Home: New York City NY Died Mar. 1971.

BEAL, ROYAL, actor; b. Brookline, Mass., June 2, 1899; s. Henry Francis and Mary Isobel (Starkweather) B.; student Harvard, 1917-18; m. Edda Frances Bennett, June 28, 1924; children—Nancy (Mrs. Conrad Ivan Gardner) Sally (Mrs. Hugh Spencer Leather). With Keith-Albee Stock Co., Boston, 1927-28; mem. road company The 19th Hole, 1928-29, Journey's End, 1929-30, Angela is Twenty-Two, 1938-39, The Doughgirls, 1943-44, others; actor N.Y. stage shows Take a Chance, 1932-33, Alley Cat, 1934, Boy Meets Girl, 1935-37, All that Glitters, 1937, The Lady Has a Heart, 1937, Papa is All, 1941, Without Love, 1942, Kiss and Tell, 1944-45, Woman Bites Dog, 1946, Parlor Story, 1947, Red Gloves, 1948, Never Say Never, 1951; with Nat. Company in Death of a Salesman, 1949-50, My Three Angels, 1953-54, No Time for Sergeants, 1955-58, Advise and Consent, 1961-62; numerous roles summer stock cos. including Skowhegan, Dennis, Bucks County Co.; acting roles TV shows, Philco, Kraft, U.S. Steel Hour, DuPont, others; motion pictures include: Boomerang, Lost Boundaries, Death of a Salesman, Anatomy of a Murder; appeared in Never Too Late, 1964; Kiss Me Kate, 1965. Trustee Equity-League Pension Fund, 1962-63. Mem. Actors Equity Assn. (chmn. house affairs, investment coms. 1961-67, treas., 1960-67). Home: Keene NH Died May 20, 1969; buried Robertson Cemetery, Chesterfield NH

BEALE, FRANK D., ry. official; b. Fredericksburg, Va., Nov. 4, 1890; C.E., U. of Va., 1915. Began with Fla. Ry., 1910; with C. & O. Ry., 1915-40; beginning as asst. section foreman, became successively asst. supervisor of track, div. engr., trainmaster, supt. Richmond Div., became asst. gen. supt., 1930; asst. v.p.-asst. to pres., C. & O., N.K.P. & P.M., 1940, operating vice pres. N.K.P. R.R., 1943, president Virginia Ry., 1944-59. Home: Norfolk VA Died Apr. 11, 1968.

BEALES, LEVERNE, statistician; b. Welshfield, O., Nov. 26, 1875; s. Cyrus L. and Sarah I. (Barber) B.; ed. pub. schs.; m. Flora Evers Durno, of Washington, D.C., Oct. 15, 1913. With U.S. Civil Service Commn., 1901-05; with Bur. of Corpns. (now Federal Trade Com.), 1906-09; with Bur. of the Census since 1909. Text writer, editor, and statistician, Census, 1913-25; chief statistician for manufactures, 1925-37, for territorial, insular and fgn. statistics since 1937. Mem. Am. Statis. Assn., Am. Econ. Assn. Home: 4124 Fifth St., N.W., Washington DC‡

BEALL, FOREST WADE, ex-govt. ofcl.; b. Nash, Okla., Jan. 30, 1910; s. James Preston and Nellie Belle (Cummins) B.; B.S., Okla. State U., 1931; m. Sadie Alice Weeks, July 17, 1938; children—James Preston, Virginia Ann. Livestock specialist Okla. State U., 1934-42; asso. editor Record Stockman and Westerner mag., 1943-44; livestock editor Farmer Stockman, Oklahoma City, 1946-48; chmn. Okla. Agrl. Stblzn. and Conservation Com., 1953-56; S.W. area dir. U.S. Dept. Agr., 1956-58, dep. adminstr. price support, 1958-61, v.p. CCC, 1958-61. Chmn. Okla. Republican State Com., 1962-63; chmn. Gov.'s Council on Agrl. Devel., 1962-63. Recipient distinguished alumnus award Okla. State U. Mem. Am. Farm Bur. Fedn., Agrl. History Soc., Okla. Hist. Soc., Okla. Cattlemen's Assn., Okla. Sheep Breeders Assn., Alpha Zeta, Farm House. Clubs: Continental Dorset, Lions Nash OK Died Sept. 27, 1967.

BEALL, JAMES GLENN, congressman; b. Frostburg, Md., June 5, 1894; student Gettysburg (Pa.) Coll.; married; 3 sons. Ins. and real estate business, Frostburg and Cumberland Md.; mem. 90th-91st congresses 6th Dist. Md. Served in Ordnance Dept., World War I. Mem. Allegany County Road Commn., 1923-30; mem. Md. State Senate, 1930-34; member 78th-82d Congresses, 6th Md. District U.S. senator from Md., 1952-65. Republican. Episcopalian. Home: Frostburg MD Died Jan. 14, 1971.

BEALS, FRANK LEE, retired army officer, educator, author; b. Morganton, Tenn., Sept. 2, 1881; s. Francis (M.D.) and Sadie Louisiana (Dawson) B.; ed. Reidville (S.C.) High Sch., George Washington U., U. Chgo.; B.S., De Paul U., 1930. A.M., 1932; m. Alice Alexandra Barnes, Apr. 17, 1909; children—Elena Louise (dec.), Bettina Byrd (Mrs. Iwersen); m. Ida Catherine Dushek, May 1, 1941 (dec. May 1972). Enlisted in U.S. Army, 1898; commd. 2d lt., Oct. 9, 1903; retired for disability in line of duty, May 1, 1908; 1st lt. retired, Oct. 30, 1916; capt. retired, Jan. 1918; maj. retired, Jan. 6, 1922. Served in Philippines, 1899-1900, 1905-06; San Francisco earthquake and fire; mil. attach., Brazil, 1909-10; comdt. Northwestern Mil. and Naval Acad., 1911-17, examining officer for Wis. state O.T.C., 1917; prof. mil. science and tactics; supr. phys. edn., high schs. Chgo., 1917-32; est. Camp Roosevelt (summer tng. camp for boys), 1919; pres. Racine (Wis.) Mil. Acad., 1930-33; asst. supt. schs., Chgo., 1935-46, supt. compulsory Edn., 1946-48. Wounded at the Battle of Big Bend, P.I., 1899. Awarded Purple Heart, 1932. Author: Topographical Primer, 1914; Squad Leaders' Note Book, 1917; Beal (e,l,s) the Ancient Name, 1929; Look Away Dixieland, 1937; Kit Carson, David Crocket, 1941; Chief Black Hawk, Buffalo Bill, 1943; The Story of Robinson Crusoe; The Story of Lemuel Gulliver in Lilliput Land; Rush for Gold, 1945; The Story of the Three Musketeers, Boswell in Chicago, 1946; The Story of Treasure Island, 1947; The Story of Moby Dick, 1949; The Patriot Silversmith, 1949; The Story of Deerslayer, 1950; Backwoods Baron, The Life Story of Claude Albert Fuller, 1951; The Story of Two Years Before the Mast, 1952; The Story of the Prince and The Pauper, 1953; American Heroes Series, 1954; Spanish Adventure Trails, 1960. Home: Eureka Springs AR Died Aug. 31, 1972.

BEALS, ROBERT DIGGS, mgmt. cons.; b. Winchester, Ind., Aug. 11, 1914; s. John H. and Nellie Edger (Diggs) B.; A.B., Colgate U., 1936; M.B.A., Harvard, 1938; m. Joanna Huttenlocher, Dec. 11, 1946; children—Joanna Jane, Diggs Huttenlocher. Asst. to v.p. Met. Life Ins. Co., N.Y.C., 1938-41, asst. to pres. Am. Express Co., N.Y.C., 1946-49; pres., dir. Film Strip-of the-Month Clubs, Inc., N.Y.C., 1949-63; treas. bus. mgr. Popular Sci. Pub. Co., Inc., N.Y.C., 1949-63, pres. Wells Fargo & Co., N.Y.C., 1963-64, chmn. bd., exec. com., 1964-67; pres., dir. Wells Fargo Armored Service Corp., N.Y.C., 1963-64; 64; v.p. Am. Express Co., Am. Express Co., Inc. (N.Y.C.), 1964-67, also gen. mgr. credit card div. world-wide, 1964-67; pres., dir. Computicket Corp. subsidiary Computer Scis. Corp., El Segundo, Cal., 1967-68; cons., 1968-71. Mem. Greater N.Y. councils Boy Scouts Am., 1958-71; mem. com. univ., relations, Maroon council Colgate U., 1961-71, also dir. Alumni Corp. Nat. dir. spl. orgns. and mailings Citizens for Eisenhower and Nixon, 1952; mem. planning bd., bus. devel. com. Briarcliff Manor, 1970-71. Served to comdr. USNR, 1940-46. Recipient commendation Sec. Navy. Mem. Harvard Bus. Sch. Assn. (exec. council 1963-66), Phi Beta Kappa, Alpha Tau Omega. Republican Presbyn. (elder). Clubs: Harvard, Wall Street (N.Y.C.). Home: Briarcliff Manor NY Died Nov. 11, 1971; buried Winchester IN

BEAN, CHARLES HOMER, psychologist; b. Petersburg, Mahoning Co., O., Feb. 28, 1870; s. R. C. and Jennie C. (Stevenson) B.; grad. Ohio Normal U., Ada, O., 1895; A.B., U. of Neb., 1899; grad. work, U. of Chicago; Ph.D., Columbia, 1912, additional year at Columbia, 1914-15; m. Caroline Champion Lamont (Ph.B., U. of Chicago), of Rockford, Ill., Sept. 7, 1904; 1 son, Kenneth Lamont. Taught at Ind. State Normal Sch., Terre Haute, Ind., 1903-14; prof. psychology and edn. La. State U., since 1915. Fellow A.A.A.S.; mem. Am. Psychol. Assn., Am. Assn. Univ. Profs. Democrat. Conglist. Wrote: Starvation and Mental Development, 1909; The Curve of Forgetting, 1912; How English Grammar Has Been Taught in America, 1914; An Ethical Code for Teachers, 1924; The Bright Child as a State Asset, 1924; The Psychological Factor in Vocational Education, 1927; Job-Analyzing Athletics, 1927; Is Mathematics Cultural?, 1928; An Unusual Opportunity to Investigate the Psychology of Language, 1931; The Psychology of Adherence to the Old and of Acceptance of the New, 1933. Home: 2015 Government St., Baton Route LA‡

BEAR, FIRMAN EDWARD, univ. prof.; b. Germantown, O., May 21, 1884; s. Ira Frank and Emily (Harris) B.; B.Sc., Ohio State U., 1908, M.Sc., 1910; Ph.D., U. Wis., 1917; D.Sc. (honorary) Rutgers U., 1954; m. Mary Helen Judy, July 6, 1911; children—Firman E., Jr., Robert Judy. Head soils dept. U. W.Va., 1914-16, Ohio State, 1916-29; indsl. research Stickstoff Syndicat, Berlin, Germany, 1927; dir. agrl. research Am. Cyanamid Co., New York, N.Y., 1929-38; sci. editor Country Home mag., Crowell Pub. Co., New York, N.Y., 1938-40; prof. agrl. chemistry and chmn. soils dept., Rutgers U., New Brunswick, N.J., 1940-54, professor emeritus, 1954-68. Fellow A.A.A.S., American Society of Agronomy (pres. 1949), Soil Conservation Soc. (pres. 1950); mem. American Chemical Society, Soil Science Society of Am. (pres. 1943), International Society of Soil Science, Phi Beta Kappa, Sigma Xi, Alpha Zeta. Republican. Author: Soils and Fertilizers, 1924, revised edition 1953; Theory and Practice in Use of Fertilizers, 1929, rev. edit. 1938; Chemistry of the Soil, 1955, rev. edit., 1964; Earth—The Stuff of Life, 1962; Soils in Relation to Crop Growth, 1965. Editor-in-Chief Soil Science, 1940-65. Home: New Brunswick NJ Died Apr. 6, 1968; buried Germantown OH

BEARCE, HENRY WALTER, physicist; b. Hebron, Me., Oct. 5, 1881; s. Herrick Mellen and Mary (Murch) B.; student Hebron Acad., 1897-1901; B.S., U. of Me., 1906; m. Kate Merrill, Dec. 1, 1907; children—Louis Merrill (dec.), Roger Mellen. Instr. physics, U. of Me., 1906-08; lab. asst. Nat. Bur. of Standards, 1908-09, asst. physicist, 1911-16, asso. physicist, 1917-19, senior and prin. physicist 1936-45, chief Div. Weights and Measures, 1940-45; owner and operator of apple orchards, Hebron, Maine, since 1945; Nat. Bur. Standards Rep. at Internat. confs. on standardization of screw threads, Paris, London, 1919, London, 1944, Ottawa, 1945; sec. Nat. Screw Thread Committee, 1918-32; member of Annual Assay Commission, 1926,

38, 41, 43, chmn., 1938. Elected Rep. rep. Me. Legislature, 1950, 1952. Member Adv. com. World Calendar Assn.; mem. Philol. Soc. of Washington, Washington Acad. of Science, Phi Beta Kappa, Sigma Alpha Epsilon. Club: Cosmos (Washington). Contbr. to Ency. Brit., 14th edit.; revised sect. on weights and measures, Marks Mech. Engrs. Handbook, 1941 and earlier edits.; cooperating expert Internat. Critical Tables, Vol. III, 1928. Author of Nat. Standard Petroleum Oil Tables; also of numerous tech. papers and bulletins. Home: Hebron ME Died June 24, 1968; buried Hebron Community Baptist Ch., Hebron ME

BEARCE, RALPH KING, school prin.; b. at Turner, Me., Apr. 29, 1875; s. Mellen Addison and Olive (Smith) B.; A.B., Colby Coll., 1895, A.M., 1902; m. Ellen Mary Bradford, July 9, 1902. Taught dist. schs., Me., 1890-1, 1894; submaster Rockland (Me.) High Sch., 1895-9; instr. Powder Point Sch., Duxbury, Mass. 1900-1; instr., 1901-4, prin., July 1, 1904-July 1, 1912, Conn. Lit. Instn., Suffield, Conn.; headmaster Powder Point Sch., Duxbury, Mass. July 1, 1912-—. Address: Duxbury MA‡

BEARDSLEY, GUY ERASTUS, ret. v.p. Aetna, Ins. Co.; b. Coventry, N.Y., Dec. 14, 1874; s. Benjamin Franklin and Anna Elizabeth (Guy) B.; grad. Sheffield Scientific Sch. (Yale), 1896; m. Jane R. Hills, Dec. 2, 1903; children—John Hills, Guy Erastus, Jr., Roxanne Willis. With Aetna Insurance Co., 1896-1902; special agt. Nat. Union Fire Ins. Co., Pittsburgh, 1902-03; state agt. Home Ins. Co., states of Conn. and R.I., 1903-05; spl. agt. Aetna Ins. Co., 1905-07; asst. sec., 1907-19, v.p. 1919-40; ret. v.p. World Fire and Marine Insurance Company, Piedmont Fire Ins. Company, Century Indemnity Co., Standard Insurance Company of New York; director Aetna Ins. Co., World Fire and Marine Ins. Co., Century Indemnity Company, Standard Ins. Co. of N.Y., Phoenix State Bank and Trust Co.; pres. Cedar Hill Cemetery Corporation; trustee and mem. exec. com. Soc. for Savings. Trustee Hartford Seminary Foundation. Mem. Theta Xi. Congregationalist. Clubs: Hartford, University, Hartford Golf (Hartford); Yale (New York). Home: 153 Oxford St., Hartford 5. Office: 670 Main St., Hartford 15 CT‡

BEARDWOOD, JOSEPH THOMAS, JR., physician; b. Phila., May 15, 1896; s. Joseph Thomas and Margaret (MacLaughlin) B.; A.B., U. Pa., 1917, M.D., 1921; m. Doris Annesley Miller, Nov. 12, 1924; children—Joseph Thomas III, Deborah Mary (Mrs. James B. Lynch), Donald Matthew. Intern, chief resident Presbyn. Hosp., Phila., 1921-23, now cons. metabolic diseases; practice of medicine, Phila., 1923-—, specializing metabolic diseases and diabetes, 1926-—; prof. metabolic diseases U. Pa. Grad. Sch. Medicine, 1936-—, also dir. dept. metabolic diseases and endrocrinology Graduate Hospital, Philadelphia; chief metabolic service Abington Hosp., 1931-42, med. dir., 1943-64. Mem. President's com. in employment physically handicapped. Recipient Banting Meml. medal Am. Diabetes Assn., J. Howard Reber medal Phila. Metabolic Assn.; award Merit, Alumni Soc. William Penn Charter Sch., 1969. Diplomate Am. Bd. Internal Medicine. Fellow A.C.P.; mem. Am. Diabetes Assn. (chmn. com. on employment; pres. 1940-42), Phila. Metabolic Assn. (founder), Phila Coll. Physicians, Sigma Xi. Clubs: Huntingdon Valley Country (Abington, Pa.); University, Union League (Phila.). Author: Simplified Diabetic Management, 6th edit., 1954. Contbr. articles med. publs. Home: Philadelphia PA Died Apr. 11, 1970.

BEASLEY, RONALD STOREY, headmaster; b. Eng., July 11, 1900; s. Henry and Mary (Storey) J; student Royal Mil. Coll., Sandhurst, Eng., 1918; B.A., Cambridge (Eng.) U., 1922, M.A., 1935; LL.D., (hon.), Washington U., St. Louis, 1959; m. Jean Edwards, July 25, 1923; 1dau., Jean (Mrs. Donald B. Read). Came to U.S., 1923, naturalized, 1936. Instr., Hill Sch., Pottstown, Pa., 1923-27; head history dept. Asheville, (N.C.) Sch., 1927-28, Groton (Mass.) Sch., 1928-49; headmaster Mary Inst., St. Louis 1949-69. Vice pres. Ednl. Council for Responsible Citizenship, 1965-66, chmn., 1967-68. Trustee St. Luke's Hosp., St. Louis, 1961-67. Mem. Headmasters Assn., Country Day Headmasters Assn. (v.p., 1960-61, pres. 1967-68), Ind. Sch. Assn. Central States (pres. 1965-66), Cum Laude Soc. (dep. pres. gen. 1966-69, pres. gen 1969). Clubs: University, Burns, Round Table (St. Louis). Old Lyme CT Died Aug. 20, 1969; buried Old Lyme CT

BEATON, KENNETH CARROL, writer; b. Stayner, Ont., Oct. 30, 1871; s. Donald John and Mary (Ingersoll) B.; grad. high sch., Orillia, Ont.; m. Martha Hayward Nelson of Minneapolis, Minn., Oct. 5, 1896 (dec.); m. 2d, Florence Wood Clark, of Los Angeles, Sept. 12, 1923; step-children—Betsy Ann, Perry Wood. Began newspaper work at 18; became editor of The Star, Seattle, Wash.; started column under title of Ye Towne Gossip"; with Post Intelligencer, Seattle, 1914-15; with Hearst Service since 1915, writing under initials K.C.B." Episcopalian. Clubs: Lambs (New York); Family (San Francisco). Author of books, Ye Towne Gossip and I Thank You. Home: 2716 Westwood Av., Los Angeles CA*‡

BEATTY, ALFRED CHESTER, mining engr.; b. N.Y.C., Feb. 7, 1875; s. John Cuming and Hetty (Bull) B.; M.E., Columbia, 1898; D.Sc., Birmingham, Eng., 1938, LL.D., 1939; m. Grace Madeline Rickard, Apr. 18, 1900 (dec.); children—Ninette, Alfred Chester; m. 2d Edith Dunn, June 21, 1913 (dec. 1952). Went to Eng., 1913, naturalized, 1933. Dir. Am. Metal Co., Ltd. Awarded Columbia U. Medal, 1933; Egleston medal by Engring. Alumni, 1948; Gold Medal of Instn. Mining and Metallurgy, 1935. Decorated Grand Cordon of Order of St. Sava (Yugoslavia); Comdr. Order of Leopold II (Belgium), Fellow Soc. Antiquaries; mem. Am., London C.'s of C., Am. Inst. Mining and Metall. Engrs., Am. Soc. in London, Automobile Assn., Bibliog. Soc., Egypt Exploration Soc., Inst. Metals, Instn. Mining and Metallurgy, Royal Philatelic Soc., Pilgrims, L'Union Interllie (Paris). Clubs: Roxburghe; Travellers (Paris, France). Collector Oriental and Western manuscripts. Address: 10 Ailesbury Rd., Dublin, Eire; also Baitel-Azark, Mena Cairo Egypt‡

BEATTY, CLARA SMITH (MRS. JESSE O. BEATTY), civic and polit. worker; b. Reno; d. Robert Norrison and Sarah (Richards) Smith; student U. Utah, 1908-09; B.A., U. Nev., 1914; m. Jesse O. Beatty, Sept. 23, 1914 (dec. Sept. 1914); children—Robert Norrison, John Orville. Mem. Nev. Bd. Charities and Pub. Welfare, 1929-36. Sec.-treas. Women's Republican Club, 1927-28; state vice chmn. Nev. State Rep. Central Com., 1936-50; del. Rep. Nat. Conv., 1948. Trustee Imlay Sch. Dist. Nev., 1915-20; bd. dirs. Tb Assn. Washoe County, Nev., 1932-40, dir. A.R.C., 1932-40, March of Dimes, 1934. Mem. Nev. Hist. Soc. (pres. dir.), League Women Voters (state pres. 1924), Bus. and Profl. Women's Club, Delta Delta Delta, Delta Kappa Gamma (hon.). Club: Quota. Home: Reno NV

BEATTY, HENRY RUSSELL, coll. pres., machine mfg. exec., cons. mgmt. engr.; b. Eastport, Me., May 14, 1906; s. Harry Hamilton and Susan (Ferguson) B.; B.S., U. Me., 1927; M. Adminstrv. Engring., N.Y.U., 1945; D. Engring., Stevens Tech., Northeastern U., 1962; Doctor Engring. University of Maine, 1963; m. Alice C. Van Schagen, Feb. 14, 1934; 1 son, Robert C. Supr. indsl. engring. Gen. Electric Co., 1927-33; salesman Remington Rand, 1933-34; prodn. supt. Holtzer Cabot Electric Co., 1934-37; prof., asst. to pres., dean engring. Pratt Inst., 1937-53; pres., trustee Wentworth Inst., Boston, 1953-71; pres., trustee Wentworth Coll. Tech., 1970-72; cons. mgmt. engr., 1944-72; cons. Coll. Petroleum Minerals, Saudi Arabia, 1968-72. Dir. Reed & Barton Co., N.J. Machine Corp. of N.H., N.J. Packaging Corp. Mem. Mass. Health and Ednl. Facilities Authority; mem. adv. bd. Greater Boston Salvation Army. Mem. sci. edn. adv. com. NSF. Trustee Endicott Jr. Coll., Gordon Coll. Chmn. Corp. Open Ch. Found. Registered profl. engr., N.Y., N.J., Mass., Me. Fellow Am. Soc. M.E., Assn. Ind. Colls. and Univs. Mass. (sec.-treas. 1967-71); mem. Nat. Soc. Profl. Engrs., Engring. Soc. New Eng. (past pres.), Mass. Schoolmasters Club (past pres.), Am. Soc. Engring. Edn., Project Bd., A.A.A.S., Am. Nuclear Soc., Boston C. of C. Conglist. (trustee). Mason, Rotarian. Clubs: Congregational (pres.), Executives (Boston). Revised: Principles of Industrial Management (L.P. Alford), 1951. Home: Quincy MA Died Sept. 26, 1972.

BEATTY, HUGH GIBSON, otolaryngologist; b. Washington Court House, O., Sept. 12, 1880; s. Talcott and Olga Forrester (Evans) B.; certificate in Pharm. Chemistry, Ohio State U., 1904, M.D., 1910; studied U. of Vienna; unmarried. Practiced as pharmacist, Columbus, O., 1904-10, physician since 1910; with Ohio State U. since 1914, prof. otolaryngology, 1929-51, prof. emeritus since 1951; mem. staff ear, nose and throat depts., University St. Francis and Children's hosps., Grant Hospital, Mount Carmel and White Cross Hospital; consultant, Columbus State, Vets. (Chillicothe) Hosps. Lt., M.C., U.S. Army, World War I. Fellow Am. Med. Assn., Am. Laryngol. Assn., Am. Broncho-Esophagolog. Soc., Am. Laryngol., Rhinol. and Otol. Soc., Am. Coll Surgeons, Internat. College Surgeons; mem. Am. Acad. Ophthalmology and Otolaryngology, Am. Bd. Otolaryngology, Am. Bd. of Plastic Surgery, Am. College of Allergists, Sons of Am. Revolution, Soc. of Colonial Wars, Phi Kappa Psi, Alpha Kappa Kappa. Mason (32 deg., Shriner). Clubs: Faculty, University, Columbus, Athletic, City. Contbr. on med. topics. Home: Columbus OH Died Aug. 31, 1971; interred Washington Court House OH

BEATTY, JAMES HELMICK, judge; b. Lancaster, O.; s. John and Delilah J. (Beery) B.; A.B., Ohio Wesleyan U., 1859, A.M., 1861; 1st lt. 4th Iowa Battery, 1863-5; m. Mary J. Caldwell, of Hamilton, O., Dec. 13, 1870. In law practice, Lexington, Mo., 1865-72, Salt Lake City, 1872-82, Hailey, Ida., 1882-9, Boise City, Ida., 1890-1; U.S. atty., Utah, 1882; mem. Territorial Council of Ida., 1886-7; Constl. Conv., 1889; chief justice Supreme Ct. of Ida., 1889-91; U.S. dist. judge, Dist. of Ida., 1891-1907; resigned. Republican. Address: Boise City ID‡

BEATTY, JAMES LAUGHEAD, cons. engr.; b. Uniontown, Pa., Nov. 29, 1893; s. John Calvin and Anna (Laughead) B.; B.S., Pa. State Coll., 1915; m. Maude Hewitt, June 30, 1920 (dec.); m. 2d, Rubie Rae

Hill, July 7, 1924 (dec.); children—Billie Rae (Mrs. C. C. Cook), James Lamar, Valerie Ann (Mrs. John Thomas). Chemist, plant engr. Aetna Explosives Co. (Ind.), 1915-17; asst. supt. Gen. Explosives Co., Joplin, Mo., 1917-18; chief inspr. explosives Ordnance Dept. U.S. Army, 1918-20; engr. for sales dept. Charleston Indsl. Corp. (W.Va.), 1920-21; testing engr. Southwestern Portland Cement Co., El Paso, 1922-23; asst. city engr., El Paso, 1923-24; owner, mgr. El Paso Testing Labs., 1924-27; insp. constrn. Coolidge Dam, Indian Irrigation Service, 1927-28; research chemist Union Oil Co., Oleum, Cal., 1928-38; asst. research engr. found. investigations, San Francisco-Oakland Bay Bridge, 1931-33; materials testing engr., jr. to asso., div. hwys., State of Cal., 1933-47, asso. material testing engr., 1950-51; sr. engr. materials and found. research, Pacific Islands Engrs., Guam, 1947-50; chief field investigation br. engring. div. Okinawa Engring. Dist., 1951-54; supervising civil engr., Mil. Air Transport Service, Andrews AFB, Md. and Scott AFB, Ill., 1954-65; cons. civil engr., Berkeley, Cal., 1965-68. Registered profl. engr., Cal., Pa., Ariz. Fellow Am. Soc. C.E.; mem. Am. Platform Assn., Am. Society Mil. Engrs. Am. Soc. Testing Materials, Am. Chem. Soc., Air Force Assn. Home: Berkeley CA Died May 11, 1968.

BEAUCHAMP, EMERSON, former lt. governor of Ky. Died Apr. 1971.*

BEAUDOIN, L. RENE, Canadian Govt. ofcl.; b. Montreal, Can., May 5, 1912; B.A., U. Montreal, 1935; m. Margaret L. Wespiser; children—Robert, Marlene, Pierre, Michel. Created Queen's Counsel, 1952; mem. Parlimanet constituency Vaudreuil-Soulanges, Que., from 1945; mem. all spl. coms. House of Commons, 1945-49, dep.-chmn. coms. of whole, 1949, dep. speaker, chmn. com. of whole, 1952-53, speaker, 1953-57, mem. Privy Council, from 1957. Canadian del. UN, 1947; del. Commonwealth Parliamentary Assn. to New Zealand and Australia, 1951, Colombo, Ceylon, 1952; rep. Canadian govt. inaugural flight Trans-Canadian Airline, Montreal to Paris, 1951; del. Queen Elizabeth's Coronation, 1953. Mem. Commonwealth Parliamentary Assn. (chmn. exec. com. Canadian br. 1951), Canadian, Montreal bar assns., Old Boys Assn. St. Laurent Coll. (past pres.). Liberal (v.p. Nat. Liberal Fedn. 1949-—). Catholic. Home: County Vaudreuil-Soulanges PQ Died Feb. 1970.

BEAUMONT, EDMOND ECKHART, banker; b. Little Rock, Oct. 28, 1892; s. Eckhart Lucius and Sophie (Kohler) B.; ed. pub. schs., Little Rock; m. Irene Hutton, Oct. 28, 1912; 1 dau., Muriel Ruth (Mrs. S. Wade Mallett). Vice chmn. bd. Nat. Bank, Little Rock. Home: Little Rock AR Died July 20, 1968.

BEAVER, SANDY, educator; b. Augusta, Ga., Oct. 5, 1883; s. Sandy and Savannah (Webb) B.; student U. Ga., 1899-1903; holds A.B., LL.D., Pd.D.; married Annice Lowry, Feb. 17, 1912; children—John Lowry, Louise, Lucile. Instr., Univ. Sch., Stone Mountain, Ga., 1903-12; pres. Riverside Mil. Acad., 1913-69. Mem. and twice chmn. Georgia's Bd. of Regents. Pres. and chmn. exec. com. Assn. Mil. Colls. and Schs. Lt. col., U.S. Reserves (ret.); brig. gen. (Ga.), ret. Mem. staffs of five govs. of Ga. and Florida; decorated by Cuban Government; recipient of Horatio Alger Award. Member Phi Beta Kappa. Democrat. Presbyn. Rotarian. Home: Gainesvillle GA Died Dec. 7, 1969.

BEBERMAN, MAX, educator; b. N.Y.C., Aug. 20, 1925; s. Israel and Lillian (Miller) B.; B.S. in Math., City Coll. N.Y., 1944; A.M.; Tchrs. Coll., Columbia, 1949, Ed.D., 1953; m. E. F. Chapman, Jan. 18, 1947; children—Lynne, John, Philip (dec.), Alice, Martin, Ruth, Mary, James, Sarah. Tchr. math. and sci. Nome (Alaska) High Sch., 1946-48; tchr. math. Riverdale Country Day Sch., N.Y.C., 1949-50; instr. math. Tchrs. Coll., Columbia, 1949-50; tchr. math., instr. edn. U. Ill. High Sch., 1950-54; asso. prof. edn. Fla. State U., 1954-55; asso. prof. edn. U. Ill., Urbana, 1955-58, prof., 1958-71. dir. Curriculum Lab., 1965-71, educational director Computer-based Education Research Laboratory, 1966-71. Inglis lectr. Harvard 1958. Dir. U. Ill. Com. on Sch. Math, 1955-71. Mem. Nat. Council Tchrs. Math., Am. Math. Soc., Math. Assn. Am., A.A.A.S., Central Assn. Sci. and Math Tchrs., Phi Delta Kappa. Author: (with others) Algebra, Course 1 and Algebra, Course 2, 1955, High School Mathematics Units 1-11, 1960-63, Algebra, First Course, 1962, Algebra with Trigonometry, Second Course, 1962, High School Mathematics Course 1, 2 and 3, 1964, 65, 66, Math Workshop, 1964, 65, 66. Contbr. numerous articles to profl. publs. Home: Champaign IL Died Jan. 24, 1971; cremated.

BECHTEL, EDWARD AMBROSE, educator, b. Media, Pa., Oct. 23, 1867; s. George K. and Mary (Bechtel) B.; A.B., Johns Hopkins, 1888; univ. scholar, same, 1889; fellow U. of Chicago, 1898-99, Ph.D., 1900; LL.D., Tulane, 1938; m. Edith Lyon, Sept. 3, 1902; children—George, Mary Edith. Prof. classical langs., Tulane U., since 1908, and dean Coll. of Arts and Sciences, 1918-37, dean emeritus since 1937. Mem. Am. Philol. Assn., Classical Assn. of Middle West and South. Club: Round Table (New Orleans). Author:

Sanctae Silviae Peregrinatio, 1902; Livy—the War with Hannibal, 1905. Contbr. on philol. and ednl. topics. Home: 6125 Pitt St., New Orleans LA‡

BECK, BROOKS, lawyer; b. N.Y.C., Feb. 4, 1918; s. Harry Brooks and Rachel (Walker) B.; grad. Lawrenceville Sch., 1937; B.A., Amherst Coll., 1941; LL.B., Columbia, 1948; m. Emily Marshall Morison, June 1, 1946; children—Cameron Winslow, Gordon Morison, Emily Marshall. Admitted to N.Y. bar, 1949, Mass. bar, 1950; practiced in N.Y.C., 1948-49, Boston, 1949-69; asso. Burns, Currie, Walker & Rich, 1948-49; asso. Hill & Barlo wand predecessor firm, 1949-54, partner, 1954-69; teaching fellow Boston U., 1954. Mem. Finance Com., Canton, Mass., 1954-60. Trustee Mass. Gen. Hosp. Served to lt. comdr. USNR, 1941-45, 51-53. Clubs: St. Botolph, Somerset (Boston). Home: Canton MA Died Aug. 22, 1969; buried Mt. Auburn Cemetery, Cambridge MA

BECK, CLAUDE SCHAEFFER, surgeon; b. Shamokin, Pa., Nov. 8, 1894; s. Simon and Martha (Schaeffer) B.; A.B., Franklin and Marshall Coll., 1916, D.Sc. (hon.), 1937; M.D., Johns Hopkins Univ., 1921; m. Ellen Manning, May 26, 1928; children—Mary Ellen, Kathryn Schaeffer, Martha Ann. House officer, Johns Hopkins Hosp., 1921-22; Meml. Cemetery, Chicago ILCabot fellow in research surgery, Harvard, and asso. surgeon Peter Bent Brigham Hosp., Boston, 1923-24; Crile fellow in surgery, Western Reserve Univ., Cleveland, 1924-25, various positions dept. of surgery since 1925, prof. neurosurgery, 1940-51, professor of cardiovascular surgery since 1951; with University Hospitals since 1924, asso. surgeon specializing in surgery of the heart since 1933; chief consultant neurosurgery, Crile Veterans Hosp., Cleveland, since 1945; visiting neurosurgeon, Cleveland City Hosp.; cardiac consultant Mt. Sinai Hospital, Cleve. Colonel, M.C., U.S. Army as surgeon consultant Fifth and Sixth Service Commands, 1942-45; awarded Legion of Merit, 1945. Spl. consultant Surgery Study Group, Nat. Institutes of Health since 1949. Fellow A.C.S. Mem. Am. Surgical Assn., Assn. for Thoracic Surgeons, Soc. Clinical Surgery, Am. Soc. for Exptl. Pathology, A.M.A., Am. Heart Assn., Am. Bd. of Surgeons, Am. Bd. Thoracic Surgeons (founders group), Eastern and Central surgical socs.; Cleveland Surgical Soc. (pres.), Cleveland Heart Soc. (pres.). Club: Halsted Contbr. about 125 chpts. and articles in med. books and jours. Home: East Cleveland OH Died Nov. 1971.

BECK, ROBERT MCCANDLASS, JR., army officer; b. Westminster, Md., May 9, 1879; s. Robert McCandlass and Amelia (Stieg) B.; B.S., U.S. Mil. Acad., 1901, Gen. Staff Sch., France, 1918, Army War Coll., 1926; distinguished grad., Sch. of the Line, 1921; m. Jessie Hamilton, Nov. 18, 1908 (dec. 1956); m. 2d, Mary Kelly Mayer, Nov. 1, 1958. Commd. 2d lt., Cavalry, U.S. Army, 1901 and promoted through grades to brig. gen., 1936, maj. gen., 1938. Served in Philippines, 1903-05, and 1909-11; participated in Aisne-Marne, Oise Aisne and Meuse Argonne offensives, World War; with Army of Occupation, Germany, 1918-19; exec. officer War Plans Div. of Gen. Staff, 1920; instr. in Cav. Sch., 1921-23; instr. Command and Gen. Staff Sch., 1926-30; instr. Army War Coll., 1931-35; comdg. gen. 2d Cav. Brig., 1936-38; asst. chief of staff, Operations and Training Div., War Dept. Gen. Staff, 1938-39, retired 1939. Awarded D.S.M.; Croix de Guerre with Palm, Officer Legion of Honor (French). Lutheran. Mason. Club: Army and Navy (Washington). Home: Washington DC Died July 4, 1970; buried Arlington Nat. Cemetery, Arlington VA

BECKER, CHARLES E., pres., The Franklin Life Insurance Co.; b. West Bend, Ia., Nov. 13, 1896; s. Jacob Paul and Caroline Elizabeth (Mackey) B.; student Creighton University, 1915-18, Doctor of Laws (honorary), 1954; married Winifred Crouch, Aug. 2, 1922; children—Charles Fulton, Jacquelyn Ann, Marylyn and Carylyn (twins). Chief exec. officer Franklin Life Ins. Co., Springfield, Ill.; chmn. exec. com. Greatamerica Corp., Dallas. Mem. Pres.'s Council Creighton U., Omaha, Neb.; mem. nat. bd. trustees Loretto Heights Coll., Colo. Named mem. Ill. Bus. Hall of Fame, 1972. Clubs: Athletic, Union League (Chicago), Sangamo, Illini Country, Elks (Springfield, Ill.). Home: Springfield IL Died June 25, 1968; buried Calvary Cemetery, Springfield IL

BECKER, CHARLES W(ASHINGTON), business exec.; b. Chicago, Aug. 7, 1896; s. Charles Valentine and Laura (McNair) B.; ed. U. of Chicago, class of 1919; m. Pauline Hayward, Sept. 8, 1920; children—Hayward Charles, Barbara Ann (Mrs. Wesley E. Behel), Laurie Morgan. Successively bank messenger, mem. financial and foreign financial depts., treas. office, sec. office, foreign and gen. accounting depts., asst. to vice pres. of by-product sales, Wilson and Co., 1918-32, sales mgr. of hair and insulation div., 1932-46, vice pres., 1946-47, vice pres. in charge of sales of hair and insulation div., research and tech. div., from 1947; vice pres., executive committee, director Wilson Sporting Goods Co. Served as pilot, U.S. Naval Air Corps Res., World War I. Mem. Psi Upsilon. Republican. Methodist. Clubs: Chicago Athletic Assn. (dir.); Indian Hill (Winnetka, Ill.). Northfield IL Died June 30, 1971.

BECKER, ELIZABETH H. (MRS. RICHARD F. BECKER), civic worker; b. Evansville, Ind., July 12, 1913; d. Charles Edwin and Daisy (Smith) Harman; student DePauw U., 1931-33; A.B., Evansville Coll., 1935; postgrad. U. Mich., 1937-38; m. Richard F. Becker, June 17, 1939; children—Richard H., Philip L., Sarah R. Librarian, Evansville, 1935-36; English faculty Bosse High Sch., Evansville, 1937-40; English tchr. Friends Sch., Balt., 1943-44; v.p., dir. Davidson-Amos, Inc. Active Boy Scouts Am., Girl Scouts; mem. Wm. Henry Harrison High Sch. Bd., 1962-63. Bd. dirs. Vanderburgh County Christian Home, 1956-58. Dir. com. Ind. State Tea, Continental Congress, Washington, 1961-70, chairman Indiana State Tea, 1966-67. Member Daughter of Colonial Wars, D.A.R. (vice regent 1962-70, chmn. Americanism com.; soloist state meml. service), Welborn Hosp. Aux., Women's Assn. Evansville Pub. Mus., Women's Guild Philharmonic Orch. Assn., Jr. League Evansville, Internat. Platform Assn., Alpha Phi. Mem. Christian Ch. (bd. dirs. Womens Christian Service Council 1954-55, 63-70, historian 1963-70). Home: Evansville IN Died Jan. 6, 1970.

BECKER, FLORENCE HAGUE (MRS. WILLIAM A. BECKER), pres. gen. D.A.R.; b. Westfield, N.J.; d. Ainsworth James and Susie (Baker) Hague; A.B., Smith Coll., Northampton, Mass., 1909; studied Columbia, 1911; L.H.D., Lincoln Memorial U.; m. William A. Becker, June 4, 1919. Mem. Nat. Soc. Founders and Patriots Am., Women's Symphony Soc. of Daytona Beach (pres. 1964-68), N.E. Women (pres. 1954-57), Patriotic Women Am., Inc. (nat. pres.), Daus. Am. Colonists, Daus. of Colonial Wars, Colonial Dames of Am. Daus. of 1812, Nat. Soc. Daughters American Revolution (pres. gen.), Holland Dames of America. Presbyterian. Club: Ormond Beach Woman's (pres.). Contbr. to D.A.R. Mag. Nat. historian Daus. Colonial Wars. Home: Daytona Beach FL Died 1971.

BECKER, JAMES HERMAN, business exec.; b. Chgo., Dec. 11, 1894; s. Abraham G. and Kate (Friedman) B.; A.B., Cornell, 1917; m. Hortense Koller, June 4, 1928; children—Jane, Kate; With A. G. Becker & Co., Inc., Chgo., 1921-70, dir. 1926-70, pres. 1947-61, chmn., 1961-70; dir. City Stores Co., Cook Coffee Co., Cleve., H. Elkan & Company, Chicago, Enterprise Paint Manufacturing Co., Gutmann & Co., Midas-Internat. Corp., H. Elkan & Company, Cyclops Corp., Parents' Mag. Enterprises, Inc. Served as 1st lt. U.S. Army, 1917-19, with Am. Relief Adminstrn. overseas unit, 1919; mem. European staff Joint Distribution Com., 1919-20, dir. European orgn., 1920. Clubs: Standard, Tavern, Mid-Day (Chgo.); Lake Shore Country (Glencoe, Ill.); Recess (N.Y.C.); La Quinta (Cal.) Country. Home: Highland Park IL Died Oct. 19, 1970.

BECKER, LAWRENCE, lawyer; b. Finnentrop, Westphalia, Germany, Aug. 10, 1869; s. Eberhard and Margaret (Alvers) B.; came to U.S., 1879; student Valparaiso (Ind.) U., 1892-4, Sch. of Law, same, 1896; m. Agnes D. Eaton, of Deer Park, LaSalle Co., Ill., Sept. 8, 1898. Cattleman, Mont., 1889-95; began law practice at Hammond, Ind., 1896; now pres. Becker & Tapper Realty Co. City atty., Hammond, 1898-1902; mayor of Hammond, 1904-11 (resigned); judge Superior Court of Lake Co., Ind., 1911-14; solicitor of the Treasury, by appmt. of Pres. Wilson, since Mar. 1, 1915. Del. Dem. Nat. Conv., 1912 (com. on rules). Mem. Pub. Library Bd., Hammond, 1903-15; chmn. legislative com. Municipal League of Ind., 1905-11. Mem. Am. Polit. Science Assn., Am. Acad. Polit. and Social Science, Am. Shropshire Sheep Breeders' Assn. Mason; Odd Fellow; Elk. Club: Hammond Country. Home: Hammond, Ind. Address: 4201 Fessenden St., Washington DC‡

BECKER, SHERBURN MERRILL, mayor; b. Milwaukee, Nov. 13, 1876; s. Washington B.; ed. pub. schs., Milwaukee, and Belmont Sch., Cambridge, Mass.; m. Milwaukee, 1899, Irene Booth Smith. Supervisor, 1st ward; Milwaukee, 1902-4, alderman, 1904-6; mayor, Milwaukee, Apr., 1906-Apr., 1908; Republican. Pres. Hansen-Schmidt Tobacco Co., etc. Clubs: Milwaukee, Milwaukee Athletic, Country, Fox Point Golf, Automobile, Milwaukee Yacht, etc. Residence: 87 Prospect Av. Address: City Hall, Milwaukee WI‡

BECKET, WELTON DAVID, architect; b. Seattle, Aug. 8, 1902; s. Hugh F. and Evangeline (McDonald) B.; A.M. U. Wash., 1927; student Fontainbleau Sch. Fine Arts, France, 1928; m. Fay Kastner, July 24, 1935; children—Bruce, Welton M. Practicing architect, 1929-69; co-partner with Walter Wurdeman (dec.), Los Angeles, 1932-49; pres. Welton Becket & Asso., 1949-69; offices Los Angeles, San Francisco, Houston, N.Y.C.; cons. architect on housing; architect notable pub. structures, including General Petroleum, Prudential Bldg., N.Y. Life Ins. Bldg., Mt. Sinai Hosp., Police Facilities Bldg. (Los Angeles), Bullock's (Pasadena and Westwood, Cal.), Hallmark Card Factory (Kansas City, Mo.), Ford Div. Offices (Dearborn, Mich.), Gulf Oil Co., Scott Paper Co. (Phila.), Kaiser Center (Oakland, Cal.), Nat. City Bank of N.Y. (Sao Paulo, Brazil), U.S. Naval Hosp. (San Diego, Cal.), Los Angeles Meml. Sports Arena, Am. Embassy (Warsaw, Poland), hotels for Hilton Hotel chain, numerous shopping centers in U.S. and other countries, Bethlehem Steel (San Francisco), Travelers Ins. (Los Angeles), Humble Oil & Refining (Houston), Bendix Corp. (Cal.), So. Cross Hotel (Melbourne, Australia), Los Angeles Music Center for Performing Arts; coordinating architect Century City (Los Angeles), Cullen Center (Houston), Xerox Corporate Hdqrs., Rochester, N.Y., John F. Kennedy Civic, Cultural and Ednl. Center, Gulf Life Ins. Co., Jacksonville, Fla., Tishman Airport Center, Los Angeles, Exchange Park, Dallas, Hartford Nat. Bank & Trust Co., Conn., Worcester (Mass.) Downtown Redevel., Mutual Benefit Life Bldg., Universal Land Co. Tower, San Francisco; supervising architect U. Cal. at Los Angeles campus, 1948-69, exec. architect med. center, 1948-69. Personal adviser to sec. air force on design Air Force Acad. Fellow A.I.A. (93 regional, rat, hemispheric awards). Author numerous articles. Home: West Los Angeles CA Died Jan. 16, 1969; buried Washell Meml. Park, Seattle WA

BECKETT, PERCY GORDON, consultant; born Quebec, Can., Dec. 17, 1882; s. Thomas and Naomi Anne (Molson) B.; ed. Fettes Coll., Edinburgh, Scotland, and Sch. of Mines, Camborne, Cornwall; D.Sc. (honorary), University of Arizona, 1957; unmarried. Engr. Copper Queen Consol. Mining Co., Bisbee, Ariz., 1904-06, Cananea, Mex., 1906-07; supt. Capillitas Copper Co., Argentina, S.A., 1907-08; engr. Phelps Dodge & Co., Ariz., 1908-12; gen. mgr. Old Dominion Co., Globe, Ariz., 1912-17; asst. to pres. Phelps Dodge Corp., New York, 1917-20; gen. mgr. and v.p. Phelps Dodge Corp., Ariz., 1920-37, vice president, 1937-46, director, 1940-60; pres. and director Apache Powder Company, 1929-49. Mem. Mining and Metall. Soc., Am. Inst. Mining and Metall. Engrs., Am. Mining Congress. Republican. Episcopalian. Home: Phoenix AZ Died Jan. 20, 1973.

BECKHAM, CLIFFORD MYRON, entomologist; b. nr. Mobile, Aug. 4, 1915; s. Charles Edward and Cornelia Edith (Campbell) B.; B.S., Auburn U., 1941; M.S., Ohio State U., 1947, Ph.D., 1951; m. Marie Calderaro, May 30, 1942; children—Linda, Stephen, Bruce. Head dept. entomology Ga. Expt. Sta., Coll. Agr., U. Ga. Expt., 1948-71, chmn. div. entomology, 1950-71. Served with USAAF. 1942-46. Mem. Entomol. Soc. Am., Ga. Entomol. Soc. Home: Griffin GA Died Apr. 18, 1971; buried Oak Hill Cemetery, Griffin GA

BECKLER, WILLIAM ALEXANDER, railway official; b. Letart Falls, Meigs Co., O.; s. Jacob L. and Georgia Anne (Alexander) B.; pub. sch. edn. Clerk ticket office, C., H.V.& T. Ry., Middleport, O., 1886-7; ticket agt., 1887-9; traveling pass. agt., C., St. P.& K.C. Ry., 1889-93; northern pass. agt., 1894-1908, asst. gen. pass. agt., 1908-10, gen. pass. agt., July 1, 1910-—, Queen & Crescent Route. Clubs: Queen City, Cincinnati Business Men's, Cincinnati Country. Office: Ingells Bldg., Cincinnati OH‡

BECKMAN, HENRY FREDERICK, M.D., obstetrician; b. Kendallville, Noble County, Ind., Mar. 5, 1876; s. Louis and Charlotte (Brust) B.; M.D., Northwestern U., 1904; m. Helen R. Kunz, June 30, 1908. Interne Chicago Lying-in Hosp., 1904-05; practice as physician, Indianapolis, Ind., since 1905; prof. obstetrics, Ind. U. Sch. of Medicine since 1928; chief of staff in obstetrics, Indianapolis City Hosp.; staff mem. Meth. Hosp., St. Vincents Hosp., Coleman Hosp. Served as chmn. Med. Advisory Bd., No. 57, during World War. Fellow Am. Coll. Surgeons; diplomate Am. Bd. Obstetrics and Gynecology; mem. A.M.A., Ind. State Med. Soc., Marion County Med. Soc. Lutheran. Address: 25 E. Ohio St., Indianapolis IN‡

BECKMAN, L. J., sec. Cities Service Oil Co. Address: Bartlesville OK

BECKMAN, NILS ARVID TEODOR, lawyer; b. Stockholm, Sweden, Oct. 30, 1902; s. Knut Anton and Ruth (Hammarstedt) B.; jur. cand. U. Stockholm, 1923, jur. dr. honoris causa, 1953; m. Sigrid Karlsson, June 4, 1927; children—Sven, Vera, Lars. Admitted to bar, Sweden, 1923, practiced in Stockholm, 1923-72; with Ct. Appeals, Stockholm, 1941-47; vice-atty. gen., 1944-47; judge Supreme Ct., 1947-63, pres., 1963-69. Mem. Commn. for Criminal Law Reform, 1937-53; pres. Commn. for Rent Law Reform, 1957-61. Decorated knight comdr. grand cross Swedish Order No. Star. Mem. Swedish Assn. Criminologists (pres. 1959-69), Swedish Assn. Against Heart and Lung Diseases (v.p. 1952-68). Author: Criminality and Social Defence in Sweden, 1947; Children's Liability to Damages, 1956. Cases in Swedish Family Law, 1954, 60, 65, 68; Cases in International Law, 1959; Swedish Criminal Law, 1964, 69. Home: Stockholm Sweden Died Jan. 22, 1972.

BECKMAN, THEODORE N., educator, cons. economist; b. Russia, Sept. 3, 1895; s. Nahum and Pearl (Treistman) B.; B.Sc. in Bus. Adminstrn., Ohio State U., 1922, Ph.D., 1924; m. Esther G. Baker, July 27, 1920 (dec. Sept. 1961); children—Gloria June, Marilyn Adelle, Joanne; m. 2d, Sarah Martin Langue, Mar. 15, 1962. Instr. econs. and sociology Ohio State U.,

1921-22, instr. bus. orgn., 1922-24, asst. prof., 1924-27, asst. prof. marketing, 1927-29, asso. prof., 1929-32, prof., 1932-66, prof. emeritus, 1966-73. Instr., Columbus chpt. Nat. Inst. Credit of Nat. Assn. Credit Men, 1921-25; dir. wholesale application program Allied Food Com., Louisville, 1929; in charge wholesale census of distbn. Bur. of Census, 1929-32; cons. expert in charge wholesale census of Am. bus., 1933-35; adviser to com. on elimination of waste in distbn. Dept. of Commerce, 1934-36; cons., Atty. Gen.'s Office, State of Fla., 1935; dir. Washington Indsl. Loan Corp., 1931-37; vis. prof. U. Colo., summers 1939-40; cons. Wage and Hour div. U.S. Dept. Labor, 1940, Nat. Def. Adv. Commn., 1940; chief cons. Office Civilian Supply, War Prodn. Bd., 1942; cons. Atty. Gen.'s Office, State of Ohio, 1954-55; served as 2d lt. AUS, World War II. Named Marketing Exec. of Year, Sales and Marketing Execs. Internat., 1962; recipient Distinguished Teaching award Ohio State U., 1962. Fellow Internat. Inst. Arts and Letters; mem. Am. Econ. Assn., Am. Assn. U. Profs., Am. Marketing Assn. (past v.p., past dir., Paul D. Converse award 1959, central Ohio chpt. award 1960), Am. Statis. Assn., Newcomen Soc., Ohio State U. Alumni Assn., Distbn. Research and Edn. Founds. (hon. chmn. 1968-73), Beta Gamma Sigma, Tau Delta Phi, Mu Beta Chi. Jewish religion. Clubs: Cosmos (Washington); Winding Hollow Country; Faculty (Columbus). Author: (with W.R. Davidson) Marketing, 8th edit., 1967; (with N.H. Engle and R.D. Buzell) Wholesaling, 3d edit., 1959; (with R.S. Foster) Credits and Collections: Management and Theory, 8th edit., 1969; (with S.F. Otteson) Cases in Credits and Collections, 1949. Contbr. articles to encys. and profl. jours. Spl. cons. G. and C. Merriam Co. on Webster's Dictionaries. Home: Columbus OH Died Apr. 20, 1973.

BECKNER, LUCIEN, geologist; b. Winchester, Ky., Dec. 29, 1872; s. William Morgan and Elizabeth (Taliaferro) B.; ed. Centre Coll., Danville, Ky., U. of Ky., Transylvania Coll., Lexington, Ky.; studied law Centre Coll.; m. Marie Daveiss Warren, of Danville, Aug. 14, 1894; children—Jean Warren, Elizabeth Taliaferro, Marie Warren. Editor Sun-Sentinel and Winchester (Ky.) Sun, 1904-12; asso. editor Filson Club Quar., 1927-36; editor Tobacco News, 1908, and Clark Co. Republican, 1915-16; admitted to Ky. bar, 1895; geologist for oil and gas cos.; civil engr.; commr. for Ecuador to Pan-Am. Expn., Buffalo, N.Y., 1901. Capt. Inf. Ky. Militia. Fellow A.A.A.S.; mem. Ky. Acad. of Science (past pres.), Appalachian Geol. Soc., Am. Inst. Mining Engrs., Ky. State Park Commn., Ky. Ednl. Assn., Ky. Ornithol. Soc., Ky. State Hist. Soc. (life), Ky. State Bar Assn., Kappa Alpha; councillor Boy Scouts of America. Dir. Louisville Free Pub. Museum. Republican. Mason (K.T., Shriner). Clubs: Filson, Astronomy, Beckham Bird. Home: 411 Belgravia Court, Louisville KY‡

BEDARD, PIERRE (PIERRE-ARMAND BEDARD DE LA PERRIERE), cultural consultant; born in Lynn, Mass., May 23, 1895; s. J. Armand and Rose Louise Chandler (Valiquet) B.; A.B., Harvard University, 1917; LL.D., Ripon College, 1949; Doctor of Letters, Middlebury College, 1954; married Caroline Baker Pryor, June 30, 1932; m. 2d, Gertrude King Winter, January 10, 1948. With American Shipping Board, Marseille, Bordeaux, 1920; asst. bunkering mgr., London, 1921-22; auditor, Rotterdam, 1922-23; The Bankers Trust Company, New York City, 1923-25; business mgr. Famous Players Lasky, 1925-27; asst. treas. and production mgr. Gloria Swanson Productions, 1927-29; producer educational and scientific films, Harvard Film Foundation, 1929; dir. French Inst. U.S. 1929-52; pres. Parsons Sch. Design, 1952-58, cons., 1958-63; dir., chmn. exec. com. French & Co., 1959-68; chmn. exec. com. Cartier, Inc., 1963-67, radio news analyst France, CBS, 1937-40; Am. counselor to French Mil. Mission, Washington, 1943-44. Mem. hon. bd. advisors Ft. Ticonderoga Mus.; mem. adv. bd., sec. adv. com. on arts for the John F. Kennedy Center for the Performing Arts, Washington; chairman executive com. Nat. La Fayette Bicentennial Com., 1957; pres. P.R. Cultural Center. Dir., secretary gen. and dir. lectures Fed. of French Alliances in U.S. and Canada, 1935-42; sec. 6th Cong. of French Lang. and Lit., N.Y. City, Apr. 1936, 7th Congress, N.Y. World's Fair, 1939. Served with Batt. A, Mass. N.G., Mexican Border, 1916; American Field Service, Apr.-Oct. 1917; 2d lt., O.R.C., later 1st lt. U.S. Army, 1917-19; assistant secretary and member of staff of Gen. Tasker H. Bliss, Am. mil. rep., Supreme War Council, Versailles, France. Decorated Commander French Legion of Honor. Mem. national selection com. on Fulbright Awards (1951-54). One of founders, treas., Lycee Francais de New York, 1935-40; mem. exec. com., bd. trustees Free Europe Univ. in Exile. Former pres., chmn. exec. com. France-America Soc.; hon. chmn. bd. dirs. Fedn. French Alliances in U.S. Mem. Order of Lafayette (charter mem., dir.), Council on Fgn. Relations, Soc. Les Amis d'Escoffier (pres. found.), Am. Inst. Interior Designers, Am. Soc. French Legion of Honor, Am. Legion (Paris post). Clubs: Century, Knickerbocker (N.Y.C.); Newport Reading Room, Clambake (Newport R.I.). Home: New York City NY Died Dec. 2, 1970.

BEDDOWS, CHARLES ROLAND, ret. utility exec.; b. Phila., Feb. 1, 1895; s. Charles W. and Fanny M. (Bower) B.; student Wharton Sch., U. Pa., 1918, Temple U. Sch. Accounts and Finance; m. Bertha Cooper, 1919; 1 son, Charles Roland. Treas. Niagara Hudson Power Corp.; 1929; gen. auditor Allied Power & Light Co., 1929; pres., treas. Penn-Western Service Corp., 1935-49; controller Am. Electric Power Corp., 1927-34; v.p., controller Iowa Pub. Service Co., 1949-58, vice chmn., controller, 1958-61, ret. Served as cpl., U.S. Army, World War I. Mem. Controllers' Inst. Home: Westfield NJ Died Aug. 1972.

BEDFORD, HENRY CLARK, college pres.; b. Bradford Co., Pa., Dec. 19, 1875; s. Sylvester and Elizabeth Ann (Rathbun) B.; grad. Houghton (N.Y.) Coll., 1902; A.M., Ohio Northern U., Ada, 1906; A.B., Oberlin (O.) Coll., 1910; m. Nellie M. Crow, Nov. 22, 1902. Prof. Greek, Houghton Sem., 1900-15; pastor Wesleyan M.E. Ch., Filmore, N.Y., 1907-10; pres. Wesleyan Meth. Coll., Central, S.C., 1915-19; pres. Marion (Ind.) Coll., 1919-22; prof. religious edn., Penn Coll., and pastor College Friends Ch., Oskaloosa, Ia., 1922-25; minister First Friends Ch., Richmond, Ind., 1925-29; v.p. and dean Penn Coll., 1929-30, pres., 1931-34. Mem. Rochester Presbytery of Presbyn. Churches since 1936. Home: West Webster NY‡

BEDFORD, PAUL, lawyer; b. Wilkes-Barre, Pa., June 24, 1875; s. George Reynolds and Emily Lindsley (Fuller) B.; B.S., Princeton, 1897; LL.B., U. of Pa., 1900; m. Gertrude Turner Vaughn, Nov. 24, 1915. Admitted to Pa. bar, 1900, and since in practice of law, Wilkes-Barre; partner Bedford, Waller, Griffith, Darling & Mitchell; asst. dist. atty., Luzerne Co., Pa., 1913-15; pres. bd. for assessment and revision of taxes of Luzerne County, Pa., 1922-31; vice pres. and dir. Miners Nat. Bank; dir. Del. & Hudson Co. President Wilkes-Barre branch Pa. Assn. for Blind, 1918-28; pres. Community Welfare Fedn., 1933-35, gen. campaign chmn., 1943; mem. U.S. Alien Enemy Bd. Middle Dist. Pa., from 1941; mem. Legal Aid Com., from 1942; pres. Home for Friendless Children; pres. Osterhout Free Library, Mercy Hosp. Trustee Princeton U.; president trustees First Presbyn. Ch. Fellow Am. Soc. C.E., Canadian Inst. Mining and Metallurgy; mem. Am. Coll. Trial Lawyers, American, Pennsylvania State and Luzerne County (pres. from 1943) bar assns., Am. Museum Natural History, Nat. Geographic Soc., Newcomen Soc. of England, Zeta Psi. Clubs: University, Princeton (New York); Princeton (Philadelphia); Westmoreland (Wilkes-Barre). Home: Wilkes-Barre PA Died Aug. 16, 1967.

BEDFORD, SCOTT ELIAS WILLIAM, sociologist; b. Winterset, Ia., Mar. 7, 1876; s. Winfield Scott and Jennie (Wilmore) B.; A.B., Baker U., Baldwin, Kan., 1902, A.M., 1903; fellow in sociology, U. of Chicago, 1908-11; (L.H.D., U. of Vt., 1911); m. Gussie Mae Taggart, of White City, Kan., June 8, 1905. Prof. history, Baker U., 1902-05, also prin. acad. same univ.; prof. sociology, Miami (O.) U., 1908-11; asst. prof. sociology, 1911-16, asso. prof. since 1916, U. of Chicago; now research sec. United Charities of Chicago. Asso. editor Am. Jour. Sociology since 1911; mng. editor publs. of Am. Sociol. Soc., 1912-20. Specialist in gen. edn., War Plans Div., War Dept., 1919-20; asst. consultant, 2d Corps Area, War Dept., 1920-21. Mem. Am. Sociol. Soc. (sec.-treas., 1912-20), Am. Civic Assn., Am. Econ. Assn., Am. Statis. Assn., Nat. Conf. Social Work, Nat. Housing Assn., Nat. Municipal League. Clubs: City (Chicago); Delta Tau Delta, Tau Kappa Alpha. Wrote: Labor Legislation of Kansas; American Cities; Readings in Urban Sociology; also various mag. articles. On staff of lecturers Redpath Lyceum Bur. Address: Chicago IL‡

BEEBE, KENNETH JOHN, ednl. counselor; b. Battle Creek, Mich., Oct. 12, 1889; s. John Frederick and Agnes Laverna (Chadbourne) B.; student U. Chgo., 1909-10, 13, U. Ill., 1911-12, Columbia 1919, Queens Coll., 1942; L.H.D., Drake Coll., 1968; m. E. Margaret Screaton, Nov. 11, 1939; children—Isabelle Laverna, Lynn Agnes. Ednl. guidance office, N.Y.C., 1913-70; pres. Beebe Advt. Agy., N.Y.C., 1960-70. Air raid warden, comdr. Forest Hills N.Y., 1951-52. Recipient certificate pub. service N.Y. State, 1958, Bronze plaque I Mens Assn. of U. Ill., 1968. Mem. Am. Schs. and Colls. Assn. (pres. 1940-70, pres. Horatio Alger awards com. 1951-70), S.A.R., Tau Kappa Epsilon. Conglist. (deacon). Clubs: Rockefeller Center Luncheon, Columbia University Illini (N.Y.C.); West Side Tennis (Forest Hills); Timber Trails. Author: Opportunity Still Knocks, 1956, 13th ann. edit., 1968; Forest Hills NY Died Mar. 21, 1970.

BEEBE, RAYMOND NELSON, lawyer; b. Wever, Ia., May 9, 1890; s. Warren Edgar and Arletta Elizabeth (Liddle) B.; B.A., State U. of Ia., 1912; J.D., U. of Chicago, 1915; m. Evalene Porter Babcock, 1919 (deceased); m. second, Martha Mead August, 1964. Was supt. of schs., Wyoming, Ia., 1912-13; admitted to Ill. bar 1915 and practiced in Chicago until 1917; asst., trial dept., Fidelty & Casualty Co. of New York (Chicago office), 1915-16; trial atty., Hoyne, O'Connor & Irwin, Chicago, 1916-17; prof. law, Chicago Law Sch., 1916-17; gen. counsel, examiner claims for Minn. and adjacent territory, Fidelty & Casualty Co., 1917-18; atty., trial examiner, Federal Trade Commn., Washington, D.C., 1918-19; practiced in Washington, 1921-71; formerly partner Davies, Richberg, Beebe, Landa & Richardson and predecessor firms; counsel with Scott W. Lucas, Friedman & Mann. Member American, D.C. bar associations, Delta Sigma Rho, Phi Alpha Delta. Democrat. Clubs: Metropolitan, University, Burning Tree, Gulf Stream Golf (Fla.); Coral Ridge Country (Ft. Lauderdale, Fla.). Home: Shady Side MD Died Mar. 7, 1971.

BEEBE, FREDERICK SESSIONS, pub. co. exec.; b. Utica, N.Y., Feb. 20, 1914; s. Henry R. and Dora Mertice (Sessions) B.; A.B., Dartmouth, 1935; LL.B., Yale, 1938; m. Liane Petzl-Basny, Aug. 5, 1939; children—Walter H., Michael. Admitted to N.Y. bar, 1938; partner firm Cravath, Swaine & Moore, N.Y.C., 1950-61; chmn. bd. Washington Post Co., owners Washington Post, Newsweek mag., TV and radio stas., 1961-73; dir. Allied Chem. Corp., Bowaters Mersey Paper Co., Ltd., S.E. Bancorp., Inc., Tri-Continental Corp. Mem. Council Fgn. Relations; trustee Com. Econ. Devel. Mem. Am. Bar Assn., Bar Assn. City of N.Y. Clubs: Metropolitan, University (N.Y.C.). Home: New York City NY Died May 1973.

BEECHER, GEORGE ALLEN, bishop; b. Monmouth, Ill., Feb. 3, 1868; s. Benjamin J. and Mercy Ann (Boland) B.; student U. of Neb., 1886-89; Phila. Div. Sch., 1889-92, D.D., 1912; m. Florence I. George, June 22, 1893 (dec.); children—Pauline H. (dec.), Mrs. Ruth Brian, George S. (dec.), Mary (dec.), Mrs. Elizabeth McNeil, Sanford Dent. Deacon, 1892, priest, 1893, P.E. Ch.; missionary, Sidney, Neb., 1892-95; rector North Platte, Neb., 1895-1903; Kearney, 1903-04; dean Trinity Cathedral, Omaha, 1904-10; consecrated bishop of Western Neb., Nov. 30, 1910. Trustee Bishop Clarkson Memorial Hosp., 1906-47, Brownell Hall (both Omaha) 1906-47; pres. Pine Ridge Hist. Assn., 1938-46; retired since 1943. Chaplain 5th Regt., Neb. N.G., 1906-16. Charter mem. Am. Inst. Criminal Law and Criminology; mem. Am. Prison Assn., Internat. Prison Assn., Neb. Humane Soc. (v.p.), Child Labor Com.; mem. State br. Com. for Treatment of Cancer. Mason (33 deg.), Elk (life mem.). Editor: Story of St. Mark's Pro-Cathedral Paris, 1945. Home: 919 N. St. Joseph Av., Hastings NE‡

BEEKMAN, FREDERICK WARREN, clergyman; b. Newbury, Mass., Feb. 14, 1871; s. Garret and Elizabeth (Cosgrave) B.; A.B., Amherst Coll., 1893; LL.B., Boston Univ., 1896; B.D., Episcopal. Theol. School, Cambridge, Mass., 1905; D.D., St. John's Coll., 1920, Amherst College; married Margaret Auchmuty Mackay, March 2, 1916. Practiced law, Dayton, O., 1895-1903; ordained deacon and priest, P.E. Church, 1905; rector Trinity Church, Woburn, Mass., 1906-08, St. Peter's Church, Uniontown, Pa., 1908-12; dean Nativity Pro-Cathedral, Bethlehem, Pa., 1912-17; dean American Pro-Cathedral of the Holy Trinity, Paris, France, 1918-48, dean emeritus since 1948. Chairman of the exec. com. American Churches in Europe and dep. gen. Convention Episcopal Ch. in U.S., 1919-46. Founder Am. Students and Artists Center, Paris, pres. since 1937; founder Am. Battle Cloister, Paris, 1923. Mem. Am. Library Bd. of Paris, 1919-37; mem. bd. govs. Am. Hosp. of Paris since 1918. Sponsor of Fight for Freedom, 1940-41; spl. preacher and speaker for Defend America, Bundles for Britain, Brit. War Relief, 1940-41; lecturer at U.S. Army Camps, 1942. Capt., 1st Ohio Cav., comdg. Troop F, Spanish-Am. War, 1898. Chaplain-dir. Am. Soldiers and Sailors Club and Canteens, Paris, 1917-19. Chaplain American Legion, Paris Post No. 1. Decorated Commander Legion of Honor (France); Officer Order of the White Eagle (Serbia). Mem. Beta Theta Pi. Republican. Mason. Clubs: University, American, St. Cloud Country (Paris). Author: A Dean's Diary (Europe-America, 1938-1943). Home: 261 Boulevard Raspail, Paris France‡

BEERS, BARNET WILLIAM, army officer, ret.; b. Petosky, Mich., July 18, 1896; s. William and Lucy Ethel (Kennedy) B.; student U. Ill., 1918; m. Marie Caroline Ball, Sept. 11, 1946. Served as officer U.S. Army, 1917-19; bldg. constrn. engr., 1921-31; prodn. engr. Eastman Kodak Co., 1931-39; reentered U.S. Army, 1940, advanced through grades to col., staff officer, dir. security div. 2d Service Command, Governor's Island, N.Y., 1940-44; chief civilian def. survey team U.S. Strategic Bombing Survey, Germany, Eng., Japan, 1944-46; with War Dept. gen. staff, sec. War Dept. Civil Def. Bd., 1946-47; exec. officer civil def. planning Office Sec. Def., 1947-48, asst. for Civil Def. Liaison, 1949-51, Asst. for Civil Def. Office Sec. Def., 1951-53; retired; now adminstr., Capitol Area Br. of FCDA, 1956-62; spl. liaison officer, OCBM, Washington Chmn. bd. trustees Nat. Inst. for Def. Moblzn. Recipient Legion of Merit. Army Commendation Medal with two oak leaf clusters. Mason. Home: Chevy Chase MD Died July 27, 1971.

BEETLE, DAVID HAROLD, editorial writer, author, columnist; born Edgartown, Martha's Vineyard Island, Mass., June 5, 1908; s. Frank Wasson and Susan (Phillips) B.; A.B., Hamilton Coll., 1930; m. Gladys Elizabeth Small, July 8, 1937 (div. Oct. 1955); 1 son,

David H.; m. 2d, Patricia Gibson, Jan. 2, 1958; children—Christopher G., Karen A. Reporter Utica Daily Press, 1930-33, state editor, 1933-36, columnist, 1936-39; dir. public relations, editor Alumni Review, Hamilton Coll., Clinton, N.Y., 1939-54, instr. English, 1941-43, cons. pub. relations, 1954-55; legislative corr. N.Y. State, Gannett Newspapers, Inc., 1944-55; editor editorial page Albany (N.Y.) Knickerbocker News, 1955-56, editor, 1956-60; special correspondent, editorial writer Gannett Newspapers, Albany, 1961-72. Cons. N.Y. State Dept. Edn., 1964-72; mem. N.Y. State Commn. History, 1959, Recipient Order Orange-Nassau (Netherlands). Mem. N.Y. State Legislative Corr.'s Assn., N.Y. State Soc. Newspaper Editors, Phi Beta Kappa. Conglist. Clubs: National Press (Wash.); Torch. Adirondack Mountain, University (Albany, N.Y.). Author: West Canada Creek, 1946; Along the Oriskany, 1947; Up Old Forge Way, 1948; The New York State Citizen, 1955. Contbr. articles to nat. mags. Home: Castleton-on-Hudson NY Died July 30, 1972.

BEGG, JAMES THOMAS, ex-congressman; b. Allen Co., O., Feb. 16, 1877; s. John and Mary Ellen (Kalb) B.; B.Sc. Wooster U. (now Coll.), 1903; m. Grace Carey Mohler, of Bluffton, O., Aug. 26, 1903;children—Mrs. Frances Eleanor Harreld, James T. (dec.). Supt. schs., Columbus Grove, O., 1905-10, Ironton, 1910-13, Sandusky, 1913-17; resigned and became connected with the Am. City Bur., Sept. 1, 1917; mem. 66th to 70th Congresses (1919-29), 13th Ohio Dist. Associated with Otis & Co., investment bankers, 1929-31; with Sweeney & James, advertising, since 1931; with Meldrum & Fewsmith, advertising, since 1932. Presbyn. Mason, K.P., Elk. Chamber of Commerce organizer and lecturer. Home: 2665 Endicott Road. Office: Cuyahoga Bldg., Cleveland OH‡

BEGGS, GERTRUDE HARPER, educator; b. at Pleasant Hill, Mo., Feb. 27, 1874; d. Francis S. and Sarah O. (Norman) B.; Drury Coll., Springfield, Mo., 1889-91; A.B., U. of Denver, 1893 (LL.D., 1914); Ph.D., Yale, 1904; studied Am. Sch. Classical Study at Athens, 1912. Teacher of Latin, Denver High School, 1894-8; prof. Greek, Earlham Coll., Richmond, Ind., 1904-5, U. of Denver, 1905-14; social dir., U. of Mich., 1915-17; dean of women, U. of Minn., since Sept., 1917. Mem. Am. Philol. Assn., Archaeol. Inst. America, Pi Beta Phi. Methodist. Author: The Four in Crete, 1915. Home: 1105 6th St. S.E., Minneapolis MN‡

BEGICH, NICHOLAS JOSEPH, congressman; b. Eveleth, Minn., Apr. 6, 1932; s. John and Anne (Martinich) B.; student Eveleth Jr. Coll., 1950; B.A., St. Cloud State Coll., 1952; M.A. in Ednl. Adminstrn. and Polit. Sci., U. Minn., 1954; postgrad. U. N.D.; m. Pegge Jendro, Dec. 29, 1956; children—Nichelle, Nicholas J., Thomas, Mark, Stephanie, Paul. Tchr., St. Cloud (Minn.) High Sch., 1952-56; boys' counselor West Anchorage High Sch., Anchorage, 1956-57; dir. student personnel Anchorage Sch. Dist., 1957-59; prin. Ursa Minor Sch., Ft. Richardson, Alaska, 1959-63; supt. schs., Ft. Richardson Sch. System, 1963-68; mem. Alaska Senate, 1963-71, minority whip, 1967-71; mem. 92d Congress from Alaska at large, 1971-72. Mem. Nat. Compact of Edn., 1967; instr. Am. govt. U.S. history U. Alaska, Anchorage, 1956-68. Life mem. P.T.A. Chmn., Kennedy-Johnson campaign, Anchorage, 1960. Recipient Community Service award V.F.W., 1964; Human Rights award N.A.A.C.P., 1965. Mem. N.E.A. (life), Alaska, Ft. Richardson (past pres.) edn. assns. Home: Anchorage AK Died Oct. 1972.

BEGLEY, ED, actor; b. Hartford, Conn., Mar. 25, 1901; s. Michael Joseph and Hannah (Clifford)B.; student parochial schools; married Amanda Huff, April 1, 1922 (died 1957); children—Thomas Allene, Eddie; m. 2d, Dorothy Bates, June 7, 1961 (div. Jan. 1963); m. 3d, Helen Jordan; 1 dau., Maureen K. Radio actor, 1931-43; Broadway shows include Land of Fame, 1943, Get Away, Old Man, 1944, Pretty Little Parlor, 1945, All My Sons, 1947, All Summer Long, 1954, Inherit the Wind, 1955 (star role, 1957), Look Homeward Angel, 1958, Advise and Consent, 1960; recordings (with Melvyn Douglas, Vincent Price and Carl Sandburg) Great American Speeches, 1958; Leaves of Grass, 1964, Favorite American Poems, 1966, also others; was actor in 21 movies, 1947-51, later ones include Patterns, 1955; 12 Angry Men, 1956; Sweet Bird of Youth, 1962; The Unsinkable Molly Brown, 1964; appearances West Coast plays include What Price Glory, 1948, John Loves Mary, 1949, Hogan's Goat, Dublin, 1966. Guest prof. of drama Syracuse U. Recipient Donaldson award, 1955, Variety award, 1955, Tony award, 1956, Kraft award, 1955, Sylvania award, 1956; Lambs award, 1947; Muse award, 1958, Acad. Award for best supporting actor in Sweet Bird of Youth, 1962; congratulatory resolutions City of Hartford, 1963; Distinguished Service award Otterbein Coll. Mem. The Lambs, Masquers, Hollywood Comedy Club, The Academy of Motion Picture Arts and Sciences. Mil. Order Purple Heart (hon. mem. motion picture chpt.). Home: Northridge CA Died Apr. 1970.

BEGOLE, GEORGE DAVIS, ex-mayor; b. Kirksville, Mo., May 28, 1877; s. Davis W. and Lydia (Stanford) B.; student high sch. and Central Business Coll.; m. Ethel Waldo, June 1, 1927; children—Lydia, Archie S., Marybelle, Carroll. Supt. of supplies Denver Pub. Schs., 1910-15; sec. to mgr. of safety, 1916-19; accountant of City and County of Denver, 1919-21, elected auditor, term 1921-31; mayor of Denver, term 1931-35. Nat. committeeman of Denver Council of Boy Scouts of America; past pres. Municipal Finance Officers' Assn. of U.S. and Can. Republican. Protestant. Mason. Clubs: Athletic, Rotary. Home: 1575 Monroe St., Denver CO‡

BEHYMER, ARTHUR LIVINGSTONE, ex-postmaster; b. Clermont Co., O., June 15, 1869; s. Barrington and Sarah Elizabeth (McDonald) B.; ed. pub. schs., Clermont Co., and Nat. Normal U., Lebanon, O., 1 term; m. Mabelle L. Shipman, of Cleveland, O., Dec. 3, 1927. Taught sch. 1887-88, then chief clerk in charge of districts out of Cincinnati and asst. div. supt. Ry. Mail Service in charge dept. Cincinnati Chamber Commerce, (1918-19); executive secretary Yellow Pine-Wholesalers' Association, 1920-21; postmaster of Cincinnati, 1922-33; apptd. comptroller sales tax div. Ohio State Treasury Dept., Jan. 1, 1935. Director Norwood-Hyde Park Bank & Trust Co. Member Federal Business Assn. Cincinnati (ex-pres.); ex-pres. Nat. Assn. of Postmasters of the U.S.; dir. Cincinnati Chamber of Commerce. Republican. Mason (33 deg.). Clubs: Kiwanis (ex-pres.), Cincinnati (dir.), Hyde Park Business (ex-pres.). Home: 1117 Herschel Av., Cincinnati OH‡

BEINECKE, EDWIN JOHN, business exec.; b. N.Y. City, Jan. 6, 1886; s. Bernhard and Johanna Elizabeth (Weigle) B.; ed. Philips Acad., Andover, Mass., 1901-03; grad. Yale Coll., 1907; D.H.L. (hon.), Bowdoin, 1950, Dr. Humane Letters; m. Linda Louise Maurer, Apr. 22, 1909; children—Sylvia L. (wife of Dr. John N. Robinson) Edwin John. Pres. Henry Maurer & Son, 1921-23; pres., chmn. bd. Sperry and Hutchinson Co., 1923-67, also dir.; dir., pres. chmn. U.S. Realty & Improvement Co., 1936-42; chmn. bd. Plaza Hotel Co., 1936-42; chmn. bd. George A. Fuller Co., 1941-56, dir., 1941-65; chmn. bd. Patent Scaffolding Co., 1957-61; dir. Hotel Waldorf Astoria Corp., Mfrs. Hanover Trust Co. N.Y.C. (hon.). Served as capt. construction div., U.S. Army, World War I; dep. commr. Am. Red Cross in Great Brit., World War II. Awarded Medal of Freedom. Past chmn. council fellows Pierpont Morgan Library, Yale Library Assos. Mason. Clubs: Com. of 25 (Palm Springs, Cal.), Bath and Tennis, Everglades (Palm Beach), Yale, Lawyers, Whitehall, Regency Whist, Marco Polo, Fifth Avenue, Grolier (N.Y.C.); Westchester (N.Y.) Country; Blind Brook (Port Chester, N.Y.); Portland, Savile (London). Home: Greenwich CT Died Jan. 21, 1970; buried Kensico Cemetery, Valhalla NY

BEINECKE, FREDERICK WILLIAM, advt. exec.; born N.Y.C., Apr. 12, 1887; s. Berhnard and Johanna Elizabeth (Weigle) B.; student Phillips Andover Acad.; Ph.B., Sheffield Sci. Sch., Yale, 1909; m. Carrie Sperry, Nov. 14, 1912; children—William S., Richard S. Insp. Bethelehm Steel Corp., South Bethlehem, Pa., 1909-10; asst. supr. N.Y.C. R.R., N.Y.C., 1910-11; chief engr. Red Hook (N.Y.) Light & Power Co., 1911-14; partner Washington Engine Works, N.Y.C., 1914; asst. supt. Tex. Corp., N.Y.C., 1914-19; pres. Studebaker Sales Co., Newark, 1919-29; partner Coady, Beinecke & Co., N.Y.C., 1929-32; pres. Houghton & Dutton, Boston, 1933-36; v.p. Sperry & Hutchinson Co., 1938-71, dir., chmn. exec. committee. Served as captain in U.S. Army, World War I. Established Beinecke Rare Book and Manuscript Library, Yale, 1963. Mason. Clubs: Manhattan, Metropolitan, Grolier, Yale (N.Y.C.); Wyantenuck New York City NY Died Aug. 1971.

BELANGER, JOHN W., elec. co. exec.; b. New Bedford, Mass., Mar. 24, 1901; s. William E. and Margaret (Wright) B.; student Franklin Tech. Inst., Boston, 1918-19, Wharton Sch. Pa. U., 1936-38; m. Anna Nordgren, Nov. 10, 1924. With Gen. Electric Co. since 1917, student test course, Lynn, Mass., 1917-18, v.p. def. products group, Schenectady, 1951-54; exec. v.p. indsl. products & lamp group, 1954-55; exec. v.p. indsl. components & materials group, 1955-58, vice president apparatus sales division, 1958-60, v.p. customer relations, 1960-63. Trustee emeritus Union Coll. Mem. bd. mgrs., Ellis Hosp., Schenectady. Mem. Am. Soc. Naval Engrs., Soc. Naval Architects and Marine Engrs., Newcomen Soc. Eng. Clubs: Mohawk Golf, Mohawk (Schenectady); Edison (Rexford, N.Y.); Pinnacle (N.Y.C.). Home: Rexford NY Died Sept. 24, 1968; buried Memories Garden, Schenectady NY

BELCHER, EDWIN NEWTON, JR., oil co. exec.; b. Miami, Fla., Aug. 10, 1913; s. Edwin Newton and Margaret (Cannon) B.; student U. Fla., 1937; m. Virginia Groos, June 29, 1936; children—Edwin Newton III, Gary Lee. Mgr. Belcher Constrn. Co., Miami, 1937-71, Belcher Towing Co., Miami, 1940-71; pres., chmn. bd. Belcher Oil Co., Miami, 1948-71; dir. First Nat. Bank Miami, Fla. East Coast Ry.; operating partner Oolite Rock Co. Bd. dirs. So. States Indsl. Council. Mem. Sigma Alpha Epsilon. Home: Coral Gables FL Died Nov. 27, 1971.

BELCHER, JAMES ELMER, educator; b. Millville, Mo., Oct. 30, 1885; s. James Henry and Lydia (Dotson) B.; A.B., Okla. U., 1922, A.M., 1924; grad. work, U. of Chicago, 1929; m. Blanche Martin, Aug. 7, 1917; children—Myra Lael (Mrs. Homer B. Brown, Jr.), James Elmer. Public sch. teacher in Okla., 1907-20; mem. faculty, chemistry dept., Okla. Univ., from 1922, prof. of chemistry from 1948. Mem. Am. Chem. Soc., Okla. Acad. of Sci., Phi Beta Kappa, Alpha Chi Sigma. Mem. Church of Christ (elder). Author: A Course in Qualitative Analysis (with Guy Y Williams), 1938; Experiments and Problems for College Chemistry (with Dr. J.C. Colbert), 1928; Properties and Numerical Relationships of the Common Elements and Compounds (with Dr. J.C. Colbert), 1928, Scripture and Science Harmonized by the Scientific Method, 1970. Home: Norman OK Died May 5, 1972; buried IOOF Cemetery, Norman OK

BELDEN, WILLIAM BURLINGAME, steel co. exec.; b. Grand Rapids, Mich., June 15, 1902; s. William Patch and Laila (Burlingame) B.; grad. Univ. Sch. Cleve., 1921; A.B., Cornell U., 1926; LL.B., Western Res. U., 1931; m. Sarah Jean Vliet, July 22, 1931; children—Sally V. (Mrs. Dudley D. Yost), Jean B. (Mrs. Thomas F. Tuttle), Nancy L. (Mrs. Carlton C. Coolidge). Admitted to Ohio bar, 1932; associate of firm of Belden Young & Veach, 1931-36; legal dept. Republic Steel Corp., 1931-42, asst. counsel, 1942-52, asst. sec., 1945-59, sec., from 1959. Bd. mgrs. Boys' Club of Cleve.; com. fiscal advisers YWCA; trustee Univ. Sch. Cleve. Mem. Nat. Bus. Aircraft Assn. (founding chmn.), Am., Ohio, Cleve. bar assns., Delta Upsilon, Phi Delta Phi, Sigma Delta Chi. Clubs: Union, Tavern, Kirtland Country (Cleve.). Home: Cleveland Heights OH

BELDING, DAVID LAWRENCE, teacher; b. Dover Plains, N.Y., July 24, 1884; s. Charles Walter and Ellinor (Frost) B.; A.B., Williams Coll., 1905; A.M., Harvard, 1915, M.D., 1914; M.D., Boston U., 1913; m. Isabel Wheeler, Aug. 18, 1915; children—Helen Wheeler (Mrs. Manson Meads), Ellinor Frost, Elizabeth Suzanne (Mrs. Leroy L. Eldredge, Jr.). Biologist, Mass. Fish and Game Commn., Mass. Dept. Conservation, Div. Fisheries and Game, 1905-33; cons. biol., Div. Fisheries and Game since 1923; asso. Biological Bd. of Can., 1931-33; pathologist Mass. Memorial Hosps., Boston, Mass., 1915-17, bacteriologist, 1923-26, dir. of laboratories, 1926-40; research asso. Evans Memorial Hosp., 1919-45; asst. prof. bacteriology, Sch. of Medicine, Boston U., 1921-23, asso. prof., 1923-26, prof. bacteriology and pathology, 1926-36, prof. bacteriology and exptl. pathology, 1936-49, emeritus, 1950; asso. Woods Hole Oceanographic Instn., 1950-70; lectr. Bowman Gray Sch. Medicine, 1953. Cons., Cape Cod Hosp., Norfolk County Hosp. Adv. bd. Cape Cod Nat. Seashore. Served with Med. Corps, U.S. Army, 1917-19, disch. with rank of capt. Mem. sch. com., Hingham, Mass., 1924-36, mem. bd. of health, 1934-35. Mem. salmon commn., Province of Quebec, Can. Mem. Soc. Am. Bacteriologists, Soc. Exptl. Pathologists, Am. Assn. Pathologists and Bacteriologists, Am. Bd. Pathology, A.M.A., Mass. Med. Assn. (mem. legislative com. 1944-51); Soc. Exptl. Biology and Medicine, Am. Fisheries Soc. (pres. 1929-30), Am. Acad. Arts and Scis., Phi Beta Kappa, Phi Sigma Kappa. Mason. Author: Textbook of Medical Bacteriology, 1938; Textbook of Clinical Parasitology, 1942; Basic Clinical Parasitology, 1958. Home: Hingham MA Died Dec. 5, 1970; buried Hingham Cemetery.

BELDING, DON, retired advt. co. ofcl.; b. Grants Pass, Ore., Jan. 23, 1898; s. William P. and Mollie (Dowell) B.; B.S., U. Ore., 1919; m. Eunice Louise Hodges, June 9, 1919; children—Don, Barbara; m. 2d, Alice Louise Freter, Mar. 28, 1942. Mgr., Western Union, Klamath Falls, Ore., 1919-21; publisher, Klamath Record, 1921-22; with Lord & Thomas, Los Angeles, 1923-43, v.p., mgr., 1938-43; chmn. bd. Foote Cone & Belding, Los Angeles, since 1943, chmn. exec. com., 1951-57, retired, 1957; chmn. exec. com. Eversharp, Inc., 1965-67, vice chmn. bd., 1967-69; dir. Gen. Am. Corp., Orange Radio, Inc. Dir. Epileptic Found., Community for Positive Living; pres. Crippled Childrens Soc. of So. Cal. Past pres. Los Angeles Bd. Airport Commn.; v.p. Nat. Monument Commn.; founder, chmn. bd. Freedoms Found. Valley Forge; vice chmn. Nat. Arthritis and Rheumatism Found.; past council of trustees U.S. Army Assn. past civilian aide to sec. of army for So. Cal. Past dir. War Advt. Council (N.Y.), Mchts. and Mfrs. Assn. (Los Angeles), Los Angeles C. of C. Named layman of year by Arthritis and Rheumatism Found., 1958, recipient top advt. industry award, 1962; D.S.M. Served as radio sgt. CAC, 1st Army, World War I; overseas, France, 9 mos. Mem. Defense Orientation Conference Assn. (pres. 1962), Advt. Assn. of West (past pres.). Mason. Clubs: California, Los Angeles, Los Angeles Yacht (Los Angeles). Home: Pacific Palisades CA Died Jan. 16, 1969.

BELDOCK, GEORGE J., judge; b. 1904; student St. Lawrence U. Admitted to N.Y. State bar, 1925; presiding justice Appellate div. N.Y. State Supreme Ct., 2d Dept., Bklyn.; v.p. Bklyn. Law Sch. Mem. Am. Bar Assn. Home: Brooklyn NY Died Mar. 15, 1970.

BELFOUR, C(AMPBELL) STANTON, foundation dir.; born Crafton, Pa., July 6, 1906; s. Geter C.S. and Isabelle (Stanton) B.; student Blair Acad., Blairstown, N.J., Carnegie Inst. Tech.; A.B., U. Pitts., 1928, M.Litt., 1936; L.H.D., Waynesburg College 1952; LL.D., Geneva College, Beaver Falls, Pa., 1958, U. Pitts., 1962; D.C.S., Elizabethtown Coll., 1959; Litt. D., Washington and Jefferson Coll., 1963, Seton Hill Coll., 1967; L.H.D., Thiel Coll., 1967; m. Hilda Haskett, Aug. 16, 1934; children—Jane (now Mrs. J. C. Abbott), and Joan Befour. Assistant registrar U. Pitts., 1928-30, asst. dir. U. extension div., also summer sessions, evening classes, 1930-42, lectr. history extension div., 1947-51; exec. sec. Pa. Forensic and Music League, 1930-42; mgr. Stephen Foster Meml., Pitts., 1937-42; exec. sec. Pa. Speech Assn., 1939-42; dir., sec. Pittsburgh Found from 1945; cons. Howard Heinz Endowment, from 1948, Irene Heinz and John L. Given Found., 1957-62; exec. sec. Pitcairn-Crabbe Found. since 1950. Vice president of Council on Founds., 1966-68. Sec. Allegheny County Bd. Pub. Assistance, 1948-54; Pa. chmn. White House Conference on Aging, 1960-61. Member Pitts. Board of Education 1954-65; dir. Pitts. Symphony Soc. Served as lieut. comdr. USNR, 1942-45. Mem. Council on Founds. (v.p.), Pa., Western Pa. (trustee, pres.) hist. socs., Pa. Fedn. of Hist. Soc. (pres. 1959-61), Pa. Sch. Music Assn., Omicron Delta Kappa (past nat. pres.), Phi Alpha Theta (past nat. pres.,), Phi Delta Kappa, Pi Sigma Alpha. Mason (32 deg.; past master). Republican. Presbyn. Club: Press (Pitts.). Author: Centennial History of Shadyside Presbyterian Church, 1967. Contbr. articles profl. jours. Home: Pittsburgh PA Died Nov. 29, 1969.

BELK, HENRY, newspaper columnist, coll. trustee; b. Monroe, N.C., May 8, 1898; s. Robert Lee and Lula (Raoe) B.; A.B., Duke, 1923; m. Lucile Marie Bullard, Oct. 7, 1923; 1 dau., Marie (Mrs. Edgar L. Lipton) (dec.). Publicity dir. Trinity Coll. of Duke, 1920-23; instr. English, publicity dir. Wake Forest Coll., 1923-25; lectr. journalism New Rochelle (N.Y.) Coll., 1924-25; editor Goldsboro (N.C.) News, 1926-29; mng. editor Goldsboro News-Argus, 1929-55, editor, 1949-68; editor emeritus, columnist editorial page, 1968-72; columnist Greensboro Daily News, 1956-72. Mem. President's Com. Employment Physically Handicapped, 1960-72, N.C. Citizens Commn. Better Schs., 1957-72, vice chmn., 1962-72; trustee East Carolina U., 1947-72, chmn. 1963-64; mem. N.C. Gov.'s Study Com. Vocational Rehab. Sec. N.C. R.R. Bd., 1942; mem. Commn. Monument 3 Native N.C. U.S. Presidents, 1945-48; mem. Gov. Aycock Meml. Commn., 1949-67; life member of adv. bd. Goldsboro Salvation Army. Bd. dirs. Bib. Recorder, 1959-62, North Carolina Baptist Homes for the Aging, 1963-67, Wayne County (N.C.) Coll. Aid, Inc., 1954-72. Named Foremost Handicapped Man of Year in N.C., Gov. Com. Employment Handicapped, 1960; recipient Citizenship award Goldsboro Rotary Club, 1956. Mem. N.C. (pres. 1950-51), Eastern N.C. (pres. 1944) press assns., Goldsboro Jr. C. of C. (hon. life mem. 1957), A.P. Council N.C. (pres. 1953; hon. plaque 1964), Am. Soc. Newspaper Editors, N.C. Lit. and Hist. Assn. (hon. life mem.; pres. 1962-63), Sigma Delta Chi, Alpha Phi Gamma. Baptist. Mason, Elk. Home: Goldsboro NC Died Oct. 20, 1972.

BELL, ARCHIE, author; b. Geneva, O., Mar. 17, 1877; s. Samuel A. and Sarah Jane (Soden) B.; ed. pub. schs.; unmarried. Critic and traveling corr. for Am. newspapers and mags. since 1905. Author: Seralmo, 1902; The Bermudian, 1908; The Clyde Fitch I Knew, 1910; The Spell of the Holy Land, 1915; The Spell of Egypt, 1916; The Spell of China, 1917; A Trip to Lotus Land, 1917; Sunset Canada, 1918; King Tutankhamen, 1923; Mary of Magdala, 1925; The Spell of Caribbean Islands, 1926. The Spell of Ireland, 1928. Home: 1540 E. 85th St., Cleveland OH‡

BELL, DANIEL WAFENA, retired comml. banker, civic ofcl.; b. Kinderhook, Ill., July 23, 1891; s. Daniel Morgan and Otis (Hardy) B.; LL.B., Nat. U., Washington, 1924; B.C.S., Southeastern U., 1927, Hon. LL.D., 1957; M.A. (hon.), Princeton, 1940; m. Sarah Agnes Killeen, June 22, 1921; 1 dau., Mary Kathleen. Stenographer, bookkeeper Treasury Dept., 1911, accountant in charge fgn. loans, 1919-20, exec. asst. to asst. sec. Treasury, 1920-24, asst. commr. accounts and deposits, 1924-31, commr. accounts and deposits, 1931-35, asst. to sec. Treasury financial and accounting matters, 1935-40, also acting dir. budget, 1934-39, under sec. Treasury, 1940-45; pres. Am. Security & Trust Co., Washington, 1946-59, chmn. bd., 1954-62, also dir.; dir. Nat. Press Bldg. Corp., Washington Gas Light Co. Mem. Decontrol Bd., 1946; spl. ambassador to Philippines, 1950; temp. chmn. pub. adv. bd. Mut. Security Adminstrn., 1952. Treas. John F. Kennedy Center for Performing Arts; mem. nat. exec. bd. Boy Scouts Am.; chmn. trustees Retirement Fund, Am. Nat. Red Cross. Bd. dirs. Columbia Hosp. for Women, Maderia Sch.; bd. trustees Brookings Instn. Served with U.S. Army, 1918-19. Decorated Legion Honor (France); recipient Silver Antelope award, 1954, Silver Beaver 1955, Silver Buffalo, 1956 (Boy Scouts Am.); Distinguished Service award Lions Club Philippines, 1950, Cosmpolitan Club D.C., 1956, D.A.V.; Gold Heart award Variety Club D.C., 1961; Brotherhood award Nat. Conf. Christians and Jews. Mem. Am. Bankers Assn. Methodist. Clubs: Metropolitan, Nat. Press, Chevy Chase, Sulgrave, Alfalfa (Washington); Ponte Vedra (Fla.); Farmington (Va.) Country. Home: Washington DC Died Oct. 3, 1971; buried Parklawn, Rockville MD

BELL, GEORGE MAXWELL, publisher; b. Regina, Can., Oct. 13, 1911; s. George Melrose and Edna (Parkin) B.; B.Com., McGill Univ., 1932; m. Suzanne Staples (div.); children—Diane, Chester (dec.), Gretchen, Paul. Pub. The Albertan (newspaper), Calgary, Alberta, 1943-71. Liberal. Presbyterian. Mason (Shriner). Club: Ranchmen's. Home: Calgary Alberta Canada Died July 19, 1972; buried Okotoks, Alberta Canada

BELL, GRAHAM BERNAT, psychologist, educator; b. Dobbs Ferry, N.Y., July 4, 1923; s. Edgar Isaac and Louise (Bernat) B.; B.A. with honors, Conn. Wesleyan U., 1947; M.A., Northwestern U., 1950, Ph.D., 1952; m. Carol A. Gramer, June 17, 1949; children—Geoffry Edward DeRevere, Karla Louise, Victoria, Graham. Asst. prof. La. State U., 1951-54, asso. prof., 1954-56, asst. dir. psychol. clinic, 1951-56; research scholar U.S. Ednl. Found. in Australia, 1955; prof., chmn. psychology dept. Pomona Coll., 1956-68; prof. Claremont Grad. Sch. and Research Center, 1956-68; sr. lectr. U. Osmania (Fulbright fellow under U.S. Ednl. Found. of India, 1963-64; vis. lectr. Univ. of Lille (France), 1964. Certified psychologist, Cal. mem. Western, Am., Cal. psychol. assns., Sigma Xi, Delta Upsilon. Home: Claremont CA Died Oct. 23, 1968.

BELL, HUGH MCKEE, coll. prof.; b. Frostburg, Pa., July 9, 1902; s. Frank W. and Mary (Smitten) B.; A.B., Willamette U., 1926; A.M., Stanford U., 1928, Ph.D., 1941; m. Eva Tacheron, June 14, 1928. Banker, Monmouth and Corvallis, Oregon, 1919-22; exec. sec. (Monmouth) Ore. Normal Sch., 1926-27, Stanford, 1927-28; teacher of psychology, dean lower dir., Chico (Calif.) State Coll., 1928-42, prof. psychology, 1956-67, dean of students, 1946-56; visiting prof. psychology, U. Maine, summer, 1954; vis. prof. U. Minn., summers 1938, 47, Denver U., summer 1956; vis. prof. ednl. psychology U. Wash., summer 1960, 66; cons. counseling psychology Office Edn., 1962-63; cons. Cal. Dept. Mental Hygiene, 1962-63; cons. Portland pub. schs. in counseling and guidance, 1959; faculty rep. Far Western Conf., 1959-60. Mem. Wesley Found. bd. Chico State Coll. Served as capt. U.S. Army, 1942-45; training specialist, Vets. Adminstrn., Washington, 1945-46, now cons. Mem. Cal. State Psychology Examining Com., 1957-67, chmn., 1958-59. Mem. Cal. Council Ednl. Research, 1948-64; mem. bd. dirs. Jour. Counseling Psychology, 1964-67; president Chico Family Service Assn., 1957. Fulbright lectr. U. Exeter (England), 1967. Recipient distinguished univ. awards. Diplomate Am. Bd. Examiners in Profl. Psychology. Mem. Shakespeare Soc. Am., Cal. Psychol. Assn. (pres. 1954), American Coll. Personnel Assn. (v.p. and mem. exec. council), Am. Psychol. Assn. (pres. div. of counseling and guidance), Nat. Vocational Guidance Assn., Western Psychological Association (pres. 1965-66), California Educational Research Association (pres.), Sigma Xi, Kappa Delta Pi, Pi Gamma Mu. Author: Theory and Practice of Personal Counseling, 1939; Adjustment Inventory (student form), 1934, rev. 1962, (adult form), 1938; School Inventory, 1936; Personal Preference Inventory, 1948. Contbr. numerous articles in ednl. publs. Methodist. Home: Chico CA Died Dec. 25, 1967.

BELL, (HAROLD) IDRIS, author; b. Epworth, Lincolnshire, Eng., Oct. 2, 1879; s. Charles Christopher and Rachel (Hughes) B.; ed. Oriel Coll., Oxford (Eng.) U., also univs. Berlin, Halle; M.A.; LL.D., Liverpool; D.Litt. (hon.) univs. Wales, Mich., Brussels; m. Mabel Winifred Ayling, 1911; children—Idris Christopher, Ernest David (dec.), John John Rhys. Asst. in dept. manuscripts Brit. Mus., 1903, dep. keeper manuscripts, 1927, keeper manuscripts, Egerton librarian, 1929-44; hon. reader in papyrology Oxford U., 1935-50, hon. fellow Oriel Coll., 1936-67. Recipeint Cymmrodorion medal for services to Welsh lit., 1946; mem. Order Brit. Empire, companion of Bath; created knight, 1946. Mem. Brit. Acad. (pres. 1946-50), Egypt Exploration Soc. (v.p. 1945-67), Hon. Soc. of Cymmrodorion (pres. 1947-53, v.p. 1953-67), Soc. for Promotion Roman Studies (pres. 1937-45, v.p. 1945-67), Soc. for Promotion Hellenic Studies (v.p. 1930-67), Internat. Council for Philosophy and Humanistic Studies (v.p. 1949-52), Internat. Assn. Papryologists (pres. 1947-55, hon. pres. 1955-67), numerous other learned socs. Author: Catalogue of Greek Papyri in the British Museum, Vol. III (with F. Kenyon), Vols. IV, V; Jews and Christians in Egypt, 1924; Oxyrhynchus Papyri, Part XVI (with B.P. Grenfell, A.S. Hunt), 1924, Part XIX (with E. Lobel, E. P. Wegener, C. H. Roberts), 1948; (with W. E. Crum), Wadi Sarga, 1922; Juden und Griechen im romischen Alexandreia, 1926; (with T. C. Skeat) Fragments of an Unknown Gospel, 1935; Egypt from Alexander the Great to the Arab Conquest, 1948; Cults and Creeds in Graeco-Roman Egypt, 1953. Editor, translator numerous vols. of Welsh lit. Address: Aberystwyth Wales Died Jan. 1967.*

BELL, JAMES WARSAW, college dean; b. Pontotoc County, Miss., Jan. 4, 1869; s. Dr. John Allan and Margaret Catherine (Mosley) B.; Ph.B., U. of Miss., 1898, A.M., 1910; studied summers, University of Michigan, 1906, also at University of Chicago and Columbia, also at Columbia, 1916-17; m. Sophia L. Boyd, Nov. 15, 1899; children—Margaret Elizabeth (wife of Dr. N.S. Dickson), James Warsaw, Jr. (dec.), Dr. Catherine Boyd (wife of Dr. Chester Colwell Brummett). Teacher in rural schools of Miss., 1887; prin. high school, Jackson, 1894-97, Jefferson County High Sch., Fayette, Miss., 1902-03; supt. schs. Water Valley, 1898-1902; asso. prof. pedagogy and high sch. visitor, U. of Miss., 1903-04; prof. mathematics, Miss. Indsl. Inst. and Coll., Columbus, Miss., 1904-07; asso. prof. mathematics, 1907-09, professor of economics and political Science, 1910-44; head dept. of economics since 1944. Dean School of Commerce and Business Adminstrn., 1917-41, dean emeritus since 1941, University of Miss. Served with Y.M.C.A., 6th Italian Army, at the front, Sept. 1918-Jan. 1919; awarded Diploma of Merit by Intendencia Generale Italiano, also Croce al Merito di Guerra. Mem. Am. Acad. Polit. and Social Science, Southern Econ. Assn., Miss. Teachers' Assn. (pres. 1910-11), Delta Psi. Presbyterian. Mason, Odd Fellow. Author: (with Grady Guyton and R. L. Sackett) Mississippi Retail Sales Tax—How It Works, 1933; Government and the Voter. Home: University MS‡

BELL, JOHN LEWIS, mfg. exec.; b. Marion, Ind., June 21, 1913; s. George A. and Alice R. (McCulloch) B.; student Ind. U., 1931-34; grad. So. Bus. U., Miami, Fla., 1938; m. Lauvonnia C. Kinder, Feb. 6, 1937; children—George McCulloch, John Lewis, Alice Melinda. Treas., gen. mgr., Bell Fibre Products Corp., Marion, 1938-54, pres.; chmn. bd. Marion Nat. Bank, Marion Nat. Corporation; vice president, mem. bd. directors Tenn. River Pulp & Paper Co., Counce. Clubs: Surf, Bath, Indian Creek Country (Miami Beach, Fla.); Key Largo (Fla.) Anglers; Meshingomesia Country, Mecca. Home: Marion IN

BELL, JOSEPH A(SBURY), physician; b. Trinidad, Colo., Mar. 27, 1904; s. Joseph C. and Bessie (Sherman) B.; M.D., U. Colo., 1929; M.P.H., Johns Hopkins, 1937, Dr. P.H., 1948; m. Margaret Nichols, Sept. 26, 1927; children—Margaret Joan, Shirley May. Intern U.S. Marine Hosp., San Francisco, 1929-30, resident, 1932-33; practice medicine, from 1930; commd. USPHS, 1930, med. dir., 1947; chief lab. infectious diseases NIH, Bethesda, Md. Mem. commn. on influenza Armed Forces Epidemiol. Bd.; mem. expert adv. panel on internat. quarantine WHO. Served with U.S. Army, 1943-45. Decorated Legion of Merit. Recipient Distinguished Service medal USPHS, 1962. Diplomate Nat. Bd. Med. Examiners, Am. Bd. Preventive Medicine; mem. Am. Epidemiol. Soc. (pres. 1952). Author scientific reports on studies infectious diseases. Home: Bethesda MD Died Oct. 29, 1968; buried Parklawn Meml. Park, Rockville MD

BELL, JOSEPH MILLIGAN, banker; b. Augusta, Ga., Sept. 15, 1876; s. John and Emily Margaret (Milligan) B.; ed. pub. schs.; m. Helen Iredell Jones, of Columbia, S.C., June 14, 1900; children—Joseph Milligan, John, Helen Iredell. Began as out-door clk. Carolina Nat. Bank, Columbia, 1889, elected cashier, 1913, pres. Jan. 1923; Carolina Nat. Bank, Bank of Charleston and Norwood Nat. Bank (Greenville, S.C.) consolidated, Mar. 1926, under name of South Carolina Nat. Bank, of which is v.p.; sec., treas., dir. Domestic Building & Loan Co. Mason (Shriner). Democrat. Episcopalian. Club: Forest Lake. Home: 1007 Bull St. Office: 1401 Main St., Columbia SC‡

BELL, MAJOR TOWNSEND, lawyer; b. Tenaha, Tex., Dec. 4, 1897; s. Seaton and Martha Elizabeth (Sterrett) B.; LL.B., U. Tex., 1923; m. Phoebe Lovell Bone, Aug. 12, 1933; children—Richard McCreary, Thomas Sterrett. Admitted to Tex. bar, 1923; dist. atty., Shelby, Panola and Rusk Counties, Tex., 1924-26; asso. Orgain & Carroll, Beaumont, Tex., 1926-30; partner Orgain, Carroll & Bell, Beaumont, 1930-45; partner Orgain, Bell & Tucker 1945-69, sr. partner, 1965-69; mem. Tex. Civil Jud. Counsel, 1944-47. Bd. dirs. Tex. So. U., Tex. Law Enforcement and Youth Found., U. Tex. Sch. Law; adv. bd., research fellow Southwestern Legal Found. Fellow Am. Coll. Probate Counsel, Am. Bar Found.; mem. Fedn. Ins. Counsel (past v.p.), State Bar Tex. (past pres.), Internat. Assn. Ins. Counsel. Democrat. Baptist. Clubs: Beaumont TX Died Mar. 1, 1969; buried Forest Lawn Meml. Park, Beaumont TX

BELL, RAE FLOYD, steel products; b. Bonus, Ill., Apri. 19, 1887; s. Raleigh and Julia (Winkler) B.; A.B., U. of Wis., 1912; m. Rose Boyd Crelly, Jan. 7, 1915; children—Robert Rae, John Stanley. Began as traveling auditor Internat. Harvester Co., 1912; sec. and mgr. Kaukauna (Wis.) Pulp Co., 1916-20; v.p. Kieckhefer Paper Co., Milwaukee, 1918-19; also pres. Bell-Kieckhefer Co., Waukesha, 1918-19; sec. and mgr. Kieckhefer Container Co., Delair, N.J., 1920-23; 1st vice-pres. A. O. Smith Corp., Milwaukee, 1923-45, chmn. bd., 1945-56. Mem. Beta Theta Pi, Beta Gamma Sigma, Delta Sigma Rho, Phi Beta Kappa, Phi Beta Kappa Assos. Baptist. Club: University (Milwaukee). Home: Chandler AZ Died Apr. 25, 1968; buried Wisconsin Meml. Park, Milwaukee WI

BELL, WILLIAM CONSTANTINE, utility exec.; b. San Antonio, May 9, 1890; s. Thad C. and Katharine (Carothers) B.; student U. of Tex., 1906-07; B.S., U. of Calif., 1910; m. Mildred Cross, June 5, 1911; 1 dau., Mildred Elizabeth. Began as electrician with U.S. Army Transport Service, 1909; with Sierra-San Francisco Power Co. and Pacific Gas & Elec. Co., 1910-11; successively purchasing agt., chief engr., and gen. mgr. Va. Ry. & Power Co. (now Va. Elec. & Power Co.), 1911-27; gen. mgr. Narragansett Elec. Co., 1927-28; v.p. N.E. Power Assn., 1928-42, and officer or dir. of subsidiaries; pres. and trustee Mass. Utilities Associates, and officer or dir. of subsidiaries, 1928-42; pres., dir. United Illuminating Co., 1942-58, chmn., dir., 1958-66; dir. First Nat. Bank & Trust Co.; trustee Conn. Savs. Bank. Clubs: Quinnipiack, New Haven Lawn, Graduates (New Haven). Home: CT Died Feb. 23, 1966; buried Grove St. Cemetery, New Haven CT

BELLAMAH, JEANNE LEES (MRS. DALE JOHN BELLAMAH), business exec.; b. Pratt, Kans.; d. Clifford and Gladys M. (Jones) Lees; grad. high sch.; m. Dale John Bellamah, June 26, 1939. Sec., treas., dir. Dale Bellamah Rentals. Inc., Hobbs, N.M., 1952-70, Mountain States Investment Corp., N.M., Tex., Colo., 1952-70, Dale Bellamah Land Co., Inc., N.M., Tex., 1954-70, Mountain States Insurers, Inc., N.M., Tex., Colo., 1957-70, Dale J. Bellamah Corp., N.M., Tex., 1958-70, Princess Jeanne Shopping Center, Inc., Albuquerque, 1958-70, Los Altos Shopping Center, Inc., Albuquerque, 1960-70, Princess Jeanne West, Inc., Albuquerque, 1960-70, Northdale Shopping Center, Inc., Albuquerque, 1961-70, Dale Bellamah Homes Tex., Inc., El Paso, Lubbock, Tex., 1961-70, Avalon Homes, Inc., Las Vegas, Nev., 1962-70, Mountain States Life Ins. Co. Am., N.M., Tex., Colo., 1962-70, Eastdale Shopping Center, Inc., Albuquerque, 1963-70, Bellehaven Shopping Center, Inc., Albuquerque, 1965-70, Manzano Shopping Center, Inc., Albuquerque, 1965-70, sec. Skyline Motel Corp., Pueblo, 1966. Pres., All Faiths Receiving Homes, Inc., Albuquerque, 1961-62. Mem. Nat. Assn. Home Builders, Internat. Council Shopping Centers, Mortgage Bankers Assn. Roman Catholic. Clubs: Poco de Dinero (treas. 1965), Green Thumb Garden (treas. 1966), Four Hills Country (Albuquerque). Home: Albuquerque NM Died Apr. 19, 1970.

BELLAMY, FRANCIS RUFUS, author, editor; b. New Rochelle, N.Y., Dec. 24, 1886; s. Rufus W. and Charella (Tappen) B.; Williams Coll., 1904-05; Cornell Univ., 1906; m. Estelle Zimmer; m. 2d, Virginia Mackall (nee Woods), 1927; children—Rufus, Jane; m. 3d, Ruth Fletcher (d); m. 4th, Virginia Woods Bellamy, 1970. Engaged in farming, 1907-11; salesman for Grosset & Dunlap, New York, 1912-15; Washington editor Red Cross Mag., 1917-18; European corr., 1918-19; editor and pub. Outlook Mag., 1927-32; exec. editor New Yorker. 1933; editor and pub. Fiction Parade, Golden Book Mag., 1935-38; editor Scribner's Commentator, 1939-40; pub. relations, pub. cons.; spl. Washington corr. Reader's Digest, 1941-55; pres. University Publishers, Inc. from 1958; director Asso. Coll. Presses, N.Y.U., 1955-58. Member Sigma Phi. Democrat. Mem. Unitarian Ch. Author: The Balance, 1917; A Flash of Gold, 1922; March Winds, 1924; Spanish Faith, 1926; We Hold These Truths, 1942; Blood Money, 1947; The Strange Blooming, 1948; Private Life of George Washington, 1951; Atta, 1953; What About Maisie? (a play, with Ruth Bellamy), 1953; Pledge of Allegiance; A Promise to Our Country, 1961; How to Keep Out of Jail, 1966; also short stories, plays and articles; editor: Conversations Across the Nation, 1954. Home: Castine ME Died Feb. 2, 1972; cremated.

BELLAMY, RAYMOND (FLAVIUS), univ. prof.; born Moorefield, Ind., Oct. 21, 1885; s. Edward Fletcher and Clara (Anderson) B.; A.B., Evansville Coll., 1910; A.M., Clark U., 1913, Ph.D., 1917; m. Laura Cole Brooks, June 15, 1911; children—Raymond Edward, Dorothy Elizabeth (Mrs. G. Doniford Bridges), Mary Eleanor. Instr. physics and chemistry Evansville Coll., 1910-12; prof. edn. and psychology Emory and Henry Coll., 1913-15; prof. sociology and edn. McKendree Coll., 1917-18; prof. sociology and head of dept. Fla. State U. since 1918, retired as head of dept., 1950, now prof. sociology. Awarded Silver Beaver, Boy Scouts of Am., 1943. Mem. Am. Sociol. Soc., A.A.A.S., Southern Sociol Soc. (council mem.; vice pres.), Fla. Acad. Scis. (sec.-treas. 1942-45; pres. 1941-42), Fla. Ednl. Assn., Phi Kappa Phi, Alpha Kappa Delta. Methodist. Co-author: Society Under Analysis, 1942; Social Control, 1947. Contbr. numerous articles to psychol., sociol. and ednl. and lit. jours. Holder patent on gas generator for chem. labs. Home: Tallahassee FL Died July 4, 1970.

BELLATTY, CHARLES E., prof. of advertising; b. Ellsworth, Me., June 4, 1877; s. Charles A. and Carrie L. (Collins) B.; grad. high sch., Ellsworth, 1896; post-grad. course, same, 1897; student journalism, Bowdoin Coll., Brunswick, Me., 1898-1900; advertising course Pilgrim Pub. Assn., Boston, 1911-12; m. Nellie L. Franklin, June 19, 1907; children—Ruth J. (Mrs. Edward D. MacDonald), Elizabeth F. (Mrs. Herbert M. Allen), Barbara P. (Mrs. Ralph T. Smith). Newspaper corr., 1895-98; editor Ellsworth Enterprise, 1900-01; with advertising department, H. B. Humphrey Company of Boston, Mass., 1901-17; dir. Mass. Health Com., 1918-19; counsellor U.S. Vets. Bureau, 1920-25; with Boston U. since 1913, prof. and head of dept. advertising, Coll. of Business Administration, 1919-43, professor emeritus since 1943, instr. house organ editing since 1948; instr. advt., Portland Jr. Coll. Bus. Adminstrn., 1933-38; instructor in advertising, Weylister School, Milford, Conn., since 1936; instr. in advertising through correspondence courses in cooperation with 250 colleges and high schools since 1933; director Advisory Service for Students of Advertising, 1940-46; editor of University Club News, 1927-30; Criticism, Suggestion, and Advice, since 1927; The Business Manager, 1930-31, Simplex Pennant since 1943. Member American Marketing Assn., Society for the Advancement of Edn., Am. Business Writing Assn., Beta Gamma Sigma, Alpha Delta Sigma, Alpha Kappa Psi, Delta Sigma Phi, Zeta Psi. Clubs: Advertising (hon. life mem.), Bowdoin. Wrote corr. course in advertising for Mass. Dept. of Education. Home: 25 Wolcott Rd., Watertown 72 MA‡

BELLINGER, MARTHA FLETCHER, author; b. Alstead, N.H., Apr., 21, 1870; d. Jarvis and Martha Ann (Shaw) Fletcher; grad. Mt. Holyoke Coll., Mass., 1892; m. Franz Bellinger, Ph.D., of New York, July 19, 1898. Author of prize play, A Woman's Sphere," in New York World contest, 1910 (prod. 1911-12, by Henry B. Harris). Author: The Stolen Singer, 1911. Address: 50 Morningside Drive, NY‡

BELLIS, LEON ROBERT, profl. diamond jewelry appraiser; b. Elizavetgrad, Russia, Mar. 25, 1910; s. Harry J. and Rachel (Levinsky) B.; came to U.S., 1923, naturalized, 1928; student U. Pa., 1928-30; m. Bobbye Aronowitz, Oct. 23, 1943; children—Jac, Marlene. Salesman, Pitts. Triangle Co., 1930-42; owner Leon R. Bellis & Co., Wholesale Jewelers, New Orleans, 1945-59; owner Central Appraisal Bur., Chgo., 1959; pres. Central File and Identification Bur., Chgo. Served to 1st lt. AUS, 1942-45. Recipient Gavel for outstanding profl. achievement Am. Soc. Apprisers, 1960, Appreciation award, 1962. Sr. mem. Am. Soc. Appraisers (dir. Ill., past pres. Greater Chgo. chpt.). Mason (Shriner); mem. B'nai B'rith. Author: Too Much for Too Little, Tech. Valuation Mag. Lectr. on secrets of diamond expert; inventor system fingerprinting and indentification diamonds. Chicago IL Died Apr. 5, 1972; buried Montefiore Cemetery, Philadelphia PA

BELLMAN, LAWRENCE STEVENS, architect; b. Toledo, O., Feb. 29, 1876; s. William Henry and Charlotte (Meredith) B.; student Toledo (O.) Manual Training Sch., 1890-94; Certificate of Proficiency, U. of Pa. Sch. of Architecture, 1899; m. Virginia Houston, Dec. 22, 1903; 1dau., Mary Lawrence (dec.). Draftsman with George S. Mills, Toledo, O., 1895-99, designer, 1899-1912; partner Mills, Rhines, Bellman & Nordhoff, Toledo, O., 1912-40, pres., 1940-44; partner Bellman, Gillett & Richards, Toledo, O., 1944-48; retired. Fellow Am. Inst. Architects; mem. Ohio and Mich. socs. architects, Toledo Metropolitan Planning Com., Toledo Chamber of Commerce. Club: Toledo. Home: 828 West Woodruff Av., Toledo, O. and 30 Pueblo Vista, Santa Barbara, Calif. Office: 518 Jefferson Av., Toledo 8 OH‡

BELT, WILLIAM BRADLEY TYLER, b. Richmond, Va., Aug. 1, 1871; s. Thomas H. and Maria (Tyler) B.; ed. Racine (Wis.) Coll.; m. Cecelia Mary Willis, Oct. 11, 1893; 1 dau., Dorothy T. (Mrs. Francis S. Gaines, dec.). Began with Northwestern Bell Telephone Co., 1889, becoming pres., 1919, now retired; president Nat. Security Insurance Co. since 1939; director Northwestern Bell Telephone Company, U.S. Nat. Bank. Mem. Telephone Pioneers of America (past pres.), S.A.R. Episcopalian. Mason (32 deg.). Clubs: Omaha, Omaha Country. Home: 320 S. Elmwood Rd., Omaha NE*‡

BELYAYEV, PAVEL IVANOVICH, cosmonaut; b. Vologada region, USSR, June 26, 1925; grad. Mil. Air Acad.; m. Tatiana Philipovna; children—Irina, Ludmilla. Served as fighter pilot, World War II; now col.; comdr. spaceship Voskhod 2 in two man orbital flight, 1965. Mem. Communist Party. Address: Moscow USSR Died Jan. 1970.*

BEMIS, HAROLD MEDBERRY, naval officer (ret.); b. Oshkosh, Wis., July 15, 1884; s. Eric Eugene and Sarah Elizabeth (Storr) B.; B.S., U.S. Naval Acad., 1906; grad., Naval War Coll., 1934; m. Hazel Haynes, Nov. 20, 1926. Commd. ensign U.S. Navy, Sept. 12, 1906, advanced through grades to rear adm., Jan. 10, 1941; ret. from active service upon reaching statutory retirement age, Aug. 1, 1946; pres. and chmn. of bd., Compania Anonima Venezolana Lummus, Caracas, Venezuela, 1947-53. Awarded D.S.M., Victory medals (World Wars I and II), Am. Defense and Am. Campaign medals, Star of Calderon (Ecuador). Clubs: Army Navy (Washington), Chevy Chase (Md.), Caracas Country, Americano (Venezuela). Home: Washington DC Died Feb. 1970; buried Arlington Nat. Cemetery, Arlington VA

BENCHOFF, ROBERT J(OHNSTON), acad. pres.; b. Woodstock, Va., Feb. 8, 1909; s. Howard Johnston and Kathryn (Mahon) B.; A.B., Franklin and Marshall Coll., 1932; LL.B., Harvard, 1935; m. Jean Rebecca Sine, May 6, 1943; children—Rosalie Jean, Gretchen Rebecca, Robert Johnston II. Asst. headmaster Massanutten Acad., Woodstock, 1935-52, acting headmaster, 1952-54, became headmaster, 1955, pres.; dir. Massanutten Bank of Shenandoah Valley, N.A. Bd. dirs. Am. Symphony Orch. League, Inc.; pres. Shenandoah County Meml. Hosp.; chmn. Shenandoah Valley Music Festival Com., Inc. Comdr., USNR, ret. Mem. Va. Assn. Prep. Schs. (past pres.), Assn. Mil. Colls. and Schs. U.S. (past pres.), Phi Beta Kappa, Kappa Sigma. Mem. United Ch. of Christ. Clubs: Rotary (past pres.), Harvard of Va. Address: Woodstock VA Died May 29, 1968.

BENDA, HARRY JINDRICH, educator; b. Liberec, Czechoslovakia, Oct. 28, 1919; s. Robert and Elisabeth (Frank) B.; B.A., Victoria Univ. Coll., Wellington, New Zealand, 1950; M.A. with 1st class honors, U. New Zealand 1952; Ph.D., Cornell U., 1955; m. Eva Susan Bloch, Apr. 13, 1950; children—Peter Martin, Susan Rebecca. Came to U.S., 1952, naturalized, 1960. Jr. lectr. polit. sci. Victoria Univ. Coll., 1950-52; instr. govt. Cornell U., 1954-55; asst. prof. history U. Rochester, 1955-59; mem. faculty Yale, 1959-71, prof. history, 1966-71; vis. lectr. Fgn. Service Inst., Washington, 1967-71; cons. in field, 1960-71. Founding dir. Inst. S.E. Asian Studies, Singapore, 1968-69. Mem. Am. Hist. Assn., Assn. Asian Studies (bd. dirs. 1967-70), Council Fgn. Relations, Asia Soc., Royal Inst. Linguistics and Anthropology. Author: The Crescent and the Rising Sun: Indonesian Islam During the Japanese Occupation, 1942-45, 1958; also articles. Home: North Haven CT Died Oct. 26, 1971.

BENDER, JACK I., chmn. bd., pres. Blake Constrn. Co. Home: Washington DC Died Dec. 8, 1966.

BENDER, MELVIN T., lawyer; b. Albany, N.Y., Dec. 19, 1877; s. Matthew and Louise (Thomas) B.; student Union Coll., 1900; Ph.B., Albany Law Sch., 1902; m. Katherine Wagoner, June 21, 1904; children—Eleanor, Louise (Mrs. Waldo Dresser). Admitted to N.Y. bar, 1903; gen. counsel N.Y. State Automobile Assn., 1902-36; dir., counsel Albany Automobile Club, 1910-40; atty. Nat. Savs. Bank of Albany since 1928; counsel Socony Vacuum Co., Ry. Express Agy., Guardian Life Ins. Co., Matthew Bender & Co.; trustee Nat. Savs. Bank of Albany. Trustee Albany Acad. for Girls since 1921. Mem. Alpha Delta Phi (former trustee). Mem. First Ch. in Albany (former trustee and v.p. bd. trustees). Club: University (past dir.) (Albany). Home: 108 South Lake Av. Office: 109 State St., Albany 1 NY‡

BENDER, WALTER, business exec.; b. Warsaw, O., 1891. Chairman bd. Gen. Fireproofing Co.; director Ohio Edison Co., 1st Fed. Savs. & Loan, Union Nat. Bank; pres. Asso. Hosp. Service, Inc., Dir., vice pres. Youngstown U., dir. C. of C. Mason. Odd Fellow. Home: Youngstown OH

BENDER, WILBUR JOSEPH, found. exec.; b. Elkhart, Ind., Oct. 15, 1903; s. George Louis and Elsie (Kolb) B.; student Goshen Coll., 1921-23; A.B., Harvard, 1927, A.M., 1931; LL.D. (hon.), Cedar Crest Coll., 1951. Harvard, 1961; m. Laura Bradshaw Fay, June 2, 1934 (dec.); children—Sarah Fay (Mrs. Yglesias), Barbara Fay, David Bowman; m. 2d, Eloise Bergland Wade, February 21, 1964. Tchr., Goshen (Ind.) pub. schs., 1923-25, Northside Sch., Williamstown, Mass., 1927-29; instr. history Harvard, 1931-36, asst. dean, 1931-35, counsellor for vets., 1945-47, dean of coll., 1947-52, dean admissions and financial aids, 1952-60, lectr. history, 1952-60; instr. history Phillips Acad., 1936-42, 44-45; dir. Com. of Permanent Charity Fund, Inc., community found., Boston, 1960-69. Mem. Gov. Mass. Commn. Investigate Crime and Corruption, 1963-65; trustee Mass. Bd. Higher Education. Mem. bd. dirs. United Fund of Greater Boston; vice president, director, Council on Founds.; trustee State Colls. of Mass., Radcliffe Coll., Cambridge, Mass., Phillips Acad., Andover, Charity of Edward Hopkins. Served as lt. (s.g.) USNR, 1943-44. Mem. Am. Assn. U. Profs., Harvard Alumni Assn. (dir.), Phi Beta Kappa. Clubs: Tavern, Thursday Evening, Cambridge. Home: Cambridge MA Died Mar. 31, 1969; buried Phillips Acad. Cemetery, Andover MA

BENDIX, ELLA CROSBY (MRS. ELLA CROSBY BENDIX), educator; b. Spring City, Tenn.; d. James Oliver and Mary Eliza (Darwin) Crosby; B.S., U. Tenn., 1938; M.A., Columbia Tchrs. Coll. 1950; Ph.D., Cornell U., 1958; m. Carlos Magana Bendix, Nov. 22, 1960 (div. Oct. 1966). Tchr. home econs. Glenville, N.C., 1938-39; dir. activities Home Demonstration Clubs and 4H Clubs, Scott and Claiborne counties, Tenn., 1939-42; 1947-49; home econs. adviser USOM, Cochabamba, Bolivia, 1952-55, Rio Grande do Sul, Brazil, 1955-57, Haiti, 1958-60, Chile, 1960-61; prof. home econs. Radford (Va.) Coll., 1965-66; dean Indiana (Pa.) U. Sch. Home Econs., 1967-69. Mem. Am. Home Econs. Assn., Am. Assn. U. Women, Federation Internationale de L'Enseignment. Home: Indiana PA Died July 16, 1969; buried Spring City Cemetery, Spring City TN

BENEDICT, C. HARRY, metallurgist; b. Pittsburgh, Pa., Sept. 24, 1876; s. Joseph and Hannah (Goldsmith) B.; B.S., Cornell U., 1897; D.Sc., Mich. Coll. of Mines, 1932; m. Lena Manson, Feb. 4, 1902; children—Manson, William S. Metallurgist for Calumet & Hecla Consol. Copper Co., 1898-1949; lecturer on hydro-metallurgy, Mich. Coll. of Mines, since 1919; mem. bd. control Mich. Coll. Mines and Metall. since 1952. Mem. Am. Inst. Mining and Metall. Engrs. (v.p. 1948-51, director, 1952-—; recipient of Robert H. Richards Award, 1954), Mining and Metall. Soc. Am. (dir. 1947), Am. Chem. Soc., Am. Inst. Chem. Engring. Democrat. Jewish religion. Mason. Author: Red Metal. Inventor of ammonia bleaching process for copper. Home: Lake Linden MI‡

BENEDICT, COOPER PROCTER, ex-govt. ofcl.; b. Glendale, O., Feb. 16, 1907; s. Cleveland Keith and Olivia (Procter) B.; grad. Hill Sch., 1925; B.A., Princeton, 1929; m. Laura De Lamater, Apr. 14, 1934; children—Cleveland Keith, Elizabeth Hasbrouck. Advt. dept. Procter & Gamble Co., 1930-49; advt. dir. Thomas Hedley & Co., Ltd., Brit. subsidiary Procter & Gamble Co., 1945-49; dep. asst. sec. def., properties and installations, Washington, 1958-61; owner and operator farm. Mem. W.Va. Republican Finance Com., 1952-53, vice chmn., 1963-64, chmn., 1964; Rep. candidate for U.S. Ho. of Reps. from 2d dist. of W.Va., 1962, for U.S. Senate, 1964. Episcopalian. Rotarian. Club: W.Va. Press (Charleston). Home: Lewisburg WV Died June, 1968.

BENEDICT, GEORGE WYLLYS, university prof.; b. Burlington, Vt., Jan. 12, 1872; s. George Grenville and Katharine Almira (Pease) B.; A.B., U. of Vt., 1893; U. of Freiburg, 1895-6; A.M., Harvard, 1897, Ph.D., 1899; m. Jane Lois Simpson, of Burlington, Vt., Dec. 27, 1899. Instr. English, Phillips Acad., Andover, Mass., 1893-5; instr. English, 1899-1901, asst. prof., 1901-6, asso. prof. since 1906, Brown U. Mem. Sigma Phi (Alpha of Vt.), Loyal Legion. Clubs: University, Metacomet Golf. Address: 16 John St., Providence RI‡

BENEDICT, SAMUEL DURLIN, clergyman; b. Poynette, Wis., May 15, 1871; s. Samuel Serenus and Debbie Desire (Brayton) B.; A.B., Hillsdale (Mich.) Coll., 1904; LL.B., Kent Coll. of Law, Chicago, 1907; student Western Theol. Sem., Chicago, D.D., Volant (Pa.) Coll., 1906; LL.D., Morris-Brown Coll., Atlanta, Ga., 1908, Norwich U., 1909; Dr. Bio-Psychology, Taylor Sch. of Bio-Psychology, Chattanooga, Tenn., 1926; unmarried. Ordained priest Evangelical Catholic Ch. (Old Catholic Ch.), 1903; consecrated bishop 1921; elected archbishop and primate, 1926. Founder and grand chief templar Ancient Order Christian Templars; founder and internat. pres. Internat. Order Christian Latols. Mem. bar Supreme Court of U.S., also supreme court of Ind. and Calif. Address: PO Box 643, New York NY‡

BENEDICT, WAYNE LECLAIRE, lawyer; b. Geneva, Neb., June 2, 1906; s. Carl M. and Lila (Plantz) B.; A.B., U. Neb., 1927; J.D., DePaul U., 1943; m. Edyth Emerson, Aug. 23, 1951. Research chemist Universal Oil Products Co., 1928-38, asst. mgr. patent dept., 1938-44; admitted to Ill. bar, 1943, D.C. bar, 1949; practice in Danville, Ill., 1944-48, Washington, 1948-71; mem. firm Burns, Doane, Benedict, Swecker & Mathis, 1948-71; specializing in patent, trade mark, unfair competition. Mem. Am. Bar Assn., Bar Assn. D.C., American Judicature Association, Am. Patent Law Association, Am. Chem. Soc., A.A.A.S. Home: Silver Spring MD Died June 19, 1971.

BENEDIKTSSON, BJARNL, prime minister Iceland; b. Reykjavik, Iceland, Apr. 30, 1908; s. Benedikt Sveinsson and Gudrun (Petursdottir) B.; LL.B., U. of Iceland, 1930; student constitutional law, Berlin, 1930-32; m. Sigridur Bjornsdottir (dec. July 10, 1970). Prof. of law U. of Iceland, 1932-40; mayor of Reykjavik, 1940-47; mem. of Parliament from 1942; del. to UN gen. assemblies, 1946-48-49; mem. Central Com., Ind. Party 1936-70, chmn., 1961-70; chmn. Fgn. Affairs Com., 1946-47; minister for Foreign Affairs, 1947-53; minister for justice and edn., 1953-56, chief editor Morgunbladied 1956-59; minister for justice and industries, 1959-63; prime minister Iceland, 1963-70. Died July 10, 1970.

BENIOFF, HUGO, scientist; b. Los Angeles, Sept. 14, 1899; s. Simon and Alfrieda (Widerquist) Hamilton B.; B.A., Pomona Coll., 1921; Ph.D., Cal. Inst. Tech., 1935; m. Alice Silverman, Feb. 27, 1928; children—Paul, Dagmar (Mrs. E. Friedman), Elena (Mrs. Richard Slusser); m. 2d, Mildred Lent, Oct. 31, 1953; 1 dau., Martha Gwen. Asst. Mt. Wilson Obs., 1917-21, seismol. research Carnegie Inst. Washington 1923-24; staff seismol. lab. Cal. Inst. Tech., 1934-68, prof. 1950-64, seismology prof. emeritus, 1964-68; research engr. Submarine Signal Co., 1939-45, Baldwin Piano Co., 1946-62; mem. Ad Hoc Group on Detection Nuclear Explosions; mem. panel on seismic improvement Dept. State; mem. adv. com. for geophysics Air Force Office Sci. Research; chmn. cons. bd. for earthquake analysis Cal. Dept. Water Resources; consultant, Nat. Sci. Found., 1953; research on stress strain characteristics and structure of earth's crust. Recipient Arthur L. Day award Geol. Soc. America; William Bowie medal Am. Geophysical Union, 1965. Fellow Am. Academy of Arts Science, A.A.A.S., Geological Soc. Am.; mem. Nat. Acad. Sci., Am. Phys. Soc., Acoustical Soc. Am., Am. Geophys. Union, Seismol. Soc. Am., Royal Astron. Soc., Phi Beta Kappa. Patentee seismographs. Home: Mendocino CA Died Feb. 29, 1968; buried Mendocino CA

BENJAMIN, A. CORNELIUS, prof. philosophy; b. Grand Rapids, Mich., Aug. 25, 1897; s. Cornelius Adrian and Anna (De Baum) B.; student Grand Rapids (Mich.) Jr. Coll., 1916-18; A.B., U. Mich., 1920 A.M., 1921, Ph.D., 1924; student Sorbonne U., 1930, Cambridge U., 1931; m. Katharine May Loomis, Mar. 29, 1923. Asst. in mathematics U. of Mich. 1920-21, asst. in philosophy, 1921-22, fellow, 1922-23; asst. in philosophy, U. of Ill., 1923-24, instr., 1924-26, asso., 1926-28, asst. prof. philosophy 1928-32; Guggenheim fellow, 1930-31; asst. prof. philosophy U. of Chicago, 1932-43, asso. prof., 1943-45; John Hiram Lathrop prof. philosophy U. Mo. at Columbia, 1945-66, prof. emeritus philosophy, 1966-68, chmn. of department, 1945-56; vis. prof. philosophy Baylor U., Spring 1961; editorial bd. Philosophy of Science, 1941-68. Fellow A.A.A.S.; member Western Division Am. Philos. Association (sec.-treas. 1934-36, vice pres. 1942-45, pres. 1947-48, chmn. nat. bd. of officers 1948), Am. Assn. Univ. Professors, Philosophy of Sci. Assn., Mo. Philos. Assn. (pres. 1948-49), Southwestern Philos. Conf., Alpha Pi Zeta, Sigma Xi. Author: Logical Structure of Science (Kegan Paul, London, Eng., 1936), Introduction to the Philosophy of Science 1937; Operationism, 1955; Science, Technology and Human Values, 1965; contbr. to profl. and tech. publs. Home: Columbia MO Died Oct. 19, 1968.

BENNARD, GEORGE, evangelist; b. Youngstown, O., Feb. 4, 1873; s. George and Margaret (Russell) B.; ed. pub. schs.; m. Araminta Behler, of Greencastle, Pa., Feb. 25, 1895; children—Zoe (dec.), Fay George, John Paul. Apptd. officer Salvation Army, 1892, interdenom. evangelist, U.S. and Can., since 1907; became connected with faculty of Chicago Evangelistic Inst., in city mission work and evangelism, 1912. Republican. Methodist. Composer and compiler: Heart and Life Songs, 1912; Sweet Songs of Salvation, 1915; Divine Praise, 1928; Bernard's Melodies, 1930; The Story of the Old Rugged Cross, 1931; Full Redemption Songs, 1933. Home: Hermosa Beach, Calif. Address: Albion MI‡

BENNER, RAYMOND CALVIN, chemist; b. Minneapolis, Minn., May 13, 1877; s. Webster and Clara Ellen (Hoak) B.; B.S. in chemistry, U. of Minn., 1902; M.A., U. of Wis., 1906, Ph.D., 1909; m. Lillian Brownell Stebbins, of Minneapolis, June 8, 1908; children—Eleanore, Priscilla, Mary. Instr. Mich. Agrl. Coll., 1902-03; U. of Wis., 1903-06; asst. prof. chemistry, U. of Ariz., 1906-11; prof. electrometallurgy, U. of Pittsburgh, 1911-13; dir. Fremont (O.) Labs. of the Nat. Carbon Co., 1913-25; research engr. Gen. Chemical Co., N.Y. City, 1925-26; dir. research, Carborundum Co., Niagara Falls, N.Y., since 1926. Chemist Wis. Geol. Survey, 1903-06; in charge of smoke investigation, Pittsburgh, 1911-13; mem. U.S. Assay Commn., 1912-13. Mem. Am. Chem. Soc., A.A.A.S., Am. Inst. Mining and Metall. Engrs., Am. Ceramic Soc., British Ceramic Soc., Am. Refractories Inst., Alpha Chi Sigma, Acacia, Chemists' Club (New York); Niagara Falls Chamber of Commerce. Mason. Democrat. Conglist. Contbr. many articles on metall. and tech. subjects. Granted over 200 patents in field of chemistry. Home: 640 College Av., Niagara Falls NY‡

BENNER, WALTER MEREDITH, constrn. engr.; b. Belle Plaine, Ia., June 26, 1907; s. Ira G. and Mable (Falls) B.; student Belle Plaine Bus. Coll., 1926, Poly. Tech., Long Beach, 1927-30; m. Edna Alice Butcher, Dec. 26, 1928; 1 dau., Dolores Mae. Surveyor Stone & Webster Engring. Co., Boston, 1927-33, constrn., 1935-47; project engr., irrigation supt., Central Pub. Power and Irrigation Dist., Holdrege, Neb., 1947-67. Registered profl. engr., Neb. Mason (32 degree). Presbyn. Address: Holdrege NB Died June 22, 1967.

BENNERS, AUGUSTUS, lawyer; b. Greensboro, Ala., May 13, 1872; s. Alfred Hatch and Margaret Chadwick (Jones) B.; B.A., Southern U., Greensboro, 1891; studied law pvtly.; unmarried. Admitted to Ala. bar, 1893; practiced at Birmingham since 1893; sr. partner Benners, Burr, McKamy & Forman since 1917; firm counsel for Tenn. Coal, Iron & R.R. Co., Am. Steel & Wire Co., Am. Bridge Co., Republic Steel Co., Bessemer Coal, Iron & Land Co., Ala. Fuel & Iron Co., I.C. R.R., Birmingham Southern R.R. and many other corps.; dir. Birmingham Southern R.R. Mem. Ala. State and Birmingham bar assns., Kappa Alpha. Democrat. Episcopalian. Clubs: Mountain Brook Country, Birmingham Country. Home: 2762 Hanover Circle. Office: Brown-Marx Bldg., Birmingham AL‡

BENNETT, ALBERT ARNOLD, mathematician, b. Yokohama, Japan, June 2, 1888; s. Albert Arnold and Mela Isabelle (Barrows) B.; came to U.S. in 1902; A.B., A.M., Brown Univ., 1910, Sc.M., 1911; Ph.D., Princeton, 1915; studied univs. of Paris, Gottingen, Bologna and Chicago; m. Velma McAfee Ely, June 17, 1922; one daughter, Betsy Bennett Miller. Instructor Princeton Univ., 1914-16; adj. professor U. of Tex., 1916-21, asso. prof., 1921-25; prof. and head of dept., Lehigh U., 1925-27; prof. mathematics, Brown U., from 1927. Editor in chief, Math. Monthly, 1923; mathematics editor Prentice-Hall, Inc. Student 1st O.T.C., Leon Springs, Tex., and Ft. Monroe, Va.; commd. capt. C.A.R.C., Aug. 15, 1917; trans. to ordnance, June 1918; hon. discharged Jan. 15, 1919; mathematics and dynamics expert, Ordnance Corps, June 1919-Sept. 1921; maj. Ordnance Corps, A.U.S., 1942-46, lt. col., 1946. Member Am. Math. Soc., Math. Assn. America (trustee 1922, v.p. 1925, 33), Am. Academy Arts and Sciences, Progressive Edn. Assn. (adv. council, 1933), A.A.A.S., Am. Assn. Univ. Profs., Am. Soc. Engring. Education, Assn. Computing Machines, Assn. Symbolic Logic (council), 1935, Assn. Teachers Math. New England (president 1941), Nat. Council Teachers of Math., Institute Math. Statistics, Rhode Island Sch. Design (Corp. mem.), Phi Beta Kappa, Sigma Xi, Delta Upsilon. Author: Introduction to Ballistic (Ordnance Dept. U.S.A.), 1921; Tables for Interior Ballistics (same), 1922; (with C.A. Baylis) Formal Logic, 1939. Address: Providence RI Died Feb. 17, 1971.

BENNETT, ANDREW CARL, naval officer; b. Goodland, Kan.; s. Andrew Pierce and Harriet Winefred (Kirkpatrick) B.; grad. U.S. Naval Acad., 1912; past grad. student various service schools; m. Jessie Crawford Biggam, Oct. 16, 1920; children—Betty Duff (wife of Lt. Donald Francis Banker, U.S.N.), Anne Douglas (wife of Lt. Charles Francis Helme, Jr., U.S.N.). Commd. ensign, U.S. Navy, 1912, advancing to rear adm., 1942; comd. submarines and submarine units, 24 yrs. also served in battleships and cruisers; comd. U.S.S. Savannah (light cruiser), 1940-42; unit comdr., Oran, Algeria, area of invasion of North Africa, Nov. 8, 1942; comdt. 8th Naval Dist., hdqrs. in New Orleans, La. since 1943. Decorated Navy Cross, also 6 campaign medals (U.S.); Legion of Honor (France). Mason (32 deg., Scottish Rite, Shriner). Clubs: Army-Navy Country (Washington, D.C.); Boston (New Orleasn, La). Home: Carmel CA Died 1972.

BENNETT, ARTHUR ELLSWORTH, clergyman; b. Elgin, Ill., Dec. 5, 1865; s. Charles Wesley and Sarah Jane (Clark) B.; B.S., Kan. Normal Coll., 1889, A.B., 1890; Pd.M., Normal Sch. of N.M., 1898; Pd.D., New York Univ., 1905; LL.D., Upper Iowa U., 1936; m. Mary Ann Steeley, Sept. 1, 1891; 1 son, Rev. A. Vincent. Prin. public schools, Wheatland, N.D., 1885-88; supt. schs., Lisbon, N.D., 1891-92; supervisor of teacher training, Kan. Normal Coll., 1892-95; v.p. Normal Sch. of N.M., 1895-99; dean Sch. of Edn., Upper Ia. U., 1899-1913; dean Highland Park Coll., 1913-16, Des Moines Coll., 1917-18; prof. ednl. psychology and dir. extension div. Sch. Religious Edn., Boston U., 1918-25; dean education, Des Moines Univ., 1925-31; pres. Upper Iowa U., 1931-36; pastor Immanuel Meth. Ch., Des Moines, since 1936. Lecturer and conductor teachers inst., commencement orator. Fellow Am. Genetic Society; mem. N.E.A., Pi Kappa Delta, Sigma Nu. Republican. Methodist. Mason, Odd Fellow. Author: The Rational Method in Geography, 1917; Laboratory‡

BENNETT, CHARLES WILBUR, former pres. Am. Sheet and Tin Plate Co.; b. Sylvester, Wis., Aug. 9, 1870; s. James Rush and Emily Adelaide B.; U. of Wis., 1888-92; m. Eleanore Robertson Park; 1 dau., Helen Adelaide (Mrs. King R. H. Nelson). Began as worker Marinette Iron Works, West Duluth, Minn., 1892; mech. dept., World's Columbian Expn., 1893; with Ill. Steel Co., Joliet, 1894-96; with Am. Tin Plate Co., Elwood, Indiana, from 1897, and Am. Sheet and Tin Plate Co., Pittsburgh, Pa., from 1906 until retirement, 1936, was pres. of both cos. Republican. Mason. Clubs: Duquesne, Pittsburgh Athletic, University, Pittsburgh Country, Fox Chapel Golf. Home: 119 Hoodridge Drive, Mt. Lebanon, Pa. Office: Frick Bldg., Pittsburgh PA‡

BENNETT, CLARENCE F., ex-chmn., The Stanley Works; b. New Milford, Conn., May 13, 1872; s. Franklin and Almira (Hine) B.; ed. pub. schs.; m. Blanche Elizabeth Hellyar, July 18, 1907; children—Marian, Helen. Began with The Stanley Works, mfrs. tools and hardware, New Britain, Conn., 1891, pres., 1923-40, later chmn. bd.; North & Judd Mfg. Co.; trustee New Britain Trust Co. Republican. Conglist. Clubs: New Britain, Shuttle Meadow. Now retired. Home: New Britain CT‡

BENNETT, DONALD MENZIES, educator, b. Milw., Nov. 24, 1897; s. William Chase and Jean Louise (Menzies) B.; B.A., U. Wis., 1921, M.A., 1922, Ph.D., 1926; m. Irene Marie Schubring, Aug. 7, 1922; 1 son Robert Menzies. Asst. physics U. Wis., 1920-22, 24-26; instr. U. Colo., 1922-24; asst. prof. physics U. Louisville, 1926-29, asso. prof., 1929-44, professor heading engineering physics, 1944-56, acting head department of physics, College of Arts and Sciences, 1953-56; head, 1956; technical aide to dir. radiation lab. Mass. Inst. Tech., 1944; research participant Oak Ridge Nat. Labs., 1950. Regional counseler in physics for Kentucky. Member Louisville Engring. and Sci. Socs. Council (v.p.

1953-55), Ky. Assn. Physics Tchrs. (past pres.), Am. Phys. Soc., Am. Acoustical Soc., A.A.A.S., American Association University Professors, Kentucky Academy of Science, American Assn. Physics Teachers, Phi Beta Kappa, Sigma Xi, Sigma Tau, Phi Mu Alpha, Kappa Delta Pi, Sigma Pi Sigma, Phi Kappa Phi, Alpha Epsilon Delta. Club: Torch (pres. 1956-57) (Louisville, Ky.). Author: Fundamentals of Physics, 1936; Physical Basis of Music, 1956. Home: Louisville KY Died Nov. 7, 1971; inurned Columbarium, Resthaven Meml. Park and Cemetery, Louisville KY

BENNETT, EUGENE DUNLAP, lawyer; b. Newton Kan.; s. Dr. George Dunlap and Nellie (Akin) B.; LL.B. Hastings Coll. Law, U. Cal., 1920; m. Gertrude Douglass, Dec. 29, 1926. Practiced law, San Francisco, 1920-68; partner Pillsbury, Madison & Sutro, 1936-68; chief dep. U.S. atty. No. Dist. Cal., 1925-27; counsel Cal. Dept. Fish and Game, 1927-33; civilian aide to sec. of army, 1950-68. Mem. U.S. Commn. on Jud. and Congl. Salaries, 1953-54; chmn. U.S. sect. Inter-Am. Tropical Tuna Commn.; commr. Pacific Marine Fisheries Commn., 1948-59; nat. trustee Ducks Unlimited. Served as 1st lt. Inf. World War I, col. inf., World War II. Fellow Cal. Acad. Scis. (trustee 1950-67), Am. Coll. Trial Lawyers; mem. Am. (chmn. sect. internat. and comparative law 1961-62), Cal., San Francisco bar assns., National Rifle Association (dir.), Am. Bar Foundation, American Judicature Society (director 1959-64), Am. Legion. Clubs: Pacific Union, St. Francis Yacht, Olympic, Press, Union League, Commonwealth, Stock Exchange (San Francisco). Home: San Francisco CA Died Dec. 16, 1968; buried Cypress Lawn Meml. Park, Colma CA

BENNETT, HARRIET, mgr. Congressional Information Bur.; b. Rome, Ga., Feb. 7, 1871; d. William A. and Harriet J. Tubbs; grad. Rome Female Coll., 1888; m. Henry T. Graves, of Ga.; children—Katharine, Harriet; m. 2d, Claude Nathaniel Bennett, of Washington, June 30, 1915 (died June 13, 1926). Mem. D.A.R., U.D.C. Clubs: Women's City, Arts, Southern Soc. of Washington, Washington Readers Club. Home: 2227 20th St. N.W., Washington DC‡

BENNETT, JAMES WILLIAM, JR., educator; b. Asheville, N.C., July 20, 1920; s. James William and Noreen (Alexander) B.; A.B., Maryville (Tenn.) Coll., 1941; M.S., U. Tenn., 1950; Ph.D., U. Fla., 1955; m. Ruth Maxine Russell, June 10, 1942; children—James William III, Keith R. With Aluminum Co. Am., 1941-42, Tenn. Eastman Corp., 1946-49; instr. Auburn U., 1950-51; prof., head marketing and transp. econs. faculty U. Tenn., 1952-72. Served with AUS, 1942-45. Mem. Am. Soc. Traffic and Transp. (dir. edn., bd. dirs.) So. Econ. Assn. Home: Maryville TN Died July 31, 1972; buried Grandview Cemetery, Maryville TN

BENNETT, LAWRENCE, lawyer; b. Lincoln, Neb., June 1, 1888; s. Charles Edwin and Margaret Gale (Hitchcock) B.; A.B., Cornell U., 1909; LL.B. cum laude, Harvard, 1912; m. Edith Pine, Oct. 15, 1924; 1 son, John Pine. Admitted to N.Y. bar, 1912, since practiced in N.Y.C.; partner Milbank, Tweed, Hadley & McCloy, and predecessors, from 1922. Dir. Gen. Telephone Co., 1935-39, Nat. Fuel Gas Co., 1938-43. Mem. Cornell University Council, 1950-60. Fellow American Bar Foundation; member of American, New York State bar assns., Am. Law Institute, Bar Association of the City N.Y., Phi Beta Kappa, Delta Upsilon. Clubs: University, Century Assn. (N.Y.C.); Silver Spring Country (Ridgefield, Conn.). Home: Ridgefield CT Died May 15, 1970.

BENNETT, MELBA BERRY (MRS. FRANK HENRY BENNETT), author, civic leader; b. Los Angeles, Aug. 2, 1901; d. William Henry and Edna (Bush) Berry; student Stanford, 1922; m. Frank Henry Bennett, May 11, 1921; children—Clarence J., Ethel Deborah (Mrs. Ralph B. Busch, Jr.). Lectr. lit. and politics to profl. groups and students, 1935-70. Chmn. nurses aid service Torney Gen. Hosp., Palm Springs, Cal., 1943-46, recipient award, 1945; chmn. U.S.O., 1942-45, recipient award, 1945; mem. Palm Springs Sch. Bd., 1948-57. Mem. Riverside County Republican Central Com., 1949-59. Trustee, Welwood Murray Meml. Library, Palm Springs, 1950-64; bd. dirs. Child Devel. Center, 1967; exec. com. Occidental Coll. Library, 1967-70, Recipient plaque for war service Ferrying Command, 1944; also recipient Award of Merit, 1966; Lit. award Commonwealth Club of Cal., 1966. Mem. Palm Springs Hist. Soc. (pres. nat. council), Alpha Phi. Republican. Episcopalian. Author: Robinson Jeffers and the Sea, 1936; Often I Wonder, 1939; In Review, 1946; Palm Springs Garden Book, 1957; Famous Libraries of Europe, 1958, 59, 64, 66, 67, 68; The Stone Mason of Tor House, 1966. Editor: Robinson Jeffers Quar. News Letter. Home: Palm Springs CA Died 1970.

BENNETT, RAWSON, cons. engr.; b. Chgo., June 16, 1905; s. Rawson and Cora A. (Jones) B.; B.S., U.S. Naval Acad., 1927; M.S. in Elec. Engring., U. Cal., 1937; m. Mary F. Wyman, 1931 (dec.); children—Rawson, Sally Ann; m. 2d, A. Louise Holmes, 1949; children—Holmes, Gregory. Commd. ensign USN, 1927, advanced through grades to rear adm., 1956; electronics dir. design Bur. Ships, 1943-46; comdg. officer, dir. Navy Electronics Lab., San Diego, Cal., 1946-50; dir. electronics prodn. resources Dept. Def., 1950-51; head minesweeping Bur. Ships, 1951-53, asst. chief electronics, 1954-56; chief of Naval Research, Washington, 1956-61; sr. v.p., dir. engring. Sangamo Electric Co., Springfield, Ill., 1961-63; cons. engr., 1963-69; dir. Washington Assos., Inc. Registered profl. engr., Cal. Fellow A.A.A.S., Am. Inst. Aeros. and Astronautics, I.E.E.E., Arlington VA Died Dec. 8, 1968.

BENNETT, W(ILLIAM) R(EECE), Dem. Nat. Committeeman; b. Jasper, Tenn., Nov. 28, 1875; s. William Merritt and Nancy (Hicks) B.; student Pryor Inst., Jasper, Tenn., 1888-94, also business colls.; m. Lora Lankester, July 30, 1894; children—Edwin Keith, William Reece, Margaret Lankester (Mrs. M. Murray Orinstein). Began as stenographer, Chattanooga, Tenn., 1894; became clerk Q.M. Dept., U.S. Army, Puerto Rico, 1898; made disbursing officer Legislative Assembly of Puerto Rico, 1903; apptd. sec. to Exec. Council of P.R., 1905; owner of photograph supply store, 1907-11; apptd. U.S. marshal, Dist. of P.R., 1915, and chief of police of P.R., 1922; went into real estate and ins. business, P.R., 1924; became merchant, 1934, now mgr. Union Mutual Life Ins. Co. of Portland, Me.; prin. owner Palm Beach Store, San Jaun P.R.; pres. Swiggett, Inc., Miramar Apt. House Co. Dem. Nat. Committeeman for P.R. 1940-71. Mem. Union Club, San Juan. San Juan PR Died Oct. 20, 1971.

BENNETT, WILLIAM RAINEY, clergyman, lecturer; b. Cynthiana, Ind., Mar. 22, 1869; s. William Thomas and Martha Emily (Carter) B.; A.B., Union Christian Coll., Merom, Ind., 1893; studied U. of Chicago; B.D., Chicago Theol. Sem., 1898; m. Ethel Clark of Clarinda, Ia., Oct. 27, 1897; children—Martha King, Wendell C., Wm. Rainey. Ordained Congl. ministry, 1898; pastor Darlington, Wis., 1898-1903, Temple Ch., Marion, Ind., 1904-09; pastor Liberal Ch., Elgin, Ill., since 1927; lyceum lecturer on business and edn. Mem. Internat. Lyceum and Chautauqua Assn. Republican. Author: Fighting Blood That Wins. Home: Elgin, Ill. Office: Kimball Bldg., Chicago IL‡

BENNION, MILTON, teacher; b. Taylorsville, Utah, June 7, 1870; s. John and Mary T. (Turpin) B.; B.Sc., U. of Utah, 1897; student U. of Chicago, 1898; M.A., Columbia, 1901, U. of Wis., 1912-13, Univ. of Calif., 1924; hon. Ed.D., U. of Utah, 1931; m. Cora Lindsay, June 22, 1898; children—Claire (Mrs. Wm. L. Jones), Maurine (Mrs. E.L. Folsom), Milton Lindsay, Wayne Lindsay (dec.), Lowell Lindsay, Ruth (dec.), Grant Madison, Frances (Mrs. Elmo R. Morgan), Margaret (dec.), Vaughn Lindsay. Principal Southern Branch Utah State Normal School, 1897-1900; assistant professor education, University of Utah, 1901-02; asst. professor philosophy same, 1902-04, prof. since 1904, and dean Sch. of Edn., July 2, 1913-July 1941, vice pres., 1940-41. Mem. State Bd. of Edn., Utah, 1898-1900. General superintendent L.D.S. Sunday Schools, 1943-49; editorial writer The Instructor since 1949. Chairman Utah State Welfare Commn., 1921-23; chmn. com. on character edn., Nat. Council of Education and N.E.A. (1921-25); chmn. Group D, Internat. Ideals, World Conf. on Edn., San Francisco, 1923. Fellow A.A.A.S.; mem. N.E.A. (life), Nat. Council of Edn. (1915-39), Western Philos. Assn., Phi Kappa Phi, Phi Delta Kappa. Independent. Mormon. Author: Citizenship, An Introduction to Social Ethics, 1917, revised edit., 1925; Moral Teachings of the New Testament, 1928; Revised edition 1945. New Frontiers for American Youth, 1939. Home: 2391 Seventh East St., Salt Lake City 6. Office: 50 N. Main St., Salt Lake City 1 UT‡

BENNION, SAMUEL OTIS, editor; b. Taylorsville, Utah, June 9, 1874; s. John R. and Emma Jane (Terry) B.; ed. pub. schs., Taylorsville; m. Charlotte Towler, Aug. 25, 1898; children—Burvidge Donald, Donetta (Mrs. Robert F. Hilton). Missionary of Mormon Ch., Independence, Mo. (Central States Mission), mission term 1904-34; presiding officer of mission for 6 states, 1906-34; editor and business mgr. Deseret News since April 1934; mem. exec. com. of bd. of dirs. Deseret Book Store; mem. First Council of Seventy (gen. authority of Ch. of Jesus Christ of Latter-Day Saints). Dir. Provo Reservoir Water Users Co., Utah; pres. Utah Lake Distributing Canal Co.; membership dir. Bennion Sheep & Ranch Co., Cokeville, Wyo. Mem. Salt Lake City Chamber of Commerce (bd. govs. 1935-38), Salt Lake City Exec. Com. Boy Scouts; former v.p. Independence, Mo., Chamber of Commerce (twice). Republican. Clubs: Rotary, Knife and Fork. Home: 1759 Yalecrest Av. Office: 47 East South Temple, Salt Lake City UT*‡

BENSON EMANUEL MERVYN, art educator; born N.Y.C., Oct. 22, 1904; s. Aaron and Ida (Halpern) B.; B.A., Dartmouth, 1927, M.A., Columbia, 1928; m. Gertrude Ackerman Rothchild, May 30, 1930; children—Sheila (Mrs. Leslie Okin), Jonathan M. Writer for newspapers, periodicals, 1927-35; asso. editor Magazine of Art, 1933-38; chief div. edn. Phila. Museum Art., 1936-53; dean Phila. Museum Coll. of Art, 1953-65; senior researcher New York University, from 1965. Mem. N.E.A., Com. Art. Edn. Author: Problems of Portraiture, 1936; John Marin: The Man and His Work, 1935; also publs. issued by museums. Home: East Hampton NY Died June 1, 1971.

BENSON, GEORGE EDWARD, v.p., treas. Youngstown Sheet & Tube Co.; b. Pittsburgh, Apr. 26, 1875; s. Robert and Mary (Burgess) B.; ed. high sch.; m. Nellie Ackerman, Jan. 2, 1906. Credit mgr. Nat. Tube Co., Pittsburgh, 1909-12, treas., 1912-23; v.p. Union Trust Co., Pittsburgh, 1923-30; v.p., treas. Youngstown (O.) Sheet & Tube Co. 1932-47; also officer various subsidiaries; ret., 1947; now pub. relations exec. Union National Bank of Youngstown. Republican. Presbyterian. Clubs: Duquesne (Pittsburgh); Youngstown. Home: 291 Park Av., Youngstown OH‡

BENSON, HENRY KREITZER, indsl. chemist; b. Lebanon, Pa., Jan. 3, 1877; s. William Frank and Catherine (Kreitzer) B.; A.B., Franklin and Marshall Coll., Lancaster, Pa., 1899, A.M., 1902, D. Sci., same coll., 1926; studied Johns Hopkins Univ., 1903-04; Ph.D., Columbia Univ., 1907; m. Eva A. Ronald, June 15, 1905; children—William Ronald, Margaret Elizabeth, Henry K., Betty. Prof. indsl. chemistry and chemical engineering, U. of Washington, 1905-47, professor emeritus since 1947; dir. research, I. L. Loucks' Laboratories, Inc., Seattle, 1949; former administrative head chem. dept. With U.S. Bureau of Soils, 3 summers; with U.S. Bur. Foreign and Domestic Commerce, as comml. agent, 1914, studying lumber by-products; state dir. with U.S. Naval Advisory Bd., 1916. Served as capt. research sect. of nitrogen div. of Army Ordnance, July 6, 1918-Feb. 20, 1919. Chmn. div. chemistry and chem. technology, Nat. Research Council, Washington, D.C., 1931-32. Del. Internat. Chem. Conf., Rome, Italy, 1938; chmn. Washington State Chemurgic Com. since 1942; Mem. Tech. Assn. of the Pulp Paper Industry, Am. Chem. Soc., Am. Inst. Chem. Engrs., Am. Legion (dist. comdr. 1923), Sigma Xi, Tau Kappa Epsilon, Phi Lambda Upsilon. Republican. Mem. Congl. Ch. Mason. Author: Industrial Chemistry, 1913; By-Products of the Lumber Industry, 1915; Chemical Utilization of Wood, 1932; Potential Chemical Industries of Washington, 2 vols., 1936. Contbr. of some 90 articles to tech. jours. Home: 6027 Princeton Av., Seattle 5 WA‡

BENSON, HENRY PERKINS, cotton waste mcht.; b. Salem, Mass., Dec. 30, 1866; s. George W. and Elizabeth F. (Poole) B.; student Salem (Mass.) High Sch., 1881-85; Mass. Inst. Tech., 1885-86; m. Rebecca A. Brodhead, Jan. 11, 1893; children—Rosamond (Mrs. James J. Storrow), Ruth (Mrs. John Pickering), Rebecca (Mrs. Paul T. Haskell). Asso. with A. Emerson Co., cotton waste mchts., Boston, Mass., since 1886, pres. and dir. since 1917; dir. Sweetland Waste Co.; director of the Naumkeag Steam Cotton Co.; dir. and mem. exec. com. Naumkeag Trust Co. Served as mem. City Council, Salem, Mass., 1902-03, Bd. of Health, 1905, alderman, 1906-12, mayor, 1916-17. Trustee Salem Hosp. Republican. Episcopalian. Clubs: Union, Eastern Yacht (Boston); Billiard (Salem). Home: 7 Hamilton St., Salem, Mass. Office: 48 Franklin St., Boston MA‡

BENSON, SALLY, author, playwright; b. St. Louis, Sept. 3, 1900. Author or co-author screenplays: Shadow of a Doubt; Anna and the King of Siam, 1946; Come to the Stable, 1949; No Man of Her Own, 1950, others. Author books: Junior Miss; Meet Me in St. Louis, others. Contbr. short stories popular mags. Died July 19, 1972.

BENSON, WILBUR EARLE, univ. dean; b. Wakefield, Va., Aug. 3, 1921; s. Richard Henry and Ada (King) B.; A.B., George Washington U., 1951, M.B.A., 1952, Ph.D., 1960; student Inst. Chartered Financial Analysts, 1967-69; m. Margaret Elizabeth Benson, Feb. 9, 1946; children—Alan Earle, Janet Marie, Robert Gordon. Asst. prof. George Washington U., 1952-60; asso. prof. U. Ga., 1960-65; prof., asso. dean Fla. Atlantic U., 1965-68; prof., dean U. Akron, 1968-70; prof., dean Clarkson Coll. Tech., 1970-71; investment and tax cons.; writer, pub. Dir. Cleve. Trust Co. Mem. Potsdam Welfare Bd., 1970-71; mem. Presdl. Manpower Study Commn., 1969. Adviser Potsdam Meml. Hosp. Served with USNR, 1942-46. Decorated Purple Heart. Mem. Am. Finance Assn., Assn. Decision Scis., Financial Analysts Fedn. Home: Potsdam NY Died June 23, 1971; buried Blandford Cemetery, Petersburg VA

BENSWANGER, WILLIAM EDWARD;, b. New York, Feb. 22, 1892; s. Edward B. and Kathryn (Cleere) B.; grad. Central High Sch., Pittsburgh, 1911; m. Eleanor F. Dreyfuss, June 29, 1925; 1 son, William Dreyfuss. Insurance business, 1911-31; in baseball from 1931; pres., treas. and dir. Forbes Field Co.; dir. Nat. League; formerly president of Pittsburgh Baseball Club; director Oakland Branch, Peoples-Pittsburgh Trust Co. Served in Air Service (balloon), U.S. Army, 1918. Dir. Pittsburgh Symphony Soc. Mem. Pittsburgh Chamber of Commerce, Pittsburgh Concert Society (past pres.), Music Guild of Pittsburgh (director), Art Society, The Pennsylvania Society of N.Y., Am. Legion; hon. mem. Phi Epsilon Pi. Republican. Mason, Elk. Clubs: Rotary, Variety, Civic, Islam Grotto, Hungry, Concordia,

Musicians, Aero, Amen Corner (past pres.). Has written extensively on music; annotator Pittsburgh Symphony, from 1926. Home: Pittsburgh PA Died Jan. 15, 1972; buried Pittsburgh PA

BENTHIN, HOWARD ARTHUR, retail chain store exec.; b. Pitts., Mar. 3, 1907; s. Ferdinand Henry and Lydia (Hoffman) B.; B.S.C., State U. Ia., 1929; grad. Advanced Mgmt. Program, Harvard, 1956; m. Irène Paula Hutter, May 18, 1935; 1 son, Theodore Charles. With Sears, Roebuck & Co., 1934-68, v.p., comptroller, 1962-68, also dir.; dir. Sears Roebuck Acceptance Corp., Sears Bank & Trust Co., Chgo., Simpson-Sears, Ltd., Toronto, Ont. Can., Homart Devel. Co., Sears Roebuck de P.R.; dir., asst. sec. Sears Roebuck Pty., Ltd. Bd. dirs. Central Du Page Hosp., Winfield, Ill., Sears Roebuck Found. Mem. Delta Sigma Pi, Beta Gamma Sigma. Home: Wheaton IL Died May 18, 1968.

BENTLEY, ALVIN MORELL, congressman; b. Portland, Me., Aug. 30, 1918; s. Alvin Morell and Helen Webb (Patterson) B.; A.B., U. Mich., 1940, M.A., 1963; D.Sc. (hon.), Cleary Coll., Mich., 1949; LL.D., Olivet Coll., Mich., 1955, Nazareth Coll., Mich., 1965; D.Hum., Lawrence Inst. Tech., Mich., 1966; m. Arvilla Peterson, June 27, 1940; children—Alvin M., Helen A., Michael D.; m. 2d, Arvella Duescher, Nov. 8, 1952; children—Clark Henry, Ann Marie. Fgn. service officer, Mexico City, 1942-44, Bogota, Colombia, 1945-46, Budapest, Hungary, 1947-49, Rome, Italy, 1949-50; v.p. Lake Huron Broadcasting Co., Saginaw, Mich. from 1952; free lance newspaper, radio work, 1950-51; dir. Owosso Mfg. Co.; mem. 83d-86th Congresses, 8th Congl. Dist. Mich. Del. State Rep. Conv., 1950-52. Established Alvin M. Bentley Found., 1961; bd. regents U. Mich., 1966-69. Mem. Nat. Conf. Citizenship (dir.), Internat. Council for Christian Leadership (exec. com.), Theta Delta Chi. Mason (33 deg., K.T., Shriner), Elk. Clubs: Rotary (hon.), Optimist, Nat. Exchange. Home: Owosso MI Died Apr. 10, 1969; buried Oak Hill Cemetery, Owosso MI

BENTLEY, HARRY CLARK, sch. pres.; b. Harwinton, Conn., Feb. 28, 1877; s. George Daniel and Sarah Louise (Blakeslee) B.; prep. edn., Robbins Prep. Sch., Norfolk, Conn., Eastman Bus. Coll., Poughkeepsie, N.Y.; B.C.S., New York U., 1903; C.P.A., Vt., Mass., Conn. and Calif.; m. J. Belle Crapser, Dec. 25, 1897; children—Ina Mai, Belle Louise. Was teacher of comml. subjects, 1897-98; proprietor Winsted (Conn.) Bus. Coll., 1898-1901; pub. accountant, N.Y. City, 1901-08; chief accountant, corps. in N.Y. and N.J., 1908-11; asst. prof. secretarial studies, Simmons Coll., Boston, 1911-13; dean of Sch. Commerce and Finance, Northeastern U., 1913-16; prof. accounting and head of dept., Boston U. Sch. of Bus. Adminstrn., 1916-17; founder, 1917, since pres. Bentley Sch. of Accounting and Finance, Boston. Mem. Am. Inst. Accountants, Nat. Assn. Cost Accountants. Republican. Protestant. Author: Corporate Accounting and Finance, 1908; Science of Accounts, 1911; Massachusetts C.P.A. Questions and Answers, 1927; Bibliography of Works on Accounting by American Authors, 2 vols., 1935. Boston MA‡

BENTLEY, RICHARD, lawyer; b. Elmhurst, Ill., June 5, 1894; s. Cyrus and Elizabeth (King) B.; prep. edn. Francis W. Parker Sch. Chicago, and Hill Sch., Pottstown, Pa.; A.B., Yale, 1917; LL.B., Northwestern University, 1921; LL.D., John Marshall Law Sch., 1956; m. Phoebe Wrenn Norcross, Dec. 9, 1922; children—Cyrus, III (dec.), Alice Wrenn (Mrs. Samuel M. Rinaker, Jr.), Barbara (Mrs. Robert G. Myhrum), Richard Norcross. Admitted to Ill. bar, 1922, practiced in Chgo.; mem. Bentley & Bentley, 1922-23, Cassels, Potter & Bentley, 1923-51, later Tenney, Bentley, Howell, Askow & Lewis. Served as 2d lt. to captain, Inf., U.S. Army, 1917-18; capt. U.S.N.R., chief legal assistance Office Judge Adv. Gen. Navy, Washington, 1943-46. Mem. Ill. State Bd. Law Examiners, 1935-39; trustee Berea (Ky.) Coll.; pres. Francis W. Parker Sch., 1932-38; pres. Chicago Nursery and Half-Orphan Asylum, 1940-43; pres. Chicago Council Fgn. Relations, 1940-41; v.p. The New World Found. Mem. Chgo. Bar Assn. Found. (pres. 1960-62), Am. Law Inst., Am. Judicature Soc., Am. (ho. of dels. 1950-52, 54-60, 61-70, bd. editors jour. 1947-70, editor-in-chief of journal 1961-70), Illinois, Chicago (president 1954-55) bar assns., Psi Upsilon, Phi Delta Phi, Scroll and Key. Clubs: Law (pres. 1958-59), Commercial, Legal (president 1934-35), Chicago Literary. Commercial, University; Onwentsia; Huron Mountain (Mich.). Home: Lake Forest IL Died June 8, 1970.

BENTON, WILLIAM, publisher; b. Mpls., Apr. 1, 1900; s. Charles William and Elma Caroline (Hixson) B.; grad. Shattuck Sch., Faribault, Minn., 1917; student Carleton Coll., 1917-18, LL.D., 1961; A.B., Yale 1921; LL.D., U. Louisville, 1948, Bard Coll. 1951, Mont. State Coll. 1957, Knox Coll. 1960, Brandeis U., Dartmouth, U. Notre Dame, 1968; m. Helen Hemingway, June 12, 1928; children—Charles, Helen (Mrs. Helen B. Boley), Louise Hemingway, John Hemingway. With advt. agy. Lord & Thomas, until 1929; co-founder Benton & Bowles, N.Y., advt. agy., pres., 1929-35, chmn. bd., until 1936, then ret. from bus.; v.p. U. Chgo., 1937-45, asst. to chancellor, 1945, trustee 1946; asst. sec. of state, Washington, 1945-47; U.S. senator from Conn., 1949-53; chmn. bd. Ency. Brit. and Ency. Brit. Ednl. Corp. (formerly Ency. Brit. Films), 1943-73; U.S. mem. exec. bd. with rank of ambassador UNESCO, Paris, France, 1963-68. Adv. com. Co- ordinator Inter-Am. Affairs, 1939-45; vice chmn. bd. trustees Com. Econ. Devel., 1942-45, exec. com. bd. trustees, 1958-63, now bd. mem., vice chmn. U.S. Commn. of Inter-Am. Devel. 1943-45; chmn. U.S. delegations to numerous internat. confs. Mem. platform com. Democratic Nat. Conv., 1952, 56, 64, 68, 72, mem. drafting subcom., 1952, 56, 64, 68. Trustee U. Conn., 15 yrs., U. Bridgeport, U. Chgo. (life), Brandeis U., Hampton Inst. (hon.) Carleton Coll. (hon.), Shattuck Sch. (emeritus); bd. dirs. Fair Campaign Practices Com., Eleanor Roosevelt Inst., Kennedy Library Corp., William Benton Found. (chmn.), Am. Assembly (Columbia) (hon.), Am. Shakespeare Festival Theatre and Acad., Cradle Soc., Inst. Internat. Edn., Wadsworth Atheneum (hon.); v.p. Nat. Book League, London; hon. patron World Congress Univ. Presidents. Recipient Ann. award of honor HIAS, 1952; Distinguished Service medal Sch. Journalism, Syracuse U., 1960. Distinguished Honor award Dept. State, 1967; 1st William Benton medal U. Chgo., 1968; Human Relations award Am. Jewish Com., 1968; Kajima Peace award, 1969; Nat. Human Relations award Nat. Conf. Christians and Jews, 1969; Key to Freedom award Hadassah, 1966. Hon. fellow Weizmann Inst. Sci., Israel, 1970; Distinguished Pub. Service award Conn. Bar Assn., 1971; Chubb fellow Yale, 1972; decorated grand cross Nat. Order So. Cross (Brazil); Order of Star of Soliadrity 1st Class (Italy). Mem. Am. Legion. Cleve. Conf., Council Fgn. Relations Yale Polit. Union (hon.), Am. Fgn. Service Assn. (hon.), Bus. Com. for Arts. Clubs: Chicago; Fairfield (Conn.) Country; Yale, University, River (N.Y.C.); Pequot Yacht (Southport, Conn.); Metropolitan (Washington); Paradise Valley Country (Phoenix); Union Interalliee (Paris). Author: This Is the Challenge, 1958; The Voice of Latin America, 1961; The Teachers and the Taught in the U.S.S.R., 1966. Contbr. to mags. Home: Southport CT Died Mar. 18, 1973.

BENZ, MARGARET GILBERT (MRS. LUKE L. BENZ), educator; b. Yakima, Wash., May 25, 1899; d. Horace Mark and Marian (Richey) Gilbert; A.B., U. Wash., 1922; Ph.D., Columbia U., 1940; m. Luke L. Benz, Sept. 5, 1928 (dec. May, 1967); children—Mark Gilbert, Marion Louise (Mrs. Lee Harrison III). Exec. sec. Los Angeles chpt. A.R.C., 1927-28; exec. sec. Child Devel. Inst., Columbia U., N.Y.C., 1934-37; prof. sociology, N.Y.U., 1938-67. Named one of Golden Dozen Tchrs., Washington Sq. Coll., N.Y.U., 1966, 67. Mem. Tri-State Council Social Work (pres. 1965-66), Nat. Assn. Marriage Counselors (sec. elect 1967), Groves Conf. on Marriage and the Family, Child Study Assn. Am., Soc. Sci. Study of Sex, Nat. Assn. Social Workers, E. Sociol. Soc, Am. Assn. U. Profs., Council of Social Work Edn., Alpha Kappa Delta. Home: Armonk NY Died May 28, 1967.

BENZEL, CHARLES FREDERICK, SR., pvt. and spl. investments mgr.; b. Bedford, Ind., June 19, 1905; s. Frederick W. and Maude E. (Campbell) B.; B.S. cum laude, Ind. U., 1927; m. Janet Bass, Nov. 22, 1927; children—Charles Frederick, John E. Asst. v.p. and gen. mgr. Gimbel Bros., Milw., 1928-33; officer, dir. Mayflower Assos., Inc., 1933-40, Pilgrim Exploration Co., 1936-47; v.p., dir. Rockland Corp., from 1940, La Floresta Perdida, Inc., from 1940, Florell Corp., from 1940, Clifton Park Manor, 1948-52, Hetherington, Inc., 1941-58, All Am. Aviation, 1943-44, Continental Research Corp., 1950-59, United Funds, Inc., 1956-59; pres., dir. Del. Chem. Engring. Co., 1954-68; pres., exec. v.p., dir. Del. Chem. Engring. Corp. (Delfi Am., Inc.), 1964-68, exec. v.p. Blue Ridge Mut. Fund, 1964-68; dir. Piasecki Helicopter, 1947-49, Waddell & Reed Inc., 1952-57, Welex Corp., 1949-55, Coral Drilling Co., 1954-67. Officer, trustee Robert Earll McConnell Found., 1937-42; pres., trustee Averell-Ross Found., 1958-68. Mem. Nat. Security Indsl. Assn. (trustee, life mem.), Beta Gamma Sigma, Delta Sigma Pi, Phi Gamma Delta (Western Conf. medal 1927). Clubs: Wall Street (N.Y.C.); University, Wilmington Country (Wilmington). Mem. P.E. Ch. (treas. 1950-56). Address: Wilmington DE

BERCKMANS, BRUCE, retired industrialist; b. N.Y.C., July 14 1901; s. Gustav Bruce and Estil (FitzRandolph) B.; A.B., Princeton, 1922; LL.B., LaSalle U., 1925; m. Hildegarde Aldrich Luedke, Dec. 27, 1923 (dec. June 1961); children—Nancy (Mrs. Matthew Krystl), Bruce (USMC); m. second, Mary Elizabeth Chamberlin, February 21, 1962. Service manager Ohio Motors, 1922-25; asst. treas., comptroller Princeton Athletic Assn., 1924-25; sec.-treas. Union Bond & Mortgage Co., 1926-29; asst. to pres., sales mgr. Huber Ink Co., 1937-38; acting dir. U.S. Bur. Fgn. and Domestic Commerce, 1938-39; v.p. sales and advt., dir. Piel Brewing Co., 1940-42; with F. & M. Schefer Brewing Co., 1943-49, successively asst. to pres., sec., v.p., 1943-47, exec. v.p., 1947-49, dir., 1944-49; v.p., dir. Schaefer Brewing Co., 1944-49; pres., mng. dir. Berkmans deWeert Found., Detroit, 1950-55; pres., dir. Frankenmuth Brewing Co., Detroit, 1950-55; pres., chmn. Internat. Breweries, Inc., Detroit, 1955-64; now dir.; dir. Iroquois Beverages, Buffalo, So. Brewery, Tampa, Old Dutch Brewery, Findlay, O., Phoenix Brewery, Buffalo, Bavarians Brewing Co., Cin. Chmn. N.Y. State Legal Complaince Com., 1947-49, N.Y. State Brewers Labor Com., 1947-49; past chmn. employee relations com. U.S. Brewers Found.; war fund chmn. Middletown chpt. A.R.C., 1942-44, exec. vice chmn. Monmouth County chapter, A.R.C., 1944-45. Served with USNRF, 1916-20. Decorated Grand Cross and Star, Am. Internat. Acad., 1959; Knight Hospitaler of St. John at UN 1959. Episcopalian. Clubs: Princeton (N.Y.C.); Fox Hounds (Monmouth County); Athletic; Buffalo; Buffalo Yacht; Tampa (Fla.) Yacht; Hundred, Recess, Detroit Athletic (Detroit). Home: Detroit MI Died Dec. 18, 1968; buried Kensico Cemetery, Valhalla NY

BERG, DOUGLAS SPEARMAN, advt. account exec.; b. Duluth, Minn., Apr. 12, 1924; s. Harold S. and Ada (Carpenter) B.; student Duluth Jr. Coll., 1947; B.B.A., U. Minn., 1948; m. Joyce Lurene Lyons, Dec. 16, 1949; children—Diana, Kevin, Laurel, Douglas Lyons. With I.F.I. Advt. Agy., Duluth, Minn., 1949-68, account exec., 1948-52, partner, 1952-68. Cons. econs. and marketing. Served with USNR, 1943-45. Mem. C. of C. Presbyn. Mason. Clubs: Kiwanis, Toastmasters. Home: Duluth MN Died Dec. 16, 1968.

BERG, KAJ, zoologist; b. Aarhus, Denmark, May 13, 1899; s. Aage and Marie (Soerensen) B.; ed. Aarhus; Cand. mag., Copenhagen (Denmark) U., 1925, Ph.D., 1931; m. Agnete Odum, 1947; children—Torsten, Asger. Dir. freshwater biol. inst., prof. Copenhagen U., 1939-69. Mem. Soc. for Conservation of Natural Scenery, Natural History Soc. Denmark, Royal Danish Soc., Sci. Editor: Folia Limnologica Scandinavia. Research and publs. on limnology, reprodn. and respiration. Home: Hillerod Denmark Died Mar. 14, 1972; buried New Cemetery, Hillerod Denmark

BERG, LOUIS, psychiatrist, author; b. London, Eng., June 19, 1901; s. Samuel and Ida B., brought to U.S. 1904, naturalized, 1919; A.B., Columbia 1920; M.D., Jefferson Med. Coll., Phila., 1923; grad. study U. Vienna, 1926; m. Lisa Conlin; adopted children—Leslie Lanham Berg, Wendy Lee Berg, Michael David Berg. Intern. Beth David Hosp., N.Y.C., 1923-24; resident Montefiore Hosp., 1924-25; asst. physician Manhattan State Hosp. for Insane, 1924-25; Dist. med. Supr. Dept. of Health, N.Y.C., 1929-72; physician to N.Y. Dept. of Correction, Welfare Island, 1928-35; part-time instr. of edn., New York U., 1929-34; med. dir. Henry Meinhard Meml. Health Center 1931-72. Medico-legal expert, lectr., 1934-72; asso. in neuro-psychiatry Beth David Hosp.; neuro-psychiatrist to the army induction station, Grand Central Palace, N.Y.C., 1943-—; mem. impartial specialist panel in neurology Workmens Compensation Bd. Bd. visitors Highland State Tng. Sch. Boys. Served in inf., U.S. Army, 1918. Diplomate Am. Bd. Psychiatry and Neurology. Fellow Royal Soc. Health; mem. A.M.A., N.Y. State, N.Y. County med. socs., Am. Psychiat. Assn. Mason. Author: (Novels) Prison Doctor; 1931; Prison Nurse, 1934; Devils Circus, 1934; Twilight Comes Early, 1939; other and later books include: The Human Personality; Sex, Methods and Manners (with Robert Treat), 1953; Psychiatry for the Layman, 1963; The Velvet Underground (with Michael Leigh) 1964. Contbr. articles in field to mags. Address: New York City NY Died Oct. 1, 1972.

BERGAN, GERALD T., 1892; ed. St. Viator's Coll., Bourbonnais, Ill. Was vicar gen. Peoria diocese and pastor St. Mary's R.C. Cathedral; apptd. bishop of Des Moines, Ia., 1934, to succeed the late Bishop Thomas W. Drumm; promoted to archepiscopal see of Omaha, Feb. 1948; archbishop of Omaha; ret. Address: Omaha NE Died July 12, 1972; buried Calvary Cemetery, Omaha NE

BERGEL, EGON ERNEST, educator; b. Vienna, Austria, Nov. 6, 1894; J.D., U. Vienna, 1918; M.A., Harvard, 1941, Ph.D., 1942; m. Emma Jahoda, Apr. 7, 1923; children—Susanne (Mrs. John Blair Mitchell), Ernest W. Came to U.S., 1938. naturalized, 1944. Prof. sociology Friends U., Wichita, Kan., 1942-44; control editor O.W.I., 1944-45; housing specialist Devel. Bd., Montclair, N.Y., 1946; asso. prof. sociology Whitman Coll., Walla Walla, Wash., 1946-47; prof. sociology, chmn. dept. social scis. Springfield (Mass.) Coll., 1947-62; prof. sociology C.W. Post Coll. of L.I. U., 1962-69; vis. prof. U. Vienna, 1962. Mem. Am., Eastern sociol. socs., Am. Assn. U. Profs. Author: Urban Sociology, 1955; Social Stratifcation, 1960; contbr. articles to profl. jours. Home: New York City NY Died Oct. 24, 1969.

BERGEMANN, GUSTAV ERNST, clergyman; b. Dodge County, Wis., Aug. 9, 1862; s. Ludwig and Wilhelmine (Schulze) B.; Northwestern Coll., Watertown, Wis., 1879-85; Luth. Theol. Sem., Milwaukee, Wis., 1885-87; m. Emma Anger, Oct. 31, 1887; children—Edward (dec.), Selma, Hans (dec.), Margarete. Ordained ministry Evang. Luth. Ch., 1887; pastor Trinity Ch., Bay City, Mich., 1887-92, St. Paul's Ch., Tomah, Wis., 1892-99, St. Peter's Ch., Fond du Lac, Wis., since 1899. Pres. bd. dirs. Evang. Luth. Theol. Sem., Thiensville, Wis. Formerly pres. Evang. Luth. Jt. Synod of Wis. and Other States. Home: 229 E. 2d St., Fond du Lac WI*‡

BERGER, MAURICE WIBERT, merchant; b. N.Y.C., July 5, 1906; s. Jay William and Caroline (Brooks) B.; Litt.B., Rutgers U., 1928; student Yale Law Sch., 1928-30; m. Barbara Ruth Freund, Nov. 26, 1936; 1 dau., Brooke Carol. Mdse. mgr. Stern Bros., N.Y.C., 1930-36; mdse mgr. Gimbel Bros., Milw., 1936-45, gen. mdse mgr., 1945-56; v.p., dir. Gimbel Bros., Inc., N.Y.C., from 1956, exec. head Gimbels, Milw., from 1956; dir. First Wis. Bankshares Corp. Regent Marquette U.; president of board of trustees Milw. Art Center; trustee Milw. Art Inst. 1st lt. USAAF, World War II. Mem. Downtown Assn. (past president, dir.), Better Bus. Bur. (past president), Greater Milw. Committee (v.p.). Home: Fox Point WI Died July 25, 1968.

BERGH, LILLIE D'ANGELO, voice teacher; b. in New York; ed. in Germany; grad. in music at Royal School of Wurtemberg, also grad. Stuttgart Conservatory of Music; studied 3 yrs. in Italy; sang in concert (soprano) in leading European cities; established and now conducts a school of singing in New York. Author of several textbooks on the voice. Has conducted 120 concerts and large musicales in N.Y.; lecturer for Bd. Edn, N.Y.; gives song recitals and lectures on musical subjects before colleges, schools, clubs, etc. Mem. D.A.R.; v.-p. Woman's Philharmonic Soc., N.Y.; v.-p. State Music Teachers' Assn, N.Y.; mem. Nat. Federation Musical Clubs. Clubs: College Woman's N.Y. Press Woman's. Studio: Carnegie Hall, NY‡

BERGMAN, WALTER JAMES, business exec.; b. N.Y.C., Jan. 14, 1904; s. Simon and Anna (Bloch) B.; student Wharton Sch. Commerce and Finance, U. Pa., 1922-25; LL.D. Drury Coll. 1954; m. Leona Lefferts, June 19, 1927; 1 dau., Virginia B. Edelman. With Lily-Tulip Cup Corp., N.Y.C., 1929-68, 1st v.p., 1929-43, exec. v.p., 1943-46, pres., 1946-62, chmn. chief exec. officer, 1962-68; pres. Lily Cups, Ltd., Toronto, Can., 1946-62, dir., 1946-68; v.p., trustee Thanks to Scandinavia, Inc.; dir. Owens-Ill., Inc.; founder College Point Nat. Bank (N.Y.), 1927, dir., 1927-29; adv. com. 45th St. br: Chase Manhattan Bank of N.Y.; pres., dir. Red River Paper Mill. Inc.; dir. First Multifund of Am., Inc. Vice pres. Am. Jewish Com.; pres.; dir. Sydenham Hosp., 1939-41. Trustee Drury Coll., 1954-68, hon. life trustee; trustee Population Reference Bur.; nat. trustee Nat. Conf. Christians and Jews; chmn. bd. trustees Henry Nias Found.; bd. dirs. Speech Rehab. Inst. Mem. Nat. Dairy Council (dir. at large 1958-60). Clubs: Beach Point Yacht, Harmonie, Pinnacle. Contbr. chpt. Top Mgmt.'s Use of Outside Services. Home: New York City NY Died Sept. 11, 1972; buried Ferncliff Cemetery, Hartsdale NY

BERGSTROM, GEORGE EDWIN, architect; b. Neenah, Wis., Mar. 1876; s. George O. and Alice (Smith) B.; prep. edn., Philips Acad., Andover, Mass.; student Sheffield Scientific Sch. (Yale U.); B.S. in Architecture, Mass. Inst. Tech., 1899; m. Nancy Evans Kimberly, May 9, 1902; children—Alice Cheney, George Edwin. With Tower & Wallace, architects and engrs., N.Y. City, 1899-1901; mem. Parkinson & Bergstrom, Los Angeles, Calif., 1902-13; practice alone since 1913. Became pres. Los Angeles Housing Commn., 1916; pres. Allied Architects Assn., Los Angeles, 1921-33; editor Uniform Bldg. Code, State of Calif., 1928-39; chief consulting architect, U.S. War Dept., 1941; chief architect The Pentagon, War Dept. Building, Washington, D.C., 1942, chief architect, Pasadena Civic Auditorium, Los Angeles Co. Hosp., L.A. Hall of Justice, L.A. Mus. Hist., Science and Art. Mem. Newcomen Soc. Eng. (Am. br.). Dir. A.I.A., 1921-27, treas. 1927-39, pres. 1939-41. Republican. Mason. Clubs: California, Los Angeles Athletic (dir.), Los Angeles Country, California Yacht, Rivera Country (dir.); Pacific Coast (dir.).‡

BERKOWITZ, ABRAM, lawyer; b. Bklyn., Apr. 15, 1892; s. Morris and Bessie (Douglas) B.; student Northeastern U., 1915; LL.B., Boston U., 1916, LL.D., 1962; m. Minna Kroll, Dec. 7, 1917 (dec. Nov. 1947); children—Leonard K., Dorothy (Mrs. Harvey White); m. 2d, Jean Sholkin, Jan. 31, 1963. Admitted to Mass. bar, 1915, since practiced in Boston; with Ropes & Gray, 1907-—, legal asso., 1916-30, mem. firm, 1930-—; dir. Emile Bernat & Sons Co., Fabreeka Products Co., Zayre Corp. Trustee, past pres. Beth Israel Hosp., trustee Combined Jewish Philanthropies Greater Boston; co-trustee Jacob Ziskind Trust for Charitable Purposes. Served with Q.M.C., U.S. Army, 1917-18. Fellow Brandeis U. Mem. Am., Mass., Boston bar assns., Am. Soc. Technion (dir. Boston chpt.). Jewish religion (trustee temple). Clubs: Palm Beach (Fla.) Country; Belmont (Mass.) Country; Down Town. Home: MA Died May 1973.

BERLACK, HARRIS, lawyer; b. Phila., July 18, 1898; s. Louis and Pauline (Cohen) B.; B.S. cum laude, Harvard, 1920, LL.B., cum laude, 1922; m. Edith Ann Raden, July 20, 1923 (dec. 1968); children—H. Ronald, Evan R. Admitted to N.Y. bar, 1922, Fla. bar, 1926; practice in W. Palm Beach, Fla., 1926-27, N.Y.C., 1922-68; mem. firm Berlack, Israels & Liberman, 1946-68; participant reorgn. corporations; specialist in investment law. Dir. Postal Telegraph Co., 1940-44, Hugh W. Long and Co., Inc., 1954-59, Welch Grape Juice Co., Inc., 1945-65. Pres. Ossining (N.Y.) Taxpayers Assn., 1934-40; mem. Ossining City Charter Commn., 1948-49; mem. Ossining War Council and SSS, 1942-45. Bd. govs., chmn. fgn. affairs com. Am. Jewish Com., 1962-66; bd. dirs. Conf. Jewish Social Studies, 1939-68; mem. nat. council Am. Joint Distbn. Com., 1959-68. Served with U.S. Army, 1918. Mem. Am., N.Y. State, N.Y. County bar assns., Bar Assn. City N.Y., Am. Law Inst., Am. Legion (past post comdr.), Phi Beta Kappa. Club: Harvard (N.Y.C.). Contbr. legal jours. Home: New York City NY Died Dec. 3, 1968; buried Ferncliff Crematory, Ardsley NY

BERLAGE, HENDRIK PETRUS, geophysicist; b. Amsterdam, Netherlands, Oct. 24, 1896; s. Hendrik Petrus and Marie (Bienfait) B.; student Eidg. Techn. Hochschule, Zurich, Switzerland, 1915-19, D.Tech. Scis., 1924; student U. Leyden (Netherlands), 1920-22; m. Elisabeth Smits, Apr. 28, 1924; children—Elisabeth (Mrs. Kamerbeek), Cornelia (Mrs. Van der Want), Francisca (Mrs. Seutter), Cecilia (Mrs. Leeuwe). Sci. asso. Royal Magnetic and Meteorol. Obs., Batavia, Netherlands, East Indies, 1925-46, dir., 1946-51; dir. Meteorol. and Geophys. Service, Netherlands Indies (later Republic of Indonesia), 1946-51; 1st sci. asso., dir. research in climatol. dept. Royal Netherlands Meteorol. Inst., De Bilt, Netherlands, 1951-62; asso. prof. gen. geophysics U. Indonesia, 1948-51; asso. prof. meteorology, climatology, oceanography U. Utrecht (Netherlands), 1954-66. Recipient Rosscha medal, Indonesia; decorated officer Order Orange Nassau, knight Order Netherlands Lion. Mem. Royal Netherlands Acad. Scis. Author: Het Onstaan van het Zonnestelsel, 1956; also articles. Research on fluctuations of metoeorl. elements throughout world of a few years, especially So. Oscillation, origin of solar system. Home: Utrecht Netherlands Died 1968.

BERLE, ADOLF AUGUSTUS, lawyer; born at Boston, Mass., Jan. 29, 1895; s. Adolf Augustus and Augusta (Wright) B.; A.B., Harvard, 1913, A.M., 1914, LL.B., 1916; LL.D., Oberlin, Wesleyan, Columbia, Detroit Yankton; Hon. D., University of Brazil, University of the Andes, University Aix-Marseilles; married to Beatrice Bend Bishop, December 17, 1927; children—Alice Bishop (Mrs. Clan Crawford), Beatrice (Mrs. Dean Winston Meyerson), Peter Adolf. Practiced law, Boston, 1916-17, N.Y.C., from 1919; partner Berle & Berle; professor of corporation law Columbia Law School, 1927-64, professor law emeritus, 1964; lecturer at Air War Coll., from 1951; mem. bd. dirs. SuCrest, N.Y.C., Twentieth Century Fund, N.Y.C., Ecole de L'Europe Libre, France; spl. counsel RFC, 1933-38; chamberlain of N.Y.C., 1934-38; asst. sec. of state, 1938-44; U.S. ambassador to Brazil, 1945-46; chairman task force on Latin America, 1961; also consultant to Secretary of State, 1961-62. Del. U.S. Govt. to Inter-Am. Conf., for Maintenance of Peace, Buenos Aires, 1936-37. 8th Pam Am. Conf., Lima, Peru, 1938, Pam Am. Conf., Habana, 1940; pres. Internat. Conf. Civil Aviation, Chgo., 1944, and chmn. U.S. delegation. Served from pvt. to 1st lt. inf. O.R.C., 1917-19; expert on staff Am. Decorated Order of the Southern Cross (Brazil); Order of Merit of the Republic of Italy. Commn. to Negotiate Peace with Germany, 1918-19. Mem. Phi Beta Kappa. Clubs: Army and Navy (Washington); Pilgrims, Harvard, Century, Players, Anglers. Author: Studies in the Law of Corporation Finance, 1928; Cases and Materials in the Law of Corporation Finance, 1930; (with Dr. G. C. Means) The Modern Corporation and Private Property, 1932; Liquid Claims and National Wealth (with Victoria J. Pederson), 1934; New Directions in the New World, 1940; (with Prof. Wm. C. Warren) Business Organization: Corporations, 1948; Natural Selection of Political Forces, 1950; The 20th Century Capitalist Revolution, 1954; Tides of Crisis, 1957; Power Without Property, 1959; The American Economic Republic, 1963; The Three Faces of Power, 1967; Power, New York City NY Died Feb. 1971.

BERLINER, HENRY ADLER, engring. exec.; b. Washington, Dec. 13, 1895; s. Emile and Cora (Adler) B.; student Cornell U., Mass. Inst. Tech.; B.S. in Mech. Engring., Harvard, 1918; m. Josephine Mitchell, Sept. 15, 1921; children—Josephine (Mrs. George Vargas), Cora Ann (Mrs. R. Cunningham), Henry Adler. Helicopter research, 1919-26; pres. Berliner Aircraft, Washington, 1926-29; v.p. prodn. Berliner-Joyce Aircraft Co., 1929-30; chmn. Engring & Research Corp., Riverdale, 1930-54; pres., chmn. bd. Tecfab, Inc., Beltsville, Md., 1955-62. Served from private to sergeant A.S. Signal Corps., 1917-19; maj. to col., U.S. Army, 1942-44. Awarded Distinguished Service Medal by USAF, Hon. Comdr. Brit. Empire. Fellow Inst. Aeros. Clubs: Army-Navy, University (Washington); Wings, Nat. Press. Patentee in field, also metal working machinery, home appliances and constrn. Home: DC Died May 1970; buried Rock Creek Parish Cemetery, Washington DC

BERMAN, EUGENE, painter, designer; b. Russia, Nov. 4, 1899; s. Gustave and Lydia (Manassevitch) B.; student schools in Petrograd. Berlin, Munich, 1911-14; art edn. in Russia, 1914-18, also Paris and Italy; m. Ona Munson, 1950. Came to U.S., 1937, naturalized, 1944. Leader Neo Romantic Movement since exhbn., Paris, 1925; Guggenheim fellow, 1947, 49. Exhibited since 1930, most of maj. museums and galleries in U.S. and Paris; designed settings and costumes for operas and ballets, U.S. and Europe; works permanently exhibited at Metropolitan and Mus. of Modern Art, N.Y.C., Fogg Art Museum, Cambridge, Mass., Vassar, Smith colls., museums in Boston, Balt., Hartford; also many pvt. collections; executed murals pvt. homes. Mem. Nat. Inst. Arts and Letters. Home: New York City NY Died Dec. 14, 1972.

BERMAN, PHILIP GROSSMAN, ophthalmologist, otolaryngologist; b. Lawrence, Mass., Feb. 12, 1900; s. Harris and Mary (Grossman) B.; M.D. cum laude, Tufts University, Medford, Mass., 1925; m. Anna Fidler, 1921; 1 son, Charles Samuel. Interne Roxbury Hosp., Boston, Mass., 1925; St. John's Hosp., Lowell, Mass., 1926; instr. Tufts Med. Sch., 1929-33; resident surgeon Boston City Hosp. for diseases of eye, ear, nose and throat, 1926-27; senior visiting surgeon St. Joseph's Hosp., Lowell, Mass., 1933; cons. surgeon Isolation Hosp., Lowell, Mass., 1934; vis. surgeon Boston City Hosp., Beth Israel Hosp., Boston, Mass., 1927-33; ex-pres. staff St. Joseph's Hosp., Lowell, Mass., mem. exec. com. and chief dept. eye, ear, nose and throat; dir. Concord Hardware Co., Canada Dry Bottling Co., Springfield, Mass. Trustee George A. Berman Trust. Diplomate Am. Bd. Ophthalmology. Fellow A.C.S., Am. Acad. Ophthalmology and Otolaryngology, N.E. Ophthal. Soc., N.E. Otol. Soc., Oxford Ophthal. Congress (Eng.); mem. Middlesex N. Dist. Med. Soc. (past pres.), chmn. com. on pub. relations, chmn. com. on mediation, A.M.A., Mass. Med. Benevolent Soc. (trustee), Societe Francaise D'Ophthalmologie (France). Mason (32 deg.). Clubs: Vesper, Country, Yorick (Lowell). Editor Middlesex North Bull. Home: Lowell MA Died Sept. 18, 1968; buried Temple Emanuel Cemetery, Lawrence MA

BERMINGHAM, ARTHUR THOMAS, paper mcht.; b. Beloit, Wis., Mar. 9, 1884; s. John Costello and Catherine (Maloney) B.; ed. parochial schs.; m. Charlotte Chmelik, May 15, 1912; children—Charlotte Elizabeth (Mrs. E. L. Todd), Arthur Thomas, Mary Ann (Mrs. B. E. Bates). Successively post office clerk, clerk Rodman Engring. Corp., wholesale paper salesman; corporater Bermingham & Prosser Co., 1915, pres., 1915-47, also pres. Bermingham & Prosser Co. of Mo., 1923-47; chmn. bd. amalgamated cos., Bermingham & Prosser Co., 1947-61; pres. 1020 West Adams Bldg. Corp., 1946-61. Roman Catholoc. Clubs: Chicago Athletic; Irish Fellowship, Butterfield Country; Park (Kalamazoo, Mich.). Home: River Forest IL Died Feb. 22, 1969.

BERNARD, FRANK BASIL, banker; b. New Antioch, O., Nov. 10, 1886; s. John William and Clara Matilda (Thatcher) B.; A.B., U. Mich., 1912; LL.D., Ball State U., 1962; m. Gladys Rockwell Jenney, Apr. 3, 1915 (dec. 1959); children—Jean, Alice, Nelle Corinne; m. 2d, Leah C. Isenbarger, Feb. 28, 1964. Began as clk. Mchts. Nat. Bank, Muncie, Ind., apptd. mgr. savs. and investment dept., 1913, v.p., 1916, pres., 1923-46, vice chmn. bd. dirs.; vice chmn., dir. Am. Nat. Bank & Trust Co., Muncie; former chmn. bd. Citizens Banking co. (Anderson); dir. Muncie-Fed. Savs. & Loan Assn. Sec., treas., v.p. and pres. Muncie C. of C.; v.p. Ind. Bankers' Assn., 1929, pres., 1930; mem. exec. council Am. Bankers' Assn., 1931. Treas., Ball State Tchrs. Coll.; v.p., dir. Ball Meml. Hoop., Ball State Tchrs. Coll. Found.; dir. Ball Bros. Found., George and Frances Ball Found. Mem. Ind. War Finance Com., 7th Fed. Res. Dist. Republican. Presbyterian. Mason (32 degree). Clubs: Rotary (Muncie), Indiana-Columbia (Indpls.). Home: Muncie IN Died May 9, 1970; buried Elmridge Muncie IN

BERNARD, HUGH ROBERTSON, b. Robertson Co., Tenn.; s. Josiah C. and Sarah (Eatherly) B.; ed. Mt. Juliet High Sch., Wilson City, Tenn.; (D.D., Mercer U.); m. Mary Elizabeth Weatherly, of Athens, Ga., Aug., 1867. Pvt. 45th Tenn. Regt., Brown's Tenn. Brigade, Western Army of the South, Civil War; wounded at Resaca, Ga., May 14, 1864. Supt. schs., Clarke City, Ga., 20 yrs.; supt. Northeastern R.R. of Ga. 15 yrs.; began to preach, 1878; editor Southern Advance 4 yrs.; auditor Mission Bd. of Bapt. Conv. of Ga., 1906-—. Democrat. Author: Work Once Delivered to the Saints, 1906. Home: 252 Peeples St. Office: 1008 Candler Bldg., Atlanta GA‡

BERNARD, LAWRENCE JOSEPH, lawyer; b. Duluth, Minn., June 10, 1905; s. William Lawrence and Ida Philomene (La Belle) B.; student Stetson U., De Land, Fla., 1924-29, LL.B., 1929; m. Barbara Hines, June 20, 1929 (dec. Oct. 1961); children—Dona (Mrs. Harold S. Jensen), Lawrence Joseph, Mary Barbara; m. 2d, Alma V. Scott, March, 1966. Admitted to Florida bar, 1929, bar of U.S. Supreme Court, 1935, D.C. bar, 1945; in private practice, De Land, 1929-33; asst. to gen. counsel N.R.A., Washington, D.C., 1933-35; spl. asst. to gen. counsel, U.S. Treasury Dept., 1935-38, asst. gen. counsel, 1938-42; in pvt. practice, 1945-68. Served as commander, U.S.C.G., 1942, captain, 1943-45. Kappa Phi. Clubs: Burning Tree (pres. 1967-68), Congressional Country (Washington). Home: Washington DC Died Feb. 16, 1968; buried Arlington Nat. Cemetery, Arlington VA

BERNATOWICZ, ALBERT JOHN, educator; b. Worcester, Mass., Mar. 8, 1920; s. Wladislaw Julius and Frances (Lankinis) B.; A.B., Clark U., 1948; M.A., U. Mich., 1950, Ph.D., 1953; m. Belle Keeney, Sept. 8, 1951; children—Lynn, Elizabeth. Instr. biology U. Ore., 1953-55; asst. prof., asso. prof., prof. gen. sci. U. Hawaii, 1955-71. Served to capt. AUS, 1942-46. Mem. Bot. Soc. Am., Am. Soc. Limnology and Oceanography, Am. Phycol. Soc., Phi Beta Kappa, Sigma Xi. Contbr. articles in field to profl. jours. Home: Honolulu HI Died May 31, 1971.

BERNE, ERIC LENNARD, psychiatrist, author; b. Montreal, Can., May 10, 1910; s. David Hillel and Sara (Gordon) B.; B.A., McGill U., 1931, M.D., C.M., 1935; student N.Y.C. Psychoanalytic Inst., 1941-43, San Francisco Psychoanalytic Inst., 1947-56; children—Ellen, Peter, Ricky, Terry, Robin Way, Janice Way (Mrs. Michael Farlinger). Intern Yale Psychiat. Clinic, 1936-38; clin. asst. psychiatry Mt. Sinai Hosp., N.Y.C., 1941-43; attending psychiatrist, mental hygiene clinic VA Hosp., San Francisco, 1950-56; pvt. practice, N.Y.C. and Norwalk, Conn., 1940-43, San Francisco, Carmel, Cal., 1946-70; cons. to surgeon gen. U.S. Army, 1951-56; adj. psychiatrist Mt. Zion Hosp., San Francisco, 1952-70; lectr. psychiatry U. Cal. Med. Sch., 1960-70; cons. group therapy McAuley Clinic, San Francisco, 1962-70. Served to maj., M.C., AUS, 1943-46. Diplomate Am. Bd. Psychiatry and Neurology. Fellow American Psychiatric Association (life member); member of the International Transactional Analysis Association (chairman board of trustees); corr. member Indian Psychiat. Society. Author: The Mind in Action, 1947; Layman's Guide to Psychiatry and Psychoanalysis, 1957; Transactional Analysis in Psychotherapy, 1961; The Structure and Dynamics of Organizations and Groups, 1963; Games People Play, 1964; Principles of Group Treatment, 1966; The Happy Valley, 1968. Home: Carmel CA Died July 1970.

BERNE-ALLEN, ALLAN, chem. engr., educator; b. S.I., N.Y., Aug. 13, 1902; s. Allan and Harriet Anna (Mallory) Berne-A.; B.S.E., U. Mich., 1924; Chem.E., Columbia, 1933. Ph.D., 1936; m. Helen Louise Kelsey, June 24, 1926. Research development tech. service Standard Oil Co. N.J., 1924-31. Vacuum Oil Co. (now Mobile Oil Co.), 1931-32; research, development, tech. asst. operation E.I. du Pont de Nemours & Co., Inc., 1934-47; prof. mech. engring. U. Cal. at Berkeley, 1947; prof. head dept. chemical engineering Clemson Agricultural College, 1948-55, profl. engr., 1955-69. Charter mem. bd. dirs. Fats and Protein Research Found., 1962-66. Served as maj. C.W.S., AUS, 1942-46; ret. lt. col. Reserves. Registered profl. engr., N.Y., S.C. Fellow Am. Inst. Chemists, A.A.A.S.; member Am. Oil Chemists' Soc., Am. Chem. Soc. (chmn. Va. sect 1941), Am. Inst. Chem.E., Am. Soc. Engring. Edn., Am. Assn. U. Profs., Va. Acad. Sci. Fla. Academy of Sciences, Res. Officers Assn. (pres. Staunton Va. 1936-37, pres. Gulf Coast chpt. 1958-59), Mil. Order World Wars, N.Y. Acad. Scis., Sarasota Power Squadron, Sigma Xi, Phi Lambda Upsilon, Phi Kappa. Phi, Phi Gamma Delta. Mason (past master). Clubs: Chemists (N.Y.C.); Army and Navy (Washington); Sarasota (Florida) Yacht; Michigan Union (Ann Arbor); Fla. N.; Highlands (N.C.) Country. Contbr. tech. mags. Patentee in field. Home: Sarasota FL Died Apr. 15, 1969; Meml. Army Marker in New Drop Moravian Cemetery.

BERNHARD, DOROTHY LEHMAN, welfare; b. New York, N.Y., Apr. 22, 1903; d. Arthur and Adele (Lewisohn) Lehman; grad. Horace Mann Sch., New York, N.Y., 1920; student Wellesley Coll., 1921-22; m. Richard J. Bernhard, July 2, 1924; children—Robert Arthur, William Lehman. Welfare worker, 1922-69. President Arthur Lehman Counseling Service, Social Legislation Information Service. Past vice pres. Jewish Child Care Association, 1940-42; past pres. Y.M.H.A. (now Asso. YM and YWHA's of N.Y.C.), 1942-47; mem. N.Y. State Bd. Social Welfare, 1942-47; former vice chmn. Millinery Stablzn. Commn.; mem. bd. adv. com. N.Y.U. Inst. Fine Arts; chmn. adv. com. Hunter Coll. Sch. Social Work; bd. dirs. N.Y. Assn. New Ams., Citizens' Com. for Children N.Y.C., Inst. Internat. Edn. (vice chairman). Child Welfare League Am. (v.p.), New York Philharmonic; trustee Fedn. Jewish Philanthropies; treas., N.Y. State Assn. Councils and Chests, N.Y. State Welfare Conf. (p.p.). Mem. Am. Pub. Welfare Assn., Council Social Work Education, National, Internat. councils social work. Clubs: Women's City, Wellesley, Cosmopolitan (N.Y.C.). Home: New York City NY Died Mar. 6, 1969.

BERNHARD, WILLIAM, ins. exec.; b. Whitestone, L.I., N.Y., June 1, 1897; s. Nicholas and Sophia (Wachman) B.; ed. pub. schs.; m. Helen Conroy, Jan. 4, 1924. With Gen. Accident Ins. Co., N.Y.C., 1913—, asst. U.S. mgr., 1949-51, joint gen. mgr., 1951-53, dep. gen. atty., from 1953; exec. v.p., dir. Potomac Ins. Co., Washington, from 1951; dir. Pa. Gen. Ins. Co. Home: Great Neck NY Died Dec. 27, 1970; buried Framingham MA

BERNHEIMER, CHARLES SELIGMAN, social worker; b. Phila., Nov. 13, 1868; s. Seligman and Betty (Loeb) B.; Ph.B., U. of Pa., 1887, Ph.D., 1896; married. Secretary Jewish Publication Soc., Phila., 1890-1906; asst. head worker, Univ. Settlement, New York, 1906-10; supt., Hebrew Ednl. Soc., Brooklyn, Sept. 15, 1910-19, Bur. of Jewish Social Research, 1919-20; social survey dir. Jewish Welfare Board since 1921; mem. editorial bd. Jewish Social Service Quarterly; editor The Jewish Center. Mem. program com. Nat. Assn. Jewish Center Workers; mem. Nat. Conf. Jewish Social Welfare, Am. Sociol. Soc., Am. Jewish Hist. Soc. Author: The Russian Jew in the United States, 1905; Boys' Clubs (with J. M. Cohen), 1914. Contbr. to various periodicals. Home: 98 Riverside Drive, New York NY‡

BERNSTEIN, JACOB LAWRENCE, lawyer; b. Paterson, N.J., May 18, 1902; s. Max and Miriam (Chakaim) B.; LL.B., N.Y.U., 1924; m. Rose Levenson, July 31, 1931; children—Claire Sollitto, Kathe Alice Kowalski. Admitted to the New Jersey State bar, 1924, to practice before U.S. Supreme Ct., 1957; pvt. practice Paterson, 1924-70; editor Passaic County (N.J.) Reporter, 1950-57, N.J. State Bar Journal, 1957-70, editor-in-chief, 1957-70. Atty. for Fair Lawn, N.J., 1948-49; chmn. Bd. of adjustment, Fairlawn, 1958-59. Fellow Internat. Acad. Law and Sci.; mem. Am. Acad. Polit. and Social Sci., Am., N.J. bar assns., Am. Judicature Soc., Authors League Am., Inc. Contr. articles to popular mags. Home: Hackensack NJ Died Jan. 9, 1970.

BERRES, ALBERT JULIUS, labor official; b. Washington, D.C., Dec. 29, 1873; s. Joseph and Mary Margret (Gensler) B.; ed. parochial schs., Washington, D.C.; m. Annie Elisabeth Riley, of Boise City, Ida., June 30, 1902. Sec.-treas. Metal Trades Dept., Am. Federation of Labor, from 1908. Mem. Shipbuilding Labor Adjustment Bd. during World War; mem. exec. bd. Patternmakers' League N.A.; mem. continuation com. Internat. Conf. on Labor and Religion; mem. Navy Dept. Wage Revising Bd. Now industrial sec., Motion Picture Producers of America. Catholic. Office: 1680 N. Vine St., Los Angeles CA*‡

BERRIEN, CORNELIUS ROACH, banker; b. Montclair, N.J., May 30, 1873; s. Cornelius and Margaret Elizabeth (Price) B.; B.A., Wesleyan U., Middletown, Conn., 1896, M.A., 1926; m. Grace Eleanor Beardmore, of Boonton, N.J., July 3, 1898; children—John Beardmore, Janet (Mrs. Donald H. Parsons), Stephen, Elizabeth (Mrs. D. Anthony D'Esopo), Geoffrey. Reporter Evening Sun, N.Y. City, 1898-1906, editorial writer, 1906-09, financial editor, 1909-13; financial editor The Sun, 1913-16; asst. sec. Central Trust Co. of New York (now Central Hanover Bank & Trust Co.), 1916-17, v.p., 1917-38; retired, 1938. Mem. Phi Beta Kappa. Republican. Methodist. Clubs: Players; Upper Montclair Country. Home: 160 Lorraine Av., Upper Montclair, N.J. Office: 70 Broadway, New York NY‡

BERRIGAN, THOMAS JOSEPH, editor; b. Allumette Island, Que., Can., Oct. 11, 1904; s. Patrick and Margaret (Ryan) B.; A.B., St. Michael's Coll., Univ. Toronto, 1926; Litt.D., Niagara U.; m. Florence Glynn, July 16, 1929; children—Paul, Patrick, Thomas, Mary, Michael. Reporter Niagara Falls Gazette, 1927-46, editor, 1946-70. Mem. Am. Soc. Newspaper Editors, N.Y. State Soc. of Newspaper Editors, Niagara Falls Chamber of Commerce. Roman Catholic. Clubs: Niagara, Gyro, Niagara Falls Country. Home: Lewiston NY Died Dec. 26, 1970; buried Niagara Falls, Ontario Canada

BERRY, CECIL RALPH, banker; b. Scranton, Pa., Aug. 25, 1895; s. J. M. and Emma J. (Van Gorden) B.; student Kissick Inst., Bklyn.; grad., sch. banking Rutgers U., 1935; m. Lena Belle Corson, June 25, 1919; cashier Hop Bottom (Pa.) Nat. Bank, 1916-18, cashier, 1918-25; pres. Citizens Nat. Bank, Waverly, N.Y., 1925-41, v.p., dir., 1941-55; pres., dir. Bloomfield Bank & Trust Co., 1938-52; chmn. exec. com. Nat. Newark & Essex Banking Co., Newark, 1952-57, dir.; pres., dir. Towanda Sand & Gravel Co., Inc. (Pa.); dir. Schering Corp., Bloomfield, N.J. Home: Bloomfield NJ Died Nov. 1968.

BERRY, EDWARD WILLARD, geologist; b. Passaic, N. J., Nov. 24, 1900; s. Edward Wilber and Mary (Willard) B.; A.B., Johns Hopkins, 1924, Ph.D., 1929; m. Dorothy Everett Pidgeon, Oct. 12, 1925; children—Mary-Susan (Mrs. E.P. Robare), Edward Lewis, Samuel Stedman. Micropaleontologist Internat. Petroleum Co., Negritos, Peru, 1925-28; instr. geology Ohio State U., 1929-36; faculty dept. geology Duke 1936-68; prof. emeritus, 1967-68; cons. geologist coal and oil. Mem. council 21st Internat. Geol. Congress, 1960; prof. geology U. Malaya, Kuala Lampur, 1961-62. Fellow Geol. Soc. Am., Geol. Soc. London, A.A.A.S.; mem. Geol. Soc. South Africa, Geog. Soc. New Zealand, Assn. Geology Tchrs., Pan Am. Inst. Mining Engring. and Geology, Am. Geophys. Union, Am. Assn. Petroleum Geologists, geol. socs., France, Switzerland, Peru, Mexico, Am. Inst. Mining Metallurigal Engineers, N.C. Academy Science (pres. 1957-58), Yorkshire Geol. Soc., Carolina Geol. Soc. (sec.-treas. 1937-67), Paleontological Inst., Paleontological Assn. (London). Sigma Xi, Kappa Sigma. Mem. Soc. Friends, Contbr. tchr. jours. Editor: Southeastern Geologist. Home: Corpus Christi TX Died May 10, 1968; buried Clearbrook VA

BERRY, FRANK, hydraulic firm exec.; b. Saltillo, Tenn., Aug. 25, 1904; s. James Jefferson and Mary (Smith) B.; spl. student U. Tenn., 1921-26; m. Beverly Cozette Spencer, Nov. 24, 1935; children—Frank II, Vicki Elise. Chief erection, maintenance Fairbanks Morse Diesel, 1926-33; supt. heavy constrn. Nat. Park Service, 1933-39; cons. engr. hydraulics, 1939-43; dir. research Corinth (Miss.) div. Reynolds Metals Co., 1943-47; founder Berry Motors, Inc., 1947, pres., chmn. bd., 1947-52; dir. research Berry Hydraulics, 1952-60; founder Differential Hydraulics, Inc., Corinth, 1960, pres., chmn. bd., 1960-66; founder Kinematicks, Inc., Pickwick Dam, Tenn., 1966, pres., asst. chmn. bd., 1966-69; mem. Hammontree & Assos., Nashville. Hydraulic cons. power transmissions. Named Man of Year, Corinth Lions Club, 1945. Mem. Soc. Automotive Engrs., Am. Mgmt. Assn., Sigma Phi Epsilon (chmn. bd. housing corp.). Methodist. Mason (32 degree). Club: Hillandale Country. Contbr. articles to publs. Patentee in field. Home: Corinth MS Died Apr. 5, 1969.

BERRY, LILLIAN GAY, prof. Latin; b. Wabash, Ind., July 14, 1872; d. Thomas Jefferson and Mary Margaret (Bowers) B.; A.B., Ind. U., 1899, A.M., 1905; fellow in Latin, U. of Chicago, 1905-07; unmarried. Instr. in Latin, Ind. U., 1902-04, asst. prof., 1904-07, asso. prof., 1907-19, prof. since 1919. Mem. N.E.A., Am. Classical League (councilor), Am. Philol. Assn., Am. Assn. Univ. Profs., Classical Assn. of Middle West and South (pres. 1931-32), Phi Beta Kappa, Pi Lambda Theta, Eta Sigma Phi. Writer: The Americanization of America; Pictures from Roman Life; Berry and Lee Latin—Second Year (textbook). Home: Bloomington IN‡

BERRY, RAYMOND HIRST, lawyer, also banker; b. Hackensack, N.J., Aug. 4, 1897; s. John N. and Julia E. (Blair) B.; A.B., Yale, 1920, L.L.B., 1924; student Sorbonne, Paris, France, 1920-21; m. Justine Wilborg, June 24, 1921; children—Alice (Mrs. Lee Stone), Helga (Mrs. Berry Ashe), Daphne (Mrs. Ian H. C. Bradley), Sylvia (Mrs. Arthur McCready). Admitted to N.J. bar, 1925, Cal. bar, 1945; practice law, Newark, 1925-38; pres. Shasta County Bank, Burney, Cal., 1952-71; also chairman of the board; vice president, gen. mgr. Scott Lumber Co., Inc., Burney, 1938-68. Chmn. Shasta County Republican Central Com., 1952-54, 60-66; California delegate Republican Natl. Conv., 1964. Served with U.S. Army, 1917-18. Named Ky. col., 1961. Mem. Forest Products Research Soc. (pres. 1960-61). Nat. Forest Products Assn. (dir.), Western Wood Products Assn. (dir. 1952-68), Soc. Am. Foresters, Am. Forestry Assn., Am. Legion, Am., Cal., N.J. bar assns., Burney C. of C. (twice past pres.), Phi Beta Kappa. Presbyn. (chmn. trustees 1950-58, bd. session 1957-58). Clubs: Yale (N.Y.C.); Essex (Newark); University, Olympic, Cal. Tennis (San Francisco). Home: Burney CA Died Feb. 28, 1971; buried Burney Cemetery, Burney CA

BERRY, WILLIAM H., ins. co. exec.; b. Aurora, Ill., 1908; ed. Ill. Inst. Tech., 1929. Exec. v.p. Continental Ins. Cos.; v.p. Fidelity & Casualty Co., Seaboard Fire & Marine Ins. Co., Fireman's Ins. Co., Newwark, Nat.-Ben Franklin Ins. Co., Pitts., Comml. Ins. Co., Newark. Home: Summit NJ Died June 15, 1972.

BERRYMAN, JAMES THOMAS, cartoonist, illustrator; b. Washington, June 8, 1902; s. Clifford Kennedy and Kate Gaddls (Durfee) B.; student George Washington U., 1920-23, Corcoran Art Sch., 1921-22; m. Louise Marble Rhees, Oct. 23, 1926; 1 son, Rhys Morgan. Reporter N.M. State Tribune, 1923-24; staff artist Washington Star, 1924-30, polit. cartoonist since 1941, editorial illustrator, 1930-33; sports cartoonist Evening Star amd Sporting News, 1934-41; mag. illustrator, 1936-66; polit. cartoonist King Features Syndicate, 1944-66; writer, illustrator mag. and news articles; tchr. graphic arts, Southeastern U., 1937-38; cartoonist for Assn. Am. R.R.'s from 1948; pub. dir. art Nat. Rifle Assn., 1941-48. Recipient awards from N.Y. World's Fair, Infantile Paralysis Found., War Bond Com. (U.S. Treas.). A.R.C. Wash. Central H.S. Alumni Assn., Freedoms Found., 1949, 50, 51, 62; D.S.M., Am. Legion, 1950, Medal for Merit, 1951; Nat. Cartoonist Society award, 1950; Pulitzer prize for cartoon, 1950; National Headliners Award, 1953. Honorary life member of the National Rifle Assn., life member Culver Military Acad. Fathers; mem. Delta Tau Delta, Sigma Delta Chi. Presbyterian. Clubs: Nat. Press, Gridiron, Chevy Chase, University, Alfalfa. Contbg. editor Am. Motorist. Home: Osprey FL Died Aug. 12, 1971; buried Sarasota Meml. Park, Sarasota FL

BERRYMAN, JOHN, author; b. McAlester, Okla., Oct. 25, 1914; s. John Allen Smith and Martha (Little) B.; student South Kent Sch.; A.B, Columbia University, 1936; B.A., Clare College, Cambridge, 1938, also Master of Arts, in 1968; Rockefeller fellow humanities, 1944-46; Hodder fellow Princeton, 1950-51; Guggenheim fellow, 1952-53; m. Eileen Patricia Mulligan, Oct. 24, 1942; m. 2d, Ann Levine; 1 son, Paul; m. 3d, Kathleen Donahue; children—Martha, Sarah. Faculty Wayne State U., 1939-40, Harvard, 1940-43;

instr. English, lectr., fellow creative writing Princeton, intermittently, 1943-49; lectr. U. Wash., 1950; Elliston lectr. poetry Univ. Cin., 1952; later Regents professor University Minn., Mpls. Recipient first prize for Imaginary Jew, Kenyon-Doubleday, 1945; Guarantors, Levinson prizes Poetry Mag., 1948; Shelley Meml. award, 1949; Am. Acad. award, 1950; The Harriet Monroe Poetry Prize, U. of Chicago, 1957; Pulitzer prize for poetry, 1965; Academy of American Poets fellowship, 1966, also received National Book award, 1968. Member of National Institute Arts and Letters, Phi Beta Kappa. Author: Poems, 1942; The Dispossessed (poems), 1948; Stephen Crane, 1950, Homage to Mistress Bradstreet, 1956; 77 Drean Songs, 1964; Short Poems, 1967; Berryman's Sonnets, 1967; His Toy, His Dream, His Rest, 1968; The Dream Songs, 1969; Delusions, Etc., 1972; (novel) Recovery, 1973. Editor: Unfortunate Traveller (T. Nashe). Contbr. to Five Young Am. Poets, 1940; Best American Short Stories, 1946; A Little Treasury of American Prose. verse, anthologies. Contbr. lit. criticism to profl. publs. Home: Minneapolis MN Died Jan. 7, 1972; buried Resurrection Cemetery, St Paul MN

BERSELL, PETRUS OLOF IMMANUEL, ch. exec.; b. Rock Island, Ill., May 6, 1882; s. Anders O. and Uma B. (Lagerlund) B.; A.B., Augustana Coll., 1899; B.D., Augustana Theol. Sem., 1906; D.D., Augustana Coll. and Theol. Sem., 1930, Gustavus Adolphus Coll. 1962; L.H.D., Luther Coll., 1938; LL.D., Upsale Coll., 1945; Th.D., Uppsala U., Sweden, 1948; m. Emelia F. Bergh, Aug. 20, 1908 (dec. Dec. 1958); children—Eleanor Sara (Mrs. Earl Andersen), Ralph Bergh. Instr. Luther Coll., Wahoo, Neb., 1899-1900, Mich. Pub. Schs., 1901-03, Augustana Coll., 1904-05; ordained to ministry Lutheran Ch., 1906; pastor in Chicago Heights, Ill., 1906-11, Chgo., 1911-13, Ottumwa, Ia., 1913-35; v.p. Ia. Conf. of Augustana Luth. Ch., 1923-28, pres., 1928-35; pres. Augustana Evang. Luth. Ch., 1935-51, pres. Emeritus, 1951-67. Pres. Nat. Luth. Council, 1941-45; chmn. Luth. Service Commn., 1941-63; mem. central com. World Council of Chs., 1948-61; mem. exec. com. Luth. World Fedn., 1948-52; mem. Joint Commn. on Luth. Unity, 1955-62. Bd. dirs. Augustana Coll., Augustana Theol. Sem., Augustana Book Concern, numerous ch. and inter-ch. bds. and commns. Decorated comdr. Royal Order of North Star 1st Class (Sweden), comdr. Order of Lion (Finland). Editor: Lutheran Men, 1924-26, The Lutheran Brotherhood Bond, 1930-67. Contbr. to ch. publs. Address: Minneapolis MN Died May 1, 1967.

BERSTED, ALFRED, mfg. exec.; b. Chgo., June 7, 1898; s. Martin and Julia B.; student pub. schs.; m. Grace Hamberg, Aug. 1923; 1 dau., Ruth. Pres. Bersted Mfg. Co., Fostoria, O., 1919-49; v.p. McGraw Edison Co., Chgo., 1949-57, exec. v.p., 1957-60, pres., 1960-67, chmn. Bd., chief exec. officer, 1967-72. Address: Elgin IL Died Feb. 28, 1972.

BERTOLET, WILLIAM S(CHAEFFER), M.D.,; b. Oley, Pa., June 27, 1875; s. John B. and Amanda (Schaeffer) B.; A.B., Franklin and Marshall, 1897; M.D., U. of Pa., 1900; D.Sc., Albright Coll., 1934, Franklin and Marshall, 1935; m. Mary E. Herbine, June 27, 1905; children—John H., Mary. Began practice at Reading, Pa., 1900; med. dir. and chief on med. service Reading Hosp.; dir. Berks County Trust Co. Chmn. Med. Advisory Bd., Reading, 1917-18. Trustee Franklin and Marshall Coll. Mem. A.M.A., Am. Coll. Physicians, Phi Beta Kappa, Sigma Xi. Mem. Ref. Ch. Mason. Home and Office:244 N. 5th St., Reading PA‡

BERTRAM, HELEN (LULU MAY BURT), operatic singer; b. Tuscola, Ill., 1869; ed. Indianapolis pub. schs.; studied music Indianapolis and Coll. of Music of Cincinnati; m. Signor Tommasi; 2d, E. J. Henley, 1893 (died); 3d, E. J. Morgan (died 1906). Sang at Indianapolis as Yum Yum in Mikado" and in Ermine"; took stage name of Helen Bertram and appeared in New York as Josephine in Pinafore"; soon after joined Emma Abbott's Co., playing Filina in Mignon," 1888; later appeared in light operas and with McCaull Opera Co.; was prima donna with the Bostonians," and with Carl Rosa Opera Co. at Covent Garden Theater, London; later appeared in The Tar and the Tartar," Foxy Quiller," Peggy from Paris," A War Time Wedding," LaBasoche," Clover," The Black Hussar," Amorita," Miss Helyett," The Prince of Pilsen," The Serenade," Robin Hood," Prince Annanias"; created part of Jack Horner in the Gingerbread Man," 1905-6.‡

BERTSCH, HOWARD, govt. ofcl.; b. Corvallis, Ore., Nov. 30, 1909; s. Benjamin F. and Nevva (Cropper) B.; B.S., Ore. State Coll., 1931, grad. student, 1932-33; M.S. Kan. State U., 1932; m. Ellen Fox, Apr. 10, 1947; 1 son, C. Thomas. Asst. dairy husbandry Ore. State Coll., 1933-34; field officer rural rehab. Resettlement Adminstrn. and Farm Security Adminstrn., Ore., 1934-43; charge farm ownership program Farm Security Adminstrn., Ore., Wash. State, Ida., Alaska, 1943-47; loan officer farm ownership div. FHA, Washington, 1947-49; dir. real estate div., 1949-54, adminstr., 1961-69; dir. program devel. Rural Housing Alliance, 1969; cons. Govt. Iran, also financial adviser Devel. Bank and Agrl. Bank of Iran, Ford Found., 1954-61. Decorated Order of Crown (Iran), 1958. Home: Alexandria VA Died Nov. 1969.

BESHLIN, EARL HANLEY, congressman; b. in Warren Co., Pa., Apr. 28, 1870; grad. high sch., Warren, Pa. Admitted to Pa. bar, 1893, and began practice at Warren; borough solicitor 4 yrs.; mem. 65th Congress (1917-19), 28th Pa. Dist. Democrat. Home: Warren PADied Aug. 1971.

BESLEY, FRED WILSON, state forester; b. Vienna, Va., Feb. 16, 1872; A.B., Md. Agrl. Coll., 1892; M.F., Forest Sch., Yale, 1904; hon. D.Sc., Md. State Coll. (now U. of Md.), 1914; m. Bertha Simonds, Sept. 17, 1899 (died Jan. 29, 1936); children—Florence Jean (Mrs. S. Proctor Rodgers), Arthur Kirkland, Helen, Lowell. Teacher in public schools, Va., 1892-1902; forest asst. U.S. Forest Service, 1904-06; state forester of Md. since 1906. Dr. Am. Forestry Assn., Md. Development Bureau. Mem. Soc. Am. Foresters. Democrat. Presbyterian. Club: Torch (Baltimore). Home: 303 Wendover Rd. Office: 1411 Fidelity Bldg., Baltimore MD‡

BESS, ELMER ALLEN, educator; b. Franklin, Ind., Aug. 18, 1869; s. George W. and Alice (Ritchey) B.; A.B., Centre College of Kentucky, 1897; studied law, 1891-3; Lane Seminary, 1893-5; grad. Kentucky Theol. Sem., 1897; (D.D., Emporia Coll., Kan., 1907, Lenox Coll., Ia., 1907); m. Emma Caughey, of Seville, O., Mar. 4, 1892. Ordained Presbyn. ministry, 1897; stated supply Ashland, Kan., 1897; pastor Trinidad, Colo., 1898-1901, Independence, Kan., 1901-7, Clinton, Ia., 1907-13; head of State U. of Iowa dept. of Presbyn. Bd. of Edn., 1913-18; commr. Nat. Service Commn. Presbyn. Ch., 1917-18; pres. Macalester Coll., St. Paul, Minn., since 1918, also head of dept. of vocation; dir. McCormick Theol. Sem. Democrat. Mason (32 deg.). Author: Our Master's Church, 1900; Twenty-Five (with Emma Caughey Bess), 1917; Vocation and Human Nature, 1922. Contbr. to ednl. and religious periodicals on vocational subjects. Address: Macalester College, St Paul MN‡

BESSON, WALDEMAR MAX, educator; b. Stuttgart, Germany, Nov. 20, 1929; s. Richard and Mina (Schlecht) B.; Ph.D., U. Tubingen (Germany), 1954; m. Margrit Lutz, Mar. 29, 1955; children—Matthias, Christian. Asst. prof. U. Tubingen, 1958-61; dir. Inst. Polit. Sci., U. Erlangen-Nurnberg, 1961-66, dean philos. faculty, 1965; prof. polit. sci., U. Konstanz (Germany) 1966-71; pro-rector, 1966-67; columnist, TV commentator. Bd. dirs. Second German TV System. Mem. Internat. P.E.N. Club. Author: Die politische Terminologie Franklin D. Roosevelts, 1955; Friedrich Ebert, Verdienst und Grenze, 1963; Grundzuge der amerikanischen Aussenpolitik von Roosevelt bis Kennedy, 1964; Die Grossen Machte, 1966; Die Aussenpolitik der Bundesrepublik 1949-69, 70. Home: Litzelstetten Federal Republic of Germany Died June 12, 1971; buried Konstanz, Germany.

BEST, HARRY, sociologist; b. Millersburg, Ky., Dec. 23, 1880; s. Isaac Reynolds (M.D.) and Sallie (Barbee) B.; A.B. Centre Coll., 1901, LL.D., 1937; M.A., George Washington U., 1902; M.A., Gallaudet Coll., 1902, Litt D., 1944; M.A., Columbia, 1908, Ph.D. 1914; LL.B., N.Y. Law Sch. 1912; LL.D., U. Ky. Successively instr. state schs. for deaf, Neb., Wash. and Ala. and N.Y. Instn. for Instrn. of Deaf and Dumb, until 1912; resident worker. Univ. Settlement, New York, 1912-19; connected with American Red Cross, 1919; prof. sociology, U. of Ky., from 1919. Dir. of survey Columbia Instn. for the Deaf, Gallaudet College, under Federal Security Agency, 1946. Pres. Ky. Conf. for Social Work, 1928, 38; mem. bd. or adv. com. Citizens Conf. Internat. Econ. Union, Nat. Civil Service League, Osborne Assn. Prison Reform. Mem. Committee to Defend America by Aiding the Allies. Recipient award American Found. for the Blind, 1954. Fellow A.A.A.S., Am. Assn. on Mental Deficiency; mem. Am. Social. Soc., Am. Acad. Polit. and Social Sci., Kappa Alpha; hon. mem. Conv. Am. Instrs. of Deaf, Am. Assn. Instructors of the Blind, Am. Association of Workers for Blind. Consultant U.S. Census Bur., Social Security Bd. Democrat. Presbyn. Author: Blindness and the Blind in the United States, 1932; Deafness and the Deaf in the United States, 1943; Crime and Criminal Law in the United States 1960. Census Bur., publs.; articles in encys. Home: Lexington KY Died Feb. 23, 1971; buried Millersburg Cemetery, Millersburg KY

BEST, JAMES MACLEOD, lawyer; b. Watertown, S.D., Nov. 1, 1903; s. Robert and Jessie Isabella (MacLeod) B.; A.B., Carleton Coll., 1925; J.D., U. Chgo., 1927; m. Katherine Denning; 1 son, James Reynolds. Admitted to Ill. bar, 1928; mem. firm Balhatchet & Best, Chgo., 1928-31; asso. firm Kirkland, Fleming, Green, Martin & Ellis, Chgo., 1931-32; atty. for RFC charge litigation in Chgo., 1932-35; atty. Quaker Oats Co., 1935-46, gen. counsel, 1946-55; engaged in investments and cons., 1956-70. Pres. bd. trustees Unified Sch. Dist., 1960-61. Mem. Am. (sec. div. food, drug and cosmetic law 1948-55), Ill., N.Y. State, Chgo. (bd. mgrs. 1946-48) bar assns., U.S. Trade-Mark Assn. (dir. 1948-55, pres. 1952-53), Clan MacLeod Soc., Isle of Skye (Scotland) Law Club, Legal Club, Phi Alpha Delta. Presbyn. Clubs: University (Chgo.); Executives (dir. 1950-52); Economic. Author papers on Paradise CA Died July 22, 1970.

BEST, JOHN G(ARVIN), mfr.; b. Elkhart, Ind., Apr. 20, 1921; s. Floyd C. and May (Garvin) B.; B.S., Tri-State Coll., Angola, Ind., 1946, D.Eng., 1959; m. Barbara Moore, Mar. 1, 1949; children—John, Mary, David, Sally, Thomas, James, Patricia, Nancy, Catherine. Began with Chicago Telephone Supply Corporation, Elkhart, Indiana, successively technician, engr., pres., 1949-60; name changed to CTS Corp., chmn. bd., 1960-70; dir. St. Joseph Valley Bank, Nat. Nugrape, Inc., Elkhart Hotel Corp. Dir., past pres., past chmn. Midwest region, bd. dirs. Jr. Achievement Elkhart County; mem. nat. budget and consultation com., lay trustee St. Mary's Coll., Notre Dame, Ind.; dir. Oaklawn Found. Mental Health; trustee Elkhart Urban Renewal, Tri-State Coll.; past pres. United Fund of Elkhart County. Recipient distinguished service award Jr. C. of C., 1955. Mem. I.E.E.E., C. of C. (past v.p.). Roman Catholic (trustee; past pres. Holy Name Soc. K.C. (4th deg.). Clubs: City (dir.), Elcona Country (past pres.), Chicago Athletic, Executives, Ind. Soc. Home: Elkhart IN Died Dec. 14, 1970.

BESTIC, JOHN BRERETON, air force officer; b. Fargo, N.D., Aug. 18, 1915; s. Arthur Edward and Anna (Doleshy) B.; student U. Minn., 1933-35; B.S., U.S. Mil. Acad., 1939; m. Frances Leona Powell, Oct. 18, 1939; children—John Brereton, Philip Brereton, Jeffrey Brereton. Commd. 2d lt. U.S. Army, 1939, advanced through grades to maj. gen. USAF, 1961; assigned New Guinea, Philippines, Okinawa, Japan, World War II; staff Hdqrs. Army Air Forces, Pentagon, 1946-49; dep. dir. communications and electronics Joint Chiefs Staff, 1949-50; chief communications electronics SAC, 1950-57; comdr. Pacific Area Airways and Air Communications Service, 1957-58; dep. dir. communications-electronics Hdqrs. USAF, 1958-61, dir. telecommunications, 1961-62; dep. dir. Nat. Mil. Command System, Hdqrs. Defense Communications Agency, Washington, 1962-67; comdr. electronic systems div. Air Force Systems Command, Bedford, Mass., 1967-68; v.p. corporate operations MACRO Systems Assos., 1968-69. Decorated Legion Merit with 1 oak leaf cluster. Mem. Armed Forces Communications and Electronics Assn. (v.p.), Club: SAC Aero (pres. Offutt AFB, Neb., 1955). Contbr. articles to mags. in field. Home: Corona Del Mar CA Died Dec. 6, 1969; buried Pacific View Meml. Park, Newport Beach CA

BESTON, HENRY, author; b. Quincy, Mass., June 1, 1888; B.A., Harvard 1909, M.A., 1911; studied U. of Lyons, France, 1 year; Litt.D., Bowdoin Coll., U. Me.; m. Elizabeth Coatsworth, June 18, 1929; children—Margaret Coatsworth, Catherine Maurice. Mem. editorial staff Atlantic Monthly Co.; editor The Living Age, 1919-23; with Am. Field Service attached to French Army, 1915-16; with U.S. Navy, 1918. Recipient Thoreau Emerson medal Acad. Arts and Scis., 1954; Outermost House (Cape Cod, Mass.) dedicated as Nat. Lit. Monument, 1964. Mem. Portland (Me.) Soc. Natural History, Josselyn Bot. Soc. Me., Audubon Soc., P.E.N., Vets. U.S. Submarine Service Assn., Am. Legion, Phi Beta Kappa (hon.). Clubs: Authors' (London), The Grange, Maine Guild of Herbalists. Author: Full Speed Ahead, 1919; Firelight Fairy Book, 1919 (school edit. same with preface by Theodore Roosevelt, 1921); Starlight Wonder Book, 1923; The Book of Gallant Vagabonds, 1925; The Sons of Kai, 1926; The Outermost House, 1928, London, 1929; (Armed Services edit., 1945); Herbs and The Earth, 1935; American Memory, 1937; The Runaway Tree, 1941; The St. Lawrence River in the Rivers of America" series, 1942; (Armed Services edit., 1944); Northern Farm, 1948; White Pine and Blue Water, 1950. Hon. editor Nat. Audubon Mag. Contbr., Human Events, to Brit. edit. The St. Lawrence, 1951. Home: Nobleboro ME Died Apr. 15, 1968; buried Chimney Farm Burying Ground, Nobleboro ME

BESTROM, LEONARD L., supt. schools; b. Grand Rapids, Mich., Sept. 3, 1904; s. Charles and Jennie (Keillor) B.; B.S., Western Mich. U., 1930; M.A., U. Mich., 1938; m. Harriet Catherine Keeling, Aug. 29, 1943. Supt. schs., Baroda, Mich., 1930-33, Memphis, Mich., 1933-40, Ravenna, Mich, 1940-44, Brown City, Mich., 1944-49, Harbor Beach, Mich., 1949-55, Mason Couty at Ludington, Mich., 1955-69. Mem. Mich. Assn. Sch. Adminstrn., County Sch. Adminstrn. Assn. (past pres.), Mich. Edn. Assn., Mich. Assn. Adminstrs. Spl. Edn., Phi Delta Kappa. Lion, Rotarian. Home: Ludington MI Died Jan. 9, 1969; interred Lakeview Cemetery Ludington MI

BETHELL, FRANK HOPKINS, b. Newburg, Warrick Co., Ind., Sept. 6, 1870; s. Union and Eva Maffett (Parrett) B.; ed. high sch., Evansville, Ind., Evansville Business Coll., Brooklyn Inst. Arts and Sciences; m. Florence, d. Gen. Albert Hartsuff, U.S.A., July 6, 1901; children—Frank H., Janet. Formerly pres. Bell Telephone Co. of Pa., and was officer or dir. many other telephone cos. Mem. Bronx Parkway Commn. Elected 1st pres. Village of Scarsdale, N.Y., 1915. Home: Richbell Road, Scarsdale, NY

BETTEN, CORNELIUS, prof. emeritus; born Orange City, Ia., Nov. 13, 1877; s. Antonie J. and Mary (Rhynsburger) B.; A.B., Lake Forest Coll., 1900, M.A.,

1901, D.Sc., 1923; Ph.D., Cornell U., 1906; m. Myrtle Alice Sherer, Sept. 8, 1906; (died December 16, 1948); children—Robert S., Cornelius, Jr.; m. Mrs. Beatrice Hobson Argetsinger, Aug. 17, 1951. Prof. of biology at the Lake Forest College, 1907-15; sec., registrar, 1915-20, vice dean res., instrn., 1920-22, dir. res. instrn., 1922-40, acting dean, 1924-26, 1931-32, N.Y. State Coll. agr. at Cornell U.; dean faculty, 1932-45, prof. entomol., emeritus since 1945. Fellow A.A.A.S., Entomol. Society America, mem. Gamma Alpha, Sigma Xi, Phi Kappa Phi, Alpha Zeta. Author: The Trichoptera of New York State, 1934; (with M. E. Mosely) The Walker Types of Trichoptera in the British Museum, 1941. Home: 177 Woodland Rd., Asheville NC‡

BETZ, ROBERT MILTON, judge; b. Gallipolis, O., May 22, 1911; s. Clarence O. and Mabel (Chick) B.; Ohio U., 1930-33, Ohio State U., 1933-35, Ohio No. U., 1937-38; m. Sara J. Field, Dec. 1, 1937; 1 son, Robert M. Pros. atty. Gallia County, O., 1942-48; judge Common Pleas Court, Gallia County, 1948-69. Mem. Ohio Ho. of Reps., 1937-41. Mem. Gallia County Bar Assn. Episcopalian. Elk, Mason (32 degree). Club: Gallia County Gun. Home: Gallipolis OH Died Apr. 20, 1969.

BEUGLER, EDWIN JAMES, civil engr.; b. Williamsport, Pa., Feb. 28, 1869; s. James M. and Catherine E. (McCollum) B.; grad. high school, Williamsport, Pa., 1888; studied Lowell Inst., Mass. Inst. Tech.; m. Helen W. White, of Phila., Pa., Oct. 21, 1891; children—Dorothy, Helen White, Isabel Watson. Ry. constrn. and operation, Bloomsburg & Sullivan R.R., 1888-90; with engring. dept. Phila. & Reading R.R., 1891-93; constrn. dept. N.Y.,N.H. & H. R.R., 1893-1903; resident engr., Boston Terminal Co., H. R.R., 1893-1903; resident engr., Boston Terminal Co., 1903-05; with Westinghouse, Church, Kerr & Co. as civ. engr., mng. engr., chief engr. and consulting engr., 1905-20; v.p. and chief engr. The Foundation Co., 1920-23; consulting practice, 1923-—. Mem. Am. Soc. C.E., Am. Ry. Engring. Assn., Boston Soc. C.E., Engring. Inst. of Can., Soc. of Am. Mil. Engrs. Clubs: Railroad, Point o' Woods Yacht, Southington Country. Home: Cheshire CT‡

BEUTEL, ALBERT PHILLIP, ret. business exec.; b. Cleve., Nov. 13, 1892; s. William C. and Sophie (Harjes) B.B.S., Case Sch. Applied Sci. Cleve., 1914, Ph.D., 1942; m. Belle Armstrong, Apr. 16, 1916; children—Phillip R., Betty Ann (Mrs. E. B. Hanley), Richard A. Engring. draftsman Dow Chem. Co., Midland, Mich., 1914-21, pipe shop supt., 1921-31, spl. asst. to pres. later asst. gen. mgr., 1931-40, v.p., dir. govt. dept., mem. exec. com. Dow Chemical Co., until 1971; v.p. dir. Dowell division Dow Chemical Co. Midland; dir. First City Nat. Bank (Houston). Bd. dirs. Tex. A. and M. Coll. Fellow Am. Soc. M.E.; mem. Am. Chem. Soc., Am. Petroleum Inst., Am. Inst. Chem. Engrs., Soc. Chem. Industry (Am. sect.). Mason. Home: Lake Jackson TX Died Nov. 27, 1972.

BEVAN, CHARLES FREDERICK, physician; M.D., Sch. of Medicine, U. of Md., 1871; dean and prof. principles and practice of surgery and clin. and gen. urinary surgery. Coll. Phys. and Surg., Baltimore. Address: College of Phys. and Surg., Baltimore MD‡

BEVERIDGE, ANDREW BENNIE, lawyer; b. Jellico, Ky., Sept. 28, 1915; s. Andrew and Annie (Bennie) B.; B.S. in Elec. Engring. U. Md., 1936; J.D., George Washington U., 1941; m. Elizabeth Griffith, Aug. 19, 1939; children—Susan W. (Mrs. Pericles G. Perikles), Lynn A. Admitted to D.C. bar, 1941 also U.S. Supreme Ct.; patent atty. Gen. Elec. Co., 1947-51; partner firm Browne, Beveridge & DeGrandi, and predecessors, Washington, 1951-72. Served to lt. col. USAAF, 1941-46; col. Res. (ret.). Mem. Am. (chmn. sect. patent, trademark and copyright law 1970-71), D.C. (chmn. sect. patent, trademark and copyright law 1963-64), Fed. bar assns., Am. Patent Law Assn., Internat. Assn. for Protection Indsl. Property, Canadian Patent and Trademark Assn., Order of Coif, Tau Beta Pi, Omicron Delta Kappa. Democrat. Presbyn. Rotarian. Clubs: Prince George Country (pres. 1965, 67, dir.) (Landover, Hyattsville MD Died Feb. 10, 1972; buried St. John's Cemetery, Beltsville MD

BEVERIDGE, KUHNE, sculptor; b. Springfield, Ill., Oct. 31, 1877; d. Philo J. and Ella B.; g.d. ex-Gov. John L. Beveridge; pupil of William Rudolph O'Donovan, N.Y., and Rodin, Paris; m. Charles Coghlan, Oct. 25, 1893 (now deceased); 2d, at London. William B. Branson, of Johannesburg, Transvaal, Aug. 25, 1903. Exhibited at Nat. Acad., New York Royal Acad., London, Salon Champs de Mars, Paris, Paris Expn., 1900. Hon. mention, Paris, 1900.*‡

BEVIS, HOWARD LANDIS, educator; born Bevis, Hamilton County, O., Nov. 19, 1885; s. Edgar and Cara (Corson) B.; A.B., U. Cin., 1908, LL.B., 1910; S.J.D., Harvard, 1920; LL.D., U. Cin., 1940, Western Res. U., 1940, Kent (O.) State Coll., 1942, U. Toledo, 1945, Baldwin-Wallace Coll., 1945, U. N.M., 1946, U. Hawaii, 1947, Morris Harvey Coll., 1955, Bowling Green State U., 1955, Ohio State U., 1955, Bradley U., Mich. State U.; m. Alma D. Murray, June 30, 1914; 1 son, Murray. Admitted to Ohio bar 1910; associated with Judge Stanley Struble, 1910-11; mem. Isaacs and Bevis, 1911-12, in practice alone, 1912-18; prof. law Stanford, summer 1921; prof. law U. Cin., 1921-31; dir. finance of Ohio, 1931-33; judge Ohio Supreme Court, 1933-34; dir. finance State of Ohio, 1935; prof. law and govt. Harvard, 1935-40; pres. Ohio State U., Columbus, 1940-56, retired; chmn. President's Committee on Scientists and Engrs., Washington, 1955-59; dir. City Nat. Bank & Trust Co.; chmn. bd. Fed. Home Loan Bank. Chief legal sect. finance div. A.S., U.S. Army, 1918-19. Secretary Charter Amendment Com., Cin., 1926; mem. Ohio Relief Commn., 1932-33. Chmn. Franklin County War Finance Com., 1942-45; vice chairman, Labor Legislation Commission, 1947-48. Mem. S.A.R., Ohio, Cin. bar assn., Am. Law Inst.; Assn. Am. Law Schools, Am. Acad. Arts and Scis., Newcomen Soc., Order of Coif, Phi Beta Kappa, Omicron Delta Kappa, Phi Alpha Delta. Democrat. Methodist Mason (33 deg.). Clubs: Rotary, Columbus, Faculty, Kit-Kat, Crichton, Torch. Author: Cochran's Law Lexicon (3d edit.), 1924; Bevis' Ohio Law Quizzer, 1926. Co-author: Private International Law in Ohio Jurisprudence, 1933; Public Law (vol. 3 in National Law Library), 1939. Contbr. to Harvard Business Review, law and other profl. and popular mags. Home: Columbus OH Died Apr. 28, 1968.

BEWLEY, LUTHER BOONE, educator; b. Mosheim, Tenn., Apr. 28, 1876; s. Joseph Brown and Lucretia (Easterly) B.; A.B., Maryville Coll., 1901, A.M., 1916, LL.D., 1921; m. Eleanor Gertrude Morris, Aug. 16, 1919; 1 dau., Virginia Morris. Went to Philippines as teacher, 1902; advanced through various positions to supt. schs., Manila, 1914; dir. of edn. P.I., since 1919. Regent U. of Philippines; mem. Playground and Recreation Commn. of P.I., etc. Mason (32 deg., Shriner), Elk. Clubs: Rotary, Golf, Army and Navy, Baguio Country, Polo. Home: Manila PI‡

BEYEA, HERBERT WRITER, newspaper exec.; b. Howells, N.Y., Mar. 3, 1895; s. George and Emma (Newkirk) B.; student pub. schs.; m. Helen Elizabeth Collins, Feb. 8, 1921; 1 dau., Mary Jane (Mrs. Bartholomew J. D'Elia). Sec. Cone, Lorenzen & Woodman, newspaper reps., 1914-19; with Hearst Newspapers, from 1919, gen. mgr. Hearst Advt. Service, 1943-56, pres. Hearst Advt. Service, Inc. N.Y.C. from 1956, chmn. bd. Hearst Corp. Dir. Hearst Found., Inc., William Randolph Hearst. Served as chief petty officer USN, 1917-19. Clubs: Metropolitan, Westchester Country, New York Athletic (N.Y.C.). Home: New York City NY Died Feb. 7, 1972; buried Gate of Heaven, Hawthorne NY

BIBBY, JAMES HARRY, ins. exec.; b. Cambridge Md., Oct. 31, 1897; s. Mark O. and Eleanor (Briley) B.; student U. Md. Law Sch., 1917-18. With U.S. Fidelity & Guaranty Co., Balt., from 1921, successively underwriter, casualty dir., v.p., 1921-55, exec. v.p., from 1955; dir. Fidelity & Guaranty Ins. Underwriters, Inc., Del Mar Company, Fidelity Insurance Company of Canada. Clubs: Maryland, Merchants (Balt.). Home: Baltimore MD Died Sept. 1970.

BIBERMAN, HERBERT J., writer, dir.; b. Phila., Mar. 4, 1900; ed. U. Pa.; M.A., Prof. Baker's 47 Workshop, Yale; m. Gale Sondergaard. Dir. N.Y. plays for Theatre Guild, including Roar China, Miracle at Verdun, Green Grow the Lilacs, Valley Forge; dir. films One Way Ticket, Meet Nero Wolfe, Road to Yesterday; dir., author original and screenplay The Master Race, Slaves; producer Abilene Town; collaborator original story New Orleans; dir. Salt of the Earth; author book Salt of the Earth-—the Making of aFilm; dir., author original and screenplay Slaves. Recipient award as dir. best fgn. film L' Academe du Cinema, Paris, for Salt of the Earth, 1956. Mem. Phi Epsilon Pi, Beta Gamma Sigma. Home: New York City NY Died June 30, 1971.

BICKEL, KARL AUGUST, editor; b. Geneseo, Ill., Jan. 20, 1882; s. William August and Emily (Anderson) B.; educated Stanford University; m. Helen Madira Davis. Editor Grand Junction, Colo., Daily News, 1908-13; with United Press, 1913-35, pres., 1923-35; apptd. mem. Press Div., Office Co-ordinator Inter-American Affairs (Pan Am. relations) Oct. 1940; mem. operating com. Ringling Mus.; mem. Fla. bd. of Parks, Historic Memorials, 1949-53. Clubs: University (Tampa, Florida); Metropolitan, Nat. Press (Wash.); Longboat (Fla.) Cabana; Sarasota (Fla.) Country. Author: New Empires—The Newspaper and Radio, 1930; The Mangrove Coast, 1941. Home: Sarasota FL Died Dec. 11, 1972.

BICKEL, SHLOMO, journalist, author; b. Uscieczko, Poland, June 8, 1896; s. Isaak and Bertha (Gefner) B.; LL.D., State U. Czernowitz, Rumania, 1922; m. Yetta Shaefer, Mar. 6, 1923; 1 son, Alexander M. Came to U.S., 1939, naturalized, 1944. Practice law, Bucharest, Rumania, 1922-39; mem. staff, columnist literary critic Yiddish Daily The Day-Jewish Journal, N.Y.C., 1940-—. Sec. bd. dirs. Inst. for Jewish Research, 1952-—, vice pres. exec. com., also chmn. Commission for Research. Served as lt., Austrian Army WWI. Recipient H. Leivick prize Congress for Jewish Culture, 1968. Mem. Congress for Jewish Culture (gen. council, 1948-—, adminstrn. com. 1958-—), Farband Internat. Assn. Poets, Playwrights, Editors, Essayists and Novelists (president Yiddish br. 1956-59), Yiddish Writers Union. Author: In Sich un Arumsich, 1936; A Shtot mit Yidn, 1943; Detaln un Sachkaklen, 1943; Di Yiddishe Essay, 1946, Yidn Davenen, 1948; Essayen fun Yiddishen Troier, 1948; Drei Brider Zenen Mir Gewen (winner Libman Hersch Literary prize 1957), 1956, Shreiber Fun Mein Dor, Vol. I, 1958, Vol. II, 1965 (winner F. Bimko lit. prize, N.Y., also Jacob Fichman prize for literary work, Tel Aviv), Vol. III, 1970; Rumenie, 1961; Family Ortschik, 1967 (winner Z. Ganapolski literary prize 1968). Editor: Zukunft, Jewish lit. monthly, 1964. Home: NYC NY Died Sept. 3, 1969.

BICKELHAUPT, GEORGE BERNARD, pub.; b. Edwardsville, Ill., Aug. 27, 1875; s. George Bernard and Lucy (Yates) B.; ed. Edwardsville pub. and high schs.,; m. Edith Chase Molen, July 8, 1902; children—Jess, George B., Helen (Mrs. David Smith), Edith (Mrs. Gordon Murray). Helper to shipping clerk N. O. Nelson Mfg. Co., Edwardsville, 1891-93; worked in drug store, Edwardsville, 1893; successively with Moffett & West, wholesale druggists, St. Louis, St. Louis Republic, counter clk., advt. solicitor and gen. utility man, 1893-1904; circulation mgr. Minneapolis Journal, 1904-24, business mgr., 1924-36; v.p. and gen. mgr. Minneapolis Tribune, 1936-40; pres. and pub. Minneapolis Tribune; pres. Minn. Tribune Co., Manistique Pulp & Paper Co., Manistique Light & Power Co., W. J. Murphy Co., Minn. Broadcasting Corp. (WTCN); dir. Mutual Holding Co. since 1940; pub. Minneapolis Daily Times and dir. Minneapolis Star Journal and Tribune Co. since 1941. Independent Republican. Mason (Shriner). Clubs: Minneapolis, Minneapolis Athletic, Minikahda, Rotary, Automobile (Minneapolis). Home: Bloomington Minn. Minneapolis MN*‡

BIDDINGER, NOBLE LYCESTER, investment banker; b. Bartholomew County, Ind., Sept. 3, 1909; s. John W. and Gertrude (Evans) B.; A.B., Ind. U., 1933; m. Eleanor Lynch, Aug. 1, 1936; children—John Wesley, Ann (Mrs. Mark Murphy), Joyce (Mrs. Gary Gilliam), David Lee, Stephen Byron. Sales dept. City Securities Corp., 1934-42, sales mgr., 1942-46, v.p., dir., 1946-51, executive vice president, director, 1951-62, president, 1963-71; treas., dir. Llanhurst Manor Realty Corp.; v.p., dir. Quaker City Realty Corp.; dir. Standard Life Ins. Co. Ind. Dir. banking and finance div. Am. Road Builders' Assn., 1957-59. Pres. Indpls. Christmas Com., 1959; hon. mem. Indpls. Citizens Sch. Com.; hon. dir. Crossroads Rehab. Center, Indpls. Dir., mem. exec. com. Nat. Com. for Study Revenue Bond Financing bd. dirs. Central Ind. Better Bus. Bur., 1949-61, pres., 1957-58; bd. dirs. Starlight Musicals, Indpls., chmn., 1964-71; dir., mem. devel. com. Winona Hosp. Found., 1963-71; bd. dirs. Indpls. Hosp. Devel. Assn., mem. adminstrv., exec. coms., 1967-68; dir. Cath. Youth Orgn. Marion County, 1963-71; dir. Brebeuf Prep. Sch. Council, 1967-71, Park Sch., 1960-71. Recipient distinguished service award Indpls. Jr. C. of C., 1946; Zora G. Clevenger award Ind. U., 1967. Mem. Indpls. Better Bus. Bur. (pres. and dir.), Ind. U. Alumni Assn. (pres. 1955-56), Nat. Assn. Securities Dealers (mem. dist. 8 com. 1966-68), Indpls. Jr. (pres. 1945), Indpls. (chmn. tax legislation com. 1953) C.'s of C., Indiana University Alumni Assn. (pres. 1947-49), Athenaeum Turners, Sigma Chi (pres. 1948, treas. Lambda chpt. 1950-53). Republican. Presbyn. (trustee 1960-63, 65-67). Mason (Shriner). Clubs: Athletic, Bond (pres. 1961), Meridian Hills Country (v.p., dir. 1953-54, 65-67), Columbia (Indpls.), Gyro. Home: Indianapolis IN Died Sept. 2, 1971; buried Crown Hill Cemetery.

BIDDLE, ALEXANDER, corp. ofcl.; b. Phila., Apr. 4, 1893; s. Alexander Williams and Anne (McKennan) B.; grad. Groton (Mass.) Sch., 1912; A.B., Harvard, 1916; student U. Pa. Law Sch., 1917; m. Margaret Scull, Sept. 12, 1917; children—Alexander Williams, David Scull. With Charles D. Barney & Co., investment bankers, 1919-31, partner, 1930-31; pres. Pa. Economy League, 1935-42; exec. v.p. Phila.-Balt. Stock Exchange, 1946-64; pres. Phila.-Balt.-Washington Stock Exchange and Stock Clearing Corp., Phila., 1964-65, cons., 1965-73. Bd. dirs. Invest in Am. Nat. Council. Served as 2d lt., F.A., U.S. Army, 1917-19; lt. col. AUS, 1943-46; ETO. Clubs: Philadelphia, The Rabbit, Gulph Mills Golf, Midday (Phila.). Home: Bryn Mawr PA 19010 Died Feb. 8, 1973.

BIDDLE, CHARLES J., ret. lawyer; b. Andalusia, Pa., Mar. 13, 1890; s. Charles and Letitia (Glenn) B.; A.B., Princeton, 1911; LL.B., Harvard, 1914; m. Katharine J. Legendre, Feb. 10, 1923; children—Charles, James. Admitted to Pa. bar, 1914, practiced law, Phila., from 1914, partner firm Drinker, Biddle & Reath, from 1924; trustee Phila. Sav. Fund Soc.; gen. counsel Phila. Contributionship for Ins. of Houses from Loss by Fire, Drexel Inst. Tech., other instns. Trustee Drexel Inst. Tech., John and Mary R. Markle Found.; chmn. bd. Overbrook Sch. for Blind. Served with U.S.A.A.F., also French Army Air Force in pursuit aviation, 1917-18. Decorated D.S.C., Letters of Commendation from Comdr. in Chief A.E.F., Purple Heart, French Legion of Honor and Croix de Guerre with 4 Palms, Belgian

Order of Leopold. Mem. Am. Pa., Phila., Bucks County bar assns., Am. Soc. French Legion of Honor, others. Episcopalian. Author: Way Andalusia PA Died May 1973.

BIDDLE, CLEMENT MILLER, SR., corp. exec.; b. Phila., Pa., Aug. 22, 1876; s. Clement M. and Lydia (Cooper) B.; direct descendant of William and Sarah Biddle who emigrated in 1681 to William Penn's colony; student Friends Central Sch., Phila., Swarthmore Coll.; m. Grace A. Brosius, 1900; children—Mrs. Lewis Sims Ayars, Jr., Mrs. Patrick M. Malin, Clement M., Jr., Mrs. Robert V. Schembs. Chairman board and director Biddle Purchasing Company, New York. Trustee Swarthmore College; director Boys' Clubs of America, Inc.; founder in 1912 and chmn. bd. Boy's Club of Mount Vernon, N.Y., Inc.; founder, 1932, Girls' Club of Mt. Vernon, N.Y. Mem. Am. Friends' Service Com.; served in European (Quaker) child feeding, 1920-21; mem. Religious Soc. of Friends. Republican. Home: Bronxville, N.Y. Office: 280 Broadway, New York 8 NY‡

BIDDLE, FRANCIS, lawyer, former atty. gen. of the United States; b. in Paris, France, May 9, 1886; s. of Algernon Sydney and Frances (Robinson) Biddle; brought to America in infancy; student Haverford (Pa.) Sch., 1895-99, Groton (Mass.) Sch., 1899-1905; B.A., cum laude, Harvard, 1909, LL.B., cum laude, 1911; LL.D., La Salle Coll., Boston U., 1942; Drexel Institute, Hobart and William Smith Colleges, 1943; m. Katherine Garrison Chapin, Apr. 27, 1918; children—Edmund Randolph, Garrison Chapin (dec.). Admitted to Pa. Bar, 1912; private sec. to Justice Holmes, U.S. Supreme Court, 1911-12; associate Biddle, Paul & Jayne, Phila., 1912-15, Barnes, Biddle & Myers, Phila., 1917-39; special asst. U.S., atty., Eastern Dist. Pa., 1922-26; Class C dir. Fed. Reserve Bank, 1938-39, dep. chmn., 1938-39; chief counsel Joint Com. to investigate Tenn. Valley Authority, 1938-39; judge U.S. Circuit Court of Appeals, 3d Circuit, 1939-40; solicitor general of U.S., 1940; attorney gen. of U.S., Sept. 1941-June 30, 1945; U.S. member International Military Tribunal, 1945-46. Former mem. Permanent Court of Arbitration. Admitted to practice before Supreme Court of the United States, 1927. Served in U.S. Army, Oct. 23-Nov. 29, 1918. Chmn. Phila. Branch Foreign Policy Assn., 1924-39; chmn. Nat. Labor Relations Bd., 1934-35; mem. Gov. Pinchot's Commn. on Special Policing in Industry, 1934; mem. Phila. County Board of Law Examiners, 1923-32; mem. bd. of Pub. Edn., Phila., 1936-39; chmn. national com. Am. Civil Liberties Union. Mem. Franklin Delano Roosevelt Memorial Commission; mem. bd. trustees Twentieth Century Fund (N.Y.). Hon. bencher. Inner Temple (London, England), 1946; Four Freedoms award, 1942; Order of Merit, Italy, 1954. National chmn. Ams. for Democratic Action, 1950-53; del. at large from Pa. Nat. Dem. Conv., 1944, delegate from D.C., 1952. Democrat. Mem. Am. Acad. of Arts and Sciences. Clubs: Cosmos (Washington, D.C.); Philadelphia, Legal (Phila.); Coffee House (N.Y.C.). Author: Llanfear Pattern, 1927; Mr. Justice Holmes, 1942; Democratic Thinking and the War, 1944; The World's Best Hope, 1949; The Fear of Freedom, 1951; A Casual Past, 1961; Justice Holmes, Natural Law and the Supreme Court, 1961; In Brief Authority, 1962. Contbr. to legal publs. Home: Washington DC also Wellfleet MA Died Oct. 4, 1968.

BIDWELL, PERCY WELLS, economist, author; b. Manchester, Conn., July 19, 1888; s. James C. and Clara J. (Woodbridge) B.; A.B., Yale, 1910, A.M., 1912, Ph.D., 1915; m. Anna Cabot Almy, June 8, 1915; children—John, Mary A., Anne W., Charlotte A., Samuel (dec.). Asst. prof. econs. Yale, 1918-21; economist U.S. Tariff Commn., Washington, D.C., and Brussels, Belgium, 1922-30; adviser to American delegation at World Economic Conference, Geneva, 1927; European rep. U.S. Tariff Commn., 1927-29; professor of economics, University of Buffalo, 1930-38; director of studies Council on Foreign Relations, 1938-53, research associate, 1953-58, director, research projector undergraduate education in international relations. Trustee World Peace Foundation. Member. Phi Beta Kappa. Democrat. Club: Century Assn. (N.Y.C.). Author: Tariff Policy of the United States, 1933; Our Trade with Britain, 1938; The Invisible Tariff, 1939; What the Tariff Means to American Industries, 1957; Undergraduate Education in Foreign Affairs, 1962; (with Harold J. Tobin) Mobilizing Civilian America, 1940, Economic Defense of Latin America, 1941, A Commercial Policy for the United States, 1945; (with J. Falconer) History of Agriculture in the Northern United States; also articles. Home: Bridgeport CT Died Aug. 4, 1970; buried St. Joseph's of Arimathia, Elmsford NY

BIEBER, SIDNEY, business man; b. Washington, D.C., May 24, 1874; s. Samuel and Johanna (Gans) B.; ed. pub. schs. and Spencerian Business Coll.; unmarried. Paymaster Naval Militia of D.C., with rank of lt., 1898. Fire marshal of D.C., 1901-05; apptd. by Rep. Nat. Com. a chmn. Bd. of Elections for D.C., Dec. 1907; del Rep. Nat. Conv., Chicago, 1908. In real estate business. Club: National Press. Home: 630 St. Office: Evans Bldg., Washington DC‡

BIERI, BERNHARD HENRY, naval officer; b. Walnut Lake, Minn., June 24, 1889; s. Bernhard and Elsie (Schild) B.; B.S., U.S. Naval Acad., 1911; grad. U.S. Naval War Coll., 1936; m. Elsie Genther, June 27, 1913; children—Bernhard, John Genther, David, Robert, James. Commd. ensign, U.S. Navy, 1911, advancing through the grades to vice adm., 1945; served in U.S. ships, Delaware, 1911-12, Nashville, 1913, Montana, 1914, Virginia, 1914-15, Texas, 1915-19 and 1929-30, Utah, 1928, Altair, 1933-35; comd. U.S.S. Corry, 1921-25; staff comdr. Battleships, 1938, Battle Force, 1939; staff comdr. in chief U.S. Fleet, 1939-40; comd. U.S. Chicago, 1941-42; staff comdr. in chief U.S. Fleet, 1942-45, this period including duty with Allied Comdr. North African Invasion Forces and Supreme Comdr. Allied Forces in Europe; dep. chief Naval Operations, 1945-46; comdr. U.S. Naval Forces in Mediterranean, 1946-48; comdt. 11th Naval Dist., 1948-49; rep. U.S. chief naval operations, on mil. staff Com. of Security Council, U.N., 1949-51. Decorated service bars, Mexican, World War I. Pacific, European-African fronts, World War II. Home: Bethesda MD Died Apr. 10, 1971; buried Arlington Nat. Cemetery.

BIGELOW, MASON HUNTINGTON, lawyer; b. Utica, N.Y., Feb. 11, 1888; s. Dana Williams and Katherine (Huntington) B.; A.B., Amherst Coll., 1909; LL.B., Columbia, 1912; m. Elisabeth Macdonald, 1911 (dec. 1946); children—John, David, Katharine (Doman); m. 2d, Ruth Miles Kinsey, 1946 (dec. March 1964). Admitted to New York Bar, 1912, mem. law firm Gould & Wilkie, New York City, 1915-67. Director Nat. Soc. Prevent-Blindness, pres., 1940-58, chmn. bd., 1958-67, hon. chmn., 1967-71, member of exec. com., from 1934; mem. exec. com. Nat. Health Council, 1946-57; trustee Am. Found. Blind, 1942-58, Ophtalmol. Found., 1945-61, N.Y. Assn. Blind (Lighthouse), 1952-60. Mem. Am. N.Y. State (chmn. exec. com. 1941-47, v.p. 1947, pres. 1948), bar assns., Assn. Bar N.Y.C. (v.p. 1944-46, exec. com. 1940-41), Civil Service Reform Assn. (executive committee), Alumni Columbia Law Sch. (standing committee, president alumni association 1944-46, board alumni visitors 1935-54), New York State Hist. Soc., Alpha Delta Phi. Clubs: Century, University, Pilgrims, Down Town (N.Y.C.). Home: New York City NY Died Feb. 6, 1971; buried St. James, Long Island NY

BIGELOW, ROBERT MANSFIELD, shoe machinery mfr.; b. Natick, Mass., Oct. 12, 1906; s. William Reed and Mary Louise (Bigelow) B.; B.S., Mass. Inst. Tech., 1927; m. Helen Miller, Mar. 23, 1929; children—Martha Ann, Jane Gibbs. With Hobart Mgf. Co., Troy, O., 1927-29; with United Shoe Machinery Corp. (now USM Corp.), Boston, 1929-68, asst. dir. research, 1947-55, dir. research, 1955-61, v.p., dir. 1959-68. Mem. Alpha Tau Omega. Unitarian. Home: Wellesley Hills MA Died May 21, 1970.

BIGHAM, MADGE ALFORD, writer; b. La Grange, Ga., Sept. 30, 1874; d. Rev. Robert Williams and Charlotte Eliza (Davies) B.; student Lucy Cobb Inst., Athens, Ga., Middle Ga. Mil. and Agrl. Coll., Milledgeville, La Grange (Ga.) Female Coll.; B.S., Ga. Woman's Coll., Covington, 1896; grad. stu. Atlanta Kindergarten Normal. Prin. Atlanta Free Kindergarten, Madge A. Bigham Private Kindergarten. Author: Tales of Mother Goose Village, 1904; Blackie, 1905; Merry Animal Tales, 1906; Little Folks Land, 1907; Overheard in Fairyland, 1909; Fanciful Flower Tales, 1910; Within the Silver Moon, 1911; The Wishing Fairies, 1915; More Mother Goose Village Stories, 1922; The Bad Little Rabbit, 1927; The Cry Baby Chicken, 1927; Sonny Elephant, 1930; Tales of Peanut Town, 1931. Home: 503 Peeples St. S.W., Atlanta GA‡

BILDERSEE, ADELE, educator; b. N.Y.C., Sept. 4, 1883; d. Barnett and Flora (Misch) Bildersee; A.B., Hunter Coll., 1903; A.M., Columbia, 1912, Ph.D., 1932; L.H.D. honoris causa, Brooklyn College, 1955. Teacher in pub. schs., New York, 1901-06, teacher English dept. Hunter Coll., High Sch., 1907-10, instr. English, advancing to asst. prof., 1910-26, dir. summer session, 1919-21, dir. establishment of Brooklyn branch, rank of acting dean and asso. prof., 1926-30 (this branch became Women's Div. of Brooklyn Coll., 1930); acting dean, 1930-32, dean and prof., 1933-38, dean of students and professor, 1938-54, professor and dean emeritus, 1954-71, director of admissions Bklyn. Coll., 1944-54. Dir. Brooklyn Assn. Mental Health. Dir. Jewish Hosp. Bklyn. Mem. Assn. U. Women, Brooklyn Jewish Community Council (director), joint Distribution Committee (nat. council), English Grad. Union (Columbia University), Jewish Acad. Arts and Scis., New York Academy of Public Education, Phi Beta Kappa, Kappa Delta Pi. Democrat. Author: The Hidden Books, Selections from the Apocrypha, 1957. Home: Brooklyn NY Died 1971.

BILLHARDT, FRED A., cable mfg. co. exec.; b. Cleve., July 14, 1908; s. Gustav Adolph and Louise (Grittner) B.; B.S. in Mech. Engring., Ohio State U., 1934; m. Thelma Ruth Pohle, June 5, 1931; children—Martha (Mrs. Joseph May), Carol (Mrs. Robert Crafts, Jr.), Carl. With Aluminum Co. Am., subsidiaries, 1934-68, pres., dir. Alcoa Steamship Co., Inc., 1960-63, Rome Cable Corp., 1963-68. Registered profl. engr., Ark. Mem. Soc. Naval Architects and Marine Engrs. Club: Duquesne (Pitts.). Home: Rome NY Died 1968.

BILLINGS, FREDERIC CHURCH, manufacturer; b. Utica, N.Y., Oct. 21, 1864; s. Charles Ethan and Frances (Heywood) B.; ed. high sch.; m. Mary Elizabeth Parker, Feb. 1893; 1 dau., Frances Heywood (Mrs. William M. Newsom). With Billings & Spencer Co., mfr. machinery and tools, Hartford, since 1886, v.p. and supt., 1890-1916, pres. and treas., 1916-37, chmn. bd. since 1937. Mem. Conn. N.G., 1884-89, paymaster, 1887-89. Mem. Am. Soc. M.E. Republican. Conglist. Clubs: Hartford, Question (Hartford). Home: 330 Laurel St. Office: 1 Laurel St., Hartford CT‡

BILLINGS, FREDERICK HORATIO, educator; b. Chicago, Ill., May 26, 1869; s. Horatio Gilbert and Emily Amelia (Bowers) B.; grad. Calif. State Normal Sch., 1890; A.B., Stanford U., 1896; A.M., Harvard, 1897; Ph.D., U. of Munich, 1901; post grad. work, University of Wisconsin, Massachusetts Institute of Technology and Harvard Medical School; m. Louise Massey, Aug. 15, 1893; children—Frances Augusta, Bertha Mae. Prof. botany and bacteriology, La. State U., 1901-1907; asso. prof. botany and bacteriology, U. of Kan., 1907-13; prof. bacteriology, 1913-17; prof. botany and bacteriology, U. of Redlands, Calif., 1921-40. Fellow A.A.A.S.; mem. Sigma Xi, Alpha Epsilon Delta. Republican. Presbyterian. Mason (past comdr. K.T.; past high priest, R.A.M.). Author: Laboratory Exercises in Bacteriology, 1914. Contbr. numerous papers on researches in botany and bacteriology. Home: 260 High Drive, Laguna Beach CA‡

BILLINGS, J(OHN) HARLAND, educator; b. Orono, Can., Apr. 4, 1888; s. Samuel Martin and Evaline Elizabeth (Swanston) B.; B.A.Sc., U. of Toronto, 1912; S.M., Mass. Inst. Tech., 1915, Harvard, 1915; Eng.D., Drexel Institute of Technology, 1959; m. Anna Sibylla Stonehouse, Sept. 29, 1915; children—Julia Evelyn, Jean Harland (Mrs. Curtis A. Grundberg), John Kimball. Asst. engr., Can. Machinery Corp., 1912-13; instr. mech. engring., U. of Missouri, 1913-14, Johns Hopkins, 1915-16; lecturer in machine design, U. of Toronto, 1916-19; prof. and head dept. of mech. engring., Drexel Inst. Tech., Phila., from 1919, acting dean Engring. Sch., 1944-45; engring. cons. U.S. Army Ordnance, Bur. Ships, USN. Gage prodn. rep. Imperial Munitions Bd. Ottawa, Can., Apr.-Oct. 1917. Fellow A.A.A.S.; mem. Am. Soc. M.E. (chmn. Phila. sect. 1928-29), Soc. Promotion Engring. Edn. (chmn. Mid-Atlantic sect. 1944), Tau Beta Pi, Pi Tau Sigma, Phi Kappa Phi. Club: Llanerch Country. Author: Applied Kinematics, 1943; Mechanics and Design of Machines, 1951. Home: Broomall PA Died Sept. 29, 1971; buried Valley Forge Gardens, King of Prussia PA

BILLINGS, STEPHEN ELLSWORTH, editor; b. Ripton, Vt., Oct. 18, 1909; s. S. Jason and Blanche A. (Newton) B.; ed. pub. schs.; m. Antonietta Sannino, June 25, 1945; children—Bianca, Marcia, Patricia. Mem. staff Barre (Vt.) Daily Times, 1928-37, 45-72, editor editorial page, 1945-72, also book editor; state news editor Rutland (Vt.) Herald, 1937-41. Pres. Ward Five P.T.A., 1960. Sec. Barre (Vt.) Republican Com., 1947-72. Served with AUS, 1942-45, ETO. Mem. Barre C. of C. (dir.), Poetry Soc. Vt., Vt. Hist. Soc. Methodist (steward). Home: Barre VT Died Aug. 26, 1972.

BINCH, WILFRED REESE, lawyer; b. Toronto, Ont., Can., July 1, 1896; s. Reese C. and Laura (Hendricks) B.; student Victoria Coll., U. Toronto; LL.B., Osgoode Hall Law Sch.; m. Betty Bowie Garner, June 10, 1933; children—Martha, James. Called to Ont. bar, 1921, created queen's counsel, 1945; mem. firm McMillan, Binch, Stuart, Berry, Dunn, Corrigan & Howland, and predecessor, Toronto. Dir. Algoma Steel Corp., Ltd., Can. Vinegars Ltd., Houdaille Industries, Inc., G.H. Wood & Co. Ltd. Clubs: Toronto Golf; Royal Canadian Yacht, National. Home: Thornhill Ontario Canada Died Sept. 18, 1967; interred Mount Pleasant Cemetery, Toronto Ontario Canada

BINFORD, RAYMOND, college pres.; b. Carthage, Ind., July 15, 1876; s. Josiah and Margaret Fell (Hill) B.; B.S., Earlham Coll., Ind., 1901; M.S., U. of Chicago, 1906; Ph.D., Johns Hopkins, 1912; m. Helen Bills Titsworth, June 18, 1913; children—Anna Naomi, Richard Titsworth, Frederick Harrison, Mary Margaret. Prof. biology, Guilford Coll., N.C., 1901-14, also research at Fisheries Lab., Beaufort, N.C., 4 summers; prof. zoology, Earlham Coll., 1914-18; also instr. zoology, Marine Biol. Lab., Woods Hole, Mass., summers 1912-17; pres. and prof. zoology, Guilford Coll., N.C., 1918-34, pres. emeritus since 1934; prof. biology, William Penn College, Ia., 1948. Director Buck Creek. Civilian Public Service Camp, Marion, N.C., 1941-43, dir. internat. good will projects at Toluca and Cuantla, Mexico, for Am. Friends Service Com., 1946-47. Convener and 1st pres., N.C. Coll. Conf., 1921; chmn. bd. edn. of Five Years Meeting of Friends in America, 1929-45. Fellow A.A.A.S.; mem. Carolina Geological Soc.; Am. Soc. Zoologists, 1912-30, Phi Beta Kappa. Independent Democrat. Author of a syllabus on phys. science for freshman in coll. and of several articles on edn. pub. in religious jours. and booklets; co-author of an outline study for elders in Soc. of Friends. Home: Guilford College NC‡

BINGHAM, GEORGE HUTCHINS, judge; b. Littleton, N.H., Aug. 19, 1864; s. George Azro and Eliza I. (Woods) B.; A.B., Dartmouth Coll., 1887, LL.D., 1917; LL.B., Harvard, 1891; m. Cordelia P. Hinckley, Oct. 29, 1891. Practiced at Littleton and Manchester, N.H., 1891-1902; asso. justice Supreme Ct. of N.H., 1902-13; U.S. circuit judge, since 1913. Democrat. Home: 251 N. Bay St., Manchester NH‡

BINGHAM, GUY MORSE, lecturer, humorist; b. Orwell, O., Dec. 26, 1872; s. Lucius A. and Sarah Elizabeth (Morse) B.; B.S. Ohio Northern U. spl. courses at Harvard; m. Helen A. Noble, Aug. 18, 1897. Formerly supt. pub. schs.; in recruiting service U.S. Army, World War; sent to Europe by Y.M.C.A. after the Armistice and served in Eng., France and Germany; lecturer on nat. polit., ednl. and business topics before clubs, business orgns. and teachers' convs.; specialist in social, moral and business problems. Mem. Pi Gamma Mu. Republican. Presbyterian. Mason (K.T.). Wrote: Principles of Success, Vocational Guidance Charts. Home: Wilmington, O. Address: 2309 N. Curtis Rd., Arlington VA‡

BINGHAM, MILLICENT TODD (MRS. WALTER V. BINGHAM), geographer, author; b. Washington, D.C., 1880; d. Prof. David and Mabel (Loomis) Todd (father an astronomer and mother an author); A.B., Vassar, 1902; studied univs. of Paris, Grenoble, Berlin and at Harvard; M.A., Radcliffe Coll., 1917, Ph.D., 1923; Litt.D., Dickinson Coll., Carlisle, Pa., 1952. Amherst (Mass.) College, 1957; Universitetets Venner, U. Oslo Norway, 1958; married Walter V. Bingham, 1920. Instr. French, Vassar Coll., 1902-04, Wellesley, 1906-07; accompanied father on his scientific expdns. to Singapore, Singkep, Siam, Philippines, Japan, Tripoli, Peru, Chili and Russia; traveled widely in Europe, Asia, Africa, N. and S. Am. With Army Edn. Corps, 1918; lecturer on geography of France, U. Grenoble, 1919; on urban geography, Columbia U., 1928-29; on geography, Sarah Lawrence Coll., Bronxville, N.Y., 1929. Mem. Internat. Geog. Congress, Paris, 1931. Fellow Am. Geog. Soc.; mem. Phi Beta Kappa, Soc. Geografica de Lima (Peru), Internat. Soc. Woman Geogs., Wash. Lit. Soc. Epis. Club: Cosmopolitan (New York). Author: Life of Mary E. Stearns, 1909; Peru Land of Contrasts, 1914; Geography of France (co-author), 1919; La Floride du sud-est et la ville de Miami, 1932, also translated into English; Ancestors' Brocades. The Literary Debut of Emily Dickinson, 1945; Emily Dickinson a Revelation, 1954; Emily Dickinson's Home, 1955. Editor: Bolts of Melody. New Poems of Emily Dickinson, 1945. Translator: Principes de Geographie Humaine, Vidal de la Blache, 1926. Established Walter Van Dyke Bingham Lectureship, 1954; est. Todd Wildlife Sanctuary, Hog Island, Muscongus Bay, Me., 1935, presented it to Nat. Audubon Soc., 1960; presented her entire collection of Emily Dickinson manuscripts, poems, and letters to Amherst Coll., 1956-57; presented Mabel Loomis Todd Forest to Amherst Coll., 1961; presented collection of artifacts from astron. expdns. and 1st installment of family archives to Yale, 1964. Washington DC Died Dec. 1968.

BINGHAM, WHEELOCK HAYWARD, store exec., b. Boston, Nov. 28, 1907; s. George Mears and Lilla Harding (Mackay) B.; student Harvard; m. Evelyn Marguerite Feakes, May 25, 1934; children—Wheelock Richard, Betsy (Mrs. Richard A. Volonte); m. 2d, Josephine Wren Carrillo, Jan. 25, 1964. Pres., dir. R. H. Macy & Co., Inc., N.Y.C.; dir. Bank of Am., Nat. Surety Corp., N.Y.C., Am. Ins. Co., Newark. Mem. adv. com. Ship's Store, U.S. Navy, 1950. Served to capt. USNR, 1943-46. Decorated Legion of Merit. Episcopalian. Mason (K.T.). Clubs: Harvard (N.Y.C.); Pacific Union (San Francisco); Country (Burlingame, Cal.). Home: Southbury CT Died May 12, 1972.

BINGHAM, WILLIAM J., ednl. adminstr.; b. Norristown, Pa., Aug. 8, 1889; s. Robert and Martha (Clyde) B.; grad. Phillips Exeter Acad., 1912; A.B., Harvard, 1916; m. Florence Patee, May 29, 1917; children—William J., Richard I. Banking, Houston, 1919-20; head track coach and asst. grad. treas. Athletic Assn., Harvard, 1920-22, dir. athletics and chmn. com. on regulation athletic sports, 1926-51, chmn. faculty athletic com. 1951; with Department of Defense, Washington, 1951-52; president and treas. Ernest Monnier, Inc., importers, Boston, 1922-37; dir. Cambridge Trust Co. Dir. Boston Garden, Harvard Coop. Soc. Nat. Football Hall of Fame. Chmn. Am. Olympic Track Com. and Olympiad (1936-Berlin); sec. Nat. Collegiate Football Rules Com., 1932-43, chmn., 1943-50; also pres. various sports coms., 1927-51). Served as pvt. to capt. U.S. Army, 1917-19; maj. to col., 1942-45, dir. security and intelligence First Service Command. Decorated Croix de Guerre, Legion of Merit. Clubs: Harvard (Boston and N.Y. City), Faculty (Harvard). Home: Marlboro NH Died Sept. 7, 1971.

BIN ISHAK, INCHE YUSOFF, head of state of Singapore. Died Nov. 1970.*

BINKLEY, ALMOND M(ADISON), educator, horticulturist; b. Franktown, Colo., May 23, 1900; s. Henry M. and Elizabeth (Davies) B.; B.S., Colo. State Univ., 1922; M.S., Ia. State Coll. (research fellow), 1923; grad. study Cornell, 1934-35; m. Alma Irene Harrington, July 22, 1932. Insp. fruit and vegetables Colo. Bur. Markets, 1923-24; research agriculturist Am. Beet Sugar Co., Rocky Ford, Colo., 1924-28; asso. prof. Colo. State Univ., Fort Collins, 1928-35, head horticulture and chief horticulturist Colo. Agri. Exptl. Sta. from 1939; Colo. state horticulturist, 1935-42; collaborator Bur. Plant Industry, U.S. Dept. Agr. from 1939. Attended Internat. Horticulture Congress, London, Eng., 1930. Served as pvt., inf. S.A.T.C., 1918. Mem. Am. Soc. Hort. Sci., A.A.A.S., Am. Potato Assn. Am. Carnation Soc. (hon.), Phi Kappa Phi (hon.), Tri-Beta (hon.), Sigma Phi Epsilon. Mason, Elk. Author tech. research, and popular articles. Home: Ft Collins CO Died Nov. 20, 1970; interred Fairmount Mausoleum, Denver CO

BINKLEY, CHRISTIAN KREIDER, author, educator; b. Millersville, Pa., Aug. 6, 1870; s. P. F. and Catherine (Kreider) B.; grad. Millersville State Normal Sch., 1892, Stanford Univ., 1899; m. 1894, Mary Engle Barr, Lititz, Pa. Teacher English lit., Cogswell Poly. Coll., San Francisco, since 1900. Author: Sonnets and Songs for a House of Days, 1902 R10; Nature-Lure, 1903 A16. Address: Mountain View CA‡

BINKLEY, WILLIAM CAMPBELL, prof. history; b. Newbern, Tenn., Apr. 30, 1889; s. Frederick Mills and Sarah Ola (Dixon) B.; A.B., U. of Calif., 1917, M.A., 1918, Ph.D., 1920; LL.D., Tulane, 1965; m. Vera B. McGlothlin, Dec. 31, 1913; children—Vera Loraine (Mrs. Chase C. Mooney), Barbara Mae (Mrs. Allen Truex), Marion Frances (Mrs. Edmond H. Kalmon). Assistant in history, University of California, 1917-20, chief asst., 1919-20; instr. polit. science, U. of Tex., 1920-21; asst. prof. history, Colorado Coll., 1921-23, asso. prof., 1923-25, prof., 1925-30; prof. history and head of dept. of history, Vanderbilt Univ., 1930-53; prof. history Tulane U., 1953-63, 67-70; Distinguished prof. history U. Houston, 1966-67. Lectr. summer sessions University of Texas, University of Colorado and University of Iowa. Mem. Am. Hist. Assn., Miss. Valley Hist. Assn. (board of editors, 1935-38; mem. exec. council, 1940-63; pres. 1944-46) Southern Hist. Assn. (bd. editors, 1934-38; mem. exec. council 1942-53; president 1950), Tex. State Hist. Assn., Tenn. Hist Soc. Author: The Expansionist Movement in Texas, 1925; The Texas Revolution, 1952. Editor: Official Correspondence of the Texan Revolution, 2 volumes, 1936. Joint Editor: New Spain and the West, 1932. Editor Tenn. Hist. Quarterly, 1941-43; editor Journal of Southern History, 1943-49; Miss. Valley Hist. Review, 1953-63. Home: New Orleans LA Died Aug. 19, 1970; interred Lake Lawn Mausoleum, New Orleans LA

BINNICKER, RICHARD JOHNSON, banker; b. Flemington, Fla., Nov. 29, 1874; s. James Lawrence and Louisa (Johnson) B.; ed. pub. schs.; m. Lois Efland, Nov. 7, 1907; children—Louisa, Richard Johnson, (dec.), Ruth. In railroading work, 1892-1902; began as bookkeeper, First Nat. Bank, Tampa, Fla., 1902, rose through various positions to pres., chairman of bd., retired from active service 1950. Democrat. Baptist. Home: 50 Bahama Circle, Office: First Nat. Bank, Tampa FL‡

BINNS, ARCHIE, author; b. Port Ludlow, Wash., July 30, 1899; s. Frank and Atlanta Sarah (McWha) B.; A.B., Stanford U., 1922; m. Mollie Windish, Sept. 14, 1923 (dec. 1954); children—Jacqueline, Georgia (now married); married second, Ellen Losey Goins, 1955; children—Richard, Thomas, Ellen Atlanta, Margaret Sarah. Formerly newspaper reporter, Washington corr. for Scripps-Howard newspapers and editor Leonard Scott Pub. Co.; tchr. creative writing U. Washington, 1950-56; asso. prof. creative writing Western Washington College Education, Bellingham, 1957-59. Served in U.S. Army, 1918; commd. 2d lt. F.A. Res., 1923. Mem. Authors League; Hammer and Coffin. Author books including: The Timber Beast, 1944; You Rolling River, 1947; The Radio Imp, 1950; Secret of the Sleeping River, 1952; Sea in the Forest, 1953; Sea Pup, 1954; Mrs. Fiske and the American Theatre, 1955, The Enchanted Islands, 1956; The Headwaters, 1957; Might Mountain, 1940; Lightship, 1934, The Laurels are Cut Down, 1936; Northwest Gateway, 1960; Sea Pup, Again, 1965; Peter Skene Ogden, Fur Trader, 1967. Address: Sequim WA Died June 28, 1971.

BIN-NUN, DOV, educator; b. Klintzi, Russia, Jan. 7, 1910; s. Joshua and Leah (Malkov) Bin-N.; came to U.S., 1929, naturalized, 1935; A.B., Chapman Coll., 1937; M.A., N.Y.U., 1938; Ph.D., U. So. Cal., 1952; m. Rose Moskowitz, Sept. 9, 1939; 1 dau., Judith (Mrs. David Roy Barthold). Instr. Hebrew, Menorah Center, Los Angeles, 1938-41; head survey dept. Richmond (Cal.) Shipyards, 1942-45; staff mem. Bur. Jewish Edn., Los Angeles, instr. Hebrew U. Judaism, Los Angeles, 1946-54; prof. Hebrew lang., lit. Hebrew Union Coll., Jewish Inst. Religion, Los Angeles, 1954-68; lectr. Hebrew, U. So. Cal., 1960-68. Served with AUS, 1944-45. Mem. Soc. Bibl. Lit. and Exegests, Am. Assn U. Profs., Los Angeles Soc. for Jewish Research, Central Conf. Am. Rabbis, Hebrew Tchrs. Fedn. Los Angeles (chmn. 1939-41), Los Angeles Council Tchrs. (sec. 1939-41), Alpha Kappa Delta. Author pamphlet Curriculum for the One-Day a Week School, 1953. Home: Los Angeles CA Died Apr. 27, 1968.

BIRCH, DAVID ROBERT, consul; b. at Phila., Mar. 15, 1876; ed. Friends' Central Sch., Phila., and Ardmore High Sch. Newspaper reporter to 1902; consul at Malaga, 1902-7, Genoa, 1907-8, Alexandria, June 10-July 1, 1908; v. consul-gen., Genoa, 1908-12; consul, Bahai, Aug. 22, 1912-—. Address: Am. Consulate, Bahai Brazil‡

BIRD, ANNA PENNOCK, psychologist; b. at Drumore, Lancaster Co., Pa.; d. Hadley and Lydia (Phillips) Pennock; ed. Millersville (Pa.) State Normal Sch.; taught in pub. schs.; studied kindergarten in Phila.; m. Charles L. Bird. of Toledo, O., 1903. Opened kindergarten, Lancaster City, Pa., Apr. 16, 1883, connected with it a school to retain the pupils up to the high school grades; also conducted teachers' training classes in connection; removed to Toledo, 1894, and soon after began teaching classes, private pupils, and lecturing on practical psychology. Author: Creative Force in Vegetable, Animal and Human World; Inside Our Own Doors; A Key to Success; The Thought Circle; Thoughts and Words. Address: Toledo OH‡

BIRD, PAUL PERCY, mechanical engr.; b. Kalamazoo, Mich., Mar. 24, 1877; s. Charles H. and Mary A. (Warrant) B.; M.E., Cornell U., 1900; m. Elizabeth Hyatt, of Toledo, O., June 20, 1908. With Newport News (Va.) Shipbuilding Co., 1900-3; instr. in marine engring. Cornell U., 1904; steam engr., Ill. Steel Co., S. Chicago, 1904-7; smoke insp., City of Chicago, 1907-11; mech. engr. with Commonwealth Edison Co., Chicago, May, 1911-1913. Mem. Assn. of Commerce Com. on Smoke Prevention with Electrification of Ry. Terminals, Chicago. Pres. Internat. Assn. for Prevention of Smoke, 1910; mem. Am. Society Mech. Engrs., 1907, Nat. Electric Light Assn., Western Soc. of Engrs., Delta Tau Delta. Presbyn. Clubs: University, Exmoor Country. Office: 111 W. Monroe St., Chicago IL‡

BIRD, REMSEN DU BOIS, educational consultant; b. N.Y.C., Jan. 3, 1888; s. Edward and Mary (Dunham) B.; A.B., Lafayette Coll., 1909, D.D., 1919; B.D., Princeton Theol. Sem., 1912; student U. Berlin, 1913; LL.D., Pomona Coll., 1937, Albany Coll., 1938, U. Cal.; L.H.D., U. So. Cal., 1940; m. Helen McClure, May 6, 1914. Instr. Princeton Theol. Sem., 1913-15; prof. ch. history San Francisco Theol. Sem., 1915-21; pres. Occidental Coll., 1921-46, retired 1946, now life trustee; cons. Della Records, 1946-48. Mem. bd. Carmel Foundation; ednl. cons. Beaudette Labs.; dir. S. Cal. Symphony Assn.; director World Affairs Council No. Cal.; spl. rep. Pres., Fund for Adult Edn. in Europe, 1952; cons. building Monterey Peninsula Coll., 1947; dir. Western Com. Inst. Internat. Edn.; chairman of board of trustees Monterey Inst. Foreign Studies; bd. dirs. Monterey Peninsula World Affairs Council, 1951-53; chmn. citizens adv. com. Army Lang. Sch.; vice chmn. citizens advisory com. 6th Army. Chairman state adv. com. Nat. Youth Adminstrn., 1935-38; pres. Los Angeles City Planning Commn., 1943. Pres. Carmel Art Assn. Assn., 1949. Pres. Assn. Colls. and Univs. Pacific S.W., 1933-34; pres. Assn. Am. Colleges, 1941; trustee Beaudette Biological Foundation. Decorated Star of Solidarity (Italy). Member Cooperative Research Organization, Academy of Political and Social Science (pres. Pacific N.W. Center, 1929-30), Defense Lang. Inst. (chmn. acad. council from 1964), Cal. Assn. Adult Edn. (pres. 1932-37), Phi Beta Kappa, Delta Upsilon. Democrat. Presbyn. Clubs: Sunset, Old Capital University (Pasadena). Address: Carmel CA Died Apr. 9, 1971.

BIRD, WALLACE SAMUEL, Canadian provincial govt. ofcl.; b. Marysville, N.B., Can., Dec. 7, 1917; s. Charles Edwin and Catherine (Yeomans) B.; student pub. schs.; LL.B., St. Thomas U., 1968; D.Com.Sc., U. Moncton, 1968; LL.D., U. N.B., 1968; D.C.L., Mt. Allison U., 1969; m. Phyllis M. Bailey, June 4, 1941; (dec. Dec. 1970); children—Richard, Nancy, David, Michael. With Mussens, Ltd., Fredricton, N.B., 1946-71, dir., 1951-71, exec. v.p., 1959-71; pres. Mack Maritime Distbrs., Ltd., Atlantic (Mussens), Ltd. Pres., chmn. bd. dirs. N.B. Devel. Corp., 1966-71. Lt. gov. Province of N.B., 1968-71. Chmn. bd. govs. Beaverbrook Art Gallery, 1968-71. Mem. Fredericton Bd. Trade (past pres.). Decorated Knight of Grace of Order of St. John of Jerusalem, 1968. Mason (Shriner, Jester). Clubs: Fredericton Golf, Fredericton Curling. Home: Fredericton NB Canada. Died Oct. 2, 1971.

BIRKENMEYER, CARL BRUCE, ins. co. exec.; b. Edgerton, Wis., Nov. 26, 1909; s. Charles Wilhelm and Jessie Inez (Kelly) B.; student U. Wis., 1927-30; m. Mary Jane Perry, Sept. 30, 1933; children—Ann Jane (Mrs. Gerald Ryles), Susan Eleanor (Mrs. Matthew Maury). Began career with the United Pacific Ins. Co., Seattle and Los Angeles, 1931-42, exec. v.p., Tacoma, 1955-62, pres., 1962-70, also dir.; asst. vp., Am. Asso. Inc. Cos., Portland, Ore., also Seattle, 1942-55; pres., dir. UniPac Corp., Cascade Ins. Co., United Pacific Life

Ins. Co.; dir. Nat. Bank of Wash., Tacoma, Van Waters & Rogers, Inc. Home: Tacoma WA Died Feb. 21, 1970.

BIRNBAUM, MARTIN, art critic; born Miscolcz, Hungary, May 10, 1878; son Leopold and Mary (Brown) B.; brought to U.S., 1883, naturalized 1899; A.B., Coll. City of N.Y., 1897, A.M., Columbia, 1898, LL.B., 1901; also music edn. Nat. Conservatory Music,; M.A. (hon.), Asia Inst. Admitted to N.Y. bar, 1901, and practiced in New York, 1901-10; mgr. Berlin Photographic Co., 1910-16; mem. firm. Scott & Fowles, Art dealers, N.Y. City, 1916-26; ethnol. and artistic research in Asia, Africa, South Seas, etc. and writing from 1926; arranged for art exhibitions in U.S. of foreign artists, also wrote catalogs in connection with exhibitions, 1910-20. Member bd. trustees Professional Children's Sch. Decorated Commendatore of Royal Crown of Italy in recognition of service in connection with Biennial Art Exhbns., Venice, 1932. Mem. Amis de l'Ecole Francaise d'Extreme Orient, World Federalists; editorial board of the World Government News. Clubs: The Explorers (New York City); Bohemians. Author: Introductions: Painters, Sculptors and Graphic Artists, 1919; Oscar Wilde: Fragments and Memories, 1920; Arthur Rackham (in collaboration with F. Coykendall), 1922; John Singer Sargent: A Conver-sation Piece, 1940; Beardsley et Wilde, 1939; Vanishing Eden, 1942; Jacovleff and other Essays, 1946; Angkor and the Mandarin Road, 1952; The Last Romantic, 1960; author of brochures on art. Contbr. Natural History, Asia, International Studio Art in America, others. Mem. Phi Beta Kappa. Address: New York City NY Died July 1970.

BISCH, LOUIS EDWARD, neuropsy..iatrist; b. Bklyn., Mar. 10, 1885; s. Otto George and Dorothea Louise B.; A.B., Columbia, 1907, Ph.D., 1912, M.D., 1911; m. Henriette B. Bousquet; children—Barbara, Betty. Interne Manhattan State Hosp., N.Y. City, 1911-13; physician Clearing House for Mental Defectives, 1912-15, N.Y. Neurol. Inst., 1912-16; instr. neuropathology, N.Y. Post-Grad. Med. Sch., 1914-15; consulting neurologist, N.Y. City Children's hosps. and schs., 1913-15; lecturer and asso. in ednl. psychology, Teachers Coll., and lecturer psychology, Columbia, 1913-16; prof. of neuropsychiatry, N.Y. Polyclinic Med. Sch. and Hosp. 1926-63; organizer and dir. Psychopathic Lab. N.Y.C., 1916, Mental Hygiene Clinic, Norfolk, Va., 1918-19; cons. specialist in neuropsychiatry USPHS Hosp. 45, Biltmore, N.C., 1921-22; med. dir. Hillcrest Manor. Organizer, 1917, and dir. psychopathic div. 5th Naval Dist., U.S.N.R.F. until 1919. Fellow A.M.A.; mem. Eugenics Research Assn., Am. Psychiatric Assn., N.Y. State, N.C. med. socs., A.A.A.S., Authors' League of America, Am. Anthropol. Assn., N.Y. Acad. Clubs: Lotos (New York); Authors' (London, Eng.). Author several books, including: Your Nerves, 1945; Cure Your Nerves Yourself, 1953, also sci. paper and contbr. to mag. Home: New York City NY Died 1963.

BISHOP, BRUCE CLAY, lawyer; b. Chattanooga, Jan. 31, 1919; s. Jacob Walter and Ola (McGaughey) B.; B.B.A., U. Chattanooga, 1940; postgrad. George Washington U. Law Sch., 1940-41; LL.B., Stetson U., 1946; m. Dorothy Pepiot, Apr. 26, 1944; children—Bruce Clay, Beverly, Leslie. Admitted to Tenn. bar, 1947, practiced in Chattanooga, 1947-68; mem. firms Thomas, Folts & Brammer, 1947-48, Folts, Bishop & Thomas, 1949-62, Bishop, Thomas, Leitner, Mann & Milburn, 1962-68. Corporate dir. Indsl. Water Chems., Inc., Chamberlain-Realtors, Inc., Smith Elevator Co., Inc. (all Chattanooga). Mem. adv. council U. Chattanooga, 1964-68; active United Fund campaigns. Commr. Town of Signal Mountain, 1959-63. Served to comdr. USNR, 1941-46. Decorated D.F.C. with three oak leaf clusters, Air medal with twelve oak leaf clusters. Mem. Fedn. Ins. Counsel, Internat. Soc. Barristers, Internat. Acad. Law and Sci., Fla. Bar, Bar Assn. Tenn., Phi Alpha Delta, Pi Kappa Alpha. Democrat. Baptist (deacon, Sunday sch. supt. 1960-68). Rotarian (v.p. 1960). Clubs: Mountain City, Signal Mountain Golf and Country (Signal Mountain, Tenn.). Contbr. articles to profl. publs. Home: Signal Mountain TN Died Dec. 1, 1968.

BISHOP, DAVID HORACE, coll. prof.; b. Newbern, Va., Aug. 20, 1870; s. Benjamin William Shields and Julia Anne (Goodykoontz) B.; A.B., Emory and Henry Coll., 1891, LL.D., 1930; fellow Vanderbilt U., 1895-97, M.A., 1897; studied U. of Chicago, Columbia U. and British Museum; m. Mary Hartwell Somerville, Jan. 14, 1914; children—Ella Vasser, Mary Hartwell (Mrs. Beckett Howorth, Jr.), Martha Somerville. Instructor English, Vanderbilt University, 1897-98; professor English and history, Polytechnic Coll., Ft. Worth, Tex., 1898-99; prof. English, Millsaps Coll., Jackson, Miss., 1900-04, 1930-32; prof. English, U. of Miss., 1904-30, and since 1932, vice chancellor, 1932-35, dean of faculty, 1936-46, dean of Grad. School, 1936-40; dean emeritus of Graduate School, since Sept. 1946; prof. English summers, George Peabody Coll., Nashville, 1914, U. of N.C., 1935. In service overseas with Y.M.C.A., 1918-19, as lecture sec. for United Kingdom, London, acting dir. instrn. in English in A.E.F., Paris, and prof. English, A.E.F. Univ. Beaune, France. Mem. Modern Lang. Assn. America, Sigma Alpha Epsilon, Omicron Delta Kappa, Phi Beta Kappa. Democrat. Methodist. Author: The Father of the Wartons, 1917; Wordsworth's Heritage: Racedown or Grasmere, 1935; The Origin of The Prelude," 1941. Contbr. to lit. and scholarly periodicals. Home: University MS‡

BISHOP, GEO(RGE) LEE, farmer; b. Osage, Tex., Oct. 9, 1870; s. David Rubin and Maggie (Lee) B.; Baylor U., Tex., 1890-92; m. Ella Phillips, of Crawford, Tex., Oct. 16, 1906; 1 dau., Alta Mary. Moved to Okla., 1899; mem. Okla. State Bd. of Agr., 1904-06; mem. Okla. State Council of Defense, World War; served as agrl. adviser, State Exemption Bd.; dist. agt. U.S. Dept. Agr., 2 yrs. Pres. Okla. Crop Improvement Assn., 1920-25, Okla. Farm Bur., 1921-23; asso. editor Okla. Farmer, 1914-23; pub. dir. Okla. Cotton Growers' Assn., 1925-28; now mgr. Houston office Okla. Cotton Growers' Assn. Democrat. Home: Oklahoma City OK‡

BISHOP, HUBERT KEENEY, civil engr.; b. Warsaw, N.Y., June 26, 1870; s. James E. and Castern Gertrude (Keeney) B.; grad. high sch., Warsaw, 1889; C.E., Cornell U., 1893; m. Anna S. Tubbs, Sept., 1899. Asst. city engr., Hudson, N.Y., 1893-95; asst. engr. N.Y. State Canals, and engr. in charge surveys and constrn., 1895-99; supt. pub. works, Hudson, 1899-1905; chief engr. for C. C. Vermeule, N.Y. City, 1905-07; expert N.Y. State Highway Dept., 1907-09, 1st dep., 1909-11; chief engr. Hawaii Loan Fund Commn., 1911-12; supt. pub. works Ty. of Hawaii, 1912-13; chief engr. Hawaii Waihole Water Co., Honolulu, 1913-14; cons. practice, with C. C. Vermeule, N.Y. City, 1914-16; dist. engr. U.S. Pub. Roads, Washington, D.C., 1916-18; chief engr. Ind. State Highway Commn., 1918-21; chief Div. of Constrn., U.S. Bur. Pub. Roads (Pub. Roads Adminstrn.), 1921-43; dep. commr. 1943-44, in charge Federal highway work in Hawaiian Islands since 1944. Republican. Mason. Mem. Am. Soc. C.E. Home: Moana Hotel Office: Federal Bldg., Honolulu HI‡

BISHOP, SAMUEL A., r.r. ofcl. (ret.); b. Brownsville, Tenn., July 21, 1874; s. Samuel A. and Ida (Peebles) B.; student Christian Bros. Coll., St. Louis; widower; 1 dau., Zuriel. With S.P. Co., 1894-1944, ret. 1944; dir. Tide Water Asso. Oil Co. Master Mason. Clubs: Jonathan, Kiwanis (Los Angeles). Home: 1552 Irving Av., Glendale 1 CA‡

BISHOPP, FRED CORRY, entomologist; b. Virginia Dale, Colo., Jan. 14, 1884; s. Thomas Barton and Harriet Caroline (McKay) B.; B.S., Colo. State Coll., 1902, M.S., 1926; grad. student Southern Meth. U., 1923-24; Ph.D., Ohio State U., 1932; m. Eulalie Virginia Spencer, Dec. 9, 1908; children—Harriett Eloise, Fred Thomas, Howard Spencer (dec.), Hazel Eulalie. Teaching fellow zoology and entomology, Colo. Agri. Coll., 1902-03; asst. prof. entomology and zoology, Md. Agrl. Coll., 1903-04; special field agt. Bureau Entomology, U.S. Dept. Agr., 1904-08, asst. entomologist, 1908-11, entomologist, 1911-26, chief Div. of Insects Affecting Man and Animals, 1926-41, asst. chief of bureau in charge research 1941-53; dir., coordinator fed., state and industry sponsored research on bollworm Oscar Johnston Cotton Found., 1953; Dept. State adviser to agr. minister Egypt, 1956; mem. Dept Agr. delegation to World Agr. Fair, New Delhi, India, 1959. Decorated His British Majesty's Medal for service in the cause of freedom. Fellow of American Public Health Associations A.A.A.S., Entomol. Soc. America (v.p. 1932); mem. Am. Assn. of Economic Enthomologists (pres. 1937), Am. Soc. of Parisitologists (pres. 1938), Washington Acad. Sciences, Enthomol. Society of Washington (pres. 1932), American Society Tropical Medicine and Hygiene, Acad. Trop. Medicine, Am. Mosquito Control Assn. (v.p. 1952), Biol. Soc. Washington, Am. Found. for Tropical Medicine. Phi Kappa Phi, Sigma Xi. Presbyn. Editor section on Insects Affecting Animals and Sanitary Entomology of Biol. Abstracts. Author of numerous bulletins and articles on Entomology. Home: Silver Spring MD Died May 8, 1970; buried Inglewood Cemetery, Inglewood CA

BISSELL, CHARLES SPENCER, banker; b. Suffield, Conn., Oct. 18, 1893; s. Charles Chauncy and Clara Julia (Spencer) B.; Ph.B., Yale Sci. Sch., 1915; m. Dorothy Fuller, May 10, 1919; children—Charles Spencer, Sumner F., Mrs. Theodore D. Olmstead. Pres. Suffield Savs. Bank, 1961-69; dir. Travelers Ins. Companies, First Nat. Bank, Suffield. Pres. trustees Suffield Acad. Mem. Conn. Hist. Soc. (pres.). Author: Antique Furniture in Suffield, Conn. (award of merit for best book local history Am. Assn. State and Local History 1956), 1956. Home: Suffield CT Died Sept. 1969.

BISSELL, CLAYTON LAWRENCE, army officer; b. Kane, Pa., July 29, 1896; s. Thomas Francis and Isabelle (Collins) B.; LL.B., Valparaiso U. Law Sch., 1917; student Air Corps Tactical Sch.; Command and Gen. Staff Sch.; Chem. Warfare Sch.; Army War Coll.; Navy War Coll.; m. LeClair Gaillard, June 3, 1925; 1 dau., LeClair. Began as pvt. 1st class, Aviation Sec. Signal Corps, 1917, and advanced through the grades to maj. gen., 1943. Served with 148th Fighter Squadron, comd. 638th Fighter Squadron in France and in Coblentz with U.S. Army of Occupation. Awarded D.S.C., D.S.M. and Silver Star (U.S.), Distinguished Flying Cross (United States), Air Medal, Order of British Empire, British Distinguished Flying Cross, Order of Crown of Italy, Italian War Cross, Polonia Restituta, Order of Merit (Chile), Abdon Calderon (Equador). Inspected fgn. aviation in Eng., France, Germany, Italy, Holland, 1921; asst., General Billy Mitchell, 1921-24; advance officer first round the world flight, U.S. to Japan and Greenland to U.S. with Stilwell in China, 1941-42; commanded 10th Army Air Force, 1942-43. Chief Army Air Force Intelligence 1943, Asst. Chief of Staff, G-2 in charge of Intelligence U.S. Army, 1944 to end of war; Mil., Mil. Air Attache, Am. Embassy, London, 1946-48. Author: History U.S. Army Air Corps, 1923. Home: Sewanee TN Died Dec. 23, 1972; buried Arlington Nat. Cemetery.

BISSELL, MARY TAYLOR, physician; b. at Brooklyn; d. E. E. L. and Mary J. (Perkins) Taylor; A.B., Vassar, 1875; M.D., Woman's Med. Coll. of N.Y. Infirmary, 1881; m. Willard Parker Bissell, 1876 (died 1878). Prof. hygiene Woman's Med. Coll., 1891-5; exec. sec. N.Y. State Consumers League, 1907-11. Mem. Woman's Medical Soc., Women's Univ. Club, N.Y. State Med. Soc. Established a rest house for semi-invalids at Marlboro, 1912. Author: Household Hygiene, 1890; Physical Development and Exercises for Women, 1892; A Manual of Hygiene, 1894. Also various articles in mags. Address: Women's University Club, 106 E. 52d St., New York NY‡

BISTLINE, FRANCIS M., lawyer; b. Ransom, Kan., Mar. 25, 1896; s. John M. and Martha (Shellenberger) B.; B.S., U. Idaho, 1917; LL.B., Northwestern U., 1920; m. Anne Glindemann, Aug. 16, 1921; 1 dau., Beverly Barbara. Admitted to Idaho bar, 1920; law clerk, Supreme Court of Idaho, 1921-23; in pvt. practice of law, Pocatello, Ida., 1923-69; spl. lectr. income tax law and real estate Ida. State Coll., 1951-63, lectr. income tax, real estate and bus. law, 1954-69; charter incorporator, dir. Pocatello Nat. Bank. State rep. Ida. legislature, 1937, 39, 41, 45, speaker, 1941; charter pres. Ida. Assn. for UN, 1954-55. Mem. Democratic Nat. Com., Ida., 1944-48. Served with U.S. Army, World War I. Dist. gov. Ida. Dist. of Lions Internat., 1936-37. Mem. Ida. Hist. Soc. (trustee), Am. Legion (post comdr.), Banncock County Hist. Soc. (pres.), S.A.R. (pres. Ida.), Phi Alpha Delta, Sigma Nu. Mason (32 deg., Shriner), Elk, Lion. Home: Pocatello ID Died Jan. 20, 1969.

BIXBY, KENNETH ROBERTS, engring. co. exec.; b. Belfast, N.Y., Sept. 10, 1891; s. Charles H. and Alice M. (Vaughan) B.; student pub. schs., Belfast; m. Ila O. Mosher, Oct. 14, 1913; children—Carmaleta (Mrs. Kenneth Danner), Marjorie L. (Mrs. Irving T. Gillick), Roger A., Donald L.; m. 2d, Virginia M. Kelley, June 27, 1940; 1 son, Richard K. Rodman, chairman, instrument man Erie R.R. Co., son, Richard K. Rodman, chairman, instrument man Erie R.R. Co., 1908-10; asst. supt. Miles-Tighe Contracting Co., Easton, Pa., 1910-12; supt. Ferguson and Edmondson Co., Pitts., 1912-18, P.J. Joyce Co., Pitts., 1921-22, Winston & Co., N.Y.C., Richmond, Va., 1922-23, Kehota Mining Co., Pitts., 1923-26, Harmeyford Coal Co., New Straitsville, O., 1926-27, Sunlight Coal Co., Booneville, Ind., 1927-28; drafting and party chief A.J. Hazlep, profl. engr., 1918-19; engr. Wickersham-Campbell Coal Co., Zanesville, O., 1919-21; gen. mgr. Midland Electric Coal Corp., Indpls., 1929-35, v.p., gen. mgr., 1935-47; pres. Ken Coal Co., Galesburg, Ill., 1947-55; mgr. K.R. Bixby-Trustee, Galesburg, 1934-69; chmn. bd. Wedge Wire Corp., Wellington, O., 1956-69; gen. mgr. Bixby-Zimmer Engring. Co., Galesburg, 1939-69; partner Ken Co., Galesburg, 1955-69; pres. Bix Co., Wellington, 1963-69, Prairie Steel Co., Havana, Ill., 1959-69; owner K.R. Bixby Oil Co., Owensboro, Ky., 1957-69; dir. Gen. Concrete Products, Inc., Mayfield, Ky., Antipol Corp., Galesburg, Martin Labs., Inc., Owensboro, 1st Galesburg Nat. Bank & Trust Co. Registered profl. engr., Ill. Mem. Am. Mining Congress, Nat., Ill. socs. profl. engrs., Ill. Mining Inst., Galesburg C. of C. Mason. Clubs: Sarasota Bay Country, Field (Sarasota, Fla.); Tri City Traffic (Moline, Ill.); Galesburg, Galesburg Executives, Knox County Country, Soangetaha County (past pres.) (Galesburg). Patentee in field. Home: Galesburg IL Died Jan. 7, 1969; interred Galesburg IL

BIXER, EDMOND P., curtain mfr.; b. N.Y.C., Mar. 15, 1899; s. Herman and Hannah (Petzal) B.; grad. high sch. Pres., dir. Bartmann & Bixer, Inc., curtain mfrs., N.Y.C.; dir. United Mchts. & Mfrs., Inc. Served with USNR, World War II. Clubs: Turf and Field; Lambs, Athletic (N.Y.C.). Home: New York City NY Died Apr. 13, 1972.

BIXLER, EDWARD CLINTON, coll. pres.; b. Westminster, Md., Feb. 1, 1877; s. Uriah and Sarah A. (Myers) B.; A.B., Western Md. Coll., 1901, hon. A.M., 1905; Ph.D., U. of Pa., 1909; studied at Johns Hopkins, 1901-03; m. Margaret Burkhart Englar, of New Windsor, Md., Dec. 29, 1910; 1 dau., Ruth Cassell. Tutor Western Md. Prep. Sch., 1903-04; ordained to ministry Ch. of the Brethren, 1910; prof. ancient langs., Elizabethtown (Pa.) Coll., 1906-08; pres. and prof. ancient langs., Manchester (Ind.) Coll., 1910-11; prof.

ancient langs., Bridgewater (Va.) Coll., 1911-13; prof. ancient langs. and edn., Blue Ridge (Md.) Coll., since 1913, pres. 1927-37, emeritus since 1937; dir. New Windsor (Md.) State Bank. Mem. Carroll County Bd. of Edn. Democrat. Home: New Windsor MD‡

BIZE, LOUIS A., banker; b. Columbus, Ga., Nov. 12, 1871; s. Daniel R. and Mary (Louis) B.; A.B., Lagola Coll., Baltimore, Md.; M.D., Baltimore Med. Sch., 1894; m. Corinne Trice, of Tampa, Fla., Oct. 15, 1901; children—John T., Ruth, Louis, Corinne. Practiced medicine at Tampa, Fla., beginning 1895; pres. Citizens Bank & Trust Co., Tampa, 1913, now chmn. bd.; chmn. bd. Citizens Mortgage & Bond Co., Citizens Security Co.; pres. Citizens Nebr. Av. Bank, Bank of Ybor City (Tampa), Morris Plan Co. (Tampa), Bradenstown (Fla.) Bank & Trust Co., Bank of Pasco County (Dade City, Fla.), First State Bank (Ft. Meade, Fla.); chmn. bd. First Bank & Trust Co. (Sarasota, Fla.). Democrat. Methodist. Mason, K.P., Elk. Rotarian. Home: 819 Bayshore Blvd. Office: Citizens Bank & Trust Co., Tampa FL‡

BLACK, HAROLD ALFRED, lawyer; b. San Francisco, June 20, 1895; s. Alfred Pressly and Fannie Jean (Lyne) B.; A.B., U. Cal. at Berkeley, 1917, J.D., 1921; m. Ella Kathryn Stone, Mar. 4, 1924; children—Donald Pressly, Robert Lincoln. Admitted to Cal. bar, 1921; asso. firm McCutchen, Black, Verleger & Shea, and predecessors, Los Angeles, 1923-40, partner, 1940-68, of counsel, 1968-70. Sec. Iricon Agy., Ltd., 1957-68. Bd. directors Travelers Aid Soc. of Los Angeles; trustee Haynes Found. Served as 1st lt., inf., U.S. Army, 1917-19. Recipient St. Thomas More award Loyola Law Sch., Low Angeles, 1968. Fellow Am. Bar Found.; mem. Law Institute, American (council legal education section 1959-63), also mem. Los Angeles County (past pres.) bar assns., State Bar Cal. (chmn. com. bar examiners 1954; past gov., v.p., treas. 1965-66, chmn. com. on legal edn. 1968), Town Hall (past president and member of the hon. bd.), Maritime Law Assn., Los Angeles World Affairs Council (dir.), Phi Beta Kappa, Phi Delta Phi, Kappa Sigma. Mason Clubs: California, University, Propeller (pres. 1948) (Los Angeles); Chancery. Home: Los Angeles CA Died Sept. 4, 1970.

BLACK, HUGO LA FAYETTE, jurist, b. Harlan, Clay County, Ala., Feb. 27, 1886; s. William La Fayette and Martha Ardella (Toland) B.; ed. pub. schs., Ashland, Ala., LL.B., University of Alabama, 1906; married Josephine Foster, February 1921 (deceased December 1951); children—Hugo La Fayette, Sterling Foster, Martha Josephine; married second Elizabeth Seay DeMeritte, Sept. 11, 1957. Began practice Ashland, Alabama, 1906-07, Birmingham, Alabama, from 1907; served as police judge 18 months, 1910-11; solicitor (prosecuting attorney) Jefferson County, Ala., 1915-17; in gen. practice, Birmingham, 1919-27; U.S. Senator from Ala. 2 terms, 1927-37; apptd. asso. justice U.S. Supreme Court, 1937-71. Entered 2d O.T.C., Ft. Oglethorpe, Ga., Aug. 3, 1917; commd. capt. F.A.; served in 81st F.A. and as adj. 19th Arty. Brigade. Home: Alexandria VA Died Sept. 25, 1971; buried Arlington Nat. Cemetery, Arlington VAArty. Brigade. Home: Alexandria VA Died Sept. 25, 1971; buried Arlington Nat. Cemetery, Arlington, VA

BLACK, MRS. MADELEINE ELMER;, b. Zanesville, O.; d. Dr. F. M. and Louise (Newton) Powell; grad. Ill. Coll. and Athenaeum; m. Elmer Ellsworth Black, of Chicago, Apr. 26, 1893 (died 1909). Mem. exec. com. Am. Peace and Arbitration League; mem. Am. Peace Soc., Am. Acad. Polit. and Social Science, Nat. Municipal League, Acad. Polit. Science, Church Peace League America (founder, 1st v.p.), N.Y. Terminal Market Commn., League for Polit. Edn., woman's dept. Nat. Civic Federation, Nat. Com. on Prison Labor (exec. mem.), Free Industrial School for Crippled Children (life mem.), N.Y. Woman's League for Animals, Nat. Soc. Patriotic Women America, Woman's Forum, Woman's Rep. Club of State of N.Y., Atlantic Union, Soc. Am. Women in London; 3d v.-p. N.Y. City Federation Woman's Clubs, 1916. Ex-pres. Editorial Review Co. Clubs: Eclectic, Woman's Press, Twilight, Rubinstein (New York); Chicago Woman's Athletic, Chicago Woman's (Chicago); Lyceum (London). Author: Civilize the Nations (brochure), 1910; A Municipal Terminal Market System (treatise), 1912. Home: Waldorf-Astoria, New York NY‡

BLACK, MELVILLE, ophthalmologist; b. Washington, Ia., Mar. 15, 1866; s. George (M.D.) and Louisa Jane (Melville) B.; M.D., Bellevue Hosp. Med. Coll., New York, 1889; interne Manhattan Eye and Ear Hosp., 1889-91; m. Ada Eleanor Cole, Apr. 2, 1896. Practiced in Denver since 1891; prof. ophthalmology, med. dept., U. of Colo.; now emeritus; ophthalmologist to St. Luke's, Children's and Colo. Gen. hosps. Fellow Acad. Ophthalmology and Oto-laryngology; Am. Coll. Surgeons; mem. A.M.A., Colo. State Med. Soc. (ex-pres.), and Med. Soc. City and County of Denver, Colo. Ophthal. Soc. Clubs: Denver, Mile High. Home: Denver Club. Office: Metropolitan Bldg., Denver CO‡

BLACK, NEWTON HENRY, educator; b. Putney, Vt., May 3, 1874; s. Newton Horace and Frances (Blanchard) B.; Phillips Exeter Acad., Exeter, N.H., 1892-93; A.B., Harvard, 1896, A.M., 1906; student U. of Berlin, 1912-13, Cambridge U., England, 1930-31; m. Elizabeth A. Herrmann, Aug. 3, 1918; children—Elizabeth Spalding (Mrs. W. J. Emlen), Margaret Persis (Mrs. Stephen A. Richardson). Teacher of science, St. George's Sch., Newport, R.I., 1896-98; High Sch., Concord, N.H., 1898-1900; Roxbury Latin Sch., Boston, 1900-24; asst. prof. edn., Harvard, 1924-32, asst. prof. of physics, 1932-40, asst. prof. emeritus since 1940, also dir. Harvard Univ. Summer Sch., 1932-34. Lecturer, U.S.N. Communication School, 1942-43, navy V-12, 1943-44. Fellow A.A.A.S., Am. Phys. Soc.; mem. Am. Inst. E.E., Coll. Entrance Exam. Bd., 1906-22. Rep. Conglist. Author: Lab. Manual in Physics, 1913; Revised Edition Jackson's Elementary Electricity and Magnetism, 1919; Laboratory Experiments in Chemistry, 1920, 27, 36; Laboratory Experiments in Practical Physics, 1923; Introductory Course in College Physics, 3d edit., 1948. Co-author: Black and Davis' Practical Physics, 1913-22, 29, 38; Black and Conant's Practical Chemistry, 1920, 27; Black and Davis' New Practical Physics, 1929; Black and Conant's New Practical Chemistry, 1936; Black and Weaver's Laboratory Experiments and Workbook in Physics, 1938; Black and Davis' Elementary Practical Physics, revised, 1949. Home: 21 Follen St., Cambridge 38, Mass.; also South Tamworth NH‡

BLACK, NORMAN DAVID, JR., newspaper pub.; b. Grand Forks, N.D., Mar. 27, 1913; s. Norman David and Cora (Powers) B.; student Univ. of N.D., 1933-34; B.S.C., Northwestern Univ., 1935; m. Margaret Jane Shotwell, Oct. 20, 1937; children—Nancy Jane, Mary Margaret. In newspaper bus. from 1935; pub. The Fargo (N.D.) Forum from 1944; vice pres. and treas. Forum Publishing Company, 1944-51, president 1951-69; president WDAY, Incorporated, 1960-69; pres. Dakota Photo Engraving Co.; dir. Merchants Nat. Bank and Trust Company, First Bank Stock Corporation, Minneapolis. Member of Sigma Chi. Delta Sigma Pi, Sigma Delta Chi. Republican. Roman Catholic. Elk. Club: Rotary. Home: Fargo ND Died Sept. 25, 1969; buried Riverside Cemetery, Fargo ND

BLACK, S(AMUEL) BRUCE, ins. co. exec. b. Fort Atkinson, Wis., Mar. 8, 1892; s. Robert B. and Margaret (Scott) B.; student Ripon (Wis.) Coll., 1908-10; A.B., U. Wis., 1913; LL.D. (hon.), U. Me., 1949; L.H.D. (hon.), Tufts U., 1957; m. Adele Bergner, 1917;children—Robert Bruce, Wallace Gordon, Donald Thomas. Asst. statistician, Industrial Commn. of Wis., 1913-15; actuary Am. Mut. Liability Ins. Co., 1915-17; treas. Liberty Mut. Ins. Co., 1917-19, v.p. and actuary, 1919-22, v.p. and gen. mgr., 1923-24, president, 1924-56, chmn. bd. 1956-62, honorary chmn., 1962-66, v.p., treas. Liberty Mutual Fire Insurance Co., 1923-24, v.p., gen. mgr., 1925-41, pres., 1942-57, chmn. bd., 1957-62, hon. chairman, 1962-66; dir. exec. com. Boston Mfrs. Mutual Fire Ins. Co.; dir. Mutual Boiler Ins. Co. Trustee National Safety Council, Eastern States Exposition, Northeastern University, Ripon College; bd. dirs. Med. Found., Inc.; hon. chmn. emeritus Nat. Planning Council Colls. and Univs. Fellow American Acad. Arts and Scis.; mem. Nat. Assn. Mut. Casualty Cos. (ex-pres.; gov.), Am. Mut. Alliance (ex-pres.), Nat. Assn. Mut. Automotive Ins. Cos. (ex-pres.), Casualty Acturial Society of America (charter), Artus (U. Wis.), Newcomen Soc. Eng., American Guernsey Cattle Club. Clubs: Algonquin, Commercial, Brae Burn Country. Home: Waban MA Died Dec. 7, 1968; buried Pepperell MA

BLACK, WILLIAM HARMAN, lawyer; b. Forsyth, Ga., June 10, 1868; s. Eugene Pinckerd B.; ed. public schools and Boys High Sch., Atlanta, Ga.; unmarried. Admitted to N.Y. bar; was special asst. corporate counsel, New York City, acting dist. atty. New York, and justice Supreme Court of N.Y.; now in practice of law. Vice chmn. Nat. War Labor Bd. during World War. Decorated Comdr. Order of the Crown of Italy. Pres. Ga. Soc. in New York and N.Y. Southern Soc. Baptist. Mason. Club: Metropolitan (New York). Author: How to Conduct a Criminal Case, 3d edit., 1935; Law of Stock Exchanges, Customers and Brokers, 1939; Our Unknown Constitution; If I Were a Jew. Radio speaker. Address: 160 Central Park S., New York NY*‡

BLACKBURN, ARMOUR JENNINGS, univ. dean; b. Danville, Va., May 3, 1903; s. William Solomon and Ella Louise (Jennings) B.; A.B., Howard U., 1926; M.A., Columbia, 1937, Ed. D., 1948; m. Mary Helen McKay, Aug. 30, 1938. Prin. elementary sch., Rowland, N.C., 1926-27; instr. English, E.E. Smith High Sch. Fayetteville, N.C., 1927-29, prin. 1929-40; field agt. Howard U., 1940-47, dir. student activities, 1947-49, dean of students, 1949-70. Mem. Pres.'s Exec. Com. Employment of Handicapped; mem. admissions team African scholarship program Am. Univs. and Colls. in W. Africa. Mem. N.E.A., Nat. Assn. Student Personnel Administrs., Am. Coll., So. personnel assns., Am. Adminstrs., American College Personnel Assn., Am. Vocational Guidance Assn., Am. Assn. Coll. Registrants and Admission Officers, Internat. Platform Assn., N.A.A.C.P. (member executive committee Washington chapter), American Acad. Polit. and Social Sci., Nat. Acad. Polit. Sci., Internat. House Assn., Phi Delta Kappa, Kappa Delta Phi, Omega Psi Phi. Baptist. Home: Washington DC Died Mar. 28, 1970.

BLACKBURN, FREDERICK GEORGE, corp. exec.; b. Pitts., Mar. 11, 1892; s. William W. and Harriet (Bloom) B.; A.B., Yale, 1914; B.S., Carnegie Inst. Tech., 1928; m. Madelaine F. Walton, June 2, 1923 (dec. Sept. 28, 1945); children—Madelaine W. (Mrs. E. S. Lewis), Harriet Elizabeth (Mrs. Moses Taylor); m. 2d, Maxwell D. Church Blair, Oct. 24, 1947. Metallurgist Carnegie Steel Co., 1915-29; partner Moore, Leonard & Lynch, 1929-32; v.p. City Deposit Bank &Trust Co., 1932-35, pres., 1935; v.p. Union Trust Co. of Pitts., 1935-46, Mellon Nat. Bank and Trust Co., 1946-57; pres. Tremarco Corp., 1956-67; mem. bd. mgrs. Homewood Cemetery; dir. Haugh & Keenan Storage & Transfer Co.; trustee Dollar Savs. Bank. Dir. Western Pa. Sch. for Blind Children; trustee Carnegie Inst., Carnegie-Mellon Univ., Child Guidance Center, Chatham Coll. Mem. Carnegie Hero Fund Commn., adv. bd. Salvation Army. Vice chmn. Pitts. Sinking Fund Commn. Served as 1st lt. U.S. Army F.A., 1917-19. Mem. Phi Beta Kappa, Alpha Delta Phi, Wolf's Head (Yale). Republican. Presbyn. (elder). Clubs: Pittsburg Golf, Duquesne (Pitts.); Yale (N.Y.C.); Pittsburgh PA Died Apr. 25, 1972.

BLACKBURN, WILLIS CLIFFORD, petroleum geologist; b. nr. Union Grove, Wis., Apr. 5, 1903; s. Roy Lindsey and Nellie (Moyle) B.; B.A., U. Tex., 1926; m. Annie Lenora Whitmire, June 19, 1930; 1 dau., Susie Ann (Mrs. William Martin Boyce). Exploration geologist to sr. exploration geologist Humble Oil & Refining Co., Houston, 1926-55, div. geologist, Ala., Ga., Fla., 1955-59; cons. geology, from 1959. Mem. Am. Assn. Petroleum Geologists, Soc. Econ. Paleontologists, Permian Basin Pioneers (charter), Southeastern Geol. Soc. (past pres.), Sigma Gamma Epsilon. Club: Skyline Country (Mobile, Ala.). Author: The Hilbig Oil Field. Address: Mobile AL Died Sept. 15, 1967; buried Houston TX

BLACKBURNE, MARY FRANCES, author; b. Manchester, N.H., Apr. 20, 1874; d. Clark and Clara M. Blaisdell; grad. Cambridge Training Sch., 1895; m. Edward Best Blackburne, Mar. 17, 1917; 1 son, Edward Francis. Taught in Brockton, Mass., 1896-1901, Medford, 1901-12. Author: Polly and Dolly, 1909; Tommy Tinker's Book, 1911; Cherry Tree Children, 1912; Twilight Town, 1913; Pretty Polly Flinders, 1914; Bunny Rabbit's Diary, 1915; Pine Tree Playmates, 1925; (with sister, Etta Austin Blaisdell McDonald); Child Life, 1899; Child Life in Tale and Fable, 1899; Child Life in Many Lands, 1900; Child Life in Literature, 1900; The Child Life Primer, 1901; The Blaisdell Spellers, 1901; The Child Life Fifth Reader, 1902; Boy Blue and His Friends, 1907; Mother Goose Children, 1916; Rhyme and Story First Reader, 1918; Pine Tree Playmates, 1925. Home: Waban MA‡

BLACKER, DANIEL JAMES, educator; b. Starke, Fla., Oct. 13, 1873; s. Daniel and Ann (Crosby) B.; A.B., Stetson U., De Land, Fla., 1909, D.D., 1918; A.B., U. of Chicago, 1909, A.M., 1911; B.D., 1912; m. Florence E. Jackson, of Lake Helen, Fla., Aug. 12, 1917. Ordained Bapt. ministry, 1910; pastor Irving Park Ch., Chicago, 1910-12; prof. Stetson U., 1913-20; pastor Williamsburg, Va., 1920-22; prof. psychology and philosophy, William and Mary Coll., 1920-22; pres. Shorter Coll., Maplehurst, Rome, Ga., since 1923. Mem. Omicron Delta Chi, Delta Theta Chi. Home: Maplehurst, Rome GA‡

BLACKFORD, KATHERINE M(ELVINA) H(UNTSINGER), character analyst; b. West Mineral, Kan., Mar. 18, 1875; d. Henry and Catherine (Schock) Huntsinger; ed. high sch., Columbus, Kan.; M.D., Coll. Phys. and Surg. (now Keokuk Med. Coll.), Keokuk, Ia., 1898; post-grad. work, Dearborn St. Med. Sch. and Hosp., Chicago, 1899; m. Everett F. Blackford, of Rochester, N.Y., June 1, 1899 (dec.); m. 2d, Arthur Newcomb, of New York, Nov. 28, 1912. Began practice of medicine at Rochester, N.Y.; research travel and lecturing, 1903-11; joined Emerson Engineers as employment and personnel specialist, 1912; individual practice, 1913, now retired; pres. Blackford Pubs., Inc. Mem. Authors' League America, League of Am. Pen Women. Club: Woman's Nat. Republican. Author: Employer's Manual, 1912; The Job, the Man, the Boss (with Arthur Newcomb), 1914; The Science of Character Analysis by the Observational Method, 1914; Analyzing Character (with Arthur Newcomb), 1916; Reading Character at Sight, 1918; The Right Job (2 vols.), 1924. Office: 50 E. 42d St., New York NY‡

BLACKMAN, EDWARD BERNARD, educator; b. Boston, Nov. 8, 1916; s. Samuel and Ethel (Dalins) B.; A.B., Harvard, 1938, S.T.B., 1941, Ph.D., 1947; m. Gloria Cutler, Aug. 22, 1948; 1 son, Robert Wells. Faculty Mich. State U., 1949-—, prof. Am. thought and lang., 1958-62, asst. to dean basic coll., 1956-58, head dept. Am. thought and lang., 1958-62, professor edn., 1962-70, chmn. dept. higher edn., 1963-64, dir. univ. pres. 1953-62, asst. dean. Univ. College, 1964-70.

Cons., examiner N. Central Assn. Colls. and Secondary Schs. Ford fellow 1955-56. Mem. Assn for Higher Edn., Phi Kappa Phi. Co-editor: The Basic College of Michigan State, 1955; Curriculum Building in Gen. Edn., 1960. Home: East Lansing MI Died Oct. 15, 1970.

BLACKMARR, FRANK HAMLIN, M.D.; b. Rouseville, Pa., Feb. 16, 1871; s. Hamlin L. and Mary C. (Gray) B.; Allegheny Coll., Meadville, Pa.; B.S., U. of Chicago, 1893; M.D., Hahnemann Med. Coll., Chicago, 1897; m. Catherine Strong, of Oil City, Pa., June 22, 1899. Practiced in Chicago, since 1897; specializes in X-Ray therapy, radium therapy, electro therapy. Dir. New York Radium Inst.; fellow A.M.A.; mem. Mo. Med. Soc., Radiological Soc. of N. America, Am. Chem. Soc., Ill. State and Chicago med. socs., Ill. and Chicago Homoe. med. socs., Western Electro-Therapeutic Assn., Western Soc. Engrs., Am. Med. Assn. of Vienna, Sigma Alpha Epsilon. Mason (32 deg. Shriner). Clubs: Unanimous (New York); Illinois Athletic (life), Press (life), Chicago Athletic, Medinah Athletic (life), Chicago Motor, South Shore Country (life). Home: 7350 Phillips Av. Office: 25 E. Washington St., Chicago IL‡

BLACKMER, HENRY M., chmn. board Midwest Refining Co.; b. Worcester, Mass., July 25, 1869; s. Francis T. and Abbie E. (Daniels) B.; ed. high sch., Worcester; married; children—Myron Kerr, Mrs. Margaret Kistler. Began practice of law at Colorado Springs, Colo., 1891; dist. atty. Colo. Springs, 1893-96; organized Cripple Creek R.R. and chmn. bd. until 1916; pres. Internat. Trust Co., 1911-13; v.p. Midwest Oil Co., 1913-14; elected pres. Midwest Refining Co., 1915, now chmn. bd. Chmn. Rocky Mountain div. of Nat. Petroleum War Service Com.; dir. Am. Petroleum Inst. Clubs: Denver, Denver Country; El Paso Country, Cheyenne Mountain Country (Colorado Springs); Metropolitan (New York). Home: 975 E. 7th Av. Office: First National Bank Bldg., Denver CO‡

BLACKWELL, OTTO BERNARD, telephone engr.; b. Bourne, Mass., Aug. 21, 1884; s. Edwin Alston and Abbie G. (Walker) B.; B.S., Mass. Inst. Tech., 1906; m. Elsie Eldredge, July 2, 1917; children—Edwin Alston, Anne Louise Wood. Engring. dept. Am. Telephone & Telegraph Co., 1906-14, transmission and protection engr., 1914-19, transmission development engr., 1919-34; dir. of transmission development Bell Telephone Labs., Mar. 1934-June 1935, mgr. staff depts., June 1935-Dec. 1936, v.p. 1937-44; asst. v.p. Am. Telephone & Telegraph Co. 1944 to 1949. Fellow Am. Inst. E.E., Inst. Radio Engrs., Acoustical Soc. America; mem. A.A.A.S., Am. Physical Soc. Clubs: Salmagundl. Inventor, patentee in devel. of telephone. Home: Planadome NY Died Oct. 21, 1970.

BLAESS, AUGUST F., civil engr.; b. Ann Arbor, Mich., Jan. 6, 1871; s. Albert F. and Catherine (Guenther) B.; B.S. in Engring., U. of Mich., 1895; m. Daisy M. Kemper, of Baltimore, Md., 1919; 1 daughter, Helen. Rodman, chainman and instrumentman Detroit & Mackinac R.R., 1895; with I. C. Ry. since 1897, successively as track apprentice, section laborer, 1897-98, rodman and instrumentman, track elevation work, Chicago, 1898-99, instrumentman and asst. engr. constrn. dept., 1899-1902, track supervisor, 1902-05, roadmaster, 1905-10, asst. engr. maintenance of way, 1910-13, dist. engr., 1913-14, engr. maintenance, 1914-25, chief engr. since Feb. 1, 1925. Mem. Am. Ry. Engring. Assn., Western Soc. C.E. Republican. Clubs: Chicago Engineers', South Shore Country. Home: 6807 Paxton Av. Office: 135 E. 11th Pl., Chicago IL‡

BLAIN, HUGH MERCER, SR., public relations counsellor; b. Christiansburg, Va., Dec. 26, 1874; s. Rev. Daniel (D.D.) and Mary Louisa (Mercer) B.; B.A., Washington and Lee University, 1894, M.A., from same, 1895; Ph.D., University of Va., 1901; m. Mary Moore Winston, of Waynesboro, Va., June 26, 1901; children—Elizabeth Winston, Hugh Mercer, Martha Randolph. Prof. English, La. State U., 1907-11; organized dept. of journalism there, 1912, and continued as prof. English and journalism until 1920; mng. editor State-Times, Baton Rouge, La., 1917-20; mgr. Associated Rice Millers of America (advertising), 1920-23; prof. journalism, Tulane U., 1923-25. Dir. La.-Miss. Com. on Pub. Utility Information, 1923—; with Pub. Relations Dept. New Orleans Pub. Service, 1925—. Mem. Modern Lang. Assn. America, Am. Assn. Teachers of Journalism, New Orleans Acad. Sciences, Phi Beta Kappa, Delta Tau Delta, Sigma Delta Chi, etc. Democrat. Presbyn. Mason, Elk. Clubs: Round Table, Audubon Golf. Author: Verb-Syntax of Anglo-Saxon Chronicle, 1901; Literature in the High School, 1910; Essential Servants of Civilization, 1924; A Near Century of Public Service in New Orleans, 1927. Home: 322 Hillary St. Office: Hibernia Bank Bldg., New Orleans LA‡

BLAINE, HELEN LOUISE TOWNSEND, dentist; b. St. Paul, Feb. 18, 1920; d. Orie P. and Louise (Ross) Townsend; B.M.E., U. Okla., 1942; R.N., St. Luke's Hosp., Kansas City, Mo.; certificate pub. health nursing U. Minn., 1958; D.D.S., U. Mo., Kansas City 1965; M.S., University Pa., 1968; m. William H. Blaine, Jr., July 16, 1949 (div. Feb. 1956). Registered nurse, 1947-65; supervisory nurse Tripler Army Hosp., Honolulu, 1952-53, Kaueohe Marine Corps Air Sta., Hawaii, 1953-55; pub. health nurse Anchorage, Alaska, 1958-60; instr. practical nursing Kansas City Bd. Edn., 1960-61; dental trainee Lancaster (Pa.) Cleft Palate Clinic, 1965-66; research fellow U. Pa., Phila., 1966-68; faculty U. Mo., Kansas City, 1968-72. Member of Omicron Kappa Upsilon, Alpha Omega, Sigma Alpha Iota (chpt. pres. 1941-42), Delta Gamma. Republican. Presbyn. Home: Kansas City MO Died Mar. 3, 1972; buried Forest Cemetery, Oskaloosa IA

BLAINE, JAMES GILLESPIE, banker; b. N.Y. City, Jan. 10, 1888; s. James Gillespie and Mary Nevins (Bull) B.; A.B., Harvard, 1911; LL.D., Washington and Jefferson Coll., Washington, Pa., 1932; D.C.S., N.Y.U., 1950; m. Marian Dow, Mar. 9, 1911 (deceased); children—Richard Gillespie, Charles Gillespie, Elisabeth (deceased), James G. III (dec.); m. 2d, Countess Irina Woronzow-Daschkow, June 20, 1936. Vice pres. Liberty Nat. Bank and N.Y. Trust Co., 1919-27; pres. Fidelity Trust Co., 1927-30, co. changed to Marine Midland Trust Co. of N.Y., pres. 1930-54, chairman of board, 1955-59, honorary chairman, dir., from 1960; director Marine Midland Trust Co. Hon. chairman Federation of Protestant Welfare Agencies; hon. v.p. Community Service Soc. N.Y. Chief of E.C.A. Mission to Belgium and Luxembourg, 1948-49. Mem. N.Y. State C. of C. (pres. 1948-50), The Pilgrims. Republican. Episcopalian. Mason. Club: Links. Home: Stuart FL Died Nov. 1969.

BLAIR, EDWIN FOSTER, lawyer; b. Weatherford, Tex., Dec. 15, 1901; s. Wiley and Josephine M. (Foster) B.; A.B., Yale, 1924, LL.B. cum laude, 1928, M.A., 1946; m. Rosemary Kane, Apr. 14, 1925; children—Roderic (dec.), Mary Kane, Kathleen, Edwin James, Rosanne. Instr. Yale Law Sch., 1928-29; asso. Davis, Polk, Wardwell, Gardiner & Reed, 1929-40; own law firm. 1940-42; partner Blair, Polk & Ogden, 1942-45. Blair & Reed, N.Y.C., 1952-68; dir., mem. exec. com. Union Bag-Camp Paper Corp.; dir. Canada Dry Corp., Mohasco Industries, Inc., Holly Sugar Corp.; dir., chmn. bd. T.A.D. Jones & Co., Inc.; mem. adv. bd. 30 Broad St. branch Chem. Corn Exchange Bank. Fellow Yale Corp.; trustee Hotchkiss Sch., Fairfield Country Day Sch., Mus. Art, Sci. and Industry, N.Y. Heart Assn.; dir. Rip van Winkle Found., Boys Club of Bridgeport, Gaylord Farm Sanitorium. Fairfield Community Chest, World Vets. Fund. Yale Football Y Assn. Fellow Branford Coll., Yale; chmn. exec. com. Yale Law Sch. Assn. Mem. Republican Finance Com., 1958-59 (mem. budget com. 1959). Mem. Am. N.Y. State bar assns., Bar Assn. City of N.Y., N.Y. County Lawyers Assn., N.Y. C. of C., Phi Beta Kappa, Order of Coif. Clubs: Links, Yale, N.Y. Yacht, Down Town Assn. (N.Y.C.); University (Bridgeport, Conn.); Madison Beach (gov.; Madison, Conn.); Mory's Assn. (gov.); New Haven Lawn, Graduates (New Haven); Pequot Yacht (Southport, Conn.). Home: Fairfield CT Died Nov. 6, 1970; buried Oakland Cemetery, Dallas TX

BLAIR, EUGENIE (MRS. ROBERT L. DOWNING), actress; b. Columbia, S.C.; acted child parts; 1st appearance in adult roles with John T. Raymond; supported Mrs. D. P. Bowers at St. Louis, and later was leading lady with James O'Neil and Frederic Warde; m. Robert L. Downing, actor, and has since taken leading female roles in his. co.‡

BLAIR, HENRY ALEXANDER, physiologist; b. Winnipeg, Manitoba, Can., Jan. 6, 1900; s. Edward and Isabella (MacFarlane) B.; B.S., U. of Manitoba, 1925; M.S., 1927; Ph.D., Princeton U., 1930; m. Eva Andrews, Aug. 4, 1926; children—Shirley Isabelle, Barbara Elizabeth, Henry Alexander Blair. Came to U.S., 1927, naturalized, 1942. Demonstrator, physics, U. of Manitoba, 1924-27; lecturer, mathematics, Manitoba Agrl. Coll., 1926-27; research asst. physics, Princeton U., 1927-29; instr. biophysics, Western Reserve Med. School, 1930-32; instr. physiology, U. of Rochester, 1932-34, asst. prof., 1934-40, asso. prof., 1940-48, prof. since 1948, dir. dept. radiation biology, and U. of Rochester Atomic Energy Project. Mem. tech. information panel A.E.C. Served with C.E.F., 1918-19. Mem. Radiation Research Soc., Am. Phys. Society, Am. Physiol. Society, Society for Experimental Biology and Medicine, A.A.A.S., Am. Inst. of Physics, Sigma Xi. Editor: Biological Effects of External Radiation, 1954. Mem. editorial bd. Jour. Neurophysiology, 1945-55, Am. Jour. Physiology, 1953-56, Jour. Applied Physiology, 1953-56. Sec. AEC com. on fellowships in indsl. medicine. Home: Rochester NY Died Nov. 4, 1971.

BLAIR, HERBERT FRANCIS, director of research; born Canton, Illinois, May 31, 1875; son Reverend James G. and Mary K. (Scofield) B.; B.S., Northwestern U., 1899; Univ. of Gottingen, 1905-06; A.M., Columbia, 1917, Ph.D., 1937; m. Nellie Martha Ober, Aug. 2, 1905; children—Mary Margaret (Mrs. Reginald Hunt), Jean Elizabeth (Mrs. Dwight McCracken, dec.), Helen Edith (Mrs. Stanley Croshie), Herbert Francis. Teacher public schools until 1903; teacher geography, Duluth State Normal School, 1903-08; supt. schs., Hibbing, Minn., 1909-14, Schenectady, N.Y., 1914-16; with Federal Bd. for Vocational Edn. and Veterans' Bur., 1918-23; prof. sch. administration, Boston U. Sch. of Edn., 1924-42; dir. research, Mass. Teachers Fed. since 1943. Methodist. Editor of Education (mag.), 1931-40. Home: Middleboro MA‡

BLAIR, JACK F., lawyer; b. Durand, Wis., May 1, 1931; s. Fred O. and Alena (Oesterreicher) B.; B.B.A., U. Minn., 1953; LL.B., 1956; student Wis. State Coll., 1949-51; m. Marilyn Christie, Apr. 18, 1958; children—Michael John, Linda Jean, David James, Roger Jeffrey. Admitted to Minn. bar, 1956, D.C. bar, 1957, Cal. bar, 1961; trial atty. U.S. Dept. Justice, Washington, 1956-58, tax div., 1958-60; atty., asst. chief U.S. Attys. Office, So. Dist. Cal., Los Angeles, 1960-62; practiced in Upland, Cal., 1962-70; mem. firm Beloud, Althouse, Blair, 1962-65, Jack F. Blair, 1965-70. Mem. Upland Civic Center Devel. Com., 1964; mem. exec. com. Old Baldy council Boy Scouts Am., 1963-70, vice chmn., 1965. Pres. U. Minn. Young Republicans Club, 1952-53; v.p. Young Republicans State of Minn., 1954-56; finance chmn. Quimby for Assembly, Western San Bernardino County, 1966. Bd. dirs. West Eng United Fund. Mem. Am., Cal. trial lawyers, Fed., Am., San Bernardino County, Western San Bernardino County (pres. 1965-66, dir. 1966-67) bar assns., Western San Bernardino County Legal Air Soc. (pres. 1963-64), State Bar Cal., Upland C. of C. Democrat. Kiwanian (pres. 1967, dir. 1963-70). Home: Upland CA Died Feb. 16, 1970.

BLAIR-SMITH, ROBERT M., lawyer; b. Nashville, Oct. 6, 1906; s. Hugh and Trevania (Dallas) Blair-S.; A.B., Harvard, 1928, LL.B., 1931; m. Jean Lithgow Foss, Sept. 22, 1934; children—Pamela (Mrs. Kenneth J. Northcott), Hugh. Admitted to N.Y. bar, 1932, Pa. bar, 1944; with firm Milbank, Tweed, Hope & Webb, N.Y.C., 1931-38; staff atty. SEC, 1938-42, head opinion writing office, 1942-45; asso. Schnader, Harrison, Segal & Lewis, Phila., 1945-47, partner, 1948-68. Sec. ABC Consol. Corp. and subsidiaries, 1951-68; sec., gen. counsel Strick Holding Co. and subsidiaries, 1966-68; trustee Fund Astrophys. Research, Inc., 1936-68, pres., 1957-68. Reporter uniform state securities act. Nat. Conf. Commrs. Uniform State Laws, 1947-53; adv. com. study states securities regulation Harvard Law Sch., 1954-56. Mem. Am. (chmn. com. state regulation securities 1949-57), Pa., Phila. (chmn. com. orgn. and operations corps., partnerships and sole traders 1965-66), Fed. bar assns., Am. Law Inst., Assn. Bar City N.Y. Clubs: Nat. Lawyers (Washington); Midday, Socialegal, Juristic Soc., Harvard (Phila.). Contbr. legal jours. Home: Philadelphia PA Died Jan. 21, 1968.

BLAISDELL, GIDEON MOORES, pharm. co. exec.; b. East Orland, Me., May 19, 1918; s. Austin Chanley and Grace (Moores) B.; certificate Bentley Coll. Accounting and Finance, 1938; B.B.A. cum Laude, Northeastern U., 1950; m. Mary Catherine Sarkey, Sept. 28, 1947; children—David, Anne, Jeanne, Elizabeth, Thomas, Br. cashier Jewel Tea Co., Peoria, Ill., 1939, Johnstown, Pa., 1939-40; jr. accountant G.D. Kilnapp, C.P.A., Quincy, Mass., 1945-46; sr. accountant Charles F. Rittenhouse & Co., C.P.A.'s, Boston, 1946-50; asst. to treas. Norwich Pharacal Co. (N.Y.), 1950-53, asst. treas., 1953-56, controller, 1956-62, treas., 1962-69, dir., mem. exec. com., 1964-69; v.p., controller, dir. successor firm Morton-Norwich Products, Inc.; dir. Norwith Pharmacal Co. de Peru. Chmn. finance com. United Fund, 1959-64; mem. finance com. Chenango Meml. Hosp., 1960-69. Served with USAAF, 1940-45. C.P.A., Mass. Gold medal man, 1948. Mem. Financial Execs. Inst. (pres. Syracuse chpt. 1963-64, nat. dir. 1964-68), Am. Mgmt. Assn., Am. Inst. C.P.A.'s Mass. Soc. C.P.A.'s. Republican. Methodist. Elk. Clubs: Tower Lost Pond. Home: Wilmette IL Died May 7, 1971; buried Blue Hill Cemetery, Braintree MA

BLAISDELL, WARREN CARL, govt. ofcl.; b. Fairhaven, Mass., Apr. 4, 1911; student Boston U., 1928-30; m. Catherine Frances Kelleher, Feb. 21, 1938; children—Allan Carl, Susan Ellen, Linda Catherine. Various adminstrv. positions Civilian Conservation Corps, 1933-44; exec. officer U.S. Maritime Service Gulf Coast Upgrade Schs., 1944-45; adminstrv. analyst, asst. adminstrv. officer communication, office facilities programs Bur. Budget, 1945-46; asst. adminstrv. officer Exec. Office Sec., Navy Dept., 1946-47; dir. operating services standardization div. Office Sec. Def., Washington, 1947, acting asst. comptroller for mgmt. engring., 1950-52, dir. fiscal mgmt. staff, 1952-54; chmn. Nat. Mil. Establishment Interdepartmental Adminstrv. Services Bd., 1948; chmn. Nat. Mil. Establishment Adminstrv. Mgmt. Council, 1949-50; asst. dir., dir. budget Office Asst. Sec. Def., Washington, 1954-59, dep. comptroller financial, operating mgmt., 1959-61, dep. asst. sec. def., 1961-65; mgmt. cons., Washington, 1966-69; comptroller Def. Communication Agy., Washington, 1969-70. Served as officer in the United States Maritime Service during World War II. Home: Alexandria VA Died Feb. 26, 1970; buried Mt. Comfort Cemetery, Alexandria VA

BLAKE, FREDERIC COLUMBUS, prof. physics; b. Decatur, Ill., Oct. 30, 1877; s. Christopher Columbus and Rachel Ellen (Beam) B.; Ph.B., U. of Colo., 1901; univ. fellow, Columbia, 1903-04, John Tyndall fellow, 1904-07, Ph.D., 1905; studied Cambridge U., Eng., 1905-06, Berlin, 1906-07; m. Edith Sherwin Adams, Aug. 20, 1907 (died 1931); m. 2d, Jane Snow Hinkley, Apr. 23, 1933. Asst. prof. physics, Ohio State University, 1907-12, prof. since 1912; prof. of physics, emeritus since 1946. Pres. Academic Bd., U.S. Army Sch. of Mil. Aeronautics, Ohio State U., Nov. 1917-Sept. 1918. Fellow, Am. Physical Soc.; mem. Am. Assn. Physics Teachers, Sigma Xi, Phi Beta Kappa. Author: papers on X-ray diffraction and curved crystal spectrographs. Home: 1581 N Grand Oaks Av., Pasadena 7 CA‡

BLAKE, GEORGE H., utilities exec.; b. Harrison, N.J., 1884; grad. New York Univ., 1906; m. Caroline Rittenhouse; 1 son, William H. Pres., mem., exec. com., dir. Public Service Electric & Gas Co., Public Service Coordinated Transport and Public Service Interstate Transportation Co. (all Newark, N.J.); mem. exec. com., dir., West Hudson Nat. Bank of Harrison, N.J.; dir., New York & Long Branch R.R. Co. Home: West Orange NJ Died Oct. 6, 1971.

BLAKE, HAROLD HAMILTON, banker; b. Newton, Mass., Nov. 24, 1873; James M. and Mary H. (Brown) B.; grad. Newton High Sch., 1892; m. Margaretta Logan, Apr. 14, 1904; 1 dau., Barbara (Mrs. Norris H. Robertson). With New Hampshire Savs. Bank, Concord, since 1924, trustee, 1924-36, chmn. investment com., 1938-52, pres., 1952-53; pres. Loan and Trust Savs. Bank, 1936-38; dir. Nat. State Capitol Bank, Concord, 1910-53, Rumford Printing Co. Trustee John H. Pearson Trust, Margaret Pillsbury Gen. Hosp., Concord Hosp., 1910-50. Republican. Conglist. Home: 123 School St. Office: 97 N. Main St., Concord NH‡

BLAKE, JOHN CHARLES, educator; b. Ottumwa, Ia., May 31, 1873; s. Christopher Columbus and Rachel (Beam) B.; B.S., U. of Colo., 1901; Ph.D., Yale, 1903; m. Jennie Archibald, of Trinidad, Colo., July 21, 1904; children—Charles Archibald, Mabel Myrtle, Frances, Ruth, Helen. Research asso. in physical chemistry, Mass. Inst. Tech., 1903-05; asst. physicist, Nat. Bur. Standards, 1905-06; head dept. of chemistry, Agrl. and Mech. Coll. of Tex., 1906-13, also chem. engr.; head dept. of chemistry, Hahnemann Med. Coll., Chicago, since 1913, dean 1921-22; dean Gen. Med. Coll. (successor to Hahnemann Med. Coll.), 1922-24. Mem. Am. Chem. Soc., Am. Inst. of Chemists, Sigma Xi, Pi Upsilon Rho. Author: General Chemistry, Theoretical and Applied, 1913; General Chemistry Laboratory Manual, 1913. Contbr. numerous articles to Jour. Am. Chem. Soc. Home: 6615 Kimbark Av., Chicago IL‡

BLAKELY, BERTHA ELIZA, librarian; b. Campton, N.H., Jan. 13, 1870; d. Quincy and Gertrude (Sykes) B.; B.L., Mt. Holyoke Coll., 1893 B.A., 1898; student New York State Library Sch. 1893-94. Librarian N.J. State Normal and Model Schs. Library, 1894-95; asst. librarian Mt. Holyoke Coll. Library, 1895-1901, librarian, 1901-36, librarian emeritus since 1936. Mem. A.L.A., Am. Assn. Univ. Women, Foreign Policy Assn., Phi Beta Kappa. Conglist. Address: Mt. Holyoke College, South Hadley MA‡

BLAKELY, GEORGE, army officer; b. in Pa., July 5, 1870; grad. U.S. Mil. Acad., 1892, Arty. Sch., 1896. Commd. 2d lt. 2d Arty., June 11, 1892; 1st lt., Feb. 13, 1899; capt. Arty. Corps, May 8, 1901; maj. Coast Arty. Corps, Mar. 8, 1909; lt. col., Aug. 25, 1915; insp. gen., Nov. 1, 1915; col., 1917; brig. gen. N.A., Aug. 5, 1917. Apptd. comdr. 61st Field Arty. Brigade, Camp Bowie, Ft. Worth, Tex., Sept. 1917; comdr. S. Atlantic Coast Arty. Dist., July-Oct. 1918; comdr. 38th Arty. Brigade, A.E.F., France, Oct. 1918-Feb. 1919; comdr. N. Pacific Coast Arty. Dist., Mar.-June 1919. Address: War Dept., Washington DC‡

BLAKEMORE, ARTHUR HENDLEY, surgeon; b. Senora, Va., July 2, 1897; s. John Edward and Mary Virginia (Fallin) B.; B.S., Coll. of William and Mary, 1918; M.D., Johns Hopkins, 1922; m. Catharine Rundlet, Jan. 13, 1927; 1 son, Rundlet. Resident house officer, surgical, Johns Hopkins Hosp., 1922-23; asst. resident surgeon, Henry Ford Hosp., 1923-24; completed surg. training Roosevelt Hosp., New York, N.Y., 1924-26; surgeon Cardova Gen. Hosp., U.S. marine surgeon, territorial commr. of health, Cardova, Alaska, 1926-27; attending surgeon, asst. chief of clinic, Vanderbilt Clinic, Columbia Presbyterian Med. Center, City of N.Y., 1928-32; mem. attending surg. staff, Presbyn. Hosp. of City of N.Y. since 1932; instr. surgery, Coll. of Phys. and Surg., Columbia U., 1930-42, asst. prof. clin. surgery, 1942-46, asso. prof. from 1946. Condr. series of studies in heart and blood vessel surgery; Dept. of Surgery, Presbyn. Hosp., since 1930. Mem. A.M.A., Am. Bd. Surgery, Johns Hopkins Surg. Assn., N.Y. Surg. Soc., Am. Surg. Assn., Internat. Soc. Surgery, So. Surg. Association, The Halsted Society, French Academy Surgery, Phi Beta Kappa, Alpha Omega Alpha. Clubs: Century Association (New York City); Apawamis (Rye, N.Y.). Contbr. articles to profl. jours. Home: Larchmont NY Died Oct. 8, 1970.

BLAKEY, ROY GILLISPIE, economist; b. Shelbina, Mo., Apr. 27, 1880; s. Frederic Glendi and Minora (Gillispie) B.; student U. of Mo., 1900-01; Ph.B., Drake U., 1905, LL.D., 1940; M.A., U. Colo., 1910; Ph.D., Columbia, 1912; m. Gladys McAlpine Campbell, Aug. 1, 1917. Reporter Daily Camera, Boulder, Colo., later Rocky Mountain News, 1908-09; special agt. N.Y. State Food Investigating Commn., 1912; assistant prof. economics, Cornell U., 1912-15; asst. prof. economics U. Minn., 1915-18, asso. prof., 1918-19, prof., 1919-48, prof. emeritus since 1948; vis. prof. U. Cal. at Los Angeles, 1948-51, U. Hawaii, 1949. Now holds chair of pub. finance Faculty of Polit. Sci., State U. of Turkey, Ankara; also lectr. Turkish Army Intelligence Div., and gen. adivser or cons. Mut. Security Adminstrn. and University Research and Activities. Dir. Bureau Research and Statistics, Minn. State Tax Commn., 1916; economist and trade specialist U.S. War Trade Bd., 1918; economist and asso. dir. Savs. Div. U.S. Treasury Dept., 1918-19; Inst. of Economics, Brookings Instn., 1927-28; cons. N.C. State Tax Commn., 1928-29; tax adviser to gov. W. Va., 1930; dir. Minn. tax survey, 1931-32; dir. tax and pub. expenditure div. Minn. and U.S. Dept. of Agr. land utilization survey, 1933. Mem. finance com. Mpls. Survey Commn., 1929-31; mayor's Tax Com., 1931-33; tax cons., gov. of Minn. 1932-35; mem. Gov's Com. on Liquor Control and Taxation, 1933; econ. analyst U.S. Treasury Dept., 1934; tax adviser Minn. Edn. Assn., 1934; mem. Minn. State Planning Bd., 1934-35; chief Econ. Research Div. of U.S. Bur. Fgn. and Domestic Commerce, 1935-37; chmn. Minn. Income Study, State Resources Commn., 1938-42; Cons. St. Louis Inst. for Govt. Research 1943; tax and research cons. Council of State Govts., 1943-44, Fedn. Tax Adminstrs., 1944, Utah State Tax Study Com., 1945. Cons Nat. Resources Planning Bd., 1939-42; mem. adv. tax com. U.S. Civil Aeronautics Bd., 1944-45; chmn. Mpls. Mayor's Commn. on Taxation and Finance, 1945-48. Past pres. Minn. Statis. Assn., Minn. State Tax Assn. Fellow Royal Econ. Soc., Royal Hist. Soc.; mem. Am. Econ. Assn., Nat. Tax Assn. (v.p. 1942-43, pres. 1943-44), Beta Gamma Sigma, Phi Beta Kappa, Lambda Chi Alpha, Alpha Kappa Psi. Author books, relating to field, latest being: Sales Taxes and Other Excises (with Gladys C. Blakey), 1945; also brochures and numerous articles. Editor, asso. editor or cons. editor various tech. publs. in field, 1920-36; co-author, co-editor studies and publs. Dept. Commerce, 1935-37. Address: Minneapolis MN Died June 1, 1967.

BLAKSLEE, JAMES I., ex-4th asst. postmaster-gen.; b. Mauch Chunk, Pa., Dec. 17, 1870; s. Alonzo Potter and Lizzie Crellin (Bond) B.; ed. Cheltenham Mil. Acad., Ogontz, Pa.; Hill Sch., Pottstown, Pa.; m. Henrietta Bunting, of Mauch Chunk, Pa., Dec. 17, 1901. Various railroad positions; owner elec. light and power plant, Lehighton, Pa.; chmn. Carbon Co. (Pa.) Dem. Com. 10 yrs.; mem. Pa. Ho. of Rep., 1907-9; Dem. nominee sec. internal affairs, Pa., 1910; sec. Dem. State Exec. Com., Pa., 1911-13; del. (and sec. Pa. delegation) Dem. Nat. Conv., Baltimore, 1912; apptd. 4th asst. postmaster-gen. Mar. 17, 1913; del. at large Dem. Nat. Conv., San Francisco, Calif., 1920; 2d lt. Co. E. 8th Regt. Pa. Vol. Inf., Spanish-Am. War. Mem. S.R., Spanish War Veterans, Episcopalian. Mason (32 deg.), Elk. Clubs: Art (Phila.), Army and Navy (Washington, D.C.), Rotary (Lehighton, Pa.). Home: 3200 17th St N.W., Washington DC‡

BLALOCK, JESSE MARION, newspaper publisher; b. Carrollton, Ga., May 10, 1898; s. Edward Caloway and Frances (Butler) B.; ed. pub. schs., Carrollton, Ga., Newman (Ga.) High Sch., and U. of Ga.; m. Frances Nolan, Mar. 10, 1920; children—Jesse Marion, Barbara Frances Foster. Pres., treas. The State Record Co., 1943-62, then chmn. bd., chmn. exec., finance coms.; pres., pub. emeritus The State and The Columbia Record; dir., mem. exec. com. Liberty Life Ins. Co.; dir., mem. common trust com-Citizens & Southern Nat. Bank of S.C.; dir. Bestway Express Gen. chmn. Spartanburg (S.C.) Community Chest, 1936, pres., 1936-37; gen. chmn. Columbia Community Chest, 1944, president, 1946; president Columbia Chamber of Commerce, 1948; president Columbia YMCA; member of the board of directors Salvation Army; chmn. Richland County Historic Preservation Commn.; bd. dirs. So. Indsl. Relations Conf. Served with U.S. Navy, World War I. Mem. S.C. Press Assn. (pres. 1947-48), Associated Press, Am. Newspaper Pubs. Assn., Southern Newspaper Pubs. Assn. (dir. 1941-45, 48-51), So. Graphic Arts Assn, (dir. 1938-47), (hon. life) Mid-Atlantic Circulation Mgrs. Assn. (pres. 1927-28), Columbia Mchts. Assn. (pres. 1942-43), Am. Legion, Sigma Delta Chi, and Chi Psi fraternities. Independent Democrat. Baptist. Mason (K.T., Shriner), Knight of Pythias (grand chancellor, S.C. 1936-37), Odd Fellow (grand master S.C. 1936-37), Lion (dist. gov. 1940-41), Clubs: Columbia Executives, Navy League, Palmetto (Columbia); Forest Lake Country. Home: Columbia SC Died June 15, 1970; buried Greenlawn Meml. Park, Columbia SC

BLALOCK, U(RIAH) BENTON, ex-pres. Am. Cotton Coop. Assn.; b. at Norwood, N.C., Apr. 26, 1873; s. Merritt E. and Hettie (Staton) B.; ed. Trinity Coll. (now Duke U.), Durham, N.C., 1892-94; m. Monte Christian, Jan. 6, 1906; children—Monte, Ben; m. 2d, Besie Dunlap, Sept. 18, 1918; 1 son, David. Formerly engaged in farming, merchandising, cotton buying; v.p. and gen. mgr. N.C. Cotton Growers Cooperative Assn., 1922-34; pres. Am. Cotton Cooperative Assn., 1930-33; pres. Blalock Motor Sales Company, Wadesboro, N.C.; dir. Carolina Mortgage Co., Stanly Cotton Oil Co. Pres. and dir. Anson Mutual Electrical Corpn., Wadesboro. Mem. N.C. Gen. Assembly, 1939. Democrat. Methodist. Mason (Shriner), K.P. Club: Rotary. Home: Wadesboro NC‡

BLAMER, DEWITT, naval officer; b. Independence, Ia., Jan. 20, 1872; grad. U.S. Naval Acad., 1891. Ensign, July 1, 1893; lt. jr. grade, Mar. 3, 1899; lt., July 6, 1899; lt. comdr., July 18, 1905; comdr., Mar. 4, 1911; capt., Aug. 29, 1916. Served on Alliance and Apache, Spanish-Am. War, 1898; in charge navy recruiting sta., Chicago, 1905-6; navigator St. Louis, 1906-8; exec. officer Milwaukee, 1908-9; with Bur. of Equipment, Navy Dept., 1909-10; in charge 9th Light House Dist., Chicago, 1910-11; comd. Paducah, 1911; exec. officer Wisconsin, 1911-12; comd. Buffalo, 1912-13; capt. of yard, Navy Yard, Puget Sound, Wash., 1913-15; at Naval War Coll., Newport, R.I., 1915-16; comd. Birmingham, 1916; chief of staff, destroyer force, Atlantic Fleet, 1916-17; comdg. U.S.S. Seattle, 1917-18; chief of staff, cruiser and transport force, Atlantic Fleet, 1917-19; chief of staff, Asiatic Fleet, 1919-20. Address: Navy Dept., Washington DC‡

BLANCH, ARNOLD, artist; b. Mantorville, Minn., June 4, 1896; s. Louis and Bertha (Adler) B.; student Mpls. Sch. Fine Arts, 1915-17, Art Students League, N.Y., 1919-21; m. Lucille Lundquist, 1922 (div. 1939). Artist, 1922-68; asso. with Woodstock (N.Y.) Artists Colony, 1923-68; instr. in painting Cal. Sch. Fine Arts, San Francisco, 1930-31, Art Students League N.Y., 1935-39, 47-59, Colorado Springs Art Center, 1939-41, Art Students League summer sch., Woodstock, 1947-68; vis. artist U. Minn., 1949, Clearwater Art Center (Fla.), 1950-68, U. Hawaii, 1955; artist in residence Joslyn Mus., Omaha, 1964; Ford grant vis. artist Bridgeport (Conn.) U., 1965. Exhibits; 1-man shows N.Y., 1926, 29, 33, 38, 42, 45, 50, 54, 58, Assn. Am. Artists, 1940, 54, Walker Art Center, 1952, Krasner Gallery, 1958-68, Norton A. Gallery West Palm Beach, 1961; 40 year retrospective N.Y. State U., New Paltz. Recipient 1st prize painting, San Francisco Art Assn., 1931; purchase prize, San Francisco Legion of Honor Mus. 1931; Norman Waite Harris medal, Chgo., 1932; Guggenheim fellow, 1933; Beck gold medal Pa. Acad. Fine Arts, 1938; 3d prize, Carnegie Internat., 1938. 1st Prize Nat. Ceramics Exhbn., Syracuse, 1940, 51; Joseph Martinson Meml. award Art U.S.A., 1959; purchase prize Du Pont Mus., 1960; best in show Albany (N.Y.) Mus., 1960; 1st prize in oil Albany Mus., 1967, Berkshire Art Assn., 1967. Served in U.S. Army, World War. Mem. Painters, Sculptors, Gravers Soc. Am. (former pres.). Am. Artists Congress (exec. council), Asso. Am. Artists (dir.), Am. Watercolor Soc. Author: Painting for Enjoyment, 1946; Boardman Robinson, The Teacher (chapter in Boardman Robinson's biography), 1946; Gouache, 1946; Arnold Blanch (monograph), 1946. Home: Woodstock NY Died Oct. 23, 1968.

BLANCHARD, ARTHUR HORACE, cons. engr.; b. Providence, R.I., Feb. 10, 1877; s. Horace Kennedy and Caroline Potter (Hill) B.; Providence High Sch.; C.E., Brown U., 1899; A.M., Columbia, 1902; m. Mary Temple Burt, of Providence, June 17, 1902; 1 son, Gerald Geoffrey. With highway dept., Providence, Am. Bridge Co., and in gen. consulting work, 1896-1903; dep. engr. State Bd. Pub. Rds. R.I., 1903-10; instr., asst. prof. and asso. prof. civ. engring., Brown U., 1899-1911; prof. highway engring., Columbia U., 1911-17, prof. highway engring. and highway transport, U. of Mich., Aug. 1919-27. Cons. highway engr., Oct. 1910—; mem. Advisory Commn. on State Highways, N.Y., 1912; consulting highway engr., Board Water Supply, to commr. public works of Borough of Manhattan, Mich., N.Y., and Pa. State Highway depts., Dominion of Can. and Nat. Highways Assn.; mem. Advisory Bd. on Highways, N.Y. State Dept. of Efficiency and Economy; chief Bur. of Pub. Works, Army Overseas Ednl. Commn., Feb.-June 1919. Consulting transport engineer and highway traffic control consultant, 1926—. United States reporter to Internat. Road Congresses, 2d at Brussels, 1910, 3d at London, 1913, 4th at Seville, 1923, 5th at Milan, 1926; U.S. rep. Internat. Com. on Standard Tests for Highway Materials, 1914. Episcopalian. Fellow A.A.A.S. (sec. sect. engring., 1913); mem. Am. Soc. C.E., Society Automotive Engineers, Institute of Transport of Great Britain, Societe des Ingenieurs Civils de France, Engring. Inst. of Can., Inst. of Traffic Engrs., Internat. Assn. for Testing Materials, Internat. Assn. Road Congresses, Am. Soc. Municipal Engineers, Nat. Highways Assn.; pres. Am. Road Builders' Assn., Nat. Highway Traffic Assn., Internat. Traffic and Transport Assn., Internat. Inst. of Transport; ex-dir. Nat. Pedestrians' Assn.; mem. highway research bd. Nat. Research Counsel; mem. Delta Tau Delta, Sigma Xi, Phi Kappa Phi, etc. Clubs: Michigan Union, University (Providence); Union Interalliee of Paris. Co-Author (with H. B. Drowne): Highway, 1910-12; Highway

Engineering, 1913. Asso. editor on highways, American Civil Engineers Pocket-Book, 1913; Elements of Highway Engineering, 1915. Editor-in-Chief, American Highway Engineers' Handbook, 1919; Internat. Highway Transport Handbook; Internat. Highway Traffic Control Handbook; Internat. Highway Engineers' Handbook. Contbr. on engring. topics. Address: Box C, Edgewood Station, Providence RI‡

BLANCHARD, FERDINAND QUINCY, clergyman; b. Jersey City, N.J., July 23, 1876; s. Edward Richmond and Anna Winifred (Quincy) B.; A.B., Amherst, 1898; B.D., Yale Div. Sch., 1901; D.D., Amherst, 1918, Oberlin, 1919; m. Ethel Hebard West, June 19, 1901; children—Edward, Virginia (Mrs. C. Becker). Ordained Congl. Ministry, 1901; pastor Southington, Conn., 1901-04, East Orange, N.J., 1904-15, Euclid Av. Ch., Cleveland, O., since 1915. Mem. Bd. of Edn., Southington, 1902-04; pres. Bd. of Edn., East Orange, 1912-15. Trustee Fisk University (Nashville, Tenn.). Mem. bd. trustees Family Service Assn., Cleveland; mem. executive committee Cleveland Red Cross; former moderator Congregational Christian Churches of U.S.A.; mem. Society of Mayflower Descendants, Delta Kappa Epsilon fraternity. Republican. Clubs: Alathian, Union (Cleve.). Wrote hymns: O Child of Lowly Manger Birth; Before the Cross of Jesus, and others. Home: 1686 Lee Rd., Cleveland Heights 18. Address: Euclid Avenue Congregational Church, Cleveland 6‡

BLANCHARD, HAROLD HOOPER, coll. prof.; b. Sherborn, Mass., Jan. 11, 1891; s. Joseph Hooper and Julia Ann (Coolidge) B.; A.B., Clark Coll., Worcester, Mass., 1916; A.M., Harvard, 1921, Ph.D., 1921; Frederick Sheldon traveling fellow (Harvard), U. of Paris, 1921-22; m. Roberta Page Newton Ray, Mar. 29, 1938; children—Mrs. John S. Wurts, Jr., Mrs. Henderson Inches, Jr., Mrs. John H. Hoagland, Jr. Tchr. English, Middletown (Conn.) High Sch., 1916-18; instr. in English, Princeton, 1922-25; prof. English, Coll. of Wooster (Ohio), 1925-27; asst. prof. English, Tufts Coll., Medford, Mass., 1927-31, prof. English lit. 1931, head dept. English, 1939-57, Fletcher prof., from 1939. Mem. Modern Lang. Assn., Mediaeval Acad. Am., Am. Assn. Tchrs. Italian, Emerson Soc., Thoreau Soc., Nuttall Ornithol. Club, Mass. Audubon Soc., (asso.) Am. Ornithologists' Union, Dante Soc. Am., Renaissance Soc. America, Phi Beta Kappa. Editor: Prose and Poetry of the Continental Renaissance in Translation, 1949, rev. edit., 1955. Home: Winchester MA Died Sept. 4, 1971; buried Lyman Center Cemetery, Lyman NH

BLANCHARD, LAFAYETTE RANDALL, editor; b. Chadron, Neb., Apr. 23, 1889; s. Dr. Randall Huron and Margaret Maria (Bowers) B.; student U. of Neb., 1907-10; m. Beula Charlotte Miner, Jan. 30, 1914; 1 son, Robert Miner. Reporter Neb. State Jour., 1911-14 and 1915-18; United Press corr. and bur. mgr., 1914-15 and 1918-21; news editor Syracuse Jour., 1921-29; mng. editor Rochester Journal, 1929-33; with Gannett Co., Inc., Rochester, 1933-57; mng. editor, Democrat and Chronicle, 1934-36; mng. editor, Times-Union, 1936-41; dir. news and editorial offices, Gannett newspapers, 1941-47; gen. exec. editor, Gannett Newspapers and editor Rochester Democrat & Chronicle, 1947-57. Mem. Asso. Press Mng. Editors Association (pres. 1951), Am. Soc. Newspaper editors. Republican. Mason. Clubs: Oak Hill, Rochester. Home: Ojai CA Died May 10, 1970; buried Nordhoff Cemetery, Ojai CA

BLANCHARD, MURRAY, engineer; b. Peru, Ill., July 25, 1874; s. Murray and Helen A. (Dolliver) B.; B.S. in C.E., Univ. of Mich., 1898, C.E., 1903; m. Alice H. Fish, Feb. 6, 1902; 1 dau., Helen (dec.). Has operated extensively in the U.S. and Can. as engr. water power development, also as hydraulic engr.; with engring. dept. Pa. R.R. as asst. engr. on tunnel in N.Y. City, 1905-09; hydraulic engr. State of Ill., Div. of Waterways, 1920-30; prin. engr. U.S. Engring. Dept., 1930-31; cons. engr., Chicago, 1930-33; engr. U.S. Pub. Works Adminstrn., 1933-37; engr. U.S. Engring. Dept. since Feb. 1, 1938. Served in World War as major engrs. U.S. Army, 1917-19. Mem. Am. Soc. C.E. (life), Western Soc. Engrs., Soc., Am. Mil. Engrs., Am. Legion. Republican. Conglist. Clubs: Univ. of Mich., Chicago Engineers'. Home: 132 Peck St. Office: U.S. Engineer Office, Sault Ste Marie MI‡

BLANCHARD, RALPH HARRIS, exec.; b. Niagara Falls, N.Y., June 27, 1895; s. Herman Kingsley and Alice Amanda (Tucker) B.; A.B., Cornell U., 1917; m. Margaret Huntington Hooker, June 30, 1924 (div. 1944);children—Sara (Mrs. Robert Erickson), Susan (Mrs. Bliss); married 2d, Grace Alma Godolphin. Employe The National Carbon Company, Niagara Falls, N.Y. 1919; asst. to pres. Nat. Thrift Bond Corp., New York, N.Y., 1920-21; bank employe, Power City Trust Co., Niagara Falls, N.Y., 1921-24; exec. sec. Community Chest, Niagara Falls, N.Y., 1924-28; administrative dir. Community Chests and Councils, Inc., New York, N.Y., 1928-43, exec. dir. 1943-60. Served as pvt., 9th Co., Coast Defenses of Chesapeake Bay, 1918; commd, 2d lt., Coast Arty. O.R.C., Fortress Monroe; Va., 1918. Vice pres. Nat. Information Bur., United Def. Fund; pres. Nat. Health and Welfare Retirement Assn., 1951-65, cons., 1965-72; pres. Nat. Conference Social Work, 1948-49. Mem. Nat. Assn. Social Workers, Delta Sigma Rho, Am. Legion. Club: University (New York). Home: Bronxville NY Died May 6, 1972; cremated, inurned Columbarium Christ Church, Bronxville NY

BLANCHARD, RAOUL, educator; b. Orleans, France, Sept. 4, 1877; s. Charles Leon and Emilienne (Badinier) B.; grad. Lycees Orleans, Louis le Grand, Paris, 1897; Ecole Normale Superieure, Paris, 1900; Doctor Honoris causa, U. Gand, Quebec, Montreal, 1932, 38, 52; m. Jane de Lauwereyns de Rosendale, Apr. 10, 1901; children—Henriette (Mrs. Tocanne), Guillaume, Antoinette (Mrs. Henry), Colette (Mrs. Mignotte). Prof. geography U. Grenoble, France, 1906-48, dean faculty letters, 1944-48; prof. Harvard, 1928-36, U. Montreal, 1946-49, summer sch., Columbia, 1921, U. Chgo., 1927, U. Cal. at Berkeley, 1932, Middlebury Coll., 1936, U. Quebec, 1952; now adj. to commr. of Republic of Lyon Region. Founder, dir. Inst. Alpine Geography, 1906, also of Rev. of Alpine Geography, 1913. Decorated Commandeur de la Legion de'Honneur, Commandeur de la Couronne de Belgique. Mem. Am. Acad. Arts and Scis. (hon.), Gesellschaft fur Erdkunde zu Berlin, Societa Geografica Italiana, Geog. socs. of Zurich, Stockholm, Belgrade, Bruxelles, Deputazione Sualpina. Rotarian (president 1945). Author 12 vols. about the Western Alps, Sevres (Seine et Oise) France‡

BLANCKE, WILTON WENDELL, foreign service officer; b. Phila., June 29, 1908; s. Wilton Wallace and Cecil Whittier (Trout) B.; A.B., Haverford Coll., 1929; m. Frances Elizabeth Nichol, Feb. 13, 1952. Joined N.W. Ayer & Son, Inc., 1929, art study, Paris, France, 1932, art dir., Buenos Aires, Argentina, 1933; fgn. service auxiliary U.S. Embassy, Buenos Aires, 1942; assigned to U.S. Polit. Adviser, Berlin, Germany, 1945; fgn. service officer, June 1946, 2d sec. embassy, Habana, Cuba, 1948; consul, prin. officer, Hanoi, Vietnam, 1950; officer in charge Burma Affairs, Dept. of State, 1953-55; counselor of embassy, Vientiane, Laos, 1955-57; consul gen. Frankfurt, Germany, 1957-60; 1st United States A.E. to the Republic of Chad, 1960-61, to the Republic of Congo (Brazzaville), the Central African Republic and Gabonese Republic; fgn. service insp. Phi Beta Kappa. Home: Washington DC Died 1971.

BLANCO-FOMBONA, RUFINO, Venezuelan diplomat, writer, publisher; b. Caracas, June 17, 1874. Consul of Venezuela and Peru in Phila., 1894; attache in The Hague, 1896; consul of Dominican Republic in Boston, 1899; consul in Amsterdam, 1901-04; became gov. of Amazonas, 1905; sec. to Chamber of Deputies, 1909; imprisoned for opposition to Juan Gomez, 1909-10, became exiled, 1914; founded publishing house America, in Madrid, Spain, 1915; civil gov. of Navarre, Spain, 1934-37; pres. State of Miranda, 1937-39; became minister of Spain to Uruguay, 1939. Author of numerous books published in Spain; many translated into English, Swedish, French, Italian, Russian. Contbr. to La Voz and El Sol of Madrid. Address: Legacion de Venezuela, Montevideo Uruguay*‡

BLANDFORD, JOHN BENNETT, JR., pub. adminstr.; b. N.Y.C., Aug. 19, 1897; s. John Bennett and Emily (Gould) B.; M.E., Stevens Inst. Tech., Hoboken, N.J., 1919; special studies Nat. Inst. Pub. Adminstrn., N.Y. City; hon. Dr. Engring., Stevens Institute of Tech., 1945; m. Ruth Brownlow, Apr. 19, 1926. Engr. The Texas Co. in N.Y., Va., Tex., 1920-22; staff mem. Nat. Inst. Pub. Adminstrn., 1922-23; asst. to city mgr., Petersburg, Va., 1923-24; dir. research Newark (N.J.) Chamber of Commerce, 1924-26; dir. Cincinnati Bureau Governmental Research, 1926-31; mem. President's Emergency Com. for Employment, 1931; dir. pub. safety, City of Cincinnati, 1931-33; asst. to chmn. Tenn. Valley Authority, 1933-34, coordinator and sec. of board, 1934-37, gen. mgr., 1937-39; asst. director U.S. Bureau of the Budget, 1939-42; administrator, Nat. Housing Agency, 1942-46, also mem. War Manpower Commn. and President's Com. for Congested Prodn. Areas; adviser to Govt. of China, 1946-47; cons. on govt. relations, 1947-48; dep. chief E.C.A. Mission to Greece, 1948-50; ambassador, U.S. rep. adv. com. U.N. Relief and Works Agy. for Palestine refugees, 1950-51, dir., 1951-53; cons. Govt. P.R., pub. adminstr. Clearing House on survey pub. adminstrn. 20 Latin Am. Republics, 1954-72. With U.S. Naval Aviation Service, World War I. Recipient Medal Merit from Pres. Truman, 1946; hon. fellow Pantios Coll. of Polit. Sci., Athens; hon. citizenship and gold medal, City of Athens, 1949; Grand Comdr. Royal Order of Phoenix, Greece, 1949. Affiliated mem. Internat. Mgrs. Assn.; asso. mem. Govtl. Research Assn.; mem. Am. Sect. Internat. Inst. Adminstrv. Sciences. Clubs: Cosmos, National Press (Washington). Home: McLean VA Died Jan. 1972.

BLANDING, ALBERT HAZEN, ret. Nat. Guard officer; b. Lyons, Iowa, Nov. 9, 1876; Abram Ormsby and Sarah Ann (Nattinger) B.; grad. East Florida Seminary (now part of U. of Fla.), 1894; LL.D., University of Florida, 1942; m. Mildred M. Hale, June 1, 1908; children—Sarah Elizabeth, Mildred Louise (Mrs. J. H. Yarborough), William Norris. Mine supt. and asst. mgr. with Dutton Phosphate Co., 1896-1910; est. and operated lumber and naval stores business, 1910-16; with Consol. Lumber Co., 1919-22, Fla. Citrus Exchange, 1922-33; chief U.S. Nat. Guard Bureau, Feb. 1, 1936 to Jan. 31, 1940; lt gen. Fla. Nat. Guard; retired, Nov. 9, 1940. Coordinating dir., Action Divisions and chmn. Division of Civil Protection, State Defense Council of Florida. Mem. bd. of Control of State Instns. of Higher Learning (Fla.), 1922-36; Fla. State Plant Bd., 1922-36, Capt., maj., lt. col. and col. Fla. Nat. Guard, 1899-1917; duty on Mexican border, 1916-17; mustered into U.S. Army, 1917, as brig. gen. and served in France, World War, 1918-19; apptd. maj. gen. of the line, N.G., U.S., 1924. Awarded D.S.M.; active State Service medal, Florida Cross. Incorporator of the Am. Legion and 1st dept. comdr. of Fla. Democrat. Mason, Elk. Clubs: Army and Navy (Washington, D.C.), Kiwanis. Address: Tallahassee FL Died Dec. 1970.

BLATT, WILLIAM M(OSHER), lawyer, writer; b. Orange, N.J., Apr. 29, 1876; s. Joseph Henry and Louise (Singer) B.; ed. pub. schs. and under tutors; Franklin medalist; LL.B. cum laude, Boston U., 1897; spl. course, Harvard, 1914-15; honorary Litt.D., Calvin Coolidge Coll., 1948; m. Lucy Romberg, Apr. 3, 1911; children—Hester M., Josephine, Louise. Admitted to Mass. bar, 1897, to bar U.S. Supreme Court, 1920; formerly pub. adminstr.; mem. Legal Advisory Bd., World War; prof. med. jurisprudence, Coll. of Physicians and Surgeons, 1930-48; lecturer on drama and literature; lecturer Boston U. Law Sch., 1931-39; lecturer on law, Bentley Sch. of Accounting and Finance, 1942-43; professor of Law, Portia Law Sch., 1943-49; asst. attorney region No. 1, Nat. War Labor Bd., 1945-46. Mem. Am. Law Inst., Boston Univ. Alumni Assn., Boston U. Law Sch. Assn. (pres. 1932), Mason. Club: New Century. Author articles in law jours. and popular mags.; numerous plays, also one-act plays, monologues, sketches and epigrams. Asso. editor Corpus Juris, 1924. Home: 29 Dighton St. Office: 18 Tremont St., Boston‡

BLATTEIS, SIMON RISEFELD, physician; b. Silesia, Austria, Mar. 27, 1876; s. Max and Sarah (Risefeld) B.; brought to U.S., 1882, naturalized 1897; student Coll. of Physicians and Surgeons, Columbia U., 1893-94; M.D., Bellevue Hosp. Med. Coll., 1898; m. Minnie Levison, Nov. 4, 1900 (dec. 1957); children—Victor Louis, Eleanor Miriam (Mrs. Edward A. Werner). Began practice in 1898; med. insp., New York Dept. of Health, and acting chief Div. of Epidemiology. 1915-17; pathologist in chief, Brooklyn Jewish Hosp., 1906-18, visiting physician, 1920-35; clinical prof. medicine, 1924-32, L.I. Coll.; prof. clinical med., 1932-41; emeritus prof. clinical med. 1941, L.I. Coll. of Medicine; physician-in-chief, Jewish Hosp., 1935-41, also consulting physician and cons. pathologist; cons. physician Adelphi Hosp., 1930; cons. physician Beth-El Hosp.; lecturer in medicine, clinical prof. med., N.Y. Univ. Med. Coll., 1900-40. Diplomate American Bd. of Internal Medicine. Fellow Am. Coll. of Physicians; mem. Am. Medical Soc., N.Y. Academy of Medicine, Harvey Society, Phi Delta Epsilon. Mason. Home: Miami Beach Died June 11, 1968.

BLATTENBERGER, RAYMOND, govt. ofcl.; b. Phila., Jan. 19, 1892; s. William Nora (French) B.; student Temple U., 1909-13; Dr. Engineering (hon.), Lehigh University, 1958; m. Harriet Coles Schubert, Apr. 24, 1914; children—Raymond Walter, John William. Pressman William Mann & Co., Phila., 1904-05; asst. plant supt. Keystone Pub. Co., 1914-17; sales staff Edward Stern Co., 1917-35, plant mgr., 1935, v.p. charge prodn., 1935-38, v.p. charge sales, labor, trade relations, 1938-53; pub. printer U.S. since 1953. Mem. indsl. relations com. Typothetae of Phila., 1935-37, v.p., 1937-38, pres., 1939-41; pres. United Typothetae of Am., 1942. Mem. Nat. Assn. Photo-Lithographers. Home: Washington DC Died Apr. 26, 1971; interred Harleigh Cemetery, Camden NJ

BLAUSTEIN, JACOB, business exec. b. Balt., Sept. 30, 1892; s. Louis and Henrietta (Gittelsohn) B.; student Lehigh U. L.H.D. (hon.); L.H.D., Hebrew Union Coll., 1957; LL.D., Morgan State College, Baltimore, 1958, Jewish Theological Seminary in America, 1960; Dr. Polit. Sci., Wilberforce University, 1959; married Hilda Van Leer Katz, June 10, 1925. Co-founder with father Am. Oil Co., 1910 (merged with Pan-Am. Petroleum & Transport Co., 1933), pres., 1933-37, now dir., mem. exec. com.; pres. Mexican Petroleum Corp. (Me.), 1933-37, dir., exec. com.; exec. v.p. Pan-Am. Petroleum & Transport Co., 1933-37, dir., mem. exec. com.; dir., mem. exec. com. Pan-Am. Refining Corp., Pan-Am. Pipe Line Co., Pan-Am. Prodn. Co., Mexican Petroleum Corp. (Ga.), Pan Am. Gas Co., Lord Baltimore Filling Stations, Inc.; pres., dir. Am. Trading & Prodn. Corp.; dir., adv. com. Union Trust Co. (Md.), U.S. Fidelity Guaranty Co.; former pres. Overseas News Agy.; director Standard Oil Company (Indiana). Consultant American delegation U.N. Conf., San Francisco, 1945; chmn. Am. delegation Conf. Jewish Orgns., London, 1946; chmn. Am. Jewish Com. delegation Paris Peace Conf., 1946; co-chmn. Consultative Council Jewish orgns. ESOCOC; member U.S. delegation 10th Gen. Assembly UN. Director former pres. Asso. Jewish Charities, Balt.; dir. Am. joint distbn. com. United Service for New Americans, Am. Fund for Israel Orgns., Am. Assn. U.N., Nat. Conf. Christians and Jews, Weizman Inst. Sci.; pres. Am. Jewish Com.; dir. Council Jewish Fedns. and Welfare Funds, United Negro Coll. Fund, Balt. Symphony Orchestra. Pres. Louis and Henrietta Blaustein, Found. Jacob and Hilda Bluestein Found.; gov. Hebrew U. Jerusalem; trustee Harry S. Truman Library; director Am. Heritage Foundation, Commission on Health Careers. Member President Truman's National Advisory board on Mobilization Policy; acting chairman marketing committee, member supplies and distribution com., and joint use facilities com. U.S. Petroleum Adminstrn. for War, World War II; mem. nat. petroleum council, oil and gas div. U.S. Dept. Interior; v. chmn. Nat. Citizens Com. for U.N. Day; v.p. Jewish Restitution Successor Orgn; mem. presidium Conf. on Jewish Claims against Germany. Mem. Internat. Assn. Iranian Art and Archaeology (trustee). Clubs: Phoenix Suburban (Balt.); Bankers, Harmonie (N.Y.C.). Home: Pikesville MD Died Nov. 15, 1970.

BLAUVELT, BRADFORD, mfg. co. exec.; b. N.Y.C. Sept. 22, 1906; s. Everett Theodore and Josephine (Matthews) B.; grad. Seton Hall Prep. Sch., 1925 certificate Pace Coll., 1930; m. Eleanor Glenck, June 22, 1935. Accountant, Warner Bros., N.Y.C., 1927-29, United Color and Pigment, Newark, 1929-33; accountant Am. Type Founders, Inc., subsidiary Daystrom, Inc., 1933-44, chief accountant, 1941-46, comptroller, 1946-49, v.p., dir., 1947-49; comptroller Daystrom, Inc., Murray Hill, N.J., 1949-54, v.p. internat., 1954-60; sr. v.p. Daystron div. Schlumberger Ltd., Murray Hill, N.J., 1960-66; ret., 1966; dir. Thomson-Nat. Press. Mem. C. of C., Holland Soc., Am. Ordnance Assn., Navy League U.S., Am. Mgmt. Assn., N.A.M. Club: Essex. Home: Forked River NJ Died Feb. 5, 1969; buried Good Luck Cemetery,Lanoka Harbor, Forked River NJ

BLAUVELT, MARY TAYLOR, author, lecturer; b. Clinton, N.J., 1869; d. Rev. I. Alstyne and Caroline (Taylor) Blauvelt; A.B., Wellesley Coll., 1889, A.M., 1892; fellow at Oxford Univ., England, 1895-97. Prof. of Greek, Elmira (N.Y.) Coll., 1892-95; prof. of history, Rockford (Ill.) Coll., 1898-1900; teacher of history, Miss Porter's Sch., Farmington, Conn., 1903-16; lecturer on internat. affairs, N.Y., N.J. and N.E., 1916-28. Mem. Fgn. Policy Assn., League of Women Voters, Non-Partisan League of Nations Assn., Assn. Am. Univ. Women, Phi Beta Kappa. Clubs: Wellesley, College. Author: Development of Cabinet Government in England, 1903; In Cambridge Backs, 1911; Solitude of Letters, 1913; Ultimate Ideals, 1917; Oliver Cromwell—A Dictator's Tragedy, 1937. Contbr. to Review of Reviews, Am. Jour. Sociology, The Bookman. Home: Milner Hotel, Hartford CT‡

BLAYNEY, T(HOMAS) LINDSEY, educator; b. Lebanon, Ky., Dec. 3, 1874; s. Rev. John McClusky and Lucy Weisiger (Lindsey) B.; A.B., Centre Coll., Ky., 1894, A.M., 1897; univs. Gottingen, Geneva, Grenoble and Faculty of Lit., Florence; Ph.D., U. Heidelberg, 1904; LL.D., Southwestern U., Loyola University, New Orleans, University of Notre Dame, 1923, Austin (Texas) College, 1926, Centre Coll., Ky., 1947; m. Gertrude South, Sept. 9; 1896 (dec. 1945);children—Lucy L. (dec.), John McC., Lindsey; m. 2d, Dr. Ida Walz Kubitz, Mar. 24, 1948. Expdn. interior Morocco, 1899; vice consul, Mannheim, Germany, 1901-04; prof. modern langs., and history European art Central U. Ky., 1904-12; prof. German, William M. Rice Inst., Houston, 1912-24; pres. Tex. State Woman's Coll., 1924-26; dean Carleton Coll., 1926-45, chmn. dept. German, 1926-46. Chmn. first Houston City Planning Commn.; as pres. Houston Art League, planned, negotiated for present site Houston Mus. Art, and self-perpetuating bd. trustees. Am. Albert Kahn fellow to Orient, 1914-15. Served from maj. to lt. col. AEF, 1917-19. Decorated Croix de Guerre with palm (2), Officer Legion of Honor (France); Hon. Officer Chasseurs Alpins; Order White War Eagle, Serbia; Chevalier Order St. Sauveur (Greece); Comdr. Order Crown of Italy; 6 citations for D.S.M., Order Purple Heart (United States), American Legion del. 17th Congress FIDAC, Warsaw; del. Internat. Ednl. Congress, Heidelberg. Mem., fellow nat. and internat. orgns., Rice U. Alumni Assn. (hon.). Vice pres. Am. Fed. Arts, 1910. Presbyn. Mason, Rotarian (hon.), Author: Thomas Moore, Ein irisch-galischer Dichter, 1906 Ideals of Orient, 1916; To Our Country (verse series); Am. Ideals and Traditions. Contbr. Am., fgn. and lit. press. Pioneered history of art Am. Colls. and univs. Article on Philippine independence credit with slowing down Congressional action. Home: Marine on St Croix MN Died Mar. 13, 1971; buried Frankfort Cemetery, Frankfort KY

BLEAKLEY, WILLIAM FRANCIS, lawyer; b. Verplanck, Cortlandt, N.Y., Nov. 11, 1883; s. Angelo and Mary A. (Drennan) B.; LL.B., Cornell U., 1904; m. Anna S. Martin, June 28, 1911; children—William Francis, James Robert, Margaret Mary. Admitted to N.Y. bar, 1905; city judge of Yonkers, N.Y., 1918-22; county judge, 1922-28; judge N.Y. Supreme Court, 1928-36; resigned to run for gov. on the Rep. ticket; defeated and returned to private practice; mem. firm Bleakley, Platt, Schmidt, Hart & Fritz; member board of directors of Companion Life Ins. Co., county exec. Westchester County, 1939-41; apptd. counsel Joint Legislative Com. of State of N.Y. on Reapportionment; Moreland Commr. (apptd. by Gov. Lehman, re-apptd. by Gov. Dewey) to investigate adminstrn. of Workmen's Compensation Law. Vice-pres. Constitutional Conv., 1938. Pres. Cornell Law Assn. Mem. N.Y. State Bar Assn. (v.p. and pres. judicial sect.). Republican. Catholic. Elk, K.C. Yonkers NY Died 1969.

BLEGEN, CARL WILLIAM, archeologist; b. Minneapolis, Minn., Jan. 27, 1887; s. John H. and Anna B. (Olsen) B.; B.A., Augsburg Sem., Minneapolis, 1904, U. of Minn., 1907; B.A., Yale, 1908, Ph.D., 1920, hon. M.A., 1927; student Am. Sch. of Classical Studies, Athens, Greece, 1910-13; honorary doctorate, University of Oslo (Norway), 1951, Thessalonike (Greece), 1951, U. Athens, 1963; D. Litt., Oxford, 1957; LL.D., U. Cin., 1958; L.H.D., Hebrew Union College, Jewish Inst. Religion, 1963; Litt.D., Cambridge U., 1963; m. Elizabeth Denny Pierce, July 11, 1924 (dec. 1966). Sec. Am. Sch. Classical Studies, 1913-20, asst. dir., 1920-26, actg. dir., 1926-27; professor classical archeology Grad. Sch. Arts and Sciences, University of Cincinnati 1927-57, prof. emeritus, 1957-71, Distinguished Service prof. emeritus, 1969-71, became fellow, 1927; head department of classics, 1950-57; field dir. University of Cincinnati Archaeol. Expdn., Turkey and Greece; on leave of absence, with Office of Strategic Services, Washington, 1942-45; cultural relations attache, American Embassy, Athens, Greece, 1945-46; dir. Am. Sch. Classical Studies, Athens, 1948-49. With the Am. Red Cross in Greece, 1918-19. Recipient gold medal Archaeological Inst. Am., 1965, gold medal Soc. Antiquaries of London, 1966, Gold medal from University of Cincinnati, 1969. Corresponding fellow of British Academy. Fellow American Academy of Arts and Sciences; mem. Am. Philos. Soc., Am. Philol. Assn., Archeol. Inst. Am., Am. Assn. Univ. Profs., German Archeol. Inst., Archaeol. Soc. Athens (hon. v.p.), Soc. Promotion of Hellenic Studies, London, England (honorary), Royal Soc. Letters of Lund (Sweden), Swedish Royal Acad. Letters, History and Antiquities, Norwegian Academy of Science and Letters, also Phi Beta Kappa (honorary), Sigma Xi. Lutheran. Clubs: Literary, University (Cinn.); Yale (New York); Cosmos (Washington). Author: Korakou, AA Prehistoric Settlement near Corinth, 1921; Zygouries, A Prehistoric Settlement in the Valley of Cleonae, 1928; Acrocorinth (with R. Stillwell, O. Broneer and A. Bellinger), 1930; Prosymna, the Helladic Settlement Preceding the Argive Heraeum (with Elizabeth Blegen), 1937; Troy, Vol. I (with J.L. Caskey, M. Rawson, J. Sperling), 1950, Troy, Vol. II (with J.L. Caskey and M. Rawson), 1951, Vol. III, 1953, Vol. IV (with C. Boulter, J. L. Caskey, M. Rawson), 1958; Troy and the Trojans, 1963; (with M. Rawson) The Palace of Nestor at Pylos, Vol. I, 1966, Vol. III, 1973. Contbr. archaeal. publs. Home: Athens Greece Died Aug. 24, 1971; buried Athens Greece

BLEICH, CLEMENTS HARRY, food co. exec.; b. Jackson, Tenn., Dec. 1, 1911; s. Clements Harry and Serena (McCutchen) B.; B.S., Washington U., St. Louis, 1934; m. Betty Jane Jess, Oct. 18, 1941; children—John North, Susan McCutchen. With Cal. & Hawaiian Sugar Refining Corp., 1935-60, v.p., 1955-60; v.p., dir. Dole Corp., 1961-66; v.p. marketing Sunshine Biscuits, Inc., Long Island City, N.Y., 1966-69; pres. Cal. Agrl. Specialties div. Heggblade-Marguleas-Tenneco Inc., Indio, Cal., 1969-70, Cal-Date Co. subsidiary Heggblade-Marguleas-Tenneco Inc., 1970-72. Dir. Rod McLellan Co. Served to lt. comdr. USNR, 1942-46. Mem. Sigma Chi. Republican. Episcopalian. Clubs: Bohemian (San Francisco); Union League (N.Y.C.); Marrakesh Country (Palm Desert, Cal.). Home: Palm Desert CA Died July 21, 1972.

BLENDER, DOROTHEA KLOTZ, lawyer, publisher; b. Carthage, Ill., Nov. 25, 1908; d. William and Meda (Klotz) Blender; student Bradley U., 1926-29; Ph.B., U. Chicago, 1930, J.D., 1932. Admitted to Ill. bar, 1932; editor Commerce Clearing House, Inc., pubs. law reports, N.Y.C., Chgo., Washington, 1932-36, pub. relations mgr., 1940, asst. pres., 1939-56, v.p. 1957-72. Mem. Am. Assn. Law Libraries, Spl. Libraries Assn., Am. (ho. of dels. 1954-56), Chgo. bar assns., Women's Bar Assn., Ill. (president 1947-48), National Assn. Women Lawyers (pres. 1952-54, exec. bd. 1948-56, 2d v.p. 1950-51, 1st v.p. 1951-52), Kappa Beta Pi. Editor of Women Lawyers Jour., 1948-50. Home: Glenview IL Died Oct. 10, 1972.

BLESSING, EDGAR M., lawyer; b. Wadena, Ind., Aug. 21, 1876; s. George A. and Margaret J. B.; grad. Ind. State Normal Sch., Terre Haute, Ind., 1899; student Cornell U., summer 1900; LL.B., U. of Mich., 1904; m. Geraldine M. White, of Danville, Ind., Oct. 5, 1905. Admitted to Ind. bar, 1905, and began practice at Danville; served as pros. atty.; mem. Pub. Service Commn. of Ind. 2 1/2 yrs.; solicitor P.O. Dept., Washington, D.C., Oct. 1, 1923-Sept. 15, 1925 (resigned); resumed practice at Danville. Republican. Methodist. Mason (32 deg., Shriner), K.P. Clubs: Athletic, Columbia, Country. Home: Danville IN‡

BLESSING, RILEY ANDREW, lawyer; b. nr. Letart, W.Va., Dec. 11, 1875; s. Calvin Thomas and Sarah Josephine (Board) B.; student Spencer (W.Va.) Normal Sch., 1897-98; LL.B., George Washington U., 1906; m. Delitha May Van Matre, Apr. 21, 1897; children—Leolia Genevieve (Mrs. Curtis M. Young), Beulah Gay, Robert Leslie. School teacher, 1894-1900; clerk to county sheriff, 1900-02; admitted to D.C. and W.Va. bars, 1906; admitted to practice before U.S. Supreme Court, 1911; mem. firm Butz & Blessing, Washington, D.C. 1907-11, Musgrave & Blessing, Point Pleasant, W.Va., since 1912; mem. Lee, Blessing & Steed, Charleston, W.Va., 1933-45; retired from active practice of law, 1949. Treasurer Republican County Com., 1902-04; mem. W.Va. Senate, 1912-16; asst. state tax commr., 1917-20; asst. attorney gen. W.Va., 1921-33. Mem. Am., W.Va. State and Local bar assns.; life mem. Columbia-George Washington Alumni Assn. Republican. Baptist; sec. Ohio Assn. of Independent Baptist Churches 1933-46. Home: 1 Buena Vista Pl. Office: Union Bldg., Charleston WV Buena Vista Pl. Office: Union Bldg., Charleston WV‡

BLETHEN, FRANK ALDEN, executive newspaper publishing company; born Seattle, Washington, January 6, 1904; s. Clarance Brettun and Frances (Hall) B.; student St. Martin's Coll., 1918, Augusta Mil. Acad., 1920-23; A.B., U. Wash., 1927; children—Frances Hall, Joan Middleton, Florence Diane, Francia A. (by former marriage). Joined Seattle Times, 1926, dir., from 1937—. pres., 1949—. Mem. Sigma Delta Chi, Phi Gamma Delta, Scabbard and Blade. Clubs: Rainier, Washington Athletic, Seattle Golf (Seattle); Bohemian (San Francisco). Home: Seattle WA Died Jan. 26, 1967.

BLEWER, CLARENCE FREDERICK, investment banker; b. Newark Valley, N.Y., Sept. 29, 1907; s. George Francis and Cora (Livingston) B.; B.S., Cornell U., 1928; m. Inez Hoover, Dec. 9, 1930; 1 dau., June Marie (Mrs. Loyd Andrew Kelly). Partner, Blewer, Heitner, & Glynn, St. Louis, 1945-55; v.p. Blewer, Glynn & Co., St. Louis, 1955-64; v.p., mgr. Midwest div. G. H. Walker & Co., St. Louis, 1964-68. Mem. Investment Bankers Assn. Am. (bd. govs. 1964-66), St. Louis Soc. Financial Analysts, Alpha Zeta. Presbyn. Clubs: Noonday, University (St. Louis). Home: Olivette MO Died 1968.

BLICHFELDT, EMIL HARRY, mgr. Chautauqua Press; b. Brooklyn, N.Y., Mar. 19, 1874; s. Harold William and Mary Ann (Allen) B.; A.B., Wesleyan U., Conn., 1900; m. Eva Graham Potter, of Saratoga Springs, N.Y., Sept. 12, 1903. Began as clk., bookstore, Middletown, Conn., 1900; teacher in Mexico, 1901-4; with Intercontinental Corr. U., Washington, D.C., 1904-5; head publication dept. Ft. Wayne (Ind.) Electric Works, 1905; ednl. corr. Macmillan Co., pubs., 1906; head extension office Chautauqua Instn., 1906-14; mgr. publication dept. same, 1914-19; asst. mgr. advertising, Fort Dearborn Nat. Bank, Chicago, 1920-—. Mem. Am. Civic Assn., Delta Kappa Epsilon. Prohibitionist. Methodist. Author: A Mexican Journey, 1912; revised edit. of same, 1919, as one of four textbooks Chautauqua Home Reading Course. Contbr. to mags. Home: Chautauqua, N.Y. Address: Fort Dearborn Nat. Bank, Chicago IL‡

BLISS, GEORGE LAURENCE, business exec.; b. Rogers Park, Ill., Mar. 5, 1896; s. George Harvey and Robina Margaret (Mount) B.; grad. high sch., Northampton, Mass., 1914; B.S. in econs., U. Pa., 1919 (as of 1918); m. Corinne Constance Sawyer, June 1, 1921; children—George Donald, Arthur Sawyer (dec.), Janet. With Fisk Rubber Company, Chicopee Falls, Mass., and N.Y. City, 1919-22; assistant to president Franklin Soc. for Home-Building and Savings, N.Y. City, 1922-23, v.p., 1923-32; exec. v.p. Fed. Home Loan Bank of N.Y., 1932-34, pres., 1934-41, (on leave as dep. gov. Fed. Home Loan Bank System, Washington, D.C., 1936-37, director 1954-57, vice chairman, 1955-57; president Century Fed. Savings and Loan Assn., N.Y.C., 1941-65, chmn. bd., dir., 1946-65; pres., mng. dir. Council Mut. Savs. Instns., from 1966; Mem. Pres. Eisenhower's Advisory Com. on Housing, 1953; mem. task force on lending agencies Commn. on Orgn. Exec. Branch of Government, 1954-55. Officer candidate, 1st O.T.C., Ft. Niagara, New York, 1917; 2d lt., 1st lt., and captain, 316th Inf., 79th Div., U.S. Army, 1917-19; with A.E.F., July 1918-May 1919; cited for gallantry in action, 1918; 1st lt., captain and maj., 71st Inf., N.Y. Nat. Guard, 1921-28; maj. lt. col., col., 17th Inf., N.Y. Guard, 1940-46; col. 71st Inf., N.Y.N.G., 1946-47; brig. general N.Y. Guard Reserve. President Metropolitan League Savings Assn., 1928-29, N.Y. State League of Savings and Loan Assns., 1931-32; chmn. accounting div. U.S. Savs. and Loan League, 1934-40, chmn. legislative com., 1950-54, director, 1956-58, mem. exec. com., 1958-61; vice chmn. Nat. Thrift Com., 1943-63; mem. council of International Union Bldg. Sec., 1956-58. Fellow Royal Society of Arts (London, Eng.); mem. American Savings and Loan Inst., (pres. 1930-31), Am. Finance Assn., Nat. Association Business Economists, American Legion, 316th Inf. Assn. (pres. 1941-42),

Internat. Benjamin Franklin Soc. (pres. from 1948). Republican Conglist. Clubs: Army-Navy (N.Y.C., also Washington); University of Pennsylvania (N.Y.C.); Rotary. Home: Mount NY Deceased.

BLISS, HARDING, educator; b. St. Louis, July 14, 1911; s. Carl Crider and Elizabeth (Harding) B.; B.S., U. of Ill., 1932; Ph.D., Yale, 1935; m. Gretchen Elizabeth Evans, Feb. 12, 1941. Dir. semi works, Rohm & Haas Co., Phila., 1935-37; asst. prof. chem. engring., U. of Pa., 1937-39; asst. prof., Yale, 1939-42, asso. prof., 1942-47, prof. chem. engring., 1947-71. Cons. State Water Commn., Nat. Def. Research Commn., World War II. Recipient Yale Engring. Assn. award for meritorious service to Yale U., 1971. Mem. Am. Inst. Chem. Engrs. (former editor jour.), Am. Chem. Soc., Sigma Xi, Tau Beta Pi. Contbr. sects. and chpts. in books; articles chem. publs. Home: Mt Carmel CT Died July 27, 1971.

BLISS, HENRY EVELYN, librarian, author; b. N.Y. City, Jan. 29, 1870; s. Henry Hale and Evelina Matilda (Davis) B.; student N.Y. City pub. schools and Coll. of the City of N.Y., 1885-88; m. Ellen de Koster, of New York, June 1, 1901; children—Enid Evelyn (deceased), Margaret de Koster (Mrs. Wolcott Coit Treat). John Hale, Conrad de Koster. Became teacher, 1890; librarian College of the City of N.Y., 1891-1940. Mem. Seaman's Church Inst.‡

BLISS, LOUIS DENTON, electrical engr.; b. Newburgh, N.Y., July 31, 1871; s. Rev. Emerson William and Sarah Pauline (Denton) B.; ed. pvt. and pub. schs., Pa. and N.J., and Columbian (now George Washington) U.; m. Mabel Stickney, of Washington, Nov. 20, 1895; children—Dorothy (dec.), Donald S., Katharine. In elec. work at Phila., 1888-89; gen. agt., United Edison Mfg. Co., New York, 1889-90; pres. Bliss Engring. Co., Washington, 1890-93; founded, 1893, and since pres., Bliss Electrical School, Washington, D.C. Mem. Town Council, Takoma Park, 1920-21. Dir. Takoma Park Bank, Nat. Metropolitan Bank. Fellow Am. Inst. E.E.; asso. mem. Edison Pioneers; mem. Nat. Assn. Stationary Engrs. (life). Has developed more than 50 copyrighted tests used in his sch. Clubs: Federal Schoolmen's (pres. 1918-19), Cosmos, University. Author: Theoretical and Practical Electrical Engineering, 1921. Home: Takoma Park DC‡

BLISS, LOUIS G., minerals exec.; b. Rahway, N.J., June 17, 1907; s. Frank H. and Lulu (Ganong) B.; B.S., Rutgers U., 1929, M.S., 1931; m. Margaret Nola, Feb. 22, 1935; 1 son, Stephen M. Grad. asst. Rutgers U., 1931-33; sales research engr. Foote Mineral Co., Phila., 1933-36, sales mgr., 1938-52, v.p. charge sales, 1952-56, pres., 1956-60, pres., chmn. bd., pres., 1961-67, pres., chief exec. officer, 1968, pres., chmn. bd., chief exec. officer, 1968-70, chmn. bd., chief exec. officer, 1970-72, also dir.; sales dept. Meckling Bros., also Gen. Chemical Co., Camden, N.J., 1936-38. Mem. bd. dirs., also exec. com. Phila. Mfrs. Mutual Ins. Co., Mfg. Chemists Assn. Mem. Am. Chem. Soc. Home: Fort Washington PA Died Nov. 11, 1972.

BLISS, WILLIAM CARPENTER, lawyer; b. East Providence, R.I., July 6, 1874; s. George Newman and Fannie A. (Carpenter) B.; A.B., Brown U., 1896; A.M., 1898; LL.B., U. of Mich., 1901; unmarried. Admitted to R.I. bar, 1901, and began practice at Providence. Served as ensign, U.S. Navy, Spanish-Am. War; lt. R.I. Naval Militia, 1899-1903, lt. comdr., 1903-04, comdr., 1904-15. Clk. Dist. Court, 7th Jud. Dist. R.I., 1904; mem. R.I. Ho. of Rep., 1908-11 (speaker, 1911); mem. commn. on Revision of Taxation Laws of R.I., 1910-12; became chmn. R.I. Pub. Utilities Commn., 1912; mem. firm of Bliss & Walsh. Home: 940 Taunton Av., East Providence. Office: 505 Industrial Trust Bldg., Providence RI*‡

BLISS, WILLIAM J., corp. exec., lawyer; b. Bklyn., 1915; ed. Sch. Commerce, N.Y.U., 1949; LL.B., Bklyn. Law Sch., 1958. Vice Pres., sec., gen. counsel Amcorp Nat. Services, Inc.; sec., gen. counsel, dir. Am. Match Co., Boatel, Inc., Crotty Bros., Inc.; asst. sec., dir. Canadian Book Wholesale Co., Ltd. Mem. N.Y. Bar. Home: Garden City NY Died May 1973.

BLOCH, MONROE PERCY, lawyer; b. N.Y.C., June 2, 1894; s. Sol M. and Rose (Strasburger) B.; A.B., Yale, 1915; LL.B., Harvard, 1919; m. Muriel Bamberger, June 1, 1925 (dec. Dec. 1941); 1 dau., Barbara (Mrs. Joseph A. Dammann) (dec. 1960); m. 2d Marjorie K. Rosenbaum, Aug. 26, 1943; 1 step-dau., Jane R. (Mrs. Richard Koff). Admitted to N.Y. bar, 1920, and practiced in N.Y.C.; partner firm Brush & Bloch, from 1935. Dir. So. Natural Gas Co., Waitt & Bond, Inc., Frederic R. Harris, Inc., Internat. Man-made Fibers, 480 Park Ave. Corp. Pres., counsel Honest Ballot Assn. Bd. dirs. Hamilton-Madison House. Served as ensign USNRF, World War I. Mem. Am., N.Y. State bar assns., Bar Assn. City N.Y., N.Y. County Lawyers Assn., Phi Beta Kappa. Clubs: City Midday, Century Country, Harvard, Nat. Republican, Yale (N.Y.C.). Home: New York City NY Died May 1970.

BLOCK SAMUEL WESTHEIMER, lawyer; b. St. Joseph, Mo., Feb. 14, 1911; s. Samuel and Oliva (Westheimer) B.; grad. Worcester (Mass.) Acad., 1929; A.B. Yale, 1933: LL.B., Harvard, 1936; m. Jean Friedberg, Nov. 7, 1940; children—Samuel Westheimer, Elizabeth, William Harry. Admitted to Illinois bar, 1936; associate law firm Jenner & Block and predecessors, Chgo., 1936-48, partner, 1948-70; chief counsel, service trades br. OPA, 1941-42. Dir. Weyenberg Shoe Co., Mid-Am, Nat. Bank of Chgo., Bowers Printing Ink Co. Trustee sec. Michael Reese Hosp. and Med. Center, Chgo.; bd. directors, adv. bd. Hyde Park Neighborhood Club, Chgo. Served to capt. AUS, 1943-45. Mem. American College of Trial Lawyers, American, Illinois. Chicago bar associations. Bar Assn. City N.Y. Democrat. Jewish religion. Clubs: Standard, Tavern, Quadrangle (Chgo.). Home: Chicago IL Died Oct. 28, 1970.

BLOCKER, DAN, actor; b. Bowie County, Tex., 1929; s. Shack and Mary Blocker; ed. Tex. Mil. Inst., Hardin-Simmons U.; M.A., Sul Ross State Coll.; postgrad. U. Cal. at Los Angeles; m. Dolphia Parker, 1952; children—Danna and Debra (twins), David, Dennis. Formerly sch. tchr. in Sonora, Tex., Carlsbad, N.M.; later substitute tchr. Glendale (Cal.) High Sch.; actor NBC-TV weekly series, Bonanza, 1959-72. Served with 45th Div. AUS, 1950-52; Korea. Democrat. Address: Hollywood CA Died May 1972.

BLODGETT, FRANCIS BRANCH, theologian; b. Oakfield, N.Y., Feb. 27, 1875; s. Alva John and Catherine (Burt) B.; B.A., Hobart Coll., Geneva, N.Y., 1899, D.D., 1932; B.D., Episcopal Theol. Sch., Cambridge, Mass., 1902; S.T.B., Harvard, 1904; m. Mary Elizabeth Gove, Dec. 28, 1909; children—Catherine Cordelia, Mary Elizabeth. Deacon, 1902, priest, 1903, P.E. Ch.; rector Ch. of Our Redeemer, Lexington, Mass., 1902-04; canon All Saints Cathedral, Albany, N.Y., 1904-05; instr. in O.T. Gen. Theol. Sem., 1906-08. prof., 1908-21; dean Cathedral of St. Paul, Erie, Pa., since 1921. Home: 129 W. 6th St., Erie PA*‡

BLODGETT, FRANK DICKINSON, educator; b. Cortland, N.Y., Mar. 29, 1871; s. Alonzo Dwight and Eleanor (Dickinson) B.; grad. State Normal Sch., Cortland, 1889; A.B., Amherst Coll., 1893, A.M., 1896, LL.D., 1918; m. Helen Marguerita Wilcox, Oneonta, N.Y., Aug. 18, 1897; (she died June 22, 1932); children—Marguertia (dec.), Dorothy (Mrs. Herbert S. Lauck), Edward Dickinson, Richard Sheridan; m. 2d, Bertha Sheridan Jones, of Garden City, New York, July 12, 1933. Teacher Latin and Greek, Normal Sch., Oneonta, 1893, teacher logic and pedagogics, same, 1906-15; president Adelphi College, Garden City, N.Y., 1915-37; mayor of Oneonta, 1912-14. Mem. New York State Exam. Bd., 1934-37. Mem. N.E.A., N.Y. State Teachers' Assn., Nat. Inst. Social Sciences, N.E. Soc. of Brooklyn, Phi Beta Kappa, Delta Kappa Epsilon, Pi Gamma Mu. Mem. L.I. Chamber Commerce. Republican. Conglist. Address: 112-42 176th St., St Albans NY‡

BLODGETT, HUGH CARLTON, psychologist, educator; b. Zamora, Cal., Nov. 21, 1896; s. Carlton Salmon and Esther Cornelia (Heard) B.; A.B., U. Cal. at Berkley, 1921, Ph.D., 1925; m. Georgia Colombat, Sept. 20, 1926 (dec. July 1932); children—Joan, Carlton Colombat; m. 2d, Yvonne Bledsoe, Sept. 9, 1933; 1 dau., Carol Yvonne. Teaching fellow U. Cal. at Berkeley, 1922-23, research asst., 1923-25; research asst. Stanford, 1925; teaching asst. Harvard, 1926-27; instr. Lehigh U., 1927-28; faculty U. Tex., Austin, 1928, prof. psychology, 1944-69, prof. emeritus, 1969-72, chmn. dept., 1948-50, 60-62, research scientist def. research lab., 1951-64, radiobiol. research lab., 1957-64; vis. scientist Bekhterev Inst. of Brain, Leningrad, USSR, 1932; vis. prof. U. Cal. at Los Angeles, 1950; participant Mercury space project S.A.M., NASA, 1959-60. Served to ensign U.S. Navy, 1917-19. Fellow Am. Psychol. Assn. (council reps. 1949-51); mem. Tex. (pres. 1954), S.W. psychol. assns., Psychonomic Soc., A.A.A.S., Sigma Xi. Contbr. to profl. jours. Home: Austin TX Died Oct. 15, 1972.

BLODGETT, THURSTON P(OND), investment exec.; b. Bucksport, Me., Apr. 10, 1899; s. Benjamin P. and Mary H. (Young) B.; grad. Phillips-Andover Acad., 1917; A.B., Yale, 1921; M.B.A., Harvard, Cambridge, Massachusetts, 1923; m. Dorothy H. Leach, May 19, 1923 (dec. March 1961); 1 son, Peter Edward; m. 2d, Margaret C. Mangan, May 18, 1966. Research asst. Harvard Com. on Econ. Research, pub. Harvard Econ. Service, 1923-29; with Tri-Continental Corp., N.Y.C., 1929-71, v.p., 1930-64, dir., 1938-71; v.p., dir. Broad Street Investing Corp., Union Service Corp., Whitehall Fund, Tri-Continental Financial. Bd. dirs. YMCA of Greater New York; trustee R.I. Sch. Design. Episcopalian (vestry). Clubs: University, Grolier, Pilgrims, Church (N.Y.C.); Hope, (Providence). Home: New York City NY Died Oct. 1, 1971; buried Bucksport, ME

BLOEDEL, JULIUS HAROLD, lumberman; b. Fond du Lac, Wis., Mar. 4, 1864; s. Henry and Helena (Maurer) B.; student U. of Mich., 1881-83; m. Mina Prentice, Oct. 20, 1898; children—H. Prentice, Lawrence H., Charlotte V. Began as mgr. Samish Lake Logging Co., 1890; sec. 1891, later pres., Blue Canyon Coal Mining Co.; pres. Fairhaven Nat. Bank, 1895; organizer 1898, and secretary and manager Lake Whatcom Logging Co., also Larson Lumber Co., 1901; now chairman Bloedel Donovan Lumber Mills, Bloedel, Stewart & Welch, Ltd.; director Pacific National Bank. Chairman Fir Production Bd. during war period of 1918, supplying Pacific Coast lumber for war purposes. Pres. West Coast Lumbermen's Assn., 1915-16; former dir. for Wash. of Chamber Commerce of N.A. Republican. Episcopalian. Mason (32 deg.). Clubs: Rainier, University, College, Seattle Golf and Country. Home: 1137 Harvard Av. N. Office: 1411 Fourth Av., Seattle WA‡

BLOOMBERG, MAXWELL HILLEL, orthopedic surgeon; b. Rovna, Russia, Feb. 24, 1899; s. Benjamin and Bessie (Kuperman) B.; student Tufts U., 1918-20, M.D., 1924; m. Leah Plutzik, June 30, 1930; 1 dau., Reva. Intern, Beth Israel Hosp., Boston, 1924-25; resident Jewish Hosp., Bklyn., 1925-27, U. Ia. Steindler Clinic, 1927-28; practice orthopedic surgery, Boston, 1928-38, 68; chief orthopedics VA, Pitts., 1938, 42, orthopedic surgeon, East Orange, N.J., 1964-68. Served to lt. col. AUS, 1942-46; ETO. Diplomate Am. Bd. Orthodic Surgeons; Fellow Internat. Coll. Surgeons; mem. Mass. Med. Soc., A.M.A., So. Med. Soc., Am. Med. Writers Assn., Am. Geriatric Soc., Assn. Mil. Surgeons U.S., Pan Am. Med. Soc., New Eng. Med. Soc., Am. Physicians Fellowship Com. of Israeli Med. Assn. Author; Orthopedic Bracing, 1964; also orthopedic articles. Patentee in field. East Orange NJ Died Oct. 9, 1968

BLOOMER, MILLARD J., publisher; b. in New York, Feb. 6, 1870; s. Theophilus J. and Malvina Devoe (Wakeman) B.; Coll. City of New York, class of 1888; m. Nellia Adams Crist, of New York, June 18, 1898. Pub. New York Progressive (official N.Y. Co. Com. paper); Bronx Co. Progressive; Harlem Local-Life and 4 other uptown newspapers; pres. Home Life Pub. Co., Bloomer Lime Co., Harlem & Bronx Merc. Agency, Inc.; dir. various corpns. Organizer various business, improvement and other orgns. Mem. Am. Civic Alliance (v.-p.), Actors' Ch. Alliance, Am. Playgoers, Internat. Soc. of the Orient and Occident; pres. Harlem Patriotic Soc.; exec. sec. Soc. Associated Club Presidents of New York City. Progressive. Recruiting officer with rank of capt., Spanish-Am. War, recruiting more men than any other person in state of N.Y. Club: Press. Author: What Shall I Eat? 1890; The Housewife's Manual. Pub. of Town Tips" (annual guide and street dir. of New York); Beautiful New York; maps of New York, etc. Home: 213 W. 125th St. and 240th St. and Van Cortland Park, E. Offices: 217 W. 125th St., 154 Nassau St. and NY‡

BLOOMFIELD, ARTHUR COLLIER, broker; b. Jackson, Mich., Dec. 30, 1873; s. Charles Cunningham and Sarah L. (Collier) B.; A.B., U. of Mich., 1895, LL.B., 1896; m. Kate Smith, June 10, 1905; children—Arthur Collier, Charles Collier, David Dwight. Treas. Hayes Wheel Co., 1908-26; v.p. Nat. Union Bank, Jackson, 1918-28, pres., 1928-30; v.p. Longyear Mesaba Land & Iron Co.; joint mgr. E.A. Pierce & Co. Mem. bd. Kingswood Sch., Cranbrook, Mich. Mem. Delta Kappa Epsilon. Clubs: Jackson City, Jackson Country; Little Harbor Club (Harbor Springs, Mich.); Detroit Club. Home: 750 W. Michigan Av., Jackson MI‡

BLOOMINGDALE, SAMUEL JOSEPH, merchant; b. N.Y. City, June 17, 1873; s. Lyman G. and Hattie (Collenberger) B.; B.S., Columbia, 1895; m. Rita Goodman, June 1, 1916; children—Susan Jane (Mrs. Richard C. Ernst), Louise G. (Mrs. Edgar M. Cullman). Honorary chmn. bd. Bloomingdale Bros., N.Y. City; dir. Federated Dept. Stores, First Avenue Assn.; pres. Bloomingdale Bros. Realty Co., Lyman G. Realty Corp. Trustee Montafiore Hosp. Member Retail Dry Goods Association, National Retail Dry Goods Assn., N.Y. State Chamber Home: New York City NY Died May 10, 1968.

BLOSSOM, FRANCIS, engr.; b. N.Y. City, Oct. 17, 1870; s. Josiah B. and Grace Parish (Ludlam) B.; ed. Poly. Inst., New York, 1880-87; C.E., Sch. of Mines (Columbia), 1891; m. Madeline Buck, Feb. 27, 1900; children—Dudley Buck, June (Mrs. H. P. Moon). Design and construction industrial railway equipment, and assistant engineer gas plant construction, 1891-93; engineer and department mgr. Westinghouse, Church, Kerr & Co., 1892-99; mem. Sanderson & Porter, engrs., offices in New York, Chicago and San Francisco, since 1899. Chmn. bd. apptd. by sec. of war to review and report on constrn. work War Dept., 1918; mem. Constrn. Adv. Com. apptd. by sec. of war, 1940, to recommend firms qualified for handling Army constrn. projects World War II. Alumni trustee Columbia Univ., 1935-41; trustee N.Y. Med. Coll., Flower and Fifth Av. hospitals, N.Y. City. Mem. Am. Soc. C.E., Am. Inst. E.E., (honorary) Am. Soc. M.E., Alpha Delta Phi. Clubs: University, Columbia Univ., City Midday, Alpha Delta Phi, (New York). Home: 784 Park Av., N.Y. City 21. Office: 52 William Street, New York City 5‡

BLOUGH, EARL, chem. engr.; b. LaGrange, Ind.; May 23, 1876; s. Samuel Snyder and Minnie (Finley) B.; A.B., U. Ind., 1899, LL.D. (hon.), 1931; grad. student

Cornell U., 1902-05; D.Sc. (hon.), U. Pitts., 1919; m. Mary Maclean Thompson, July 29, 1908; 1 dau., Frani (Mrs. Curt Muser). Tchr. science, LaGrange, Ind., 1899-1900, Iron Mountain, Mich., 1900-02; with lab. Oliver Mining Co., Iron Mountain, 1902; v.p., dir. Aluminium, Ltd. from 1928; pres. Aluminium Labs., Ltd., 1935-48. Clubs: Univ. (N.Y.C.); Sakonnet Golf, Warren's Point Beach (Little Compton, R.I.). Home: Tiverton RI Died Dec. 13, 1971; buried Union Cemetery, Little Compton RI

BLOUGH, SANFORD P., telephone co., exec.; b. Johnstown, Pa., Oct. 27, 1920; s. Edward and Carrie Etta (Blough) B.; B.S., Susquehanna U., Selinsgrove, Pa., 1942; m. Margaret C. Harman, July 3, 1946; children—Sandra Carol, Janet Lynn. With comptrollers dept. Bell Telephone Co. Pa., 1946-65; data systems adminstrn. Am. Tel. & Tel. Co., 1965-67; v.p., comptroller Bell Telephone Co. Va., 1967-69, Diamond State Telephone Co., 1967-69. Mem. Financial Execs. Inst., Phila., Pa. U.S. chambers commerce. Home: Berwyn PA Died Oct. 5, 1969.

BLUE, FREDERICK OMAR, lawyer; b. Grafton W.Va., Nov. 25, 1872; s. George Frederick and Mary Martha (See) B.; ed. high sch. and under tutors; m. Margaret Jarvis Ice, Nov. 26, 1895. Began practice at Philippi, W.Va., 1893, also engaged in banking; asso. in practice at Philippi with Arthur S. Dayton, 1908-11; mem. Blue, Dayton & Campbell; dir. Charleston Nat. Bank. Mem. W.Va., Senate, 1906-10; state tax commr. of W.Va., 1911-17, also chief insp. and supervisor pub. offices of W.Va., 1911-17; mem. W.Va. Mining Strike Commn., 1912-13; state commr. of Prohibition of W.Va., 1914-17, successfully conducting litigation to Supreme Court of U.S. sustaining Webb-Kenyon Law. Mem. Am. Bar Assn., Nat. Tax Assn. Republican. Baptist. Mason (33 deg., Shriner). Author: When a State Goes Dry, 1916. Home: 853 Edgewood Drive. Office: Security Bank & Trust Bldg., Charleston WV‡

BLUE, JOHN HOWARD, surgeon; b. Montgomery, Ala., Aug. 31, 1877; s. John H. and Mary W. B.; B.S., U. of Ala., 1896; M.D., Coll. Physicians and Surgeons (Columbia), 1901, LL.D., Univ. of Alabama, 1942; m. Anna Pelzer, April 20, 1910. Practiced at Montgomery since 1905; attending surgeon St. Margaret's Hospital; surgeon L.&N. R.R., Seaboard R.R., Western of Alabama R.R. Fellow American Coll. Surgeons; mem. Am. and Ala. State med. assns., Sigma Nu, Omicron Delta Kappa, Phi Beta Kappa. Democrat. Methodist. Home: 300 Felder St. Office: 201 Montgomery St., Montgomery AL*‡

BLUGERMAN, LEE N. (LEONID), cons.; b. Russia, May 25, 1899; s. N. and A. (Krasnovska) B.; B.S., U. Wash. 1928; m. Mary R. Truitt, Nov. 9, 1931; children—Richard, Robert and Bruce (twins). Came to U.S., 1921, naturalized, 1932. Engr. United Engineers & Constructors, Inc., 1928-36; mgr. Red Lion plant Phila. Budd Co., 1936-52; v.p. mfg. Crane Co., Chgo., 1952-58, dir., 1955-58; v.p. Lester B. Knigh & Assos., Inc., Chgo., 1958-59; mgmt. cons., 1959-72. Home: Narbeth PA Died 1972.

BLUM, HARRY, chmn. bd. James B. Beam Distilling Co., 1933-67. Home: Chicago IL Died Oct. 3, 1971.*

BLUM, WILLIAM, chemist; b. Phila., Pa., Dec. 28, 1881; s. Jacob and Catherine (Hoffman) B.; B.S., U. of Pa., 1903; Ph.D., 1908; m. Willetta Carr Baylis, Sept. 20, 1910; 1 son, William. Instr. in chemistry, U. of Utah, 1903-08, asst. prof., 1908-09; with U.S. Bureau of Standards, Washington, 1909-52, chemist 1918-52; cons. to numerous cos., Dept. Def., CIA. Member American Chemical Society, A.A.A.S., Washington Acad. Sciences, Electrochem Society (awarded Acheson medal, 1944); hon. mem. Am. Electroplaters' Society, Sigma Xi. Awarded medal Institute of Chemists, for distinguished governmental service," 1926. Awarded Edward Goodrich Acheson gold medal and prize for achievement in electrochemistry, Oct. 1944. Chairman Citizens Committee, Section 4, Chevy Chase, Maryland, 1916-26. Presbyn. Clubs: Chemists (New York); Cosmos (Washington). Author: (with G. B. Hogaboom) Principles of Electroplating and Electroforming, 1924, 2d edit., 1930; also articles on analytical and electro chemistry. Home: Chevy Chase MD Died Dec. 7, 1972.

BLUMBERG, HYMAN, labor union ofcl.; b. Lithuania, 1885; s. Moses and Hannah (Herman) B.; brought to U.S., 1889, naturalized, 1889; m. Bessie Simons, Oct. 20, 1907; children—Ethel (Mrs. Zwickel), Phillip I. Co-founder, mgr. joint bd. Amalgamated Clothing Workers Am., Balt., 1916-22, mem. gen. exec. bd. from 1916, exec. v.p., N.Y.C., from 1946; exec. v.p. Amalgamated Ins. Co., from 1942; dir. Amalgamated Bank of N.Y., from 1923. Amalgamated rep. Q.M.G., assisting uniform prodn., 1941-45; U.S. rep. I.L.O. Conf., 1938, 45; mem. Men's Clothing Authority, Nat. Recovery Adminstrn., 1933-35; state chmn. Am. Labor Party, 1946-48. Pioneer establishment union welfare programs. Home: New York City NY Died Oct. 17, 1968; buried Westchester Hills Cemetery.

BLUME, FRED H., judge; b. Audubon, Ia., Jan. 9, 1875; s. William and Lena (Blume) B.; Ph.B., State U. of Ia., 1898; m. Blanche Alexander, June 1920. Admitted to Ia. bar, 1899, and practiced at Audubon; city atty., 1899-1904; pros. atty. Audubon County, Ia., 1900-04; moved to Sheridan, Wyo., 1904; mem. Wyo. Ho. of Rep., 1907-09, Senate, 1909-13; city atty. Sheridan, 1907-10; asso. justice, Supreme Court of Wyo., 1921-31, chief justice, 1927-31; re-elected Justice, 1930, for term 1931-39, chief justice, 1937-39; re-elected as justice for terms 1939-47, and 1947-55; chief justice, 1945-47. Mem. Riccobono Seminar of Roman Law, Phi Beta Kappa. Mason, K.P. Home: Cheyenne WY‡

BLUMENFIELD, SAMUEL M., educator, rabbi; b. Letichev, Russia, Sept. 13, 1901; s. Max and Fanny (Waxman) B.; B.S., College City of N.Y., 1925; M.A., Columbia, 1926; M.H.L. and Rabbi, Jewish Inst. of Religion, 1930, D.H.L., 1944, Dr. of Divinity (honorary), 1957; married to Rose Mazel, Jan. 8, 1930; children—Tamar Ephrimina, Rena Sarah, Naomi Judith. Ednl. dir. Jewish Communal Center, Brooklyn, N.Y., 1925-29; instr., extension dept., Teachers Inst., Jewish Theol. Sem. of America, 1926-30; dir. Dept. of Youth and Ednl. Bd. of Jewish Edn., Chicago, Ill., 1930-34; dean and dir. Coll. of Jewish Studies, Chgo., 1934-47, became pres., 1947, also prof. of edn.; former dir. edn. and culture dept. The Jewish Agy.; prof. Hebrew culture Hofstra Univ., 1968-72; lectr. U. Chgo., 1935 Roosevelt U., 1947, New Sch. for Soc. Research, N.Y. City; cons. on commn. on tchr. edn. and religion of Am. Assn. Colls. for Teacher Edn., 1953-72; ednl. consultant World Conf. of Jewish Orgns.; consultant World Jewish Education conference. Mem. War Labor Bd., 1941-43. Pres. Nat. Council for Jewish Edn., Chicago Rabbinical Assn. Honorary president Soc. for Advancement of Hebrew Culture; chmn. Jewish Book Month Council, Army, Nvay com. U.S.O. Author: Master of Troyes—a study of Rashi, the Educator, 1946; Maimonides, the Educator; Education in the American Jewish Community. Contributor Ency. Brit., British Book of the Year, 1954-72, American Educators Ency., Great Jewish Personalities, also to various ednl. and religious publs. Home: Brooklyn NY Died 1972.

BLUMENSCHINE, LEONARD G., mfg. exec.; b. Buffalo, 1894. Chmn. Rit Products Corp.; chmn., pres. Best Foods, Inc., div. Corn Products Co. mem. financial and mdse. com., dir. Diamond Match Co. Home: New York City NY

BLUNT, HUGH FRANCIS, clergyman, author: b. Medway, Mass., Jan. 20, 1877; s. Patrick and Ann (Mahon) B.; student St. Laurent Coll., Montreal, 1893-96; Ph.B., St. John's Sem., Boston, 1901; LL.D., U. of Notre Dame, 1920. Ordained Catholic priest, 1901; chief editorial writer Boston Pilot, 1911-19; editor Sacred Heart Review, 1917-20; pastor St. John's Ch., Cambridge, Mass., since 1929. Awarded Marian poetry prize, 1919, Catholic press poetry prize, 1929. K.C., Cath. Order of Foresters. Democrat. Created Domestic Prelate by Pope Pius XII, 1944; censor of books, diocesan consultant, Archdiocese of Boston; member Board Free Public Library Commrs. of Mass. Author: The Heart Aflame, 1947; Savers of Homes, 1948. Writer and composer of 6 hymns in honor of The Little Flower." Address: 2254 Mass Av., Cambridge MA‡

BLY, ELEANOR SCHOOLEY, bacteriologist; b. Montgomery, Pa., May 30, 1907; d. Joseph G. and Mabel (Fowler) Schooley; B.A., Bucknell U., 1928, M.S., 1937; Ph.D. in Bacteriology, Pa. State U., 1954; m. Earl W. Bly, Jan. 30, 1942 (dec. July, 1944). With Phila. Zool. Soc., Phila., 1928-29; mem. bacteriology dept. Bucknell U., Lewisburg, Pa., 1929-49; bacteriologist Williamsport (Pa.) Hosp., 1949-69. Mem. social services Watsontown (Pa.) Guild, 1930-54; active YWCA. Mem. Soc. Am. Bacteriologists, Am. Soc. Microbiology, D.A.R., Delta Delta Delta. Club: Soroptomist (Williamsport). Home: Williamsport PA Died July 4, 1969.

BLYDE, LEWIS J(OHN) N(EWBERY), assn. executive; B. Hitchin. Hertfordshire, Eng., June 20, 1889; s. Arthur William and Mercy (Hale) B.; stu. schs. of Eng.; m. Lillian Clark, March 20, 1926 (dec. Feb. 1940); 1 son, Lewis John Newbery; m. 2d, Ella Muriel Reakes, July 4, 1942. Came to U.S., naturalized, 1945. Banker, United Kingdom, Can., 1904-14; banker Bank of Montreal, Can., 1919-20, Mexico, 1920-23, N.Y.C., 1923-24; export, import exec. Kemsley Millbourn & Co., N.Y.C., 1924-32; investment exec. J. R. Timmins & Co., N.Y.C., 1933-40; exec. sec. Brit. War Relief Soc., 1940-43; sec. Brit. Commonwealth C. of C. from 1945; mgr. British Trade Promotion Centre, N.Y.C., from 1954. Awarded King's Medal for services with Brit. War Relief Soc., 1946; hon. mem. Order Brit. Empire. Mem. Pilgrims Soc. U.S., Canadian Soc., St. George's Soc., Newcomen Soc. Club: English Schools and Universities (N.Y.C.). Home: Darien CT Died Jan. 1970.

BLYNN, LLOYD ROSS, writer; b. Phila., Sept. 7, 1875; s. Harry and Ida (Ross) B.; ed. Swarthmore Coll., 1888-91; Ph.B., U. of Pa., 1893; read law 2 yrs.; m. Lucy Miller, of New York, Jan. 27, 1903. On staff Philadelphia North American, 1901-2; asso. editor The Ladies Home Journal, 1902-6, Philadelphia Evening Bulletin, 1906-8; city editor, Philadelphia Evening Times, 1908-9; head of newspaper div., advertising dept. of the United Gas Improvement Co., Phila., 1910-15; mgr. since Apr., 1915, publicity and promotion dept. of the Hearst publs., including New York American, Evening Journal, Boston American, Chicago Examiner, Chicago American, San Francisco Examiner, Los Angeles Examiner, Atlanta Georgian, Cosmopolitan, Hearst's Magazine, Harper's Bazar, Good Housekeeping, Motor, and Motor Boating. Seaman Pa. Naval Battalion, 1895; capt. and q.-m. 13th Regt. Arty., N.G.N.Y., 1900-1, Mem. Soc. Colonial Wars, S.R. Clubs: Pen and Pencil, Orpheus, Puritan, Racquet and Tennis, Nat. Arts. Contbr. stories, etc., to newspapers and mags. Home: 15 Gramercy Park. Office: William and Duane Sts., NY‡

BOARDMAN, GEORGE HENRY, cons. photographer, columnist; b. Chgo., May 2, 1902; s. Henry Francis and Lillian (Fitzpatrick) B.; student Tenn. Mil. Inst., 1920; m. Eva M. Reid, Feb. 20, 1951 (div.); 1 dau., Lolita (Mrs. Harold Aubry Burch); m. 2d, Dawn Dodd, Mar. 23, 1962. Pvt. photographic studio, Canoga Park, Cal., 1939-69; cons., to photographic schs., product mfrs., publs., 1957-69; author regular Weekly Polit. column, Gazette-Telegraph, Colorado Springs, Colo., Santa Ana (California) Register, 1959-69; also cons. economist and the regular columnist several daily newspapers Freedom Newspaper chain; dir. Philosophic Research Unltd., Chloride, Ariz. Mem. Photographic Inst. Am. (past pres.), Club: Lake Mohave Ranch Ariz.). Address: Chloride AZ Died Apr. 20, 1969.

BOARDMAN, HAROLD SHERBURNE, educator; b. Bangor, Me., Mar. 31, 1874; s. James A. and Marilla M. (Leighton) B.; B.C.E., Me. State Coll., 1895; grad. student, Mass. Inst. Tech., 1896, Civil Engr., Univ. of Me., 1898, Dr. Engring., 1922; LL.D., Colby, 1927; Dr. Engring. R.I. Coll., 1928; LL.D., Bates Coll., 1929; m. Caroline A. Hilton, July 24, 1897 (died 1910); m. 2d, Nellie Frances Mann, July 2, 1912; children—James Alden, Rosemary (dec.). Tutor in drawing, U. of Me., 1896-99; draftsman Union Bridge Co., Pa., 1899-1900, Am. Bridge Co., Pa., 1900-01; instr. in civ. engring., 1901-03, asso. prof., 1903-04, prof. and head of dept., 1904-26, dean Coll. of Tech., 1910-26, acting pres., 1925-26, pres. 1926-34, U. of Me. (retired). While mem. of engring. faculty was actively engaged in many important hydrographic, structural, hydraulic and highway projects and active in professional and ednl. socs. Chmn. engring. sect. Assn. Land Grant Colleges, 1922-23. Served as chairman Me. Liquor Commn., 1937-41. Cadet maj. Coburn Cadets, Me. State Coll., 1894-95; Capt. Co. G, N.G.S.M., Edn. (vice pres. 1923-24; pres. 1930-31), Maine Assn. 1898-99. Mem. Am. Soc. C.E., Am. Soc. for Engring. Engineers, Beta Theta Pi, Tau Beta Pi, Phi Kappa Phi, Phi Beta Kappa, Scabbard and Blade. Republican. Mason (32 deg.). Home: 172 Main St., Orono ME‡

BOATRIGHT, MODY COGGIN, educator, writer; b. Colorado City, Tex., Oct. 16, 1896; s. Eldon and Frances Ann (McAulay) B.; B.A., W. Tex. Coll., 1922; M.A., U. Tex., 1923, Ph.D., 1932; m. Elizabeth Reck, Aug. 26, 1925; 1 dau., Frances (Mrs. William E. Bridges); m. 2d, Elizabeth Keefer, Sept. 12, 1931; 1 son, Mody Keefer. Asso. prof. English, Sul Ross State Coll., Alpine, Tex., 1923-26; faculty English, U. Tex., from 1926-—, prof., from 1950-—, chmn. dept., 1952-61. Mem. Am. Studies Assn., Am., Tex. folklore socs., Tex. Inst. Letters. Author: Tall Tales from Texas, 1934; Gib Morgan, Minstrel of the Oil Fields, 1945; Folk Laughter on the American Frontier, 1949; also numerous articles, coll. textbooks. Editor publs. Tex. Folklore Soc., from 1945-—. Home: Austin TX Died Aug. 20, 1970.

BOATWRIGHT, GERTRUDE FLOYD HARRIS, educator; b. Abingdon, Va.; d. Dr. William Anderson Harris (distinguished Southern educator) and Victoria M. (Gordon) H.; A.B., Wesleyan Female Inst., Staunton, Va.; supplemented education with travel, courses of lectures, etc.; m. James Sampson Boatwright, of Columbia, S.C.; 1 dau., Gertrude Harris (Mrs. William Graham Claytor). Lady prin. Wesleyan Female Inst.; v.p. Virginia Coll. for Girls and Women, since Sept. 1893. Christian Scientist. Member of Colonial Dames of Va.; life mem. Internat. Longfellow Soc.; chmn. Red Cross Naval Auxiliary, Roanoke, Va.; mem. Va. Hist. Soc., Sulgrave Instn., Kenmore Assn., Edgar Allan Poe Shrine, Richmond (charter mem.). Mem. Va. War History Commn.; 1st pres. woman's br. and dir. woman's div. Chamber of Commerce, Roanoke; lt. Roanoke Red Cross Canteen; asso. mem. Thursday Morning Music Club; hon. mem. College Club; mem. Woman's Federation of Clubs of Va.; 1st v.p. Assn. of Commerce, Civics Div.; ex-pres. Local League Women Voters, now mem. State Bd. of Dirs.; mem. Conservation of Peace Soc., League of Nations Non-Partisan Assn., Liberal League of America, Internat. Foundation for Peace, Nat. Travel League, Nat. Forestry Assn., Shakespeare Assn., Societe Academique d'Histoire Internationale, Assn. of Va. Sch. and Colls.; del. to Pan Am. Conf. Women Voters, Nat. League Women Voters, Conf. on Governmental Efficiency, 1921; chmn. Va. Pageant Association. Club: Woman's of Roanoke (v.p.). Address: Virginia College, Roanoke VA

BOAZ, HIRAM ABIFF, bishop; b. Murray, Ky., Dec. 18, 1866; s. Peter Maddox and Louisa Ann (Ryan) B.; ed. Sam Houston State Normal Sch., Huntsville, Tex., 1885-87; B.S., Southwestern U., Georgetown, Tex., 1893, M.A., 1894, LL.D., 1935; studied Columbia, 1915-17; D.D., Ky. Wesleyan Coll., 1906; LL.D., Centenary Coll., 1926, Southern Methodist U., 1938; m. Carrie Odalie Browne, Oct. 2, 1894; children—Ruth (Mrs. C. A. Penniman), Edith (Mrs. Prentiss M. Terry), Mary Louise (Mrs. Graham Hall). Licensed to preach, 1889; ordained ministry M.E. Ch., S., 1891; pastor Mulkey Memorial Ch., Ft. Worth, Tex., 1894-97, 1st Ch., Abilene, Tex., 1897-99, 1st Ch., Dublin, Tex., 1899-1902; pres. Polytechnic Coll., Ft. Worth, 1902-11; v.p. Southern Meth. U., Dallas, 1911-13; pres. Tex. Woman's Coll., Ft. Worth, 1913-18; sec. Ch. Extension Bd., M.E. Ch., S., 1918-20; pres. Southern Meth. U., 1920-22; elected bishop M.E. Ch., S., 1922, and assigned to superintend ch. work in China, Japan, Siberia and Manchuria; in charge Ark. and Okla. Confs. of M.E. Ch., S., 1926-30, Tex., N. Tex. and N.W. Tex. Confs., 1930-34; W. Tex., Central Tex., N.W. Tex., N.M. and Tex. Mexican Confs., 1934-38; retired from active service, May 1938. Mem. Meth. Ecumenical Conf., London, 1921. Mem. Soc. Colonial Wars (Va.), Kappa Alpha, Theta Phi. Democrat. Mason (York Rite, Scottish Rite, Shriner). Clubs: Dallas Country; River Crest (Ft. Worth). Author: Fundamentals of Success; The Essentials of an Effective Ministry; Thomas Boaz Family in America. Home: Dallas TX‡

BOBB, BYRON ARTHUR, surgeon; b. Richland Center, Wis., July 16, 1870; s. Martin L. and Mary J. (Wulfing) B.; student Dak. Wesleyan U., 1887-91, LL.D., 1935; M.D., Northwestern U., 1894; Post-Grad. Hosp., Chicago, 1 yr.; m. Mae E. Spink, Sept. 23, 1896. Practiced at Mitchell since 1894; mem. firm Bobb & Bobb. Served as maj. Med. R.C., chief of surgical service, Base Hosp. 111, Bordeaux, France, 1918-19. President board of trustees Dakota Wesleyan University. Fellow American College of Surgeons; mem. American, S.D., S. Minn., Sioux Valley and Mitchell District medical association. Mason. Clubs: Kiwanis, Country. Home: 351 Heather Heights, Monrovia CA‡

BOBER, SAM HENRY, former govt. ofcl.; b. Borzova, Ukraine, Nov. 14, 1891; s. Benjamin and Hannah (Sonenschein) B.; came to U.S. 1906, naturalized, 1911; grad. Baron de Hirsch Agrl. Sch., Woodbine, N.J., 1912; student agr. Mich. State U., 1913, S.D. State Coll., 1916, Harvard, 1937; D.Sc., S.D. State U., 1966; m. Rose Stolar, Apr. 13, 1916 (dec. Dec. 1968); children—Louis, Mira Lee (Mrs. Henry Goldstein), Jack; m. 2d, Rachel Silverman, Oct. 1968. Sci. asst. animal husbandry U.S. Dept. Agr., 1916-23; grower, distbr. field seeds; mem. Fed. Farm Credit Bd., 1955-62. Chmn. adv. com. U.S. Expt. Farm, 1948-67, Nat. Farm Loan Assn., 1950-54; chmn. dirs. adv. com. Fed. Land Bank of Omaha, 1950-54. Chmn. war drives Butte County chpt. A.R.C., 1940-45. Candidate for Congress, S.D., 1952. Bd. govs. Agrl. Hall of Fame. Recipient 1st prize for alfalfa Internat. Grain Shows, 1927, 52, other prizes State Crop Improvement Shows, S.D. Fairs. Mem. Am. Farm Bur. Fedn., Newcomen Soc. N.A., Nat. Planning Assn. (nat. council, nat. agrl. com.), Aberdeen Angus Breeders Assn., S.D. Crop Improvement Assn. Contbg. editor: Dakota Farmers, 1919-22. Home: Tucson AZ Died Jan. 7, 1973.

BOCK, HAROLD PATTENDON, ret. hotel exec.; b. London, Eng., Aug. 27, 1901; s. Henry Joseph and Elizabeth Harriet (Pattendon) B.; student pvt. schs., Belgium, Austria; m. Dorothy Celeste Hazard, June 3, 1933; 1 son, Philip Hazard. Came to U.S., 1926, naturalized, 1932. Employee hotels, Austria, 1916-26; with Berkeley-Carteret, Asbury Park, N.J., 1926-27, Drake Dorset hotels, N.Y.C., 1927-30, Carlyle, N.Y.C., 1930-44; gen. mgr. Homestead, Hot Springs, Va., 1945-49, Bismarck Hotel, Chgo., 1949-56, Sheraton Hotel, Chgo., 1956-58, Sheraton-East Hotel, N.Y.C., 1958-66; v.p. Sheraton-Ambassador Corp., 1958-66, Carlyle Hotel N.Y.C., 1967-71. Mem. Am., Internat., N.Y.C. (food rationing chmn. during World War II) hotel assns. Clubs: Hotel Execs. (past pres.), Ye Host's Square, Fort Dearborn-Chicago Camera (past pres.), Tavern. Home: CT Died Dec. 3, 1972.

BODDE, JOHN R., banker; b. Detroit, Mich., Feb. 12, 1872; s. Frank and Adelaide (Cramer) B.; ed. parochial schs., Detroit, and Detroit Coll. (now U. of Detroit); unmarried. Began with Peoples Savings Bank, Detroit, Mich., 1889; with same and successors until retired; now v.p. and treas. H. A. McDonald Creamery Co.; v.p. McDonald, Moore & Hayes, Inc. Republican. Catholic. Clubs: Detroit, Players, Detroit Boat (Detroit); Essex County Golf and Country (Essex, Ont., Can.). Home: 3001 Seminole Av. Office: Penobscot Bldg., Detroit MI‡

BODDINGTON, ERNEST FEARBY, journalist, dramatist; b. Teddington, Eng., Apr. 17, 1873; s. Richard and Emily (Crick) B.; Uxbridge Coll.; local examinations, Cambridge U.; m. Agnes Singleton, Montreal, Can., Apr. 22, 1895 (died Jan. 16, 1917); m. 2d, Lillian May Bevan, of N.Y. City, May 3, 1919; children—Clement, Hilary, Sister Agnese, Margaret, Ethel. Came to U.S., 1890, naturalized citizen, 1902. Began as reporter Montreal Star, 1893; city editor Montreal Herald, 1895-97; telegraph editor Brooklyn (N.Y.) Eagle, 1897-98, dramatic critic and editorial writer, 1898-1900; Sunday editor New York Times, 1901-02; later with New York World, New York Evening Post and New York Evening Mail; mng. editor Binghamton (N.Y.) Press, 1907-08; editor in chief Columbus (O.) News, 1909-10; gen. mgr. Regina (Sask., Can.) Daily Province and Evening Province and Standard, 1912-14; dir. publicity, Canadian Belgian Relief Fund, 1914-15; in publicity dept., U.S. Liberty Loans, New York, 1917-19; asso. dir. press dept. Nat. Catholic Welfare Conf., 1921-26. Winner of Phila. Public Ledger editorial contest, 1916. Club: Nat. Press. Author: (play) The Heretic, 1903; also dramatic version of Mary Johnston's To Have and To Hold, 1901, and Audrey, 1902. Contbr. to The Commonweal, Dictionary of Am. Biography, etc. Home: 1012 13th St. N.W., Washington DC‡

BODELL, DAVID EUGENE, mfg. exec.; b. Dodgeville, Wis., Feb. 25, 1933; s. Robert O. and Jeanette (Kettwig) B.; B.S., U. Ill., 1958; m. M. Diane Bracy, Nov. 7, 1953; children—Gregory Scott, Kurt David. Accountant Haskins & Sells, Chgo., 1958-60; controller Modern Drop Forge Co., Blue Island, Ill., 1960-68. Served with AUS, 1953-56. C.P.A. Ill. Mem. Am. Inst. C.P.A.'s Ill. Soc. C.P.A.'s, Forging Industry Assn., Kappa Sigma. Club: Flossmoor Country. Home: Homewood IL Died Apr. 1, 1968.

BODER, BARTLETT, banker; b. Troy, Kan., Jan. 5, 1885; s. Louis and Fannie (Quimby) B.; student Saint Joseph (Missouri) Schools, 1903; student, London, Paris, and Berlin, 1911-14; m. Vira Price, Apr. 26, 1930 (dec. Sept. 1959); m. 2d, Mary Louise Wallace, Dec. 24, 1960, Bank clk., 1903-05, 1907-08; reporter St. Joseph News-Press, 1905-07; reporter St. Joseph Gazette, 1915-17, editorial writer, 1919; pres. Missouri Valley Trust Co. 1931—, also dir.; trustee of Harris Trust & Savings Bank, Chicago, St. Joseph Light & Power Co., from 1946; v.p. Tootle-Lacy Nat. Bank, 1949. Pres. St. Joseph Mus. Student Ft. Riley (Kan.) Training Camp, 1917; commd. 2d lt., 1917; with 127th and 104th F.A., A.E.F.; organized 35th Div. Tank Co., 1923; retired 1935, as lt. col. on 35th Division Staff. Handled Missouri financing for building river bridge at Rulo, Neb., 1938. Originated name, Missourissippi, for world's longest river, July 7, 1942. Chmn. 1st Dist. Missouri State Council of Defense, 1941-45. Mem. President's Washington Conf. on Fire Prevention, 1947. City assessor, 1920-23; city comptroller, 1930-32; police commr., 1932-33. Decorated Knight of Red Cross of Constantine. Mem. Missouri Archeological Soc. (trustee, 1957), American Legion (state vice-comdr. 1927), Forty and Eight (director Nat. Voiture Activities, 1946), Soc. Mayflower Descs., State Hist. Soc. Mo. (v.p.). Sons Revolution, Central Overland Pony Express Assn. (pres. 1959-61). Episcopalian. Mason (Shriner), Nat. Sojourner, Royal Order Jesters. Clubs: St. Joseph Auto (president 1939-40), Benton and St. Joseph Country. Author articles in France-Amerique on history of the early French west of the Mississippi River, 1947; also historical and geographical articles in English. Home: St. Joseph MO Died Jan. 8, 1967.

BODINE, A(LDINE) AUBREY, photographer; b. Balt., July 21, 1906; s. Joel Goode and Adele Louise (Wilson) B.; student St. Paul's Sch., Balt., 1918-23, Md. Inst. Art, 1930-34; m. Annette Florence Tait, Nov. 24, 1944; 1 dau., Jennifer Beatty. Joined Balt. Sun, 1924, became photographic dir., 1949; pres. Bodine Assos., publishers, from 1951; lectr. various fields photography; one man exhbns. Balt. Mus. Art, Eastman Exhbn. Hall, Mariners' Mus., Newport News, Va., also various univs.; photographs in permanent collection Smithsonian Instn., Met. Mus. Art, Detroit Mus. Art, Toronto Mus. Art, Seattle Mus. Art, Balt. Mus. Art. Recipient 1st prize Popular Photography contest, 1948; named newspaper photographer of the year Ency. Brit.-Nat. Press Photographers Assn. contest, 1957. Hon. fellow Photog. Soc. Am.; fellow Nat. Press Photographers Assn.; mem. Hist. Soc., S.A.R., Kappa Alpha Mu. Author: My Maryland, 1952; Chesapeake Bay and Tidewater, 1954; Baltimore and Annapolis, 1957; The Face of Maryland, 1961; The Face of Virginia, 1963. Home: Ruxton MD Died Oct. 28, 1970; buried Greenmount Cemetery, Baltimore MD

BOECKLIN, ROLAND, educator; b. Fiesole, Italy, Sept. 29, 1900; s. Carlo and Nadia (von Gringmuth) B.; diploma Colonial Inst., Florence, Italy, 1922; Ph.D., Yale, 1935; m. Peg Pitman, June 16, 1941; 1 son, Arnold P. Came to U.S., 1923, naturalized, 1929. Instr. German and Latin, Eastern prep. schs., 1936-46; asso. prof. U. Mass., Ft. Devens, 1946-48; asso. prof. Ohio Wesleyan U., Delaware, 1948-54, prof., 1954-71, prof. emeritus, 1971-72, Found. prof. lang. and lit., 1954-71, chmn. dept. classics, 1948-71. Cons. Ohio State U. Research Found., 1963. Mem. Modern Lang. Assn., Classical Assn. Middle West and South, Am. Philol. Assn., Am. Assn. U. Profs. Home: Delaware OH Died Aug. 5, 1972; interred Cimitero degli Allori, Florence Italy

BOEGNER, MARC, clergyman; b. Epinal, France. Feb. 2, 1881; s. Paul and Jenny (Fallot) B.; Licencie en droit, and Docteur en theologie, U. of Paris; D.D., univs. of Edinburgh and Prague; married. Ordained priest, Reformed Ch. of France, 1905; prof. theology Missionary Coll. of Paris, 1911-18; pastor Reformed Ch. of Passy, Paris, from 1918. Pres. Federation protestante de France from 1929; pres. Nat. Council of Reformed Ch. of France from 1938; one of presidents World Council of Churches, 1948; mem. Institut de France, 1946; Lenten lecturer annually over Nat. Radio since 1928. Officer Legion of Honor. Author: Dien l'eternal tourment des hommes; Jesus Christ; Qu'est-ce que l'Eglise; L'Eglise et les question du temps present; Qu'est-ce qu'un Chretien? le Probleme de l'Unite Chretienne. Home: Paris France Died Dec. 18, 1970.*

BOEHM, EDWARD MARSHALL, sculptor; b. Balt., Aug. 21, 1912; s. Edward D. and Elsie (Bonnert) B.; student U. Md., 1935-38; m. Helen F. Franzolin, Oct. 29, 1944. Mgr., exhibitor cattle in Balt. to 1950; established Boehm Pottery, Trenton, N.J., 1950, dealing in fine porcelain sculpture; porcelains represented in permanent collections Met. Museum Art, Houston and Memphis art museums, Los Angeles County Mus., N.J. Museum, Smithsonian Inst., La. Museum, Buckingham Palace, Elysee Palace, Royal Ont. Mus. Toronto, The Vatican, The White House, Academy Natural Sciences of Philadelphia. Served with USSAF, World War II. Mem. N.Y. Zool. Soc., Audubon Soc. Collects song and game birds for exhbns. in schs., as live models. Home: Titusville NJ Died Jan. 30, 1969.

BOERICKE, GARTH WILKINSON, physician; b. San Francisco, Calif., Aug. 12, 1893; s. William and Kate (Fay) B.; student U. Cal., 1912-14; M.D., U. Mich., 1918; m. Aurilla Mae Shively, May 30, 1923; m. 2d, Martha Kloeren, June 28, 1958. Interne San Francisco General Hospital, 1918-19; instr. in internal medicine, U. Mich. Homeo. Med. Sch., 1919-21; asst. clin. prof. homeopathy, U. Cal., 1921-26; prof. materia medica and therapeutics, Hahnemann Med. Coll., Phila., 1926-60, prof. emeritus, 1960-68, formerly dir. Hering Research Lab. Mem. Am. Inst. Homeopathy (past pres. exec. sec. 1959-63), Pa. State Homeo. Association (pres. 1935), Beta Theta Pi Alpha Sigma. Democrat. Swedenborgian. Club: Hahnemann. Author: Principles of Homeopathy, 1929. Editor Jour. Am. Inst. Homeopathy, 1960-64. Home: Lansdowne PA Died Jan. 8, 1968; buried George Washington Meml. Park, White Marsh PA

BOERNSTEIN, RALPH A(UGUSTUS), fgn. service officer; b. Washington, Feb. 13, 1893; s. Henry N. and Charlotte (Schlegel) B.; student pub. schs., Washington; also pvt. tutors; m. Myra Dickey, Mar. 19, 1921; 1 son, Robert Charles. Sec. to congressman, 1916; vice consul, Fiame, 1917, Oslo, Norway, 1917-19, Port au Prince, 1919-20. Barbados, W.I., 1920-21, Rome, Italy, 1921-26; consul, Malmo, Sweden, 1927-30, Naples, Italy, 1930-34, Montreal, 1937-39, Yarmouth, N.S., 1941-42, Vancouver, 1943-48, Port Elizabeth, S. Africa, 1948-49; 1st sec. Am. Embassy, Copenhagen, Denmark, 1949; consul gen., Belfast, Ireland, 1951-53; with Dept. of State, 1926, 34, 42. Presbyn. Club: Malone Golf (Belfast). Home: Washington DC Died Mar. 15, 1969; buried Congressional Cemetery, Washington DC

BOESCHENSTEIN, HAROLD, mfr.; b. Edwardsville, Ill., July 21, 1896; s. Charles and Bertha (Whitbread) B.; A.B., U. Ill., 1920; hon. degrees Bowling Green (O.) State U., Defiance Coll., Juniata Coll., Clemson Coll., Oberlin Coll., U. Toledo; m. Mary Elizabeth Wade, Mar. 30, 1922; children—William Wade, Nancy Ann (Mrs. Hart Fessenden), Harold. With Edwardsville (Ill.) Nat. Bank, 1920, Ill. Terminal R.R., Alton, Ill., 1921; various adminstrv. positions Ill. Glass Co., also subsidiaries and affiliates, 1921-26 v.p., 1926-29, (merger Ill. Glass Co. and Owens Bottle Co. 1929), v.p., gen. sales mgr. sales mgr. Owens-Ill. Glass Co., Toledo, 1929-33, v.p., gen. mgr., dir., 1934-38, pres. dir. Owens-Corning Fiberglas Corp., Toledo, 1938-63, chmn. bd., 1963-67, chmn. exec. com., dir., 1967-72; chmn. bd. Fiberglas Can. Ltd., Owens-Corning Fiberglas Columbia, S. Am., Owens-Corning Fiberglas Europe, S. Am.; dir. Dow Jones & Co., Inc., Nat. Distillers & Chem. Corp., Edwardsville (Ill.) Nat. Bank & Trust Co., Asahi Fiber Glass Co. Ltd., Tokyo, Vitro Fibras, S. Am., Mexico City. Mem. WPB, 1942-45, vice chmn. operations, 1943-45; bus. council U.S. Govt., 1951-72, chmn., 1954-56; chmn. Pres. adv. com. on Soviet Econ. Competition, 1957; mem. adv. com. on Army orgn., 1953. Pres. Toledo Mus. Art; co-chmn. A.R.C. Fund Raising Campaign, 1969-70. Trustee Am. Mus. Natural History (N.Y.), Stanford Research Inst., Rutherford B. Hayes Found., other civic and philanthropic orgns.; bd. dirs. U. Ill. Found. Served to lt. U.S. Army, 1917-19. Decorated Pres.'s Medal for Merit, 1946; recipient Distinguished Citizens citation Denison U. 1956; Distinguished Illini, U. Ill., 1961; Certificate of Appreciation, U.S. Army, 1953; Distinguished Service award Treasury Dept., 1968. Mem. Sigma Chi, Sigma Delta Chi. Episcopalian. Clubs: Links, University, (N.Y.C.); Metropolitan, 1925 F Street (Washington); University (Chgo.); Pacific-Union, Bohemian (San

Francisco); Toledo, Toledo Country; Belmont, Carranor Hunt and Polo (Perrysburg, O.); Cypress Point (Pebble Beach, Cal.). Home: OH Died Oct. 23, 1972; buried Perrysburg OH

BOGAN, LOUISE, writer; born at Livermore Falls, Maine, August 11, 1897; d. Daniel Joseph and Mary Helen (Shields) Bogan; educated Mount St. Mary's Academy, Manchester, New Hampshire, 1907-09, and Girls' Latin School. Boston, Mass., 1910-15, Boston Univ., 1915-16; L.H.D., Western College for Women, 1956; Litt.D., Colby College, June 1960; married Curt Alexander, September 4, 1916 (died 1920); 1 daughter, Mathilde; m. 2d, Raymond Holden, July 10, 1925 (div. 1937). Winner of John Reed memorial prize, Poetry—A Mag. of Verse, 1930; Helen Haire Levinson memorial prize, same, 1937. Fellow John Simon Guggenheim Memorial Foundation, 1933 and 1937. Fellow in American Letters, Library of Congress, 1944; Chair of Poetry, Library of Congress, 1945-46; vis. lecturer, U. of Wash., 1948. U. Chicago, 1949, U. Arkansas, 1952, Salzburg Seminar in American studies, 1958; visiting professor Brandeis University, 1964-65. Member National Inst. Arts and Letters. Winner Harriet Monroe Poetry Award (U. Chicago), 1948; grant from Nat. Inst. Arts and Letters, 1951, Bollingen Prize in Poetry, 1955; awarded Academy of American Poets fellow, 1959; Creative Arts award in Poetry, Brandeis U. 1962; National Endowment for the Arts award, 1967. Member American Academy of Arts and Letters. Author: Body of This Death, 1923; Dark Summer, 1929; The Sleeping Fury, 1937; Poems and New Poems, 1941; Achievement in American Poetry 1900-1950, 1951; Collected Poems. 1923-53, 1954; Selected Criticism, 1955; The Blue Estuaries; Poems 1923-68, 1968; A Poet's Alphabet, 1970. Contbr. verse, criticism, fiction to New Republic, The New Yorker, The Nation, Poetry—A Mag. of Verse. Co-translator: The Journal of Jules Renard, 1964; The Glass Bees, 1961; Elective Affinities (Goethe), 1964; The Sorrows of Young Werther and Novella (Goethe), pub. posthumously, 1971. Editor: (with W. J. Smith) The Golden Journey, 1965. Home: New York City NY Died Feb. 4, 1970.

BOGART, WALTER THOMPSON, educator; b. Erie, Colo., Mar. 9, 1906; s. Walter Scott and Elizabeth Howard (Anderson) B.; A.B., U. Cal. at Los Angeles, 1930; M.A., Stanford, 1931, Ph.D., 1948; m. Mildred Josephine Marshall, Nov. 26, 1933. Instr. polit. sci. Stanford, 1935-37, Middlebury (Vermont) Coll., 1937-38, asst. prof., 1938-39, asso. prof., 1939-49, prof. since 1949, chmn. dept. from 1939, Jermain Prof. Polit. Economy, from 1952, chairman, Division of Social Sciences, from 1956. Selectman Town of Weybridge, Vermont, 1951-54; mem. legislative commn. to study Lease Lands, 1957-58; mem. adv. com. Little Hoover Commn., 1957-58; cons. to Gov. Vt., 1962; mem. from Vt., New Eng. Bd. Higher Edn., 1967-68. Served with USAAF, 1941-46; now col. Air Force Reserve (ret.). Decorated Am. Defense Medal, American Theater Ribbon, ETO Ribbon, Victory Medal. Mem. Am. Polit. Sci. Assn., Am. Assn. U. Profs., Res. Officers Assn., Alumni Assn. U. Cal. at Los Angeles, Theta Chi. Mason. Author: The Vermont Lease Lands, 1950. Home: Weybridge VT Died Oct. 6, 1968; buried Arlington Cemetery, Washington DC

BOGER, GLEN ALVIN, coop. exec.; b. Fulton County, O., Oct. 16, 1891; s. Alvin and Edith (Todd) B.; B.S., Ohio State U., 1915; m. Sarah E. Strait, Feb. 6, 1917; children—Evelyn (Mrs. Glenn Rink), Elizabeth (Mrs. Frank Eby). Organizer Lehigh Valley Coop. Farmers, 1933, pres. gen. mgr. from 1933; chmn. First Nat. Bank of Allentown, from 1954. Mem. Fed. Farm Credit Bd., 1956-—. Home: Allentown PA Died Jan. 29, 1968; buried Salisbury Hills Cemetery, Allentown PA

BOGER, ROBERT FORRESTER, pub. co. exec.; b. Parkersburg, W.Va., Dec. 27, 1900; s. Cyrus Maxwell and Bertha (Forrester) B.; student Marietta (O.) Coll., 1921; m. Muriel Robinson, 1925 (dec. 1956); 1 dau., Lydia; m. 2d, Elizabeth Rodgers, Oct. 20, 1956. With McGraw-Hill Publs., div. McGraw-Hill, Inc., N.Y.C., Boston, 1928-68, pub. Aviation Week, 1946-53, Engring. News-Record and Constrn. Methods & Equipment, 1948-64, v.p. adminstrn., 1964-66, exec. asst. to pres., 1966-68, also dir., dir. Dolphin Inc., Dimensions in Living Inc., Minotte E. Chatfield Co., Eugene Baehr Co., Stamford, Conn. Mem. Constrn. Writers Assn. Clubs: Santa Barbara (Cal.) Kennel; Am. Kennel (del.), Engineers (N.Y.C.); Sachem's Head Yacht (Guilford); Madison (Conn.) Winter; Nat. Press (Washington). Home: Guilford CT Died Dec. 11, 1968.

BOGERT, WALTER LAWRENCE, teacher of singing, baritone; b. Flushing, N.Y., Dec. 7, 1864; s. Henry A. and Mary Bowne (Lawrence) B.; A.B., Columbia, 1888, A.M., 1889, LL.B., 1890; student Conservatory of Music of America, 1894-98; grad. Inst. of Mus. Art, New York, 1908; studied singing with P. A. Rivarde, George Henschel, W. N. Burritt, A. Freni; violin with Eduard Mollenhauer; theory with Max Spicker and Percy Goetchius; piano with Rafael Joseffy and August Fraemcke; unmarried. Admitted to N.Y. bar, 1890, and practiced in N.Y. City; instr. in harmony, Nat. Conservatory of Music, 1894-1901; lecturer for Univ. Extension Soc., 1904-06, Am. Inst. Applied Music, 1908-11, 1918-21; instr. Inst. of Mus. Art, 1907-09; lecturer on music for N.Y. City Bd. of Edn., 1900-17; mus. dir. Pan-Am. Conf. of Bishops of P.E. Ch., Washington, D.C., 1903; mus. dir. People's Inst., N.Y. City, 1909-14; lecturer on history and appreciation of music, at Sch. of Music, Yale, 1920-21. Has given 550 song recitals in eastern cities. Trustee Queens Borough Pub. Library, 1900-09; mem. and treas. Com. of 3 in charge of erection of Carnegie libraries in Borough of Queens since 1901. Pres. Peter Minuit Corp., 1942-44. Conducted experiments at Ward's Island, New York, State Hosp. for Insane as to the therapeutic value of music, 1900. Member board dirs. Russian Symphony Society, 1904. Member New York Singing Teachers Association (pres. 1915-18), N.Y. State Music Teachers' Assn. (pres. 1913; chmn. program com. 1912, 18, 19), N.Y. Oratorio Soc. (bd. of dirs. 1917-21), Am. Academy Teachers of Singing (sec. 1922-42), Citizens' Union, Alumni Assn. of Grad. Schs. of Columbia U. (pres. 1939), Delta Phi, etc. Clubs: Century (trustee, com. on lit., 1920-22; com. on admissions, 1926-30), Barnard (pres. 1918-25), The Bohemians (dir. 1918-23, sec. 1923-43). Author of articles on Voice" in mus. and other mags. Consultant auditioner on Fed. Music project, New York City, since 1935; received prizes as amateur photographer; has more than 200 pictures on file in New York Pub. Library and Library of Columbia U. Home: 25 Claremont Av., New York NY‡

BOGGESS, ARTHUR CLINTON, prof. economics; b. Catlin, Ill., Mar. 2, 1874; s. Enoch Perry and Mary Elizabeth (Austin) B.; grad. high sch., Catlin, 1892; grad. Ill. State Normal U., Normal, Ill., 1900; A.B., U. of Ill., 1902; studied U. of Wis., 1902-04, fellow in Am. history, 1903-04; Harrison scholar in Am. history, U. of Pa., 1904-05, reader in European history, 1905-06, Ph.D., 1906; m. Ina Vivia Gould, of Forest Grove, Oregon, September 30, 1908 (she died December 7, 1929). Was acting professor of history, U. of Colo., summer 1905, same, Ill. State Normal U., 1906; prof. history and economics, Pacific U., Forest Grove, Ore., 1906-10; same, Lucknow (India) Christian Coll., 1910-15; prof. economics, Baldwin-Wallace Coll., Berea, O., since 1916. Y.M.C.A. sec. for S.A.T.C., Baldwin-Wallace Coll., 1918. Methodist. Author: The Settlement of Illinois (1778-1830), 1908; First Days in India, 1912. Editor The Lucknow Collegian, 1911-15, the Khaukab-i-Hind, 1912-14. Contbr. to mags. Home: Berea OH‡

BOGGS, EARL HUFFNER, univ. adminstr.; b. Orton, W.Va., June 3, 1905; s. Scott and Susan (Stump) B.; A.B., Glenville (W.Va.) State Coll., 1931; M.A., W.Va. U., 1938; Ph.D., George Peabody Coll., 1949; PeD. (hon.), Morris Harvey Coll., 1958. Chmn. grad. com. Sch. Edn., U. Va., 1951-55; dean Longwood Coll., Farmville, Va., 1955-60; dean Coll. Edn., W.Va. U., 1960-65, dir. admissions, asst. to pres. univ., 1965-72. Bd. visitors Ft. Eustic Transp. Sch. Named Alumnus of Year, Glenville State Coll., 1961. Mem. N.E.A., Nat. Soc. Coll. Tchrs. Edn., Am. Assn. Sch. Adminstrs., Phi Delta Kappa (Distinguished Service award ednl. service Va. 1957). Address: Morgantown WV Died Sept. 16, 1972; buried Alderson WV

BOGGS, FRANK CRANSTOUN, army officer; b. Swedesboro, N.J., Mar. 16, 1874; s. George Brenton and Hannah Garrison (Thompson) B.; grad. Pub. High Sch., Norristown, Pa., 1890; grad. U.S. Mil. Acad., 1898; m. Marianne Thomson, of Norristown, Pa., June 23, 1900. Commd. 2d lt. engrs., U.S.A., Apr. 26, 1898; 1st lt., Feb. 7, 1900; capt. Apr. 23, 1904; major., Feb. 27, 1911; lt. col., Corps of Engineers U.S.A., May 15, 1917; colonel N.A., Aug. 5, 1917. Quartermaster battalion engineers and Post Willets Point, N.Y., 1898-9; local charge fortification work near Tampa, Fla., 1899-1900; with battalion engrs. and at Engr. Sch., Willets Point and Washington, D.C., 1900-2; adj. engr. battalion, Washington, D.C., and P.I., 1902-4; local charge fortification works, P.I., 1904-5; local charge constrn. dam Monongahela River, Pa., 1906-7; charge Wheeling District, engr. dept., 1907-8; gen. purchasing officer and chief Washington office, Isthmian Canal Commn. 1908-16; in charge U.S. Engring. Dist., Montgomery, Ala., 1916; in charge Engr. Depot and engr. purchasing officer at San Antonio, Tex., 1916-17; comdg. 315th Engrs., at San Antonio and in France, 1917-18; in charge engr. depots and engr. purchasing officer in France for A.E.F., 1918; duty with Gen. Staff, Washington, 1919-—. Episcopalian. Mem. Am. Soc. C.E., Engrs. Club (Washington), Nat. Geog. Soc. Club: Army and Navy. Address: War Dept., Washington DC‡

BOGGS, THOMAS HALE, congressman; b. Long Beach, Miss., Feb. 15, 1914; s. William Robertson and Claire Josephine (Hale) B.; B.A., Tulane U., 1935, LL.B., 1937; m. Corinne Claiborne, Jan. 22, 1938; children—Barbara Rowena (Mrs. Paul Eugene Sigmund), Thomas Hale, Corinne (Mrs. Steven Roberts). Admitted to La. bar, 1937, general practice civil law, 1943, 46; mem. 77th Congress, 80th to 92d Congresses from 2d La. Dist., mem. banking and currency com., 1946-48, ways and means com., 1949-71, joint com. on internal revenue taxation, 1961-71, joint econ. com., 1957-72, chmn. subcom. on fgn. econ. policy, 1957-72, dep. whip, 1955-61, majority whip, 1962-71, majority leader U.S. Ho. of Reps., 1971-72. Vice chmn. Democratic Nat. Com., 1956-72; parliamentarian Dem. Nat. Conv., 1964, chmn. platform com., 1968. Mem. Pres.'s Commn. on Causes and Prevention of Violence; mem. Pres.'s Commn. on Assassination of President Kennedy, 1964. Served with USNR, World War II. Recipient Cunningham award International House, 1958. General manager Tulane U. Alumni Assn., 1937-40; mem. Family Service Soc. of New Orleans. Mem. Am., La., New Orleans bar assns., New Orleans C. of C., Am. Judicature Soc., S.A.R., Am. Legion, Am. Vets. World War II, Internat. Assn. Ports and Harbors (hon.), Phi Beta Kappa, Beta Theta Pi, Omicron Delta Kappa. Democrat. Roman Catholic. K.C. Club: Congressional (Washington). Home: New Orleans LA Died Oct. 1972.

BOGOSIAN, ARES GEORGE, aerospace co. exec.; b. Providence, Apr. 7, 1915; s. Armen D. and Aven (Sebastian) B.; B.S. in Mech. Engring., U. R.I., 1938; M.S. in Aero. Engring., Mass. Inst. Tech., 1941; m. Claire Beverly Janick, Oct. 6, 1943; children—Armen James, Gale Ruth. Project engr. Instrumentation Lab., Mass. Inst. Tech., 1946-53; mil. operations research analyst Lockheed-Burbank (Cal.), 1953-56; head SAGE evaluation group Rand Corp., Santa Monica, Cal., 1956-57; dir. systems dept. Am. Standard & San. Corp., Norwood, Mass., 1957-60; gen. mgr. advanced engring. concepts div. Epsco, Inc., Cambridge, Mass., 1960-62; gen. mgr. systems mgmt. div. Kollsman Instrument Corp., Elmhurst, N.Y., 1962-67; dir. mgmt. systems Harry Belock Assos., Inc., Great Neck, N.Y., 1967-69. Mem. electronic com. hwy. research bd. Nat. Acad. Sci.-NRC, 1962-69. Served to lt. comdr. USNR, 1942-46. Mem. Inst. Nav., Small Bus. Assn. New Eng., Mass. Inst. Tech. Alumni Assn. Club: Amesbury (Mass.) Golf and Country (dir.). Editor, co-author: (with Adolph, Bassett and Taub) Research in Neurology, 1961. Home: Huntington Bay NY Died Sept. 6, 1969.

BOHAN, PETER THOMAS, M.D.; b. Keithsburg, Ill., Jan. 16, 1874; M.D., Rush Med. Coll., Chicago, 1900. Practiced at Kansas City, Mo., since 1900; prof. clin. medicine, U. of Kan. Sch. of Medicine. Fellow Am. Coll. Phys., A.M.A.; mem. Mo. State Med. Assn. Home: The Walnuts. Office: Med. Arts Bldg., Kansas City MO*‡

BOHEN FREDERICK OWEN, mag. publisher; b. Waseca, Minn., May 25, 1895; s. Thomas Thaddeus and Amelia Francis (McLaughlin) B.; student N.Y. U., 1923; LL.D., Drake U., 1956; m. Mildred Meredith, Nov. 26, 1919; 1 dau., Barbara Meredith (Mrs. Friedl Pfeifer). Asso. Mpls. Jour., Mpls. Tribune, St. Paul Daily News, Portland Ore. Jour., Des Moines Capital, 1909-21; with Meredith Corp. (formerly Meredith Pub. Co.), Des Moines, 1921-73, gen. mgr., 1927-28, pub., gen. mgr., 1928-73, pres., chief exec. officer, 1929-65-66, chmn. bd., until 1973; dir. Central Life Assurance Co., Des Moines, Allis-Chalmers Mfg. Co., Milw., C., R.I. & D. R.I.&&D. Ry. Co. Mem. Bus. Council Washington, 1954-73. Bd. dirs. Nat. 4-H Service Com. Chgo., Greater Des Moines Com.; trustee Midwest Research Inst., Kansas City, Mo., Hawley Welfare Found., Des Moines, Thunderbird Grad. Sch. Internat. Mgmt., Phoenix; trustee, mem. exec. com. Drake U., Des Moines, 1929-73; pres., bd. dirs. Meredith Found., 1956-73. Bohen Found., 1958-73; bd. govs. Ia. State U. Found., Ames, 1959-73, bd. dirs., 1967-73; bd. dirs. Advt. Council (industries adv. com.), N.Y.C., Washington. Rotarian. Clubs: Wakonda, Des Moines, Embassy (Des Moines); Chicago, International, Tavern (Chgo.); Minneapolis; Marco Polo (N.Y.C.); Paradise Valley Country (Phoenix). Home: Des Moines IA Died Feb. 17, 1973.

BOHLMAN, HERBERT WILLIAM, economist; b. Hortonville, Wis., Dec. 23, 1896; s. Henry H. and Emilie (Schroeder) B.; A.B., Lawrence Coll., 1919; A.M., U. of Wis., 1922, Ph.D., 1936; m. Mary Edna McCaull, Sept. 10, 1924; 1 son, Herbert McCaull. Teacher high sch., 1919-21; asst. in economics, U. of Wis., 1921-24; asst. prof. economics, Drake U., 1924-27, prof., from 1927, dean grad. div., 1940-54, dean bus. adminstrn., 1954-64. Research economist 20th Century Fund, N.Y., 1934-35; sr. and prin. economist Office of Price Admnstrn., Washington, 1942-45. Mem. U.S. Naval Reserve, 1918-19. Chmn. Polk County Consumers' Council, 1934. Mem. Am. Econ. Association, Phi Beta Kappa, Beta Gamma Sigma, Alpha Epsilon Pi, Pi Gamma Mu, Delta Sigma Pi. Conglist. Mason (Shriner). Author: The Cost of Distributing Consumer Goods, 1936; Labor Market in Iowa, 1937; Our Economic Problems (with Edna McCaull Bohlman), 1942, Problems of Democracy, 1964; Insuring Your Life, Income and Property; Knowing How to Budget and Buy; Understanding Consumer Credit; Investing Your Savings; The Law for You. Home: Des Moines IA Died Jan. 8, 1968.

BOHN, DONALD GEORGE, physician; b. Gt. Bend, N.D., Jan. 30, 1921; s. George and Ruth (Stenson) B.; M.D., U. Minn., 1946; m. Yvonne Delores Kvan, July 9, 1949; children—Robert, Merry. Intern, Mpls. Gen. Hosp., 1945-46, former resident and fellow, mem. active staff, until 1971; hon. staff Met. Med. Center, Mpls.;

clin. asso. prof. U. Minn., Mpls. Served to capt., M.C., AUS, 1953-55. Diplomate Am. Bd. Internal Medicine. Mem. A.M.A. Home: Minneapolis MN Died May 17, 1971; buried Ft. Snelling Cemetery.

BOHR, FRANK, consular service; b. Wathena, Kan., Oct. 5, 1877; s. of Matthias and Agnes (Wank) B.; grad. Kan. State Normal Sch., Emporia, 1904; A.B., U. of Mich., 1907; m. Mildred E. Lombard, of Edna, Labette Co., Kan., July 5, 1911; children—Elizabeth Jane, David F. Apptd. asst. in consular service, Washington, D.C., 1908; dep. consul gen., Berlin, Germany, 1909-11; v. and dep. consul gen., Santo Domingo, Dominican Republic, 1911-13; v. consul, Zurich, Switzerland, 1913-18, consul, Cienfuegos, Cuba, 1919-25, Mexicali, Mexico, 1925-32, Sault Sainte Marie, Can., 1932-35; retired. Republican. Club: Rotary Internat. Home: 516 N. 7th St., Ann Arbor MI‡

BOIES, WILLIAM ARTEMAS, physician; b. Longmeadow, Mass., Apr. 10, 1871; s. William Ely and Elizabeth Phelps (Wright) B.; ed. Springfield (Mass.) Collegiate Inst.; M.D., New York Homoe. Coll., 1896; m. Charlotte Devol, of New Albany, Ind., Oct. 29, 1901. Mem. Am. Inst. Homoeopathy, Southern Homoe. Assn., Knox Co. Med. Soc., Alpha Sigma. Republican. Presbyn. Home: 1820 W. Clinch Av. Office: 507 W. Church Av., Knoxville TN‡

BOK, CARY WILLIAM, publisher; b. Merion, Pa., Jan. 25, 1905; s. Edward William and Mary Louise (Curtis) B.; B.A., Williams Coll., Williamstown, Mass., 1926; student Oxford (Eng.) U., 1927-29; m. Helene Boericke, June 18, 1935 (div. Jan. 1961); children—Anthony Shannon, Gordon Dennis; m. 2d, Agnes Margaret Curtis, December 5, 1961. Sr. vice pres. The Curtis Publishing Company, Pres. Curtis Inst. of Music, Mary Louise Curtis Bok Found.; bd. govs. Nature Conservancy. Congregationalist. (treasurer). Clubs: Corinthian Yacht (Phila.); Camden (Me.) Yacht. Home: Camden ME Died Dec. 29, 1970; buried Rockport ME

BOLAND, JOHN PETER, clergyman; b. Buffalo, N.Y., Apr. 27, 1888; s. John J. and Mary (Sullivan) B.; student St. Bonaventure's Coll., Allegany, N.Y., 1904-05, hon. LL.D., 1929; Ph.D., Propaganda Coll., Rome, Italy, 1907, J.C.D., 1909, D.D., 1911; LL.D., Manhattan Coll., 1942, Hobart Coll., 1952; ordained R.C. priest in Rome, June 10, 1911; assistant pastor, Blessed Sacrament Ch. and later St. Brigid's Ch., Buffalo, 1911-17; adminstr. St. Anthony's Ch., Lackawanna, N.Y., June-July 1917; pastor St. Lucy's Church, Buffalo, 1917-37, and St. Columba's Church Buffalo, 1928-37; pastor St. Thomas Aquinas Ch. since 1942; chmn. N.Y. State Labor Relations Bd., July 1937-June 42; director National Labor Relations Bd. for Buffalo area, 1934-37; mem. New York State Board of Mediation from 1947. European rep. War Relief Services, Inc., Nat. Catholic Welfare Conf., 1944-45. Judge of Matrimonial Court, Buffalo diocese; diocesan director of hospitals from 1919; director of Buffalo (New York) Diocese Labor College. Named as Domestic Prelate to his Holiness Pius XII, with title of Rt. Rev. Monsignor, May 1945. Grand Commander Order SS. Maurice and Lazarus (Italy) Nov. 1945; Grand Comdr. Order Orange-Nassau (Netherlands) 1948; named by Pius XII Prothonotary Apostolic, 1954. Contbr. of articles on labor problems to periodicals. Home: Buffalo NY Died June 30, 1968; buried Holy Cross Cemetery, Lackawana NY

BOLES, H(ENRY) LEO, author, editor; b. near Gainesboro, Tenn., Feb. 22, 1874; s. Henry J. and Sarah (Smith) B.; student Dibrell (Tenn.) Normal Sch.; B.S., Burritt Coll., Spencer, Tenn., 1900, A.M., 1913; B.A., Nashville Bible Sch., 1906; M.A., Vanderbilt, 1920; D.D. Southern School of Divinity, 1927; m. Ida May Meiser, Sept. 23, 1906; 1 son, Leo L. Taught in pub. schs. Tenn., Tex., Fla., several years; prof. mathematics and philosophy, 1906-13, pres., 1913-20 and 1923-32, now in Bible dept. and sec. bd. of dirs., David Lipscomb Coll. (formerly Nashville Bible Sch.). Evangelist, 1920-22; editor Gospel Advocate, 1922-23, and since 1930; also editor Advanced Quarterly. Mem. Internat. Council Religious Edn. (uniform lesson com.). Mem. Church of Christ. Author: New Testament Teaching on War, 1922; Instrumental Music in Christian Worship, 1926; Unfulfilled Prophecy (with R. H. Boll), 1928; Eldership of Churches of Christ, 1931; Biographical Sketches of Gospel Preachers, 1932; Bible in Questions, 1935. Editor of Notes on International Sunday School Lessons, 1927; Commentary on the Gospel According to Matthew, 1936; Commentary on Luke, 1939; Commentary on Acts, 1941; The Holy Spirit, 1942. Address: 4100 Granny White Rd., Nashville TN*‡

BOLES, JOHN, screen actor and singer; b. Greenville, Tex., 1896; s. John Monroe and Mary Jane (B); A.B., U. of Texas, 1917; m. Marcelite Dobbs, June 21, 1917; children—Frances Marcelite, Janet. Played on the legitimate stage, 1923-26 in support of leading stars; motion picture actor, 1926-1948; best known pictures are: Back Street, Life of Vergie Winters, Wild Gold, Music in the Air, Stella Dallas, Fight for Your Lady, Romance in the Dark, Curly Top, Littlest Rebel (in support of Shirley Temple), Desert Song, Rio Rita, Only Yesterday, Seed, Craig's Wife; in oil bus., San Angelo, Tex. Served in France in Intelligence Dept., U.S. Army, World War I. Mem. Beta Theta Pi. Presbyterian. Home: San Angelo TX Died Feb. 27, 1969.*

BOLLES, FRANK CRANDALL, army officer (ret.); b. Elgin, Ill., Sept. 25, 1872; s. Elisha and Harriett (Crandall) B.; student Mo. Sch. of Mines, 1890, C.E., 1922; grad. U.S. Mil. Acad., 1896; distinguished grad., Army Sch. of Line, 1915; grad. General Staff Sch., 1920; also grad. Army War Coll., 1921; m. Irene H. Pettit, Jan. 14, 1909; children—Frank Crandall, Seaman P., Elizabeth L., Henrietta, Jonathan. Commd. 2d lt., U.S. Army, 1896; promoted through grades to maj. gen., 1935. Served in Spanish-Am. War, Filipino Insurrection; wounded in action, Battle of Jaro, P.I., Jan. 13, 1899, battle of Tangalan, P.I., Feb. 1900; comdr. 39th U.S. Inf., France, World War; gassed during the 2d Battle of the Marne, 1918, and wounded at Bois de Septarges, Sept. 28, 1918; comdr. 30th Inf., Presidio, San Francisco, 1925-28; comdg. gen. at Ft. D.A. Russell, Wyo., 1928-29; comdg. gen. at Ft. Stotsenburg, P.I., 1929-31; comdg. gen. at Fort Sheridan, Ill., 1931-35; comdg. gen. of Fort Sam Houston, 1935; comdg. gen. of 7th Corps Area, Omaha, Neb., 1935-36; retired; pres. Union State Bank South San Antonio, Tex., since July 19, 1937. Awarded D.S.C. for gallantry in action in battle of Jaro, P.I., 1899; citations for gallantry in action at assault of Moro position in crater at Bud Dajo; awarded D.S.C. and Oak Leaf Cluster for service in France; D.S.M. (U.S.); Croix de Guerre with Palm, and Chevalier of Legion of Honor (France); D.S.M. (State of Mo.), 1936. Mem. Am. Legion. Baptist. Mason. Elk. Clubs: Rotary, Kiwanis, Army and Navy. Sojourners. Author: Economy in Military Administration, 1928; Back to the Land, 1933. Address: 117 Geneseo Rd., San Antonio TX‡

BOLLING, GEORGE MELVILLE, philologist, linguist; b. Baltimore, Apr. 13, 1871; s. William Nicholls and Hannah Lamb (Bonham) B.; A.B., Loyola Coll., Baltimore, 1891; Ph.D., Johns Hopkins, 1896; m. Irene Johnson, of Baltimore, Sept. 8, 1898. Began as instr. Sanskrit and comparative philology, 1895, later till 1913, prof. Greek and Sanskrit langs. and lits., Catholic U. of America; Henry E. Johnston, Jr., scholar, Johns Hopkins, 1913-14; prof. Greek, Ohio State U. since 1914; lecturer in Linguistic Inst., 1928-31. Mem. Am. Philol. Assn., American Oriental Soc., Archaeol. Inst. America, Soc. for Promotion Hellenic Studies, Linguistic Soc. America (pres. 1932), Beta Theta Pi. Gold cross of the Knights of the Redeemer (Grecian), for services in connection with the boundaries of Thrace at the close of the World War, 1919. Democrat. Author: The External Evidence for Interpolation in Homer, 1925. Editor (in conjunction with J. von Negelein) of the Parisistas of the Atharvaveda (Leipzig), 1910-11. Contbr. tech. articles relating chiefly to the Homeric question. Editor Publs. of Linguistic Soc. of America since Columbus OH‡

BOLSTER, STANLEY MARSHALL, lawyer, trustee; b. Boston, Mass., Mar. 21, 1874; s. Solomon A. and Sarah Jane (Gardner) B.; student Roxbury Latin Sch., 1888-93; A.B., Harvard, 1897, LL.B., 1900; m. Lucy C. Daniell, June 12, 1902; children—Marshall G., Richard D., Catherine M. Admitted to the bar of Mass., 1900, gen. practice of law, Boston; pres. and dir. Yuba Consolidated Gold Fields, Calif., since 1919, Capital Dredging Co., San Francisco, Calif., since 1919; treas. and dir. Aetna Portland Cement Co., Bay City, Mich., since 1920. Dir. Nat. Rockland Bank of Boston. Trustee of estates. Trustee and vice pres. Inst. for Savings in Roxbury and Its Vicinity; pres. and trustee Forest Hills Cemetery, Boston. Past treas. Newton (Mass.) Hosp. Mem. Am. and Boston bar assns. Republican. Conglist. Club: Brae Burn Country, West Newton, Mass. (past dir. and treas.). Home: 29 Exeter St., West Newton, Mass. Office: 50 Congress St., Boston 9 MA‡

BOLTON, ELMER KEISER, chemist; b. Phila., June 23, 1886; s. George and Jane (Holt) B.; A.B., Bucknell U., 1908, hon. D.Sc., 1932; A.M., Harvard, 1910, Ph.D., 1913; student Kaiser Wilhelm Inst. fur Chemie, Berlin, 1913-1915; D.Sci. (honorary), U. Del.; m. Marguerite L. Duncan, December 6, 1916; children—Duncan G., Marjorie L., Elmer K. With E. I. du Pont de Nemours and Co. 1915-51, successively asst. mgr. Lodi Works, mgr. organic div. of chem. dept., dir. chem. sect. of dyestuffs dept., asst. chem. dir. of chem. dept., 1929-30, chem. dir., 1930-51; retired, 1951; mem. tech. advisory panel on materials Dept. of Def. Trustee Bucknell U.; bd. mgrs., The Wilmington Institute Free Library. Mem. Nat. Acad. of Sciences, Am. Chemical Soc. (dir., 1940-43), Am. Inst. Chem. Engrs., Sigma Xi, Phi Kappa Psi, Alpha Chi Sigma. Recipient Chemical Industry Medal, 1941, Perkin Medal, 1944; Willard Gibbs gold medal, Am. Chem. Soc., 1954. Clubs: Wilmington, Wilmington Country, du Pont Country, Harvard. Home: Wilmington DE Died July 30, 1968.

BOLTON, FREDERICK ELMER, university prof.; b. Tomah, Wis., May 9, 1866; s. Edwin Latham and Rosaline (Cady) B.; grad. State Normal Sch., Milwaukee, 1890; B.S., U. of Wis., 1893, M.S., 1896; student U. of Leipzig, 1896-97; fellow, Clark U., 1897-98, Ph.D., 1898; m. Olive A. Foster, Aug. 23, 1893 (died June 5, 1934); m. 2d, Helen Rose Coldwell, Feb. 26, 1938. Teacher dist. schs., Wis., 1885-87; prin. Tunnel City (Wis.) graded sch., 1887-88, Fairchild High Sch., 1890-91; prin. schs., Kaukauna, Wis., 1893-95; prof. psychology and edn., State Normal Sch., Milwaukee, 1898-1900; asst. prof. edn., U. of Ia., 1900-01, prof. and head dept. of edn., 1901-12, dir. summer session, 1901-10, sec., 1910-12, dir. sch. of edn., 1906-12; prof. edn., dean college of edn., U. of Wash., 1912-28, prof. of education and dean emeritus since 1928, dir. summer sessions, 1913-25, lecturer summer session, Univ. of Wis., 1899; prof. of edn., summers, U. of Chicago, 1913, U. of Calif., 1925, U. of Hawaii, 1930, U. of Tex., 1940, Syracuse U., 1941. Asso. editor School Review, 1906-12; asso. editor Am. School Education; contbr. editor Nation's Schs., 1916-32. Chmn. Com. to Revise Sch. Laws of Iowa, 1907-09; chmn. Accrediting Com. Higher Instns., N.W. Assn. of Secondary and Higher Schools, 1920-40; former mem. advisory council, Simplified Spelling Bd.; mem. gen. advisory bd. Soc. for Visual Edn.; former mem. edn. com. Inst. of Pacific Relations. Mem. N.E.A., Nat. Soc. Scientific Study of Edn., Nat. Soc. Coll. Teachers of Edn. (sec., 1904-10), Am. Soc. Ednl. Research, Am. Psychol. Assn.; fellow A.A.A.S. Author: The Secondary School System of Germany, 1900; Principles of Education, 1910; Everyday Psychology for Teachers, 1923; Adolescent Education, 1931; History of Education in Washington, 1935; The Beginning Superintendent, 1937; Educational Sociology, 1941. Home: 4514 16th Av. NE, Seattle WA‡

BOLTON, HERBERT EUGENE, historian, explorer; b. Wilton, Wis., July 20, 1870; s. Edwin Latham and Rosaline (Cady) B.; B.L., U. of Wis., 1895, post-grad. in history, 1896-97; Harrison fellow in history, U. of Pa., 1897-99, Ph.D., 1899; LL.D., St. Mary's Coll., and Catholic U. of America, 1929; D.Litt., U. of San Francisco, 1930; LL.D., U. of Toronto, 1932; L.H.D., Marquette U., 1937; LL.D., U. of N.Mex., 1937, U. of Calif., 1942; Lit.D., Univ. of Pa., 1940, Univ. of Wis., 1945; m. Gertrude James, Aug. 20, 1895. Instr. history, 1901-05, adj. prof., 1905-08, asso. prof., 1908-09, University of Texas; prof. Am. history, Stanford, 1909-11; prof. Am. history, U. of Calif., 1911-31, Sather prof. of history, 1931-40, chmn. of dept. history, 1919-40, Sather prof. emeritus since 1940, lecturer in history, 1942-44, faculty research lecturer, 1917; dir. Bancroft Library, 1916-40; Bernard Moses Memorial lecturer, U. of California, 1941. Investigator Mexican archives, summers 1902-06; investigator history native tribes, Texas, for U.S. Bur. Ethnology, 1906-12; on commn. for Carnegie Instn. to prepare report on U.S. history materials in Mexican archives, 1907-11; research in Mexican archives many summers since 1911; traveling fellow in Europe for Native Sons of Golden West and Del Amo Foundation, summer 1931. Mem. Hist. Manuscripts Commn. of Am. Hist. Assn., 1914-16, bibliography com., 1916-17, exec. council, 1917; mem. Calif. Hist. Survey Commn., 1915-24; mem. Nat. Advisory Bd. H.A.B.S., 1933; mem. advisory board National Parks Service since 1933; mem. national committee Franklin D. Roosevelt Library, 1938; lecturer Lowell Inst., Boston, Dec. 1920-Jan. 1921; hon. prof. history, Universidad de Santiago, Chile, since 1939; prof. honoria, Univ. de Mexico, 1945; prof. history, Internat. summer sch., Mexico, 1946. Member California commission representing Nat. Statuary Hall, 1930-31, Hist. commn. to promote canonization of Father Junipero Serra, Lima Geographic Society, American Historical Assn. (1st v.p. 1931; pres. 1932; pres. Pacific Coast Branch, 1915-16), Southwest Soc. Archaeol. Inst. of America, Hispanic Soc. America, Am. Philos. Soc., Philos. Society of Texas; fellow Society American Historians, Texas Historical Association, American Geographical Soc.; mem. Academia Real de la Historia since 1928; mem. Sociedad Cientifica Antonio Alzate (Mexico), Sociedad Mexicana de Geografia y Estadistica, Sociedad Chihuahuense de Estudios Historicos; Am. Antiq. Soc.; corr. mem. Academia Colombiana de Historia, Junta de Administracion de la sociedad Chilena de Historia y Geografia; mem. U.S. com. to aid Nat. Library of Peru, Library of Congress Policy Planning Com. since 1946, Phi Beta Kappa, Theta Delta Chi. Hon. mem. New Mexico Historical Society, Native Sons of Golden West. Author: Guide to Materials for United States History in the Archives of Mexico, 1913; Texas in the Middle Eighteenth Century (U. of Calif.), 1915; Colonization of North America (with Thomas Maitland Marshall), 1920; The Spanish Borderlands, 1921; The Debatable Land (with M. Ross), 1925; Palou and His Writings, 1926; A Pacific Coast Pioneer, 1927; The History of the Americas—A Syllabus, 1928; Anza's California Expeditions (1774-76), 5 vols., 1930; Outpost of Empire (awarded gold medal, Calif. Commonwealth Club), 1931; The Padre on Horseback, 1932; Rim of Christendom (awarded gold medal, California Commonwealth Club), 1936; Cross, Sword and Gold Pan, 1936; Drake's Plate of Brass, 1937; Wider Horizons of American History, 1939; Cultural Cooperation With Latin America, 1940. Editor: Athanase de Mezieres 1914; Spanish Explorations in the Southwest, 1542-1710, 1915; Kino's Memoirs, 2vols., 1919; Spain's Title to Georgia, 1925; Palou's Noticias de la Nueva California, 4 vols., 1926; Crespi's Pacific Coast Diaries, 1927. Co-editor: The Pacific

Ocean in History, 1916; Southwestern Historical Quarterly. Advisory editor Hispanic American Hist. Rev. since 1917. Writer of numerous monographs on history of Spanish America; contbr. of Tex. articles to Handbook of American Indians, 1907-10. Decorated Comendador de la Real Orden de Isabella Catolica, by King of Spain, 1925; Comendatore dell' Ordine della Corona d'Italia. Attended Pan-Am. Conf., Lima, 1938; del. of Am. Nat. Com. to First Conf. on Intellectual Cooperation, Santiago, Chile, 1939; del. to 3d Assembly, Pan-Am. Inst. of Geography and History, Lima, Peru, 1941. Mem. Coronado Internat. Monument Commn. to Mexico, July 1942. Traveled widely in western hemisphere and Europe. Address: Univ. of Calif., Berkeley CA*‡

BOLTON, (JOHN) WHITNEY (FRENCH), writer; b. Washington, July 23, 1900; s. Henry Simon and Lydah Elizabeth (French) B.; student pvt. schs. Mexico City, Mexico; student Staunton Mil. Acad., 1912-19, U. Va., 1919-21; m. Frances Schiff; 1 son, Whitney French; m. 2d Nancy Coleman, Sept. 16, 1943; children—Grania Theresa and Charla Elizabeth (twins). By-line reporter, drama reporter N.Y. Herald-Tribune, 1924-28; drama critic, columnist N.Y. Morning Telgraph, 1928-38, drama critic from 1949; publicity dir. Warner Bros. and Columbia Pictures, 1941-46; personal asst. to David O. Selznick, film producer, 1946-49; syndicated columnist McNaught Syndicate, Inc., from 1949. Commentator MBS. Mem. N.Y. Drama Critics Circle, London Drama Critics Circle (hon.). Author: (novel) The Rosewood Jail, 1953; (play) Save The Pieces, 1932; also screenplays and short stories. Home: New York City NY Died Nov. 1966.

BOMANN, GEORGE ATKINS, fabrics exec.; b. Brooklyn, Aug. 5, 1864; s. Joseph and Mary Emma (Burns) B.; student pub. schs. of Brooklyn; widower; children—Mrs. F. Hamilton Dyckman, Mrs. Robert F. DeGraff, Mrs. Celia B. Becker, George Atkins, Donald. Asso., J. H. Thorp & Co., Inc., N.Y. City, since 1880, pres. since 1921. Decorated Societa Nationale D'Encouragement au Bien gold medal (France). Mem. Father and Sons Golf Tournament Assn. (charter mem.). Clubs: Metropolitan (N.Y. City); Tin Whistles (golf) (Pinehurst, N.C.). Home: Croton Lake Rd., Katonah, N.Y. Office: 250 Park Av., New York City 17 NY‡

BONCI, ALESSANDRO, operatic tenor; b. Cesena, Italy, 1870; ed. Rossini Conservatory, Pesaro, Italy, and Conservatory, Paris. Appeared in small part in Verdi's Falstaff" at Royal Theatre, Parma, 1885, later in l'Puritani" at La Scala, Milan; sang 10 seasons in Florence, also at Naples and Palermo; received with great favor in Berlin, Vienna, St. Petersburg, Madrid, Paris, and frequently at Buenos Aires. Engaged at Manhattan Opera House, New York, 1906; made concert tour through U.S., 1912; with Chicago Grand Opera Co., season of 1912-13; later with Met. Opera Co., New York, Commendatore della Corona d'Italia, conferred by King of Italy; Singer of the Chamber," to King of Spain; and many other decorations. Address: Care Metropolitan Opera Co., NY

BOND, AHVA J. C., univ. dean; b. Roanoke, W.Va., May 23, 1875; s. John C. and Elizabeth (Schiefer) B.; A.B., Salem (W.Va.) Coll., 1903; B.D., Alfred Sch. of Theology, 1907; student Southern Baptist Theol. Sem., Louisville, Ky., 1914-15; D.D.; m. Ora Van Horn, June 17, 1903 (died, 1938); children—Elizabeth Elsie (Mrs. Evert Pearcy), Winifred Virginia (Mrs. John R. Spicer), Mary Josephine (Mrs. Donald E. Lewis), Wilna Van Horn (Mrs. Dwight E. Wilson). Nellie Mae (Mrs. William Parry), Ahvagene Leora (Mrs. F. Kenyon Clarke); m. 2d, Mrs. Agnes K. Clarke, 1940. Ordained to ministry of Baptist Ch.; pastor, Milton Junction, Wis., 1908-13, Salem, W.Va., 1913-19; forward movement dir. Seventh Day Bapt. Gen. Conf., 1919-24; pastor, Plainfield, N.J., 1924-35; dean. Sch. of Theology, Alfred (N.Y.) U. since 1935. Leader ecumenical Sabbath promotion American Sabbath Tract Soc. Seventh Day Bapt. Educational Society. Mem. Society Am. Church History. Author: The Challenge of the Ministry, 1919; Reconstruction Messages, 1919; Sabbath History, 1922; The Sabbath, 1925; When I Was a Boy, 1928. Home: 33 S. Main St. Alfred NY‡

BOND, CHARLES GROSVENOR, ex-congressman; b. Columbus, O., May 29, 1877; s. William W. and Frances (Currier) B.; Ohio State U., 1892-96, LL.B., 1899; m. Bertha Paterson, of Columbus, June 27, 1905. Practiced law, Columbus, 1899-1903; moved to Brooklyn, N.Y., 1903; now mem. Bond & Strouss. Pres. Bay Parkway Nat. Bank of Brooklyn; counsel and dir. Seventh Nat. Bank of New York; dir. Lloyd's Casualty Co. Mem. 67th Congress (1921-23), 8th N.Y. Dist. Republican. Pres. Ohio State U. Assn., 1921-23; mem. Phi Delta Theta, Phi Delta Phi, Brooklyn Chamber Commerce, Ohio Soc., etc. Clubs: Phi Delta Theta (New York); Union League, University (Brooklyn). Home: 1701 Elmore Pl., Brooklyn, N.Y. Office: 7 Dey St., New York NY‡

BOND, (FREDERIC) DREW, financial and scientific writer; b. Philadelphia, Pa., May 22, 1876; s. Francis Strong and Rosalie (de Solms) B.; prep. edn., pvt. schs. and La Salle Coll.; B.S., U. of Pa., 1899; m. Anna Louise Minford, Oct. 23, 1905; 1 son, Wolcott; m. 2d, Annette Dembitz, Apr. 3, 1920. Newspaper reporter, copy reader and city editor, Philadelphia and New York City, 1899-1905; financial consultant since 1910; associate with late Isaac M. Cate, in his successful readjustment of Am. Locomotive Co., 1913-16; mem. stockholders' com. Sealshipt Oyster System, 1913; chmn. stockholders' com. Am. Hide & Leather Co., 1915-17. Active leader Municipal League, Philadelphia, Pa., 1899-1901; served as Sec. Am. Defense League, 1914-15. Fellow A.A.A.S.; mem. Am. Civil Liberties Union, Authors' League of America. Author: Stock Prices, 1911; The Need of Currency Reform, 1911 (brochure distributed by Nat. Citizens' League for the Promotion of Sound Banking System); Readjustments and Reorganizations, 1926; Stock Movements and Speculation, 1928; Success in Security Operations, 1931; The Third Way, 1945. Winsted CT‡

BOND, HORACE MANN, ednl. adminstr.; b. Nashville, Nov. 8, 1904; s. Dr. James and Jane (Browne) B.; A.B., Lincoln U., Pa., 1923, LL.D., 1941; A.M., U. Chgo., 1926, Ph.D., 1936; LL.D., Temple U., 1952, Grinnell Coll., 1970; m. Julia Agnes Washington, Oct. 11, 1930; children—Jane Marguerite (Mrs. Moore), Horace Julian, James George. Head dept. of edn., Langston U., Okla., 1924-27; dir. of extension, Ala. State Coll., 1927-28; instr. dept. Social Sci. Fisk U., Nashville, 1928-29, asst. prof., 1932-34, head and prof., dept. of edn., 1937-39; dean Dillard U., New Orleans, 1934-37; research asst. Julius Rosenwald Fund, 1934-37; pres. Fort Valley State Coll., Ga., 1939-45; pres. Lincoln U., 1945-57, pres. hon., 1957-72; dean Sch. Edn., Atlanta U., 1957-66, dir. bureau of ednl. and social research, 1966-72; summer lectr. Tuskegee Inst., Ala., 1929, Garrett Biblical Inst., Evanston, Ill., 1943. Mem. Joint Army and Navy Com.; staff mem. UNESCO seminar, Ashbridge, Eng., summer 1948; ednl. survey West Africa, 1949, 60-61. Chmn. bd. Am. Soc. African Culture; mem. bd. dirs. Southeastern Ednl. Corp. Recipient Ednl. Research Assn. Am. award for book, Education in Alabama; A Study in Cotton and Steel, 1940; Susan Colver Rosenberger prize for outstanding thesis in social science, U. of Chicago, 1936. Author: The Education of the Negro in the American Social Order, 1934; Education in Alabama, A Study in Cotton and Steel, 1936; The Search for Talent. Contbr. profl. jours. Home: Atlanta GA Died Dec. 1972.

BOND, JAMES LESLIE, educator; b. nr. Haynesville, La., July 16, 1877; s. James Joseph and Mary Caroline B.; A.B., Hendrix Coll., Conway, Ark., 1900; m. Fearn Clark, of Milan, Tenn., Sept. 29, 1903. Prin. or supt. schs. for a number of yrs.; deputy state supt. pub. instrn., Ark., 1908-12; state supervisor of rural schs., Ark., 1912—. Mem. M.E. Ch., S. Mem. Ark. State Teachers' Assn. (sec., 1911—). Home: 1721 West 22d St. Office: State Capitol, Little Rock AR‡

BOND, WILLARD FAROE, state relief adminstr.; b. Harrison County, Miss., Feb. 22, 1876; B.A., Peabody Coll. for Teachers, Nashville, Tenn., 1902; m. Susie Graham, June 25, 1905. Began as teacher in common schs., 1893; prin. high schs. at Purvis, Miss., and Wiggins, Miss., until 1912; prof. history and Latin, Miss. Normal Coll., 1912-16; state supt. edn., Miss., 1916-36; now adminstr. State Welfare Program. Mem. Nat. Council of State Supts. of Edn. (pres. 1932-33). Democrat. Baptist. Home: Jackson MS‡

BONDS, ARCHIBALD, U.S. attorney; b. Pond Spring, Ga., Jan. 29, 1876; s. John F. and Elizabeth T. (Hall) B.; Emory Coll., Oxford, 1897-98; U. of Ga., 1898-99; m. Ora M. Camp, of Chickamauga, Dec. 11, 1900; children—Charlotte Elizabeth McClendon, Archibald Camp. Moved to Ind. Ty., 1900; mayor of Chelsea, 1904-05; county judge, Rogers Co., Okla., 1907-11; mem. Okla. Ho. of Rep., 1913-14; spl. asst. U.S. atty., Eastern Dist. of Okla., 1914-17; U.S. atty. same dist., Dec. 1919—. Mem. Sigma Nu. Democrat. Mem. M.E. Ch., S. Home: 520 N. 14th St. Office: Manhattan Bldg., Muskogee OK‡

BONDURANT, EUGENE DUBOSE, physician; b. near Greensboro, Ala., Jan. 26, 1862; s. James William and Evelyn (DuBose) B.; student Avery Sch. and Southern U., Greensboro; M.D., U. of Va., 1883; grad. study Heidelberg and Vienna, 1890-91, Edinburgh and London, 1911; m. Annie Laurie Prince, Apr. 19, 1899. Asst. physician, Manhattan Hosp., N.Y. City, 1884-85; asst. phys., Bryce Hosp., Tucaloosa, Ala., 1886-90, asst. supt., 1892-97; prof. nervous and mental diseases, U. of Ala. Sch. of Medicine, 1897-1915, dean, 1911-15; one of condrs. of Inge-Bondurant Sanatorium, Mobile, Ala. Served as maj., later lt. col., Med. Corps., U.S. Army, comdg. officer Gen. Hosp., Dansville, N.Y., 1917-19; col. Med. Res. Corps, U.S. Army, since 1925. Trustee Ala. Insane Hosp. 20 yrs. Fellow A.A.A.S.; mem. A.M.A., Am. Psychiatric Assn., Am. Neurol. Assn., Med. Assn. State of Ala., Kappa Alpha (Southern). Democrat. Episcopalian. Clubs: Athelstan, Mobile Country, Alba Hunting and Fishing. Assn. editor and contbr. to Sajous' Analytic Cyclopedia of Practical Medicine; also contbr. to medical journals. Home: 1600 Government St., Mobile AL‡

BONE, ALFRED RUFUS, JR., airline exec.; b. Chicago, Jan. 25, 1907; s. Alfred R. and Estelle Kennedy (Aldrich) B.; A.B., Bethany (W.Va.) Coll., 1928; m. Lois Mitchell, Jan. 20, 1933. With Am. Airlines and predecessor cos., 1928-72, asst. to v.p., sales, 1937-39, western sales mgr., 1940-44, regional v.p., Los Angeles, 1944-72. Mem. Beta Theta Pi. Clubs: California, Annandale Golf, Bohemian (San Francisco). Home: Pasadena CA Died 1972.

BONE, HOMER TRUETT, U.S. senator, judge; b. Franklin, Ind., Jan. 25, 1883; s. James Milton and Margaret Jane Demaree B.; m. Blanche Sly, Jan. 25, 1919. Admitted to bar, 1911; elected to Washington State Legislature, 1923; elected U.S. senator for term 1933-39; re-elected Nov. 8, 1938, for term ending 1945; resigned as senator, Nov. 1944; to become judge of U.S. Court of Appeals for the Ninth Circuit with hdqrs. at San Francisco, 1944-54. Honorary mem. Order of the Coif, Gamma Eta Gamma. Address: San Francisco CA Died Mar. 1970.

BONELL, BENJAMIN WALTER, clergyman, educator; b. Eau Claire, Wis., May 6, 1867; s. James and Hannah M. (Loftus-Stocks) B.; grad. Falls River Normal Sch., Beloit Acad.; student Beloit Coll.; B.D., Nashotah House, 1895, D.D., 1922; M.A., Matthews Hall, Denver, Colo.; grad. Colo. State Teachers Coll., 1911; Ph.D., St. John's, 1936; m. Agnes Battelle Bailey, June 7, 1898 (now dec.); children—Hannah Elisabeth, Agnes Battelle, Benjamin Walter (dec.). Deacon and priest, P.E. Ch., 1895; rector St. Andrew's Ch., Manitou, Colo., 1899-1909, Trinity Ch., Greeley, 1909-23; founder, 1913, since pres. St. John's Coll.; chaplain American Ch., Tokyo, Japan, 1929-30. Del. to Gen. Conv. 4 times; exam. chaplain Diocese of Colo.; hon. canon St. John's Cathedral, Denver. Founder Manitou Library, 1906, Bonell Home for Aged, Greeley, Colo., 1937. Red Cross worker, World War. Mem. Phi Alpha Theta. Republican. Mason, Lion. Author: (pageants) Christmas Eve, 1920; Feast of Lights, 1920; Pastice, 1930; A Maori Fairytale, 1935; A Short Story of the Church, 1937; The Tombs of Kosai. Traveled in Asia, 1930, South America, 1933, Windsor CO‡

BONFILS, HELEN G., newspaper exec.; b. Peekskill, N.Y., Nov. 26, 1889; d. Frederick and Belle Bonfils; ed. pvt. sch., Forest Glen, Md.; m. George Somnes, 1936 (dec. 1956); m. 2d, Edward Michael Davis (div. 1971). With Denver Post, 1933-72, chmn. bd., until 1972. Active numerous civic orgns.; founder Bonfils Theatre, Bonfils Tumor Clinic, Belle Bonfils Blood Bank (all Denver). Address: Denver CO Died June 6, 1972.*

BONHAM, KENNETH ARLINGTON, business exec.; b. Des Moines, Ia., Mar. 17, 1903; s. John Rhule and Rilla May (Jolly) B.; student Ia. State, 1923-24, Drake Univ., Des Moines, Ia., 1924-25; m. Hazel Olive Booth, Nov. 25, 1926; children—Bonnie Dean, Barbara Lee. Salesman F. W. Fitch Co., Des Moines, Ia., 1925-28; merchandising mgr., Dispatch Pub. Co., Columbus, O., 1928-33; sec. treas., Druggists Supply Corp., New York, N.Y., 1933-37; exec. editor Am. Druggist, Hearts Mags. Inc., New York, N.Y., 1937-38, editor, 1938-41, bus. mgr. and co-pub., 1941-43; exec. vice pres. The Emerson Drug Co., Balt., 1943-45, pres., chmn. exec. com., 1945-51; pres., chmn. bd., dir. Alkalithia Co., 1944-51; dir., chmn. bd. Bromo-Seltzer, Ltd., Toronto, 1945-51; asst. to pres. Am. Home Products Corp., N.Y.C. 1951-57, exec. v.p., 1960-72; pres. Whitehall Labs. div. Am. Home Products Corp., New York City NY Died 1972.

BONNER, CAMPBELL, univ. prof.; b. Nashville, Tenn., Jan. 30, 1876; s. Jesse Willis and Frances (Campbell) B.; A.B., Vanderbilt, 1896, A.M., 1897; A.M., Harvard, 1898, Ph.D., 1900; U. of Berlin, winter, 1900-01; traveled and studied in Greece and Italy, 1901; m. Ethel Howell, Sept. 29, 1903; children—Frances Campbell (Mrs. J. B. Titchener), Sue Grundy (Mrs. C. C. Walcutt). Prof. Greek, Peabody Coll. for Teachers, U. of Nashville, 1901-07; jr. prof. Greek, U. of Mich., 1907-12, prof. Greek lang. and lit., 1912-46; now emeritus. Mem. Am. Philol. Assn. (pres. 1933), Classical Assn. Middle West and South (pres., 1918-19), Archaeol. Inst. Am., Mich. Acad. Sci., Arts and Letters (pres., 1923-24); fellow Am. Acad. of Arts and Sciences; corr. fellow British Acad.; mem. Am. Philos. Soc.; mem. managing com. Am. Sch. Classical Studies at Athens, annual prof., 1927-28. Mem. Phi Beta Kappa. Author: A Papyrus Codex of the Shepherd of Hermas, 1933; The Last Chapters of Enoch in Greek, 1937; The Homily on the Passion by Melito, Bishop of Sardis, 1940; Studies in Magical Amulets, 1949. Contributor on classical philology, papyrology and history of religions. Home: 1025 Martin Place, Ann Arbor MI‡

BONNER, JOHN WOODROW, gov. Mont.; b. Butte, Mont., July 16, 1902; s. Patrick and Kathleen (Kelly) B.; A.B., LL.B., U. Mont., 1928; m. Josephine Martin, Feb. 3, 1929; children—Jacqueline, Josephine, Patricia, Wilma Jean, Thomas John. Teacher athletic dir. Mont. pub. schs., 1921-23; admitted to Mont. bar, 1928, practicing in Butte, 1928-29; atty. State Highway Commn., 1929-36; atty. and sec. State Bd. Railroad

Commn., Pub. Service Commn.; Mont. Trade Commn., 1936-40; elected atty. gen. of Mont., Jan. 5, 1941; elected gov. Mont. 1949-53; asso. justice Mont. Supreme Ct., 1968-70. Commd. major, Judge Advocate General's Dept. U.S. Army Reserve; lt. colonel; assigned as Staff Judge Advocate 104th Inf. Div.; maj. J.A.G.D. Res., May, 1942; served as exec. officer, asst. staff judge adv., acting staff judge dv. 1st U.S. Army. Apptd. chief of War Crimes 1st Army, Apr. 1945; discharged with rank of col., Dec. 10, 1945. Former mem. Bd. of Edn., Mont.; former sec.-treas. State Democratic Central Com.; former chmn. Lewis and Clark County Democratic Central Com.; past pres. Mont. Law Sch. Alumni Assn., State Reserve Officers Assn., Lewis and Clark County Chapter Reserve Officers Assn. Past State Comdr. Vets. Fgn. Wars of U.S. (1947-48). Mem. Lewis and Clark Bar Assn., Mont. Bar Assn. (past pres.), Phi Delta Phi, Sigma Phi, Epsilon; former ex-officio mem. Am. Law Inst. Democrat. Roman Catholic. Elk, Eagle. Author: Handbook on Eminent Domain, 1933. Home: Helena MT Died Mar. 28, 1970; buried Arlington Nat. Cemetery, Arlington VA

BONNER, PAUL HYDE, author; b. Bklyn., Feb. 14, 1893; s. Paul Edward and Theodora Wilson (Hall) B.; student Adelphi Acad., Bklyn., Poly. Prep. Sch., Bklyn., Phillips Exeter Acad.; student Harvard, 1915; m. Lilly M. Stehli, Apr. 30, 1917 (dec. Jan. 1962);children—Paul Hyde, John Tyler, Henry Stehli, Anthony Edmonde; m. 2d, Elizabeth McGowan, Jan. 10, 1963. Vice pres., gen. mgr., dir. Stehli & Co., Inc., textile mchts., 1919-31; central field commr. Office Fgn. Liquidation, State Dept., 1946; spl. adviser U.S. ambassador to Rome on economics of peace treaty, 1947-51. Served as 2d lt. U.S. Army, 1917-19; from maj. to col., USAAF, 1941-46. Episcopalian. Clubs: Union, The Brook (N.Y.C.); The Travellers (Paris); Rotary (Sommerville, S.C.). Author: S.P.Q.R., 1954; Hotel Talleyrand; Excelsior; The Glorious Morning; With Both Eyes Open; Aged in the Woods; Amanda; The Art of Llewellyn Jones, 1959; Ambassador Extraordinary, 1962. Home: Charleston SC Died Dec. 15, 1968.

BONNEY, WILBERT LOWTH, consular service; b. Fairmont, Minn., May 20, 1872; s. Henry H. and Marcella (Lowth) B.; Ph.B., Hamline U., 1893; U. of Leipzig, 1895-96; studied law 2 yrs.; m. Vena Dunlap, of Minneapolis, Minn., Nov. 28, 1894. In employ of Security Bank, Minneapolis, Minn., 1890-95; with packing house, Chicago, 1897-98; in real estate business, Chicago, 3 yrs.; clk. office of Corps of Engrs., U.S.A., Chicago, 1899-1910; consul at San Luis Potosi, Mexico, 1910-16; duty Dept. of State, Washington, 1916-17; consul at Rosario, Argentina, 1917-24, at Edinburgh, Scotland, 1924-27, Georgetown, British Guiana, since July 1927. Club: University (Washington). Home: Santa Ana, Calif. Address: American Consulate, Georgetown British Guiana‡

BONTEMPS, ARNA WENDELL, author; b. Alexandria, La., Oct. 13, 1902; s. Paul Bismarck and Marie Carolina (Pembroke) B.; prep. edn., San Fernando (Cal.) Acad., 1917-20; A.B., Pacific Union Coll., 1923; A.M., U. Chgo., 1943; L.H.D., Morgan State Coll., 1969; m. Alberta Johnson, Aug. 26, 1926; children—Joan Marie, Paul Bismark, Poppy Alberta, Camille Ruby, Constance Rebecca, Arna Alex. Tchr. pvt. schs., 1923-38; librarian Fisk U., Nashville, Tenn., 1943-65; prof. U. Ill., Chgo. Circle, 1966-69; lectr., curator Yale, 1969-73. Julius Rosenwald fellow, 1938-39, 42-43. Awarded Crisis poetry prize, 1926; Alexander Pushkin poetry prize, 1926,27; Opportunity (jour. of Negro Life) short story prize, 1932; Jane Addams Children's Book Award, 1956. Mem. P.E.N., Authors League, Dramatists Guild, Sigma Pi Phi, Omega Psi Phi, Phi Mu Alpha. Editor: Golden Slippers, An Anthology, 1941; Father of the Blues (by W. C. Handy), 1941. Author numerous books latest publs.: Black Thunder, 1936, reissued 1968; Story of the Negro, 1948; The Poetry of the Negro (anthology, co-editor with L. Hughes), 1949; Chariot in The Sky, 1951; Story of George Washington Carver, 1954; Lonesome Boy, 1955; The Book of Negro Folklore (anthology, co-editor with L. Hughes), 1958; Frederick Douglass: Slave- Fighter-Freeman, 1959; One Hundred Years of Negro Freedom, 1961; American Negro Poetry, 1963; Personals, 1964; Famous Negro Athletes, 1964; (with J. Conroy) Anyplace But Here, 1966 (Dow award Soc. Midland Authors 1967); Hold Fast to Dreams, 1969; Great Slave Narratives, 1969; Free at Last: the Life of Frederick Douglass, 1971; Young Booker. Co-author with Countee Cullen: (play) St. Louis Woman, 1946. Editor: American Negro Poetry, 1963. Home: Nashville TN Died June 4, 1973.

BOODELL, THOMAS J., lawyer; b. Harvard, Ill., June 15, 1906; s. John H. and Annette Cullen) B.; LL.B., U. Ill., 1929; m. Mary Elizabeth Houze, Oct. 4, 1933; children—Thomas J., Mary H. (Mrs. R. Donald Prescott, Jr.), William C., Leslie Jane (Mrs. Charles D. Floro). Admitted to Ill. bar, 1929, pvt. practice law, 1929-72; sr. partner firm Boodell, Sears, Sugrue & Crowley, and predecessor firms, 1949-72; sec., dir. various corps. Bd. dirs. Am. Bar Endowment, 1969-72. Fellow Am. Bar Found. (chmn. 1964-65); mem. Am. (chmn. standing com. on regional meetings 1959, 61, 62, chmn. com. to cooperate with A.M.A. 1964, 65, assembly del. 1960-69, standing com. profl. ethics 1968-72, chmn. scope and correlation of work com. 1969-72), Ill., Chgo. (bd. mgrs. 1951-53, 63-67, pres. 1965-66) bar assns., Nat. Conf. Lawyers and Bankers (chmn. conf. 1958-72), Am. Judicature Soc., Law Club Chgo., Chi Psi (trustee ednl. trust), Phi Delta Phi. Clubs: University, Mid-Day, Saddle and Cycle (Chgo.); Skokie Country (Glencoe, Ill.); Seven Lakes Country (Palm Springs, Cal.). Home: Chicago IL Died 1972.

BOOG, CARLE MICHEL, painter and illustrator; b. Sursee, Lucerne, Switzerland, June 27, 1877; s. Michel Johann and Anna (Glanzmann) B.; came to U.S., 1881, naturalized, 1894; studied Art Students League, New York, 1896-1902, also student Ecole de Beaux Arts, Paris, and pupil of Leon Bonnat, 1902-05; unmarried. First exhibited in the Salon des Artists Francaise, Paris, 1904, and since rep. in exhibitions at the Nat. Acad. of Design, Phila., Pa. Acad. Fine Arts, Corcoran Gallery, Washington, D.C., N.Y. Watercolor Soc., N.Y. Watercolor Club, Brooklyn Mus. Permanently represented in Museum of City of New York, Hist. Museum, Bennington, Vt., and Fine Arts Dept., U. of Neb. Mem. faculty of Newark (N.J.) Pub. Sch. of Fine and Indsl. Art. Democrat. Club: Salmagundi (New York). Illustrator of numerous books, child histories, etc. Studio: 206 Parkville Av., Brooklyn 30 NY‡

BOONE, ARTHUR UPSHAW, clergyman; b. Elkton, Ky., Sept. 7, 1860; s. Higgason Grubbs and Martha Maria (Edwards) B.; ed. pub. schs. and Southern Bapt. Theol. Sem., Louisville, Ky.; D.D., Union U., Jackson, Tenn., 1900; m. Eddie B. Cooke, Apr. 30, 1891; children—William Cooke, Martha Maria (Mrs. Frank Hartwell Leavell); m. 2d, Ida McIntosh, June 9, 1927. Ordained Bapt. ministry, 1887; pastor, Elkton, Leitchfield and Smith's Grove, Ky., 1887-91, Clarksville, Tenn., 1891-98, 1st Ch., Memphis, Tenn., 1898-1930; interim pastor First Bapt. Ch., Tulsa and Shawnee, Okla., and Nashville, Tenn., Shelbyville, Tenn., Montgomery, Ala., Tampa, Fla., 1931; pastor Baptist Memorial Hospital since January 1937. President Tenn. Baptist Convention, 1903-09; trustee Southern Bapt. Theol. Sem.; dir. Bapt. Memorial Hosp., Memphis; Trustee Union U., Tenn., 1900-10. Home: 41 N. Bellevue, Memphis TN‡

BOONE, HENRY BURNHAM, author; b. Fall River, Mass., May 8, 1872; s. John H. and Charlotte M. M. (Wrightington) B.; A.B., Williams Coll., 1893; U. of Va. Law Sch., 1895; m. Francesca Brown, of Charlottesville, Va., Sept. 25, 1896. Has practiced law, but since 1899 devoted entirely to lit. work. Author: Eastover Court House (with Kenneth Brown, q.v.), 1901; Redfields Succession (with same), 1903; The Career Triumphant, 1902. Address: West Cairns," Charlottesville VA‡

BOORD, CECIL ERNEST, research dir.; b. Veedersburg, Ind., June 29, 1884; s. Rev. John Summerbell and Rose Ann (Campbell) B.; grad. high sch., Veedersburg, 1904; B.A., Wabash Coll., 1907; M.A., Ohio State U., 1909, Ph.D., 1912; m. Augusta Corinne Brown, Aug. 20, 1913; 1dau., Mary Elizabeth (Mrs. Kenneth W. Greenlee). With Ohio State U. since 1907; successively fellow in chemistry till 1909, asst. in chemistry, 1909-12, instr., 1912-13, asst. prof., 1914-24, prof., 1924-51, research prof. of chemistry, 1951-54, emeritus, 1954, still in active service as dir. Air Research and Development Command project on oxidation of hydrocarbons. Mem. Nat. Research Council, 1924-26; mem., contbr. 3d World Petroleum Congress, The Hague, 1951. Dir. program of pure hydrocarbon research under the sponsorship Am. Petroleum Inst. and Ohio State U. Research Found. since 1938. Served as civilian dir. Ohio State U. Field Station, research div., Gas War Service, 1917-19. Recipient Joseph Sullivant Medal, Ohio State U., 1950-56. Dir. Ohio State U. Research Found., 1955-58. Fellow A.A.A.S., O. Acad. Sci.; mem. Am. Chem. Soc., Am. Petroleum Inst. (awarded Scroll 1954), N.Y. Acad. Sci., Am. Assn. Univ. Profs., Sigma Xi, Phi Lambda Epsilon, Gamma Alpha, Alpha Chi Sigma, Phi Beta Kappa. Republican. Presbyterian. Clubs: Faculty, Torch. Author: (with Wallace R. Brode and Roy G. Bossert) of Lab. Outlines for Organic Chemistry. Coinventor (with others) Chemistry of Petroleum Hydrocarbons, 1954; Knocking Characteristics of Pure Hydrocarbons, Mechanism of the Oxidation of Hydrocarbons, 1958. Coinventor (with Wallace R. Brode and Charles D. Hurd) of Molecular Models. Contbr. to chem. jours. and of chapters in Annual Survey of American Chemistry, Vols. VII, 1932; VIII, 1933, and in The Science of Petroleum, 1938. Home: Columbus OH Died Nov. 3, 1969; buried Union Cemetery, Columbus OH

BOOTH, BRADFORD ALLEN, educator; b. Pitts., Apr. 9, 1909; s. Bradford Allen and Margaret (Youngson) B.; B.S., Allegheny Coll., 1930, Doctor of Letters, 1960; Master of Arts, Harvard University, 1932, Ph.D., 1935; married Josephine Conduitte, June 10, 1939; children—Barbara Allen, Celia Belle, Carol Lee. Instr. U. Tenn., 1935-36; instr. U. Cal., Los Angeles, 1936-40, asst. prof., 1940-48, asso. prof., 1948-54, professor, 1954-68, chairman department of English, 1965-68; founder and editor Nineteenth-Century Fiction, 1945-68; vis. prof. U. Minn., 1952. Com. on lit. selection Huntington Hartford Found., 1953-68. Grantee Am. Council Learned Societies, 1944, Am. Philos. Soc., 1947; recipient Guggenheim fellowship, 1960-61. Faculty athletic rep. Pacific Coast Conference, 1956-59; faculty athletic rep. Athletic Assn. Western Univs., 1959-68, president, 1962-63; v.p., mem. council Nat. Collegiate Athletic Assn., 1965-68. Mem. Modern Lang. Assn. (editorial cons. publs.), Nat. Council Tchrs. English, Coll. English Assn., Phi Kappa Psi. Author: A Cabinet of Gems, 1938; Galt's Gathering of the West, 1939; The Tireless Traveler, 1941; Trollope's Autobiography, 1947; Letters of Anthony Trollope, 1951; Trollope's North America, 1951; Anthony Trollope: Aspects of His Life and Art, 1958; also articles scholarly jours. Home: Los Angeles CA Died Dec. 1, 1968.

BOOTH, CHARLES ARTHUR, mfr.; b. Southbridge, Mass., Dec. 31, 1876; s. William and Catherine Wood (Dole) B.; grad. Worcester (Mass.) Acad., 1894, Worcester Poly. Inst., 1898; m. Mabel Louise Morse, of Southbridge, Sept. 12, 1902 (died May 4, 1907); children—Theodore Harrington, William Wood; m. 2d, Gertrude Pratt Thompson, of Milford, Mass., Nov. 11, 1911. Instr. in physics, Williston Acad., Easthampton, Mass., 1898-1900; jr. engr., Buffalo (N.Y.) Forge Co., 1900, sales engr., 1901-02, asst. sales mgr., 1903-07, sales mgr., 1907-29, vice pres. since 1922. Mem. Am. Soc. M.E., Am. Soc. Heating and Ventilating Engrs., Engring. Soc. Buffalo. Republican. Presbyn. Clubs: Rotary, Buffalo, Buffalo Athletic, Buffalo Canoe. Home: 142 Summit Av. Office: 490 Broadway, Buffalo NY‡

BOOTH, CLARENCE MOORE, ry. official; b. Marietta, O., Dec. 14, 1876; s. Henry J. and Eliza G. B.; grad. high sch., Toledo, O., 1894; m. Mrs. Jannette Davis Wilson of Detroit, Mich., June 15, 1923; stepson, Edward Wilson. Began as clk., Flint & Pere Marquette R.R. (later P.M. R.R.), 1894, and continued as traveling freight agt., 1896-99, commercial agt., at Toledo, 1899-1903; gen. eastern freight agt. same rd. and C., H. & D. Ry., at New York, 1903-06; asst. gen. freight agt., P.M.R.R., at Chicago, 1906-09; gen. freight agt., same rd., at Detroit, 1909-20, freight traffic mgr., 1920-29, traffic mgr. since 1929. Republican. Protestant. Clubs: Transportation, Detroit Athletic, Detroit Golf. Home: 1941 Wellesly Drive. Office: General Motors Bldg., Detroit MI‡

BOOTH, EDWIN PRINCE, clergyman, educator; b. Pittsburgh, Pa., Apr. 26, 1898; s. Harry John and Ella Montgomery (Youngson) B.; A.B., Allegheny Coll., 1919, D.D., 1939; S.T.B., Boston U., 1922, Ph.D., 1929; student Berlin (Germany) U., 1925-26; Litt.D., Lincoln Memorial University; S.T.D., Oklahoma City U., 1964; L.H.D., Simpson Coll.; married Elizabeth Fehr, June 15, 1922; children—Edwin Bray (killed in action, Germany, Mar. 24, 1945), Harry Fehr, Francis. Ordained to ministry M.E. Ch., 1922; pastor The Community Church, Islington, Mass. since 1922; instructor in church history, Boston U., 1924, prof., 1925-63, emeritus, 1963-69; prof. history Curry Coll., Milton, Mass., 1963-69. Lectr.; appeared on TV programs Dateline Boston, We Believe. Served as 2d lieut., U.S. Inf., 1918, World War I. Mem. Am. Soc. Church History, American Assn. of Biblical Instrs., Am. Academy of Arts and Sciences, Soc. Bibl. Lit. and Exegesis, Inst. Religion in Age of Sci. (1st pres.), Friends of Albert Schweitzer (recipient Albert Schweitzer medal), Friends Boston Symphony Orch. Sigma Alpha Epsilon. Methodist. Clubs: Authors, Lincoln (Boston); Editor: New Testament Studies, 1942; Religion Ponders Science, 1964; editorial bd. Lygon. Author: An Eighteenth Century Newspaper, 1931; Martin Luther—Oak of Saxony, 1938; Letters to Live By, 1948; (article) Let Them Rest in Peace; From Experience to Faith, 1951; The Greater Church, 1951; One Sovereign Life, 1965. Home: Islington MA Died Dec. 26, 1969; buried Margraten Military Cemetery, Holland

BOOTH, FRANKLIN, illustrator; b. Indiana, 1874; s. John and Susan Emily (Wright) B.; ed. Quaker Acad., Westfield, Ind.; student Art Inst. Chicago, 1900; m. Beatrice Wittmack, 1923. Began writing and drawing for Indianapolis News, 1899; with Munsey's publs., New York, 1904-05; traveled in Europe, spending most of time in Spain, painting, 1906; settled in New York, 1907; has made many illustrations for Scribner's, Harper's, Collier's, Ladies' Home Journal, etc. Mem. Soc. Illustrators, Guild of Free Lance Artists. Socialist. Christian Scientist. Home: 58 W. 57th St., New York NY*‡

BOOTH, ISAAC WALTER, ry. official; b. Phila., Pa., Apr. 1, 1883; s. Isaac Johnson and Helen Alois (Cullen) B.; graduate Chester (Pa.) Comml. Coll., 1900-01, U. of Pa. Evening Sch., 1911-14; m. Myrtle T. Crossan, June 7, 1916; children—John Filbert (dec.), Robert Emrey. With Norfolk and Western Ry. at Phila., 1902-58, successively as stenographer and clerk, 1902-09, chief clerk, 1909-14, asst. sec. and cashier, 1914-20, sec. and asst. treas., 1920-36, v.p. and sec. 1936-38, v.p., 1939-58; dir. Norfolk and Western Ry. Co. and subsidiaries, Phila. Nat. Bank, Mutual Fire, Marine and Inland Ins. Co., Guarantee Co. of N. America (Phila.

branch), Phila. Beneficial Saving Fund Soc.; dir. Pocahontas Land Corp., Virginia Holding Corp. Former v.p., pres., mem. exec. com. Ry. Treasurers Assn. Mem. Pi Delta Epsilon, Newcomen Society. Republican. Episcopalian. Mason. Clubs: Union League. Old York Road Country (Jenkintown, Pa.); Pine Valley Golf; Roanoke (Va.) Country. Home: Jenkintown PA Died Nov. 16, 1970; buried Lawnview Cemetery, Rockledge, Philadelphia PA

BOOTH, NEWELL SNOW, bishop; b. Belchertown, Mass., June 14, 1903; s. Charles Edwin and Elisabeth Mary (Snow) B.; A.B., Boston U., 1924, S.T.B., 1927, S.T.M., 1930, D.D. (hon.), 1956; Ph.D., Hartford Sem. Found., 1936; S.T.D. (hon.), Dickinson Coll., 1964; m. Esma Rideout, Dec. 28, 1925; children—Newell Snow, Esma-Marie. Ordained to ministry Methodist Ch., 1926; pastor in Bryantville, W. Duxbury, New Bedford and Freetown, Mass., 1926-30; missionary to Congo, 1930-43, 44-64; head Africa dept. Hartford Sem. Found., 1943-44; bishop assigned to Africa, 1944-64. Harrisburg, Pa. area, 1964-68. Trustee Lycoming College; trustee Dickinson Coll., bd dirs. Wesley Theol. Sem. Mem. Nat. Geog. Soc., Nat. Council Churches of Christ in U.S.A., Internat. African Inst., Meth. World Council, Phi Beta Kappa, Beta Chi Sigma. Author: Serving God in the Sunday School, 1934; The Cross Over Africa, 1944; Africa South of the Sahara, 1958; also numerous articles. Home: Harrisburg PA Died May 17, 1968; buried Belchertown MA

BOOTH, ROBERT HIGHMAN, army officer; b. Washington, Feb. 20, 1905; B.S., U.S. Mil. Acad., 1930; m. Constance May Ralston; children—Constance R., Barbara L., Robert Highman. Commd. lt. U.S. Army, 1930, and advanced through grades to maj. gen., 1956; chief Def. Atomic Support Agy., Washington. Home: Ft George G Meade MD Died 1972.

BOOTHE, GARDNER LLOYD, banker; b. Alexandria, Va., June 1, 1872; s. William J. and Mary (Leadbeator) B.; grad. Potomac Acad., Alexandria, 1889; B.L., U. of Va., 1893; m. Eleanor Harrison Carr, Feb. 7, 1906; children—Armistead Lloyd, Gardner Lloyd. Admitted to Va. bar, 1893, and since in practice at Alexandria; now as div. counsel So. Ry. Co.; dist. counsel Richmond, Fredericksburg & Potomac R.R. Co.; gen. counsel A.B. & W. Rapid Transit Co.; pres. First Nat. Bank of Alexandria; City atty., Alexandria, 1895-1901. Trustee Protestant Episcopal Theol. Sem. of Va., Episcopal High Sch. of Va. Mem. advisory com. Mt. Vernon Ladies Assn. of the Union. Mem. Alpha Tau Omega, Raven Soc. Episcopalian. Democrat (mem. state central com.; chmn. 8th Congressional Dist. com.). Club: University (Washington). Home: 711 Princess St. Office: 108 N St. Asaph St., Alexandria VA‡

BOOTHROYD, SAMUEL LATIMER, astronomer; b. Loveland, Colo., Aug. 10, 1874; s. Philip Henry and Edith Margaret (Latimer) B.; B.S., Colo., A.&M. Coll., 1893, M.Sc., 1904; U. of Colo., 1 semester, 1893-94, U. of Chicago, 1894-95, Cornell U., 1904-08; m. Alice Bell, Jan. 12, 1898; children—Philip Douglass, Robert Samuel, Lucy Elizabeth, Mary Alice. Prof. mathematics and astronomy, Mt. Morris (Ill.) Coll., 1895-97; asst. astronomer, Lowell Obs., Flagstaff, Ariz., 1897-99; asso. prof. physics, engring., Colo. A.&M. Coll., Ft. Collins, 1902-04; instr. civil engring., Cornell U., 1904-08, asst. prof. topographic and geodetic engring., 1908-12; asso. prof. mathematics and astronomy, U. of Wash., 1912-17, asso. prof. astronomy, 1917-21; prof. astronomy and geodesy, Cornell U., 1921-42, prof. emeritus, June 30, 1942; teacher navigation, Naval Training Sta., Cornell U., Nov. 1942-Sept. 1945. In charge field work, Ariz. Meteor. Expdn., Harvard, Cornell, Lowell Obs., Flagstaff, 1931-32. Asst. surveyor Alaskan Boundary Commn., summers 1905-09; teacher of navigation, Naval Training Sta., U. of Wash., during World War I. Fellow A.A.A.S.; The Meteoritical Society; life member of Astronomical Soc. Pacific, Am. Astronomical Soc., Am. Assn. Variable Star Observers, Sigma Xi, Phi Kappa Phi. Conglist. Co-author: Manual of Astronomy. Contributor to publications of Dominion Astrophys. Obs., Victoria, B.C. Head of expdn. to secure ultra-violet spectra of stars at Mountain Station of Lowell Obs., 1933, using aluminum coated mirrors first made at Cornell U. Selected by Alumni of Colo. A. and M. Coll. as honor alumnus for 1946. Home: Warley Place RD 1, Ithaca NY‡

BORCH, GASTON, composer; b. in Guines, P.d.C., France, Mar. 8, 1871; s. Christopher and Emma Hennequin B.; ed. in schs. in Sweden; studied 3 yrs. under J. Massenet and later under Joh. Svendsen in conducting and score reading. Has led the Amsterdam Symphony Orchestra, Brussels Opera Orchestra, 1868, Societe Symphonique, Lille, France, Crystal Palace Orchestra, London, Harmonie Royale, Antwerp, Gewerbehaus Orchestra, Dresden, and was regular conductor of the Kristiania Philharmonic Soc., and of the Musikforeningen of Bergen, Norway, as well as many others. Engaged with Theodore Thomas Orchestra as cellist, 1899; now at first stand with Pittsburgh Orchestra; conductor of different European orchestras, 1906-7, as guest-conductor; is recognized in Europe as an authority on Wagner and the Russian School; 1st performances in Europe and America of Genevieve de Paris, 1906; conducted the Grieg Jubilee Concert, New York, Apr. 21, 1907. Composer of many songs, cantatas, anthems, etc., of pieces in great number for piano, organ, violin, cello, and orchestra, and of Silvio, a music drama in one act, and of Ostenfor Sol, a fairy opera, both performed in Europe; composed 3d symphony for orchestra; published 18 songs, 1906-7. Address: Care G. Schirmer, 35 Union Sq., NY‡

BORCHARDT, SELMA MUNTER, lawyer, educator; b. Washington, D.C.; d. Newman and Sara (Munter) Borchardt; B.S. in Edn., Syracuse U., 1919, A.B., 1922; LL.B., Washington Coll. of Law, 1933; A.M., Catholic U., 1937. Dir. teacher training, Montgomery County, Md., 1920, supervisor rural schools, 1921; instr. Washington Coll. of Law, 1934-47; admitted to Washington (D.C.) bar, 1934, Supreme Court of U.S., 1944; practiced law in Washington, D.C., from 1934. Exec. sec. Tchrs. Union D.C.; chairman education com. Greater Washington Central Labor Council. Dir. Inst. on World Problems from 1941. Inst. on World Studies from 1946. Mem. U.S. Nat. Commn. on UNESCO, 1945-51; mem. Commrs. Youth Council director Washington Self Help Exchange, 1935-42; member legislative conference, AFL; member of standing committee on education AFL-CIO. mem. Women's Joint Congressional Com.; cons. to Mut. Security Adminstrn., Europe, 1952; del. internat. teachers conf., Copenhagen, 1952. Mem. Am. Fedn. Teachers (v.p. 1924-35 and from 1942; chmn. com. on internat. relations from 1927), World Fedn. Edn. Assns. (dir. 1927-46, v.p. for Americas 1937-46, chmn. sect. on social adjustment through edn., Toronto 1927, Geneva 1929, Denver 1931, Dublin 1933, Oxford 1935, Tokyo 1937, Rio de Janeiro 1939, Havana 1940), Women's Bar Association (mem. board directors). Author (studies for A.F. of L.) Who Selects Our Textbooks, 1926; The Relation of School Attendance Laws and Child Labor Laws, 1930; Labor's Program for the Prevention of Juvenile and Youth Delinquency, 1943; (studies for World Federation Edn. Assns.) The Teaching of International Cooperation in the Secondary Schools of the United States, 1945; The Structure and Work of the International Teacher Organizations 1945; Getting and Keeping Children in School, 1954; A Citizen's Responsibility for the Education of Children and Youth, 1954; Program for Accelerated Training of Earlier School Drop Out, 1960; Balancing the Rights of the Individual and the Rights of Society, 1960. Home: Washington DC Died Jan. 31, 1968.

BORCHERS, CHARLES MARTIN, congressman; b. Lockville, Fairfield Co., O., Nov. 18, 1869; common sch. edn.; taught sch. 7 yrs.; read law in office of Albert G. Webber, Decatur, Ill.; m. Alice Bowman, June 28, 1905. Admitted to Ill. bar, 1897; practiced, Decatur; mayor, Decatur, 1909-11; mem. 63d Congress (1913-15), 19th Ill. Dist.; Democrat. Home: Decatur IL‡

BORDEN, DANIEL LERAY, surgeon; b. Ft. Douglas, Utah, Oct. 25, 1887; s. William Cline and Jennie E. (Adams) B.; M.D., distinction, Geo. Washington U., 1912, B.S., 1916, A.M., 1917; m. Pauline S. Stone, Oct. 20, 1917; children—Wm. Liscum, Charles Stone, Richard LeRay. Asso. in surgery, George Washington U., 1912-14, associate professor surgery, 1914-41; clin. prof. surgery, 1941-53, emeritus 1953; attending surgeon George Washington U. Hosp., Doctors Hosp.; chairman Med. Bd. of Licensure, D.C.; dir. Fed. Storage Co. Col. ret. Med. R.C. Trustee George Washington U. Served in World War I and II. Fellow American Board of Surgery, Am. Coll. Surgeons, Southern Surg. Assn.; mem. Am. Med. Assn., D.C. Medical Soc. (president, 1940), George Washington Med. Soc. (pres. 1929), Washington Surg. Soc., Am. Legion, Delta Tau Delta, Phi Chi, Omicron Delta Kappa, Sigma Xi, etc. Republican. Presbyterian. Mason (32 deg., Shriner). Clubs: Chevy Chase, Metropolitan, (Washington, D.C.), Crescent Yacht (commodore, 1936-38) Chaumont, N.Y. Contbr. on med. subjects. Pioneer in motion picture photography of surgical operative technique. Home: Washington DC Died Dec. 10, 1969; buried Chaumont NY

BORDEN, HOWARD SEYMOUR, merchant; b. N.Y. City, Apr. 27, 1876; s. Matthew Chaloner and Harriet Minerva (Durfee) B.; A.B., Yale, 1898; m. Edith Caroline Curtis of Orange, N.J., Feb. 1, 1900. With Am. Printing Co., Fall River, Mass., since 1898, now v.-p. and treas.; mem. firm M. D. Borden & Sons, dry goods. Dir. Lincoln Nat. Bank. Republican. Conglist. Clubs: University, Merchants, Automobile of America, Rumson Country, New York Yacht. Home: Oceanic, N.J. Office: 90 Worth St., New York NY‡

BORDEN, MARY (MARY BORDEN SPEARS), author; b. Chicago, Ill., 1886; d. William and Mary Borden; ed. Vassar Coll.; m. 2d, Brig. Gen. Edward Louis Spears, of London, Eng., 1918. Equipped and directed Mobile Hosp. in France, 1915-18. Decorated Legion of Honor, French Red Cross. Mem. Ch. of England. Author: The Romantic Woman, 1919; Jane, Our Stranger, 1922; Three Pilgrims and a Tinker, 1924; Jericho Sands, 1925; Four O'clock, 1926; Flamingo, 1927; Jehovah's Day, 1928; The Forbidden Zone, 1929. Home: London Eng Died Dec. 2, 1968.

BORDEN, WILLIAM SILVERS, ins. exec.; b. Groveville, N.J., Feb. 1, 1893; s. Edward and Susan M.M. (Lewis) B.; A.B., Princeton, 1915; m. Lida M. Scheidnagel, Dec. 28, 1920; children—William Silvers, Barbara Louise (Mrs. William F. Floyd), Walter Johnson. Social worker Essex County Children's Aid Soc., 1915-17; examiner N.J. Civil Service Commn., 1919; pres. W.S. Borden Co., ins. and real estate, Trenton, 1920-68. chmn., from 1968; dir. finance Mer-County, 1922-31. Sec. Trenton and Mercer County Meml. Bldg. Commn., 1931-62; chmn. Trenton Central Planning Bd., 1960-68. Pres. Del. Valley United Fund, 1954; adv. bd. Mercer St. Friends Center. Chmn. Mercer County County Rep. Com., 1939-49; mem. N.J. Rep. Com., 1949-53. Trustee, Rutgers U., 1944-58. Served as capt. F.A., U.S. Army, 1917-19. Mem. Trenton Council Human Relations (exec. bd.). Mason. Clubs: Terrace (Princeton, Trenton NJ Died June 16, 1971; buried Groveville M.E. Cemetery.

BORDNER, HARVEY ALBERT, supt. schs.; b. Mt. Aetna, Pa., Apr. 9, 1872; s. Tilon J. and Rebecca (Shreffler) B.; student Pa. State Normal Sch., Kutztown, Pa.; A.B., Ind. U., 1896; post-grad. work same univ.: m. Maude Ethel Martin, of Bloomington, Ind., Jan. 29, 1902. Supt. schs., Philippine Islands, 1902-15, successively at Bayombong, Malolos, San Fernando, Lingayen; supt. Philippine Normal Sch., Manila, 1915-18; supt. city schs., Manila, since 1918. Republican. Mem. Christian (Disciples) Ch. Mason (32 degrees). Club: Rotary (Manila). Home: 5146 Broadway, Indianapolis IN‡

BORGER, HUGH DONALD, former utility exec.; b. Edgewood, Pa., Sept. 22, 1905; s. William Edward and Alice Annetta (McCune) B.; student Duquesne U., U. Pitts.; m. Gladys Ellerton, 1935; 1 dau., Nancy Jean. With Pepples Natural Gas Co., Pitts., 1922-70, chief accountant, 1934, asst. treas. 1934-42, treas., dir., 1942-51, v.p. 1951-54, exec. v.p. 1954-55, pres. 1955-70, ret.; exec. v.p. operations Consol. Natural Gas Co., 1963-64, pres., 1964-66, chmn. chief exec. officer, 1966-70; dir. Pitts. Nat. Bank. Mem. Allegheny Conf. on Community Devel. Bd. dirs. Suburban Gen. Hosp. Mem. Am. Gas Assn. Presbyn. Address: Sewickley PA

BORGERHOFF, ELBERT BENTON OP'TEYNDE, educator; b. Cleve., June 17, 1908; s. Joseph Leopold and Elisabeth (Guerard) B.; B.A., Princeton, 1930, Ph.D., 1934; m. Cornelia Cuyler Newlin, June 14, 1947; children—Jane Cuyler, Elisabeth Guerard, Ledlie Newlin. Faculty Princeton, 1930-68, successively instr. dept. romance langs. and lit., asst. prof., asso. prof., prof., 1952-68, dir. Christian Gauss seminars in criticism, 1952-57, 65-66, Class of 1900 prof. French, 1956-68. Author: Liberal Theory and Practice in the French Theatre, 1680-1757, 1936; The Freedom of French Classicism, 1950, 2d edit., 1968. Contbr. articles periodicals. Home: Princeton NJ Died June 30, 1968; buried Princeton Cemetery, Princeton NJ

BORHEGYI, STEPHAN FRANCIS DE, educator, museum dir.; b. Budapest, Hungary, Oct. 17, 1921; s. Francis E. and Hildegard (Geiger) de Borhegyi; Doctor of Philosophy summa cum laude from the Royal Peter Pazmany U., Budapest, 1946; postdoctoral fellow U. Ariz., 1948-49, Yale, 1951-52; m. Suzanne Catherine Sims, July 5, 1949; children—Ilona-Maria, Stephan E., Carl, Christopher. Came to U.S., 1948, naturalized, 1955. Instr. class. archaeology Peter Pazmany U., 1946-47, asst. prof., asst. curator mus., 1947-48; asso. prof. anthropology San Carlos U., Guatemala, 1949-51; asst. prof. anthropology U. Mo., 1952; asst. prof. anthropology, mus. dir. U. Okla., 1954-59; dir. Milwaukee Pub. Mus., 1959-69; prof. dept. anthropology U. Wis. at Milw., 1959-69. Served as 1st lt. Mounted Arty., Royal Hungarian Army, 1941-44. Recipient diploma of merit for reorgn. Guatemalan Mus. (Rep. of Guatemala), 1951. Fellow Royal Anthrop. Assn. Gt. Britain and Ireland, Am. Anthrop. Assn., Soc. Am. Archaeology, Sociedad de Geographia de Guatemala; mem. Mountain Plains Museums Assn. (past pres.), Am. Assn. Museums (councilor), Central States Anthrop. Soc. (pres.), Midwest Museums Assn. (v.p.), Internat. Council Museums (U.S. del. to com. on ethnography museums, sec. U.S. nat. com. on ethnographical research and museums). Home: Milwaukee WI Died Sept. 27, 1969; cremated.

BORING, EDWIN GARRIGUES, psychologist; b. Phila., Pa., Oct. 23, 1886; s. Edwin McCurdy and Elizabeth Garrigues (Truman) B.; M.E., Cornell, 1908, A.M., 1912, Ph.D., 1914; hon. A.M., Harvard, 1942; Sc.D., University of Pa., 1946; D.Sc., Clark University, 1956; married Lucy May Day, June 18, 1914; children—Edwin Garrigues, Frank Henry, Mollie Day, Barbara (dec. 1950). Asst. psychol., 1911-13, instructor, 1913-18, Cornell; psychological examiner, rank of capt., Camp Upton, N.Y., 1918; in Surgeon General's Office, Washington, 1918-19; prof. exptl. psychology and dir. Psychol. Lab., Clark U., 1919-22; asso. prof. psychology Harvard, 1922-28 prof., 1928-56, Lowell TV lectr., 1956-57, Edgar Pierce professor 1956-57, emeritus, 1957-68. Phi Beta Kappa visiting scholar, 1958-59, director of the psychology laboratory, 1924-49. Hon. pres. XVII Internat. Congress of Psychology, 1963.

Fellow A.A.A.S., Soc. Exptl. Psychologists, Am. Acad. Arts and Scis.; mem. Nat. Acad. Scis., Am. Psychol. Assn. (sec. 1920-22; council 1920-25; pres. 1928), Am. Philos. Soc., Brit. Psychol. Soc. (hon.), Soc. Franc de Psychol. (hon.), Society Espanol. de Psichol. (hon.), Soc. Ital. di Psicol. Scient. (hon.). Author: A History of Experimental Psychology, 1929, 2d edit., 1950; The Physical Dimensions of Consciousness, 1933; Sensation and Perception in the History of Experimental Psychology, 1942; Psychologist at large, 1961; History, Psychology and Science, 1963; (with R.J. Herrnstein) Source Book in the History of Psychology, 1965. Coeditor: Psychology: A Factual Textbook, 1935; Introduction to Psychology, 1939; Psychology for the Fighting Man, 1943; Psychology for the Armed Services, 1945; Foundations of Psychology, 1948. Editor: Contemporary Psychology, 1956-61; asso. editor Basic Books, 1961-68. Contbr. numerous articles to psychol. jours. Home: Cambridge MA Died July 1, 1968.

BORLAND, CHAUNCEY BLAIR, real estate exec.; b. Chgo., Nov. 26, 1878; s. John Jay and Harriet (Blair) B.; grad. Lawrenceville (N.J.) Sch., 1897; A.B., Harvard, 1901, postgrad. Law Sch.; m. Belle McCullough, June 23, 1904; children—Harriet, Beatrice, Martha. With John H. Wrenn & Co., 1902-03, No. Trust Co., Chgo., 1903-04; in charge of Borland properties and bldgs., Chgo., 1904—, also mgr., pres. Borland Mfg. Co.; partner Betts Borland & Co. Mem. Chgo. Crime Commn. Trustee Presbyn.-St. Lukes Hosp. Episcopalian. Clubs: Harvard (Chgo., N.Y., Boston); Chicago, Commercial, University, Chicago Athletic (Chgo.); New York Yacht. Home: Chicago IL Died Oct. 17, 1972; cremated.

BORN, MAX, physicist; b. Breslau, Germany (now Poland), Dec. 11, 1882; s. Gustav and Margaret (Kauffmann) B.; student Breslau, Heidelberg, Zurich univs.; Ph.D., Goettingen U., 1907; D.Sc. (hon.), Bristol U., Eng., 1928; M.A., Cambridge U., Eng., 1933; D.Sc. (hon.), Bordeaux U., 1948, Oxford U., 1954; Dr. rer. nat., Freiburg U., 1957, Berlin U., Frankfurt U.; LL.D., Edinburgh U., 1957; Dr. Ing. (hon.), Stuttgart Tech. U., 1960; D.Sc. (hon.), Oslo U., 1961, Brussels University, 1961; Dr. rer. nat. (honorary), Frankfurt University, 1964; m. Hedwig Ehrenberg, August 2, 1913; children—Irene (Mrs. Newton John), Margaret (Mrs. Pryce), Gustav V.R. Privat-docent, Goettingen U., 1909, prof., 1921; guest lectr. U. Chgo., 1912; prof. U. Berlin, 1915, Frankfurt University, 1919, Goettingen, 1921; guest lecturer at Massachusetts Inst. Tech., 1925; Stokes lectr. Cambridge U., Eng., 1933; guest prof. Indian Inst. Science, Bangalore, 1935-36; prof. natural philosophy, Edinburgh, Scotland, 1936-53, emeritus, 1953-70. Decorated Stokes medal, Cambridge, 1934; Macdougall-Brisbane and Gunning-Victoria Jubilee prize, Royal Soc. Edinburgh, 1945, 1950; Max Planck medaille, Germany, 1948; Hughes medal Royal Soc. London, 1950; Freedom City of Goettingen, 1953; Nobel prize, 1954; Grotius Medal, Munich, 1956. Fellow Royal Society of Edinburgh, Royal Society of London: mem. acads. Berlin, Goettingen, Copenhagen, Stockholm, Moscow, Dublin, Am. Acad. Arts and Scis., Nat. Acad. Sci. Author many books and articles, mostly on theoretical physics. Home: Bad Pyrmont Germany Died Jan. 5, 1970; buried Gottingen Germany

BORNSTEIN, YETTA LIBBY FRIEDEN (MRS. HARRY BORNSTEIN), artist; b. Waynesboro, Pa.; d. Samuel and Anna (Hoffman) Frieden; student Coll. William and Mary, 1959-61, also pvt. instrs.; m. Harry Bornstein, Jan. 25, 1941; children—Carol Eileen, Joan Adrienne. Tchr. art Hebrew Acad. Norfolk, 1962-68, Jewish Community Center, Norfolk, 1961-68. One-man shows Norfolk Mus. Arts, 1960, 20th Century Gallery, Williamsburg, Va., 1961, Sta. WAVY-TV, 1962, Design Assos. Gallery, Greensboro, N.C., 1962, N.Y. World's Fair, 1965; 1-man show touring U.S., 1966; numerous local shows; exhibited in group shows Tidewater Artists, Norfolk Mus., 1958-63, Va. Mus. Fine Arts, 1959, 61, 63, Valentine Mus., Richmond, 1960, 20th Century Gallery, 1960-62, 94th and 95th Am. Watercolor Soc., 1961, 62, Nat. Assn. Women Artists, 1961-63, 26th and 28th Butler Inst. Am. Art Anns., 1961, 63, Riverside Mus., 1962, 20th and 21st Ann. Exhbns. Audubon Artists, 1962-63, Denver Mus. Arts, 1963, Watercolor U.S.A., Springfield, Mo., 1962, Argentina, 1963, Scotland, 1963, Eng., 1964, France, 1965-66, Mexico, 1965, U.S., Can., 1965-66, also others; represented in permanent collections Bellaire Gallery, Crittendon, Va., 20th Century Gallery, Winston-Salem (N.C.) Gallery Fine Arts, Va. Mus., Richmond, Norfolk Mus. Arts, Temple Israel. Recipient numerous awards for paintings, latest being Purchase prize Joe and Emily Lowe 1st Nat. Painting Exhbn., 1963. Mem. Nat. Assn. Women Artists, Tidewater Artists Assn. (v.p. 1959-61, Charral award 1961, watercolor prize 1962, best in show award 1963), Audubon Soc., Am. Watercolor Soc. Address: Norfolk VA Died Dec. 8, 1968.

BORTZ, EDWARD LEROY, physician; b. Greensburg, Pa., Feb. 10, 1896; s. Adam Franklin and Anna Margaret (Wineman) B.; student Pa. State Coll., 1915-17; A.B., Harvard, 1919; M.D. Harvard Med. Sch., 1923; LL.D., honorary, Hahnemann Med. Col., 1948; grad. work pathology, U. of Vienna, Erdheim's Clinic, Vienna and Christeller's Clinic, Berlin, 1925-26; D.Sc., Pennsylvania Military College, 1950; m. Margaret Sophia Welty, December 27, 1926; 1 son, Walter Michael. Interne Lankenau Hosp., 1923-25; spl. work pathology, Mayo Clinic, 1925, U. of Ill. Med. Sch., 1925; instr. dept. of pathology, U. of Pa. Sch. of Medicine, 1930-32; asso. prof., medicine, Grad. Sch. of Medicine, U. of Pa., from 1932, chief med. service B, Lankenau Hospital, 1932-61, senior consultant in medicine, from 1961, pres. med. staff, from 1949. Diplomate of American Bd. Internal Medicine, 1937. Mem. Coll. of Physicians of Phila., Am. Coll. Physicians (gov. Eastern Pa.; regent), A.M.A. (chmn. council on sci. assembly 1944-47; chmn. on nat. emergency service 1946-47; in charge sci. program Centennial Celebration, Atlantic City, 1947; v.p. 1946; pres. 1947), Am. Clin. and Climatol. Assn., Phila. County Med. Soc. (life mem.; pres. 1940-41), Pa. State Med. Soc., (hon.) Alpha Omega Alpha; fgn. corr. mem. Soc. of Internal Medicine of Med. Assn. of the Argentine. Hon. med. cons. to surgeon gen. of U.S. Navy; mem. med. adv. bd. Nat. Resources Security Bd.; cons. Council on Nat. Emergency Med. Service; advisor to the White House Conference on Aging. Awarded meritorious service medal Comonwealth of Pa. for work on pneumonia commn. of State Med. Soc., 1939; Gold medal by Am. Geriatrics Society, 1960; American Medical Writers' Association. 1961; award International Congress on Aging, Vienna, 1966. Served as pilot, Army Air Corps, World War I; capt., M.C., U.S.N., with marines in Iwo Jima, and in atomic bomb area. World War II. Mem. Am. Geriatrics Soc. (pres. 1960-61). Presbyn. Author: Diabetes Control; Creative Aging, 1963; also articles on nutrition, metabolism and geriatrics. Editor: The Cyclopedia of Medicine, Surgery and Specialties; Bala Cynwyd PA Died Feb. 24, 1970.

BOSLEY, WILLIAM BRADFORD, lawyer; b. Livonia, N.Y., May 9, 1865; s. Daniel Bradford and Margaret Matilda (Milliman) B.; A.B., Yale, 1892, LL.B., 1894; m. Cornelia Charlotte Walsworth, July 18, 1893; children—Bradford Walsworth, Ruth (Mrs. Sidney D. Peterson, dec.); m. 2d, Margaret Albertine Cosgro, July 7, 1908; m. 3d, Jeannette Ethel Doub, Nov. 16, 1935. Admitted to Calif. bar, 1894; asst. prof. law, Hastings Coll. of the Law, 1895-99; in gen. practice, 1894-1903; head of law dept. Calif. Gas and Electric Corp., 1903-07. Pacific Gas and Electric Co., 1906-22, gen. counsel, 1922-44, spl. counsel, 1944-48; retired since 1948. Trustee Samuel Merritt Hospital; director Hastings College of the Law. Mem. Calif. State and Am. bar assns. Clubs: University, Pacific Union, Commonwealth (Calif.). Home: 1904 Broadway, San Francisco 9‡

BOSS, BENJAMIN, astronomer; b. Albany, N.Y., Jan. 9, 1880; s. Lewis and Helen M. (Hutchinson) B.; A.B., Harvard, 1901; m. Marguerite M. Guy, Aug. 30, 1906 (died 1919); children—Marguerite, Elizabeth; m. 2d, Helga S. Nordstrom, Aug. 7, 1923; 1 dau., (Helga) Lucinda. Asst. Dudley Obs. Albany, N.Y., 1901-05, U.S. Naval Obs., Washington, 1905-06; dir. U.S. Naval Obs., Tutuila, Samoa, 1906-08; mem. expdn. to observe solar eclipse at Flint Island, 1908; sect. Dept. Meridian Astrometry, Carnegie Instn., Washington, 1908-12, acting dir., 1912-15; acting dir., Dudley Obs., 1912-15; dir. Dept. Meridian Astronomy, Carnegie Instn., Washington, 1915-39; dir. Dudley Obs., 1915-56. Editor Astron. Jour. 1912-41. Mem. Am. Astron. Soc., A.A.A.S. Club: University. Specialized in determination of star positions and motions. Pub. General Catolog of 33342 Stars, 1937. Address: NY Died Oct. 18, 1970.

BOSS, HENRY M., lawyer; b. at Providence, R.I., Sept. 13, 1875; s. Henry M. and Emma J. (Wilbur) B.; student Brown U.; LL.B., Yale, 1899; m. Louise J. Gifford, Oct. 20, 1906; children—Betsey, Mary Louise. Admitted to R.I. bar, 1900, and began practice at Providence; U.S. atty., R.I. Dist., 1929-34. Mem. Zeta Psi. Republican. Episcopalian. Clubs: Agawam Hunt, Hope. Home: 125 Lloyd Av. Office: Turks Head Bldg., Providence RI‡

BOSWORTH, CHARLES WILDER, lawyer; b. Springfield, Mass., Aug. 28, 1871; s. Henry Wilder and Mary Elizabeth (Hall) B.; A.B., Yale, 1893; m. Mrs. Rachel Rising Woods, 1917. Admitted to bar, 1894, and began practice at Springfield; formerly pres. and chmn. bd. Union Trust Co.; now dir. Springfield St. Ry. Co.; trustee of Proprietors of Springfield Cemetery Assn. Mem. Phi Beta Kappa. Home: 70 Chestnut St. Office: 182 State St., Springfield MA*‡

BOSWORTH, EDWIN CARPENTER, univ. dean; b. Foxboro, Mass., Mar. 13, 1890; s. Arthur H. and Annie Frances (Marsh) B.; Ph.B., Brown U., 1911, M.C.S. (hon.), 1927; m. Lucinda Eliza Jeffrey, May 15, 1912; children—Lucinda Caroline, Anne Frances (Mrs. Robert S. Beall), Ruth Margaret (Mrs. Chester C. Hustead). Prof. mathematics Leland U., New Orleans, 1911; prof. commerce Detroit YWCA, 1912-14; dean Pace Inst. of Accountancy, Detroit, 1914-17, Washington, 1917-22; with Benjamin Franklin U., 1925-71, dean, 1926-71. Mem. Mayflower Soc., Am. Accounting Assn., Phi Beta Kappa, Phi Alpha Delta, Sigma Phi Epsilon. Republican. Presbyn. Co-author: Manual of Charting, 1923. Home: Washington DC Died Oct. 22, 1971; buried Foxboro MA

BOTKIN, HAROLD MITCHELL, communications exec.; b. Galesburg, Ill., Apr. 15, 1906; s. James Symington and Rose (Mitchell) B.; B.S., Knox Coll., 1928; student Columbia, 1953; m. Julia Emma Bishop, May 5, 1933; children—Jean (Mrs. William Duncan), Suzanne (Mrs. Ranulf Ueland), James Waldron. Various assignments long lines dept. Am. Tel. & Tel. Co., N.Y.C., 1928-53, asst. dir. operations, 1954. asst. v.p., 1955, v.p. internat. services, until 1970. Pres. Cuban Am. Tel. & Tel. Co., Eastern Tel. & Tel. Co., Transoceanic Communications, Inc., Transoceanic Cable Ship Co., Inc., Transpacific Communications, Inc.; dir. Communications Satellite Corp. Adviser to sec. Dept. of Def., 1954; asst. dir. ODM, 1955. Decorated Legion of Merit (France); Third Order Merit (Japan, awarded posthumously). Mem. Armed Forces Communications and Electronics Assn. Home: Red Bank NJ Died Nov. 8, 1970; buried Fairview Cemetery, Red Bank NJ

BOTSFORD, FLORENCE HUDSON;, b. Cairo, Ill.; d. Sandford and Marietta (Boyd) Topping; studied piano with William H. Sherwood, voice with Achille Errani, New York; grad. Mt. Caroll Sem.; also studied in Europe; m. Charles Hull Botsford, 1892 (died 1930); children—Rosamond, Willard H. Compiler or editor: Folk Songs of Many Peoples (2 vols.), 1921-22; Picture Tales from the Italian, 1929; Russian Folk Songs, 1930; Botsford Collection of Folk Songs (3 vols.), 1930-31. Home: 611 W. 114th St., New York NY‡

BOTTHOF, WALTER E., publisher; b. Chgo., Nov. 16, 1888; s. William B. and Alma (Stockmar) B.; honorary alumnus Northwestern University, Illinois; m. Elsa Laury Botthof, Apr. 2, 1914; children—Charles Laury, Sherley Marie. Organized Standard Rate & Data Service Inc., Detroit, Mich., 1919, pres., 1919-43, pub., 1943-59, chmn. bd., 1943-69; pub. Media/scope, 1957-63; dir. d.i. Offset Corp., Nat. Register Pub. Co. Dir., chmn. edn. com. Mag. Pubs. Assn., 1958-65; chmn. edn. com. Asso. Bus. Publs.; mem. edn. com. Nat. Bus. Publs.; mem. bus. paper advt. com. Advt. Council. Mem. Northwestern U. Assos., alumni fund council Northwestern U. Recipient Joseph Medill award Northwestern U., 1962; Honor medal award U. Mo., 1965; hon. alumnus Northwestern U. Clubs: Chgo. Athletic Assn., Executives, Mid-Am., Tavern (Chicago); Westmoreland Country (Wilmette, Ill.); Carlin (Manitowish Waters, Wis.). Author: Threads of Gold, 1955; Malahinis in Hawaii, 1957; Night in St. Thomas, 1958. Speaker pub. and advt. industries. Home: Wilmette IL Died July 10, 1971.

BOUATTOURA, TEWFIK, diplomat of Algeria; b. Algeria, Jan. 30, 1936; student philosophy; m. Officer in the Army of Nat. Liberation, 1957-58; mem. Provisional Govt. Republic Algeria, 1958-62; minister armed forces, 1959-60; polit. sec. for Afro-Asian affairs, 1960; polit. sec. for Arab affairs, then ambassador to Ghana; at this time also Algerian del. numerous internat. confs. and meetings; after independence mem. Algerian delegation to XVII session Gen. Assembly UN; dep. dir. Office Minister Fgn. Affairs, 1963, dir. polit. affairs 1963-64; permanent rep. Algeria to UN Security Council, 1964-70, pres. Econ. and Social Council, 1966. Died Aug. 6, 1970; buried Boubsila Cemetery, Kouba Algiers Algeria

BOUCHER, ANTHONY (PSEUDONYM FOR WILLIAM ANTHONY PARKER WHITE), writer; b. Oakland, Cal., Aug. 21, 1911; s. James Taylor and Mary Ellen (Parker) W.; student Pasadena Jr. Coll., 1928-30; A.B., U. So. Cal., 1932; A.M., U. Cal., 1934; m. Phyllis Mary Price, May 19, 1938; children—Lawrence Taylor, James Marsden. Writer mystery stories, 1934-68; theater editor United Progressive News, Los Angeles, 1935-37; mystery book editor San Francisco Chronicle, 1942-47, Ellery Queen's Mystery Magazine, 1948-50, 58-68; fantasy reviewer Chicago Sun-Times, 1949-50; mystery reviewer N.Y. Times Book Review 1949-68; sci-fantasy reviewer N.Y. Herald Tribune Book Rev., 1951-63; editor The Magazine of Fantasy and Science Fiction, 1949-58, True Crime Detective, 1952-53; radio writer, 1945-48 (Sherlock Holmes, Gregory Hood, etc.); with Golden Voices, radio KPFA, 1949-68, Invitation to Opera, KQED-TV, 1960. Mem. Nat. Collegiate Players, Mystery Writers of America (winner award for best U.S. mystery criticism 1946, 50, 53, nat. pres. 1951), Baker Street Irregulars, Phi Beta Kappa. Democrat (state central com., 1946-50). Roman Catholic. Author: The Case of The Seven of Calvary, 1937; The Case of The Crumpled Knave, 1939; The Case of the Baker Street Irregulars, 1940; The Case of The Solid Key, 1941; The Case of The Seven Sneezes, 1942; Far and Away, 1955; (as H. H. Holmes) Nine Times Nine, 1940; Rocket to The Morgue, 1942; The Compleat Werewolf and Other Stories, 1969. Compiler: The Pocket Book of True Crime Stories, 1943; Great American Detective Stories, 1945; Four-and-Twenty Bloodhounds, 1950; The Best from Fantasy and Science Fiction, ann. 1952-58; A Treasury of Great Science Fiction, 1959; Best Detective Stories of the Year, 1963-68. Contbr. to mags. and anthologies. Home: Berkeley CA Died Apr. 29, 1968.

BOUCICAULT, RUTH BALDWIN HOLT (MRS. AUBREY BOUCICAULT), actress, author; b. at

Belmont, Mass.; d. Gustavus C. and Frances Ann (Payne) Holt; ed. pub. schs.; grad. Emerson Coll. of Oratory, Boston, 1895; m. Aubrey Boucicault, of London, Eng., Dec. 21, 1906. Has played in leading parts in repertoires of Richard Mansfield, Otis Skinner, Grace George, Mary Mannering, and Margaret Anglin, modern society plays, Shakespeare; appeared in Greek drama, at Berkeley, Cal., with Margaret Anglin, 1915. Author: The Substance of His House, 1914; The Rose of Jericho, 1920. Address: 23 Blenheim Rd., St. John's Wood, London England‡

BOUCKE, EWALD AUGUSTUS, prof. German; b. Bremerhaven, Germany, Aug. 15, 1871; s. Frederick William and Bertha (Geburek) B.; grad. Gymnasium, Bremerhaven, 1890; studied, univs. of Jena, Breslau and Freiburg; Ph.D., Freiburg, 1894; m. Florence Perkins Benedict, of New York, Oct. 10, 1896. Instr. in German, 1898-06, asst. prof., 1906-11, jr. prof., 1911-12, prof., 1912-—, U. of Mich. Mem. Modern Lang. Assn. America. Author: Wort und Bedentung in Goethe's Sprache, 1901; Goethe's Weltanschauung auf historischer Grundlage, 1907. Home: 901 Oakland Ave., Ann Arbor MI‡

BOUDINOT, JANE J., author; b. at Newark, N.J.; d. Judge Elias E. and Jane Mary (Kip) B.; pvt. sch. edn.; unmarried. Mem. Hist. Soc. of N.J., Rocky Hill Assn., Princeton, N.J., Colonial Dames of America (bd. of mgrs. standing com. on publ., 2d v.-p.), Huguenot Soc., Nat. Geog. Soc. Author: Life and Letters of Elias Boudinot (commissary-gen. of prisoners under Washington, pres. Continental Congress), 2 vols., 1896. Contbr. to Magazine of History, newspapers, etc. Address: 136 E. 16th St., NY NY‡

BOUILLON, LINCOLN, cons. engr.; b. Seattle, Feb. 12, 1900; s. Alfred Victor and Mary (Young) B.; student U. Wash., 1919-20, Tulane U., 1920; B.S. in Elec. Engring., U. Pa., 1923, Mech. Engr., 1938; m. Louise Huntington Richards, Sept. 12, 1925; 1 son, Richard. With Gen. Electric Co., 1923-24, Stone & Webster Co., Seattle, 1924-25, Josiah C. Moore, Seattle, 1926-31; owner and/or sr. mem. cons. engring. firms, 1931-65; chmn. bd. Bouillon, Christofferson & Schairer, Seattle, 1965-66. Guest speaker Heating, Ventilating and Air Conditioning Conf., London, Eng., 1962. Served as pvt. U.S. Army, 1918; served to lt. comdr. USNR, 1943-45. Registered profl. engr., Wash., Ore., Ida. Fellow Am. Soc. Heating, Refrigerating and Air Conditioning Engrs. (bd. dirs. 1962-66, pres. 1966-67); mem. Am. Soc. M.E., Nat. Soc. Profl. Engrs. (Engr. of Year award Puget Sound region 1966), Delta Kappa Epsilon, Tau Beta Pi, Eta Kappa Nu. Mason (Shriner). Clubs: Seattle Yacht, Rainier (Seattle); Outrigger Canoe (Honolulu). Home: Mercer Island WA Died Sept. 30, 1966; buried Sunset Hills Cemetery, Bellevue WA

BOULDIN, VIRGIL, judge; b. Princeton, Ala., Oct. 20, 1866; s. John and Mary (Collins) B.; student Burritt Coll., Spencer, Tenn., 1 yr., Winchester (Tenn.) Normal Coll., 1886; B.Sc., Cumberland U., Lebanon, Tenn., 1889; LL.D., Howard Coll., Birmingham, Ala, 1929; m. Irene Jacoway, June 12, 1895: children—Elizabeth (Mrs. T. U. Crumpton), John, Walter. Began practice at Scottsboro, Ala., 1889; chmn. Dem. Exec. Com., Jackson County, 1890-92; mem. Ala. Ho. of Rep., 1896; mem. Dem. State Exec. Com., 1907-10, 1915-16; asso. justice Supreme Court of Ala. since 1923. Retired May 1, 1944; now supernumerary judge of Alabama. Private, Co. I, 2d Ala. Regt., Spanish-Am. War, 1898. Mem. bd. trustees Howard Coll., Birmingham, Ala. Member board of trustees Alabama College from 1895 to 1911; 1923 to 1924. Mem. Am. and Ala. State bar assns., Beta Theta Pi. Democrat. Baptist. Club: (hon. mem.) The Thirteen" (Montgomery, Ala.). Home: Scottsboro AL‡

BOURKE-WHITE, MARGARET, photographer; born New York, N.Y., June 14, 1906; d. Joseph and Minnie Elizabeth (Bourke) White; student Columbia, 1922-23, U. Mich., 1923-25, A.F.D. (hon.), 1951; A.B., Cornell, 1927; Litt.D. (hon.), Rutgers U., 1949; married Everett Chapman, 1925; married 2d, Erkskine Caldwell, 1939 (divorced 1942). Industrial photographer, 1927-71. Photographed American industries including steel, mining, farming, railroads, shipping; (Canada) newsprint; (Germany) AEG, I. G. Farben. (South America) coffee; (airplane) Trans Western Airways, Eastern Airlines; Pan Am. Airways. Brazil. Has taken photographs in 34 countries including Arctic region; Asso. editor Fortune Mag., 1929-33. Life Mag., 1936-71. U.N. war corr. in Korea for Life Mag., 1952. Accredited war correspondent-photographer for Life Mag. to the U.S. Air Forces in Great Britain, North Africa and Europe, 1942-45. Photomurals for Aluminum Co. Am., 1933; Lehigh Portland Cement Co., 1938. Awards: 1st prize, Cleve. Mus. Art, 1928, Art Dirs. Club, N.Y., 1920; American Woman of Achievement Award, 1951; 2d ann. ASMP-U. Miami Photojournalism Conf., 1958. Rep. in Library of Congress, Bklyn. Mus., Cleve. Museum of Art. Mus. of Modern Art, New York. Author: Eyes on Russia, 1931; U.S.S.R., A Portfolio of Photographs, 1934; You Have Seen Their Faces (with Erskine Caldwell), 1937; North of the Danube (with Erskine Caldwell), 1939; SayCaldwell), 1941; Shooting the Russian War (text & photographs), 1942. They Called It Purple Heart Valley, 1944; Dear Fatherland. Rest Quietly 1946: Halfway to Freedom, A Study of the New India, 1949; A Report on The American Jesuits (with Father John Lafarge), 1956; Portrait of Myself, 1963. Home: Darien CT Died Aug. 27, 1971.

BOURLAND, CAROLINE BROWN, prof. Spanish; b. Peoria, Ill., June 4, 1871; d. Benjamin Langford Todd and Clara (Parsons) B.; A.B., Smith Coll., Northampton, Mass., 1893; fellow in Romance langs., 1898-9, scholar in Romance langs., 1899-1900, Mary E. Garrett European fellow, 1900-1, Ph.D., 1905, all of Bryn Mawr Coll., Pa.; unmarried. Instr. in Spanish, 1902-6, asso. prof., 1906-13, prof., Sept., 1913-—, Smith Coll. Asso. mem. Hispanic Soc. America, New York. Author: Boccaccio and the Decameron in Spanish and Catalan Literature (thesis for degree of Ph.D.), 1905. Contbr. on lit. subjects. Address: 10 West St., Northampton MA‡

BOUTON, EMILY ST. JOHN, author; b. New Canaan, Conn.; d. Daniel Webb and Almina (St. John) B.; grad. Sandusky (O.) High Sch., 1857; unmarried. Was high sch. teacher in Milan and Tiffin, O.; teacher English lit. Central High Sch., Chicago, 2 yrs.; later in high sch. in Toledo; lit. and household editor Toledo Blade, 1879-1907; newspaper and mag. writer and lecturer. Author: Health and Beauty, 1883; Social Etiquette, 1884; Life's Gateways, 1897; The Life Joyful, 1910. Hon. pres. Writers' Club, 1923, after 10 yrs. as pres. Address: 2139 Glenwood Ave., Toledo OH‡

BOUTON, S(TEPHEN) MILES, writer, lecturer; b. Blockville, Chautauqua County, N.Y., Sept. 24, 1876; s. Harry B. and Almina M. (Lewis) B.; grad. Eastern High Sch., Washington, D.C., 1894; grad. work, same, 1894-95; LL.B., Albany Law Sch., 1899; spl. studies U. of Berlin, 1911-12, 1925-27; m. Frieda Dorothea Kleinsang, Nov. 11, 1903; children—S. Miles, Noel Lewis. Admitted to N.Y. bar, 1899, and practiced at Jamestown; on staff Meadville (Pa.) Star, 1903-04, Oil City Times, 1904-05, Buffalo Express, 1905-09; with Associated Press, 1909-19; at New York office, 1909-11; transferred to Berlin, Germany, 1911; with German armies on various fronts as war corr., 1914-16; in charge Associated Press bureau at Stockholm, Sweden, 1916-19; in Petrograd summer of 1917; first enemy corr. to enter German after armistice; Berlin corr., N.Y. World, N.Y. Times and Baltimore Sun, 1920-34; ordered by the Hitler govt. to leave Germany in June 1934. Mem. Jamestown (N.Y.) Bar Assn. Clubs: Norden (Jamestown, N.Y.); Overseas Press. Unitarian. Author: And the Kaiser Abdicates—the German Revolution, 1920; Das Ende der Grossmacht Deutschland, 1922; Chiefly Concerning Garet Garret (brochure), 1923; A Watcher in the North; Der Wahn des Alkoholverbots, 1925. Contributor to American and Scandinavian periodicals. Chief editorial writer The Post-Journal, Jamestown, N.Y. Home: Ashville NY‡

BOUTWELL, JOHN M(ASON), engr.; b. St. Louis, May 1, 1874; s. Henry Thatcher and Helen Grace (Willis) B.; A.B., Harvard, 1897, B.S., 1898, M.S., 1899; m. Esther G. Miner, Jan. 22, 1910; m. 2d Ruth Crellin, Sept. 28, 1922; 1 dau., Jean Miner (Mrs. Joseph B. Paul). Tchr. dept. ecology Harvard, 1896-1900; geologist U.S. Geol. Survey, 1898-1908; cons. mining geologist, examiner econ. possibilities of mines in U.S., Mexico and S.A., since 1908; cons. Metals Res. Co. (R.F.C.), 1942-44. Mem. nat. council Boy Scouts Am. Emeritus fellow Geol. Soc. Am., A.A.A.S.; mem. Soc. Econ. Geologists (pres. 1944, counsellor, mem. com. on Penrose medal), Am. Inst. Mining and Metall. Engrs. (dir. 1937-43), Mining and Metall. Soc. Am. (counsellor), Wash. Geol. Soc., Wash. Acad. Sci., S.A.R., Soc. Mayflower Descendants (founder Utah soc., gov. 1948-53). Clubs: Harvard (N.Y.C. and Boston); Alta (Salt Lake City). Author reports. Address: 105 E.S. Temple St., Salt Lake City 1‡

BOUTWELL, PAUL WINSLOW, educator; b. Lyndeborough, N.H., Feb. 6, 1888; s. Benjamin Jones and Louise Elizabeth (Knight) B.; B.S., Beloit Coll., 1910; A.M., U. Wis., 1912, Ph.D., 1916; m. Clara Gertrude Brinkhoff, June 12, 1915; children—Roswell Knight, Clara Barnes (Mrs. Leslie Paul Bunker, Jr.) Paul Winslow. Tchr. high sch., Mankato, Minn. 1910-11; instr. State Tchrs. Coll., summers 1911-15 instr. U. Del., 1916-17; asst. chemistry U. Wis. 1912-16, instr. agrl. chemistry, 1917-18, asst. prof. 1918-20; asso. prof. Beloit (Wis.) Coll., 1920-21, prof., head dept. chemistry from 1921, faculty athletic rep., 1923-52; research, prodn. div. synthetic chemistry Eastman Kodak Co., 1928. Fellow A.A.A.S.; mem. Am. Chem. Soc., Wis. Acad. Scis., Arts and Letters (v.p. 1936-39, pres. 1939-42), Am. Assn. U. Profs., Phi Beta Kappa, Sigma Xi, Gamma Alpha, Delta Sigma Rho, Omicron Delta Kappa, Sigma Chi. Republican. Conglist. Contbr. chem. Beloit WI Died Feb. 22, 1971.

BOUVIER, MAURICE, steamship offl.; b. St. Louis, Mo., July 14, 1862; s. Leopold and Emma (Bennett) B.; student St. Francis Xavier Coll., New York, until 1879, Coll. City of New York, 1879-80; m. Henrietta Jenkins O'Donovan, Jan. 17, 1894. Began, 1880, in employ of W. R. Grace Co., ocean transportation, New York, now dir. of co. Mem. com. on food protection, U.S. Food Adminstrn., World War. Mem. Delta Kappa Epsilon. Catholic. Clubs: India House, Delta Kappa Epsilon, New York Yacht. Home: 580 Park Av. Office: 7 Hanover Sq., New York NY‡

BOVING, ADAM GIEDE, entomologist; b. Saby, Denmark, July 31, 1869; s. Niels Orten Mathias and Otilia Louise Augusta (Giede) B.; A.B., U. of Copenhagen, 1889, M.S., 1894, Ph.D., 1906; m. Anna Kirstine Christensen, of Copenhagen, Jan. 31, 1916; 1 son, Bent Giede. Came to U.S., 1913, naturalized citizen, 1918. Asst. curator entomol. div. Zool. Mus., Copenhagen, 1902-13; zoologist, govt. expdn. to Iceland, 1908; entomologist, U.S. Bur. Entomology, Washington, D.C., 1913-39; sr. entomologist; retired July 31, 1939. Fellow Entomol. Soc. Am.; mem. A.A.A.S., Entomol. Soc. Washington (pres. 1923-24), Biol. Soc. Washington, Washington Acad. Science (v.p. 1924-30); honorary member Copenhagen Entomol. Society; corr. member Vanamo," Finnish Zool.-Bot. Soc. Decorated Golden Cross Knights of Dannebrog. Author: Donaciinlarvernes Naturhistorie, 1906; Larvae of Coleoptera (with F. C. Craighead), 1931. Contbr. on entomol. subjects. Home: 221 Rock Creek Church Rd., Washington DC‡

BOVING, CHARLES B(RASEE), clergyman; b. Harrisonville, Mo., Nov. 26, 1871; s. George Joseph and Mary Stuart (Cordell) B.; A.B., Westminster Coll. (Mo.), 1891, A.M., 1895, D.D., 1909; grad. Princeton Theol. Sem., 1895; m. Mary Louise Woodbridge, of Marshall, Mo., Nov. 6, 1895; children—Louise Woodbridge (Mrs. George W. Baumhoff, Jr.), Eleanor Russell (Mrs. D. Franklin Manning). Ordained Presbyn. ministry, 1893; pastor, Lamar, Mo., 1893-98; pastor-at-large Lafayette-Springfield, Mo., 1898-99, Webb City, Mo., 1899-1905, Hannibal, Mo., 1905-11; pres. Westminster Coll., 1911-14; pastor Bowling Green, Ky., 1914-18; Moberly, Mo., 1918-24, Sidney St. Ch. (now Peters Memorial), St. Louis, Mo., 1924-27; field rep. Presbyn. Bd. of Pensions, Phila., 1927-39. Trustee Westminster Coll., 1919-27; state pres. Mo., Christian Endeavor Union, 1907-08, pastor counsellor, 1919-27. Minister of Visitation, East Liberty Presbyn. Ch., Pittsburgh, Pa., 1939. Mem. Beta Theta Pi. Republican. Mason (32 deg.). Address: 372 S. Highland Av., Pittsburgh PA‡

BOW, FRANK TOWNSEND, legislator; b. Canton, O., Feb. 20, 1901; s. Charles Clinton and Anna (Withrow) B.; LL.D., Ohio No. U., 1961, Mount Union Coll., 1963; m. Caroline Denzer, May 12, 1923; children—Robert Lee, Joseph Withrow. Admitted to Ohio bar, 1923; practiced at Canton. Mem. Ohio State Rep. Com., 1945-46; counsel to Congl. Com. investigating publicity and propaganda 80th Congress, 1947-48, to Select Com. 80th Congress investigating F.C.C., 1948; mem. 82d-92d Congresses, 16th Dist. Ohio Mem. bd. regents Smithsonian Instn. Served as war corr. Ohio 37th Div., World War II; PTO. Mem. Ohio Bar Assn. (v.p. 1944-46, exec. com. 1946-50), Sigma Pi. Republican. Presbyn. Elk. Home: Canton OH Died Nov. 1972.

BOWEN, ARTHUR JOHN, educator; b. Neponset, Ill., Jan. 12, 1873; s. William and Sarah Jane (Norton) B.; B.A., Northwestern U., 1897 (LL.D., 1914); post-grad. work, Columbia, 1904-5; m. Nora Jones, of Neponset, Ill., Aug. 11, 1897. Student of Chinese lang., 1897-12; teacher Nanking U., to 1903, acting pres., 1903-4; dist. supt., Kiangsi Dist., 1907-9; pres. U. of Nanking (union of three instns.), since Feb. 1, 1910. Treas. Central China Mission, 1901-5; pres. East China Ednl. Assn., 1916, 17. Clubs: University, American University, Nanking Assn., Chinese-Am. Assn. (treas.). Address: Care The University of Nanking, Nanking China‡

BOWEN, ELIZABETH DOROTHEA COLE, author; b. Dublin, Ireland, June 7, 1899; d. Henry Cole and Florence (Colley) Bowen; ed. Downe House, Downe, Kent, Eng.; D. Litt. (hon.), Trinity Coll., Dublin, 1949; m. Alan Charles Cameron, Aug. 4, 1923. Author short stories, novels, essays published since 1923. Comdr. Order of Brit. Empire Mem. American Acad. Arts and Letters (hon.). Author: Encounters, 1923; Ann Lee's, 1926; The Hotel, 1927; The Last Sept., 1929; Joining Charles, 1929; Friends and Relations, 1931; To the North, 1932; The Cat Jumps, 1934; The House in Paris, 1935; The Death of the Heart, 1938; Look at All those Roses, 1941; Bowen's Court, 1942; Seven Winters, 1943; The Demon Lover, 1945; The Heat of the Day, 1949; Collected Impressions, 1950; Shelbourne Hotel, 1951; A World of Love, 1955; A Time in Rome, 1960; W.W. Heath, 1961; Afterthoughts, 1962 (essays); Little Girls, 1964; Good Tiger, 1965; A Day in the Dark, 1965; Eva Trout, 1968. Home: Kilderory County Cork Ireland Died Feb. 22, 1973.

BOWEN, IRA SPRAGUE, astronomer; b. Senece Falls, N.Y., Dec. 21, 1898; s. James Henry and Philinda May (Sprague) B.; A.B., Oberlin Coll., 1919, D.Sc., 1948; postgrad. U. Chgo., 1919-21; Ph.D., Cal. Inst. Tech., 1926; Ph.D., U. Lund, 1950; Sc.D., Princeton, 1953; m. Mary Jane Howard, July 12, 1929. Asst. in physics U. Chgo., 1919-21; instr. physics Cal. Inst. Tech., 1921-26, asst. prof., 1926-28, asso. prof.,

1928-31, prof. 1931-45; dir. Mount Wilson Obs., 1946-64, Palomar Obs., 1948-64, Distinguished Service staff mem., 1964-69. Morrison research asso. Lick Obs., 1938-39. S.A.T.C., 1918. Recipient Potts medal Franklin Inst., 1946; Ives medal Optical Soc. Am., 1952. Mem. Nat. Acad. Sci. (Draper medal 1942), Am. Philos. Soc., Am. Acad. Arts and Scis. (Rumford Premium 1949), Am. Astron. Soc. Astron. Soc. Pacific (asso., Bruce medal 1957), Royal Astron. Soc. (Gold medal Altadena CA Died Feb. 6, 1973.

BOWEN, JOHN CAMPBELL, lt. gov. Province of Alberta; b. Metcalfe, Ont., Can., Oct. 3, 1872; s. Peter and Nancy (Poapst) B.; student Branden Coll., Branden, Manitoba, 1897-1903, McMaster U. (Toronto), 1902; LL.D., U. of Alberta, 1940; m. Edith Oliver, Oct. 25, 1905; children—Margaret Gwendolyn (wife of Capt. Francis Neal), Emma Ruth. Baptist minister, 1900-12; insurance business, Mutual Life of Can., 1918-37. Mem. Legislature of Alberta, 1921-26, leader of Liberal Party; lt. gov., Province of Alberta, since 1937. Chmn. bd. dirs. Brandon Coll., 1929-43. Served as capt., C.E.F., 1915-18, World War I; hon. col., Can. O.T.C., U. of Alberta. Clubs: Mayfair Golf and Country, Edmonton Golf and Country, Edmonton. Mem. Liberal Party. Baptist. Address: Legislature Bldg., Edmonton AB Canada‡

BOWERS, EDISON LOUIS, univ. prof; b. Massillon, O., May 24, 1898; s. Frank Samuel and Nellie (Klinglesmith) B.; A.B., Heidelberg Coll., Tiffin, O., 1922, M.A., Ohio State U., 1923, Ph.D., 1928; University of California, 1925; L.H.D.; Heidelberg College, 1950; Social Science Research fellowship for study abroad, 1930-31; m. Elizabeth Charlotte Hass, Sept. 12, 1922. Asst. in economics, Ohio State U., 1923, instr., 1925-28, asst. prof., 1928-32, asso. prof., 1932-41, prof. from 1941, chmn. of dept. of economics 1939-63; statistician Ohio Vocational Rehabilitation Service, 1924; dir. Western and Southern Life Insurance Co. Mem. Ohio Advisory Council on Unemployment Compensation from 1937, chairman, 1948-62; member National War Labor Board (public member of fifth region), 1943-45; member Ohio Disability Insurance Commission, 1950-51. Trustee Am. Institute for Property and Liability Underwriters; member administrative board The S.S. Huebner Found. for Ins. Edn.; mem. Council ednl. advisers Am. Coll. Life Underwriters. Mem. Am. Econ. Assn., Am. Statistical Assn., Am. Assn. of U. Profs., Am. Assn. U. Teachers of Insurance (past president), American Finance Association, also Phi Beta Kappa, Beta Gamma Sigma, Pi Kappa Delta, Delta Sigma Rho. Clubs: Faculty (Columbus, O.); Queen City (Cincinnati). Author various books and articles on economics and insurance. Joint editor Richard D. Irwin Insurance Series. Home: Columbus OH Died June 11, 1971; buried Homer OH

BOWERS, ROBERT GRAVES, college pres.; b. Princeton, Dallas Co., Ark., Sept. 3, 1869; s. James A. and Martha (Sasser) B.; Little Rock Conf. Training Sch., Fordyce, Ark.; Ouachita Coll., Ark., 1894-9, A.B., 1899; (D.D., Baylor U., Tex., 1910); m. Blanche Wynne, of Orlando, Ark., Oct. 25, 1899. Ordained Bapt. ministry, Sept. 10, 1898; pastor Malvern, Ark., 1898-1900, Lulling, Tex., 1900-1, Columbus St. Bapt. Ch., Waco, Tex., 1901-6; missionary sec. Ark. Bapt. State Conv., 1906-8; ed. sec. same, 1908-11; pres. Ouachita Coll., June 1911—. Mem. State Mission Bd. and Bd. of Ministerial Edn., Ark Bapt. State Conv. Address: Arkadelphia AR‡

BOWES, THEODORE F., lawyer; b. Moshannon, Pa., Dec. 12, 1904; s. Maines J. and Nancy (Fleming) B.; Ph.B., Dickinson Coll., 1927; LL.B., Syracuse U., 1936; m. Erna E. Hofmann, Aug. 7, 1948. Admitted to N.Y. bar, 1936; asst. to pres. Bankers Investment Trust, 1928-31; prof. law Syracuse U., 1936-41, 46-53; v.p., gen. counsel Onondaga Aviation Corp., 1940-41; gen. counsel Inst. Indsl. Research, Syracuse U., 1952-53; U.S. Atty., No. Dist. N.Y., 1953-61; commr. N.Y. State Public Service Commn., from 1961. Trustee N.Y. Ct. of Appeals Library, from 1948. Served as col., USAAF, 1942-46. Decorated Legion of Merit. Mem. Am., N.Y. bar assns., Order of the Coif, Phi Delta Theta, Phi Delta Phi. Methodist. Mason. Club: Syracuse University. Contbr. articles profl. jours. Home: Syracuse NY Died Jan. 8, 1967.

BOWIE, WALTER RUSSELL, clergyman, author; b. Richmond, Va., Oct. 8, 1882; s. Walter Russell and Elizabeth Halsted (Branch) B.; grad. Hill Sch., Pottstown, Pa., 1900; B.A., Harvard, 1904, M.A., 1905; B.D., Theol. Sem. in Va., 1908, D.D., 1938; D.D., Richmond Coll., 1915; S.T.D. Syracuse U., 1933; m. Jean Laverack, Sept. 29, 1909; children—Jean Laverack, Beverley Munford, Elisabeth Halsted, Walter Russell. Ordained deacon Protestant Episcopal Ch., 1908, priest, 1909; rector Emmanuel Ch., Greenwood, Va., 1908-11, St. Paul's Ch., Richmond, 1911-23, Grace Ch., N.Y.C., 1923-39; prof. practical theology Union Theol. Sem., N.Y.C., 1939-50, dean students, 1945-50; prof. homiletics Theol. Sem. in Va., 1950-55, spl. lectr., 1956-69; lectr. Phila. Div. Sch.; Lyman Beecher lectr. Yale Div. Sch., 1935; Hale lectr. Seabury-Western Theol. Sem., 1939. Mem. Commn. on World Conf. Faith and Order; del. Gen. Conv. P.E. Ch., 1916, 19, 22, 34, 37. Dir. So. Edn. Found.; mem. bd. Nat. Hosp. for Speech Disorders, N.Y.C. Chaplain of Base Hosp. 45, World War I. Mem. Phi Beta Kappa. Author numerous books, including: The Children's Year (sermons for children), 1916; The Master, a Life of Jesus Christ, 1928; The Story of the Bible, published in 1934; The Bible Story for Boys and Girls, New Testament, 1951; The Bible Story for Boys and Girls, Old Testament, 1952; Preaching, 1954; The Story of the Church, 1955; Lift Up Your Hearts, 1955; Christ Be With Me, 1958; I Believe in Jesus Christ, 1959; The Living Story of the New Testament, 1959; Jesus and the Trinity, 1960; Men of Fire, 1961; Women of Light, 1963; The Living Story of the Old Testament, 1964, The Compassionate Christ, 1965 (Religious Book Club choice); What Is Protestantism?, 1965; See Yourself In The Bible, 1967; Where You Find God, 1968; (autobiography) Learning to Live, 1969. Asso. editor The Interpreter's Bible. Home: Alexandria VA Died Apr. 23, 1969; buried Virginia Theological Seminary, Alexandria VA

BOWLES, GILBERT, missionary; b. Stuart, Ia., Oct. 16, 1869; s. Ephraim and Elizabeth (Epperson) B.; A.B., Penn Coll., Oskaloosa, Ia., 1898, A.M., 1899, Litt.D., 1938; spl. work, U. of Chicago, 1900; grad. New York Sch. of Philanthropy (now N.Y. Sch. of Social Work), 1909; LL.D., Whittier Coll., 1917; LL.D., Haverford Coll., 1938; m. Minnie M. Pickett, Dec. 31, 1898; children—Herbert Epperson, Helen Joy (dec.), Gordon Townsend. Teacher, Penn Coll., 1899-1901; missionary, Soc. of Friends, Tokyo, Japan, since 1901. Chmn. trustees Friends' Girls' Sch., Tokyo, Japan, 1901-41. Mem. exec. com. Internat. Service Bur. of Japan, 1917-24; del. London All Friends Conf., 1920, Phila. Friends World Conf., 1937. An organizer Japan Peace Soc.; asso. with Sch. of Japanese Lang. and Culture as an organizer, sec., chmn. bd. trustees and acting dir., 1927-29, 1934-35; mem. Am. Assn. of Tokyo, Am.-Japan Society, Asiatic Society of Japan (mem. council); sent by exec. com. of Federated Missions, with rep. of Japanese Ch. Fed. to investigate Korean situation, 1919; rep. Am. Friends' Service Com. in China, India and Europe, 1930-31. Author: Jamaica and Friends Missions, 1899. Address: 141-Chrome, Mita Dai Machi, Shiba, Tokyo Japan‡

BOWLEY, ARTHUR LYON, statistician; b. Bristol, Eng., Nov. 6, 1869; s. Rev. James William Lyon and Maria (Johnson) B.; student Christs Hosp., London, 1879-88; B.A., Trinity Coll., Cambridge, 1892, M.A., 1895, Sc.D., 1913, hon. fellow, 1938; D.Sc., Manchester, 1926; D.Litt. (hon.), Oxford, 1895, D.Litt., 1944; m. Julia Hilliam, Mar. 26, 1904; children—Ruth Nicholson, Agatha, Marian. Lectr., U. Coll., Reading, 1900-19, London Sch. Economics and Polit. Sci., U. London, 1895-1915, prof. statistics, 1915-36, emeritus since 1936; acting dir. Inst. Statistics, Oxford, 1940-44. Decorated C.B.E., 1937, Knight Bachelor, 1950. Fellow Royal Statis. Soc. (president 1938-40, hon. v.p. since 1941), Royal Econ. Soc. (v.p., 1942); mem. Internat. Statis. Inst. (treas. 1929-36, 1947-49, hon. pres., 1949). Author: Elements of Statistics, 1902; Wages and Income in the United Kingdom since 1860, 1937; The Mathematical Groundwork of Economics, 1924; Editor: Studies in the National Income, 1924-38, 1944. Home: Marley Hill, Haslemere, Surrey England‡

BOWMAN, CHARLES HENRY, educator; b. Davenport, Ia., Nov. 19, 1873; s. John R. and Mary A. (Gabbert) B.; Ph.B., M.S., State U. of Ia., 1894; m. Minnie P. Schansenbach, of Ogden, Utah, Aug. 4, 1903. Began as instr. in physics, at State U. of Iowa. Pres. Mont. State Sch. of Mines, 1906-19. Mem. Am. Inst. Mining and Metall. Engrs. Home: Langhorne PA‡

BOWMAN, CRETE DILLON (MRS. JOHN W. BOMAN), civic worker; b. Sterling, Ill., Mar. 28, 1906; d. Paul W. and Crete (Blackman) Dillon; ed. Shipley Sch., 1924-27; m. John W. Bowman, June 21, 1928; children—Crete (Mrs. Bowman Harvey), Jon, Timothy (dec.), Diana (Mrs. Michael Neely). Chmn. women's aux. Community Gen. Hosp. Gift Shop, Sterling, Ill., 1956-61, head buyer, 1956-64, mem. Women's Aux. Bd., 1956-61; mem. program and bldg. coms. St. Timothy's Chapel, Southern Cross, Anaconda, Mont. Bd. dirs. McCormick Theol. Sem., Chgo., 1961-67, Salvation Army; chmn. bd. dirs. Presbyn. Nursery Sch., Sterling, 1957-68. Mem. bldg. com. YWCA; mem. Sts., Hwys., and Bridges Com. Presbyn. (pres. women's assn). Home: Sterling IL Died Sept. 15, 1968.

BOWMAN, HOWARD H(IESTAND) M(INNICH), ednl. admn.; b. Lancaster, Pa., Nov. 3, 1886; s. Andrew Minnich and Kate Howard (Hiestand) B.; desc. of John Bowman, pioneer Swiss settler in Lancaster County, Pa., 1712, B.Ph., Franklin and Marshall Coll., Lancaster, 1913, M.Sc., 1914; Ph.D., U. of Pa., 1917; m. Edna Katherine Lockwood, July 28, 1928 (deceased 1960). Began career as instructor Franklin and Marshall College, 1913-14, Pa. Sch. of Horticulture, Ambler, 1915; asst. U. of Pa., 1916-17; prof. Heidelberg Coll., Tiffin, O., 1917-18; at U.S. Army Md. Sch., Washington, D.C., 1918-1919; prof. biology Toledo U., 1919-57, head dept. biology and pre-medical div. emeritus, 1957; dir. med. edn. Toledo Hosp., 1957-63. Insp. Ohio Bureau of Plant Industry, 1945-48. Mem. executive committee Toledo Pub. Health Council. Vice chmn. Mich. Acad. Science, 1935, mem. council, 1935-36. Fellow Assn. Am. Genealogists, Am. Geneal. Soc., Am. Assn. for Advancement Science, Ohio Acad. Sci. (v.p. 1924; chmn. finance com. 1940, pres. 1946-47); mem. Am. Assn. Univ. Prop. (pres. Toledo Chapter, 1947), Am. Genetic Assn., Am. Bot. Soc., Am. Physiol. Soc., Field Nature Soc., Mich. Acad. Science, American Heart Association (sec. bd. dirs. N.W. Ohio chpt.), Ohio Heart Assn. (pres. 1953-54), Sons of the American Revolution, Sigma Xi, Kappa Psi, Pi Kappa Alpha, Phi Kappa Phi; hon. mem. Toledo Acad. Medicine. Republican. Episcopalian. Mason. Club: Torch. Wrote: Botanical Ecology of the Dry Tortugas, 1918; A Manual of Botany, 1930; Work Book for General Biology, 1939; Ecology and Physiology of the Red Mangrove for Proc. American Philos. Soc., 1917; Brochure on Internship at Toledo Hospital. Contbr. to tech. journs.; author of papers on Eastern Pa. history and genealogy. Collaborator editorial bd. Biol. Abstracts, 1925-45. Home: Toledo OH

BOWMAN, JAMES CLINTON, business exec.; b. Silverton, Colo., Mar. 14, 1903; s. Clinton A. and Mabel T. (Gifford) B.; B.S., U. of Colo., 1924; m. Helma Stephenson, Jan. 19, 1936; children—James Clinton, Bernadetta, Kenneth Horace, Stephen Alexander, Dianne Edna. Senior vice president and director C. & S. Ry. Co., Mountain States Tel. & Tel. Co., Denver-U.S. National Bank. Mem. Beta Theta Pi. Mason, (32 deg., Shriner), Clubs: Rotary Denver Athletic, Cherry Hills Country, Denver Press. Home: Golden CO Died Oct. 27, 1971.

BOWMAN, JOSEPH MERRELL, JR., govt. ofcl.; b. Valdosta, Ga., June 23, 1931; s. Joseph Merrell and Martha (Stanley) B.; LL.B., Emory U., 1957; m. Mary Isabella Nichols, Dec. 19, 1953; children—Joseph N., Mary B., Henry H. Admitted to Ga. bar, 1958; legislative asst. to Congressman Flynt, Jr., 1958-59; partner Kennedy, Kennedy, Seay &Bowman, Barnesville, Ga., 1959-62; Congl. liaison officer Dept. Labor, 1962-63; dep. asst. to sec. treasury Congl. liaison, 1963-64; asst. to sec. treasury Congl. relations, 1964-68; asst. sec. treas., 1968-72; mem. firm Corcoran, Foley, Youngman & Rowe. Mem. bd. visitors Emory U. Served to capt. USAF, 1952-56. Mem. Am., Ga., D.C. bar assns., Phi Delta Theta, Phi Delta Phi. Democrat. Methodist. Home: Alexandria VA Died May 16, 1972; buried Culpepper Nat. Cemetery, Culpepper VA

BOWMAN, KARL MURDOCK, physician; b. Topeka, Nov. 4, 1888; s. Homer Caleb and Isabelle Susanna (Murdock) B.; A.B., Washburn Coll., 1909, D.Sc., 1953; M.D., U. Cal. at Berkeley, 1913, LL.D., also Dr. J. Elliott Royer award, 1964; m. Eliza Abbott Stearns, Aug. 18, 1916 (dec. 1957); children—Richard Stearns, Thomas Elliot, Murdock Stearns, Walter Murdock; m. 2d, Anna Lowrey, July 18, 1959. Intern Children's Hosp., Los Angeles, 1913, Seton Hosp., N.Y.C., 1914, Roosevelt Hosp., N.Y.C., 1915, Bloomingdale Hosp., White Plains, N.Y., 1915-17, 19-21; chief med. officer Boston Psychopathic Hosp., 1921-36; asst. prof. psychiatry Harvard Med. Sch., 1921-36; dir. div. psychiatry Bellevue Hosp., N.Y.C., 1936-41; prof. psychiatry N.Y.U. Coll. Medicine, 1936-41; prof. psychiatry U. Cal. Sch. Medicine, San Francisco, 1941-56, prof. emeritus, 1956-73, med. supt. Langley Porter Clinic, San Francisco, 1941-56; vis. prof. U. Philippines Coll. Medicine, 1954-55; dir. div. mental health for Alaska, also supt. Alaska Psychiat. Inst., Anchorage, 1964-67. Sent to China by WHO to assist govt. China in setting up Nat. Psychiat. Inst., Nanking, 1947; cons. USPHS, Office Surgeon Gen., U.S. Army, U.S. Navy, USAF, VA; mem. com. neuropsychiatry NRC, 1944-47; dir. Cal. Sexual Deviation Research, 1950-54; mem. nat. health adv. com. USPHS, 1948-50; mem. profl. adv. com. Office Vocational Rehab., 1944-50; trustee Nat. Com. Mental Hygiene, 1944-47; mem. adv. bd. psychiatry A.R.C., 1938-50. Served as capt., M.C., U.S. Army, World War I; lt. comdr. USNR, 1935-52; ret., 1952. Diplomate in psychiatry Am. Bd. Psychiatry and Neurology (dir. 1943-46, 50-51). Fellow Am. Psychiat. Assn. (life fellow, pres. 1944-46), Physician Philippines (hon.), Am. Coll. Psychiatrists; hon. life mem. Philippine Mental Health Assn.; mem. Cal., San Francisco med. socs., N.Y., Mass. psychiat. socs., A.A.A.S., Boston Soc. Psychiatry and Neurology (sec.-treas. 1933-36), New Eng. Soc. Psychiatry, Assn. Research Nervous and Mental Disease (1st v.p. 1938, 41), Sigma Xi, Phi Delta Theta, Alpha Omega Alpha. Author: Personal Problems for Men and Women, 1931; also numerous articles. Asso. editor Geriatrics, Quar. Jour. Studies on Alcohol, 1942-73. Address: San Francisco CA Died Mar. 2, 1973.

BOWN, RALPH, physicist, cons. engineer; b. Fairport, N.Y., Feb. 22, 1891; s. Gardner W. and Bertha (Bruner) B.; Cornell U., M.E., 1913, M.M.E., 1915, Ph.D., 1917; m. Alma Crawford, June 28, 1919; children—Ralph, Crawford. Instr. in physics, Cornell U., 1913-17; with Am. Telephone & Telegraph Co., dept. of development and research, engaged in development of radio broadcasting and transoceanic comml. radiotelephony, 1919-34; dir. radio research, Bell Telephone Labs., N.Y.C. 1934-45, dir. TV research, 1938-46, dir. research 1946-51, v.p. research, 1951-54, v.p., 1954-56, ret.; cons. N.W. Ayer & Son, Inc., from 1956. Served at lt. later capt., Signal Corps, U.S. Army, 1917-19. Mem. Radar Division, Nat. Defense Research Com.; member Nat. Television Systems Com., 1940-41; expert consultant to secretary of war, 1941. Awarded Morris Liebmann Memorial prize by Institute of Radio Engineers, 1926, Medal of Honor, 1949, Founder's award, 1961. Fellow Am. Phys. Soc., Inst. Radio Engrs. (v.p. 1925; pres. 1926; dir.), Acoustical Soc. Am., Am. Inst. Elec. Engrs., A.A.A.S.; mem. Sigma Xi, Eta Kappa Nu, Gamma Alpha. Author of several technical papers; patentee. Address: Millburn NJ Died July 29, 1971; buried Old Brick Church, Bradevelt NJ

BOWRA, CECIL MAURICE, educator; b. Kiukiang, China, Apr. 8, 1898; s. Cecil Arthur Verner and Ethel Fleay (Lovibond) B.; B.A., Cheltenham Coll., New Coll., Oxford U., 1922, M.A., 1923, D.Litt., 1937; D. es Lettres, Sorbonne. Paris, 1950, U. Aix-Marseille (France), 1953; LL.D., St. Andrews (Scotland) U., 1959; Litt.D., Trinity Coll., Dublin, Ireland, 1949, Hull University, 1959, University of Wales, 1961. Harvard University, 1963; D.Litt., Columbia University. N.Y.C., 1967, U. Teheran, 1971; D.C.L., Oxford U., 1970. Fellow Wadham Coll., Oxford U., 1922-38, warden, 1938-70, vice chancellor univ., 1951-54, prof. poetry, 1946-51; E. C. Norton prof. poetry Harvard, 1948-49. Pres. British Acad., 1958-62. Served with R.F.A., British Army, World War I; France and Flanders. Created knight batchelor, 1951; companion Honour, 1971. Hon. mem. Am. Academy of Arts and Letters, National Institute of Arts and Letters, Royal Irish Academy. Author: Tradition and Design in the Iliad, 1931; Greek Lyric Poetry, 1936; Sophoclean Tragedy, 1944; The Heritage of Symbolism, 1943; Heroic Poetry, 1952; The Greek Experience, 1959; Primitive Song, 1962; Pindar, 1964; Memories, 1966; Landmarks in Greek Literature, 1966; Periclean Athens, 1971; On Greek Margins, 1970; Homer, pub. posthumously, 1972. Address: Oxford England Died July 4, 1971; buried St. Cross Oxford

BOWRON, FLETCHER, ret. judge; b. Poway, Cal., Aug. 13, 1887; s. Samuel and Martha (Hershey) B.; student U. Cal. at Berkeley, 1907-09, U. So. Cal. Law Sch., 1909-11; m. Irene Martin, Sept. 16, 1922 (dec. Jan. 4, 1961); 1 son, Barrett; m. 2d, Albine Power Norton, Nov. 18, 1961. Admitted to bar, 1917, practiced in Los Angeles, 1919-22; dep. corp. commr. State of Cal. 1923-25; exec. sec. to gov. Cal., 1925-26; judge Superior Court, Los Angeles, 1926-38, 56-62; compiler recent history Los Angeles, U. Cal. at Los Angeles, 1962-68; elected mayor of Los Angeles at recall election, Sept. 16, 1938; re-elected 1941, 45, 49. With 144th F.A., and later Mil. Intelligence Div., U.S. Army, 1917-18. Decorated Knight Order St. Olav (Norway); Orden del Aguila Azteca (Mexico); Orden el Merito (Chile); comdr. Order Orange-Nassau (Netherlands); Medalle Vermeille Reconnaissance Nationale (France); Star Italian Solidarity, 2d class (Italy); comdr Orderde la Couronne de Chene (Luxembourg). Mem. Los Angeles County Bar Assn., Conf. Cal. Judges, U.S. Conf. Mayors (past trustee), League Cal. Cities (past pres.), Am. Municipal Assn. (past pres.), Native Sons Golden West, Delta Chi. Republican. Methodist. Mason Kiwanian. Clubs: Jonathan, Greater Los Angeles Press (life). Home: Los Angeles CA Died Sept. 11, 1968; buried Inglewood Park Cemetery, Los Angeles CA

BOWYER, JOHN WILSON, prof. English; b Lexington, Va., Nov. 21, 1901; s. Logan Samuel and Mary Virginia (Potter) B.; B.A., Washington and Lee U., 1921. Howard Houston fellow, 1921-22, M.A., 1922; Stedman fellow, Harvard, 1925-26. Dexter traveling fellow, summer 1927, Ph.D., 1928; student in Europe, summers 1929-31: m. Lora B. Boarman, June 7, 1931; children—Mildred (Mrs. Bill Roy Norvell), Denis. Instr. English Va. Polytechnic Inst., 1922-23, assistant professor, 1923-24; acting professor of English, Coll. of Charleston, S.C., 1924-25; instr. in English and tutor in div. of mod. languages. Harvard, 1927-28; asso. prof. English, Southern Meth. U., Dallas, Tex., 1928-32, professor English, 1932-68, chmn. dept. 1960-63. Mem. Modern Lang. Assn. America. Am. Assn. Univ. Profs., Texas Inst. Letters, S. Central Modern Lang. Association, Texas Conf. Coll. Tchrs. of English. Phi Beta Kappa (asso.), Phi Eta Sigma, Delta Upsilon. Sigma Upsilon, Kappa Phi Kappa. Methodist. Editor and author: (with C. H. Thurman) Annals of Elder Horn, 1929; (with John O. Beaty) Famous Editions of English Poets, 1931; (with John O. Beaty, David L. Clark, and J. L. Neu) Form and Style, 1935; (with John Lee Brooks) The Victorian Age, 1938; (with G. Bond, I. Herron, J. Brooks) Better College English, 1950; The Celebrated Mrs. Centlivre, 1952; Rev. edit. Victorian Age, 1954. Contbr. of studies in literary history. Home: Dallas TX Died Feb. 1, 1968.

BOX, JOHN CALVIN, ex-congressman; b. Houston Co., Tex., Mar. 28, 1871; s. John J. W. and Susan A. (Morris) B.; ed. dist. schs. and Alexander Inst., Kilgore, Tex.; m. Mina Hill, Lufkin, Tex., June 1, 1893. Began practice of law at Lufkin, Tex., 1893; removal to Jacksonville, 1897; mem. firm Willson, Box & Watkins; judge County Ct., Cherokee Co., Tex., 2 terms, 1898-1901; mayor of Jacksonville 2 terms; served as chmn. Dem. Co. Com. and mem. Dem. State Com., Tex.; mem. 66th to 71st Congresses (1919-31), 2d Tex. Dist. Democrat. Methodist. Mason. Home: Jacksonville TX‡

BOXLEY, CALVIN PEYTON, lawyer; b. Butler, Mo., Nov. 6, 1901; s. Clark C. and Dott Edna (Ash) B.; student U. Mo., 1920-21; LL.B., U. Okla., 1925; m. Ruth Embry, Sept. 24, 1930; children—John Embry, Joan Elizabeth (Mrs. Jack Edward White). Admitted to Okla. bar, 1925, since practiced Oklahoma City; mem. firm Crowe, Boxley, Dunlevy, Thweatt, Swinford & Johnson, 1932-66. Mem. Am. (Okla. chmn. membership com. of corp. banking and bus. law section), Okla. bar assns., American Judicature Society, Phi Alpha Delta, Alpha Sigma Phi (past grand council). Methodist. Mason; Order of DeMolay (mem. Legion of Honor). Clubs: Men's Dinner, Beacon, American Business (past pres.) (Oklahoma City). Home: Oklahoma City OK Died Dec. 19, 1966; buried Rosehill Burial Park, Oklahoma City OK

BOYAJIAN, SETRAK KRIKOR, chemist; b. Harpute, Armenia, Turkey, Nov. 9, 1889; s. Krikor Heroian and Kohar (Samueian) B.; student Euphrates Coll. (Harpute), 1904-06; U. Wis., 1910-13; M.A., Clark U., 1914; research student Boston U., 1923-26, Harvard, 1924-33. Came to U.S., 1906, naturalized, 1915. Proprietor, research dir. Precision Testing Labs., Worcester, Mass., 1920-70. Cons. chemist, 1920-70. Served as 1st lt. Ordnance Res. Corp., 1917. Mem. Am Chem. Soc., A.A.A.S. Club: Harvard (Worcester, Mass.). Patentee in field. Home: Hudson MA Died Jan. 19, 1970; buried Woodlawn Cemetery, Wellesley MA

BOYCE, CHARLES MEREDITH, investment bankers; b. Balt., Feb. 8, 1920; s. Fred Grayson and Sophie (Meredith) B.; A.B., Yale, 1942; grad. sch. banking Rutgers U., 1952; m. Lila Jones, Oct. 3, 1942; children—Charles Meredith, Lila Capen, Elizabeth Barker. With Merc.-Safe Deposit and Trust Co., Balt., 1946-61, v.p., 1954-60, exec. v.p., 1960-61; partner Robert Garrett & Sons, Balt., 1961-64; exec. v.p. Robert Garrett & Sons, Inc., Balt., 1964-67, pres., 1967-69; dir. Can. Dry-Frostie Corp., F. Bowie Smith & Son, Inc., Baltimore & Annapolis R.R., All American Engring Co. city council, Balt., 1951-55, city treas., 1959-63. Treas., trustee Peabody Inst.; trustee Union Meml. Hosp., Samuel Ready Sch.; overseer Goucher Coll. Served from pvt. to maj., inf., AUS, 1942-46. Mem. Investment Bankers Association. Clubs: Maryland, Elkridge, Merchants. Home: Baltimore MD Died Mar. 31, 1969; buried Druid Ridge Cemetery.

BOYD, ALFRED, civil engineer; b. Evansville, Ind., January 7, 1872; s. Abram and Bettie (Jones) B.; B.S. in C.E., Washington U., 1894; m. Alice Sloan Dimmick, Aug. 31, 1910; children—Alice Louise, Alfred Gordon. Engaged in water supply and structural engring., Mo., Ill. and Ohio, 1895-1906; instr. civ. engring., U. of Neb., 1907-10; prof. civ. engring., Okla. Agrl. and Mech. Coll., Sept. 1910, dean sch. of engring., Sept. 1914-June 1920; prof. civil engineering, U. of N.D.; 1920-44. Mem. Am. Soc. Civil Engr., Sigma Tau, Sigma Alpha Epsilon, Phi Kappa Phi. Address: Middle Brook MO‡

BOYD, DARRELL SULLY, lawyer; b. N. Tonawanda, N.Y., Nov. 12, 1889; s. George A. and Anna F. (Wagstaff) B.; A.B., Wesleyan U., Middletown, Conn., 1910; grad. study Columbia, 1910-11; LL.B., Northwestern U., 1913; m. Emily F. Matz, June 25, 1921; children—Charlotte McNitt, Denman, Darrell. Admitted to Ill. bar, 1913, and began practice at Chgo.; mem. firm Bell, Boyd, Lloyd, Haddad & Burns, and predecessors, 1918-71. Mem. bd. directors of L.C.N. Closers of Canada, Ltd., First National Bank Winnetka. Trustee Wesleyan U. Mem. Am., Chicago bar assns., Law Club, Phi Beta Kappa, Phi Nu Theta, Phi Delta Phi, Order of the Coif. Republican. Episcopalian. Clubs: University, Indian Hill, Attic. Home: Winnetka IL Died July 10, 1971.

BOYD, EDWIN FORREST, physician and surgeon; b. Fresno, Cal., Nov. 10, 1889; s. John D. and Margeret L. (Goree) B.; A.B., Stanford U., 1915, M.D., 1919; m. Ethel C. Ostrander, July 29, 1914; 1 son, Edwin Forrest. Began practice in 1919; sr. mem. staff Hollywood Presbyn. Hosp., chief of staff, 1942; sr. attending staff Los Angeles Gen. Hosp. Surg. for Presbyn. Bd. Fgn. Missions for Southern Calif. Sr. Surg. U.S. Res. Public Health Service. Founder, mem. Los Angeles Civic Light Opera Assn. Fellow Internat. Coll. Surgeons; mem. A.M.A., Hollywood Acad. Medicine, Los Angeles County Med. Soc., Am. Soc. Tropical Med., Calif. State Med. Assn., Radiol. Safety Soc., Stanford Assos. (bd. dirs.), Crossroads Operations, Wilshire Y.M.C.A., Nu Sigma Nu, Del. to Gen. Assembly Presbyn. Ch. in U.S.A., Detroit, 1943. Republican. Presbyterian. Mason (Shriner). Clubs: Los Angeles Breakfast, University, Kiwanis, Town Hall. Contbr. articles to medical jours. World traveler, lecturer and photographer. Home: Hollywood CA Died 1971.

BOYD, GEORGE ADAMS, ins. co. exec.; b. Middletown, N.Y., Oct. 4, 1898; s. Frederick Newton and Grace Cooper (Adams) B.; A.B., Cornell U., 1921; m. Helen Gurnee Green, June 23, 1928; 1 dau., Margaret Deborah. Statistician, Am. Tel. & Tel. Co., 1921-26; investment analyst Continental Ins. Co., N.Y.C., and affiliates, 1926-28, asst. sec., 1928-54, v.p., 1954-60, exec. v.p., 1960-72; exec. v.p Fidelity-Phenix Ins. Co.; exec. v.p., dir. Niagara Fire Ins. Co., Fidelity

& Casualty Co. of N.Y.; exec. v.p. Firemen's Ins. Co. of Newark, and affiliates, Yorkshire Ins. Co. and affiliate; trustee United States Trust Co. (New York City); dir. Niagara Ins. Co. (Bermuda), Ltd., Afco, Inc., Cafo, Ltd., Nypen Corp. Trustee Skidmore Coll. Mem. Ins. Fedn. N.Y., Ins. Soc. N.Y., Phi Beta Kappa. Presbyn. Clubs: University, Bankers Am. (N.Y.C.). Author: Elias Boudinot, Patriot and Statesman, Middletown NY Died Mar. 11, 1972.

BOYD, HARRY HUTCHESON, dramatist; b. at Newry, Co. Down, Ireland, May 22, 1869; s. Hutcheson and Jessie (Smyth) B.; ed. mil. coll., Isle of Jersey, English Channel; unmarried. Author: A Citizen's Home (play in 4 acts, prod. Majestic Theatre, New York, Oct. 4, 1909; (with Geraldine Bonner) Sauce for the Goose (comedy). Translator: Du Bois L'Education de Soi-meme. Address: 52 W. 39th St., NY‡

BOYD, JAMES CHURCHILL, civil engr.; b. St. Louis, Mo., Aug. 19, 1871; s. Samuel Stillman and Harriet E. (Churchill) B.; student Mass. Inst. Tech., 1889-92; m. Ada Yerxa, Sept. 5, 1895. Engr. on location and constrn. of railroad, sewer and waterworks, 1891-97; div. engr. in charge design and constrn. Boston Elevated Ry., including terminal stas. and shops, 1897-1902; engr. in charge new constrn. and maintenance, Bangor & Aroostook R.R., 1902; with Westinghouse, Church, Kerr & Co. as cons. engr., chief engr., and v.p. and dir., 1902-20; v.p., treas. and dir. F. H. McGraw & Co., New York, 1929-31; now consulting engr., private practice, Portland, Me. V.p. and dir. Nat. Bank of Commerce; director The Boyd Corp.; dir. Thomas Laughlin Co., Portland, Me. Home: 231 Woodfords St., Portland, Me. Office: 35 Exchange St., Portland ME‡

BOYD, LOUISE ARNER, explorer, author; b. San Rafael, Cal., Sept. 16, 1887; d. John Franklin and Louise Cook (Arner) Boyd; ed. Miss Stewart's Sch., San Rafael, Miss Murison's Sch., San Francisco; hon. LL.D., U. Cal., 1939, Mills Coll., 1939. Explorer of East Greenland; explorer polar region, N.E. and West Greenland (Spitzbergen and Franz Josef Land); flew pvt. chartered plane over North Pole, 1955. Decorated Chevalier Legion of Honor (France), St. Olaf of Norway (1st fgn. woman to receive award); awarded Andree plaque by Swedish Anthropol. and Geog. Soc.; Cullum gold medal Am. Geog. Soc., medal of King Christian Xth of Denmark; certificate of Appreciation, U.S. Army; made hon. citizen City of San Rafael. Mem. Royal Hort. Soc. (London), Am. Polar Soc. (hon., dir.), Cal. Acad. Sci. (hon.), Am. Soc. Photogrammetry, Am. Geog. Soc. (council), Assn. Pacific Coast Geographers, Brit. Glaciological Soc., Am. Hort. Soc., Soc. Woman Geographers, Cal. Bot. Soc., Nat. League Am. Pen Women, Geog. Soc. Phila. (hon.), Colonial Dames Am., Sigma Delta Epsilon. Republican. Episcopalian. Clubs: San Francisco Garden (hon.); Burlingame (Cal.) Country, Marin Garden (hon.); Colony (N.Y.); Garden of Am. (mem.-at-large). Author: Fiord Region of East Greenland, 1935; Polish Countrysides, 1937; Coast of Northeast Greenland. Contbr. to Geog. Rev. Office: San Francisco CA Died Sept. 1972.

BOYD, MARY BROWN SUMNER (MRS. MARK BOYD), author; b. N.Y. City, Aug. 6, 1876; d. Charles Porter and Abigail Anna (Prince) Sumner; A.B., Barnard Coll. (Columbia), 1900; m. Mark Boyd, of London, Eng., 1913; 1 son, Sumner. Was made mem. of staff of Survey Mag., 1909; sec. data dept. Nat. Am. Woman Suffrage Assn., 1915-18; on editorial staff The Woman Citizen, 1917-19; chmn. of research, Leslie Woman Suffrage Commn., 1917-19; mng. editor Birth Control Rev. since 1924; chmn. research com. League of Women Voters, 1918-19. Formerly mem. exec. com. Twilight Sleep Assn. Author: Painless Childbirth, 1915; The Woman Citizen, 1918. Home: 87 Bedford St., New York, N.Y.; also Hudson OH‡

BOYD, PAUL PRENTICE, univ. dean; b. Cameron, W.Va., Feb. 26, 1877; s. Milton Robin (M.D.) and Florence Virginia (Talbott) B.; A.B., Oberlin, 1898; M.A., Cornell U., 1905, Ph.D., 1911, LL.D., Park College, Parkville, Missouri, 1942; m. Cleona Belle Matthews, Aug. 2, 1906; children—Virginia Drue, Martha Elizabeth. Teacher pub. schs., Isle St. George, O., 1898-99, teacher mathematics, Park Coll. Acad., Parkville, Mo., 1899-1903; prof. mathematics and astronomy, Park Coll., 1903-04; fellow in mathematics, Cornell U., 1905-06; prof. mathematics, Hanover (Ind.) Coll., 1906-12; prof. mathematics, U. of Ky., 1912-1947, head of dept. 1913-1947, dean coll. arts & sciences, 1917-47, acting pres., 1917. Pres. Interstate Oratorical Association, 1911-12; chmn. bd. of trustees Lees Junior College; chmn. Kentucky com. Postwar Higher Edn., 1943-45. Fellow A.A.A.S.; mem. Am. Math. Soc., Math. Assn. America, Ky. Ednl. Assn., Ky. Acad. of Science (pres., 1919-20), Ky. Assn. Colls. and Secondary Schs. (sec. 1929-47), Southern Assn. Colls. and Secondary Schs. (sec. com. on postwar edn. 1943-45), N.E.A., Phi Beta Kappa, Sigma Xi, (pres. Ky. chapter, 1921-22), Phi Delta Kappa, Pi Mu Epsilon, Pi Gamma Mu, Sigma Delta Chi, Omicron Delta Kappa, Phi Sigma Kappa. Democrat. Presbyterian. Mason. Club: Lexington Executive (pres. 1944-45). Co-author: Boyd, Davis & Rees' Analytic Geometry, 1922; Boyd and Downing's Brief Course in Analytical Geometry, 1946. Contbr. to mags. on ednl. subjects. Home: 119 Waller Av., Lexington KY‡

BOYD, RALPH E., mfg. co. exec.; b. Orrville, O., 1900. Chmn., dir. Galion Iron Works & Mfg. Co. div. Jeffrey-Galion Inc.; chmn. Galion Mfg. of Can., Ltd.; dir. Jeffrey Co., Gen. Hydraulics Co., Galion (Pty.) Ltd., Jeffrey-Galion Mfg. Co., First Nat. Bank Mansfield. Home: Bucyrus OH Died Dec. 23, 1971; buried Galion OH

BOYD, RALPH GATES, lawyer; b. Chelmsford, Mass., Oct. 30, 1901; s. Richard Turnbull and Jennie (Gates) B.; A.B. cum laude, Harvard, 1922, LL.B., 1925; m. Dorothy Louise Koch, Apr. 2, 1932; 1 son, Douglas. Admitted to Mass. bar, 1926, since practiced in Boston; asso. firm Dunbar, Nutter & McClennen (now Nutter, McClennen & Fish), 1925-34, partner, 1934-54, own practice, and partner firm Boyd & MacCrelish, 1954-61; partner firm Boyd, MacCrellish & Weeks, 1962-72; pres. West Point Mfg. Co., 1950-51, also chmn. bd. dirs. subsidiary and affiliated textile cos.; gen. counsel United-Carr Inc., 1929-65, also dir.; chmn. bd. dirs. Davis-Furber Machine Co.; dir. Roger Boyd, Inc., W. J. Connell Co.; dir., clk. Bankers Service Co. Mem. Beacon Hill Archtl. Com., 1964-71. Mem. nat. bd. dirs. Arthritis and Rheumatism Found., also mem. nat. exec. com., trustee gen. counsel Mass. chpt.; trustee, treas. France G. Lee Found. Served as pvt. Jr. Co., S.A.T.C., 1918; maj. to col., U.S. Army, 1941-46, col., brig. gen. JAGC, U.S. Army Res. 1947-61; ret., 1961. Decorated Legion of Merit, Commendation ribbon, Am., Asiatic, E.T.O. ribbons, Battle star for No. France. Mem. Am. Bar Assn. (chmn. sect. corp., banking and bus. law 1950-51, mem. Ho. of Dels. 1948-52, chmn. com. lawyers in Armed Forces, 1952-53, chmn. com. Mil. Justice, 1953-56; mem. adv. com. to U.S. Mil. Appeals, 1952-72; mem. Judge Advs. Assn. (pres. 1947, dir. 1946-57), Mass. State, Boston bar assns., Assn. U.S. Army (pres., dir. Mass. Bay chpt.). Republican. Conglist. Clubs: Union Algonquin, Harvard, Fort Hill, Downtown (Boston); Harvard (N.Y.C.). Author wartime legislation and Army regulations and manuals; also articles. Home: Boston MA Died Mar. 31, 1972; buried Mt. Auburn Cemetery, Cambridge MA

BOYD, ROBERT, shorthand school; b. Russell, Ont., Canada, Apr. 10, 1870; s. Robert and Anna (Corscadden) B.; high sch., Ottawa, Can.; grad. Toronto, U., 1896. Founder and head of the Boyd Sch., Chicago. Author: The Boyd Shorthand Instructor; Boyd Letter Writer; Boyd Shorthand Dictionary; Boyd Phrase Book; Scientific Touch Typewriting. Home: Atlantic Hotel. Office: 64 W. Randolph St., Chicago IL‡

BOYD, WILLIAM (HOPALONG CASSIDY), actor; b. nr. Cambridge, O., June 5, 1895; s. Charles W. and Lida Alberta (Wilkins) B.; student pub. schs. Cambridge, O.; m. Elinor Fair; m. 2d Dorothy Sebastian; m. 3d Grace Bradley, June 5, 1937. Motion picture actor since 1919; played leading role in The Volga Boatman, 1926; appeared in King of Kings, 1927, Two Arabian Knights, 1928; starred in Skyscraper, The Leatherneck, Officer O'Brien, The Painted Desert; in title role of Hopalong Cassidy series since 1934, in series films, starring on nat. TV. program since 1949; in Bar 20, 1943, Texas Masquerade, 1944. Riders of the Deadline, 1944; formed Hopalong Cassidy Prdns., 1945; co-producer The Devil's Playground, 1946, other prdns. include: Fool's Gold; Unexpected Guest; Lost Canyon; Border Vigilantes; Stick to Your Guns; made radio debut, Jan. 1950; appears as figure of Hopalong Cassidy in syndicated comic strip and comic books. Participated in Armed Forces Radio Service Show; made transcriptions for forces during World War II. Address: Beverly Hills CA Died 1972.

BOYDEN, FRANK LEAROYD, headmaster; b. Foxboro, Mass., Sept. 16, 1879; s. Benjamin Franklin and Anna Wales (Cary) B.; A.B., Amherst, 1902, A.M., 1922; A.M., Williams, 1924, Yale, 1926; Sc.D., Colgate, 1930; Pd.D., N.Y. State Coll. for Teachers, 1931; LL.D., Wesleyan U., 1933, Kenyon Coll. 1937; L.H.D., Amherst Coll., 1935, Bowdoin Coll., 1936, Williams Coll., 1936, Princeton, 1940, Dartmouth, 1949, Trinity, 1952, Penn, 1968; LL.D., Harvard, 1947, Lehigh University, 1951, University of Massachusetts, 1957, St. Anselm's, 1963, Ripon Coll., 1963; Litt. D., Tufts, U., Medford, Mass., 1947; Doctor of Pub. Service, Denver U., 1952; Ed.D., Suffolk, 1967; Litt. D., Boston U., 1970; m. Helen Childs, June 27, 1907; 3 children—John Cary, Theodore Childs, Elizabeth. Headmaster of Deerfield (Massachusetts) Acad., 1902-68. Mem. Sec. of Navy's Civilian Adv. Com., World War II; mem. Jamestown-Williamsburg-Yorktown Commn. Chmn. bd. trustees U. Mass., 1960-70; trustee at various times of numerous instns., including Amherst Coll., Andover-Newton Theol. Sch., Cushing Acad., Deerfield Acad., Mass. Tng. Sch., Nichols Coll., Stoneleigh-Burnham Sch., Suffield Acad., Vt. Acad., Historic Deerfield, Inc., Franklin County Pub. Hosp., bd. dirs. Franklin County YMCA; chmn. Franklin County chpt. A.R.C., 1920-58. Recipient Shattuck Centennial citation for service to secondary edn., 1958; Commonwealth Mass. citation, 1967; citation Pres. U.S., 1967; Distinguished American award Nat. Football Found. and Hall Fame, 1971; gymnasium at U. Mass. named in his honor; professorship established in his honor at U. Mass.; numerous other honors and awards. Mason. Republican. Clubs: Amherst, Century, Yale, Princeton (N.Y.C.); Harvard, Tavern (Boston). Home: Deerfield MA Died Apr. 25, 1972; buried Laurel Hill Cemetery, Deerfield MA

BOYER, FRANCIS, pharm. mfg. exec.; b. Penllyn, Pa., June 21, 1893; s. Henry Conover and Nathalie C. (Robinson) B.; student Groton Sch., 1912, Harvard, 1912-15, Cambridge (Eng.) U., 1919; LL.D., Hahnemann Medical College, 1956, Univ. of Pa., 1961; D.Sc., Trinity Coll., 1961; L.H.D., Jefferson Med. Coll., 1965, Pa. Mil. Colls., 1966; m. Marian Angell Godfrey, July 6, 1950;children—(by previous marriage) Markley Holmes, Mary Robinson. Began in circulation dept. Curtis Pub. Co., 1915; advt. dept. Phila. Public Ledger, 1916; with Smith Kline & French Labs., pharm. mfrs., Phila., 1919-72, became asst. to pres., 1926, exec. v.p., 1936, pres., 1951, chmn. bd., 1958-66, dir.; mem. of the board of directors of The Philadelphia Contributionship. Mem. bd. advisers Nat. Fund for Medical Education. Mem. bd. mgrs. Wistar Institute Anatomy and Biology; formerly mem. nat. adv. com. Arthritis and Metabolic Diseases Council; dir. Project Hope, 1958-61; mem. Harvard Bd. Overseers, 1958-64; mem. Harvard overseers com. to visit Peabody Mus. and dept. anthropology, 1966-72; associate trustee, member board med. education and research University Pennsylvania 1960-72. Served as 1st lieutenant F.A., U.S. Army, 1917-19. Fellow Royal Soc. Medicine London (hon.); mem. Pharmaceutical Manufacturers Association (director, 1958-65), Phi Beta Kappa. Clubs: Philadelphia, Harvard (Phila.). Author articles profl. jours. Home: Ardmore PA Died May 21, 1972.

BOYKIN, FRANK WILLIAM, ex-congressman, business exec.; b. Bladon Springs, Alabama, February 21, 1885; s. James Clark and Glo Ermenia (Ainsworth) B.; ed. pub. schs.; m. Ocllo Gunn, Dec. 31, 1913; children—Frances Ocllo, Frank William (dec.), James Robert and John Gunn (twins), Richard Ainsworth. Began as clerk in store at Fairford, Ala., later store mgr.; started own business as mfr. ry. crossties; entered lumber and naval stores business, Malcolm, Ala.; now identified extensively with real estate, farming, livestock, timber, lumber and naval stores in southern Ala., with hdqrs. at Mobile; elected representative to 74th Congress, 1st Alabama District, July 30, 1935, to fill unexpired term of John McDuffle, resigned; mem. 75th to 87th Congresses, 1936-62, same dist.; exec. v.p. Tensaw Land and Timber Co. Served as official of shipbuilding cos. at Mobile and Pensacola, Fla., during World War I; president Loyalty League of Alabama and Miss. Democrat. Methodist. Mason (32 deg., Shriner), Moose, Woodman, Elk, Eastern Star. Home: Mobile AL Died Mar. 12, 1969; buried Pinecrest Cemetery, Mobile AL

BOYLE, LEO MARTIN, adj. gen. of Illinois; b. Chicago, Ill., July 20, 1899; s. Frank E. and Margaret (Callahan) B.; grad. Cath. schs., Chgo.; m. Anna Marie Boyle, July 4, 1931 (dec.); one son, George Anthony. Served with U.S. Army, 1917-19; 2d lt., inf., 1924, advancing through the grades to maj. gen., 1945; the adjutant general, chief of staff, Mil. and Naval Dept., State of Ill., 1940-69. Decorated Silver Star for gallantry during World War I. Roman Catholic. Home: Springfield IL Died May 3, 1969.

BOYLEN, MATTHEW JAMES, mining exec.; b. Weston, Ont. Can., Aug. 10, 1907; s. James G. and Dorothy (Baker) B.; D.C.L., U. N.B., 1954; D.Sc., Sacred Heart U., Bathhurst, N.B., 1957; m. Dorothy Pearson, May 30, 1936; children—James A., Phillip E., Dorothy E. Chmn. Advocate Mines, Ltd., Coniagas Mines, Ltd.; pres., dir. Northern Can. Mines Ltd., Satellite Metal Mines Ltd., Consol. Rambler Mines Ltd. (all Toronto); dir. Guaranty Trust Co., Brunswick Mining and Smelting Corp. Ltd. Canadian Bd. govs. Mt. Allison U., Sackville, N.B.; dir. Queensway Hosp., Toronto. Mem. United Ch. of Canada. Clubs: Granite, Royal Canadian Yacht; (Toronto); Seigniory (Que.); Canadian (N.Y.C.); Jockey (Ontario); Indian Creek Golf (Miami, Fla.); Key Largo Anglers (Fla.). Home: 35 Kingsway Crescent Toronto Ontario Canada Died July 7, 1970.

BOYLON FRANCIS OSCAR, paper co. exec.; b. Ada, Mich., Jan. 12, 1912; s. Thomas C. and Pauline (Feutz) B.; B.S. in Mech. Engring., U. Mich., 1934; night student Wharton Sch. of U. Pa.; corr. student Am. Mgmt. Assn.; m. E. Marjorie Lindsey, Nov. 19, 1937; children—James L., Kathleen A. Engaged in paper business, 1934-70; with Crown Zellerbach Corp., 1948-70, pres., chief exec. officer, 1969-70; dir. Bank of Cal., St. Francisville Paper Co. Home: San Francisco CA Died Feb. 17, 1970.

BOYNTON, CHARLES ALBERT, judge; b. East Hatley, Compton County, P.Q., Can., Nov. 26, 1867; s. Alpheus S. and Jane Grannis (Cook) B.; B.S., Glasgow (Ky.) Normal U., 1888; LL.B., U. of Mich., 1891; m. Laura Bassett Young, Nov. 1, 1897; children—Ben Lee, Charles Albert, James Edward (dec.). Admitted to Tex. bar, 1891; to practice before Supreme Court of U.S., 1914; practiced in Waco, Tex.; apptd. by President Theodore Roosevelt U.S. atty., Western Dist. of Tex., 1906; re-apptd. by President Taft, 1910 (resigned), 1912; mem. law firm Sleeper, Boynton & Kendall; apptd. by President Coolidge U.S. dist. judge, Western Dist. Tex., Dec. 16, 1924. Mem. Rep. State Exec. Com. of Tex. for a number of years; del. to Rep. Nat. Conv., 1896, 1900, 1904 (chmn. Tex. delegation), 1908 and 1920, Rep. nominee for gov. 1918. Episcopalian. Home: 716 W. Yandell Boul. Address: US Court House, El Paso TX‡

BOYNTON, CHARLES HOMER, clergyman, educator; b. Lake Side, Wayne Co., N.Y.; s. Lorenzo Robinson and Harriet M. (Northrup) B.; grad. Brockport State Normal Sch., 1880; A.B., U. of Rochester, 1886; B.D., Gen. Theol. Sem., 1899; Ph.D., New York U., 1889; D.D., U. of the South, 1922; m. Frances H. Cogswell, of Rochester, N.Y., June 1, 1892; children—Richard (dec.), James Breck, Martha Cogswell, Charles Francis. Deacon, 1889; priest, 1890, P.E. Ch.; curate Christ Ch., Rochester, N.Y., 1889; rector St. Michael's Ch., Geneseo, N.Y., 1890-1909; professor homiletics and pedagogy, General Theological Seminary, 1909-29 Commr. to Turkey and Armenia, Mar.-July 1919, also June-Aug. 1923; in the Orient, 1926. Lecturer summer schs., Wellesley, Mass., Geneva, N.Y., Princeton, N.J., Sewanee, Tenn., and Racine, Wis.; chmn. Provincial Commn. of Religious Edn. of N.Y. and N.J.; mem. Dept. of Religious Edn. P.E. Ch., 1913-25; dep. to Gen. Conv., 1907; dir. religious edn., St. Paul's Ch., Englewood, N.J., 1914-25. Mem. Alpha Delta Phi, Phi Beta Kappa, National Arts Club. Republican. Mason. Home: Williamstown MA‡

BOYNTON, HENRY WALCOTT, writer; b. Guilford, Conn., Apr. 22, 1869; s. George Mills and Julia (Holmes) B.; A.B., Amherst, 1891, A.M., 1893; m. Lucia Griswold Merrill, 1893 (died 1899); children—Merrill Holmes, Oliver Griswold; m. 2d, May Whittemore, 1908; 1 son, John. Head dept. of English lit., Phillips Acad., Andover, Mass., 1892-1901; since then a professional writer. Chief reviewer for Atlantic Monthly, 1901-04; contbr. various periods, to Nation, Bookman, Independent, Outlook, N.Y. Sun, etc. Mem. Psi Upsilon. Clubs: Authors (New York); Rhode Island Country. Author: Life of Washington Irving, 1901; The Golfer's Rubaiyat, 1901; Bret Harte, 1903; (with T. W. Higginson) A Reader's History of American Literature, 1903; Journalism and Literature, 1904; Guenever—a Romantic Play, 1905; The World's Leading Poets, 1911; James Fenimore Cooper, 1931; Annals of American Book-Selling, 1932. Editor: Selections from Carlyle, 1895; Tennyson's The Princess, 1896; Milton's Paradise Lost, 1897; Goldsmith's The Vicar of Wakefield, 1899; Pope's The Rape of the Lock, etc., 1901; Mrs. Ewing's Jackanapes, etc., 1902; Miss Martineau's The Prince and the Peasant, 1902; Pope's Complete Poetical Works (Cambridge edit.), 1902; Selected Poems for Secondary Schools, 1911; Carlyle's Essay on Burns, 1922; Tennyson's Idylls of the King, 1923; Longfellow's Tales of a Wayside Inn, 1925. Contbr. to American Writers on American Literature," 1931 Home: Upper Longfield, Bristol RI‡

BOZELL, HAROLD VEATCH, elec. engineer; b. Beloit, Kan., May 31, 1886; s. Charles Fremont and Olive Arletta (Veatch) B.; B.S. in E.E., U. of Kan., 1908, E.E., 1915; m. Isadel Read Heath, Nov. 22, 1910; children—Mrs. Elizabeth Louise Forrest, Joan Virginia (dec.). Head of elec. engring. dept., U. of Okla., 1908-16, also cons. engr.; asst. prof. elec. engring., Yale, 1916-21, also editor Electric Ry. Jour., New York, 1920-21; First editor Bus. Transportation, 1922; editor Electrical World, 1922-25; connected with Bonbright & Co. investments, 1925-32; dir. and pres. General Telephone Corp.; dir. Gen. Pub. Utilities Corp. (N.Y.), The North Electric Company, Galion, O., Roanwell Corp., N.Y.C., N.E. Electronics Corp., Concord, N.H. Capt. Signal Corps., Oklahoma National Guard, 1913-16; in charge signal training Com. on Edn. and Spl. Training, World War, also with Com. on Spl. Problems of Naval Cons. Bd., World War, and dir. Okla. industrial survey 1916; mem. telephone operations industry adv. bd. W.P.B., World War II. Named to Hall of Fame, Ind. Telephone Pioneer Assn., 1970. Fellow Am. Inst. E.E.; mem. Sigma Xi, Tau Beta Pi, Beta Theta Pi. Republican. Methodist. Rotarian. Clubs: Bankers, Down Town Athletic, Univ., Yale (N.Y.); Larchmont Shore, University, Bonnie Briar Country (Larchmont). Home: Larchmont NY Died Nov. 27, 1972.

BRACH, FRANK VINCENT, confectioner; b Jan. 9, 1891; s. Emil J. and Kathryn M. (Cunningham) B.; grad. in bus. adminstrn., De Paul U., 1908; m. Helen Marie Vorhees, Dec. 22, 1951. A founder E. J. Brach & Sons, Chgo., 1904, dir., 1917-70, pres., 1951-70. Recipient certificate of quality excellence Montgomery Ward & Co., 1965, plaque Ben Franklin Stores, 1966, Candy Kettle award, 1966; named dean candy industry Nat. Candy Wholesalers Assn., 1966. Mem. Nat. Confectioners Assn. (1st hon. conv. chmn. 1965). Republican. Clubs: Chicago Athletic, Illinois Athletic (Chgo.); Bob-O-Link (Highland Park, Ill.); Oakmont (McHenry, Ill.); Indian Creek (Miami Beach, Fla.). Home: Glenview IL Died Jan. 29, 1970; buried Unionport Cemetery, Unionport OH

BRACKEN, JOHN, leader Progressive Conservative Party Can., 1942-48; b. Seeley's Bay, Ont., Can., June 22, 1883; s. Ephraim and Alberta (Gilbert) B.; ed. Brockville Collegiate Institute, Ont. Agrl. College; B.S.A., U. Ill.; LL.D., U. Manitoba, 1927, U. Saskatchewan, 1930; m. Alice Wylie Bruce, 1909; children—John Bruce, Alan Douglas, William Gordon, George Murray. Prof. field husbandry, U. of Saskatchewan, 1910-20; pres. Manitoba Agr. Coll., U. of Manitoba, 1920-22; active in furthering interests of farmers; became mem. Manitoba Legislature as mem. Progressive Party, later Liberal-Progressive Party; premier of Manitoba and pres. exec. council 1922-42; leader of the Progressive Conservative Party 1942-1948; elected to Can. House of Commons, constituency of Neepawa, Manitoba, June 1945. Mason. Mem. United Ch. Clubs: Manitoba (Winnipeg, Can.); Rideau Manotick ON Canada Died Mar. 18, 1969; buried Rideauvale Cemetery, Kars Ontario Canada

BRACKETT, E(LMER) E(UGENE), engr.; b. Jamesburg, N.J., Nov. 22, 1876; s. Benjamin Franklin and Annie Eliza (Lary) B.; B.Sc. in Elec. Engring., U. of Neb., 1901; m. Minnie Burt Guile, Sept. 17, 1903; children—Mary (Mrs. Leo Barnell), Ruth (dec.), Annie L. (Mrs. Charles B. Heal), Elmer Eugene, Jane J. (wife of Dr. Elbert T. Phelps). Installation, operation and management of small pub. utilities in midwest, 1901-06 and 1911-12; instr. elec. engring. U. of Pa., 1907-10; instr. agrl. engring., advancing to prof., U. of Neb., 1913-47, chmn. dept. 1928-47, retired as emeritus prof., 1947; prin. U. of Neb. Trades Sch. (Vets. Rehabilitation), 1922-24. Mem. Neb. Bd. Tractor Test Engrs., 1919-47, chmn., 1928-47; former asso. Am. Inst. Elec. Engrs. Registered professional engr., Neb. Served as 1st lt., U.S. Army Air Service, 1918-19; overseas, France and Italy. Mem. Soc. Agrl. Engrs. (pres. 1940), Neb. Engring. Soc., Am. Soc. Engring. Edn., Neb. Reclamation Assn., Lincoln C. of C., Y.M.C.A., Farm House, Am. Legion, Sigma Xi, Gamma Sigma Delta. Republican. Presbyterian. Mason. Clubs: Engineers (past pres.), Rotary (Lincoln). Home: 6053 25th Rd. N., Arlington, Va. Office: University of Nebraska, Arlington VA‡

BRACKETT, FRANK PARKHURST, astronomer; b. Provincetown, Mass., June 16, 1865; s. S. H. and Mary (Thomas) B.; A.B., Dartmouth Coll., 1887, A.M., 1890, Sc.D., 1927; hon. fellow, Clark U., 1902-03; m. Lucretia Burdick, Aug. 15, 1889 (died 1937); children—Mary Amanda (dec.), Frederick Sumner, Frank Parkhurst. Instr. mathematics and astronomy, 1888-90, prof. mathematics, 1890-1924, prof. astronomy, 1924-33, dir. observatory, 1908-33, prof. emeritus since 1933, chmn. of faculty, 1927-30, Pomona Coll., Calif.; also chmn. faculty Claremont Colls., 1930-32. Prof. mathematics, U. of Calif., summer 1910, mem. Smithsonian Astron. Expdn. to Africa, 1911, to Mt. Whitney, 1913; sec. Local Exemption Bd., 1917-18; dir. Solar Eclipse Expdn. to the Isthmus, Santa Catalina Island, 1923, to Ramm's Ranch and Honey Lake, Calif., 1930. Trustee C.R.B. Ednl. Foundation, Belgian Am. Ednl. Foundation. Fellow A.A.A.S.; mem. Am. Math. Soc., Math. Assn. of America, Astron. Soc. America, Royal Astron. Soc. Can., Sigma Xi, Phi Beta Kappa. Lecturer and writer on astron. subjects. Am. del. of Commn. for Relief in Belgium, Province of Brabant, 1916. Author: History of San Jose Rancho, 1919; The Challenge of the Ages; Granite and Sage Brush. Home: Box 433, Balboa Island, Calif. Office: 11044 Kling St., N Hollywood CA‡

BRACKETT, HAVEN DARLING, univ. prof.; b. Southbridge, Mass., Sept. 16, 1876; s. George and Frances Louisa (Darling) Brackett; A.B., Amherst College, 1898; M.A., Harvard University, 1902, Ph.D., 1904; m. Marion Louise Gaillard, June 15, 1918. Master in Greek, Mercersburg (Pennsylvania) Academy, 1898-99, Lake Forest (Illinois) Academy, 1899-1900; submaster, Boston Latin School, 1900-01; lecturer in Greek history, Radcliffe College, 1903-04; instr. and asst. prof. Greek and Latin, 1904-12, prof. Greek lang. and lit., 1912-20; professor Greek and Latin, Clark University, 1920-46, professor emeritus since 1946. Chairman Worcester People's Forum, 1938-40. Member Am. Philol. Assn., N.E. Class. Assn., Phi Beta Kappa, Delta Upsilon. Episcopalian. Mason. Home: 138 Elm St., Worcester MA‡

BRACKETT, LEDRU JOSHUA, mfr.; b. Harper's Ferry, W.Va., Mar. 29, 1873; s. Nathan Cook and Nancy Louise (Wood) B.; A.B., Bates Coll., 1894; m. Anna Cordelia Hicks, Dec. 23, 1897; children—Anthony Hicks, Nathan Cook (dec.), Truman Hicks. Newspaper and advt. business many yrs., now pres. Durand Co., Brigham's, Inc., and Dorothy Muriel's. Mem. Mass. Rep. State Com., 1911-12. Mem. Boston Chamber Commerce. Clubs: Algonquin, Brae Burn Country. Home: 4 Gloucester St., Boston. Office: 40 Ames St., Cambridge MA‡

BRADDOCK, ROBERT LOUIS, ins. exec.; b. Franklin Ind., Oct. 2, 1911; s. E. Yost and Ruth M. (Stephens) B.; A.B., Wittenberg Coll., Springfield, O., 1934; m. Mary Alice Krueger, Oct. 30, 1936. Casualty underwriter Travelers Ins. Co., 1934-51; exec. v.p. Gen. Reinsurance Corp., 1951-60, pres., 1960-70, dir.; v.p., dir. N. Star Reinsurance Corp., 1955-60, pres., 1960-70, dir.; dir. Guaranty Reinsurance Company, Limited, Nassau, Herbert Clough, Incorporated, General Reinsurance Life Corporation. Served as lt. (j.g.) USN, World War II. Member Ins. Soc. N.Y., Insurance Fedn. N.Y., Beta Theta Pi. Clubs: California, Hartford, Casualty and Surety of N.Y., University, Bankers of America, Innis Arden Golf; Winged Foot. Home: Old Greenwich CT Died Sept. 21, 1970.

BRADFORD, KARL SLAUGHTER, army officer; b. Washington, D.C., June 28, 1889; s. Ben Boyland and Nellie Irene (Harvey) B.; student U. of Va., 1906-07; B.S., U.S. Mil. Acad., 1911; grad. Machine Gun Officers Sch., Ecole Speciale Militaire, St. Cyr, France, Cavalry Sch., Command and Gen. Staff Sch. and Army War Coll.; m. Loraine Allen Sickel, Dec. 27, 1917; 1 daughter, Sally Harvey (Mrs. Richard Peck, Jr.). Commissioned 2d lt., U.S. Army, 1911; promoted through grades to brig. gen., 1941; served at various times in 2d, 3d, 4th, 15th and 26th Cavalry Regts.; comdr. 1st Cavalry Brigade, Fort Bliss, Tex., 1941-43; instr. U.S. Mil. Acad., 1914-18, and Cavalry School, 1934-36. Member Cavalry Board, 1921-25. Dep. pres. War Dept. Manpower Bd., 1943-46. Retired since Dec. 1946. Awarded Legion of Merit. Mem. Soc. of the Cincinnati, Beta Theta Pi. Clubs: Army and Navy, Army and Navy Country (Washington). Editor of Cavalry Jour., 1926-27. Home: Washington DC Died Aug. 1972.

BRADFORD, ROBERT D., former refinery exec.; b. Salt Lake City, April 29, 1903; s. Robert H. and Nettie (Davis) B.; B.S., U. Utah, 1924, M.S., 1925; m. Ethel Mays, Feb. 14, 1929; children—Suzanne (Mrs. Fred R. Mason), Robert D. Research chemist Utah Copper Co., 1925, metallurgist Garfield Smelter, Am. Smelting & Refining Co., 1926-28, asst. to gen. mgr. western dept., 1929, ore dept., N.Y.C. office, 1930-35, asst. mgr. southwestern dept., 1936-39, mgr. East Helena plant, 1940-41, southwestern dept., 1942-46, Selby plant, 1947-48, Utah dept., 1949-50, gen. mgr. western dept., 1951, v.p., 1952-59, exec. v.p., 1959-63, pres., 1963-69, also dir., ret. 1969. Mem. Am. Inst. Mining Metall. Petroleum Engrs., Mining and Metall. Soc. Am., Canadian Inst. Mining and Metallurgy, Sci. Research Soc., Sigma Xi, Theta Tau, Pi Kappa Alpha. Clubs: Mining (N.Y.C.); Westchester Country Greenwich CT Died Feb. 25, 1973.

BRADLEY, CHARLES HARVEY, corp. exec.; b. Dubuque, Ia., Apr. 20, 1899; s. Charles Harvey and Katherine (Wetherbee) B.; grad. Phillips Andover Acad., 1917; A.B., Yale, 1921; LL.D., Butler U., 1969; m. Carolyn Coffin, Jan. 14, 1922; children—Charles Harvey, Barbara (Mrs. J.W. Walker), Katherine Wetherbee (Mrs. W.B. Moseley). With Fletcher Trust Co., Indpls., 1921-24; cashier subsidiary 16th St. State Bank, 1922-24; sec.-treas. W.J. Holliday & Co., 1927-32, pres., 1932-55, co. became div. Jones & Laughlin Steel Corp., 1955, chmn. adv. bd. warehouse div., Indpls., 1955-60, dir.; pres. Shorewood Corp., 1960-62; chmn. exec. com., vice chmn. bd. dirs. P.R. Mallory & Co., Inc., Indpls., 1963-64, chmn. bd., 1964-68, also dir; pres. Monarch Steel Co., Hammond, Ind., 1951-55; dir. P.R. Mallory Internat., Ransburg Electrocoating Corp., Indpls., Jones & Laughlin Steel Corp., Ind. Nat. Bank, Ind. Bell Telephone Co., Ind. Gas Co., I.C. R.R., I.C. Industries. Vice pres. Indpls. Bd. Aviation Commrs.; pres. Indpls. Hosp. Devel. Corp. Chmn. bd. dirs. Community Hosp. Indpls; mem. alumni bd. Yale; gov. Crown Hill Cemetery. Served with USMC, 1917-18. Mem. Ind. (past pres.), Indpls. (dir.) chambers commerce, Employers Assn. Ind. (pres. 1937), Sportsman's Pilot Assn. Delta Kappa Epsilon. Episcopalian. Clubs: Indianapolis Athletic (dir.), Woodstock, Columbia, University (Indpls.); Chicago. Home: Indianapolis IN Died Sept. 1, 1972; buried Crown Hill Cemetery, Indianapolis IN

BRADLEY, HENRY STILES, clergyman; b. Jackson County, Ga., Mar. 22, 1869; s. Henry Stiles and Susan Celina (Jackson) B.; A.B., Emory Coll., Ga., 1890; post-grad. courses in biology, Brooklyn Inst. Arts and Sciences, Cold Spring Harbor, N.Y., 1896, and Marine Biol. Laboratories, Woods Hole, Mass., 1897; D.D., U. of Ga., 1904; m. Mary Emma Stafford, of Barnesville, Ga., Nov. 1, 1893. Mem. N. Ga. Ann. Conf. M.E. Ch., S., 1891-1905; adj. prof. natural sciences, 1890-95, prof. biology and geology, 1896-1901, v.p., 1899-1901, Emory Coll.; pastor Trinity Ch., Atlanta, Ga., 1901-05, St. John's Ch., St. Louis, 1905-09, Piedmont Congl. Ch., Worcester, Mass., 1909-20, State St. Congl. Ch., Portland, Me., 1920-1928. Ex-chaplain 19th Regt., Mass. S. G., rank of capt. Mem. Phi Delta Theta. Mason (32 deg.); ex-Grand Chaplain Grand Lodge of Mass. Author: Christianity as Taught by Christ, 1905. Address: Care National Bank of Commerce, 465 Congress St., Portland ME‡

BRADLEY, HERBERT EDWIN, lawyer, traveler; b. Brooklyn, Ont., Can., Dec. 20, 1874; s. Thomas and Margaret (Bradshaw) B.; ed. Whitby Collegiate Inst. (Ont.), U. of Mich., 1900; spl. student Northwestern U., 1901; m. Mary W. Hastings, June 21, 1910; children—Alice Hastings, Mary Lee (dec.). Began practice in Chicago, 1901; formerly mem. firms MacChesney & Bradley, and MacChesney, Becker & Bradley, now alone. Trustee Chicago Zoological Soc.; life mem. and trustee Chicago Acad. Sciences. Mem. Geog. Society of Chicago (pres. 1933-34). Republican. Mason. Clubs: Explorers (New York); University Club of Chicago, Casino, Arts, Adventurers, Camp Fire, Lake Zurich Golf, The Wayfarers. Big game hunter, traveler and explorer; accompanied Carl E. Akeley of Am. Museum Natural History to Belgian Congo, Africa, for gorillas, 1921-22; made second trip to Africa, 1924; took first expdn. through country west of Lake Edward; in Sumatra and Indo-China for tigers, 1925; 3d expdn. to Africa, studying Pygmies and Mangbetou tribes, 1930-31. Home: 5344 Hyde Park Blvd. Office: 30 N. La Salle St., Chicago IL‡

BRADLEY, J. KENNETH, lawyer; born Newark, New Jersey, March 10, 1903; son of James Peters and Minerva B. Bradley; A.B., Columbia University, 1925, LL.B., 1927. Admitted to Conn. bar, 1927, mem. Pullman, Comley, Bradley & Reeves, Bridgeport, Connecticut, also Stamford, Connecticut, mem. Ho. of Reps., Conn. Gen. Assembly, 1929, 1933; mem. State Senate, 1935, 37; judge Westport Town Ct., 1931-37. Nat. chmn. Young Republicans, 1935-37; dir. Young Republican activities for Rep. Nat. Com., 1940-44; mem. Rep. Nat. Com. 1940-48; chmn. Conn. Rep. State Central Com., 1936-44. Mem. State Bar Assn. Conn. (pres.), Am. Coll. Trial Lawyers, Internat. Assn. Ins. Counsel, Delta Upsilon. Mason (32deg, Shriner, Jester). Clubs: Algonquin, University, Black Rock Yacht, Longshore, Hartford. Home: Owenonke Park CT Died 1969.

BRADLEY, LAURA MAY THOMPSON (MRS. WILLIAM PICKERING BRADLEY), author, editor; b. St. Louis.; d. Jay Hill and Emma (Hannam) Thompson; ed. Pa. State U. extension, pvt. tutors; m. William Pickering Bradley, Nov. 11, 1908 (dec. June 1962); children—Lois (Mrs. Edgar Fraser Sadd), William Pickering. Editor poetry page Pitts. Lantern, 1943, The Congress Lantern, 1941, Periscope page Tri-State Clubwoman, 1940, The Potter's Wheel, Pitts. Poetry Soc., 1939-59; tchr. poetry technique and appreciation to adults Pitts. Congress of Clubs. Mem. Pitts. (past pres.), London, Sewickley (founder) poetry socs., Nat. League Am. Pen Women. Mem. Order Eastern Star. Clubs: Fair Oaks Women's (past pres.), Woman's Club Sewickley Valley), Sewickley Music. Author: West Woods, 1967. Home: Sewickley PA Died Apr. 21, 1970.

BRADLEY, ROBERT STOW, capitalist; b. Meriden, Conn., Feb. 22, 1855; s. William Lambert and Frances Martina (Coe) B.; A.B., Harvard, 1876; m. Leslie Newell, Dec. 15, 1881 (died Mar. 25, 1919); children—Robert Stow (dec.), Mrs. Rosamond Rheault, Mrs. Leslie Cutler, Mrs. Frances Chase (dec.). Began, 1876, with Bradley Fertilizer Co., founded by father, and became pres. 1894; this co. was absorbed, 1899, by Am. Agrl. Chem. Co., of which became 1st v.p. and chmn. exec. com. Republican. Unitarian. Home: 411 Commonwealth Av., Boston, and Pride's Crossing, Mass. Office: 92 State St., Boston MA‡

BRADLEY, THOMAS J., congressman-lawyer; b. New York, Jan. 2, 1870; grad. Coll. of City of New York, 1887; taught in public schools of New York, 1887-91, at same time attending University Law School (grad. 1889); deputy asst. dist. att'y Co. of New York, 1891-5; member of Congress since 1897 from 9th N. Y. dist.; present term expires 1901; Democrat. Home: 54 Lewis St., New York. New York NY Washington Address: Riggs House.Riggs House.‡

BRADLEY, WALTER PARKE, chemist; b. Lee, Mass., July 7, 1862; s. George Franklin and Mary Alverson (Freeman) B.; A.B., Williams Coll., 1884; U. of Gottingen, Germany, 1884-86, 1888-89, A.M., Ph.D., 1889; Sc.D., Wesleyan U., 1914; m. Adelaide Bartlett Huntting, June 26, 1888; 1 child, Marian Huntting. Prof. chemistry, Wesleyan U., Conn., 1893-1914; dir. General Lab., U.S. Rubber Co., 1912-13, research chemist same, 1914-19; pres. Bradstone Rubber Co., 1919-38. Dir. 1st laboratory in U.S. for research at extreme low temperatures. Mem. Phi Beta Kappa, Zeta Psi, Sigma Xi. Author: They Made Him Christ, 1942. Contbr. to scientific mags. on liquefaction of permanent gases, critical temperature, etc. Home: 196 College St., Middletown CT‡

BRADSHAW, DE EMMETT, insurance exec.; b. Izard Co., Ark., Jan. 5, 1869; s. David Carroll and Emily Frances (Meredith) B.; B.S., Nat. Normal U., Lebanon, O., 1891; LL.B., Ark. Law Sch., Little Rock, 1894; m. Nellie Gertrude Shorthill, Mar. 26, 1895; children—Melba Shorthill (Mrs. John B. Dawson), Ellen Frances (Mrs. Mason S. Zerbe). Admitted to Ark. bar, 1894; practice of law, Little Rock, 1894-1916, Omaha, 1916-32; gen. atty. Woodmen of World Life Ins. Soc., 1916-32; pres., 1932-43, now chmn. bd., chmn. investment com.; dir. Omaha Nat. Bank, Western Union Telegraph Co., Am. Dist. Telegraph. Mem. bd. regents U. Omaha, 1935-38; King of Ak-Sar-Ben, 1935, mem. bd. govs., 10 yrs. Mem. Fraternal Investment Assn. (organizer), Neb. State,

Ark. (sec.) bar assns., Am. Judicature Soc., Newcomen Soc. Democrat (chmn. city com., Little Rock; mem. state com. from Pulaski Co.). Methodist. Woodmen of the World (head consul, Ark., La., Miss., also dir., 1899), Mason (32 deg., Shriner). Clubs: Omaha, Country, Athletic (Omaha). Author: My Story, 1941. Home: 102 S. 51st Av., Omaha 3. Office: Insurance Bldg., Omaha 2 NE‡

BRADSHAW, FREDERICK JOSEPH, JR., hosp. adminstr.; b. Kiating Sze, China, Aug. 24, 1904 (parents Am. citizens); s. Frederick Joseph and Martha (Philp) B.; B.A., U. Redlands, 1927; B.M., Northwestern U. Med. Sch., 1931, M.D., 1932; m. Edna Margaret Biersdorfer, Dec. 14, 1931;children—Edna Joan (Mrs. Lyle Edward Miller), Frederick Joseph III. Intern, Cal. Hosp., Los Angeles, 1931, Cedars of Lebanon Hosp., Los Angeles, 1932; resident Community Hosp., Long Beach, Cal., 1932-33; med. officer VA, Palo Alto, Cal., 1938-39, St. Cloud, Minn., 1939-41; chief neuropsychiat. service Barnes Gen. Hosp., Vancouver, Wash., 1941-44; asst. clin. dir., instr. neuropsychiatry VA Hosp., Coatesville, Pa., 1946-47; chief profl. services VA Hosp., Gulfport, Miss., 1947-51; mgr. VA Hosp., Ft. Meade, S.D., 1951-57; chief of staff VA Hosp., Tomah, Wis., 1958-63; med. dir. Brentwood Hosp. VA Center, Los Angeles, 1964-71; asst. clin. prof. psychiatry U. Cal., Los Angeles. Served to col. M.C., AUS, 1941-46. Fellow Am. Coll. Physicians, Am. Psychiatric Assn.; mem. A.M.A. Home: Canoga Park CA Died Jan. 6, 1971; inurned Columbarium, Veterans Administration Cemetery, Los Angeles CA

BRADSHAW, JEAN PAUL, lawyer; b. Iberia, Mo., Mar. 27, 1906; s. John O. and Maude (Benage) B.; A.B., University of Missouri, 1927, LL.B., 1929; married to Catherine Ann Brandt, October 17, 1929; children—Paul Ludwig, William Brandt. Admitted to Missouri bar, 1928; asst. atty. Mo. Hwy. Commn., 1929-35; mem. firm Bradshaw and Fields, Lebanon, Mo., 1935-50, Neale, Newman, Bradshaw & Freeman, Springfield, Mo., 1951-70; sr. v.p., gen. counsel Ozark Air Lines, Inc., 1959-68, chmn. bd., 1968-70. Republican nominee gov. Mo., 1944, U.S. senator, 1964. Mem. Am., Mo., Greene County bar assns., Phi Delta Phi, Beta Theta Pi, Delta Sigma Rho. Conglist. Odd Fellow. Home: Springfield MO Died July 30, 1970; buried Maple Park Cemetery, Springfield MO

BRADSHAW, MICHAEL, editor; b. Goldsboro, N.C., June 18, 1903; s. Michael and Mary (Whitehurst) B.; A.B., Trinity Coll. (now Duke Univ.), 1923, A.M., 1925; student Harvard, 1926-28; m. Margaret Booth, June 23, 1934; children—Deborah, Michael, James. Instr., Univ. of Tex., 1928-33; city editor, Durham (N.C.) Morning Herald, 1933-36; state editor, Raleigh (N.C.) News and Observer, 1936; editor, Danville (Va.) Register, 1936-37; editorial writer, Dayton (O.) Herald, 1939-43, editor, 1943; asso. editor, Pittsburgh (Pa.) Post-Gazette, 1943-45; editor, Toledo (O.) Blade, from Nov. 1945; covered internat. confs. for Block newspapers at San Francisco, 1945, Paris, 1946, Rio de Janeiro, 1947. Mem. Sigma Delta Chi, Alpha Tau Omega. Co-author: A Goodly Company, 1934. Home: Maumee OH Died Oct. 17, 1971.

BRADT, PETER EDWARD, III, lawyer; b. St. Charles, Mich., June 4, 1907; s. Peter Edward and Edith (Van Riper) B.; student Detroit Inst. Tech. and Detroit Coll. Law, 1929-33; LL.B. with honors, Detroit Coll. Law., 1933; m. Emily Elizabeth Fodor, Dec. 23, 1939 (div. Dec. 1967); children—Daniel Joseph, Storm Vander Zee; m. 2d, Mary Meaker Danhausen, Mar. 16, 1968; 1 dau, Mary Rachel; 1 stepdau., Cindy Sue Danhausen. Staff mem. Detroit Law Review, 1932-33; admitted to Mich. bar, 1933; pvt. practice, Detroit and St. Charles, 1933-38, Port Huron 1951-68; assistant attorney general, Michigan, 1939-47, 49-51, chief dep. attorney gen., 1947-48; lectr. on case orgn. 9th Annual Inst. on Advocacy, U. of Mich., 1958. Mem. State Bar Com. on Civil Procedure, 1955-59; mem. Joint Com. on Mich. Procedural Revision, 1956-59; mem. com. on character and fitness, 1953-62; chmn. St. Clair County Bar Com. on Unauthorized Practice, 1956, 59; chmn. State Bar Little Hoover subcommittee of Com. on Legislation and Law Reform, 1952. Served with U.S. Navy, 1926-29, AUS, World War II. Mem. American, Michigan State, St. Clair Co. (chmn. com. court rules, 1959-60) bar assns., Mich. Assn. Pros. Attys. (past sec.). Mason. Home: Port Huron MI Died Nov. 4, 1968; buried Riverside Cemetery, St Charles MI

BRADY, FRANCIS M., army officer; b. Yonkers, N.Y., July 7, 1896; grad. Air Service Pilots Sch., and Observation Sch., 1921, Tactical Sch., 1923, Command and Gen. Staff Sch., 1931, Army War Coll., 1936; rated command pilot, combat observer. Commd. 2d lt., Inf., U.S. Army, Oct. 1917; transfered to Air Corps as capt., 1925; advanced through the grades to brig. gen., Feb. 1942; Gen. Staff Corps, 1938-39; served as 2d and 1st lt., Inf., World War I; decorated Distinguished Service Cross, Silver Star, Purple Heart. Address: Miami Beach FL Died Oct. 1969.*

BRADY, JAMES COX, business exec.; b. West End, N.J., July 28, 1907; s. James Cox and Elizabeth Jane (Hamilton) B.; grad. Canterbury Sch., New Milford,

Conn., 1925; A.B., Yale, 1929; m. Eliot Chace, July 5, 1929; children—Nicholas F., Elizabeth H., James C., Eliot. Pres. and dir. Brady Security & Realty Corp., N.Y.C., from 1941; chmn. bd., dir. Purolator Products, Inc.; former dir. Chrysler Corp., Chairman of the bd. of trustees N.Y. Racing Assn. Trustee Somerset (N.J.) Hosp. Comdr. USNR, from 1945. Mem. Greater N.Y. Racing Assn. (past exec. v.p., trustee, member executive committee), Chi Psi, Scroll and Key. Clubs: Jockey (vice chairman also the steward), Yale, Racquet and Tennis, The Links (N.Y. City); Essex Fox Hounds (Peapack, N.J.); Yale Graduate (New Haven); Sommerset Hills Country. Home: Far Hills NJ Died May 1971.

BRADY, THOMAS FRANCIS, journalist; b. Keokuk, Ia., Aug. 30, 1915; s. Joseph Lajus and Sara (Barney) B.; B.A., U. Cal. at Los Angeles, 1936; student U. Paris (France), 1951-52; m. Elizabeth Pallette, Mar. 30, 1946; children—Elizabeth, Thomas Francis. Corr., N.Y. Times, 1942-43, 46-70, assigned India, 1962-65, Middle East, 1965-68, met. staff, 1968-70; dir. information UN mission for Tunisia and Libya, 1970-72. Served with AUS, 1943, with USNR, 1944-46. Died Apr. 4, 1972.

BRADY, THOMAS PICKENS, state supreme ct. asso. justice; b. New Orleans, Aug. 6, 1903; s. Thomas and Jane Tullia (Smith) B.; A.B., Yale, 1927; LL.B., U. Miss., 1930; m. LaVerne Holmes, July 23, 1929; children—Thomas Pickens, Bruce Holmes. Instr. sociology U. Miss., 1929-30; admitted to Miss. bar, 1930; mem. firm Brady, Dean & Hobbs, Brookhaven, 1930-38; judge Circuit Ct., 14th Dist. Miss., 1950-63; asso. justice Miss. Supreme Ct., 1963-73. Dir. Brookhaven Bank & Trust Co., 1930-73, atty., 1947-50; pres. Brookhaven Investment Co., 1934-44; v.p. Arcade Theater, Inc., 1935; pres., atty. Brookhaven Leader Co., 1942-57; dir., atty. Miss. Compress Co., 1947-61. Commr. pub. safety, dir. Miss. Hwy. Safety Patrol, 1940-43, chmn. hwy. traffic adv. com. to War Dept., 1942-43; awards judge Freedoms Found., 1966. Nat. Chmn. speakers' bur. States' Rights Democratic Com., 1948, mem. Dem. Nat. Com., 1960-64; del. Dem. Nat. Conv., 1940, 48, 60; chmn. Miss. Dem. Nominating Com., 1960; mem. exec. com. City of Brookhaven, 1932-53. Bd. dirs. Whitworth Coll., 1962. Recipient Distinguished Service citation Miss. Legislature, 1956. Mem. Miss. State Bar (v.p. 1954-55), Miss. Gun Collectors Assn. (pres. 1957), Am. Newcomen Soc., Abraham Lincoln Assn. Am. Judicature Soc., S.A.R. First Families of Miss., Sons Colonial Govs., U. Miss. Alumni Assn. (dir. 1962-64), Co. Mil. Collectors and Historians, Eta Sigma Phi, Phi Delta Phi, Zeta Psi, Omicron Delta Kappa, Eta Sigma Phi. Baptist. Mason (32, K.T., Shriner). Clubs: New Orleans Athletic, Boston (New Orleans). Author: South at Bay, 1948; Black Monday, 1954. Home: Jackson MS Died Jan. 31, 1973.

BRADY, WILLIAM, writer, M.D.; b. Canandaigua, N.Y., Mar. 26, 1880; s. Andrew E. and Ellen (Farell) B.; M.D., U. of Buffalo, 1901; m. Cora May McGuire, 1904; children—Elizabeth, Helen. Began practice at Buffalo, 1901; writer of health column, syndicated in daily and Sunday newspapers throughout U.S. and Can., since 1914; former editor Medical Pickwick; contbr. to med. press. Author: Personal Health; Little Lessons in the Ways of Health. Home: Beverly Hills CA Died Feb. 25, 1972.

BRAGG, EDWARD MILTON, prof. naval architecture and marine engring.; b. Chicopee, Mass., Feb. 22, 1874; s. Warren Sylvester and Mary Charlotte (Shores) B.; B.S., Mass. Inst. Tech., 1896; m. Helen Elizabeth Brooks (M.D.), July 2, 1907; children—Martha Shores (Mrs. John Clarke Moore), Edward Brooks; m. 2d, Marion Olive Wood, June 21, 1932. Assistant Instructor Mass. Inst. Tech., 1896-1900; draftsman at William Cramp & Sons, Philadelphia, Pa., William R. Trigg Company, Richmond Virginia, New York S. B. Co., Camden, N.J., 1900-03; with Newport News Shipbuilding & Drydock Co., 1907-08; instr. naval architecture and marine engring., U. of Mich., 1903-45, now prof. emeritus. Mem. Soc. Naval Architects and Marine Engrs., Inst. of Naval Architects, Royal Soc. of Arts, Sigma Xi, Phi Kappa Phi. Home: 1056 Ferdon Rd., Ann Arbor MI‡

BRAGG, SIR (WILLIAM) LAWRENCE, physicist; b. Adelaide, South Australia, March 31, 1890; s. William Henry and Gwendoline (Todd) B.; student St Peters Coll., Adelaide, 1900-05; Adelaide U., 1905-08; B.A., M.A., Trinity Coll., Cambridge, 1912; D.Sc. (hon.), Dublin, Leeds, Manchester, Lisbon, Paris, Brussels, Liege, Durham; Ph.D. (hon.), Cologne; LL.D., St. Andrews; m. Alice Hopkinson, Dec. 10, 1921; children—Stephen, David, Margaret, Patience. Fellow and lectr. Trinity Coll., 1914-19; prof. physics Manchester U., 1919-37; dir. Nat. Phys. Lab., 1937-38; prof. exptl. physics Cambridge, 1938-53; past director The Royal Institution, London, England. Awarded Barnard Medal, 1914; Nobel Prize, 1915; Roebling Medal by Mineral. Soc. Am., 1948. Decorated, Companion of Honour, Officer Brit. Empire; Mil. Cross; comdr. Order Leopold of Belgium. Fellow Royal Soc., Inst. of Physics; hon. mem. Swedish, Dutch Nat. acads. sci., Am. Philos. Soc., Chinese Phys. Soc., Royal Acad. Belgium, Societe Francaise de Mineralogue et

Cristallographic, Academie Nazionale dei Lincei, Rome. Author: The Crystalline State, 1934; Electricity, 1936; Atomic Structure of Minerals, 1937; (with G.F. Claringbull) Crystal Structures of Minerals, 1965. Address: London England also Waldringfield Suffolk England Died July 1, 1971.

BRAINARD, MORGAN B., JR., ins. co. exec.; b. 1906; grad. Kent (Conn.) Sch.; A.B., Yale. With Aetna Life Affiliated Cos., 1927-60, v.p., treas., 1956-57, sr. v.p., treas., 1957-60, also dir.; dir. Aetna Casualty Co., Standard Fire Ins. Co., Conn. Bank and Trust Co., Arrow Hart and Hegeman Electric Co., Hartford Courant, Fafnir Bearing Co. Address: Hartford CT Died May 1960.

BRAINERD, HENRY DEAN, SR., physician; b. San Francisco, Dec. 3, 1914; s. Herbert K. and Myrtle (Healy) B.; A.B., U. Cal. at Berkeley, 1935, M.D., 1939; m. Harriet Edwards Hall, Jan. 29, 1955; children—Henry Dean, Alan, Karen, David, Eleanor. Intern, San Francisco Hospital, 1938-39, chief of U. Cal. medical service, 1951-56, 64-67; resident U. Cal. Hosp., 1939-40, 41-42, physician in chief, 1956-64; resident Boston City Hosp., 1940-41; instr. to asso. prof. medicine U. Cal., 1942-55, William Watt Kerr professor clinical medicine, 1955-69; chmn. dept. medicine U. Cal. Med. Sch., 1956-64; cons. infectious diseases Children's Hosp., San Francisco; cons. Letterman Gen. Hosp., Oak Knoll Naval Hosp.; cons. medicine Ft. Miley VA Hospital. Diplomate Am. Bd. Internal Medicine (chmn. 1965-67). Fellow A.C.P.; mem. Western Assn. Physicians, Western Soc. Clin. Research, A.M.A., A.A.A.S., Sigma Xi, Alpha Omega Alpha, Nu Sigma Nu, Alpha Delta Phi. Club: Rafael Racquet. Home: Kentfield CA Died Mar. 18, 1969.

BRAMKAMP, JOHN MILTON, clergyman; b. Cincinnati, O., Dec. 21, 1867; s. Lewis Christian and Anna Catherine (Belmer) B.; A.B., Wittenberg Coll., Springfield, O., 1890, A.M., 1893, D.D., 1911; B.D., Wittenberg Theol. Sem., 1893; m. Sarah S. Breckenridge, Jan. 31, 1895; children—Lewis Breckenridge, Mary Garver (Mrs. J. L. Gutermuth). Ordained Luth. ministry, 1893; pastor, New Castle, Ind., 1893-96, Bellevue, Kentucky, 1896-1906, Calvary Ch., Chicago, 1906-21; pres. Ill. Synod. United Lutheran Ch. in America, 1921-31; pres. Bd. Home Missions and Ch. Extension of Ill. Synod, 1931-32; pastor Emmanuel Lutheran Ch., Maywood, Ill., 1932-45, ret. Pres. Miami Synod of General Synod, Evang. Luth. Ch., 1904-05; pres. Northern Ill. Synod, 1913-15; recording sec. Bd. of Home Missions and Ch. Extension, United Lutheran Ch. in America, 1922-27, Western sec. transportation com. 1923-1948. Editor of S.S. Dept., Lutheran World, 1897-1900, Chicago Lutheran Advocate, 1912-19. Mem. Beta Theta Pi. Republican. Home: 6220 Rogers Park Pl., Cincinnati 13, OH‡

BRANCH, HOUSTON, writer, editor, orgn. exec.; b. St. Paul, March 5, 1905; son of Doctor Uriah and Hannah (Swanson) B.; ed. in pub. and private schs.; m. Mildred E. Clark, Jan. 13, 1942 (dec. July 1957); 1 daughter, Victoria Elaine. Writer for films, Hollywood, Cal., 1926-68; expert consultant on training films, U.S. Army Signal Corps, 1942-43; founder and dir. Am. Library Foundation, organized to secure books and libraries for bookless rural sch. children—editor The Sportsman's Handbook; editor tech. publs. Marquardt Corp., 1959-63; exec. dir. Acad. Applied Sci., 1963-68. Mem. A.L.A., Authors League Am., Motion Picture Acad. Arts and Scis., Screen Writers Guild, Am. Rocket Soc. Author: (stories and screen plays) about 80, The Booby Prize, Feather in His Crown, The Peabodys, of Boston; (novels with Frank Waters), Diamond Head, 1948; River Lady, 1942; booklets pub. Am. Library Foundation: Two Gifts of Books; Give Rural Youth an Equal Chance; American Pilgrimage; The Story of Horace Mann, 1937; Dynamic Living, 1950; (ednl. films) Of Space and Time, 1959, This is California, 1959; Into Polar Orbit, 1959; Submarine Safari, 1959; The Polaris Story, 1961; Wings at Work—The Story of Business Aviation, 1966; Francis W. Davis, Inventor of Power Steering, 1967. Home: Cambridge MA Died Jan. 27, 1968.

BRAND, HARRISON, JR., association exec.; b. Ilion, N.Y., Aug. 24, 1891; s. Harrison and Marion S. (Eaton) B.; B.S., U.S. Mil. Acad., 1914; m. Helen McCumber, Apr. 21, 1917; 1 son, Harrison; married 2d, Emily Hambrock, June 21, 1960. Commissioned 2d lieut. and advanced through grades to lt. col., Engrs. Corps, U.S. Army, 1914-19; lt. col. Engineers reserve, 1920-32, col., 1932-42, colonel, Army of United States, retired, 1951; federal tax practice, 1920-25; admitted to D.C. bar, 1925; mem. firm McCumber and Brand, Washington, 1925-33; mem. D.C. Pub. Utilities Comm., 1927-29; pvt. practice of law, 1933-37; in charge of supply for W.P.A. of New York, N.Y., 1937-38, purchase of construction equipment, federal W.P.A., 1938; exec. sec. Washington (D.C.) Board of Trade, 1938-41; with the Aerospace Industries Association of America, Inc., and predecessors, Washington, D.C., since 1941, secretary-treasurer, since 1944. Member Washington Board of Trade. National Aeronautic Association, Soc. American Military Engineers (honorary life member;

director or officer 1923-37). Mason. Clubs: Army and Navy (Washington); Chevy Chase (Md.). Home: Washington DC

BRAND, LOUIS, mathematician, educator; b. Cin., Sept. 27, 1885 s. Louis William and Josephine (Zingsheim) B.; Ch.E., U. Cin., 1907, E.E., 1908, A.M., 1909, Doctor of Science (honorary), 1956; Ph.D., Harvard University, 1917; m. Lulu Edith Shinkle, Aug. 14, 1915; children—Sara Josephine (Mrs. Oliver Marcy), Martha Louise (Mrs. Bruce Raymond). Head dept. mathematics and mechanics, coll. engring. U. Cin., 1919-56, head dept. mathematics, 1935-56, prof. emeritus, 1956-71; Whitney vis. prof. Trinity Coll., 1956-57; M.D. Anderson professor of mathematics University of Houston, Tex., 1957-71; vis. prof. University of Brazil, 1963. Fellow A.A.A.S., Ohio, Tex. acads. scis.; mem. Am. Math. Soc., Am. Math. Assn., Sigma Xi, Tau Beta Pi, Phi Kappa Phi. Author math. textbooks, latest being Differential and Difference Equations, 1967; also articles Houston TX Died Jan. 27, 1971.

BRANDON, SAMUEL GEORGE FREDERICK, educator; b. Portsmouth, Eng., Oct. 2, 1907; s. Samuel James and Lilian (Aldridge) B.; student Coll. of the Resurrection, Mirfield, Yorks, Eng., 1927-32; M.A., U. Leeds, 1937, D.D., 1943; M.A., Manchester U.; m. Ivy Ada Miles, Sept. 29, 1934; children—Mark Miles (dec.), David Lawton. Anglican orders, Diocese of Exeter, 1932-39; with Royal Army Chaplains Dept., 1939-51; prof. comparative religion Manchester U., from 1951, pro-vice chancellor, from 1967. Named Hon. Chaplain of Forces. Mem. Internat. Assn. for History of Religions (Brit. rep., mem. exec. com.), Old Testament Soc., Folklore Soc., Royal Asiatic Soc., Internat. Soc. for Study Time, Studiorum Novi Testamenti Societas. Author: The Fall of Jerusalem and the Christian Church, 1951; Time and Mankind, 1951; Man and his Destiny in the Great Religions, 1962; Creation Legends of the Ancient Near East, 1963; History, Time and Deity, 1965; Jesus and the Zealots, 1967; The Judgment of the Dead, 1967; The Trial of Jesus of Nazareth, 1968; Religion in Ancient History, 1969. Editor, contbr. Ancient Empires, 1969. Editor, chief contbr. Dictionary of Comparative Religion, 1970. Home: Knutsford Cheshire England Deceased.

BRANDT, ALLEN DEMMY, engr.; b. Mountville, Pa., Nov. 8, 1908; s. Charles G. and Mary Bella (Demmy) B.; B.S. in Civil Engring. (White, Carnegie scholar), Pa. State Coll., 1931, M.S. in San. Engring., Harvard, 1932, D.Sc. (Rockefeller Found. fellow), 1933; B.S. in Law, LaSalle Extension U., 1954; m. Ella Nora Snavely, June 23, 1933; children—Patricia Ella, Barry Allen, Frederick Thomas. Dir. indsl. hygiene research Wilison Products, Inc., Reading, Pa., 1933-40; chief, engring. sect., indsl. hygiene div. USPHS, Washington, 1940-42; asst. chief indsl. hygiene br. safety and security div. Office Chief of Ordnance, War Dept., Chgo., 1942-45; research fellow, assigned by USPHS to research lab. Am. Soc. Heating and Ventilating Engrs., Cleve., 1945-46; chief indsl. hygiene dept. Bethlehem Steel Co. (Pa.), 1946-60, mgr., indsl. health engring., 1960-67, mgr. environmental quality control, 1967-71. Cons. environmental engring. problems; vis. lectr. indsl. hygiene engring. Harvard; chmn. Pa. Air Pollution Commn.; mem. council tech. advisers N.Y. Air Pollution Control Bd.; past chmn. Environmental Engring. Engring. Intersoc. Bd. Past pres. Bethlehem Area council Boy Scouts Am. Recipient certificate of commendation U.S. Army; Richard Beatty Mellon award Air Pollution Control Assn., 1971. Named adm. Navy Great State of Neb. Registered engr., Pa., Ohio. Fellow A.A.A.S.; mem. Am. Soc. Heating, Refrigerating and Air Conditioning Engrs., Am. Indsl. Hygiene Assn. (past pres., Cummings Meml. award), Am. Standards Assn. (mem. 3 coms. dealing with air sanitation and ventilation), Phi Kappa Phi, Tau Beta Pi, Delta Omega, Chi Epsilon. Republican. Club: Saucon Valley Country. Author: Industrial Health Engineering, 1947; also papers on phases of air sanitation, indsl. hygiene, ventilation chpts. in tech. handbooks. Home: Bethlehem PA Died Oct. 2, 1971; buried Meml. Park, Bethlehem PA

BRANDT, CARL GUNARD, educator; b. Ludington, Mich., Sept. 20, 1897; s. Charles H. and Mary (Carlson) B.; LL.B., U. Mich., 1921, L.M., 1922. Admitted to Wis. bar, 1922, Ill. bar, 1929, practiced in Chgo., 1929-32; mem. faculty, dept. of speech U. Mich., 1920-28, prof. English and chmn. dept. English, coll. of engring., lectr. in speech, coll. of lit., sci., and the arts, 1937-69, bus. mgr. Oratorical Assn. Lecture Course, 1933-69. Mem. Speech Assn. Am., Am. Soc. for Engring. Edn., Delta Sigma Rho, Delta Theta Phi. Presbyn. Mason. Co-editor: Selected American Speeches on Basic Issues. Home: Ann Arbor MI Died Jan. 2, 1969; buried Ludington MI

BRANDT, GEORGE LOUIS, foreign service officer; b. Washington, D.C., Sept. 23, 1892; s. Frederick Ferdinand and Cora Jane (LaDane) B.; ed. Business High Sch., Washington, 1907-09, George Washington U., 1913-14; m. Eva Emily Finotti, Jan. 15, 1920 (dec.); children—Eva Daphne, Eleanor Jane, Joan Marie; married 2d Eva Taylor, July 26, 1952. Student interpreter, Constantinople, Turkey, 1915-16, Cairo, Egypt, 1916-19; vice-consul at Alexandria, Egypt, 1919-22; consul, Messina, Italy, 1922-24; asst. chief visa office, Dept. of State, 1924-27, chief, 1927-28; consul Beirut, Syria, 1928-30, Cologne, Germany, 1930-32, Genoa, Italy, 1932-33; assigned to Dept., 1934-38; consul at Mexico City, Mex., 1938; tech. adviser, meeting of Intergovernmental Com. on Political Refugees, Evian, France and London, 1938; adviser to Commonwealth Govt. of the Philippines on immigration matters, 1938-39; adminstrn. officer, Special Div., Sept. 1, 1939; chief, Jan. 2, 1941; 1st sec. at Berne, Switzerland, Dec. 17, 1941; exec. asst. to asst. sec. of State, Apr. 21, 1942; consul general, Naples, Italy, supr. consul gen. for all Am. Consulor Offices in Italy, 1944 ret. 1949. Mem. promotion panels USIA, 1957. Awarded Medal of Freedom. Mem. Diplomatic and Consular Officers Ret. Mason; mem. Order Eastern Star. Address: Shady Side MD Died June 15, 1971; buried Woodfield Cemetery, Galesville MD

BRANDT, HARRY, motion picture exec.; b. N.Y.C., Feb. 22, 1897. Film salesman World Pictures Corp.; co-founder Times Picture Corp., 1934; co-founder, sec. Film Alliance of U.S., 1939; pres., Brandt Theatre Circuit, N.Y.C.; v.p., dir. Cornwall Press, Inc.; dir. Am. Book-Stratford Press, Inc.; dir. Trans-Lux Corp., Movielab Film Labs, Ind., Fairbanks-Whitney Corp. Nat. chmn. Sixth War Loan Drive. Mem. bd. Will Rogers Meml. Hosp., Am. Theatre Wing, Theatre Authority. Mem. Motion Picture Pioneers (mem. bd.), Ind. Theatre Owners Assn. (pres., 1933-72), Council of Motion Picture Orgns. (exec. com.). Clubs: Lambs, Variety, Lotos. Home: New York City NY Died 1972.

BRANNER, MARTIN MICHAEL, cartoonist; b. New York, New York, December 28, 1888; educated in public schools and high school, New York City; married Edith Fabbrini, Aug. 21, 1907 (dec.); children—Bernard Donald, Robert Jay. Played in stock, repertoire, vaudeville, 1907-20; cartoonist, comic strip, Louie, the Lawyer; Pete and Pinto (N.Y. Sun and Herald); Winnie Winkle, the Breadwinner (Chicago Tribune-N.Y. News Syndicate). Elk (New London). Rotarian. Club: Lambs, Cartoonists Soc. of Am. (N.Y.C.); Toastmasters International (New London, Conn.). Home: Waterford CT Died May 19, 1970; buried Maple Grove Cemetery, Kew Gardens NY

BRANSON, TAYLOR, band leader; b. Washington, D.C., July 31, 1881; s. James Taylor and Serena Moore (Arnold) B.; ed. pub. schs.; studied violin with Capt. William H. Santelmann, former leader U.S. Marine Band; clarinet with Andres Coda; composition with Arthur Tregina; m. Marie Quill, of Washington, June 1, 1909; children—Mary Serena, Albert Edward, Anne Marie, James Taylor, Ellen Marie. Enlisted in U.S. Marine Band, 1898; apptd. 2d leader, 1920, leader, May 1927-Feb. 1940; solo violinist, 1907-40; leader Gridiron Club orchestra, from 1912. Catholic. Composer of pieces for band and orchestra. Home: Washington DC Died Nov. 1969.

BRANTON, JAMES RODNEY, clergyman, educator; b. Hathorn, Miss., May 28, 1906; s. Simon Leon and Martha Eulora (Fortenberry) B.; A.B., Miss. Coll., 1926; Th.M., Southwestern Bapt. Theol. Sem., 1929; postgrad. U. Berlin (Germany), 1930-31; Ph.D., U. Chgo., 1934; m. Elizabeth Dana, Aug. 5, 1933; children—Dana Sue, James Rodney, Beth Ella. Ordained to ministry Bapt. Ch., 1926; instr. N.T. interpretation and Greek, Southwestern Bapt. Theol. Sem., 1929-30; teaching and research fellow U. Chgo., 1932-34; instr., acting chmn. classical langs. U. Okla., 1934-36; prof. religion Linfield Coll., 1936-38, Coll. Social Sci., U. Ore., 1938-41; John B. Trevor prof. N.T. interpretation Colgate Rochester (N.Y.) Div. Sch., 1941-67; lectr., mem. Nat. Christian Mission to Univs., 1939-67. Mem. Soc. Bibl. Lit. and Exegesis. Contbr. Interpreter's Dictionary of the Bible, 1956; articles profl. jours. Home: Rochester NY Died Sept. 12, 1967.

BRASSERT, HERMAN ALEXANDER, consulting engr.; b. London, Eng., Jan. 24, 1875; s. Charles Alexander and Marie (Stein) B.; student Latin and Greek Sch., Freiburg, Baden, Germany, 4 yrs., Sch. of Mines, Leoben, Austria, 1 yr.; grad. Metallurgical engr., Coll. Mining and Metallurgy, Berlin, 1896; m. Sarah Maury Childs, May 1902 (died Nov. 1907); 1 son, Charles Alexander; m. 2d, Ethel Mohr, Oct. 6, 1909; children—William Ewing, James Elton. Came to the U.S. Oct. 1897. Worked six months at Warrick Furnaces, Pottstown, Pa.; asst. supt. and supt. Edgar Thomson Blast Furnaces, Carnegie Steel Co., Pittsburgh, 1898-1905; in charge of blast furnaces for Ill. Steel Company, Chicago Dist., 1905-16; charter mem. U.S. Steel Corp. Coke Committee; asst. gen. supt. South Works, Ill. Steel Company, 1916-18; organized and became chmn. bd., 1918-22, Freyn-Brassert Co., engineers; also vice pres. Miami Metals Co. of Chicago. Established cons. engineering business as H.A. Brassert, Inc. in 1922, and organized H.A. Brassert & Co., Chicago, cons. engineers, 1925; now chairman board and president with offices New York, Pittsburgh; organized British Company, H.A. Brassert & Co., Ltd.; also president and director various other companies. Internationally known for contribution to development of the modern blast furnace and for many improvements to iron and steel plants and processes; contributed ten technical papers these subjects. Designed and constructed plants in this country and abroad; modernized plants and methods; created new industries in many parts of the world. Mem. Am. Iron & Steel Institute, Mining and Metall. Engineers, Blast Furnace and Coke Assn.; British Iron & Steel Inst.; iron and steel institutes and engineering societies of other countries. Clubs: University (Chicago), Duquesne (Pittsburgh); Uptown (New York). Home: Nettleton Farm, Washington, Conn.; also 1165 Fifth Av., N.Y.C. Office: 69 E. 42d St. N.Y.C.; also 210 Blvd. of the Allies, Pitts‡

BRASTED, ALVA JENNINGS, army chaplain, ret.; b. Findley Lake, N.Y., July 5, 1876; s. Nathan Russell and Adaline (More) B.; B.S., Des Moines College, 1902; B.D., Chicago U., 1905; LL.D., Sioux Falls Coll., 1946; m. Ada Crocker, June 15, 1910; children—Mary Frances, Robert Crocker, Donald More. Student pastor Wauconda (Ill.) Bapt. Ch., 1902-05; ordained to ministry Bapt. Ch., 1905; pastor Lisbon, N.D., 1905-10, Montevideo, Minn., 1910-12, Ft. Dodge, Ia., 1912-13; 1st lt. chaplain U.S. Army, 1913; capt., 1920, maj., 1927; lt. col., 1933, apptd. chief of chaplains, U.S. Army, with rank of col. term Dec. 23, 1933-Dec. 22, 1937. Member of John More Association, Sons of Am. Revolution, Am. Legion. Republican. Mason (32 deg.); Soujourner. Author of articles and pamphlets on the work of chaplains in the regular army and Civilian Conservation Corps.; (books) Service to Service Men; For Victorious Living; AZ You Were. Home: 204 MacArthur Rd., Alexandria VA‡

BRAUCHER, FRANK, publishing exec.; b. Lincoln, Ill., Dec. 22, 1884; s. Frank S. and Katherine (O'Donnell) B.; ed. De Pauw U.; m. Lucile Bruen, Oct. 15, 1913; children—Marjorie, Joan. Engaged in newspaper work until 1908; Western rep. Review of Reviews, 1908-10; Western mgr., Chicago, Scribner's Mag., 1910-15; joined Crowell Pub. Co., N.Y. City, 1915; v.p. and dir., 1922-37; vice pres. and dir. Station WOR, New York, 1937-41; pres. Periodical Pub. Assn., from 1941, Mag. Advt. Bur., from 1942, Publishers Information Bur., Inc., from 1948. Clubs: Scarsdale Golf, Advertising of New York, Tavern. Home: New York City NY Died Sept. 1968.

BRAUDE, JACOB MORTON, justice; b. Chgo., Dec. 13, 1896; s. Emil and Anna (Kaplan) B.; A.B. cum laude. U. Mich., 1918; grad. study Northwestern, 1919; J.D., U. Chgo., 1920; m. Adele Covv Englander, Feb. 22, 1946; children—Ann Englander, Jane (Mrs. Jane E. Berkson). Admitted to Ill. bar, 1920, since practiced in Chgo.; counsel Nat. Jewelers Bd. Trade, 1927-33; asst. atty. gen. State of Ill., 1933-34; judge Municipal Ct. Chgo., 1934-56; judge Circuit Cts. Ill., Cook County, 1956-70, chief justice, 1960-61; presiding judge Chgo. Boys' Ct., 1938-45; asso. dir. finance State of Ill., 1933-34. Mem. Citizens Com. on Parole; bd. dirs. Jewish Children's Bur., Big Bro. Assn. Ill., Juvenile Protective Assn.; pres. Portal House Clinic for Treatment Alcoholics, Chgo. Com. Alcoholism; del.-at-large Chgo. Council Social Agys.; v.p. Chgo. Conf. for Youth; mem. Chgo. adv. bd. Nat. Council Family Relations; adv. bd. World Youth, Nat. Assn. for Gifted Children, St. Leonard's House; citizens com. Loyola U.; chmn. Chgo. div. Am. Jewish Com., chmn. bd. Judge Bishop Bernard J. Sheil Youth of Year Award, 1952-70; pres. orgn. which sponsors Am. Boys' Commonwealth, Deborah Boys' Club, Albany Park Boys' Club, Camp Wooster; nat. v.p. Com. for Advancement Am. Judaism, 1954-55. Served as 2d lt. F.A., United States Army, 1918. Recipient citation for pub. service U. Chgo. Alumni Assn., 1967; award for meritorious service and understanding urban problems Chgo. City Colls. Mem. International Platform Association, The Authors Guild, The Authors League, also member American, Ill. Chgo. bar assns., Am. Judicature Soc., Chgo. (pres.), Ill. (pres. 1950) acads. criminology, Soc. Midland Authors, Decalogue Soc., Ill. Soc. for Mental Hygiene (v.p.), Mil. Order World Wars, Am. Legion, 40 and 8, Beta Phi. Democrat. Jewish religion. Mason (past master). Clubs: City, Standard (Chgo.). Author: I Like Bad Boys, 1939; Speaker's Ency. of Stories, Quotations and Anecdotes, 1955; Braude's Second Ency. of Stories, Quotations and Anecdotes, 1957; Braude's Handbook of Humor for All Occasions, 1958; New Treasury of Stories for Every Speaking and Writing Occasion, 1959; Speaker's Ency. of Humor, 1961; Lifetime Speaker's Ency., 2 vols., 1962; Quips, Quotes and Anecdotes, 1963; Braude's Treasury of Wit and Humor, 1964; Complete Speaker's and Toastmaster's Library (9 vols.), 1965; Complete Speaker's and Writer's Index, 1966; Braude's Handbook of Stories for Toastmasters and Speakers, 1967; Braude's Source Book for Speakers and Writers, 1968; Braude's Guide for Public Speakers and Source Book for Ideas, 1969; The Complete Art of Public Speaking, 1970; Speaker's and Toastmaster's Handbook of Anecdotes By and About Famous Personalities, pub. posthumously, 1971. Contbr. encys. and mags. Lectr. juvenile delinquency. Home: Chicago IL Died Dec. 24, 1970; buried Chicago IL

BRAUER, JOHN CHARLES, educator; born Sterling, Neb., Sept. 6, 1905; s. John Thomas and Mary Ann

(Ross) B.; D.D.S., U. Neb., 1928, A.B., 1934, M.Sc., 1936; student U. Mich., summer 1932; m. Dora Lee Stewart, June 20, 1932; 1 son, James Stewart. Practiced as dentist, Orleans, Neb., 1928-30; instr. operative dentistry, pedodontics, preventive dentistry U. Neb., 1930-36; dir De Los L. Hill, Jr., Meml. Children's Dental Clinic, prof. pedodontics, orthodontics and preventive dentistry, Atlanta Southern Dental Coll., 1936-38; head dept., prof. preventive dentistry and pedodontics, dir. bur. dental hygiene State U. Ia., 1938-42; dir. postgrad. dental edn., exec. officer dept. pedodontics U. Wash. Sch. Dentistry, 1947-50; dean, U. N.C. Sch. Dentistry, 1950-66; sec. Dental Found of N.C., Inc., from 1950; lectr. numerous dental socs., U.S. and Can. Cons. to asst. sec. def. for manpower Dept. Def., from 1958, USPHS, from 1960, W.K. Kellogg Found., Council on Dental Edn., from 1961; studies dir. Com. on Instnl. Cooperation, Big 10 Univs. Commd. 1st lt., Dental Corps, U.S. Army Res., 1928; lt. col., asst. to Maj. Gen. Robert H. Mills, dental div. and chief dental standards br., Surg. Gen. Office, 1942-46. Decorated Legion of Merit. Recipient O. Max Gardner award U. N.C., 1963 Fellow Am. Coll. Dentists; mem. Am. Dental Assn., Am. Soc. Dentistry for Children, Internat. Research Assn., Am. Acad Pedodontics (pres. 1949, chmn. 1946), Sigma Xi, Tau Kappa Epsilon, Omicron Kappa Upsilon, Delta Sigma Delta. Author: Dentistry for Children, 1939. Co-author, co-editor: Dentistry for Children, rev. edit., 1964; The Dental Assistant, rev. edit., 1964. Editor (with Sturdevant, Barton, Harrison) The Art and Science of Operative Dentistry, 1968. Contbr. articles to jours. Address: Carmel CA Died Apr. 9, 1971.

BRAUN, WERNER, microbiologist; b. Berlin, Germany, Nov. 16, 1914; s. Simon and Edith (Brach) B.; Ph.D., U. Gottingen, 1936; m. Barbara Melnikow, June 7, 1942; children—Renee, Stephanie, Robin. Came to U.S., 1936, naturalized, 1941. Guest investigator U. Mich., 1936-37; research asso. dept. zoology U. Cal. at Berkeley, 1937-42, asso. dept. vet. sci. Expt. Sta. Coll. Agr., 1942-48; med. bacteriologist, chief variation br. Chem. Corps Biol. Labs., Camp Detrick, Frederick, Md., 1948-55; prof. microbiology Inst. Microbiology, Rutgers U., New Brunswick, N.J., 1955-72; cons. U.S. Army Chem. Corps, 1955-68; USPHS, 1956-72, U.S. Dept. of Def., 1960-68, NSF, 1967-70; bd. sci. counselors Nat. Inst. Allergy and Infectious Diseases, NIH, 1966-69, chmn. bd. sci. counselors, 1968-69, vis. scientist, 1970-72; I.M. Lewis lectr. U. Tex., 1951; vis. prof. U. P.R. Med. Sch., 1957, 59, 60, 61, 63, 65, 67, 68; NIH research fellow, Israel, Paris, also vis. prof. Hebrew U., Hadassah Med. Sch., Jerusalem, 1962-63; vis. scientist Weizmann Inst., Israel, Pasteur Inst., Paris, Karolinska Inst., Stockholm, 1969-70; O. Stark lectr. Miami U., Oxford, O., 1971. Recipient Barnett Cohen award. Soc. Am. Bacteriologists, 1954; superior accomplishment award Chem. Corps, U.S. Army, 1954. Fellow Am. Acad. of Microbiology (pres. 1968-69), A.A.A.S.; mem. Theobald Smith Soc. (pres. 1957-58), Sci. Research Soc. Am., Am. Soc. Microbiology, Am. Assn. Immunologists, Genetics Soc. Am., Soc. Exptl. Biology and Medicine, Soc. Gen. Microbiology, Sigma Xi, Phi Sigma. Author: Bacterial Genetics, 1953, 2d edit., 1965. Editor several sci. books. Contbr. articles to sci. jours. Home: Princeton NJ Died Nov. 19, 1972.

BRAY, HAROLD BRYAN, banker; b. Farmersville, Ill., Dec. 6, 1896; s. Michael Emerson and Elizabeth Boyd (Graham) B.; student Walton Sch. Commerce, Chgo.; m. Sallie Margaret Crabb, Nov. 4, 1920; children—Harold Bryan, Barbara Keating (Mrs. Edward Chamberlin Robertson), Graham Davis. With Continental Ill. Nat. Bank & Trust Co., Chgo., 1914-20, Goodyear Tire & Rubber Co., Akron, O., 1920-23; v.p. Peoples Trust & Savs. Bank, Chgo., 1923-32, Harris Trust & Savs. Bank, Chgo., 1932, sr. v.p., until 1961. Served with USN, 1917-18. Clubs: Chicago, Mid-Day, Bankers (Chgo.); Skokie Country. Home: Glencoe IL Died Dec. 1969.

BRAYTON, ISRAEL, lawyer; b. Fall River, Mass., Aug. 5, 1874; s. Hezekiah Anthony and Caroline Elizabeth (Slade) B.; A.B., Harvard, 1896, LL.B., 1899; m. Ethel M. Chace, Jan. 10, 1912; children—Charlotte, Philip Sherman, Roswell. Admitted to Mass. bar, 1899, and since practiced in Fall River, (except 1923-30); chairman of the board Sagamore Mfg. Co.; president Durfee Mills; vice president Union Savings Bank; dir. B.M.C. Durfee Trust Co.; treas. Lincoln Mfg. Co., 1923-30. Representative Mass. Gen. Court, 1909-10; alderman City of Fall river, 1910-14. Treas. Frank S. Stevens Home for Boys, Incorporated (Fall River). Treasurer Trustees Fall River High Sch. Alumni Scholarships. Mem. Am., Mass., Bristol Co., Fall River bar assns. Clubs: Harvard (Boston); Harvard, Quequechan (Fall River); Acoaxet (Westport Harbor, Mass.). Home: 618 Rock St. Office: 216 Granite Block, Fall River MA‡

BRAZEAU, THEODORE WALTER, lawyer; b. Wisconsin Rapids, Wis., Mar. 12, 1873; s. Stephen and Margurite (Brady) B.; B.L., U. of Wis., 1897, LL.B., 1900; m. Harriet Pickett, Aug. 31, 1904; children—Bernard C., Richard S. Admitted to Wis. bar, 1900 and since practiced in Wisconsin Rapids; dir. Consol. Water Power & Paper Co., Prentiss-Wabers Products Co.; pres. Central Cranberry Co. Dist. atty. Wood Co., 1904-06; state senator Wis., 1907-11; del. Nat. Rep. Conv., 1909. Mem. Am. and Wis. bar assns., Wis. State Hist. Soc. (life mem.). Home: 1230 3d St. S. Office: Mead &Witter Bldg., Wisconsin Rapids WI‡

BREADY, CHARLES J., clergyman; b. Northport, Mich.; s. John A. and Frances (Carpenter) B.; A.B., Hillsdale (Mich.) Coll., 1900; A.M., Hope Coll., Holland, Mich., 1902; student U. of Mich., 1904-05; m. Lois C. Nickerson, Sept. 10, 1910; 1 son, John Charles. Began as newspaper reporter; ordained ministry M.E. Ch., 1907; successively pastor Chicago, Rockford, Ill., Aurora, Ill., Galesburg, Ill., First M.E. Ch., Omaha, Neb.; now pastor St. Paul's Ch., Cedar Rapids. Traveled in Russia, 1932, 1934, contb. articles to newspapers. Author: Red Alley (novel), 1938. Home: 1328 3d Av., Cedar Rapids IA‡

BRECHT, ROBERT PAUL, educator; b. Lancaster, Pa., Apr. 25, 1899; s. Milton Josiah and Mary Mehaffey (Wolfe) B.; B.S., U. Pa., 1922, A.M., 1925, Ph.D., 1931; m. June Dalbey Heller, Sept. 5, 1925; children—Robert Paul, Barbara June (Mrs. Benjamin Dawson, Junior), Mary Suzanne (now Mrs. Richard Mowry). Began as instructor industry Wharton Sch. Finance and Commerce, U. Pa., 1922-34, asst. prof., 1934-41, asso. prof., 1941-42, prof. industry, 1942-66, emeritus, 1967-70, chmn. geography and industry dept., 1941-58, mem. labor relations council, 1947-56; research asso. indsl. research dept, U. Pa., 1931; research cons. Work Project Adminstrn.-Nat. Research Project, 1936; lectr. management Pub. Service Inst., Department of Pub. Instrn., Commonwealth Pa., 1941-44; chmn. arbitrators Millville Mfg. Co., Textile Workers of America, from 1938; director several companies, 1956-62. Impartial chmn. adjustment bd. N.Y. Shipbldg. Corp., 1936-47, Phila. Knitted Outerwear Industry, from 1947; chmn., mem. various industry coms. Dept. of Labor, 1941, 43; pub. panel mem. 3d Regional War Labor Bd., 1943-45; spl. mediation rep. Nat. War Labor Bd., 1942-43; mem. panel of arbitrators Fed. Mediation and Conciliation Service; panel mem. N.J. Bd. Mediation, from 1959, Supervising Referees Election Inst., from 1959; research asso. Financial Execs. Research Inst., from 1960. Recipient Leffingwell medal Nat. Office Mgmt. Assn., 1948. Mem. Acad. Mgmt. (pres. 1941), A.I.M., Am. Assn. of University Profs., Nat. Academy of Arbitrators, The National Office Management Association (president 1951-52), Kappa Sigma. Author: Philadelphia Upholstery Wearing Industry (with Balderston, Hussey, Palmer and Wright), 1932; Management of an Enterprise (with Balderston, Karabasz and Riddle), 1937, rev., 1949; Practical Office Management (with Wylie and Gamber), 1937. Mem. cons. and adv. bd. Funk & Wagnalls New Standard Ency., 1947-50; mem. editorial cons. and advisers Harper & Bros. New Ency., 1955-60. Contbr. profl. jours. Home: Media PA Died May 21, 1970; buried Greenwood Cemetery, Lancaster PA

BREEDING, GLENN EDWARD, lawyer, business exec., builder; b. Green Forest, Ark., Apr. 28, 1911; s. Kit Carson and Nancy Susie (Satterfield) B.; student Hills Bus. Coll., 1933, Nat. Salesmen Tng. Assn., 1934; LL.B., Okla. Coll. Law. 1936-38, 1950-51; m. Gladys Irene Tipton, June 27, 1932; 1 son, Gerald L. Admitted Okla. bar, 1951; self-employed transp. bus., 1938-49; builder, land developer, real estate, 1950-68; exec. officer in closely held corps. and family partnerships engaged in shopping centers, multi-family housing and comml. properties. Mem. bd. numerous civic and community orgns.; dir. YMCA, 1955-68. Named Outstanding YMCA Layman of Year, 1957. Mem. C. of C. (dir.), Home Builders (dir.). Methodist. Mason (Shriner); Rotarian (charter mem. Midwest City). Home: Midwest City OK Died Apr. 3, 1968.

BREEN, WILLIAM JOHN, JR., former yacht broker; b. Boston, Sept. 23, 1904; s. William John and Frances Carrie (Boileau) B.; student Worcester Poly. Inst., 1927; m. Parker Goodwin, Mar. 16, 1946. With N.W. Ayer & Son, Inc., Phila., 1929-40, Gen. Aniline & Film Corp., N.Y., 1941-42; account exec. Young & Rubicam, Inc., N.Y.C., 1943-46; account exec. Sherman & Marquette, Inc., N.Y.C., 1947-51; v.p. mgmt. account supr., mgr. account service div., vice chmn. plans rev. bd. McCann-Erickson, Inc., N.Y.C., 1952-59; sr. v.p., mgmt. account supr. Lennen & Newell, Inc., N.Y.C., 1959-60; pres. William J. Breen, Inc., Ft. Lauderdale, Fla., yacht brokers, 1961-71; partner Brenn-Fisher & Assos. Clubs: Seawanhaka Corinthian Yacht (Oyster Bay, N.Y.); Coral Reef Yacht (Miami). Home: Fort Lauderdale FL Died Apr. 30, 1971.

BREES, HERBERT JAY, army officer, bank president; b. Laramie, Wyoming, June 12, 1877; s. Daniel Hickey and Cora (Andrews) B.; B.S., University of Wyoming, 1897, LL.D., 1939; honor graduate U.S. Inf. and Cav. School, 1903, Staff College, 1905, Army War College, 1907; m. Elizabeth Porter Nicholson, July 28, 1926. Commissioned 2d lieutenant, U.S. Army, May 23, 1898; advanced through grades to colonel, July 1, 1920; brig. gen., Nov. 1, 1930; maj. gen., May 2, 1936; lt. gen., Oct. 1, 1940; retired June 30, 1941; pres. Nat. Bank of Fort Sam Houston, San Antonio, Texas, since July 1, 1941. Participated in Spanish-American War, Philippine Insurrection, Mexican Border, World War in Vosges Sector, St. Mihiel, Meuse-Argonne and Ypres-Lys campaigns; chief of staff, 91st div., Sept. 1917-Oct. 1918, 7th Army Corps, 1918-June 1919. Awarded D.S.M., Silver Star (U.S.); Officier Legion of Honor (France). Clubs: Army and Navy, Army Navy Country; San Antonio (Tex.) Country. Address: 310 Arcadia Place, San Antonio 9 TX‡

BREHM, CLOIDE EVERETT, univ. pres.; b. Newville, Pa., Mar. 23, 1889; s. John Joseph and Tirzah Belle (Heffelfinger) B.; B.S. in Agr., Pa. State Coll., 1911, D.Sc. (hon.), Clemson Coll. S.C., 1936; LL.D., Gettysburg Coll., 1949, Roanoke Coll., 1954; m. Ruth Dapp, Dec. 25, 1912; children—John Frederick, Alice Jean (Mrs. Perry J. Williamson). Instr. in horticulture, Purdue U., 1911-13; internat. corr. schs., 1913-14; horticulturist Greer's, Phila., 1914-17; specialist in horticulture, Agrl. Extension Service, U. of Tenn., 1917, marketing economist, 1917-20, asst. dir., 1920-36, dir., 1936-43, dean, College of Agr., 1943-46; acting pres. Univ. of Tenn., 1946-48, pres. 1948-59. Dir. Nashville br. Atlanta Fed. Reserve Bd. Pres. Knoxville Navy League. Mem. Bd. Edn., United Lutheran Ch. Dir., Mid-South Cotton Assn., Tenn. Livestock Commn. Co. Dir. Williams Henson Orphanage for Boys. Mem. Alpha Zeta; Phi Kappa Phi, Delta Sigma Phi, Omicron Delta Kappa, Epsilon Sigma Phi. Lutheran (chmn. ch. council St. Johns Luth. Ch.). Mason. Club: Rotary. Home: Knoxville TN Died july 25, 1971; buried Highland Meml. Cemetery, Knoxville TN

BREIDENTHAL, JOHN W., banker; b. Kansas City, Kan., Nov. 4, 1911; s. Willard J. and Mary (Gray) B.; student U. Kan., Kansas City Law Sch.; m. Mary Ruth Pyle, Feb. 11, 1939; children—Julie (Mrs. Henry C. Gold), Nancy, Mary Ann (Mrs. Scott A. Nordheimer), Susan Jane. With Riverview State Bank, 1933-38, 40-42, chmn. bd., 1957-62; asst. cashier Victory State Bank, 1938-40, now dir.; vice chmn. bd., chmn. exec. com. Security Nat. Bank, Kansas City, Kan., 1962-66, chmn. bd., pres., 1966-72; adv. dir. Turner State Bank; dir. Victory State Bank, Fort Riley Nat. Bank, ERC Corp., Employers Reins. Corp., Gas Service Co., Kan. Bankers Surety Co., Kan. & Mo. Ry. & Terminal Co., Ortmeyer Lumber Co., Wyandotte Hotel Co. Chmn. Greater Kansas City Flood Protection Planning Commn.; chmn. dist. 5, Water Resources Assn. Mem. Pres.'s Adv. Com. on Mo.-Ark. Basins Flood Control and Conservation; mem. adv. council Kansas City FAA. Trustee Midwest Research Inst., Ottawa U.; bd. dirs. Central Indsl. Dist. Assn., Civic Council Greater Kansas City, 1st v.p., exec. bd. Agrl. Hall Fame. Served to maj., cav., AUS, 1941-46, PTO; brig. gen. Kan. N.G. Mem. Am. Royal Assn. (exec. com.), Assn. U.S. Army, N.G. Assn. U.S., Newcomen Soc., Mil. Order World Wars, 35th Div. Assn. (exec. com.), Am. Legion. Rotarian. Clubs: Kansas City (Kan.); Ft Leavenworth (Kan.) Officer's Open Mess; Richards-Gebaur Officers; Terrace; Victory Hills Golf and Country; Garden of the Gods (Colorado Springs). Home: Kansas City KS Died Jan. 4, 1972.

BREIDENTHAL, MAURICE LAUREN, JR., banker; b. Kansas City, Kan., May 2, 1916; s. Maurice L. and Louise (McCurry) B.; B.S., U. Kan., 1938; m. Berdean Bastian, Mar. 2, 1939; children—Marilyn Ann, Maurice Lauren III. With Security Nat. Bank, Kansas City, Kan., 1939-71, pres., 1958-71; dir. Parsons Comml. Bank (Kan.). Bd. dirs. Greater Kan. Corp. Pres. Kansas City (Kan.) United Community Fund; mem. lay adv. bd. Providence Hosp., Kansas City; trustee Episcopal Diocese Kan. Served to lt. (j.g.) USNR, 1943-45. Mem. Am. Kan. (chmn. ins. com. 1963-71) bankers assns., Am. Inst. Banking, Robert Morris Assos., Kansas City (bd. dirs.), Kan. (bd. dirs.) chambers commerce, Delta Sigma Kappa, Phi Delta Theta. Kiwanian. Clubs: Terrace, River (Kansas City). Home: Kansas City KS Died Feb. 16, 1971; interred Highland Park Cemetery.

BRENDLINGER, MARGARET ROBINSON, educator; b. Port Perry (now Braddock), Pa., Sept. 22, 1873; d. Peter Franklin and Hannah Emily (Brown) B.; grad. Yonkers (N.Y.) High Sch.; A.B., Vassar, 1895; post-grad. work, Yale (winter), 1898-99, Vassar (winter), 1900-01; unmarried. Taught in pvt. sch. 4 yrs., in pub. high sch. 2 yrs.; lived in Phila. 7 yrs. with no professional work, but interested in club work and in study of endl. problems; prin. Hillside Sch., Norwalk. (inc. as Hillside Country School, 1934), 1908-38, retired on 30th anniversary. Presbyterian. Mem. Am. Assn. Univ. Women (ex-pres. Norwalk br. and of state fed. same), Nat. Assn. Prins. of Schls. for Girls, Vassar Alumnae Assn., League of Women Voters. Day Nursery, United Nations Assn. Fgn. Policy Assn., Phi Beta Kappa. Clubs: Woman's City (Norwalk) (founder and hon. pres.); Women's University, Vassar (Phila.). Address: Plaza Hall, 4301 Chestnut St., Philadelphia 4 PA‡

BRENKE, WILLIAM CHARLES, prof. mathematics; b. Berlin, Germany, Apr. 12, 1874; s. Frederick Martin and Wilhelmina (Kloepper) B.; brought to U.S., 1882; A.B., U. of Ill. 1896, M.S., 1898; Ph.D., Harvard, 1907; m. Kate Read, Aug. 16, 1898; children—Katherine (Mrs. R.T. Dunstan), Bernice. Instr. mathematics and astronomy, U. of Ill., 1896-1904; instr. in mathematics and astronomy, Harvard, 1905-07; successively asst. prof., asso. prof. and prof. math., U. of Neb., 1907-44, emeritus since 1944; chmn. dept. math. and astronomy, 1934-43. Member American Math. Soc., Math. Assn. of America, Nat. Council of Math. Teachers Am. Soc. for Engring. Edn., Am. Assn. Univ. Profs., A.A.A.S., Deutshe Mathematiker Vereinigung, Sigma Xi. Presbyterian. Author: Advanced Algebra and Trigonometry, 1910; Algebra, First Course (with Edith Long), 1913; Plane Geometry (with same), 1916; Elements of Plane Trigonometry, 1917; Advanced Algebra, 1917; Calculus (with E.W. Davis), 1918. Contbr. articles on mathematics and astronomy. Home: 1250 S. 21st St., Lincoln NB‡

BRENNECKE, ERNEST, educator; b. N.Y. City, Feb. 16, 1896; s. Ernest and Anna (Beck) B.; A.B., Columbia, 1917, A.M. 1919, Ph.D., 1926; m. Julia Conklin, Mar. 15, 1947; m 2d, Lucille Donovan. Mem. faculty Columbia, 1920-69, asst. prof. English, 1936-42, asso. prof., 1942-50, prof., 1950-69; chmn. dept. English, Finch Jr. Coll., N.Y., 1938-46; spl. lectr. U.S. Mil. Acad., 1937, 1939; staff writer and editor; N.Y. World (Sunday editor, 1921-28); organist and choirmaster, Trinity Luth. Church, N.Y. City, 1917-44. Served with U.S.N.R., 1917-18. Mem. Modern Lang. Assn., Am. Guild Organists, Nat. Council Tchrs. English, Shakespeare Assn. Am., Am. Assn. U. Profs. Author: Thomas Hardy's Universe, 1924; Magazine Article Writing (with D. L. Clark), 1929, 1942; John Milton the Elder and His Music, 1938; John Badwin, A Singing Man of Windsor, 1939. Home: New York NY Died Apr. 3, 1969.

BRENNER, MORTIMER, lawyer; b. Bklyn., July 5, 1889; s. Jacob and Louise (Blumenau) B.; B.A., Columbia, 1910; LL.B., 1912; m. Sylvia Freehof, June 27, 1915; children—Louise (Mrs. L. Franklyn Lowenstein), Janet F. (dec.), Naomi (Mrs. Paul Pascal). Admitted to New York bar, 1912; since practiced in N.Y.C.; member firm Cook, Nathan & Lehman, later Lehman, Rohrlich, Solomon & Heffner, 1921-69. Co-chmn. joint adv. com. Synagogue Council Am. and Nat. Community Relations Adv. Council, 1945-69. Former pres. United Jewish Aid Socs. of Bklyn., Bklyn. Council of Social Planning, Kings County Council State Commn. Against Discrimination, Bklyn. Human Rights Conf.; bd. dirs. Jewish Family Welfare Service, Bklyn. Jewish Community Council. Mem. Bklyn. (past chmn. grievance com.), N.Y. State bar assns., N.Y. County Lawyers Assn. (chmn. com. uniform state laws). Jewish Brooklyn NY Died July 1, 1969; buried Mt. Carmel Cemetery, Jamaica LI NY

BRENNER, OTTO, trade union exec.; b. Hannover, Germany, Nov. 8, 1907; s. Otto Friedrich and Anna (Giessler) B.; m. Martha Brenner, Aug. 6, 1931; 1 dau., Heike (Mrs. Lother Pinkall). Electrician; active metal workers union and Social Dem. Party; arrested and imprisoned, 1933-35; active reviving union movement, 1945; regional dir. Industrie-Gewerkschaft Metall. Hannover, 1947, co-pres., 1952-56, pres., 1956-72, pres. Internat. Metalworkers Fedn., 1961-72; mem. exec. council German Fedn. Trade Unions, 1954-72, econ. and social council European Econ. Community, 1961-72. Dep. Social Democratic Party Diet Lower Saxony, 1951-52. Author: Gewerkschafters Dynamik in unserer Zeit, 1964; Japan. Reisebericht eines Gewerkschafters, 1967; Fur eine bessere Welt, 1970. Home: Frankfort/Main Federal Republic of Germany Died Apr. 15, 1972.

BRENTON, WOODWARD HAROLD, banker; b. Dallas Center, Ia., Feb. 27, 1899; s. Charles R. and Carrie Alicesta (Woodward) B.; A.B., Ia. State Coll., 1920; m. Etta Spurgeon, 1921; children—Mary Elizabeth, William Henry, Carolyn Ruth, Sarah Jane, Charles Robert, Junius Clyde, Juliette. Began in banking business, Dallas Center, 1920; v.p. Ia. Nat. Bank, Des Moines, 1929, later merged into Iowa-Des Moines Nat. Bank and Trust Co., of which was pres., 1931-34; v.p. and treas., dir. Northwest Bancorporation, Minneapolis until 1941, chmn. Brenton Bros., Inc., and Brenton Banks, Incorporated; chmn., dir. numerous Ia. banks; farming and banking; dir. Bankers Life Co., Employers Mutual Casualty Co. Trustee Com. Econ. Devel. Treas. Rep. Nat. Com., 1954-58. Trustee Ia. Meth. Hosp., Ia. State U. Found. Served in USN, World War I. Mem. Am. (pres. 1952-53), Ia. (pres. 1946-47) bankers assns., Newcomen Soc. Eng., Delta Tau Delta (nat. pres. 1948-50). Presbyn. Mason. Clubs: University (Chgo.); Des Moines. Wakonda (Des Moines). Home: Des Moines IA Died Sept. 30, 1968; buried Dallas Center IA

BRES, EDWARD SEDLEY, cons. civil engr.; b. New Orleans, Sept. 15, 1888; s. Joseph Ray and Sara Ella (Hughes) B.; B.E. in Civil Engring., Tulane U., 1910, C.E., 1931; m. Ann Elizabeth Todd, Sept. 7, 1917; children—Edward Sedley (officer U.S. Army), Elizabeth (Mrs. Samuel D. G. Robbins). In engring. work, harbors, flood control, dredging, docks, highway constrn., New Orleans and State of La.; mem. Eustis & Bres, 1910-17; cons. engr. and contractor, 1919-26; mem. Scott & Bres, cons. and contracting engr., 1926-41. Served from lt. to maj. C.E., AEF, U.S. Army, 1917-19; col. C.E. Res., 1927, reentered Army, 1941, brig. gen., 1945, maj. gen., 1946; ret., 1950; cons. and regional engr. U.S. Army constrn. projects, 1941; dep. chief engr. U.S. Army Forces in Australia, 1942-43; regulating officer Office of G.H.Q., S.W. Pacific Forces, 1942-44; duty Gen. Staff Corps, Washington, 1945-50; mem. N.G. Res. policies com., 1945; exec. for Res. and R.O.T.C. affairs, 1945-47; mem. sec. of army personnel bd., 1947-50. Chmn. La. Com. for Trade Recovery, 1933; La. del. Nat. Rivers and Harbors Conf., 1935; mem. adv. bd. Soil and Foundation Survey, New Orleans and vicinity, 1935; mem. La. State Bd. Engring. Examiners, 1941; mem. housing code rev. com. D.C., 1954-55. Mem., chmn. Battle of New Orleans Sesquicentennial Celebration Commn., 1963 (apptd. by pres.). Mem. Tulane Athletic Council, 1937-40. Decorated Legion of Merit with oak leaf cluster, World War I Victory medal with 3 stars, World War II Victory medal, Asiatic-Pacific medal with 4 stars, and other medals. Recipient Freedom Found. award, 1965. Nat. dir. Soc. Am. Mil. Engrs. 1941; nat. pres. Res. Officers Assn. of U.S., 1939-40, pres. New Orleans chpt., 1930, La. dept. 1932, IV Corps area council, 1934-35; dir. Navy League of U.S., 1953. Mem. Am. Soc. C.E. (life mem., past pres. La. sect., past nat. dir.), La. Engring. Soc. (hon. mem., past pres.), Am. Legion, Tulane Alumni Assn. (sec. 1915, pres. 1941), Soc. War of 1812, Mil. Order World Wars, Delta Kappa Epsilon (nat. hon. pres. 1951), Theta Nu Epsilon, Kappa Delta Phi, Delta Tau Omega, Omicron Delta Kappa, Scabbard and Blade. Clubs: Boston (New Orleans); Army and Navy, Cosmos, Post Mortem (Washington). Home: New Orleans LA Died Sept. 24, 1967; buried Arlington Nat. Cemetery, Arlington VA

BRESLICH, ERNST RUDOLPH, teacher; b. Germany, August 30, 1874; son of Louis Friedrich and Hermine (Kummer) B.; A.B., Baldwin-Wallace Coll., Berea, O., 1898; A.M., U. of Chicago, 1900; m. Marie D. Christiansen, Dec. 25, 1901; children—Paul, Erna, Herman, Golde. Came to U.S., 1890, naturalized, 1896. Head of dept. of mathematics, Univ. High Sch. (U. of Chicago), since 1912; asso. prof. teaching of mathematics, Dept. of Edn., University of Chicago, associate professor emeritus since 1939. V.p. Nat. Council of Teachers Mathematics, 1939. Member Phi Delta Kappa; hon. mem. Central Assn. of Science and Mathematics Teachers, 1940. Baptist. Author: Breslich logarithmic Tables and Mathematical Formulas, 1917; Mathematics for Junior Colleges, 1919; Slide Rule (with Charles A. Stone), 1929; Technique of Teaching Mathematics in Secondary Schools, 1930; Problems Related to Teaching Secondary School Mathematics, 1931; Administration of Mathematics in Secondary Schools, 1933; Algebra, 1934; Plane Geometry, 1935; Solid Geometry, 1935; Plane and Spherical Trigonometry (with Chas. A. Stone), 1945. Chicago IL‡

BRESNAHAN, THOMAS F., army officer; born Mass., July 4, 1892; B.S., Middlebury Coll., Vt., 1917; grad. Inf. Sch., 1924, Command and Gen. Staff Sch., 1938; commd. 2d lt. Inf., Aug. 1917; advanced through the grades to brig. gen., Sept. 1943; acting comdt. Army War Coll., 1943. Decorated D.S.C., Purple Heart with oak leaf cluster. Home: Fitchburg MA Died 1971.

BRESTELL, RUDOLPH EMILE, clergyman; b. New York, N.Y., July 4, 1873; s. Major Charles and Maud Henrietta (Thacher) B.; prep. edn., Hayden Acad., N.Y. City; B.A., St. Stephen's Coll., Annandale, N.Y., 1895; M.A., 1898; B.S.T., Gen. Theol. Sem., 1898; D.D., St. Stephen's Coll. of Columbia U., 1929; m. Bessie Maud Craske, Nov. 9, 1899. Deacon, 1898, priest, 1899. P.E. Ch.; curate Ch. of the Advocate, Phila., Pa., 1898-1901; rector Trinity Ch., Ambler, Pa., 1901-03; curate St. Martin's in the Field, Wissahickon Heights, Phila., 1903-04; curate St. Paul's Ch., Camden, N.J., 1904-05, rector, 1905-36, rector emeritus since 1941. Member National Guard New York, 1891-94; chaplain 3d Infantry, N.J. N.G., 1906-13. Examining chaplain and diocese sec. Bd. of Missions, N.J.; del. Gen. Conv. P.E. Ch., 7 times since 1913. Trustee Cathedral Foundation, St. Stephen's Coll. (Columbia U.) Mem. Phi Beta Kappa, Sigma Alpha Epsilon. Republican. Home: Merchantville NJ‡

BRETT, ALDEN CHASE, mfg. exec.; b. Abington, Mass., Nov. 10, 1889; s. William C. and Clara J. (Johnson) B.; B.S., U. Mass., 1912, LL.D., 1954; m. Katherine S. Blanchard, Sept. 1, 1915; children—Helen B. (Mrs. Thacher), Barbara S. (Mrs. Patterson), Dorothy A. (Mrs. Anderson), Janice H. (Mrs. Mead). With Hood Rubber Co. div. B. F. Goodrich Co., Watertown, Mass., 1920-55, treas., 1929-55; chmn. Boston Mut. Life Ins. Co.; pres., dir. Arrow Mut. Liability Ins. Co., 1924-59; partner Colonial Cranberry Company; advisory board State Street Bank & Trust Company, director Boston Mutual Life Insurance Company. Assistant dir. purchases WPB, Washington, 1941-42, dep. coordinator for rubber, 1942. Mem. nat. council Boy Scouts Am., 1945. Pres., dir. U. Mass. Bldg. Corp., 1939-59; trustee U. Mass.; mem. Mt. Auburn Hosp. Corp., Cambridge; chmn. development com. Wheelock Coll., 1959-60. Mem. Nat. Cranberry Assn. (treas., dir.), Asso. Industries of Mass. (exec. com., dir.), Cranberry Inst. (dir.), Kappa Sigma. Republican. Unitarian. Mason. Clubs: Down Town (Boston); Eastward HoDied Mar. 6, 1970; buried Mt. Vernon Cemetery, North Abington MA

BRETT, HOMER, consular service (retired); b. Scooba, Kemper County, Miss., Sept. 1, 1877; s. Matthew Josephus and Sarah (Casteel) B.; ed. Wall & Mooney Acad. (Franklin, Tenn.) and Mississippi Agrl. and Mechanical Coll.; m. Ona Bell Wellborn Oct. 17, 1911 (died Apr. 17, 1939; children—Wellborn (dec.), Lt. Homer Brett Jr. (U.S.N.R.), Julia Wellborn (wife of Lt. Comdr. G.M. Rouzee). In U.S. postal service 10 years and postal service of Isthmian Canal Commn., 1907-11; apptd. consul at Muskat, Arabia, Aug. 19, 1911; consul at Teneriffe, 1913-15, La Guaira, Venezuela, 1915-19, Caracas, 1919-20, Tacna, Chile, 1920, Arica, Chile, 1920-21, Iquique, 1921-23, Bahia, Brazil, 1923-26, Nottingham, Eng., 1926-28, Milan, Italy, 1928-34, Rotterdam, Holland, 1934-37; consul gen. and 1st sec. of Embassy, Lima, Peru, since Oct. 1937; retired May 1, 1941. Sergt. 1st Miss. Vol. Inf., 1898; has been lt., capt., maj. and lt. col. Miss. Nat. Guard, retired, 1907. Decorated Order of Liberator, 3d class, by Govt. of Venezuela. Fellow Am. Geog. Soc.; mem. Acad. of Polit. Science. Author: Blueprint for Victory, 1942. Rotarian. Home: Alameda CA‡

BREWBAKER, CHARLES WARREN, ch. official; b. State Line, Pa., Oct. 18, 1869; s. Abraham Rush and Mary Elizabeth (Sourbeck) B.; grad. W.Va. Normal and Classical Acad., Buckhannon, 1890; Ph.B., Western Coll, Toledo, O., 1892, Ph.M., 1896; B.D., Union Bibl. (now Bonebrake Theol.) Sem., Dayton, O., 1896; grad. study Wooster (O.) Coll., 1898-99; A.M., Otterbein Coll., 1902, D.D., 1914; PhD., Ill. Wesleyan U., 1905; grad. study Yale, 1911-12; D.D., Western Leander Clark Coll., 1914; S.T.D., Temple U., 1920; m. Nellie M. Snoke, Aug. 30, 1899; children—Mary Elizabeth (Mrs. John Ruskin Howe), Virginia Luella (Mrs. Robert Copeland). Ordained ministry U.B. Ch., 1893; pastor Hagerstown Circuit, Md. Conf., 1896-98, 1st U.B. Ch. Canton, O., 1898-1904, Chambersburg, Pa., 1904-11; asso. pastor 1st Ch. of Christ, New Haven, Conn., 1911-12; pastor Salem U.B. Ch., Baltimore, Md., 1912-13; gen. sec. S.S. and Brotherhood Work, U.B. Ch., 1913-1929; dir. Bur. of Evangelism, U.B. Ch., 1929-33; pastor Fairview Ch., Dayton, O., 1933-39. At present giving time to writing on Christian education and educational evangelism topics. Mem. adult section Internat. Council Religious Edn.; mem. Dept. Evangelism, Fed. Council of Churches of Christ in America. Mem. Phi Kappa Phi, Pi Gamma Mu. Author: The Sunday School in Action, 1914; The Devotional Life of the Sunday School Worker, 1917; A Program for Sunday School Management, 1922; Christian Growth and Conduct, 1922; Progressive Training Course (Parts III, IV), 1923; Adult Program in the Church School, 1925; Adventurous Youth, 1930; Evangelism and The Present World Order, 1932; Christian Life for Catechism— Older Boys and Girls; The Adult Bible Teacher and Leader. Contbr. to Religious Telescope, Otterbein Teacher, and to various religious periodicals. Home: 926 Manhattan Av., Dayton OH‡

BREWER, OBY T., business exec.; b. Atlanta, Ga., Dec. 19, 1893; s. William David and Dura Elizabeth (Jackson) B.; ed. pub. schs. of Atlanta, Ga.; m. Jewel Folks, May 17, 1917; children—Betty, Oby T. Asso. with George Muse Clothing Co., Atlanta, 1919-71, pres., 1944-71. Chmn. Atlanta chapter Am. Red Cross, 1941-46. Mem. Atlanta Retail Merchants Assn. (pres. 1945-46), Atlanta Humane Soc. (pres.), High Museum of Art. Democrat. Methodist. Mason (Shriner). Clubs: Atlanta Civitan (treas. Civitan Internat., 1941-44, vice pres., 1944-47), Atlanta Athletic. Home: Atlanta GA Died Nov. 16, 1971.

BREWER, WILLIS, ex-congressman, planter; b. Ala.; entered C. S. army at 18 yrs. of age; engaged in journalism; later practiced law; is now aplanter; treas. Lowndes Co., Ala , 1871; State auditor, Ala., 1876-80; mem. legislature, 1880-2 and 1890-4; State senator, 1882-90 and 1894-7; presidential elector, 1892; mem. Congress, 1897-1901, 5th Ala. dist; Democrat. Address: Hayneville AL‡

BREWSTER, RAYMOND, editor; b. Ironton, O., May 27, 1906; s. John Wesley and Margaret May (Macklin) Brewster; A.B., Marshall Coll., Doctor of Literature (honorary); married Esther Christine McCormick, Feb. 3, 1932; children—Timothy Drake, John Macklin. Asso. with Huntington (W.Va.) Publishing Co., 1927-72, v.p., exec. editor, dir.; editor-in-chief, Herald Dispatch, Huntington, 1938-72. Mem. W. Va. State. Bd. of Edn., 1941, 46; apptd. mem. reconstituted Bd. of Edn., 1947, pres., 1947-62; mem. exec. com., Huntington and Tri-State councils, Boy Scouts of Am., past pres., Family Service; W. Va. member of National Econ. Council, dir. Huntington Y.M.C.A. Mem. A.P. Mng. Editors, Sigma Delta Chi, Am. Soc. Newspapers Editors, Nat. Conf. Editorial Writers, W.Va. Newspaper Council, Southern Newspaper Pubs. Association, W.Va. State Chamber of Commerce (executive com.), Kappa Alpha, Order of the South, Omicron Delta Kappa. Republican. Methodist. Elk. Club: Rotary (dir.). Home: Huntington WV Died May 8, 1972; buried Ridgelawn Cemetery, Huntington WV

BREYER, HENRY W. JR., corp. exec.; b. Phila., Aug. 15, 1904; s. Henry W. and Edith (Scott) B.; student Penn. State Coll.; m. Margaret McKee, Oct. 24, 1929;

1 son, Henry W. 3d. Pres., Breyer Corp.; dir. Breyer Ice Cream Co. (Phila.), Nat. Dairy Products Corp. Pres., Breyer Found. Home: Bryn Mawr PA Died July 1, 1972.

BRICKEN, CARL ERNEST, composer; b. Shelbyville, Ky., Dec. 28, 1898; s. Bird E. and Lillie M. (Martin) B.; A.B., Yale U., 1922; studied composition under Scalero and piano under Leopold and Bert, David Mannes Sch.; studied under Cortot (Paris) and Weisse (Vienna); m. Dorothy Moran, Dec. 17, 1927; children—Anne. C. Alexander. Tchr. of piano, David Mannes Sch., 1925-29; tchr. theory Inst. of Mus. Art, 1929-30; chmn. music dept. U. Chgo., 1931-38; dir. Sch. Music, U. Wis., 1938-44; mus. dir. and conductor Seattle Symphony, 1944-48; prof. theory and composer in residence Sweet Briar Coll., also chmn. dept. music, now prof. emeritus. Awarded Pulitzer prize, 1929; Guggenheim fellowship, 1930-31. Mem. Am. Assn. U. Profs., Am. Musicological Soc., Am. Composers Alliance. Methodist. Rotarian. Clubs: Elizabethan (Yale). Composer of two ballads for baritone, Edward, Lord Randall, Songs from Emily Dickinson; miscellaneous songs; Daniel Boone (legend for orch.); The Prairie Years; 2d Sonata for Violin and Piano; Making of a River (music for film); Symphony No. 1, d minor, Symphony No. 2, f minor; Symphony No. 3, a Maj., The Travelled Sea (for women's voices); Sonata for Violin and Piano; Piano Sonatas Nos. 1 and 2; incidental music to the Trojan Woman; For the Time Being (Christmas oratorio); others. Home: Sweet Briar VA Died Jan. 25, 1971.

BRIDGE, GERARD, clergyman, educator; b. Crabtree, Pa., Jan. 30, 1873; s. Valentine F. and Mary (Felbaum) B.; A.M., St. Vincent Coll., Beatty, Pa., 1898. Joined Benedictines, 1893; ordained priest R.C. Ch., 1898; teacher of oratory and Latin, St. Vincent Coll. since 1898, dir., 1918-23, dean, 1923-27, alumni sec. and treas., 1927. Democrat. Compiler of History of St. Vincent Archabbey; Sixty Selections from Shakespeare; College Chimes. Author of Shakespeare's Catholicity in Hamlet, and monographs on vocations. Address: St. Vincent College, Beatty PA

BRIDGMAN, HELEN BARTLETT (MRS. HERBERT L. BRIDGMAN), writer; b. Milwaukee, Wis.; d. Frederick Kinlock and Sophia Pamela (Fuller) Bartlett; ed. pub. schs.; m. Herbert L. Bridgman, of Brooklyn, N.Y., Sept. 7, 1887 (died Sept. 24, 1924). For many yrs. contbr. musical criticisms, sketches, stories to newspapers; has traveled widely in N. and S. America, Europe, Asia and Africa, contributing articles to Brooklyn Standard Union. Author: Gems, 1916; Within My Horizon, 1920; The Last Passion, 1925; Conquering The World, 1925. Home: 604 Carlton Av., Brooklyn NY‡

BRIERLEY, WILFRID GORDON, pomologist; b. Dover, N.H., Sept. 9, 1885; s. Benjamin and Harriet (Tarbuck) B.; student U. of N.H., 1901-03; B.S.A., Cornell U., 1906; M.S., Washington State Coll., 1913; grad. student U. Minn., 1925-28; Ph.D., Mich. State Coll., 1930; m. Beulah R. Wellman, June 30, 1914; 1 son, W. Gordon. Instr. in horticulture Washington State Coll., 1909-13; asst. prof. horticulture U. Minn., 1913-17, asso. prof., 1917-37, professor since 1937. Mem. Am. Soc. Hort. Sci., Am. Soc. Plant Physiologists, Minn. Hort. Soc. (hon. life mem.), Alpha Zeta, Alpha Gamma Rho, Gamma Sigma Delta, Gamma Alpha, Sigma Xi. Author of numerous bulls., tech. papers and popular articles on behavior of fruit plants. Home: St Paul MN Died Dec. 17, 1970.

BRIGGS, FRANK RICHMOND, shoe mfr.; b. Taunton, Mass., June 9, 1874; s. Marshall Dexter and Mary M. (Bliss) B.; ed. high sch., Taunton; grad. Nat. Inst. Pharmacy, Chicago, Ill., 1891; m. Sarah Estelle Irish, of Boston, Mass., Oct. 12, 1905; 1 dau., Betsy Weeks. Entered drug business, Taunton, 1889; partner firm Ripley & Briggs, retail druggists, 1893-95; traveling salesman Thomas G. Plant Co., shoe mfrs., Boston, 1895-97, dept. mgr., 1897-1905, vice pres., 1905-11, treas., later chmn. bd. until 1927; pres. Frank R. Briggs Co., Newburyport, since 1928. Mem. Nat. Shoe Mfrs. Assn. (ex-pres.). Republican. Unitarian. Mason (K.T.), K.P. Clubs: Algonquin, Boston Athletic, Boston Boot and Shoe (Boston); Tedesco Country (Swampscott, Mass.); Brae Burn (Newton, Mass.). Home: 198 Dean Rd., Brookline, Mass. Office: 102 Merrimac St., Newburyport MA‡

BRIGGS, GEORGE ERNEST, lumber mcht.; b. at Sheldonville, Mass., May 3, 1873; s. Rev. Thomas P. and Sarah Jane (Chamberlain) B.; ed. common schs., Mass.; m. Effie L. Backer, of Melrose, Mass., Apr. 8, 1900. Began with Charles River Nat. Bank, 1889; with Lee, Higginson & Co., Boston, 1898-07; pres. Lexington Lumber Co., since Feb. 1, 1907; trustee Lexington Savings Bank. Mem. Mass. Ho. of Rep. from 29th Middlesex Dist., 1913-14. Chmn. bd. Am. Bapt. Foreign Mission Soc., 1910-12; trustee Newton Theol. Instn., etc. Progressive. Club: Boston City. Home: Lexington MA‡

BRIGGS, THOMAS HENRY, educator; b. Raleigh, N.C., Jan. 25, 1877; s. John D. and Florence (Dunn) B.; A.B., Wake Forest (N.C.) Coll., 1896, Litt.D., 1919; postgrad. U. Chgo., 1898-99, 1900-01; Ph.D., Columbia, 1914; D.H.L., 1954; m. Helen Hoyt Harriman, 1902; children—Thomas Henry IV, Barbara Winde; m. 2d, Ruth G. Sugnet, 1941. Tchr., Elizabeth City, N.C., Princeton-Yale Acad., Chgo.; prof. English, John B. Stetson U.; tchr. English, Eastern Ill. State Normal Sch.; with Tchrs. Coll. Columbia, from 1912, prof. edn., 1920-42, emeritus, 1942-71; dir. consumer edn. study Nat. Assn. Secondary-Sch. Prins.; chmn. bd. Council for Advancement of Secondary Edn., from 1954. Chmn. com. on reorientation of secondary edn., reviewing com. N.E.A. and nat. com. on research in secondary edn.; chmn. faculty com. Tchrs. Coll., World Congress on Edn. for Democracy. Del. to Pan Am. Seminars on Secondary Edn., Santiago, Chili, 1954. Fellow A.A.A.S.; mem. Phi Beta Kappa, Kappa Alpha, Kappa Delta Pi. Democrat. Author: Poetry and Its Enjoyment; Opera and Its Enjoyment; other ednl. books and mag. articles. Home: Meredith NH Died Aug. 12, 1971.

BRIGGS, WALTER OWEN, JR., business exec.; b. Detroit, Mich., Jan. 20, 1912; s. Walter Owen and Jane (Cameron) B.; student Canterbury Prep Sch., New Milford, Conn.; B.S., Georgetown Univ., 1934; m. Laura Manly, June 28, 1934; children—Walter Owen, III, Basil Manly, James Rodney. Pres., Briggs Sales Corp. (now Meridian Industries, Inc.), Lake Wales, Fla.; v.p., dir. Detroit Football Co., Fife Electric Supply Co.; pres., dir. Erie Lands, Inc.; dir. Briggs Mfg. Co.; formerly pres. Detroit Baseball Co.; formerly v.p., dir. Detroit Football Co.; exec. v.p., asst. gen. mgr. Briggs Mfg. Co. Former mayor City of Bloomfield Hills, Mich. Dir. Boys Clubs of Detroit; overseer William Beaumont Hosp.; alumni senate Georgetown U. Served from 2d lt. to lt. col. USAAF, 1941-45. Mem. Detroit Urban League, Detroit Indsl. Safety Council, Boy Scouts Am., Detroit Bd. of Commerce, United Found., Old Newsboys, Vets. Fgn. Wars, Mil. Order World Wars, Newcomen Soc., Am. Legion. Elk. Clubs: Touchdown (Washington); Economic, Adcraft, Detroit Athletic (Detroit); Aero of Mich., Bloomfield Open Hunt, The Hundred, Lambs, Variety, Bloomfield Hills Country. Home: Bloomfield Hills MI Died July 3, 1970.

BRIGHAM, GERTRUDE RICHARDSON (VIKTOR FLAMBEAU), writer, lecturer; b. Lexington, Massachusetts; d. Eli Howard and Augusta (Richardson) Brigham; student Mass. Normal Art Sch., Boston, 2 yrs.; special study, Boston U., and Harvard and Columbia universities; A.B., George Washington U., 1913, A.M., 1914, Ph.D., 1916; visited Europe for literary and art study, 1912-14, also 1922-27; including northern Africa, later China, Japan, Near East, Egypt, 1932-40, Russia, Greece, Mexico, Cuba. Began teaching in district school of Mary who had a little lamb," Sterling, Mass.; engaged in industrial orgn. with Filene Cooperative Assn., Boston, 1901-07; with Smithsonian Instn. of Washington, 1910-21; with La France Mag., N.Y. City, Jan.-June 1921; instr. in history of art, George Washington U., 1916-29; lecturer, Trade Union Coll., 1920-23; with Nat. Art Center, 1922-24; art editor Washington Herald, 1921-26, Washington Post, 1922-24; associate professor Lingnan University, Canton, China, 1924-25. Director Cross Art School, 1945. Member S. Atlantic Modern Language Association (secretary Eng. div.), Anson K. Cross Art School Alumni Assn. (nat. sec.), Archaeol. Soc. Washington, Art and Archaeology League (sec.), Washington Soc. Fine Arts, Assn. Ga. Artists, Southern States Art League. Clubs: Writers (founder), Columbian Women (George Washington University), Art Promoters (founder), National Press, Brenau Faculty Club ex-pres.; Gainesville Business and Professional Women's (v.p.), Alpha Delta (nat. pres.); Hall County Women's Dem. Club (parliamentarian). Author: The Study and Enjoyment of Pictures, 4th edition, 1932; Red Letter Days in Europe, with a glimpse of Northern Africa; (brochure) In Memoriam, Sven Magnus Gronberger; Story of David Edstrom; Ellen Key's Message to the Labor Movement; also Viktor Flambeau Travel Series (newspaper articles), series on Russia; Literary Women of 1812; The Business Woman's Role Today; Writing and Selling the Short Story; How to Draw and Paint, 1945; art criticism and miscellaneous revs. and contbns. to Art and Archaeology, Public Affairs, Sonnet Sequences, Atlanta Constitution, Atlanta Jour., Brenau Alchemist, Delta Zeta Lamp, and broadcasting. Editor: Life of Rear Admiral George Collier Remey, U.S. Navy. Home: Portland ME Died Feb. 1971.

BRIGHAM, HAROLD FREDERICK, librarian; b. Newark, N.J., May 25, 1897; s. William Clarence and Anna M. (De Chapin) B.; A.B., Princeton, 1921; certificate, Library Sch. of New York, Pub. Library, 1922; spl. courses U. of Chicago; m. Rose Shuler, June 8, 1921; children—Harold Frederick, Ann Shuler, Owsley Haskins. With Free Pub. Library, Trenton, N.J., 1912-16; Princeton Univ. Library, 1916-17 and 1919-21; war service with A.L.A., 1917-19; cataloger, Rutgers Univ. Library, 1921-23; librarian New Brunswick (N.J.) Pub. Library, 1922-25; research asst., A.L.A., Chicago, 1925-27; librarian Carnegie Library, Nashville, Tenn., 1927-31; librarian Free Pub. Library, Louisville, Ky., 1931-42; dir. Ind. State Library since 1942; lecturer U. of Louisville, 1931-37. With U.S. N.R.F., 1918. Pres. Y.M.C.A. Southern Area Council, 1939-40, chmn. bd., 1941-42; mem. Y.M.C.A. Nat. Council and Nat. Board, 1941-48; director Louisville Y.M.C.A., 1933-42, Indianapolis Y.M.C.A. since 1943 (pres. 1947-48); president Indiana State YMCA, from 1959. Recipient Race Relations award, Indianapolis Church Fedn., 1952. Mem. A.L.A. (pres. pub. libraries div. 1951-52, 2d v.p. 1956), Indpls. Ch. Fedn. (pres. 1955-57), Indianapolis Literary Club (president 1957-58), Ind. State Assn. Adult Edn. (dir.), Ind. Library Assn. (dir.), Ind. Hist. Soc., others. Presbyn. Contbr. on profl. subjects. Home: Indianapolis IN Died Mar. 15, 1971.

BRILES, CHARLES WALTER, educator; b. at Thomasville, N.C., Feb. 24, 1873; s. Millard Fillmore and Sallie (Lopp) B.; Litt.B., U. of N.C., 1896; post-grad. work, U. of Tex., summer, 1905; m. Maggie Cox, of Gainesville, Tex., June 18, 1901. Teacher in pub. schs. of Tex., 1896-05; supt. city schs., Muskogee, Okla., 1905-9; prin. East Central State Normal Sch., Ada, Okla., since 1909. Democrat. Methodist. Has assisted largely in standardizing and unifying the work of the higher ednl. instns. of Okla. Address: Ada OK‡

BRILL, GEORGE MACKENZIE, cons. engr.; b. Poughquag, N.Y., Mar. 24, 1866; s. Thomas and Mary J. (Hurd) B.; M.E. from Cornell U. in 1891, M.M.E., same 1905; m. Achsah A. Quick, June 1, 1892; children—Elliot M., G. Meredith, Roland C.; m. 2d, Edith Seaman Brill, June 4, 1932. Research engr., Solvay Process Co., Syracuse, 1891-96; chief engr. Solvay Process Co., Detroit, 1896-97; cons. engr. Solvay Process Co., 1904-14; gen. engr., Swift & Co., Chicago, 1897-1900; cons. practice, Chicago, 1900-13, engrng. investigations abroad, 1910, 12, 13; chmn. bd. engrs., smoke suppression, Chicago, 1907-12; mem. Jury of Awards and chmn. of jury covering gen. machinery, San Francisco Expn., 1915; joined staff of Guggenheim Bros. as cons. mech. engr. early in 1917, but resigned to enter mil. service; commd. maj. O.R.C., July 1917, and in charge of plant facilities in office of acting chief of ordnance to Apr. 1918; in charge requirements sect. of Emergency Fleet Corp., representing it on War Industries Bd., later cons. engr. for the corp.; determined condition and value of ships requisitioned by President Wilson, Aug. 3, 1917, upon which claims had not been settled, Jan. 1, 1919; cons. practice, N.Y. City, since 1919. Fellow A.A.A.S., Am. Geog. Soc., Am. Soc. M.E. (past v.p.), Sigma Xi. Republican. Home: 19 Kingston Av., Poughkeepsie NY‡

BRILL, HARVEY CLAYTON, chemist; b. Preble County, O., Dec. 29, 1881; s. John and Matilda (Velte) B.; A.B., Miami U., 1908; Ph.D., U. of Mich., 1911; m. Gertrude Davidson, June 17, 1913; 1 dau., Elizabeth. Asst. prof. chemistry, Miami U., 1911-13; organic chemist Bur. of Science, Manila, P.I., 1913-16; chief Div. of Organic Chemistry, same, 1916-18; member Food and Drugs Board, P.I., 1914-17; prof., head dept. chemistry, Miami U., from 1918. Chem. engr. Fellow A.A.A.S., Ohio Acad. Sci., Am. Institute Chemists; mem. American Chemical Society, Deutsche Chemische-Gesellschaft, Phi Sigma Kappa, Sigma Xi, Phi Lambda Upsilon, Phi Beta Kappa, Pi Gamma Mu. Democrat. Presbyterian. Author many papers dealing with original investigations in organic chemistry. Home: Oxford OH Died Jan. 11, 1972; buried Oxford Cemetery.

BRIND, CHARLES ALBERT, lawyer; b. Albany, New York, Sept. 16, 1897; s. Charles Albert and Mary Eleanor (Gordon) B.; A.B., Union Coll., 1919; LL.B., Albany Law Sch., 1922; LL.D., Keuka Coll., Keuka Park, New York, 1941; J.D., Union U., 1968; L.H.D., N.Y. Sch. Tech., 1970; m. Laura Stuart Hutchison, June 9, 1923; children—Charles Albert, III (dec.), David Hutchison, Nancy Virginia (Mrs. William L. Wallace). Admitted to N.Y. bar, 1922, U.S. bar, 1952; claim dept. United Traction Co., 1920-23; asso. atty. N.Y. Dept. Edn., Albany, 1923-33, prin. atty. and dir. div. of law, 1933-40; gen. counsel, State Dept. of Edn., and U. of the State of N.Y., 1940-68, also N.Y. State Bd. Regents, N.Y. State Tchrs. Retirement System, 1940-68, Dormitory Authority N.Y.; v.p., dir., George R. Cooley, Inc., investments; past pres. Northeastern N.Y. Med. Service, Inc.; lectr. State Coll. for Tchrs. at Albany, Union Coll., Hofstra Coll., Cornell University; lectr. N.Y. State law Tchrs. Coll., Columbia U., Syracuse U. Trustee The Philatelic Foundation. Past pres. Assn. of State Civil Service Employees. Member Legislative Commn. on extension of civil service to local units of govt.; pres. Associate Hosp. Service of Capitol Dist. of N.Y.; mem. bd. govs. Albany Hosp. Served in O.T.C., Camp Zachary Taylor, Louisville, Ky., 1918. Member board directors Albany Training School for Practical Nurses; mem. Council of Sch. Supts. (Cities and Villages); mem. board visitors Union U. School of Nurses; pres. Blue Cross. Mem. Alumni Assn. of Delta Chi (vice president), Albany County Bar Assn., New York State Teachers Assn., Delta Chi, Phi Beta Kappa (past pres. Upper Hudson chpt.). Presbyn. (trustee). Mason. Club: Ft. Orange Stamp (past pres.). Editor State Employee, 1935-42. Contbr. to ednl. jours. Author: (with A. K. Getman) Story of State Government (N.Y.), 1942. Home: Albany NY Died Oct. 7, 1970; buried Albany Rural Cemetery.

BRINKEN, CARL ERNEST, composer; b. Shelbyville, Ky., Dec. 28, 1898; s. Bird E. and Lillie M. (Martin) B.; A.B., Yale U., 1922; studied composition under Scalero and piano under Leopold and Bert, David Mannes Sch.; studied under Cortot (Paris) and Weisse (Vienna); m. Dorothy Moran, Dec. 17, 1927; children—Anne, C. Alexander. Tchr. of piano, David Mannes Sch., 1925-29; teacher theory, Inst. of Musical Art, 1929-30; chmn. music dept., U. of Chicago, 1931-38; dir. School of Music, U. of Wis., 1938-44; musical director and conductor Seattle Symphony, 1944-48; prof. theory and composer in residence Sweet Briar Coll., also chmn. dept. music, later prof. emeritus. Awarded Pulitzer prize, 1929; Guggenheim fellowship, 1930-31. Mem. Am. Assn. U. Profs., Am. Musicological Soc., Am. Composers Alliance. Methodist. Rotarian. Clubs: Elizabethan (Yale). Composer of two ballads for baritone, Edward, Lord Randall, Songs from Emily Dickinson; misc. songs; Daniel Boone (legend for orchestra); The Prairie Years; 2d Sonata for Violin and Piano; Making of a River (music for film); Symphony No. 1, d minor, Symphony No. 2, f minor, Symphony No. 3, a Maj., The Travelled Sea (for women's voices); Sonata for Violin and Piano; Piano Sonatas Nos. 1 and 2; incidental music to the Trojan Woman; For the Time Being (Christmas oratorio); others. Home: Sweet Briar VA Died Jan. 25, 1971.

BRINKMAN, OSCAR H., editor, lawyer; b. Mansfield, O., Mar. 13, 1893; s. Harry and Clara (Heller) B.; student Georgetown U., 1912-13; LL.B., Kansas City Sch. of Law, U. of Kansas City, 1920; m. Isabel Mary Galbraith, Dec. 26, 1914; children—Claire Louise, Constance. Admitted to bar, Mo., 1920, D.C., 1926, Mass., 1939; practiced law in Kansas City, Washington and Boston, 1920-49; spl. counsel for U.S. Senate in various legislative investigations; drafted pioneer bill regulating sale of securities passed by Senate; writer, asst. editor LaFollette's Weekly Mag., 1910; state editor Milwaukee Journal, 1911; writer numerous articles on polit. and econ. subjects for metropolitan newspapers, syndicates including N.Y. Herald Tribune, N.Y. Times, 1925-33; editor Babson's Washington Forecast, 1944-52; editor-in-chief Business Digest and Forecast, 1954-69; editor Current Features Syndicate; editor Rental Housing mag., 1961-63; exec. sec. Nat. Apt. Owners Assn., 1961-63, practice law, 1963-69. Trial and appeals attorney, N.L.R.B., and regional atty. (New England), Interstate Commerce Commn., 1938-43. Mem. bar supreme courts of U.S., Mo., Dist. of Columbia and Mass. Author: America's Choice: Freedom or Slavery, 1956. Home: Alexandria VA Died July 18, 1969; buried Mt. Comfort Cemetery, Alexandria VA

BRISBIN, CLARENCE FRANKLIN, pioneer telephone executive; b. Greenville, Pa., Oct. 12, 1871; s. James Montgomery and Martha (Showers) B.; ed. pub. and select schs., and Picketts Sch. of Commerce, Phila.; m. Marion Perry, of Brooklyn, Pa., Jan. 9, 1902. Began active career with James Humphrey & Son, lumber mchts., Greenville; with W. T. Craig & Son, lumber, Greenville, 1885-94; mgr. flour mill of A. D. Mead & Son, Du Bois, Pa., 1894-95; installer and inspector Central Dist. and Printing Telegraph Co., Du Bois, 1895-97; first solicitor Central Pa. Telephone & Supply Co., Scranton, 1897-1900, local mgr., 1900-02; after merger with Pa. Telephone Co. served as div. supt., Wilkes-Barre, 1902-07; after merger with Phila. Bell Telephone Co. forming the Bell Telephone Co. of Pa. was dist. plant supvr. at Wilkes-Barre, 1907-10, dist. mgr. 1910-19, div. mgr., at Harrisburg, 1919-21; genl. connecting co. supervisor at Phila. in charge relations with state and federal govts., railroads, connecting and independent telephone cos., 1921-27; from formation of N.J. Bell Telephone, 1927, served as v.p. in charge personnel and pub. relations, retired, 1932. One of best known telephone pioneers; active in early telephone socs. which were forerunners of employees training courses now conducted throughtout Bell System. Director Bur. of Civilian Relief Am. Red Cross, of Wyoming Valley, World War; dir. and nat. councillor Mfrs. Council (N.J.); dir. and v.p. N.J. State Chamber of Commerce. Mem. H. G. McCully Chapter Telephone Pioneers of America. Mason. Clubs: Essex, Downtown, Newark Athletic (Newark); Braidburn Country (Madison). Home: 305 West End Av., New York NY‡

BRISCOE, BIRDSALL PARMENAS, architect; b. Harrisburg, Tex., June 10, 1876; s. Andrew Birdsall and Annie Frances (Payne) B.; student San Antonio Acad., Tex. A. and M. Coll., U. Tex.; m. Ruth Dillman, 1927. Pres., Birdsall P. Briscoe, Houston, 1906-71; specializing in residences. Served to maj., inf. U.S. Army, World War I. Fellow A.I.A. Author: (fiction) In the Face of the Sun, 1935, Spurs from San Isidro, 1951. Contbr. tech. articles, short stories to nat. mags. Home: Houston TX Died Sept. 18, 1971; buried Oakhill Cemetery, Goliad TX

BRISCOE, ROBERT PEARCE, naval officer; b. Centreville, Miss., Feb. 19, 1897; s. Pearce Tonstil and Alice Letitia (Ware) B.; B.S., U.S. Naval Acad., 1918; student Marion Inst., 1914-15; m. Katherine Norwood Lewis, Aug. 22, 1923. Commd. ensign U.S. Navy, 1918, advanced through grades to admiral, 1956; served in destroyer convoy escort duty, Europe, World War I; served Near East, 1919-21; asst. engring. officer, U.S.S. West Va., 1926-29; instr., U.S. Naval Acad., 1929-31, 1934-37; China duty, 1931-33; navigation officer, U.S.S. Miss., 1937-39; asst. dir. Naval Research Lab., 1939-41; comdr. U.S.S. Prometheus, Destroyer Squadron 5, U.S.S. Denver, Amphibious Group 14, 1942-44; staff comdr. in chief, U.S. Fleet, 1944; comdr. Operational Development Force, 1945-48; comdr. amphibious force Atlantic Fleet 1950; comdr. 7th Fleet, Korea, 1972; comdr. naval forces, Far East, 1952-54, dep. chief naval operations, 1954-56; comdr. in chief Allied Forces So. Europe, 1956-59, rank adm. Decorated Navy Cross, D.S.M., Legion of Merit with gold star, commendation ribbon, citation from sec. of navy. Mem. Newcomen Soc. Presbyn. Home: Liberty MS Died Oct. 14, 1968; buried Arlington Nat. Cemetery, Arlington VA

BRISKIN, SAMUEL JACOB, motion picture exec.; b. Russia, Feb. 8, 1897; s. Benjamin and Rose (Buchman) B.; brought to U.S., 1898, derivative citizen; student Coll. City N.Y., 1916-17; m. Sara Myers, July 27, 1918; children—Gerald, Bernard. With Brisken, Sohn & Feiman, C.P.A.'s, 1918-20, C.B.C. Film Sales Corp., 1920-26; with Columbia Pictures Corp., 1926-36, 38-42, 58-68 v.p., dir. until 1968. with RKO Radio Pictures, 1936-38, Liberty Films, Inc., 1945-50, Paramount Pictures Corp., 1950-57; chmn. bd. TelAutograph Corp.; bd. dirs. Screen Gems, Inc. Spl. advanced gifts div. Community Chest. Trustee bd. dirs., pres. Cedars of Lebanon Hosp., Mt. Sinai Hosp. (both Los Angeles). Served from major to lt. col. Signal Corps, AUS, 1942-45. Decorated Legion of Merit. Mem. Screen Producers Guild. Western Harness Racing Association. Jewish religion. Mason. Club: Hillcrest Country Los Angeles CA Died Nov. 14, 1968; buried Hillcrest Meml. Park and Mausoleum.

BRISTOL, THEODORE LOUIS, pub. utility exec.; b. Ansonia, Conn., Apr. 25, 1870; s. Charles Edward and Frances Ellen (Bartholomew) B.; student Phillips Exeter Acad., 1888-89; B.A., Yale, 1893; m. Florence M. Espe, Oct. 5, 1893; children—Theodore L., Jr., Frances Bartholomew (Mrs. Stanley Gordon Seccombe), Florence (Mrs Lardner Hancock Shull), Elleda (Mrs. William Rives Wilson), John Thorvald (dec.). Pres. Ansonia (Conn.) Water Company; dir. Ansonia Nat. Bank; Birmingham Water Co., Connwood, Inc Served on state council of national defense, World War. Member New Haven Grays (independent mil. orgn.). Rep. Conn. legislature, 1903; pres. Ansonia Bd. of Public Works, 1913-14. Chmn. Julia Day Nursery; chmn. Ansonia Community Chest; dir. Griffin Hosp.; director Conn. and Ansonia chambers of commerce. Member Connecticut Water Works Assn. (ex-pres.), N.E. Water Works Assn. (ex-pres.), Conn. Forest and Park Assn. (ex-pres.), Am. Water Works Assn., Conn. Soc. of Civil Engrs., Industrial Association of Lower Naugatuck Valley, Ansonia Chapter of Am. Red Cross (Chmn.), Delta Kappa Epsilon, Wolf's Head (Yale). Republican. Conglist. (trustee 1st Ch., Ansonia). Mason. Club: Graduate. Home: 67 N. Cliff St. Office: 354 Main St., Ansonia CT‡

BRISTOW, LOUIS JUDSON, hosp. supt.; b. Timmonsville, S.C., Jan. 19, 1876; s. James Tazewell and Elizabeth (Blackwell) B.; Th.G., Southern Bapt. Theol. Sem., Louisville, Ky., 1901; m. Caroline Winkler, Oct. 29, 1902; children—Gwen (Mrs. Bruce Manning), Louis J., Caroline (Mrs. J. P. Riley). Ordained ministry Baptist Ch., 1901; pastor at Wedgefield, S.C., later at Marion, S.C., until 1905; editor Baptist Press, Greenwood, 1905-06; pastor Williamston, 1907-10, Abbeville, 1910-15, 1918-21; founder and supt. S.C. Baptist Hosp., Columbia, S.C., 1915-18, Ala. Bapt. Hosp., 1921-24, Southern Bapt. Hosp., New Orleans, 1924-47, ret.; founder Good Samaritan Hosp., Selma, Ala. (for Negroes), 1922. Served as lt. inf., S.C. Vols., Spanish-Am. War; adj. 3d Batn.; col. chief of Ordnance, gov.'s staff, S.C., 1899-1900. Trustee Anderson Coll.; v.p. Southern Bapt. Conv., 1925-27 and 1937-38; mem. Hosp. Commn. Southern Bapt. Conv.; mem. Am. Hosp. Assn., Am. Protestant Hosp. Assn., Southern Bapt. Hosp. Assn. Democrat. Mason, K.P. (G.C. for S.C., 1918-19, Supreme Rep. 1919-24). Rotarian (pres. New Orleans Club, 1936-37, dist. gov. 1948-49). Author: Healing Humanity's Hurt, 1926; Hosp. Stories, 1932; Why Christian Hospitals?, 1933. Home: 4501 Magnolia St., New Orleans LA‡

BRITTIN, LEWIS HOTCHKISS, engineer; b. Derby, Conn., Feb. 8, 1877; s. Edwin and Mary (Hotchkiss) B.; prep. edn., Gunnery and Ridge schs., Washington, Conn.; student Harvard, 1897-99; m. Arna Torkelson, 1919 (died July 25, 1935). Engineer Newhall Engineering Co., Sierra Madre Land & Lumber Co.; mgr. Nat. Lamp Div. of Gen. Electric Co.; v.p. and gen. mgr. Northwestern Terminal, Minneapolis; founder, vice pres. and gen. mgr. Northwest Airways, Inc.; consultant, Bureau Foreign and Domestic Commerce, U.S. Dept. of Commerce; cons. and collaborator, U.S. Dept. Agr.; cons. Bur. Fgn. and Domestic Commerce, N.Y. Bd. Trade, dir. Edward S. Evans Transportation Research, Washington, D.C. Pres. Chicago Air Traffic Assn.; v.p. St. Paul Assn.; mem. bd. govs. and cons. Aeronautical Chamber Commerce; pres. Nat. Assn. of State Aviation Officials; chmn. Minn. Aeronautics Commn.; dir. Airport Program, Dept. Commerce, State of Minn.; dir. Independent Air-Freight Assn. Cons. aeronautical engr. Cpl. Batt. A, 1st Mass. Vols., Spanish-Am, War; lt. col., assigned duty Gen. Staff, U.S. Army, World War; chmn. Minn. State Defense Com. Mem. Sons of Am. Revolution, Soc. of War of 1812, Sigma Alpha Epsilon, Pi Eta Soc. (Harvard). Clubs: Harvard (New York); Minnesota (St. Paul); Minneapolis (Minn.). Home: 1445 Ogden St., N.W. 813 Arlington Bldg., 1025 Vermont Av., N.W., Washington 5‡

BRIZZOLARA, RALPH DOMINIC, steel co. exec.; b. Chgo., Oct. 28, 1895; s. Charles Anthony and Louise Mary (Segale) B.; ed. pub. schs., Chgo.; m. Florence M. Hurley, Sept. 19, 1925; children—Robert F., Charles A., Nancy (Mrs. Lorenz). Editing engr. Western Electric Co., Chgo., 1915-17; engr. Am. Steam Conveyor Corp., 1917-18, Am. Steel Foundries, Chgo., from 1919, asst. chief engr., 1928-31, chief engr., 1931-43, v.p., 1943-61; sec., dir. Chgo. Bears Football Club, Inc., from 1933, acting pres., 1942-45, dir.; dir. Danly Machine Spltys., Onsrud Machine Co.; chmn. bd., dir. Poor & Co., 1962-65, chief exec. officer, 1962-64. Trustee Barat Coll. until 1970. Served with USNR, 1918-19; cons. to chief of ordnance, Dept. Army, 1950. Fellow Am. Soc. M.E. Clubs: Tavern, Chicago, Chicago Athletic Assn. Home: Chicago IL Died Aug. 3, 1972; buried Calvary Cemetery, Evanston IL

BROADBENT, JAMES THOMAS, dir. Standard Coated Products Co.; b. nr. Manchester, Eng., Mar. 17, 1875; s. Thomas and Mary (Booth) B.; ed. pub. schs. and Victoria Hall Tech. Sch., Eng.; came to U.S., 1896, naturalized, 1905; student Lowell, Mass., Tech. Sch., 1897-99; m. Marietta Cryer, of New Bedford, Mass., June 10, 1902. Instr. New Bedford (Mass.) Textile Sch., 1899-1902, Fall River Textile Sch., 1904-08; in charge textile div. Mississippi Agricultural and Mechanical College, 1 yr., 1902-03; director Standard Coated Products Co. Mem. Commn. sent to Europe in interests of World's Cotton Conf., 1919. Fellow Textile Inst.; mem. Nat. Assn. Cotton Mfrs., Am. Assn. Cotton Mfrs., Textile Research Council, Textile Associates, Textile Club, Arkwright Club. Mason (32 deg., K.T.). Club: New Bedford (Mass.) Country. Home: 1522 Caton Av., Brooklyn, N.Y. Office: 40 Worth St., New York NY‡

BROCK, HENRY IRVING, writer; b. Amherst, Va., Aug. 4, 1876; s. Henry Clay and Mary Carter (Irving) B.; A.B., Hampden-Sidney (Va.) Coll., 1895, A.M., 1896, hon. Litt.D., 1925; m. Nelly Grattan Morton, Oct. 1, 1908; 1 dau., Georgiana Mary. Teacher, prep. schs. Va. and Tenn., 1896-99; reporter Chattanooga (Tenn.) Times, 1899-1900; reporter and writer, New York Times, 1900-06, exchange and foreign editor, 1906-11; editor Saturday Magazine, New York Evening Post, 1912-17; asst. editor New York Sunday Times, 1919-24; polit. editor Unpartizan Review, 1919; writer for N.Y. Times since 1924. Capt. Air Service, U.S. Army, 1918-19. Clubs: Century, Players. Author: A Little Book of Limericks, 1947. Home: 776 Lexington Av., New York; and Bleak Hill, Comorn, Va. Address: New York Times, Times Square, NYC‡

BROCK, LARRY, govt. official; b. Platte County, Neb., Aug. 16, 1906; s. John and Mary (Moeller) B.; Ph.G., U. Neb., 1929; m. Roenna Utemark, 1929; children—Anjenean (Mrs. Harold Tell), Betty (Mrs. Charles Soderberg), Jacqueline (Mrs. Richard Rosenbohm), Judith (Mrs. William Gibson). Member of the Eighty-Sixth Congress, 3d District Nebraska; asst. adminstr. Farmers Home Adminstrn., 1961-68. Mem. Neb. Hwy. Adv. Commn., 1950-53. Chmn. Neb. Democratic Com., 1954-56. Mem. Neb. Livestock Feeders Assn. (past pres.), Nat. Livestock Feeders Assn. (past pres.), Neb. Rural Electric Assn. (v.p. 1956), Better Neb. Assn. (exec. com.). Home: Wakefield NB Died Aug. 28, 1968; buried Wakefield NB

BROCK, LORING STEWART, steel co. exec.; b. William, Ont., Can., Apr. 8, 1911; s. William Albert and Melissa (McInroy) B.; came to U.S., 1924, naturalized, 1926; student U. Cal. at Los Angeles, 1927-28; grad. Exec. Devel. Program, Stanford, 1954; m. Bernice Geneva Erickson, Mar. 4, 1937; children—Carolyn Jean, Marilyn Sue, David L. Salesman Columbia Steel Co., Los Angeles, 1935-45; mgr. sales Columbia Geneva Steel div. U.S. Steel Corp., Los Angeles, 1945-51, dist. v.p. sales, Salt Lake City, 1951-55, dir. product devel. U.S. Steel Corp., Pitts., 1955-57, mgr. plate and structural steel sales, 1957-60, pres. U.S. Steel Products div., N.Y.C., 1960-65, v.p. U.S. Steel Internat. 1965-68, pres., 1968-71. Home: Bronxville NY Died 1971.

BROCK, THOMAS SLEEPER, clergyman, educator; b. Bridgeboro, N.J., Jan. 22, 1874; s. James Edwards and Suanna (Sleeper) B.; Ph.B., Ill. Wesleyan U., 1898; grad. New Brunswick (N.J.) Theol. Sem., 1908; B.D., Temple U., 1911, S.T.D., 1912; m. Carrie R. Iszard, Apr. 8, 1897; children—C. Lester, Dorothy Mae; m. 2d, Harriet G. Harper, March 15, 1932. Ordained ministry M.E. Ch., 1898; pastor successively at Lambertville, Burlington, Vineland, Camden and Atlantic City, N.J.; supt. of Trenton District; prof. homiletics, Sch. of Theology, Temple U., 1924-41; now pastor Calvary

Meth. Ch., Lake Worth, Fla. Mem. Phi Beta Kappa, Delta Kappa Epsilon. Republican. Mason. Home: 207 S. O St., Lake Worth FL‡

BROCKWAY, GEORGE A., retired mfr.; b. Homer, N.Y., Mar. 26, 1863; s. William N. and Edith (Hine) B.; ed. high sch.; married 1888; children—William N. (dec.), G. Russell (dec.). Founder, 1912, Brockway Motor Truck Corp., Cortland, N.Y.; retired, 1929; v.p. Homer (N.Y.) Nat. Bank, First Nat. Bank, Cortland, N.Y. Vice-pres. Cortland Hosp.; pres. Children's Home; pres. Home for Aged Women. Republican. Mason. Clubs: Cortland (N.Y.) Country; Century (Syracuse); Surf (Miami Beach, Fla.). Home: 19 W. Court St., Cortland, N.Y.; and 2054 N. Bay Rd., Miami Beach, Fla. Office: 60 Main St., Cortland NY

BRODERICK, CARROLL JOSEPH, banker; b. Balt., Oct. 1, 1905; s. John William and Katherine (McKew) B.; eve. student Balt. City Coll., 1922-26, Balt. Coll. Commerce, 1930-34; m. Agnes Marie Daily, Apr. 8, 1940; 1 son, John Carroll. With O'Neil and Co., Balt., 1920-21; with Savs. Bank Balt., 1921-72, sr. v.p., treas., 1965-72; instr. accounting Balt. Coll. Commerce Eve. Sch., 1950-72. Served to lt. comdr. USNR, 1941-46. Home: Baltimore MD Died 1972.

BRODHEAD, GEORGE LIVINGSTON, physician; b. New Orleans, Oct. 14, 1869; s. Augustus Wackerhagen and Sarah Blandina (Trumpbour) B.; grad. Ulster Acad., Kingston, N.Y., 1886; med. prep. course, Cornell U., 1886-88; M.D., Coll. Phys. & Surg. (Columbia), 1891; m. Frances Louise Clark, June 2, 1897; 1 daughter, Mrs. Katharine Livingston Fiske. Mem. house staff, Mt. Sinai Hosp., 1891-93; pvt. practice, 1894-95; resident physician, Sloane Hosp., 1895-97; instr. in obstetrics, Coll. Phys. and Surg., 1895-97; N.Y. U. and Bellevue Hosp. Med. Coll., 1899-1917; prof. obstetrics, New York Post-Grad. Med. Sch. and Hosp., 1899-1916; cons. obstetrician, Knickerbocker, Jewish Maternity, Lutheran, Union, Bronx Maternity hosps., St. Agnes Hosp. (White Plains, N.Y.), Jamaica Hosp. (Jamaica, N.Y.), United Hosp. of Portchester, Letchworth Village, St. Luke's Hospital, Newburgh, N.Y. Mem. A.M.A., N.Y. State Med. Soc., N.Y. County Med. Soc., New York Acad. Medicine, New York Obstet. Soc., Soc. Med. Jurisprudence, Phi Gamma Delta, Phi Alpha Sigma, etc. Republican. Episcopalian. Club: Hosp. Graduates. Author: Approaching Motherhood, 1925; also numerous med. monographs. Home: 580 Park Av., New York 21 NY‡

BRODSKY, PAUL, psychologist; b. Vienna, Austria, Nov. 12, 1900; s. Leo and Olga (Fleischer) B.; M.A., Federal Tchrs. Coll., Vienna, Austria, 1936; postgrad. Tchrs. Inst., Vienna, Austria, 1936-37, U. Cal. at Los Angeles, 1945-48, U. So. Cal., 1946; m. Margareth Waldmann, Nov. 30, 1928. Came to U.S., 1939, naturalized, 1945. Asso. to Prof. Alfred Adler, Vienna, 1925-37; radio, TV speaker, head child Guidance Clinic, Vienna, 1929; tchr. pub. schs., Vienna, 1937-39; instr. Tchrs. Inst. Los Angeles Bd. Edn., 1946; dir. Sunset Play Corner Day Nurseries, Los Angeles, 1948-65; acting dir. Alfred Adler Counseling Center, 1962-70; instr. U. Cal. Edn. Extension; tchr. adult edn. Los Angeles County and City Schs., 1950-54, Beverly Hills Unified Schools; lectr., instr. Alfred Adler Soc., 1958-59, 61-62; vis. prof. Oregon State U., Corvallis. Mem. Am., Cal., Los Angeles County psychol. assns., Am. Soc. Adlerian Psychology, Group Psychotherapy Assn. So. Cal., Alfred Adler Soc. Los Angeles, Inst. Individual Psychology. Author various children's songs. Author articles pub. profl. jours. Address: Los Angeles CA Died Sept. 9, 1970.

BROGAN, FRANCIS ALBERT, lawyer; b. Dewitt, Ia., Dec. 6, 1860; s. Francis and Anne (Cummins) B.; student St. Benedict's Coll., Atchison, Kan., 1878-80; A.B., Georgetown Coll., 1883; LL.B., Harvard Law Sch., 1885; m. Maude Haskell Perley, Oct. 17, 1888; children—Dr. Albert Perley, Maurice Perley. Admitted Kan. bar, 1885; in practice at Emporia, Kan., 1885-88, Omaha, Neb., since 1888; local atty. A.T. & S.F. Ry. Co., 1885-88; sr. mem. firm Brogan, Ellick, Shoemaker and Fitzgerald; gen. atty. in Neb. for Mo. P. Ry. Co., 1910-12, for Western Union Telegraph Co. since 1909; atty. Omaha Live Stock Exchange since 1913. President Omaha Chamber of Commerce, 1920; mem. Omaha Sch. Bd., 1916-20. Mem. Omaha Bar Assn. (pres. 1905), Neb. State Bar Assn. (pres. 1909), Am. Bar Assn. (v.p. for Neb. 1911). Republican. Clubs: Omaha, Omaha Country. Home: 516 N. 51st St., Omaha. Office: Insurance Bldg., Omaha NE‡

BROGAN, JAMES M., clergyman, educator; b. Co. Clare, Ireland, Dec. 24, 1869; s. John and Judith (Minogue) B.; came to U.S., 1890; joined Soc. of Jesus (Jesuits), 1893; student Desmet Sem., Ida., 1893-95, St. Ignatius Coll., Mont., 1898-99; M.A., Gonzaga U., Spokane, Wash., 1901; studied theology, Immaculate Conception Coll., Montreal, Can., 1903-07; ascetic theology, Tronchiennes, Belgium, 1911-12. Teacher Gonzaga High Sch., Spokane, 1895-98; prof. Latin, English and mathematics, 1901-03, prof. mathematics and philosophy, 1907-09, Seattle Coll.; prof. history of philosophy and physiology, St. Joseph's Coll., Phila., 1909-10; prof. Latin, Greek and English, St. Peter's Coll., Jersey City, N.J., 1910-11; preacher during Lent, at Oxford, Eng., 1912; dir. of studies, Loyola Coll., Los Angeles, Calif., 1912-13; pres. Gonzaga U., 1913-20; pastor St. Joseph's Ch., Seattle, 1920-21; prof. ethics Grad. Sch. Gonzaga U., 1921-22; pastor St. Francis Xavier Ch. and supt. Loyola High Sch., Missoula, Mont., 1922-24; dean Coll. of Arts & Sci., philosophy and edn., 1927-30, prof. ascetic theology for priests of the Soc. of Jesus since 1930. Active in war work during World War; compiled Pledge of Americanism" which was widely adopted in U.S. Chmn. Pacific Northwest Assn. of Presidents of Univs., Colls. and Normal Schs., 1917-18. Author: Ethical Principles for the Character of a Nurse, 1922. Address: Manresa Hall, Port Townsend WA‡

BROMLEY, CHARLES DUNHAM, lawyer; b. Boulder, Colo., Nov. 19, 1899; s. Charles Clark and Theresa (Dunham) B.; LL.B., U. Colo., 1924; m. Priscilla Price, Aug. 19, 1924 (div. 1929); 1 son, Charles P.; m. 2d, Sarah W. Wendelken, June 30, 1932; children—James F., John C. Admitted to Colo. bar, 1924; practice in Denver, 1930-68; mem. firm Bromley & Myers, 1946-68. Mem. Colo. Supreme Ct. Bd. Law Examiners, 1959-62. Del. Republican. Nat. Conv., 1924, alternate del., 1952; sec. Rep. Congl. Com. 2d Congl. Dist., 1924-30. Bd. regents U. Colo., 1928-34, 50-68. Served with U.S. Army, World War I; served to col USAAF, World War II; PTO. Decorated Legion of Merit, Bronze Star medal, commendation ribbon. Mem. Vets Fgn. Wars (judge adv. Colo. 1958-63), Chi Psi, Phi Alpha Delta. Mason. Home: Denver CO Died Jan. 8, 1968.

BRONFMAN, SAMUEL, business exec.; b. Brandon, Man., March 4, 1891; s. Ekiel and Minnie (Elman) B.; ed. pub. and high schs., Brandon and Winnipeg, Man.; LL.D., U. Montreal, 1948, U. Waterloo, 1961, Brandon U., 1969; m. Saidye Rosner, June 22, 1922; 2 sons, 2 daus. Began in hotel business at age of 18; purchased large hotel in Winnipeg at age 21, operater of same, 1912-15; asso. with father and brothers in operating a string of hotels in various Can. provinces; later operating inter-provincial mail order liquor business throughout the Dominion, to 1922; pres. Globe Bedding Co. Ltd., Winnipeg, from 1921; organizer Distillers Corp., Ltd., 1924, became pres.; pres. Distillers Corp.-Seagram, Ltd., Thomas Adams Distillers, Ltd., Vancouver, B.C., Seagram Overseas Corp., Ltd., Four Roses Distilleries, Ltd., Globe Bedding Co., Ltd., Winnipeg; dir. Joseph E. Seagram and Sons, Limited, Waterloo, Calvert of Canada Limited; member of the board Quebec Heart Found.; dir. Canadian Mental Health Assn.; asso. mem. Central council Can. Red Cross Soc.; mem. Can. gen. council Boy Scouts Assn.; v.p. World Jewish Congress, chmn. N.Am. Sect.; past pres., chmn. bd. govs. Can. Jewish Congress; pres. Can.-Israel Corp., Can.-Israel Securities Ltd., Can.-Israel Devel., Ltd., United Jewish Relief Agys., Jewish Publ. Soc. Am.; v.p. Nat. Found. Jewish Culture; hon. pres. Jewish Community Services; mem. adv. council Sch. of Commerce. McGill U. Mem. war tech. bd. NRC. Mem. Order St. John of Jerusalem (comdr. br.), Orthodox Jewish religion. Mason; mem. B'nai B'rith. Clubs: Canadian (Montreal); Montefiore; Elm Ridge Golf and Country; Century (Westchester, N.Y.). Home: Westmont Montreal PQ Canada Died July 1971.

BRONSON, WILLIAM HOWARD, publisher, lawyer, radio and TV exec.; b. Dadeville, Ala., July 10, 1912; s. George A. and Meige (Berkstresser) B.; student Alabama Poly. Inst., 1929-30; B.A., U. Ala., 1933; grad. study Harvard, 1933-34; LL.B., La. State U., 1938, J.D., 1968; m. Lillian Francez, July 9, 1935; children—William H., and Susan Francez (now Mrs. E.S. Croft III). Admitted to La. bar, 1938, practiced in Shreveport, 1938-40; with firm Tucker, Bronson & Martin, 1940-52; pres., pub., dir. Shreveport Times; pres., dir. Monroe (La.) News Star, Monroe Morning World, radio stas. KWKH, Shreveport, Radio Broadcasting, Inc., Shreveport, Louisiana, also the Tri State Broadcasting System, Inc., Shreveport, 1952-72; pres. Newspaper Prodn. Co. (agts. Shreveport Times, Shreveport Jour.), 1953-72; chmn. bd., dir. Ark. TV Co., Inc. (TV sta. KTHV, Little Rock), 1952-72; dir., mem. exec. com. of bd. dirs. Kansas City So. Ry.; dir., mem. exec. com. Kansas City So. Industries, Inc., La. & Ark. Ry.; dir. Shreveport Engraving Co., Inc. Mem., Trustee Shreveport Obs., 1963-65; exec. com., dir. organizer Council Better La., 1962-72; pres. bd. trustees Southfield Sch., 1949-50; mem., vice chmn. La. Coordinating Council for Higher Edn., 1969-72; trustee S.W. Research Inst., San Antonio, La. Council Econ. Edn., Pub. Affairs Research Council La.; dir. La. State Fair Assn. Mem. Nat. Planning Assn. (nat. council). Shreveport C. of C. (dir.; 1st v.p. 1959), Newcomen Soc., Sigma Delta Chi. Episcopalian (former vestryman). Clubs: Shreveport (dir.), Shreveport Country (pres. 1958); Boston (New Orleans); Fairway Farm Hunt (San Augustine, Tex.); Press (Dallas). Home: Shreveport LA Died Nov. 18, 1972.

BROOKE, BEN C., physician; b. Helena, Mont., 1872; s. Dr. B. C. and Sarah J. B.; ed. common and high schs.; grad. Bellevue Hosp. Med. Coll., 1896; married. Began practice 1896; ex-coroner, co. physician and sec. co. bd. health Lewis and Clarke Co., Mont.; pres. Mont. State Med. Assn. Surgeon St. Peter's, St. John's and County hosps. and Florence Crittenden Home. Address: Helena MT‡

BROOKE, MARY MYRTLE, coll. prof.; b. Canton, Ga., May 31, 1872; d. George Washington and Mary Elizabeth (Dial) Brooke; Brad. Peabody Coll., Nashville, Tenn., 1891; A.B., U. of Nashville, 1892; grad. student U. of Nashville, 1893, U. of Tenn., 1902-03, Sch. of the South, summers, 1902, 03, 04, U. of Chicago, 1906-09, 1911, Columbia, 1908, 13, 14; A.M., Columbia 1914. Taught in pub. schs., Ga. and La., 1894-1908; prof. edn., and head dept. of psychology and sociology, Alabama Coll., Montevallo, 1908-23, head dept. of sociology since 1923. Baptist. Mem. Am. Sociol. Soc., Soc. of Country Life, Am. Fed. of Child Study, Conf. of Social Work. Ala. State Edn. Assn. Home: Montevallo AL‡

BROOKE, WILLIAM ELLSWORTH, university prof.; b. Minier, Ill., Oct. 7, 1870; s. John P. and Rebecca A. (Reynolds) B.; B.C.E., U. of Neb., 1892, A.M., 1896; m. Helen Frances Langer, of West Point, Neb., Aug. 22, 1898. Fellow and asst. in mathematics, U. of Neb., 1894-97; prof. mathematics, Omaha High Sch., 1897-1901; instr. mathematics, 1901-05, asst. prof., 1905-07, prof. mathematics and mechanics since 1907, U. of Minn., also head of dept. of mathematics and mechanics and head dept. drawing and descriptive geometry. Emeritus prof. mathematics and mechanics, June, 1939. Mem. Am. Math. Soc., Circolo Matematico di Palermo, Deutschen Mathematiker Vereinigung, Soc. Promotion of Engring. Edn.; fellow A.A.A.S.; mem. Am. Soc. Mech. Engrs. Author: Plane and Spherical Trigonometry (with George N. Bauer), 1907; Engineering Mechanics (with H. B. Wilcox), 1929; Intermediate Algebra (with H. B. Wilcox), 1938. Home: 416 Walnut St., S.E., Minneapolis MN‡

BROOKS, ALFRED MANSFIELD, university prof.; b. Saginaw, Mich., July 19, 1870; s. George Byron and Abby Davis (Mansfield) B.; A.B., Harvard, 1894, A.M., 1899; studied Mass. Inst. Tech. Sch. of Architecture, 1894-95 (hon. A.M., Ind. U., 1911); m. Ruth Bryce Steele, of Indianapolis, Aug. 30, 1910. Instr. fine arts 1896-99, asst. prof., 1899-1904, asso. prof., 1904-06, jr. prof., 1906-07, and prof., Indiana Univ., 1907-22; now prof. emeritus, Swarthmore Coll. Author: The Newell Fortune, 1906; Somes House, 1909; Architecture and the Allied Arts, 1913; Dante, How to Know Him, 1916; Notes on Drawing and Engraving, 1919; Our Architectural Debt to Greece and Rome, 1923; Architecture, 1927. Editor: Great Artists and Their Works by Great Masters, 1919; Letters of John Ruskin to William Ward, 1921; Readings in Art Appreciation, 1930. Contbr. articles on architecture, painting, etc., to various mags. Home: The Brick House, Gloucester MA‡

BROOKS, CHARLES HAYWARD, lawyer; b. Auburn, Calif., Nov. 23, 1859; s. Julius Philander and Sarah (Gambell) B.; grad. Montpelier (Vt.) Meth. Sem., 1879; m. Jane M. Lillie, June 22, 1886. Practiced at Wichita, Kan., 1887; chmn. bd. and counsel Wichita Union Stock Yards Co.; counsel First Nat. Bank; dir. Union Stock Yards Nat. Bank. Republican. Unitarian. Mason (32 deg., K.T.). Man—the Story of Man's Conquest of Mental Illness, 1937; Mind Explorers, 1939; also author various monographs. Office: 25 W. 54th St., New York NY‡

BROOKS, CLARENCE RICHARD, lawyer; b. Detroit, Apr. 17, 1901; s. Richard E. and Ellen (Walters) B.; S.B., Harvard, 1926, LL.B., 1931; m. Virginia M. Jerguson, May 14, 1927; children—Philip A., Alan F., Ellen W., Richard C., Barbara A. Admitted to Mass. bar, 1932; practiced in Springfield, Mass., 1932-70; mem. firms Small and Brooks, 1932-41, Brooks and Wallace, 1942-55, Brooks, Wallace & Pillsbury, 1956-64, Brooks and Wallace, 1964-66, Brooks and Brooks, 1967-70. Dir. R.E. Phelon Co., Inc., East Longmeadow, Mass., Sterling Radiator Co., Inc., Westfield, Mass., Hampden Glazed Paper & Card Co., Holyoke, Mass.; trustee, dir. Carlos Ruggles Lumber Co., Springfield. Mem. Springfield City Council, 1936-40. Trustee Horace Smith Fund. Mem. Am., Mass. Hampden County bar assns. Republican. Conglist. Clubs: Colony, University (Springfield); Longmeadow (Mass.) Country; Boothbay Longmeadow MA Died May 12, 1970.

BROOKS, FREDERICK A., agrl. engr.; b. Mpls., May 1, 1895; s. Morgan and Frona (Brooks) B.; B.Elec. Engring., U. Ill., 1917, M.E., 1927; Sc.D., Mass. Inst. Tech., 1920; m. Margaret H. Ward, Sept. 7, 1922; children—Audrey M. (Mrs. Preble Stolz), Emily F. (Mrs. Robert E. Lynde), Deborah A. (Mrs. Arthur Corra), Brenda D. (Mrs. Vinson Jester). Airplane designer Curtiss Aeroplane & Motor Corp., Buffalo, 1917-18; asst. engr. Dunlop Tire & Rubber Corp., Buffalo, 1920-21; sales engr. Hall-Scott Motor Car Co., Berkeley, Cal., 1923-25; chief engr. Johnson Gear Co., Berkeley, 1925-28; asst. to chief engr. Byron Jackson Co., Los Angeles and Berkeley, 1930-31; mem. faculty U. Cal. at Davis, 1931-67, research agrl. engr., prof. emeritus, 1962-67. U.S. del. UNESCO-Australia symposium on arid zone climatology, 1956; collaborator

U.S. Forest Service div. forest fire research, 1953-67. Guggenheim fellow, 1959; recipient Cyrus Hall McCormick medal, 1960. Life fellow Am. Soc. M.E.; fellow Am. Soc. Agrl. Engrs.; mem. Am. Meteorol. Soc. (award bioclimatology 1966), Am. Geophys. Union, Sigma Xi. Contbr. numerous articles profl. jours. Spl. research parallel-beam measurement atmospheric radiation over short paths with hohlraum chilled with liquid nitrogen and through whole atmosphere simultaneously with spl. radiosonde flights; project leader extensive field research frost protection; coop. field expts. eddy transfers of momentum, heat, moisture over 12-acre irrigated turf surfaces. Author: An Introduction to Physical Microclimatology, 1960. Home: Davis CA Died Mar. 10, 1967.

BROOKS, GERALDINE, teacher; b. at Phila., June 26, 1875; d. late Elbridge Streeter and Melissa (de Baun) B.; ed. Adelphi Acad., Brooklyn, Somerville (Mass.) High Sch.; A.B., Radcliffe Coll., 1908; unmarried. Head of English dept., Leominster (Mass.) High Sch., 1908-12. Teacher of English in Plainfield (N.J.) High Sch., Sept., 1912—. Clubs: Boston Authors, Boston College, New York Women's University, New York Radcliffe. Author: Dames and Daughters of Colonial Days, 1900; Dames and Daughters of the Young Republic, 1901; Romances of Colonial Days, 1903; Dames and Daughters of the French Court, 1905. Address: 316 W. 6th St., Plainfield NJ‡

BROOKS, HENRY LUESING, U.S. dist. judge; b. Louisville, Dec. 9, 1905; s. Horace G. and Amelia (Luesing) B.; A.B., U. Wis., 1927; LL.B., Jefferson Sch Law, 1929; m. Christine Clarke, Oct. 29, 1930; children—Henry Luesing, Peggy C. (Mrs. Robert B. Beale, III), and Tommy C. Admitted to Ky. bar, 1928; engaged in practice of law, Louisville, 1929-54; judge Jefferson Circuit Ct., 1946-48; faculty Jefferson Sch. Law, 1948-52; U.S. dist. judge, Louisville, 1954-71. Mem. Ky. State Bd. Bar Commrs., 1950-54. Served as lt. USNR, 1943-46. Mem. Sigma Chi, Phi Delta Phi. Mason (32 deg., Shriner). Home: Louisville KY Died 1971.

BROOKS, JOHN G(AUNT), mfg. exec.; b. Chgo., Jan. 9, 1913; s. Overton and Emmilgene (Wortsman) B.; student Northwestern U., 1930-36; m. Ann. Malcolm, Oct. 30, 1941; children—William Blair, Robert Malcolm. With Commonwealth Edison, 1930-36, Zenith Radio Corp., 1936-42, Majestic Radio Corp., 1946-47; with Ekco Products Co., 1947-54, v.p., 1950-54; pres., dir. Siegler Corp., Los Angeles, 1954-62; chmn. of the board and chief executive officer of Lear Siegler, Inc., Santa Monica, 1962-71, pres., 1964-71; dir. Royal Industries, Mattel, Inc., Aircraft Builders Counsel, Inc. Campaign chmn. Los Angeles County Heart Assn.; vice chmn. Nat. UN Day, 1960. Gov. Henrotin Hosp., Chgo.; regent St. John's Hosp., Santa Monica; asso. Cal. Inst. Tech.; founding mem. Claremont Coll.; trustee City of Hope, U. So. Cal., Cal. Council Econ. Edn. Served to capt. USAAF, 1942-46. Mem. Aerospace Industries Assn. (gov.), N.A.M. Air Force Assn., Navy League, U. So. Cal. Assos., U.S. C. of C. (dir., marine resource adv. panel). Clubs: Bel Air Country (Los Angeles); The California, Los Angeles Country. Home: Los Angeles CA Died Jan. 15, 1971; buried Holy Cross Cemetery, Los Angeles CA

BROOKS, LAURANCE WADDILL, lawyer; b. Baton Rouge, June 22, 1900; s. Claude Morley and Pennie (Overton) B.; B.A., La. State U., 1920, LL.B., 1922, J.D., 1968; m. Neveda Stokes, Aug. 12, 1925; children—Neveda Merlyn (Mrs. William A. Norfolk), Laurance Waddill. Admitted to La. bar, 1922, U.S. Supreme Ct., 1946, other fed. cts.; practiced in Baton Rouge, 1922-71; counsel firm Taylor, Porter, Brooks & Phillips, and predecessors, 1925-71; spl. asst. to atty. gen. La.; dir. emeritus La. Nat. Bank of Baton Rouge. Dir. Baton Rouge Port Devel. Assn., 1948-50, Council Better La., 1963-71; mem. Pub. Affairs Research Council La., 1964-71. La. Civil Service League, 1964-71. Asst. clk. La. Ho. of Reps., 1920-26; asst. sec. La. Senate, 1928. Mem. La. State U. Found., 1964-71. Served as 2d lt., inf., U.S. Army, World War I. Fellow Am. Coll. Trial Lawyers; mem. Am., La. (chmn. ins. sect. 1955, legislative com. 1956-58; gov. 1963-65), Baton Rouge (pres. 1950), Internat. (patron 1963-71) bar assns., Internat. Assn. Ins. Counsel, La. State Law Inst. Council (dir. 1964-71), Baton Rouge C. of C. (pres. 1954), Mil. Order World Wars, Am. Legion, La. Def. Council, Kappa Alpha, Phi Delta Phi, Sigma Delta Chi. Democrat. Episcopalian (past sr. warden). Mason, Elk (past exalted ruler Baton Rouge). Clubs: Knife and Fork (charter, 1st pres. 1951), Baton Rouge Country City (Baton Rouge); Boston (New Orleans). Home: Baton Rouge LA Died Dec. 27, 1971; interred Roselawn Meml. Park.

BROOKS, LAVERNE W., state supt. public instruction; b. Bloomington, Wis., Nov. 27, 1875; s. Jesse and Josephine (Hayden) B.; A.B., Lawrence Coll., Appleton, Wis., 1903, A.M., 1915; Ed.D. (hon.), U. of Wichita (Kan.), 1928; m. Ethel M. Bates, June 9, 1907;children—Emerson Hayden, LaVerne Alden, Robert Wright. Teacher Wis. State Sch. for Blind, Janesville, 1903-04, Janesville High Sch., 1904-05; supervising principal, Necedah (Wis.) pub. schs., 1905-07; supt. Tomahawk (Wis.) pub. schs., 1907-09; supervising principal, North Dist. Manitowoc (Wis.) pub. schs., 1909-10; principal Manitowoc (Wis.) Central High Sch., 1910-11, Racine (Wis.) High Sch., 1911-19; prin. Wichita High Sch., East and North; dir. secondary edn., acting supt. schs., Wichita, Kan., 1919-45; state supt. pub. instrn., State of Kan., since 1946. Chmn. scholarship board Nat. Honor Soc.; sec. Kan. State Sch. Fund Commn.; chmn. Kan. Sch. Retirement Bd.; sec. Kan. Safety Council; mem. Exec. Council of Kan.; past pres. Nat. Assn. Secondary Sch. Principals, Kan. State Teachers Assn. Mem. Phi Beta Kappa, Phi Delta Kappa. Home: 618 Lindenwood Av. Topeka KS‡

BROOKS, NED, radio, TV commentator; b. Kansas City, Mo., Aug. 13, 1901; s. John B. and Jennie (Cadle) B.; B.S., Ohio State U., 1924; m. Mary Curry Jeannot, Jan. 14, 1928; children—Ned (dec.), Martha Jane (Mrs. Francis B. Donovan, Jr.). Began as newspaperman, 1924; city editor Youngstown (O.) Telegram, 1926-27, mng. editor, 1928-32; corr. Scripps-Howard Newspaper Alliance, 1932-47; commentator, NBC, 1947-66; nat. affairs editor Three-Star Extra (NBC radio), 1947-65; moderator Meet the Press (NBC-TV, radio). Elected mem. of Standing Com. of Washington Corrs., 1940-42, 1943-44, chmn., 1943-44. Exec. sec. Raymond Clapper Meml. Assn., Washington, 1944. Mem. Radio Corrs. Assn., J. Russell Young Sch. Expression, Phi Kappa Tau, Sigma Delta Chi, Pi Delta Epsilon, Sphinx Soc. Clubs: Gridiron, Nat. Press, Alfalfa (Washington); Chevy Chase (Md.). Shared Alfred I. du Pont Found. citation for radio news program, 1952; radio news reporting citations, Freedoms Found., 1954, 55, 58, 59. Author: Winning the Pacific, 1945. Home: Chevy Chase MD Died Apr. 13, 1969.

BROOKS, NEIL, lawyer, govt. official; b. near Selmer, Tenn., Sept. 11, 1906 s. Joseph Mansel and Mary Elizabeth (Wood) B.; student Birmingham-Southern Coll., 1923-24; J.D., U. of Tenn., 1928; LL.M., George Washington U., 1936; m. Geneva Bass, Mar. 2, 1940. Admitted to Tenn. bar, 1928, to U.S. Supreme Ct. bar, 1934, D.C. bar, 1939; in pvt. practice, Selmer, 1928-33, mem. firm Wood and Brooks; atty., R.F.C., Washington, 1933-37 with U.S. Dept. Agr. since 1937, chief atty. in charge marketing div., 1945-48, in charge of litigation, 1948-69, asso. solicitor, 1948-55, asst. gen. counsel, 1955-69; also special assistant to attorney general of U.S., 1948-55, special attorney, 1955-69. Member President's Conference on Adminstrv. Procedure, 1953-54. Recipient Superior Service award from sec. of agr., 1958; Distinguished Service award U.S. Sec. Agr. and N.Y. Commr. Agr., 1953, Mem. Am. Judicature Soc. American Fed., Tenn. bar assns., Phi Alpha Delta. Baptist. Editor: Tenn. Law Rev., 1927-28; contbr. 1954 Yearbook on Agr. Author articles to various profl. jours. Home: Washington DC Died Dec. 26, 1969; buried Pine Ridge Cemetery, Lawrence MS

BROOKS, PHILLIPS MOORE, astronautics co., exec.; b. Independence, Cal., Feb. 18, 1908; s. Willis Moore and Wilhelmina (Singlaub) B.; student U. Cal., Los Angeles, 1931-34; A.B., U. Cal., Berkeley, 1935; Ph.D., Leland Stanford U., 1943; m. Jean Woodworth Smith, Aug. 21, 1941; 1 son, Phillips Robertson. Scientist Bikini Sci. Resurvey Group, USAF, 1947; head dept. bacteriology, botany, physiology, Riverside (Cal.) Coll., 1947-49; asst. prof. aviation physiology U. So. Cal., Los Angeles, 1949-51; chief nuclear safety analysis group Nuclear Div., Martin Co., Balt., 1960-62; staff physiologist McDonnell Douglas Corp., St. Louis, 1962—. Lectr. physiology dept. Ohio State U., Columbus, 1958-59; lectr. Washington U., St. Louis, 1963-65, cons. dept. radiation physics, 1965—; vice chmn. space simulator safety operations subcom. Aerospace Industries Assn. Am., St. Louis, 1962. Served to lt. col., USAF, 1943-47, 52-60. Recipient Huntington Meml. Library scholarship U. Cal., 1933-34; Am. Smelting and Refining Corp., fellowship, Stanford U., 1935-38. Mem. A.A.A.S., Am. Inst. Aeronautics and Astronautics, Health Physics Assn., Aerospace Indsl. Life Scis. Assn., Aerospace Physiologist Assn., Aerospace Bioenvironmental Engring. and Scis. Assn., Aerospace Med. Assn., Air Force Assn., Nat. Sojourners, Inc., Am. Inst. Biol. Scis., Sigma Xi, Chi Phi. Contbr. articles to profl. jours. Home: Creve Coeur MO Died Dec. 17, 1967.

BROOKS, WILLIAM E., clergyman; b. Phila., Pa., Aug. 9, 1875; s. John and Sarah Jane (McDevitt) B.; A.B., Westminster Coll., New Wilmington, Pa., 1900, Litt.D., 1935; A.M., Princeton, 1904; grad. Princeton Theol. Sem., 1904; D.D., Lafayette, 1916, Univ. of Dubuque, 1916; LL.D., Waynesburg (Pa.) Coll., 1938; m. Jeanette Steele Stewart, Oct. 12, 1904; children—S. Stewart, Jeanette Steele (Mrs. Frederick H. Thompson), Margaret Hamilton (Mrs. Walter E. Wright). Ordained Presbyn. ministry, 1904; pastor East Kishacoquillas Ch., Reedsville, Pa., 1904-09, 1st Ch., Allentown, Pa., 1909-24, 1st Ch., Morgantown, 1924, West Virginia, 1924-48, pastor emeritus since 1948. Director Army Y.M.C.A. and acting chaplain, Camp Crane, 23 mos., 1917-19; nat. chaplain U.S. Army Ambulance Service Assn.; mem. Gen. Council Presbyn. Church, U.S.A., 1929-35; pres. W.Va. Council of Social Welfare, 1931-32; vice-pres. Upper Monongahela Valley Assn., 1935-48. Fellow Society of American Historians; member Newcomen Society of England, Phi Beta Kappa. Recommended for D.S.M. Author: Lee of Virginia; Grant of Appomattox. Contributing editor The Presbyterian Banner, 1927-35. Contbr. poems and articles to leading mags. Home: Bridge Rd., Orleans MA‡

BROOME, HARVEY, lawyer, assn. ofcl.; b. Knoxville, Tenn., July 15, 1902; s. George William and Adeline (Smith) B.; A.B., U. Tenn., 1923; LL.B., Harvard, 1926; m. Anne Pursel, June 29, 1937. Student sec. YMCA at Wayne U., Detroit, 1929-30; admitted to Tenn. bar, 1925; law clk. Judge Xen Hicks, U.S. Ct. of Appeals, 6th Circuit, 1930-49; mem. law firm Kramer, Dye, McNabb & Greenwood, Knoxville, 1949-58; law clk. U.S. Dist. Judge, Knoxville, Tenn., 1958-68. Pres. The Wilderness Soc.; trustee Robert Marshall Wilderness Fund. Mem. Izaak Walton League, Nat. Parks Assn., East Tenn. Hist. Soc., Bar Assn. Tenn., Tenn. Outdoor Writers Assn. (hon. life mem.). Clubs: Smoky Mountains Hiking; Sierra. Author: Harvey Broome: Earth Man, Some Miscellaneous Writings, 1970; Faces of the Wilderness, 1972. Home: Knoxville TN Died Mar. 8, 1968.

BROSNAHAN, PATRICK EDWARD, clergyman; b. Port Byron, N.Y., Aug. 21, 1876; s. Maurice and Sarah (Henvy) B.; ed. coll., Denison, Ia., Servite Prep. Sem., N. Milwaukee, Wis.; Univ. of Propaganda Fide, Rome, 1900-07, Ph.B., S.T.B., S.T.L., from same. Ordained priest R.C. Ch., 1906; teacher of philosophy, theology and canon law, Servite Sem., Chicago, 1906-11, Servite Sem., Milwaukee, Wis., 1911-23, also gave missions and conducted retreats; founder, and editor Messenger of Our Lady of Sorrows, 1912-20; Provincial Superior of Servite Order in U.S., 1923-29, reelected, 1933-36, reelected for fourth term, 1936-39. Formerly regent of studies in Servite instns. in U.S.; founded Servite Institutions in Detroit, Mich., St. Louis, Mo., Belen, N.M., Hillside, Ill., Sanctuary of Our Sorrowful Mother, Portland, Ore. Home: Belen NM‡

BROUGHER, J(AMES) WHITCOMB, clergyman; b. Vernon, Ind., Jan. 7, 1870; s. Frederick Christopher and Euphemia Ryker (Cumley) B.; B.A., Calif. Coll., Oakland, 1891, M.A., 1894; grad. Rochester Theol. Sem., 1894; D.D., Carson and Newman Coll., 1901, Berkeley Div. Sch., 1926, Bates Coll., 1930; LL.D., Linfield Coll., 1926, Denison U., 1927; married Corinna S. Morse, July 28, 1891 (died 1939); children—Verna Isabelle (Mrs. Walter Saint, Jr.), Rev. Russell Morse, Corinna Morse (Mrs. Norman A. Buist), Rev. James Whitcomb, Jr.; m. 2d, Margaret T. Wood, 1945. Ordained Bapt. ministry, 1894; pastor 1st Ch., Paterson, N.J., 1894-1900, 1st Ch., Chattanooga, Tenn., 1900-04. White Temple, Portland, Ore., 1904-10, Temple Ch., Los Angeles, 1910-26, First Ch., Oakland, Calif., 1926-30, Tremont Temple, Boston, 1930-35; associate pastor of First Baptist Church, Glendale, Calif., 1935-45; interim pastor of Tremont Temple, Boston, 1946-47. President Am. Bapt. Publ. Society, Phila., 1913-17; mem. Exec. Com. Northern Bapt. Conv., 1917-23, and since 1925; pres. Northern Bapt. Conv., 1926-27; trustee Bapt. Div. Sch., Berkeley, Calif., 1926-30, Gordon College of Theol. and Missions, 1930-35. Mem. Am. Baptist Foreign Mission Bd., 1927-39, Southern Calif. Baptist Conv. Board; mem. Gen. Council, Northern Bapt. Conv., 1941-47. Hon. trustee Redlands Univ. Mason (32 deg., K.T.); grad. chaplain emeritus, Royal Arch Masons State of Calif. Hon. mem. St. Paul's Royal Arch Ch. and Aleppo Shrine, Boston, Mass.; hon. mem. Kiwanis, Optimist, Exchange clubs, Los Angeles Breakfast and Advertising Clubs. Author: Life and Laughter, 1950. Home: 115 N. Jackson St. Address: P. O. Box 711, Glendale 5 CA‡

BROUGHTON, LESLIE NATHAN, teacher; b. Delhi, New York, October 3, 1877; s. Charles Henry and Lydia Anne (Houghtaling) Broughton; graduate Delaware Acad., Delhi, N.Y., 1896; A.B., Union U. 1900, A.M., 1910, Litt.D., 1945; Ph.D., Cornell U., 1911; m. Rose C. Fenton, June 22, 1904. Vice prin. high sch., Pulaski, 1901-03; instr. English, Peekskill Mil. Acad., 1903-04; prin. high sch., Victor, N.Y., 1904-06; instr. in English, Cascadilla Sch., Ithaca, 1906-10; with Cornell U, since 1910, asst. prof. English, 1916-31, professor English, 1931-45; professor emeritus since 1945. Mem. Modern Language Association America, Modern Humanities Research Association, Am. Assn. for the Advancement of Science, Am. Assn. of Univ. Profs., Phi Beta Kappa, Pi Gamma Mu. Republican. Meth. Editor: Model Paragraphs, 1921; Selections from Edmund Burke, 1925; Wordsworth and Reed—the Poet's Corr. with his American Editor, 1933; Sara Coleridge and Henry Reed, 1937; Some Letters of the Wordsworth Family Now First Published, 1942. Editor in chief: A Concordance of the Poems of John Keats, 1917; A Concordance of the Poems of Robert Browning (2 vols.), 1924-25. Author: The Theocritean Element in the Works of William Wordsworth, 1920; The Wordsworth Collection—A Catalogue, 1931; A Supplement to the Catalogue of the Wordsworth Collection, 1942. Asso. editor of Ann. Bibliography English Lang. and Lit. (Cambridge, Eng.), 1931-41 Address: 931 N. Tioga St., Ithaca NY

BROUILLETTE, T. GILBERT, art dealer, cons.; b. Warrensburg, Mo., Aug. 2, 1906; s. T. William and Bessie M. (Trumbull) B.; B.A., Westminster Coll., 1928; postgrad. architecture, mus. direction Harvard, 1929-30, 1933-34. Asso., Ehrich-Newhouse Galleries, N.Y.C., 1935-36; asso. Acquavella Galleries, N.Y.C., 1945-50; dealer, art cons., N.Y.C., 1950-60, Falmouth, Mass., 1961-70; organizer old masters exhbns. Denver Art Mus., 1955, Brooks Meml. Art Gallery, Memphis, Tenn., 1952, Wichita (Kan.) Art Assn. Galleries, 1946, 48, 54, Staten Island Mus., 1955, 58, Moravian Coll., Bethlehem, Pa., 1948, Mus. Fine Arts, Little Rock, 1955, Mint Mus. Art, Charlotte, N.C., 1957, Okla. Art Center, Oklahoma City, 1946, 54, 65. Served to capt. USAAF, 1942-45. Mem. Coll. Art Assn. Am., Am. Fedn. Arts, Am. Assn. Museums, Soc. Archtl. Historians, Alumni Assn. Harvard Grad. Sch. Design, Falmouth Hist. Soc., Beta Theta Pi. Presbyn. Club: N.Y. Athletic (N.Y.C.). Address: Falmouth MA Died Jan. 24, 1970.

BROULLIRE, JOHN MERLIN, govt. ofcl.; b. Iron Mountain, Mich., July 2, 1917; s. Peter Joseph and Minnie (Grossbusch) B.; student U. Mich., 1936-38; B.B.A., U. Tex., 1941; m. Mary Theresa Sullivan, Feb. 18, 1950; children—John Christopher, Joseph Michael, Mary Patricia, James Mark, Frances, Marie. Financial analyst SEC, 1941-55; regional supt. FHLB, 1955-66; dep. dir. Fed. Savs. & Loan Ins. Corp., 1966-—; cons. AID, El Salvador, 1963-64; mem. savs. and loan thesis rev. bd. Grad. Sch., U. Ind., 1967. Mem. Beta Alpha Psi, Delta Sigma Pi, Beta Gamma Sigma. Club: Univ. Mich. Alumni (Washington). Home: Hyattsville MD Died Apr. 30, 1972; buried Gate of Heaven Cemetery, Silver Spring MD

BROWDER, EARL (RUSSEL), author, lecturer; born Wichita, Kansas, May 20, 1891; son of William and Martha (Hankins) B.; formal edn. ended with 3d grade; law course at corr. school, 1914; m. Raissa Berkman, Sept. 1926; children—Felix, Andrew, William. Gen. Sec. Pan-Pacific Trade Union Secretariat (hdqrs. in Hankow and Shanghai, China), 1927-28; gen. sec. Communist Party, U.S., 1930-44; expelled from Communist Party, 1946. Candidate for Pres. of U.S. on Communist ticket, 1936, 1940. As result of opposition to entrance of U.S. in World War I, was sentenced and imprisoned in Leavenworth, 1919-20 (full pardon 1933); sentenced to prison for 4 yrs. for passport irregularity, 1940 (sentence commuted by President Roosevelt after 14 mos. in Atlanta prison). Club: Internat. Workers Order. Author: Communism in the United States, 1935; What Is Communism?, 1936; The People's Front, 1938; Fighting for Peace, 1939; The Second Imperialist War, 1940; The Way Out, 1941; Victory—and After, 1942; Teheran, 1944; American Marxists and the War, 1945; War or Peace with Russia, 1947; World Communism and U.S. Foreign Policy, 1948; In Defense of Communism, 1949; Keynes, Foster & Marx, 1950. Home: Yonkers NY Died June 27, 1973.

BROWER, ALFRED SMITH, ednl. adminstr.; b. Randolph County, N.C., Mar. 23, 1892; s. Rufus A. and Mary L. (Smith) B.; A.B., Duke, 1912, pvt. student law; m. Bessie H. Crouse, July 28, 1932; children—Blanna (Mrs. M. W. Harris, Jr.), Billie C. (Mrs. J. H. Coman, Jr.). Financial, statis. sec. N.C. Dept. Edn., 1912-20, dir. div. finance and certification, 1920-24; comptroller N.C. State Coll., 1924-31; dir. div. purchase and contract State of N.C., 1931-36; adminstrv. asst. Duke, 19 7-47, bus. mgr., comptroller, 1947-57, treas., 1957-62. Dir. Burham Bank & Trust Co. Mem. N.C. Bd. Edn., 1944-55, chmn., 1956-57. Mem. adv. budget commn., N.C., 1937-44; dir., v.p. Hosp. Care Assn. N.C. Mem. Carolinas-Va. Purchasing Agts. Assn. (pres. 1936), Eastern So. assns. coll. and univ. bus. officers, Kappa Sigma, Omicron Delta Kappa. Presbyn. Clubs: Hope Valley Country, Kiwanis Durham NC Died Sept. 20, 1968; buried Maplewood Cemetery, Durham NC

BROWN, AARON SWITZER, ambassador; b. Pontiac, Mich., Apr. 15, 1913; s. Guy Carlton and Millie Belle (Switzer) B.; student Cranbrook Sch., Bloomfield Hills, Mich., 1927-31; A.B., Princeton, 1935; m. Dorothy Park, Aug. 8, 1936; children—Dorothy (Mrs. Don Kilgore), Barbara (Mrs. Charles W. Hewitt). Reporter Pontiac Daily Press, 1936-37; apptd. fgn. service officer, July 2, 1937; vice consul Mexico City, 1937-38, 3d sec. (later 2d sec.), Dublin, 1943-45, 2d sec. Bogota, Columbia, 1945-47; attached to Office of the Sec., Dept. of State, 1939-43; attached to Div. Fgn. Service Planning, Dept. of State, 1947-49, asst. to dir. exec. secretariat, 1949-50, spl. asst. dep. under-sec., 1950-51; counselor of embassy, Bangkok, 1951, Lisbon, 1954; dep. dir. of personnel, Dept. of State, 1956; dep. asst. sec. for personnel, 1958-61; ambassador Nicaragua, 1961-67. Mem. Am. Fgn. Service Assn. Club: Cloister Inn (Princeton, N.J.); Princeton (N.Y.). Home: Lyme NH Died Feb. 22, 1969; buried Lyme NH

BROWN, ALBERT EDMUND, music educator; b. Derby, England, Dec. 9, 1874; s. Samuel and Elizabeth (Frost) B.; came to U.S., 1886; ed. pvt. schs., Eng., and pub. schs., United States; student Inst. of Music Pedagogy, Northampton, Mass.; Mus.D. honoris causa, N.Y. Coll. of Music, 1933; m. Martha Elizabeth Taylor (pianist), of Easthampton, Mass., June 15, 1898; 1 dau., Doris Elizabeth (Mrs. Frederick J. Ranlett, Jr.). Baritone and leader of singing; dir. dept. of music, State Normal Sch., Lowell, Mass., 1910-19; mem. faculty, Chautauqua Instn., 1912-13, Boston U., 1916-17; studio for professional singers, Boston, 1912-24; has appeared in many recitals, U.S. and Eng.; condr. music N.E.A. Conv., Dept. of Superintendence, Atlantic City, N.J., 1920, Washington, D.C., 1926, Cleveland, 1929, State Teachers' Assn., Mo., 1921, Neb., 1921, La., 1924, Rep. Nat. Conv., Chicago; dir. division of music, Ithaca (N.Y.) Coll. An organizer War Camp Service, U.S.A., 1917-19. Asso. editor Musical Courier, New York. Mem. Eastern Supervisors' Conf. (1st pres.), Nat. Supervisors' Conf. Republican. Mason (32 deg., K.T., Shriner), Elk, Rotarian. Sinfonian. Lecturer and writer on musical subjects. Home: Albany Country Estates, East Greenbush NY‡

BROWN, ALBERT SIDNEY, mem. Dem. Nat. Com.; b. Perry, Mo.; s. William Campbell and Martha Dunn (Muldrow) B.; A.B., U. of Mich., 1892; student U. of Mich. law dept. and Kent Coll. of Law; m. Mary Evelyn Melville, of Salt Lake City, Utah, Jan. 3, 1912; children—Campbell Lee, Jean (Mrs. Robert Chez), Kenneth Melville, Marian, William Sidney. Admitted to Ill. bar, 1893; was pres. Brown Sch. of Correspondence; now sales manager Utah Oil Refining Co., Salt Lake City, Utah. Mem. Dem. Nat. Com. for Utah. Pres. Salt Lake City Chamber of Commerce. Mem. Beta Theta Pi, Phi Delta Phi. Presbyn. Home: 553 3d Av. Office: Federal Bldg., Salt Lake City UT‡

BROWN, ALFRED HODGDON, lecturer; b. at Brooklyn, N.Y., Apr. 8, 1871; s. of George Washington and Mary Elizabeth (Stainburn) B.; B.A., N.Y. U., 1892, M.A. in Greek and philosophy, 1894; Gen. Theol. Sem., New York, 1892-3; m. Mrs. Fanny Gray Merrick-Norton, of Newton Centre, Mass., Nov. 4, 1911. Clergyman P.E. Ch., 1894-05, and rector of old St. Paul's, Tivoli-on-Hudson, Ch. of Messiah, Providence, R.I., St. John's, Delhi, N.Y.; head master, St. John's Sch., Santa Barbara, Cal., 1901-4; Unitarian minister, Newton Centre, Mass., 1906-8; lecturer and writer on drama, 1906-—. Mem. council, Brooklyn Inst. Arts and Sciences; pres. of Dept. of Dramatic Art. Staff lecturer on drama, Am. U. Extension Soc., Phila., and Extension Div. of Chicago U.; also at Columbia U.'s extension. Mem. Delta Chapter Psi Upsilon. Progressive. Club: University (Brooklyn). Author (plays): Slander; The Exile. Home: Jamaica Estates, Jamaica, N.Y. Office: Brooklyn Institute, Academy of Music, Brooklyn‡

BROWN, ALFRED SEELY, educator; b. Washington, Sept. 24, 1906; s. Horace Seely and Nellie Constance (Raynal) B.; Chem.E., Rensselaer Poly. Inst., 1926; Ph.D., Yale, 1929; m. Mary Abigail Ring, June 14, 1934; children—Abigail Anne Seely, John Raynal Seely. Instr. chemistry Yale, 1929-31; NRC fellow Rockefeller Inst., 1931-33; mem. faculty Colgate U., 1934-42, 46-68, prof. chemistry, 1948-68, chmn. dept., 1959-67; dir. research Skenandoa Rayon Corp., Utica, N.Y., 1942-46, cons., 1933-34, 36-42, 46-62. Mem. exec. bd. Chamber Music Soc. Utica. Mem. Am. Chem. Soc., A.A.A.S., N.Y. Acad. Scis., Sigma Xi. Club: Fort Schuyler (Utica). Patentee in field. Home: Hamilton NY Died Aug. 15, 1968; buried Colgate Cemetery, Hamilton NY

BROWN, ALVIN (MCCREARY), business exec.; b. Washington, D.C., Dec. 17, 1893; s. Sherman Josiah and Genevieve (McCreary) B.; A.B., George Washington U., 1914; LL.B., 1916; m. Lyle Virginia Rush, July 25, 1918; children—Alan Rush, Virginia Lyle, Stephen Jeffry. Vice pres. and treas. Moline Implement Co., 1925-29; asst. to dir. of the budget, 1933; asst. adminstr., N.R.A., 1933-35; v.p. West Virginia Coal and Coke Corp., 1937-39; with Johns-Manville Corp., New York City, since 1940, v.p. and dir. since 1946; vis. lectr. on orgn. Mass. Inst. Tech. 1946-51. Fellow Academy of Management (president 1957). Author: Organization: A Formulation of Principle, 1945; Organization of Industry, 1947; The Armor of Organization, 1953. Home: Washington DC Died Feb. 1972.

BROWN, ANN MARY MAROTHY (MRS. ERNEST M. BROWN), city ofcl.; b. Pukanec, Czechoslovakia, Sept. 19, 1900; d. John and Anna (Hloska) Marothy; came to U.S., 1907, naturalized, 1910; student pub. schs., Kenosha, Wis.; m. Ernest M. Brown, May 3, 1919 (dec. May 1954); 1 dau., Rothymay (Mrs. Lyle F. Chapman). Bookkeeper E. R. Clarke & Co., Coldwater, Mich., 1918-20; bookkeeper, credit mgr. Woodward & Sons, Coldwater, 1928-36; treas. City of Coldwater 1939-46, 54-64, clk., 1947-49. Chmn. mayor exchange day Mich. Week, Coldwater chmn., co-chmn., 1965, chmn. Branch County, 1956, Coldwater chmn., 1957, chmn. hospitality day, 1958, 61, chmn. our livelihood day, 1959, 60, 64, our heritage day, 1968; chmn. hospitality div. Greater Coldwater Centennial, 1961; initiated, chmn. Art Display, 1956-64. Active worker various VA Hosps., 1921-32, part time, 1932-68; pres. Am. Legion Aux., Coldwater, 1923-24, chmn. Americanism com., 1942-58, 61-68; comdr. D.A.V. Aux., Coldwater, 1959-60, chmn. Americanism com., 1956-59, 61-68, exec. active Community Fund dirs., 1928-68, legislative chmn. dept. Mich., 1964, 65; br. county campaign dir. Nat. Found.-March of Dimes, 1965-68; citizens adv. com. City of Coldwater, Mich., 1965-68; mem. Community Coll. Feasibility Study Com., 1966. Conv. sec. Coldwater Rep. Com., 1938-68, Branch County Rep. Com., 1938-68; civic participation chmn. Bus. and Profl. Women's Club, 1964, legislative chmn., 1967-68; chmn. Branch County chpt. Nat. Found. 1964-65; vice chmn. City Rep. Women's Club, 1964-65. Recipient outstanding citizen award Coldwater C. of C., 1958; named outstanding citizen Bus. and Profl. Women's Club, 1957. Presbyn. (treas. Sisterhood 1930-41, 58-61, 66-68). Mem. 8 and 40 (La Demi Chapeau I 1965-66, Chapeau 1967-68). Club: Coldwater Art (treas. 1956-59). Home: Coldwater MI Died Oct. 28, 1968.

BROWN, BURDETTE BOARDMAN, clergyman, ednl. welfare worker; b. Andover, N.Y., Oct. 28, 1871; s. Anson D. and Esther J. (French) B.; A.B., Alfred U., 1890, A.M., 1891, D.D., 1913; grad. Chautauqua (N.Y.) Sch. Physical Edn., 1895; studied Wesleyan U., Conn., New York U.; B.D., Yale, 1898; m. Antoinette F. Fullerton, of New Haven, Conn., 1899. Teacher pub. schs., 1892-95; dir. summer schs. physical training, Silver Lake Assembly, N.Y., 1894-96. Ordained M.E. ministry, 1898; pastor successively Pleasant Valley, Middlefield, and Hartford, Conn., until 1904, then Port Washington, and Mamaroneck, N.Y., until 1913. Sec. and supt. child welfare activities, M.E. Ch., since 1911; inaugurated Epworth League Inst., New Haven, 1903; initiated, 1911, Meth. Child Welfare Soc. (systematized management in behalf of neglected and destitute children), and in 1922 founded the Child Welfare Soc. (work to be carried on in pub. and pvt. schs. along lines of right conduct, good manners and dramatic method in moral edn.); mem. Source Research Council. Elected a founder of Sch. of Philosophy, U. of Southern Calif. Home: 817 New York NY‡

BROWN, CHARLES WILSON, geologist; b. Overton, Neb., Aug. 11, 1874; s. Rev. Henry Wheaton and Abbie E. (Wilson) B.; student Boston U., 1896-97; Ph.B., Brown U., 1900, A.M., 1901; student Grad. Sch., Harvard, 1903-04; m. Anne Taft Peirce, June 10, 1908. With U.S. Geol. Survey, 1902-08; prin. high sch., Warren, R.I., 1901-03; instr. geology, Lehigh U., S. Bethelehem, Pa., 1904-05; instr., asst., asso. prof., prof. geology, and head dept., Brown U., 1905-40; emeritus prof. since 1940; supt. Natural Resources Survey of R.I., 1909-13; v.p. R.I. Ice Co. Fellow Geol. Soc. America, Am. Geog. Soc., Seismol. Soc. America, A.A.A.S., Am. Inst. Mining and Metall. Engineers; mem. Providence Engineer Soc., Am. Geophys. Union, Sigma Xi. Clubs: University, Art, Agawam Hunt (Providence); Joint author of Penobscot Bay (Me.) Folio (U.S. Geol. Survey), 1907. Writer of geol. and geog. bulls., articles and reviews. Home: 37 Barnes St., Providence RI‡

BROWN, CYRUS JAY, educator; b. Eastland Co., Tex., Apr. 7, 1875; s. Charles James and Virginia (Heidel) B.; grad. La. State Normal Sch., 1902; m. Berenice Marie Carter, of New Orleans, Aug. 7, 1907. Teacher and prin. various schs. in La.; supt. schs., Iberville and Ascension parishes; state supervisor of rural schs. (now chief state rural sch. supervisor), and prof. rural education, State U. of La., Dec. 1, 1909-—. Methodist. Mem. N.E.A., Southern Assn. State Rural Sch. Supervisors (pres. 1916), Conf. on Edn. in the South, Nat. Assn. of State Supervisors and Inspectors of Rural Schs. (pres. 1917). Author of elementary course of study now in use in La. Address: 710 Main St., Baton Rouge LA‡

BROWN, DAVID ABRAHAM, b. Edinburgh, Scotland, Nov. 3, 1875; s. Morris and Charlotte (Levy) B.; brought to Detroit, Mich., 1880; ed. pub. schs.; Dr. of Hebrew Laws, Hebrew Union Coll., 1928; m. Paula Kahn, Nov. 3, 1904 (died Feb. 1, 1924); children—Rosalie Agnes, Carolyn Elizabeth; m. 2d, Pearl Kroll, May 21, 1940. Began in coal business, 1896, later head of Brown & Brown Coal Co., Detroit; chmn. bd. Broadway Nat. Bank & Turst Co., N.Y. City; pres. Broadway Nat. Co., N.Y. City, 1929-30; pres. People's Ice Co., Detroit, 1903-10; pres. General Necessities Corp., Detroit, 1911-29; pres. David A. Brown, Inc., N.Y. City; pres. and pub. The American Hebrew, 1930-35. Nat. chmn. Am. Jewish Relief Campaign, 1921-22, United Jewish Campaign, 1925-28; chmn. finance com. Hebrew Union Coll.; chmn. finance com. Union of Hebrew Congregations, 1924-35; mem. bd. Am.-Jewish Joint Distribution Com., 1920-37, Palestine Economic Corp., 1926-36; mem. Jewish Agency for Palestine; pres. Am. Friends of China; U.S. chmn. China Famine Relief, 1928-33. Mem. United Spanish War Vets. Jewish religion. Received Gottheil medal for distinguished service, 1927. Home: 149 Burlingame Av. Office: 3115 Cadillac Tower Bldg., Detroit 26 MI‡

BROWN, EDGAR, botanist; b. Ontario County, N.Y., Sept. 25, 1871; s. Amos C. and Emma L. (Smith) B.; Ph.B., Union Coll., N.Y., 1895; m. Harriet V. Tefft, Aug. 14, 1902; m. 2d, Elizabeth D. Gould, June 6, 1934. Botanist in charge seed testing labs. U.S. Dept. Agr., 1902-38, principal botanist. Mem. Washington Acad. Science, Phi Gamma Delta, Sigma Xi. Mem. Soc. of Friends. Club: Cosmos. Author of bulls. Dept. of Agr. Home: Mount Airy MD‡

BROWN, EDITH, art teacher; b. Wolfville, N.S., 1874; d. John Lothrop and Elizabeth (Whidden) B.; ed. Acadia Sem. to 1890; grad. Boston Mus. of Fine Arts Sch., 1895; unmarried. Teacher of clay modeling and drawing in Miss Pierce's pvt. sch., Brookline, Mass., Miss Hazard's pvt. sch., Boston. Dir. N. Bennet St. Industrial Sch., Boston. Dir. and designer S.E.G. Bowl Shops, Boston, since 1908. First illustrating done for The Churchman about 1899. Mem. Copley Soc., Boston. Illustrator: Folk-Lore Stories and Proverbs (Miss S. E. Wiltse), 1900; Wonderfolk in Wonderland (Edith Guerrier), 1903; Stella's Adventures In Starland (Elbridge H. Sabin), 1907; The Cheerful Cricket (Jeanette Marks), 1907. Address: 18 Hull St Boston‡

BROWN, EDWARD VAIL LAPHAM, oculist; b. Morrison, Ill., Aug. 15, 1876; s.George H. and Margaret (Lapham) B.; S.B., U. of Chicago, 1902; M.D., Hahnemann Med. Coll., 1897; post-grad. work, Berlin and Vienna; M.D., Rush Med. Coll., 1898; m. Frieda Muench Kirchoff, Aug. 10, 1912; children—Edward Kirchoff, Bradford Barnes, Nancy, Donald Augustus Kirchoff, David Vail Lapham. Interne Ill. Charitable Eye and Ear Infirmary, 1899; attending oculist, Presbyn. Hosp., 1900-17, and since 1942, Cook County Hosp., 1913-19; asst. prof. of eye pathology, Univ. of Chicago, 1907-17; asst. prof. ophthalmology, Rush Med. Coll., 1907-17; prof. ophthalmology and head of dept., U. of Ill. Coll. of Medicine, 1917-26; prof. ophthalmology U. of Chicago, 1926-42; Rush prof. of ophthalmology, University of Illinois College of Medicine, 1942-46; dir. Ill. Soc. for the Prevention of Blindness, Hadley Correspondence School for the Blind. Trustee, Provident Hospital. Member of Provident Medical Associations (pres.), A.M.A., Am. Ophthal. Soc., Chicago Ophthal. Soc., Inst. of Medicine, Chicago. Republican. Protestant. Clubs: University, Quadrangle, Indian Hill, Arts. Home: 529 Cedar, Winnetka, Ill. Office: Peoples Gas Bldg., Chicago IL

BROWN, EDWIN PIERCE, food container mfr.; b. George, N.C., Oct. 18, 1903; s. Walter Jay and Loula Mae (Vaughan) B.; A.B., Guilford Coll., 1926; m. Dorothy Heath, Nov. 26, 1932; children—Edwin Pierce, Hannah Heath, Dorothy May (Mrs. Robert M. Shoffner), Andrew Vaughan. Pres. Am. Timber Products Co. div. Ga.-Pacific Corp., Roanoke Valley Oil Co., Murfreesboro, N.C., Farmers Cold Storage Co., Moorestown, N.J., Roanoke-Chowan Gas & Furniture Sales, Murfreesboro, Northeastern Oil Co., Murfreesboro and Weldon, N.C., Brown & Parker, Inc., BP Service Stas., Inc., Murfreesboro; dir. Va. Electric & Power Co., Richmond, Farmers Bank of Woodland, N.C., also Murfreesboro, Carolina Tel. & Tel. Co., Tarboro, N.C., Wachovia Bank & Trust Co., Raleigh. Past mem. N.C. Banking Commn. Pres. Roanoke-Chowan Hosp., Ahoskie, N.C., Pine Forest Rest Home for Aged, Potecasi, N.C.; dir. N.C. Found. Church Related Colls.; trustee Guilford Coll.; mem. endowment com., bd. advisers Chowan Coll., Murfreesboro. Mem. Am. Veneer Package Assn. (past pres.), N.A.M. (past dir.), Newcomen Soc. North America. Mem. Soc. Friends (rep. Friends World Conf., Oxford, Eng. 1952). Clubs: Rotary, Beechwood Country. Home: Murfreesboro NC Died Apr. 14, 1972; buried Murfreesboro NC

BROWN, ELMER, pres. Internat. Typographical Union. Home: Indianapolis IN Died Feb. 1968.

BROWN, ELZEAR JOSEPH, r.r. exec.; b. St. Joseph, Mo., Dec. 1, 1900; s. Maurice J. and Julia (Dalton) B.; student Christian Bros. Coll., St. Joseph, Mo., 1917, St. Patrick's Acad., Chgo., 1919; m. Alice Louise Hair, Apr. 5, 1934; children—Mary Alice, John Paul, James. With C.,B.&Q. R.R., 1919-67, successively yard clk., sect. foreman, extra gang foreman, roadmaster, dist. engr. maintenance, asst. div. supt., engr. track, asst. chief engr., 1919-55, chief engr. Burlington Lines, 1955-66, assistant vice president operations, 1966-67. Mem. Am. Ry. Engring. Assn. (pres. 1960), Roadmasters and Maintenance of Way Assn. (pres. 1947), Am. Ry. Bridge and Bldg. Assn., Chgo. (pres. 1936), St. Louis maintenance of way clubs, Western Railway Club Chgo. Home: LaGrange IL Died Jan. 3, 1968.

BROWN, FRANK XAVIER, lawyer; b. N.Y.C., Oct. 18, 1914; s. Frank X. and Emma (Knorr) B.; A.B., Fordham U., 1935; LL.B., Georgetown U., 1940; m. Catherine A. Toomey, Jan. 4, 1947. Admitted to D.C. bar, 1940; spl. asst. Office Undersec. War, 1939-41; asst. gen. counsel War Assets Adminstrn., 1947-49, Gen. Services Adminstrn., 1949-50; asst. gen. counsel Dept. Def., 1950-54, dir. procurement supply and distbn., 1954-56; partner Cox, Langford & Brown, Washington, 1956-68. Served from lt. to col. AUS, 1942-46. Mem. Am. Bar Assn., Bar Assn. D.C. Republican. Roman Catholic. Clubs: Army-Navy, Lawyers, Nat. Aviation. Home: Washington DC Died May 1, 1968.

BROWN, FRANKLIN STEWART, civil engr.; b. Chgo., Oct. 22, 1909; s. Charles Dickerson and Martha May (Swaney) B.; B.S. in Civil Engring., U. Ill., 1931; m. Aura Frances Clark, June 9, 1934; children—Charles Clark, Gail Frances, Richard Alan. With C.E., U.S. Army, 1931-46, 48-62, chief engring. div. No. Pacific, Portland, Ore., 1952-62; chief gen. engring. div. Panama Canal, 1946-48; chief bur. power FPC, from 1962, also chief engr.; staff dir. Nat. Power Survey. Registered profl. engr., Ore. Fellow Am. Soc. C.E. (pres. Ore. 1962); mem. U.S. Com. Large Dams (chmn. 1964-65), Nat. Soc. Profl. Engrs., Soc. Am. Mil. Engrs., P.I.A.N.C., Internat. Commn. Large Dams (chmn. com. dam failures). Home: McLean VA Died May 3, 1970.

BROWN, FREDERICK WALWORTH, author; b. Ann Arbor, Mich., Dec. 31, 1875; s. Rev. Frederick Thomas and Anna Eliza (Bates) B.; A.B., Princeton, 1897, A.M., 1898; read law in offices of Holden & Buzzell, Chicago; m. E. Virginia Hynson, of Baltimore, Oct. 12, 1905. Admitted to bar, 1901; practiced at Chicago, 1901-4; mag. writer, 1904-8; examiner U.S. Civil Service Commn., Washington, 1908—. Mem. A.A.A.S., Am. Anthropol. Assn. Progressive Republican. Presbyn. Author: Dan McLean's Adventures, 1911; also many stories in mags. Home: 2124 P St., N.W., Washington‡

BROWN, FREDERICK WINFIELD, govt. ofcl., physicist; b. Enid, Okla., July 2, 1908; s. Winfield Scott and India Mae (Graham) B.; B.S., U. Ill., 1928, M.S., 1930, Ph.D., 1932; student U. Cal., 1934-35; m. Jouita Ramirez, Aug. 25, 1935 (dec. 1956); children—Frederick W., Anita Marilyn; m. 2d, Betty Ellen Boylan Rees, Dec. 27, 1957; children—David Charles Rees, Suzanne Elizabeth, Scott Joseph. Instructor and research associate at Univ. Cal., U. Kansas City (Mo.), Cal. Inst. Tech., 1934-40; physicist U.S. Bur. Mines, Pitts., 1940-46; research specialist North Am. Aviation, Inc., Los Angeles, 1946-49; tech. dir. Naval Ordnance Test Sta., China Lake, Cal., 1949-54; dir. Boulder Labs., Nat. Bur. Standards, Boulder, Colorado, 1954-63; scientific attache American Embassy, Buenos Aires, Argentina, 1963-65; chief planning analyst Environmental Sci. Services Adminstrn., U.S. Dept. Commerce, Washington, 1965-67; chief scientist, tech. dir. Sanders Assos., Inc., Reston, Va., 1967-69; pres. Internat. Systems Engring. Corp., Springfield, Va., 1969-70. Fellow American Physical Soc., A.A.A.S., I.R.E.; mem. Am. Mathematical Society, Research Soc. Am. Clubs: Cosmos (Washington); Rotary (Boulder). Author tech. publs. Home: Rockville MD Died Oct. 24, 1970.

BROWN, FREDRIC, novelist; b. Cin., Oct. 29, 1906; s. Karl Lewis and Emma Amelia (Graham) B.; student pub. schs. of Cin., also Oxford U.; m. Elizabeth Charlier, Oct. 11, 1948; children—(by previous marriage) James Ross, Linn Lewis. Author: The Fabulous Clipjoint (winner Edgar Allen Poe award Mystery Writers of Am., Inc., 1947), 1947; The Dead Ringer, 1948; Murder Can Be Fun, 1948; The Bloody Moonlight, 1949; What Mad Universe, 1949; The Screaming Mimi, 1949; Compliments of a Fiend, 1950; Here Comes a Candle, 1950; Night of the Jabberwock, 1950; Death Has Many Candle, 1950; Night of the Jabberwock, 1950; Death Has Many Doors, 1951; The Far Cry, 1951; Space On My Hands, 1951; We All Killed Grandma, 1952; The Deep End, 1952; Mostly Murder, 1953; The Lights in the Sky are Stars, 1953; Madball, 1953; His Name Was Death, 1954; Angels and Spaceships, 1954; The Wench is Dead, 1955; Martians, Go Home, 1955; The Lenient Beast, 1956; Rogue in Space, 1957; One For The Road, 1958; The Office, 1958; Honeymoon in Hell, 1958; The Late Lamented, 1959; Knock Three-One-Two, 1959; The Mind Thing, 1961; Nightmares and Geezenstacks, 1961; The Murderers, 1961; The Five Day Nightmare, 1962; The Shaggy Dog and Other Murders, 1963; Mrs. Murphy's Underpants, 1963; Daymares, 1968; Paradox Lost and 12 Other Great Science-Fiction Stories, 1973. Mem. Mystery Writers of Am. Home: Tucson AZ Died Mar. 12, 1972.

BROWN, GEORGE GARVIN, business exec.; b. Louisville, Feb. 11, 1912; s. Owsley and Laura Lee (Lyons) B.; student U. of Va.; m. Gertrude Polk Brown, Feb. 17, 1940; 3 children. Asst. sec. Brown-Forman Distillers Corp., Louisville, 1934-38, v.p., 1938-45, exec. v.p., 1945-51, pres., 1951-69, chmn., 1966-69; dir. 1st Nat. Bank. Episcopalian. Clubs: Country, River Valley, Pendennis (Louisville) Saddle and Sirloin (Chicago); Farmington Country (Charlottesville, Va.); Key Largo (Fla.) Anglers. Home: Prospect KY Died Mar. 6, 1969; buried Cane Hill Cemetery.

BROWN, GEORGE ROWLAND, III, clergyman; b. Stewart County, Ga., July 6, 1867; s. George Rowland, II, and Martha Jane (Hightower) B.; student Western Md. Coll., Westminster, Md., 1885-87; A.B., Bowdon (Ga.) Coll., 1888; D.D., Kansas City (Kan.) U., 1904; m. Edith May Adamson, Feb. 28, 1889; children—George Rowland, IV, Edith May (Mrs. George Hering Armacost), Helen Marguerite (Mrs. Weaver McTyeire Marr), Robert Adamson. Ordained to ministry Meth. Prot. Ch., 1888; pastor successively at Bowdon, Ga., Montgomery, Ala., Inwood, L.I., N.Y., Grafton, W.Va., Harrisville, W.Va., Morgantown, W.Va., High Point, N.C., Reidsville, N.C.; pastor Liberty, N.C., since 1938. Pres. W.Va. Conf., 1903-04; mem. of 10 gen. confs., 1892-1936; sec.-treas. Bd. of Ministerial Edn., 1908-17; v.p. of exec. com. Meth. Protestant Ch., 1936-39; del. to Meth. Uniting Conf., Kansas City, Mo., 1939; elected mem. Judicial Council of Meth. Ch., May 8, 1939. Democrat. Mason. Rotarian. Editor W.Va. Protestant, 1893-96; asst. editor Meth. Recorder, Pittsburgh, 1905-07. Contbr. to church publs. Home: Liberty NC‡

BROWN, GEORGE WOODFORD, neuropsychiatrist; b. Culpeper, Va., Dec. 10, 1868; s. James Richard and Elizabeth (Bickers) B.; student U. of Va., 1887-88; M.D., Coll. Phys. and Surg. (now U. of Md.), 1893; studied Med. Dept., U. of Va., 1894; m. Josephine Watts, June 19, 1895 (died June 30, 1924); children—Thelma Josephine, Lucille Woodford (Mrs. Walter Scott Chisholm) Interne Baltimore City Hosp, 1893; gen. practice in Va., 1895-1911; supt. Eastern State Hosp. of Va. Mar. 1911-Sept. 1943; mem. Med. Coll. of Va., dept. neuropsychiatry since 1937; lecturer in clin. psychology. Coll. of William and Mary, since 1921, in med. jurisprudence, 1924; dir. and mem. exec. com. Peninsula Bank & Trust Co., Williamsburg. Cons. neuropsychiatrist and mem. Med. Adv. Bd., World War I; chmn. Med. Advisory Bd. 13A, World War II; neuropsychiatrist, Armed Forces Induction Center, Richmond, Va., Nov., 1943-July 1946; mem. Gov's. Adv. Bd. of Mental Hyg. since 1918. Diplomate Am. Psychiatric Assn. (councilor); mem. A.M.A., Tri-State Med. Soc., Med. Soc. of Va., S.A.R. Democrat. Baptist. Mason. Home: 9 Indian Springs, Williamsburg VA‡

BROWN, HARRY JOE, motion picture dir.-producer; b. Pitts., Sept. 22, 1893; s. Nathan and Anna Brown; student U. Mich., 1909-10; LL.B., U. Syracuse, 1915; m. Dorothy Gray, Sept. 1, 1953; 1 son, Harry Joe. Stage and screen actor, dir., producer Warner Bros., Paramount Pictures, Pathe, R.K.O.; pres. Federal TV Prodns., Producers Actors Corp., 1944-72, Murphy Brown Prodns., Sage Prodns. Served as capt., inf., U.S. Army, World War I. Mem. Am. Legion, Screen Producers Guild, Motion Picture Alliance, Motion Picture Arts and Scis. Elk. Clubs: Masquers (pres. 1954-58), Friars (dir.) (Hollywood); Pioneers, Lambs (N.Y.C.); Tamarisk Country; Hillcrest Country; Variety. Home: Beverly Hills CA Died Apr. 28, 1972.

BROWN, HENRY DANIELS, museum dir.; b. Albion, Mich., May 28, 1910; s. Herbert Mason and Lorain Clare (Smith) B.; A.B., Albion Coll., 1933, LL.D., 1963; M.A., University Mich., 1939, grad. student, 1940-41, 46; H.H.D., Wayne State University, 1964; m. Helen Monroe Langworthy, June 12, 1934; children—Barbara Joanne (Mrs. Joseph Zikmund, II), Shirley Jean (Mrs. Philip R. Beltz). Asst. curator Mich. Hist. Collections, U. Mich., 1937-46; asst. dir. Detroit Hist. Mus., 1946-47, dir., 1947-70; coordinating dir. Detroit Historical Soc., 1947-70. Pres. Detroit Adventure, Inc. Trustee Great Lakes Maritime Institute. Recipient of Chevalier des Palmes Academiques, 1963; Henry D. Brown Fund ann. meml. lecture Local Hist. Conf., 1973-—. Mem. Hist. Society Michigan (past pres.), Am. Assn. Museums (past mem. council past sec., chmn.), Am. Assn. State and Local History (council, past pres.), Midwest Mus. Conf. (past pres.), Am. Hist. Assn., Orgn. Am. Historians, Detroit Ednl. TV Found. (past chmn. gen. com., mem. bd. trustees). Detroit Association. Gt. Lakes Maritime Assn. (trustee), Internat. Afro-Am. Mus., Assn. Study Negro Life and History, Phi Beta Kappa (past pres.), Phi Mu Alpha, Phi Kappa Phi. Clubs: Prismatic, Economic, Detroit Press, Detroit; Algonquin. Editor Detroit Hist. Soc. Bull., 1947-—. Home: Detroit MI Died Feb. 2, 1970; buried Albion MI

BROWN, HENRY MATTHIAS, clergyman; b. Georgetown, D.C., Oct. 26, 1867; s. Joseph Thomas and Jennie Catharine (Buckey) B.; B.S. and C.E., New York U., 1886, A.B., 1890, A.M., 1892; grad. Union Theol. Sem., 1893; D.D., New York U., 1907; m. Adele Frances Bedell, Nov. 20, 1894; children—Philip Tenney, Randolph Bedell. In practice as civ. engr., Washington, D.C., New Rochelle, and New York, 1886-93; ordained Congl. ministry, 1894; stated supply, Pelhamville, N.Y., 1893-94; pastor of Christ Ch. (now called Pilgrim Ch.), New York, Jan. 1, 1894-1921, Federated Churches of Dana, Mass., 1921-38; Hardwick, Mass., Community Church, 1939, 1944. Mem. council New York U., 1908-21. Republican. Mem. Phi Beta Kappa, Delta Phi. Editor of New York University Alumni Catalogue, Vol. I, 1905, Vol. II, 1906. Home: 16 Serpentine Drive, New Rochelle NY‡

BROWN, HERBERT DANIEL, industrial relations consultant; b. nr. Ft. Madison, Ia., Feb. 1, 1870; s. Daniel Truesdale and Maria Dean (Foster) B.; ed. public schools; m. Harriet Chedie Connor, of Burlington, Ia., July 29, 1897; children—Constance Connor, Beatrice (dec.). Entered service of U.S. Govt. as spl. examiner, Bur. of Corpns., 1905; asst. actuary in charge work of Joint Congressional Commn. on Fidelity Bonds, 1910; accountant on President Taft's Commn. on Economy and Efficiency, 1914; chief Div. of Efficiency, U.S. Civil Service Commn., 1913; chief U.S. Bur. of Efficiency, by apptmt. President Wilson, 1916-33. Mem. Federal Bd. of Actuaries. Fellow Casualty Actuarial Soc. America. Author: Savings and Annuity Plan for Retirement of Superannuated Civil Employees, 1911, Civil Service Retirement in Great Britain and New Zealand, 1910; Civil Service Retirement in New South Wales, Australia, 1910. Club: Cosmos. Home: Glenora Yates Co NY‡

BROWN, JAMES BARRETT, plastic surgeon; b. Hannibal, Mo., Sept. 20, 1899; s. Albert Sydney and Evelyn (Segsworth) B.; M.D., Washington U., 1923, D.Sc., 1970; m. Bertha Phillips Phillips, Sept. 30, 1946; children—Jane Hamilton, Frances Reith; (by previous marriage)—James Barrett, Charles Sydney. Interne and assistant resident surgical service, Barnes and Childrens' Hospital, 1923-25; engaged in private practice of plastic surgery, Saint Louis, Missouri, since 1925; professor clin. surgery, School of Medicine, Washington U., 1948-68, prof. emeritus plastic surgery, 1968-71; prof. maxillo-facial surgery, Sch. of Dentistry from 1936; mem. surg. staff, Barnes, St. Louis Children's, St. Luke's, Jewish, Deaconess and DePaul hosps., St. Louis Mo. consultant surgeon, Shriners. Barnard Free Skin & Cancer, Ellis Fischel State Cancer Hosps., and others; cons. surgeon M.P. & Frisco R.R.; cons. plastic surg. USAF; consultant Los Alamos Medical Center. Served as colonel, M.C., U.S. Army, 1942-1946; chief consultant plastic surgery, E.T.O., 1942-43; chief plastic surgeon, Valley Forge Gen. Hosp., 1943-45; senior consultant plastic surgery U.S. Army, 1945-46; sr. civilian cons. plastic surg., U.S. Army, Office Surgeon Gen.; chief cons. plastic surg., U.S. Vets. Adminstrn. Decorated Legion of Merit; Am. Design Award, Lord & Taylor, 1944; Alumni Citation, Washington U., 1955; award Am. Assn. Plastic Surgeons, 1967, Modern Medicine, 1968; Certificate Merit, St. Louis Med. Soc., 1969; James Barrett Brown vis. professorship established in his honor Washington U., 1969. Diplomate Am. Bd. Surgery (founders group), Am. Bd. Plastic Surgery (founders group), Fellow A.C.S. (v.p. 1959-60), Am. Assn. Plastic Surgeons (hon.; pres. 1954); mem. Am., Southern, Western (vice president 1955, president 1958), Central surg. assns., Am. Assn. Surg. Trauma. Assn. Mil. Surgs., Am. Society of Plastic and Reconstructive Surgery, International Society of Surgeons (Brussels), Assn. of Medical Consultants, World War II, Surgeons' and Halsted clubs, Am. Soc. Surgery Hands, Society Head and Neck Surgeons, Phi Delta Theta, Nu Sigma Nu, Alpha Omega Alpha. Presbyterian. Clubs: Grolier (New York City); University (St. Louis). Co-author: Skin Grafting, 1958; Plastic Surgery of the Nose, 1951; Neck Dissections, 1957; Surgery of Face, Mouth and Jaws, 1954; Post-Mortem Homografts, 1960; (with Dr. Thomas Zaydon) Early Treatment Facial Injuries, 1964; other books on plastic surgery. Editorial bd. Excerpta Medica, Amsterdam; and others. Contbr. chpts. textbooks and articles in surg. jours. and other sci. publs. Home: St. Louis MO Died Mar. 18, 1971; interred Oak Grove Mausoleum, St. Louis MO

BROWN, JAMES WRIGHT, JR., consultant; b. Chicago, Jan. 1, 1902; s. James Wright and Sarah (Wilson) B., ed. Bordentown (N.J.) Military Acad.; U. of Mo. Sch. of Journalism; m. Thelma Ann Pitz, Mar. 25, 1925 (dec.); 1 dau., Matil; 2nd m. Sally Jeannette Brown, Nov. 8, 1930; children—Anne Elizabeth, Jane Wright. Consultant Editor & Publisher Co. Mem. Sigma Chi, Sigma Delta Chi. Episcopalian. Mason (past master). Home: Gaithersburg MD Died Nov. 16, 1970.

BROWN, JOE EVAN, actor; b. Holgate, O., July 28, 1892; s. Matthias and Anna (Evans) B.; ed. pub. schs.; m. Kathryn Frances McGraw, Dec. 24, 1915; children—Don Evan, Joe LeRoy, Mary Elizabeth Ann, Kathryn Frances. Began as circus acrobat, 1902; with burlesque and vaudeville, 1916-19, with musical comedies, 1919-27, including Listen Lester," Greenwich Village Follies," Capt. Jinks," etc.; in motion pictures since 1927, leading roles in Crooks Can't Win," 1st silent picture, Painted Faces," 1st talking picture, etc.; movie Some Like It Hot, 1959. Member of the Actors Equity Assn.; hon. mem. Los Angeles High Sch. Alumni Assn., Blue C" S Soc. (U. of Calif.) Episcopalian. Mason (Shriner), Elk. Clubs: Masquers (Hollywood); Mayfair (Los Angeles); Beach (Santa Monica); Lambs (New York). Home: Los Angeles CA Died July 6, 1973.

BROWN, JOEL BASCOM, asso. justice; b. Somerville, Ala., May 18, 1872; s. George Robinson and Sarah (Morris) B.; ed. pub. schs., and coll., at Hartsells, Ala.; m. Minerva Heidelberg, Nov. 24, 1898 (died May 25, 1939); children—James Edmond, William Thomas; married 2d Mrs. Rebecca Knight Odum, Nov. 9, 1941. Admitted to Ala. bar, 1892, practiced at Cullman; judge Ala. Ct. of Appeals, 1914-19 (presiding judge 2 yrs.); asso. justice Supreme Ct. of Ala., 1919-21 and since 1926, re-elected November 1950, for term ending Jan. 1957. President Bd. of Education, Cullman, 1910-14. Democrat. Methodist. Home: 539 S. Perry St. Office: Judicial Bldg., Montgomery AL‡

BROWN, JOHN BERNIS, educator, biochemist; b. Rock Falls, Ill., Dec. 25, 1893; s. Frank T. and Kathryn (Robb) B.; B.S., U. Ill., 1915, M.S., 1917, Ph.D., 1921; m. Bertha G. States, Oct. 9, 1918; children—Phyllis Margery (Mrs. John Buchanan), Franklin S. Asst. chemistry U. Ill., 1915-21; asso. chemistry and pharmacology U. Pa., 1921-23; research chemist Swift & Co., Chgo., 1923-24; successively asst. prof., asso. prof., prof. and chmn. dept. physiol. chemistry and pharmacology Ohio State U., 1924-64, prof. emeritus, 1964-69, dir. Inst. Nutrition and Food Tech., 1950-64. Mem. Ohio Nutrition Com., from 1950; fat com. agrl. bd. NRC, from 1955, fat com. food and nutrition bd., 1956-58; oilseeds adv. com. Dept. Agr., from 1957; mem. biochemistry test com. Nat. Bd. Med. Exam., 1953-57. Mem. Grandview Heights Library Bd., from 1950; governor's adv. com. on atomic power, Ohio, 1956-57. Served as 2d lt., U.S. Army, 1918-19. Mem. Am. Inst. Nutrition (treas. 1956-59), Am. Soc. Biol. Chemistry, Am. Chem. Soc., Inst. Food Technologists, Sigma Xi (pres. Ohio 1946), Phi Lambda Upsilon. Methodist (chmn. bd. trustees). Mason. Clubs: Mercator, Ohio State U. Faculty (past pres.) (Columbus). Editor physiology sect. Chem. Abstracts, 1940; editorial bd. Jour. Am. Oil Chemists Soc., 1952-56. Home: Columbus OH Died Nov. 21, 1969; buried Union Cemetery, Columbus OH

BROWN, JOSEPH ALLEINE, railway official; b. Tampa, Fla., Jan. 31, 1874; s. John Matthews and Emma Garland (Penick) B.; ed. pub. and high schs., Austin, Tex., student, U. of Tex., 1891; m. Louise Zimpleman Jones, Nov. 14, 1899; 1 son, Hart. Began as stenographer in treas. office M-K-T R.R., Dallas, 1896; successively stenographer, gen. clk., rate clk. gen. freight office, Palestine, Tex., 1897-1903; commercial agt. Internat. Great Northern R.R., Dallas, 1903-07; chief clk. traffic dept. Gulf Coast Lines, Beaumont, Tex., 1907-10; asst. gen. freight agt., gen. freight agt. and freight traffic mgr. Gulf Coast Lines, Houston, 1910-26; asst. v.p. M.P. System Lines, St. Louis, 1927-41, v.p. and chief traffic officer. Oct. 1941-June 1, 1944; retired. Protestant. Clubs: Missouri Athletic, Traffic (St. Louis); Union League (Chicago); Houston, Houston Turnverein (Houston, Tex.). Home: 3618 Burlington St., Houston TX‡

BROWN, JUNIUS CALVIN, lawyer; b. Apex, N.C., Dec. 2, 1886; s. James Gaston and Cornelia (Hunter) B.; A.B., Wake Forest Coll., 1913, LL.B., 1913; student Grenoble U. (France), 1918; m. Eliza Ray Pratt, Feb. 9, 1921. Admitted to N.C. bar, 1913; practiced in Madison, 1913-17; mem. firm Brown and Trotter, Reidsville, N.C., 1927-37, Brown, Scurry, McMichael, Griffin and Rankin, attys. at law, Reidsville, Madison, N.C., 1952-63; atty. Rockingham County, N.C., 1930-52; counsel City of Madison 1914-67. State senator, N.C., 1923-24; mem. exec. com. Democratic party N.C. and Rockingham County, N.C., 1924-28. Served with U.S. Army, 1917-18. Donor scholarships in honor of wife Wake Forest Coll., 1958. Mem. Am., N.C., Rockingham bar assns., Am. Judicature Soc., S.A.R., Am. Legion, V.F.W. Democrat. Baptist. Mason (Shriner). Home: Wakeham NC Died Dec. 30, 1968; buried Riverview Cemetery, Madison NC

BROWN, (HERMAN) LARUE, lawyer; b. Louisville, Ky., Dec. 17, 1883; s. George Herman and Nelly (LaRue) B.; A.B., Harvard, 1904, LL.B., 1906; m. Dorothy Browning Kirchwey, Nov. 23, 1915; 1 dau., Eleanor LaRue (dec.). Mem. Brown, Field & McCarthy, Boston. Assistant reporter of decisions, Mass Supreme Ct., 1908; chmn. Mass. Minimum Wage Commn., 1912-14; spl. counsel Mass. Pub. Service Commn.; spl. counsel for U.S. in Shoe Machinery and other Sherman Act and Clayton Act cases, 1914-22; asst. atty. gen. of U.S., 1918-19; gen. solicitor U.S.R.R. Administration, 1919-21, spl. counsel, 1921-25; counsel truck div. Nat. Automobile Chamber of Commerce, 1926-33; counsel to the federal and state authorities in prosecution of banking frauds, 1932-34; chmn. Laundry and Retail Stores Minimum Wage Bds., 1936, Jewelry Bd., 1939; Hotel and Restaurant Bd., 1941; mem. Jewelry Industry Com., Wages and Hours Act, 1940. Consultant Office of Defense Transportation, 1942; spl. rep. of the Atty. Gen. of U.S., and asst. to the Ambassador, U.S. Embassy, London, England, 1943-46. Vice chmn. Public Franchise League; vice chmn., Regional Loyalty Bd. 1947-53; A.D.A. (chmn. Mass. chpt. 1953-55); pres., Voluntary Defenders Com., Incorporated; chmn. Massachusetts Defenders Committee, 1960-62, 1965-66; chmn. Friends of Framingham Reformatory, 1948-52; mem. bd. trustees Civic Edn. Found., Inc. Mem. Atty. Gen.'s Adv. Com. on Civil Rights, 1958-62. Member American, Boston (chmn. committee on the Bill of Rights 1956) bar assns. Democrat. Mason. Home: Boston MA Died Apr. 3, 1969.

BROWN, LOUIS M(YRON), pencil mfr.; b. Atlanta, Aug. 25, 1896; s. W. M. and Lucy J. (Thomason) B.; student Marist Coll., Atlanta; m. Lorena A. Brotherton, Aug. 2, 1917; children—Louis Myron, Rena A. (Mrs. C. W. Rogers). Manager of the Southern School Book Depository, 1916-23; with Eberhard Faber Pencil Co., Bklyn., 1923-63, beginning as Canadian rep., successively advt. mgr., asst. sales mgr., sales mgr., gen. sales mgr., v.p. charge sales, exec. v.p., dir., pres., 1952-63; pres. Eberhard Faber Internat., Ltd.; pres., dir. Eberhard Faber Pencil Co. of Canada, Ltd., Eberhard Faber Premium Sales Co., Inc., Eberhard Faber Toy & Game Co., Inc., Faber Pan-Am., Ltd.; pres. Graphite Pencil Co., Inc.; dir. Industria Colombiana de Lapices, S.A. (Cali, Columbia). Dir. Hosp. Service Assn. Northeastern Pa. Mem. Nat. Stationery and Office Equipment Assn., Bklyn. C. of C., Wholesale Stationers Assn., Pencil Industry Export Assn. (pres.), Lead Pencil Mfrs. Assn. (dir.). Mason. Clubs: Westmoreland (Wilkes-Barre, Pa.) N.Y. Athletic. Home: Dallas PA Died Jan. 16, 1969.

BROWN, M(ARY) BELLE, physician; b. Troy, O.; d. Daniel and Eliza (Telford) B.; ed. Oxford (O.) Female Coll.; M.D., N.Y. Med. Coll. and Hosp. for Women, 1879. Lecturer on chemistry, 1879, lecturer and demonstrator of physiology, 1880-9, prof. diseases of women, 1889-1903, clin. prof. diseases of women since 1904, N.Y. Med. Coll. and Hosp. for Women; sec. of faculty, 1889-98, dean, same since 1898. Mem. Am. Inst. Homoeopathy, N.Y. State Homoe. Med. Soc., N.Y. Co. Homoe. Med. Soc. Address: 30 W. 51st St., New York‡

BROWN, MANUEL NICHOLAS, corrections adminstr.; b. Aug. 8, 1910; B.A., Grinnell Coll., 1934; M.A., U. Ia., 1937; Ph.D., U. Portland, 1951; m. Margaret Lee Brady, Apr. 2, 1938; children—Kathryn (Mrs. Allan Harrison), Christopher L., Carolyn F. (Mrs. Ronald Lewis), Craig N. Corrections officer various branches U.S. Bur. Prisons, 1940-48; chief counseling psychologist VA Hosp., Vancouver, Wash., 1948-54; chief psychologist and acting asso. warden for treatment Minn. State Prison, Stillwater, 1954-56; asso. warden treatment Penitentiary of N.M., Santa Fe, 1956; dir. N.M. Bd. Probation and Parole, Santa Fe, 1956-69; dir. adult probation-parole div. N.M. Dept. Corrections, 1969-72, chmn. designate N.M. adult parole hearing bd. Instr. psychology and sociology U. Portland (Ore.), 1950-51, Coll. of Santa Fe, 1956-63, N.M. Highlands U. Las Vegas, 1965, U. N.M., Santa Fe and Los Alamos, 1964-—; vis. expert UN Asia and Far East Inst. for Prevention of Crime and Treatment of offenders, Tokyo, Japan, 1967-68. Cons. state vocational rehab. divs. Wash., Ore., N.M., N.M. Boys Sch., Springer, North Rio Grande (N.M.) Sheltered Workshop. Mem. N.M. Bd. Psychologist Examiners, 1963-65; N.M. rep. Gov.'s Com. on Juvenile Delinquency, 1963-72; mem. exec. com. Gov.'s Policy Bd. Law Enforcement. Served with USMCR, 1943-45. Recipient Distinguished Alumni award Grinnell Coll., 1969. Wolfe Meml. fellow in philosophy U. Neb., 1934. Meml. fellow in philosophy U. Neb., 1934-35. Mem. N.M. Psychol. Assn. (past pres.), Am. Psychol. Assn., Am. Correctional Assn., Nat. Council on Crime and Delinquency (cons.), Western Probation Parole and Correctional Assn. Cons., English editor Japan's Summary of the White Paper on Crime, 1967, 1968. Home: Santa Fe NM Died Jan. 20, 1972.

BROWN, MARK A., banker; b. Fairmont, Ind., Mar. 11, 1889; s. Will F. and Lillian (Dean) B.; ed. Wabash College, Crawfordsville, Ind., 1911; m. Hannah Coxon, Mar. 11, 1914; children—Betty B. Landwer, Nancy B. Cruttenden. Reorganized and financed the J. M. Leach Mfg. Company, Kokoma, Indiana; organized the Kokomo Automotive Co. in 1919; handled the financing of the Shell American Petroleum Company, Kokomo, Indiana in 1922; reorganized the Globe Stove & Range Co., of Kokomo, 1922, now the Globe Am. Corp., also dir.; v.p., gen. mgr. Cole Mfg. Co., Chicago, 1924-26; v.p., Harris Trust & Savings Bank, Chicago, 1928, exec. v.p. and dir., 1946-50, pres. 1950, ret. 1954; dir., mem. exec. com. Chgo., Rock Island & Pacific R.R. Co.; dir. Bell & Howell Co., Am. Radiator & Standard Sanitary Co., The Kelvie Press, Medallic Art Company. Trustee Wabash College. Financial adv. War Prodn. Bd., 1942. Lt., F.A., World War I. Mason, Elk. Clubs: Chicago, Commodore, Mid-Day, University, Commercial, Chicago Yacht (Chgo.); Bob o' Link, Glenview; Canadian. Home: Wilmette IL Died Apr. 2, 1968.

BROWN, MAXINE MCFADDEN (MRS. JACK T. BROWN), educator; b. Portales, N.M., Jan. 9, 1917; d. Tollie Ward and Mable (Gruhn) McFadden; diploma Shannon West Tex. Meml. Hosp. Sch. Nursing, San Angelo, Tex., 1938; student U. Colo., summers 1947-48, 55, Sul Ross State Coll., Alpine, Tex., summer 1949; B.S., Incarnate Word Coll., 1950; M.Ed., West Tex. State U., 1954; postgrad. U. Tex., summer 1958, Tex. Technol. Coll., 1959, East Tex. State Coll., 1963; m. Jack T. Brown, Apr. 8, 1939 (dec. Jan. 1945); 1 son, James Max. Indsl. nurse Big Lake Oil Co., Texon, Tex., 1938-39; nurse supr. Shannon West Tex. Meml. Hosp., 1943-49, instr. Sch. Nursing, 1946-49; dir. health services, instr. health edn. West Tex. State U., Canyon, 1950-54; guidance counselor at San Angelo Central High Sch., 1954-64, asst. dir. admissions Lindenwood Coll., at St. Charles, Missouri, 1964-67; asst. dean women W. Tex. State U., Canyon, 1967-68; dean women Angelo State Coll., San Angelo, Texas, 1968-69. Mem. exec. com. Tex. Assn. Student Councils, 1955-56; guest speaker to local community clubs and orgns., 1950-69. Chmn. com. for sch. and coll. information, mem. exec. com. San Angelo Central High Sch. P.T.A., 1961-63. Mem. Am. Tex. (sec.-treas., exec. com. 1959-60), Dist. XI (chmn. 1957-58) personnel and guidance assns., Nat. Vocational Guidance Assn., Am. Sch. Counselor Assn., N.E.A., Nat. Assn. Women Deans and Counselors, Assn. Coll. Admissions Counselors, Am. Assn. U. Women, San Angelo Classroom Tchrs. Assn. Tex. Assn. Women Deans and Counselors, Tex. Tchrs. Assn., Am. Coll. Personnel Assn., Tex. Assn. Coll. Tchrs. Home: San Angelo TX Died Dec. 15, 1969.

BROWN, MILTON WILBERT, clergyman; b. Mt. Eaton, O., Apr. 4, 1873; s. Rev. Milton W. and Sarah

(Finney) B., B.S., Ohio Wesleyan U., 1894, M.S., 1900; M.A., Wooster Coll., 1895; studied Harvard, Emerson Coll., Lane Theol. Sem.; D.D., Maryville (Tenn.) College, 1922; LL.D., College of Ozarks, 1950; married Edith Marian Witt, Apr. 5, 1904. Ordained Presbyterian ministry, 1899; pastor Westwood Church, Cincinnati, 1899-1904, Central Church, 1904-06; lyceum and chautauqua lecturer since 1906; delivered one lecture— The Superfluous Man"—more than 1,500 times. Incorporator Milton and Edith Brown Found., 1956, Y.M.C.A. sec. Camp Pike, then dir. for Army and Navy Commn. in Hudson Valley, World War. Campaign dir. Bd. of Christian Edn. of Presbyn. Ch. U.S.A., for endowment for Presbyn. colleges. Trustee Maryville Coll.; elected pres. Press Radio Bible Service, 1936. Mem. S.A.R., Chi Phi (grand chaplain 1928-31). Author: What Is Your Life? (brochure), 1910; The Superfluous Man, 1926; So You Are Going to College, 1940; Autumn Leaves, 1945; If a Man Die, 1948; Today and Every Day, 1948; Mental Medicine in Christian Practice, 1953; The Lost Saint (a def. of Judas Iscariot), 1956. Supplies daily sentence sermon to newspapers of English speaking world. Home: 3480 Cheviot Av., Cincinnati OH‡

BROWN, OWEN CLARENCE, clergyman, editor; b. Cato, Kan., July 25, 1871; s. Israel Keys and Edith Eva (Johnson) B.; ed. Kan. Normal Coll., Ft. Scott, Kan., 1892, 97, 98; B.A., Ottawa (Kan.) U., 1902, M.A., 1909, D.D., 1919; B.D., Newton Theol. Instn., 1905; m. Lois C. Gates, of McCune, Kan., July 12, 1899; 1 son, Carl Newton. Ordained Bapt. ministry, 1899; pastor Bronson, Kan., 1899-1902, Mt. Auburn Ch., Cambridge, Mass., 1904-05, First Ch., Emporia, Kan., 1905-07; First Ch., Lawrence, Kan., 1907-17; editor adult S.S. publs., Am. Bapt. Publ. Soc., 1917-24; editor in chief, same, 1924-33, sec. dept. of religious edn., 1928-33, and exec. sec. 1933-38; retired. Republican. Home: 1801 Marshall Rd., Lansdowne, Pa. Office: 1701 Chestnut St., Philadelphia PA‡

BROWN, RAY ANDREWS, prof. law; b. Sutton, N.H., Aug. 19, 1890; s. George Lawrence and Sarah Lavinia (Andrews) B.; A.B., U. of Minn. 1913, LL.B., 1915; S.J.D., Harvard, 1923; m. Ethel Celia Linnell, June 23, 1917; 1 son, Robert Linnell. Admitted to Minn. bar, 1915, N.Y. bar, 1944, Wis. bar, 1947, U.S. Supreme Ct., 1943; in practice Mpls. and Duluth, Minn., 1915-20; asst. prof. law, U. of S.D., 1920-22; asst. prof., asso. prof., and prof. law, U. of Wis. 1923-61, emeritus prof. law, 1961-70; vis. prof. law, summers, U. of Chicago, 1930, U. of Kan., 1933, U. So. Cal., 1939, Legion Lex distinguished visiting professor, 1958, 59; lecturer in law N.Y. University law school, 1946. On leave from University of Wisconsin, with Tax Division, Department of Justice, Washington, 1943-44; attorney American Telephone & Telegraph Company, New York City, 1944-46. Member of the staff on survey of Indian affairs Brookings Instn., collaborating in report to Secretary of Interior on Probelm of Indian Administration, 1927; chmn. staff Brookings Instn. researching adminstrn. law on Indian reservations and co-author report on enforcement of law on Indian reservations, to Com. of Indian Affairs, 1930. Nat. pres. Order of Coif, 1937-40. Served as 2d lt. U.S. Army, 1918. Mem. Wisconsin State Bar Association, Sigma Chi, Phi Delta Phi, Phi Beta Kappa, Order of Coif. Baptist. Author books. Contbr. to 1969, 1971 edits. Ency. Brit., also to legal jours. Home: Madison WI Died Dec. 9, 1970.

BROWN, REYNOLDS DRIVER, lawyer; b. Newcastle, Del., May 6, 1869; s. Henry Waterston and Alice Prestman (Driver) B.; A.B., Harvard, 1890; LL.B., U. of Pa., 1894; m. Frances Brodhead Harris, of Phila., Pa., June 4, 1895 (died Feb. 7, 1925); children—Joseph Harris (dec.), Reynolds D., Delia B. (Mrs. Edwards); m. 2d, Blanche W. (Bartram) Cameron, Apr. 5, 1926 (died Nov. 1935); m. 3d, Emily T. Perry Russell, Sept. 10, 1936. Began practice with Read & Pettit, 1894; mem. firm Burr, Brown & Lloyd, 1900-10, Brown & Lloyd, 1910-20; prof. law, U. of Pa., 1897-1936. Republican. Clubs: Rittenhouse, Charleston. Home: 193 Hinckley Rd., Milton MA‡

BROWN, ROBERT ARTHUR, JR., oil exec.; b. Calgary, Alberta, Can., Mar. 20, 1914; s. Robert Arthur and Christine (McLaughlin) B.; grad. U. Alberta, 1936; m. Genevieve Mary Sulphur, Feb. 18, 1950; children—Pamela Mary, Lois Lorraine, Carolyn Genevieve. Pres., dir. Home Oil Co. Ltd., United Oils, Ltd., Calgary; dir. Trans-Can. Pipe Lines Ltd., Crown Trust Co. Home: Calgary AL Canada Died Jan. 4, 1972.

BROWN, ROBERT FREDERICK, banker; b. Astoria, L.I., N.Y., Apr. 1, 1896; s. John H. and Bertha (Hague) B.; m. Lillith Chatain, June 27, 1931 (dec. 1939); m. 2d, Ruth Murtaugh Ryan, Feb. 8, 1941; children—Donald H., Leo J. Ryan. Partner, later limited partner Kuhn, Loeb & Co., N.Y.C., 1941-71; director General American Transporation Corp., Polaroid Corp., Buckeye Pipe Line Co. Home: Ridgewood NJ Died Sept. 1971.

BROWN, W(ILLIAM) L(EE) LYONS, business exec.; b. Louisville, Ky., July 26, 1906; s. Owsley and Laura Lee (Lyons) B.; student U.S. Naval Acad., 1924-26, U. of Va., 1926-28; m. Sara Shallenberger, Aug. 13, 1935; children—William Lee Lyons, Martin Shallenberger, Owsley, Ina Hamilton. Began career with W. L. Lyons & Co., Louisville, Ky., 1928-32, mgr. branch office; sec., dir. Brown-Forman Dist. Corp., 1933-41; v.p. Brown-Forman, 1941-45, pres. chmn. bd., 1951-71. Mem. Sons Colonial Wars, Newcomen Soc. Eng., Delta Tau Delta. Episcopalian. Clubs: Everglades (Palm Beach, Fla.); Country, Pendennis River Valley, Wynn Stay (Louisville), Saddle and Sirloin (Chicago); Gulf Stream Golf, Gulf Stream Bath and Tennis. Breeder of shorthorn cattle, registered Durocs and Hampshire hogs. Home: Harrods Creek KY Died Jan. 5, 1973.

BROWN, WALTER FOLGER, ex-postmaster gen.; b. Massillon, O., May 31, 1869; s. James Marshall and Lavinia (Folger) B.; A.B., Harvard, 1892; student Harvard Law Sch., 1893-94; m. Katharin Hafer, Sept. 10, 1903. Practiced law with father at Toledo, O., 1894-1905; mem. firm of Brown, Hahn & Sanger, 1905-27; chmn. Congressional Joint Com. on Reorganization, representing the President, 1921-24; asst. sec. of commerce, Nov. 2, 1927-Mar. 4, 1929; postmaster general, March 5, 1929-March 4, 1933; associate counsel Spengler, Nathanson, Hebenstreit & Heyman, Toledo, Ohio; president Pilliod Company; director National Can Company, The Toledo Trust Company. Presdient Toledo Humane Society; chairman trustees Lucas County Child Welfare Board. Clubs: Toledo, Harvard, Bankers (New York); Metropolitan (Washington). Office: Nicholas Bldg., Toledo 4‡

BROWN, WILLARD DAYTON, clergyman; b. Seward, N.Y., Feb. 15, 1874; s. William and Irene (Moore) B.; A.B., Union Coll., Schenectady, N.Y., 1900; grad. Theol. Sem., New Brunswick, N.J., 1903; studied Teachers Coll. (Columbia); D.D., Hope Coll., Holland, Mich., 1921; m. Eva Van Woert, Apr. 19, 1896 (died Feb. 10, 1929); m. 2d, Mabel Frances Cronk, Aug. 1, 1931. Ordained ministry Reformed Church in America, 1903; pastor Middletown, N.J., 1903-05, North Reformed Ch., Passaic, N.J., 1905-20; sec. Progress Campaign Com., Reformed Ch. in America, 1919-20; gen. sec. bd. of edn., Reformed Church in America, August 1920-45, sec. emeritus since 1945; acting pastor Jay Gould Reformed Ch., Roxbury, N.Y., 1945-48, supply pastor since 1948. Mem. Publ. Council, Christian Intelligencer, Mission Field (contbg. editor); mem. Council of Ch. Bds. of Edn.; trustee Theol. Sem. Reformed Ch. in America; trustee Central Coll., Ia. Mem. Phi Beta Kappa, Delta Upsilon. Republican. Preacher at Am. Ch., The Hague, Netherlands, 1914. Author: History of the Reformed Church in America; My Confession of Faith. Home: Cupsaw Drive E., Roxbury NY‡

BROWN, WILLIAM ATWELL, JR., business executive; b. Kansas City, Mo., August 12, 1908; s. William Atwell and Louise (Kimmerle) B.; A.B., Albion Coll., 1929, LL.D., 1969; B.S., Mass. Inst. Tech., 1931; m. Ruth Jones, Dec. 21, 1934 (div.); children—Marcia (Mrs. David Richard Grismore), Mary Louise (Mrs. Frank Smith); m. 2d, Eloise Dickens Wilde, 1968. Began with Air Reduction Company, N.Y.C., 1931-35; with Liquid Carbonic Corp., Chicago, 1935-56, pres., dir., gen. mgr., 1951-56; v.p. Stewart-Warner Corp., gen. mgr. alemite and instrument div., Chgo., 1956-60; exec. v.p. Vulcan Materials Co., Birmingham, Ala., 1960-70, also dir.; pres. consumers div. Vulcan Materials Co., Chgo., 1960-70; chmn. exec. com. dir. Stanray Corp.; dir. Diversey Corp. (Chgo.). Pres. trustees Albion Coll. Past mem., Ill. Housing Board. Bd. trustees Albion Coll.; member of lay advisory board St. Elizabeth's Hospital, Chgo.; mem. bd. Duncan Medical Center YMCA. Member Internat. Acteylene Assn. (past pres.; hon. mem.), Alpha Tau Omega. Clubs: Glen View (Golf, Ill.); Skokie (Ill.) Country; Chicago, Massachusetts Institute of Technology, Builders, Tower (Chgo.); University (N.Y.C.). Home: Wilmette IL Died Mar. 27, 1970; buried Memorial Park, Evanston IL

BROWN, WILLIAM CHANNING, clergyman;b. Sherborn, Mass., Mar. 7, 1868; s. Rev. William and Salome Stephens (Williams) B.; desc. Thomas Browne, Concord, Mass., 1640; grad. Highland Mil. Acad., Worcester, Mass., 1887; studied Mass. Inst. Tech., 1887-89; grad. Meadville Theol. Sch., Pa., 1894; grad. work, Div. Sch. of Harvard, 1894-95; m. Mary Anna Brown, Aug. 4, 1897; children—Elizabeth Corelli (Mrs. H. W. Harshfield), Margaret Lord (Mrs. Robert M. Murdock). Ordained Unitarian ministry, 1895; pastor Gardner, Mass., 1895-98, Littleton, 1898-1904; field agt., 1904-05, field sec. Am. Unitarian Assn., 1905-24; pastor Wheeling, W.Va., 1924-28; minister (corr.) All Souls Unitarian Ch. since 1904. Established Open Forum, Wheeling, W.Va., 1924. Ex-chmn. sch. com., Littleton; ex-sec. Littleton Pub. Library; town clerk, Littleton, since 1930, town treas. since 1934; minister emeritus First Parish Church, Littleton, 1939. Pres. Mass. Collectors' and Treasurers' Assn., 1939. Mem. Old Colony Hist. Soc., Unitarian Hist. Soc., Littleton Hist. Soc., Am. Unitarian Assn. Club: Twentieth Century (Boston). Home: MA‡

BROWN, ZAIDEE, librarian; b. Burdett, N.Y., Oct. 27, 1875; d. Edmund Woodward and Martha Day (Coit) B.; A.B., Leland Stanford, 1898; N.Y. State Library Sch., Albany, N.Y., 1901-02; unmarried. Prin. Castelleja Hall (girls' sch.), Palo Alto, Cal., 1898-99; taught in High Sch., Pueblo, Colo., 1899-1901; asst. N.Y. State Library Sch., 1902-03; classifier and cataloguer, Pub. Library, Brookline, Mass., 1903-05, and asst. librarian, 1905-08; library organizer, Ednl. Extension Div., N.Y. State Edn. Dept., 1908-10; agt. Mass. Free Pub. Library Commn., 1910-14; librarian, Pub. Library, Long Beach, Calif., 1914-22; librarian State Teachers Coll., Montclair, N.J., since 1928. Mem. P.B.K. Conglist. Lecturer N.Y. State Library Sch., and instr. in its summer sch., 1923-26; lecturer Sch. of Library Service, Columbia U., 1927-28. Editor Lantern Lists (reading lists for libraries); editor Standard Catalog for High School Libraries and Supplement, 1926-27. Author: Library Key (an aid in using books and libraries), 1928, 3d edit. rev., 1939. Address: Upper Montclair NJ‡

BROWNE, MARGARET FITZHUGH, artist; b. Boston, Mass., June 7, 1884; d. William Maynadier and Cordelia Brooks (Fenno) Browne; student Boston Latin Sch., 1899-1903, Mass. Normal Art Sch., 1904-09, Sch. of Boston Mus. Fine Arts, 1910. Began career as portrait painter, 1910; art editor Boston Evening Transcript, 1919-20; mem. Grand Central Galleries, New York. Has painted many portraits of prominent men and women for leading social and ednl. instns., among them: King Alfonso of Spain, for N.Y. Yacht Club; Mrs. Asa Candler, Wesleyan Coll., Macon, Ga.; Samuel W. Stratton, Bur. of Standards, Washington; Elihu Thomson, Mass. Inst. of Tech., Cambridge. Awarded popular prize, N. Shore Arts Assn., Gloucester, Mass., 1925; hon. mention, Nat. Assn. Women Painters and Sculptors, Brooklyn Art Mus., 1928; special award Nat. Exhbn. of Soc. for Sanity in Art, Chicago, 1941. Apptd. mem. Art Commn. of City of Boston, 1937-42. Mem. North Shore Arts Assn. (president 1934-36), Connecticut Academy of Fine Arts, National Association Women Artists, Springfield (Illinois) Art Assn., Springfield (Mass.) Art League, Newport (R.I.) Art Assn., Boston Art Club, Copley Soc. of Boston, Allied Artists of America, N.E. Branch Soc. Sanity in Art (pres. since 1939). Author: Portrait Painting, 1933. Studio: Boston MA Died 1972.

BROWNE, PAGE, hotel comml. bldg. corp. exec.; b. Newton, Mass., Apr. 16, 1892; s. Charles A. and Edith (Guild) B.; grad. Governor Dunmer Acad., 1912; A.B., Dartmouth, 1916; m. Grace C. Fagan, June 26, 1929; children—Page, Pierce Butler. Exec. officer, dir. corps, operating 55 hotels in U.S. and Can., and various office bldgs., 1937-57; v.p., dir. Sheraton Corp. of Am. Overseer Boys' Clubs of Boston; dir., mem. exec. com. World Trade Center in N.E., Inc.; trustee, Plimoth Plantations. Served with U.S. Army in U.S. and ETO, 1917-19. Mem. C. of C. Republican. Clubs: Union (Boston); Myopia Hunt. Home: Concord MA Died Feb. 1970.

BROWNELL, ELEANOR OLIVIA, sch. principal; b. New York, N.Y., Jan. 25, 1876; d. Silas B. and Sarah S. (Sheffield) Brownell; student Brearley Sch., New York, 1889-93; A.B., Bryn Mawr Coll., 1897; grad. student Columbia, 1898-99; 2 adopted daughters, Sylvia Ann Shipley, Mary Sheffield Shipley. Mem. Local Sch. Bd., New York, 1898-1905; state and student sec. Y.W.C.A., 1905-07; prin. New School, Utica, 1908-11; prin. Shipley Sch., Bryn Mawr, Pa., since 1911; dir. Sch. of Occupational Therapy, Phila., 1931-38. Pres. Headmistresses Assn. of East, 1928-32; mem. exec. com. Dem. Women's Luncheon Club of Phila. Democrat. Mem. Soc. of Friends. Clubs: Acorn, Cosmopolitan (Phila.); Cosmopolitan, Bryn Mawr (New York). Home: Bryn Mawr PA Died Aug. 1968.

BROWNING, ELIZA GORDON, librarian; b. at Fortville, Ind.; d. Woodville and Mary Anne (Brown) B.; ed. pub. and pvt. schs. in Indianapolis; unmarried. Librarian, Indianapolis Pub. Library, 1892-1917, asst. librarian since 1917. Mem. Indiana Library Assn., A.L.A., Indiana Hist. Soc., D.A.R., Y.W.C.A., Ind. Federation of Clubs, Indianapolis Chamber of Commerce. Clubs: Fortnightly, Woman's Rotary, Portfolio. Episcopalian. Home: 3624 Guilford Av. Office: Public Library, Indianapolis IN‡

BROWNING, ROBERT TURNER, corp. exec.; b. Flint Hill, Va., July 15, 1905; s. Edgar R. and Lucy G. (Turner) B.; B.S. in Civil Engring., U. Va., 1929; m. Alice M. Wilkie, Apr. 4, 1933. Chmn., chief exec. officer Wallace & Tiernan, Inc., Belleville, N.J. Home: Verona NJ Died Feb. 20, 1969.

BROWNSON, MARY WILSON, educator; born Washington, Pa.; d. James Irwin (D.D., LL.D.) and Eleanor McCullough (Acheson) B.; A.B., Pa. Coll. for Women, 1904, Litt.D., 1920; A.M., Washington and Jefferson Coll., 1905; summer courses in U. of Chicago, U. of Wis., Oxford U., England, and at Harvard and Columbia; library research in British Mus., Bibliotheque Nationale, Paris, and Harvard U. Prof. mathematics, 1885-89, English Bible, 1898-1919, modern European hist., 1904-20 (resigned), Pa. Coll. for Women. Lecturer. Mem. Nat. Inst. of Social Sciences. Presbyn. Author: Old Testament Story (4 vols.), 1904; His Sister,

1904; Syllabus Old Testament History, 1917; Victory Through Conflict (with Vanda E. Kerst), a pageant produced at Pa. Coll. for Women, during the fiftieth anniversary of the instn., June 1920. Home: 4301 Spruce St., Philadelphia PA‡

BRUCE, ANDREW DAVIS, univ. adminstr.; b. St.L., Mo., Sept. 14, 1894; s. John Logan and Martha Washington (Smith) B.; B.S., Agr. and Mech. Coll. of Texas, 1916; LL.D., 1946; graduate Infantry School, Fort Benning, Georgia, 1924, Field Arty. School, Fort Sill, Okla., 1925, Command and Gen. Staff Sch., Ft. Leavenworth, 1933, Army War Coll., Washington, 1936, Naval War Coll., Newport, R.I., 1937; m. Roberta Kennedy, Jan. 28, 1920; children—Andrew Davis Jr., Roberta Linnell, Logan Lithgow. Commd. 2d lt., U.S. Army, June 16, 1917; advanced to lieut. gen., 1951; served as lt. col. (temp.) 2d Div., U.S. Army, in all actions of 2d Div. (Verdun defensive and Aisne-Marne, San Mihiel, Champagne, Meuse-Argonne offensives), World War I; comdg. gen. Tank Destroyer Center, Camp Hood, Tex., 1942-43; comdg. gen. 77th Inf. Div. 1943-46; in Guam, Leyte, P.I.; Kerama Rhetto Ie Shima, and Okinawa operations, occupation of Japan. Comdg. gen. 7th Infantry Div., 1946-47, occupation of Korea, dep. army comdr. 4th Army, 1947-51; comdt. Armed Forces Staff Coll., Norfolk, Va., 1951-54, ret. from Army, 1954; pres. U. Houston, 1954-56, chancellor, 1956-61, chancellor emeritus, 1961-69. Decorated Distinguished Service Cross, the Distinguished Service Medal with Oak Leaf, Navy Distinguished Service Medal, Leg. of Merit, Bronze Star, Air Medal, Commendation, Purple Heart, Victory medal (with 5 stars), Leg. of Honor, 3 Croix de Guerres (2 palms and 1 gold star), 1 Fourragere and numerous campaign ribbons. Mem. First Families of Va., S.A.R. Mason (Shriner). Home: Southern Pines NC Died July 27, 1969; buried Arlington Nat. Cemetery, Arlington VA

BRUCE, DONALD COGLEY, ex-congressman; b. Trouteville, Pa., Apr. 27, 1921; s. Rev. W. H. and May Belle (Stewart) C.; student Muskingum Coll.; m. Hope Mitchell, June 9, 1944; children—Donald, Patricia. Various position radio broadcasting industry; news commentator sta. WIRE, Indpls., 1948-57, program dir., 1957-59, bus. mgr., 1959-61; mem. 87th and 88th congresses from 11th Dist. Ind., mem. un-American activities com., edn. and labor com. Bd. dirs. Ind. chpt. Multiple Sclerosis Society. Recipient of an Americanism citation Dept. of Ind. Vets. Fgn. Wars, Am. Legion; named outstanding young man of the year Indpls. Jr. C. of C.; Distinguished Service award D.A.R.; Book of Golden Deeds, Nat. Exchange Club, numerous other awards. Republican. Lutheran. Home: Round Hill VA Died 1969.

BRUCE, H(ENRY) ADDINGTON (BAYLEY), author; b. Toronto, Can., June 27, 1874; s. John and Mary (Bayley) B.; Upper Canada Coll., Toronto; B.A., Trinity U., Can., 1895, M.A., 1896; studied University of Toronto and Harvard University; m. Lauretta Augusta Bowes, November 24, 1897 (died Aug. 8, 1941). Staff Toronto Week, 1895, Star, 1896; Am. Press Assn., New York, 1897-1903; editor New York Tribune Review, 1903-04; staff contbr. to Outlook, 1904-15; psychol. adviser Associated Newspapers, 1915-27; consultant in psychic re-education. Lecturer on psychol., ednl. and sociol. subjects. Fellow Am. Acad. Art and Sciences; Boston Browning Soc. (ex-pres.), American Society for Psychical Research, Nantucket Historical Assn., Marblehead Arts Assn.; ex-president of Boston Symposium. Clubs: Authors (ex-president), Algonquin, Faculty (Harvard). Author: The Riddle of Personality, 1908; Historic Ghosts and Ghost Hunters, 1908; The Romance of American Expansion, 1909; Daniel Boone and the Wilderness Road, 1910; Scientific Mental Healing, 1911; Woman in the Making of America, 1912; Adventurings in the Psychical, 1914; Sleep and Sleeplessness, 1915; Psychology and Parenthood, 1915; Handicaps of Childhood, 1917; Nerve Control and How to Gain It, 1918; Self-Development, 1921; Your Growing Child, 1927. Editor: The Education of Karl Witte, 1914; Mind and Health Series of Medical Handbooks, 1915-20. Translator: Pierre Leroy-Beaulieu's The United States in the Twentieth Century, 1906. Contbr. to newspapers, mags. and revs. Address: 2 Riedesel Av., Cambridge MA‡

BRUCE, LOGAN LITHGOW, clergyman, chem. cellulose co. exec.; b. Bryan, Tex., Nov. 22, 1928; s. Andrew Davis and Roberta (Kennedy) B.; A.B., Duke, 1950. Mgmt. trainee Rayonier, 1953-55, mem. prodn. planning staff, N.Y.C., 1955-56, Jesup, Ga., 1956-59, shift supt., 1959-61, mfg. mgmt., N.Y.C.; ordained to ministry Episcopal Ch., 1964; asst. St. Peter's Ch., Freehold, N.J., 1964-67, St. Paul's-in-Flatbush, Bklyn. Served with AUS, 1950-53. Mem. Sigma Chi (grand tribune 1966-67, pres. N.Y. Alumni). Home: Brooklyn NY Deceased.

BRUCKER, WILBER M(ARION), lawyer, ex-Sec. Army; b. Saginaw, Mich., June 23, 1894 s. Ferdinand and Roberta (Hawn) B.; LL.B., U. Mich., 1916; J.D. (hon.), U. Detroit, 1931; Ph.D., Hillsdale Coll., Alma Coll., 1932; LL.D., Hope Coll., George Washington U.,

U. Mich., Norwich U., Defiance (O.) Coll., Dickerson Coll.; married Clara Hantel, Aug. 18, 1923; 1 son, Wilber M. Admitted to Mich. bar, 1919; pvt. practice law, Saginaw, 1919-26; pros. atty. Saginaw County (Mich.), 1922-26; atty. gen. Mich., 1928-30, gov., 1930-32; mem. Clark, Klein, Brucker & Waples, 1937-54; gen. counsel 1st Fed. Savings & Loan Assn., Detroit, 1952-54; gen. counsel Dept. of Def., Washington, 1954-55, Secretary of the Army, Washington, 1955-61; mem. firm Brucker & Brucker, Detroit, 1961-68; dir. Fruehauf Corp., 1st Fed. Savs. & Loan Assn. of Detroit, United States Truck Company, Inc., Detroit. Bd. dirs. Freedom's Found., Valley Forge, Pa. Served with 33d Inf., Mich. N.G., Mexican Border, 1916, 1st lt. Rainbow Div., U.S. Army, 1918-19. Mem. Am. Bar Assn. (chmn. ethics com.), Nat. Assn. Rainbow Div. Vets. (pres. 1933-34), Am. Legion (co-founder Paris br.). Republican. Presbyn. Mason (K.T., most eminent grand master, 33 deg.). Home: Grosse Pointe Farms MI Died Oct. 28, 1968; buried Arlington Nat. Cemetery.

BRUCKNER, JACOB HERBERT, educator; b. Anaconda, Mont., May 14, 1905; s. Jacob H. and Minnie (Vogel) B.; B.S., Purdue U., 1930; Ph.D., Cornell U., 1935; m. Frances E. McKibben, Sept. 14, 1930; children—Bruce, Allan, Dean, Keith. Instr. Cornell U., 1930-35; farm supt. N.Y. State Conservation Dept., 1935-37; asst. prof. poultry Cornell U., 1937-40, prof. from 1940, head dept., 1940-65. Fellow Poultry Sci. Assn. (pres. 1959), Am. Assn. Advancement Science, Evolution Society, Sigma Xi, Phi Kappa Phi, Alpha Zeta, Alpha Gamma Rho. Republican. Co-author: Poultry Management, 1952. Home: Ithaca NY Died Feb. 26, 1970.

BRUENING, HEINRICH, univ. prof.; b. Muenster Germany, Nov. 26, 1885; s. Friedrich Wilhelm and Bernhardine (Beringhoff) B.; ed. U. of Munich, U. of Strassburg, U. of Bonn (Ph.D.), London Sch. of Economics; LL.D., Brown U., 1937; hon. A.M., Oxford U., 1938. Came to U.S., 1935. Prussian Ministry of Welfare, 1919-21; polit. and econ. advisor to Christian Trade Unions, 1921-30; member German Reichstag, 1924-33; chancellor German Reich, 1930-32; lecturer Oxford Univ., 1937-1938; lecturer, Harvard, from 1937, Littauer prof. of pub. administrn., 1939-52; prof. polit. sci. U. Cologne, 1951-55. Served in German Army during World War. Decorated Iron Cross, 2d and 1st class. Roman Catholic. Home: Norwich VT Died Mar. 30, 1970; buried Munster, Westfalen Germany

BRUERE, ROBERT WALTER, author, specialist in industrial relations; b. at St. Charles, Mo., Jan. 6, 1876; s. John Ernst and Cornelia (Schoeneich) B.; A.B., A.M., Washington U.; post-grad. work, Univs. of Berlin and Chicago; m. Martha S. Bensley, Oct. 28, 1907. Instr. German and French, South Side Acad., Chicago, English, U. of Chicago, 1899-1904; lecturer on Am. literature and municipal govt., Rand School of Social Science, New York, 1908-09; gen. agt., N.Y. Assn. for Improving Condition of Poor, 1907-09; mem. bd. of Arbitration, Dress and Waist Industry, 1915-17; dir. Bur. of Industrial Research, New York, 1917-23; asso. editor The Survey, 1923-28; research sec. J. C. Penney Foundation, 1928-30. Mem. bd. of dirs. Taylor Soc., 1919-20; treas. and mem. bd. of govs. Personnel Research Fedn., 1921; mem. fact finding commn. to Japan and China of Inst. Religious and Social Research, 1930-31; chmn. Cotton Textile Nat. Industrial Relations Bd. (under NRA); apptd. by President Roosevelt, mem. Camden Bd. of Arbitration, 1935; U.S. govt. del. Preparatory Tech. Meeting of Prin. Maritime Countries, Geneva, 1935; U.S. govt. del. and chmn. U.S. delegation 21st and 22d sessions Internat. Labor Conf., Geneva, 1936. Commissioner of Conciliation, U.S. Dept. of Labor, 1937-38; chmn. Maritime Labor Board, July 6, 1938-June 30, 1942. Mem. U.S. Technical Mission to Brazil, 1943. Chmn. bd. Palisades Pub. Sch., 1932; mem. Vocational Edn. and Extension Bd. of County of Rockland, N.Y., 1930-39. Clubs: Cosmos (Washington); Town Hall (New York). Author: (with wife) Increasing Home Efficiency, 1912; (with Joseph D. Eggleston) The Work of the Rural School, 1913; The Coming of Coal, 1922; The Man with a Thousand Partners, 1931. Home: Sneden's Landing Palisades NY‡

BRUHN, CARL, formerly pres. Internat. Press Assn.; b. Stockholm, June 28, 1869; s. Carl Wilhelm and Johanna (von Bruun) B.; grad. Stockholm Coll., 1887; studied Stockholm Poly., 1888-89; m. Sigrid Helena Wessman, of Jonkoping, Sweden, Dec. 24, 1906 (died May 3, 1928). Came to U.S., 1903, naturalized, 1912. Founder, 1905, and was pres. Internat. Press Assn.; ex-pres. Saratoga Estates. Organized relief bureau, 1919, and sent over $2,000,000 worth of food and clothing to Central Europe, later operating in Russia. Investigated emigration, conditions in Europe, summer 1921, for U.S. Ho. of Rep. Com. on Immigration and Naturalization; colonizer and explorer in Latin America 1892-97. Founded in 1914 El Hispano Americano." Del. to Prog. Conv., 1912. Mem. Met. Mus. Art. Served as lt. Nicaragua Army and promoted capt. at Battle of Masaya, 1896; spl. rep. of Costa Rica Gov. to the Royal Swedish Jubilee and Exhbn., Stockholm, Sweden, 1897. Commander of Order of Bolivar; Prussian Red Eagle,

4th class. Mem. American Tree Assn.; hon. mem. Swedish Glee Club, Brooklyn, N.Y., International Hunters (273), London, England. Author: Suecia, 1895; Rosas Negras, 1899; Stanna Hemma, 1916; Neutral Sweden, 1917; Das Gelahmte Deutschland, 1919; Hundlif i Amerika, 1923. Contbr. many articles to newspapers. Translator of Owen Wister's The Virginian, into the Swedish. Home: 1717 Av. P, Brooklyn, NY*‡

BRUMBAUGH, GAIUS MARCUS, physician, genealogist; b. Huntington County, Pa., May 7, 1862; s. Andrew Boelus, M.D., and Maria Baer (Frank) B.; M.E., Juniata Coll., 1879, M.S., 1898, Litt.D., 1926; M.D., Howard Univ., 1885; M.D., Univ. of Georgetown, 1888; m. Catherine Elliott Brown, Oct. 1, 1889; children—Charles Andrew (dec.), Marcus Morton (dec.), Elliott Frank. In Washington, D.C., 1882; asst. chief bur. animal industry, Dept. of Agr., 1894-99; mem. 3d bd. U.S. Pension Examining Surgeons (sec.), 1899-1914; lecturer materia medica, Nat. Training Sch. for Nurses (Sibley Hosp.), 1897-1911; pres. bd. trustees Juniata coll., pres. emeritus, 1948. Republican. Mem. Ch. of the Brethren. Mem. Pa. German Soc., Am. Med. Assn., Med. Society of D.C. Author: Genealogy of the Brumbach Families, 1913; Genealogy of the Fouse Families (Brumbaugh and Fouse); Maryland Records: Colonial, Revolutionary, County and Church, Vol. I, 1915, Vol. II, 1928; Revolutionary Records of Maryland, Part I (Brumbaugh & Hodges), 1924; Lancaster County (Pa.) Tax Lists (with Dr. Albert H. Gerberich), 1933; Revolutionary War Records, Vol. I, Virginia, 1936; First Census of Kentucky, 1790 (with Charles Brunk Heinemann), 1940. Editor The Nat. Geneal. Soc. Quarterly; mng. editor and co-author Lists of Swiss Emigrants in the 18th Century to the American Colonies (Faust and Brumbaugh), Vol. I, 1920, Vol. II, 1925. Home: 1954 Biltmore St. N.W. Office: 905 Massachusetts Av. N.W., Washington 1 DC‡

BRUMBY, FRANK HARDEMAN, naval officer; b. Athens, Ga., Sept. 11, 1874; s. John Wallis and Arabella (Hardeman) B.; grad. U.S. Naval Acad., 1895; m. Isabelle Truxtun, June 4, 1907; children—Isabelle Truxtun, Frank Hardeman. Commd. ensign U.S. Navy, July 1, 1897; promoted through grades to rear admiral Sept. 8, 1927, vice admiral in command of Scouting Force, May 1933-June 1934; admiral in command of Battle force June 15, 1934 to April 1, 1935; retired Oct. 1, 1938. Served as capt. (temp.), World War; comdr. U.S.S. Kansas, 1920-21, U.S.S. New Mexico, 1924-26. Episcopalian. Club: New York Yacht. Home: Athens GA*‡

BRUMLEY, BENJAMIN BASIL, live stock breeder and feeder; b. McComb, O., Mar. 7, 1875; s. Joseph and Phillipina (Leffler) B.; student Ohio Northern U., 1893-95; m. Iva Dell Van Sickle, Mar. 29, 1901; 1 son, Donald Richard. Taught sch. in Ohio, 1891-1902; farming since 1902. One of organizers, 1930, and since dir. Nat. Live Stock Producers Assn., pres. since 1939; pres. and dir. Nat. Live Stock Pub. Assn., Nat. Feeder & Finance Corp., Producers Live Stock Credit Assn. (Columbus, O.); pres. and dir. Producers Livestock Co-op. Assn. (Columbus) since 1934; pres. Toledo Tri-State Stock Yards Co., Toledo. Chmn. emergency com. which defeated Bigelow amendment to Constitution of State of O., 1939. Chmn., Joint Live Stock Com. (representing all livestock producing assns.), 1942-46; dir. and member exec. com., Nat. Council of Farmer Co-ops. since 1936. Master Farmer, State of Ohio, 1930. Mem. Farm Bureau, Nat. Grange, Future Farmers Club of Ohio (hon.). Republican. Methodist. Odd Fellow. Home: McComb, O. Office: 139 N. Clark St., Chicago 2‡

BRUNDAGE, CHARLES EDWIN, investment counsel; b. East Orange, N.J., May 20, 1895; s. John Norman and Martha Elizabeth (Riker) B.; A.B., Dartmouth, 1916, M.C.S., 1917; postgrad. (fellow) Carnegie Inst. Tech., 1917, Ecole des Hautes Etudes Sociales, Paris, France, 1919; m. Edna Thompson, May 25, 1922; children—Robert Peter, June, John Edwin. Asst. personnel mgr. Celluloid Co., Newark, 1919-21; examiner Fed. Res. Bank of N.Y., Washington, 1921-22, Guaranty Co. of N.Y. 1922-23; asso., gen. partner Scudder, Stevens & Clark, 1923-31; gen. partner firm of Brundage, Story & Rose, from 1932; dir. Fluid Dynamics, Inc., Hanover Twp., N.J.; trustee Union Dime Savs. Bank, N.Y.C., Chmn. bd. trustees Canaan (N.H.) Coll. Served with 15th Engrs., U.S. Army, 1917-19. Mem. Investment Counsel Assn. Am., Phi Beta Kappa. Clubs: Bankers of Am., Weavers; Shongum. Dartmouth (N.Y.C.); Dover NJ Died July 28, 1972; interred Rosedale Cemetery, Orange NJ

BRUNE, FREDERICK W., former judge; b. Baltimore, Md., Oct. 15, 1894; s. Frederick William and Blanche (Shoemaker) B.; ed. Gilman Country Sch., Baltimore, 1904-09, University Sch., Baltimore, 1909-11, Johns Hopkins U., 1911-12; A.B., Harvard Coll., 1915; LL.B., Harvard Law Sch. 1920; LL.D., U. Md., 1965; m. Mary Washington Keyser, Jan. 22, 1921; children—Frederick William, Jr., Caroline Fischer, (dec.). Law clk. for Osborne I. Yellott, 1920-22; admitted to Md. bar, 1921, and began pvt. practice of law in Baltimore; asst. U.S. Atty., Md., 1923-24; partner, Coleman, Fell, Morgan &

Brune, 1923-27, Morgan & Brune, 1927. Semmes. Bowen & Semmes. 1928-54; chief judge Ct. Appeals, Md., 1954-64; chmn. Md. Com. Revision Motor Vehicle Laws, from 1964; chmn. nat. conf. Judicial Councils, 1955-58; mem. exec. council Conf. Chief Justices, 1955-58. Trustee, Goucher College, Union Meml. Hosp., Md. Sch. for the Blind. Mem. City Service Commission, 1937-46, Charter Revision Commn., 1944-46. War Price and Rationing Bd., 1942-45 (all Baltimore). Mem. Commn. on General Corp. Laws, of Md., 1948-50. Served with Ambulance Service; sergt. Intelligence Service, World War I. Recipient John C. Merriam, Irwin S. Cobb and Rupert Hughes Memorial award of merit, 1958. Fellow of the American Bar Foundation (life); mem. Am. (chmn. com. on jurisprudence and law reform, 1947-48), Md. (pres. 1947-48), and Baltimore (pres. 1940), bar assns., Am. Law Inst., Am. Judicature Soc., Maritime Law Assn., Am. Acad. Pub. Affairs, Md. Historical Soc. (v.p. 1963-65). Order of Coif (honorary), Alpha Delta Phi. Past chmn. for Md. spl. com. Improving Adminstrn. of Justice; mem. Council of Sec. of Corpn., Banking and Merc. Law 1946-49 (Am. Bar Assn.); mem. standing com. on Rules of Practice and Procedure apptd. by Ct. of Appeals of Md., 1946-54; mem. Md. Tax Survey Com., 1949-50. Clubs: Maryland Elkridge, Merchants (Balt.); Harvard (Boston and N.Y.C.). Home: Baltimore MD Died Feb. 19, 1972; buried St. Thomas Churchyard, Garrison Forest MD

BRUNER, RAYMOND ALPHONSE, sci. editor; b. Indpls., Sept. 6, 1900; s. Alphonse and Sarah (Barnett) B.; grad. Charles E. Emmerich Manual Tng. High Sch., Indpls., 1918; m. Louise Katherine Eisele, Nov. 22, 1937; children—Madelin, Sylvia (Mrs. Charles Shapley), Suzanne. Chemist, Citizens Gas Co., Indpls., 1920-22; asst. Ind. mgr. and Cleve. mgr. United Press, 1922-28; feature writer A.P., 1928-32; sci. writer, art editor Cleve. News, 1932-41; engaged in pub. relations, 1941-51; pub. relations dir. Western Res. U., 1944-48, 49; engaged in farming, 1951-53; sci. editor Toledo Blade, from 1953. Recipient Grady award Am. Chem. Soc., 1968, Morse award Am. Psychiat. Assn., 1967, A.A.A.S.-Westinghouse Co. award, 1966, Cetalin award A.M.A., 1966, spl. writing award Toledo Dental Soc., 1966, Toledo Acad. Medicine, 1969. Home: Toledo OH Died Sept. 13, 1970.

BRUNER, WILLIAM EVANS, ophthalmologist; b. Columbia, Pa., Jan. 8, 1866; s. Abram and Sarah Jane (Breneman) B.; Dickinson College, Carlisle, Pa., 1yr.; A.B., Wesleyan U., Middletown, Conn., 1888, A.M., 1891, D.Sc., 1928; M.D., U. of Pa., 1891; m. Lydia S. Clark, Feb. 18, 1897; children—Williams Evans (dec.), Clark Evans. Began as clin. asst. in ophthalmology 1894, clin. prof., 1912-15, prof. ophthalmology, 1915-36, emeritus, Med. Dept., Western Reserve U.; visiting ophthalmologist St. Vincent's Hosp., 1898-1917, Lakeside Hosp., 1912-36; consulting ophthalmologist, St. Vincent's Hospital, 1917-34, Rainbow Hosp., 1920-36, Maternity and Babies' and Children's hospitals; ex-mem. advisory bd. Ohio State Commn. for the Blind, Cleveland Soc. for the Blind; oculist to U.S. Pension Bur. Maj. Med. Corps, U.S. Army. Mem. Am. Ophthal. Soc., Am. Acad. Ophthalmology and Oto-Laryngology, A.M.A., Cleveland Med. Soc. (ex-pres.), Cleveland Med. Library Assn. (ex-pres.), Phi Beta Kappa, Alpha Delta Phi, Sigma Nu; fellow Am. Coll. Surgeons. Republican. Presbyn. Clubs: Union, Rowfant, Mayfield, Pasteur, Cleveland Ophthalmologic. Contbr. articles to med. jours. Collaborator Am. Jour. Ophthalmology, 1918-24. Home: 13515 Shaker Blvd., Cleveland 20. Office: Guardian Bldg Cleveland 14 OH‡

BRUNIA, WILLIAM FRANS, investment exec.; b. nr. Des Moines, Ia., May 17, 1893; s. Frans W. and Alice I. (Roorda) B.; student Ia. Tchrs. Coll., 1921, Central Coll., 1923; m. Ena M. Heemstra, Feb. 28, 1916; children—Alice (Mrs. F. Melvin Proudfit), Frank W., Marion W., Nathan W., Catherine (Mrs. James Maurer), William. Farmer, 1916-20, 24-27; tchr. grade schs., 1920-24; elec. contractor, mfr. Brunia Electric, 1927-42, wholesaler, 1942-68; owner Brunia Investments, Des Moines, Ia., 1962-68. Dir. Des Moines Area Fair Tax Assn., 1962-68. Mem. Econ. Club Des Moines. Republican. Unitarian. Mason (Shriner). Home: Des Moines IA Died June 27, 1968.

BRUNSCHWIG, ALEXANDER, surgeon, gynecologist; b. El Paso, Tex., Sept. 11, 1901; s. Felix and Pauline (Harris) B.; B.S., U. of Chicago, 1923, M.S., 1924; M.D., Rush Med. Coll., 1927; post grad. work, Strasbourg, and Paris, France; M.D. (honorary), Laval U., P.Q., Can.; Doctoris Honoris Causa. U. Strasbourg (France), 1959, University of Montpellier, University Bordeaux; married Lea Naye, June 16, 1926; children—Louise (Mrs. Paul Sivak), Roxane (Mrs. Bruno Pavia). Practice Chgo., from 1928; Nat. Research fellow, Strasbourg, 1930-31; surg. staff U. Chgo. Clinics, became prof. surgery U. Chgo., 1940; attending surgeon, chief gynecol., dept. Meml. Hosp. for Treatment Cancer and Allied Diseases; became prof. clin. surgery Cornell U. Coll. Med., 1947; cons. gynecologist, surgeon New York Infirmary; consulting surgeon at New York Polyclinic Hosp. Paris civilian cons. U.S. Govt., 1942-46; mem. Unitarian Service Com. Medical Teaching Missions to Czechoslovakia, 1946, Austria, 1947. Served as lt. (j.g.) USN, 1926-27. Awarded Medal of Charles U. of Prague, 1946; Order of White Lion of Czechoslovakia; Medal, U. Brussels (Belgium); Officer Legion of Honor (France); Gold Medal, Societie des Journees Medicales de Bruxelles; medal U. Bologna (Italy), Lucy Wortham James award, James Ewing medal; Ann Langer Cancer Research Found. Award, 1968. Fellow American College Surgeons, International College Surgeons (hon.), Am. Surgical Association; hon. or corr. member medical and professional socs. various foreign countries; member Society Clinical Surgery, Soc. U. Surgeons, A.M.A., Soc. Pelvic Surgeons, N.Y. Cynecol. Soc., Academie de Chirurgie Paris. Author: The Surgery of Pancreatic Tumors; Radical Surgery in Advanced Cancer of the Abdomen; L'exenteration pelvienne, 1964; also articles med. jours. Home: Pelham NY Died Aug. 7, 1969; buried Ferncliff, Hartsdale NY

BRUNSCHWIG, ROGER E., mfg. co. exec.; b. Argenteuil, France, July 14, 1891; s. Achille and Blanche (Picard) B.; student French Mil. Sch.; Baccalauret of Arts, French schs.; m. Zelina Comegys, June 25, 1938. Partner, Brunschwig & Fils, mfrs. in France of decorative fabrics, N.Y.C., from 1925; pres. Brunschwig & Fils, Inc. Pres., Union of French Facial Wounded. Served with French Army, 1909-21; with Free French Forces, 1940-46; col. inf. Army Res. Decorated grand cross Legion of Honor, Croix de Guerre (2) (France); Croix de Guerre (Belgium); Legion of Merit, Bronze Star medal (U.S.). Author: Historical Studies of the French Revolution and Empire Periods. Home: New York City NY Died Dec. 7, 1972.

BRUNSON, MAY AUGUSTA, coll. dean; b. Mobile, Ala., Sept. 1, 1909; d. Charles Augustus and May Leila (Davidson) Brunson; A.B. magna cum laude (Algernon Sidney Sullivan award), Judson Coll., 1935; M.A., Columbia U. Tchrs. Coll., 1945, Frank Ross Chambers fellow, 1952-53, Ed.D., 1957. Dir. publicity Judson Coll., Marion, Ala., 1935-38, dir. admissions, instr. English, 1938-42, dean students, 1942-46; instr. English U. Ala., summer 1946; counselor for women, asst. prof. orientation U. Miami, Coral Gables, 1946-54; asso. dean women, asso. prof. orientation, 1954-55; dean women, professor education, 1955-70. Chmn. regional interviewing bd. Tchr. Exchange Program U.S. office Health, Welfare & Edn., 1955-70. Recipient Judson Coll. outstanding alumnae award, 1960; Dade County (Fla.) recipient Theta Sigma Phi Community Headliner award, 1963. Member of Assn. Coll. Honor Socs. (council 1958-61, 67-70, executive committee 1968-70), So. College Personnel Assn. (historian 1958-61), Fla. Assn. Deans and Counselors (pres. 1950-52), Nat. Assn. Deans Women (sec. u. sect. 1950-52), Nat. Assn. Women Deans and Counselors (nat. treas.), Am. Assn. U. Women, Am. Personnel and Guidance Assn., Am. Coll. Personnel Assn. (mem. senate 1963-64). Fla. College Personnel Assn. (president 1966-67), Assn. Coll. Honor Soc. (exec. com. 1968-69), Florida Personnel and Guidance Association, Assn. Higher Edn., N.E.A., Kappa Delta Pi, Pi Lambda Theta, Alpha Lambda Delta (treas. nat. council 1957-66, national president 1966-70), Gamma Alpha Chi, Mortar Board. Congregationalist. Author: Guidance: An Integrating Process in Higher Education 1959; (with others) Introduction to College, 1958. Home: Coral Gables FL Died Apr. 20, 1970.

BRUNSWICK, MARK, educator, composer; b. N.Y.C., Jan. 6, 1902; s. Emanuel and Cecile (Blumgart) B.; ed. Horace Mann Sch., Phillips Exeter Acad.; pvt. study with Rubin Goldmark, Ernest Bloch, Nadia Boulanger; m. Natascha Artin. Head composition dept. Greenwich House Music Sch., N.Y.C., 1938-42; chmn. music dept. Coll. City N.Y., 1946-64. Mem. bd. Young Audiences. Chairman Nat. Com. Refugee Musicians, 1937-41. Mem. Internat. Soc. Contemporary Music (pres. U.S. sect. 1941-50), Am. Composers Assn. (vice pres. 1967-68), College Music Assn. (pres. 1953). Composer: String Quartet, 1926; Lysistrara-Suite for Orchestra and Chorus, 1930; Fantasia for Viola Solo, 1932; B Flat Symphony, 1945; (choral symphony) Eros and Death, 1954; Seven Trios for String Quartet, 1956; Septet, 1957; Doublebass Quartet, 1958; Four Songs, 1964; Five Madrigals, 1965; Air with Toccata for Princeton NJ Died May 26, 1971.

BRUSH, FREDERIC (LOUIS), M.D.; b. Susquehanna, Pa., Jan. 13, 1871; s. Addison G. and Cora (Stoddard) B.; grad. Delaware Lit. Inst., Franklin, N.Y., 1892; M.D., New York Univ. Med. Coll., 1896; m. Emma Sutcliffe, 1901 (died 1910); m. 2d, Florence Bullen, 1912. House surgeon, New York Post-Grad. Hosp., 1898; practiced in Boston, 1900-08; supt. New York Post-Grad. Med. Sch. and Hosp., 1908-12; med. dir. since 1912, The Burke Foundation; consultant in planning and orgn. of various instns. Asst. surgeon, rank of lt., U.S.N.R.F., on active duty Apr. 1917-May 1919. Trustee Assn. for Prevention and Relief of Heart Disease; member Am. Hosp. Assn., Am. Forestry Assn., Nat. Grange, Am. Legion, Assn. Military Surgeons, etc. Club: City (New York). Author: (poems) Susquehanna; also papers on hosp. and med. topics and country life; stories, essays and poems in mags. Address: White Plains NY‡

BRUSH, HOWARD GRAFTON, business exec.; b. Buffalo, July 6, 1903; s. Samuel S. and Fanny Boice (Snider) B.; B.S., U. Pa., 1927; m. Sybil Reppert, Sept. 21, 1932; 1 son, Howard Grafton. Pub. accountant Ernest & Ernest, 1927-34, Price Waterhouse & Co., 1938-42; controller Motor Products Corp., 1942, treas., 1943, v.p., 1944-47; with Brown Co., Berlin, 1948-54, treas., v.p., 1950-54; v.p. charge finance Gt. Northern Paper Co., 1954-68. Active Boy Scouts of Am. C.P.A., N.Y., Mich. Mem. Am. Inst. Accountants, Financial Execs. Inst. Rep. Unitarian. Clubs: Northeast Harbor Fleet, Mount Desert Yacht; Union League (N.Y.C.). Home: Mt Desert ME Died Aug. 19, 1971; buried Somesville ME

BRUSH, MURRAY PEABODY, educator; b. Zanesville, O., Apr. 17, 1872; s. Edmund J. and Judith Dodge (Peabody) B.; A.B., Princeton, 1894; Ph.D., Johns Hopkins, 1898; studied Sorbonne and College de France, 1895-96; m. Charlotte M. Kinney, June 14, 1899; children—Eleanor Peabody (Mrs. Edward A. Cudahy), Murray Peabody. Instructor in French, Ohio State U., 1898-99; instr., asso., asso. prof. and prof. and dean of the college faculty, Johns Hopkins, 1899-1919; dir. of Tome School, Port Deposit, Md., 1919-32; headmaster Calif. Prep. School, Ojai, 1932-49, ret. Officier d'Academie (France). Rep. Presbyterian. Mem. Modern Lang. Assn. America, Alpha Delta Phi, Phi Beta Kappa, Omicron Delta Kappa, Society Colonial Wars, Cum Laude Society, University Club of Los Angeles. Editor: Isopo Laurenziano (doctor's dissertation), 1899. About's La Mere de la Marquise, 1903; Ysopet III of Paris, 1907; Esopo Zuccarino, 1911; Moliere's Femmes Savantes, 1911; Maupassant's Contes Choisis, 1916. Home: Ojai CA‡

BRUSH, WILLIAM WHITLOCK, civil engr.; b. Orange, N.J., July 28, 1874; s. Clinton Ethelbert and Eliza Thomson (Whitlock) B.; B.S., New York, U., 1893, C.E., 1894, M.S., 1895; m. Jean Evelyn Mitchell, Apr. 28, 1897; 1 son, John Mitchell. Engr. on water supply for Brooklyn, N.Y., 1894-1907; engr. with Bd. of Water Supply, on Catskill system, 1907-09; dept. engr. Bd. of Water Supply, on design of city aqueduct system, 1909-10; dep. chief engr. Bur. Water Supply Dept. of Water Supply, Gas and Electricity, N.Y. City, 1910-17; apptd. acting chief engr. same, July 1917, dep. chief engr., 1919, chief engr., 1927; retired, 1934; editor Water Works Engring., 1934. Designed system of delivery of Catskill water to the five boroughs of N.Y. City. Mem. of Council of New York Univ. Hon. mem. Am. Water Works Assn. (ex-pres. and treas.); mem. Am. Soc. C.E., Munic. Engrs. of N.Y. (ex-pres.), Am. Pub. Health Assn., Alumni Assn. Arts and Engineering of New York U. (ex-pres.) Gamma Chapter Delta Phi; hon. mem. N.E. Water Works Assn. Republican. Mem. Dutch Ref. Ch. Club: Engineers, Town Hall. Contbr. tech. papers on engring. subjects. Home: Hotel Drake, 440 Park Av., New York 22. Office: 24 W. 40th St., New York 18 NY‡

BRUTON, JOHN FLETCHER, lawyer; b. Wentworth, Rockingham County, N.C., May 29, 1861; s. David Rasbury and Margaret G. (Nixon) B.; prep. edn. Bingham Sch., N.C., 1879-81; student U. of N.C., 1884; m. Hattie Tartt Barnes, Nov. 15, 1887; children—John Barnes, Howard Barnes. Admitted to N.C. bar, 1884, and began practice at Wilson; v.p. N.C. Home Ins. Co.; dir. Carolina Telephone & Telegraph Co.; chmn. bd. N.C. Joint Stock Land Bank; dir. Federal Reserve Bank of Richmond, 1914-25; mem. Federal Advisory Council of Federal Reserve Bd., 1926-28. Mem. N.C. State Advisory Banking Commn., 1931. Col. 2d Regt., N.C.N.G., 1893-98; mayor of Wilson, 1894-96; chmn. Wilson County Bd. of Edn. Pres. bd. trustees Duke U., Durham, N.C. Pres. Wilson County Bar Assn.; mem. Am. and N.C. bar assns., Alpha Tau Omega, Phi Beta Kappa, Omicron Delta Kappa. Democrat. Methodist. Odd Fellow (past grand master). Home: Wilson NC‡

BRYAN, SHELDON MARTIN, painter, sculptor; b. Jacksonville, Fla., June 15, 1916; s. Jacob Franklin and Olive (Gibson) B.; student Phoenix Art Inst., 1936; Grand Central Art Sch., 1938; Art Students League N.Y., 1946-50; m. Caroline Eugenie Barnett, July 9, 1947; children—Caroline Gibson, Olive Madeleine. One man show Sagittarius Gallery, Cummer Gallery of Art; exhibited in group shows at Nat. Acad. Design Ann., Emily Lowe Award Ann., Salmagundi Club Ann., Fla. Fedn. Art Ann.; represented in permanent collections at Cummer Gallery Art, Independent Life Ins. Co. Served with USAAF, 1941-45. Mem. Artist Equity Assn. N.Y. Clubs: Salmagundi; Florida Yacht (Jacksonville, Fla.). Home: New York City NY Died Nov. 7, 1968.

BRYAN, WINFRED FRANCIS, clergyman; b. Bryan's Mill, Tex., May 9, 1872; s. William Gaston and Emma Aurelia (Moody) B.; M.A., Southwestern U., Georgetown, Tex., 1895; D.D., Asbury Coll., Wilmore, Ky., 1924; m. Emma Belle Cullum, June 1, 1897; children—Ruth Aurelia (wife of Dr. E. S. Kane), Inez Sophronia, Marvin Pierce, William Gaston, Marjorie Elizabeth (wife of Dr. Orion Thompson), Dorothy (Mrs. E. B. Miller, Jr.). Ordained M.E. Ch., S., 1895; successively pastor Oak Lawn (Dallas), Lannius,

Emberson, Blossom, Ervay Street Ch., Dallas, Wichita Falls, Whitewright, Sulphur Springs, until 1911; presiding elder Paris Dist., 1911-15; pastor Marlin, 1915-18; presiding elder Jacksonville Dist., 1918-19; pastor Tyler, 1919-23; presiding elder Marlin Dist., 1923-24; pastor First Ch., Austin, 1924-29; presiding elder Decatur Dist., 1929-31; presiding elder Tyler Dist., 1931-34; pastor First Ch., Galveston, 1934-38. Dist. supt. Huntsville District, 1938-42; dist. superintendent Houston District, 1942-44; asso. pastor First Methodist Ch., Houston, 1944-49. Delegate to Gen. Conf. M.E. Ch., S., 5 times, and to Ecumenical Conf. of World Methodism, London, 1921, 31; conf. missionary sec. West Texas Conf., M.E. Ch., S., 1924-29; del. to North Am. Home Mission Conf., Washington, D.C., 1930; del. to Gen. Conf. of M.E. Ch., S., 1934; chmn. finance com. Gen. Conf. 1934; del. Sesquicentennial Conf. of Am. Methodism, Baltimore, 1934; vice chmn. Gen. Conf. Commn. on Budget, 1934-38, chmn. since 1938; del. to Missionary Council of M.E. Ch., S., Washington, 1936; del. to Uniting Conf. (chmn. com. on membership and temporal economy), Kansas City, 1939; chmn. com. that wrote Financial Plan for Meth. Ch., 1939; del. Gen. conf. Meth. Ch., 1940; vice chmn. com. on Ministry; chmn. legislative com. for Commn. on World Service and Finance; vice chmn. Commn. on World Service and Finance, 1939-42, chmn. 1942-44. Mem. commn. to formulate post-war program, for the Meth. Ch. in U.S., 1943; mem. Meth. Emergency Commn., 1941; mem. advisory council Am. Bible Soc., 1940-44; mem. Nat. Inter-Faith Com. for Aid to the Democracies, 1941; chmn. dist. supts. of Texas Conf., 1938-44; chmn. commn. on expense, Jurisdictional Conf., Methodist Church, 1940; vice chairman committee on Episcopacy; chairman committee on American Bible Society; executive secretary Board of Superannuate Endowments and Homes of Methodist Church since 1949. Delegate to Jurisdictional Conf. Meth. Ch., 1940-44, to Gen. Conf. Meth. Ch., 1944. Trustee Southwestern U., 1908-30; pres. Ministerial Alliance, Austin, 1929. Ministerial Alliance, Galveston, 1936. Mem. Pi Gamma Mu, Kappa Sigma. Mason (K.T., Shriner), Kiwanian. Received 146 members into ch. on one Sunday while pastor at Tyler. Traveled extensively in Europe, Asia and Africa. Home: 4905 Jackson, Houston TX ‡

BRYANS, HENRY BUSSELL, cons. engr.; b. Phila., Mar. 26, 1886; s. Henry M. and Ella (Lonergan) B.; A.B., Central High School, Phila., 1903; B.S. in mech. engring., U. of Pa., 1907; m. Ada Matilda Trinkle, May 1, 1911; children—Henry Trinkle, Robert Trinkle. Began as engr. United Gas Improvement Co., 1907; gen. supt. Phila. Suburban-Counties Gas & Electric Co., 1927-28, asst. gen. mgr. Phila. Electric Co., 1928-29, v.p. in charge operations, 1929-38, exec. v.p., 1938-47, dir., 1940-52, pres., 1947-52; v.p., dir. United Engrs. & Constructors, Inc., 1952-55; dir. mem. exec. com. Bellevue-Stratford Hotel; dir. Baldwin Securities Corp.; mem. bd. mgrs. emeritus Western Sav. Fund Soc. of Phila. Mem. electrical utility Def. Adv. Council, 1950-51. Life trustee past chmn., mem. finance, investment and devel. coms., exec. bd. U. Pa. Fellow Royal Soc. Arts, Manufacturers and Commerce; mem. Am. Standards Assn. (past pres.), Am. Soc. M.E., I.E.E.E., Franklin Inst. (bd. mgrs., past chmn., mem. finance com., past mem. exec. com.), Pa. Elec. Assn. (past pres.), Elec. Assn. Phila. (past pres.), Hist. Soc. Pa., Newcomen Soc., Pa. Soc. N.Y. Republican. Presbyterian. Mason. Clubs: Engineers, Union League (past pres.), Midday (Phila.); Penn., Sunday Breakfast. Home: Bryn Mawr PA Died May 1973.

BRYANT, ANNA BURNHAM, author; b. Exeter, N. H.; d. John Cleveland and Caroline A. Burnham; ed. Bradford Acad., Salem Normal Sch., Radcliffe Coll.; m. 1898, Rev. Albert Bryant. Editor and writer of books for young people; contb'r to young people's mags. Author: Fussbudget's Folks, 1884 P8; Wellspring Series, 1884 P8; Lake View Series, 1884 P8; Rock-a-By Series, 1891 P8; The Bunker Hill Failure, 1897 P8; Sunny Hour Series, 1899 P8; Holly Berry Series, 1899 P8; The Christmas Cat, 1902 P8. Address: Boston‡

BRYANT, EUGENE, lawyer; b. Atlanta, Nov. 12, 1902; s. Wade Hampton and Mamie (Robinson) B.; student Ga. Sch. Tech., 1921-25; LL.B., Furman U., 1927; m. Harriet Pullen, Nov. 5, 1929; children—Edith (Mrs. E. L. Smith), Eugenia (Mrs. Frank P. McGowan, Jr.), Wade H. Admitted to S.C. bar, 1928, practiced in Greenville; with Haynsworth, Perry, Bryant, Marion & Johnstone, 1926-69. Dir. So. Bank & Trust Co., Fountain Inn, S.C., United Family Life Ins. Co., Atlanta. Chmn. Greenville County chpt. A.R.C., 1937-38; pres. Greater Greenville Community Chest, 1942; pres. Greenville YMCA, 1950, dir., 1969; pres. Greenville Community Council, 1956. Trustee Greenville County Found. Mem. Am., S.C., Greenville County (past pres.) bar assns., Am. Judicature Soc., Greenville C. of C. (past pres.), Alpha Tau Omega. Baptist (deacon). Club: American Business (past pres.) (Greenville). Greenville SC Died Sept. 11, 1969; buried Woodlawn Meml Park, Greenville SC

BRYANT, HENRY EDWARD COWAN, newspaper man; b. Mecklenburg Co., N.C., Jan. 3, 1873; s. Henry and Julia (Parks) B.; B.Sc., U. of N.C., 1895; m. Eva Sumner, of Lincolnton, N.C., Feb. 1, 1900; 1 dau., Mrs. Harold W. Northcutt. Reporter Charlotte (N.C.) Observer, 1895-1910; with Missoulian, Missoula, Mont., 1910-11; Washington corr. New York World, 1911-31, Raleigh News and Observer (Raleigh, N.C.), etc. Presbyn. Club: Gridiron (Washington, D.C.). Author: Tar Heel Tales, 1910; Biographical Sketch of Joseph Pearson Caldwell, Journalist; A Little Despot; also articles and stories in mags., treating of farm and outdoor life. Home: 3551 Springland Lane. Office: Munsey Bldg., Washington DC‡

BRYANT, SARA CONE, author; b. Melrose, Mass., Jan. 4, 1873; d. Dexter and Dorcas Anne (Hancock) B.; A.B., Boston U., 1895; diplomas from Frau Doktor, Hempel Normal Sem., Berlin, Ind Am. Home Sch. of Berlin, 1896; m. Theodore Franz Borst, Mar. 9, 1908; children—Elizabeth, Bryant, James Bryant. Engaged in journalism and writing short stories for mags., 1897-1900; teacher of English and lecturer on poetry, Simmons Coll., Boston, 1904-06; lecturer on story telling in Lucy Wheelock Kindergarten, Boston, 1907; also has lectured on same subject in principal cities of United States. Mem. Phi Beta Kappa, Kappa Kappa Gamma. Club: Women's City Club of Boston. Author: How to Tell Stories to Children, 1905; Stories to Tell to Children, 1907; Stories to Tell the Littlest Ones, 1915; I Am an American, 1918; New Stories to Tell Children, 1923; The Story Reader, Books I and II, 1924; Gordon and His Friends, 1925; The Magic Flute, 1926; Gordon in the Great Woods, 1928; Story Reader, 1929. Address: 93 Hancock Av., Newton Centre MA‡

BRYDEN, WILLIAM, retired army officer; b. Hartford, Conn., Feb. 3, 1880; s. George and Florence Andrews (Bliss) B.; B.S., U.S. Mil. Acad., 1904; m. Ellen Barry, Oct. 26, 1912; children—Ellen (wife Lt. Col. Alexander D. Surles). Marion (wife Lt. Col. F. W. Moorman). Commd. 2d lt. U.S. Army, 1904, served as officer all grades until promoted to maj. gen., 1940. Decorated D.S.M. with two oak leaf clusters. Mem. Am. Legion, The Newcomen Soc. Clubs: Army and Navy, Army and Navy Country. Address: Washington DC Died 1972.

BRYSON, OLIVE FLORA, college pres.; b. Clinton, S.C., Jan. 26, 1875; d. Matthew Henry and Martha Ann (Leake) B.; prep. edn., Presbyn. Acad. of S.C. (Clinton) and pvt. and high schs.; B.S., Holbrook Normal Coll., Fountain City, Tenn., 1900; S.B., U. of Chicago, 1916, A.M., 1921. Began as teacher pub. schs., S.C., 1897; prin. graded sch., Whitney, S.C., 1903-04, high sch., Stanford, Ky., 1904-05; teacher science and psychology, Millersburg (Ky.) Coll., 1905-09, science and German, Miss. Synodical Coll., Holly Springs, Miss., 1909-11; prof. chemistry and biology, Martha Washington Coll., Abingdon, Va., 1911-14; prof. biology and health, Radford (Va.) Teachers' Coll., 1914-28; pres. Centenary Coll., Cleveland, Tenn., since 1928. Mem. A.A.A.S., Va. Biologists, Va. Acad. Science, Pi Gamma Mu. Democrat. Mem. M.E. Ch., S. Home: Cleveland TN‡

BUCHANAN, DAVID H., army officer; b. Marion, Va., May 8, 1907; s. B.F. and Eleanor Fairman (Sheffey) B.; student Greenbrier Mil. Sch., Lewisburg, W.Va., 1920-24; B.S., U.S. Mil. Acad., 1929; grad. Inf. Sch., 1936;, Nat. War Coll., 1951; m. Katherine Pritchett, Nov. 29, 1929; 1 dau., Cynthia Dee. Commd. 2d lt. U.S. Army, 1929, advanced through grades to maj. gen., 1956; company officer 16th Inf., Governor's Island, N.Y., 45th Inf., P.I., 31st Inf., Manila, 20th Inf., Ft. Francis E. Warren, Wyo.; instr. equitation Inf. Sch., 1936-39; comdr. Hawaiian Div. Pack Train, Schofield Barracks, T. H., 1939; successively div. asst. chief staff G-4, bn. and regtl. comdr. 161st Inf., regt. comdr. 27th Inf. Regt., 25th Inf. Dv., Pacific, World War II; Army instr. Air U., Maxwell Field, Ala., 1946-49; sec. Gen. Staff, Army Ground Forces, Ft. Monroe, Va., 1949-51; chief Joint War Plans G-3, Dept. Army 1951, asst. chief Plans Div. G-3, Dept. Army Gen. Staff, 1952; mem. standing group, North Atlantic Treaty Mil. Com., Washington, 1952; dep. standing group liaison officer North Atlantic Council, 1953-56; chief staff Fifth Army Hdqrs., Chgo., 1956-57; comdg. gen. 1st Inf. Div., Ft. Riley, Kan., 1957-58; chief M. I. Assistance & Adv. Group, Korea, 1958-59; dep. insp. gen. U.S. Army, 1959-61; chief staff U.S. Continental Army Command, 1962, ret., 1962; cons. Research Analysis Corp., 1963-70. Decorated D.S.M., Silver Star, Legion of Merit, Bronze Star Medal, Purple Heart, Combat Inf. Badge, Liberation Philippines. Presbyn. Clubs: Circle Inter-alliee (Paris, France); Army and Navy (Washington). Home: Washington DC Died Jan. 1, 1972; buried Arlington Nat. Cemetery, Arlington VA

BUCHANAN, SCOTT, foundation cons.; b. Sprague, Wash., Mar. 17, 1895, s. William Duncan and Lillian Elizabeth (Bagg) B.; A.B., Amherst Coll., 1916, student Balliol College; Rhodes scholar (Massachusetts) Oxford University, England, 1919-21; Ph.D., Harvard, 1925; m. Miriam Thomas, Feb. 5, 1921; 1 son, Douglas. Instr. in Greek, Amherst Coll., 1917-18; asst. in philosophy, Harvard, 1922-24; instr. in philosophy, Coll. City of N.Y., 1924-25; asst. dir., People's Inst., New York, N.Y., 1925-29; asso. prof. philosophy, U. of Virginia, 1929-30, prof., 1930-36; chmn. com. on the liberal arts, U. of Chicago, 1936-37; dean, St. John's Coll., Annapolis, Md., 1937-47; dir. Liberal arts, Inc., Pittsfield, Mass., 1947-49; trustee Found. World Govt., 1948-58; prof. philosophy, chmn. dept. religion, philosophy, Fisk U., 1956-57; cons. Fund for the Republic, 1957-68; founding mem., sr. fellow Center for Study Dem. Instns., 1957-68; visiting lectr. Christian Gauss Seminar, Princeton, 1956. Served as ensign, U.S.N.R.F., 1918. Mem. Am. Math. Assn., Am. Philosophical Assn., Delta Upsilon. Author: Possibility, 1926; Poetry and Mathematics, 1929; Symbolic Distance, 1931; The Doctrine of Signatures, 1937; Essay in Politics, 1953; Embers of the World, 1970; The Truth in the Sciences, 1972; also numerous papers on law and Bill of Rights. Home: Santa Barbara CA Died Mar. 25, 1968; buried Jeffersonville VT

BUCHANAN, W. C., business exec.; b. Johnstown, Pa., 1888; 2 sons. Pres., dir. Globe Steel Tubes Co., Milw.; pres., mem. exec. com., dir. Allis-Chalmers Mfg., until 1952, mem. exec. com., dir., 1952-62; dir., chmn. exec. com. Kearney & Trecker Co., Milw.; dir., mem. exec. com. Ind. Steel Products Co., Chgo.; dir. Milw. Gas Light Co. Mason (Shriner). Home: Peoria IL Died Feb. 27, 1968.

BUCHER, JOHN EMERY, chemist; b. Hanover, Pa., Aug. 17, 1872; s. Jacob F. and Elizabeth (Emery) B.; A.C., Lehigh U., 1891; Ph.D., Johns Hopkins, 1894; Sc.D., Brown U., 1917; m. Alcista Howard, of Milford, Mass., 1896. Instr. organic chemistry, Tufts Coll., 1894-97; asso. prof. chemistry, R.I. Coll., 1897-1901; same, Brown U., 1901-15, prof. and head of dept., 1915-17; with Penman-Littlehales Chem. Co., 1917-20. Mem. Naval Consulting Bd., World War. Mem. Civil Legion. Republican. Contbr. numerous articles in professional jours. Inventor of process for nitrogen fixation, and processes for mfr. of magnesium, beryllium and aluminium. Consulting chemist, New York. Home: 57 Davenport St., North Adams, Mass. Address: P.O. Box 401, Norwalk CT‡

BUCK, ELLSWORTH BREWER, bus. exec.; b. Chicago, July 3, 1892; s. Orlando Jacob and Lillian Louisa (Brewer) B.; B.S., Dartmouth Coll., 1914, M.A., 1939; LL.D., Wagner Coll., 1941; m. Constance Tyler, Apr. 12, 1919; children—Orlando John (deceased), Nancy (Mrs. Nancy B. Burger). Began as an apprentice with William Wrigley Jr. Co., Chicago, 1914-16, asst. purchasing agent, 1916-17; lab. asst. L.A. Dreyfus Co., 1919-20, treas. 1920-25, vice pres. and treas., 1925, pres. and treas., 1925-32, chmn. bd. 1932-57, also dir.; vice president, dir. Thunder Mountain Ranch Company; elected to 78th Congress from 11th dist. New York, at special election June 6, 1944; elected to 79th Congress from 16th dist., Nov. 7, 1944; to 80th Congress, 1946; mem. com. on edn. and labor which wrote Taft-Hartley law; did not seek reelection to 81st Congress; dir. Office of Trade, Investment and Monetary Affairs, Foreign Operations Administration, 1954; public advisor U.S. delegation to UN Economic and Social Council, Geneva, Switzerland, 1955. Chairman Rep. County Com., Richmond County, N.Y., 1951-52; del. Republican National Conv., 1952. Chmn. Code Authority for Chewing Gum Industry, NRA, 1933-35. Served as ensign USN, World War I. Formerly mem N.Y. Bd. of Edn. (pres. 1942-44); former trustee Am. Museum Natural History, Staten Island Hosp., Staten Island Acad., former v.p. Staten Island Community Chest. Past trustee Wagner Coll., S.I., N.Y. Mem. Staten Island Zool. Soc. (trustee), Delta Tau Delta. Republican. Clubs: New York Yacht, India House, Richmond County Country, Dartmouth College (N.Y.C.). Address: Crivitz WI also Staten Island NY Died Aug. 1970.

BUCK, FOSTER, mfg. co. exec.; b. Creston, Mont., Oct. 30, 1904; s. Charles L. and Christine (Norlander) B.; B.S. in Elec. Engring. with honors, Mont. State Coll., 1929; M.S., U. Pitts., 1931; m. Hattie E. Beeman, June 22, 1929; children—Richard, Raymond, Norman, Ruth (Mrs. Charles Cummings). Design engr. Westinghouse Co., 1929-31; instr. elec. engring. N.D. State Coll., 1931-36; teaching fellow U. Wash., 1936-37; research engr. Internat. Harvester Co., Chgo., 1937-42; chief engr. Franklin Photog. Industries, Chgo., 1942; owner Buck Mfg. Co., North Aurora, Ill. Chmn. Lisle (Ill.) Sch. Bd., 1940-43. Mem. Am. Soc. E.E. Republican. Conglist. (Sunday Sch. tchr.). Club: Optimist (Aurora). Patentee in field. Home: Aurora IL

BUCK, HARRY LAMBERT, elec. supplies mfr.; b. Phila., 1911; s. Henry L. and Sarah G. (Simmington) B.; B.S. Electrical Engring., Drexel Inst. Tech., 1934, Dr.Engring. (hon.), 1965; m. Mary Esther Oman, Oct. 18, 1935; children—Harry Lambert, Richard S., Thomas A. With I-T-E Imperial Corp., Phila., 1935-72, treas., 1946-55, v.p., gen. mgr., 1955-60, exec. v.p., 1960-67, chmn. exec. com., 1967-72, pres., 1967-68, vice chmn. bd., 1968-72; dir. I-T-E Circuit Breaker (Can.), Ltd., Toronto, Canadian Porcelain Co., Ltd., Hamilton, Ont., Bd. dirs. Goodwill Industries of Phila.; bd. dirs. S.E. Pa. Devel. Fund; trustee Hahnemann Med. Coll. and Hosp.; vice chmn. bd. trustees Drexel U. Mem. Am. Mgmt. Assn., I.E.E.E. (gov.), Franklin Inst. Pa., Newcomen Soc. N.A. Club: Sunday Breakfast, Union League (Phila.) Home: Bryn Mawr PA Died July 8, 1972; buried Arlington Cemetery, Drexel Hill PA

BUCK, PEARL SYDENSTRICKER (MRS. RICHARD J. WALSH), author; b. Hillsboro, W.Va., June 26, 1892; d. Absalom and Caroline (Stulting) Sydenstricker; A.B., Randolph-Macon Woman's Coll., Lynchburg, Va., 1914; M.A., Cornell U., 1926; M.A., Yale, 1933; Litt.D., W.Va. U., 1940, St. Lawrence U., 1942; LL.D., Howard U., 1942; L.H.D. (hon.), Lincoln U., 1953, Women's Med. Coll. Pa., 1954, U. Pitts., 1960, Bethany Coll., 1963; Mus.D. (hon.), Combs Coll. Music, Phila., 1962; H.H.D. (hon.), W.Va. State Coll., 1963; L.H.D., Bethany Coll., 1963, Hahnemann Hosp., 1966; Litt.D., Del. Valley Coll., 1965; LL.D., Muhienberg Coll., 1966; L.H.D., Rutgers U., 1969; m. Johr Lossing Buck, May 13, 1917; children—Carol, Janice; m. 2d, Richard J. Walsh, June 11, 1935 (dec. May 1960); adopted children—Richard, John, Edgar Sydenstricker, Jean C., Henriette, Mary Chieko, Johanna Michiko, Theresa. Tchr. U. Nanking (China), 1921-31, Southeastern U., Nanking, 1925-27, Chung Yank U., Nanking, China, 1918-30. Chmn. bd. Welcome House, Inc., 1956; Pearl S. Buck Found., 1964. Awarded Pulitzer prize, 1932; William Dean Howells medal, 1935; Nobel award in lit., 1938; Skinner award Women's Nat. Book Assn., 1960; Pa. Award for Excellence, Gov.'s Com. 1000,000 Pennsylvanians, 1968; Phila. Club Advt. Women award, 1969; ELA award in Lit., 1969. Mem. Am. Acad. Arts and Letters, Nat. Inst. Arts and Letters, Phi Beta Kappa, Kappa Delta. Club: Cosmopolitan (New York). Author: East Wind-West Wind, 1930; The Young Revolutionist, 1931; The Good Earth (Pulitzer prize), 1931; Sons, 1932; The First Wife and Other Stories, 1933; All Men Are Brothers (translation of the Chinese classic Shul Hu Chuan), 1933; The Mother, 1934; A House Divided, 1935; House of Earth, 1935; The Exile, 1936; Fighting Angel, 1936; This Proud Heart, 1935; The Patriot, 1939; The Chinese Novel, 1939; Other Gods, 1940; Stories for Little Children, 1940; Today and Forever, 1941; Of Men and Women, 1941; Dragon Seed, 1942; American Unity and Asia, 1942; The Chinese Children Next Door, 1942; What America Means to Me, 1943; The Water-Buffalo Children, 1943; The Promise, 1943; The Dragon Fish, 1944; (with James Yen) Tell the People, 1945; Yu-Lan, Flying Boy of China, 1945; Portrait of a Marriage, 1945; (with Masha Scott) Talk about Russia, 1945; Pavilion of Women, 1946; (with Erna von Pustau) How It Happens, 1946; Far and Near, 1947; The Big Wave, 1948; Peony, 1948; (with E.S. Robeson) American Argument, 1949; Kinfolk, 1949; One Bright Day, 1950; The Child Who Never Grew, 1950; God's Men, 1951; The Hidden Flower, 1952; Come My Beloved, 1953; My Several Worlds, 1954; The Beech Tree, 1955; Imperial Woman, 1956; Letter From Peking, 1957; Christmas Miniature, 1957; American Triptych, 1958; (with Carlos P. Romulo) Friend to Friend, 1958; Command The Morning, 1959; Christmas Miniature, 1959; The Christmas Ghost, 1960; Fourteen Stories, 1961; A Bridge for Passing, 1962; The Living Reed, 1963; Welcome Child, 1963; The Joy of Children, 1964; The Big Fight, 1965; (with Gweneth Zarfoss) The Gifts they Bring, 1965; Death in the Castle, 1965; (with Theodore F. Harris) For Spacious Skies, 1966; The Time is Noon, 1967; Matthew, Mark, Luke and John, 1967; To My Daughters, With Love, 1967; The New Year, 1968; The Three Daughters of Madame Liang, 1969; The Good Deed and Other Stories of Asia, Past and Present, 1970, numerous other books. Address: Danby VT Died Mar. 6, 1973.

BUCK, RAYMOND ELLIOTT, lawyer, ins. exec.; b. Ft. Worth, July 13, 1894; s. Raymond H. and Eula E. (Blackmore) B.; student Tex. Christian U., 1911-13; LL.B., U. Tex., 1917; m. Katherine Camp, Dec. 8, 1921; children—Raymond Elliott Buck (deceased), Katherine Camp Buck (Mrs. McDermott). Admitted to Tex. bar, 1919, since in general practice as member Buck & Buck; city atty., Ft. Worth, 1920-22; gen. counsel, dir. So. Air Transport, 1928-30; president Midway Airport Corp., 1948-52; associate gen. counsel Am. Airlines, Inc., from 1929; dir., gen. counsel Trinity Life Ins. Co., 1934-35; dir., gen. counsel Comml. Standard Ins. Co., 1935-43, chmn., gen. counsel, from 1943, pres., from 1952; chmn., past pres., gen. counsel, chmn. exec. com. Comml. Standard Fire & Marine Co., from 1952, Comml. Standard Life Ins. Co., from 1955, Comml. Standard Title Ins. Co., from 1958; owner, operator Raymond E. Buck Ranch & Cattle Co., from 1938; asso. gen. counsel Convair, div. Gen. Dynamics Corp., from 1941; pres. Bucco Homes, Inc., from 1950, Tarrant Land Co., from 1954; v.p., dir. Geyser Corp., from 1964; dir., sec., mem. exec. com. Ft. Worth Air Terminal, Inc., from 1948; dir. Continental Nat. Bank, Forth Worth, vice chairman of bd., mem. exec. com., from 1967. Active mem. internat. bd. electors Ins. Hall of Fame, 1962-65; co-chmn. U. Tex. Internat. Ins. Seminar, bd. govs. Internat. Invitational Ins. Seminar, 1965-66; mem. ins. adv. council and planning commn. U. Tex., U. Tex. Council Bus. Adminstrn. Foundation. Mem. the Governor's Post War Planning Committee on Taxes and Aviation, 1944-47; member of Texas War Bonds Com., 1942-45; director of Ft. Worth Better Bus. Bur., Tex. Technological College Found. Chmn. Young Democrats Tex., 1931-35; finance chmn. Tex. Democratic Party, 1942; Tex. chmn. Jefferson Day Dinner, 1941-42; chmn. Tex. Dem. Conv., 1956; mem. Dem. Adv. Council, 1955. Lay council St. Joseph's Hosp.; citizens council Scott and White Meml. Hosp.; sponsoring com. Nat. Jewish Hosp. at Denver. Served as capt., inf., U.S. Army, 1917-19; AEF in France. Mem. Am., Tex. bar assns., First Officers Tng. Camp Assn. (pres. 1952-53), Texas Univ. Alumni Assn. of Ft. Worth (president 1925), Ft. Worth C. of C. (dir. from 1957, pres. 1962-63), Texas Christian University Ex-Student Assn. (pres. 1949-50), Am. Assn. UN (pres. Ft. Worth from 1964). Clubs: Forth Worth (gov. 1946-57, dir., exec. com.), Town, River Crest Country, Ridglea Country, Admirals (Ft. Worth). Home: Ft Worth TX Died Mar. 27, 1971; interred Greenwood Masoleum, Ft Worth TX

BUCK, WALTER E., pres., treas. Tex. Consol. Oil Co.; pres. Am. Distilling Co. of Cal.; chmn. bd. Nat. Ice & Cold Storage Co.; exec. v.p., dir. Am. Distilling Co., v.p., dir. Am. Comml. Alcohol Corp., Hakalau Plantation Co., Honolulu Plantation Co., dir. Consumers Ice Co. (Sacramento, Cal.), N. Am. Oil Co., City Ice Delivery Co., San Francisco Bank, Anglo-Cal. Nat. Bank of San Francisco, Matson Naviation Co., Oceanic S.S. Co., Pacific Nat. Life Assurance Co., Foremost Dairies, Inc., Foremost Food & Chem. Co., First Western Bank & Trust Co., Firstamerica Corp. Pres., trustee Cal. Palace of Legion of Honor. Home: San Francisco CA Died Sept. 24, 1966.

BUCKINGHAM, BURDETTE ROSS, educationist; b. Riverhead, N.Y., Dec. 9, 1876; s. George A. and Emily D. (Parks) B.;. B.A., Wesleyan U., Conn. 1899, M.A., 1900; Pd.B., State Normal Coll., Albany, N.Y., 1901; Ph.D., Teachers Coll. (Columbia), 1913; Ed.D. from Miami U., 1924; m. Bertha I. Hawkins, Aug. 21, 1901 (deceased 1948); children—George H. (dec.), Leroy H., Burdette H., Inez P.; m. 2d, Edith M. Smith, May 5, 1949. Prin. pub. sch., Northport, N.Y., 1901-04; lectr. edn., mem. faculty Harvard Grad. School of Education, 1928-33; editor with Ginn & Co. since 1928; partner, 1936-39; dir. 1940-46. Member N.E.A. (life), Nat. Soc. Study of Edn. (dir.), Ednl. Research Assn. (twice pres.), Am. Psychol. Assn., A.A.A.S., Nat. Research Council (div. anthropology and psychology), Internat. Assn. Torch Clubs (twice pres.), Psi Upsilon, Phi Beta Kappa, Sigma Xi. Republican. Methodist. Mason. Author: Elementary Arithmetic, Its Meaning and Practice, 1947. Writer numerous articles on phases ednl. research and elementary education. Editor Jour. Ednl. Research, 1920-28, Ednl. Research Bull., 1922-28. Home: 33 Chatham Circle, Wellesley Hills, Mass. Office: Statler Office Bldg., Boston‡

BUCKINGHAM, DAVID EASTBURN, veterinarian; b. Wilmington, Del., Mar. 21, 1870; s. David Eastburn and Sara (Van Trump) B.; grad. high sch., Wilmington, Del., 1888; V.M.D., U. of Pa., 1893; m. Roberta Randall, of N.Y. City, Dec. 8, 1897. Practiced at Washington, D.C., since 1893; insp. and veterinarian Q.-M. General's Office, U.S.A., 1898-1900, and 1916; organizer and dean George Washington U. Coll. of Vet. Medicine, 1908-18; organizer, and pres. Bd. Vet. Med. Examiners, D.C., 1909-12; made disease investigation of foxes, Alaska, for U.S. Biol. Survey, 1924; spl. distemper investigation, Paris, London, Belgium, Switzerland and Holland; consulting toxicologist, Insecticide Div. of U.S. Bur. Chemistry and Soils; propr. Hosp. for Animals; veterinarian to D.C. Republican. Baptist. Mason. Club: Rotary. Home: 3108 Hawthorne St. N.W. Office: 2115 14th St. N.W., Washington DC‡

BUCKINGHAM, EDWARD TAYLOR, lawyer;b. Metuchen, N.J., May 12, 1874; s. Walter Taylor and Helen Emeline (Tolles) B.; A.B., Yale, 1895, LL.B., 1897; m. Bessie L. R. Budau, June 3, 1903; children—Russell Budau (dec.), Edward Taylor Jr. Admitted to Conn. bar, 1897; city clerk, Bridgeport, Conn., 1901-09, mayor, 1909-11, 1929-31, 1931-33; mem. Bd. of Edn., Bridgeport, 1928-31; workmen's compensation commr., State of Conn., 1913-28, 1933-43. Ex-pres. Bridgeport Bar Assn., Yale Alumni Assn. of Fairfield County; pres. Conn. Recreation Assn.; mem. Bridgeport C. of C.; hon. mem. Vets of Fgn. Wars, Disabled Am. Vets., Nat. Naval Vets. of U.S. Mem. Bd. of Recreation, 1921-29, Conn. Motor Club (v.p.), Bridgeport Kiwanis Club (past pres.). Democrat. Conglist. Mason, Elk, Redman. Club: Bridgeport Sportsman (pres.). Home: 2255 Main St. Office: 955 Main St., Bridgeport CT*‡

BUCKLAND CHARLES CLARK, mfg. exec.; b. Cranston, R.I., July 30, 1899; s. Edward Grant and Sally Tyler (Clark) B.; A.B., Yale, 1922; m. Helen Beall Bradley, Dec. 29, 1928; children—Edward Grant 2d, Katharine Scott. With Minneapolis Honeywell Regulator Co. since 1931, sec., 1932, dir. from 1937, v.p. and sec. from 1951. Clubs: Minneapolis, Minikahda (Mpls.). Home: Wayzata MN Died May 26, 1968.

BUCKLE, JOHN FRANKLIN, fgn. service officer; b. Salt Lake City, Sept. 22, 1920; s. John Vivian and Gladys Elizabeth (Frink) B.; A.B., U. Utah, 1941; postgrad. Harvard Law Sch., 1941, Fletcher Sch. Internat. Law and Diplomacy, 1942, U. Cal., 1946; M.A., Sch. Advanced Internat. Studies, 1948; m. Eva Roberta Kratzer, Aug. 30, 1942 (div. 1956); children—Eve Roberta, Michele L.; m. 2d, Mary Jane Vinson, Jan. 1957; children—John Franklin, Guy Jerome. With Bur. Economic Affairs, United States Dept. of State, Washington, 1948-50, Bur. European Affairs, 1952-56; 1st. sec. of embassy, counsul American Embassy, Madrid, Spain, 1956-57; officer in charge of economic affairs, Northern Africa, Bur. African Affairs, 1957-62; 1st sec., chief econ. sect. Am. embassy, Lisbon, Portugal, until 1966; assigned Nat. War Coll., 1966-67; sr. regional adviser Office Regional Affairs, Bur. Nr. East and S. Asian Affairs, 1967-68; dir. Office Maritime Affairs, Bureau Economic Affairs, 1968-69. Served as capt. USMC, 1942-46, PTO, as maj., 1950-52. Korea. Mem. Sigma Nu. Mason. Home: Washington DC Died Sept. 18, 1969.

BUCKLEY, JAMES R., congressman; b. Nov. 18, 1870. V.p. Universal Granite Quarries; Dem. nominee for clk. Superior Court of Cook Co., Ill., 1908; mem. City Council, Chicago, 1910; del. Dem. Nat. Conv., 1908, 12, 16; mem. 68th Congress (1923-25), 6th Ill. Dist. Home: 3517 5th Av., Chicago IL‡

BUCKLEY, MAY, actress; b. at San Francisco, Cal., Dec. 15, 1875. First appeared on stage in child's part, in May Blossom," San Francisco; toured with Lawrence Barrett and Edwin Booth 2 yrs.; joined stock co. at Alcazar Theatre, San Francisco, and won first success as Loey Tsing in The First Born'" debut in London, Eng., at Globe Theatre, Nov. 1, 1897, again in London, in A Man of the World," at Comedy Theatre, 1905; has played in One Summer's Day," The Manxman," Cameo Kirby," The Little Damozel," etc.*‡

BUCKLIN, GEORGE AUGUSTUS, consul; b. West Hartford, Mo., Oct. 5, 1875; s. George Augustus and Mary Ann (Williamson) B.; Southwest Kansas Coll., 1893-95; in law office, 1895-97; A.B., U. of Okla., 1903; A.M., Yale, 1904; m. Emeline Wood Porter, of Peterboro, Ont., Can., Aug. 17, 1904. Registrar, 1900-03, prof. and head dept. economics and sociology, 1904-06, U. of Okla.; Am. consul at Glauchau, Germany, 1906-08, at San Luis Potosi, Mex., 1908-10; consul gen. at Guatemala City, Guatemala, 1910-14; consul at Bordeaux, France, Feb. 1914-Oct. 1919, where was in charge of many spl. war actvities in conjunction with U.S. mil. and naval operations; detailed to assist in Consulate-General, Paris, Oct. 1919-20; consul, in charge of Coblenz office of the Am. Commn., Oct. 1920-May 1922; consul, Acapulco, Mexico, 1922-24, Victoria, B.C., Can., 1924-34; consul gen. Wellington, New Zealand, 1934-37. Mem. Phi Beta Kappa. Address: Dept. of State, Washington DC‡

BUCKMAN, HENRY HOLLAND II, cons. civil engr.; b. Jacksonville, Fla., Oct. 25, 1886; s. Henry Holland and Sarah Caruthers (Allison) B.; B.S., Harvard, 1908; postgrad. student univs. Berlin, Leipzig, also Royal Tech. Coll., Charlottenburg; m. Mildred Regester, Apr. 26, 1911; children—Allison Caruthers (Mrs. B. Bassett), Henry Holland III, Yardley Drake. Mineral exploration, 1908, in Mongolia, 1909-15; designed, constructed 1st comml. electric furnaces in U.S., 1915-22; discovered rare earth, radioactive mineral deposits of Fla., developing for comml. uses 1915-22; dir. exploration for tin ores in fgn. countries, developed uses for titanium, made surveys for stream salinity and meteorological research and for nonmetallic minerals of Ala., Ga., Fla., 1922-68; cons. engr., specializing in river and harbors, stream pollution, inland navigation and transportation, canalization, 1934-68; engring. counsel Ship Canal Authority Fla., 1948-68; engring. counsel Fla. Inland Navigation Dist.; dir., vice chmn. project com. Nat. Rivers and Harbors Congress, 1939-68, pres., 1961. Tech. counsel com. fgn. affairs on strategic materials, U.S. Ho. of Reps., 1935-36; cons. Chem. Warfare Service, World War II, to Dept. of State at London Internat. Tin Conf., 1946. Mem. Am. Soc. C.E. (corp.). Jacksonville Hist. Soc. (past pres.), Sigma Alpha Epsilon. Protestant Episcopalian. Clubs: Harvard (past pres. Fla.; past v.p. asso. clubs). Author reports and documents. Home: Orange Park FL Died Mar. 5, 1968; buried Evergreen Cemetery, Jacksonville FL

BUCKNELL, HOWARD, JR., corp. exec. (ret.); b. Philadelphia, Feb. 17, 1899; s. Howard and Marie Ethel (Harlan) B.; student Chateau de Rosy (Rolle, Switzerland), 1912-13, Fleet Sch. (Hendersonville, N.C.), 1914-19, U. of Ga., 1916-18; m. Lucy Barrow Taylor, Apr. 19, 1922; children—Howard, III, John Addison Cobb. Student interpreter, China, 1919-21; vice consul, Chungking and later Peking, 1921; vice consul and interpreter, Changsha, 1921, Canton, 1922-24; asst. mixed-court assessor, Shanghai, 1924-25, senior, same, 1925-27; became secretary Diplomatic Service, 1927; 3d sec. Peking, 1927-29; rep. Am. minister to China in regard to Provisional Court, Shanghai, 1929-30; 2d sec., Panama, 1930-32, Belgrade, 1932-34; Dept. of State, Washington, D.C., 1934-36; press officer Inter-Am. Conf. for Maintenance of Peace, Buenos Aires, 1936; asst. chief div. current information, 1937; consul, Geneva, 1937-39; consul, later consul gen., Barcelona, 1939-40; 1st sec., consul gen., counselor of Embassy, Madrid, 1940; asst. chief div. current information, Dept. of State, 1940-43; minister counselor of Embassy, London, 1944; resigned, 1945; vice pres. International Telephone & Telegraph Corp., 1945-49; retired. Clubs: National Press, Army-Navy, Congressional Country (Washington, D.C.). Home: Athens GA Died June 22, 1971; buried Oconef Hill Cemetery, Athens GA

BUDA, JOSEPH, textile co. exec.; b. Lodz, Poland, Dec. 20, 1917; s. Herman and Maria (Gross) B.; grad textile technician, Ecole de Textiles, Tournai, Belgium, 1938; m. Miriam Boreustein, Dec. 22, 1946; children—Henry Michael, David Newton. Came to U.S., 1948, naturalized, 1952. With textile bus., Lodz, 1938-39; with Beaunit Mills, Inc., N.Y.C., from 1948, dept. mgr., 1953-61, v.p. charge elastic operations, from 1961. Mem. Textile Salesmens Assn., Assn. Textile Technicians. Home: Syosset LI Died Nov. 19, 1962

BUDD, EDWARD G., JR., business exec.; b. Philadelphia, Pa., Mar. 23, 1902; s. Edward G. and Mary Louisa (Wright) B.; B.S., Wesleyan U., 1923; m. Ruth P. Blydenburgh, June 13, 1925; 1 dau., Mary Francenia; m. 2d, Althea de Baun, Nov. 23, 1960. With The Budd Company, Phila., 1923-71, dir., 1938-71, exec. v.p., 1943-46, pres., later chmn., chief exec., until 1967; dir. Tasty Baking Co.; trustee Greenfield Real Estate Investment Trust; Bell Telephone Co. of Pa.; mem. bd. trustees Penn Mut. Life Ins. Co. Mem. bd. mgrs. Savs. Fund Soc. of Germantown; trustee Phila. Coll. Art, Phila. Mus. Art. Clubs: Phila. Country, Rittenhouse (Phila.). Home: Bryn Mawr PA Died May 20, 1971; buried West Laurel Hill Cemetery, Bala-Cynwyd PA

BUDD, NATHAN P., coll. dean; b. Reading, Kan., Apr. 29, 1911; s. Charles Albert and Ethel (McKeehen) B.; B.S. in Edn., Kan. State Teachers Coll., Emporia, 1946; M.A., U. Colo., 1949, Ed.D., 1956; m. Helen Raikes, Dec. 28, 1941; children—Michael Nathan, Pamela Sue, Joan Elizabeth. Tchr. country schs., Kan., 1930-35, elementary schs., Kan., 1935-37; tchr. math., coach Osage City (Kan.) Jr. High Sch., 1937-40; jr. high sch. prin., Stafford, Kan., 1946-48; mem. faculty Kan. State Tchrs. Coll., 1949-71; dean instrn., 1957-71; visiting prof. Univ. Minn., summers 1964-67. Served to capt. AUS, 1942-46. Mem. Am. Personnel and Guidance Assn. (pres. U. Colo. 1956), N.E.A., Kan. Tchrs. Assn., Emporia C. of C., N. Central Assn. Acad. Deans, (pres. 1966-67), Phi Delta Kappa, Kappa Delta Pi, Blue Key. Methodist (ofcl. bd.). Rotarian. Editor: The Faculty Role in Working with Students as Persons, 1965; Assessment of Teacher Competencies, 1964; The Teacher Education Program as a Total Institutional Responsibility, 1966; Improving Instruction, 1967. Home: Emporia KS Died Nov. 28, 1971; buried Meml. Lawn Cemetery, Emporia KS

BUDENZ, LOUIS FRANCIS, journalist; b. Indianapolis, Ind., July 17, 1891; s. Henry Joseph and Mary Gertrude (Sullivan) B.; student St. Xavier's Coll., Cin.; St. Mary's Coll.; LL.B., Indpls. Law School, Indianapolis, 1912; m. Margaret D. Rodgers; children—Julia, Josephine (now Mrs. Donald A. Palermo), Justine, Joanna. Began as asso. editor The Carpenter, organ of United Brotherhood of Carpenters and Joiners, 1912-13; asst. dir. Central Bur. of Central Verein, St. Louis, Mo., 1913-14; sec. St. Louis Civic League, 1914-19; franchise expert, Fed. Electric Rys. Commn., 1920; publicity dir. Am. Civil Liberties Union, 1920-21; editor The Labor Age, 1921-31; organizer for special situation, A.F. of L. unions, 1927-34; leading strikes in Kenosha, Wis., 1928, Nazareth, Pa., 1929, Paterson Silk, 1930, Toledo Auto Lite, 1934; tried 21 times in labor disputes and acquitted 21 times; labor editor, The Daily Worker, 1935-37; editor Midwest Daily Record, Chicago, 1937-40; pres. and mng. editor The Daily Worker, 1940-45; prof. econ., Notre Dame U., 1945-46; prof. econ. Fordham U., 1946-56, ret.; adviser on Communist research to Cardinal Cushing, 1959-63; prof. Seton Hall U., 1952; witness for govt. in numerous Communist trials; columnist Nat. Cath. Welfare Conf. News Service, 1948-63. Mem. Am. Econ. Assn., Am. Acad. Polit. and Social Science, Acad. Polit. Sci. Roman Catholic. Author: This Is My Story, 1946; Men Without Faces, 1950; The Cry is Peace, 1952; The Techniques of Communism (textbook), 1953; Ex-Red (in newspaper syndicated series), 1954; The Bolshevik Invasion of the West, 1965. Contbr. articles to nat. mags. Home: Newport RI Died Apr. 27, 1972; buried St. Columba's Cemetery, Middletown RI

BUDROW, LESTER RUSK, mining engr.; b. Ogden, Ia., Mar. 17, 1877; s. William C. and Rebecca (Beauchamp) B.; Ph.B., State U. of Ia., 1897; spl. course, Sch. of Mines of Mo., Rollo, Mo., 1898-9; m. Ruth Niles, of San Diego, Cal., Nov. 20, 1906. With M. Guggenheim Sons or affiliated cos., 1899-05; general supt. Tiro General Mine, Charcas, S.L.P., Mexico, 1905-7; gen. supt. Cia Metalurgica de Michoacan, Angangneo, Mex., 1907-8; mgr. Michoacan & Pacific Ry. & Mining Co., 1908-9; gen. mgr. Tigre Mining Co., Yzabal, Sonora, Mexico, Nov., 1909—; v.-p. Hunter Av. Realty Co., Kansas City, Mo.; gen. mgr. The Tigre Mining Co., S.A., Esqueda, Sonora, Mex. Mem. Am. Inst. Mining Engineers, 1902, Beta Theta Pi. Club: American (Mexico City). Home: 2346 3d St., San Diego, Cal. Office: Douglas AZ‡

BUEHLER, ALBERT CARL, mfg. exec.; b. Chicago, June 20, 1897; s. Carl and Rose (Stupp) B.; student U. of Illinois, 1919; m. Fern Davis;children—Carl, Barbara, Bert, Rose. With Victor Comptometer Corporation, Chgo., 1920-71, pres., 1932-64, chief executive officer, 1964-71, chmn. bd., 1932-71. Mem. Kappa Sigma. Clubs: Athletic, Chicago (Chicago); Barrington Hills Country (Barrington, Ill.). Home: Barrington IL Died Sept. 1971.

BUEHLER, ALFRED GRETHER, educator, tax economist; b. Swanton, O., May 10, 1900; s. John J. and Louise (Grether) B.; A.B., Heidelberg Coll., 1922, L.H.D., 1950; A.M., Yale, 1923, Ph.D., 1930; m. Marian Sheffer, Sept. 8, 1925; children—Philip G., Gretchen H. Asst. prof. bus. adminstrn. Lawrence Coll., 1924-25; asst. prof. econs., then asso. prof. U. Vt., 1925-39; asso. prof. pub. finance U. Pa., 1939-42, prof., from 1942, dir., founder U. Pa. Pub. Finance Center, from 1962. Tax cons. to fed., state, local govts.; chmn. Pa. Tax Study Com., 1951-55; mem. Conn. Tax Study Commn., 1957-59; vice chmn. Pa. Tax Adminstrn. Study Com., 1963-66. Mem. Phila. Citizens Budget Com., from 1953; chmn. U. Pa. Ann. Tax Conf. Trustee Tax Found. Served with U.S. Army, WW I. Recipient Pa. medal for distinguished service, 1955. Mem. Nat. Municipal League, Tax Inst. America (mem. adv. council, pres. 1950), National Tax Association (pres. 1951-52), Am. Econ. Assn., Am. Finance Assn., Internat. Inst. Pub. Finance, Am. Polit. Sci. Assn. Am. Acad. Polit. and Social Sci., Am. Assn. U. Profs., N.E. State Tax Ofcls. Assn. (hon.), Phi Beta Kappa, Tau Kappa Alpha, Pi Kappa Delta, Lambda Alpha. Baptist. Author: General Sales Taxation, 1932; Public Finance, 1936, 3d edit., 1948; The Undistributed Profits Tax, 1937; other books on taxation and govt. finance. Contbr. to Ency. Social Scis., also articles to profl. jours. Home: Devon PA Died Jan. 12, 1970.

BUELL, ROBERT CATLIN, JR., banker; b. Hartford, Conn., Aug. 11, 1911; s. Robert Catlin and Elizabeth (Goodrich) B.; B.A., U. Va., 1936; grad. Stonier Grad. Sch. Banking, 1952; m. Mary Easter Stilson, Aug. 17, 1940; 1 dau., Mary Buell (Mrs. Frank E. Bassett). With Hartford Nat. Bank (Conn.), 1936-70, sr. v.p., 1960-64, exec. v.p., 1964-70, corporator Savings Bank of New London; dir. Hartford National Bank & Trust Company, Pres., dir. Greater New London (Conn.) C. of C., 1950. Campaign chmn. United Fund Southeastern Conn., 1963-64; pres. Lawrence & Meml. Benefactors Soc., 1961. Trustee Lawrence & Meml. Hosp., 1958-70, v.p., 1962; bd. dirs. Newington Hosp. Crippled Children, 1964-70, Marine Hist. Asnn., 1959; bd. corporators Hartford Hosp., 1965-70, St. Francis Hosp., 1966-70; bd. dirs. Elmcrest Manor, Inc., 1952-70; corporator Inst. Living; trustee, treas. Health Care Facilities Planning Council Greater Hartford; Served to 1st lt. AUS, 1942-46. Mem. Conn. C. of C. (dir.), Zeta Psi. Clubs: Thames (New London); Hartford. Home: West Hartford CT Died Apr. 25, 1970; buried Old St. Andrews Ch., North Bloomfield CT

BUETOW, HERBERT P(AUL), mfg. exec., banker; b. St. Paul, Jan. 25, 1898; s. Charles A. and Henriette (Ramlow) B.; A.B., U. of Minn., 1921; LL.D., Valparaiso (Ind.) University, 1964; m. Luella R. Witt, June 24, 1924; 1 dau., Shirley J. Office boy Waldorf Paper Co., St. Paul, 1913-16; accountant St. Paul Athletic Club, 1916-18; staff accountant Bishop-Brissman & Co., 1918-20, sr. accountant City of St. Paul, 1920-21; staff accountant State of Minnesota, 1922-25; auditor Minnesota Mining & Mfg. Co., 1926-35, controller 1935-39, treas., 1939-49, exec. v.p., 1949-53, pres., 1953-63, chmn. finance com., 1963-68, also dir.; pres., dir. SPH Hotel Co., from 1963; dir. 1st Trust Co., St. Paul; pres. 1st Merchants State Bank, 1948-55, chmn., from 1955; dir. 1st Nat. Bank, Theo. Hamm Brewing Co., several Minn. Mining & Mfg. Co. subsidiaries; trustee Minnesota Mutual Life Ins. Co. Decorated Comdr. Order Lion and White Rose (Finland); recipient U.S. Chamber of Commerce Great Living Am. award, 1961. Mem. adv. council Nat. Bus. Aircraft Assn., Inc., 1955-59. Mem. St. Paul C. of C. (chmn. bd. 1965), Nat. Indsl. Conf. Bd., Controllers Inst. Am. (nat. dir. and v.p. 1945-48, trustee, mem. adv. council Controllership Found., 1952-53). Clubs: Union League (Chgo.); Midland Hills Country, Pool and Yacht, St. Paul Athletic, Town and Country, Minnesota. Home: St Paul MN Died Jan. 8, 1972; buried Elmhurst Cemetery, St. Paul MN

BUGG, BENJAMIN LAMAR, ry. executive; b. Palo Alto, Miss., Aug. 8, 1869; s. Thomas Elliott and Emma (Shotwell) B.; edn. high sch. and under private instrn.; m. Mabel Dodd, Mar. 15, 1892; 1 dau., Mildred (dec.). Terminal agt. Central of Ga. Ry., at Savannah, 1901-07; gen. agt. Old Dominion S.S. Co., Norfolk, Va., 1907-10; traffic mgr. Norfolk Southern Ry., 1910-12; apptd. asst. gen. mgr., A.B.&A. Ry., 1912, gen. mgr., 1916, v.p. and gen. mgr. 1917, pres., 1920, receiver, 1921-26; pres. Atlanta, Birmingham & Coast R.R., 1927-45; retired July 1, 1945. Commissioned lieutenant colonel, engineers, United States Army, May 22, 1918; sailed for France in command 66th Regt. Engineers, June 30, 1918; comd. camps Gron. Raymond, St. Pierre des Corps and 20th Grand Div. Transportation Corps; discharged May 29, 1919. Chevalier Legion of Honor (French). Mem. Am. Ry. Engring. Assn., Soc. Am. Mil. Engrs. Baptist. Scottish Rite Mason, Shriner. Home: 34 Inman Circle, N.E., Atlanta GA‡

BUGG, LELIA HARDIN, author; b. at Ironton, Mo., of Southern ancestry; grad. Ursuline Acad., Arcadia, Mo.; studied under pvt. masters for lit., history and music; spl. course in philosophy and modern langs., Trinity Coll., Washington; spent 2 yrs. in study and travel in Europe; unmarried. Author: The Correct Thing for Catholics, 1893; A Lady, 1894; Correct English, 1895; Orchids—A Novel, 1896; The Prodigal's Daughter, 1898; The People of Our Parish, 1899. Contbr. to mags. Address: Wichita KS‡

BUGGELLI, BLANCHE SWETT (MOWRY), author; b. Garland, Me., Jan. 4, 1870; d. Henry A. and Mary Marilla (Preble) Swett; grad. high sch., Gloucester, Mass., 1887; m. Arthur May Mowry, July 5, 1888, at Gloucester, Mass.; 2d, Rev. Giuseppe Buggelli, Jan. 1, 1913. Head worker House of Good Will, E. Boston, Mar., 1908-Jan., 1913. Mem. Presbyn. Ch. Co-Author: First Steps in the History of England, 1902; American Heroes and Heroism, 1903; American Pioneers, 1905; Essentials of American History, 1906. Address: 345 Chestnut St., Detroit‡

BULEY, R. CARLYLE, historian, univ. prof.; born Georgetown, Ind., July 8, 1893; s. David Marion and Nora (Keithley) B.; A.B., Ind. U., 1914. A.M., 1916; Ph.D., U. of Wis., 1925; Litt.D., Coe College, Cedar Rapids, Ia., 1958; m. Esther Giles, June 21, 1919 (died 1921); m. 2d, Evelyn Barnett, Aug. 5, 1926. Teacher history, Delphi and Muncie (Ind.) high schs., 1914-18; head dept. and asst. prin. Springfield (Ill.) High Sch., also prin. Knights of Columbus evening schs., 1919-23; asst.-instr. U. of Wis., 1923-25; instr. advancing to prof. Am. history Ind. University, Bloomington, 1925-64, prof. emeritus, 1964-68. Served as pvt. advancing to sgt. 1st class, U.S. Army, 1918-19. Mem. Am., Miss. Valley hist. assns., Ind., Ohio hist. socs., Republican. Author: The Political Balance in the Old Northwest, 1926; The Old Northwest Pioneer Period, 1815-1840 (2 vols.) (Pulitzer prize in history, 1951), 1950; The American Life Convention—A Study in the History of Life Insurance (2 vols.) (Elizur Wright award 1954), 1953; The Equitable Life Assurance Society of the United States, 1859-1959, 1959; The Equitable Life Assurance Society of the United States 1859-1964, 2 vols., 1967. Co-author: The Midwest Pioneer—His Ills, Cures and Doctors, 1945. Editor: The Indiana Home, 1947. Home: Bloomington IN Died Apr. 25, 1968; buried Beech Grove Cemetery, Muncie IN

BULL, ALFRED CASTLEMAN, banker; b. Austin, Tex., Dec. 20, 1893; s. Richard Platt and Margaret (Castleman) B.; grad. Austin Acad., 1912; B.S., Tex. A. and M. Coll., 1916; m. Edna Hazlewood, July 2, 1924 (dec. 1943); 1 son, Richard Hazlewood; m. 2d, Alice Archer, Oct. 20, 1951. Partner, Bull & DeViney, gen. ins. agy., 1919-25; v.p., dir. Tex. Bank & Trust Co., Austin, 1926-33; v.p., dir. Am. Nat. Bank, Austin, 1936-61, chmn. bd., 1961-67. Mem. Tex. Library and Hist. Com., 1940-44; chmn. Travis chpt. A.R.C., 1945-46. Mem. sch. bd., Austin, 1938-43. Served as capt., inf., U.S. Army, 1917-19. Mem. Austin C. of C. (pres. 1934), Am. Bankers Assn. Episcopalian. Mason (33 deg.). Clubs: Austin, Austin Country. Home: Austin TX Died Dec. 27, 1967; buried Oakwood Cemetery, Austin TX

BULL, GEORGE MAIRS, cons. civil engr.; b. Troy, N.Y., Mar. 15, 1873; s. Rice C. and Catharine (Johnson) B.; C.E., Rensselaer Poly. Inst., 1897; Dr. Engring., Colo. Sch. of Mines, 1938, U. of Colo., 1940; m. Sara E. Baker, June 1, 1910. Asst. engr. on contract work reconstructing original Erie Canal, 1897-98; employed by C.&W. Ry. Co. and located the foundation of Boone Viaduct across Des Moines River, 1899-1900; returned to Troy, N.Y., 1900; deputy city engr., Troy, N.Y., 1900-03, in charge of constrn. and maintaining municipal structures; resident engr. in office N.Y. State Barge Canal, 1903-06; with J. G. White Engring. Corp., 1906-09; engr. Arnold Co. of Chicago, 1909; private practice as cons. engr., Denver, 1910-18; developing Pub. Works Program for Denver, Colo., 1920-33; apptd. state engr. P.W.A., Colo., 1933, state dir. P.W.A., 1935-37, regional dir. for 7 southwestern states, 1937-40; in private practice as cons. engr., 1940; returned to service with the Office of Prodn. Management, 1941, as field rep. in the southwestern states; later apptd. regional dir. P.W.A. Defense Construction Program in the Rocky Mountain States; in 1943 appointed Colo. state dir. Office of Price Administration; returned to private practice as cons. engr., 1945. Served as 1st class private, 1st Vol. Engrs., 1898-99; lt. comdr. Civil Engr. Corps, U.S. Naval Res., 1918-22. Mem. Am. Soc. Civil Engrs., Colo. Soc. Engrs., Rensselaer Soc. of Engrs. Presbyterian. Club: Denver Athletic. Home: 3910 Perry St., Denver CO‡

BULLARD, DANIEL R., corp. exec.; b. Opelika, Ala., Apr. 6, 1894; s. Charles Clarence and Carrie (Fisher) B.; A.B., LL.B., Houston Law Sch., 1928; C.P.A., Internat. Accounting Soc., 1929; m. Eleonore Rau, Dec. 26, 1921; children—Daniel R., William C. With Weil Bros., Montgomery, Ala., 1913-17, Anderson Clayton Co., 1919-21, Humble Oil & Refining Co., 1921-24; with Mound Co., Houston, from 1924, chmn. bd., from 1955; with Fidelity Oil & Royalty Co., Houston, 1924 from pres., 1931-55; dir. Bank of Southwest, Houston. Bd. govs. William Marsh Rice U., 1953-61, trustee, 1961; bd. dirs. Tex. Med. Center, 1956; sr. pres., trustee

Robert A. Welch Found., 1952. Served to lt. col., inf., U. S. Army, 1917-19. Mem. Tex., Houston bar assns., Tex. Soc. C.P.A.'s, Photog. Soc. Am. Clubs: River Oaks Country, Ramada; St. Charles Bay Hunting. Home: Houston TX Died Apr. 16, 1972; interred Ch. of St. John the Divine, Houston TX

BULLARD, EDWARD CLARKE, ret. business exec.; b. Bridgeport, Conn., Mar. 13, 1896; s. Dudley Brewster and Alice Anna (Clarke) Bullard; student Curtis Sch., Brookfield Centre, Conn., 1906-10, Univ. Sch., Bridgeport, 1910-14; M.E., Yale, 1917; m. Ruth Leslie Johnson, June 28, 1920; children—Brewster Leslie, David Edward. Asso. with The Bullard Co., mfrs. machine tools, Bridgeport, 1919-73; past dir. New Haven R.R., Northeastern Steel Co., So. New Eng. Telephone Co. Rolock, Inc., Conn. Nat. Bank of Bridgeport. Served in Ordnance Dept., U.S. Army, World War I. Mem. Am. Soc. M.E., S.A.R., Sigma Xi, Phi Sigma Kappa. Conglist. Mason. Home: Southport CT Died Jan. 10, 1973; buried Fairfield CT

BULLARD, ROBERT FELTON, govt. ofcl.; b. Nashville, Ga., Sept. 10, 1908; s. Adrian E. and Mattie (Tygart) B.; student bus. adminstrn. U. Ga., 1925-27, accounting Ga. Carolina Bus. Coll., 1928, agrl. econs. N.C. State Coll., 1941; m. Lyda Grace Hutchinson, Apr. 9, 1939; 1dau. Rebecca. Tchr. Berrien County (Ga.) pub. schs., 1929-34; co. agt., 1935-37; with A.A.A., Berrien Co., 1938-45; dist. supr. Fed. Crop Ins. Corp., Ga., 1946-48, field underwriter Southeastern states, 1949-51, sales mgmt. div., Washington, 1952-53, area dir. Southeastern states, 1953-69. Home: Nashville GA Died Jan. 6, 1969; buried Westview Cemetery, Nashville GA

BULLEN, PERCY SUTHERLAND, newspaper man; b. Hastings, Eng., Mar. 21, 1868; s. late Capt. Richard Edward B. (of Royal Navy) and Laura Emma (Attwood) B.; g.s. Admiral Sir Charles B., in comd. H.M.S., Britannia at Battle of Trafalgar; ed. St. Anne's Streatham Hill, London; m. Bertha, d.late Richard Clark, of London, Eng., Aug. 4, 1898; children—Daisy Gertrude, Percy S., Norman S., Kenneth S., Godfrey S. Has traveled largely in Europe and Morocco; war corr. in Egypt and South Africa during Boer War; visited British front in France in 1916, as guest of the British government; represented newspapers in London, Paris, Rome and Berlin; staff corr. London Daily Telegraph, 1895-1934. Organizer and hon. sec. Dollar Christmas Fund for destitute Belgians, 1915, over 300,000 being contributed; raised 15,000 as Am. contribution to Dickens' Centennial Memorial, London; also $5,000 Am. gift to memorial of Scott, the Arctic explorer. Chairman of League of Remembrance for Celebration of Armistice Day. Fellow and corr. sec. Inst. Journalists, London; pres. of Assn. of Foreign Press Correspondents in U.S.A., 1919; fellow Royal Colonial Inst.; hon. sec., 1926-31, Am. Shakespeare Foundation, working in cooperation with British Committee to rebuild and endow the Shakespeare Memorial Theatre, Stratford-on-Avon. Officier de l'Instruction Publique (France); the Verdun Medal inscribed For Service to France"; Chevalier Order of Leopold II (Belgium); Chevalier Order of Redeemer (Greece); Cavaliere of the Order of the Crown (Italy); Queen Victoria Medal S. African War; awarded first medal conferred upon a foreign corr. by U. of Mo. (Dept. of Journalism), 1930. Author of various brochures, relating to the European war; contbr. on mil. and naval topics, etc. Address: care National City Bank, Long Beach NY‡

BULLOCK, CHANDLER, life insurance; b. Worcester, Mass., Aug. 24, 1872; s. Augustus George and Mary (Chandler) B.; A.B., Harvard, 1894, LL.B., 1897; m. Mabel Richardson, Oct. 17, 1900; children—Margaret (Mrs. Edward C. Thayer), Rose (Mrs. Roger W. Converse), Noeline (Mrs. Oliver S. Chute), Vera (Mrs. George S. McElroy). Admitted to Mass. bar, 1897, and began practice as atty. State Mut. Life Assurance Co. at Worcester, gen. counsel, 1903, v.p., 1920-27, pres., 1927-42, chmn. bd. 1942-49, now hon. chmn.; trustee Worcester Five Cents Savs. Bank; dir. Worcester Co. Electric Co., Worcester County Trust Company, Boston & Albany R.R., Providence & Worcester R.R. Chmn. of a dist. Selective Service Board, World War I. Past mem. bd. trustees Worcester Pub. Library; dir. Worcester Traveler's Aid Soc.; dir. Worcester Children's Friend Soc. Mem. Am. Antiquarian Soc. (treas., mem. council), Worcester Chamber Commerce (pres. 1943-44). Repbulican. Episcopalian. Mason. Clubs: Shakespeare, Bohemian. Harvard Club (Boston). Home: 41 Server St. Office: State Mutual Life Assurance Co., Worcester‡

BULMAN, JOHN NOEL THOMPSON, lithographer; b. Winnipeg, Manitoba, Can., Dec. 25, 1900; s. William John and Lily (Thompson) B.; grad. Royal Mil. Coll., Kingston, Ont.; m. Ruth Odell Antliff, June 3, 1925; children—Ruth Elizabeth (Mrs. George Frederick Bondar), William John Antliff, Nancy Jean (Mrs. Antony Kingsmill Stephens). Began career as an apprentice plate maker Lithographic Trade, 1920-25; supt. Bulman Bros., Ltd., 1925-30, sales mgr. 1934-38, pres., gen. mgr., 1938-71, chmn. of the board, 1964-71; dir. Norfield-Bulman Ltd., Winnipeg; dir. Bulloch's Ltd., Cable Ltd., Wawanesa Mut. Ins. Co., Wawanesa Mutual Life Ins. Co., Western Business Forms, Ltd. Mem. bd. regents United Coll. Past pres. Canadian Mfrs. Assn., Manitoba div. Canadian Red Cross Soc. Mem. United Church of Can. Clubs: Manitoba; Rotary (past pres.) (Winnipeg); National Travel (N.Y.C.). Home: Winnipeg Died 1971.

BUMGARNER, RAY QUINCY, hosp. supt.; b. Wauneta, Kan., Nov. 8, 1902; s. Walter A. and Emma (Goode) B.; student Marquette U., 1922-23, U. Wis. at Milw., 1940-41; m. Thelma E. Leyden, Oct. 16, 1945; 1 son, Ray Quincy. Engaged in pvt. business, 1923-40; bus. adminstr. Milw. County instns., 1940-46; with VA, 1946, dir. VA Center, Dayton, O., 1959. Pres. Met. Hosp. Fedn., Dayton, 1967; chmn. adv. com. hosp. facilities Dayton Hosp. Planning Council, 1968; mem. exec. com., interagy bd. U.S. Civil Service Examiner So. Ohio, 1968; chmn. Fed. Exec. Assn., 1968. Served to capt. AUS, 1943-46. Decorated Army Commendation medal; recipient awards D.A.V., Am. Legion, V.F.W. Fellow Am. Coll. Hosp. Adminstrs. Club: Walnut Grove Country (Dayton). Home: Dayton OH Died Aug. 3, 1972.

BUMSTEAD, CHARLES W., pres. and dir. George W. Helme Co., New York, N.Y.; b. Jersey City, N.J., 1873. Home: Helmetta, N.J. Office: George W. Helme Co., 9 Rockefeller Plaza, New York 20 NY*‡

BUNCHE, RALPH JOHNSON, U.N. ofcl. b. Detroit, Mich., Aug. 7, 1904; s. Fred and Olive Agnes (Johnson) B.; A.B., U. C.L.A., 1927; A.M., Harvard U., 1928, Ph.D., 1934; post-doctoral work in anthropology and colonial policy, Northwestern U., London Sch. of Economics and U. of Capetown, South Africa, 1936-37; numerous honorary degress; married to Ruth Ethel Harris, June 23, 1930; children—Joan Harris, Jane (dec.), Ralph Johnson. Ozias Goodwin fellow, Harvard Univ., 1929; Rosenwald fellowship, Europe, Eng., N. and West Africa, 1931-32; Social Sci. Research Council post-doctoral fellowship in Europe, South and East Africa, Malaya and Netherlands Indies, 1936-38; staff mem. Carnegie Corp's. Survey of Negro in America, 1939. Asst. in polit. science, U. of Cal. at Los Angeles, 1925-27; instr. polit. science, Howard U., 1928-29, asst. prof., 1929-33, asst. to pres., 1930-31, asso. prof., 1933-38, prof. since 1938, head of dept., 1929-50; co-dir. Inst. of Race Relations, Swarthmore, 1936; professor government Harvard, 1950-52; senior social science analyst in charge of research on Africa and other colonial areas, British Empire sect., Office of Strategic Services, 1941-44, deputy chief Near East-Africa sect., 1943, chief Africa sect., June 1943-Jan. 1944; with the Department of State, 1944-47; adviser, U.S. Delegation, 27th Session International Labour Conference, Phila., April, 1945; asst. sec., U.S. Delegation, Dumbarton Oaks, Aug.-Oct., 1944; adviser U.S. Delegation, U.N.C.I.O., San Francisco, Mar.-June, 1945, U.S. Delegation, exec. com. U.N., London, Sept.-Nov., 1945; U.S. Delegation, 28th Session Internat. Labour Conf., Paris, Oct., 1945, U.S. Delegation Gen. Assembly, U.N., London, Jan., 1946; Presidential appointment U.S. Commr., Caribbean Commn., Sept., 1945-June 1947; U.S. Commr., West Indian Conf. (2d session), St. Thomas, Virgin Islands, Feb.-Mar., 1946; director, Div. Trusteeship, UN, 1946-48, principal dir. Dept. Trusteeship, 1948-54, under-sec., 1955; under sec. for speical political affairs UN, 1958-67, undersecretary general, from 1968. Principle secretary, U.N. Palestine Commn., 1948; acting U.N. Mediator on Palestine, 1948, 1949; UN spl. Rep. in Congo, 1960, United Nations Mission to Yemen, 1963. Prof. govt. Harvard 1950-52. Mem. bd. of higher edn. N.Y.C., 1958-64. Trustee Oberlin College; mem. bd. overseers Harvard, 1960-65. Recipient of Spingarn medal by Nat. Assn. for Advancement of Colored People, 1949; Nobel Peace Prize, 1950; Theodore Roosevelt Assn. Medal of Honor, 1954; Third Order of St. Frances Peace Award, 1954, Presidential Medal of Freedom (U.S.A.), 1963. Member Polit. Sci. Assn. (past pres.), Am. Philos. Soc. Home: Kew Gardens NY Died Dec. 9, 1971; buried Woodlawn Cemetery, Bronx NY

BUNGE, HELEN LATHROP, school administrator; b. LaCrosse, Wis., Oct. 11, 1906; d. George W. and Sarah (Wheeler) Bunge; A.B., U. of Wis., 1928, Diploma in Nursing, 1930; M.A.; Columbia, 1936, Ed.D., 1950. Faculty U. of Wis. Sch. Nursing, 1931-40; asst. prof. nursing Frances Bolton Sch. of Nursing, Western Reserve U., 1942, asso. prof. nursing, 1943-46, prof. and dean of nursing 1946-53; exec. ofcr., Inst. Research and Servce in Nursing Edn., Tchrs. Coll., Columbia, 1953-59; dir. sch. nursing, asso. dean sch. nursing U. Wis., 1959-67, dean, 1967-70. Mem. Phi Beta Kappa, Pi Lambda Theta, Alpha Kappa Delta, Gamma Phi Beta. Address: Madison WI Died Apr. 12, 1970.

BUNKLEY, JOEL WILLIAM, JR., educator; b. Washington, Nov. 12, 1916; s. Joel William and Sally (Williams) B.; A.B., Coll. William and Mary, 1938; LL.B., U. Miss., 1946; postgrad. Yale, 1950; m. Rubye Barnes, Mary 16, 1942; 1 son, Joel William III. With U.S. Dept. Commerce, 1938-40; admitted to Miss. bar, 1946; prof. law, dean U. Miss. Sch. Law, 1946-71. Commr. on Uniform State Laws, 1969-71. Served to lt. comdr. USNR, 1941-45. Mem. Miss. State Bar, Am. Bar Assn., Phi Delta Phi, Omicron Delta Kappa. Episcopalian. Rotarian Author: Divorce and Separation in Mississippi, 1957. Home: University MS Died Sept. 30, 1971.

BUNN, EDWARD BERNARD, clergyman, educator; b. Balt., Mar. 25, 1896; s. Sebastian Philip and Philomena (Fortmann) B.; A.B., Loyola Coll., Baltimore, 1917; student St. Andrew-on-Hudson, M.A., 1921; Woodstock College, Maryland, 1921-30; Ph.D., Gregorian U., Rome, Italy, 1930; hon. LL.D., Fordham U., 1938, Brandeis University, Waltham, Mass., 1958, Notre Dame U., Wheeling Coll., Seattle U., Boston Coll., Coll. Holy Cross, 1964, Nat. U. Ireland, 1965, Gannon Coll., Erie, Pa., 1965; L.H.D., Am. U., 1964, St. Joseph's Coll., 1965, Georgetown U., 1968; Ed.D., Catholic University of America, 1968; Litt.D. (hon.), George Washington University, Washington, 1964. Entered Soc. Jesus, 1917; ord. R.C. priest, 1929. Asst. prof. Eng. lit., Fordham U., 1923-26; dean of boys, Brooklyn (N.Y.) Prep. Sch., 1930-31; asso. prof. systematic and adolescent psychology, Canisius Coll., Buffalo, N.Y., 1931-34; asso. prof. systematic and adolescent psychology and asst. dir. Child and Adolescent Guidance Clinic, Fordham U., 1934-38; pres. Loyola Coll., Baltimore, 1938-47; regional dir. studies of colls. and univs. of Md. province, 1944-52; regent dental and nursing shcs. Georgetown U., 1948-52, became president university, 1952, chancellor, 1964-72; regional director studies Maryland province Soc. Jesus. Former chmn. panel Regional War Labor Bd., Md. Ednl. Conf. Postwar Orgn. Trustee of Loyola Univ., Baltimore; chmn. emeritus bd. trustees Consortium Univs. Wash. Met. Area. Decorated Comdr.'s Cross Order Merit (Germany); Order of Merit Rank of Grand Cross (Peru); Grand Gold Badge of Honor (Austria). Member of Jesuit Edn. Assn. (mem. exec. com.), Nat. Catholic Ednl. Association, Association for Higher Education, N.E.A., Assn. Am. Colls., Am. Council on Edn., Newcomen Soc. Club: Cosmos (Washington). Author, producer of pageants, Spirit of Canasa," Civilization." Address: Washington DC Died June 18, 1972; buried Jesuit Community Cemetery, Georgetown U., Washington DC

BUNN, EDWARD SCHAIBLE, mfg. co. exec.; b. E. Hartford, Conn., May 1, 1906; s. Benjamin F. and Nettie B. (Howard) B.; B.S., Yale, 1929, M.S., 1931; m. Elizabeth H. Quinn, June 12, 1934; 1 son, Edward Schaible. With Revere Copper and Brass Inc., 1932-69, gen. mgr. research and devel. dept., 1960-61, v.p. research and devel. center, 1961-69. Mem. Am. Soc. M.E., Am., Soc. Testing Materials, Am. Inst. Mining and Metall. Engrs., British Inst. Metals, Rome C. of C., Sigma Xi. Clubs: Yale (N.Y.C.); Rome, Teugega Country (Rome). Co-author: Copper and Copper Base Alloys, 1943. Home: Rome NY Died Apr. 26, 1969; buried Hillside Cemetery, East Hartford CT

BUNN, PAUL AXTELL, physician, educator; b. Lorain, O., Dec. 9, 1914; s. Paul C. and Lois (Axtell) B.; A.B., DePauw U., 1936; M.B., U. Cin., 1940, M.D., 1941; m. Elizabeth Maxwell, June 14, 1941;children—Barbara (Mrs. Philip H. Howard), Paul Axtell, Mary Elizabeth. Intern, Univ. Hosps. of Cleve., 1940-41; resident in Tb, U. Mich. Hosp., Ann Arbor, 1941-42, resident in internal medicine, 1942-43; instr. medicine Cornell U. Coll. Medicine, N.Y.C., 1943-46, asst. in pharmacology, 1944-46, asst. prof. medicine, 1946-47; asst. physician out-patient dept. N.Y. Hosp., 1943-46, physician, 1946; asst. to chief Tb div. Central Office, VA, Washington, 1946-47; asso. prof. medicine State U. N.Y. Coll. Medicine at Syracuse, 1947-56, prof., 1956-70, acting chmn., 1967-70; asso. attending physician Syracuse Meml. Hosp., 1948-56, attending physician, 1956-70; attending physician Syracuse Univ. Hosp., 1947-70; cons. in internal medicine VA Hosp., Syracuse, 1953-70, St. Joseph's Hosp., Syracuse, 1957-70, Chenango Meml. Hosp., Norwich, N.Y., 1957-70; asso. dir. medicine Syracuse City Hosp., 1948-56; med. dir. Gen. Electric Co., Syracuse, 1970. Mem. panel on infectious diseases Com. on Revision U.S. Pharmacopeia, 1956-70. Mem. DeWitt (N.Y.) Central Sch. Dist. No. 11 Bd. Edn., 1950-56; v.p. DeWitt Community Assn., 1957-58; mem. DeWitt Planning Commn., 1957-60. Bd. dirs. Onondaga Health Assn., 1954-60; bd. visitors Roswell Park Meml. Inst., Buffalo, 1959-70. Diplomate Am. Bd. Internal Medicine. Fellow A.C.P. (gov. 1967-70), N.Y. Acad. Medicine; mem. Am., N.Y. (pres. 1954-55) Trudeau socs., N.Y. State, Onondaga County med. socs., Syracuse Acad. Medicine (pres. 1960), A.A.A.S., Am. Fedn. Clin. Research, Am. Soc. for Clin. Investigation, Am. Clin. and Climatol. Assn., Alpha Omega Alpha, Alpha Tau Omega, Nu Sigma Nu. Clubs: Onondaga Golf and Country, Thursday Night, Interurban. Assoc. editor: Cornell Conferences on Therapy, Vol. II, 1947, N.Y. State Jour. Medicine, 1956-70; abstractor Infectious Diseases, Excerpta Medica Found., 1952-70. Contbr. De Witt NY Died May 26, 1970; buried Oakwood Cemetery Syracuse NY

BUNNELL, STERLING HAIGHT, mech. engr.; b. Stratford, Conn., Jan. 30, 1871; s. Rufus William and Catharine Mary (Sterling) B.; Ph.B., Yale, 1891; M.E., 1893; m. Rebecca Lapham Peterson, Oct. 17, 1900;children—Charles Sterling, Elizabeth Lapham (Mrs. Edwin Marshall Deery). Began as with various manufacturing companies, 1893-99; engineer mgr., 1899-1916; chief engr., R. Martens & Co., N.Y. City, 1916-22; cons. engr., N.Y. City, 1922-27; with indsl. department Nat. City Co., N.Y. City, 1928-32; vice president George S. Armstrong & Co., Inc., financial consultants and indsl. engrs., 1932-51; staff mem. Stanford Research Inst., since 1951. Fellow American Soc. M.E.; mem. Franklin Inst., Nat. Geog. Soc., Yale Eng. Assn. Trustee Sterling Park and Community House. Republican. Episcopalian. Clubs: Yale (New York); Housatonic Boat and Cupheag (Stratford, Conn.), Technical writer, author. Address: 2225 Main St., Stratford CT‡

BUNTING, CHARLES HENRY, pathologist; b. La Crosse, Wis., May 22, 1875; s. Charles Hood and Florence Josephine (Smith) B.; B.S., U. of Wis., 1896, fellow in biology, 1896-97; M.D., Johns Hopkins U., 1901; m. Carlotta Mary Swett, June 19, 1907; children—Elizabeth (Mrs. John V. A. Fine), Henry. Served as medical house officer, Johns Hopkins Hosp., 1901-02; asst. demonstrator in pathology, U. of Pa., 1902-03; instr. and asso. in pathology, Johns Hopkins, 1903-06; pathologist, Bay View Hosp., Baltimore, 1903-06; professor pathology, University of Virginia, 1906-08; prof. pathology, U. of Wis., 1908-45, professor emeritus, since 1945; lecturer in pathology, Yale Medical Sch., since 1945. Fellow A.A.A.S., Am. Assn. Pathologists and Bacteriologists; mem. Assn. Am. Physicians; mem. Soc. Exptl. Biology and Medicine, Chicago Pathol. Soc., Am. Assn. of Anatomists, Am. Assn. for Cancer Research, Am. Soc. Exptl. Pathology, Beta Theta Pi, Nu Sigma Nu, Alpha Omega Alpha, Sigma Xi, Phi Beta Kappa; hon. mem. Milwaukee Surg. Soc. Wis. Acad. of Arts and Science, State Hist. Soc. of Wis., Soc. of Mayflower Descendants. Contbr. articles on gen. pathol. subjects, especially in hermatology, on anemias, pernicious anemia, Hodgkin's disease. Home: 139 Armory St., Hamden, 11, Conn. Office: 310 Cedar St., New Haven CT‡

BURBA, EDWIN HESS, army officer; b. Crowder, Okla., Feb. 18, 1912; s. Joseph L. and Estella B. (Hess) B.; B.S. in Bus. Adminstrn., U. Okla., 1933; grad. Army War Coll., 1954; m. Margaret Elizabeth Monk, Jan. 1, 1934; children—Lallie C. (Mrs. John A. Sheard), Edwin Hess, Margaret E. (Mrs. Clarence T. Babbitt), Alonzo R., Joseph C. Commd. 2d lt. F.A. Res., 1933; sec.-treas. Burba Auto Supply Co., McAlester, Okla., 1933-34; commd. 2d lt. U.S. Army Res., 1935, transferred to Regular Army, 1946, advanced through grades to maj. gen., 1963; co. comdr., dist. staff officer Civilian Conservation Corps, 1935-40; battery and battalion comdr.. arty. 1st Armored Div., 1940-43; operations officer, comdr. Combat Command B, 8th Armored Div., 1944-45; various troop staff assignments, 1945-50; mil. asst. to undersec. army, 1950-52; chief staff 3d Inf. Div., Korea, 1953; exec. officer Office Asst. Sec. Army, 1955-58; combat command comdr. 4th Armored Div. and 7th Army Tng. Center in Germany, 1958-60; dep. operations officer Joint Chiefs Staff, 1960-62; comdg. gen. 2d Armored Div., 1963-64; chief joint MAAG, Korea, 1965-66; project mgr. US/FRG Main Battle Tank-70, 1966-68; deputy CG 1st Army, 1968-70. Decorated Silver Star, Legion of Merit with 2 oak leaf clusters, Bronze Star with oak leaf cluster, Purple Heart, Combat Inf. badge, Army Commendation ribbon; Cezch War Cross of 1939; Croix de Guerre with palm (France and Belgium), Mem. Alpha Tau Omega. Democrat. Presbyn. Mason. Home: Ft. Geo. G. Meade MD Died Oct. 1970; buried Arlington Nat. Cemetery, Washington DC

BURCH, ALBERT, mining engr.; b. Peru, Neb., Jan. 8, 1867; s. Hiram and Mary (Brisbin) B.; studied Neb. State Normal Sch., 1877-80; Pawnee City (Neb.) Acad., 1880-81; York (Neb.) Coll., 1882-83; m. Mary Louise Aylesworth Stewart, Jan. 1, 1891 (died Dec. 8, 1931); m. 2d, Marguerita Adaline Dinsmore Backus, Nov. 5, 1932; children—Mary Beryl (wife of Max T. Smith, M.D.), Irma Louise (Mrs. E. A. Pond), Alberta (deceased). Surveyor in Utah, 1889-92; U.S. dep. mineral surveyor, 1890-96; supt. Bullion Beck & Champion Mine, Utah, 1893-94; supt. Bunker Hill & Sullivan Mine, Ida., 1897-1901, mgr., 1901-03; cons. practice since 1904; mgr. Plymouth Mine, Calif., 1911-16, Goldfield Consolidated Mine, Nev., 1911-14; mem. firm Burch, Caetani & Hershey, cons. engrs., San Francisco, 1912-19; war mineral service, U.S. Bureau Mines, 1918; mem. Burch, Hershey & White, San Francisco, 1919-25; cons. engr. Mountain Copper Co., Ltd.; cons. engr. Lewis Investment Co.; cons. engr., mining div. of The Pacific Company. Mem. bd. of control Ore. Dept. of Geology and Mineral Industries; mem. Ore. State Sanitary Authority. Mem. Am. Inst. Mining and Metallurgical Engrs. Republican. Mason (32 deg., K.T., Shriner), Odd Fellow. Home: Black Oak Ranch, Medford OR*‡

BURCH, H(UBERT) WENDEL, editor; b. Bloomington, Ind., Aug. 26, 1908; s. Audrey R. and Ethel L. (Williams) B. A.B., U. Cal., 1929; m. LaVerne A. Blundell, July 6, 1933; children—Richard N., Barbara J. With United Press Internat., 1931-70, beginning as newsman, successively assigned various bureaus, 1931-51, dir. fgn. services, 1951-59, dir. internat. services, 1959-70. Mem. Delta Upsilon, Episcopalian. Home: Forest Hills NY Died Feb. 9, 1970; buried Mountain View Cemetery, Reno NV

BURCH, HENRY REED, economist; b. Phila., Pa., Feb. 5, 1876; s. Charles Edward and Eva Anna (Reed) B.; A.B., Central High Sch., Phila., 1893; grad. Sch. of Pedagogy, Phila., 1894; B.S., U. of Pa., 1900, Ph.D., 1903; univs. Halle and Jena, 1906; m. Mary Grier Stewart, of Phila., July 23, 1902; 1 dau., Eleanor Stewart. Instr. English, 1903-04, prof. history and economics, 1904-06, head dept. history and economics, 1906-12, Central Manual Training Sch., Phila.; head dept. commerce and history, West Phila. High Sch. for Boys, 1912-26; head dept. history and social science, Overbrook High Sch., Phila., 1926—. Mem. commn. on Reorganization of Secondary Edn. in U.S. Mem. N.E.A., Am. Acad. Polit. and Social Science, Pa. State Edn. Assn., Nat. Com. for Teaching Citizenship, Nat. Council for the Social Studies, Nat. Economic League, Assn. Hist. Teachers of Middle States and Maryland (vice president 1922-23). Episcopalian. Clubs: University (Phila.); Salmagundi (New York). Author: Conditions Affecting Suffrage in the Colonies, 1903; Elements of Economics (with Scott Nearing), 1912; American Social Problems (with S. H. Patterson), 1918; American Economic Life, 1921; Problems of American Democracy (with S. H. Patterson), 1922. Home: 5208 Drexel Rd., Philadelphia PA‡

BURCHARD, ERNEST FRANCIS, mining geologist; b. Independence, Kan., May 20, 1875; s. George W. and Alice (Boyd) B.; student Lehigh U., 1897; B.S., Northwestern U., 1900, M.S., 1903; Sc.D., U. of Ala., 1935; m. Frances Elizabeth Baker, June 18, 1910 (died Jan. 1931). Instr. chemistry and geology, Sioux City (Ia.) High Sch., 1900-03; asst. geologist Wis. Geol. and Nat. Hist. Survey, 1903; on geologic staff of U.S. Geological survey, 1904-05; geologist in charge sect. non-metal resources, 1915-17, sect. iron and steel metals, 1917-44, prin. geologist, 1942-45, ret. 1945; sr. geologist, Geol. Survey of Ala., since 1945; cons. geologist, Bur. Bus. Research, Univ. of Ala., Tenn. Valley Authority, Ky. Geol. Survey, 1947; field work on iron ores, structural materials in all parts of the U.S. Organized World War I studies of U.S. Geol. Survey of reserves of ferro-alloy metals, 1917; mem. commn. to study chrome and manganese ores of Cuba, 1918; in petroleum fields of P.I., 1920, Argentina and Bolivia, 1922; made studies of iron ore reserves for Argentine Govt. and reconnaissance of iron and manganese ore fields of Brazil, 1925, Venezuela, 1929. Fellow Geol. Soc. America; mem. Am. Inst. Mining and Metall. Engrs. (chmn. com. on mining geology, 1924-27), Soc. Economic Geologists, Geol. Soc. Washington, Phi Beta Kappa, Sigma Xi, Phi Kappa Psi. Episcopalian. Author: Geology of Dakota County, Nebraska; Geology of Lancester-Mineral Point, Wis. (with U.S. Grant); Iron Ores of the Birmingham District, Ala., Red Iron Ores of East Tennessee, Northeast Alabama and Northwest Georgia, Marble Resources of Southeast Alaska, Chrome and Manganese Ores of Cuba, Bauxite in Mississippi; Iron Ore in Misiones Territory, Argentina, The Iron Ore Situation in the South, The Pao Deposits of Iron Ore, Venezuela, Geological Exploration for Iron Ore Deposits, Fluorspar Deposits in Western States, The Sources of Ores of Iron and Ferro-alloy Metals, The Iron Ore Situation in the Western States and in California; National reserves and production of iron ore; Conservation of Iron Ore.; Red Iron Ore Outcrops in Northeast Alabama (with Thos. G. Andrews)—in bulletins of Federal and state geological surveys and tech. mags. Contbr. many other papers on geol. and economic subjects. Address: 3403 Lowell St., Washington 16‡

BURDEN, HARRY P., educator; b. Lynn, Mass., Feb. 25, 1890; s. Robert H. and Lizzie B.; B.S., U. Me., 1912; M.S., Harvard, 1928; m. Lunetta A. McPhetres, June 7, 1915; 1 son, Robert P. Instr. civil engring. Tufts Coll., 1913-19, asst. prof., 1919-21, asso. prof., 1922-29, prof., 1930-35, dean engring., prof. civil and san. engring., 1936-57. Chmn. planning bd. City of Somerville, Mass. Member Am. Soc. Engring. Edn., Boston Soc. Civil Engrs., N.E. Water Works Assn., N.E. Sewage and Indsl. Wastes Assn., Am. Soc. C.E., Sigma Xi, Tau Beta Pi, Sigma Pi Sigma. Home: Medford MA Died Oct. 1972.

BURDETTE, CLARA BRADLEY (MRS. ROBERT J. BURDETTE), clubwoman; b. E. Bloomfield, N.Y., July 22, 1855; d. Albert H. and Laura (Coville) Bradley; ed. Syracuse U., 1872-76 (Phi Beta Kappa); LL.D., Mills College, Calif., and Syracuse Univ.; m. N. Milman Wheeler, July 24, 1878 (died Dec. 6, 1886); 1 son, Roy Bradley Wheeler (deceased); m. 2d, Presley C. Baker, June 4, 1890 (died Sept. 5, 1893); m. 3d, Robert J. Burdette, Mar. 25, 1899 (died Nov. 19, 1914). Active in woman's club organ, and in philanthropic work; 1st pres. Calif. Fedn. Woman's Clubs; was chmn. bd. of trustees Gen. Fedn. Woman's Clubs, v.p., 1902-04, now hon. vice-pres., corr. for foreign and territorial clubs 12 years; past pres. Pasadena Hosp. Assn., Woman's Civic League of Pasadena, Pasadena Bd. of Nat. Needlework Guild of America. Builder and donor of Maternity Wing to Pasadena Hosp. Trustee Mills Coll. (Calif.), vice chmn. bd. trustees, 1922-37, hon. mem. for life; trustee Syracuse U. (vice chmn.), Calif. Coll. in China (vice chmn); v.p. and chmn. finance com. Auditorium Co., Los Angeles; member Nat. Com. for Fed. Dept. of Edn.; mem. Advisory bd. Calif. Prep. Sch. for Boys (Covina); mem. Calif. Inst. Associates; mem. Nat. Com. of Nat. Welfare Assn., also Calif. Com. of same assn. Associate dir. food conservation for Calif. under Federal Food Adminstrn.; mem. State Com. on Soldiers' Employment and Readjustment; was field sec. for Calif. of Nat. Council Defense; served as chmn. Com. on Reorganization of Gen. Fed. Women's Clubs. Mem. Am. Social Science Assn., Archeol. Inst. of America, Council Internat. Relations, N.E.A. (life), Nat. Kindergarten Assn., Nat. Conversation Assn., Am. Social Hygiene Assn., Nat. Welfare Foundation, Nat. Com. on Calendar Simplification, Internat. Assn. Policewomen, Am. Green Cross, Calif. Council Adult Edn., Los Angeles Center of Am. Acad. Polit. and Social Science, Calif. Bot. Gardens in Los Angeles (gov. bd.), Los Angeles br. Am. Assn. Univ. Women (councillor), Del. Rep. Nat. Com., Chicago, 1920. Vice-pres. Board of Pilgrimage Play Assn., Los Angeles; mem. bd. Los Angeles La. Fiesta Assn. Clubs: Women's Athletic of Los Angeles (pres. emeritus), Ebell (hon.), Friday Morning (hon.), Ruskin Art (hon.). Author of books and contbr. to daily press and mags.; lectured on social and ednl. questions. Home: Hotel Huntington, Pasadena CA‡

BURDICK, DONALD LANGWORTHY, anesthesiologist; b. Ashaway, R.I., Apr. 1, 1900; s. William H. and Nellie I. (Langworthy) B.; B.Sc., Alfred U., 1922; M.A., Columbia, 1924; M.D., Albany Med. Coll., 1938; m. Winifred M. Stevenson, Nov. 22, 1953. Instr. biology Washington Sq. Coll., N.Y.U., 1923-25; asst. prof. biology Southwestern U., 1926; prof. biology Alfred U., 1927-29; asst. prof. biology Union Coll., Schenectady, 1930-32; instr. anatomy Albany Med. Coll., 1933-34; intern United Hosp., Port Chester, N.Y., 1938-39, resident, 1939-40; resident anesthesiology Bellevue Hosp., N.Y.C., 1940-42; instr. anesthesiology N.Y.U.-Bellevue Med. Coll., 1945, asst. clin. prof., 1946-56, asso. clin. prof., 1957-62; asst. dir. anesthesiology Doctors Hosp., N.Y.C., 1944-45, dir., 1946-67. Served as pvt. U.S. Army, 1918-19. Diplomate Am. Bd. Anesthesiology (pres. 1956-57, dir. 1948-62). Fellow Am. Coll. Anesthesiology (chmn. 1946-50); mem. Am. (editor newsletter 1945), N.Y. State socs. anesthesiology, A.M.A., Internat. Research Soc. Anesthesiology, Med. Soc. County N.Y., Am. Soc. Clin. Hypnosis, N.Y. Acad. Medicine, Alpha Omega Alpha. Author articles and papers. Home: New York City NY Died Nov. 12, 1967; buried Oak Grove Cemetery, Ashaway RI

BURFORD, CYRUS EDGAR, urologist; b. Girard, Ill., Aug. 20, 1876; s. Giles McKenzie and Elizabeth Ellen (Hamilton) B.; Ph.B., LL.D., Central Coll., Fayette, Mo., 1899; M.D., Marion Simms Beaumont Med. Coll., St. Louis U., 1902, Zeugniss, U. Vienna, 1912; m. Katherine Lloyd Humber, June 15, 1899 (dec.); children—Ada Margaret (Mrs. George Osburn Cutter), Edgar H. (dec.). Intern St. Louis City Hosp., 1902-03; instr. St. Louis U. Med Sch., asst. to Dr. Bransford Lewis, urologist, 1904-10; postgrad. work European clinics, 1912; prof., dir. urology dept. St. Louis U., from 1922; urologist, Columbia (Mo.) State Cancer, Firmin DesLoge, St. Mary's, St. Luke's, Mo. Baptist, Bethesda Gen., Jewish hosps., Shriners Hosp. Crippled Children; ret. Pres. bd. curators Central Coll. (chmn.). Diplomate Am. Bd. Urology. Fellow A.C.S., Am. Assn. Genito-Urinary Surgeons (past pres.); mem. Am. Urol. Assn. (past pres.), St. Louis Med. Soc. (past pres.), Mo. Med. Assn. (past pres.), St. Louis Surg. Soc. (past pres.), St. Louis Urol. Assn. (past pres.), Sigma Alpha Epsilon, Phi Beta Pi, Alpha Omega Alpha. Mason (32 deg.). Clubs: Contemporary of St. Louis (bd. dirs.), University, Glen Echo Country, Automobile of Mo. (dir.). Contbr. chpt. to Christopher's Surgery. Author papers on kidney and bladder surgery. Home: St Louis MO Died July 10, 1972; interred Oak Grove Mausoleum, St Louis MO

BURGEE, CLYDE ELMORE, educator; b. Hagerstown, Md., Feb. 21, 1894; s. Amon and Mary Elizabeth (Engleman) B.; A.B.; Western Md. Coll., 1914; A.M., Johns Hopkins, 1920, spl. grad. courses econs., 1940; m. Lois Ellen Montgomery, Aug. 31, 1930; children—Mary Jane, Michael Buford. Prof. econs. U. Mont., 1920-27, Rider Coll., 1929-30; mem. faculty Bucknell U., 1930-70, chmn. dept. econs. and bus. adminstrn., 1951-58, Charles P. Vaughan prof. econs., 1954-64, prof. econs. emeritus, 1964-70. Mem. Am. Accounting Assn., Alpha Tau Omega, Phi Mu. Meth. Episcopalian. Home: Lewisburg PA Died Sept. 12, 1970; buried Frederick Meml. Cemetery, Frederick MD

BURGER, WILLIAM HENRY, civil engr.; b. Caribou, Colo., May 2, 1874; s. Henry and Caroline (Mohr) B.; B.S., U. of Colo., 1896, post-grad. work, 1896-97; m. Elizabeth L. Shotwell, of Evanston, Ill., Aug. 7, 1912; children—William H(enry), Elizabeth Marie. Instr., U. of Colo., 1896-97; with engring. corps, Colo. & N.W. Ry., 1897-99; aide and asst., U.S. Coast and Geod. Survey, 1899-1910; asst. prof. civ. engring., 1910-15, prof., 1915-39; professor of civil engring. emeritus since 1939, Northwestern U. Consultant, precision and geod. surveys. Author: Measurement of Flexure of Pendulum Supports with the Interferometer; Biographical Memoir of John F. Hayford. Fellow A.A.A.S., American Geophysical Union; mem. Sigma Xi, Delta Tau Delta. Home: 1220 Noyes St., Evanston IL‡

BURGESS, CHARLES MCFETRIDGE, mfg. exec.; b. Evanston, Ill., Jan. 22, 1896; s. Frank A. and Mary E. (McFetridge) B.; student sch. engring. U. Wis.; m. Ruth Mary Kendall, Feb. 1, 1918; children—Frank K., Robert C. With Burgess-Norton Mfg. Co., Geneva, 1920-69, supt., 1921-22, pres., 1922-57, chmn., 1957-69. Mem. Ill. Commn. Higher Edn., 1943-45, Ill. Commn. Youthful Offenders, 1945-49; nat. field adviser Small Bus. Adminstrn., 1954-56; mem. Ill. Toll Hwy. Commn., 1956-63, chairman, 1959-63. Delegate Republican National Convention, 1944, 52. Served as 1st lt. F.A., U.S. Army, 1917-19; as capt. F.A., Ill. N.G. Officers Res. Corps, 1919-28; industry chmn. integration com. for tank track prodn. Ordnance Dept., 1942-44, 51-59. Mem. Nat. Standard Parts Assn. (dir. 1927-29, president 1931), Soc. Automotive Engrs., Am. Legion (past co. and post comdr.), V.F.W., Vets. World War I, Sigma Alpha Epsilon. Elk. Clubs: Lions (Geneva, Ill.); Aurora Country, Phoenix (Aurora); Union League (Aurora, Ill.; Chgo.). Home: IL Died Mar. 26, 1972.

BURGESS, JOHN ALBERT, mining engr.; b. St. John, N.B., Can., May 30, 1876; s. Rev. Joshua Chase and Mary Helen (Noble) B.; brought to U.S., 1883; B.S., U. of Calif. Coll. of Mining, 1906; m. Florence Helen DuBois, Sept. 25, 1907; children—Eleanor, John DuBois, Peter DuBois. Chief engr. and geologist, Tonopah Mining Co. of Nev., 1906-11; supt. Nevada Wonder Mining Co., Wonder, Nev., 1911-16; gen. mgr. United Eastern Mining Co., Oatman, Ariz., 1916-20; cons. engr. and geologist San Francisco, 1920-33; gen. mgr. Carson Hill Gold Mining Corp., 1933-43; agent Metals Res. Co., Yosemite Tungsten Project, 1943; gen. supt. U.S. Smelting Exploration, S.A., a subsidiary co. of U.S. Smelting & Refining Co. and cons. geologist Cia de Real del Monte y Pachuca, 1926-27; cons. engr. Mayflower Associates, New York, 1929; pres. Mother Lode Mining Assn. 1940-41. Brought into successful operation Nevada Wonder Mine (silver), United Eastern Mine (gold) and Carson Hill Mine (gold). Mem. Am. Inst. Mining and Metall. Engrs., Mining and Metall. Soc. of America; Sigma Xi. Republican. Presbyterian. Contbr. to Economic Geology, Mining Sonora CA‡

BURGESS, PHILIP, civil engineer; b. Newtonville, Mass., Dec. 1, 1876; s. Charles Arthur and Adelaide Louise (Kimball) B.; B.S., Mass. Inst. of Tech., 1899; m. Amy II, Jones, June 26, 1913; 1 dau., Anne Kimball. Employed as asst. engr. by C. W. Leavitt, New York, 1899-1900, City of Philadelphia, 1900-01, Jersey City Water Supply Co., 1901-03, Hering & Fuller, 1903-04, City of Cincinnati, 1904-05; spl. asst. engr. Ohio State Bd. of Health, 1906-10; mem. Burgess & Niple and pres. Burnip Constrn. Co. since 1910; dir. Consumers Water Co., Shenango Valley Water Co. Pres. bd. trustees, Broad St. Presbyterian Ch. Mem. Am. Soc. C.E., Am. Waterwks. Assn., New Eng. Waterworks Assn. Republican. Presbyterian. Clubs: Athletic (past president), Engrs., Columbus Country. Author: Water Purification in Ohio, 1910. Contributor many articles in professional journals; as associate water consultant assisted in preparation of Report on Ohio River Basin to National Resources Commn., 1936. Home: R.F.D., Lancaster Rd., Granville. Office: 568 E. Broad St., Columbus 15 OH‡

BURGESS, ROBERT WILBUR, statistician; b. Newport, R.I., July 25, 1887; s. Isaac Bronson and Ellen (Wilbur) B.; grad. Morgan Pk. Acad., 1905; A.B., Brown U., 1908, hon. Sc.D., 1948; Rhodes scholar, 1908-11; B.A., Oxford U., 1910; Ph.D., Cornell 1914; m. Dorothy Cross, Jan. 1, 1925; children—Mary Ellen, Dorothy (Mrs. H. M. Baird Voorhis), Margaret (Mrs. Charles W. Cammack, 3d). Instr. mathematics Purdue, 1911-12; asst. mathematics Cornell, 1912-14, instructor, 1914-16; instr. mathematics, Brown University, 1916-17, assistant professor, 1919-25; statistician and economist, Western Electric Co., 1924-52; cons. statistics from 1952; dir. Bur. of Census, Dept. Commerce, 1953-61. Served as first lieutenant, O.R.C., duty at Washington, D.C., Oct. 1917-May 1918; 1st lt., capt., maj. N.A., duty with statistics br. Gen. Staff, Washington, May 1918-Sept. 1919; maj. O.R.C., 1919-29. Fellow Am. Statis. Association (v.p. 1939); member Conference of Business Economists, Population Assn. Am., Am Econ. Assn., Econometric Soc., Brown Engring. Association (pres. 1942), Economic Principles Commission N.A.M. Delta Upsilon, Phi Beta Kappa and Sigma Xi. Baptist. Clubs: Brown University (N.Y.C.); Cosmos (Washington); Huguenot Yacht. Author: Introduction to Mathematics of Statistics; chapter on research for gen. administration in Scientific Management in Am. Industry. Contbr. math. or statis. articles in Am. Jour. Mathematics, Physical Rev., Am. Oxonian, Encyclopedia Britannica, etc. Home: Pelham NY Died May 27, 1969.

BURGESS, MRS. SAMUEL ROSTRON, b. Ogden, Utah; d. James X. Allen, M.D.; grad. high sch., St. Louis, Mo., 1875; m. Samuel Rostron Burgess, 1876 (died, 1918). Learned chess under father; won title of Woman's Chess Champion of the United States," 1907, defeating Mrs. C. P. Frey, of Newark, N.J., by score of 4 1/2 to 1 1/2; in response to challenge, 1908, defeated Mrs. Natalie Nixdorff, of New York, score of 4 to 1. Hon. mem. St. Louis Chess Club. Active ch. worker. Home: 5920 Etzel Av., St Louis MO‡

BURGIN, SAMUEL H. C., clergyman; b. Ridgeway, Mo., Sept. 7, 1871; s. Henry S. and Sarah E. (McCammon) B.; ed. Woodland Coll. (Independence, Mo.), Central Coll. (Fayette, Mo.), and by pvt. study; D.D., Southwestern U., Georgetown, Tex., 1914; m. Lora E. Miller, of Kansas City, Mo., Oct. 18, 1899 (died Aug. 22, 1913); children—Herschel Steele, Ruth Evangeline, Miller Strange; m. 2d, Elizabeth Kilpatrick, of Corinth, Miss., Mar. 11, 1916. Ordained minister, M. E. Ch., S., 1897; pastor Campbell St. Ch. (now Institutional, of Kansas City, Mo.), St. Paul, Butte, Mont., Windsor, Mo., Centenary Chapel (Fayette, Mo.), Travis Park Ch., San Antonio, Tex., 1909-10; presiding elder San Antonio Dist., 1910-14; pastor Trinity (later First Ch.), Dallas, Tex., 1914-20 (projected movement for erection of new First Ch.); exec. sec. Gen. Bd. Ch. Extension, M.E. Ch., S., Louisville, Ky., 1920-22; became pastor Laurel Heights Ch., San Antonio, Tex., 1922. Mem. bd. trustees Westmoreland Coll., San Antonio; three times mem. Gen. Conf. M.E. Ch., S. Mason (32 deg., K.T., Shriner); Past Grand Orator and Past Grand Chaplain*‡

BURGIN, WILLIAM GARNER, educator, lecturer; b. Mayhew, Miss., July 4, 1892; s. Daniel Augustus and Nancy Myrtis (Garner) B.; student Miss. Coll., Clinton, Miss., 1907-10; A.B., Colo. State Teachers' Coll., 1913, A.M., 1914; post-grad. study U. of Wis.; m. Susie Will Gunter, July 24, 1919 (now deceased); children—Nancy, William Garner, Charles Mellville (dec.); m. 2d, Florence Knight Ramond, June 2, 1929 (dec.); children—John Ramond, Jane Ramond; m. 3d, Nancy Dolfinger Henderson, Aug. 27, 1955. Was teacher pub. schs. until 1915; teacher polit. sci., high sch., Pasadena, Calif., 1915-17; spl. lecturer Telluride Assn., Calif., 1918; prof. polit. science, Miss. State Coll. for Women, Columbus, 1919-22; prof. sociology, Winthrop Coll., Rock Hill, S.C., 1922-27; dean and active pres. Dodd Coll., Shreveport, La., 1927-30; dean of men, San Bernardino (Calif.) Junior Coll., 1930-33. Organizer, and leader of San Bernardino Valley Forum, 1932-33; mem. Miss. State Senate, 23d Senatorial Dist., 1936-40; agency mgr. Investors Syndicate, Memphis 1940-43, divisional mgr. 1944-49. Baptist. Mason. Contbr. to press and mags.; lectr. on social and polit. subjects. Club: Lions (pres. 1929-30). Wrote: The Challenge of Liberalism, 1927. Home: Starkville MS Died Nov. 10, 1970.

BURKE, BILLIE, actress; b. Washington, D.C., Aug. 7, 1886; d. William E. and Blanche B.; ed. schs. in France and London, Eng.; m. Florenz Ziegfeld, Jr., Apr. 11, 1914; 1 dau., Mrs. William R. Stephenson. Made debut as singer at Pavilion Music Hall, London, 1902, as support of Edna May in The School Girl"; appeared in The Duchess of Dantzic," The Blue Moon" and The Belle of Mayfair," London, 1906; 1st dramatic engagement as leading woman in Mr. George," 1907, and Mrs. Ponderbury's Past"; John Drew's leading woman, in America, in My Wife," 1907; star in Love Watchers," Lyceum Theatre, New York, 1908, Mrs. Dot," 1910; as Suzanne Beulemans in Suzanne," at Lyceum Theatre, New York, 1911; as Colette in The Runaway," 1911; in Marriage of Convenience," 1918; starring in Caesar's Wife," 1919; in Booth Tarkington's Intimate Strangers," 1921; Rose Briar," 1923; Annie Dear," 1924; The Marquise" (by Noel Coward), 1927; Happy Husbands," 1929; Truth Game," 1930, Vinegar Tree," 1931. Has appeared in many motion pictures including Becky Sharp," My American Wife," Craig's Wife," The Bride Wore Red," Everybody Sing," Wizard of Oz," Eternally Yours." Home: Brentwood CA Died May 1970.

BURKE, DANIEL, lawyer; b. New Berlin, N.Y., Dec. 5, 1873; s. James and Mary S. (York) B.; student Oxford (N.Y.) Acad., 1885-89; A.B., Hamilton Coll., 1893, A.M., 1894; student New York U. Law Sch., 1894-95; LL.B., N.Y. Law Sch., 1896; LL.D., Hamilton College, 1936; married Kate Hull Bundy, August 20, 1901 (deceased 1945); children—James Bundy, Agnes Bundy (Mrs. Henry W. Harding), Coleman; married 2d Charlotte Greene Adams, January 6, 1951. Admitted to the New York bar, 1896; established own office, 1899; mem. firm Burke & Burke, from 1929; president of Connecticut Mills, 1921-24; former dir. Summit (N.J.) Trust Co., R.T. French Co. (former chmn.) Atlantis Sales Corp. (chmn.). Truste Hamilton Coll. (chmn. bd., 1937-45); manager American Bible Society, pres., 1944-62. Mem. Am., N.Y. State, N.Y. City bar assns., Chi Psi, Phi Beta Kappa, Phi Delta Phi. Rep. Methodist. Clubs: Wall Street (N.Y.C.). Home: Fernwood Rd NJ also Oxford NY Died Jan. 1970.

BURKE, EDMUND, lawyer; b. Buffalo, Ill., Aug. 8, 1876; s. Michael and Julia M. (Dalton) B.; student Quincy Coll., 1893-95; LL.B., U. Mich., 1898; m. Alice Trotter, Oct. 7, 1902; children—Mary B. (Mrs. John B. McCarthy), Edmund, Alice M. (Mrs. H. H. Bentley), Dorothy, Kevin (dec.). Admitted to Mich., Ill. bar, 1898; Ill. states atty., 1908-16; corp. counsel, Springfield, Ill., 1924-27; mem. Gillespie, Burke & Gillespie, from 1927; U.S. jury commr. So. Dist. Ill., from 1937; spl. asst. U.S. atty. gen. and hearing officer conscientious objector cases, 1941. Presdl. elector, 1932, 48; del. Dem. Nat. convs., 1940, 44. Mem. Am., Ill. (sr. counsellor 1948), Sangamon County bar assns. Roman Catholic. K.C. Home: Springfield IL Died July 27, 1970; interred Calvary Cemetery, Springfield IL

BURKE, EDWARD RAYMOND, ex-senator; b. Runningwater, S.D., Nov. 28, 1880; s. Patrick Dorsey and Mary (Nolan) B.; A.B., Beloit Coll., 1906; LL.B., Harvard, 1911; m. Henrietta Flinn, Dec. 28, 1911; children—Beatrice, Barbara. Admitted to Neb. bar, 1911, and in practice at Omaha; mem. 73d Congress (1933-35), 2d Neb. District; elected U.S. senator for term, 1935-41. Served as 2d lt. Air Service, U.S. Army, 1917-19. Pres. Omaha Bd. of Edn., 1927-31. Mem. Am. Bar Assn. (mem. gen. council 1928-32), Omaha Bar Assn. (pres. 1926-27). Democrat. Conglist. Home: Omaha NB Died Nov. 4, 1968.

BURKE, THOMAS A., lawyer, former senator; b. Cleve., Oct. 30, 1898; s. Thomas A. and Lillian (McNeil) B.; A.B. cum laude, Holy Cross Coll., 1920, LL.D., 1954; LL.B., Western Res. U., 1923; m. Josephine Lyon, June 25, 1924; children—Jo Ann, Barbara. Admitted to Ohio bar, 1923; asst. pros. atty., Cuyahoga County, O., 1930-36; spl. counsel to atty. gen. of Ohio, 1937; mem. firm McConnell, Blackmore, Cory & Burke, Cleve., 1937-41; dir. law, City of Cleve., 1941-44; mayor of Cleve., 1945-53; U.S. senator from Ohio, 1953-54; later partner firm Burke, Haber & Berick, Cleve. Mem. Phi Alpha Delta. K.C. Clubs: Shaker Heights (O.) Country; Cleveland (O.) Athletic. Address: Cleveland OH Died Dec. 5, 1971.

BURKETT, CHARLES WILLIAM, editor, author; b. Thornville, O., Jan. 3, 1873; s. Joseph W. and Anna (Klingler) B.; B.Sc., U. of Ohio, 1895, M.Sc., 1898; Ph.D., Lima Coll., 1900; m. Laura Anna Weisman, of Columbus, O., Dec. 27, 1900; children—Dorothy Louise, Charles William. Asst. agr., U. of Ohio, 1895-98; prof. agr., N.H. Coll. Agr., and agriculturist, N.H. Expt. Sta., 1898-1901; prof. agr., N.C. Coll. Agr., and agriculturist, N.C. Expt. Sta., 1901-06; dir. Kan. Agrl. Expt. Sta., 1906-08; investigator cereal problems in Turkey and Russia, 1907, for State of Kan.; editor Am. Agriculturist, 1908-22; editor, Macfadden Book Co., 1923-32; pres. Orange Judd Pub. Co., 1922-27; pres. True Strange Stories Pub. Co.; vice president Farmers Independence Council, 1935-—. Founder and 1st editor, 1896-98, The Agricultural Student; farmers' institute lecturer. Editor Country Life Education Series. Co-founder Alpha Zeta Fraternity; mem. Kappa Sigma, Ohio Soc. of New York (historian). Author: History of Ohio Agriculture, 1900; Agriculture for Beginners (joint author), 1903; Cotton (joint author), 1906; Our Domestic Animals; The Hill Readers (joint author), 1906; Soils, 1907; Farm Stock, 1908; The Farmer's Veterinarian, 1909; Farm Crops, 1910; First Principles of Feeding Farm Animals, 1912; Farm Arithmetic, 1913; Soils and Crops (joint author), 1913; Farm Animals (joint author), 1914; Between Two Lives, 1916. Mem. Authors' League of America. Club: Westchester Country. Home: 5121 N. Bay Road, Miami Beach FL‡

BURKHALTER, JOHN THOMAS, U.S. Pub. Health Service; b. Warrenton, Ga., Jan. 19, 1873; s. Thomas Jefferson and Anna (Scruggs) B.; A.B., Emory Coll., Oxford, Ga., 1895; student med. dept. U. of Ga., 1896-97, U. of Baltimore, 1897-98; M.D., Md. Med. Coll., Baltimore, 1899; m. Lillian Johnson, Jan. 2, 1901; children—Helen (wife of Dr. Julian A. Quattlebaum), John (dec.), Preston Brooks, Frances, Lillian (Mrs. River Worrell); m. 2d, Louise Howell, Dec. 18, 1916. Commd. asst. surgeon, U.S.P.H.S., 1900, passed asst. surgeon, 1906, surgeon, 1914, med. dir., 1930; served as med. officer in charge quarantine stations and marine hosps.; retired, 1933; asso. prof. tropical diseases, U. of Ala., 1914-20, prof. medicine, 1918-20. Former mem. bd. dirs. Health Center (Savannah); mem. Am. Red Cross (Savannah Chapter), Chatham-Savannah Tuberculosis Assn., Med. Dept. of the Corolla, U. of Ala., dedicated in his honor, 1920. Mem. A.M.A., Alpha Tau Omega. Democrat. Methodist. Club: Savannah Golf (Savannah, Ga.). Home: 704 E. 46th St., Savannah GA‡

BURKHOLDER, CHARLES IRVINE, public utilities; b. Sterling, Ill., Oct. 9, 1872; s. Christian and Mary Parsons (Irvine) B.; B.S. in E.E., U. of Wis., 1896; E.D., N.C. State Coll., 1938; m. Clara Sauter, Oct. 10, 1898. Machinist Diamond Meter Co., Peoria, Ill., 1897-98; testing dept. Gen. Elec. Co., Schenectady, 1898-1900, asst. to elec. supt., 1900-06; operating supt. Duke Power Co. (formerly Southern Power Co.), Charlotte, N.C., 1906-12, gen. mgr. since 1912, v.p. since 1917, chief engr. since 1935, dir. since 1920; trustee Duke Endowment; dir. Wateree Power Co., Western Carolina Power Co., Catawba Mfg. & Electric Power Co. Fellow Am. Inst. E.E., mem. Am. Soc. M.E., Omicron Delta Kappa, Phi Gamma Delta. Club: Country (Charlotte, N.C.). Home: 801 Ardsley Rd., Charlotte, N.C. Office: Charlotte NC*‡

BURKHOLDER, PAUL RUFUS, educator, microbiologist; b. Orrstown, Pa., Feb. 1, 1903; s. William Rankin William Rankin and Mary Ellen (Schubert) B.; A.B., Dickinson Coll., 1924; Ph.D., Cornell U., 1929; NRC fellow in botany, Harvard, 1932-33, Columbia, 1933-34; M.A. (hon.), Yale, 1944; Sc.D. (hon.), Dickinson Coll., 1949; m. Lillian Miller, Feb. 4, 1930; children—Franz M., Peter M., Karl M. Instr. botany Cornell U., 1924-28; biol. curator Buffalo Mus. Sci., 1929-32; asst. prof. Conn. Coll., 1934-37, asso. prof., 1937-38; asso. prof. U. Mo., 1938-40; asso. prof. Yale, 1940-43, Eaton prof. botany, 1944-53; chmn. dept. plant sci., 1950-53; head dept. bacteriology U. Ga., 1953-56; dir. research Bklyn. Botanic Garden, 1956-61; chmn. marine biology programs Lamont Geol. Obs. Columbia, 1961-69; vis. prof. microbiology U.P.R., Mayaguez, 1969-72. Mem. A.A.A.S., Nat. Acad. Sci., Bot. Soc. Am. (sec. 1940-45), Am. Soc. Naturalists (pres. 1948), Am. Soc. Microbiologists, Soc. Protozool., Soc. Gen. Microbiol., Torrey Bot. Club, Sigma Xi. Contbr. papers in field. Home: Madison WI Died Aug. 1972.

BURLEIGH, NATHANIEL GEORGE, educator; b. Franklin, N.H., July 10, 1889; s. Harry W. and Nannie (Burley) B.; student Phillips Exeter Acad. 1906-07; B.A., magna cum laude, Dartmouth College, 1911, M.C.S., 1912, M.A. (honorary degree), 1919; m. Theodora Tufts, Apr. 11, 1914 (dec. Apr. 3, 1948); 1 dau., Barbara (Mrs. John H. Hewitt); m. 2d, Beatrice U. Bridges, July 29, 1950. With Boston Elevated Ry., 1912-16. Winchester Repeating Arms Co., 1916-19; prof. indsl. mgmt. Dartmouth Coll., 1919-57. professor emeritus, 1957-70, acting dean Amos Tuck School, 1951-53; cons. Department of Defense, Washington, 1955; dean faculty, lecturer, Instituto Post-universitario, Turin, 1953; lecture staff U.S. Command and Staff School. Advisory committee N.H. Planning Commission; dir. service equipment div., office of operations W.P.B., 1941-45; cons. Nat. Security Resources Bd., 1948, 49. Smaller Bus. Assn. New Eng. Trustee, treas. Mary Hitchcock Meml. Hosp. Recipient Dartmouth Alumni award, 1961. Mem. N.H., New Eng. hosp. assns., Dartmouth Gen. Alumni Assn. (past 1st v.p.), Assn. for Edn. in International Business, Phi Beta Kappa, Phi Gamma Delta. Republican. Conglist. Clubs: Dartmouth (N.Y.C.); Lake Mitchell Trout (Sharon, Vt.); University (Washington); Gulquac Salmon (Plaster Rock, N.B., Can.). Home: Hanover NH Died Apr. 6, 1970.

BURLIN, PAUL, artist; b. N.Y.C., Sept. 10, 1886; s. Jack and Julia (Samuels) B.; ed. New York and London, Eng.; m. Natalie, d. late Edward Curtis, of N.Y. City, July 25, 1917; m. 2d, Margot Koop, 1925; 1 dau., Barbara; m. 3d, Helen Strauss, 1937; m. 4th Margaret Timmerman, Sept. 22, 1947. Represented in Whitney Museum of American Art and Museum of Modern Art, Denver Art museum, Nat. Collections Smithsonian Instns.; collections of Internat. Business Machines Corp., State Dept., Ency. Brit., others; pvt. collections of Sam Lewisohn, Franz Hirschland, Bernard Reis (all of N.Y.); Nathaniel Saltonstall (Boston); Morton Goldsmith (Westchester). Has exhibited at London Tri-national, International at Venice, Pitts. Internat., Corcoran Galleries, Pennsylvania Academy of Fine Arts, Museum of Modern Art (40 Living Arms., N.Y. Coliseum, 1959, retrospective exhbn. Whitney Mus., N.Y.C., 1962; 1 man show, Am. Artists, N.Y.C., 1942, 43, Downtown Gallery, 1946, 53, The Stable Gallery, 1954, St. Louis, 1954, Los Angeles, San Diego and San Francisco at Legion of Honor Museum, 1954, Poindexter Gallery, 1958, 59, Chgo. Art Inst., 1960, John Whitney Found., Borgenicht Gallery, New York City, 1963, 64, 65. vis. prof. Union Coll., Schenectady, N.Y., 1954-55; artist in residence. Recipient 1st prize , 500 Pepsi-Cola contest, 1945; 1,000 prize for art USA, 1959; Ford Found. Retrospective exhibition award, 1960; 000 Watson F. Blair award Chgo. Art Inst., 1960; H. J. Schiedt award Pa. Acad. Biennial, 1964; Marjory Peabody Waite award Nat. Inst. Arts and Letters, 1965; $5000 award Nat. Council Arts, 1968-69. Home: New York City NY Died Mar. 13, 1969; buried Batesburg SC

BURLING, EDWARD BURNHAM, lawyer; b. Eldora, Hardin County, Iowa, Feb. 1, 1870; s. Edward and Lucy (Burnham) B.; A.B., Grinnell (Ia.) Coll., 1890; A.B., Harvard, 1891; LL.B. and A.M., 1894; m. Louisa Peasley, November 9, 1902 (deceased October 1960); children—Edward, John (deceased); married 2d, Bertha Blake Jones, February 13, 1962. Admitted Ill. bar, 1895; mem. Bentley & Burling to 1915, Bentley, Burling & Kumler, 1915-17; chief counsel U.S. Shipping Bd., 1917-19; mem. Covington & Burling, Washington, 1919-66. Mem. Am. Bar Assn. Home: Washington DC Died Oct. 3, 1966; buried Cornish NH

BURLINGAME, LEONAS LANCELOT, prof. biology; b. Guernsey County, O., Aug. 25, 1876; s. Gorton and Nancy Jane (Hamilton) B.; Ph.B., Ohio Northern U., 1901; A.B., U. of Chicago, 1906, Ph.D., 1908; m. Anna Irene Lesh, Jan. 1, 1902; children—Edith Mildred, Anna Lucile (Mrs. Howard Day). Prof. biology and geology, Ohio Northern U., 1902-04; asst. in botany, U. of Chicago, 1906-08; instr. in botany, Stanford, 1908-09, asst. prof., 1909-16; asso. prof., 1916-24, professor biology, 1924-41; professor emeritus since 1941; acting professor zoology, University of Oregon, summers 1924, 25. Field asst. U.S. Department Agr., 1918. Mem. A.A.A.S., Bot. Soc. America, Genetics Soc. of America, Am. Genetics Soc., Am. Eugenics Soc., Assn. for Research in Human Heredity, Am. Naturalists, Western Naturalist, Am. Assn. Univ. Profs., Sigma Xi, Phi Beta Kappa; fellow Calif. Acad. Sciences. Author: General Biology, 1921; Heredity and Social Problems, 1940. Also numerous scientific papers. Address: 426 Jordan Hall, Stanford University, Palo Alto CA‡

BURN, BELLE SUMNER ANGIER, writer; b. Carlyle, Ill., Apr. 25, 1870; d. Albert Warriner and Josephine A. (Summer) Angier; ed. Berkeley (Cal.) High Sch.; spl. courses at U. of Cal. and U. of Southern Cal.; m. Walter Lewis Burn, of Albany, N.Y., Jan. 5, 1907. Advertising writer, 1899-1904; on staff Los Angeles Times, 1900-5, Los Angeles Express, 1905; society editor Los Angeles Evening News, 1906; now on staff of West Coast Magazine. Landscape architect since 1906; lecturer on civic improvements and gardening. Organizer of human progress clubs. Mem. Equal Suffrage League. Clubs: Woman's Press of Southern Cal., San Diego Woman's. Author: The Garden Book of California, 1907. Address: 1036 W. Washington St., Los Angeles CA‡

BURNET, DUNCAN, librarian; b. Cincinnati, June 2, 1876; s. Jacob, Jr., and Mary Scott (Duncan) B.; ed. Pomona Coll., Cal., Lehigh Univ., N.Y. State Library Sch.; student abroad, 1896-97; m. Inez Daughtry, June 29, 1912; children—Mary Scott, Duncan II, Robin Grier. On staff Cincinnati Pub. Library, 1900, Univ. of Mo. Library, 1901-04. Librarian Univ. of Ga., since Oct. 1904. Member Kappa Alpha Soc. and various professional and academic socs. Home: 375 Cloverhurst Av. Address: University of Ga., Athens GA*‡

BURNETT, CHARLES HOYT, physician, educator; b. Boulder, Colo., Mar. 7, 1913; s. Clough Turrill and Lucille (Hoyt) B.; A.B., U. Colo., 1934, M.D., 1937; M. Eda Waugh, Apr. 27, 1940; children—Grosvenor Turrill, Mark Hoyt, Margaret Jamie. Asst. resident pathology, asst. pathology Presbyn. hosp., N.Y.C., Columbia U. Coll. Phys. and Surg., 1937-38; intern Harvard med. service Boston City Hosp., 1939-40; asst. resident medicine Mass. Gen. Hosp., Boston, 1940-42, chief resident medicine, 1945-46; asst. medicine, med. sch. Harvard, 1940-42, 45-46; asst. prof. medicine Boston U. Sch. Medicine, 1947-50, asso. prof., 1950; asst. mem. Robert Dawson Evans Meml. Hosp., 1947-50, asso. mem., 1950; prof. medicine, chmn. dept. Southwestern Med. Sch., U. Tex., Dallas, 1950-51; prof. medicine University N.C., Chapel Hill, 1951-67, head dept. medicine, 1951-65; consultant Surgeon Gen.'s Office, 1946-56, 63-67; chief med. service N.C. Memorial Hospital, 1952-65; chief cons. for research Richardson Merrell, Inc., 1965-67. Mem. Nat. Board Medical Examiners medicine test committee, 1955-56, chmn. 1956. Member of sub-com. on shock Nat. Research Council, 1951-54; sci. adv. bd. Armed Forces Inst. Pathology, 1952-56; mem. adv. com. for biology and medicine AEC, 1953-58; council Nat. Inst. for Arthritis and Metabolic Diseases, 1958-62. Served as maj. M.C., AUS, 1942-46. Decorated Bronze Star Medal Fellow A.C.P.: mem. Soc. for Clin. Investigation (emeritus), Assn. Am. Physicians. A.A.A.S., Endocrine Soc., A.M.A., Am. Acad. Arts and Scis., So. Soc. Clin. Research, Assn. Am. Profs. Medicine (v.p. 1963), Alpha Omega Alpha. Author sci. articles. Home: Chapel Hill NC Died Oct. 23, 1967.

BURNETT, CHARLES HUGH, JR., bottling and food company executive; born at Seattle, Washington, May 24, 1902; son of Charles Hiram and Mary (Goodfellow) B.; B.A., U. Wash., 1924; postgrad. Harvard Law Sch., 1924-25, Harvard Bus. Sch., 1957; spl. studies Ore. State Coll., 1933-34; m. Elizabeth Clare Lindsay, Apr. 11, 1929. Asst. mgr. Laie Plantation, Oahu, Hawaii, 1927-30, Wailuku Sugar Co., (Hawaii), 1930-33; ranch mgr. Hawaiian Commercial & Sugar Co., Puunene, Hawaii, 1934-48; gen. mgr. Kahului Railroad Co. (Hawaii), 1948-65; partner Haiku Poultry Farm; pres. Maui Soda & Ice Works, Ltd. Home: Makawao HI Died July 8, 1967.

BURNETT, GEORGE JACKSON, college pres.; b. Auburn, Ky., Dec. 26, 1874; s. Joseph H. and Laura A. (Duff) B.; ed. Auburn and Bethel colls., Ky.; m. Laura Yates, of Winchester, Ky., Aug. 19, 1903. Taught in country schs., and Loudon (Tenn.) Sem.; became teacher, later v.-p., and 1903-7, pres. of Liberty Coll., Glasgow, Ky.; pres. Tenn. Coll., Murfreesboro, Tenn., since June, 1907. Pres. Tenn. Bapt. Conv., 1914-16; pres. Assn. of Tenn. Colleges, 1921-22. Home: Murfreesboro TN‡

BURNETT, JESSE MCGARRITY, college pres.; b. Del Rio, Tenn., Aug. 29, 1870; s. Jesse LaFayette M. and Henrietta Sarah (Cody) B.; A.B., Richmond (Va.) Coll., 1894; Th.M., Southern Bapt. Theol. Sem., Louisville, Ky., 1894; (D.D., Carson-Newman Coll., 1906); m. Lucile Phillips, of Pembroke, Ky., Nov. 6, 1898. Prof. Greek, 1894-12, pres., Apr., 1912—, Carson-Newman Coll. Democrat. Baptist. Mem. Beta Theta Pi. Address: Jefferson City TN‡

BURNETT LEO, advt. exec.; b. St. Johns, Mich., Oct. 21, 1891; s. Noble and Rose (Clark) B.; A.B., U. Mich., 1914; m. Naomi Geddes, May 29, 1918; children—Peter, Joseph, Phoebe. Founder, pres. Leo Burnett Co., Incorporated, 1935, founder chmn., 1967-71. Director Advertising Council 1941-71, chmn., 1962-63; trustee, mem. exec. com. Am. Heritage Found., 1953-69; dir. Better Bus. Bur. Met. Chgo., 1946-71; dir. advt. Non-Partisan Register and Vote campaign, 1952, 56. Mem. exec. bd. Com. Econ. and Cultural Devel. Chgo., 1962-69; trustee Adler Planetarium, Chgo., 1967-71; bd. dirs. Chgo. Met. chpt. Nat. Alliance Businessmen, 1968-71. Received honor award, Wartime Advt., 1945, Freedoms Found., Inc., 1949; Gold Medal award, Printers Ink, 1955; Special Merit award, N.Y. Art Directors Club, 1956; Gold Key award Copy Club N.Y., 1961; Honor award distinguished service in journalism, Sch. Journalism, U. Mo., 1963; Bus. Statesmanship award Harvard Bus. Sch. Assn. Chgo., 1963; Benjamin Franklin award Printing Industry, 1970; named Marketing Man of Yr. Chgo. chpt. Am. Marketing Assn., 1966. Republican. Clubs: University, (N.Y.); Everglades (Palm Beach, Fla.); Detroit Athletic; Minneapolis; Chicago, Racquet, Tavern, Executives, Economic, Mid America, Commercial (Chgo.) Lake Zurich (Ill.) Golf; University (Indpls.). Author: Communications of an Advertising Man, 1961. Editor, compiler: Good Citizen, 1948. Home: Lake Zurich IL Died June 7, 1971.

BURNETT, WHIT, editor, writer; b. Salt Lake City, Utah, Aug. 14, 1899; s. Benjamin James and Anna Marian (Christensen) B.; student U. of So. Cal. 1918; U. Utah, 1920; U. Cal. 1921; m. Martha Foley, 1930 (div.); 1 son, David; m. 2d, Hallie Southgate Abbett, 1942; children—John, Whitney Ann Beekman. Reporter, Salt Lake newspapers 1916; reporter on Evening Express, Los Angeles, 1918; editor Asso. Press, Los Angeles, 1919-20, San Francisco, 1921, asst. city editor, N.Y. 1926-27; city editor, N.Y. Herald, Paris edition, 1927-28; organizer Balkan news service for N.Y. Sun Fgn. Service and Consol. Press, Vienna, Austria, 1929-31; founder, with Martha Foley, of magazine, Story, Vienna, 1931, transferred magazine to New York, 1933; with J.B. Lippincott Co. 1939-49, E.P. Dutton, other cos. 1949-73; editor Scholastic Press, until 1971; instr. advanced short story, Columbia U., 1936-43. Queens Coll., 1940, Hunter Coll., 1957-58; editor Hawthorn Books, N.Y.C., 1958-61; editor (with Hallie Burnett) Story Mag., Story Press, 1942-65; mem. editorial bd. Story (acquired by Scholastic Mags., Inc.), 1966, dir. Story's Coll. Creative Awards Contest, 1966-71. Charter Member Anglo-Am. Press Assn. Vienna, Overseas Press Club, N.Y., gov., 1963-67, 71; chmn. nat. awards com. 1966-67, 69, 70, sec. of P.E.N., Am. Center, 1944-46. Editor (with Martha Foley): A Story Anthology, 1933, Story in America, 1934; The Flying Yorkshireman, novellas, 1937. Editor: This Is My Best, anthology of 93 of America's greatest living authors, 1942; Two Bottles of Relish, a book of strange stories, 1942; The Seas of God, great stories of the human spirit, 1944; Time To Be Young, 1945; The Story Pocket Book, 1945; American Writers Today (with C.E. Slatkin), 1947; Story: The Fiction of the Forties, and Sextet (with Hallie Burnett), 1949, 51; The World's Best, 1950; Story, No. 1, 2, 3, 4 (with Hallie Burnett) 1951-54; editor and collaborator on This Is My Best, radio series, 1944-45. Author: The Maker of Signs (short stories), 1934, The Literary Life and the Hell With It (essays), 1939; Immortal Bachelor, The Love Story of Robert Burns (with John Pen), 1942; contbr. articles and stories to mags. Editor: This Is My Best Humor, 1955; The Spirit of Adventure, 1956; Animal Spirits, 1956; This is My Philosophy, 1957; The Spirit of Man, 1958; Firsts of the Famous, 1962; (with Hallie Burnett); Best College Writing, 1962, Prize College Stories, 1963, The Stone Soldier, 1964, The Modern Short Story in the Making, 1964, Story Jubilee, 1965; Story: The Yearbook of Discovery, 1968, 69, 70, 71, That's What Happened to Me, 1969; This Is My Best, 1970; Black Hands on a White Face, 1971. Home: Wilton CT Died Apr. 1973.

BURNHAM, E(NOCH) LEWIS, ret. banker; b. Phila., Jan. 27, 1883; s. George, Jr., and Anna G. (Lewis) B.; student Havorford Sch., 1897-99; A.B., Harvard, 1904; C.E., Cornell, 1907; m. Cora B. Sellers, Oct. 9, 1909; children—Alan, Joan (Mrs. Thomas Spencer). With Hooker Electrochem. Co., Niagara Falls, N.Y., 1907-09, dir. from 1925; confidental sec. George Burnham, Jr., Phila., 1914-24; executor, trustee numerous estates from 1924; dir. Berwyn Nat. Bank from 1914, pres., 1949, chmn. bd. from 1950. Exec. sec. War Camp Community Service, Waco, Tex., World War I; Vol. Port Security Force, U.S. Coast Guard Res., Phila., World War Ii. Pres. Phila. Bur. Municipal Research, 1924-42, Pa. Sch. Social Work, 1920-43. Mem. bd. edn. for social work U. of Pa. Mem. A.A.A.S., Franklin Inst. Phila., Phi Delta Theta. Clubs: Harvard (N.Y. City, Phila.); University, Franklin Inn (Phila.). Berwyn PA Died Apr. 1969.

BURNHAM, FREDERICK E(DWIN), financial exec.; b. Loda, Ill, June 3, 1906; s. John and Louise (Spears) B.; student pub. schs., Ill.; m. Ruth Ellen Klepinger, Oct. 23, 1934; children—Frederick Edwin, Jean Louise. Pub. acct. Allen R. Smart & Co., C.P.A.'s, Chgo., 1927-33, mgr. Dayton office, 1933-35; gen. acct. United Aircraft Corp., East Hartford, Conn., 1936-45; controller, treas., dir. Colt's Mfg. Co., Hartford, 1945-49; v.p., controller Freuhauf Trailer Co., Detroit, 1950-53, financial v.p., 1953-56, exec. v.p., 1956-57; executive v.p. George L. Nankervis Co., 1958; financial cons., 1958-59; financial v.p. Chance Vought Corporation, 1959-61; pres., dir. Master Consol., Inc., Dayton, O., from 1962; dir. Brady Mfg. Co. Ky. col. C.P.A., Ill. Mem. Am. Inst. C.P.A.'s, Financial Execs. Inst., Nat. Assn. Accountants. Home: Dayton OH Died Feb. 11, 1970; buried White Chapel Meml. Park, Troy MI

BURNHAM, FREDERICK WILLIAM, clergyman; b. Chapin, Ill., May 7, 1871; s. Dr. John Kirby and Laura A. (Woodward) B.; student Whipple Acad., Jacksonville, Ill., 1889-90; A.B., Eureka (Ill.) Coll., 1895, LL.D., 1915; student U. of Chicago, summer 1902; m. Cenie Allison, Oct. 2, 1895. Ordained ministry Christian (Disciples) Ch., 1896; pastor Carbondale, Ill., 1896, Charleston, Ill., 1896-1901, Decatur, Ill., 1901-06, Springfield, Ill., 1907-14, Wilshire Blvd. Ch., Los Angeles, Calif., 1914; pres. Am. Christian Missionary Soc., 1915-31; pres. United Christian Missionary Soc., 1919-30; pastor University Park Christian Ch., Indianapolis, Ind., 1930-31. Seventh St. Ch., Richmond, Va., 1931-46; now retired, but serving rural churches. Member executive committee Federal Council of Chs. of Christ in America (chmn. exec. com. 1920-24); rep. of Disciples of Christ on Advisory Council of Am. Bible Soc., 1931-36. Pres. Ill. Christian Endeavor Union, 1904-06; sec. Assn. for Promotion of Christian Unity, 1910-14; rep. to World Conf. on Faith and Order, Geneva (visited France, Switzerland, Germany, Denmark, Norway, England and Scotland), 1920, Universal Conf. on Life and Work, Stockholm, 1925, Oxford Conf. Church, Community and State, 1937; pres. Foreign Missions Conf. of N.A., 1927-28, visited Alaska, 1918, Puerto Rico, 1923; special envoy to All Russian Evang. Union, Leningrad; 1925, visited capitals of Europe, Palestine, Egypt and Near East. Fraternal delegate to chs. of New Zealand and Australia and visited missions of India, P.I., China and Japan, 1928-29; pres. Virginia Christian Missionary Conv., 1935. Member Va. Council of Churches. Chairman com. appointed by Governor to advise with conscientious objectors. Former national dir. Boy Scouts America; former chaplain Richmond Chapter S.A.R. Mason (32 deg., K.T., Prelate St. Andrews Commandery 13). Author: A Missionary Tour of Alaska, 1919; Unification, 1927. Va. corr. to Christian Century. Contbr. to Expositor. Churches built during pastorates at Decatur and Springfield. Home: Stratford Hills, R.F.D. No. 9, Richmond VA‡

BURNHAM, HUBERT, architect; b. Chicago, Ill., Sept. 7, 1882; s. Daniel Hudson and Margaret (Sherman) B.; grad. Chicago Manual Training Sch. and Phillips Acad. Andover, Mass; grad. U.S. Naval Acad., 1905; grad. Ecole des Beaux Arts, Paris, 1912; m. Vivian Cameron, June 24, 1908; children—Cherie (Mrs. Lawrence Kendall Morris), Margaret (mrs LeGrow). Mem. D.H. Burnham & Co. (founded by father), Chicago, 1910-12, Graham, Burnham & Co., 1912-17, re-established firm of D. H. Burnham & Co., 1917, Burnham Bros., Inc., 1928. Burnham Bros. & Hammond, Inc., 1933, now Burnham & Hammond; firm designed the Burnham, Bankers, Carbide and Carbon, Engring. and Medical and Dental Arts Bldg., Chicago, So. wing and boiler house Evanston (Ill.) Hosp., Presbyn.-St. Lukes Nurses Home, Chgo., Argo Elementary Sch., Meml. Hosp., Springfield, Ill. Past chmn. Evanston City Plan Commn. Ret., 1955. Lt. U.S. Navy, World War; aviation constrn. work in France 14 mos. Fellow Am. Institute of Architects; member Society Beaux Arts Architects, Chicago Archtl. Club. Republican. Club: Glen View. Mem. Archtl. Commn. Chicago World's Fair Centennial Celebration, 1933. Home: Chicago IL Died Dec. 31, 1968; buried Graceland Cemetery, Chicago IL

BURNHAM, WALTER HENRY, advt., pub. relations exec.; b. Providence, Aug. 31, 1886; s. Walter Willcutt and Grace Edith (Warner) B.; A.B., Brown U., 1908; m. Anne H. Edwards, Apr. 21, 1917; children—Margrette Louise (Mrs R. Manning Brown, Jr.), Anne Warner (Mrs. William B. Moore), Phoebe Barber (Mrs. E. J. White, Jr.). With Carlisle, Mellick Co., N.Y.C., 1908-11, Richmond Dorrance & Co., Providence, 1911-12; salesman Potter, Choate & Prentice, N.Y.C., 1912-14; dept. Mgr. Crompton Richmond Co., N.Y.C., 1914-17; sec. Doremus & Co., N.Y.C., 1919, v.p., 1932-46, hon. vice chmn., dir. until 1962. Dir., Elizabeth Gen. Hosp., 1925-35, also Social Welfare Soc. Elizabeth. Served as capt., U.S. Army, World War I. Mem. Delta Kappa Epsilon. Clubs: Yacht (Bay Head, N.J.); Tiger Inn (Princeton, N.J.). Home: Bay Head NJ Died June 1, 1968.

BURNITE, CAROLINE, librarian; b. in Caroline Co., Md., Jan. 2, 1875; d. Emery and Annie K. (Holmes) B.; grad. Easton (Md.) High School, 1892; grad. Pratt Inst. Library Sch., Brooklyn, 1894; unmarried. Asst., Schermerhorn Library, Brooklyn, 1894; librarian Equitable Assurance Soc. of U.S., 1895; librarian Tome Inst., Port Deposit, Md., 1895-01; asst., Carnegie Library, Pittsburgh, 1902-4; dir. Children's work, Pub. Library, Cleveland, 1904-—. Instr. Western Reserve Library Sch. Mem. A.L.A. (council, 1912-—). Ohio Library Assn. (pres., 1911-12). Contbr. to library periodicals. Address: 45 The Plaza, Cleveland‡

BURNS, ANNA LETITIA, editor; b. Mansfield, O.; d. Dr. James and Anna (Wiley) Miller; ed. pvt. schs.; m. Capt. Andrew Marion Burns (died 1894). Since 1894 lit. editor W. A. Wilde Co., Boston and Chicago publishers. Mem. Ohio Woman's Press Assn., New England Woman's Press Assn., D. A. R. Clubs: Boston Authors', New England Woman's. Home: 112 Newbury St., Boston‡

BURNS, DAVID, actor; b. N.Y.C., June 22, 1902; s. Harry and Dora Burns; student pub. schs.; m. Mildred Todd. Appeared Broadway plays, Oklahoma, South Pacific, Two's Company, Make Mine Manhattan, A Hole in the Head, The Music Man, A Funny Thing Happened on the Way to the Forum, Hello Dolly, The Price, Sheep on the Runway, Lovely Ladies, Kind gentlemen; motion pictures include Knock on Wood, Deep in My Heart, It's Always Fair Weather, Let's Make Love, Who is Harry Kellerman and Why is He Saying Those Terrible Things about Me; in Broadway prodn. Do Ri Me. TV appearances NBC, CBS. Served with AUS, 1942-43. Recipient Tony award, 1958, 62, Emmy award, 1971. Home: New York City NY Died Mar. 12, 1971.

BURNS, EDWARD MCNALL, ret. educator, author: b. Burgettstown, Pa., Feb. 18, 1897; s. James McNall James McNall and Lucy (Gilliland) B.; student Washington and Jefferson Coll., 1917-18; A.B., U. Pitts., 1925, A.M., 1927, Ph.D., 1935, LL.D., 1962; student U. Chgo., 1926-29; m. Marie K. Bentz, June 29, 1936; 1 dau., Eleanor W. Asst. in polit. sci. U. Pitts., 1925-27; instr. history and polit. sci. Rutgers, 1928-31, asst. prof. history, 1931-41, asso. prof., 1941-47, prof. history 1947-51, prof. polit. sci., 1951-62, emeritus, 1962-72, chmn. dept. history and polit. sci. 1950-51, chmn. dept. polit. sci., 1951-62, sec. faculty Coll. Arts and Scis., 1943-62; lectr. Vanderbilt U., summer 1963, U. Cal. at Santa Barbara, 1964-65; lectr. South Orange-Maplewood (N.J.) Adult Sch., 1935-40; Fulbright prof. U. Berlin, 1959-60; James Taylor lectr. S.W. Tex. State Coll., 1966. Recipient Distinguished Research award Rutgers Research Council, 1957. Mem. Am. Hist. Assn., Am. Polit. Sci. Assn., Am. Assn. U. Profs., Phi Beta Kappa, Tau Kappa Alpha, Phi Alpha Theta. Author: James Madison, Philosopher of the Constitution, 1938; Western Civilizations, Their History and Their Culture, 1941; David Starr Jordan: Prophet of Freedom, 1953; The American Idea of Mission, 1957; Ideas in Conflict, 1960; The Counter Reformation, 1964; (with Phillip L. Ralph) World Civilizations, 1955. Home: Santa Barbara CA Died July 14, 1972.

BURNS, HENDRY STUART MACKENZIE, company dir.; b. Aberdeen, Scotland, April 28, 1900; s. John Stuart and Anne (Mackenzie) B.; ed. Robert Gordons Coll., Scotland, 1914-17; B.Sc., Aberdeen Univ., 1922; B.A., Cambridge Univ., 1925; m. Dorcas Jackson, Jan. 24, 1929; children—Peter Mackenzie, Michael Jackson. Came to U.S., 1926. Geophysicist, Shell Oil Co., Calif., 1926, transferred to mfg. and supplies dept., 1927, asst. to div. mgr., Seattle, 1928-32, assistant gen. sales mgr., 1932-34, gen. sales mgr., 1934-36, gen. mgr. Shell Co. of Colombia, S.A., 1936-46; senior v.p., Shell Oil Co., Inc., N.Y., 1946-47, pres. 1947-60; dir. Ampex Corp., General Dynamics Corp. Dir., Am. Petroleum Inst. Trustee National Safety Council. Mem. Saint Andrews Soc. (N.Y.), Burns Soc. Conservative. Clubs: Pacific Union (San Francisco), Racquet and Tennis, Links (N.Y.C.); Piping Rock L.I.); Whites New York City NY Died Oct. 21, 1971.

BURNS, HOWARD FLETCHER, lawyer; b. Lockport, N.Y., Oct. 25, 1888; s. William Treat and Ella Louise (Marsh) B.; student Lewis Inst., Chicago, Ill, 1906-08; A.B., Amherst Coll., 1912; LL.B., Harvard Univ., 1916; LL.D. (honorary), Cleve. State U. (formerly Fenn Coll.), 1961; m. Mary Leaycraft Strong, Dec. 9, 1916 (died Dec. 20, 1922); m. 2d, Elna Margareta Anderson, Sept. 3, 1924; children—Allen Anderson, Howard Marsh. Admitted to Ohio bar, 1917; associated with M.B. and H.H. Johnson, Cleve., 1916-17, with White, Johnson, Cannon & Neff, Cleve., 1917-21; practiced individually, 1921-27; partner in firm, Baker, Hostetler & Sidlo, and successor firms, Baker, Hostetler, Sidlo & Patterson and Baker, Hostetler & Patterson, 1928-68; dir. Eudy & Assos., Inc. Mem. American Law Institute (council mem., mem. exec. com.); mem. vis. com. Western Res. Law Sch. 1958-68; alumni council Amherst Coll., 1957-62; trustee Hawken Sch., Cleve.; trustee Mt. Holyoke Coll., 1950-60, pres. bd. trustees, 1958-60; member board of trustees Cleve. Inst. of Music, Mus. Arts Association, Fenn Coll., 1952-65. Fellow Am. Bar Found., Am. Coll. Trial Lawyers; mem. Assn. of Bar N.Y.C., Am. (chmn. com. on fed. judiciary 1949-53), Ohio, Cleve. (pres. 1958-59), Inter. Am. bar assns., Am. Judicature Soc., Jud. Conf. 6th Circuit (life), Harvard Law Sch. Association (member of the council 1957-61). Clubs: Amherst, Century Assn. (N.Y.C.); Tavern, City, Kirtland Country, Mid-Day, Union (Cleve.). Home: Cleveland OH Died Dec. 19, 1968.

BURNS, ROBERT EDWARD, univ. pres.; b. Flat River, Mo., July 26, 1909; s. John L. and Stella Lee (DeGrant) B.; A.B., Coll. of the Pacific, 1931, A.M., 1946; LL.D., Williamette U., 1947; m. Grace Weeks, Oct. 6, 1934; children—Bonnie Jean, Ronald Robert. Field sec., Coll. of the Pacific (name changed to University of Pacific, 1961), 1931-32, alumni and placement sec., 1932-36, registrar, 1936-41, registrar and asst. to pres., 1942-46, pres., 1946-71. Del. Quadrennial Gen. Conf. Methodism, 1952, 56, 60, 64, 68. Mem. Cal. Centennial Commn., Cal. State Park Commn. Past chmn. Independent Coll. Funds Am. Mem. Cal. Conf. Social Work (past pres.), Nat. Assn. Schs. and Colls. Meth. Ch. (past pres.), Independent Colleges of Northern California (past president), Western College assn. (past pres.), Cal. Hist. Soc., Assn. Am. Colls. (mem. commn. coll. adminstrn.), Assn. Ind. Cal. Colls. and Univs. (pres.), Phi Kappa Phi, Pi Gamma Mu, Phi Delta Kappa, Rho Lambda Phi, Alpha Epsilon Rho, Phi Mu Alpha, Pi Kappa Delta, Methodist (mem. univ. senate, nat. bd. edn.). Mason (33 deg., Shriner; past grand chaplain Cal.). Clubs: Rotary, Commonwealth (sec.); Bohemian (San Francisco). Address: Stockton CA Died Feb. 13, 1971.

BURNS, ROBERT EMMETT, orthopedist; b. Wisconsin Rapids, Wis., May 6, 1895 s. Walter Hamilton and Delia Barbara (Meulemans) B.; B.S., U. of Wis., 1917; M.D., U. of Pa., 1919; m. Charlotte Joslin Calvert, M.D., Sept. 16, 1930; children—Thomas Calvert, Charlotte Ann, Mary Ellen. Interne St. Mary's Hosp., Madison, Wis., 1919-21, Hosp. for Ruptured and Crippled, New York, 1921-22; fellow in orthopedic surgery Mayo Clinic, 1922-23; resident instr., asst. and asso. prof. of orthopedic surgery, U. of Wis., 1923-30, prof., from 1930; chief orthopedic service U. Hosps., U. Wis., from 1930. Fellow A.C.S.; mem. A.M.A., Clin. Orthopedic Soc. (past pres.), Am. Acad. Orthopedic Surgeons, Am. Orthopedic Assn., Alumni Assn. of Hosp. for Ruptured and Crippled. Assn. of Resident and Ex-resident physicians of Mayo Clinic, Internat. Orthopaedic Society. Catholic. Home: Madison WI Died Sept. 8, 1969; buried Wisconsin Rapids WI

BURR, FREEMAN F., geologist; b. Medford, Mass., Mar. 7, 1877; s. Horace Freeman and Susan Lydia (Sawyer) B.; B.S., Harvard, 1900; student Yale, 1908; A.M., Columbia, 1913; m. Lois Southwick Ives, June 30, 1904; children—Richard Southwick, Barbara (Mrs. Horton Flynt), Foster Ives (dec.), Jean (Mrs. Alexander F. Smith), Horace Freeman. Science teacher high and prep. schs., 1900-04; instr. State Normal Sch., New Haven, 1904-12; lecturer, instr. Barnard Coll. (Columbia U.), 1912-15; geol. to Me. State Commns., 1914-22; head dept. geol., St. Lawrence U., 1922-31; Me. State geol., 1935-46; retired; part time biology, Allendale Sch., Rochester, N.Y. Mem. Augusta City Council, 1921-22. Past pres. Knox Acad. of Arts and Sciences; mem. Me. Mineral, Soc. Republican. Unitarian. Author: Maine State Reports; also science and nature articles. Home: Sunrise Farm, Wayne ME‡

BURR, GEORGE L(INDSLEY), business exec.; b. Phoenixville, Pa., Aug. 29, 1889; s. William Hubert and Caroline Kent (Seelye) B.; A.B., Harvard, 1910; C. E., Columbia, 1912; m. Susan Sturgis Strong, May 13, 1913 (dec. 1918); children—William F., R. Peters; m. 2d, Priscilla Munroe Reynolds, Jan. 5, 1920; 1 son, Benjamin. Civil engineer Interborough Rapid Transit Co., N.Y. City, 1912; civil engr. Stone & Webster, Inc., Keokuk, Ia., 1912-13, Houston and Dallas, 1913-16; employee Guaranty Trust Co., N.Y. City, 1916-19, vice pres., 1919-27; partner Lazard Freres, 1927-40; dir. United Corp. Trustee, James Found. N.Y., Inc. Mem. N.Y. State Banking Bd., 1933-43. Mem. N.Y. State Soc. Cin. Club: Harvard (N.Y.C.). Home: Dobbs Ferry NY Died Mar. 7, 1971.

BURR, HAROLD S(AXTON), coll. prof.; b. Lowell, Mass., Apr. 10, 1889; s. Hanford Montrose and Clara Helen (Saxton) B.; student Springfield Coll. (Y.M.C.A.), 1907-08; Ph.B., Sheffield Sci. Sch. (Yale), 1911; Ph.D., 1915; m. Jean Forrest Chandler, Dec. 27, 1911; 1 son, Peter Saxton. Asst. instr. in anatomy, later instr., Yale U., 1914-19, asst. prof., 1919-26; Sterling fellow, 1926-27, asso. prof., later prof., 1926-33, E.K. Hunt prof. of anatomy, 1933-58, E. K. Hunt prof. anatomy emeritus, 1958-73. Mem. A.A.A.S., Am. Association of Anatomists, Am. Neurol. Assn., Conn. State Med. Soc., Lyme Art Assn., Sigma Xi. Republican. Conglist. Clubs: Graduate (New Haven), Yale (New York); Beaumont Med. History, Nathan Smith. Home: Old Lyme CT Died Feb. 17, 1973.

BURR, HENRY TURNER, educator; b. Medford, Mass., Apr. 29, 1874; s. Horace F. and Susan L. (Sawyer) Burr; grad. State Normal School, Bridgewater, Mass., 1896; S.B., Harvard, 1899, S.M., 1900; m. Ada M. Harding, of Westfield, Mass., Aug. 15, 1901. Asst. in geology and geography, Harvard, 1897-1900; instr. in science, State Normal Sch., New Britain, Conn., 1900-4; prin. State Normal Sch., Willimantic, Conn., since 1904. Address: 122 Windham St., Willimantic CT‡

BURRAGE, CHAMPLIN, author, archaeologist; b. Portland, Me., Apr. 14, 1874; s. Henry Sweetser and Caroline (Champlin) B.; A.B., Brown U., 1896, hon. A.M., in absentia, 1905; studied univs. of Berlin and Marburg, and traveled widely in Europe, 1899-1901, Oxford U., 1906-15; B.Litt., Oxford, 1909; hist. research in English libraries, 1901-15; m. at Oxford, Florence Dwight Dale, of Montclair, N.J., Sept. 3, 1907. Librarian Manchester Coll., Oxford, 1912-15; librarian John Carter Brown Library (Brown U.), and mem. faculty of Brown U., 1915-17; hist., archaeol. and philol. research in Am. libraries and museums, 1915-20; temporarily on staff Mus. of Fine Arts, Boston, summer

1923 and winter 1923-24. Corr. mem. N.E. Hist.-Geneal. Soc.; mem. Archaeol. Inst. America, Bibliog. Soc. America, Delta Kappa Epsilon, Phi Beta Kappa. Author: A New Year's Guift by Robert Browne, 1588, 1904; The Church Covenant Idea, 1904; The True Story of Robert Browne (Oxford Univ. Press), 1906; The Retraction of Robert Browne, 1907; New Facts Concerning John Robinson, 1910; The Early English Dissenters in the Light of Recent Research (Cambridge Univ. Press), 1912; John Penry, the So-Called Martyr of Congregationalism, 1913; Nazareth and the Beginnings of Christianity, 1914; John Pory's Lost Description of Plymouth Colony, 1918; An Answer to John Robinson, of Leyden, 1920; The Minoan Hieroglyphic Inscriptions, I; The Phaestos Whorl, 1921 (reprinted from Harvard Studies in Classical Philology, Vol. 32, 1921; this brochure is believed to contain a considerable number of first readings from the prehistoric Cretan inscriptions); Studies in the Hieroglyphic Inscriptions and Pictographs of Minoan Crete and Neighboring Countries and Islands; also contbr. hist. articles in English Historical Review, American Jour. of Theology, Harvard Theol. Review, etc. Collector Henry S. Burrage collection, Colgate U. library, relics of mound builders of Ohio (Muskingum valley and Blennerhassett island regions) and the Burrage collection of Cretan Antiquities, 1927-—. Compiler and editor Seaman's Handbook for Shore Leave, 1st edit., 1919 (for U.S. Shipping Bd.). Made Minoan and Hittite investigations in the Ashmolean Mus., British Mus. and museums of Athens and Candia; also made first archaeol. visit to Crete, 1926-27, 2d visit 1927. Home: 5 Brookline MA‡

BURRAGE, DWIGHT GRAFTON, college prof.; b. Pittsford, Vt., Aug. 3, 1873; s. Joseph and Mary Eliza (Closson) B.; A.B., Amherst, 1897, A.M., 1899; studied summers in six univs.; Ph.D., U. of Neb., 1920; unmarried. Teacher high sch., Amherst, Mass., 1897-99; prin. high sch., Jaffrey, N.H., 1899-1902; prin. Peacham (Vt.) Acad., 1902-06; instr. Greek and Latin, Doane Coll., Crete, Neb., 1906-09, prof. since 1909. Mem. Am. Classical League, Classical Assn. Middle West and South, Archaeol. Inst. of America, Phi Beta Kappa, Phi Kappa Psi. Author: Educational Progress in Greece During the Minoan, Mycenaean, and Lyric Periods, 1921. Home: Crete NE‡

BURRELL, DAVID DE FOREST, clergyman; b. Chicago, Ill., June 29, 1876; s. David James and Clara Sergeant (de Forest) B.; A.B., Yale, 1898; B.D., Princeton Theol. Sem., 1901, fellow, 1903; D.D., U. of Dubuque, 1918; m. Margaret Yonker North, Apr. 29, 1905; children—Elizabeth North, Margaret de Forest, Catharine. Ordained ministry Presbyn. Ch., 1901; asst. pastor 1st Presbyn. Ch., Germantown, Pa., 1901-02; instr., Princeton Theol. Sem., 1903-04; pastor 1st Presbyn. Ch., La Porte, Ind., 1904-07, South Orange, N.J., 1908-18; prof. English Bible, Dubuque (Ia.) Coll., 1918-20; pastor Westminster Presbyn. Ch., Dubuque, 1920-23, 1st Presbyn. Ch., Williamsport, Pa., 1923-41, retired 1941; interim pastor, First Presbyn. Ch., Greensburg, Pa., since Apr. 1943. Pres. Presbyn. Pub. Co. Dir. Lord's Day Alliance of U.S.A. Mem. N.J.N.G., 1917-18. Mem. Delta Kappa Epsilon. Republican. Author: Letters From the Dominie, 1916; Belligerent Peter, 1920; David James Burrell, a Biography, 1929; also wrote booklets: The End of the Way; The Gift; How They Came to Bethlehem; The Lost Star; The Hermit's Christmas Greensburg PA‡

BURRELL, GEORGE W., engring. exec.; b. Andes, N.Y., 1871; s. George and Jeanette (Dowie) B.; ed. Ohio State U.; m. Evelyn A. Jones, 1894; children—Dr. Arthur B., Lucille (Mrs. Crowder), Franklin B. Entered employ of Cleveland Rolling Mills, 1887, and after attending Ohio State U. returned as draftsman, later in charge of physical testing dept.; master mechanic Ironton Structural Steel Co., 1896; joined The Wellman Engring. Co. as draftsman, 1898, pres., 1928-37, chmn. bd., 1937-54, now cons. Pres. C. of C., 1936-37; mem. bd. mgrs. Y.M.C.A. Mem. Associated Industries of Cleveland. Clubs: Mid-Day (Cleveland); Canterbury Golf. Home: 1875 Page Av., East Cleveland, O. Office: 7000 Central Av., Cleveland 4 OH‡

BURRIS, QUINCY GUY, univ. dean; b. Danville, Ill., Feb. 1, 1901; s. Q. D. and Nancy (Russell) B.; B.A., U. Ill., 1924, M.A., 1927, Ph.D., 1930; m. Alice Archbold, Aug. 22, 1925; children—Natalie. Assistant professor English, Milliken U., Decatur, Illinois, 1930-32, Eastern Illinois Coll., 1932-38; prof.; head dept. English, N.M. Highlands U., Las Vegas, from 1938, dean of university, 1952, vice president of university, from 1961. Consultant Ministry of Edn., La Paz, Bolivia, 1946-47. Mem. sch. bd., Las Vegas. Mem. Phi Beta Kappa. Author: Richard Doddridge Blackmore: His Life and Novels, 1930; Translation: The Towers of Manhattan, 1945. Home: Las Vegas NM Died July 31, 1971.

BURROUGHS, W(ILLIAM) DWIGHT, journalist; b. Lynchburg, Va., Feb. 19, 1871; s. Henry Alexander and Elizabeth Carter (Miller) B.; ed. pub. schs.; m. Jennie Gertrude Simpson, of Baltimore, Apr. 29, 1895. On staff Baltimore World, 1892, Herald, 1892-1906, News, 1908-—. Publicity dir. Greater Baltimore Expn. and Jubilee Commn., 1906; sec. Md. Home-Coming Assn., 1907-—; sec. Md. Senate Library Com., 1908; commr. from Md. Legislature to Va. in re joint oyster legislation, 1908. Democrat. Presbyn. Mem. Am. Philatelic Soc., Baltimore Stamp Club, Soc. Army and Navy Confed. States in Md. Clubs: West Arlington Country, Journalists. Author: Jack, Jr., The Giant Killer, 1908; The Wonderland of Stamps, 1910. Home: West Arlington, Md. Office: Munsey Bldg., Baltimore‡

BURROWES, ARTHUR VICTOR, editor; b. Sedalia, Mo., Dec. 23, 1893; s. Evans Barkalow and Teresa (Moore) B.; grad. Sedalia (Mo.) High Sch., 1913; L.H.D. (hon.), St. Benedicts College, Kan., 1951; m. Helen Ann Cooney, June 12, 1926; children—Mary Helen, Arthur, Teresa (Mrs. A. Lee Bloomingdale, Jr.), Madeleine (Mrs. Earle Eugene Sanders, Jr.), Betty Rose (Mrs. Thomas J. Morrison), Janet Alice (now Mrs. Lawrence Schiesl). With St. Joseph (Missouri) News-Press, 1913-68, editor, 1939-68; editor and director News-Press and Gazette. Member executive committee Missouri Pub. Expenditures Survey, Inc.; v.p. St. Joseph Library Bd. Named outstanding citizen of St. Joseph by K.C., 1955; recipient citation for 50 years on same newspaper Gov. John M. Dalton, 1963, Outstanding Community Activities citation Fraternal Order Eagles. Mem. Am. Soc. Newspaper Editors, Nat. Geog. Soc., Acad. Missouri Squires, Sigma Delta Chi. Republican. Roman Catholic. Home: St. Joseph MO Died July 25, 1968; buried Mount Olivet Cemetery, St. Joseph MO

BURROWS, DANIEL CHAPEL, newspaper editor; b. Indianapolis, Jan. 17, 1898; s. William R. and Minnie (Chapel) B.; student New Mexico Mil. Inst., 1918-20, U. of New Mexico, 1922-26; m. Lenore Hanks, 1930 (divorced 1943); 1 son, William Chapel Burrows; m. 2d Mary A. Mathewson, 1951 (dec.). Reporter, sports editor, Albuquerque Journal, 1923-28; reporter, sports editor, Albuquerque Tribune, 1928-31, mng. editor, 1931-44, editor 1944-69. Vice pres. N.M. State Tribune Co., 1944-66. Mem. N.M. Bd. Finance; mem. exec. com. Bataan Meml. Hospital; member board Albuquerque Tech. Vocational Instn. Elected to New Mexico Newspaper Hall Fame, 1969. Member of the American Legion, Am. Soc. Newspaper Editors, N.M. Press Assn. (past pres.), Sigma Chi, Sigma Delta Chi. Presbyn. Elk. Contbr. to various fact-detective mags. Home: Albuquerque NM Died Mar. 30, 1971.

BURSE, WALTER MORRILL, lawyer; born Pittsfield, Me., June 1, 1898; s. Alonzo H. and Nellie M. (Burton) B.; A.B., Brown U., 1920; LL.B., Harvard, 1923; J.D. (hon.). Suffolk University, Boston, 1954; m. Elizabeth G. Luck, July 3, 1935; 1 son, Richard Luck. Admitted to Mass. bar, 1923; asso. law firm Lyne, Woodworth & Evarts, 1923-27, mem. firm, 1927-30; sr. partner Burse, Carpenter, Jackson & Roland from 1930; president. Suffolk University, 1948-54. Director Scott Linotyping Co., Scott Monotype Co., Boston Bldg. Material Co.; treas. N.E. Concrete Masonry Mfrs. Assn. Trustee, treas. Suffolk Univ.; dir. N.E. Sch. of Art. Mem. Officers Training Sch., 16th Training Bn., Field Arty., World War I. Mem. Alpha Delta Phi, Delta Sigma Rho. Universalist. Club: Nat. Exchange of Boston (pres.). Home: Hull MA Died Aug. 1970.

BURSUM, HOLM O., ex-senator; b. Ft. Dodge, Ia., Feb. 10, 1867; s. Frank O. and Marie (Hilton) B.; ed. pub. schs.; m. Lula M. Moore, Aug. 3, 1898; children—Claire Irvin, Ruth Mildred, Holm O., Betty. Moved to N.M., 1881, and engaged in stock raising; mem. Territorial Senate, 1899-1900; del. Rep. Nat. Conv., 1904, 08, 12, 28 (chmn. of N.M. delegation; made seconding speech in behalf of Vice President Curtis); chmn. Territorial Central Com., 1905, 11; mem. Constl. Conv., 1910 (Rep. floor leader); ex-mem. Rep. Nat. Com.; apptd. U.S. senator, Mar. 11, 1921, and elected, Sept. 20, 1921, for unexpired term (1921-25) of Albert B. Fall; nominated for U.S. senator and defeated, 1924. Mem. Com. on Conservation and Administration of Pub. Domain. Republican. Home: Socorro NM‡

BURT, AUSTIN, electrical engr.; b. at Detroit, June 20, 1870; s. Horace Eldon and Lillie (Higgins) B.; g.g.s. William Austin Burt, inventor of solar compass; studied U. of Wis. and U. of Minn.; M.E., Cornell U., 1900; m. Mary Ellen Bartlett, of Cedar Falls, Ia., Jan. 18, 1898. Mgr. Cedar Falls (Ia.) Electric Light Co., 1900-2, Waterloo & Cedar Falls Gas & Electric Co., 1902-5; gen. supt., 1905-11, mgr., 1912, Citizens Gas & Electric Co., Waterloo and Cedar Falls. V.-p. Waterloo Pub. Library; pres. Waterloo Bd. of Edn. Republican. Conglist. Fellow Am. Inst. Elec. Engrs., 1912; mem. Am. Gas Inst. (dir.), Ia. Elec. Assn. (past pres.), Ia. Gas. Assn. (past pres.), Ia. Hist. Soc., S.A.R. (pres. Bunker Hill Chapter), Sigma Xi, Phi Gamma Delta. Mason, K.P. Clubs: Country, Town Criers (Waterloo), Rotary, University (Chicago). Address: Waterloo IA‡

BURT, JOSEPH BELL, prof. pharmacy; b. Woodland, Ill., Sept. 8, 1895; s. James Marion and Olive Jane (Fuller) B.; Ph.C., and B.S., Purdue U., 1920; M.S., U. of Wis., 1927, Ph.D., 1935; m. Marie Frances Clifford, June 5, 1918. With Coll. of Pharmacy, U. of Neb., since 1920, as instr. in pharm., 1920-21, asst. prof., 1921-25, asso. prof., 1925-29, prof. since 1929, chmn. dept. since 1925, dean since 1946. On leave of absence, Oct. 1943-Feb. 1946, as chief, Surg. and Accessory Health Supplies Sect., later dir. Chem., Drugs and Health Supplies Div. Office Civilian Requirements, War Prodn. Bd., Washington, D.C. In 1st R.O.T.C., Ft. Benj. Harrison, May, 1917; commd. 1st lt., U.S. Army, assigned to Mil. Police, 84th Div., also instr. O.T.C., Camp Zachary Taylor; with A.E.F.; disch. Aug., 1919. Awarded scholarship, U. of Wis., 1934-35. Mem. U.S. Pharmacopoeial Revision Com. since 1940; mem. Pharm. Syllabus com. as rep. of Am. Assn. Colls. of Pharmacy. Fellow A.A.A.S.; mem. Am. Phar. Assn., Am. Chem. Soc., Neb. Pharm. Assn., Neb. Acad. Science, Am. Assn. Univ. Profs., Sigma Xi, Phi Sigma, Rho Chi (nat. pres. 1942-43), Phi Delta Chi, Delta Sigma Phi, Scabbard and Blade. Mem. Christian Ch. Mason. Author of A Lab. Study of the Fundamental Process of Pharmacy, 1925. Co-author, with H. M. Burlage, C. O. Lee and L. W. Rising, of Fundamental Principles and Processes of Pharmacy, 1944. Co-author (with H.M. Burlage and L. Wait), Rising Laboratory Manual for Principles and Processes of Pharmacy, 1946. Editor of Pharm. Archives. Contbr. to Jour. Am. Pharm. Assn. Home: 811 Elmwood Av., Lincoln 8 NB*‡

BURTIN, WILL, designer; b. Cologne, Germany, Jan. 27, 1908; s. August and Gertrude (Sieger) B.; student Kolner Werkschulen, 1927-30; m. Hilda Munk, Apr. 12, 1932 (dec., Oct. 1960); 1 dau., Carol; m. 2d, Cipe Pineles Golden, Jan. 28, 1961; 1 stepson, Tom. Came to U.S., 1938, naturalized, 1943. Designer exhbns. and graphic projects, Germany, 1930-38; free-lance designer, N.Y.C., 1938-43; tchr. exptl. design Pratt Inst., Bklyn., 1939-43; art dir. Fortune mag., 1945-49; designer for industry and govt., N.Y.C., 1949-72; design dir., cons. Upjohn Co., Kalamazoo, 1950. Program chmn. Internat. Design Conf., Aspen, Colo., 1954-56, Vision 65, World Communication Congress; speaker numerous design confs. in U.S. and fgn. countries, 1948-72; pres. International Congress Communication Arts and Scis.; v.p. International Com. Graphic Design Association, London. Served with the United States AAF 1943-44; with OSS, 1944-45. Recipient numerous medals and awards from N.Y. Art Dirs. Club, Detroit Art Dirs. Clubs, Am. Inst. Graphic Arts. Mem. Am. Inst. Graphic Arts (past dir.), Am. Soc. Indsl. Designers, Alliance Graphique Internationale (pres. Am. sect.), Soc. Typographers and Artists (hon.), N.Y. Art Dirs., Am. Society Information Sci., Package Designers Council. Club: New York Type Dirs. Club. Designer The Cell, The Brain, Chromosone exhbn., Upjohn Co., 1958-64, also Atom in Action for Union Carbide Corp., 1960. Home: Stony Point NY Died Jan. 18, 1973.

BURTON, EDGAR GORDON, corp. exec.; b. Toronto, Can., 1903; m. Clayton Callaway; children—Mary Alice (Mrs. A. K. Stuart), Anne (Mrs. J. Duncan Smith, Edgar Gordan, C. Merrill. Chmn., pres. Simpsons, Ltd., Toronto; dir. Simpsons-Sears, Ltd., Toronto; v.p., dir. Canadian Imperial Bank Commerce, Brazilian Traction, Light & Power Co., Ltd. (all Toronto); dir. Can. Permanent Trust Co., Johns-Manville Corp. (N.Y.C.), Procter & Gamble Company (Cincinnati), Sears, Roebuck & Company (Chgo.), Am. Airlines, Inc. Decorated comdr. Order Brit. Empire. Home: Toronto ON Canada Died May 8, 1968; buried King City Cemetery, King Ontario Canada

BURTON, LAURENCE V(REELAND), consultant; b. Aurora, Ill., Apr. 15, 1889; s. Charles Pierce and Cora Lena (Vreeland) B.; B.S., U. Ill., 1911, M.S., 1914; Ph.D., Yale University, 1917; m. Isabel Clegg, Aug. 17, 1921 (deceased on August 12, 1965). With Libby, McNeil & Libby, 1915-17, 22-24, Nat. Canners Assn., 1919-21, Ill. Canners Assn., 1921-22, Foulds Milling Co., 1924-28, McGraw-Hill Pub. Co., 1928-47; exec. dir. Packaging Inst., N.Y.C., 1947-55, cons. food processing and packaging, from 1955; contbg. editor Package Engring. Leader 2-man Reverse Flow team under ECA invited by Anglo-Am. Council on Prodn. to visit Eng., 1951. Served as pvt. to 1st lt. San Corps, World War I; corr. SWPA, 1944, Combined Intelligence Objectives Survey, 1945. Recipient Internat. award Inst. Food Technologists, 1957. Mem. Am. Soc. Testing Materials, Tech. Assn. Pulp and Paper Industry, Inst. Food Technologists (pres. 1941-42), Am. Chem. Soc., Soc. Am. Microbiologists, Am. Assn. Cereal Chemists, Packing Inst., Met. Bakery Prodn. Men's Assn., N.Y. Acad. Scis., Soc. for Investigation of Recurring Events, Phi Kappa Sigma, Phi Tau Sigma. Club: Yale (N.Y.C.). Author: Week-End Painter, 1948. Contbr. profl. jours. Home: Scarsdale NY Died July 9, 1970.

BURTON, ROBERT ALLEN, college pres.; b. Willisburg, Ky., Oct. 1, 1878; s. Capt. John Wells and Miranda Alice (Hale) B.; A.B., Ky. Mil. Inst., 1895; student Ky. U. three years, Centre Coll., Danville, Ky., 1899; A.M., Bethany U., 1900; m. Hattie Eloise Weymouth, of New Orleans, La., Sept. 24, 1902; 1 son, Robert Allen. Represented Ky. U. in State oratorical contest, 1897; editor The Cadet, 1896-98; supt. Shelby Co. (Ky.) Schs. 3 years; comdt. cadets, Ga. Mil. Acad., one year; same, Ky. Mil. Inst. two years; supt. Jefferson Mil. Coll., three years; same Tennessee Mil. Inst., two years; assisted in Presbyn. ednl. campaigns in Ia. and Ill., 1923-25; pres. Ogden Coll., Bowling Green, Ky., 1925-27; counselor Whitman Coll., Walla Walla, Wash., 1927-28; pres. Tex. Mil. Coll., Terrell, Tex., since 1928. Capt. 2d. Ky. Inf. two yrs.; assigned to O.T.C., San

Antonio, Tex., 1917-18. Member Kappa Alpha, Pi Gamma Mu. Democrat. Presbyn. Mason (K.T.). Clubs: Lions, Filson (Louisville, Ky.). Address: Terrell TX‡

BURTON, VIRGIL LEE, food broker; b. Hamburg, Mo., Nov. 30, 1901; s. George J. and Ellen (Yahn) B.; student pub. schs.; m. Lena Schall, June 30, 1921. Owner grocery store, St. Charles, Mo., 1920; store mgr., supr. Kroger Co., St. Louis, 1922, 1925-35, produce buyer, dist. mgr., 1935-40, grocery buyer, sales mgr., advt. mgr., merchandiser, 1940-48; food broker, pres. Burton Brokerage Co., Springfield, Mo., 1948-67; pres., chmn. bd. Jiffy Investment Co., Inc., Springfield, Mo., 1960-67. Mem. Modern Woodman. Republican. Mem. Evangelical Ch. Mason (32 deg., K.C.C.H., Shriner). Home: Springfield MO Died Nov. 22, 1967.

BURWELL, JOHN T(OWNSEND), JR., mfg. co. exec.; b. Millwood, Va., Dec. 24, 1912; s. John T(ownsend) and Rosalie Leslie (Wheat) B.; B.S., Mass. Inst. Tech., 1934, M.S., 1936, Ph.D. in Physics, 1938; m. Katharine G. Despard, June 21, 1947; children—John Townsend III, Leslie Bond, George Harrison IV. Teaching fellow physics Mass. Inst. Tech., 1937, research asso., 1939-42, asst. prof. mech. engring., then asso. prof., 1946-51; research physicist research lab, U.S. Steel Corp., Kearny, N.J., 1937-39; tech. mgr. Horizons, Inc., Cleve., 1951-53, asso. dir. research, 1953-55, v.p., 1955-56; dir. research Am. Radiator & Standard San. Corp., 1956-62, v.p. research, 1962-69. Mem. subcom. lubrication and wear NACA, 1942-51; cons. Office Naval Research, 1946-51. Served with USNR, 1942-46. Fellow Am. Phys. Soc.; mem. Am. Soc. M.E., Bldg Research Inst. (acting pres. 1967), N.J. Council Research and Devel. (mem. bd.), National Planning Association (national council), New Jersey Council for Research and Devel. (dir.), N.Y. Acad. Scis., Newcomen Soc., Sigma Xi. Clubs: Engineers (N.Y.C.); Cosmos (Washington); Nassau (Princeton, N.J.). Editor: Mechanical Wear, 1950. Home: Chester NJ Died Mar. 11, 1971; buried Old Chapel, Millwood VA

BURWELL, WILLIAM RUSSELL, business exec.; b. Providence, R.I., Mar. 23, 1894; s. William Chamberlain and Frances Weeden (Knowles) B.; A.B., Brown U., 1915, A.M., 1916, LL.D., 1950; Rhodes scholar, Oxford U., B.A., M.A., 1920, Ph.D., 1921 (first Am. to receive this degree); Sc.D. (hon.), Case Inst. Tech.; 1950; m. Marion Aubrey Eaton, June 3, 1922; children—Robert Winsor, Anstis M. (Mrs. Russell Gifford), Richard Eaton. Inst. math. and navigation, Brown U., 1918-19; asst. prof. math., Univ. of Tenn., Jan.-June, 1922; dean of freshmen and asst. prof. mathematics, Brown U., 1922-26; investment banker, 1926-37; chmn. bd. Brush Development Co. and pres. and dir. Brush Laboratories Co., 1937-52; vice chmn., dir. Clevite Corp., 1952-71; pres. Brush Electronics Co., 1952-55; director Asso. Industries (past pres.); exec. com., director Wheeling Steel Corporation; member board of dirs. Brown & Sharpe Mfg. Co., Clevite Corp. Mem. Bratenahl Village Council, 1952-56. Trustee Council on World Affairs, Cleve. (past pres.), Cleve. Inst. Music (past pres.); board of fellows Brown University; trustee Musical Arts Assn., Play House Found. (v.p.); past chmn. Cleve. Commn. Higher Edn. War worker, Council of Nat. Defense and War Industries Bd., Wash., 1917-18. Mem. Am. Math. Soc., Math. Assn. Am., American Association Rhodes Scholars (director), Phi Beta Kappa Assos., Phi Beta Kappa, Sigma Xi, Zeta Psi. Republican. Baptist. Clubs: University (former pres.), Philosophical (former pres.); Mayfield Country, Fifty (Cleve.) Home: Cleveland OH Died 1971.

BUSBEE, CHARLES MANLY, army officer; b. Raleigh, N.C., July 3, 1893; s. Charles Manly and Elinor (Cooper) B.; B.S., U.S. Mil. Acad., 1915; grad. Command and Gen. Staff Sch., 1926, Army War Coll., 1930; m. Elizabeth C. White, July 9, 1917; 1 son, Charles Manly, Jr.; m. 2d, Lou Taylor Uline, Dec. 26, 1926; children—John Taylor, Willis Uline; m. 3d, Elizabeth Divers, July 3, 1957. Commd. 2d lt., F.A., U.S. Army, June 12, 1915, and advanced through grades to brig. gen., July 25, 1942, ret., 1954. Served in Mexican Campaign, 1916-17, World War I, and with Occupation Forces in Germany after World War II. Decorated Bronze Star, Silver Star, campaign medals. Club; Army and Navy Country (Washington, D.C.). Home: Rocky Mount VA Died Jan. 19, 1970; buried Arlington Nat. Cemetery, Arlington VA

BUSBEE, JACQUES, artist; b. Raleigh, N.C., May 20, 1870; s. Charles Manly and Lydia (Littlejohn) B.; ed. Horner's Mil. Acad., Oxford, N.C., and under private tutors; studied at Nat. Acad. Design, Art Students' League, Chase Sch., all of N.Y. City; m. Juliana Royster, Nov. 3, 1910. Portrait painter. Sent to Roanoke Island by N.C. Hist. Commn., 1907, to paint settings along the coast of N.C., for Jamestown Expn.; became interested in the Jugtown community and found the people to be descendants of the English Staffordshire potters; has renounced his profession as a portrait painter to train the younger members of the community in pottery, and organize a folk-craft centre. Address: Steeds NC‡

BUSBEY, KATHERINE GRAVES, writer; b. Brooklyn, Mar. 16, 1872; d. Horace and Annie A. (Hall) Graves; Smith Coll., class '94; m. L. White Busbey, June 10, 1896. Writer on econ. subjects, contributing articles to various periodicals; sent abroad by Dept. of Commerce and Labor, 1910, to study the problem of the life of the English factory woman; also contributes short stories to Saturday Evening Post, Ladies' Home Journal, Harper's Monthly, Good Housekeeping, etc. Mem. Com. on Pub. Information, 1917-18, Veterans' Bur., 1918-19. Author: Home Life in America, 1910; Biography of Uncle Joe Cannon, 1927. Address: 900 19th St., Washington DC‡

BUSCH, HENRY MILLER, educator; b. N.Y. City, Sept. 24, 1894; s. Casper Henry and Annie (Miller) B.; student Coll. City of New York, 1913-16; B.S., Columbia, 1926, A.M., 1927, grad. work summers, 1927-30; m. Lucy Locken Young, Mar. 13, 1916; 1 son, David Clarendon. Boys work dir., East Side Y.M.C.A., N.Y. City, 1916-20; asst. field work dir. Union Theol. Sem., 1920-27; asst. prof. group work, sch. applied social scis., Western Reserve U., 1927-28, asso. prof., 1928-30, prof. adult edn., asst. dir. and head extension div. Cleve. Coll. of Western Res. U., 1930-36, prof. sociology, 1936-63, prof. emeritus, 1964-70; indsl. cons. conf. methods; vis. prof. Carnegie Inst. Tech., Columbia U., Colo. Coll. Edn., univs. Denver, Hawaii, So. Cal., Syracuse. Foreman Grand Jury, Cuyahoga County, 1937. Executive dir. Nat. Com. on Postwar Immigration Policy, N.Y. City, 1944-45. Mem. Ohio adv. com. U.S. Commn. on Civil Rights; mem. U.S. Rivers and Harbors Conf. Fellow Population Reference Bureau, American Sociol. Assn.; mem. Am. Arbitration Assn., Am. Assn. U. Profs. (past chmn. Western Res.), Family Service Assn., Nat. Council Family Relations, Population Assn. of Am., Am. Acad. Polit. and Social Sci., A.A.A.S., Soc. Study Social Problems, Ams. for Dem. Action (hon. chmn., past chmn. Cleve. chpt., mem. nat., state, local bds.), Alpha Kappa Delta, Theta Kappa Sigma. Democrat. Unitarian. Club: City of Cleveland (past pres.). Author: Leadership in Group Work, 1934; Conf. Methods in Industry, 1949. Home: Cleveland Heights OH Died Nov. 1970.

BUSH, PRESCOTT SHELDON, former U.S. senator; bus. exec.; b. Columbus, O., May 15, 1895; s. Samuel Prescott and Flora (Sheldon) B.; M.A., Yale, 1917; m. Dorothy Walker, Aug. 1921; children—Prescott Sheldon, George Herbert Walker, Nancy (Mrs. Alexander Ellis, Jr.), Jonathan James, William Henry Trotter. Partner Brown Bors., Harriman & Co., 1930-72; formerly dir. C.B.S., Prudential Ins. Co. Am.; resigned all corporate directorships. Nat. campaign chmn. U.S.O., 1942; chmn. National War Fund Campaign, 1943-44; chairman Conn. Rep. Finance Com., 1948, del-at-large Rep. Nat. Conv. Served as capt. F.A., AEF, 1917-19. U.S. senator Conn., 1952-63. Trustee Westminster Choir Coll. Mem. U.S. Golf Assn. (pres. 1935). Republican. Episcopalian. Home: Greenwich CT Died 1972.

BUSH, ROBERT R(AY), psychologist, educator; b. Albion, Mich., July 20, 1920; s. Ray N. and Selma P. (Gottslich) B.; B.S. in Elec. Engring., Mich. State Coll., 1942; Ph.D. in Physics, Princeton, 1949. Research engr. RCA Labs., Princeton, N.J., 1942-45; instr. physics Princeton, 1948-49; postdoctoral fellow Social Sci. Research Council-NRC, Harvard, 1949-51, lectr. social psychology, 1951-52, asst. prof. social relations, 1952-56; asso. prof. applied mathematics N.Y. Sch. Social Work, Columbia, 1956-58; prof. psychology U. Pa., 1958-71, past chmn. dept. Mem. com. on math. tng. social scientists Social Sci. Research Council; mem. fellowship evaluation bd. Nat. Sci. Found., 1956, 57, chmn., 1958-59. Mem. Child Welfare League Am. (research adv. com. 1957-71), Am., Eastern psychol assns., Am. Statis Assn., Psychometric Soc., Psychonomic Soc. Address: Philadelphia PA Died Jan. 5, 1971.

BUSHBY, WILKIE, lawyer; b. Shoreham, Vt., Sept. 11, 1897; s. James Cloud and Jessie M. (Wilkie) B.; A.B., Yale, 1918; LL.B., Harvard, 1921; m. Laura Cheney, July 5, 1924; children—James Cheney, Anne Kimberly (Mrs. Wm. J. Roome, 2d). Admitted to N.Y. bar, 1921, D.C. bar, 1947, various cts.; mem. Dewey, Ballantine, Bushby, Palmer & Wood, and predecessors, N.Y.C., 1921-71; mem. firm, 1928-71. Nat. chmn. Harvard Law Sch. Fund, 1950-52; nat. pres. Harvard Law Sch. Assn., 1957-59. Vis. com. Harvard Law Sch., 1949-56; mem. Yale Alumni Bd. Served to capt. F.A., U.S. Army, 1918. Mem. Am., N.Y. State, N.Y.C., N.Y. Co. bar assns., Am. Law Inst., Am. Judicature Soc., Harvard Law Sch. Assn. of N.Y.C. (past pres.), Phi Beta Kappa, Delta Kappa Epsilon, Elihu. Republican (mem. Conn. finance com.; chmn. Greenwich finance com. 1947-52; presidential elector from Conn., 1948). Clubs: Round Hill (Greenwich, Conn.); Racquet and Tennis, Anglers, Down Town, Yale, Wall (N.Y.C.); Amabelish Fish and Game (P.Q.); Ekwanok Country (Manchester, Vt.); Stratton Mountain Country (Vt.). Home: Greenwich CT Died 1971.

BUSHEE, FREDERICK ALEXANDER, college prof.; b. Brookfield, Vt., July 21, 1872; s. William Aldrich and Emily Jane (Clapp) B.; B.Litt., Dartmouth, 1894; A.M., Harvard, 1898, Ph.D., 1902; Paine fellow of social science, 1899-1901; studied Paris and Berlin, 1900-01; Hartford (Conn.) Sch. of Sociology, 1895-96; resident South End House, Boston, 1894-95, 1896-97; m. Bertha Julia Fellows, of Cambridge, Mass., Sept. 2, 1902. Instr. in history, 1902-03, asst. prof. economics and sociology, 1903-08, prof., 1908, Clark Coll., also instr. in economics and sociology, Clark Univ., 1905-08; prof. economics and sociology, Colorado Coll., 1910-12; prof. same since 1912; acting dean Sch. of Business Administration, U. of Colo., 1912-32. Conglist. Mem. Am. Sociol. Soc., Psi Upsilon, Delta Sigma Pi, Pi Gamma Mu, Phi Beta Kappa, Am. Econ. Assn., Am. Assn. for Labor Legislation, Am. Assn. Univ. Profs. Author: Principles of Sociology, 1923; Social Organization, 1930; Economics, Sociology and the Modern World, 1935. Asst. editor and contbr. to Socialism in Theory and Practice. Home: Boulder CO‡

BUSHNELL, DAVID I., JR., anthropologist; b. St. Louis, Mo., Apr. 28, 1875; s. David I. and Belle (Johnston) B.; ed. in St. Louis and abroad. Asst. in archaeology, Peabody Mus., Harvard, 1901-04; in Europe, 1904-07, studying collections in various museums and associated in field exploration in Italy and Switzerland. Fellow A.A.A.S., Royal Anthropol. Inst. of London; mem. Anthropol. Soc. of Washington, Washington Acad. Sciences, Va. Hist. Soc., Minn. Hist. Soc., Phi Beta Kappa; hon. mem. La. Hist. Soc. Episcopalian. Author: The Sloane Collection in the British Museum, 1906; Ethnological Material from North America in Swiss Collections, 1908; Archaeological Investigations in Ste. Genevieve County, Missouri, 1914; The Five Monacan Towns in Virginia, 1607, 1930; also bulls. of Bureau of Ethnology, The Choctaw of Bayou Lacomb, Louisiana, 1909; Villages of the Algonquian, Siouan, and Caddoan Tribes West of the Mississippi, 1922; Burials of the Algonquian, Siouan, and Caddoan Tribes West of the Mississippi, 1927. Club: Cosmos. Address: Care Smithsonian Institution, Washington DC‡

BUSHNELL, HENRY DAVIS, lawyer; b. Parker's Landing, Pa., May 28, 1875; s. John and Susan Frances (Sellers) B.; A.B., Harvard, 1898; LL.B., N.Y. Law Sch., 1900; m. Edith Taber Johnson, June 3, 1903 (died May 17, 1904); 1 dau., Edith Johnson (deceased; Mrs. Maynard L. Harris); m. 2d, Helen Sprague Martin, Oct. 19, 1907; children—Daniel, Francis Martin. Admitted to N.Y. bar, 1900; also admitted to bar U.S. Supreme Court; practiced in various offices, N.Y. City, 1900-03; asst. atty. South Penn Oil Co., Pittsburgh, Pa., 1903-12; gen. counsel The Buckeye Pipe Line Co., Northern Pipe Line Co., N.Y. Transit Co., Inc. (comprising northern group of pipe lines) 1912-48, retired. Trustee Montclair (N.J.) Art Association 1918-24. Mem. American Bar Association, Washington Assn. of N.J., Conglist. Clubs: Harvard (N.J.); Montclair Golf. Contbr. to jours. Home: 59 Afterglow Av., Montclair, N.J. Office: 30 Broad St., New York NY‡

BUSHNELL, MADELINE VAUGHAN (ABBOTT), editor; b. Cambridge, Mass., Feb. 20, 1871; d. Rev. Edward Abbott, D. D.; ed. Cambridge public schools, Radcliffe and Bryn Mawr Colls.; A.B., Bryn Mawr, 1893; 2d sec. to dean, Bryn Mawr Coll., 1893-4, and sec., 1894-8; asso. editor Literary World, 1898-9; m. Oct. 6, 1899, Charles Elmer Bushnell. Home: 1836 Pine St., Philadelphia‡

BUSICK, ADRIEN FOWLER, lawyer; b. Louisa County, Va., Apr. 29, 1879; s. John Bedelle and Elizabeth Goodwin (Tate) B.; ed. in Va. private schs.; LL.B., Georgetown U., Washington, D.C., 1911; m. Georgie Breckinridge Rust, Oct. 16, 1904; children—Adrien Fowler, Cornelia Elizabeth (Mrs. Gilman Baker Allen), John Rust, George Cabell. Newspaperman, 1900-04; admitted to D.C.; bar, 1911, and practiced in Washington, D.C.; atty. for Fed. Trade Commn., 1915-17, and mem. of its Auxiliary Bd. of Review, 1917-18, chmn. Bd. of Review, 1919-20, actg. chief counsel, 1920-21, asst. chief counsel appellate work, 1921-29, appearing in all U.S. circuit courts of appeals and U.S. Supreme Court in defense of orders of the Commn.; resumed private practice, 1929, of counsel Davies, Richberg, Tydings, Landa and Duff. Mem. Am. Bar Assn. Democrat. Episcopalian. Mason. Home: Culpeper VA Died 1969.

BUTCHER, THOMAS WALTER, educator; b. Macomb, Ill., July 3, 1867; s. Boman R. and Adaline (Vail) B.; A.B., Univ. of Kansas, 1894; A.M., Harvard, 1904; U. of Berlin, 1908-09; LL.D., Coll. of Emporia, 1922; m. Mary Peck, July 3, 1900; children—Thomas Peck, Walter Whitmore, Mary Louise. Prin. high sch., Wellington, 1894-97, Sumner County (Kan.) High Sch., 1897-1906; pres. Central State Normal Sch., Edmond, Okla., 1906-08; supt. city schs., Enid, Okla., 1909-13; pres. Kan. State Teachers' College, Emporia, 1913-43, emeritus since 1943. Mem. and sec. Internat. Jury of Awards on Social and Indsl. Betterment, St. Louis Expn., 1904; pres. Kan. State Teachers' Assn., 1905, Okla. State Teachers' Assn., 1911, Nat. Council of Normal School Pres. and Principals, 1919-20. Republican. Conglist. Gov. 12th Dist. Rotary Internat., 1924-25. Home: Emporia KS‡

BUTLER, CHARLES WILLIAM, clergyman; b. Caro, Tuscola County, Mich., May 13, 1873; s. Robert A. and Angeline (Russell) B.; ed. private study; studied with Bd. of Edn. Detroit Conf. of Meth. Ch.; D.D., John Fletcher Coll., 1924; m. Catherine Cronkright, 1892 (died 1918); children—Grace Arena (Mrs. Ellwood B. Hencks), Helen Edith (Mrs. Andrew D. Cupp), Blanche Angeline (dec.), Celia Catherine (wife of Rev. L. L. Collins); m. 2d, Selma Schilling, Sept. 12, 1921; 1 dau., Ruth Elizabeth. Ordained to ministry Meth. Ch., 1896; pastor in Detroit Conf., 1891-1906; pres. Cleveland Bible Inst., 1921-36; pres. Nat. Assn. for Promotion of Holiness, 1927-42; pres. Kletzing College, formerly John Fletcher Coll., University Park, Ia., 1936-46. Spl. lectures in Seminary and College work. Trustee Asbury Theology Sem., Kletzing McLaughlin Memorial Foundation. Editor of The Christian Witness, 1933-47. Contbr. to religious publs. Address: 2222 N. La Salle Gardens, Detroit MI‡

BUTLER, ELMER GRIMSHAW, biologist; b. Parish, N.Y., Feb. 13, 1900; s. Frank Alexander and Elizabeth Jane (Grimshaw) B.; A.B., Syracuse U., 1921; A.M., Princeton U., 1925, Ph.D., 1926; hon. Sc.D., Syracuse U., 1941; m. Eleanor Brill, June 30, 1927. Instr. zoology, U. of Vt., 1921-23; fellow in biology, Princeton U., 1923-26, instr. biology, 1926-28, asst. prof., 1928-31, asso. prof., 1931-37, Class of 1877 prof. of zoology, Princeton U., 1937-60, Henry Fairfield Osborn prof. biology, from 1960, chmn. dept. biology, 1933-48. Asso. editor, Journal of Morphology, 1941-43; mng. editor, 1946-54. Mem. editorial board Journal of Experimental Zoology, American Zoologist, also Biological Bulletin, 1955-58; cons. editor Developmental Biology. Mem. vis. com. for the biological sciences Johns Hopkins. Trustee Asso. Univs., Inc. (Brookhaven National Laboratory). Chmn. Am. Inst. Biol. Scis., 1949-50; chmn. cell biology study sect. Nat. Insts. Health, 1959-72. John Simon Guggenheim Fellow, 1950. Fellow International Institute Embryology, A.A.A.S., New York Acad. Sci.; mem. Am. Soc. Zoologists (pres. 1956-57); Am. Soc. Naturalists, Am. Assn. Anatomists, Soc. for Exptl. Biol. and Medicine, Soc. for Growth and Development (pres. 1951-52), American Society for Cell Biology, Marine Biological Laboratory, Woods Hole (trustee), Bermuda Biol. Station, Am. Philos. Society, Mt. Desert Island Biol. Lab., Internat. Soc. Cell Biology, Phi Beta Kappa, Sigma Xi, Phi Kappa Psi. Presbyn. Club: Nassau (Princeton). Author sci. articles on normal and experimental embryology, including development of blood-vascular system in man and other mammals, effects of X-radiation on embryonic development, studies on regeneration. Home: Princeton NJ Died Feb. 23, 1972; buried Parish NY

BUTLER, FRANK OSGOOD, chmn. bd. Butler Co.; b. Chicago, Ill., April 22, 1861; s. Julius Wales and Julia (Osgood) B.; student pub. schs. of Chicago; m. Fannie Maud Bremaker, June 10, 1886. With J. W. Butler Paper Co., Chicago, since 1879; v.p., 1890, pres. since 1913; chmn. bd. Butler Co., pres. Butler Bros. Development Co., Chicago, Seven-Eleven Ranches, S.D.; retired from active participation in paper industry. Mem. Soc. Colonial Wars. Clubs: Union League (Chicago); Hinsdale Golf, Oakbrook Polo, Hinsdale Hounds (hunt club) (Hinsdale); Everglades, Seminole Old Guard (Palm Beach, Fla.); Hot Springs (S.D.) Country, Union Interalliee (Paris). Home: Hot Springs, S.D. Office: 223 W. Monroe St., Chicago IL‡

BUTLER, HAROLD LANCASTER, musician; b. Silver City, Ida., June 18, 1874; s. Gilbert Lancaster and Frances (Gilpin) B.; A.B., Valparaiso (Ind.) U., 1895, LL.B., 1896; grad. Gottschalk Lyric Sch., Chciago, 1897; studied with Sauvage (New York), Blasco (Milan), Dubulle (Paris); m. Florence Higgins, May 23, 1898; 1 dau., Florence Vale. Dir. music dept., Valparaiso U., 1899-1903; dir. vocal dept., Syracuse U., 1903-05, 1907-15; dean Sch. of Fine Arts, U. of Kan., 1915-23; dean Coll. of Fine Arts, Syracuse U., since 1923. Principal basso, Castle Sq. Opera Co., 1897-99, and sang in 16 grand operas. Mem. Music Teachers Nat. Assn. (pres. 1926-28), Am. Acad. Teachers of Singing, Nat. Assn. of Presidents of State Music Teachers' Assn., Nat. Assn. Schs. Music and Allied Arts (pres. 1928-31). Republican. Episcopalian. Mason (32 deg.). Rotarian. Has given over 500 recitals in N.Y. and Middle West. Home: 732 Ostrom Av., Syracuse NY‡

BUTLER, JAMES ORVAL, sch. adminstr.; b. Butler, Okla., May 8, 1928; s. James Grady and Opal (Duncan) B.; B.S., Southwestern State Coll., Weatherford, Okla., 1950; M.Ed., U. Okla., 1955, Ed.D., 1965; m. Tomasina Pair, Nov. 20, 1948; children—James Steven, Janet Kay. Tchr., sch. adminstr. Okla. Pub. Schs., 1950-61; tchr. Colorado Springs (Colo.) Pub. Schs., 1961-64, sch. adminstr., 1964-69. Lectr. edn. Cragmoor Center, U. Colo., Colorado Springs, 1965-66. Chmn. advancement com. Silver Cloud dist. Boy Scouts Am., 1966-67. Served with AUS, 1946-47, 50-51. Mem. N.E.A., Colo. Edn. Assn., Nat., Colo. depts. elementary sch. prins., Phi Delta Kappa. Home: Colorado Springs CO Died June 18, 1969.

BUTLER, ROBERT PAUL, lawyer; b. Prairieville, Mich., Dec. 25, 1883; s. Robert W. and Bertha E. (Watson) B.; A.B., Cornell U., 1905; M.A., Trinity Coll., Hartford, Conn., 1906; m. Emily Joslyn, June 4, 1910; children—Joslyn, Philip Gale. Began as newspaper reporter, 1906; clk. Common Pleas Ct., Hartford County, 1913-16; admitted to Conn. bar, 1915, and in practice at Hartford; mem. Butler, Volpe, Garrity & Sacco; asst. corp. counsel, City of Hartford, 1918-20, corporation counsel, 1922-24; U.S. dist. atty. for Conn., 1934-45. Mem. Am. and Conn. bar assns., Delta Psi. Democrat. Conglist. Club: University. Home: West Hartford CT Died Feb. 1971.

BUTLER, THOMAS BALDWIN, business exec.; b. Towson, Md., Feb. 10, 1899; s. Thomas Baldwin and Sophia (Stockdale) B.; student Univ. of Md. Law Sch., 1922; m. Louise V. Waters, June 27, 1923; children—Thomas B., Howard Lee, Josephine Waters. Clerk, Safe Deposit and Trust Co. of Baltimore (Md.), 1915-32, sec. 1932-35, vice pres. 1935-42, pres., from 1942, chmn. bd., chief exec. officer Mercantile-Safe Deposit and Trust Co., until 1968; chmn. exec. com., dir. L. & N. R.R. Co., Atlantic Coast Line Co., Seaboard Coast Line R.R. Co.; dir. Fidelity & Guaranty Life Ins. Co., U.S. Fidelity & Guaranty Co., Alico Land Devel. Co. Dun & Bradstreet, Inc., A.S. Abell Co., Commercial Credit Co., Mt. Vernon Mills, Inc., A. E. Staley Mfg. Co. Bd. trustees Johns Hopkins Hosp., Johns Hopkins U., Children's Hosp. Sch., Inc., Good Samaritan Hosp.; mem. pres.'s bd. Loyola Coll., Balt.; finance com. Cath. Univ. of Am. Episcopalian. Clubs: Elkridge, Maryland; Augusta National Golf (Augusta, Ga.); Union League (N.Y.C.). Home: Baltimore MD Died May 20, 1968.

BUTTERFIELD, ERNEST WARREN, educator; b. Weathersfield, Vt., June 7, 1874; s. Stephen Warren and Sarah Josephine (Mudgett) B.; A.B., Dartmouth, 1897; LL.D., New Hampshire Coll., 1921; Ed.D., R.I. State College, 1926; LL.D., Bates College, 1930; m. Edith May Thompson, July 30, 1902; children—Richard David, Stephen Ernest, Priscilla, Dorothy. Prin. high sch., Bethlehem, N.H., 1897-99, Groveland, Mass., 1899-1902, Laconia, N.H., 1902-06, Dover, N.H., 1906-11; supt. schs., Dover, 1911-16; dep. supt. pub. instrn., N.H., 1916-17; commr. of edn., N.H., 1917-30; commr. of edn., Conn., 1930-38; supt. schs., Bloomfield, Conn., since 1938; mem. faculty Bates Coll., summer 1939-40. Mem. advisory com. Peabody Inst. of Natural Science; chmn. Conn. Pub. Library Com. Mem. N.E.A. (ex-v.p.), Nat. Council of Edn., N.E. Supts., Assn. (ex-pres.), Am. Assn. School Adminstrs., Council Chief State Sch. Officers (ex-pres.), Phi Beta Kappa, Kappa Kappa Kappa, Kappa Phi Kappa. Conglist. Mason. Rotarian. Asso. editor The Clearing House; advisory editor Connecticut Circle, also New England Jour. of Edn. Home: West Hartford, Conn. Office: CT‡

BUTZER, ALBERT GEORGE, clergyman; b. Buffalo, N.Y., July 19, 1893; s. Louis and Minnie (Betz) B.; A.B., Northwestern Coll., Naperville, Ill., 1915; student Evang. Theol. Sem., Naperville, 1915-17; B.D., Union Theol. Sem., N.Y.C., 1920; D.D. Middlebury (Vt.) Coll., 1929, Hamilton Coll., 1945; LL.D., McMaster University, Hamilton, Ontario; m. Katharine Coe, Sept. 6, 1921; children—Albert George, Marjorie Betty, Clayton Coe. Ordained ministry Presbyn. Ch., 1921; pastor West Side Presbyn. Ch., N.J., 1921-32, Westminster Ch., Buffalo, 1932-62, minister emeritus, 1962-67; teacher The Buffalo Sem. and Nichols Sch., Buffalo. Schaefer lectures, Yale University Div. Sch., 1938. Mem. exec. com. Community Chest of Buffalo; capital expenditures com. City Buffalo; member Buffalo City Planning Board. Served as chaplain 103d Inf., 26th Div., AEF, France and 16th Inf., 1st Div., Army of Occupation, Germany, 1918-19. Recipient Distinguished Service award University of Buffalo, 1956; chancellor's medal Univ. of Buffalo, 1964. Chaplain Buffalo Police Dept., Judges and Police Execs., Conf. of Erie Co. Dir. Auburn Theol. Sem. Named Nat. Presbyterian Church Preacher for 1959. Mem. Phi Alpha Tau Club: Buffalo. Author: You and Yourself (sermons), 1932; One Little Red Animal: Stories for Children, 1965. Contbr. to The Interpreter's Bible, 1951. Home: Buffalo NY Died Nov. 28, 1967.

BUXTON, CHARLES LEE, obstetrician and gynecologist; b. Superior, Wis., Oct. 14, 1904; s. Edward Timothy and Lucinda (Lee) B.; B.S., Princeton, 1927; M.D., Columbia, 1932, Med. Sc.D., 1940; M.A. (honorary), Yale, 1954; m. Helen Morgan Rotch, Sept. 3, 1938 (div.); children—Timothy, Anthony, Edward, Lucinda; m. 2d, Margaret P. Mithoefer. Intern Bassett Hosp., Cooperstown, N.Y., 1932-33; fellow endocrinology, med. sch. Harvard, 1933-34; resident Sloane Hosp. for Women, 1934-38, dir. endocrine clinic, 1938-54, asso. attending obstetrician, 1947-54; instr. obstetrics and gynecology Coll. Phys. and Surg. Columbia, 1938-46, asso. prof., 1947; prof. obstetrics and gynecology, 1954-69, chmn. dept., sch. med. Yale, 1954-66; member consulting staff William W. Backus Hosp., Norwich, Conn., Charlotte Hungerford Hosp., Torrington, Conn., Meriden (Conn.) Hosp., New Britain (Conn.) Gen. Hosp., Stamford (Conn.) Hosp. Hartford Hosp., Sharon Hosp. Served as comdr. USNR, 1942-45. Recipient of Albert Lasker award, 1965. Diplomate Am. Bd. of Obstetrics and Gynecology (dir.). Fellow Am. College of Obstetrics and Gynecology; (first vice president 1963-1964, chairman district I, 1961-64); mem. A.M.A., Am. Endocrine Soc., Am. Soc. Study Sterility (pres. 1959-60, dir.), Am. Assn. Obstetricians and Gynecologists, New England, New Haven obstet. socs., Am. Gynec. Soc., Conn. Obstetrics Soc. (pres. 1955-56), Soc. Obstetricians and Gynecologists of Can., Assn. Profs. Gynecology Soc. Gynecol. Investigation, Sociedad Esterilidad Brasileria, Sociede de Obstetricia e Gynecologia de Brasil Soc. Royal Belge de Gynecologei etd' Obstetrique, Brit. Society for Study Fertility, Sigma Xi. Presbyterian. Author, co-author books on gynecology, endocrinology and sterility; contbr. med. jours. Asso. editor Jour. Fertility and Sterility. Home: New Haven CT Died July 7, 1969.

BUXTON, ROBERT WILLIAM, educator, surgeon; b. Joplin, Mo., Oct. 3, 1909; A.B., U. Kan., 1931, M.D., 1936; M.S., U. Mich., 1943; D.Sc. (hon.), Franklin and Marshall Coll., 1962. Intern Strong Meml. Hosp., Rochester, N.Y., 1936-37, asst. resident surgery, 1938-39; resident surgery Genesse Hosp., Rochester, 1939-40; resident surgery Strong Meml. Hosp., 1940-41; resident thoracic surgery U. Mich. Hosp., 1941-42; mem. faculty U. Mich. Sch. Medicine, 1942-55; prof. surgery, chmn. dept. U. Md. Sch. Medicine, 1955-70. Home: Baltimore MD Died Apr. 14, 1970; buried Baltimore MD

BUZBY, GEORGE CARROLL, publisher; b. Phila., Apr. 19, 1897; s. George H. and Nina (Carroll) B.; A.B., Princeton, 1920; m. Jean Pearson, June 21, 1924, 1 son, George Carroll. Joined Chilton Co., Phila., 1920, beginning as salesman, successively bus. mgr., pub., v.p., 1920-56, pres., 1956-66, chmn., from 1966, also chief executive officer; director of Newton Falls Paper Company (N.Y.). Member Com. of 70, Phila. Trustee Free Library Phila. Served with Am. Field Service, 1917, as 1st lt., U.S. Marine Corps, 1918-19. Home: Philadelphia PA Died Aug. 1970.

BYARS, LOUIS THOMAS, physician; b. Alma, Ark., Dec. 24, 1906; s. Louis Thomas and Rebecca Eleanor (Lake) B.; B.S., U. of Ark., 1928; M.D., Washington U., St. Louis, Mo., 1932; m. Alabama Dalton, Sept. 1, 1937; 1 dau., Caroline Dalton (Mrs. Robert Morisseau). Asst. resident surgeon Barnes Hosp., St. Louis, 1932-34; plastic surgeon, 1934-69; asso. prof. in clinical surgery, Washington U. Sch. of Med.; consultant in plastic surgery Vets. Adminstrn. since 1945; mem. staff or courtesy privileges 10 St. Louis hosps. Diplomate Am. Bd. Plastic Surgery. Fellow Am. Coll. of Surgeons. Mem. A.M.A., Mississippi Valley Med. Soc., American Surgical Assn., Am. Society Plastic and Reconstructive Surgery, Am. Assn. Plastic Surgeons, Western Surg. Assn., Southern Surg. Assn., Alpha Omega Alpha, Lambda Chi Alpha, Phi Beta Pi, Phi Beta Kappa. Author: (with others) Cancer of Face and Mouth, Diagnosis, Treatment and Surgical Repair, 1941. Contbr. to med. jours. Home: St Louis MO Died Aug. 8, 1969; buried St. Louis MO

BYERS, JOHN WINFORD, architect; b. Grand Rapids, Mich., Mar. 22, 1875; s. James Albion and Sarah Elizabeth (Durbar) B.; grad. high sch., Grand Rapids, 1894; B.S. in E.E., U. of Mich., 1898; S.B., Harvard, 1899; post grad. work same univ.; m. Mrs. Harriet Hale Staley, of Pittsburgh, Pa., June 30, 1915; stepson, Thomas Fulton Staley (dec.). With U.S. Commn., Paris Expn., 1900-01; instr. in French and English, North Am. Acad., Montevideo, Uruguay, S.A., 1901; instr. and part owner Hitchcock Mil. Acad., San Rafael, Calif., 1902-10; head of Romance lang. dept., Santa Monica High Sch., 1910-20; organized group of native Mexicans for making handmade roofing and floor tiles and adobe mud bricks and adapting same to modern construction. Protestant. Club: Brentwood Country. Contbr. articles on adobe constrn. Home: 2034 La Mesa Drive. Office: 246 26th St., Santa Monica CA‡

BYERS, WALTER LOUIS, surgeon; b. Cedar Rapids, Ia., June 30, 1910; s. Edward Jacob and Mary Ellen (Fenton) B.; M.D., U. Ia., 1938; m. Barbara Jean Hood, July 21, 1952; children—Kathleen (Mrs. Richard A. Larson), David, Laura, Robert. Intern St. Mark's Hosp., Salt Lake City, 1938-39; resident Highland-Alameda County (Cal.) Hosp., 1945-47, later coordinator vascular surgery; resident Samuel Merritt Hosp., 1947-49; chief surgeon emergency surg. service Alameda County Med. Instns. Bd. dirs., mem. exec. com. Oakland Boys Club; bd. dirs. Alameda County chpt. A.R.C., 1968-69. Served to maj., M.C., AUS, 1940-46. Decorated Bronze Star; recipient Good Govt. award Alameda County, 1965. Diplomate Am. Bd. Surgery. Fellow A.C.S., Am. Coll. Chest Physicians, mem. A.M.A. Republican. Methodist. Mason. Club: Commonwealth of Cal. Address: Oakland CA Died Sept. 14, 1970; buried Chapel of Chimes, Oakland CA

BYINGTON, SPRING, actress; b. Colorado Springs, Colo.; d. Edwin Lee and Helene (Cleghorn); student pub. schs., pvt. tutors; m. Roy Carey Chandler; children—Phyllis Helene (Mrs. William Baxley), Lois Irene (Mrs. W. Hembold). Actress stage, motion pictures, radio and TV; motion pictures include You Can't Take it With You, Louisa, Angels in the Outfield, Please Don't Eat the Daisies. Radio and TV program December Bride; role in weekly TV series Laramie. Home: Hollywood CA Died Sept. 7, 1971.

BYNNER, WITTER, author; b. Brooklyn, N.Y., Aug. 10, 1881; s. Thomas Edgarton and Annie Louise (Brewer) B.; A.B., magna cum laude, Harvard, 1902; Litt.D., University of New Mexico, 1962. Asst. editor McClure's Magazine, lit. editor McClure, Phillips & Co., 1902-06; advisory editor with Small, Maynard & Co., 1907-15. Instr. English, S.A.T.C., U. of Calif., 1918-19. Contbr. to many mags. Lecturer on poetry and kindred subjects. Phi Beta Kappa poet, Harvard University, 1911, University of California, 1919, Amherst College, 1931. President Poetry Society of America, 1920-22, S.W. regional v.p. (gold medal, 1954); chancellor Acad. Am. Poets. Mem. Santa Fe City Planning Commn., 1945-47. Recipient Boylston and Bowdoin prizes. Harvard. Mem. Nat. Inst. Arts and Letters, Am. Humanist Assn. (hon. life)Clubs: Signet (Cambridge); New England Poetry (hon.); Book of California (honorary life member San Francisco); The Players, Harvard (N.Y.). Author: (verse) Young Harvard, 1907; (plays) Tiger, 1913; The Little King, 1914; (verse) The New World, 1915; (play) Iphigenia in Tauris, 1915 (verse) Grenstone Poems, 1917; A Canticle of Praise, 1919; The Beloved Stranger, 1919; A Canticle of Pan, 1920; Pins for Wings (under pseudonym Emanuel Morgan), 1920; A Book of Plays, 1922; (verse) Caravan, 1925; (play) Cake, published in 1926, The Pamphlet Poets, published in 1927; (prose) The Persistence of Poetry, 1929; (verse) Indian Earth, 1929; (verse) Eden Tree, 1931; (verse) Guest Book, 1935; Selected Poems, 1936; (verse) Against the Cold, 1940; Take Away the Darkness, 1947; (prose) Journey with Genius, Recollections and Reflections Concerning the D. H. Lawrences, 1951; A Book of Lyrics, 1958; New Poems 1960; (verse) with Arthur D. Ficke, und pseudonyms, Emanuel Morgan and Anne Knish) Spectra, 1916; (with Julia E. Ford) Snickerty Nick, 1919. Translator: (verse) A Book of Love (from the French of Charles Vildrac), 1923; The Jade Mountain (with Kiang Kang-hu; verse from Chinese poets of T'ang dynasty), 1929; (verse) The Way of Life According to Laotzu, 1944; Iphigenia in Tauris, (new version in Euripides II (play); 1956. Editor: Sonnets of Frederick Goddard Tuckerman, 1931; editor, translator numerous poems of Tang dynasty. Home: Santa Fe NM Died June 1, 1968.

BYNUM, MARSHALL FRANCIS, banker, mortician; b. Chgo., Feb. 26, 1912; s. George S. and Alma (Branch) B.; ed. pub. schs., Chgo., also Worsham Sch. Embalming, Chgo.; m. Gloria I. Anglin, Mar. 17, 1965; children by previous marriage—Marsha F., Marshall Francis. Propr., Charles S. Jackson Co. Inc., Chgo., 1936-69; founder, dir. Service Fed. Savs. & Loan Assn, Independence Bank Chgo. Treas. Chgo. br. N.A.A.C.P., 1962-69; commr. Chgo. Park Dist., 1967-69. Bd. dirs. Harvard-St. George Sch., 1960-69. Playground in Washington Park named in his honor by Chgo. Park Dist., also Chgo. Pub. Sch. Served with AUS, 1942-44. Home: Chicago IL Died Nov. 2, 1969; buried Graceland Cemetery, Chicago IL

BYRD, HARRY CLIFTON, univ. pres.; b. Crisfield, Md., Feb. 12, 1889; s. William Franklin and Sallie May (Sterling) B.; B.S., U. of Md., 1908; post grad., law studies, George Washington U., Georgetown U., Western Md. Coll.; LL.D., Washington Coll., 1936; LL.D., Dickinson Coll., 1938; D.Sc., Western Md. Coll., 1938; m. Katherine Turnball, Dec. 27, 1913; children—Harry Clifton, Evelyn Westover, William, Sterling. Instr. English and history, Univ. of Md., 1912-13, dir. athletics, and football coach, 1913-34, asst. to pres., 1918-32, v.p., 1932-35, actg. pres., July 1935-Feb. 22, 1936, pres., 1936-54. Mem. Draft Bd., World War; trustee, Longfellow Sch. for Boys. Mem. bd. of dirs. Md. Farm Bur. Fedn.; mem. Am. Assn. Sch. Adminstrs., Base Ball Writers Assn. of Am. (hon.), Am. Geog. Soc., Md. Acad. of Science, Md. Hist. Soc., Am. Acad. of Polit. and Social Science, Grange, Washington Bd. of Trade, Phi Kappa Phi, Pi Delta Epsilon, Omicron Delta Kappa, Pi Sigma Alpha, Sigma Alpha Epislon. Demo. Meth. Mason (Shriner); Moose. Clubs: Univ. (Baltimore, and Washington, D.C.); Rotary, Maryland Soc. of Washington, Merchants, Baltimore Press (Baltimore); Vansville Farmers' (Md.). Home: College Park MD Died Oct. 1970.

BYRER, CHARLES EMORY, religious educator; b. nr. Canton, O., July 10, 1870; s. John Michel and Sarah (Werner) B.; A.B., Otterbein Coll., 1897, A.M., 1901; student Div. Sch. of Kenyon Coll., 1897-1900, D.D., 1922, D.C.L., 1940; m. Rose A. Bower, June 24, 1897. Ordained deacon P.E. Ch., 1900; priest, 1901; served chs., Cambridge, O., 1900-02, Mechanicsburg, O., 1902-05. rector Ch. of the Good Shepherd, Columbus, 1905-10, Christ Ch., Springfield, O., 1910-22; prof. ch. history, Div. Sch. Kenyon Coll., 1922-26, dean and prof. systematic theology, 1926-40; retired July 1940. Mason. Home: 15 East Lane Ave., Columbus OH‡

BYRER, HARRY HOPKINS, lawyer; b. Philippi, W. Va., Apr. 20, 1877; s. Frederick Samuel and Isabella (Woods) B.; student W.Va. Wesleyan Coll., 1897-1900; studied law in law office of J. H. Woods, Philippi, West Virginia, 1900-02; m. May Griffin, November 19, 1903;children—S. Woods, Virginia, John G., Catherine Armentrout, and Harry Hopkins, Jr. Admitted to W.Va. bar, 1902; prosecuting attorney Barbour County, W.Va., 1909-14; asst. U.S. atty., Northern Dist. W.Va., 1914-22; B.&O.R.R.Co. since 1936. Trustee W.Va. Wesleyan Coll., 1910-19. Mem. Am. Bar Assn., (pres.), Berkeley County Bar Assn. Clubs: Rotary (past pres.). Democrat. Methodist. Home: Martinsburg WV‡

BYRNE, ALICE HILL, educator; b. Lancaster, Pa., Aug. 28, 1876; d. John Hill and Mary Ann (Reinhold) B.; B.E., Millersville State Normal Sch., 1894; A.B., Wellesley, 1908 (Phi Beta Kappa); Ph.D., Bryn Mawr, 1918. Teacher of Greek and Latin, Union High Sch., Coleraine, Pa., 1894-96, 1899-1900, Mrs. Blackwood's Sch., Lancaster, 1896-99, 1900-01, Miss Stahr's Sch., afterwards the Shippen Sch., Lancaster, 1901-09, Miss Hills' Sch., Phila., 1909-11, Baldwin Sch., Bryn Mawr, 1911-17; prof., Western Coll., Oxford, O., 1917-20, dean since 1920. Member Ref. Ch. in U.S. Mem. Am. Philol. Assn., Archaeol. Inst. America, Wellesley Shakespeare Soc., Phi Beta Kappa. Home: Western College, Oxford OH‡

BYRNE, AMANDA AUSTIN;, b. Lewisburg, W.Va., Apr. 28, 1866; d. Dr. Samuel Hunter and Mary Copeland (MacPherson) Austin; student Lewisburg Female Inst. (now Greenbrier Coll. for Women), 1875-84; m. William Eston Randolph Byrne, June 12, 1889; children—George Austin, Marie Louise (Mrs. Lester L. Sheets), Barbara Linn (Mrs. Daniel N. Mohler), Charlotte Virginia (Mrs. Robt. B. Mesmer), William Eston Randolph. Long active in United Daughters of the Confederacy, pres. Charleston chapter, 1924-27 and since 1942, pres. W.Va. div., 1917-22, corr. sec. gen., 1919-21, recording secretary gen., 1922-23, 1st v.p. gen., 1925-27, pres. gen., 1931-33; pres. Charleston Y.W.C.A., 1926-31; registrar National Society Colonial Dames Resident in W.Va., 1904-36, pres., 1936-42, elected hon. pres. in 1942. President Woman's Auxiliary Synod of W.Va. Presbyterian Church U.S., 1934-36. Democrat. Clubs: Charleston Women's (pres. 1931-32), Charleston Women's Democratic, Women's Kanawha Literary. Home: 1422 Quarrier St., Charleston WV‡

BYRNE, SISTER MARIE JOSE, college pres.; b. New York, N.Y., Aug. 13, 1876; d. George Philip and Louise Abigail (Kingsland) Byrne; A.B., Coll. of St. Elizabeth, Convent, N.J., 1902; A.M., Columbia, 1909, Ph.D., 1915; Litt.D. (honorary), St. Peter's College, 1949; mem. Sisters of Charity. Instructor Greek and Latin, Coll. of St. Elizabeth, 1902-05 and 1906-08, prof. Latin and Greek, 1910-21, dean 1921-40, pres. since 1940. Mem. Am. Assn. of Univ. Women, National Education Association, Classical League, Classical Association of Atlantic States. Translator: Considerations on Eternity (from Latin), 1920. Author: Prolegomena to an Edition of Decimus Magnus Ausonius, 1916. Address: College of St. Elizabeth, Covent Station NJ‡

BYRNES, ALLEN WILLIAM, psychiatrist; b. Lake Park, Ia., Mar. 20, 1910; s. Roscoe Conklin and Anna (Leese) B.; B.S., M.D., State U. Ia., 1934; m. Elizabeth Earley, Dec. 25, 1934; children—Eva Ann (Mrs. James Elmer), Barbara Jean (Mrs. Paul Reddington). Intern, Ia. Meth. Hosp., Des Moines, 1934-35; pvt. practice medicine, Traer, Ia. 1936-37; physician Civilian Conservation Corps, Ia., 1938-40; physician VA Hosp., Ft. Custer, Mich., 1940-42, chief continued treatment service, 1946-49; chief neuropsychiat. sect. VA Hosp., Dayton, O., 1949-52, chief phys. medicine and rehab. service VA Hosp., Downey, Ill., 1952-54, VA Hosp., Danville, Ill., 1954-58; chief staff VA Hosp., St. Cloud, Minn., 1958-61; dir. VA Hosp., Knoxville, Ia., 1961-63, VA Hosp., Battle Creek, Mich., 1963-67. Served with M.C., AUS, 1942-46; ETO, NATOUSA. Decorated Bronze Star. Diplomate Am. Bd. Psychiatry and Neurology. Mem. Am. Psychiat. Assn., Acad. Religion and Mental Health, Law-Sci. Found. (founding mem.), Am. Acad. Forensic Scis., Am. Legion, V.F.W., D.A.V. Mason (Shriner) Address: Sun City AZ Died Nov. 3, 1971.

BYRNES, JAMES FRANCIS, former U.S. sec. state, ex-gov. S.C.; b. S.C.; son of James Francis and Elizabeth E. Byrnes; educated public schools; married Maude Busch, May 2, 1906. Admitted to bar, 1903; editor Journal and Review, Aiken, 1903-07. Official court reporter 2d Circuit, S.C., 1900-08; solicitor, 2d Circuit, S.C., 1908-10; member 62d to 68th Congresses (1911-25), 2d S.C. District. Engaged in practice of law, Spartanburg, 1925-31; elected U.S. Senator, 2 terms, 1931-43; apptd. justice U.S. Supreme Court, June 1941, resigned from U.S. Supreme Court, Oct. 3, 1942, to accept appointment as dir. economic `stabilization, resigned; apptd. dir. of war mobilization, May 27, 1943, resigned, 1945; sec. of state, July 1945-47; resigned Jan. 20, 1947. Gov. of S.C., 1951-55. Ind. Democrat. Author: Speaking Frankly; All in One Lifetime. Home: Columbia SC Died Jan. 24, 1972; buried Trinity Episcopal Churchyard, Columbia SC

BYRNES, ROBERT DENNISON, newspaperman; b. Norwich, Conn., Nov. 9, 1900; s. Perry and Mary (McGee) B.; B.S., Trinity Coll., Hartford, Conn., 1922; m. Dorothy Seymour, Sept. 8, 1923; 1 son, Robert Seymour. Reporter Norwich Bull., 1917-18; with Harford Courant, from 1920, successively coll. corr., reporter, state editor, polit. editor, 1920-43, Washington corr., from 1943. Mem. Congl. Standing Com. of Correspondents, 1949-51. Mem. White House Correspondents Assn., Pi Gamma Mu. Episcopalian. Club: National Press (Washington). Home: Arlington VA Died July 20, 1969; buried Columbia Gardens Cemetery, Arlington VA

BYRON, ROBERT BURNS, JR., game mfg. exec.; b. Chgo., Sept. 13, 1916; s. Robert Burns and Helen (Manchester) B.; grad. high sch.; m. Doris Bloom, Feb. 28, 1963; children—Laura, Barbara. Copy writer, retail sales supr. Montgomery Ward & Co., Chgo., 1938-41; copy writer, media dir. C. Wendel Muench & Co., advt. agy., 1946-47; outdoor advt. buyer, account exec., media dir., v.p., account supr. Young & Rubicam, Inc., 1947-63; v.p. Pacific Outdoor Advt. Co., Los Angeles, 1963-64; v.p., media dir. Wolf, Krautter, Inc., Chgo., 1964-66; v.p., sec. The Fyanes Corp., Chgo., 1966-69. Devel. director of Lawrence Hall, Inc., Chgo., past pres. Served to capt. Signal Corps, AUS, 1941-46. Decorated Bronze Star medal. Mem. Western Advt. Golf Assn., Lawrence Hall Alumni Assn. (past pres.). Home: Des Plaines IL Died Nov. 13, 1969; interred Memory Gardens, Arlington Heights IL

CABELL, CHARLES PEARRE, business cons.; b. Dallas, Tex., Oct 11, 1903; B.S., U.S. Mil. Acad. 1925; grad. Air Corps Primary Flying Sch., 1931, Advanced Flying Sch., observation course, 1931, Command and Gen. Staff Sch., 1940; Army and Navy Staff Coll., 1943; m. Jacklyn DeHymel, 1934; children—Charles, Catharine, Ben. Commd. 2d lt., F.A., A.U.S., 1925, advanced to general (U.S.A.F), 1958; served successively as asst. chief operations sect., tng. and operations div., as chief, photo unit, and as chief, tech. coordination br., Office of Chief of Air Corps, Wash., D.C., 1941-42; mem. advisory council Hdqrs. Army Air Forces, Washington, D.C., 1942-43; assigned 8th Air Force, European Theater of Operations, Oct. 1943, comdr. combat wing, Dec. 1943; dir. of plans, U.S. Strategic Air Forces, Apr.-July 1944; mil. air adviser to U.S. representative on European Adv. Commn., London, May-July 1944; dir. operations and intelligence, Mediterranean Allied Air Forces, July 1944-May 1945; chief strategy and policy div. of air plans, Hdqrs. A.A.F., Washington, 1945; dep. and U.S. air representative on mil. staff com. of UN N.Y., 1946-47; dir. of intelligence, Hdqrs., USAF, Washington, 1948; dir. Joint Staff, Joint Chiefs of Staff, 1951; dep. dir. Central Intelligence, 1953-62; business cons. Awarded D.S.M., Legion of Merit, Air Medal (Oak-Leaf Cluster), Distinguished Flying Cross, Bronze Star; Distinguished Intelligence medal; Hon. Comdr. Brit. Empire, Officer French Legion of Honor, Croix de Guerre; mem. Order of St. Laurice and Lazarus of Italy. Home: Arlington VA Died May 25, 1971; buried Arlington Nat. Cemetery.

CABLE, EMMETT JAMES, college prof.; b. Eldora, Hardin Co., Ia., Nov. 12, 1875 s. George Cable and Sarah E. (Kammary) C.; B.A., Cornell Coll., Mt. Vernon, Ia., 1900, M.S., 1905; studied U. of Chicago, 1903-05; Ph.D., State U. of Ia., 1917; m. Laura Elizabeth Van Horn, of Albion, Ia., Aug. 30, 1905; 1 son, Emmett Van Horn. Began as teacher, rural sch., Ia., 1896; in charge grammar grade, Hubbard, Ia., 1897-98; supt. Twp. High Sch., Albion, Ia., 1900-03; instr. geography, 1906-08, prof. since 1908, head of dept. natural science since 1917, Ia. State Teachers Coll. Mem. Ia. Acad. Sciences, Sigma Xi, Phi, Beta Kappa. Methodist. Mason. Home: Cedar Falls IA‡

CABLE, JOHN L., ex-congressman; b. Lima, O., Apr. 15, 1884; s. Davis J. and Mary (Harnley) C.; L.B., Kenyon Coll., 1906; LL.B., George Washington U., 1909; hon. M.C.L., Kenyon; m. Rhea Watson, Dec. 9, 1910; children—Mrs. Alice C. Hayes, Davis Watson. Began practice law at Lima, 1909; admitted to practice in Ohio courts, Dist. Court, U.S. Court of Appeals and Supreme Court of U.S.; pros. atty., Allen County, O., 2 terms, 1917-21; mem. 67th and 68th Congresses (1921-25), 71st and 72d Congresses (1929-33), 4th Ohio Dist.; author of federal laws granting independent citizenship to women, also Federal Corrupt Practices Act; spl. counsel to atty. gen. of Ohio and Reconstruction Finance Corp., in liquidation of Lima First Am. Trust Co., 1933-37; dir. Pangles Master Market, Inc. Republican presdl. elector, 1936. Govt. appeal agt. Selective Service Board 2, Lima, 1948-71; Allen Co. chmn. A.R.C. Roll Call Com., 1939-40; chief Civilian War Services, Lima and Allen Co., O., 1943-44. Mem. Am., Ohio State and Allen County bar association. Member of the Episcopalian Church. Mason. Author: The Rights and Responsibilities at Railway Grade Crossings; Am. Citizenship Rights of Women; Denaturalization—The Alien in War Time. Contbr. to newspapers and mags. Home: Lima OH Died Sept. 14, 1971.

CABOT, TED, U.S. dist. judge; b. Hobe Sound, Fla., Feb. 5, 1917; s. Frederick Mortimer and Sallie Belle (Crenshaw) C.; LL.B., U. Miami (Fla.), 1953; m. Louise Morris Cook, June 28, 1947; children—Nathalie Ann, Bruce, Sallie, Louise, Mary Beth. Engaged in accounting, Ft. Lauderdale, Fla., 1936-44; clk. circuit ct. Broward County, Fla., 1945-53; admitted to Fla. bar,

1953; pvt. practice, Ft. Lauderdale, 1953-59; mem. Fla. Senate from Broward County, 1954-58; circuit judge Broward County, 1959-66; U.S. dist. judge So. Dist. Fla., 1966-71. Democrat. Presbyn. (trustee). Home: Ft Lauderdale FL Died Dec. 4, 1971; buried Lauderdale Meml. Park, Ft Lauderdale FL

CADDY, EDMUND HARRINGTON HOMER, lawyer; b. Brooklyn, N.Y., Oct.9, 1902; s. Edmund Harrington and Georgia Irene (Homer) C.; prep. edn. Blair Acad., Blairstown, N.J.; A.B., Columbia Univ.; LL.B., New York Law Sch.; m. Glenna Corrine Garratt, M.D., June 1, 1927; children—Edmund Harrington Homer, John Garratt, Glenna Irene. Private practice, 1932-35; asst. prof. law, N.Y. Law Sch., 1935; prof. law and asst. dean, 1937, acting dean, 1938, dean, 1939-41; asst. corp. counsel, Div. Appeals, 1942; N.Y. State asst. atty. gen. in charge of N.Y. offices, counsel to various state agencies including N.Y. State Racing Comm., Jan. 1943-June 1944; counsel to N.Y. State Commr. of Housing 1944-47; dean, prof. law N.Y. Law Sch., 1947-49; pvt. practice law, 1949-70. Mem. N.Y. County Lawyers Assn. (dir. 1945-51; chmn. com. on publs., editor Bar Bull.), Alpha Chi Rho, Phi Delta Phi. Clubs: Union League (Bklyn.); Metropolitan; Church. Home: Brooklyn NY Died June 1970.

CADE, GEORGE NEWTON, educator; b. Patterson, Ill., Aug. 3, 1876; s. James David and Nancy Catherine (Hill) C.; grad. high sch., Patterson, 1897, Ill. State Normal U., 1910; B.S., U. of Chicago, 1917, M.A., 1918; m. Flora Belle Moore, of Springfield, Ill., Aug. 1, 1912. Supt. Cerro Gordo (Ill.) pub. schs., 1910-12; critic teacher, 1912-13, prin. training sch., 1913-16, Ill. State Normal U.; asst. supt. schs., Springfield, Ill., 1918-21; prof. edn., U. of Ark., since 1921, also dir. training sch. for teachers since 1921. Mem. N.E.A., Ill. and Ark. State teachers' assns., Research Assn. U. of Ark., Phi Delta Kappa, Kappa Delta Pi. Republican. Baptist. Mem. Ancient and Beneficent Order of Red, Red Rose. Club: Lion. Co-Author: Arithmetics for Today (with Prof. Robert F. Anderson), 1931. Home: Fayetteville AR‡

CADWALADER, THOMAS FRANCIS, lawyer, b. nr. Jenkintown, Pa., Sept. 22, 1880; s. John and Mary Helen (Fisher) C.; student Episcopal Acad., Phila., Pa., 1889-96, St. Paul's Sch., Concord, N.H., 1896-97; A.B., U. of Pa., 1901; LL.B., University of Maryland, 1903; married Elizabeth Middleton Read, November 23, 1911 (died June 27, 1952); children—Thomas Francis, Mary Helen, Anne Cleland, Benjamin Read. Admitted to Md. bar, 1903; practiced as partner in Cadwalader & Whitman, later Cadwalader, Whitman & Mason, Baltimore, 1903-16; practiced alone since 1919; trustee or agt. of various estates, individuals and charitable funds administered in Phila.; dir. Baltimore & Phila. Steamboat Co., 1904-35, pres., 1930-35; trust officer, First Nat. Bank of Baltimore, 1943-45. Served Mexican border with Troop A, First Md. Cav. and in 5th Md. Inf.; mem. First R.O.T.C., Ft. Myer, Va., 1917; 2d lieutenant cavalry, 1st lieutenant and captain field artillery, Camp Lee and Camp Zachary Taylor. Trustee University of Pennsylvania (1928-43), Hannah More Academy (Reisterstown, Md.), St. Paul's Sch. for Boys (Brooklandwood, Md.). Church Home and Hospital of City of Baltimore, St. Andrew's School, Middletown, Del. Mem. Md. State, Harford County and Baltimore City bar assns., Delta Phi, Phi Beta Kappa. Episcopalian (del. to Gen. Conv. P.E. Ch., 1943, 46, 49, 52). Club: University (Phila.) Home: Joppa MD Died Feb. 24, 1970.

CADWELL, CHARLES STEWART, ret. mfg. exec.; b. Havana, Cuba, May 11, 1901 (parents U.S. citizens); s. Walter S. and Lillian (Barron) C.; student U. Ill. 1923; m. Louise Bielby, June 12, 1926; children—Patricia L. (Mrs. J. H. Stocker), Nancy L. (Mrs. R. G. Rettig), Charles S., James Burton. With Automatic Electric Company Chicago, 1923-58, beginning as govt. contract sales mgr. successively fgn. sales mgr., gen. sales mgr., v.p., sales mgr., v.p., gen. mgr., pres., 1923-55, also a dir.; dir. Automatic Electric (Can.) Ltd., Automatic Electirc Sales (Can.), Ltd. Bd. govs. Community Meml. Gen. Hosp., La Grange, Ill. Mem. Ind. Pioneer Telephone Association (pres. Chicago chpt. 1964), Am. Soc. Naval Engrs., Def. Orientation Conf. Assn., Chgo. Natural History Mus., Army Signal Assn., Phi Kappa. Roman Catholic. Clubs: Chicago, Ill. (Chgo.); La Grange La Grange IL Died Mar. 1972.

CADY, JOHN HUTCHINS, architect; b. Providence, Jan. 17, 1881; s. John H. and Mary T. (Eddy) C.; Ph.B., Brown U., 1903, M.F.A. (hon.), 1958; student Mass. Inst. Tech., 1904-06, Atelier Duquesne, Paris, 1908. Pvt. practice architecture, Providence, 1908—; planning cons. Nat. Planning Bd., 1934, assigned R.I. Planning Bd., 1935-37; restored historic R.I. houses. Mem. Providence Plan Commn., 1917-44, chmn., 1929-44. Pres. Proprietors Swan Point Cemetery, from 1931. Served with Officers Tng. Sch.; 1918. Fellow A.I.A. (pres. R.I. 1943-45; R.I preservation officer com. preservation historic bldgs. 1954); mem. Am. Planning and Civic Assn., Soc. Preservation N.E. Antiquities, R.I. Hist. Soc., English Speaking Union, Nat. Trust for Hist. Preservation, Soc. Archtl. Historians, Providence Preservation Soc., World Affairs Council, Soc. Colonial Wars, Alpha Delta Phi. Clubs: Arts, Brown, Players (Providence); Appalachian Mountain. Author: Rhode Island Boundaries, 1936; Walks Around Providence, 1942; Highroads and Byroads of Providence, 1948; The Civic and Architectural Development of Providence, 1957. Contbr. articles hist. subjects to mags. Home: Providence RI Died Sept. 27, 1967.

CADY, WALTER GUYTON, educator; b. Providence, Dec. 10, 1874; s. John Hamlin and Mary Tabitha (Eddy) C.; Ph.B., Brown U., 1895, A.M., 1896, D.Sc., (Hon.), 1938; student U. Berlin, 1897-1900, Ph.D. 1900; m. Kathrin Olive Miller, July 3, 1903 (died July 11, 1909); 1 son, Willoughby M. (dec.). Magnetic Observer U.S. Coast and Geod. Survey, 1900-02; instr. physics Wesleyan U., 1902-03, asso. prof. 1903-07, prof., 1907-46, prof. emeritus 1946—; research asso. Cal. Inst. Tech., 1951-55. Mem. div. phys. scis. Nat. Research Council, 1935-38. Served as lt. comdr. USNRF., ret. 1939. Awarded Duddell medal, Phys. Soc. London, 1936. Fellow A.A.A.S., Am. Phys. Soc., Inst. Radio Engrs. (Morris Liebmann Meml. prize 1928; chmn. bd. editors of proceedings 1929; pres. Inst. 1932), Am. Acad. Arts and Scis.; mem. Am. Assn. Phys. Tchrs., Am. Assn. U. Profs. (council 1938-40), Alpha Delta Phi, Phi Beta Kappa, Sigma Xi. Author: Piezoelectricity, 1946; also articles in field. Asso. editor Physical Rev., 1924-26, Jour. Opt. Soc. Am., 1938-41. Home: 3350 Calvert Rd Pasadena 8 CA‡

CAESAR, DORIS, sculptor; b. N.Y.C., 1893; student Art Students League, 1910-13, Archipenko Sch. Art, 1925-30. One man shows Weyhe Gallery, 1933, 35, 37, 47, 53, 58, 58, Curt Valentine Gallery, 1943, Brown Gallery, Boston, 1956, Howard U., 1958, Whitney Mus. Am. Art, 1959; rep. permanent collections Addison Gallery Am. Art, Busch Reisinger Mus., Cleve. Mus., Colorado Springs Art Center, Dayton Art Inst., Wellesley Coll., Ft. Worth Art Assn., Howard U., Williams Coll., Mpls. Inst. Art, Phila. Mus., U. Del., U. Ia., U. Minn., Wadsworth Atheneum, Whitney Mus. Am. Art, others; also pvt. collections. Mem. Sculptors Guild, Archtl. League N.Y., Nat. Assn. Women Artists, Audubon Artists. Home: Litchfield CT Died Sept. 1971.

CAGLE, FRED RAY, scientist; b. Marion, Ill., Oct. 9, 1915; s. Fred and Agnes (Guiney) C.; B.E., So. Ill. Normal U., 1937; M.S., U. Mich., 1938, Ph.D. (univ. fellow, 1941-42, Rackham fellow, 1942-43), 1943; m. Josephine Alexander, June 18, 1938; children—Fred Ray, Mary Jo. Instr. zoology, critic teacher, Univ. High Sch., So. Ill. Normal U., Carbondale, 1938-39, dir. museum, asst. prof. zoology, 1939-46, instr. gen. biology course for teachers, 1939-40; vis. lecturer zoology, Tulane U., 1946, asso. prof. zoology, 1946-49, prof. zoology, 1949-63, chmn. dept., 1955-59, research coordinator, 1959-63, v.p. planning, 1963-65, v.p. instnl. devel., 1965-68; dir. Audubon Conservation Camp, summers 1948, 49. Mem. U.S. Commn. for UNESCO; cons. NASA, USPHS, Biol. Sci. Commn. Project, 1963-68, Sci. in Policy Devel. Countries, 1963-68. mem. sci. and tech. com. Library of Congress, 1962-68. Bd. dirs. Gulf U. Research Corp., Nat. Acad. Sci.-NRC Council Biol. Information. Served as aviation physiologist, capt., USAAF, 1943-45; India, PTO. Recipient Alumni Achievement award So. Ill. U., 1965. Fellow Herpetologists League, A.A.A.S.; mem. S.W. Assn. Naturalists, Am Soc. Naturalists, Nat. Council U. Research Adminstrs., Am. Assn. Icthyologists and Herpetologists (v.p. 1953-55), Am. Soc. Mammalogists, Wildlife Soc., Soc. Study Evolution, Soc. Systematic Zoology, Ecol. Soc. Am., Netherlande Assn. Herpetologists, Brit. Herpetology Soc., Am. Inst. Biol. Scis. (bd. govs. 1957-62, exec. com. information 1960-63, chmn. internat. com. 1961-68, chmn. com. transl. 1959-61), Conf. Biol. Editors (exec. sec. 1957-63), Am. Assn. U. Profs., Nat. Conf. Adminstrv. Research (program com. 1967), Fedn. Internationale de Documentation, Am. Council Edn. (chmn. com. sponsored projects 1966-68), U. Research Assn. (dir.), Gulf South Research Inst. (dir.), Sigma Xi (pres. Tulane chpt. 1963-64), Phi Sigma. Club: Cosmos. Author reptile sect. Vertebrates of N. Am.; also articles. Home: New Orleans LA Died Aug. 8, 1968.

CAHILL, ARTHUR JAMES, artist; born San Francisco, Cal., May 15, 1878; son John and Mary (Snow) C.; ed. pub. schs., Eureka, Calif., Jesuit Brothers schs., San Jose, Calif.; studied art, San Francisco, N.Y., Paris; m. Irene Cazeaux, Oct. 5, 1918 (died 1943);children—James Arthur, Richard John. Artist, San Francisco Chronicle, San Francisco Examiner, New York World, San Francisco Call, 1892-1906; illustrator Saturday Evening Post, Ladies' Home Jour., Cosmopolitan, etc., New York, 1906-10; art editor Sunset Mag. and Southern Pacific R.R., San Francisco, 1910-15; portrait painter since 1915. Works: (oil portraits) President Hoover, Washington, D.C.; Gen. John J. Pershing and John McLaren, Palace of Legion of Honor, San Francisco; Gov. James Rolph, Jr., for City of San Francisco; William May Garland, Los Angeles Museum of Art; Robert G. Sproul, president University of California; Col. Seeley Mudd, California Inst. of Tech.; Professor Henry Moose Stephens and Dr. Ernest C. Moore, U. of Calif.; Archbishop John J. Cantwell, Los Angeles Sem.; Mr. and Mrs. Allen C. Balch, Cornell U.; Dr. Robert A. Millikan, Calif. Inst. Tech.; A. P. Gianinni, Bank of America; numerous others; portraits in Bohemian and Family clubs, San Francisco California Club, Los Angeles. Mem. Los Angeles Art Assn., San Francisco Art Assn. Mem. of Final Jury of Art at the Calif. Art Exhibition, World's Fair, 1939. Republican, Roman Catholic. Clubs: Bohemian, Family (San Francisco); California, Sunset. Home: San Francisco CA Died Apr. 10, 1970.

CAIN, GEORGE R., pharm. exec.; b. Noblesville, Ind., Sept. 9, 1910; s. Rolly Morton and Dersie Alberta (Myers) C.; A.B., Williams Coll., 1933; m. Jane Gent, Oct. 20, 1934; children—Denis G., Tyler R., Michael G. Group dept. rep. Equitable Life Assurance Soc. of U.S., 1933-37; gen. ins. broker W. A. Alexander & Co., Chicago, 1937-40; in sales dept. Abbott Labs., North Chicago, 1940-47, dir. and administrv. asst. to pres., 1947-50, dir. from 1947, exec. v.p., chmn. exec. com., 1950-58, pres., 1958-67, chmn. bd., 1962-72; dir. Abbott Universal, Ltd., Ill. Bell Telephone Co., Internat. Harvester Co., Continental Ill. Nat. Bank & Trust Co. Chgo., Skil Corp., Standard Oil Co. (Ind.). Trustee Northwestern U.; hon. dir. Evanston Hosp.; dir. Pharm. Mfrs. Assn. Mem. Northwestern U. Assos., Phi Gamma Delta. Republican. Episcopalian. Mason. Clubs: Commonwealth, Mid-America, Chicago, Commercial (Chgo.); Glen View (Golf, Ill.); Old Elm (Ft. Winnetka IL Died July 2, 1972.

CAKE, RALPH HARLAN, savs. and loan assn. exec.; b. Portland, Ore., June 26, 1891; s. William M. and Lulu (Riley) C.; A.B., U. Ore., 1913; LL.B., Harvard, 1916; m. Katherine Myers, Apr. 6, 1963; children—by previous marriage Martha, Ralph Harlan. With Equitable Savs & Loan Assn., Portland, 1922-73, v.p., 1933-38, pres., 1938-64, chmn. bd., 1964-68, chmn. finance com., 1968-73, also dir.; dir. Ore. Portland Cement Co., Hayden Island, Inc., Gerber Legendary Blades. KATU, Portland, Ore., Panama Canal Co.; sr. partner firm Cake, Jaureguy Hardy, Buttler & McEwen, 1938-73. Pres. Portland Rose Festival Assn., 1938, Multonomah Civic Stadium Assn., 1936. Mem. Republican Nat. Com. for Ore., 1940-52. Mem. U.S. Savs. and Loan League (pres. 1942-43), U. Ore. Alumni Assn. (pres. 1937-38), Phi Delta Gamma (trustee 1964-66, pres. 1952-53, pres. ednl. found. 1970-73). Clubs: Waverly Country, Multonomah Athletic, Arlington, University (Portland); University (N.Y.C.); Capitol Hill (Washington). Home: Portland OR Died Mar. 18, 1973.

CALDER, HELEN BARNETSON, missionary sec.; b. Hartford, Conn., Jan. 29, 1877; d. George and Margery (Patterson) C.; B.A., Mt. Holyoke Coll., 1898; studied Hartford Theol. Sem. Teacher Western Coll., Oxford, O., 1898-99; sec. Y.W.C.A., Hartford, 1899-1902; sec. Y.W.C.A., Mt. Holyoke Coll., 1902-05; sec. Woman's Bd. of Missions Congl. Ch., 1905-27; sec. A.B.C.F.M., 1927-32; in Europe, 1927-28; del. to Jerusalem Conf., 1928. Visited mission field as mem. deputation of Federation of Women's Bds. of Foreign Missions of N. America, 1919-20; visited China, 1935, 36. Chmn. Foreign Missions Conf. of N. America, 1930. Home: Auburndale, Mass. Office: 14 Beacon St., Boston MA*‡

CALDER, HUGH GORDON, petroleum exec.; b. Little Rock, Ark., Sept. 11, 1902; s. Christopher and Sophia M. (Calder) C.; student U. Tex., 1920-23; m. Gladys Edwards, July 23, 1927; children—Lorayn, Joan, Hugh. Auditor various cos. in Cuba, Mexico and Tex., 1923-26; co-owner Fox-Calder Motor Co., McAllen, Tex., 1926-27; asst. comptroller Fed. Water Service Corp., N.Y. City, 1927-29; sec., treas. and dir. Internat. Public Service Corp., N.Y. City, 1930-34, sec., comptroller, 1932-34; v.p., treas. and dir. Scranton-Spring Brook Water Service Co., Wilkes-Barre, Pa., 1935-37; v.p., treas., dir. So. Natural Gas Co., Birmingham, Ala., 1937-47; pres. So. Prodn. Co., Inc., Shreveport, La., 1947-53, dir.; then ind. oil producer and cons. Mem. Tex. Mid-continent Oil and Gas Assn. (dir.), Delta Theta Phi. Presbyn. Clubs: Shreveport (La.); Shreveport Shreveport LA Died Dec. 21, 1970; buried Shreveport LA

CALDER, ROBERT SCOTT, clergyman, educator; b. Seaforth, Ont., Dec. 22, 1870; s. George (M.D.) and Mary (Scott) C.; A.B., Washington and Jefferson Coll., 1893, A.M., 1895; grad. Western Theol. Sem., Pittsburgh, Pa., 1897; studied U. of Leipzig, Germany; Ph.D., Grove City (Pa.) Coll., 1912; (D.D., Bellevue (Neb.) Coll., 1911); m. Katharine Graham Calder, of Pittsburgh, Apr. 24, 1900. Instr. in classics, Washington and Jefferson Coll., 1893-6; ordained Presbyn. ministry, 1897; pastor Conemaugh, Pa., 1897-1903, Monessen, Pa., 1903-6; dean and prof. philosophy and edn., Bellevue (Neb.) Coll., 1906-11; prof. philosophy and Bible, and coll. pastor, Grove City (Pa.) Coll., 1911-17, Lindenwood Coll., St. Charles, Mo., since Sept., 1917. Address: St Charles MO‡

CALDERON GUARDIA, RAFAEL ANGEL, ex-President of Costa Rica; b. San Jose de Costa Rica, Mar. 10, 1900; s. Dr. Rafael Calderon Munoz and Ana Marie Guardia Mora; student at Colegio Seminario of Costa Rica; medical studies at Univ. of Louvain in Belgium and Universite Libre of Brussels, receiving med. degree, 1927. Successively interne, asst. surgeon, head of clinic and chief surgeon, Hosp. of San Juan de Dios, San Jose; mem. faculty of medicine, Nat. Univ. of Costa Rica; mem. bd. dirs. Duran Sanatorium; vice-pres. Liga Anti-Cancerosa (League against Cancer); served as vice-pres. and later pres. of City of San Jose; also successively as rep., vice-pres. (1935-37), and pres. (1938-39), of Costa Rican Congress; elected President of Costa Rica as mem. Rep. Nat. party, Feb. 11, 1940, served until 1944; ambassador to Mexico, 1957-62. Roman Catholic. Address: San Jose Costa Rica Died June 11, 1970.*

CALDWELL, J. G., clergyman; born at St. Louis, June 16, 1913; s. James G. and Sarah Elizabeth (Hobson) C.; A.B., Univ. of Redlands, 1936, B.D., Divinity Sch. of Pacific, 1939. Ordained to ministry of Episcopal Ch., Sept., 1939, and served as vicar St. Bartholomew's Parish, Los Angeles, 1939-43, of Emmanual Parish, El Monte, 1941-43; rector Mount Calvary Parish, Los Angeles, 1943-61. Home: Los Angeles CA Died Sept. 7, 1971.

CALDWELL, JOHN LIVY, college pres.; b. at Rome, Ga.; s. Rev. John McKnitt Madison and Caroline Elizabeth (Livy) C.; A.B., Princeton, 1870; Union Theol. Sem., Va., 1871-3; Princeton Theol. Sem., 1873-4, grad., 1874; (D.D., Central U. of Ky., 1888); m. Rilma Sanders, of St. Mary's Parish, La., June 8, 1881. Ordained Presbyn. ministry, 1874; pastor Independence, Mo., Pleasant Hill, Mo., and Liberty, Mo., 1874-76, 1st Ch., Bowling Green, Ky., 1876-91, 1st Ch., New Orleans, 1891-3, 1st Ch., Pine Bluff, Ark., 1893-1905; pres. Queens Coll. (for women), formerly Presbyn. Coll. for Women, 1911-18; again pastor 1st Ch., Bowling Green, Ky., 1920—. Mayor Pine Bluff, 1906. Trustee Arkansas Coll. Mem. Am. Whig Soc., Beta Theta Pi. Mason (K.T.). Address: 1253 State St., Bowling Green KY‡

CALDWELL, MARY LETITIA, educator; b. Bogota, Columbia, Dec. 18, 1890; dau. Milton Etsil and Susanna (Adams) Caldwell; A.B., Western Coll., 1913; A.M., Columbia, 1919, Ph.D., 1921; unmarried. Instr. in chemistry, Western Coll., 1914-15, asst. prof., 1915-17, asso. prof., 1917-18; univ. fellow in chemistry Columbia, 1920-21, instr. in chemistry, 1922-29, asst. prof., 1929-43, asso. prof. 1943-1948; prof. from 1948. Recipient Gavvan medal, 1959. Fellow A.A.A.S., N.Y. Acad. Sci.; mem. Am. Chem. Soc., Am. Inst. Nutrition, Am. Soc. Biol. Chemists, Am. Assn. U. Profs., Am. Geog. Soc., Sigma Xi. Presbyn. Republican. Author sci. papers in sci. profl. jours. Home: New York City NY Died July 1, 1972; buried South Salem OR

CALDWELL, ORESTES HAMPTON, editor, elec. engineer; b. Lexington, Kentucky, Mar. 8, 1888; s. William Hampton, M.D., and Flora V. (Weed) C.; prep. edn., Dr. Duhrings Sch., Charlottenburg, Germany, and Shortridge High Sch., Indianapolis, Ind.; B.S. in E.E., Purdue, 1908, E.E., 1931, Dr. of Engring., 1933; m. Mildred Hope Bedard, Sept. 9, 1914; children—Joan Hope (Mrs. Edward Schempp), Mary Jane (Mrs. Robert E. Nickerson). Asso. editor Electrical World, 1910-17; editor Electrical Merchandising, 1916-29, Radio Retailing, 1925-35, Electronics, 1930-35, Radio Today, 1935-48, Radio and Television Retailing, 1941-52, Electronic Industries, 1942-54, Tele-Tech, 1946-52; federal radio commr., 1927-29; vice president, treas. Caldwell-Clements, Incorporated; chmn. bd., treas. Caldwell-Clements Manuals Corp.; partner Electronic Development Assos.; Nat. Broadcasting Co. commentator on weekly programs, Radio Magic." Chmn. Indsl. Relations Committee Armed Forces Communication Association, New York Section; mem. Nat. Color-Television Standards Committee; mem. com. on ednl.-television station awards. Fellow Institute of Radio Engineers; Fellow Am. Inst. E.E. (chmn. N.Y. sect. 1931-32); member Am. Standards Assn. (chmn. civilian-radio committee), N.Y. Elec. Society (first v.p. 1931-32; pres. 1932-34), Radio Pioneers (treas., 1st vice pres.), Am. Mus. Natural History (vice chmn. com. on planetarium), Epsilon Chi, Tau Beta Pi, Amateur Astronomers Assn. (pres. 1936-38). Trustee N.Y. Museum of Science and Industry. Club: Indian Harbor Yacht. Home: Cos Cob CT Died 1967.

CALHOUN, RALPH EMERSON, mining engr.; b. Rockmart, Ga., Jan. 8, 1906; s.William A. and Mildred E. (Davitte) C.; student N. Ga. Agrl. Coll., Dohlonegg, 1923-26; m. Mary J. Pickett, Nov. 10, 1931;children—William Mitchell, Robert Lewis, Ann. Rodman, engring. dept. Am. Zinc Co. of Tenn., 1925-28; resident engr. Jarnigon Property, Jefferson City, Tenn., 1928-29; supt., Joplin, Mo., 1929-31; engring. dept., Tenn., 1932, supt. of mines, Joplin, 1933-36; gen. supt. Am. Zinc Lead & Smelting Co., Metaline Falls, Wash., 1936-42, Joplin, 1942, asst. dist. mgr. charge mining, exploration engr., 1946, mgr. Colo. operations, 1946-49, Southwestern rep., 1949-54, Western mgr., 1954-59, mgr. mines, 1959-65, v.p., St. Louis, 1965-68. Mem.Am. Inst. Mining Engrs., Mo. Soc. Profl. Engrs., Pi Kappa Alpha. Home: Mascot, Tenn and St. Louis MO Died Oct. 6, 1968; buried Mount Hope Cemetery, Joplin MO

CALKINS, JAMES E., lawyer; b. Lowell, Ind., Oct. 6, 1877; s. James C. and Euphemia (Leach) C.; LL.B., U. of Ga., 1901; m. Lucy Black Yerger, Oct. 10, 1907. Began practice of law at Fernandina, Fla., 1901; gen. counsel Fla. R.R. Commn., 1919-25. Capt. Fla. State Troops, 1904-12. Mem. Fla. Ho. of Rep., 1906-10; mem. Fla. State Senate, 1910-26, pres. of Senate, 1919-21, mayor of Fernandina, Fla., 1916-20. Democrat. Mason. Clubs: Miami City; Century, Biltmore Country (Coral Gales). Compiler: Revised General Statutes of Florida, 1920. Home: 446 Navarre Av., Coral Gables FL

CALKINS, RAYMOND, clergyman; b. Buffalo, N.Y., Aug. 10, 1869; s. Wolcott and Charlotte Grosvenor (Whiton) C.; A.B., Harvard, 1890, A.M., 1895; student Harvard Divinity Sch., 1893-95; D.D., Bowdoin Coll., 1907, Grinnell Coll., 1914; m. Emily Blackwell Lathrop, Sept. 14, 1899. Master in Belmont (Calif.) Sch. for Boys, 1890-91; Seth Richards prof. modern langs., Ia. (now Grinnell) Coll., 1891-93; instr. German, Harvard, 1893-95. Ordained Congl. ministry, 1896; asst. pastor First Ch. of Christ, Pittsfield, Mass., 1896-1903; pastor Pilgrim Memorial Ch., Pittsfield, 1897-1903, State St. Ch., Portland, Me., 1903-12; pastor First Ch., Cambridge (Congl.), 1912-40, emeritus. Mem. Phi Beta Kappa. Author: Substitutes for the Saloon (in series on Liquor Problem, edited by the Com. of Fifty), 1901; The Christian Idea in the Modern World, 1918; The Social Message of the Book of Revelation, 1920; The Christian Church in the Modern World, 1925; The Eloquence of Christian Experience, 1927; Jeremiah the Prophet, 1929; The Holy Spirit, 1930; The Life and Times of Alexander McKenzie, 1935; Religion and Life, 1935; How Jesus Dealt With Men, 1941; Children's Sermons, 1942; The Romance of the Ministry, 1944; Daniel Evans, Teacher, Preacher, Theologian, Editor, 1944; The Modern Message of the Minor Prophets, 1947. Co-editor: Hymns of the Church, 1912. Home: 19 Berkeley St., Cambridge MA‡

CALLAHAN, JEREMIAH JOSEPH, coll. pres.; b. Bay City, Mich., Jan. 7, 1878; B.A., Pittsburgh Coll. of the Holy Ghost (now Duquesne U.), 1897, LL.D., 1923; studied Holy Ghost Apostolic Coll. (Cornwells Hgts., Pa.), Gregorian U. (Rome). Ordained priest R.C. Ch., 1904. Began teaching at Duquesne U., 1897; prof. St. Mary's Sem., Norwalk, Conn., 1906-1912; pastor Notre Dame Ch., Chippewa Falls, Wis., 1912-17; pres. Holy Ghost Coll., Cornwells Hgts., Pa., 1917-30; pres. Duquesne U. 1930-40; pastor St. Augustine Ch., Isle Brevelle, La., 1940-68. Ind. Democrat. Author: Euclid or Einstein (Vol. I), 1932; The Science of Language: Vol. I, The Science of Grammar, 1938, Vol. II, Word Study, 1939. Home: Pittsburgh PA Died Oct. 11, 1969; buried Sacred Heart Cemetery, Morrilton AR

CALLAHAN, WILLIAM PAUL, JR., pathologist; b. Sept. 20, 1917; s. William Paul and Catherine C.; B.S., Notre Dame U., 1939; M.D., Washington U., St. Louis, 1943; m. Jo Anne Aylward, June 19, 1941; children—Patricia (Mrs. Berry), Catherine (Mrs. Mandigo), William Paul, Michael. Intern, Washington Univ., St. Louis, 1943-44, asst. pathologist, 1943, instr. pathology, 1943-45, asso. pathologist, 1944-45; mem. staff St. Francis Hosp., Wichita Kans., 1947-48, dir. labs., 1948-66; founder, dir. Callahan Labs., Wichita, 1966-71. Chmn. Midwest Div., Field Survey Project for Lab. Assts.; med. dir. Kans. Certified Lab. Assts. Program; dir. cerivcal cytology screening program for the indigent of Kans.; cons. in field. Dir. fund raising Univ. Notre Dame Found., Kansas. Served M.C. AUS from lt. to capt., 1945-47. Diplomate Am. Bd. Pathology. Mem. A.M.A., Am. Soc. Clin. Pathologists (bd. Schs. of Med. Tech.), Am. Assn. Pathologists and Bacteriologists, Internat. Acad. Pathology, Coll. Am. Pathologists (rep. Kans.), Kans. Soc. Pathologists (sec.-treas.). Home: Wichita KS Died Aug. 16, 1971. Buried Old Mission Mausoleum Wichita KS

CALLANDER, WILLIAM FORREST, economist; b. N. Gower, Ont., Can., June 14, 1880; s. Alexander Stirling and Mary Jane (Trimble) C.; LL.B., Georgetown U., Washington, D.C., 1912; spl. studies U. of Wis., 1915-16, George Washington U., 1912-24; D.Sc. (hon.), U. Fla., 1958; m. Helen Edith Wright, Dec. 9, 1904; children—Ronald Charlton, Charles Stirling, Mary Helen. Came to U.S., 1898, naturalized, 1903. Began as court reporter; asst. adminstr., Agrl. Adjustment Adminstrn; chmn. U.S. Crop Reporting Board, 1937-42; Southern regional statistician, 1942-44; chief statistician for agr., U.S. Bureau of Census, Washington, D.C.; asst. chief in charge statistics Bureau of Agricultural Economics, also chmn. crop reporting bd., 1945-50; visiting lectr., acting dir. statistical center U. Fla., 1950-52, statis. cons. 1952-58. Mem. Am. Statis. Assn., Am. Farm Econ. Assn. Methodist. Contbr. tech articles to mags. Home: Alexandria VA Died Dec. 1968.

CALLCOTT, WILFRID HARDY, educator, author; b. Guadalupe County, Tex., Nov. 12, 1895; s. George Hardy and Mary (Ireland) C.; A.B., Southwestern U., Georgetown, Tex., 1919; A.M., Columbia, 1920, Ph.D., 1926; Litt.D., Southwestern U., 1958; Erskine Coll., 1964; m. Grace Otter, 1925 (dec. 1929); 1 son, George Hardy; m. 2d, Rebecca Anderson, 1932; children—Nancy Anderson, Frank Dobson, Thomas Anderson, Mary Ireland. Instr. extension teaching, Columbia, 1921-23; asso. prof. history, U. S.C., 1923-29, prof. history, 1929-69, dean Graduate School, 1944-60, dean faculty, 1955-60, dean university, 1960-62; pres. Coker Coll., 1968-69; vis. prof. history, Duke U., 1935-36, U. Tex., 1962-63; prof., Duke U. U. of N.C., and U. of Tex.; Albert Shaw lecturer on diplomatic history, Johns Hopkins U., 1942; sr. Fulbright lectr. Oxford University, 1963-64. Served in U.S. Army Air Corps, 1917-19. Sec. Conf. Deans of Southern Graduate Schools, 1948-53, president, 1954-55; mem. grad. commn. Bd. Control for Southern Regional Education, 1949-51; mem. exec., adminstrv. coms., So. Fellowship Fund. Mem. Am., So. and S.C. hist. associations, Am. Acad. Polit. Social Sci., Phi Beta Kappa. Democrat. Methodist. Club: Kosmos. Author several books, latest: The Rise of the Hemisphere Policy of the United States, 1967; also spl. lectures. Home: Columbia SC Died Sept. 20, 1969; buried Elmwood Cemetery, Columbia SC

CALLENDER, GEORGE RUSSELL, pathologist, army officer; b. Everett, Mass., May 13, 1884; s. Thomas Russell and Martha Ellen (Bemis) C.; grad. Mt. Hermon (Massachusetts) Sch., 1903; M.D., Tufts College Medical School, 1908, Sc.D. (honorary), 1954; graduate Army Medical School, 1913; married Gladys Foster Moore, August 28, 1913 (dec. 1969); children—Janet (Mrs. Merrill Buffington), George Russell, Gladys Catherine (Mrs. R. L. Gellein). Instr. pathology and bacteriol., Tufts Med. Sch., 1909-12; commd. 1st lt. M.R.C., U.S. Army, 1912, 1st lt. M.C., 1913, advanced through grades to brig. gen., 1945; chief of lab. Army Gen. Hosp., Ft. Bayard, N.M., 1913-15, Hawaiian Dept., 1916-18; asst. Div. of Lab. and Infectious Diseases, Surgeon Gen's. Office, 1918, chief, 1919; asst. curator Army Med. Mus., 1919-20, curator, 1920-22, 1924-28; mem. Med. Dept., Research Bd., Manila, 1922-24, pres., 1922-23; pres. Philippine Leprosy Research Bd., 1923-24; adviser in pathology, Philippine U. Med. Sch., 1923-24; instr. pathology Army Med. Sch., 1924-32; prof. gross pathology Georgetown U. Med. Sch., 1925-28; chief lab. 8th Corps Area, 1932-35; pres. Army Med. Research Bd., Canal Zone, 1935-38; pathologist, Army Med. Center, 1939; asst. comdt. Med. Dept., Professional Service Schs., 1940-45, comdt., 1946, retired, 1946; dir. pathology VA, 1947-59; advisor Gorgas Meml. Inst. Organizer, 1930, American Registry Pathology; mem. adv. bd. Armed Forces Inst. Pathology, until 1967. Served in Mass. N.G., 1907-12; 1st lt., M.C., 1911-12. Awarded Sternberg Medal, 1913; The Strong Medal, 1946; D.S.M., 1945; U.S.A. Typhus Com. Medal, 1946; Medale de la Reconnaisance Francaise, 1947. Diplomate Am. Bd. Pathology, Am. Bd. Preventive Med. Pub. Health Fellow A.C.P.; member A.M.A., Am. Assn. Pathologists and Bacteriologists (pres. 1930), Am. Soc. Tropical Med. (pres. 1933), Internat. Assn. Med. Mus. (pres. Am. and Canadian sect. 1932), Am. Acad. Tropical Medicine (pres. 1954) Armed Forces Inst. Pathology (sci. advisory bd.), Walter Reed Memorial Association, Am. Urol. Assn., Association of Mil. Surgeons of U.S., International College of Surgeons, com. on pathology Nat. Research Council, Nat. Adv. Cancer Council, Am. Found. Trop. Med., A.P.H.A., Acad. of Medicine of Washington, Massachusetts Society of Cincinnati, Alpha Kappa Kappa. Mason. Club: Army and Navy (Washington, D.C.). Wrote Pathology of the Acute Respiratory Diseases (Vol. XII, The Med. Dept., U.S. Army in World War), 1929—Co-author of Malaria in Panama." Contributor technical articles to jours. Home: Washington DC Died Feb. 26, 1973.

CALLER, MARY ALICE, teacher English language and literature Ala. Conf. Female Coll., Tuskegee, Ala., since 1877; b. Clarke Co., Ala.; g.d. Col. James C. (prominent in history of Ala., 1802-19); grad. Centenary Coll., 1866; taught there 1872-4; presiding teacher Marion Sem., 1875-6. Author: A Literary Guide for Home and School, 1891. Residence: (Summer) Avondale Ala. (Winter) Tuskegee AL‡

CALLERY, FRANCIS ANTHONY, investments; b. Pittsburgh, Pa., Aug. 14, 1898; s. James Dawson and Marcella (Howley) C.; prep. edn., Newman Sch., Hackensack, N.J., 1912-16; war diploma, Princeton, 1920; married Virginia R. Annan, December 6, 1924; children—Roberdeau (Mrs. Arthur B. DuBois), Joanne Dawson (Mrs. T. P. Heffelfinger II), James; m. Holly Simonds. Various positions Marland Oil Co., Ponca City, Okla., 1919-21, Ladenburg, Thalmann & Co., N.Y.C., 1921-23, 25-32, Guinnes,, Mahon & Co., London, Eng., 1923-24, Mellon Nat. Bank, Pitts., 1924-25; partner Emanuel & Co., N.Y.C., 1932-41; v.p., dir. Consol. Vultee Aircraft Corp., San Diego, Cal., 1942-46; asso. with Lehman Bros., Investment bankers, 1946-59, partner 1946-58; oil producer, Houston, from 1944; Clubs: University, Seawanhaka, Corinthian Yacht, Quiet Birdmen. Brook, Union (N.Y.C.); Bayou, Ramada (Houston). Home: NY Died Dec. 24, 1971; buried Pittsburgh, PA

CALLOWAY, WALTER BOWLES, ry. official; b. Harrison, O., Dec. 28, 1873; s. Thomas Bond and Anna (Bowles) C.; ed. Wabash Coll., Ind., 1890-91; m. Wilma Rhine, of Cincinnati, O., Oct. 6, 1903; children—Arthur Bond, Catherine. Began with C.,C.,C.&St.L. Ry., 1891;

various positions, pass. dept., same rd., 1894-98; division clk., 1898-1900, chief rate clk., 1900-01, adv. mgr., 1901-02, gen. pass. dept. C., H.&D. Ry.; asst. gen. pass. agt. Cincinnati, Richmond & Muncie R.R., at Richmond, Ind., 1902-03; gen. pass. agt. Chicago, Cincinnati & Louisville R.R., at Cincinnati, 1903-04; asst. gen. pass. agt., same rd., and C., H.&D. Ry., 1904-05; gen. pass. agt., C., H.&D. Ry., 1905-11; asst. gen. pass. agt., Mar., Sept. 1911, gen. pass. agt., 1911-16, B.&O. Southwestern R.R.; apptd. pass. traffic mgr. B.&O. R.R., 1917; gen. pass. traffic mgr. B.&O. R.R. and Alton R.R. since Feb. 1, 1934. Mem. Phi Kappa Psi. Republican. Presbyn. Clubs: Chesapeake, Merchants. Home: 3810 Fenchurch Rd., Baltimore. Office: B.&O. Bldg., Baltimore MD‡

CALVER, GEORGE WEHNES, physician; b. Washington, D.C., Nov. 24, 1887; s. Dr. Thomas and Elizabeth (Wehnes) C.; M.D., George Washington U., 1912; m. Jessie Willits, Mar. 15, 1916; children—Jessie Carleton (wife of Captain Paul F. Dickens, U.S.N.), Georgianna Elizabeth (wife of Capt. Eldon C. Swanson, U.S.N.). On active duty as naval med. officer, from 1913; commd. rear adm. M.C., USN, 1945, later vice adm.; with Naval Hosp., Washington, D.C., 1913, naval med. sch., Naval Sta., Guam, 1914-15, Naval Sta., Cavite, P.I., 1915-16, Yangtze River Patrol, 1916, Naval Hosp., Yokohoma, Japan, 1916-17, Charleston, S.C., 1917-19, U.S.S. Bridgeport, 1919-22; Naval Hosp. and Hosp. Corps Training Sch., 1922-25, U.S.S. Henderson, 1925-27; visiting surgeon U.S. Naval Dispensary, Washington, D.C., 1927-28; attending physician Congress of the U.S., 1928-66; dir. research lab. Naval Med. Research Institute, Bethesda Naval Medical Center, from 1966; consultant internal medicine and med. research Nat. Naval Med. Center; trustee Worcester Found. Research, Southwest Foundation for Research (San Antonio). Honorary consultant for Army Medical Library. Diplomate Bd. Internal Medicine. Fellow A.C.S., A.C.P., Am. Coll. Cardiology (trustee, pres. 1958-59), Am. Geriatrics Soc., A.A.A.S.; member A.M.A., D.C., George Washington U., Pam Am. (past president), Southern med. socs., Am. Heart Assn., Assn. Mil., Surgeons U.S., Medical Library Assn., Endocrine Soc., Pan Am. Med. Soc. (pres.), Laurentian Hormone Conf., Phi Chi. Mason. Clubs: International Medical, Carabao, Washington Clinical, Army-Navy Country, Chevy Chase (Washington): New York Yacht. Home: Washington DC Died Feb. 27, 1972; buried Arlington Nat. Cemetery, Arlington VA

CALVER, HOMER NORTHUP, health edn., pub. relations; b. N.Y.C., Nov. 22, 1892; s. William Louis and Mary Ella (Northup) C.; B.S. in Sanitary Engring., Mass. Inst. Tech., 1914; m. Hulings Elizabeth Lappe, Apr. 17, 1922; children—Cornelia and Judith Margaret. Hydrographic asst. Metropolitan Sewage Commission, New York City, 1913; asst. prof. hygiene, N.Y. U. Med. Sch., 1928-32; sec. pub. health com. of the Paper Cup and Container Inst., 1934-58, sec. pub. relations com., 1942-58; editor Health Officers News Digest, 1936-57; vis. prof. pub. health Am. U., Beirut, 1957, 59. Secretary Am. Mus. of Health, Inc., 1938-54; director Health exhibits N.Y. World's Fair, 1939 and 1940; consultant in health edn.; coordinator of Inter-Am. Affairs, 1943-46; mem. nat. adv. com. on emergency feeding FCDA; vice president nat. citizens com. WHO. Secretary-treasurer of Empire State Health Council. With American Ambulance in France, 1915; 1st lieutenant and captain Sanitary Corps, U.S. Army, 1917-19; asst. san. insp. 89th Div., Camp Funston, Kan.; comdr. 89th Div. Mobile Field Lab.; lecturer A.E.F. Univ., Beaune, France; captain Sanitary Officer Reserve, 1919-20. Recipient of the Ling Medal, 1930. Fellow of American Public Health Assn. (governing council, 1931-37; vice-chmn. Pub. Health Edn. Sect., 1934-36, chmn., 1936-37; chmn. com. on scientific exhibits 1932-42); fellow Royal Soc. Promotion Health (hon.), Am. Med. Writers Assn.; mem. S.R., Soc. Am. Bacteriologist, Pub. Relations Soc. Am., Soc. Pub. Health Educators, Kappa Sigma, Delta Omega. Club: University (N.Y.). Home: Clinton Corners NY Died Sept. 15, 1970.

CALVERT, PHILIP POWELL, entomologist; b. Phila., Jan. 29, 1871; s. Graham and Mary S. (Powell) C.; grad. Central High Sch., Phila., 1888; studied U. of Pa., 1888-89, 1891-95, Ph.D., 1895; Berlin, 1895-96, Jena, 1896; m. Amelia C. Smith, 1901. Instr. zoology, 1897-1907, asst. prof., 1907-12, prof., 1912-39, emeritus since 1939, U. of Pa. (studying natural history in Costa Rica on leave of absence, 1909-10). Asso. editor Entomological News, 1893-1910, editor 1911-43. Fellow A.A.A.S., mem. council Academy Natural Sciences of Phila., since 1897; pres. Am. Entomol. Society (Phila.), 1899-1915; pres. Entomol. Soc. America, 1914; mem. Limnological Soc. of Am., Am. Soc. Zoologists, Am. Soc. Naturalists, Ecol. Soc. America, Am. Philos. Soc., Am. Soc. Trop. Medicine, Sigma Xi. Known as student of the Odonata (Dragonflies). Contbr. to the sect. Odonata in Biologia Centrali-Americana (edited by F. D. Godman, F.R.S.), 1901-08; also catalogues and numerous articles on the Odonata of various regions. Author: (with Amelia S. Calvert) A Year of Costa Rican Natural History, 1917. Home: Box 14, PA‡

CALVERT, RICHARD CREAGH MACKUBIN, business man; b. College Park, Md., Dec. 31, 1872; s. of Charles Baltimore and Eleanor (Mackubin) C.; B.S., Md. Agrl. Coll., 1890, postgrad. work to 1892; Johns Hopkins, 2 yrs., 1890-92; (hon. E.E., Md. Agrl. Coll., 1913); m. Zoe Ammen, d. of Maj. Gen. George W. Davis, U.S.A., Oct. 18, 1906. Worked several yrs. in shops of Gen. Electric Co., Lynn, Mass., and Schenectady, N.Y.; went to Brazil twice, to Venezuela and to India for Gen. Electric Co.; asst. chief elec. engr. Mysore State Govt., 1904-10; purchased controlling interest in water, electric and ice cos. of Oxford, N.C., 1911; later sold electric co.; now pres. Oxford Ice Co., Oxford Water Co. Commd. officer Bangalore (India) Rifle Vols., 1905-10. Democrat. Episcopalian. Mason. Club: Granville Commercial. Address: Oxford NC‡

CALVERT, ROBERT, patent atty., chemist; b. Milford, Mo., Mar. 15, 1889; s. William Samuel and Martha Ann (Newkirk) C.; A.B., U. Okla., 1909, A.M., 1910; S.M., U. Chgo, 1912; Ph.D., Columbia, 1914; m. Mary Power Siggers, Mar. 6, 1922; children—Robert, Carol (dec.), George Edward. Instr. chem. U. Okla., 1909-11, Columbia, 1913-15; chemist and research lab. dir. E. I. du Pont de Nemours & Co., 1915-20; asst. prof. chemistry U. So. Cal., 1921-22; research lab. dir. Celite Products Co., 1922-24; prof. indsl. chemistry U. Md., 1925-26; chief chemist Van Schaack Bros. Chem. Works, Chgo., 1926-31; patent atty. Johns-Manville Corp., 1931-38, cons., 1938-41, patent atty., 1941-58; patent atty. Borden Company, 1958-64; professor industrial chemistry American University Beirut, 1951-52. Distinguished Service citation University Oklahoma, 1965; American Institute Chemists' Freedman Patent Found. award, 1966. Mem. Del. Chemists Soc. (chmn. 1917), N.J. Chem. Soc. (vice chmn. 1920), Am. Chem. Soc. (vice chmn. Chgo. sect. 1931; chmn. N.Y. sect. 1940), Tech. Soc. Council of New York (pres. 1950-51), N.Y. Patent Law Assn., Japan Patent Attorneys Assn. (hon.), Ret. Chemists Assn. N.Y. (pres. 1965-66), Phi Beta Kappa, Beta Theta Pi, Phi Lambda Upsilon, Sigma Xi. Republican. Conglist. Clubs: Chemists (N.Y.); Scarsdale (N.Y.) Golf. Author: Diatomaceous Earth, 1930; Patent Practice and Management, 1950; Winds of Opportunity (autobiography), 1969. Editor; Ency. Patent Practice and Invention Mgmt., 1964. Home: Scarsdale NY Died June 26, 1969.

CALVERT, WILLIAM JEPHTHA, M.D.; b. Lexington, Ky., Oct. 7, 1871; s. Henry Clay and Rebecca (Downing) C.; A.B., Ky. U. (now Transylvania U.), 1893; post-grad. work Ky. State Agrl. and Mech. Coll. (now U. of Ky.), 1893; M.D., Johns Hopkins, 1898; m. Edith U. Geery, of Warrensburg, Mo., 1912; 1 son, William Geery. Was first lt. and asst. surgeon U.S.A., 1899-1902; prof. pathology, Washington U., 1902-03; prof. clin. pathology, U. of Mo., 1903-09; prof. medicine, Baylor U. Med. Sch., Dallas, Tex., 1909-11; prof. preventive medicine, U. of Mo., 1911-13; prof. clin. medicine, Baylor U. Medical School, 1913-19. Mem. Bd. of Health, Manila, P.I., 1899-1901, Dallas, Tex., 1915 (resigned). Mem. Sigma Xi, Scabbard and Blade. Contbr. numerous articles to med. jours. Address: care First National Bank, Dallas TX‡

CALVIN, HENRIETTA WILLARD (MRS. JOHN H. CALVIN), home economist; b. Jonesboro, Ill., Aug. 11, 1865; d. Henry Webb and Alice (Condon) Willard; student Washburn Coll., B.S., Kan. State Agricultural Coll., 1886, LL.D., 1925; Pd.D., Temple University; LL.D., Purdue U., 1937; m. John H. Calvin, June 16, 1886 (dec.); children—John Willard, Paul Henry, Mrs. Ruth Yoke, David (dec.), Catherine (dec.), Benjamin Willis, George Fairchild. Librarian Kansas State Agrl. Coll., 1901-03; prof. domestic science, same, 1903-08; prof. home economics, Purdue U., 1908-12; dean home economics and prof. domestic science, Ore. Agrl. Coll., 1912-15; specialist in home economics, U.S. Bur. Edn., 1915-22; dir. of home economics, Phila. public schs., 1922-36. Lecturer at N.E.A. Chautauquas, farmers' insts., etc. Democrat. Baptist. Contbr. on ednl. topics and on cooperation in county, state and national relief projects. Home: 465 Bellevue Av., Oakland CA‡

CAMERON, ADAM KIRK, business exec.; b. Arthur, Ont., Can., 1874. Chmn. bd. and dir. Eastern Steel Products, Ltd., St. Laurence Paper Mills, Ltd., Lake St. John Power & Paper Co., Ltd. (all Montreal); pres. St. Lawrence Corp., Montreal; dir. Brompton Pulp and Paper Co. (Montreal), Canadian Wirebound Boxes, Ltd., W.D. Heath & Sons, Ltd., A. B. Ormsky Company, Ltd. (all of Toronto), Eastern Trust (of Halifax, Nova Scotia), Siscoe Gold Mines. President of the Montreal Chamber of Mines; vice president of Investment Found. Mason. Home: 834 Landsdowne Av., Westmount, Que., Can. Office: Eastern Steel Products, Ltd., 1335 De Lormier Av., Montreal PQ Canada*‡

CAMERON, ALBERT BARNES, architect; b. Raleigh, N.C., Oct. 21, 1925; s. John Stanley and Rosanna (St. George) C.; B. Arch., N.C. State U., 1952; m. Marjorie Louise Deaton, Aug. 30, 1946; children—Teresa Louise (Mrs. Randall Boyd Hartzoge), Deborah Deaton, Valori Nan, Albert B, Jr. Archtd. design cons. N.C. Dept. Pub. Instrn., 1949-50; architect A. G. Odell, Jr. Assos., 1952-59; architect and owner Cameron Assos., architects, 1959-66; architect, pres. Cameron, Little & Assos., Charlotte, N.C., Associates, 1966-67. Mem. A.I.A., Constrn. Specifications Inst., Charlotte C. of C., Central Charlotte Assn. Club: Charlotte Atletic. Home: Charlotte NC Died Nov. 18, 1967.

CAMERON, CHARLES RAYMOND, consular service; b. York, N.Y., June 25, 1875; s. John and Catherine (McDougall) C.; A.B., Cornell, 1898 (Phi Beta Kappa); unmarried. Mercantile business, 1898-1901; entered Philippine Civil Service, 1901; supt. schs., Moro Province and Province Mindanao and Sulu; asst. to dept. gov., dept. sec. and treas.; census asst. Capt. Aviation Sect. Signal Corps U.S.A., World War, 1917-18; maj. Air Service, 1918-19. Consul at Tacna, Chile, 1919-20, Pernambuco, Brazil, 1920-23, Tokyo, 1923-25; assigned to the Department of State, 1925; consul at Sao Paulo, Brazil, 1930-33, at Habana, Cuba, 1934-36, at Osaka, Japan, 1936-37, at Tokyo, Japan, since 1937. Chairman U.S. delegation to Second International Coffee Congress, Sao Paulo, May-June 1931. Author: Sulu Writing—an Explanation of the Sulu Arabic Script as Employed in Writing the Sulu Language of the Southern Philippines; also numerous magazine articles. Address: Dept. of State, Washington DC‡

CAMERON, D(ONALD) EWEN, psychiatrist; b. Bridge of Allan, Scotland, Dec. 24, 1901; s. Duncan and Margaret Isabel (Conacher) C.; M.B., Ch.B., U. Glasgow, 1924, M.D. with distinction, 1936; D.P.M., U. London, 1926; m. Jean Carruthers Rankine, Aug. 5, 1933; children—Duncan Hume, Airlie A. C., D. Stuart, James R. Intern, resident surgeon Glasgow Mental Infirmary, 1924-25; asst. physician Glasgow Royal Mental Hosp., 1925-26; Henderson research scholar in psychiatry Johns Hopkins, 1926-28; volontairarzt Burgholzli Clinic, Zurich, Switzerland, 1928-29; physician charge reception unit Province Mental Hosp., Brandon, Man., Can., 1929-36; sr. research psychiatrist Worcester (Mass.) State Hosp., 1936-37, resident dir. research, 1937-38; prof. neurology and psychiatry Albany Med. Coll., also neurologist and psychiatrist in chief Albany Hosp., 1938-43; prof. chmn. dept. psychiatry McGill U., also psychiatrist in chief Royal Victoria Hosp., dir. Allan Meml. Inst. Psychiatry, Montreal, 1943-67; cons. psychiatrist Montreal Gen. Hosp.; dir. psychiatry and aging research labs. VA Hosp., Albany, N.Y., 1964-67; research professor of psychiatry Albany Med. Coll., 1964-64. Mem. expert adv. panel mental health WHO, 1952-67; mem. bd. examiners Am. Psychiat. Assn., 1938-39, bd. psychiat. examiners State N.Y., 1941-43. Hon. president Manfred Sakel Found. Diplomate Am. Bd. Psychiatry and Neurology. Fellow N.Y. Acad. Medicine, Am. Psychiat. Assn. (pres. 1952-53), Royal Coll. Physicians and Surgeons Can.; hon. fellow Am. Geriatrics Soc.; member A.M.A., Brit., Que. Indsl., Canadian medical assns., World Fedn. Mental Health, Royal Medico-Psychol. Assn. (hon.), A.A.A.S., Assn. Research Nervous and Mental Disease, Que. Psychiat. Assn. (pres.), American Psychopath. Assn. (pres. 1962-63), World (pres. 1961-66), Canadian, Que. (pres. 1956-57) psychiat. assns., Soc. Biol. Psychiatry pres. 1965-66). Author: Objective and Experimental Psychiatry, 1935; Remembering, 1947; Life is for Living, 1948; General Psychotherapy: Dynamics and Procedures, 1950; Psychotherapy in Action, 1968. Contbr. profl. Loudonville NY Died Sept. 8, 1967; cremated.

CAMERON, HAROLD WILLIAM, business exec.; born Aberdeen, Wash., Oct. 26, 1902; s. William T. and Laura (Sutherland) C.; student Stanford, 1921-23; A.B. magna cum laude U. Wash., 1926; children—Anne (Mrs. B.A. Ekren), Carol (Mrs. J.A. Fleury, Junior). C.P.A., Haskins & Sells, 1927-29; investment analyst Pacific Northwest Co., Seattle, 1929-40, v.p., 1940-45, exec. v.p., 1945-64; dir. Equity Fund, Inc., Seattle, 1932-67, asst. treas., 1932, sec., 1933, v.p., 1934-50, pres., 1950-61; chmn. bd. Pacific Resins & Chems., Inc., Seattle, 1962-65; vice president United Pacific Corp., Seattle, 1954, senior vice president, 1954-67; dir. Pacific Am. Corp., 1960-66, pres., 1965-66; sr. v.p. VWR United Corp., Seattle, 1967-70. Mem. Washington Soc. C.P.A.'s, N.Y. Soc. Security Analysts, Phi Beta Kappa, Phi Kappa Psi, Beta Gamma Sigma, Alpha Kappa Psi. Republican. Methodist. Clubs: Seattle WA Died Feb. 6, 1970; buried Seattle WA

CAMERON, TURNER CHRISTIAN, JR., fgn. service officer; b. Faunsdale, Ala., Sept. 5, 1914; s. Dr. Turner Christian and Louise Chadwich (Minge) C.; A.B., U. Ala., 1936; A.M., La. State U., 1937; Ph.D., Princeton, 1940; married to Dorothy Drake. Instructor at Sweet Briar Coll., 1940-42; div. assistant, div. comml. policy Department of State, 1942-44; apptd. fgn. service auxiliary officer, 1944, fgn. service officer, 1947; sr. econ. analyst Am. Embassy, Paris, 1944-47, 2d sec. and consul, 1947-50; 2d sec. Am. Embassy, Belgrade, Yugoslavia, 1950, 1st sec. 1951; 1st sec., cons., Saigon, Phnom Penh and Vientiane, 1953, 54; consul, Hanoi, 1954; 1st sec. Seoul, 1955; Officer-in-charge Swiss Benelux Affairs, Dept. of State, 1956-58; dep. dir. Office Western European Affairs, Dept. of State, Washington,

1958-60, dir. office S. Asian Affairs, 1962-65; counselor Am. Embassy, Colombo, Ceylon, 1960-62, Am. embassy, Stockholm, Sweden, 1965-69, charge d'affaires, 1969-70; diplomat-in-residence U. S.C., 1970-71. Home: Faunsdale AL Died Dec. 24, 1971; buried Greenwood Cemetery, Montgomery AL

CAMILLO, MICHAEL FRANCIS, physician; b. Middletown, N.Y., May 22, 1928; s. Frank and Louise B. Camillo; M.D., State U. N.Y., Syracuse, 1953; m. Marian A. Flood, Aug. 23, 1952; children—Michael, Christopher, Mark Lynne. Intern, State U. N.Y. Med Center Hosps., Syracuse, 1953-54, asst. resident, 1954-55, 57-59, chief resident in surgery, 1959-60; asso. attending surgeon Morton Meml. Hosp., Middletown; cons. surgeon Middletown State Hosp. Served to capt., M.C., AUS, 1955-57. Diplomate Am. Bd. Surgery. Fellow A.C.S.; mem. A.M.A., N.Y. State Med. Soc., Mid-Hudson Surg. Soc., Phi Beta Kappa, Alpha Kappa Kappa. Roman Catholic. Home: Middletown NY Died Mar. 15, 1971; buried Middletown NY

CAMMACK, JOHN WALTER, b. Orange County, Va., Apr. 28, 1875; s. George Walter and Mary Jane (Pidgeon) C.; student Fredericksburg (Va.) Coll.; B.A., U. of Richmond, Va., 1900, M.A., 1901, D.D., 1914; Th.M. Southern Bapt. Theol. Sem., Louisville, Ky., 1903; Ph.G., U. of Va., 1904; m. Bessie Clay Hagan, June 14, 1905. Ordanied Bapt. ministry, 1904; pastor Onancock, Va., 1904-07, Buckhannon, W.Va., 1907-10; asso. editor Religious Herald, Richmond, 1910-15; sec. Bapt. Edn., Commn. of Va., 1915-24; sec. Edn. Commn. Southern Bapt. Conv., 1914-19; exec. sec. Edn. Bd. Southern Bapt. Conv., 1924-27; pres. Averett Coll., Danville, Va., 1927-36; pastor Fork Union, Va., 1936-43; Oakwood Av. Ch., Richmond, Va., since 1942. Trustee Fork Union Mil. Acad. and Bluefield Coll. Pres. Southern Bapt. Edn. Assn.; v.p. Am. Assn. of Junior Colls.; mem. N.E.A., Council of Ch. Schs. of the South, Sigma Phi Epsilon. Mason (Shriner). Clubs: University (Richmond); Rotarian; Ruritan. Home: 9444 Sierra Bonita Circle, Phoenix

CAMP, THOMAS RINGGOLD, engineer; b. San Antonio, Nov. 5, 1895; s. Harmon Clark and Mildred Stella (Dashiell) C.; B.S., Tex. A. and M. Coll., 1916; M.S., Mass. Inst. Tech., 1925; Sc.D. (hon.), Clarkson Inst. Tech., 1970; m. Margaret Alice Evans, June 15, 1925; children—Frances, John, Emilie (Mrs. R. F. Stouffer). Practicing engineer, Tex., N.C., N.Y., N.J., 1916-29, hydraulic, san. engr. since 1921; asso. prof. san. engring., Mass Inst. Tech., 1929-44; consulting engr., 1944-1971; founded Camp Dresser & McKee, Boston, 1947. Served with U.S. Army, 1917-19. Received Boston Soc. C.E. san. sect. prize, 1941, hydraulic, 1944, Desmond FitzGerald medal, 1949; Karl Emil Hilgard prize, Am. Soc. C.E., 1941. J.C. Stevens hydraulic prize, 1945, J. James R. Croes medal, 1947; N.E. Water Works Assn. Dexter Brackett meml. medal, 1943, 56, Fuller award, Am. Water Works Assn., 1955; Rudolph Hering medal, Am. Soc. C.E., 1956, Friedman award 1964, C.E. Clemens Herschel award, 1970. Samuel A. Greeley award, 1969, posthumously awarded J.C. Stevens award, 1972; New Eng. award Engring. Socs. of New Eng., 1963, Distinguished Service award Nat. Clay Pipe Inst., 1966. Registered profl. engr., Mass., Me., Conn., Vt., R.I., N.H., Pa., N.Y., N.C. Diplomate Am. Acad. Sanitary Engrs., 1955. Fellow Am. Pub. Health Assn.; mem. Am. Soc. C.E. (hon.), Boston Soc. C.E. (pres. 1950; hon.), N.E. (pres. 1950; hon.), Am. water works assns., N.E. Sewage Works Assn. (pres. 1947), Am. San. Engring. Intersoc. Bd. (founder, chmn. 1956-62), Am. Inst. Cons. Engrs., Water Pollution Control Fedn. (hon. mem.; fedn. established Thomas R. Camp medal 1964), Sigma Xi, Tau Beta Pi. Author profl., tech. articles. Mem. adv. com. 1962. Revision USPHS Drinking Water Standards. Patentee in field. Author: Water and Its Impurities, 1963. Address: Boston MA Died Nov. 15, 1971.

CAMPBELL, ALEXANDER MORTON, lawyer, member Democratic National Committee; born Coldwater, Ohio, April 14, 1907; son of Samuel T. and Elsie C. (Bolman) C.; student Olivet Coll., 1925-27; LL.B., Indiana U., 1930; m. Eleanor E. Church, July 5, 1935; 1 son, Thomas Morton. Practicing atty., Fort Wayne, Ind., 1930-35; asst. U.S. atty., Northern Dist. of Ind., 1935-41, U.S. atty., 1941-48; asst. attorney Gen. U.S., 1948-50. Dem. National committeeman from Indiana, 1960. Trustee Indiana U.; dir. Ind. U. Found., Boys Clubs of Am. Chmn. Allen Co. Dem. Com., 1934-36; nat. pres., Ind. U. Alumni Assn., 1939-40. Awarded Neizer Debating Trophy, Ind. U., 1929, Nat. Keystone award, Boys Clubs Am. Mem. Ind. Saddle Horse Assn. (pres. 1957), Tau Kappa Alpha, Delta Chi, Delta Theta Phi. Mason, Elk, Moose, Eagle. Mem. Christian Ch. Clubs: Chicago Lake Shore; Indianapolis Athletic; Ft. Wayne Country, Ft. Wayne Press; Kiwanis, Quest. Author: Building Our Defenses, World Order through Law; The Christian Evangelist; The Choice Before Civilization. Home: Coesse IN Died Jan. 4, 1968.

CAMPBELL, BRUCE JONES, retail merchandising exec.; b. in Flagstaff, Ariz., Aug. 20, 1912; s. William Alexander and Mina B. (Jones) C.; B.S. in Bus. Adminstrn., U. So. Cal., 1934, M.B.A., 1939; m. Susanne Margaret Jones, Aug. 10, 1940; children—Barbara Jones, Robert William. Partner Campbell & Guill, pub. accountants, 1946-50; supervising auditor Cal. Bur. Milk Control, 1946-50, chief, 1950-52; controller Golden State Co., Ltd., 1952-54; controller Foremost Dairies, San Francisco, 1954-56, v.p., comptroller, 1956-59, financial v.p., 1959-61; financial v.p., treas. Food Giant Markets, Inc.; v.p. dir. Meyenberg Old Fashion Products Co., Giant Realty Co. Served as maj. AUS, 1941-46. Mem. Financial Execs. Inst., Cal. Soc. C.P.A.'s. Methodist. Mason. Home: Whittier CA Died May 26, 1968.

CAMPBELL, CHARLES KING, corp. exec.; b. Westerly, R.I., Dec. 22, 1911; s. Clifford W. and Effie (King) C.; student Choate Sch., 1928-30; Ph.B., Brown U., 1934; m. Phyllis Lord, Mar. 17, 1939; children—Sally Lord, Judith King, Charles King. Vice pres., dir. IBM World Trade Corp., N.Y.C., 1952-70; dir. Am. Brazilian Assn., Inc. Mem. bus. adv. council U. Mass. Mem. Pan Am. Soc., U.S. Inter-Am. Council, Council for Latin Am. (trustee), Am. Soc. Friendship with Switzerland (dir.), Argentine-Am. (dir.), Netherlands (dir.), German Am. (pres.) chambers commerce, Peruvian Am. Assn. (pres.), Sales and Marketing Execs. Internat. (sec.-treas.), Newcomen Soc. Clubs: Brown, University, Wee Burn Country. Home: Darien CT Died Mar. 7, 1972.

CAMPBELL, DOAK SHERIDAN, univ. pres.; b. Tate, Scott County, Ark., Nov. 16, 1888; s. Edward S. T. and Elizabeth DeWitt (Hunsucker) C.; B.A., Ouachita Coll., Arkadelphia, Ark., 1911; A.M., George Peabody Coll. for Teachers, 1928, Ph.D., 1930; LL.D., Quachita University, 1937; LL.D., Stetson University, 1942; LL.D., Florida Southern, 1946; m. Helen Gray Smith, May 28, 1913 (died 1938); children—Doak Sheridan, Elizabeth Caroline; m. 2d, Edna Simmons, Feb. 5, 1941. Supt. Columbus (Ark.) State High Sch., 1911-14; state sec. Baptist Young Peoples Union and Religious Edn. Assn., 1914-16; v.p. Central Coll., Conway, Ark., 1916-20, pres. 1920-28; with George Peabody Coll., 1928-41, as asst. in school adminstrn., 1928-29, asso. dir. surveys and field studies, 1929-34, dir., 1934-41, dean grad. sch. and sr. coll., 1938-41, bd. trustees, 1954-73; pres. Fla. State U., 1941-57. Mem. exec. com. So. Regional Edn. Bd., 1954-73; consultant President's Advisory Com. on Education, 1937-38; mem. exec. com. Curriculum Commn. of Southern Assn. Colls. and Secondary Schs.; mem. exec. com. Soc. for Curriculum Study, 1938, chmn. 1939; pres. Southern Assn. Colleges and Secondary Schs., 1946-47; mem. Tenn. Bd. Edn., 1935-41; mem. Sunday School Board Southern Baptist Convention, American Educational Research Association, American Assn. Univ. Profs., Am. Council on Edn. Com. on Surveys. Democrat. Baptist. Mason. Author: A Critical Study of the Stated Purposes of the Junior College, 1930; Curriculum Development (with H. L. Caswell), 1935; Readings in Curriculum Development (with H. L. Caswell), 1937; Social Studies and the American Way of Life, 1941; also several reports and bulletins. Home: Tallahassee FL Died Mar. 23, 1973.

CAMPBELL, DONALD FRANCIS, actuary; b. East River, St. Mary's, N.S., Can., Apr. 26, 1867; s. George and Ellen Esther (Gunn) C.; B.A., Dalhousie Coll., Halifax, N.S., 1890; B.A., Harvard, 1894, M.A., 1895, Ph.D., 1898; m. Lou Rena Bates, Mar. 28, 1906 (died July 4, 1939); children—Donald Francis, Elizabeth Bates (Mrs. L. T. Arthur). Instructor mathematics, Harvard, 1897-1900; prof. and head dept. mathematics, Armour Inst. Tech., Chicago, 1900-27. Lecturer on ins., Northwestern U., 1909-11; sec. and actuary Illinois Pension Laws Commissions of 1916 and 1918; actuary, Pension Laws Commission of Milwaukee, 1921; deputy examiner of Pension Funds to which public moneys are contributed, 1929-30; president of Bates Laboratories, Inc., of Chicago. Member Am. Math. Soc.; fellow Am. Institute Actuaries, Am. Assn. Advancement of Science. Author: The Elements of the Differential and Integral Calculus, 1904; A Short Course in Differential Equations, 1907; A Short Course in Life Insurance, 1909. Actuary in charge of the preparation of bills for the following annuity and benefit funds for public employees which are now laws: Policemen of Milwaukee; Firemen of Milwaukee; Sheriffs of Milwaukee; Policemen of Chicago; Firemen of Chicago; Municipal Employees of Chicago; County Employees of Cook County; Sanitary District Employees; Peoria Police; Park Employees of Chicago; Park Policemen of Chicago; Laborers' and Retirement Board Employees of Chicago; Municipal Court and Law Department Employees of Chicago; Election Commissioners' Employees of Chicago. Home: 1209 Hinman Av., Evanston, Ill. Office: 3542 N. Clark St., Chicago 13‡

CAMPBELL, E(RNEST) RAY, lawyer, newspaper exec.; b. Cameron, N.C., May 19, 1895; s. Duncan Ray and Catherine Glascock (Muse) C.; B.S., Davidson Coll., 1914, LL.D., 1946; LL.B., U. of Colo., 1922; m. Bertha Handlan, June 14, 1947; 1 dau., Jean Ray. Teacher and athletic coach, Charlotte (N.C.) High Sch., 1914-17; admitted to Colo. bar, 1922; president The Denver Post; member board directors First National Bank, Denver. Served as pvt. 2d lieutenant, 1st lt., Arty., with A.E.F., May 1917-Feb. 1920. Regent U. of Colo., 1932-44. Apptd. by Governor of Colo., 1933, as mem. com. to study form of state govt. and submit administrative code for reorganization of departments. Member of the board of Presbyterian Hospital. Mem. Am. Bar Assn., Denver Bar Assn., Newcomen Soc., Chi Psi, Phi Beta Kappa, Order of Coif, Sigma Delta Chi. Democrat. Presbyn. Mason. Clubs: Mile High, Denver Denver CO Died Apr. 25, 1971.

CAMPBELL, EDWARD HALE, naval officer; b. South Bend, Ind., Oct. 4, 1872; s. Myron and Abbie Johnson (Fifield) C.; grad. U.S. Naval Acad., 1893; m. Lilian, d. George Henry Strong, Aug. 30, 1899; children—Edward S., Georgiana. Ensign, July 1895; promoted through grades to judge advocate gen. of navy with rank of capt., 1907; capt. 1918; service at Pacific, Asiatic, S. Am. and Atlantic stations; chief of staff, comdr. Battle Force, Pacific Fleet, 1921; comdg. U.S.S. Pennsylvania, 1922, Navy Yard, Mare Island, Calif., 1923-24; with Bureau of Navigation, Navy Dept., Washington, D.C., 1924-25; judge advocate gen. with the rank of rear adm., 1925-29; comdr. Special Service Squadron, 1929-30; comdt. 13th Naval District and Puget Sound Navy Yard, Bremerton, Wash., 1931-34; comdr. Scouting Force, with rank of vice-admiral, 1934-35; comdt. 12th Naval Dist., San Francisco, 1935-36; retired, Nov. 1, 1936. Club: Rainier (Seattle). Address: Overlake Drive, Medina WA‡

CAMPBELL, ELMER GRANT, biology; b. Fairburn, Ga., Feb. 11, 1876; s. William Jackson and Sarah Elizabeth (Smith) C.; A.B., Hiram (O.) Coll., 1905; M.S., Purdue U., 1914; Ph.D., U. of Chicago, 1923; m. Elizabeth Fisher, Oct. 24, 1904; 1 son, Elbert Grant. Teacher, prin. and dir. biology, high schs., Ind. and Mich., 1907-12; instr. in biology, Purdue, 1912-15; asst. prof. botany, Tex. State Coll., 1915-18; head of dept. agrl. botany, Purdue U., 1919-27; became dean of men and head of biology dept., Transylvania Coll. and Coll. of the Bible, Lexington, Ky., 1927, head of institution, 1928-32; became dean of men and head of botany, Oglethorpe U., 1932; head of human biology and dean of students, U. of Ga., Atlanta Div., 1933, now research associate. Mem. Am. Assn. Advancement of Science, Sigma Xi, Phi Kappa Tau, Alpha Kappa Psi. Democrat. Mem. Christian (Disciples) Ch. Mason. Author: General Elementary Botany, 1929, rev. edit., 1941; Phantoms (nature sketches), 1940; Life's Temples (biology text), 1942; Man and Others. Contbr. research and academic papers. Home: 810 Virginia Circle N.E. Office: 24 Atlanta GA‡

CAMPBELL, H. DONALD, banker; b. Danville, Ill., Jan. 11, 1879; s. Thomas Jefferson and Emma Luella (English) C.; A.B., U. Minn., 1902, LL.B., 1904; m. Alice E. Calmus, Mar. 15, 1919. Bus. mgr. Independent Telephone Co., Seattle, 1906-12; asst. sec., sec., v.p., dir. Wash. Mut. Savs. Bank, Seattle, 1912-17; dir., sec., treas., later v.p. Merc. Trust Co., N.Y.C, 1917-22; v.p., dir. Seaboard Nat. Bank, N.Y.C., 1922-29; exec. v.p., trustee Equitable Trust Co., N.Y.C., 1929-30; v.p., dir. Chase Nat. Bank, N.Y.C., 1930-34, pres., dir., 1934-46, vice chmn. bd., 1946-47, chmn. trust com. of bd. dirs., 1947-55; dir. other corps. Bd. dirs. Leonard Wood Meml.; trustee Stevens Inst. Tech. Mem. Beta Theta Pi. Republican. Clubs: University, India House, Links, River (N.Y.C.); Wianno (Mass.). Home: New York NY Died Feb. 3, 1969; buried Danville IL

CAMPBELL, JAMES HOBART, public utility exec.; b. Jackson, Mich., Oct. 18, 1910; s. Birum Gould and Helen May (Chapel) C.; B.S.M.E., Purdue U., 1933; student Mass. Inst. Tech. (Alfred P. Sloan fellow), 1939-40; D. Engring. (honorary), Purdue U., 1964; m. Jane Hewett, June 11, 1936; children—Bruce Hobart, James Birum, Scott Richard. Power engr., Consumers Power Co., Lansing, Mich., 1933-39; power engr., Ohio Edison Co., Youngstown, 1940-42; asst. to division mgr. Consumers Power Co., Grand Rapids, Mich., 1946-47, division mgr., 1947-49, asst. to pres., 1949-50, v.p., Jackson, Mich., 1950-56, sr. v.p. Consumers Power Co., 1956-60, president, chief operating officer, 1960-72, also dir.; dir., v.p. mem. exec. com. Power Reactor Devel. Co.; dir. Nat. Bank of Jackson, Tecumseh Products Co. (Mich.), Hayes-Albion Corporation. Vice pres., dir. Atomic Indsl. Forum. Chmn. Nat. Assn. Electric Cos., 1962-63. Served from 1st lt. to lt. col., Fifth Army, AUS, 1942-46; ETO. Mem. Am. Gas Assn. (director), Newcomen Society, Beta Theta Pi. Clubs: Town, Country, Rotary (Jackson); Metropolitan (Washington). Student history of Am. Revolution. Home: Jackson MI Died Jan. 24, 1972; buried Campbell Cemetery, Parma MI

CAMPBELL, JAMES WATSON, college pres.; b. Warren, Pa., Sept. 14, 1872; s. George W. and Mary D. C.; C.E., Allegheny Coll., 1893 (D.D., 1912); B.D., Drew Theol. Sem., 1899; A.M., Harvard, 1908; Ph.D., Boston U., 1909; m. Edith M. Payne, of Cherry Creek, N.Y., Jan. 4, 1898. Ordained M.E. ministry, 1895; pastor Cherry Creek, 1894-6, Corry, Pa., 1899-1903, New Castle, Pa., 1903-6, Newtonville, Mass., 1908-16; pres. Simpson Coll., 1916-19. Mem. Phi Beta Kappa. Traveled in Egypt and Palestine, 1896. Contbr. to religious press; lecturer on ednl. and patriotic subjects. Home: Indianola IA‡

CAMPBELL, JOHN THOMAS, banker; b. Jacksonville, Ga., Oct. 6, 1876; s. William Parker and Susannah (Willcox) C.; ed. pub. schs.; m. Nettie Lee Cook, Nov. 19, 1903; children—Elizabeth, Martha. Began as clerk Darien (Ga.) Bank, 1892, subsequently asst. cashier, Merchants Bank, McRae, Ga.; successively cashier, v.p. and pres. Bank of Manatee (now First Nat. Bank), Bradenton; dir., v.p. Guarantee Abstract Company; dir., sec.-treas. Bradenton Home Builders Corp.; pres. and dir. First National Company, Bradenton; treasurer South Florida Museum; director, First National Bank of Tampa, Florida. Chairman Manatee County (Florida) Liberty Loan Drives, World War; now Manatee County chmn. U.S. Defense Savings Committee. President Florida Bankers' Assn., 1935-36. Democrat. Methodist. Mason, Shriner. Club: Bradenton Country. Home: 1603 3d Av., Bradenton FL‡

CAMPBELL, L. J., company exec.; b. Washington, Oct. 27, 1906; s. Louis Joseph and Winifred (Mitchell) C.; B.C.S., N.Y.U., 1930; m. Dorothy Hanschka, Jan. 10, 1929. C.P.A., N.J., 1931-42; comptroller Firestone Aviation Products Div., 1942-44; asst. treas., dir. G & A Aircraft, Inc., 1944-45; asst. treas., asst. sec. Firestone Steel Products Co., Akron, O., 1945-51, v.p., 1951-52, pres., 1952-58; v.p. Firestone Tire & Rubber Co., 1958-68, dir., 1966-68. Mem. S.A.R. (past pres. Lafayette chpt.). Episcopalian. Clubs: Portage Country, (Akron); Detroit Athletic. Home: Akron OH Died Dec. 12, 1968; buried Akron, OH

CAMPBELL, LEROY WALTER, bank exec. Cons. Chem. Bank N.Y. Trust Co., N.Y.C., mem. adv. bd. Midtown area; mem. finance com., dir. Sun Chem. Corp.; dir. Colgate-Palmolive Co.; dir., mem. exec. com. Napier Co. (Meriden, Conn.). Home: Scarsdale NY Died Jan. 19, 1967.

CAMPBELL, OSCAR JAMES, JR., prof. emeritus; b. Cleve., Aug. 16, 1879; s. Oscar James and Frances Amelia (Fuller) C.; student U. Mich., 1898-1900; A.B., Harvard, 1903, A.M., 1907, Ph.D., 1910; Harvard traveling fellow to univs. Copenhagen, Berlin, Paris, London, also Oxford U.; m. Emily Lyon Fuller, Sept. 10, 1907 (dec.); children—Eunice Clark (Mrs. Robert Goodale), Katharine, Emily Fuller (Mrs. George Meyer), Robert Francis. Instr. English and law U.S. Naval Acad., 1904-06; successively instr. English, asst. prof., asso. prof. U. Wis., 1911-21; prof. English, U. Mich., 1921-35; prof. English, Columbia, 1936-50, prof. emeritus, 1950-70; vis. prof. English, Harvard, 1929; research asso. Henry E. Huntington Library, 1934-38; vis. prof. Yale, 1946-47; adminstr. Columbia Arts Center Program. Fellow Am. Acad. Arts and Scis., Am. Assn. for UN (pres. Manhattan chpt.), ANTA (bd. Greater N.Y. chpt.), Nat. Council Arts and Govt. (exec. com.), Phi Beta Kappa, Delta Kappa Epsilon. Clubs: Century; Harvard (N.Y.C.); Columbia Faculty. Author: Comedies of Holberg, 1914 (trans. three plays of Holdberg 1916); The Position of the Roods en Witte Roos in the Saga of Richard III, 1919; The Teaching of English in American Colleges and Universities, 1934; Troilus and Cressida, 1938; Shakespeare's Satire, 1943; The Living Shakespeare, 1949. Editor: The Sonnets, Songs and Poems of Shakespeare for Schocker Books, 1965; A Midsummer Night's Dream; The Reader's Shakespeare Ency. Home: New Orleans LA Died June 1, 1970; buried Lake View Cemetery, Cleveland OH

CAMPBELL, ROY DAVIES, lawyer; b. Cotton Plant, Ark., March 24, 1872; s. W. P. C.; grad. Ark. Coll., Batesville, 1893; law dept., Univ of Ark., 1895; unmarried. Practices Little Rock; mem. Ho. Reps., Ark., 1901; Democrat. Address: 303 E. 15th St., Little Rock AR‡

CAMPBELL, THOMAS A., mining co. exec.; b. Mar. 29, 1897; s. Andrew P. and Ellen (Murphy) C.; Ph.B., Yale, 1919; m. Carroll Southern Whipple, July 31, 1928; children—Jean Carroll, Thomas Andrew. Chemist, metallurgist Remington Arms Co., Bridgeport, Conn., 1919-25; chemist, metallurgist Chile Exploration Co., Chuquicamata, Chile, 1925-30, asst. reduction plant supt., supt., 1930-36, asst. gen. mgr., 1936-41, gen. mgr., 1941-46, v.p., N.Y.C., 1946-48; v.p., mng. dir. Chile Exploration Co. and Andes Copper Mining Co., Santiago, Chile, 1948-52, exec. v.p., N.Y.C., 1952-57; v.p. Anaconda Co., N.Y.C., 1956-57, v.p. charge Latin-Am. affairs, 1957-62, v.p. fgn. bus. and metal sales policy, 1963-—; pres. Anaconda Sales Co., N.Y.C., 1956-62, now dir.; dir., v.p. Andes Exploration Co. of Maine; pres., dir. Tooele Valley Ry. Co.; dir. Anaconda Am. Brass Co., Brit. Am. Metals Co., Ltd., Greene Cananea Copper Co., Internat. Smelting &Refining Co., Chile Copper Co., Potrerillos Ry. Co., Santiago Mining Co., Chile Steamship Co., Chile Exploration Co., Andes Copper Mining Co. Bd. dirs. Am. Zinc Inst., Pan Am. Soc. U.S., Nat. Fgn. Trade Council. Decorated Order of Merit of Order Bernardo O'Higgins. Mem. Am. Inst. Mining and Metall. Engrs., U.S. Inter-Am. Council, Mining and Metall. Soc. Am., Yale Engring. Soc. Clubs: Yale, University (N.Y.C.); Union (Santiago). Home: New York City NY Died July 15, 1972.

CAMPBELL, WALLACE EDWIN, direct sales exec.; b. East Charleston, Pa., Sept. 30, 1896; s. Eugene Coolidge and Hattie (Calkins) C.; B.A., Syracuse U., 1919; m. Bertha Anna Cole, Sept. 15, 1918 (dec.); 1 son, Wallace Cole; m. 2d, Dorothy Elizabeth Lilie, Jan. 15, 1938; children—Charles Lilli, Bruce Calkins. With Fuller Brush Co., Hartford, Conn., 1916-65, beginning as salesman, successively mgr. Syracuse br. office, asst. to pres., Hartford, asst. sec., sec., mem. bd., v.p., 1916-56, 1st v.p. charge pub. relations, indsl. relations, personnel and procurement, 1956-65; dir. Riverside Trust Co., Insurance City Life Co. (both Hartford); industry adv. com. Fed. Res. Bank of Boston. Rep. from West Hartford, Conn. Legislature, 1942-45; mem. Conn. Finance Adv. Com., 1943-46; Republican Town Chmn., West Hartford, 1946-49. Chmn. Nat. Better Business Bureau, New York City; president, director Connecticut Blue Cross; member board, executive committee Council State Chambers; director Conn. Forest and Park Assn. Mem. Nat. Assn. Direct Selling Cos. (sec.), Am. Brush Mfrs. Assn. (past pres.), Conn. C. of C. (chmn.), N.A.M. (economy com.), Pub. Relations Soc. Am., Sigma Alpha Epsilon. Pi Delta Epsilon. Republican. Episcopalian. Mason (32 deg., K.T., Shriner). Home: West Hartford CT Died Apr. 29, 1968.

CAMPBELL, WALTER GILBERT, b. Knox County, Ky., Nov. 8, 1877; s. Charles Christopher and Sallie (Hoskins) C.; A.B., State U. of Ky., 1902; LL.B., U. of Louisville, 1905; m. May Ashby Lambert, Nov. 29, 1916. Began practice of law as mem. Campbell & Young, Louisville, 1905, retained to look after interests of Ky. Expt. Sta. in enforcing state food and drug laws in vicinity of Louisville; chief insp. Bureau of Chemistry, U.S. Dept. Agr., 1907-14; upon reorganization of Bur. Chem., Jan. 1, 1914, promoted to chief of Eastern food and drug inspection dist.; made asst. chief of Bureau of Chemistry, Dec. 1, 1916; designated acting chief, July 15, 1921; apptd. dir. regulatory work, U.S. Dept. Agr., Oct. 1, 1923; chief of Food and Drug Adminstrn., U.S. Dept. of Agr., Feb. 1, 1933-40; commr. of food and drugs, Fed. Security Agency 1940 to 1944. Voluntarily retired. Conglist. Mem. Phi Delta Theta, Phi Beta Kappa. Clubs: University, Chevy Chase, Washington Golf and Country (Washington). Home: 700 North Wayne St., Arlington, Va. Address: Food and Drug Administration, Washington DC‡

CAMPBELL, WAYNE, univ. prof.; b. Waterville, Kan., May 9, 1872; s. William Parker and Mary Elizabeth (Wayne) C.; grad. Wamego (Kan.) High Sch., 1886, Fulton-Trueblood Coll. of Oratory, Kansas City, 1890; m. Theresa Stern, Aug. 1, 1923; 1 dau., Isla Mary. Began in printing trade in office of father, publisher Waterville Telegraph; teacher dist. sch. nr. Westmoreland, Kan., 1887; entertainer with Lyceum Bur., and barnstorming actor with repertory and stock cos., 1891-92; appeared with first class cos., 1900-13; leading and character actor from 1915; head of drama dept. Oklahoma City Univ. since 1922. Author and producer annual pre-dawn Easter play, Life, Lord of Death, 1937-43, annual passion play, Via Crucis, produced in Masonic Temple, Guthrie, since 1940, annual city-wide Christmas play, Goodwill to Men, since 1937. Author: Acting and Play Production, 1931. Writer and producer radio programs, The Poet's Hour, station WKY, 1920-22; Among Our Neighbors, 1935-38; You and I, 1939-40; Wayne Campbell Presents, 1940-41; College Daze, 1942-43. Methodist. Mason (32 deg.). Home: 1517 24th St., Oklahoma City OK‡

CAMPBELL, WILLIAM PURNELL, editor Cincinnati Post; b. Maysville, Ky., Oct. 20, 1869; ed. public schools and Prof. Werntz's Naval Acad. Prepr. School, Annapolis, Md.; m. Mamie Heaverin, Augusta, Ky. Sec. Union Bethel Sunday School, one of the largest in the world. Home: 741 Scott St., Covington, Ky. Office: Post Cincinnati‡

CAMPBELL, WILLIAM WILSON, banker; b. Forrest City, Ark., Feb. 9, 1889; s. Silas Calvin and Jessie (Griggs) C.; student Eastman Coll., Poughkeepsie, N.Y., 1908-09; LL.D. (hon.), U. Ark., 1949; m. Victoria Mann, Dec. 14, 1916; children—William Mann Ann. President of the First National Bank of Eastern Arkansas, Forrest City, 1923-54, chmn. bd., chief exec. officer, 1954-70; dir. Arkansas Power and Light Corporation, Federal Reserve Bank, Memphis, First Arkansas Development Finance Corporation; mem. fed. adv. council, Eighth Fed. Res. Dist., St. Louis Fed. Res. Bank chairman of regional adv. committee to comptroller of currency Eighth National Bank Region. State chairman Ark. War Finance Com.; mem. cotton adv. com. Commodity Credit Corp., Washington; adv. com. R.F.C., Little Rock, Ark.; chmn. state highway finance adv. com.; mem. Memphis and Ark. Bridge Commn., 1945, Hoover panel on loan agencies, 1954; vice chmn. Ark. Indsl. Development Commn.; mem. White House Conf. on Edn. Trustee Arkansas Coll., Forrest City Library; dir. Ark. Crippled Children's Hosp.; dir., trustee Ark. Tb Sanatorium; mem. So. Presbyn. Gen. Assembly's Bequest Com.; chmn. Presbyn. Found. Investment Com. Synod Arkansas; mem. Ark. Com. for Salk Inst.; state chmn. Ark. Farmers Home Adminstrn. U.S. Dept. Agr. Recipient Hon. Life Membership award 4-H Clubs; Man of Year in Service to Ark. Agr., Progressive Farmer, 1951. Mem. Soil Conservation Society of America (hon.), Ark. C. of C. (dir.), Mid-South Fair Assn. Memphis (dir.), Am. Bankers Assn. (mem. exec. council; chmn. agrl. commn., pres. nat. bank div., chmn. state adv. com. U.S. Savs. Bank div.), Ark. Bankers Assn. Presbyn. Mason (33deg). Clubs: Rotary, Young Bus. Men's (Forrest City). Home: Forrest City AR Died May 28, 1970.

CAMPELLO, COUNT SOLONE DI, lawyer, educator; b. Arrone, Umbria, Italy, Oct. 2, 1871; s. Francesco and Maria (Marchetti) di C.; student Univ. of Rome, 1891-2, grad. Univ. of Macerata, 1894. Admitted to bar in Rome, 1895, judge of the Pretura, Rome, 1896; came to U.S., Oct., 1897; dir. Soc. for Protecttion of Italian Immigrants of Boston; lectures to Italian residents. Prof. Italian lang. and lit., Amherst Coll. Summer Sch., 1900; prof. same Smith Coll., 1902; unmarried. Founder and president Societa Dante Allghieri Circolo Italiano di Boston. Contb'r to Italian mags. and newspapers. Admitted to Mass. bar, Nov. 13, 1903. Address: 319 Washington St., Boston‡

CANADA, JOHN WILLIAM, editor; b. Summerfield, N.C., Dec. 14, 1871; s. William and Elizabeth (Strader) C.; A.B., U. of N.C., 1896, grad. work, 1896-1900; m. Verona Keener, Jan. 13, 1910; 1 dau., Jane Verona. Engaged in ind. newspaper work, 1900-05, weekly and spl. corr., Tex., 1905-11; editor and pub. Southland Farmer, 1911-26; organizer Nat. Farm Loan Assns., 1917, sec.-treas. 1917-35; organizer Houston Agrl. Credit Corp., 1923, sec.-mgr., 1923-35; editor The Milk Producer (dairy jour.) since 1936; organizer and pres. since 1936, Milk Producers Fed. Credit Union, Dir. Houston Agrl. Credit Corp., 1923, Port City Packinghouse, Port City Stockyards. Mem. Phi Beta Kappa. Democrat. Methodist. Author: Life at Eighty (an autobiography) 1951. Breeder of registered Jersey cattle; began direct shipment of gardenias by mail, 1929. Home: La Porte TX

CANADA, ROBERT OWEN, JR., retired naval med. officer; b. Grottoes, Va., July 16, 1913; s. Robert Owen and Mary Patterson (Crawford) C.; grad. Augusta Mil. Acad., Ft. Defiance, Va., 1931, M.D., U. Va., 1937; m. Julia Dent Salter, July 16, 1938; 1 son, Robert Owen III. Intern U. Va. Hosp., 1937-38; commd. lt. (j.g.) U.S. Navy, 1938, advanced through grades to rear adm., 1964; med. officer oiler U.S.S. Salinas, 1940-41; sr. med. officer U.S.S. Pasadena, 1944-45; then shore assignments naval hosps. Charleston, S.C., Oakland, Cal., Portsmouth, Va., Sampson, N.Y., Fitzsimons Gen. Hosp., Denver; comdg. officer U.S. Naval Hosp., Jacksonville, Fla., 1961-62, Bethesda, Md., 1962-65; dep. surg. gen., asst. chief Bur. Medicine and Surgery, Navy Dept., 1965-68; comdg. officer Nat. Naval Medical Center, Bethesda, 1968-69; ret., 1969; mem. staff Greenbrier Clinic, White Sulphur Springs, W. Va., 1969-—. Decorated Legion of Merit. Diplomate Am. Bd. Internal Medicine. Fellow A.C.P. (gov. for Navy), Am. Coll. Chest Physicians; mem. Am. Clin. and Climatol. Assn., Am. Thoracic Soc., A.M.A. Home: Lewisburg WV Died Dec. 6, 1972; buried Arlington Cemetery, Washington DC

CANDEE, CHARLES LUCIUS, clergyman; b. Milwaukee, Wis., Jan. 16, 1874; s. William Sprague and M. Cecilia (Smith) C.; B.A., Princeton, 1895, M.A., 1898; grad. Princeton Theol. Sem., 1898; D.D., Dubuque (Ia.) Coll. and Sem., 1916; LL.D., Coll. of the Ozarks, 1934; m. Elizabeth L. Browne, May 18, 1899; children—Alice Beaver (Mrs. C. F. Backus), William Sprague. Asst. minister 4th Presbyn. Ch., Chicago, 1899-1900; ordained Presbyn. ministry, 1901; pastor Riverton, N.J., 1901-08. Am. Ch., Frankfort-on-the-Main, Germany, 1908, Westminster Ch., Wilmington, Del., 1909-25, pastor emeritus since 1938. Special preacher in military camps and under Y.M.C.A. during World War; special preacher Am. Ch., Paris, summer 1923. Moderator Presbytery of Monmouth, 1907, Presbytery of Newcastle, 1912, Synod of Baltimore, 1924-25; mem. Presbyn. Gen. Assembly 4 times to 1942. Mem. Presbyn. Bd. of Ministerial Relief and Sustentation, 1915-28; mem. bd. trustees Synod of Baltimore; pres. bd. of trustees New Castle Presbytery, chmn. legal com., 1940. Apptd. mem. Del. State Bd. of Charities, 1928, pres., 1931-39; apptd. mem. State Commn. for the Blind, 1929, and Special Commn. to Draft Old Age Pension Law for Del., 1930; pres. Permanent Old Age Welfare Commn. of Del. since 1931. Republican. Clubs: Country (Wilmington); Newcomen mem. bd. of dirs. Family Society, Y.M.C.A., Wilmington (1931-43). Mem. exec. com. Del. Com. of Am. Soc. for Cancer Control. Author: (brochures) The English Bible; John Calvin. Contbr. to newspapers and religious periodicals. Home: 1006 Westover Rd., Wilmington 79 DE‡

CANDLER, HENRY E., realtor; b. Detroit, Mar. 7, 1870; s. William R. and Eleanor (Van Dusen) C.; student Mich. Mil. Acad.; A.B., U. Mich., 1892, LL.B., 1894; m. Pearl Boyer, Oct. 5, 1904; 1 son, Joseph Boyer. Admitted to Mich. bar, and practiced in Detroit; pres. Candler Realty Co.; dir. Burroughs Adding Machine Co., 1929-49. Clubs: Detroit, Country, University (Detroit); Everglades (Palm Beach, Fla.). Author: A Century and One, 1933. Home: 265 Lakeshore Rd., Grosse Pointe Farms, Mich. Office: 1716 Ford Bldg., Detroit 26 MI*‡

CANDLER, SAMUEL CHARLES, merchant; born Oxford, Ga., Dec. 9, 1895; s. Warren Akin and Sarah Antoinette (Curtright) C.; A.B., Emory U., 1916; m. Mary Frances Godfrey, Nov. 29, 1917; children—Caroline (Mrs. Lowry W. Hunt), Frances (Mrs. Frances C. Shumway). Pres., Godfrey's Warehouse, Madison, Ga., 1937-70, ret. chmn. bd. Mem. Southeastern Jurisdictional Conf., 1948, 52, member comm. on chaplains, 1948-64. Trustee emeritus Emory University, Atlanta, Georgia; ret. trustee Wesleyan Christian Advocate, Salem Camp Ground. Served as capt., inf., U.S. Army, World War I. Mem. Am. Legion, Kappa Alpha. Mason. Clubs: Atlanta Athletic. Home: Madison GA Died Feb. 10, 1973.

CANDLER, THOMAS SLAUGHTER, judge; b. Blairsville, Ga., Dec. 15, 1890; s. William Ezekiel and Elizabeth (Haralson) C.; A.B., Young L. G. Harris Coll., Georgia, 1913; B.L. Univ. of Ga., 1915; m. Augusta Beulah Cook, April 26, 1916; children—Sarah (Mrs. Jason B. Gilliland), Nelle (Mrs. Walter J. D. McNeil), Thomas Slaughter. Admitted to Ga. bar, 1915; engaged in gen. practice of law, Bairsville, Ga., 1915-39; U.S. Commr., 1927-39; Judge of Superior Court, Northeastern Judicial Circuit, 1939-45; associate justice Supreme Court of Ga., 1945-65, presiding justice, 1965-66, emeritus, 1967-71. Trustee Young L. G. Harris Coll.; chmn. Bd. of Edn., Blairsville, Ga.; chmn. Dem. exec. com., Union County, Ga., 1920-39; lt. col. on staff of Gov. Ellis Arnall; mayor, Blairsville, Ga. Mem. Ga., Atlanta, Northeastern Judicial Circuit and Union bar assns., Ga. Hist. Soc. (past pres.), Peace Officers Assn., Blue Key. Methodist. Mason. Odd Fellow, Woodman of the World. Clubs: Gridiron, Capital City. Home: Blairsville GA Died Sept. 15, 1971; interred Union Meml. Gardens.

CANJAR, LAWRENCE NICHOLAS, coll dean.; b. Pitts., Mar. 5, 1923; s. Michael and Catherine (Kosturic) C.; B.S., Carnegie Inst. Tech., 1947, M.S., 1948, D.Sc., 1951; m. Patricia McWade, Aug. 4, 1951; 1 son, Robert Michael. Mem. faculty Carnegie Inst. Tech., 1951-65, asso. prof. chem. engring., 1954-59, prof. chem. engring., 1959-65, asso. dean Coll. Engring. and Sci., 1962-65; dean Coll. Engring., U. Detroit, 1965-72; prin. cons., research chem. engr. Research Project 44, Am. Petroleum Inst., 1952-72; partner Asso. Chem. Engrs., 1955-61; cons. L'Air Liquide, Montreal, Que., 1951-59. Mem. ecumenical commn. Archdiocese of Detroit, 1968-72. Served with C.E., AUS, 1942-45. Recipient Teaching award Carnegie Inst. Tech., 1954; Pro Eclesia et Pontifice award Pope Paul, 1964. Mem. Am. Inst. Chem. Engrs., Am. Chem. Soc., Am. Soc. Engring. Edn. (Western Electric teaching award 1968), Am. Soc. M.E., Engring. Soc. Detroit (dir. 1968-72), Sigma Xi, Tau Beta Pi, Pi Mu Epsilon, Phi Kappa Phi, Eta Kappa Nu, Omega Chi Epsilon, Pi Kappa Alpha, Theta Tau. Home: Detroit MI Died Nov. 6, 1972; buried Mt. Olivet Cemetery, Detroit MI

CANNAN, ROBERT KEITH, organization exec.; b. Fowler, Cal., April 18, 1894; son of David and Mary (Cunningham) C.; B.Sc., University of London (England), 1914, M.Sc., 1923, D.Sc., 1929; married Catherine Ann Smith, Aug. 4, 1920; 1 dau., Cecily (Mrs. Henry M. Selby); m. 2d, Hildegard Wilson, Aug. 21, 1953. Asst. biochemistry U. London, 1919-23; Rockefeller traveling fellow in United States, 1924-25; lecturer, U. of London, 1925-30; prof. chemistry N.Y.U., 1930-52; vice chmn., div. med. scis. Nat. Research Council, 1952-53, chairman 1953-67; spl. asst. to pres. Nat. Acad. Sciences, 1967-70. With B.E.F., France, 1914-19; lt. 2d East Lancashire Regt., 1914-15; capt. 66th Div. Trench Mortar, 1916-19. Mem. Nat. Acad. Scis. Clubs: Cosmos (Washington); Century Assn., (N.Y.). Home: Washington DC Died May 24, 1971.

CANNON, CHARLES A., chmn. bd. dirs. Cannon Mills Co., Cannon Mills, Inc., N.Y., Cabarrus Bank & Trust Co., Concord, N.C.; pres. Wiscassett Mills Co., Albemarle, N.C., Social Circle Cotton Mill Co. (Ga.), Imperial Cotton Mills, Eatonton, Ga.; sr. dir. N.Y. Life Ins. Co.; gov. Fed. Res. Bank of Richmond. Hwy. commr. State of N.C. Trustee N.C. Med. Care Commn., Sanitorium Commn., Davidson Coll., U. N.C. Duke U.; chmn. bd. dirs. Cabarrus Meml. Hosp. Hon. fellow Am. Assn. Hosp. Adminstrs.; mem. Am. Cotton Mfrs. Assn. (chmn. bd. govs.), Am. Textile Mfrs. Inst. (chmn. cotton policy com.), N.C. Textile Mfrs. Assn. (pres., chmn. employment security com.), Am. Hosp. Assn. (hon. mem.). Address: Kannapolis NC Died Apr. 2, 1971; buried Oakwood Cemetery, Concord NC

CANNON, CORNELIA JAMES (MRS. WALTER BRADFORD CANNON), author; b. St. Paul, Minn., Nov. 17, 1876; d. Henry Clay and Frances Linda (Haynes) James; A.B., Radcliffe Coll., 1899; L.H.D., Wheaton Coll., 1928; m. Walter Bradford Cannon (M.D.), of Cambridge, Mass., June 25, 1901; children—Bradford, Wilma, Linda, Marian, Helen. Began as writer of articles on social and economic subjects in Atlantic Monthly, Harper's, North Am. Review, etc., 1918. Pres. Massachusetts Mothers' Health Council. Mem. Authors' League America, League of Women Voters, Mass. Parent-Teacher Assn. Unitarian. Author: The Pueblo Boy, 1926; Red Rust, 1928; The Pueblo Girl, 1929; Heirs, 1930; Lazaro in the Pueblos, 1931; The Fight for the Pueblo, 1934. Home: 12 Prescott St., Cambridge MA‡

CANNON, GRANT GROESBECK, editor, writer; b. Salt Lake City, May 6, 1911; s. Joseph Jenne and Florence (Groesbeck) C.; student Latter Day Saint Coll., 1927-30, U. Utah, 1933; m. Josephine Winslow Johnson, Apr. 5, 1942; children—Terence Martin, Jane Ann, Carol Lynn. Archeologist, Zion Nat. Park, 1933-34, Utah State Museum, 1934-35, Smithsonian Instn., 1937; field examiner NLRB, Washington and Cincinnati, 1937-47; editor, writer for the Farm Quarterly, Cincinnati, 1948-69. Mem. Clermont County (O.) Bd. Health, 1960-64. Served with USAAF, 1942-46. Mem. Am. Agrl. Writers Assn. Mem. Soc. of Friends. Club: Literary (Cin.). Author: Great Men of Modern Agriculture. Home: Cincinnati OH Died Feb. 22, 1969.

CANNON, WILLIAM CORNELIUS, lawyer; b. Andover, N.Y., Dec. 8, 1873; s. Patrick and Mary (Delaney) C.; Ph.B., Alfred U., 1894; LL.B., Harvard, 1900; LL.D. (honorary), Alfred University, 1926, Seton Hall Coll., 1936, Canisius College, 1954; m. Edith Dormer, Sept. 8, 1908 (dec. 1965); 1 son, John Dormer. Admitted to bar, N.Y.; mem. Davis Polk Wardwell Sunderland & Kiendl; dir. Salisbury Bank & Trust Co. (Conn.), 775 Park Av., Inc. Dir. Empire State Found. Ind. Liberal Arts Colleges, New York; hon. chmn. bd. Alfred Univ. Candidate for presdl. elector N.J. Dem., 1924; alternate del. at large N.J., Dem. Nat. Conv., 1928. Mem. State Bd. Instns. and Agencies, N.J., 1925-44. Mem. Am., N.Y. State, N.Y. County, and N.Y. City Bar Assns., American Law Institute, American branch International Law Society (hon. vice pres.), Harvard Law Sch. Assn., Am. Judicature Soc., Am. Soc. Internat. Law. Knight of Malta. Clubs: Harvard (N.Y.), Union, Broad St., Wall St. Home: New York City NY Died Dec. 1971.

CANSE, JOHN MARTIN, writer and theologian; b. Orland, Ind., Feb. 20, 1869; s. John A. and Hannah (Scripture) C.; Ph.B., DePauw U., 1899, D.D., 1918; m. Bessie Ruth Herrick, Aug. 15, 1900. Entered M.E. ministry in 1894; ordained elder, M.E. Ch., 1898; pastor successively of churches at South Whitley, Jolietville, Bunker Hill, Logansport, Ft. Wayne (all of Ind.), Seattle, Wash., Vancouver, Olympia, Centralia, until 1926; supt. Bellingham dist., 1914-21; pres. Kimball Sch. Theology, Salem, Ore., 1926-30; pastor Montesano, Washington, 1930-33. Curator Wash. State Hist. Soc. since 1917; exec. sec. Puget Sound Hist. Soc. since 1908; pres. Hist. Soc. Pacific Northwest Conf. since 1929. Mem. Gen. Conf. M.E. Ch., 1916, alternate, 1920. Chmn. Portland (Ore.) Bd. 2, Selective Service. Mem. Salem Chamber Commerce, Phi Kappa Psi, pres. Robert Gray Memorial Assn. Republican. Rotarian. Author many hist. publs. since 1930, latest are: The Twain (anthology), 1949; Circuit Riders of the Northwest, 1951. Contbr. religious jours. Home: 3324 N.E. 18th Av., Portland OR

CANTER, HOWARD VERNON, prof. classics; b. Winchester, Va., Mar. 8, 1873; s. James Hiram and Sarah Ann (Wise) C.; A.B., Washington and Lee U., 1896 (Beyers scholarship, 1894); Ph.D., Johns Hopkins, 1904, fellow, 1900, fellow by courtesy, 1903; m. Edna Hopkins Maloy, of Baltimore, Md., Sept. 2, 1905; 1 son, Howard Vernon. Instr. in Latin and Greek, Notre Dame Coll. of Md., 1902-05; asst. prof. Latin, U. of Mo., 1905-09; asso., asst. prof. and asso. prof. classics, U. of Ill., 1909-20, prof. since 1920; asst. dean Coll. Liberal Arts and Sciences, 1915-26. Regional dir. Y.M.C.A., 7th Italian Army, 1918-19. Mem. Am. Philol. Assn., Classical Assn. Middle West and South, Phi Beta Kappa. Awarded Gold Service Medal (Italy). Presbyterian. Club: University. Author: Sallust's Jugurthine War, 1911; The Defeat of Varus and the Frontier Policy of Augustus, 1915; Index Verborum Senecae Tragici, 1918; Rhetorical Elements in the Tragedies of Seneca, 1925. Contbr. to Am. Jour. Philology, etc. Home: 101 Chalmers St., Champaign IL‡

CANTILO, JOSE MARIA, Argentine diplomat; b. Buenos Aires, Argentina, Aug. 23, 1877; s. Francisco and Herminia (Botet) C.; student Sorbonne and Faculty of Law, Paris; m. Rosa Martinez Chas; children—Enrique, Herminia, Maria Cristina. Entered foreign service of Republic of Argentina, 1906, becoming 2d sec. of legation, Rome (Quirinal); 1st secretary of legation, Rio de Janeiro, 1908-10; charge d'affaires, Brazil, 1910; sec. to the President of Argentina, 1910-12; became asst. sec. of foreign affairs, 1912; minister to Paraguay, 1916-19; envoy extraordinary and minister plenipotentiary to Portugal, 1919-27, to Switzerland, 1927-31; ambassador to Uruguay, 1932-33, to Italy, 1933-38; minister of foreign relations and public worship, Argentina, 1938-41. Awarded Grand Cross of the Orders of Christ of Portugal; Sun of Peru; Merit of Chile; Southern Cross of Brazil; Grand Officer de la Legion d'Honneur (France); Commander of Orders of Pius IX of Holy See and of Charles III of Spain. Mem. Argentine delegation to League of Nations several times; mem. commn. which attempted to solve the Saar problem; mem. prep. commn. for Internat. Disarmament Conf.; Argentine rep. to Administrative Council, Internat. Labor Office, Geneva; mem. Internat. Peace Conf., Buenos Aires, 1936; Argentine del. to Pan-Am. Conf., Lima, Peru, 1938. At Pan-Am. Conf. of 1938 at Lima he proposed a plan of hemisphere solidarity, making all Latin Am. countries joint guarantors of Monroe Doctrine. Home: Juncal 739, Buenos Aires Argentina

CANTRALL, ARCH MARTIN, lawyer; b. Danville, Ky., Aug. 30, 1896; s. Charles McKee and Ann (Wood) C.; A.B., W.Va. U., 1922, LL.B., 1925; m. Grace Maxwell, Sept. 27, 1933; children—Carrie Annabelle (Mrs. Stuart R. Waters), Rebecca Jane. Admitted to W.Va. bar, 1925; partner Stathers & Cantrall, Clarksburg, 1925-58, 59-67; chief counsel Internal Revenue Service, 1958-59; dir. The Lowndes Bank (Clarksbury, W.Va.), Security Savings & Loan Company of Fairmont (W.Va.), Guaranty Savings & Loan Co. (Charleston, W.Va.). Mem. W.Va. State Bar, (pres. 1951), Am. Law Inst., Fed., Am. bar assns., Assn. Bar City N.Y. Author legal articles. Home: Clarksburg WV Died June 9, 1967; buried Marshville Cemetary, Harrison County WV

CANTRIL, (ALBERT) HADLEY, psychologist; b. Hyrum, Utah, June 16, 1906; s. Albert Hadley and Edna Mary (Meyer) C.; B.S., Dartmouth Coll., 1928; grad. work univs. Munich and Berlin, 1929-30; Ph.D., Harvard, 1931; LL.D. (hon.), Washington and Lee U., 1949; Sc.D. (hon.), Dartmouth Coll., 1960; m. Mavis Lyman, June 18, 1932; children—Albert Hadley, Mavis Ann. Instr. sociology Dartmouth Coll., 1931-32; instr. psychology Harvard, 1932-35; asst. prof. edn. Tchrs. Coll., Columbia, 1935-36; asst. prof. psychology Princeton, 1936-67, asso. prof., 1937-44, prof., 1944-53, Stuart prof., chmn. dept. psychology, 1953-55, research asso. dept. psychology, 1955-69, asso. dir. Radio Project, 1937-39, dir. office pub. opinion research, 1939-57, sr. counsellor, chmn. bd. Inst. for Internat. Social Research, 1955-69. Expert cons. U.S. sec. of war and O.W.I., 1942-45; consultant The White House, 1955-56. Dir. UNESCO Tensions Project, 1948. Pres. Research Council, Inc.; pres. Inst. for Asso. Research. Recipient Exceptionally Distinguished Achievement award Am. Assn. Pub. Opinion Research, 1966. Guggenheim fellow, 1949. Mem. Am. Psychol. Assn., Soc. Psychol. Study Social Issues (past pres.), Eastern Psychol. Assn. (pres. 1949-50). Author: Psychology of Radio (with Gordon Allport), 1935; The Invasion from Mars, 1940; The Psychology of Social Movements, 1941; Gauging Public Opinion, 1944; Psychology of Ego-Involvements (with M. Sherif), 1947; Understanding Man's Social Behavior, 1947; Tensions that Cause Wars, 1950; The Why" of Man's Experience, 1950; (with William Buchanan), How Nations See Each Other, 1953; The Politics of Despair, 1958; (with C. H. Bumstead) Reflections on the Human Venture, 1960; Soviet Leaders and Mastery over Man, 1960; Human Nature and Political Systems, 1961; The Pattern of Human Concerns, 1965; The Human Dimension: Experiences in Policy Research, 1967; (with Lloyd A. Free) The Political Beliefs of Americans, 1967. Editor: Public Opinion 1935-46, 1951; The Morning Notes of Adelbert Ames, Jr., 1960. Contbr. numerous articles to profl. jours. Adv. editor Princeton NJ Died May 28, 1969.

CAPEN, EDWARD WARREN, sociologist; b. Jamaica Plain, Mass., Sept. 24, 1870; s. of Samuel Billings and Helen Maria (Warren) C.; B.A., Amherst College, 1894; D.D., 1935; grad. Hartford Theol. Sem., 1898; Columbia, 1898-1901, Ph.D., 1904; m. Lydia Elizabeth Sanderson, Oct. 6, 1904. Lecturer on spl. phases of sociology, Hartford Theol. Sem., 1902-15; Thompson lecturer on missions, 1909, 11, 12, 14, 17, 18; in hist. researches for A.B.C.F.M., 1904-07; in spl. sociol. and missionary research in the far East, 1907-09; mem. commn. (preparation of missionaries) World Missionary Conf., Edinburgh, 1910, Internat. Commn. on Training Schs. for Missionaries, 1910-22, Bd. of Missionary Preparation for U.S. and Can., 1911-22; sec. 1911-19; instr. sociology, 1911-14, asso. prof., 1914-17, prof., dean, 1919-39, emeritus since 1939, Kennedy Sch. of Missions; asst. recording sec, A.B.D.F.M. 1915-44. Chairman training sch. sect. of Religious Edn. Assn., 1919-20; chmn. Assn. of Insts. engaged in Missionary Training, 1920-22; ordained Congl. minister, May 13, 1912; lecturer on missions, L. H. Severance Foundation, Western Theol. Seminary, Pittsburgh, 1912. Mem. Am. Sociol. Soc., etc.; fellow Royal Anthropol. Inst. of Great Britain. Mem. Phi Beta Kappa. Clubs: Authors' (London); Congregational, University, City (Hartford); Psi Upsilon, Amherst (New York). Author: Historical Development of the Poor Law of Connecticut (Columbia U. series), 1905; Sociological Progress in Mission Lands, 1913. Contbr. The History of Connecticut Institutions, in History of Connecticut in Monographic Form, 1925; also many articles and pamphlets on missions. Editor: Preparation for Missionary Work in Japan, 1915; Presenting Christianity to Hindus, 1917. Home: 80 Sherman St., Hartford 5 CT

CAPERS, WALTER BRANHAM, clergyman; b. Greenville, S.C., Aug. 8, 1870; s. Bishop Ellison and Charlotte Rebecca (Palmer) C.; student South Carolina Coll., Columbia, S.C., 1887-90; grad. Virginia Theol.

Sem., 1897; D.D., University of the South, 1917; m. Louise Drane Woldridge, of Columbia, Tenn., June 29, 1904; children—Walter Woldridge, Charlotte. In newspaper work 4 yrs.; deacon, 1897; priest, 1898, P.E. Ch.; rector John's Memorial Ch., Farmville, Va., 1897-1901, St. Peter's Ch., Columbia, Tenn., 1901-11; pres. Columbia Inst., 1906-18; in charge Trinity Ch., New Orleans, 1918-19; rector St. Andrew's Ch., Jackson, Miss., since 1919. Deputy to Gen. Conv. P.E. Ch. from diocese of Tenn., 1907-10; same from diocese of Miss., 1922-28. Mem. Sigma Alpha Epsilon. Democrat. Mason. Club: Century (Columbia). Author: The Soldier-Bishop, Ellison Capers, 1912. Home: Jackson MS‡

CAPLES, RUSSEL B., metals exec.; b. Glasgow, Mo., Dec. 16, 1888; s. Russel B. and Agnes (Watts) C.; B.S., Mo. Sch. Mines, 1910, D.Engring., 1948; m. Bernice Barker, Feb. 17, 1917; children—Agnes Lucy, George Barker. With Anaconda Co., 1910-59, beginning as employee testing and research depts., gen. lab. reduction works, successively asst. supt. electrolytic zinc plant, asst. supt. and supt. Great Falls (Mont.) zinc plant, asst. supt., asst. gen. supt. and gen. supt. Great Falls reduction dept., mgr. reduction dept., 1910-53, pres. Anaconda Aluminum Co., N.Y.C., 1953-58, v.p. charge metall. operations The Anaconda Co., N.Y.C., 1955-59; dir. Am. Brass Co., Anaconda Aluminum Co., Anaconda Wire & Cable Co., Andes Copper Mining Co., Chile Copper Co., Chile Exploration Co., Greene Cananea Copper Co., Golden Reward Mining Co., Internat. Smelting & Refining Co., Potrerilles Ry. Co., Santiago Mining Co., Tooele Valley Ry. Co., First Nat. Bank (Great Falls). Mem. adv. com. on zinc Def. Minerals Adminstrn. Mem. Am. Inst. Mining and Metall. Engrs. (dir.), Am. Zinc Inst. (dir.), India House, Mining Club. Home: New York City NY Died Feb. 1968.

CARBONARA, E(MIL) VERNON, educator, ins. co. exec.; b. Gravina, Italy, Apr. 16, 1897; s. Frank Paul and Vita Maria (Nuzzi) C.; Indsl. Chem. Engr., Pratt Inst., Bklyn., 1921: postgrad. N.Y.U., also Sch. of Ins., N.Y.C. (pres. 1st life ins. tng. course 1927); m. Olive Ann Herzberg, July 28, 1925; 1 son, Douglas Purdy. Came to U.S., 1908, naturalized, 1918. Research chem. engr., sales mgr. John Johnson Co., 1921-26, with Fraser Agy., 1926-27; sales mgr. J. Elliot Hall Agy. of Penn Mut. Life Ins. Co., 1928-29; owner operator gen. ins. and life ins. office, N.Y.C., 1930-68; formerly tchr. navigation Seamen's Ch. Inst., N.Y.C., aerial navigation N.Y. Aerial Acad., mathematics Pratt Inst., Bklyn., ins. Am. Savs. and Loan Inst., N.Y.C.; instr. ins. banking and finance dept. N.Y.U., 1954, adj. asst. prof., 1955, adj. asso. prof., 1959-61, adj. prof., 1961-65, former mem. faculties Sch. Commerce, Grad. Sch. Bus. Adminstrn. Conservative Party candidate for lt. gov. N.Y. State, 1962; mem. exec. com. Conservative Party N.Y. C.L.U., C.P.C.U. Recipient Outstanding Service award Air Force R.O.T.C., 1964, the alumni medal for 1965, Pratt Institute. Member Am. Soc. C.L.U.'s, Soc. C.P.C.U.'s, Ins. Soc. N.Y., Am. Finance Assn., Albert Gallatin Assos. of N.Y.U., N.Y. U. Arnold Air Soc. (named honorary colonel 1966), Am. Assn. U. Profs., Am. Econ. Association, Pratt Inst. Alumni of Chem. Engring. and Chemistry, N.Y.U. Alumni Assn., American Acad. Polit. and Social Science, United States C. of C., Life Underwriters Assn. N.Y., N.Y. Assn. Health Underwriters, Air Force Assn., American Legion, Association of the United States Army (honorary member), Sigma Eta Phi, Omega Iota Pi, Delta Sigma Pi, Phi Alpha Kappa, Iota Nu Sigma, Beta Alpha Psi. Clubs: The Lawyers', N.Y.U. Men in Finance, N.Y. University, N.Y. University Faculty, Varsity of N.Y. University (N.Y.C.); Rockville Country. Lectr. in field. Contbr. articles to profl. publs. E. Vernon Carbonara Seminar Room at N.Y.U. Grad. Sch. Bus. Adminstrn. named in his honor, 1959. Home: Rockville Centre NY Died June 13, 1968; buried Nassau Knolls, Port Washington NY

CARD, ERNEST MASON, judge; b. Monroe, Jasper Co., Ia., May 17, 1877; s. Mason Lewis and Mattie A. (Langan) C.; grad. high sch., Tacoma, 1896; A.B., Stanford, 1901; LL.B., Cornell U., 1904; m. Jessie V. Johnson, of Eau Claire, Wis., Aug. 5, 1908; children—Janet, Ernest M. Admitted to bar, N.Y. State and State of Wash., 1904, and began practice at Tacoma; justice municipal court, Tacoma, 1905-09; judge Superior Court, Wash., 1909-26; v.p. Northwestern Mfg. Co.; sec. Local Investment Co. Mem. Am. and Wash. State bar assns. Republican. Congregationalist. Mason, Elk, Moose. Compiler: Washington Laws, 1910. Home: 2907 S. 9th St. Address: Court House, Tacoma WA‡

CARDENAS, LAZARO, former President of Mexico; b. Jiquilpan, Michoacan, Mexico, May 21, 1895; s. Damasco and Felicitas (del Rio) C. (both descendants of Tarascan Indians). Began as printer's apprentice; organized coop. printing co. at age of 17; joined Revolutionary Movement, 1913; enlisted in Gen. Calles' forces under Obregon; took part in movement against Carranza, 1920; fought against de la Huerta, 1923, Escobar, 1929; gov. of State of Michoacan, 1928-32; pres. Nat. Revolutionary party, 1930; became minister of interior, 1931, minister war and marine, 1933; resigned to become candidate for presidency; President of Mexico, 1934-40; inaugurated 6-year plan providing agrarian reforms to distribute land to peasants; also organized coop. farms and set up credit system; during his administration oil properties were nationalized, education was extended and secularized, govt. and church were at peace; by law he was not eligible for re-election, and succeeded by Gen. Manuel Avila Camacho, 1940; named comdr. all Mexican forces on Pacific Coast, including airplanes and gunboats, July 1942. Address: Mexico Died Oct. 19, 1970.*

CARDIFF, IRA D., botanist; b. Stark Co., Ill., June 20, 1873; s. Edward Austin and Latrobe R. (Sellon) C.; B.S., Knox Coll., 1897; U. of Chicago, 1902-4; Ph.D., Columbia, 1906; m. Myrtle Sherman, of Galesburg, Ill., Aug. 14, 1902. Teacher and prin. pub. schs., Ill., 1897-1901; asst. in botany, Columbia, 1904-6; asst. prof. botany, 1906-7, prof., 1907-8, U. of Utah; prof. botany, Washburn Coll., Topeka, Kan., Sept., 1908-12; prof. plant physiology and bacteriology, 1912, head of dept. of botany and dir. State Expt. Sta., Washington State Coll., 1913—. Dir. Washburn Summer Sch., 1909-12; prof. botany, U. of Kan. Summer Sch., 1911-12. Mem. 6th Ill. Inf., Spanish-Am. War, 1898, in P.R. Fellow A.A.A.S.; mem. Utah Acad. Science (pres., 1908), Kan. Acad. Science. Contbr. Bot. Gazette, Bull. Torrey Bot. Club, Plant World, etc. Home: 302 Oak St., Pullman WA‡

CAREY, CHARLES IRVING, lawyer; b. Westmoreland Co., Va., Apr. 2, 1884; s. William Jett and Maria Louisa (Eichelberger) C.; A.B., William and Mary Coll., Williamsburg, Va., 1905; LL.B., Washington and Lee U., Lexington, Va., 1909; m. Arline Smith, Oct. 29, 1914; children—Charles Irving, William Hart, Jack Smith. Admitted to Va. bar, 1909, Ga. bar, 1909, Fla. bar, 1924, also to practice before federal courts and Supreme Court of U.S.; sr. partner Carey & Harrison, St. Petersburg, Fla., 1934-70; mem. Fla. legislature, 1933. Former trustee Darlington Prep. Sch. for Boys, Rome, Ga. Mem. Am., Fla. bar assns., St Petersburg Bar Assn. (pres. 1927), Phi Beta Kappa Assos., Phi Delta Phi, Phi Beta Kappa, Theta Delta Chi. Episcopalian. Kiwanian. Home: St Petersburg FL Died June 7, 1970.

CAREY, JAMES WILLIAM, consulting civil and elec. engr.; b. Duluth, Minn., Aug. 28, 1892; s. Peter and Marie (Nichols) C.; ed. various schs. of Minn., Ohio, N.Y.; m. Sally B. Lofthus, Dec. 5, 1942. Transitman on railroad constrn. work, State of Washington, 1908-09; constrn. engr. building railroads, docks, power and sewer systems for Pacific Coast Steamship Co., Pacific Coast Coal Co., Pacific Coast R.R. Co., 1909-15; charge valuation work of Pacific Coast R.R. Co. of Wash. and Pacific Coast Ry. Co. of Calif. for Interstate Commerce Commn., 1915-17; constrn. engr., various positions, 1919-21; constrn. engr. transmission lines, Stone & Webster Engring. Corp., 1921-22; chief engr., State of Wash. Dept. Pub. Works and Tax Commn., Wash., 1922-28; cons. engr., Portland, Ore., and Tacoma, Wash., engaged in valuation, reports on water power sites, etc., including present Bonneville power site; outlined present public service laws Oregon, 1928-33; chief engr. Department Public Service, Wash., 1933-36; state engr. in charge construction. Fed. P.W.A., State of Wash., 1936-38; cons. civil and elec. engr., Seattle and Tacoma., Wash., 1938-43; member of firm of James W. Carey & Associates, Carey & Kramer, consulting engineers; member U.S.-Alaskan Internat. Highway Commn., 1938-54; member National Rivers and Harbors Congress. Served as officer U.S. Naval Reserve Force, World War, 1917-19; engaged as consulting engr. rebuilding City of Renton, Wash., as defense matter; new streets, water and sewer system, sewage disposal plant, 1944; designed Des Chutes Basin Project, dam, spillway; Tolt River Dam for Seattle Water Supply; design for USN, largest drydock in world, Bremerton, Wash. with N.Y. firm); co-designer met. sewage project City of Seattle; engaged in work with Hydro-Electric Project, Sitka, Alaska; widely known in electric light, power, water, sewerage and sewage disposal appraisals. Mem. Soc. Am. Military Engrs., Washington Soc. Profl. Engrs. (pres. 1942; nat. vice pres., 1944), Am. Legion, Forty and Eight, Seattle Exec. Assn., Seattle C. of C., Am. Water Works Assn., Northwest Sewage Assn., Am. Concrete Inst., Am. Arbitration Assn., Cons. Engrs. Assn., Nat. Rivers and Harbor Congress; past pres. Alaska-Yukon Pioneers. Mason (K.T.). Clubs: Rainier, Blue Ridge (past pres.), Washington Athletic, Arctic, Engineers (Seattle). Author numerous engring. papers. Home: Seattle WA Died Aug. 2, 1969.

CAREY, JOHN JOSEPH, architect; b. Washington, Feb. 9, 1894; s. Hugh Joseph and Mary (Brenan) C.; student George Washington U., 1915-18, 19-20; B.S. in Archtl. Engring., Cath. U. Am., 1922; m. Esther L. Jones, July 19, 1924; 1 dau., Patricia (Mrs. Francis H. Thompson). Practice architecture, Washington, 1923-25, Fla., 1925-26, Mobile, Ala., 1926-71; prin. works include Bishop Toolen High Sch., 1928, Allen Meml. Home, 1929, U.S. Fed. Bldg., 1934, Municipal Airport Terminal, 1949, Cath. Boys Home, 1950, McGill Inst., 1952, Weinacker's Super Market, 1952, Restoration of Cathedral, 1955, St. John's Episcopal Church, 1956, Little Flower Ch., 1958, St. Mary's Home, 1961, Indian Springs Elementary Sch., 1963 (all Mobile), Sacred Heart Church, Pensacola, Florida, 1967. Mem. Bd. Registration Architects Ala., 1931-37, 55-64, chmn., 1956-64. Vice pres., dir. Cath. Maritime Club Mobile, 1945-71. Served with USMC, World War I; AEF in France. Named knight St. Gregory, 1960; recipient Alumni award Cath. U. Am., 1961. Emeritus fellow A.I.A. (pres. Ala. 1951, dir. 1952; chmn. Gulf Coast regional jud. com. 1961, nat. jud. com. 1962-64). Club: Mobile Country. Address: Mobile AL Died July 13, 1971; buried Catholic Cemetery, Mobile AL

CARGILL, FRANK VALENTINE, publications exec., editor; b. Port Huron, Mich., Mar. 31, 1885; s. William Rice and Luvia (Powers) C.; student, courses Sch. Commerce, Northwestern, 1906-12, 1932-34; m. Muriel Wilson, Aug. 8, 1916 (dec); m. 2d, Mildred Hanson; children—William Rice, III, Barbara Ruth. Subscription mgr. Jour. A.M.A., 1906-08, established biog. records of physicians, 1909-12, field orgn. work A.M.A., 1912-16, dir. membership records and circulation jour., also nine other publs., 1951-55; editor Am. Med. Dir., 1909-55, established supplement Report Service, 1927-55; circulation mgr. Todays Health, formerly Hygeia, 1923-53; owner Mildred Cargill's Fashions for Children, Highland Park, Ill., 1955-71. Mem. Circulation Round Table of Chgo., Direct Mail Assn., Med. Soc. Exec. Conf. Republican. Mason (Shriner). Author numerous articles on direct mail, also Highland Park IL Died Oct. 5, 1971; buried North Shore Gardens of Memories, North Chicago IL

CARGILL, OSCAR, teacher and editor; b. Livermore Falls, Me., Mar. 19, 1898; s. Carrol David and Rose (Farrington) C.; B.S., Wesleyan U., 1922; Stanford U., 1924-25; Ph.D., Columbia U., 1930; D.Litt., N.Y. U., 1967; L.H.D., Ohio U., 1968; m. Gladys Gertrude Lermond, June 14, 1924; children—Elizabeth Anne, Marcia Jean. Instr. English, Mich. State Coll., 1922-23; Marietta Coll., 1923-25; New York U., 1925-27, 1928-30; Cutting traveling fellow, Columbia U., 1927-28; asst. prof. English, New York U., 1930-36, prof., 1945-66, chmn. dept. English, 1949-63, head grad. dept. English, 1956-63; McGuffey vis. prof. English at Ohio V., 1966-67; distinguished lectr. Nat. Council Tchrs. Eng., 1968-69; cons. Internat. Inst. Edn., from 1953; co-sponsor 1st closed-circuit TV composition expt. Fund for Advancement Edn., 1955-56; dir. Am. Civilization Program since 1948; lecturer Pelham Adult School, 1939-40; visiting prof., N.J. State Teachers Coll., Montclair, 1940-41, U. So. Cal., summer 1957. Am. specialist State Dept., Japan, summer 1962. Mem. bd. dirs. N.Y.U. Press, Inc., 1957-65. Dir. W.P.A. Index to Am. Periodicals, N.Y. City, 1932-39. Consulting editor, English texts, The Macmillan Co., 1935-63; general editor Gotham Library, from 1959; mem. editorial board Garrett Press, from 1969. Mem. poetry jury National Book Award, 1954. Mem. Am. Studies Assn., Modern Language Association (representative Copyright Bill from 1965), Nat. Coll. Tchrs. English, Phi Beta Kappa. Author and co-author several books, including Drama and Liturgy, 1930; Highways in College Composition, (with H. A. Watt), 1930; Intellectual America (Vol. I: Ideas on the March), 1942; New Highways in College Composition (with H. A. Watt and William Charvat), 1943; Novels of Henry James, 1961; Toward a Pluralistic Criticism, 1965. Editor: Walt Whitman's The Wound Dresser, 1949; Walt Whitman's Leaves of Grass, 1950; Thoreau's Selected Writings on Nature and Poetry, 1952; The Wolfe-Watt, Correspondence (with T. C. Pollock), 1953; Henry James' Daisy Miller and Washington Square, 1956, (with J. W. Bennett and V. Hall) Studies in the English Renaissance Drama, 1959; (with N. B. Fagin and W. J. Fisher) O'Neill and His Plays, 1961; The Ambassadors, 1962, Portrait of a Lady, 1963 (Henry James); The Octopus (Frank Norris), 1963. Contributor essays, revs. to mags., article on American literature to Crowell-Collier Ency., Collier's Yearbook, 1960-68. Home: Upper Montclair NJ Died Apr. 18, 1972.

CARIAS ANDINO, TIBURCIO, President of Honduras; b. Tegucigalpa, Honduras, Mar. 15, 1876; student Coll. of Tegucigalpa; law degree, Central U., Tegucigalpa, 1898. Began in politics, 1891; later became prof. mathematics, Colls. of Tegucigalpa; took part in Honduran revolution, 1893, 1894, 1930 (given title, Gen. of Brigade); later given title, General, by Nat. Congress; became mem. Nat. Congress, and also comdr. and polit. gov. of several depts.; elected President of Honduras, 1933, term extended by Nat. Congress to 1943, in 1936, and to 1949, in 1941. Address: Tegucigalpa Honduras*‡

CARLILE, WILLIAM BUFORD, postmaster; b. Lebanon, Ky., Jan. 21, 1870; s. Charles Robert and Mary Prudence (Spalding) C.; ed. pvt. schs. (Lebanon), St. Mary's Coll. (Ky.), and Louisville Business Coll.; m. Virginia Fontaine, of Memphis, Tenn., Apr. 26, 1893. Entered ins. business, 1890, and was apptd. spl. agt., traveling from home office of Mutual Life Ins. Co. of New York; was made insp. of agencies for U.S. and Can., 1896, and removed to Chicago, 1899, to organize the western spl. dept.; mgr. Chicago agency, same company, 1900-17; postmaster of Chicago since Mar., 1917. Democrat. Clubs: Chicago, Chicago Athletic, South Shore Country, Chicago Golf, Chicago Yacht, Mid-Day. Office: The Post Office, Chicago IL‡

CARLISLE, HELEN GRACE, novelist; b. N.Y. City, June 19, 1898; prep. edn., Morris High Sch., N.Y. City; student Alfred (N.Y.) U., 1917-18; m. Harry Carlisle, of London, Eng., Mar. 10, 1919; children—Peter Carlisle, Christopher Carlisle; m. 2d, James Malcolm Reid, Aug. 16, 1932; 1 son, James Malcolm, III. Volunteer nurse with Quakers in France, 1919; employed in business offices, New York, London and Paris, 1919-26; on stage, 1927-28; writer since 1928. Clubs: New Canaan (Conn.); Authors League (New York). Author: See How They Run, 1929; Mothers Cry, 1930 (filmed, translated into French, Italian, German, etc.); Together Again, 1931; We Begin, 1932; Wife, 1934 (also translated); The Wedding Dress, 1936 (filmed); The Merry Merry Maidens, 1937 (filmed and translated). Contbr. fiction to mags. Home: New York City NY Died Apr. 1968.

CARLISLE, HOWARD BOBO, lawyer; b. Spartanburg, S.C., Jan. 23, 1867; s. John Wilson and Louisa (Bobo) C.; B.A., 1st. honor, Wofford Coll., Spartanburg, South Carolina, 1885, LL.D. (honorary), 1949; LL.B., Vanderbilt University, 1887 (founder's medal for best standing in law dept.); m. George F. Adam, Mar. 16, 1892;children—Mrs. Sophie Bean, Louisa Bobo, Howard Bobo, George Adam, Robert Marsden. Practiced at Spartanburg since 1890; mem. Carlisle, Brown & Carlisle (firm in same family since 1825); mem. S.C. Senate, 1906-16; chmn. Senate judiciary com. 9 yrs., introduced state-wide prohibition law, Torrens land system, 1st marriage license bill for S.C., negotiable instrument law, and a race-track gambling act. Trustee Wofford Coll. (chmn. bd.), Converse Coll. Mem. Spartanburg Chamber of Commerce (pres. 3 terms). Mem. Am. and S.C. bar assns., Commercial Law League America, Chi Phi; hon. mem. Phi Beta Kappa. Democrat. Methodist. Home: Spartanburg SC

CARLSON, ANDERS JOHAN, educator, engr.; b. St. Peter, Minn., Aug. 3, 1894; s. John Sven and Mary Mathilda (Anderson) C.; B.S., U. Minn., 1916, C.E., 1917, M.S., 1925; Ph.D., U. Cal., 1929; m. Louise Josephine Thorson, Sept. 26, 1925; children—Anders Johnston, John Stanley, Mary Louise (Mrs. Gerald L. Hanes). Instr. sch. mines U. Minn., 1917-19, asst. prof., 1919-26; cons. engr., mine expert Minn. Tax Commn., 1918-26; research asst., jr. research fellow Am. Petroleum Inst., 1927-31; lectr. coll. mining U. Cal., 1926-30, asso. prof., 1930-42, prof. petroleum engring., 1942-43, prof. petroleum engring. div. mineral tech., from 1943, chmn. div., 1949-53. Ednl. supr. ESMWT, 1941-45; operations analyst USAAF, 1945. Profl. petroleum engr., Cal. Mem. Am. Petroleum Inst., A.A.A.S., Am. Chem. Soc., Sigma Xi, Tau Beta Pi, Alpha Sigma Phi, Sigma Rho, Pi Epsilon Tau, Scabbard and Blade. Clubs: Engrs. (Mpls.); Faculty (Berkeley); Univ. (Oakland, Cal.). Author research paper Inorganic Environment in Kerogen Transformation, 1937. Home: Berkeley CA Deceased.

CARLSON, CHESTER, b. 1906. Inventor. Xerox copier, also leading stockholder Battelle Corp. Address: NYC NY Died Sept. 1968.

CARLSON, E(RNEST) LESLIE, clergyman, educator; b. Chicago, Ill., Oct. 14, 1893; s. Patrick Edward and Emma (Bengtson) C.; student Southern Ill. Normal U., Carbondale, 1912; student Moody Bible Inst., Chicago, 1914-16 (diploma in music); Th.M., Southwestern Baptist Theol. Sem., Fort Worth, Tex., 1920, Th.D., 1936; A.B., Tex. Christian U., 1921, A.M., 1928; m. Edna S. Massey, Sept. 16, 1917; (dec. Jan. 22, 1956); children—Ernest Leslie, John Edward; Edna Louise, Benjamin Eugene; m. 2d. Marjorie Smyth, Feb. 8, 1957. Pub. Sch. tchr., 1912; gospel singer, 1914-17; ordained to ministry of Bapt. Ch., 1917; held various pastorates, Tex., 1919-43; prof. O. T. Intro., Interpretation and Hebrew, Southwestern Bapt. Theol. Sem., 1921-64; lectr. and cons. in Bibl. study and archaeology; study and research Bibl. manuscripts and versions Europe, 1955-56, 58, Near East, 1925, 55; research and field work in archaeology and manuscripts, Mexico, summer 1960, archeol. research, field work Near East, Europe, 1962. Mem. Soc. Biblical Literature and Exegesis. Am. Oriental Soc., Am. Schs. Oriental Research, Am. Academy of Religion, Soc. O. T. Study (Eng.). Mason. Author: Elementary Hebrew, 1938, rev. edit., 1956; Confirming the Scripture, 1941. Co-author: The Prophet Micah, 1949; Monuments and the Old Testament, 1958. Cons. editor: Bakers Bible Atlas, 1961; O. T. editor Wycliffe Bible Ency.; gen. editor Bible Helps Used in Bibles. World Pub. Co., 1965-67; asso. editor The Biblical World (Baker), 1966. Home: Ft Worth TX Died Dec. 12, 1967; buried Laural Land Cemetery, Fort Worth TX

CARLSON, GUNARD OSCAR, steel co. exec.; b. McKessport, Pa., Jan. 2, 1895; s. Frank Oscar and Mathilda (Swanson) C.; student Carnegie Inst. Tech., 1913-14; student Drexel Inst. Tech., 1916-17, D.Sc. (hon.), 1958; LL.D., Pa. Military College, 1964; m. Margaret Bailey Berry, Nov. 30, 1917; children—Gunard Berry (dec.), Barbara Ann (Mrs. A. Frederick Travaglini), Nancy Jean (Mrs. Benjamin Bacharach). Chmn. bd. dirs. G. O. Carlson, Inc., Thorndale, Pa., 1947-69, v.p., dir. The Nat. Bank of Coatesville (Pa.), 1942-69; director and member of executive committee Industrial Valley Bank & Trust Company. Chmn. Chester County Area Airport Authority, 1957-69; active Boy Scouts Am. Mem. Rep. State Com., 1958-69. Chmn. bd. dirs. Coatesville Hosp., 1958-69; pres. bd. trustees Perkiomen Sch., Pennsburg, Pa., 1944-69; pres. bd. dirs. Bradford (Mass.) Jr. Coll., 1959-69; trustee Schwenkfelder Library, Pennsburg, Pa., 1946-69; trustee Drexel Inst. Tech., Pa. Mil. Coll.; bd. govs. Am. Swedish Historical Found.; established The Gunard Berry Carlson Meml. Found., 1957. Recipient Benjamin Rush award Chester County Med. Soc., 1959; Benjamin Rush award Med. Soc. State Pa., 1959; Chester County Soc. Profl. Engrs. award, 1961; Medal of Honor Daus. Am. Revolution, 1962. Profl. engr., Pa. Mem. Nat. Soc. Profl. Engrs., Am. Mil. Engrs., Am. Soc. M.E., Am. Soc. Metals, Swedish-Italian Archeology Soc. (life), Pa. Society (Chester County chmn.), Union League Phila., The Swedish Colonial Soc., Newcomen Soc. Republican. Presbyn. Mason. Clubs: Coatesville (Pa.) Country; Concord (Pa.) Country; Whitford (Pa.) Country; Wilmington (Del.) Country; Engineers (N.Y.C.); Union League (Phila.); Radley Run Country. Address: Thorndale PA Died Apr. 5, 1969.

CARLSON, HARRY JOHAN, architect; b. St. Paul, Minn., Nov. 8, 1869; s. John M. and Christina (Monson) C.; student Mass. Inst. Tech., 1888-92, Atelier Duray, Paris, France, 1892-94; hon. A.M., Bates College, Lewiston, Me., 1928; m. Carrie Elizabeth Cornforth, Apr. 8, 1896; children—John Edwin, Elizabeth Hunnewell, Catherine Cornforth, Harrison Cornforth. With W.S. Sampson & Co., contractors, 1894-96; practiced architecture alone, 1896-1903; Coolidge & Carlson, 1903-50, ret. Built coll. and office bldgs., chs., residences, etc. Formerly lectr. architecture Mass. Normal Art Sch. Trustee Newton Center Savs. Bk.; dir. Fuel Engring. Co. Inc. (v.p.). Life mem. Corp. Mass. Inst. Tech.; mem. Alumni Council Mass. Inst. Tech. (pres. 1922-23), Boston Soc. Architects (ex-sec. and mem. exec. com.; v.p. 1922), Boston Chamber of Commerce (dir.; mem. exec. com.); mem. bd. overseers and finance com. Bates Coll.; pres. Mass. Library Aid Assn. (chmn. Finance Com.). Archtl. adviser Mass. State Library Commn.; past Boston sec. Am. Acad. in Rome; former mem. bd. visitors architectural sch., Harvard. Fellow A.I.A. Baptist. Clubs: Neighbors, University, Charles River Golf. Home: Bradford Court, Newton Centre MA

CARLSON, LOREN DANIEL, physiologist, educator; b. Davenport, Ia., May 5, 1915; s. Frank Daniel and Esther (Lind) C.; B.S., St. Ambrose Coll., 1937; Ph.D., U. Ia., 1941; Ph.D. honoris causa, U. Osio (Norway), 1969; m. Marion Dudley Gross, June 7, 1941; children—Eric Daniel, Christopher Dean, Allen David, Katherine Dudley. Research asso. cellular physiology dept. zoology U. Ia., 1941-42; instr. zoology U. Wash., 1945, asst. prof. to prof. physiology and biophysics, 1946-60; prof., chmn. dept. physiology and biophysics U. Ky. Coll. Medicine, 1960-66; chief of scis. basic to medicine U. Cal. at Davis, 1966-72, asso. dean curriculum and research devel., 1971-72. Mem. sci. adv. bd. to USAF, 1957-62. Served to maj. USAAF, 1942-46. Decorated Legion of Merit; recipient USAF Exceptional Civilian Service medal, 1962; John Jeffries award Am. Inst. Aeros. and Astronautics, 1968, Outstanding Achievement award Office Aerospace Research, Dept. Air Force, 1970. Asso. fellow Inst. Aeros. and Astronautics; fellow Aerospace Med. Assn., Am. Acad. Arts and Scis.,; mem. Am. Physiol. Soc. (pres. 1968-69), Fedn. Am. Socs. Exptl. Biology (pres. 1969-70), Soc. Exptl. Biology and Medicine, Am. Soc. Zoologists, A.A.A.S., Internationalis Astronautica Academia, Sigma Xi. Contbr. articles to sci. jours. Home: Davis CA Died Dec. 12, 1972.

CARLSON, T(HORGNY) C(EDRIC), educator; b. St. Peter, Minn., Jan. 17, 1893; s. John Sven and Mary Mathilda (Anderson) C.; A.B. with distinction, U. of Minn., 1915; student Oxford U., 1919, Yale, 1943; m. Rosemary Crate, July 2, 1917; children—Thorgny Cedric, Eugene Cedric, Rosemary (Mrs. Charles Rufus McNair, Jr.), Joel Henry. Registrar, U. of Ark., 1915-17, exec. sec., 1921-23, bus. mgr. since 1923, treas. since 1925, sec. bd. trustees since 1927, v.p. for finance, since 1946; accountant, Barnsdall Oil Co., 1920-21. Mem. Governor's Commn. on Reorganization of State Govt., Ark., 1950. Served with U.S. Army, 1917-20, served in France with 7th Div.; disch. as capt., Inf.; major, Specialist Reserve, U.S. Army, 1943-45, chief fiscal officer, Rhineland Province Mil. Govt. Detachment, 1944-45. Advisor on student war loan program, U.S. Office Edn., 1941, advisor War Dept. on coll. training contracts, 1942. Mem. Assn. Coll. and Univ. Bus. Officers (pres., 1933), Ark. Hist. Assn., Phi Beta Kappa, Scabbard and Blade, Alpha Sigma Phi, Grey Friars (Univ. Minn.). Home: Fayetteville AR Died Mar. 1970.

CARLSTON, KENNETH S., prof. of law; b. Grand Haven, Mich., July 11, 1904; s. Charles and Nina Mae (Smith) C.; B.B.A., Univ. of Wash., 1926; M.A., American Univ., 1928; LL.B., Yale, 1933; m. Margaret O. Hall, Mar. 30, 1934; children—Peter Kenneth, James Scott. Admitted N.Y. bar, 1935, Ill. bar, 1955; atty. Mexican Claims Commns., Washington, D.C., 1928-31, Mitchell, Taylor, Capron & Marsh, New York, N.Y., 1933-38, Shell Union Oil Corporation and related companies at New York, N.Y., 1938-46; professor of law at University of Ill. from 1946; United Nations Legal Secretariat, 1950; mem. U.N. legal secretariat, 1952, 53. Member American Soc. of Internat. Law, American Arbitration Association (member of national panel of arbitrators), American Society for Legal and Polit. Philosophy, Internat. Law Assn., African Law Society, Law and Society Association, Internat. Assn. for Philosophy of Law and Social Philosophy, Order of Coif, Pan Xenia, Phi Beta Kappa, Beta Gamma Sigma. Author: The Process of Internat. arbitration, 1946; Law and Structures of Social Action, 1956; Law and Organization in World Society, 1962; Social Theory and African Tribal Organization, 1968. Contbr. law jours. Specialist internat. law and arbitration, antitrust, jurisprudence. Home: Ocean Shores WA Died Sept. 9, 1969; buried Lake View Cemetery, Seattle WA

CARLTON, CALEB SIDNEY, lawyer; b. New Albany, Miss., Nov. 26, 1915; s. Landon Kimbrough and Esther Catherine (Hall) C.; student Mississippi Delta Jr. Coll., 1934-35, 35-36; LL.B., U. Miss., 1939; m. Corrie Anne Campbell, Jan. 28, 1938; children—Anne Campbell (Mrs. Don Eldridge Gorton, Jr.), Carolyn Hall, Sidney Catherine. Admitted to Miss. bar, 1939; jr. title atty. U.S. Engrs., 1939-40; claims mgr. for Miss., State Farm Mut. Auto Ins. Co., 1940-41; atty. OPA, Jackson, Miss., also Atlanta, 1942-46; partner Carlton & Henderson, Sumner, Miss., from 1946. Vice pres. Conf. Local Bar Assns., Miss. State Bar, 1956-57, pres., 1957-58; commr. Miss. State Bar, 1957-61. Past exec. sec. W. Tallahatchie Devel. Assn. Trustee, v.p. Miss. Bar Found., Inc. Mem. Miss. State Bar (chmn. lawyers bus. affairs com. 1958-61, 1st v.p. 1961-62, pres. 1962-63), Am. Judicature Soc., Tallahatchie County Bar Assn., Phi Alpha Delta, Beta Theta Pi. Rotarian (past pres. Sumner). Contbr. articles law jours. Note editor Miss. Law Jour., 1938-39. Home: Sumner MS Died June 1966.

CARLTON, DOYLE ELAM, lawyer; b. Wauchula, Fla., July 6, 1885; s. Albert and Martha (McEwen) C.; A.B., Stetson U., 1910, also LL.D.; A.B., U. Chgo., 1910, LL.D., 1912; LL.B., Columbia, 1912; LL.D., U. Fla., 1933; L.H.D., Fla. South Coll., 1953, U. Tampa, 1953; m. Nell Ray, Aug. 30, 1912; children—Martha (Mrs. David Ward), Mary (Mrs. W. J. Ott), Doyle Elam. Admitted to Fla. bar, 1912, practiced in Tampa; partner firm Carlton, Fields, Ward, Emmanuel, Smith & Cutler, 1912-72; city atty., Tampa, 1926-28. Mem. Pres. Eisenhower's Commn. Civil Rights, 1957-61, Pres. Kennedy's Nat. Agrl. Adv. Commn., 1961-63; pres. Pan Am. Commn. of Tampa. Mem. Fla. Senate, 1917-19; gov. of Fla., 1929-33. Trustee, chmn. Stetson U. Named Outstanding Citizen of Tampa, Civitan Club, 1954. Mem. Am., Fla., Tampa, Hillsborough County bar assns., Fla. C. of C. (past pres.), Com. of 100. Baptist. Tampa FL Died Oct. 25, 1972; buried Myrtle Hill Cemetery, Tampa FL

CARLTON, FRANK TRACY, economist; b. Mantua, O., Dec. 22, 1873; s. George Washington and Chloe M. (Hotchkiss) C.; B.S., Case Sch. Applied Science, Cleveland, 1895, M.E. (in absentia), 1899; summer sch. U. of Mich., 1898, 1900; Cornell U., 1901; U. of Chicago, 1902, 03; A.M., U. of Wis., 1905, Ph.D., 1906; LL.D. from Albion (Mich.) Coll., 1932; m. Nellie G. Chittenden, July 5, 1898. Teacher, Toledo U. Sch., 1896-1904; fellow in economics, U. of Wis., 1904-06; prof. economics and history, 1906-15, prof. economics and sociology, Albion Coll., 1915-19; prof. economics, DePauw U., 1919-27, leave of absence, 1925-26, serving as prof. economics U. of Ill.; prof. economics, Case Sch. of Applied Science, 1927-44, professor emeritus (in residence) since 1944; visiting professor Western Reserve University, 1946; lecturer in economics, Western Reserve Univ. Graduate School, 1931-40; lecturer in economics Cleveland Coll., Western Reserve U., 1940-41; prof. economics, U. of Ill., summer, 1914, Columbia, 1923, Bay View Summer Sch., 15 summers, 1918-47, prof. of economics, U. of Southern Calif., summer, 1927. Western Reserve, summers, 1929, 30. Sec. Mich. Child Labor Com., 1908-19; Albion Charter Commn., 1914-15; mem. Cleveland Bd. Edn. (com. in citizenship training), 1934-35. Pres. Mich. Acad. Science, 1918-19 (v.p. 1912-18); mem. Am. Assn. Univ. Profs., American Economic Association, American Statistical Association (president of Cleveland Chapter, 1937-38). Unitarian. Mason. Author: Economic Influences upon Educational Progress in the United States (1820-50), 1908; Education and Industrial Evolution, 1908; The History and Problems of Organized Labor, 1911 and 1920; The Industrial Situation, 1914; Elementary Economics, 1919; Organized Labor in American History, 1920; Economics, 1931; Labor Problems, 1933; chapter Labor, Vol. VI, History of the State of Ohio, 1942; also contbr. numerous articles to econ. and ednl. jours. Address: Case Inst. of Technology, Cleveland 6 OH‡

CARLYLE, IRVING EDWARD, lawyer; b. Wake Forest, N.C., Sept. 20, 1896; s. John Bethune and Dora (Dunn) C.; A.B., Wake Forest College, 1917, student law sch., 1920, LL.D., 1953; student U. of Virginia,

1920-22; LL.D., University of North Carolina, 1968; m. Mary Belo Moore, October 20, 1928; children—Elizabeth (Mrs. Robert D. Byerly, Jr.), Mary (Mrs. Hugh B. Campbell, Jr.). Admitted N.C. bar, 1920; practiced law, Winston-Salem, N.C., 1922-71; associated with firm Manly, Hendren & Womble, 1923-71; becoming partner and remaining as partner in firm under present name, Womble, Carlyle, Sandridge & Rice. Served as 2d lt., F.A., U.S. Army, World War I. State representative N.C., 1941, 43, 45, 51; state senator last three terms; N.C. del.-at-large to Dem. Nat. Conv., 1952, 56. Mem. N.C. Adv. Budget Commn., 1945-46, Bd. Law Examiners, 1936-49; apptd. by gov. to N.C. State Bd. Pub. Welfare, 1948-63; chmn. N.C. Ednl. Radio and Television Commn., 1953-71; chmn. Gov's. Commn. Edn. Beyond High Sch., 1961-62; mem. N.C. State Constitutional Study Commn., 1968. Trustee Wake Forest Univ. (pres. 1946-65), Goucher Coll., E. Carolina U. Recipient Medallion Merit, Lake Forest U., 1969. Mem. Am., N.C. (pres.), Forsyth County (pres.) bar assns., Am. Judicature Soc. (mem. so. regional council), Phi Beta Kappa, Delta Psi, Omicron Delta Kappa, Phi Delta Phi. Clubs: Torch, Forsyth Country (Winston-Salem). Home: Winston-Salem NC Died June 5, 1971.

CARLYLE, WILLIAM LEVI, agricultural scientist; b. Chesterville, Ont., Can., Sept. 22, 1870; s. Thomas and Nancy (Thom) C.; Ont. Agrl. Coll., 1889-92; B.S. in agr. U. of Toronto, 1892; M.S., Colo. Agrl. Coll., 1905; m. Inez M. Fairbanks, of Herman, St. Lawrence Co., N.Y., July 7, 1896. Instr. dairying, Ont. Agrl. Coll., 1893; lecturer, live stock and dairy husbandry extension dept., U. of Minn., 1893-7; prof. animal husbandry, U. of Wis., 1897-1903; prof. agr., 1903-5, dean of agr., 1905-9, Colo. Agrl. Coll.; expert in animal husbandry, U.S. Dept. Agr., 1905-9; supt. in charge live stock div., Alaska-Yukon-Pacific Expn., 1909; dean Coll. of Agr. and dir. Expt. Sta., 1910-15, acting pres., Feb., 1913-May, 1915, U. of Ida.; dean of agr. and dir. Expt. Sta., Okla. Agrl. and Mech. Coll., since 1915. Dir. Western Live Stock Show, Portland, Ore.; mem. Internat. Live Stock Show, Chicago, Nat. Live Stock Show, Denver. Has judged live stock at leading state and nat. shows since 1900. Presbyn. Clubs: Saddle and Sirloin (Chicago). Author bulls. and ann. reports Wis. Expt. Sta., 1898-1904, Colo. Expt. Sta., 1904-7; contbr. to Stillwater OK‡

CARMICHAEL, JOHN HUGH, lawyer; b. Cairo, Ill., Feb. 2, 1868; s. Isaac Hugh and Minerva (Beck) C.; ed. pub. and pvt. schs., Paris Acad., Logan Co., 1887-90; taught sch., 1890-92; LL.B., U. of Ark., 1894; m. Amelia Parker, Jan. 10, 1893 (died May 1, 1931); children—Mrs. Lentes Moore, Mrs. Camille Herndon (dec.), Mrs. Celeste Bean, Lt. Comdr. John Hugh (U.S.N.); m. 2d, Mrs. L. M. Beauchamp, May 20, 1933. Admitted to bar 1893; acting dean law, University of Arkansas, 1898-1900. Candidate for chief justice Supreme Court, Arkansas; appointed special counsel for state in suit against car companies; mem. State Dem. Central Com., 1900-02; has served as spl. judge in Supreme, Chancery and Circuit courts; sec. and mem. bd. to examine applicants for admission to practice in Supreme Court, 1908-10; mem. law firm Carmichael & Hendricks; dean Law Dept., U. of Ark., 1900-15; since dean Ark. Law Sch. Mem. Am., Ark. State (pres. 1918-19) and Little Rock bar assns., del. Universal Congress Lawyers and Jurists, St. Louis, 1904. Methodist. Democrat. K.P., W.O.W. Club: Lakeside Country (pres. 1935). Author: An Arkansas Border Incident; The Coulter Case. Compiled (with W. F. Coleman), Supplemental Digest of City Ordinances of Little Rock, Ark., 1893. Teacher of men's Bible class, 35 years. Home: Route 4, Little Rock. Office: Pyramid Bldg., Little Rock AR

CARNAHAN, A.S.J., former ambassador; b. Ellsinore Mo., Jan. 9, 1897; s. Robert Thompson and Orlena (Boxx) C.; B.S. in Edn., Southeast Mo. State Tchrs. Coll., Cape Girardeau, 1926; M.A., U. Mo., 1932; m. Mary Kathel Schupp, May 27, 1925; children—Robert Eldon, Melvin Eugene. tchr. rural sch., 1914; later served successively as tchr. elementary grades in town sch., prin. high sch.; held sch. adminstrv. positions in Carter, Reynolds and Shannon Counties, Mo., 1926-44; mem. 79th, 81st to 86th Congresses, 8th Mo. District. U.S. del. 12th Gen. Assembly UN; former U.S. ambassador to Sierra Leone. Served with USN, World War I. Democrat. Baptist. Mason. Home: Ellsinore MO Died Mar. 24, 1968; buried Carson Hill Cemetery.

CARNAHAN, DAVID HOBART, prof. Romance langs.; b. Dixon, Ill., Nov. 16, 1874; s. David Franklin and Sarah Anna (Dobbins) C.; A.B., U. of Ill., 1896, A.M., 1898; Ph.D., Yale, 1905; student, Sorbonne, Paris, 1898-99, U. of Chicago, 1899-1900; m. Mabel C. Johnson, of Arkadelphia, Ark., June 19, 1909; children—Margaret Lucy, Sarah Elizabeth, Frank Neil. Asst. in Romance langs., U. of Chicago, 1899-1900; prof. modern langs., U. of Ida., 1900-01; asst. prof. Romance langs., 1901-03, 1905-06, asso. prof., 1906-17, prof. since 1917, U. of Ill., also acting head of dept. 6 years, head of dept. 1927-39, and asst. dean for foreign students, 1920-22. Member Modern Lang. Assn. America, Am. Assn. Univ. Profs., Sigma Chi, Phi Beta Kappa. Conglist. Author: The Prologue in the Old

French and Provencal Mystery, 1905; Poesies de Maistre Eloy du Mont, 1907; Jean D'Abundance, His Life and Works, 1909; The Ad Deum Vadit of Jean Gerson, 1917; French Review Grammar, 1920; Spanish Review Grammar (with A. Seymour), 1923. Reviser: Fraser and Squair French Grammar, 1931. Home: 607 W. Nevada St., Urbana IL‡

CARNAP, RUDOLF, educator; b. Wuppertal, Germany, May 18, 1891; s. Johannes S. and Anna (Dorpfeld) C.; student U. Freiburg Baden, Jena; Ph.D., U. Jena, 1921; Sc.D. (hon.), Harvard, 1936; LL.D. (hon.) U. of Cal. at Los Angeles, 1963; H.L.D. (hon.), U. of Mich., 1965; Ph.D. (honorary), Univ. of Oslo (Norway), 1969; m. Elizabeth Ina von Stoger, 1933 (dec. 1964). Came to U.S., 1935, naturalized, 1941. Instr. philosophy U. Vienna (Austria), 1926-31; prof. natural philosophy German U., Prague, Czechoslovakia, 1931-35; prof. philosophy U. Chicago, 1936-52; prof. philosophy University of California at Los Angeles, 1954-62, research philosopher, 1962-70; vis. prof. Harvard, 1940-41. Fellow Am. Academy of Arts and Sciences, British Academy (corresponding); mem. Am. Philosophical Assn., Assn. Symbolic Logic, Philos. Sci. Assn. Author: Der Raum, 1922; Physikal. Begriffsbildung, 1926; Der Logische Aufbau der Welt, 1928; Scheinprobleme der Philosophie, 1928; Abriss der Logistik, 1929; The Unity of Science, 1934; Logische Syntax der Sprache, 1934; Die Aufgabe der Wissenschaftslogik, 1934; Philosophy and Logical Syntax, 1935; Logical Syntax of Language, English translation, 1937; Foundations of Logic and Mathematics, 1939; Introduction to Semantics, 1942; Formalization of Logic, 1943; Meaning and Necessity, 1947; Logical Foundations of Probability, 1950; The Continuum of Inductive Methods, 1951; Einfuhrung in die symbolische Logik, 1954; Introduction to Symbolic Logic and its Applications, 1958; Induktive Logik und Wahr-Scheinlishkeit, 1958; Philosophical Foundations of Physics, 1966; The Logical Structure of the World, 1967; A Basic System of Inductive Logic, 1971; also book chpts., articles. Writings collected in The Philosophy of Rudolf Carnap (editor Paul A. Schilpp), 1963. Home: Los Angeles CA Died Sept. 14, 1970.

CARNEGIE, T(HOMAS) MORRIS(ON), b. Pittsburgh, Pa., Jan. 6, 1874; s. Thomas M. and Lucy (Coleman) C.; ed. St. Paul's Sch., Concord, N.H.; student, Columbia Law Sch.; m. Virginia D. Beggs, Oct. 25, 1898. Dir. Carnegie Foundation for Advancement of Teaching, Boomer & Co. Clubs: Racquet and Tennis, etc. Home: 400 Park Av., New York NY‡

CARNEY, WILLIAM ROY, independent investor; b. Chgo., Sept. 15, 1889; s. William J. and Teresa (Cunningham) C.; grad. U. of Chicago, 1912; grad. Sch. of Mil. Aviation, Champaign, Ill., 1918; m. Marie M. Murphy, Jan. 19, 1919; children—Jean, William J., J. Otis, Peter Roy. Began as bookkeeper Saylor Coal Co., 1913; became dir. Wright Coal Co., 1915; pres. Superior Flake Graphite Co.; v.p. Carmac Coal Co.; dir. Poor & Co., v.p. and dir. Dolese & Shepard Co. Served in Aviation Sect., Signal Corps, later, Air Service. V.p. Assn. Cath. Charities, Clubs: Chicago, Onwentsia, Shoreacres, Midday, Attic, Old Elm, Coleman Lake. Home: Lake Forest IL Died Mar. 17, 1973.

CARPENTER, AARON EVERLY, mfg. exec.; b. Woodbury, N.J., Aug. 1, 1883; s. Charles Everly and Florence Rebecca (Browne) C.; A.B., U. Pa., 1906; m. Elizabeth Ryder Williams, 1904 (div.); children—Florence (Mrs. Carpenter Murray), Aaron Everly (dec.); m. 2d, Edythe Aramantha Anderson, July 6, 1914 (dec.). With E. F. Houghton & Co., Phila., mfr. oils, leathers, 1905-69, being successively fgn. rep., treas., 1st v.p., pres. and gen. mgr., chmn. bd., 1950-69; editor The Houghton Line; mem. conseil d'administration Societe des Produits Houghton; dir. E. F. Houghton & Co. of Can., Ltd., E. F. Houghton & Co. of Eng., Ltd., Edgar Vaughan & Co., Ltd., Birmingham, Eng. Bd. mgrs. Germantown Dispensary and Hosp.; trustee Phila. Mus. Art. Served as capt. inf. A.E.F., World War I; maj. USAAF, World War II. Fellow Royal Geog. Soc., St. Andrews Soc., Newcomen Society England; mem. Sigma Alpha Epsilon. Mason (K.T.), National Sojourner. Clubs: Bay Head (New Jersey) Yacht; Racquet, Army and Navy (Washington, D.C.); Manasquan River Marlin and Tuna (Brielle, N.J.); Philadelphia Country; Germantown (Pa.) Cricket. Home: Philadelphia PA Died May 15, 1969.

CARPENTER, ALLEN HARMON, head master; b. Minneapolis, Sept. 5, 1876; s. Albert Nathaniel and Arra Alfaretta (Harmon) C.; student Carleton Coll., 1894-5; A.B., Adelbert College (Western Reserve U.), Ohio, 1898, A.M., 1899; Harvard, 1899-1902, A.M., 1899; m. Phyana Hulbert Haskell, of Ashtabula, O., June 29, 1904. Head of history dept., Pomfret Sch., and athletic coach, Pomfret Center, Conn., 1902-5; head master The College Sch., Kenilworth, Ill., since 1905. Mem. Am. Hist. Assn., Nat. Geog. Soc., N. Central Academic Assn., Delta Upsilon, Phi Beta Kappa. Republican. Congregationalist. Clubs: Harvard, Minnesota, Delta Upsilon (Chicago). Contbr. hist. and ednl. articles to mags. and revs. Address: The College School, Kenilworth IL‡

CARPENTER, CHARLES COLCOCK JONES, bishop, university chancellor; born in Augusta, Georgia, September 2, 1899; s. Rev. Samuel Barstow and Ruth Berrien (Jones) C.; grad. Lawrenceville School, 1917; A.B., Princeton U., 1921; D.D., 1947; B.D., Va. Theol. Sem., 1926, D.D., 1938; LL.D., U. of Ala., 1938; D.D., U. of the South, 1938; m. Alexandra Morrison, Nov. 21, 1928; children—Charles C. J., Douglas Morrison, Ruth Berrien and Alexandra (twins). Ordained to ministry P.E. Ch. Dec. 1925; rector Grace Ch., Waycross, Ga., 1926-28; archdeacon of Ga., 1928-29; rector St. Johns Ch., Savannah, Ga., 1929-36; rector Ch. of the Advent, Birmingham, Ala., 1936-38; consecrated bishop of Ala., June 24, 1938; chancellor, University the South, Sewanee, 1961-67. Served as 2d lt. Inf., U.S. Army, 1918; capt., chaplain, 118th F.A., Georgia National Guard, 1931-36. Trustee U. of the South. Mem. Soc. Colonial Wars, Soc. of the Cin., Princeton Quadrangle Club, Newcomen Society (American Branch). Mem. Nat. Council, P.E. Church, 1943-49. Club: Mountain Brook. Democrat. Home: Birmingham AL Died June 28, 1969; buried Church of the Advent, Birmingham AL

CARPENTER, CLARENCE, state ofcl.; b. Meriden, Conn., Mar. 11, 1906; s. Ernest Charles and Nettie (Hale) C.; A.S., New Haven Coll., 1940; m. Helen A. Gerte, Mar. 20, 1960 (dec. Dec. 1963); 1 son, William Hale. Chief accountant Dahl Oil Co., Norwich, Conn., 1946-52; with State Employees Retirement System, State of Conn., 1952-68, chief, Hartford, 1959-68. Bd. dirs. State Employees Credit Union, 1958-68, pres., 1965-66. Bus. mgr. Mark Twain Masquers, 1954. Served with AUS, 1943-45. C.P.A., Conn. Mem. Soc. Govtl. Accountants (pres. 1962-63), Conf. State Social Security Adminstrs. (v.p. 1967-68), Nat. Conf. State Retirement Adminstrs. (sec. 1964-65). Home: Hartford CT Died May 3, 1968.

CARPENTER, COY CORNELIUS, medical educator; b. Carpenter, N.C., Apr. 24, 1900; s. Rufus Jackson and Betty (Rogers) C.; B.A., Wake Forest (N.C.) Coll., 1922; M.D., Syracuse U., 1924; m. Dorothy Mitten, Oct. 23, 1926; children—Harry Mitten, Coy Cornelius. Began practice medicine, 1924; instr. pathology, asst. attending pathologist U. Hosp., Syracuse U., 1924-25, resident physician, instr. clin. medicine, 1925-26; pathologist various hosp. in N.C., 1926; prof. pathology Bowman Gray Sch. Medicine, Wake Forest U., 1926-70, prof. emeritus, 1970-71, dean, 1936-60, v.p. med. affairs, 1960-68, v.p. emeritus med. affairs, 1968-71; Fulbright lectr. pathology Fouad U. Faculty Medicine and Ibrahim U. Faculty Medicine, Cairo, Egypt, 1953-54. Diplomate Am. Bd. Pathology. Fellow A.M.A.; mem. N.C., Forsyth County med. socs., Assn. Am. Med. Colls., Winston-Salem C. of C., Nu Sigma Nu, Alpha Omega Alpha. Democrat. Baptist. Clubs: Rotary, Old Town. Home: Winston-Salem NC Died Nov. 7, 1971.

CARPENTER, EDWARD CHILDS, author; b. Phila., Pa., Dec. 13, 1872; s. of Edward P. and Fannie (Childs) C.; m. Helen Alden Knipe, June 1, 1907. Financial editor Phila. Inquirer, 1905-16. Pres. Dramatists' Guild of Authors' League America, 1922-23 and 1929-36. Clubs: Coffee House, Players (New York). Author: The Chasm, 1903; Captain Courtesy, 1906; The Code of Victor Jallot, 1907; The Easy Mark, 1912. Plays: The Dragon-Fly (with John Luther Long), prod. Phila., 1905; Captain Courtesy, dramatization, Los Angeles, 1906; Remembrance, Chicago, 1906; The Barber of New Orleans, New York, 1909; The Challenge, Washington, 1911; The Tongues of Men, New York, 1913; The Cinderella Man, New York, 1916, London, 1918; The Pipes of Pan, 1917; The Three Bears, New York, 1917; Bab, dramatization of Mary Roberts Rinehart's novel, New York, 1920; Pot-luck, New York, 1921; Connie Goes Home, New York, 1923; The Bachelor Father, New York, 1928, London, Berlin, Budapest, 1929; Whistling in the Dark, 1932; Melody, 1933; Order Please, 1935. Address: The Salt Box, New Hartford CT‡

CARPENTER, FANNY HALLOCK, lawyer; b. Rainbow, Conn.; d. Rev. Thomas Henderson and Eliza (Hallock) Rouse; Mills Coll., Cal.; LL.B., New York U. Law Sch., 1896; m. Philip Carpenter, of Bath, N.H., Sept. 3, 1880 (died July 23, 1919). Practiced law, New York, 1897—. Conglist. Dir. Women's Bar Assn., Gen. Federation Women's Clubs, 1906-10 (pres. N.Y. State Federation, 1903-5). Clubs: Sorosis (pres. 1907-11), Nat. Soc. N.E. Women, Women Lawyers'. Has traveled extensively in U.S., Can., Europe and S. Sea Islands. Home: Pelham Manor, N.Y. Office: 111 Broadway, New York NY‡

CARPENTER, FRANK WATSON, b. Corinth, N.Y., June 16, 1871; s. Franklin and Amanda M. (Watson) C.; grad. High Sch., Saratoga Springs, 1885; studied law under Judge Charles S. Lobingier (q.v.); m. Lucia Rolschau, of Omaha, July 1, 1893. Pvt. and corpl. 8th U.S. Inf., non-commd. staff officer U.S.A., 1889-95; civ. service employee, War Dept., 1895-8; pvt. sec. to comdg. gen. 4th U.S. Army Corps, 1898; chief clk. hdqrs. Gen. Lawton in Philippines and 1st Div. 8th Army Corps, 1899-1901; pvt. sec. to U.S. mil. gov. of P.I., 1901; chief clk. Exec. Bur. Philippine Govt., 1902-4; asst. exec. sec., 1904-8, exec. sec., Feb. 1,

1908-Dec. 15, 1913; govt. Depts. of Mindanao and Sulu, Govt. P.I., Dec. 16, 1913—. Clubs: Army and Navy, University (Manila). Address: Zamboanga PI‡

CARPENTER, FRED WARNER;, b. Sauk Centre, Minn., Dec. 12, 1873; s. Ira M. and Eva A. (Wright) E.; ed. pub. schs. of Duke Co., Calif., Lakeport (Calif.) Acad.; law course, U. of Minn.; unmarried. Admitted to bar, in Minn. and Calif., 1898; stenographer to Charles S. Wheeler, of law firm of Bishop & Wheeler, San Francisco, 1898-1900; resigned to go to P.I., as stenographer to William H. Taft, being made his pvt. sec. when he was inaugurated as gov., 1901; accompanied Gov. Taft to Rome, in 1902, in connection with friars' lands controversy; went to Washington, D.C., as his private sec. when he was made Secretary of War, 1904, accompanying him on his trips to P.I., 1905 and 1907; resigned from War Dept., July 10, 1908; secretary to President Taft, Mar. 5, 1909-May 26, 1910; E.E. and M.P. to Morocco, May 1910-Sept. 1912, to Siam, Sept. 12, 1912-Dec. 1913. Republican. Episcopalian. Mem. Delta Chi. Author: Verses from Many Seas, 1914. Home: San Anselmo CA‡

CARPENTER, JAMES D., lawyer; b. Woodbury, N.J., Feb. 10, 1885; s. James D. and Harriet (Fish) C.; grad. Brown Coll. Prep. Sch., 1905; LL.B., U. Pa. 1909; m. Emily M. Atkinson, Oct. 17, 1912 (dec. Jan. 1960); children—Emily A. (Mrs. Lawrence Pratt), William A., Frances H. (Mrs. Albert E. Betteridge, Jr.); m. 2d, Mildred L. Pearson, 1961. Practiced in Newark; s.r. mem. firm Carpenter, Bennett & Morrissey; U.S. Commr. Jersey City, 1910-1920; spl. asst. atty. gen. N.J., prosecuting jury fixers and racketeers at Paterson, 1933-34. Mem. N.J. Crime Commn., 1934; tchr. law Fordham Law Sch., 1915-25. Bd. dirs. Jersey City YMCA, 1947-52, pres., 1952-61. Fellow Am. Bar Found. (recipient 50 Year award from fellows 1965); mem. Internat. (patron), Am. (ho. of dels. 1951-72), Inter-Am., N.J. (pres. 1933-34), Hudson County (pres. 1923), Essex County bar assns., Assn. Bar City N.Y., N.Y. County Lawyers Assn. Democrat. Conglist. Clubs: Lawyers (N.Y.C.); Upper Montclair Country; Essex. Home: Montclair NJ Died Aug. 9, 1972; buried Mt. Hebron Cemetery, Upper Montclair NJ

CARPENTER, ROBERT WILFRED, broadcasting exec.; b. Elizabeth, N.J., Sept. 30, 1909; s. Hugh Tabler and Eleanor (Servoss) C.; student pub. schs., Roselle Park, N.J.; m. Isabelle Struthers, Sept. 15, 1934; children—Barbara, Robert, Heather. Accounting and sales positions CBS, 1934-43; sta. relations MBS, from 1945, v.p. dept., from 1956. Supply dir. A.R.C., Morocco, N. Africa, 1943-45. Club: Inn's Arden Golf (Old Greenwich). Home: St Croix VI Died Feb. 3, 1970.

CARPENTER, WILLIAM WESTON, sch. adminstrn.; b. Lawrence, Kan., Mar. 2, 1889; s. William Thomas and Helen Eva (Weston) C.; A.B., U. of Kan., 1912, A.M., 1917; studied U. of Ariz.; Ph.D., Columbia, 1926; m. Doris Melvina Cotey, Dec. 27, 1914; children—Barbara Cotey, William Weston, Edward Thomas. Teacher of science high schs. of Ariz., and head of Science dept., Phoenix Union High Sch., until 1920; dean Phoenix Jr. Coll., 1920-23; prof. of teaching physical science, George Peabody Coll. for Teachers, Nashville, Tenn., 1925-27, prof. sch. administration, 1927-28; prof. edn., U. of Mo. from 1928. Educational Reorganization advisor, Japan, 1948-50. Served as 2d lt. inf., U.S. Army, World War; 1st lt. Ariz. National Guard. Received Silver Beaver award, Boy Scouts America. Past chmn. research com. Am. Assn. of Jr. Colleges. Mem. N.E.A. (life mem.), Am. Assn. Univ. Profs., Assn. for Higher Edn., Am. Ednl. Research Assn., Nat. Soc. for Study of Edn., Nat. Council Schoolhouse Constrn., Phi Delta Kappa, (past nat. secretary), Kappa Delta Pi. Democrat. Presbyn. Author: Certain Phases of the Administration of High School Chemistry, 1925; (with John Rufi) The Teacher and the School; (with John Rufi) The Teacher and Secondary School Administration, 1931; (with Ralph Yakel) State and National School Administration, 1931, revised, 1934, 37, 39, revised by William Weston Carpenter, 1951, 54; (with L. G. Townsend) Community School Administration, 1936, revised 1948, 1951; (with W. E. Rosentengel) Community School Finance Problems, 1936, revised 1939; (with N.E. Viles) Community School Building Problems, 1934, revised 1940; The Organization and Administration of The Junior College, 1939; (with G.H. Marshall and Clara W. Marshall) The Administrator's Wife, 1941; Schoolhouse Planning and Construction 1946; Suggestions for Procedure for Missouri Boards of Education (with A. G. Capps and L. G. Townsend), 1950, rev., 1956; (with A. G. Capps) selected Readings, State and National School Administration, 1951, rev., 1954; Evaluating The Educational Services in the Local School District (with A. G. Capps and L. G. Townsend), 1955; Local School Administration in Action (with L. G. Townsend), 1956; Titles of Dissertations in Edn. Accented by U. of Mo. 1916-58 (with A. G. Capps), 1958. Home: Columbia MO Died Sept. 28, 1968.

CARR, ALBERT ZOLOTKOFF, writer, govt. ofcl.; b. Chicago, Jan. 15, 1902; s. Leon and Fannie (Ogus) Z.; B.S., U. Chicago, 1921; A.M., Columbia, 1926; student London Sch. Economics, 1936; m. Anne Kingsbury, Dec. 13, 1943. Editor, Business Training Corp., 1927-30; asst. to pres., Tradeways, Inc., 1931-33; author of books and contbr. to Sat. Eve. Post, Harpers mag., Cosmopolitan, Life, This Week, 1931-41; asst. to chmn. W.P.B., 1942-44; economic adviser, White House staff, 1944-46; consultant to Inter-Allied Reparation Agency, Brussels, Belgium, 1946-47, 1949, to President Truman, 1948-52; mem. W.P.B. Mission to Eng., 1943, to China, 1944; mem. White House Mission to Pres. of China, 1945, of Inter-Allied Reparations Mission to Germany, 1947. Awarded Order of Victory of Republic of China, 1945. Author: Juggernaut: The Path of Dictatorship, 1939; Men of Power, 1940, rev., 1956; America's Last Chance, 1940, Napoleon Speaks, 1941; Truman, Stalin and Peace, 1950; How to Attract Good Luck, 1952; The Black Kitten (winner 1st prize, Queen's Awards 1955); The Coming of War, 1960; John D. Rockefeller's Secret Weapon, 1962; The World and William Walker, 1963; A Matter of Life and Death: How Wars Get Started or Are Prevented, 1966; Business As A Game, 1968; (pseudonym A.B. Carbury) The Girl With the Glorious Genes, 1968. Home: Truro Cape Cod MA Died Oct. 28, 1971; buried Truro, Cape Cod MA

CARR, EMMA PERRY, emeritus prof. of chemistry; born Holmesville, Ohio, July 23, 1880; d. Edmund Cone and Anna Mary (Jack) Carr; student O. State 1898-99, Mt. Holyoke, 1899-1901; B.S., U. of Chicago, 1905, Ph.D., 1910; D.Sc., Allegheny Coll., 1939, Russell Sage Coll., 1941. Engaged as asst. in chemistry, Mount Holyoke Coll., 1901-04; grad. asst. U. of Chicago, 1904-05; instr. chemistry, Mount Holyoke Coll. 1905-08, Mary E. Woolley fellow U. of Chicago 1908-09, Loewenthal fellow, 1909-10; asso. prof and joint chmn. dept. chemistry, Mount Holyoke Coll., 1910-13, chmn. dept. chemistry and prof., 1913-46; visiting prof., Inst. of Chemistry, Nat. U. of Mexico 1944; research Queens U. (Belfast, Ireland), 1919; U. of Zurich, 1925; official del. to Internat. Union Pure and Applied Chemistry at Bucharest, 1925; Alice Freeman Palmer fellow research at Univ. of Zurich, 1929-30; official del. to Internat. Chem. Union at Lucerne, Switzerland, summer, 1936. Fellow A.A.A.S.; Fellow American Physical Society; member American Chemical Society (councillor, 1932-37), American Assn. Univ. Profs., Am. Assn. Univ. Women, Phi Beta Kappa, Sigma Xi. Iota Sigma Pi, Sigma Delta Upsilon. Received grants from Nat. Research Council, 1930 and 1934, Rockefeller Foundation, 1935 and 1937; honored by Garvan gold medal award, Am. Chem. Soc., 1937. Methodist. Club: Cosmopolitan, (New York). Contbr. sci. articles to chem. publs. and socs. Home: Evanston IL Died 1972.

CARR, IRVING J., army officer; b. Chippewa Falls, Wis., May 29, 1875; s. Joseph Shannon and Ella (Wentworth) C.; C., Pa. Mil. Coll., Chester, 1897; grad. Inf. and Cav. Sch., 1907, Army Signal Sch., 1909, Army Staff Sch., 1920, Army War Coll., 1921, Army Industrial Coll., 1926; m. Margaret Lisle Halley, Apr. 25, 1912 (deceased 1932); m. 2d, Betty Guinn, Mar. 17, 1942. Commd. 2d lieut. inf., U.S. Army, July 9, 1898, advanced through grades to maj. gen., July 1, 1931; chief of staff, Hawaiian Div., 1921-25; dir. Army Industrial Coll., 1926-30; exec. to asst. sec. of war, 1931; chief signal officer, July 1, 1931-Dec. 31, 1934; retired Dec. 31, 1934. Served in the Philippine Islands, 1899-1902, 1903-05, 1909-11; with Punitive Expdn. to Vera Cruz, Mexico, 1914; signal officer 2d Div., 4th Army Corps and 3d Army, France, World War. Awarded silver star citation for gallantry in action against insurgents, Magalang, Luzon, P.I., 1899; meritorious service citation certificate by comdg. gen. A.E.F., for service as chief signal officer; Officer Order of Black Star (France); Purple Heart. Club: Chevy Chase (Md.). Washington DC‡

CARR, LAWRENCE, theatrical producer; b. Ocean Grove, N.J., Dec. 24, 1917; s. John and Eva (Asay) C.; student Am. Acad. Dramatic Art, N.Y.C., Princeton. Producer (with Robert Fryer) By the Beautiful Sea, The Desk Set, Shangri-La, Auntie Mame, Redhead, There Was a Little Girl, Advise and Consent, Hot Spot, A Passage to India, Roar Like a Dove; pres. Fryer, Carr and Harris, Inc., N.Y.C.; actor with Old Vic Theatre Co., Eng., Century Theatre, N.Y.C., summer stock in Cleve., Ogunquit, Me., Dennis, Mass., numerous TV· shows; also stage mgr., summer theatre dir.; producer Sweet Charity, 1966; Mame, 1966. Home: New York City NY Died Jan. 17, 1969.

CARR, LELAND WALKER, judge; b. Livingston County, Mich., Sept. 29, 1883; s. Eli French and Eva (Walker) C.; grad. Mich. State Normal Coll., 1903; LL.B., U. of Mich., 1906; LL.D. (honorary), Michigan University, 1946; m. Irene Lindow, August 6, 1913; children—Dorothy (Mrs. R. W. Houvener), Ruth (Mrs. J. R. Carney), Clarice (Mrs. J. R. Dawson), Leland. Admitted to Mich. bar, 1906. Prin. High Sch., Marine City, Mich., 1906-07; supt. of schs., 1907-09; supt. of schs., Ely, Nevada, 1909-11; in gen. practice of law, Ionia, Mich., 1911-13; asst. atty. gen. of Mich., 1913-19; legal advisor Mich. State Highway Dept., 1919-21; Ingham County (Mich.) circuit judge, 1921-45; justice Supreme Ct. Mich., 1945-63, chief justice, 1962-63. Republican. Methodist. Home: Lansing MI Died May 30, 1969; buried Evergreen Cemetery, Lansing MI

CARR, OSSIAN ELMER, city manager; b. Saegerstown, Pa., Sept. 7, 1876; s. Alfred and Chloe (Stebbins) C.; B.S. in Engring., Allegheny Coll., Meadville, Pa., 1900; m. Nora B. Gentry, of Portland, Ore., Aug. 10, 1912. With U.S. Coast and Geodetic Survey, 1900-03, B. &O. R.R., 1903-05; constrn. filtration plant, Pittsburgh, Pa., 1905-06; constrn. at Olongapo, P.I., 1906-08; earthwork computation, Seattle, Wash., 1908-09; asst. supt. Hawthorne Av. Bridge, Portland, Ore., 1909-11, engr. in charge underground survey, Cincinnati, O., 1911-13; city mgr. Cadillac, Mich., 1913-15, Niagara Falls, N.Y., 1915-17, Springfield, O., 1917-19, Dubuque, Ia., 1919-25, Ft. Worth, Tex., 1925-31, Oakland, Calif., 1931-33; Public Works Adminstrn. inspection engr. for California, Nevada and Arizona 1933-37; now dir. mgr. Insurance Securities, Inc., of Oakland, Calif. Fuel administrator, Niagara Falls, World War. Mem. Am. Soc. C.E., Nat. Municipal League, City Managers' Assn. (dir.). Congregationalist. Mason. Club: San Francisco Commonwealth. Home: 5915 Morago Av., Oakland, Calif. Office: 414 13th St., CA‡

CARR, STERLING DOUGLAS, lawyer; b. Monterey Co., Calif., Nov. 25, 1876; son of John Sterling and Florida Nichols (Carr) C.; grad. Belmont (Calif.) Sch., 1895; student U. of Calif. 2 yrs.; LL.B., from Columbia Law School, 1900; m. Mary Grayson Hinckley, July 18, 1927. Was admitted to Calif. bar, 1900, and began practice at San Francisco; U.S. atty. Northern District of Calif., July 11, 1924-Sept. 30, 1925. Mem. Delta Kappa Epsilon. Republican. Episcopalian. Clubs: Pacific Union, Commonwealth. Home: 2100 Green St. Office: 2406 Russ Bldg., San Francisco CA‡

CARR, WILBERT LESTER, prof. Latin; b. Leon, Ia., Aug. 15, 1875; s. William Mack and Sabra Ella (Rilea) C.; A.B., Drake U., Des Moines, Ia., 1898, A.M., 1899 and LL.D., 1937; fellow in Latin, U. of Chicago, 1902-05; m. Ada Wallace, June 10, 1911; children—William Wallace, Mary Eleanor, Wilbert Lester, Elizabeth Ley. Instr. in Latin and Greek, Drake U., 1899-1902; teacher of Latin and Greek, Univ. High Sch. (U. of Chicago), 1905-06, Shortridge High Sch., Indianapolis, Ind., 1906-09; teacher of Latin, University High Sch., 1909-20; asst. prof. Latin, Oberlin (O.) Coll., 1920-24; asst. prof. Latin, U. of Mich., 1924-26, asso. prof., 1926-29, prof., 1929-30; prof. Latin, Teachers Coll. (Columbia), 1930-42, now emeritus; visiting prof. Latin, Colby College, 1942-49. Member American Classical League (pres. 1931-37), Classic Assn. New England, Am. Philol. Assn., Phi Beta Kappa. Republican. Mem. Baptist Church. Mason. Club: Men's Faculty. Author: Development of Language (with H. F. Scott), 1921; The Teaching of Elementary Latin (monograph), 1929; also chapter in Vol. XII of The Classroom Teacher, 1927; The Living Language: A Latin Book for Beginners (with G. D. Hadzsits), 1933; The Living Language: A Second Latin Book (with G. D. Hadzsits and H. E. Wedeck), 1934; Language and Its Growth (with H. F. Scott and G. T. Wilkinson), 1935; Latin Poetry (with Harry E. Wedeck), 1940; Article on Latin in Ency. of Educational Research, 1941. Editor: Parsons' and Little's First Latin Lessons, 1926; Little and Parsons' Second Latin Lessons, 1927; Pharr's Aeneid of Vergil, 1930; Wedeck's Third Year Latin, 1931; Poteat's Selected Letters of Cicero, 1931; Rogers, Scott and Ward's Caesar Augustus, 1935; Poteat's Selected Letters of Pliny, 1937; Maxey's Acta Muciorum, 1942; Brown's Modern Latin Conversation, 1943; asso. editor Classical Outlook since 1938. Contbr. to Classical Journal, Classical Weekly, Classical Outlook, School and Society. Home: 9 West St., Waterville ME‡

CARRICK, ALICE VAN LEER (MRS. PRESCOTT ORDE SKINNER), b. Nashville, Tenn., Aug. 1, 1875; d. Samuel Pulsifer and Mary Florence (Clark) Carrick; ed. Lewis Sch., Roxbury, Mass., and Girls' Latin Sch., Boston; m. Prescott Orde Skinner of Hanover, N.H., July 10, 1901; children—Margaret, John Carrick, Alicia Prescott. Began writing for magazines, 1900; now mem. editorial staff of Antiques"; lecturer on old furniture and domestic life of the past. Mem. N.H. Hist. Soc., Essex Inst., Salem, Mass. Chmn. Dem. Women's Orgn. for N.H., 1932—; chmn. for N.H. of Women's Orgn. for Nat. Prohibition Reform, 1932—. Episcopalian. Author: Kitty-Cat Tales, 1907; Collector's Luck, 1919; The Next-to-Nothing House, 1922; Collector's Luck in France, 1924; Collector's Luck in England, 1926; (collaboration) Mother Goose for Antique Collectors, 1927; Shades of Our Ancestors, 1929; Collector's Luck in Spain, 1930. Contbr. to Country Life, House Beautiful, Good Housekeeping, etc. Home: Webster Cottage, Hanover NH‡

CARROLL, AUGUSTUS JOHN, assn. exec.; b. Seneca Falls, N.Y., Oct. 6, 1907; s. John F. and Alice C. (Coleman) C.; m. Agnes E. Houman, Oct. 19, 1940; children—Kathleen A., Patrick L. With N.Y. Dept. Correction, 1929-45, prison bus. mgr. Auburn, N.Y., 1938-45; with N.Y. Edn. Dept., 1945-63, forestry coll. bus. dir., Syracuse (N.Y.) U., 1945-48; with State U. N.Y. Med. Center, Syracuse, N.Y., 1949-63, bus. officer, 1949-63; financial cons., dir. studies med. coll. financing Assn. Am. Med. Colls., Evanston, Ill., 1957-63, asst. dir. div. operational studies, dir. studies ednl. costs in hosps., 1963-68. Mgmt. and financial cons. to med. colls. and univs., hosps., USPHS, Nat. Insts. Health, Nat. Sci. Found., U.S. VA, Rockefeller Found., med. and dental assns., Canadian med. colls., health adv. bds. and mgmt. cons. firms, 1963-65. Mem. Nat. Assn. Ednl. Buyers, Eastern Assn. Coll. and U. Bus. Officers. Roman Catholic. Democrat. Author: A Study of Medical College Costs, 1958. Contbr. articles to profl. jours. Home: Evanston IL Died Apr. 10, 1968.

CARROLL, CAROLINE MONCURE BENEDICT (MRS. MITCHELL CARROLL), archaeologist; b. Belair Plantation, La.; d. Judge E. D. and Caroline (Moncure) Benedict; A.B., Wells Coll., 1891; studied in Europe, 1893-94, later studied archaeology at Athens, Rome, Sch. Am. Research (Santa Fe, N.M.), Am. Sch. Prehistoric Research, Western Europe 1925; Central European Research, 1926; m. Dr. Mitchell Carroll, Sept. 6, 1897 (died Mar. 3, 1925); children—Mitchell Benedict, Randolph, Fitzhugh, Charles Doyal. Lecturer in current history, Nat. Cathedral Sch. for Girls, 1909-10; lecturer in archaeology, Chautauqua Summer Sch., 1914-16; lecturer in archaeology, George Washington U., 1925-1932 (succeeding husband); mem. editorial staff and bd. dirs. Art and Archaeology (monthly mag.). Active worker in Liberty Loan Campaign. Non-resident. mem. Woman's Bd. of Santa Fe; recorder bd. of mgrs. Sch. of Am. Research and State Mus., Santa Fe. Hon. life mem. Archaeol. Soc. Washington (sec. dir. and trustee), Art and Archaeol. League (pres.), Internat. Soc. Woman Geographers (member exec. council, chmn. Washington group), Fondation Egyptologique, Brussels, Anthropol. Soc. Washington, Am. Assn. Univ. Women, Lit. Soc. Washington, English-Speaking Union, Italy America Soc., Am. Classical League, Columbian Women (ex-pres.), Phil Beta Kappa (mem. Washington assn.). Del. Internat. Congress Univ. Women, Paris, 1922, Congress French A.A.S., Liege, 1924; U.S. del. 21st Internat. Congress Americanists, The Hague and Goteborg, 1924, Congress of Fed. Archaeology and History, Bruges, 1925; del. Pan American Inst. Geography and History, 1935, Internat. Fedn. Univ. Women Conf., Cracow, Poland, 1936; U.S. del. Am. Scientific Congress, Washington, 1940. Episcopalian. Clubs: Washington (bd. govs.), Arts, Nat. Club Am. Assn. Univ. Women. Author: Story of Flora MacDonald, 1914; Historical Sketches of Kashmir, 1915. Contbr. to mags. Research work in Southern Europe, 1928-29, Eastern Europe, 1930, 31, Baltic lands, 1936, Mexico, 1937. Home: 2320 Twentieth St., N.W. Office: 315 Southern Bldg., Washington DC*‡

CARROLL, DUDLEY DEWITT, prof. economics; b. Mizpah, N.C., July 28, 1885; s. DeWitt Valentine and Sallie Ann (Lewis) C.; grad. Mountain View Inst., Mizpah, 1903; A.B., Guilford Coll., N.C., 1907; A.B., Haverford (Pa.) Coll., 1908; A.M., Columbia, 1916; m. Eleanore Dixon Elliott, June 27, 1918; children—Dudley DeWitt, Marshall Elliott, Eleanor Hillyard, Donald Cary. Principal of Mountain View Inst., 1908-09; instr. history and economics, Guilford Coll., 1909-14, dean, 1912-14; asst. prof. economics, Hunter Coll., New York, 1917-18; Kenan prof. economics Univ. of N.C., 1918-56, dean Sch. Bus. Adminstrn., 1919-50, dean emeritus, 1950-71, head department economics and commerce, 1920-46, Kenan traveling prof., 1924-25. Pres., dir. Orange County Bldg. & Loan Assn.; dir. Bank of Chapel Hill (now NCNB Corp.). Mem. corp., Haverford Coll. Mem. Am. Econ. Assn., Southern Econ. Chapel Hill NC Died Nov. 30, 1971; buried Chapel Hill NC

CARROLL, FRANCIS X., coal co. exec., b. N.Y.C.; m. Lucy Sullivan; children—Michael Francis, Francis X., Mary Colleen. Vice pres., later pres. Met. Petroleum Corp., Oradell, N.J.; adv. bd. South Roanoke br. First Nat. Exchange Bank; pres. dir. Virginia Iron, Coal & Coke Co. Former mem. Roanoke Airport Com.; chmn. Roanoke Valley Brotherhood Week; area chmn. Radio Free Europe; chmn. exec. com. Va. Port Authority. Bd. dirs. Roanoke Symphony Soc. Served with AUS, World War II. Recipient Nat. Brotherhood citation Nat. Conf. Christians and Jews. Mem. Roanoke Valley C. of C. (dir.). Roman Catholic. Address: Roanoke VA Died July 7, 1971; buried St. Andrew's Catholic Cemetery, Roanoke VA

CARROLL, HORACE BAILEY, editor, educator; b. nr. Gatesville, Tex., Apr. 29, 1903; s. J. Speed and Lena O. (Russell) C.; ed. So. Meth. U., summer 1920. McMurray Coll., 1924-25; A.B., Tex. Tech. Coll., 1928, M.A., 1928; Ph.D., Tex. U., 1935; m. Mary Joe Durning, June 3, 1935; 1 son, Joe Speed. Instr., Tex. Tech. Coll., 1928-29, asso. prof., 1929-30, 1931-32; instr., Tex. U., 1930-31, Tex. Wesleyan Coll., 1933-34; prof. Lamar Coll., 1934-35, Hillsboro Coll., 1935-36, West Tex. State Coll., 1936-37, Eastern N.M. Coll., 1937-38, N. Tex. Agrl. Coll., 1938-40, 1941-42; asso. prof. history U. Tex., 1942-46, prof., 1946-66, also dir. research in Tex. history taught summers, Texas U., W. Tex. State Coll., N. and E. Tex. State Tchrs. Coll., Tex. Coll. Mines and Metallurgy; asso. dir. Tex. State Hist. Assn., 1940-41, acting dir., 1942-46, dir., 1946-66; nat. chmn. Overland Mail Centennial Com.; hist. advisor Nat. Cowboy Hall of Fame; editor Southwestern Hist. Quar, Jr. Historian; regional editor Am. Heritage. Fellow Royal Geog. Soc.; mem. Panhandle-Plains Hist. Soc. (asso. editor Panhandle-Plains Hist. Rev.), Am., Miss. Valley hist. assns., Am. Assn. State and Local History (mem. publs. adv. bd., v.p.), Tex. Folklore Soc., Bibliog, Soc. Am., Hist. Soc. in U.S. and Can., Soc. Am. Historians, Phi Alpha Theta, Pi Gamma Mu, Alpha Chi. Fellow Tex. State Hist. Assn. Awarded Rockefeller Grant-in-Aid, 1942. Democrat. Episcopalian. Mason (32 deg., Shriner). Clubs: Headliners, Austin Rod and Gun. Edited Guadal P'a, 1941; Three New Mexico Chronicles (with J. V. Haggard), 1942; Texas County Histories; A Bibliography, 1943; The Texan Santa Fe Trail, 1951; Texas History Theses: A Check List (with Milton R. Gutsch), 1954: (with Frances Nesmith and Mary Jane Gentry) The Story of Texas, 1962. Mng. editor The Handbook of Texas, 1952. Pioneered Jr. Historian Clubs. Home: Austin TX Died May 12, 1966.

CARROLL, LEO G., actor; b. Weedon, Eng., 1892; m. Nancy De Silva, 1927; 1 son, William. First appeared in English prodn. Liberty Hall, 1908; Broadway appearances: The Vortex, 1925, Green Bay Tree, 1935, Two Bouquets, 1938, You Never Can Tell, 1948; Someone Waiting, 1956; role in Angel Street, 1941-44, Late George Apley, 1945-46; motion pictures include Wuthering Heights, 1939, Waterloo Bridge, Rebecca, 1940, Spellbound, House on 92d Street, 1945, Paradine Case, 1948, The Swan, 1956; also The Barretts of Wimpole Street, Forever Amber, Father of the Bride, Strangers on a Train, Snows of Kilmanjaro, We're No Angels, North by Northwest, Desert Fox, Bad and the Beautiful, Young Bess, The Parent Trap, others; played role of Cosmo Topper, television series, 1953; co-star Going My Way TV series, The Man from U.N.C.L.E., 1964-67. Home: Hollywood CA Died Oct. 1972.

CARROLL, LOUIS FRANCIS, lawyer; b. Davenport, Ia., May 31, 1905; s. Edward John and Lydia (Keller) C.; B.A., U. Ia., 1927; J.D., State U. Ia., 1929; m. Lina Katharine Sidney, July 18, 1930; children—Michael Edward, Sidney Ann (Mrs. David Peter Knapp), Mary Lydia, Terence John, Timothy Thomas. Admitted to N.Y. bar, 1930, since practiced in N.Y.C.; partner firm Willkie, Farr and Gallagher, New York City, and predecessors, 1941—. Mem. Am., N.Y. State bar assns., Assn. Bar City N.Y., N.Y. County Lawyers Assn., Am. Judicature Soc., Phi Beta Kappa, Order of Coif, Delta Sigma Rho, Delta Upsilon. Republican. Roman Cath. Clubs: Wall Street (N.Y.C.); St. Andrews Golf (Hastings-on-Hudson, N.Y.); Larchmont Yacht. Home: Larchmont NY Died Oct. 25, 1971; buried Gate of Heaven, Valhalla NY

CARROLL, MONROE SPURGEON, provost; born San Saba, Tex., Feb. 4, 1898; s. James William and Mary Catherine (Smythe) C.; A.B., Baylor, U., 1921; Harvard Univ. Gen. Edn. Board Fellow, 1946; A.M., Brown U., 1926; Ph.D., U. of Chicago, 1937; m. Eulalie Trice, Dec. 27, 1922; 1 son, Richard Alan. Employed in accounting office, Baylor U., 1921-22; assistant, later associate and professor Baylor Sch. of Business, 1926-37, chairman and prof. finance, indsl. mgmt., 1937-68, dean univ., 1948-55, provost, 1955-68; vis. prof. So. Ill. U., 1945. Pres. S.W. Area council YMCA, dir. Waco YMCA; mem. bd. Waco U.S.O.; mem. Merit System Council, State Tex.; exec. com. Tex. Personnel Conf. Del. White House Conf. on Edn. Served in USN, 1918-19. Mem. Tex. Personnel Mgmt. Assn. (state adv. com.), Southwestern Social Sci. Assn., American Assn. U. Teachers of Insurance, Pi Gamma Mu, Delta Sigma Pi, Beta Gamma Sigma. Democrat. Baptist. Mason, Rotarian (chairman international service committee Waco). Author: Budgetary Control and Accounting for Social Agencies. Contbr. profl. publs. Home: Waco TX Died Nov. 21, 1968; buried Oakwood Cemetery, Waco TX

CARROLL, PAUL VINCENT, dramatic author; b. Dundalk, Ireland, July 10, 1900; ed. Dublin and Glasgow; widower; 3 daus., 1 son. Tchr. math. and English, Scotland, 1921-37; dramatic author, 1937-68. Author: (plays prod. N.Y.C., London and Dublin) Things That are Caesar's (Abbey Theatre prize play 1930), 1931, Shadow and Substance (Case award Ireland 1936, N.Y.C. Critic's award 1937), 1937, The White Steed (N.Y.C. Critic's award 1938), 1938, The Old Foolishness, 1942, The Strings, My Lord, Are False, 1943, The Wise Have Not Spoken, 1944, The Wayward Saint, 1955, The Devil Came from Dublin, 1949; Irish Stories and Plays, 1958; (play) Farewell to Greatness, 1967. Roman Cath. Home: Kent England Died Oct. 20, 1968; buried Plaistow Lane Cemetery, Bromley Kent England

CARROLL, PHIL, cons. indsl. engr.; b. Bucyrus, O., June 20, 1895; s. Phil and Martha Ada (Couts) C.; B.S. in Elec. Engring., U. Mich., 1918, M.E., 1940; m. Margaret Birdsell, Mar. 20, 1920; children—Margaret Birdsell (Mrs. L. Terry Finch), Jeane Durrell (Mrs. Thomas G. Custin), Phil III, Patricia Anne (Mrs. Martin H. Buchler, III). Engaged in r.r. work, track constrn., automatic signals, summers 1911-17; with Westinghouse, East Pittsburgh, 1919, timestudy Krantz Mfg. Co. (Westinghouse), Bklyn., 1921-22, Westinghouse, Mansfield, O., 1922-23; with Hydraulic Pressed Steel Co., Cleve., 1923-24; a founder Dyer Engrs., Inc., Cleve., 1924, engr., chief engr., v.p. in charge operations, 1924-40; own bus. specializing in timestudy, wage incentive, cost control, 1940-71. Lectr., Newark Coll. Engring., Stevens Inst. Tech., univs. Pa., Mich., Wis., Conn., N.Y. Chmn., Maplewood (N.J.) Planning Bd., 1965-69; mem. indsl. engring. adv. com. U. Mich. Served with Signal Corps, adv. com. U. Mich. Served with Signal Corps, U.S. Army, 1918. Awarded Gilbreth medal in 1950, Indsl. Incentive award, 1953, Distinguished Alumnus, U. Mich., 1953. Fellow Am. Soc. M.E. (Gantt medal bd. 1949-53, chmn. mgmt. div. 1954, chmn. gen. engring. dept., mem. bd. tech. 1962-63), Internat. Acad. Mgmt. (Frank and Lillian Gilbreth award 1970), Am. Inst. Indsl. Engrs. (regional v.p. 1956), Gilbreth award 1970), Am. Inst. Indsl. Engrs. (regional v.p. 1956), Soc. for Advancement Mgmt. (Distinguished Service award N.J. chpt. 1958, nat. sec. 1947, nat. treas. 1948-49, nat. sec. 1947, nat. treas. 1948-49, v.p. membership 1955-57, 1st v.p. 1957, pres. 1958, chmn. bd. 1959; mem. Wallace Clark Bd. Award 1960-66, chmn. 1962); mem. N.J. Tech. Socs. Council (pres. 1951), U.S. Adv. Group on European Productivity, Am. Mgmt. Assn., Nat. Soc. Profl. Engrs., Acad. Mgmt. Republican. Methodist (ofcl. bd.). Mason. Author: Timestudy for Cost Control, 1938; Timestudy Fundamentals for Foremen, 1944; Discussion Leaders Manual, 1948; How to Chart Data, 1950; rev., 1960; How to Control Production Costs, 1952; How Foremen Can Control Costs, 1955; Better Wage Incentives, 1957; Cost Control Through Electronic Data Processing, 1958; Profit Control, 1962; Overhead Cost Control, 1964; Practical Production and Inventory Control, 1966. Contbr.: Foremen's Handbook, 1943, 66; Industrial Engineering Handbook, 1956; profl. jours., encys. in field. Editorial bd. Advanced Mgmt. and Supervision. Home: Maplewood NJ Died Oct. 23, 1971.

CARROON, FRANK, normal univ. pres.; b. Lafayette, Ind., Oct. 10, 1869; s. Andrew and Mary (Tully) C.; grad. Ind. State Normal Sch., Terre Haute, 1894; A.B., Ind. U., 1902; A.M., U. of Denver, 1913; grad. study Stanford, 1919; m. Elsie Scudder, of Edwardsport, Ind., Aug. 18, 1900; children—Dorothea (Mrs. Willis Barnes), Frank Scudder, Elsie Frances. Teacher in country schs. until 1894; prin. twp. grade schs., 1894-1902; head dept. English, Columbus (Ind.) High Sch., 1902-04; ward prin., Roswell, N.M., 1904-08; instr. in English, high sch., Roswell, 1908-09; prof. English and history, N.M. Normal U., East Las Vegas, N.M., 1909-10, prof. psychology and dean, 1910-23, pres., 1923-31, now dir. of extension and pub. relations. Pres. N.M. State Teachers Assn., 1926. Presbyn. Mason. Club: Rotary Internat. Home: 1015 Lincoln Av., Las Vegas NM‡

CARSE, ELIZABETH, educator; b.N.Y. City, 1875; d. John and Marian (Bisland) C.; A.B., Hunter Coll., N.Y. City, 1893; A.B., Cornell, 1895; A.M., Columbia, 1910; also Master's diploma from Teachers Coll.; studied Oxford and Cambridge, Eng. Instr., Teachers Coll. (Columbia), 1895-1903; prin. Charlton Sch., N.Y. City, 1903-12; prin. Northrop Collegiate Sch., Minneapolis, Minn., since 1915. Mem. N.E.A., Dept. of Superintendence, Minn. N.E.A., Nat. Assn. Principals Schs. for Girls, N. Central Assn. Schs. and Colleges, Am. Assn. Univ. Women, Alliance Francaise, Cornell Alumnae, Kappa Alpha Theta, Minn. Soc. Fine Arts, League of Women Voters. Presbyn. Clubs: Woman's, Symphony, Women's University (New York). Contbr. to ednl. mags. Home: 2418 Pillsbury Av. Address: 511 Kenwood Parkway, Minneapolis MN‡

CARSON, CLIFFORD, army officer; b. N. Greenfield, Ohio, Apr. 4, 1876; s. Leonard W. and Laura B. (Conn) C.; B.S., U.S. Mil. Acad., 1900; graduate, Gen. Staff Sch., 1922, Sch. of the Line, 1921, Cav. and F.A. Sch., 1904, Coast Arty. Sch., 1916; unmarried. Commd. 2nd lt., U.S. Army, 1900, and advanced through grades to col. (temp. arty.), 1918; prof. mil. sci. and tactics, Va. Poly. Inst., 1916-17, 1919-20; service in France as maj., lt. col., and col., 6th Art'y, as commander, Tractor Arty. Schs., AEF and with Inspector Gens. Dept., 1917-1919; ret. (own request), 1922; active duty, recruiting service, Knoxville and Chattanooga, Tenn., 1926-28. Recipient D.S.M., in France, 1919. Hon. Alumnus, Va. Poly Inst., 1920. Home: Mount Dora FL‡

CARSON, JAMES S., business exec.; b. Detroit, Mich., Dec. 9, 1874; s. George and Eleanor Carson; grad. Calif. State Normal Coll., San Jose, 1894; m. May Emerson, June 30, 1903; children—James Emerson, Mary Carter. Prin., Alviso (Calif.) Sch., 1894; chief Associated Press Bureau, Republic of Mexico, 1906-16; made S.A. survey trip for Asso. Press, 1916-17; asst. gen. mgr. and gen. sales mgr., Nat. Paper and Type Co., 1917-23; pub. relations rep. for Latin America, Electric Bond and Share Co., 1923-32; vice pres. in charge pub. relations American and Foreign Power Co. since 1932; director, American and Foreign Power Co., Inc.; director Colonial Trust Co., vice chairman board since January 3, 1949. Chmn. exec. com., dir. Av. of the Americas Assn., Inc.; dir. Mexican C. of C. in the U.S., Peruvian Am. Assn., Inc.; mem. bd. advisers Indsl. Coll. of the Armed Forces (Washington); mem. bd. overseers Sch. of Advanced Internat. Studies; chmn. adv. bd. United States Marketing Council, Incorporated. Decorated Order of Merit (Republic of Ecuador).

National councillor American Chamber of Commerce of Mexico; pres. and mem. bd. Argentine-Am. C. of C.; v.p. and mem. bd. Colombian-Am. C. of C., Ecuadorean-American Assn., Inc.; mem. foreign commerce dept. com. C. of C. of U.S.; v.p. and chmn. U.S. com. Inter-Am. Comml. Arbitration Commn.; mem. bd. and exec. com. Nat. Fgn. Trade Council (chmn. fgn. trade edn. com.); v.p. and mem. council Pan Am. Soc. of U.S., Inc.; mem. bd. Am. Arbitration Assn., Am. Asiatic Assn., Am.-Brazilian Assn., Bolivarian Soc. of U.S., Inc., Chile-Am. Assn., Cuban C. of C. in U.S., Inter-Am. Safety Council, Inc. Clubs: India House, Downtown Athletic (New York); National Press (Washington). Home: Knolltop, Closter Dock Rd., Closter, N.J. Office: 1230 Av. of the Americas at 48th St., NY City 20 NY‡

CARSON, JESSIE M(AY), librarian; b. Bellevue, Pa., Mar. 29, 1876; d. Thomas Craig and Sarah Reed (Longmore) C.; diploma Carnegie Library Sch., Pittsburgh, Pa., 1903; unmarried. Children's librarian, Carnegie Library, Pittsburgh, 1901-07; head of children's dept. Tacoma (Wash.) Pub. Library, 1907-14; asst. supervisor of work with children, New York Pub. Library, 1914-17; relief work with Am. Com. for Devastated France, 1917-20; dir. library work, same, June 1920-Apr. 1924. Mem. A.L.A., New York Library Assn., Assn. des Bibliothecaires Francaises. Club: Am. Women's (Paris). Home: Bronxville NY‡

CARSON, JOHN HARGADINE, gas co. exec.; b. Camden, N.J., Jan. 12, 1911; s. William H. and Matilda (Hollinger) C.; B.S., Mich. Coll. Mining and Tech., 1932; M.S., Case Inst. Tech., 1933; m. Mabel Stull, Nov. 25, 1939; children—Christine M. (Mrs. William J. Bruner). John Hargadine. With East Ohio Gas Co., Cleve., 1933-64, dir., 1949-64, v.p., 1950-56, v.p., gen. mgr., 1956-58, v.p. operations, 1958-64; sr. v.p., dir. Consol. Natural Gas Service Co., Inc., Pitts., 1964-72; dir. Consolidated Natural Gas Co. Registered profl. engr., Ohio. Mem. U.S.A. Standards Inst., Am. Gas Assn., Cleve. Engring. Soc., Newcomen Soc. N.Am., Pitts. C. of C. Home: Pittsburgh PA Died 1972.

CARSON, MATTHEW VAUGHAN, JR., corp. exec.; b. Cleburne, Tex., Nov. 12, 1910; s. Matthew Vaughan and Mary (Brady) C.; LL.B., U. Tex., 1934; m. Gwendolyn Strieber, Nov. 30, 1933; 1 son, Matthew Vaughan III. Admitted to Tex. bar, 1934, U.S. Supreme Ct. bar, 1949; practiced law, 1934-40; adminstrn. Oil Import Adminstrn., Washington, 1957-60; dir. Office Oil and Gas, Dept. of Interior, 1958-61; vice president of Sinclair Refining Co., Washington, 1961-65; corporate sec. Sinclair Oil Corp., N.Y.C., 1965-69; v.p. Sinclair Oil & Gas Co., Tulsa, 1966-69. Served with USNR, World War II; captain USN (ret.). Decorated Legion of Merit (U.S.); Medal Naval Merit (Spain). Recipient Distinguished Service medal from United States Department of Interior, 1961. Member Texas State Bar, Internat. Petroleum Assn. Home: Sea Island GA Died Oct. 26, 1971; buried Arlington Nat. Cemetery, Arlington VA

CARSON, WILLIAM PIERCE, ednl. adminstr.; b. Saluda, S.C., May 14, 1894; s. Thomas Coleman and Sallie (Padget) C.; B.A., Furman U., 1913; Ph.B., U. Chgo., M.A., 1916; Ph.D., Columbia, 1925; m. Dahlia Caudell, Sept. 1, 1917; 1 son, William Pierce. Prof. English, La. Coll., 1916-45; vis. scholar U. N.C., 1945-46; prof. English, Ark. Tech., 1947; dean instrn. Mary Hardin-Baylor Coll., 1947-50; dir. Sch. Arts and Scis., Memphis State Coll., 1951-60, tchr. Shakespeare, 1960-65; vis. prof. Union U., Jackson, Tenn., 1965-66. Served with 27th Div. AEF, World War I. Mem. Tenn. Edn. Assn., N.E.A. Democrat. Baptist (deacon). Clubs: Kiwanis (pres. 1945) (Pineville, La.); Rotary (pres. 1950) (Belton, Tex.). Home: Memphis TN Died Mar. 20, 1971; buried Memphis Meml. Park, Memphis TN

CARTER, ALBERT PAINE, lawyer; b. Newton, Mass., Dec. 13, 1873; s. Henry H. and Lydia A. (Paine) C.; A.B., Harvard, 1894, LL.B., 1897; m. Elizabeth C. Cheney, Nov. 7, 1899; children—Mrs. Elizabeth C. Miner, Mrs. Martha A. Hill. Admitted to Mass. bar, 1897, and since practiced at Boston; pres. John Carter & Co., Inc.; dir. Samson Cordage Works; trustee of Franklin Savings Bank, City of Boston. Dir. Stone Inst., and Newton Home for Aged People, Newton Upper Falls, Mass. Mem. Am. and Mass. bar assns., Bar Assn. City of Boston. Republican. Swedenborgian. Clubs: Harvard, Algonquin, Brae Burn Country. Home: 104 Highland Av., Newtonville, Mass. Office: 25 Pemberton Sq., Boston MA

CARTER, GEORGE CALVIN, state manager Dun & Bradstreet, Incorporated; b. Boston, Massachusetts, Jan. 28, 1876; s. John V. and Josephine S. (Rowe) C.; ed. public and high schools, Brockton, Massachusetts; m. Kate E. Batchelder, Aug. 19, 1902; children—Theodore Batchelder, Robert Eugene, James Burnham, Dorothy Withington. With Dun & Bradstreet, Inc., since May 1, 1893. Secretary and treasurer, New Hampshire Manufacturers Association, 1922-33; pres. Manchester C. of C., 1932-34; Mem. N.H. Hist. Soc., Am. Assn. Indiologists (pres.), Manchester Hist. Assn., Manchester Hist. Group (pres.). Rep. Bapt. (pres. Merrimack St. Bapt. Soc.) Mason (32 deg.). Kiwanian. Club: Executives. Writer and lecturer on colonial and Indian history. Author: Captain Samuel Morey; The Edison of His Day; Walter Kittredge, Minstrel of the Merrimacks. Industrial New Hampshire; over 100 spl. articles on New Hampshire. Address: 22 Hazel St., Manchester NH‡

CARTER, HODDING, editor, pub., author; b. Hammond, La., Feb. 3, 1907; s. William Hodding and Irma (Dutartre) C.; B.A., Bowdoin Coll., 1927; student journalism, Columbia, 1927-28, Tulane University, 1928-29, Harvard, 1939; M.A. (honorary) Harvard, 1947; Litt.D. (honorary), Bowdoin College, 1947; L.H.D. (hon.), Washington U., 1954, Protestant Episcopal Theological Seminary, 1965; H.H.D., Coe Coll.; 1958; LL.D., Allegheny Coll.; married Betty Werlein, October 14, 1931; children—William Hodding III, Philip Dutartre. Teaching fellow at Tulane University, 1928-29; reporter New Orleans Item-Tribune, 1929; night bureau mgr., United Press, New Orleans, 1930; mgr. Asso. Press Bureau, Jackson, Miss., 1931-32; started Daily Courier, Hammond, La., editor, pub., 1932-36; started Delta Star, Greenville, Miss., editor, pub., 1936-38; editor, pub. Delta Democrat-Times, Greenville, Miss., from 1939; newspaper editor PM, 1939; civilian aide to sec. of army, 1952-60; writer in residence Tulane University, 1962-68. Trustee of George Peabody Coll. for Tchrs., 1952-65; mem. bd. of overseers Bowdoin College; member National Citizens Council Better Schs.; board visitors Tulane U., 1953-62; mem. Pulitzer Prize Adv. Bd., 1951-61. Joined Nat. Guard, 1938; pub. Dixie, 31st div. paper, Camp Blanding, Fla., 1940; Army Bur. of Pub. Relations, Washington, D.C., 1940-41; editor: Stars and Stripes, Yank, Middle East edits., Cairo, Egypt; ret. as maj., 1945; awarded War Dept. citation, 1946. Received Nieman fellowship for newspapermen, Harvard, 1939, Guggenheim fellowship, 1945, Pulitzer prize 1946, Southern Literary Award, 1945; fellow Sigma Delta Chi, 1954; William A. White Foundation national citation of journalistic merit, 1961; recipient Bowdoin Prize, 1963; First Fed. award, 1968; Journalism Alumni award Columbia U., 1971. Mem. American Society Newspaper Editors. Author: Civilian Defense of the United States (with Col. R. Ernest Dupuy), Lower Mississippi, 1942; The Winds of Fear, 1945; Flood Crest, 1947; John Law Wasn't So Wrong, 1949; Southern Legacy, 1950; Gulf Coast Country (with Anthony Ragusin), 1951; Where Main Street Meets the River, 1953, Robert E. Lee and The Road of Honor, 1954, Marquis De Lafayette, Bright Sword for Freedom, 1958; The Angry Scar, 1959, So Great a Good, 1955; Doomed Road of Empire, 1962; First Person Rural, 1963; The Ballad of Catfood Grimes and Other Verse, 1964; So the Heffners Left McComb, 1965; The Commandos of World War II, 1966; Their Words Were Bullets, 1969; Man and the River: the Mississippi, 1970. Contbr. to mags. Home: Greenville MS Died Apr. 4, 1972; buried Greenville Cemetery, Greenville MS

CARTER, JAMES FRANCIS, naval officer; b. St. Clair, Pa., Mar. 25, 1869; grad. U.S. Naval Acad., 1891. Ensign, July 1, 1893; lt. jr. grade, Mar. 3, 1899; lt., May 26, 1900; lt. comdr., June 3, 1906; comdr., July 1, 1911; capt., July 1, 1917. Served on Mayflower, Spanish-Am. War, 1898; in charge 12th Lighthouse Dist., 1906-8; navigator Georgia, 1908-11; supervisor New York Harbor, 1912; duty at Navy Yard, N.Y., 1912-14; comd. Castine, 1914-16; Navy Yard, Phila., 1916; apptd. comdr. Alabama June 9, 1916. Home: Pottsville PA‡

CARTER, WILBERT JAMES, business exec.; b. Wallace, N.C., Oct. 24, 1902; s. Newton Hill and Lutie (Boney) C.; B.S., N.C. State Coll., U. of N.C., 1923; Dr. Textile Sci., 1943; m. Christine Brooks, Jan. 16, 1927 (died Jan. 18, 1949); children—Nancy Christine (Mrs. Ralph Hoyt), Dorothy (Mrs. Francis E. Price), Wilbert James; m. 2d Jane Schlendorf Bradley, Nov. 25, 1950; m. 3d, Brent Woodson Holderness, 1966; stepchildren—Charles, Brent, Hayes, Thomas. With Erlanger Cotton Mills, Lexington, N.C., 1924-25; asst. supt. and asst. to Col. Eugene Holt, Lawrence S. Holt & Sons, Burlington, N.C., 1925-27, became partner, treas. and mgr. N.C. Silk Mills, 1927; vice pres. in units of Burlington Mills Corp. until 1936; exec. v.p. S. Slater & Sons, Inc., Slater, S.C., also v.p. and treas. Cleveland Cloth Mills of Shelby, N.C., 1936-37; formed Carter Fabrics Corp., 1937, becoming pres. and treas.; the companies headed by him became divs. and subsidiaries of J. P. Stevens & Co., Inc., 1946; v.p. J. P. Stevens & Co., Inc., 1946-50, exec. v.p., then chmn.; president Carter Operating Group. Pres. (an organizer) N.C. Textile Found., Inc. Mem N.Y. So. Soc., Sigma Phi Epsilon. Presbyterian. Clubs: Rotary, Greensboro Country (Greensboro); Everglades, Bath and Tennis (Palm Beach, Fla.). University (N.Y.). Home: Greensboro NC Died July 13, 1972.

CARTER, WILLIAM CURTIS, business executive; b. Homer, Ill., Oct. 10, 1881; s. James Franklin and Emily Amanda (Melcer) C.; B.S., U. of Ill., 1902; m. Maye Corbin, June 10, 1911; children—Marian Elizabeth (Mrs. Francis Kenneth Ratcliff), William Gilbert. With Link-Belt Co. 1902-48, successively, draftsman, engring. dept. supervisor, constrn. supt., plant supt., plant gen. mgr., v.p. in charge of production, executive vice pres., pres. 1942-46, chmn. executive committee, 1946-48. Mason. Club: South Shore Country (Chicago, Ill.). Home: Castle Park MI Died Mar. 16, 1970; buried Holland MI

CARTER, WILLIAM V., army officer; b. Fort Lowell, Ariz., Jan. 30, 1883; s. Maj. Gen. William Giles Harding and Ida (Dawley) C.; B.S., U.S. Mil. Acad., 1904; m. Helen C. Hunter, Aug. 14, 1907 (now dec.); 1 son, William H. (dec.); m. 2d, Margaret B. Woodbury, Jan. 5, 1921; children—Woodbury, Leigh, David Giles. Commd. 2d lt., U.S. Army, 1904, and advanced through the grades to brig. gen., 1940; began service in the cavalry; transferred to Adj. Gen. Dept., 1922; later in charge personnel bureau; retired, Aug. 31, 1942. Awarded Victory medal, World War. Club: Army and Navy Country (Washington, D.C.). Home: Westerly RI Died Jan. 1971.

CARTY, ROLAND KENNETH, corp. exec.; b. Midland, Ont., Can., Jan. 5, 1919; s. Roland Dennis and Kenina (Morrison) C.; B.Com., Queen's U., 1941; m. Catherine Elizabeth Matheson, Sept. 26, 1942;children—Roland Kenneth, Donald John, Robert Matheson, William George, Douglas Alan, Carolyn Elizabeth. With Canadian Gen. Electric Co., 1941-42, 46-48, 52-55, dist. mgr., Toronto, Ont., 1952-55; sec.-treas. Canadian Allis Chalmers, Montreal, Que., 1949-51; with Canron, Ltd., Montreal, 1955-72, v.p. finance, 1962-65, exec. v.p. finance, 1965-72. Bd. dirs. Que. div. Canadian Nat. Inst. Blind. Served to flight lt. RCAF, 1942-45. Mem. United Ch. Can. Clubs: Canadian, University St. James's (Montreal). Home: Mount Royal Quebec Canada Died Mar. 15, 1972; interred Georgeville Quebec Canada

CARY, HARRY FRANCIS, gen. passenger agt.; b. Augusta, Ga., Nov. 28, 1874; s. Silas Jennings and Annie LaFitte (Parker) C.; ed. Houghton Inst. and Central Grammar Sch., Augusta; m. Catherine Cornell, of Macon, Ga., Nov. 8, 1900. Cashier for Austin Mullarkey, mcht., Augusta, 1886-88; clk., later stenographer, Augusta br. Bradley Fertilizer Co., 1889-95; stenographer, Internat. Expn., Atlanta, Apr.-Oct. 1895; with Southern Ry. Co. since 1895, traveling passenger agt., Atlanta, May-Dec. 1898, Macon, Ga., 1898-1901, Fla. passenger agt., 1901-02, dist. passenger agt., 1902-04, chief clk., Gen. Passenger Dept., Washington, D.C., 1904-06, asst. gen. passenger agt., Washington, 1906-09, gen. passenger agt., Washington, 1909-26, Cincinnati, O., since 1926. Mason (32 deg., Shriner). Methodist. Home: 2415 Maplewood Av., Mt. Auburn, Cincinnati, O. Office: Southern Railway Bldg., Cincinnati OH‡

CARY, LUCIAN, writer; b. Hamlin, Kan., Jan. 1, 1886; s. Charles Preston and Myra Treat (Pugsley) C.; student U. of Wis., 1902-06 except 1yr. Beloit (Wis.) Coll., 1905, U. of Chicago, 1907-08; m. Augusta Stromme, 1906; children—Lucian, Peter, Michael. Instr. English, Wabash Coll., Crawfordsville, Ind., 1908-10; reporter Chicago Tribune, 1910-12; lit. editor Chicago Evening Post, 1913-14; acting editor The Dial, Chicago, 1914; with Collier's Weekly, 1916-17; staff corr., 1918-19. Author: (novels) The Duke Steps Out; One Lovely Moron; The Duke Comes Back; The Little Champion; Second Meeting. Contbr. to mags. Home: Colebrook CT Died Sept. 1971.*

CASADAY, L(AUREN) W(ILDE), economist, educator; b. Santa Cruz Co., Cal., July 3, 1905; s. Charles H. and Susie (Proctor) C.; A.B., U. Cal. at Los Angeles, 1927; Ph.D., U. Cal. at Berkeley, 1937; m. Ruth Marian Peiffer, June 28, 1929; children—Claire Helen (Mrs. Wagner), Carol Sue (Mrs. William T. Baker). Teaching fellow econs. U. Cal., 1928-31; prof. econs. U. Santa Clara (Cal.), 1932-37; acting statistician Office of Cal. State Labor Commr., San Francisco, 1934; asso. economist Cal. Emergency Relief Administrn., 1934-35; vis. lectr. econs. U. Hawaii, 1937-38; economist U.S. Maritime Labor Bd., Washington, 1938-41; sr., prin., chief econ. analyst Office of Internat. Finance, Treasury Dept., 1941-49, during which time served as chief Brit. Empire sect., Washington 1944-45, U.S. Treasury attache, spl. asst. to ambassador to Ct. of St. James, U.S. Embassy, London, Eng., 1941-44; asst. U.S. Treasury attache U.S. Embassy, Chungking, China, Aug.-Oct. 1945; financial adv., chief financial adv. to comdg. gen. U.S. Armed Forces and Mil. Govt., Seoul, Korea, Nov. 1945-May 46; asst., acting and U.S. Treasury attache U.S. Embassy, Nanking, China, and U.S. Consulate-Gen., Shanghai, 1946-49; dir. bur. bus. and pub. research, prof. econs. U. Ariz. 1949-69. Mem. Tucson Airport Authority, 1954-69; mem. Pima County (Ariz.) Planning and Zoning Commn.; state-wide adv. bd. and dollar development com. Greater Ariz., Inc., Phoenix, central planning com. for community development Pima Co. Council Social Agencies, Tucson since 1950; chmn. research adv. com. Pima Co. and City of Tucson planning depts., mem. Statewide Com. to Foster Bus.-Industry-Educators Cooperation, So. Ariz. Steering Com. 1951-69. Mem. tech. secretariat International Monetary Conf., Bretton Woods, N.H., July 1944; mem. Joint Commn. Econ. and Financial Problems, Joint Conf. between U.S. Occupation Authorities, South Korea and U.S.S.R. Occupation

Authorities, North Korea, held in Seoul, Mar.-Apr. 1946; U.S. rep. U.S. Treasury Spl. Mission to Siam, Feb.-Mar. 1946; econ. adv. to U.S. del. to Shanghai Conf. U.N., Econ. Commn. for Asia and Far East, Shanghai, June-July 1947. Recipient distinguished service award for achievement in econ., govt., and outstanding pub. service, Chapman Coll., Chapman Coll. Alumni Assn., 1953. Mem. Tucson C. of C., American Econs. Assn., Western Govtl. Research Assn., Am. Soc. Pub. Adminstrn., Phi Kappa Phi, Beta Gamma Sigma, Alpha Kappa Psi, Phi Gamma Delta. Author articles, govt. bulls. and reports. Home: Tucson AZ Died Mar. 27, 1969.

CASADESUS, ROBERT, concert pianist, composer; b. Paris, France, Apr. 7, 1899; studied harmony and piano, Paris Conservatory; m. Gaby Lhote; children—John (dec.), Guy, Therese. Soloist with orchestras and recitalist throughout Europe and North Africa, Mexico, S.Am., Palestine, Japan, and in about 2000 concerts, throughout U.S. First concert in U.S. with N.Y. Philharmonic Symphony Orch., Arturo Toscanini, conductor, 1935; gen. dir. Am. Conservatory of Fountainbleau, France, 1948-72. Awarded first prize, piano, Paris Conservatory, 1913, first prize, harmony, 1919; Diemer prize, 1921; Comdr. Order of Leopold (Belgium); comdr. of Legion of Honor (France); comdr. Order Orange-Nassau (Netherlands); gold medal World's Fair, Paris, 1937; Brahms medal, Hamburg, Germany, 1958. Composer numerous concertos, quartettes, trios, sonatas and pieces for piano; 7 symphonies; Paris France Died Sept. 19, 1972.

CASE, ALBERT HERMON, mining engr.; b. Cambridge, Lenawee County, Mich., June 1, 1875; s. Marion and Mary Stirling (Ladd) C.; B.S. in Mech. Engring., Michigan State College, 1902, D.Eng., 1945; Co-University, 1905; D.Sc. (honorary), Tampa University, 1950; married Sarah B. S. Avery, August 14, 1906. Superintendent of Cliff Mine, Ophir, Utah, 1906-07, with various Lewisohn interests since 1907, as superintendent Santa Fe Gold & Copper Mining Co., general manager Tennessee Copper Co., S. A. Gold & Platinum Co.; v.p., dir. Tampa Southern Ry. Co., numerous mine examinations in U.S., Can., Alaska, Colombia and Panama. Trustee Tampa Univ. Dir. Lyons Fertilizer Co., Medal for Achievement, Col. University, 1947. Mem. Am. Inst. Mining and Metall. Engrs., S.A.R., Alpha Tau Omega, Tau Beta Pi, Sigma Xi. Democrat. Episcopalian. Mason (32 deg.). Club: Rotary (Tampa). Home: 1314 Rugby Rd., Charlottesville VA

CASE, ERMINE COWLES, paleontologist; b. Kansas City, Mo., Sept. 11, 1871; s. Theodore Spencer and Julia (Lykins) C.; A.B., A.M., U. of Kan., 1893; M.S., Cornell U., 1894; Ph.D., U. of Chicago, 1895, m. Mary Margaret Snow, of Lawrence, Kan., June 24, 1899; children—Francis Huntington, Theodore Johnston. Instr. chemistry, U. of Kan., 1893-94; instr. paleontology, U. of Chicago, 1895; prof. geology and phys. geography, State Normal Sch., Milwaukee, Wis., 1897-1906; asst. prof. hist. geology and paleontology, 1906-08; jr. prof., Sept. 25, 1908-12, prof., 1912-—, U. of Mich. Research asso. Carnegie Instn. of Washington. Fellow A.A.A.S., Geol. Soc. America, Paleontol. Soc.; mem. Washington Acad. Science, Am. Soc. Mammalogists, Am. Soc. Naturalists, Paleontolog. Gesellsch., Mich. Acad. Science, Sigma Xi, Phi Delta Theta. Author: Geology and Physical Geography of Wisconsin. Contbr. numerous papers and 9 monographs, mostly on vertebrate paleontology. Home: Ann Arbor MI‡

CASE, FRANCIS OWEN, mining exec.; b. Chattanooga, Tenn., Dec. 9, 1894; s. Frank Luther and Minnie Lee (Magee) C.; student Cornell, Mass. Inst. Tech., Northwestern U.; m. Winifred Alice Williams, Nov. 12, 1925; 1 son, Robert O. Chem. engr. Cornell, 1912-16; with N.J. Zinc Co., 1916-17, 1919-21, Depew, Ill., 1922-42; mgr. Midwest dist. Anaconda Copper Mining Co., Chicago, 1921-72; gen. mgr. Basic Magnesium, Inc., Los Vegas, Neb., 1942-45; asst. to pres. Anaconda Copper Mining Co., N.Y. City, 1945-48, vice-pres., 1948; v.p., dir. Anaconda Wire & Cable Co. 1947-72; pres., dir. Anaconda Aluminum Co., 1952-72; president Glen Alden Corp., Feb. 1953-72; dir. American Brass Company, Delaware Laackawanna Coal Company. Appointed member lead pigment mfg. industry, com. W.P.B., 1941; mem. Selective Service Bd., Chicago, 1941-42; consultant Def. Minerals Adminstrn., Bur. Mines, Interior Dept. Washington. Res. mil. aviator U.S. Signal Corps., 1917-19. Mem. Am. Chem. Soc., Am. Inst. Chemists, Inc., Anthracite Inst. (dir.), Loyal Legion, Am. Legion, Alpha Chi Sigma. Republican. Conglist. Clubs: Cornell (Chgo., & N.Y.), Metropolitan (Washington). Author tech. articles in profl. mags. Home: Wilkes Barre PA Died Feb. 1972.

CASE, HAROLD CLAUDE, clergyman, coll. pres.; b. Cottonwood Falls, Kan., May 20, 1902; s. Harry Claude and Rose (Kiger) C.; B.A., Baker U., 1923, D.D. (honorary), 1934; Doctor of Divinity (honorary), Pacific School Religion, 1951; S.T.B., Boston U., 1927; grad. study Harvard, 1923-24, Garrett Theol. Sem., 1927-33; Litt.D., Huston-Tillotson Coll., 1944; Sc.D., R.I. Coll. Pharmacy and Allied Scis., 1953; LL.D., W.Va. Wesleyan College, 1954, Northeastern University, 1954, Tufts University, 1955, Temple University, Brandeis University, Pratt Inst., 1961, Pasadena Coll., 1964; Ed.D., Franklin Pierce Coll., 1966; m. Phyllis Elizabeth Kirk, June 27, 1927; children—Harold Robert, Phyllis Rosanna (Mrs. Victor Kazanjian), David (dec.). Ordained to ministry Meth. Ch.; instr. Southwestern Coll., 1927-28; pastor N. Shore Ch., Glencoe, Ill., 1928-33, First Meth. Ch., Topeka, 1933-38, Elm Park Ch., Scranton, Pa., 1938-45, First Meth. Ch., Pasadena, Cal., 1945-51; pres. Boston U., 1951-67, pres. emeritus, 1967-72. Dir. Sterling Drug Inc.; dirs. adv. bd. State Street Bank & Trust Co. Mem. Univ. Senate, Meth. Ch. Co-founder Religion in Higher Edn. Found., 1946. Trustee N.E. Deaconess Hosp.; chmn. bd. Council on Religion and Internat. Affairs, bd. dirs. Glochet Mountain Rehab. Center, 1967-72. Hon. dir. Alexander Graham Bell Assn. for Deaf, Inc. Mem. Am. Acad. Arts and Scis., Phi Beta Kappa, Delta Tau Delta, Pi Kappa Delta, Beta Gamma Sigma, Pi Gamma Mu. Mason. Clubs: Algonquin, University (Boston). Author: A Year of Special Parties, 1927; The Prophet Jeremiah, 1953. Home: Annisquam MA Died Feb. 20, 1972; buried Mt. Adnah, Annisquam MA

CASE, J(AMES) HERBERT, banker; b. Elizabeth, N.J., Aug. 20, 1872; s. Samuel Pyatt and Susan (Thorn) C.; educated Lansley (Elizabeth) School; LL.D., Elmira College, 1931, Colgate Univ., 1942; married Alice Needham, Sept. 28, 1898; children—Everett Needham, James H. (dec.), Elizabeth Parker (Mrs. Hamilton Robinson) (dec.). Successively sec. and vice pres. Plainfield Trust Co., 1902-17; v.p. Farmers Loan & Trust Co., N.Y. City, 1912-17; dep. gov. Federal Reserve Bank, N.Y. City, 1917-1930, chmn. bd., 1930-36; partner R. W. Pressprich & Co., N.Y. City, 1936-40; cons. to pres. City Bank Farmers Trust Co., 1941-54; dir. City Bank Farmers Trust Co., Lehman Corp. of N.Y., Witherbee Sherman Corp., until 1957. American mem. of Netherlands Purchasing Commn., 1940-42. Trustee, chmn. finance com., Ministers and Missionaries Benefit Bd. of Northern Baptist Conv., 1922-47, financial cons., from 1947. Director of National War Fund, 1942-46. Pres., Assn. Community Chests Am., 1930-33, treas., 1936-46; trustee and chmn. com. on finance and investment, Elmira Coll., 1929-31; mem. Sch. Bd., Pub. Library and Sinking Fund Commn. of City of Plainfield. Decorated Medal of Merit, Comdrs. Cross with Stars, Order of Polonia Restituta, 1924. Republican. Baptist. Clubs: Union League (bd. govs.), Downtown Assn. (N.Y. City). Author: Desirability of Commercial Paper as Banking Investment: Report to U.S. Treasury on British Short-term Financing. Home: Plainfield NJ Died Aug. 4, 1972.

CASE, LORENZO DOW, clergyman; b. at Watertown, N.Y., Jan. 25, 1872; s. Edward E. and Lorain (Weese) C.; St. Lawrence U., Canton, N.Y., 1900; grad. Canton Theol. Sch., 1906; (D.D., Lombard Coll., Galesburg, Ill., 1907); m. Inez Ladd, of Victor, N.Y., Oct. 26, 1897. Ordained Universalist ministry, 1896; pastor, Rome, N.Y., 1895-1900, Albany, 1900-6, St. Paul's Ch., Chicago, since 1906. Trustee Lombard Coll. Progressive. Mem. Beta Theta Pi, Phi Beta Kappa. Club: University. Address: 3006 Prairie Av., Chicago‡

CASE, MAURICE, educator; b. Rheims, France, July 4, 1910; s. Zevall and Dina (Zilbone) S.; B.S., Coll. City N.Y., 1932; postgrad. N.Y. Sch. Social Work, 1933-35; M.A., N.Y.U., 1955, Ed.D., 1963; m. Phyllis Eleanor Shapiro, Jan. 18, 1936; children—Stephen Michael (killed in action), Robert Ian. Supr., adminstr. N.Y.C. Dept. Welfare, 1932-42; sr. social worker N.Y. State Dept. Social Welfare, 1942-45; mgr. recreation Camping Services N.Y. Assn. F/T Blind, 1945-65; lectr., asst. prof. City Univ. N.Y., 1965-66; prof., chmn. dept. State U. N.Y., 1966-67, prof. sociology, chmn. div. gen. edn., 1967-68. Bd. dirs. N.Y.C. Assn. Sr. Centers. Mem. Acad. Certified Social Workers, Am. Recreation Soc., Am. Assn. U. Profs., Am. Assn. Social Workers, Phi Delta Kappa (honor service key). Author: Recreation For Blind Adults, 1965. Home: New York City NY Died May 2, 1968.

CASE, RALPH E., indsl. engr.; b. Rowayton, Conn., Apr. 25, 1887; s. Elmer E. and Katie E. (Petty) C.; E.E., Rensselaer Poly. Inst., 1912; m. Mildred Fleming, June 30, 1917; children—Carolyn F. (Mrs. Renwick Tweedy), Renwick E. Engr. Crooker Wheeler & Co., Ampere, N.J., 1912-14; engr. R.U.V. Co., Norwalk, Conn., 1914-17; engr. Spicer Mfg. Co., South Plainfield, N.J., 1919-23; partner Stevenson, Jordan & Harrison, 1923-62; chmn. bd. Case & Co., N.Y.C., 1962-69; dir. Glen Alden Corp., Ivan Sorvell, Inc., Flexible Tubing Corp.; corporator of South Norwalk Savs. Bank; adv. bd. City Trust Co. Served as ensign USNRF, 1918-19. Mem. National Assn. Cost Accountants. Clubs: N.Y. Yacht, Cruising of America (N.Y.C.); Norwalk Yacht, Off Soundings, Essex Yacht. Home: Durham CT Died Feb. 1969.

CASESA, PHILIP ROBERT, physician, hosp. adminstr.; b. Argrigento, Sicily, Italy, June 6, 1909; s. Gerlando and Marie (Florio) C.; came to U.S., 1910, naturalized, 1920 student L.I.U., 1927-29, Tufts Coll., 1929-30; M.D., Boston U., 1934; m. Rose Giammaivo, Dec. 11, 1938; children—Marie, James. Rotating intern St. Elizabeth's Hosp., Boston, 1934-35; gen. practice medicine, Bklyn., 1935-42; med. officer VA Facility, Waco, Tex., 1942-44, VA Hosp., Columbia, S.C., 1944; med. officer, chief outpatient services VA Hosp., Bronx, N.Y., 1946-47; asst. chief med. officer, chief med. officer VA Outpatient Clinic, VA Regional Office, Bklyn., 1947-56; mgr. VA Outpatient Clinic, Bklyn, 1956-60; dir. VA Hosp., Bklyn. 1960-73; chief med. con. bur, disability determinations N.Y. State Dept. Social Services; adj. prof. biology, cons. in med. tech. C.W. Post Coll., Greenvale, N.Y. Mem. subcomm. gen. community relations Fed. Exec. Bd., 1965; pres. Better Bklyn. Com., Bklyn. Hall of Fame. Served to maj., M.C., AUS, 1944-46. Recipient award for dedicated med. service to vets. Italian Hist. Soc. Am., 1961. Fellow Am. Coll. Chest Physicians, Am. Coll. Hosp. Adminstrs.; mem. A.M.A., N.Y. State, Kings County (hosp. and profl. relations com.) med. socs., Am., N.Y. State, Bklyn. socs. internal medicine, Am. Legion. Address: Brooklyn NY Died Mar. 18, 1973.

CASEY, DANIEL VINCENT, journalist; b. Crawfordsville, Ind., March 14, 1874; grad. Univ. Notre Dame, 1895; instr. English composition, Univ. Notre Dame, 1895-6; subsequently entered journalism and held various positions as reporter and corr.; sp'l corr. in the field during Spanish-Am. war for Chicago Record. Residence: Crawfordsville IN‡

CASHIN, JOHN MARTIN, judge; b. Kingston, N.Y., Aug. 31, 1892; s. Martin J. and Catherine (Kelliher) C.; LL.B., Cornell U., 1915; m. Carolyn Markle, Dec. 9, 1928. Admitted to N.Y. bar, 1916; city treas., Kingston, 1922; asst. U.S. atty., 1922-25; counsel Fed. Prohibition Adminstrn., N.Y.C., 1925-26; corp. counsel, City of Kingston, 1935-41; county judge Ulster County, N.Y., 1943-55; U.S. judge Southern Dist. of N.Y., 1955-65. Mem. N.Y. State, Ulster Co. bar assns., Phi Delta Phi. Home: Kingston NY Died Oct. 21, 1970.

CASHMAN, EDWIN JAMES, corp. exec.; b. Owatonna, Minn., Oct. 26, 1904; s. Thomas Edward and Margaret (Laughlin) C.; student Georgetown U., 1922-24, U. Minn., 1925-27; m. Mary McNally, Sept. 27, 1930 (dec. 1961); children—Marilyn (Mrs. Gabriel Nahas), Edwin, Tyrone, Kathleen, Victoria; m. 2d, Lorraine Dale, Apr. 30, 1963. Sales exec. George A. Hormel & Co., Austin, Minn., 1928-35; pres. Doughboy Industries, Inc., New Richmond, Wis., 1936-66, chmn. 1966-67; chmn. Combustion Products Corp., 1965-70, Energy Transmission Corp., 1965-70; vice president, director Cashman Nurseries, Owatonna, Minn., 1940-70, Midwest Radio & TV, Inc., Mpls., 1952-70; dir. Mid Continent Broadcasting, Minn. Tribune Co.; former treas., dir. Minn. Wis. Dairy Queen, Inc. Mem. exec. com. St. Paul region Boy Scouts Am. Mem. Chi Psi. Home: Deming NM Died Mar. 16, 1970.

CASSADY, JOHN HOWARD, naval officer; b. Spencer, Ind., Apr. 3, 1896; s. William Franklin and Samantha (Haxton) C.; ed. Spencer (Ind.) High Sch., and Army and Navy Prep. Sch., Annapolis, Md.; grad. U.S. Naval Acad., 1918; m. Sallie Dold, Feb. 3, 1925; children—John Howard, William Francis. Commd. ensign, U.S. Navy, 1918, and advanced through the grades to rear adm., 1943; served in U.S. ships Cassin, Olympia, Wilkes, Truxton, McCormack, Colorado, Aroostook, Saratoga, Ranger, Virginia, Yorktown and Wasp; designated naval aviator, 1927; asst. naval attache and naval attache for air, Am. Embassy, Rome, Italy, 1937-39; operations officer on staff of commander aircraft, Atlantic Fleet, 1940-41; chief of staff of to commander of operational training command, Jacksonville, Fla., 1941-42; dir. aviation training div. Bureau of Aeronautics, Navy Dept., Mar.-Aug. 1943; comdg. officer, U.S.S. Saratoga, 1943-44; asst. dep. chief of naval operations (air) Navy Dept., Washington, D.C., 1944-45; comdr. carrier div. Atlantic Fleet, 1945-47; assistant chief of naval operations for air, 1947-49; comdr., air fleet, Jacksonville, Fla., from 1949. Decorated Legion of Merit with gold star, Victory Medal World War I with destroyer clasp, Am. Defense Service Medal with fleet clasp, Am. Area Campaign Medal, Asiatic-Pacific Area Campaign Medal with 4 stars, Victory Medal World War II (U.S.), Order British Empire, Comdr. of Bath (Gt. Britain), Order of the Phoenix (Greece). Home: Boca Raton FL Died Jan. 30, 1969.*

CASSADY, MORLEY FRANKLIN, journalist; b. Shelby, Ia., Oct. 23, 1900; s. George Alvin and Albertha (Dixon) C.; student U. of Neb., 1918-20; U. of N.M., 1920-22; A.B., U. of Denver, 1923; m. Phyllis Hunter, Feb. 25, 1926. Reporter and editorial writer on various newspapers in N.M. and Ariz., 1920-23, on Rocky Mountain News, Denver, 1923-24, Omaha Bee, 1925-26, New Orleans Item, 1926-30; feature editor for Associated Press, N.Y. City, 1930-33; associate editor The American Progress, New Orleans, 1933-36; free lance writing, 1936-39; feature writer, The Bulletin, Phila., 1939-47; European corr., Paris, 1947-55, editorial writer, 1955-58, assistant editor Evening and Sunday Bulletin, 1958-61, editor editorial page, 1961-65; free-lance magazine, newspaper writing, 1965-68; correspondent Evening Bulletin and North

American Newspaper Alliance in Europe and the Aleutians (16 mos.) 1943-45. Received Nat. Headliners Club award for newspaper feature writing, 1942; Freedom medal (U.S.A.); Medaille de la Liberation (France). Mem. Am. Assn. Newspaper Editors, Alpha Delta (Univ. N.M.). Clubs: Franklin Inn, Pen and Pencil, National Press; Anglo-American Press (Paris). Author: (with Phyllis Hunter Cassidy) Spellbinder (play), 1935; (with John Klorer and S. S. Field) On Such a Night (motion picture), 1938; The Marshall Plan and How it Works, 1949; The Defense of Europe, 1951; A Statement of Faith, 1957. Contbr. to Saturday Evening Post, Coronet, Liberty, Reader's Digest, Passing Show (London). Home: Philadelphia PA Died Sept. 16, 1968.

CASSADY, THOMAS GANTZ, mfg. co. exec.; b. Owen County, Ind., Jan. 5, 1896; s. Otto Ezra and Edith (Gantz) C.; student U. Chgo., 1914-16; m. Elizabeth Harrison, Sept. 1, 1923. Mgr. Mpls. office George H. Burr & Co., 1921-26; partner McGowen, Cassady & White, Chgo., Mpls., Detroit, 1926-41; partner Farwell Chapman & Co., Chgo., 1946-53; v.p., chmn. bd., chmn. exec. com. Chamberlain Mfg. Corp., Elmhurst, Ill., 1953-72. Mng. trustee Thomas G. Cassady Found. Served with French Air Force, 1916-18; from lt. comdr. to capt., USNR, 1941-45. Decorated D.S.C. with bronze oak leaf, Legion of Merit; Croix de Guerre with 3 palms and gold star, Comdr. Legion d'Honneur (France); Belgian Mil. medal. Republican. Club: Onwentsia (Lake Forest). Home: Lake Forest IL Died July 7, 1972; buried Lakewood Cemetery, Minneapolis MN

CASSEL, JOHN H., editorial cartoonist; b. Nebraska City, Neb.; s. Job W. and Mary (Harmon) C.; student Doane Coll., Crete, Neb., 1892-94; studied Art Institute Chicago; m. Louise Anderson. Illustrated and cartooned for Ram's Horn, Chicago, later for Life, Puck, Judge, also book illustrator; formerly cartoonist N.Y. Evening World and Brooklyn Daily Eagle; now free lance work. Mem. Illustrators' Assn., Artists' Guild. Republican. Clubs: Dutch Treat, Salmagundi. Home: 2 W. 67th St., New York 23, N.Y.; Silvermine," New Canaan, Conn. Studio: 67 W. 67th St., New York 23 NY‡

CASSIDY, JAMES H., congressman; b. Cleveland, Oct. 28, 1869; s. James H. and Mary Grace (Brown) C.; ed. pub. schs. and business coll.; LL.B., Baldwin U., Berea, O., 1901; m. Elizabeth Handiges, of Cleveland, Nov. 24, 1903. Admitted to bar, 1901; mem. firm of Lang, Cassidy & Copeland; clk. Rivers and Harbors Com., U.S. Ho. of Rep., 1902-9 (resigned); elected to 61st Congress (1909-11), 21st Ohio Dist., Apr. 20, 1909, to succeed Theodore E. Burton, resigned; Republican. Baptist. Mem. Ohio Bar Assn. Clubs: Cleveland Athletic, Tippecanoe, Western Reserve. Home: 2063 E. 88th St. Office: 1019 Williamson bldg., Cleveland OH‡

CASSON, HERBERT NEWTON, editor; b. at Ontario, Can., Sept. 23, 1869; s. Rev. Wesley and Elizabeth (Jackson) C.; grad. Victoria Coll., 1892; m. Lydia Kingsmill Commander (q.v.), 1899. On editorial staff New York World till 1904; on staff Munsey's Magazine, 1905-6; independent work for a number of mags., and lecturing since 1906. Ex-pres. Brooklyn Philos. Assn. Wrote: Romance of Steel, 1907; Romance of the Reaper, 1908; Life of Cyrus Hall McCormick, 1909; History of the Telephone, 1910; Salesmanship, 1911; Horse, Truck and Tractor, 1912; Axioms of Business, 1914; Factory Efficiency, 1916; Human Nature, 1917. Propr. The Efficiency Magazine, and Sheldon Sch. Pres. London Publicity Club. Address: The Dell, Church Rd., Upper Norwood, S.E., London England‡

CASTELLANI, ALDO (COUNT OF CHISIMAIO), physician; b. Florence, Italy, Sept. 8, 1877; s. Ettore and Violante (Giuliani) C.; M.D., U. of Florence, 1899; studied U. of Bonn, London Sch. of Tropical Medicine; m. Josephine Ambler Stead, of Yorkshire, Eng., Jan. 2, 1906; 1 dau., Jacqueline (wife of Sir Miles Lampson). Hon. physician to the King of Greece and Crown Prince and Princess of Italy. Mem. Foreign Office Royal Soc's. First Sleeping Sickness Commn., Uganda, Africa, 1902-03; prof. pathology, later prof. tropical medicine, Ceylon Med. Coll., 1903-15, also dir. Bacterial Inst., lecturer on dermatology, etc.; prof. tropical medicine, Royal U. of Naples, 1915-19, also lt. col. Italian Med. Service and mem. Internat. Sanitary Commn.; lecturer London Sch. Tropical Medicine and dir. tropical medicine, Ross Inst., 1919-33; prof. tropical medicine, Tulane U., 1926-30; prof. tropical medicine, Royal U. of Rome, 1930-71; prof. tropical medicine La. State U. Med. Sch., 1932-71; surgeon gen. and inspr. gen. for Italian Army, Ethiopian War, 1935-36. Made the fundamental discovery in elucidation of etiology of sleeping sickness, 1902; discoverey in Ceylon, the micro-organism which causes yaws; described the organisms causing certain new diseases; etc. Fellow Royal Coll. Physicians, London, Royal Soc. Tropical Medicine, London, Am. Coll. Phys., Royal Soc. Medicine. Decorated Knight Comdr. of St. Michael and St. George (British); Grand Cross Crown of Italy; Officier Legion of Honor (French); Grand Cross Order of Civil Merit (Spain); Grand Cross Order of St. Sava and Officer White Eagle (Jugo Slavia); created Hereditary Count by King of Italy for services in Ethiopian War. Catholic. Clubs: Atheneum (London); Travellers (Paris); Caccia (Rome). Author: (with Dr. Albert Chalmers), Manual of Tropical Medicine, 4th edit. by Castellani, 1940; Fungi of Fungal Diseases (lectures), 1927; Climate and Acclimatization, 1930, 2d edit., 1938; also about 400 contributions on medical subjects. Editor of Journal of Tropical Medicine and Hygiene (London). Address: New Orleans LA Died Oct. 1971.*

CASTELLOW, BRYANT THOMAS, ex-congressman; b. on farm, Quitman Co., Ga., July 29, 1876; s. William Franklin and Mary (Gay) C.; student Mercer U., Macon, Ga., 1894-95; B.L., U. of Ga., 1897; m. Ethel McDonald, of Cuthbert, Ga., June 28, 1911 (died 1927); 1 dau., Gertrude. Admitted to Ga. bar, 1897; now mem. firm King & Castellow; elected mem. 72d Congress (1931-33) to fill unexpired term of Charles R. Crisp; mem. 73d and 74th Congresses (1933-37), 3d Georgia District. Served as captain Georgia State Militia, 1899-1902. Democrat. Baptist. Mason. Home: Cuthbert GA‡

CASTELNUOVO-TEDESCO, MARIO, composer, b. Florence, Italy, Apr. 3, 1895; s. Amedeo and Noemi (Senigaglia) Castelnuovo-T.; ed. Cherubine Royal Inst. Music, Florence; student piano with Edgardo del Valle de Paz, Composition with Lidelbrande Pizzetti. Came to U.S. under Italian antisemetic program, 1939; composer motion picture sound tracks under pseudonyms, 1939-40. Mem. Los Angeles Conservatory Music, Acad. Motion Picture Arts and Scis. Composer: (piano) Cielo de Settembre, 1910; (opera) La Mandragola (winner Nat. Contest for Opera in Italy), 1925; Symphonic Variations, 1928; (opera) Bacca in Toscana, 1931; (ballet) Birthday of the Infanta, 1942; (violin concerto) The Prophets, 1932; The Lark for Violin and Piano, 1930; (motion picture sound tracks) And Then There Were None, 1944, Time Out of Mind, 1947, The Loves of Carmen, 1948, Everybody Does It, 1949; (orchestral works) Overture to a Fairy Tail, 1940, Indian Songs and Dances, 1949; (overture) Much Ado About Nothing, 1953; Quintet for Guitar and String Orchestra, 1950; Platero and I: 5 pieces (sonata for guitar) Homage to Boccherini. Died June 1968.

CASTER, GEORGE BROWN, savs. and loan assn. exec.; b. Leon, Ia., Sept. 21, 1894; s. Joseph A. and Olive (Brown) C.; A.B., U. Cal., 1916; LL.B., Columbia, 1920; m. Bernice A. Browning, Mar. 3, 1948. First v.p., founding dir. Coral Gables Fed. Savs. & Loan Assn. (Fla.), 1934, pres., 1938-66, chmn. bd. 1966-72; real estate broker, 1926-72; ins. agt., 1930-72; pres., dir. Caster Ins. Agy., Inc., 1956-72. Served to 1st lt. U.S. Army, World War I; AEF in France. Mem. U.S., Fla. (past pres.) savs. and loans leagues, Greater Miami Ins. Bd. (past v.p., mem. exec. com.), Coral Gables Bd. Realtors (past pres.), Coral Gables C. of C. (past v.p., dir.), Sigma Chi (past pres. Miami alumni chpt.). Rotarian (charter, past pres. Coral Gables), Elk (charter trustee, hon. mem.). Clubs: Century (past pres.), Riviera Country (Coral Gables). Home: Coral Gables FL Died Mar. 14, 1972.

CASTLE, JOHN H., JR., corp. exec.; b. 1916; B.A., Yale, 1938; M.B.A., Harvard; married. Pres. Wilmont Castle Co., 1940-59; exec. v.p. Ritter Corp., 1959-65; exec. v.p. Ritter-Pfaudler Corp., 1965-68, also dir.; dir. Erdle Perforating Co., Security Trust Co., Hard Mfg., Rochester Telephone Inc. Home: Rochester NY Died Oct. 1968.

CASTLE, KENDALL BROOKS, lawyer; b. Philadelphia, Pa., May 13, 1868; s. John Harvard and Marie Antoinette (Arnold) C.; prep. edn., Model Sch. and Collegiate Inst., Toronto, Ont., Can.; B.A., Toronto U., 1889, U. of Rochester, 1889; student Harvard Law Sch., 2 yrs.; m. Louise Brown, Nov. 15, 1894 (dec.); children—Newton Brown, Kendall Brooks; m. 2d, Mary Dugan, July 16, 1931. Admitted to bar of N.Y. State, 1892, practicing at Rochester; senior member Castle & Fitch (now Castle, Fitch, Swan & Dividio), since 1921; chmn. board of directors, R. J. Strasenburg Co.; v.p. and dir., Stecher-Traung Lithographic Co.; counsel and director, International Talc Co., Oswegatchie Light & Power Co.; dir. Wilmot Castle Co. Dir. Genesee Hosp.; trustee Rochester Inst. of Tech., U. of Rochester (hon.). Mem. Am., N.Y. State and Rochester bar assns. Republican. Baptist. Clubs: University (N.Y.C.). Home: 17 Buckingham St. Office: Union Trust Bldg., Rochester 14 NY‡

CASTON, SAUL, symphony condr.; b. New York, N.Y., Aug. 22, 1901; s. Louis and Rose (Gusikoff) Kaszhdan; student private school, N.Y. City; Mus.D. (honorary), University of Denver, 1949; married Selma Amansky, Mar. 26, 1930; 1 dau., Marise (Mrs. Martin Zerobnick). Became 2d trumpet player Phila. Orchestra, 1918, 1st trumpet player, 1923; apptd. trumpet instr., Curtis Inst., Phila., 1924; apptd. associate condr. Phila. Orchestra, 1936, condr. Reading Symphony Orchestra, 1941; assisted Mr. Stokowski in formation of All-Am. Youth Orchestra, 1940, and conducted on tour, 1941; special consultant on music, Fort McArthur, Jan.-Feb. 1941. Condr. Hollywood Bowl, 1952, Phila. Orchestra, 1948, 52. Conducted first full ballet performance in U.S. of Ravel's Daphnis and Chloe, 1936. Condr. and mus. dir. Denver Symphony Orchestra since 1945; sometime guest condr. NBC Orchestra, Nat., Los. Angeles, Cin., Grant Park, Vienna, Heidelberg, Bad Piermont, Germany Symphonies, Robin Hood Dell; condr., head orch. and trumpet depts. N.C. Sch. Arts, Winston-Salem, 1965-70. Received 1st Hartmann-Kuhn Award, Phila.; Juvenile Ct. award, outstanding service to youth, 1955; UN Com. for Colo. award, 1958; Regis Coll. Civis Princeps award, Nat. Music Council condrs. award, 1960. Mem. A.S.C.A.P. Home: Winston-Salem NC Died July 28, 1970; buried Baltimore MD

CASTRO, AMERICO, univ. prof. emeritus; b. Rio de Janeiro, Brazil, May 4, 1885, s. Antonio and Carmen (Quesada) C.; ed. University of Granada, 1900-05, University of Paris, 1905-08; Ph.D., University of Madrid, 1913; hon. Ph.D., Univ. Poitiers, 1935, U. of Paris, 1936, U. of Rio de Janeiro, 1946; m. Carmen Madinaveitia, 1911; children—Carmen, Luis. Prof., U. of Madrid, 1915, visiting prof. Univ. of Buenos Aires, 1923-24, 1936-37, Columbia U., 1924, Univ. of Berlin, Germany, 1930-31, prof. Univ. of Wis., 1937-39, University of Texas, 1939-40, Princeton since 1940 now emeritus; hon. prof. U. of La Plata, Chile, Mexico; spl. prof. Spanish, U. Houston, 1955-56, now prof. Adviser John Simon Guggenheim Memorial Foundation, 1938-46. Member Academia Argentina de Letras. Hispanic Soc. Am. Officer de la Legion d'Honneur. Author books including: Espana en su historia, 1948; scholar editions of Spanish classic authors (Quevedo, Tirso de Molina, Rojas Zorrilla); Aspectos del vivir hispanico, 1949. Iberoamerica, 1953; The Structure of Spanish History, 1953; Dos Ensaynos, 1956; Santiago de Espana, 1957; Hacia Cervantes, 1957; Santiago de Espana, 1958. Contbr. articles Am. French, German, Spanish and S. Am. pubs. Home: Princeton NJ Died July 1972.

CASTRO, HECTOR DAVID, diplomat; b. San Salvador, El Salvador, Central America, Apr. 22, 1894; s. David and Teresa (Gomar) C.; Dr. Law and Polit. and Soc. Science, Nat. U. of El Salvador, 1915; m. Elena Cromeyer, Oct. 3, 1915; children—David Alejandro Francisco, Elena Alicia, Hector Emilio; Ricardo Benjamin, Teresa de Jesus. Dist. atty. San Salvador, 1917; judge, civil and criminal law, Dist. of Nueva San Salvador, 1917-18, judge San Salvador City, civil and commercial law, 1918-19; undersec. Ministries of Finance and War of El Salvador, 1919-20; consul, Liverpool, Eng., May-Nov. 1920; sec. Legation, Washington, D.C., 1920-22, charge d'affiares, 1922-27; undersec. for foreign relations, 1927-28; del. to 6th Am. Internat. Conf. Havana, Cuba, 1928; dir. gen. of Income Tax Bur., 1928-29; prof. of international law (pub. and private), Nat. Univ. of El Salvador, 1928-33; minister for foreign affairs, 1931; rector Nat. Univ. of El Salvador, 1933; E.E. and M.P. of El Salvador to Uruguay, 1933-34; chief Salvadoran delegation to 7th Am. Internat. Conf. at Montevideo, 1933; E.E. and M.P. of El Salvador to U.S., 1934-43, ambassador, 1943-44, A.E. and P., 1945-61. Served as del. to meeting of consultation of Foreign Ministers of Am. Republics, Rio de Janeiro, 1942; gov. of Internat. Monetary Fund and Internat. Bank for Reconstruction and Finance, 1944; chief, Salvadoran delegation to United Nations Conf. for Internat. Orgn., San Francisco, 1945; del. to meetings of the council of U.N.R.R.A.; acting chmn. delegation of El Salvador to Gen. Assembly of U.N., New York, 1946; del. El Salvador to U.N. Spl. Com. on Palestine, New York, 1947; chmn. El Salvador del. to 2d session Gen. Assembly U.N., 1947, to 9th Internat. Am. Conf., Begota, Colombia, 1948; chmn. El Salvador del. to 3d session U.N. Gen. Assembly, Paris, France, 1948, 4th session, N.Y., 1949; del. to second part of 3d session, Gen. Assembly of U.N., N.Y., 1949, 5th session, Paris, 1951-52; chmn. El Salvador delegation to Japanese Treaty Conf., San Francisco, 1951; del. Internat. Wheat Council. Washington, 1953; pres. council of the Organization of Am. States, Washington, 1953; del. Tenth Inter-Am. Conf., Venezuela, 1954. Recipient several fgn. decorations. Home: San Salvador El Salvador Died Apr. 1, 1973.

CASWELL, IRVING A., lawyer; b. at Anoka, Minn., Feb. 25, 1870; s. Albert J. and Martha (Hayden) C.; LL.B., U. of Minn.; m. Mary Dunbar Woodbury, June 3, 1897; 1 son, Dwight Woodbury. Owner Anoka Herald, 1892-1902. Successfully managed campaigns in Minn., for Theodore Roosevelt, 1912, Cummins, 1916, Wood, 1920. Mem. Rep. Nat. Com., 1912 and 1920-24; collector of customs, Port of Minneapolis, 1924-31. Served as 1st lt. Co. B, 3d Minn. Nat. Guard; 1st lt. Co. K, 14th Vol. Inf., Spanish-Am. War. Mem. S.A.R. Mason (32 deg.), life member Shrine, Elk. Home: Jefferson Court Hotel, Orlando FL‡

CATES, CLIFTON BLEDSOE, Marine Corps officer; b. Tiptonville, Tenn., Aug. 31, 1893; s. Willis Jones and Martha (Bledsoe) C.; LL.B., U. of Tenn., 1916; grad. Field Officers' Course, Marine Corps Schs., Army Indsl. Coll., Army War Coll.; m. Jane Virginia McIlhenny, Oct. 7, 1920; children—Clifton Bledsoe (lt. comdr. U.S.N.), Ann Willis. Commd. 2d lt., Marine Corps, 1917, advancing through the grades to major general

1944; promoted to rank of general, 1948; served with 96th Company, 2d Battalion, 6th Marines, 2d Div., Jan. 1918-Sept. 1919; participated at Verdun sector, Aisue defensive, Bouresches and Belleau woods, Aisne Marne offensive, Marbach sector, St. Mihiel offensive, Blanc Mont sector, Meuse-Argonne offensive; with Army of Occupation in Germany; twice wounded during World War I; commander, 1st Marine Regiment, 1st Marine Division, Guadalcanal, Solomon Islands, August-December, 1942; comdt. Marine Corps Schools, Quantico, Va., 1943-44; participated Saipan and Tinian offensives, July 1944-August 1944, Iwo Jima Operation, February-March, 1945; comdg. gen. 4th Marine Div., July 1944-Nov. 1945; comdg. gen. Marine Barracks and Marine Corps Schools, Quantico, Va., June 1946-Dec. 1947. Appointed commandant of the Marine Corps, 1948; comdt. Marine Corps Schools, Quantico, since 1952. Decorated Navy Cross, Distinguished Service Cross (Army) with oak leaf, Distinguished Service Medal with gold star, Legion of Merit, Silver Star with oak leaf, Purple Heart with oak leaf, Presidential citation with 3 stars, Victory Medal with 5 bronze stars, World War II Victory Medal, Army of Occupation of Germany, Marine Corps Expeditionary, Yangtze, China and Am. services, Asiatic-Pacific Area Medal with 5 bronze stars (U.S.), Legion of Honor, Croix de Guerre (3) with 2 palms and 1 gold star, Fourragere (France). Comdr. Order Orange of Nassau with Crossed Swords (Netherlands). Mem. Phi Gamma Delta, Phi Alpha Delta. Clubs: Army and Navy, Army-Navy Country, Alfalfa (Washington); Chevy Chase. Address: Quantico VA Died June 6, 1970.

CATES, GORDON DELL, advt. exec.; b. Logansport, Ind., July 18, 1906; s. John M. and Grace (Cohee) C.; student (scholarship), Cin. Conservatory of Music, 1926-27; grad. Culver Mil. Academy, 1928; student journalism Columbia, 1928-30; married Jeanne Winifred Dubrell Crump, Mar. 17, 1945; children—Paula Jeanne, Gordon Dell; 1 dau. by previous marriage, Theo Merrill. Copy chief, McCann-Erickson Agency, Cleveland, 1932-39; vice president Young & Rubicam Agency, 1942-47, also general manager broadcast division, 1942-45; v.p. Lennen & Mitchell Agency, 1947-51; sr. v.p. successor corporation Lennen & Newell, Inc., 1953-63; sr. v.p. Maxon, Inc., advt., 1963-70; asso. Newspaper 1, 1968-70; vice president Biow Agency, 1951-53. Founder, also leader, of the floating Dixieland Jazzband, amateur group devoted to charity orgns. Sr. writer nat. award campaigns Standard Oil of Ohio. Mem. Am. Assn. Advt. Agencies (broadcast com.). Clubs: New York Yacht; Larchmont Yacht; Storm Trysail. Contbr. nat. mags. including The New Yorker. Home: Larchmont NY Died June 2, 1970; buried Kensico Cemetery, Valhalla NY

CATES, WALTER THRUSTON, comml. orgn. exec.; b. Burlington, N.C., Apr. 28, 1913; s. Claud Holt and Ella Lee (Cheek) C.; student U. N.C., 1931-32, Southeastern Institute for C. of C. Executives, 1942-47; m. Martha Fonville, June 12, 1932; children—George E., Jeanie (Mrs. Rodney O. Siggelkow). Sales mgr. Alamance Motors, Burlington, 1932-41; mgr. Burlington C. of C., 1941-44; Macon (Ga.) C. of C., 1945-52; exec. v.p. Ga. C. of C., Atlanta, 1952-71; pres. Empress Hosiery Corp., Atlanta, 1943-71; instr., pres., dean of faculty S.E. Inst. Comml. Orgns. Execs., U. N.C., 1951-59. Mem. Regional Export Expansion Council, Gov.'s European Trade Mission, 1962. Mem. Selective Service Bd., 1941-45, adv. bd. Salvation Army, from 1961. Mem. Am. C. of C. Execs. State Economy Study Commn., Sigma Phi Epsilon. Baptist. Elk, Mason, Kiwanian. Home: Atlanta GA Died Dec. 13, 1971; buried Arlington Cemetery, Atlanta GA

CATHCART, THOMAS EDWARD (TOM CATHCART), editor; b. Chgo., Aug. 12, 1894; s. Alexander and Mary (Elliot) C.; ed. pub. schs., Chgo. and Phila., and Wharton Sch. of Finance and Commerce (U. Pa.); m. Elizabeth Swanson, Jan. 15, 1920; 1 son, Tom. Began as apprentice mechanic, 1912, later sales engr. Standard Roller Bearing Co., advt. mgr. Vim Motor Truck Co., Packard Motor Car Co.; promotion mgr. Crowell Pub. Co., 1922-29; spl. editorial work, 1929; editor Country Home, 1930-34, editorial dir., 1935; dir. promotion This Week mag., 1935-44, mgr. newspaper relations, 1946-48, vice president and director from 1949, exec. vice president, 1957-60; pres. Newspaper and Magazine Special Services. Served as 1st lt. inf., Motor Transport Corps, U.S. Army, 1917; capt., attached to hdqrs. 1918-19. Republican Episcopalian. Clubs: Nat. Press (Washington); Old Lyme Country and Beach (Lyme, Conn.). Home: Lyme CT Died Dec. 31, 1968; buried Hamburg Cemetery, Lyme CT

CATHLES, LAWRENCE MACLAGAN, chmn. North Am. Reassurance Co.; b. Edinburgh, Scotland, July 21, 1877; s. John and Emily Sarah (Lawrence) C.; grad. George Watson's Coll., Edinburgh, 1893; m. Esther Findlater Robertson Bain, July 29, 1905; children—Dorothy (Mrs. John Kenchington), Lawrence M., Henry Moir. Came to United States, 1903, naturalized, 1911. Began in insurance business, Edinburgh, 1895; asst. actuary, Provident Savings Life Assurance Soc., 1903-05; actuary, Franklin Life Ins. Co., 1905-08, sec. and actuary, Southwestern Life Ins. Co., 1908-20; v.p. and actuary, Southland Life Ins. Co., 1920-23; pres. North Am. Reassurance Co., 1923-48; now chmn. board Fellow Faculty of Actuaries in Scotland; fellow Royal Soc. Arts, Soc. Actuaries; asso. mem. Inst. Actuaries (London). Independent. Episcopalian. Mason (32 deg., Shriner). Clubs: Union League, Scarsdale Golf. Home: Cragswold, Garth Rd., Scarsdale, N.Y. Office: 161 E. 42d St., New York City 17 NY‡

CATLIN, WARREN BENJAMIN, prof. economics; b. Nemaha, Neb., Nov. 3, 1881; s. Norman Bull and Mary Ann (Adams) C.; grad. Nebraska State Normal School, Peru, 1899; A.B., U. of Neb., 1903; Ph.D., Columbia, 1927; unmarried. Teacher of English, high sch., Hamburg, Ia., 1903-04, Dubuque, Ia., 1904-06; instr. in economics and politics, Cornell U., 1909-10; asst. prof. economics and sociology, Bowdoin Coll., 1910-12, Daniel B. Fayerweather prof. economics and sociology and head of dept. 1912-52. Public panel member for War Labor Board, Region I. Mem. Am. Econ. Assn., Am. Acad. Polit. and Social Science. Acad. Polit. Science, Am. Management Assn., Phi Beta Kappa. Conglist. Club: Town and College. Author: The Labor Problem in the United States and Great Britain, 1926, revised edit., 1935. Co-editor: Yearbook of American Labor: War Policies, 1945. Contbr. to Am. Econ. Review; also article on Hours of Labor in Ency. Britannica; labor articles in Ency. of Religion, 1945. Home: Brunswick ME Died July 10, 1968.

CAULDWELL FREDERIC WADSWORTH, newspaper corr.; b. Watkins, N. Y., Sept. 23, 1873; s. James A. C.; academic ed'n Owego, N. Y.; grad. in 1892; unmarried. Washington corr. Hartford (Conn.) Courant, and Buffalo (N.Y.) Courier. Address: 1403 F St., Washington‡

CAUTHORN, JOSEPH LURTON, newspaper publishing co. exec.; b. Mexico, Mo., August 12, 1882; s. Columbus Hill and Sarah A. (Scott) C.; student pub. schs. Mexico, Mo.; m. Grace Wulff Wright, Sept. 1, 1918 (dec. 1924); step-daughter, Jean Wulff Wright Cannon (dec.); married 2d, Janis Jewett, November 11, 1929. Reporter Mexico (Mo.) Intelligencer, 1904-06; reporter Mexico (Mo.) Ledger-Reporter, 1906-07; reporter San Diego (Calif.) Sun, 1907-08, circulation mgr., 1908-10; circulation mgr. Los Angeles Record, 1910-13, gen. circulation mgr., 1915; business mgr., 1915-16; circulation mgr. San Francisco Daily News Co., Ltd., 1913-15, gen. circulation mgr., 1915, bus. mgr., 1918-29, gen. bus. mgr., 1929-40, pres., 1925-59; gen. business mgr. Denver (Colo.) Rocky Mountain News, 1927-29. Democrat. Clubs: Olympic, Press-Union League, Advertising, Bohemian, St. Francis Yacht, San Francisco CA Died Apr. 3, 1969.

CAVAGNARO, JAMES FRANCIS, banker; b. Greenwich Village, N.Y., Sept. 1, 1883; s. Agostino and Clorinda (Valente) C.; student pub. schs., N.Y.C.; m. Victoria Louise Cavagnaro, Jan. 28, 1909; children—James Francis, Louise Victoria, Victoria Agosta, Angela Irene (Mrs. J. O. McManus). Freight clk. Hirzel Feltmann Co., 1904-05; cashier Savoy Trust Co., 1905-12; v.p. East River Nat. Bank, 1912-28 (absorbed by Bank of Am.); v.p. Bank of Am., 1928-31; v.p., N.Y. rep. Bank of Am. Nat. Trust & Savs. Assn., 1931-45; v.p., N.Y. rep. Trans-America Corp., San Francisco, 1931-49, chmn., 1949-53, now dir.; dir. Hall Scott, Inc. (Berkeley), Occidental Life Ins. Co. (Los Angeles), Pacific Nat. Fire Ins. Co., San Francisco, Am. Surety Co., N.Y.C. Home: San Mateo CA Died Nov. 16, 1970.

CAVAGNARO, ROBERT JOHN, newspaperman; b. Ridgewood, N.J., Dec. 3, 1905; s. John Baptiste and Victoria M. (Cella) C.; student Seton Hall Prep. Sch., South Orange, N.J.; m. Elizabeth Boye Carson, Sept. 24, 1932; children—Margo V. (Mrs. Gerald L. Manton), Sandra Elizabeth, Peter John. News assignments weekly and daily newspapers, Ridgewood, Hackensack and Paterson, N.J., also Internat. News Service, White Plains, N.Y. and N.Y.C., 1924-30; news staff A.P., 1930-69, successively staff, Newark and N.Y.C. chief bur., Newark, news editor Rocky Mountain div., Denver, gen. sports editor, N.Y.C., 1930-48, now gen. exec. N.Y.C. Mem. Sigma Delta Chi (nat. pres. 1958, chmn. bd. dirs., exec. council 1959). Home: Greenwich CT Died Sept. 11, 1969.

CAVALIERI, LINA (MRS. LUCIEN MURATORE), operatic soprano; b. Rome, Italy, 1874; studied music under Mme. Mariani-Mase; m. Lucien Muratore, opera singer. Debut in Lisbon, Portugal, 1900; debut in America at Manhattan Opera House, 1906. Home: Eze France*‡

CAVAN, MARIE (MARY CAWEIN), operatic soprano; b. N.Y. City, Feb. 6, 1889; ed. pub. schs.; studied for opera under Mlle. Rose Marie Hellig, New York, and Charles W. Clark, Paris, France; later studied with Franz Emerich, Berlin; m. Otakar Marak, Czech tenor, of Prague, Dec. 19, 1917. First attracted attention as soprano, Trinity M.E. Ch., New York; operatic debut as Irma in Louise," with Chicago Opera Co., Nov. 9, 1910; with same co., 1911-12; at Stadt Theatre, Hamburg, Germany, until 1914; Nat. Theatre, Prague, 1914-18; returned to New York. Roles include Mimi in La Boheme," Tosca in Tosca," Minnie in Girl of the Golden West," Carmen in Carmen," Santuzza in Cavalleria Rusticana," Nedda in Pagliacci," Suzanne in Secret of Suzanne," etc. Address: NYC NY Died Mar. 1968.

CAVANAGH, C. J., assn. exec.; b. Santa Margarita, Cal., Dec. 11, 1908; s. William E. and Josephine (Asberry) C.; ed. Cal. Poly. Sch., U. Cal. at Davis, U. Hawaii; m. Georgia Durden, June 19, 1937; 1 dau., Louise. Tchr. high sch., Honolulu, 1934-37; acting mgr., investigator Nat. Ins. Reference Agy., 1937-40; with Liberty House, Honolulu, 1940-62, asst. gen. supt. 1951-53, gen. supt., 1954-62; exec. v.p. Hawaii C. of C., 1963-72. Pres., Honolulu Retail Bd., 1963; mem. Regional Export Expansion Council, U.S. Army Adv. Com. Mem. exec. bd. Honolulu council Boy Scouts Am. Served with U.S. Army, 1930-37; to lt. col. AUS, 1941-45. Mem. Friendly Sons St. Patrick. Mem. Union Ch. Rotarian. Clubs: Pacific, Oahu Country. Home: Honolulu HI Died Sept. 12, 1972.

CAVANAUGH, JOHN WILLIAM, lawyer; b. Chgo., Mar. 28, 1906; s. Edward Bernard and Harriette (Shinners) C.; A.B., Notre Dame U., 1928; LL.B., Chgo.-Kent Coll. Law, 1935; m. Jane Stude, June 27, 1942;children—Ann, Mary Elizabeth, Jane, Margaret Kim, John William. Admitted to Ill. bar, 1935; with trust dept. Continental Ill. Nat. Bank & Trust Co., Chgo., 1929-34. Northern Trust Co., Chgo., 1934-36; with firm McDermott, Will & Emery, Chgo., 1936-69. Trustee Dominican Coll., Racine, Wis., Marquette University, Milwaukee, Wis. Member American, Illinois, Chicago, D.C. bar assns. Clubs: Mid-Day, Knollwood, Chicago, University (Chgo.); Milwaukee; Saddle and Cycle. Home: Winnetka IL Died 1969.

CAWLEY, EDGAR MOORE, pianist; b. Pyrmont, O., Feb. 26, 1871; s. John W. and Mary E. C.; ed. Cincinnati Conservatory of Music and at Leipzig, Germany; m. Leipzig, Sara Scorgie, 1896. Instr. piano, Cincinnati Conservatory of Music, 1887-92; dir. Indianapolis Conservatory of Music since 1897. Clubs: Maennerchor, Business Men's Club of Indianapolis, Board of Trade. Home: 310 N. Delaware St., Indianapolis IN‡

CAYTON, HORACE ROSCOE, writer, sociologist, cons.; b. Seattle, Apr. 12, 1903; s. Horace Roscoe and Susie (Revels) C.; A.B., U. Wash., 1931; grad. student U. Chgo., 1931-35; spl. tng. Inst. Psychoanalysis, 1945; grad. student N.Y.U., 1956; m. Ruby Jordan, Dep. sheriff, Seattle, 1929-31; instr. econs. Fisk U., 1935-36; research asst., instr. dept. anthropology U. Chgo., 1936-37; fellow Julius Rosenwald Fund, 1937-39; dir. Parkway Community House, Chgo., 1940-49; UN corr. Pitts. Courier, 1952-54; lectr. dept. sociology Coll. City N.Y., 1957-58; spl. asst. Commr. Welfare, N.Y.C., 1958-59; research asst. geriatric mental illness Langley Porter Clinic, 1959-60; staff internat. survey corrections Inst. Study Crime and Delinquency, Berkeley, Cal., 1961-62; writer, researcher, 1962-63; program coordinator univ. ext., U. Cal., 1963-64, project dir. study Negro marketing theory Inst. Bus. and Econ. Research, U. Cal. at Berkeley, 1965-70. Bd. dirs. Council Social Agencies, Chgo.; sec., mem. bd. dirs. Parkway Community House, 1944-48. Co-recipient Anisfield-Wolf award for Black Metropolis, book on race relations pub. 1945; named outstanding race relations book of year New York Pub. Library, 1945. Mem. Soc. Social Research, Am. Sociol. Soc., Soc. Midland Authors, Inst. Psychoanalysis, Alpha Kappa Delta, Zeta Phi. Independent. Author. (with George S. Mitchell) Black Workers and the New Unions, 1935; (with St. Clair Drake), Black Metropolis, 1945; Long Old Road, 1965. Contbr. mags., jours.; book reviews to newspapers. Home: Santa Cruz CA Died Jan. 1970.

CECIL, GEORGE W., advt. exec.; b. Phila., Nov. 3, 1891; s. George W. and Eleanor (Farley) C.; student pub. schs. Phila.; m. Florence A. Gerwig, Apr. 30, 1917. Advt. writer, news room editor Phila. Record, 1911-14; with George A. Deatel Advt. Agy., Balt., 1914-17; copywriter N.W. Ayer & Son, Inc., Phila., 1917-36, head copy dept., 1936-45, v.p., dir., 1936-67; wrote advt. campaigns which introduced Canada Dry and Ford Model A (won 000 Bok award Harvard Bus. Sch. 1927); writer advt. for Ford, 1927-40, Am. Tel & Tel. Co. mag. since 1931. Awarded Gold Medal for essay, 1909, Silver Medal, 1910; also advt. awards. Clubs: Racquet, North Hills Golf (Phila.), Author 5 advertisements: The 100 Greatest Advertisements (Julien Watkins), 1949 and 1959. Contbr. advt. publs. Home: Philadelphia PA Died July 6, 1970.

CEDERBERG, WILLIAM EMANUEL, prof. mathematics; b. Upsala, Seden, Jan. 26, 1876; s. Rudolph and Charlotte (Fleur) C.; brought to U.S., 1895; B.A., Augustana Coll., Rock Island, Ill., 1900; Ph.B., Yale, 1902; student Brown U., Providence, R.I., 1902-03; student Goettingen, Germany, 1905-07; Ph.D., U. of Wis., 1922; m. Martha M. Sievers, June 9, 1923; children—Rita Charlotte, Enid Augusta. Instr. Brown U., Providence, R.I., 1902-03; prof.

mathematics, Augustana Coll. since 1908. Mem. Am. Math. Soc., Math. Assn. Am., A.A.A.S. (fellow), Sigma Xi. Lutheran. Author: On the Solution of Differential Equations of a Double Pendulum, 1923. Home: 2542 22 1/2 Av. Office: Augustana Coll., Rock Island IL‡

CEDERGREN, HUGO, assn. exec.; b. Gefle, Sweden, July 26, 1891; s. Axel W. and Augusta (Peterson) C.; student Lund (Sweden) U., 1910-15; m. Elsa Bernadotte, Sept. 18, 1929. Sec., YMCA, Stockholm, 1919-21, gen. sec., 1921-24; sec.-gen. Swedish Nat. YMCA, 1924-45; pres., 1952-62, hon. pres. 1962-71; European dir. War Prisoners' Air YMCA, 1941-47; asso. gen.-sec. world com. YMCA, 1946-53; v.p. World Alliance YMCA, 1955-61, hon. life mem. 1961-71. Home: Stockholm Sweden Died July 10, 1971.

CEHRS, CHARLES HAROLD, educator; b. Akron, O., Sept. 15, 1918; s. Glenn P. and Florida (Staib) C.; B.S., U. Akron, 1940; M.S., Ore. State Coll., 1949; M.E., U. Cal. at Berkeley, 1953; m. Elizabeth Virginia Webb, Jan. 25, 1946 (dec. Apr. 18, 1970); children—David Charles, Donna Roberta. Engring. designer Boeing Aircraft Co., Seattle, 1940-47; teaching fellow mech. engring. Ore. State Coll., 1947; asst. prof. engring. Fresno State Coll., 1948-51, 53-55, asso. prof., 1955-59, prof., 1959-70, chmn. engring. dept., 1957-63; asst. research engr., lectr. mech. engring. U. Cal. at Berkeley, 1951-53. Registered profl. engr., Cal., Ohio. Mem. Am. Soc. M.E., Am. Soc. Engring. Edn., Nat. Soc. Profl. Engrs. Presbyn. Club: Sierra (Fresno). Home: Fresno CA Died Apr. 18, 1970; buried Academy Cemetery, Academy CA

CELENTANO, WILLIAM C., mayor; b. New Haven, Jan. 23, 1904; s. Frank and Antonette (DeMartino) C.; m. Marian T. Piontek; 1 son, William C. Sec.-treas. Celentano Funeral Home. Mem. bd. alderman, 21st Ward, New Haven, 1930-40, 44-45; mayor of New Haven, 1946-53. Republican. Roman Catholic. K.C., Elk, Eagle. Clubs: Union League, Quinnipiack, Amity (New Haven). Home: New Haven CT Died Nov. 14, 1972; buried St Lawrence Cemetery, West Haven CT

CELL, JOHN W(ESLEY), coll. prof.; b. Kansas City, Mo., Mar. 29, 1907; s. John Franklin and Mary Florence (Musson) C.; A.B., U. of Ill., 1928, A.M., 1929, Ph.D., 1935; m. Mary Louise Keith, Apr. 3, 1931; children—John Whitson, Howard Robert, Mary Linn. Part time instr. in mathematics U. of Ill., 1928-29, 1933-35; asst. prof. mathematics School of Engring., Southern Methodist U., 1929-32; instr. mathematics N.C. State Univ., 1935-36, asst. prof., 1936-38; asso. prof., 1938-46, prof., 1946-67, chmn. dept. mathematics, 1957-67, dir. research project, 1952-59, director of applied math. research group, 1959-67; prof. mathematics, rocket research, Aberdeen Proving Grounds, 1944-45. Fellow A.A.A.S.; mem. Society of Indsl. and Applied Mathematics, Am. Math. Soc., Math. Assn. Am., Am. Soc. Engring. Edn., Am. Inst. Aeros. & Astronautics, Am. Ordn. Assn., Engineering Science Society, Phi Kappa Phi, Sigma Xi, Pi Mu Epsilon. Democrat. Baptist. Author: Engineering Problems Illustrating Mathematics, 1943; Analytic Geometry, 1951. Researcher in applications of mathematics in engring., in ballistics, operational mathematics, and in visual aids in teaching mathematics. Home: Raleigh NC Died Nov. 9, 1967.

CELLA, JOHN G., realtor, investment exec.; b. St. Louis, May 26, 1909; s. Charles J. and Harriet (Gallagher) C.; student U. Mo., 1931; m. Geneva Carter, Aug. 8, 1964; children by previous marriage—Charles J., Eloise (Mrs. John D. Lipscomb). Pres. So. Real Estate & Financial Co., St. Louis, 1940-68, Oaklawn Jockey Club, Hot Springs, Ark., 1940-68, Am. Theatrical Co., St. Louis, 1940-68, Mid City Real Estate Co., St. Louis, 1940-68; dir. Nat. Gypsum Co., Union Electric Co., Thoroughbred Racing Assn. Co-chmn. entertainment com. St. Louis Bicentennial, St. Louis C. of C. Bd. dirs. Ark. Crippled Childrens Hosp., Crippled Childrens Non-Sectarian Hosp. Boston. Clubs: University, Racquet, Old Warson Country (St. Louis); Buffalo, Buffalo Tennis. Home: St Louis MO Died Sept. 23, 1968.

CERF, BENNETT ALFRED, book publisher; b. New York, N.Y., May 25, 1898; s. Gustave and Fredericka (Wise) C.; A.B., Columbia, 1919; Litt.B., Columbia School of Journalism, 1920; m. Sylvia Sidney, 1935 (div. 1936; m. 2d, Phyllis Fraser, 1940; children—Christopher Bennett, Jonathan Fraser. Vice president Boni and Liveright, publishers, 1923-25; founded Modern Library, Incorporated, 1925, pres., 1925-70; founded Random House, Inc., 1927, pres., 1927-65, chmn., 1965-70, chmn. bd., sr. editor, 1970; dir. Bantam Books, 1945-67; dir. RCA, Inc., Alfred A. Knopf, Inc. Panelist on What's My Line, 1952-66. Mem. Peabody Awards committee, 1950-67, 69-70, chmn. com., 1955-67. Recipient Distinguished Service award New York Philanthropic League, 1964. Served in O.T.C., Camp Lee, Va., 1918. Mem. Pi Lambda Phi, Phi Beta Kappa, Phi Delta Epsilon. Clubs: Dutch Treat, Overseas Press. Author: Try and Stop Me, 1944; Laughing Stock, pub. 1945; Anything for a Laugh, 1946; Shake Well Before Using, 1948; Laughter, Inc., 1950; Good for a Laugh, 1952; Ency. of American Humor, 1954; Life of the Party, 1956; Reading for Pleasure, 1957; The Laugh's On Me, 1959; Out on a Limerick, 1960; Riddle-De-Dee, 1962; Laugh Day, 1965; Treasury of Atrocious Puns, 1968; Bennett Cerf's Sound of Laughter, 1970; Stories to Make You Feel Good, 1971. Contbg. editor King Features, others. Home: New York City NY Died Aug. 27, 1971.

CHADWICK, E. WALLACE, lawyer; born Vincennes, Indiana, January 17, 1884; s. William Burtch and Margaret (Moore) Chadwick; A.B. Univ. of Pa., 1906, LL.B., 1910; married Alice Cambern. President judge, Orphans Court of Delaware County, 1945. Mem. 80th Congress (1947-49), 7th Pa. Dist. Mem. law firm Chadwick, Curran, Petrikin & Smithers, Chester, Pa. President J. Lewis Crozier Library; director Delaware County National Bank. Member Delaware County Bar Assn. (past pres.), Phi Beta Kappa, Republican. Clubs: Chester Rotary, Union League of Phila. Home: Delaware County PA Died Aug. 1969.

CHADWICK, HENRY DEXTER, physician; b. Boscawen, N.H., Jan. 2, 1872; s. Jeremiah Clough and Eliza (Austin) C.; M.D., Harvard, 1895; m. Edith Nichols Clark, May 24, 1898; children—Maurice Place (U.S. Army), Barbara. House officer, surg. service, Boston City Hosp., 1895-96; began practice at Waltham, Mass., 1896; mem. staff Waltham Hosp.; bacteriologist, Waltham Bd. of Health, 1898-1905; supt. Vt. Sanatorium for Tuberculosis, Pittsford, 1907-09; supt. Westfield (Mass.) State Sanatorium, for tuberculous children, 1909-29; tuberculosis controller, Detroit Health Dept., 1929-33; Mass. Commn. Pub. Health, 1933-38; med. dir. Middlesex County Sanatorium, 1938-41; med. dir. Cambridge (Mass.) Sanatorium, 1942-47; retired. Acting asst. surg., U.S. Mil. Hosp., Ponce, Porto Rico, 1898; capt. Mass. Vol. Militia, 1899; mem. bd. tuberculosis examiners, Camp Bartlett, Westfield, 1917, U.S. Vol. Med. Service Corps, 1918. Acting dir. Div. of Tuberculosis, Mass. State Dept. Pub. Health, 1927; lecutrer post grad. medicine, U. of Mich., 1931-33; lecturer in medicine Harvard, lecturer Harvard Sch. Pub. Health; retired, 1946. Mem. White House Conf. Child Health and Protection. Member National Tuberculosis Assn. (pres. 1939), American Sanatorium Association (president eastern sect. 1928; v.p. 1929; pres. 1930), Mich. Tuberculosis Assn. (pres. 1932, 33), Am. Climatol. and Clin. Assn., Mass. Med. Soc., Mass. Tuberculosis League (pres. 1942-45), Hampden County Tuberculosis and Public Health Association (pres. 1928), American Public Health Association, Massachusetts Public Health Assn. (president 1940, 41), Boston Trudeau Soc., S.A.R., Westfield C. of C. (1st pres. 1920). Conglist. A Pioneer in tuberculosis investigation among children; orginator of Ten Yr. Program" (now known as the Chadwick Clinics) in Mass., providing for examination of sch. children. Author: The Modern Attack on Tuberculosis (with Dr. A. S. Pope), 1942. Contbr. of articles on tuberculosis and pub. health to med. periodicals. Home: Worcester Lane, Waltham MA‡

CHADWICK, LEE SHERMAN, mfr.; b. East Braintree, Vt., Feb. 26, 1875; s. Eugene H. and Emeline Sarah (Farnsworth) C.; B.S. in M.E., Purdue, 1899; m. Ethelyn Pearl Rogers, July 1900; children—Eugenia Pearl (wife of Dr. R. M. Wansbrough), Herbert Lee, Winfield Scott. Pioneer in auto industry, building first exptl. auto in Boston, 1899, while in charge of Boston Ball Bearing Co.; supt. Searchmont Motor Co., Phila., to 1903, when he founded Fairmount Engine Works, became Chadwick Engring. Co., Phila., 1903-11; cons. engr. Cleveland Foundry Co. (became Cleveland Metal Products Co.), 1912-17, successively dir. and asst. gen. mgr., v.p. and pres. 1921 when company name was changed to Perfection Stove Co., v. chmn. bd. 1922-45, chmn. bd. since 1945. Mem. Am. Society M.E., Mass. Soc. Mayflower Descendents, Nat. Hist. Soc., N.E. Hist. and Geneol. Soc., Nat. Geographic Soc., Canadian Camp Fire Club. Clubs: Shaker Heights Country; Cleveland Gun; Dover Boy Gun; Sportsman's of Am. (Chicago); Okaboji Indian Shooting; Boston Hills Country. Rep. Protestant. Author: Balanced Employment, 1933 (booklet); Balanced Labor, 1931. Home: 2719 Wicklow Road, Shaker Heights 20, O. Office: 7609 Platt Av., Cleveland 4 OH‡

CHAFFE, HENRY HANSELL, lawyer; b. New Orleans, La., Nov. 26, 1877; s. William Hamilton and Ellen (Hansell) C.; A.B., Tulane U., 1898, LL.B., 1900; m. Mary Ewing, Dec. 7, 1907 (died Mar. 15, 1939). Admitted to La. bar, 1900; mem. law firm Terriberry, Butler & Chaffe, 1900-01; in private practice, 1902-03; asso. with Denegre & Blair, 1903-13; mem. Denegre, Leovy and Chaffe, 1913-42; Chaffe, McCall, Bruns, Toler & Phillips, 1942-47; Chaffe, McCall, Toler & Phillips, since Jan. 1948. Mem. bd. trustees John M. Bonner Memorial Home. Mem. Am., La. State and New Orleans bar assns., Maritime Law Assn., Alpha Tau Omega, Order of Coif. Democrat. Episcopalian. Clubs: Boston (pres.) New Orleans Country, Lake Shore (New Orleans). Home: 1431 Josephine St. Office: Whitney Bldg., New Orleans 12 LA‡

CHAISSON, JOHN ROBERT, marine corps officer; b. Swampscott, Mass., Sept. 27, 1916; s. Joseph and Annie Josephine (Donovan) C.; A.B. cum laude, Harvard, 1939; m. Marguerite Martin, Feb. 22, 1946; children—Joseph M., Dorothy (Mrs. Robert Jones), Jane, Thomas M. Commd. 2d lt. USMC, 1941, advanced through grades to lt. gen., 1971; assigned 1st Marine Div., 1942-45, 53-54; chief staff USMC, 1971-72; ret., 1972; dep. dir. regulations AEC, 1972. Decorated D.S.M., Silver Star, Legion of Merit, Bronze Star, Navy Commendation medal. Home: Washington DC Died Sept. 20, 1972; buried Arlington Nat. Cemetery, Arlington VA

CHALMERS, ALLAN KNIGHT, assn. exec., author; b. Cleveland, O., June 30, 1897; s. Andrew Burns and Lillian Mary (Knight) C.; A.B., Johns Hopkins, 1917; B.D. Yale, 1922; D.D., Syracuse U., 1932; LL.D., Am. International Coll., 1932; D.D., Vt. U., 1941; m. Frances Kinghorn, June 15, 1922 (dec.); 1 dau., Elizabeth (Mrs. Gustave Todrank). Tchr. Gilman Sch., Baltimore, Md., 1918-19; ordained ministry Congl. Ch., 1922; minister Broadway Tabernacle Congl. Ch., New York City, 1930-48; professor Preaching and Applied Christianity, Boston University School of Theology, 1948-62, prof. emeritus, 1962-72; exec. president N.A.A.C.P. Legal Def. & Ednl. Fund, N.Y.C., 1962-72. Shepard lecturer on preaching, Bangor Seminary, 1941. Served with Foyer de Soldat, French Army, 1917-18, Motor Transport Corps, U.S. Army, 1918. Trustee Talladega U., Berea Coll. Chmn. Scottsboro Defense Com. Mem. exec. com. Federal Council of Chs., gen. council Congl. and Christian Chs., 1931-40; moderator N.Y. State Congl. Church, 1940-42; mem. bd. dirs. exec. com. Religion and Labor Foundation, Am. Civil Liberties Union, N.A.A.C.P., N.A.A.C.P. Legal Def. Soc. (president), Fellowship of Reconciliation; co-chmn. Fair Employment Practice Council; member Alpha Sigma Phi, Omicron Delta Kappa. Awarded Medaille de la Grande Guerre (France), Verdun medal; recipient Alper award Am. Civil Liberties Union, 1963. Clubs: Century Assn.; Appalachian Mountain, Athaneum (Boston). Author: books including: The Commonplace Prodigal, 1934; Candles in the Wind, 1947; High Wind at Noon, 1948; They Shall Be Free, 1951, That Revolutionary—Christ, 1957. Home: New York City NY Died Jan. 1972.

CHALMERS, HARVEY 2D, author; b. Amsterdam, N.Y., Sept. 11, 1890; s. Arthur Augustus and Emma Appleton (Curtis) C.; A.B., Yale, 1913; m. Ruth Elizabeth Warren, Sept. 11, 1914; children—Arthur A., Shirley (wife of Dr. George H. Carter). President of Harvey Chalmers & Son Inc. Consultant to New York State Dept. of Edn. Served with A.U.S., World War I; disch. with rank of 2d lt. Member of Beta Theta Pi. Republican. Episcopalian. Clubs: N.Y. Fencers, Yale (N.Y. City); Corinthian Yacht (Marblehead, Mass.); Antlers Country (Amsterdam, N.Y.). Author: West to the Setting Sun, 1943; Drums Against Frontenac, 1949; Joseph Brant: Mohawk, 1955; Birth of the Erie Canal, 1960; Last Stand of the Nez Perce: Destruction of a People, 1962; How the Irish Built the Erie, published 1964; Tales of the Mohawk, published 1967. Contributor to Northeast Sportsman, also Field & Stream, Am. Field, Nat. Sportsman, Hunting and Fishing, Outdoors, Field and Stream Reader, 1935-42. Lectr. on N.Y. State and N.E. hist. and Indian wars, govt. and way of life. Research student; source material of Indian cultures and contacts with white prople and Brit. and Am. Development in Mohawk Valley. Home: Amsterdam NY Died Oct. 6, 1971; buried Amsterdam NY

CHAMBERLAIN, ARTHUR VAN DOORN, lawyer; born Rochester, N.Y., Apr. 28, 1891; s. Philetus and Elizabeth (Van Doorn) C.; student U. Rochester, 1910-11; LL.B., Syracuse U., 1914; m. Helen F. Mason, Feb. 18, 1915; 1 son, Philetus Mason. Admitted to N.Y. bar, 1915; sr. mem. Chamberlain, Page & D'Amanda, Rochester, 1915-71, sr. mem. Chamberlain, D'Amanda, Bauman, Chatman & Oppenheimer, specializing trial, appellate, surrogate law. Dir. Found. N.Y. State Bar Assn., Inc. Mem. Monroe Co. Legal Adv. Bd. of Draft Bd., 1917-18. Mem. bd. visitors Syracuse U. Coll. Law (exec. com.). Chmn. N.Y. Lawyers Com. to Support Ct. Reorgn., 1959. Recipient award of merit Syracuse U. Coll. Law Alumni Assn., 1959. Fellow Am. Coll. of Trial Lawyers, American Bar Foundation; member Federation of Bar Associations of Western N.Y. (council), N.Y. State (pres. 1951-52), Am. (past mem. house of delegates), Monroe County bar associations, Nat. Conf. Bar Pres. (past chmn.), Am. Judicature Soc. (dir. 1962-65), Rochester Art Gallery, Rochester Civic Music Assn., Justinian Soc., Phi Delta Phi, Delta Kappa Epsilon. Republican. Presbyn. Mason. Clubs: Oak Hill Country (Rochester, N.Y.); Longboat Beach (Sarasota, Fla.). Home: Honeoye Falls NY Died Mar. 18, 1971.

CHAMBERLAIN, CLARKE E., dentist; born Aurora, Neb., Apr. 23, 1895; s. Thad and Clara E. (Silloway) C.; student Bradley Coll., Peoria, Ill., 1915; D.D.S., Chicago Coll. Dental Surgery, 1918; m. Martha J. Kasjens, Sept. 18, 1918; children—Clarke Wilton, Mary Jeanette (Mrs. George Dickison), Dorothy Ann (Mrs. Richard Millikan). In general practice dentistry and periodontia, Peoria, specializing in peridontia. Mem. Ill. State Bd. Dental Examiners 1941-50. Fellow American College of Dentists; member American Academy Periodontology (sec.), Am. Bd. Periodontology, Omicron Kappa Upsilon, Delta Sigma Delta. Mason (32deg). Home: Peoria IL Died Dec. 12, 1970.

CHAMBERLAIN, MRS. HOPE SUMMERELL;, b. Salisbury, N.C., June 21, 1870; d. Joseph John and Ellen Hannah (Mitchell) Summerell; Mary Baldwin Sem., Staunton, Va., 1886-87; studied etching under Armin Hansen, Monterey, Calif.; Litt.D. from University of North Carolina, 1932; m. Joseph R. Chamberlain, June 23, 1891 (died 1926); children—Mary Mitchell (wife of Prof. A.R. Moore), Jesse Mack, John Summerell, Joseph Redington, and (adopted) Joseph Stickney, Julius Joscelyn, Melissa Ervilla. Chmn. legislative com. State Fed. Women's Clubs which effected establishment, 1917, of Samarcand Manor, state reformatory for women, of which was sec. and trustee, 1917-20; chmn. Women's Council Nat. Defense and food administrator, Wake Co., N.C., 1917-20. Lecturer in English lit., French and Am. history; etcher. Head of Pegram House, Women's Coll., Duke U., 1931. Mem. N.C. Soc. Colonial Dames America. Author: History of Wake County, 1922; Old Days in Chapel Hill, 1926; This Was Home," 1938. Address: Chapel Hill NC‡

CHAMBERLAIN, JOSEPH SCUDDER, prof. chemistry; b. Hudson, O., Mar. 7, 1870; s. William Isaac and Lucy Jones (Marshall) C.; B.S., Ia. State Coll., 1890, M.S., 1892; Ph.D., Johns Hopkins, 1899; grad. study U. of Berlin, 1908-09; student Oxford Univ. (Eng.), 1930-31; m. Mary Cole Brauns, June 23, 1903; 1 dau., Lucy Marshall. Grad. asst. in chemistry, Ia. State Coll., 1890-92, asst., 1894-97; instr. in chemistry, Oberlin (O.) Coll., 1899-1901; research asst. to Prof. Ira Remsen, Johns Hopkins, 1901; asst. chemist, U.S. Dept. Agr., 1901-03, chemist, 1903-08; asso. prof. chemistry, Mass. State Coll., 1909-13, prof. organic and agrl. chemistry since 1913, head chemistry dept., 1928-34, Goessmann prof. 1934-40; emeritus since 1940. Fellow A.A.A.S., Am. Inst. Chemists; mem. Am. Chem. Soc., N.E. Assn. Chemistry Teachers (pres. 1928-30), Phi Beta Kappa, Sigma Xi, Phi Kappa Phi, Delta Tau Delta. Democrat. Episcopalian. Author: Organic Agriculture Chemistry, 1916; Text book of Organic Chemistry, 1921. Co-editor: Chemistry in Agriculture (with C. A. Browne), 1926. Home: Mt. Pleasant, Amherst MA‡

CHAMBERLAIN, LUCY JEFFERIES, univ. prof.; b. Natchez, Miss., July 12, 1893; d. Edward Norman, Sr., and Jane Raymond (Jefferies) Chamberlain; student New York Sch. of Social Work, 1921-23, Sch. of Journalism, Columbia U., 1925-26; B.S., New York U., 1927, A.M., 1930, Ph.D., 1932; m. Rhys Evans Ryan, Sept. 19, 1924. Engaged in business, Jacksonville, Florida, 1912-18; editorial assistant Milbank Memorial Fund, New York, 1928-29; lecturer, dept. sociology and anthropology, Washington Square Coll. of Arts and Science, New York U., 1928-29, asst. prof., 1929-30, asso. prof., 1930-43, prof. since 1943, mem. administrative com., dept. sociol. and anthropol., 1939-40, chmn., 1941-48, chmn. dept. of sociology and anthropology since 1948, also chmn. com. on admissions, and lecturer, Graduate Sch. of Pub. Adminstrn. 1953-58. Executive secretary Lafayette County chapter Am. Red Cross, Darlington, Wis., summer 1922, Shiawassee County chapter, Owosso, Mich., summer 1923; special rep., nat. hdqrs., summer 1924. Lecturer in sociology, U. of Florida, summer sch., 1924; lecturer nat. bd. Y.W.C.A., summers 1929, 1930; lecturer and consultant Nat. Council Jewish Women, Brooklyn, N.Y., 1926-27; executive secretary, Flatbush (Brooklyn, N.Y.) Community Center, 1924, 1925; consultant Jewish Social Service Bur., Brooklyn, 1926. Dir. Lower East Side Met. Area Study (N.Y. City), sponsored by New York U. and U.S. Dept. of Interior, 1931-35. Served as sec. U.S. Base Hosp. No. 43, A.E.F., Blois, France; sec. to comdg. officer U.S. Hosp. Center, Savenay, France; sec. Camn Hosp. No. 69, Bourges. France, 1918-19. Member Alumni Council Assn., N.Y. Sch of Social Work, Columbia, 1941-45, treas. and chmn. finance com., 1942-44, mem. curriculum com., 1946-47. Mem. Am. and Eastern sociol. socs., Am. Assn. Social Workers, Am. Anthron. Assn., N.Y. State Conf. Social Work, Nat. Conf. Social Work; asso. mem. Am. Assn. Schs. of Social Work; com. on Preprofessional Edn. for Social Work, 1947-49; mem. N.Y. State Conf. on Preprofl. Edn. for Social Work; orgn. com., 1947, exec. com., 1948; Am. Council on Edn., Conf.-Inst. for Social Scientists, 1947; mem. National Board Rev. of Motion Pictures, Foreign Policy Assn., White House Conf. on Child Health and Protection (1930), Pi Lambda Theta, Alpha Kappa Delta, Trigonoi. Woman's Auxiliary, Am. Inst. Mining and Metal. Engrs. Episcopalian. Clubs: Essex Fells (N.J.) Country; New York University Faculty (mem. bd. dirs. and exec. com., 1946-47, house com., 1945-47). Contbg. editor: Case Studies in Community Organization, 1928. Contbr. articles and book revs. to professional publs. Home: New York City NY Died May 22, 1969.

CHAMBERLIN, GEORGE ELLSWORTH, consul gen.; b. Woodstock, Conn., February 17, 1872; s. Edward Chandler and M. Jane (Kinney) C.; ed. Woodstock Acad. and Eastman Bus. Coll., Poughkeepsie; m. Grace Anna Stone, of Somerville, Mass., Sept. 7, 1911. Engaged in piano mfg. business, 1893-98; in wholesale shoe business, Boston and New York, 1905; clk., Singapore Consulate Gen., 1905-06; v. and dep. consul-gen. at same place, 1906-10; consul, Swatow, China, [illegible]-June [illegible]910, Cork, Ireland, 1910-14, Georgetown, British Guiana, Apr. 24, 1914-Sept. 22, 1919, Glasgow, Scotland, 1919-32; consul gen. same, June 5, 1924; transferred to Halifax, Nov. 1932; retired Dec. 31, 1935. Presbyn. Mason. Home: Oneonta NY‡

CHAMBERLIN, STEPHEN J., army officer; b. Spring Hill, Kan., Dec. 23, 1889; s. Clark and Minnie (Hare) C.; B.S., U.S. Mil. Acad., 1912; grad. Inf. Sch., 1924, Command and Gen. Staff Sch. (hon. grad.), 1925, Army War Coll., 1933; m. Sarah Chapman Shanks, Mar. 2, 1918; children—Sarah Shanks, Stephen Jones. Commd. 2d lt., U.S. Army, 1912, and advanced through the grades to lieut. general, 1943; served with regt. at San Francisco, El Paso, Philippines, 1912-17; chief troop movement sect., Port of Embarkation, Hoboken, N.J., 1917-18; with 16th Div., General Staff, Camp Kearney, Calif., then chief passenger traffic sect., Office of chief Embarkation Service; asst. chief of staff, Port of Embarkation, Hoboken, N.J., and at Gen. Staff Coll., Washington, D.C., 1918-20; transportation officer, Panama Canal Dept., and with regiment and brigade, 1920-23; with regt., Fort McPherson, Ga., 1923; instr. Nat. Guard, Staunton, Va., 1925; Office, Chief of Inf., Washington, D.C., 1926-30; with regt., Fort McPherson, Ga., 1930-32; asst. chief of staff, G-3, Hawaii Dept., 1933-36; R.O.T.C. duty, Los Angeles high schools, 1936-38; chief Constrn. Div., G-4, War Dept. Gen. Staff, 1938-41; G-4 and chief of staff, U.S. Army Forces, Australia, 1942; G-3, Southwest Pacific Area, U.S. Army Forces Pacific, 1942-45; dep. chief of staff and acting chief of staff, U.S. Army Forces, Pacific and for Supreme Comdr. for Allied Powers, 1945-46; dir. Intelligence, Dept. of the Army, 1946-48; comdg. gen. 5th Army, Chicago. Awarded D.S.M. with 3 Oak Leaf Clusters, Navy Distinguished Service Cross, Silver Star, Phillipine Distinguished Service Star; Order British Empire, Al Merito Militarde, Chile; Odu Nile Grand O, Egypt; Order de la Couronne arec Palme, Croix de Guerre, Belgium; Order of Orange of Nassau with Swords, Netherlands; Egyptian O'Ordre d'Ismail de 28eme classe; French Officer Legion of Honor. Home: Laguna Hills CA Died Oct. 23, 1971; buried Arlington Nat. Cemetery.

CHAMBERLIN, WILLIAM H(ENRY), writer; b. Brooklyn, N.Y., Feb. 17, 1897; s. Ernest V. and May E. (McClintock) C.; grad. Penn Charter Sch., Phila., 1913, Haverford (Pa.) Coll., 1917; m. Sonya Trosten, Mar. 31, 1920; 1 dau., Nadyezhda (Mrs. Klaus Epstein). Asst. mag. editor, Philadelphia Press, 1917-18; asst. book editor, New York Tribune, 1919-22; Moscow corr. The Christian Science Monitor, 1922-34; chief Far Eastern corr. of same in France, 1939-40. Independent writer and lecturer, Haverford Coll., Yale U. and Civil Affairs Training School, Harvard University, since 1940; contbg. editor, The New Leader; editorial contributor, The Wall Street Journal, since 1945. Member of the Academy of Political Sci., Phi Beta Kappa. Author: Soviet Russia, 1930; The Soviet Planned Economic Order, 1931; Russia's Iron Age, 1934; The Russian Revolution, 1917-21, 1935; Collectivism—A False Utopia, 1937; Japan Over Asia, 1937 (revised edit., 1939); The Confessions of an Individualist, 1940; The World's Iron Age, 1941; The Russian Enigma: An Interpretation, 1943; Canada Today and Tomorrow, 1942; America: Partner in World Rule, 1945; The European Cockpit, 1947; America's Second Crusade, 1950; Beyond Containment, 1953; The Evolution of A Conservative, 1959; Appeasement: Road to War, 1962; The German Phoenix, 1963; contributor of articles to the Readers Digest, Human Events, The Russian Review and others; contbr. biographical essays to Saturday Rev., 1965-67. Home: Cambridge MA Died Sept. 12, 1969; buried Mt. Auburn Cemetery, Cambridge MA

CHAMBERS, CHARLES AUGUSTUS, horticulturist; b. Portland, Me., Feb. 22, 1873; s. Joseph Augustus and Maria (Charles) C.; ed. pub. schs., Ark. and La.; m. Alice Roland, of Oakland, Cal., Oct. 6, 1913. Trained in horticulture under George C. Roeding, of Cal.; connected with nursery business in Fresno, 1891—; with Fancher Creek Nurseries 10 yrs.; sec.-treas. Fresno Nursery Co., 12 yrs.; later mgr. nursery dept. of Luther Burbank Co., of San Francisco; now industrial agt. Memphis, Dallas & Gulf Ry. Co. Regarded as an authority on hort. and agrl. topics on Pacific Coast. Democrat. Unitarian. Mem. Pacific Coast Assn. of Nurserymen, Nat. Geog. Soc. Contbr. hort. articles and widely known as writer of humorous stories and feature writer for agrl. press. Address: 1630 3d St., San Diego CA‡

CHAMBERS, FRANCIS T., JR., cons. alcoholism; b. Phila., Pa. Mar. 21, 1897; s. Francis T. and Nanette (Schuyler) C.; grad. Cloyne Sch., Newport, R.I., 1917; m. Jean Knox, 1922; children—Francis Taylor, Catherine (Mrs. Gideon Boericke). Consultant on alcoholism Institute of Pennsylvania Hosp.; vis. lectr. Grad. Sch. Medicine U. Pa. Mem. Mental Health Assn. Southeastern Pa. Cpl. Vol. 1st City Troop, World War. Rep. Episcopalian. Club: Philadelphia. Author: Alcohol: One Man's Meat (with E. A. Strecker), 1938; The Drinker's Addiction, 1968; also articles profl. jours. Home: Horsham PA Died Oct. 30, 1969; buried St. Thomas Church, Whitemarsh PA

CHAMBERS, LENOIR, newspaper editor; b. Charlotte, N.C., Dec. 26, 1891; s. Joseph Lenoir and Grace Singleton (Dewey) C.; grad. Woodberry Forest (Virginia) Sch., 1910; A.B., University of North Carolina, 1914, LL.D., 1960; student Columbia U. Sch. of Journalism, 1916-17; m. Roberta Burwell Strudwick, Sept. 15, 1928; children—Robert Strudwick Glenn (stepson), Elisabeth Lacy. Teacher Woodberry Forest Sch., 1914-16; Washington staff New Republic News Service, 1917; dir. U. of N.C. News Bureau, 1919-21; staff Greensboro (N.C.) Daily News, successively as reporter, city editor, asso. editor, 1921-29; asso. editor Norfolk Virginian-Pilot, 1929-44; editor Norfolk Ledger-Dispatch, 1944-50; editor Norfolk Virginian-Pilot, 1950-61; pres. Norfolk Forum, Inc., 1943-46, also director; mem. Am. Soc. of Newspaper Editors. Served as 1st lt. inf., U.S. Army, with A.E.F., 1917-19. Trustee Woodberry Forest Sch., Norfolk Acad., Norfolk Public Library; chmn. parent's adv. bd. Sweet Briar Coll., 1957-58. Recipient Pulitzer Prize for editorial writing, 1960. Mem. Cum Laude Soc., Acad. Polit. Sci., National Conference of Editorial Writers, Sigma Alpha Epsilon, Phi Beta Kappa, Ind. Democrat. Clubs: Virginia, Norfolk Yacht and Country. (Norfolk). Author: Stonewall Jackson, 1959; Salt Water & Printer's Ink, 1967. Home: Norfolk VA Died Jan. 10, 1970; buried Forest Lawn Cemetery, Norfolk VA

CHAMBERS, VICTOR JOHN, educator; b. Rochester, N.Y., Nov. 18, 1869; s. Robert Wright and Mina (Jones) C.; B.S., U. of Rochester, 1895; Ph.D., Johns Hopkins, 1901; m. Elizabeth Stanley, June 15, 1903; children—Victor S., Charles R. Instr. in organic chemistry, Columbia, 1901-08; prof. chemistry, U. of Rochester, since 1908, head of dept. since 1908, and dean of grad. studies since 1935; retired, 1940. Mem. Am. Chem. Soc., Delta Kappa Epsilon, Phi Beta Kappa, Sigma Xi. Presbyterian. Home: 1300 Clover St., Brighton NY*‡

CHAMBLESS, JOHN ROBERT, confection co. exec.; b. Georgetown, Ga., July 13, 1911; s. Jesse Eugene and Geraline (Hatfiedl) C.; student pub. schs.; m. Frances Eugenia Haines, June 2, 1932; children—Robert Eugene, James Louis. With Tom 1944-58, v.p. charge finance, sec., 1958-72; sec.-treas. Muscogee Sales Corp., Columbus, 1951-72; dir., sec.-treas. Dixie Confections Inc. Columbus, 1944-47; mem. adv. Columbus Bank & Trust Co., 1961. Sec.-treas. Walter Alan Richards Found., Inc., Columbus, 1956-72. Mem. Nat. Assn. Accountants, Ga., Columbus chambers commerce. Methodist. Clubs: Lions, Columbus Country, Executives (Columbus). Home: Columbus GA Died Apr. 28, 1972; interred Park Hill Cemetery, Columbus GA

CHAMBLISS, CHARLES EDWARD, agronomist; b. Petersburg, Va., Aug. 20, 1871; s. David Lewis and Lucy Jane (Mann) C.; B.S., U. of Tenn., 1892, M.S., 1894; m. Lucy Page Smith, June 11, 1896; children—Charles Edward, Bathhurst Lee. Instructor zoology and entomology, U. of Tenn., and entomologist, Tenn. Agrl. Expt. Sta., 1894-1900; state entomologist, Tenn., 1900-01; asso. prof. zoology and entomology, Clemson Coll., and entomologist S.C. Agrl. Expt. Sta., 1901-07; state entomologist of S.C., 1907-08; agronomist in charge of rice investigations, U.S. Dept. of Agr., 1908-30, in Puerto Rico, 1917-19, in Dominican Republic, 1918-19, in Cuba for Tropical Plant Research Foundation, 1927, in charge rice technology and botany, 1930-41, collaborator since 1941. Fellow A.A.A.S.; mem. Am. Soc. Agronomy, Bot. Soc. Washington (sec. 1913-20; pres. 1920), Biol. Soc. Washington (pres. 1933-36), Washington Acad. Sciences (v.p. 1934-36; pres. 1939), Sigma Alpha Epsilon, Phi Kappa Phi. Club: Cosmos. Home: 1833 Kilbourne Pl., Washington DC‡

CHAMLEE, MARIO, operatic tenor; born Los Angeles, May 29, 1892; son of Samuel (M.D.) and Clara E. Chamlee; honorary M.M., University of Southern California, 1924; studied voice with Achille Alberti, Los Angeles, repertoire with Ricardo Dellera, New York; Master of Music, Univ. of Southern Calif., 1924; m. Ruth Miller (singer), Oct. 2, 1919; 1 son, Archer Mario. Mem. faculty, Coll. of Music Univ. of So. Calif. Appeared with small opera cos. for several yrs.; nat. debut, as Cavaradossi, in La Tosca," with Farrar and Scotti, Met. Opera House, New York, Nov. 22, 1920; toured with Scotti Opera Co.; scored notable successes in Lucia," Rigoletto," Butterfly," Faust" and Manon"; debut Manon" and Marouf," Paris, 1929, in Marouf," Brussels, 1929; with Met. Opera Assn., 1937. Served with 77th Div., N.Y. troops, with A.E.F. in France, 18 mos., 1917-19. Mem. The Argonne Players". Dir. Chamlee Studios, Los Angeles. With U.S.O. units, entertainment of soldiers, World War II. Club: Bohemian (San Francisco). Home: 8118 Hollywood Blvd., Los Angeles 46 CA‡

CHAMOVE, ARNOLD S., ophthalmologist. fgn. govt. ofcl.; b. Portland, Ore., June 21, 1902; s. Samuel and Sophia (Adler) C.; B.S., U. Ore., M.D., 1928; m. Elyse Shirek, Mar. 25, 1938; children—Arnold Shirek, Sherry (Mrs. Victor B. Levit). Intern, S.P. Gen. Hosp., San Francisco; resident U. Vienna, 1931; practice medicine specializing in ophthalmology; consul gen. for Ethiopia,

San Francisco, 1964-71. Trustee Pacific U. Decorated Gold Star of Honor (Ethiopia), 1970. Fellow Internat. Coll. Surgeons, All India, Pan-Am. ophthal. socs.; mem. Oxford U. Ophthal. Congress, Ophthal. Soc. U.K. Home: San Francisco CA Died Mar. 1, 1971.

CHANCEL, LUDOVIC, French diplomat; b. Jan. 1, 1901; ed. Lycee Carnot and Faculty Law, U. Paris. Comml. attache, Brazil, 1929; consul Shanghai and Tallinn, 1939, later at Bucharest; del. French Nat. Com. in E. Africa, 1941; counsellor to Arab Govt., later dir. Arabian Affairs, 1944; consul gen., N.Y.C., 1946-51, minister, 1951-52; ambassador to Iraq, 1952-54; del. to French Residency Gen., Morocco, 1954-56; ambassador to S. Africa, 1956-58; chief to protocol Ministry Fgn. Affairs, 1958; ambassador to Czechoslovakia, 1961-64; diplomatic adviser to Govt., 1964-67. Decorated comdr. Legion d'Honneur, comdr. Arts Paris France Deceased

CHANDLER, ALFRED N(OBLIT), economist, publicist; b. Wilmington, Del., Aug. 27, 1858; s. George and Sarah Rebecca (Cain) C.; ed. North East Classical Sem., North East, Md.; bachelor. Telegrapher, operating Phila.-Chicago quadruplex, until 1880; with Robert Glendinning & Co., stock brokers, Phila., 1880-93, making a study of economics and finance. An organizer, 1884, and pres., 1884-89, Henry George Club of Phila., 1st club of that name, and forerunner of others of the name in different parts of the world; organizer, 1887, and served as sec. and treas. Pa. Ballot Reform Assn. to secure legislation to enact Australian secret ballot, finally enacted in all the states in U.S.; mem. lecture staff of Wharton Sch. of Economics and Commerce, U. of Pa., 1890-93; engaged in promotion of pub. utilities, New York and Phila., from 1893. Assisted, 1894, in organizing cavalry co. which developed into the 2d Troop, Phila. City Cav.; a founder of Aero Club of America (N.Y. City), 1905, and the first member to obtain a balloon, the Initial," in which made a number of ascensions; organizer, 1906, and served as pres. Aero Club of Phila.; pres. Automobile Club of Phila., 1906-08. Winner of many yachting prizes. Author: Land Robbery in America, 1942. Home: Roseville, Newark NJ‡

CHANDLER, ANNA CURTIS, story teller; b. Brunswick, Me.; d. Fred Wellington and Marilla Turner (Curtis) C.; B.A., Wellesley, 1909; studied same coll., 1910, later at Columbia; costume class, Eric Pape Art Sch., Boston; m. Harry B. Brainerd. Became connected with photograph dept. of Library of Met. Mus. of Art, New York, 1910; began telling illustrated stories in Lecture Hall of the Museum, 1916; instr. and story teller at Museum, in charge of work with elementary schs. Mem. Am. Federation Art, Am. Assn. Museums, Nat. League of Story Tellers, College Art Assn. Baptist. Clubs: Wellesley, Three Arts, Knickerbocker Story Tellers' Club. Author: Magic Pictures of the Long Ago, 1918; More Magic Pictures of the Long Ago, 1919. Home: New York City NY Died Oct. 21, 1969; buried Nichols NY

CHANDLER, ELBERT MILAM, civil engr.; b. Santa Cruz, Cal., Apr. 11, 1886; s. Milam and Jessie (Peck) Chandler; B.S. in civil engring., U. of Calif., 1907; m. Winifred V. Goodrich, Sept. 26, 1907 (dec. Aug. 1944); children—Dorothy (Mrs. Donald Ballard), Milam (dec.), Geneva (Mrs. Orin Tapert), Benson, Travis; married 2d, Frances Simas, April 21, 1946. Manager and engineer Burbank Irrigation Project, Eastern Washington, 1908-17, chief engr. Naches Selah Irrigation Dist., Yakima Valley, 1917-19, in charge of design and construction of 11 lined tunnels, etc.; chief engr. for State Reclamation Bd. in charge of surveys and designs for irrigation, drainage and flood control projects, 1919-21; acting secretary American Soc. of Civil Engrs., New York, 1921-22; private practice as civil engr. from 1922; prin. project, design, constrn. Hood River Interstate Bridge over Columbia River, also reconstrn. made necessary by constrn. Bonneville Dam. Chmn. Olympia Planning Commission, 1926-38, and 1940-46; past pres., Thurston Co. Taxpayers Assn.; pres. Ore.-Wash. Bridge Co.; pres. Security Properties, Inc. Life mem. Am. Society of Civil Engineers (past pres. Western Wash. sect.), Washington Irrigation Inst. (past pres.). Republican. Mason. Home: Olympia WA Died Apr. 27, 1968.

CHANDLER, GEORGE GARVIN, lawyer; b. Tacoma, Wash., Aug. 23, 1890; s. George Garvin and Joan Alice (Christie) C.; grad. Haverford Sch., 1907; A.B., Yale, 1912, Larned fellow in English, 1913; LL.B., Harvard, 1917; m. Ann G. Howell, May 11, 1935; children—Alice Christie, George Garvin III. Admitted to Pa. bar, 1919; asso. Roberts & Montgomery, 1919-29; partner Montgomery, McCracken, Walker & Rhoads, Phila., 1929-65; prof. torts Temple U., 1924-27; asst. to Hon. Owen J. Roberts, 1924-30; spl. atty. Commonwealth of Pa., 1930-32, 52-55. Trustee Haverford Sch., 1950-63. Served with AEF, 1917-19, lt. col. AUS, 1943-45. Decorated Legion of Merit. Mem. Am., Pa., Phila. bar assns., Harvard Law Sch. Assn. Phila. (pres. 1953-54), Mil. Order Fgn. Wars (comdr. Pa. 1954-55), Phi Beta Kappa, Psi Upsilon Beta. Clubs: Union League Whitford-Exton PA Died Jan. 14, 1973.

CHANDLER, KATHERINE, writer; b. San Francisco, California; d. of William Sylvester and Catherine (Comerford) Chandler; A.B., Leland Stanford Jr. University, 1900. Proprietor and mgr. Deer Park Springs, Lake Tahoe, Calif., 1908-26. Mem. Am. Assn. Univ. Women, Women's City Club of S.F.; Calif. Spring Blossom and Wild Flower Assn. (a founder; pres. 1927-29), Phi Beta Kappa; chmn. Establishment Garden of Shakespeare's Flowers, Golden Gate Park, 1927-29; dir. flower shows, San Francisco, 1925-30. Democrat. Catholic. Clubs: Women's City, San Francisco Stanford Women's. Author: Habits of California Plants, 1903; In the Reign of Coyote, 1905; The Bird-Woman of the Lewis and Clark Expedition, 1905; As California Wild Flowers Grow, 1922; Stories of Wild Flowers Children Love, 1923. Contbr. to mags. Home: 113 Duncan St., San Francisco CA‡

CHANDLER, KENT, mfg. exec.; b. Chicago, Apr. 15, 1892; s. Elisha Eldred and Cornelia Miller (Kent) C.; B.S., U. Chicago, 1913; m. Grace Emeret Tuttle, June 15, 1918; children—Kent, Emerson Tuttle (dec.), Henry Tuttle, Bruce, Nora Farwell. With East St. Louis Cotton Seed Oil Co., 1913-15; with Armour & Co., Chicago, 1915-17, plant supt., Sioux City, Ia., 1917, asst. mgr. fgn. dept., Chicago, 1919-22; investment banking, 1922-34; with A. B. Dick Co., Chgo., 1934-72, sec., 1939-57, sometime vice chmn. exec. com., dir., dir. Am. Metal Products Co., Marshall Field & Co., Pres. Chgo. Fair 1950. Alderman and mayor, Lake Forest, Ill., 1930-40; mem. Chicago Plan Commn., 1935-39; dir. Chicago Regional Planning Assn., 1938-45; dir. Chicago chpt. A.R.C., 1932-47. Mem. Alpha Delta Phi. Republican. Presbyn. Clubs: Chicago, Commercial (Chicago); Onwentsia (Lake Forest). Home: Lake Forest IL Died Oct. 14, 1972; buried Lake Forest Cemetery, Lake Forest IL

CHANDLER, PHILIP, newspaper exec.; b. Los Angeles, Feb. 17, 1907; s. Harry and Marian (Otis) C.; student U. So. Cal., 1926-30; m. Alberta Williamson, Oct. 12, 1933; children—Bruce, Corinne, Jeffrey, Stephen. Circulation agt. Los Angeles Times, 1928-30, asst. gen. mgr., 1936-45, prodn. mgr., 1937-41, v.p., 1941, v.p., general manager, 1945-58, executive vice pres., 1958-61, chmn. bd., 1961-68; vice president Rancho Santa Anita, Inc.; v.p., dir. Chandlis Securities Co.; chmn. bd. Pubs. Paper Co.; dir. Times-Mirror Broadcasting Co. Pres. Los Angeles Times Charities, Inc.; v.p., trustee Pfaffinger Found.; v.p. Boys' Club; Found.—So. Cal.; dir. Los Angeles Times Boys Club member board of trustees Mirror Charities; mem. exec. bd. Salvation Army, Boy Scouts Am. Trustee Claremont Mens Coll. Recipient Sally award Salvation Army, 1964. Clubs: Valley Hunt, Town (Pasadena, Cal.); Flat Rock (Idaho); San Gabriel Country; Irvine Coast Country. Home: Pasadena CA Died May 22, 1968; buried Forest Lawn Cemetery.

CHANDLER, RALPH BRADFORD, newspaper publisher; b. Akron, O., Nov. 25, 1891; s. James Davenport and Sarah (Bardsley) C.; educated high school, Akron, Ohio. Advertising manager for Cincinnati Post, 1914-21; pres. Birmingham (Ala.) Post, 1921-26; pub. Greenville (S.C.) Piedmont, 1926-27; pres. and pub. Mobile Press and Register, 1929-69, pub. emeritus, chmn. bd., 1969-70. Established Chandler Found. for citizens of Mobile. Home: Mobile AL Died Mar. 30, 1970; buried Chapel of The Pines Mausoleum, Pine Crest Cemetery, Mobile AL

CHANEL, GABRIELLE (BONHEUR) (COCO), fashion designer; b. nr. Issoire, Auvergne, France, 1883. Began early career as milliner; creator simplicity of style for women's fashions in hats and dresses, 1920-38, 54-71; mfr. textiles, costumes jewelry; inventor and mfr. perfume. Home: Paris France Died Jan. 10, 1971.*

CHANEY, STEWART, stage designer; b. Kansas City, Mo., June 23, 1910; s. Lee Stewart and Ruby (Shoop) C.; student Yale, 1926-28; studied painting under Andre L'Hote, Paris. Designer plays, including: The Old Maid (Pulitzer Prize play), 1935; Hamlet, 1936; Life With Father, 1939; Twelfth Night, 1940; Voice of the Turtle, 1943; The Late George Apley, 1944; Jacobowsky and the Colonel, 1944; Embezzeled Heaven, 1944; Winter's Tale, 1946; I Know My Love, 1949; The Moon Is Blue, 1951; Late Love, A Girl Can Tell, Sherlock Holmes (all 1953); Faust (Gounod's opera, Covent Garden, London), 1938; The Rivals (Old Vic, London), 1938; Bad Seed also Into Thin Air (London, 1955); Hidden River, 1957; designer ballets, Apollon Musagete (Stravinsky-Balanchine, American Ballet Theatre) 1937; Vienna: 1814 (Weber-Massine Ballet-Russe de Monte Carlo), 1937; Schumann Concerto (Schumann-Nijanska, Ballet Theatre), 1951; designer technicolor films Up In Arms, 1943, A Kid From Brooklyn, 1945; producer Am. Nat. Theater and Acad. prodn. The House of Bernarda Alba, 1951. Guggenheim fellowship for study European theatre, 1937. Mem. New York City NY Died Nov. 1969.

CHANG, HSIN-HAI, educator, author; b. Shanghai, China, June 24, 1900; s. Tung-sen and Shen (Shen-shib) C.; student Tsinghua Coll., 1916-18; A.B. John Hopkins, 1919; M.A., Harvard, 1920, Ph. D., 1923; m. Siang-mei Han, Feb. 28, 1927; children—Yi-an (Mrs. Wenchung Chou), David Ping-chung. Came to U.S., 1941, naturalized, 1964. Prof. Tsinghau Coll. and Nat. U., Peking, 1923-26; prof., chmn. dept. Western lit., dean coll. Liberal Arts, Nat. Central U., Nanking, 1926-27; prof. v.p. Kwanghua U., 1927-28; sr. counsellor, dir. European and Am. Dept., Chinese Ministrv Fgn. Affairs 1928-33; envoy extraordinary, minister plenipotentiary Republic of China to Portugal, Poland and Czechoslovakia, 1933-37; prof. Western lit. Kwanghua U., 1937-40; lectr. in U.S. on China's war effort, 1941-45; spl. asst. to Chinese Fgn. Minister, 1943; research prof. L.I. U., 1950-53; vis. prof. Adelphi Coll., 1954-56; prof. English lit. and Asian culture Fairleigh Dickinson U., 1956-69, prof. emeritus, 1969-73. Dir. China Inst. London. del. to Universal Postal Congress 1933; dir. Chinese UN Assn., 1947-48; China's chief del. Congress World Fedn. UN Assn., Geneva, 1948; participant as faculty for Pacific-Asia Seminar sponsored by Inst. on Man and Sci. and East-West Center, Honolulu, 1966; invited by Senate Fgn. Relations Com. to testify on U.S.-China relations, 1966. Trustee Tsinghua U., Peking, 1927. Decorated Order of the Nile (Egypt). 1933; Order of the Briliant Jade (China), 1936. Mem. Royal Asiatic, Social and Political Sci., Am. Oriential Soc., Acad. Soc., Am. Acad. Polit. Sci., Am. Assn. Asian. Studies. Club: Harvard (N.Y.C.) Author: Letters form a Chinese Diplomat, 1941; The Fabulous Concubine (novel) 1956 (transl. into French, German, Swedish); Within the Four Seas; 1958; America and China; A New Approach to Asia, 1966 (transl. into Italian); Matthew Arnold and the Humanistic View of Life, Contbr. articles to scholarly jours. Home: Great Neck NY Died Feb. 1973.

CHAPIN, CORNELIA VAN AUKEN, sculptor; b. Waterford, Conn.; d. Lindley Hoffman and Cornelia Garrison (Van Auken) Chapin; ed. pvt. schs.; unmarried. Has exhibited since 1930; studied with Mateo Hernandez, Paris. Exhibited Internat. Expn. Art and Technique, Paris, 1937 (won 2d Grand Prize, class stone sculpture), World's Fair, New York, 1939-40, San Francisco Golden Gate Internat. Expn., 1939, Brooklyn (N.Y.) Museum, Modern Museum (Washington), Art Centre (Oganquit, Me.), Salon des Tuileries, Salon d'Automne, Paris, Fairmont Park Art Assn., Internat. Sculpture Show, Phila. Museum, Pa. Acad. (Philadelphia), San Francisco Art Museum, Montclair (New Jersey) Museum, Springfield Art Museum; private collections Paris, London, New York, Philadelphia, Washington; Christ the King," high altar of Cathedral St. John the Divine, N.Y. City; Giant Frog," Rittenhouse Square, Phila. Mem. sculpture jury Contemporary Art Exhibit N.Y. World's Fair, 1939; sculpture chmn. N.Y. Met. Area, National Art Week, 1941; work invited for 3d Internat. Exhbn. of Sculpture, Philadelphia, 1949; sculptor mem. N.Y.C. Art Commission, 1951-53. Works in leading museums and national parks. Fellow National Sculpture Soc. (sec. 1942-45; chmn. library and research com. of council), Academician National Academy Design; mem. Soc. Salon d'Autmore, Paris, 1936, Allied Artists Am., Inc., Artists for Victory (Sculpture chmn., 1942). Dir. Kips Bay Boys' Club, N.Y. City, Lectures widely on Carving Direct from Life, Some Tales and Tools. Clubs: Cosmopolitan, National Arts, Architectural League of New York. Address: Lakeville CT Died Dec. 4, 1972. V1973I

CHAPIN, E(DWARD) BARTON, lawyer; b. Warwick Neck, R.I., July 13, 1885; s. Edward Pike and Cornelia Ann (Smith) C.; grad. Phillips Acad., Andover, Mass., 1903; A.B., Yale, 1907; LL.B., Harvard, 1910; m. Jeannette Ogden Thomas, June 19, 1915; children—Edward Barton, Melville. Admitted to Mass. bar, 1909, since practiced in Boston; partner firm Warner, Stackpole, Stetson & Bradlee, and predecessors, 1917-67. Dir. Bird & Son, Inc., E. Walpole, Mass., 1945-65, mem. exec. com., 1945-64; dir., mem. trust com. Merchants Nat. Bank, Boston, 1944-60, mem. exec. com., 1953-60; dir. New Eng. Merchants Nat. Bank, Boston, 1961-62, adv. dir., 1962-67, mem. trust com., 1961-67; trustee William Underwood Co., Watertown, Mass., 1953-67; corporator Andover Savs. Bank, 1932-67, trustee, 1945-60. Fuel adminstr., Andover, World War I; appeal agt. Andover dist. Draft Bd., World War II. Bd. dirs. Boston Legal Aid Soc., 1934-55; trustee, clk. bd. Abbot Acad., Andover, 1920-34, trustee, pres. bd., 1934-52. Mem. Am., Mass., Boston bar assns. Conglist. Clubs: Union, Yale (Boston). Home: Andover MA Died Nov. 9, 1967; buried Spring Grove Cemetery, Andover MA

CHAPLIN, JAMES CROSSAN, banker; b. Pittsburgh, Pa., Sept. 7, 1863; s. James Crossan and Martha (Harris) C.; student, Pritchet Inst., Glasgow, Mo., 1875-79, Duffs Coll., Pittsburgh, 1880-81; m. Fannie Campbell, Feb. 5, 1891 (dec.); children—James Crossan, David C. Messenger, Citizens Nat. Bank, 1881-91; with Fidelity Title & Trust Co., 1891-1902; became v.p. Colonial Trust Co., 1902, chmn. of bd., Jan. 1941; dir. Pittsburgh Railways Co., Union Colleries. Mason. Clubs: Duquesne, Allegheny County, Edgworth. Home: 305 Frederick Av., Sewickley, Pa. Office: Colonial Trust Co., Wood St., Pittsburgh PA

CHAPLINE, VANCE DUNCAN, naval officer; born Red Cloud, Neb., Sept. 19, 1887; s. William Ridgely and

Henrietta (Duncan) C.; student U. of Neb., 1904-05; B.S., U.S. Naval Acad., 1909; m. Marion Pilsbury, Aug. 9, 1938; children by previous marriage—Dorothy Drake (Mrs. Richmond D. Fitzgerald), Frances Drake; step-daughters, Cynthia Billings Morgan (Mrs. William C. Wilcox), Frances Pilsbury Morgan (Mrs. Charles C. Hartigan). Commd. ensign, U.S. Navy, 1911, and advanced through the grades to rear admiral; comd. destroyers operating out of Brest, France on Troop Convoy, World War I; dir. Fleet Maintenance Div., Office of Operations, Navy Dept., Washington, World War II; retired Nov. 1, 1946; asst. to the pres. Marine Transport Lines Inc., 1946-54. Decorated Navy Cross, Legion of Merit (U.S.), officer Legion of Honor (France), Hon. Comdr. Mil. Div. Order of British Empire. Mem. U.S. Naval Acad. Alumni Assn. Clubs: Army and Navy, Army-Navy Country (Washington); N.Y. Yacht; Chevy Chase Country; Propeller Club of Amrica. Home: Washington DC Died Aug 1970.

CHAPMAN, DANIEL KNOWLTON, broker; b. Greenwich, Conn., July 31, 1904; s. Edwin N. and Charlotte F. (Knowlton) C.; ed. Pomfret Sch.; A.B., Williams Coll., 1926; m. Carroll H. Ferguson, Jan. 14, 1928; children—Daniel K., Diana F. Partner Chisholm and Chapman, 1927-41, Francis I. du Pont & Co., 1941-69; mem. Chgo. Bd. Trade, Westchester Rep. County Committeeman; chairman Rep. Town Com., Newcastle, N.Y., 1958-59. Dir. Boys Club, Mt. Kisco, N.Y., 1941-50; alumni trustee, Williams Coll., 1945-50, permanent trustee, 1963-69. Member of Society of Alumni, Williams Coll. (exec. com. 1945-50, v.p. 1958-61, pres. 1961-63), Delta Kappa Epsilon (pres., trustee Epsilon chpt. 1956-62), Gargoyle Soc. Clubs: Bedford Golf & Tennis, Broad St., Williams (N.Y.; gov., pres., 1947-50). Home: Mt. Kisco NY Died June 24, 1969; buried Putnam Cemetery, Greenwich CT

CHAPMAN, DWIGHT WESTLEY, JR., psychologist; b. South Bend, Ind., June 4, 1905; s. Dwight Westley and Carrie Ethel (Carpenter) C.; A.B., Harvard, 1927, Ph.D., 1930; Sheldon Traveling fellow U. Leipzig, 1927-28; m. Harriet Nye, Sept. 27, 1930; m. 2d, Elisabeth Halsted Bowie, June 30, 1942; children—David Dwight, Judith Carpenter (Mrs. Joseph Dixon), Michael Beverley. Instr., tutor psychology Harvard, 1930-36; psychologist statistician, psychopathic clinic Recorder's Ct., Detroit, 1936-37; instr. psychology Columbia, 1937-38; tchr. psychology Bennington (Vt.) Coll., 1938-42; study dir., div. program surveys Dept. Agr., 1942, research dir., 1943-44; personnel assessment staff OSS, 1945; dir. nat. surveys div. Office Civilian Requirements, 1946; asst. research dir. Washington Post, 1946-47; asso. Washington Sch. Psychiatry, 1947-51; prof. psychology, chmn. dept., Vassar Coll., 1952-68, prof. emeritus psychology, 1968-73; vis. prof. psychology U. Mich., 1951-52; panel dir. com. on human resources Research and Devel. Bd., 1947-48, dep. exec. dir., 1949, exec. dir., 1950-52; co-chmn. com. on Disaster Studies, NRC, 1955-57. Mem. Am. Psychol. Assn., Soc. Psychol. Study Social Issues. Phi Beta Kappa. Author: (with G.W. Baker) Man and Society in Disaster, 1962. Home: Poughkeepsie NY Died Apr. 11, 1973.

CHAPMAN, GEORGE HERBERT, civil engr.; b. Chgo., Dec. 9, 1898; s. George Orlando and Nellie (Cross) C.; diploma Chgo. Tech. Coll., 1922-26; m. Mary Lucille McNamara, Oct. 20, 1921; 1 son, Gerald McNamara. Project engr. Allen & Garcia Co., Chgo., 1946-48; chief engr., v.p. Mines Engring. Co., Chgo., 1949-54; sr. civil engr. Paul Weir Co., Chgo., 1954-61; pvt. practice cons. engring., Chgo., 1961-67. Served as maj. AUS, 1943-46. Named officer Order of Leopold II (Belgium). Registered profl. engr., Ill., Mich., W. Va.. Mem. Nat., W.VA. socs. profl. engrs., Am. Soc. C.E., Am. Inst. Mining Engrs., Ill. Mining Inst. Presbyn. Mason. Home: Arlington Heights IL Died Dec. 29, 1967.

CHAPMAN, JOHN (ARTHUR), journalist; b. Denver, Colo., June 25, 1900; s. Arthur and Lillian Mathewson (Eddy) C.; student U. Colo., 1916-17, 17-18, Columbia, 1919-21; H.H.D. (honorary), University of Denver; married Georgia Christina Anderson, July 31, 1923; 1 dau., Karin. Reporter Denver Times, 1917-19, The News, N.Y., 1920-23; mgr. Paris bureau Pacific and Atlantic Photos, 1924-26; reporter The News, 1926-29, dramatic editor from 1929; conductor of column Mainly about Manhattan, 1931-40; Hollywood corr., 1940-42; drama critic, 1943-71; lectr. drama N.Y.U., 1956-57. Mem. N.Y. Drama Critics Circle (pres. 1949-51), Sigma Phi Epsilon. Clubs: Dutch Treat (pres. 1943-71), Silurians (N.Y.C.); Editor, Best Plays and Yearbook of Drama, 1947-53; Theatre, 1953-56; Broadway's Best, 1957-60; Tell It to Sweeney, aHistory of the N.Y. Daily News. Co-editor: Best Plays of Westport CT Died Jan. 19, 1972; buried CO

CHAPMAN, JOHN MARTIN, economist; b. Big Otter, W.Va., Jan. 15, 1887; s. John Bunyan and Sarah (Mollahan) C. student Marshall Coll., Huntington, W.Va., 1907-10, W.Va. U., 1912-14; A.B., Ind. U., 1917; student U. of Wis., summer 1917; A.M., Columbia, 1920, Ph.D., 1923; m. Mary Kathryn Gibson, Aug. 22, 1928; children—Barbara Lee (Mrs. Richard Sorich), Mary Anne. Prin. high sch. Masontown, W.Va., 1912-16; instr. New York U., 1920-22; with Federal Reserve Bd., 1920-21; research div., Bureau of Foreign and Domestic Commerce, summer, 1923; lecturer, Sch. of Business, Columbia, 1922-23, asso. prof. of banking, 1944-53, prof., 1953-55; adviser to State Banking Dept., Charleston, W.Va., 1929-30; tech. and economic adviser State Banking Bd., Columbus, O., 1933-34; sr. research asst. Nat. Bureau of Econ. Research, 1938-39; exec. v.p. Council Applied Economics, New York, 1937-39; econ. adviser Bank of America Nat. Trust and Saving Assn., 1939-43; chairman, Am. Economist Council for Study of Branch Banking 1939-70. Served as chief petty officer U.S.N.R., 1917-21, on active duty Sept., 1917-July, 1919. Member American Economic Association, American Marketing Assn. (mem. com. on consumer credit), Alpha Kappa Psi, Gamma Sigma. Club: Columbia University. Author: Fiscal Functions of Federal Reserve Banks, 1923; Problems in Money, Credit and Banking (with R. B. Westerfield), 1927; Contemporary Banking (with H. P. Willis and R. W. Robey), 1933; The Concentration of Banking, 1934; The Banking Situation (with H. P. Willis), 1934; The Economics of Inflation (with H. P. Willis), 1935; Commercial Banks and Consumer Instalment Credit (with associates), 1940; Banking Facilities for Bankless Towns (S. D. Southworth), 1941; Branch Banking (with R. B. Westerfield), 1942. Contbr. to banking and econ. jours. Home: Paterson NJ Died Dec. 15, 1970.

CHAPMAN, KATHARINE HOPKINS, author; b. Selma, Ala., Mar. 4, 1872; d. Thomas Holmes and Mary Elizabeth (Glass) Hopkins; grad. Shorter Coll., Rome, Ga., 1889; Lake Chautauqua, N.Y., 1904; m. Dr. John Thomas Chapman, of McKinley, Ala., Oct. 8, 1891. Author: Love's Way in Dixie, 1905; The Fusing Force, 1911; also short stories in various mags. Address: 219 Lapsley St., Selma AL‡

CHAPMAN, LEVI S(NELL), lawyer; b. Fayetteville, N.Y., Oct. 15, 1865; s. Nathan Randall and Martha Maria (Tibbits) C.; prep. edn., Fayetteville Union Sch.; student Whitestown (N.Y.) Acad., 1884-85; A.B., Syracuse U., 1889; m. Lucia Louise Pattengill, Nov. 30, 1892 (died June 15, 1932); children—Mrs. Ella Louise Cady, Charles Randall, Mrs. Lucia Maria Beadel; m. 2d, Maudie Lorena Stone, June 17, 1933. Admitted to New York bar, 1891, beginning as member firm Newell & Chapman, Syracuse; now member firm Chapman, Newell & Crane; pres., sec. and treasurer North Am. Holding Corp., organized to carry on benevolences of late George H. Maxwell; organizer, 1899, Morningside Cemetery, now pres. Morningside Cemetery Assn.; organizer, 1909, dir. and atty., 1909-23, City Bank Trust Co. (now merged with First Trust & Deposit Co.); chmn. bd. Pierce, Butler & Pierce Mfg. Corp., 1916-24. Clk. Bd. U.S. Gen. Appraisers, N.Y. City, 1891-92; mem. N.Y. Gen. Assembly, 1895. Pres. Am. Bapt. Pub. Soc., 1921-22; trustee Syracuse U. (ex-v.p. bd.), Syracuse Y.M.C.A. (ex-pres.); trustee Rochester Theol. Sem. many yrs. Mem. Am., N.Y. State and Onondaga County bar assns., S.A.R., Phi Beta Kappa, Delta Upsilon. Republican. Mason. Home: 321 Westcott St., Syracuse 10; also Pennsylvania Hotel Annex, St. Petersburg, Fla. Office: City Bank Bldg., Syracuse 2 NY‡

CHAPMAN, W(ILBERT) M(CLEOD), ichthyologist, writer; b. Kalama, Washington, Mar. 31, 1910; s. Albert Bradford and Ivy Myrtle (McLeod) C.; B.S., U. of Wash., 1932, M.S., 1933, Ph.D., 1927; m. Mary Elizabeth Swaney, Mar. 22, 1935; children—Lewis McLeod, Alan Bruce, Jane Elizabeth, Thomas Malcolm, Jonathan Emery, Kathryn Ann. Scientific assistant with the International Fisheries Commn., 1933-35; biologist, Wash. State Dept. of Fisheries, 1935-41; aquatic biologist, U.S. Fish and Wildlife Service, 1941-42; oyster biologist, Wash. State Planning Council, 1942; curator of fishes, Calif. Acad. of Sciences, 1943-47; sr. fisheries specialist in charge Fisheries Project, Bd. of Econ. Warfare, South Pacific, 1943-44; dir., Sch. of Fisheries, U. of Wash., 1947; spl. asst. to under sec. of state, U.S. Dept. of State, 1948-51; dir. of research American Tunaboat Assn., 1951-70. Fellow, Calif. Academy of Sciences, John S. Guggenheim Memorial Foundation; mem. Inst. of Food Technologists, Am. Soc. of Ichthyologists and Herpetologists (bd. of govs., pres., West. Div., 1940), Oceanographic Soc. of Pacific, A.A.A.S., Pacific Fishery Biologists, Western Soc. of Naturalists. Methodist. Author: Fishing in Troubled Waters, 1948. Contbr. numerous articles on fish and fisheries to Scientific and popular periodicals, since 1932. Home: San Diego CA Died July 1970.

CHAPMAN, WILLIAM EDGAR, foreign service officer (retired); born Mt. Pisgah, Arkansas, February 1, 1877; son of Charles Arnold and Alice (Blevins) Chapman; LL.B., Washington College of Law, 1914; LL.M., National University, 1915; married Maurine Eva Oleson, Feb. 12, 1906 (now dec.); 1 dau., Clara Alice; m. 2d, Alice Bertha Moerner, Sept. 19, 1929; 1 son, Robert Lane. Mem. Company B, 33d Regiment, U.S. Vols., in Philippines, 1899-1901; teacher and asst. supt. schs., P.I., 1901-08; editor Iloilo Enterprise; clerk War Dept., Washington, D.C., 1909-10; asst. supt. State, War and Navy Dept. bldgs. Washington, D.C., 1910-16; admitted to D.C. bar, 1915; apptd. consul and assigned to Dept. of State, 1916; consul to Nogales, Mex., Jan.-May 1917, Guaymas, May 1917, Mazatlan, 1917-25, Sault Ste. Marie, Can., 1925-26, Torreon, 1926, Puerto Mexico and Monterey, 1927, Cali, Colombia, 1928-30, North Bay, Can., 1930-32, Bilbao, Spain, 1932-37; 2d sec. of Embassy, Madrid, 1937; consul, Gibraltar, 1938-40; retired June 30, 1940. Mem. United Spanish War Vets and various clubs including Royal Yacht Club of Gibraltar. Norman OK‡

CHAPPELL, MATTHEW N(APOLEON), psychologist; b. Wakefield, R.I., July 26, 1900; s. William Henry Hazzard and Grace Mary (Stillman) C.; B.S., R.I. State Coll., 1924; grad. student training course, Westinghouse Elec. Mfg. Co., 1924-25, Ph.D., Columbia, 1929; m. Arlene Jane Brown, Dec. 24, 1931; 1 dau., Suzanne (Mrs. Finch). Elec. engr. Brooklyn Edison Co., N.Y. City, 1925-26; instr. in extension, Columbia U., 1927-29, 1936-38, dept. of psychology, 1929-36; sr. staff psychologist, The Psychol. Corp., 1938-39, and 1947-50; research dir. C. E. Hooper, Inc., radio audience research, 1939-41; pvt. consultant to bus. industry and research orgns., 1941-47; chmn. dept. psychology, Hofstra Univ., 1950-61, dir. psychol. workshop, now emeritus; cons. to bus. and industry; treas. Am. Inst. Sci. Communications, Inc., 1966-68; clin. cons.; developed and presented TV program People, for National Education Television Center. Diplomate in business and industrial psychology, Am. Bd. Examiners in Prof. Psychology. Licensed profl. psychologist in New York State. Dir. research projects in rehab. alcoholics. Fellow div. bus. and indsl. psychology, Am. Psychol. Assn.; fellow N.Y. Acad. Sci.; mem. Am. Assn. U. Profs., Eastern, N.Y. State, Nassau Co. (pres. 1953-54), psychol. assns., A.A.A.S., Sigma Xi, Alpha Epsilon Delta. A pioneer in process" conception of psychol. therapy. Author: In the Name of Common Sense, Worry & Its Control, 1938; Back to Self Reliance, 1939; Radio Audience Measurement, 1941; Worry and Its Control, 1961. Contributor articles in sci. and trade mags. Home: Massapequa NY Died Feb. 10, 1968; buried Raymond Hill Cemetery, Carmet NY

CHARBONNEAU, LOUIS HENRY, lawyer; b. Detroit, Jan. 21, 1897; s. Louis Israel and Mary Ellen (Cadieux) C.; LL.B., U. Detroit, 1920; m. May Ellen Young, Feb. 6, 1922; children—Frank L., Louis H., Mary Helen (Mrs. Bruce Mellett), Ann Elizabeth (Mrs. Stephen Pobutski), Michael J. Admitted to Mich. bar, 1920; asst. v.p. Union Trust Co., 1920-30; v.p. Detroit Life Ins. Co., 1931-35; practice of law, Detroit, 1936-60, 66-71; dean and professor University Detroit (Michigan) School of Law, 1960-66. Served as 1st lt. U.S. Army, World War I; from lt. col. to brig. gen., AUS, World War II. Decorated Bronze Star Medal (U.S.); Croix de Guerre (France); Fourragerre (Belgium). Mem. State Bar of Mich. (commr.), Am., Detroit (past pres., director) bar assns., Am. Legion. Mil. Order World Wars, Mil. Order Fgn. Wars. Delta Theta Phi. Roman Catholic. K.C. Home: Grosse Pointe Park MI Died Aug. 13, 1971; buried Mt. Olivet Cemetery, Detroit MI

CHARIPPER, HARRY A., educator; b. N.Y.C., July 7, 1900; s. Adolph and Hannah (Breier) C.; B.S., N.Y.U., 1926, M.S., 1927, Ph.D., 1929; Litt.D., Long Island University, 1958; m. Else-Marie Holzman (M.D.), Apr. 17, 1926; 1 son, Bret Adolph. On teaching staff N.Y.U., from 1926, becoming head of all-univ. dept. biology; biologist dept. of labs. Beth Israel Hospital, N.Y.C.; cons. on acad. placement fgn. students Inst. Internat. Edn., N.Y.C. Bd. dirs. Jewish Culture Found., N.Y.U. Fellow N.Y. Zool. Soc., A.A.A.S., N.Y. Acad. Scis., Gerontological Soc., Inc., Am. Inst. Biol. Scis. Am. Soc. Geriatrics, N.Y. Acad. Medicine (asso.); mem. Am. Assn. Anatomists, Am. Soc. Zool., Am. Physiol. Soc., Assn. Study Internal Secretions, Soc. Exptl. Biol. and Medicine, Harvey Soc., Nat. Sci. Tchrs. Assn., Jewish Acad. Arts and Sci., Am. Mus. Natural History (corr. mem.), N.Y. Zool. Soc. (research asso.), Sigma Xi. Jewish religion. Author: The Microscope and Its Use, 1943; also articles med. and sci. jours. Home: Rockaway Beach NY Died Nov. 17, 1971.

CHARLES, FRANCES, author; b. San Francisco, Apr. 10, 1872; d. Henry A. and Martha G. C.; ed. San Francisco grammar and high schs.; unmarried. Employed in Southern Pacific R.R. office, San Francisco, for 4 yrs. At age of 16 wrote her first book. Author: Siftings from Poverty Flat, 1889; In The Country God Forgot, 1902; The Siege of Youth, 1903; The Awakening of the Duchess, 1903; Pardner of Blossom Range, 1906. Address: 370 26th Av., San Francisco‡

CHARLTON, CHARLES MAGNUS, clergyman; b. Maynard, Mass., Oct. 12, 1877; s. Emmanuel Carlson and Bellona Maria (Fisk) C.; student Wesleyan Acad., Wilbraham, Mass., and Boston Univ.; S.T.B., Boston U., 1898; m. Lucia Sarah Chamberlain, June 17, 1904 (deceased); children—Frances Lincoln, Newell Chamberlain, Lucia Woodruff; m. 2d, Jessie M. Caddoo. Ordained M.E. ministry, 1898; minister in Vt. conf., 1898-1901; appointed by Pres. Theodore Roosevelt, chaplain U.S. Navy, Oct. 17, 1901; served in P.I. and on

Asiatic Sta., 1901-04; Naval Training Sta., Newport, R.I., 1904-06; U.S.S. Georgia, 1906-09; Navy Yard, Norfolk, Va., 1909-10; Navy Yard, Boston, 1910-13; U.S.S. Nebraska, 1913-15; training sta., Newport, R.I., 1915-17; U.S.S. Pennsylvania, 1917; with U.S. Marines, A.E.F., 1917-19; participated in Belleau Woods, Chateau Thierry, Soissons and St. Miheil operations; Navy Yard and Prison, Portsmouth, N.H., June 1, 1919-Nov. 21, 1921 (resigned); former rector Christ Ch. Parish (Protestant Episcopal), Providence, R.I.; later asso. rector St. Stephens Parish, Lynn, Mass., St. Mark's Ch., Boston; and Gloucester, Mass.; now chaplain and dir., Seamen's Club of Boston. Trustee National Sailor's Home, Duxbury, Mass. Mem. North Sea Mine Force Assn., Mil. Order World Wars, Appalachian Mountain Club. Nat. chaplain-in-chief, Commandery N. and M.; order of Spanish-Am. War and comdr. Mass. Commandery; Mass. Dept. chaplain of V.S.W.V. Mason (32 deg.). Home: 176 Marlborough St. (B 16) Boston, Mass.; and Gloucester MA‡

CHARNAUX-GRILLET, RAYMOND PAUL, mfg. co. exec.; b. Pontarlier, France, Nov. 1, 1922; s. Henry G. and Mary (Bourgeois) Charnaux-G.; B.Sc., U. Besancon (France), 1941, certificate physics, 1943; M.B.A., U. Toronto, 1954; m. Helga Haas, Oct. 26, 1957; children—Hubert, Elizabeth, Lisa-Anne. Came to U.S., 1954, naturalized, 1960. Vice chmn., dir. Joy Mfg. Holding, SA, Luxembourg; v.p. Joy Mfg. Co., Pitts.; pres. Joy Internat., S.A., Panama; dir. Joy-Sullivan Ltd., London, Eng., Joy-Ville-Gozet, S.A., Paris, France. Mem. I.E.E.E. Address: Brussels Belgium

CHARNOCK, DONALD AUSTIN, physician; b. Vancouver, B.C., Can., Sept. 25, 1893; s. George Austin and Sarah (Johnson) C.; A.B., U. Cal. at Berkeley, 1921; M.D., Harvard, 1925; m. Gretta Jane Gibson, July 9, 1929; 1 dau., Lois Jane (Mrs. James E. Stickler). Intern Univ. Cal. Hosp., San Francisco, 1925-26; grad. tng. urology U. Cal. Hosp., 1925-29; pvt. practice urology, Los Angeles, 1929-68; chief div. urology Childrens Hosp., Los Angeles, 1942-60, sr. physician, 1960-68; prof. urol. surgery, head dept., U. So. Cal. Sch. Medicine, 1957-59. Mem. Adv. Bd. for Med. Specialists, 1962. Served with U.S. Army, 1917-18. Diplomate Am. Bd. Urology (pres. 1962). Fellow A.C.S.; mem. Am. (ho. dels.), Cal. (pres. 1957) med. assns., Los Angeles Acad. Medicine, (pres. 1958-59), Am. Assn. Genito-Urinary Surgeons, Am. Urol. Assn. (exec. com.). Contbr. articles profl. jours. Los Angeles CA Died June 16, 1968; buried Forest Lawn Meml. Park

CHASE, EUGENE PARKER, coll. prof.; b. New Britain, Conn., Apr. 19, 1895; s. Charles Francis and Elizabeth Hance (Parker) C.; A.B., Dartmouth, 1916; Rhodes scholar from N.H. to Magdalen Coll., Oxford U., B.A., 1919; M.A., Harvard, 1921, Ph.D., 1924; M.A., Oxford, 1938; m. Ann Frances Hastings, June 30, 1923; children—Elisabeth Huntington (Mrs. John Morris Trimmer), Katharine Safford (Mrs. John Packer Sibun). Instructor in history Massachusetts Institute of Technology, 1919-20; tutor Harvard, 1921-23; asst. prof. history and govt., Wesleyan U., Conn., 1923-26, U. of Vt., summer, 1926; asso. prof. govt., Lafayette Coll., 1926-29, prof. from 1929, then Fred Morgan Kirby prof. civil rights, also head of dept. of govt. and law; visiting professor, University of Virginia, 1950-51; with Dept. of State, Washington, D.C., 1943-46; lectr. Sch. Am. Studies, Nice, France, summer 1953; Fulbright lecturer in France, 1956. Member of American Polit. Science Assn., Am. Hist. Assn., Fgn. Policy Assn., Am. Assn. Univ. Profs. (mem. council 1942-45), Phi Beta Kappa (sec. Lafayette chpt. since 1929, senator united chpts. from 1946), Theta Chi. Democrat. Episcopalian. Club: Cosmos (washington). Editor and translator of Barbe-Marbois's Our Revolutionary Forefathers, 1929. Author: Democratic Governments in Europe—England, 1938; Government in Wartime Europe—England, 1942; United Nations in Action, 1950. Member of the board of editors Am. Polit. Science Rev., 1942-45. Contbr. to mags. and periodicals. Home: Hebron CT Died Jan. 23, 1972.

CHASE, H. STEPHEN, banker; b. San Jose, Cal., Jan. 16, 1903; s. Stephen Harold and Katherine Emily C.; A.B., Stanford, 1925; M.B.A., Harvard, 1927; m. Mary Bonar, Feb. 4, 1930; children—Judith (Mrs. James Ludwig), Stephanie (Mrs. William MacColl). With Wells Fargo Bank Am. Trust Co. (formerly Am. Trust Co.), 1927-68, with various brs., 1927-40, v.p., mgr. Sacramento dist., 1940-55, sr. v.p., San Francisco, 1955-60, exec. v.p., 1960-64, president, 1964-66, chmn. bd., 1966-68; dir. Cal. Western States Life Ins. Co. (Sacramento), S.H. Chase Lumber Co. (San Jose). Member California Highway Commission, 1951-58. Clubs: The Family (San Francisco), Pacific Union, San Francisco Golf, Merchants Exchange (San Francisco). Home: San Francisco CA Died Oct. 15, 1969.

CHASE, HAROLD STUART, realty developer; b. Boston, July 23, 1890; s. Hezekiah Griggs and Nina Wheeler (Dempsey) C.; B.S., U. Cal. at Berkeley, 1912; m. Gertrude Boyer, July 28, 1917; 1 dau., Barbara (Marchioness of Landsdowne) (dec.); stepchildren—Gertrude (Mrs. Raoul Schumacher). Business career with H. G. Chase Real Estate, Santa Barbara, Cal., 1912-70; pres., dir. La Cumbre Mut. Water Co., Laguna Blanca Water Co., Castro Valley Ranch, Inc., Dune Lakes, Ltd.; chmn. adv. bd. Security-First Nat. Bank, Los Angeles, Santa Barbara br., dir., 1924-70; dir. Burroughts Corp., 1929-70. Mem. Santa Barbara Earthquake Relief Com. of 15, 1925; chmn. Pres.'s Unemployment Relief Com., Santa Barbara, 1931-32, v.p., dir. Community Chest, 1931-39, 45-46, War Chest, 1942-44; mem. U.S. Treasury Def. Savs. Com. for So. Cal., 1941; asso. adminstr. War Savs. Staff for So. Cal., 1942; So. Cal. War Finance Com., 1942-46; chmn. Santa Barbara Co. Def., War and U.S. Savs. Bonds Coms., 1941-49; mem. adv. com. U.S. Treasury Savs. Bonds Dir., So. Cal., 1946-49. Pres. 1952-66 (dir. 1946-70) Santa Barbara Mus. Natural History; dir. Santa Barbara Cottage Hosp., 1927-70, pres., 1958-66, chmn. of bd., 1966-70; pres. Knapp Coll. Nursing, 1958-66, chmn. bd., 1966-70, Santa Barbara Found., 1947-49, trustee, 1941-70; trustee Meml. Cancer Found. Santa Barbara, 1950-62, Jefferson Endowment Fund, 1953-70. Served as capt. inf., U.S. Army, WW I. Mem. Duck Hunters Assn. of Cal. (honorary life member of board of directors), Santa Barbara C. of C. (dir. 1925-27, hon. life pres., 1946-70), Cal. Alumni Assn., Beta Theta Pi. Republican. Episcopalian. Clubs: Detroit; Bohemian (San Francisco); Bankers' of America (New York City); Valley Montecito, Montecito Country, University (honorary life member), also mem. Santa Barbara, Coral Casino Beach, Cabana, Kennel (pres. Santa Barbara); La Cumbre Golf and Country (mem. bd. dirs. 1957-70). Home: Santa Barbara CA Died Apr. 26, 1970.

CHASE, HARRIE BRIGHAM-CHASE, judge; b. Whitingham, Vt., Aug. 9, 1889 s. Charles Sumner and Carrie Emily (Brigham) C.; prep. edn. high sch., Wilmington, Vt., and Phillips Exeter (N.H.) Acad.; student Dartmouth College, 1908-09, Boston University School Law, 1910-12; LL.D., Dartmouth Collge, 1939; m. Mina Annis Gilman, Mar. 7, 1912; children—Madeline Harriet, Alice Natalie, Dana Charles. Admitted to Vt. bar, 1912, and began practice at Brattleboro; mem. firm Chase & Chase, 1912-19; state's atty., Windham County, Vt., Feb.-May 1919; judge, Superior Court, Vt., 1919-27, chief judge, 1926-27; asso. justice, Supreme Court, Vt., 1927-29; judge, United States Court of Appeals, 2nd Judicial Circuit, 1929-53, chief judge, 1953-54. Trustee Brattleboro Retreat. Mem. Am. and Vt. State bar assns., Chi Phi, Phi Delta Phi. Republican. Universalist. Mason, Odd Brattleboro VT Died Nov. 17, 1969.

CHASE, JESSIE ANDERSON, author; b. Cincinnati, May 6, 1865; d. Rev. James M. and Elizabeth (Robbins) Anderson; A.B., Smith Coll., 1886; m. at Duluth, Minn., Robert S. Chase, Sept. 15, 1897; children—Elizabeth Le Baron, Charles Chauncey (dec.), Josephine Leverett (dec.). Club: College (Boston). Author: Sixty Composition Topics, 1894; A Study of English Words, 1897; Three Freshmen, 1898; Mayken, 1902; A Daughter of the Revolution, 1910; Chan's Wife, 1919; A New Study of English Words, 1929; Paul Revere, Junior, 1932. Address: 53 Snow Hill St., Boston MA‡

CHASE, JOHN CALVIN, socialist organizer; b. Gilmanton, N.H., May 27, 1870; s. Levi M. and Lynthia E. Chase; ed. common schs. of Milton Mills and Barnstead, N.H.; m. 1906. Shoemaker since 1882. Joined trade union movement at 16, became a Socialist at 21, elected in 1898 mayor of Haverhill on socialist ticket; reelected 1899; first socialist mayor elected in America; chmn. Nat. Conv. Social Dem. Party at Indianapolis, 1900; socialist party candidate for gov. of Mass., 1901, 02, of N.Y., 1906; asst. nat. sec. socialist party, 1908-10; now state sec. Socialist Party of Neb. Address: 3 Rohrbough Bldg., Omaha‡

CHASE, MARY ELLEN, author, educator; b. Blue Hill, Me., Feb. 24, 1887; d. Edward Everett and Edith (Lord) C.; B.A., U. of Me., 1909; M.A., U. of Minn., 1918, Ph.D., 1922; Litt.D., U. of Maine, 1929, Bowdoin College, 1933, Northeastern U., 1948, Smith College, 1949, Wilson Coll., 1957; LL.D., Goucher Coll., 1960; L.H.D., Colby College, 1937. Instr. English, Univ. of Minn., 1918-22, asst. prof., 1922-26; asso. prof. English lit. Smith Coll., 1926-29, prof. 1929-55, prof. emeritus, 1955-73. Mem. Phi Beta Kappa. Episcopalian. Author numerous bks. including: Dawn in Lyonesse, 1938; Jonathan Fisher; Maine Parson, 1948; The Plum Tree, 1949; Abby Aldrich Rockefeller, 1950; Readings from the Bible, 1952; Recipe for a Magic Childhood, 1952; The White Gate, 1954; Life and Language in the Old Testament, 1955; The Edge of Darkness, 1957; Sailing the Seven Seas, 1958; Donald McKay and the Clipper Ships, 1959; The Lovely Ambition, 1960; The New England Fishing Fleets, 1961; The Psalms for the Common Reader, 1962; The Prophets for the Common Reader, 1963; The Edge of Darkness, 1964; A Journey to Boston, 1965. Contbr. stories and reviews to New York Times, N.Y. Herald Tribune, Atlantic Monthly, Yale Review, etc. Home: Northampton MA Died July 31, 1973.

CHATFIELD, WILLIAM HAYDEN, merchant and mfr.; b. Cincinnati, O., Jan. 26, 1893; s. Albert Hayden and Helen (Huntington) C.; student St. Mark's Sch., Southboro, Mass., 1907-10; A.B., Harvard, 1914; m. Elizabeth Wolcott Henry, Oct. 14, 1916; children—Henry Houston, Frederick Huntington, Helen Huntington, Charles Wolcott, John Snowden. Pres. Chatfield and Woods Co. from 1929; also president Chatfield Paper Corporation, Clements Paper Company, The Scioto Paper Co.; chmn. Chaftield & Woods Co. Pa., Union Paper & Twine C. of O., Union Paper & Twine Co. of Mich.; dir. Cin. Equitable Fire Ins. Co., Emery Industries, Incorporated. Served as capt. 309th Inf., A.E.F., World War I. Dir. Cincinnati Community Chest, Children's Home. Trustee, Cincinnati Inst. of Fine Arts. Clubs: Camargo, Queen City (Cincinnati). Home: Madeira OH Died Sept. 11, 1970; buried Spring Grove Cemetery, Cincinnati OH

CHEATHAM, ELLIOTT EVANS, educator; b. Savannah, Ga., July 13, 1888; s. Elliott Evans and Sarah Frances (Swoll) C.; A.B., U. Ga., 1907; LL.B., Harvard, 1911; LL.D., Boston U., 1942, Oglethorpe U., 1951, Columbia, 1960, Emory U., 1966; D.C.L., University of New Brunswick, 1954; married Ida May Blount, May 20, 1914. Practiced law Atlanta, 1911-14, 1919-24; faculty Atlanta Law Sch., 1913-14; atty. dept. of justice and asst. U.S. atty., 1914-17; prof. law Emory U., 1921-24, U. Ill., 1924-26, Cornell U., 1926-29, Columbia, 1929-57; vis. prof. law U. Istanbul, 1957-58, Harvard, 1958-59; prof. law Hastings Coll. Law, 1959-60; prof. law Vanderbilt U., Nashville, 1960-68, research prof. law, 1968-72; lectr. Hague Acad. Internat. Law, 1960; Carpentier lecturer Columbia University, 1963. Recipient Research award Fellows Am. Bar Found., 1972. Mem. Am. Bar Assn., Bar Assn. City of New York, Association of American Law Schools (pres. 1942), Institut de Droit Internat. (associate member). Democrat. Author: Cases on the Legal Profession 1955; A Lawyer When Needed, 1963; (with Maurice Rosenberg, Erwin N. Lawyer When Needed, 1963; (with Maurice Rosenberg, Erwin N. Griswold, Willis L. M. Rease) Cases on Conflict of Laws; (with L. Ray Patterson) The Profession of Law, 1971; also articles various law revs. Home: Nashville TN Died Jan. 12, 1972; buried Nashville TN

CHEATHAM, OWEN ROBERTSON, corp. exec.; b. Lynchburg, Va., July 9, 1903; s. Walter Beverly and Sally Fenton (Franklin) C.; grad. Hargrave Mil Academy, Chatham, Va., 1921; student Va. Polytech. Inst., University of Ga.; LL.D., Presbyn. Coll., U. Portland, Lewis and Clark Coll.; Doctor Science, Clemson University, D.C.L., U. South; m. Celeste Wickliffe, September 5, 1928; children—Mary Fenton (Mrs. Roland R. Comerford), Celeste (Mrs. Albert Kennerly). With Porter Bros., Maben, West Virginia, and Portland, Oregon, in 1922; treasurer, Dolan Lumber Company, Lynchburg, Virginia, 1924-27; founded Georgia-Pacific Corporation in Augusta, Ga., 1927, president, 1927-57, chmn., 1957-67, hon. chmn., chairman exec. committee, 1968-70, dir. subsidiaries; dir. Bank of Am. NT & SA, San Francisco. Del. 10th Internat. Congress Sci. Orgns. Vice chmn. Nat. Fund Med. Edn.; bd. dirs. Boys Club Am., Met. Opera Assn., Giannini Found. Trustee Ind. Coll. Funds Am., Ga.-Pacific Found. Owen Cheatham Found., American Episcopal Ch. Riviera, Nice, France; member nat. com. Association of Episopal Colls.; fellow of the Virginia Mus. Fine Arts; mem. scientific adv. bd. Center for Advanced Studies in Scis., U. Va. Decorated Cross Order Naval Merit, Spanish Navy, 1957. Mem. Royal Soc. Arts, Va. Soc. (dir.), Chi Psi. Episcopalian. Clubs: Bath and Tennis, Everglades (Fla.); Links Brook, River, Deepdale Golf (N.Y.C.); Augusta Assembly, Augusta Nat. Golf (Ga.); Arlington, Waverley Country (Portland, Ore.). Home: Portland OR Died Oct. 24, 1970; buried Presbyterian Church Grounds, New Concord, Campbell County VA

CHEAVENS, DAVID ANDERSON, educator, journalist; b. Kansas City, Mo., Dec. 3, 1907; s. John Self and Katherine (Herndon) C.; A.B., Baylor U., 1933; m. Alice Elizabeth Dawson, June 3, 1934; children—Katherine (Mrs. Mac Hargrove), Alice (Mrs. Robert M. Baird), Joseph, Martha (Mrs. Larry Kvols). Reporter, El Paso (Tex.) Post, 1923-25, Waco (Tex.) News Tribune, 1925-26, U.P., Buenos Aires, Argentina, 1927-29, N.Y. Morning Telegraph, 1930-31; mng. editor Marshall (Tex.) News Messenger, 1933-35; reporter, Austin (Tex.) statehouse corr. A.P., 1935-61; prof. journalism, chmn. dept. Baylor U., from 1961; lectr. journalism U. Tex., 1948-61. Charter mem., chmn. Tex. Bapt. Pub. Relations Adv. Com., 1947-61; dir. Bapt. Standard Pub. Co., from 1961. Baptist (deacon). Author: (with Mrs. Cheavens) (novel) As Love Knows How, 1952; also articles. Home: Waco TX Died Dec. 8, 1970; buried Oakwood Cemetery, Waco TX

CHEFFEY, JOHN HOWARD, physician, naval officer; b. Smithfield, O., Oct. 17, 1916; s. Windsor H. and Zana M. (Galbraith) C.; B.S., U. Pitts., 1938; M.D., Jefferson Med. Coll., 1942; m. Ruby E. Marshall. Commd. lt. (j.g.) U.S. Navy, 1942, advanced through grades to rear adm., 1968; intern U.S. Naval Hosp., Portsmouth, Va., 1942-43; jr. med. officer in U.S.S. Gen. H.W. Butner, 1944-45; resident in surgery U.S. Naval Hosp, Bainbridge, Md., 1945-46; mem. staff U.S. Naval Hosp, Chelsea, Mass., 1946; resident in orthopedic surgery U.S. Naval Hosp., Chelsea, Mass., 1946-48; tng. in children's orthopedics Alfred I. DuPont

Inst., Wilmington, Del., 1948; staff U.S. Naval Hosp., Bethesda, Md., 1949-50, chief orthopedics, 1953-56, 58-64; officer in charge E Co., 1st Med. Detachment, 1st Marine Div., Fleet Marine Force, 1950-51; chief orthopedic surgery U.S. Naval Hosp., Key West, Fla., 1951-53; chief orthopedic service U.S. Naval Hosp., Yokosuka, Japan, 1956-58; asst. chief Bur. Medicine and Surgery for Personnel Control and Planning, Navy Dept., Washington, 1964-66; asst. for personnel to dep. asst. sec. def. Dept. Def., Washington, 1966-57; comdr. U.S. Naval Hosp., Newport, R.I., 1967-69, U.S. Naval Hosp. and Hosp. Corps Sch., Great Lakes, Ill., 1969-70, also dist. med. officer 9th Naval Dist., 1969-70. Decorated Legion of Merit. Diplomate Am. Bd. Orthopedic Surgery. Fellow Am. Acad. Orthopedic Surgeons; mem. A.M.A. Home: Barnesville OH Died May 17, 1970; buried Arlington Nat. Cemetery, Arlington VA

CHEHAB, FUAD, pres. of Lebanon; b. Lebanon, Mar. 19, 1902; ed. St. Cyr; France; m. Rose Noiret. Joined French Army, promoted by Vichy French to comdr. Lebanese bn., French Army of Levant; chief New Army of Lebanon, 1945; acting pres. of Lebanon, 1952, pres., 1958-64; defense minister of Lebanon, Suez Crisis. Roman Catholic. Address: Beirut Lebanon Died Apr. 1973.

CHEKIB BEY, E. E. and M. P. from Turkey to U.S., apptd. 1900; b. Constantinople; s. Mustapha Sureya Pacha (vizir of the Empire) and Nesrin Hamin; studied Turkish, Arabian, Persian, French languages, math. science, polit. economy, finance, sciences and law, at home under pvt. tutors; m. Firdews Hanim. Entered Imperial Ottoman Gov't service as mem. of secretaryship, Council of State; mem. Foreign Corr. Bureau; acting gov. Vilayet of Siwas; received rank of Saliseh, Sanich, etc.; imperial comm'r to Montenegro; dir. Bureau of Cipher, 3 yrs.; 1st sec. to a sp'l Extraordinary Embassy to London; decorated 3d class of Osmanieh and promoted chief Bureau of Legal Counsellors of the Sublime Porte; Turco-Bulgarian Comm'r to revise organic laws of Eastern Roumelia; decorated 2d class Medjidieh; promoted to civil rank of Oula, 1st class, receiving Grand Cordon of the Osmanieh. Imperial Ottoman Comm'r, St. Louis Exp'n; Imperial del. 8th Internat. Geog. Congress (hon. v.-p.); apptd. Councilor of State (Civil Sect.), Constantinople; comdr. Order of Danilo (Montenegro); Grand Cordon of Sun and Lion (Persia). Address: 1810 Calvert St., N.W., Washington‡

CHEN, YI, Chinese govt. ofcl.; b. nr. Chengtu, Szechwan, China, 1902; student U. Communications, Shanghai; govt. scholarship for study chemistry in France; married, 2 children. While student in France, assisted formation Paris br. Chinese Communist Party, regular mem. Communist Party, 1923-72, mem. central com.; adjutant Szechwan warlord, also magistrate; founder Chungkin newspaper; mem. polit. br. Chinese Army, 1927, comdr. 1st detachment New Fourth Army, 1938-41, acting comdr., 1941-46, comdr., 1946; head People's Liberation Army of Eastern China, 1947, reorganized forces as Third Field Army, 1949, comdr., 1949, also comdg. gen. East China Mil. Area; mayor of Shanghai, 1949-58; mem. Chinese Communist delegation 19th Soviet Party Congress, 1952; marshall, mem. Nat. People's Congress, 1955, later vice premier of the republic; delivered policy speech 8th Party Congress of Chinese Communists, 1956, full mem. Politburo, 1956; dep. chmn. Nat. Def. Council, 1956-58; fgn. minister Communist China, 1958-72. Pres. Nat. Assn. for Eliminating Illiteracy in China, 1956. Address: China Died Jan. 1972.

CHENERY, CHRISTOPHER TOMPKINS, corp. exec.; b. Richmond, Va., Sept. 16, 1886; s. James Hollis and Ida Burnley (Taylor) C.; student Randolph-Macon Coll.; B.S. in Engring., Washington and Lee University, 1909; LL.D., Randolph Macon College, 1964; m. Helen Clementina Bates; children—Hollis Burnley, Margaret Emily, Helen Bates. Chmn. bd. So. Natural Gas Co., now chmn. emeritus; dir. Offshore Company. Trustee Washington and Lee Univ. Served as capt., later maj., engrs., U.S. Army, World War I. Mem. Am. Soc. C.E., New England Geneal. Sco., Acad. Polit. Sci., Am. Waterworks Assn., Inc., Newcomen Soc., N.Y. So. Soc., Va. Hist. Soc., Va. Thoroughbred Assn., Phi Beta Kappa, Phi Delta Theta, Phi Beta Kappa Assos., Omicron Delta Kappa. Clubs: City Midday, Jockey, Madison Sq. Garden, Turf and Field, Recess, Pinnacle (N.Y.C.); American Yacht, Shenorock Shore (Rye, New York); Pelham Country, Boulder Brook, Union Leaggue, Deep Run Hunt, Country of Virginia, Commonwealth. (Richmond); Metropolitan (Washington); Mt. Brook (Birmingham, Ala.); Blind Brook (Purchase, N.Y.); Everglades. Home: Pelham Manor NY Died Jan. 1973.

CHENERY, WILLIAM ELISHA, laryngologist; b. Wiscasset, Me., June 14, 1864; s. Elisha (M.D.) and Harriet Ann (Grose) C.; prep. edn., Boston Latin Sch.; A.B., Boston U., 1887; M.D., Harvard U., 1890; D.S., Boston University, 1938; Dr. Humane Letters, Tufts College, 1945; studied in Europe, Freiburg, Vienna, and Berlin; m. Marion M. Luse, Oct. 14, 1896. Prof. laryngology, Tufts College Med., now emeritus prof.; consultant in nose, throat and ear dept. Boston Dispensary, also of Roxbury and Booth hosps., Walter E. Fernold State Sch. and Forsyth Dental Infirmary for Children; consultant in laryngology, New England Deaconess Hosp.; mem. staff N.E. Bapt. Hosp.; chief surgeon med. staff, Aleppo Temple; lecturer dental hygiene Forsyth Dental Infirmary. Volunteered for service with U.S. Med. Corps, Sept. 24, 1918. Fellow Am. Laryngol., Rhinol. and Otol. Soc., N.E. Otolaryngol. Soc., Am. Acad. Ophthalmology and Oto-Laryngology, Am. Coll. Surgeons; mem. A.M.A., Mass. Med. Soc., Mass. Soc. Examining Physicians, A.A.A.S., S.A.R. (Boston chapter), Ancient and Honorable Arty. Co. of Mass., Nat. Geog. Soc., Harvard Brotherhood of Brookline, Theta Delta Chi, Phi Chi, Phi Beta Kappa. Mem. exec. com. and trustee Boston Univ.; ex-pres. Boston Methodist Social Union, Interchurch Fellowship; co-founder and ex-pres. Friends of China, Inc. (Sino-Am. Soc.), Boston; v.p., Boston Industrial Home; treas. New England Com. for Relief in China. Republican. Methodist; trustee and chmn. finance com. St. Marks Ch., Brookline. Mason (32 deg., K.T.). Clubs: Boston City, University, Harvard, Algonquin, Appalachian Mountain, Tufts College Masonic, Kiwanis of Brookline, Cosmopolitan. Address: 377 Commonwealth Av., Boston MA

CHENEY, BENJAMIN AUSTIN, physician, surgeon; b. Joliet, Ill., June 10, 1867; s. Benjamin Hicks and Sarah (Austin) C.; A.B., Yale, 1888, M.D., 1890; student U. of Vienna, 1890-91; m. Lillian Clark Farrel, Jan. 11, 1905; children—Alton Austin, Charles Brooker. Chmn. bd. and pres. Grace Hosp., New Haven, since 1929; mem. bd. govs. and consulting staff, Charlotte Hungerford Hosp., Torrington, Conn.; mem. med. advisory bd. Neuro-Psychiatric Inst., Hartford; cons. staff, Griffin Hosp., Derby. Mem. bd. dirs. New Haven Bank. Companion Mil. Order of Loyal Legion. Fellow Am. Coll. Surgeons; mem. Conn. Acad. Arts and Sciences, Am. Med. Assn., New Haven County Med. Assn. (past pres.), New Haven City Med. Assn. (past pres.), Conn. State Med. Soc., Soc. Colonial Wars of Conn., Psi Upsilon, Nu Sigma Nu, Am. Guernsey Cattle Club. Republican. Episcopalian (jr. warden Trinity Ch.). Mason (32 deg.). Clubs: Rotary, Graduate, Lawn (New Haven); Sanctum (Litchfield). Breeder of Guernsey cattle. Home: 755 Prospect St., New Haven; (country) Falcon's Flight Farms, Litchfield, Conn. Office: 265 Church St., New Haven CT‡

CHENEY, FRANK, JR., silk mfr.; b. Manchester, Conn., Aug. 14, 1860; s. Frank and Susan Jarvis (Cushing) C.; Mass. Inst. Tech., 1882; m. Florence W. Wade, Jan. 6, 1897; 1 dau., Frances Virginia. Formerly chmn. bd. Cheney Bros., silk manufacturers; pres. Savings Bank of Manchester; dir. Phoenix Mutual Life Ins. Co., Phoenix State Bank & Trust Co. of Hartford, Hartford Electric Light Co. Mem. Conn. Ho. of Rep., 1905-09. Republican. Address: 20 Hartford Rd., Manchester CT*‡

CHENEY, FRANK WOODBRIDGE, silk mfr. Treas. and dir. Cheney Bros., silk mfrs.; pres. and dir. S. Manchester R. R. Co.; dir. Central New England R. R. Co., Hartford & Conn. Western R. R. Co., New England R. R. Co., New York, New Haven & Hartford R. R. Co., Poughkeepsie Bridge R. R. Co., Rockville R. R. Co., Nat. Fire Ins. Co., Conn. Mutual Life Ins. Co., Hartford Steam Boiler Inspection & Ins. Co. Address: S Manchester CT‡

CHENOWETH, DAVID MACPHERSON, brewery exec.; b. Montreal, Can., Apr. 1, 1917; s. Walter Richard and Dora (Burgess) C.; B.A., McGill U., 1938; m. Clare Buck, Aug. 9, 1947; children—David, Richard, Brian, Christopher, John. With Pepsi-Cola Co. of Can., 1938-53, pres., 1950-53, also dir.; exec. v.p. Molson Breweries, Ltd., Montreal, 1954-66, pres., 1966-69, also dir.; dir. Sicks' Rainier Brewing Co. Mem. Naval Officers Assn., Montreal Bd. Trade, Delta Upsilon. Home: Westmount Que Can Died Mar. 1969.

CHENTUNG, LIANG-CHENG, SIR, K. C. M. G., LL. D., E. E. and M. P. to U. S., Peru, Cuba, Mexico, since 1902; grad. Phillips Acad., Andover, Mass. Served attache Chinese Legation, U. S., 1886-9; 2d sec. sp'l. mission to Japan, 1895; 1st sec. embassy to Diamond Jubilee, London, 1897; 1st sec. sp'l. mission to Berlin, 1901; 1st sec. sp'l. mission to London, 1902. (K. C. M. G.; LL.D., Amherst, 1903). Address: 2001 19th St., Washington DC‡

CHERRY, CHARLES, actor; b. Greenwich, Kent, Eng., 1874; s. James Frederick and Lady Emily C.; ed. St. Paul's Coll., London; Chatham House Coll., Ramsgate, Kent; unmarried. Made debut at 18; played for a number of yrs. in England, with John Hare; then in the U.S., for Henrietta Crosman, Elsie de Wolfe, Mary Mannering, and for 5 yrs. with Maxine Elliott; starred in The Bachelor," The Spitfire," The Seven Sisters," Thy Neighbor's Wife," Scandal," etc. Clubs: Whist, Players (New York); Green Room (London). Address: 19 W 54th St., New York NY‡

CHESNUTT, NELSON ALEXANDER, musician; b. Phila., Pa., June 1, 1872; s. Frank Lewis and Kate (MacNichol) C.; ed. public schools, under pvt. tutors and spl. studies, U. of Pa.; studied music under masters; m. Elizabeth Clarke, Mar. 12, 1896 (died Nov. 20, 1928); children—Nelson A., Marjorie Clarke (Mrs. Edmund G. S. Flannigan); m. 2d, Helen Mayhew, Aug. 8, 1930; 1 son, William Alexander. Began study of piano at age of 5; organist Westminster Presbyn. Ch., Phila., at 10, later accompanist for vocalists and violin in Phila. and other cities; organist and choirmaster various chs.; numerous appearances in oratorio and concert; dir. vocal dept. Combs Conservatory of Music, Philadelphia, 1912-34. Musical director Philadelphia Consistory A.A.S.R. Mem. Music Teachers' National Association, Musical Fund Society, St. Andrew's Society of Philadelphia. Republican. Methodist. Mason (33 deg.); hon. mem. Supreme Council A.A.S.R. for Northern Jurisdiction. Clubs: Orpheus, Music Art. Contbr. to the Etude and other musical jours. Home: 205 Long Lane, Upper Darby PA‡

CHESTER, JOHN NEEDELS, civil and mech. engr.; b. Columbus, O., Sept. 24, 1864; s. Hubert and Melvina S. (Needels) C.; B.S., U. of Ill., 1891, M.S. and C.E., 1909, M.E., 1911. Began as field supt. Nat. Water Supply Co., 1891; constrn. engr. Am. Debenture Co., Chicago and New York, 1892-94; sales engr. Henry R. Worthington Co., New York, 1894-99; chief engr. Am. Water Works Electric Co., Pittsburgh, Pa., 1899-1906; gen. mgr. Epping-Carpenter Pump Co., Pittsburgh, 1906-11; founder, 1911, J. N. Chester, Engrs., head 1911-41, retired; pres. Edgeworth and Fayette City water cos., Jamestown Water Co. Mem. bd. dirs. U. of Ill. Foundation. Mem. Am. Soc. C.E. (former v.p. and dir.), Am. Soc. Mech. Engrs., Engrs. Soc. Western Pa. (pres. 1929), Am. Water Works Assn., American Pub. Health Assn. Methodist. Club: Duquesne. Inventor of apparatus for water filtration. Contbr. to tech. publs. Collector of rare books and manuscripts. Visited every continent, every state of the U.S., every province of Canada, and practically every European country many times. Home: 4200 Center Av., Pittsburgh PA*‡

CHESTER, K(ENNETH) STARR, scientist, biologist; b. Turner's Falls, Mass., July 21, 1906; s. John Daboll Webster and Alice Josephine (Starr) C.; S.B., Boston Univ., 1928, S.M., 1929; S.M., Harvard, 1930, Ph.D., 1931; Harvard Sheldon fellow Switzerland, 1931-32; children—Desire Packer (now Mrs. Greenidge), Lois Faxon (now Mrs. Sousa). Research fellow Rockefeller Inst. Med. Research. Princeton, 1932-37; prof. and head dept. botany and plant pathology, Okla. A. and M. Coll., 1937-48, dir. coll. research found., 1944-48; supervisor Battelle Meml. Inst., Columbus, O., 1948-54, cons., 1954-55; tech. adviser Alton Box Board Co. (Ill.), 1955-63; prof. biology Ohio Northern Univ., Ada, 1964-69; v.p. and chmn. research com., council for Agrl. and Chemurgic Research; chmn. Internat. Commn. on Plant Diseases Losses, in coop, with UNESCO. Fellow A.A.A.S.; mem. Am. Phytopath. Soc., Ohio Forestry Assn. (pres. 1955; hon. v.p.); adviser Pres. Bipartisan Commn. and Indsl. Use Agrl. Products, 1956. Mem. American Pulpwood Association, Phi Beta Kappa, Sigma Xi, Pi Gamma Mu. Author: Nature and Prevention of Plant Diseases, 1942; The Cereal Rusts, 1946; Selected Writings of N.J. Vavilov (Russian trans.), 1951; Plant Disease Losses: Their Appraisal and Interpretation, 1950; Papermaking Raw Materials. Contbr. numerous scientific articles in professional and popular pub's. Home: Ada OH Died Feb. 26, 1969.

CHESTON, RADCLIFFE, JR., bus. exec.; b. Phila., Feb. 28, 1889; s. Radcliffe and Eugenia (Morris) C.; B.S., U. of Pa., 1910; m. Sydney Helen Ellis, 1916; children—George Morris, Sydney; m. 2d Frances Drexel Fell, 1925; 1 dau., Frances Drexel. With Edward B. Smith &Co., 1910-19, partner, 1919-37, Smith, Barney & Co., 1937-45, limited partner, 1945-65. Dir. Pa. Glass Sand Corp., N. Pa. R.R. Co. Mem. Zool. Soc. Phila. (pres.). Mem. St. Thomas' Ch. Clubs: Rabbit, Racquet, Gulph Mills Golf, Philadelphia (Phila.). Home: Gwynedd Valley PA Died Mar. 21, 1968; buried St. Thomas Ch., Whitemarsh PA

CHETTA, NICHOLAS JOHN, physician; b. New Orleans, June 9, 1916; s. John W. and Evelyn (Blood) C.; grad. Loyola U. of South; M.D., La. State U., 1941; m. Josie Delaune, June 9, 1942; children—Carol Ann, Constance Jo, Nicholas John. Chief externe Hotel Dieu, New Orleans, 1939-40, intern, chief intern, 1941, examining physician Sch. of Nursing, 1941-42; house surgeon French Hosp., New Orleans, 1944-47; prof. anatomy, physiology Sch. Nursing, Mercy Hosp., New Orleans, 1947-68, physician, 1947-68, pres. hosp. staff, 1958; physician New Orleans Baseball Club, 1947-68; med. dir. New Orleans Recreation Dept., 1947-68; asso. prof. dept. pathology La. State U. Med. Sch., 1951-68; gen. instr. surg. clinics Charity Hosp., 1950-68; physician City of New Orleans, 1950-68; med., legal adviser Cts. of Parish of Orleans, 1950-68; coroner, Parish of Orleans, 1950-68; pvt. practice New Orleans, 1942-68; lectr. forensic medicine Tulane U., 1951-68; cons. path. FAA. Dir. First Homestead & Savs. Assn., Nat. Am. Ins. Co., Nat. Am. Corp., LaPlace Corp., Bank of La. Head statis. div. Civil Def., Parish of Orleans, 1950-68; examining physician VA, 1948-68; bd. dirs. New Orleans Cerebral Palsy Unit, 1951. Served as lt., M.C., 64th Gen. Hosp., 1942-44. Fellow Am. Acad. Forensic Medicine; mem. A.M.A., Assn. Am.

Physicians, Nat. Coroners Assn. (pres. 1953, dir. 1954-68). Internat. Coll. Surgeons, Am. Acad. Gen. Practice, La. Assn. Pathologists, World (founding mem.), So., Orleans Parish med. assns., New Orleans Grad. Med. Assembly, La. Med. Soc. (pres. 1968-69), Am. Legion, Assn. of Commerce. Clubs: New Orleans Athletic, Metairie Country, Young Men's Business, Mid-City Kiwanis (past pres.) (New Orleans). Home: New Orleans LA Died May 25, 1968.

CHETWOOD, CHARLES HOWARD, surgeon; b. Elizabeth, N.J., Oct. 1869; s. Bradbury C. and Eleanor (Keyes) C.; M.D., Bellevue Hosp. Med. Coll. (New York U.), 1887; (LL.D., Fordham U., 1911); m. Jeannette Campbell Mecke, 1891; m. 2d, Mary Foley, 1918. Interne Bellevue Hosp., 1887-89; prof. genito-urinary surgery, New York Polyclinic and Hosp., 1897; visiting surgeon, Bellevue Hosp., 1899; consulting surgeon, St. John's Hospital, L.I. City, 1903, Knickerbocker Hospital, White Plains Hospital, Nassau Hospital, Mineola, N.Y., Bellevue Hospital, 1923; attending urologist and dir. of service, French Hosp., 1920, sec. and v.p. med. bd., 1930-33; sec. faculty, N.Y. Polyclinic Med. Sch. and Hosp., 1903-09; apptd. mem. Pub. Hospitals Commn., New York, 1906. Served as mem. surgeon general's com. on venereal diseases, World War, also as chmn. home unit, New York Polyclinic. Mem. Am. and N.Y. State med. assns., N.Y. County Med. Soc. (pres. 1920), Societe Internat. d'Urologie, Am. Med. Soc., Vienna; corr. mem. Deutsche Gesellschaft fur Urologie. Fellow N.Y. Acad. Medicine, Am. Coll. Surgeons. Clubs: Century, Princeton, Knollwood Country, Nantucket Yacht. Author: Compend of Genito-Urinary Diseases, 1892; Venereal Diseases (Keyes and Chetwood), 1900; Text-Book on Genito-Urinary Surgery, 1911; Practice of Urology, 1913, 4th edit., 1927. Home: 160 Henry St., Brooklyn, N.Y. Office: 25 Park Av., New York NY*‡

CHEVALIER, MAURICE (AUGUSTE), stage and film actor, entertainer; born Paris, September 12, 1888; s. Victor Charles and Josephine (Vanden-Boosche) C.; ed. schs. in Paris; married, 1926, marriage dissolved, 1935. Made debut at 12 yrs. of age as singer-entertainer in cafes, concert and music halls, Paris; later toured in provinces; appeared with Mistinguette at Folies-Bergeres, Paris, 1909; made London debut in revue, 1919; dir. Alhambra-Maurice Chevalier, Paris, 1956; has appeared in revues, operettas and in one-man show in important theatres, Paris and London, and on tour in Argentina, United States, Canada, Scandinavia, and throughout Europe, from 1919; in one-man show, Songs and Impressions, N.Y.C., 1958, 63, 65, 68; has introduced songs, made records, appeared on radio and television programs. Actor in American films including: The Love Parade, The Playboy of Paris, One Hour With You, The Beloved Vagabond, Folies Bergeres, Love in the Afternoon, Gigi (1958); Count Your Blessings, Can-Can, Pepe, Fanny, also acted in The Castaways and Monkeys Go Home; starred in French films including: With a Smile, 1939; Man of the Hour, 1940; Le Silence est d'Or (shown in U.S. under title, Man About Town), 1947 and film Black Tights which was produced in 1962. Decorated Chevalier Legion of Honor, Croix de Guerre with palm (France), Order of Leopold (Belgium) Officer Legion of Honor, Officer Merite Nat.; recipient spl. award for contbn. to show business, Academy of Motion Picture Arts and Sciences, 1959; special Tony award, in 1968. Served with French Army, World War I; in retirement in Paris during German Occupation, World War II. Mem. Academie des Vins de Bordeaux. Author: Ma Route et Mes Chansons (autobiography); With Love, 1960. Home: Marnes-La-Coquette Hauts-De-Seine France Died Jan. 1, 1972; buried Marnes-La-Coquette, France*

CHEWNING, EDMUND TAYLOR, clay products producer; b. Bowling Green, Va., June 23, 1889; s. William Samuel and Ella (Thornton) C.; student pub. schs.; m. Caroline Cupler Mosher, May 15, 1918. With Washington Evening Star, 1906-11; cashier Nat. Fireproofing Co., 1911-16; v.p., treas. Asher Fireproofing 1916-18; gen. mgr. Pa. Fireproofing Co.; pres. Continental Clay Products Co., Martinsburg, W.Va., 1920-70, United Clay Products Co., 1921-70, United Brick Corp., (both Washington), 1930-70, United Clay & Supply Corp., 1935-70; dir., mem. exec. com. Riggs Nat. Bank; dir. John Hancock Mutual Life Ins. Co., Armour & Co. Mem. Washington Bd. Trade, Md. Racing Commn., 1953-70. Mason. Clubs: Chevy Chase, Columbia Country (Chevy Chase, Md.); Rotary, University, Metropolitan, Alfalfa (Washington); Lyford Cay Country (Nassau, Bahamas); Bald Peak Colony (N.H.). Home: MD Died Oct. 12, 1970; buried St. James Ch., Lothian MD

CHEZ, JOSEPH, lawyer; b. Richmond, Ia., Jan. 24, 1869; s. Wencel and Barbara C.; LL.B., Georgetown U., 1897; LL.M., Nat. U. Law Sch., 1898; m. Jessie May McCorkle, May 16, 1900. Admitted to Ind. bar, 1897; in practice at Ogden since 1902; atty. gen. of Utah since Jan. 1, 1933. Trustee State Industrial Sch. Democrat. Presbyterian. K. of P. Club: Lions. Home: Ogden UT*‡

CHICHESTER, SIR FRANCIS, author, air and sea navigator; b. Sept. 17, 1901; ed. Marlborough Coll. Emigrated to New Zealand, 1919; dir. Godwin Chichester Aviation Co., Ltd., 1927-30; 2d person to fly solo Eng. to Australia, 1929; first East to West solo flight from New Zealand to Australia across Tasman Sea, 1931 (Johnston Meml. trophy for navigation); 1st long distance solo seaplane flight, New Zealand to Japan, 1931; cruising flight in Puss Moth with one passenger, Sydney to London via Peking, 1936; chmn. Francis Chichester Ltd., map and guide pubs., 1945—; dir. Straight Aviation Tng. Ltd., 1946-49; record solo East-West Crossing, Plymouth to N.Y.C., 1962; 2d in 2d solo trans-Atlantic yacht race, 1964; solo cruise So. Atlantic route in Gypsy Moth, 1967, Warden Guild Air pilots and Air Navigation, 1960; first true circumnavigation of world via Cape of Good Hope, Cape of Leewin, Cape of Horn, 1966-67; one-stop global circumnavigation at record speed in Gypsy Moth IV, 1967; record speed solo sailing in Gypsy Moth V, 1971; v.p. Inst. Navigation, 1964. Trustee Nat. Maritime Mus., 1965-70. Comdr. Order British Empire, 1964; created knight, 1967; winner 1st singlehanded trans-Atlantic Yacht race, 1960; recipient Yachtsman of Year trophy, 1960; Blue Water medal Cruising Club Am., 1960, 67; Gold medal Brit. Inst. Navigation, 1961, Silver Globe award, 1967; Gold medal Australian Inst. Navigation, 1967; Gold medal Guild Yachting Writers, 1967; Superior Achievement award Am. Inst. Navigation, 1967; Gold medal Royal Geog. Soc., 1967; Marconi Meml. Gold medal Vet. Wireless Operators Assn., N.Y.C., 1967; Hon. life mem. Royal Yacht Squadron (spl. bronze medal 1967); mem. Royal Geog. Soc. (v.p. 1970). Author of: Navigation Notes for Instructor and Students, 1941-43; Solo to Sydney, 1930; Seaplance Solo, 1932; Ride on the Wind, 1937; The Spotters Handbook, 1940; Astro Navigation, 1940; Pinpoint the Bombers, 1941; Star Recognition, 1941; The Star Compass; The Sun Compass; Alone Across the Atlantic, 1962; Atlantic Adventure; The Lonely Sea and the Sky, 1964, Along the Clipperway; The Romantic Challenge; Gipsy Moth Circles the World, 1967; How to Keep Fit, 1969. Clubs: Royal Aero; Royal Air Force Yacht; Yacht (hon., spl. centenary award) (France); Royal Ocean Racing; Ocean Cruising; Royal Cruising (medal for seamanship); Royal Western Yacht (Plymouth); Royal London Yacht; Royal Thames Yacht. Address: London England Died Aug. 26, 1972.

CHILDS, EDWARD POWELL, educator; b. at Jonesville, Mich., Apr. 15, 1870; s. Edwin William and Helen (Force) C.; student U. of Mich., 1890-1; B.S., Denison U., Ohio, 1894; student, Harvard Summer Sch., 1894; m. Sada Hart, of Huron, O., June, 1895. Prof. mathematics, Fargo, (N.D.) Coll., 1891-3; instr. mathamatics, 1893-4, acting prof. physics and chemistry, 1894-5, Denison U.; instr. science, Pueblo (Colo.) High Sch., 1895-8; prof. physics and mathematics, 1898-1901, dean, 1899-1901, U. of N. Mex., prin. high sch., Newark, O., 1901-7; pres. Normal and Collegiate Inst., Asheville, N.C., 1907-16; asst. dept. edn. U. of Wis., Jan. 16-Apr. 1917; pres. Cumberland U. since Apr. 1917. Mem. Phi Gamma Delta. N.E.A., etc. Presbyterian. Mason. Address: Lebanon TN‡

CHILDS, HARWOOD LAWRENCE, educator; b. Gray, Me., May 1, 1898; s. Herman Andrew and Eudora (Whittemore) C.; A.B., Dartmouth, 1919; M.A., 1921; Ph.D., U. of Chicago, 1928; m. Willa Patricia Whitson, June 28, 1922; children—Elizabeth Ann (Mrs. Arthur Edward Rowse), Margaret Frances (Mrs. Richard Stoll Armstrong), Martha (Mrs. Lyman Edwin Sproul, Jr.). Instr. of pub. speaking, Dartmouth Coll., 1919-20, instr. economics, 1920-21; asst. prof. economics, Syracuse U., 1922-24; asso. prof. govt., Coll. of William and Mary, 1925-27; prof. govt. and head dept. polit. science, Bucknell U., 1928-31; asso. prof. politics, Princeton U., 1932-46, prof. since 1946; on leave as regional specialist. Overseas Branch. O.W.I., Washington, D.C., 1943-45; lectr. School Pub. Adminstrn., Rio de Janeiro, 1953-54; vis. lectr. on Haynes Found., U. So. Cal., spring 1957. Research asst. Nat. Industrial Conf. Bd., N.Y. City, 1924; Social Science Research Council fellow for study in Germany, 1931-32; Guggenheim fellow for study in Germany, 1937; founder, 1st editor Public Opinion Quar., pub. Princeton U., 1937-41, editor, 1964-72. Mem. Enemy Alien Hearing Bd., Dist. of N.J., 1942-43. Alumni trustee. Tilton Sch. Mem. Am. Assn. Univ. Profs., Am. Political Science Assn., Alpha Chi Rho, Delta Sigma Rho, Phi Beta Kappa. Served in USN, 1918. Author: Public Opinion—Nature, Formation, Role, 1965. Author, editor, translator various publs.; contbr. articles. Home: Princeton NJ Died June 1972.

CHILDS, PRESCOTT, foreign service officer; b. Holyoke, Mass., Dec. 2, 1898; s. Thomas Southworth and Eliza Porter (Prescott) C.; A.B., Yale, 1922; m. Roberta Lewis, June 20, 1931; children—David Lewis, William Prescott. Entered foreign service, 1924; first secretary Embassy and consul gen., Habana, Cuba, 1946; consul gen., Bombay, 1950; consul gen., Antwerp, 1952-58. Served as pvt. Tank Corps, U.S. Army, 1918. Clubs: The Crocks (Barbados, British West Indies); Jangada (Fortaleza, Brazil); Yale (N.Y.C.); University (Washington). Home: Farmington CT Died June 20, 1969.

CHILES, JAMES ALBURN, prof. modern langs.; b. Franklin Co., Mo., Mar. 6, 1877; s. Alburn and Emma Laura (Drace) C.; A.B., Central Coll., Mo., 1895; A.M., Vanderbilt, 1898; Ph.D., U. of Ill., 1908; student U. of Leipzig and Sorbonne, Paris; m. Marie Therese Duenckel, of St. Louis, Mo., 1905; 1 son, James Alburn. Asst. in French and German, Vanderbilt, 1897-99; instr. German, Washington U., 1900-01, U. of Ill., 1905-10; prof. modern langs., Southern U., 1910-13; instr. German, U. of Wis., 1913-14; prof. modern langs. and head of dept., Wofford Coll., since 1914. Mem. Modern Lang. Assn., America, South Atlantic Modern Lang. Assn., Am. Assn. Teachers of French, Am. Assn. Teachers of German, Delta Phi Alpha (nat. pres.), Sigma Nu. Democrat. Mem. M.E. Ch., S. Author: German Prose Composition, 1914; German Composition and Conversation, 1931. Home: Spartanburg SC‡

CHILLMAN, JAMES, JR., educator, museum dir., architect; b. Phila., Pa., Dec. 24, 1891; s. James Henry and Clara Emma (Miller) C.; B.S., U. of Pa., 1913, M.S., 1914; student Pa. Acad. of Fine Arts, 1915-16, Am. Acad. in Rome, 1919; m. Dorothy Dawes, July 2, 1923; children—Helen, Dawes. Instr. in drawing, U. of Pa., 1914-16; instr. in architecture, Rice Univ., Houston, Tex., 1916-19, asst. prof., 1922-45. asso. prof., 1945-47, prof., 1947-61, trustee prof., 1961-72, Agnes Cullen Arnold prof. fine Arts, 1970-72; dir. Mus. Fine Arts, Houston, 1924-53, emeritus, 1953, also life trustee; also cons. architect, Houston, 1924; lectr. arch., Summer Sch., U. Pa., 1925-29; past lectr. Intercollegiate Tours, Boston; lectr. Woman's Inst. of Houston. Past mem. staff of art lectrs. The Bur. of Univ. Travel, spending 14 summers in Europe and 8 in Mex. Chmn. archtl. com., Tex. Med. Center, Houston. Decorated Stella della Solidarieta (Italy), 1956; Brown award for excellence in teaching, Rice U. Fellow in arch., Am. Acad. Rome, 1919-22, A.I.A., 1950. Fellow emeritus A.I.A.; mem. Tex. Fine Arts Assn. (past pres.; v.p., dir.), So. States Art League (past pres.), Am. Assn. Museum Am. Fedn. Arts. Archtl. Soc. U. Pa., Am. Assn. Art Mus. Dirs. Houston Philos. Soc. (past pres.). Presbyn. Kiwanian. Clubs: Faculty (Rice Inst.) University (Houston). Contbr. to art and architecture publs. Holder of Carl Schurz Memorial Foundation Fellowship for research work in German speaking countries of Europe, summer of 1936. Radio program Art is Fun, sta. KTRH, Houston, 1950-59. Home: Houston TX Died May 13, 1972.

CHILTON, CECIL HAMILTON, engineer, economist; b. N.Y.C., Sept. 25, 1918; s. Claudius Lysias and Clara Caroline (Weidmann) C.; B.S., Auburn U., 1939; M.S., Carnegie-Mellon U., 1940; m. Florence Edna Zitzman, Oct. 1, 1941; children—Edward Morgan, Margaret Arnold (Mrs. W. Owen BeMent). Chem. engr. Mobil Oil Corp., 1940-41, E.I. duPont de Nemours & Company, 1941-50; editor McGraw-Hill, Inc., 1950-66, editor-in-chief Chem. Engring., 1959-66; tech. economist Battelle Meml. Inst., Columbus, 1966-72. Recipient Am. Bus. Press editorial achievement award, 1966. Mem. Am. Inst. Chem. Engrs. (dir. 1971-72), Am. Assn. Cost Engrs. (award of merit, pres. 1962-63), Am. Society for Engring. Edn. Mem. Ch. of Nazarene. Editor: Cost Engineering in the Process Industries, 1960; co-editor: Chemical Engineers' Handbook, 1963, 5th edit., 1972. Home: Columbus OH Died Nov. 13, 1972; buried Union Cemetery, Columbus OH

CHILTON, THOMAS HAMILTON, chem. engr.; b. Greensboro, Ala., Aug. 14, 1899; s. Claudius Lysias and Mabel Cecilia (Pierce) C.; student Starke's U. Sch., Montgomery, Ala., 1910-13, Lanier High Sch., Montgomery, Ala., 1914-15, U. Ala., 1915-16, Columbia U., 1917-22. Chem. Engr., 1922; D.Sc. (hon.) U. Del., 1943; m. Cherridah McLemore, June 29, 1926 (dec. Mar. 1969); children—Thomas McLemore, Daniel Tanner; m. 2d, Elizabeth Crafs Rinehart, Jan. 2, 1971. Research chemist F.J. Carman, N.Y.C., 1922-25; chemist; chem. dept. Exptl. Sta., E.I. du Pont de Nemours & Co., Wilmington, Del., 1925-30, group leader, chem. engring. research, 1930-35, asst. div. head, tech. div., engring. dept., 1935-38, dir. tech. div., 1938-45, mgr. devel. engring. div., 1945-46, tech. dir. devel. engring. div., 1946-58, tech. adviser, 1958-59; Regent's prof. U. Cal. at Berkeley, 1959-60; Fulbright lectr. Japan, 1960-61; vis. prof. U. New S. Wales, Australia, 1961, U. Del., 1963-64, Cal. Inst. Tech., 1965, U. Va., 1965-66, Biria Inst. Tech., Pilani, Rajasthan, India, 1967, U. Wash. at Seattle, 1968, U. Ala., spring 1969, U. Mass., Amherst, fall 1969, U. P.R., spring 1970, U. Natal, Durban, South Africa, fall 1970; Fulbright lectr. France, 1961-62; Neely vis. prof. Ga. Inst. Tech., 1962-63. Recipient Presdl. Certificate of Merit, 1948; Chandler medal Columbia, 1939, Univ. medal, 1950; Egleston medal Columbia Engring. Sch. Alumni Assn., 1943; Founders award Am. Inst. C.E., 1958. Mem. adv. bd. for books in chem. engring. John Wiley & Sons, 1939-59. Mem. Am. Inst. Chem. Engrs. (pres. 1951), Am. Chem. Soc. (bd. editors Monographs 1938-57), Am. Soc. Engring. Edn., A.A.A.S., Sons of Am. Revolution, Automobile License Plate Collectors Assn., Nat. Acad. Engring., Sigma Xi, Tau Beta Pi, Phi Lambda Upsilon, Omega Chi Epsilon. Presbyn. (elder 1944-50). Clubs: University and Whist (Wilmington,

Delaware); Chemists (N.Y.C.). Author: Strong Water, 1968. Section editor for Indsl. Chemistry, Chem. Abstracts, 1945-51. Contbr. profl. publs. Address: Wilmington DE Died Sept. 15, 1972.

CHINARD, GILBERT, prof. French; b. Chatellerault, France, Oct. 17, 1881; s. Hilaire and Marie (Blanchard) C.; student College de Chatellerault, Lycee de Poitiers, Universite de Bordeaux, Sorbonne; B.L., Poitiers, 1899, Licencie es lettres, 1902; LL.D., St. John's, 1934; m. Emma Blanchard, 1908; children—Lucienne Gilberte, Francis Pierre. Instr. in French, Coll. of the City of New York, 1908, Brown U.; 1908-12, U. of Chicago, summer 1912; asso. prof. and prof. of French, U. of Calif., 1912-19, Columbia, summer 1919; prof. French and comparative lit., Johns Hopkins, 1919-36; became mem. Walter Hines Page Sch. Internat. Relations, 1925; at U. of Calif., 1936-37; Pyne prof. of French lit., Princeton, 1937-50, emeritus, 1950-72; Inst. for Advanced Study, Princeton, 1950; Newberry Library Guggenheim fellow, 1952. Mem. Am. Antiquarian Soc., Modern Language Assn. America, Am. Philos. Soc., Philol. Assn. Pacific Coast (pres. 1918), Societe des Americanistes de Paris; corr. mem. L'Institut Academie des Sciences Morales et Politiques; Laureat de l'Academie Francaise, 1914; Laureat de l'Institut, 1951. Guggenheim fellow 1952; comdr. Legion d'Honneur. Author L'Exotisme americain dans la litterature francaise, au XVI siecle, 1911; L'Amerique et le reve exotique, 1913; L'Exotisme americain dans loeuvre de Chatteaubriand, 1918; La doctrine de l'Americanisme, 1919; Volney et l'Amerique; Les amities americaines de Madame d'Houdetot, 1923; Jefferson et les Ideologues, 1925; Les Refugies Huguenots en Amerique, 1925; Destutt de Tracy, de l'Amour, 1926; Les Amities Francaises de Jefferson, 1927; The Literary Bible of Thomas Jefferson, 1928; Jefferson, The Apostle of Americanism, 1928. Editor: The Commonplace Book of Thomas Jefferson, 1926; The Letters of Jefferson and Du Pont de Nemours, 1931; Un Francais en Virginie, Chateaubriand les Natchez, 1932; Honest John Adams, 1933; Diderot Supplement au Voyage de Bougainville, 1935; Le Voyage de Laperouse en Alaska et sur les cotes de Californie, 1937; Origines historiques de la Doctrine de l'Isolement aux Etats-Unis, 1937; George Washington as the French knew him, 1940; Billardon de Sauvigny, Washington, 1941; Chamfort, La Jeune Indienne, 1945 En lisant Pascal, 1948; L'homme contre la nature, 1949; Morelly, Code de la Nature, 1950; Ode'rahi, 1950. Editor Institut Francais de Washington from 1928; editor The French American Review from 1948. Mem. Phi Beta Kappa. Home: Princeton NJ Died Feb. 8, 1972; buried Princeton NJ

CHING, CYRUS STUART, cons. labor management relations; b. Prince Edward Island, Can., May 21, 1876; s. John and Miranda (Stuart) C.; student Prince of Wales Coll., Charlottetown, P.E.I., Can. 1893-96, Charlottetown Business Coll., 1896-97; LL.B., Northeastern Univ., Boston, 1912; LL.D., Dartmouth College, 1942, Northeastern University, 1946, Temple University, 1950, Bowdin College, 1953, Colby College, 1954; married Anna MacIntosh, July 10, 1912 (deceased); married 2d, A. Mildred Vergosen, Nov. 10, 1943. Came to United States, 1900, naturalized 1909. Began as motorman, Boston Elevated Railroad, 1901, became supt. of equipment, 1903, asst. to pres., 1912; with U.S. Rubber Company, 1919-47, supervisor of indsl. relations, 1919-29, dir. indsl. and pub. relations 1929-47; dir. Fed. Mediation and Conciliation Serv., 1947-52; established office Cyrus S. Ching Assos., con. bus., 1952; chmn. Wage Stabilization Bd., Oct. 1950-Apr. 1951, on leave from Fed. Med. and Conciliation Service; indsl. member National Regional Labor Bd. (N.R.A.), 1933; mem. advisory council on indsl. relations, Nat. Indsl. Conf. Board, 1925-31, and 1940-47; appointed, March 1941, by President Roosevelt, mem. Nat. Defense Mediation Bd.; mem. Nat. War Labor Bd. 1942-43; mem. Business Council, Dept. of Commerce, 1942-67; chmn. China-Am. Council of Commerce and Industry, 1944-47; chmn. Atomic Energy Labor Relations Panel, 1953-67. Lectr. indsl. relations Dartmouth, Yale, Harvard, Vassar, University of Pa. Admitted to Mass. bar, 1912; pres. Am. Management Assn., 1928-29. Republican. Mason. Club: Garden City (N.Y.) Country. Contbr. to jours. Home: Washington DC Died Dec. 27, 1967; buried Naugatuck CT

CHIPERFIELD, ROBERT BRUCE, congressman; b. Canton, Ill., Nov. 20, 1899; s. Burnett Mitchell and Clara (Ross) C.; prep. edn. Phillips Exeter Acad., N.H., 1916-18; student Knox Coll., Galesburg, Ill., 1918-19; A.B., Harvard, 1922; student Harvard Law Sch., 1922-24; LL.B., Boxton U., 1925; m. Catherine Newbern (dec.), July 1, 1930; children—Robert, Virginia; m. 2d Eunice K. Anderson, 1963. Admitted to Ill. bar, 1925; mem. Chiperfield & Chiperfield; mem. 76th to 87th Congresses, 19th Illinois District. Mem. Am. Legion, Forty and Eight, Phi Delta Theta, Phi Delta Phi. Repbulican. Mason. Elk, Eagle, Moose. Home: Canton IL Died Apr. 9, 1971; buried Greenwood Cemetery, Canton IL

CHIRUG, JAMES THOMAS, advt. co. exec.; b. Boston, July 22, 1906; s. Michael and Martha Mabel (Ames) C.; B.S., Mass. Inst. Tech., 1927, M.S., 1929; postgrad. Harvard Sch. Bus. Adminstrn., 1928; m. Ruth E. French, Dec. 27, 1951; children—James Thomas, Jane Ames. Organizer, partner K.R. Sutherland Co. (now Sutherland-Abbott Co.), Boston, 1931-33; organizer James Thomas Chirurg Co., Inc., Boston, N.Y.C., 1933, pres. 1937-55, chmn. bd. dirs., 1956-60; vice chmn. Chirurg & Cairns, Inc., N.Y.C., Boston, Hartford, Conn., 1960-67, chmn. 1968-69, dir., 1969-73; chmn. CMC & C, Inc., N.Y.C., 1964-69, Asso. advt. faculty Simmons Coll., 1948; trade adviser U.S. Dept. Commerce Trade Mission, Egypt, 1960. Founder, James Thomas Chirurg Advt. Fellowship, Harvard Grad. Sch. Bus. Adminstrn., 1953; study reduction war factory absenteeism Brit. Govt., 1942; advt. agy. chmn. Mass. Gov.'s Council on Oil Conservation, 1948; chmn. publicity Community Fund, Greater Met. area, 1946; vice chmn. bd. govs. council Worcester Disaster Relief. 1953; chmn. Danvers Indsl. Devel. Com., 1956. Recipient Jacobs award as Boston's Outstanding Advt. Man, Jr. Advertising Club, Boston, 1957. Mem. Am. Assn. Advt. Agys. (adv. bd., nat. com. pub. relations 1952), Nat. Indsl. Advertisers Assn. (pres. Boston 1949), U.S. C. of C. (nat. com. pub. relations, 1953), Lambda Chi Alpha (Achievement award for leadership in advt and pub. relations 1968). Republican. Conglist. Mason. Clubs: Advertising University (Boston): Union League (N.Y.C.): Salem (Mass.) Country. Author: So You're Going to Choose an Advertising Agency. Home: Danvers MA Died May 1973.

CHISHOLM, JULIAN J., M.D.; grad. Med. Coll. S.C., 1850; prof. emeritus, eye and ear diseases Univ. of Md.; ex-pres. Ophthal. Sect. Internat. Med. Congress; surgeon-in-chief Presby'n Eye, Ear and Throat Charity Hosp.; ex-mem. Am. Med. Assn., etc. Address: Petersburg VA‡

CHITWOOD, OLIVER PERRY, educator, author; b. Franklin County, Va., Nov. 28, 1874; s. Henry Clay and Gillie Anne (Divers) C.; A.B., William and Mary Coll., 1899, LL.D., 1926; Ph.D., Johns Hopkins, 1905; Litt.D., Concord Coll., 1962; m. Agnes Cady, December 17, 1910; children—Henry Cady, Elizabeth Anne (Mrs. J. C. Appel). Librarian, William and Mary College, 1898-99; headmaster Richmond (Virginia) Academy, 1902-03; fellow in history, Johns Hopkins, 1904-05; professor history and economics, Mercer University, 1905-07; professor history, W.Va. Univ., 1907-46, emeritus, 1946-71; instr. history, Johns Hopkins, summer 1922; vis. prof. history, Ohio State U., summer 1938, U. of N.C., summer 1941; visiting professor John B. Stetson Univ., 1949-51. Received Vandalia award W.Va. Univ., 1963. Mem. Am., Southern, W.Va. hist. assns. Phi Beta Kappa. Democrat. Baptist. Author: Justice in Colonial Virginia, 1905; The Immediate Causes of The Great War, 1917; A History of Colonial America, 1931, rev. edit. 1962; John Tyler, Champion of the Old South, 1939. Joint author: Makers of American History, 1904; A Short History of the American People, Vol. I, rev. edit. 1962; Vol. II, rev. edit. 1962; The United States: From Colony to World Power, 1949, rev. edit. 1954; Richard Henry Lee: Statesman of the Revolution, 1968; also 3 student manuals on U.S. history, 1956-57. Home: Morgantown WV Died Feb. 3, 1971; buried Oak Grove Cemetery, Morgantown WV

CHOATE, AUGUSTA, educator; b. Cochran, Pulaski County Ga., Nov. 27, 1874; d. Augustus Edward and Adnah Celestia (Penick) Choate; A.B., Vassar, 1899, A.M., 1900. Teacher pub. schs., Atlanta, Ga., 1893-96, Mt. Hope Pvt. Sch., Fall River, Mass., 1900-01; tutor Baldwin Sch., Bryn Mawr, Pa., Oct.-Dec. 1901; teacher English, Central High Sch., Washington, D.C., Jan.-June, 1902; teacher English, Baldwin Sch., also head of English dept. and asst. in adminstrn., 1902-16; teacher English, Liggett Sch., Detroit, Mich., 1916-17; asso. prin. Miss. Guild and Miss Evans Sch., Boston, 1918-20; owner and prin. Choate Sch. (for girls), Brookline, Mass., since 1920. Mem. Phi Beta Kappa. Address: 1600 Beacon St., Brookline 46 MA*‡

CHOUINARD, CARROLL, public relations consultant; born in Eau Claire, Wisconsin, December 19, 1907; son of Franklin Benjamin and Kathryn Marie (Reichel) C.; B.E., U. Wis., 1929, M.A., 1931; postgrad. U. Ill., 1933-34, 36-37, 60-62; m. Florence Mary Damisch, Sept. 14, 1935; children—Jeffrey Carroll, Paul Lewellyn. Editor Ill. State Natural Hist. Survey, 1931-38; univ. editor, dir. publicity U. Neb., 1939-41; pub. relations writer Swift & Co., Chgo., 1941-43; dir. pub. relations Marshall Field & Co., Chgo., 1943-44; prodn. mgr. World Book Ency., 1944-48; pub. relations dir. Chgo. Assn. Commerce and Industry, 1948-50; pres. Carroll Chouinard Pub. Relations, Chgo., 1950-55; mng. editor Am. Peoples Encyclopedia, 1955-56, exec. editor, 1956-58, editor-in-chief, 1959; pub. relations cons., 1960-72; journalism lectr. Northwestern U., 1946-50 stylist, typographer. Fellow Newspaper Fund, 1961, 62. Mem. Am. Assn. Handwriting Analysts (a founder), Sigma Delta Chi, Beta Phi Theta. Moose. Clubs: Chicago Press, Chicago Headline, Wisconsin (Chgo.). Author: An Introduction to Professional Handwriting Analysis. Editor books, monographs in biol. scis. Home: Lombard II. Died Feb. 13, 1972.

CHOUINARD, MRS. NELBERT MURPHY, art educator; b. Montevideo, Minn., Feb. 9, 1879; d. Lea and Ruth Helen (Lawrence) Murphy; student Windom Inst., Montevideo, Pratt Inst., N.Y.C., 1889-1904; M. Horace A. Chouinard, Apr. 15, 1916 (dec. Sept. 1918). Supr. arts Mpls. pub. schs. 1888-89; tchr. S. Orange (N.J.) pub. schs., 1904-05, Batcheolar Art Sch., Pasadena, Cal., 1905-06; founder Chouinard Art Inst., Los Angeles, 1921, pres., dir., 1924-61. Home: South Pasadena PA Died July 9, 1969; buried Mountain View Cemetery Pasadena CA

CHREITZBERG, AUGUSTUS MCKEE, banker; b. Spartanburg, S.C., May 20, 1874; s. Rev. Hilliard Francis and Addria Eugenia (Kirby) C.; A.B., Wofford Coll., Spartanburg, 1895; m. Cema Sitton, of Autun, S.C., Apr. 12, 1911; children—Cema Sitton, Leila Eugenia, Mary Jo, Augustus McKee. Began as bookkeeper in jewelry store, Spartanburg, 1895; instr. Wofford Fitting Sch., 1897-99; bookkeeper, First Nat. Bank, Spartanburg, 1899; cashier, same, 1907, v.p., 1909, pres., 1914-Jan. 1930, pres. Mechanics' Bldg. and Loan Assn., Spartanburg. Trustee Wofford Coll., Converse Coll. Mem. Chi Psi. Democrat. Methodist. Home: 245 Hampton Av., Spartanburg SC‡

CHRIST, HARDING SIMON, editor; b. Shamokin, Pa., Dec. 6, 1903; s. Charles Frailey and Jennie (Ludlow) C.; A.B., U. Akron, 1925; M. Litt., Columbia, 1929; m. Hildegarde Zillioux, Sept. 25, 1930;children—Lois Marie (Mrs. Du Perow), Harding James. Pres. Am. Newspaper Guild Cleveland, 1942; counsellor journalism Ohio Newspaperwomens Assn., 1948-49; lectr. journalism Am. Press Inst., Columbia U., 1949-51; reporter Akron (O.) Times-Press, 1926; reporter N.Y. Times, 1927-28; with Cleveland Press, 1929-69, mng. editor, 1948-69; tchr. journalism Lorain County Community Coll., 1969. Mem. C. of C. Mem. Am. Newspaper Pubs. Assn., Am. Soc. Newspaper Editors, Sigma Delta Chi, Phi Kappa Tau. Club: Mid-Day (Cleve.). Home: Rocky River OH Died Mar. 18, 1971; buried Lakewood Park Cemetery.

CHRISTENBERRY, ROBERT KEATON, ret. bus. exec.; b. Huntingdon, Tenn., Jan. 27, 1899; s. William Calvin and Rebecca Arminta (Keaton) C.; ed. by pvt. tutors; student George Washington U.; m. Edna Joan LeRoy, Aug. 14, 1929; children—Robert Keaton, Sally Joan. Entered Foreign Service, State Dept., as vice consul, Vladivostok, Siberia, 1919, later at Santo Domingo, Dominican Republic, then mem. staff Washington (D.C.) Herald and Florida Times Union, dep. hotel commr., State of Fla., 1926-29; public relations dir. Hotel Winton, Cleveland, 1929-31; dir. of sales and promotion Book-Cadillac Hotel, Detroit, 1931-32; manager Jefferson Hotel, Peoria, 1932-34; gen. mgr. Hotel Roosevelt, Pittsburgh, 1934-35; v.p. Hotel Astor, N.Y.C., 1935-44; pres., mng. dir., 1944-45; chmn. bd. Clinton Trust Co., 1946-47; v.p., mng. dir. Sheraton Astor Hotel to 1955; cons. Webb & Knapp, Inc., real estate developers, 1954-55; pres. chmn. bd. Ambassador hotel, N.Y.C., 1955-64, Ambassador Internat. Corp., 1957-58. Postmaster City of New York, 1958-66. Chairman ECA Mission to Ireland, 1950; spl. ambassador of President of U.S. to inauguration of Pres. Storessner of Paraguay, 1954. Chmn. bd. Damon Runyon Meml. Fund of Cancer Research; chmn. N.Y. State Athletic Commn., 1951-54. USMC, World War I, and served overseas with 1st and 2d divs.; civilian cons. on recreation and housing facilities in Germany, Austria and Italy, France, also cons. food and beverage operations, World War II; maj., N.Y. State Guard, 1943-44. Mem. Nat. Assn. Postmasters, Nat. League Postmasters, Com. Econ. Devel., Disabled Am. Vets., Hotel Greeters Assn., Am. Legion, Vets. Fgn. Wars, Fla. State (hon.), Ft. Lauderdale (hon.) hotel and motel assns., Hotel Assn. N.Y.C. (hon. mem., dir.), Broadway Assn. (past pres.), Catholic Actors Guild. Republican. Presbyn. Mason. Clubs: Lambs, Ye Hosts Square (past pres.), (N.Y.C.); National Press Tavern (Washington); Le International. Address: Fort Lauderdale FL Died Apr. 1973.

CHRISTENSEN, PARLEY PARKER, lawyer; b. Weston, Ida., July 19, 1869; s. Peter and Sophia M. C.; A.B., U. of Utah, 1890; LL.B., Cornell U., 1897; unmarried. Prin. schs., Grantsville, Utah, 1890-95; county supt. schs., Toole Co., Utah, 1892-95; sec. Utah Constl. Conv., 1895; pros. atty. Salt Lake Co., Utah, 2 terms, 1901-06; mem. Utah Ho. of Rep., 1910-12; arbitrator street car strike, Salt Lake City, 1916; permanent chmn. Com. of 48," Chicago, 1920; candidate of Farmer Labor Party for Pres. of U.S., 1920; settled at Chicago, Jan. 1921, in practice of law. Unitarian. Mem. Universala Esperanto Asocio. Toured world, 1921-22; studied social and economic conditions in Europe, 1926-27; Progressive candidate for U.S. Senate in Ill., 1926. Home: Morrison Hotel, Chicago IL‡

CHRISTENSON, WALTER E., newspaper editor; b. Craig, Neb., Aug. 19, 1899; s. Andrew and Bingta (Johnson) C.; A.B., Univ. of Neb., 1919; m. Doris Thetge, Jan. 4, 1925; 1 son, Douglas A. Asst. prof. of journalism, Univ. of Mont., 1919-21; editor The New Northwest, Missoula, Mont., 1921-28; joined staff of Omaha (Neb.) World-Herald, 1928, mng. editor,

1935-39, asso. editor, 1939-42, editor, 1942-68; pres. The World Pub. Co., Omaha, 1955-66. Served in U.S. Coast Arty., 1918. Home: Omaha NB Died Jan. 7, 1969.

CHRISTIAN, GEORGE BUSBY, JR., secretary to late President Harding; b. nr. Marion, O., Mar. 25, 1873; s. George Busby and Lydia (Morris) C.; C.E., Pa. Mil. Coll., Chester, Pa., 1896 (M.A. 1921); m. Stella Farrar, of Shelby, O., 1897; children—Warren Wilson, John Farrar. Began, 1896, in employ of Norris, Christian Lime & Stone Co., Marion, and advanced to gen. mgr.; gen. sales mgr. White Sulphur Stone Co., Marion, 1907-15; pvt. sec. to Senator Warren G. Harding, 1915-21, to President Harding, Mar. 4, 1921. Trustee Girls' Industrial Sch., Delaware, O. Mem. Ohio Soc. of Washington, D.C.; hon. mem. Sigma Soc. of Coll. of Secretarial Science of Boston U. Republican. Presbyn. Mason (K.T., Shriner). Clubs: Chevy Chase, Columbia. Home: 2649 Connecticut Av., Washington DC‡

CHRISTIAN, JOHN L., chem. co. exec.; b. Oxford, Ala., Dec. 17, 1910; s. Manning G. and Carrie (Smith) C.; B.S., Ala. Poly. Inst., 1931; student Columbia, 1931-32, Harvard U. Grad. Sch. Bus. Adminstrn., 1948; m. Claudia Maybank, June 12, 1935 (dec.); children—Josephine Maybank, Carolyn Rhett; m. 2d, Mary Whitney Eversole, May 31, 1953; stepchildren—John, Susan. With Monsanto Co., from 1933, plant mgr. Columbia (Tenn.) plant, 1946-47, gen. mgr. phosphate div., St. Louis, 1948-51, v.p. phosphate div., 1951-59, v.p. inorganic chems. div., 1959-60, v.p. mfg., dir., mem. exec. com., from 1960, then sr. v.p. operations, dir. Member Manufacturing Chemists Assn. (dir.), Am. Chem. Soc., Assn. Am. Soap and Glycerine Producers (mem. bd.), Nat. Plant Food Inst., Am. Inst. Chem., Engrs. Clubs: Noonday, Racquet, Old Warson Country, Deer Creek. Home: Ladue MO

CHRISTIANSEN, EDWARD S., IV, metal mfr.; b. Northampton, Mass., June 19, 1909; s. Edward Smith and Mary Ethel (Oldham) C.; A.B., Case Western Res. U., 1933; m. Mary Catherine Badger, May 21, 1938; children—Karen Christiansen Davis, Edward Smith V, William Earl. Mem. sales dept. Stewart Die Casting Corp., Chgo., 1933-34; sales mgr. Nat. Smelting Co., Cleve., 1935-38; organizer, v.p., dir. Aluminum and Magnesium, Inc., Sandusky, O., 1939-41; v.p., sales mgr., dir. Apex Smelting Co., Chgo., 1941-44; organizer, pres., chmn. bd. Magnesium Co. Am., E. Chicago, Ind., 1944-62, Christiansen Corp., Oak Park, Ill., 1944-62, Indsl. Smelting Corp., Chicago Heights, Ill., 1946-62, Aluminum Alloyer's Can., Ltd., 1952-62, Magcoa, Ltd., 1954-62; chmn. bd. Equipment Co. Am., Hialeah, Fla., 1962-72; consul for Sweden, Miami, Fla., 1956-63. Founder, pres. Magnesium Assn., 1943-46. Bd. dirs. Met. Miami YMCA; bd. govs. Com. of 100, Miami Beach, Fla.,; past bd. dirs. United Fund, Mental Health Soc., Cancer Inst., Opera Guild, Hist. Assn. So. Fla.; adv. bd. Fla. Meml. Coll. Named Man of Year in Light Metals Industry, 1951. Mem. Execs. Assn. Greater Miami, World Bus. Council, Delta Kappa Epsilon. Mason (32, Shriner) Clubs: Coral Reef Yacht (founding commodore 1955), Two Hundred (Miami); Century (past bd. govs.) (Coral Gables). Home: Coral Gables FL Died Oct. 13, 1972.

CHRISTOL, CARL, univ. prof. (surname changed from Christophelsmeier); b. at Henstorf, Lippe, Germany, May 18, 1872; s. Simon and Amalia (Bornemeier) C.; came to U.S., 1889; A.B., U. of Neb. 1899, A.M., 1902; studied Sorbonne, Paris, 1902-03, U. of Heidelberg, summer semester, 1903; U. of Berlin, 1903-05, Ph.D., 1905; m. Winifred Quimby, June 4, 1912; children—Carl Quimby, Eugene Whitney, Max Stanton, Robert Geer. Prof. history, Lawrence Coll., Appleton, Wis., 1906-07; asso. prof. history, U. of Neb., 1907-08; research work, Cornell U., 1908-09; head dept. history and polit. science, U. of S.D., 1909-29, and history since 1929; dir. Gurney Seed & Nursery Co., The House of Gurney, Yankton, S.Dak., 1921-40. Mem. Am. Soc. of Internat. Law, Am. Acad. Polit. and Social Science, Am. Assn. Univ. Profs., State Educational Assn. of S.D. (life), S.D. History Teachers' Assn. (founder, pres. 19 yrs.), Hist. Soc. of S.D. (life), Vermillion Chamber of Commerce, Pi Gamma Mu; faculty adv., U.S.D. Internat. Relations Club since 1926; pres. S.D. Fedn. of Garden Clubs, 1945-48. President Dept. of Higher Edn. of State Ednl. Assn. of South Dakota, 1923-27. Awarded silver Beaver, Nat. Council Boy Scouts of America for distinguished service to boyhood." Republican. Conglist. Mason (K.T.). Author books, also articles and studies on hist. topics. Home: Forest Hill Vermillion SD

CHRYSLER, MINTIN ASBURY, botanist; b. Berlin, Ont., Can., Aug. 25, 1871; s. Edgar and Sarah (Green) C.; B.A., U. of Toronto, 1894; certificate, Ont. Normal Coll., 1894-95, grad. student, 1902-03, fellow in botany, 1903-04; Ph.D., U. of Chicago, 1904; m. Clara Belle Van Duzen, of Grimsby, Ont., Sept. 15, 1910; 1 son, Sidney Van Duzen, Science master, Toronto Junction Collegiate Inst., 1895-1902; asst. in botany, Marine Biol. Lab., summer 1904; on bot. survey of Md., summers 1904-05; asst. in botany, 1904-05, instr., 1905-07, Harvard; asso. prof. botany, 1907-10, prof., 1910-11, prof. biology, 1911-23, U. of Me.; asso. prof. botany, Rutgers U., 1923-—. Fellow A.A.A.S. mem. Bot. Soc. America, Torrey Bot. Club. Conglist. Mason. Joint Author: Plant Life of Maryland, 1910. Home: 208 Lawrence Av., New Brunswick NJ‡

CHUBB, THOMAS CALDECOT, author; b. East Orange, N.J., Nov. 1, 1899; s. Hendon and Alice Margaret (Lee) C.; prep. edn., St. Paul's Sch., Concord, N.H., 1913-18; B.A., Yale, 1922; m. 2d, Caroline Parker Smith, June 22, 1929 (dec.); m. 3d, Edith Onions, July 1, 1938; children—Russell Parsons, Mary Alice Victoria (Mrs. Gerald Wolsfelt), Rosamond Caldecot (Mrs. Hillyer M. Young). Connected in editorial capacity with various magazines, 1923-24; with the New York Times, 1925-29. Served with U.S. Naval Reserves, 1918. With Office of Strategic Services, 1942-45; chief port section, 1944, consultant, 1944-45; director Greenwich (Conn.) Broadcasting Co. Mem. Merritt Pkwy. Commn., 1955-59, sec., 1957-59; mem. Conn. Commn. on the Arts, from 1965. Winner John Masefield prize, 1920, Albert Stanborough Cook prize, 1921 (both Yale University). Trustee Chubb Foundation, Victoria Foundation, Incorporated, Rosemary Hall Found., Inc., Yale Library Assos., director of the Greenwich C. of C., 1947-50; vice chmn. Conn. chpt. Committee to Defend America, 1940-41, chmn. Greenwich chpt., 1941. Mem. Greenwich Bd. Estimate and Taxation, 1960-64; mem. Greenwich Dem. Town Com., 1953-64; Conn. mem. Dem. Nat. Finance Committee, 1960; delegate to Democratic Nat. Convention, 1956, 60. Fellow of Timothy Dwight College, Yale Univ. Fellow Am. Geog. Soc.; mem. Poetry Soc. Am. (exec. bd. 1956), Alpha Delta Phi. Clubs: Indian Harbor Yacht, Royal Bermuda Yacht, Belle Haven, Beachton Yacht, Florida-Georgia Field Trial; Yale, New York Yacht (New York City, New York); Elizabethan and the Chi Delta Theta (New Haven). Democrat. Author: The White God and Other Poems, 1920; Kyrdoon (poem), 1921; The Life of Giovanni Boccaccio, 1930; Ships and Lovers (verse), 1933; Cliff Pace and Other Poems, 1936; Aretino: Scourge of Princes, 1940; My Daughter's World, 1941; A Time to Speak (verse), 1943; Cornucopia: Poems 1919-53; If There Were No Losses, 1957; The Byzantines, 1959; The months of the Year (verse), 1960; Slavic Peoples, 1962; The Northmen, 1964; Dante and His World, 1967; The Letters of Pietro Aretino, 1967; The Venetians; Merchant Princes, 1968. Contbr. to mags. Address: Greenwich CT also Thomasville GA Died Mar. 20, 1972; buried Springwood Plantation, Thomasville GA

CHUJOY, ANATOLE, editor; b. Riga, Latvia, Apr. 4, 1894; s. Jacob and Braina (Rubin) C.; grad. law sch. U. Petrograd, 1918. Came to U.S., 1924, naturalized, 1930. Contbr. editor Am. Dancer, 1933-36; mng. editor Dance mag., 1936-41; editor, pub. Dance News, 1942-68; awarded diploma for meritorious research and fruitful activities in realm of dance Archives Internationales de la Danse, Paris, 1950. Author: Ballet, 1936; Symphonic Ballet, 1937; The Dance Encylopedia, 1949; New York City Ballet, 1953. Translator, editor: Fundamentals of the Classic Dance (Vaganova), 1946. Editor: Fokine, Memoirs of a Ballet Master, 1961 Dance Ency., 1967. Contbr. articles profl. publs. Home: New York City NY Died Feb. 24, 1969; buried Westchester NY

CHUPP, CHARLES DAVID, plant pathologist; b. Millersburg, Elkhart County, Ind., June 2, 1886; s. Levi N. and Margaret Rebecca (Weaver) C.; A.B., Wabash Coll., Crawfordsville, Ind., 1912; Ph.D., Cornell U., 1916; m. Nora Mae Scrugham, Aug. 23, 1913; children—Karl Richard, William Howard, Frank Marsh, John Paul. Asst. in plant pathology, Cornell, 1912-14, instr. 1914-16; acting prof. botany, Wabash Coll., 1916-17; instr. plant pathology, Cornell, 1917-19, asst. prof., 1919-27, prof., 1927-54; prof. emeritus, 1954-67; on leave at Rutgers U., 1926-27; visiting prof., Puerto Rico, 1946-47. Recipient Superior Service award U.S. Dept. Agr., 1954. Member A.A.A.S., American Mycological Soc., Am. Phytopathol. Soc. (councilor 1937-38; v.p. 1939; pres. 1940, recipient Award of Merit 1964), Sigma Xi, Sigma Phi. Methodist. Mason. Author: Manual of Vegetable-Garden Diseases, 1925; (with other) Vegetable Diseases and Their Control, 1960. Contbr. numerous articles to scientific jours. Has been working on monograph of fungus genus, cercospora, 30 yrs.; studied European herbaria, especially at London and Berlin, summer 1938. Home: Ithaca NY Died Nov. 9, 1967; buried East Lawn Cemetery, Ithaca NY

CHURCH, RANDOLPH, educator; b. Phila., Apr. 1, 1904; s. Warren Randolph and Mary (Laros) C.; A.B., Amherst Coll., 1926; A.M., U. Pa., 1930; Ph.D., Yale, 1935; m. Helen Van Nuys, Apr. 26, 1929; children—Robert F., Alan W. Instr. in math. Am. U. Beirut, Syria, 1926-29, Peddie Sch., Hightstown, N.J., 1930-31, Yale, 1932-35, U.S. Naval Acad., 1935-38; asst. prof. U.S. Naval Postgrad. Sch., 1938-42, asso. prof., 1946-47, prof. math. and mechanics, 1947-67, chmn. dept., 1947-67. Consultant in prep. refresher course series U. Calif., 1947-48. Commd. U.S.N.R., 1938; active duty, 1942-46. Awarded Navy Commendation ribbon. Mem. Am. Math. Soc., Math. Assn. Am., Assn. for Computing Machinery, Inst. Math. Statistics, Nat. Speleological Society, American Soc. Engineering Edn., Econometric Society Canadian Mathematical Congress, Society for Indsl. and Applied Mathematics, Inst. Radio Engrs., Societe Mathematique de France, Indian Math. Soc., Am. Assn. U. Profs., A.A.A.S., Sigma Xi, Phi Delta Theta. Presbyn. Contbr. articles and reviews in profl. jours. Home: Monterey CA Died Feb. 8, 1969.

CHURCHILL, EDWARD DELOS, surgeon; b. Chenoa, Ill., Dec. 25, 1895; s. Ebenezer Delos and Maria A. (Farnsworth) C.; B.S., Northwestern U., 1916, A.M., 1917; M.D. cum laude, Harvard, 1920; Dr. Honoris Causa, of Algiers, 1944; D.Sc., Princeton, 1947, U. Ala., 1959, Harvard, 1961; LL.D., Queen's U., 1954; m. Mary Lowell Barton, July 7, 1927; children—Mary Lowell, Frederick Barton, Edward Delos, A. Coolidge. Student intern Faulkner Hosp., Boston, 1919-20; surg. intern Mass. Gen. Hosp., 1920-22, resident, 1922-23, chief West Surg. Service, 1931-48, chief Gen. Surg. Services, 1948-72; asso. surgeon and dir. Surg. Research Lab., Boston City Hosp., 1928-30; asst. in surgery Harvard, 1922-23, Alumni asst. in surgery, 1923-24, instr. surgery, 1924-28, Moseley traveling fellow, 1926-27, asso. prof. surgery, 1928-31, John Homans prof. surgery, 1931-62, emeritus, 1962-72. Adv. med. bd. Am. Hosp., Paris, 1957-72; mem. adv. council Shiraz Med. Center, Nemazee Hosp., Iran, 1957-72; charter mem. sci. adv. bd. Walter Reed Inst. Research, Washington, 1958. Served in Med. Res., U.S. Army, 1918, 1st lt., 1924-29; col. M.C., cons. surgeon N. African and Mediterranean theatres, 1943-46. Decorated Legion of Merit, 1944; European Theater Service medal with 4 bronze battle stars; Cross of Knight Legion of Honor, 1953; War medal of Brazil; comdr. Order Crown of Italy; hon. officer Mil. Div. Order Brit. Empire, 1945; D.S.M., 1946; officer de l'Ordre National du Cedre (Lebanon). Chmn. med. adv. com. to sec. of war, 1946-48; vice chmn. task force, Fed. Med. Services, Commn. on Orgn. Exec. Br. Govt., 1948-49, 1953-55; mem. Armed Forces Med. Adv. Com. to Sec. Def., 1948-51; chmn. com. on surgery NRC, 1946-49; sr. civilian cons. in thoracic surgery to Surgeon Gen., 1953-72; cons. to Surgeon Gen., 1954-55; mem. edit. bd. Annals of Surgery. Fellow Royal Coll. Surgeons Eng. (hon.), Royal Coll. Univ. Surgeons Denmark (hon.), Am. Acad. Arts and Sci.; lectr. Royal Coll. Physicians and Surgeons (Can.); mem. Am. Assn. for Thoracic Surgery (pres. 1948-49), Am. Bd. Surgery Founders' Group (mem. bd. 1937-49), A.C.S., A.M.A., Am. Soc. for Clin. Investigation (emeritus 1941-72), Am. Surg. Assn. (pres. 1946-47), Assn. Mil. Surgeons U.S., Internat., New Eng. Boston, Excelsior (hon.) surg. socs., Halsted Club, Mass. Med. Soc., No. Pacific Surg. Assn. (hon.), Soc. Clin. Surgery (pres. 1949-50), Soc. U.S. Med. Cons. in World War II, Trudeau Soc., Korean Communications Zone Med. and Dental (hon.), 38th Parallel Med. Soc. of Korea (hon.), So. Honshu Med. Soc., Alpha Omega Alpha, Sigma Xi, Delta Tau Delta; hon. mem. U.S. and fgn. surg. socs. Presbyn. Clubs: Tavern, Century Assn., Harvard (Boston and N.Y.C.), Aesculapian. Home: Belmont MA Died Aug. 28, 1973.

CHURCHILL, GEORGE MORTON, prof. history; b. Elmwood, Mass., Jan. 23, 1874; s. Warren Keen and Elizabeth Hervey (Josselyn) C.; A.B., Boston U., 1896; student Bridgewater (Mass.) State Normal Sch., 1896-97; A.M., George Washington U., 1909, Ph.D., 1914; m. Mary Josephine Solyom de Antalfa, of Bethesda, Md., Apr. 2, 1910; children—Elizabeth Sarah, Warren Solyom de Antalfa, Morton Vincent. Teacher, Lawrence Acad., Groton, Mass., 1897-98; law clk., Harris & Barker, Brockton, Mass., 1898-1904; cataloguer and classifier, in charge social and polit. science, Library of Congress, 1904-20; part-time instr. in history, George Washington U., 1908-13, asst. prof. part-time, 1914-20, full time, 1920-22, prof., 1922-39, prof. emeritus since 1939. Chmn. East Bridgewater Sch. Com., 1899-1904. Mem. Am. Hist. Assn., Phi Beta Kappa, Beta Theta Pi. Republican. Unitarian. Mason. Clubs: Cosmos, Federal Schoolmen. Editor: Library of Congress Classification Schedules H and S (social sciences and agriculture), 1910-20. Home: Bethesda MD‡

CHURCHILL, LIDA A., author; b. Harrison, Md.; d. Josiah and Catherine (Hilton) C.; orphaned in childhood; self educated; unmarried. Learned stenography and telegraphy; was telegraph operator at Northbridge, Mass.; began journalism, Boston, 1896; wrote for Boston Globe, Herald, Transcript, New York Independent, Observer, Collier's, Delineator, Cosmopolitan, etc. Asst. editor Success, 1897-1902, when retired to devote attention to gen. lit. work. Author: My Girls; Interweaving; The Magic Seven, 1901; The Magnet, 1903; The Master Demand, 1908; The Truth About Our Dead, 1917. Originator and leader of the Internat. Hearts Desire Circle. Address: 523 W 122d St., New York NY‡

CHURCHMAN, PHILIP HUDSON, coll. prof.; b. Burlington, N.J., Sept. 23, 1874; s. Horace and Edith Anna (Woolman) C.; A.B., Princeton, 1896, A.M. 1903; post-grad. work, univs. of Paris and Grenoble, France; Ph.D., Harvard, 1908; m. Mary Colchester Morgan, Oct. 5, 1910; children—Frances (Mrs. J. Ross Hunter,

Jr.), Elizabeth (Mrs. R. B. George), Carolyn. Master in Chestnut Hill Acad., Phila., 1897-99; instr. in French, Princeton, 1900-04, French and Spanish, U.S. Naval Acad., 1904-05, Romance langs., Harvard, 1906-08; asst. prof. Romance langs., 1908-11, prof. and head of Romance lang. dept., 1911-20, Clark Coll.; prof. Romance langs., Clark U., since 1920, professor emeritus since Oct. 1, 1944; visiting professor University of Chicago, summer quarter, 1912. Mem. Modern Lang. Assn. America, Phi Beta Kappa; mem. Simplified Spelling Bd. Presbyterian. Author: La Alegria del Capitan Ribot, 1906; An Introduction to the Pronunciation of French, 1906; Espronceda's Blanca de Borbon, 1907; Byron and Espronceda, 1909; Beginnings of Byronism in Spain, 1910; Exercises on French Sounds, 1911; First Phonetic French Course (with E. F. Hacker), 1921; Scott's Influence in Spain (with E. A. Peers), 1922; French Literature in Outline (with C. E. Young), 1928; The Phonetic Gateway to French, 1928; A First Book in French (with L. L. Atwood and A. R. Racine), 1935; Manuel de la Litterature Francaise (with J. P. LeCoq and C. E. Young), 1936. Home: 20 Institute Rd., Worcester MA‡

CHUTE, A(ARON) HAMILTON, economist and prof.; b. Toledo, O., Oct. 30, 1891; s. George Maynard and Grace Belle (Hamilton) C.; B.A., U. of Mich., 1916; M.A., O. State U., 1931, Ph.D., 1935; m. Ruth Lyle Wells, June 30, 1917; children—George Merrill, Elizabeth Marie. Business executive in machine tool firm, Ohio, 1918-22, department stores, Ohio, 1922-29; instructor, Ohio State University, marketing research asso. Bur. Bus. Research, 1930-36; asst. prof. and later asso. prof., Sch. Bus. Adminstrn., U. of Minn., lecturer, Coll. Pharmacy, marketing cons. in Cooperative Bus. Research Sta., 1936-46; training specialist Compliance Branch War Food Adminstrn., Washington, D.C., 1943-45; prof. marketing, U. of Toledo, O., 1946-47; prof. retailing Coll. Bus. Adminstrn. U. Tex., from 1947; retailing specialist Bur. Bus. Research, 1947-57. Vis. prof. So. Meth. U., 1964-65, Fresno State U., 1965-68. With U.S. Army, Information and Edn. Br. as civilian employee U.S. War Dept., Biarritz (France) Am. U., 1945-46. Mem. Am. Mktng. Assn., Am. Econ. Assn., A.A.A.S., Am. Assn. U. Profs., Am. Statis. Assn., Southwestern Social Sci, Assn., Am. Acad. Polit. and Social Sci., Phi Beta Kappa, Beta Gamma Sigma, Delta Sigma Pi. Independent. Conglist. Mason. Author books including: Business Management Handbook, 1952; The Pharmacist in Retail Distribution, 1953, rev. edit. 1960. Home: Austin TX Died Aug. 19, 1968; interred Capital Meml. Gardens, Austin TX

CILLEY, C. C., treas., Northrup Corp. Home: South Pasadena CA Died Sept. 27, 1969.

CIMIOTTI, GUSTAVE, artist; b. New York City, Nov. 10, 1875; s. Gustave and Louise (Wenzlik) C.; grad. Verona (N.J.) pub. schs.; studied at Art Students' League, 1895-99, and with H. S. Mowbray, J. C. Beckwith, Kenyon Cox, New York, Academie Julian and Delecluse Acad., 1900, and with Benjamin Constant, Paris; m. Evelyn E. Moreland. Exhibited at Society Am. Artists, Nat. Acad. Design, Corcoran Gallery, etc., former dir. Newark School of Fine and Industrial Art. Received Ranger Fund 1500, 1929. Mem. Grand Central Art Galleries, Salmagundi Club. Studio: 51 W. 10th St., New York NY‡

CIOCCO, ANTONIO, biostatistician; b. Columbus, O., May 1, 1908; s. Michael and Gelsomina (Ferraro) C.; Sc.D. (economics), U. Naples (Italy), 1930; Sc.D. (hygiene), Johns Hopkins, 1936; m. Augusta Kershaw, Feb. 16, 1942; 1 dau., Angela. Research asso. otology Johns Hopkins Sch. Medicine, 1930-35, asso. biology Sch. Hygiene and Public Health, 1936-39; biometrician, pub. health adminstr. U.S.P.H.S., Washington, 1939-49; prof., head dept. biostatistics U. Pittsburgh Grad. Sch. Pub. Health, 1949-69, professor of biostatistics, 1969-72; sometimes cons. U.S.P.H.S., United States Children's Bur., Rockefeller Found., War Manpower Commn., Nat. Security Resources Bd. Mem. Am. Pub. Health Assn., Biometrics Soc., Soc. Research in Child Development, Am. Soc. Human Genetics, A.A.A.S. Roman Catholic. Author monographs, contbr. articles various jours. dealing with investigations fields deafness, physical growth and development, human genetics, etc. Home: Pittsburgh PA Died Jan. 5, 1972; buried Gate of Heaven Cemetery, Silver Spring MD

CLAIRE, RICHARD SHAW, accountant; b. Wirt, N.Y., Jan. 31, 1907; s. William Lee and Hazel (Coats) C.; A.B., Alfred U., 1927; M.B.A., U. Mich., 1932; m. Eleanor Pratchett, Oct. 26, 1940; children—Edward William, Robert Lee. Mem. staff Arthur Andersen & Co., N.Y.C., 1936-39, audit mgr., Chgo., 1945-47, partner, 1947-69; asst. dir. research Am. Inst. C.P.A.'s, N.Y.C., 1939-40; asso. prof. accounting Harvard Grad. Sch. Bus. Adminstrn., 1940-45. Mem. exec. bd. Chgo. council Boy Scouts Am. Trustee, Village of Glencoe (Ill.), 1960-69. C.P.A. numerous states. Mem. Am. Inst. C.P.A.'s (v.p. 1960), Ill. Soc. C.P.A.'s (pres. 1957-58), Am. Accounting Assn. (v.p. 1952). Home: Glencoe IL Died Nov. 26, 1969; buried Pinelawn NY

CLANCY, JOHN W., judge; became judge U.S. Dist. Ct. of N.Y., southern dist., 1936, chief judge, until 1959. Home: New York City NY Died Mar. 4, 1969.

CLAPP, EARLE HART, forester; b. North Rush, N.Y., Oct. 15, 1877; s. Edwin Perry and Ermina Jane (Hart) C.; student Geneseo (N.Y.) Normal Sch., Cornell U., 1902-03; A.B., U. of Mich., 1905, D.Sc., 1928; m. Helen Adele Roberts, Oct. 15, 1908; children—Stewart, Helen Ermina. Asst. in forest service, U.S. Dept. Agr., 1905, chief of office forest management, 1908, asso. dist. forester, 1909-12, forest insp., 1912-15, asst. forester in charge research, 1915-35, asso. chief of forest service, 1935-44; except when acting chief forest service, 1940-42; organized research bureau; planned and helped obtain legislation to insure planwise development of research commensurate with nat. needs, resulting in 12 regional forest expt. stas. and further development of a nat. forest products lab.; as acting chief formulated Fed. legislation leading towards nation-wide forestry, with primary emphasis on pub. regulation of forest practices on privately owned land and greatly increased pub. ownership. Fellow Soc. Am. Foresters (twice v.p.); mem. Soc. Forestry Finland (corr.), Sigma Xi. Clubs: Cosmos (Washington); U. of Mich. Union (Ann Arbor, Mich.). Author: National Program of Forest Research, 1926, Supervised report A National Plan for American Forestry," 1933; The Western Range, A Great but Neglected National Resource," 1936; also various other govt. reports. Contbr. to forestry jours. Home: 6802 Meadow Lane Chevy Chase 15 MD‡

CLAPP, JOHN MANTLE, editor; b. at Orange, N.J., Sept. 16, 1870; s. of Oliver Martin and Lois Antoinette (Comstock) C.; A.B., Amherst Coll., 1890, A.M., 1893; U. of Chicago, 1895; m. Margaret Linton Paterson, of Buffalo, N.Y., June 18, 1896. Instr. in English, 1890-04, prof., 1894-9, Ill. Coll.; asst. prof. English, 1899-1904, asso. prof., 1904-06. Ind. U. prof. English, Lake Forest (Ill.) U., 1906-16, with the Ronald Press Co., N.Y., since 1916. Mem. Modern Lang. Assn. America, Delta Upsilon, Phi Beta Kappa. Congregationalist. Editor: Amherst Memories (with A. B. MacNeill), 1890; Select Orations from American History (with S. B. Harding), 1909. Author: Talking Business, 1920. Address: 20 Vesey St., New York NY‡

CLAPP, VERNER WARREN, librarian; b. Johannesburg, Union of S. Africa (parents U.S. citizens), June 3, 1901; s. George Herbert and Mary Sybil (Helms) C.; A.B., Trinity Coll., 1922; grad. study Harvard, 1922-23; m. Dorothy Devereux Ladd, Aug. 24, 1929; children—Nancy Priest (Mrs. Joseph H. Roe, Jr.), Verner Warren, Judith Ladd (Mrs. James F. Bromley). With Library of Congress, Wash., 1923-56, dir. administrative dept., 1940-43, dir. acquisitions dept., 1943-47, chief asst. librarian, 1947-56; president Council on Library Resources, Inc., 1956-67, consultant, 1967-72; director of Forest Press, Incorporated, 1954-72, pres., 1962-72; librarian U.N. Conf. Internat. Orgn., San Francisco, 1945; chmn. U.S. Library Mission to Japan, 1947-48; mem. Nat. Adv. Commn. on Libraries, 1966-67. Mem. A.L.A. (Lippincott Medal 1960), Spl. Libraries Assn., Canadian, D.C. library assns., Bibliog. Soc. Am., Bibliog. Soc. Can., Am. Inst. Graphic Arts, Phi Beta Kappa, Sigma Nu. Clubs: Grolier; Cosmos (Washington). Author: United Nations Ednl., Sci., Cultural Orgns. Report Bibliog. Services, 1950; The Future of the Research Library, 1963; Copyright—A Librarian's View, 1968; also articles and reports profl. jours. Home: Chevy Chase MD Died June 15, 1972; buried Wappingers Falls NY

CLARK, ANNE KINNIER, educator; b. Wilmington, N.C., July 18, 1874; d. James M. and Sarah (Kinnier) Forshee; ed. pvt. schs., Wilmington; grad. Tileson Normal Sch., Wilmington; m. Henry John Clark, of Aberdeen, Scotland, and Boston, Mass., 1892 (died 1914). Took charge, 1914, of Clark Sch. of Business Administration, Boston, which was founded by husband, and now at head two schs. same name, at Boston and Quincy, Mass. Home: 1087 Boylston St., Fenway, Boston MA‡

CLARK, BERT BOONE, M.D.; b. Galva, Ill., Sept. 23, 1872; s. Charles Wesley and Rilla (Clarke) C.; M.D., New York Homoe. Med. Coll. and Flower Hosp., 1899; m. Blanche MacCorristen, of N.Y. City, Oct. 1, 1907. Prof. medicine, New York Coll. for Women, since 1905; phys. to Hahnemann, Metropolitan, Broad Street hosps. Mem. Am. Inst. Homoeopathy, Homoe. Med. Soc. State of N.Y., Acad. Pathol. Science, Homoe. Med. Soc. County of N.Y., Dunham Club, Clinical Club, Alpha Sigma. Mason. Home: 170 W. 73d. St., New York NY‡

CLARK, CAROLINE RICHARDS, educator; b. at Northampton, Mass.; d. Joseph Cook and Lydia Anne (Burt) C.; early edn., Northampton; student of langs., Gottingen, Germany, and Paris, France, 3 yrs.; later traveled, and studied in Paris and Germany, 2 yrs.; diploma, Sorbonne, Paris, 1892; (A.M., Oxford (Ohio) Coll., for Women, 1895); unmarried. Teacher Prospect Hill Sch., Greenfield, Mass., 1887-91; dean Oxford Coll. for Women, 1892-5; prin. Prospect Hill Sch., 1896-07; prin. (with Dr. David A. Kennedy), of Dearborn-Morgan Sch., Orange, N.J., 1907-11, owner and prin. same since 1911. Lecturer on history of art, and French and German lit. Conglist. Mem. Alliance Francaise (pres., 1912-14, now hon. pres.); mem. Head Mistresses' Assn. Club: Woman's (Orange). Address: 91 Main St., Orange NJ‡

CLARK, CHARLES CLEVELAND, statistician, meteorologist; b. Washington, D.C., Mar. 6, 1875; s. Ezra Wescote and Sylvia (Nodine) C.; student Columbia U.; LL.B., Phila. Law Sch. (Temple Coll.), 1899; LL.M., Columbia, 1900, D.C.L., 1901; m. Mary Duncan Swingle, July 12, 1905; children—Charles Cleveland, Robert Duncan, Mary Elizabeth, Anita. Asso. statistician in charge Bur. of Statistics, Dept. of Agr., Washington, D.C., 1906-08, also chmn. crop-reporting bd.; statistician Internat. Inst. Agr., Rome, Italy, 1909, 1910; chief clk. U.S. Dept. Agr., 1911-13; exec. asst. U.S. Weather Bur., 1913-14; asst. chief same since 1915. Represented U.S. in organizing Internat. Inst. Agr., at Rome, Italy, 1908. Mem. bar States of Pa. and Wash. and of Washington, D.C. Mem. Am. Statis. Assn., Am. Meteorol. Soc., Loyal Legion, Columbia Hist. Soc., Am. Forestry Assn., Inst. of Aeronautical Sciences. Clubs: University, Torch, Federal, Congressional Country (Washington, D.C.). Author various bulls., and monographs on statis. and crop reporting subjects. Home: 21 W. Irving St., Chevy Chase MD‡

CLARK, DERRAL LEROY, assn. exec.; b. nr. Almond, Wis., July 25, 1907; s. John Roy and Nellie (Sanders) C.; A.B., Lawrence Coll., 1928; M.A., State U. Ia., 1937; m. Rhoda Murphy, July 29, 1937 (dec. July 29, 1963); m. 2d, Antoinette Strege, June 16, 1965. Teacher public schools, Marinette, Wis., 1929-40; bus. director public schools, Wauwatosa, Wis., 1940-58; exec. sec. Milw. Assn. Ins. Agts., 1958-67; v.p. Road Aid of Wis., Inc.; pres. Nat. Conf. Met. Ins. Bds., 1962. Pres. Milw. Civic Alliance, 1958-59. Recipient Distinguished Service award Wauwatosa Civic Alliance, 1958. Mem. Wis. C. of C., Milw. Assn. Commerce, American Soc. Association Executives, Wis. Conf. Christians and Jews. Kiwanian (gov. Wis.-Upper Mich. dist. 1958; chairman international committee 1956, 60, 62, internat. trustee 1965-67). Mason (32 degree, Jester, Shriner). Home: Wauwatosa WI Died June 18, 1967.

CLARK, EDWARD BRAYTON, newspaper man; b. Utica, N.Y.; s. Erastus and Frances (Beardsley) Clark; grad. Free Academy, Utica; cadet U.S. Mil. Acad., 1879-81; m. Eliza Frances Obee, of Highland Park, Ill.; one daughter, Frances Clark Devereux (deceased). Enlisted in United States Army, 1887, and served as non-commissioned officer and instr. of recruits, and later with 6th U.S. Inf.; assisted in raising an Ill. regt. for Spanish-Am. War and commd. capt. by Ill. legislature (services of regt. not required). Began newspaper work as reporter, Boston Herald, 1882; reporter and spl. article and editorial writer in Chicago, 1890-1903; Washington corr. Chicago Evening Post, 1903-31; was corr. in field in Sioux Indian war, 1890-91, in Garza uprising, Tex., 1892, in France, 1915. An organizer, 1897, and v.p. Ill. Audubon Soc. for Protection of Birds; life mem. Franklin Inst.; mem. permanent orgn. West Point Class of 1884. Republican. Episcopalian. Clubs: Gridiron, Nat. Press, Army and Navy, Overseas Writers; The Tavern (Chicago). Contbr. newspapers and mags. on polit. and natural history topics; wrote interview with Theodore Roosevelt, on The Nature Fakers," for Everybody's Mag. Commd. capt., N.A., Dec. 18, 1917; major, July 1918; lt. col., R.C., Aug. 18, 1919; col., O.R.C., 1923; with A.E.F. in France 5 months; participated in two major mil. operations. Decorated Chevalier Legion of Honor (France), wife awarded same decoration. Home: 2100 Massachusetts Av., Washington DC‡

CLARK, FELTON GRANDISON, univ. pres.; b. Baton Rouge, La., Oct. 13, 1903; s. Joseph Samuel and Octavia (Head) C.; student Southern U., Baton Rouge, Louisiana, 1920-22; A.B., Beloit Collge; Beloit, Wisconsin, 1924, LL.D., 1946; M.A., Columbia Univ., 1925, Ph.D., 1933; m. Allen Knighten, Aug. 22, 1958. Instr. Wiley Coll., 1925-27, So. U., 1927-30; instr., Howard U., Washington, D.C., 1931-33; dean of college, Southern University, 1934-37, pres., 1938-70. Director National Survey of Vocational Education and Guidance of Negroes; member Nat. Conf. Problems Edn. of Negroes, Bd. Fgn. Scholarships (Fulbright); mem. adv. com. Grad. Fellowship sect. Div. Higher Edn., U.S. Office Edn., Survey Fed. Programs Higher Edn.; cons. Ednl. Policies Commn.; pres. Land Grant Coll. Pres'. Conf., 1940-41; mem. La. Dept. of Instns. Advisory Com. on Juvenile Delinquency; mem. La. Dept. of Welfare Advisory Com. on Coordinating Ch. and Welfare Agencies; adv. bd. to registrants, East Baton Rouge Parish; state coordinator of Civilian Defense Activities among Negroes; head Negro div. State Speakers Bur.; chmn. Negro div. East Baton Rouge Parish War Bond Com.; mem. adv. panel on ednl. statistics U.S. office of Edn. Active YMCA, v.p. nat. council N.A., 1955-56, 61, mem. World Council 1961, internat. com., 1961, mem. Am. delegation to Geneva meeting, 1961, member commission on racial relationships, 1964, mem. Blue Ridge Assembly Bd., mem. Am. delegation World Centennial, Paris, 1955. Gubernatorial rep. 50th Anniversary Celebration of founding of Mound Bayou, 1937, Am. Negro Expn., Chicago, 1940, Miss. River Discovery Expn., Memphis, 1940. Gubernatorial rep. Nat. Freedom Day, Phila., 1945. Awarded Gen. Edn. Bd. fellowship, 1932-33. Mem. Assn. Colls. and Secondary Schs. for Negroes (pres. 1944-45), A.A.A.S., Am. Acad. Polit. and Social

Sci., N.E.A., Am. Assn. Sch. Adminstrs., Am. Assn. Land Grant Colls. and State Universities (mem. exec. com. 1960-62), Am. Sociol. Society, Kappa Phi Kappa, Pi Gamma Mu, Alpha Phi Alpha, Phi Beta Kappa, Phi Beta Delta, Alpha Kappa Mu, Betta Kappa Chi, Kappa Delta Pi, Alpha Phi Omega, Sigma Pi Phi. Baptist. Mason (33 deg.), Elk. Mem. editorial staff Jour. Negro Edn. Home: Baton Rouge LA Died July 5, 1970; buried Southern University, Baton Rouge LA

CLARK, FRED, actor; b. Lincoln, Cal., 1914; ed. Stanford. m. Benay Venuta; m. 2d, Gloria Clark. Motion picture appearances include Ride the Pink Horse, Sunset Boulevard, How to Marry a Millionaire, Daddy Long Legs, Court Martial of Billy Mitchell, Birds and the Bees, How to be Very Popular, Miracle in the Rain, Solid Gold Cadillac, Back from Eternity, Joe Butterfly, The Mating Game, Visit to a Small Planet, It Started with a Kiss, Don't Go Near the Water, Bells are Ringing; Broadway appearance in Absense of a Cello, 1965; TV appearances on The Burns and Allen Show, Milton Berle Show, The Double Life of Henry Fyfe. Home: Hollywood CA Died Dec. 5, 1968.

CLARK, FRED GEORGE, found. exec.; b. Cleve., Nov. 2, 1890; s. Frederick George and Mary Angeline (Winter) C.; student Kenyon Coll., Gambier, O., 1909-13; LL.D., Morningside Coll., Sioux City, Ia.; m. Margaret L. Moore, June 26, 1915 (div. Dec. 1931); m. 2d, Sibyl Young Hine, Jan. 16, 1932 (div. Sept. 1948); m. 3d, Diana M. Brodie, Dec. 18, 1948. Oil tester Fred G. Clark Co., oil refining, Cleve., 1913, office mgr., 1914-16, salesman, 1916-17, v.p., 1920-24, pres., 1924-32; pres. Conewango Refining Co., Warren, Pa., 1926-32; pres. Clark, Curtin & Norton, Inc., ins., N.Y., 1932-65; organizer, nat. comdr. Crusaders against Nat. Prohibition, 1929-33; nat. radio broadcaster for econ. enlightenment, 1933-36; established, chmn. bd. Am. Factfinders, 1936; founder, chmn. bd. Am. Econ. Found., ednl. research, 1939-72; moderator radio program, Wake Up Am., 1939-46. Served as capt. U. S. Army, in charge all lubricating oil purchases for U.S. Army, 1917-18. Mem. Soc. Colonial Wars, Huguenot Soc., Colonial Lords of Manors in Am., Nat. Inst. Social Scis., Psi Upsilon. Clubs: Racquet and Tennis, Sky, River (N.Y.C.); Atlantic Beach (L.I.). Author: Magnificent Delusion, 1940: (with Richard S. Rimanoczy) How We Live, 1944; Money, 1946; How To Be Popular Though Conservative, 1948; How to Think About Economics, 1952; What Every Supervisor Should Know About the Principles of Economics, 1960; Where the Money Comes From 1961; editorials. Composer, Wake Up America, 1932. Lectr. Home: New York City NY Died Jan. 7, 1973; buried Lake View Cemetery, Cleveland OH

CLARK, FREDERICK HUNTINGTON, mining engr.; b. Minneapolis, Minn., Apr. 13, 1877; s. John Bates and Myra Almeda (Smith) C.; student Amherst, 1895-96, Worcester Poly. Inst., 1896-97, law dept. U. of Minn., 1897-98; M.E., Sch. of Mines (Columbia), 1907; m. Eleanor Phelps, Dec. 30, 1908; children—Eunice, Eleanor. Engr. El Oro Mining & Ry. Co., 1907; mgr. San Cayetano Mines, Ltd., and consulting engr. various companies, 1908-10; field engr. Gen. Development Co., 1910-13; gen. practice since 1913; v.p. Peninsula Development Corp. (Bradentown, Fla.); now gen. mgr. and dir. The Trans-Lux Movie Ticker Corp., New York. Engr. U.S. Shipping Bd. and Emergency Fleet Corp. until June 1917. Originated plan for construction of emergency fleet of wooden vessels to meet war crises in shipping. Mem. Minn. N.G., 1897-98. Mem. Delta Kappa Epsilon, Tau Beta Pi, Sigma Psi. Club: University. Home: 35 Fifth Av. Address: 24 State St., New York 4 NY‡

CLARK, FREDERICK M., seedsman; b. Milford, Conn., Nov. 24, 1874; s. Everett Byran and Charlotte E. (Woodruff) C.; ed. Hopkins Grammar Sch., New Haven, Conn.; Wesleyan Acad., Wilbraham, Mass.; m. Anna Clark Platt, of Milford, Conn., Dec. 9, 1897; children—Merritt, Josephine King, Donald Newton, Newton Platt (dec.). In wholesale seed business at New Haven, Conn., since 1892; v.p. and dir. Associated Seed Growers, Inc. (founded by father) until 1938; dir. Milford Trust Co.; has developed many new and improved standard varieties of seeds. Republican. Conglist. Mason (32 deg.). Rotarian. Home: Milford CT‡

CLARK, FREDERICK PAREIS, planning consultant; b. Tillson, N.Y., July 7, 1908; s. Leon and Grace Darling (Pareis) C.; student Kingston (N.Y.) High Sch., 1922-26; B.Arch., Cornell, 1933; m. Jane Ashworth Mason, Oct. 26, 1935; children—Frederick Pareis, Bruce Munroe, Douglas Mason. Planning engr., Fairfield Co., Conn., Planning Assn., 1933-34; town planner, Montclair, N.J., 1934; planning consultant N.E. Regional Planning Commn., 1934-36; state planning dir. N.H. State Planning and Development Commn., 1936-41, exec. dir., 1941-42; secretary N.H. State Land Use Board, 1936-42; planner new town of Hill, N.H., 1939-41; vis. lectr. on city and regional planning, Mass. Inst. Tech., 1940-42; mem. City Planning Bd., Concord, N.H., 1938-42; planning dir. Regional Plan Assn., Inc., N.Y.C., 1942-44, 45-52, cons., 1952-55; spl. adviser Plan for Rezoning, N.Y.C., 1948-49; bd. cons. Eno Found. for Hwy. Traffic Control, 1952-61; chmn. gov.'s adv. com. replanning flood-damaged communities Conn., 1955; cons. Naugatuck Valley Regional Study, Conn., 1955-58; vis. lectr. Columbia, 1947-51, Cornell Univ., 1955-60. Chmn. City Planning Commn., Rye, N.Y., 1947-64; bd. directors Westchester County Planning and Housing Council, 1958-61; consultant UN Headquarters Commission, 1946; U.S. Nat. Security Resources Bd., 1948-49; U.S. Gen. Servs. adminstrn., 1950-51, U.S. Housing and Home Finance Agy., 1952, numerous cities on planning. Served as lt., U.S.N.R. on active duty, 1944-45. Awarded De Molay Legion of Honor, 1942. Mem. Am. Inst. Planners (nat. president 1952-54), International Federation Housing and Planning (U.S. rep. standing com. profl. planners 1962-64, co-opted council mem. 1966-68), Am. Society Planning Ofcls. (mem. bd. dirs. 1966-68), Internat. Soc. City and Regional Planners, Am. Soc. Consulting Planners, Tau Beta Pi, Sigma Alpha Epsilon, Gargoyle Soc., Lambda Alpha Presbyn. Home: Rye NY Died May 16, 1968.

CLARK, FRIEND EBENEZER, prof. chemistry; b. New Martinsville, W.Va., Aug. 21, 1876; s. Josephus and Lina (Russell) C.; B.S., W.Va. U., 1898; Ph.D., Johns Hopkins, 1902; studied U. of Chicago, U. of Berlin; D.Sc., W.Va. Wesleyan Coll., 1941, Centre Coll., 1950; m. Emma May Hanna, June 29, 1911; children—Josephus Browne, Samuel Friend. Instr. chemistry, W.Va. U., 1902-03, Pa. State Coll., 1903-05; prof. chemistry, Centre Coll., Ky., 1905-14; prof. chemistry, W.Va. Univ., 1914-47, head dept., 1919-47, prof. emeritus since June 30, 1947; prof. chem., in charge organic and indsl. chem., Davis and Elkins Coll., Elkins, W.Va., since 1947; chmn. Grad. Council since 1935. Fellow A.A.A.S., Chemical Soc. (London); mem. Am. Chem. Soc., Sigma Xi, Phi Kappa Psi, Phi Beta Kappa. Democrat. Presbyterian. Mason. Home: 649 Spruce St., Morgantown, W.Va.; and Elkins WV

CLARK, GEORGE HARLOW, explorer; b. Hyde Park, Mass., Feb. 21, 1871; s. Theodore E. and Ellen A. C.; grad. Brookline (Mass.) High Sch., 1887; m. Estelle May Baker, of San Francisco, Mar. 21, 1900. With Lookout Mountain exploring expdn., 1890-1; naturalist Peary Polar expdn., 1893-4; companion of Lt. R. E. Peary throughout journey over the Greenland Ice Cap, 1894, and during sledge journeys over frozen sea, 1893-4; leader of several minor expdns. in Arctics; comdr. N. Alaskan expdn., 1898-99-1900; associated in expdn. to interior of Labrador, 1902. Charter mem. Polar Research Club; mem. Geog. and Arctic Club of America, Folk-Lore, Antiquarian, Anthropol. and Natural History socs., Sons of Veterans, etc. Contbr. to scientific jours. and mags. Address: Winthrop MA‡

CLARK, GEORGE LINDENBERG, chemist; b. Anderson, Ind., Sept. 6, 1892; s. Ralph Bliven and Olive (Burnett) C.; B.A., DePauw U., 1914; M.S., U. of Chicago, 1914, Ph.D., 1918; Sc.D., DePauw U., 1937; m. Mary Mason Johnson, June 19, 1919; children—Mary Ann (dec.), Ralph Burnett, George Mason, Jean Louise, Carolyn Johnson. Instr. in chemistry, DePauw U., 1914-16, 19; asso. prof. chemistry, Vanderbilt, 1919-21; nat. research fellow, Harvard, 1921-24; asst. prof. applied chm. research, Mass. Inst. Tech., 1924-27 (installed and directed first industrial X-ray research lab.); prof. chemistry U. Ill., 1927-53; research prof. analytical chemistry, 1953-60, emeritus 1960, vis. prof. DePauw U., 1961; chmn. Merchants Property Ins. Co. of Ind.; dir. Clark-Mchts., Inc. Mem., past chmn. Concert and Entertainment Bd., U. Ill., 1934-36, 38-51; mem. Nashville Symphony Orch., 1920-21, U. Ill. Symphony Orch., 1938-44. Served as lt. C.W.S., Am. U. Expt. Sta., 1918. Fellow A.A.A.S.; mem. Am. Chem. Soc., (Mobile-Pensacola sect. award, 1952), Am. Crystallographic Assn., Am. Inst. Chemists, Radiol Soc. Am., Am. Soc. Testing Materials (Marburg Meml. lectr. 1927), Phi Beta Kappa, Phi Beta Kappa Associates, Sigma Xi, Phi Lambda Upsilon, Beta Theta Pi, Alpha Chi Sigma; founder, Electron Microscope Soc. Am., 1943. Methodist. Mason (32 deg., K.T.). Clubs: Nat. Exchange, Torch, University. Author: Applied X-Rays, 1926, 4th edit., 1955; also many papers in chem. and physical jours. Awarded Grasselli medal, 1932; Mehl. medal, 1944; Orton Lectureship award, 1946. Editor-in-chief Ency. of Chemistry, 1957, co-editor 2d edit., 1965; editor: Supplement, 1958. Editor Ency. Spectroscopy, 1960, Microscopy, 1961; Ency. X-Rays and Gamma Rays, 1963. Home: Urbana IL Died Jan. 8, 1969; buried Eastlawn Cemetery, Urbana IL

CLARK, GEORGE LUTHER, prof. law; b. Waynesville, O., February 19, 1877; s. Horace Mann and Mary Ellen (Coon) C.; A.B., Kenyon Coll., Gambier, O., 1896; LL.B., Ind. U., Bloomington, Ind., 1899; LL.B., Harvard, 1902, S.J.D., 1913; m. Mary Craig Mathers, June 25, 1902; 1 son, George Mathers; m. 2d, Helen Ackert Miles, July 21, 1938. Instructor law, Stanford, 1902-04; prof. law, U. of Ill., 1904-09, U. of Mich., 1909-12, U. of Mo., 1913-21, U. of Cincinnati, 1924-25, New York U., 1925-43, U. of Kansas City, 1947-50, John Marshall Law School, Chicago, since 1950. Member firm of Cravath, de Gersdorff, Swaine & Wood, N.Y. City, 1942-43. Mem. Phi Beta Kappa, Phi Delta Phi, Order of the Coif. Republican. Contbr. on legal topics. Author books. Editor publs. including: Cases on Common Law Pleading; Summary of American Law, 1947. Home: 241 Sixth Av., NYC 14

CLARK, GRENVILLE, laywer; b. N.Y.C., Nov. 5, 1882; s. Louis Crawford and Marian de Forest (Cannon) C.; A.B., Harvard, 1903, LL.B., 1906, LL.D., 1951; LL.D., Princeton, 1951, Dartmouth, 1953; m. Fanny Pickman Dwight, Nov. 27, 1909; children—Mary Dwight, Grenville, Louisa Hunnewell; m. 2d, Mary Brush, January 1, 1965. Admitted New York State bar, 1906, began practice with Carter, Ledyard & Milburn, N.Y.C.; mem. Root, Clark & Bird, and successor firms, 1909-46; counsel to Cleary, Gottlieb, Steen and Hamilton, 1954. Afounder Mil. Tng. Camps Assn., 1915-16; chmn. Nat. Emergency Com. for Selective Service, 1940-41; chmn. Citizens Com. for Nat. War Service, 1944-45. Served from maj. to lt. col. Adj. Gen.'s Dept., U.S. Army, 1917-18. Decorated D.S.M.; awarded Theodore Roosevelt Meml. Medal, 1940; gold medal Am. Bar Assn., 1959; 2d Ann. Publius award N.Y. Met. Com. of United World Federalists, 1965. Member of Pres. and Fellows Harvard College, 1931-50; member American Bar Association (chairman committee bill of rights 1938-40), Assn. Bar City of N.Y., N.Y. Law Inst., United World Federalists (v.p.), Phi Beta Kappa. Clubs: Century, Downtown Assn., Somerset Author: A Plan for Peace, 1950; (with L. B. Sohn): World Peace through World Law, 1958, rev. edit., 1960; also articles on civil govt., world orgn. and legal subjects. Home: Dublin NH Died Jan. 12, 1967.

CLARK, HAMILTON BURDICK, press assn. official; b. Syracuse, N.Y., Oct. 18, 1869; s. Charles Neukerck and Frances (Burdick) C.; ed. St. John's Mil. Acad., Manlius, N.Y., Pa. Mil. Coll., Chester; m. Sarah Gray, of Toronto, Can., June, 1900. Was mgr. San Francisco News; circulation mgr. Seattle Star; gen. mgr. Pubs. Press Assn., Scripps-McRrae Press Assn., Scripps News Assn.; trustee Seattle Star, Pueblo Sun; dir. San Francisco News; chmn. bd. dirs. United Press Assns. Mem. Soc. of the Cincinnati. Home: Chula Vista, San Diego Co., Cal. Office: Park Row Bldg., New York‡

CLARK, HENRY BENJAMIN, business exec.; b. near Walworth, Wis., Apr. 15, 1874; s. James Dallas and Adelia Violet (Church) C.; Ph.B., Beloit (Wis.) Coll., 1895; B.S., U.S. Mil. Acad., 1899; grad. Army Staff Coll., 1905, Army War Coll., 1920; m. Lena Sefton Wakefield, Nov. 20, 1912; children—James Dallas, Henry B., Jr. Commd. 2d lt., U.S. Army, 1899, and advanced through grades to col., 1921; served with China Relief Expdn. (Boxer Rebellion), 1900, Philippine Insurrection, 1900-02, Moro Expedition, Mindanao, 1902, A.E.F., France, 1918; on War Department General Staff, 1921-22; ret., 1922; vice pres. Sefton Mfg. Corp., Chicago, 1922-25, pres., 1925-28; dir. Container Corp. of Am. since 1931; retired. Mem. Beta Theta Pi. Republican. Presbyn. Mason. Clubs: Union League (Chicago); Army-Navy (Washington); Cuyamaca (San Diego). Home: 3810 Narragansett Av., San Diego 7 CA

CLARK, HENRY HUNT, art educator; b. Haverhill, Mass., Sept. 15, 1875; s. Herbert Appleton and Ella Amelia (Fletcher) C.; Mass. Inst. Tech., class of 1898, Sch. Mus. Fine Arts (Boston), 1899; studied abroad, and pupil of Dr. Denman W. Ross; m. Florence Raymond Hackett, July 14, 1908; 1 son, Raymond Appleton. Teacher of theory of design, Boston, 1898-1903; head of dept. decorative design, R.I. Sch. of Design, 1902-13; instr. Sch. Mus. Fine Arts, Boston, 1913-20, dir. dept. of design, 1920-31; supervisor of instrn., Mus. of Fine Arts, Boston, 1925-31; dir. Cleveland (O.) Sch. of Art since 1931. Mem. Copley Soc., Soc. of Arts and Crafts (Boston), Boston Soc. of Artists, Art Assn. (Cleveland). Unitarian. Address: 11441 Juniper Road, Cleveland OH*‡

CLARK, JAMES EDWARD, petroleum exec.; b. Ojai, Cal., June 25, 1909; s. R. E. and Alice (Barnett) C.; student Santa Clara U., 1926-28; A.B. in Engring., Stanford, 1932; student advanced mgmt. program Harvard, 1948; m. Fern Bounds, 1934; children—Patricia, Linda, James II, Leslie. With Shell Oil Co., 1932-67, engring. assignment Cal., 1932-37, prodn. operations, 1937-44, spl. exploration assignment in China, 1947, successively div. supt., div. mgr. Ventura, div. mgr. Casper, Wyo., prodn. mgr. Denver area, 1947-53, v.p. exploration and prodn. Midland area, 1954-57, v.p. prodn. head office N.Y.C., 1958-61, exec. v.p. charge exploration and prodn., 1961-67. Home: Ojai CA Died Dec. 27, 1970; buried Ivy Lawn Cemetery, Ventura CA

CLARK, JAMES G., prof. mathematics, William Jewell Coll., since 1873; b. in Va.; grad. Univ. of Va.; m. 1st, Jennie Hume, Portsmouth, Va.; 2d, Kate Mason Morfit, Baltimore. Was asst. prof. mathematics Univ. of Va., and later prof. mathematics Columbian, Washington, until 1871; chmn. of faculty, William Jewell Coll., 1883-92. Author: Elements of the Infinitesimal Calculus (a text-book), 1875; History of William Jewell College, 1892; etc. Address: Liberty MO‡

CLARK, JANET HOWELL, scientist; b. Balt., Jan. 1, 1889; d. William Henry and Anne Janet (Tucker) Howell; A.B., Bryn Mawr Coll., 1910; Ph.D., Johns Hopkins, 1913; m. Admont Halsey Clark, July 9, 1917 (dec. Oct. 1918); 1 dau., Anne Janet (Mrs. Peter Picard Rodman). Lectr. physics Bryn Mawr Coll., 1914-15; instr. physics Smith Coll., 1916-17; instr. Johns Hopkins, 1918-20, asst. prof. physiology, 1920-22, asso. prof., 1922-35, lectr. physiology, 1935-38; prof. biophysics, dean Coll. for Women U. Rochester, 1938-52; lectr., researcher Johns Hopkins, 1952-69. Mem. bd. trustees Bryn Mawr Sch., 1952-58, St. Paul's Sch. for Girls, 1958-69. Huff fellow Bryn Mawr Coll., 1913-14; Am. Assn. U. Women Sarah Berliner fellow, 1915-16. Mem. Am. Assn. U. Women (chmn. internat. grants com., 1953-59), Internat. Fedn. U. Women (chmn. fellowships com. 1960-69), Am. Physical Soc., Am. Optical Soc., Am. Physiological Soc., Radiations Research Soc., A.A.A.S., Phi Beta Kappa, Sigma Xi. Author: Lighting in Relation to Public Health, 1924; also articles in profl. jours. Home: Baltimore MD Died Feb. 12, 1969.

CLARK, JOHN LEWIS, clergyman; b. Decatur, Ill.; s. Milton and Sarah Ann (Lee) C.; A.B., Lincoln (now James Millikin) U., Lincoln, Ill., 1891; A.M., New York U., 1892; Union Theol. Sem., 1894; m. Marie Louise Campman, June 2, 1894. Ordained Cumberland Presbyn. ministry, 1890; student pastor Cuyler Chapel, Brooklyn, 1892-95; asst. pastor Marble Collegiate Ch., New York, 1895-98; pastor 1st Cumberland Presbyn. Ch., Chicago, 1898-1900; moderator Chicago Presbytery, also commr. to Gen. Assembly, 1899; asso. pastor 4th Presbyn. Ch., New York 1901, Bushwick Av. Congl. Ch., Brooklyn, since 1906. Sec., treas. Alpha Chapter Patriotic League of America, 1895-98; sec. N.Y. Anti-Saloon League, 1900-10; sec. exec. com. 20th Century National Gospel Campaign, 1901-02; pres. Bushwick-Ridgewood-Glendale Ministers Assn.; mem. bd. mgrs. Am. Tract Sec.; mem. bd. dirs. Brooklyn Bible Soc. Chaplain Vet. Assn., 13th Regt. and 245th C.A., N.Y. Nat. Guard. Mem. Am. Soc. Comparative Religions, Delta Upsilon. Pres. N.Y. Classis, 1897. Mason, Chaplain Long Island Grotto, Knight of Pythias, Modern Woodman. Republican. Clubs: Crescent Athletic, Clergy, Congregational. Home: 26 Linden St., Brooklyn NY *

CLARK, JOSEPH JAMES, retired naval officer; born in Pryor, Okla., November 12, 1893; s. William Andrew and Lillie Belle (Berry) C.; student Okla. A. and M. Coll., 3 1/2 yrs.; grad. U.S. Naval Acad., 1917; children—Mary Louise, Catherine Carol; m. 4th, Olga Choubaroff. Commissioned ensign, USN, 1917, advancing through grades to admiral; comdr. of 7th Fleet, USN, retired, 1953; chmn. bd. Hegeman Harris, Inc., New York City. Decorated two D.S.M.'s (Navy), D.S.M. (Army), Navy Cross, Silver Star, Commendation Ribbon. Clubs: N.Y. Yacht, Larchmont Yacht, N.Y. Athletic; Chevy Chase; Long Island. Home: New York City NY Died July 1971.

CLARK, JULIAN JEROME, banker; b. Clarkton, N.C., Mar. 7, 1907; s. Eric Conrad and Margaret (Cromartie) C; A.B., Davidson Coll., 1927; student Stonier Grad. Sch. Banking, Rutgers U., 1945; m. Mary Mackey Hough, Aug. 10, 1936; children—Julian Jerome, William M. With N.C. Nat. Bank (formerly Am. Trust Co), Charlotte, 1927-71, asst. treas., 1941, asst. sec., 1942-46, asst. v.p. and asst. sec., 1946-47, v.p., asst. sec., 1947-56, sr. v.p., 1956-57, president, 1967-71; dir. Am. Commercial Agy., Charlotte, Am. Bank & Trust Co., Monroe, N.C., Bus. Devel. Corp of N.C. Mem. John Motley Morehead Scholarship Dist. Com. Bd. commrs. Charlotte Meml. Hosp.; bd. dirs. YMCA, Goodwill Industries of Charlotte; trustee Davidson Coll. Mem. Robert Morris Assos. (nat. dir.), N.C. Bankers Assn. (legislative com.). Presbyn. (elder). Club: Charlotte City (dir., pres.). Home: Charlotte NC Died 1971.

CLARK, LINWOOD L., congressman; b. Aberdeen, Md., Mar. 21, 1876; s. Daniel H. and Sarah J. (Greenland) C.; grad. Milton Acad., Baltimore, Md., 1900; A.B., American U., Harriman, Tenn., 1902; LL.B., U. of Md., 1904; m. Linnie Habersank, of Baltimore, July 24, 1907; children—Charles Hoffman, Catherine L., John Marshall. Admitted to Md. bar, 1904, and practiced since at Baltimore. Mem. 71st Congress (1929-31), 2d Md. Dist. Mem. Md. State Bar Assn., Bar Assn. Baltimore City. Republican. Methodist. Moose. Home: 3802 Sequoia Av. Office: 1st Nat. Bank Bldg., Baltimore MD‡

CLARK, LLOYD MONTGOMERY, educator; b. Roslindale, Mass., Apr. 4, 1895; s. Irving Montgomery and Lucy (Powers) C.; grad. Phillips Exeter Acad., 1913; A.B., Amherst Coll., 1917; D.Sc., Washington-Jefferson Coll.; m. Ella Wilson, Nov. 30, 1923; 1 son, Roger Montgomery. Mem. research dept., H.K. McCann Co., N.Y. City, 1916-17, 1919-20; built Norwood Airport, Mass., 1931; a founder Clark-Hooper, Inc., 1934, and served as chmn. bd. dirs.; a founder L. M. Clark, Inc., 1938, chmn. bd. and pres., 1938-69; chmn. bd. and pres. Kiskiminetas Springs Sch., Saltsburg, Pa., 1941-69; started Kiski Plan of Study, 1944, started study langs. in fgn. countries, resigned as headmaster of Kiski in 1957. Enlisted in the U.S. Navy, April 1917, commd. ensign, Sept. 1917, served overseas in command of submarine chaser No. 255, on U.S.S. Yacoma and U.S.S. Wadena. Mem. Phi Kappa Psi. Club: Amherst (founder, N.Y.C.). Author: Selection and Education of our Most Capable Youth. Home: Clearwater Beach FL Died Nov. 7, 1969.

CLARK, PAUL DENNISON, pediatrician; b. Woodstock, Vt., Nov. 27, 1901; s. Homer Pearley and Martha (Dana) C.; M.D., U. Vt., 1926; m. Elizabeth Kelton, July 10, 1929; children—Elizabeth (Mrs. J. Dean Clewley), John D. Intern Mary Fletcher Hosp., 1926-27, later attending pediatrician; sr. intern Children's Hosp., Detroit, 1927-28, med. resident, 1928-29; attending pediatrician Bishop De Goesbriand Hosp., Fanny Allen Hosp., Winooski, Vt. Asst. prof. clin. pediatrics emeritus U. Vt. Served to col. M.C., AUS, 1942-45. Diplomate Am. Bd. Pediatrics. Mem. Am. Acad. Pediatrics, Northeast Pediatric Soc. Home: Burlington VT Died June 5, 1969; buried Burlington VT

CLARK, PAUL FOSTER, ins. exec.; Dayton, O., Nov. 19, 1892; s. Joseph Dayton and Lulu Helen (Foster) C.; student Staunton Mil. Acad. and Denison U.; B.S., U. Pa., 1915, LL.D., 1947; D.Sc., Lowell Technological Institute, 1957; m. Anna Quast, Feb. 19, 1917; children—Jean Clark Boas, Paul Foster (killed in action, Italy, Oct. 6, 1944). Asso. state agt. John Hancock Mut. Life Ins. Co., 1917-21, gen. agt. Boston Agy., 1921-38, v.p., 1938-44, dir. 1941-65, hon. dir., 1965-73, pres., 1944-57, chmn. bd., 1957-63; dir. Armour & Co., S.A.L. R.R. (hon.), Am. Research & Devel. Corp., Boston-Old Colony Ins. Cos., Sheraton Corp. of Am., John Hancock Mut. Life Ins. Co. Dir. Life Ins. Med. Research Fund. Trustee Lahey Clinic, Boston U., Garland Jr. Coll.; v.p. New Eng. Bapt. Hosp.; mem. corp. Northeastern U. Fellow Am. Academy of Arts and Scis.; mem. Am. Soc. C.L.U. (pres. 1934-35), Nat. Association of Underwriters (pres. 1928-29, trustee 1930-36), American College of Life Underwriters (chmn.), Beta Gamma Sigma (hon.), Phi Delta Theta, Mason (32 deg.). Clubs: Chicago, Algonquin, U. of Pennsylvania, Commercial-Merchants (Boston, Mass.); The Country (Brookline); Varsity (Phila.); Yeamans Hall (Charleston, S.C.); Bald Peak (dir., past pres.) (Melvin Village, N.H.). Home: Brookline MA Died Jan. 1973.

CLARK, ROBERT BRUCE, Presby'n clergyman; b. Newark, N.J.; s. William H. and Elizabeth S. (Munn) C.; grad. Amherst, 1876; Union Theol. Sem., 1879; pastor 1st Ch., Goshen, N.Y.; pres. Goshen Library and Hist. Soc.; organizer and musical dir. Goshen Vocal Soc.; organizer and mem. bd. dirs. Goshen Light & Power Co. Now pastor Presby'n Ch., Bay Ridge, Brooklyn. Address: Goshen NY‡

CLARK, WALTER VANTILBURG, writer; b. East Orland, Me., Aug. 3, 1909; s. Dr. Walter Ernest and Euphemia Murray (Abrams) C.; A.B., U. of Nevada, 1931, M.A., 1932; M.A., U. of Vermont, 1934; Litt. D., Colgate University, Hamilton, N.Y., 1958, University of Nevada, Reno, Nevada, 1969; m. Barbara Frances Morse, Oct. 14, 1933 (dec. Nov. 1969); children—Barbara Ann, Robert Morse. Teacher of English, dramatics and sports in public school, Cazenovia, N.Y., 1935-45; was asso. prof. English, Mont. State U., lectr.; past tchr. English, coach Va. City High School; tchr. writer's workshop U. Ia., 1951-52, Mont. State U., 1954-56; prof. creative writing San Francisco State Coll., 1956-62; writer in residence U. Nev., Reno, 1962-71; also tchr. summer writer's confs. at univs. Utah, Wyo., Mont., Omaha Missouri. Fellow in fiction Center Advanced Studies, Wesleyan University, Middletown, Conn., 1960-61. Winner O. Henry Short Story Award, 1945. Member American Civil Liberties Union, Western History Association, Western Literature Association (honorary life), Phi Kappa Phi. Club: Sierra. Author: The Ox Bow Incident, 1940 (produced as movie by 20th Century-Fox); The City of Trembling Leaves, 1945; The Track of the Cat, 1949 (produced as movie 1954); The Watchful Gods, 1950. Contbr. to periodicals, including Atlantic Monthly, Accent, The New Yorker, The Nation. Sat. Eve. Post, Yale Rev., Virginia Quarterly Rev., others. Home: Virginia City NV Died Nov. 10, 1971; buried Virginia City NV

CLARK, WILLIAM HENRY, banker; b. St. Louis, Nov. 9, 1909; s. Arthur P. and Elizabeth (Haigh) C.; B.A., De Pauw U., 1932; M.B.A., Northwestern U., 1952; m. Alice M. Hein, Aug. 27, 1938; 1 dau., Carolyn E. With First Nat. Bank & Trust Co., Evanston, Ill., 1933-69, successively messenger, teller, asst. cashier and v.p., exec. v.p., pres., 1960-68, vice chmn., 1968-69, dir., 1960-69. Pres. United Community Services, Evanston, Ill., 1963-65. Dir. St. Francis Hosp., Evanston, 1959-69. Served to capt. AUS, 1943-45. Mem. Evanston C. of C. (pres. 1960-62), Chgo. Bankers Club, Chgo. Economic Club, Northwestern U. Assos., Delta Kappa Epsilon. Republican. Episcopalian. Clubs: University, Rotary (officer), Westmoreland Country, John Evans (Northwestern U.). Home: Evanston IL Died Dec. 18, 1969.

CLARK, WILLIAM R., exec. editor Newark News. Address: Newark NJ Deceased.

CLARK, WILLIAM SMITH II, univ. prof.; b. Baltimore, Md., Sept. 13, 1900; s. Hubert Lyman and Frances Lee (Snell) C.; grad. Phillips Acad., Andover, Mass., 1917; A.B., magna cum laude, Amherst Coll., 1921; A.M., Harvard 1924, Ph.D., 1926; m. Gladys Louise Hathaway, June 26, 1926; children—Stirrat Holman, Penelope Frances. Asso. missionary, A.B.C.F.M., student work and teaching Hokkaido Imperial U., Sapporo, Japan, 1921-23; instr. English, Amherst Coll., 1926-31; asst. prof. English, U. Cincinnati, 1931-37, asso. prof., 1937-40; research as Guggenheim fellow in Irish stage history, British Isles, 1939; vis. prof. summer sch. Johns Hopkins, 1940; prof. U. Cincinnati, 1940-59, head English dept., 1943-66, Nathaniel Ropes prof. of comparative literature, 1959-69; ednl. mission to Japan under auspices U.S. Dept. State, Japanese Ministry Edn. and Hokkaido Univ., 1956; ednl. specialist U.S. Dept. of State, Japan, 1960. Served S.A.T.C., Amherst Coll., 1918. Awarded The Sachs prize, Cin. Inst. Fine Arts, 1948. Mem. Am. Assn. Univ. Prof., Modern Lang. Assn., Phi Beta Kappa, Omicron Delta Kappa, Chi Phi, Sigma Delta Rho. Republican. Congretational-Presbyterian. Clubs: MacDowell Society, Literary (Cincinnati). Editor: Dramatic Works of Roger Boyle, Earl of Orrery, 2 volumes, 1937. Author: Chief Patterns of World Drama, 1946; The Early Irish Stage: The Beginnings to 1720, 1955; The Irish Stage in the County Towns: 1720 to 1800, 1965. Publisher: James Russell Lowell; Essays, Poems, Letters (Odyssey) 1948; Extensive travel in Asia and Europe. Home: Cincinnati OH Died July 16, 1969; buried Amherst MA

CLARKE, HANS THACHER, educator, biol. chemist; b. of Am. parents, Harrow, Eng., Dec. 27, 1887; s. Joseph Thacher and Agnes (Helferich) C.; B.Sc., Univ. Coll., London, 1908, D.Sc., 1914; grad. study U. of Berlin, 1911-13; Sc.D., U. Rochester, 1953, Columbia, 1957; m. Frieda Planck, October 8, 1914 (dec. Aug. 1960); children—Eric, John, Rebecca, Heidi; m. 2d, to Flora de Peyer, July 1963. Demonstrator in chemistry, Univ. Coll., 1908-09, lecturer in stereochemistry, 1910-11, asst. in chemistry, 1913-14; research organic chemist, Eastman Kodak Co., Rochester, N.Y., 1914-28; prof. biol. chemistry, Coll. Physicians and Surgeons, Columbia U., 1928-56, prof. emeritus, 1956; lecturer Yale, 1956-64; research guest Boston Children's Hosp., 1964-72; science attache American Embassy, London, 1951-52. Fellow Inst. Chemistry of Great Britain, Chem. Soc. London, Univ. Coll. (London); mem. Nat. Acad. Science, Am. Philos. Soc., Am. Chem. Soc., Am. Soc. Biol. Chem. (pres. 1947-49), Harvey Soc. (pres. 1942-44). Club: Century. Author: Organic Analysis, 1911; Introduction to Study of Organic Chemistry, 1914. Editor: Organic Syntheses, 1921-32; The Chemistry of Penicillin, 1949, asso. editor Jour. of Am. Chem. Soc., 1928-38; mem. editorial com. Jour. of Biol. Chemistry, 1930-37, mem. editorial board, 1937-51, 53-58. Home: Cambridge MA Died Oct. 21, 1972; buried Scotland CT

CLARKE, J. CALVITT, welfare dir.; b. Brooklyn, N.Y., June 30, 1887; s. Joseph Calvitt and Ella (Hamilton) C.; Doane Acad. of Denison U., 1908; Meadville Theol. Sch. Chicago, 1913; Washington and Jefferson Coll., M.A., 1916; D.D., Oskaloosa Coll., 1917; S.T.B., Western Theol. Sem., Pittsburgh, Pa., 1918; student war course Internat. Y.M.C.A.; m. Helen Caroline Mattson, Dec. 8, 1913; children—Helen Jeanne (Mrs. H. E. Wood, Jr.), J. Calvitt IV. Y.M.C.A. dir. Russian troops in France, 1918; asso. state dir. Near East Relief, Pittsburg, Pa., 1919; made survey of famine situation, Russian Caucasus, Armenia, Greece, Turkey, 1920; asso. regional dir. Near East Relief, Pittsburgh, Pa., 1920-21; campaign consultant North Central Region Near East Relief, Milwaukee, Wis., 1922-23; state dir. Near East Relief, Cleveland, O., 1924-26; Southern dir. Near East Relief, Richmond, Va., 1927-30; nat. sec. and Southern dir. Golden Rule Foundation, Richmond, Va., 1931-33; southern dir. Save the Children Fund, Richmond, 1934-37; campaign work Am. Foundn. for Blind and other organizations, 1937-38; founder China's Children Fund (now Christian Children Fund), 1938, internat. dir., 1938-64; founder Clarke College Tokyo, Japan, Clarke High Sch., Alwaye Settlement, India; founder, bd. dirs. Christian Children's Fund Can., Children, Inc.; bd. mem. Jiai Nomura (Japan); mem. com. Seoul Children's Home (Korea); hon. mem. bd. S.O.S. Kinderdorf Internat. Decorated Order Cultural Merit Nat. Medal (Korea); Cravat Brilliant Star, (Nationalist China); Order Sacred Treasure, 4th Class (Japan). Author several novels. Contbr. to mags. and profl. publs. on religious, social and internat. relations. Presbyn. (mem. Presbytery). Home: Richmond VA Died July 17, 1970; buried Hollywood Cemetery, Richmond VA

CLARKE, JAMES AUGUSTINE, editor; b. at Bowling Green, Ky., July 21, 1871; s. James Kelly and Martha Ann (Hines) C.; A.B., U. of Rochester, N.Y., 1894; grad. Rochester Theol. Sem., 1897; (D.D., McMinnville Coll., 1906); m. Emily Adeline Brown, of Wallingford, Conn., June 20, 1907. Ordained Baptist ministry, 1898; pastor 1st Ch., Wallingford, Conn., 1897-03; editor Pacific Baptist, 1904—; propr. The Pacific Bapt. Pub. Co., The Telephone Register Pub. Co. Mem. Delta Upsilon, Phi Beta Kappa. Address: McMinnville OR‡

CLARKE, JOE ALEXANDER, banker; b. Albany, Tex., Mar. 13, 1897; s. Archibald A. and Virginia P. (Jones) C.; student Reynolds Presbyn. Coll., 1913; grad. Grad. Sch. Banking, New Brunswick, N.J., 1948; m. Mary E. Whatley, Nov. 15, 1941; 1 foster dau., Mary (Mrs. Ross Harper). Asst. cashier Albany Nat. Bank, 1919-29, cashier, 1929-32; cashier, then v.p. and cashier First Nat. Bank, Albany, 1932-46, dir., from 1932—; v.p. Ft. Worth Nat. Bank, 1946-59, exec. v.p., 1959—. Mem. Am. (v.p. Tex. 1950-51), Tex. (pres. 1956-57) bankers assns., West-Central Tex. Oil and Gas Assn. (pres. 1940). Home: Ft Worth TX

CLARKE, RICHARD WILTON, editor; b. Chicago, Ill., Aug. 3, 1896; s. Arthur LaTelle and Emma Margaret (Jenkins) C.; student Hackley Sch., Tarrytown, N.Y., 1909-10 and 1912-13, Morgan Park Acad., Morgan Park, Ill., 1910-12, U. of Munich, 1913-14, U. of Grenoble, 1914; A.B., Harvard Coll., 1918; m. Mabel McElliott, Jan. 14, 1922 (died Feb. 24, 1951); children—Lucia McElliott (deceased), Constance Margaret, Mary Cecile; m. 2d, Mrs. Joy Wright, Mar. 23, 1959. Reporter Chicago Examiner, 1915, Chicago Herald, 1916; picture editor New York News, 1919-21, Sunday editor, 1922; rotogravure and asst. Sunday editor The World, N.Y. City, 1922-30; automobile editor New York News, 1930-32, Sunday editor, 1932-39, mng. editor, 1939, exec. editor, 1946-61, editor, 1961-71; member of board of directors A.P., 1952-61, vice pres., 1960-61; member board trustees McCormick-Patterson Trust; pres. Chgo. Tribine-N.Y. News Syndicate, Inc.; dir. News Syndicate Co., Inc. Served as 1st lt. inf. U.S. Army, 1917-19; with 331st Machine Gun Bn., 86th Div. 1917-18. Home: New York City NY Died Feb. 26, 1971; buried White Plains NY

CLARKE, THURMOND, United States district judge; born at Santa Paula, California, June 29, 1902; the son of Robert M. and Edna (Thurmond) C.; student Stanford University, 1920-23; grad. U. So. Cal. Law sch.; m. Frances Corbet, 1924 (dec.); 1 dau., Frances (Mrs. John H. Rae, Jr.); m. 2d, Athalie R. Irvine, Sept. 1944. Admitted to Cal. bar, 1927; dep. dist. atty. Los Angeles County, 1927-29; dep. city atty. Los Angeles, 1929-32; municipal judge Los Angeles, 1932-35; judge Superior Ct., County of Los Angeles, 1935-55; judge United States Dist. Ct., Central District of California, 1955-71, chief judge, 1966-70, sr. judge, 1970-71. Member American, Los Angeles County bar associations, State Bar Cal., Zeta Psi, Phi Delta Phi. Republican. Episcopalian. Mason. Clubs: Bohemian (San Francisco); Native Sons of Golden West (Pasadena Parlor); California (Los Angeles); Valley Hunt, Annandale Golf (Pasadena) Newport Harbor Yacht; Eldorado Country (Palm Desert); Irvine Country; Club de Cazay Pesca Las Cruces (La Paz, Baja, Cal.); Club 33 (Disneyland). Home: Pasadena CA Died Feb. 28, 1971; buried Carpenteria Cemetery, Ventura County CA

CLARKIN, FRANKLIN, newspaper man; b. Blackstone, Mass., Jan. 31, 1869; s. Mitchell and Elizabeth (Rafger) C.; m. Clara Hobart Cross, Oct. 14, 1896. Asso. editor Providence Sunday Journal, 1891; war corr. New York Evening Post, Spanish-Am. War, 1898. Russo-Japanese War, 1904; exec. sec. City Club of N.Y., 1910-11; N.Y. rep. Boston Transcript, 1912-18; mgr. U.S. Govt. Com. on Pub. Information at Tchita, Siberia, 1918-19; vice-consul for U.S. State Dept. in Siberia, 1919-21; mem. staff Sunday New York Times, 1924-38; now retired. Pre-Mayflower Pilgrim researches, Leyden (Holland) University library, 1940; collaborating Writers War Board, 1942-45. Mem. Authors' League America, Authors' Club of London. Home: 26 Blackstone Blvd., Providence RI‡

CLARKSON, JAMES A(NDREW), educator; b. Newburyport, Mass., Feb. 7, 1906; s. Edward Hale and Alice Channing (Batchelder) C.; A.B., Dartmouth, 1929; A.M., Brown U., 1933, Ph.D., 1934; member Inst. Advanced Study, 1934-36; Nat. Research Council fellow Inst. Advanced Study, also Princeton, 1935-36; m. Jessie Murdoch McIntosh, June 14, 1930. Instr. Phillips Andover Acad., 1929-30; instr. U. Pa., 1936-40, asst. prof., 1940-47, asso. prof., 1947-48; prof., chmn. mathematics dept. Tufts U., 1948-69, Robinson prof., 1949-70. Exec. sec. div. mathematics Nat. Research Council, 1951-55. Chmn. board trustees Medford Public Library. Served as operations analyst hdqrs. 8th A.F.. U.S.A.A.F., 1943-45. Medal of Freedom, USAAF, 1948. Mem. Dansk Matematisk Forening, Am. Math. Soc., Math. Assn. Am., Am. Assn. U. Profs., Phi Beta Kappa, Sigma Xi, Sigma Pi Sigma. Republican. Unitarian. Contbr. West Medford MA Died June 6, 1970; buried Dover NH

CLARKSON, ROBERT LIVINGSTON, banker; born at Sewaren, New Jersey, July 26, 1892; son of Robert Goodhue and Emily Hartman (Wright) C.; educated Horace Mann Sch. and Trinity Sch., N.Y.C.; m. Cora G. Shields, June 2, 1923; children—Robert Livingston (dec.), Bayard D., Peter S. (dec.). Began as bookkeeper, Herrick, Hicks & Colby; later in bond dept. Effingham Lawrence & Co. and with Alexandre & Burnett, became mem. firm; began with Chase Securities Corp., 1919, v.p., 1921-25, vice chmn. exec. com., 1925, also asst. to pres. Chase Nat. Bank, 1925; vice chmn. bd. Chase Nat. Bank, 1926-28, pres., 1928-29, again vice chmn. bd., 1929; pres. Chase Securities Corp., July 1931; pres. The Chase Corp., May 1933-Mar. 1934; chmn. bd. Amerex Holding Corp., 1935, pres., chmn., 1936-50; chmn., exec. com. Am. Express Co. and Am. Express Co., Inc., 1935-60, chmn. finance com., exec. com., 1960-65; pres. Smith, Kirkpatrick & Co., Inc., 1966-65, chmn. bd., 1935-69; chmn. bd. Clarkson Industries, Inc., 1968-69; dir. RAC Corp., Highfield Mfg. Co., 550 Park Av. Corp., G. Schirmer, Inc.; dir., exec. com. Nat. Aviation Corp.; dir., mem. exec. com., chmn. retirement com. 20th Century-Fox Film Corp.; dir., chmn. retirement bd., exec. com. National Distillers and Chem. Corp. Trustee Musuem City N.Y. Served from seaman to ensign USN, World War I. Member of New York C. of C., Colonial Lords of Manors Am. (exec. com., treas.), Descs. Signers of Declaration of Independence, Mil. Order of World Wars (N.Y.), Soc. of the Cincinnati N.Y. (treas., del. Gen. Soc., trustee), English Speaking Union, St. Nicholas Soc. (life), Am. Legion, Bayville Athletic Assn. (hon.), Navy League U.S., Soc. N.Y. Hosp., Pilgrims of U.S. Republican. Clubs: Union, Recess, Turf and Field, Creek, Piping Rock, The Links. Home: Bayville NY Died Mar. 4, 1969.

CLARY, WILLIAM WEBB, lawyer; b. Northfield, Minn., Oct. 15, 1888; s. Smith B. and Anna (Lathrop) C.; B.A., Pomona Coll., 1911, M.A., 1917, LL.D., 1956; pvt. law studies; D.H.L., Claremont Grad. Sch., 1964; m. Elizabeth A. Foss, June 20, 1914; children—William Webb, Everett Burton, Mary Virginia (Mrs. Garry W. Meeker). Admitted to Cal. bar, 1912; dep. pub. defender Los Angeles County, 1914-18, dep. county counsel, 1918-20; spl. counsel Los Angeles County Flood Control Dist., 1920-21; asst. atty. Cal. R.R. Commn., 1921-23, with O'Melveny & Myers, Los Angeles, 1923-71, partner, 1925-56, of counsel, 1956-71; v.p., dir. Clary Corp. Spl. asst. atty. gen. State of Cal., 1945-47; mem. Cal. Code Commn., 1944-45. Mem. bd. fellows Claremont U. Center, 1928-71, chmn., 1953-63, hon. mem., 1963-71, acting pres., 1963. Trustee Pomona Coll., 1952-62, hon. trustee, 1962-71; trustee Harvey Mudd Coll., 1955-64, hon. trustee, 1964-71; trustee Pitzer Coll., 1963-65, hon. trustee, 1965-71; bd. dirs. Friends of Huntington Library, 1939-71; pres., 1940-50. Mem. Am., Cal., Los Angeles county bar assns. Clubs: Lincoln (dir., pres. 1956-58), California, Sunset, Zamorano (Los Angeles, Cal.); Twilight (Pasadena, Cal.). Author: B. Franklin, Printer and Publisher, 1935; Japan; The Warnings and Prophecies of Lafcadio Hearn, 1943; How Abe Lincoln Went to Oxford, 1948. Contbr. articles to mags. Established at Honnold Library, Claremont Coll., collection of 4000 books on Oxford U. and its colls. Home: Pasadena CA Died Oct. 13, 1971.

CLAS, ANGELO ROBERT, architect; b. Milw., Feb. 13, 1887; s. Alfred Charles and Louise (Wick) C.; grad. E. Div. High Sch., Milw., 1905; B.S. in Architecture, Harvard, 1909; m. Norma Huette, Oct. 12, 1910 (dec. 1963); 1 dau., Mary Louise (Mrs. Delmar W. Holloman); m. 2d, Alice Beier Nicholson, 1965. Began as architect in Milw., 1908; engaged in mfg. business, Sheboygan, Wis., also Toledo, 1909-23; manufactured truck and tractor motors and shells during World War; traveled abroad, 1924; partner D.H. Burnham & Co., architects, Chgo., 1924-26, W.W. Ahischlager, 1927-29, Holabird & Root, 1929-34; apptd. mem. housing div. Fed. Emergency Adminstrn. of Pub. Works, Washington, 1934, dir. of housing, 1935-36; asst. adminstr. pub. works, 1936-37; now cons. Clas, Riggs, Owens & Ramos. Recent work: Fed. Loan Agy., Internat. Bank for Reconstrn. and Devel., YMCA Addition, Washington Statler Hotel, Wyatt Bldg. (winner 1952 Archtl. award of Merit); large scale housing devels. in Md., Va., Pa. and Tenn.; office bldg. Govt. of India, also Nat. Rifle Assn., Phillip Murray, IMF bldgs. of Washington (winner 1959 Archtl. award of Merit). Recipient Bronze award for outstanding contbns. to architecture of Nat. Capitol, Bldg. Stone Inst.; bronze medal Am. Heart Assn., 1965. Fellow A.I.A.; mem. Washington Bldg. Congress, Honolulu Acad. Arts, Delta Upsilon. Mason. Methodist. Club: Harvard, Outrigger Canoe. Home: Honolulu HI Died Dec. 4, 1970; interred Wildwood Cemetery, Sheboygan WI

CLAUSEN, JENS (CHRISTIAN), research botanist; b. North Eskilstrup, Denmark, Mar. 11, 1891; s. Christen Augustinus and Christine (Christensen) C.; M.A., U. Copenhagen, 1921, Ph.D., 1926; Doctor of Agr. (hon.), University of Uppsala, 1957; m. Anna Hansen, October 28, 1921 (deceased August 24, 1956). Came to the United States, 1931, naturalized, 1943. Farmer, 1905-15; tchr. secondary schools, 1910-16, 18-20; research asst., dept. genetics Royal Agrl. and Vet. Coll., Copenhagen, Denmark, 1921-31; research fellow Internat. Edn. Bd., U. Cal., 1927-28; staff dept. plant biology Carnegie Inst. of Washington, Stanford, Cal., 1931-69; lectr. U. Copenhagen, 1936, universities of Brazil, 1953, Messenger lecturer Cornell, 1950, U. Chgo., Wash. State U., 1961, Vanderbilt U., 1962; prof. biology Stanford U., 1951-69; vis professor genetics, University Cal. at Davis, 1963-64. Trustee Berkeley Bapt. Div. Sch., 1950-61. Served with Arty. Corps, Denmark Army, 1916-18. Recipient Mary Sope Pope medal of botany. Cranbrook Inst. Sci., 1949; certificate of merit Botanical Soc. Am., 1956; decorated Knight of Dannebrog (Denmark), 1961. Fellow Bot. Soc. Edinburgh (hon.), California Academy of Sciences, American Academy of Arts and Sci., A.A.A.S.; mem. Soc. Study Evolution (pres. 1956), Royal Swedish Acad. Sci., Nat. Acad. Genetics Soc. Am., Am. Soc. Agronomy, Royal Danish Acad. Sci. and Letters. Republican. Baptist. Author: Experimental Studies on the Nature of Species I-III (with D. D. Keck and William M. Hiesey) 1940-48, IV (with William M. Hiesey), pub. 1958 Stages in the Evolution of Plant Species, 1951. Author sci. articles on hybridization, race ecology, plant evolution, world forest compositions. Home: Palo Alto CA Died Nov. 22, 1969.

CLAUSON, IVY P. STEWART (MRS. EDWIN CLAUSON), artist, civic worker; b. Kremming, Colo., Aug. 19, 1905; d. and Etna Mae (Grindle) Stewart; B.A., Colo. State Coll., 1927; m. Edwin Clauson, Aug. 28, 1927; 1 dau., Sonja Kay. Pharmacist, Gilbert-Bishop Drug Co., Greeley, Colo., 1927-32, Clauson Drug Co., Ault, Colo., 1932-43; mgr., pharmacist Sunnyside Pharmacy, Ault, 1943-44; exhibited in group shows Ault Fall Festival, 1965-67, 1st Nat. Bank, Greeley, 1966, Longmont China Guild Show, 1967, Colo. Federated Women's Club Conv., Estes Park; represented in permanent collections Ault Pub. Library, Ault Pub. Sch. Mem. Weld County Cancer Soc., 1965-67, trustee, 1967-70; chmn. art exhibit and tea Cancer Benefit, 1966; chmn. art dept. Ault Fall Festival, 1967. Mem. Colo. Fedn. Womens Clubs, China Workshop Guild, Alpha Gamma Delta. Republican. Conglist. (active ch. work). Mem. Order Eastern Star. Club: Ault CO Died Mar. 13, 1970.

CLAY, HENRY BREVARD, broadcasting exec.; b. Atlanta, Dec. 9, 1918; s. Clifford Charles and Zerelda Battle (Martin) C.; student U. Ga., 1936-37; B.A. cum laude, Vanderbilt U., 1941; m. Helen May Ewing, July 19, 1945; children—Helen, Virginia, Kathryn, Henry Brevard. With So. Bell Tel. & Tel. Co., 1936-37; mgr. radio sta. WLAY, Muscle Shoals, Ala., 1946-47; gen. mgr. KWKH, Shreveport, 1947-52, exec. v.p., gen. mgr., 1952-67; director of Times Publishing Company, Ltd., Monroe News Star World Publishing Company, International Broadcasting Corporation, Radio Broadcasting, Inc., Arkansas Television Company. President Goodwill Industries, Shreveport, 1953; general chairman United Fund Drive, Shreveport; mem. Com. of 100. Bd. dirs., gen. chmn. capital funds drive YMCA; bd. dirs. TV Information Office. Served as lt. comdr. USNR, World War II. Named young man of the year, Shreveport, 1952; named Louisiana Broadcaster of the Year, 1965. Mem. Nat. Assn. Broadcasters (chmn. 1954-55, TV bd. 1960-61), Vanderbilt Alumni Assn. (director, local president 1959-60), American Legion (state commander 1952-53, member national pub. relations commn. 1958-67, nat. exec. committeeman for La. 1963-67, chmn. La. pub. relations commission), C. of C. (pres. 1956-57, dir. 1964-67), La. Association Broadcasters (dir. 1959), Pub. Affairs Research Council La. (bd. trustees, exec. com.), So. States Indsl. Council (dir.), Sigma Alpha Epsilon. Episcopalian (vestryman). Club: Holiday in Dixie-Ambassador (chmn. 1966-67, dir.). So. Golden Glove champion, 1940. Home: Shreveport LA Died Aug. 1, 1967.

CLAY, JOHN CECIL, artist, illustrator; b. Ronceverte, Greenbrier Co., W. Va., Apr. 2, 1875; s. Gen. Cecil and Anna Wood (Kester) C.; ed. Friends Sch., Washington; studied drawing at Students' League, Washington, 1895-6, receiving scholarship to New York Art Students' League, for best work done in school; studied drawing, art Students' League, New York, 1897-8; mem. Bd. of Control during latter year; m. Greenwich, Conn., June 22, 1904, Marie Deschapelles Bauduy. First professional work done for The Saturday Evening Post. Phila., 1899; since then work has appeared in all leading mags. Episcopalian. Club: The Players. Designed and arranged books of his drawings: In Love's Garden, 1904; The Portfolio of Celebrated Actresses, 1905; The Portfolio of Authors, 1906; The Lovers Mother Goose, 1907. Residence: Ronceverte, Manaroneck, N.Y. Studio: 7 W. 30th St., New York NY‡

CLAYBOURN, JOHN GERONOLD, civil engineer, consultant on marine development and dredging; b. Albert Lea, Minn., May 23, 1886; s. John Bethel and Ellen (Clink) C.; grad. high sch., Albert Lea; student College of Engineering, University of Minnesota, 3 yrs., B.S. (hon.), 1964; m. Elsie Kathryn Grieser, Sept. 1, 1928. Served as rodman, levelman and transitman Isthmian Canal Commn., 1910-14; with dredging div. of Panama Canal since 1914, jr. engr., 1917-18, asst. engr. 1919-20, supt. of div., 1921-48, mem. Gov.'s staff, 1924-48, salary bd., 1926-48; retired; cons. engr. on marine developments, nav., rivers, harbors, canals; cons. on harbor developments, Colombia and Venezuela, 1949; collaborator on design of Diesel electric and turbo-driven suction dredges, Diesel electric tugs, floating electric compressor, floating electric grader, floating electric relay booster plant; original design and lay-out of new dredging div. hdqrs. and townsite Gamboa, Canal Zone, 1924-36; cons. engr. Dique Canal, Colombia, 1917, harbor development at Puntarenas, Costa Rica, 1925-46, 48; Aguadulce,

Panama, 1926; Trans-Fla. Ship Canal, 1933, Panama Harbor, 1940-44, 46-48; study and layout docks and warehouses, Colon, 1948; reconnaisance covering Inland Waterway of Guatemala for I.B.E.C Tech. Service Corp., New York City, 1949; consultant for Inland Water Transport, Government of Union of Burma, 1951-53. Mem. commission for revision Colombian Code covering vessel construction and navigation, 1955-56. Mem. Pres.'s Club, U. Mich. Decorated Commendador, 1945, Gran Official, 1946, La Orden Vasco Nunea de Balboa (Panama). Mem. American Soc. Civil Engrs., Society of American Military Engineers, Tau Beta Pi. President of Gamboa Civic Council, 1937-48; pres. gen. com. Canal Zone Civic Councils, 1939-41; pres. The Panama Canal Employees' Mutual Benefit Assn., 1943-48, Minn. Club of Canal Zone, 1942-47. Mason (K.T. and Red Cross of Constantine, Shriner). Clubs: Union, Panama City, Panama Golf, Gamboa Golf and Country (pres. 1937-47). Author: Dredging on the Panama Canal, 1931; The Dredging Division of The Panama Canal, Its Function, Organization and Equipment, 1937; Evolution of the Panama Canal, 1944; Streamlining the Panama Canal for Maximum Safety and Unlimited Capacity, 1946; Suggested Methods and Equipment, Dredging and Mining for Convering the Present Locktype Canal to Sea Level, 1947. Contbr. to Mil. Engr., The Dock and Harbor Authority, London. Home: Ann Arbor MI Died June 26, 1967; buried Graceland Cemetery, Albert Lea MN

CLAYPOLE, EDITH JANE, asst. in physiology Cornell Univ. Med. School, 1899-1901; b. Bristol, England, 1870; d. Dr. E. W. C.; grad. Buchtel Coll., Akron, O., Ph.B., 1892; M.S., Cornell, 1893; entered med. course Cornell, 1899; studied at Mass. Inst. Technology, 1893-4; held Wellesley Coll. table at Woods Holl Biol. Sta., summer of 1895-6; instr. zoology, Wellesley, 1894-9; acting head of dept., 1896-8. Instr. biology, Throop Poly. Inst., Calif., 1901-02; pathologist, Los Angeles, Calif., since 1902; M. D., Univ. of Southern Calif., 1904. Mem. Sigma Xi; fellow A.A.A.S., Am. Micros. Soc. Contb'r to periodicals. Address: Pasadena CA‡

CLAYPOOL, J(OHN) GORDON, physician; b. Kansas City, Kan., Oct. 8, 1916; s. Charles William and Ruby (Larey) C.; A.B., U. Kan., 1939, M.D., 1941; m. Martha Roena Tillman, June 30, 1938; children—John Mark, Martha Ann. Asst. instr. anatomy U. Kan. Med. Sch., 1938; mem. teaching staff student health service Kan. State Coll., 1946-47; preceptor gen. practice U. Kan. Med. Sch., 1949-55, research fellow in medicine, 1955-56; practice medicine, specializing in internal medicine, Howard, Kan. Dir. Howard Nat. Bank (Kan.). Breeder Hereford cattle, buffalo. Trustee Kan. Blue Shield, 1963-67, v.p., 1967; trustee 4 County Mental Health Assn. Served as capt. M.C., AUS, 1944-46. Diplomate Am. Bd. Internal Medicine. Fellow A.C.P.; mem. A.M.A., Kan. (mem. council 1960-63, v.p. 1967), Greenwood County (pres. 1965), Elk County (sec.-treas., 1948-67) med. socs. Methodist. Contbr. papers in hemodynamics, other tech. studies to profl. jours. Home: Howard KS Died Sept. 22, 1967.

CLAYTON, PHILIP THOMAS BYARD, clergyman; b. Queensland, Australia, Dec. 12, 1885; s. Reginald Byard Buchanan and Isabel (Sheppard) C.; scholar St. Paul's Sch., London, 1897-1905; M.A., Exeter Coll., Oxford U., 1909; D.D. (Lambeth), 1954. Ordained to ministry Ch. of Eng., 1910; curate of Portsea, 1910-14; opened Talbot House, Poperinghe, 1915; chaplain, tutor Service Candidates Sch., Knutsford, Eng., 1919; vicar All Hallows-by-the-Tower, 1922-72; founder Toc H, social service fellowship, 1922; chaplain to The Queen; hon. chaplain to Lord Bishop of London; sr. chaplain to Brit. Petroleum Oil Co., Port of London Authority. Served as chaplain Brit. Army, World War I, Anglo-Saxon Tanker Fleet and Mcht. Navy, World War II. Decorated Companion of Honour, Mil. Cross Fellow Soc. Antiquaries. Clubs: Royal Automobile, London Press. Author: Encaustic Mediaeval Tiles, 1910; The Work of a Great Parish, 1912; Tales of Talbot House, 1919; Plain Tales from Flanders, 1929; Earthquake Love, 1932; Letters from Flanders, 1932; Pageant of Tower Hill, 1933. Home: London England Died Dec. 15, 1972.

CLEARY, JAMES MANSFIELD, writer; born Hubbell, Neb., Jan. 19, 1887; s. Michael T. and Kate (McPhelim) C.; B.A., U. of Ill., 1906; LL.B. Northwestern University (Chicago), 1909; married Evelyn Morency, June 22, 1916; children—Marguerite (Mrs. C. J. Remien), Mary E. (Mrs. W. A. Sundlof), Jeanne (Mrs. F. W. Goessling), Dorothy Anne (Mrs. Lathrop G. Hoffman), James M., Jr., Michael. Chemist Corn Products Co., Chicago, 1902-03; law clerk, Bastrup & O'Neill, Chicago, 1906-07; reporter, editor, advertising solicitor, exec., Chicago (Ill.) Tribune, 1907-25; gen. sales mgr., Studebaker Corp., South Bend, Ind., 1925-32; pres., White Co., Cleveland, O., 1932-33; v.p. Roche, Williams & Cleary, Inc., advt. agency, 1933-59; special research and Cleary, Inc., advt. agency, 1933-59; special research and writing Chgo. Tribune, from 1959. Mem. Illinois Public Aid Commission, from 1959. Trustee U. of Ill., 1937-43, pres. of board, 1941-42; cons. War Dept., Washington, 1943-44; spl. asst. to adminstr., E.C.A., Washington, 1948-49, Chmn. Chicago com., United China Relief; dir. Chicago Press Veterans, Cath. Charities, Conf. Christians and Jews; dir., past pres. Irish Fellowship Club, Chgo. Democrat. Roman Catholic. Home: Winnetka IL Died Mar. 4, 1972.

CLEASBY, HAROLD LOOMIS, univ. prof.; b. Hartford, Conn., July 22, 1876; s. William Henry and Alice Frances (Porch) C.; A.B., Trinity Coll., 1899, A.M., 1901; A.M., Harvard, 1902; Ph.D., 1904; Harvard traveling fellow in Europe, 1904; unmarried. Tutor in classics, Trinity Coll., 1899-1901; instr. Latin, Amherst, 1905-08; asst. prof. and asso. prof. Latin, Syracuse U., 1908-18; asso. prof. classics, Hunter Coll., New York, 1918-19; prof. Roman archaeology, Syracuse U., 1920-24; prof. classical archaeology and Italian, same univ., since 1924. Mem. Archaeol. Inst. America, Am. Philol. Assn., Phi Beta Kappa, Alpha Chi Rho, Phi Kappa Phi. Republican. Unitarian. Collaborator on Place's Beginning Latin, 1919; Place's Second Year Latin, 1923. Home: 805 Comstock Av., Syracuse NY‡

CLEAVELAND, AGNES MORLEY, author; b. Cimarron, N.M., June 26, 1874; d. William Raymond and Ada (McPherson) Morley; student Friends Central Sch., Phila.; student U. of Mich., 1893-95; B.A., Stanford U., 1899; m. Newton Cleaveland, Dec. 23, 1899; children—Norman, Loraine (Mrs. George M. Keffer), Agnes Morley, Mary (Mrs. Claus Wohlers). Active in community and civic affairs, writing, lecturing, radio broadcasting; has seen development of N.M. from Wild West." Republican. Author: No Life for a Lady, 1941 (received prize award, Life in America Series). Contbr. short stories to popular mags., newspapers, etc. Address: 2532 Cedar St., Berkeley CA*‡

CLEE, GILBERT HARRISON, mgmt. cons.; b. Providence, Dec. 20, 1912; s. Lester Harrison and Katherine (Steele) C.; grad. Newark Acad., 1931; B.A., Wesleyan U., 1935; m. Virginia Mitchell, Sept. 7, 1936; children—Deborah, Hillary. With Norman S. Taber & Co., 1936-42, 46-47, partner, 1939-47; staff Internat. Bank for Reconstrn. and Development, 1947-49; asso. McKinsey & Co., N.Y.C., 1949-50, prin., 1950-53, partner, 1953-56; dir. McKinsey & Company, Inc., 1956-68. Trustee, pres. bd. Wesleyan U. Lt. comdr. USNR, 1942-46. Mem. Mil. Order Fgn. Wars, Phi Beta Kappa, Delta Tau Delta. Club: Bedford (N.Y.) Golf and Tennis. Home: Mt Kisco NY Died July 28, 1968; buried Indian Hill Cemetery, Middletown CT

CLEGG, CECIL HUNTER, judge; b. Sion Mills, County Tyrone, Ireland, June 9, 1873; s. Joseph and Elizabeth (Clark) C.; prep. edn., Owen Sound (Can.) Collegiate Inst.; B.A. with honors, Toronto U., 1897; studied law in offices of Gen. Charles H. Toll, Denver, Colo., 1897-99; m. Jessie Magdalene Johnston, of Toronto, May 11, 1903. Began practice at Denver, 1899; moved to Nome, Alaska, 1900; asst. U.S. atty. 3d Div., Alaska, 1903-07, 4th Div., 1908-12; city atty., Fairbanks, 1918; became judge U.S. Dist. Court, 4th Dist., Alaska, and 3d Dist., 1921. Suggested pub. observance of Oct. 18 as Alaska Day, also erection of monument to William H. Seward, at Seward, Alaska. Four-minute speaker, World War; food administrator, 1917-18. Grand President Pioneers of Alaska, 1919. Republican. Episcopalian. Mason (32 deg., Shriner), Elk. Home: Valdez AK*‡

CLELAND, RALPH ERSKINE, botanist; b. Le Claire, Ia., Oct. 20, 1892; s. Charles Samuel and Edith Eleanor (Collins) C.; A.B., U. of Pa., 1915, M.S., 1916, Ph.D., 1919, Sc.D., 1958; LL.D., Hanover College, 1957; Sc.D., Ind. U., 1970; married Elizabeth Prentice Shoyer of East Orange, N.J., June 11, 1927; children—William Wallace, Robert Erskine, Charles Frederick. Asst. in botany, U. of Pa., 1915-16, Harrison fellow, 1916-18; instr. biology, Goucher Coll., 1919-20, asst. prof., 1920-23, asso. prof., 1923-30, prof., 1930-38, chmn. of dept., 1937-38; prof., chmn. botany dept. Ind. U., 1938-58, dean of Grad. School, 1950-58, Distinguished Service prof. botany, 1958-63, Distinguished Service prof. botany emeritus, co-dir. aerospace applications center, 1963-68; instructor botany Marine Biol. Lab., Woods Hole, 1925; editor plant cytology, Biol. Abstracts (trustee, 1943-48); cons. Nat. Sci. Found.; editor in chief Am. Jour. of Botany, 1940-46. Mem. U.S. Nat. Commn. for UNESCO, 1958-60; mem. of the program committee U.S. Nat. Com., 1958-60. Pvt., arty., U.S. Army, with A.E.F., 1918-19. Rec. John F. Lewis award, Am. Philos. Soc., 1937, J. S. Guggenheim traveling fellowship, 1927-28. Fellow A.A.A.S. (mem. council 1932-37, v.p. 1944), Ind. Acad. Sci. (pres. 1959), Am. Acad. Arts and Scis.; mem. Nat. Research Council (chmn. div. biol. and agr. 1948-51), Bot. Soc. Am. (pres. 1947), Genetics Society of Am. (v.p. 1955, pres. 1956), Nat. Acad. Scis. (chmn. Pacific sci. bd.), Nat. Assn. Biology Tchrs., Am. Soc. Naturalists (sec. 1938-40, pres. 1942), Am. Inst. Biol. Sci. (chmn. 1948-49), Soc. Study Evolution, Am. Philos. Soc. (v.p. 1965-68), Genetics Soc. Japan (hon. fgn. mem.), Bot. Soc. Korea (hon. life), Deutsche Botanische Gesellschaft (corresponding member), Phi Beta Kappa, Sigma Xi. Presbyterian. Author: Oenothera Cytogenetics and Evolution, 1971. Contbr. numerous articles to scientific jours. Home: Bloomington IN Died June 11, 1971.

CLEMEN, RUDOLF ALEXANDER, coll. prof.; b. Halifax, N.S., June 11, 1893; s. Leopold and Harriet Byron (Taylor) C.; A.B., Dalhousie U., 1913, M.A., 1914; M.A., Harvard, 1915, Ph.D., 1926; m. Margaret May Jones, Dec. 29, 1923; children—Arthur Taylor, Rudolf Alexander. Instr. history and economics, Purdue U., 1917-18, Northwestern U., 1918-21; sec. to pres. Northwestern U., 1918-19; asso. editor The National Provisioner, 1921-23; economist Ill. Merchants Trust Co., 1923-26; asso. dir. Armour & Co.'s Livestock Bur., 1926-30; asso. chief Social Science, Century of Progress Expn., 1930-32; pres. Whitman Coll., Walla Walla, Wash., 1934-36; lecturer economics and business, Univ. of Wash., 1936; prof. economics, American University, 1937-42. Mem. Am. Econ. Assn., Am. Hist. Assn., Am. Polit. Science Assn., American Assn. Univ. Professors. Ordained Presbyterian ministry, June 11, 1933. Clubs: Cosmos (Washington, D.C.); University (Evanston, Ill.), Author: American Livestock and Meat Industry, 1923; By Products in the Packing Industry, 1927. Editor of Century of Progress Series. Contbr. Ency. of Social Sciences and Dictionary of Am. Chevy Chase MD Died Dec. 1969.

CLEMENT, FRANK GOAD, ex-gov. Tenn.; b. Dickson, Tenn.; June 2, 1920; s. Robert Samuel and Maybelle (Goad) C.; student Cumberland U., Lebanon, Tenn., 1939; LL.B., Vanderbilt U., 1942; m. Lucille Christianson, Jan. 6, 1940; children—Robert Nelson, Frank Goad, James Gary. Admitted to Tenn. bar, 1941; practice in Nashville and Dickson, Tenn., 1946-50; with FBI, 1941-43; chief counsel Tenn. Utilities Commn., 1946-50; gov. of Tenn., 1953-59, 63-66; practice law, 1967-69. Former chairman of the Southern Govs. Conf., mem. exec. com., 1956; past chmn. So. Regional Edn. Bd. Keynote speaker Democratic Nat. Conv., Chgo., 1956. Chmn. bd. Cordell Hull Found. Internat. Edn., 1955-59. Served to 1st lt. AUS, World War II. Named outstanding young man, Tenn. Jr. C. of C., 1948; One of Nations Ten Outstanding Young Men by U.S. Jr. C. of C., 1953; recipient spl. service award So. Psychiatric Assn., 1958, spl. award Nat. Assn. Mental Health, 1958. Mem. Am. Legion (comdr. Tenn. dept. 1948-49), Dickson Co. Jr. C. of C., Sigma Alpha Epsilon, Phi Delta Phi. Democrat. Methodist Mason (32, Shriner), Kiwanian. Club: Young Dem. Tenn. (pres. 1946-48). Home: Brentwood TN Died Nov. 4, 1969; buried Dickson County Meml. Gardens, Dickson TN

CLEMENTE, ROBERTO WALKER, profl. baseball player, humanitarian; b. Carolina, P.R., Aug. 18, 1934; student Julio Coronado Bezcarrondo Coll.; m. Vera Zavala, Nov. 14, 1964. Mem. Pitts. Pirates Profl. Baseball Team, 1955-72. Lifetime batting average of. 317; 4-times Nat. League batting champion; 12 times on All-Star Team; 3000 hits, 12 Gold Glove awards; named Most Valuable Player, 1966; recipient Babe Ruth award, 1971. Home: Pittsburgh PA Died Dec. 31, 1972.

CLEMENTS, EDITH SCHWARTZ, ecologist, illustrator; b. Albany, N.Y., d. George and Emma G. (Young) Schwartz; B.A., U. of Neb., 1898, Ph.D., 1906; m. Frederic E. Clements, 1899. Fellow in German, U. of Neb., 1898-1901, asst. in botany, 1903-07; instr. botany, U. of Minn., 1909-13; investigator and illustrator, Carnegie Institution, Washington, D.C., 1918-41. Mem. Sigma Xi, Phi Beta Kappa, Kappa Alpha Theta fraternities. Author: Relation of Leaf Structure to Physical Factors, 1905; Rocky Mountain Flowers (with husband), 1913, 19; Flowers of Mountain and Plain, 1913, 19; (monograph) Herbaria Ecadium Californiae, 1914; (booklet) Wild Flowers of the West, 1927; Flower Families and Ancestors (with husband), 1928; Flowers of Coast and Sierra, 1929; Flower Pageant of the Midwest, 1939; Flowers of Prairie and Woodland, 1947. Editor: Dynamics of Vegetation, 1949. Illustrator: La Jolla CA Died June 30, 1971.

CLEVA, FAUSTO, conductor; b. Trieste, Italy, May 17, 1902; s. Giacomo and Fortunata (Canarutto) C.; student Trieste Conservatory Music, Conservatorio Verdi of Milan; D. Music, Coll. Music Cin., 1949; m. Irene Ghedini, June 20, 1931; children—Maria, Wally. Came to U.S., 1920, naturalized, 1931. Asst. conductor, conductor principal theatres, Italy, 1916-20; asst. conductor, chorus master, later conductor Met. Opera Co., 1920-42; conductor, musical dir. Cin. Summer Opera, 1934-71; gen. mgr. Chgo. Civic Opera, 1944-46; conductor San Francisco Opera Co., 1942-44, 49-55, Met. Opera Co., 1950-71; symphony guest condr. various seasons U.S., Can., S.A., Italy, Sweden, Havana, Empire Festival Ellenville N.Y., Edinburgh Festival, 1959, Greek Attica theater, 1971. Decorated commendatore Stella Della Republica Ialiana, 1958; gran officiale della Republica Italiana; Golden Cross of Greece; honored for 50 years of association with Met. Opera by bd. dirs. Home: New York City NY Died Aug. 6, 1971; buried Cimitero Israelitico, Trieste, Italy

CLEVELAND, AUSTIN C(ARL), educator; b. Knoxville, Ia., Dec. 20, 1889; s. Talcot Easton and Ora May (Oreutt) C.; A.B., Phillips U., Enid, Okla., 1917, B.S., 1922; student Yale, 1919-20; M.A., U. of Chicago,

1924; student Columbia summer 1930; Ed.D., Stanford, 1933; student U. of So. Calif., summer 1937; extension 1938-39, summer 1940, U. of Okla., summer 1945, U. of Calif. at Los Angeles, summer 1947; m. Hazel Harned, August 16, 1925; 1 dau.; Ina Mae. Teacher and coach Conway Springs (Kan.) High Sch., 1917-18; asst. in economics Yale, 1919; prin. and coach Scott City (Kan.) High Sch., 1920-21, Instr. Phillips U. summers 1921-23, 25; head history dept. and asst. coach Neodesha (Kan.) High Sch., 1921-23; ast. in psychophysical research U. of Chicago, 1923-25; prof. end., dir. of summer sch., soccer coach, Friends U., Wichita, Kan., 1925-32; asst. in citizenship research Stanford, 1933-34; vis. teacher in social science Antelope Valley High Sch. and Jr. Coll., Lancaster, Calif., 1933; registrar Taft (Calif.) High Sch. and Jr. Coll., 1934-37; prof. psychology and philosophy Fullerton (Calif.) Jr. Coll., 1937-40; asso. prof. psychology and edn. Oklahoma City U., 1940-46, dean of students, 1941-46, head dept. psychology, 1953-60, dir. div. social studies, 1950-60, prof. emeritus, 1960-70, prof. psychology, part-time 1960-65; prof. sociology Oklahoma City Southwestern Coll., 1968-70. Counselor, Salvation Army, 1960-70. Mem. Hazen Found. Conf., Colo. Springs, 1952. Fellow Oklahoma Acad. of Sciences; member American Association of Univ. Profs., Nat. Com. for Mental Hygiene, N.E.A., Okla. Ednl. Assn., Nat. Soc. Study Edn., Okla. Psychol. Assn. (pres. 1954), So. Soc. Philosophy and Psychology, S.W. Sociol. Soc., Phi Delta Kappa, Sigma Phi Epsilon. Republican. Methodist. Home: Oklahoma City OK Died Jan. 19, 1970; buried Memorial Park Cemetery.

CLEVELAND, LEMUEL ROSCOE, zoologist; b. Newton County, Miss., Nov. 14, 1892; s. Daniel Frank and Donna (Taylor) C.; B.S., U. of Miss., 1917; U. of Chicago, 1919-20; Sc.D., Johns Hopkins U. Sch. of Public Health, 1923; m. Mabel Bush, Mar. 27, 1925; 1 dau., Margaret Elaine; m. 2d, Dorothy Eleanor Colby, June 17, 1936; 1 son, Bruce Taylor. Asst. prof. protozoology, Harvard Med. Sch., 1925-36, asso. prof. zool., 1936-46, prof. biol., 1946-59, prof. emeritus, 1959-69. Mem. Am. Acad. Arts and Sci., Am. Acad. Tropical Med., Am. Soc. Zool., Am. Soc. Parasitol., Am. Naturalists, Gamma Alpha, Sigma Xi. Contbr. to scientific jours. Home: Boston MA 2Died Feb. 12, 1969.

CLEVELAND, REGINALD MCINTOSH, advertising mgr.; b. N.Y. City, Nov. 6, 1886; s. Treadwell and Evelyn Spaulding (McIntosh) C.; A.B., Yale, 1908; m. Denise Fisher Goodhue, Dec. 9, 1911; children—Evelyn McIntosh (Mrs. John N. Warren), Charles Goodhue, Reginald McIntosh, Denise Goodhue (Mrs. Roger J.S. Jensen). Reporter and exchange editor, New York Evening Post, 1909-12; automobile editor, asst. city editor, New York Times, 1912-16; asso. editor, Vanity Fair, 1916-20; aviation editor, New York Times, 1929-37, automobile editor, 1937-41, indsl. advt. mgr., 1941, asst. to nat. advt. mgr.; pres. Am. Museum of Safety, 1951, also trustee. Pres. Greater N.Y. Safety Council; dir. Nat. Safety Council. Trustee Citizen's Traffic Safety Bd. Gov. Flight Safety Found. Mem. adv. Com. Acad. Aero. Am. corr. for Interavia, Geneva, Switzerland, internat. tech. news chronicle of aviation, 1935-41. Twice received 2d award, hon. mention. Comml. Investment Trust Safety awards for editorials on safety; among prize winners 4 different years, Transcontinental and Western Air newspaper writers awards for editorials on air transport, New York Times. Mem. Soc. Colonial Wars, Inst. Aeronaut. Scis., Wings, German Shepard Dog Am., Phi Beta Kappa, Aviation Writers Assn., Zeta Psi. Author: Cop, Chief of Police Dogs, 1926; Guard, Son of Cop, 1931; Young America's Aviation Annual (with Frederick P. Graham), 1940-41, 1941-42, 1942-43; America Fledges Wings, 1942; The Aviation Annual for 1944 (with Frederick P. Graham), 1943, Air Transport at War, 1946; The Road Is Yours (with S.T. Williamson), 1951. Contbr. to Sci. Am., Country Gentleman, Parents, Boys Life. Home: Randolph Center VT Died Apr. 1971.

CLEVELAND, TREADWELL, JR., editor; b. Plainfield, N.J., May 19, 1872; s. Treadwell and E. S. (McIntosh) C.; ed. Harvard, 1892-4; traveling abroad and teaching, 1894-5; A.B., Williams Coll., 1897; post-grad. work, A.M., Columbia, 1898; fellow in psychology, Clark U., 1900-01; m. Margaret T. Boulger, of Washington, Nov. 1, 1899. Asst., Div. of Forestry (now Forest Service), U.S. Dept. of Agr., 1899-1900; editorial staff, New York Evening World, 1903-05. Socialist. Author: A Night with Alessandro, 1904. Address: Forest Service Dept. Agr., Washington DC‡

CLEVELAND, WILLIAM DAVIS, merchant; b. Houston, Tex.; s. William Davis and Tina (Latham) C.; A.B., U. of the South, 1893, Yale, 1894; m. Julia May Morse, Apr. 29, 1903. Mem. firm William D. Cleveland & Sons, wholesale grocers and cotton factors. Address: Commerce & Fannin St., Houston TX‡

CLEVEN, NELS ANDREW NELSON, prof. of history; b. Lake Mills, Ia., Dec. 21, 1874; s. Nels Grovum and Turina (Sanders) C.; Ph.B. and Ed.B., U. of Chicago, 1906; Ph.D., U. of Munich, 1913; also student U. of Berlin, U. of Paris, U. of Grenoble, U. of Bonn, U. of Calif., Columbia; m. Hilma A. Willd, of Hoffman, Minn., June 8, 1912. Taught in pub. schs., 1894-1918; asst. prof. history and politics, U. of Ark., 1919-21; with U. of Pittsburgh since 1921, prof. of history since 1927; visiting prof. history, U. of W.Va., summer 1929, George Washington U., summer 1932. Current history asso. Current History Mag., 1928-29; research asso. in history in Bolivia for Carnegie Instn. of Washington, 1930-31. Research asst. Bur. of Research, War Trade Bd., Washington, 1918-19. Official del. of U. of Pittsburgh to Hist. Congress of Rio, 1922, to Bolivarian Congress of Panama, 1926, Congress of Hist. Sciences, Oslo, 1928, 7th Am. Scientific Congress, Mexico City, 1935. Founder Phi Alpha Theta (bat. hon. history fraternity), permanent hon. pres. Mem. Am. Hist. Assn., Hist. Soc. of Western Pa., Hist. Assn. of Pa., Com. on Latin-Am. Research, Acad. of Polit. Science, Hispanic Am. Hist. Conf., Inter-Am. Hist. Commn., Hispanic Soc. of America, Delta Sigma Pi, Delta Sigma Phi, Scabbard and Blade. Mason. Clubs: Hungry (Pittsburgh), Civic (Allegheny County). Translator: Simon Bolivar; An Introduction to a Study of His Political Ideals, 1930. Lecturer and writer. Author: Readings in Hispanic American History, 1927. Home: 4303 Andover Terrace Pittsburgh PA*‡

CLIFFORD, CHARLES P., sr. v.p. Farmers and Merchants Savs. Bank Mpls. Home: Minneapolis MN Died June 26, 1971.

CLIFFORD, ELMER LAURENCE, advertising mgr.; b. Maiden Rock, Wis., June 17, 1874; s. Villeroy Eugene and Zoe (Huestis) C.; B.A., U. of Minn., 1895; m. Margaret A. O'Brien, of Minneapolia, Sept. 9, 1902. Became connected with newspaper business, Minneapolis, 1899; advertising mgr. Minneapolis Journal, since Feb. 9, 1912. Strong advocate of movement for clean advertising" in newspapers; writer and lecturer. Republican. Mem. Theta Delta Chi. Clubs: Minneapolis Athletic, University, Lafayette, Interlachen, Elks. Home: 2125 Olive Av. S. Office: The Journal, Minneapolis‡

CLIFFORD, LESLIE FORBES, heating and ventilating engr.; b. Reedsburg, Wis., July 18, 1913; s. Cecil Leslie and Margaret (Forbes) C.; student Intermountain Coll., 1932-33; A.B., Mont. State U., 1936; grad. study U. Minn., 1943-44, Ill. Inst. Tech., 1946-47, Northwestern U., 1949-50, 52-53; m. Almira Rita Santell, Dec. 26, 1953. Head music dept. Ronan (Mont.) High Sch., 1936-37; asst. prin. Inverness (Mont.) High Sch., 1937-38; Flathead Co. (Mont.) ednl. supervisor, W.P.A., 1938, zone supervisor edn., 1938-40, Mont. State librarian, edn. and recreation, 1940-41; sales engr. Holland Furnace Co., 1941-42; application engr. Cardox Corp., Chgo., 1942-43; prof. Chgo. Tech. Coll., 1943-45, head refrigeration and air conditioning dept., 1944-45; mech. engr. Skidmore-Owings & Merrill, 1945-46, asst. chief mech. engr., 1946-47; research engr. Assn. Am. R. Rs., 1947-49; organized, 1944, pres. Clifford-Johnson & Asso., 1944-66; cons. Vern E. Alden Co., U. Chgo.; chief cons. engr. Horozon Corp.; adminstrv. engr. William A. Pope Co.; cons. engr. U. Chgo., Ragnar Benson, Inc. Pres. Industry's Profl. Tng. Registered profl. engr.; licensed ins. broker. Mem. Nat. Assn. Practical Refrigerating Engrs., Am. Assn. Engrs., Am. Soc. Heating Refrigerating and Airconditioning Engrs., Chgo. Tech. Socs. Council, Nat. Assn. Power Engrs., Refrigeration Service Engrs. Soc., Mont. State Alumni Assn. (pres. Chgo. chpt.), Eagle, Associate editor Nat. Engr., 1951-52, editor-in-chief, 1952-55; pres. Forbes Pubs., Inc., 1955-66; editor, LISTEN, High Fidelity and FM Guide, 1955-65. Author several manuals and numerous tech. articles. Home: Riverside IL Died Oct. 5, 1966; buried Bronswood Cemetery, Oakbrook IL

CLIFFORD, REESE F(RANCIS), bus. exec. ret.; b. Frankfort, Ky., Sept. 6, 1891; s. Frank L. and Nancy E. (Ward) C.; student So. Ill. Normal Sch., 1907-10; m. Genevieve D. Doughterty, Jan. 10, 1910; children—Janellen (Mrs. Norbert A. Huebsch), Reese Francis Clifford, Jr. With Western Electric Co., Hawthorne, Ill., 1910-14, sect. chief, officer service orgn., 1914-25, asst. clerical supt., 1925-27, plant supt., 1929-38, div. mgr., 1938-41, supt. plant, Kearny, N.J., 1927-29, works mgr., 1942-52, personnel dir., N.Y.C., 1941-42, v.p. Western area, Chgo., 1952-56, ret., dir.; pres., dir. Mfrs. Junction Ry. Co.; mem. bd. dirs. Teletype Corp., Teletypesetter Corp. Mem. N.J. State, Newark C.'s of C., Chgo. Assn. Commerce. Home: Pelican Lake WI Died Dec. 8, 1971; buried Holy Family Catholic Cemetery, Elcho WI

CLINE, HOWARD FRANCIS, govt. ofcl., historian; b. Detroit, June 12, 1915; s. Francis E. and Sarah L. (Orr) C.; S.B. magna cum laude in History, Harvard, 1939, A.M. Frederick Sheldon Prize fellow 1939-40, Social Sci. Research pre-doctoral fellow 1942-43, 1943, Ph.D. in History, 1947; m. Mary A. Wilson, June 14, 1941; children—Ann E., Sue L. Asst. dean coll. Harvard, 1943-47, registrar coll., 1945, asst. counsellor for vets. univ., 1945-46, Woodbury Lowery traveling fellow, 1946, exec. sec. Com. Internat. and Regional studies, 1946-47, instr. history, 1947; instr. history Yale, 1947-49; asst. prof. history Northwestern U., 1949-52; dir. Hispanic Found., Library Congress, Washington, 1952-71; U.S. Govt. rep. II Internat. Colloquium on Luso-Brazillian Studies, Sao Paulo, 1954; adviser U.S. delegation VI Gen. Assembly, Pan Am. Inst. Geography and History, Mexico, 1955, II Cultural Council, Orgn. Am. States, Lima, Peru, 1956; Am. Council Learned Societies rep. III Internat. Colloquium on Luso-Brazilian Studies, Lisbon, Portugal, 1957; adviser U.S. delegation IV Consultation, Commn. on History, Cuenca, Ecuador, 1959, national mem. Commn. on History, 1960-68; vice chmn. U.S. Delegation IV Interam. Cultural Council, 1959; mem. exec. com. commn. Latin Am. Anthropology NRC, 1956-59. Decorated Commander Order Isabel la Catolica. Mem. Am. Hist. Assn. (exec. mem. com. guide to hist. lit. 1956-60), Anthrop. Soc. Washington, Conf. Latin Am. History (chmn. 1963, distinguished service award 1972), Societe des Americanistes (France), Latin American Studies Association (sec. 1966-67), Hispanic Soc. of Am. (corresponding mem.), Am. Acad. Franciscan History (asso.), Phi Beta Kappa. Club: Cosmos. The United States and Mexico, 1953; Mexico: Revolution to Evolution, 1940-60, 1962; also numerous articles. Editor: Latin American History: its study and teaching, 1967; Handbook of Middle American Indians, Vols. XII-XV. Bd. editors: Hispanic Am. Hist. Rev., 1957-62; editorial bd. Middle Am. Indians Handbook, 1958-71. Home: Arlington VA Died June 1, 1971; buried Fairview Cemetery, Westford MA

CLINE, LEWIS MANNING, educator; b. Duncan, Okla., Sept. 25, 1909; s. Edgar Betel and Leila (Sims) C.; B.S., U. Tulsa, 1931; M.S., U. Ia., 1934, Ph.D., 1935; m. Grace Ellen Shaw, Nov. 27, 1935; children—Ellen Sperling, Catherine Arlene, Charles Harry. Instr. geology U. Tulsa, 1931-32; research asst. U. Ia., 1932-35; instr. Tex. A. and M. Coll., 1935-36; instr. Ia. State Coll., 1936-37, asst. prof., 1938-42; mem. Ia. Geol. Survey, summers 1936-42; dist. geologist Standard Oil Co. Tex., 1943-45; faculty U. Wis., 1946-71, prof. geology, 1947-71, chmn. dept., 1960-65; cons. Natural Gas Pipeline Co. Am., 1940-42, Ia. Ins. Commn., 1939-41, Mobil Oil Research Lab., 1957-61, also other cos.; distinguished prof. Tex. Tech. Coll., 1952-53. Recipient Lew Wentz prize U. Tulsa, Lowden prize U. Ia. Fellow Geol. Soc. Am. (rep. Am. Stratigraphic Commn. 1957-60, chmn. publs. com. 1965, mem. council 1966-71, tech. program chmn. nat. meeting 1970); mem. Paleontol. Soc. Am. (chmn. nominating com. 1962), Am. Geol. Inst. (mem. geol. orientation study 1962-63, chmn. publs. com. 1966-71), Internat. Assn. of Sedimentalogy, Am. Assn. Petroleum Geologists (dist. rep. 1958-59, distinguished lectr. 1965), Soc. Econ. Paleontologists and Mineralogists (president 1965, chairman publications committee 1965), editor of Journal of Sedimentary Petrology 1961-64, Sigma Xi (sec.-treas. Iowa State College 1940-42), (president Univ. of Wisconsin chapter 1965-66), Gamma Alpha (v.p. U. Ia. 1934-35). Republican. Methodist. Rotarian (chmn. fellowship com. Madison 1951, Uthrotar com., Madison, 1959, vice president of Madison chpt. 1964-65). Author: Late Paleozoic Rocks of the Quachita Mountains, 1960. Editor, contbr.; Guidebook to Ouachita Mountains, 1956. Co-editor, contbr.; Geology of Ouachita Mountains, a symposium, 1959. Home: Madison WI Died Mar. 10, 1971; buried Forest Hill Cemetery, Madison WI

CLINE, THOMAS SPARKS, clergyman; b. Woodstown, N.J., Sept. 25, 1877; s. Philip and Anna (Sparks) C.; grad. Pennington (N.J.) Sem., 1897; A.B., Wesleyan U., Conn., 1901; B.D., Berkeley Divinity Sch., Conn., 1905, D.D., 1924; m. Lois Golder Clute, Sept. 6, 1905;children—Philip Arthur, Anna Katharine (Mrs. Roy W. Miner, Jr.), Lois Golder (Mrs. Bernard P. Ireland). Deacon and priest, P.E. Ch., 1905; in charge St. Barnabas' Ch., Berlin, N.H., 1905-09; curate St. Stephen's Ch., Boston, 1909-13; rector Grace Ch., Mt. Airy, Phila., 1913-24; prof. pastoral theology, Gen. Theol. Sem., New York, also rector St. Peter's Ch., New York, 1924-28; prof. pastoral theology and asst. dean, Berkeley Div. Sch., 1928-30, rector Christ Ch., Watertown, Conn., 1931-48, rector emeritus; lecturer at Berkeley Divinity School. Commd. chaplain 1st lt. U.S. Army, July, 1917; assigned to 19th Engrs., later to 16th Inf., 1st Div. served in France, Aug., 1917-Feb., 1919. Mem. Bd. of Exam. Chaplains, Diocese of Pa., 1920-24, Diocese of N.Y., 1925-29, Diocese of Conn., 1931-39 (mem. Standing Com. Diocese of Conn., 1935-43, president 1939-43; dep. to Gen. Conv. P.E. Church, 1934, 37, 40, 46; archdeacon Litchfield Archdeaconry, 1939-44. Mem. Phi Beta Kappa, Alpha Delta Phi. Republican. Mason. Home: Woodbridge CT Died June 2, 1968.

CLINTON, FRED S., surgeon; b. Okmulgee, Okla., Apr. 15, 1874; s. Charles and Louise (Atkins) C.; ed. schs. of Creek Nation; Young Harris Coll., Ga.; grad. Kansas City Coll. Pharmacy, 1896; M.D., Univ. Med. Coll., Kansas City, 1897; m. Jane C. Heard, of Elberton, Ga., Apr. 15, 1897. Practiced at Tulsa, Okla., since 1896; organized first hosp. and training sch. for nurses, Tulsa; founder, 1915, pres. and chief of staff, 1915-25, Oklahoma Hosp.; local surgeon M., K. & T. R. R.; was surgeon St. L. & S. F. Ry. 25 yrs.; div. surgeon M. V. Ry.; formerly chief surgeon Tulsa St. Ry. Co. (one of organizers, dir., sec.); surgeon Sand Springs Ry. Co.;

with Dr. Bland drilled first commercial oil well in Okla. Surgeon S.A.T.C., Kendall Coll., Tulsa, and mem. Dist. Bd. No. 2, during World War. Fellow Am. Coll. Surgeons; mem. Am., and Tulsa Co. med. socs., Southern Med. Assn., Am. Hosp. Assn., Am. Assn. Ry. Surgeons (pres. 1927), Okla. State Hosp. Assn. (organizer and pres., 1919-26; com. on hosps., 1915-28; hon. life pres., 1927—), Santa Fe Ry., Med. and Surg. Soc. (pres. 1925), Okla. State Med. Assn. (one of promoters Indian Ty. Med. Assn. which has been merged; chmn. com. on contract and industrial medicine, 1926-28), Tulsa Council of Hosps. (pres.), Med. Vets. World War (charter mem. and a founder); Midwest Hosp. Assn. (twice v.p.; pres. 1928-29; life mem. Okla. Hist. Soc.; hon. mem. Hyechka Club; del. from Okla. to Internat. Congress on Tuberculosis, Washington, D.C., 1908; mem. Bd. U.S. Pension Examiners 25 years, sec., later pres. for 10 years. Mem. bd. of stewards and Building Com. Boston Av. M.E. Church, South. Mason. One of founders of Kendall Coll. (now U. of Tulsa). Invited to admission in Okla. Hall of Fame. Home: 230 E. Woodward Boul. Office: Wright Bldg., Tulsa OK‡

CLIPPINGER, DONALD ROOP, educator; b. Dayton, O., Jan. 14, 1905; s. Walter G. and Sara (Roop) Clippinger; B.S., Otterbein Coll., 1925, LL.D., 1957; M.S., Ohio State U., 1926, Ph.D., 1936; m. Florence Vance, Aug. 30, 1927; children—Richard, Miriam Jo, William, Donald (dec.). Asst. prof. chemistry Otterbein Coll., 1926-28, Ohio U., 1928-36, asso. prof., 1936-42, prof. chemistry, 1942-67, chmn. dept. chemistry, 1946-51 dir. grad. Coll. 1951-53, dean grad. coll., 1953-65, prof. chemistry 1965-67. Pres. Athens (O.) City Board Edn., S.E. Ohio Sch. Board Assn., and Ohio Sch. Bd. Assn.; sec., editor proceedings Midwest Conf. on Grad. Study and Research, 1950-65; councillor Am. Chem. Soc. Fellow Ohio Acad. Sci. (exec. vice pres.); mem. Ohio Edn. Assn., Sigma Xi, Phi Kappa Phi, Phi Lambda Upsilon. Methodist. Author: Laboratory Program for General Chemistry, 1946, rev., 1954; Manual of Quantitative Analysis, 1948. Contbr. Handbook of Chemistry. Home: Athens OH Died Oct. 5, 1967; buried Greenville OH

CLOSE, CHARLES MOLLISON, ins. exec.; b. N.Y.C., Nov. 5, 1903; s. Charles M. and Carrie B. (Scott) C.; student pub. schs.; m. Marion B. Young, Apr. 24, 1926; children—Charles M. III, John C. With Home Ins. Co., 1921-24, N.Y. Fire Ins. Rating Orgn., 1925-26, Henderson Agy., Herkimer, N.Y., 1927-28; with Great Am. Ins. Co., N.Y.C., from 1928, successively asst. sec., sec., v.p., 1928-55, exec. v.p., from 1955; director Great American Insurance Company. Mem. Silver Bay Assn. (trustee). Mason. Clubs: Drug and Chemical (N.Y.C.) Glen Ridge Country. Home: Glen Ridge NJ Died Apr. 14, 1965; buried Mohawk Cemetery, Mohawk NY

CLOSE, JAMES WILLIAM, lawyer; b. Denver, Apr. 3, 1909; s. Henry Francis and Rose (Youk) C.; Ph.B., Regis Coll., Denver, 1931; LL.B., Cath. U. of Am., 1934; m. Jane Winburn, Dec. 29, 1934; children—Henry, Mary Jane, Betty Anne, Nancy Lou, Jeannie, John, Patricia. Admitted to D.C. bar, 1934, Ill. bar, 1944; counsel RFC, 1934-44; gen. counsel War Damage Corp., 1942-44; partner Wilson & McIlvaine, Chgo., from 1944; bd. directors of Hibbard, Spencer, Bartlett & Co., Evanston, Ill. Mem. Am., Ill., Chgo. bar assns. Home: Wilmette IL Died Mar. 3, 1972; buried All Saints Cemetery, Des Plaines IL

CLOSE, LYMAN WITHROW, steel co. exec.; b. Omaha, Mar. 25, 1892; s. Dorr Ralph and Helen (Withrow) C.; M.E., Armour Inst. Tech., 1915; m. Helen Caroline Englehart, Feb. 14, 1953; children—Alvin Ralph, Thomas Arthur, John Dorr. Tchr. YMCA sch., now Fenn Coll., Cleve., 1916-17; engr. Standard Parts Co., Cleve., 1917-19; chief engr. Book Bearing Co., 1919-25; v.p., dir. Toledo Pressed Steel Co., 1925-68. Trustee Flower Meml. Hosp., Toledo. Mem. Delta Tau Delta. Republican. Presbyn. Mason (K.T.). Clubs: Toledo, Kiwanis. Died May 1968.

CLOTHIER, ROBERT CLARKSON, educator; b. Phila., Jan. 8, 1885; s. Clarkson and Agnes (Evans) C.; ed. Haverford Sch., 1894-1903; Litt.B., Princeton, 1908, LL.D., 1932; LL.D., U. of Pittsburgh and Tusculum Coll., 1932, Dickinson Coll., 1933, New York Univ., 1935; Lafayette Coll., 1938; Litt.D., Temple U., 1934; LL.D. U. Del., 1950, U. State of N.Y., 1951, Rutgers U., 1952, University of Rhode Island, 1952; m. Natalie Wilson, June 24, 1916; children—Agnes Evans (Mrs. Charles P. Whitlock), Arthur Wilson (deceased), Robert C. With Curtis Publishing Co. Phila., 1910-17; v.p. The Scott Co., Philadelphia, 1918-23; asst. headmaster Haverford Sch., 1923-29; dean of men, U. Pitts., 1929-32, pres. Rutgers U., 1932-51, pres. emeritus, 1951-70. Dir. Mut. Benefit Life Ins. Co., Pub. Serv. Gas & Electric Co., Newark, Delaware and Bound Brook R.R. Company. Member Committee on Classification of Personnel, Washington, and A.E.F., World War I; commissioned lt. colonel. President of the New Jersey State Constitutional Conv. 1947. Mem. Dutch Reform Church. Clubs: Century Assn., University (N.Y. City and Phila.). Author: Personnel Management Haverford PA Died Mar. 1970.

CLOUCHEK, EMMA OLDS, Rep. nat. committeewoman; b. Carlton, Ore., Mar. 3, 1877; d. Nelson Harvey and Phebe (Livengood) Olds; grad. Oregon State Normal Sch., 1901; m. Dr. Henry Walker Clouchek, June 14, 1904. Teacher in pub. schools, Ore., 1894-1904. Republican nat. committeewoman for Idaho since 1931. Mem. bd. regents, Coll. of Idaho, Caldwell, Ida. County chmn. United Service Orgns. council; mem. bd. War Fund Drive; chmn. exec. com. Salvation Army; 3d vice pres. Idaho Pub. Health Assn. Mem. D.A.R. Mem. Order Eastern Star, Daughters of Nile. Clubs: Womens Business and Professional, Twentieth Century (Twin Falls). Home: 327 Fifth Av., E., Twin Falls ID*‡

CLOUD, JOHN HOFER, prof. physics; b. Clinton, Ill., Oct. 24, 1871; s. Albert D. and Anna (Hofer) C.; B.S., Valparaiso U., 1893, A.B., 1896; studied U. of Chicago; A.M., Johns Hopkins, 1917; Ph.D., Ind. U., 1921; m. Luemma F. Williams, of Athens, Ill., Aug. 16, 1899; children—Albert Williams, Arthur Franklin, Robert Rowland; m. 2d, Grace Williams, of Athens, Ill., Sept. 5, 1910. Prof. physics and mathematics, Valparaiso U., 1897-1917; prof. physics and head of dept., Oklahoma Agrl. and Mech. Coll. since 1920. Teacher of radio, U.S.A., at Ind. U., 1918. Mem. A.A.A.S., Okla. Acad. Science, Central Assn. Science and Math. Teachers, Am. Assn. Univ. Profs., Sigma Xi, Phi Kappa Phi, Alpha Sigma Delta, Alpha Epsilon, Phi Beta Pi. Democrat. Rationalist. Author: Five books on scientific subjects. Home: Stillwater OK‡

CLOUGH, MERRILL H., pub. co. exec.; b. Sharpsburg, Ia., Feb. 21, 1919; s. Raymond S. and Helen (King) C.; student Drake U., 1939-40, N.Y. U., 1941-42; B.B.A., U. Tex., 1948; m. Louise Henry, Nov. 24, 1940; children—Thomas N., Nancy J. Vice pres., controller Cowles Communications, Inc., N.Y.C., 1948-72, dir., 1967-72. Served to 1st lt. USAAF, 1943-45. Methodist. Clubs: Huntington Yacht; Lloyd Harbor (N.Y.) Yacht. Home: Huntington NY Died May 1972.

CLOUGH, PAUL WISWALL, physician, emeritus prof.; born Portage, Wis., Sept. 27, 1822; son Willoughby G. and Elsena (Wiswall) C.; B.S., Univ. of Wis., 1903; M.D., Johns Hopkins, 1907; m. Mildred Clark, Sept. 5, 1916; children—Paul Clark, Eleanor Wiswall. Resident physician Johns Hopkins Hosp., 1913-16, asso. prof. medicine, Johns Hopkins Univ., 1916-19; asso. prof. med. Univ. of Md., since 1923; asst prof. emeritus medicine, Johns Hopkins University asst. vis. physician and vis. physician Johns Hopkins Hosp., since 1921; physician in charge diagnostic clinic, Johns Hopkins Hosp., since 1928. Fellow A.C.P. Mem. Am. Soc. Clin. Investigation, Assn. Am. Physicians, Phi Beta Kappa, Alpha Omega Alpha, Sigma Xi. Acting editor Annals Internal Medicine, 1942-46. Author books including: Haematology and Animal Parasitology (with E. R. Stitt and Sara E. Branham) tenth edit., 1947. Home: 24 E. Eager St., Balt 2

CLOW, ALLAN BOWMAN, chem. mfr.; b. St. Paul, Mar. 14, 1906; s. Willard and Louise (Anderson) C.; A.B., Carleton Coll., 1928; M.C.S., Dartmouth, 1931; m. Esther del Valle, Oct. 26, 1933; children—Conchita, Mary Ann, James. With Am. Cyanamid Co., N.Y.C., 1933-68, successively dept. sales mgr., asst. to gen. mgr. Calco Chem. div., exec. dir. Lederle Labs. div., gen. mgr. Fine Chemicals div., gen. mgr. farm and home div., 1933-57, v.p. Am. Cyanamid Company, 1957-65, exec. v.p., 1965-68, also dir. Clubs: University (N.Y.C.); Bay Head (N.J.) Yacht; Manasquan River Golf. Home: Mantoloking NJ Died July 19, 1968.

CLUBB, MERREL DARE, educator; b. Chattanooga, Oct. 30, 1897; s. Merrel Dare and Lizzie Thompson (Graham) C.; B.A., Pomona Coll., 1920; Ph.D., Yale, 1924; m. Edith Josephine Jordan, June 22, 1920; children—Merrel Dare, William Graham, Roger Lane. Asst. prof. English Miami (Ohio) U., 1924-29; prof. English Texas Christian U., 1929-38; asst. prof. Stanford, 1933-34; prof. head dept. English Okla. Agrl. and Mech. Coll., 1938-46; prof. U. of Kan., 1946-70, chmn. dept. English, 1946-50; prof. U. of Texas, summers 1930, 35; writer music reviews Fort Worth (Texas) Star Telegram, 1930-38. Mem. Modern Lang. Assn. Am., Am. Assn. U. Profs., Phi Beta Kappa. Editor: Christ and Satan: An Old English Poem, 1925. Home: Lawrence KS Died Feb. 20, 1970.

CLUETT, SANFORD LOCKWOOD, civil and mechanical engr.; b. Troy, N.Y., June 6, 1874; s. Edmund and Mary Alice (Stone) C.; student Albany (N.Y.) Acad., 1889; grad. Troy Acad., 1894; C.E., Rensselaer Poly. Inst., 1898, D.Eng., 1952; D.Sc., Russell Sage Coll., 1958; m. Camilla E. Rising, Feb. 1916; children—Gregory Stone, Sanford Lockwood, Camilla Trent, Marvin Vaughan. With Walter A. Wood Mowing & Reaping Machine Co., Hoosick Falls, N.Y., successively as chief engr., asst. supt., v.p. and v.p. and gen. supt., 1901-19; with Cluett, Peabody & Co., Inc., Troy, N.Y., 1919-68, in charge engring. and research until 1944; dir. from 1921, vice pres. from 1927; trustee Troy Savings Bank; director Albany & Vermont R.R. Co., Saratoga & Schenectady Railroad Company. Member board directors Troy Orphan Asylum. Enlisted as private, Nat. Guard N.Y., 1897, later N.Y. Vol. Inf.,

Spanish Am. War; trans. to 1st U.S. Vol. Engrs., June 1898; promoted lt. and capt.; served in Porto Rican campaign; again with N.G.N.Y., 1904-17, advancing to maj. Signal Corps.; Reserve list, May 11, 1917. Designed one-horse and two-horse vertical lift mowing machines; steel work for Govt. locks on Big Sandy River, Kentucky, 1900; valves for St. Andrews Rapids locks, Manitoba; etc. Trustee, v.p. Rensselaer Poly. Inst. Received Modern Pioneer award N.A.M.; Longstreth medal Franklin Inst., Holley medal Am. Soc. M.E., 1952. Fellow Am. Numis. Soc., Am. Soc. M.E.; hon. mem. Rensselaer Soc., Soc. Engrs.; mem. N.Y. State Hist. Assn., Franklin Institute, Mil. Order of Foreign Wars, Society Colonial Wars, Founders and Patriots America, Sons of the Revolution, Army Ordnance Association, U.S. Naval Institute, Soc. Am. Mil. Engrs., U.S. Inst. for Textile Research, Sigma Xi, Chi Epsilon. Republican. Episcopalian. Clubs: Troy, Troy Country; Univ., New York Yacht (N.Y.C.); Bath and Tennis, Everglades (Palm Beach, Fla.). Inventor of Sanforized process, Clupak (extensible paper). Home: Palm Beach FL Died May 17, 1968; buried Troy NY

CLUETT, W. SCOTT, b. Williamstown, Mass., June 16, 1912; grad. Hotchkiss Sch., Williams Coll., 1935. Sr. v.p., dir. Drexel Harriman Ripley, Inc., N.Y.C.; v.p., dir. Middlebrook Farm, Inc. Served to maj. USAAC, 1942-46. Decorated Bronze Star. Mem. Investment Bankers Assn. Am., Nat. Assn. Securities Dealers (gov.). Clubs: Bond (gov.), University (N.Y.C.). Address: Wilton CT Died Oct. 25, 1971.

CLUFF, HARVEY H., lawyer; b. Provo City, Utah, Oct. 24, 1872; s. Samuel S. and Frances A., (Worsley) C.; Master of Accounts, Brigham Young U., Provo, Utah, 1895; LL.B., Highland Park Coll., Des Moines, Ia., 1901, LL.M., 1902 (1st prize, oratorical contest, 1901, 02); m. Freda Barnum, Oct. 11, 1900 (deceased); children—Bernice (Mrs. I. G. Bishop), Mrs. Frances A. Josephs; m. 2d, Matilda S. Roby, Aug. 31, 1929. Reared on farm; Mormon missionary, W.Va., Eastern Ky. 3 yrs.; worked way through college; admitted to Utah Bar, 1902; mem. firm Booth & Cluff, Provo, 1902-09; sec. State Bd. of Insanity, 1906-08 and 1912-16; dist. atty. 4th Jud. Dist., Utah, 1908-12; chmn. Rep. County Com., Utah County, 1917-20; attorney general of Utah, 2 terms, 1921-29; director Tantic Delmar Mining Co., N. Tintic Mining Company. Member Utah National Guard, 1917-21. Trustee Industrial Sch. of Utah, Deaf and Blind Sch. of Utah. Mem. Nat. Assn. Attys. Gen. (pres. 1924-25; chmn. exec. com.). Past grand master and past grand rep. I.O.O.F.; Elk. Home: 963 Wilson Ave. Office: 710 McIntyre Bldg., Salt Lake City UT

CLYDE, GEORGE DEWEY, gov. Utah; b. Springville, Utah, July 21, 1898; s. Hyrum Smith and Elenore Jane (Johnson) C.; B.S., Utah State U. Agr. and Applied Sci., 1921; M.S., U. Cal., 1923; m. Ora Packard, Sept. 10, 1919; children—Ned P., Ruth (Mrs. Elmer D. Landsaw), Bruce, Jerald Reid, Mary Ann. Cons. engr.; faculty Utah State U. Agr. and Applied Sci., 1923-45, dean Sch. Engring. 1935-45, dir. Engring. Exptl. Sta., 1939-45; chief div. irrigation engring. and water conservation Soil Conservation Service, Dept. Agr., 1945-53, chief engr., 1953-56, adv. com. soil and water conservation, 1956-72; gov. Utah, 1957-72. Mem. U.S. delegation 4th Pan-Am. Conf. on Agr., 1950. Dir. Utah Water and Power Bd.; commr. Interstate Streams for Utah; mem. Utah State Water Conservation Comm.; mem. Upper Colorado River Commn., Bear River Commn., Columbia River Commn., Pacific Interagency Com., Columbia Basin Interagency Com., Mo. Basin Interagency Com. Mem. Am. Soc. C.E., Nat. Reclamation Assn., Western Snow Conf. Mem. Ch. of Jesus Christ of Latter Day Saints. Clubs: Rotary (hon.), Kiwanis. Home: Salt Lake City UT Died Apr. 1972.

CLYDE, NORMAN ASA, explorer western mountains; b. Phila., Apr. 8, 1885; s. Charles and Isabelle (Purvis) C.; A.B., Geneva Coll., Beaver Falls, Pa., 1909, Sc.D., 1939; postgrad. U. Wis., 1910, U. Cal., 1911-13; postgrad. in English, U. Cal. at Berkeley, 1923-24, in edn. U. So. Cal., 1926. Tchr. high schs. N.D., Utah, Ariz., Cal., 1898-10; engaged in solitary mountaineering, exploring (over 1000 ascents, 200 1st ascents including new routes), 1910-72, in various mountain ranges and peaks including Sierra Nevadas (Cal.), Cascades (Wash. and Ore.) Selkirks (B.C., Can.), Canadian Rockies (Alta., B.C. and Yukon, Can.), Tetons (Wyo.), Colo. Rockies, Wasatch Mountains (Utah), Sawtooth Range (Ida.), Sierra Madre (So. Cal.), Mt. Whitney, North Palisade (both in Sierra Nevadas), Beartooth Range (Mont.), Wind River Range (Wyo.), Salmon Alps (Cal.), Sierra San Pedro Martir (Baja, Cal.); much individual exploratory climbing in Glacier Park, Mont. (36 peaks in 36 days), 1926; cons. A.C., U.S. Army, on various occasions; collector zool. specimens U. Cal.; guide, climbing leader Sierra Club base camp, summers; ascents with Sierra Club (Glacier Park Canadian Rockies), Seattle Mountaineers (Canadian Rockies, No. Cascades of Wash. State), Alpine Club Can. (Selkirks). Recipient Distinguished Service award Geneva Coll., 1962. Mem. Nat. Rifle Assn., Cal. Acad. Scis. (wildlife observer 1943-72). Clubs: Sierra (San Francisco); American Alpine; Appalachian (corr.). Expert on high altitude flora and fauna (Hudsonian and Arctic Alpine zones of Sierra

Nevada), geol. history and structure of mountain ranges of Western U.S., ski mountaineering. Classical scholar, linguist. Author: Close Ups of the Sierra, 1961; also over 300 articles on various phases of mountains, trout fishing, camping, wild life, other subjects, pub. in various mags., newspapers including Field and Stream, Touring Topics, Westward, Sierra Club Bull., Am. Alpine Jour., Nat. Motorist, Sports Afield. Made several rescues of lost mountain climbers, dead and alive, locating them by knowledge of the terrain, sometimes after other searchers had given up. Numerous mountain features in the Sierra named after him including Clyde's Minaret, Clyde's Spires, Clyde's Ledge, Clyde Meadow, Clyde Peak. Address: Inyo County CA Died Dec. 23, 1972.

CLYMER, R(EUBEN) SWINBURNE, author, physician; b. Quakertown, Pa., Nov. 25, 1878; s. Lewis and Emma (Stevenback) C.; M.D., D.O., Coll. of Medicine and Surgery, Chicago, 1902; m. Laura Edith Bowers, Dec. 30, 1898 (dec.); m. 2d, Gertrude Lucy Cosgrove, Nov. 9, 1932. Founder, Philos. Pub. Co., 1900, Royal Frat. Assn., Inc. 1909, Beverly Hall Corp., 1921, Beverly Hall Found., 1941, Confederation of Initiates, 1929; co-founder and dir. gen. La Federation Universelle des Ordres, Societes et Fraternites des Initiates, Internat., 1939; The Academy, Comparative Religion and Philosophy, 1941; dir. gen. Ch. of Illumination. Supreme Grand Master, Fraternitas Rosae Crucis, Priests and Princes of Melchizedek and Merged Occult Fraternities; Past Most Venerable Grand Master, Supreme Council Brotherhood of America. Mason (Scottish and York rites and allied bodies; Shriner); mem. Royal Order of Scotland, Red Cross of Constantine; hon. mem. Orden Constructores Masones (Pan-Am.); Respectable Logia, Rosa de America (Panama). Clubs: Lehigh Valley, Lehigh Country. Author books, from 1902, latest being: Prenatal Culture, 1950; Mastership, 1951; The Teachings of the Masters, 1952; Ritual, Church of Illumination, 1952; Interpretation of St. John, 1953; Christic Teachings, 1954; Occult Science—Hidden Forces, 1954, Philosophic Initiation, 1955; The Master Initiate, 1956; Hidden Teaching of the Initiate Masters, 1957; The Age of Treason, 1958; Nadoure, Prietess of the Magi, 1958; Your Health and Sanity, 1958; Philosophy of Immortality, 1959; Spiritual Initiation, 1961; The Coming Masters, 1961. Home: Quakertown PA Died June 1966.*

CLYNE, CHARLES F., lawyer; b. Maple Park, Ill., July 26, 1877; s. J. and Mary (Fitzgerald) C.; Ann Arbor High Sch.; LL.B., U. of Mich., 1902; unmarried. Began practice, Aurora, Ill., 1904; city atty., Aurora, 1906-11; spl. asst. atty. gen., Ill., 1912; mem. Ill. Ho. of Rep., 1913-14; U.S. atty. Northern Dist., Ill., 1914-23, conducting numerous Sherman anti-trust cases; apptd. by President as mem. Commn. Investigation and Preparation of Legislation Concerning U.S. Courts, 1923. Del. Dem. Nat. Conv., 1920. Mem. Am. Bar Assn. Democrat. Clubs: Union League, Iroquois. Home: 4194 Clarendon Av., Chicago IL‡

CLYNE, JAMES FRANCIS, JR., cement co. exec.; b. Bklyn., Mar. 1, 1927; s. James Francis and Mildred deS. (Cogan) C.; B.A. cum laude, U. Notre Dame, 1949; LL.B., N.Y. U., 1953, student Grad. Sch. Bus. Adminstrn., 1953-54; m. Eileen T. O'Shea, Aug. 5, 1950; children—James Francis III, Kathleen Ann, Michael Eugene, Patricia Eileen, Elizabeth Mary, Moira Jean. Admitted to N.Y. bar, 1954; with firm Chadbourne, Parke, Whiteside & Wolff, N.Y.C., 1953; with Lone Star Cement Corp., N.Y.C., 1953-—, asst. sec., 1958-61, corp. sec., 1961-—, gen. counsel, dir., officer subsidiaries. Served with USNR, 1945-46. Mem. Am. Soc. Corp. Secs., Shareholders Relations Soc. Home: Rockville Centre NY Died. Apr. 22, 1971; buried Holy Cross Cemetery, Brooklyn NY

COASH, LOUIS E., circuit judge; b. Saginaw, Mich., Jan. 1, 1904; s. Peter and Ida (Patterson) C.; student Alma Coll., 1922-24; LL.B., U. Detroit, 1927; m. Dorothy R. Rigney, Feb. 8, 1930; 1 dau., Mary Ann. Admitted to Mich. bar, 1927; practiced in Detroit, 1928-34, Lansing, Mich., 1934-41; municipal judge City of Lansing, 1941-45; circuit judge 30th Jud. Dist. Circuit, Mich., 1945-68. Mem. Ingham County (past pres.), Mich. bar assns., Mich. Judges Assn. (past pres.), Delta Theta Phi. Roman Catholic. Clubs: Lansing City, Lansing Press, Lions (Lansing). Home: Lansing MI Died Mar. 28, 1968.

COATE, ALVIN TEAGUE, business exec.; b. Dayton, O., Nov. 15, 1870; s. Abijah J. and Mary (Miles) C.; tutored by Prof. Jacob Kessler, Heidelberg Univ., 1892-96; m. Evelyn May Alexander, Apr. 15, 1896; 1 dau., Mary Miles (Mrs. Roy Evans Houtz). Founded Ins. Audit & Inspection Co., Indianapolis, Ind., 1901, pres. since 1901; recorded minister Soc. of Friends, 1928; a founder and trustee, Friends Fiduciary Corp., 1947. Del. World Council of Chs., Edinburgh, Scotland, 1937; chmn. bd. trustees, Friendsville (Tenn.) Acad., 1908-35; chmn. finance com. Quaker Hill Foundation; chmn. exec. com. Social Agencies (county); mem. exec. com. Ind. Council on Religion in Higher Edn., mem. exec. Com. Bd. Edn. of Five Years' Meeting of Friends, exec. com. Fed. Council of Chs. Mem. bd. Japanese Relocation Citizens' Com. Mem. Midwest Council on Internat. Relations (pres.), Am. Friends' Service Com. (dir.), John Herron Art Assn., Hoosier Art Salon. Republican. Mason (Scottish rite). Club: Columbia. Author: Beyond Democracy, The Johnson Lecture for Five Years' Meeting of Friends, 1940. Chmn. pub. bd. Five Years' Meeting of Friends since 1913. Home: 2451 Broadway, Indianapolis. Office: Hume Mansur, Bldg., Indianapolis 4 IN‡

COATES, ROBERT MYRON, writer, art critic; b. New Haven, Conn., Apr. 6, 1897; s. Frederick and Harriet (Davidson) C.; B.A., Yale, 1919; m. Elsa Kirpal, Feb. 3, 1927 (div. Jan. 1946); m. 2d, Astrid Peters, June 14, 1946. Mem. Internat. Art Critics Assn., Nat. Inst. Arts and Letters. Clubs: P.E.N., Century Assn. Author: The Eater of Darkness, 1929; The Outlaw Years, 1930; Yesterday's Burdens, 1933; All the Year Round, 1943; The Bitter Season, 1946; Wisteria Cottage, 1948; The Farther Shore, 1955; The Hour After Westerly, 1957; The View From Here, 1960; Beyond the Alps, 1961; The Man Just Ahead of You, 1963; South of Rome, 1965. Contbr. to Whither, Whither, a Symposium, 1930; The American Caravan IV, 1931; also articles and fiction to The New Yorker, others. Home: Old Chatham NY Died Feb. 1973.

COBB, BRUCE BENSON, ednl. sec.; born Whitewright, Tex., Sept. 28, 1874; s. John William and Eleanor Morelza (Durham) C.; A.B., U. of Tex., 1910, M.A., 1928; m. Ita Coulton Cobb, June 30, 1910. Teacher rural schs., Fannin County, Tex., 1893-95; prin. elementary sch., Denton, Tex., 1899-1900; teacher Latin, pvt. schs., Waxahachie, 1900-02, Wynnewood, Okla., 1903-05; supt. pub. schs. Gatesville, Tex., 1904-08, Marshall, 1910-15, Waco, 1915-35. Sec.-treas. Tex. State Teachers Assn., 1935-50. Member N.E.A. Tex. State Teachers Assn., Horace Mann League, Phi Beta Kappa. Democrat. Presbyterian. Home: Claude TX‡

COBB, CHARLES WELLINGTON, lawyer; b. Gilroy, Cal., Aug. 15, 1871; s. Robert and Anna (McGregor) C.; pub. and high schs., Cal.; San Jose (Cal.) Law Sch.; m. Mariedna Snell, of Berkeley, Cal., June 30, 1910. Admitted to Cal. bar, 1897; mem. firm of Cobb & Rea, San Jose, 1897-1906; removed to San Francisco, 1906, and mem. firm of Heney (Francis Joseph, q.v.) & Cobb, 1906-11; spl. counsel for State of Cal., engaged in San Francisco graft prosecutions, 1906-09; apptd. by President Taft asst. atty. gen. of U. S., May, 1911, and assigned to Dept. of Interior, retired, Sept. 15, 1913. Republican. Methodist. Clubs: Bohemian (San Francisco), Sainte Claire (San Jose). Home: 10 Lafayette Sq., Washington‡

COBB, DUDLEY MANCHESTER, JR., physician, surgeon; b. Cleve., Aug. 13, 1907; s. Dudley Manchester and Maude (Van Wyck) C.; B.S., Andrews U., 1935; M.D., Loma Linda U., 1937; m. Alethea May Usborne, Aug. 20, 1929 (dec. Apr. 1971); 1 son, Dudley Manchester III. Rotating intern White Meml. Hosp., Los Angeles, 1937-38; practice in Los Angeles, 1937-72; sr. staff mem. Cal. Luth. Hosp., 1947-72, chmn. gen. practice sect., 1963-64; sr. cons. staff Resthaven Psychiat. Hosp., 1963-67; med. dir. Los Angeles County Sheriff's Dept., 1970-72. Mem. area 5186 FCDA, 1946; chmn. med. div. Los Angeles Community Chest, 1959; mem. exec. bd. Cancer Prevention Soc., 1958-67, Diplomate Nat. Bd. Med. Examiners. Mem. Am. (chmn. sect. gen. practice 1964-65, chmn. physicians adv. com. TV, radio and motion pictures 1963-65, alternate del. 1961-68, del. 1970), Cal. (del. 1960-63, 67-68, 70-72, chmn. uniform ins. claims com. 1960, 63, 67-68, mem. reference com. C, 1971), Los Angeles County (pres. sect. gen. practice 1956, councillor 1957, 1st pres. met. area dist. 1, 1959, chmn. cancer quackery com. 1957-59) med. assns., Am. (chmn. TV, radio and motion pictures subcom. 1961-65, del.), Cal. (pres. 1968-69, ho. of dels., bd. dirs. acads. gen. practice, Cal. Physicians Service (trustee 1957-63, exec. com. 1957-63, chmn. med. Policy com. 1959-61, chmn. editorial com. 1962), Alumni Assn. Loma Linda U. Sch. Medicine (pres. 1971-72), Los Angeles World Affairs Council, Los Angeles C. of C., Res. USPHS Assn. Ret. Surgeons (life), Nat. Rifle Assn. (life), Navy League, Clubs: Jonathan, Breakfast, Town Hall, Press, Los Caballeros (charter) (Los Angeles). Home: Inglewood CA Died Oct. 28, 1972.

COBB, JOHN ROBERT, orthopedic surgeon; b. N.Y.C., Feb. 28, 1903; s. Robert S. and Winifred A. (Powers) C.; A.B., Brown U., 1925: grad. study Harvard, 1925-26; M.D., Yale, 1930, Med. Sc.D., Columbia, 1936; m. Louise W. Tower, Sept. 3, 1932; children—Joan, Robert Tower, Allen Tower. Surg. intern, advancing to acting resident orthopedic surgery New Haven Hosp., 1930-34; asst. attending orthopedic surgeon to attending orthopedic surgeon Hosp. for Special Surgery, 1939-64, consultant ortnopedic surgery, from 1964; asst. vis. orthopedic surgeon to vis. orthopedic surgeon Sea View Hospital, S.I., 1937-64; assistant vis. orthopedist, Willard Parker Hosp., 1946-48, asso. vis. orthopedist, 1948-55; asso. attending surgeon in orthopedics N.Y. Hosp., from 1951; orthopedic cons. Eastern N.Y. Hosp., St. Charles Hosp., Port Jefferson, N.Y., Castle Point V.A. Hosp., Beacon, N.Y.; teaching fellow orthopedic surgery Hosp. for Ruptured and Crippled, 1934-39; adj. prof. dept. orthopedic surgery, fractures, N.Y. Polyclinic Med. Sch. and Hosp., 1946-48, prof. orthopedic surgery, from 1948, clin. instr. orthopedic surgery Columbia U. Coll. Phys. and Surg., 1936-49; asst. prof. clin. surgery in orthopedics Cornell U. Med. Sch., 1951-57, asso. prof. clin. surgery (ortho.), from 1957. Fellow N.Y. Acad. Medicine; mem. World, Am. med. assns., Association Am. Medical Colleges, Am. Orthopedic Assn., Am. Acad. Orthopedic Surgeons, N.Y. State, Co. med. socs., Sociedade Brasileira de Ortopedia e Traumatologia (hon.), Societe Internationale de Chirurgie Orthopedique et de Traumatologie, Mass. Soc. Mayflower Descendants, Am. Geriatrics Soc., Am. Medical Writers Assn., Alpha Omega Alpha. Address: Cornwall-on-Hudson NY Died Mar. 24, 1967.

COBB, LLOYD JOSEPH, lawyer; b. New Orleans, July 19, 1904; s. William Holmes and Katherine Mary (Salter) C.; LL.B., Tulane U., 1924; m. Mireille LeBreton, 1934; 1 dau., Mary. Admitted to La. bar, 1924; asso. Milling, Godchaux, Saal & Milling, 1924-26; practiced in New Orleans, 1928-72; partner firm Cobb & Wright, 1949-72; asst. to gen. counsel Pan Am. Petroleum Corp., 1926-28, gen. counsel, 1928, and to successor firm Pan Am. So. Corp., 1948-72; founder Marydale Products Co., Inc.; pres. New Orleans Internat. Trade Mart. Recipient Thomas A. Cunningham award, 1952; hon. consul Dominican Republic, 1956, 57. Club: Internat. House (pres. 1949-51). Pioneered dehydration sweet potatoes for cattle feed, for food for mil. use, World War II; developer model grassland farming operation Marydale Farm nr. St. Francisville, La., 1944. Home: New Orleans LA Died Nov. 27, 1972.

COBLEIGH, WILLIAM MERRIAM, dean emeritus of engring., Montana State Coll.; b. Haverstraw, N.Y., Sept. 7, 1872; s. William and Julia Adelaide (Merriam) C.; E.M., School of Mines, College of Montana, 1894; A.M., Columbia University, 1899; m. Esther Rose Cooley, August 7, 1901; children—Winifred Merriam (wife of Dr. Robert K. Curry), Arthur Cooley (dec.), Lois Esther (Mrs. William H. McCall, Jr.), Norman Blake (dec.). Instr. chemistry, Mont. State Coll., 1894-99, asst. prof., 1899-1902, prof., 1902-15, prof. chemical engineering, 1915-42, dean of engineering, 1929-42, acting pres., 1942-43, dean emeritus of engineering since 1943. Director division of water and sewage, Montana State Board of Health, 1910-22, cons. engr. since 1923; state chemist Mont. Oil Commn., 1919-29. Fellow A.A.A.S.; mem. Am. Inst. of Chem. Engrs., Mont. Soc. of Engrs., Soc. for Promotion of Engring. Edn. (council 1933-35), Am. Chem. Soc., Am. Water Works Assn., Newcomen Soc., Tau Beta Pi, Alpha Chi Sigma, Phi Kappa Phi, Sigma Xi, Kappa Sigma. Republican. Presbyterian. Mason. Clubs: Chamber of Commerce, Kiwanis, Bozeman MT‡

COCHRAN, ARCHIBALD PRENTICE, metal fabricator; b. Louisville, Mar. 28, 1898; s. Heywood and Margaret (Lee) C.; B.S., Mass. Inst. Tech., 1920; m. Polly Zimmer, May 5, 1936; children—Polly Walker, Margaret Lee. Workman Reynolds Metal Co. (formerly U.S. Foil Co.), Louisville, 1920-39, v.p., 1934; pres. Cochran Foil Co., 1939-70, also dir.; pres. and dir. Anaco da Aluminum Co.; chmn. bd. Anaconda Am. Brass Co.; dir. Anaconda Wire & Cable Co., Spindletop Research Inc., Kentuckiana TV, Inc., First Nat. Bank, Ky. Trust Co., First Kentucky Co., Louisville Cement Co.; regional dir. Liberty Mutual Ins. Co. Trustee U. Louisville; bd. dirs., past pres. YMCA. Mem. Aluminum Assn. (pres., dir.), C. of C. (pres., dir. 1954). Episcopalian. Clubs: University (N.Y.C.); Country, Pendennis, River Valley, Wynn-Stay. Home: KY Died May 2, 1970; buried Cave Hill Cemetery, Louisville KY

COCHRAN, HOMER PIERCE, banker; b. Plainfield, N.J., Sept. 11, 1906; s. Henry J. and Nannette (Pierce) C.; student Princeton, 1925-29; m. Elisabeth Nash, March 14, 1930; children—Fergus, Thomas, James. With Scudder, Stevens & Clark, 1929-31, Fed. Res. Bank of N.Y., 1931-35; with Morgan Guaranty Trust Co., N.Y.C. (merger of J.P. Morgan & Co. and Guaranty Trust Co.), 1935-69, asst. v.p., 1946-50; v.p., 1950-65, sr. v.p., 1965-69; dir. Vulcan Materials Co.; trustee Franklin Savs. Bank, Provident Loan Soc. Presbyn. Home: Plainfield NJ Died Feb. 8, 1969.

COCHRAN, JAMES HARVEY, educator; b. Abbeville, S.C., Sept. 14, 1913; s. Harvey Nickles and Leona (Greene) C.; B.S., Clemson A. and M. Coll., 1935; M.S., Ia. State Coll., 1936, Ph.D., 1946; m. Mildred Viola Batson, Aug. 28, 1940; children—Andrew, Sandra, Jennifer. Research entomologist E. I. DuPont De Nemours & Co., Wilmington, Del., 1938-42, 46-47; asso. entomologist S.C. Expt. Sta. in charge fruit and nut research, 1947-53; head entomology and zoology dept., prof., state entomologist Clemson Coll., 1953-69. Served from 2d lt. to maj., AUS, 1942-46. Mem. S.C. Entomol. Soc. (pres. 1955), S.C. Acad. Sci., Entomol. Soc. Am., S.C. Pest Control Assn., Sigma Xi, Alpha Zeta, Phi Kappa Phi, Gamma Sigma Delta (pres. chpt. 1961). Kiwanian. Home: Clemson SC Died May 9, 1969; buried Upper Long Cane Cemetery, Abbeville SC

COCHRAN, JEAN CARTER, author; b. Mendham, N.J., Nov. 24, 1876; d. Israel Williams and Anne (Carter) C.; ed. Miss Dana's Sch.; unmarried. Mem. Authors' League America, League of Women Voters, D.A.R. Presbyn. Club: Monday Afternoon. Author: The Rainbow in the Rain, 1912; Foreign Magic, 1919; The Bells of the Blue Pagoda, 1922; Church Street, 1923. Contbr. series of articles on Chinese Women, etc., to the Outlook. Home: Plainfield NJ‡

COCHRANE, F(RANCIS) DOUGLAS;, b. Prides Crossing, Mass., June 28, 1877; s. Alexander and Mary Russell (Sullivan) C.; prep. edn. Groton (Mass.) Sch.; A.B., Harvard, 1899; m. Ramelle McKay Frost, of Charleston, S.C., Dec. 17, 1908; children—Alexander, Mary McKay, Ramelle, F. Douglas. Began as clk. with Stone & Webster, 1900; with Eastern Exploration Co., 1903-06; then with Cochrane Chem. Co.; founder Cochrane, Harper & Co., investment bankers; later chmn. bd. N.E. Oil Refining Co. Home: 257 Commonwealth Av., Boston MA*‡

COCKE, WILLIAM RUFFIN COLEMAN, lawyer; b. Montgomery, Ala., Dec. 31, 1884; s. William Ruffin Coleman and Clara Vernon (Pollard) C.; student Episcopal High School, Virginia, 1898-1901, Va. Mil. Inst., 1902-04, U. Va., 1904-09; m. Alice Watts DuBose, Oct. 7, 1909; children—William Ruffin Coleman, Breckinridge DuBose (dec.), (twins) Dudley DuBose and Alice Barraud (Mrs. Edward Howard Goodwin). In gen. practice law, Seattle, 1909-13, Birmingham, 1913-29; mem. firm Cabiness, Johnston & Cooke, representing railroads and other utilities and industrial concerns; gen. counsel Seaborad Air Line Ry. Co., 1929-30, counsel for receivers, 1930-46; mem. firm, Williams, Cocke, Worrell & Kelly. Member of Am., Va., Norfolk and Portsmouth (pres. 1954) bar assns., Am. Law Inst., Kappa Alpha, Phi Delta Phi. Democrat. Clubs: Princess Anne Country, Virginia. Home: Norfolk VA Died Mar. 12, 1967; buried Bremo Bluff VA

COCKRELL, ROBERT SPRATT, lawyer; b. Livingston, Ala., Jan. 22, 1866; s. Augustus William and Susan (Spratt) C.; B.A., U. of Va., 1887, M.A., 1888, LL.B., 1891; m. Courtney, d. late Gov. David S. Walker, of Florida, Oct. 28, 1903; children—Elizabeth, William, Robert, Caroline. Admitted to Fla. bar, 1891; justice Supreme Court of Fla., Dec. 1, 1902-Jan., 1917; resumed practice in firm Cockrell & Cockrell, Jacksonville, Fla.; retired prof. law, U. of Fla. Mem. Phi Delta Theta, Phi Kappa Phi, Phi Delta Phi, Phi Beta Kappa. Home: Gainesville FL*‡

COCKS, ORRIN GIDDINGS, social service; b. Augusta, Mich., May 12, 1877; s. Charles Willets and Orpha Pelton (Ives) C.; A.B., Union U., 1898, D.D., from same, 1928; B.D., Union Theological Sem., 1901; post-grad. work, Columbia; m. Evelyn G. O'Loughlin, June 27, 1908;children—Orrin Giddings, Robert Stuart, Laura Wilder, Mary Ives. Ordained Presbyn. ministry, 1901; asst. pastor Central Ch., Brooklyn, 1901-02; pastor and asso. pastor, Sea and Land Ch., New York, 1902-08 (trustee 1908-21); service sec. New York Fedn. of Chs., 1908-14; advisory sec. Nat. Bd. of Review of Motion Pictures, 1914-22. Sec. Nat. Commn. for Better Films, 1917-22. War work with Commn. on Training Camp Activities and War Camp Community Service, 1917-18. Awarded Silver Beaver, Boy Scouts of America, 1937. Dir. Boy Scouts of America, Bd. of Edn. (South Orange, N.J.), 1st Presbyn. Ch., Wellsboro, Pa. Mem. Phi Beta Kappa, Kappa Alpha. Mason. Moderator Northumberland Presbytery, 1936. Lecturer. Author: The Social Evil and Methods of Treatment, 1911; Engagement and Marriage, 1912; also many pamphlets, pub. addresses on sex questions and Wellsboro PA‡

CODD, LEO A., editor; b. Balt., Apr. 20, 1895; s. John and Amelia (Dittmar) C.; A.B., Loyola, 1916; A.M. Georgetown U., 1923, LL.B., 1922, LL.M., 1923, L.H.D., 1964; m. Gertrude Jane Callahan, Dec. 27, 1919. Asst. sec. Am. Ordnance Assn., 1923, sec., 1928, exec. v.p., 1940-64; editor Ordnance mag., 1928-65, contbg. editor, 1945-71, instr., Georgetown Coll., 1917, Cyrus Fogg Brackett lectr., Princeton, 1937. Served as chemist, Ordnance Dept., U.S. Army, World War 1; exec. asst. to chief of ordnance, AUS, World War II; capt., Ordnance Res., 1920, col. 1943-71. Decorated Legion of Merit. Mem. D.C., Md. bar assns. Roman Catholic. Clubs: Army and Navy (Washington); University (N.Y.). Author: American Industry and the National Defense, 1937. Lectr. in U.S., Can. and Eng. Home: Washington DCDied Sept. 4, 1971; buried Oak Hill Cemetery, Washington DC

CODDINGTON, HERBERT GUIBORD, clergyman; b. Cazenovia, N.Y., Feb. 6, 1865; s. Rev. Wellesley Perry (S.T.D.) and Louisa (Guibord) C.; A.B., Syracuse, 1886, D.D., 1905, LL.B., 1914; Gen. Theol. Sem., 1886-88; m. Leone Adelle Fitch, Dec. 12, 1888 (died Apr. 1930); 1dau., Dorothy (wife of Colonel H. S. Robertson); m. 2d, Mrs. Cora Willard Frederick, Dec. 29, 1931. Deacon, 1888, priest, 1889, P.E. Ch.; rector St. John's Ch., Marcellus, N.Y., 1888-91, Grace Ch., Syracuse, 1891-1931, rector emeritus of Grace Church since 1931. Established St. Philip's Ch., Syracuse, 1896, St. John's Ch., Phoenix, N.Y., 1903; exam. chaplain, Diocese Central N.Y., 1909-37, mem. standing com., 1920-36, chmn. 1930-36; chaplain of Hosp. of Good Shepherd, Syracuse, N.Y., 1906-29; mem. bd. trustees St. John's Mil. Sch., 1893-1920; dep. Gen. Conv., 1904-19, 28. Mem. Nat. Hist. Assn., N.Y. State Hist. Association, New England Historic Genealogical Society, Onodaga Co. Hist. Assn. (past pres.), Church Hist. Society (Episcopal), Garrett (Md.) County Hist. Soc., Archaeol. Inst. America, Izaak Walton League America, S.A.R. (N.Y. State chaplain, 1941-48), A.A.A.S., Phi Beta Kappa, Psi Upsilon. Mason. Republican. Clubs: University Automobile, Carlowden Golf and Country. Author: The Coddington Family, 1907; Coddington Records, 1920; Coddington Records No. 2, 1930. Miscellaneous Addresses. Home: 88 Dayan St., Lowville NY‡

CODDINGTON, MERRILL FRANKLIN, state supt. schs.; b. Parker, S.D., Sept. 11, 1901; s. William Stewart and Edna (Smith) C.; B.A., Dakota Wesleyan U., 1924; M.A., U. S.D., 1942; Doctor of Education, Sioux Falls College, 1960; m. Evelyn Squier, Aug. 3, 1927; children—William Squier, Kenneth Earl. Teacher in South Dakota, from 1926-58; speech instr. Pierre (S.D.) Sr. High Sch., 1926-31; supt. schs., Tulare, Letcher, then Centerville, S.D., 1931-58; state supt. pub. instrn., Pierre, S.D., 1958-67. Named hon. state farmer S.D. State Future Farmers Am., 1959. Mem. N.E.A., S.D. Ednl. Assn., Hickory Stickers (chmn. 1947), S.D. Am. Bapt. Conv. (pres. 1948-49), Baptist. Mason, Rotarian. Home: Pierre SD Died Jan 20, 1967; buried Parker SD

CODE, JAMES A., JR., telephone co. exec., ret. army officer; b. San Francisco, Jan. 17, 1893; s. James Arthur and Katherine (Shaw) C.; B.S., U.S. Mil. Acad., 1917; M.S., Yale, 1920, E.E., 1933; postgrad. Ohio State U., 1920-23, U. Cal., 1934-38; m. Isabelle Elizabeth Black, Jan. 17, 1929. Commd. 2d lt., C.A.C., U.S. Army, 1917, and advanced to capt., 1930; maj. S.C., 1932, lt. col., 1940, col., 1941; brig. gen., dep. chief signal officer, 1942, maj. gen., asst. chief signal officer, 1942-45; chief signal officer, ETO (France), 1945; ret. 1945. Chmn. bd. Telephone Services, Inc.; dir., v.p. Asso. Tel. & Tel. Co. (Wilmington, Del.); chief exec. Gary Group; v.p., dir. Anglo-Canadian Telephone Co., Automatic Elec. Co. (1946), Internat. Automatic Elec. Corp., Pan-Am. Tel. & Tel. Co., Continental Telephone Co., Dominican Dir. Co., Can., Tex., Home and Citizens Telephone Cos., Allied Syndicate, Inc., Gen. and Telephone Investments, Inc., Ohio Consol., Ill. Telephone Co.; v.p., dir. Gary Services and Investment Co., Tel. Bond & Share Co., Linwood Investment Co., Antel Services, Ltd., Asso. Telephone Services Ltd.; dir. various other telephone cos.; v.p., trustee Pt. Roberts & Gulf Telephone Co.; cons. Automatic Electric Co., Diablo Labs., 1963, Lenkurt Electric Co., 1959. Decorated Bronze Star medal, D.S.M.; Croix de Guerre, L'Ordre de la Legion d'Honneur (France), Commandeur de l'Ordre de la Couroune (Belgium). Asso. mem. Am. Inst. E.E.; sr. mem. Inst. Radio Engrs.; mem. Armed Forces Commn., Am. Soc. Legion of Honor, West Point Soc., Yale Alumni Assn., Army Athletic Assn., Assn. Grads. U.S.M.C., Am. Signal Corps Assn., Am. Legion, Mil. Order of World Wars, S.A.R., Scabboard and Blade, Pi Tau, Pi Sigma. Republican. Episcopalian. Clubs: Olympic; Army and Navy; Lake Shore: South Shore Country; Chicago; University. Address: Palo Alto CA Died Oct. 29, 1971.

CODEL, MARTIN, publisher; b. Duluth, Minn., May 18, 1902; s. Maurice and Sarah C.; A.B., U. of Mich., 1924; post-grad. work 1924-25; m. Ella April, July 1, 1927; children—Sureva (Mrs. Paul Y. Seligson), Martha, Nancy (dec.), Richard. Began career as reporter for the Duluth News-Tribune, 1917-18, Hibbing (Minn.) Tribune, 1918-21; U. of Mich. corr. Detroit Journal, 1921-22, Detroit News, 1922-25; with Asso. Press, New York, 1925-26, U.S. Daily, Washington, D.C., 1926-28, N. Am. Newspaper Alliance, 1928-30; organizer, 1930, and mgr. Radio News Bur.; founder, 1931, and pub. until 1944 of Broadcasting Magazine; dir. of information for Mediterranean Area for American Red Cross 1943; founder and publisher Television Digest and Electronics Reports, 1945-59; consultant on television and radio, 1959-73. Member advisory com. Inst. for Edn. by Radio and TV, Ohio State U. Surveyed African TV potentials, RCA, 1960; surveyed European, Latin America TV for Time-Life, 1961-62, television in Asia, 1963, Europe, 1964-66; consultant to various organizations on foreign radio-TV Adviser U. Wis. Hist. Soc. Asso. I.R.E.; mem. Phi Sigma Delta, Sigma Delta Chi. Clubs: Nat. Press, Overseas Writers. Author: Radio and Its Future, 1930. Home: Lewes DE Died Mar. 20, 1973.

CODMAN, EDMUND DWIGHT, lawyer; b. Boston, Dec. 2, 1864; s. Robert and Catherine C. (Hurd) C.; A.B., Harvard, 1886; m. Annie M. Briggs, of Boston, June 21, 1898. Admitted to Mass. bar, 1894, and since practiced in Boston. Home: 141 Beacon St. Office: 38 Kilby St. Boston MA*‡

COE, ALBERT BUCKNER, clergyman; b. Henderson, N.C., Apr. 16, 1888; s. Samuel Walker and Laura (Buckner) C.; A.B., Western Md. Coll., Westminster, 1909; B.D., Yale Divinity Sch., 1922; student summer sessions Johns Hopkins Univ, and Cambridge (Eng.) University; D.D., Yankton (S.D.) College, 1930, Western Maryland College, 1942, Yale, 1955; m. Katharine Chalmers, June 21, 1921; children—Chalmers, Buckner, Anstey. Pastor Broadway Winterhill Congl. Ch., Somerville, Mass., 1922-25, Second Congl. Ch., Waterbury, Conn., 1925-30, First Congl. Ch., Oak Park, Ill., 1930-49; pres. Mass. Congl. Conf. and Missionary Soc., 1949-58. Mem. exec. com. Gen. Council Congl. Christian Chs., 1936-42; dir. Chicago Congl. Union, 1931-49; mem. Federal Council Commn. on Bases for Just and Durable Peace; del. to first assembly of World Council of Churches, Holland, 1948, 2d assembly, Evanston, Ill., 1954, Internat. Congretationa Council; St. Andrews, Scotland, 1953; past pres. Ch. Fedn. Greater Chicago; president, Mass. Council of Churches, 1955-57; mem. executive council United Church of Christ. Trustee Andover-Newton Sem., Talladega (Alabama) College, Berea (Kentucky) College, Lady Doak College, India. Served as lieutenant of artillery, U.S. Army, in France and Germany, World War I. Moderator Ill. State Conf. of Congl. Christian Ch., 1944-46, Gen. Council Congl. Christian Chs. in U.S.A., 1954-56. Mem. Congl. Christian Deputation to Missionary Work, India, Near East, 1945-46. Club: Congl. (Boston). Author: Born For Victory; Let Us Pray, 1952. Home: Columbus OH Died Feb. 21, 1970.

COE, WESLEY ROSWELL, biologist; b. Middlefield, Conn., Nov. 11, 1869; s. Henry Seth and Hannah (Bailey) C.; grad. Conn. Agrl. Coll., 1888, Meriden (Conn.) High Sch., 1889; Ph.B., Sheffield Scientific School (Yale), 1892, Ph.D., 1895; D.Sc. (hon.) Yale, 1947; investigator University of Wurzburg, 1895-96, Naples, 1896; married Charlotte Eliza Bush, July 25, 1905. Assistant in biology, Sheffield Scientific School, 1892-95; instructor biology, Yale University, 1895-1901, assistant prof. comparative anatomy, 1901-07, prof. biology, 1907-38, prof. emeritus since 1938; curator zool. collections, Peabody Mus., 1914-26. Research associate, Scripps Institute of Oceanography. Mem. sci. expedns. to Alaska. Fellow A.A.A.S. (v.p.; chmn. Sec. F, 1930); mem. Am. Soc. Naturalists, Am. Soc. Zoologists (pres. 1940), Am. Assn. Anatomists, Am. Genetic Society, N.Y. Zool. Soc., Conn. Acad. Arts and Scis. (fellow), San Diego Hist. Soc. (pres. 1946-47, pres., 1947-48). Has written over 100 monographs and papers on biol. and anat. subjects, chiefly on morphology and embryology of invertebrates, regeneration, and change of sex in animals. Asso. editor Am. Jour. of Science, 1917-44. Journal of Morphology, 1928-30. Address: Osborn Zoological Laboratory, Yale University, New Haven CT‡

COE, WILLIAM ROGERS, found. exec.; b. N.Y.C., Mar. 22, 1901; s. William Robertson and Mai Huttleston (Rogers) C.; student U.S. Naval Acad., 1924; LL.D., U. Wyo, 1956; m. Clover Simonton, Mar. 31, 1923; children—William Robertson, II, Michael Douglas. With J.A. Sisto & Co., N.Y.C., 1923-24; r.r. security analyst Nat. City Co. of N.Y.C., 1923-34; head r.r. buying dept. Harriman Ripley & Co. (formerly Brown, Harriman & Co.), 1934-41; v.p., dir. treas. Va. Ry. Co., N.Y.C., 1942-56, chmn. exec. com., 1956-60; pres. Planting Fields Found.; pres., trustee Coe Found. Clubs: Piping Rock (L.I.): Seawanhaka-Corinthian Yacht. Home: Oyster Bay NY Died May 26, 1971.

COESTER, ALFRED, univ. prof.; b. Bridgeport, Conn., Sept. 30, 1874; s. Charles and Belinda (Whitney) C.; A.B., Harvard, 1896; A.M., Ph.D., 1905; student U. of Berlin, 1894-95; m. Belle Haven, July 7, 1898 (now dec.); m. 2d, Amalie Bostelman, September 15, 1939. Teacher Commercial High Sch., Brooklyn, N.Y., 1905-20; mem. faculty Stanford U., since 1920, prof. Spanish-Am. lit. since 1928. Spl. investigator U.S. Dept. of State in Chile, Argentina, Brazil, during World War. Decorated Cavalier Order of Isabel the Catholic. Corr. mem. Academia Hispano-Americana de Ciencias y Artes (Cadiz, Spain), Academia de Bellas Artes (Valladolid, Spain). Academia Nacional de la Historia (Buenos Aires), Colombian Academy of Letters. Mexican Academy of Letters, U.S. del. to celebration of 4th centenary founding of Bogota, 1938. Mem. Hispanic Soc. America, Am. Assn. Teachers of Spanish (sec.-treas. 1917-26), Modern Lang. Assn. America. Pan-American Soc. (San Francisco Br.). Republican. Clubs: Harvard (N.Y. City). Author: A Spanish Grammar. 1912; The Literary History of Spanish America, 1916, 2d edit., 1928, translated into Spanish, 1929; A Year of Spanish, 1930; A Tentative Bibliography of The Belles—Letters of The Argentine Republic, 1933; Argentine Nationality; Its Political and Literary Expression 1949. Editor: Cuentos de la America Espanola, 1920; An Anthology of the Modernista Movement in Spanish America, 1924; La Hechizada, by F. Santivan, 1929. Contbr. articles to Hispania, offical jour. Am. Assn. Teachers of Spanish; editor of Hispania, 1926-41. Home: 616 Foothill Rd. Stanford University, CA‡

COFER, JOHN DALY, lawyer; b. Gainesville, Tex., Mar. 11, 1898; s. Robert Emmet and Corinne (Able) C.; A.B., U. Tex., 1919, LL.B., 1921; M. George Hume, Sept. 28, 1922; children—George Hume, Patricia (Mrs. Frances A. Brogan, dec.). Admitted to Tex. bar, 1921, practiced in Austin, 1921-71; spl. justice, Supreme Ct., Tex., 1928; spl. counsel Anti-Trust Litigation, Tex., 1931-38. Mem. Nat. Democratic Advisory Committee Tex., 1952-56; chief counsel United States Senate Preparedness Investing Sub-Committee, 1956. Entered the U.S. Army, 1942; mil. gov., Fuerth-Rothenburg, Bavaria, 1945-46; member Gen. Mil. Govt. Ct., Bavaria, 1945-46. Charter mem. World Peace through Law Center. Awarded Ribbon, World War I; 2 Theatre. Occupation ribbons; 4 Battle Stars, Bronze Star medal, World War II. Mem. Am., Tex., Travis Co. bar assns., Delta Sigma Rho, Sigma Nu. Austin TX Died Feb. 28, 1971; buried Oakwood Cemetery, Austin TX

COFFEE, HARRY BUFFINGTON, ex-congressman; b. Sioux County, Neb., Mar. 16, 1890; s. Samuel Buffington and Mary Elizabeth (Tisdale) C.; A.B., U. of Neb., 1913; m. Katharine Newbranch Douglas, Nov. 30, 1935. Began in real estate and ins. business, Chadron, Neb.; organized Coffee Cattle Co., Inc., 1915, pres. until 1950; mem. 74th to 77th Congresses 5th Neb. Dist. Chmn. bd. Union Stock Yards Co. of Omaha; pres. South Omaha Terminal Ry. Co. Served as 2d lt. AS, U.S. Army, World War I. Home: Omaha NE Died. Oct. 1972.

COFFEN, T. HOMER, physician; b. Minneapolis, Minn., July 16, 1877; s. Charles William and Emma F. (Cook) C.; B.S., Penn Coll., Oskaloosa, Ia., 1901, M.S., 1904; M.D., Johns Hopkins Univ., 1906; post grad. study, Vienna, 1913-23, 31, Berlin, 1913, Paris, 1913, London, 1923-31; m. Lena West, Dec. 17, 1906; children—Charles West, Margaret (Mrs. Margaret C. White). Instr. in pathology and medicine, N.Y. Post-Grad. Med. Sch. and Hosp., 1906-13; instr. clin. pathology Cornell Med. Sch., New York, N.Y., 1909-13; attending physician, Out Patients Dept., 2d div., Bellevue Hosp., New York, 1909-13; instr. in medicine Univ. of Ore. Med. Sch., 1914-18, in charge Dept. of Medicine, 1924-29, clin. prof. of med. since 1924. Served as capt. med. corps U.S. Army, 1918-19. Fellow Am. Coll. of Physicians (gov. 1924-40, regent 1940-46, 3d vice pres, since 1946), A.M.A. Mem. Am. Heart Assn. (treas. 1938-43), Ore. Med. Assn., Multnomah County Med. Soc., N. Pacific Soc. Internal Medicine. Republican. Protestant. Club: Pacific Interburban Clinical. Home: 2857 N.W. Shenandoah. Office: Standard Ins. Bldg., Portland OR*‡

COFFEY, GEORGE NELSON, agriculturalist; b. Patterson, N.C., Jan. 17, 1875; s. Elijah and Mary Ann (Nelson) C.; Ph.B., U. of N.C., 1900; M.S., George Washington Univ., 1907, Ph.D., 1911; m. Clara Estella Kean, Apr. 22, 1914. Assistant in geological laboratory, Univ. of N.C., 1899-1900; scientist, soil survey, Bur. of Soils, U.S. Dept. Agr., as asst., 1900-4, in charge, 1904-05, in charge soil classification and correlation, 1905-9, in charge, Great Plains Div., July, 1909-July 1911; asst. in charge soil survey, Ohio Expt. Sta., July 1, 1911-Dec. 1912; asso. in charge Div. of Soil Tech., same, Dec., 1912-Feb., 1915; asst. state leader for county farm advisers, U. of Ill., 1915-17, state leader, 1917-22; sec. Wayne County Abstract Co., May 1922-—. Lecturer on soils of Univ. of N.C., Feb. 1905; has made exhaustive study of classification and correlation of soils of U.S. and constructed soil maps and written reports upon numerous areas in N.C., Ohio, Ill., Pa., Ia., Kan., N.D., S.D., and Tex.; assisted Ontario Agrl. Coll. in beginning soil survey of Ont., May-June, 1915. Pres. Am. Soc. Agronomy, 1909 (chmn. com. of 15 mem. to secure a more uniform system of soil classification and nomenclature for soils of U.S. and Can.). Mem. Am. Title Assn., Ohio Title Assn. (v.p. 1923). Mason, Rotarian. Home: Wooster OH‡

COGGESHALL, CHESTER, physician; b. Champaign, Ill., Apr. 27, 1909; s. Trovalo Chester and Jessie (McCann) C.; student Knox Coll., 1926-27, U. Chgo., 1927-29, Cambridge (Eng.) U., 1930-31; B.S., U. Ill., 1933, M.D., 1936; m. Marion Frances Campbell, June 7, 1938; children—John Campbell, Susan Campbell (Mrs. George P. Adinamis), Sarah Campbell (Mrs. Gene P. Stute), Marion Campbell (Mrs. Don P. Schmidt). Intern, Presbyn.-St. Luke's Hosp., Chgo., 1936-37, resident in medicine, 1937, sr. attending staff medicine, until 1970; Joslin fellow diabetes New Eng. Deaconess Hosp., Boston, 1938-39, sr. attending staff medicine Cook County Hosp., Chgo., 1946-51; asso. medicine Northwestern U., 1946-70; asst. clin. prof. medicine U. Ill. Med. Sch., 1970; med. dir. Arthur Andersen & Co. Med. cons. various indsl. corps. Served to lt. col., M.C., USAAF, 1942-46. Diplomate Am. Bd. Internal Medicine. Mem. Am., Chgo. (founder, dir.) diabetes assns., Chgo. Med. Soc., Am. Heart Assn., Chgo. Inst. Medicine, A.A.A.S., A.M.A., Am. Legion, Sigma Xi, Beta Theta Pi. Home: Chicago IL Died June 2, 1970; buried Glen Oaks Cemetery, Westchester IL

COGGS, THEODORE WASHINGTON, lawyer; b. Muskogee, Okla., Sept. 26, 1916; s. Isaac M. and Eula (Brown); B.A., Howard U., 1940; LL.B., U. Wis., 1948; m. Pauline Redmond, May 9, 1942; 1 son, Gregory. Admitted to Wis. bar, 1948-68, practiced in Milw.; mem. firms Dorsey & Coggs, 1954-56, Coggs & McCormick, 1956-63, Theodore W. Coggs, 1963-65, 67-68, Coggs & Pitts. 1965-67. Pres., Milw. N.A.A.C.P., 1949-51, Milw. Northside YMCA, 1948-68; mem. Milw. County Safety Commn., 1950-68, commr. Boy Scouts Am., 1955-68. Mem. nat. steering com. Am. Vets. Com. Lawyers for Johnson-Humphrey, 1963. Bd. dirs. North Side Hosp., Milw., Wis. br. Am. Vets. Com., Milw. com., pres., 1966. Served as 1st lt. AUS, 1940-45. Recipient E. Francis Stratford award nat. Bar Assn.; Human Relations award B'nai B'rith, 1949; Citation of Merit, Milw. Sch. Bd., 1964. Mem. Nat. (pres. 1965), Am., Wis., Milw. bar assns., Kappa Alpha Psi (pres. 1950-52). Baptist (legal counsel 1948-68). Elk. Home: Milwaukee WI Died June 12, 1968.

COGHILL, WILLIAM HAWES, metall. engr.; b. Roseville, Ill., Mar. 14, 1876; desc. James Coghill who came from Eng. to Va. 1664; s. John Waller and Elisabeth (Tucker) C.; student Shurtleff Coll., Alton, Ill., 1892-94, 1896-97; E.M., Colo. Sch. of Mines, 1903; m. Maria Robinson, May 16, 1906; children—Elizabeth, William Waller, Robert Gregory. Began as public sch. teacher, 1894; engr. Albuquerque (N.M.) Land & Irrigation Co., 1897-98; asst. mine surveyor, Bisbee, Ariz., 1901-02, 1903-04; asst. engr. Calumet & Ariz. Mining Co., Bisbee, 1904-05, Tamarack Mining Co., Calumet, Mich., 1905-06; gen. engring. work N.M., and Joplin, Mo., 1906-07; asst. prof. mining and metallurgy, Northwestern U., 1907-14; cons. engr. El Paso, Tex., 1914-15; prof. mining and metallurgy and head dept. chem. engring., Ore. State Agrl. Coll., Corvallis, Ore., 1915-17; metallurgist U.S. Bur. of Mines, Seattle, Wash., Golden, Colo., Platteville, Wis., Miami, Okla., 1917-25; supervising engr. in charge of ore dressing sect., U.S. Bur. Mines, Rolla, Mo., 1926-37; prin. engr. nonmetals div., U.S. Bur. Mines and supervising engr. Southern Expt. Sta., U. Ala., 1938-45; chief, Tuscaloosa div. Metall. branch, U.S. Bureau of Mines 1945, retired Dec., 1945. Milling research St. Joseph Lead Co., Bonne Terre, Mo., 1946-47; ret. Mem. American Inst. Mining and Metall. Soc. of Am., A.A.A.S., Sigma Xi, Tau Beta Pi. Club: Rotary. Author: many papers and govt. bulls. on cyaniding, flotation, concentration and grinding. Home: 145 W. Lincoln Av., Delaware OH‡

COHEN, ABRAHAM, university prof.; b. Baltimore, Sept. 11, 1870; B.A., Johns Hopkins, 1891, fellow in mathematics, 1893-94, Ph.D., 1894; student at Sorbonne, Paris, 1894-95; married; 1 dau., Inez Teress. Instr. mathematics, 1895-98, asso., 1898-1914, asso. prof., 1914-26, prof. since 1926, Johns Hopkins; lecturer summers, U. of Colo., 1916-25. Co-editor Am. Journal of Mathematics since 1899; asso. editor Am. Math. Monthly, 1916-17. Fellow A.A.A.S.; mem. Am. Math. Soc., Math. Assn. America (pres. Md.-Va.-D.C. Sect.), Phi Beta Kappa, Johns Hopkins Chapter Sigma Xi. Author: Elementary Treatise on Differential Equations, 1906; The Lie Theory of One-parameter Groups, 1911; Differential and Integral Calculus, 1925. Home: 233 E. University Pkwy., Baltimore MD‡

COHEN, ANDREW BENJAMIN, Brit. govt. ofcl.; b. Berkhamsted, Eng., Oct. 7, 1909; s. Walter Samuel and Margaret (Cobb) C.; student Malvern Coll., 1923-28; B.A. with first class honors, Trinity Coll., Cambridge U., 1931; m. Helen Stevenson, Apr. 24, 1949; 1 son, Richard. With Brit. Colonial Office, 1932-68; served in Malta, 1940-43; head Central, later East Africa dept., 1943-47; asst. undersec. state in charge African div. Colonial Office, 1947-51; gov., comdr. in chief Uganda, 1952-57; permanent rep. U.K. to UN Trusteeship Council, 1957-61; dir. gen. Dept. Tech. Cooperation, 1961-64; head Dept. Overseas Devel., 1964-68. Decorated Order Brit. Empire, knight comdr. St. Michael and St. George, knight comdr. Royal Victorial Order. Home: London Eng Died June 17, 1968.

COHEN, DOLLY LURIE (MRS. A. B. COHEN), club woman, civic worker; b. Punxsutawney, Pa.; d. Michael and Rachael (Harris) Lurie; student pub. schs.; student Actual Bus. Coll., Akron, Ohio; m. Abraham B. Cohen (dec. Apr. 1960); 1 son, Ralph. Mem. Pres. Eisenhower's Com. Employment Physically son, Ralph. Mem. Pres. Eisenhower's Com. Employment Physically Handicapped; founder, life pres. Ohio Orphans' Mothers and Dads Club; charter pres. Greater Cin. chpt. auxiliary, campaign chmn. Muscular Dystrophy Assns. of Am.; former Hamilton County chmn., CARE; former dir. Camp Fire Girls, Jewish Consumptive Relief, Hon. Citizen Girls' Town; mem. dormitory com. Hebrew Union Coll.; charter trustee Magnetic Springs Found.; only woman mem. Nat. Football Found., Hall of Fame. Contbr. to scholarship funds Washington and Lee U.; originated Excellence in Teaching award, U. Cin., 1962. Active Cin. Symphony Orchestra, Fine Arts Assn., Children's Dental Care Found., Am. Cancer Soc., Cath. Charity Ball, City of Hope, Bonds for Israel; life mem. YMCA; mem. Pres.'s Com. Employment Handicapped; mem. People-to-People Program Handicapped; gen. chmn. art. com. B'nai B'rith, U. Cin.; life mem. of pres.'s com. Ohio State Univ. Named Ky. Col. Recipient Pop Warner award for service to youth, 1965. Mem. Ohio State U. Asso. Alumni Assn. (life), Ohio Patrol (hon.), Fraternal Order Police (hon.). Club: President's (life mem.) (U. Cin.). Home: Cincinnati OH Died June 4, 1970.

COHEN, HARRY, physician; b. Austria, Oct. 1, 1885; s. Samuel and Betty (Holzer) C.; brought to U.S., 1885, naturalized, 1892; M.D., Cornell, 1907; J.D., Calvin Coolidge College, 1958; married to Flora Levy, 1921; children—Robert H., Curtis, Michael S. Curtis. Intern Beth Israel Hosp. 1907-10; med. insp. N.Y.C., Health Dept., 1912-13; on staff Sydenham Hosp., 1913-16; attending surgeon Peoples Hosp., 1914-35; chief surg. clinic Beth Israel Hosp., 1915-30, asso. surgeon 1934-46; cons. surgeon Columbus Hosp.; staff other hosps.; vice chancellor Chatham Hill Coll. and Divinity Sch.; chancellor Philathea College (London, Ont., Can.); v.p. St. Andrews Coll., London, editor-in-chief Am. Jewish Lit. Found.; cons. surgeon N.Y.C. SSS; provost Am. Internat. Acad. Decorated Knight Order St. John of Jerusalem, Order of Malta, Vasco Nuzez de Balboa (Panama), Nichan-Iftaker (Tunis), White Lion (Czechoslovakia), Cross of Loraine, Renaissance (France), Legion of Honor (Cuba), St. Michael (Holland), Crown of Stuart (Scotland), Crown of Italy, Sta. Maurizzio and Lazzaro (Italy), Knights Templar (Germany), Constantine the Great (Pope Pius XII); named Father of the Jerusalem Acad. Medicine; established in his name Ann. Lectureship in Surgery; hon. pres. 3d Med. and Dental Congress, Oaxaca, Mexico, 1956. Diplomate Internat. Bd. Surgery. Fellow A.C.S., Internat. Coll. Surgeons, Internat. Coll. Proctology, Am. Geriatric Soc.; mem. Am. Med. Writers Assn., Nat. Council Bus. and Profl. Men, Inc. (president), The Jewish Forum Assos. (pres.), Am. Hist. Soc., Am. Assn. Abdominal Surgs., Am. Jewish Hist. Soc., N.Y. State, N.Y. Co. med. socs., A.M.A. Beth Israel Alumni Assn. (past pres.), N.Y. Physicians Soc., Eastern Med. Soc. (past pres.), Fedn. for Support Jewish Philanthropic Socs. (a founder), Am. Jewish Physicians Com. (a founder),Am. Physicians Fellowship Soc. (exec. com.), A.A.A.S., N.Y. Acad. Scis., Jerusalem Acad. of Medicine (chmn. bldg. com.). Democrat. Jewish relgn. Clubs: Power Squadron, Navigators (N.Y. City). Author numerous articles med. jours. Asso. editor of American Jewish Cyclopedia, 1945-56; editor-in-chief American Jews: Their Lives and Achievements, 1958; co-editor Jews in the World of Science, 1957. Author: Simon Bolivar and the Conquest and Liberation of South America, 1956; The Religion of Benjamin Franklin, 1956. Chmn. com. sci. and medicine Ency. Hebraica. Inventor of clamp tourniquet, and other med. instruments. Home: New York City NY Died Jan. 29, 1969.

COHEN, IRVIN JOSEPH, hosp. adminstr.; b. Bklyn., June 5, 1908; s. Louis J. and Anna S. (Cohen) C.; Ph.G., U. Md., 1926, M.D., 1930; m. Elsa Bondy Kaufman, Sept. 2, 1928; children—Barbara Louise (Mrs. Thomas Noel Casselman), Abby Ruth (Mrs. Marius Clarke Smith). Intern, Mass. Gen. Hosp., 1930-31; asst. resident pediatrics Children's Hosp., Phila., 1931-32; resident pediatrics Beth-El Hosp., Bklyn., 1932-33; exec. physician Bklyn. Hebrew Orphanage, 1933-35; practice medicine, specializing in pediatrics, Bklyn., 1935-42; asst. chief, chief profl. services VA Hosp., Bronx, N.Y., 1946-52; dir. VA Hosp., Balt., 1952-54; dir. hosps. VA., Washington, 1954-56, dir. hosps., clinics, 1956-59, asst. chief med. dir. profl. services, 1959-62; exec. v.p. Maimonides Med. Center, Bklyn., 1962-70; prof., chmn. health care and hosp. adminstrn. program Coll. Health Related Professions, State U. N.Y. Downstate Med. Center, 1967-70; VA rep. Intrgovtl. Working Group on Aging, 1956-59; VA rep. Fed. Council Aging, 1959-60; cons. Welfare Fedn. Cleve., 1961-66, Social Security Administrn., Washington, 1965-70; adv. council for extended care services VA, 1966-70; adv. com. on comprehensive ambulatory care N.Y. City Department of Health, 1967-70. Mem. joint com. Am. Hosp. Assn. and Nat. Assn. Social Workers. Served to maj., M.C., AUS, 1942-46. Recipient Meritorious Service award VA, 1959, Exceptional Service award, 1961. Diplomate Am. Bd. Pediatrics. Fellow A.C.P.; mem. A.M.A., Am., Greater N.Y. (bd. govs. 1965-68) hosp. assns., Nat. Assn. Social Workers (chmn. joint com. 1963-69), Am. Pub. Health Assn. Home: Rockville MD Died Oct. 29, 1970; cremated.

COHEN, PAUL, indsl. products mfg. exec.; b. N.Y.C., Jan. 24, 1917; s. Reuben and Anne (Frank) C.; B.A., Bklyn. Coll., 1936; student Acad. Advanced Traffic and Traffic Mgrs. Inst., N.Y.U., 1937-40; m. Shirley Schwartz, Sept. 1, 1940; children—Carol, Laura, Rebecca. Asst. gen. mgr. Hudson Pulp & Paper Corp., 1936-45; dir. purchasing Hygrade Food Products Corp., 1945-47; founder, pres. Tech. Tape Corp., now chmn.; pres. W. Ralston, Inc., 1950-68; pres., chmn. bd. dirs. Detroit Indsl. Products Corp., 1963-68; v.p., treas. A. J. Armstrong Co.; treas. A. J. Armstrong Co. of Ohio. Founder Muscular Dystrophy Assn. Am., 1950, pres., 1950-53, 63-68. Recipient Citizens award N.Y. Soc. Medicine, 1962. Mem. Allied Graphic Arts, Inc. (treas.). Author: Continental Freight Guide, 1943. Home: Harrison NY Died Apr. 25, 1968.

COHEN, PAUL PINCUS, lawyer, industrialist; b. Ellicottville, N.Y., Mar. 26, 1896; s. Isaac Henry and Sarah (Kallet) C.; A.B., magna cum laude, Harvard, 1916, LL.B. cum laude, 1918; Doctor of Laws, Niagara University, 1967; m. Frances Proskauer; 1 dau., Virginia Alice. Admitted to N.Y. bar 1918; sec. to U.S. circuit ct. judge, 1918; asso. law firms, N.Y.C., 1919, Niagara Falls, 1921-26; mem. Franchot Runals Cohen Taylor &

Mallam and predecessor firms, 1927-50, Cohen Fleischmann Augspurger Henderson & Campbell, Buffalo and Niagara Falls, 1951-53, Cohen, Swados, Wright, Hanifin & Bradford, 1953-71; counsel various nat. and internat. firms; chmn. Creo-Dipt Co. Inc., mfrs. stained shingles, N. Tonawanda, N.Y., Vancover, B.C., 1937-71; mem. Niagara Falls adv. bd. Marine-Midland Trust Co. of Western N.Y.; dir. Niagara Share Corp. Mem. council N.Y. State University Coll. at Buffalo, 1966-67; mem. bd. trustees Niagara University, 1968-71. President Old Fort Niagara Assn. Mem. nat. exec. com. Am. Jewish Com., 1955-71; chmn. Niagara Council World Affairs, 1956-71; v.p. Niagara Arts Council. Decorated Silver Medal of Honor (France), 1958. Mem. Am., N.Y. State, local county bar assns., Phi Beta Kappa. Jewish religion. Clubs: Niagara, Westwood Country, Harvard. Sponsor first Am. reciprocal income tax treaty, U.S. and Can., 1937. Author numerous articles on govt. and finance. Home: Buffalo NY Died Aug. 8, 1971.

COHON, MORRIS, investment broker; b. N.Y.C., June 22, 1904; s. Benjamin and Rachel (Silver) C.; B.S. in Chem. Engring., Mass. Inst. Tech., 1925; postgrad. Law Sch. Columbia, 1926-29; m. Ruth Fidler, June 1938; children—Peter, Elizabeth. Statistician, 1929; established investment firm, 1935; sr. partner Morris Cohon & Co., N.Y.C., 1935-71; pres. Hudson & Manhattan R.R. Co., 1949-50; pres. Englewood Antiques Corp. (N.J.). Mem. Nat. Assn. Security Dealers, N.Y. Security Dealers Assn., American-Internat. Charolais Assn. Author: The Broker-Dealer-Customer Problem-A Study of Dealer's Profits, Broker's Commissions and the Trend of Regulation, 1945; A Study of the Dealer-Customer Relationship, 1946; An Analysis of the New Issue Problem, 1960. Home: Englewood NJ Died July 26, 1971.

COHU, LA MOTTE T., corp. exec., b. N.Y. City, Sept. 23, 1895; s. Henry Moore and Annabelle (Turck) C.; A.B. Princeton Univ., 1917; Doctor of Laws, Whittier College, 1955; married Didi Muus Aug. 30, 1924; children—Anne, Marit June, Renee. Security salesman, 1918-21; partner Myron S. Hall Co. and Hall, Cohu Bros. Co., 1921-33; pres. Air Investors, Inc., 1930-39; pres. Aviation Corp., 1931-32; pres. Am. Airways (now Am. Airlines), 1931-32; pres. American Airplane & Engine Corp., 1931-32; director North Am. Aviation, Inc., 1933-34; dir. Transcontinental Air Transport, 1933-34, Northrop-Hendy Co., Hoffman Radio Corporation, Salsbury Motors, Inc., Los Angeles Chamber of Commerce; mem. exec. com., Transcontinental and Western Air, Inc., 1933-47, pres. 1947-48; director Eastern Air Transport, 1933-34, Air Assos., 1930-33; chmn. bd. and gen. mgr. Northrop Aircraft, Inc., Hawthorne, Calif., 1939-47; pres., gen. manager Consolidated Vultee Aircraft Corporation, 1948, vice chmn. bd., 1952-53; dir., mem. exec. com. Gen. Dynamics Corp., 1953-57; chmn. bd. of dirs. Cohu Electronics, Inc. (formerly Kay Lab.), 1954-68; dir. Garrett Corp., Eastern Industries. Pres. San Diego Community Chest, 1955-56. Trustee Whittier Coll., 1956. Served as ensign, USNRF, World War I. Quaker. Clubs: Princeton, Rancheros Visitadores. Home: Rancho Santa Fe CA Died Sept. 10, 1968.

COIT, JOHN CLARKE, ex-pres. U.S. Radio & Television Corpn.; b. Missouri Valley, Ia., June 22, 1872; s. Dr. George William and Anna (Armstrong) C.; attended high sch., Mo. Valley, to 1890; m. Mary K. Sargent, 1897; children—George S., Elisabeth (wife of Lt. Comdr. Paul C. Crosley, U.S.N.). Began career as stockroom boy, 1890; pres. Lee, Coit, Andreesen Hardware Co., 1917-24, Simmons Hardware Co. (St. Louis), 1924-29, U.S. Radio & Television Corpn., 1929-33; became chmn. bd. Gen. Household Utilities Co., 1933; now retired; was also pres. Radio Mfg. Assn. Democrat. Episcopalian. Mason (32 deg.). Clubs: Union League, Tavern. Address: Florida Theatre Bldg., St Petersburg FL‡

COIT, JOHN KNOX, educator; b. Charlotte, N.C., Feb. 12, 1872; s. Julius Thornwell and Dovey Jane (Knox) C. Textile mfg. and part time sec. of City Y.M.C.A., Salisbury, N.C., 1888-97; field worker in Christian Edn., Gen. Assembly Presbyn. Ch. in U.S., covering State of N. C., 1898-1902; student Bible Teachers Training Sch. (now Bibl. Sem. of New York), 1903-06; D. D., U. of Ga., 1930; m. Rebecca Isabella Galloway, of Toronto, Canada, Oct. 11, 1906; children—John McIver (dec.), John Knox. Missionary pastor, Rock Hill, S.C., 1905-07; licensed to preach by Bethel Presbytery, Sept. 1906; ordained as evangelist, by same, Apr. 1907; installed as pastor Nacoochee Presbyn. Ch., Apr. 1918. Served as supt. Nacoochee Inst., Santee, Ga., 1909-28; asso. supt. Rabun Gap—Nacoochee Sch., 1928-34, vice pres. since 1934. Home: Rabun Gap GA‡

COKE, JAMES L., judge; b. Marshfield, Coos County, Ore., Aug. 31, 1875; s. John S. and Mary E. (Moore) C.; ed. in Ore. and Calif.; m. Effie Riley, Mar. 11, 1913; children—Philip L., Virginia Nahl, James H. Began practice at Marshfield, Ore., 1896; elected county atty., County of Maui, T.H., 1908; elected territorial senator, City and County of Honolulu, 1912; apptd. by President Wilson circuit judge, 1st Circuit, Honolulu, Nov. 16, 1916; apptd. asso. justice Supreme Court of Hawaii, Jan. 8, 1917; apptd. by President Wilson chief justice Supreme Court of Hawaii, Mar. 12, 1918 for 4-yr. term; retired from bench Apr. 1922, and resumed practice at Honolulu; apptd. by President Roosevelt, chief justice Supreme Court of Hawaii, June 18, 1934, and reappointed by President Roosevelt, Aug. 5, 1939. Clubs: Outrigger, Oahu Country. Democrat. Mason (32 deg., Shriner, Jester). Home: 3649 Nuuanu Av., Honolulu HI‡

COKE, JOHN STORY, lawyer; b. Morristown, Tenn., Aug. 21, 1867; s. John Stephen and Mary Elizabeth (Moore) C.; ed. pub. schs. and under pvt. tutors; m. Annie Laurie Anderson, May 27, 1903; children—John Morton, Virginia. Admitted to Ore. bar, 1893, and began practice at Portland; moved to Marshfield, Ore., 1893, and practiced there until 1909; judge Circuit Court, 2d Dist. of Ore., 1909-23; U.S. atty. for Ore., 1923-25. Mem. bd. regents Ore. Normal Schs., 1920-25. Republican. Episcopalian. Mason (32 deg., Shriner) K.P. Clubs: Arlington, Portland Golf. Home: 2868 N.W. Cumberland Rd. Office: Yeon Bldg., Portland OR

COKER, ROBERT E(RVIN), biologist; b. Society Hill, Darlington County, S.C., June 4, 1876; s. William Caleb and Mary Ervin (McIver) C.; S.C. Coll., 1892-93; B.S., U. of N.C., 1896, M.S., 1897; Ph.D., Johns Hopkins Univ., 1906; Doctor of Science, Univ. of South Carolina, 1948; m. Jennie Coit, Oct. 11, 1910; children—Robert Ervin, Coit McLean. Asst. in biology, 1895-97; prof. zoology, U. of N.C., 1922-39, Kenan prof. zoology, 1939-53, now emeritus, chmn. div. natural scis., 1935-44, chmn. bd. trustees Chapel Hill Schools, 1935-1947; mem. Council on Human Relations, A.A.A.S., 1939-41; collaborator U.S. Forest Service, 1939-41; consultant U.S. Public Health Service and mem. Nat. Advisory Com. on Gerontology, 1940-42; chairman Survey of Marine Fisheries of N.C., 1946; director U. of N.C. Inst. of Fisheries Research, 1947-48, chairman executive committee, 1948-50. O. Max Gardner award (for service in organization of Fisheries Survey and Institute), 1950. Delegate to Peruvian Government to 4th Internat. Fisheries Congress (v.p.), Washington, 1908. Fellow A.A.A.S., Chgo. Acad. Scis.; member Am. Fisheries Soc., Ecological Soc. Am. (president 1937), Am. Soc. Zoologists (pres. 1941), North Carolina Academy Science (president 1941), Elisha Mitchell Scientific Society (president 1929-30), Limnological Society of America (vice-pres. 1935, pres. 1938), Assn. S.E. Biologists, Society Syst. Zoology, Sigma Xi, Phi Beta Kappa, Chi Psi; corr. member Davenport (Ia.) Acad. Science. Mason. Author: The Great and Wide Sea, 1947 (Mayflower award); various papers relating to oyster culture, fisheries and guano industry of Peru, mussels, copepods, etc. Home: Chapel Hill NC

COLACCI, MARIO, educator, author; b. Boiano, Italy, Oct. 11, 1910; s. Joseph and Cristina (Carnevale) C.; S.T.D., Pontifical Roman Major Sem., 1932; student Pontificium Institutum Biblicum, Rome, 1933-35; Litt.D., U. Naples, 1940; m. Maria C. Pizzuto, Apr. 28, 1950; children—David, Irving, Miriam. Came to U.S., 1949, naturalized, 1955. Prof. Hebrew, N.T. Greek, Pontifical Regional Sem., Benevento, Italy, 1935-40; prof. Latin, Classic Greek, philosophy, Italian, history Mario Pagano Coll. and Normal Inst. P.Elena, Campobasso, Italy, 1941-49; prof. N.T. Greek and Theology, Augsburg Coll. Mpls., 1952-68; lectr. Luther Theol. Sem., St. Paul, 1959-68; ordained to ministry Luth. Ch. Author: L'Inferno di Dante Alighieri, 1947; Christian Marriage Today, 1958; The Doctrinal Conflict between Roman Catholic and Protestant Christianity, 1962. Contbr. articles to Minneapolis MN Died Mar. 7, 1968.

COLBERT, CARL CATO, corp. exec.; b. Richland, Ga., Nov. 12, 1892; s. William E. and Emma C. (Jenkins) C.; student pub. schs. of Richland, So. Bus. U., Atlanta; m. Irene Purvis, Dec. 23, 1913; children—Kathryn (Mrs. Geo. C. Buchanan), Ralph C. With Nehi Corp., 1914-68, beginning as stenographer and bookkeeper, president, 1940-55, chmn. bd., 1955-56, consultant, 1956-68; dir. First Nat. Bank of Columbus. Baptist. Clubs: Rotary (past-pres.). Home: Columbus GA Died July 4, 1968; buried Riverview Cemetery, Columbus GA

COLBERT, CHARLES FRANCIS, JR., corp. exec.; b. Pitts., s. Charles Francis and Philomena (Dischner) C.; ed. Cathedral Sch. Ill., Shurtleff Coll., Ill.; m. Marie Louise Benford, Jan. 12, 1911 (dec. Jan. 1931);children—Jane Elizabeth (Mrs. Eugene Scott), Dorothy Benford (Mrs. Ralph H. Irwin). Richard Gary, Margaret L. (Mrs. William J. Gehweiler) (dec.), Patricia (Mrs. Emmett E. Robinson); m. Mildred Frances Allen, Oct. 27, 1955; 1 son, Charles Francis III. Engaged in coal, coke and alloys bus., Pitts., Charleston, S.C., Calvert, Ky. and Niagara Falls, N.Y., 1908; chmn., cons., Pitts. Metall. Co. div. Air Reduction Co. of N.Y., also dir. parent co.; chmn. adv. bd. Mfrs. & Traders Trust Co., Niagara Falls. Mem. Am. Iron and Steel Inst., Nat. Security Soc., Palm Beach Round Table. Clubs: Duquesne (Pitts.); Niagara Falls; Country, Pinnacle (N.Y.C.); Palm Beach Civic, Beach, Everglades (Palm Beach, Fla.); Youngstown (N.Y.) Yacht; Royal Canadian Yacht (Toronto, Ont.). Home: Youngstown NY Died Aug. 28, 1971; buried Allegheny County Meml Park, Allison Park PA

COLBERT, LEO OTIS, hydrographic and geodetic engr; b. Cambridge Mass., Dec. 31, 1883; s. P. John and Margaret (Byrnes) C.; B.S. in C.E., Tufts Coll., 1907, hon. Sc.D., 1939; m. Florentine Odou, Sept. 12, 1912; children—Mary Louise (Mrs. Raphael A. Neale), Jeanne (Mrs. William L. Doonan). With U.S. Coast and Geodetic Survey, 1907-50, on various survey parties; comdg. officer on survey ships, 1912-17; chief sect. vessels in Washington office, 1919-28; director of coast surveys in P.I., 1928-30; comdg. officer ship "Oceanographer," 1931, 32; chief div. of charts, 1933-38; dir. with rank of rear adm., 1938-50, ret. U.S. rep. Joint Colorado River Boundary Commns. Ariz.-Cal. Mem. adv. council Princeton University Department Civil Engring., Am. Con. on Surveying and Mapping. Hon. trustee Woods Hole Oceanograhic Instn. Awarded Dept. of Commerce Exceptional Service Citation; USC & GS Meritorious Service Ribbon, 1950; Gold medal by Society Am. Mil. Engrs., 1959. Fellow Arctic Inst. N.A.; mem. Am. Soc. C.E. (honorary member), Newcomen Soc. of North Am., Soc. Am. Mil. Engrs. (dir., past pres.), Am. Geophys. Union, Inst. Nav., Am. Shore and Beach Preservation Assn. (past pres.) Nat. Geog. Soc. (life trustee), Alpha Tau Omega, Tau Beta Pi. Clubs: Adventurers (Honolulu); Army and Navy. Home: Washington DC Died Dec. 23, 1968.

COLBY, IRVING HAROLD, govt. ofcl.; b. Booque, S.D., Mar. 6, 1908; s. Charles E. and Julia H. (Bly) C.; B.S., S.D. State U., 1931; m. Frances U. Ryland, Feb. 20, 1935; 1 dau., Carole. Served with U.S. Army, 1933-35; engr. S.D. State Hwy., Pierre, S.D., 1936-40, 46-68, emergency planning engr. Served to lt. col. AUS, 1941-46. Mem. Nat. Soc. Profl. Engrs., V.F.W., Am. Legion. Lutheran. Mason, Elk. Home: Pierre SD Died June 15, 1968.

COLBY, WALTER FRANCIS, physicist; born Rockford, Mich., July 28, 1880; s. Joshua and Sarah (Massie) C.; A.B., U. of Mich., 1901, Ph.D., 1909; grad. study U. Vienna, 1901-04; post doctoral study U. Munich, 1910-11, U. Copenhagen, 1922, U. Hamburg, 1921; m. Martha Guernsey, 1930. Mem. faculty U. Mich., 1909-44, prof. physics, 1919-44; staff Mt. Wilson Obs., 1914-15; dep. chief Office Sci. Research and Development, 1944-45; became dir. intelligence, U.S. AEC, 1948; asst. dir. Office Sci. Personnel, Nat. Acad. Scis., from 1953. Mem. Am. Phys. Soc. Club: Cosmos. Home: Washington DC Died July 1970.

COLBY, WILLIAM EDWARD, lawyer, b. Benicia, Calif., May 28, 1875; s. Gilbert Winslow and Caroline Amelia (Smith) C.; student Bowens Acad., Berkeley, Calif.; U. of Calif. 2 yrs.; LL.B., Hastings Coll. of Law (U. of Calif.), 1898; LL.D., Univ. of Calif., 1937, Mills Coll., 1937; m. Rachel Vroonan, Oct. 18, 1902 (deceased); children—Henry Vrooman, Gilbert Winslow; married 2d Helen Leach Flemming, 1951. Practiced, San Francisco, since 1898; associated with Curtis Hollbrook Lindley (dec.); specializes in mining law, former lecturer on law of mines and waters, U. of Calif., lecturer on law of mines, Stanford U., greatly interested in conservation of forests and assisted in drafting a forest fire law for Calif.; for a number of years was forest fire law for Calif.; for a number of years was associated with John Muir in work of conservation natural scenery, chiefly nat. parks; chmn. Calif. State Park Commn., 1927-37. Mem. Am. Alpine Club, Boone and Crockett Club (asso.); one of presidents d'honneur Internat. Congres l'Alpinism, Monaco, 1920; councilor Save the Redwoods League; mem. Phi Delta Phi, Order of the Coif. Club: Sierra (hon. pres.). Author publs. including: The Law of Oil and Gas; Mining Law in Recent Years. Republican. Home: 2901 Channing Way, Berkeley 4, Cal. Office: Mills Tower, San Francisco

COLE, BETTY JOY, librarian; b. Roselle, N.J., Mar. 18, 1898; d. Stepehn Edgar Cole and Elizabeth Rosina (Johnson) C.; ed. Laurel Sch., Cleve.; B.A., Sweet Briar Coll.; M.A., Columbia. Instr. chemistry Winthrop Coll. 1925-27; technician Skin and Cancer Hosp., N.Y.C., 1927-28; research chemist, Calco Chem. div. Am. Cyanamid Co., Bound Brook, N.J., 1929-30, librarian, 1930-63. Chmn., Council Nat. Library Assn., 1948-49. Bd. dirs. Plainfield Pub. Library. Recipient Spl. Library Assn. Hall of Fame Award, 1963. Mem. Aslib, Am. Chem. Soc. (Chem. literary sect.), Spl. Libraries Assn. (pres.; chmn. sci. tech. group 1938-39; chpt. pres. 1939-41; chmn. Com. Three, 1943-44; chmn., publs. governing com., 1945-46; dir. 1943-46; pres. 1946-47; chmn. awards com., 1948-49), Soc. Mayflower Descs. Republican. Episcopalian. Author: Library vs. Laboratory as Basis for Research; Finding Facts for Chemical Clientele; Chemical Libraries. Address: Plainfield NJ Died Dec. 21, 1970.

COLE, CHARLES H., corpn. exec.; b. Boston, Mass., Oct. 30, 1871; s. Charles H. and Mary Lyon (Ball) C.; grad. English High Sch., Boston, 1888; m. Grace F. Blanchard, of Brookline, Mass., July 1910. Clk., later cashier, office of several mining cos., Boston, 1888-98;

treas. U.S. Smelting Co., Centennial Eureka Mining Co., Am. Zinc, Lead & Smelting Co., 1898-1900; mgr. and dir. Coeur d'Alene mines, Murray, Ida., 1900-06; police commr., Boston, 1905-07; in mining business, 1907-12; fire commr., Boston, 1912-14; adj. gen., Mass., 1914-16; in mining business, 1917; became treas. Bay State Film Co., 1919; president Colbres Chemical Co., United States Chemical Co. Enlisted as pvt. and advanced through grades to 1st lt., Mass. N.G., 1890-1905, col. and insp. gen. rifle practice for Mass., 1905, resigned, 1906, and reenlisted as pvt., 1906, advancing through grades to brig. gen., 1914, resigned 1916; reenlisted as pvt., World War, 1917, later capt.; apptd. brig. gen. U.S.A., Aug. 1917; overseas, 1917-19; in battles of Apremont, Zivray-Marvoisin, Chateau-Thierry, St. Mihiel, Meuse-Argonne. Del. at large to Dem. Nat. Conv., 1924, 28 and 32; was adjutant gen., chief of staff, Commonwealth of Mass., Jan. 7, 1937. Dem. candidate for gov. of Mass., 1928. Chmn. State Racing Commn., 1934-35; now chmn. Mass. State Bd. of Conciliation and Arbitration. Unitarian. Clubs: Algonquin (Boston); Manhattan (New York). Home: 34 Gloucester St. Office: 329 Newbury St., Boston MA*‡

COLE, CHARLES NELSON, college dean; b. Bunker Hill, Ill., Mar. 3, 1871; s. Luther Elliot and Sarah Catherine (Stout) C.; A.B., Ill. Wesleyan U., 1894; A.M., U. of Ill., 1897; Ph.D., Harvard, 1901; m. Mabel Stewart, of Champaign, Ill., Aug. 29, 1899; children—Kenneth Stewart, Robert Hugh. Instr. Greek and Latin, Prep. Sch., U. of Ill., 1895-97; instr. Latin, Cornell, 1899-1902; asso. prof. Latin, 1902-04, prof. Latin lang. and lit., 1904-36, dean Coll. Arts and Sciences, 1911-36, Oberlin Coll.; retired Aug. 31, 1936. Prof. Latin, summer sch., Cornell, 1903, summer session, Ohio State U., 1910. Home: Oberlin OH‡

COLE, CYRUS W(ILLARD), naval officer (ret.); b. Marshall, Mich., June 21, 1876; s. Willard Churchill and Mary Underhill (Weeks) C.; B.S., U.S. Naval Acad., 1899; student U.S. War Coll., 1923-24; m. Julia Anna Busby, June 8, 1908; 1 s., Cyrus Churchill. Commd. ensign, U.S. Navy, Jan. 28, 1901, and advanced through grades to rear admiral, 1932; commanded U.S. Naval Transports, 1918, Squalus Salvage Unit, May-Sept. 1939; Command Submarine Force, U.S. Fleet 1934-36; ret. July 1, 1940. Pres. Calif. State bd. of pilot commrs. for San Diego since June 1942. Awarded Navy Cross, World War I; Navy D.S.M. (Squalus rescue and salvage), 1939. Republican. Clubs: San Diego (Calif.). Carabao. Hobby: sculpture. Home: 2878 Rosecrans Blvd., San Diego 6 CA‡

COLE, FELIX, foreign service officer; b. St. Louis, Mo., Oct. 12, 1887; s. Theodore Lee and Kate Dunn (Dewey) C.; student U. of Wis., 1905; A.B., Harvard, 1910; LL.D., George Washington U., 1928; m. T. Imshenetzkaya, Oct. 10, 1916; 1 dau., Marian; m. 2d, Marilla C. Cole (cousin), Sept. 22, 1928 (died Aug. 28, 1939); children—Marilla Callender, Catherine Dewey. Began as reporter Boston Herald, 1911, continuing until 1913; in automobile business, St. Petersburg, Russia, 1913-14 publisher there, 1914-15; in U.S. foreign service, 1915-49; charge d'affaires, Monrovia, Liberia, 1944; became minister to Ethiopa, 1945; ambassador to Ceylon, 1948; assigned State Dept., 1950. Mem. Order of Coif, Psi Upsilon, Phi Beta Kappa. Club: University (Washington). Home: Montclair NJ Died July 1969.

COLE, FRANKLIN, investment counsel; b. Towson, Md., Feb. 24, 1897; s. William Purrington and Ida Estelle (Stocksdale) C.; student Johns Hopkins, 1919; m. Jane Eleanor Irvin, June 1, 1927; 1 dau., Jane Irvin (Mrs. Peter D. Bunzel). Pres., dir. Franklin Cole & Co., Inc., N.Y.C., 1944-68; dir., mem. exec. com. United Merchants & Mfrs., Inc., 1964-68. Treas., trustee Marine Hist. Assn., Mystic, Conn., 1959-60, pres., trustee, 1961-68; bd. mgrs. Seamen's Ch. Inst., N.Y.C., 1962-68. Served as ensign USNRF, 1917-19. Mem. S.A.R. Episcopalian. Mason. Clubs: Plainfield Country, Log Cabin Gun (Plainfield); Wall Street, Union League (N.Y.C.); Edgartown (Mass.) Yacht. Home: Plainfield NJ Died Apr. 1968.

COLE, GEORGE CLARENCE, educator; b. at Logan, Ind., Oct. 15, 1872; s. John Arnold and Rebecca J. (Boatman) Kohl; ed. Ind. State Normal Sch., 1895-1902; m. Tillie A. Lorenz, June 1, 1909; children—Mary Rebecca, Georgia Irene. Teacher grade schs., 1890-96; prin. high sch., Lawrenceburg, Ind., 1897-1907; supt. schs., Dearborn Co., Ind., 1907-30; state supt. instrn., Ind., term 1930-34; v.p., bus. mgr. Ind. State Teachers' Coll., Terre Haute, since 1934. Democrat. Mason (32 deg., Grand H.P. Grand Chapter R.A.M. of Ind.). Home: 1444 S. 6th St., Terre Haute IN‡

COLE, HAROLD MERCER, lawyer; b. Montclair, N.J., Dec. 10, 1905; s. Harry Mercer and Julie (Young) C.; A.B., Brown U., 1929; LL.B., Harvard, 1932; m. Eleanor Kountze, June 3, 1933; 1 dau., Eleanor Estabrook; m. 2d Barbara Chisholm Scott, June 30, 1948. Admitted to N.Y. State bar, 1932, practiced in N.Y.C.; partner in the firm, Cole & Deitz, 1942-72; spl. dep. asst. dist. atty. on staff Thomas E. Dewey, 1935-37; asst. dist. atty. New York County, 1938-41; chmn. bd. Allegheny River Mining Co.; dir. Am. Australian Fund, Inc., Amoskeag Co., Exeter Fund, Inc., Exeter Second Fund, Inc., Exeter Third Fund, Inc., W.L. Morgan Growth Fund, Gemeni Fund, Inc., Santa Cruz Industries, Inc., Arthur T. Walker Estate Corp., Windsor Fund, Incorporated, also dir. First Investors Life Ins. Co., McCandless Corp., Standard-Thomson Corp., N.Y. Adv. Com. of Am. Mut. Liability Ins. Co. Dir. Wellington Fund. Served as lt. USNR, 1943-45. Mem. Assn. Bar City of New York, Newcomen Soc. in North Am. Republican (spl. counsel to chmn. national com. 1946-48; treas. N.Y. Co. Com. 1949-53). Clubs: National Republican, Union League, Leash Indian Harbor Yacht, Edgartown Yacht, Down Town Assn., River (New York); University (Washington); Montclair (N.J.) Golf; Edgartown Golf. Home: New York City NY Died Jan. 1972.

COLE, HOWARD WARE, lawyer; b. Marblehead, Mass., June 27, 1898; s. Leland Howard and Mary Abby (Roundy) C.; A.B., Dartmouth, 1919; LL.B., Harvard, 1922; m. Doris W. Enslin, Sept. 15, 1925; children—Rosamonde E. (Mrs. George R. Little), Natalie W. (Mrs. Gordon R. Hamilton, Jr.), Roger E. Admitted to Mass. bar, 1922; practiced in Boston, 1922-72; mem. Brickley, Sears & Cole. Dir. New Eng. Electric System. Del. nat. council YMCA, 1940-60, chmn. bd. Mass. YMCA, 1957-72; bd. mgrs. Am. Bapt. Fgn. Mission Soc., 1936-58. Chmn. bd. trustees Andover Newton Theol. Sch., 1965-69; trustee Bapt. Home Mass., pres. 1970-72. Mem. Mass. Bible Soc. (pres. 1965-72), Am., Mass., Boston bar assns., Am. Trial Lawyers Assn., Am. Judicature Soc. Home: Beverly MA Deceased.

COLE, LAWRENCE THOMAS, clergyman; b. Ann Arbor, Mich., Apr. 24, 1869; s. Nelson B. and Elizabeth H. (Felch) C.; A.B., U. of Mich., 1892; A.M., 1896; B.D., Gen. Theol. Sem., 1896; Ph.D., Columbia Univ., 1898; D.D., St. Stephen's Coll., 1905, General Theological Seminary, 1934; unmarried. Deacon, 1895, priest, 1896, P.E. Ch.; scholar Ch. Univ. Bd. of Regents, 1895-98; rector St. John's Crawfordsville, Ind., 1898; archdeacon Diocese of Michigan City, Ind., 1899; warden St. Stephen's Coll., 1899-1903; rector Trinity Sch., New York, 1903-37; retired. Author: The Basis of Early Christian Theism, Vol. 11, No. 3, of Columbia University Contributions to Philosophy, Psychology and Education, 1898. Home: 38 E. 37th St., New York NY‡

COLE, RUFUS, M.D.; b. Rowsburg, O., Apr. 30, 1872; s. Dr. Ivory S. and Ruth (Smith) C.; B.S., U. of Mich., 1896; M.D., Johns Hopkins, 1899; D.Sc., U. of Chicago, 1927, National U. of Ireland, 1933; m. Annie Hegeler, of LaSalle, Ill., Jan. 2, 1908; children—Camilla (Mrs. John Staige Davis, Jr.), Elizabeth, Mary (Mrs. Alton Childs). Resident house officer, asst. resident phys. and resident phys., Johns Hopkins Hosp., Baltimore, 1899-1907; asst. instr. and asso. in medicine, Johns Hopkins U., 1901-09; became dir. Hosp. of the Rockefeller Inst., New York, 1909, retired 1937; mem. emeritus Rockefeller Inst. for Med. Research; former mem. Bd. Scientific Dirs., Internat. Health Div., Rockefeller Foundation. Foreign mem. Danish Soc. of Internal Medicine; mem. Assn. Am. Physicians (pres. 1931), Nat. Acad. Sciences, Am. Assn. Advancement Clin. Research, Am. Assn. Pathologists and Bacteriologists, A.M.A., N.Y. Acad. Medicine, Phi Beta Kappa, Nu Sigma Nu. Contbr. to Osler's System of Medicine and Nelson System of Medicine; also articles in med. and scientific jours. Clubs: Century, University, Grolier (New Mount Kisco NY*‡

COLEMAN, ARCH, ex-first asst. postmaster gen.; b. Detroit, Mich., May 29, 1877; s. Silas Bunker and Rebecca (Backus) C.; ed. Chappaqua (N.Y.) Inst., Heidelberg, Germany, and high sch., Detroit; m. Annieclare Northrop, June 7, 1899; children—Archie Frederick, Ruth Northrop, Priscilla Northrop. Began as clk. in coal office, Minneapolis, Minn., 1896; organized City Fuel Co., 1910. Chmn. Rep. Co. Com. Hennepin Co., Minn., 1917-22; mem. State Senate, 1919-22; postmaster of Minneapolis, 1922-29; apptd. 1st asst. postmaster gen., July 1, 1929, resigned, Mar. 4, 1933; now sec.-treas. Edwards Co., Sanford, N.C. Republican. Episcopalian. Mason (K.T., Shriner). Clubs: Traffic, Minneapolis Athletic, Minneapolis Golf. Home: Sanford NC‡

COLEMAN, CORNELIUS CUNNINGHAM, clergyman; b. Aberdeen, Miss., Aug. 26, 1877; s. George Clarence and Annie Billups (Cunningham) C.; A.B., from Bethel Coll., 1898; Th.M., Southern Baptist Theol. Sem., Louisville, Ky., 1901; D.D., Simmons U., 1908; m. Juliet Cox, June 7, 1905; children—Juliet Cox, Cornelia Cunningham. Ordained Southern Bapt. ministry, 1899; pastor West Washington, D.C., Ch., 1901-05, First Ch., San Antonio, Tex., 1905-09, First Ch., Abilene, Tex., 1909-12; western sec. Foreign Mission Bd., Southern Bapt. Conv., 1912-14; pastor Citadel Sq. Ch., Charleston, S.C., 1914-25, First Ch., Durham, N.C., 1925-29, Grace Ch., Richmond, Va., 1929-44. Ministry-at-large, interim pastorates, and Bible conferences, since 1944. Led religious work campaigns in Army and Navy camps during the World War. Mem. Foreign Mission Board of Southern Bapt. Conv.; has served as trustee, various periods, Simmons Univ., Southern Bapt. Theol. Sem., Wake Forest Coll., Southwestern Bapt. Theol. Sem. Wake Forest Coll., Southwestern Bapt. Theol. Sem. Mem. Sigma Alpha Epsilon. Has specialized in denominational work, evangelism and church building. Home: 938 Twentieth St., Stuart Gardens, Newport News VA‡

COLEMAN, JOHN SHIELDS, banker; b. Jasper, Ala., Nov. 13, 1894; s. E.W. and Nancy (Shields) C.; student U. Ala. 1912-23, LL.B. 1915; student spl. session Harvard Grad. Sch., 1929; m. Gertrude Davidson, July 7, 1921 (dec. 1924); m. 2d, May Steiner, Apr. 28, 1928 (dec. 1970); 1 son John Shields; m. 3d, Dorothy H. Morrow, July 14, 1970. Admitted to Ala. bar, 1915; asso. with Tillman, Bradley & Baldwin, 1920-26; mem. Bradley, Baldwin, All & White, 1926-37; pres. Birmingham Trust Nat. Bank, 1937-58, now mem. bd.; Chmn. banking div. War Finance Com. for Ala.; chmn., dir. Jefferson County chpt. A.R.C. (chmn. drive 1944), Birmingham and Jefferson County Community Chest (Chmn. drive 1941, pres. 1951-52). Served as 2d lt. 7th Div., U.S. Army, 1918; AEF. Mem. Birmingham C. of C. (pres. 1941). Am. Bankers Assn. (exec. com. nat. bank div. 1956-57, chmn. 1957-58, pres. 1959-60), Newcomen Soc. Eng., S.A.R., Soc. Colonial Wars, Delta Kappa Epsilon. Presbyn. Democrat. Mason (32 Shriner). Clubs: Links (N.Y.C.); Redstone, Downtown Birmingham Country, Club. Home: Birmingham AL Died Mar. 11, 1972.

COLEMAN, RALPH PALLEN, illustrator; b. Philadelphia, Pa., June 27, 1892; s. William Herr and Anna M. (Pallen) C.; student Central High Sch., Phila., 1907-10, Sch. of Industrial Art, Phila., 1910-13; m. Florence L. Haeberle, June 2, 1917; 1 son, Ralph Pallen. Began as illustrator, 1913; illustrator for various magazines. Illustrated stories for Somerset Maughm, F. Scott Fitzgerald, Rex Beach, Booth Tarkington, Clarence Buddington Kelland, others; 17 paintings for Donald F. Irvin's Life of Jesus, 1951; paintings for churches, The Eternal Christ," 1942; Christ of the Upward Way," 1944, murals, Go Forth and Serve," 1944; Christ by the Sea of Galilee," 1948; The Nativity," 1948; Christ Calling," 1948; Benediction," 1948; Come Unto Me," 1948; Sermon on the Mount," 1949; (mural) Washington at White-Marsh," 1950; The Good Shepherd, 1955; large paintings include Christ and the Children," 1960, Madonna and Child," 1962, Holy Family at Grace," 1962, Resurrection," 1962, Compassionate Christ," 1963, Feed My Sheep," 1964; stained glass windows include Jesus and Little Child. Mary and John at the Cross, 1956; 23 scenes from life of Christ in ten stained glass windows of Grace Presbyn. Ch., Jenkintown, 1958; (painting) The Savior, 1954; 64 Old and New Testament paintings for a new edition of The Bible, 1957; lectr. on Life of Jesus with slides of over 100 own paintings; 42 color paintings in Hurlbut's Story of the Bible; 55 color paintings in The Way, The Truth and The Life; portraits of Army officers and gen., Armory, Phila., grand master Pa. Masonic Temple, Phila. Dir. Over-the-Counter Securities Fund, Inc. Mem. board governors YMCA, Philadelphia. Served with Marine Camouflage Dept., World War I. Mem. Huguenot Soc. Pa., Nat. Soc. Mural Painters. Presbyn. Home: Jenkintown PA Died Apr. 3, 1968; buried George Washington Meml. Park, Whitemarsh PA

COLEMAN, STEWART P., ret. bus. exec.; b. Corpus Christi, Tex., June 22, 1899; s. Charles Edwin and Margaret (Gill) C.; B.S., Rice Inst., Houston, Tex., 1920; M.S., Mass. Inst. Tech., Cambridge, Mass., 1921, D.Sc., 1930; m. Jane Cochran, Nov. 5, 1930; children—Nancy Jane, Margaret Stewart. With Humble Oil & Refining Co., Houston, 1920-33; with Standard Oil Co. (N.J.), 1933-61, head coordination and econs. dept., 1945, v.p., dir., 1955-61, retired. Chairman working subcom. Committee on Petroleum Economics, Petroleum Industry War Council, 1942-43; director program division Petroleum Administration for War, 1943-45. Member Military Petroleum Adv. Bd.; trustee National Industrial Conf. Board, 1953-61. Mem. Am. Inst. Chem. Engrs., Am. Chem. Soc., A.A.A.S., Am. Petroleum Inst. Clubs: University, River, Economic (New York); Rockaway Hunting; Bayou, Petroleum Houston Houston TX Died Nov. 13, 1969; buried Glenwood Cemetery, Houston TX

COLEMAN, WILLIAM JOHN, clergyman; b. Lisbon, N.Y., May 12, 1851; s. John and Mary (Glass) C.; A.B., Geneva Coll., 1875, A.M., 1890, D.D., 1901; D.D., Wheaton Coll., 1902; m. S. Elizabeth George, 1879;children—John, Paul, George Slater, William Carithers (killed in battle, France, 1918), Mary Slater. Ordained ministry Reformed Presbyn. Ch., 1879; pastor McKeesport, Pa., 1879-81; lecturer on nat. reform, 1881-86; pastor Utica, O., 1886-87; prof. polit. philosophy, Geneva Coll., 1887-92; pastor Allegheny Reformed Presbyn. Ch., Pittsburgh, Pa., 1892-1924. Moderator Ref. Presbyn. Synod, 1905; chmn. and lecturer witness com., Reformed Presbyn. Ch., since 1924; prof. pastoral theology, Reformed Presbyn. Sem., since 1928. Home: Millvale, R.R. 4, Pittsburgh PA‡

COLFORD, WILLIAM EDWARD, educator; b. Brooklyn, May 9, 1908; s. William Martin and Helen Elizabeth (Gee) C.; A.B., Coll. City of N.Y.,1929; A.M., Columbia, 1933, Ph.D., 1942, post doctoral studies in

Latin Am. edn., 1946-71; student U. of Madrid, 1932, U. of Mexico, 1934; m. Eugenia Sutton Wade, Aug. 23, 1943; children—Elizabeth Esperance, Robert Wade, Christopher William. Mem. Faculty Coll. City of N.Y. since 1929, prof. Romance langs. since 1948, head dept. Romance langs., 1950-52, asst. director of summer session, 1952-57, asst. dean curriculum guidance, 1957-62. Lt., Inf., O.R.C., 1929-39; instr., interpreter Command and Gen. Staff Sch., U.S. Army, serving with Brazilian Army group, 1943-45. Awarded Medal of Commendation, U.S. Army, 1945. Mem. Am. Assn. Teachers of Spanish and Portuguese, Am. Assn. U. Profs., Columbia U. Alumni Assn. of Union County, N.J., Brazilian Cultural Soc. (N.Y. City), Mexican Inst. Linguistic Investigation (Mexico City), Phi Beta Kappa Assos., Phi Beta Kappa. Author: Juan Melendez Valdes, a Study in the Transition from Neoclassicism to Romanticism in Spanish Poetry, 1942; classic Tales from Spanish America, 1962; New York: Gateway to U.S.A., 1954, rev. edit., 1963; Classic Tales from Modern Spain, 1964; also translator. Contbr. articles to profl. periodicals. Home: Elizabeth NY Died Aug. 13, 1971; buried Rosedale Cemetery Linden NJ

COLIE, ROSALIE LITTELL, educator; b. N.Y.C., June 18, 1924; d. Frederic Runyon and Rosalie (Hall) Colie; A.B. Vassar Coll., 1944; M.A., Columbia, 1946, Ph.D., 1950. From instr. to asso. prof. Barnard Coll., 1948-61; asso. prof. history Wesleyan U., Middletown, Conn., 1961-63; prof. history and English, U. Ia., 1963-66; prof. English, U. Toronto, 1968-69; Nancy Duke Lewis prof. Brown U., 1969-72. Fulbright fellow, 1952, 67-68; Howard fellow, 1958-59; Guggenheim fellow, 1959-60, 67-68; fellow Am. Council Learned Socs., 1948. Mem. Am. Assn. U. Women. Author: Some Thankfulnesse to Constantine, 1956; Light and Enlightment, 1957; Paradoxia Epidemica, 1966; My Echoing Song, 1970. Home: Old Lyme CT Died July 7, 1972; buried Evergreen Cemetery, Morristown NJ

COLKET, EDWARD BURTON, ry. official; b. Philadelphia, Pa., Jan. 10, 1873; s. William Walker and Jane Frances (Hoxsie) C.; student Wm. Penn Charter Sch., Phila., 1883-89; B.S., U. of Pa., 1893, M.E., 1894; m. Bessie Lippincott, of Phila., Feb. 12, 1918; 1 dau., Jane Hoxsie. Successively with Baldwin Locomotive Works, Standard Steel Works, Self Clinching Nail Works; pres. Phila. City Passenger Ry. Co., 1908-40; also formerly pres. Phila. & Darby Ry. Co.; pres. Chestnut Hill R.R. Co.; mgr. Phila., Germantown & Norristown R.R. Co. Mem. Welcome Soc. of Pa., S.R. Republican. Presbyterian. Home: 5237 Wissahickon Av., Philadelphia PA‡

COLLENS, CLARENCE LYMAN, electrical manufacturing executive; b. Cleveland, Ohio, Mar. 19, 1875; s. Charles Terry Collins and Mary Abby (Wood) C.; Ph.B., Sheffield Scientific Sch., Yale, 1896, E.E., Sch. of Mines, Columbia Univ., 1897; D.Eng. (honorary), Fenn College, 1954; married Clara Ransom Latimer, December 12, 1906;children—Emilie Robb (Mrs. Grenville Strong Sewall), Clarence Lyman (dec.), Jonathan Latimer, Granger Hall. Asst. supt. Hartford Electric Light Co., 1897-99; supt., v.p., gen. mgr., Internat. Acheson Graphite Co., Niagara Falls, N.Y., 1899-1906; supt. Canadian Plant, Niagara Power Co., 1906-07; pres., dir. Reliance Electric and Engring. Co., Cleve., 1907-44, dir., chmn. board, 1945-55. Delegate to meeting of the International Electro-Chemical Commission, Geneva, Switzerland, 1922, London, England, 1924. Awarded McGraw Medal for cooperative effort in electrical manufacturing industry. Trustee Fenn Coll., Cleve. Member Am. Inst. of Electrical Engrs., Cleveland Engring. Soc., Sigma Xi, Delta Psi. Clubs: Yale (New York City), Kirtland, Mayfield, Union (Cleveland). Home: Cleveland Heights OH Died Mar. 24, 1972.

COLLIER, JOHN, b. Atlanta, May 4, 1884; son of Charles A. and Susie (Rawson) C.; ed. Columbia and Woods Hole, 1902-05, College de France, 1906-07; m. Lucy Wood, Oct. 20, 1906; children—Charles Wood, Donald, John; m. 2d, Laura Thompson, August 25, 1943; married third, Grace E. Volk, January 26, 1957. Began as social worker with immigrants, 1905; civic secretary People's Inst., New York, 1909-19; dir. community orgn. state of Calif., 1919-20; dir. social science training, State Teachers Coll., San Francisco, 1921-22; exec. sec. Am. Indian Defense Assn., Inc., 1923-33; commr. of Indian Affairs, 1933-45; mem. Indian Arts and Crafts Bd., 1934-45; dir. Nat. Indian Inst., U.S.A., 1945-50, U.S. del. governing bd. Inter-Am. Inst. the Indian, Mexico City, 1942-51. Adviser to U.S. del. 1st session Gen. Assembly, London, 1946; prof. sociol. and anthropology College of City of New York, 1947-54, professor emeritus, 1954-68; vis. prof. anthropology Knox Coll., Galesburg, Ill., 1955-56. President Institute Ethnic Affairs, Washington, D.C. Founder and secretary National Board Review for Motion Pictures, 1910-14; director Training School for Community Workers, 1915-19. Edited American Indian Life (mag.), 1926-33. Author: The City Where Crime Is Play, 1931; The Indians of the Americas, 1947; America's Colonial Record, 1947; Patterns and Ceremonials of the Indians of the Southwest, 1949; On the Gleaming Way, 1962; From Every Zenith, 1963. also verse. Address: Ranchos de Taos NM Died May 8, 1968; buried Ranchos Presbyn. Mission Ch. Cemetery, Ranchos de Taos NM

COLLIER, MARIE ELIZABETH, soprano; b. Ballarat, Australia, Apr. 16, 1927; d. Thomas Robinson and Ann-Marie (Bechaz) C.; grad. high sch.; m. 1952; three sons, 1 dau. Australian debut, 1954; appeared in prin. parts in Italian and Slavic operas at Covent Gardens, 1957, also Sadler's Wells and Cardiff, S.Am., 1961, U.S.A., 1962. Address: London Eng Died Dec. 8, 1971.

COLLIN, HARRY E., business exec.; b. Tontogany, O., Dec. 4, 1885; s. Robert J. and Alice E. (Hannah) C.; ed. Ohio State U.; m. Selma G. Gardner, Oct. 8, 1913. With Northern Nat. Bank, Toledo, O., 1906-12; with Citizens Securities Co., 1912-20; sr. partner Collin Norton & Co., Toledo, 1920-64; asso. Clark, Dodge & Co., Inc. (merger with Collin, Norton & Co.), 1964-72; dir., mem. exec. com., Canrad Precision Industries, Inc., Owens Ill. Glass Co.; dir. numerous other cos., including Clinton Foods Corp. Mason (33, Shriner). Mem. C. of C. Clubs: Toledo, Country (Toledo); Bankers (N.Y.); Recess (Detroit); Buttonwood (N.Y.C.). Home: Toledo OH Died Sept. 11, 1972.

COLLINGS, JOHN AYRES, airline exec.; b. Washington County, Va., Apr. 6, 1903; s. John and Rachel (Farris) C.; ed. pub. schs.; m. Esthma Basham, Dec. 23, 1926. Test pilot Ford Motor Co., 1925-28; chief pilot Transcontinental Air Transport, 1928-29; with Trans World Airlines, 1929-59, div. supt., 1929-39, superintendent operations, 1939-42, v.p. operations, 1942-51, exec. v.p., 1951-57, sr. cons. to bd. dirs. and pres., 1957-59, dir., 1942-59; asst. to pres. United Aircraft Corp., 1959-67. Served as pilot, U.S. Army, 1922. Clubs: Conquistadores del Cielo; Hartford Golf (Conn.); Farmington Country (Charlottesville, Va.). Home: Salem VA Died Jan. 16, 1971.

COLLINS A(RCHIE) FREDERICK, elec. physicist; b. South Bend, Ind., Jan. 8, 1869; s. Capt. Thomas Jefferson and Margaret Ann (Roller) C.; ed. pub. schs. and old U. of Chicago; m. Evelyn Bandy, June 28, 1897; 1 son, Virgil Dewey. Invented the wireless telephone, 1899; gold medal, Alaska-Yukon-Pacific Expn., 1909; invented rotating oscillation arc, 1909; discovered effect of electric waves on brain cells, 1902; formulated neutron theory of the ether, 1937. Lecturer New York Bd. Edn., 1900-10; technician Collins Wireless Telephone Co., 1904-10; scientific corr. New York Herald, 1901-03; editor: Collins Wireless Bulletin, 1908-10. Fellow Royal Astron. Society (Great Britain). Member of the American Heart Association. Clubs: Royal Aero of United Kingdom, Authors (London). Author: Wireless Telegraphy, Its History, Theory and Practice, 1905; and over 97 other books on arithmetic, astronomy, aviation, business, chemistry, electricity, gardening, internal combustion engines, hobbies, magic, mechanics, metallurgy, microscopy, motor cars, motor boating, natural history, optics, philately, physics, photography, shooting, submarines, tops and gyroscopes, tractors, travel, wireless telegraphy and telephony, television, invention, etc., and over 500 articles in encys. and Am., English and French tech. papers and mags. Home: The Antlers, Congers, Rockland County, N.Y. and Jacksonville FL‡

COLLINS, ALFRED MORRIS, retired mfr.; b. Phila., Pa., May 3, 1876; s. Henry Hill and Edith Earl (Conrad) C.; A.B., Haverford (Pa.) Coll., 1897; m. Mrs. Helen Wilson Glenn, Sept. 6, 1928; stepchildren—Helen, Thomas F., Harry W., Shirley. With A. M. Collins Mfg. Co., cardboard and photographic mounts, 1897-1929, v.p. and gen. mgr., 1899-1929. Mem. 1st Troop Phila. City Cav., 1905-12; commd. maj. Ordnance U.S.A., Jan. 1918. Fellow Royal Geographical Society; patron Field Museum Natural History (Chicago); hon. life mem. Acad. Natural Sciences, Zoological Society (Philadelphia), Am. Museum Natural History (New York); mem. Alumni Assn. Haverford Coll. (pres. 1917-18), Phila. Geog. Soc. (pres. 1922, 25, 26, 27, 29, 31), Main Line Citizen's Assn. (pres. 1916-21). Polo player and big game hunter; in charge hunting and scientific expdn. to Brit. E. Africa, in interest of Acad. Natural Sciences, Phila., 1911-12; made hunting trip through Alaska, N.E. Siberia and as far north as Wrangel Island, 1914; a dir. of Collins-Day S. Am. expdn., traveling 4,000 miles across S. Am., in interest of Am. Mus. Natural History, N.Y., and the Field Museum, Chicago, 1916; sent expdn. to W. Africa, in interest of Smithsonian Instn. of Washington, 1917; led Central African expdn. in interest of Field Mus. Chicago, 1923-24; expdn. to Tanganyika and S. Africa, 1928; now pres. San Luis Valley Land & Cattle Co. Republican. Episcopalian. Clubs: Wilderness (pres.), Explorers, Penn Athletic, Boone and Crockett, Racquet, Phila. Barge, Phila. Country, Merion Cricket, Bryn Mawr Polo. Home: Crestone CO‡

COLLINS, CHARLES E., stockman; b. Topeka, Kan., July 18, 1869; s. Charles and Lorettea (McMillon) C.; ed. pub. schs.; m. Mary Smethers, July 20, 1893; children—Don, Georgie B., Pauline C. Has engaged in cattle raising since 1891; pres. Kit Carson (Colo.) State Bank, O. M. Franklin Serun and Production Credit Corpn., both of Denver. Home: Kit Carson CO‡

COLLINS, CONRAD GREEN, physician; b. New Orleans, Apr. 23, 1907; s. Charles and Amelie Marie (Haydel) C.; B.S., Tulane, 1926, M.D., 1928, M.S., 1931; m. Louise Carroll, Oct. 9, 1935; children—Louise Carroll, Conrad G., Claudia Elizabeth. Intern Touro Hosp., New Orleans, 1928-29; asst. resident obstetrics and gynecol. Touro Infirmary, 1929-30, and 1930-31; pvt. practice splty., New Orleans, from 1931; sr. vis. surgeon Charity Hosp. of La. from 1938; sr. consultant Hotel Dieu, Vets. Hosp., U.S. Marine Hosp., Flint Goodridge and Sara Mayo hosps. Instr. gynecol. and lab., Sch. Med., Tulane, 1931-32, asst. prof. gynecol., 1932-38, asst. prof. clin., obstet. and gynecol., 1938-45, prof., chmn., 1945-50, chmn. dept. gynecol., 1949-50, prof., chmn. dept. obstet. and gynecol., from 1950; nat. cons. obstet. and gynecol. Surgeon Gen., USAF, 1952-62. Served as maj., U.S.A., 1942-46; Asiatic-Pac. Theatre, 1942-43, European Theatre, 1944-45. Diplomate Am. Bd. Obstetrics and Gynecol.; fellow A.C.S., mem. A.M.A., Am. Assn. Obstetrics and Gynecology, Am. Coll. Obstetricians and Gynecol., Am. Gynecol. Soc., Sigma Psi. Club: American Gynecological; Boston (New Orleans). Home: New Orleans LA Died Dec. 15, 1971.

COLLINS, GEORGE W., congressman; b. Chgo., Mar. 5, 1925; student Northwestern U.; m. Cardiss Robertson; 1 son, Keith. Various positions Cook County Sheriff's Dept., Municipal Ct. System, Bd. Health; pres. Lawndale Youth Commn.; bd. dirs. Greater Lawndale Conservation Commn.; mem. 91st and 92d Congresses from 6th Dist. Ill. Served with C.E., AUS, World War II; PTO. Mem. Profl. and Businessmens Assn. Democrat. Baptist. Address: Chicago IL Died Dec. 8, 1972.

COLLINS, HENRY W., corp. ofcl.; b. South Yarmouth, Mass., 1903; grad. Fordham U.; m. Clarinda Collins; children—William H., Patricia. President, chmn. Celotex Corp.; vice chmn. Jim Walters Corp.; dir. South Shore Oil & Devel. Co., New Orleans. Home: Northbrook IL Died Mar. 1971.

COLLINS, JAMES H(IRAM), author; b. Detroit, Mich., Nov. 3, 1873; s. William H. and Mary (Mappelbeck) C.; ed. pub. schs. to 14; m. Lillian Gertrude Keyes, of Montreal, Quebec, Canada, 1903 (now deceased); children—Esther Mappelbeck (Mrs. Willfred H. Mennell), and Lillian Mary; m. 2d, Elizabeth McCaully, of Washington, D.C., 1918. Learned printer's trade and traveled as journeyman, also with circus; made trips of business investigation to Europe as corr. Saturday Evening Post, 1907 and 1910, and corr. Philadelphia Public Ledger 8 months, in South America, 1919; editor Southern Calif. Business (mag. of Los Angeles Chamber of Commerce; now discontinued), 1930-39; now free-lance author. Vol. with U.S. Food Administration, associated with Com. of Pub. Information, publn. dept., 1917, Emergency Fleet Corpn., and finally as asst. to Edward N. Hurley of U.S. Shipping Bd., 1918. Author: Human Nature in Selling Goods, 1909; The Art of Handling Men, 1910; The Great Taxicab Robbery, 1912; Straight Business in South America, 1920; The Story of Canned Foods, 1924. Address: 6608 Cahuenga Terrace, Hollywood CA‡

COLLINS, JOSEPH, neurologist; b. Brookfield, Conn., Sept. 22, 1866; s. P. H. and M. F. C.; ed. U. of Mich., 1884-85; M.D., New York U., 1888; post-grad. student Frankfort, Germany; unmarried. Phys. to Neurol. Inst.; prof. neurology, New York Post-Grad. Med. Sch., 1897-1909; visiting phys., City Hosp., 1894-1908. Alvarenga prize, Coll. Physicians, Phila. 1897. Mem. Assn. Am. Physicians, Am. Neurol. Assn. (pres. 1902-03), N.Y. Acad. Medicine, Am. Med. Assn., N.Y. Neurol. Soc. (ex-pres.). Clubs: Century, Charaka. Author: The Faculty of Speech, 1900; Diseases of the Brain, 1899; Diseases of the Nervous System, 1900; Pathology of Nervous Diseases, 1901; The Sympathetic Nervous System, 1905; The Way with the Nerves, 1911; Sleep and the Sleepless, 1912; My Italian Year, 1919; Idling in Italy, 1920; The Doctor Looks at Literature, 1923; Taking the Literary Pulse, 1924; The Doctor Looks at Biography, 1925; The Doctor Looks at Love and Life, 1926; The Doctor Looks at Doctors, 1927; The Doctor Looks at Marriage and Medicine, 1928; The Doctor Looks at Life and Death, 1931. Address: 36 E. 72d St., NY*

COLLINS, MARK, lithographing co. exec.; b. Vancouver, B.C., Can., Nov. 8, 1912; s. Mark George and Margaret (Greer) C.; B.A., B. Commerce, U.B.C., 1934; M. Madeline Phae Van Dusen, Sept. 25, 1937; children—Marcia (Mrs. D. H. Rothery), Elaine (Mrs. D. L. Killam). With H. R. MacMillan Export Co. Ltd., 1934-35, Canadian Transp. Co. Ltd., 1935-36; with B.C. Packers Ltd., 1936-42, asst. prodn. mgr., 1940-42; with Smith Lithograph Co. Ltd., Vancouver, 1945-70, pres., gen. mgr., 1945-70; board directors MacMillan, Bloedel Ltd., Mercantile & Gen. Reins. Co. Can. Ltd., Ocean Cement & Supplies Ltd.; mem. Vancouver adv. bd. Can. Trust Co. Mem. B.C. Aviation Council. Mem. senate U. B.C., 1960-63; mem. senate and bd. govs. Simon Fraser U., 1967-70. Navigator Royal Canadian Air Force, 1942-45. Mem. Lithographic Tech. Found. (past dir.). Alumni Assn. U. B.C. (past pres.). Clubs: Vancouver, Shaughnessy Golf, Rotary (Vancouver). Home: Vancouver British Columbia Canada Died Apr. 21 1970.

COLLINS, PAUL FISK, air transportation; b. Wooster, O., April 22, 1891; s. Joseph Victor C.; grad. U. of Wis., 1916; m. 2d, Florence Potter, March 15, 1941; children—Paul L. (lt., U.S. Air Corps), Paula P. Pilot U.S. Air Mail Service, 1921-29; gen. supt. Transcontinental Air Transport, 1929-30; v.p. in charge of operations Ludington Airlines, 1930-32; pres. Nat. Airways, Boston-Maine Airways, Northeast Airlines, 1933-41, chmn., 1941-43, pres., chmn. 1944, formerly chmn. bd., chairman advisory committee, 1958-65; pres. and treas. Fibermold, Inc., Woburn, Mass. Served as lt. United States Army Air Corps, 1917-19. Awarded presidential Certificate of Merit, 1948. Member American Legion, Kappa Sigma. Author of series of aviation stories in Liberty mag., 1928-29. Home: Van Nuys CA Died Mar. 1971.

COLLINS, ROSS ALEXANDER, ex-congressman; b. Collinsville, Miss., Apr. 25, 1880; s. Nathaniel Monroe and Rebecca J. (Ethridge) C.; A.B., Ky. U., 1900; LL.B., U. of Miss., 1901; LL.D., Transylvania U., 1930; m. Alfreda Grant, Nov. 2, 1904; children—Jane (Mrs. Thomas P. Corwin), Madison M. Began practice at Meridian, Miss., 1901; elected atty. gen. of Miss., 1911; reelected, 1915; candidate for gov., Dem. primaries, 1919; mem. 67th to 73d Congresses (1921-35) and 75th, 76th and 77th Congresses (1937-43), 5th Miss. Dist. Candidate for nomination to U.S. Senate, 1934, also for nomination to fill vacancy after death of Senator Pat Harrison, 1941, and for full term following. As chmn. Mil. Appropriation, during early 30's and later, wrote, spoke and fought for mechanized weapons; credited with bringing into being the Flying Fortress. Hon. mem. Am. Library Assn. Club: Cosmos (Washington, D.C.). Episcopalian. Mason. Home: Meridian MS Died July 14, 1968.

COLLINS, ROY CHARLES, lawyer; b. Newark, July 22, 1903; s. Charles Abram and Mary (Finley) C.; student Rutgers U., 1921-22, LL.B., 1931; student Columbia, 1923-24; m. Doris Pauline Rose, Oct. 16, 1926;children—James Pittenger, Peter Rose. Admitted to N.J. Bar, 1932, U.S. Supreme Ct., 1951; practice in Newark, 1932-71; sr. partner firm Collins and Toner, 1960-71. Dir. Great Atlantic and Pacific Tea Co., Inc. Past dir. mem. finance com. Bloomfield (N.J.) Coll. Mem. Am., Essex County bar assns. Presbyn. (pres. trustees). Clubs: Essex, Down Town (Newark). Home: Maplewood NJ Died Feb. 21, 1971; buried St. Stephens Cemetery, Millburn NJ.

COLM, GERHARD, economist; b. Hannover, Germany, June 30, 1897; s. Emil and Olga (Strassburger) C.; Dr. Rer. Pol., Freiburg U., 1921; student U. Munich, 1920, U. Berlin, 1921, 1923; Dr. Rer. Pol. h.c., University of Frankfurt, 1961; Dr. h.c., New Sch. for Social Research, 1964; m. Hanna Nicolassen, Sept. 11, 1922 (dec. Mar. 1965) children—Peter, Anne, Stine, Claus; m. 2d, Mascha Gilde, April 11, 1966. Came to United States, 1933, naturalized 1939. Economist with the Fed. Statistical Bureau, Berlin, 1921-27; instr. Inst. World Economics, Kiel U., 1927, asst. prof., asso. prof. economics, dir. research div., 1927-33; prof. econs. New Sch. Social Research. N.Y.C., 1933-39; fiscal expert Dept. Commerce, Washington, 1939-40; professorial lectr. George Washington U. 1940-62; prin. fiscal analyst, fiscal div. Bur. Budget asst. chief fiscal div., 1940-46; economist Council Econ. Advisers, Exec. Office of Pres., 1946-52; chief economist Nat. Planning Assn., 1952-68; spl. mission Am. Mil. Govt. to Germany, for preparation plan of financial reform, 1946. Recipient Bernard Harms prize Inst. World Econs., 1964. Mem. Am. Econ. Assn., International Phenomenology Society. Author: Economic Consequences of Recent American Tax Policy (with Fritz Lehmann), 1938; Who pays the Taxes (with Helen Tarasov), 1940; The American Economy in 1960 (with Marilyn Young), 1952; Essays in Public Finance and Fiscal Policy (with Helen O. Nicol), 1955; The Economy of the American People (with Theodore Geiger). Published 1958, 3d edit., 1967, reports Contbr. articles profl. publs. Home: Chevy Chase MD Died Dec. 25, 1968.

COLMAN, JAMES DOUGLAS, health services exec.; b. N.Y. City, 1910; s. Cecil and Margaret (Plenderleith) C.; M.E., Cornell, 1932; spl. student Johns Hopkins, 1939-41; m. Ruth E. Baldwin, 1935; children—Ann Elizabeth, Jane Carol. Mgr. med. hosp. and dental div. N.J. Emergency Relief Adminstrn., 1932-35; exec. sec. Hosp. Council of Essex Co., N.J., 1935-37; also exec. dir. Hosp; Service Plan of N.J.; exec. dir. Md. Hosp. Service, Inc. and Md. Med. Service, Inc., 1937-51; v.p. Johns Hopkins U. and Hosp., 1951-57; v.p., sec. Nat. Blue Cross Assn., 1957-60, chmn. exec. com., 1966-72; pres. Asso. Hosp. Service of N.Y., 1960-72; lectr. pub. health adminstrn. John Hopkins, 1942-59, Columbia, 1958-72. Chmn. Nat. Blue Cross Commn., 1947-50; sec.-treas. Commn. Chronic Illness, 1949-52, treas., 1952-56; treas. Nat. Tb Assn., 1957-64; mem. bd. dirs. Nat. Health Council, 1962-72, pres., 1967-68; mem. Fed. Hosp. Council, 1967-72; vice chmn. N.Y. Hosp. Rev. and Planning Council, 1966-72. Fellow Am. Pub. Health Assn.; mem. Am. Statis. Assn., Am. Hosp. Assn. (trustee, 1963-66; recipient Kimball award 1965). Clubs: University (N.Y.C.), Maryland (Balt.). Home: Scarsdale NY Died Dec. 8, 1972.

COLTON, DON BYRON, ex-congressman; b. Mona, Juab Co., Utah, Sept. 15, 1876; s. Sterling D. and Nancy A. (Wilkins) C.; grad. commercial dept. Brigham Young U., Provo, Utah; LL.B., U. of Mich., 1905; m. Grace Stringham, of Vernal, Utah, June 17, 1908; children—Mera, Alice, Glade Byron, Gwen Mary. Began practice at Vernal, 1905; mem. Colton Bros., ranchers and sheep raisers; pres. Vernal Express Pub. Co. Mem. Utah Ho. of Rep., 1903, Senate, 1915-19; receiver U.S. Land Office, Vernal, 1905-14; mem. 67th to 72d Congresses (1921-33), 1st Utah Dist. Pres. bd. Uintah Academy. Republican. Mem. Ch. of Jesus Christ of Latter Day Saints. Home: Vernal UT*‡

COLTON, ETHAN THEODORE, Y.M.C.A. worker; b. Palmyra, Jefferson County, Wis., Nov. 22, 1872; s. of Harvey T. and Jane (Congdon) C.; B.A., Dakota Wesleyan U., 1898, LL.D., 1929; p. grad. work, U. of Chicago and Columbia U., m. Caroline Quigg, Oct. 11, 1900; children—Ethan Theodore, Elizabeth G. (dec.), Marjorie Congdon. Teacher prep. dept. Dakota Weslayan U., 1898-99; executive for Y.M.C.A., War Prisoners Aid in camps of the U.S., 1943-46. Mem. Internat. Com. of Y.M.C.A.; dir. Tolstoy Found. Mem. Phi Kappa Phi. Methodist. Author books including: The Russia We Face Now. Home: 109 Haddon Pl., Upper Montclair NJ

COLTON, JULIA M., author; b. New York; d. Francis and Sarah E. C.; ed. Packer Collegiate Inst.; occasional contributor to St. Nicholas and other mags. Author: Annals of Switzerland, 1897 B5; Annals of Old Manhattan, 1902 B27. Address: Mansion House Brooklyn NY‡

COLUM, PADRAIC, poet, dramatist; b. Longford, Ireland, Dec. 8, 1881; s. Padraic and Susanna (MacCormack) C.; ed. pub. schs.; Litt.D., Columbia, 1958, Trinity Coll. (Dublin, Ireland), 1958; m. Mary Gunning Maguire, 1912 (dec.). Came to U.S., 1914. Mem. Acad. Irish Letters (pres.), Am. Acad. Arts and Letters. Catholic. Author: Wild Earth (poems), 1907; A Boy in Eirinn, 1913; Three Plays, 1916; The King of Ireland's Son, 1916; The Adventures of Odysseus and the Tale of Troy; The Boy Who Knew What the Bird Said, 1918; The Girl Who Sat by the Ashes, 1919; The Children of Odin, 1920; The Boy Apprenticed to an Enchanter, 1920; The Golden Fleece, 1921; The Children Who Followed the Piper, 1922; Castle Conquer, 1923; Dramatic Legends (poems), 1922; The Island of the Mighty, At the Gateways of the Day (Hawaiian Stores), 1924; The Voyagers, The Forge in the Forest, The Bright Islands (Hawaiian Stories), 1925; The Road Round Ireland, 1926; Creatures (verse); The Fountain of Youth, 1927; Balloon, a comedy in four acts; Orpheus—Stories from the Mythologies of the World, 1929; Poems, 1932; A Half-Day's Ride—A Book of Essays, 1932; The Big Tree of Bunlahy (stories), 1933; The Legend of Saint Columba, 1935; The Story of Lowry Maen (narrative poem), 1937; Where the Winds Never Blew and the Cocks Never Crew, 1940; The Frenzied Prince, 1943: Anthology of Irish Verse, 1948; A Treasury of Irish Folklore, 1954; The Flying Swans, 1957; Arthur Griffith and the Origins of the Irish Free State, 1958; Our Friend James Joyce, 1958; Legends of Hawaii, 1960; Ourselves Alone, 1960; Poet's circuits (collection of poems of Ireland), 1960; Roofs of Gold (poetry anthology), 1964. Lectr. Recipient Acad. Am. Poets award, 1952; Gregory medal, Irish Acad. Letters, 1953; Regina Medal, Cath. Library Assn., 1961; Boston Arts Festival Poet, citation, 1961; Georgetown U. 175th Anniversary Medal of Honor, 1964. Address: New York City NY Died Jan. 11, 1972; buried Dublin, Ireland.

COLVIN, JAMES G., lead and zinc mining co. exec.; b. N.Y.C., Aug. 5, 1905; s. James and Margaret (Peacock) C.; ed. N.Y. U.; m. Hope Madeline Hoelzer, Nov. 30, 1940; children—James G., II, John S., Donald P., Jocelyn Patricia. Auditor, Price, Waterhouse & Co., 1928-29; with St. Joseph Lead Co., N.Y.C., 1929-68, successively asst. comptroller, comptroller, treas., v.p., until 1968. Dir. Compania Minerales Santander. Trustee, chmn. finance com. No. Westchester Hosp. Mem. Am. Mining Congress (tax com.), Financial Execs. Inst., N.Y. State Soc. C.P.A.'S, Am. Inst. Mining Metal. & Petroleum Engrs. Republican. Episcopalian. Mason. Club: Rockefeller Center Luncheon (N.Y.C.). Home: Pleasantville NY Died Feb. 18, 1968.

COLVIN, W. H. JR., steel exec.; b. Chicago, Ill., May 20, 1897; s. W. H. and Bessie (Small) C.; student Cornell University, 1916-20; married Grace Ellett, September 3, 1921 (died January 4, 1949); 1 daughter, Caroline; married 2d Allis N. Ferguson, July 11, 1952. Clerk Harris Trust and Savings Bank, Chicago, Illinois, 1921-25; manager W. H. Colvin Company, Chicago, Illinois, 1925-57; v.p. Oklahoma Power and Water Co. Tulsa, Okla., 1927-30; partner Pynchon Co., Chicago, Ill., 1930-31; sec.-treas. Rotary Electric Co., Detroit, Mich., 1932-36, pres., 1937-45; pres. Crucible Steel Co. of Am., 1945-54, ret., then member board of directors; also director Central and Southwest Corp.; member board directors National Biscuit Co. Clubs: Racquet, River (N.Y.C.) Home: Sarasota FL Died Apr. 22, 1972.

COMAN, EDWIN TRUMAN, banker; b. Kankakee, Ill., May 25, 1869; s. Daniel Franklin and Rosilla (Thresher) C.; U. of Mich., 1885-87 and 1888-89; LL.B., Washington and Lee U., Lexington, Va., 1890; m. Ruth Martin, of Carrollton, Mo., Mar. 10, 1897; children—Edwin T., Robert M., Catherine; m. 2d, Eva R. Freeland, 1926. Admitted to practice in Virginia, Illinois and Washington; moved to State of Wash., 1894; practiced at Colfax, 1894-97; pres. Marin County Nat. Bank and Marin County Savings Bank, San Rafael, Calif.; v.p. of Mercantile Trust Co., of Calif; pres. Exchange Nat. Bank, Spokane, Wash., 1907-21; organized and was pres. State Bank of Plummer, State Bank of Worley (Idaho), Bank of Endicott (Wash.), State Bank of Wilbur (Wash.); pres. Bank of Farmington (Wash.), Nat. Bank of Palouse (Wash.), 1912-20; dir. Spokane br. of Federal Reserve Bank, 1915-19; vice pres. American Trust Co.; retired. State senator, Washington, 1918-22; pres. Bd. Regents, State Coll. of Wash., 1915; pres. Chamber of Commerce, Spokane, 1909. Mem. Liberty Loan and various war committees. Director Marin County chapter Am. Red Cross, Marin Co. Tuberculosis Assn. (treas.); pres. San Rafael Chamber Commerce. Pres. Wash. State Bankers' Assn., 1905; mem. exec. council Am. Bankers' Assn., 1914-15 and 1916; mem. Phi Kappa Psi. Republican. Episcopalian. Mason (32 deg., Shriner), Elk. Clubs: Spokane, University; Arctic (Seattle); Rotary (president), Marin Golf and Country, Shrine Club, San Rafael Club (San Rafael). Home: San Rafael CA‡

COMBS, EVERETT RANDOLPH, Dem. Nat. Committeeman; b. Russell County, Va., Jan. 18, 1876; s. John Williams and Jane (Kiser) C. student Tazewell (Va.) Coll., 1896-97; m. Rassa Candler, Mar. 24, 1897;children—Nell (Mrs. Joseph A. Leslie, Jr.), Willie A., Dorothy (Mrs. Paul P. Spring), Cecil G., Earl B. Carlton E., Bernice, Roberta, Nancy. Farmer and schoolteacher, 1899-1912; clerk Circuit Court, Russell County, Va., 1912-28; state comptroller, 1928-38; clerk Senate of Va., 1940-48, chmn. State Compen. Com., 1928-38, 1942-45; Va. del. at large, Dem. Nat. Conv., 1932, 40, 44, Dem. Nat. committeeman from Va. since 1940. Baptist. Mason. Club: Commonwealth. Home: 3109 Noble Av. Office: State Capitol, Richmond VA*‡

COMFORT, CHARLOTTE WALRATH, former headmistress; b. Ft. Plain, N.Y., Mar. 22, 1903; d. Alton Alphonso and Charlotte (Barber) Walrath; A.B., Vassar Coll., 1924; m. Lowell R. Comfort, Sept. 8, 1928; children—Joan (Mrs. H. Alden Johnson, Jr.), Robert. Tchr., Warrenton (Va.) Country Sch., 1924-25; with Miss Hewitt's Sch., 1925-69, headmistress, 1942-69. Bd. dirs. Profl. Children's Sch., 1954-58, hon. dir., 1958-69; trustee The Hewitt Sch., 1969-73. Mem. Nat. Assn. Prins. Schs. Girls, Headmistresses Assn. East (council 1957-60, pres. 1960-62, hon. mem. 1969-—), Guild Ind. Schs. N.Y. (pres. 1956-58). Club: Cosmospolitan (N.Y.C.). Home: Sarasota FL Died Jan. 22, 1973.

COMINSKY JACOB R(OBERT), publisher; b. Rochester, N.Y., April 11, 1899; s. Marcus and Rebecca (Maxon) C.; A.B., U. Rochester, 1920; Litt. D., Ithaca Coll., 1968; m. Roslyn Weisberg, Oct. 29, 1929. U. of Rochester corr. for Democrat & Chronicle, 1916-20, reporter, 1920-25, city editor, 1925-28; Rochester corr. for Asso. Press and feature writer, Sunday edition New York World, 1920-28; mem. bus. staff New York Times, 1928-42, nat. advt. mgr., 1935-36; exec. v.p., charge Sat. Rev., 1942-68, treas., dir., 1942, pub., 1952-68, v.p., McCall Corp., N.Y.C., 1961-68. Mem. of board trustees University Rochester, 1956-59. Recipient Alumni Gold Key for distinguished postgrad. work U. Rochester, 1945, cited for distinguished service to publishing, 1952. Mem. Greater N.Y. Alumni Assn. (bd. govs.), Soc. Genesee, Phi Beta Kappa, Delta Rho. Clubs: University of Rochester (dir.), Nat. New York City NY Died Aug. 2, 1968; buried Syracuse NY

COMPTON-BURNETT, IVY, novelist; b. London, Eng.; d. James and Katharine (Rees) Compton-B.; B.A. with honours in Classics, Royal Holloway Coll.; D.Litt., Leeds U., 1960. Recipient James Tait Black Meml. prize, Edinburgh, Scotland, 1956; comdr. British Empire, 1951. Fellow Royal Soc. Lit. Author: Pastors and Masters, 1925; Brothers and Sisters, 1929; Men and Wives, 1931; More Women than Men, 1933; A House and its Head, 1935; Daughters and Sons, 1937; A Family and a Fortune, 1939; Parents and Children, 1941; Elders and Betters, 1944; Manservant and Maidservant, 1947; Two Worlds and Their Ways, 1949; Darkness and Day, 1951; The Present and the Past, 1953; Mother and Son, 1955; A Father and His Fate, 1957; A Heritage and its History, 1959; The Mighty and Their Fall, 1961; A God and His Gifts, 1963. Home: London Eng. Died Aug. 1968.

COMSTOCK DANIEL FROST, physicist, engineer; b. Newport, R.I., Aug. 14, 1883; s. Ezra Young and Nellie Preston (Barr) C.; S.B., Mass. Inst. Tech., 1904; studied U. of Berlin, 1905, U. of Zurich, 1905-06, U. of Basel, 1906, Ph.D., studied U. of Cambridge, Eng., 1906-07, under J.J. Thomson; m. Joan Barton, June 30, 1925; children—Daniel Frost, Charles Barton. Apptd. to teaching staff, Mass. Inst. Tech., 1904, instr. in theoretical physics, 1905-10, asst. prof., 1910-15, asso.

prof., 1915-17; directed scientific work on development of means for detection of hostile submarines, World War I, president Comstock & Wescott, Inc., Engrs. 1912-14; v.p. Kalmus, Comstock & Wescott, Inc., engrs., 1914-25; dir. of scientific work on, and principal inventor of the process for producing Motion Pictures in natural color known as the Technicolor process, developed by Kalmus, Comstock & Wescott, Inc., for the Technicolor Motion Picture Corp., during 1914-25; v.p. Technicolor Motion Picture Corp., 1918-25; pres. Comstock & Westcott, Inc., 1925-67, chmn. bd., 1967-70; engaged almost exclusively with research and development on war projects during World War II; now engage in industrial research. Pres., treas., dir. Stator Co., co-inventor of new refrigeration process owned by same. Member National Advisory Council to Committee on Patents, Ho. of Reps., 1939. Fellow Am. Academy Arts and Sci., Am. Physical Society; mem. Am. Chemical Society. Club: St. Botolph (Boston). Author: Nature of Matter and Electricity (with L.T. Troland), 1917. Contbr. original research articles on modern theory of electricity and optics to Am. and English tech. jours. Home: Cambridge MA Died Mar. 2, 1970; buried Mt. Auburn Cemetery, Cambridge MA

COMSTOCK, ELTING HOUGHTALING, univ. prof.; b. Milwaukee, Wis., June 26, 1876; s. Everett G. and Victorine (Houghtaling) C.; B.S., U. of Wis., 1897; scholar, Cornell U., 1897-98; fellow, U. of Chicago, 1898-99; teaching fellow, U. of Wis., 1899-1900, M.S., 1907; m. Myrtle T. Wade, Aug. 1, 1900 (died July, 1929); children—Everett Wade, John Elting; m. 2d, Gladys E. Mitchell, Dec. 26, 1932. With U. of Minn. since 1906; prof. mine plant and mechanics, Sch. of Mines, 1908-35; administrative head Sch. of Mines and Metallurgy, 1935-44, prof. emeritus since July 1944. Council scout commissioner, Boy Scouts of Am. Fellow A.A.A.S.; mem. Am. Soc. Mech. Engrs., Am. Inst. Mining and Metall. Engrs., Soc. for Promotion Engring. Edn. Theta Tau, Acacia, Alpha Phi Omega. Republican. Methodist. Mason (33 deg., K.T., Shriner). Club: Campus. Home: Dyscom Farm, Monticello MN‡

COMSTOCK, HARRIET THERESA, author; b. Nichols, N.Y.; d. S. Alpheus and Jean A. (Downey) Smith; acad. edn. Plainfield, N.J.; m. Philip Comstock, 1885; children—Philip S., Albert. Has been writing, since 1895, short stories, in mags. and books, principally for children. Author: Molly, the Drummer Boy, 1900; Cedric, The Saxon, 1901; A Boy of aThousand Years Ago, 1902; A Little Dusky Hero, 1902; Tower or Throne, 1902; When the British Came; Then Marched the Brave; The Queen's Hostage (novel), 1907; Janet of the Dunes (novel); Joyce of the North Woods (dramatized); Camp Brave Pine, 1913; A Son of the Hills, 1913 (dramatized); The Place Beyond the Winds, 1914 (dramatized); The Vindication, 1916; The Man Thou Gavest, 1917; Mam'selle Jo, 1918; Unbroken Lines, 1919; The Shield of Silence, 1921; Glen of the Mountains, 1922; At the Crossroads, 1922; The Tenth Woman, 1923; Out of the Clay; Joline; Penelope's Web, 1928; The Piper's Price, 1929; Fate Is a Fool, Strange Understanding, 1933; The Mark of Cain, 1935; Fool, Strange Understanding, 1933; The Mark of Cain, 1935; Sacrifices of Love, 1936; Can This Be Wrong?, 1937; Lori—Daughter of Kit, 1937; The Road Beyond, 1939; Windy*‡

CONANT, ERNEST BANCROFT, lawyer; b. Enfield, N.H., May 21, 1870; s. Washington Irving and Fanny Ann (Skinner) C.; A.B., Harvard, 1895, LL.B., 1898; m. Alice Widney, of Alpha, Ill., June 26, 1906. Admitted to Mass. bar, 1898, and practiced in Boston until 1903; lectured on legal subjects, evening sch. of Boston Y.M.C.U., 1900-03; engaged in gen. practice, Chicago, and prof. torts, damages and evidence, Ill. Coll. of Law, Jan. 1-Aug. 1903; prof. law and dean, Washburn Coll. Sch. of Law, Topeka, Kan., 1903-07; prof. law, U. of Neb., 1907-13, U. of the Philippines, Manila, 1913-17, Washington U., 1917-35 (emeritus). Prof. law, U. of Mich., summer, 1912. Mem. Philippine Library Bd. Mem. exec. com. Philippine Amateur Athletic Fed., 1913-16; business mgr. Far Eastern Olympic Games, Shanghai, May 1915. Mem. Am. Bar Assn., Far Eastern Bar Assn., Phi Delta Phi. Mason (32 deg.). Episcopalian. Contbr. cyclopedia and legal mag. articles. Address: Poe Av., Overland, St Louis County MO‡

CONARD, HENRY SHOEMAKER, botanist; b. Phila., Pa., Sept. 12, 1874; s. Thomas Pennington and Rebecca Savery (Baldwin) C.; B.S., Haverford, Coll., Pa., 1894, M.A., 1895; Ph.D., U. of Pa., 1901; Johnston scholar, Johns Hopkins, 1905-06; Sc.D., Grinnell, 1944, Haverford, 1945; m. (E) Laetitia Moon, Apr. 13, 1900; children—Elizabeth M., Rebecca S., Alfred F. Teacher of science, Westtown Sch., 1895-99; instr. botany, U. of Pa., 1901-05; prof. botany, Grinnell Coll., 1906-44, retired since June 1944; research professor State Univ. of Iowa since 1944. Instr. in plant ecology, Summer Sch., L.I. Biol. Assn., Cold Spring Harbor, L.I. Fellow A.A.A.S., Ia. Acad. Science. Mem. Bot. Soc. America, Sullivant Moss Soc., Am. Mycological Soc., Ecological Soc. of America, American Assn. Univ. Profs., Phi Beta Kappa (Haverford); Sigma Xi (U. of Pa.). Mem. Soc. of Friends (orthodox). Author: Waterlilies, 1905; Waterlilies and How to Grow Them (with Henry Hus), 1907. Translator and Editor: (with G. D. Fuller) Plant Sociology (by J. Braun-Blanquet), 1932. Ranger-naturalist, Yellowstone Park, summers, 1924-26. Grinnel IA‡

CONDE, BERTHA, author; b. Auburn, N.Y.; d. Samuel Lee and Elizabeth L. (Collier) C.; B.A., Smith Coll., 1895; theol. study, Free Church Coll., Glasgow, Scotland, and travel in Orient, 1906. Teacher biology, Elmira (N.Y.) Coll., 1895-97, student sec., Am. Com. of Y.W.C.A., 1898-1905; sr. student sec. Nat. Bd. Y.W.C.A., 1906-20; mem. Gen. Exec. Com. World's Student Christian Federation, 1907-20; mem. exec. com. Student Vol. Movement for Foreign Missions, 1906-20; lecturer on Christian apologetics and missions for Nat. Bd. Y.W.C.A. since 1920. Visited leading univs. and colls. of America, Europe and Orient in behalf of Christian and social service, and enlisted many students. Organized Central Club for Nurses, N.Y. City; led commn. to S. America to study women's work, 1919; lectured 6 mos. to leadership groups in Egypt, Turkey, Syria and Palestine, 1927. Mem. Authors' League America, Pen and Brush Club. Author: The Business of Being a Friend, 1916; The Human Element in the Making of a Christian, 1917; A Way to Peace, Health and Power, 1925; Spiritual Adventuring, 1926; What's Life All About?, 1930; Spiritual Adventures in Social Relations, 1930. Address: care Chase Nat. Bank, 40 W. 34th St., New York NY‡

CONDRON, THEODORE LINCOLN, cons. engr.; b. Washington, D.C., Apr. 16, 1866; s. Rev. George M. and Abbie (Smith) C.; B.S., Rose Poly. Inst., 1890, M.S., 1892, C.E., 1918, D.Engr. (hon.), 1947; m. Grace E. Layman, June 9, 1896; children—George Tolman, Helen (Mrs. Charles E. McGuire), Arnold Layman. Retired; formerly mem. Condron & Post, designers of railroad and highway bridges, factories and warehouse buildings of reinforced concrete and steel. Advisory engr. Reconstruction Finance Corp. on Tacoma Narrows Suspension Bridge, 1938-39. Awarded Chanute medal by Western Soc. Engrs., 1905. Mem. Structural Engrs.' Commn., State of Ill. Mem. Am. Soc. C.E. (dir. 1923-25), Am. Ry. Engrs. Assn., Am. Soc. for Testing Materials, Western Soc. Engrs. (v.p. 1899; hon. mem. 1945). Republican. Conglist. Clubs: Union League, Engineers; (hon. mem. 1938). Home: 212 S. Scoville Av., Oak Park IL‡

CONFREY, EDWARD ELZEAR (ZEZ), composer, author; b. Peru, Ill., Apr. 3, 1895; s. Thomas J. and Margaret (Brown) C.; student Chicago Musical Coll., 1911-12; m. Wilhelmina Beaumont Matthes, Mar. 15, 1932;children—Paul, Thomas. Writings have appeared chiefly under pseudonym, ZEZ; toured U.S. with own orchestra; made numerous recordings for Victor, Q.R.S. Compositions include: Kitten on the Keys, 1921; Stumbling, 1921; Dizzy Fingers, 1923; (song) Sittin' on a Log, 1935; Concert Etude, 1930; (miniature opera) Thanksgiving (libretto and music), 1947; Four Candy Pieces; Globetrotter Suite; Tin Pan Symphony. Author: Musical Alphabet Rymes: Boomerang Suite, Three Little Oddities; Buffoon; Dancing Shadow; Valse Mirage. Roman Catholic. Home: Lakewood NJ Died Nov. 22, 1971.

CONGDON, HARRIET RICE, seminary pres.; b. Montour Falls, N.Y., Dec. 25, 1876; d. Hiram Ward and Flora Ann (Potter) C.; A.B., Mount Holyoke Coll., 1898; grad. study, Oxford, Eng., 1900-01, U. of Mich., 1908-10; unmarried. Prof. Latin and GreeK, Western Coll. for Women, Oxford, O., 1903-07; dean of women, Hillsdale (Mich.) Coll., 1910-14; dean Wilson Coll., Chambersburg, Pa., 1916-18; pres. Monticello Sem., Godfrey, Ill., since 1918. Presbyn. Clubs; Wednesday, College (St. Louis). Address: Godfrey IL‡

CONGER, ALBERT C., coll. pres.; b. Van Buren, Ark., May 13, 1920; s. Eli E. and Blanche (Shehan) C.; B.A. in Natural Sci., Hendrix Coll., 1942; M.A. in Psychology, U. Wyo., 1949; m. Ethel Mai Robertson, Nov. 26, 1947; 1 son, Rex E. Tchr. pub. high sch., Muskogee, Okla., 1947-48; dir. extension center U. Wyo., 1949-50, 1950-51; dean Eastern Wyo. Coll., 1951-67, pres., 1967-68. Mem. Wyo. Community Coll. Commn. Served with AUS, 1942-46. Mem. N.E.A., Phi Delta Kappa. Mason; mem. Order Eastern Star. Home: Torrington WY Died Sept. 7, 1968; buried Torrington WY

CONGER, (SEYMOUR) BEACH, III, journalist; b. Berlin, Germany, Mar. 1, 1912 (of Am. parents); s. Seymour Beach and Lucile (Bailey) C.; B.A., Univ. Mich., 1932; m. Marion Cunningham, July 8, 1938; children—Seymour Beach, Susan Garvin (Mrs. John R. Gullotta, Jr.). Research and publicity dir., The Crusaders, Detroit, Mich., 1932-33; foreign editor World Letters, Inc., 1933-36; (took yearly expedition to write weekly geography letters to U.S. schools, visiting every continent except polar regions); reporter New York Herald Tribune, 1936-39, foreign correspondent 1939-41, news editor, 1942-46, managing editor's department, 1946-56, editorial writer, 1956-62, Sunday news editor, 1962-66; with gen. books dept. Reader's Digest, 1966-69; was forced to leave Berlin by German government, November, 1939, corr. in Paris, 1939-40, covered German invasion of Holland, later to Budapest, Bucharest, Athens, after expulsion from Hungary. Fellow of the American Geographic Society; member Anglo-American Press. Assn. of Paris, Zeta Psi, Phi Eta Sigma, Sigma Delta Chi, Veterans of Amsterdam. Republican. Episcopalian. Clubs: Zeta Psi, University of Mich. (N.Y. City). Author artices in numerous Am. and fgn. mags. Home: Pleasantville NY Died Jan. 6, 1969; buried Wellfleet MA

CONGER JOHN LEONARD, educator; b. Silver City, Ia., July 10, 1876; s. Daniel Lampson and Caroline (Wilkinson) C.; U. of Neb., 1896-98; B.A., U. of Mich., 1904, M.A., 1905; Ph.D., U. of Wis., 1907; LL.D., Knox Coll., 1937; m. Ada Greenwood, June 22, 1904; children—James G., Amy Louise, Virginia. Head department of history and government, Knox College, Galesburg, Illinois, 1907-45, professor emeritus since 1945. Served as prof. Am. history summer sessions, at U. of Ill., U. of Mich., U. of Wash., U. of Calif., U. of Ia., Harvard and U. of Minn.; exchange prof., Knox Coll. to Harvard, 1923-24. Mayor of Galesburg, 1915-17. Mem. Am. Hist. Assn., Miss. Valley Hist. Assn., Phi Beta Kappa (Mich.), Phi Beta Kappa of Knox Coll. (charter mem.). Democrat. Conglist. Home: 428 S. Cedar St. Galesburg IL‡

CONKLIN, JOHN F., army officer; b. Kansas, Apr. 20, 1891; B.S., U.S. Mil, Acad., 1915; grad. Engr. Sch., 1921, Command and Gen. Staff Sch., 1927, Army War Coll., 1934. Commd. 2d lt., U.S. Army, 1915, and advanced through the grades to brig. gen., 1945. Decorated Distinguished Service Medal, Legion of Merit, Bronze Star. Home: Westmoreland Hills MD Died Jan. 25, 1973.

CONLEY, CLYDE, state govt. ofcl. State auditor, Ky. Address: Frankfort KY Died Mar. 1969.

CONNELLY, EMMA MARY, author; b. near Louisville, Ky.; d. John D. and Mary Anne (Thatcher) C.; ed. pvt. sems., Georgetown and Louisville, Ky.; unmarried. Began lit. work at lit. editor and paragraphist on Louisville Courier-Journal; since 1880 has lived chiefly in New York; contbr. serials and short articles to various periodicals. Author: Tilting at Windmills, 1888; Story of Kentucky (Story of the States Series), 1891; In China Land (pamphlet). Address: 41 E. 29th St., New York‡

CONNELLY, JOHN R., congressman; b. Brown Co., Ill., Feb. 1870; s. Arthur and Sarah Jane C.; ed. common schs., and Salina (Kan.) Normal U.; m. Lillian Souders, of Colby, Kan., June 17, 1896. Went to Kan. at 18; began teaching sch. at 19; county supt. schs., Thomas Co., Kan., 1895-9; owner and editor Colby Free Press since 1897; candidate for Congress on Dem. ticket, 1908 (defeated); mem. 63d to 65th Congresses (1913-19), 6th Kan. Dist. Mason; K.P. Home: Colby KS‡

CONNER, BRUCE, artist; b. McPherson, Kan., Nov. 18, 1933; B.F.A., U. Neb.; student U. Wichita, (with Reuben Tam) Bklyn. Mus. Sch., Kansas City Art Ints. and Sch. Design, U. Colo. Exhibited one-man shows including: Alan Gallery, 1960, 61, 63, 64; Batman Gallery, San Francisco, Ferus Gallery, 1963; Robert Fraser Gallery, London, Eng., 1964; group shows including: U. Ill., 1961; Mus. Modern Art, 1961; Whitney Mus. Am. Art, 1962-63; The Hague, Netherlands, 1964, others; represented in permanent collections Mus. Modern Art, San Francisco Mus. Art. Home: San Francisco CA Deceased

CONNER, FOX, army officer (ret.); born Slate Springs, Miss., Nov. 2, 1874; s. Robert H. and Nannie (Fox) C.; grad. U.S. Mil. Acad., 1898, Staff Coll., 1906, Army War Coll., 1908; m. Virginia Brandreth, June 4, 1902; children—Betty Virginia, Fox Brandreth, Florence Slocum. Commd. 2d lt. 2d Arty., Apr. 26, 1898; advanced through grades to lt. col. May 15, 1917; col. (temp.) Aug. 5-Dec. 5, 1917; brig.-gen. (temp.), Aug. 23, 1918; brig.-gen. regular army, April 27, 1921; maj. gen. U.S. Army, Oct. 20, 1925. At Ft. Adams, R.I., 1898, Havana, Cuba, 1900; comd. 123d Co., Coast Arty., at Ft. Hamilton, N.Y., 1901-05; detailed to Gen. Staff, 1907; arrived in France, June 1917; with Insp. Gen.'s Dept. A.E.F., served as mem. Operations Sect. Gen. Staff G.H.Q., A.E.F., and asst. C. of S. for Operations; comdr. Hawaiian Dept., 1928-30, First Corps Area, 1930-38. Address: Brandreth NY‡

CONNER, WALTER THOMAS, clergyman, educator; b. Cleveland County, Ark., Jan. 19, 1877; s. Philip Orlander and Frances (Monk) C.; A.B., Baylor U., 1906, A.M., 1908, D.D., 1920; B.D., Rochester Theol. Sem., 1910; Ph.D., Southern Bapt. Theol. Sem., 1931; m. Blanche Ethel Horne, June 4, 1907; children—Mary Irene, John Davis, Arnette, Blanche Ray, Neppie Leo, Sarah Frances. Ordained Bapt. ministry, 1899; prof. systematic theology, Southwestern Baptist Theological Seminary since Sept. 1910. Mem. Southwest Society for Biblical Study and Research, Pi Gamma Mu. Democrat. Author: System of Christian Doctrine, 1924; Gospel Doctrines, 1925; The Resurrection of Jesus, 1926; Teachings of Mrs. Eddy, 1926; Doctrines of Pastor Russell, 1926; The Epistles of John, 1929; Revelation and God, 1936; Personal

Christianity, 1937; The Christ We Need, 1938; The Faith of the New Testament, 1940; The Gospel of Redemption, 1945; The Work of the Holy Spirit, 1949. Contbr. to Southwestern Jour. Theology. Southwestern Evangel. Asso. editor Review and Expositor. Lecturer at Bible conferences and summer assemblies. Home: 4378 McCart St., Fort TX‡

CONNIFF, FRANK, journalist; b. Danbury, Conn., Apr. 24, 1914; s. Andrew Conniff; student U. Va., 1932-33; married Aug. 25, 1951; children—Anthony, Michael, Frank, Rex, Lucy. Sports writer Dambury News Times, then mem. staff N.Y. Jour. Am.; nat. editor Hearst Newspapers, 1958-66; editor World-Journal Tribune, N.Y.C., 1966-67; author syndicated column East Side, West Side; formerly general director Hearst Headlines Service; war corr. in Africa, Italy, Germany, also Korean war. Democratic candidate for U.S. Ho. of Reps., 1964. Recipient George Holmes award for overseas reporting, 1944, 47; co-recipient Pulitzer prize for interview with Premier Khruschev, 1955. Roman Cath. Clubs: Overseas Press (best fgn. reporting award 1958; past bd. govs.) (N.Y.C.). Home: New York City NY Died May 25, 1971.

CONNIFF, PAUL R., clergyman, educator; b. Oneida, N.Y., Dec. 22, 1871; s. Thomas and Ellen (Kelly) C.; student Fordham Coll., N.Y. City, 1888-90; A.B., Woodstock (Md.) Coll., 1897, A.M., 1898. Joined Soc. of Jesus (Jesuits), 1893; ordained priest R.C. Ch., 1907; v.-p. Brooklyn Coll., 1910, Fordham U., 1911; prof. dogmatic theology, Woodstock Coll., 1912-15; v. prin. Canisius High Sch., Buffalo, N.Y., 1915; pres. Gonzaga Coll., Washington, D.C., since 1916, also pastor St. Aloysius Ch. Home: 19 I St. N.W., Washington DC‡

CONNOR, EDWARD, govt. ofcl.; b. Chgo., Apr. 3, 1908; s. Daniel McGovern Sebastian and Jeannette (Guildersma) C.; B.A., U. Notre Dame, 1930; m. Hilda Radermacher, 1930; children—Edward, Michael, Patricia. Admitted to Ind. bar, 1935, Mich. bar, 1951; with Fed. Agys., 1935-43, successively county supr. adult edn. Pub. Works Agy., analyst community needs War Pub. Services Div., Pub. Works Adminstrn., with Chgo. Regional office, War Manpower Comm.; exec. dir. Future Detroit, Inc., Citizens Housing and Planning Council, 1943-48; mem. Detroit's Common Council, 1948-67; judge Recorders Ct., 1966. Mem. Wayne County Bd. Suprs., 1948-58, 64-65, chairman of the board, 1954-58; supervisor of Inter-County Com., 1954-57; sec. southeastern Mich. Met. Community Research Corp., 1954-60, cons., 1960-63; mem. exec. bd. Detroit Met. Area Regional Planning Commn., 1947-67, chmn., 1952; mem. Fed. Adv. Commn. Intergovtl. Relations, 1959-67. Mem. Surgeon Gen.'s adv. com. on urban health affairs, 1963-65, mem. Nat. Adv. Environmental Health Com. Mem. Mich. State Assn. Suprs. (chmn. bd. dirs. 1963-67), Nat. Assn. County Ofcls. (1st v.p., director), Am. Fedn. Tchrs. Moose, Elk, K.C. Club: Notre Dame Alumni. Home: Detroit MI Died Feb. 18, 1967.

CONOVER, (JAMES) MILTON, educator; b. South Harrison Twp., N.J., Aug. 16, 1890; s. Samuel S. and Atlantic Dean (Moore) C.; Ph.B., Dickinson Coll., 1913, Sc.D., 1933; M.A. in Polit. Sci., U. Minn., 1916; M.A., Harvard, 1934; postgrad in politics univs. of Oxford, Munich and Paris (Inst. of Urbanism); LL.B., Vanderbilt U., 1955, J.D., 1969. Corr., Boston Herald, 1908-09; tchr. pub. schs., Swedesboro, N.J., 1909-10, St. Matthew's Episcopal Sch., Burlingame, Cal., 1913-15; admitted to Ind. bar, 1916; bill draftsman Ind. Legislature, 1917; fellow polit. sci. Ind. U., 1916-17; instr. govt. U. Pa. and Camden YMCA, 1919-20, N.Y. U., 1922-24, 46-47; mem. faculty govt. Yale, 1924-35, asso. prof., 1930-35; seminarian Princeton U. and Dropsie Coll. for Hebrew and Cognate Learning, Phila., 1938-39; investigated Indian and French communities in Can., 1941-42; resident researcher Cath. U. Am., Washington, 1942-43; research Middle Am. Research Inst., New Orleans, 1943-44; legal practice, Chgo., 1944-45; law adjudicator U.S. VA, Newark, 1946-48; seminarian in law Columbia, 1948-53; lectr. finance Rutgers U., 1949; mem. faculties of social sci. and law Seton Hall U., 1947-68, asso. prof. law, 1955, prof. law, 1960-68, prof. emeritus law, 1968-72; exec. sec. N.J. Assn. Pvt. Colls. and Univs., 1958-60. Served as pvt. 3d N.J. Inf., 1917, later cpl. 104th Engrs., 29th Div.; commd. 2d lt. inf., Camp Lee, Va.; with 42d (Rainbow) Div. in Argonne drive; convoy officer Army of Occupation, Germany; diplomatic courier to Am. Commn. to Negotiate Peace, Paris, operating in Finland, Lithuania, Poland, Czechoslovakia, Italy and Greece; del. Founders' Conv. of Am. Legion, Paris, 1919; mem. staff Inst. for Govt. Research, Brookings Instn., Washington, 1921-22, asso., 1922-32; visited numerous countries and fgn. univs.; mil.-polit. observations in Europe, mid-Asia and Africa, journeying mainly by land from France to Mongolia and Korea via Siberia, 1929-30, Germany to India and Arabia via Khyber Pass, 1935-37, Latin-Am., finishing journey mainly by land from Alaska to Strait of Magellan, 1939-40; studied Negro self-govt. in Haiti, 1940-41; explored wildlife conditions North of Arctic Circle, 1971; pres. Am. Immigrant Inst. Conn., affillie Nat. Inst. of Immigrant Welfare, 1934-35. Recipient Bernard J. McQuald Distinguished Service Medal Seton Hall U., 1969. Mem. Royal Soc. Tchrs. (London), Holland Soc. of N.Y., Huguenot Soc. of N.J., Swedish Colonial Soc., Van Kouwenhoven-Conover Family Assn., Soc. Colonial Wars, Am., Fed., Inter-Am. bar assns., Order of Founders and Patriots of Am., Assn. Princeton Grad. Alumni, S.A.R., Delta Theta Phi, Phi Kappa Psi, Grange (7), Oxford Soc. Pi Gamma Mu. Club: Harvard. Author: The General Land Office, 1923; The Federal Power Commission, 1923; The Office of Experiment Stations. 1924; Working Manual of Original Sources in American Government, 1924; Working Manual of Civics, 1925; co-author Political Theory, 1959. Contbr. to legal and social sci. publs. Home: Mullica Hill NJ Died May 6, 1972; buried Swedesboro NJ

CONROY, THOMAS MICHAEL, investment banker; b. Cin., Apr. 1, 1896; s. Andrew J. and Mary Elizabeth (Clements) C.; ed. Hughes High Sch., Franklin Sch., Brown U.; m. Olga Marie Nugent, Apr. 27, 1927; children—Thomas Michael, Edwin Nugent, Olga (Mrs. James H. Stoehr, Jr.). Vice pres., dir. A. J. Conroy Co., Cincinnati, 1920-25, Globe-Wernicke Co., Cincinnati, 1925-30; sec., treas., dir. Cincinnati Baseball Club Co. 1932-70; with Central Trust Co., Cin., 1930-61, sr. v.p., v.p. finance, exec. coms., now dir.; investment banker W.E. Hutton & Co., Cincinnati, O., 1962-70. Mem. bd. of trustees, and president Thomas J. Emery Meml.; chmn. finance com., trustee Cin. Music Hall Assn.; mem. Cin. Adv. Com. Airports. Mem. adv. council Boys Clubs Cin. Served with U.S. Navy, World War I; lt comdr., U.S.N.R.F. Awarded Navy Cross; Chevalier Del Ordre Saviour of Greece. Mem. A.I.M., Mil. Order World Wars (life), Psi Upsilon. Clubs: Question (Detroit); Commercial, Bankers, Queen City, Camargo, Miami, Commonwealth, Cincinnati Country (Cin.). Home: Cincinnati OH Died Mar. 13, 1970; buried Spring Grove Cemetery, Cincinnati OH

CONSIDINE, JAMES W(ILLIAM), corp. exec.; born Washington, Jan. 24, 1908; s. James Leo and Marie Calfernia (Bell) C.; B.C.S., Benjamin Franklin U., 1928; LL.B., Columbus University, Washington, 1938; married Carrie Estelle Layton, February 9, 1929; children—Carrie Marie (Mrs. E. L. Haan), Catherine Lee (Mrs. Martin S. Kilsdonk), Jane Myrtle (Mrs. Ralph Lemon), James W., Linda Anne (Mrs. Thomas J. Fitzsimmons III). Admitted to practice before U.S. Supreme Court bar, also admitted to D.C. bar, 1938; treasurer Defense Homes Corp., Washington, 1940-43, Metals Reserve Co., 1943-45; asst. treas. Reconstrn. Finance Corp., 1944-47, controller, 1948-50, became asst. to dir., 1948; asst. treas. Fed. Nat. Mortgage Assn., 1938-45, controller and asst. to dir. 1948-67, v.p., 1967-71; became asst. to pres. Gar Wood Industries, Inc., Wayne, Mich., sec.-treas., dir., mem. exec. com., until 1967. Pres. Long Lake Shore Civic Assn. C.P.A., D.C. Mem. Am. Bar Assn., Am. Ordnance Assn., Mich. Soc. C.P.A.'s, Am. Soc. Corporate Secs., Sigma Delta Kappa. K.C. Home: Alexandria VA Died Mar. 31, 1971; buried Gate of Heaven Cemetery, Silver Spring MD

CONSTANGY, FRANK ALAN, lawyer; b. Atlanta, Feb. 23, 1911; s. Harry and Mamie (Cohen) C.; A.B., U. Ga., 1929, J.D., 1930; m. Eleanor Smullyan, Nov. 4, 1931; 1 dau., Carolyn (Mrs. Richard S. Wasser). Admitted to Ga. bar, 1930, since practiced in Atlanta; mem. firm Walker, Kilbridge & Constangy, 1933-35; mem. dress code authority and millinery code authority NRA, 1933-35; S.E. regional atty. Social Security Bd., 1936-38; S.E. regional atty. FSA, 1938-41; regional dir. operations S.E. War Manpower Commn., 1941-45; chmn. industry mem. S.E. War Labor Bd., S.E. Wsb, 1944-46; sr. partner Constangy & Prowell, 1945; prof. constl. law Woodrow Wilson Coll. Law 1933-44; gen. counsel Tufted Textile Mfrs. Assn., Carpet and Rug Inst. Am. Dir. Murray Ohio Mfg. Co. Participant Nat. Labor Relations Conf., 1945; chmn. Bd. of Rev., Employment Security Agy. of Ga., 1950-71; mem. Gov.'s staff, Govs. Griffin, Arnall and Sanders of Ga., 1945-50, 62-66; mem. Adv. Council on Employment Security Legislation 1945-71; mem. Ga. Commn. Aging, 1962-70 mem. adv. bd. Vets. Re-employment Rights. Recipient Merit award for war time service Pres. Truman, 1946. Mem. Am. (mem. Ho. of Dels., past chmn. labor relations law sect.) Ga., Atlanta bar assns., Tau Epsilon Phi, Omicron Delta Kappa. Republican. Jewish religion. Clubs: Commerce, Standard (both Atlanta). Contbr. articles profl. jours. Home: Atlanta GA Died Apr. 11, 1971.

CONWAY, ALBERT, justice; b. Bklyn., Apr. 3, 1889; s. Joseph P. and Jane Lucille (Flanagan) C.; ed. St. Johns Coll., Bklyn., LL.D., 1932; LL.B., Fordham U., 1911, LL.D., 1930; LL.D., Syracuse U., 1949, Manhattan Coll., 1951, Brooklyn Law School, 1957, New York Law School, 1956, Union College (Schenectady, New York), 1957; D.C.L., N.Y.U., 1955; m. Irene M. Hewitt, Apr. 17, 1917 (died May 5, 1929); children—Alberta Irene (Mrs. Edwin M. Jones), Elaine Margaret (Mrs. Edward J. McLaughlin), Hewitt, Lois Jane (Mrs. Ralph E. Crabill, Jr.); m. 2d, Alice O'Neil, Sept. 19, 1933. Admitted to New York bar, 1910. and began practice at Brooklyn. Asst. dist. atty. Kings County, 1913-20; professor equity jurisprudence St. Lawrence University, Brooklyn Law School, 1918-19; candidate for attorney general, state of New York, 1928; supt. of insurance, in Cabinet of Gov. Roosevelt, N.Y., 1929-30; apptd. county judge, Kings County, by Gov. Roosevelt, 1930, elected to same office, 1930; elected justice New York Supreme Court, 1931 (after being nominated by both the major parties); assigned to Appellate term of Supreme Ct., Oct. 1937; assigned by Gov. Lehman, 1939, to hold extraordinary term of Supreme Court for Erie County involving municipal affairs of Buffalo; apptd. by Governor Lehman an associate judge of the Court of Appeals of New York, January 1940; elected to same office after nomination by both major parties, 1940; chief judge, Court of Appeals of N.Y., 1954-60; offical referee Court of Appeals of New York, 1960-62; justice Supreme Ct. of State of N.Y. 1962-66. Trustee Brooklyn Inst. Arts and Sciences, Brooklyn Law Library, Grant Monument Assn.; vice chmn., past pres. Brooklyn Council, Boy Scouts of America; member of regional executive committee, Region 2, (New York and New Jersey). Mem. Bill of Rights Commemorative Soc. (past v.p.), Nat. Probation and Parole Assn. (past trustee), Conf. Chief Justices of States (chmn. 1958-59), Am. Law Inst., Am., N.Y., Bklyn. (past trustee) bar assns. Assn. Bar City N.Y., Lawyers Club, Delta Theta Phi. Democrat. Catholic. Clubs: Authors' (London); Century (N.Y.C.); Cathedral, Rembrandt, Brooklyn; Fort Orange (Albany). 1969; buried St. John's Cemetery, Middle Village NY

CONWAY, HERBERT, plastic surgeon; b. Ft. Wayne, Ind., June 25, 1904; s. James Francis and Irene (McCarthy) C.; student Miami U., 1921-24; B.S., U. Cin., 1929, M.S., 1932, M.B., 1928, M.D. (Taft fellow in surgery 1928-29), 1929, D. Sc. (hon.), 1969; m. Frances Gallagher, Nov. 7, 1936; children—Karen, Richard William, Catherine Lanning. Asst. resident surgeon Cin. Gen. Hosp., 1929-32; asst. resident surgeon New York Hosp., 1932-33, asst. attending surgeon, 1935-42, attending surgeon, attending surgeon in charge plastic surgery, 1945-69; instr. surgery Cornell U. Med. Coll., 1932-35, asst. prof. surgery, 1935-45, asso. prof. clin. surgery, 1945-55, prof. clin. surgery, 1955-69; cons. plastic surgeon VA Hosp., Bronx, N.Y., 1945-69; cons. plastic surgery White Plains (N.Y.) Hosp., Bellevue Hosp., Hosp. Spl. Surgery; cons. plastic and reconstructive surgery Health Center, Inc., N.Y.C., 1950-69; cons., lectr. plastic surgery St. Albans (N.Y.) Naval Hosp., 1957-69; 1st vis. prof. Found. Am. Soc. Plastic and Reconstructive Surgery to Latin Am. (Brazil), 1965; guest prof. U. Cal. at Los Angeles, 1965; guest prof. N.Y.U. Med. Center, 1966, V.H. Kazanjian lecturer, 1966. Board of directors of Goodwill Industries, New York Society Crippled Children Adults; rep. Acad. Surgery of Peru to American College of Surgeon, 1950-69; pres., trustee Found. Am. Soc. Plastic and Reconstructive Surgery, 1960-61; spl. State Dept. lectr. India, Saudi Arabia, Pakistan, Lebanon, 1962-63. Served as lt. col. M.C., AUS, 1942-45; chief plastic surgery Lovell Gen. Hosp.; chief surg. service 116th Sta. Hosp., Port Moresby, New Guinea, 54th Gen. Hosp., Hollandia, New Guinea, Batanges, P.I.; plastic surg. cons. S.W. Pacific area. Decorated Bronze Star; hon. surgeon Police Dept. City N.Y.; Colles medal Royal Coll. Surgeons Ireland. Diplomate Am. Bd. Plastic Surgery (chmn.), Am. Bd. Surgery, Mem. New York State, N.Y. County med. socs., New York Regional Soc. of Plastic Surgeons (pres.), A.M.A., N.Y. Acad. Medicine, N.Y. Surg. Soc., N.Y. Soc. Electromicroscopists, N.Y. Cancer Soc., Am. Surg. Assn., Soc. Univ. Surgeons, Internat. Soc. Surgery, Soc. Med. Cons. World War II, Mont Reid Surg. Soc., Am. Soc. Surgery of the Hand, Society Head and Neck Surgery, British Association Plastic Surgeons, A.C.S., American Academy Compensation Medicine (chairman plastic surgery sect. 1949-69), Pan Am. Med. Assn. (chmn. plastic surgery sect. 1952-59), Am. Assn. Plastic Surgeons (trustee 1954-57, president 1960-61), American Soc. Plastic and Reconstructive Surgery (chmn. pub. relations com. 1954-57), Sigma Delta Chi, Delta Upsilon, Alpha Kappa Kappa; hon. mem. Faculty Medicine U. Chile, Acad. Surgery of Chile, Chilean Soc. Plastic and Reconstructive Surgery, Acad. Surgery of Peru, Hollywood Med. Assn., Argentine Med. Assn., French Society of Plastic Surgery, also hon. mem. Argentine Assn. Plastic Surgery. Knights of Malta. Clubs: University (N.Y.C.); Larchmont Yacht; Westchester Country; Everglades, Bathing and Tennis and Seminole Golf (Palm Beach, Fla.). Editor Transplantation Bull.; U.S. editor Revista Latino Americana de Cirurgia Plastica; asso. editor Jour. of Surgery, N.Y. State Jour. of Medicine, Plastic and Reconstructive Surgery, 1956-66. Home: Larchmont NY Died Aug. 25, 1969; buried Gate of Heaven, Valhala NY

COOK, ALICE RICE, educator; b. Bridgewater, Mass., June 24, 1899; d. Ernest L. and Georgiana (Wrisley) C.; B.A., Smith Coll., 1921; M.A., Radcliffe Coll., 1924; fellow Columbia, 1934-35. Instr. English, secondary and higher edn., 1921-30; pres. E. L. Cook Brick Co., 1927-47; dean Briarcliff Jr. Coll., 1930-34; instr. self-evaluation N.Y.U., 1938-1942; supervisor employee relations, counseling dept. Arma Corp., 1943-45; director of Human Relations Center, City Coll. N.Y., 1951-57; founder, director of Human Relations Center, New School Social Research, 1951-66. Mem. Am. Assn. U. Women, League Women Voters, Delta Kappa Gamma. Unitarian. Club: Personnel (N.Y.C.). Home: New York City NY

COOK, ANDREW BRUCE, newspaper editor; b. Rahway, N.J., Oct. 19, 1898; s. Clarence Jeheil and Anna Marie (Chambers) C.; student U. Richmond, 1921; m. Grace Alverta Bare, Apr. 1, 1923; 1 dau., Elizabeth (Mrs. John Schlicting); m. 2d, Ida Marie Schmidt, Sept. 16, 1961. Reporter, Richmond Times-Dispatch, Balt. Am., Elizabeth (N.J.) Jour., Elizabeth Times and Tri-City News, Bradenton, Fla., 1921-28; editor semi-weekly Rahway (N.J.) Record, 1923-25; editor, pub. This Week in Venice, Sarasota, Fla., 1925-27; Land of Manatee, Bradenton, Fla., 1926-27; with Hudson Dispatch, Union City, N.J., 1928-69, mng. editor, 1941-60, editor, 1960-69. Served to 2d lt. U.S. Army, 1918. Mem. Am. Legion. Baptist. Rotarian (hon.) Mason. Home: Fort Lee NJ Died June 30, 1969.

COOK, CHARLES EMERSON, writer; A.B., Harvard, 1893. With Boston Budget, 1893-6; since in New York; head of press dept. David Belasco's theatrical enterprises. First pres. The Friars; mem. Delta Upsilon. Author: (comic operas) The Rose of the Alhambra; Red Feather (music by DeKoven). Address: Belasco Theatre New York‡

COOK, CLINTON DANA, educator, chemist; b. St. Johnsbury, Vt., Feb. 20, 1921; s. Clinton Dana and Anna Francis (Kubavec) C.; S.B., Mass. Inst. Tech., 1942; M.S., U. Vt., 1948; Ph.D. in Chemistry, Ohio State U., 1951; m. Alice Maclaren Fisher, May 21, 1944; children—Dana, Allison, Polly, Timothy, Cynthia. Group leader chemistry Gen. Electric Co., W. Lynn (Mass.) works, 1942-46, supervising chemist liquid dielectrics sect., Pittsfield, Mass., 1951-52; instr. chemistry U. Vt., 1946-48; asst. instr., research fellow Ohio State U., 1948-51, vis. grad. prof. chemistry, summer 1959; faculty U. Vt., 1952-69, prof. chemistry, 1959-69, chairman dept. chemistry, 1960-63, became dean of faculties, 1963, v.p. acad. affairs, 1965-69, chmn. premed. adv. sect. 1956-60; cons. organic chemistry U.S. Rubber Co., 1956-59; cons. NSF Instnl. Programs, 1965-—. Trustee St. Johnsbury (Vt.) Acad. Mem. Am. Chem. Soc., Sigma Xi (pres. Vt. chpt. 1956), Phi Lambda Upsilon. Contbr. articles profl. jours. Home: Burlington VT Died June 25, 1969.

COOK, EDWARD NOBLE, former physician; b. St. Paul, Aug. 21, 1905; s. Edward and Jessie Gertrude (Noble) C.; B.A., U. Minn., 1926, B.S., 1927, B. Medicine, 1928, M.D., 1929, M.S. in Urology, 1935; m. Jean Elizabeth Moore, June 14, 1934; children—Margaret (Mrs. C.M. Berndt, Jr.), Edward Noble, Nancy (Mrs. L. Bruce Nelson). Intern, Kings County Hosp., Bklyn., 1929-30; mem. staff Mayo Found., U. Minn., from 1930-72, prof. urology, from 1958-72; staff Mayo Clinic, 1935-70, cons. urology, 1935-70; cons. urology Meth., St. Mary's hosps.; spl. research infections urinary tract, transurethral surgery; ret., 1970. Served as lt. M.C., USN, 1939-47. Mem. Am. Urol. Assn., A.M.A. (sec. sect. urology 1946-49), chmn. sec. 1949-50), Societe Internationale de Chirugie, Minn. Med. Assn., Olmsted County Med. Soc., Sigma Xi, Delta Upsilon, Alpha Kappa Kappa. Clubs: Country, Rochester MN Died July 26, 1972; buried Oakwood Cemetery, Rochester MN

COOK, GEORGE ROY, utility co. exec.; b. Springfield, Ill., Sept. 16, 1907; s. William Roy and Marie (Ruch) C.; B.S., U. Ill., 1929. With Central Ill. Pub. Service Co., Springfield, 1929-73, asst. treas., 1951-58, treas., asst. sec., 1958-61, v.p., sec., 1961-73. Home: Springfield IL Died May 1973.

COOK, H. EARL, banking exec.; b. Bucyrus, O., June 19, 1886; s. Frederick J. and Rosa (Wagner) C.; extension courses, La Salle Inst., Chicago, 1925-27, O. State U., 1930-31; m. Edna Ehmann, Oct. 27, 1908; children—Martha Elizabeth (Mrs. Robt. Downard), Ruth (Mrs. John F. Shaner), Harold Earl. Teacher, Bucyrus, 1906-07; with 2d Nat. Bank, Bucyrus, 1907-43, teller, asst. cashier, cashier, dir., pres., 1929-43; supt. banks of O., Columbus, 1943-47; dir. Fed. Deposit Insurance Corp., Washington, 1947-57, chmn., 1953-57; director Plains Exploration Co., Denver, 1931-57, v.p. 1940-57, chairman board, 1957; bank consultant member faculty Central States School Banking Madison, Wis. Pres. Bucyrus C. of Co., 1924-25 Sch. Bd., 1928-40; mem. Civilian Defense Staff, Bucyrus, 1941-45. Trustee Central Hosp. Assn., Columbus, 1940-47; mem. Ohio Banking Adv. Bd., 1941-43. Mem. Am. (pres. nat. bank div. 1938-39), Ohio (chmn. 1935-36, pres. 1938-39), bankers assns., Nat. Assn. Suprs. State Banks (2d v.p., 1946-47). Republican. Evangelical Church. Mason (33 deg., Shriner), Red Cross of Constantine, Royal Order of Scotland. Clubs: Nat. Press (Washington), Rotary, Elks (Bucyrus); Sphinx. Home: St. Louis MO Died Apr. 3, 1971; buried Bucyrus OH

COOK, JOHN HENRY, lawyer; b. Jasper Co., Miss., Feb. 27, 1874; s. Marshall and Susan (Mounger) C.; grad. high sch., Heidelberg, Miss., 1895; m. Annie Griffith, of Silver Creek, Miss., June 1900; children—Celia Anna (Mrs. R. B. Davis), Vivian, Marshall, Rebecca, John Henry, Virgil Griffith, Frederick Milton, Robert Morehead. Postmaster, Ellisville, Miss., 1899-1906; admitted to Miss. bar, 1902, and began practice at Pascagoula; U.S. marshal Northern Dist. of Miss., 1922-25; U.S. dist. atty. same dist. since Dec. 22, 1925. Mem. Miss. State Bar Assn. Republican. Methodist. Mason (Shriner), Elk. Home: 204 Sharkey St. Address: Federal Bldg., Clarksdale MS‡

COOK, PETER, JR., bus. exec.; b. San Francisco, 1898; s. Peter and Julia (Mastin) C.; U. Cal., 1920, m. Mary West, Sept. 9, 1920 (dec. Jan. 29, 1969); children—Julia (Mrs. Doty), Marion (Mrs. Tilton). Dir. Western Pacific R.R. Company, Wells Fargo Bank, Emporium Capwell Company, Pacific Tel. & Tel. Company. Served in Armed Forces World War I. Home: Rio Vista CA Died July 4, 1970.

COOKE, ARTHUR BLEDSOE, foreign service officer of United States, retired; b. Melton's, Louisa County, Va., June 15, 1869; s. George Washington and Sallie Farrar (Anderson) C.; B.A., U. of Virginia, 1895, Ph.D., 1901 (for work at U. of Va. and Gottingen); m. Stella Viola Crider, Sept. 26, 1899; children—Katherine Anderson (Mrs. W. G. Davies), Stella Virginia (dec.), Karl Arthur (dec.), Mary Clifton (Mrs. G. P. Wickham Legg), Arthur Louis, Earle Truesdale. Prof. German and French, Wofford Coll., Spartanburg, S.C., 1895-1908; dir. dept. European civilization and langs., Throop Coll. of Tech., Pasadena, Calif., 1908-10; dir. Summer School same coll., 1909; Am. consul, Patras, Greece, 1910-19, Swansea, Wales, 1919-26, Plymouth, Eng., 1926-34. Hon. mem. U. of Va. Chapter Phi Beta Kappa, 1910. Democrat. Methodist. Author: Nature-Sense in the German Lyric, 1901; Essays on Work and Life, 1904; With the Tourist Tide, 1907. Contbr. on lit. topics. Home: 3111 First Av., Richmond, Va. Address: care Dept. of State, Washington DC‡

COOKE, CHARLES MAYNARD, JR., naval officer; b. Ft. Smith, Ark., Dec. 19, 1886; s. Charles Maynard and Sarah Bleeker (Luce) C.; B.S., U. of Ark., 1905; B.S., U.S. Naval Acad., 1910; m. Lesley Temple, April 30, 1913 (died 1917); children—Lesley (dec.), Anne Bleeker; m. 2d, Mary Louise Cooper, Oct. 5, 1921; children—Mary Maynard, Carol Ridgely, Charles Maynard, III. Commd. ensign, U.S. Navy, 1912 and advanced through the grades to admiral, 1946; commanded Submarines E-2, R-2. S-5, Submarine Division 11, Battleship Pennsylvania; commandant, Naval Station, Guantanamo; Fleet war plans officer, U.S. Fleet, 1936-38; asst. chief of staff, comdr. in chief, U.S. Fleet, 1942-45. Chief of Staff to Comdr. in chief U.S. Fleet, Sept. 1944-Oct. 1945; deputy chief Naval Operations, 1945; comdr. 7th Fleet, 1946-48, retired May 1, 1948. Awarded D.S.M., Victory Medal (World Wars I and II); Hon. Knight Comdr. Mil. Order of Most Excellent Order of British Empire. Officer dans l'Ordre de la Legion d'Honneur, French Republic. Mem. U.S. Naval Inst. Club: Army and Navy (Washington, D.C.). Home: Sonoma CA Died Dec. 24, 1970.

COOKE, HARRISON RICE, banker; b. Honolulu, Oct. 11, 1908; s. Clarence Hyde and Lily (Love) C.; student Yale, 1928-30; m. Dorothea Sloggett, Apr. 7, 1931. With Bank of Hawaii, 1930-34; v.p., sec. Cooke Trust Co., Honolulu, 1934-41; pres. Honolulu Sporting Goods Co., 1946-73; chmn. Bank of Hawaii, 1963-73; pres. Molokai Ranch Ltd., 1958-73, Molokai Electric Co., 1961-73. Trustee, v.p. Honolulu Acad. Arts. Served to comdr. USNR, 1941-45. Decorated Bronze Star. Home: Honolulu HI Died Feb. 9, 1973.

COOKE, JOHN DANIEL, educator; born Beloit, Kan., May 26, 1892; s. Edwin Willis and Sarah Arminda (Shutts) C.; A.B., Stanford U., 1914, A.M., 1915, Ph.D., 1924; m. Grace Steinberger, Aug. 15, 1917; (dec. 1945); 1 dau., Marianne Whitehead; married 2d Mariam Bailey Parr, April 15, 1950. Assistant in Greek, Stanford U., 1913-15; instr. English, Kan. State Agrl. Coll., 1915-17; instr. comparative and English lit., U. of Colo., 1917-19; asst. prof. of Eng., Wash. State Coll., 1919-20; asst. prof., prof. English, U. of So. Calif., 1920-60, dept. head, 1930-38, chmn. div. humanities, 1938-59., ednl. dir., Naval Flight Prep. Sch., 1943; dean summer sessions, 1945-60, now emeritus, acting dean grad. sch., 1956-58. Mem. Am. Assn. U. Professors, Modern Lang. Assn. Am., Pacific Coast Philol. Assn., Phi Beta Kappa (chmn. essay contest Southern Calif. Alumni 1930-36), Phi Delta Kappa, Phi Kappa Phi, Alpha Phi Epsilon. Catholic. Mason. Club: Am. College Quill (high chancellor 1934-36). Editor: Minor Victorian Poets, 1928; Essays for the New America (with M. C. Struble), 1930; English Literature of the Victorian Period (with Lionel Stevenson), 1949. Home: Palm Desert CA Died June 1972.

COOLEY, ANNA MARIA, prof. household arts; b. New York, Sept. 16, 1874; d. Charles Wallace and Emma (Davin) Cooley; grad. New York Normal Coll., 1893; grad. Jenny Hunter Kindergarten Training Sch., New York, 1894; Barnard Coll., 1896; B.S., Teachers Coll. (Columbia) and Bachelor's diploma for teaching household arts, 1903. Prin. domestic art and domestic sci., Hackley Manual Training Sch., Muskegon, Mich., 1904; instr., U. of Tenn., summer sessions, 1905-07; asst. household arts, 1904-05, tutor, 1905-06; instr., 1906-10, asst. prof., 1910-17, asso. prof., 1917-23, prof., 1923-41, professor emeritus since 1941. Teachers College (Columbia University). Presbyterian. Mem. Am. Home Economics Assn., N.E.A., Am. Assn. Univ. Women, Nat. Inst. Social Science, Am. Acad. Polit. and Social Sciences. Clubs: Home, Economics, Household Arts, American Women's. Author: Occupations for Little Fingers (with Elizabeth Sage), 1905; Domestic Art in Woman's Education, 1910; also Household Arts Text-Books, Vol. I, Shelter and Clothing, Vol. II, Foods and Management (Kinne and Cooley), 1913; textbooks for rural communities, Vol. I, Food and Health, Vol. II, Clothing and Health, Vol. III, The Home and the Family, 1916; Household Arts for Home and School (Cooley & Spohr), Vols. I and II, 1920; Teaching Home Economics (in collaboration), 1920 Home: 501 W. 120th St., New York NY‡

COOLEY, ARTHUR HENDERSON, banker; b. South Deerfield, Mass., May 7, 1875; s. James D. and Candace E. (Henderson) C.; ed. pub. and high schs., Hartford; m. Jessie W. Wheeler, of Springfield, Mass., 1902. Began in employ Am. Nat. Bank, Hartford, 1892; with Security Trust Co., 1899-1919, advancing to asst. treas.; pres. Mutual Bank & Trust Co. since 1919; v.p. Plimpton-Hills Corpn. Mem. Am. Inst. Banking. Republican. Episcopalian. Clubs: City, Rotary, Hartford Advertising, Automobile, Sequin Golf. Home: 54 Bishop Rd., West Hartford. Office: 75 Pearl St., Hartford CT‡

COOLEY, CHARLES PARSONS, banker; b. Hartford, Conn., Feb. 25, 1867; s. Francis B. and Clarissa A. (Smith) C.; A.B., Yale, 1891; m. Zaidee Whitman, Jan. 9, 1901; children—Charles Parsons, Paul Whitman. Engaged in banking bus. since 1896; dir. Hartford Nat. Bank & Trust Co., Smyth Mfg., Co., Aetna Ins. Co., Conn. Gen. Life Ins. Co., Hartford Steam Boiler Inspn. Ins. Co., Hartford Gas Co., Landers, Frary & Clark; chmn. bd. Soc. for Savings. Mem. S.A.R., Soc. Colonial Wars, Delta Kappa Epsilon (Phi Chapter). Republican. Conglist. Clubs: Hartford, Hartford Golf; University (New York); Graduate (New Haven). Home: 1093 Prospect Av., West Hartford, Conn. Office: 31 Pratt St., Hartford CT*‡

COOLEY, ETHEL HALCROW (MRS. JOHN B. COOLEY), ex-mem. Rep. Nat. Com.; b. Nowesta, N.D., June 22, 1888; d. John and Elizabeth (Manson) Halcrow; A. B., U. of N.D., 1914; grad. Wesley Coll., 1914; m. John Booth Cooley, May 12, 1917 (dec.); children—Madeline Ethel (Mrs. W.O.S. Sutherland, Jr.), Mary Elizabeth (deceased), Dorothy Frances (Mrs. Joseph S. Massee). Farm editor for Grand Forks (N.D.) Herald, 1920-30, Watertown (S.D.) Pub. Opinion, 1933-47; comml. mgr. radio sta. KLPM, Minot, N.D., 1936-56; president Minot Broadcasting Company, Inc., 1958-70; lobbyist for pure seed legislation, establishing state seed dept., N.D., 1929, S.D., 1933; member national board field advisers Small Business Administration; assistant director Dakota Playmakers, U. of N.D., 1912-19, acting dir. univ. extension div., 1916-18, N.D. rep. Republican Nat. Com. 1948-61. Mem. Independent Voters Assn. (chmn. women's div., N.D., 1928-33), Minot Assn. Commerce, N.D. Press Women, Nat. Fedn. Press Women, Nat. Soc. Arts and Letters, Columbia Sheep Breeders Assn. Am., Quota Internat., Am. Legion Auxilliary, N.D. Fed. Women's Clubs. Methodist. Clubs: Women's Country (Minot). Home: Minot ND Died Aug. 31, 1970; buried Memorial Park, Grand Forks ND

COOLEY, ROBERT ALLEN, entomologist; b. Deerfield, Mass., June 27, 1873; s. Alfred A. and Charlotte Maria C.; B.S., Mass. Agrl. Coll., 1895; studied entomology under Prof. C. H. Fernald, of Mass. Agrl. Coll.; D.Sc., Mont. State Coll., 1936; m. Edith M. Cooley, June 7, 1899 (died Aug. 1920); children—Charlotte Packard (Mrs. Gray D. Dickason), Robert Allen (dec.), Genevieve (Mrs. Kenneth M. McIver); m. 2d, Elsie Eddy Jolliffe, Aug. 13, 1925. Prof entomology, Mont. Coll., and entomologist, Mont. Experiment Sta., 1899-1931; state entomologist, Mont., 1903-31; leader of African tick parasite expdn., 1928; entomologist U.S.P.H.S., 1931-41, sr. entomologist from 1941. Fellow A.A.A.S.; mem. Assn. Econ. Entomologists. Republican. Presbyn. Home: Hamilton MT Died Nov. 16, 1968.

COOLIDGE, HERBERT, author; b. at Natick, Mass. Nov. 30, 1875; s. Francis and Sophia (Whittemore) C. Riverside (Cal.) High Sch. 1 yr.; spl. student in sociology and economics, Stanford U., 5 yrs., 1899-04 m. Harriett Henrietta Brown, of Palo Alto, Cal., June 28, 1904. Sec. Y.M.C.A., Stanford U., 1903-4; home missionary, Pitt River Indians, Shasta Co., Cal., 1904-6 pub. health work, for Cal. State Bd. of Health, 1907-11 Began writing fiction, 1903. Progressive. Conglist Clubs: Quadrangle, English (Stanford U.). Author Pancho McClish, 1912. Home: 1848 Emerson St., Palo Alto CA‡

COOMBE, HARRY E. (JAMES), business, exec.; b Cincinnati, Nov. 4, 1888; s. Harry H. and Lida (Greenwald) C.; B.A., Yale, 1910; m. Mary Anderson Jan. 27, 1923; children—Vachel Anderson, Mary Anderson. Machinist, Wm. Powell Co., Cincinnati 1910-12, salesman, 1912-17, asst. to pres., 1920-26 v.p., 1926-40, became pres., gen. mgr., director, 1940 chmn. bd. gen. mgr., chief exec.; director Philip Cary Manufacturing Co., Robert A. Cline, Inc., Randall Co., 1st Nat. Bank of Cin., Cincinnati Baseball Club Co., Baldwin-Lima-Hamilton Co., Procter & Gamble Co. Trustee The Children's Home. Served as capt., F.A., U.S. Army, 1917-19; overseas 1918-19. Clubs: Queen City, Camargo, Cincinnati Country, Twenty Nine, Racquet, Commercial, Commonwealth (Cin.); University (N.Y.C.); Misquamicut (Watch Hill, R.I.). Home: Cincinnati OH Died Mar. 7, 1969.

COOMBS, HARRISON S., pediatrician; b. Cornwall, Pa., Apr. 15, 1921; s. Robert Duncan and Harriet (Lord) C.; M.D., Tufts U., 1945; m. Elizabeth Gaskill, July 1, 1944; children—Lee (Mrs. William Earl Benjamin), Harrison S., Christine, Stephen Gaskill. Intern Salem (Mass.) Hosp., 1945-46; pediatric asst. resident Boston Floating Hosp., 1948-50; dist. physician, also pediatric teaching fellow Boston Dispensary, 1950; courtesy staff Stamford (Conn.) Hosp., St. Joseph Hosp., Stamford; attending staff Norwalk Hosp., 1952; chief sch. physician New Canaan sch. system, 1951-71. Trustee Natural Sci. for Youth Found., 1970-71; bd. dirs., also co-founder Genesis, Inc., bd. dirs. New Canaan Nature Center, 1960-71, pres., 1960-62, also co-founder. Served to capt. M.C., AUS, 1946-47. Diplomate Am. Bd. Pediatrics. Mem. A.M.A., Am. Acad. Pediatrics (chmn. by-law com. Conn. chpt. 1971), Northeast Pediatric Soc., New Canaan Field Club (charter), Nat., New Canaan (dir. 1951-71, pres., 1957-59) Audubon socs., Am. Mus. Nat. History, New Canaan Hist. Soc. Episcopalian. Home: New Canaan CT Died May 22, 1971; buried Lakeview Cemetery, New Canaan CT

COONEY, JAMES D., lawyer; b. Arlington, Ia., May 19, 1893; s. James and Ellen (Newton) C.; LL.B., State U. of Iowa, 1915; m. Portia Belvel Evans, June 28, 1916; 1 son, James Evans. Admitted to Iowa bar, 1914, and entered into gen. practice at West Union, Ia.; pros. atty., 1916-17 and 1920-21; judge Dist. Court, 13th Judicial Dist. of Ia., 1922-26; atty. for Wilson & Co., Inc., packers, 1926-30, v.p. 1930-53, pres., 1953-60, chmn., chief exec. officer, 1960-63; also dir.; dir. Wilson Sporting Goods Co., Mid-Am. Nat. Bank, Upper-Avenue Nat. Bank Bd. dirs. Herbert Hoover Found. Served with AF, U.S. Army, 1917-18. Mem. Northwestern Assos., Newcomen Soc., Phi Alpha Delta. Republican. Methodist. Clubs: Chicago, Economic Casino, Glenview; Tucson Country. Home: Chicago IL Died May 10, 1971; buried Des Moines IA

COONLEY, PRENTISS LOOMIS, manufacturer of machinery; b. Chicago, July 10, 1880; s. John Clark and Lydia Arms (Avery) C.; student University School, Chicago, 1898; graduate Chicago Latin Sch., 1899; A.B., Harvard, 1903; m. Mary Lord, Nov. 15, 1905 (died July 3, 1944); children—Alice Lord (Mrs. Milton P. Higgins, Eleanor Kavanaugh; m. 2d, Katharine Rogers Sullivan, December 21, 1945 (dec. 1961). Salesman Link-Belt Co., Chicago, 1905-11, v.p., 1911-25; pres. H. W. Caldwell & Son Co., later Caldwell-Moore, 1921-25; pres. C. B. Live Stock Co. and subsidiaries of Chicago, 1907-17; founder and treas., Electric Steel Co., Chicago, 1916-25; dir. Chicago Trust Co., 1906-25; v.p. Walworth Co., New York, 1925-32; became connected with NRA, June 1934 and served successively as dep. adminstr., div. adminstr., code adminstrn. dir., and as dir. Div. of Business Cooperation until Sept. 30, 1935; asst. to chairman of the business advisory council for the U.S. Dept. Commerce, 1938-39; consultant to mgt., 1940-71. With C.W.S. as assistant mgr. army gas defense plant, Long Island City, N.Y., rank of lt. col., World War. Trustee and v.p. Austen Riggs Foundation, Stockbridge, Mass. (pres. 1939, chmn. 1943-46). Republican. Clubs: Metropolitan, Burning Tree (Washington). Home: Washington DC Died Aug. 15, 1970; buried Worcester MA

COONS, ARTHUR GARDINER, educator; b. Anaheim, Calif., June 13, 1900; s. Richard LaSalle and Mary Ella (Gardiner) C.; A.B., Occidental Coll., Los Angeles, 1920; A.M., U. Pa., 1922, Ph.D., 1927, Sc.D. in Econs., 1957; LL.D., Lewis and Clark Coll., 1946, Wm. Jewell College, 1949; Pomona College, 1951, U. Cal., 1958, Whittier College, 1964, U. So. Cal., 1964, Claremont Grad. Sch., 1965, Occidental Coll., 1965; L.H.D., U. of Judaism, 1962, U. Santa Clara, 1966; m. Mary Edna Palmer, Feb. 9, 1927; 1 son, Arthur Gardiner. Instr. of econ., Wharton Sch., Univ. of Pennsylvania, 1920-22; teacher, Anaheim (Calif.) Union High Sch., 1922-23, Fullerton (Calif.) Union High Sch. and Jr. Coll., 1923-24; instr. econs. U. Cal. at Los Angeles, 1924-25; and 1926-27; asst. prof. econ., Occidental Coll., 1927-30, asso. prof., 1930-36; prof., 1936-38, exec. sec. to pres., 1927-31, dean of men, 1931-38, dean faculty, prof. econs., 1943-46, pres., 1946-65, pres. emeritus, 1965-68; prof. econs. Claremont Colls., 1938-43, dir. studies, 1941-42; vis. prof. and research fellow Cal. Coll. in China Found., 1933-34; research asso. Haynes Found., 1939-44. Dir. Los Angeles br. Fed. Res. Bank San Francisco, Cal. state price exec., OPA, 1942-43, asso. regional price exec. and Los Angeles dist. price officer, 1943; consultant Nat. Resources Planning Bd., 1940-41; adviser to chief, U.S. Reparations Mission to Japan, 1945-46. Trustee Haynes Found., Los Angeles, College Entrance Exam. Bd., 1961-64. Bd. dirs. Assn. Am. Colls., 1952-57, pres., 1956; bd. dirs. Council Financial Aid Edn., Los Angeles World Affairs Council; pres. Coordinating Council Higher Edn. in Cal.; president Ind. Colls. Southern Cal., Inc., 1958-60; v.p. National Council Chs., 1957-60; mem. Pres's Com. on Edn. Beyond High Sch., 1956-57; chmn. Master Plan Survey Higher Edn. Cal., 1959-60. Decorated hon. comdr. Order Brit. Empire. Mem. Western Coll. Association (pres. 1946-47), Pacific Southwest Acad. (pres. 1936-38, 1939-40), Pacific Coast Econ. Assn. (pres. 1940; editor Proceedings 1937-39), Am. Econ. Assn., Am. Acad. Polit. and Social Sci. (editor supplements to Annals, 1932-33, 35, 37, 39), Social Sci. Research Conf. (Pacific Coast Group; president, 1941), Tau Kappa Alpha, Pi Gamma Mu, Phi Beta Kappa. Presbyn. Clubs: Town Hall of Los Angeles (1st v.p. 1940, 48, 49, pres. 1950), University, California (Los Angeles); Twilight (pres. 1957-58), University (Pasadena). Author: The Foreign Public Debt of China, 1930; Economic Reconstruction in China (pamphlet) 1934; An Economic and Industrial Survey of the Los Angeles and San Diego Areas, 1941.; Crises in California Higher Education, 1968. Contbr. to tech. and sci. publs. Home: Newport CA Died July 26, 1968; buried Pacific View Meml. Park, Newport Beach CA

COONS, JAMES EPHRAIM, educator; b. Hanesville, Ont., Can., Nov. 1, 1877; s. John and Rhoda Ann Cross; brought by parents to U.S., 1878; A.B., Ohio Wesleyan U., 1906, A.M., 1908, D.D., 1926; S.T.B., Boston Univ., 1909; grad. study Harvard U., 1910-11; LL.D. from Boston U., 1935; m. Mabel Ida MacIntosh, Jan. 1, 1900; 1 son, John Warren. Ordained ministry M.E. Ch., 1906; pastor chs. in Ohio and Mass. until 1921; supt. Lynn Dist., 1921-26; pres. Ia. Wesleyan Coll., Mt. Pleasant, 1928-35; headmaster Tilton (N.H.) Sch. since July 1935; pres. Tilton Jr. Coll. Trustee N.E. Conf.; dir. Meth. Ministers Ins. Co.; del. to Gen. Conf. M.E. Ch., 1924. Was vice-pres. Ia. Coll. Presidents Assn. Mem. Sigma Phi Epsilon. Mason. Clubs: University, Boston Clerical, Boston Itinerants, Mt. Pleasant Rotary, Mt. Pleasant Golf, Tilton Rotary (pres. 1930-40). Home: 45 School St., Tilton NH‡

COOPER, ARMWELL LOCKWOOD, lawyer; b. Willow Grove, Del., Nov. 15, 1870; s. Thomas Broadaway and Emily (Marvel) C.; ed. Wesley Coll. Inst., Dover, Del., and Kan. Normal Coll., Fort Scott; m. Caroline M. Ley, Nov. 14, 1899 (dec.); children—Dorothy Emily (dec.), Gertrude Caroline (Mrs. Robert C. Searle); m. 2d, Blanche A. Green, July 9, 1927. Admitted to Missouri bar, 1895, and began practice at Kansas City; mem. Cooper, Neel & Sutherland; gen. Mo. Orpheum Co., Mercantile Home Bank & Trust Co.; dist. atty. M.K.&T. Ry. Col., a.d.c., staff Gov. Herbert S. Hadley. Mem. Mo. State Senate, 1906; county counselor, Jackson County, Mo., 1915-23; mem. charter commn., Kansas City, Mo., 1925. Mem. Internat., Am. and Kansas City bar assns., Mo. State Bar Assn. (elected pres. Oct. 1935). Democrat. Episcopalian. Mason, K.P., Elk. Club: Kansas City Athletic. Home: Hotel Continental. Office: Commerce Bldg., Kansas City MO

COOPER, CYRIL BERNARD, dept. store exec., b. Faversham, Eng., Jan. 24, 1898; s. William and Annie May (Marsh) C.; came to U.S., 1908, naturalized, 1914; B.A., Occidental Coll., 1920; student Harvard Grad. Sch. Bus. Adminstrn., 1920-21; m. Esther Mae Brown, June 1, 1926; m. 2d, Maudie Prickett. With Bullock's, Inc., Los Angeles, 1931-60, mdse. mgr., 1935-60, dir., 1960-71. Bd. dirs. Goodwill Industries So. Cal., Pasadena Symphony Assn., Arcadia Methodist Hosp. So. Cal.; past trustee Occidental Coll.; past pres. Pasadena Community Chest and Council. Mem. Pasadena C. of C. (pres.), Pasadena Merchants Assn. (past pres.), Occidental Coll. Alumni Assn. (past pres.), Alpha Tau Omega. Republican. Methodist. Clubs: Annandale Golf, Twilight (Pasadena). Home: Pasadena CA Died May 12, 1971.

COOPER, EDWARD NATHAN, economist; b. Cleve., June 5, 1912; s. Aaron and Fannie (Koppelman) C.; B.A. magna cum laude, Harvard, 1934, M.B.A., 1938; m. Evelyn Sternberg, July 7, 1946; children—Louis Franklin, Harry Allan. Research asst. Harvard, 1935-36; economist FHA, 1938-40; asst. to dir. St. Lawrence Seaway Survey, U.S. Dept. Commerce, 1940-41; economist, asso. div. dir. OPA, 1941-46; dep. asst. adminstr. NHA, 1946-47; intelligence research officer and exec. Dept. State, 1947-56; fgn. service officer, 1956-62, 1st sec. Am. embassy, London, 1958-61; econ. adviser Harvard U. Adv. Group, Dacca, East Pakistan, 1962-65; econ. cons., pvt. bus., Bethesda, Md., 1965-71. Mem. Am. Econ. Assn., Phi Beta Kappa. Home: Bethesda MD Died Oct. 21, 1971.

COOPER, ELIZABETH (MRS. CLAYTON SEDGWICK COOPER), author; b. Homer, Ia., May 10, 1877; d. Benten and Frances Hunt; normal, high and pvt. schs.; m. 2d, Clayton Sedgwick Cooper, of New York City, Feb. 3, 1912. Lived 10 years in Shanghai, China; has made extensive trips in the Far East, two trips around the world, studying especially status of women in Oriental lands; at Greenwich Settlement, N.Y. City, and work with the Immigration Commn., 1908-09; editor of Woman's Dept., Educational Foundations (magazine), 1915-16. Founder of the American Woman's Club, in Shanghai, China—the first American woman's club outside the U.S., founder-pres. Miami Beach Woman's Club; pres. Homemakers Club, Miami, Fla. Member Disciples of Christ. Author: The Market for Souls, 1910; My Lady of the Chinese Courtyard, 1914; The Women of Egypt, 1914; Living Up to Billy, 1915; Drusilla with a Million, 1916; The Harim and the Purdah, 1916; The Heart of O Sono San, 1917; My Lady of the Indian Purdah, 1927; What Price Youth, 1929; also Japanese one-act play entitled Sayonara," prod. Maxine Elliott. Contbr. to mags. Home: Sarasota FL‡

COOPER, FRANK EDWARD, lawyer; b. Detroit, July 3, 1910; s. Frank Lee and Edith (Ruehle) C.; A.B., U. Mich., 1931, J.D., 1934; m. Margaret E. Hayes, June 27, 1936; children—Frank, Edward, William. Admitted to Mich. bar, 1934, since practiced in Detoit; asso. firm Beaumont, Smith & Harris, 1934-68, partner, 1943-68; prof. law U. Mich., 1950-68. Recipient Ross award Am. Bar Assn., 1942. Mem. Am. Bar Assn. (chmn. adminstrative law), Episcopalian. Author: Adminstrative Agencies and the Courts, 1951; Effective Legal Writing, 1953; (with E. B. Stason) Cases on Administrative Law, 1957; The Lawyer and Adminstrative Agencies, 1957; Living the Law, 1958; Writing in Law Practice, 1963; State Adminstrative Law, 1965; also numerous articles in legal periodicals. Faculty editor U. Mich. Prospectus, a Jour. of Law Reform. Home: Grosse Pointe Farms MI Died Feb. 16, 1968; buried Columbarium of Christ Episcopal Ch., Grosse Pointe Farms MI

COOPER, GLADYS, actress; b. Lewisham, Eng.; d. Charles William Frederick and Mabel (Barnett) Cooper; m. Herbert Buckmaster, Dec. 12, 1908; children—John, Joan; m. 2d, Sir Neville Pearson; 1 dau., Sally; m. 3d, Philip Merivale, Apr. 30, 1937. Profl. debut Theater Royal, Colchester, Eng., 1905; 1st London appearance Vaudeville Theater, 1906; appeared The Playhouse, London, 1916. Gaiety Theater, 1921; actress mgr. The Playhouse, 1927-33; Broadway debut in The Shining Hour, 1934; appeared in plays including Call It a Day, 1936. The Morning Star, 1942, Indifferent Shepherd, 1950, Relative Values, 1951, A Question of Fact, 1953, The Chalk Garden, 1956; motion pictures include White Cliffs of Dover, 1944, Love Letters, 1945, Green Years, Green Dolphin Street, 1947, Madame Bovary, 1949, Rebecca, Song of Bernadette, Separate Tables. Recipient Acad. Motion Picture Arts and Scis. award, 1952. Mem. Church of Eng. Address: Pacific Palisades CA Died Nov. 17, 1971.

COOPER, HAROLD, architect; b. Montreal, Can., Jan. 9, 1915; s. David and Frieda (Harlig) Kupferberg; B.Arch., McGill U., 1937. Came to U.S., 1938, naturalized, 1947. Archtl. designer William Ginsberg, cons. engrs., N.Y.C., 1937-41, asso., 1945-53, partner, 1953-69 (firm now William Ginsburg & Assos.); designer Frederic R. Harris, Engrs., N.Y.C., 1941-43. Served as lt. Royal Canadian Naval Res., 1943-45. Fellow Am. Soc. C.E.; mem. Royal Inst. Brit. Architects, A.I.A., N.Y. Soc. Architects. Home: Scarsdale NY Died Nov. 30, 1969.

COOPER, HERMAN CHARLES, chemist; b. Glen Ellyn, Ill., Nov. 22, 1875; s. Lawrence Charles and Emma Parthenia (Yalding) C.; Ph.B., Beloit Coll., 1896; U. of Gottingen, 1896-97, Heidelberg, 1897-1900, various colls. of Paris, 1899; independent research worker, U. of Chicago, 1899-1900; m. Agnes Kent Packard, of Stratford, Conn., June 20, 1905; children—Elizabeth Packard, Lawrence Carleton, Cynthia Pamelia. Teacher chemistry, Lincoln (Neb.) High Sch., 1900-01; instr. chemistry, Syracuse U., 1901-03; research asso. phys. chemistry, Mass. Inst. Tech., 1903-04; asst. prof. chemistry, 1904-06, asso. prof., 1906-12, prof. 1912-18, Syracuse U.; asst. prof., Coll. City of New York, 1918-20; factory mgr. Acids Mfg. Corpn., 1920-22; research dir. Bauer & Black, Chicago, 1923-24; v.p. Glen Ellyn State Bank, since 1925. Mem. Am. Chem. Soc. (pres. Syracuse sect., 1909-10), Am. Electro-chem. Soc. (chmn. N.Y. sect., 1922-23, Chicago sect., 1925); Am. editor Holleman-Cooper Textbook of Inorganic Chemistry, 1902, 05, 08, 11, 16, 20, 26. Author: Laboratory Manual of Elementary Chemistry, 1917. Contbr. research Glen Ellyn IL‡

COOPER, ISABELLE MITCHELL, librarian; b. Troy, N.Y.; d. William Scobie and Sarah Maria (Veis) C.; grad. Emma Willard Sch., Troy, N.Y., 1894; grad. Teachers Coll. (Columbia), 1899; A.B., Barnard Coll. and Teachers Coll., 1901; A.M., Columbia, 1912; student New York Pub. Library Training Class, 1904-05; B.L.S., N.Y. State Library Sch., 1908. Instr. New York Pub. Library Training Class, 1905-07; asst. branch librarian New York Pub. Library, 1908-09; instr. State U. of Ia. Summer Library Sch., 1909; reference librarian Newark (N.J.) Pub. Library, 1909-10; instr. Dept. of Library Science, Simmons Coll., Boston, 1910-13; librarian Dept. of Sociology and Municipal Reference, Brooklyn (N.Y.) Pub. Library, 1913-16; librarian in charge Central Circulation, New York Pub. Library, 1916-24, also instr. New York Pub. Library

Sch., 1916-17, and absent on leave in France with Am. Com. for Devastated France, 1920-21; editor A.L.A. Cat. 1926 at A.L.A. hdqrs., Chicago, and Library of Congress, 1924-1926; on Library Survey Coms., Oakland, Calif., and Queens Borough, N.Y. City, 1927; visiting lecturer in book selection, Sch. of Librarianship, U. of Calif., 1927; cons. librarian and supervisor of staff instruction, Queens Borough Pub. Library, Jamaica, N.Y., since 1927. Mem. A.L.A., N.Y. State Library Assn., N.Y. Spl. Libraries Assn., New York Library Club, Am. Woman's Assn., etc. Baptist. Compiler: Dictionary Catalogue of the First 505 Volumes of Everyman's Library (with Margaret A. McVety), 1910. Address: The Queens Borough Public Library, Jamaica NY‡

COOPER, JOHN GORDON, ex-congressman; b. England, Apr. 27, 1872; s. Joseph and Mary (Toy) C.; brought to America, 1880; ed. pub. schs., Youngstown, O.; m. Elizabeth M. Harries, of Youngstown, Mar. 7, 1896. Began work at 13 in steel mills, Youngstown; became locomotive fireman Pa. R.R., 1896, eng., 1900-15; mem. Ohio Ho. of Rep., 1911-15; mem. 64th to 74th Congresses (1915-37), 19th Ohio Dist. Republican. Mason, K.P., I.O.O.F. Methodist. Mem. Brotherhood of Locomotive Engrs. Home: Youngstown OH‡

COOPER, MERIAN C., motion picture dir., producer, author; b. Jacksonville, Fla., Oct. 24, 1894; s. John C. and Mary (Coldwell) C.; ed. Lawrenceville Sch., U.S. Naval Acad., 1911-14; m. Dorothy Jordan; children—Mary Caroline, Elizabeth T., Richard. Advanced to capt. U.S. Army, World War I, pilot aviation France, later lt. col. Kosciusko Squadron, Poland, traveled widely in Orient, Africa making moving pictures, as newspaper, mag. corr.; exploration in Arabia, Iran; co-dir., co-author, co-producer motion pictures, Grass, Chang, Four Feathers; sole creator, co-producer, co-author King Kong; producer Flying Down to Rio, Last Days Pompeii, Little Women, Lost Patrol, and others; producer (with John Ford); Three Godfathers, Fort Apache, She Wore a Yellow Ribbon, Wagonmaster, Rio Grande, Quiet Man; co-dir., co-producer (with Lowell Thomas) This Is Cinerama; exec. producer The Searchers; dir., co-producer The Best of Cinerama, 1962. Exec. producer with RKO Studios, Hollywood, 2 yrs.; pres. Argosy Pictures Corp., 1946-56, Merian C. Cooper Enterprises, Inc., 1958-73; v.p. Cinerama Prodn. Corp. Was early supporter civilian aviation, former dir. Pan Am. World Airways, Western Airlines, Gen. Aviation, others. Served as col. USAAF, 1942-45, staff China Air Task Force, 1942, 5th Air Force, New Guinea, 1943-45; to brig. genl. Air Force, 1950. Clubs: Explorers, Brook, Boone and Crockett (N.Y.C.), Daedalians (San Antonio). Recipient Acad. Motion Picture Arts and Scis. spl. award motion picture innovator, 1952. Author: (with Edward A. Salisbury) The Sea Gypsy, 1924; Grass, 1925; Things Men Die For, 1927; (with Edgar Wallace) King kong, 1932. Home: Coronado CA Died Apr. 1973.

COOPER, PRENTICE, former gov. Tennessee; b. Shelbyville, Tenn., Sept. 28, 1895; s. William Prentice and Argentine (Shofner) C.; student Vanderbilt U., 1914-15; A.B., Princeton, 1917; LL.B., Harvard, 1921; hon. LL.D., Lincoln Memorial Univ., 1940; hon. LL.D., Muhlenberg Coll., 1942; Hartwick College 1943; married Hortense Powell, 1950; children—William Prentice III, James Hayes Shofner, John Norment Powell. Admitted to Tennessee bar, 1922; attorney general of 8th Judicial Circuit, 1925-26; practiced at Shelbyville and Lewisburg, Tenn., and served as city atty. of both municipalities; member Tenn. Ho. of Reps., 1923; member Tenn. State Senate, 1937; became gov. of Tenn. Jan., 1939, elected for 3d term Nov. 1942. United States Ambassador to Peru, 1946-48, as ambassador aided in settlement of $83,000,000 debt of Peruvian government to U.S. owing for 16 years. President Tennessee's Constl. Convention, 1953. Organized Duck River Electric Membership Corp. Mem. gen. bd., mem. policy com. dept. internat. affairs National Council of Churches, 1956-58; member executive com. United Lutheran Ch. in America. Served as master gunner, Fort Monroe, Va., World War I; finished training with rank of 2d lt. Chmn., Southern Governors' Conference, Southern Gov.'s Freight Rate Com. chmn. Tenn. delegation Dem. Nat. Conv., 1944. Mem. Am. Legion (State Comdr. Tenn., postwar planning commn.). Mem. Tenn. Bar Assn., Acad. Polit. Sci., Phi Delta Theta. Democrat. Lutheran. Clubs: Belle Meade Country, Cumberland (Nashville); University (N.Y.). Home: Shelbyville TN Died May 18, 1969; buried Jenkins Chapel, Lutheran Church Cemetery.

COOPER, WADE HAMPTON, banker; b. Mullins, S.C., Dec. 5, 1874; s. Noah B. and Lucinda (Jenerette) C.; ed. pub. and pvt. schs., S.C. and Tenn.; studied law, Nashville, Tenn.; LL.D., Ohio Northern U., 1929; Litt.D., Lincoln Memorial U., 1929; m. Caroline Binkley, Aug. 1898 (died 1927); children—Josh W., Bryant S. Admitted to Tenn. bar, 1897, and practiced at Nashville until 1910; with U.S. Savings Bank, Washington, D.C., since 1910, formerly president; formerly pres. Commercial National Bank, Continental Trust Company (Washington, D.C.); pres. Bureau of National Literature (New York City), Hanover

Investors, Incorporated (New York City); dir. other corpns. Colonel on staff of Gov. A. A. Taylor and Gov. Henry H. Horton, of Tenn., and Gov. Flem D. Sampson, of Ky. Vice pres. and trustee Lincoln Memorial Univ.; trustee American U., Washington, D.C., Baxter (Tenn.) Sem.; former chmn. Goodwill Industries, Boston. Mem. Am. Society of Internat. Law, Am. Acad. Polit. Science, Am. Peace Soc. Archaeol. Soc. Washington, Am. Bankers Assn., Columbia Hist. Soc., Am. Bible Soc., English-Speaking Union of U.S., S.A.R. Methodist. Clubs: National Press, University, Congressional Country. Donor many scholarships to poor boys and girls. Lecturer on Lincoln. Home: 1722 Massachusetts Av. N.W. Office: 2100 14th St. N.W., Washington DC‡

COOPER, WILLIAM GOODWIN, naval officer; b. Savannah, Ga., July 22, 1903; s. Albert Sidney and Katherine (Falli) C.; student Ga. Inst. Tech., 1921-22; B.S., U.S. Naval Acad., 1926; student Nat. War Coll., 1950-51; m. Lois Luther, Oct. 19, 1929; children—William Goodwin, Ann, John L. Commd. ensign USN, 1926, designated naval aviator, 1929, vice adm.; comdr. U.S.S. McCalla, U.S.S. Charles J. Badger, Destroyer Div. 98, World War II; successively comdr. Destroyer Squadron 9, U.S.S. Newport News, Destroyer Flotilla 6; Naval Base, Guantanamo; deputy controller USN; commander Anti-Submarine Defense Force, United States Atlantic Fleet, Norfolk, 1958-71. Awarded Navy Cross, Bronze Star Medal. Mem. Naval Inst. (sec. 1948-50, editor proc. 1948-50, dir. 1950-51), Phi Gamma Delta. Clubs: New York Yacht (N.Y.C.); Army-Navy Country (Arlington, Va.). Died Mar. 1971.

COPASS, BENJAMIN ANDREW, clergyman, educator; b. Clementsville, Tenn., May 29, 1865; s. Charles Wesley and Lucinda (Bowman) C.; ed. Willette (Tenn.) Acad.; B.A., Bethel Coll., Russellville, Ky., 1890, M.A., 1893, D.D., 1898; studied Southern Bapt. Theol. Sem., 1891-94, Univ. of Chicago, 1919; m. Cloantha Williams, May 29, 1894 (died Nov. 1902); children—Cloantha, Benjamin A., Charles Williams (dec.), Lucile; m. 2d, Crickett Keys, Sept. 12, 1904; children—Mike K., Jack (dec.), Mary (dec.). Ordained Bapt. ministry, 1889; pastor Clinton, Ky., 1894-96, Los Angeles, Calif., 1896-98, Marksbury, Ky., 1898-1901, Waxahachie, 1901-06, San Marcos, 1906-12, Denton, 1912-13; asst. sec. Executive Bd. Bapt. Gen. Conv. of Tex., 1914-18; prof. O.T. interpretation, Southwestern Bapt. Theol. Sem., since 1918. Mem. Tex. Hist. Soc., Phi Gamma Delta. Democrat. Mason. Author: The Message of Hosea, 1906; A Manual of Old Testament Theology, 1925; Theology in Hebrew Words, 1934; One God, 1935; Amos, 1938; Isaiah, Prince of Old Testament Prophets, 1943. Home: Seminary Hill TX*

COPE, QUILL EVAN, college pres.; b. White County, Tenn., Mar. 28, 1912; s. Rogers and Dora (Breeding) C.; B.S., Tenn. Poly. Inst., 1933; M.A., George Peabody Coll., 1936, M.Ed., 1949; Ed.D., N.Y.U., 1952; M. Mary Kate Smith, Nov. 29, 1939; children—John Rogers, James Carl. Elementary tchr. White County, Tenn., 1932-33, high sch. tchr., 1933-38, supt. schs., 1938-43; field rep. U.S. Office Edn., 1946-47; prin. White County High Sch., 1947-51; instr. Tenn. Poly Inst., 1949-51; part-time instr N.Y.U., 1951-52; asso. prof. edn. U. Tenn., 1952-53, head dept. continuing and higher edn., 1968. state commr. edn., Tenn., 1953-58; pres. of Middle Tennessee State College, 1958-68. Mem. So. Regional Edn. Bd. Mem. Nat., Tenn. edn. assns. Am. assn. U. Profs., Assn. Am. Sch. Adminstrs., Am. Legion, Phi Delta Kappa. Mason (32 deg.). Mem. Church of Christ. Rotarian. (president 1963-64, Murfreesboro, Tenn.). Club: Civitan (past pres.) (Sparta, Tenn.). Home: Murfreesboro TN Died Sept. 24, 1968.

COPELAND, ARTHUR H(ERBERT), SR., mathematician, educator; b. Rochester, N.Y., June 22, 1898; s. Albert E. and Jenny M. (Morris) C.; A.B., Amherst Coll., 1921; M.A., Ph.D., Harvard, 1926; m. Dorothy Eleanor West, June 16, 1925; 1 son, Arthur Herbert. Instr. math. Harvard, 1922-23, Rice Inst. 1924-28; asst. prof. math. U. Buffalo, 1928-29, U. Mich. 1929-37, asso. prof., 1937-42, prof. math., 1942-68, prof. emeritus, 1968-70; research worker Office Naval Research project, 1947-49, project dir., 1949-54; Guggenheim Memorial Found. fellow, 1935-36. Fellow Institute Math. Statistics; mem. Am. Math. Soc., Math. Assn. Am., Sigma Xi, Phi Beta Kappa, Phi Delta Theta. Home: Ann Arbor MI Died July 6, 1970; cremated.

COPELAND, EDWIN BINGHAM, botanist; b. Monroe, Wis., Sept. 30, 1873; s. Herbert Edson and Alice (Bingham) C.; A.B., Leland Stanford Jr. U., 1895; student Leipzig, 1895-96; Ph.D., U. of Halle, 1896; studied U. of Wis., 1896-97, 1898, U. of Chicago, 1901-02; m. Ethel Faulkner, of Chico, Calif., Dec. 19, 1900; children—Herbert Faulkner, Mary Faulkner, Alice Bingham, Charles Faulkner, John Bingham. Asst. prof. botany, Ind. U., 1897-98, State Normal Sch., Chico, Calif., 1899; asst. prof., 1899-1900, prof. botany, 1900-01, W.Va. U.; instr. botany, Stanford U., 1901-03; botanist, Philippine Govt., 1903-08; supt. Philippine Agrl. Sch., 1908-09; dean Coll. of Agr., and prof. plant physiology, U. of the Philippines, 1909-17; in charge herbarium, U. of Calif., 1928-32; established Los Banos Economic Garden, 1932; retired as dir. of same and as

tech. adviser in agr., Philippine Govt., 1935. Mem. Phi Gamma Delta. Mason. Author: Philippine Agriculture, 1908; The Coco-nut, 1914; The Ferns of Borneo, 1917; Rice, 1924; Natural Conduct, 1928; Fiji Ferns, 1929; also some 140 pieces of bot. research. Home: Chico, Berkeley CA‡

COPLAND, DOUGLAS BERRY, economist, diplomat; b. Timaru, New Zealand, Feb. 24, 1894; s. Alexander and Annie (Loudon) C.; M.A., Canterbury Coll., 1915; D.Sc., U. New Zealand, 1925; Litt.D., U. Melbourne, 1933, Queensland U., 1935, Harvard, 1936; LL.D. McGill University, 1949. Clark University, Carleton U., Univ. of B.C., 1954, U. Adelaide, 1958, U. Tasmania, 1958, Australian National Univ., 1967; D.C.L., Bishops U., 1955; m. Ruth Jones, Jan. 28, 1919; children—Joyce (Mrs. D. J. Tier), Rosemarie MacNeil. Lectr. history, econs.,dir. tutorial classes U. Tasmania, 1917, prof. 1920-24; Sidney Myer prof. commerce, dean faculty commerce U. Melbourne, 1924-44, chmn. professorial bd., 1934-37, Truby Williams prof. economics, 1944-45; chmn. State Econ. Com. of Victoria, 1938-45, commonwealth prices commr., 1939-45; commr. Victorian State Savs. Bank, 1940-45; econ. cons. to Prime Minister, 1941-45; Australian minister to China, 1946-48; first vice chancellor Australian National University, 1948-53; high commr. for Australia, Can., 1953-56; first principal for Australian Administrative Staff College, from 1956-60; mem. bd. dirs. Ansett Transport Industries. Founder Com. for Econ. Devel. Australia; pres. Nat. Council for Balanced Devel.; Beatty lectr. McGill U., 1961, Australian del. UN, 1946, 53, 54, chmn. Econ. Com. UN, 1954-55, pres. ECOSOC, 1954-55; leader of Australian Trade Mission to Canada, 1960. Decorated Companion St. Michael and St. George, Knight Comdr. Brit. Empire; recipient coronation medals. Mem. Am. Philos. Soc., Australian and New Zealand Association. Advancement Science (pres. 1952). Club: The Melbourne (Australia). Author: Australia and the World Crisis, 1934; The Road to High Employment, 1945; The Australian Economy, 1947; Towards Total War, 1942; Back to Earth in Economics, 1948; Inflation and Expansion, 1951; The Adventure of Growth, 1960; The Changing Structure of The Western Economy (Beatty Lectures McGill U.), 1963. Editor: Giblin: the Scholar and the Man, 1960. Co-editor several books on Australian economic policy. Contbr. articles Victoria Australia Died Sept. 27, 1971.

COPPER, JOSEPH BENJAMIN, steel co. exec.; b. Lexington, Va., Oct. 31, 1905; s. James McCown and Rosa May (Miller) C.; B.S., in Elec. Engring., Washington and Lee U., 1928; m. Betty Dunn, May 31, 1941; 1 son, Joseph Benjamin. With Am. Tel. & Tel. Corp., 1929-31, Merck & Co., 1931-32; pres., owner Interstate Produce Co., N.Y. and N.J., 1932-35; indsl. engr. Western Elec. Co., 1933-35; with U.S. Steel Corp., 1935-68, asst. to exec. v.p. personnel services, 1958-61, v.p. personnel and compensation, 1961-68. Mem. Am. Iron and Steel Inst., Phi Gamma Delta. Republican. Presbyn. Clubs: Allegheny Country, Edgeworth (Sewickley). Home: Sewickley PA Died May 23, 1968; buried Sewickley Cemetery

COQUILLETTE, ST. ELMO, banker; b. Linn County, Ia., Apr. 4, 1890; s. Daniel L. and Carrie (Whitney) C.; ed. pub. schs. of Linn County, Ia.; m. Bernice Grout, Sept. 27, 1913; children—Janet Whitney (Mrs. Robert S. Wray), James Elmo. With Merchants National Bank, Cedar Rapids, since 1910, successively as clerk, asst. cashier, v.p., pres., chmn. bd., from 1946, chmn. exec. com., from 1966; director Ia. Nat. Mut. Ins. Co., Cedar Rapids, J.S. Cook Co., Ia. Electric Light & Power Co., Ia. Mfg. Co., City Nat. Bank Cedar Rapids. Trustee, Cornell Coll., Mt. Vernon, Ia. Mem. Cedar Rapids C. of C. (past pres.), Republican. Presbyn. Mason (32 deg., Shriner), Elk. Home: Cedar Rapids IA Died Jan. 10, 1971; buried Cedar Rapids IA

CORAM, JOSEPH A., copper miner; b. St. John, N.B.; A.B., Gagetown Coll., 1874; m. Cora E. Work, of Bangor, Me., 1877; 2d, Margaret J. Harrington, of New York. Agt. of Northwestern Life Ins. Co. in Can., and later engaged with father in lumber exporting business; began in soap business at Bangor, 1876, and removed the business to Lowell, Mass.; became interested in mica mining in N.H.; 1878; later in real estate business, Minneapolis, Minn.; went to Butte, Mont., 1886, and organized the Butte & Boston Mining Co.; pres. Alvarado Consolidated Mines Co., Davis-Daly Copper Co.; dir. Middlesex Safe Deposit & Trust Co., Bingham Consolidated Mining & Smelting Co., etc. Home: Newton Center, Mass. Office: 60 State St., Boston MA‡

CORBE, ZENAN M., clergyman; b. Middle Point, O., Oct. 6, 1876; s. William Howard and Mandane Adeline (Calhoun) C.; prep. edn., Morgan Park Acad., Chicago; student U. of Chicago; grad. Chicago Luth. Sem., 1900; D.D., Gettysburg Coll., 1927; m. Caroline Christine Cramer, June 20, 1900 (deceased); children—Capt. Hubert Anthony, Miriam (dec.), Lois Anna Ellen. Engaged in farming until 1890; ordained ministry United Luth. Ch., 1899; pastor at St. Mark's Ch., Chicago, Ch. of Transfiguration, Philadelphia, Ch. of Transfiguration, New York, until 1922; exec. sec. Bd. of W. I. Missions of United Luth. Ch. in America, 1922-27;

treas. and sec. dept. ch. extension and finance, Bd. of Am. Missions, 1927-34, now exec. sec. Editor of Ecclesia Plantanda. Democrat. Home: 1 Nancy Blvd., Merrick, L.I. Office: 231 Madison Av., NY City 16 NY*‡

CORBETT, GAIL SHERMAN (MRS. HARVEY WILEY C.), sculptor; b. Syracuse, N.Y.; d. of Frederick Coe and Emma Jane (Ostrander). Sherman; ed. pub. and pvt. schs.; Art Students' League, New York, 1895; Beaux Arts, Paris, France, 1900; pupil of Augustus Saint Gaudens; m. Harvey Wiley Corbett, architect, June 28, 1905; children—Jean, John Maxwell. Prin. works; Hamilton S. White Memorial, Syracuse, 1905; Kirkpatrick Memorial Fountain, Syracuse, 1908; bronze doors, Springfield (Mass.) municipal group, 1913; portrait of Washington, George Washington Masonic Memorial, Alexandria, Va.; Leeds Memorial, Tarrytown; Constance Witherby Memorial Providence, R.I. Mem. Nat. Sculpture Soc., Nat. Assn. Women Painters and Sculptors. Studio: 443 W. 21st St., New York 11 NY‡

CORBETT, ROBERT JAMES, congressman; b. Avalon, Pa., Aug. 25, 1905; s. Samuel James and Martha (Henderson) C.; A.B., Allegheny Coll., 1927; A.M., U. of Pittsburgh, 1929; student Columbia, summer, 1929; LL.D., Allegheny Coll., Meadville, Pa., 1965; m. Ruthe Ethel McClintock, May 24, 1926; one dau., Eleanor Louise (Mrs. Dunbar). Instr. of history, Coraopolis (Pa.) Sr. High Sch., 1929-39, Pitts. Acad. Evening Sch., 1938; mem. 76th to 82d Congresses, 30th Pa. Dist., 83-87th Congresses, 29th Pa. Dist.; member of 88th-91st Congresses 18th Dist. Pa.; youngest sheriff of Allegheny County, 1941-45; former editor, pub. North Pittsburgh Times; owner profl. basketball team P.Hs. Raiders, 1940s. U.S. rep. NATO Parliamentarians Conf., 1957-60, awarded Wallace research fellowship in history, U. of Pittsburgh, 1927-29. Mem. Pa. State Edn. Assn., Nat. Forensic League, Civic Club of Allegheny County, Bellevue C. of C., Phi Delta Theta, Delta Sigma Rho, Phi Alpha Theta. Republican. Presbyn. Elk, Moose, Eagle. Clubs: Kiwanis, Lions. Home: Pittsburgh PA Died Apr. 25, 1971; buried Union Dale Cemetery, Pittsburgh PA

CORBIN, ALVIN LEROY, govt. ofcl.; b. Washington, Mar. 5, 1913; s. George Alvin and Elton S. (Weaver) C.; student George Washington U., 1931-37; LL.B., Washington Coll. Law, 1939; m. Frances Josephine Eichholz, June 10, 1940 (dec. Sept. 1957); children—Alvin LeRoy, Lucille E.; m. 2d Lilly Vaughn Smith, May 3, 1958. Messenger, Govt. Printing Office, 1930-31, apprentice printer, 1931-35, linotype operator, 1935-40; admitted to D.C. bar, 1940; examiner Bur. Motor Carriers, ICC, Washington, 1940-47, examiner Bur. Formal Cases, 1947-51, sr. examiner, hearing examiner Commr. Richard F. Mitchell's staff, 1951-59, Commr. Clyde E. Herring's staff, 1959-61, asst. dir. Bur. Rates and Practices, 1961-62, dir. bur., 1963-69. Scout master Nat. capital area council Boy Scouts Am., 1950-58. Served to lt. comdr. USNR, 1942-46. Mem. Phi Sigma Kappa; Delta Theta Phi. Burtonsville MD Died Oct. 29, 1969; buried Arlington National Cemetery, Washington DC

CORBIN, ARTHUR LINTON, JR., lawyer; b. Cripple Creek, Colo., Apr. 13, 1902; s. Arthur Linton and Bernice (Lockhead) C.; A.B., Yale, 1923, LL.B., 1926; m. Ihrene Olson, June 3, 1939 (dec.). Admitted to Conn. bar, 1926, practiced New Haven, 1926-69; mem. firm Gumbart, Corbin Tyler & Cooper, 1952-69, counsel to firm, 1954-69; became v.p. and dir., The New Haven Water Co., 1950, then pres.; mem. board of directors The So. Conn. Gas Co., The First New Haven Nat. Bank, Pond Lily Co.; trustee Nat. Savs. Bank. Mem. Conn. Water Resources Commission, 1955-57. A trustee of Quinnipiac College. Member of Am., Conn., New Haven bar assns., Phi Delta Phi, Order of Coif. Rep. Clubs: Hartford; Graduate, Quinnipiack, New Haven Country, New Haven Lawn (New Haven); Yale (New York). Home: New Haven CT Died Oct. 8, 1969.

CORCORAN, BREWER, author; b. Springfield, Mass., Mar. 11, 1877; s. of Luke and Harriet (Brewer) C.; ed. St. Paul's Sch., Concord, N.H.; student Williams Coll., 1897-98; m. Carolyn Upson, Oct. 8, 1901. Mem. editorial staff Springfield Republican, 1899-1911; dir. Springfield Safe Deposit & Trust Co., Springfield Five Cent Savings Bank, G. & C. Merriam Co. Dir. Conn. Valley Hist. Soc., Springfield Cemetery. Home for Aged Men; v.p. Springfield City Library Assn.; mem. Delta Psi. Author: The Bantam, 1912; The Road to Le Reve, 1916; The Barbarian, 1917; The Boy Scouts of Kendallville, 1918; The Boy Scouts of the Wolf Patrol, 1920; The Princess Naida, 1921; The Boy Scouts at Camp Lowell, 1922; Follow the Ball, 1927. Capt., mil. intelligence div., Gen. Staff, U.S. Army, 1918. Home: 95 Maple St., Springfield, Mass.; (summer) Vineyard Haven MA‡

CORDON, GUY, U.S. senator; b. Cuero, Tex., Apr. 24, 1890; s. Jacob and Caroline Tabitha (Terry) C.; ed. public schools and self-study; m. Ana Lucille Allen; children—Allen, Margaret Anne (wife of Col. Plin A. Laurance). Practicing law, Roseburg, Ore., 1920-69; apptd. to interim vacancy in U.S. Senate caused by death of Charles L. McNary, Mar. 1944; elected for unexpired term, Nov. 7, 1944; reelected Nov. 1948, for the term ending 1955. Republican. Home: Roseburg, OR Died June 8, 1969; buried Roseburg Meml. Gardens.

COREY, ALFRED ADAMS, JR., iron and steel mfr.; b. North Braddock Borough, Pa., Jan. 4, 1878; s. Alfred Adams and Adaline (Fritz) C.; ed. pub. schs.; m. Amelia S. Rose, of Braddock, Pa., Dec. 7, 1897; children—David K., Adaline. Apprentice, machine shops Homestead Steel Works, Carnegie Steel Co., 1893-95, Ill. Steel Co., Chicago, 1895-96, again Homestead Steel Works until 1900; mill positions, including asst. supt. structural mill and asst. supt. open hearth dept., 1900-04; supt. open hearth department rolling mills, North Sharon Plant, Carnegie Steel Co., 1904-06; gen. supt. Donora (Pa.) Steel Works and Furnaces, Union Steel Co., 1906-09; asst. gen. supt. Homestead Steel Works, Munhall, Pa., Carrie Furnaces, Rankin, Pa., Schoen Steel Wheel Works, McKees Rocks, Pa., 1909-14; gen. supt. same, 1914-19; pres. Cambria Steel Co., Johnstown Water Co.; v.p. Midvale Steel and Ordnance Co., Union Coal and Coke Co., 1919-23; pres. and dir. Vanadium Corpn. of America, Southern Mineral Products Corpn., 1923-35; now retired; dir. Gen. Refractories Co. (Phila.). Republican. Methodist. Mason (32 deg., K.T., Shriner). Clubs: Links, Recess (New York); Racquet (Phila.); Duquesne (Pittsburgh). Home: 111 E. 56th St., New York NY‡

COREY, JAMES WILLIAM, company exec.; b. Rutland, Vt., Aug. 9, 1891; s. John F. and Elizabeth (O'Brien) C.; m. Miriam Preston, June 16, 1917; 1 dau., June Louise. Successively draftsman, engr., salesman several elec. machinery builders; v.p. in charge sales, dir. Reliance Electric & Engring. Co., Cleve., 1938-44, pres. 1944-57, chmn. bd., from 1957; pres. Reliance Electric & Engring. Can., Ltd. Trustee Fenn Coll. Mem. Nat. Indsl. Conf. Bd., Assn. Iron and Steel Engr., N.A.M. National Electric Mfrs. Association, Am. Mgmt. Assn., Asso. Industries Cleve. (pres.), C. of C. Mem. Christian Ch. Clubs: Midday, Canterbury Golf, Union (Cleve.); Welland (Ont., Can.). Contbr. tech. publs. Holds patents on elec. devices. Home: Shaker Heights OH Died Aug. 19, 1970.

COREY, ROBERT BRAINARD, chemist; b. Springfield, Mass., Aug. 19, 1897; s. Fred Brainard and Caroline Louise (Heberd) C.; Ch.B., University of Pittsburgh, 1919, Doctor of Science (honorary), 1964; Ph.D., Cornell, 1924; m. Dorothy Gertrude Paddon, July 7, 1930. Instr. analytical chemistry, Cornell, 1923-28; asst. in biophysics, Rockefeller Inst. Med. Research, 1928-30, asso., 1930-37; research fellow, Calif. Inst. Tech., 1937-38, sr. research fellow in structural chemistry, 1938-46, research asso., 1946-49, professor of structural chemistry, from 1949; civilian with the OSRD, 1942-45, Bureau of Ordnance, U.S. Navy, 1945-46. Fellow John Simon Guggenheim Found., 1951-53. Member Nat. Acad. Scis., Am. Chemical Soc., A.A.A.S., Am. Crystallog. Assn., Sigma Xi, Phi Kappa Phi, Phi Lambda Upsilon, Alpha Chi Sigma. Contbr. articles to scientific jours. Home: Pasadena CA Died Apr. 23, 1971; buried Glenwood Cemetery, Homer NY

COREY, STEPHEN JARED, clergyman; b. Rolla, Mo., Apr. 29, 1873; s. Ambrose Brookmire and Maria Fidelia (Henry) C.; student Mo. Sch. of Mines; A.B., U. of Neb., 1898; student Rochester Theol. Sem., 1898-1901, awarded B.D., by successor, Colgate-Rochester Div. Sch., 1929, as of 1901; LL.D., Transylvania Coll., 1914; D.D., Culver-Stockton Coll., 1934; m. Edith C. Webster, Oct. 1, 1901; children—Helen D. (dec.), Stephen Maxwell, Julia Edith, John Pershing. Ordained ministry Christian (Disciples) Ch., 1898; student pastor Waterloo, Neb., 1897-98; pastor Rochester, 1898-1903; sec. N.Y. Christian Missionary Soc., 1903-05, Foreign Christian Missionary Soc., 1905-19; sec. United Christian Missionary Society, Indianapolis, Ind., 1919-20, vice-pres., 1920-30, president, 1930-38; president College of the Bible, Lexington, Kentucky, 1938-April '45, president emeritus, since 1945; instructor in missions, College of The Bible; chaplain U.S. Public Health Hospital (Narcotic); member. International Missionary Council, com. on reference and council of Fgn. Missions Conf. of N.A., World Conf. on Christian Work for S.A. Trustee Nanking (China) U., Union Theol. Sem., Nanking (China), Fed. Christian Colls. and Univs. (China), Collegio Ward. Buenos Aires. Author: Missions in the Sunday School, 1910; Among Central African Tribes, 1912; Among Asia's Needy Millions, 1915; Among South American Friends, 1925; The Preacher and His Missionary Message, 1930; Missions Matching the Hour, 1931; Beyond Statistics, or The Wider Range of World Missions, 1937. Contbr. to World Call. Home: 330 Cochran Rd., Lexington KY‡

COREY, WENDELL REID, actor; b. Dracut, Mass., Mar. 20, 1914; s. Milton Rothwell and Julia Ried (MacKenney) C.; m. Alice Nevin Wiley, Nov. 19, 1939; children—Lucy Robin, Jonathan Wendell, Jennifer Julia, Bonnie Alice Elsie. Actor Broadway plays, including Dream Girl, 1946, Voice of the Turtle (London company with Margaret Sullavan), 1947, (Nat. company) Caine Mutiny Court Martial, 1954-55, Jolly's Progress, 1959; numerous motion pictures, latest being The Wild North, The Accused, No Sad Songs, Big Knife, The Rack, Loving You, Alias Jesse James; star TV shows, also TV series Harbor Command. Peck's Bad Girl, Westinghouse Playhouse, Eleventh Hour series; president of the Los Angeles Home Entertainment Corporation. Member of the Santa Monica City Council. Member Academy of Motion Picture Arts and Scis. (pres.), Legion of Honor, Order DeMolay, Acad. TV Arts and Scis. (nat. trustee, bd. dirs.), Screen Actors Guild (dir.). Home: Santa Monica CA Died Nov 8, 1968; buried Becket MA

CORFMAN, ELMER ELLSWORTH, lawyer; b. Toledo, Ia., Mar. 2, 1863; s. John and Catherine (Hufford) C.; pub. schs.; LL.B., U. of Mich., 1890; m. Ivy G. Loar, June 8, 1898; children—Mrs. Aileen Baxter, Mrs. Betty Ottenstein. Practiced at Provo, Utah, 1890-1917; justice Supreme Court of Utah, 1917-23; mem. and chmn. Pub. Utilities Commn. and Pub. Commn. of Utah, 1923-37; mem. Utah Constitutional Conv., 1895. Democrat. Conglist. Mason (33 deg., Scottish Rite). Home: 1231 E. 3d So. St., Salt Lake City UT‡

CORKERY, FRANCIS E., Coll. pres.; b. Springfield, Ill., Jan. 17, 1903; s. Thomas J. and Elizabeth H. (Kennedy) C.; A.B., Gonzaga U., 1925, A.M., 1927; Ph.D., St. Louis U., 1934. Entered Jesuit Order, 1920; ordained priest Roman Cath. Ch., 1934. Prof. of English lit., Gonzaga U., 1928-31; pres. Seattle Coll., 1936-45; pres. corp. Seattle Coll.; pres. Gonzaga U., Spokane, Wash., 1945-57. Mem. Council Advisors U.S. Office Edn. Mem. bd. Pioneer Ednl. Assn. Pub. mem. War Labor Bd., 12th Region, K.C. Home: Spokane WA Died Apr. 23, 1969.

CORLETT WEBSTER DAVID, business exec.; b. Oak Park, Ill., Aug. 3, 1891; Walter Robert and Evelyn (Craig) C.; M.E., U. of Mich., 1913; m. Helen Katherine Ehrman, May 29, 1917; children—Webster David, Barbara, Helen Katherine, Edwin Hart. With Chicago (Ill.) Screw Co. since 1913, successively as draftsman, foreman, asst. supt., supt., factory mgr., v.p., sec., pres.; v.p. Standard Screw Co., Chicago, 1930 to Sept. 19, 1945, chairman, from 1945; also chmn. bd. dirs. Standard Screw Co.'s subsidiaries, Chicago, Ill., Elyria, Ohio, and Hartford, Conn. Republican. Universalist. Clubs: Country (Oak Park, Ill.); Tennis (River Forest, Ill.). Home: River Forest IL Died May 29, 1971; buried Forest Home Cemetery, Forest Park IL

CORLISS, LELAND MARCHANT, physician; b. Gloucester, Mass., July 5, 1905; s. William Dale and Leonette (Burnham) C.; M.D., Tufts Coll., 1932; postgrad. surgery, U. Edinburgh (Scotland), 1934-35; m. Eleanor Nelson, June 6, 1934; children—Leland Marchant (dec.), Gardner Burnham. Intern Meml. Hosp., Worcester, Mass., 1932-34 resident New Eng. Med. Center, Boston, 1935-36, Community Hosp., Rumford, Me., 1936-37; sch. physician, also engaged in gen. practice, Paris, Me., 1937-42; med. examiner Oxford County, Me., 1939-42; med. dir. Denver pub. schs., 1949-70; Mem. Paris Sch. Bd., 1939-42; initiated pure tone hearing test for pre-schoolers, 1955; a developer pre-sch. vision test, 1955; mem. sci. and research com. Colo. Heart Assn., 1952-70; charter mem., bd. dirs. Colo. Soc. Prevention Blindness, 1956-70; mem. Colo. Adv. Com. Polio, 1955-70; speaker Internat. Conf. Health and Health Edn., 1962; cons. Forsyth Conf. Dental Health Edn., 1963; lectr. seminar Sch. Pub. Health Harvard; cons., group leader USPHS; charter member Joint Com. on School and College Health. Bd. dirs. Colo. div. Am. Cancer Soc. Dir. Meridian (Mut.) Fund, Inc. Recipient Distinguished Service awards Colo. Health Fair, 1961, Am. Sch. Health Assn., 1963, Howe award Am. Sch. Health Association, 1967. Served to lt. comdr. USNR, 1942-47; ETO, Mem. Internat. Union Health Edn., Am. Nat. Council Health. Edn. Pub. (research com), Am. Sch. Health Assn. (life, pres. 1960-61), World, Am. (group chmn. nat. conf. physicians and schs. 1949-70) med. assns., Me., Mass., Colo., Denver med. socs., Colo. Pub. Health Assn., Colo. Health Careers Council, Nat. Colo. edn. assns., Colo. Schoolmasters Assn., Ret. Officers Assn., U.S. Naval Acad. Found., Phi Chi. Republican. Member of the Universalist Church. Mason (32 deg.), Shriner). Author: The School Physician in the Athletic Program (lecture with audio-visual aids), 1962. Co-author of high school health textbook. Producer: About Your Life, sex education filmstrip, 1958. Contbr. articles profl. jours. Home: Denver CO Died Sept. 18, 1970; buried Gloucester MA

CORMENY, ALVIN E(UGENE), coll. pres.; b. Springfield, Ill., Aug. 27, 1912; s. Alvin Eugene and Gladys (Collins) C.; A.B., Illinois Coll. 1933; LL.B., Cornell U., 1936; m. Meredith Storr, Dec. 31, 1936; children—Jon, Susan, William, James. With Chadbourne, Hunt, Jaeckel & Brown, attys., N.Y.C., 1936-41; gen. counsel N.Y. Shipbuilding Corp., and asso. cos., 1941-50; v.p. N.Y. Shipbldg. Corp., 1950-53; pres. Worcester (Mass.) Poly. Inst. from 1953. Mem. Soc. Naval Architects and Marine Engrs., S.A.R. Mason. Home: East Setauket NY Died Feb. 22, 1973.

CORNELIUS, CHARLES LE SUEUR, lawyer; b. Nashville, Tenn., June 16, 1888; s. William Robinson and Lily (Le Sueur) C.; A.B., Vanderbilt U., 1910; A.M., Columbia U., 1912, LL.B., 1913; m. Elizabeth Currey, Sept. 4, 1914 (divorced); children—Charles L., Elizabeth (Mrs. W. O. Collins, Jr.), William (dec.), Jan (deceased), Lillian (Mrs. Robert K. Sharp); m. 2d, Mary E. Fleming, Feb. 1, 1936; 1 dau., Mary Fleming (Mrs. Barton D. Schmitt). Admitted Tenn. bar, 1912, practicing at Nashville; asst. atty. gen. of Tenn., 1918-25, atty. gen., Aug.-Oct. 1926. Mem. Tenn. State Senate, 1931. Mem. Am., Tenn., Nashville (pres. 1941-42) bar assns., American Automobile Assn. (dir. 1937-45), Delta Kappa Epsilon, Phi Delta Phi. Democrat. Episcopalian. Mason (32 deg., Potentate of Shrine, 1932-33). Clubs: Exchange (pres. 1927), Belle Meade Country; Colemere, Cumberland. Shrine (pres. 1943). Nashville TN Died Dec. 26, 1968.

CORNELIUS, RALPH E., banker; b. Lawrence, Pa., May 28, 1869; s. William and Mary (Swisher) C.; grad. Rayen High Sch., Youngstown; m. Helen Arms, of Youngstown, 1906. Began as collector Second Nat. Bank, Youngstown, 1886, advancing to cashier; bank merged with First Nat. Bank of which was asst. cashier, and was made cashier after affiliation of First Nat. Bank and Dollar Savings & Trust Co., also serving as trust officer of latter; later pres. Mahoning Nat. Bank and Mahoning Savings and Trust Co.; now retired. Republican. Home: 212 Broadway, Youngstown OH‡

CORNELL, (SARAH) HUGHES, physician, author; b. Fairhaven, Ill.; d. James Andersen and Annie Elizabeth (Haines) Hughes; ed. by pvt. tutor; M. D., Cooper Med. Coll., San Francisco, 1892. Practiced medicine, 1893-6; contb'r to The Argonaut, Youth's Companion, McClure syndicate, New York Evening Post, etc. Clubs: Woman's (San Jose); Sequoia (San Francisco). Author: Kenelm's Desire, 1906 L6. Address: Sequoia Club, 1565 Bush St., San Francisco‡

CORNELL, JOSEPH, artist; b. Nyack, N.Y., Dec. 24, 1903; s. self-taught. One-man exhbns. include Julien Levy Galleries, N.Y.C., 1932, 33, 39, 40, Hugo Gallery, N.Y.C., 1946, Copley Gallery, Hollywood, Cal., 1948, Charles Egan Gallery, 1949, 50, Allan Frumkin Gallery, Chgo., 1953, Stable Gallery, 1957, Bennington Coll., 1959; three-man exhbn. Richard Feigen Gallery, Chgo., 1960; group exhbns. include Fantastic Art, DADA, Surrealism Mus. Modern Art, 1936, Exposition Internat. du Surrealisme, Galeries des Beaux Arts, Paris, France, 1938, Art of This Century, N.Y.C., 1942, Carnegie Inst., 1958, Art. of Assemblage, Mus. Modern Art, 1961, Whitney Mus. ann., 1962; rep. permanent collections Mus. Modern Art, Whitney Mus. Home: Flushing NY Died Dec. 1972.

CORNELL, WALTER STEWART, physician; b. Phila., Pa., Jan. 3, 1877; s. Watson and Mary Ella (Hurtt) C.; B.S., U. of Pa., 1897, M.D., 1901, D.P.H., 1922; m. Mabel Bremer Kuhn, 1922. Engaged in private practice of medicine, 1902-12; dir. of med. inspection of public schs., Phila., 1912-43; lecturer in anatomy, U. of Pa. Med. Sch., 1902-26; lecturer in hygiene, Univ. of Pennsylvania, 1919-56; formerly asst. professor of public health and preventive medicine, Temple University Med. Sch.; chmn. exec. com. and dir. Pub. School Health Fund, Phila. Maj. in Med. Corps, U.S. Army, 1917-19; 1t. col., then col., Med. Reserve Corps, and surgeon 79th Div., 1919-35. Member American Public Health Association, A.M.A., Am. Sch. Health Assn., Phila. Coll. of Physicians, Phi Beta Kappa, Delta Tau Delta, Alpha Mu Pi Omega, Sigma Xi. Republican. Presbyterian. Mason. Club: Union League (Phila.). Author: Handbook of Osteology, 1909; Health and Medical Inspection of School Children, 1912. Former editor: Diabetic Digest. Home: Philadelphia PA Died Mar. 21, 1969; buried West Laurel Hill Cemetery, Philadelphia PA

CORNICK, PHILIP H., govtl. research; b. Mascoutah, Ill., Nov. 5, 1883; s. Dr. Boyd and Louise (Postel) C.; B.S. (chemistry), Univ. of Tenn., 1903; grad. work in polit. sci., Columbia, 1917, New Sch. for Social Research, 1919; m. Frieda Elizabeth Mylecraine, Apr. 15, 1920; children—Roger Philip, Louis. Chemist, assayer, govt. ofcl., 1904-21; mem. research staff Bur. Municipal Research, Nat. Inst. Pub. Adminstrn., Inst. of Pub. Adminstrn., N.Y., 1921-50; spl. assignments for North Jersey Transit Commn., 1926-29, N.Y. State Planning Council, 1936-38, Fed. Housing Adminstrn., 1940-42, Mass. Spl. Commn. on Real Estate Taxation and Related Matters, 1943-45; occasional lecturer on property tax and land use problems, Columbia, Cornell, Harvard, Mass. Inst. Tech. and Wayne Univs. Mem. bd. trustees, Robert Schalkenbach Foundation since 1932. Mem. com. on taxation President's Conf. on Home Bldg. and Home Ownership, 1931; consultant Nat. Resources Planning Bd. (mem. local planning com., 1938-39, mem. land com., 1938-42); chmn. Charter revision commn. City of Yonkers, 1944. Mem. Govtl. Research Assn. (chmn. exec. com., 1940), Nat. Municipal League (mem. council 1940, 46), Tax Inst. (mem. adv. council, 1945), affiliate mem. Am. Inst. Planners, Sigma Alpha Epsilon. Democrat. Author: several books on finance; Research Report in Report of Mass. Spl. Commn. on Real Estate Taxation and Related Matters, 1945. Occasional contbr. to Nat. Municipal Rev., Public Finance, etc. Home: Yonkers NY Died Oct. 24, 1971.

CORNING, HOBART M., supt. schools; b. Elyria, O., Nov. 25, 1889; s. Hobart Erastus and Pluma (Royce) C.; A.B., Dickinson Coll., Carlisle, Pa., 1911, A.M. in English, 1912; A.M. in Adminstrn., Columbia, 1931; Ed.D. (honorary), Colorado College; D.Sc., Dickinson College, 1953; married Florence Kisner, Mar. 17, 1913; children—Catherine Alvaretta (Mrs. Harold R. Packard), Hobart M. Teacher English, Johnstown (Pa.) High Sch., 1911-13; supt. schools, Newport, Pa., 1913-17, Trinidad, Colo., 1917-27, Colorado Springs, Colo., 1927-40, Omaha, Neb., 1940-46; apptd. Supt. Schools, Washington, D.C., March 1946; ret., 1958; served as member faculty, summers, U. of Missouri, Denver U., Colo. State Teachers Coll. Mem. N.E.A. (life), Am. Assn. Sch. Adminstrs., Boy Scouts of Am. (mem. exec. bd.), Nat. Conf. Christians and Jews, Nat. Council Chief State Sch. Officers, Commn. on Licensure (v.p.), Phi Delta Kappa, Kappa Delta Pi, Sigma Alpha Epsilon, 96 Club. Mason (33 deg.). Clubs: Rotary; Cosmos (Washington), Author: After Testing, What?, 1926. Home: Washington DC Died Aug. 1970.

CORNWELL, ALFRED L., business exec.; b. Pulaski, N.Y., 1884. Became treas. F.W. Woolworth Co., 1932, exec. v.p., 1944, pres., 1946-53, chmn. bd., 1953-56, also dir.; dir. Woolco Realty Corp. Home: Brookfield Center CT Died Aug. 4, 1968; buried Woodlawn Cemetery, Sandy Creek NY

CORRELL, CHARLES J., radio writer, producer; performer under title of Andy"; b. Peoria, Ill., Feb. 3, 1890; s. Joseph Boland and Anna (Fiss) C.; m. Alyce McLaughlin, Sept. 11, 1937; children—Dorothy Alyce, Barbara Joan, Charles James, Jr., John Joseph, Richard Thomas. Began as newsboy; learned bricklayers' trade under father; played piano in movie theatres; asso. with Freeman F. Gosden in promotion of amateur theatricals; under the title of Sam 'n' Henry" the partners broadcast for Radio Station WGN, 1925-27; partners transferred to Radio Station WMAQ, 1927, broadcasting under title of Amos 'n' Andy." With Nat. Broadcasting Co., 1929-39; Columbia Broadcasting System, 1939-43; National Broadcasting Co., 1943-48, CBS from 1948. Home: Beverly Hills CA Died Sept. 1972.

CORROTHERS, JAMES DAVID, clergyman, author, lecturer; b. Calvin, Cass Co., Mich., July 2, 1869; s. James Richard and Maggie (Churchman) C.; is of Negro, Indian and Scotch-Irish blood; mother died the day he was born; attended sch. South Haven, Mich., 1874-83; worked in lumbering, saw mill, as hotel hand, coachman, sailed the lakes one season; then had bootblack's chair in barber's shop; encouraged by Henry D. Lloyd, the author, and Frances E. Willard, who helped him, and working to assist paying his expenses, attended Northwestern Univ., 1890-3. Ordained to ministry, Sept., 1894; Baptist. Contb'r to mags., prose and verse. Author: The Black Cat Club, 1902 F3. Address: S Haven MI‡

CORRY, EDGAR CLAYTON, lawyer; b. Des Moines, Mar. 25, 1912; s. Edgar C. and Anna Marie (Kirk) C.; A.B., U. Ia., 1934, J.D., 1936; m. Florence C. Hagenah, Feb. 12, 1943; children—Lawrence Dunsworth, Sheila Carlstedt, David John. Admitted to Ia. bar, 1936, Ill. bar, 1951; practice in Des Moines, 1936-42, 46-47; corp. counsel State of Ia., 1948-51; gen. counsel, v.p., dir. Mather Stock Car Co., Chgo., 1951-55; v.p. North Am. Car Corp., Chgo., 1955, sec., 1956, gen. counsel, 1961, dir., 1961-68; exec. v.p., 1963-68; dir., sec. Nat. Tank Car Co., Chgo., 1956, treas., 1960; sec., dir. North Am. Car (Can.), Ltd., 1963. Comdr. Ia. dept. AMVets, 1946-47, nat. comdr., 1947-48, pres. bd. trustees AMVets Nat. Service Found. Mem. fed. adv. com. on employment security Sec. Labor, 1948-52; exec. com. White House Conf. on Children and Youth, 1960. With vets. div. nat. hdqrs. Republican party, 1948. Served with USNR, 1942-46; lt. comdr. exec. reservist O.E.P. Mem. Am., Ill., Ia., Chgo. bar assns., Delta Upsilon, Delta Theta Phi. Presbyn. Clubs: University (Chgo.); Skokie Country, Skokie Valley Skating (pres.). Home: Glencoe IL Died Oct. 9, 1968.

CORSON, HARRY HERBERT, ins. agt.; b. Nashville, Oct. 7, 1898; s. Harry Herbert and Sadie Clare (McGuire) C.; student The Hill Sch., 1912-15, Duncan Sch., Nashville, 1915; A.B., Vanderbilt U., 1920; m. Mary Phillips, 1927 (dec. 1960); children—Clare C. Armistead, Harry Herbert III. Operated real estate and ins. bus., Nashville, 1921-27; mng. partner Davis, Corson & Armistead and predecessors, 1928-63; chmn. Corson & Armistead, Inc. Maj. gen. Tenn. N.G. (ret.). Mem. various ins. orgns., Sword and Cutlass (chancellor), Am. Legion Founders, Am. Legion, V.F.W., S.A.R., The Holland Soc. Episcopalian. Home: Nashville TN Deceased.

CORTNEY, PHILIP, President Coty, Inc. and Coty Internat. Grad. elec. engr. Univ. of Nancy, France; Doctor of Laws (honorary), Hamilton Coll.; m. Marcelle Denya. Began in steel business, exporting from France and Belgium; became dir. of Banque Transatlantique; with Coty 1940-60, now pres. Coty Inc. and Coty Internat. Trustee U.S. Inter-Am. Council; dir. Nat. Indsl. Conf. Bd. Decorated Comdr. Legion of Honor (France). Fellow N.Y. Acad. Sci.; mem. U.S. council Internat. C. of C., Am. Society French Legion of Honor (v.p.). Author: The Economic and Political Consequences of Lord Keynes' Theories (essay); The Economic Munich. Home: Geneva Switzerland Died June 1971.

CORTRIGHT, ERNEST EVERETT, coll. pres.; b. Middletown, N.Y., Aug. 28, 1873; s. Bowdewine S. and Harriet (Clark) C.; student Allegheny Coll., Yale U.; M.A., New York U., 1922; married Viola Van Gordon; children—Enid, Bernice, Estelle; married 2d, Eva Van Fleet, July 10, 1948. Teacher, Mt. Hope, N.Y., 4 yrs., 1894-98; prin. schs., Harriman, N.Y., 6 yrs., 1898-1904, supt. schs., Cornwall-on-Hudson, 6 yrs., 1904-10; at Bridgeport, Conn., since 1911, successively as prin. Shelton Sch., City Normal Sch., asst. supt. schs., supt. schs., 1922-25; asst. prof. of edn., Sch. of Edn., New York U., 1925-27; pres. Jr. Coll. of Conn., Bridgeport, 1927-46, pres. emeritus since 1946. Ex-pres. New England Jr. Coll. Council, Conn. State Teachers Assn., Conn. Jr. Teachers Conf.; mem. Founders Soc. America. Conglist. Mason. Rotarian. Club: University. Extensive contbr. on ednl. subjects. Home: 52 Wikon St., Bridgeport 29. Office: 1001 Fairfield Av., Bridgeport 5 CT‡

CORWIN, GEORGE B., gen. sec. Gen. Orgn. Religious Soc. Friends. Home: Philadelphia PA Died July 23, 1972.

CORY, ABRAM EDWARD, clergyman; b. Osceola, Ia., Aug. 13, 1873; s. Nathan Edward and Margaret (Connoran) C.; B.A., Eureka (Ill.) Coll., 1894; M.A., Drake U., Des Moines, Ia., 1898; grad. work, Columbia, and Union Theol. Sem.; D.D., Drake, 1914; LL.D., Eureka, 1915; m. Bertha Adkins, Sept. 30, 1895. Served in China 15 yrs., as missionary in secretarial and ednl. work; gen. work for Disciples of Christ in America since 1912; sec. Foreign Christian Missionary Soc., Men and Millions Movement; mem. exec. com. Federal Council Churches of Christ; asso. sec. Interchurch World Movement of N. America; sec. United Christian Missionary Soc. of Disciples of Christ; vice pres. Internat. Christian Endeavor Soc.; mem. exec. com. World's Christian Endeavor Society. Was pastor Gordon St. Ch., Kingston, N.C., dir. adv. Pension Fund Disciples of Christ; retired; adj. prof. missions, Sch. of Religion, Butler U. Pres. Internat. Conv. Disciples of Christ, 1923-24. Acting chaplain 1st U.S. Inf. in Philippines, 1900; served overseas for Y.M.C.A., 1918. Mem. Am. Assn. Univ. Profs., Theta Phi. Mason. Author: The Trail to the Hearts of Men, 1916; Think Peace, 1916; Out Where the World Begins, 1921; Voices of the Sanctuary, 1930. Home: 2407 N. Delaware St., Indianapolis IN‡

CORY, CHARLES EDWARD, prof. philosophy; b. Thornburg, Ia., 1878; s. Freeman and Sarah Catherine (Hamilton) C.; A.B., Drake U., 1901, A.M., 1902; A.M., Yale, 1903, Ph.D., 1905; S.T.B., Harvard, 1907; m. Dr. Harriet S. Stevens, of St. Louis, Mo., Aug. 25, 1918. Mem. faculty, Washington U., since 1907, prof. philosophy since 1920. Mem. Am. Philos. Assn., Phi Beta Kappa. Conglist. Home: 6157 Pershing Av., St Louis MO‡

CORY, HARRY THOMAS, engineer; b. Lafayette, Ind., May 27, 1870; s. Thomas and Carrie (Stoney) C.; B.M.E., Purdue U., 1887 (first to receive degree in electrical engineering), B.C.E., 1889, Dr. Engring., 1929; M.C.E., Cornell, 1893, M.M.E., 1896; m. Ida (Judd) Hiller, Oct. 4, 1911; children—Thomas Judd, Clarence Richard and John Harry (twins, both dec.). Asst. engr. A.&M. Ry., 1888; asst. city engr. Lafayette, Ind., 1889; dep. county engr. Tippecanoe County, Ind., 1890-92; prof. civ. engring., U. of Mo., 1893-98; in Europe, 1898; prof. civ. and sanitary engring., U. of Mo., 1898-1900; dean Coll. of Engring. and prof. civ. engring., U. of Cincinnati, 1900-03; on leave of absence, 1901-03, with Mex. Central, Tex. & Pacific and S.P. railroads; asst. to gen. mgr. S.P. Co., July 1904-May 1905; in personal charge of diverting Colo. River from running to Salton Sea, 1906-07; asst. to pres. associated Harriman lines in Ariz. and S.P.R.R. in Mex., May 1905-Apr. 1911; gen. mgr. and chief engr. of the Calif. Development Co. and La Sociedad de Riego y Terrenos de la Baja California, April 1906-Dec. 1910; consulting engr. at San Francisco, 1909-17; dir. gen. foreign relief, Am. Red Cross nat. hdqrs., 1917-18; cons. engr. of U.S. Reclamation Service on soldier's land settlement plan, 1918-20; Am. mem. Internat. Nile Projects Commn. for the Egyptian and Sudanese govts., Cairo, Egypt, and Khartum, Sudan, Jan.-Sept. 1920; cons. engr. San Francisco, Calif., 1920-21; cons. engr. Los Angeles, Calif., and also for the U.S. Reclamation service, 1921-23; chief of engring. Palos Verdes project, Redondo Beach, Calif., 1922-24; chief engr. Guadalquivir marismas desalting and irrigation project, Seville, Spain, 1925-27; cons. engr. Muluya Valley irrigation project. French and Spanish Morocco, 1926; cons. engr. Los Angeles, Calif., since 1928; advisory engr. Los Angeles Agency, R.F.C., 1932-34; advisory com. on R.F.C. earthquake rehabilitation loans,

1933-34; mem. Passamaquoddy Bay Tidal Power Project Commn., 1934-35; cons. engr. Soil Conservation Service, U.S. Dept. Agr., Albuquerque, N.M., and Washington, D.C., 1935-40, supervising engineer, Defense Plant Corp., U.S. Govt., 1941-42; manager Los Angeles Office Bureau of Economic Warfare, 1942-43; consulting engr., Los Angeles, Calif., since 1943. Member Laymen's Advisory Council of National Conference of Jews and Christians. Life member American Society C.E. (Thomas Fitch Rowland prize 1914), Phi Delta Theta, Theta Nu Epsilon, Sigma Xi, Tau Beta Pi, Chi Epsilon, Kappa Phi Sigma. Mason (K.T., 32 deg., Shriner). Clubs: Bohemian (San Francisco); University, Los Angeles Athletic (Los Angeles). edn., (with T. Cory) Manual of U.S. System of Land Surveying, 1888; Imperial Valley and Salton Sink, 1915; Democratization of Family Planning, 1940; also atlases of Boone (1888), Clay (1890) and Tippecanoe (1892) counties, Ind. Contbr. tech. reports, scientific papers and mag. articles. Home: Los Angeles Athletic Club. Office: 431 W. 7th St., Los Angeles CA‡

CORYELL, CHARLES DUBOIS, chemist; b. Los Angeles, Feb. 21, 1912; s. William Harlan and Florence Elizabeth (Cook) C.; B.S., Calif. Inst. Tech., 1932, Ph.D., 1935; m. Meta Patricia Seward, Dec. 6, 1930 (div. 1936); 1 daughter, Patricia Louise Huber; m. 2d, Grace Seeley, Dec. 2, 1937 (dec. May 1965); dau., Julie Esther; m. 3d, Barbara Buchman, Mar. 30, 1969. Research asst. Calif. Inst. Tech., 1935-38; instr. chemistry Deep Springs Jr. Coll., Deep Springs, Calif., 1937-39; mem. staff, chemistry dept. U. of Calif. at Los Angeles, instr., 1938-40, asst. prof., 1940-44, asso. prof., 1944-45 (on leave, 1942-45); chief fission products sect., Metall. Lab., U. of Chicago, 1942-43, Clinton Labs., Oak Ridge, Tenn., 1943-46; prof. chemistry Mass. Inst. Tech., 1946-71. Consultant to AEC Laboratories, 1946-71. Louis Lipsky fellow Weizmann Inst. Science, Rehovoth Israel, 1953-54. Mem. board inc. Midwest Bus. Inst., Utopia Coll., 1947-68; mem. adv. bd. Williams-Waterman Fund, 1947-68; trustee Windham Coll., 1963-71, Mark Hopkins Coll., 1966-71. Guggenheim fellow, Fulbright lectr., Paris, 1963. Fellow Am. Nuclear Soc., Council for A Livable World, Am. Acad. Arts and Scis., Am. Phys. Soc., Am. Association for Advancement of Science; mem. Am. Chem. Soc., United World Federalists, Internat. Sci. Found., Fedn. Am. Scientists, Sigma Xi, Tau Beta Pi. Author numerous articles for sci. publs. Editor: Radiochemical Studies: The Fission Products, 1951. Home: Lexington MA Died Jan. 7, 1971.

COSGRAVE, JOHN O'HARA, II, artist; b. San Francisco, Oct. 10, 1908; s. Charles O'Malley and Margaret Mary (Mahoney) C.; student Marin Jr. Coll., 1926-29, U. Cal., 1929-30, Acad. Andre Lhote, 1932; m. Mary Eliza Silva, 1952. Illustrator books, mag. and book covers from 1933. Recipient Brooklyn watercolor prize, 1942. Club: The Dutch Treat (New York City, New York). Illustrator: Log of Columbus; the Sacramento; Wind, Sand and Stars; A Man Named Grant; The Long Ships Passing; The Days of Ofelia, Come In, The Monogahela, The Salt Rivers of the Massachusetts Shore; Carry on Mr. Bowditch; Old Creole Days; Listen for a Lonesome Drum; jacket illustrations The Cruel Sea, The Captain. Author-illustrator; America Sails the Seas; Clipper Ship. Home: Pocasset MA Died May 9, 1968.

COSGROVE, EMILIE DOHRMANN (MRS. JOHN CHARLES COSGROVE), civic worker; b. San Francisco, Feb. 19, 1912; d. Frederick W. and Emilie (Plagemann) Dohrmann; A.B., Stanford, 1933; student Bryn Mawr Coll., 1933-34; m. John Charles Cosgrove, Nov. 30, 1935; children—Carole Jane, Julie Dohrmann, John Frederick. Dir. Jr. League, Los Angeles, 1949-52, chmn. pub. affairs com. 1949-51, chmn. nominating com. 1951-52, recording sec. 1961-62. Trustee Stanford U., 1964-66. Mem. So. Cal. Symphony Assn. (jr. philharmonic com. 1943-56), St. Brendans Mother's Guild (dir. 1946-56, v.p. 1953-56), Kappa Kappa Gamma, Phi Beta Kappa. Republican. Roman Catholic. Clubs: Marlborough School Mothers (dir. 1952-55, pres. 1953-54), Stanford Mothers (dir. 1958-60). Home: Los Angeles CA Died Mar. 7, 1969; interred Santa Barbara CA

COSTELLO, WILLIAM ALOYSIOUS, news corr., counsellor internat. affairs, amabassador; b. St. Paul, Mar. 5, 1904; s. Edward A. and Hilda Marie (Swanson) C.; A.B. cum laude, U. of Minn., 1935; m. Helen Welch Murchie. Mar. 30, 1935; children—Patricia B. Malzan. Catherine J. Simmons. Newspaperman on Minneapolis Journal, Minneapolis Tribune, Honolulu Star-Bulletin and Omaha World-Herald, 1929-41; radio corr. Columbia Broadcasting System, Chicago and Wash., 1941-46, Far East news dir. based in Tokyo, 1946-51; White House corr. CBS, 1952-53; counsellor internat. affairs, 1955-58; White House correspondent MBS, 1958-65, nat. corr., 1966-67; U.S. ambassador to Trinidad-Tobago, 1967-69; lecturer. President Radio-Television Correspondents Assn., 1955. Member Association Radio-TV News Analysts (vice president 1954-55, 63-67), Acad. Political Sci., Overseas Writers, Assn. for Asian Studies, American Political Science Association, White House Correspondents Assn., Sigma Delta Chi, Phi Beta Kappa. Clubs: Nat. Press (Washington); Overseas Press (N.Y.C.). Author: Democracy vs. Feudalism in Post-War Japan, 1948; The Facts About Nixon, 1960. Contbr. various mags. Home: Tobago WI Died June 20, 1969; buried at sea.

COSTIGAN, JOHN EDWARD, artist; b. Providence, Feb. 29, 1888; s. John Henry and Hanna (Cronin) C.; ed. pub. schs.; self-taught in art; m. Ida Blessin, June 1919; children—John Edward, Rosella Josephine, Elizabeth Mary, Danny M., Ida May. Awarded numerous prizes and medals for paintings and etchings, 1920-—, latest being Henry B. Shope Prize, Soc. Am. Etchers and Litho. Engravers Exhbn., 1948, 56; 2d prize Balt. Water Color, 1951, 52, 1st 1956; Barry-Stevens award Am. Water Color Soc. Ann. Exhbn., 1953; citation Am. Artist Mag., 1956; Mary Trueblood Whitney Meml. award Am. Water Color Soc., 1958; Emily Lowe award, 1962; medal of merit Syndicate Mags., 1968; Benjamin Clinedienst Meml. medal Artists Fellowship, 1971. Figure and landscape artist. Represented in Art Inst. Chgo., Met. Mus. N.Y.C., Library of Congress, Washington, various other museums, pvt. collections, Smithsonian Instn. traveling exhbn., 1968-70. Murals U.S. Post Office and Agr. Bldg., Stewart, Va.; U.S. Post Office, Girard, O., Rensselaer, Ind., IBM collection Am. art; Rochester (N.Y.) Mus.; Wellesley Coll. collection water colors; Frye Mus., Seattle. Served as pvt. Pioneer Inf. Co., U.S.A., overseas 9 mos. World War I. N.A., 1928. Recipient Gold Medal, Nat. Art Club Exhbn., 1954; 62; second popular prize Ogunquit (Maine) Art Center, 1958; Water Color Purchase prize Butler Intstitute of American Art, 1962. Member Allied Artists Am., Soc. Animal Painters and Sculptors, Guild Am. Painters, Soc. Am. Etchers, Phila. Soc. Etchers, Prairie Print Makers, Am. and N.Y. water color clubs, Artists Fellowship. Clubs: Salmagundi, Nat. Arts, Kit Kat, Lotus (New York). Home: Orangeburg NY Died Aug. 5, 1972; buried Nanuet NY

COTNAREANU, LEON, bus. exec.; born Romania, Apr. 27, 1891; s. Iancou and Anna (Drumann) C.; grad. U. Leipzig, Germany, 1912; m. Yvonne Le Baron, Aug. 25, 1933. Steel bus. and export from France, Belgium, Luxemburg, 1922; founded elec. equipment and time control, Cotna, Versailles, France, 1927; chmn. Coty, Eng., Ltd., 1939-70; dir. Coty, Inc. and Coty Internat., 1937-70, treas., 1947-70, chairman of the board of directors, 1956-70; asso. pub. newspaper Le Figaro, Paris, 1933-40; dir. The Foundation Co. Awarded Legion of Honour (France). Clubs: Yachting de France, Golf de St. Cloud (Paris). Author: The Alternative, 1941; Suites Francaises, 1944. Home: Geneva Switzerland Died Jan. 1970.

COTTERILL, GEORGE FLETCHER, consulting civil engr.; b. Oxford, Eng., Nov. 18, 1865; s. Robert and Alice (Smith) C.; came to U.S., 1872; grad. (valedictorian) Montclair (N.J.) High Sch., 1881; m. Cora Rowena Gormley, Feb. 19, 1890 (died Feb. 26, 1936); children—Ruth Eileen (dec.), (adopted) Marjorie Alice (Mrs. Paul J. Avery). Studied engineering with James Owen, civ. engr., Essex County, N.J., 1881-83; landscape engring., Arlington Cemetery. Hudson County, N.J., 1883-84; moved to Seattle, Wash., 1884, and since engaged in various lines of engring.; asst. city engr., Seattle, 1892-1900, spl. duties development city water supply and harbor platting; gen. engring. practice Seattle and N.W. since 1900; mem. Wash. State Irrigation Commn., 1903-05; mem. Seattle City Planning Commn., 1926-28; specialty landscape platting, municipal plans, etc.; chief engr. Wash. State Highway Dept., 1916-19. Charter mem. and first sec., 1902-03, Pacific Northwest Soc. Engrs. Dem. nominee for mayor of Seattle, 1900; for rep. in Congress, 1902 and 1916; mem. Wash. Senate, 1907-11; Dem. direct primary nominee for U.S. Senate, 1908, 10, 20; mayor of Seattle, Wash., 1912-14; commr. Port of Seattle, 1922-34; federal cons. to Wash. State Planning Council, 1934-35; cons. engr. State Dept. of Conservation and Development and liaison supervisor for state sponsor of U.S. Works Progress Adminstrn. Flood Relief Projects, 1935-36; consultant engr. State Dept. Social Security and Federal Work Projects Administration on Water Resources Research, 1937-39; supervisor U.S. Works Projects Adminstrn., Island County, Washington, 1940-41; cartographer asst. King County assessor, 1943-47. Dir. Am. Assn. Port Authorities, 1927-34; also of Assn. of Pacific and Far East Ports, 1927-30. Active in temperance reform, especially through Good Templars; sec. G.L. of Washington, 1889-90; rep. Internat. Supreme Lodge, 1893, and all sessions to 1930; U.S. Nat. Chief Templar Internat. Order of Good Templars, 1905-13, and internat. counselor, 1899-1902, and 1908-30; U.S. national counselor, 1936-39; Grand Chief Templar, Wash. Grand Lodge since 1945; U.S. del. 12th, 14th and 16th Internat. congresses against alcoholism, London, 1909, Milan, 1913, Lausanne, 1921. Mem. Washington State Pioneers Assn. (historian 1940-41, pres. 1942-43). Public speaker, writer and extensive traveler in Europe and America. Congregationalist. Mason (K.T., Shriner). Club: Seattle Press (life). Wrote: Puget Sound—The Mediterranean of the Pacific, 1927; The Climax of a World Quest, 1928; also various papers relating to Pacific Ocean and world commerce. Designed New World Map, Pacific Planisphere Projection, 1929. Home: 2020 E. 65th St., Seattle WA‡

COTTRELL, WILL REA, JR., iron co. exec.; b. Townley, Ala., Oct. 26, 1918; s. Will Rea and Alice (Guthrie) C.; student U. Ala., 1938-42. With Woodward Corp. (Alabama), 1936-68, sec.-treas. Woodward Co. div. of Mead Corp., Birmingham, Ala., 1968-72. Home: Birmingham AL Died Mar. 14, 1970; buried Birmingham AL

COUDERT, AMALIA KUSSNER, miniature painter; b. Terre Haute, Ind., Mar. 26, 1873; d. Lorenz Kussner; ed. mainly by pvt. governess and tutor; studied, 1883-90, St. Mary's of the Woods, Indiana; m. at New York, Charles du Pont Coudert, July 3, 1900. Began artistic career in New York, 1892; went to London, 1896, and painted the King (then the Prince of Wales), and most of the highest aristocracy of Eng.; in 1899 was summoned to Russia to paint the Emperor and Empress and the Grand Duchesses Vladimir and Ellen; in autumn of 1899 went to S. Africa to paint Hon. Cecil Rhodes. Address: 53 W. 48th St., New York‡

COUDERT, FREDERIC RENE, JR., ex-congressman, lawyer; b. N.Y.C., May 7, 1898; s. Frederic Rene and Alice T. (Wilmerding) C.; A.B., Columbia, 1918, LL.B. (Kent scholar), 1922; m. Paula Murray, Oct. 1931. Admitted to N.Y. bar, 1923, since practiced in N.Y.C.; mem. firm Coudert Bros., 1924-72; asst. U.S. atty. So. Dist. N.Y., 1924-25. Rep. candidate for dist atty. N.Y. County, 1929; mem. N.Y. State Senate, 17th Dist., 1939-46, Ho. of Reps., 17th Dist. Manhattan, 1946; mem. 80th to 85th U.S. Congresses, 17th N.Y. Dist. chmn. subcom. Rapp-Coudert Legislative Com. to Investigate Pub. Ednl. System; chmn. N.Y. Lawyers Committee against Jones Act, 1929; mem. temporary state commn. on govtl. operations N.Y.C., 1959-61. Served with U.S. Army, 1917-18, AEF; 1st lt. 105th U.S. Inf., 27th Div. Decorated Chevalier Legion of Honor (France); recipient U. medal for distinguished pub. service, Columbia, 1941. Mem. Am., N.Y. State bar assns., Assn. Bar City N.Y., N.Y. County Lawyers Assn., Fedn. French Alliances U.S. (pres. 1965-72). Clubs: Sky, Century, Pilgrims, Racquet and Tennis, Piping Rock, Seawanhaka, Corinthian Yacht, N.Y. Yacht. Home: New York City NY Died May 21, 1972; buried Gold Spring Cemetery, Oyster Bay NY

COUEY, JAMES HENRY, JR., newspaper exec.; b. Macon, Ga., Sept. 16, 1923; s. James Henry and Mary Beatrice (Turner) C.; m. Elizabeth Brown, September 19, 1945; children—Mary Bryn (Mrs. E.R. Daniel III), Caryn Sue (Mrs. G.E. Broten), James Henry III. With The Birmingham (Alabama) News, 1941-61. Sunday editor, 1950-55, asst. mng. editor, 1955-56, asst. gen. mgr., 1957-60, v.p., gen. mgr. Birmingham News Co., 1960-61; v.p., gen. mgr. Tampa (Fla.) Tribune and Times, 1961-66, pres., pub., 1966-68; exec. v.p. Hawaii Newspaper Agy., Inc., from 1968; pub. Honolulu Star Bull., 1971. Served with AUS, 1943-46. Episcopalian. Home: Honolulu HI Died June 22, 1971; buried Atlanta GA

COUGHLAN, ROBERT EDWARD, JR., lawyer; b. Balt., Mar. 3, 1899; s. Robert Edward and Nellie Aurelia (Wheatley) C.; A.B., St. John's Coll., Annapolis, Md., 1920; LL.B., U. Md., 1924; m. Margaret Wagner, Oct. 15, 1924; children—Margaret Nourse, Robert Edward III. Admitted to Md. bar, 1928; adjuster Md. Casualty Co., 1920, corr. claim dept., 1920-25, asst. mgr. property damage claim div., 1925, mgr., 1925-28, mgr. Balt. claim div., 1929-33; trial counsel, 1933-44; sr. partner Lord, Whip, Couglan & Green, 1944-71. Mem. bd. dirs. Legal Air Bur., Roland Park Civic League. Served with U.S. Army, 1918. Fellow Am. Coll. Trial Lawyers; mem. Am., Md., Balt. (pres.) bar assns., Fedn. Ins. Counsel, Maritime Law Assn., Trial Table Law Club (past pres.), Barrister's Law Club (past pres.), Balt. C. of C., Am. Judicature Soc., Kappa Alpha. Democrat. Episcopalian. Mason. Clubs: Merchant's, Center. Baltimore MD Died Mar. 5, 1971; buried Druid Ridge Cemetery, Baltimore MD

COULSON, EDWIN RAY, educator; b. Shinston, W.Va., May 11, 1899; s. John and Caroline V. (Tetrick) C.; A.B., U. Cal., Los Angeles, 1926; M.A., U. So. Cal., 1929; m. Ruby Marguerite Wheeler, Aug. 22, 1925; children—Margaret (Mrs. Walter William Thompson), Carolyn (Mrs. Harry Handler), Mary (Mrs. John McClelland). Reporter, Los Angeles Herald Express, 1920-22; English tchr., Cal., 1928-29; head English dept. Santa Monica City Coll., 1929-64, dir. summer session, 1942, 46; lectr. U. Cal. at Los Angeles, 1949-55, 61, Middlebury Coll. Bread Loaf Sch. English, summer 1951. Mem. library bd. City of Santa Monica, 1954-66. Mem. Modern Lang. Assn., Coll. English Assn. (v.p. regional div. 1954), Am. Assn. U. Profs., Phi Delta Kappa. Co-editor: Thought and Form in the Essay, 1933. Author: (with Richard Webb) Sidney Lanier, Poet and Prosodist 1941. Contbr. to poetry mags. Home: Santa Monica CA Died Sept. 21, 1969; inurned Woodlawn Cemetery, Santa Monica CA

COULTER, SIDNEY BEECH, lawyer; b. Frederiksted, St. Croix, Virgin Islands, Dec. 11, 1897; s. Frank and Emily (Beech) C.; LL.B., Syracuse U., 1924; m. Mildred Soper, Sept. 2, 1924; children—Robert F., Elizabeth Emily (Mrs. Edward L.

Mueller), John R. Admitted to N.Y.bar, 1924, since practiced in Syracuse; mem. firm Coulter, Fraser, Carr, Ames, Bolton, 1958-68; claims adjuster, atty. Md. Casualty Co., Balt., 1929-35; atty. Town of Geddes, N.Y., 1943-59 spl. dist. atty., 1960-68. Chmn. Onondaga County Charter Commn., 1960-63. Trustee Onondaga Community Coll., 1961-68. Fellow Am. Coll. Trial Lawyers; mem. Am. Arbitration Assn. (mem. panel), Am., N.Y. State, Onondaga County (recipient Distinguished Lawyer award 1968) bar assns., Phi Delta Phi, Phi Kappa Phi. Episcopalian (vestryman 1928-58, jr. warden 1958-62, sr. warden 1962-68). Home: Syracuse NY Died Aug. 9, 1968; buried Syracuse NY

COULTHARD, GEORGE WILLIAM, lawyer; b. Modale, Ia., May 21, 1916; s. David Lloyd and Ruth (Mintun) C.; B.S.C., Creighton U., 1937; J.D., U. Ia., 1939; m. Lena Silvagni, Aug. 8, 1942 (dec. 1955); 1 dau., Karen Jane; m. 2d, Diane Crandall, Sept. 5, 1957; children—Leslie, William, James. Admitted to Ia. bar, 1939, Nev. bar, 1945; spl. agt. FBI, 1939-45; practiced in Las Vegas, 1946-72. Mem. Nev. Bd. Bar Examiners, 1948-51, Legislative Counsel Bur., Nev. Legislature, 1951-54. Vice pres., dir. Las Vegas Valley Water Dist., 1950-57; active Boys Club Clark County. Mem. Nev. Legislature from Clark County, 1951-54. Mem. State bar Nev. (pres. 1964), Am., Ia., Clark County (pres. 1952) bar assns., Las Vegas C. of C. (dir. 1965-67), Gamma Eta Gamma. Elk. Home: Las Vegas NV Died July 25, 1972.

COUNTRYMAN, J. E., food processor; b. Lindenwood, Ill., Jan. 4, 1903; s. Floyd M. and Marian (Pullin) C.; student Cornell Coll., U. Ill.; m. Bernice Smith, Sept. 15, 1924; children—Jacquelyn (Mrs. J. Countryman Hoganson), James. Dir., Del Monte Corp., San Francisco, Wells Fargo Co., Wells Fargo Internat., Wells Fargo Bank, Transam. Corp., Planning Research Corp., Dillingham Corp. Mem. U. Ill. Found.; mem. adv. council Sch. Bus. Adminstrn., U. Santa Clara. Trustee Cal. Council for Econ. Edn.; bd. dirs. No. Cal. Industry-Edn. Council; bd. regents U. of Pacific. Mason (Shriner). Clubs: St. Francis Yacht, San Francisco Golf; Bohemian; Pacific Union. Home: San Francisco CA Died July 29, 1972; buried Cypress Lawn Cemetery, San Francisco CA

COURANT, RICHARD, mathematician, educator; born Lublinitz, Poland, January 8, 1888; s. Siegmund and Martha (Freund) C.; student U. of Breslau (Germany), U. of Zurich (Switzerland); Ph.D., U. of Goettingen (Germany), 1910; E.D., Technische Hochschule (Darmstadt); Sc.D., Case Inst. Tech., 1958, N.Y.U., 1958; D.E., Technische Hochschule, Aachen, Germany, 1958; m. Nerina Runge, Jan. 1919; children—Ernest David, Gertrude A. Elizabeth, Hans Wolfgang Julius, Marianne Leonore. Came to U.S., 1934, naturalized, 1940. Asst. and instr. of mathematics, U. of Goettingen, 1910-14; prof. of mathematics, U. of Muenster, 1919-20; prof. of mathematics and dir. of Math. Inst., Goettingen, 1920-33; lecturer, U. of Cambridge, Eng., 1933-34; prof. of mathematics and head mathematics dept. N.Y.U., 1934-58, prof. emeritus, science adviser, from 1958; also dir. Inst. Mathematical Scis. Served in German Army, 1914-19. Decorated Knight Comdr. Order of Merit (Fed. Republic of Germany; recipient Navy Distinguished Pub. Service award, 1958. Mem. Am. Math. Soc., A.A.A.S., American Physical Society, National Academy Sciences, New York Academy Sciences, Math. Assn. Am., American Philos. Soc., Accademia Nazionale dei Lincei, Acad. Scis. USSR, Royal Netherlands, Acad. Sciences and Letters, Akademie der Wissenschaften (Goettingen), Royal Danish Acad. Sci. and Letters, Sigma Xi. Club: Cosmos. Author textbooks including: (with H. Robbins) What is Mathematics?, 1941; Supersonic Flow and Shock Waves (Interscience), (with K. O. Friedrichs), 1948; Methods of Mathematical Physics (Wiley) (Interscience) (with D. Hilbert), vol. I, 1953, vol. II, 1962. Home: New Rochelle NY Died Jan. 27, 1972.

COURTIS, STUART APPLETON, teacher; b. Wyandotte, Mich., May 15, 1874; s. William Munroe and Lizzie Easton (Folger) C.; ed. Detroit Central High Sch. and Detroit Business Univ. to 1894; Mass. Inst. Tech. 2 yrs.; spl. studies, summers, U. of Chicago and Columbia U.; B.S., Teachers Coll., Columbia, 1919, M.A., 1921; Ph.D., U. of Mich., 1925; m. Margaret Alice Weber, June 12, 1901; children—William Stuart (dec.), Joseph Weber, Thomas Maybury, Walter Folger. Head of dept. of science and mathematics, Liggett Sch., Detroit, 1898-1914; dir. ednl. research, Detroit pub. schs., 1914-19; dir. of instrn. and dean, Detroit Teachers Coll., 1920-24; educational consultant, Detroit public schools, 1924-31, Hamtramck public schools, Michigan, 1926-30, Culver Mil. Acad., 1930-35; prof. Sch. of Edn., U. of Mich., 1921-44, prof. emeritus since 1944; professor edn., School of Edn., Wayne U., Detroit, 1931-44. Originator of Courtis standard tests," a system of measuring efficiency of school work; member staff of experts, Hanus Committee on School Inquiry, New York, 1911, the Gary Survey, 1916, New York Survey, 1924; in charge of testing work, Boston public schools, 1912. Fellow A.A.A.S. (sec. sect. L, 1913-17; pres. 1918-19, 1932-33). Mem. Nat. Assn. Dirs. Ednl. Research (pres. 1917-18), Nat. Soc. for Scientific Study of Edn., Coll. Teachers of Edn. (sec. 1925-31), Phi Kappa Phi. Episcopalian. Author: Then and Now in Education (with Otis W. Caldwell); Why Children Succeed; The Measurement of Growth; A Picture Dictionary for Children (with Mrs. G. Walters); also various bulls. and magazine articles. Lecturer. Address: 9110 Dwight Av., Detroit 14 MI‡

COURTNEY, THOMAS J(AMES), lawyer; b. Chicago, Ill., Dec. 23, 1894; s. James R. and Catherine (Hussey) C.; ed. Visitation Grammar Sch. and St. Rita's High Sch., Chicago; LL.B., Chicago Kent Coll. of Law, 1926; m. Kathryn Foley, July 19, 1917; 1 dau., Rita Marie. Sergt. at arms and sec. City Council, Chicago, 1922-27; began practice of law, Chicago, 1926; mem. Ill. Senate, 1926-32; state's atty. of Cook County, 1932-45; judge Circuit Court, 1945-64. Mem. Chicago Bar Assn., Ill. State Bar Assn., Am. Legion, Forty and Eight, Knights of Columbus. Democrat. Club: Bob O' Link Golf. Home: Chicago IL Died Dec. 1971.

COURVILLE, CYRIL BRIAN, physician; b. Traverse City, Mich., Feb. 19, 1900; s. Philip Albert and Emma Amelia (Kroupa) C.; student Cedar Lake (Mich.) Acad., 1915-16; A.B., Emmanuel Missionary Coll., Berrien Springs, Mich., 1921; M.D., Coll. of Med. Evangelists, Loma Linda and Los Angeles, Calif., 1925; M.Sc. in embryology U. of So. Calif., 1930; D.M.S., Teijo University, Tokyo, Japan; married Margaret Louise Farnsworth, June 10, 1939. Instr. in anatomy Loma Linda University, Loma Linda, 1926-29, prof. neurology since 1934, head sect. nervous diseases; vol. asst. neurosurg. clinic Dr. Harvey Cushing, 1927; resident neurology and nerosurgery Los Angeles Co. Gen. Hosp., 1929-33, dir. Cajal Lab. Neuropathology, 1934-68; consultant neuropathology, Los Angeles County coroner White Meml. Hosp., Los Angeles. Founder, organizer med. cadet corps, 1935, organized 47th Gen. Hosp., 1937. Diplomate Nat. Bd. Med. Examiners; fellow Am. Acad. Neurology; mem. Cal., Los Angeles County med. assns., Am. Neurol. Assn., Am. Acad. Forensic Scis., Am. Acad. Cerebral Palsy, Los Angeles Neurological Society, Am. Assn. Neuropathologists, British Anthropological Association. Republican. Adventist. Author sci. books, including Commotio Cerebri, 1953; Effects of Alcohol in the Nervous System of Man; contributor to the Study of Cerebral Anoxia, 1953, Forensic Neuropathology, 1964, others. Author and editor, Medical Cadet Corps Training Manual, 1942, 43. Author essays and articles profl. jours. Home: Pasadena CA Died Mar. 22, 1968; buried Forest Lawn, Glendale CA

COVELL, LOUIS CHAPIN, army officer; b. at Grand Rapids, Mich., June 22, 1875; s. Elliott Franklin and Laura (Chapin) C.; grad. Grand Rapids High Sch., 1893; m. Florence Davidson, of Grand Rapids, June 12, 1906. Began as salesman, Macy Co., Grand Rapids, 1900, and became sales mgr.; organizer, 1915, and pres. The Covell-Hensen Co., advertising and printing. Enlisted as pvt. Mich. N.G., Apr. 6, 1892; served as capt. Co. H, Mich. Vol. Inf., Spanish-Am. War; advanced to brig. gen. Mich. N.G., Feb. 7, 1917; brig. gen. N.A., Aug. 5, 1917; assigned as comdr. 63d Inf. Brigade, 32d Div.; hon. discharged, Feb. 17, 1919. Now mgr. Reynolds-Chrysler Co., Flint, Mich. Mem. Am. Legion, S.A.R., Mil. Order Foreign Wars. Republican. Conglist. Mason (K.T.). Home: 408 E. First St., Flint MI‡

COVENEY, CHARLES CARDEN, architect; b. Boston, Mass., Nov. 28, 1874; s. Charles John and Augusta Emma (Kehaile) C.; ed. pub. schs.; tech. edn. received in the office of Charles Brigham, architect, Boston, supplemented by travel and study in Europe, 1898, 1902, 04, 06, and 11; has specialized in ecclesiastical art; m. Caroline J. Hobbs, Oct. 14, 1921 (she died Sept. 2, 1936). Began as draftsman and later chief draftsman in the office of Charles Brigham, Boston, 1891-96; mem. Brigham, Coveney & Bisbee, 1906-19; practicing alone since Jan. 1, 1920. Firm was architect of Memorial ch. group and high sch. bldg., Fairhaven, Mass.; Christian Science Ch., Boston; Messiah Home, New York; etc. Specializes in ch. architecture; architect many ch. bldgs. in Diocese of Mass. and elsewhere. Mem. A.I.A., 1908-36; mem. Am. Eccles. Soc.; mem. Trustees of Donations of Diocese of Mass., Trustees Boston Episcopal Charitable Soc., 1920-35; mem. Diocesan Bd. Edn., 1918-21; provisional deputy to Gen. Conv. Protestant Episcopal Ch., 1922-28; mem. Diocesan Council, 1920-33. Mem. Commn. on Ch. Architecture of Providence of N.E., deputy to Synod of the Province various times. Republican. Episcopalian; mem. corn. Parish of the Advent and past pres. Eccles. Soc. same; past pres. Episcopalian Club of Mass. Mason (K.T.). Home: 91 Bay State Rd. Office: 184 Royalston St., Boston MA*‡

COVER, RALPH, lawyer and inventor; b. Carrol Co., Md., June 13, 1892; s. Harry Fisher and Dora May (Hiteshew) C.; A.B., Western Md. Coll., Westminster, Md., 1910; LL.B., Harvard, 1913; m. Anna Saulsbury Fisher, Dec. 11, 1919; 1 son, Paul Fisher; m. 2d, Edna Arnold, Apr. 10, 1943. Admitted to Md. bar, 1913; asso. with Bond, Robinson & Duffy, Balt., 1913-15; mem. firm Smith & Cover, 1915-17; pvt. practice, Westminster, Md., 1930-69; chmn. bd. United Company, engaged in development and mfr. of inventions, machines and methods employed in food processing industry, Westminster, Md., 1914-69; pres. The United Products Co., licensor of canning methods and processes. Served as asst. sec. priorities com., War Industries Bd., World War I. Mem. Am., Md. bar assns., Old Guard Soc. of Canning Industry, Am. Inst. Food Technologists (charter mem.). Club: Illinois Athletic (Chicago), Inventor various machines and methods employed in food processing industry; dir. tech. experts in development of such machines and methods; writer tech. articles. Home: Westminster MD Died Sept. 6, 1969.

COVERT, CHARLES EDWARD;, b. Maspeth, N.Y., July 3, 1872; s. Henry Aldrich and Amy Elizabeth (Betts) C.; ed. pub. and private schools; m. Magdalene F. Vanderveer, Mar. 15, 1900; children—Frances Elizabeth, Florence V., Charles Aldrich. Began as clk., 1st Nat. Bank, Brooklyn, N.Y., 1889; trust officer, Williamsburgh Trust Co., Brooklyn, 1904-08, asst. sec., 1908-09, sec., 1909-11; vice pres. U.S. Title Guaranty Co., Brooklyn, 1911-20, pres., 1920-26; became v.p., dir. and mem. exec. com. N.Y. Title & Mortgage Co., 1926, now retired. Mem. N.G.N.Y. 6 yrs. Republican. Conglist. Clubs: The Brooklyn (Brooklyn); Lawyers (New York); Garden City Country. Home: Old Westbury NY‡

COWAN, SAMUEL KINKADE, editor, author; b. Nashville, Tenn., Jan. 8, 1869; s. Samuel and Jennie (Patterson) C.; grad. Montgomery Bell Acad., Nashville, 1888; studied Vanderbilt U., 1888-92; m. Floy Pascal, of Nashville, Oct. 16, 1902; children—Samuel Kinkade, Pascal. Gen. newspaper work, Nashville, 1893-98; asso. editor Nashville American, 1898-1901; editor Southern Lumberman, 1901-14; magazine and newspaper syndicate writer since 1914; editorial staff Literary Digest since 1922. Author: Sergeant York and His People, 1922. Home: 69 E. 176th St., New York NY‡

COWARD, NOEL PEIRCE, playwright, actor; London (Teddington), England, Dec. 16, 1899; s. Arthur Sabin and Violet (Vetch) C.; educated privately. Appeared first on stage 1910. Author: (plays) The Young Idea, 1920; The Rat Trap, 1921; I'll Leave It to You, 1922; Hay Fever, 1924; Fallen Angels, 1925; The Vortex, 1925; Easy Virtue, 1926; The Queen Was in the Parlor, 1926; The Marquise, 1927; This Year of Grace, Bitter Sweet, 1929; Private Lives, 1930; Cavalcade, 1931; Words and Music, 1932; Design for Living, 1933; Conversation Piece, 1934; Point Valaine, 1935; Tonight at Eight-Thirty, 1936; Operette, 1938; Nude with Violin; Present Laughter; South Sea Bubble; Look After Lulu; (musical comedy) The Girl Who Came to Supper; Waiting in the Wings, 1960; Sail Away, 1965; also Suite-in Three Keys, 1966; made motion picture appearances in Our Man in Havana, Surprise Package, Bunny Lake is Missing; books include Collected Sketches and Lyrics, 1931; Present Indicative, 1937; To Step Aside, 1939; In Which We Serve (motion picture; dir., also took leading part); author Blithe Spirit (motion picture) 1942; TV appearances in This Happy Breed, Blithe Spirit. Together with Music; author: Future Indefinite, 1954; Present Indicative; Pomp & Circumstance, 1960; Pretty Polly, 1965. Frequently on radio. Address: Montreux Switzerland Died Mar. 26, 1973.

COWDEN, JOHN BRANDON, author, evangelist; b. nr. Petersburg, Tenn., June 15, 1876; s. John (M.D.) and Mary Hannah (Leonard) C.; L.I. and A.B., Peabody Coll. for Teachers, Nashville, Tenn., 1901; post-grad. work in the Bible, Transylvania U., Lexington, Ky., 1904-05; m. Lillian Smallman, Oct. 26, 1910; children—Charles Magness, John Smallman, Frederic Eugene. Teacher prep. sch. until 1904; ordained ministry Disciples of Christ, 1904; pastor Detroit, Mich., 1904-07, McMinnville, Tenn., 1908-13, Tullahoma, Tenn., 1914-18; Christian unity evangelist, 1918-32; editor Tennessee Christian (monthly), 1923. Democrat. Author: Christian Worship, 1920; Paul's Plan for Christian Unity, 1922; St. Paul on Christian Unity, 1923; Christian Unity and Open and Close Membership, 1925; Thinking Toward Christian Unity, 1927; The Firm Foundation of God, 1929; Worshipping Toward Christian Unity, 1930; Unity In His Name, 1932; The Southern Cowdens, 1933; The House of Magness, 1937; St. John's Christ, 1939; A Robert Browning Anthology, 1943. Home: West Nashville TN*‡

COWDEN, ROBERT E., JR., lawyer, corp. exec.; b. Dayton, O., Sept. 15, 1910; s. Robert E. and Erma (Shupe) C.; A.B., Dartmouth, 1932; LL.B., U. of Mich., 1935; m. Susannah Brown, Mar. 1, 1939; children—Martha Brown, Rober E., III, Ann Duddleson, John Alexander. Admitted to Ohio bar, 1935; pvt. practice law as partner Cowden, Cowden & Crew, 1936-43; sec., v.p., gen. counsel Nat. Cash Register Co., Dayton, 1943-68; central adv. bd. dirs. Mut. Boiler Machinery Ins. Co. Mem. bd. dirs. National Cash Register Company, The Winters National Bank & Trust Company, Dayton, Firemans Mutual Ins. Company (Providence). Mem. bd. trustees Western Coll. for Women, Miami Valley Hosp., Dayton. Mem. Am., Ohio State and Dayton bar assns. Republican.

Episcopalian (sr. warden). Clubs: Lawyers, Buz Fuz, Moraine Country (Dayton). Home: Dayton OH Died July 21, 1968; buried Woodland Cemetery, Dayton OH

COWELL, ALFRED LUCIUS, newspaper man; b. Woodland, Cal., Mar. 17, 1870; s. A. H. and Emeline C.; grad. San Joaquin Valley Coll., 1892; B.D., Union Bibl. Sem., Dayton, O., 1895; m. Alice K. Gingrich, June 23, 1896. Pres. San Joaquin Valley Coll., 1895-7; prin. Lodi (Cal.) High Sch., 1897-8, Siskiyou Co. High Sch., 1898-9; reporter, 1899-1900; asst. editor, 1900-2, editor, 1902-11, Stockton Mail; editor Modesto News, 1911-12; exec. sec. Irrigation Districts Assn. of Cal., 1912-13; asst. dir. of congresses, Panama-Pacific Internat. Expn., 1913-15; sec. Irrigation Districts Assn. of Cal., 1916—. Home: 420 E. Magnolia St., Stockton CA‡

COWELL, SYLVESTER E., bus. exec.; b. Fayette County, Pa., Mar. 15, 1893; s. Charles C. and Flora L. (Eneix) C.; teaching certificate, Calif. State Teacher's Coll., 1912; B.Sc., Washington and Jefferson Coll., 1918; m. Laura L. Butler, Sept. 28, 1921; children—Robert E., Margaret Ann. In coal and gas bus., 1919-21, ins. bus., 1921-26; owner ice plant, 1926-30; sales mgr. Western Ice and Utilities Co., 1930-33; gen. mgr. and dir. Victor Brewing Co., 1933-36; sales mgr. Eberhardt and Ober Brewing Co., 1937-47; exec. v.p. and dir., Pittsburgh Brewing Co., pres., chmn. bd., chmn. exec. com.; dir., 2d v.p., United States Brewer's Found. Member of Pa. Brewers Assn. (dir.), Pa. Soc., Pitts. Athletic Assn., Alpha Tau Omega. Mason. Home: Pittsburgh PA Died Mar. 31, 1970; buried Allegheny County Memorial Park, Pittsburgh PA

COWEN LAWRENCE, bus. exec.; b. N.Y.C., 1907.. Past chmn. chief executive officer Schick, Incorporated; secretary, treasurer, dir. Lionel-Essex International Corp. (both N.Y.C.); dir. Airex Mfg. Co., Inc., Airex Corp., E. L. Waterman Co. Home: New York City NY Died July 1970.

COWGER, WILLIAM OWEN, past mayor; b. Hastings. Neb., Jan. 1, 1922; s. Rolla Henry and Catherine (Combs) C.; student Tex. A. and M. Coll., 1939-40; B.A., Carleton Coll., 1943; m. Cynthia Thompson, Mar. 19, 1945; children—Cynthia Combs, David Garvin. With Thompson & Cowger Co., Inc., real estate mortgage, Louisville, 1946-71, pres., 1948-71; mayor City of Louisville, 1961-66; mem. 90th, 91st Congress, 3d Congl. Dist. Ky., 1966-70; Chmn. for Ky., Crusade for Freedom, 1955-57; chmn. Louisville A.R.C. blood program, 1956-57. Republican chmn. 3d Congl. Dist. Ky., 1956-71; mem. Kentucky Republican Central Committee, 1956-71. Bd. dirs., president Kentucky Municipal League; board directors Louisville Urban League, Louisville Internat. Center, Louisville chpt. A.R.C., Louisville chpt. United Cerebral Palsy Assn. Served to lt. (j.g.) USNR, World War II. Named one of 3 outstanding young men in Ky., 1955. Mem. Inter-Am. Municipal Organization (president), American Municipal Association (executive com.), Mortgage Bankers Assn. Am., Louisville Mortgage Bankers Assn. (pres. 1954-55), Louisville Jr. C. of C. (pres. 1953-54), Louisville Real Estate Bd. Presbyn. (past deacon). Clubs: Louisville Country, Pendennis (Louisville). Home: Louisville KY Died Oct. 2, 1971; buried Cave Hill Cemetery, Lousiville KY

COWLES, WILLIAM HUTCHINSON, newspaperman; b. Sands Point, N.Y., July 23, 1902; s. William Hutchinson and Harriet Bowen (Cheney) C.; student Thacher Sch., Ojai, Calif., 1918-20; B.A., Yale, 1924; LL.D., Whitworth Coll., Spokane, Wash., 1954; m. Margaret Paine, Dec. 3, 1930; children—William Hutchinson, 3rd, James Paine, Margaret (Mrs. Daniel A. Stein), Agnes Cowley (Mrs. Shepley W. Evans). Various positions in Cowles Pub. Co. (pubs. daily and Sunday Spokesman-Rev., Wash. Farmer-Stockman, Ore. Farmer-Stockman, Ida. Farmer-Stockman, Utah Farmer-Stockman, semi-monthlies), 1918-71, pres., 1946-68, pub., 1946-70, chmn., 1968-71; various positions Spokane Chronicle Co. (pubs. Spokane Daily Chronicle, Spokane Weekly Chronicle), 1918-71, pres., 1935-68, chmn., 1968-71; pres. Mont. Farmer-Stockman, Inc., Gt. Falls (pubs. Mont. Farmer-Stockman), 1963-68, publisher, 1963-70, chairman, 1968-71; dir. A.P., 1952-61, Inland Empire Paper Co. (Millwood, Wash.); pres. Agrl. Pubs. Assn. 1939-40; dir. Inter-Am. Press Assn., 1950-71, pres., 1960. Mem. Region 11 exec. com. Boy Scouts Am., 1950-71. Trustee Whitworth Coll., 1960-71. Recipient Silver Antelope award Boy Scouts Am., 1962. Mem. Pacific N.W. Newspaper Assn. (exec. com. various periods 1936-69), Sigma Delta Chi, Psi Upsilon. Republican. Conglist. Clubs: Spokane, Spokane Country; Chicago University; Elihu (New Haven). Home: Spokane WA Died Aug. 12, 1971.

COX ALONZO BETTIS, cotton expert; b. Hamilton County, Ill., Apr. 2, 1884; s. Van Buren and Manerva (Compton) C.; A.B., U. of Tex., 1911; A.M., 1914; Ph.D., U. of Wis., 1920; LL.D., Abilene (Texas) Christian Coll., 1938; m. Sue Merle Shepperd, Aug. 21, 1911 (now dec.); children—Bettis Merle, Enola Jean, Sue Shepperd; m. 2d, Irene Shannon Breazeale, Mar. 1, 1933. Asst. U. of Tex., 1917-18, in charge div. farm and ranch economics, Agrl. Expt. Sta., 1919-22, prof. of business adminstration since 1926, organizer, dir. bureau of business research, 1926-42; professor of cotton marketing, cotton research U. Tex. since 1926. Chairman fgn. markets com. Tex. State-wide Cotton Committee since 1940; apptd. mem. Research Planning Group of Social Science Research Council, 1941; spl. consultant on cotton price fixing for U.S. govt., 1943. Rep. Am. Cotton Shippers in nat. and internat. affairs, 1945; mem. U.S. Govt. com. to study merchandising of cotton and cotton products 1945; organizer and permanent supervisor, Cotton Econ. Research, 1947. Fellow A.A.A.S.; fellow Council Am. Geog. Soc.; member American Farm Economics Assn., American Statistical Association, Southwestern Polit. and Social Science Association, American Economic Association. Mem. Tex. Postwar Planning Commission, 1943; bd. dirs. Gulf Southwest Indsl. and Agrl. Conf., 1944. Democrat. Mem. The Ch. of Christ. Club: Lions. Author: Cotton Markets and Cotton Merchandising, 1948, rev. 1952; The Cottonseed Crushing Industry in its National Setting, 1949. Author sect. on cotton Ency. Brit., 1952. Visited all European countries as research econ. for Edward T. Robinson & Son, of Havre, France, 1928; apptd. by Lions Internat. to study bus. cycles of U.S., 1933. Invited to address Internat. Cotton Congress, Prague, 1935, Cairo, 1937, 52. Home: Austin TX Died Dec. 25, 1968.

COX, C(LARENCE) BROWN, clergyman, educator; b. Knoxville, Tenn., Apr. 18, 1873; s. Rev. George H. (D.D.) and Nannie E. (McPherson) C.; A.B., N.C. Coll., Mt. Pleasant, N.C., 1895, A.M., 1897; B.D., Luth. Theol. Sem., 1898; D.D., Wittenberg Coll., Springfield, O., 1924; m. Cordelia E. Spangler, of Gettysburg, Pa., 1898 (died 1911); children—Catherine Cordelia; m. 2d, Blanch Mearig Kuhlman, of Norfolk, Va., 1912; children—Elizabeth, Martha, C. Brown, Mary, Alfred Bard (dec.). Ordained Luth. ministry, 1898; pastor Asheville, N.C., 1898-1900, Greenville, Tenn., 1900-03, Burlington, N.C., 1903-11, Norfolk, Va., 1911-14; pres. Marion Junior Coll. since 1916. Pres. Luth. Synod of Va., 1922-26; del. United Luth. Ch. America since 1918. Democrat. Kiwanian. Home: Marion VA‡

COX CHANNING HARRIS, ex-govenor; b. Manchester, N.H., Feb. 28, 1879; s. Charles Edson and Evelyn (Randall) C.; A.B., Dartmouth, 1901, LL.D., 1922; LL.B., Harvard, 1904; LL.D., Tufts, 1922; m. Mary Emery Young, Feb. 18, 1915; 1 dau., Nancy. Began practice of law at Boston, 1904; mem. Mass. Ho. of Rep., 1910-15 (speaker 1915-18); lt. gov. of Mass., 1919-20, govenor, 1921-22, and 1923-24, Chmn. Mass. Delegation to Rep. Nat. Convs., 1924-28; chmn. Mass. Committee on Pub. Safety 1940-68. President Old Colony Trust Co.; dir. United Fruit Co., Revere Sugar Co., First Nat. Bank of Boston, Boston Herald Traveler Co., U.S. Smelting & Refining Co.; trustee Boston Five Cents Savings Bank, Boston Pub. Co. Trustee Boston Univ., Wheaton Coll., N.E. Conservatory of Music; dir. Boston Children's Friend Soc., Boys' Camp, Inc.; mem. bd. Deaconess Hosp. Dir. Boston Chamber of Commerce; trustee Mass. Soc. Prevention of Cruelty to Animals, Mass. Humane Soc. Pres. Boston Council of Boy Scouts of America, Travelers Aid Society of Boston, Beacons Soc. Mem. Trinity Church (vestryman). Clubs: Algonquin, Union, University, Brookline Country, Cohasset Country, Cohasset Yacht. Home: Boston MA Died Aug. 20, 1968; buried Forest Hills Cemetery Jamaica Plain MA

COX, CREED FULTON, army officer; b. Bridle Creek, Va., June 12, 1877; s. Melville B. and Martha (Fulton) C.; grad. U.S. Mil. Acad., 1901; m. Mrs. Margaret Kennedy Ross, Aug. 12, 1925 (died July 15, 1934). Commissioned 2d lt. cavalry, U.S. Army, Feb. 2, 1901; transferred to arty., promoted through successive grades to col. Served in Philippines, 1902-04; Cuba, 1906-07; assigned to Army Staff Coll., 1908-09; prof. mil. science and tactics, Shattuck Sch., Minn., 1909-12; instr. cav. various state nat. guards, 1914-17; instr. Sch. of Fire, Ft. Sill, Okla., 1917-18; with A.E.F. in France, May 1918-Jan. 1919; comdg. 13th F.A., Aisne-Marne, 77th F.A., St. Mihiel and Meuse-Argonne, barrage grouping 26th Div. and 4th Div.; gen. staff A.E.F., to war's close; War Dept. exec. staff, 1919; mil. observer S. Russia, Turkey, Bulgaria, 1920-21; mil. attache Germany, Holland, Denmark, Norway, Sweden, 1921-24; pres. F.A. Bd., 1926-28; assigned to Army War Coll., 1929; asst. to chief Bur. Insular Affairs, 1929-32; comdg. 8th F.A. Regt., T.H., 1932-33; chief Bureau of Insular Affairs, with rank of brig. gen., May 1933-May 1937; retired, Sept. 30, 1937; adviser to President of P.I., 1938-39. Awarded D.S.M. (U.S.). Address: Independence VA‡

COX, EDWARD WESTON, banker; b. Brunswick, Maine, Sept. 6, 1865; s. Augustus F. and Tryphena (Jones) C.; ed. pub. schs., Portland Me.; m. Lena Prince, Nov. 14, 1888; children—Margaret P., Eleanor W. Chmn. bd. First Portland Nat. Bank, Me. Bonding & Casualty Co.; pres. Portland & Ogdensburg R.R.; dir. Union Mutual Life Ins. Co., Mason, Elk. Home: 111 West St. Office: 396 Congress St., Portland ME*

COX GARFIELD V., educator; b. Fairmount, Ind., May 4, 1893; s. Milton Theodore and Martha Elizabeth (Petty) C.; student Fairmount Acad., 1908-13, Earlham Coll., Richmond, Ind., 1913-15; A.B., Beloit (Wis.) Coll., 1917, LL.D., 1946; Ph.D., U. Chicago, 1929; m. Jeannette Wade, Aug. 30, 1917; children—Phyllis Jean, Marilyn Lois, Lowell Wade. Prof. pub. speaking, Wabash Coll., 1917; instr. bus. adminstrn., U. of Chicago, 1920-25, asst. prof., 1925-29, asso. prof. of bus. econ., 1929-30, prof. of finance, 1930-36. Robert Law prof. finance, 1936-58, professor emeritus, 1958-70, acting dean School of Business 1942-45, dean, 1945-52; chairman of the board of directors of South East Nat. Bank, 1935-58. Trustee of Earlham College, 1954-58. Served under American Friends Service Committee in war relief and reconstrn., France, 1918-19. Chmn. Midwest Br. Am. Friends Service Com., 1946-55. Mem. Am. Finance Assn. (p.p.). Am. Econ. Assn., Am. States Assn. (ex-pres. Chgo.), Am. Assn. U. Profs., Phi Beta Kappa, Delta Sigma Rho, Beta Gamma Sigma, Sigma Pi. Mem. Soc. of Friends. Club: Quadrangle (ex-pres.). Co-author: Forecasting Business Conditions, 1927. Author: An Appraisal of American Business Forecasts, 1930. Home: Claremont CA Died Feb. 9, 1970.

COX, (CHARLES) HUDSON BAYNHAM, lawyer; b. London, Eng., Oct. 25, 1909; s. Harry Jasper and May Helena (Baynham) C.; came to U.S., 1927, naturalized, 1936; ed. Uppingham, Eng.; A.B. summa cum laude, Stanford, 1932; LL.B. scholarship ranking, Harvard, 1935; m. Elizabeth Maitland Knapp, Dec. 1, 1936; children—Douglas Marshall, Cecily Maitland. Asso. law firm Newlin and Ashburn, Los Angeles, 1935-43; counsel, Bur. of Ships, Navy Dept., 1946, asst. gen. counsel, Navy Dept., 1946-47, gen. counsel, 1947-49; member firm Newlin, Tackabury and Johnston 1949-61, resident partner in Santa Cruz, Cal. Served as lt., U.S. Naval Reserve, 1943-46. Mem. Calif. State Bar Assn., Phi Beta Kappa. Republican. Protestant Episcopal. Clubs: L.A. Athletic (Los Angeles); University (Washington). Author: Renegotiation of Government Contracts. Home: Santa Cruz CA Died Nov. 18, 1968.

COX, ISAAC JOSLIN, univ. prof.; b. West Creek, Ocean County, N.J., Nov. 19, 1873; s. Walter Scott and Almeda (Joslin) C.; A.B., Dartmouth, 1896, research in Archivo General, City of Mexico, summer 1898-1911; U. of Tex., 1900, U. of Chicago, 1901, U. of Wis., 1902; fellow Am. History, U. of Pa., 1902-04, Ph.D., 1904, research fellowship, 1911-12; m. Grace Elizabeth Yost, July 11, 1899. Teacher and v.-prin. San Antonio (Tex.) Acad., 1896-1902; instr. history, 1904-06, asst. prof., 1906-12, asso. prof., 1912-19, U. of Cincinnati; prof. history, Northwestern U., 1919-41, prof. emeritus since 1941; visiting prof. U. of Chile, 1943, Louisiana State University, 1943-46; Trinity University, San Antonio, Texas, 1947-48; Newberry Library Fellowship, 1946-47; Shaw lectureship, Johns Hopkins U., 1911-12. Life member Ohio Archaeol. and Hist. Society; pres. Ohio Valley Historical Assn., 1909-10; fellow Texas State Hist. Association; member American Historical Association (mem. exec. council, 1937-41), Miss. Valley Hist. Assn. (pres. 1914-15), Doheny Research Foundation, in Mexico, 1918, Phi Beta Kappa, Phi Delta Theta; corr. mem. Chicago Hist. Soc. Presbyterian. Clubs: City (Chicago); University (Evanston, Ill.). Author: The Journeys of La Salle and His Companions (2 vols.), 1905; The Early Exploration of Louisiana, 1906; The West Florida Controversy, 1798-1813, 1918; Nicaragua and the United States, 1927. Ec Desarrollo de la Democracia Norte Americana, 1943 (Univ. of Chile Press); W. B. Seeley, Founder San Antonio Academy, 1948. Translator: Estudio de la Historia de Chile (by Luis Galdames), 1944. Editorial work on New Internat. Ency., 1903; contbr. encys. Americana and Britannica, Am. Hist. Review, Dictionary Am. Biography, etc.; actively engaged on a series of frontier studies covering the early relations between Spain and the U.S.; lecturer on Inter-Am. relations. Home: 2611 Hartzell St., Evanston IL‡

COX, JOCELYN MERIDITH NOLTING (MRS. ROWLAND COX III), county ofcl.; b. Plainfield, N.J., Sept. 28, 1900; d. John Paul and Fannie R. (Dryden) Nolting; student pub. schs., Plainfield; m. Rowland Cox III, Sept. 10, 1925 (dec. Jan. 7, 1942); 1 son, Rowland IV. Clk., teller, chief bookkeeper State Trust Co., Plainfield, 1920-25; bookkeeper 1st Nat. Bank, Fontana, Cal., Fontana Union Water Co., Fontana Producers, 1st Nat. Bank, Cucamonga, Cal., 1926-29; reporter, bookkeeper, office mgr. Fontana Community News, 1929-32; reporter Ontario (Cal.) Herald, 1932-33; various positions, 1933-35; bookkeeper Barbee and Traub Ins., Fontana, 1935-37; from clk. to asst. auditor San Bernardino County, San Bernardino, Cal., 1937-59, auditor, controller, from 1959. Sec., San Bernardino County Employees' Retirement Bd.; chmn. A.I.D. campaign, 1965; mem. San Bernardino County Boundary Commn.; bd. dirs. Am. Cancer Soc.; mem. supervisory com. San Bernardino County Employees' Credit Union, 1951-57. Mem. Cal. Auditor's Assn. (legislative com., spl. dist. com.). Democrat. Episcopalian. Home: Fontana CA Deceased.

COX, LEILYN MUNNS, ins. co. exec.; b. Ft. Bayard, N.M., Oct. 28, 1903; s. Herbert F. and Carey (Munns) C.; A.B., Coll. Emporia, 1926; children—Leilyn S., Shirley L. (Mrs. Kenneth W. Seefeld). With accounting firm, Philippines, 1926-37; with Employers Ins. Co., 1938-72, dist. audit supr., N.Y.C., 1940-44, comptroller, 1944-49, v.p., comptroller, Wausau, Wis., 1949-69, financial adminstr., 1969-72. C.P.A., Wis., Cal., P.I. Mem. Nat. Assn. Accountants, Financial Execs. Inst. Am. (past pres. Milw.), Adminstrv. Mgmt. Assn., Am. Inst. C.P.A.'s, Wis. Soc. C.P.A.'s, Ins. Accounting and Statis. Assn. (past pres.), Soc. Advancement Mgmt., Am. Mut. Ins. Alliance. Author: Introduction to Accounting and Partnership Accounting in the Philippines, 1935. Contbr. profl. jours. Home: Wausau WI Died Feb. 25, 1972; buried Lakeview Cemetery, Oshkosh WI

COX, LESTER EDMUND, mfr.; b. Republic, Mo., Aug. 22, 1895; s. James M. and Amanda Belle (Brittain) C.; student Southwest Mo. State Coll., 1914; student Drury Coll., 1915-16, LL.D. (hon.), 1953; m. Mildred Belle Lee, Aug. 9, 1918; children—Virginia (Mrs. Lynn E. Bussey), Lester L., Cathryn (Mrs. Jack E. Lipscomb). Tchr. rural sch., Prairie View, Mo., 1914; salesman Langenberg Milling & Grain Co., Republic, Mo., 1916-17, sales mgr., 1917; v.p., gen. mgr. M & W Motor Co., 1919-21; v.p. Martin Bros. Piano Co., 1921-27; pres. Ozark Motor & Supply Co., 1927-68; chmn. bd. Radio Sta. KWTO, Springfield, Mo., since 1932, WTMV, East St. Louis, 1935-40; v.p. KCMO, K.C., 1935-54, Springfield Credit Bur., 1935-52; chmn. KOAM, Pitts., Kan., 1935-68; chmn. Ozark Tractor & Implement Co.; pres. Mod. Tractor & Supply Co., Okla. City, Ozark Mfg. & Supply Co., 1932-68, Superior Advertising Co.; pres. Pioneer Outdoor Advt. Co., Mo. Warehousing Co.; dir. Ozark Air Lines, Inc. Chmn., Mo. Div. Commerce, 1960. Bd. dirs. So. Meth. U., Dallas, 1949-61; bd. curators U. Mo., 1951-63; pres. bd. trustees Burge Protestant Hosp., renamed Lester E. Cox Med. Center in his honor, 1969. Mem. Mo. Bd. Health, 1967-68. Served as 1t. A.C., U.S. Army, World War I. Awarded place Hall of Fame and Philanthropy, Meth. Ch., 1953. Mem. Mil. Order World Wars, Friends of Land, Radio Pioneers, Newcomen Soc. Eng. in N.A., C. of C. (past pres. and dirs.), Am. Legion, Acad. Mo. Squires, Lambda Chi Alpha (Nat. Order of Achievement award 1966). Meth. Clubs: Shriners Crippled Childrens', Kansas City, Hickory Hills Country (Springfield, Mo.), Nat. Press (Washington). Home: Springfield MO Died Aug. 14, 1968; buried Springfield MO

COX, LINTON A., lawyer; b. Azalia, Ind., Sept. 2, 1868; s. William and Sarah Jane (Newsom) C.; Ph.B., Earlham Coll., Richmond, Ind., 1888; LL.B., U. of Mich., 1890; m. Elizabeth Harvey, June 19, 1890; children—Thomas Harvey, Katherine, Addison Harris, Linton A., Frank H., Eleanor, William E. Admitted to Ind. bar, 1890, and since practiced at Indianapolis; sr. partner firm of Cox & Cox (Linton A. Cox and Thomas Harvey Cox); mem. Ind. State Senate, 1906-10; mem. governing com., Indianapolis Bd. of Trade since 1915. Mem. Ind. State and Indianapolis bar assns., Phi Delta Phi. Republican. Mem. Soc. Friends (Quaker). Clubs: Ind. Soc. of Chicago; Columbia (Indianapolis). Home: 3202 Central Av. Office: 156 E. Market St., Indianapolis IN*

COX, LOUIS SHERBURNE, judge; b. Manchester, N.H., Nov. 22, 1874; s. Charles Edson and Evelyn Mary (Randall) C.; A.B., Dartmouth Coll., 1896; LL.B., Boston Univ. Sch. of Law, 1899, LL.D., Boston Univ., 1936; J.S.D., Suffolk University, 1950; student Harvard Med. Sch., 1896-97; m. Mary I. Fieles, Oct. 22, 1902; children—Randall Truell, Dorothy. Admitted to Mass. bar, 1899 and began practice in Boston; removed to Lawrence, 1900; mem. Mass. Senate, 5th Essex Dist., 1906; postmaster, Lawrence, 1906-14; dist. atty. Eastern Dist. of Mass., 1915-18; justice Mass. Superior Court, 1918-37; Mass. Supreme Judicial Court, 1937-44; Mass. Judicial Council since 1944. Served as captain, Battery C. Massachusetts National Guard, 1910-13; colonel Mass. State Guard, 1918-20. Mem. Am. Mass. and Boston bar assns., N.H. Hist. Society (trustee), Phi Beta Kappa, Kappa Kappa Kappa, Phi Delta Phi, Sphinx. Republican. Conglist. Mason (32 deg.), Odd Fellows, Elk, Grange. Club: University (Boston). Author: Cox Families; A Pease Family. Home: 7 Lowell St., Lawrence MA

COX, NELLIE I. MCMASTER (MRS. WILLIAM COX), journalist; b. Jacobsburg, O.; d. Charles A. and Suie (Lucas) McMaster; student Coshocton Bus. Coll., 1926; m. William S. Cox, Aug. 6, 1944. Classified advt. mgr. Coshocton (O.) Tribune, 1943-68, weekly advt. column Here 'N' There with Nell, 1947-68, writer feature advt. page Shutter Gems, 1966-68. 1st sec. Ohio Classified Clinic, 1957, pres., 1968. Mem. Coshocton Bus. and Profl. Women's Club (Woman of Year 1966), Ohio Select List Classified Advt. Mgr. Assn. (pres. 1954), Am. Legion (pres. West Lafayette, O. aux. unit 1948), West Lafayette Progressive Guild (pres. 1937), West Lafayette Sorosis (charter), Plainfield, Coshocton Pomona granges. Methodist (supt. jr. dept. 1928-48, mem. Women's Soc. Christian Service, Together Class). Home: West Lafayette OH Died July 24, 1968.

COX, OSCAR LARKEN, banker; b. Bakers Corner, Ind., Sept. 29, 1877; s. Paris and Mary (Ferguson) C.; grad. Pacific College, Newberg, Oregon, 1898; m. Lulu Mae Buddemer, Feb. 26, 1902; children—Louis Larken, Marjorie Mary. Pres. Union Bank of Commerce Co., Cleveland, O., since 1938. Pres. Union Properties, Inc. Home: 2931 Sedgewick Rd., Shaker Heights, O. Office: 917 Euclid Av., Cleveland OH*‡

COX, W(ILLIAM) ROWLAND, mining engr.; b. Salt Lake City, Utah, May 29, 1872; s. William Judson and Johanna M. (O'Farrell) C.; U. of Denver Business Coll.; student Mo. Sch. of Mines, 1893-96, hon. E.M., 1911; m. Gertrude Potter, May 25, 1907; children—Harriet, Barbara, Potter. Mine and mill supt., Aspen, Colo., 1897-1902; gen. mgr. Silver Lake Mines, Silverton, Colo. 1903-05; asst. gen. supt. mining dept. Guggenheim Exploration Co. and Am. Smelters Securities Co., hdqrs. Aguascalientes, Mexico, 1905-07; mem. Spurr & Cox, Inc., 1908-10; consulting practice. Mem. Am. Inst. Mining and Metall. Engrs., Mining and Metall. Soc., Canadian Inst. Mining and Metall. Engrs., Tau Beta Pi. Catholic. Office: 120 Broadway, New York NY*‡

COX, WALLY, actor; b. Detroit, Dec. 6, 1924; s. George Wallace and Eleanor Frances (Atkinson) C.; student City Coll. N.Y., N.Y. U.; one child. Propr. silversmith shop, N.Y.C., 1946-48; monologue comedy Village Vanguard, 1948, Blue Angel, Manhattan, 1949-50; appeared mus. revue Dance Me A Song, Royale Theater, N.Y.C., 1940; entertainer Persian Room, N.Y. Plaza Hotel, also radio, TV shows, 1950-51; discless disc jockey Sta. WNEW, 1951; appeared in TV prodn. The Copper; comedy actor Mr. Peepers, NBC-TV, 1952-55; guest appearances numerous TV series; performer TV show Hollywood Squares; actor summer theater prodns. Three Men on a Horse; comedy actor Adventures Hiram Holiday NBC-TV, 1956-57; appeared in motion pictures Yellow Rolls Royce, Morituri, Fate Is the Hunter, Spencers Mountain, State Fair, The Bedford Incident, A Woman for Charlie. Served with inf. AUS, World War II. Recipient Peabody award for Mr. Peepers performances, 1953. Author plays, short stories, My Life as a Small Boy, 1961; Ralph Makes Good, 1966. Address: New York City NY Died Feb. 16, 1973.

COYLE, DAVID CUSHMAN, cons. engr.; b. North Adams, Mass., May 24, 1887; s. John Patterson and Mary Allerton (Cushman) C.; A.B., Princeton, 1908; C.E., Rensselaer Poly. Inst., 1910; m. Isadore Douglas, Sept. 3, 1914 (died 1927); children—Anne Douglas, John Patterson, Lawrence Thompson; m. 2d Chalice Kelly, Dec. 8, 1934 (died 1940); m. 3d, Doris Porter, Dec. 17, 1949. Began with Gunvald Aus Co., cons. engrs., N.Y.C., 1910; practicing under own name, 1930-69. Mem. Tech. Bd. of Review, PWA, 1933-35; cons. various govt. agencies, Washington, 1935-42, 1945-53, London, 1942-45. Club: Cosmos (Washington). Author about 12 books 1932-69, including: The American Way (recipient Harpers prize), 1938; The U.S. Political System, 1954; The United Nations, 1955; Conservation, 1957; Ordeal of the Presidency, 1959. Address: Washington DC Died July 15, 1969.

COYLE, FRANK J., stock exchange exec.; b. N.Y. City, Feb. 14, 1900; s. Frank J. and Alice (Sperbeck) C.; student pub. schs. Hasbrouck Heights, N.J.; m. Doris Bennett, Jan. 27, 1923; children—Barbara (Mrs. Kiffin), Norma (Mrs. William A. Siebenheller). Became member of staff N.Y. Stock Exchange, 1922, v.p. from 1948. Commr. Boro of Hasbrouck Heights, N.J. Served USMC, 1918, U.S. Army, 1918-19. Mason. Home: Hasbrouck Heights NJ Died Oct. 26, 1971.

COZIER, ROBERT V., U.S. atty. for Idaho since Dec. 18, 1897; b. Wapakoneta, O., Oct. 20, 1869; s. B. F. W. and Zelora A. C.; grad. Simpson Coll., Indianola, Ia.; attended St. Louis Law School; m. Shoshone, Ida., Dec. 2, 1892, Lena M. Fife. Went west in 1891, commenced practice of law at Blackfoot, Ida.; represented Bingham, Bannock and Fremont counties in State legislature, 3d session, lower house; was elected speaker same; moved to Moscow, 1895; Republican; Methodist. Address: Moscow ID‡

CRAFTS, LELAND WHITNEY, educator; b. Boston, July 10, 1892; s. Albert E. and Mary H. (Wilkinson) C.; B.S., U. N.H., 1915; M.A., Clark U., 1920; Ph.D., Columbia, 1927; m. Edith L. Honigman, Aug. 16, 1927; 1 dau., Valery. Instr. English and German U. N.H., 1916-17; instr. psychology U. Colo., 1921-24; instr. psychology Washington Sq. Coll. of N.Y.U., 1925-27, asst. prof., 1928-31; asso. prof., 1932-45, prof. 1946-57, head dept., 1949-57. Served as capt. F.A., U.S. Army, 1917-19. Fellow Am. Psychol. Assn.; mem. N.Y. State Psychol. Assn., Sigma Xi. Author: Recent Experiments in Psychology (with T. C. Schneirla, E. E. Robinson, R. W. Gilbert; rev. edit.), 1950. Contbr. articles profl. jours. Home: Red Bank NJ Died Jan. 23, 1968; buried Fairview Cemetery, Red Bank NJ

CRAFTS, SARA JANE, teacher; b. Cincinnati d. Jesse and Jane C. Timanus; ed. pub. schs., Cincinnati, acad. at Davenport, Ia., and Ia. Coll.; m. Rev. Wilbur Fisk Crafts (q.v.), May 1, 1874. Taught in Normal Coll. of Minn. 5 yrs.; since 1874 instr. in Sunday Sch. normal insts. and state Sunday school convs.; organizer International Primary Union of S.S. Teachers; supt. S.S. Dept., World's W.C.T.U., 25 years. Instr. and lecturer at Chautauqua assemblies; writer of temperance lessons for Nat. Temperance Soc., S.S. lessons for Christian Herald, 14 1/2 yrs.; contbr. to S.S. papers. Traveled in Europe, 1880, Orient and Palestine, 1904, Japan, China, Korea and Australia, 1907, Norway, Sweden, and Iceland, 1910. Started the organization of Sunday schs. in Iceland, 1913. Author: Open Letters for Primary Teachers; Primary Normal Outlines; The Infant Class (with Edward Eggleston); Songs for Little Folks and Little Pilgrim Songs (with Jenny B. Merrill); Plain Uses of the Blackboard (with her husband), 1881; Course in Esperanto; Intoxicants and Opium; World Book of Temperance (both with her husband), 1908. Washington DC‡

CRAGUN, JOHN WILEY, lawyer; b. Ogden, Utah, Dec. 8, 1906; s. Wiley G. and Joanna D. (Seaman) C.; A.B., George Washington U., 1932, J.D., 1934; m. Hazel Gabbard, Sept. 5, 1931 (div.); children—Joanna (Mrs. Sigmund Gordon), Kathryn (Mrs. Harry T. Grace, Jr.); m. 2d, Hilda Henderson, Dec. 30, 1957 (dec. October 1964); m. 3d, Priscilla A. Martin, December 8, 1965. With U.S. Govt., 1926-31; admitted to D.C. bar, 1934, Va. bar, 1943; law clk. Justice Sutherland, U.S. Supreme Court, 1934-38; practice law, Washington, 1938-69; partner Ernest L. Wilkinson, 1940-45, Wilkinson, Cragun, and Barker, 1945-69; gen. counsel Nat. Grange, various Indian tribes, Farm Roads Found.; Coop. Agri. Services, Inc., 1951-69; lectr. in law of civil procedure, George Washington U., 1948-49; mem. nat. conf. lawyers and C.P.A.'S, 1956-58; cons. pres.'s Conf. on Adminstrv. Procedure, 1953-54; mem. com. of experts Survey of Legal Profession, 1950-53. Mem. Am. (mem. House Delegates, 1956-60; chmn. adminstrv. law sec., 1952-54, mem. council, 1954-61, chmn. standing com. facilities law library Congress 1961-63; mem. com. profl. relations, 1954-61; mem. standing com. on legislative drafting 1965-69), Fed., D.C. Fed. Power bar assns., Am. Judicature Soc. Clubs: Torch, National Lawyers, University. Founder, rec. sec. Soc. Appropriate Recognition of Elegant Mixed Metaphors. Home: Washington DC Died Mar. 31, 1969; buried Ogden Cemetery, Ogden UT

CRAIG, EDWIN WILSON, insurance exec.; b. Pulaski, Tenn., Mar. 8, 1893; s. Cornelius Abernathy and Margaret (Sinclair) C.; ed. Wallace U. Sch., Branham and Hughes Prep. Sch.; attended Vanderbilt U., 1915; m. Elizabeth Wade, Nov. 4, 1916; children—Elizabeth (Mrs. William Weaver, Jr.), Margaret Ann (Mrs. Walter M. Robinson, Jr.), Cornelius Abernathy II. With National Life and Accident Insurance Company, Nashville, Tennessee, 1913-69, pres. 1943, chmn. bd. 1953-65, hon. chmn. corp., chmn. exec. com., 1965-69; chmn., chief exec. officer WSM, Inc.; dir. NLT Corp. Past chmn. Inst. Life Insurance. Past pres. Life Insurers Conf.; ex-mem. exec. com., Am. Life Conv.; past mem. bd. Health Ins. Assn. Am., United Givers Fund; mem. exec. com., v.p. Davidson County chpt. A.R.C.; past mem. bd. Vanderbilt U. Hosp. Mem. Nat. Assn.Broadcasters (past mem. bd. and exec. com.; chmn. com. to reorganize under paid execs.; 1937; chmn. clear channel broadcasting service 1934-69), Ins. Econs. Soc. Am. (exec. com.), Tenn. Taxpayers Assn. (dir., mem. exec. com.), Phi Delta Theta. Mem. West End Methodist Church (steward) (Nashville). Club: Belle Meade (past pres.) (Nashville). Chief exec. Nat. Life and Accident Ins. Co. radio station WSM. Home: Nashville TN Died June 26, 1969; buried Mt. Olivet Cemetery, Nashville TN

CRAIG, HARDIN, college prof.; b. Owensboro, Ky., June 29, 1875; s. Robert and Mary Jane (McHenry) C.; A.B., Centre Coll., 1897, Litt.D., 1937; A.M., Princeton, 1899, Ph.D., 1901; U. Chgo., summers, 1900, 01; Exeter Coll. Oxford, Eng., 1902-03; Dott. dell' Universita di Padova, 1922; F.R.S.L., 1948; Doctor of Letters, U. Ky., 1950; m. Gertrude Carr, Sept. 4, 1906 (died July 8, 1941); 1 son Hardin Craig. Charles Scribner fellow in Eng., Princeton U., 1899-1901; instructor in English, 1901-05, Edgerstoune preceptor in English, 1905-10, Princeton; prof. English, Univ. of Minn., 1910-19; on leave for mil. service, 1917-19; grad. 1st R.O.T.C., Ft. Snelling, Minn.; 2d 1t., Q.M.C., N.A.; capt. Q.M.C., disch. Dec. 30, 1918; maj. Q.M.R.C., 1919-28; prof. English and head of dept., State U. of Ia., 1919-28; prof. English, Stanford University, 1928-42; prof. of English, University of North Carolina, 1942-49; research associate, Henry E. Huntington Library and Art Gallery, 1930-33; visiting prof. English, U. of N.C., winter 1935, State University of Iowa, summers 1937-43; Stockton Axson Memorial lecturer, Rice Institute, 1943; Walker-Ames professor, Univ. Washington, 1944; visiting prof. English, U. Mo., 1949-60; scholar in residence Stephens Coll., 1960-63, Centre Coll., 1964-67. Mem. Modern Language Assn. Am. (mem. exec. com. 1935-38), Linguistic Soc. America, Modern Humanities Research Assn., Mediaeval Academy America, Am. Assn. University Professors, Kappa Alpha, Phi Beta Kappa. Democrat. Presbyn. Author: Recent Literature of the English

Renaissance, 1925-50; Shakespeare, 1931; The Enchanted Glass, 1936; Literary Study and the Scholarly Profession, 1944; An Interpretation of Shakespeare, 1948; Freedom and Renaissance, 1949; The Written Word and Other Essays, 1953; English Religious Drama of the Middle Ages, 1955; New Lamps for Old, 1960; Woodrow Wilson at Princeton, 1960; A New Look at Shakespeare's Quartos, 1961; Centre College of Kentucky, 1967. Editor: Two Coventry Corpus Christi Plays, 1902; Little Masterpieces of Poetry (with Dr. Henry Van Dyke), 1906; Richard II (Tudor Shakespeare), 1912; Childe Harold's Pilgrimage, and other Poems by Byron, 1913; Works of John Metham, 1916; Selections from Swift (Modern Students' Library), 1923; Poe, Representative Selections, 1935; Stanford Studies in Language and Literature, 1941; The Complete Works of Shakespeare, 1951; editor Philological Quarterly, 1922-28. Contributor to magazines and learned periodicals. Address: Houston TX Died Oct. 13, 1968; buried Ashby MA

CRAIG, JAMES EDWARD, editor; b. Norborne, Mo., Oct. 8, 1881; s. Rev. Jesse Thomas Jefferson and Kathleen (O'Donoghue) C.; ed. pub. schs. and high schs., Maryville and King City, Mo.; student U. of Mo., 1901-05; m. Jessie Caroline Hall, June 6, 1911; 1 dau., Mary Caroline (Mrs. Frank R. Nichols). Began as printer's apprentice, 1894; reporter successively with Kansas City (Mo.) Journal, Star, Post, St. Louis (Mo.) Republic, 1907-11; reporter and editorial writer, St. Louis Post-Dispatch, 1911-18; city editor St. Louis Globe-Democrat, 1918; mng. editor Brownsville (Tex.) Herald, 1920; city editor and dramatic critic N.Y. Evening Mail, 1921-24; editorial writer N.Y Sun, 1925-43, chief editorial writer, 1940, and editor of the editorial page, 1943-50; mng. editor Protestant World, 1950. Mem. James Gordon Bennett Memorial Fund Corp., Delta Tau Delta, Trustee Park Avenue Christian Church, New York City. Clubs: Masonic, Silurians (New York). Author: History or Freemasonry (with H. L. Haywood), 1927, also of numerous essays and articles, including Masonic Outlook prize essay, 1925. New York City NY Died Mar. 1970.

CRAIG, PALMER HUNT, electrical engineer and physicist; b. Cheviot, O., Jan. 10, 1901; s. Charles Harry and Florence Irene (Hunt) C.; A.B. with honors, U. Cin., 1923; M.A. (Hanna grad. fellow), 1924, Ph.D., 1926; m. Hedwig Feltner, Apr. 5, 1927; children—Palmer Hunt, Marian Jean. Prof. physics, head of dept., dean of coll. of pre-engring., Mercer U., 1926-27; chief physicist, Premier Lab. Co., Inc., New York, 1927-29; research physicist, consulting engr., Harris Hammond Interests, New York, 1929; v.p. and dir., lab. of the Crason Corp., New York, 1929-30; v.p. and dir., lab. of Invex, Inc. (patent holding company developing, marketing his inventions) 1930-50; head of dept. elec. engring., U. of Fla., 1941-46; supervisor, War Research Lab., U. of Fla., 1943-46; chief engineer of radio station WRUF, 1943-47; radio supervisor State of Fla., under Federal E.S.M.W.T. program, 1942-45; associate technical director Pan American Technological and Manufacturing Corp., Miami; pres., dir. research Invex, Inc. Miami; cons. engineer; dir. electronics research lab., prof. engring. U. Miami, 1947-51; cons. engr. and physicist; with ICA, U.S. Dept. State, Indian Inst. Sci., Bangalore, India, 1957-59, guest prof. electronics, 1957-59; prof. electronics on fgn. assignment, U. Wis., 1957-59; tech. dir. Electronic & Chem. Research, Inc., Newark; cons. Airpax Electronics, Inc., Ft. Lauderdale, Fla.; U.S. del. Indian Sci. Congress, Madras, 1958, del., leader, Delhi, India, 1959, lectr. throughout India, Orient, Asia, Middle-East, Europe; dean of scis. and mathematics, also dir. indsl., govt. relations Fla. Atlantic U., Boca Raton, Fla.; 1961-66, dean emeritus, 1966-67; cons. to electronics corps. Mem. exec. com. S. Fla. Edn. Center; member com. on Oceanographic research Fla. U. System; cons. Broward County Bd. Public Instrn. Registered profl. engr. Recipient Naval Ordnance Award for Civilian Service; bldg. named in his honor Fla. Atlantic U. Fellow I.E.E.E., Am. Phys. Society, A.A.A.S.; I.R.E. (post chmn. Miami sect.), Am. Inst. Elec. Engrs.; mem. Fla. Engring. Soc. (life sr.), Fla. Acad. Sci. (sr.); Fla. Soc. Profl. Engineers (senior mem., past president of Miami chapter); member of Phi Beta Kappa, Sigma Xi, Sigma Tau, Omicron Delta Kappa, Sigma Phi Epsilon. Clubs: Coral Gables Country; Rotary; Bangalore (India). Author of numerous technical articles; inventor many electronic devices, including the Craig System of Television. Holder of over 40 issued patents. Contbr. articles on physics, electronics and electricity, in World Book Ency. Home: Boca Raton FL Died Apr. 7, 1967; interred Forest Lawn Meml. Gardens Mausoleum, Pompano Beach FL

CRAIG, ROBERT S(PENCER), assn. exec.; b. Savannah, Ill., Mar. 16, 1905; s. Harry C. and Grace (Thompson) C.; student U. Dubuque, 1923-25; m. Thelma Coile, June 14, 1947; children—John, Nessly, Robert, Christaine. Pres. Greenleaf, Inc., Detroit, 1930-41; v.p., gen. mgr. Territorial Motors, Honolulu, 1947-49; partner Hawaiian Economic Service, Honolulu, 1950-57; mng. dir. Robert S. Craig Asso., Honolulu, 1957-62; exec. dir. Downtown Improvement Assn.; pres. Pacific Research Corp. Mem. edn. committee of Traffic Safety Council; mem. Mayor's Citizen's Adv. Com. Community Renewal Program; mem. Mayor's Advisory Council on Urban Renewal; advisory council International Training Agency Center for Cultural and Technical Interchange between East and West. President Volunteer Service bur. Mental Health Assn., 1955-56, pres. assn., 1958-59; chmn. Govs. Conf. on Edn., Hawaiian dels. White House Conf. on Edn., 1955-56. Trustee Joint Council on Econ. Edn., Hawaii Council on Economic Education. Served from 1st lt. to lt. col., AUS, 1942-47. Mem. C. of C. Honolulu, Am. Marketing Assn., Internat. Downtown Exec. Assn., Urban Land Inst. Hawaiian Acad. Scis. Republican. Conglist. Home: Honolulu HI

CRAIG, WALLACE, zoologist, psychologist; b. Toronto, Can., July 20, 1876; s. Alexander and Marion (Brookes) C.; B.S., U. of Ill., 1898, M.S., 1901; Ph.D., U. of Chicago, 1908; m. Mrs. Mima Davis Jenness, Oct. 12, 1904. Prof. philosophy, U. of Me., 1908-22; lecturer, psychology, Harvard, 1922-23, librarian, bio-physics, 1923-27; engaged in research since 1929. Fellow A.A.A.S.; mem. Am. Philos Assn., Am. Psychol. Assn., Boston Soc. Nat. History, Sigma Xi, Phi Kappa Phi, Phi Sigma. Author: Song of the Wood Pewee, a study of bird music, 1943. Contbr. on animal behavior, psychology. Address: 18 Martin St., Cambridge MA‡

CRAIG, WALTER, television-radio cons.; b. St. Louis, Dec. 5, 1900; s. Frank E. and May (Goodrich) C.; student Westminster Coll., Fulton, Mo., 1918; m. Margaret Guthrie Gray, Sept. 13, 1946; 1 dau., Patricia Anne. Vaudeville Actor, Keith and Orpheum Circuits, 1920-22; juvenile leads musical comedy, Broadway and road, 1923-29; dir. programs World Broadcasting System, N.Y.C. 1930-32; independent radio prodn., 1933-38; radio dir. Street & Finney, Inc., N.Y.C. 1939-40; dir. programs radio sta. WMCA, N.Y. City, 1940-42; radio dir. Benton & Bowles, Inc., 1943-45, v.p. in charge radio, 1945-47, v.p. in charge radio and television 1948-53; v.p. advt. dir. Pharmaceuticals Inc., 1953-54; partner Norman, Craig & Kummel, Inc., 1955-60, TV cons., 1960-72; pres. First Fla. Funding Corp., Sarasota, Fla., 1961-67; creative dir. Hansen-Rubensohn-McCann-Erickson, Sydney, Australia, 1967-69; dir. Guaranteed Weather, Inc. Mem. Sarasota C. of C. Am. Assn. of Advt. Agencies (chmn. radio and TV prodn. com., 1948-53), Assn. Nat. Advertisers, Dramatists Guild, Author's League, Clubs: Sarasota Yacht; Athletic (N.Y.C.); American Nat. (Sydney). Lectr. in TV N.Y. U., 1947-59. Home: Sarasota FL Died July 5, 1972.

CRAIGHILL, GEORGE BOWDOIN, SR., lawyer; b. Bel Air, Md., Dec. 2, 1882; s. James B. and Margaret (Smith) C.; B.A., U. of South, 1903; LL.B., Georgetown U., 1906; m. Julia A. Lippitt, June 29, 1910 (dec. 1964); children—George Bowdoin, Margaret (Mrs. Karl R. Price). Admitted to D.C. bar, 1906, mem. firm Craighill, Mayfield & McCally (formerly McKaney, Flannery & Craighill), 1920-72; mem. faculty George Washington U., 1939-49, emeritus prof. law 1953-72. Chancellor, Episcopal Diocese of Washington, 1948-61. Member of American Bar Association, Bar Association D.C., Order of Coif. Phi Beta Kappa. Clubs: Lawyers (past pres.), Rotary (Washington); Chevy Chase (Md.) (past secretary, board governors); Metropolitan (D.C.). Home: Washington DC Died Oct. 13, 1972.

CRAM, WILLARD GLIDEN, church official; b. Doudton, Ky., Dec. 11, 1875; s. Edward Thomas and Margaret Elizabeth (Grace) C.; B.S., Asbury Coll., Wilmore, Ky., 1898; D.D., Asbury, 1910; LL.D., Kentucky Wesleyan, 1926; married Rosella Hogan, June 6, 1900; children—Newton McDonald (deceased), Willard Winston, Donald Hogan, Margaret Simmons, Ensign Kendall Hutchinson (deceased). Ordained ministry M.E. Church, South, 1902; missionary to Korea, 1902-17; associate director gen. Missionary Centenary Movement (campaign for 35,000,000), 1917-20; active in Centenary Revival, under Bd. of Missions in Korea, 1920-22; directing sec. Centenary Movement, 1922-26; gen. sec. Bd. of Missions, M.E. Ch. South, 1926-40; exec. sec., Joint Division Education and Cultivation, Board of Missions and Ch. Extension of the Meth. Ch., since 1940; mem. of Gen. Conf. M.E. Ch., S., 5 times. Trustee Scarritt Coll. for Christian Workers. Mem. Commn. on Union of the Meth. Chs. Mem. of the Uniting Conf. of the Meth. Ch., Kansas City, Mo., April, 1939. Secretarial mem. Gen. Conf. Meth. Ch., Atlantic City, April, 1940. Mem. Southeastern Jurisdictional Conf. Meth. Ch., Asheville, N.C., May, 1940; mem. gen. conf. Meth. Ch., Kansas City, Mo., 1944; sec. Commn. on Interdenominational Relations, Meth. Ch. Mem. Bd. of Translation of Bible in Korean Lang., 1905-10; editor Korean Messenger, 1910-15. Author: Methodism and Kingdom Extension. Address: 150 Fifth Av., New York NY*

CRAMER, FREDERIC, clergyman, educator; b. Germany, Dec. 29, 1874; s. Frederick B. and Fredericka (Becker) C.; brought to U.S., 1888; A.B., U. of Cincinnati, 1896; post-grad. work same coll. and Hebrew Union Coll., 1896-7; student Drew Theol. Sem., 1899-1901, univs. Halle, and Berlin, 1904-6; A.M., Baldwin-Wallace Coll., Berea, O., 1910; (D.D., Central Wesleyan Coll., Warrenton, Mo., 1915); m. Amelia Wehman, of Cincinnati, 1902. Ordained ministry M.E. Ch., 1904; pastor Mt. Healthy, O., 1906-08, Davenport, Wash., 1912-13; prof. philosophy, Willamette U., 1908-12, Baldwin-Wallace Coll. since 1913. Home: Berea OH‡

CRAMER, JOHN FRANCIS, educator; b. Kansas City, Mo., Sept. 13, 1899; s. John Lyman and Josephine (Coffman) C.; A.B., Willamette U., Salem, Ore., 1920, A.M., 1921; Ed.M., U. of Ore., 1932; Ed.D., 1937; m. Mabel Osterling, May 30, 1922; children—John Francis, William Donald and Richard Seldon. Science teacher for high schools located in Milton-Freewater and La Grande, Ore., 1920-24; principal high sch., Coquille, Ore., 1924-27; city supt. schs., Bandon, Ore., 1927-29, Grants Pass, Ore., 1929-34, The Dalles, Ore., 1935-37, Eugene, Ore., 1937-44; dir., gen. extension div., Oregon State System Higher Edn., 1944-55, dean, 1944-55; pres. Portland State Coll., 1955-58, prof. edn., 1958-67; vis. lectr. Hong Kong, 1958-59; vis. lectr. ednl. adminstrn. U. of Melbourne, 1951. Pvt., U.S. Army, 1918; officer Res. Corps, Chem. Warfare Service, 1926-43; active duty Civilian Conservation Corps, 1934; active service Edn. Branch, Special Service Div., 1943. Mem. Northwest Institute of International Affairs. Recipient of the medal Silver Beaver, Boy Scouts of Am.; received Carnegie grant to visit Australia and New Zealand, 1934-35. Mem. Nat. Edn. Assn., Am. Assn. Adult Edn., Phi Delta Kappa. Republican. Presbyterian. Mason (32 deg.), Rotarian. Clubs: City, University (Portland). Author: (with G. S. Brown) Contemporary Education, 1956, 2d edit., 1965; 2 books on Australian edn. Home: Portland OR Died Oct. 12, 1967; buried Willamette Nat. Cemetery, Portland OR

CRAMP, ARTHUR JOSEPH, b. London, Eng., Sept. 10, 1872; s. Joseph and Mary (Jackson) C.; prep. edn., Sir Walter St. John's Sch. (London) and Maryville (Mo.) Sem.; M.D., Wis. Coll. Physicians and Surgeons, Milwaukee, Wis., 1906; m. Lillian Caroline Torrey, of Skidmore, Mo., Sept. 1, 1897. Teacher of sciences in high schs., 1894-98, and prin. schs., 1898-1902; asst. in chemistry, Wis. Coll. Physicians and Surgeons, 1905-06; dir. Bur. of Investigation, A.M.A., 1906-35. Fellow A.M.A.; member Society of Medical History of Chicago, Inst. of Medicine of Chicago, Royal Inst. Pub. Health, Chicago Ornithol. Soc., Phi Rho Sigma. Club: Chicago Literary. Author: Nostrums and Quackery (Vol. I), 1911; (Vol II), 1921; Vol. III) 1936; also many pamphlets and articles in mags. Home: Ft Lauderdale FL‡

CRAMPTON, GEORGE S., ophthalmologist; b. Rock Island, Ill., Mar. 10, 1874; s. Richard and Martha (Betty) C.; M.D., U. of Pa., 1898; m. Hazel Smedes, May 16, 1907. Practiced at Phila., Pa., since 1898; prof. emeritus ophthalmology, Grad. Sch. U. of Pa.; adjunct opthalmologist to Pa. Hosp. Served as dir., Field Hosps., 28th Div., U.S. Army, rank of lt. col., 1918-19. Fellow A.M.A., Coll., Phys. of Phila.; mem. Am. Ophthal. Soc., Illuminating Engring. Soc. (ex-nat. pres.), Franklin Inst. Republican. Episcopalian. Home-office 2031 Locust St., Philadelphia 3 PA‡

CRAMTON, LOUIS C., lawyer, legislator; born Lapeer County, Mich., Dec. 2, 1875; s. George W. and Josephine Bird (Osmun) C.; student U. of Mich., 1894-95; LL.B., Law Dept., U. of Mich., 1899; Doctor of Laws (honorary), Alma (Mich.) Coll., 1937, Howard University, 1945; married Fame Kay, April 28, 1903 (dec. 1950); m. 2d Alice Cary White, May 28, 1951. Practiced law, Lapeer, 1899-1905; member 63d to 71st Congresses (1913-31), 7th Michigan District; active in expansion of national park systems; also in development of Indian health and education and Negro edn.; spl. atty. to sec. of Interior, 1931-33; circuit judge, 1934-41; mem. Mich. Ho. of Reps. 1949-50, 51-52, 53-54. Decorated Order of the White Eagle (Serbia), 1918; Order of Holy Redeemer (Greece), 1918; awarded Silver Beaver, Boy Scouts Am. Vice-president Tall Pine Council Boy Scouts (Shiawassee, Genesee and Lapeer counties); president Lapeer County Youth Council. Member State Bar Michigan, Detroit Society Geneal. Research, Society Preservation Virginia Antiquities (life) Michigan Soc. Mayflower Descendants, Mich. Hist. Soc., Detroit Hist. Soc., Lapeer County Hist. Soc. (pres.), Lapeer Rotary (past pres.; dist. gov., 1942-43; chmn. com. on constn. and by-laws, 1943-44; chmn. com. on Insts. of Internat. Understanding, 1946-47. Republican (del. to Rep. Nat. Conv., 1940). Presbyterian. Mason. Odd Fellow (Past Grand Master). Commentator Radio Station WMPC, Lapeer, since 1934. Home: 711 Pearl St. Office: Lapeer Savings Bank Bldg., Lapeer MI

CRANDALL, CLIFFORD WALDORF, univ. prof. and lawyer; b. Argentine, Mich., Nov. 17, 1874; s. Jesse Milton and Susan Maria (Harrington) C.; B.S., Adrian (Mich.) Coll., 1896, LL.D., 1937; LL.B. U. of Mich., 1899; m. Cora Augusta Davin, Aug. 27, 1901 (died Dec. 4, 1912); 1 son, John Milton; m. 2d, Kathleen Lorne Blain, July 8, 1914. Admitted to Mich. bar, 1899; practiced law with Wolcott & Moore, Port Huron, 1899-1900. Cady & Crandall, 1900-13; prof. law U. of Fla. since 1913, acting dean, 1947-48. Mem. Fla. State Bar Assn. Democrat. Episcopalian. Author: Florida Common Law Practice, 1928 (supplement, 1940). Home: Box 2383 University Station, Gainesville FL‡

CRANDALL, LEE SAUNDERS, zoologist; b. Sherburne, N.Y., Jan. 26, 1887; s. Charles Spencer and Ada (Harwood) C.; grad. Utica (N.Y.) Prep. Sch., 1907; student Cornell U. Med. Coll., 1907-08; Columbia, 1908-09; m. Celia Mary Dowd, Jan. 15, 1910; 1 dau., Sylvia. Asst., dept. of birds, N.Y. Zool. Park, 1908-11, asst. curator, 1911-19, curator, 1920-43, gen. curator, 1943-52, emeritus. Mem. sci. expeditions of New York Zoological Society to British Guiana, 1909, Costa Rica, 1914, New Guinea, 1928-29. Fellow New York Zool. Soc., N.Y. Acad. Science, Am. Ornithologists Union; mem. Linnaean Soc., Am. Soc. Mammalogists, Am. Soc. Icthyologists and Herpetologists; corr. mem. Zool. Soc., London. Author: Pets and How to Care for Them, 1917; Paradise Quest, 1931. Contbr. many articles and papers on natural history. Home: Bronxville NY Died June 25, 1969.

CRANDALL, SHANNON, merchant; b. Colusa, Calif., Mar. 25, 1871; s. Giles Griswold and Lucretia Little (Fifield) C.; ed. pub. schs., San Francisco, Calif.; m. Katherine Whitney, of San Francisco, Calif., Oct. 1901; children—Shannon, Frances Whitney. In wholesale hardware business since 1887; with Calif. Hardware Co. since 1897, pres. since 1918; dir. Security-1st Nat. Trust & Savings Bank. President Nat. Wholesale Hardware Assn. Pres. Los Angeles Chamber Commerce, 1929. Republican. Mason. Clubs: California, Beach, Midwick Country. Home: 173 N. Las Palmas Av. Office: 500 E. 1st St., Los Angeles CA‡

CRANE, CHARLES P., public utility exec., b. Annapolis, Md., Aug. 26, 1888; s. John Giles and Mary Louisa (Moffett) C.; grad. McDonogh Sch., Baltimore, 1905, student, Johns Hopkins, 1916; m. Louise Curtis Withgott, Feb. 29, 1936. With B. & O. R.R., Baltimore, 1905-09; in office chief of gen. staff, U.S. War Dept., 1909-10. With Consolidated Gas Electric Light & Power Company (now Baltimore Gas & Electric Company), Baltimore, 1910-72, vice pres., 1938, exec. vice pres., dir. 1946-50, pres. 1950-57, chmn. bd. 1957-60, chmn. exec. com., 1961-72; dir. First National Bank, U.S. Fidelity & Guaranty Co. Served in U.S. Naval Reserve, as exec. officer, U.S.S. Wanderer (lt.), staff officer Adm. Halstead, 1917-19. Mem. Am. Gas Assn., Md. Hist. Soc., Sons of Am. Revolution, Edison Elec. Institute (dir.). Mason. Clubs: Annapolis Yacht, Engineers of Baltimore, Maryland, Merchants, Baltimore Country, Gibson Island (Md.). Home: Baltimore MD Died May 31, 1972.

CRANE, EARL H(OWARD), mfg. exec.; b. Griffin, Ga., Oct. 1, 1901; s. David A. and Lela II. (Hart) C.; student U. Ga., 1920-23; m. Lillian Orlin, Aug. 15, 1926. Bond salesman S. W. Straus Co., 1923-25; independent bond broker, 1925-26; salesman, sales mgr. Mather & Co., Chgo., 1927-35; sales exec. Carrier Corp., N.Y.C., Newark, N.J., Syracuse, 1936-39; pres., chmn. Iroquois China Co., Syracuse, 1939-57; treas., dir. Allen Jigger Corp., 1946-67. Mem. Sales Mgrs. Assn. Am., N.A.M., Mfrs. Assn. Syracuse. Mason (Shriner). Club: Rotary, Syracuse Yacht. Home: Syracuse NY Died 1967.

CRANE, JASPER ELLIOT, mfr.; b. Newark, N.J., May 17, 1881; s. Edward Nichols and Cordelia (Matthews) C.; A.B., Princeton, 1901, M.S., 1904; student Mass. Inst. Tech., 1903-04; m. Olive E. Crow, Oct. 24, 1908; children—Cordelia C. Speakman, Helen C. Rupert, Catherine C. Welling. With the Arlington Co., Arlington, N.J., 1901-15; with E. I. dupont de Nemours & Co., 1915-46, vice pres., 1929-46; dir. Du Pont Co., D. Van Nostrand Co.; chmn. Temporary Emergency Relief Commn. of Del., 1932-34; alumni trustee Princeton U., 1939-43. Trustee, Found. for Econ. Edn. Dir. Wilmington YMCA, Del. Hosp. Chmn. United Community Fund No. Del. 1946-50. Member American Chemical Society, Institute of Chemical Engineers, Society of Chemical Industry. Republican. Presbyterian (elder Westminister Ch. mem. gen. council Presbyn. Ch. in U.S.A., 1939-45; chmn. finance com., 1941-45, Pilgrims Soc. Colonial Wars. Clubs: Wilmington, Wilmington Country; University, Princeton, Chemists' (New York). Home: Wilmington DE Died Dec. 1, 1969; buried Lower Brandywine Cemetery.

CRANE, JAY EVERETT, ret. banker and oil exec.; b. Newark, Sept. 13, 1891; s. William A. and Elizabeth P. (Hopping) C.; m. Amy Berthe Nagel, May 19, 1917; 1 dau. Barbara A. (Mrs. J. C. Tobin), Formerly dep. gov., chmn. bd. Fed. Res. Bank of N.Y.; v.p., dir. Standard Oil Co., 1935-57; financial cons.; dir. A. & P., Empire Trust Co., French American Banking Corporation. Club: University. Home: Orange NJ Died Apr. 11, 1973.

CRANE, LAWRENCE GORDON, clergyman; b. Detroit, Oct. 4, 1929; s. Charles Leroy and Mary Helen (Holmes) C.; A.B., Tex. Christian U., 1952; B.D., Vanderbilt U., 1955; postgrad. Hebrew U., Jerusalem, Israel, 1963; m. Sarah Anne Pledger, Feb. 21, 1958; children—Wendy, Carol Faith, Lawrence Gordon. Ordained to ministry Christias Ch. (Disciples of Christ), 1954; minister Christian chs., Tennessee Colony, Tex., 1948-52, Rochester, Ky., 1952-55, asso. minister, Birmingham, Ala., 1955-57, Chattanooga, 1957-67; minister Madison Av. Christian Ch., Covington, Ky., 1967-70. Counselor, Sci. Marriage Found. Mellott, Ind.; mem. Covington-Kenton County Commn. on Human Rights. Bd. dirs. No. Ky. Assn. for Retarded Children. Recipient Barton W. Stone award, 1955. Mem. Disciples of Christ Hist. Soc., Nat. Conf. Christians and Jews, Israel-Am. Cultural Soc. Inter-Univ. Com. Ft Mitchell KY Died Feb. 19, 1970.

CRANE, OSCAR W., airlines co. exec.; b. Eufaula, Okla., 1904. Treas. Braniff Airways, Inc. Home: Oklahoma City OK Died July 15, 1969; buried Memorial Park, Oklahoma City OK*

CRANE, RONALD SALMON, prof. English b. Tecumseh, Mich., Jan. 5, 1886; s. Theodore H. Bricena (Chadwick) C.; A.B., U. of Mich., 1908; Ph.D., U. of Pa., 1911, D.H.L., 1966; Dr. of Humane Letters, U. Michigan. 1941; D.Lit., Northwestern U., 1963; married Julia L. Fuller, June 20, 1917; children—Barbara Chadwick (Mrs. William M. Gibson), Ronald Fuller. Instructor English, 1911-15, assistant professor, 1915-20, associate professor, 1920-24, Northwestern U.; asso. prof. English, 1924-25, prof. 1925-50, chmn. dept. of English, 1935-47, distinguished service prof. English, 1950-51, emeritus from 1951, U. Chgo.; vis. prof. Alexander lectr. U. Toronto, 1952; vis. prof. Cornell U., 1952-53, 57, Carleton College, 1953, U. of Oregon, 1954, Stanford, 1954-55, Ind. U., 1955-56, U. Fla., 1958 Northwestern U., 1959, N.Y.U., 1960-61, U. Rochester, 1962, U. Ia., 1963, U. Chgo., 1963-66. Corr. fellow Brit. Acad.; mem. Modern Lang. Assn., Am. (v.p. 1931-32), Am. Acad. Arts and Scis., Phi Beta Kappa, Bibliog. Soc. (London); v.p. Commn. internationale d'histoire litteraire moderne, 1929-35. Club: Quadrangle. Editor: (with W. F. Bryan) The English Familiar Essay, 1916; (with F.B. Kaye) A Census of British Newspapers and Periodicals, 1620-1800, 1927. New Essays by Oliver Goldsmith, 1927; A Collection of English Poems 1660-1800, 1932; (with others) Critics and Criticism, Ancient and Modern, 1952; The Languages of Criticism and the Structure of Poetry, 1953; The Idea of theHumanities, 2 vols., 1967. Contbr. to Modern Philology, Romanic Review, Modern Language Notes, etc. Managing editor Modern Philology 1930-52. Home: Chicago IL Died Aug. 27, 1967; buried Tecumseh MI

CRANE, WALTER RICHARD, mining engr.; b. Grafton, Mass., Feb. 5, 1870; s. Richard Reed and Arethusa Thorndyke (Barret) C.; grad. Franklin (Neb.) Mil. Acad., 1891; A.B., U. of Kan., 1895, A.M., 1896; Ph.D., Columbia, 1901; m. Margaret M. Gray, Dec. 28, 1898; children—Dorothy G., Margaret E., Aldyth C. Asst. in chemistry, U. of Kan., 1896; asst. to prin., Beloit High Sch., 1896-98; dir. manual training, city schs., Janesville, Wis., 1898-99; asst. geologist, Univ. Geol. Survey of Kan., 1893-1905; asst. prof. mining, U. of Kan., 1900-05; gas expert, Univ. Geol. Survey of Kan. and U.S. Geol. Survey, 1902-05; mem. faculty, Sch. of Mines, Columbia, 1905-08; dean Sch. of Mines and prof. mining, Pa. State Coll., 1908-18; mining engr., U.S. Bur. of Mines, 1918-33. Mem. State Commn. for Establishment U.S. Mining Expt. Sta. at Pittsburgh, 1913-18; war minerals investigation, U.S. Bur. of Mines, 1918-19; chief engr. War Minerals Relief Commn., Dept. Interior, 1920; apptd. supt. Southern Mining Expt. Sta., U.S. Bur. Mines, Birmingham, Ala., 1921; then supervising research engr., U.S. Bur. Mines until 1933; now cons. mining engr. Mem. Am. Inst. Mining and Metall. Engrs., Coal Mining Inst. America, Sigma Xi, Tau Beta Pi, Arctic Brotherhood. Republican. Congregationalist. Author: A Treatise on Gold and Silver, 1908; Index of Mining Engineering Literature, 1909; Ore Mining Methods, 1910; also French and Russian edits.; also writer of numerous pub. monographs, papers and reports on mining and kindred subjects. In Alaska, investigating the coal resources of that territory, 1912 and 1913. Address: P.O. Box 453 Oakland CA‡

CRANE, WINTHROP MURRAY, JR., paper mfr.; b. Dalton, Mass., Sept. 12, 1881; s. W. Murray and Mary (Benner) C.; student Hill Sch., Pottstown, Pa.; A.B., Yale, 1904; m. Ethel G. Eaton, Feb. 9, 1905; children—Barbara (Mrs. George Monaghan), Winthrop Murray, III, Arthur Eaton. Entered family paper mills, 1904; pres. and gen. mgr., Crane & Co., 1923-52, chmn. board. Served as lt. colonel, U.S. Army, World War I. Trustee Mem. Skull and Bones (Yale). Republican. Conglist. Clubs: Yale (New York); Yale (Boston). Home: Dalton MA Died Mar. 28, 1968; buried Dalton MA

CRANNELL, ELIZABETH KELLER SHAULE (MRS. WINSLOW CRANNELL), writer, anti-suffragist; b. Sharon Springs, N.Y.; d. Solomon and Elizabeth (Keller) Shaule; ed. pvt. schs.; m. Winslow Crannell, of Albany, N.Y., Oct. 3, 1870 (died 1908). First woman to appear against extension of suffrage to women; addressed Rep. Nat. Conv., St. Louis, 1896, in opposition to female suffrage plank in party platform, conv. refusing to endorse the plank, appeared before Dem. Nat. Conv., Chicago, 1896, against female suffrage, conv. also refusing to embody female suffrage in its platform; organized anti-suffrage assns. in S.D., Wash. and Ore. and toured the country several times in opposition to female suffrage; addressed N.Y. Legislature annually, 1896-1911, in opposition to female suffrage. An organizer, 1892, and pres. Albany Assn., mem. exec. com. Pittsburgh Assn., and mem. Nat. Assn. Opposed to Woman Suffrage. Mem. Nat. Indian Assn. (exec. bd.), Albany Indian Assn. (ex-pres.), Albany Hist. and Art Soc., Dana Natural History Soc. (ex-president), Consumer's League, Authors' League America, Mohawk Chapter D.A.R. (charter mem. and 1st historian), etc. Episcopalian. Founder and editor Indian Advocate, also of the Anti-Suffragist; founder and 1st editor Church Record. Home: 9 Hall Pl., Albany NY‡

CRANSTON, EARL, educator and clergyman; b. Denver, Colo., Jan. 30, 1895; s. Earl Montgomery and Florence Terry (Pitkin) C.; A.B., Dartmouth Coll., 1916; B.D., Drew Theol. Sem., 1920; grad. study, Union Theol. Sem., 1924-26; M.A., Columbia U., 1925; Ph.D., Harvard, 1931; m. Mary Mildred Welch, Jan. 28, 1929; children—John Welch, Margaret Brayton, Florence Pitkin. Ordained Meth. ministry, 1920; religious and ednl. work for Meth. Mission, Peking, China, 1920-21, in Taianfu, 1921-22, in Chengtu, 1922-24; teacher West China U., 1926-28; instr. Boston U., 1928-30; acting head, dept. of history, State Teachers Coll., Buffalo, N.Y., 1930-31; asst. prof. history, Colgate U., 1931-34; chmn. history and polit. science, University of Redlands, 1934-44; dir. of social sciences, 1942-44; Phillips Professor of Religion, Dartmouth College, 1944-49; dean School of Religion, U. So. Calif., 1949-56; dean So. Cal. School of Theology, 1956-60; prof. humanities Claremont Men's College, 1960-61; exchange preacher in England and Scotland, 1933; lecturer, 7th Internat. Congress of Hist. Sciences. Warsaw, Poland, 1933; vis. lectr. ch. history. Pacific Sch. Religion, 1940, Boston U., 1961-62; vis. prof. history U. Redlands, 1963-66; lectr. humanities Scripps Coll., 1958-59; lectr. history U. Cal., Riverside, 1967-68. Leader seminar in Middle East Riverside, 1967-68; vis. prof. history State Poly. Coll., Pomona, 1969. Leader seminar in Middle East Ariz. Conf. of Methodist Ch. Army Y.M.C.A. sec., Washington, D.C., 1917-18; PVT. U.S. Army Ambulance Service, Italy, 1918-19. Received Italian War Cross, 1919; posthumously awarded with wife Distinguished Service award U. Redlands Alumni award, 1970. Mem. American Historical Association, American Council of Institute of Pacific Relations, National Association of Biblical Instructors, Ch. Fedn. Los Angeles (v.p., 1955-56), Phi Beta Kappa (pres. so. Cal. alumni, 1951-53), Delta Sigma Rho. Republican. Mason. Author: Swords or Plowshares, 1937; The Way Out (with others), 1939; A new World Through Racial Understanding (pamphlet), 1944; also articles in various periodicals. Home: Claremont CA Died Oct. 12, 1970; buried Oak Park Cemetery, Claremont CA

CRAVEN, THOMAS, writer; b. Salina, Kan., Jan. 6, 1889; s. Richard Price and Virginia (Bates) C.; student Salina (Kan.) High Sch., 1901-05; A.B. Kan. Wesleyan U., 1908; m. Aileen St. John-Brenon (writer), Aug. 25, 1923; 1 son, Richard. Began as newspaper reporter, 1910, later night clerk, A.T. & S.F. & S.F. Ry.; instr. U. of Puerto Rico, 1913-14; author, lecturer, art critic, book reviewer, free lance writer since 1914. Editor: A Treasury of Art Masterpieces, 1939; A Treasury of American Prints, 1939. Served as 2d class seaman U.S. Navy, 1918. Ind. Democrat. Author: Men of Art, 1931; Modern Art, 1934; The Story of Painting, 1943. Editor: Life of Benvenuto Cellini, 1937: Cartoon Calvalcades 1943. Died Feb. 1969.Cartoon Cavalcades 1943 Died Feb. 1969.‡

CRAVEN, TUNIS AUGUSTUS MACDONOUGH, radio engineer; b. Phila., Pa., Jan. 31, 1893; s. T. A. and Harriet Baker (Austin) C.; prep. edn. St. Paul's Sch., Baltimore, Md., 1902-08; grad. U.S. Naval Acad., 1913; m. Josephine La Tourette, Sept. 25, 1915; children—Eugenie La Tourette, Tunis Augustus Macdonough, Jr.; m. 2d, Emma Stoner, Dec. 1931; 1 son, Thomas Tingey; m. 3d, Margaret Preston, Dec. 1963; m. 4th, Emma Stoner, Mar. 1971. Commd. ensign U.S.N., 1913, radio officer, 1913-23; chief radio research and design section Bureau of Engineering, 1923-26; tech. adviser Internat. Radio-telegram Conf., Washington, 1927; resigned from navy, 1930, to enter private practice as cons. engr.; chief engr. Fed. Communications Commn., 1935-37; commr., 1937-44; senior executive and technical adviser Cowles' broadcasting stations, 1944-49; partner, Craven, Lohnes and Culver, cons. radio engrs., 1949-57; mem. FCC, 1957-63; consulting radio engineer, 1963—. Fellow Inst. Radio Engineers; member of U.S. Naval Inst., Mil. Order Loyal Legion of the U.S. Episcopalian. Clubs: Nat. Press (Washington, D.C.); Army and Navy Country; Ends of the Earth Club, Kilocycle Wave Length Club. Home: McLean VA Died May 31, 1972.

CRAVENS, DU VAL GARLAND, educator; b. Ft. Smith, Ark., Apr. 20, 1875; s. Col. William Murphy and Mary Eloise (Cravens) C.; B.S. in Mechanical Engring., A. and M. Coll. of N.M., Mesilla Park, N.M., 1898; post-grad. work, same coll., 1899; M.A., U. of the South, 1916; m. Florence Eileen Fain, of Bristol, Tenn., June 21, 1905; children—DuVal, William Murphy, John Fain, Mary Virginia, Thomas Rutherford. Govt. supervisor schs., Vega Baja, P.R., 1899-1900; instr. St.

Albans Sch., Radford, Va., 1900-04; sr. master Money Sch., Murfreesboro, Tenn., 1904-08; headmaster Carlisle Mil. Acad., Arlington, Tex., 1908-10; asso. headmaster Murfreesboro Sch. for Boys, 1910-12; supt. Sewanee Mil. Acad. since 1912. Mem. Kappa Alpha. Democrat. Episcopalian. Mason. Clubs: Civitan. Home: Sewanee TN‡

CRAVENS, KENTON ROBINSON, banker; b. Salina, Kan., June 7, 1904; s. Richard Price and Crudenia (Poston) C.; A.B., University of Kansas, 1925; married Vivian Crouch, May 28, 1927; children—Susan, Kenton (deceased). Vice pres. Cleveland Trust Co., 1938-43 (on leave 1941-42); became v.p., dir. Mercantile Trust Co., (formerly Mercantile-Commerce Bank & Trust Co.), St. Louis, 1943, pres., 1954-62, chmn. bd., 1962-67, chmn. exec. com., from 1967; chmn. bd. Eagle Rubber Co., from 1940; adminstr. RFC, Washington, 1953-54; dir. Am. Zinc Company, Granite City Steel Company, Interco Inc. Home: St Louis MO Died Sept. 16, 1971.

CRAVENS, OSCAR HENRY, banker; b. Center Valley, Ind., Dec. 1, 1869; s. William Reece and Sarah (Bray) C.; student Indiana U., 1886-88, Central Normal Coll., Danville, Ind., 1888-91; m. Bertha Miers, Dec. 7, 1898. Established Bloomington World, 1892, editor and pub. to 1926; postmaster, Bloomington, 1913-22; pres. Monroe County State Bank since 1927; also pres. Mutual Bldg. and Loan Assn. Police commr. of Bloomington, 1930-34; code rep. of Monroe County Com. for NRA; state senator, Indiana, term 1936-40. Mem. bd. trustees Indiana Sch. of Religion; past pres. Bloomington Chamber of Commerce, Indiana Democratic Editorial Assn. Mem. Indiana Bankers Assn., Phi Gamma Delta. Democrat. Presbyterian. Mason, Modern Woodman, Rotarian (gov. 20th dist. 1933-34). Home: Bloomington IN‡

CRAWFORD, ANGUS, city ofcl.; b. Cleve., June 12, 1928; s. John Alexander and May (Arthur) C.; student Williams Coll., 1946-47, Western Reserve U., summer 1948; B.A., Grinnell Coll., 1951; postgrad. U. Pa., 1951-52; m. Doris Janaan Wilts, Sept. 9, 1951;children—Ellen Jane, Howard Angus. Personnel dir., adminstrv. asst., Eau Claire, Wis., 1952-55; city mgr., Iowa Falls, Ia., 1955-58, North Bend, Ore., 1958-63, Berkeley, Mo., 1963-66, Oshkosh, Wis., 1966-70. Mem. adv. bd. Salvation Army, Oshkosh, Wis. Mem. Internat. City Mgrs. Assn., Am. Soc. for Pub. Adminstrn., Am. Pub. Works Assn., Kappa Alpha. Conglist (trustee). Mason. Home: Oshkosh WI Died Nov. 1970.

CRAWFORD, EARL STETSON, artist; b. Phila., Pa., June 6, 1877; s. Franklin Matthew and Florence A. (DePuy) C.; ed. Sch. of Industrial Art, Phila.; Pa. Acad. Fine Arts; Delacluse and Julian acads., and Ecole Nationale des Beaux Arts, Paris; also in Munich, London, Rome, Florence and Venice; m. Brenetta Bimm Herrman, of Toledo, O., and New York, Jan. 14, 1903; 1 dau., Brenetta De Puy. Connected with Sch. of Applied Design for Women, New York, 1912-17, instr. advanced classes, life, book cover designs, composition; has served as art dir. several publs.; portrait painter and mural decorator, also designer stained glass windows various chs.; mural work in U.S. govt. bldgs., San Francisco; giving practically entire time since 1923 to etching, principally French, Belgian and Italian subjects. Represented in various collections of prints throughout Europe, Australia and New Zealand. Formerly member National Guard Pa.; mem. Nutley Shade Tree Commn. 5 yrs. Fellow Soc. Am. Illustrators; mem. Nat. Assn. Portrait Painters (sec. since 1912), Am. Legion, Imperial Three Arts Club (London); societaire Societe Arts et Belles Lettres, Societe Lyonnaise des Beaux Arts; asso. mem. Societe Nationale des Beaux Arts (Paris). Entered O. T. C., Plattsburg, N.Y., May, 1917; commd. lt. Q.M.C., N.A., and on active duty with 77th Div., Camp Upton, L.I., 1917; transf. to Camp Johnston, Fla., later to Hdqs. Southern Dept., San Antonio, Tex.; served until Oct. 25, 1919. Republican. Episcopalian. Mason. Home: The Atrium, Mentone, Alpes Maritimes, France Address: Care Guaranty Trust Co., Paris France‡

CRAWFORD, FINIA GOFF, former vice-chancellor Syracuse U., ednl. cons.; b. Cameron Mills, N.Y., June 16, 1894; s. Eugene and Mary (Goff) C.; graduate of Canisteo Academy, 1911; Ph.B., Alfred U., 1915, LL.D., 1933; A.M., U. of Wis., 1916, Ph.D., 1922; LL.D., St. Lawrence U., 1952; Syracuse University, 1959; L.H.D., Yeshiva University, 1959; m. Marian Elliott, Dec. 23, 1917; children—Jean, Richard Asst. profl. polit. science, Syracuse U., 1919-21, prof., 1921-24, professor, School of Citizenship and Public Affairs 1924-59, dean, College of Liberal Arts, 1938-50; vice-chancellor 1942-59; retired; dir. Youth Development. Center, 1958-61, mem. advisory council, 1961-65; taught summers at Stanford, Alfred U.; dir. Unity Mutual Life Ins. Co. Citizens Nat. Bank (Wellsville, N.Y.). Trustee Power Authority State N.Y., 1958-65. Trustee Alfred U., chairman, 1963-73. Served in 331st Machine Gun Bn., U.S. Army, 2d lt. and 1st lieutenant, War Plans Division, Gen. Staff, 1917-19. Mem. Am. Polit. Science Assn., Nat. Municipal League, Am. Assn. Univ. Profs., and American Legion.

Democrat. Methodist. Clubs: Faculty; also the Century (Syracuse, New York). Author: Handbook of the Agencies of Economics Mobilization of the United States for the War of 1917 (joint author); The Electrical Utilities, A Crisis in Public Control (with W. E. Mosher), 1929; State Government, 1931; Readings in American Government, 1927, revised edition, 1933; Public Utility Regulation (with W. E. Mosher), 1933; Our Government Today, 1935. Author of pamphlet, Administration of the Gaosline Tax in the United States, 1927, rev. edit.; 1930, 1932, 1936; Motor Fuel Taxation in the United States, 1939, etc. Home: Andover NY

CRAWFORD, JACK RANDALL, author, educator; b. Washington, D.C., Apr. 1, 1878; s. Theron C. and Inez R. (Joyce) C.; B.A., Princeton U., 1901, M.A., 1903; m. Clarissa Connell, of Erie, Pa., July 2, 1903 (died 1908); 1 dau., Clarissa; m. 2d, Dorothy Gabain, of The Manor House, Bushey, Hertfordshire, Eng., June 26, 1909; children—Pamela, Elizabeth. Asso. English, Yale, 1909-46, prof. emeritus, 1946-68. Member Commission on English, College Entrance Examination Board. Fellow Timothy Dwight College. Member Phi Gamma Delta, Chi Delta Theta. Aurelian Soc., The Pundits. Episcopalian. Clubs: Elizabethan, Graduates, Lawn (New Haven); Yale (N.Y.). Author: Lovely Peggy (play), 1910; Robin of Sherwood (play), 1911; Community Drama and Pageantry (with Mary P. Beegle), 1916; I Walked in Arden (novel), 1922; What to Read in English Literature, 1928; The Philosopher's Murder Case, 1931. Edited: Hamlet, As You Like It, and Richard III; (with T. H. Dickinson) Contemporary Plays, 1925. Home: New Haven CT Died Aug. 7, 1968; buried Madison Garden.

CRAWFORD, JOHN FORSYTH, prof. philosophy; b. Damascus, Syria, Nov. 16, 1871; s. John and Mary Beattie (Stewart) C.; came to U.S., 1885; student Union Coll., Schenectady, N.Y., 1891-93; A.B., Princeton, 1895, A.M., 1897; studied univs. of Halle and Berlin, 1895-96; B.D., McCormick Theol. Sem., 1910; Ph.D., U. of Chicago, 1913; m. Bertha Adams, of Grinnell, Ia., June 25, 1901; children—John A., Martha H., Grenville (dec.). Demonstrator of experimental psychology at Princeton University, 1896-97; ordained to Baptist ministry, 1900; entered Congl. ministry, 1907; pastor 1st Bapt. Ch., Beaver Dam, Wis., 1900-04; prof. philosophy and edn. Grand Island (Neb.) Coll., 1904-07; prof. psychology, U. of Neb., summers, 1906-07; prof. philosophy and psychology, Tabor (Ia.) Coll., 1907-12; prof. philosophy, U. of Chicago, summers, 1913, 14, 15; prof. philosophy, Beloit Coll. since 1913; exchange prof. philosophy, U. of Texas, 1933-34. Mem. Am. Philos. Assn., Phi Beta Kappa. Author: The Relation of Fact and Inference in Mill's Logic, 1913. Contbr. to Essays in Philosophy, 1929. Home: 726 Milwaukee Road, Beloit WI‡

CRAWFORD, JOSEPH E(MANUEL), ry. official; b. San Diego, Calif., Dec. 1, 1876; s. Joseph U. and Harriet (Henriques) C.; B.S. in civil engring., U. of Pa., 1895; m. Alice Marion Christeson, May 15, 1904. Draftsman and designer Pencoyd (Pa.) Iron Works, 1895-1903; with N.&W. Ry. since 1903, as bridge engr., 1903-14, chief engr., 1914-24, gen. mgr., 1924-36, vice-pres. in charge of operation 1936-39, vice-president, assistant to president, 1939-41, retired Jan. 1, 1942. Member Am. Soc. Civil Engrs., Am. Ry. Engrs. Assn., Psi Upsilon. Republican. Episcopalian. Clubs: University (Phila.); Shenandoah, Roanoke Country (Roanoke, Va.). Home: 645 Wellington Av., Roanoke VA*‡

CRAWSHAW, FRED DUANE, educator; b. St. Paul, Minn., Mar. 19, 1874; s. Frank and Mary (Dunnaway) C.; grad. Mechanics Arts High Sch., St. Paul, 1891; grad. St. Paul Business Coll., 1892; B.S., Worcester Poly. Inst., 1896, M.E., 1909; grad. work, U. of Chicago, summer session, 1900, and by correspondence; m. Wilhelmina Blanche Story, of Peoria, Ill., Sept. 12, 1899. Chmn. manual arts, Central High Sch., Minneapolis, 1896-97; instr. in manual arts, Bradley Poly. Inst., Peoria, Ill., 1897-03; also prin. Franklin Sch. and manual arts advisor, Peoria, and instr. in Bradley Poly. Inst. summer sessions, 1903-8; asst. dean Coll. of Engring., U. of Ill., 1908-10; chmn. Dept. of Manual Arts, and prof. manual arts, U. of Wis., 1910-17; pres. academic board, U.S. School of Military Aeronautics, U. of Ill., 1917-19; prof. industrial edn., and asst. to dir. Engring. Expt. Sta., U. of Ill., arts, U. of Wis., 1919-20. Supervising editor, manual arts and vocational edn. dept., Scott, Foresman & Co., Chicago and New York. Pres. Western Drawing and Manual Training Assn., 1913, Wis. Sch. Arts and Home Econ. Assn., 1914-16; mem. N.E.A., Nat. Assn. for Promotion Industrial Edn., Phi Gamma Delta. Mem. Bd. of Commerce, Madison. Republican. Conglist. Author: Problems in Furniture Making, 1902; Problems in Wood Turning, 1905; Metal Spinning, 1910; Manual Arts for Vocational Ends, 1912; Problems in Mechanical Drawing (part author), 1908; Furniture Design for Schools and Shops, 1914; Mechanical Drawing for Colleges and Universities (part author), 1915; Mechanical Drawing for Secondary Schools (part author), 1916. Now in ins. business. Home: 304 Bigelow St., Peoria IL‡

CREAGER, CHARLES E., ex-congressman; b. Montgomery Co., O., Apr. 28, 1873; s. of William O. C.; pub. sch. edn.; m. Lizzie J. Fleenor, of Dayton, O., Feb. 23, 1896. Entered newspaper business at Dayton, O., 1894; formerly reporter at Dayton and Columbus, O., city editor Columbus Press-Post, state corr. Cincinnati Times-Star; editor Daily Leader, Marietta, O., 1902-4; sergt.-major 4th Ohio Vol. Inf., Spanish-Am. War, 1898, Porto Rico Campaign; mem. 61st Congress (1909-11), 3d Okla. Dist.; Republican. Address: Muskogee OK‡

CREECH, OSCAR, JR., physician, univ. dean; b., Nashville, N.C., Nov. 14, 1916 s. Oscar and Martha (Gulley) C., student Wake Forest Coll., 1933-37; M.D., Jefferson Med. Coll., 1941; m. Dorothy B. Creech. Intern Charity Hosp., New Orleans, 1941-42; resident Tulane Surg. Service, 1945-49; asst. instr. dept. surgery Tulane Med. Sch., 1946-49, now William Henderson prof. surgery, chmn. dept.; instr. to asso. prof. dept. surgery, Baylor U. Coll. Medicine, 1949-55; now dean Sch. Medicine, Tulane U. Served maj., 9th Inf. Div., AUS, 1942-46. Diplomate Am. Bd. Thoracic Surgery, Am. Bd. Surgery, Mem. A.M.A., Am. Surg. Soc., Soc. U. Surgeons, Soc. Vascular Surgery, Am. Assn. Thoracic Surgery, Soc. Soc. Clin. Research, Soc. Exptl. Biology and Medicine, Sigma Xi, Alpha Omega Alpha. Home: New Orleans LA Died Dec. 22, 1967; buried Ahoskie NC

CREED, THOMAS PERCIVAL, univ. chancellor; b. 1897; s. C. J. Creed; B.A. in Lit. Humanities, (Classical scholar), Pembroke Coll., Oxford (Eng.) U., 1922, M.A., 1925; LL.D. (hon.), Leicester (Eng.), 1965; m. Margaret Brewis, 1928; one son, two daus. Called to bar Lincoln's Inn; with Sudan Polit. Service, 1922; dist. judge, 1926; judge to Iraq cts under Anglo-Iraq Jud. Agreement, 1931, then additional judge Baghdad; pres. of cts., Kirkuk, 1932, Moeul, 1934; judge High Ct., Khartoum, Sudan, 1935; chief justice of The Sudan, 1936-41; mem. legal sect. Sudan Govt., also mem. gov. gen.'s council, 1941-47; periodically acting gov.-gen.; chief rep. Sudan Govt. at hearing of Egyptian case, UN Security Council, 1947; sec. King's Coll., London, Eng., 1948-51; prin. Queen Mary Coll., U. London, 1952-67, dep. vice chancellor of univ., 1958-61, vice chancellor of univ., 1964-67; coopted mem. senate, 1968-69. Mem. Commonwealth, Scholarship Commn.; hon. bencher Lincoln's Inn, 1967-69. Chmn. forest of dean com. Forestry Commn., 1955, Collegiate Council, 1955-57, Burnham Com., 1958-65. Served with Brit. Army, 1915-19. Decorated Medal of Commendation; comdr. Order British Empire, 1943; created knight, 1946; comdr. Order of Nile, 1939; hon. fellow Pembroke Coll., 1950. Club: Athenaeum. Home: London England Died May 11, 1969.

CREEL, ROBERT CALHOUN, fgn. service officer; b. Kansas City, Mo., Sept. 25, 1913; s. James Randall and Margaret Emerson (Davis) C.; A.B. summa cum laude, Harvard, 1934; LL.B. cum laude, 1938; married to Mariana Mears Evans, January 21, 1956; children—Elizabeth Calhoun and Margaret Evans. Admitted to N.Y. bar, 1939; Richard Sheldon prize fellowship for travel, Europe, 1934-35; atty. Root, Clark, Buckner & Ballantine, N.Y.C., 1938-41; chief counsel, dir. legal div. European hdqrs., area dir. for Europe, Washington hdqrs. Office Fgn. Liquidation Commr., Dept. of State, 1946-47; commd. fgn. service officer, consul career; sec. Diplomatic Service, July 1947; 2d sec., consul, Bucharest, Rumania, 1947-50, 1st sec. embassy New Delhi, India, 1950-51, also Katmandhu, Nepal; chief polit. affairs div. Berlin Element, Office U.S. High Commr. for Germany, 1952-54; detailed Nat. War Coll., 1954-55; officer-in-charge, German Polit. Affairs, Dept. State, 1955-58; counselor embassy, dep. chief mission, Beirut, Lebanon, 1958-61; counselor Am. embassy, dep. chief mission, Vientiane, Laos, 1961-62; dir. Office German Affairs, Dept. State, 1962-64; dep. asst. sec. of state for European affairs, 1964-65; U.S. consul general, Munich, Germany, 1965-70. Served as pvt. to lt. col. U.S. Army, 1941-46; with 101st Cav., 212th CA.C., N.Y.N.G. 1938-41. Mem. Assn. Ex-Mems. Squadron A. Phi Beta Kappa. Clubs: Metropolitan, Chevy Chase (Washington); Harvard (N.Y.C.). Home: Washington DC Died Oct. 1970.

CREESE, WADSWORTH, banker; b. Green Creek, N.J., 1883. President and trust officer First National Bank and Trust Co., Woodbury, N.J.; dir. Pitman (N.J.) Nat. Bank & Trust Co., People's Bldg. & Loan Association, New Jersey Bell Telephone Company. Member national board of field advisers Small Bus. Adminstrn., Region III, Phila. Mason (Shriner). Home: Woodbury NJ

CRENSHAW, OLLINGER, historian, coll. prof.; born College Park, Ga., May 9, 1904; s. Hansell and Carrie Proctor (Ollinger) C.; A.B., Washington and Lee U., 1925, A.M., 1926; Ph.D., Johns Hopkins, 1945; m. Marjorie Burford, June 22, 1939; 1 son, Albert Burford. Instr. in history Washington and Lee U., 1926-29, asst. prof. history, 1930-41, asso. prof., 1941-47 (leave absence for research, 1945-47), prof. history, 1947-70, head dept., 1962-69; instr. govt. Coll. of William and Mary, summers 1929, 30; lecturer in hist. U. of Wis., summer 1948; lecturer in history U. of Va., summer

1966; vis. prof. history (summers) W.Va. U., 1950, Johns Hopkins U., 1952; Ernest J. King prof. of Maritime History, U.S. Naval War College, Newport, Rhode Island, 1956-57. Mem. Am., So. (exec. council 1952-54), Organization of American Historians, also Phi Beta Kappa, Phi Gamma Delta. Democrat. Episcopalian. Clubs: Cosmos (Washington); Johns Hopkins (Baltimore). Author: The Slave States in the Presidential Election of 1860, 1945; General Lee's College; The Rise and Growth of Washington and Lee University, 1969. Contributor articles and revs. to hist. jours.; specialist in Old South, Civil War, Am. and Am. Diplomatic intellectual history. Voluntary tennis coach, Washington and Lee Univ., 1934-41. Home: Lexington VA Died Mar. 19, 1970; buried Stonewall Jackson Cemtery, Lexington VA

CRESON, LARRY BARKLEY, justice; b. Memphis, Jan. 17, 1906; s. Robert Franklin and Etta (Thomas) C.; student Memphis U. Sch., grad. Vanderbilt U., 1928. LL.B., 1929; m. Gertrude Jean Hooper, Aug. 29, 1934; children—Jean Edrington (Mrs. Allen Cooper Dell), Larry Barkley. Admitted to Tenn. bar, 1929; practiced in Memphis, 1930-65; past mem. firm Laughlin, Watson, Creson, Garthbright & Halle; associate justice Supreme Court of Tennessee, chancellor Chancery Court of Shelby County, Tenn., 1947-54. Past member board trust Vanderbilt U. Served as lt. comdr., air combat intelligence, USNR, World War II. Mem. Vanderbilt Alumni Assn. (dir., past pres., Memphis), Am., Tenn., Memphis and Shelby County, (pres. 1960-61) bar assns., Sigma Alpha Epsilon, Phi Delta Phi. Home: Memphis TN 38103 Died June 19, 1972; buried Calvary Cemetery, Memphis TN

CRESWELL, HARRY I. T., mil. attache; b. Mar. 11, 1891; B.S., Va. Mil. Inst., 1913; grad. advance course, Inf. Sch., 1930, Command and Gen. Staff Sch., 1933. Commd. 2d lt., Inf., 1916; promoted through grades to lt. col., Sept. 22, 1938; now mil. attache, Tokyo, Japan. Address: care Am. Embassy, Tokyo Japan‡

CREWS, LESLIE F., business exec., management cons.; b. New Canton, Ill., Nov. 19, 1896; s. Seneca Watson and Ida May (Sigler) C.; grad. Gem City Bus. Coll., Quincy, Ill., 1917-18; A.B., LaSalle U., 1922; m. Elvira Rach, Sept. 28, 1921; children—Virginia Lee Lofquist, Leslie F. Buyer, Marshall Field & Co., wholesale, Chicago, 1919-21; mem. staff Arthur Young & Co., C.P.A.'s, Chicago, 1921-28; with Montgomery Ward & Co., 1928-49; vice pres. and controller, 1931-33, 45-47, v.p., dir. research, 1948-49; engaged in mgmt. consultancy, 1949-52; v.p., cons. Gamble-Skogmo, Inc., Mpls., 1953, v.p. charge finance. 1954-60, sr. v.p., 1960-65, controller, director, member executive committee, 1954-68, president, chairman of board, 1965-68; chairman board, chief exec. officer Western Land Corp.; dir. Midland National Bank, Mpls., Minn.; director of consumer goods price control Indiana, Illinois, Wisconsin, 1951-52. Officer 329th Field Remount Squadron, World War I. Member International Platform Association, American Legion. Presbyn. Mason (Shriner). Clubs: Edina Country, Minneapolis, Minneapolis Athletic (Mpls.); International (Chgo.). Lectr., writer on evolution in distbn. Home: Edina MN Died 1968.

CRIDLAND, CHARLES, pub. co. exec.; b. Phila., Mar. 5, 1915; s. George Shober and Estelle (Heyland) C.; B.A., U. Pa., 1936; M.B.A., Drexel Inst. Tech., 1949; m. Margery McKay, Nov. 23, 1939; children—Jean (Mrs. John O'Connor), Ruth (Mrs. William A. Brunneli), George. With Matheison, Aitken, C.P.A.'s, Phila., 1936-46; instr. Drexel Inst. Grad. Sch., 1940-61; treas. David McKay Co., 1946-49, pres., 1950; treas. Thomas Nelson, Inc., Camden, N.J., 1950-62, pres., 1962-67, chmn. bd., treas., 1967-70, financial cons., 1970-72; pres. dir. Thomas Nelson & Sons, Toronto, Ont., Can., 1965-68, chmn. bd., 1968-69. Treas. Community Nursing Service of Delaware County, Pa., 1952-62. Served to lt. (s.g.) USNR, 1942-45. C.P.A., Pa. Home: Camden NJ Died Sept. 29, 1972.

CRIPPEN, LLOYD KENNETH, life ins. exec.; b. Jackson, Mich., Jan. 4, 1895; s. Henry Delos and Etta (Davis) C.; student Albion Coll., 1916-17; A.B., U. Mich., 1921; m. Amy Louise Darte, Apr. 21, 1923; children—Kenneth Darte, Davis Allan. Joined Acacia Mut. Life Ins. Co., Washington, 1921, asst. actuary, 1921-32, actuary, 1932-37, v.p., actuary 1937-61, v.p., from 1961. Member Life Office Mgmt. Assn. (v.p. 1943-44, pres. 1944-45), Soc. Actuaries, Middle Atlantic Actuarial Club, Phi Beta Kappa. Mason. Home: Washington DC Died Nov. 27, 1967; buried Rock Creek Cemetery, Washington DC

CRISS, NEIL LOUIS, ins. exec.; b. Sac City, Ia., Aug. 13, 1886; s. James L. and Villa (Wadell) C.; M.D., Creighton U., 1912. With Mutual Benefit Health & Accident Assn., 1910, treas., sr. v.p., med. dir., dir., 1923-66, v.p., med. dir., United Benefit Life Ins. Co., 1926-66 (now Mut. of Omaha Ins. Co.). Mem. Am. Legion. Clubs: Happy Hollow, Omaha Athletic, Elks. Home: Omaha NB Died Apr. 23, 1966; buried Forest Lawn Cemetery Omaha, NB

CRIST, BAINBRIDGE, composer; b. Lawrenceburg, Ind.; Feb. 13, 1883; s. Kendall and Maley (Bainbridge) C.; LL.B., George Washington U., 1906; student Paul Juon, Berlin, Claude Landi, London, Franz Emerich; m. Florence Libbey, Nov. 16, 1909; 1 son, Bainbridge. Admitted to Mass. bar, 1906, practiced in Boston, 1907-12; tchr. singing, Boston, 1915-21, Washington, 1922-23, Florence, Paris, Lucerne, 1923-27. Composer of (symphonic works): La Morte Amoureuse; American Epic, 1620; The Night Remembered; Hymn to Nefertiti; A Leave-Taking; The Parting; Hindu Rhapsody; Festival Overture; Souvenir de Ballet; Egyptian Impressions; Pregiwa's Marriage (ballet); Le Pied de la Momie (ballet); Japanese Nocturne; (songs): Coloured Stars; Leile, Chinese Mother Goose Rhymes; Remember; Into a Ship, Dreaming; Love's Offering; Fairyland; The Mocking Fairy; Evening; By a Silent Shore; Knock on the Door; Noontime; Mistletoe; (choruses); To a Waterfowl; I Come Once More; They Saw the Light; O, My Soul, Awake; He Shall Sustain Thee; Christ, The Only Light; Kate Kearny; (piano): Fantasie in D Major; Egyptian Impressions; Oriental Dances; Nautch Dance; Retrospections; In a Swiss Toy Shop. Mem. Soc. Composers, Authors and Publishers. Mem. Soc. Friends. Club: Friday Morning Music (Washington). Author: The Art of Setting Words to Music, 1945. Editor, revisor: German Diction (by Eva Wilcke), 1929. Contbr. articles to mus. pubs. Home: Washington DC also South Yarmouth MA Died Feb. 7, 1969.

CRITTENDEN, CHRISTOPHER, state ofcl.; b. Wake Forest, N.C., Dec. 1, 1902; s. Charles Christopher and Ethel (Taylor) C.; A.B., Wake Forest Coll., 1921, A.M., 1922, Litt.D., 1956; Ph.D., Yale, 1930; LL.D. (honorary), University North Carolina, 1961, Wake Forest Coll.; m. Janet Quinlan, Sept. 1930; children—Christopher, Robert Hinton, Ann Lane. Prin., pub. sch., Roxobel, N.C., 1922-23; instr. of history, Yale, 1924-25; instr. of history, U. of N.C., 1926-29, asst. prof., 1930-35, dir. N.C. State Dept. of Archives and History (formerly the N.C. Hist. Commn.) since 1935 (on leave, 1946-47, serving as asst. dir. World War II Records project Nat. Archives, Washington); state director, Hist. Records Survey, 1936-37; regional dir. Survey of Fed. Archives, 1936-37; chmn. Conf. of Hist. Socs., 1938-40; pres. Am. Assn. for State and Local History, 1940-42; mem. Am., So. hist. assns., N.C. State Lit. and Hist. Assn. (sec.), soc. Am. Archivists (past pres.), N.C. Folk-Lore Soc., N.C. State Art Soc., N.C. Archeol. Soc. (past pres.), Nat. Trust for Historic Preservation, Phi Beta Kappa (pres. county chpt. 1958-59). Baptist. Club: Watauga (pres. 1956-58). Author, editor histories of N.C. Compiler, editor: Historical Societies in the United States and Canada: A Handbook, 1944. Editor N.C. Hist. Rev., 1935-69. Contbr. articles and reviews to jours. Home: Raleigh NC Died Oct. 13, 1969.

CRITZ, HUGH, educator; b. Starkville, Miss., Dec. 21, 1876; s. Wiley Haman and Nancy America (Moon) C.; B.S., Miss. Agrl. and Mech. Coll. (now Miss. State Coll.), 1896; m. Julia Georgene Gillespie, of Starkville, Miss., Aug. 24, 1899; children—Hugh Melville, Wiley Gillespie, Julia Moon. Teacher in pub. schs., 1896-1902; bookkeeper and head clerk M. L. Smith Co., 1902-03; supt. schs., Starkville, Miss., 1903-06; teacher Miss. Agrl. & Mech. (now Miss. State) Coll., 1906-10, asst. prof. agronomy, 1910-14, dean Sch. of Edn. and registrar, 1914-16, dir. service bur., 1923-25, pres. since 1930; pres. Bolton (Tenn.) Coll., 1916-18, State Agrl. Sch. (now Ark. Polytech. Coll.), Russellville, 1918-23; industrial commr. Miss. Power & Light Co., 1925-30. Mem. Miss. Edn. Assn., Blue Key. Methodist. Mason. Rotarian. Home: State College MI‡

CRITZ, RICHARD, judge; b. Starkville, Miss., Oct. 16, 1877; s. George Edward and Ella C.; student Southwestern U., Georgetown, Tex., 1894-96; m. Nora Lamb, Jan. 18, 1906; children—James Richard, Genevieve (Mrs. J. T. Atkin), Chauncey Edward Ellanora. Admitted to Tex. bar, 1902; practiced at Granger, Tex., 1902-10; city atty., 1906-10; county judge 1910-18; returned to pvt. practice at Taylor, Tex., 1918-26; mem. Tex. State Commn. of Appeals, 1927-35; asso. justice Tex. Supreme Court since 1935. Democrat. Methodist. Mason, K.P. Address: 1602 W. Lynn St., Austin TX*

CROCKER, EDWARD SAVAGE, foreign service officer; b. Fitchburg, Mass., Dec. 20, 1895; A.B., Princeton U., 1918; student Columbia U. Law Sch., 1921-22; m. Lispenard Seabury, May 12, 1923; children—Lispenard Seabury, Katharine Winthrop (dec.). Assistant secretary of Am. del., Conf. on Central Am. Affairs, Washington, 1922-23; apptd. 3d sec., San Salvador, 1923, Warsaw, 1924, Rome, 1925, Budapest, 1926, Stockholm, May 1929; apptd. 2d sec., Stockholm, Oct. 1929, Tokyo, 1933; apptd. 1st sec., Tokyo, 1938; interned in Japan, Dec. 7, 1941-June 17, 1942; returned to U.S. on evacuation vessel, Aug. 25, 1942; apptd. 1st sec., Lisbon, Dec. 1942, counselor, 1944-47; counselor, Warsaw, Poland, 1947 charge d'affaires ad interim, Apr.-Oct. 1948; ambassador to Iraq 1948-52, cons. faculty Air War Coll., Ala., 1952-53, Naval War Coll., Newport, R.I., 1953-55. Served USN, 1917-19. Clubs: Century, Racquet and Tennis, Princeton (New York), Metropolitan, Chevy Chase (Washington). Home: Kittery Point ME Died Apr. 7, 1968.

CROCKETT, ALBERT STEVENS, writer, publicist; b. Solomons, Md., June 19, 1873; s. William Handy and Ada Augusta (Stevens) C.; A.B., Western Md. Coll., 1891; A.M., 1894; studied Harvard; m. Dolores Newkirk Tousey, d. the late Dr. Charles T. Newkirk, June 6, 1905. Teacher pvt. schs. and coll., 1891-99; reporter Phila. Times and Phila. Inquirer, 1899, 1900; N.Y. corr. London Daily Telegraph, 1901; published account of automobile tour of Europe, 1902; chartered steam yacht to cover finish of Internat. Yacht Race for German Kaiser's Cup, 1905; corr. N.Y., Hearld, London and Paris, also spl. corr. and interviewer, South America, 1901-09; columnist N.Y. Sun, until 1912, originator column, Heard in Hotel Corridors, forerunner of syndicated New York columns of later years; interviewer and feature writer with the New York Times, 1912-15 (also served as special corr. in Orient made survey and report on conditions in the Philippines with bearing on ability of the islands to exercise self-govt.), spl. corr., Cuba, 1921; made surveys of European countries for various magazines, 1920-29; v.p., gen. mgr. Bryant Advt. Corp., 1919; editor World Traveler and pres. World Traveler Pub. Co., 1920-24; editorial dir., chmn. bd. Nomad Mag. Pub. Co., 1927-29; news editor Waldorf Astoria, 1915-17 and 1925-29. Clubs: Dutch Treat, Overseas Press, Author numerous books, including: Ghosts of the Old Waldorf, 1929, Peacocks on Parade, 1931; Old Waldorf Bar Days, 1931; Old Waldorf-Astoria Bar Book, 1934. Recipient first prize in Overseas Press Club of America contest for story of newspaper work, 1945. Home: New York City NY Died Nov. 1969.

CROMIE, WILLIAM JAMES, physical instr.; b. New Castle, Pa., Oct. 27, 1875; s. Robert and Annie (Beck) C.; ed. pub. schs. and Y.M.C.A. and Harvard summer schs.; Sc.D., 1920; m. Erma Gertrude Apple, of New Castle, Pa., Aug. 4, 1898; 1 dau., Erma Kathryn. Phys. dir. Y.M.C.A., New Castle, Pa., 1896, Aurora, Ill., 1897-98, Easton, Pa., 1899-1902, Germantown, Phila., 1903-04, 1905-06; instr. in gymnastics, 1907-12, in physical edn., 1913-16, acting dir. phys. edn., 1915-16, asst. dir., 1919-25, asst. dir. and asst. prof. phys. edn. since 1925, U. of Pa.; also dir. summer sch. course in phys. edn., U. of Pa. Instr. R.O.T.C. in U. of Pa., 1917; attended Bayonet and P.T. Sch., Ottawa, Can., 1918; instr. Central Bayonet and Physical Training Sch., S.A.T.C., Princeton U.; athletic dir. Camp Eustis, Va., 1918; instr. U. of Pa. S.A.T.C. and Naval Unit. Mem. Am. Physical Edn. Soc., Soc. Physical Edn. in Colls., Phi Epsilon Kappa, Sigma Pi. Republican. Presbyn. Mason. Author: Keeping Physically Fit, 1915; Gymnastics in Education, 1925; Volley Ball in School and College, 1937; also series of 12 pamphlets on phys. exercises for promotion of health; 325 group contests for army, navy and school, 1918. Contbr. to Outlook, Saturday Evening Post, Woman's Home Companion, American Magazine, etc. Home: 5324 Reinhard St., West Philadelphia PA‡

CROMMELIN, HENRY, naval officer; b. Montgomery, Ala., Aug. 11, 1904; s. John Geraerdt and Katherine Vasser (Gunter) C.; student U. Ala., 1920-21; B.S., U.S. Naval Acad., 1925; m. Sally Huntress Clendening, July 14, 1934; children—Diane, Henry, Sally, Harriet, Commd. ensign U.S.N., 1925, advanced through ranks to rear adm., 1952; assigned battleships, destroyers, 1925-33, 1936-40; staff U.S., Naval Acad., 1933-36; bur. personnel Navy Dept., 1940-42, 1945-46; comdr. destroyer division, destroy-Atlantic, 1947-48; attached Naval Base, Guantanamo Bay, Cuba 1950-51; comdr. cruiser U.S.S. Des Moines 1950-51; staff, comdr. in chief Pacific, 1951-52; asst. chief naval operations personnel, 1952-56; comdr. Battleship Div. 2, 1956-57; comdr. naval base, Newport, R.I., from 1957. Decorated Silver Star, Bronze Star with combat V. Club: Army-Navy Country (Washington). Home: Montgomery AL Died Mar. 1971.

CROMWELL, ARTHUR DAYTON, prof. agriculture; b. Oakland Valley, Ia., Sept. 29, 1869; s. Frank C. and Elizabeth (Clinesmith) C.; student Hastings (Neb.) Coll., 1890-93; U. of Neb., 1894; studied U. of Chicago, U. of Pa.; hon. M.Ph., Humboldt (Ia.) Coll., 1912; m. Sarah E. Wright, of Fort Dodge, Ia., June 25, 1895; children—Seymour B., Helen, Gertrude. Formerly mgr. Chester Co. (Pa.) Farm Bur. (now mem. exec. com.); prof. agr. and edn., Humboldt Coll., Ia., 1896; sent by Dept. of Agr. to teach agr. to teachers in Porto Rico, 1912; head of rural dept. of State Teachers Coll., West Chester, Pa., also prof. of agriculture and rural sociology. Republican. Conglist. Author: Practical Child Study, 1896; Student's United States History Outline, 1900; Agriculture and Life, 1915; Alfalfa for New England, 1915; Alfalfa and Other Legumes, 1916. Lecturer on agrl. and sch. topics. Home: West Chester PA‡

CROMWELL, FREDERICK, govt. ofcl.; b. Prescott, Ariz., Feb. 23, 1909; s. Frederick N. and Alice M. (Hooper) C.; A.B., U. Ariz., 1935; A.M., Stanford, 1937; library certificate, U. Cal., 1938; m. Elizabeth McPhee Wright, July 18, 1942; children—Sallie Elizabeth (Mrs. Cromwell Griffin), Eleanor, Carol. Asst. librarian Eastern Wash. Coll. Edn., Cheney, 1938-39, U. Ariz., 1939-42, librarian, 1942-52; dir. U.S. Information Service libraries, Spain, 1952-56; public affairs officer, Sevilla, 1956-57; cultural affairs attache Am. Embassy, Bogota, Colombia, South America, 1958-59; with Dept. State, Washington, 1960-64; dir. American Cultural Libraries, Japan, 1964-67; asst. cultural affairs officer USIS, Paris, 1967-69. Director American Library Association International Relations Office, Washington, 1947-48 (on leave from U. Ariz.). Fellow U. Chgo. Grad. Library Sch., 1946. Mem. A.L.A. (council 1945-50, 1952-56), Phi Beta Kappa, Phi Kappa Phi, Phi Gamma Delta. Editor of Arizona Quarterly (review of lit., history and folklore), 1945. Home: Tucson AZ Died Feb. 5, 1969.

CROMWELL, MICHAEL JENKINS, importer; b. nr. Balt., Oct. 25, 1901; s. William Kennedy and Sally (Franklin) C.; A.B., Johns Hopkins, 1923; m. Maria McEvoy, Aug. 17, 1929; children—Michael Jenkins, P. McEvoy, Maria (Mrs. Linton S. Marshall Jr.), Anne, Kitty. Clk., Merchant & Minero S.S. Co., 1924-27; real estate salesman Roland Park Co., 1927-30; pres. P. J. McEvoy, Inc., Balt., 1930-68; chmn. Loyola Fed. Savs. & Loan Assn., 1950-68; advisory dir., mem. trust com. Maryland National Bank; director Baltimore Equitable Soc. Dir. Balt. Hearing Society, 1953-68; trustee Provident Hosp., 1951-68, Johns Hopkins U., 1956-68; chmn. adv. bd. Mercy Hosp.; dir. Balt. Assn. Commerce. Served as capt. USMC Res., 1943-44. Decorated Knight of St. Gregory. Mem. S.R. Democrat. Roman Catholic. Home: Lutherville MD Died Apr. 30, 1968.

CRONE, FRANK LINDEN, educator; b. Kendallville, Ind., July 19, 1875; s. John S. and Ella (Weaver) C.; A.B., Ind. U., 1897, A.M., 1921; m. Luetta V. Stahl, of Avilla, Ind., Jan. 21, 1911. Teacher high schs. until 1901; went to P.I. as teacher pub. schs., 1901, becoming asst. dir. edn., P.I., 1909-13, dir. edn., 1913-16; in charge ednl. dept. Gen. Brokerage Co., Grand Forks, N.Dak., 1917-18; rep. Bur. War Trade Intelligence, San Francisco, Calif., 1918-19; dir. schoolhouse constrn., 1921-24, regional dir. instrn., 1921-22, dir. gen. of instrn., 1922-24, for Peruvian Govt.; with D.C. Heath and Co., since 1925. Fellow Royal Geog. Soc.; mem. Phi Beta Kappa, Phi Delta Kappa, S.R. Home: Kendallville, Ind. Address: 1600 Monument Av., Richmond VA‡

CRONE, R. BERTRAM, college pres.; b. Cedar County, Ia., Jan. 7, 1871; s. Henry and Rebecca A. (Arnold) C.; Ph.B., State U. of Ia., 1897; student State U. of Ia. Coll. of Law 1 yr.; (LL.D., Coe Coll., Cedar Rapids, Ia., 1917); m. Elizabeth H. Hulsebus, of Burlington, Ia., July 26, 1899. Teacher country schs., 1890-3; prin. schs., Churdan, Ia., 1897-8, Fonda, 1898-9; supt. schs., Tipton, Ia., 1899-03, Washington, 1903-8, Ft. Dodge, 1908-12; pres. Hastings Coll. since July 15, 1912; mem. N.E.A., Neb. State Teachers' Assn., Neb. Peace Soc. (v.-p.). Presbyn. Mason. Home: Hastings NE‡

CRONEIS, CAREY, educator, geologist; b. Bucyrus, Ohio, Mar. 14, 1901; s. Frederick William and Nell (Garner) C.; B.S., Denison U., 1922, D.Sc., 1945; M.S., U. of Kan., 1923; Ph.D., Harvard, 1928; LL.D., Lawrence College, 1944, Beloit College, 1954; D.Sc. (honorary), Ripon College, 1945; D.Eng. (honorary), Colorado School of Mines, 1949; L.H.D. (honorary), Tampa University, 1964; D.Sc., Tex. Christian U., 1965, Tex. Tech., 1967; D.Sc., Beloit College, 1968; married to Grace Williams, on September 15th, 1923; children—Christine (Mrs. Wm. C. Sayres), Catherine (Mrs. Theodore Alfred). Instructor in geology at Kansas, U. of 1922-23, Ark. U., 1923-25, Harvard and Wellesley Coll., 1927-28; geol. surveys Ark., Kan., Ill.; asst. prof. geology, U. of Chicago, 1928-31, asso. prof., 1931-41, prof. 1941-44, also curator paleontology, Walker Mus., U. of Chicago, 1928-44; pres. Beloit (Wis.) Coll. 1944-54; provost, Harry C. Wiess prof., Rice University Houston 1954-60, acting pres., 1960-61, chancellor, 1961-71; cons. Nat. Defense Research Com., 1943-44. Mem. Beloit Coll.-Logan Mus. Expdn. to Colombia, 1947. Designed geology sect., Mus. of Science and Industry, Chicago; in charge geology sect. (1933), and chief of basic sciences (1934), A Century of Progress Expn., Chicago. Mem. com. math., physics, engring. sciences, Nat. Scientific Found., 1954-56; mem. sci. information council NSF, from 1969. Mem. com. on edn. Internat. Geophysical Year. Mem. panel sci. and tech. manpower Pres.' Sci. Adv. Com., 1962-64; adv. com. grad. edn. U.S. Office of Edn., 1964-66. Pres. bd. dirs. Gulf Univs. Research Corp., 1964-66. Mem. academic bd. U.S. Naval Acad.; chmn. Houston City Charter Com. Bd. dirs. Grad. Research Center S.W.; chmn. bd. educators United Educators, Chicago, American Society Oceanography. Erasmus Haworth award University of Kansas, 1952, Distinguished Alumni award, 1962; citation, Govt. Guatemala, 1956; Sidney Powers award Am. Assn. Petroleum Geologists, 1967; also Founder's medal of Austin College, 1968. Trustee Kinkaid Sch.; dir., former chmn. bd. Houston Mus. Contemporary Art; dir. Nat. Hist. Mus. Houston; v.p. Nat. Space Hall Fame, Houston, 1968; chmn. edn. subcom. Tex. Constn. Revision Com. Fellow A.A.A.S., Geol. Soc. of America, Am. Geol. Inst. (pres. 1951-52), American Association Petroleum Geologists, The Academy of Texas (charter mem.), Paleontology Society Am. (v.p. 1937), Houston C. of C. (past dir.), Houston Symphony Soc. (dir.), Houston Council World Affairs (pres. 1962-63), National Association Geology Teachers (pres. 1959-60), Society Econ. Paleontologists and Mineralogists (pres. 1940-41), Chicago Literary Club, Phi Delta Theta, Phi Beta Kappa, Sigma Xi, Phi Eta Sigma, Omicron Delta Kappa. Mason. Clubs: River Oaks Country, The Houston Petroleum (honorary). Editor of the Harper &Brothers Geoscience Series since 1941; associate editor of the Journal of Geology, 1930-45. Author: Paleozoic Geology of Arkansas; Down to Earth (with W. C. Krumbein); also numerous scientific articles and reviews. Home: Houston TX Died Jan. 22, 1972.

CRONYN, GEORGE WILLIAM, dramatist; b. Anderson, Ind., July 12, 1888; s. William and Carrie B. (Chittenden) C.; student Harvard, 1909-11, Cornell U. Agrl. Coll., 1912, Columbia, 1906-08, 1916-17; B.A., Columbia, 1916, M.A., 1917; m. Allura Miller, of Mt. Hood, Ore., Mar. 15, 1914; children—Kathleen, Marshall, George, Naissa. In charge art dept. Hebrew Sheltering Guardian Soc., Pleasantville, N.Y., 1912-13; rancher, Hood River, Ore., 1913-14; stage mgr., scene designer, Little Theatre Co., Indianapolis, Ind., 1915-16; teacher English, De Witt Clinton High Sch., N.Y. City, 1916-17; prof. English and drama, U. of Mont., 1924-25; was teacher of English and Drama, Oakland Tech. High Sch.; with Willy Pogany Studio, 1927. Exhibited paintings at Portland, (Ore.) Art Musuem, 1914, John Herron Art Inst., Indianapolis, 1915, San Francisco Expn., 1915, Internat. Exhbn. of Scenic Design, New York, 1926. Author: Poems, 1914; The Greaser, one-act play, prod. at Cort Theatre, New York, Dec. 1914; The Sandbar Queen, one-act play, prod. by the Washington Square Players, New York, 1917-18; Civic Christmas Pageant, play, prod. St. Paul, Minn., Dec. 1919. 49 (novel), 1925. Edited The Path on the Rainbow (Indian Poems), 1918; Raoul, the Troubadour (drama), 1922; one-act plays (Frank Shay), 1920-27. Home: Bronxville NY Died May 1969.

CROOKS, ALEXANDER RICHARD, tenor; b. Trenton; s. Alexander Struthers and Elizabeth (Gore) C.; ed. high sch., Trenton; Mus.D., Temple U., Lafayette Coll.; m. Mildred Wallace Pine, July 23, 1921; children—Patricia, Richard. Began as boy soprano soloist in ch.; made debut as boy soprano with Mme. Schumann-Heink, Asbury Park, N.J., 1910; debut as tenor with N.Y. Symphony Orch., Walter Damrosch, condr., 1922; European concert tours, 1924-38; operatic debut in Tosca, Hamburg (Germany) Opera, 1927; debut Met. Opera, N.Y.C., 1933; concert tour of Australia, New Zealand and Tazmania, 1936. Served as cadet flying officer, Air Service, U.S. Army, World War I. Episcopalian. Home: Portola Valley CA Died Sept. 29, 1972.

CROOKS, RICHARD M., corp. exec.; b. Seabright, N.J., 1905. Vice pres., dir. Thompson & McKinnon, Auchincloss, Inc. N.Y.C. Trustee N.Y. Stock Exchange Gratuity Fund. Home: Brielle NJ Died Jan. 29, 1973.

CROSAS, ANDRES BERNARDINO, judge; b. of Am. parents, San Juan, P.R., Apr. 4, 1877; s. Eduardo Esteban and Ellen Elizabeth (Graham) C.; A.B., St. John's Coll. (now Fordham U.), Fordham, N.Y., 1897; student New York Law Sch., 1897-1900; m. Amanda Munoz Sassot, of Malaga, Spain, July 25, 1912. Admitted to N.Y. bar, 1900, bar of Porto Rico, 1900; referee in bankruptcy, 1901-8; apptd. spl. asst. atty. gen. of P.R. for Dist. of Humanacao, 1902; U.S. commr., 1909-10; atty. for P.R. Irrigation Service, 1910-16; judge Dist. Court of P.R., Dist. of Aguadilla, since July 11, 1916; mem. Dem. Nat. Com. for P.R., 1916-20. Catholic. Elk. Home: Aguadilla PR‡

CROSBY, EDWIN L., administrator; b. Rochester, N.Y., Aug. 18, 1908; s. Edwin Lorenzo and Alice H. (Hammond) C.; A.B., Union Coll., 1929; M.D., Albany Med. Coll., 1933; M.P.H., Johns Hopkins U., 1936, Dr. P.H., 1937; D.Sc. (honorary), Union College, N.Y., 1955; m. Harriet O. O'Neil, May 20, 1930; children—Ruth, Ann, Sue. With N.Y. State Dept. of Health, Albany, 1935-39; asst. prof. biostatistics, preventive med. adjunct prof. pub. health adminstrn., dir. Johns Hopkins Hosp., 1946-52; dir. Joint Commn. on Accreditation of Hosps., 1952-54; chmn. Nat. Intern Matching Plan; pres. Adv. Bd. for Med. Specialties, 1960-63; pres. Am. Hosp. Assn., Chgo., 1952-53, chief exec. officer, 1954-72. Mem. adv. bd. Salvation Army. Diplomate Am. Bd. of Preventive Medicine and Pub. Health. Fellow Am. Pub. Health Assn., Am. Coll. Hosp. Adminstrs., A.M.A.; mem. Internat. Hosp. Fedn. (pres. 1963-67), Nat. Health Council (pres. 1964). Contbr. to hosp. and med. jours. Home: Winnetka IL Died Feb 20, 1972.

CROSBY, EVERETT NATHANIEL, personal bus. mgr.; b. Roslyn, Wash., Apr. 5, 1900; s. Harry L. and Catherine C. (Harrigan) C.; student Gonzaga U.; m. Florence George Guthrie, May 9, 1939; 1 dau., Mary Sue (Mrs. Charles D. Shannon, Jr.). Mgr., Bing Crosby, 1929-72; pres. Bing Crosby Enterprises, Everett Crosby Prodns.; v.p. Northwest Leasing Corp.; dir. Astor Pictures, N.Y.C., Sprayfoil Corp., Mpls.; sec. Crosby Investment Co. Served with AEF, World War I. Address: Los Angeles CA Deceased.

CROSBY, WILLIAM HUGH, mfr.; b. Unionville, Ont., Can., Aug. 3, 1862; s. Hugh Powell and Harriet (White) C.; ed. high sch. and Normal Sch., Ont.; m. Emma Newton, 1890. Naturalized citizen, 1888. Chmn. bd. The Crosby Co., sheet metal stamping; chmn. bd. Molin Corp. Alderman, Buffalo, 2 yrs. Mem. District Bd. No. 3, Western Federal Dist., 1917-18, World War. Republican. Conglist. Clubs: Buffalo, Canoe (Buffalo). Address: 170 Franklin St., Buffalo NY‡

CROSLAND, JOHN EVERETT, mgmt. cons.; b. Bennetsville, S.C., Jan. 3, 1902; s. Jack Weatherly and Annie Cole (Everett) C.; grad. Clemson A. and M. Coll., 1923; m. Geneva Evelyn Stroud, Oct. 29, 1938. With Pacific Mills, from 1923, beginning with tng. course, Lawrence, Mass., successively asst. foreman Lyman Div. Finishing Plant, foreman, asst. supt., supt., v.p., gen. mgr., 1923-55, v.p., gen. mgr. Lyman Printing & Finishing Co., Lyman, S.C., 1955-57, management consultant, from 1957. Served as executive committeeman for Spartanburg County, State Dem. Com., 1948-52; mem. Spartanburg County Bd. Control, 1954-—. Club: Lyman Democratic (pres. 1946-—). Home: Lyman SC Died June 1, 1971; buried Wood Meml. Park, Greer SC

CROSS, E(THAN) A(LLEN), educator, author; b. Campbell Hill, Ill., July 22, 1875; s. Thomas J. and Minnie D. (Carson) C.; student Southern Illinois University, 1893-95; A.B., U. of Ill., 1905; A.M., U. of Chicago, 1906; Ph.D., Columbia, 1926; Litt.D., U. of Colo., 1939; L.H.D., Colo. State Coll. of Edn., 1940; m. Mae Miller, June 27, 1899; children—Carl Allen (dec.), Neal Miller. Prof. lit. and English 1906-41, dean, 1917-26, vice pres., 1926-31, head div. of lit. and languages, 1933-40, emeritus since 1941, Colo. State Coll. of Edn., Greeley; instr. Air Corps Tech. Training Command, Greeley, Colo., 1942-43; prof. English lit., U. of Colo., 1943-44, Atlanta Univ., summer 1945. Mem. Nat. Council Teachers of English (president, 1939-40), also Phi Beta Kappa. Conglist. Author: The Short Story, 1914; (with Nellie Margaret Statler) Story-Telling, 1917; The Little Grammar, 1922; The Cross English Test, 1923; The Little Book of English Composition, 1925; Fundamentals in English, 1925; A Book of the Short Story, 1934; World Literature, 1935; Teaching English in High Schools (with Elizabeth Carney), 1939. General editor 7 vols., Literature: a series of anthologies, 1943-47; Wings for You (for the C.A.A.), 1942. Contbr. to ednl. jours., lit. mags. and revs. Home: 1916 Glenmere Blvd., Greeley CO‡

CROSS, JOHN W(ALKER), lawyer; b. Sheldon, Mo., Aug. 29, 1902; s. John William and Sarah Juliza (Warnick) C.; B.S., Kan. State Tchrs. Coll., 1924; LL.B., George Washington U., 1931; m. 2d, Agnes Hoerner, Sept. 24, 1963; children by previous marriage—Carol, John Earle. Sec. C. of C., Dodge City, Kan., 1924-27; sec. Hon. Clifford Hope, mem. Congress, 1928-31; admitted to D.C. bar, 1930; partner Denning & Cross, Washington, 1931-47, Cummings, Stanley, Truitt &Cross, 1947-55, Cross, Murphy & Smith, 1955-71; gen. counsel Govt. Services, Inc., Washington, 1934-71; counsel Air Transit Services, Inc., Washington: dir., Washington counsel Nat. Airlines, Inc of Miami, Fla., 1938-71; Washington counsel Boyce-Harvey Machinery Co., Baton Rouge. Mem. Am., D.C. bar assns., Kappa Delta Pi, Delta Tau Delta, Delta Theta Phi, Pi Kappa Delta. Republican. Presbyn. Clubs: Metropolitan, Congressional Country, Nat. Aviation, Capitol Hill, International (Washington). Home: Bethesda MD Died Oct. 1971.

CROSS, LEWIS JOSEPHUS, chemist; b. Hoosick Falls, N.Y., Oct. 15, 1874; s. Waite J. and Hannah M. (Scriven) C.; A.B., Cornell, 1909, Ph.D., 1912; m. Jessie B. Kerr, of Adams, Mass., Dec. 23, 1915. Asst. prof. chemistry, 1912-14, prof. 1914-23, Cornell U.; research chemist N.Y. State Dept. Farms and Markets since 1923. Developed process of pectin mfr. Editor Cornell Chemist, 1912-14. Mem. Am. Chem. Soc., Sigma Xi, Gamma Alpha. Republican. Presbyn. Mason. Home: 933 E. State St., Ithaca NY‡

CROSS, OLIVER HARLAN, congressman; b. Eutaw, Ala., July 13, 1870; s. James F. and Margarett (Dunlap) C.; A.B., U. of Ala., 1891, studied Law Sch., 1892-93; m. Mary Watt, of Waco, Tex., Apr. 24, 1907; children—Harlan Watt, Mary Augusta. Teacher, pub. schs., Union Springs, Ala., 1891-92; admitted to N.M. bar, 1893, and began practice at Deming; moved to McGregor, Tex., 1894; city atty., McGregor, 1895-96; moved to Waco, Tex., 1896; asst. county atty., McLennan Co., Tex., 1898-1902, dist. atty., 1902-06; retired from practice, 1917, and devoted time to farming interests. Mem. Tex. Ho. of Rep., 1900; mem. 71st to 74th Congresses (1929-37), 11th Tex. Dist. Member Delta Kappa Epsilon. Democrat. Presbyn. Mason, Odd Fellow. Clubs: Karem, City. Home: Overlook Place, Waco TX‡

CROSS, WALTER SNELL, C.S. practitioner; b. Fitchburg, Mass.; s. Charles A. and Sarah F. (Wright) C.; student Phillips Acad., Andover, Mass., 1900, Yale, 1904; m. Ruth Chadwick Crosby, June 26, 1920. Christian Sci. practitioner, Baltimore, 1906-18, com. on publ. for State of Md., 1915-18, practitioner, Fitchburg,

Mass. since 1920, pres. The Mother Ch., The First Church of Christ Scientist, Boston, 1950. Chaplain, U.S. Army, World War I. Member Psi Upsilon, Skull and Bones (Yale). Club: Yale (Boston). Address: Fitchburg MA Died June 8, 1971.

CROSSLAND, PAUL MARION, physician; b. Wayne, Neb., June 8, 1904; s. George Washington and Mary Katrina (Schonlau) C.; student Wayne State Tchrs. Coll., 1922-25; A.B., U. Minn., 1926, M.B., 1930, M.D., 1931; postgrad. (fellow) Stanford Sch. Medicine, 1951-52; m. Harriet Kent Dueringer, Sept. 20, 1959; 1 son by previous marriage, William. Commd. lt. (j.g.), M.C., USN, 1930, advanced through grades to capt., 1948; intern U.S. Naval Hosp., San Diego, 1930-31; resident in surgery U.S. Naval Hosp., Newport, R.I., 1939; sr. med. officer U.S. Lend Lease Base, Argentia, Nfld., 1941, USS Montpelier, 1942-43; base med. officer Russell Island, 1943-44; exec. officer U.S. Naval Hosp., Sampson, N.Y., 1944-45; 1st med. officer in command U.S. Naval Hosp., Guantanamo Bay, Cuba, 1946-48; resident in dermatology N.Y. Poly. Med. Sch. and Hosp., 1949-51; practice medicine specializing in dermatology, Santa Rosa, Cal., 1952-69; lectr. dir. dermatology Stanford, Palo Alto, Cal., 1951-53, clin. instr., 1953-55, asst. clin. prof., 1955-59, associate clinical professor, 1959-65, clinical professor dermatology, 1965-69; courtesy staff Meml. Hosp., Santa Rosa; active staff Community Hosp., Santa Rosa, 1952-69, chief dept. dermatology and syphilology, 1955, 58, 60, 62, 65, 67, skin clinic and tumor bd. cons., 1952-68, chmn. pharmacy com., 1957-68, exec. com., 1957-59; courtesy staff Warrack Hosp., Santa Rosa, 1960-69, Stanford Hosp., Palo Alto, 1952-68; staff Presbyn. Hosp., San Francisco, 1961-69. Crossland Lab. at Stanford U. dedicated in his honor, 1970. Diplomate Am. Bd. Dermatology, dermatology sect. Pan Am. Med. Assn. Fellow Am. Acad. Dermatology (dir. 1960-63, chmn. com. nominations 1957, 59, membership com. 1958-63, dir. spl. grad. course 1958-65, mil. affairs com., 1963-64, chmn. com. ionizing radiations 1960-69; mem. Am., Cal (chmn. sect. dermatology 1965-66) med. assns., Internat. Soc. Tropical Dermatology, Am. Dermatol. Assn., Sonoma County Med. Soc., Pacific, San Francisco dermatol. socs., Soc. Investigative Dermatology, Am. Cancer Soc. (dir. Sonoma County br. 1956-68), Acacia, Phi Beta Pi. Republican. Methodist. Mason (32 degree). Author: (with A.C. Cipollaro) X-rays and Radium in the Treatment of Diseases of the Skin, 1967. Contributor articles to med. jours., pamphlets. Home: Santa Rosa CA Died Sept. 30, 1968; buried Memorial Park, Santa Rosa CA

CROSSLEY, ARTHUR WEBSTER, engr.; bus. exec.; b. Somerset, Colo., Dec. 16, 1908; s. George Lewis and Sarah Elizabeth (Jowett) C.; B.S., Franklin Inst., 1928; LL.B., Southeastern U., 1939; LL.M., M.P.L., 1940, B.C.S., 1941; m. Margaret M. Neu, Oct. 15, 1932; children—Anne Jowett, Jane Elizabeth, Susan Margaret. Engr. Dennison Mfg. Co., 1928-30, Washington Gas Light Co., 1930-33, H.J. Saunders (cons. engr.), Washington, 1933-34, Pub. Utilities Commn., D.C., 1935-38; asst. dir., chief engr. Pub. Works, D.C., 1938-40, dir., 1940-41; asst. gen. mgr. Potomac Electric Co., 1941-48; treas. Diamond Alkali Co., 1948-55; dir. finance Theo. Hamm Brewing Co., St. Paul, Minn., 1956-60, v.p. finance, 1960-68, sec., dir., 1965-68; chmn. bd. Marquette Corp., from 1969. Served as col. chemical corps AUS, 1942-45. Decorated Legion of Merit with oak leaf cluster, Commendation medal with 2 clusters. Mem. A.I.M. Club: Army-Navy (Washington). Home: Burnsville MN Died Apr. 2, 1971; buried Fort Snelling Nat. Cemetery, Minneapolis MN

CROSSLEY, JAMES JUDSON, lawyer; b. Crawford Township, Madison County, Ia., Aug. 31, 1869; s. John Wesley and Cynthia Jane (Hardy) C.; Des Moines Coll., Ia; A.B., State U. of Ia., 1891, A.M., 1897; post-grad. study, Yale, 1897-99; LL.B., U. of Ia. Law Sch., 1900; m. Cherry L. Hyde, Aug. 10, 1910 (dec. July 3, 1932); children—Helen, Jane Hannah, Alice Cherry; m. 2d, Minerva K. Brouillette Brown, May 1, 1934 (dec. Nov. 20, 1944); step-children—Helen, Edwin. Supt. public schools, Madison County, Iowa, 1894-98; began practice at Winterset, Ia., June 6, 1900; mem. Ia. State Senate, sessions, 1900, 02, 04, 06, 07; U.S. atty. 4th Div. of Alaska, 1908-14; resumed practice at Portland, Ore., 1914. Republican. Capt. Co. G, 55th Regt. Iowa Nat. Guard, 1901-04; capt. Co. C, 162d Inf., with A.E.F. 18 mos. in France, Belgium and Germany; was in Champagne, Oise-Aisne and Argonne offensives; promoted to lt. col.; served with 41st (Sunset"), 42d (Rainbow"), and 6th (regular) divs. Comdr. Portland Post No. 1, Am. Legion, 1922. Mem. Am. Bar Assn., Ore. State Bar (vice-pres.), 1941-42, Vets. of Foreign Wars, Mil. Order World War, Am. Legion, Phi Delta Phi. Conglist. Mason (32 deg.), O.E.S. (past patron), Alaskan Sourdoughs. Home: 3916 N Concord Av. Office: American Bank Bldg., Portland OR*

CROSSLEY, ROBERT PIERCE, magazine editor; b. near Council Bluffs, Iowa, January 1st 1914; son Bruce William and Mary Mitchell (Wilson) C.; graduated in printing Los Angeles Trade-Tech. Jr. College, 1931; B.S., Iowa State Univ., 1939; m. Mary Elizabeth

Hansen, Sept. 5, 1937; children—Sheila Mary, Margaret Jane. Editor, pub. Denison (Ia.) Review, 1939-45; asso. editor, dir. family life dept. Better Homes and Gardens, 1946-51; lectr. mag. journalism Ia. State Univ., 1948-51; editor Household, 1951-57; editorial dir. Capper's Farmer, 1952-55; Better Living editor McCall's magazine, 1957-58, executive editor, 1958-60; exec. editor Woman's Day, 1960; editor Popular Sci., 1962-64; dir. Popular Science Publishing Co., 1963-64; mag. cons., free-lance writer 1965; editor Popular Mechanics magazine, from 1966. Served as lieutenant (j.g.) with USNR, 1944-46, signal officer U.S.S. Concord. Member American Agrl. Editors Assn., Sigma Delta Chi, Alpha Zeta, Gamma Sigma Delta, Phi Kappa Phi, Cardinal Key. Home: Stamford CT Died Feb. 6, 1972; buried Council Bluffs IA

CROSSMAN, JEROME KENNETH, lawyer, corp. exec.; b. Gainesville, Tex., Sept. 14, 1896; s. Bernard and Sarah (Goodman) C.; LL.B., U. Tex., 1918; m. Pauline Gans, Sept. 8, 1920; children—Betty, Stanley. Admitted to Tex. bar, 1917; with firm Scurlock, Crossman & Dale, Wichita Falls, Tex., 1918-19; private practice of law, Dallas, Texas, 1919-72. Dir. Republic National Bank of Dallas, Lomas & Nettleton Financial Corp., Inc., Gt. Am. Res. Ins. Co. Pres. Dallas Citizens Interracial Association. Mem. bd. govs. Menninger Foundation; trustee Tex. Research Found., Southwestern Legal Found.; dir. Nat. Conf. Christians and Jews, Dallas Theatre Center, Inc., Greater Dallas Planning Council, Educational Television Foundation, Texas Psychiatric Found., Children's Devel. Center, Dallas Council World Affairs; adv. council W.A.I.F.; mem. adv. council Girl Scouts Am., Citizens Charter Assn.; chmn. bd. Dallas Heart Assn., 1950-54. Dir. Children's Hosp. of Tex.; trustee, v.p. Nat. Jewish Hosp., Denver. Mem. Tex. State adv. com. Civil Rights Commn. Recipient Linz award for outstanding civic work in Dallas, 1954, Headliner of Year award Press Club Dallas, 1954. Mem. Am., Dallas bar assns., State Bar Tex., Dallas C. of C. (pres. 1954-55, dir.). Jewish religion (temple trustee). Home: Dallas TX Died 1972.

CROTT, HOMER DANIEL, lawyer; b. Oakland, Cal., Mar. 15, 1899; s. Daniel and Mary Frances (O'Connor) C.; A.B., U. Cal., 1920, J.D., 1922; LL.M., Harvard, 1923; LL.D., Trinity Coll., U. Dublin (Ireland); L.H.D., Cal. Western U., 1964; m. Ida Hull Lloyd, May 12, 1934; children—Daniel Lloyd, Mary Elizabeth, Anne Lloyd, Peter Lloyd. Asst. to dir. Chabot Obs., Oakland, Cal., 1917-22; with Gibson Dunn & Crutcher, L.A., 1923-72, mem. firm, 1930-72; spl. asst. to U.S. Atty. Gen., 1953-55; lectr. on legal profession Law Sch. U. So. Cal., 1952-63; dir. Lloyd Corp. Ltd., Parkview Apts. Trustee emeritus Claremont U. Center; dir. I.N. and Susannah H. Van Nuys Found., 1943-72, pres., 1945-70; dir. and Southwest Mus.; mem. council fellows Pierpont Morgan Library, 1959-62; chmn. bd. trustees Henry E. Huntington Library and Art Gallery, 1957-72. Dir. emeritus Los Angeles World Affairs Council. Fellow Am. Bar Found.; mem. Internat., Inter-Am., Am. (chmn. sect. on legal edn. 1959-60), Los Angeles County bar assns., State Bar Cal. (pres. 1950-51), A.A.A.S., Am. Law Inst. (com. legal edn. 1948-51, mem. council, 1956—). Am. Soc. Internat. Law, Am. Judicature Soc. (dir., v.p. 1953-59), Assn. Ind. Cal. Colls. and Univs. (trustee 1955-63), Assn. Bar City N.Y., Inst. Jud. Adminstrn., Inc., Council Fgn. Relations, Los Angeles Com. Fgn. Relations, Am. Acad. Social Sci., Honnold Library Soc. (dir.), Astron. Soc. Pacific, Selden Soc. (council mem.) (London), Stair Soc. (Edinburgh), Cal., So. Cal. hist. socs., Order of Coif, Tau Kappa Epsilon. Republican. Clubs: California, Chancery, Sunset (pres. 1956) Stock Exchange, Town Hall, Zamarano, Jonathan; Harvard (So. Cal.; N.Y.); Grolier, (N.Y.C.); Commonwealth (San Francisco); Valley Hunt, Athenaeum (Pasadena). Author: Glimpses of Don Quixote and La Mancha, 1963. Home: San Marino CA Died Mar. 29, 1972.

CROUCH, SYDNEY JAMES LEONHARDT, clergyman; b. Perth, West Australia, Aug. 20, 1889; s. Charles James and Maryann Naomi (Hall) C.; came to U.S., 1913, naturalized, 1930; student Scotch Coll., Perth, 1910; Biblical Sem., N.Y. City, 1913-15; B.D., Hartford Theol. Sem., 1922; Th.D., Union Theol. Sem., Richmond, Va., 1937; L.H.D., Clemson Agrl. Coll., 1959; m. Katy Austin, Nov. 13, 1916; children—Alexander Charles, Douglas Sydney. Sec. fgn. dept. Internat. Com. of Y.M.C.A., Egypt and Palestine, 1915-18, World War I.; in charge survey of Mohammedan North Africa, Internchurch World Movement, N.Y. City, 1919-20; ordained to ministry of Congl. Church, 1922; pastor, Westminster, Vt., 1922-25, Fort Hill Presbyn. Ch., Clemson Coll., S.C. 1925-69; head dept. of Bible Clemson Coll., 1929-69, prof. internat. relations, 1937-69, chmn. com. on ethics and religion, 1940-69. Moderator Synod of South, 1942. Recipient Algernon S. Sullivan award Clemson Coll. 1957, Distinguished Service Scroll of Honor, 1957, named hon. alumnus, 1958. Hon. mem. Blue Key. Presbyterian. Mason. Book reviewer, Interpretation, Richmond, 1938-69. Mem. gen. assembly's adv. com. on Christian Edn., Presbyn. Ch., U.S., 1936-69. Home: Clemson SC Died Aug. 13, 1969; buried Cemetery Hill, Clemson U., Clemson SC

CROUSE, MARY ELIZABETH, author; b. at Phila., Pa., Nov. 3, 1873; d. Henry William and S. Jennie (Thornton) C.; ed. pvt. schs., Phila. and N.J., Packer Collegiate Inst., 1899-1901, Adelphi Acad., 1901-3, and supplemented by travel, U. S. and abroad. Author: Vigiliae, 1896 X1; Algiers, 1906 P12. Address: Greenwich CT‡

CROWDER, RENDER LEWIS, JR., banker; b. Durand, Ga., Aug. 22, 1905; s. Render Lewis and Elizabeth (Rutherford) C.; student Columbia, 1926-27; m. Sylvia Edgington, Feb. 19, 1932; children—Grace E. (Mrs. T. N. Sutton), Caroline Sue (Mrs. W. P. Dowling). Auditor, Johns-Manville Co., 1928-29; with credit dept. Gulf Oil Co., 1930-31; engaged in publicity for radio stas., Tulsa, 1931-32; credit mgr. Mid-Continent Oil Co., Tulsa, 1933-34; cashier First Nat. Bank, Tonkawa, Okla., 1934-54, pres., 1954-68, also dir.; dir. First Nat. Bank, Ponca City, Okla. Mem. President's Com. Employment Handicapped, 1963-68. Mayor of Tonkawa, 1949-56. Mem. Okla. State Regents for Higher Edn., 1960-68, chmn., 1963-64. Served with AUS, World War II. Decorated Purple Heart with 2 oak leaf clusters. Mem. Tonkawa C. of C. (pres. 1937-38), Am. Legion (past post comdr.), V.F.W. Presbyn. Tonkawa OK Died May 24, 1968.

CROWDER, THOMAS REID, physician; b. at Sullivan, Ind., Feb. 6, 1872; s. Robert H. and Juliet M. (Reid) C.; Ph.B., DePauw U., 1894; M.D., Rush Med. Coll., Chicago, 1897; U. of Vienna, 1902-3; m. Edith Warner Cadwallader, of Titusville, Pa., Oct. 26, 1905 (died 1906). Interne, Cook Co. Hosp., 1897-8; fellow in pathology, 1899, instr. in medicine, 1900-3, instr. in surgery, 1904-5, Rush Med. Coll.; supt. sanitation, The Pullman Co., 1905—. Mem. A.M.A., Am. Pub. Health Assn., Ill. Med. Soc., Chicago Med. Soc., Chicago, Pathol. Soc., Phi Gamma Delta, Phi Beta Kappa, Nu Sigma Nu. Republican. Protestant. Clubs: University, Quadrangle. Home: Quadrangle Club. Office: Pullman Bldg., Chicago‡

CROWELL, GRACE NOLL (MRS. NORMAN H. CROWELL), poet; b. Inland, Ia., Oct. 31, 1877; d. Adam and Sarah Elizabeth (Southern) Noll; hon. Litt.D., Baylor University, Waco, Texas; m. Norman H. Crowell, Sept. 4, 1901; children—Dean Hillis, Reid Kendrick, Norton Barr. Writer of verse from 1906. Republican. Methodist. Mem. Poetry Soc. Tex., Dallas Pen Women. Club: Wednesday Study. Author several books, the latest of which are: Apples of Gold, A Child Kneels to Pray, 1950; Meditations, 1951; Bright Harvest, 1952; Little Boy Down the Lane, 1952, Moments of Devotion, 1953; Journey into Dawn (poems), 1955; My Book of Prayer and Praise (poems for children), 1955; Come See A Man, 1956; Proofs of His Presence (devotional book), 1958; also Vital Possessions (devotional book), 1960; God's Masterpieces (devotional book), 1963, Let the Sun Shine In, 1970. Poet laureate of Tex., 1935-37; chosen by Golden Rule Found. as Am. Mother for 1938. Honor poet of Poetry, Week, 1938. Selected by Am. Pubs. as one of ten outstanding American Women of 1938. Home: Dallas TX Died Mar. 31, 1969; buried Sparkman-Hillcrest Meml. Park, Dallas TX

CROWLEY, JOHN DENNIS, clergyman, educator; b. Boston, Dec. 20, 1915; s. Cornelius J. and Helen (Mc Gonigle) C.; A.B., Boston Coll., 1942, M.A., 1943; Licentiate in Philosophy, Weston Coll., 1943, S.T.L., 1947; Ph.D., Pontifical Gregorian U., Rome, Italy, 1965. Ordained priest Roman Catholic Ch., 1946; missionary, Jamaica, 1947-49; asst. prof. Fairfield (Conn.) U., 1950-54, asso. prof. philosophy, 1966-69; asso. prof. philosophy Holy Cross Coll., Worcester, Mass., 1954-66, chmn. dept., 1961-64. Lectr. philosophy Boston Coll., 1956-59; extra-mural tutor U. West Indies, 1947-49. Mem. Am. Cath. Philos. Assn., Jesuit Philos. Assn., Metaphys. Soc. Am., Am. Assn. U. Profs. K.C. (4 deg.). Address: Fairfield CT Died June 24, 1969.

CROWLEY, LEO T., corp. ofcl.; b. Milton Junction, Wis.; s. Thomas Franklin and Catherine Elizabeth (Ryan) C.; student pub. schs., Madison, Wis. Pres. Gen. Paper & Supply Co., from 1917; chmn. bd. Standard Gas & Electric Co., 1939-47, Phila. Co., 1942-48, Wis. Pub. Service Corp., from 1948; 1st chmn. FDIC, 1934-45; served as Alien Property Custodian, mem. Pres. Roosevelt's cabinet, 1942-43; head Office Econ. Warfare, 1943. Fgn. Econ. Adminstrn., 1943-45; chmn. C.M., St. P. & P. Ry., 1945-63, and from 1966, also dir., chmn. finance com. Mem. Phi Beta Kappa. Democrat. Roman Catholic. Clubs: Chicago, Duquesne. Home: Madison WI Died Apr. 15, 1972; buried Resurrection Cemetery, Madison WI

CROWTHER, CYRIL IRWIN, found. exec.; b. Yonkers, N.Y., Sept. 4, 1895; s. John Henry and Mary Eliza (Irwin) C.; B.A., N.Y.U., 1920; postgrad. Columbia, N.Y.U.; m. Olive Maria Van Rensselaer, Apr. 22, 1922; children—Olive Van Rensselaer (Mrs. Richard Stuart Baird), Joan Eltonhead (Mrs. Rolf Charles Walther), Virginia Van Rensselaer (Mrs. Robert Wing Langhans), Cyril Irwin, Florence Louise (Mrs. Emil Albert Tessin II). Asst. comptroller Near East Relief, 1920-30; asst. comptroller Near East Found.,

1930-45, comptroller, 1945-57, exec. dir., 1957-58, also dir.; past president, trustee Leonard Wood Memorial for Eradication of Leprosy, Am. Leprosy Found., 1958-68. Cons. accounting and finance, bus. and philanthropic orgns. Served with USN, 1917-19. Mem. Internat. Leprosy Assn., Pi Kappa Alpha, Delta Iota Delta. Home: Jamaica NY Died Oct. 28, 1968; buried Oakland Cemetery, Yonkers NY

CROY, HOMER, author; b. on farm near Maryville, Mo., Mar. 11, 1883; s. Amos J. and Susan (Sewell) C.; student in school of journalism U. Mo.; hon. degree, U. Mo., 1956; m. Mae Belle Savell, Feb. 1915; 1 dau., Carol. Began on country newspapers; later reporter on city papers; made trip around world taking motion pictures. Author of numerous books, from 1918, including, West of the Water Tower, 1923; They Had to See Paris (which became Will Rogers' first talking motion picture); also wrote others of Will Rogers' movies; among most recent books: Jesse James Was My Neighbor, 1949; Wheels West, the Story of the Donner Party, 1955; Last of the Great Outlaws, the Story of Cole Younger, 1956; The Lady from Colorado, 1957; Trigger Marshall; Our Will Rogers; He Hanged Them High: The Story of Judge Parker; Star Maker: The Story of D.W. Griffith. Contbr. to New York City NY Died May 1965; cremated.

CRUCHAGA-TOCORNAL, MIGUEL, ambassador; b. Santiago de Chile, May 5, 1869; s. Miguel Cruchaga and Maria Tocornal; ed. U. of Chile, Santiago; LL.D., Catholic U. of Chile, 1929; m. Elvira Matte, May 7, 1893 (died, 1925). In practice of law at Santiago, 1889-91; capt. in Constitutional Army, Civil War, 1891; solicitor of Ministry of Finance, 1891-95; mem. Govt. Board of Solicitors, 1895-1900; prof. pub. and pvt. internat. law, U. of Chile, 1891-1900; mem. House of Deputies, Depts. of Victoria and Melipilla, 1900-06; rep. Chile at Latin American Scientific Congress, Montevideo, 1902; minister of finance, 1904-05; prime minister with portfolio of Ministry of Interior, 1905-06; minister to Argentina and Uruguay, 1908-13, to Germany and Netherlands, 1913-20; ambassador to Brazil, 1923-25; chmn. Chilean delegation to First World Conf. on the Codification of Internat. Law, The Hague, 1930; A.E. and P. to U.S., 1926-27 and since 1931; pres. German-Mexican, Spanish-Mexican, and Italian-Mexican Mixed Claims Commns., since 1926; neutral mem. for U.S., of Permanent Arbitration Commn. between Spain and U.S.; neutral umpire U.S.-Panama Claims Commn. Mem. Am. Soc. Internat. Law, Institut de Droit Internat. de Bruxelles; hon. mem. Faculty Law of U. of La Plata (Argentina). Decorated Crown of Prussia (first class); Red Cross of Germany; Grand Cross of St. Gregory the Great (Papal). Club: Club de la Union (Santiago, Chile). Author: Droit International, 2 vols., 1893; Germany Before and After the War, 1922; Brasil en su primer centenario, 1923. Address: Chilean Embassy, 2154 Florida Av., Washington DC‡

CRULL, HARRY EDWARD, educator; b. Chgo., Feb. 7, 1909; s. Roy and Janette (Ostrom) C.; A.B., U. Ill., 1930; A.M., 1931, Ph.D., 1933; m. Edna Hale, Sept. 3, 1932; children—Janet Lee, Royale, Harry. Lectr. Adler Planetarium, Chgo., 1933-34; prof. math. and head dept. Park Coll., Parkville, Mo., 1934-47, dean, 1946-47; head math. dept., prof. math. and astronomy Butler U., 1947-65, also dir. Univ. Coll., 1948-54, J.L. Holcomb Obs., 1954-65; prof. astronomy State U. N.Y., Albany, 1965-72, dir. Henry Hudson Planetarium, 1965-72. Served with USNR, 1942-46. Mem. Math. Assn. Am., Am. Astron. Soc., Ind. Acad. Sci., Phi Beta Kappa, Sigma Xi. Home: Guilderland NY Died Apr. 25, 1972; buried Arlington Nat. Cemetery, Washington DC

CRUTCHFIELD, WILLIAM GAYLE, surgeon; b. Henry County, Ky., Sept. 28, 1900; s. Pinkney H. and Amanda (Malin) C.; A.B., U. Ky., 1923; M.D., Johns Hopkins, 1927; m. Theresa Salzsieder, Nov. 2, 1929; children—Emma Lou (Mrs. Davis), Jean Hartford (Mrs. Echols), William Gayle, Intern, Woman's Hosp., Balt., 1927-28; surg. house officer Peter Bent Brigham Hosp., Boston, 1928-29; resident neurol. surgery Med. Coll. of Va., Richmond, 1930-33, asst. prof. neurol. surgery, 1935-41; prof. neurol. surgery U. Va., Charlottesville, 1941-72, also chmn. dept. neurol. surgery, 1941-69; neurol. cons. U.S. Naval Med. Center, NIH, Bethesda, Md., VA Hosp., Richmond. Named hon. Ky. col. Mem. Am., So. med. assns., So. Surg. Assn. (v.p. 1951), So. Neurosurg. Soc. (pres. 1956), Harvey Cushing Soc. (v.p. 1956), Va. Neuropsy. Soc. (pres. 1935), Soc. Neurol. Surgeons, Kappa Alpha, Nu Sigma Nu, Alpha Omega Alpha. Clubs: Farmington Country, Farmington Hunt (Charlottesville, Va.). Author articles in med. jours. Introduced Skeletal Traction for treatment of neck injuries 1933. Home: Charlottesville VA Died Oct. 31, 1972; buried Monticello Meml. Park, Charlottesville VA

CRUTHCER, LEWIS PINKERTON, physician; b. Ducker Station, Woodford County, Ky., Jan. 30, 1874; s. Rev. Samuel Williams and Virginia Louise (Pinkerton) C.; pub. schs., Louisville, Ky., and Belton, Mo.; prep. dept., Center Coll., Danville, K.; M.D., Durham Med. Coll., Chicago, 1897; Hahnemann Coll. (Kansas City U.), 1904; ad eundem degree M.D., Hahnemann Med. Coll. and Hosp., Chicago, 1907; m. Edith Nichol, Dec. 13, 1900; 1 dau., Esther. In drug business, 1889-93; prof. materia medica and diseases of children, Hahnemann Med. Coll. (Kansas City U.), 1900-12, and registrar same, 1910-11. First v.p. and editor Nat. League for Med. Freedom, 1911-12; mem. and pres. Calif. State Board of Edn., 1932-41. Mem. Christian (Disciples) Ch. Mem. Am. Inst. Homeopathy, Mo. Inst. Homeopathy (ex-pres.), Mo. Valley Homoe. Med. Assn. (ex-pres.), Southern Homeopathic Med. Assn., Los Angeles County Homeopathic Med. Soc. (pres.), Calif. State Homoe. Med. Soc. (pres., 1927-28), Phi Alpha Gamma. Asso. editor Medical Century. Pres. Long Beach Bd. Edn., 1915-19; chmn. Long Beach Chapter Am. Red Cross during World War I. Long Beach 3 CA‡

CRYDERMAN, MACKIE MACINTYRE (MRS. CLIFFORD WILLIAM CRYDERMAN), artist; b. Dutton, Ont., Can.; d. John Horton and Adda Elvira (Delong) M.; student Winnipeg (Ont., Can.) Sch. of Art, Ontario (Toronto, Can.) Coll. of Art, Detroit Soc. Arts and Crafts; m. Clifford William Cryderman, Feb. 19, 1927. Dir. art H. B. Beal Tech. and Comml. High Sch. (name changed H. B. Beal Secondary Sch.), London, Ont., Can., 1927-62; exhibited in one man shows U. Western Ont., London Pub. Library and Art Mus., Shute Inst. London, Richard Cranch Library; exhibited in numerous group shows in London, Montreal, Toronto and Ontario (all Can.); represented in permanent collections Sir Wilfred Laurier Sch., Medway High Sch., Victoria Hosp., McCormick Home (all London); print selected for exhbn. Habitat, Expo '67, Montreal, Que., Can. Bd. govs. Fanshawe Coll. of Applied Arts and Tech., London, 1966-69. Named Woman of Achievement, London Bus. and Profl. Women's Club, 1964. Mem. Can. Painter Etcher Engravers Assn., Western Art League, Can. Handicraft Guild, Am. Craftsmen, London Art Mus. (women's art com.). Executed two ceramic murals Park Towers Dining Club, London, 1962. Address: London ON Can. Died Nov. 19, 1969.

CSATORDAY, KAROLY, Hungarian diplomat; law grad. U. Budapest; m. Klara Varga; 3 sons, 1 dau. With Hungarian diplomatic service, 1948-—; served in Holland, 1949-51, China, 1951-55, Vietnam, 1955; chief of protocol Ministry Fgn. Affairs, Budapest, 1956-60; ambassador to Japan, 1960-62; head permanent mission of Hungarian People's Republic to UN, 1962-71, chmn. polit. and security com., 1965, v.p. Gen. Assembly, 1966-71, mem. Security Council, 1968-69, pres., 1969; dep. fgn. minster of Hungary, 1971-72. Address: Budapest Hungary Died July 23, 1972.

CUDAHY, MICHAEL FRANCIS, meat packer; b. Milwaukee, Wis., May 27, 1886; s. Patrick and Anna (Madden) C.; A.B., U. of Wis., 1909; m. Mrs. Alice Dickson Pinto, July 15, 1921 (died 1942); 1 son, Richard Dickson. Actively identified with packing business, 1910-70; chmn. Cudahy Bros. Co., 1960-69, name changed to Patrick Cudahy, Inc. Captain Qm. Corps, U.S. Army, World War I. Founder Patrick and Anna M. Cudahy Fund (for charitable purposes). Catholic. Clubs: Milwaukee, University. Home: Milwaukee WI Died May 20, 1970.

CUDLIP, MERLIN A., steel co. exec.; ed. U. Mich. Chmn., chief exec. officer, dir. McLouth Steel Corp., Detroit. Home: Detroit MI Died Sept. 23, 1968.

CULBERTSON, JAMES GORDON, lawyer; b. Stanley, Wis., Nov. 3, 1903; s. Clarence R. and Mary Lillian (McCaffrey) C.; A.B., U. Wis., 1925, LL.B., 1927; M. Frieda Schmidt, Nov. 3, 1928; children—Jean Lillian (Mrs. John Rumbold), Lois Carlotta (Mrs. James Callahan), Mary Kathryn. Admitted to Wis. bar, 1927, Ill., 1928; partner Hinshaw, Culbertson, Moelmann, Hoban & Fuller, Chgo., 1934-69. Dir. and sec. various corps. Dir. Glencoe Pub. Library, 1947-53, pres., 1950-52, Trustee Ravenswood Hosp. Mem. Internat. Am., Ill., Chgo. bar assns., Am. Judicature Soc., Chgo. Law Inst. Alpha Tau Omega, Phi Delta Phi. Presbyn. Mason. Clubs: Skokie Country (pres. 1952-53) (Glencoe, Ill.); Executives, University (Chgo.); Law. Home: Glencoe IL Died May 1, 1969.

CULBERTSON, WILLIAM, clergyman; b. Philadelphia, Pa., Nov. 18, 1905; s. William, Jr., and Lydia Barnes (Roper) C.; S.B., Temple U., Phila., 1939; B.D., Reformed Episcopal Theol. Sem., Phila., 1939, D.D., 1939; LL.D., Bob Jones University, Greenville, S.C., 1948; m. Catharine Havilla Gantz, Mar. 16, 1929; children—Joy Anne, William Robert, Paul Gantz, Ruth Catharine. Ordained deacon, Reformed Episcopal Ch., 1927; presbyter, 1928; consecrated bishop, 1937; rector Grace Ch., Collingsdale, Pa., 1927-30; St. John's-by-the-Sea, Ventnor, N.J., 1930-33; Atonement, Germantown, Phila., 1933-42; Episcopacy; New York and Phila. Synod, Reformed Episcopal Church, 1937-42; lecturer Ref. Episcopal Theol. Sem., 1929-42, dean Moody Bible Inst., 1942-47, acting pres. and dean of edn., 1947-48, president 1948-1971, Chancellor 1971. Trustee Ref. Episcopal Theo. Sem., Philadelphia, 1930-71. Member of the North American Council, China Inland Mission, 1940-71; asst. editor Episcopal Recorder, 1932-37, asso. editor, 1937-71; editor Moody Monthly, 1947-71. Mem. Evang. Theol. Soc. Home: Chicago IL Died Nov. 16, 1971.

CULIN, ALICE MUMFORD (MRS. STEWART CULIN), artist; b. Phila., Jan. 30, 1875; d. Joseph Pratt and Mary (Eno) Mumford; g.d. Edward William Mumford, artist, of Newport, R.I.; studied in Paris, France, 1897-1900, Spain, 1901-02; m. Jacob Clarence Roberts, Apr. 28, 1905 (died 1910); 1 dau., Penelope Roberts; m. 2d, Stewart Culin, Apr. 11, 1917 (died 1929). Exhibited at the Salon, Paris, 1900; Ville de Yant, 1901; Earl's Court, London, 1902; N.A.D.; Pa. Acad. Fine Arts, etc. Mary Smith prize, Pa. Acad., 1906, 10; bronze medal, San Francisco Expn., 1915. Has painted portraits of many prominent men and women in U.S. Episcopalian. Address: Coconut Grove FL‡

CULLEN, FREDERICK JOHN, physician, med. cons.; born Kokomo, Indiana; son of John and Mildred (Ristley) C.; Ph.G., Winona Coll. Pharmacy, Indianapolis, 1907; M.D., U. Colo., 1913; m. Marie Eloise Stone, Aug. 1, 1936. Gen. practice medicine, State of Washington, 1914-16 and 1919-29; chief, drug control div., Food and Drug Adminstrn., Washington, 1929-34; exec. v.p. and med. dir. Proprietary Assn., Washington, 1934-56; cons. to Proprietary Drug & Pharm. Industries, 1956-68; former professorial lectr. Sch. Pharmacy George Washington U. Served M.C., U.S. Army, 1916-19; retired with rank of maj. Recipient Purple Heart, Silver Star with palms. Registered pharmacist and physician, Wash. state. Past pres. Nat. Drug Trade Conf.; hon. mem. Can. Proprietary Assn., Am. Found. for Pharm. Edn.; sec. Therapeutic Research Found. Mem. George Washington U. Med. Soc., Med. Alumni Assn. U. Colo., Am. Pharm. Assn., Association of Military Surgeons of U.S., Am., National Capitol orchid socs., Disabled Am. Vets., Disabled Officers Assn., Am. Med. Writers Assn. Am. Legion. Clubs: Army and Navy, Congressional Country (Washington); Farmington Country (Charlottesville, Va.). Author: Your Medicine Chest; also articles on Fed. and state laws in field drugs. Home: Washington DC Died June 10, 1968; buried Arlington Nat. Cemetery, Arlington VA

CULLEN, THOMAS ERNEST, clergyman, educator; b. Charlottetown, P.E.I., Can., Sept. 20, 1874; s. Patrick and Mary (Campbell) C.; student Prince of Wales Coll. and St. Dunstan's U., Can.; B.A., Ottawa U., 1898, Ph.D., 1922; studied St. Paul Sem., St. Paul, Minn., 1898-1902. Ordained priest R.C. Ch., 1901; pastor Pro Cathedral of St. Mary, Minneapolis, Minn., 1904-20; pres. Coll. of St. Thomas, St. Paul, since Aug. 15, 1921. K.C. Clubs: Skylight, Informal, Minneapolis Athletic. Address: College of St. Thomas, Cleveland and Summits Avs., St Paul MN‡

CULLMAN, HOWARD S(TIX), civic leader; born in N.Y. City, Sept. 23, 1891; s. Joseph F. and Zillah (Stix) C.; grad. Phillips Exeter (N.H.) Acad., 1909; A.B., Yale U., 1913; LL.D., Syracuse U., 1947, N.Y.U., 1952, Columbia, 1954; LL.D., Rutgers U., 1959, Hamilton Coll., 1963, Philippine Womens' University, 1967; m. to Elsie Gottheil, Mar. 9, 1915 (dec.); children—Hugh, Paul Thomas; m. 2d, Marguerite Wagner; children—Marguerite, Brian. Commissioner of Port of New York Authority, 1927-72, chmn., 1945-55, hon. chmn., 1955-72. Pres., Cullman Bros., Inc., N.Y.C.; chmn. bd. Chanin Bldg.; director several corps., including adv. bd. Philip Morris Inc., dir. Nat. Distillers and Chem. Corp. Commnr. gen. Brussels Internat. Exhbn., 1958. Honorary trustee Fordham Univ. Pres. Tobacco Mchts. Assn.; chmn. bd. Beekman Downtown Hosp.; trustee Nat. Fund for Med. Edn. Decorated grand officer L'Ordre de Leopold (Belgium); comdr. Order of St. Sylvestre (Pope John XXIII); Presdl. Medal of Merit (P.I.); recipient silver medal for distinguished service U.S. Dept. State, 1967. Club: Lotos (past pres.). Home: New York City NY Died June 1972.

CULLOM, WILLIS RICHARD, clergyman, educator; b. Halifax County, N.C., Jan. 15, 1867; s. Joseph J. and Mary E. (Johnson) C.; A.M., Wake Forest (N.C.) Coll., 1892; Th.M., Southern Bapt. Theol. Sem., Louisville, Ky., 1895, Th.D., 1903; D.D., Richmond Coll., 1915; m. Fannie Farmer, June 2, 1897; children—Edward Farmer, Elizabeth Peter, Nancy Frances, Sarah Virginia. Ordained missionary Bapt. ministry, 1888; prof. Bible, Wake Forest Coll., since 1896. Gen. mgr. million dollar campaign for Bapt. schs. in N.C., June 1, 1918-July 1, 1919; state organizer for Bapt. 75 million campaign, in N.C., July 1, 1919-Jan. 1, 1920; dir. of Mobile Schs. for N.C. Bapt. State Conv., Jan. 1, 1920-Sept. 1, 1920; resumed work as prof. of Bible, Wake Forest Coll., Sept. 1, 1920, acting dean, 1922-23. Dean Bapt. Summer Sch. for Ministers, Raleigh, N.C., 1926-38, emeritus since June 1, 1938. Mem. of Edn. Commn. of the Southern Bapt. Conv. since 1928, chmn., 1930-31. Home: Wake Forest NC*‡

CULVER, CHARLES BEACH, artist, writer; b. Chicago Heights, Ill., May 30, 1908; s. Frank Henry and Millie (Bornholt) C.; student Wicker Sch. Fine Art, Detroit, 1926-30, Cranbrook (Mich.) Acad., 1930-31; m. Florence Helen Morrow, Oct. 25, 1935;

children—Sara Roxana, Eric Charles. Art critic Detroit Free Press, 1966-67; head watercolor dept. Art Sch. of Soc. Arts and Crafts Detroit, 1960-67; twenty-two one-man exhbns. in Detroit, 1935-67; five one-man shows in N.Y.C., 1951-67; exhbt. nat. and internat. exhbns., 1937-67; rep. permanent collections Detroit Art Inst., Whitney Mus., New Britain (Conn.) Mus., Worcester (Mass.) Mus., Flint (Mich.) Art Inst., Cranbrook Mus., Ill. State Mus., Dearborn (Mich.) Art Inst., Butler Inst. Am. Art, Middlebury (Vt.) Coll., IBM Corp., Lever House, N.Y.C., Albion (Mich.) Coll., U.S. Embassy, Brazil, Northwestern Mich. Coll., Central Mich. Coll., also pvt. collections. Recipient Field and Hartwig purchase prize Mich. Annual Exhbn., 1935, Albert Kahn watercolor prize, 1942, first prize watercolor div., 1949, 2 awards for picture Ducks and Geese, 1963; first prize watercolor div. Ill. State Mus., 1950; gold medal of honor Audubon Artists 9th annual exhbn., 1951; purchase prize Butler Inst. annual exhbn., 1957, first prize watercolor div., 1962, watercolor prize, 1966; top award watercolor div., 1966; gold medal show prize Scarab Club, 1962; Albert Kahn watercolor prize Mich. Ann. Exhbn., 1966. Club: Scarab (Detroit). Editor: Topic and Talk, 1960—. Home: Huntington Woods MI Died Sept. 22, 1967; buried Bellaire, MI

CUMINGS, EDGAR ROSCOE, geologist; b. North Madison, O., Feb. 20, 1874; s. Charles and Rebecca A. (Sullivan) C.; A.B., Union College (N.Y.), 1897; grad. study Cornell U., 1897; fellow Yale University, 1901-03, Ph.D., 1903; Sc.D., Union College, 1912; m. Frances Lois Crowther, June 28, 1905; children—Edith Katharine, Edgar Crowther. Instr. paleontology, 1898-1903, asst. and asso. prof. and head dept. geology, 1903-09, prof. and head dept. geology since 1909, professor emeritus since 1944, secretary faculty, 1913-20, acting dean Graduate School, 1914-19 and 1923, Ind. University. Author of numerous papers on geology and paleontology with spl. reference to the stratigraphy of the Ordovician formations of N.Y. and Ind., the development, morphology and phylogeny of Brachiopoda and Bryozoa, Silurian of the Michigan Basin region, and the structure of ancient coral reefs. Fellow A.A.A.S., Geol. Society of America (v.p. 1931), Paleontol. Soc. America (v.p. 1928; pres. 1931), Ind. Acad. Science (pres. 1925); mem. Am. Assn. Univ. Professors (council 1916-19 and 1923-26), Phi Beta Kappa, Sigma Xi. Home: Painesville OH‡

CUMMINGS, MARSHALL BAXTER, college prof.; b. N. Thetford, Vt., Dec. 2, 1875; s. Harlan Page and Alpha Maria C.; B.S., U. of Vt., 1901; M.S., U. of Me., 1904; Ph.D., Cornell, 1909; m. Lura Alice Bugbee, of Hartford, Vt., Aug. 24, 1910. Instr. horticulture and botany, U. of Me., 1902-07; instr. horticulture, Cornell U., 1907-09; prof. horticulture, U. of Vt., 1909—. Mem. Am. Pomol. Soc., A.A.A.S., Am. Assn. Hort. Science, Am. Assn. Plant and Animal Breeders, New England Bot. Club, Sigma Xi, Alpha Zeta, Gamma Alpha. Republican. Conglist. Home: 230 Loomis St., Burlington VT‡

CUMMINGS, MARVIN EARL, sculptor; b. Salt Lake City, Utah, Aug. 13, 1876; s. M. E. and Ardelle (Clawson) C.; ed. in Salt Lake pub. schs., Salt Lake Bus. Coll. and acad. at Logan, Utah; student Mark Hopkins Art Inst., San Francisco; pupil of Douglas Tilden; student Beaux Arts, Paris, 1900-03; m. Lupe Rivas, of San Francisco, June 7, 1905. Prof. sculpture Hopkins Inst. and Univ. of Calif. Executed numerous statues in and around San Francisco. Principal work, Commodore Sloat Monument, Monterey, Calif. Chmn. advisory com. artists and architects, Bd. of Park Commrs., San Francisco (mem. bd. 1904-28); trustee Calif. Palace of Legion of Honor, M.H. de Young Memorial Mus. Home: 3966 Clay St., San Francisco CA‡

CUMMINS, CLAUDE, dredging exec.; b. Cookville, Tenn., Mar. 4, 1872; s. William Gailbreth and Irene (Sims) C.; B.S., U. of Tenn., 1894; m. Jeannie Gloster Rowan, Feb. 12, 1891; 1 son, Claude Rowan. Civil engr. sewer and drainage work, New Orleans, 1895-96; with New York Dredging Co. on construction work, 1896-97; with San Francisco Bridge Co., 1897-1900; Puget Sound Bridge & Dredging Co., 1900-04; served Standard Dredging Co. of New York in various capacities since 1904, pres. since 1932. Home: 1068 University Av., Palo Alto, Calif. Office: 80 Broad St., New York NY‡

CUMMINS, CLESSIE LYLE, engine co. exec.; b. Honey Creek, Ind., Dec. 27, 1888; s. Francis M. and Josephine E. (Ed) C.; ed. Columbus (Ind.) schs.; m. Ethel M. McCoy, May 18, 1910 (dec. 1925); children—Brainard L., Beatrice M., Mary E., Joseph W., George T., m. 2d, Estella M. Feldmann, Oct. 8, 1926; 1 son, Clessie Lyle. With Am. Motors Co., Indpls., 1904-08; final tester, insp. Marmon Motor Car Co., Indpls., 1908-12; organizer, pres. Cummins Machine Works, Columbus, 1912-18; organizer, pres. Cummins Engine Co., Columbus, 1918-48, chmn. bd., 1948-50, dir., 1948-54, hon. chmn. bd., 1950-54. Mem. WPB, 1942-44. Mem. Soc. Automotive Engrs. (v.p., 1935), Am. Soc. M.E. Inventor first automotive diesel. Home: Sausalito CA Died Aug. 18, 1968; buried Columbus IN

CUNNINGHAM, BENJAMIN FRAZIER, physician; b. Gloucester, Mass., Jan. 30, 1869; s. Augustus F. and Mary E. (Martin) C.; Ph.B., Tufts Coll., 1891; M.D., Harvard Med. Sch., 1894; m. Clara I. Shaw, of Woodstock, N.B., 1895. Carney Hosp., Boston, 1894-5; Cripple Creek, Colo., 1895-07, Reno, Nev., since 1907; mem. Reno Bd. of Health. Mem. Sch. Bd., Cripple Creek, Colo., 1904-07. Mem. A.M.A., Nev. State Med. Assn. (pres., 1911-12), Washoe Co. Med. Soc. (pres., 1909-10), Harvard Alumni Assn., Tufts Coll. Alumni Assn., Delta Upsilon. Mason. Democrat. Club: Commercial. Commd. capt. Med. R.C., 1917. Home: Reno NV‡

CUNNINGHAM, BURRIS BELL, educator; b. Springer, N.M., Feb. 16, 1912; s. Charles Chapman and Lora (Beall) C.; B.S., U. Cal., Berkeley, 1935, Ph.D., 1940; m. Irene Charlotte Metcalf, Aug. 1, 1936 (div. 1964); children—Susan M., Bruce J., Joseph M.; m. 2d, Juliana B. Weaver, July 8, 1964. Asst. sect. chief Manhattan Project, Chgo., 1942-46; asst. prof. chemistry, asso. prof. U. Cal., Berkeley, 1946-53, prof., 1953—. Mem. U.S. delegation to Geneva Conf. on Peaceful Uses of Atomic Energy, 1955. Guggenheim fellow, 1956. Mem. A.A.A.S., Am. Chem. Soc., Fedn. Am. Scientists, N.Y. Acad. Sci. Home: El Cerrito CA Died Mar. 28, 1971.

CUNNINGHAM, C. FREDERICK, business exec.; b. Paterson, N.J., June 17, 1889; s. Robert Hudson and Camilla Jane (Miller) C.; M.E., Stevens Inst. Tech., Hoboken, N.J.; m. Gertrude Wells Oliver, Sept. 30, 1916;children—J. Oliver, Anna Gertrude (Mrs. Russel H. Downey, Jr.), Frederica (Mrs. John S. Warriner). Indsl. engr. 1910-16; asst. gen. mgr. U.S. Cartridge Co., Lowell, Mass., 1916-18; works mgr. Oliver Chilled Plow Works, South Bend, Ind., 1918-29; director The National Bank of South Bend, National Bank & Trust Co.; dir. Walter Heller & Co. Republican. Presbyterian. Clubs: Chicago, University (Chicago); Indiana, Country (South Bend). Home: South Bend IN

CUNNINGHAM, FRANK HARRISON, writer; b. Roanoke, Va., Mar. 13, 1911; s. Frank Henry and Ruby Grayson (Lawrence) C.; A.B., Washington and Lee U., 1932; M.A., Litt.D., Sequoia U., Washington and Lee U., 1932; M.A., Litt. D., Sequoia U., 1951; Ph.D., St. Andrew's Coll. (London), 1953; H.H.D., Fremont Coll., 1953; LL.D., Coll. Seminarians, 1955; Dr. Journalism, Burton Coll., 1956. Dr. Edn., 1957; Ph.D., U. West, 1957; Lit. Dr., Evergreen U., 1958; Dr. Eng. Lit., Phoenix U., Italy, 1958; Litt. D., Trinity So., 1960; L.H.D., Intercollegiate U., 1961; Ps.D., Chatham Hill Co.; H.H.D., London Inst., Hong Kong, 1969; Dr. Fine Arts St. Olav's Acad., Sweden, 1968; Ph.D., No. Pontifical Acad., 1968; Dr. History, Internat. Montezuma U., 1968; Dr. Fine Arts and Letters, U. Libre Asia 1968; Doctor of Journalism, Internat. Acad., Eng., 1969. Formerly asso. editor Screen Digest, Hollywood editor Fgn. Press syndicate, Sartain syndicate; rep. Richmond Times-Dispatch Sunday Mag.; syndicate movie column; writer film radio program; gen. journalistic work, hdqrs. Santa Monica, 1942-72; asst. chief staff Civil War Press Corps, 1959-72; asst. to pres. Sequoia U., 1952-55; v.p. Sequoia U., Fremont Coll., 1955-58; dir. Sequoia U. Press, 1955-58; editorial staff Cal-Press Features, 1963-65; spl. press rep. Millionaire magazine, 1965-67; asso. editor, mem. adv. bd. Confederate Echoes Mag., 1970-72. Hon. pres. No. Pontifical Acad., 1968-72. Co-chmn., George Wallace for President Com., Los Angeles, 1966-72. Fellow, Andhra Research U., 1952, Sequoia Research Inst., 1963; literary grantee Confederate Caucus Eng., 1961. Recipient awards including Fight Communism Com. award of merit, 1958; Congress of Freedom Liberty award, 1959; decorated Knight Commander Order of Crown of Thorns; Cross of Lorraine (France); certificate of appreciation Korean Consulate Gen., 1966; Knight honor Sovereign and Royal Order Piast; numerous other fgn. and Am. awards. Served with AUS, 1941. Fellow Am. Artists West, Internat. Inst. Arts and Letters (life); mem. Internat. Platform Assn., Commanding Armies West Confederate High Command (gen.), Confederate Hist. Soc. (Eng.), Nat. Soc. Arts and Letters (Santa Monica v.p. 1958-65), Gettysburg Battlefield Preservation Assn. (hon. state chmn. 1960-72), Am. Edn. Assn., (hon. dir. 1966), Count Dracula Soc. (gov., hon. nat. chmn. 1969, pres.'s award 1969, Montague Summers award), Soc. Protection Individual Freedom (chmn.), Congress of Freedom, Liberty and Property (nat. bd.), Soc. Pan Am. Culture (bd.), S.C.V. (Cal. comdr. 1964-72), Order of Stars and Bars (So. Heritage award) Delta Upsilon, Sigma Delta Chi, Pi Delta Epsilon. Clubs: Manuscripters of Los Angeles (hon. life mem.; past pres.). Author: Sky Master—The Story of Donald Douglas, 1943 (Manuscripters Club award 1944); Big Dan, 1946 (winner Nat. R.R. Assn. The Railfan. award 1947): (with William R. White), Red Rock II, 1950 (winner Leash & Collar Mag. award) (with Pat Barham), Operation Nightmare, 1953; General Stand Watie's Confederate Indians, 1959 (Confederate High Command award); Knight of the Confereracy—Gen. Turner Ashby, 1960. Contbr. articles in nat. mags. Home: Los Angeles CA Died Apr. 21, 1972.

CUNNINGHAM, HORACE HERNDON, educator; b. Warren, Ind., Jan. 20, 1913; s. James William and Margaret (Settle) C.; A.B., Atlantic Christian Coll., 1936; M.A., U. N.C., 1940, Ph.D.,1952; m. Mary Shaw Robeson, Dec. 19, 1942; children—Anne Chalmers, Margaret Settle, Jama Rhett. Tchr. history, high schs., Lucama and Greenville, N.C., 1936-42; instr. history, polit. sci. N.C. State Coll., 1946-47; parttime instr. social sci., history U. N.C., 1947-52, lectr. summer sch., 1952, 58; chmn. dept. social scis. Elon Coll., N.C., 1952-65, dean of coll., 1957-61, William S. Long prof. history, 1961-65; professor of history University of Ga., 1965-69. Dir. Hist. Soc. of So. Convention Congl. Christian Chs., pres. N.C. and Va. Laymen's Conf., 1957-59; pres. Laymen's Fellowship So. Conv. Congl. Christian Chs., 1960-64. Chmn. planning and zoning commn., Town of Elon Coll., 1956-57, mem. bd. commrs., 1960-62. Served with USAAF, 1942-46. Fellow Society American Historians; member Am., So., Mississippi Valley historical assns., Historical Society North Carolina, Pi Gamma Mu (vice chancellor Southeastern region). Democrat. Mem. Disciples of Christ Ch. Author: Doctors in Gray, 1958; Field Medical Services at the Battles of Manassas, 1968. Home: Elon College NC Died Nov. 5, 1969; buried Magnolia Cemetery, Elon College NC

CUNNINGHAM, JOHN CHARLES, physician; b. Boston, Mar. 5, 1910; s. John Joseph and Rose Millicent (Murphy) C.; student Holy Cross Coll., 1927-29; A.B., U. Vt., 1931, M.D. cum laude, 1935; m. Sarah Evalyn Odell, June 20, 1942; children—John Charles James Michael, Elizabeth Ann, William Lawther, Barbara Rose. Rotating intern St. Francis Hosp., Hartford, Conn., 1936-37; eye resident Eye Inst., Columbia-Presbyn. Hosp., N.Y.C., 1937-40; instr. ophthalmology N.Y.U., 1940-41; clin. practice, Dubuque, Ia., 1941-42; prof. ophthalmology U. Vt., 1946-71, chmn. dept. eye, nose and throat, 1956-71; attending surgeon ophthalmology Mary Fletcher Hosp., pres. staff, 1951; attending surgeon Bishop DeGoesbriand Hosp., Burlington; ophthal. cons. Heaton, Plattsburg, Ticonderoga, Vt. State hosps.; instr. postgrad. courses Am. Acad. Ophthalmology, Chgo.; ophthal. rep. Vt. State Med. Soc. to Pub. Health Com. Served as 1st lt. M.C., U.S. Army, 1935-36, capt. M.C. USAAF, 1942-46; chief ophthalmology AAF Regional Hosp., Wright-Patterson Field, Dayton, O., 1943-46. Diplomate Nat. Bd. Med. Examiners, Am. Bd. Ophthalmology. Fellow American College of Surgeons: member American Academy of Ophthalmology, N.E. Ophthal. Soc., Pan-Am. Ophthal. Assn., Assn. Research Ophthalmology, C. of C. (past dir.), Am. Assn. Ophthalmology (trustee), Assn. Univ. Profs. Ophthalmology, Vt. Ophthalmol. Soc. (pres.), Nu Sigma Nu, Sigma Nu. Roman Catholic. Home: Burlington VT Died June 19, 1971; buried Resurrection Park, South Burlington VT

CUNNINGHAM, JOHN HENRY, surgeon; b. Chelsea, Mass., Apr. 30, 1877; s. John H. and Frances E. (Prouty) C.; Lawrence Scientific Sch. (Harvard), 1897-99; M.D., Harvard Med. Sch., 1902; m. Theresa Van der Heuvel Ingersoll, Oct. 8, 1914; children—John Henry, Colin McAllister, Ingersoll. Practiced at Boston since 1903; surgeon Boston City Hosp. and Long Island Hosp.; cons. surgeon several hospitals; now also asso. genito-urinary surgeon of the Harvard Grad. School of Medicine. Private Spanish-Am. War, 1895-1901; vol. attached to surgeon-general's office, com. of four in charge of venereal diseases, U.S. Army, throughout World War I. Fellow Am. Coll. of Surgeons; mem. A.M.A., Mass. Medical Society, Suffolk District Medical Soc., Chicago Medical Society, Am. Association Genito-Urinary Surgeons (pres. 1920-21), Am. Urol. Assn., N.E. Br. Am. Urol. Assn. (pres. 1922-25), N.E. Surg. Soc., Internat. Urol. Assn., Clin. Soc. Genito-Urinary Surgeons (pres. 1935), Eugene Field Soc., New Eng. Natural History Soc., Am. Soc. of Ichthyologists and Herpetologists, etc. Clubs: Charaka, Harvard, University, Harvard U. Faculty, Travelers, St. Botolph (Boston); Beverly Yacht; Harvard, University (New York); Country (Brookline); Club of Odd Volumes. Author: (with Frances S. Watson) Genito-Urinary Diseases (text book), 1908; also of sect. on Urology, Ochsner's System of Surgery and Lewis' Practice of Surgery. Editor Year Book of Urology. Home: 53 Seaver St., Brookline, Mass. Office: 46 Gloucester St., Boston MA

CUNNINGHAM, JULIAN W., army officer; b. Blairsville, Pa., May 1, 1893; s. Samuel Howard and Julia (Zimmers) C.; A.B., George Washington Univ., 1915, law sch., 1916-17; m. Margaret L. McGarry, June 27, 1925; children—Julian W. Jr. (deceased), Gary Craig. Commd. 2d lt. Cav., July 1917, and advanced through the grades to brig. gen., Sept. 1943. Mem. Phi Gamma Delta, Theta Delta Chi, Phi Delta Phi. Mason. Home: Alexandria VA Died Aug. 1972.

CUNNINGHAM, THOMAS MAYHEW, lawyer; b. Savannah, Ga., Jan. 30, 1869; s. Henry Cumming and Virginia Waldburg (Wayne) C.; B.Ph., U. of Ga., 1888; m. Lilla Clifford Woodbridge, Nov. 29, 1893. Admitted to Ga. bar, 1890, and began practice at Savannah; connected with legal dept. Central of Ga., Ry. Co. 1892, gen. counsel 1921-48, now director; director Ocean S.S.

Co. of Savannah; president Chatham Savings and Loan Co., Atlanta Towing Co., Lawton & Cunningham. Episcopalian. Home: 1918 Drayton St. Office: 26 Bryan St. E., Savannah GA

CUNNINGHAM, WILFRED HARRIS, banker; b. Phila., Pa., Apr. 18, 1871; s. William and Mary Jane (Craig) C.; ed. pub. schs.; wife deceased; 1 dau., Elizabeth Barry. Began as clk. Kurtz Bros., bankers and brokers, Phila., 1888, mem. of firm, 1913—; dir. Lake Superior Corpn., 1916, later pres.; now v.p. and dir. Shreveport-El Dorado Pipe Line Co.; dir. North Md. Coal Mining Co. Republican. Presbyn. Clubs: Merion Cricket, Art. Home: Rosemont, Pa. Office: 1421 Chestnut St., Philadelphia PA‡

CUNNINGHAM, WILLIAM JAMES, univ. prof.; b. St. John, N.B., Can., Apr. 29, 1875; s. William A. and Jennie (Smith) C.; ed. pub. schs., St. John, and at Boston Y.M.C.A.; tech. edn. while in railroad service, including r.r. engrng. course Internat. Corr. Sch.; hon. A.M., Harvard Univ., 1921, hon. D.Sc., Clarkson Coll. of Technol., 1946; m. Emily Hutchison McDuffee, Sept. 3, 1901 (died June 29, 1928); 1 son, Ross McDuffee; m. 2d, Ethel Gertrude Hoyle, Aug. 10, 1929. With Canadian Pacific Railway, 1892-95, B.&A. R.R., 1895-98, N.Y., N.H.&H. R.R., 1898-1900, Lackawanna R.R., 1900-07, B.&A. R.R., 1907-13, N.Y., N.H.&H. R.R., 1913-14, B.&Me. R.R., 1914-16; last period service as asst. to pres.; asst. prof. transportation, Harvard, 1910-15; prof. trans-portation, 1916-46, prof. emeritus since 1946. Asst. dir. of operations, U.S. R.R. Adminstrn. 1918-19. Mem. Am. Econ. Assn., Am. Ry. Engrng. Assn., N.E. Railroad Club (pres. 1917-18), Traffic Club of N.E. (pres. 1928-29), Newcomen Soc.; fellow Am. Acad. Arts and Sciences. Republican. Episcopalian. Clubs: Harvard (Boston, Massachusetts). Home: 15 Fernald Dr., Freedom NH

CUNZ, DIETER, educator; b. Hoechstenbach, Germany, Aug. 4, 1910; s. Paul and Hedwig (Silbersiepe) C.; student Humanistisches Gymnasium Wiesbaden, 1920-29; Ph.D., U. Frankfurt, 1934; unmarried. Came to U.S., 1938, naturalized, 1944. Newspaper work in Switzerland, 1935-38; instr. German, U. of Md., 1939-43, asst. prof., 1943-47; asso. prof., 1947-49, prof. German, 1949-57, chmn. dept. German, Ohio State U., 1957-69; resident dean U. of Md. Fgn. Study Center, Zurich, 1947-48. Dir. Carl Schurz Meml. Found., Phila. Recipient Officers Cross of Merit (Republic of Germany), 1962. Mem. Modern Language Association of America, American Assn. Teachers German, Soc. History of Germans in Maryland (secretary 1944-56), Phi Beta Kappa. Lutheran. Author: The Maryland Germans, A history, 1948, 2d edit., 1972; German for Beginners, 1958, 2d rev. edit., 1965. Editor: Ricarda Huch's Der Letzte Sommer, 1963; They Came From Germany, pub. 1966; Jung-Stilling's Lebensqeschichte, 1968. Editor annual bibliography Americana-Germanica, 1945-60. Contbr. to One America; also articles on history of German immigration into the U.S. in various jours. Home: hington OH Died Feb. 17, 1969.

CURL, ROBERT FLOYD, clergyman, educator; b. Winfield, Ala., July 3, 1897; s. Levi Slaten and Daniel Catherine (Logan) C.; A.B., So. Meth. U., 1931; A.M., Perkins Sch. Theology, 1932; D.D., Southwestern U., 1949; m. Lessie Waldene Merritt, June 8, 1922; children—Mary Gessner (Mrs. Norris A. Kurio), Robert Floyd. Ordained to ministry Meth. Ch., 1922; pastor in Alice, Bastrop, Brady, Del Rio, Kinsville, Mesquite, Harlandale, San Antonio (all Tex.), 1922-41; dist. supt., McAllen, Austin and San Antonio dists., 1941-47, 53-57; exec. sec. S.W. Tex. Conf., 1947-53; prof. ch. adminstrn., dir. field work Perkins Sch. Theology, Dallas, 1957-63, emeritus, 1963-71; supt. McAllen dist., 1963-65; supt. San Antonio district, 1965-67; pastor 1st Meth. Ch., Ozona, Tex., 1967-69; pastor Hunt (Tex.) United Meth. Ch., 1969-71. Mem. Uniting Conf. of Methodism, 1939; mem. Gen. Conf. Meth. Ch., 1940, 44, 48, 52, 56; mem. Council on World Service and Finance, 1944-56, jud. council, 1956-64; mem. gen. bd. Nat. Council Chs. Christ in Am., 1963; pres. Tex. Meth. Planning Commn., 1948-51, Tex. Met. Student Movement, 1950-57; del. World Meth. Council, Oslo, Norway, 1961. Mem. Tex. Council Chs. (pres. 1953-56), Alpha Theta Phi, Eta Sigma Pi. Democrat. Mason, Rotarian. Author: Southwest Texas Methodism, 1952. Home: Kerrville TX Died July 1, 1971; buried Center Point Cemetery, Center Point TX

CURLEY, WALTER J., corp. exec.; b. Pitts., July 13, 1897; s. John D. and Margaret (Deere) C.; grad. St. Mary's High Sch.; student spl. night courses; hon. degree Duquesne U.; m. Marguerite C. Cowan, June 16, 1920 (dec.); 1 son, Walter Joseph. With Pa. R.R. 3 years, Pure Oil Co., 4 years; president Curley Land Company; dir. Willers & Son, Thomas Petroleum Transit, also Crescent Brick Co., Nat. Can Co. Served as 1st lt., 42d rainbow Div. overseas, W.W. I; ret. as maj. U.S. Inf. Res. Corps. Mem. Am. Petroleum Inst., Am. Iron and Steel Inst. Republican. Roman Catholic. Clubs: Duquesne, Rolling Rock, Fox Chapel Golf (Pitts.); Army-Navy, Metropolitan (Washington). Home: Pittsburgh PA Died Dec. 1970.

CUROE, PHILIP R(APHAEL) V(INCENT), educator; b. New York, N.Y., Oct. 24, 1892; s. Daniel J(oseph) and Catherine (Meredith) C.; B.S., Coll. of City of New York, 1913; A.M., Columbia, 1915, Ph.D., 1926; m. Anne Edwina Keller, Sept. 5, 1917; 1 dau., Phyllis Ann. Teacher of mathematics, Townsend Harris Hall, New York, 1914; tutor in edn. Coll. of City of New York, 1914-17; with Hunter Coll., New York, since 1917, successively as instr., asst. prof., asso. prof., and now prof. of edn., chmn. dept. of edn. since 1939. Mem. N.E.A., Am. Assn. Univ. Profs., N.Y. Acad. of Pub. Edn., Phi Beta Kappa. Roman Catholic. Author: History of Education, 1921; Principles of Education, 1926; Educational Attitudes and Policies of Organized Labor, in the U.S., 1926; Recent Trends in Education, 1932. Contbr. to School Review, School and Society and other journals. Contbr. of 12 articles to Ency. of NYC NY Died Feb. 24, 1969.

CURRAN, KENNETH JAMES, educator; b. Chgo., Nov. 29, 1903; s. Samuel Hair and Mary (Orr) C.; B.S., Princeton, 1925, M.A., 1926, Ph.D., 1941; m. Elizabeth Hare, July 24, 1930. With fgn. sales Americo-Persian Devel. and Trading Corp., 1926-30; asst. to plant mgr. Standard Brands, Inc., 1930-36; instr. econs. Princeton, 1938-41, asst. prof., 1941-50; prof. econs., head dept. econs. and bus. adminstrn. Colo. Coll., Colorado Springs, 1950-63, acting dean, 1963-64. dean coll., from 1964. Served from capt. to lt. col., AUS, 1943-46. Decorated Bronze Star medal; Cavalleria d'Italia. Mem. Am. Econ. Assn., Am. Marketing Assn., Rocky Mountain Social Sci. Assn., Am. Assn. U. Profs. Unitarian. Author: Excess Profit Taxation, 1943. Editorial staff Journal of Marketing, 1953-63. Home: Colorado Springs CO Died Aug. 3, 1971.

CURRIER, GEORGE HARVEY, publisher; b. Derry, N.H., May 7, 1875; s. George C. and Ione (Wood) C.; ed. pvt. schs., Dallas, Tex.; m. Frances Cummins, of Seattle, Wash., June 22, 1903. Pub. Woman's World (monthly mag.). Clubs: Chicago Athletic, Calumet, Press, South Shore Country. Home: Deerfield, Ill., and 4357 Grand Boul., Chicago. Office: 107 S. Clinton St., Chicago IL‡

CURRIER, RAYMOND PILLSBURY, assn. exec.; b. Malden Mass., May 16, 1891; s. George Cushman and Lydia Frances (Mitchell) C.; A.B. magma cum laude with honors in English, Harvard, 1912, A.M. in English lit., 1920; student Andover-Theol. Sch., 1912-13; m. Edith Alberta Gould, June 30, 1913; children—Laurence Meredith, Robert Newton, Gwendolyn (Mrs. E. B. Jamieson), Lloyd Randolph. Member American Baptist Mission, teacher English Baptist College, Rangoon, Burma, 1913-19, 20-23; secretary University Y.M.C.A., Bloomington, Indiana, 1924-26; asso. prof. Franklin Coll., 1926-30; ednl. sec. Student Vol. Movement for Fgn. Missions, 1930-34; asso. N.Y. area, 1934-50, exec. 1950-54, adminstrv. sec. Am. Leprosy Missions, Inc., 1954-58, gen. sec., 1958-60. Member Fellowship of Reconciliation, War Resisters' League, Phi Delta Kappa. Mem. Soc. of Friends. Contbr. poems to mags. Home: Cronton-on-Hudson NY Died Mar. 1973.

CURRY, ALLEN, lawyer; b. Fairfield, Ill., Feb. 20, 1871; s. Charles Wesley and Elizabeth (Carson) C.; ed. pub. schs., Wayne Co., Ill., and Hayward Coll., Fairfield; studied law in office of Bunch & Bonham, Fairfield; m. Mattie Day, of Fairfield, Apr. 6, 1895; children—Irene, Mrs. Pauline Funk, Chauncey Christman, Enid, Charles Marshal, Glenna Mary. Teacher pub. schs. of Ill. 9 yrs.; admitted to Mo. bar, 1901, and began practice at Salem; pros. atty. Perry Co., Mo., 7 1/2 yrs., 1909-18, except 2 1/2 yrs.; city atty. Perryville, 1908-18; editor and mgr. The New Republican Era (weekly newspaper), 1914-21; asst. U.S. atty. Eastern Dist. of Mo., under James E. Carroll, 1922-23; U.S. atty. same dist., by apptmt. of President Harding, reapptd. by President Coolidge, since Apr. 11, 1923, term ending May 17, 1928. Republican. Mem. Christian (Disciples) Ch. Home: 5117 Garfield Av. Office: Federal Bldg., St Louis MO‡

CURRY, JAMES ROWLAND, educator; b. Wooster, O., Dec. 29, 1903; s. William R. and Edna (Smith) C.; B.S., Dartmouth Coll., 1925; Ph.D., Johns Hopkins, 1930; m. Leota DeVore, July 24, 1939. Lumber business, 1925-26; research in chemistry and physics, Kaiser Wilhelm Inst. and Univ. of Berlin, 1930-32, at Technische Hochschule in Darmstadt, 1933; research asst., Columbia, 1934-35; instr., Williams Coll., 1935-39, asst. prof., 1939-43, asso. prof., 1943, prof. and chmn. chemistry dept., 1946-47, Ebenezer Fitch prof. and chmn. dept. since 1947; spl. research asso., Radio Research Lab., Harvard, 1943-45; with Office of Scientific Research and Development, 1943-45. DuPont Fellow, 1929-30; German American Exchange Fellow, 1930-31. Fellow A.A.A.S.; mem. Am. Chem. Soc., Am. Phys. Soc., Inst. Radio Engrs., Phi Beta Kappa, Sigma Xi, Gamma Alpha, Theta Chi. Clubs: Faculty, Williams (N.Y.C.). Contbr. scientific papers. Home: Williamstown MA Died Apr. 5, 1968; buried Westlawn Cemetery, Williamstown MA

CURTIS, ASAHEL, photographer; b. Le Sueur Co., Minn., Nov. 5, 1874; s. Johnson Asahel and Ellen (Sheriff) C.; ed. pub. schs.; m. Florence E. Carney, Nov. 27, 1902; children—Whitney A., Walter M., Marjorie L., Ellen J. News photographer, Alaska and Yukon, 1897-99, Seattle, Wash., 1900-06; commercial photographer, Seattle, since 1906. Chmn. Rainier Nat. Park Advisory Bd. since 1911; chmn. Wash. State Development Com. Mem. Am. Alpine Soc., Nat. Econ. League, Seattle Chamber Commerce (dir.), Wash. State Good Roads Assn. (pres.). Republican. Contbr. mag. articles on mountaineering. Home: 626 Belmont St., N. Seattle. Office: Colman Bldg., Seattle WA‡

CURTIS, EDWARD GILMAN, lawyer; b. Somerville, Mass., Dec. 11, 1886; s. Edward Bissell and Mary Augusta (Colson) C.; student Worcester Acad., 1903-05; A.B., Harvard, 1909, LL.B., 1912; m. Mary Helen Seelbach, Oct. 28, 1920; children—Mary Gilman (Mrs. John R. Brooks), Anne Raquet (Mrs. J. Wayne Fredericks), Eleanor Colson (Mrs. Jan S. F. van Hoogstraten), Edward Morey. Admitted to Massachusetts bar, 1912, New York bar, 1922; law practice, Boston, 1912-17; apptd. spl. asst. to Atty. Gen. U.S., in charge def. of U.S. in patent litigation, 1919-21; pvt. practice law, specializing in patents, N.Y. City, 1922-70; sr. mem. Curtis, Morris & Safford since 1948. Mem. Bronxville (N.Y.) Sch. Bd., 1940-43. Trustee Worcester (Mass.) Acad., 1945-48. Served as 1st lt. Ordnance, U.S. Army, Europe and U.S., 1917-19; maj. to lt. col. Res. Corps. Mem. Am. Legion (post comdr. 1931), Am. Bar Assn., New Eng. Soc., Sigma Alpha Epsilon. Mason (K.T.). Clubs: Union League, Harvard (N.Y. City); Am. Yacht (Rye, N.Y.). Home: Bronxville NY Died Mar 20, 1970.

CURTIS, EDWARD GLION, JR., fgn. service officer; b. St. Louis, Sept. 8, 1909 s. Edward Glion and Isabel (Wallace) C.; A.B., Washington U., 1930; Diploma, Cesare Alfieri Inst., Florence, Italy, 1935; m. Mary-Ellen Chivvis, Sept. 20, 1936; children—Mary Glasgow (Mrs. Curtis Kamman), Edward Glion, Frank Bradford, and Susan Harker. Appointed foreign service officer, 1935; vice consul, Budapest, Hungary, 1935-36, Wellington, N.Z., 1937-40, Port au Prince, Haiti (also 3d sec. of legation), 1940-43, 2d sec. of legation, 1943-44; 2d sec. of embassy, also vice consul, Madrid, Spain, 1944-47, consul, 1947; consul and 2d sec. of embassy, The Hague, 1947-50, econ. officer, 1950; consul Zurich, Switzerland, 1950-54; 1st sec. and consul, Panama, 1954-56; counselor and dep. chief of mission, Managua, 1956-57; assigned Dept. of State, 1957-68; consul gen., counselor, dep. chief mission Portau-Prince, 1962. Mem. Am. Fgn. Service, Eagle Scout Assn., Phi Delta Theta, Pi Mu Epsilon. Home: Fennville MI Died Apr. 16, 1968; buried Pier Cove MI

CURTIS, GEORGE MARTIN, II, former bus. exec.; b. Clinton, Ia., Aug. 8, 1905; s. George L. and Frances (Wilcox) C.; student Hotchkiss Sch., 1920-23; A.B., Yale, 1927; LL.D., Parsons Coll.; m. Louise Scully, Oct. 3, 1931 (dec. 1953). With Curtis Cos., Inc., Clinton, 1928-34, traveling sales rep., 1935-40, sec., 1938-47, v.p., sec., 1947-50, exec. v.p., 1950-51, pres., 1951-61, chmn. bd., pres., 1959-61, chmn. bd., 1961-66, ret. Mem. staff lumber code authority NRA, Washington, 1934. Trustee Parsons Coll., Fairfield, Ia., 1959-65, 69-72. Mem. Nat. Ponderosa Pine Woodwork Assn. (past pres.), N.A.M. (past dir.), U.S. C. of C. (past nat. counselor). Presbyn. Mason Clubs: Clinton (Ia.) Country: Tavern (Chgo.) Home: Clinton IA Died July 27, 1972.

CURTIS, HOWARD JAMES, physiologist; b. Lansing, Mich., Dec. 11, 1906; s. Harvey Lincoln and Anna (Puffer) C.; B.S., U. Mich., 1928; A.M., Swarthmore Coll., 1929; Ph.D., Yale, 1932; Rockefeller fellow Johns Hopkins Sch. Medicine, 1938-40; m. Dorothy Albert, Aug. 27, 1932; children—Brian Albert, Richard Harvey, Barbara Ann. Biophysicist, The Biol. Lab., Cold Springs Harbor, N.Y., 1932-35; asso. in physiology Coll. Physicians and Surgeons, Columbia, 1935-38, asst. prof. physiology, 1941-43, asso. prof., 1946-47; prof. of physiology and head physiology dept. Vanderbilt U. Med. Sch., 1947-50. Med. cons. to AEC, 1946-72; cons. in radiobiol. to USPHS, 1946-72, chmn. radiation study sect., 1955-72; mem. Nat. Com. on Radiation Protection; mem. sci. council of Am. Cancer Soc., 1956; cons. in radioisotopes to VA, 1948-72. Del. Atoms for Peace Conf., Geneva, 1958. Active in adv. capacity in formulating nat. legislation of atomic energy and on NSF; mem. Nat. Council Radiation Protection, 1962-72. Mem. NRC (mem. space sci. bd. 1959-72, mem. com. on growth; chmn. com. on radiobiology); v.p. Radiation Research Soc., 1956; chmn. biology dept. Brookhaven Nat. Lab., 1950-72. Mayor of Village of Shoreham, N.Y. Mem. bd. of sci. councilors Nat. Inst. Neurol: Diseases and Blindness, 1958-72. Mem. L.I. Biol. Assn. (dir.), Am. Phys. Soc., Am. Physiol. Soc., Harvey Soc., A.A.A.S., N.Y. Acad. Sci. Author: (with J.H. Lawrence) Advances in Medical Physics, Vol. II, 1949; (with F. M. Liver) Biophysical Research Methods, 1949; (with Philip Bard) Medical Physiology; Biological Mechanisms of Aging. Editor: Physiological Reviews, 1951. Contbr. research articles to sci. publs. Home: Shoreham LI NY Died Sept. 13, 1972.

CURTIS, JESSE WILLIAM, jurist; b. San Bernardino, Calif., July 18, 1865; s. William Jesse and

Frances Sophia (Cowles) C.; Ph.B., U. of Southern Calif., 1887, LL.D., 1926; LL.B., U. of Mich., 1891; LL.D., Southwestern U., 1928; m. Ida Lucinda Seymour, of San Bernardino, June 23, 1892; children—Frances (dec.), Margaret (Mrs. Harris Marshall Chadwell), Jesse William, Helen Seymour (Mrs. J. B. Shepordson). Admitted to Calif. bar, 1891, and began practice at San Bernardino, mem. firm Curtis, Oster & Curtis, later Curtis & Curtis and Curtis & McNabb; dist. atty. San Bernardino County, 1899-1903; judge Superior Court, San Bernardino County, 1915-23; justice Dist. Court of Appeal, 1923-26; appointed justice Supreme Court, Calif., 1926, elected same year for term 1926-38, reelected for terms, 1938-50; retired Jan. 1945; now practicing with son, firm name Curtis & Curtis. Trustee U. of Redlands, Berkeley Div. Sch. Received Asa Call achievement trophy, given annually to alumnus of U. of So. Calif. who has brought the greatest honor to his alma mater, 1934. Mem. Native Sons of Golden West, Am. Bar Assn., S.R., Order of the Coif, Phi Delta Phi, Phi Beta Kappa. Democrat. Baptist. Mason (K.T.). Clubs: Commonwealth (San Francisco); Athletic (Los Angeles). Home: 380 17th St., San Bernardino CA‡

CURTIS, VIVIAN CRITZ, clergyman; b. Noxapater, Miss., Feb. 13, 1876; s. Benjamin Flowers and Cherry Leland (Shirley) C.; ed. under pvt. instrs. and Louisville (Miss.) Normal Sch.; D.D., Asbury Coll., Wilmore, Ky., 1929; m. Letha Annie Fleming, Sept. 7, 1898; children—Annie Mae (Mrs. H. B. McGee), Gladys (Mrs. Gordon McIntyre), Vivian (Mrs. W. W. Caldwell, Jr.), Virginia (Mrs. Marshall Lang). Ordained ministry M.E. Ch., 1902; pastor successively at Starkville, McCool, Artesia, Coldwater, Kosciusko and Lexington (all in Miss.) until 1917; presiding elder Greenville (Miss.) Dist., 1917-20; pastor Greenwood, Miss., 1921-24, Starkville, 1925-29, Clarksdale, 1930-31; presiding elder Columbus (Miss.) Dist., 1932-35; then pastor of the First Church, Aberdeen, Miss., 1st Ch., Louisville, Miss., First Meth. Ch., West Point, Miss.; now dist. supt., Columbus District. Director New Orleans Christian Advocate. Del. to Ecumenical Conf., London, Eng., 1921, Atlanta, Ga., 1931. Chmn. of delegations, Gen. Conf., 1926-30; sec. com. on unification of Southern and Northern M.E. chs., 1926-30; del. to Gen. Conf. of M.E. Ch., S., 1934; Uniting Conf. Meth. Church, Kansas City, 1939; Southeastern Jurisdictional Conf., Asheville, N.C., 1940; mem. Com. of Appeals Southeastern Jurisdiction, Nashville, Tenn. Trustee Methodist Orphanage, Jackson, Miss. Democrat. Mason (Shriner), Odd Fellow, K.P. Home: 924 Third Av. N., Columbus MS‡

CURTIS, WILLIAM FULLER, artists; b. Staten Island, N.Y., Feb. 25, 1873; s. Samuel Bridgeham and Louise (Fuller) C.; ed. St. Austin's Sch., Staten Island, Columbian Prep. Sch., Washington; studied art, 1890-93, first in pvt. studio of Julius Rolshoven and two winters at Academie Julian under Jules Lefebvre and Tony Robert Fleury; unmarried. Since 1893 professionally engaged as artist-painter. Awarded silver medal, La. Purchase Expn., 1904. Home: Ashfield MA‡

CURTIS, WINTERTON CONWAY, zoologist; b. Richmond, Me., Nov. 4, 1875; s. William Conway and Fanny Mary (Norton) C.; A.B., Williams, 1897, A.M., 1898, Sc.D., 1934; Ph.D., Johns Hopkins, 1901; m. Marion Hitchcock Peck, Sept. 5, 1902; 1 son, William Dwight. Instr. on staff, Marine Biol. Lab., Woods Hole, Mass., 1899-1903; in charge of the Invertebrate course, 1908-11; instr. zoology, 1901-04, asst. prof. 1904-08, prof. since 1908, acting dean, College of Arts and Science, 1939, dean of same 1940-45, dean and professor emeritus since 1946; director of instruction Armed Forces, 1943-44, University of Mo.; scientific assistant U.S. Bur. Fisheries, 1907-10. Visiting prof. Keio U., Tokio, 1932-33. Expert witness, Scopes trial, Dayton, Tenn., 1925. Mem. Nat. Research Council (div. biology and agr., 1924-26; chmn. same, 1930-31, mem. exec. bd., 1935-38); pres. Union of Am. Biol. Socs., 1931-35; trustee Marine Biol. Lab., Woods Hole, Mass., 1923-35, and since 1937. Fellow A.A.A.S. (v.p. sect. F, zoology, 1926); member American Society Zoologists (sec. 1913, pres. 1932), American Society of Naturalists, Phi Beta Kappa, Sigma Xi, Phi Gamma Delta. Has made investigations in embryology, morphology, parasitism in platoda and mollusca and in effects of radiations upon animals, also in humanistic aspects of biol. science. Club: Faculty (Univ. of Mo.). Author: Science and Human Affairs, 1922; Laboratory Directions in General Zoology, 1938, 48. Textbook of General Zoology (both with Mary J. Guthrie), 1938-47. Asso. editor Jour. of Morphology and Physiology, 1927-29. Home: 210 Westmount Av., Columbia MO‡

CURTISS, LAWRENCE MEREDITH, investment co. exec.; b. Des Moines, Apr. 9, 1903; s. Charles Clinton and Minnie (Olson) C.; B.S. in Econs., Ia. State Coll., 1925; m. Frances Haynes, May 12, 1934; children—Constance (Mrs. Jay Quisenberry), Craig H., Judith, (Mrs. Wesley L. Metts). With Am. Investment Co., and subsidiaries, from 1928, mgr., supr., v.p. Boston div., 1938-49, v.p. charge operations St. Louis, 1948-54, 1st v.p., 1954-59, pres., 1959-64, chmn. bd., from 1964, also dir. Exec. com. St. Louis Better Bus. Bur. Mem. Nat. Consumer Finance Assn. (dir. 1951, chmn. exec. com., pres. 1957-58). Clubs: Clayton, Bath and Tennis (St. Louis). Home: St. Louis MO Deceased.

CUSHING, EDWARD HARVEY, physician; b. Cleveland, O., March 17, 1898; son of Edward Fitch and Melanie (Harvey) C.; A.B., Yale, 1919; M.D., Harvard, 1923; m. Bobbie Guyer, Nov. 28, 1942; children—Patsy Melanie (Mrs. N. Lawrence Niles), Barbara Ellen (Mrs. Charles H. Gibbs, Jr.). Instructor in medicine, Columbia, 1926-28; asst. clin. professor Western Reserve U., 1938-46; asso. clin. prof. George Washington U., 1946-48; asst. chief med. dir. for research and edn. Vets. Adminstrn., 1946-52; dep. asst. sec. of def. for health and medicine, 1955-61. Vice pres. B.G. Olson Co.; dir. Middleburg Nat. Bank. Mem. Nat. Research Council, 1942-45, 46-49. Served as lt., F.A., U.S. Army, 1918-19; capt., Med. Corps, U.S.N.R., 1940-70. Member United States Typhus Commn., 1943-44, (awarded medal), Decorated Commander Legion of Honor (Philippines); Vermeil Medaille d'Honeur de Service de Sante Militaire (France). Diplomate American Board of Internal Medicine, American Board of Cardiology. Fellow A.C.P.; mem. Clin. and Climatol, Assn., A.A.A.S., Central Soc. Clin. Research, Am. Soc. Tropical Diseases, Royal Soc. Medicine. Clubs: Tavern (Cleve.); Army and Navy, Metropolitan, Cosmos (Washington); Hamilton St. (Balt.). Home: Washington DC Died Nov. 15, 1969; buried Lake View Cemetery, Cleveland OH

CUSHING, GEORGE HOLMES;, b. Goshen, O., May 3, 1873; s. Matthew and Mary (Wade) C.; grad. high sch., Springfield, O., 1892; m. Ciel Adams Crooke, of Louisville, Ky., Feb. 28, 1904; 1 dau., June. Reporter on Republic Times, Springfield, 1893-96; city editor, The Gazette, Springfield, 1896-97, The Herald, Dayton, O., 1897-98; asst. city editor Ohio State Journal, Columbus, 1898-99; marine and railroad editor The Leader, Cleveland, 1899-1903; financial editor Cleveland Leader, 1903-07; editor The Black Diamond, 1907-19; mng. dir. Am. Wholesale Coal Assn., 1919-22; pub. Cushing's Survey since 1922. Patented a projecting lamp, 1926; perfected automobile headlight, 1927. Republican. Presbyn. Address: 500 26th St. N.W., Washington DC‡

CUSHING, HERBERT HOWARD, physician; b. Toungoo, Burma, June 5, 1872; s. Josiah N. and Ellen H. C.; spl. scientific course Brown U., 1891-3; M.D., U. of Munich, 1898; M.D., Jefferson Med. Coll., Phila., 1899; also studied at Heidelberg, Giessen and Glasgow; m. Claudia D. Thompson, of Phila., Apr. 8, 1901. Demonstrator histology and embryology, Jefferson Med. Coll., 1901-2; dir. histol. and embryol. laboratories Woman's Med. Coll. of Pa. since 1899. Author: Cushing's Compend of Histology, 1903. Translator: Boehm, Davidoff and Huber's Histology, 1900. Address: 5710 Market St., Philadelphia‡

CUSHING, RICHARD CARDINAL, born Boston, Aug. 24, 1895; ed. Boston Coll. and St. Johns Sem., Boston. Ordained priest Roman Cath. Ch., 1921; pastor, Archdiocese of Boston, 1921-39; active in propagation of Faith Soc., 1922-39; consecrated auxiliary bishop of Boston, titular bishop of Mela, 1939; archbishop of Boston, 1944-70; named cardinal by Pope John XXIII, Dec. 1958. Episcopal director national Cath. Welfare Conf., youth dept., 1947-70. Recipient numerous awards for civic, relief and youth work. Decorated Officer Legion of Honor; Prior Knights of Holy Sepulchre; Grand Cross Order of Merit (Fed. Republic Germany), 1957. Member of the American Academy Arts and Scis. Author articles on moral, social and eccles. questions. Home: Boston MA Died Nov. 2, 1970.

CUSHMAN, HORACE O., army officer; b. Ill., Jan. 4, 1893; grad. Inf. Sch., Officers Course, 1928, Command and Gen. Staff Sch., 1936, Army War Coll., 1938; m. Kathleen O'Neill; 2 sons, 2 daus. Commd. 2d lt. Inf., Apr. 1917, and advanced through the grades to brig. gen., Oct. 1942; served as 2d lt. to capt., Inf., World War I; Gen. Staff Corps, 1939-40; ret. 1953. Address: Fort Devens MA Died Nov. 1972.

CUSHMAN, ROBERT EUGENE, polit. scientist; b. Akron, O., Mar. 27, 1889; s. Sylvanus Dustin and Estelle Caroline (Hodgman) C.; A.B., Oberlin, 1911; Ph.D., Columbia University, 1917; Litt.D., Oberlin College, 1946; married Clarissa White Fairchild, Dec. 25, 1916;children—Robert Fairchild, John Fairchild. Instr. in history and civics, Oberlin Acad., 1911-13; instr. polit. science, U. of Ill., 1915-18, assoc., 1918-19; asso. prof. polit. science, U. of Minn., 1919-22, prof., 1922-23; prof. govt., Cornell U. since 1923, head dept., 1923-46, Goldwin Smith prof. govt. 1929-57; dir. Cornell Research in Civil Liberties 1943-57; vis. prof. polit. sci., Vanderbilt Univ., 1957-58. Mem. staff of President's Com. on Administrative Management, 1936. Trustee Cornell U., Wells Coll. Fellow Am. Acad. Arts and Sci.; mem. Am. Philos. Soc., Am. Political Science Assn. (pres. 1943), Sigma Phi Epsilon, Phi Beta Kappa, Phi Kappa Phi, Phi Delta Phi. Democrat. Conglist. Author several profl. studies. Editor: Constitutional Decisions, 1925. Editor-in-chief: Documentary History of Ratification of Constitution, 1958-69. Mem. bd. editors American Political Science Review 1923-48. Contributor to law reviews. Home: Ithaca NY Died June 10, 1969.

CUTTER, MRS. GEORGE ALBERT (FLORENCE MAXIM CUTTER), composer; b. Brooklyn, June 4, 1873; d. Sir Hiram Stevens and Louisa Jane (Budden) Maxim; sister of Hiram Percy M.; ed. grammar and high schs., Hyde Park, Mass., 1884-92; grad. N.E. Conservatory of Music (pianoforte dept.), 1895; m. George Albert Cutter, May 1, 1913; 1 dau., Patricia (dec.) Composer: (pianoforte music) Ten Little Tonal Fancies, 1901; The Holidays, 1902; Half-a-dozen Wonderfuls, 1904; Boy Roy and His Friends, 1905; Fairy Tales in Tone, 1906; The Dancing School in Noah's Ark, 1906; Nature's Little Carols, 1906; Ten Teddy Bears (operetta), 1907; The Little Ghost of Halloween; April Fool (operetta), 1898; The County Fair. Plays: L'Enfant Terrible; Ann is Chic but Is She Safe? Address: Dedham MA‡

CUTTING, CHARLES SUYDAM, naturalist; b. New York, N.Y., Jan. 17, 1889; s. Robert Fulton and Helen (Suydam) C.; prep. edn. Groton Sch., 1903-09; A.B., Harvard, 1912; m. Helen McMahon, 1932 (dec. 1961); m. 2d, Mary Pyne Filley, Apr. 8, 1964. Trustee Robert F. Cutting Estate from 1913; field work on expdns. to Central Asia for Am. Museum Natural History, Field Museum of Natural History, Chicago, Pitt River Museum of Oxford, Eng. Trustee Am. Museum Natural History, New York Zool. Soc. Hon. fellow Field Museum of Natural History, Chicago. Served as 1st lt., U.S. Army during World War; with A.E.F. in France 15 months. Performed active duty abroad as lt. col., U.S. Army. Decorated Croix Noire (French), Croix de Guerre with Gold Star, Honorary Comdr. Most Excellent Order of British Empire. Member of Bombay Natural History Society, Royal Geog. Soc., Royal Central Asia Soc. (all Brit.); Himmalyan Club. Republican. Episcopalian. Clubs: Knickerbocker, Brook, Racquet (New York). Author: The Fire Ox and Other Years, 1940; also series of articles pub. by Am. Museum Natural History. Home: Bernardsville NJ Died Aug. 24, 1972.

CUTTING, WINDSOR COOPER, physician; b. Campbell, Cal., July 30, 1907; s. Theodore A. and Mary Elizabeth (Cooper) C.; A.B., Stanford, 1928, M.D., 1932; m. Mary E. Weaver, May 3, 1935; children—Cecil Cooper, John Weaver, David Windsor, Ann Ely, April Bourne, Susan Mary Atwood. Intern, sch. medicine Stanford, 1931-32, asst. resident medicine, 1932-34, resident, 1934-35, asst. prof. therapeutics, 1938-41, asso. prof., 1941-46, prof. therapeutics, 1946-50, exec. prof. pharmacology and therapeutics, 1950-54, prof. pharmacology, 1954-58, prof. exptl. therapeutics, 1958-64, dean, 1953-57; dir. Pacific Biomed. Research Center, U. Hawaii, 1964-66, dean Sch. Med., 1966-71. NRC fellow in medicine Courtauld Inst. Biochem., London, Eng., 1935-36; fellow med. and pharmacology Johns Hopkins, 1936-38. Mem. A.M.A. (council on drugs 1950-62), Am. Soc. Pharmacology and Exptl. Therapeutics, Soc. Exptl. Biology and Med., Am. Soc. Cancer Research, Cal. Acad. Med., U.S. Adopted Names Council (chmn. 1961-72). Author: Manual of Clinical Therapeutics, 1943, rev. edit., 1948; Actions and Uses of Drugs, 1946; Handbook of Pharmacology, 1962, rev. edits., 1964, 67, 69, 72. Exec. com. U.S. Pharmacopeia, 1950-60, bd. dirs., 1960-70, Annual Revs., Inc., 1959-70. Editor Annual Review Pharmacology, 1959-70. Contbr. profl. jours. Home: Haleiwa HI Died May 29, 1972; cremated.

CUTTLE, FRANCIS, pres. Riverside Water Co.; b. Montreal, Can., Sept. 25, 1864; s. George and Martha (Oborne) C.; came to U.S., 1881, naturalized 1887; ed. pub. schs.; m. Mae Penrose, Sept. 13, 1890; children—Richard F., Ted Penrose, Kenneth O. Began as a newsboy in Montreal, later laborer; zanjero, Riverside, Calif., 1887; supt. Riverside Water Co., 1888-1904, pres. since 1904. Mem. Water Conservation Assn. (pres.), State Bd. Forestry; mem. State Water Conservation, 1911-15. Advocated for years forest conservation out of which developed Civilian Conservation Corps camps. Republican. Mason. Club: Rotary. Home: 3207 Orange St. Office: 3596 Main St., Riverside CA*‡

DACOSTA, ALBERT LLOYD, singer; b. Amsterdam, N.Y., Mar. 21, 1928; s. Joseph Lewis and Violet (DaCosta) Sochin; Mus.B., Julliard Sch. Music; m. Jean Rower, May 27, 1946; children—Albert, Mary Beth, Christopher, Jonathan and Jennifer (twins), Gregory. Debut Metropolitan Opera, N.Y.C., 1954; appeared in Tristan, 1954-55, leading roles in Miestersinger, Boris Godonov, Rosencavelier, 1955-56; (Met. Opera); Wozzeck, Pagliacci, Parsifal, Electra; concerts Columbia Artists; European appearances, 1962-67, including Otello, Cologne, Germany. Served with USNR 1944-46. Home: Jamaica VT Died Nov. 7, 1967.

DADMUN, FRANCES MAY, author; b. Marlborough, Mass., Sept. 17, 1875; d. William E. and Marion R. (Estabrook) D.; B.A., Wellesley, 1899, M.A., 1901. Teacher and lecturer history of art, Norwich (Conn.) Art Sch., 1903-4, Swarthmore Coll., 1905-9, Tuckerman Sch., Boston, since 1922. Dir. religious edn. (Unitarian) in 4 parishes in Mass., 1909-20. Mem. Alpha Kappa Chi. Author: Living Together, 1915; Children of the Father, 1916. Home: 27 Linnaean St., Cambridge MA‡

DAGGETT, ATHERN PARK, educator; b. Springfield, Mo., Jan. 10, 1904; s. William Athern and Evelina (Park) D.; A.B., Bowdoin Coll., 1925; A.M. Harvard, 1928, Ph.D., 1931; m. Catherine Jordan Travis, Sept. 4 1936; children—William, Ellen (Mrs. Glatter). Instr English, Lafayette Coll., 1925-27; summer faculty U. Maine, 1930; instr. gov. Bowdoin Coll., 1930-31, 32-34, asst. prof., 1934-40, asso. prof., 1940-46, prof. 1946-73, William Nelson Cromwell prof. constl., internat. law and govt., 1951-73, acting pres. of coll., 1967-68; instr. polit. sci. Dartmouth Coll., 1931-32; adj. prof. polit. sci. Randolph-Macon Woman's Coll., 1932; vis. prof. polit sci. Brown U., 1948-49; summer faculty Columbia, 1953. Trustee Bangor Theol. Sem. Mem. Am. Soc. Internat. Law (exec. council 1940-43), Am., N.E. (exec. com. 1953-54, pres. 1956-57) polit. sci. assns., Congl. Christian Conf. Maine (pres. 1946-47), Phi Beta Kappa. Conglist. Home: Brunswick ME Died Jan. 20, 1973; buried Pine Grove Cemetery, Brunswick ME

DAGGY, MAYNARD LEE, educator; b. Greencastle, Ind., Nov. 27, 1874; s. Charles White and Ella (Lee) D.; Ph.B., DePauw U., 1896; studied Ind. Law Sch., Indianapolis, U. of Chicago, and Sch. of Expression, Boston; m. Marie Jay Stone, June 6, 1905; m. 2d, Alma G. Forsythe, Sept. 4, 1920. Instr. English, State Sch. for the Blind, Jacksonville, Ill., 1896-97; admitted to bar, Indianapolis, 1898, and practiced 1 yr.; instr. English high sch., Mt. Vernon, Ill., 1899-1900, high sch., Fond du Lac, Wis., 1900-01; instr. rhetoric and oratory, U. of Wis., 1901-04; asst. prof. rhetoric and oratory, U. of Wash., 1904-09, asst. prof., 1909-11, head of dept. of pub. speaking and debate, 1911; lecturer since 1895; treas. Redpath-Priest Lyceum Bureau, 1911-13; western supt. Chautauqua Mgrs. Assn., 1913-14,; asso. mgr. Edwards Lyceum Bureau, 1917-19; exec. sec. Am. Community Assn., Chicago, 1922-23; spl. extension lecturer, univs. of Wis., Minn. and Kan., 1917-23; asso. prof. speech, and head of dept. State Coll. of Wash., Pullman, 1923-25, prof. and head of dept., 1923-47; prof. emeritus since 1947; lecturer, City College of New York, summer 1938. Pres. Northwest Speech Conf., 1930-31, Wash. State Speech Assn., 1933-34. Charter mem. Internat. Lyceum Assn.; mem. Phi Gamma Delta, Delta Sigma Rho, Pi Gamma Mu, Nat. Collegiate Players (former pres.), Sigma Tau Delta, Alpha Psi Omega, Corda Fratra, Nat. Assn. Teachers of Speech, Western Assn. Teachers of Speech, The Thespians (hon.), Nat. Collegiate Radio Guild, Chamber of Commerce. Club: Kiwanis. Author: The Principles of Public Speaking, 1900; The Principles of Dramatic Reading, 1910. Asso. editor Players' Mag. Home: 304 Howard St., Pullman WA‡

DAHL, FRANCIS W., cartoonist; b. Wollaston, Mass., Oct. 21, 1907; s. J. Frank and Mildred (Boyd) D.; m. Louise C. Bartlett, June 4, 1933; children—Jane, Francis W., Jr. (dec.), Linda. Daily cartoons, Boston Herald Traveler, 1930-73; with Boston Globe, 1973. Author: (books) Left Handed Compliments, 1941; Dahl's Cartoons, 1943; What More Dahl? 1944; Dahl's Boston, 1946; Dahl's Brave New World, 1947; Birds, Beasts and Bostonians, 1954. Address: Boston MA Died May 7, 1973.

DALBY, ZACHARY LEWIS, lawyer; b. Farmville, Va., Sept. 21, 1870; s. John Anderson and Ann Churchill (Lewis) D.; student Hampden-Sydney Coll., Va., 1890-93; B.S., Columbian (now George Washington) U., 1898; LL.B., National U. Law Sch., Washington, D.C., 1901, LL.M., 1902; m. Dorothy Eva Juteau Bowles, Apr. 2, 1900; children—Dorothy Louise (Mrs. Basil Meigs), Henry Bowles, Helen Churchill (Mrs. Abner W. Biberman). With N. & W.R.R., Roanoke, Va., 1884-87; stenographer and sec. to pres. Sloss Iron & Steel Co., Birmingham, Ala., 1887-90; with various railroads until 1894; with U.S. Govt., 1894-1909, various capacities, becoming Indian inspector; admitted to bar, Dist. of Columbia, and practiced in Washington, 1909-17; legal work for U.S. Govt. since 1917, chief counsel U.S. Employees Compensation Commn. administering Federal Workmen's Compensation laws since 1928. Served as corpl. Co. K, D.C. Inf. Vols., May. to Sept. 1898, Spanish-Am. War; participated in Santiago Campaign and present at surrender of Santiago; volunteered but not accepted for World War; lt. col. Finance Reserves, U.S. Army, since 1925. Democrat. Christian Scientist. Home: 1615 Longfellow St., N.W. Office: 8th and E Sts., N.W., Washington DC‡

DALE, COUDOASHIA BERNICE WATTS (MRS. LUTHER W. DALE), librarian; b. Mexia, Tex.; d. Marshall Henry and Ora (Cleveland) Watts; B.S., Huston-Tillotson U., 1941; M.S., Emporia State Tchrs. Coll., 1961; postgrad. Denver U., 1952-58; m. Luther William Dale, June 7, 1958. Tchr. elementary schs., Parsons, Kan., 1945-58; asst. librarian Parsons (Kan.) Jr. Coll., 1958-59; librarian East High Sch., 1959-62; librarian Parsons Jr. High Sch., 1962-69. Trustee Parsons Pub. Library, 1965-69. Mem. League Women Voters, Am. Assn. U. Women (publicity chmn. 1962-65), Am., Kan. library assns., Kan. Assn. Sch. Librarians, Faculty Wives (pres. 1964-69), Christian Women's Fellowship (pres. 1960-69), Delta Sigma Theta (treas. 1954-60, asst. sec. 1964-69). Mem. Christian Ch. Mem. Order Eastern Star. Club, Jewel Art (v.p., dist. dir. 1965-69). Home: Parsons KS Died July 13, 1969.

DALE, EDWARD EVERETT, research prof. history; b. Keller, Tex., Feb. 8, 1879; s. John Franklin and Mattie Counts (Colley) D.; grad. Central State Tchrs. Coll., Edmond, Okla., 1909; A.B., U. of Okla., 1911; A.M., Harvard, 1914, Ph.D., 1922; m. Rosalie Gilkey, July 18, 1919; 1 son, Edward Everett. Cowboy and ranchman, 1896-1901; tchr. country sch., 1902-06; supt. schs., Headrick, 1906-07, Roosevelt, 1910, Blair, Okla., 1912-13; instr. in history, U. of Okla., 1914-24, prof. history and head dept., 1924-42; graduate prof. history, 1942-43; dir. Frank Phillips collection, 1927-52; research prof. history, from 1943, later research prof. history, emeritus; Fulbright lectr. in history U. Melbourne, Australia, 1953; vis. prof. history U. Houston, 1954-55, M.D. Anderson prof. history, 1958-59. Collaborator in hist. research, U.S. Dept. Agr. 1925; mem. Indian Survey Commn., U.S. Inst. for Govt. Research, 1926-27. Trustee Frank Phillips Fund of U. of Okla., Mary E. Laing Scholarship Fund. Mem. Agrl. Hist. Soc. (pres. 1925-27), Am. Miss. Valley (pres. 1936-37), So. Okla. hist. assns., Okla. State Folk Lore Assn. (ex-pres.), Ark, Ill. State Ind. hist. socs., Tex. Inst. of Letters Phi Beta Kappa, Acacia. Democrat. Mason. Clubs: Authors' Twentieth Century (Boston); Zamorano (Cal.). Author: Territorial Acquisitions of the UsS., 1912; Tales of the Teepee, 1919; (with J.S. Buchanan) A History of Oklahoma, 1924; The Prairie Schooner and Other Poems, 1929; The Range Cattle Industry, 1930; Cow Country, 1942. Compiler: Letters of Lafayette, 1926; Readings in Oklahoma History (with J. L. Rader), 1930; Frontier Trails, 1930; A Rider of the Cherokee Strip, 1936; Cherokee Cavaliers (with Gaston Litton), 1939; History of U.S. (with D. L. Dumond and E. B. Wesley), 1948; History of Oklahoma (with M. L. Wardell), 1948; Oklahoma, The Story of a State, 1949; The Indians of the Southwest, 1949; (with J. D. Morrison) Pioneer Judge, 1958; Frontier Ways, 1960; The Cross Timbers: Memories of A North Texas Boyhood, 1966; The Vanquished Prairie, 1973. Home: Norman OK Died May 28, 1972; buried I.O.O.F. Cemetery, Norman OK

DALE, SIR HENRY HALLETT, scientist; b. London, Eng., 1875; s. C. J. Dale; Scholar, Leys Sch., Coutts-Trotter Student Trinity Coll., Cambridge; St. Bartholomew's Hosp.; George Henry Lewes student, Sharpey Scholar, U. Coll., M.A., M.D., D.Sc., LL.D.; m. 1904; one son (deceased), two daughters. Director of Wellcome Physiological Research Lab., 1904-14; mem. Gen. Med. Council, 1927-37; dir. Nat. Inst. for Med. Research, Hampstead, 1928-42; Crown nominee to Ct. of London U., 1939-50; Fullerian prof. Royal Instn., 1942-46; Croonian lectr. Royal Soc., 1919, Herter Lectures, Balt., 1919, Harvey lectures, N.Y.C., 1919, 37, Croonian lectr. Royal Coll. Physicians, 1929; Dohme lectures, Balt., 1933, Welch lectures, N.Y.C., 1937, Pilgrim Trust lecture, Philadelphia, 1946; chairman Wellcome Trust, 1938-60. Mem. sci. adv. commn. to War Cabinet, 1940-47, chairman, 1942-47 Knighted, 1932. Decorated Medal of Freedom with Silver Palm (U.S.A.); Orden Pour le merite (Fed. Republic Germany); Order of Merit, Grand Cross Order Brit. Empire; recipient Nobel prize (with O. Loewi), 1936. Fellow of the Royal Society (president 1940-45); fellow Royal College of Physicians; fgn. asso. Nat. Acad. Sci. U.S.A. Clubs: Athenaeum. Author articles profl. jours. Home: Cambridge England Died Aug. 1968.

DALEY, WILLIAM RAYMOND, investment banker; b. Ashtabula, O., Sept. 26, 1892; s. Flory and Margaret (Coade) D.; A.B., Adelbert Coll., Western Res. U., 1915; LL.B., Western Res. U., 1917; m. Florence Catherine Doran, Nov. 20, 1920; children—Kathleen, Jane. Admitted to Ohio bar, 1917; asso. with Bulkley, Hauxhurst, Inglis & Saeger, Cleveland, 1917-28, partner, 1925-28; with Otis & Co., investments, 1928-71, pres., dir., 1931-71; ltd. partner Milw. Brewers Baseball Co.; chmn. Reading Co.; trustee U.S. Realty Investments; dir. Murray Ohio Mfg. Co., also various corps. Trustee Catholic Charities Corp.; chmn. Cleve. Opera Assn. Mem. bd. lay trustees U. Notre Dame. Served as sgt. Machine Gun Co., 331st Inf., later lt. 27th F.A. 1917-18; mem. Troop A, 107th Cav., 1919-23. Mem. Investment Bankers Assn. (gov. 1937-39), Cleve. Bar Assn., Pi Kappa Alpha, Delta Theta Phi, Order of Coif. Roman Catholic. Clubs: Seminole Golf (Palm Beach, Fla.); Union, Mayfield Country, Pepper Pike Country (Cleve.); Pinnacle, Marco Polo (N.Y.C.). Home: Cleveland OH Died Oct. 21, 1971; buried Calvary Cemetery, Cleveland OH

DALLENBACH, KARL M., psychologist; b. Champaign, Ill., Oct. 20, 1887; s. John J. and Anna Caroline (Mittendorf) D.; B.A., U. of Ill., 1910; M.A., U. of Pittsburgh, 1911; Ph.D., Cornell U., 1913; m. Ethel Leila Douglas, Aug. 22, 1914; children—John Wallace, Elizabeth Ann, Frederick Douglas. Asst. in psychology, U. of Ill., 1909-10; fellow in psychology, U. of Pittsburgh, 1910-11, Sage fellow, Cornell U., 1911-12; instr. in psychology, U. of Ore., 1913-15, Ohio State U., 1915-16, Cornell, 1916-18, 1919-21; asst. prof. Cornell U., 1921-30, prof., 1932-45. Sage prof. psychology, 1945-48; distinguished professor of psychology, University of Texas, from 1948, chmn. dept., from 1950; visiting prof. Columbia, 1930-32. Capt., U.S. Army, 1918-19, O.R.C., 1919-42, 1946-48, lt. col., Adj. Gen.'s Dept., Army of U.S., 1942-46, ret., 1948. Asso. and business editor Am. Jour. Psychology, 1921-25, editor from 1926. Chmn. emergency com. in psychology, The National Research Council, 1940-46. Fellow A.A.A.S. (v.p., chmn. Sec. I, 1940); mem. Am. Psychol. Assn. (dir. 1928-30, 1951-54, pres. div. I, 1951), Soc. of Exptl. Psychologists, Am. Assn. Univ. Profs., Southern Soc. Philosophy and Psychology (council member 1952-55, president 1954), Texas Psychological Assn., Eastern Psychol. Assn. (dir. 1937-38; pres. 1939), Psychometric Soc., Am. Legion, Sigma Xi, Phi Kappa Phi, Phi Delta Kappa, Delta Upsilon, Nu Sigma Nu, Psi Chi, Acacia. Republican. Mason. Club: Rotary. Author articles and monographs on psychology. Editor: Washburn Commemorative Volume, 1927; General Index, Am. Jour. Psychology, vols. 1-30, 1926; vols. 31-50, 1942; Golden Jubilee Volume, Am. Jour. Psychology, 1937. Home: Austin TX Died Dec. 23, 1971; buried Champaign IL

DALSIMER, SAMUEL, advt. exec.; b. N.Y.C., Nov. 13, 1908; s. Nathan Samuel and Carolyn (Baum) D.; student Cornell U., 1930; m. Shirley Marjorie Wasch, Jan. 17, 1935; children—James Samuel, Andrew Samuel. Copywriter, account exec., Husband & Thomas Co., 1932-36; v.p. Brown & Thomas, 1936-40; v.p. Cecil & Presbrey, Inc., 1940-54, exec. v.p., 1954-55; v.p., mem. exec. com., supr. Grey Advt. Agy., Inc., 1955-61, exec. v.p., 1961-64, vice chmn. bd., 1964-69. Program mgr. OWI, 1944-45; chmn. nat. program com. and nat. commr. Anti-Defamation League of B'nai B'rith, 1955; nat. chmn. Anti-Defamation League, 1969. Home: New York City NY Died Aug. 22, 1969.

DALSTROM, OSCAR FREDERICK, engineer; b. Wyanet, Ill., Aug. 15, 1871; s. Anders John and Anna Christina (Jacobson) D.; grad. Fremont (Neb.) Normal Sch., 1895; student civ. engring. course, U. of Neb., 1897-98; C.E., Rensselaer Poly. Inst., 1901; unmarried. Teacher dist. and village schs., 1894-97; draftsman and shop inspector, bridge dept., Pa. Steel Co., 1901-03 and 1904-06; draftsman Scherzer Rolling Lift Bridge Co., 1903-04; draftsman Riverside Bridge Co., Martin's Ferry, O., Apr.-Dec. 1904; with C. & N.W. Ry. Co. since 1906, draftsman bridge dept. until 1909, chief draftsman same dept., 1909-17, engr. of bridges since 1917. Mem. Am. Soc. C.E., Am. Ry. Engring. Assn., A.A.A.S., Western Soc. Engrs. Republican. Club: Engineers. Home: 4109 N. Paulina St. Office: 400 W. Madison St., Chicago IL‡

DALTON, ALBERT CLAYTON, army officer (ret.); b. Lafayette, Ind., Oct. 2, 1867; grad. Inf. and Cav. Sch., Ft. Leavenworth, Kan., 1895, Gen. Staff Sch., 1920, War Coll., 1921; m. Caro Gordon, 1907. Pvt., corpl. and sergt. Co. A, 22d Inf., Jan. 18, 1889-Aug. 1, 1891; 2d lt. 22d Inf., July 31, 1891; promoted through grades to brigadier-gen. Q.M.C., Dec. 8, 1922. Participated in Cheyenne Indian Campaign, 1890, Sioux Campaign, 1891, Santiago Campaign, 1898, Philippine Campaign, 1899-1902; with Army of Cuban Occupation, 1907-09, Vera Cruz Expdn., 1914; on Mexican border, 1916-17; organized Expeditionary Depot, Phila., Sept.-Oct. 1917; gen. supt. Army Transport Service, New York, Nov. 1, 1917-Nov. 5, 1918; comdr. 18th Inf. Brig., 9th Div., Nov. 6, 1918-Feb. 5, 1919; duty in France, May-Aug. 1919; apptd. asst. q.m. gen., Washington, D.C., Dec. 8, 1922; retired, July 7, 1926; apptd. pres. U.S. Shipping Bd. Merchant Fleet Corp., July 8, 1926, later v.p. and gen. mgr. same. Awarded Silver Star for gallantry in action, 1899; D.S.M. for World War service; decorated with Grand Officer Crown of Rumania. Home: 4000 Washington DC‡

DALTON, JOHN M(ONTGOMERY), lawyer; b. Vernon Co., Mo., Nov. 9, 1900; s. Fred A. and Ida Jane (Poage) D.; LL.B., U. Mo., 1923; LL.D., Drury College, University of Missouri, Westminster College, William Jewell College; m. Geraldine Hall, Nov. 22, 1925; children—John Hall, Julia Hall. Admitted to Mo. bar, 1923, practiced, Kennett, Mo., 1923-52; city counselor, Kennett, 1944-53; legislative counsel Mo. Rural Electrification Coop. Assn., 1951-52; atty. gen. Mo., 1952-60; governor Missouri, 1961-65; practice of law, Jefferson City, Mo., 1965-—. Chmn., Fed. Home Loan Bank, Des Moines, Ia. Mem. bd. visitors U. Mo., 1949-53; trustee Westminster Coll., The School of the Ozarks; member bd. curators Stephens Coll. Mem. Nat. Assn. Attys. Gen. (past pres.), Am. Coll. Trial Lawyers, Phi Delta Phi, Phi Gamma Delta. Democrat. Presbyn. Mason. Club: Lions (gov. Mo. 1931-32). Home: Jefferson City Died July 7, 1972; buried Oak Ridge Cemetery, Kennett MO

DALTON, WILLIAM, mech. engr.; b. Albany, N.Y., Sept. 12, 1869; s. Philip W. and Harriet A. D.; M.E., Cornell, 1890; m. Ida M. Hill, of Nashville, Sept. 3, 1895; m. 2d, Sylvia Loines, of Schenectady, N.Y., 1929. Began in machine shop, Buffalo, N.Y., 1890; chief engr. Am. Locomotive Co., 1902-16; gen. mgr. Washington (D.C.) Steel & Ordnance Co., 1916-18; with Gen. Electric Co., Schenectady, N.Y., since 1918. Mem. Am. Soc. Mech. Engrs. Home: R.D. No. 2, Schenectady NY‡

DALY, SISTER CECILIA, educator; b. Bklyn., Jan. 14, 1905; d. Timothy W. and Margaret (Burke) Daly;

Ph.B., De Paul U., 1945, M.A., 1956; postgrad. Marquette U., 1957, Fordham U., 1958. Tchr. elementary schs., Mobile, Ala., Donaldsville, La., 1923-47; tchr. Laboure High Sch., St. Louis, 1947-57; chmn. dept. history Marillac Coll., St. Louis, 1957-70, prof. history. Tchr., Adult Edn. Program, Kinlock, Mo., 1965-66. Mem. Ma. Hist. Assn., Nat. Council Social Studies, Am. Geog. Assn. Home: St Louis MO Died Oct. 31, 1968.

DALY, JOHN FIDLAR, physician, educator; b. Overton, Neb. Oct. 12, 1905; s. William H. and Jessie Huff (Fidlar) D.; B.S., Knox Coll., 1926, student Northwestern U. Sch. Medicine, 1926-28; M.D., U. Pa., 1930; m. Catharine Gardette Maury, Mar. 15, 1930. Intern Hosp. of U. Pa., 1930-32; gen. practice of medicine, 1932-40; grad. tng. in dermatology Columbia-Presbyn. Med. Center, N.Y.C., 1946-49; prof. dermatology, chmn. div. U. Vt., from 1949; pvt. practice specializing dermatology, Burlington, Vt., from 1949. Served as maj. M.C., AUS, 1940-46. Decorated Silver Star. Diplomate Am. Bd. Dermatology and Syphilology. Fellow Am. Acad. Dermatology and Syphilology; mem. A.M.A. Canadian Dermatol. Assn., New Eng., Montreal dermatol. socs. Home: Hivesburg VT Died Jan. 16, 1969; buried Village Cemetery, Hivesburg VT

DAMBACH, CHARLES ARTHUR, educator; b. Cleve., Dec. 31, 1911; s. Frederick and Alida (Carpenter) D.; B.S.A., Ohio State U., 1937, M.S., 1941, Ph.D., 1945; m. Christine Kibler, Aug. 21, 1937; children—Charlou Emily, George Ernest, Charles Frederick. Biologist, asst. regional biologist U.S. Soil Conservation Service, 1934-42; dir. conservation curriculum Ohio State U., 1942-50, dir. Natural Resources Inst., 1955-68; dir. Sch. Natural Resources, 1968-69; chief Ohio div. wildlife Dept. of Natural Resources, 1950-55. Adviser com. on agrl. pests NRC; mem. sci. adv. com. Great Lakes Fish Commn.; exec. sec. Ohio Biol. Survey; chmn. Ohio chpt., counselor Nature Conservancy; trustee Ohio Conservation Found. Fellow A.A.A.S., Ohio Academy of Scis., Soil Conservation Soc. Am.; mem. Ecol. Soc. Am., Soc. of Am. Foresters, Outdoor Writers Am., Izaak Walton League Am., Wildlife Soc. (pres. 1958-60), Conservation Edn. Assn., Internat. Assn. Fish, Game and Conservation Commns., Sigma Xi, Gamma Sigma Delta. Home: Worthington OH Died Oct. 30, 1969; buried Union Cemetery, Columbus OH

DAME, ELIZABETH L., exec. sec.; b. Titusville, Pa., Aug. 6, 1904; d. Alan Grant and Louise (Fiely) Dame; grad. Bryant-Stratton Coll., 1924; student Villa Maria Coll., 1937-38, N.Y. U., summer 1948. With Guardian Life Ins. Co., Buffalo, 1926-27, Titusville Forge Co., 1927-32; sec. to pres. 2d Nat. Bank, Tutusville, 1932-37; sec. to bishop Episcopal Diocese, See City, Erie, Pa., 1937-49; exec. sec. Trinity Episcopal Ch., Tulsa, 1949-52; owner Pub. Stenography Office, Tulsa, 1952-57; sec. to dir. nursing USPHS Hosp., Mt. Edgecumbe, Alaska, 1957-59; sec. to supt. Mt. Edgecumbe (Alaska) High Sch., 1959-63; exec. sec. with asst. area dir. Bur. Indian Affairs, Juneau, Alaska, 1963-68. Sec., Tulsa chpt. Arthritis and Rheumatism Nat. Found., 1954-57; sec.-treas. Nat. Fedn. Fed. Employees, Mt. Edgecumbe, 1962-63. Mem. D.A.R., (chpt. sec. 1966-68, state sec. 1964-66, state hist. chmn. 1967-68), Nat. Secs. Assn. Episcopalian. Clubs: Soroptimist (corr. sec. 1967-68). Home: Juneau AK Died 1968.

DAME, J. FRANK, educator; b. Farmington, N.H., Dec. 2, 1905; s. Walter S. and Ethel M. (Young) D.; diploma Bay Path. Inst., 1925; B.S., N.Y.U., 1930; Ed.M., Temple U., 1934, Ed.D., 1938; m. Florence Pedrick, November 18, 1928; children—Margaret Anne, Robert Frank, John Walter. Began as a high school teacher in Upper Darby, Pa., 1925-42; supr. business edn., pub. schs. of Washington, 1942-45; dir. bus. edn. Temple U., 1945-46, Bloomsburg (Pa.) State Tchrs. Coll., 1946-47; dir. edn. Nat. Office Mgmt. Assn., 1947-48; prof. bus. edn. Fla. State U., 1948-61, dean sch. bus. 1951-53; pres. Jones Bus. Coll., from 1961. Author: Exploratory Business Training (rev. 1961); Guidance in Business Education (rev. edit.), 1953; Typewriting Techniques and Shortcuts, 1948 (rev. 1961); Transcription Office Practice, 1957. Home: Winter Park FL Died Oct. 30, 1969.

DAMESHEK, WILLIAM, physician, hematologist, editor; b. Voronezh, Russia, May 22, 1900; s. Isadore and Bessie (Muskin) D.; brought to U.S., 1902, naturalized, 1921; M.D., Harvard, 1923; m. Rose Thurman, Oct. 14, 1923; 1 dau., Elinor Thurman (Wife of Dr. Seymour Reichlin). Intern, Boston City Hosp., 1923-25, asst. blood lab., 1925-28; chief blood lab. Beth Israel Hosp., Boston 1928-39; sr. physician, hematologist, dir. blood research lab. New Eng. Center Hosp., Boston, 1939-69; cons. hematologist Lynn. Waltham, Mt. Auburn, Malden, U.S. V.A. hosp.; consultant Surgeon-Gen., U.S. Army; successively asst., instr., asst. prof., prof. medicine Tufts University Sch. of Medicine, 1925-67, professor emeritus, 1967-69; extraordinary prof. medicine at National Univ., Mexico, 1945; prof. medicine, honoris causae, U. Santiago, Chile; grad. lectr. hematology in many countries in Europe, South Am. and the Orient. Awarded Certificate of Merit, A.M.A., 1945, Silver medal, 1951; Claude Bernard medal University of Montreal, 1950; Premia Ferrata, Rome, 1958; decorated Commander Order of Carlos Finlay (Cuba). Fellow A.M.A., A.C.P., A.A.A.S., Am. Soc. Clin. Investigation, Internat. Soc. Hematology (pres. 1954-56), Am. Soc. Immunology, Am. Soc. Exptl. Pathology; Am. Acad. Arts and Scis., N.Y. Acad. Scis.; mem. Greater Boston Med. Soc. (pres. 1933), Peruvian Soc. Pathology (hon.), Am. (pres. 1964), Italian, Swiss, Chilean, French, European societies hematology (hon.), Chilean Soc. Internal Medicine, Soc. Exptl. Biology and Medicine. Club: Harvard (Boston). Author: Leukopenia and Agranulocytosis, 1944; Hemolytic Syndromes, 1945; Spleen and Hypersplenism, 1947; Chemotherapy of Leukemia and Leukosarcoma, 1949; Leukemia, 1958; also numerous articles medical jours. Co-author: Hemorrhagic Disorders, 1955. Founder and editor-in-chief Blood, the Jour. of Hematology, 1945-69; Home: New York City NY Died Oct. 1969.

DAMON, FRANK HARDY, educator; b. Buenos Aires, S.A., July 20, 1870; s. Capt. Mason and Joan (Hardy) D.; B.S., U. of Me., 1895; m. Annie Hinckley Atwood, of Hampden, Me., Dec. 30, 1896; 1 dau., Joan Atwood. Instr. U. of Me., 1893-96, Bangor High Sch., 1896-1908, Powder Point Sch., 1908-09; supt. schs., Lexington, Mass., 1909-14, Dover, N.H., 1915-17; Army ednl. work, 1917-19; pres. Damon Hall Junior Coll., Newton, since 1918. Mem. Newton Hist. Soc. (pres.), Newton Chamber of Commerce, Soc. Mayflower Descendants, S.A.R., Beta Theta Pi (pres. N.E. Assn.), Phi Kappa Phi, De Burians; hon. corr. mem. Ancient Council of Heraldry and History of France. Pres. Descendants of John Damon; dir. Edward Bangs Descendants. Conglist. Republican. Mason. Author: Life of Captain Mason Damon; John Adams, President; Manual of Short Story Writing; How to Train Your Mind, Co-Editor: Colonel Baldwin's Revolutionary Journal. Compiler: Tercentenary History of Newton, Mass. Lecturer on ednl. and hist. subjects. Home: 16 Fairmont Av., Newton MA‡

DAMON, NORMAN CLARE, traffic safety specialist; b. Gerry, N.Y., Nov. 7, 1897; s. George Clayton and Frances (Norman) D.; A.B., U. of Mich.; m. Madeleine Hoag, Sept. 6, 1922; children—Robert Bates, Norman Strong, Terry Allen. Sec. to chmn., Highway Transport Com., Council of Nat. Defense, 1917-18; sec. to pres. Hudson Motor Car Co., 1919; asst. to Washington rep., Automobile Mfrs. Assn., 1922-36; sec. coms., Nat. Conf. on Street and Highway Safety, 1924, 26, 30; sec. safety com. Automobile Mfrs. Assn., 1930-37; staff organizer and first dir. Automotive Safety Found., 1937, v.p., dir. grants, from 1942; mem. Traffic Conf. Nat. Safety Council, also mem. exec. com. edn., mem. D.C. citizens traffic bd., chmn. traffic tng. com.; mem. research com. Adv. Council to Pres. Com. for Traffic Safety. Recipient Hon. Key, Northwestern U. Traffic Inst., 1951. Hon. life mem. Nat. Sheriffs Assn.; mem. Inst. Traffic Engrs., Internat. Assn. Chiefs Police, Am. Soc. Safety Engrs., Phi Delta Theta, Sigma Delta Chi. Presbyn. Clubs: University, Corinthian Yacht, Cosmos, Press (Washington); University (Chicago). Author traffic safety articles. Asso. editor Traffic Safety Research Rev. Home: Washington DC Died Aug. 6, 1967.

DAMON, S(AMUEL) FOSTER, author; b. Newton, Mass., Feb. 22, 1893; s. Joseph Neal and Sarah Wolf (Pastorius) Damon; A.B., Harvard, 1914, A.M., 1927; A.M. (honorary), Brown University, 1943; married Louise Wheelwright, Feb. 4, 1928. Traveling fellow American Scandinavian Foundation, 1920-21; asst. in English, Harvard, 1921-27; asst. prof. English, Brown U., 1927-30; asso. prof., 1930-36, prof. from 1936; curator Harris Collection Am. Poetry, Brown, from 1929. Odist at Boston Beethoven Centenary Festival, Mar. 28, 1927. Member American Antiquarian Society, R.I. Hist. Soc., N.E. Poetry Club (hon. pres.), Providence Art Club. Clubs: Harvard, St. Botolph; Annisquam Yacht. Author: William Blake—His Philosophy and Symbols, 1924; A New Page in Blake's Milton, 1925; Astrolabe (verse), 1927; Tilted Moons (verse), 1929; Thomas Holley Chivers, 1930; The Day After Christmas, 1930; Amy Lowell, A Chronicle, 1935; The Doctrine of Job, 1950; History of Square Dancing, 1957, others. Plays: Witch of Dogtown (Russel Crouse award), 1954; Punch and Judy, 1957. Editor: Series of Am. Songs, 1936. Translator: Complete Works of Thomas Holley Chivers, Vol. I, 1957. (with others) A Book of Danish Verse, 1922. Home: Providence RI Died Dec. 25, 1971; buried Mt. Auburn Cemetery, Weston MA

DANA, FRANK M., banker; b. Prescott, Ont., Can., June 28, 1906; s. Frank C. and Margaret I. (Collins) D.; LL.B., U. San Francisco, 1928; grad. Am. Inst. of Banking; grad. Am. Bankers Assn. Grad. Sch. of Banking, Rutgers U., 1938; m. Wanda Hall, July 2, 1949; children—Randal, Scott, Leslie, Charleen. Messenger, Bank of America, 1922, asst. personel dir., 1932, asst. v.p., 1938, asst. to pres., 1942, corp. sec., 1944-46, v.p., supr. brs., 1946-51, v.p., supr. operations, 1951-59, exec. v.p., 1959-68, mem. mng. com., adv. com., dir., 1957-68. Faculty mem. Pacific Coast Banking Sch., U. Wash., 1956-68. Regent Grad. Sch. Banking Rutgers U., 1951-68, faculty mem., 1958-67; faculty Banking Summer Sch., Saint Andrews, Scotland, 1958. Recipient Leonard P. Ayres Leadership award. Stonier Grad. Sch. Banking, Rutgers U., 1965. Past pres. San Francisco chpt. Am. Inst. Banking; past dir. San Francisco Jr. C. of C.; mem. Am. Bankers Assn. (past chmn. bank mgmt. com.), Cal. Bankers Assn. (pres. 1965-66), Am. Mgmt. Assn., Assn. Res. City Bankers. Roman Catholic. Club: Commercial, The Family (San Francisco). Co-author banking texts. Home: Berkeley CA Died Nov. 28, 1968; buried Holy Cross Cemetery, Colma CA

DANE, WALTER ALDEN, lawyer; b. Newport, Vt., Feb. 4, 1882; s. Olin S. and Mabel (Robinson) D.; A.B., Univ. of Vt., 1903; student George Washington U. Law Sch., 1906-08; LL.D., Norwich U., 1937; m. Bertha A. Aldrich, Sept. 16, 1907 (dec.); children—Barbara, Harriet F., Helen R.; m. 2d, Dorothy Horne, Jan. 14, 1960. Confidential sec. to U.S. sec. of Navy, 1907-08; admitted to Mass. bar, 1912, practiced in Boston; mem Dane, Howe & Brown; special counsel Christian Science Orgn., Boston; director, general counsel John Hinckley & Son Co.; dir. counsel E. C. Schirmer Music Company; counsel, sec. Bon Marche Dry Goods Co. Member of the bar of the U.S. Supreme Court. Trustee of Newton-Wellesley Hospital, Children's Hosp., Boston. Charter member World Peace Through Law Center. Member Am., Mass. bar associations, Phi Beta Kappa, Delta Psi; asso. mem. Assn. Bar City of N.Y. Republican. Conglist. Mason (32 deg.). Clubs: Dorset Field, Union, Brae Burn Country. Home: Dorset VT Died Dec. 27, 1971; buried Pine Grove Cemetery, Newport VT

DANFORTH, CHARLES H., army officer; b. District of Columbia, Feb. 5, 1876; grad. Infantry and Cavalry Sch., 1903, Air Service Pilots Sch. and Air Service Bombardment Sch., 1921. Began as pvt. U.S.A., June 16, 1898; commd. 2d lt. inf., Feb. 2, 1901; advanced through grades to col.; chief of Air Corps, rank of brig. gen., for term 1930-34; reverted to rank of col., 1934; now retired. Address: War Dept., Washington DC‡

DANHOF, RALPH JOHN, clergyman; b. Chgo., July 28, 1900; s. John and Marie (Hoekstra) D.; A.B., Calvin Coll., 1922, Th.B., 1925; Th.D., Free U. Amsterdan, Netherlands, 1929; m. Margaret Van Dellen, Sept. 22, 1926; children—John William, Helene (Mrs. Richard DeHoek), Calvin, Roger. Ordained to ministry Christian Ref. Ch., 1929; pastor, Pella, Ia., 1929-34, Holland, Mich., 1934-45, Neland Av. Ch., Grand Rapids, Mich., 1945-56; stated clk. Christian Ref. Ch., 1945-71, also exec. sec., 1956-71. Del. to Assembly of Chs., South Africa, 1949. Home: Grand Rapids MI Died Oct. 13, 1971.

DANIEL, CHARLES WILLIAM, clergyman; b. Monticello, Ark., May 6, 1874; s. William Dudley and Effie (Clayton) D.; M.A., Union University, Jackson, Tenn., 1894; LL.D. from same, 1933; student Southern Baptist Theol. Sem., 1894-96; D.D., Ouachita Coll., Ark., 1900; m. Alice Calhoun, Feb. 11, 1897; children—Tyler (Mrs. F. D. Burge), Effie Clayton (Mrs. T. B. Washington). Ordained Baptist minister, March 27, 1893; pastor, Texarkana, Texas, 1896-97, successively at Pine Bluff, Arkansas, Covington, Kentucky, Fort Worth, Tex., First Ch., Atlanta, Ga., to 1927, First Ch., Richmond, 1928-34, 1st Ch., Eldorado, Ark., 1934-44. Past pres. exec. com. Southern Baptist Convention. Home: 1109 W. Peachtree St., Atlanta GA‡

DANIEL, J. MCTYEIRE, prof. education; b. Walhalla, S.C., Dec. 4, 1896; s. Joseph Luther and Letitia (Smith) D.; A.B., Wofford Coll., Spartanburg, S.C., 1917; A.M., U. of South Carolina, 1929; Ed.M., Harvard, 1931, Ed.D., 1935; m. Frances Gibson, Aug. 8, 1923. Prin. high sch., Abbeville, S.C., 1918-22; supt. pub. shcs., Conway, S.C., 1922-26; state high sch. supervisor, State Department of Edn., Columbia, S.C. 1926-32; professor education U. of South Carolina, Columbia, S.C., since 1932. Supervisor of Merit System (part-time), State Dept. Pub. Welfare. Mem. Am. Assn. U. Profs., S.C. Edn. Assn., So. Assn. Colls. and Secondary Schs. (commn. research and service 1949-54, chmn. from 1954; state chmn. secondary sch. commn. 1959—), National Soc. Coll. Tchrs., Phi Beta Kappa, Phi Delta Kappa, Kappa Phi Kappa, Pi Gamma Mu. Clubs: Kosmos, Torch, Wardlaw (Columbia). Author: Excellent Teachers, Their Qualities and Qualifications, 1944. Co-author: South Carolina, Economic and Social, 1945. Home: Columbia SC Died Oct. 21, 1970; buried Rosemont Cemetery, Newberry SC

DANIEL, RICHARD POTTS, lawyer; b. Jacksonville, Fla., July 13, 1880; s. Col. James Jaquelin and Emily Isabel (L'Engle) D.; ed. Jacksonville pub. schs.; student U. of the South, Sewanee, Tenn., 1896-98, Washington and Lee U. Law Sch., 1900-01; m. Mary Goff Palmer, June 10, 1911 (dec. 1951); children—Mason (Mrs. Edward W. Barrett), Jaquelin James, Mary Palmer (Mrs. Overton Thompson, Jr.). Admitted to Florida bar, 1902; practiced in Jacksonville, 1902-68; mem. firm Daniel, Mitchell & Higgins counsel Fla. State Road Dept., 1937-41; mem. Jacksonville City Council,

1908-11. Major judge advocate, Fla. Nat Guard, 1910-16; mem. U.S. Selective Service Bd., 1917-18; capt. Mil. Intelligence Div., U.S. Army, 1918-19. Past chmn. Civilian Adv. Com. for Naval Officer Procurement; mem. Ration Bd. Dir., chmn. endowment fund Daniel Meml. Home for Children; pres. Jacksonville Asso. Charities, 1916-18, Jacksonville Hist. Society, 1945-46; pres. Jacksonville Art Museum, 1953-56, also trustee; chmn. Duval Co. Welfare Bd., 1923-31; mem. Civil Service Bd., Duval Co., 1942-43; dir. So. Regional Council; mem. trustees Jacksonville Public Library; past president of Florida Historical Society; founder Jacksonville Urban League which created R. P. Daniel award good citizenship. Member of the Florida (honored for 50 years practice 1963) and Jacksonville bar assns., Kappa Alpha (Southern). Demo. Episcopalian. Clubs: Florida Yacht, River. Home: Jacksonville FL Died June 4, 1968; buried Evergreen Cemetery, Jacksonville FL

DANIELL, FRANCIS RAYMOND, journalist; b. New Haven, Conn., Oct. 22, 1901; s. Francis Guild and Maude Louise (Mazeine) D.; ed. Rutgers U., 1919-23; m. Blanche Elizabeth Naylor, June 13, 1924 (divorced);children—Curtis Guild, Elizabeth Lake; m. 2d, Tatiana Long, Nov. 22, 1941. Began as reporter 1923; successively on New York Herald, Associated Press, New York Post; with New York Times, 1929-67, chief London corr., 1939-45, and dir. New York Times, Ltd., London; chief, Berlin bureau, 1945-46; European corr. N.Y. Times Sunday Dept., 1946-49; chief London corr., 1949-53; corr. Canadian Times, 1953-67. Recipient Distinguished Alumnus Medal, Rutgers U. Mem. English Speaking Union, Delta Kappa Epsilon. Episcopalian. Clubs: D K E (N.Y. City); American Correspondents, Press (London). Author: Civilians Must Fight, 1941. Contbr. chapter Land of the Free" to We Saw it Happen, 1938; contbr. to mags. Home: Ottawa ON Canada Died Apr. 12, 1969.

DANIELS, FARRINGTON, prof. chemistry; b. Minneapolis, Minn., Mar. 8, 1889; s. Franc Burchard and Florence Louise (Farrington) D.; B.S., U. of Minn., 1910, M.S., 1911; Ph.D., Harvard, 1914; D.Sc., Univ. Rhode Island, University Minnesota, University Dakar, U. Louisville, University Wis.; m. Olive M. Bell, Sept. 15, 1917; children—Farrington, Florence Mary (Drury), Miriam (Ludwig), Dorin. Instr. in chemistry, Worcester (Mass.) Poly. Inst., 1914-17, asst. prof., 1917-18; electrochem. U.S. Nitrogen Research Lab., Washington, 1919-20; asst. prof. chemistry, U. of Wis., 1920-24, asso. prof., 1924-28, prof., 1928-59, emeritus, 1959-72, chmn. dept. chemistry 1952-59, research Solar Energy Laboratory, Engineering Expt. Sta.; prof. chemistry Stanford, summer 1930; George Fisher Baker non-res. lecturer chemistry, Cornell Univ., Feb.-June 1935; vis. scholar Cranbrook Institute Sci., 1968. Dir. metall. lab., U. of Chicago, 1945-46; chmn. bd. govs., Argonne Nat. Laboratory, 1946-48. Served as 1st lt., U.S. Chem. Warfare Service, 1918. Recipient Outstanding Achievement award U. Minn., 1950, Norris award for excellence in teaching, 1957, Distinguished Service Citation U. Wis., 1972. Guggenheim fellow, 1952. Fellow A.A.A.S. (chmn. chem. sect. 1937, 1947); mem. Am. Chem. Soc. (pres. 1953; Willard Gibbs Medal; Priestley medal), Nat. Acad. Scis. (vice president 1957-61), Am. Acad. Arts and Scis., Geochemical Society (president 1958), American Philosophical Society, Solar Energy Society (president 1964-66), Sigma Xi (president 1965-66), Phi Beta Kappa, Alpha Delta Phi, Alpha Chi Sigma. Conglist. Author: Mathematical Preparation for Physical Chemistry; Chemical Kinetics; Direct Use of the Suns Energy. Co-author: Physical Chemistry; Experimental Physical Chemistry; Challenge of Our Times: Solar Energy Research. Research chem. kinetics, nitrogen oxides, thermoluminescence of crystals, atomic energy and solar energy. Home: Madison WI Died June 24, 1972.

DANIELS, JOHN KARL, sculptor; b. Norway, May 14, 1875; s. Daniel Jakobsen and Beret Martha (Jensen) D.; prep. edn., Mechanic's Arts High Sch., St. Paul; m. Hazel Cecelia Bimer, Feb. 5, 1910 (div.); children—Elizabeth Cecelia, Mahlon, Karl. Rep. by portrait statues of Alexander Wilkin, Gen. John B. Sanborn, Senator Knute Nelson (all at Minn. state capitol, St. Paul); monuments at Andersonville, Ga., Little Rock, Ark., Memphis, Tenn., Nashville, Tenn., Jefferson Barracks, Mo., Shiloh battlefield, etc. Awarded 3 gold medals and 5 first awards, Recent work, figures for Washington Park water tower, Pioneer Monument, Minneapolis, Charles M. Babock Memorial, Elk River, Minn., 12 1/2 ton granite Bison (single handed) Minneapolis, portrait bust of Dr. W. J. Mayo, University of Minn.; bronze statue of George Washington, Austin, Minn.; mem. bronze tablets of Ernest G. Wold and Cyrus F. Chamberlain for the Wold-Chamberlain Airport, Minneapolis. Hon. mem. Am. Inst. Architects. Protestant. Club: Professional Men's. Home: 1430 Spruce St. Studio: 1900 La Salle Av., Minneapolis MN‡

DANIELS, JOSEPH J., lawyer; b. Indpls. Apr. 13, 1890; s. Edward and Virginia (Johnston) D.; A.B., Wabash Coll., 1911; LL.B. cum laude, Harvard, 1914; m. Katharine A. Holliday, June 20, 1918 (dec. Apr. 1935); 1 dau., Katharine (Mrs. L.I. Kane); m. 2d, Robertine B. Fairbanks Apr. 2, 1945; 1 stepson, Michael B. Fairbanks (dec.). Practiced in Indpls., 1914-67, ret., 1967; counsel firm Banker & Daniels; dir. Electric Steel Castings Co.; hon. dir. Nat. Starch & Chem. Corp. Hon. gov. Riley Hosp.; bd. corps. Crown Hill Cemetery, Indpls. Served from 1st lt. to capt. U.S. Army, 1917-1919. Mem. Phi Beta Kappa, Phi Beta Kappa Assos., Beta Theta Pi. Clubs: Indianapolis Literary, University (Indpls.). Home: Indianapolis IN

DANNER, ARTHUR VINCENT, oil co. exec.; b. Vevay, Ind., Nov. 12, 1911; s. A. V. and Effie M. (Morrison) D.; student Ind. U., 1929-30; B.S. in Chemistry, George Washington U., 1936; LL.B., N.Y.U., 1940; m. Frances Tillinghast, Feb. 14, 1943; 1 son, Arthur Vincent. Patent examiner U.S. Patent office, 1934-36; patent agt. Allied Chem. & Dye Corp., 1936-37; patent agt., patent atty. Socony-Vacuum Oil Co., Inc., 1937-44, contract negotiator on loan to U.S. Govt., chief process sect. Office Petroleum Coordinator, Petroleum Adminstrn. for War, 1942-44; patent atty., 1944; exec.v.p. Houdry Process Corp., 1944-48; mgr. process promotion Socony-Mobil Oil Co., Inc., 1948-56, sr. v.p., director charge engineering and research, 1959-60, exec. v.p., dir., 1960-63, sr. v.p., dir. bus. devel., catalysts and licenses, 1963-67; pres. Mobil Petroleum Co., 1960-62; v.p., dir. Mobil Overseas Oil Co., Inc., 1956, pres., 1956-59. Mem. Am. Petroleum Inst., Phi Delta Phi, Alpha Chi Sigma, Delta Upsilon. Clubs: Racquet (Phila.); Pinnacle (N.Y.C.); Tokeneke (Darien, Conn.). Home: Sarasota FL Died Nov. 20, 1969.

DAPPING, WILLIAM OSBORNE, editor, newspaper and radio exec.; b. New York City, June 12, 1880; s. William and Mathilda (Lauterbach) D.; grad. Clinton Liberal Inst. and Hackley Sch.; A.B., Harvard, 1905; m. Ina May Fairchild, June 3, 1911. Former managing editor, secretary and treasurer of the Auburn (New York) Citizen-Advertiser; sec. treas., Auburn Pub. Co.; pres., radio sta. WMBO AM-FM, 1938-60. Pres., N.Y. State Fish, Game and Forest League, 1931-32; mem., N.Y. State Conservation Council; chmn. Auburn War Council. World War II; pres. elector, Democratic party, 1932, 36, 40, 44, 48, 52, 56, 60, 64; del. Dem. National Convention, 1936; delegate Democratic State Convention, 1954. Director George Jr. Republic Assn. Awarded Pulitzer prize for reporting, 1930, gold watch, Asso. Press, 1930. Fellow, Am. Geog. Soc.; mem. Am. Ordnance Assn., N.Y. State Pubs. Assn. (pres., 1947; chmn. dept. of purchase and supply), N.Y. State Asso. Dailies (pres., 1932), N.Y. State Newspaper Pubs. Safety Group (chmn. No. 167) N.Y. State Compensation Fund, N.Y. State Asso. Press (pres., 1930-43), N. Y. State Soc. Newspaper Editors, Am. Soc. Newspaper Editors, Am. Newspaper Pubs. Assn., Asso. Press, Sigma Delta Chi. Democrat. Universalist. Elk. Clubs: Kiwanis, Torch, Harvard of N.Y.C., Silurian, Lotos, Overseas Press (N.Y.C.); Harvard Varsity (Cambridge, Mass.); Nat. Press (Washington); Owasco Country; Auburn Golf and Country. Home: Auburn NY Died Aug. 1, 1969; buried Fort Hill Cemetery, Auburn NY

DARGAN, HENRY MCCUNE, educator; b. Charleston, S.C., July 10, 1889; s. Edwin Charles and Lucy Augusta (Graves) D.; student Tharp-Brownell Sch., Louisville, 1904-07; A.B., Mercer U., 1910; student grad. sch., U. of Calif., 1910-11; A.M., Harvard, 1912, Ph.D., 1914; unmarried. Instr. in English, U. of N.C., 1914-20, asst. prof., 1920-23, prof. of English, Darmouth Coll., 1923-57, Willard prof. rhetoric and oratory, 1946-57, emeritus, 1957-70. Served with U.S. Army, 1917-19. Mem. Modern Lang. Assn. Am., Am. Assn. U. Profs., Phi Delta Theta. Home: New York City NY Died Aug. 1970.

DARGAN, OLIVE TILFORD, author; b. Grayson County, Ky.; d. Elisha Francis and Rebecca (Day) Tilford; ed. U. of Nashville and Radcliffe Coll., Cambridge, Mass.; hon. Litt.D., U. North Carolina, 1924; m. Pegram Dargan. Taught sch. in Ark., Mo., Tex., and Can. until marriage; since living at New York, Boston, in the Carolinas and abroad. Charter mem. Poetry Soc. America; hon. mem. Radcliffe Club (New York). Author: Semiramis and Other Plays (Carlotta, The Poet), 1904, 08; Lords and Lovers and Other Dramas (The Shepherd, The Siege), 1906; The Mortal Gods and Other Dramas (A Son of Hermes, Kidmir), 1912; Path Flower and Other Poems, 1914; The Cycle's Rim, 1916; Flutter of the Gold Leaf (with Dr. Frederic Peterson), 1922; Lute and Furrow, 1922; Highland Annals, 1925; Call Home the Heart (under pseud. of Fielding Burke), 1932; A Stone Came Rolling (same pseudonym), 1935; From My Highest Hill (under own name), 1941; Sons of the Stranger (Fielding Burke), 1947; The Spotted Hawk, 1958. Winner of $500 prize, Southern Soc. of New York, for best book by Southern writer, 1916; also Belmont-Ward Fugitive prize, 1924. Asheville NC Died Jan. 22, 1968.

DARGEON, HAROLD WILLIAM, physician; b. N.Y.C., May 7, 1897; s. William Joseph and Florence (Kinghorn) D.; M.D., Albany Med. Coll., 1922; m. Muriel Mosher, Sept. 21, 1926; 1 dau., Jill Elizabeth. Intern 4th div. Bellevue Hosp., N.Y.C., 1922-24; attending in pediatrics St. Luke's Hosp., N.Y.C., 1924-29, asst. attending pediatrician, chief clinic, 1929-33, chief Tb clinic, 1929-33, asso. attending pediatrician, 1933-48, attending pediatrician, 1949-60, cons. pediatrician, 1960-70; asst. attending physician Knickerbocker Hosp., N.Y.C., 1924-29, dir. pediatrics, 1941-45; asst. pediatrician N.Y. Nursery and Children's Hosp., 1926-29; asst. attending physician Willard Parker Hosp., 1926-29; asst. attending pediatrician N.Y. Foundling Hosp., 1933-36; pediatrician Meml. Hosp. for Cancer and Allied Diseases, N.Y.C., 1935-46, attending pediatrician, 1946-62, chmn. dept. pediatrics, 1960-62, attending pediatrician emeritus, 1962-70; attending pediatrician St. Vincent's Hosp., 1948-51; cons. pediatrician Monmouth Meml. Hosp., Long Branch, N.J., 1949-70, House of Calvary, 1948-70, Lawrence Hosp., Bronxville, N.Y., 1954-70, Strang Clinic, Meml. Center, 1954-63, Fitkin Hosp., Neptune, N.J., 1958-70, Misericordia Hosp., Bronx, N.Y., 1958-70, N.Y.C. Dept. Health, 1961-70, N.Y. Infirmary, 1964-70, Riverview Hosp., Red Bank, N.J., 1968-70, Point Pleasant (N.J.) Hosp., 1969-70; spl. cons. USPHS, 1965-70; instr. pediatrics Columbia Coll. Phys. and Surg., 1931-46; asst. prof. clin. pediatrics Cornell U. Med. Coll., N.Y.C., 1947-51, asso. prof., 1951-61, clin. prof., 1961-63, clin. prof. emeritus, 1963-70. Otto Faust lectr. Albany Med. Coll., 1961; lectr. in U.S. and fgn. countries. Served with U.S. Army, 1917-18; to comdr., M.C., USNR, 1942-44. Recipient Hon. Alumni award Albany Med. Coll., 1969. Diplomate Am. Bd. Pediatrics. Mem. A.M.A., N.Y. State, New York County, N.Y. Celtic (pres. 1949) med. socs., Am. Acad. Pediatrics (past chmn. com. on tumor registry), Am. Radium Soc. (v.p. 1960, Janeway medal 1963), James Ewing Soc. (medal 1963), N.Y. Acad. Medicine, N.Y. Otolaryng. Soc., Bellevue Hosp. Alumni Assn. (pres. 1952), Alpha Omega Alpha. Roman Catholic. Author: Tumors of Childhood, 1960; (monograph) Reticuloendothelioses in Childhood, 1966. Editor, contrbr. Cancer in Childhood, 1940. Contbr. articles to med. jours. Pioneer in pediatric oncology. Home: Sea Girt NJ Died Oct. 29, 1970; buried Gate of Heaven Cemetery, Hawthorne NY

DARLING, ARTHUR BEEBE, banker; b. Waterville, N.Y., Dec. 19, 1873; s. Josiah Cook and Frances Lamercia (Beebe) D.; grad. Cazenovia (N.Y.) Sem., 1891; A.B., Wesleyan U., Conn., 1895; A.M., Harvard, 1901; m. Lonelle Stoddard Walker, Feb. 17, 1909. Teacher, Cazenovia (N.Y.) Sem. and Centenary Collegiate Inst., Hackettstown, N.J., until 1903; asst. cashier Redfield (S.D.) Nat. Bank, 1904-07; farm loan business, Redfield, 1907-13; v.p. Western Nat. Bank, Mitchell, S.D., 1913-18, also sec. S.D. Bankers' Assn., 1915-18; v.p. Security Nat. Bank, Sioux City, Ia., 1918-23, pres. 1923-28; v.p. and chmn. exec. com. Toy Nat. Bank, and v.p. Farmers Loan & Trust Co., 1928-33; trustee operating Central West Pub. Service Co., 1934-39; broker, Los Angeles, 1939-40. Was on exec. com. American Red Cross and Liberty Loan Drives, and as four-minute man. Ex-pres. Sioux City Chamber Commerce, Sioux City Clearing House Assn.; trustee Methodist Hosp. Mem. Psi Upsilon. Republican. Methodist. Mason (K.T. 32 deg.). Clubs: Sioux City Country, Rotary. Home: 235 Harrison St., East Orange, N.J. Office: Weston Electrical Instrument Newark NJ‡

DARLING, ARTHUR BURR, educator; b. Wichita, Kan., Dec. 28, 1892; s. Howard Wetmore and Marietta (Upson) D.; student Fairmount Acad. Wichita, 1907-10, Phillips Acad., Andover, 1910-12; A.B., Yale U., 1916; A.M., Harvard U., 1920, Ph.D., 1922; m. Susan Lambert Flahive, of Quincy, Mass., June 24, 1920; children—Susan Lambert, Arthur Burr (dec.), Sarah, Martha. Instr. Phillips Acad., Andover, 1917-18, 33-56; instr. Simmons Coll., Boston, 1921-22; instr. Yale U., 1922-29, asso. prof. history, 1929-33; historian CIA, Washington, 1952-54; current history asso. New York Times, 1924-28. Served as ensign, U.S.N.R.F., 1918. Mem. Am. Hist. Assn., Phi Beta Kappa, Zeta Psi. Club: Graduate (New Haven). Author: Political Changes in Massachusetts, 1824-1848, 1925; The Public Papers of Francis G. Newlands, 1932; An Historical Introduction to the Declaration of Independence, 1932. Contbr. to Dictionary of Am. Biography, Ency. Britannica, Am. Hist. Review, Current History and The Am. Scholar. Address: Paris France Died Dec. 1971.

DARLING, HERBERT FRANKLIN, constrn. contractor; b. White Plains, N.Y., May 1, 1904; s. Benjamin F. and Florence (DeMille) D.; B.S., Dartmouth, 1926, M.Sc., 1927, C. E. Thayer Sch. Engring., 1927; m. Bertha Wilson, Sept. 9, 1927; children—Herbert Franklin, Virginia Wilson. Partner Connelly Bros., gen. contractors, 1937-38, pres., 1938-41; gen. contractor, Williamsville, N.Y., 1941—. Trustee Buffalo Sem.; trustee Colby Junior College, New London, N.H.; member board overseers Thayer Sch. Engring. Mem. Contracting Employers Assn. Buffalo (pres.), Soc. C.E., Am. Soc. Mil. Engrs., Dartmouth Soc. C.E., Hist. Soc. Buffalo, Nat. Sci. Mus. Buffalo. Clubs: Buffalo, Buffalo Athletic, Country of Buffalo. Home: Eggertsville NY Died Nov. 5, 1968; buried Williamsville Cemetery, Williamsville NY

DARLING, JOSEPH ROBINSON;, b. Chicago, Mar. 19, 1872; s. Joseph and Lillie (Robinson) D.; ed. Chicago and France; m. Charlotte Kelsey, of Chestnut Hill, Phila., Pa., Aug. 8, 1907; children—Joseph Warren, Janet, Carlota, Albert. Began in ranching and orange growing, Calif., 1890; later r.r. engring. work; opened up West Indian orange industry (Jamaica) for United Fruit Co., 1902-04; concessionist for same co. in Latin America, 1904-05; made reconnaissance of the northeastern coast of Nicaragua, and southern coast of Honduras, latter for construction of r.r. to develop banana industry; secured options on prin. oil fields of Ecuador, Peru and Chile for Gulf Refining Co., Pittsburgh. With Dept. of Justice, 1908-14; prepared cases involving alleged violations of anti-trust law on part of Pacific Coast Plumbing Supply Assns., Standard Sanitary Mfg. Co. (bath tub"), Motion Picture Patents Co., Internat. Harvester Co., etc.; prohibition enforcement officer, Southern California, 1927; promoter of Martin Johnson South African Expedition motion pictures, 1928. Broke up Santo Domingo revolution by imprisoning Generals Morales, Jimenez, Torribio at San Juan, Porto Rico, etc. Holds non-professional transcontinental auto record; in 1915 and 1925, awarded silver medal by Motor" for the trip; lectured on War of Nations," 1914-15; spl. rep. for Fox Film Corpn. in Great Britain, Europe, Australasia, S. America and the Far East, 1915-19. Awarded Chinese decoration for famine relief work, 1919; research work in connection with invasion of the Mediterranean fly in Fla., 1929-30; in re barberry bush and Japanese beetle in Ohio, 1931. Republican. Mason. Clubs: Chevy Chase (Washington, D.C.); Authors' (London). Author: Darling on Trusts and Combinations, 1915; (brochures) Commercial Latin America; Romance of the Moving Pictures; Standardized Mah Jong; Super Trusts and Combinations; The Mediterranean Fly; also brochure for U.S. Med. Dept. on use of tryparsomide in the treatment of Epidemic Encephalitis (sleeping sickness) as applied successfully in Central Africa, 1933. Home: Kew Gardens, Long Island NY*‡

DARLING, LOUIS, JR., author, illustrator; b. Stamford, Conn., Apr. 26, 1916; s. Louis and Llanceley (Lockwood) D.; student Art Students League, N.Y.C., also pupil of Frank V. DuMond and Frank Reilly; m. Lois MacIntyre, June 3, 1946. Served with USAAF, 1941-45. Recipient John Burroughs medal John Burroughs Meml. Assn., 1966. Mem. A.A.A.S., Ecol. Soc. Am., Animal Behavior Soc., Am. Ornithologists Union, British Ornithol. Union, Am. Inst. Biol. Scis., Cat Boat Assn. Club: Coffee House (N.Y.C.). Author, illustrator: Greenhead, 1954, Seals and Walruses, 1955, Penguins, 1956, Kangaroos and Other Animals with Pockets, 1958, The Gull's Way, 1965; author, illustrator: (with Mrs. Darling) Before and After Dinosaurs, 1959, Sixty Million Years of Horses, 1960, The Science of Life, 1961, Bird, 1962, Turtles, 1962, Coral Reefs, 1963, The Sea Serpents Around Us, 1965; (with Lois Darling) A Place in The Sun, 1968; also allus. 65 books for other authors including Silent Spring, The Appalachians, Henry Huggins series for children. Home: Old Lyme CT Died Jan. 21, 1970.

DARLING, ROBERT ENSIGN, fuse mfr.; b. Rye, N.Y., Sept. 19, 1904; s. Robert and Julia Whiting (Ensign) D.; grad. Westminster Sch., 1922; A.B., Yale, 1926; m. Virginia Kusterer, July 2, 1935; children—Robert Ensign, Elizabeth Conant (Mrs. George C. White), Julia Whiting (Mrs. Robert N. Spahr). With Ensign-Bickford Company, Simsbury, Conn., 1926-69, successively with traffic dept., asst. sec., sec., v.p. and sec., exec. v.p., dir., pres., 1926-60, chmn. bd., 1960-69; dir. Canadian Safety Fuse Co., Hartford Nat. Bank &Trust Co., Simsbury Bank & Trust Co. Travelers Insurance Company. Mem. board directors Hartford Hospital; trustee Westminster School (Simsbury), Ethel Walker Sch. (Simsbury), Hartford Sem. Found.; mem. bd. trustees Wadsworth Atheneum. Mem. Alpha Delta Phi. Methodist. Clubs: Hartford, Hartford Golf; East Haddam (Conn.) Fish and Game; Gulfstream Golf, Simsbury CT Died Nov. 24, 1969.

DARLING, SID L(OUIS), trade assn. exec.; born West New York, N.J., Aug. 9, 1894; s. John Sidney and Abigail Bates (Crossley) D.; student N.Y.U. Law Sch., 1914-16; m. Mabel Elizabeth Burridge, Sept. 22, 1920; children—Bruce Burridge, Laird Burridge (dec.). Began as law student, clk. Marshall VanWinkle, Jersey City; then credit mgr. Republic Rubber Co., credit dept. B.F. Goodrich Rubber Co.; asst. treas. George Borgfeldt & Co., N.Y. City; then exec. vice president Nat.-Am. Wholesale Lumber Assn. Mem. Nat. Distbn. Council, U.S. Dept. Commerce. Served from private to capt. U.S. Army, 1917-19, Mem. Am. Soc. Assn. Execs., Nat. Assn. of Wholesalers (Washington trustee), N.Y. Lumber Salesmen's Assn. (hon.), Hoo-Hoo, Delta Chi. Republican. Presbyn. Mason (32 deg., K.T., Shriner). Club: Nylta (N.Y. City). Author articles in lumber trade jours. Home: Leonia NJ Died Aug. 6, 1971; buried Fairview Cemetery, Fairview NJ

DARNTON, ELEANOR CHOATE, writer, editor; born Phila., Pa., Jan. 1, 1907; d. Ernest and Eleanor (Townsend) Choate; student, Univ. of Pa., 1924-26, 28-29; m. Clarkson Hill, Apr. 10, 1929 (divorced, 1938); m. 2d Byron Darnton, Apr. 23, 1938 (dec. 1942); children—Robert Choate Darnton, John Townsend Darnton. Advt. and mag. writer, 1929-36; editor, You mag., 1937-38; writer, Office of War Information, 1942; reporter, Washington bur., N.Y. Times, 1943, woman's editor, 1944-45; co-founder, pres. and co-editor, Women's Nat. News Service, 1946-54; press officer The Children's Bur., U.S. Department of Health, Education and Welfare. 1954-55; information dir. Nat. Probation and Parole Association, 1956-57; women's editor Parade magazine, 1958-59; in charge editorial projects schools and mental health program Bank Street College, N.Y.C., 1960-61; mng. editor Haire Publs., N.Y.C., 1962-63; director of publs. for Arthritis Found. America, 1964-65. Civilian editorial advisor, information and edn. div., U.S. Army hdqrs., European theatre, 1945; mem., nat. bd., Y.W.C.A.; exec. com. mem., Nat. Commn. on Children and Youth; mem. bd. of dirs. Fashion Group, 1944-45. Hon. mem. Theta Sigma Phi. Protestant. Clubs: Women's Nat. Press, N.Y. Newspaper Women's. Author: The Children Grew. Editor: Gout and Purine Metabolism, 1965; Relation of Mycoplasma to Human Diseases, 1966. Home: Westport CT Died May 14, 1968.

DARR, JOHN WHITTIER, educator; b. Bucyrus, O., Sept. 2, 1888; s. George F. and Ida B. (Humiston) D.; B.L., Ohio Wesleyan U., 1910; student Union Theol. Sem., 1912-15; A.M., Columbia, 1913; m. Vera Campbell, Oct. 7, 1915; children—George C., John W., William H., G. Guthrie. Ordained to ministry Presbyn. Ch., 1915; pastor Spring St. Ch., N.Y. City, 1917-24; 1st Congl. Ch., Northampton, Mass., 1924-29; prof. religion Scripps Coll., Claremont, Calif., 1929-41, Wesleyan U., Middletown, Conn., from 1941. Home: Seattle WA Died Jan. 27, 1972; cremated, ashes interred Shadeli, Calmes Neck, Fauquier County VA

DARR, LOREN ROBERT, publisher; b. Philadelphia, Mo., Oct. 7, 1897; s. Samuel Fenton and Edna Etta (Banks) D.; law student De Paul U., 1920-21; m. Frances Vogel, Oct. 7, 1940; children—Loren Robert, Joanne. Employed Callaghan & Co., law book pubs., 1919-30; 2d v.p. Commerce Clearing House, Inc., 1930-32; exec. v.p. Found. Press, Inc., 1932-38, pres., chmn. bd., 1938-68. Club: Brooklyn. Home: Garden City NY Died Jan. 8, 1968.

DARROW, CHESTER WILLIAM, psychophysiologist; b. Ft. Plaine, N.Y., Nov. 7, 1893; s. William E. and Harriet (Mills) D.; A.B., Des Moines Coll., 1915; M.A., Oglethorpe U., 1922; Ph.D., U. Chgo., 1924; m. Ruth Rentor, 1926; children—Virginia (Mrs. Robin Oggins), Diane (Mrs. Roland Grybek), Gale (Mrs. Anthony Kaliss); m. 2d, Alice Hale Waterman, Dec. 22, 1961. With Behavior Research Fund, Inst. for Juvenile Research, Chgo., 1924-26, psychophysiologist, psychophysiol. lab., 1926-67; asso. prof. physiology U. Ill., 1950-66, asso. prof. emeritus, 1966-67. Diplomate, fellow Am. Psychol. Assn. Mem. Am., Central (pres. 1954-55) electro-encepholographic socs., Soc. for Psychophysiol. Research (pres. 1960-61), Am. Physiol. Soc., Am. Psychopath. Soc., Am. Acad. Neurology, A.A.A.S., Chgo. Neurol. Soc., Soc. Biol. Psychiatry, Psychonomic Soc., Chgo. Inst. Chicago IL Died Apr. 7, 1967.

DASHER, BENJAMIN JOSEPH, educator; b. Macon, Ga., Dec. 27, 1912; s. Benjamin Joseph and Odille (King) D.; B.S., Ga. Inst. Tech., 1935, M.S., 1945; Sc.D., Mass. Inst. Tech., 1952; m. Anne Moore Brooks, June 7, 1941; children—Benjamin Joseph III, Anne B., Preston B., Elizabeth S., David, Carole. Instr., asst. prof. elec. engring. Ga. Inst. Tech., 1940-46, asso. prof., 1952, prof. elec. engring., 1953-71, dir. Sch. Elec. Engring., 1954-69, asso. dean engring., 1969-71. Fellow I.E.E.E.; mem. Am. Soc. Engring. Edn., Nat. Soc. Profl. Engrs., Sigma Xi, Eta Kappa Nu. Home: Atlanta GA Died Dec. 13, 1971.

DASHER, CHARLES LANIER, JR., army officer; born Savannah, Ga., July 11, 1900; s. Charles Lanier and Eloise (Wilder) D.; student George Washington U., 1919-20; B.S., U.S. Mil. Acad., 1924; grad. F.A. Sch., 1930, Command and Gen. Staff Coll., 1940; m. Helen Catherine Rowzee, Feb. 10, 1925; children—Beverly Anne, Charlene Catherine. Commd. 2d lt. U.S. Army, 1924, advanced through grades to maj. gen., 1953; successively instr. tactics, instr. gunnery, exec. officer F.A. Sch., Ft. Sill, Okla., 1940-43; arty. officer 3d Armored Corps. Camp Polk, Ia., 1943; asst. arty. officer 19th Corps, 1943-44; comdg. officer 32d F.A. Brigade, 1944-45; arty. comdr. 75th Div. Arty., 1945; corps arty. comdr. 18th Corps (airborne), 1945; comdr. Rome area Allied Commd., 1945-47; mil. attache, Spain; 1947-50; asst. div. comdr. 8th Inf. Div., 1951-52; 3d Inf. Div., 1952; div. comdr. 24th Inf. Div., 1952-53; dep. comdr. 5th Army, 1954-55, U.S. Comdr., Berlin, 1955-57, Caribbean, 1958-60. Decorated D.S.M., Legion of Merit with 2 oak leaf clusters, Bronze Star medal with two oak leaf clusters. (V), Purple Heart (U.S.); Legion of Honor, Croix de Guerre with palm (France); Order of Orange Nassau (Dutch); Croix de Guerre with palm (Belgium); Ulchi Distinguished Service medal with gold star (Korea); Presdl. Unit Citation; grand officer Order of Crown (Italy); UN Service medal. Mem. Delta Tau Delta, Baronial Order Magna Charta. Home: Bethesda MD Died Oct. 31, 1968; buried Arlington Nat. Cemetery.

DASHIELL, ALFRED SHEPPARD, editor; b. Snow Hill, Md., Apr. 29, 1901; s. Erastus Seth and Sallie (Marshall) Dashiell; A.B., Princeton, 1923; married Cornelia Ringgold Ross, May 17, 1924 (died April 3, 1942); children—Cornelia Ringgold (Mrs. Dino McCurdy), Ann Marshall (Mrs. Harry Woske); married 2d, Sara Ross Skillern, May 1, 1943. Correspondent metropolitan dailies from Princeton University, 1921-23; managing editor Daily Princetonian, 1922-23; reporter Baltimore Evening Sun, summers 1922, 23; asst. editor Scribner's Mag., 1923-30, mng. editor, 1930-36; asso. editor Reader's Digest, Pleasantville, N.Y., 1936-40, mng. editor, 1940-65, vice president, 1961-67, editor special books, 1965-67; conductor of short story seminar Columbia University, 1936, 37. Trustee Village of Croton-on-Hudson, 1937-1945. Vice pres. Croton Free Library Board, 1951-55, pres., 1955-69. Clubs: Overseas Press, Princeton (N.Y.C.); P.E.N., Terrace (Princeton); Sleep Hollow Country (Searborough, N.Y.). Author: Editor's Choice, 1934; (with Henry Seidel Canby) Astudy of the Short Story, rev., 1935. Home: Croton-on-Hudson NY Died Oct. 3, 1970; buried Snow Hill MD

DATES, HENRY BALDWIN, electrical engr; b. New Britain, Conn., July 15, 1869; s. Henry Masten and Sarah E. (Baldwin) D.; B.S. in E.E., Mass. Inst. Tech., 1894; E.E., Case Sch. Applied Science; m. Harriet Burt Haskell, Dec. 29, 1896. Engr. Westinghouse Electric & Mfg. Co., 1894-96; prof. physics and elec. engring. Clarkson Sch. of Technology, Potsdam, N.Y., 1896-1903; dean Coll. Engring. and prof. elec. engring, U. of Colo., 1903-05; prof. elec. engring., Case Sch. Applied Science, 1905-38, now prof. emeritus. Fellow Am. Inst. Elec. Engrs.; mem. Illuminating Engr. Soc. (U.S.), country mem. Illuminating Engr. Soc. (London, Eng.); mem. U.S. Com. of Internat. Commn. on Illumination. Registered professional elect. engr., Ohio. Home: 3071 Euclid Heights Blvd., Cleveland 18 OH‡

DAUGHERTY, ARTHUR CORNELIUS, supt. schs.; b. Hamilton, Ill., Jan. 11, 1901; s. Cornelius T. and Anna E. (Pressly) D.; B.S., Knox Coll., 1922; M.S., M.E., U. Ill., 1943; m. Florence Ida Johnson, June 1, 1928; 1 son, Arthur C. (dec.). Tchr. high sch., Westfield, Ill., 1924-29, Casey, Ill., 1929-37; prin. high sch., Palestine, Ill., 1937-43, Dupo, Ill., 1943-56; supt. Unit Dist. 196, Dupo, 1956-68. Mem. N.E.A., Tau Kappa Epsilon, Phi Delta Kappa, Kappa Delta Pi. Presbyn. Mason. Lion. Home: Dupo IL Died Aug. 29, 1970; buried Valhalla Belleville IL

DAUGHERTY, DUNCAN W(ILMER), lawyer; born Reedy, W.Va., Sept. 15, 1895; s. David W. and Amanda (Boice) D.; student Marshall Coll., 1915-17; LL.B., George Washington U., 1922; m. Grace Jones, Oct. 22, 1924; children—Duncan W., David II., Boice N. Admitted to W.Va. bar, 1922, since practiced in Huntington, mem. Daugherty and Daugherty, 1949-69; U.S. atty. So. dist. W.Va., 1953-61. Mem. W.Va. Legislature, 1921-22. Served as cpl., AEF, U.S. Army, 1917-19. Mem. Am., W.Va., Cabell Co. (past pres.) bar assns., W.Va. State Bar (pres. 1952-53), Marshall Coll. Alumni Assn., (past pres.), Am. Legion. Republican. Meth., (trustee, mem. ofcl. bd.). Clubs: Kiwanis, Lawyers of University of Michigan. Home: Huntington WV Died Aug. 16, 1969; buried Woodmere Abbey of Remembrance, Huntington WV

DAUZVARDIS, PETRAS PAULIUS, Lithuanian diplomat; b. Lithuania, Nov. 16, 1895; s. Petras and Julija (Balciunaite) D.; student Valparaiso U., 1922; LL.B., Georgetown U., 1924; M.P.L., John Marshall Sch. Law, 1942; J.D., 1943; m. Ona Malakauskas, June 28, 1924 (dec. 1931); children—Peter V., Fabian G.; m. 2d, Josephine J. Rudis, Aug. 10, 1933. Sec. Lithuanian Roman Cath. Labor Assn., also asst. editor assn. organ, Darbininkas, Boston, 1924-25; sec. Ministry Fgn. Affairs, Lithuania, 1925; vice consul in N.Y.C., 1925-37; consul in Chgo., 1937-61, consul gen., from 1961; lectr. throughout U.S. and Can. Decorated Order Grand Duke Gediminas (2) (Lithuania); Order of Petliura (Ukraine); recipient consular medallion Loyola University, 1968. Mem. of American Society of International Law, Chgo. Council Fgn. Relations, Chgo. Assn. Commerce and Industry, Georgetown U. Alumni Assn., Lithuanian Lawyers Assn. Rotarian. Author numerous articles for newspapers, mags., encys. Address: Chicago IL Died Sept. 26, 1971; buried St. Casimir Lithuanian Cemetery, Chicago IL

DAVANT, THOMAS S., ry. official; b. Gillisonville, S.C.; ed. pub. schs. Station agt. Charlotte & S.C. R.R., Ft. Mills, S.C., 1865-9; agt. Columbia & Augusta R.R., Columbia, Jan.-June 1869; chief clk. consol. agency, Charlotte, Columbia & Augusta R.R., at Columbia, 1869-71; chief clk. for gen. frt. and pass. agt. same rd., 1871-4; gen. frt. and pass. agt., Port Royal R.R., 1874-7; asst. gen. frt. and pass. agt., Memphis & Charleston R.R., Memphis, Tenn., 1877-86; gen. frt. agt., E. Tenn., Va. & Ga. Ry., 1886-92; gen. frt. agt., Norfolk & Western R.R. and its successor the N. & W. Ry., 1892-1903; frt. traffic mgr., 1903-7, 3d v.p. and traffic mgr., 1907-12, v.p. in charge of traffic since Dec. 1, 1912, same rd. Apptd. asst. to regional dir., Pocahontas Region, U.S. R.R. Administration, at Roanoke, Va., June 1, 1918. Address: Roanoke VA‡

DAVENPORT, GEORGE WILLIAM, bishop; b. Brandon, Vt., Aug. 14, 1870; s. Rev. Willard Goss and Mary (Converse) D.; A.B., Hobart Coll., S.T.D., 1920; D.D., U. of Vt., 1921; student Md. Theol. Sch., also Gen. Theol. Sem., 1896; m. Jennie Platt Briggs, Sept. 24,1896; children—Eleanor Curtis, Willard Platt, George William. Deacon, 1893, priest, 1896, P.E. Ch.; in charge Ch. of St. John the Baptist, Baltimore, Md., 1893-95; asst. St. Mathew's Ch., N.Y. City, 1895-96; rector Ch. of the Resurrection, Richmond Hill, L.I., 1896-99, Ch. of the Redeemer, Astoria, L.I., 1899-1902, St. James' Ch., Danbury, Conn., 1902-12, provincial sec. 1st Province, 1912-15; rector St. Paul's Ch., Burlington, Vt., 1915-19; consecrated bishop, Sept. 15, 1920; retired, Nov. 7, 1938. Mem. Phi Kappa Psi. Mason. Home: 529 S. Putney Av., San Gabriel CA‡

DAVENPORT, LOUIS M., hotel man; b. Pawnee City, Neb., July 14, 1868; s. John S. and Minnie E. (Taylor) D.; ed. pub. schs., San Francisco, Calif.; m. Versus E. Smith, Aug. 30, 1906; 1 son, Lewis M. Settled at Spokane, 1889, and established a restaurant, out of which grew the Davenport Hotel, erected 1914; pres. Davenport Hotel, Inc.; vice-pres. Old Nat. Building Co., dir. Old National Bank & Union Trust Co. Vice-pres. Spokane Park Board. Mem. United Air Lines' 100,000 Mile Club. Clubs: Spokane City and University, Spokane Country. Home: Davenport Hotel, Spokane WA‡

DAVENPORT, WALTER, journalist; b. Talbot County, Md., Jan. 7, 1889; s. John and Mary Elizabeth (Dillon) D.; ed. in prep. schs.; student U. of Pa., 2 yrs.; m. Barbara Scollard Brown, Oct. 16, 1919; children—Michael, Anthony. Mem. original staff, Liberty Mag., 1923-24; gen. journalistic writer, specializing in politics, Collier's magazine, 1925, asso. editor 1925-46, editor, 1946-48, became asso. editor and columnist 1948. Served as capt., 111th Infantry, 28th Div., A.E.F., during World War I. Clubs: The Players, Dutch Treat (New York); National Press (Washington). Author: Power and Glory: The Story of Boies Penrose, 1931; (with James C. Derieux) Ladies, Gentlemen and Editors, 1960. Home: Southern Pines NC Died Dec. 9, 1971; cremated.

DAVIDSON, DONALD (GRADY), educator, writer; b. Campbellsville, Tenn., Aug. 18, 1893; s. William Bluford and Elma (Wells) D.; grad. Branham and Hughes Sch., Springhill, Tenn., 1909; A.B., Vanderbilt U., 1917, A.M., 1922; Litt.D., Cumberland Univ., 1946, Washington and Lee Univ., 1948; L.H.D., Middlebury (Vt.) Coll., 1965; m. Theresa Julienna Sherrer, June 8, 1918; 1 dau., Mary Theresa. Faculty dept. English, Vanderbilt, 1920—, professor of English, 1937-64, professor emeritus, 1964-68; literary editor Nashville Tennessean, 1924-30; editor weekly column The Critics Alumnac, also book page, Memphis Commercial Appeal, Knoxville Jour., 1928-30; faculty Bread Loaf Sch. English, 1931-63. State chmn. Tenn. Fedn. for Constl. Govt., 1955-59. Served from 2d lt. to 1st lt., inf., U.S. Army, 1917-19. Mem. Am. Folklore Soc., Am. Acad. Polit. and Social Sci., So. Atlantic Modern Lang. Assn., Tenn. Hist. Soc., Phi Beta Kappa, Alpha Tau Omega. Author: (poetry) An Outland Piper, 1924, The Tall Men, 1927, Lee in the Mountains, 1938; The Attack on Leviathan: Essays on Regionalism and Nationalism, 1938; The Tennessee, Vol. I, 1946, Vol. II, 1948; Twenty Lessons in Reading and Writing Prose, 1955; Still Rebels, Still Yankees, and other Essays, 1957, rev. edit., 1972; (with Sidney E. Glenn) Readings for Composition, rev. edit., 1957; Southern Writers in the Modern World, 1958; American Composition and Rhetoric, revised edition, 1959; The Long Street (volume of poems), 1961; The Spyglass: Views and Reviews, 1924-30, 1963; Concise American Composition and Rhetoric, 1964, 5th edit., 1967; Poems, 1922-1961, 1966. Editor: British Poetry of the 1890s, 1937; Selected Essays and Other Writings (John Donald Wade), 1966. Editorial adv. bd. Modern Age:A Conservative Review, 1957-68. The Intercollegiate Review, 1965-68. Contbr. periodicals. Home: Nashville TN Died Apr. 25, 1968; buried Nashville TN

DAVIDSON, JOSEPH G., chemical corporation executive; b. N.Y. City, Feb. 7, 1892; s. John Wellington and Theresa (Gahan) D.; A.B., U. of Southern Calif., 1911, A.M., 1912; Ph.D., Columbia, 1917; m. Madeleine E. Scheuerer, June 20, 1935. Chemist Chapala Gold Mining Co., Mexico, 1912-13; mem. chemistry dept. Los Angeles Jr. Coll., 1914-16; Columbia, 1916-17; asso. Mellon Inst., 1919-23; employee Carbide & Carbon Chem. Corp., 1923, mgr. chem. sales, 1925-30, gen. sales mgr., 1930-32, vice-pres. 1932-44, pres., 1944-54, chmn. bd., 1954-58; chmn. Canadian Resins & Chems., Ltd., 1953-58, dir., 1941-58; v.p. Union Carbide & Carbon Corp.; v.p. Bakelite Corp., 1939-53; dir. Warren Wire Co., Vt., Vt. Bank & Trust Co., Bennington, Vt., Nat. Life Ins. Co. of Vt. Pres. Conn. River Valley Watershed Council. Trustee Bennington (Vt.) Hosp., pres., 1960-67; trustee University of Vermont. Served as 1st lt. chem. warfare U.S. Army, 1917-18. Recipient Soc. Chem. Industry medal, 1955. Home: Manchester VT Died Oct. 9, 1969; buried Dellwood Cemetery, Manchester VT

DAVIDSON, JOSEPH QUENTIN, lawyer; b. Ft. Valley, Ga., Oct. 11, 1905; s. Joseph Elijah and Belle (Aultman) D.; B.A. magna cum laude, U. Ga., 1926; LL.B. summa cum laude, Mercer U., 1929; m. Maude Ray Adams, Sept. 28, 1929; children—Barbara Lynette (Mrs. Lee H. Henkel, Jr.), Joan Elaine (Mrs. George W. Mize), Joseph Quentin. Admitted to Ga. bar, 1929; asso. Slade & Swift, Columbus, Ga., 1929-31; partner Swift, Pease, Davidson & Chapman, and predecessor, 1931-69. Dir. United Oil Corp., Columbus, Ga. Bd. edn., Muscogee County, Ga.; mem. bd. publs. Methodist Ch., mem. bd. pensions, bd. hospital and homes South Ga. Conf. Meth. Ch. Past pres. United Givers; bd. dirs. Columbus YMCA, local chpt. A.R.C.; local adv. council Salvation Army; chmn. bd. mgrs. City Hosp.; v.p., trustee South Ga. Meth. Home for Aging, Americus, Ga.; trustee Mercer U., Columbus Coll. Found., Inc. Recipient Algernon Sidney Sullivan bronze Medallion and certificate Mercer U., Walter F. George Sch. Law faculty medal. Fellow Am. Coll. Probate Counsel; mem. Columbus C. of C. (chmn. edn. com.), Phi Beta Kappa, Phi Kappa Phi, Sigma Upsilon, Phi Alpha Delta, Delta Tau Delta. Methodist (mem. ofcl. bd.). Elk. Clubs: Rotary (past pres.), Columbus Executives, Country (v.p., mem. governing bd.) (Columbus). Home: Columbus GA Died Apr. 7, 1969; buried Parkhill Cemetery, Columbus GA

DAVIDSON, LAURA LEE, author; b. Baltimore, Md.; d. Spencer and Laura Lee (Burwell) D.; grad. Baltimore Kindergarten Training Sch., 1895, post-grad. work, same sch., 1897; studied English, Goucher Coll. and English composition, summer course, Cornell U. Dir. Henshaw Free Kindergarten, Baltimore, 1897, Light Street Free Kindergarten, 1898-1901; teacher pub. schs., Baltimore, since 1901. Democrat. Episcopalian. Club: Woman's Literary (hon.). Author: A Winter of Content, 1922; Isles of Eden, 1924. Home: 1608 Bolton St., Baltimore MD‡

DAVIDSON, LOUCRETIA ISOBEL, b. Mt. Vernon, O., Oct. 17, 1869; d. John William and Eliza Ellen (Underwood) D.; grad. high sch., La Porte, Ind., 1889, Kindergarten Training Sch., 1890; student U. of Chicago, 1898-1902; diploma Sloyd Sch., Chicago, 1904; B.S., Teachers Coll. (Columbia), 1907. Formerly teacher elementary schs.; supervisor elementary schs., Baltimore County, Md., 1905-17; state supervisor elementary schs., Wis., 1920-23; dir. elementary edn., Elizabeth, N.J., since 1923. Mem. N.E.A., Dept. of Superintendence Primary Council and Nat. Soc. Administrative Women same, Nat. Assn. Univ. Women, N.J. State Teachers' Assn. Baptist. Club: Woman's (Elizabeth). Lecturer in univs. and before teachers' institutes. Author: Real Stories from Baltimore County History (with others), 1917; Busy Brownies at Work; at Play, 1918; Lincoln Readers (with C. J. Anderson), 1923; Reading Objectives (with C. J. Anderson), 1925; etc. Home: La Porte, Ind. Address: Elizabeth NJ‡

DAVIDSON, MARY BLOSSOM, (MRS. CHARLES S. DAVIDSON), dean of women; b. Red Bluff; Litt.B., Univ. Calif., 1906; m. Charles S. Davidson; 1 son, Dr. Charles S. Asst. dean of Women, U. Cal. at Berkeley, 1911, asso. dean of women, 1930, dean of women, 1941-51. Mem. Am. Assn. Univ. Women, Nat. Association Deans of Women, Calif. Assn. Women Deans and Vice Principals, Kappa Kappa Gamma. Presbyn. Republican. Club: Town and Gown. Home: Berkeley CA Died Nov. 11, 1968.

DAVIES, GEORGE REGINALD, sociologist; b. Abingdon, Eng.; Feb. 3, 1876; s. George Hicks and Gertrude Mary (Barnes) D.; brought to America, 1885; A.B., Des Moines (Ia.) Coll., 1899, A.M., 1908, grad. State Normal Sch., Valley City, N.D., 1906; U. of Wis., summers, 1909, 10; Ph.D., U. of N.D., 1914; m. Margaret Van Woert Whipple, Dec. 19, 1901; 1 dau., Edith Winifred. Prin. high sch., Denison, Ia., 1899-1900; dep. county supt. schs., Ransom County, N.D., 1901; prin. schs., Hankinson, N.D., 1902-04; prin. high sch., Lisbon, N.D. 1904-05, Consol. Sch., Amenia, 1905-10; instr. State Normal Sch., Valley City, 1910-12; instr. and asso. prof. sociology, U. of N.D., 1913-19; asst. prof. Economics, Princeton U., 1919-21; prof. sociology, U. of N.D., 1921-28; prof. statistics, Coll. of Commerce, U. of Ia., since 1928; visiting lecturer economics, Grinnell Coll., 1948-49; cons. statistics, U. Minn., summer 1951. Fellow A.A.A.S.; mem. Am. Statis. Assn., Am. Econ. Assn. Author several books including: The Drift Toward Socialism, 1952; also articles on ednl. economic and sociol. subjects. Home: 130 Grove St., Iowa IA

DAVIES, THOMAS STEPHEN, physician; b. Detroit, May 1, 1883; s. Thomas and Isabelle (Bow) D.; B.S. in Mech. Engring., U. Mich., 1907; postgrad., 1914; M.D., Wayne U., 1919; m. Isabella Huntington Jacobs, Dec. 2, 1908; 1 dau., Florence Huntington (dec.). Intern, Woman's Hosp., Detroit, 1919-20; vis. pediatrician Herman Kiefer Hosp., 1920-23; physician Detroit Children's Hosp. out-patient dept., 1923-43; commr. health Grosse Pointe-Harper Woods, 1943-50; dept. health commr. Wayne Co. Health Dept., Grosse Pointe, 1950-67. Mem. Detroit Pediatric Soc. (Recognition certificate 1965), Wayne Co. Med. Soc. Episcopalian. Clubs: Detroit Curling, Detroit Lawn Bowling, Detroit Boat. Home: Grosse Pointe MI Died Nov. 6, 1967.

DAVIS, A. M., lawyer; b. N.Y.C., 1883; A.B., Columbia, 1904, LL.B., 1906. Admitted to N.Y. bar, 1906; mem. firm Davis, Gilbert, Levine and Schwartz, N.Y.C. Mem. Assn. Bar City N.Y., Am., N.Y. State bar assns., N.Y. County Lawyers Assn., Phi Beta Kappa. Address: New York City NY Died Nov. 13, 1971; buried Bayside Cemetery, Ozone Park NY

DAVIS, ARLENE (MRS. MAX T. DAVIS), aviatrix, assn. exec.; b. Cleve., Mar. 2; d. Philip and Anna (Hepp) Palsgraff; student Central Radio Sch., Kansas City, Mo., Sundorph Aero. Sch., Cleve., Western Res. U.; student Baldwin-Wallace Coll., 1951-64; m. Max T. Davis, Feb. 4, 1928. Received pvt. pilot license, 1931, multi-rating land and sea instrument rating to fly blind, 1937; winner first all-women's air race, 1934; instr. instrument flying army trainees, 1943; nat. chmn. adv. com. Wing Scouts of Girl Scouts Am., 1946-49; bd. dirs. Nat. Aero. Assn., 1952-64, sec. 1954-64; U.S. del. Fedn. Aeronatique Internationale, 1954-64. Vice pres., treas. Peerless Packing Co., Cleve. Chmn. Operation Skywatch for Ohio, Va., Pa.; mem. bd. Ohio Aviation Planning Com., 1949-64; chmn. vols. Ground Observer Corps of Cuyahoga County, O.; exec. com., mem. bd. Ohio Safety Council; vice chmn. Nat. Model Plane Contest. Ohio aviation chmn. citizens for Eisenhower Com. First v.p. Cleve. Boys Sch., Hudson, O., 1956-64; mem. bd. Friendly Inn for Underprivileged Children, Cleve.; mem. bd. sr. advisers Nat. Intercollegiate Air Meet. Recipient Paul Tissandiar diploma Monaco, internat. citation, 1961; named woman of yr. aviation Women's Nat. Aero. Assn.; hon. angel U.S. Air Force R.O.T.C.; mem. Mach Buster's Club (exceeding speed of sound USAF F-100 F Super Sabre). Mem. Cleve. Fedn. Women's Clubs (dir. aviation 1954-64), Nat. Aero. Assn. (hon. life), Soc. Women Engrs. (life), Profl. Race Pilots Assn., Soaring Club Am., Am. Helicopter Soc., Acad. Model Aero. (adminstrv. leader, ofcl. contest dir.), Ninety-Nines (internat. v.p. 1951-52), Zonta Internat., Delta Zeta (Woman of Year award 1960), Alpha Eta Rho. Compiler Wing Scout Manual, 1949. Home: Cleveland OH Died July 3, 1964.

DAVIS, ARTHUR NEWTON, dental surgeon; b. Piqua, O., Jan. 1, 1879; s. John Franklin and Georgiana Frances (Wright) D.; D.D.S., Chicago Coll. Dental Surgery (Lake Forest U.); m. London, Eng., Helen Winifred Proctor, Aug. 30, 1904 (dec.); 1 dau., Frances Annette; m. 2d, Mrs. Irene Atkins Myers, 1941. Practiced Chicago, 1902-03; went to Berlin, Germany, 1903, and associated in practice with Dr. A. H. Sylvester, continuing until his death, 1905, then practiced alone; numbered among patients the Kaiser and his family; returned to U.S., 1918, and settled in N.Y. City. Mem. Am. Dental Soc. of Europe, Nat. Dental Assn., First Dist. Dental Soc. of N.Y. City, N.Y. Acad. Dentistry. Mason. Author: The Kaiser as I Know Him, 1918. Home: 930 Fifth Av. Office: 745 Fifth Av., New York NY‡

DAVIS, ARTHUR VINING, officer corps; b. Sharon, Mass., May 30, 1867; s. Perley B. and Mary Frances (Vining) D.; A.B., Amherst, 1888; m. Elizabeth Hawkins, Mar. 1912. Chmn. bd. Aluminum Co. of America; director Mellon National Bank & Trust Co. Aluminum Goods Mfg. Co., Can. Life Assurance Co., Bucyrus-Erie Corp., Am. Brake Shoe Co., Hotel Waldorf Astoria Corporation. Member Psi Upsilon. Republican. Episcopalian. Clubs: Pittsburgh, Duquesne; Metropolitan, Union (New York). Home: Duquesne Club, Pittsburgh, Pa. Office: 960 Fifth Av., N.Y.C.; also 801 Gulf Bldg., Pitts.; and Alfred I. duPont Bldg., Miami 32 FL‡

DAVIS, BERNARD GEORGE, pub., educator; b. Pitts., Dec. 11, 1906; s. Charles and Sarah (Harris) D.; student U. of Pa., 1923-24; Columbia, summer 1926; B.S. U. of Pitts., 1927; m. Sylvia Friedman, Nov. 20, 1930; children—Joel, Carol. Editor of Pitt Panther, U. of Pitts., 1926; sec.-treas. Assn. of College Comics of the East, 1926-27; v.p. and dir. Ziff-Davis Publishing Co., 1936-46, pres., 1946-57; pres. Davis Publs., Inc., 1957-67, chmn., 1967-72. Mag. pub. rep. Am. Council Edn. Journalism, 1960-66; dir. internat. programs U. Palm Beach, Fla., 1969-72. U.S. del. Civil Air Patrol. Internat. Cadet Exchange Program Conf., Lisbon, 1955, Lima, 1956. Mem. Mag. Pub. Assn. (mem. bd. dirs. 1955-68, treas., 1959-67), Sigma Delta Chi. Club: Ocean Beach. Home: Palm Beach FL Died Aug. 27, 1972.

DAVIS, BRINTON BEAUREGARD, architect; b. Natchez, Miss., Jan. 23, 1872; s. Jacob Brinton and Mary (Gamble) D.; student, Eustic Acad., Jefferson Coll.; m. Clara Gwyn Benbrook, Feb. 23, 1889 (dec.); children—Gladys, Mildred. Draftsman in offices in New York, Chicago, and St. Louis; private practice in Louisville, Ky., since 1903. Served in Spanish-Am. War. Mem. Louisville Comml. Club, Louisville Convention and Publicity League, Bd. of Trade, City of Louisville Planning and Zoning Commn., Ky. Soc. of Professional Engrs. Fellow A.I.A.; mem. Am. Soc. of Planning Officials, Vets. of Foreign Wars. Mason, K.T. Home: 4600 Southern Parkway. Office: Washington Bldg., Louisville KY‡

DAVIS, CHARLES ERNEST, JR., newspaperman; Urbana, Ill., Sept. 17, 1916; s. Charles E. and Inez Ellen (White) D.; student pub. schs., Balt.; m. Dorothy Robinson, Apr. 1939; children—Diane, Christopher, Charles III; m. 2d, Jean Jacobsen, July 1954;children—Richard, Jean. Staff writer Albany (N.Y.) Times-Union, 1937-43, N.Y. Jour.-American, 1943-45. Washington Post, 1945-50, Washington Times-Herald, 1950-53, Los Angeles Examiner, 1953-62, Los Angeles Times, 1962-68. Cons. Sec. Interior, 1955-56. Co-recipient Pulitzer prize for local news reporting, 1943; Theta Sigma Phi Matrix Table award for best Los Angeles news story, 1956. Club: Los Angeles Press. Home: Glendale CA Died Feb. 10, 1968; buried Glenhaven Cemetery San Fernando CA

DAVIS, CHARLES MOLER, ret. geographer, educator; b. Denver, Dec. 11, 1900; s. Charles Moler and Margaret Bigger (Porter) D.; A.B., U. Mich., 1925, A.M., 1926, Ph.D., 1935; m. Margaret Beal, Oct. 31, 1931. Instr. in geography, U. Mich., 1931-38, asst. prof., 1938-42, asso. prof., 1945-49, prof., 1949-71, prof. emeritus, 1971-72, chmn. dept. geography, 1956-66. Vis. prof. U. Cal. at Los Angeles, summer 1947, U. Tex., summer 1951, also U. Wash., summer 1963; Fulbright research scholar, Australia, 1952; geographer, Inst. for Fisheries Research, 1931-32; asst. land negotiator, U.S. Biol. Survey, 1935; Carnegie vis. prof. U. Hawaii, 1962; sect. organizer 10th Pacific Science Congress, Honolulu, 1961; geographer U.S. Geol. Survey, 1966-67, mem. NRC Com. on Remote Sensing Adv., 1966-72; dir. Inst. on Remote Sensing for Geographers. Served from lt. comdr. to capt., USNR, 1942-60; plans officer, Spl. Air Task Force, U.S. Fleet, 1943-44; mem. acad. library adv. bd. USAF Acad., 1958. Chmn. com. on geog. field techniques NRC, 1949-53; mem. com. adv. to geog. br. Office of Naval Research, 1949-51. Recipient Carnegie Corp. grant-in-aid, 1939-40. Mem. Assn. of Am. Geographers (del. to Nat. Acad. Science-NRC 1959-62), Mich. Acad. Sci., Phi Kappa Phi, Phi Sigma, Chi Gamma Phi, Delta Tau Delta. Club: University (Ann Arbor). Contbr. articles on geog. subjects to profl. mags. Home: Ann Arbor MI Died Nov. 26, 1972.

DAVIS, CLAUDE JEFFERSON, educator; b. Asheville, N.C., Dec. 22, 1923; s. Hardee Thrumond and Ethel (Deaton) D.; B.A., U. Tenn., 1949, M.A., 1951, Ph.D., 1957; postgrad. U. Ala., 1949, U. Ky., 1950, U. Cal., Los Angeles, 1950-51; m. Lucile Mulkey, June 9, 1950; children—Terence Jerome, Teresa Susanne. Fellow So. Regional Tng. Program in Pub. Adminstrn., 1949-50; prin. Fontana Dam Elementary Sch., 1951-52; instr., research asso. dept. polit. sci., U. Tenn., 1954-57; research asst. Bur. for Govt. Research, W.Va. U., Morgantown, 1957-61; dir., prof. polit. sci. Cons. to W.Va. state and local governments. Served with USAAF, 1943-46. Mem. Pi Sigma Alpha. Baptist. Editor, author: (with others) West Virginia State and Local Government, 1963; also author monographs on W.Va state and local govt. Editor, W.Va. Govt. Home: Morgantown WV

DAVIS, CLIFFORD, congressman; b. Hazlehurst, Miss., Nov. 18, 1897; s. Odom A. and Jessie (Ott) D.; LL.B., U. of Miss., 1918; m. Carolyn Leigh, June 7, 1922; children—Clifford, Barbara Leigh, Ray. Began as pvt. sec. to mayor of Memphis, Tenn., 1920; judge Municipal Court, Memphis, 1924-27, vice-mayor and commr. of pub. safety, 1928-40; mem. 76th-82d Congresses 10th Tenn. Dist., 83rd-88th Congresses, 9th Dist.; mem. coms. on pub. works, flood control, others. Trustee Bapt. Meml. Hosp., Memphis. Mem. Sigma Alpha Epsilon. Democrat. Baptist. Mason (Shriner), Moose, Elk, A.H.E.P.A. Home: Memphis TN Died June 1970.

DAVIS, DAVID WILLIAM, ex-gov.; b. Wales, Apr. 23, 1873; s. John Wynn and Frances (Lewis) D.; brought to U.S. in infancy; ed. pub. schs. until 12; m. Florence O. Gilliland, Sept. 19, 1894 (died Mar. 17, 1903); m. 2d, Nellie Johnson, Apr. 5, 1905; children—Margaret Ruth (wife of Capt. Daniel Stubbs), Comdr. David William, Ltd. Comdr. Donald J. Coal miner at 12 years of age; clerk, Dawson, Iowa, at 16; clk., later mgr. Farmers' Cooperative Assn., Rippey, 1892-99; cashier Bank of Rippey, 1899-1905; cashier Dayton (Wash.) Nat. Bank, 1905-06; organizer, and pres. First Nat. Bank, American Falls, Ida., 1907; del. Rept. Nat. Convention, Chicago, 1912; joint owner American Falls Press; mem. Idaho Senate, 1912-14; gov. of Ida., 2 terms, Jan. 6, 1919-Jan. 4, 1923; spl. asst. sec. of Interior, 1923; U.S. Commr. of Reclamation, 1923-24; dir. of finance, Bur. of Reclamation, 1924-26; resigned to engage in mining; pres. Orango Corp. of Fla., Orlando Fla. Chairman War Loans Finance Com., for Ida., World War. Pres. Ida. State Bankers' Assn., 1918. Honarary life mem. G.A.R., Dept. of Idaho. Republican. Orlando FL‡

DAVIS, E. ASBURY, merchant; b. Somerset County, Md., Aug. 24, 1870; s. Francis A. and Sallie (Long) D.; Baltimore City Coll., 1885; m. Jennie Conradt, Oct. 20, 1892; children—Francis A., Allan C., Hamilton C., Clara A., Virginia. Partner F. A. Davis & Sons, and Washington Tobacco Co. Pres. U.S. Fidelity & Guarantee Co.; v.p. Old Dominion Tobacco Co. Home: Warrington Apts., Balt. Office: 119 S. Howard St., Baltimore MD*

DAVIS, EDWARD E., U.S. dist. atty., Ariz. Office: Phoenix AZ Died June 2, 1969.

DAVIS, EDWIN G., lawyer; b. Samaria, Ida., July 9, 1874; s. Thomas J. and Elizabeth (Williams) D.; grad. U.S. Mil. Acad., 1900; m. Elsie Poll, of Salt Lake City, Utah, July 23, 1900. Served in Philippines, 1900-1; instr. law, U.S. Mil. Acad., 1903-7; capt. U.S.A., retired, Feb. 28, 1910; maj., lt. col. and col. J.A. Gen.'s Dept., Washington, D.C., World War. Rep. candidate for gov. of Ida., 1916, for U.S. senator, 1920; U.S. dist. atty. for Ida. since Jan. 1, 1922. Episcopalian. Elk. Kiwanian. Author: A Text Book of Constitutional Law, 1905. Home: Boise ID‡

DAVIS, ELMER JOSEPH, supt. Better Government Assn.; b. N. Eaton, Lorain Co., O., Apr. 9, 1869; s. Thomas Jefferson and Mary Naomi (Brooks) D.; ed. Avalon (Mo.) Coll.; m. Mary Minton Smith, Nov. 27, 1894; children—Nelson Louis, Rollo Joseph, James Brooks, Raymond Hoyt, William Mead. Engaged as sash and door mfr., 1893-1907. Pres. Englewood Law and Order League, 1905-10; one of founders of Chicago Law and Order League and County Voters' League; assisted in movement to close saloons in Chicago on Sunday; supt. Chicago Dist. Anti-Saloon League of Ill., 1911-23; organizer, 1923, and since supt. Better Government Assn. of Chicago and Cook Co. Mem. bd. Chicago Ch. Federation since 1918. Mem. Disciples of Christ. Club: City. Home: 156th and Le Claire. Office: 189 W. Madison St., Chicago IL‡

DAVIS, GAYLORD, lawyer; b. Lincoln, Neb., Sept. 16, 1897; s. Walter Clyde and Minerva (Caldwell) D.; A.B., U. Neb., 1920; LL.B., Columbia, 1925, M.S., 1925; m. Susan Scott, July 4, 1925; 1 dau., Susanne Davis Newsberry. Instr. accounting U. Neb., 1920-21, Sch. Bus. Columbia, 1921-25; admitted to N.Y. bar, 1926, practiced in N.Y.C., 1925-46; with firm Root, Clark, Buckner & Ballantine, 1925-28; asso. firm Cadwalader, Wickersham & Taft, 1928-46, mem. firm, 1942-46; gen. counsel, treas., sec. Am. Enka Corp. (N.C.), 1946-50, gen. counsel, treas., v.p., 1950-54, financial v.p., gen. counsel, 1954-62. Mem. bd. dirs. Asheville Symphony Soc.; gen. agt. in U.S.A. Algemene Kunstzijde Unie N.V. of Arnhem Holland, 1947-67. Mem. bd. Wachovia Bank and Trust Co., Asheville, N.C., 1952-67. Pres., dir. Asheville Community Concert Assn., Inc. Trustee N.C. Symphony Soc. Inc.; dir. Bus. Found. N.C., Inc., 1959-64. Mem. C. of C., Am., N.C. bar assns., Soc. Mayflower Descendants, Newcomen Soc. of Eng., Phi Beta Kappa, Beta Gamma Sigma, Phi Kappa Psi, Sigma Delta Chi, Alpha Kappa Psi, Sr. Hon. Soc. Innocents (U. Neb.). Republican. Mason (32 deg.). Clubs: University (N.Y.C.); Biltmore Forest Country, Mountain City (Asheville, N.C.). Home: Asheville NC Died June 26, 1972; buried Calvary Cemetery, Fletcher NC

DAVIS, GEORGE THOMPSON BROWN, author; b. nr. Staunton, Ill., July 4, 1873; s. Rev. James Scott and Elizabeth Amelia (Rogers) D.; B.A., Lake Forest (Ill.) Univ., 1894; grad. McCormick Theol. Sem., 1898; m. Rose Helen Fox, Nov. 20, 1934. Assistant editor Ram's Horn, 1894-1901; manager Davis Literary Syndicate, 1901-04; evangelist since 1904. Internat. sec. Pocket Testament League, 1912-24; condr. of various campaigns to distribute the New Testament. Presbyterian. Author: D.L. Moody—The Man and His Mission, 1899; Metlakahtla, 1903; When Christ Was Here, 1904; Torrey and Alexander, 1905; Twice Around the World with Alexander, 1907; Korea for Christ, 1910; The Pocket Testament League Around the World, 1910; Winning the World with the Bible, 1912; China's Christian Army, 1925; Adventures in Soul-Winning, 1929; Fulfilled Prophecies that Prove the Bible, 1931; Caleb Maccabee, 1934; Rebuilding Palestine According to Prophecy, 1935; Seeing Prophecy Fulfilled in Palestine, 1937; Jewels for Messiah's Crown, 1939; When the Fire Fell, 1945. Conducted Pocket Testament League evang. campaign Brit. and American military camps, 1914-19; made tour of world to promote world-wide Bible revival, 1921-25; conducted campaign to distribute one million Testaments in China, 1925-28; conducted one million testaments campaign for Latin Am., 1928-31, also for students in the U.S. and Canada, 1931-34; campaign for quarter million Testaments for people of Philippine Islands, 1934-37; campaign for million Testaments for Jewish people since 1937. Home: 2012 W. Tioga St. Address: 1505 Race St., Philadelphia PA‡

DAVIS, HALLIE FLANAGAN, prof. drama; b. Redfield, S.D., Aug. 27, 1890; d. Frederic Miller and Louisa Bertha (Fischer) Ferguson; Ph.B., Grinnell (Ia.) Coll., 1911; A.M., Radcliffe Coll., 1924; Dr. Humane Letters, Williams Coll., 1941; m. John Murray Flanagan, Dec. 25, 1912 (died 1918); children—John Murray (dec.), Frederic Fionn; m. 2d, Philip Haldane Davis, Apr. 26, 1934 (died 1940); stepchildren—John Dwelle Davis and Joanne Plympton Davis (twins), Helen Dwelle Davis. Production asst. to Prof. G.P. Baker, Harvard University, 1923-24; dean Smith Coll., 1942-46; prof. drama and dir. Smith Theatre, since 1946; artist-in-residence, Dartington Hall Sem., Eng., 1950. Received Guggenheim Fellowship to study comparative theatre styles in 12 European countries, 1926-27 (first woman to receive this award); later studied theatre in Greece, Africa and other countries; made theatre survey in Mexico for Inst. of Current World Affairs, summer 1943. Mem. Nat. Association University Professors, National Theatre Conf., Am. Nat. Theatre and Acad., Phi Beta Kappa. Author: Dynamo: The Story of a College Theatre, 1942; (play) Atomic Energy (with Sylvia Gasell and Day Tuttle), 1948; others. Contbr. periodicals. Address: Poughkeepsie NY Died Aug. 1969.

DAVIS, HARRY ELLERBE, educator; b. Little Mountain, S.C., Aug. 25, 1905; s. Braxton Bragg and Ada (Boland) D.; A.B., U. S.C., 1927; M.A., Columbia, 1940; D.F.A. (hon.), Catawba Coll., Salisbury, N.C., 1962; m. Anne Mallard Osterhout, Aug. 29, 1965. Dir., Town Theatre, Columbia, S.C., 1929-31; mem. faculty U. N.C. at Chapel Hill and staff Carolina Playmakers, U. N.C., 1931-68, prof. dramatic art, 1949-68, chmn. dept., 1958-68, dir. Carolina Playmakers, 1958-68; mem. profl. groups summers Surry (Me.) Playhouse, 1930, 31, Island Theatre, Nantucket, Mass., 1934, 35, The Lost Colony, Manteo, N.C., 1938, 40; dir. Unto These Hills, Cherokee, N.C., 1950-67, producer, 1967-68. Mem. adv. bd. Inst. Outdoor Drama, Chapel Hill, N.C., 1963-68. Served with AUS, 1942-46. Mem. Cherokee Hist. Assn. (bd. dirs. 1950-68), Southeastern (past pres.), Nat. theatre confs., Am. Ednl. Theatre Assn. (past bd. dirs.), ANTA. Author articles in field. Home: Chapel Hill NC Died Sept. 15, 1968; buried Chapel Hill Cemetery.

DAVIS, HARVEY HENRY, educator; b. Corydon, Ia., Dec. 15, 1894; s. Winfield Scott and Ida Belle (McVay) D.; student Drake U., 1916-19, Ia. State Coll., summers 1919, 20; A.B., A.M., State U. of Ia., 1923, Ph.D., 1928; LL.D. (honorary), Bowling Green State University; m. Frances Wadle, June 1, 1922; 1 son, Philip Wadle. Rural sch. teacher and supt. various towns in Ia., 1913-22; supt. schs., Carrollton, Ill., 1923-24; dir. div. of records and statistics, St. Louis (Mo.) Pub. Schs., 1924-28; auditor Ohio State Dept. of Edn. and asst. prof. sch. adminstrn., Ohio State U., 1928-31, asso. prof. sch. adminstrn., 1931-35, prof. of edn., 1935-63, chmn. dept. of education, 1937-42; v.p., 1942-48; exec. dean, div. research and training, dean grad. coll. State U. Ia., 1948-50. provost, 1950-63; cons. on higher edn., various states, 1963-69; Nat. University Kingdom Jordan, summer 1965. Dir., chmn. bd. First Nat. Bank, Iowa City. Mem. academic adv. bd. U.S. Marine Acad., 1953-59, exec. bd. N. Central Assns. Colls. and Univs.; commn. on colls. and univs. N. Central Assn. Colls. and Secondary Schs., 1949-55; mem. advisory com., Armed Forces Edn. Program com., 1950-53; asso. dir. project research in univs., U.S. Office of Edn., 1936; research associate Am. Council Edn., 1937; participated in sch. surveys at Cleveland, O., and elsewhere. Served as color sgt. engrs., U.S. Army, 1918; part time cons. War Dept., 1943. Mem. Am. Assn. Sch. Adminstrs., Ia. Hist. Soc. (dir.), Am. Assn. Higher Edn. (pres. 1952-53), Am. Legion, Phi Delta Kappa. Mason. Contbr. articles to ednl. jours. Home: Iowa City IA Died June 8, 1969; buried Oakland Cemetery, Iowa City IA

DAVIS, HAYNE, lawyer; b. Statesville, N.C., Nov. 2, 1868; s. Hayne and Mary (Pearson) D.; A.B., U. of N.C., 1888; unmarried. Began practice of law at Knoxville, Tenn., 1890; mem. Williams, Henderson & Davis, 1891-94; in practice at New York since 1904. Sec. Dem. State Exec. Com. of N.C., 1888. Contbr. to periodicals on internat. questions. Press representative of Interparliamentary Union, 1904; authority on internat. polit. organization; advocate of a Union of Nations in the likeness of the Am. Union of States; founder of Am. Peace and Arbitration League; sec. Am. delegation to 13th and 14th Inter-Parliamentary Confs. Home: 2647 Broadway, New York NY‡

DAVIS, HELEN CLARKSON MILLER, (MRS. HARVEY NATHANIEL DAVIS), ednl. adminstr.; b. Roselle, N.J., May 9, 1879; d. Charles Dexter and Julia (Hope) Miller; ed. pvt. schs., St. Timothy's Sch., Catonsville, Md. (now Stevenson, Md.); L.H.D., Middlebury Coll., 1956; spl. student Tchrs. Coll., Columbia; m. Harvey N. Davis, Feb. 8, 1935; stepchildren—Suzanne Courtonne (Mrs. Thomas J. Durham), Louisa Frederika, Marian (Mrs. Bliss Woodruff), Nathaniel. Tchr. pvt. sch., mem. bd. dirs. Miss Spence's Sch. (now Spence Sch.), N.Y.C., 1914-18. asso. prin., 1924-29, headmistress, trustee, 1929-32; organizer, dir. tng. sch. for women war workers YMCA, N.Y., 1918, dir. personnel, chief womens bur. YMCA, Paris, 1919, met. sec. YWCA, N.Y.C., 1920-24; mem. Nat. Com. on Prisons and Prison Labor, 1916-18; alternate mem. sub-com. Experts for Instrn. of Youth League of Nations, Geneva, Switzerland, 1931; mem. bd. dirs. Am. Assn. for UN, 1945-50; mem. Nat. Edn. Com. League of Nations Assn. (now Am. Assn. for the UN), 1921-52, chmn. 1922-41; mem. nat. commn. for UNESCO, 1950-52; mem. Presbyn. Bd. Fgn. Missions, 1914-32; mem. bd. trustees Internat. House, N.Y.C., 1924-50, now trustee emerita; mem. bd. dirs. Near East Found., 1935-65; dep. liaison officer between World Assn. Girl Guides and Girl Scouts, London and the UN, 1958-60; mem. Stanley Fellowship com. Stevens Inst. Tech.; mem. Soc. Mayflower Descs. Democrat. Presbyn. Author: Religious Liberty in the Near East, 1938;

Constitutions, Electoral Laws and Treaties of States in the Near and Middle East, 1947, rev. 1953. Address: New York City NY Died Dec. 25, 1968.

DAVIS, HERBERT SPENCER, zoologist; b. Oneida, N.Y., Mar. 28, 1875; s. Edson Warburton and Anna Maria (Griswold) D.; Ph.B., Wesleyan U., Conn., 1899; Ph.D., Harvard, 1907; m. Raynor Nicolson Harris, Aug. 12, 1912; 1 dau., Muriel Griswold. Instr. zoology, 1901-04, asst. prof., 1904-06, Wash. State Coll.; prof. zoology, U. of Fla., 1907-22; pathologist U.S. Bur. Fisheries since 1922. in charge aquicultural investigations. Cons. Oregon Game Commn., 1945-47; retired Sept. 1947. Mem. A.A.A.S., Am. Soc. Zoologists, Ma. Micros. Soc., Alpha Delta Phi. Congregationalist. Home: Claiborne MD‡

DAVIS, HOWLAND SHIPPEN, trustee; b. Seabright, N.J., Sept. 5, 1886; s. Howland and Anna Elizabeth (Shippen) D.; A.B., Harvard, 1908; LL.D. (honorary), Bard College, 1960; married Laura Suffern Livingston, Sept. 26, 1914; children—Howland, Catherine Livingston (Mrs. Oliver Gordon Stonington). Clerk, Blake Brothers and Co., New York, N.Y., 1908-15, partner, 1915-38; officer, New York Stock Exchange, 1938-48; executive vice pres., 1940-48; trustee Bank for Savings (New York), The Grant Foundation; member bd. directors W. T. Grant Company (New York). Past mem. Tivoli Bd. Edn. Trustee Bard Coll. Served as private, advancing to major, Headquarters 77th Division, A.E.F., World War I. Chairman Taconic (New York) State Park Commission; chmn. bd., Leake and Watts Children's Home (N.Y. City); manager New York Institute for Edn. of Blind; v.p. Fedn. Protestant Welfare Agys. N.Y. Mem. St. Paul's Ch. (vestryman). Clubs: Down Town Assn., Union (N.Y.C.). Home: Tivoli NY Died July 15, 1969; buried St. Paul's Ch., Tivoli NY

DAVIS, HUGH ORTON, educator; b. Nacogdoches, Tex., Aug. 30, 1899; s. Hugh Barclay and Martha (Orton) D.; A.B. cum laude, Baylor U., 1925; A.M., Harvard, 1930, Ph.D., 1941; certificate U. Va., 1944; m. Martha Malvenia Edwards, June 26, 1929; 1 son, Hugh Edward. Prin., Cleveland (Tex.) High Sch., 1919-21; supt. schs. Dayton, Tex., 1921-24, Mertson, Tex., 1925-27; head dept. social scis. Winthrop (Mass.) High Sch., 1928-41; analyst Joint Army, Navy and Air Intelligence Div., Washington, 1946-48; asso. prof. sociology Baylor U., Waco, Tex., 1948-53; prof. social scis. Okla. Baptist U., Shawnee, 1953-64; prof., chmn. of div. social sciences Oral Roberts U., Tulsa, 1964-68. Cons. family relationships and juvenile problems, 1953-68. Oklahoma's Institutes on Juvenile Problems, 1957-68. Dir. Winthrop dist. Boy Scouts of America, 1928-37; director Winthrop drives A.R.C., 1928-32; Baylor U. rep. United Fund, Waco, Tex., 1948-53; v.p. Okla. Heart Assn.; mem. Tulsa and Okla. State Community Relations Commn. Sponsor of Okla. Bapt. U. Federated Republican Club, 1957-64. Served with U.S. Army, 1918; with AUS, 1941-46; ETO. Decorated Bronze Star; recipient certificate of appreciation Am. Heart Assn., 1959, 61, 63. Fellow Am. Sociol. Assn.; mem. Nat. Council Family Relations, Am. Acad. Polit. and Social Sci., Urban League, Southwestern Social Sci. Assn., Am. Assn. U. Profs., Am. Legion, Ret. Officers Assn., Pi Gamma Mu, Phi Alpha Delta. Republican. Baptist. Mason. Rotarian (v.p. Shawnee 1962-63). Author: America's Trade Equality Policy, 1942; articles and book revs. Home: Friendswood TX Died Mar. 1, 1969.

DAVIS, J. F., banker. chmn. bd. First Nat. Bank of Omaha. Chmn. bd. Aksarben-Clarkson Hosp., Creighton U. Indsl. Found., Joslyn Art Mus. Home: Omaha NB Died Mar. 23, 1972.

DAVIS, J(OHN) LIONBERGER, lawyer, banker; b. St. Louis, Missouri, Oct. 2, 1878; s. John D. and Marion Scott (Lionberger) D.; prep. edn., Smith Acad., St. Louis and Lawrenceville (N.J.) Sch.; A.B., Princeton, 1900; student law dept., Harvard; LL.B., St. Louis Law Sch., 1903; m. Julie M. Vietor, Nov. 1, 1906; children—Marion Lionberger (Mrs. B. F. Hobart Cale), Anne Vietor (Mrs. J. Douglas Streett II), George Vietor, J. Lionberger, Jr. Admitted to Mo. bar, 1903; chmn. bd. Security Nat. Bank S.&T. Co., 1921-47; alumni trustee Princeton U. Mng. dir. for Alien Property Custodian during World War I. Chmn. com. on Debt. Adjustment, The Twentieth Century Fund (1937); former chairman Mayor's Commn. on Unemployment; ex-chmn. New Constn. Assn. of Mo.; ex-mem. Code Commn. of Mo.; ex-pres. St. Louis Chamber of Commerce. Former chmn. St. Louis Chapter, Am. Red Cross, Mem. U.S. Territorial Memorial Commn., English-Speaking Union (pres. St. Louis Chapter). Publisher, St. Louisian. Pres. Mo. Inst. for Administration of Justice. Clubs: University (pres. 1922), Princeton, Noonday, Round Table, St. Louis Country; University, Coffee House (New York). Founder and chmn. J.L.D. Art Trust (1947). Home: Princeton NJ Died Apr. 1973.

DAVIS, JAMES SHERMAN, educator; b. Troy, Ala., Feb. 16, 1918; s. John Sherman and Sally (Simpson) D.; B.S., Birmingham-So. Coll., 1941; M.A., U. Wis. 1948, Ph.D., 1952; m. Mary Lou Overall Mar. 14, 1941; children—Beatrice Anne, James Sherman. Research asst. zoology U. Wis., 1946-51; mem. faculty U. Tenn. Med. Units, Memphis, 1952-69, prof. anatomy, 1963-69, asst. dean basic med. scis., 1965-68, asso. dean, 1968-69; head research career sect. Nat. Inst. Gen. Medicine (spl. cons. to dir. 1965-66), NIH, 1964-65. Served to 1st lt. USAAF, 1942-45. Decorated Air medal. Mem. Am. Assn. Anatomists, Endocrine Soc., Am. Soc. Zoologists, Am. Assn. Med. Colls., So. Soc. Anatomists, Sigma Xi. Home: Memphis TN Died Apr. 29, 1969.

DAVIS, JESS HARRISON, coll. pres.; b. Columbus, O., July 29, 1906; s. Willard Ellsworth and Winifred (Jones) D.; B.S., Ohio State U., 1928. M.S., 1933, D.Sc., 1956, St. Lawrence U., 1949; D.Eng., Clarkson Coll. Tech., 1951, Newark Coll. Engring., 1963; LL.D., Rutgers, 1954; m. Dorothy Carrigan, 1928 (dec. 1969); 1 dau., Sarah Louise (Mrs. Edward S. Boslow, Jr.); m. 2d, Mary Grattan Roper, July 1970. Student engr., asst. to maintenance supt. Ohio Bell Telephone Co., Columbus, 1928-29; mech. engr. Atmospheric Nitrogen Corp., Hopewell, Va., 1929; instr. mech. engring. Clarkson Coll., Potsdam, N.Y., 1929-31, asst. prof., 1931-36, asso. prof., 1936-40, prof. heat power and exptl. engring., 1947, pres. 1948; pres. Stevens Inst. Tech., Hoboken, N.J., 1951-72; prof., chmn. dept. mech. engring Speed. Sci. Sch., U. Louisville, 1944-46; mech. engr. Ala. Power Co., 1936, Am. Locomotive Co., 1937, Central N.Y. Power Co., 1940, Foster Wheeler Corp., 1941; cons. engr. Hydraulic Controls, Inc., 1942, N.Y. Air Brake Co., 1943-45, D.M. McBean, 1945-47, DeWolfe Furnace Corp., 1945-47; dir. Philip Morris, Inc., Pub. Service Electric & Gas Co., Nat. Biscuit Co., Prudential Ins. Co. Am., 1st Jersey Nat. Bank, Carrier Corp., Bethlehem Steel Corp., Pennwalt Corp. Commr., Port of N.Y. Authority, 1952-59. Registered Profl. engr., N.J., N.Y., Ky. Mem. Engrs. Council Profl. Devel., Am. Soc. M.E.s (bd. tech. 1954, Richards award 1952), Am. Soc. for Engring Edn., Am. Soc. Testing and Materials, Ky. Soc. Profl. Engrs., Louisville Adv. Com. on Smoke Abatement (chmn. 1944-45), Sigma Xi, Tau Beta Pi, Pi Mu Epsilon. Clubs: University, Engineers (N.Y.C.); Saucon Valley Country (Bethlehem, Pa.). Home: Hoboken NJ Died Sept. 17, 1972; buried Charlottesville VA

DAVIS, JOHN KER, fgn. service officer; b. of Am. parents, Soochow, China, Mar. 5, 1882; s. John Wright and Alice Irene (Schmucker) D.; B.A., Wooster U. (now Coll.), 1904, M.A., 1908, LL.D., 1941; m. Mary Isabelle Murphy, May 29, 1912; children—Mary Shannon, John Spencer. Pvt. sec. and tutor in China 3 yrs.; instr. in Chinese Govt. Coll. 1 yr.; apptd. dep. consul gen., Shanghai, Apr. 14, 1910; student interpreter, 1912-13; dep. consul gen., Shanghai, 1913; v. and dep. consul gen., Canton, 1913-14; v. and dep. consul, Chefoo, 1914-15; consul, Antung, 1915-19, Nanking, 1919-27; first sec. of Legation, Peking (in charge of Chinese Secretariat), 1927-28; consul gen. (on detail), London, 1928-30; consul general, Seoul, Chosen, 1930-34, at Vancouver, B.C., Can., 1934-39, at Warsaw, Poland, Jan.-Sept., 1939; on detail at Oslo, Norway, Oct. 1939-Jan. 1940; at Dublin, Ireland, Feb.-July, 1940; chief of Office of Philippine Affairs, Dept. of State, Dec. 1, 1940-Aug. 1942; retired, Aug. 1942. Was in charge of American official mission which rescued American and European captives from Lincheng bandits in China, 1923; in charge of evacuation of Nanking Am. colony during anti-foreign attack, Mar. 24, 1927; in charge of protection of Americans during siege of Warsaw, Poland, and of their evacuation, Sept. 1939. Mem. Beta Theta Pi, Phi Beta Kappa. Presbyterian. Home: West Vancouver British Columbia Canada Died July 12, 1969; cremated.

DAVIS, JOSEPH SMITH, electronics engr.; b. Balt., July 15, 1923; s. Joseph S. and Theresa (Mueller) D.; student U. Balt., 1941-42, Johns Hopkins, 1948-53, U. Cin., 1962-64, Miami U., 1964-65; m. Dorothy Gough Fiege, Feb. 28, 1942; children—Cheryl D., Kevin B. Asst. foreman Bethlehem Fairfield Shipyard, Balt., 1942-43; supr. Bendix Radio, Towson, Md., 1948-56; product supr. Whirlpool Corp., Marion and Hamilton, O., 1956-62; sr. engr. Aeronca Mfg. Corp., Middletown, O., 1962-65; project supr. Access Corp., Cin., 1965-67; project supr. Philco-Ford Corp., Connersville, Ind., 1967-68. Served with AUS, 1943-46. Registered profl. engr. Ohio. Mem. I.E.E.E., Instrument Soc. Am., Ohio Soc. Profl. Engrs. (chpt. dir. 1965). Presbyn. Home: Hamilton OH Died May 18, 1969; buried Parkwood Cemetery, Baltimore MD

DAVIS, MALCOLM MCTEAR, editor; b. St. Louis, Sept. 2, 1921; s. Dr. Arthur Jobe and Elizabeth Crawford (McTear) D.; student U. Ga., 1939-40, N.Y.U., 1947-48. Various positions Atlanta Constitution, 1940-41; travel writer Am. Express, N.Y.C., 1946-48, spl. corr., 1948; contbr. researcher Information Please Almanac, 1947, 50, compiler, arranger world travel sect. 1947 edit.; editor co. mag. Going Places, 1947-48; roving corr. Brit. Travel Assn., 1948; asso. editor Am. Soc. Travel Agts. News, 1948-49; editor Let's Go, 1949-50, Travel, 1950-73. Served as yeoman USNR, 1942-45. Recipient spl. Lafayette medal, France, 1957, named hon. Tar Heel by Gov. N.C., 1968. Mem. Soc. Am. Travel Writers, Drama Desk, N.Y. Travel Writers Assn. (pres. 1963-66), Am. Soc. Mag. Editors. Contbr. to Our Navy, 1944, The Smart Traveler, ann. yearbooks Am. Peoples Ency., 1953-58, World Book Ency., 1934-64, Readers Digest, travel publs., gen. mags. Home: New York City NY Died 1973.

DAVIS, MICHAEL MARKS, med. adminstr.; b. N.Y.C., Nov. 19, 1879; s. Michael Marks and Miriam Maduro (Peixotto) D.; A.B., Columbia, 1900, Ph.D., 1906; L.H.D. (hon.), Howard University, 1965; m. Janet Hayes, June 5, 1907 (deceased Mar. 23, 1950); children—Paul Sprague, Burnet Maduro, Michael Marks; m. 2d Alice L. Taylor, Jan. 7, 1951. Sec. Peoples Inst., N.Y. City, 1904-09; dir. Boston Dispensary, 1910-20; organizer pay clinic for people of moderate means, Boston, 1913; sec. com. on Dispensary Development, N.Y. City, 1920-27; consultant in hosp. organization and medical administration, 1920-71; organizer pay clinic, Cornell Med. Coll., N.Y. City, 1921; dir. med. services, Julius Rosenwald Fund, Chgo., 1928-36; professorial lecturer, University of Chicago, 1932-36; chmn. Com. on Research in Med. Economics, 1937-48. Fellow Am. Pub. Health Assn., Am. Coll. Hosp. Administrators (hon.); mem. Am. Hosp. Assn., A.A.A.S., Am. Sociol. Soc., Am. Public Welfare Assn., National Organization for Public Health Nursing, S.A.R.; chairman Health Program Conference, 1944; consultant on health studies United States Social Security Administrn.; chairman executive committee, Committee for The Nation's Health, 1946-56. Club: National Arts (New York). Author: Gabriel Tarde An Essay in Sociological Theory, 1906; Psychological Interpretations of Society, 1909; (with Dr. A.R. Warner) Dispensaries, 1917; Immigrant Health and the Community, 1919; Clinics, Hospitals and Health Centers, 1927; Hospital Administration A Career, 1929; Paying Your Sickness Bills, 1931; (with C.R. Roem) The Crisis in Hospital Finance, 1932; Public Medical Services, 1937; America Organizes Medicine, 1941; Medical Care for Tomorrow, 1954. Editor, Medical Care (quarterly), 1941-44; contbr. to Harper's, New Republic, Modern Hospital, etc. Michael M. Davis lectures established at U. Chgo., 1963. Home: Chevy Chase MD Died Aug. 19, 1971; buried Camp Margaret, Lake Memphremaqog, Quebec Canada.

DAVIS, NEAL BALBACH, physician; b. Omaha, Oct. 3, 1926; s. Edwin and Dorothy (Balbach) D.; student Swarthmore Coll., 1943-44, Harvard, 1945; M.D., U. Neb., 1950; m. Jean Leman; children—Daphne, Neal, Gail, Nancy, Daniel, Andrew, Joan. Intern, Charles T. Miller Hosp., St. Paul, 1950-51; fellow in urology Mayo Clinic, Rochester, Minn., 1951-53; resident in urology Kansas City (Mo.) Gen. Hosp., 1955-56; asso. staff Clarkson, U. Neb. hosps.; courtesy staff Children's, Methodist hosps.; attending staff VA Hosp.; sr. staff Lutheran Hosp. (all Omaha); asso. U. Neb. Served with M.C., USAF, 1953-55. Diplomate Am. Bd. Urology. Mem. A.M.A. Home: Omaha NB Died July 27, 1969; buried Forest Lawn Cemetery, Omaha NB

DAVIS, OLIVE BELL, author, lectr.; b. Milledgeville, Ga.; d. Charles Milton and Olive (Bell) Davis; student Arlington Hall Jr. Coll., Washington, 1938-39, U. Ga., 1939-40, Ga. State Coll., 1955-56. Writer feature articles mag. sect. Atlanta Jour.-Constitution, 1951-53; coms. sec. Senate Ga., 1958-64; lectr., 1959-69. Mem. Rabun Gap-Nacoochee Jr. Guild, 1943-69, Atlanta Symphony Jr. Guild, 1945-69, Ga. Art Commn., 1967-69. Bd. dirs. Atlanta Music Club. Mem. D.A.R. (past pres.), Magna Charta Soc., U.D.C., Dixie Council Authors and Journalists, Nat. League Am. Pen Women, Ga. Writers Assn. (past v.p.), Atlanta Writers Club, Alpha Delta Pi. Methodist. Clubs: Atlanta Debutante, Theatre Atlanta Guild, Variety of America, Tent 21. Author: Exodus: 20, 1959; Between Two Novels, 1965; (plays) An Evening With O.B.D., 1966. Contbr. book revs. to newspapers. Address: Atlanta GA Died May 11, 1969; buried Arlington Cemetery, Atlanta GA

DAVIS, PAUL (ALEXANDER), columnist; b. Falconer, N.Y., Mar. 30, 1896; s. Murray Herschel and Laura Julia (Cooke) D.; ed. Falconer pub. schs.; m. Edna Erla McClane, Apr. 15, 1925. Falconer corr. for Jamestown (N.Y.) Evening Journal, 1916; on news staff, Jamestown Morning Post, 1916-20; asst. city editor, Jamestown Evening Journal, 1920-23; reporter, St. Petersburg (Fla.) Evening Independent, 1923, city editor, 1924-47, mng. editor, 1947-51; columnist St. Petersburg Morning Times from 1951; news editor, Havana (Cuba) Post, 1925, 30; covered 2d Bikini bomb test for Evening Independent, 1946. Served U.S. Army, Camp Dix, N.J., 1917-18. Mem. United World Federalists, C. of C. Democrat. Methodist. Club: Florida Legislative Correspondents' Assn. (pres. 1943-45). Home: St Petersburg FL Died Apr. 26, 1971; cremated.

DAVIS, PAUL HAZLITT, broker; b. Crawfordsville, Ind., May 29, 1889; s. Jospeh L. and Frances (Hall) D.; Ph.B. in Commerce and Adminstrn., of U. of Chicago, 1911; m. Dorothy Milford, June 24, 1913 (dec. Nov. 1964); children—Paul Hazlitt, Jr., Patricia Davis Bethke, Milford Hall; m. 2d, Suzanne D. Davis, Jan. 16, 1965. With bond dept. Colonial Trust & Savings Bank, 1911-12, John Burnham and Co., 1912-16; senior partner Paul H. Davis & Company, 1916-53.

Hornblower & Weeks, 1953-69; dir. Borg-Warner Corporation, Arvin Industries Inc.; advisory dir. Amphenol Electronic, Inc.; pres. Chgo. Stock Exchange, 1931-33; gov. N.Y. Stock Exchange, 1935-41; v.p. Investment Bankers Association of America, 1939-41. Trustee Illinois Institute of Technology since 1932, A Century of Progress Expn., Chicago, 1934-35. Served in Co. I, 3d Regt., Illinois Res. Militia, World War; also in Red Cross and Liberty Loan activities. Mem. Art Inst. Chicago, Field Museum of Natural History, Chicago Historical Society, Delta Upsilon. Mason (32 deg.). Clubs: The Adventurers, Attic, Chicago, Union League. Home: Glenview IL Died Dec. 17, 1969.

DAVIS, PHILIP, real estate attorney, ednl. film producer; b. Moteleh, Russia, June 12, 1876; s. Dave Ben and Rachel Leah Chemerinsky (changed to Davis upon arrival in U.S., 1890); ed. Hull House (social settlement), Chicago, 1890-98; Lewis Inst., 1898-99; U. of Chicago, 1899-1901; A.B., Harvard, 1903; LL.B., Boston U., 1914; m. Belle Shomer, July 16, 1904; children—Frances Parsons, Phyllis Bella. Nat. organizer Internat. Ladies' Garment Workers, Am., 1903-05; supervisor Boston Newsboys' Republic and Boston Newsboys' Court (Boston pub. schs.), 1906-12; dir. nationwide study Boy Problem," under Nat. Fedn. of Settlements, 1913-15; dir. $50,000 campaign, Mass. Credit Union, 1916; head worker Civic Service House, Boston, 1911-17. Served as supt. employment and welfare dept. Am. Internat. Shipbuilding Corp., Hog Island, Pa. Field lecturer, United Americans of State of Me.; ednl. and indsl. motion picture producer; dir. Community Motion Pic. Bur. of N.E.; pres. Nat. Motion Picture Bur., Inc., 1914-40; Russian War Relief worker, 1943-45; builder, mgr., Washington Apt. Hotel. Author: Street-Land, 1914; (with Mabel Hill) Civics for New Americans, 1915. Editor: (with Maida Herman) The Field of Social Service, 1914; Immigration and Americanization (with Bertha Schwartz), 1919. Producer: New England in Motion Pictures; Jack Spruce, or Life in the Northern Woods; From Wool to Cloth; Forbidden Waters (featuring U.S. Coast Guard Service); The Romance of Palestine (talking motion picture); Marching On (talking motion picture on the garment industry). Home: Washington Apartments, Brighton MA‡

DAVIS, RICHARD HALLOCK, government official; b. Jamestown, N.Y., Feb. 7, 1913; s. Alfred Cookman and Ethel (Falconer) D.; grad. Phillips Exeter Acad., 1931; A.B., Princeton, 1935; M.B.A., Harvard, 1937; area study, Russian Inst., Columbia University, 1949-50; married Harriet Kingsland Robbins, May 31, 1952; one daughter, Cynthia Elinor; 1 step dau., Anne Robbins Schlapp. Fgn. service officer Dept. State, 1938-72; vice consul, Hamburg, 1938-39, Tsingtao, 1940-42; 3d sec., Chungking, 1942-43, New Delhi, 1942; 2d sec., Moscow, 1943-46, 1st sec., 1948-49; asst. chief Eastern European div., Dept. of State, 1946-48, officer in charge U.S.S.R. Affairs, Office Eastern European Affairs, 1950-53; counselor of embassy, Vienna, and asst. dept. high commr. for Austria, 1953-55; mem. Policy Planning Staff Dept. of State, 1955-57; minister-counselor embassy, Moscow, 1957-59; dir. Office Soviet Union Affairs, 1959-60; dep. asst. sec. of state for European Affairs, 1960-62, sr. dep. asst., 1962-72. Died Mar. 1972.

DAVIS STURGISS BROWN, educator; b. Newark, Ohio, Sept. 9, 1877; s. Lucius Edgar and Estella Ann (Brown) D.; A.B., Ohio Wesleyan U., 1907; A.M., Ohio State U., 1912; Ph.D., U. of Pa., 1920; m. Alice Margaret Wolfe, Aug. 15, 1907; children—Sturgiss Wolfe, Alice Brown, Mary Slocum, Edgar Forsman. Teacher, high sch., Groveport, 1900-02; supt. village schs. in Minn., 1907-14; dean Coll. of Edn., Ohio Northern U., 1914-16; lecturer, Ursinus Coll., Collegeville, Pa., 1916-17, Swarthmore Coll., 1917-18; prof. ednl. administration, University of Pittsburgh, 1918-33; supt. of schools, Champion, Ohio, 1933-35; Sabbatical year, 1932-33, at Yale; ednl. director Canal Winchester Ohio Bank since 1939. Founder and chmn. bd. of editors Sch. of Education Jour. Served as capt. Mil. Band, Ohio Wesleyan. Mem. N.E.A., Nat. Soc. for Study of Edn., Coll. Teachers of Edn., Phi Delta Kappa, Kappa Delta Pi. Methodist. Contbr. to Jour. Ednl. Research, High Sch. Teacher; review manuscripts of Am. Book Co. Address: Bexley Station, R.D. 5, Columbus OH‡

DAVIS, WALLACE MCRAE, banker; b. Moline, Ill., Nov. 13, 1898; s. William Wallace and Elizabeth (McRae) D.; student Purdue U., 1916-17; LL.B., Jefferson Sch. of Law, Louisville, 1923; m. Leona Mae Knoderer, June 27, 1923; children—Wallace M., Warren B. Messenger, Citizens Nat. Bank, Louisville, 1919-20, asst. cashier, 1926-30, asst. vice pres., 1930-32, vice pres., 1932-49, exec. v.p. Citizens Fidelity Bank and Trust Co. (formerly Citizens Union Nat. Bank) 1949; pres., dir. Hibernia Nat. Bank, New Orleans 1949-65, chmn. bd., 1965-66; dir. New Orleans & Northeastern R.R. Co. Instr. F.A. Central O.T.S., 1918-19. Presbyn. Clubs: New Orleans Country, Pickwick, Lake Shore, Boston; Metropolitan (N.Y.C.). Home: New Orleans LA Died Nov. 25, 1966; buried Metairie Cemetery, New Orleans LA

DAVIS WILLIAM H., sheriff Allegheny County, Ga. Died Feb. 15, 1970.

DAVIS, WILLIAM HARPER, psychologist, librarian; b. Phila., Dec. 10, 1877; s. William and Alice (Hoff) D.; certificate in biology, U. of Pa., 1895; A.B., Princeton, 1900; post-grad., Columbia, 1900-4; unmarried. Asst. in psychology, Columbia, 1900-3; instr. philosophy and psychology, 1904-5, asst. prof. in charge of dept., 1905-7, Lehigh U.; asst. in biology, U. of Pa. Summer Sch., 1894; sec. gen. psychology, Internat. Congress Arts and Sciences, St. Louis Expn., 1904; librarian to Public Service Corpn. of N.J., Newark, since Sept., 1915. Fellow A.A.A.S. (sec. council 1907), New York Acad. Sciences; mem. A.L.A., Spl. Libraries Assn., N.Y., N.J., Pa. Library assns., Am. Electric Ry. Assn., Nat. Commercial Gas Assn., Nat. Electric Light Assn., Am. Psychol. Assn. (sec.-treas. 1904-8), N.E.A., Am. Soc. Naturalists, Am. Anthrop. Assn., Am. Philos. Assn., New York Zool. Soc., Phila. Zool. Soc., Am. Peace Union, Drama League, Soc. Jud. Settlement Internat. Disputes, Society Promotion of Liberal Studies, Browning Soc. of Phila., Gesellschaft fur positivistische Philosophie (Berlin), etc. Contbr. essays and reviews. Republican. Clubs: Philobiblon, Princeton, Plays and Players, N.Y. Library, Newark Traffic; Royal Socs. (London). Address: Public Service Corpn., Newark NJ‡

DAVIS, WILLIAM HOLMES, b. Petersburg, Va., Feb. 25, 1873; s. Joseph Claiborne and Mary Eleanor (Holmes) D.; A.B., Randolph-Macon Coll., 1892; m. Mary Freer Matthews, of Holly Springs, Miss., Sept. 1, 1898; children—William Holmes, Joseph Claiborne. Headmaster and owner, Weldon (N.C.) Univ. Sch., 1892-93; prin. and owner, Univ. Sch., Rocky Mount, N.C., 1894-98; prin. Randolph-Macon Inst., Danville, Va., 1898-1906; supt. pub. instrn., Danville, 1905-08; headmaster The Danville Sch. for Boys, 1908-18. Pres. Hampton Roads Maritime Exchange, 1920-21; pres. Va. Forwarding Corpn., 1923; spl. rep. Norfolk Port Commn. in Eng., 1923. Contbr. to mags. and newspapers since 1901. Democrat. Methodist. Mem. Kappa Alpha. Home: Norfolk VA‡

DAVISON, EDWARD, poet; b. Glasgow, Scotland, July 28, 1898; s. Robert and Evelyn Mary (Ford) D.; foundation scholar, St. John's Coll., Cambridge Univ., Eng., 1921, B.A., 1921, M.A., 1925; hon. Litt.D., U. of Colorado in 1934; m. Natalie Eva Weiner, April 27, 1926 (dec. 1959); children—Peter Hubert, Lesley (Mrs. Forrest Perrin); married second to Rose Landver, July 26, 1960. Editor Cambridge (England) Review, 1920-22; editor The Challenge, London, 1922-24; general mgr. The Guardian, London, 1924-25; came to U.S., 1925; prof. English literature, Vassar Coll., 1926-27; editor The Wits' Weekly," Saturday Review of Literature, 1928-30; engaged in lecturing, 1925-70. John Simon Guggenheim Memorial fellow in poetry, Europe, 1930; visiting prof. English lit., U. of Miami, Fla., 1934-35; dir. Writers' Conf. in the Rocky Mtns., Boulder, Colo., 1935-42; prof. English lit., U. of Colo., 1935-46. Served as ordinary seaman, advancing to paymaster sub-lt. Brit. Royal Naval Div., 1914-18; expert cons. to Sec. of War, 1943; commd. major, A.U.S., 1943 (Army Edn. and Information Div.); lt. col., dir. Army's re-edn. program for enemy prisoners of war, Provost Marshal Gen.'s Office, 1944-46. Awarded Army Commendation, Legion of Merit, 1946. Apptd. George M. Laughlin prof. English lit. and chmn. Eng. dept., Washington and Jefferson Coll., Washington, Pa., 1946, dean of college, 1947-49; prof. English, dean Sch. Gen. Studies, Hunter Coll., City U. N.Y., 1953-68, dean and professor emeritus, 1968-70. Member Poetry Society America (pres. 1955-56), Cum Laude Society (honorary). Author: Poems, 1920; Poems by Four Authors (collaborator), 1923; Harvest of Youth, 1925; Some Modern Poets, 1927; The Heart's Unreason, 1931; The Ninth Witch, 1932; Nine Poems, 1937; Collected Poems, 1940. Editor: Cambridge Poets, 1914-20, 1921. Home: New York City NY Died Feb. 8, 1970.

DAVISON, MRS. HENRY POMEROY, philanthropist; b. Bridgeport, Conn., Feb. 2, 1871; d. Frederick and Mary (Baldwin) Trubee; ed. Miss Salisbury's Sch., Pittsfield, Mass., and Rye (New York) Seminary, Doctor of Humanities, Adelphi College; m. Henry Pomeroy Davison, Apr. 13, 1893 (died May 6, 1922); children—Alice (Mrs. Artemus L. Gates), Frances (Mrs. Ward Cheney), F. Trubee, Harry P. Active in philanthropic, civic and social work. Mem. board trustees, Presbyn. Med. Center, including Presbyn., Babies, Sloane Maternity hosps., Vanderbilt Orthopedic Clinic, Neurol. Inst. and Eye Inst.; v. chmn. Presbyn. Nursing Com.; hon. chmn., mem. exec. com. and bd. mgrs. Am. Red Cross, Nassau County Chapter; hon. mem. bd. dirs., Y.W.C.A., City of New York; trustee and acting mayor, Village of Lattingtown, L.I.; v.p., Nat. Inst. of Social Sciences (mem. council and exec. com.); hon. chmn. Women's Com. of the Farmers Fedn. of North Carolina. Received Gold Medal, Nat. Institute Social Sciences. Episcopalian. Club: Cosmopolitan (N.Y.C.). Home: Peacock Point, Locust Valley, L.I., N.Y.; also 2 E. 67th St., New York NY‡

DAVISON, HOMER R(EESE), trade assn. exec.; b. Marshall, Ill., Mar. 29, 1899; s. Burns M. and Mary (Quick) D.; student Culver Mil. Acad., 1914-15; B.S., U. Ill., 1921; m. Elna Mary Magnuson, Oct. 2, 1928; children—Linda Ellin (Mrs. Conrad Bishop), O. Christopher Abbott. Livestock commissioner for the Chicago Live Stock Exchange, 1921-24; dir. assn. mgmt. Am. Meat Inst., 1924-25, v.p., 1927-57, pres., 1957-72; dir. Am. Meat Inst. Found., 1944-72, v.p., 1944-57, pres., 1957-72; v.p., dir. Mfrs. Coop. Assn., 1941-72. Mem. President's Nat. Agrl. Adv., Commn., 1953-57. Mem. exec. com. Inst. Animal Agr., Purdue U.; chmn. Nat. Food Conf. Com., 1957-60; v.p., sec., dir. Nat. Food Conf. Assn., Inc., 1960-72. Mem. S.A.R., Chi Phi. Mason (32 deg., Shriner). Club: Saddle and Sirloin (Chgo.). Home: Cadillac MI Died June 1972.

DAVISON, WILBURT CORNELL, pediatrician; b. Grand Rapids, Mich., Apr. 28, 1892; s. William L. (D.D.) and Mattie E. (Cornell) D.; A.B., Princeton, 1913; Sr. Demy (Rhodes scholar 1913-16), Magdalen Coll., Oxford, Eng., 1915-17; B.A., Oxford U., 1915, B.Sc., 1916, M.A., 1919; M.D., Johns Hopkins, 1917; D.Sc., Wake Forest Coll., 1932; LL.D., U. N.C., 1944, Duke, 1961; m. Atala Thayer Scudder, June 2, 1917; children—William Townsend, Atala Jane Scudder Levinthal, Alexander Thayer. Instr., asso. prof., acting head dept. pediatrics, asst. dean, Johns Hopkins Med. Sch., 1919-27; asso. pediatrician, acting pediatrician in charge, editor Bull. Johns Hopkins Hosp., 1919-27; dean, James D. Duke prof. pediatrics Duke Sch. Medicine, 1927-61; cons. Womack Army Hosp; mem. medico adv. bd. CARE; trustee Duke Endowment; v.p. bd. dirs. Doris Duke Found. Mem. div. med. scis. NRC, vice chmn. 1942-43; cons. office Surgeon Gen., U.S. Army; adv. group Armed Forces Med. Library; mem. com. on vets. med. problems; mem. com. atomic casualties NRC; mem. med. adv. com. N.C. Bd. Mental Health; mem. med. adv. panel Oak Ridge Inst. Nuclear Studies; mem. council chief cons. VA; mem. dean's com. Durham VA Hosp.; mem. N.C. gov.'s working com. Research Triangle Devel. Council, N.C. Nuclear Energy Adv. Com; dir. Playtex Park Research Inst.; med. adv. com. Research Found.; nat. adv. com. Chronic Disease and Health of Aged; trustee Ednl. Council Fgn. Med. Grad.; mem. Civilian Health and Med. Adv. Council; chmn. OSD Hosp. Planning Group. Served with AEC, 1914-15. France, Serbia; capt. M.C., U.S. Army AEF, 1917-19; served to col. AUS. Recipient Alvaranga prize, 1917. Master A.C.P.; mem. Am. Acad. Pediatrics, Am. Coll. Clin. Adminstrn. (hon.), Am. Pediatric Soc., Soc. for Pediatric Research, Am. Soc. Clin. Investigation, N.C. Pediatric Soc., Am. Acad. Gen. Practice (hon.), Assn. Pediatricians de Guatemala (hon.), Phi Beta Kappa, Sigma Xi, Omicron Delta Kappa, Alpha Omega Alpha (pres.). Democrat. Methodist. Clubs: Cosmos (Washington). Hope Valley Country, Roaring Gap Yacht. Author: Pediatric Notes, 1925; (with S.A. Waksman) Enzymes; 1926; The Compleat Pediatrician, 1934, 38, 40, 44, 46, 49, 57, 61. Contbr. articles to profl. jours. Home: Roaring Gap NC Died June 26, 1972; cremated.

DAVOL, RALPH, writer, painter; b. Taunton, Mass., 1874; s. Ezra and Arabella Malvina (White) D.; ed. Harvard, class of 1896 (non-grad.); studied art, Washington, D.C., and Providence, R.I. Has been cartoonist and spl. writer for various publs.; mem. Mass. Ho. of Rep., 1908, 09. Past trustee Curry School of Expression, also Public Library, and Playground Commission, Taunton; gave public playground to city of Taunton, 1911. With War Trade Bd., Washington, 1918. Mem. Plattsburg Mil. Training Camp, 1916; mem. Co. B., 5th Regt. D.C. Nat. Guard, 1918; with Co. D, 14th Inf., Mass. State Guard, during Boston police strike, 1919. Clubs: Cosmos (Washington); National Arts (New York). Author: Two Men of Taunton; American Pageantry; Raw Products of Africa; Animals Speak French. Painter of hist. subjects. Mus. Compositions include: Hands Around the Globe; Rainbow in Tears; You My Friend Me, and others. Contbr. Dictionary Am. Biography. Now working in sculpture. Home: Taunton MA Died Apr. 25, 1966.

DAWE, HELEN CLEVELAND, educator; b. Concord, N.H., April 2, 1909; d. Harry and Hilda Foster (Goddard) Dawe; A.B., Smith Coll., 1931; M.A., U. Minn., 1932; Ph.D., State U. Ia., 1940. Research asst. Inst. Child Welfare, U. Minn., 1931-32, 33-34; preschool tchr. Child Welfare Research Sta., State U. Ia., 1934-36, research asst., 1936-39; instr. dept. child development Ia. State Coll., 1939-40, asst. prof., 1940-41; prof. home econs., chmn. dept., dir. nursery sch. U. Wis., 1941-71. Mem. Wis. Adv. Com. Early Childhood Edn. Mem. Am. Home Econ. Assn., Nat. Assn. for Edn. Young Children, Midwest Assn. Edn. Young Children, Soc. Research in Child Development, Nat. Council Family Relations. Episcopalian. Club: Altrusa. Author: (with Updegraff et al) Practice in Preschool Education, 1938. Home: Madison WI Died Apr. 9, 1971; buried Beacon NY

DAWES, IRVING D., business exec.; b. Somerville, Mass., Mar. 12, 1892; s. Henry Laurens and Minnia Walton (Goodwin) D.; grad. Harvard Coll., 1912, Sch. Bus. Adminstrn., 1914; m. Corinne Lee Thies, June 23, 1917; children—Richard Irving (lt. U.S.N.R.), Phyllis

Corinne. C.P.A., Mass., 1917. Began as comptroller or treas. in various lines, automotive textile, paper and bag industries; treas. Martin-Parry Corp., York, Pa.; comptroller Virginia-Carolina Chem. Corp., 1930, chief accounting officer, dir. Bag Division, later vice president, treas. and dir.; dir. Tobacco By-Products & Chem. Corp., Fidelity Chem. Co., Blackstone Guano Co. (subsidiaries of Va.-Carolina Chem. Corp.), Algonquin Chemical Company, St. Louis. Mem. Controllers Inst. of Am. (former chmn. of com. on tech. information and research); dir. Nat. Tax Equality Assn., Va. Assn. Bus. Men, Inc. Formerly chmn. cost accounting com. Nat. Fertilizer Assn.; formerly pres. First Unitarian Ch. of Richmond, Southern Neighbors Fellowship of Liberal Chs.; past vice pres. Am. Unitarian Assn.; past v.p. chpt. A.R.C. Mem. Harvard Alumni Assn. (past v.p.). Republican. Unitarian. Clubs: Harvard (past pres.); Country Club of Va. Author numerous articles on accounting and bus. subjects. Home: Richmond VA Died Feb. 10, 1968.

DAWSON, ALBERT FOSTER, ex-congressman; b. Spragueville, Ia., Jan. 26, 1872; s. Thomas and Alice (Foster) D.; student U. of Wis. 1 yr., later George Washington U.; m. Phoebe R. De Groat, of Clinton, Ia., June 21, 1893; children—Loleta, Claribel, Olive, Albert D., Eugene. Began publication Preston (Ia.) Advance, 1891; city editor Clinton (Ia.) Herald, 1894; sec. to Congressman G. M. Curtis, 1895, to Senator W. B. Allison, 1899; now pres. Dawson, Howe & Dawes, Inc., of Davenport. Mem. 59th to 61st Congresses (1905-11), 2d Ia. Dist. Republican. Active in Liberty Loan Campaign, 1917. Home: 2905 Middle Rd., Davenport IA‡

DAWSON, CHARLES I., ex-judge; b. Logan County, Ky., Feb. 13, 1881; s. S. N. and Frances D.; ed. Bethel Coll., Russelville, Ky., Univ. of Ky., and Bowling Green Business Coll.; m. Eleanor Hopson, 1905; children—Eleanor, Jean Maxwell, Richard. Admitted to bar, 1905; began practice at Russellville, 1905; moved to Pineville, 1906; mem. Ky. Ho. of Rep., 1906; county atty., Bell County, Ky., 1910-20; atty. gen. of Ky., term Jan. 1920-Jan. 1924; U.S. dist. judge, Western Dist. Ky., from 1925-35; in practice of law at Louisville since July, 1935; mem. firm Bullitt, Dawson & Tarrant. Rep. nominee for gov. of Ky., 1923. Republican. Mem. Christian (Disciples) Ch. Mason. K.P., Elk, Woodman. Home: Anchorage KY Died Apr. 24, 1969; buried Cave Hill Cemetery, Louisville KY

DAWSON, CLAUDE IVAN, consular service; b. Burlington, Ia., Oct. 23, 1877; s. Noble Edmund and Laura Frances (Gerry) D.; ed. high sch., Washington, D.C.; studied law Georgetown U. 1 yr.; m. Theodosia Brock, of S.C., Mar. 29, 1902; 1 son, Edwin Albert. With treasury dept. of insular govt. of P.R., 1899-1904; sec. of a traction co. in S.C., 1904-08; examiner, Interstate Commerce Commn., 1908-10; consul at Puerto Cortes, Honduras, 1910-12, Valencia, Spain, 1912-15, Tanipico, Mexico, 1915-21; consul agent assigned to Mexico City, Nov. 28, 1921, to Stockholm, Sweden, Aug. 1, 1924, Rio de Janeiro, Nov. 16, 1926, now at Barcelona, Spain. Pvt. D.C. Militia 2 yrs.; sergt. Co. G. 1st D.C. Vols., May-Nov. 1898. Home: Anderson, S.C. Address: American Consulate-General, Barcelona Spain‡

DAWSON, JAMES FREDERICK, landscape architect; b. Jamaica Plain, Mass., Jan. 13, 1874; s. Jackson Thornton and Mary (McKenna) D.; grad. high sch., West Roxbury, Mass., 1893; spl. landscape course, Harvard, 1894-96; study abroad, 1900-02, 1904; m. Hazel Lease, June 4, 1913; children—Jackson Thornton, James Frederick, Robert Fletcher, Jane Lease. Began as plantsman, Olmsted Bros., landscape architects, Brookline, Mass., 1896, asso. mem. firm, 1906-22, mem. firm since 1922. Prin. works: Park work, Essex Co., N.J., Watertown, N.Y., Seattle and Spokane, Wash., Portland, Ore.; Seattle Expn., 1906-09, San Diego Expn., 1911; St. Francis Wood, San Francisco; Palos Verdes Estates, nr. Los Angeles, Calif.; State Capitol grounds, Olympia, Wash., and Montgomery, Ala.; Grove City (Pa.) Coll.; Russell Sage Coll. and Emma Willard Sch. for Girls, Troy, N.Y.; Fort Tryon Park, N.Y. City; also grounds of many other schools, parks, pvt. estates and country clubs all over U.S. Mem. U.S. War Housing Commn., Newville Island, Pa., 1918. Fellow Am. Soc. Landscape Architects (mem. Boston and Pacific Coast chapters); mem. Palos Verdes Art Jury. Episcopalian. Clubs: Harvard, Nat. Arts (New York); Horticultural (Boston). Home: Sherborn, Mass. Office: 99 Warren St., Brookline MA‡

DAWSON, MARION LINDSAY, lawyer; b. Scottsville, Va.; s. George Washington and Sarah May D.; B.L., Richmond Coll., 1894; m. Alice Taylor, of Nattallburg, W.Va., 1903; children—Elizabeth, Nutall (dec.), Marion Lindsay, Taylor, John Wyatt, Thomas Raven, George Kisty. Began law practice at Richmond, Va., 1895; chmn. Dem. Exec. Com., Richmond, 1895-98; judge adv. gen. of Va., 1898-1900; mem. Suffolk Co. (N.Y.) Dem. Com., 1906-10; moved to Brooksville, Fla., 1912; mem. Fla. Ho. of Rep., 3 terms, 1916-19; mgr. conservative Dem. campaign through which Cary A. Hardee was elected gov., 1919; author of Budget Bill taking effect in State of Fla., 1921; apptd. sec. to gov. but resigned to become state equalizer of taxes. Mem. Nat. Econ. League. Mem. Va., N.Y. and Fla. State bars, Pi Kappa Alpha. Presbyn. Mason, K.P., Elk, Red Man. Speaker and writer on economic and governmental topics. Mem. Fla. advisory council, Yenching U., China. Home: Brooksville FL*‡

DAWSON, WILLIAM, foreign service officer; b. St. Paul, Aug. 11, 1885; s. William and Maria (Rice) D.; B.A., U. of Minn., 1906; studied Ecole Libre des Sciences Politiques, Paris; m. Agnes Balloch Bready, June 8, 1926. Apptd. v. and dep. consul-gen., St. Petersburg, 1908; A.E. and P. Panama, 1939-41, Uruguay, 1941-46; vet. 1946. Polit. adviser U.S. delegation U.N. Gen. Assembly sessions, 1946, 47, and to U.S. delegation Rio de Janeiro Conf., 1947; U.S. rep. with rank of ambassador on governing bd. Pan Am. Union, 1947-48. Mem. Chi Psi. Episcopalian. Clubs: Cosmos (Washington). Home: Washington DC Died 1972.

DAWSON, WILLIAM L., congressman; b. Albany, Ga., Apr. 26, 1886; s. Levi and Rebecca (Kendrick) D.; A.B., magna cum laude, Fisk U., Nashville, 1909; studied law Chicago-Kent Coll. of Law; LL.B., Northwestern U. Sch. of Law; m. Nellie W. Brown, Dec. 20, 1922; children—William L., Jr., Barbara Ann. Admitted to Ill. bar, 1920, and practiced in Chicago; became alderman 2d Ward, Chicago, 1933. Apptd. vice chairman Democratic National Com. Mem. 78th to 91st U.S. Congresses from 1st Ill. Dist.; chmn. House com. on exec. expenditures, 1949-70, mem. D.C. Com., chmn. govt. operations com. Served at 1st lt. AEF, U.S. Army, 1917-19. Mem. Am. Legion, Disabled Am. Veterans, Alpha Phi Alpha. Mason (33 deg.), Elk. Home: Chicago IL Died Nov. 9, 1970.

DAY, CLIVE, univ. prof.; b. Hartford, Conn., Feb. 11, 1871; s. Thomas M. and Ellen C. (Pomeroy) D.; ed. Hartford pub. Schs.; A.B., Yale, 1892; U. of Berlin, 1892-93; Yale, 1893-95; Ph.D., 1899; univs. Berlin and Paris, 1898-99; m. Elizabeth Dike Lewis, June 30, 1904; children—Margaret, Ellen. Instr. history and economics, U. of Calif., 1895-98; instr. economics, Sheffield Scientific Sch., 1899-1900; instr. history, Yale, 1900-02, asst. prof. economic history, 1902-07, prof., 1907-36, since emeritus. Chief of Balkan Div. of Am. Commission to Negotiate Peace, Paris, 1918-19. Foreign mem. Koninklijk Instituut voor de Taal-Land-en Volkenkunde van Nederlandsch-Indie; corr. mem. Bataviaasch Genootschap van Kunsten en Wetenschappen. Fellow Am. Acad. Arts and Sciences. Author: Policy and Administration of the Dutch in Java, 1904; History of Commerce, 1907; History of Commerce of the U.S., 1925; Economic Development in Modern Europe, 1933. Address: 44 Highland St., New Haven CT‡

DAY, CYRUS LAWRENCE, educator; b. N.Y.C. Dec. 2, 1900; William S. and Emily H. (Lawrence) D.; student Phillips Exeter Acad., 1916-18, Mass. Inst. Tech., 1918-20; B.S., Harvard, 1923, Ph.D., 1930; A.M., Columbia, 1925; m. Camilla Downing, Sept. 3, 1935; children—Benjamin D., Margaret W. Instr. English, U. Tex., 1925-26; Sheldon treveling fellow, Harvard, in Eng. and France, 1930-31; grantee Am. Council Learned Societies, Eng., 1935; asst. prof. English, U. Del., 1931-37, asso. prof. 1937-46, prof., 1946-68; vis. prof. U. Cal., summer 1947; cons. Webster-Merriam Co. Mem. selection com. Dist. V, Woodrow Wilson Nat. Fellowship Found., 1958-59. Mem. Am. Assn. U. Profs., Modern Lang. Assn. (chmn. Group VII, 1948), Bklyn. Inst. Arts and Scis., Bklyn. Bot. Gardens, Del. Edn. Assn., Phi Sigma Kappa, Phi Kappa Phi. Republican. Episcopalian. Club: Newark (Del.) Country. Author: Sailors Knots, 1935; The Art of Knotting and Splicing, rev. edit., 1955. Editor: Songs of Dryden, 1932; Songs of D'Urfey, 1933. Compiler: (with E. B. Murrie) English Song-Books, 1651-1703, a Bibliography, 1940. Contbr. articles profl. jours. Newark DE Died July 1968.

DAY, KARL S., airline exec.; b. Ripley County, Ind., May 30, 1896; s. Franklin Groves and Edith (Schmolsmire) D.; B.A., Ohio State U., 1917; m. Margaret Raine, Oct. 16, 1925; children—John Franklin, Nancy (Mrs. Howard M. Trowern, Jr.). Served from 2d lt. to lt. gen., USMC and USMC Res., 1917-57; operations mgr. Curtiss-Wright Flying Service, 1929-32; with Am. Airlines, Inc., 1932-62, successively instrument instr., pilot, check pilot, asst. flight supt., flight supt., 1932-46, dir. flight dispatch, 1946-62. Marine Corps mem. Res. Forces Policy Bd., 1954-57; pres. Marine Corps Res. Officers Assn., 1953-56, chmn. bd. dirs., 1961-68, chmn. emeritus, 1968-73. Died Jan. 19, 1973; buried Arlington National Cemetery.

DAY, KENNETH, otologist; b. Pittsburgh, Pa., Apr. 8, 1896; s. Ewing Wilbur and Annie (Mosier) D.; A.B., Princeton, 1917; M.D., John Hopkins, 1921; m. Ruth Piper, October 9, 1935; one daughter, Elizabeth Anne (Mrs. Norwell B. Browne, Jr.). Resident of Massachusetts Eye and Ear Infirmary, 1923-24; in private medical practice, specializing in otology, Pittsburgh, Pa., since 1924; asst. prof. otology, U. of Pittsburgh, 1930-40, associate professor, 1941-49, prof. otology, dept. chmn., 1960-61, emeritus, 1962-68, dir. audiology, 1949-68; consultant Pittsburgh Eye and Ear Hosp.; consultant Childrens Hosp., Elizabeth Steele Magee Hosp. Trustee, Western Pa. Sch. for Deaf. Served with R.O.T.C., 1917; with Med. Res., 1917-18. Recipient Distinguished Service award, Pa. Academy of Ophthalmology and Otolaryngology, 1960. Mem. Am. Otol. Soc. (pres. 1951), Am. Laryngol., Rhinol. and Otol. Soc. (president 1955), Pitts. Academy Medicine (pres. 1952). Clubs: Longue Vue, University (Pitts). Contbr. to med. jours. Home: Pittsburgh PA Died Sept. 9, 1968.

DAY-LEWIS, CECIL, writer, educator; b. Ballintubber, Ireland, Apr. 27, 1904; s. Rev. F. C. and Kathleen Blake (Squires) Day-L.; student Sherborne School, Wadham College, Oxford; D.Litt. (honorary), Exeter University; D.Litt., U. Hull, 1969, Trinity Coll., Dublin, 1968; m. Constance Mary King, 1928 (div. 1951);children—Sean Francis, Nicholas Charles; m. 2d, Jill Angela Henrietta Balcon, 1951; children—Lydia Tamasin Day-Lewis, Daniel Michael Blake Day-Lewis. Assistant master at Summer Fields, Oxford, 1927-28, Larchfield, Helensburgh 1928-30, Cheltenham Coll., 1930-35; editor books and pamphlets Ministry of Information, 1941-46; Clark lectr. Trinity Coll., Cambridge, 1946-51; professor poetry Oxford U., 1951-56; Charles Eliot Norton professor of poetry Harvard University, 1964-65; also writer detective novels under pseudonym Nicholas Blake. Dir. Chatto & Windus, pubs. Vice president of the London Library. Decorated commander Order Brit. Empire; companion of lit. Royal Soc. of Literature; honorary fellow Wadham College, Oxford, 1968. Named Poet-laureate of Gt. Britain, 1968. Fellow Royal Society Literature (vice pres.); mem. Am. Academy Arts and Letters (hon.), Irish Acad. Letters. Author: Collected Poems, 1954; A Hope for Poetry; Overtures to Death; Word Over All; Poetry for You; The Poetic Image; Poems, 1943-47; An Italian Visit, Pegasus, The Gate, The Buried Day, various others. Translator of books, including the Georgics of Virgil; The Aeneid of Virgil; The Eclogues of Virgil. Home: London England Died May 22, 1972; buried Stinsford Churchyard, nr. Dorchester, Dorset England

DAYTON, HUGHES, physician; b. Philadelphia, Pa., May 13, 1873; s. William Berrian and Cornelia (Hughes) D.; Ph.B., Sheffield Scientific Sch. (Yale), 1894; M.D., Coll. Phys. and Surg. (Columbia), 1898; m. Amy Edna Albert, Feb. 10, 1915. Began practice, 1898; asso. attending phys., New York Hosp., 1908-19; cons. phys. United Hosp., Portchester, N.Y., since 1913; attending phys. House of Relief, 1916-19, Grasslands Hosp., 1924-29 (cons. phys. since 1929), Tarrytown (N.Y.) Hosp., 1925-35 (cons. phys. since 1935). Mem. Soc. Cincinnati. Republican. Episcopalian. Author: Practice of Medicine (in Medical Epitome Series), 1905, 5th edit, 1928. Address: Irvington-on-Hudson NY‡

D'AZAMBUJA, LUCIEN HENRI, astronomer; b. Paris, France, Jan. 28, 1884; s. Antonio and Blanche (Gagniot) D'A.; D.Sc.; m. Marguerite Roumens, July 4, 1935. Joined Observatoire de Meudon, 1899, named titular astronomer, 1938; titular astronomer astrophysics sect. Observatoire de Paris. Laureat de l'Institut, 1915, 27, 35, 43, Societe Astronomique de France, 1932, 48. Mem. Societe Astronomique de France (pres. 1949-51), Conseil des Observatoires Astronomiques, Federation des Societes Francaises de Physique, Comite Francais de Radio-Electricite Scientifique, Bur. Longitudes (corr.), Research and publs. on structure of solar chromosphere and evolution of protuberances. Home: Salies-de-Bearn (P.-A.) France Died July 18, 1970.

DEAK, FRANCIS, fgn. service officer, educator; b. Ujvidek, Hungary, Mar. 5, 1899; s. Emery and Ilona (Kozma) D.; student Inst. Tech., Budapest, 1920-22, L'ecole des sciences politiques, Paris, 1924-25; LL.D., U. Budapest, 1925; S.J.D., Harvard, 1927; m. A. Patricia O'Quin, Aug. 1, 1936. Came to U.S., 1925, naturalized, 1939. Asst. to Hon. Judge John Bassett Moore, 1927-28; lectr., asst., later asso. prof. law Columbia, 1929-47; vis. prof. Sch. Internat. Studies, Geneva, Switzerland, Carnegie Internat. Inst., Paris, 1937-38; lectr. Acad. Internat. Law, The Hague, 1939; mem. League of Nations Copyright Study Group, 1937-39; spl. atty. Office of Gen. Counsel, Treasury Dept., 1937-40; spcl. mission, U.S. Govt., overseas, 1943-45; regional civil air attache to Switzerland, Austria, Germany, Bulgaria, Czechoslovakia, Hungary, Rumania, Yugoslava, 1945-50; chief aviation policy staff State Dept., 1950-52; 1st sec. Embassy, polit. officer Office U.S. Spl. Rep. in Europe, Paris, 1952-53; counselor of embassy for econ. affairs U.S. embassy, Rome, 1953-58; UN advisor to Asst. Sec. of State Econ. Affairs, from 1958; prof. internat. law Rutgers U., New Brunswick, N.J. dep. dir. USOM. Mem. Am. Soc. Internat. Law, Acad. Polit. Sci., Fgn. Service Assn. Author: The Hungarian-Rumanian Land Dispute, 1928; Neutrality: Its Economics, History and Law (with Dr. Philip C. Jessup), 1937; Neutrality Laws and Regulations, 1776-1939 (with Dr. Philip C. Jessup), 1939; Turkey at the Straits (with Dr. James T. Shotwell), 1940; Hungary at the Paris Peace Conference, 1942; articles in legal publs. Died Jan. 21, 1972.

DEAKIN, GERALD, communications exec.; b. Birmingham, Eng., Feb. 14, 1883; s. James Edward and Lily Mary (Tarbolton) D.; student Acad. Armour Inst. Tech., 1898-1902; m. Marguerette Burton, Feb. 26, 1907; 1 son, Gerald Edward. Asst. chief engr. Pacific Telephone &Telegraph Co., San Francisco, 1904-10; asst. chief engr. Bay Cities Home Telephone Co., 1910-11, chief engr., 1911-12; asst. European chief engr. Western Electric Co., Antwerp, Belgium, 1912-25; also chief engr. Bell Telephone Mfg. Co., 1919-25; asst. tech. dir. Internat. Telephone & Telegraph Corp., 1925-32, later v.p. and gen. tech. dir., now v.p., chief engr.; v.p. Le Materiel Telephonique, Paris, France, 1925-28; v.p. and dir. Internat. Standard Elec. Corp. dir. Fed. Telephone & Radio Corp., 1941-70. Home: Sands Point NY Died Sept. 10, 1970; buried Chicago IL

DEAL, ERASTUS CHARLES, officer public utility cos.; b. Gainesville, Ga., Nov. 15, 1876; s. Columbus Lafayette and Mary Olivia (Stringer) D.; grad. high sch., 1893; student business sch., Brockton, Mass.; m. Carrie Wahl, Mar. 5, 1902; children—Lois Lafayette, Erastus Charles. With Ga. Electric Light Co. (now Ga. Ry. and Power Co.), Atlanta, 1895-98; operating and constrn. work, Stone and Webster, pub. utility operators, 1899-1904; with Public Service Corp. of N.J., as chief engr. Bergen County Gas and Electric Co. and supervisor corp.'s properties in Central N.J., 1904-09; gen. mgr. Public Service Co. of N.C., 1909-11; with J. G. White &Co., as v.p. and gen. mgr. Augusta Aiken Ry. and Electric Corp. and Ga. Carolina Power Co., 1911-14; simultaneously, 1914-17, pres. Yadkin Constrn. Co., v.p. and gen. mgr. N.C. Public Service Co., Salisbury-Spencer Ry. Co., Carolina & Yadkin R.R. Co., Delaware County Power Co., Henry County Light & Power Co., Tacoma Water Co., Interstate Public Service Co., Galena Water Co.; chief engr. W. N. Coler & Co.; gen. mgr. Trinidad Electric, Transmission, Ry. & Gas Co., Springfield Gas &Electric Co. and Springfield Traction Co., 1917-22; with Electric Bond and Share Co., as v.p. and gen. mgr. Campania Cubana de Electricidad and 12 subsidiary cos., and Phoenix Utility Co., Cuba, 1922-24; on staff of pres. Federal Light & Traction Co., 1924-26; spl. supervisor Nat. Public Service Corp., New York, 1926-27; pres. Peoples Light & Power Co., N.Y., Green Mountain Public Service Co., Vt., Tex. Public Service Co., Tex., Arizona Edison Co., Ariz., Wis. Hydroelectric Co., Wis., Calif. Public Service Co., Calif. Gen. Power & Light Co., N.Y., Miss. Public Service Co., Miss., West Coast Power Co., Ore.-Wash., Western States Utilities, Ala. Public Service Co., Ala., Trojan Engring. Corp., N.Y.; chmn. of bd. Pinnacles Development Co., Va.; pres. Campania de servicios, Mexico, 1927-32; chmn. bd. Am. Natural Gas Co., N.Y., pres., Oklahoma Natural Gas Co., Okla., Natural Gas Engring. Co., Okla., Natural Gas Producers Corp., Okla., Okla. Natural Gas Bldg., Okla., Onaga Royalty Corp., Okla., Philokla Gas Co., Okla., Texakan Oil Corp., Okla.; v.p. Quinton Natural Gas Corp.; v.p. Trojan Engring. Corp. of Tex.; pres. of 16 other companies in various states; dir. Public Works Engring. Corp., N.Y.; dir., Power Gas & Water Securities Corp., N.Y., 1929-32; now pres. Scranton-Spring Brook Water Service Co. and several other water service companies, Scranton Gas System and Carbondale Gas Co., Pa.; dir. New York Water Service Co., N.Y.; v.p. and dir. Utility Operators Co., N.Y.; dir. Sterling Hotel Co., Wilkes-Barre, Pa. Engaged in elec. constrn. work, Key West, during Spanish-Am. War; mgr. elec. power utility, Colo. coal fields during World War I; ex-v.p. Nat. Electric Light Assn.; ex-pres. southeastern sect. Nat. Electric Light Assn.; ex-pres. Ga. Pub. Utility Assn.; ex-v.p. Mo. Assn. Public Utilities; dir. Pa. Waterworks Assn., Am. Gas Assn. Clubs: Scranton; Westmoreland (Wilkes-Barre, Pa.). Home: 92 W. River St., Wilkes-Barre, PA. Office: 135 Jefferson Av., Scranton PA‡

DEALEY, EDWARD MUSGROVE (TED), journalist; b. Oct. 5, 1892; s. George Bannerman and Olivia (Allen) D.; A.B., U. of Tex., 1913; A.M., Harvard, 1914; student Sch. Bus. Harvard, 1914-15; m. Clara MacDonald, Mar. 1, 1916 (dec.); children—Edward Musgrove (dec.), Joseph MacDonald, Clara Patricia; married 2d, Mrs. Trudie Kelley, June 29, 1951. Reporter on Dallas News, 1915-20, staff corr., 1920-24, Sunday editor and editorial writer, 1924-28; dir. A. H. Belo Corp., pubs. Dallas Morning News and Texas Almanac, 1926-69, asst. to publisher, 1928-32, v.p., 1932-40, pres., 1940-69, chmn., 1960-69, pub., 1964-69; mem. conf. and editorial boards This Week mag. Dir. Southland Paper Mills, Inc. Trustee Texas Research Found. Colonel on staff Gov. Ross Sterling, 1931-33. Major, comdg. 29th Bn., Tex. Defense Guard, 1941-42; maj. Army Specialist Corps, U.S. Army, 1942-43. First vice president Associated Press, 1948; director of the American Newspaper Publishers Association, 1940-45. Member Texas Newspaper Publishers Association (president 1935-36 and 1936-37), Southern Newspaper Publishers' Association (president 1937-38, chairman board, 1938-39), Advertising Fedn. of America (dir. 1936-41), Dallas Hist. Soc., Dallas Citizens Council, English-Speaking Union, Phi Delta Theta, Sigma Delta Chi, Order of the T (football, Texas U.). Independent Democrat. Presbyterian. Mason (33 deg.). Clubs: Athletic, Dallas Country, Skeet and Gun (Dallas), Advertising, Anglers, Leash (N.Y.C.); Koon Kreek Hunting and Fishing (Athens, Texas); Pine Island Hunting and Fishing (Lufkin, Tex.); Carmen Mountain Hunting (Coahuila, Mexico); Welsh Terrier of America (gov.). Contbr. fiction to publs. Home: Dallas TX Died Nov. 1969.

DEAN, GEORGE ADAM, entomologist; b. Topeka, Kan., Apr. 19, 1873; s. Thomas Jackson and Harriet (Reese) D.; state teachers' certificate, Kan. State Teachers Coll., 1898; B.S., Kan. State Coll., 1895, M.S., 1905; D.Sc. Southwestern College, Kansas, 1943; m. Minerva Blachly, August 30, 1903; children—Helen Elizabeth, George Thomas, Loua Marjorie, Paul McConnell, Dorothy. With Kan. State Agl. Coll. since 1902, prof. entomology, also Experiment Station entomologist, state entomologist of Kan. since 1912; sr. entomologist, U.S. Dept. Agriculture, 1923-25. Mem. Mediterranean Fruit Fly Com. Federal Fruit Fly Board. Developed heat method for control of injurious insects and the poison bait method for control of grasshoppers, cut worms and army worms. Fellow A.A.A.S., Entomol. Soc. America (pres. 1925); mem. Am. Assn. Econ. Entomologists (pres. 1921), Sigma Xi, Phi Kappa Phi, Gamma Sigma Delta. Republican. Conglist. Mason (32 deg.). Home: 1725 Poyntz Av., Manhattan KS*‡

DEAN, SARA, author; b. Boise City, Idaho, 1870; d. Peter and Isabella (Armstrong) D.; ed. at home. Has traveled widely in America, Europe, Egypt, Algeria, India, Burmah and Ceylon and the Pacific Islands. Clubs: Spinner's, of San Francisco (founder), Lyceum (London, Eng.). Author: Travers, 1907; A Disciple of Chance, 1910. Address: Lyceum Club, 128 Piccadilly, London England‡

DEAN, VERA MICHELES, editor, author, lectr.; b. St. Petersburg, Russia, Mar. 29, 1903; d. Alexander and Nadine Micheles; A.B., Radcliffe Coll., 1925; M.A., Yale, 1926; Ph.D., Harvard, 1928; LL.D., Wilson Coll., 1940; D.H.L., U. Rochester, 1943; hon. degrees Smith, Rockford, Cedar Crest, Colby, Skidmore, Monmouth colls., N.J. Coll. Women; m. William J. Dean, Aug. 9, 1929 (dec. 1936); children—Elinor (Mrs. Charles W. Wilder), William Johnson. Came to U.S., 1919, naturalized, 1928. Research asso. Fgn. Policy Assn., 1928-31, editor research publs., 1931-38, research dir., editor, 1938-51, editor Bull. and Headline series, 1951-61; vis. prof. Smith Coll., 1952-54; vis. prof. govt. U. Rochester, also dir. non-Western civilizations program, 1954-62; prof. internat. devel. Grad. Sch. Pub. Adminstrn., N.Y.U., 1962-71, mem. Center Internat. Studies, 1971-72. Recipient Radcliffe Alumni Assn. medal, 1942, Jane Addams medal, 1954; French Legion of Honor. Club: Cosmopolitan. Author books including: European Retreat, 1939; The Four Cornerstones of Peace, 1946; Russia: Menace or Promise?, 1946; The United States and Russia, rev. edit., 1970; Europe and the United States, 1950; Foreign Policy Without Fear, 1953; The Nature of the Non-Western World, 2d edit., 1966; New Patterns of Democracy in India, rev. edit., 1969; Builders of Emerging Nations, 1961; West and Non-West: New Perspectives, 1963; The United States and the New Nations, 1964; The UN Today, 1965. Contbr. jours. Home: New York City NY Died Oct. 10, 1972.

DEAN, WALTER CARLETON, organization executive; born Oakland, California, July 17, 1891; son Albert Carleton and Margaret Anne (Thomas) D.; B.A., University of California, Berkeley, 1915; m. Salome Ann Mark, Jan. 5, 1918; 1 dau., Flora May. Soil technologist Coll. of Agr., U. of Calif. at Berkeley, 1915-19; in charge seed dept. Calif. Packing Corp., San Francisco, 1919-21; land bank appraiser, 1921-23; chief appraiser Fed. Land Bank of Berkeley, 1923-27; asst. chief reviewing appraiser Farm Loan System, Washington, 1927-29; sec. Fed. Intermediate Credit Bank Berkeley, 1929-33; sec. Fed. Land Bank of Berkeley, 1929-34, v.p., 1933-44, exec. v.p., 1944-47, pres., 1947-61; vice chmn. bd. govs. Council of Cal. Growers, 1961-71; trustee Cal. Alumni Found., U. Cal. at Berkeley. Clubs: Berkeley Tennis; Commonwealth (chmn. agrl. sect.) (San Francisco); Faculty. Walnut Creek CA Died Mar. 5, 1971; buried Mountain View Cemetery, Oakland CA

DEANDRADE, ANTHONY J., pres. Internat. Printing Pressman and Assistants Union N. Am., also mem. exec. council AFL-CIO. Home: Washington DC Died Jan. 20, 1970; buried Cheshire, Conn

DEANE, CHARLES BENNETT, ex-congressman, lawyer; b. Salem Township, N.C., Nov. 1, 1898; son of John Leaird and Florence Mae (Boyette) D.; student Trinity Park Sch., Durham, N.C., 1918-20; LL.B., Wake Forest Coll., 1923, H.H.D., 1961; m. Agnes W. Cree, Oct. 15, 1927; children—Betty-Cree, Agnes Carol, Charles B., Jr. Admitted to bar of N.C., 1923; adminstrative law and banking, Rockingham, N.C., 1923-26; register of deeds, Richmond County, N.C., 1926-34; clerk Bd. of County Commrs., 1926-34; compiler U.S. Congressional Directory, Washington, D.C., 1935-39; administrative atty., hearings br., Wage & Hour Div., U.S. Dept. of Labor, Washington, D.C., 1938-39; owner, gen. ins. and adminstrv. law bus., 1940-69. Mem. 80th-85th Congresses, 8th North Caroline Dist. Chmn. Richmond Co. Dem. Executive Com., 1932-46; adv. member Rockingham local draft bd., World War II. Past pres. bd. trustees Meredith College, Raleigh; member bd. trustees Wake Forest Coll., Winston-Salem. Awarded Civitan Citizenship Cup for outstanding community activity, Rockingham, N.C. 1930 and 1937. Baptist (recording sec. N.C. Baptist Conv. 1932-59, pres., 1959-61). Club: Rockingham Civitan (charter mem., sec. 15 yrs.). Home: Rockingham NC Died Nov. 24, 1969; buried Eastside Cemetery, Rockingham NC

DEARBORN, EARL HAMILTON, research adminstr.; b. Manhattan, Kan., June 10, 1915; s. Edgar Hamilton and Gladys (Nichols) D.; A.B., U. Kan., 1938, M.A., 1940; Ph.D., U. Chgo., 1942; M.D., Johns Hopkins, 1949; m. Margaret Ann Kuchta, Dec. 24, 1943; children—Margaret K., Barbara Ann, Earl, Hamilton II, Patricia. Asst. pharmacology U. Chgo., 1940-43, instr., 1943; instr. pharmacology, exptl. therapeutics Johns Hopkins, 1943-49, asst. prof., 1949-52; prof. pharmacology, chmn. dept. Boston U., 1952-56; head dept. pharmacological research, Lederle Labs. div. Am. Cyanamid Co., Pearl River, N.Y., 1956-60, assistant director experimental therapeutics research, 1960-63, director, 1963-65, assistant director research, 1965-69; pres. therapeutics research div. Dome Labs., 1969-71; pharmacologist pres. Miles Research div. Miles Labs., Inc., 1971-73. Fellow A.A.A.S.; mem. N.Y. Acad. of Sciences, Soc. Experimental Biology and Medicine, Society of Toxicology, American Society Pharmacology and Exptl. Therapeutics, American Chemical Soc., Phi Beta Kappa, Sigma Xi, Alpha Omega Alpha, Phi Sigma. Home: Montvale NJ Died Feb. 28, 1973.

DEARING, CHARLES LEE, economist; b. Parkville, Mo., Sept. 4, 1903; s. James and Laura (Higgins) D.; student U. of N.M., 1922-24, U. of Mich., 1926-27; A.B., George Washington U., 1929; m. Mary Rulkotter, Sept. 30, 1938 (div. 1960); children—Cynthia Lee, James Frederick, m. 2d, Margaret Ladd, Nov. 12, 1970. Staff mem. Brookings Instn., Washington, 1929-57, research asst., 1929-33, research asso., 1933-45, sr. staff mem., 1945-57; asst. dep. adminstr. Nat. Indsl. Recovery Adminstrn., 1933-34; cons. U.S. Office Defense Transportation, 1942, and dir. div. review and spl. studies, 1942-44; adviser to Interim Com. on Highways California Legislature, 1945, 46; dir. transportation Task Force", Commn. on Orgn. Exec. Br. Govt. (Hoover Commn.), 1949; spl. cons. Under-sec. Commerce Transportation, 1953-54; exec. director Ill. State Toll Hwy. Commn., Chgo., 1956-62; dir. research and planning Ill. Tollway, 1962-64; economist Wilbur Smith & Assos., New Haven, 1964-67. Trustee Remedial Edn. Center, Washington, 1947-72. Mem. Am. Econ. Assn., Sigma Chi. Clubs: Kenwood Golf and Country (Bethesda, Md.); University, Corinthian Yacht (Washington); The Tavern (Chgo.). Author: National Transportation Policy (with Wilfred Owen), 1949, Toll Roads and the Problem of Highway Modernization, 1951; Industrial Pensions, 1954; Turnpike Authorities in the United States, Law and Contemporary Problems, 1961. Home: Silver Spring MD Died Aug. 15, 1972; buried Mt. Pleasant Cemetery, St. Johnsbury VT

DE BASTOS, EMIL, physician; b. Bklyn., July 18, 1931; s. Emil and Veronica (Sebest) de B.; B.S., N.Y.U., 1952, M.D. 1956; m. Emma Vendla Gustavson, June 9, 1956; children—Debra Ann, Donna Lynn, David Roy. Intern, Bellevue Med. Center, N.Y.U., N.Y.C., 1957; resident Lincoln Hosp., Bronx, N.Y., 1959-62; practice medicine specializing in obstetrics and gynecology, Lake Ronkonkoma, Hauppauge, Selden, N.Y., 1962-70; attending Smithtown (N.Y.) Gen. Hosp., St. John's Hosp., Smithtown, St. Charles Hosp., Port Jefferson, N.Y. Served to capt., M.C., AUS, 1957-59. Diplomate Am. Bd. Obstetrics and Gynecology. Fellow A.C.S., Am. Coll. Obstetricians and Gynecologists; mem. A.M.A., Suffolk County Med. Soc., Suffolk County Obstet. and Gynecol. Soc. (past sec.), Phi Beta Kappa. Home: St James NY Died Nov. 19, 1970; buried Pinelawn Meml. Park, Farmingdale NY

DE BOER, JOHN J., educator; b. Chicago, Ill., Oct. 12, 1903; s. James and Maria (Wezeman) D.; student Calvin Coll., 1919-21, Wheaton Coll., 1921-23; A.M., U. of Chicago, 1927, Ph.D., 1938; m. Henrietta Geerdes, Sept. 3, 1931; 1 son, Fredric Eugene. Teacher, English, Chicago Christian High Sch., 1923-31; dir. student teachers Chicago Teachers Coll., 1931-44; in English department Herzl Junior College, 1944-45; chmn. dept. and prof. edn. Roosevelt Coll., Chicago, Ill., 1945-47, prof. edn. U., 1947-68. Tchr. summer sessions Northwestern U., 1940-41, La. Poly. Inst., 1942, U. of Wis., 1945-47. Lecturer edn. confs., U. of Chicago, Atlanta U., Pennsylvania State Coll., Arizona State Coll., Ind. State Teachers Coll., Purdue U., San Francisco State College, Northwestern, Ind. U., U. Pitts., U. Miami, numerous sch. systems and educational organizations. Awarded Susan Colver Rosenberg prize Ednl. Research U. Chgo., 1940; W. Wilbur Hatfield award, Nat. Council Tchrs. English, 1960. Pres. Nat. Council Tchrs. English, 1942-43, Am. Edn. Fellowship, 1946-49, The Nat. Conf. on Research in English. 1951-52; chmn. Nat. Commn. on Cooperative Curriculum Planning, 1940. Chmn.

Chicago Civil Liberties Com., 1946-47; mem. bd. Nat. Conf. Christians and Jews; national chmn. Nat. Council Arts, Scis. and Professions, 1948. Cons. Coronet Ednl. Films, Grover-Jennings Films. Judge Follet Book award, 1957, 58. Author: Design for Elementary Education, 1945; Building Better English, 1948, revised, 1955; Creative Reading, 1950; Teaching Secondary English, 1951; Reading for Living, 1953; co-author The Teaching of Reading, 1960, 3d edit., 1970. Editor: Educating for Peace, 1940; The Subjects Fields in General Education, 1941; editor, The Elementary Eng. Review (official organ of Nat. Council Teacher of Eng.), past assistant editor: The English Journal; co-editor Secondary Education, 1966. Contributor of articles to Childhood Education, Educational Method, Jour. of Applied Psychology, Ednl. Adminstrn. and Supervision, Clearing House, Jour. of Speech, Cyclopedia of Modern Education and Review Ednl. Research. Chmn. com. to prepare series of lang. arts sect. Sequential Tests of Educational Progress. Home: Urbana IL Died May 21, 1969; buried Fairmount Cemetery, Willow Springs IL

DE CAMP, GEORGE, banker; b. Meigs Co., O., Feb. 20, 1869; s. John M. and Phoebe (Downing) De C.; ed. Rio Grand Coll. and Ohio U.; m. Ellen Jane Ryan, June 22, 1904. Teacher pub. schs. 5 yrs.; with First Nat. Bank, Athens, later with Athens Nat. Bank; Nat. bank examiner, 1910-18; organizer, 1918, Pittsburgh Br. of Federal Reserve Bank of Cleveland, of which was mgr., chmn. bd., also federal reserve agt.; settled in Newark, O., Sept. 1933; now pres. Licking County Bank. Republican. Baptist. Mason (32 deg.), Elk. Clubs: Union, Mayfield Country (Cleveland); Cincinnati; Duquesne (Pittsburgh). Home: Newark OH‡

DE CAPRILES, JOSE RAFAEL, lawyer, r.r. ofcl.; b. Mexico City, Mexico, Feb. 13, 1912; s. A. M. and Cristina (Treserra) de C.; LL.B., New York University, 1942, LL.M., 1954; M. Adela Casanova, July 4, 1943; children—John Robert, Charles Michael. Came to U.S., 1920, naturalized, 1936. Admitted to N.Y. bar, 1945; atty. Lehigh Valley R.R., 1945-49, claims atty., 1949-55, trial counsel, 1955-58, gen. counsel, 1958, v.p., 1959-69; pres. Ablalan Corp., Communipaw, Inc.; v.p. United Real Estate Co.; dir. Bayshore Connecting R.R., Osuasco.River Rwy., Buffalo Creek R.R. Co., Ironton R.R. Member U.S. Olympic Fencing Com., 1936-61, chmn., 1953-57; dir. U.S. Olympic Com., 1965-69. Trustee Robert Packer Hospital, Sayre, Pennsylvania. Served from pvt. to maj., USAAF, World War II. Decorated Bronze Star, Presdl. Citation; Croix de Guerre (France). Mem. Assn. Am. R.R., Am. Bar Assn., N.Y. State Assn. R.R. (exec. com.), Assn. R.R. N.J. (exec com.), Nat. Assn. R.R. Trial Counsel, Assn. ICC Practitioners, N.Y. R.R. Club, Fedn. Internat. d'Escrime (dep. pres. 1961-64), Amateur Fencers League Am. (pres. 1953-57), Fencers Club N.Y., A.I.M. Founder, editor: Am. Fencing mag. 1948-69. Mem. U.S. Olympic Fencing Team, 1936, 40, 48, 52, capt., 1956; nat. fencing champion, 1939, 46, 51; capt. Pan-Am. Sabre Team, 1955; fencing ofcl. Olympic games, Tokyo, 1964, Mexico, 1968. Home: Middletown NJ Died Feb. 21, 1969.

DECHERD, H. BEN, newspaper exec.; b. Dallas, Mar. 14, 1915; s. Henry Benjamin and Fannie (Dealey) D.; B.A. in Govt., U. Tex., Austin, 1936; m. Isabelle Thomason, Dec. 17, 1938; children—Dealey (Mrs. H. David Herndon), Robert W. With A.H. Belo Corp., pub. Dallas Morning News, Tex. Suburban Dailies and Tex. Almanac; owner radio-TV stas. WFAA, TV sta. KFDM, Beaumont, Tex., 1936, 38-72, v.p., sec., 1960-64, chmn. exec. com., 1964-68, chmn. bd., 1968-72; with Balt. Sunpapers, 1937. Past pres. Family Guidance Center, Incarnation Bay Sch., S.W. Sch. Printing, St. Marks Sch. Tex.; bd. dirs. Central Bus. Dist. Assn., Dallas Zool. Soc., Dallas Symphony Orch., Southwestern Legal Found., St. Marks Sch. Tex.; trustee Dallas Hist. Soc., Tex. Research Found. Served to lt. col., inf., AUS, 1942-46. Decorated Bronze Star. Mem. Tex. Daily Newspaper Assn. (past pres.), Phi Beta Kappa, Phi Delta Theta. Episcopalian. Clubs: City, Dallas Country, Northwood, Petroleum, Idlewild (Dallas). Home: Dallas TX Died Nov. 18, 1972.

DECKER, CLARENCE RAYMOND, univ. v.p.; b. Sioux City, Ia., Dec. 19, 1904; s. John and Agnes Teresa (Decker) Hostetler (took mother's name); prep. edn., Pillsbury Mil. Acad., Owatonna, Minn., 1919-21; A.B., Carleton College, 1925, LL.D., 1951; Ph.D., U. Chgo., 1928; LL.D., Kyung Hee U., Seoul, Korea, 1963; m. Mary Bell Sloan, June 2, 1937 (dec. Apr. 1964); m. 2d, Greta Medlinger, January 21, 1965. Instructor English, U. N.D., 1925-26, De Paul U., Chgo. (part time), 1927-28, Northwestern U. (part time), 1928-30; chmn. Eng. dept., Ill. Wesleyan U., Bloomington, 1929-31; travel and study Europe, 1931-33; U. of Berlin, 1931, vis. lectr. Eng., Western Ill. State Coll., 1933-34; chmn. Eng. dept. U. Kansas City, 1934-38, v.p. 1938, pres., 1938-53; vis. prof. Fairleigh Dickinson U., 1955-56, v.p., 1956-67; asst. dir. Mutual Security Agy., Far East, 1952. Ednl. cons. to Creole Petroleum Corp., 1954-57. Chmn. Western Mo. Crusade for Freedom, 1950; guest moderator America's Town Meeting of the Air, 1950-52, mem. Round-the-World Broadcasting Tour, 1949; mem. adv. com. UN Non-Govtl. Orgns., 1960-62; mem. adv. bd. Seaman's Church Inst., 1963-69; member executive bd. International House Association, Incorporated, 1960-62; member President's Com. White House Conf. International Cooperation, 1965. Awarded Order Aztec Eagle, Mexico, 1949. Member Poetry Society America (president 1957-61, member executive board 1957-69), Kansas City Chamber Music Society (founder, dir. 1934-53), Am. Assn. for UN (dir. Manhattan chpt.), Phi Beta Kappa Assos., Phi Beta Kappa, Sigma Chi, Delta Sigma Rho. Author: (with wife, under name Sydney Bell) Wives of the Prophet, U.S. 1935, England, 1936; The Victorian Conscience, 1952; A Place of Light (with wife), 1954; Richard Le Gallienne: aCentenary Memoir-Anthology, 1966; co-author: Southeast Asia in the Coming World, 1952; World Neighbors Working Together for Peace and Plenty, 1952. Co-editor: Modern Stories from Many Lands, 1963. Founder, ed. U. Kan. City Rev. (quarterly), 1934-53; co-editor: Lit. Rev., 1958-69. Contbr. articles and New York City NY Died Nov. 21, 1969; cremated.

DECKER, EDWARD WILLIAM, banker; b. Austin, Minn., Aug. 24, 1869; s. Jacob S. and Mary Ann H. (Smith) D.; grad. high sch., Austin, 1887; m. Susie May Spaulding, Feb. 24, 1892. Began as messenger, Northwestern Nat. Bank, Minneapolis, 1887; asst. cashier and cashier, Met. Bank, 1895-1900; cashier, 1900-03; v.p. and gen. mgr., 1903-12; pres., 1912-34, Northwestern Nat. Bank; also pres. Minn. Loan & Trust Co., 1910-18, chmn. 1918; dir. Northwestern Nat. Life Ins. Co. of Mpls. Mem. Minn. Soc. of N.Y. Republican. Conglist. Mason. Clubs: Minneapolis, Twin City Bankers'. Home: 510 Groveland Av. Office: Northwestern Bank Bldg., Minneapolis MN

DECKER, MARION EMORY, educator; b. Mansfield, Pa., June 15, 1902; s. Dana D. and Flayvilla (Ford) D.; B.S., U. Ill., 1929; M.Ed., Pa. State U., 1939; m. Clarissa Arlene Hitchcock, June 25, 1932; children—Marlene Eldena (Mrs. Charles B. Engle), Kathryn Jane (Mrs. Lewis P. G. Hart). Dir. health and phys. edn. Athens (Pa.) High Sch., 1929-34, Williamsport (Pa.) High Sch., 1934-46; dir. city playgrounds, Williamsport, 1940-45; chmn. health and phys. edn. dept. Mansfield State Coll., 1946-68, dir. athletics, 1946-68. Mem. Pa. Edn. Assn., A.A.H.P.E.R., Sigma Pi. Republican. Baptist. Mason, Kiwanian (dir.). Club: Coreycreek Golf of Mansfield (dir. 1964-68). Home: Mansfield PA Died Aug. 16, 1968.

DECKER, PERL D., ex-congressman; b. Athens Co., O., 1875; A.B., Park Coll., Parkville, Mo., 1897; LL.B., Law Dept., U. of Kan., 1899. Admitted to Mo. bar, 1900; mem. 63d to 65th Congresses (1913-19), 15th Mo. Dist. Democrat. Home: Joplin MO‡

DEES, RANDALL EUESTA, naval officer; b. Oct. 8, 1893; entered U.S. Navy, 1913, and advanced through the grades to commodore, 1943; formerly chief of staff Newport Naval War Coll. Decorated Silver Star. Address: Newport RI Died July 1972.

DEFENBACH, BYRON;, b. Rome, Wis., Dec. 5, 1870; s. Philip and Bertha (Winckler) D.; student M.E. Coll., York, Neb., 1887-89; m. Susie Wise, 1889; children—Philip Earnest (dec.), Ralph B., Leroy W.; m. 2d, Jane Adam, June 8, 1923; children—Mary Jane, James Adam, Will Sheridan. Clk., Indian Sch., Genoa, Neb., 1891; supt. Indian Sch., Ft. Belknap, Mont., 1892; in. ry. mail service, Spokane, Wash., 1893-97; asst. postmaster, Spokane, Wash., 1897-1903; in commercial lines, Ida., 1903-13; certified pub. accountant since 1917; gen. mgr. Byron Defenbach & Sons since 1919. Mayor of Sandpoint, Ida., 1905; mem. Ida. State Senate, 1913; state treas., Ida., 1927-30. Republican. Mason (32 deg., Shriner; Grand Master, Ida., 1910-11); K.P., Woodman of World. Author: Red Heroines of the Northwest, 1929. Contbr. to local and state press. Home: 1610 N. 8th St., Boise ID‡

DEFERRARI, ROY JOSEPH, coll. prof.; b. Stoneham, Mass., June 1, 1890; s. Augustino and Mary (Crovo) D.; A.B., Dartmouth, 1912; M.A. and Ph.D., Princeton; m. Evelyn Mary Biggi, Dec. 30, 1920 children—Austin John, Mary Evelyn. Instr. in Latin and Greek, Princeton, 1915-18; instr. in same, Catholic U., Washington, D.C., 1918-20, asso. prof., 1920-23, prof. since 1923, dir. summer session since 1929, dean of Grad. Sch., 1930-38, sec. gen., 1938-67. Instr. in military studies, Princeton U. Ground School, World War. Fellow Medieval Acad. America. Mem. mng. com. American Sch. Classical studies, Athens, Rome; dir. affiliation The Cath. University of Am. Mem. Am. Philol. Assn., Linguistic Soc. America, Classical Assn. Middle Atlantic States. Catholic. Author several books latest of which are: College Organization and Administration, 1947; Marian Latin Series (4 vols.), 1950-53; Lexicon, Latin-English of St. Thomas Aquinas, 1953; Early Christian Biography, 1952; Minor Works of St. Augustine, 1953; Memoirs of the Catholic University of America, 1918-1960, 1961; Theological Treaties of St. Ambrose, 1961, Editor: Catholic U. Patristic Studies (100 vols.), 1922-45; Catholic University Studies in Mediaeval and Renaissance Latin (30 vols.); Catholic Univ. Classical Studies (5 vols.); Complete Index of Summa Theologica of St. Thomas, 1956; Sources of Catholic Dogma, 1957; Latin-English Dictionary of St. Thomas, 1960. Editorial director The Fathers of the Church (50 volumes). Contbr. to Commonweal, Cath. Ednl. Rev., Classical Weekly, and others. Home: Washington DC Died Aug. 24, 1969; buried Gate of Heaven Cemetery, Wheaton MD

DEFFENBAUGH, WALTER SYLVANUS, school, management; b. at Smithfield, Pa., Dec. 17, 1872; s. of Henry and Maria (Durr) Deffenbaugh; A.B., W.Va. U., 1898; grad. work, U. of W.Va., 1905, U. of Pa. (summer) 1908, U. of Pittsburgh, 1911-13; spl. work under Dr. Earl Barnes, Chautauqua, N.Y., summer, 1912; A.M., George Washington U., 1917; m. Blanche Sturgis, Aug. 8, 1900; children—Ruth, Helen. Prin. pub. schs., Smithfield, Pa., 1898-1900, Fairchance, Pa., 1900-01; prin. high sch., Leechburg, Pa., 1901-06, Connellsville, Pa., 1906-07; supt. pub. schs., Connelsville, 1907-11, Homestead, Pa., 1911-13; chief of div. of sch. adminstrn., U.S. Bur. of Edn., 1913-17; specialist in rural edn., 1917-20; now chief Am. school system, U.S. Bureau of Edn. Mem. N.E.A., Phi Kappa Psi, Phi Beta Kappa. Mason. Clubs: Federal School Men's. Author of various bulls. on ednl. topics; contbr. to ednl. jours.; lecturer before insts. and summer schs. Home: 519 Butternut St., Tacoma Park DC‡

DE FOREST, KATHARINE, writer; b. Seymour, Conn., d. George F. de Forest; private ed'n; unmarried. Author: Paris as It Is, 1900 D6; also contributions to Scribner's, Harper's, La Revue Bleue (Paris), Harper's Bazaar. Address: 9 Rue Freycinet, Paris France‡

DEFREES, DONALD, lawyer; b. Chgo., Feb. 25, 1885; s. Joseph H. and Harriet (McNaughton) D.; Ph.B., Yale, 1905; LL.B., Harvard, 1908; m. Florence Baker, Dec. 18, 1915; 1 dau., Jean. Admitted to Ill. bar, 1908; with Defrees, Fiske, Thomson & Simmons and predecessors, 1908-68; dir. LaSalle Steel Corp., Vapor Corp. Pres. Ill. Health Found., Inc. Home: Chicago IL Died Oct. 6, 1968.

DE GAULLE, CHARLES ANDRE JOSEPH MARIE, former pres. France; born in Lille, France, Nov. 22, 1890; student Saint-Cyr Acad.; m. Yvonne Vendroux, Apr. 7, 1921; children—Philippe, Elisabeth (deBoissieu), Anne (dec.). Under-sec. Nat. Defense, 1940; chief of Free French, then pres. French Nat. Com., London and Brazzaville, 1940-42; pres. French Com. of Nat. Liberation, 1943, Provisional Govt. of the Republic, 1944-46; head chief of Armies, 1944-46; founder, pres. Rassemblement du Peuple Francaise, 1947; Premier France, 1958, Pres., 1958-69. Served as captain of French Army, 1914-18, general brigade and comdr. 4th Armoured Div., 1939-40. Author: La Discorde chez l'ennemi; le fil de l'Epee; Vers Armee de metier; La France et son Armee; Discours et Messages; Memoires de guerre; l'Appel, l'United: The War Memoirs of Charles De Gaulle, 1959. Address: Colombey-les-deux Eglises, Haute-Marne France Died Nov. 9, 1970.

DE GELLEKE, GERRIT JACOB, architect; b. Milwaukee, Wis., Aug. 19, 1872; s. Pieter and Antje (Davelaar) deG.; grad. U. of Pennsylvania, 1897; m. Sylvia W. deHeus, Sept. 27, 1906; children—Sylvia (Mrs. Gerhard M. Kuechle), Gerrit James (officer U.S. Army), Janet (Mrs. Peter Holderness Woods), Dorrit (Mrs. James Edward Cormany), Elizabeth (Mrs. Stuart Bruce Palmer). Mem. firm VanRyn & de Gelleke, architects, 1897-1936, of firm VanRyn & de Gelleke, Armstrong & de Gelleke, 1925-30; engaged in practice individually since 1936; architect, Milwaukee Sch. Bd., 1905-18; exec. architect Allied Architects of Milwaukee, architects of Parklawn, Federal Housing project, Milwaukee, 1936-44. Chmn. architects div. Wis. Registration Bd. of Architects and Professional Engrs., 1935-49, chmn. Citizens Lake Front Com. (Milwaukee), 1940-46; mem. Metropolitan Master Plan Assn. (Milwaukee), 1943-45. Dir. and mem. bd. trustees Y.M.C.A. since 1925. Vice pres. Wis. Home and Farm Sch. since 1910. Fellow A.I.A. (dir. 1934-37; mem. jury of fellows 1938-44; chmn. investment and property com. 1940-46, past pres. Wis. chap.). Mem. Dutch Reformed Church (formerly deacon). Clubs: City, Knickerbocker Society, University of Pennsylvania Alumni, Rotary (1912). Home: 1748 N. 60th St.Office: 152 W. Wisconsin Av., Milwaukee 3 WI‡

DEGLMAN, GEORGE ANTHONY, educator; b. Mankato, Minn., Mar. 13, 1877; s. Anthony and Louise (Reuther) D.; student Canisius Coll., Buffalo, N.Y., 1892-95; A.B., Campion Coll., Prairie du Chien, Wis., 1901; A.M., St. Louis U., 1910; Ph.D., Marquette U., 1916. Ordained priest R.C. Ch., 1909; joined Soc. of Jesus (Jesuits), 1895. Instr. in classics and English. St. John's Coll., Toledo, O., 1901-05; was professor of philosophy, John Carroll U., 1927-28. Rockhurst Coll., 1928-31; prof. philosophy, dean Coll. of Arts and Sciences and regent of the Corp. Colleges and the Coll. of Commerce, Creighton U., Omaha, 1931-37; prof. philosophy, chmn. division philos. and religion, student counsellor, Rockhurst College, Kansas City, Missouri, 1937-55; professor of theology, Creighton University, 1955-—. Lectr. on edn., philosophy in Mo.-Kans. area. Mem. Am. Philos. Assn., Cath. Philos. Assn.; (hon.), Ancien Institut Historique et Heraldique de France.

Democrat. Mem. Knights of Columbus. Author: Elements of Psychology, 1922. Address: Creighton University, Omaha 31 NE‡

DE GOGORZA, EMILIO EDUARDO, baritone singer; b. of Spanish parentage, at Brooklyn, N.Y., May 29, 1874; s. Julio Antonio Gomez and Maria Francisca Navarrete Y. (Romay) de G.; was taken abroad at age of 2 mos.; ed. Ecole Monge, Paris, France, and Baylis House, Salt Hill, Slough, Berks, Eng.; m. at Paris, Emma Eames, operatic soprano, July 13, 1911. Began as boy soprano in Eng.; debut in New York with Madame Sembrich's Co., Met. Opera House, 1897; soloist with leading orchestras and musical festivals, and has made many transcontinental tours as concert and recital artist; repertoire includes classic and folk songs, and solos from operas, in English, Spanish, French, Italian and German. Republican. Roman Catholic. Home: Bath, ME Address: care George Engles, Aeolian Bldg., New York NY‡

DEGROAT, GEORGE BLEWER, govt. ofcl.; b. Binghamton, N.Y., Sept. 27, 1898; s. George Steven and Frances (Blewer) DeG.; m. Helen Elizabeth Walker, July 31, 1921 (dec. Apr. 1952); children—Shirley (Mrs. Conrad Hovik), Barbara (Mrs. Thomas Watson). Various positions Erie R.R., Hornell, N.Y., Huntington, Ind., also N.Y.C., Jersey City, 1916-42; dir. rys. Japan and Korea, War Dept., 1947-48; gen. mgr. Myers Y. Cooper Co., Cin., 1948-53; transportation adviser UN Command and Econ. Coordinator, ICA, Dept. State, 1955-61; U.S. rep. UN meeting, Bangkok, Thailand, Internat. Transp. meetings, Taipei, Taiwan. Bd. suprs., bd. appointments, chmn. hwy. commn., chmn. equalization commn., chmn. laws commn. Steuben County, N.Y., 1933-42. Served to col AUS, 1942-46; assigned 3d Transportation Ry. Command, U.S. Army, 1953-55. Decorated Legion of Merit, Bronze Star, Presdl. citation (U.S.); Ulchi medals (2) (Korea). Mem. Nat. Def. Transportation Assn. (past chpt. pres.). Mason. Clubs: Cincinnati, Buckeye (Cin.). Home: Ft Lauderdale FL Died Nov. 17, 1969.

DEGROAT, HARRY DEWITT, coll. pres.; b. Owego, N.Y., Sept. 13, 1873; s. Joseph DeWitt and Adelaide Delilah (Waite) D.; student, Owego Free Acad., 1886-90; A.B., A.M., Williams Coll., 1894; Pd.D., Albany State Teachers Coll., 1921; m. Helen Louise Goodrich, June 27, 1899; children—Helen Stiles (Mrs. Charles A. Bader), Mary Adelaide (Mrs. Wendell M. Sears), DeWitt Goodrich; m. 2d, Fannie R. Metcalf, Aug. 27, 1944. Teacher of science, Lima, Ind., 1894-95; vice principal, teacher of Latin, Gouverneur, N.Y., 1895-99, supt., 1899-1904; inspector of schs. for N.Y. and L.I., for Univ. of State of N.Y., 1904-09; asst. chief of examination div., N.Y. State Edn. Dept. in charge of teachers licenses, 1909-12; prin. Cortland Normal Sch., 1912-42; pres. Cortland State Teachers Coll., 1942-43; pres. emeritus since 1943; trustee Cortland Savings Bank. Dir. Y.M.C.A. Baptist (deacon First Baptist Ch.). Mason. Co-author of Iroquois Arithmetics. Home: 100 N. Main St. Cortland NY

DEHN, ADOLF, artist, water colorist, lithographer; b. Waterville, Minn., Nov. 22, 1895; s. Arthur C. and Emilie (Haase) D.; student Mpls. Art. Sch., 1914-17, Art Students League, 1917-18; m. Virginia Lee Engleman, Nov. 12, 1947. Traveled in Germany, France and Eng. and for the most part stayed in Vienna, 1921-29; did black and white drawings and lithography entirely until 1937, later watercolors and oils. Represented in Met. Museum, Museum of Modern Art, Whitney Museum, Brooklyn Museum, N.Y. (City) Pub. Library, Library of Congress, Boston Museum, Minneapolis Museum, Honolulu Museum, Albertina Museum, Vienna, Brit. Museum, etc. Served with U.S. Army, 1918-19; instr. art in reconstruction hosp., 8 months. Awarded 1st prize, Phila. Art Alliance, 1936; Guggenheim fellowship, 1939, 51; 1st prize, Phila. Print Club, 1939; 1st prize Chicago Internat. Water Color Exhbn., 1943. Mem. Am. Water color Soc., Soc. Am. Graphic Artists, Century Assn. Author: Water Color Painting, 1945; How to Print and Draw Lithographs, 1950; Water Color, Gouache and Casein Painting, 1955. Contbr. (illustrations) to Fortune, Vanity Fair, Vogue, Harper's Bazaar, The New Yorker, Jugend, Dial, Masses; (articles) to The Arts, Time, Art News. Art Digest, Coronet. Illustrator: Selected Stories of Guy de Maupassant (Book of the Month Club), 1949. N.A. Mem. Nat. Inst. Arts and Letters. Home: New York City NY Died May 19, 1968.

DEICHMAN, CARL F., consular service; b. St. Joseph, Mo., Nov. 23, 1871; ed. pub. schs. and pvt. tutors; m. Eudora Ruth Keyes, of Peach Orchard, Ky. In business St. Louis, until 1899; with U.S. Coast and Geodetic Survey, 1899-1907; apptd. consul at Manzanillo, Mex., Mar. 30, 1907; consulat Tansui, 1908-09, Nagasaki, Japan, 1909-14, Bombay, India, Dec. 1914-Oct. 1915, Santos, Brazil, 1915-19, Valparaiso, Chile, 1919-30; apptd. consul gen., June 4, 1920; consul gen., Lisbon, Portugal, 1930-36 (retired). Decorated Order of Merit (Chile), 1922. Home: 3651 Wyoming St., St. Louis, Mo. Address: State Department Washington DC‡

DEIMLER, PAUL ELLAS, banker; b. Hummelstown, Pa., Mar. 19, 1912; s. Grover C. and Minerva (Stephenson) D.; B.S. in Econs., Lebanon Valley Coll., 1930; m. Sara Evelyn Ferguson, Aug. 28, 1940; 1 dau., Jean L. Exec. v.p., trust officer The Farmers Bank and Trust Co., Hummelston, Pa., 1934-62, v.p., trust officer, 1962-64, president, 1964-69; owner-operator Susquehannamarina, Hummelstown and Goldsboro, Pa. Secretary-treasurer, South Hanover Township; member Lower Dauphin School Board. Lutheran. Mason. Home: Hummelstown PA Died Sept. 15, 1969.

DEINES, ERNEST HUBERT, wood engraver; b. Russell, Kan., Mar. 1894; s. George J. and Katharine E. (Hein) D.; ed. Kansas City Art Inst., 1914-17, 1920-21; Academie Julien, Paris, France, 1919; unmarried. Staff artist, Kansas City (Mo.) Star, 1920-32; established studio, Kansas City, Mo., for wood engravings, printmaking, typographical design, book and magazine design and illustrations, 1932. Exhibited principal graphic art exhbns. and museums in U.S. including Contemporary Am. Art (Am.-British good will exhibition, tour of British Isles, 1944-45); represented in Exchange Exhbn. Soc. Am. Graphic Artists, Inc., Royal Soc. Painter-Etchers and Engravers London, and various art centers, 1954-55, permanent collection Met. Mus. Art, N.Y.C., 1956. Fellowship Huntington Hartford Found., California. Member regional judging committee, Graphic Art. World's Fair, N.Y., 1939. Represented in several cities U.S., also Nat. Exhibition, Library Congress (Joseph and Elizabeth R. Pennell first purchase prize, wood engraving, Mother's Horseshoe Geranium," 1943, Flowers of Westport", 1946); purchase prize Artist's Study," N.W. Printmakers Soc., 1939; in the permanent collection Museum of Art, Kansas City Society of Artists, treasurer, 1935; Salmagundi Prize for wood engraving, 1958. Huntington Hartford Fellowship Grant, 1961. Member of Hist. Soc. of Mo., Kans. State Hist. Society, Prairie Print Makers (Chicago); Print Council of America. Nat. Arts Club (N.Y.), Northwest Printmakers (Seattle), Print Club (Albany, N.Y.), Allied MacDowell Members (New York), Salmagundi Club, Audubon Artists (N.Y. City). Am. Artists Professional League (N.Y.), Am. Federation of Arts (Washington, D.C.), Academic Artists Association, Incorporated, Printmakers Society of Cal., Cal. Society of Etchers. Purchased for permanent collection of Library of Congress Monody of Evening", 1948. Associate mem. Nat. Acad. of Design, Soc. Print Connoisseurs, Soc. Am. Graphic Artists, Inc., Phila. Water Color Club, Am. Inst. Graphic Arts. Served with 109th Engrs., 34th Div., A.E.F., France, 1918. Address: Kansas City MO Died July 2, 1967.

DEITRICK, ELIZABETH PLATT, writer; b. N.Y. City, Oct. 18, 1890; d. Frank A. and Almeda E. D.; spl. student Columbia, and U. of Calif. Newspaper writer since 1910; world traveler, 1910-14; originator of Betty the Shopper," feature on Hearst papers, New York, San Francisco, etc.; wrote Best Bits," San Francisco Expn., 1915; feature writer, Los Angeles Examiner, 1916-17, San Francisco Call, since 1917, Mem. Y.W.C.A., Irish Assn. Mem. Sch. of Truth (Theosophical). Mem. Pacific Coast Feature Syndicate, Pacific Coast Pub. Co., Western Arts Assn. Clubs: Business and Professional Women's, San Francisco Advertising. Home: 1501 Leavenworth St., San Francisco CA‡

DEITZ, ARCHIBALD EDWIN, clergyman, educator; b. Berne, Albany County, N.Y., Oct. 27, 1869; s. Charles Edwin and Laura Jane (Ludden) D.; grad. Hartwick Sem., N.Y., 1886; studied theology at same sem. 2 yrs.; grad. Gettysburg (Pa.) Sem., 1892; D.D., Hartwick, 1916; m. Caroline W. Secor, Oct. 18, 1893 (died Dec. 18, 1907); children—Vernon I., Harlan S.; m. 2d, Marie Barbara Lederle, Aug. 3, 1919. Ordained ministry United Luth. Ch. in America, 1892; pastor Rhinebeck, N.Y., 1892-98, Poestenkill, N.Y., 1899-1904, Riverside, Calif., 1904-08, Ponca, Neb., 1908-11, Jersey City, N.J., 1912-20, Hartwick Sem., 1920-24, N.Y. City, 1924-28, Bellmore, L.I., N.Y., 1928-31; prof. systematic theology and N.T. exegesis, 1920-24, prof. systematic theology, Hartwick Sem., 1930-41; lecturer in dogmatics in Phila. Lutheran Theol. Sem., 1943-45. Author: The Untroubled Heart, 1896; Exploring the Deeps—Studies in Theology, 1935. Home: 127 Linden St., Bellmore, LI NY

DEJARNETTE, JOSEPH SPENCER, physician; b. Spotsylvania County, Va., Sept. 29, 1866; s. Elliott Hawes and Evelyn May (Magruder) DeJ.; M.D., Med. Coll. of Va., 1888; m. Chertsey Hopkins (M.D.), Feb. 14, 1906. Began as 3d asst. physician, Western State Hosp., Staunton, Va., 1888, supt. of hosp. since 1906. Food adminstr., Staunton and Augusta Counties, Va., World War; examiner of insane vets. of World War. Honored with banquet given by Gov. and State Hosp. Bd. for 50 years' service at Western State Hosp., 1939. Mem. Am. Psychiatric Assn. (life mem.), Tri-State Med. Soc., Va. State Med. Soc., Shenandoah Med. Soc., Augusta County Med. Soc. Democrat. Presbyterian. Sponsor of sterilization law of Va., also law for state care of idiots. Founder, 1928, and supt. DeJarnette State Sanatorium. Address: Western State Hosp., Staunton VA*‡

DEKALB, FRANCES DOUGLAS (MRS. COURTENAY DEKALB), translator; b. E. Cornwall, Conn., Nov. 19, 1870; d. Alanson Delos and Betsy Ellen (Miller) Douglas; ed. Derby, Conn.; hon. Litt.D. from U. of Ariz., 1933; m. Courtenay DeKalb, June 25, 1913. Studied racial types and langs. of Pueblo Indians, N.M., utilizing material in lectures and fiction; transcribed hitherto undeciphered diary of Padre Junipero Serra, the fundamental document of Calif. history; introduced Blasco Ibanez and Concha Espina to English readers. Charter mem. Spanish-Am. Athenaeum, Washington; hon. mem. Am. Assn. Univ. Women (1935), Southern Univ. Women's Assn., Sigma Delta Pi Fraternity; corr. mem. Real Academia Hispano Americana de Ciencias y Artes de Cadiz, Hispanic Soc. America (1934). Real Academia Sevillana de Buenas Letras; mem. Nat. League Am. Penwomen, Delta Kappa Gamma. Awarded Medella de Honor de la Instruccion Publica de Venezuela (1934). Translator: (works by Blasco Ibanez) Sangre y Arena (Blood of the Arena), 1911; Sonnica la Cortesana (English title, Sonnica), 1912; Los Muertos Mandan (The Dead Command), 1919; In the Land of Art, 1924; also (works by Concha Espina) Mariflor (La Esfinge Maragata), 1924; The Red Beacon (Dulce Nombre), 1924. Contbr. critical studies of Benito Perez Galdos, Vicente Blasco Ibanez, Concha Espina, Gregorio Martinez Sierra, G. Diaz Caneja, etc.; also in series of Pan Am. Patriots, biographies of Jose Gervasio Artigas, Benito Juarez, Juan Rafael Mora, Francisco Morazan, Bernardo O'Higgins, Simon Bolivar, Jose Marti and Miguel Larreinaga. Asso. editor of Hispania, 1930-41. Editor's Advisory Council Hispania, 1941. Home: 829 N. Tyndall Av., Tucson AZ‡

DE KAY, JOHN WESLEY, capitalist, author; b. nr. New Hampton, Ia., July 20, 1872; s. John and Mary Elizabeth (Ellsworth) D.; a descendant of family of Picardy, France; pub. sch. edn.; m. Anna May Walton, of Hot Springs, Dak., July 15, 1897. Edited, managed and owned chain of newspapers in the Black Hills of S.D. at an early age; organized the U.S. Packing Co. and the Mexican Nat. Packing Co., operating under concessions granted by Mexican Govt. Mem. Nat. Geog. Soc. Clubs: Algonquin (Boston), Nat. Arts, Lawyers', City, Authors' (New York). Author: The Men of Mexico and the Land They Love, 1906; Longings, 1908; The Weaver and the Way of Life, 1908; Judas (drama) 1910; Thoughts, 1911; Brown Leaves, 1911. Address: 334 Fifth Av., NY‡

DEKKER, ALBERT, actor; b. N.Y.C., Dec. 20, 1905; s. Albert and Grace (Ecke) D.; B.S., Bowdoin Coll., 1927; m. Esther T. Guerini, Apr. 4, 1929 (div.). First broadway appearance with Walter Hampden in Enemy of the People, 1927; other prodns. include Grand Hotel, 1931, Death of a Salesman, 1950, Andersonville Trial, 1960; numerous motion pictures, 1939-68, including Dr. Cyclops, 1941, Gentlemen's Agreement, 1948, Woman of the Town, 1942. Wake Island, 1942; (plays) Face of A Hero, 1960, Man for all Seasons, 1961-64; several television appearances, 1964; lecturer on Am. poetry and drama, 1951-68. Mem. Cal. Legislature from Hollywood, 1945-46. Mem. Alpha Delta Phi. Club: Players (N.Y.C.). Home: Hollywood CA Died May 5, 1968.

DE KRUIF, PAUL, writer; b. Zeeland, Mich., Mar. 2 1890; s. Hendrik and Hendrika J. (Kremer) de K.; B.S. U. Mich., 1912, Ph.D., 1916; m. Rhea Barbarin, Dec 11, 1922 (dec. July 1957); m. 2d, Eleanor Lappage Sept. 1, 1959. Bacteriologist, U. Mich., 1912-17 Rockefeller Inst., 1920-22; reporter for Curtis Pub. Co. 1925-71; cons. Chgo. Bd. Health, Mich. State Health Dept. Labs. Served from lt. to capt. San Corps, U.S Army, 1917-19. Mem. Mich. Med. Soc. (hon.) Collaborator with Sinclair Lewis, on Arrowsmith, 1925 Author: Our Medicine Men, 1922; Microbe Hunters 1926; Hunger Fighters, 1928; Seven Iron Men, 1929 Men Against Death, 1932; Why Keep Them Alive? 1936; The Fight for Life, 1938; Health Is Wealth, 1940 Kaiser Wakes the Doctors, 1943; The Male Hormone 1945; Life Among the Doctors, 1949; A Man Agains Insanity, 1957; The Sweeping Wind, 1962. Contbr. t Readers Digest. Home: Holland MI Died Mar. 1971.

DE LABOULAYE, ANDRE LEFEBVRE, diplomat; b Paris, France, Jan. 22, 1876; s. Rene and Clair (Musnier) de L.; graduate Ecole des Sciences Politiques licencie en droit; m. Marie Hely d'Oissel, of Paris, July 9, 1912; children—Paul, Marie-Therese, Francois Agnes. Apptd. attache of embassy, French legation Bucharest, 1900, Rome (Holy See), 1902; sec. c embassy, Washington, 1912, counsellor, 1923 counsellor of embassy, Berlin, 1924, ministe plenipotentiary, 1925; asst. polit. dir., Ministry o Foreign Affairs, Paris, 1929; ambassador to U.S. sinc 1933. Commander Legion of Honor (France). Catholic Address: French Embassy, 2400 16th St., Washingto DC‡

DELAHANTY, WILLIAM JOHN, mfg. exec. b. Por Huron, Mich., July 24, 1895; s. Christopher and Sara (Bennett) D.; student Harvard, 1948; m. Maybelle R Walz, 1920; children—William C., Marjorie A. Wit Burroughs Adding Machine Co., now Burroughs Corp 1912-60, successively chief factory clk., assistant work manager, general mgr. mfg., 1912-51, v.p. charge mfg 1951-60. A.E.F., France, 1917-19. Mem. Am Ordnance Assn., N.A.M., Detroit Bd. Commerce

Clubs: Detroit Economic, Detroit Harvard Business School. Home: Grosse Pointe Farms MI Died July 1971.

DELANEY, GEORGE PHILIP, govt. ofcl.; b. Washington, Feb. 20, 1909; s. George Patrick and Agnes E. (Connery) D.; student Emerson Prep. Sch., Washington, Mt. St. Mary's Coll., Emmitsburg, Md., Harvard, 1945-46; m. Margaret D. Mulholland, July 1947; children—Timothy, Hannah Kevin, Mary Margaret. Engaged as apprentice molder, U.S. Navy Yard, Washington, 1928-38; internat. rep., Molders Internat., Cin., 1938-42, 47-48; labor specialist, Civilian Prodn. Adminstrn., Washington, 1946-47; with Lustron Corp., Columbus, O., Mar.-July 1948; chief of mission, liaison sect., E.C.A., July-Oct. 1948; internat. rep. AFL-CIO, Washington, October 1948; now spl. asst. to sec., coordinator internat. labor affairs Dept. Labor. Workers delegate from U.S. to Internat. Labor Orgn. Served as molder, U.S. Navy, 1942-45. Mem. Internat. Molders and Foundry Workers Union. Democrat. Washington DC Died Feb. 9, 1972; buried Washington DC

DE LARGENTAYE, JEAN, govt. official; b. Pledran, France, Nov. 15, 1903; s. Jacques and Marguerite (de Langle) de L.; student, Poly. Sch., Paris, 1921-23; licencie, Faculty of Law, Paris, 1925; married Ines de Pedroso, December 15, 1945; children—Bertrand, Armand, Helene, Christine. Engineer L'Air Liquide, Inc., Paris, 1925-26, 29, 30, engineer Sad Espanola Oxigeno, Madrid, 1927-28; inspector of finance, Finance Ministry, 1931-35; insp. of finance French Treasury, 1935-39; financial attache French Embassy and Legation of Madrid and Lisbon, 1940-42, 44-45; chief of service Commissariat of Finance, Algiers, 1943-44; exec. dir. Internat. Monetary Fund, 1946-64; economic and social councillor, from 1964; mem. French Delegation, Conf. of Bretton Woods, 1944. Served as lieut., arty., French Army, 1939-40. Decorated comdr. Legion d'Honneur. Author: Translation into French of Gen. Theory of Employment, Interest and Money by J.M. Keynes, 1942. Club: Jockey (Paris) Home: Paris France Died Feb. 26, 1970; buried Ple'dran (C. du N.) Cemetery.

DELBOS, JULIUS, artist; b. London, Eng., July 22, 1879; s. Leon and Clara (Ralph) D.; licentiate Royal Acad. Music, London; unmarried. Came to U.S., 1920, naturalized, 1928. Teacher music and art. Leys Sch., Cambridge, and Uppingham Sch., England, 1914-19; instructor of art at Hunter College, New York City, Rosemary Hall, Greenwich, Connecticut. Represented in collections of Brooklyn, Yale and Toledo museums, Knoedler, Macbeth, Babcock and Ferargil galleries. Mem. Am. Water Color Soc., Conn. Acad., Washington and Baltimore water color clubs. Life mem. Nat. Arts Club. Author: Historic Cambridge, 1912. National Academician. Home: New York City NY Died Jan. 1970.

DELEUW CHARLES EDMUND, cons. engr.; b. Jacksonville, Ill., July 3, 1891; s. Oscar Anthony and Bessie Mary (Tribbey) DeL.; B.S., U. of Ill., 1912, C.E., 1916; married Martha Guthrie, Aug. 21, 1917 (dec.); 1 dau., Martha Guthrie (Mrs. Donald E. Stende); m. 2d, Ethel Buckmaster, July 29, 1927 (divorced 1948); children—Charles E., Sally (Mrs. Jon Peak) m. 3d, Sylvia Ffennell, Feb. 25, 1948 (dec. Oct. 1960); m. 4th, Emilene Brown, November 11, 1961. Chmn. bd. De Leuw, Cather & Co., cons. engrs.; transit and highway reports and plans for Chgo., Det., Los Angeles, Montreal, Toronto, Balt., Washington, Cleveland, Cin., Louisville, Boston, St. Louis, Providence, Buffalo, NY., Portland, San Francisco, Caracas, El Paso, Milwaukee, Norfolk, Oakland, Richmond, Istanbul, Sydney, Australia, Perth, Australia, New Jersey Turnpike; New York Thruway, Ohio Turnpike, Okla. Turnpike; consulting engineer for Department of Subways, City of Chicago, 1936-40, chief engr. 1941-44. Served as capt., 4th U.S. Engrs., 1917-19. Awarded D.S.C. Mem. Engring. Inst. of Can., Am. Institute Cons. Engrs., Am. Soc. C.E., Soc. Am. Mil. Engrs., Western and Ill. socs. engrs., Am. Transit Assn., Inst. Civil Engrs., Inst. Traffic Engrs., Phi Delta Theta. Clubs: University, Tavern; Mid-America. Home: Chicago IL Died Oct. 1970.

DELL, FLOYD, author; b. Barry, Ill., June 28, 1887; s. Anthony and Kate (Crone) D.; ed. high sch. (non-grad.); m. Berta-Marie Gage, Feb. 8, 1919; children—Anthony, Christopher. Reporter, Davenport, Ia., and Chicago, 1905-08; asso. lit. editor, 1909-11, lit. editor, 1911-13, Chicago Evening Post; asso. editor Masses, New York, 1914-17, Liberator, 1918-24. Author: (novels) Moon-Calf, 1920; The Briary-Bush, 1921; Janet March, 1923, revised edit., 1927; This Mad Ideal, 1925; Runaway, 1925; An Old Man's Folly, 1926; An Unmarried Father, 1927; Souvenir, 1929; Love Without Money, 1931; Diana Stair, 1932; (short stories and verse) Love in Greenwich Village, 1926; (essays) Women as World-Builders, 1913; Were You Ever a Child? 1919; Looking at Life, 1924; Intellectual Vagabondage—An Apology for the Intelligentsia, 1926; The Outline of Marriage, 1926-27; Love in the Machine Age, 1930; (biography) Upton Sinclair—A Study in Social Protest, 1927; Homecoming—An Autobiography, 1933; (one-act plays) The Angel Intrudes, 1918; Sweet-and-Twenty, 1921; King Arthur's Socks, and Other Village Plays, 1922; (3-act play with Thomas Mitchell) Little Accident (prod. by Crosby Gaige), 1928; Cloudy with Showers (3-act play, with Thomas Mitchell), prod. by Patterson McNutt, 1931; The Golden Spike (novel), 1934; Lincoln and the Democrats (with Christopher Dell), in preparation. Edited (with Paul Jordan-Smith) All-English Edit. of Burton's Anatomy of Melancholy, 1927. Editorial work for Fed. agencies, 1935-47; now in ind. lit. work. Home: Bethesda MD Died July 23, 1969.

DELL, ROGER LEROY, state supreme ct. justice; b. Bird Island, Minn., July 19, 1897; s. August Theodore and Ellen (Donohue) D.; LL.B., St. Paul Coll. of Law, 1920; m. Agnes Collier, Jan. 9, 1943. Admitted to Minn. bar, 1920; practiced in Fergus Falls, 1920-53; asso. justice Supreme Ct. of Minn., Jan. 12-July 16, 1953, chief justice from 1953. Mem., Am., Minn. bar assns. Home: Fergus Falls MN Died Mar. 8, 1966.

DELLA PIETRA, ALFONSO, surgeon; b. Waterbury, Conn., Jan. 20, 1917; s. Stefano and Giovaianina (Alfieri) Della P.; B.S., Fordham U., 1937; M.D., Georgetown Sch. Medicine, 1941; m. Helen Marie Stephenson, June 17, 1946; children—Stephen John, Richard Alfonso. Intern, St. Mary's Hosp., Waterbury, 1941-42, attending orthopedic surgeon, 1951-69, chief of staff, 1960-69; surg. resident Polyclinic Hosp. N.Y., 1942-44, clin. asst. orthopedic surgeon, 1948-51, asst. attending orthopedic surgeon, 1951, clin. prof. orthopedic surgery, traumatology, 1949-69; orthopedic resident St. Lukes Hosp., N.Y., 1944-48, asst. in orthopedic clinic, 1948-51, asst. attending orthopedic surgeon, 1951-63; asst. attending orthopedic surgeon St. Vincent's Hosp., S.I., N.Y., 1948-52; asso. attending orthopedic surgeon Sea-Hosp., N.Y., 1962; asst. clin. prof., asso. Hosp., N.Y., 1948-51; attending orthopedic surgeon Waterbury Hosp., 1951-69; cons. orthopedic surgeon Norwalk (Conn.) Hosp., 1951-69, Charlotte Hungerford Hosp., Torrington, Conn., 1960-69; state police surgeon State of Conn., 1960-69; instr. orthopedic surgery Columbia U., 1957-66; asso. vis. orthopedic surgeon Met. Hosp., N.Y., 1962; asst. clin. prof., asso. attending orthopedic surgeon N.Y. Med. Coll., 1962. Spl. cons. bone Tb, Tb Commn., State of Conn., 1955-60; chmn. med. adv. bd. Easter Seal Rehab., Waterbury, 1957-61, co-chmn. bldg. fund, 1960-61, v.p. med. adv. bd., 1961-69, pres. Rehab. Center; chmn. chief staffs conf. Conn. Regional Med. Planning. Recipient Easter Seal Rehab.-Citizens award, Conn., 1961; Achievement award in Medicine, Fordham U., 1961; knight of Malta, 1963. Fellow Internat. Coll. Surgeons (regent for Coll. Conn.), A.C.S.; mem. Conn., N.Y. med. socs., A.M.A., N.Y. Acad. Medicine, Am. Bd. Orthopedic Surgery, Am. Acad. Orthopedic Surgery, New Haven County Med. Assn. (bd. govs.), Internat. Soc. Orthopedic Surgery and Traumatology, Pan-Pacific Surg. Assn., Overseas Letters Club Orthopedic Surgery (Jordan project), Am. Med. Writers Assn., Middlebury Orthopedic Group (pres.), State Police Surgeons Conn. (chmn. Middlebury CT Died Jan. 3, 1969.

DELLA TORRE ALTA, IL MARCHESE (ALBERT-FELIX SCHMITT), artist; b. Boston, Mass., June 14, 1873; s. Theodore and Sarah Elizabeth (Heitz) S.; student Mass. Normal Art Sch., Cowles Art Sch., Sch. of the Mus. of Fine Arts, Boston; m. Esther Rhoads Stokes Cattell, of Phila., Pa., June 2, 1916. In charge art dept. Bradford (Mass.) Acad., 1903-13; instr. of life class and mem. faculty, R.I. Sch. of Design, 1912-18; established studio in Biarritz, France, 1930. Works: Symphony in Blue, The Capri Bowl, The Blue Veil, Bride and Groom, Old Trees, Psyche, Naiads, La Dame au Leopard, Musee du Louvre, Paris. Represented in exhbns. at Boston Art Club, Art Inst. Chicago, Mus. of Fine Arts (Boston), Pa. Acad. of Fine Arts, Corcoran Gallery (Washington, D.C.), Detroit Inst. of Art, Albright Gallery, Carnegie Inst., Art. Mus. (St. Louis), Worcester Art Mus. Awards: Grand Chevalier of the Order of the Holy Sepulchre, Vatican, 1934; Panama-Pacific Internat. Expn., 1915; gold star and cravate of Societe Academique d'Histoire Internationale, Paris, 1929; La grande croix de la Legion d'honneur given by the Beaux Arts to the painting in the Louvre collection, La Dame au Leopard," Paris, 1937; awarded Congressional Medal of Honor, 1938. Catholic. Studio: 58 Avenue Sarasate, Biarritz France‡

DELLPLAIN, MORSE, business exec.; b. New Orleans, Sept. 17, 1880; s. Frank X. and Mary (Ryckman) D.; student Genesee Wesleyan Sem., Lima, N.Y., 1898-1901, Syracuse U., 1901-03, D.Eng. (hon.), 1951; m. Grace Perry, Feb. 28, 1910 (dec. 1958); m. 2d, Edith Giles Bettys, June 27, 1959. Salesman engr. Westinghouse Electric & Mfg. Co., 1903-09; power engr. Syracuse Lighting Co., 1909-18; v.p., gen. mgr. No. Ind. Pub. Service Co., 1918-29, pres., 1929-34; with Welsbach Corp., Phila., 1934-68, exec. v.p., 1934-41, pres., dir. 1941-64, chmn. bd. 1964-68. Mem. Am. Inst. E.E., A.S.M.E., Illuminating Engring. Soc., Sigma Chi. Republican. Baptist. Mason (K.T., Shriner). Clubs: Midday, Merion Cricket, Union League, Engineers (Phila.); Ill. Athletic (Chgo.); University, Engineers (N.Y.C.). Home: Bryn Mawr PA Died Feb. 5, 1968.

DEL MAR, ALGERNON, mining engr.; b. New York, Mar. 3, 1870; s. Alexander (author and historian) and Emily D.; ed. public schs., San Francisco; degree A.R.S.M., Royal School of Mines, London, 1891; m. Belle Rogers, Aug. 20, 1903; children—Roger Alexander, Bruce Eugene, Walter Homer. Practiced in S. Africa, Europe, Can., U.S., Mexico; specialty stamp mill constrn. and metall. treatment of gold and base metal ores; cons. metall. engr. Mem. Am. Inst. Mining Engrs. Author: Stamp Milling, 1912; Tube Milling, 1917; and number metall. articles in tech. press. Home: 4524 Alpha St., Los Angeles CA‡

DELOACH, ROBERT JOHN HENDERSON, investigator; b. Statesboro, Ga., Dec. 21, 1873; s. Zachariah Taylor and Jane (Williams) D.; A.B., U. of Ga., 1898, A.M., 1906; m. Bessie Holland of Johnston, S.C., Apr. 2, 1900; children—Edward Lowell, Louise, Evelyn, Julia Helen. Supt. city schs., Swainsboro, Ga., 1900; prin. teacher, U.S. Indian Sch., Ft. Sill, Okla. Ty., 1900-02; prin. Statesboro High Sch., 1903-05; botanist, Ga. Expt. Sta., 1906-08; prof. cotton industry, State Coll. of Agr., Ga., Oct. 1908-13; dir. Ga. Expt. Sta., 1913-17; dir. Armour's Bur. of Agr. Research, Chicago, since 1917. Collaborator, Bur. of Plant Industry, Washington, summer 1911. Mem. Am. Ornithologists' Union, Sigma Chi (Delta Chapter), Phi Beta Kappa, 1922; fellow A.A.A.S. Democrat. Clubs: Chicago, Cliff Dwellers, Quadrangle, Saddle and Sirloin. Baptist. Author: Rambles with John Burroughs, 1912; Agriculture for the Common Schs. Writer bulls. on plant breeding and diseases, also contbr. to current mags. Some time editor agrl. dept. Atlanta Constitution. Address: Statesboro GA‡

DE LONG, IRWIN HOCH, Orientalist; b. near Bower's, Pa., May 11, 1873; s. Adam B. and Caroline (Hoch) D.; student Keystone State Normal Sch., Pa., 1889-91; Muhlenberg Coll., Pa., 1894-95; A.B., Franklin and Marshall Coll., 1898, A.M., 1901, D.D., 1928; grad. Theol. Sem. of Ref. Ch. in U.S., 1901; instr. Latin and Roman history, Perkiomen Sem., Pa., 1901-02; D.B., U. of Chicago, 1902; Thayer fellow Am. Sch. for Oriental Study and Research in Palestine, Jerusalem, 1902-03; studied univs. of Berlin and Strassburg, Germany, 6 semesters; Ph.D., Strassburg, 1905; U. of Chicago, summer quarter, 1906; m. Mary R. Meister, Oct. 10, 1907; children—Margaret Eleanor (Mrs. William G. Carrington), Dorothy Meister (Mrs. John W. Lines), Emilie Meister, May Meister (Mrs. Stanton B. Le Fever). Traveled in Palestine, trans-Jordanic countries, Egypt, Asia Minor, Greece and Constantinople, 1902-03, in Europe, 1897, 1903-06; ordained ministry Reformed Ch. in U.S., 1909; instr. O.T. science, 1906-09, professor Hebrew and O.T. science since 1909, dean since 1921, librarian, 1909-22; Theological Seminary Ref. Church in U.S.; professor emeritus since September 1943. Mason (32 deg.). President, Classis of East Pennsylvania, 1921-22. Mem. Soc. Bibl. Lit. and Exegesis, Am. Oriental Soc., Deutsche Morgenlandische Gesellschaft, Vorderasiatisch-Aegyptische Gesellschaft, Die Deutsche Orient-Gesellschaft, Zentralstelle fur Deutsche Personen und Familiengeschichte, Pa. German Soc. Author: Early Occurrences of the Family Name De Long in Europe and in America, 1924; Descendants of Otto Henrich Wilhelm Brinkman, 1925; Pennsylvania Gravestone Inscriptions, 1925; The Lineage of Malcolm Metzger Parker from Johannes Delang, 1926; Pioneer Palatine Pilgrims, 1928; My Ancestors, 1930; An Early Nineteenth Century Constitution of a Union Church, 1931; An Early Eighteenth Century Reformed Church—a Contribution to Church and Family History, 1934. Home: 637 N School Lane, Lancaster PA‡

DELSASSO, LEO PETER, physicist, educator; b. Central City, Colo., Oct. 9, 1895; s. Fortunato and Elizabeth (Bitzenhoffer) D.; A.B., U. Cal. at Los Angeles, 1925; Ph.D., Cal. Inst. Tech., 1941; m. Mary Mussen, Dec. 18, 1948. Jr. engr. Southern Cal. Edison Co., 1917-19; instr. to prof. U. Cal. at Los Angeles, 1925-51, asst. to asso. dean grad. div., 1953-59, prof. physics, 1941-63. asso. dean grad. sch., 1958-59, chmn. dept. physics, 1959-63. Served from ensign to comdr. USNR, 1941-46. Fellow Acoustical Soc. Am. (v.p. 1957), Am. Phys. Soc.; mem. Am. Assn. Physics Tchrs., Sigma Xi Research in archtl. acoustics in auditoria; designer, builder sonic depth sounder giving continuous graphical record of depth of ocean, 1927. Home: Los Angeles CA Died July 26, 1971.

DEL TUFO, RAYMOND, JR., judge; born at Newark, N.J., July 31, 1919; son of Raymond and Mary (Pellecchia) Del T.; A.B., Princeton, 1942; LL.B., Rutgers University, 1948; married Elizabeth R. Burke, 1959. Admitted to New Jersey bar, 1949; government appeal agt. SSS local draft bd., 1951-53; prof. law Seton Hall Law Sch., 1952-53; U.S. atty. dist. N.J., 1954-56; partner Lowenstein, Del Tufo, Callahan & Kean, 1956-58; asso. prof. law Seton Hall U. Law Sch., 1958-60; appointed judge, New York City, 1960—. Charter commissioner to reorganize govt. City Newark, 1953. Served with AUS, 1942-46. Mem. Am., N.J., Essex County bar assns., Holy Name Soc., YMCA, Cum Laude Soc. Newark Acad., Newark Acad. Alumni Assn. (pres. 1952-53). Clubs: Princeton (N.Y.C.);

Princeton (Oranges and Newark); Down Town (Newark); Cannon (Princeton U.). Home: East Orange NJ Died Mar. 1970.

DEL VALLE, MANUEL ANGEL, business exec.; b. San Juan, P.R., Oct. 1, 1895; s. Dr. Manuel Vicente and Maria (Buso) del V.; B.Ch.E., U. of Mich., 1916; m. Matilde Gonzalez, Aug. 8, 1919; children—Ana Matilde (Mrs. Etienne Totti, Jr.), Manuel Luis. Chief chemist, Central Plazuela, Barceloneta, P.R., 1917; served as 1st lt., capt., U.S. Inf., 1917-19; factory supt., Central Pasto Viejo, Humacao, P.R., 1919; prof., head, dept. sugar chemistry, Coll. of Agriculture and Mechanic Arts, Mayaguez, P.R., 1919-25; factory supt., gen. field and factory supt., Central Constancia, 1920-37; field mgr., asst. gen. mgr., v.p., Eastern Sugar Assos., Caguas, P.R., 1938-45, pres., 1946-57; chmn. Fajardo Eastern Sugar Assos., from 1958; pres. Sugar Service Corp.; v.p. Cia Azucarera del Toa, Toa Baja, P.R., Caribe Motors Corp., San Juan; exec. v.p. Jimenez del Vatte, Inc.; director Banco Popular de P.R., Santurce Development Co. Pres. exec. com. Presbyn. Hosp., San Juan. Mem. Assn. Sugar Producers of Puerto Rico (president), Association of Sugar Technologists of Puerto Rico, Military Order of World Wars (commander of P.R. chpt. 1950-51), Colegio de Quimicos de P.R., Tau Beta Pi, Phi Lambda Upsilon. Republican. Roman Catholic. Clubs: Rotary, U. Mich. (pres.), Bankers (Puerto Rico); Bankers of America, University (N.Y.C.). Home: Santurce PR Died 1964.

DELZELL, THOMAS WHITE, public utilities exec.; b. Chickasha, Okla., May 4, 1901; s. William Abner and Edith Mae (White) D.; student Ore. State Coll., 1919-22; married Sarah Croxton, July 17, 1925 (died April 17, 1961); children—Caryl Edith, Paul Croxton; m. 2d, Clarice Spatz, Oct. 19, 1963. With Cal. Ore. Power Co., So. Ore., No. Cal., 1922-36; asst. mgr. Klamath div. and Klamath Engring. div., Klamath Falls, Ore., 1925-32; asst. to v.p. and gen. mgr., The Calif. Ore. Power Co., Medford, Ore., 1932-36; dir. W.P.A., 1936; asst. pub. utilities commr. of Ore., 1938-39; independent trustee Portland Elec. Power Co. and subsidiary cos., 1939-51, chairman board of directors and chief executive officer Portland General Electric Company, 1948-69; bd. dirs. Edison Electric Institute. Chmn. Pacific Northwest Coms. on relations and use of electricity in agr., 1931-32, 1935 for Northwest Electric Light & Power Assn. and Ore. Reclamation Congress (chmn. finance com. latter orgn.); state finance dir. Ore. Dem. Nat. Com., 1937; asst. Dem. State chmn., 1936. Vice chairman board trustees Pacific University, Forest Grove, Oregon. Member Nat. Assn. Elec. Companies (dir. 1950-53), N.W. Elec. Light and Power Assn. (pres. 1950-51, N.A.M. (dir. 1954-56, chmn. conservation com. 1956), Newcomen Soc., Sigma Nu. Presbyn. Mason. Clubs: Waverly, Arlington, University, Multnomah (Portland, Ore.); Bohemian (San Francisco). Home: Portland OR Died Jan 21, 1969.

DEMAREST, GEORGE STUART, univ. dean; b. Roselle Park, N.J., Aug. 9, 1906; s. George L. and Ethel L. (Johnson) D.; Litt. B., Rutgers U., 1928, M.A., 1938; m. Grace Banker, June 18, 1931; children—Muriel Ann, Donald B. (dec.). Editor, Rahway (N.J.) Record, 1928-30; editor publs. Rutgers U., 1930, mem. faculty, from 1935, chmn. dept. English, 1945-58, prof. English, from 1951, dean Univ. Coll., from 1965. Mem. Am. Assn. U. Profs., Modern Lang. Assn., Theta Chi. Republican. Presbyn. Author articles. Home: Westfield NJ Died Mar. 3, 1972; buried Fairview Cemetery, Westfield NJ

DEMERS, PIERRE PAUL, ex-consul; b. in Canada, Aug. 7, 1876; s. Isaac and Adelaide (Morisette) D.; A.B., St. Joseph's Coll., N.B., 1897; LL.B., Boston U., 1902; m. Della M. Demers, of Dover, N.H., Apr. 28, 1903. Practiced at Boston and Somersworth, N.H.; mem. N.H. Ho. of Rep., 1903; consul at Port Limon, Costa Rica, 1903-5, Barranquilla, Colombia, 1905-8, Bahia, Brazil, Mar. 10, 1908-July 26, 1909; now engaged in railroading and manufacturing in Brazil. Republican. Catholic. Mem. Am. Soc. Internat. Law, Boston Bar Assn. Contbr. on economic conditions in Central and S. America. Home: Dover, N.H. Address: Bahia Brazil‡

DE MILHAU, LOUIS JOHN DE GRENON, lawyer; b. N.Y. City, July 27, 1884; s. John Jefferson (surgeon. bvt. brig. gen. U.S. Army) and Katherine Louise (Manning) de M.; A.B., Harvard University, 1906; LL.B., New York Law School, 1911; married Renee Noel Gourd, December 29, 1909; children—John Waddington, Renee D. (Mrs. de Milhau Davis), Louis John. Admitted to New York bar, 1911, and practiced at N.Y. City. Mem. Squadron A, Cadet Corps, N.Y. City, 1889-1901; mem. 9th Training Regt., Plattsburg, N.Y., 1916; capt. Signal Corps U.S. Army, Dec. 1917-Mar. 1919; capt. J.A.G.D., O.R.C., 1921; lt. col. ret. Govt. appeal agt. Local Bd. No. 133, N.Y. County, June-Dec. 1917. Trustee Inc. Village Old Brookville, L.I., N.Y., 1930-34, police justice, 1935-39. Treas. and mem. bd. mgrs. Lincoln Hall; member bd. trustees and president emeritus St. Vincent de Paul Inst., Tarrytown. Past comdr. N.Y. Commandery Mil. Order Loyal Legion; com. visitors Peabody Mus.; Univ. Mus., Harvard, 1908-21. Republican. Clubs: Harvard, Explorers (honorary mem., historian, director), End of the Earth (N.Y.C.); Army and Navy (Washington); Harvard Travelers (fellow; Boston). Mem. Harvard expdn. to Iceland, 1905; de Milhau-Harvard expdn. to S. America, 1907-09; explorations in Peru and Bolivia; donor Icelandic birds to Peabody Mus. Wrote introd. to Indians of Eastern Peru," by Farabee, 1923. Author: Sprengisandur Holiday" in Explorers Club Tales, 1937. Home: New York City NY Died 1968.

DE MILT, AIDA RODMAN, author; b. Brooklyn, Dec. 19, 1871; d. Henry Rodman and Mary Eliza (Tugnot) D.; grad., Miss Chisholm's Sch. for Girls, New York, 1899. Author: Ways and Days Out of London, 1910. Address: 535 W. 135th St., NY‡

DE MONCHY, W. H., vice chmn. bd. Holland-America Line. Address: Holland-America Line, Rotterdam Holland

DEMOS, RAPHAEL, teacher of philosophy; b. Smyrna, Asia Minor, Jan. 23, 1892; s. Stavros and Anna (Constantinidou) Demetracopoulos; A.B., Anatolia Coll., Marsovan, Asia Minor, 1910; Ph.D., Harvard; student Cambridge U., Eng., 1918-19, U. of Paris, 1928-29; m. Jean McMorran, June 19, 1936; children—John Putnam, Penelope. Came to U.S. 1913, naturalized, 1921. Asst. in philosophy, Harvard, 1916-17, instr. and tutor, 1919-26, asst. prof. and tutor, 1926-29, lecturer and tutor, 1931-34, asst. prof. and tutor, 1934-39, associate prof. 1939-45, prof. of philosophy and Alford prof. of natural religion, moral philosophy, and civil polity, 1945-62, prof. emeritus, 1962-68; vis. prof. Vanderbilt U., 1962-67; academic dir. Coll. Year in Athens, Inc., 1967-68; guest prof. philosophy McGill U., Montreal, 1963-64. Guggenheim fellowship, Paris, 1928-29; grants Rockefeller Found., 1956, Am. Philos. Association, 1959, Littauer Found., 1960. Director Anatolia College, Saloniki, Greece. Member American Academy Arts, Scis., Acad. Athens (corr.), Am. Philos. Assn., Phi Beta Kappa. Club: Harvard Faculty. Editor: Plato Selections, 1931; Complete Works of Plato, 1936. Author: The Philosophy of Plato, 1939. Home: Kifissia Greece Died Aug. 8, 1968.

DEMOTT, RICHARD HOPPER, mfg. exec.; b. Tenafly, N.J., Sept. 12, 1886; s. John Henry and Margaret Jane (Hopper) De M.; student Stevens Prep. Sch., Hoboken, N.J., 1903; M.E., Stevens Inst. Tech., 1908; m. Hazel Childs, Apr. 24, 1915 (died 1922); children—Harriet Childs (Mrs. Thomas E. Betner), Richard Warren; m. 2d, Lucille Cornish, June 5, 1924. Apprentice and supervisor centrifugal pump test, Worthington Pump Co., Harrison, N.J., 1908; draftsman Crocker Wheeler, Ampere, N.J., 1909; salesman Westinghouse Lamp Co., Bloomfield, N.J., 1910, northwest dist. mgr., Seattle, 1910-14; spl. power engr., Public Service Co., Jersey City, N.J., 1914-15; sales engr., SKF Industries, Phila., 1915-16, dist. mgr. at N.Y., 1916-20, mgr. indsl. development, 1921-23, asst. sales mgr., 1923-27, sales mgr., 1928-42, v.p. in charge of sales, 1943-50, pres. 1950-55, chmn. bd., 1955-57; v.p., asst. to pres. H. B. Maynard & Co., mgmt. cons., 1958; chmn. bd., pres. Acheson Mfg. Co., Braddock, Pa., 1958-68; former chmn. bd. Tyson Bearing Corp., Massillon, O. Hon. v.p., former pres. and dir. Exhibitors Advt. Council, Inc., N.Y.; vice chmn. exec. com. and gov. Am. Swedish Hist. Found.; mem. adminstrv. com., v.p. Phila. council Boy Scouts Am. Decorated Royal Order of Vasa (Sweden); recipient Stevens Honor award, Stevens, Inst. Tech. Mem. Anti-Friction Bearing Mfrs. Assn. (past pres. and dir.), C. of C. (past dir.), Sales Mgrs. Assn. Phila. (past pres. and dir.), Am. Mgmt. Assn. (past dir.), Pennsylvania Soc., Swedish C. of C. of U.S. (dir.), Am. Soc. Sales Execs. (exec. com.), Am. Ordinance Assn., Franklin Inst., Soc. Automotive Engrs., Assn. Iron and Steel Engrs., Am. Swedish Hist. Mus., Newcomen Soc. N.A. Presbyn. Clubs: Union League, Orpheus, Cricket (Phila.); Bayhead Yacht (N.J.); Skytop (Pa.). Home: Philadelphia PA Died Aug. 1968.

DENFELD, LOUIS EMIL, retired naval officer; b. Westboro, Mass., Apr. 13, 1891; s. Louis E. and Etta May (Kelley) D.; A.M., Naval Acad., 1912; m. Rachel Metcalf, June 5, 1915. Commd. ensign, June 1912 and advanced through grades to admiral; served in Virginia, Ark., Paducah, and N.J., 1912-17; on Destroyers Ammen and Lamberton on escort duty during World War I; comd. Destroyers Wadsworth and Brooks and Submarine S-24, 1919-29; aide to Chief of Bur. of Navigation, 1929-31; staff of Comdr. Battle Force and Comdr. in Chief, U.S. Fleet, 1931-33; Bur. of Navigation, 1933-35; comd. Destroyer Div. 11, Battle Force, 1935-37; adminstrative aide to Chief of Naval Operations, 1937-39; comd. Destroyer Div. 18 and Destroyer Squadron 1, 1939-41; special naval observer in London, Chief of Staff for Comdr. Support Force, Atlantic Fleet, 1941; asst. chief naval personnel, Bur. of Naval Personnel, Navy Dept., 1942-44; comdr. battleships, Div. 9, Pacific, 1945; chief of Naval Personnel, 1945-47; comdr.-in-chief Pacific and U.S. Pacific, 1947; chief of naval operations, and mem. Joint Chiefs of Staff, 1947-49; ret. as adm., 1950; cons. Sun Oil Co., 1950-71. Decorated D.S.M., Legion of Merit with gold star. Episcopalian. Clubs: Chevy Chase (Md.); Army-Navy, Metropolitan, Carlton, 1925 F Street. Home: Westboro MA Died Mar. 28, 1972.

DENHAM, HENRY HENDERSON, educator; b. Flint, Mich., June 27, 1870; s. Giles Leach and Eliza J. (Henderson) D.; grad. Univ. of Mich., B.S., 1893; m. June 23, 1897, Mabel Sherman, Buffalo. Instr. chemistry, Cornell, 1893-6; instr. chemistry and physics, Buffalo Central High Sch., 1896-1903; prin. Syracuse Business High Sch. since Sept., 1903. Mem. Am. Chem. Soc. Residence: 102 W. Beard Av., Syracuse NY‡

DENISE, LARIMORE CONOVER, clergyman, educator; b. Omaha, Neb., June 7, 1872; s. Jacob Conover, M.D., and Mary Clara (Collier) D.; A.B., Princeton, 1894; grad. Presbyn. Theol. Sem., Omaha, 1897, studied Western Theol. Sem., Pittsburgh, Pa., 1905; D.D., Bellevue (Nebraska) College, 1916; and Hastings (Nebraska) College, 1934; m. Bernice Evans, Oct. 28, 1902 (died Mar. 28, 1917); children—Dorothy Bernice (Mrs. H. M. Hagerman), Marguerite Meredith (Mrs. Gilbert F. Broking), Paul Larimore; m. 2d, Alma E. Dodds, Apr. 23, 1919. Ordained Presbyn. ministry, 1897; pastor Clay Center, Kan., 1897-1902, New Kensington, Pa., 1902-16; asst. gen. supt. Nat. Reform Assn., Pittsburgh, Pa., 1916-23; pres. Presbyn. Theol. Sem., Omaha, Neb., 1924-44; pastor Union Church, Lihue, Kauai, Ter. Hawaii, 1944-47; pastor Presbyn. Ch., Punta Gorda, Fla., since 1948. Moderator Synod of Neb., 1934-35; sec. Council Presbyterian Theol. Sems., 1927-43; member Board of Christian Edn., Presbyn. Ch., U.S.A., 1935-38. Mem. S.A.R. Republican. Rotarian. Home: Punta Gorda, Fla.; summer; Chautauqua NY‡

DENISON, EDWARD EVERETT, Congressman; b. Marion, Ill., Aug. 28, 1873; s. Charles H. and Mary E. (Bundy) D.; B.L., A.B., Baylor U., Waco, Tex., 1895; A.B., Yale, 1896; LL.B., LL.M., Columbian (now George Washington) U., 1899; unmarried. Admitted to Ill. bar 1899, and began practice at Marion, Ill. Mem. 64th to 71st Congresses (1915-31), 25th Ill. Dist. Republican. Home: Marion IL‡

DENISON, ROBERT FULLER, lawyer; b. Cleveland, O., Jan. 4, 1876; s. Lemuel Taylor and Sarah Louise (Fuller) D.; A.B., Williams Coll., 1897; LL.B., Columbia, 1900; m. Elizabeth Brainerd Thomson, Oct. 11, 1899 (dec.); children—Robert B., Elizabeth St. John (Mrs. Edgar Picket Hetzler); married 2d, Kathleen Townsend Dunmore, October 26, 1950. Admitted to Ohio bar, 1900, and since practiced in Cleveland; associated with Squire, Sanders and Dempsey, 1900-12, member since 1913. General attorney Wheeling and Lake Erie division R.R. Adminstrn. during World War. Mem. Cleveland Heights council since 1913, vice mayor since 1932; mem. com. on canons and standing com. of Diocese of Ohio, Diocesan Council of P.E. Ch., 1928-30. Mem. Am. Archaeol. Inst., New England Society of Cleveland (pres. 1938), Phi Delta Theta, Phi Beta Kappa, Phi Delta Phi. Republican. Mem. Protestant Episcopal Ch. (vestryman). Clubs: Union, University, Country (Cleveland). Author: A Manual for the Issuing and Sale of Ohio Bonds, 1922. Asso. editor of Page's Ohio General Code. Home: 2873 N. Park Blvd., Cleveland Heights 18, O. Office: 1857 Union Commerce Cleveland 14 OH‡

DENNEY, LAWRENCE VINCENT, ex-govt. ofcl.; b. Washington, Apr. 5, 1910; s. Harry and Mar E. (O'Connell) D.; LL.B., Columbus U., 1934, B.C.S., 1938; m. Suemary Hite, Oct. 17, 1939; children—Lawrence, Thomas, James, Edward, Susan. Adm. to D.C. bar practice; Washington, 1934-35; with audit and claims div. Gen. Accounting Office, 1935-42, atty. Office Gen. Counsel, 1942-51, asst. gen. counsel, 1951-57, dir. claims div., 1957-68. Mem. Fed. Bar Assn. Home: Washington DC Died Feb. 7, 1973.

DENNIE, CHARLES CLAYTON, physician; b. Excelsior Springs, Mo., Oct. 20, 1883; s. Arthur Doggett and Catherine (Heffley) D.; B.S., Baker U., 1908; M.D., U. of Kan., 1912; m. Glynn Bowden, July 29, 1940. Interne, Kan. City Gen. Hosp., 1912-13, Mass. Gen. Hosp., 1913-15; house officer and instr. in syphilis, Harvard Med. Sch., 1914-15; prof. of dermatology, Med. Sch., U. of Kan., from 1938, becoming prof. emeritus; clin. prof. medicine U. Mo.; dermatologist to Kansas City Gen., Mercy, St. Luke's, hosps. Served A.U.S., 1918-19; major, Med. Corps. A.E.F. Mem. Am. Bd. Dermatology and Syphilology, Am. Med. Assn., Am. Dermotol. Assn. (pres., hon. mem.), Am. Acad. Dermatology and Syphilology, Pan-Am. Med. Assn., French Soc. Dermatology and Syphilology, Brazilian (asso.), N.Y. (hon.) dermatol. assns. Author: Congenital Syphilis, 1940; A History of Syphilis, 1962; also monograph, Syphilis, 1928. Translator of Francisco Lopez de Villalobos book relating to syphilis, written 1498 (pub. in Bull. of History of Medicine). Home: Kansas City MO Died Jan. 13, 1971.

DENNING, JAMES EDWIN, film, television exec.; b. N.Y.C., Nov. 25, 1912; s. John Joseph and Estelle (McCoy) D.; A.B., Columbia, 1935, LL.B., 1938; m. Catherine E. Manton, Jan. 20, 1940; children—Peter, Anne, Jeffrey, Gale, Sara. Admitted to N.Y. bar, 1938, California bar, 1966; attorney United States Department of Justice, 1938-39; with firm Townley,

Updike & Carter, N.Y.C., 1939-44; sec., gen. counsel Press Wireless, Inc., 1944-47; dir. indsl. relations RCA Communications, Inc., 1947-51; sr. atty. NBC, Inc., N.Y.C., 1951-54, mgr., then dir. talent and program contract operations, 1955-57, v.p. talent and program adminstrn., 1957-59; vice pres. MCA-TV, Ltd., 1959-65, Universal City Studios (Col.), 1963-65, MCA Entertainment, Inc., 1965-71, cinematique, Ltd., 1965-71, Universal Television, 1966-71; v.p., dir. Gauss Electrophysics, Inc., 1967-71; v.p., dir. Saki Magnetics, Inc., 1968-71; lectr. law of corps., agy. and partnerships N.Y.U., 1946-48. Mem. exec. bd. Alfred W. Dater council Boy Scouts Am., 1952-63, bd. dirs. Darien chpt. A.R.C., 1961-62, Darien Fund, 1954-63. Mem. Rep. Town Meeting, Darien, 1951-63, moderator, 1955-58; chmn. Darien Town Govt. Study Commn., 1961-63. Mem. Darien Rep. Town Com., 1960-62. Mem. Nat. Acad. Television Arts and Scis., Assn. Motion Picture and Television Producers, Am. Arbitration Assn. (nat. panel arbitrators), Am., Beverly Hills, Los Angeles County bar assns., Los Angeles Copyright Soc., Town Hall. Club: Cave Des Roys. Home: Los Angeles CA Died Dec. 17, 1971.

DENNING, REYNOLDS MCCONNELL, educator, mineralogist; b. Fitchburg, Mass., Sept. 3, 1916; s. William Wallace and Emma (McConnell) D.; B.S., Mich. Tech. U., 1939, M.S., 1949; Ph.D. in Mineralogy, U. Mich., 1953; m. Helen Green, June 25, 1942; 1 son, William Charles. Geologist, C.E., U.S. Army, 1939-40, Ark. Geol. Survey, 1940-41; Austin F. Rogers teaching fellow, Stanford, 1941-42; geologist Patino Mines and Enterprises, Cons., Inc., Llallagua, Bolivia, 1942-45; inst., then asst. prof. Mich. Tech. U., 1945-52; mem. faculty U. Mich., 1952-67, asst. prof., 1952-56, asso. prof., 1956-61, prof. mineralogy, 1961-67; cons., lectr. in field, 1945-67. Mem., acting chmn. panel indsl. diamonds Nat. Acad. Scis.-NRC, 1956-58. Mineral denningite named for him, 1961. Fellow Mineral. Soc. Am., Geol. Soc. Am., Royal Microscopical Soc., A.A.A.S.; mem. Mineral. Assn. Can., Geochem. Soc., Am. Crystallographic Assn., Mineral. Soc. Great Britain, Mich. Acad. Sci., Research Club Mich., Sigma Xi. Presbyn. Author papers in field. Researcher, cons. in crystal optics, phys. crystallography, diamond technology and gemology. Home: Ann Arbor MI Died Nov. 1, 1967; cremated.

DENNIS, JOSEPH CHARLES, lawyer; b. Worcester, Mass., Mar. 9, 1877; s. William H. and Annie (Broadbent) D.; A.B., Harvard, 1899, LL.B., 1902; m. Eley Miles, July 17, 1912. Admitted to Mass. bar, 1902 and in practice at Boston, 1902-06; in practice at Tacoma, Wash., since 1906; mem. firm Ray & Dennis, 1908-18; corp. counsel City of Tacoma, 1920-23; atty. Pierce County Home Owners Loan Corp., 1933-34; U.S. atty. Western Dist. of Wash. since 1934; sec. and dir. State Savings & Loan Assn; sec. Miles Estate Co. Mem. Pierce County Dem. Central Com., 1916-32. Democrat. Episcopalian. Mason, Elk, Eagle. Club: University (Tacoma, Wash). Home: 1001 N. Yakima Av., Tacoma, Wash. Address: U.S. Courthouse Bldg., Seattle WA

DENNISON, HENRY STURGIS, pres. Dennison Mfg. Co.; b. Boston, Mass., Mar. 4, 1877; s. Henry B. and Emma J. (Stanley) D.; A.B., Harvard, 1899; Sc.D., U. of Pa., 1927; Doctor of Bus. Administration, U. of Mich., 1929; m. Mary Tyler Thurber, Feb. 12, 1901 (died Mar. 31, 1936); m. 2d, Gertrude B. Petri, Oct. 11, 1944. Pres. Dennison Mfg. Co., Framingham, Mass., since 1917; dep. chmn. Fed. Res. and dir. Federal Reserve Bank of Boston. Assistant director Central Bureau of Planning and Statistics, Washington. World War; ex-director service relations, U.S. Post Office Department; member President Wilson's Industrial Conf., 1919, President Harding's Unemployment Conf., 1921, Business Advisory and Planning Council of U.S. Dept. of Commerce, 1933; appointed member National Labor Board, 1934; chmn. Industrial Advisory Bd. under NRA, 1934; member National Resources Planning Board 1935-43. Member American Academy of Arts and Sciences. Club: Union (Boston, Mass.). Author: Organization Engineering, 1931; (with others) Profit Sharing and Stock Ownership for Employees, 1926; Toward Full Employment, 1938; Modern Competition and Framingham MA‡

DENNY, JAMES W., congressman, lawyer; b. Frederick Co., Va.; ed. Univ. of Va.; grad. Judge Richard Parker's Law Sch., Winchester, Va.; engaged in practice of law in Baltimore since 1868. Pres. 1st branch city council, 1882; ten yrs. mem. sch. bd.; mem. Md. legislature, 1888; mem. Congress, 1899-1901, and 1903-5, from 4th Md. dist.; Democrat. Married. Address: Baltimore MD‡

DENNY, LUDWELL, journalist; b. Boonville, Ind., Nov. 18, 1894; s. Wallace N. and Alice (Pursley) D.; ed. U. of Chicago and Meadville Theol. Sch.; m. Josephine Shryock, Nov. 6, 1917; children—Diana, Alice Josephine; married second, Dorothy Detzer, Aug. 2, 1954. Minister First Unitarian Ch., Rochester, N.Y., 1917-21; European corr. The Nation, 1922-23; news editor Federated Press, 1924; diplomatic corr. United Press, 1924-27; chief editorial writer Scripps Howard Newspaper Alliance, 1928-32, asso. editor, 1932-35; editor Indianapolis Times, 1935-39; columnist, foreign analyst Scripps-Howard Newspaper Alliance, 1939-50, fgn. editor, 1951-59, emeritus, 1960-70. Member board trustees Science Service, 1960-70. Recipient Freedom Found. Editorial award, 1953; Roy W. Howard award, 1959. Clubs: Cosmos, Overseas Writers, National Press (Washington). Author: We Fight for Oil, 1928; America Conquers Britain, 1930. Contbr. articles to Ency. Social Sciences and periodicals. Home: Monterey CA Died Oct. 1970.

DENSLOW, DOROTHEA HENRIETTA, sculptor; b. N.Y.C., Dec. 14, 1900; s. Henry Carey and Cornelia Julia (Smith) Denslow; student Art Students League, pvt. studies. Sculptor, 1915-71; works rep. Brookgreen Gardens, S.C., meml. plaque Bklyn. Jewish Hosp., fountain figure, Richmond, Va.; founder Clay Club, N.Y.C., 1928; maintained Sculpture Canteen for service personnel, World War II; founder, dir. Sculpture Center, N.Y.C., 1944-71. Mem. jury for Fulbright Sculpture award, 1958-60. Mem. Conn. Acad. Fine Arts. Home: Strousburg PA Died Apr. 25, 1971.

DENT, FREDERICK RODGERS, JR., retired air force officer; b. Mercer, Pa., Feb. 12, 1908; son Reverend Fred and Jane Margaret (Hoon) D.; B.S., U.S. Mil. Acad., 1929; A.B., St. Mary's University, San Antonio, 1930; M.S., Mass. Institute Technology, 1938; student Air Corps Engring. Sch., Wright Field, 1936, Harvard Bus. Sch. Advt. Management Program, 1947; m. Corra Lynn Robinson, Jan. 24, 1931; children—Frederick Rodgers III, Corra Lynn, David Haley. Commd. 2d lt., U.S. Army, 1929, ret. maj. gen. Air Force; instr. Kelly Field, Tex., 1931; engr. officer and armament officer, Luke Field, Hawaii, 1931-32; instr. Randolph Field, Tex., 1933; engr. officer and test pilot, Wright Field, 1938-43; chief U.S. Air Tech. Sect., Eng., 1943, comdr. 44th Bomb group, Eng., 1943-44, comdr. 95th Bomb Wing, 1944, wounded and returned to U.S.; chief aircraft div. A.A.F. Bd., Orlando, Fla., 1944-45, chief engring. br., material div. A.A.F. Hdqrs., Washington, 1945; chief, aircraft and physical requirements sub-div., Wright Field, 1945-47, chief equipment lab., 1947, asst. to chief, engring. div., 1947-48, chief operations engring. div., 1948-49, dep. chief, engring. div., 1949-50, chief, 1950-51, comdg. gen. Wright Air Development Center, 1951-52; mil. dir. production and requirements Munitions Board, 1952-53; Commander Mobile Air Materiel Area, Brookley AFB, 1953-57, ret.; program manager of missile The Martin Co., Baltimore. Decorated the Silver Star, Legion of Merit, D.S.M., D.F.C., Air medal with 1 Oak Leaf Cluster, Commendation ribbon, Purple Heart (United States); Croix de Guerre with palm (Belgium); Croix de Guerre with palm (France). Mem. com. on operating problems NACA, 1947-51. First glider pilot in Air Force. Home: Towson MD Died Sept. 11, 1969.

DENTON, J. FURMAN, banker; b. Elizabeth, N.J., 1914; grad. summa cum laude N.Y.U., 1943; m. Doris Henn; children—John F., Mrs. John J. Beck. With 1st Nat. Bank N.J., 1933-70, v.p., 1950-61, exec. v.p., cashier, 1961-70. Tchr. Seton Hall U., Am. Inst. Banking. Mem. N.J. (exec. com.), Essex County (past pres.) bankers assns. Home: Bernardsville NJ Died Mar. 1972.

DENTON, LYMAN MORSE, clergyman, educator; b. Nova Scotia, Can., Sept. 9, 1869; s. Kelsey and Mary Emily (Brooks) D.; A.B., Acadia U., 1896, A.M., 1898; B.D., Rochester (N.Y.) Theol. Sem., 1900; Th.D., Kansas City (Kan.) Bapt. Theol. Sem., 1924; D.D., Northern Bapt. Theol. Sem., Chicago, Ill., 1927; m. Agnes Stevens Merryman, of Lincoln, Neb., Sept. 3, 1901. Came to U.S., 1897. Ordained ministry Bapt. Ch., 1900; successively pastor Second Ch., Lincoln, Neb., Edgerton Place Ch., Kansas City, Kan., and First Ch., Montreal, Can., until 1916; prof. Greek interpretation and pub. speaking, Kansas City Bapt. Theol. Sem., 1916-27, pres., 1927-35; minister First Bapt. Ch., Bellflower, Calif., since 1935. Mem. Am. Research Soc., Pi Gamma Mu. Rotarian. Author: The Structure of The Book and Its Books, 1927; Travel in Europe, Palestine and Egypt, 1929. Home: La Habra CA‡

DENTON, WINFIELD K., lawyer; born Evansville, Ind., Oct. 28, 1896; s. George K. and Sara Linda (Chick) D.; A.B., DePauw U.; LL.B., Harvard; m. Grace Abernethy, Dec. 27, 1927; children—Beth (Mrs. Jim Bamberger), Mary, Sara (Mrs. D. Ong). Admitted to Ind. bar, and practiced in Evansville; prosecutor Vanderburgh County, Ind.; mem. Ind. State Legislature, caucus chmn., 1939, minority leader, 1941; mem. 81st, 82d, 84th-89th U.S. Congresses, from eighth congressional district Indiana; attorney at law Denton and Gerling. Served as 2d lieutenant, Aviation Corps, U.S. Army, World War I, from maj. to lt. col., USAAF, World War II; judge adv. gen. dept. Mem. Am. Legion, Vets. Fgn. Wars, Phi Kappa Psi. Democrat. Mason (32 deg., K.T., Shriner). Elk. Home: Evansville IN Died Nov. 2, 1971.

DE PARIS, WILBUR, orch. leader, trombonist; b. Crawfordsville, Ind., Sept. 20, 1900; s. Sidney Gibney and Frances (Hyatt) de P.; grad. Crawfordsville High Sch., 1919; m. Barbara Nickerson, Oct. 30, 1958 (div. 1968); children—Steven, Melanie, Todd, Karen. Played with father's band, 1907-17, Original Blue Rythm Band, 1931, Benny Carter, 1930, Noble Sissle, 1931-32, Teddy Hill, 1938, Louis Armstrong, 1938-49; Ella Fitzgerald, 1940-41, Duke Ellington, 1945-46; band with brother Sidney de Paris, 1944; played for Guy Lombardo, Jones Beach, N.Y., summer 1965; various shows Midwest and Toronto, Can., 1966; toured Europe, 1961; in Africa for State Dept., 1957; own band at Cannes Festival, 1960; recording artist for Atlantic Records. Mem. Sons of Indiana. Jazz composer. Address: New York City NY Died Jan. 1973.

DEPEW, JOSEPH WILLIAM, lawyer; b. Slater, Mo., Sept. 17, 1889; s. James Pendelton and Emma (Hesser) DeP.; LL.B., Ill. Wesleyan U., 1914; m. Finney Rozetta McKim; 1 dau., Johanna Audre (Mrs. Barry W. McLeane). Admitted to Ill. bar, 1914; practice in Bloomington, 1920-72; mem. firm DePew, Grimes & DePew, 1966-72; asst. states atty. McLean County, 1920-24, states atty., 1928-32; arbitration Indsl. Commn. Ill., 1946-49; mem., atty. War Price and Radion Bd., McLean County, World War II; atty. Twp. of City of Bloomington, 1937-59. Trustee, legal counsel Baby Fold, Normal, Ill., 1946-72; life mem. adv. bd. Salvation Army. Recipient Distinguished Service award City Bloomington, 1969. Served to 2d lt., inf., U.S. Army, 1917-19. Mem. McLean County Bar Assn., Am. Legion, Tau Kappa Epsilon. Republican. Mason. Home: Springfield IL Died Feb. 9, 1972; buried Oak Ridge Cemetery, Springfield IL

DEPPERMANN, WILLIAM HERMAN, pub. relations exec.; b. Indpls., May 15, 1903; s. Otto Frederick and Anna (Klotz) D.; student Ind. U.; m. Margaret Little, Sept. 17, 1937; children—William Herman, Stephen Rolfe, Daniel Robert. Reporter Indpls. Star, 1921-24; advt. mgt., publicity agt. various motion picture theaters, 1925-32; in sales promotion Western Union Telegraph Co., 1932-39; in charge of newsstand promotion Reader's Digest, 1939-42; account exec. Steve Hannagan Pub. Relations; dir. pub. relations Olin Industries, 1951-55; dir. pub. relations Link-Belt Co., 1955-61; account exec. Hill & Knowlton, Inc., 1961-71, v.p. subsidiary H & K Marketing Services Inc. Mem. pub. relations conf. Nat. Safety Council. Author: Shooter's Choice, 1952. Founder, editor, pub. Practical Pub. Relations. Home: Chappaqua NY Died Aug. 8, 1971.

DERBY, DONALD, univ. dean; b. N.Y.C., May 14, 1908; s. Chester Cawthorne and Amy (Holiday) D.; A.B., Bowdoin Coll., 1931; A.M., Harvard, 1934, Ph.D. in History, 1940; m. Cordelia Evelyn Pass, Apr. 13, 1946; children—Cordelia Evelyn, Amy Priscilla. Research, writing Nat. Archives, Washington, 1946-47; dean adminstrn., prof. history Am. U., 1947-69, v.p., dean faculties, 1960-69. Served with Signal Corps, M.I., AUS, 1942-46. Mem. Phi Beta Kappa. Contbr. articles profl. jours. Home: Washington DC Died July 10, 1969; buried GeHysburg Nat. Cemetery.

DERLETH, AUGUST (WILLIAM), author; b. Sauk City, Wis., Feb. 24, 1909; s. William Julius and Rose Louise (Volk) D.; B.A., U. Wis., 1930; m. Sandra Evelyn Winters, Apr. 6, 1953 (div. Mar. 1959); children—April Rose, Walden William. Began writing, 1922; lectr. Am. regional lit., U. Wis., 1940-43; editor, dir. Arkham House, Publishers, Mycroft and Moran, Stanton and Lee, Sauk City, Wis., spl. lectr. U. Wis., 1958-71. Recipient golden anniversary poetry award Midland Authors, 1965; governor's award for service to the creative arts, 1966. Mem. Midland Authors, The Cliffdwellers' Club, The Fortean Soc., Poetry Soc. of Am., P.E.N., Baker Street Irregulars, Am. Folklore Soc., Author's Guild, Nat. Audubon Soc., Ornithologists Union, Wis. Hist. Soc. Author numerous books, 1934-71, latest being: The Country of The Hawk, 1952; The Captive Island, 1952; Three Problems for Solar Pons, 1952; Fell Purpose, 1953; Design for Death, 1953; Empire of Fur, 1953; The Land of Grey Gold, 1954; Land of Sky Blue Waters, 1955; (poems) Rendezvous in a Landscape, 1952; Psyche, 1953; The House of Moonlight, 1953; Father Marquette and the Great Rivers, 1955; St. Ignatius and the Company of Jesus, 1956; Country Poems, 1956; The Survivor and Others (with H.P. Lovecraft), 1957; Columbus and the New World, 1957; The House on the Mound, The Mask of Cthulhu, The Moon Tenders, The Return of Solar Pons, 1958; The Mill Creek Irregulars, 1959. Editor vols. including: Beyond Time and Space, 1950; Far Boundaries, 1951; The Outer Reaches, 1951; Night's Yawning Peal, 1952; Beachheads in Space, 1952; Worlds of Tomorrow, 1953; Time to Come, 1954; Portals of Tomorrow, 1954; Wilbur The Trusting Whippoorwill (with Dwig), 1959; The Hills Stand Watch, 1960; West of Morning, 1960; The Pinkertons Ride Again, 1960; Wiconsin In Their Bones, 1961, The Ghost of Black Hawk Island, Walden West, The Reminiscenses of Solar Pons, Fire and Sleet and Candlelight, 1961; Sweet Land of Michigan, 1962; The Trail of Cthulhu, 1962; Dark Mind, Dark Heart, 1962; The Wound, 1962; Concord Rebel; A Life of Thoreau, 1962; Lonesome Places, 1962; 100 Books by August Derleth, 1963; The Shadow in the Glass, 1963; The Tent Show Summer, 1963; Countryman's Journal, 1963; When Evil Comes, 1963; Mr. George and Other

Odd Persons, 1963; The Irregulars Strike Again, 1964; Over the Edge, 1964; Forest Orphans, 1964; Wisconsin Country, 1965; The Casebook of Solar Pons, 1965; Praed Street Papers, 1965; Adventure of the Orient Express, 1965; Country Places, 1965; The House by the River, 1965; (with Mark Schorer) Colonel Markesan and Less Pleasant People, 1966; The Only Place We live, 1966; A Wisconsin Harvest, 1966; The Watcher on the Heights, 1966; A House Above Cuzco, 1967; Travellers by Night, 1967; Collected Poems, 1967; By Owl Light, 1967; Wisconsin: A Profile, 1967; Vincennes: Portal to the West, 1968; Wisconsin Murders, 1968; Walden Pond, 1968; Mr. Fairlie's Final Journey, 1968; The Prince Goes West, 1968; A Praed Street Dossier, 1968; The Wind Leans West, 1969; The Three Straw Men, 1969; Caitlin, 1969; A House Above Cuzco, 1969; Emerson, Our Contemporary, 1970; Thirty Years of Arklham House, 1970; Return to Walden West, 1970; The Landscape of the Heart, 1970; Love Letters to Caitlin, 1971; Dark things, 1971; the Chronicles of Solar Pons, 1971; Last Light, 1971; (with H.P. Lovecraft) The Watchers Out of Time and Others, 1972. Lit. editor, columnist Capital Times, Madison, Wis., 1941-71. Editor Hawk & Whippoorwill, 1960-64. Contbr. well-known mags. Home: Sauk City WI Died July 4, 1971.

DERLETH, CHARLES, JR., coll. dean; b. New York, Oct. 2, 1874; s. Charles and Annie (Taubert) D.; B.S., Coll. City of New York, 1894; C.E., Columbia University, 1896; LL.D., University of Calif., 1930; m. Emily Bush, May 19, 1904; children—Charles Edward, Dorothy. Instr. and lecturer, dept. of civ. engring., Columbia, 1896-1901; prof. of civ. engring., U. of Colo., 1901-1903; asso. prof. structural engring., 1903-07, prof. civ. engring. since 1907, dean Coll. of Civ. Engring, 1907-30, dean Coll. of Engring., 1930-42, U. of Calif. Cons. engr. U. of Calif., Alameda County, San Francisco Civic Center; chief engr. Carquinez Strait Highway Bridge; cons. engr. Oakland Estuary Tunnel, Golden Gate Bridge, San Francisco-Oakland Bay Bridge, Broadway Tunnels, Oakland, California. Mem. Am. Soc. C.E., Am. Soc. Testing Materials, Soc. Promotion Engring. Edn., Seismol. Soc. America, Internat. Assn. Testing Materials, Pacific Assn. Cons. Engrs., Am. Philos. Soc., Phi Gamma Delta, Phi Beta Kappa, Sigma Xi, Tau Beta Pi. Clubs: Engineers' (San Francisco); Claremont Country (Oakland). Home: 2834 Webster Berkeley 5 CA‡

DERR, HOMER MUNRO, engineering geologist; b. Turbotville, Pa., Feb. 5, 1877; s. John Frederick and Sarah (Houseknecht) D.; student U. of Mich., U. of Minn., Mich. Coll. of Mines; A.B., Stanford 1898; scholar in geology, Columbia, 1899, A.M., 1901; Ph.D., U. of Pa., 1903; m. Anna Laurie Stacy, Apr. 1, 1903; children—Coralie, Stacy. Asst. in physics, Columbia, 1899-1901; instr. mining engring. and geology, U. of Wyo., 1901-02; Tyndale fellow in physics, U. of Pa., 1902-03; supt. mines, Santa Margarita Gold Mining Co., Colombia, S.A., 1903-04; prof. of mathematics and civil engring. Clarkson College of Technology, 1904-06; professor civil engineering, S. Dak. State Coll., 1906-13; state engr., S. Dak., 1913-21; prof. mathematics, Ala. Poly Inst., 1921-22; prof. mathematics and engring., Southwestern Presbyn. U., 1922-25; prof. mathematics and engring., State College, West Virginia, 1925-33. Mathematician, Douglas Aircraft Co. 1942-45. Engineer S.D. Bd. of Railroad Commrs., 1908-10; sec. S.D. Highway Commn., 1917-19; mem. Commn. to Investigate Feasibility of Power Project at Big Bend (Missouri River), 1917; mem. Commn. to Report on Drainage and Prevention of Overflow in Valley of Red River of the North, 1917. Conducted survey leading to Angostura Irrigation Project (100,000 acres), in South Dakota. Mem. Am. Soc. C.E., Mathematical Association of America, Chi Beta Chi, Beta Kappa Chi. Author: Siliceous Oolites of Sweetwater County, Wyo., 1902; A Method of Petrographic Analysis, 1903; Biennial Reports of the State Engineer of S.D., 1914, 16, 18; Plane Trigonometry (with B. H. Crenshaw), 1923; Key to Plane Trigonometry, 1928; also examinations and reports on various mines in Calif., Ariz., Nev., Ida., Wyo., Colo., and Mexico. Expert rifleman," Nat. Rifle Assn. Home: 16113 S. Caress Av., Compton CA‡

DERRICK, SAMUEL MELANCHTHON, prof. economics; b. Chapin, S.C., May 13, 1896; s. Noah Samuel and Mary Aquilla (Frick) D.; A.B., Newberry Coll., 1917, M.A., U. of S.C., 1920, Ph.D., U. of N.C., 1931; m. Blanche Mildred Stuckey, Dec. 29, 1921; 1 dau., Dorothy. Prin. Ballentine pub. sch., 1917-18; U.S. Navy, June 1918-Feb. 1919; supt., Pelzer public sch., 1920-23; asso. prof., econs., Univ. of S.C., 1923-24, prof., econs., from 1924; dean Sch. Bus. Adminstrn. from 1946; vis. prof. Grad. Sch. of Bus. Adminstrn., Harvard, 1950; editor, U. Weekly News, 1925-27; research asso., S.C. Tax Commn., 1932; editorial contbr., Columbia Record, 1931-42; dir. research and statistics (part time) S.C. Unemployment Commission, 1937-43; prin. field supervisor of War Manpower Commn., Region 7, 1943-44; asso. editor, South Carolina Mag., from 1945; consultant S.C. State Planning Bd., 1939; chmn. Mediation com., S.C. dept. of labor, 1939; mem. legislative com. of 9 on S.C. revenue and taxation, 1939; mem. legislative com. of 9 on Employment Compensation, 1941; principal field supervisor of War Manpower Commn., Region VII, 1943-44; mem. City Planning Commn., Columbia; mem. Richland Co. S.C. Def. Council. Mem. Am., So. econ. assns., Phi Beta Kappa. Democrat. Lutheran. Club: Kosmos. Author hist. publ., various bulls. Home: Columbia SC Died Feb. 7, 1969; buried Greenlawn Cemetery, Columbia, S.C.

DERTHICK, HENRY J., educator; b. Bedford, O., Oct. 23, 1872; s. James Warren and Alice M. D.; grad. high sch., Bedford, O., 1887; A.B., Hiram (O.) Coll., 1897; A.M., U. of Mich., 1912; studied Columbia, 1918, 31, 42; married Perl S., Nov. 17, 1897; children—Francis Leigh, Lawrence G., Sargent F. (dec.), Roger Henry. Teacher pub. schools, Cleveland, 1890-93; minister West Boulevard Ch., Cleveland, 1897-98; teacher mountain schs., Ky., 1898-1909, mountain schs. of Tenn., 1909, 13; supt. social welfare work, Indianapolis, Ind., 1913-17; pres. Milligan Coll., 1917-40, emeritus; now pres. Facing Forward, Incorporated, a movement for vocational guidance in high schools. Travelled abroad, 1928, 30. Mem. Christian Ch. Rotarian. Home: Elizabethton TN‡

DE SALVIO, ALFONSO, coll. prof.; b. Orsara di Puglia, Italy, July 13, 1873; s. Antonio and Antonia (Terlizzi) De S.; Internat. Coll., Springfield, Mass.; A.B., Trinity, Conn., 1889; A.B., Harvard, 1902, A.M., 1903, Ph.D., 1904; student U. of Paris; m. Marion Gertrude Smith, of Hartford, Conn., July 7, 1913 (died Jan. 17, 1927). At Northwestern U. since 1904; prof. Romance lang., 1917—. Mem. Modern Lang. Assn. of America, Modern Lang. Teachers' Assn. Club: University (Evanston). Edited (with intro., notes and vocabulary) Tamayo's Lo Positivo (with Dr. Philip Harry), 1908; Fogazzaro's Pereat Rochus, 1909. Translated from the Spanish, DeQuiros' Modern Theories of Criminology, 1911, from Italian and Latin, Dialogues Concerning Two New Sciences, by Galileo Galilei (with Prof. H. C. Crew), 1914. Address: University Club, Evanston IL‡

DE SAULLES, CHARLES AUGUST HECKSCHER, former pres. U.S. Zinc Co.; b. Hutton Park, West Orange, N.J., Nov. 22, 1876; s. Arthur Brice and Catherine M. (Heckscher) deS.; Ph.B., Yale, 1899; m. Louise Hoch, of Marshall, Mich., Sept. 1905; m. 2d, Ann Barnitz, Jan. 1922. In employ N.J. Zinc Co., 1899, later gen. mgr. of South West dept. of the co.; pres. U.S. Zinc Co. until 1928. Democrat. Episcopalian. Clubs: Bankers, Yale, Racquet and Tennis. Home: The Box, Westbury, LI NY‡

DESIDERIO, ANTHONY, chmn. pres. Whippany Paper Board Co., Inc. Home: West Orange NJ Died Sept. 1970.*

DESLOGE, JOSEPH, engineer; b. St. Louis, Jan. 26, 1889; s. Firmin and Lydia (Davis) D.; A.M., St. Louis U., 1909; B.S., Mass. Inst. Tech., 1912; m. Anne Farrar, Oct. 10, 1922 (dec.); children—Joseph, Anne (Mrs. Louis Werner, II), Bernard, Zoe (Mrs. Samuel Fordyce); m. 2d, Marie Saalfrank, October 26, 1953. Pres. Killark Electric Mfg. Co. since 1913; pres. Minerva Oil Co. from 1940; v.p. Chemalloy Foundry Co. from 1945; dir. St. Joseph Lead Co. Pres. United Charities, 1942-43. Served as lt. French Army, World War I. Decorated Croix de Guerre, Legion of Honor (France); named Papal Chamberlain. Mem. Mo. Hist. Soc. (past pres.), St. Louis Acad. Sci. (past pres.), A.A.A.S., Am. Inst. Mining and Metall. Engrs., Am. Geog. Soc. Home: Florissant MO Died Mar. 11, 1971.

DESMOND, THOMAS CHARLES, retired engr.; b. Middletown, N.Y., Sept. 15, 1887; s. Thomas Henry and Katherine (Safried) D.; A.B. magna cum laude, Harvard, 1908; S.B. in C.E., Mass. Inst. Tech., 1909; L.H.D., Union Coll., 1939; m. Alice B. Curtis, Aug. 16, 1923. Engaged in constrn. work in various parts of U.S., 1909-14; pres. T. C. Desmond & Co., engrs. and contractors, N.Y. from 1914, pres. Colonial Terraces Corp. Mem. N.Y. State Senate, 1930-58. Nat. treas. Roosevelt Non-Partisan League, 1916; pres. N.Y. Young Republican Club, 1926-29; del. Rep. Nat. Conv., Kansas City, Mo., 1928, Phila., 1940; mem. N.Y. Rep. Co. Com., 1915-30. Trustee or office several profl., sci. or ednl. instns. Mem. bd. mgrs. N.Y. Bot. Garden, N.Y.C. Trustee Theodore Roosevelt Assn.; mem. nat. adv. com. White House Conf. Aging, 1959. Mem. vis. com. bd. overseers dept. of astronomy Harvard; mem. at large nat. council Boy Scouts Am.; mem. adv. bd. Inst. Nutrition Scis., Columbia, 1959; life mem. governing bd. Mass. Inst. Tech. Recipient Silver Antelope award Boy Scouts Am., 1947; Brotherhood Award, 1956, Distinguished Service award N.Y. chpt. N.Y. Soc. Profl. Engrs., 1958; 1957 annual award Gerontological Research Found.; N.Y. State YMCA youth and govt. award, 1958; 1959 Ann. War Meml. award N.Y. Young Rep. Clubs, Eloise Payne Luauer medal, Garden Club Am., 1961. Mem. Nat. Geriatrics Soc. (hon.), Am. Astron. Soc., Astron. Soc. of the Pacific, Nat. Municipal League, State Soc. Profl. Engineers, C. of C. State New York, Acad. Scis., Am. Acad. Polit. and Social Sci., Royal Astron. Soc. of Can., Harvard Engring. Soc., Am. Soc. C.E. (life), Nat. Inst. Social Scis., A.A.A.S., Phi Beta Kappa, Phi Beta Kappa Assos., Sigma Alpha Epsilon. Mason (K.T.), Elk. Clubs: Newburgh City, Powelton; University, Union League, Union, Engineers, Harvard, Technology, Tuxedo, City, Century, Explorers (N.Y.C.); Harvard (Boston). Fort Orange (Albany); Adirondack; Lake Placid. Contbr. articles to mags. Owner and developer pvt. arboretum containing nearly 800 species trees and shrubs. Recipient medal award Fed. Garden Clubs of N.Y. State, 1950; large gold medal award Mass. Hort. Soc., 1950; Mass. Inst. Tech. Silver Stein Award, 1952; N.Y. Hort. Soc. Amateur award, 1971. Address: Newburgh NY Died Oct. 7, 1972; buried Fairfield CT

DESPRES, EMILE, economist; b. Chgo., Sept. 21, 1909; s. Emile and Irma Helen (Rosenthal) D.; student Riverdale (N.Y.) Country Sch., 1922-25; S.B., Harvard, 1930, resident cons. Grad. Sch. Pub. Adminstrn., 1937-38; L.H.D., Williams Coll., 1970; m. Joanna Hitt Eakin, Dec. 22, 1939; children—Lani (Mrs. David A. Burack), John, Charles. Spl. fgn. exchange analyst Fed. Res. Bank., N.Y.C., 1930-37, Held fgn. research div., 1938-39; econ. adviser to chmn. bd. govs. Fed. Res. System, Washington, 1939-41; mem. bd. analysts, dir. econ. divs., alternate mem. joint intelligence staff U.S. Joint Chiefs Staff, O.S.S., 1941-44; adviser on German econ. affairs Dept. State, 1944-45; mem. faculty Williams Coll., 1946-61, prof. econs., chmn. dept. 1950-61; prof. econs., Stanford, 1961-73; vis. research prof. Brookings Instn., 1967-68. Mem. financial adv. mission Chinese Nat. Govt., 1941; mem. Am. del. to Potsdam Conf., 1945, office program rev. E.C.A., Paris, summer 1948; attached to Am. Embassy, Belgrade, for econ. aid program to Yugoslavia, summer 1951; fiscal and monetary advisor Pakistan Planning Bd., 1955-56, dir. Inst. Devel. Econs., Karachi, Pakistan, 1959-64. Mem. Council Fgn. Relations, Am. Econ. Assn. Club: Century Assn. Home: Portola Valley CA Died Apr. 1973.

DESSAR, LEO CHARLES, lawyer; b. Cincinnati; s. Dr. Julius H. D.; ed. in Cincinnati and Columbia Coll. Law School; admitted to N.Y. bar, 1870. Assemblyman, 1875; civil justice, 11th jud. dist., 1885; trustee Colonial Trust Co. Democrat. Author: A Royal Enchantrees, 1900. Residence: 238 W. 72d St. Office: 261 Broadway, NY‡

DESSES, JEAN, fasion designer; born Alexandrie, Egypt, Aug. 6, 1904; s. Jean Demitri and Verginie (Benachi) D.; student Alexandrie Greek Sch.; LL.B., U. Paris, Alexandrie br., 1926; unmarried. Left study of law and became designer for the Haute Couture Houses of Paris, 1926-36; opened own house, 1936; presents 2 Am. collections in addition to 4 Paris collections, N.Y. City, bi-annually. Trustee Jean Desses Societe. Recipient Knickerbocker Ball Gown of the Year Award, 1949. Mem. Council of Direction Chambre Syndical De La Couture Parisienne, Cercle Des Echanges Artistiques, Am. C. of C. in France, French C. of C. of the U.S., Inc., Chambre De Commerce Francaise D'Italie, Chambre De Commerce Francaise De Grande-Bretagne, Chambre De Commerce Francaise De Belgique, Am. Soc. Composers. Mem. Greek Orthodox Ch. Clubs: Internationaux (Paris); Yacht (Alexandrie). Home: Paris France Died Aug. 1970.

DETCHON, ADELAIDE, poet; b. in Ohio; d. Rev. Horace and Lorinda Knox (Davis) D.; ed. Cleveland and abroad; unmarried. Appeared in lyrical recitals throughout Great Britain, France, Sweden, Australia; received diamond decorations from univs. of Edinburgh, Glasgow and St. Andrew's in recognition of her spontaneous powers; gave farewell evening, World's Woman's Congress, Chicago Expn., 1893; began writing poems, 1903; 1st pub. recital, Greenacre (Me.) Coll. Comparative Religions, 1904. Interested govs., senators and leading citizens of 17 states in cause of nat. bird protection, 1903. Author: (poems) Liberty Found; The Awakening Word; The Soul's Release; The Invisible Sail; The After Story; Misunderstood; The Seeing Eye; etc. Address: 181 Sumner Av., Springfield MA‡

DETELS, MARTIN PAUL, lawyer; b. San Francisco, July 21, 1892; s. Martin Paul and Margaret (Lynch) D.; A.B., U. Santa Clara, 1912; LL.B., Stanford, 1915; LL.M., Columbia, 1916; m. Mary Janice Crooker, June 30, 1934; children—Martin Paul, Michael, Peter, Roger, Terry Stephen. Admitted to Cal. bar, 1915, N.Y. bar, 1923, Ct. Appeals 2d Circuit, 1929, U.S. Supreme Ct., 1937; practice in N.Y.C., 1923-71; average adjuster Geo. E. Billings Co., 1917, 1921; 21; asso. Bigham, Englar, Jones & Houston, 1922-25, partner, 1926-71. Police justice, Plandome, N.Y., 1945-50. Served with Signal Corps, U.S. Army, 1917-18. Mem. Am., N.Y. State bar assns., Maritime Law Assn., U.S. (past mem. exec. com.), Assn. Average Adjusters U.S. (past chmn.), Down Town Assn., Am. Legion Manhasset, The Lambs, Delta Tau Delta, Phi Alpha Delta. Roman Catholic. Clubs: India House, University Plandome NY Died Mar. 30, 1971; buried Greenwood Cemetery, Brooklyn NY

DETHMERS, JOHN R., judge; b. Plessis, Ia., Oct. 15, 1903; s. Roy P. and Agnes (DeRoos) D.; student Northwestern Classical Acad., Orange City, Ia., 1917-21; Hope Coll., Holland, Mich., 1921-24, LL.D., 1954; LL.B., U. of Mich., 1927, LL.D., 1959; J.D., Detroit College Law, 1947, LL.D., 1967; married Aleen DeJong, April 4, 1931; children—John Robert, David

Conrad, Marjorie Aleen. Admitted to Michigan bar, 1927; in practice of law, Holland, Michigan, 1927-45; pros. attorney, Ottawa Co., Mich., 1931-38; chief asst. atty. gen. of Mich., 1943-44; atty. gen. of Mich., 1945-46; apptd. Supreme Court of Michigan, 1946, first permanent chief justice, 1956-62, chief justice, 1967-70; practiced law, Muskegon, Mich., 1970-71. Chmn. Rep. State Central Com., 1942-45. Mem. Am. Bar Assn. (vice chmn. sect. jud. adminstrn. 1959-63), Am. Judicature Soc. (chmn. bd. 1961-63), Nat. Conf. Chief Justices (chmn. 1957-58), Scribes, Delta Theta Phi. Presbyn. K.P. Mason, Rotarian. Author articles in field. Home: Lansing MI Died Nov. 1, 1971.

DETWEILER, A(LBERT) HENRY, educator; b. Perkasie, Pa., Oct. 4, 1906; s. Wm. H. and Lillian M. (Myers) D.; B.Arch., U. of Pa., 1930; m. Catharine S. Bunnell, Feb. 7, 1939; children—John H., Katharine D., Alice M., Mary S. Architect and archaeologist Univ. Museum, Tell Billa, Iraq, 1930-31; student Am. Sch. Oriental Research, Jerusalem, 1932-35, archtl. fellow, 1933-35; architect and archaeologist Tell Beit Mirsim, Gerasa, Bostra, Samaria, 1933-35; Yale, Dura Europos, 1935-37; Mich., Seleucia-on-the Tigris, fall 1936; asst. on survey Mosque d'Juma, Isfahan, summer 1936; asst. in research, Yale, 1937-39; mem. faculty Cornell since 1939, prof. architecture, 1948-56; asso. dean Coll. Architecture, Cornell, 1956-70; Langley scholarship Am. Inst. Architects, Eng., 1947; acting dir. Am. Sch. Oriental Research, Jerusalem, summer 1949, dir. 1953-54, president, 1955-66, trustee, 1955-66, life trustee, 1966-70; mem. Jerusalem Sch. Com., 1951-54; vis. prof. Roman archaeology Am. Sch. in Jerusalem, Jan. 1951; Haskell lectr. Oberlin Grad. Sch. Theology, 1964; Guggenheim fellow in Italy, 1961-62; associate director of Cornell-Harvard Expdn. to Sardis, 1958-70; archaeol. adviser Cosa Expdn., Am. Acad. Rome, 1954; mem. nat. com. to decide how to salvage Abu Simbel tombs, Egypt, 1963; mem. com. to survey ancient and medieval monuments in Egypt for Am. Research Inst., Egypt, 1966; mem. U.S. nat. com. Internat. Council Monuments and Sites-Icomas, 1967-70. Fellow A.I.A.; mem. Am. Inst. Archaeology, Soc. Archtl. Historians (1st v.p.), DeWitt Hist. Soc., N.Y. State Assn. Architects. Democrat. Unitarian. Clubs: Statler (Ithaca); Cornell (N.Y.C.). Author: Manual Archaeological Surveying, 1948. Contbr. articles in profl. publs.; chpts. and drawings in books. Home: Ithaca NY Died Jan. 30, 1970; buried Perkasie PA

DEUTSCH, HENRY, lawyer; b. Minneapolis, Aug. 28, 1874; s. Jacob and Malchen Amelia (Valfer) D.; ed. pub. schs., Minneapolis; grad. Minneapolis Central High Sch., 1891, Law Sch. Univ. of Minn., LL.B., 1894, law dept. Yale, LL.M., 1895; m. Phila., May 2, 1898, Grace A. Levi. Admitted to Minn. bar, 1895, and since in practice at Minneapolis; now mem. firm Nye & Deutsch. Mem. Commercial Law League of America, Nat. Fraternal Congress, Am. Bar Assn., Minn. State Bar Assn.; del. Universal Congress Lawyers and Jurists, St. Louis, 1904. Mason (32 deg.), K. C. C. H. Club: Minneapolis Commercial (2d v.p. and dir.). Christian Scientist. Republican. Residence: 2705 Fremont Av. S. Office: N. Y. Life Bldg., Minneapolis‡

DEUTSCHER, ISAAC, author; b. 1907; ed. Cracow, Poland. Journalist, Polish Press, 1924-39; mem. Polish Communist Party, editor Communist Press, 1926-32; Polish corr., London, Eng., 1939; mem. editorial staff The Economist, 1942-49, The Observer, 1942-47, European Corr., 1946-47, The Reporter, 1949-61. Author: The Moscow Trial, 1936; Stalin—A Political Biography, 1949; Soviet Trade Unions, 1950; Russia—What Next?, 1953; Russia After Stalin, 1953; The Prophet Armed, 1954; Heretics and Renegades, 1955; Russian in Transition, 1957; Tragedie du communisme polonais entre deux guerre, 1958; The Prophet Unarmed, 1959; The Great Contest: Russia and the West, 1960; The Prophet Outcast, 1963; co-author: The Era of Violence, 1960. Editor: The Age of Permanent Revolution, 1964; Three Currents in Communism, 1964; Maoism, 1964; Unfinished Revolution: Russia 1917-67, 1967; The Non-Jewish Jew, 1968; Lenin's Childhood, 1970; Russia, China and the West, 1970; Marxism in Our Time, 1970. Home: London England Died Aug. 19, 1967.

DEVAN, HARRIET BEECHER SCOVILLE, educator; b. Norwich, Conn.; d. Rev. Samuel and Harriet Eliza (Beecher) Scoville; g. d. Henry Ward Beecher; B.A., Wellesley Coll., 1883; m. at Stamford, Conn., Spencer Cone Devan, June 19, 1888 (died 1893). Propr. and head of Catharine Aiken Sch., Stamford, Conn., since 1896. Congregationalist. Mem. D.A.R. Address: Stamford CT‡

DEVANEY, MICHAEL R., milling exec.; b. Boston, Oct. 2, 1876; s. Martin and Mary (Mitchell) D.; m. Nina Parker, June 14, 1904; children—Ruth M., John Parker. Sch. tchr., Waseca, Minn., 1898-1900; pvt. sec. G.N. Ry., 1900-02; mgr. Lyon Electric Co., Mpls., 1902-09, Occident Electric Co., 1909-47; v.p. in charge all grain divs. Russell-Miller Milling Co., Mpls., since 1947, also chmn. Mem. Winnipeg Grain Exchange, Duluth Bd. Trade, Mpls. Grain Exchange, Chgo. Bd. Trade. Club: Minneapolis Pong. Home: Hempshire Arms Hotel. Office: Midland Bank Bldg., Minneapolis 1

DEVILBISS, HOWARD P., chmn. bd. DeVilbiss Co., Toledo; dir. Toledo Trust Co. Home: Toledo OH Died Apr. 1971.

DEVINE, JAMES GASPER, army officer; born Calif., Apr. 19, 1895; grad. Coast Arty. Sch., 1924, Advanced Course, 1932. Commd. 2d lt. C.A.C., Calif. Nat. Guard, May 1915; 1st lt. and capt., Calif. Nat. Guard, World War I; advanced through the grades, U.S. Army, to brig. gen., C.A., Mar. 1943. Address: Fishers Island NY Died 1972.

DEVINE, JOHN M., ret. army officer; b. Providence, June 18, 1895; s. Patrick and Bridget (Nangle) D.; B.S., U.S. Mil. Acad., 1917; M.S., Yale U., 1922; grad. Field Arty. Sch., 1929, Command and Gen. Staff Sch., 1938; m. Anne C. Whitelegg, May 15, 1918; children—Austin, Ruth Mildred, Dorothy Anne, Donald Whitelegg. Commd. 2d lt., 1917; promoted through grades to maj. gen. (temp.), May 2, 1945, permanent, 1948; asst. prof. English, U.S. Mil. Acad., Aug. 1932-June 1936; asst. prof. mil. science and tactics, Yale U., July 1938-July 1940; with Armored Force since July 1940, overseas (Europe) with 90th Div. Arty., became comdg. gen., 8th Armored Div., Oct. 1944; comdg. gen. Universal Mil. Training Exptl. Unit, Fort Knox, Ky., 1946-47; chief of staff of Army Ground Forces, dep. chief Army Field Forces, 1948; comdg. gen. 1st Cav. Div., 1949, 9th Div., 1950; chief Information and Edn. Div., Office Sec. of Def., 1950-52, ret.; comdt. of cadets Virginia Poly. Inst., 1952-60. Awarded Bronze Star, Silver Star, Legion of Merit, Distinguished Service Medal; French Legion of Honor, Croix d'Guerre; Knight Comdr. with Swords Netherlands Order of Orange-Nassau; War Cross and Order of White Lion (Czechoslovakia). Home: Leesburg VA Died Mar. 8, 1971; buried West Point Cemetery, West Point NY

DE VOE, WALTER, author; b. near Cedar Rapids, Ia., May 11, 1874; m. Pauline Mildred Chapman, of New Cumberland, W. Va. Teacher and lecturer on psychology of religion; founder The Eloist Ministry, 1910. Editor of Inspiration (mag.). Author: Healing Currents, 1904; Mystic Words, 1905; The Doors of Life, 1909. Home: 306 Riverway, Boston MA‡

DEVOORE, ANN (MRS. REGINALD PRESCOTT WALDEN), author; b. New York, N.Y., Sept. 16, 1872; d. Ulysses Doubleday and Jane (Brevoort) Eddy; m. at Mamaroneck, N.Y., Reginald Prescott Walden, Dec. 20, 1900; children—Jorne Brevoort, Anne Townsend, Caroline Walden (Mrs. Daniel McCory), Rosamond Prescott. Author: Oliver Iverson—His Adventures During Four Days and Nights in the City of New York, in April of the Year 1890, 1899; The Whip Hand, 1897; The Stolen Saint, 1899; The Kentucky Heiress, 1898; On the Trail of a Go-Cart, 1904; His Sporting Aunt; With Molly and the Birds. Also other stories and poems. Home: Mamaroneck NY‡

DE VORE, REBECCA JANE, college pres.; b. Georgetown, O., d. David G. and Rebecca (Murray) D.; A.B., Glendale (O.) Coll., 1879; studied under pvt. tutelage at Cincinnati, New York, and Berlin, Germany; unmarried. Teacher in pub. schs., Georgetown, O., 1879-82; prof. mathematics, Glendale Coll., 1882-86; dean Oxford (O). Coll., 1886-91; prof. English, Miss Dana's Sch., Morristown, N.J., 1892-94; pres. Pa. Coll., Pittsburgh, 1894-1900; traveled and studied in Europe, 1900-01; pres. Glendale Coll., 1901-20. Actively interested in social service, Y.W.C.A., civic and polit. affairs, in promotion of movement for better speech, in the integrity of the Constitution of the U.S., and has delivered many lectures for same. First v.p. Southwest Dist. Ohio Fed. Women's Clubs: mem. League of Women Voters, D.A.R., Peace League. Democrat. Presbyn. Club: Cincinnati Woman's; founder The Colloquium (Pa. Coll.) and Glendale College Club. Home: 1814 Hewitt Av., E. Walnut Hills, Cincinnati OH‡

DE WAHA, BARON RAYMOND, diplomat; b. Luxembourg, May 16, 1877; s. Baron Mathias and Augusta (de Colnet-d'Huart) de W.; ed. Gymnase, Luxembourg; univs. of Freiburg, Munich and Paris; Dr. rerum politicarum, from U. of Munich, 1902; m. Alix de la Kethulle, of Belgium, Dec. 30, 1922. Began as charge d'affaires, at Munich, Bavaria, 1910; mem. Chamber of Deputies, Grand-duchy of Luxembourg, 1919-20; minister of agr., industry and labor, 1920-24; charge d'affaires of Luxembourg at Washington, D.C., since Sept. 12, 1920; pres. Social Ins. Corpns., and Social Ins. Instns., Grand-duchy of Luxembourg. Grand Officer Order of Leopold (Belgian); of the Crown of Italy; Comdr. Legion of Honor (French). Catholic. Author: Finanz politik der Franzosischen Revolution, 1903; Nationalokonomie in Frankreich, 1910. Address: Legation of Luxembourg, Washington DC‡

DEWART, FREDERICK WESLEY, lawyer; b. Bradford, Ontario, Canada, July 19, 1867; son of James Hartley (Doctor of Divinity) and Mary (Day) D.; A.B., Harvard Univ., 1890, A.M., 1892; LL.B., St. Louis Law School, Washington U., 1895. Began practice in St. Louis, 1894; at Spokane, Wash., 1899-1924; at Washington, D.C., 1924-37; spl. atty. with gen. counsel Bur. of Internal Revenue; spl. asst. to attorney general; tax counsel with Herzbrun & Chantry, Los Angeles, California, 1937-41; retired, 1942; with Library of Congress since 1943. Member Am. Society of Book Plate Collectors (Washington), American Book Plate Society, Shakespeare Society, The Print Makers Soc. Republican. Epsicopalian. Mason (32 deg., Shriner). Club: University (Washington). Address: 2722 Ontario Road N.W., Washington 8 DC‡

DEWEERD, JAMES A., clergyman; b. Olivet, Ill., May 23, 1916; s. Fred and Lelia Z. (Benedict) DeW.; student Marion Coll., M.A., Ball State U., 1967; A.B. Taylor U., 1937. D.D., 1949; postgrad. Cambridge U. (Eng.), 1958; m. Mildred J. Geyer, June 5, 1963. Pub. speaker evangelist, lectr. 1937-72; pres. Christian Witness Assn., editor monthly publ. The Christian Witness 1947-57; pres. Kletzing Coll. (now Vennard Coll.), 1949-51; daily broadcast and weekly TV over WLW. Cin., 1952-57; chaplain gen. S.A.R., 1969-71. Sec. bd. edn. pub. schs., Fairmount, 1946-49; chmn. Jay County (Ind.) United Fund Drive, 1969-1970, bd. dirs., 1967-72; chmn. Juvenile Delinquency Study Commn., State of Ind., 1952-56. Pres. bd. trustees Bethany (Ky.) Children's Home, 1948-57, bd. dirs., 1946-72. Served as chaplain (capt.) U.S. Army, northern France, 1943-45. Recipient Purple Heart, Oak Leaf Cluster, Silver Star; George Washington Honor award Freedoms Found., 1970. Mem. S.A.R. (Gold Good Citizenship medal 1969, Patriot's medal 1970, Minuteman award, 1971), Nat. Assn. Conf. Evangelists (v.p. 1969-72), Nat. Assn. Evangs. (mem. commn. on evangelism and spiritual life), Assn. for Advancement of Ethical Hypnosis, Internat. Platform Assn., N.E.A., Y.M.C.A., Am. Legion, Military Chaplain's Assn. Mason. Author: The Realities of Christian Experience, 1940; Memory is Bitter-Sweet, 1952; Stories My Mother Told Me, 1955; What is Worthwhile, 1970. Address: Pennville IN Died Mar. 28, 1972.

DEWESSE, ARVILLE OTTIS, physician, educator; b. Harrison County, Ind., Aug. 25, 1888; s. Marion Douglas and Emma Francis (Stevens) C.; grad. Ind. State Teachers Coll., 1911; B.S., U. of Louisville, 1918, grad. student, Ind. U., 1919-20; M.D., U. of Louisville, Med. Sch., 1924; m. Vergie Jenkins, July 18, 1911; children—Byrne, Marion Spencer, Harriette Elizabeth, James Arville. County supt. of schools, Corydon, Ind., 1911-18; instr. and asst. prof. of physiology and pharmacology, U. of Louisville Med. Sch., 1918-20, asso. prof., 1920-23, prof. 1923-24; dir. Student Health Service, Kent (O.) State U., 1924-58. Recipient of The Howe School Health Award, 1950. Fellow American Public Health Assn., American Sch. Health Assn. (executive sec.-treas. 1937-69); mem. Amer. Assn. Sch. Physicians (pres. 1933-34), Am. Student Health Assn. (chmn. health edn.in teachers colls.), Ohio Health and Phys. Edn. Assn. (governing council), Ohio Student Health Assn. (pres. 1932-34), Am. Assn. Univ. Profs., Am. Health and Phys. Edn. Assn., A.M.A., N.E.A. Democrat. Methodist. Club: Kiwanis. Contbr. to ednl. jours. Home: Kent OH Died Mar. 10, 1970; buried Standing Rock Cemetery, Kent O.

DEWEY, BYRD SPILMAN, author; b. Covington, Ky.; d. Rev. Dr. J. E. and Eliza Sarah (Taylor) Spilman; is grand-niece of Zachary Taylor ed. Maysville Ky. Acads. Maysville Coll., Maysville Inst., Sayre Inst., Lexington, Ky.; m. Frederick Sidney Dewey, Sept. 25, 1877 (died 1919). Lived during girlhood in Maysville, Ky., in Florida since December 1881. Author: Bruno, 1899; The Blessed Isle and Its Happy Families; 1907; Peter the Tramp, 1907; From Pine Woods to Palm Groves (serial), 1909; Flying Blossom, 1911; Romance of Old Lake Worth Days, 1912; The Tale of Satan, 1913; O, Youth Eternalmuch mag. and newspaper writing under pen names; editor, critic, reviewer, lecturer on conservation, especially bird protection and forestry. Home: 17 Home St., Jacksonville FL‡

DEWEY, THOMAS EDMUND, lawyer; b. Owosso, Mich., Mar. 24, 1902; s. George Martin and Annie (Thomas) D.; A.B., U. Mich., 1923, LL.M., 1937; LL.B., Columbia, 1925; LL.D., Tufts Coll., 1937, Brown U., 1938, Dartmouth, 1939, St. Lawrence U., 1941, N.Y.U., 1942, Union Coll., 1943, Alfred U., 1945, Fordham, 1946, Colgate, 1947, Hamilton Coll., 1947, Columbia, 1947, Williams Coll., 1949, St. Bonaventure, 1950, Yeshiva U., 1951, U. Rochester, 1957; m. Frances E. Hutt, June 16, 1928; children—Thomas E., John Martin. Admitted to N.Y. bar, 1926; asso. Larkin, Rathbone &Perry, 1925-27; with McNamara & Seymour, 1927-31; chief asst. U.S. atty., So. Dist. of N.Y., 1931-33, U.S. atty., 1933; pvt. practice, 1934-35; counsel to Assn. of Bar in N.Y. in removal of Municipal Justice Harold L. Kunstier, 1934; spl. prosecutor Investigation of organized Crime, N.Y., 1935-37; elected dist. atty. N.Y. County, 1937; Republican candidate for gov. State of N.Y., 1938, elected gov., 1942, reelected, 1946, 50; Rep. nominee for pres. U.S., 1944, 48; mem. law firm Dewey, Ballantine, Bushby, Palmer & Wood, N.Y.C., 1955. Awarded Medal for Excellence, Columbia U., in recognition pub. service, 1936; Cardinal Newman Distinguished Service award U. Ill., 1939, various other awards. Trustee N.Y. Heart Assn., N.Y. YMCA, Roosevelt Hosp., N.Y.C. Fellow Am. Coll. Trial Lawyers; mem. Am., N.Y. State bar assns., Assn. Bar City N.Y., N.Y. County Lawyers Assn., Council Fgn. Relations, Pilgrims, Phi Mu Alpha, Phi Delta Phi. Episcopalian. Mason (33). Clubs: Links, Blindbrook, Recess, Downtown Assn., City Midday, Hill; Augusta Nat., Indian Creek. Author: The Case Against the New Deal, 1940; Journey to the Far Pacific, 1952; Thomas E. Dewey on the Two Party System, 1966. Contbr. to mags. Home: New York City NY Died Mar. 16 1971.

DEWILDE, BRANDON, actor; b. N.Y.C., Apr. 9, 1942; s. Frederic and Eugenia (Wilson) deW.; grad. high sch. Broadway appearances include Member of the Wedding, 1950, Mrs. McThing, 1952, The Emperor's Clothes, 1953, Comes a Day, 1958; motion pictures include Shane, 1951, Member of the Wedding, 1952, Night Passage, 1956, Goodbye, My Lady, 1955, The Missouri Traveler, 1957, Blue Denim, 1959; Hud, 1963; In Harms Way, 1965; Race of Hairy Men, 1965, frequent TV appearances, including starring role in Jamie, 1953. Youngest recipient Donaldson award, 1950. Died July 6, 1972.

DEWINDT, HAROLD CLIFFORD, clergyman; b. Grand Rapids, Mich., Jan. 23, 1911; s. Justus Christopher and Amy (Tuinman) DeW.; A.B., Hope Coll., 1933; Th.B., Princeton, 1936; A.M., Columbia, 1941; D.D. (hon.), Trinity U., 1946; LL.D., Parsons Coll., 1958; m. Esther A. Maurits, June 13, 1936; 1 son, David Maurits. Ordained to ministry of Presbyn. Ch., 1936; served as minister First Ch., Morrisville, Pa., 1935-37, Webb Horton Meml. Ch., Middletown, N.Y., 1937-42, West-Park Ch. N.Y.C., 1943-53, Kirk in the Hills, Bloomfield Hills, Mich., 1953-71. Vice-moderator of N.Y. Presbytery, 1953-54; trustee ch. erection fund, Gen. Assembly of Presbyn. Ch. U.S.A., 1951-55; mem. bd. mgrs., joint dept. evangelism, Nat. Council of Chs.; mem. gen. council Synod of Mich., also Presbytery of Detroit. Clubs: Bloomfield Hills Country, Forest Lake Country, Home: Bloomfield Hills MI Died Apr. 17, 1971; inurned Garden of Kirk in the Hills.

DEWING, ARTHUR STONE, utilities exec.; b. Boston, Apr. 16, 1880; s. Charles Hamlet and Eliza Williams Stone (Paine) D.; A.B., Harvard, 1902, A.M., 1903, Ph.D., 1905; postgrad. U. Munich, Germany; m. Frances Hall Rousmaniere, June 3, 1910; children—Mary Stone (Mrs. Lloyd L. Morain), Abigail Starr (Mrs. Stuart B. Avery, Jr.), Ruth Rousmaniere (Mrs. James D. Ewing). Asst. in philosophy, Harvard, 1902-11, instr. in econ., 1911-12, 1919-20, asst. prof. econs., 1920-22, asso. prof. finance, 1922-27, prof., 1927-33; pres. Portland, Chatham, Hazardville and Jewett City Water cos., Ill. Gas Co., Eastern Ill. Gas & Securities Co., Pinetum, Inc. (N.H.), Wetmore Gas Producing Co.; pres. Granite State Gas & Elec. Co., Edward Durant Investment Co.; bd. dirs. Fall River Gas Co., Keene N.H. Sentinel Pub. Co., others; chmn. Old Colony R.R. Bondholders Protective Committee. Mem. of bd. of visitors classical art Boston Museum of Fine Arts. Fellow Am. Acad. Arts, Scis., Am. Numismatic Soc. (Greek numismatics (past pres.), Royal Numismatic Soc.; mem. The Am. Friends of Greece, Mass. Hist. Soc., N.E. Hist. Geneal. Soc., Mass. Soc. Mayflower Descs., Soc. for Preservation of N.E. Antiquities (past pres.), Archeol. Inst. Am. (past pres. Boston soc.). Republican. Author books including: Life as Reality, 1910; Corporate Promotions and Reorganization, 1914, Reprinted in American Life and Culture, 1969; Financial Policy of Corporations, 1920, 5th rev. edit. 1953; The Corporation—A Study of Its Financial Structure, 1934. Address: Cambridge MA Died Jan. 20, 1971.

DE WITT, GEORGE ASHLEY, editor; b. Appleton, Wis., Oct. 22, 1893; s. William George and Nan Frances (Philpot) D.; ed. pub. schs., Fond du Lac, Wis.; m. Ilma Henrietta Spaar, June 21, 1916; children—George Ashley, Clinton William. Began as reporter, Fond du Lac, 1909; city editor Milwaukee (Wis.) Free Press, 1911-12, mng. editor, 1912-14; successively telegraph editor, city editor, day mng. and 1935; mng. editor Washington (D.C.) Herald, 1936-39; mng. editor Washington Times-Herald, 1939-41; organized staff and became first mng. editor of Chicago Sun, 1941; returned as mng. editor Washington Times-Herald, 1942; Sunday Editor Los Angeles Examiner, 1944-46; exec. editor Chicago Herald-American, 1947-52; pres. Washington Printers, Inc., Washington, 1952-54. Clubs: Los Angeles Press, National Press. Home: St Petersburg FL Died Mar. 12, 1973.

DEWITT, JOHN DOYLE, ins. exec.; b. Sully, Ia., June 25, 1902; s. Henry and Lola Belle (Forsyth) DeW.; student Drake U., 1921-24; LL.D., 1955; LL.D. (hon.), Trinity Coll., 1962; L.H.D. (hon.), U. Hartford, 1964; m. Marjorie Aileen Everett, Oct. 3, 1927; children—John Doyle, Patricia Ann (Mrs. Brig Barnum Elliott). Claim adjuster, Travelers Ins. Cos., Hartford, Des Moines office, 1925, transferred to home office, 1927, claim examiner, 1929, asst. mgr. life, accident, and group claim dept., 1933, supervising adjuster in charge met. N.Y., 1937, asst. mgr. home office, 1939; sec. in charge all claim depts. 1943, asst. to pres. 1945, v.p., asst. to pres. Travelers Ins. Co., Travelers Indemnity Co., Travelers Fire Ins. Co., Charter Oak Fire Ins. Co., 1950-52, pres., dir., 1952-64, chmn. bd., chief exec. officer, 1964-68, chairman of the board of directors, 1964-70; pres. Eastern Life Claim Conf., 1939-40; chmn. exec. com. of International Claim Assn. 1942-43, pres., 1943-44; dir. Chase Manhattan Bank, N.A., Hartford Nat. Bank & Trust Company, Veeder Industries, Inc., also So. N.E. Telephone Co., United Aircraft Corp., Trustee Nat. Safety Council, Herbert Hoover Birthplace Found., YMCA Greater Hartford; a founder, regent U. Hartford; corporator Mt. Sinai Hosp.; corporator Saint Francis Hospital; trustee Rensselaer Poly. Inst. Conn., Inc., Hartford Grad. Center; dir. Hartford Hosp. Served in USN, World War I. Recipient of the Freedoms Found. Honor Medal award, 1950; spl. award Conn. League Hist. Socs., 1961; Drake U.'s Alumni Distinguished Service award, 1968. Fellow Am. Numis. Soc.; mem. Hartford C. of C. (Certificate of Merit award), Hartford Numis Soc. Republican. Methodist. Clubs: Hartford, Ekwanok Country, Links, Golf (Hartford); Economic, Twentieth Century, Accident and Health (N.Y.C.); Nat. Golf (Augusta, Ga.). Home: West Hartford CT Died Dec. 27, 1972; buried Fairview Cemetery, West Hartford CT

DE WOSKIN, MORRIS R., hotel broker; b. Gluckow, Russia, Aug. 27, 1903; s. Aaron and Dora (Lewandowsky) De W.; came to U.S., 1917, naturalized, 1938; student LaSalle Extension U., 1922-24. With Carson Pirie Scott & Co., Chgo., 1919, Montgomery Ward and Co., 1919, C.,M. & St.P. R.R., 1919-20; engaged in hotel bus., 1920-25; founder, St.P. R.R., 1919-20; engaged in hotel bus., 1920-25; founder, 1925, since propr. Morris R. DeWoskin & Co., hotel brokerage firm, Chgo.; chmn. bd. Executive House Inc., Chgo., 1961-70; pres. Hotel Claridge, Inc., St. Louis, 1938-70; Midwest Hotels Mgmt., Inc., St. Louis, 1938-70; Aruba Caribbean Hotel Co. (B.W.I.), 1959-70, Surinam Torarica Hotel-Casion Hotel Co. (S.A.), 1962-70; dir. First Comml. Bank Chgo. Chmn. bd. govs. Israel Bond Campaign, Chgo., 1957-58, chmn. campaign, 1955-56; pres. Chgo. chpt. Am. Friends Hebrew U. Jerusalem, 1961-70; v.p. Chgo. U. Found. Emotionally Disturbed Children, 1961-70; vice chmn. Combined Jewish Appeal Chgo., 1960-70. Bd. dirs. Jewish Theol. U. Am., Chgo. Jewish Bd. Edn.; v.p., dir. Am. Friends Hebrew U. Jerusalem. Named Chgo. Man of Year, Chgo. Israel Bond Orgn., 1956, Man of Year, Jewish Nat. Fund, 1963; recipient Aruba medal of merit award, 1960, Community Service award Jewish Theol. Sem., 1960, Community Jewish Appeal award, 1964, Am. award Chgo. Com. 100, 1964. Mem. Ill. Real Estate Bd., Chgo. Assn. Commerce and Industry, Chgo. Bd. Underwriters. Clubs: Covenant (bd. dirs.), Bryn Mawr Country (Chgo.). Home: Chicago IL Died Sept. 20, 1970.

DEWSNUP, ERNEST RITSON, economist; b. Manchester, Eng., Apr. 17, 1874; s. Joseph and Annie (Ritson) D.; B.A., Owens Coll. (Victoria U.), Manchester, 1895. M.A., 1900, Warburton research prizeman, 1902, Stanley Jevons student in economic research, 1903; studied in Paris, 1902; m. Sarah Jane Gibbs, of Swansea, South Wales, June 19, 1897. Head of dept. higher commercial edn. and Sikes lecturer in economics, Tech. Coll., Huddersfield, Eng., 1899-03; lecturer in ry. transport, U. of Manchester, Eng., 1903-4; prof. lecturer in rys. and curator Commercial Mus., U. of Chicago, 1904-7, also sec. advisory bd. ry. edn., Chicago; prof. ry. administration and head of dept. of transportation, U. of Ill., 1907-20; Chaddock prof. of commerce, U. of Liverpool, 1920—. Statis. and finance officer, Dept. of Movements and Rys., War Office, London, 1918-19. Fellow Royal Statis. Soc. of Eng.; mem. Am. Econ. Assn., Authors Club, London, University Club, Liverpool. Author: The Housing Problem in England, 1907; Railway Freight Classification, 1913. Co-Author: The State in Relation to Railways, 1912. Editor and joint author of Railway Organization and Working, 1906; contbr. on transport economics and commerce in general. Address: University of Liverpool, Liverpool England‡

DEXTER, GREGORY MUMFORD, cons. indsl. engr.; b. East Providence, R.I., Oct. 3, 1887; s. Walter Mumford and Emily O. (Potter) D.; C.E., Mass. Inst. Tech., 1908; M.E., Bklyn. Poly. Inst., 1929; m. Katie W. Jaecker, Nov. 24, 1934; children—Gregory Warren, Nancy Lee, Susan Marcy. Draftsman Hazen & Whipple, 1908-10; chief draftsman constrn. Ore. Short Line R.R., 1910-14; jr. engr. U.S. Engrs., Wheeling, W.Va., 1914-16; exec. engr. Honolulu Iron Works Co., 1916-28; engr. Peabody, Smith & Co., 1928-29; v.p. and gen. mgr. Finn, Iffland & Co., 1930-31; engring. asso. Bitting, Inc., 1932-44; in pvt. practice as cons. indsl. engr. since 1944. Fellow Am. Soc. M.E.; mem. Am. Society for Engring. Edn. Clubs: New York Athletic; Scarsdale (N.Y.) Town; Chemists. Contbr. tech. articles on mech. and chem. engring. to jours. Home: Scarsdale NY Died July 20, 1969.

DEYO, DONALD EDMUND, state ofcl., jr. coll. pres.; b. Kewanee, Ill., May 15, 1913; s. Edmund O. and Elsie M. (Searl) D. B.Ed., Ill. State Normal U., 1935; M.A., U. Mich., 1938, Columbia Tchrs. Coll., 1950; grad. student State U. Ia., Pa. State U., Yale; m. Irene G. Johnson, June 10, 1936; 1 son, Philip. Supt. schs., Woodhull, Ill., 1935-38; grad. asst. econs. Pa. State U., 1938-39; head bus. adminstrn., bursar Hillyer Jr. Coll., Hartford, Conn., 1939-43; dir. Walter Hervey Jr. Coll., N.Y.C., 1943-50; editorial dir. jr. coll. program John Wiley & Sons, pubs., 1950-53; dean Montgomery Jr. Coll., Takoma Park, Md., 1953-65; director of master plan study Mass. Board for Regional Community Colleges, Boston, 1965-72; pres. Dean Jr. Coll., Franklin, Mass., 1968-72, pres. emeritus, 1972. Mem. of Gov. Md. Commn. Higher Edn., 1957-60; pres. Md. Assn. Jr. Colls., 1957-58, jr. coll. council Middle Atlantic States, 1958-59; chmn. legislation commn. Am. Assn. Jr. Colls., 1958-59, bd. dirs., 1959-62, v.p., 1962-63, pres., 1963-64. Mem. N.E.A., Assn. Higher Edn., Am. Soc. Engring. Edn., Holland Soc. N.Y. Methodist. Home: Wellesley MA Died Oct. 11, 1972; buried Kewanee IL

DE YOUNG, CHRIS ANTHONY, educator; born Zeeland, Mich., Oct. 2, 1898; s. Christian De Jonge and Adriana (Bouwens) de Jonge; A.B. summa cum laude, Hope Coll., 1920, Litt.D., 1952; A.M., Columba, 1929; Ph.D., Northwestern U., 1932; LL.D., Lincoln (Ill.) Coll., 1949; m. Marion E. Van Drezer, Aug. 26, 1927 (deceased); m. 2d, Mary F. Leenouts, Oct. 8, 1960. Principal Hope High Sch., Madanapalle, India, 1920-24, Fort Elementary Sch., 1920-24; supt. of schs., Hudsonville, Mich., 1924-26, Zeeland, Mich., 1926-30; mem. faculty Northwestern U., 1930-34; head depts. of edn. and psychology Ill. State Normal U., 1934-43, 1952-58, dean of univ. and Grad. Sch. 1943-49, dir. of integration, 1952-58; coordinator pub. and teacher education Commission on Occupied Areas, 1949-50; Fulbright lectr. U. of Delhi, India, 1950-51; educational cons. Presbyterian Ch., Pakistan, 1955; chairman American staff at Rural Education Center, Kampong Kantout, Cambodia, 1958-60; coordinator Grand Valley College, 1960-61; examiner English, University of Madras (India), 1923; lecturer at University of Hawaii, 1963; ednl. consultant Butterworth Hospital Sch. Nursing, from 1961; chmn. Am. team to establish a tchrs. coll. in Cambodia, 1958-60. Member bd. mgrs. Cong. of Parents and Teachers (Mich. and Ill.); ednl. cons. Ill. Postwar Planning Commn., U.S. War Dept. in Germany; coordinator German-Austrian teacher edn. project Am. Assn. of Colls. for Teacher Edn.; lecturer on ednl. and internat. subjects. Bd. dirs. Vols. in Probation; chmn., trustee Grand Rapids Art Mus. trustee Grand Rapids Pub. Library, Urban Renewal, Cultural Commn., Hist. Commn., Porter Hills Retirement Home. Decorated Chevalier de Monisaraphon, Cambodia. Recipient Freedoms Found. award, 1964. Mem. Am. Assn. Sch. Adminstrs., Ill. Schoolmasters Club (past pres.), Phi Delta Kappa (emeritus). Presbyn. Clubs: Torch, Rotary. Author: American Education, 1st edit., 1942, 7th edit., 1972. Home: Grand Rapids MI Died Nov. 24, 1971; buried Zeeland MI

D'HARNONCOURT, RENE, museum director; born Vienna, Austria, May 17, 1901; s. Hubert and Julie (Mittroswky) d'H.; ed. Real Gymnasium and State University, Graz, Austria, and Technische Hochschule, Vienna, Austria; L.H.D., Dartmouth College, 1955, Columbia, 1958; Dr. Fine Arts, Univ. of New Mexico, 1964; m. Sarah Carr, May 29, 1933; one dau., Anne Julie. Came to U.S., 1931, naturalized 1939. Associate in Mexican art store, 1927; dir. exhibition of Mexican art sponsored by Am. Fedn. of Art, 1930-32; instr. art hist., Sarah Lawrence Coll., Bronxville, N.Y., 1934-37; gen. mgr. Indian arts and crafts bd. U.S. Dept. of Interior, Washington, 1937-44; chairman board, 1944-61, commissioner, 1961-66; director of the Museum of Modern Art, N.Y.C., 1949-68, counselor to bd. trustees, 1968; v.p. Mus. of Primitive Art, N.Y.C., 1957-68, acting director of art section Office Inter-American Affairs, 1941-43. Chevalier Legion d'honneur 1954; Order of Merit (German Republic), 1958; Commander Order of the Sun (Peru), 1959. Mem. American Fedn. of Art (dir.), Council Foreign Affairs, National Indian Assn., Municipal Art Society New York City (past director), National Council on the Arts, Washington. Club: Century Association. Author: Mexicana, 1931; Indian Art in the United States (with Frederic Douglas), 1941. Home: New York City NY Died Aug. 13, 1968.

D'HERELLE, FELIX, prof. bacteriology; b. Montreal, Can., Apr. 25, 1873; s. Felix and Augustine (Meert) d'H.; prep. edn., Lycee Louis le Grand, Paris; B.A., Lille, France, 1888; M.D., U. of Leiden, Holland; hon. M.A., Yale, 1928; hon. M.D., Montreal (Can.) U., 1930, Laval U., Quebec, Can., 1930; m. Mary Kerr, of France, July 11, 1893; children—Marcelle, Huberte. Director bacteriol. lab., Guatemala, 1902-06, Merida, Mexico, 1907-08; asst., Inst. Pasteur, Paris, 1908-14, chief of lab., 1914-21; lecturer U. of Leiden, 1922-23; dir. Internat. Sanitary Council of Egypt, 1923-27; prof. protobiology, Yale, 1928-34; hon. prof. University of Tiflis (U.S.S.R.), 1934. Fellow Royal Soc. Canada; member Harvey Soc., Am. Assn. Univ. Profs., Leningrad Soc. Microbiology; foreign mem. Societe de Biologie of Paris. Awarded Leewenhoek medal, Dutch Acad. Sciences, 1925; William Wood Gerhard medal, Philadelphia Pathol. Society, 1928; Shaundim medal, Institute Tropical Medicine, Hamburg, 1930; medal of Royal Asiatic Society, 1930. Author: Le Bacteriophage, 1921; The Bacteriophage, 1922; Les Defenses de l'Organisme, 1923; Immunity in Natural Infectious

Diseases, 1924; Le Bacteriophage et son cemportement, 1926; The Bacteriophage and Its Behavior, 1926; Etudes sur le Cholera, 1929; The Bacteriophage and Its Therapeutical Applications, 1929; Le phenomene de la Guerison dans les Maladies infectieuses, 1938. Discoverer of a parasite of microbes, the bacteriophage, 1917. Home: 40 Olivier de Terres, Paris France‡

DIAMOND, TOBIAS ELLSWORTH, lawyer; b. Tilsit, Germany, Mar. 18, 1876; s. Hyman and Lena (Epstein) D.; came to U.S. 1887, naturalized, 1897; student Northern Ill. Normal Sch., Dixon, 1892-93; LL.B., State U. of Ia., 1904; m. Maude Elizabeth Peck, Nov. 12, 1907; children—Marion Lou (Mrs. H. C. H. Williamson), William John, Robert Edwin, Dorothy Ruth (dec.), Fulton (dec.). Admitted to Ia. bar, June 1904; engaged principally as trial lawyer since 1905; U.S. atty. for the Northern Dist. of Ia. since Nov. 19, 1940. Del. to Nat. Dem. Convs. at Houston, Tex, 1928, Chicago, 1932, 40; hon. mem. Ia. Civilian Defense Orgn., Sheldon. Mem. Ia. State Bar Assn., State Historical Society of Iowa. Mason (32 deg., Scottish Rite, Shriner). Clubs; Sheldon Country; Kiwanis. Home: 10th and Washington Sts., Sheldon, Iowa. Address: Federal Bldg., Sioux City IA‡

DICK, HUGH GILCHRIST, educator; b. Whitehall, N.Y., Sept. 14, 1909; s. Herbert Hugh and Isabel (Hughes) D.; A.B., Union Coll., Schenectady, 1930; M.A., Cornell U., 1935, Ph.D. (Univ. fellow 1936-37), 1937; m. Frances Keeler McIntosh, June 20, 1936; 1 son, Robert M. English master Mohawk Sch., 1930-34; instr. U. Cal. at Los Angeles, 1937-42, asst. prof., 1942-48, asso. prof., 1948-53, prof. English, 1953-71, joint prof. School of Library Service, 1967-71, chmn. dept., 1960-65; vis. instr. Queens Coll., 1943; vis. asso. prof. U. N.C., 1947. Served with AUS, 1942-43. Rockefeller fellow humanities, 1947-48. Mem. Am. Council Learned Socs. (sec. Pacific Coast com. for humanities 1945-52). Modern Lang. Assn., Pacific Coast Philol. Assn., History of Sci. Soc. Author: Sir Francis Bacon, Selected Writings, 1955. Home: Pacific Palisades CA Died Dec. 31, 1971; buried Woodland Cemetery, Delhi NY

DICKEN, CHARLES ERNEST, college pres.; b. Elizabethtown, Ky., Dec. 1, 1877; s. of Charles William and Mary (Williams) D.; ed. William Jewell Coll., Liberty, Mo., 1899-1903; D.D., Ouachita Coll., 1915; LL.D., Baylor U., 1920; m. Belle H. Quick, of Raton, N.M., Dec. 24, 1906; 1 son, Albert Rockwell. Ordained Bapt. ministry, 1904; pres. Ouachita Coll., 1916-26; mgr. Home Life Ins. Co., El Dorado, Ark., 1926. Mem. Kappa Alpha Fraternity. Democrat. Mason, K.P. Home: El Dorado AR‡

DICKENSON, MELVILLE PIERCE, life ins. exec.; b. Phila., Dec. 14, 1898; s. David Stephens and Henrietta (French) D.; student Wyo. Sem. Kingston, Pa., 1913-17; A.B., Princeton, 1922; m. Sarah Christy, Apr. 7, 1923; children—Irene (Mrs. Meverell L. Good), Melville Pierce, David Stephens II. Agt. N.Y. Life Ins. Co., 1922-27; charge group dept. Prudential Ins. Co. Am., 1927-29; with Eastman Dillon, 1929-31; mem. N.Y. Stock Exchange, 1931-35; exec. sec. Princeton Endowment Fund, 1935-37; with home office Equitable Life Assurance Soc. N.Y., 1937-39, mgr., Phila., 1939-55, asst. to pres., N.Y.C., 1955-68, sr. v.p., 1956-68. Served with USN, World War I, lt. (s.g.) USNR for Air, World War II. Clubs: Pine Valley Golf of Clementon (N.J.) (gov.); Gulf Stream (Fla.) Golf (gov.), Gulf Stream Bath and Tennis; University, Links (N.Y.C.). Home: Clementon NJ Died Apr. 18, 1968.

DICKENSON, ROBERT EDWARD, clergyman, educator; b. Cross Timbers, Mo., Sept. 4, 1875; s. Robert Winfield and Catharine Jane (Williams) D.; A.B., Morrisville (Mo.) Coll., 1897, A.M., 1903; B.D., Vanderbilt, 1900; D.D., U. of Denver, 1916; m. Anne Ruby Wynne, Sept. 4, 1900; children—Anita Frances, Robert Edward, Jr. Ordained elder M.E. Ch. South, 1902; pastor Hobson Ch., Nashville, Tenn., 1900-02; missionary to Mexico and pastor Am. Ch., San Luis Potosi, 1902-04; pastor and presiding elder and dir. religious edn., Liberty, Mo., St. Joseph, Mo., Denver, Colo., Colorado Springs, Colo., Vernon, Tex., 1904-24; chaplain State Senate, Denver, Colo., 1910, 12; chaplain and dir. religious activities, and head dept. of religion in coll. of arts and sciences, Southern Meth. U., 1924-32; pastor Las Cruces, N.M., Clovis, N.M., Portales, N.M., 1932-39; pastor University Meth. Ch., Tucson, Ariz., 1939-42; pastor Garfield Community Meth. Ch., Phoenix, Ariz., 1942-45. Mem. exec. com. Federal Council Chs. of Christ in America, 1916-20 and 1928-32; mem. Commn. Tucson Hosp., 1934-38; mem. Ecumenical Conf. Methodism, Toronto, 1911; mem. Gen. Conf. M.E. Ch., South, 1914, 22, 24; mem. Gen. Sunday Sch. Bd., M.E. Ch. South, 1914-18; traveling companion with Bishop Walter R. Lambuth in the Orient and del. to World Sunday Sch. Conv. Tokyo 1920. Toured Europe, 1930; conf. missionary sec., N.Mex., 1934-38. Pres. Tucson Ministerial Association, 1940-42, Salt River Valley Meth. Ministerial Assn., Phoenix, 1942-43. Mem. Southern California Arizona Conference (member board of education, board ministerial training), vice-chmn. for Pima County, Ariz., and mem. div. of recreation and spiritual welfare of Civilian Defense Coordinating Council. Democrat. Mason, Odd Fellow, Modern Woodman. Clubs: Rotary, Kiwanis, Faculty, Civitan. Author: Alfred Tennyson and the Message of In Memoriam, The Unification of Methodism, Sketch of Bishop Walter R. Lambuth, A. Glimpse into the Life and Character of Bishop Charles B. Galloway. Address: 1423 New York Av., Alamogordo NM‡

DICKEY, CHARLES EMMET, educator; b. Brothersvalley Twp., Somerset County, Pa., Sept. 24, 1871; s. Ephraim F. and Josephine (Carns) D.; grad. California (Pa.) State Normal Sch., 1891; A.B., U. of Pittsburgh, 1919; post-grad. work, Columbia and Harvard univs.; LL.D., U. of Pittsburgh, 1932; m. Della M. Boyer, June 10, 1896; children—Paul Hamilton, Lloyd Emmet, Josephine S., Harriet Katherine. Teacher rural schs., high sch., normal sch.; supervising principal Avalon, Pa., 12 yrs., Elk Lick, 2 yrs.; asst. county supt. schs., Allegheny County, Pa., 1907-22, county supt., 1922-40; pres. Ohio Valley Building & Loan Assn. Mem. bd. dirs. Pa. Safety Council World War. Trustee Thomas Patton Institution for Boys. Mem. N.E.A., Pennsylvania State Ednl. Assn. (pres. 1926), Am. Acad. Polit. and Social Science, Phi Delta Kappa. Republican. Presbyterian. Mason (33 deg.). Club: Butler Country. Home: Cathedral Mansions, Pittsburgh 13 PA‡

DICKEY, ROBERT W(ILLIAM), educator; b. Mountain Grove, Va., May 13, 1891; s. Robert James and Martha (Jones) D.; B.S., Washington and Lee Univ., 1910, A.B., 1911, A.M., 1912; A.M., Johns Hopkins, 1915, Ph.D. (fellow in physics, 1915-16), 1916; m. Eliabeth Drury, Sept. 10, 1918; 1 son, Robert W., Jr. Instr. in physics and mathematics, Washington and Lee Univ. (Howard Houston teaching fellow, 1911-13), 1910-13, asso. prof. physics, 1916-22, asso. prof. elec. engring., 1922-24, prof. elec. engring., 1924-28, prof. of physics and elec. engring., 1928-34, McCormick prof. of physics, 1934-61, distinguished lecturer in physics, 1961-72, engring. cons. bldg. program, 1921-40 (designed and installed elec. lab.), elected prof. on Ball Foundation, 1947. Served as aeronaut. mech. engr., A.A.F., 1917-19; 2d lt., A.A.F., 1918-19. Mem. Am. Assn. Physics Teachers, Va. Acad. Scis., Phi Beta Kappa, Omicron Delta Kappa, Gamma Alpha, Phi Kappa Psi, Alpha Epsilon Delta. Episcopalian. Club: Hopkins (1913-16). Home: Lexington VA Died Mar. 24, 1972; buried Stonewall Jackson Cemetery, Lexington VA

DICKINSON, AUGUSTUS EDWIN, pres. Indiana Limestone Co.; b. Park Ridge, Ill., Mar. 8, 1869; s. Frederick and Emma (Elliott) D.; ed. Moseley Sch., Chicago; m. 2d, Maud Forbes, Jan. 29, 1927; children (by first marriage)—Augusta Edwina, Betty. Began in building stone business, Chicago, 1885; supt. Ashland Brown Stone Co., 1890-97; pres. Bedford Quarries Co., 1897-1910; pres. Consolidated Stone Co., 1910-26; pres. Indiana Limestone Co. since 1926. Chmn. Ind. War Bd., Lawrence Co., and vice chmn. Am. Red Cross, Ind., World War. Mem. Internat. Cut Stone Contractors and Quarrymen's Assn. (ex-chmn.). Republican. Episcopalian. Clubs: Union League, Rotary, Lake Shore Athletic, North Shore Golf; Bedford Country. Home: 2130 Lincoln Park W. Office: Tribune Tower, Chicago IL‡

DICKINSON, CALVIN L., chem. co. exec.; b. Wilmington, N.C., Aug. 2, 1914; s. John B. and Sallie (Duncan) D.; B.A., Wake Forest Coll., 1936; M. Chem. Engring., N.C. State Coll., 1942; m. Dorothy Dockery, Sept. 9, 1940; children—Calvin L., James D. Mgr. Houston plant organic chem. div. Diamond Alkali Co., 1951-53; with Am. Potash &Chem. Corp., 1953-70, v.p. mfg., 1963-70; v.p. mfg., engring., purchasing and distbn. Velsicol Chem. Corp., Chgo., 1970-71. Home: Chicago IL Died Jan. 11, 1971.

DICKINSON, CLARENCE, organist; b. Lafayette, Ind., May 7, 1873; s. William C. and Annis (Dougherty) D.; M.A. (hon.) Northwestern U., 1909, Mus.D., 1917; student music under Wild (Chicago), Singer and Dr. H. Reimann (Berlin), Guilmant, widor, Vierne, Moszkowski (Paris); Litt.D., Miami U., 1921; Mus.D., Ohio Wesleyan U., 1942, Gustavus Adolphus Coll., 1962; m. Helena Adell Snyder, June 15, 1904 (dec. 1957); m. 2d, Lois Stice, 1963. Organist and choir master Brick Presbyn. Ch.; 1909-59, dir. emeritus, 1959-69; founder and dir. emeritus School of Sacred Music of Union Theological Seminary, N.Y.C.; conductor the Mendelssohn Glee Club, N.Y., 1909-13, and Bach Festival, Montclair, Sunday Evening Club Choir, Orchestra Hall and Musical Art Soc., Chgo.; organist, choirmaster Temple Beth-El, N.Y.C., 1919-39; prof. sacred music, Union Theological Seminary, N.Y., 1912-45, ret. 1945. Pub. numerous Compositions including arrangements. Produced comic opera, The Medicine Man," Chicago, 1895, Boston, 1900. Composer of pieces for organ and voice; series of Sacred Choruses" (269 to date). Historical Recital Series (48 to date) and Sacred Solos (23 to date); also Storm King Symphony for organ and orchestra, 1919. Co-author (with Helen Dickinson) Excursions in Musical History, 1917; The Prince of Peace (A Nativity Play in Ancient Christmas Carols), 1919; A Book of Antiphons. 1920; Songs of the Troubadours, 1920; Technique and Art of Organ Playing, 1921; A Choirmaster's Guide, 1923; A Treasury of Worship, 1927. Editor: The Hymnal for Presbyn. Ch. of U.S., 1933, Evangelical-Reformed Hymnal, 1941; (with Paul A. Wolfe) The Choir Loft and the Pulpit, 1943. Mem. Am. Guild Organists, (founder) Hymn. Soc. of Am. (hon.) ASCAP, Am. Musicol. Soc., Am. Choral Dirs. Assn., Century Assn. N.Y., Nat. Assn. Am. Composers and Conductors. Beta Theta Pi. Clubs: Federated Music Clubs (hon.), St. Wilfrid of N.Y. Home: New York City NY Died Aug. 2, 1969; buried Caldwell NJ

DICKINSON, EDWARD EVERETT, JR., mfr. witch hazel; b. Essex, Conn., Oct. 27, 1891; s. Edward Everett and Frances Louise D.; Ph.B., Yale, 1912; m. Dorothy E. Bumford, Oct. 18, 1942; children—Edward Everett III, Alice Ben, Patricia Cobden, Alan Page. With The E.E. Dickinson Co., since beginning of active business career; pres. and treas., until 1968. Joined the US., Naval Res., June 1917; discharged as lt. j.g., Jan. 1919. Mem. Mayflower Descs., Sons of Colonial Wars, Patriots and Founders, S.A.R., Sachem Hall, Am. Legion. Mason, Odd Fellow, Elk. Clubs: Dauntless, Yacht (Essex); Yale, New York Yacht (New York); Fishers Island Yacht; Key Largo Anglers; Everglades (Palm Beach); Bal Harbour, Fishers Island Country. Home: Essex CT Died Nov. 22, 1968; buried Riverview Cemetery, Essex CT

DICKINSON, EDWARD T., JR., assn. exec.; b. Bklyn., Mar. 5, 1911; s. Edward T. and Jeannette E. (Guelpa) D.; A.B., Yale, 1932; m. Eileen M. Durning, Feb. 7, 1957; children—Mary, Edward T. III. With Bklyn. Trust Co., 1932-35; spl. agt. Fidelity & Casualty Co. of N.Y., 1935-37; on staff chmn. finance com. U.S. Steel, 1937-40; served as research asst. to chmn. bd. U.S. Steel, 1940-42; exec. dir. planning com., W.P.B., Washington, 1942-43; v.p. and dir. overseas operations World Wide Development Corp., 1946-47; v.p. in charge ednl. films United World Films, Incorporated, 1947-48; dir. Program Coordination Div., Econ. Cooperation Adminstrn., 1948-50; asst. to the joint secs. Dept. of Def., Washington, 1950-51; dep. for installations U.S.A.F., Washington, 1951; vice chmn. NSRB, Washington, 1951-53; alternate NSC 1951-53; exec. asst. to pres., Carrier Corp., 1953-55; commr. N.Y. Dept. Commerce, 1955-59; pres. N.Y. Racing Assn., 1959-69; chmn. N.Y. Bus. Development Corp., 1956, 59-61. Chmn. N.E. Interstate Water Pollution Control Commn. 1958; U.S. mem. Emergency Econ. Com. for Europe, 1945; mem. Fgn. Mil. Assistance Coordinating Com., 1949-50. Served with USMC, 1943-46. Decorated Bronze Star Medal, Knight of Malta. Democrat. Roman Catholic. Clubs: Yale, Grolier, Brook (N.Y.C.); Cosmos (Washington). Home: Garden City NY Died Feb. 2, 1969.

DICKINSON, LESTER JESSE, ex-senator; b. Derby Lucas County, Ia., Oct. 29, 1873; descendant Nathaniel Dickinson, Hadley, Mass.; s. Levi D. and Willamine (Morton) D.; B.S., Cornell Coll., Mt. Vernon, Ia., 1898., LL.D., 1936; LL.B., State U. of Ia., 1889; m. Myrtle Call, Aug. 21, 1901; children—Levi Call, Ruth Alice. Asso. in law practice with T. P. Harrington, at Algona, Ia., 1899-1934. County atty., Kossuth Co., Ia., 2 terms, 1909-13; mem. Rep. State Central Com., 1914-18; mem. 66th to 71st Congresses (1919-31), 10th Ia. Dist. U.S. senator from Ia., term, 1931-37; senior member firm Dickinson, Throckmorton, Parker, Mannheimer and Raife, Des Moines, Ia. Temporary chmn. of Republican Nat. Conv., Chicago, 1932. Trustee Cornell Coll. Mem. Phi Delta Phi. Conglist. Home: Des Moines IA Died June 4, 1969; buried Riverview Cemetery, Algona IA

DICKINSON, LUCY JENNINGS (MRS. LA FELL DICKINSON), clubwoman; b. Winchester, New Hampshire; daughter Willard Harvey and Jane (Buffum) Jennings; A.B., Mount Holyoke Coll., South Hadley, Massachusetts, 1905; LL.D., New Hampshire University, 1949; m. La Fell Dickinson, Oct. 28, 1911;children—Jane, Lucy. Upon death of father took over management of his lumber business, Winchester, N.H., also directorship in Winchester Nat. Bank, serving in this work, 1907-11. Pres. Keene (N.H.) Woman's Club, 1924-26; pres. N.H. State Fedn. Woman's Clubs, 1929-31; treas. gen. Fedn. Women's Clubs, 1935-38, first vice-pres. 1941-44; pres. Gen. Fedn. Women's Clubs, 1944-71. Mem. Am. Assn. Univ. Women, Nat. Fedn. Bus. and Professional Women's Clubs, D.A.R., Daughters Colonial Wars, Colonial Dames, League of Women Voters, Garden Club of America, Cancer Commn. of New Hampshire, Tuberculosis Society of N.H. (dir.), Nat. Cancer Soc. (dir.), D.A.R., Daughters of Colonial Wars. Republican (nat. committee Woman for N.H., 1948-52). Address: West Hartford CT Died Feb. 15, 1971.

DICKINSON, MAY BLISS, b. Amherst, Mass., July 23, 1874; d. Noah and Malah (Bliss) D.; ed. Framingham Training Sch. for Nurses and Boston U. Field supervisor, later asst. to dir. hygiene, Mass. Dept. Pub. Health, 1914-16; Red Cross worker, 1917-19; lecturer and writer. A pioneer organizer industrial welfare work, anti-tuberculosis edn., health edn., illustrated lectures, etc.; founder and dir. Mothercraft (nat. and internat. ednl. movement); mem. Am. Pub. Health Assn., Am. Child Health Assn., D.A.R.; advisor child welfare div. Gen. Fed. Women's Clubs. Republican. Episcopalian. Clubs: Woman's City, Civic, Browning (Boston). Home: Amherst, Mass. Office: Trinity Court, Boston MA‡

DICKINSON, ROBERT SMITH, flour milling co. exec.; b. Columbus, Neb., Jan. 22, 1889; s. Richard Storrs and Mary Leona (Holden) D.; B.A., Doane Coll., Crete, Neb., 1910; m. Carrie Hazel Clark, Dec. 20, 1913; children—Jean, Robert Hugh, Ann Marie, Sheila, Rae Leona. With Ravenna Mills (Neb.), 1910-20; with Con-Agra, Inc. (formerly Neb. Consol. Mills Co.), Omaha, 1920-71, chmn. bd., hon. chmn. until 1971. Home: Omaha NB Died July 12, 1971.

DICKINSON, WILLIAM HALE, JR., clergyman; b. Paris, Tex., July 20, 1913; s. William Hale and Lucy (Davidge) D.; B.A., So. Methodist U., 1935; B.D., Perkins Sch. Theology, 1946; D.D. (hon.), Tex. Wesleyan Coll., 1959; m. Nina Rebecca Sadler, June 22, 1937; children—James Walter, Lucy Ann. Ordained to ministry Meth. Ch., 1936; pastor in Tex., 1936-43; asso. charge pastoral ministry Highland Park Meth. Ch., Dallas, 1946-58, pastor in charge, 1958-72. Mem. bd. publns. Meth. Ch. Mem. planning com. Goals for Dallas; participant Am. Assembly, 1966, Pub. Affairs Inst., 1967. Bd. dirs. Timberlawn Found., Meth. Hosp., Dallas; bd. govs. So. Meth. U.; bd. trustees, exec. com. Southwestern U. Served as chaplain AUS, 1943-46. Decorated Legion of Merit, Bronze Star; Croix de Valor (Italy); named Distinguished Alumnus So. Meth. U. Mem. Blue Key. Home: Dallas TX Died Oct. 29, 1972.

DICKSON, HARRIS, author, lawyer; b. Yazoo City, Miss., July 21, 1868; s. T. H. and Harriet E. (Hardenstein) D.; common sch. edn. at Meridian and Vicksburg, Miss.; attended summer class, 1891, U. of Va.; LL.B., Columbian (now George Washington) U., 1894; m. Madeleine L. Metcalf, Apr. 24, 1906; children—Elizabeth, Madeleine. Pvt. sec. to Andrew Price, M.C., 1893-94; in law practice at Vicksburg since 1896; judge Municipal Court, Vicksburg, 1905-07. Democrat. War corr. in France for Collier's Weekly, 1917. Clubs: Country, Elks (Vicksburg); National Press, Army and Navy (Washington); Players, Dutch Treat (New York); Boston (New Orleans). Author: The Black Wolf's Breed, 1899; The Siege of Lady Resolute, 1902; She That Hesitates, 1903; The Ravanels, 1905; The Duke of Devil-May-Care, 1905; Gabrielle, Transgressor, 1906; Old Reliable, 1912; The House of Luck, 1917; Unpopular History of U.S., 1917; Old Reliable in Africa, 1920; An Old-Fashioned Senator, 1925; Children of the River, 1928; Port of Queer Cargoes, 1931; The Story of King Cotton, 1937; also Sunlover Sam stories, 1912, and Coffin Club stories, 1913; Marse Jeff Davis (Collier's), 1938. Contbr. numerous spl. articles and fiction to mags. Home: Vicksburg MS‡

DIECKMANN, JOHANNES, pres. East German Peoples' Chamber; b. Fischerhude, Dist. of Bremen, Jan. 19, 1893; ed. Bus. Coll. Berlin, univs. Berlin Giessen, Goettingen, Freiburg im Breisgau, 1913-20. Editor, gen. sec. German Peoples' Party, Osnabrueck, Duisburg and Dresden, 1919-33; mem. Parliament of Saxony, 1930-33, 46-52; leading coal mining orgns., 1933-48; minister of justice, asst. minister-pres. State of Saxony, 1948-50; asso. founder Liberal-Democratic Party of Germany, 1945, now asst. to pres.; pres. Peoples' Chamber, 1950-69; asst. to pres. Council of State 1960-69; pres. permanent German Dem. Republic delegation Internat. Conf. for peaceful solution of German Question; pres. Soc. for German-Soviet Friendship, 1963-69. Served with mil. in World War I. Recipient Hero of Work award, 2 Banners of Work awards, Meritorious Service medal, German Peace medal, others. Home: East Berlin Germany Died Feb. 1969.*

DIEFENDORF, ALLEN ROSS, physician; b. Savannah, N.Y., Dec. 21, 1871; s. Fletcher Adelbert and Susan (Quackenbush) D.; grad. Yale 1894, Yale Univ. Med. Sch., 1896; m. Jeanette Cooper, Sept. 4, 1895, New Haven. Mem. New York Neurol. Soc., Am. Medico-Psychol. Assn., Am. Bacteriol. Soc., Conn. Med. Soc., Am. Med. Assn. Now lecturer in psychiatry, Yale. Author: Clinical Psychiatry, 1902 M1. Address: Middletown CT‡

DIEFENDORF, DORR FRANK, clergyman; b. Canajoharie, N.Y., Aug. 9, 1874; s. John W. and Emma (Keller) D.; grad. Drew Theol. Sem., Madison, N.J., 1899; B.D., 1922; D.D., Dickinson Coll., 1919; m. Mabel A. Runyon, June 15, 1898; children—Robert Runyon, Katharine (dec.). Ordained ministry M.E. Ch., 1900; pastor Chatham, N.J., 1901-05, Ridgewood, 1905-07, Roseville Ch., Newark, 1907-20, Calvary, East Orange, N.J., 1920-28; contbg. editor Christian Advocates, 1928-32; lecturer on practical theology, Drew U., 1921-33, asso. prof. practical theology and applied Christianity, 1933, prof. since 1934, retired July, 1944. Mem. book com., Meth. Book Concern, 1920-28; mem. Bd. Fgn. Missions, 1920-28. Mem. Gen. Com., Dept. of Research and Ednl. Com. on Worship, and Social Service Department (Federal Council of Chs.); mem. Council for Clinical Training of Theol. Students. Clubs: Kappa Chi, Monday. Author: Christian in Social Relationships, 1922. Address: 45 Prospect St., Madison NJ‡

DIEFFENBACH, ALBERT CHARLES, clergyman and editor; b. at Manchester, Md., July 4, 1876; s. Ferdinand Albert and Jeannette Rix (Frankforter) D.; brother of Rudolph Dieffenbach; g.s. Dr. Ferdinand Dieffenbach, a leader in the Revolution in Germany, 1848, who founded Irving Coll., Md., 1858; student Baltimore City Coll.; A.B., Johns Hopkins, 1898; grad. Ref. Theol. Sem., Lancaster, Pa., 1901; D.D., Meadville (Pa.) Theol. Sch., 1918; m. Helen Albright Bertolette, Nov. 4, 1903; 1 dau., Ruth Bertolette. Ordained Ref. Ch. ministry, 1901; field missionary Ref. Ch. S.S. Bd., 1901-02; founder and pastor Ref. Ch. of Ascension, Pittsburgh, Pa., 1902-11; pastor First Unitarian Church, Hartford, Conn., 1911-18; editor The Christian Register, Boston, 1918-33; editor of religion Boston Transcript, 1933-1941; minister Unitarian Church, Newton Centre, 1927-40, now minister emeritus; minister ad interim, Unitarian Ch., Lynn, 1942-44; minister Unitarian Church of Larger Fellowship, 1944-49, now minister emeritus. Trustee and sec. Mass. Bible Society. Member of the corporation Deaconess Hospital. Delegate World Conference of Churches, Oxford, 1937. Dir. for N.E. Am. Com. for Christian Refugees, 1942-43; director war information division, Office of Civilian Defense, First Region for 1943. Chaplain (captain), First Regiment Connecticut State Guard, May-Dec. 1917. Mem. American Unitarian Association (life member), American Newspaper Guild, Phi Kappa Sigma (nat. pres., 1923-26). Clubs: University, Authors'. Author: Religious Liberty—The Great American Illusion, 1927, edit. in Braille for Library of Congress, 1928. Editor: Wayside Community Pulpit, 1944-49. Originated Religious Book Week, Boston, 1942, in which Protestants, Catholics and Jews for first time united in exhibits and meetings, since continued in other cities. Home: 3 Lincoln Lane Cambridge 38 MA‡

DIEHL, CHARLES EDWARD, clergyman, educator; b. Charles Town, W.Va., May 18, 1875; s. Albert and Christina (Nolte) D.; A.B., Johns Hopkins, 1896; M.A., Princeton, 1900; grad. Princeton Theol. Sem., 1900; D.D., Southwestern Presbyn. U., 1910; LL.D., Davidson (N.C.) College, 1926 Centre Coll. (Kentucky), 1947, U. of Chattanooga, 1949; m. Katherine Ireys, Mar. 24, 1909; 1 son, Charles Ireys. Ordained Presbyn. ministry, 1900; pastor Crescent Springs and Independence, Ky., 1900-05, Greenville, Miss., 1905-07, 1st Ch., Clarksville, Tenn., 1907-17; pres. Southwestern At Memphis, 1917-49, president emeritus since July 1, 1949, director; dir. Louisville Presbyn. Sem.; pres. Assn. of Am. Colls., 1942; sec.-treas. Southern U. Conf. 1938-47; sec. Pan-Presbyterian College union, 1940-45; chmn. Nat. Conference Church-Related Colleges, 1943. Vice-chmn. education com., Memphis Round Table Conference of Christians and Jews; moderator Synod of Tenn., 1919, and 1935-36, Gen. Assembly Presbyn. Church in U.S., May 1941-May 1942; trustee General Assembly and Presbyn. Foundn; bd. visitors U.S. Naval Acad., 1949 and 1950. Mem. Newcomen Soc., Phi Beta Kappa, Omicron Delta Kappa. Dem. Mason (32 deg., Shriner). Clubs: Rotary, Univ., Executives, Eygptians. Writer of monographs and reviews. Address: 1967 Snowden Av., Memphis 7 TN‡

DIEHL, JOHN CASPER, supt. schs.; b. Erie, Pa.; s. Frederick and Barbara C. (Doll) D.; A.B., Yale, 1887, A.M., 1903; m. Annie Belle Ingham, of Erie, Dec. 21, 1893; children—Frederick, Annabel, Samuel, Virginia. Teacher classics, Central High Sch., Erie, 1887-90, prin., 1890-1919; prin. Acad. High Sch., 1919-21; asst. supt. schs., Erie, 1921-22, supt. since 1922. Republican. Presbyn. Mason (33 deg., Shriner). Clubs: University, Shrine. Home: 510 Myrtle St. Office: Pub. Library Bldg., Erie PA‡

DIELMAN, LOUIS HENRY, librarian; b. New Windsor, Md., Jan. 16, 1864; s. Louis and Theodora (Muller) D.; A.B., New Windsor Coll., 1884; student Md. Coll. of Pharmacy; Ph.G., Phila. Coll. Pharmacy, 1885; m. Anna Good Barkdoll, Oct. 8, 1890. Cataloguer Md. State Library, 1900-04; asst. librarian Enoch Pratt Free Library, Baltimore, 1904-11; exec. sec. Peabody Inst., Baltimore, since 1912; librarian since 1927. Mem. Am. Hist. Assn., Md. Hist. Soc. Democrat. Editor and Compiler: British Invasion of Maryland, 1913. Editor of Md. Hist. Mag. (Vols, 4-32), 1909-37. Home: 1514 Park Av. Address: Peabody Institute, Baltimore MD‡

DIES, MARTIN, congressman; b. Colorado, Texas, Nov. 5, 1900; s. Martin and Olive M. (Cline) D.; student Wesley Coll. (Greenville) and U. Tex.; LL.B., Nat. U., Washington; m. Myrtle McAdams, June 3, 1920; children—Martin, Robert M., Jack. Began practice, Marshall, Tex., 1920; moved to Orange, 1922; sr. mem. Dies, Stephenson & Dies; mem. 72d to 78th Congresses, 2d Texas Dist.; mem. 83d-85th Congresses, at large; chmn. spl. com. investigate un-American activities. Democrat. Mem. Christian (Disciples) Ch. Home: Lufkin TX Died Nov. 14, 1972.

DIETER, BERTHOLD B., art dir.; b. Naperville, Ill., Oct. 15, 1909; s. Julian Michael and Bertha (Ory) D.; student North Central Coll., Naperville, 1927-29, Am. Acad. Art, Chgo., 1931-32; m. Terese Weiland, July 14, 1934; children—Frances, Berthold, Michael, Joanne, Loretta, Andrea. With advt. dept. Carson Pirie Scott & Co., Chgo., 1929-34; with Meredith Pub. Co., Des Moines, Ia., from 1934, mag., book, advt. designer, became art editor Better Homes and Gardens, 1940, editor Better Homes & Gardens, 1960, editorial dir., from 1967. Home: Des Moines IA Died Jan. 30, 1972.

DIETERLE, WILLIAM, motion picture director; b. Ludwigshafen, Germany, July 15, 1893; s. Jacob and Bertha (Doerr) D.; student Ludwigshafen, Heidelberg, Munich (Germany), Zurich (Switzerland); m. Charlotte Hagenbruch, July 15, 1921. Began as actor, 1912; appeared on stage in Heidelberg, Zurich, Munich, Berlin; became motion-picture actor, Berlin, 1921; motion-picture actor and dir., Germany, 1923-30, U.S., 1930-40; director and producer for William Dieterle Prodns., Hollywood, Calif., pres., 1940-42. Directed or produced pictures: The Life of Emile Zola, Juarez, Dr. Ehrlich's Magic Bullet, Story of Louis Pasteur, Tennessee Johnson; All That Money Can Buy, I'll Be Seeing You, Love Letters, Portrait of Jenny, Rope of Sand, September Affair, Volcano, Boots Malone, The Turning Point, Salome, Elephant Walk. Home: Canoga Park CA Died Dec. 1972.

DIETZ, GOULD COOKE, retired; b. Anamosa, Ia., May 24, 1868; s. Gould Price and Leonora Antonette (Cooke) D.; ed. high sch. and business coll.; m. Florence Putnam, Jan. 17, 1907 (died Dec. 20, 1922); m. 2d, Mrs. Alice Kountze, Dec. 20, 1930. Associated with brother, C. N. Dietz, in wholesale and retail lumber business since 1883, and with him pioneered and developed bituminous coal field of Sheridan County, Wyo.; director Omaha National Bk.; director and treasurer, Rivett Lumber & Coal Co.; dir. Blair Lumber Co., Waterloo Lumber Company; president Masonic Home for Boys; member board Child Saving Inst., Municipal Airport Board; pres. Neb. Humane Soc.; mem. exec. com. U. of Neb. Foundation, Lincoln. Delegate Republican National Convention 7 times; captain of Civilian Air Patrol; mem. notification com., nomination of Charles E. Hughes and Warren G. Harding, of Coolidge as v.p. and pres.; and Hoover and Wendell Willkie for pres.; civilian aid to sec. of war for 7th Corps Area citizens' mil. training camps, and mem. exec. com. of nat. orgn.; instrumental in orgn. Base Hosp. No. 49 and Ambulance Company No. 135 for service overseas; now serving as officer Civilian Air Patrol. Mem. board of corporation American Red Cross. Member aviation com. Sesquicentennial Internat. Expn., Phila. Trustee Nebraska Historical Society (Lincoln, Neb.), Old People's Home, Stuntz Hall for Girls. Republican. Methodist. Mason (32 deg., K.T., Shriner), Elk. Clubs: Omaha, Sojourner, Omaha Country. Made 4 trips around the world. Home: Hotel Fontenelle, Omaha NE‡

DIGGS, MARSHALL RAMSEY, lawyer; b. Paris, Tenn., Nov. 7, 1888; s. Robert Albert and Anna (Sauls) D.; A.B., Epworth U. (now Oklahoma City Univ.), 1910; LL.B., Yale, 1913; m. Alice Muse, Nov. 7, 1919; children—Helen (Mrs. Frank Quiggen), Marshall Ramsey, Alice Muse (Mrs. Chas. K. Nulsen, Jr.). Admitted to Ill. bar, 1913, Minn., 1916; practiced in Chicago, 1913-16, Minneapolis, 1916-17; organized Three Captains Co., 1919; sec. and general manager Walraven Advt. Service, 1921-28; exec. asst. comptroller of the currency, 1934-38, 1st dep., Jan. 1938; acting comptroller of currency, 1938. Served as lt., capt., U.S. Army, instr. O.T.C., 1917-19. Mem. Am. Judicature Soc. Am. Bar Assn., Phi Alpha Delta. Meth. Mason (Shriner). Clubs: Yale (N.Y.C.); Burning Tree. Yale, Metropolitan (Washington). Home: Washington DC Died Sept. 26, 1968; buried West Springfield NH

DIKE, CHESTER THOMAS, civil engr.; b. Woodstock, Ill., Aug. 13, 1870; s. Chester B. and Rose (Mayne) D.; B.C.E., Cornell Coll., Mt. Vernon, Ia., 1893, C.E., 1903; m. Bonnie Elder, Feb. 19, 1900; children—Edwin Berck, Gardner Elder. Began as chainman N.P.Ry.; chief engr. Mason City & Clear Lake Ry., 1896-97, Ia., Minn. & N.W. Ry., 1898-99; with C. & N.-W. Ry. since 1899, successively resident engr., div. engr., supt. constrn. various branches, gen. supt. Minn. and Dak. divs., asst. gen. supt. of the rd., 1918-19, asst. gen. mgr. Lines West of Mo. River, 1919-20, engr. maintenance of way, 1920-30, chief engr., 1930-34, v.p. and chief engr.; also v.p. way and structures C.,St.P.,M.&ORy., 1934-35; v.p. and chief engr. C. & N.-W. System since 1935. Mem. Western Soc. Engrs. Club: Union League. Home: 821 Ridge Av., Evanston Ill. Office: 400 W. Madison St., Chicago IL‡

DILES, DOROTHY VERNON, educator; b. Zaleski, O., Aug. 14, 1906; d. Fred Lawrence and Anna (Trace) Diles; B.A., Ohio Wesleyan U., 1929; M.A., U. Wis., 1941, postgrad. Western Res. U. Tchr., English and dramatics Birmingham (O.) High Sch., 1929-31; tchr. English and dramatics, prin. high sch., McArthur, O., 1931-34; head dept. English and drama Geneva (O.) High Sch., 1934-32; adminstr., asst. dean women Miami U., Oxford, O., 1945-46; prof. dept. English, Evansville (Ind.) Coll., 1946-47; prof. dept. English, Kent (O.) State U., 1947-67, emeritus, 1967-68. Served with USNR, 1943-45. Mem. Am. Assn. U. Women (exec. bd. 1947-68, Kent. pres. 1960-61, mem. state bd. 1962-64), Nat. Council Tchrs. English, English Assn. Ohio (mem.

com. of 88 1964-68), Coll. English Assn. Ohio, Am. Assn. U. Profs., Delta Kappa Gamma (state bd. 1959-61), Phi Delta Gamma, Phi Lambda Theta, Kappa Delta Pi, Alpha Gamma Delta (del. internat. conv. 1952, 59, chmn. chpt. exec. council 1951-60, pres. alumnae chpt. 1952-54, 62-64, province v.p. 68). Republican. Methodist. Home: Kent OH Died Sept. 8, 1968.

DILGER, WALTER LINNELL, lawyer; b. Chgo., Sept. 19, 1906; s. Robert and Lydia (Linnell) D.; LL.B., Chgo.-Kent Coll. Law, 1927; m. Doris Elizabeth Riggs, June 15, 1935; 1 son, Herbert Edgar. Admitted to Ill. bar, 1928; practice of law, Quincy, Ill., 1928-30; with Beatrice Foods Co., 1930-70, gen. counsel, 1935-70, sec., dir., 1943-70, v.p., 1955-70. Mem. Am., Ill. State bar assns., Chgo. Law Inst., Am. Soc. Corp. Secs., Delta Chi. Mason. Clubs: Executives (Chgo.). Home: Chicago IL Died Mar. 27, 1970.

DILLARD, ALLYN, lawyer, bus. exec.; b. Norfolk, Va., Feb. 2, 1905; s. George Mason and Elizabeth (Allyn) D.; LL.B., U. Va., 1927; m. Frances E. Pratt, Apr. 30, 1938; 1 dau., Frances Allyn. Admitted to Va. bar, 1927, N.Y. bar, 1929; asso. Mitchell, Capron, Marsh, Angulo & Cooney, and predecessors, N.Y. City, 1929-45; sec. Reynolds Metals Co., and affiliates, 1945-71; dir. Reynolds Metal Co., 1959-72. Pres. Richmond Area Community Council, 1957-59. Mem. Am. Soc. of Corporate Secs., Inc., Va. State Bar Assn., Newcomen Soc. N.Am., Kappa Alpha, Phi Delta Phi. Club: Country of Virginia. Democrat. Episcopalian. Home: Richmond VA Died Apr. 2, 1972.

DILLER, GEORGE E., educator; b. Pittsburgh, Mar. 7, 1906; s. Theodore and Rebecca Chambers (Craig) D.; A.B., Princeton, 1926, Ph.D., 1933; m. Constance Dorothea Weeks, June 18, 1938 (dec. Oct. 1957); children—George T., John E.; m. 2d, Angele Belval, Dec. 11, 1958. Bank clk. Paris and N.Y., 1926-30; instr. in French, Princeton, 1933-34, Rutgers U., 1934-36; instr. in French, Dartmouth Coll., 1936-38, asst. prof., 1938-47, prof. of French, 1947-69. Mem. sch. bd., Norwich, Vt., 1946-49. Served with Army Air Force, U.S., India and Guam as intelligence officer, 1942-45; disch. rank of major. Mem. Modern Lang. Assn. of Am., Am. Assn. Teachers of French, Am. Assn. Univ. Profs. Socialist. Author: several books, including La France d'autrefois et d'aujourd'hui (with Charles R. Bagley), 1951. Awarded Bronze Star medal, 1945. Home: Norwich VT Died Aug. 1969.

DILLEY, ARTHUR URBANE, writer, lecturer and adviser on Oriental rugs; b. Wilkes-Barre, Pa., Aug. 23, 1873; s. Urbane and Lydia Ann (Weber) D.; A.B., Harvard, 1897, A.M., 1899; m. Millicent Davis, June 27, 1900; children—Urbane, Richard Davis, Margaret, Raymond LL.D., Elizabeth Huntsman. Master, Taft Sch., Watertown, Conn., 1899-1903; Oriental rug merchant, Boston, 1903-13, N.Y. City since 1914; lectuer at art museums and schs., univs., clubs since 1903. Mem. Alpha Delta Phi. Club: Harvard. Author: Oriental Rugs and Carpets, 1931. Lecturer New York U. and New York School of Interior Decoration. Home: 524 Pelham Manor Rd., Pelham Manor, N.Y. Office: 32 E. 57th St., New York NY‡

DILLINGHAM, FRANCES BENT, author; b. Chelsea, Mass.; d. Isaac Snow and Frances (Bent) D.; A.B., Boston U., 1891; unmarried. Engaged as writer since 1895; contbr. poems and stories to Century, Scribner's, McClure's, Lippincott's, The Youth's Companion, St. Nicholas, etc. Author: A Proud Little Baxter, 1898; A Christmas Tree Scholar and Other Stories, 1900; The Sister (serial in N. E. Mag.), 1910-11. Now instr. English, Miss Porter's School, Farmington, Conn. Address: 81 Woodland Rd., Auburndale MA‡

DILLON, GEORGE, author; b. Jacksonville, Fla., Nov. 12, 1906; s. William and Adah (Hill) D.; Ph.B., U. of Chicago, 1927; grad. study, U. of Paris, 1933-34; unmarried. Tech. and literary translator, pubs. adviser.; editor Poetry mag., 1936-47. Served with U.S. Signal Corps, Africa, Europe, 1942-45. Mem. P.E.N., Sigma Nu, Phi Beta Kappa. Author: Boy in the Wind, 1927; The Flowering Stone, 1931 (Pulitzer prize for poetry 1932). Translator: Flowers of Evil (with Edna St. Vincent Millay), 1935. Awarded Guggenheim fellowship, 1932-33. Mem. Modern Poetry Assn. (pres.). Home: Charleston SC Died May, 1968.

DILLON, JESSE WILLIAM, govt. ofcl.; b. Dillonsmill, Va., July 15, 1904; s. Dr. Charles Lewis and Janie Elizabeth (Goggin) D.; student Fork Union Mil. Acad.; LL.B., U. Richmond, 1931; m. Margaret Knight, May 30, 1931; children—Peter L. P., Margaret Burroughs, Julie Maupin. Admitted to Va. bar; staff Dept. Taxation, Richmond, 1928-33; dist. counsel HOLC, 1933-34; dir. div. inheritance and gift taxes Commonwealth of Va., 1934-45, sec. to gov., 1945-47, sec. Commonwealth, 1945-47, state treas., 1947-57, chmn. compensation bd., 1955-57; member Va. Corp. Commn., 1957-72, chmn., 1959, now commr. Sec. Dem. Central Com. Va. Mem. bd. trustees U. Richmond, Fork Union (Va.) Mil. Acad. Mem. Delta Theta Phi, Kappa Alpha, Omicron Delta Kappa. Methodist (steward). Club: Country of Virginia. Home: Richmond VA Died Mar. 2, 1972.

DILLON, PHILIP ROBERT, editor; b. Savannah, Ga., Dec. 1, 1868; s. John Anglin and Anne (Burke) D.; ed. pub. schs. and under pvt. tutors; m. Grace Taggart Downer, May 12, 1896. With U.S. Navy, 1883-86; teacher pub. schs., Ohio, 1890-92; editor Collinwood (O.) Times, 1892; asso. editor Cripple Creek (Colo.) Crusher, 1893; reporter, Cleveland (O.) Press, 1894-98; sec. Lincoln Rep. League of Ohio, 1898-99; with publicity bur. Rep. Nat. Com., 1900; in charge publicity for Rep. County Com. N.Y. County, 1900-03; editor The Editor and Publisher, 1901-02, 1906-07, 1909-11; mem. editorial staff New York Daily News, 1904; spl. writer New York Evening World, 1911-12; mng. editor Am. Penman, 1912-21; editor Sea Stories Mag., 1922-23. Sec. Dir. Nominations League, N.Y., 1905-09; hon. sec. Paris br. English Speaking Union, 1925-26. Founder Soc. of Friends of de Grasse, 1930. Clubs: National Press (Washington, D.C.); Connaught (London, England); and Cercle l'Artistique (Nice, France). Author: The United States Flag, 1917; American Anniversaries, 1918; L'Amiral de Grasse et l'Independence Americaine, 1929. Fiction: Running the Dardanelles; Bullseye Higginson, Man o' Warsman; Plotters of the Under Sea; The Jonah of West Harbor; The Buddhism of Hogler Headstone; also (monograph) The Penmanship of New York Eighteen Years Later, 1929; short stories, essays and descriptive articles to mags. Address: Redding Ridge CT

DILNOT, FRANK, newspaper man; b. Hampshire, Eng., May 22, 1875; s. George and Elizabeth Ann (Baker) D.; ed. pvt. sch.; unmarried. Began as newspaper reporter, 1896; joined staff Central News, London, 1900; staff Daily Mail, 1902-12, visiting U.S., Can., France and Russia, and parliamentary sketch writer, 1907-12; editor Daily Citizen (organ of British labor movement), 1912-15; sent to Scandinavia by Daily Chronicle to investigate social and economic conditions, 1916; corr. for Chronicle in New York, and pres. Assn. of Foreign Correspondents in America. Chevalier of the Legion of Honour (France), 1917-19; editor London Globe, 1919. Author: The Tyrants of North Hyben, 1904; Scoundrel Mark, 1906; Love and the Forge, 1910; The Old Order Changeth, 1912; Adventures of a Newspaper Man, 1913; Lloyd George, the Man and His Story, 1917; The New America, 1919. Regarded as an authority on social and economic conditions in England. Home: 16 Sudbrooke Rd., Balham, London Eng‡

DIMNENT, EDWARD D., college pres.; b. Chicago, Ill., 1876; s. Daniel and Adelaide (Ramaker) D.; A.B., Hope Coll., Holland, Mich., 1896; student U. of Chicago, Western Theol. Sem.; Litt.D., Rutgers, 1919; L.H.D., Hope, 1919; LL.D., Central, 1919; unmarried. Prof. of Greek and economics, Hope Coll., 1898, pres. 1918—. V.p. First State Bank. Republican. Mem. Ref. Ch. America. Home: Holland MI‡

DINKINS, PHILIP M., business exec.; b. Savannah, Ga., Dec. 20, 1896; s. Tyre J. and Anna Belle (Moss) D.; B.S., Ch.E., Mass. Inst. of Technology, 1918; m. Ella Uppercu, Jan. 26, 1935; one daughter, Sarah Ann. With So. Cotton Oil Co., 1919, Zinsser & Co., 1919-21. With Dorr Co., 1921-23; with Am. Cyanamid & Chem. Corp. and predecessor, Kalbfleisch Corp., 1923-44; vice pres. and gen. mgr. Jefferson Chem. Co., 1944-46, pres., 1946-55; v.p. gen. mgr., dir. Dystuff & Chem. div., Gen. Aniline & Film Corp., 1955-58, pres., dir. corp., 1958-59, pres., chief executive officer, dir., from 1959. Mem. Am. Inst. Chem. Engrs. Clubs: Seabright Beach, Chemists' Univ. (N.Y. City), Rumson Country, Union League. Home: Red Bank NJ Died Apr. 1969.

DINSMORE, JOSEPH CAMPBELL, lawyer; b. Cin., Mar. 29, 1899; s. Frank Forbus and Mary Evelyn (Campbell) D.; A.B., Harvard, 1921, LL.B., 1924. Admitted to Ohio bar, 1925; asso. Dinsmore, Shohl & Sawyer, Cin., 1925-33; partner Dinsmore, Shohl, Barrett, Coates & Deupree and predecessors, Cin., 1934-64, Dinsmore & Dinsmore, 1964-66. Hamilton County rep. Ohio State Gen. Assembly, 1927-28, 29-30; mem. Hamilton County (O.) Republican Club. Trustee Cin. Law Library Assn., 1939-73, pres., 1965-67. Mem. Am., Ohio, Cin. (pres. 1958-59) bar assns., Cincinnatus Assn. (pres. 1932-33). Presbyn. (trustee 1942-51, pres. bd. 1943-51). Clubs: Lawyers, Country, Queen City, Racquet, Commonwealth (Cin.). Home: Cincinnati OH Died Mar. 22, 1973.

DINWIDDIE, GEORGE SUMMEY, utility exec.; b. New Orleans, Dec. 24, 1909; s. Albert Bledsoe and Caroline (Summey) D.; B.B.A., Tulane, 1937, M.B.A., 1943; m. Augusta Rosser Benners, July 2, 1929 (div. 1957); children—Mrs. Ainslie Snellings, Bruce Wayland; m. 2d, Thelma Ruth Larsen, Mar. 15, 1958. Chmn. finance com., dir. New Orleans Pub. Service Inc. Pres. and mem. Bd. of Liquidation, City Debt, New Orleans; mem. bd. commissioners Port of New Orleans. Bd. dirs. Nat. Indsl. Conf. Bd., Internat. House (New Orleans); trustee U.S. council Internat. C. of C., So. Research Inst. of Birmingham, Ala. Mem. Beta Gamma Sigma. Clubs: Boston, New Orleans Country. Home: New Orleans LA Died July 11, 1968; buried Garden of Memories, Metairie LA

DIRKSEN, EVERETT MCKINLEY, U.S. senator; b. Pekin, Ill., Jan. 4, 1896; s. Johann Frederick and Antje (Conrady) D.; student U. of Minn., 1913-17; m. Louella Carver, Dec. 24, 1927; 1 dau., Danice Joy (Mrs. Howard H. Baker, Jr.). Gen. mgr. Cook Dredging Co., 1922-25. Commr. of finance, Pekin, 1927-31; mem. 73d to 80th Congresses, 16th Ill. Dist.; U.S. senator Illinois, 1950-69, minority whip, 1957-69, minority leader, 1959-69. Mem. Ill., D.C., bars. Pvt., later 2d lt., U.S. Army, A.E.F., 1917-19. Mem. Am. Legion, Vets. of Foreign Wars. Republican. Mason, Elk, Eagle. Home: Pekin IL Died Sept. 7, 1969; buried Glendale Meml. Gardens, Pekin IL

DISNEY, ROY O., motion picture executive; b. Chgo., 1893; s. Elias and Flora (Call) D.; m. Edna Francis, Apr. 11, 1925; 1 son, Roy Edward. Chairman of board, dir. Walt Disney Prodns., Burbank, Cal. Trustee Cal. Inst. Arts. Died Dec. 1971.

DISQUE, ROBERT CONRAD, educator; b. Burlington, Ia., Mar. 14, 1883; s. Frederick Jacob and Marie Louisa (Holstein) D.; B.L., U. of Wis., 1903, B.S. in E.E., 1908; Sc.D., Northwestern, 1942; D.Eng., Stevens Inst., 1946; grad. study, U. of Pa., 1925-31; m. Laura Maud Crafts, June 14, 1921; children—Sarah Marie, Robert Otis, Helen Cushman. Teacher high sch., Burlington, Ia., 1903-05; engr., Milwaukee Electric & Ry. Co., 1908; instr. in elec. engring., U. of Wis., 1908-17; prof. elec. engring., Drexel Inst., Philadelphia, Pa., 1919-24; academic dean, 1924-32, dean of the faculty, 1932; acting president, 1943-44. Educational consultant Walter P. Murphy Foundation. Served as 1st lt. Air Service, United States Army, 1917, capt. 1918; maj. United States Res., 1918-24. Dir. School Dist. of Swarthmore. Fellow Am. Inst. E.E.; mem. Am. Society for Engring. Edn., The Newcomen Soc., Phi Beta Kappa, Sigma Xi, Tau Beta Pi, Alpha Sigma Phi, Eta Kappa Nu, Phi Kappa Phi. Democrat. Mason. Home: Swarthmore PA Died May 7, 1968.

DITZLER, CHARLOTTE WEBER, illustrator; b. Phila., 1877; student Met. Sch. of Art, New York, 1893-95; went to Munich, 1895; entered Fehr & Schmidt class, and admitted to Royal Acad. of Munich, 1898. Returned to New York, 1900; since then engaged as illustrator for mags. and books. Illustrator: The Castle of Twilight (Margaret Horton Potter); Robert Cavalier and The Flower of Destiny (William Dana Orcutt). Address: 22 W. 9th St., NY‡

DIVEN, ROBERT JOSEPH, clergyman, author: b. Davis, Pa., Dec. 8, 1869; s. Franklin and Mary Ann (Allison) D.; grad. Kellysburg (Pa.) Prep. Sch.; A.B., Grove City (Pa.) Coll., 1893, D.D., 1916; grad. Auburn (N.Y.) Theol. Sem., 1896; m. Eva Wortman, Aug. 29, 1894; children—Florence Lucile, Joseph Lyle, Robert Kenneth. Ordained ministry Presbyn. Ch. in U.S.A., 1896; pastor Otisville and New Hamburgh, N.Y., 1896-1901; missionary in Oregon, 1901-11; pastor Moreland Ch., Portland, 1911-12; missionary in Alaska, 1912-30; resident agt. Nat. Missions in Alaska, 1927-30; pastor Lebanon, Ore., 1934-36; retired, Oct. 1936. Republican. Odd Fellow; mem. Arctic Brotherhood, League of Western Writers. Author: A Daughter of the Hills, 1916; Rowdy—An Alaskan Dog Story, 1927; Tim Towser, a Story of a Little Dog and His Friends, 1929; The Black Wolf Mystery, 1931. Contbr. to St. Nicholas (mag.), Dictionary of Am. Biography and ch. publs. Home: 3238 S.E. Woodward St., Portland OR‡

DIX, OTTO, painter; b. Gera, Germany, Dec. 2, 1891; ed. art sch. Became proponent Neue Sachlichkeit (new realism), 1918; prof. State Acad. Art, Dresden, Germany, 1927-33; exhibited Degenerate Art Exhbn., 1937, Stuttgart Exhbn., 1963; represented in U.S., German and French museums, art galleries. Served in World War I; imprisoned by Gestapo in World War II. Recipient Cornelius prize, Dusseldorf, 1959, Grosses Bundesverdienstkreuz, 1959. Hon. fellow Medizinischen Akad. Carl Gustav Carus, Dresden; hon. mem. Accad. delle Arti del Disegno, Florence; mem. Acad. of Arts, West Berlin. Prin. works include war drawings and paintings, Bibl. subjects. Home: Bodensee Federal Republic of Germany Died July 25, 1969; buried Hemmenhofen Germany.

DIXON, ARMINIUS GRAY, clergyman; b. Rockingham Co., N.C., Feb. 13, 1870; s. John Franklin and Lucinda Elsebeth (Harrison) D.; A.B., Western Md. Coll., Westminster, Md., 1899; B.D., Westminster Theol. Sem., 1901; D.D., Adrian Coll., 1919; m. Mary Etta Watts, of Baltimore, Md., Oct. 28, 1902 (died July 18, 1904); m. 2d, Margaret M. Kuhns (returned missionary from Japan), May 16, 1908. Ordained ministry M.P. Ch., 1901; pastor Rocky Mount, N.C., 1901-02, Henderson, N.C., 1903; traveling sec. for N. Carolina Coll. enterprise, 1904; pastor Chestnut Ridge, N.C., 1905-06, Henderson, 1906-08, High Point, 1908-17; sec. Bd. Young People's Work, M.P. Ch., 1917-22; pres. N.C. Annual Conf. Meth. Protestant Ch. since 1922. Democrat. Home: Greensboro NC‡

DIXON, L. A., SR., mfr.; b. North Laurence, O., Sept. 1, 1898; s. Wallace Willard and Elizabeth (Pollock) D.; m. Ruth O. Shobert, July 12, 1919; 1 son, L. A. Exec.

v.p. Rockwell Mfg. Co., Pitts., also dir.; chmn. bd. AUM Corp., Jamestown, N.Y.; sr. v.p., dir. N.Am. Rockwell Corp., 1964-68. Address: Pittsburgh PA Died Aug. 10, 1972; buried DeBois PA

DIXON, WESLEY MOON, corp. exec.; b. Chicago, May 16, 1896; s. Thomas J. and Dora (Moon) D.; student Cornell U., 1914-17; m. Katherine Strawn, January 15, 1926 (dec. Oct. 17, 1958); children—Wesley M., Stewart Strawn, Thomas H.; m. 2d, Eleanor C. Kribben, June 24, 1960. Vice pres., director Cornell Wood Products Co., 1920-25; pres. Dixon Bd. Mills, 1925-28, Sefton Mfg. Corp., 1928-30; v.p., dir. Container Corp. of Am., 1930-46, pres., 1946-61, chmn. bd., pres., chief exec. officer, 1960-61, chmn. bd., 1961-63; dir. U.S. Gypsum Co. Trustee Com. Econ. Devel. Served as 2d lt. 333d F.A., World War I. Trustee Chgo. Wesley Meml. Hospital; mem., past president board of trustees Northwestern University. Republican. Member Methodist Ch. Mason (K.T.). Clubs: Chgo., Comml., Old Elm, University (Chicago); Onwentsia Golf. Home: Lake Forest IL Died Nov. 3, 1969.

DIXON, WILLIAM PALMER, investment banker; N.Y.C., Mar. 19, 1902; s. William H. and Josephine Theodora (Williams) D.; student Eton Coll., Eng.; A.B., Harvard University, 1925; m. Joan Deery, Feb. 21, 1941; children—Palmer, Peter T. With J. Henry Schroder Banking Corp., N.Y., 1926-29; partner Rhoades & Co., N.Y.C., 1929-38, Loeb, Rhoades & Co., mem. N.Y. Stock Exchange, 1938-68; dir. Loeb, Rhoades & Co., Inc., USLIFE Holding Corp. (N.Y.), also dir. U.S. Life Insurance Co. of N.Y., Am. Home Assurance Co. (N.Y.C.), Am. Internat. Life Assurance Co. of N.Y., The Lighthouse (N.Y.), Loeb, Rhoades Internat., Inc. Trustee, member finance com. Midtown Hospital, New York City; dir. American Field Service. Served as colonel USAAF, World War II, assistant chief staff 9th Air Force, 1944. Decorated Legion of Merit with Oak Leaf Cluster; Croix de Guerre with Palm (Belgium). Mem. N.Y. C. of C., Nat. Inst. Social Scis., Newcomen Soc., N.Y. Philharmonic Soc. Clubs: Recess, Racquet and Tennis, River, Harvard, Madison Sq. Garden, Marco Polo, Turf and Field, Links Golf, The Brook (New York City, N.Y.); Philadelphia (Pennsylvania); Racquet (Montreal), Racquet (Detroit); Jesters, White's, Old Etonian Racquets and Tennis (London, Eng.); Harvard Varsity (pres.) (Cambridge, Mass.), Nat. Champion U.S., Squash Racquets, 1925, 26. Home: New York City NY Died July 25, 1968; buried St. James Ch., New York City NY

DOAN, GILBERT EVERETT, metall. engr.; b. Lansdale, Pa., Jan. 16, 1897; s. William E. and Agnes Sibbald (McKinlay) D.; Chem. E., Lehigh University, 1919; Ph.D., University of Berlin, Germany, 1927; m. Alice Curtis Olney, Nov. 23, 1929; children—Gilbert Everett, Julia Alice (Mrs. Ben M. Cart), Agnes Sibbald (Mrs. Ronald Gregson). Metallographist, U.S. Naval Experiment Station, Annapolis, 1919-20; dir. research Una Welding Co., Cleveland, 1920-24; company mission to Germany, 1922-23; prof. metallurgy, Lehigh U., 1926-52, head of the dept., 1939-52; mgr. metall. research, Koppers Co., Pitts., 1952-59, cons., 1959-70; cons. U.S. Naval Research Lab., 1929; Spl. cons. Gen. Electric Co., Westinghouse, Bethlehem Steel Co, Union Carbide. Guest lecturer Franklin Inst.; exec. sec. Vol. Com. to Make Poor TV Better, 1961-70. Guest lectr. Osaka University, Kyushu Institute of Technology, Japan, Benares Univ., India, Lafayette College. Dir. Nat. Assn. Better Radio and TV. Investigator Office of Scientific Research Development, 1942-46. Awarded Lincoln gold medal for advancement of science of welding, 1943; Navy Certificate, 1947; The Stoughton Award, 1949. Member Board of Awards American Welding Society, Howe Medal Committee American Society for Metals. Del. London Conf. English Speaking Union, 1952. Fellow Royal Soc. Arts (London); mem. Newcomen Soc., and many sci. and tech. socs., Sigma Xi, Tau Beta Pi, Omicron Delta Kappa, Delta Upsilon. Author: The Principles of Physical Metallurgy 1935; Our Sons Specialize; Summer Enchantment: The New Position of Science; Science Changes the Scientist; The New American. Co-author: The Principles of Metallurgy, 1933; The Post-Scientific Era Arrives, 1965; Bradley Stoughton—Mankind Was My Business, 1966; also tech. and sci. papers. Home: Nazareth PA Died Oct. 27, 1970; buried Montgomery Square Methodist Ch., Lansdale PA

DOAN, JAMES BURTON, business exec.; b. Cincinnati, Oct. 21, 1870; s. James Burton and Genevra (Faulkner) D.; m. Gertrude Fletcher, June 7, 1898. With Am. Tool Works Co. since 1888, vice pres., gen. mgr., 1904-16, pres., 1916-36, chmn. bd. dir. since 1936; dir. First Nat. Bank of Cincinnati, Ohio Nat. Life Ins. Co., Am. Rolling Mill Co., Middletown, O. Dir. Bethesda Hosp. (Cincinnati), Childrens Home; trustee at large Methodist Church of U.S. Past mem. and officer Nat. Machine Tool Builders Assn., Nat. Metal Trades Assn., Army Ordnance Assn. of Cincinnati Area; Hist. and Philos. Soc. of Ohio, Cincinnati Metal Trades Assn., Cincinnati C. of C. Methodist. Clubs: Commercial, Optomist, Commonwealth, Cincinnati, Cincinnati Country. Home: 1845 Madison Rd., Cincinnati 6. Office: Pearl and Eggleston Av., Cincinnati OH

DOANE, RICHARD CONGDON, paper mfr.; b. Phila., Feb. 26, 1898; s. William T. and Edith (Medbury) D.; A.B., Yale, 1919; m. Mary Goodfellow, June 17, 1949. North African rep. Lamborn & Co. of N.Y., Algiers, Algeria, 1922-23; sales dept. Internat. Paper Co., N.Y.C., 1924-28, mgr. newsprint sales, 1928-38, dir. 1948-72, v.p., 1948-54, pres., 1954-59, chief executive officer, 1959-66, chmn. 1961-67; Canadian Internat. Paper Co., Montreal, Que., Can., 1938-48, dir. since 1938, gen. mgr., 1947-48; dir. Del. & Hudson Co., D. & H. R.R., Bankers Trust Co. Dir. Internat. Paper Company Foundation. Member of the Institute of Paper Chemistry (trustee). Clubs: Union League, Yale, Links; St. James, Mt. Royal (Montreal). Home: Waitsfield VT Died July 6, 1972; buried Pittsfield Cemetery, Pittsfield MA

DOANE, SAMUEL EVERETT, electrical engr.; b. Swampscott, Mass., Feb. 28, 1870; s. Capt. Edward E. and Helen M. (Nickerson) D.; grad. Swampscott High Sch., 1886; hon. E.E., Case Sch. of Applied Science, 1927; m. Marion M. Jackman, of Marlboro, Mass., Oct. 17, 1900; children—Dorothy Helen, Edward Everett. Entered employ of Thomson-Houston Electric Co., Lynn, Mass., 1886; asst. engr. Harrison (N.J.) Lamp Works of Gen. Electric Co., 1892-96, supt., 1893-94; acting engr. foreign dept. Gen. Electric Co., at Schenectady, 1896-97; supt. Bryan-Marsh Co., Marlboro, Mass., 1897-1901; chief engr. Nat. Electric Lamp Assn. (now Nat. Lamp Works of Gen. Electric Co.), 1901-30, consultant, 1930-35, retired. Fellow Am. Inst. E.E., A.A.A.S.; mem. Am. Soc. M.E.; ex-pres. Illuminating Engring. Soc. of U.S. Address: 651 State St., Bridgeport CT‡

DOBBIE, ELLIOTT VAN KIRK, educator; b. Bklyn., May 9, 1907; s. Thomas William and Amanda Mabel (Van Kirk) D.; A.B., Columbia, 1927, A.M., 1928, Ph.D., 1937; m. Mary Lorraine Kout, June 29, 1937; 1 son, William Andrew. Instr. English L.I.U., 1928-29; lectr. English, Columbia, 1934-37, instr., 1937-42, asst. prof., 1942-45, asso. prof., 1945-51, prof. since 1951; fellow Guggenheim Meml. Found., 1948-49. Mem. rationing bd. O.P.A., 1943-45. Mem. Modern Lang. Assn. Am., Linguistic Soc. Am., Modern Humanities Research Assn., Linguistic Circle N.Y., Am. Dialect Soc., Phi Beta Kappa. Author: The Exeter Book (with George Philip Krapp), 1936; The Manuscripts of Caedmon's Hymn and Bede's Death Song, 1937; The Anglo-Saxon Minor Poems, 1942; Beowulf and Judith, 1953; Asst. editor Am. Speech, 1939-40, asso. editor, 1941, 1948-—, mng. editor 1942-47. Home: New York City NY Died Mar. 23, 1970.

DOBBIN, CARROLL EDWARD, geologist; b. Jonesport, Me., Oct. 2, 1892; s. Edward Butler and Myrtie Grace (Rumery) D.; A.B., Colby Coll., 1916; hon. D.Sc., 1941; Ph.D., Johns Hopkins, 1924; D. Engineering (hon.), Colorado School of Mines, 1952; m. Catharine Dorcas Barncord, Nov. 13, 1921. Geologist U.S. Geol. Survey, 1918-59, ret. Recipient U.S. Dept. Interior Honor award, 1959. Mem. Geol. Soc. America, Am. Assn. Petroleum Geologists (v.p. 1936-37, pres., 1947-48, hon. mem. 1958-67), Rocky Mountain Geologists (pres. 1932), Am. Inst. Mining Metall. and Petroleum Engrs., A.A.A.S., Colo. Sci. Soc., Geol. Soc. Washington, Am. Geophys. Union, Colo. Engring. Council (pres., 1945-47), Colo. Soc. Engrs. (pres. 1951), Soc. Econ. Geologists, Wyo. Engring. Soc., Wyo. Geol. Assn., N.M. Geol Soc., Sigma Xi, Sigma Gamma Epsilon, Lambda Chi Alpha, Gamma Alpha, Tau Beta Pi. Mason (32 deg.). Club: Teknik. Author bulls. and profl. papers of U.S. Geol. Survey; articles to geol. jours. Home: Denver CO Died Mar. 15, 1967; cremated.

DOBBINS, HARRY THOMPSON, editor; b. Williamsburg, Blair County, Pa., Jan. 4, 1865; s. Thomas and Clarissa Sidney (Ake) D.; ed. high sch., Huntingdon, Pa.; m. Mary Lorena Highlands, Jan. 11, 1887; 1 son, Harry Sidney (dec.). Formerly journeyman printer; editor and part owner Capital Courier, Lincoln, Neb., 1886-88; joined staff of Lincoln Evening News, 1888, now The Evening State Journal, of which he was editor until consolidation with Nebraska State Journal; now asso. editor; contbr. to a number of newspapers and magazines. Mem. Rep. State Com., Neb., 2 yrs.; chmn. Lancaster County Rep. Com., 1904. Mem. First Plymouth Congl. Ch. (chmn.bd. trustees 9 yrs.). Mem. City Library, 1897-40, pres., 1930-40; mem. com. Y.M.C.A., since 1895. Mem. Am. Inter-Professional Inst., Nebraska Writers Guild, Neb. Press Assn., Lincoln Chamber of Commerce. Conglist. Home: Hotel Lincoln. Office: 904 P St., Lincoln NB‡

DOBBINS, JAMES T(ALMAGE), chemist, educator; b. Boonville, N.C., Feb. 11, 1888; s. Nathan C. and Sophronia C. (Reece) D.; A.B., U. of N.C., 1911, A.M., 1912, Ph.D., 1914; m. Lila Shore, June 20, 1917; children—Christine (Mrs. Robert W. Taylor), James Talmage. Instr., N.C. State U., 1914-18; asso. prof. chemistry U. of N.C., 1918-30, prof. chemistry, 1930-60, emeritus prof., 1960-72. Chmn., Chapel Hill City Bd. Adjustment, 1948-68. Recipient 1st Ann. Distinguished Prof. award U. N.C. Sch. Pharmacy, 1961. Mem. Am. Chem. Soc., Soc. Pub. Analysts, Sigma Xi, Alpha Chi Sigma. Democrat. Baptist (lifetime deacon). Author: Semi Micro Qualitative Analysis, 1943. Home: Chapel Hill NC Died May 13, 1972; buried Chapel Hill Cemetery, Chapel Hill NC

DOBBS, SAMUEL CANDLER, b. Carroll County, Ga., Nov. 8, 1868; s. Henry H. and Elizabeth (Candler) D.; ed. country sch.; LL.D., Emory University, Atlanta, Ga., 1928; m. Ruth Mixon, June 11, 1890; children—Samuel C., Mildred Frances (Mrs. Stewart Bird). With Coca-Cola Co., 1892, various positions from laborer to pres., elected 1919, resigned, 1920; now dir. Atlantic Steel Co., Coca-Cola Co., First Nat. Bank; chmn. bd., dir. Bank of Villa Rica (Ga.); chmn. bd. Am. Sumatra Tobacco Corp. Pres. Asso. Adv. Clubs, 1909, 10; ex-pres. Atlanta C. of C. Chairman board of trustees Reinhardt Coll. (Waleska, Ga.), Georgia Mil. Acad., College Park, Ga. Democrat. Methodist. Home: The Lichens," Lakemont, Ga. Office: First Nat. Bank Bldg., Atlanta GA‡

DOBI, ISTVAN, prime minister of Hungary; b. Szony, Komarom, Hungary, 1898. Began as agrl. worker in youth; took part in northern Carpathian campaign of Hungarian Soviet Republic, 1919; became active in Nat. Fedn. of Agrl. Laborers; joined Smallholders Party, 1933, becoming leader of agrl. laborers dept., 1934, pres. of Party, 1952-67; active in movement for Hungarian independence, a movement directed against German aggression and Hungarian sympathizers with those plans, 1942; following liberation at end of World War II, elected mem. of parliament for Smallholders Party; became minister of state, 1945, minister of agr., 1946; head of democratic wing of Smallholders Party to fight to democratize the Party, 1947; again became minister of agr., 1948; prime minister, 1948-67; pres. Presidential Council Hungarian People's Rep. Vice pres. Hungarian People's Independence Front. Home: Budapest Hungary Died Nov. 24, 1968.

DOBSON, SIR ROY HARDY, aero. engr.; b. Horsforth, Yorkshire, Eng., Sept. 27, 1891; s. Horace and Mary Ann (Hardy) D.; m. Annie Smith, 1916 (dec.); one son, one daughter. Apprenticeship T. & R. Lees, Hollinwood, Manchester, Eng.; with A.V. Roe & Co., Ltd., 1914-68, engring. depts., 1914-18, works mgr., 1919-34, gen. mgr., 1934-36, dir., 1936-41, mng. dir., 1941-68, also chmn.; chmn. Hawker Siddeley Group, Ltd., London, 1963-68, Kelvin Constrn. Co., Ltd.; former chmn. Hawker Siddeley Can., Ltd.; dir. Hawker Siddeley Aviation Limited, High Duty Alloys, Ltd., Dominion Coal Company, Ltd. Decorated commander Order of the Brit. Empire, 1942; created knight 1945, Founder mem. Lancashire Aero Club, Lancashire and Derbyshire Gliding. Hon. fellow Royal Aero. Soc.; mem. Soc. Brit. Aircraft Constructors, Ltd. (pres. 1948-49, 62-63), C. of C. Clubs: Eccentric; Royal Aero; Union (Ashton-under-Lyne); York, Royal Angelesey (Toronto); Royal Air Force, Overseas Bankers' (London). Home: Hantshire England Died July 7, 1968; buried Woodford Parish Ch., Woodford Cheshire England

DOCTOROFF, JOHN, portrait artist; b. N.Y.C., July 19, 1893; s. Benjamin and Rose (Lehman) D.; student Cooper Union Inst., N.Y.C., 1909-11, Art Inst. Chgo., 1925; m. Rose Kaufman, Nov. 30, 1916 (dec.); children—Ruth Joanne (Mrs. Charles Levy, Jr.), Marjorie Rose (Mrs. Harvey Stuart Bank). Engaged in portrait painting 1924-—; portraits commd. include those of Pres. Calvin Coolidge, Pres. Herbert Hoover, Wendell Willkie, Gen. John J. Pershing, Gov. Henry Horner, Julius Rosenwald, Gov. Alfred Landon, Lester Selig, Dr. Louis L. Mann, Edwin Markham, Frank Rathje, Ralph Budd, Arthur Rubloff, Vice Pres. Charles G. Dawes, Fred Sargent, Gov. William Stratton, Edward Eagle Brown, Foster McGaw, Arthur A. Frank, Max Epstein, Paul Harris, Col. Jacob Arvey, Dr. Morris Fishbein, Gov. Dwight H. Green, William J. Hagenah, Issac Miller Hamilton, Judge Michael L. Igoe, Oscar Mayer, Max McGraw, Ben Bohac, Dr. Willis J. Potts, Dr. Vincent O'Conner, Dr. T.K. Lawless, Soloman Smith, George Keck, and many other famous mem. Mem. All Ill. Soc. Fine Arts, Bryn Mawr C. of C. Rotarian. Designer Liberty Loan war posters. Commd. by Republican nat. com. to do campaign portraits. Home and studio: Chicago IL Died May 27, 1970.

DODD, NORRIS E., United Nations official; born Chicksaw Co., Ia., July 20, 1879; s. Edwin H. and Mary Ellen (West) D.; ed. in public schs. of Ia., Greenwood and Drew Acad.; m. Pauline Ensminger, Aug. 28, 1905; 1 dau., Mary; m. 2d, Ara Pruit, 1954. Registered pharmacist, Oregon, 1903; opened and operated drug stores, Pendleton, Pilot Rock, Baker, Haines, Wallowa, Ore., 1900-07; built and operated rural and city telephone lines also gen. store and telephone exchange, Haines, Ore., 1907-12; livestock feeding operator Coles & Dodd, Haines, Ore., 1912-33; ranch owner, Haines, Ore., since 1912; chmn. County Wheat Com., 1933, County Corn-Hog Com., 1934; chmn. Corn-Hog State Bd. Control, 1934-35, Ore. State Agrl. Conservation Com., 1936; fieldman western div. (13 states) Agrl. Adjustment Agency, 1938, asst. dir. western div., 1938-39, dir., 1939-43, chief Agrl. Adjustment Agency, Washington, D.C., 1943-45; under sec. agriculture, 1946-48; dir. gen., Food and Agr. Orgn. of U.N. (FAO), Washington and Rome, 1948-54; head U.S. delegation 2d and 3d FAO Confs., Copenhagen and Geneva; chmn. U.S. delegation Internat. Wheat Council ret., 1954. Democrat. Home: Phoenix AZ Died June 23, 1968; buried Baker OR

DODD, THOMAS JOSEPH, U.S. senator; b. Norwich, Conn., May 15, 1907; s. Thomas Joseph and Abigail Margaret (O'Sullivan) D.; Ph.B., Providence (Rhode Island) College, 1930; LL.B., Yale University, 1933; m. Grace Murphy, May 19, 1934; children—Thomas Joseph, Carolyn, Jeremy, Martha, Christopher, Nicholas. Established Nat. Youth Adminstrn. program in Conn., 1935; asst. chief civil rights sect. Dept. Justice, 1938-45; vice chmn. review bd., chief trial counsel Nuremberg Trials, Nazi war criminals, 1945-46; pvt. practice of law, Hartford, 1947-71; mem. Congress, 1st Dist. Conn., 1953-57; U.S. senator from Conn., 1959-67; mem. fgn. relations, judiciary, space coms. Decorated Presdl. citation, U.S. Medal Freedom, Order White Lion (Czechoslovakia), Comdr. Order of Merit (Italy). Author: Freedom and Foreign Policy. Home: Old Lyme CT Died May 24, 1971.

DODDS, ROBERT J., lawyer; b. nr. Pittsburgh, Oct. 20, 1877; s. Joseph Spratt and Sarah Jane (Wallace) D.; LL.B., U. Pittsburgh, 1903; m. Agnes J. Raw, Feb. 14, 1914; children—Agnes A. (Mrs. Morton Frank), Robert J. Admitted to Pa. bar, 1903, and since practiced in Pittsburgh; mem. Reed, Smith, Shaw & McClay; dir. Mesta Machine Co., Pittsburgh-Erie Saw Corp. U.S. atty. Western Dist. of Pa., 1920. Mem. Am. Judicature Society, Am. Pa. and Allegheny Co. bar assns. Clubs: Longue Vue, Duquesne, Pittsburgh Athletic Association, Law (Pitts.). Home: 1452 N. Highland Av., Pitts. 6. Office: Union Trust Bldg., Pitts 30‡

DODGE, BARNETT FRED, educator; born Akron, Ohio, Nov. 29, 1895; s. Fred Bradley and Charlotte Ida (Barnett) D.; B.S., Mass. Inst. Tech., 1917; D.Sc., Harvard, 1925; D.Sc. (hon.), Worcester Polytechnic Institute, 1956; Honorary Diplome de Docteur, University of Toulouse (France), 1961; Huesped de Honor, U. Central de Venezuela, Caracas, 1961; m. Constance Woodbury, June 5, 1918; children—Richard Woodbury, Phyllis. Chem. engineer E. I. du Pont Nemours Company, 1917-20; with Lewis Recovery Corp., Boston, 1920-22;- lecturer on chem. engring., Harvard U., 1922-25; asst. prof., Yale U., 1925-30, asso. prof., 1930-35, prof. and head of department, 1935-60, dean sch. engring., 1960-61, professor of chemical engineering, 1961-64, professor emeritus, 1964-72; lecturer Worcester Polytechnic Inst., 1922-25; official investigator for Nat. Defense Research Com., 1941-45; asso. dir. Central Engring. Lab. U. of Pa., 1943-44; tech. dir., Fercleve Corp., Oak Ridge, Tenn. (on leave from Yale); former chmn. chem. engring. dept., Yale U.; cons. to various organizations; Fulbright lectr., Univ. Toulouse, Fr., 1951; mem. Engring. Mission to Japan, Am. Soc. Engring. Edn., 1951; lecturer Univ. of Barcelona, Spain, 1954, U. Central de Venezuela (Carcaras), 1957; Fulbright lectr. U. Lille, also Cath. U. Lille (France), 1958; Ford Found. grant tchr. U. Buenos Aires, 1965-61; Sigma Xi lectr. Central and South Am., 1966; taught U. Uruguay, 1966; lectr. U. New South Wales, Sydney, Australia, 1967; Am. Acad. Sci. rep. to Yugoslavia, 1968; taught Pahlavi U., Shiraz, Iran, 1970; lectr. U.S. Bahia Blanca (Argentina), 1969. Recipient Walker award American Institute of Chemical Engineers, Warren K. Lewis award, 1963. Fellow Am. Inst. Chem. Engrs. (dir. 1939-41, 43-45, v.p. 1954, pres. 1955, chmn. com. on chem. engring. edn., 1942-47, chmn. spl. task com. for new engring. center site; rep. on Bd. United Engring. Trustees 1956-57, recipient founders award, 1962), Am. Acad. Arts and Scis.; mem. Am. Chem. Soc., American Society for Engring. Edn., Engrs. Council Profl. Development (chmn. region IV 1947-51), A.A.A.S., Sigma Xi, Tau Beta Pi. Republican. Club: Appalachian Mountain (Boston), Harvard of New Haven. Author: Chemical Engineering Thermodynamics, 1944. Contbr. to tech. jours. Home: Hamden CT Died Mar. 16, 1972.

DODGE, BAYARD, educator; b. N.Y. City, Feb. 5, 1888; s. Cleveland Hoadley and Grace (Parish) D.; B.A., Princeton, 1909, D.D., 1928; B.D., Union Theological Seminary, 1913; M.A., Columbia University, 1913; LL.D., Occidental College, 1926, Yale University, 1949; L.H.D., Am. U. Beirut, 1966; m. Mary Williams Bliss, Feb. 12, 1914; children—Grace, Margaret, David Stuart, Bayard (killed in action, France, November 22, 1944). Mem. faculty American University of Beirut, Lebanon, from 1913, pres., 1923-48, pres. emeritus since 1948; vis. prof. Columbia, 1949-55; lectr. Princeton, 1951-55; regional cultural officer U.S. Information Service, Am. Embassy, Cairo, 1955-56; vis. prof. Am. U. at Cairo, 1956; dir. Nr. East Relief (Syria and Palestine), 1920-21. Recipient Woodrow Wilson award Princeton, 1960; decorated Chevalier de la Legion d'Honneur, 1927; Merite Libanais, 1927; Merite Syrien, 1937; Grand Officer de l'Ordre Royal du Phenix, 1937; Ordre de l'Instruction Publique, Republique Libanaise, 1942; Decoration de l'Instruction Publique, Iran, 1942; Hon. Officier, Order of British Empire, 1946; Order of Cedar (Lebanon), Comdr. 1947, Grand Officer, 1948; Merite Syrien Superior Grade, 1947; Comdr. Pologna Restituta, 1947; Comdr. Order of Ismail, 1948; Order of Umayya, 1948; grand officer rank Lebanese Order of Cedars, 1972. Presbyterian. Clubs: Princeton, Century Association, Broad Street (New York). Address: Princeton NJ Died May 30, 1972; buried Princeton NJ

DODGE, LOUIS, author; b. Burlington, Ia., Sept. 27, 1870; s. Henry Lewis and Lila (Haskell) D.; ed. Quitman (Ark.) Coll.; unmarried. Began as newspaper reporter, Eagle Pass, Tex., 1893; reporter, critic and editorial writer for St. Louis papers, 1901-16. Served as pvt. and non-commd. officer 18th and 23d U.S. Ind., during Spanish-Am. War. in P.I. Democrat. Author: Bonnie May, 1916; Children of the Desert, 1917; A Runaway Woman, 1918; The Sandman's Forest, 1918; Rosy, 1919; The Sandman's Mountain, 1919; Whispers, 1920; Tawi Tawi, 1921; Everychild, 1921; Nancy; Her Life and Death, 1921; The American, 1934; Wagon Ruts (pub. in England), 1935. Home: 605 Garnet St., Redondo Beach CA‡

DODGE, SHERWOOD, advt. exec.; b. Chgo., Dec. 18, 1915; s. Adiel Yeaman and Geraldine (Hopkins) D.; A.B., U. Cal., Berkeley, 1938; m. Helen Aydelott, Oct. 15, 1938 (div.); children—Sherwood, Dorian; m. 2d, Betty Grant, July 25, 1952; one daughter, Dariel Ross. With Lord & Thomas, Chgo., 1938-42, research mgr.; with Foote, Cone & Belding, N.Y.C., 1946-57, v.p. charge marketing, 1952-57; exec. v.p. Fletcher D. Richards, Inc., N.Y.C., 1957-59; v.p., dir. marketing tiolet articles div. Colgate-Palmolive Co., 1960-63; v.p. contact supr. Young & Rubicam, N.Y.C., 1964-66; pres. Advt. Research Found., N.Y.C., 1966-68. Mem. Am. Advt. Fedn. (dir.), Copy Research Council, Market Research Council. Contbr. articles trade publs. Home: New York City NY Died July 5, 1968; buried Ferncliff Cemetery.

DODGE, WALTER PHELPS, lawyer, author; b. Beirut, Syria, June 13, 1869; s. Dr. David Stuart (q.v.) and Ellen (Phelps) D.; studied in Greece and Germany under pvt. tutors; entered Yale, 1887, but did not grad.; student Oxford U., Eng.; traveled extensively 3 yrs., admitted to bar, London, 1898, New York, Oct. 1909; m. Ida Cooke; 2d, Ethel Adlard Coles, of Staverton Court, Eng. Fellow Royal Geog. Soc. (London); member Am. Geog. Soc., S.R. Clubs: Reform, Authors', Racquet, Players. Author: Three Greek Tales, 1892; As the Crow Flies, 1893; A Strong Man Armed, 1896; The Sea of Love, 1898; Piers Gaveston, 1899; From Squire to Prince, 1901; The Real Sir Richard Burton, 1907; King Charles I, a Study, 1912; The Purple Iris, 1915; Studies of the English Sovereigns, 1918. Home: The Grange, Weatogue, Conn. Address: Reform Club, Pall Mall, S.W., London England‡

DODSON, LOREN RALPH, ins. co. exec.; b. Columbus, O., Dec. 21, 1897; s. Frank S. and Nellie (Call) D.; B.Sc., Ohio State U., 1919; m. Margaret Anderson, June 23, 1923; children—Nancy Jane (Mrs. Humphrey Sullivan, Jr., dec. Oct. 1950); Betty Louise (Mrs. John Kenneth Borton). Mem. firm Battelle & Battelle, C.P.A.'s, Dayton, O., 1919-25; sec.-treas. Conway Co., Boston and N.Y.C., 1928-34, asst. sec., 1934-59, sec.-treas., 1959; dir. Firemen's Mutual Ins. Co., Providence. Police commr., Town of Mamaroneck, 1943-57. Mem. Sigma Chi. Clubs: University (Larchmont, N.Y.); Hole-in-the Wall Golf, Naples Yacht (Naples, Fla.). Home: Naples FL also Old Lyme CT Died May 27, 1972; buried Naples Meml. Gardens, Naples FL

DODSON, MARTHA ETHEL, editor; b. Fairmount Springs, Pa.; d. Boyd Headley and Sarah (Hess) D.; B.E., Bloomsburg (Pa.) State Normal Sch., 1899; Wyoming Sem., 1901; A.B., Cornell U., 1907. In charge U.S. Immigration Commission's investigation of immigrant aid socs., 1907-09; spl. agt. Census Bur., 1910; fiction editor Housekeeper Mag., 1911-12; editor Dress Essentials, 1914; asso. editor Harper's Bazar, 1915-18; mng. editor Harper's Bazar, 1919-20; editorial staff of Ladies' Home Journal, 1921-27; exec. staff of Pacific Mills, 1927-28; sales promotion mgr. since 1929. Mem. Acad. Polit. Science, Authors' League of America, N.Y. Drama League, Kappa Kappa Gamma. Clubs: Woman's University, Pen and Brush (New York). Address: 106 E. 52d St., New York NY‡

DOHAN, EDWARD G., college pres.; b. Troy, N.Y., Jan. 12, 1870; s. Timothy and Catherine (Sheedy) D.; B.S., Villanova (Pa.) Coll., 1894, A.B., 1896, A.M., 1904; S.T.L., Rome, 1911, S.T.B., 1913 (LL.D., Duquesne University, Pittsburgh, 1915). Instr. Villanova Coll., 1896-9; ordained R. C. priest, May 27, 1899; instr. Augustinian Acad., S.I., N.Y., 1899-06; prior Augustinian Convent, New York, 1905-10; rector, Ch. of St. Nicholas of Tolentine, New York, 1906-10; pres. Villanova Coll., July 1, 1910-Sept. 17, 1917; rector St. Joseph's Ch., Greenwich, N.Y., 1917—. Home: Greenwich NY‡

DOHME, ALFRED ROBERT LOUIS, chemist; b. Baltimore, Md., Feb. 15, 1867; s. Charles E. and Ida (Schultz) D.; A.B., Johns Hopkins, 1886; Ph.D., 1889; post-grad. courses in chemistry, geology and mineralogy; U. of Berlin, lab. of Fresenius Wiesbaden, and U. of Strassburg, 1889-91, U. of Paris, 1905; m. Emma D. Blumner, Feb. 15, 1893 (dec.); m. 2d, Paula Carl, Nov. 22, 1909. In bus. as mfg. chemist, 1891-1929; pres. Sharp & Dohme, 1911-29. Instr. pharmacy, Johns Hopkins, 1901-12; sec. Nat. Com. of Revision of Pharmacopoeia of U.S. for 1900-10 at decennial conv., Washington, 1900, and mem. Committee of Revision, 1900-30; president The Lync Co., Baltimore, Md. President of the Maryland Pharmaceutical Assn., 1899-1900. Am. Pharmaceutical Assn., 1918, Baltimore Drug Exchange, 1916-18; trustee Walters Art Gallery, Gilman Country Sch. for Boys; mem. bd. dirs. Sharp &Dohme, Fidelity Trust Co.; pres. City Wide Congress, Baltimore, 1911-21; vice pres. Baltimore Museum of Art. Clubs: University, Maryland, Elkridge Country, Baltimore Country, Merchants. Home: 5204 Roland Av., Office: Baltimore Life Bldg., Baltimore 1 MD‡

DOHNANYI, ERNO (ERNEST VON DOHNANYI), pianist; b. Presburg, Hungary, July 27, 1877; s. Friedrich D.; studied with his father (an amateur cellist), Karl Forstner, Hans Koesler, and later with d'Albert. Debut at Berlin, 1897, later toured in Europe; first came to U.S. in 1900. Composer of symphonies, piano pieces, string quartets, songs.*‡

DOIG, JAMES RUFUS, newspaper advt. exec.; b. Chgo., Dec. 2, 1903; s. Rolla Wallace and Lucretia (von Klein Smid) D.; B.S., U. Cal. at Berkeley, 1928; m. Mary Coloma Jameson, Jan. 26, 1929;children—Jameson W., Naomi L. (Mrs. George Hulme), Mary Jean (Mrs. Howard H. Foster). Salesman, Cresmer, Woodward, O'Mara & Ormsbee, Inc. (formerly O'Mara & Ormsbee, Inc.), San Francisco, 1928-36, mgr., Los Angeles, 1936-40, Pacific Coast mgr., San Francisco, 1940-45, sales mgr., N.Y.C., 1945-46, v.p., dir., N.Y.C., 1946-51, pres., dir., N.Y.C., 1951-62, chmn. exec. com. 1962-69, chmn. bd., 1965-67. Clubs: Union League (N.Y.C.); Wychmere Beach (Harwichport, Mass.). Home: East Brewster MA Died Sept. 22, 1969.

DOLAN, ROBERT EMMETT, composer, conductor; b. Hartford, Conn., Aug. 3, 1908; s. Lawrence and Marion (Lynch) D.; student Loyola Coll., Montreal, Can.; m. Vilma Ebsen, June 24, 1933 (div. Jan. 1948); 1 son, Robert Emmett; m. 2d, Nan Martin, Mar. 17, 1948; 1 son, Casey Martin, Musical dir. radio programs, 1934-72, member faculty music Columbia U., 1964-72; composer, condr. Broadway prodns., 1935-72, latest being Juno, 1958-59, Foxy, 1963-64, Coco, 1969 composer, condr. Paramount Studios, Hollywood, Cal., 1941-51, prod., 1951-56; prodns. include White Christmas, 1954, Anything Goes, 1955; TV prodns. include Acad. Awards shows, 1956, 58, Aladdin, 1957, numerous specials. Recipient Exhibitor Laurel, So. Cal. Motion Picture Council, 1954, Box Office award, 1954. Mem. A.S.C.A.P., Acad. Motion Picture Arts and Scis. (past chmn. music br., bd. govs.), Screen Composers Assos. (past v.p.), Dramatists Guild, Composers and Lyticists Guild Am. Composer: (songs) Little by Little, 1929, Big Movie Show in the Sky, 1949, Talk to Me Baby, 1964; (Broadway musical comedies) Texas, Li'l Darlin', 1949, Foxy, 1964; (motion picture scores) Going My Way, Bells of St. Mary's, Three Faces of Eve, Mr. Peabody and the Mermaid, The Great Gatsby, numerous others; (TV film scores) The World of Jacqueline Kennedy, The World of Sophia Loren, The World of Jimmy Doolittle, The World of Billy Graham, The World of Maurice Chevalier, The World of Darryl Zanuck. Author: Music in Modern Media, 1967. Home: Westwood CA Died Sept. 26, 1972.

DOLAN, TOM, wildlife illustrator, author; b. Berwyn, Ill., Sept. 22, 1912; s. George William and Pearl (Plottner) D.; student pub. schs.; m. Grace Fabri, July 22, 1939; 1 dau., Dee Dee Ann. Free-lance artist, Berwyn, Ill., 1932-69; represented in permanent collections of Ency. Brit., Field Mus.; numerous pvt. collections. Dir. 1st Fed. Savings & Loan Assn., Berwyn, Ill. Commr. Berwyn Park Dist., 1948-64; mem. Berwyn City Planning Commn.; Mem. bd. dirs., Dialogue. Mem. Am. Soc. Ichthyologists and Herpetologists, Chgo. Artists Guild, Am. Fisheries Soc. Clubs: Danish, Kennicott (Chgo.). Author, illustrator: Know Your Fish, 1960. Numerous articles pub. in nat. mags. Home: Berwyn IL Died Aug. 11, 1969; buried Bronswood Cemetery, Oak Brook IL

DOLE, ARTHUR, JR., mfg. exec.; b. Chicago, Feb. 4, 1894; s. Arthur and Mary Gertrude (Burns) D.; student Cornell, 1915; m. Dorothy W. Price, Oct. 12, 1918 (dec. Mar. 1966); children—Windsor (Mrs. Glenn R. Green), Arthur, III; m. 2d, Agnes Sheridan, Jan. 14, 1967. With Hooker Glass & Paint Mfg. Co., Chgo., 1915-72, pres., 1947-58, chmn. bd., 1958-72; dir. Dole Valve Co., William Wrigley Jr. Co. Served as pilot USAAF, World War I. Trustee Chgo.-Wesley Memorial Hosp., Chgo., Ill.; member Cornell U. Council. Episcopalian. Clubs: University (Chgo.); Indian Hill (Winnetka, Ill.); Old Elm (Lake Forest, Ill.). Home: Wilmette IL Died Aug. 29, 1972.

DOLE, MARGARET FEMALD (MRS. JOHN S. DOLE), portrait painter; b. Melrose, Mass.; d. Benjamin Marvin and Grace (Fuller) Femald; student Radcliffe Coll., 1915-16, Sch. Boston Mus. Fine Arts, 1916-19; studied art under Philip L. Hale, Charles Woodbury, Jacques Maroger; m. John S. Dole, Oct. 8, 1921; children—Grace F., John Nicholas, Benjamin Prescott. One man shows Portrait Painters Gallery, N.Y., 1936, Argent Gallery, N.Y.C., 1940, Stamford (Conn.) Mus., 1954, Bruce Mus. Greenwich (Conn.), 1960, Awards Gallery, Eastchester, N.Y.; exhibited in group shows at Salon, Paris, Pa. Acad. Fine Arts,

Corcoran Gallery, N.A.D., Grand Nat. Am. Artists Profl. League (gold medal 1964), Smithsonian Inst.; mem. So. Vt. Art Center. Tchr. painting Riverdale Country Sch. for Girls, 3 yrs.; tchr. classes painting, Phila. Cape Cod, Greenwich, Conn. Mem. bd. Chapin Adoption Soc., 1938-42; vol. worker Thrift Shop of Greenwich Hosp. Recipient Albert Reid Meml. prize for best traditional painting, 1956; 1st prize oil Hudson River Museum, 1956; popular prize Greenwich Art Soc., 1956; Mary Mott Smith award N.Y. br. Nat. League Am. Pen Women, 1957, 1st prize for drawing, 1957, Best in Show, 1965, 68; Thomas Stephens award Nat. Arts Club, 1959; 1st prize for best oil portrait and 1st prize for best drawing, Nat. League Am. Pen Women, 1962, Hudson Valley Art Assn. in 1963. Fellow Internat. Inst. Arts and Letters, Royal Soc. Arts, Am. Artists Profl. League; mem. Nat. League Am. Pen Women (chmn. nat. bd.), Council Am. Artists Socs. (dir.), Acad. Artists, Daus. Am. Colonists of Greenwich (dir.), C. of C., Pen and Brush. Clubs: Contemporary (pres. 1960). Travel (Greenwich, Conn.); Catherine Lorillard Wolf Art (pres. 1962-70); Providence Art; Hudson Valley Art; Nat. Arts. Home: Byram CT Died Feb. 28, 1970; interred Putnam Cemetery, Greenwich CT

DOLOWITZ, FRANCIS MARIE FLEISHER (MRS. DAVID A. DOLOWITZ), pediatric nurse; b. Phila., June 23, 1913; d. David Teller and Fridolyn (Gimbel) Fleisher; student Wellesley Coll., 1932-33; B.Nursing, Yale Coll. Nursing, 1936; m. David A. Dolowitz, May 6, 1938; children—David Sander, Julia Louise (Mrs. William Reagan), Wilma Florence, Susan Reda, Fridolyn Gimbel III. Head pediatric nurse Flower Hosp., N.Y.C., 1936-37; research nurse, premature children, N.Y.C. Hosp., 1937-39; voluntary nurse with project Head Start, Salt Lake City, Utah. Pres. Salt Lake City sect., Nat. Council Jewish Women, 1964-65, 67-68; bd. dirs. Y.W.C.A., 1966-68, League of Women Voters, 1965-67. Mem. B'nai B'rith Women, Salt Lake Council Women, Temple B'nai Israel (sisterhood mem. and mem.). Home: Salt Lake City UT

DOMERS, HENRY RUSSELL, govt. ofcl.; b. Phila., Nov. 24, 1905; s. Henry August and Lenora (Jachimowicz) D.; LL.B., Nat. U., 1943; m. Alberta Marie Nichols, Aug. 31, 1929; 1 dau., Janet Carol (Mrs. Gilbert A. Hense). With U.S. Gen. Accounting Office, successively chief audit subdivision, Chgo., chief agency audit sect., Washington, chief audit subdivision, St. Louis, asst. to dir. corp. audits div., Washington, tech. asst. to dir. audits, Washington, dir. European br. GAO, Paris, Frances, supervisory auditor, Washington, 1935-54; exec. dir. Fed. Power Commn., 1954-59. U.S. rep., internat. bd. auditors NATO, Paris, 1953-54. Served as sgt. U.S. Army, 1927-30. Mem. Delta Theta Phi. Roman Catholic. Club: National Press (Washington). Home: Washington DC Died Jan. 1972.

DOMINICI, SANTOS ANIBAL, diplomat; b. at Carupano, Venezuela, June 19, 1869; s. Dr. Anibal and Elina (Otero) D.; ed. U. of Caracas, Venezuela, and U. of Paris, France; unmarried. Prof. and rector U. of Caracas, 1895-01; specialized in sero-therapy, and founded the Pasteur Inst. in Caracas; minister to Germany, 1909-14; mission enlarged, 1912, to include Great Britain and Belgium; spl. rep. of his govt. at coronation of King George V. of Great Britain, etc.; E.E. and M.P. from Venezuela to U.S. since Sept. 23, 1914. Address: 1406 Massachusetts Av., Washington DC‡

DOMINICK, FRED H., ex-congressman; b.Peakes, Lexington Co., S.C., Feb. 20, 1877; s. Jacob L. and Georgiana L. (Minick) D.; ed. South Carolina Coll. and Newberry Coll.; m. Alva Seger, Dec. 19, 1929; children—Joan Seger, Doris Seger. Admitted to South Carolina bar, 1898; served as law partner of Cole L. Blease, former United States senator and governor of S.C., and managed his campaigns for gov.; now mem. Dominick & Workman, Newberry, S.C. Del. to every Dem. state conv., 1900-28, except one; mem. S.C. Ho. of Rep. 1901, 02; served as city atty., Newberry, and county atty., Newberry Co.; co. chmn. Dem. Party, 1906-14; asst. atty. gen. of S.C., 1913-16 (resigned); mem. 65th to 72d Congresses (1917-33), 3d S.C. Dist. Lutheran. Mason (K.T., Shriner), Odd Fellow, Elk, Red Man. Home: Newberry SC‡

DOMINICK, JAMES ROBERT, banker; b. Houston, Miss., Dec. 9, 1863; s. Robert Neely and Mary Jane (Martin) D.; grad. U. of Miss., 1883, Ph.D., 1884; grad. Bryant & Stratton's Business Coll., St. Louis, 1885; m. Gertrude Masten, Oct. 27, 1892. With Am. Nat. Bank, Kansas City, as clerk, asst. cashier and cashier, 1886-1900; organized Traders Bank, later Traders Gate City Nat. Bank, 1900, and since served it as pres.; organized Produce Exchange Bank of Kansas City, 1908; dir. Postal Life & Casualty Ins. Co. Member Missouri Bankers Assn. (pres. 1909, member executive council, 1918-21), Bankers' Club of Kansas City (pres. 1917). Curator Central Coll., Fayette, Mo., mem. Chamber Commerce; mem. bd. trustees Drumm Inst. for Boys, Spofford Home for Children; dir. Jacob L. Loose Million Dollar Charity Fund Assn., Kansas City, Mo. Mem. Phi Delta Theta. Democrat. Methodist. Clubs: Kansas City, Blue Hills. Home: 3529 Harrison Blvd. Office: 1111 Grand Av., Kansas City MO*‡

DONAHUE, CHARLES, lawyer; b. Portland, Me., Aug. 14, 1912; s. Charles Louis and Helen Katherine (Cunningham) D.; grad. Canterbury Sch., New Mildford, Conn., 1930; A.B., Princeton, 1934; LL.B., Harvard, 1937; m. Bertha Halsted Terry, Nov. 14, 1942 (div.); children—William Halsted, Christopher Cunningham, Charles, Helen Cunningham, Peter Waldron; m. 2d, Jeanne Coleman Small, June 6, 1968. Admitted to Me. bar, 1937, D.C. bar, 1938; atty. Nat. Cath. Welfare Conf., 1938-39, Dept. Labor, 1939-43, 46-49; labor counsel U.S. Senate Majority Policy Com., 1949; asst. solicitor of labor for employment security, 1949-51, asst. solicitor of labor for legislation, 1951-52; research dir. United Assn. Plumbers and Pipefitters, 1953-61; became solicitor of labor Dept. Labor, 1961; now in pvt. practice law. Served to capt. AUS, 1943-46. Mem. Am., Fed. bar assns., U.S. Judge Advocates Assn., Indsl. Relations Research Assn., Internat. Soc. Labor Law and Social Legislation (exec. com.), Princeton Alumni Assn., Harvard Law Sch. Alumni Assn., Nat. Lawyers Club. Club: Nat. Press. Author labor law rev. articles. Home: Fenit County Kerry Ireland Died Oct. 27, 1972; buried Churchill, County Kerry Ireland

DONAHUE, CHARLES HENRY, judge; b. Milford, N.H., Dec. 7, 1877; s. John Francis and Bridget Agnes (Murphy) D.; B.L., Dartmouth Coll., 1899; LL.B., Boston U., 1901, LL.D., 1933; m. Ellen G. Teevens, June 8, 1909; children—John Teevens, Dorothy Marie, Margery Ellen, Paul. Admitted to Mass. bar, 1901; practiced in Boston, 1901-24; judge Superior Court of Mass., 1924-32; justice Supreme Judicial Court of Mass., 1932-44; resigned April, 1944. Democrat. Catholic. Home: 374 Hammond St., Chestnut Hill MA*

DONAHUE, JOHN BARTHOLOMEW, editor; b. Somerville, Mass., Nov. 14, 1900; s. Denis and Margaret (DeForest) D.; A.B., Boston Coll., 1921; m. Catherine E. Cody, June 30, 1928; children—John, Patrick, Mary Jane, Sue Ellen. Feature writer with Boston Sunday Post, Boston, Mass., 1921-24; asso. editor, Columbia, nat. K.C. pub., 1924-28, editor, 1928-65. Roman Catholic, K.C. Home: New Haven CT Died Oct. 26, 1970; buried St. Paul's Cemetery, Arlington MA

DONALD, GEORGE H., clergyman; b. Girvan, Scotland, 1876; s. Andrew Thomson and Annabel Gordon (Robertson) D.; M.A., Edinburgh U., 1896; D.D., Montreal Theol. Coll., 1926; D.D. (centenary degree), Queen's U. (Kingston, Ont.), 1943; m. Margaret Dora Alison, 1906; m. 2d, Adelaide Webster, 1925; children—John, Henry, George, James. Minister Southdean Parish, Scotland, 1905-08; Haddington Abbey, 1908-10; chaplain Scots Ch., Simla, India, 1910-13; minister World Ch. of St. Nicholas, Aberdeen, Scotland, 1913-18; Parish Ch. of Galashiels, Scotland, 1918-25; Ch. of St. Andrew and St. Paul, Montreal, since 1925. Pres. Alliance of Reformed Chs. throughout the World in the Presbyterian System. Chaplain 51st Highland Div., 1914-18; chaplain Black Watch (R.H.R.) of Canada, 1925-46. Received Victoria Decoration for long service in the army. Conservative. Presbyterian. Mason (chaplain Montreal lodge). Clubs: University (Edinburgh and Montreal); Faculty (Montreal); Mount Royal. Author: An Interpretation of Church Symbols, 1947. Home: 1523 Crescent St., Office: 3415 Redpath St., Montreal PQ Canada‡

DONALDSON, J. A., carpet mfg. exec.; b. Lenox, Ia., May 7, 1894; s. William and Sarah (Allison) D.; A.B., U. Kan., 1920; m. Charlotte Kathryn Erhardt, Sept. 7, 1926; children—Jane Ann, John Allison. Asso. Arthur Andersen & Co., 1922-29; asst. controller Colgate Palmolive-Peet Co., 1930-31; controller, v.p. Montgomery Ward & Co., 1932-39; financial v.p., dir. Butler Bros., 1940-49; v.p. finance Bigelow-Sanford Carpet Co., Inc., 1949-59, pres., dir. Schlafer Supply Co., Appleton, Wis. Mem. Financial Execs. Inst. (nat. pres. 1942, nat. dir.), Ill. Soc. C.P.A.'s, Phi Beta Kappa, Delta Sigma Rho. Republican. Presbyn. Clubs: Union League (N.Y.C. and Chgo.); Scarsdale Golf (Hartsdale, N.Y.). Home: Rutland VT Died Mar. 26, 1973.

DONALDSON, JESSE MONROE, ex postmaster gen.; b. Shelby County, Illinois, August 17, 1885; s. Moses M. and Amanda S. (Little) D.; ed. public schools and high school, Sparks Bus. Coll., Shelbyville, Ill., and teachers normal schools in Ill.; m. Nell Fern Graybil, Apr. 14, 1911; children—Helen LaVerne, Jesse Monroe, Doris Dee. Postal employee and supervisor in Illinois and Oklahoma, 1908-15; post office inspector and inspector in charge div., Chattanooga, Tenn., and Kansas City, Mo., 1915-33; dep. 2d asst. postmaster gen., Washington, D.C., 1933-36, deputy first asst. postmaster gen., 1936-43; chief post office inspector, 1943-45; first asst. postmaster gen., 1945-47, postmaster gen., 1947-53. Democrat. Methodist. Mason. Home: Washington DC Died Mar. 1970.

DONDERO, GEORGE ANTHONY, ex-congressman; b. Detroit, Dec. 16, 1883; s. Louis and Caroline (Truthern) D.; LL.B., Detroit Coll. of Law, 1910; m. Adele Roegner, June 28, 1913; children—Marion, Stanton, Robert. In practice of law 1910-68; mayor of Royal Oak, 1921-23, asst. pros. atty., 1918-26, mem. Bd. Edn., 1910-28; mem. 73d to 82d Congresses, 17th Mich. Dist., 83d-84th Congresses, 18th Dist Republican. Methodist. Mason (Shriner), Kiwanian Wiley-Dondero Ship Canal, St. Lawrence Seaway named in his honor. Home: Royal Oak MI Died Jan. 27, 1968; buried Oakview Cemetery, Royal Oak MI

DONDO, MATHURIN, univ. prof., author; b. Lorient, France, Mar. 8, 1884; s. Yves and Marie (Le Hegarat) D.; grad. Coll. de Vannes, 1903; M.A., U. of Pa., traveling fellow univs. of Paris, Rome and Granada, 1906-09; Ph.D., Columbia, 1922; m. Anna Mercer, June 14, 1913. Teacher of French lang. and lit. at U. of Wis., Columbia and Smith Coll. until 1918; dir. French instr. Camp Gordon, Ga., 1918-19; professor French, Princeton, 1919, Columbia, 1919-22; prof. French, U. Cal., 1922-48, emeritus, 1948; professor at Pa. State College, summers, 1933-37, 1939-41; visiting prof. Hunter Coll., 1933-34. Mem. Am. Assn. Univ. Profs., Authors League Am., Modern Lang. Assn. Am., Philol. Assn. Pacific Coast, Calif. Writers League, P.E.N. (San Francisco), Societe des Prof. Francais en Amerique, Am. Assn. of Teachers of French, Am. Acad. Polit. and Soc. Sci., Nat. Geog. Soc., France Forever, Pi Delta Phi, Pi Mu Iota. Officer d'Academie, 1933. Landscape painter; has exhibited in New York, San Francisco, Berkeley. Clubs: Faculty, Mask and Dagger, English. Author: Vers Libre, 1922; Pathelin et autres pieces, 1923; French Fairy Plays (with M.E. Perley), 1923; Two Blind Men and a Donkey, 1925; The Pie and the Tart, 1925; Contes Dramatiques (with E.C. Hills), 1926; The Miracle of St. Martin, 1928; Modern French Course, 1929; Every Dog Has His Day, 1929; LaFrance (with E.C. Hills), 1931; Principes de Grammaire et de Style (with F. Ernst), 1935; French Conversation, 1940; French for the Modern World (with M. Brenman), 1945; Brief French Revue Grammar (with F. Ernst), 1947; The French Faust, Henri de Saint-Simon, 1955; Les Nuits, 1956; Histoire Naturelle, 1957; La Perouse in Maui, 1959. Contbr. ednl. jours. Home: Maui HI Died Aug. 30, 1968.

DONGES, RALPH WALDO EMERSON, lawyer; b. Donaldson, Pa., May 5, 1875; s. John W. (M.D.) and Rose (Renaud) D.; grad. Rugby Acad., Phila., 1892; LL.D., Rutgers University, (South Jersey br.); married Eleanor M. Deakyne, January 5, 1945. Admitted to N.J. bar, 1897; counsellor at law since 1900; pres. Pub. Utilities Commn. of N.J., 1913-18; judge Circuit Court of N.J., 1920-30; asso. justice Supreme Court of N.J., 1930-48, judge appellate division, Superior Court, 1948-51, ret. Served as lieut. col., U.S. Army, 1918-19. Mem. Am., N.J. State and Camden County bar assns. Democrat. Episcopalian. Mason, Moose, Elk. Home: Park View Apts., Collingswood 6, N.J. Address: 709 Market St., Camden 2 NJ

DONIGER, WILLIAM, sportswear mfg. co. exec.; b. 1908; m. Beatrice Bronfman; children—Bruce, Peter, David, Patricia (Mrs. R. Goldman). Chmn. bd., chief exec. officer McGregor-Doniger, Inc., 1965-72. Jewish religion (past v.p., trustee, gov. temple). Home: Rye NY Died June 1972.

DONKIN, MCKAY, univ. adminstr.; b. Westport, Conn., Oct. 17, 1904; s. George W. McKay and Leah (Gaydenne) D.; Petroleum Engr., Colo. Sch. Mines, 1929; grad. student U. Tex., 1936, Harvard, 1937; m. Agnes Denison McLean, June 25, 1935; children—Carla Swan (Mrs. Donald C. Jenkins), Deborah (Mrs. William Wells the third). Engaged as geologist, corporation official, and oil producer in oil and petroleum engring, 1929-50; with Dept. Def., 1950-51; spl. asst. chmn. AEC, 1951-57; v.p., treas. Pa. State U., 1957-68. Served to lt. comdr. USNR, 1942-46. Clubs: Metropolitan (Washington); Rolling Rock (Ligonier, Pa.). Home: State College PA Died Mar. 17, 1968; buried Graysville Cemetery, Spruce Creek, Huntington County PA

DONNELLON, JAMES AUGUSTINE, univ. pres., clergyman; b. Niagara Falls. N.Y., Sept. 10, 1906; s. James P. and Catherine (Mahon) D.; A.B., Villanova U., 1930; postgrad. Augustinian Coll., 1930-32, Cath. U. Am., 1932-33; M.S., U. Pa., 1936, Ph.D., 1938; postgrad. Harvard Med. Sch., summer 1934, Marine Biol. Lab., Woods Hole, Mass., summers 1935-40; LL.D., LaSalle Coll., 1958; D.Sc., Merrimack Coll., 1958. With Villanova U., 1933-71, successively instr., asst. prof. biology, 1933-48, prof. biology, chmn. dept., 1948-54, pres., 1954-59. Subprior St. Thomas of Villanova Monastery, 1944-50, prior, 1950-54; mem. Phila. Diocesan Sch. Bd., 1958-71. Mem. com. on higher ednl. opportunities, Phila., 1957, Am. Inst. Med. Climatology, Inc., 1958; mem. adv. commn. Joint State Govt., 1958. Mem. Assn. Coll. Pres. of Pa., A.A.A.S., Sigma Xi. Home: Villanova PA Died Apr. 11, 1971; buried St. Mary's Collegiate Seminary Cemetery.

DONNELLY, HENRY EDMUND, bishop; b. Hudson, Mich., Aug. 28, 1904; s. Henry P. and Mary G. (Fitzpatrick) D.; A.B., Sacred Heart Sem., 1926; M.A., U. Detroit, 1936. Ordained priest Roman Cath. Ch., 1930; prof. Sacred Heart Sem., Detroit, 1930-40; dean discipline, 1936-40, rector, 1940-52, domestic prelate, 1946; pastor St. Catherine's Ch., 1952-57; consecrated titular bishop of Tymbrias, auxiliary bishop of Detroit, 1954; pastor St. Matthew's Ch., Detroit, from 1957—. Home: Detroit MI

DONNELLY, JAMES L(EONARD), assn. exec.; b. Sedalia, Mo.; s. Edward James and Mary Catherine (Campbell) D.; student U. Mo., 1910-12; LL.B., U. Mich., 1916; widower; children—Marie L. (Mrs. V.J. Cushing), Margaret Louise (Mrs. E. James Best), James Leonard, Helen Adele (Mrs. Edmund J. Goehning). With Western Cartridge Co. (now Olin Mathieson Corp.), East Alton, Ill., 1912-13, sec., sales mgr., dir., 1917-28; practiced law in Kansas City, Mo., 1916-17; exec. v.p. Ill. Mfrs. Assn., Chgo., 1928-64, chmn. exec. com., 1965-72; dir. Binks Mfg. Co., Chgo. Trustee Barat Coll. of Sacred Heart, Lake Forest. Republican. Roman Catholic. Clubs: Chicago, Union League (Chgo.); Skokie Country (Glencoe); Everglades (Palm Beach, Fla.). Home: Evanston IL Died Oct. 1972.

DONNELLY, JUNE RICHARDSON, librarian; b. College Hill, O., June 3, 1872; d. John Marshall and Anne (Moore) Donnelly; B.S., U. of Cincinnati, 1895; B.L.S., N.Y. State Library Sch., 1907. Cataloguer Pub. Library, Cincinnati, 1903-05; teacher library science, Simmons Coll., Boston, 1905-09; dir. Drexel Inst. Library Sch., Phila., 1910-12; teacher library economy, Washington Irving High Sch., N.Y. City, 1912-13; with Simmons Coll., 1913-37, prof. library science, and dir. Simmons Coll. Library Sch., to 1937, prof. emeritus since 1937. Cincinnati Charterite. Mem. A.L.A., Phi Beta Kappa. Republican. Episcopalian. Home: 4216 Delaney St., Cincinnati 23‡

DONNELLY, RICHARD CARTER, Simon E. Baldwin prof. law Yale. Home: New Haven CT

DONNELLY, WALTER JOSEPH, ex-ambassador; b. New Haven, Conn., Jan. 9, 1896; s. Henry Joseph and Elizabeth Anne Kivian; student Georgetown U., 1919-21, George Washington U., 1921, U. of Caracas (Venezuela), 1921; m. Maria Helena Samper de Donnelly, Jan. 28, 1936; children—George James, Maria Teresa, Paul, John. Began as comml. agent, United States Department of Commerce, 1923; asst. trade commr., Ottawa, Can., 1924-27; trade commr., Montreal, Can., 1927-28; comml. attache, Bogota, Colombia, 1929-32; Dept. of Commerce, Washington, D.C., 1933; comml. attache, Havana, Cuba, 1934-37, Rio de Janeiro, Brazil, 1937-45; counselor of embassy, Panama, 1945; ambassador to Costa Rica, 1947, to Venezuela, Aug. 1947; minister and first U.S. civilian high commr. to Austria; high commr. Germany, 1952; spl. rep. U.S. Steel Corp., for Central and South America., 1952-70. Served in U.S. Army, 1917-18. Roman Catholic. Club: Venezuela Country (Caracas, Venezuela). Home: Bogota Colombia Died Nov. 14, 1970.

DONOGHUE, THOMAS J., oil executive; b. Titusville, Pa., May 13, 1869; s. Cornelius C. and Catherine M. (Goodwin) D.; ed. pub. and parochial schs.; m. Mary Evangelist Sullivan, Dec. 15, 1896; children—Francis J., Gerald T., Mary Catherine. With The Texas Co., 1902-39, v.p., 1908-39, retired July 1, 1939. Democrat. Catholic. Clubs: Houston, Houston Country. Address: 17 Courtland Pl., Houston TX‡

DONOHUGH, THOMAS SMITH, church official; b. Phila., Pa., Sept. 13, 1875; s. William Johnson and Eliza Jane (Wetter) D.; ed. Swarthmore Prep. Sch. and Coll., 1888-92; LL.B., U. of Pa., 1895; student Union Theological Seminary, 1912-13; M.A., Columbia U., 1913; D.D., Dakota Wesleyan U., 1942; m. Agnes Crawford Leaycraft, June 14, 1906; children—Agnes Caroline (dec.), Crawford Edgar. Practiced law in Phila., 1895-1904; ordained ministry M.E. Ch., 1905; missionary at Meerut, India, 1904-12; sec. Personnel Dept., Bd. of Foreign Missions M.E. Church, 1913-18; asso. secretary same, 1918-46, in charge work in Central and South Africa, India, Burma, Europe, Latin Am., 1924-46; advance program, fgn. missions conf., 1947-48. Lecturer on missions and personal efficiency, Drew Theol. Sem., 1919-30. Mem. bd. dirs. Isabella Thoburn College, Lucknow, India, Ward Coll., Buenos Aires, Argentina, to 1946, Santiago (Coll.) to 1940, Washington Inst., Liberia. Knight Liberian Order of African Redemption, 1945. Republican. Mason. Home: 1055 N Kingsley Dr., Los Angeles 29. Office: 150 Fifth Av., NYC 11

DONOVAN, GEORGE FRANCIS, educator; b. Rockland, Mass., Dec. 1, 1901; s. John Joseph and Catherine (Smith) D.; A.B., Boston Coll., 1925, A.M., 1927; A.M., Harvard, 1929; Ph.D., St. Louis U., 1931; m. Margaret Mary Ryan, Sept. 7, 1931. Instr. Rockhust Coll., 1927-29; teaching fellow St. Louis U., 1929-31; pres. Webster Coll., 1931-48; br. chief ednl. and cultural relations U.S. Mil. Govt., Germany, 1948-49; adviser pub. affairs Dept. State, Wiesbaden, Germany, 1949-51; sr. adviser U.S.High Command, Germany, 1951-52; cultural affairs attache Am. embassy, India, 1952-53; dir. higher edn. program Cath. U. Am. Grad. Sch. Arts and Scis., Washington, 1954-66; chmn. dept. edn. Marquette U., Milw., from 1966, also dir. tchr. edn. from 1966. Cons. study coll. bds. trustees N.Y. State Bd. Regents, 1964-65; pres. Cath. Conf. Indsl. Problems; coordinator U.S. Peace Corps tng. program for coll. and univ. tchrs. overseas Georgetown U., summer 1964. Mem. Am., Cath. hist. assns., Am. Acad. Polit. and Social Sci., Am. Polit. Sci. Assn., Am. Assn. U. Profs., Cath. Assn. Internat. Peace, Nat. Fedn. Cath. Alumni (pres. St. Louis 1939-40, regional dir. 1940-41), Nat. Cath. Ednl. Assn. (chmn. coll. and univ. dept. Eastern regional unit, mem. exec. com. coll. and univ. dept. 1961—), N.E.A. (mem. com. on fraudulent schs. Assn. for Higher Edn. 1955-57), Alpha Sigma Nu. Democrat. Roman Catholic. Lion. Clubs: Harvard (Milw.), Serra (v.p. 1946). Author: The Pre-Revolutionary Irish in Massachusetts, 1620-1775; Developments in the Accreditation of Teacher Education in the United States, 1957; Selected Readings for the College and University Officer of Administration, 1961; The Faculty Manual in American Colleges and Universities, 1966, rev. 3d edit., 1969; Selected Annotated Readings on Accreditation in Higher Education, 1966; Vatican Council II; Challenge to Education, 1967. Co-author: The Road Ahead; Quality of College Teaching and Staff, 1961; Church-Related Boards Responsible for Higher Education, 1964. Editor: Higher Education Book Review, 1960; College and University Student Personnel Services, 1962; Selected Problems in the Administration of American Higher Education, 1964; College and University Inter-institutional Cooperation, 1965; Vatican II Council-Its Challenge to Education, 1967; (with W. Hugh Stickler) Representative Questions Asked in Comprehensive Doctoral Examinations in the Area of Higher Education, 1967. Home: Fox Point WI Died July 16, 1972; buried Sedalia MO

DONOVAN, JAMES BRITT, lawyer, educator, author; born New York City, New York, on February 29, 1916; s. Dr. John J. and Harriet F. (O'Connor) D.; A.B., Fordham University, 1937, LL.D. (honorary), 1962; LL.B., Harvard University, 1940; LL.D., Union U. Albany Law Sch., 1965, Gannon Coll., 1965; Litt.D., St. Francis Coll., 1963; L.H.D., Villanova Univ., 1963, also Bryant Coll., 1963; m. Mary E. McKenna, June 30, 1941; children—Jane Ann, John, Mary Ellen, Clare. Admitted to N.Y. bar, 1941, D.C. bar, 1951; pvt. practice of law, N.Y.C., 1940-42; asso. gen. counsel OSRD, 1942-43; partner Watters & Donovan, N.Y.C., also Washington, 1950-70; president Pratt Institute, since 1968-70; lecturer various colleges and univs. President of N.Y. Board of Edn., 1963-65; mem. Art Commn. City N.Y., 1951-61, pres. Art Assos. of Commn., 1966-68. Member governing com. Bklyn. Mus.; trustee Meth. Hosp. Bklyn., 1966-70, Bklyn. Inst. Arts and Scis. Served as comdr. USNR, 1943-46; gen. counsel OSS, 1943-45, asst. to U.S. Chief Pros. maj. war criminals, Nuremberg, 1945. Decorated Legion of Merit, Commendation Ribbon with cluster, U.S. Distinguished Service medal for intelligence; recipient Tyne award Fedn. Ins. Counsel, 1952; Gold Medal award, Greater N.Y. Ins. Brokers Assn., 1958; Humanities award Coll. Ins., 1966; Medallion of Honor (N.Y.C.); Gold medal Bklyn. Coll.; Civil Liberties award N.Y. State Bar Assn., 1961; Gold medal Xavier U., 1965; Knight Holy Sepulchre; Grand Cross Mercedarian. Fellow Am. Coll. Trial Lawyers American Soc. Internat. Law; mem. Am. (chairman insurance, negligence and compensation section 1961-62), New York State (chmn. ins. sec. 1953-54, exec. com. 1964-67) Bklyn. bar assns., Assn. Bar City N.Y. (chmn. ins. law com. 1952-55), Internat. Assn. Ins. Counsel, Authors Guild. Roman Catholic. Knight of Malta. Author: Strangers on a Bridge, 1964; Challenges, 1967; also articles in mags. and law reviews. Home: Brooklyn NY Died Jan. 19, 1970.

DONOVAN, JAMES J., coll. pres., clergyman; b. Castlefarm, Co. Limerick, Ireland, Jan. 9, 1909; s. John and Mary (Quinn) D.; M.A., St. Thomas Seminary, Denver, 1931-32; J.C.B., Catholic Univ. of Am., 1936; J.C.L., 1937; J.C.D., 1938. Ordained priest Roman Catholic Church, 1932; pro. sociology and religion Coll. of Great Falls, Mont., 1938; notarius, judge, officialis tribunal diocese of Great Falls, pres. college of Great Falls, vicar gen. of diocese, 1942-68; pastor St. Patrick's Ch., Billings, Mont., 1960-68; Domestic Prelate to His Holiness, Pope Pius XII, 1949. Mem. Community Chest Bd.; Red Cross Bd. Served as coordinator of civilian pilot training program Great Falls, World War II; chaplain to Great Falls A.A. Base. First v.p. Community Council of Cascade County, 1949-50; mem. Great Falls City Transit Commn., 1957-68. Mem. Cascade Fedn. Social Workers (pres. 1945), Nat. Cath. Edn. Assn. (chmn. western regional unit), Canon Law, Soc. Am. (pres. N.W. region 1948-49), Am. Genetic Assn., Alumni in U.S. of St. Patrick's Coll., County Tipperary, Ireland (pres. 1965-66). Knights of Columbus (state chaplain), Hibernian (state chaplain). Author: (book) The Pastor's Obligation in Pre-nuptial Investigation, 1938. Home: Billings MT Died Jan. 23, 1968; buried Holy Cross Cemetery, Billings MT

DOOLY, OSCAR EARLE, investment broker; b. Talbotton, Ga., June 5, 1900; s. Oscar Earle and Ada Belle (Lummus) D.; student Riverside Mil. Acad., Gainesville, Ga., 1917-18; m. Constance Davenport, May 16, 1923; 1 dau., Caren (Mrs. Richard L. Tatum). Pres., Oscar E. Dooly Assos., Inc., real estate, Miami, Fla., 1930-70; chmn. bd. Dooly, Gerrish & Co., investments. Chmn. finance com., past pres. Orange Bowl Com. Chmn. U. Miami. Recipient Gold Medal award of merit U. Miami. Mem. Miami, Miami Beach bds. realtors, Fla. (dir.), Miami, Miami Beach chambers commerce, Fla. Assn. Realtors, Nat. Assn. Real Estate Bds., Fla. Security Dealers Assn., Nat. Assn. Securities Dealers, Soc. Colonial Wars, S.A.R. Mason. Clubs: LaGorce Country Club (past pres.), Bath, Indian Creek Country (Miami Beach); Miami (past pres.); Bankers of Am. (N.Y.C.); Capital City (Atlanta); River (Jacksonville). Miami FL Died Sept. 12, 1970.

DOPP, KATHERINE ELIZABETH, educator; b. Belmont, Wis., d. William Daniel and Janet (Moyes) D.; graduate State Normal Sch., Oshkosh, Wis., 1888; Ph.B., University of Mich., 1893; Ph.D., U. of Chicago, 1902; unmarried. Prin. normal dept. E. Greenwich (R.I.) Acad., 1888-90; critic teacher, State Normal Sch., Oshkosh, 1893-95; prin. Training Sch., Moline, Ill., 1895-96; prin. training dept., State Normal Sch., Madison, S.D., 1896-98; dir. training normal dept. U. of Utah, 1898-99; supervisor history and nature study and teacher ednl. methods, State Normal Sch., Oshkosh, 1899-1900; instr. correspondence study, dept. philosophy, 1902-18, lecturer in edn., extension div., 1904-11, U. of Chicago. Author: The Place of Industries in Elementary Education, 1903; The Tree Dwellers, 1903; The Early Cavemen, 1904; The Later Cavemen, 1906; The Early Sea People, 1912; Bobby and Betty at Home, 1917; The Early Herdsmen, 1923; Bobby and Betty with the Workers, 1923; Bobby and Betty in the Country, 1926; Bobby and Betty at Play, 1927; The Early Farmers, 1929; Happy Road to Reading, A Basic Series of Readers Chicago IL‡

DORIGAN, HARRY WILLIAM, railroad ofcl.; b. Taunton, Mass., Nov. 23, 1895; s. William Henry and Nettie W. (McMann) D.; ed. pub. schs. also Harvard Bus. Sch.; m. Hazel M. Baldwin, Oct. 20, 1920. With N.Y., N.H. & H. R.R. Co., 1914-50, trustee, 1961-66; with C.R.R. of N.J., 1950-60, v.p. traffic, 1954-60; pres., dir. New Eng. Transp. Co., New Haven R.R. Communications Co., Providence Terminal Co., S. Manchester R.R. Co.; v.p., dir. N.Y. Connecting R.R. Co.; dir. Boston Terminal Co., Realty Hotels, Inc. Clubs: New Haven Country, Quinnipiack (New Haven). Home: New Haven CT Died 1966.

DORR, HAROLD M., univ. dean; b. Chadwick, Mich., Jan. 16, 1897; s. Foster P. and Berlie (McVicar) D.; A.B., U. Mich., 1923, A.M., 1929, Ph.D., 1933; m. H. Barbara Johnston, Apr. 29, 1932; 1 stepdau., Janette J. Prin., Lake City (Mich.) High Sch., 1923-27; supt. schs., Lake City, 1927-28; asst. in polit. sci. U. Mich., 1928-29, instr. 1929-35, asst. prof., 1935-39, asso. prof., 1939-44, prof., 1944-68, prof. emeritus, 1968-73, acting chmn., 1948, dir. summer session, 1950-67, dean of statewide edn., 1956-67. Served with O.T.C., Camp Hancock, Ga., 1918. Mem. City Charter Study Commn., Wartime Housing Commn., Selective Service Local Bd. 85, Washtenaw County; chmn. Social-Civic Com., Mich. Council on Adult Edn.; cons. and spl. adv. to numerous civic orgns. and govtl. agys.; chmn. Ann Arbor Twp. Planning Commn. Vis. expert (C.A.D.), Mil. Govt. for Germany, 1949; govtl. specialist Dept. of State (HICOG), assigned to Germany, summer 1950. Mem. Conf. Mid-West Polit. Scientists (pres. 1949-50), Am. Assn. U. Profs. (council 1951-54), Am. Polit. Sci. Assn. (com. advancement teaching), Am. Soc. Pub. Administrs., Am. Acad. Polit. and Social Sci. (spl. editor Annals, vol. 249), Mich. Acad., Schoolmasters Club, Sigma Delta Kappa, Phi Kappa Phi, Pi Sigma Alpha. Republican. Clubs: Research, Quadrangle, University, Rotary (dist. gov. 1934-55). Author books. Editor: Michigan Constitutional Convention of 1835-36; Debates and Proceedings; Governing Postwar Germany. Contbr. articles and papers to profl. jours. Home: Ann Arbor MI Died Jan. 31, 1973.

DORRANCE, STURGES DICK, advt. exec.; b. Dorranceton, Pa., July 15, 1881; s. James Ford and Elizabeth (Dick) D.; student Harry Hillman Acad., Wyo. Sem., Hotchkiss Sch.; m. Mary Grear, Mar. 28, 1912; children—Helen, Sturges Dick. Began with J. Horace McFarland Co., Harrisburg, Pa., 1900, gen. supt., 1904-06; advt. mgr. LaHacienda, N.Y.C. and Buffalo, 1906; staff Collier's Weekly, 1908; eastern advt. dir. McClure Publs., 1912; pub. Westfield (Mass.) Evening Jour., 1916; spl. rep. Internat. Mag. Co., N.Y.C., 1918; v.p. Thomas F. Logan, Inc., 1919; v.p., sec. Grandin, Dorrance, Sullivan & Co., N.Y.C., 1921; pres. Dorrance Sullivan & Co., 1924-36; pres. Brooke, Smith, French & Dorrance, Inc., 1937-41; chmn. bd., 1941-56. Home: Clearwater FL Died Nov. 26, 1968.

DORSEY, CLARENCE WILBUR, agrl. engineer; b. Kirkersville, O., July 6, 1872; s. Edwin Jackson and Mary Elma (Grove) D.; brother George Amos D. (q.v.); Litt.B., Denison U., 1894; A.B., Harvard, 1896; m. Florence May Juilliard, of Louisville, O., Dec. 28, 1898. Asst. physicist, Md. Agrl. Expt. Sta., 1896-8; in charge field work in Div. of Soils, U.S. Dept. Agr., 1898-1902; soil physicist, Bur. of Agr., P.I., 1902-3; in charge Soil Survey, Bur. of Soils, U.S. Dept. Agr., 1903-9; in pvt. practice as agrl. engr., in Cal., 1909—. Author of bulls. and papers relation to soil investigations in U.S., P.R. and P.I. Home: 520 S. St. Andrews Pl. Office: Central Bldg., Los Angeles CA‡

DORSEY, HARRY WOODWARD, govt. official; b. New Market, Md., Nov. 27, 1874; s. Dr. Harry W. and Helen (James) D.; ed. pub. schs. and night schs; m. Susie M. Naylor, Nov. 10, 1897; 1 dau., Charlotte Templeman (Mrs. Joseph S. Emmerich). Began as messenger boy Smithsonian Instn., 1888, chief clerk, 1907, adminstrv. asst. to sec. 1930, acting sec., 1934-48, retired 1948; in charge U.S. Internat. Exchange Service, 1920-48, U.S. rep. Conf. on International Exchange of Publications, League of Nations, Geneva, 1924. Democrat. Episcopalian. Home: 4107 Jefferson St., Hyattville MD‡

DORSEY, HERBERT GROVE, physicist; b. Kirkersville, O., Apr. 24, 1876; s. Edwin Jackson and Mary Elma (Grove) D.; B.S., Denison U., Granville, Ohio, 1897, M.S., 1898, Sc.D., 1938; Ph.D., Cornell Univ., 1908; m. Virginia Rowlett, June 21, 1906; children—Herbert Grove, William Rowlett. Instr. physics, U. of Me., 1898-1900; asst. prof. U. of Fla., 1901-03; instr. physics and electricity, Mechanics Inst., Rochester, 1903-04; asst. instr. physics, Cornell U., 1904-05, instr., 1905-10; engr. research br., Western Electric Co., 1910-12; research engr. Nat. Cash Register Co., 1912-16, Hammond Radio Research Lab., 1916-22, Submarine Signal Co., 1922-26; senior elec. engr. U.S. Coast and Geodetic Survey, 1926-28, prin. elec. engr. and chief research sect., 1923-46; lecturer in physics, George Washington Univ., 1947; instr. physics Capitol Radio Engring. Inst. since 1948. Invented Dorsey Phonelescope, dynamic loudspeaker, Fathometer, Sono Radio Buoy. and improved acoustics contrivances in telephone and radio fields; Sonar, the fathometer used horizontally has been employed extensively to locate enemy craft and submarines. Recipient 1st annual award, Washington Soc. Engrs., 1941. Fellow A.A.A.S., Am. Phys. Soc., Acoustical Soc. of America, Inst. Radio Engrs. (chmn. Washington sect., 1933), American Institute Elec. Engrs. (chmn. Washington sect., 1934); member American Optical Society, American Assn. Physics Teachers, Internat. Com. on Radio, Am. Geophys. Union, Am. Radio Relay League, Washington Acad. Science, Philos. Soc. of Washington, Washington Soc. Engrs., Sigma Xi, Phi Kappa Phi, Beta Theta Pi. Baptist. Club: Cosmos. Home: 3708 33d Pl., Washington 8 DC‡

DOS PASSOS, JOHN (RODERIGO), writer; b. Chicago, Ill., Jan. 14, 1896; s. John R. and Lucy Addison (Sprigg) DP.; A.B., Harvard, 1916; m. Katharine F. Smith (dec.); married Elizabeth Hamlin Holdridge; one daughter Lucy. Author: One Man's Initiation, 1919 (reprinted as First Encounter, 1946); Three Soliders, 1921; Rosinante to the Road Again (book of essays), 1922; A Pushcart at the Curb (verse), 1922; Streets of Night, 1923; Manhattan Transfer, 1925; The Garbage Man (play), 1926; Orient Express, 1927; Airways, Inc. (play), 1929; The 42d Parallel, 1930; Nineteen Nineteen, 1931; In All Countries, 1934; Three Plays, 1934; The Big Money, 1936; U.S.A., 1938; Journeys Between Wars, 1938; Adventures of a Young Man, 1939; The Ground We Stand On, 1941; Number One, 1943; State of the Nation, 1944; Tour of Duty, 1946; The Grand Design, 1949; The Prospect Before Us, 1950; Chosen Country, 1951; District of Columbia, 1952; The Head and Heart of Thomas Jefferson, 1954; Most Likely to Succeed. 1954; The Theme is Freedom, 1956; The Men Who Made the Nation, 1957; The Great Days, 1958; Prospects of a Golden Age, 1959; Midcentury, 1961; Mr. Wilson's War, 1962; Brazil on the Move, 1963; Occasions and Protests, 1964; World in a Glass, 1966; The Shackles of Power, 1966; The Best Times, 1966; The Portugal Story, 1969; Easter Island (Island of Enigmas), 1971. Recipient gold medal, fiction, Nat. Inst. Arts and Letters, 1957; Feltrinelli award for innovations in narrative style Academia Nazionale dei Lincei, Rome, Italy, 1967. Home: Westmoreland VA Died Sept. 28, 1970; buried Yedcomico Church, Westmoreland County VA

DOSTERT, LEON EMILE, educator; b. Longwy, France, May 14, 1904; s. Leon Emile and Marie (Hollet) D.; came to U.S., 1921; naturalized, 1941; student Occidental Coll., 1924-26; B.S., Georgetown U., 1928, Ph.B., 1930, M.A., 1931; graduate student Johns Hopkins, 1935-36; Litt.D. Franklin and Marshall College, 1957; LLD., Georgetown University, 1958; Litt.D. (hon.), Occidental College, 1960; children—Leon Emile (dec.), Anne Marie, Pierre, Francois; m. 2d, Bozena Henisz, May, 1965. Instr. French, Georgetown U., 1926-29, asst. prof., 1929-32, acting chmn. faculty modern languages, 1930-36, chmn. dept., 1936-41, asso. prof., 1932-36, prof., 1936-41; prof. French civilization Scripps Coll., 1941; attache French embassy, Washington, 1939-40; with O.S.S., 1942; dir. simultaneous interpretation div., U.N., 1946-47; administrative counsellor Internat. Telecommunication Union, Geneva, 1948-49; sec. gen. Internat. High Frequency Broadcast Conf., 1948-49; dir. Inst. Languages and Linguistics, Georgetown U., 1949; prof. French, chmn. dept. langs. and linguistics Occidental Coll., Los Angeles, 1963-69, prof. emeritus of langs. and linguistics, 1969-71; lang. cons. internat., U.S., fgn. govts., pvt. corps. Served from maj. to col., 1942-46; served as liaison officer to Gen. Henri Giraud, 1942-44, interpreter to Gen. Eisenhower, 1942-45; chief language div., Nurenberg Trials, 1945-46; U.S. Army Reserve Officer. Decorated U.S. Legion of Merit with cluster, Bronze Star with cluster, France Knight Legion of Honor, Croix de Guerre with Palms, Morocco and Tunisia. Mem. Modern Language Association of America, Linguistic Soc. Am., Phi Beta Kappa Assos., Phi Beta Kappa. Club: Cosmos (Washington). Editor Monograph Series on Langs. and Linguistics, 1952-56. Author: Spoken French, 1956; Francais Premier Cours, 1958; Francais, Cours Moyen; Francais, Styles Litteraires. Contbr. articles on langs. to profl. jours. Home: Pasadena CA Died Sept. 2, 1971; buried Mountain View Cemetery, Pasadena CA

DOTSON, FLOYD D., educator; b. Tuscumbia, Ala., June 19, 1909; s. John H. and Clara D. (Duncan) D.; B.S., Fla. State Coll., 1936; M.A., U. Ala., 1941; Ed.D., Columbia, 1948; m. Hettie Miller, Mar. 19, 1927; children—Helen (Mrs. Bruce Tittle), Frances (Mrs. Clifton Blackburn), James Ray, David Houston, Marjorie (Mrs. Ray House). High sch. tchr. and prin., Ala., 1926-48; dir. tchr. tng. Howard Coll., 1948-50; supr. secondary schs. Ala. Dept. Edn., 1950-55; cons. tchr. edn. ICA, Amman, Jordan, 1955-57; coordinator tchr. edn. Berry Coll., Mt. Berry, Ga., 1960-69. U. Profs., N.E.A., Ga. Edn. Assn., Kappa Phi Kappa. Mason, Lion. Home: Rome GA Died Sept. 1969.

DOTTERWEICH, JUNE (MRS. FRANK HENRY DOTTERWEICH), civic worker; b. N.Y.C., July 4, 1918; d. Walter Battle and June (Dixon) Smith; B.A., Oberlin Coll., 1939; M. Nursing, Yale, 1942; M.A., U. Md., 1944; m. Frank Henry Dotterweich, May 16, 1946. Instr. nursing arts U. Md. Hosp. Sch. Nursing, 1942-43; night supr., sci. instr. Hosp. for Women Md., 1943-44; nurse edn. cons. cadet nurse program USPHS, Washington, 1944-46. Bd. dirs. Kleberg-Kenedy Counties Tb Assn., 1949-55, head publicity, 1949-52, 2d v.p., 1952-55; organizer Kleberg County unit Am. Cancer Soc., 1947, county comdr., 1947-54, pres., 1954-55, state bd. dirs., 1953, state exec. com., 1954-56, sec. state lay activities com., 1954-56; bd. trustees Kingsville Ind. Sch. Dist., 1951-57, v.p., 1956-57; bd. dirs. Kingsville Community Chest, 1951-54, Kingsville United Fund, 1954; sec. Kingsville Community Concerts Assn., 1947-48; vice-chmn. Kingsville Pub. Library Bldg. Com., 1955-59, chmn. library bd., 1959-69. Mem. D.A.R., Am. Assn. U. Women (sec.-treas. Kingsville br. 1947-48), Tex. Fedn. Women's Clubs (pres. S. Tex. dist. 1964-66), Delta Kappa Gamma. Clubs: Woman's (chmn. health com. 1953-58, program chmn. lit. dept. 1947-49, chmn. lit. dept. 1957-59, pres. 1961-63), Faculty Wives (pres. Tex. Coll. Arts and Industries 1949-50). Home: Kingsville TX Died Jan. 17, 1969.

DOTY, WILLIAM FURMAN, consular service; b. Brooklyn, N.Y., Dec. 1, 1870; s. Clarence Samuel and Henrietta Amanda Wallace (Lamb) D.; A.B., Princeton, 1896 (honors in philosophy); studied Princeton Theol. Sem. parts of 3 yrs.; m. Elizabeth Maria Julia Thonigs, of Mitau, Courland, Russia, Dec. 21, 1913. Was Govt. teacher and agt. for Eskimo, St. Lawrence Island, Behring Strait, 1897-8 and 4 mos. in 1900; ordained Presbyn. ministry at Los Angeles, Cal. Apptd. clk., Am. Consulate, Tahiti, Society Islands, 1900; consul at Tahiti, 1902-6, Tabriz, Persia, 1906-10, Riga, Russia, 1910-13, Nassau, Bahamas, Nov. 24, 1913, now at Cardiff, Wales. Address: American Consulate, Cardiff Wales‡

DOUGHERTY, EDWARD ARCHER, actuary, ins. exec.; b. Newark, May 21, 1910; s. George Pryor and Bertha (Hurlbut) D.; A.B., Williams Coll., 1931; m. Elizabeth Freeman, Oct. 5, 1932; children—Elizabeth Lloyd (Mrs. Reginald Byrd Childers), Edward Archer Dougherty. Actuarial student with Mutual Benefit Life Ins. Co., Newark, 1932-35; actuarial student Mutual Life Ins. Co. N.Y., 1935-42, asst. treas., 1942-44; asst. actuary Union Central Life Ins. Co., Cin., 1949, actuary, 1949-57, chief actuary, 1957-69, v.p., 1968-69; dir. Cin. Equitable Ins. Co. Trustee Cin. Country Day Sch., 1954-57. Chmn. laymen's work Province V, Episcopal Ch., 1961-67, dep. gen. conv., 1955, 61, 64, 67. Served to lt. USNR, 1944-46, Fellow Soc. Actuaries; mem. Soc. Colonial Wars, Sigma Phi. Home: Cincinnati OH Died Jan. 6, 1969.

DOUGHERTY, JOSEPH P(ATRICK), bishop; b. Kansas City, Kan., Jan. 11 1905 s. Patrick and Grace (Meehan) D.; student Columbia Prep Sch., Portland, Ore., 1919-22, St. Patrick's Sem., Menlo Park, Cal., 1922-30; M.A., U. Wash., 1934; LL.D., U. Portland, Ore., 1950. Ordained priest, Roman Catholic Ch., 1930; asst. pastor St. Mary's Ch., Seattle, 1930-31; instr. St. Edward's Sem., Kenmore, Wash., 1931-34; vice chancellor Diocese of Seattle, 1934-42, chancellor, 1942-51; domestic prelate, 1951; apptd. first Bishop of Yakima, consecrated, 1951, resigned, 1969; aux. bishop of Los Angeles, 1969-70. Home: Yakima WA Died July 10, 1970; buried Calvary Cemetery, Yakima WA

DOUGHERTY, PROCTOR LAMBERT;, b. Boston, Mass., 1873; s. M. Angelo and Mary Elizabeth (Proctor) D.; B.S., Mass. Inst. Tech., 1897; m. Grace C. Holmes, Oct. 12, 1910; children—Proctor L., Frances, Elizabeth, Faith. Mgr. Otis Elevator Co., Washington, D.C., 1919-26; pres. Bd. of Commissioners of D.C., 1926-30; now cons. engr. Mem. Washington Soc. of Engrs., Washington Soc. Mass. Inst. Tech. Mem. Massachusetts Soc. Republican. Conglist. Club: University (past pres.). Home: 3723 Jenifer St. Office: National Press Bldg., Washington DC‡

DOUGHTY, WILLIAM ELLISON, clergyman; b. Jeffersonville, Sullivan County, N.Y., Feb. 2, 1873; s. Elisha Cullen and Roxanna (Keesler) D.; grad. Cortland (N.Y.) State Normal Sch., 1897; A.B., Syracuse U., 1904, D.D., 1918; m. Eveline Morgan, July 2, 1902; children—Donald Morgan, Florence Eleanor. Ordained Meth. ministry, 1903; pastor Syracuse, N.Y., 1903-05, Phelps, N.Y., 1905-06; field sec. Young People's Missionary Dept. Meth. Ch., 1906-10; sec. Laymen's Missionary Movement of the U.S. and Can., 1910-18. Editor Men and Missions, 1911-17; leader of men's convs. for years including 30 cities in nat. missionary campaign, 1915-16; exec. cons. Meth. Missionary Centenary and exec. chmn. Spiritual Resources; asso. gen. sec. Interchurch World Movement and dir. Spiritual Resources Dept., 1919-20; associate general secretary Near East Relief, 1920-29; nat. field adminstr. Near East Foundation, 1930-36, national counsellor, same, since 1938. Knighted by King George, II, of Greece, Grand Comdr. Order of the Phoenix, 1937; recipient four distinguished service awards; Nr. East Relief medal; Near East Foundation 25 year award; and others. Director American Committee of Colleges in India, 1937. Mem. Phi Beta Kappa, Phi Gamma Delta. Republican. Rotarian. Author books including: Lake Minnewaska in the Heart of the Shawangunks, 1946. Home: 142 Willow St., Roslyn Heights, L.I. N.Y. Office: 54 E. 64th St., NYC‡

DOUGLAS, CLARENCE BROWN, editor; b. Jefferson City, Mo., Oct. 19, 1864; s. George B. and Margaret Ann (Pendleton) D.; ed. pub. schs.; m. Annie Van Sycle, Apr. 29, 1889. Admitted to bar, 1896, and began practice at Ardmore, Indian Ty.; editor and pub. Muskogee (Okla.) Daily and Weekly Phoenix, 1902-08; editor Tulsa (Okla.) Spirit, 1916-21; mng. dir. Tulsa Chamber Commerce 5 1/2 yrs.; one of organizers Mayo Hotel Co., 1920, financial sec., 2 yrs.; organizer, 1922, Claremore Baths Co.; exec. officer Apartment Hotels, Inc. Former chmn. Dept. of Waterways, Flood Control, Power and Navigation of State of Okla. Active in movement for statehood of Okla.; Rep. nominee for U.S. senator, 1908; pres. Ark. River Flood Control Assn.; ex-v.p. Nat. River and Harbor Congress. Mem. Okla. Hall of Fame. Ex-pres. Okla. Memorial Assn. (sponsor Okla. Hall of Fame). Served as colonel Ind. Ty. Vol. Militia; mem. staff Govs. Cruce and Robertson; colonel on staff Governor Murray; apptd. by Gov. Marland colonel infantry Okla. Nat. Guard. Mem. Okla. Hist. Soc. K.P. Author: Prominent Men of Indian Territory, 1904; A Book of Verse, 1920; History of Tulsa and Tulsa County, 1921; Life of Tams Bixby, 1928. Organized first Indian Congress, at Muskogee, 1909, and was adopted into tribe of Pueblo Indians. Contbg. editor The El Reno American. Spl. rep. of War Dept. under Sec. Hurley assigned to inland waterways. Address: 6510 Hillcrest Oklahoma City OK

DOUGLAS OF KIRTLESIDE, LORD (WILLIAM SHOLTO DOUGLAS), Marshal of the Royal Air Force; born Oxford, Eng., Dec. 23, 1893; s. Robert Langton and Margaret (Cannon) D.; student, Tonbridge Sch., 1908-13, Lincoln Coll., Oxford (hon. fellow), 1913-14; m. Hazel Walker, 1955; 1 dau., Katharine Ann. Joined Royal Arty., trans. to R.A.F., 1914; comd. fighter squadrons, France, 1917-18; comdg. officer R.A.F., Sudan, 1929-32; instr. Imperial Defence Coll., 1932-36; dir. staff duties, Air Ministry, 1936-37, asst., chief, Air Staff, 1937-40, deputy chief, 1940, air officer comdg.-in-chief Fighter Command, 1940-42, Middle East Command, 1942-44, Coastal, 1944-45; air comdr.-in-chief, British Air Force of Occupation, Germany, 1945-46; comdr.-in-chief mil. gov. British zone in Germany, 1946-47; director of the British Overseas Air Corps, 1948-49; chairman of the British European Airways, 1949-64, chairman of Horizon Asso. Travel, Ltd., 1964-69. Decorated Knight Grand Cross, Order of the Bath, Mil. Cross, Distinguished Flying Cross, Legion of Merit (chief comdr.), Naval Distinguished Service Medal; created a peer, 1948. Mem. Internat. Transp. Assn. (pres. 1956-57). Author: Years of Combat, 1963; Years of Command, 1966. Home: Denham Bucks England Died Oct. 29, 1969; inurned RAF Meml. Ch., St. Clement Danes London England

DOUGLAS, WALTER G., chmn. bd. Music Publishers' Protective Assn., 1965. Home: New York City NY Died Apr. 1966.*

DOUGLASS, DANA CARROLL, ry. official; b. Wales, Me., Feb. 2, 1877; s. George Emery and Ella Betsey (Libby) D.; ed. pub. sch.; m. Martha Brackett, Oct. 30, 1900; 1 son, Dana Carroll. Stenographer Maine Central R.R., 1894-98, later asst. to v.p., asst. to pres., gen. mgr., 1898-1920; v.p. and gen. mgr., 1920-33; became exec. v.p. Maine Central R.R. Co., and v.p. and dir. subsidiary companies, 1933; now retired. Mason (32 deg.). Home: 296 Spring St. Office: 222 St. John St., Portland ME‡

DOUGLASS, EARL LEROY, clergyman; b. McKeesport, Pa., Aug. 22, 1888; s. Elisha Peairs and Elvira (Weddle) D.; grad. Mercersburg Acad., 1909; A.B., Princeton, 1913; grad. Union Theol. Sem., 1916, postgrad., 1923-25; D.D., Tusculum Coll., 1931, Wooster Coll., 1936; Litt.D., Catawba Coll., Salisbury, N.C., 1941; m. Lois Haler, Sept. 4, 1913; children—Elisha P., Dorothy (Allen). Ordained to ministry, Presbyn. Ch., 1917; pastor First Ch., Tonawanda, N.Y., 1917-23, Poughkeepsie, N.Y., 1925-31, Summit Ch., Germantown, Phila., 1931-45. Trustee Mercersburg Acad., 49 years; chmn. Gen. Assembly's Com. on Tercentenary of Westminster Assembly, 1942-43; chmn. Gen. Assembly's Com. to revise the Intermediate Catechism, 1944-47. Recipient George Washington Honor medal Freedoms Found. of Valley Forge. Mason. Clubs: Authors' League (N.Y.C.); Union League (Phila.); Princeton (N.Y.C., Phila.); Nassau, S.R. (Princeton). Author: Prohibition and Common Sense, 1931; The Faith We Live By, 1937; The Douglass Sunday School Lessons (35 edits. of ann. commentary on Internat. Sunday Sch. Lessons); The Douglass Devotional, 1964. Syndicates two religious features in 104 newspapers. Contbr. revs. and articles to religious mags. Home: Princeton NJ Died Sept. 26, 1972; buried Versailles Cemetery, McKeesport PA

DOUGLASS, GAYLORD WILLIAM, educator; b. Hinesburgh, Vt., July 4, 1876; s. Elvin Leroy and Phebe Merisa (Scovell) D.; B.A., Wesleyan U., Conn., 1900, M.A., 1914; m. Edith Ellen Bride, of Concord, N.H., Dec. 27, 1905. Head of history dept., Mt. Hermon (Mass.) Boys' Sch., 1900-05; prin. Berry Sch. for Boys, Rome, Ga., 1905-07, high sch., Rumford, Me., 1907-10, Murdock Sch., Winchendon, Mass., 1910-12; head master Wilbraham Acad. since 1912. Mem. Phi Nu Theta. Republican. Methodist. Rotarian. Home: Wilbraham MA‡

DOUGLASS, H(ERBERT) ELLWOOD, editor, writer; b. Rush Hill, Mo., Nov. 19, 1900; s. William Henry and Myrtle (Painter) D.; student Washington U., evenings 1919-28; m. Helen Randle, Mar. 11, 1925 (div. Oct. 1930); children—Jolie (Mrs. Robert L. Leaf, Jr.), Randle; m. 2d, Jean Harris, Sept. 15, 1934 (dec. Dec. 1950); 1 son, David E.; m. 3d, Ann Atkinson Odell, Nov. 7, 1953. Mem. news and feature staffs St. Louis Post-Dispatch, 1920-42; with Chgo. Sun, 1942-46, successively feature editor, editorial feature editor, sci. editor; mng. editor Today's Health (Hygeia), Chgo., Ill., 1947-57; mng. editor World-Wide Abstracts of Gen. Medicine. Morris Plains, N.J., 1958-66; cons. editor, writer Warner-Chilcott Labs., Morris Plains, 1966-69. Pres. St. Louis Newspaper Guild, 1938-40. Mem. Nat. Assn. Sci. Writers Home: Lebanon NJ Died Jan. 1969.

DOUGLASS, JOHN JOSEPH, ex-congressman; b. E. Boston, Mass., Feb. 9, 1873; s. John Douglass and Elizabeth (McLaughlin) D.; A.B., Boston Coll., 1893, A.M., 1896; LL.B., Georgetown U., 1896; m. Marion G. Cummings, of Boston, Nov. 25, 1925; 1 son, Paul. Admitted to Mass. bar, 1897, and since practiced at Boston; mem. Mass. Ho. of Rep. 4 terms between 1899-1913; mem. Mass. Constl. Conv., 1917-18; mem. 69th to 72d Congresses (1925-33), 10th Mass. Dist., and 73d Congress (1933-35), 11th Mass. Dist. Democrat. Home: 51 Landseer St., West Roxbury MA*‡

DOUGLASS, MABEL SMITH, coll. dean; b. Jersey City, N.J., Feb. 11, 1877; d. James Weaver and Wilhelmine Joanne (Midlige) Smith; grad. high sch., Jersey City; A.B., Columbia, 1899; Litt.D., Rutgers U., 1924; m. William Shipman Douglass, Apr. 14, 1903; children—Edith Shipman, William Shipman (deceased).Teacher, public schools, N.Y. City, 1899-1902; administrative dean N.J. Coll. for Women, Rutgers U., since founded, 1918. Mem. N.J. State Bd. of Edn. Mem. Am. Assn. Univ. Women, Phi Beta Kappa. Awarded Columbia Univ. medal, 1931. Protestant. Clubs: College (New Brunswick); College (Jersey City). Home: New Brunswick NJ‡

DOUGLASS, TRUMAN BARTLETT, clergyman; b. Grinnell, Ia., July 15, 1901; s. Truman Orville and Katherine (Bartlett) D.; A.B., Pomona Coll., 1923; A.M., Columbia, 1926; Union Theol. Sem., 1924-27; D.D., Chgo. Theol. Sem., 1936, Pomona Coll., 1952; LL.D., Grinnell Coll., 1953; L.H.D., Doane Coll., 1954, Defiance College, 1962; Litt.D., Yankton College, 1957; married Virginia Zimmerman, November 5, 1926. Ordained to the ministry of Congl. Ch., 1926; asso. pastor Union Ch., Upper Montclair, N.J., 1926-30; pastor Pilgrim Ch., Pomona, Cal., 1930-35, St. Louis, 1935-43; exec. v.p. United Church Board for Homeland Ministries, 1943-69; president Home Missions Council of North America, 1949-50. Lyman Beecher lectr., Yale, 1951; radio preacher Art of Living, NBC, 1956, Member Nat. Council Chs. (chmn. broadcasting and film commn., 1951-52; ex. bd. home missions, 1953-65, exec. bd. div. Christian life and mission, 1965-69, mem. gen. bd. 1953-69, chmn. dept. worship and arts 1955-62), World Council Chs. Club: Century (N.Y.C.). Author: Mission to Am.; Preaching and the New Reformation; Why Go to Church, 1957; The New World of Urban Man; also articles religious jours. Home: New York City NY Died May 27, 1969.

DOUTY, NICHOLAS, tenor singer; b. Phila., Pa., Apr. 14, 1870; s. Henry Browne and Helen Matilda (Barber) D.; studied singing with Aline Osgood, William Castle in U.S., Alberto Randegger, London, Guiseppe Sbriglia, Paris; hon. Mus.D., George Washington Univ., 1919; Philadelphia Musical Academy, 1929; m. Frieda Shloss, of Philadelphia, Mar. 4, 1894; children—Nicholas (dec.), Alfred, Blanche. Known as singer of Bach's music; soloist in Bach performances in New York, Chicago, Boston, Phila., Pittsburgh, Milwaukee, Montclair Bach Festival, etc.; soloist every festival Bethlehem Bach Choir for 25 years, and of many choral socs. and orchestras; also conductor. Club: Pegasus (pres.). Author: What the Vocal Student Should Know; also many articles in mags. Composer of numerous published songs, part songs, etc. on the Editorial staff Etude magazine. Editor of Oratorio Repertoire (4 vols.). Translator song, opera and oratorio texts from European langs. Home: 331 Harrison Av., Elkins Park, Pa. Studio: 1712 Chestnut St., Philadelphia PA‡

DOVE, W(ILLIAM) FRANKLIN, biologist; b. Marion, Ia., Apr. 11, 1897; s. William Franklin and Edith (Gregory) D.; B.S., Ia. State Coll., 1922; M.S., U. of Wis., 1923, Ph.D. in Genetics, 1927; m. Ruth Rebecca Stone, Sept. 5, 1933; children—Edith Felicia, William Franklin, Ellen Rebecca, Christopher Stone, John Gregory. Asst. in genetics, U. Wis., 1923-26; asso. biol., Me. Argr. Expt. Sta., U. Me., 1926-31, head dept. biology, 1931-43. Cons., Subsistence Research Br., Mil. Planning Div. O.Q.M.G., Washington, 1944; biologist in charge Food Acceptance Research Br., Subsistence Research and Devel. Lab., C.Q.M.D. (later Quartermaster Food and Container Inst. for Armed Forces, C.Q.M.D.), Chgo., 1944-45; coordinator for Food Acceptance Com. on Food Research, 1945; chief, Food Acceptance Research Branch, Q.M. Food and Container Inst. for the Armed Forces, 1946-48; biologist USPHS, (nutrition br.), also dir. food acceptance Studies Dept. Pub. Health, Coll. of Medicine, U. Ill., 1950, research asso., 1950-66, research asso. emeritus, 1966-72; adv. bd. U.S. Soil, Plant Nutrition Lab., Cornell U., 1939-42. Served AS, USN, Pensacola, Fla., 1918. Mem. A.A.A.S., Am. Soc. Human Genetics, Soc. for Study of Growth and Devel., Genetics Soc. Am., Am. Statis. Assn. (Biometrics), Inst. Food Technologists, Sigma Xi. Contbr. to sci. jours. on physiol. genetics, transplantation of tissues, artifical production of the fabulous unicorn, individual vs. group-growth and need-getting, the theory of aggrid ascendance, bio-economics, appetite levels of food consumption, food acceptance research, water and the consumer. Home: Oak Park IL Died Mar. 24, 1972; buried Mt. Vernon IA

DOVELL, RAY C., publisher; b. Hanging Rock, O., Mar. 3, 1890; s. Richard and Rachel (Jackson) D.; ed. high school; m. Louise Dooley Harris, Aug. 15, 1922; 1 son, Ray Harris. Newspaper reporter, El Paso, Dallas, Tex., Chicago, 1915-17; city editor Houston Post, 1920-24; rewrite man, asst. city editor, New York Daily Mirror, Sunday mag. writer, King Features Service, editor, Internat. Illustrated News, 1924-30; dir. pub. relations, Melville Shoe Corp., operator, John Ward and Thom McAn shoe stores, 1930-1946; founder of The History Book Club, Inc., pres., 1946-61, chmn. bd., editor in chief, 1961-68. Served in U.S. Army in France, 1918-19. Mem. N.Y. Hist. Soc. Democrat. Episcopalian. Clubs: Groiler, Players (N.Y.C.); Appalachian Mountain (Boston). Contbr. mags. and Sun. feature articles on various subjects. Home: Darien CT Died May 2, 1968.

DOWD, DAVID L(LOYD), historian, educator; b. Cleve., May 25, 1918; s. Edward A. and Winifred Pauline (Eberhard) D.; A.B., U. Cal., 1940, M.A., 1943, Ph.D., 1946; student Harvard, 1944-45, U. Paris, Ecole du Louvre, Ecole des Beaux-Arts, 1951-52; m. Lyla Elena Bylinkin, Aug. 31, 1944; children—Elizabeth Irene, Alexandra Winifred. Instr. history U. Cal., 1942-43, Lake Forest Coll., 1945-46, U. Neb., 1946-49; asst. prof. U. Fla., 1949-53, asso. prof., 1953-58, prof. history, 1958-66, asst. head dept. history, 1961-63, dir. grad. studies dept. history, 1965-66; prof. history U. Ky., Lexington, 1966-68; faculty research fellow Social Science Research Council, 1958-59; Fulbright vis. prof. U. Toulouse, France, 1960-61; faculty fellow Ford Foundation France, 1951-52, Soc. Sci. Research Council, France, 1955-56. Recipient grants-in-aid. Am. Philos. Soc., 1948, 52, 55. Mem. Am., So. (mng. editor European Newsletter 1963-68, pres. European hist. sect. 1966-67) hist. assns., Soc. French Hist. Studies, Soc. de L'Histoire de l'Art Francais, Societe de l'Histoire de France, Soc. des Etudes Robespierristes, Institut Napoleon, Fla. Acad. Sci., Am. Acad. Polit. and Social Sci., Fla. Hist. Soc., Am. Assn. U. Profs., Phi Beta Kappa, Phi Alpha Theta, Delta Epsilon. Author: Pageant Master of the Republic, 1948; Napoleon, 1957; The French Revolution, 1965; The Age of Revolution, 1770-1870, 1967. Co-author: Studies in Modern European History, 1956. Editor: Jean Ribaut, 1964. Contbg. editor: Guide to Historical Literature; Guide to Photographed Historical Material in Canada and the U.S. Mem. editorial bd. Jour. of Modern History, 1966—. Contbr. periodicals and jours. Home: Lexington KY Died Oct. 25, 1968.

DOWDALL, GUY GRIGSBY, surgeon; b. Peoria, Ill., Mar. 9, 1875; s. William Tecumseh and Delle (Mason) D.; A.B., U. of Mo., 1897; M.D., Coll. Phys. and Surg., Chicago, 1900; studied U. of Vienna, 1907; m. Winifred Warner, June 3, 1905. Began practice at Clinton, 1901; removed to Chicago, 1908; associated with Dr. John B. Murphy, 1909—; chief surgeon I.C. R.R. Co. since 1911. Republican. Episcopalian. Mem. A.M.A., Ill. State Med. Soc., Chicago Med. Soc., Beta Theta Pi, Theta Nu Epsilon, Nu Sigma Nu. Clubs: South Shore, Flossmoor Country. Home: Hotel Windermere West. Office: 5800 Stony Island Av., Chicago IL‡

DOWELL, ALVIS YATES, lawyer; b. Durham, N.C., Aug. 19, 1896; s. Rev. George J. and Tranquilla Avery (Yates) D.; B.A., Wake Forest Coll., 1917; LL.B., Nat. U., 1924; J.D., George Washington University, 1968; m. Emma Haralson Knight, Nov. 29, 1917; children—Margaret (Mrs. John P. Cochran), Alvis Yates, Josephine (Mrs. Harrison L. Hinson). Asst. prin. and coach, also instr. chemistry, physics, manual tng., Lawrence County (Ala.) High Sch., 1917; mem. examining corps U.S. Patent Office, 1918-21; admitted to D.C. bar, 1926; pvt. practice specializing in patent, trademark, copyright law 1921-70; patent counsel Servel, Incorporated. N.Y.C., 1929-34. Mem. bars U.S. Supreme Ct., Ct. Appeals, D.C., U.S. Ct. Customs and Patent Appeals, U.S. Ct. Claims. Mem. com. 40, alumni council, bd. dirs. D.C., Md. and Va. Area Alumni of Wake Forest U.; bd. visitors Law Sch., Wake Forest U.; bd. assos. Meredith Coll. Mem. Am. Soc. Heating, Refrigerating and Air Conditioning Engrs. Baptist. Clubs: Nat. Lawyers, Civitan (D.C. past pres.); Kenwood (hon. life mem.). Home: McLean VA Died May 4, 1970; buried Nat. Memorial Park, Falls Church VA

DOWLING, NOEL THOMAS, educator, lawyer; b. Ozark, Ala., Aug. 14, 1885; s. Angus and Laura Lavinia (Boswell) D.; A.B., Vanderbilt U., 1909; A.M., Columbia, 1911, LL.B., 1912, LL.D., 1954; m. Elizabeth Brown Molloy, June 19, 1918; children—Janet Cameron Brown, Elizabeth Molloy (dec. June 1972). Asst., Legislative Drafting Research Fund, Columbia, 1912-14, 16-17; prof. law U. Minn., 1919-22; asso. prof. law Columbia, 1922-24, prof. law, 1924-30, Nash prof. law, 1930-46, Harlan Fiske Stone prof. constl. law, 1946-54, emeritus, 1954-69; acting prof. law Stanford, 1925; vis. prof. law U. Va., 1940. Spl. asst. legislative counsel U.S. Senate, 1921, 27; asso. dir. Bur. War Risk Ins. (now VA), commr. mil. and naval ins., 1918-19; mem. sec. navy com. to prepare report on orgn., methods and procedures of naval courts, 1943, mem. bd., 1945. Chmn. N.Y. Mayor's factfinding bd., city bus strike, 1941. Vice pres. Riverside Ch., N.Y.C., 1941-45, pres., 1945-46, hon. trustee 1959-69; trustee, vice chmn. Nat. Child Labor Com. Served as maj., judge adv. general U.S. Army, World War I. Recipient Distinguished Pub. Service award U.S. Navy, 1948. Mem. Acad. Polit. Sci. (trustee, sec. 1936-46), Am. Univ. Union (dir. Brit. div. 1928-29), Am. Bar Assn., Assn. Bar City N.Y., Am. Law Inst., Phi Beta Kappa, Sigma Alpha Epsilon (mem. supreme council, editor The Record 1918-20). Club: Century (N.Y.C.). Author: (with Joseph P. Chamberlain, Paul R. Hays) The Judicial Function in Federal Administrative Agencies, 1942. Editor; Cases on Constitutional Law, 6th edit., 1959, (with Gerald Gunther), 7th edition, 1965. Co-editor: Cases on Public Utilties, 1926, 36; Cases on Conflict of Laws, 1936-41; Materials for Legal Method, 1946, 52; American Constitutional Law, 1954. Contbr. articles to law reviews. Home: New York City NY Died Feb. 11, 1969; buried Grove Hill Cemetery, Shelbyville KY

DOWNER, ALAN SEYMOUR, educator; b. Syracuse, N.Y., July 15, 1912; s. Harry Vincent and Mary Louese (Bliss) D.; A.B., Harvard, 1934, M.A., 1936; m. Florence Marcia Walsh, Sept. 6, 1941; 1 son, Alan Seymour. From instr. to asst. prof. English, Wells Coll., 1939-46; mem. acting company Village Hall Players, Framingham, Mass., summers 1939-42, Forbes Theatre, Rockport, Mass., 1943; mem. faculty Princeton, 1946-70, prof. English, 1957-70. chmn. dept., 1963-68; Fulbright lectr. U. Copenhagen (Denmark), 1953-54; lectr. Salzburg Seminar Am. Studies, 1959, 61; Forbes Heermans lectr. Cornell U., 1958; Edgar Stone lectr. U. Toronto, 1963; Distinguished lectr. of yr. Nat. Council Tchrs. of English, 1969. Mem. Modern Lang. Assn., Am. Soc. Theatre Research (co-founder, chmn. 1956-59), Internat. Fedn. Theatre Research, Theatre Library Assn., Am. Assn. U. Profs., Phi Beta Kappa (hon.). Club: Century Assn. Author: British Drama, 1950; Fifty Years of American Drama, 1951; The Art of the Play, 1955; Recent American Drama, 1961. Editor: 25 Modern Plays, 2d edit., 1953; American Drama, 1960; Theatre of Bernard Shaw, 1961; Shakespeare's Plays, 2d edit., 1958; King Richard III, 1959; On Plays, Playwrights and Playgoers, 1959; The Autobiography of Joseph Jefferson, 1964; The Eminent Tragedian: William Charles Macready, 1966. Editor, translator: Hedda Gabler, 1961; editor: Great World Theatre, 1964; The Memoir of John Durang, 1966; American Drama and Its Critics, 1965; The American Drama Today, 1967. Home: Princeton NJ Died Jan. 20, 1970; buried All Saints Cemetery, Princeton NJ

DOWNEY, HERMON HORATIO, clergyman; b. Akron, N.Y., Mar. 26, 1876; s. Henry and Almeda (Shell) D.; A.B., Syracuse U., 1900, D.D., 1916; S.T.B., Boston U., 1902; m. Jessie Lydia Sheffield, Nov. 27, 1902; 1 dau., Vivian Almeda; m. 2d, Mary Ellen Wyckoff, Oct. 2, 1922; children—Beverly, Bradford Wyckoff, Joanne. Ordained ministry M.E. Ch., 1903; pastor Northampton M.E. Ch., Buffalo, 1905-08, Spencer Ripley M.E. Ch., Rochester, N.Y., 1908-13, Furman St. M.E. Ch., Syracuse, 1913-23; camp pastor Camp Hancock, Ga., World War; pastor St. Paul's M.E. Ch., Wichita, Kan., 1923-25, Boulevard Temple, Detroit, Mich., 1925-31, Monroe Av. M.E. Ch., Rochester, New York, 1931-34, Furman Methodist Church, Syracuse, 1934-48, Woodlawn Methodist Church, since 1948. Trustee Cazenovia (N.Y.) Sem. Mem. Beta Theta Pi. Republican. Mason. Home: 181 Maplehurst Ave., Syracuse NY‡

DOWNING, LEWIS KING, coll. dean; b. Roanoke, Va., Jan. 2, 1896; A.B., Johnson C. Smith U., 1916, Sc.D., 1953; B.S. in Civil Engring., Howard U., 1921; B.S. Mass. Inst. Tech., 1923; M.S., U. of Michigan, 1932; D.Sc., Virginia State College, 1995; married Morease M. Chisholm, December 26, 1925; children—Charlotte C., Morease M. With Howard University, 1924-67, professor, 1938-67, became dean School of Engineering and Architecture, 1936, dean emeritus until 1967. Chairman engring. com. D.C. Commrs. Traffic Adv. Bd., 1958-—; mem. D.C. Commrs. Urban Renewal Council, 1958, D.C. Commrs. Planning Adv. Council, 1959-62; vice chmn. Washington Met. Area Joint Bd. on Sci. Edn., 1959, sec., 1960, D.C. Bd. for Registration of Professional Engineers, 1962-67. Recipient Distinguished Alumni award, Howard University, 1953, cited by N.Y. chpt. Howard U. Alumni Assn., 1957, 58. Registered civil engr., Va., 1936, D.C., 1951. Fellow Am. Soc. C.E. (dir. nat. capital sect. 1962-64); mem. Washington Acad. Sci., Am. Soc. Engring. Edn. (sec., dir. 1957-58, chmn. civil engring. div. 1959-60), Nat. Tech. Assn., Pi Mu Epsilon, Alpha Phi Alpha, Beta Kappa Chi, Tau Beta Pi. Home: Washington DC Died Oct. 19, 1967; buried Lincoln Meml. Cemetery, Washington DC

DOWNING, RUSSELL VINCENT, business executive; b. Yonkers, N.Y., Aug. 11, 1900; s. Isaac G. and Ida A. (Vincent) D.; student U. Pa., 1918, Columbia, 1919-22; m. Sally Neville Rush, Nov. 9, 1935. Asst. to pres. Tide Water Oil Sales Corp., 1920-26; asst. treas. Mag. Repeating Razor Co., 1926-28, Holmes Products, Inc., 1928-30; treas. Prudence Co., Inc., 1930-33; treas. Radio City Music Hall Corp., 1933-48, v.p., 1942-48, dir. since 1942, exec. v.p., 1948-52; pres., mng. dir. Radio City Music Hall, 1952-66; dir. Rockefeller Center, Inc., Rugoff Theatres, Inc. Trustee N.Y. Polyclinic Med. Sch. and Hosp. Mem. Met. Motion Picture Theater Assn. (dir.). Methodist (trustee). Mason. Club: Kiwanis. Home: New York City NY Died June 28, 1968.

DOWNS, LE ROY DONNELLY, congressman; b. Danbury, Conn., Apr. 11, 1900; s. Reuben J. and Grace (Donnelly) D.; student Danbury High Sch.; m. Mabel Anna Miller, Aug. 21, 1926; 1 son, William Edward. Began as newspaper reporter, 1920; pres. and treas. Sentinel Pub. Co., South Norwalk, Conn.; regional dir. information VA. Served in U.S. Army, with A.E.F., World War. Mem. Conn. Vets. Home Commn., 1931-39; city clerk, Norwalk, 1933-40; mem. 77th Congress (1941-43), 4th Conn. Dist. Mem. Am. Legion, Vets. Foreign Wars. Mason. Democrat. Protestant. Club: Shorehaven Golf (Norwalk, Conn.). Home: South Norwalk CT Died Jan. 18, 1970.

DOWS, SUTHERLAND, utility exec.; b. Cedar Rapids, Ia., July 3, 1891; s. William Greene and Margaret Burnell (Cook) D.; grad. Hill Sch., 1910; Ph.B., Yale University, 1913; LL.D., Cornell College, 1960; married Frances Daisy Mills, October 3, 1914; children—Peter, Henrietta, Sutherland. With Iowa Electric Light & Power Co., Cedar Rapids, 1913-69, successively clk. in stores dept., purchasing agt., gen. mgr., exec. v.p., 1913-41, pres., 1941-61, chairman board, chief executive officer, 1961-69; dir. Merchants National Bank, Iowa National Mutual Liability Insurance Company. Bd. trustees Coe Coll., Cornell Coll. Mem. Midwest Research Institute (Trustee). Home: Cedar Rapids IA Died Sept. 22, 1969; buried Oak Hill Cemetery, Cedar Rapids IA

DOX, CHARLES E., ins. co. exec.; b. Omaha, Dec. 3, 1906; s. William Henry and Maud (Staley) D.; B.S., U. Neb., 1929; m. Kathryn Foote, Nov. 16, 1935; children—Bonnie (Mrs. Robert Caffray), Charles E. With London & Lancashire Ins. Co., 1929-62, U.S. mgr., 1960-62; sr. v.p. Royal-Globe Ins. Companies, N.Y.C., 1962-68; dir. Am. & Fgn. Ins. Co., Globe Indemnity Co., Newark Ins. Co., Queen Ins. Co. Am., Royal Indemnity Co., Safeguard Ins. Co., Conn. Bank & Trust Co. Mem. Delta Tau Delta. Club: Scarsdale Golf. Home: Scarsdale NY Died Nov. 7, 1968; buried Ferncliff Cemetery, Hartsdale NY

DOYLE, ALBERT PRYOR EDWARD, former Dem. nat. committeeman; b. Providence, R.I., Aug. 3, 1873; s. Hugh Edward and Margaret Frances (McLaughlin) D.; ed. common sch.; m. Ave Maria Conway, Oct. 25, 1896 (dec.); children—Hugh McLaughlin, Ave Marie (wife of Capt. James Edward Dyer, U.S. Navy), Albert Aloysius, Paul Conway. Apprentice printer, E. A. Johnson Co., Providence, 1889; civil service printer, Govt. Printing Office, Washington, D.C., 1897-1909; supt., New Century Press, Washington, D.C., 1903; craftsman instr., Bureau Printing, Manila, P.I., 1909-11; with Govt. Printing Office, 1911-12; supt. Panama Canal Press, 1912-35; retired, 1935. Mem. Nat. Guard, Washington, D.C., 1898-1902. Mem. Dem. Nat. Com. since 1940. Elk, K.C. Clubs: Strangers (past mem. bd. of govs.), Rotary (past pres.; Colon). Address: Box 1468 Cristobal Canal Zone‡

DOYLE, JAMES HAROLD, lecturer; b. Decorah, Ia., Mar. 19, 1875; s. James and Ann (Holahan) D.; student Dixon (Ill.) Coll., 1894-96; grad. Marion (Ind.) Normal Sch., 1908; student U. of Chicago, summer 1912; Ph.B., U. of Wis., 1912, A.M., 1913, Ph.D., 1915; grad. Cummock Sch. of Expression, Evanston, Ill., 1916; unmarried. Served as teacher country schs., S.D., and Ill.; supt. city schs. Mont. and Ia.; mem. faculty U. of Wis. and Culver Mil. Acad.; platform speaker and writer since 1917. Author: The Call of Education, 1921; Salvaging the American Republic, 1933. Lectures: The Best Mental Attitude; Why Some People Fail and Others Succeed; The Fundamental Criterion of Education; Americanization; The Monumental Mistake in Education; Footprints of Disease. Home: Box 347, Huron SD‡

DOYLE, MARTHA CLAIRE MACGOWAN (MARTHA JAMES,"), author; b. Boston, June 16, 1869; d. Henry M. and Anne (Lande) MacGowan; grad. Boston Normal Sch., 1890; m. Boston, James R. Doyle, Feb. 16, 1896. Author: Little Miss Dorothy, 1900; My Friend Jim, 1901; Tom Winstone, Wide Awake," 1902; Jimmie Suter and the Boy's Pigeon Camp, 1906. Home: Newton Highlands MA‡

DOYLE, SISTER MARY PETER, past college pres.; b. Rockford, Ill., Oct. 29, 1898; d. Denis Patrick and Mary Margaret (Dunne) Doyle; A.B., St. Clara Coll. (now Rosary Coll.), Sinsinawa, Wis., 1920; A.M., University of Wisconsin, 1923; Dominican Sister of the Congregation of the Most Holy Rosary at Sinsinawa, Wis., 1924; summer session, U. of Iowa, 1930-31; Ph.D., Columbia, 1935; student Theodora Irvine Studio and Francis Robinson-Duff Studio for the Theatre, N.Y. City. Teacher, Hall Sch., Rockford, Ill., 1920-22; Trinity High Sch., 1924-27; Rosary College, River Forest, Ill., 1927-40, chmn. speech dept., 1929-43, dean, 1942-43, pres., 1943-49, also trustee and coordinator War Activities, 1942-43; dir. Midwest Region Catholic Theatre Conf. Mem. Nat. Assn. Teachers of Speech, Ill. Assn. Teachers of Speech, Nat. Ednl. Theatre Conf., Am. Assn. of Univ. Women, Am. Assn. of School Administrators, Nat. Catholic Ednl. Assn. (mem. exec. com., 1947). Home: Dubuque IA Died July 1971.

DOYLE, PRICE, fine arts dir.; b. nr. Redfield, Ia., Feb. 21, 1896; s. Grant and Army Jane (Lyon) D.; B.S., State Tchrs. Coll., Maryville, Mo., 1924; A.M., U. Cincinnati, 1930; Mus. D., Am. Conservatory, 1950; m. Loree Strader, Sept. 22, 1921; 1 son, R. Larry. Profl. musician, singer, condr., adjudicator, 1913-67; part time instr., Maryville Coll., 1921-23; dir. music Concord (N.C.) Schs., 1923-26; head dept. music, State Tchrs. Coll., Peru, Neb., 1926-30; dir. dept. fine arts, Murray (Ky.) State Coll., 1930-67; Mem. Nat. Assn. Schs. of Music (chmn. com. on teachers colls. since 1940; ofcl. examiners since 1940, com. on curriculum since 1943, president 1948-52), Nat. Assn. for American Composers and Conductors, Ky. Music Tchrs. Assn. (pres. 1932-34), So. Conf. for Music Edn. (v.p. 1935-37), Music Tchrs. Nat. Assn., Music Educators Nat. Conf., Am. Legion, Rotary, Phi Mu Alpha. Christian Church. Specialist in curriculum for music schs.; studies concerning curriculum for training teachers of music in pub. schs., certification for teachers of music in pub. schs., music study applied and theoretical, pvt. teachers, since 1906. Contbr. to profl. jours. Exec. sec. Phi Mu Alpha Sinfonia, 1949-67. Home: Murray KY Died May 5, 1967.

DOYLE, RHEDERICK ELWOOD, JR., electric utility exec.; b. Elkhorn, W.Va., Feb. 2, 1906; s. Rhederick Elwood and Virginia (Hawkins) D.; B.S. in Elec. Engring., Va. Poly. Inst.; grad. Advanced Mgmt. Program, Harvard; m. Opal Hackney, Dec. 7, 1934; children—Virginia Bell, Kathleen Hackney. Exec. v.p. Ind. and Mich. Electric Co.; dir. Am. Electric Power Service Corp., Ind. and Mich. Electric Co., Ind.-Ky. Electric Co., Mich. Gas and Electric Co., Twin Branch R.R. Bd. dirs. Taxpayers Research Inst.; trustee E. Central Nuclear Group. Mem. exec. com. Ind.-Purdue Found.; bd. dirs. YMCA. Registered profl. engr. Named hon. Ky. Col. Mem. Ind. Electric Assn. (bd. dirs., past pres.), Ky. Soc. Profl. Engrs., Ind., Ft. Wayne chambers commerce, Newcomen Soc., Ind. Soc. Chgo. Presbyn. (trustee). Rotarian (bd. dirs. Ft. Wayne), Mason (Shriner). Clubs: Quest; Shrine; Press; Ft. Wayne Country. Fort Wayne IN

DOYLE, RICHARD SMITH, lawyer, orgn. exec.; b. Woodstock, N.H., Jan. 8, 1889; s. Samuel W. and Nellie F. (Smith) D.; grad. Colby Acad., 1908; LL.B., Georgetown U., 1913, LL.M., 1914; student George Washington U., 1914-17; m. Anne H. Chamberlain, Nov. 29, 1919; children—Samuel C., Willis S. Admitted to D.C. bar, 1913, Md. bar, 1932, also U.S. Supreme Ct., Ct. of Claims; spl. atty. Bur. Internal Revenue, 1914-17, 20; pvt. practice law, Washington, 1920-66; partner firm Korner, Doyle, Worth & Crampton, 1944-66; Mem. Sigma Chi, 1914-66, grand consul, 1959-66; pres. Sigma Chi Found., 1947-57, Sigma Chi Corp., 1959-66. Mem. President's Conf. Adminstrv. Procedure, 1953-54; mem. judicial conf. U.S. Circuit Ct. for D.C., 1958-59. Served as 1st lt., arty., U.S. Army, 1917-19; AEF in France. Mem. Am. (chmn. com. revision rules and procedure in Ct. of Claims 1948-53), D.C. (chmn. com. adminstrv. law sect. 1941) bar assns., Mil. Order Wolrd Wars. Episcopalian. Mason (32 deg., Shriner). Clubs: Chevy Chase, Metropolitan, University, Burning Tree, Capital Yacht (Washington); Philadelphia Country. Home: Washington DC Died Aug. 23, 1966.

DOYLE, SHERMAN HOADLEY, clergyman; b. St. Clairsville, O.; s. David D. and Mary A. (Hughes) D.; A.B. Franklin Coll., New Athens, O., 1887, A.M., 1890, Ph.D., 1895; grad. Western Theol. Sem., Pittsburgh, 1890 (D.D., Franklin, 1902); m. Effa M. Parrish, of New Athens, O., Nov. 7, 1889. Ordained Presbyn. minstry, 1890. Club: Union League (Phila.). Editor: Presbyterian Home Missions, 1905; also editor Christian Endeavor Dept. of Am. Press Assn., New York, 1894-—. Address: 4720 Springfield Av., Philadelphia PA‡

DOYLE, THOMAS HENCHION, judge; b. Worchester County, Mass., Dec. 21, 1863; s. John and Johanna (Henchion) D.; ed. pub. schs.; m. Rosa O'Neill, Aug. 3, 1893; 1 dau., Mrs. John Francis Martin. Admitted to Kan. bar, 1887; mem. Ho. of Rep., Okla. Ty., 1897-1901; nonpartisan joint statehood del. from Okla. and Ind. Tys. to 57th, 58th and 59th Congresses, 1901-07; del.-at-large and chmn. Okla. del. Dem. Nat. Conv., Denver, 1908; hon. v.-chmn. Okla. del. Dem. Nat. Conv., Baltimore, 1912; asso. justice Court of Appeals, Okla., Jan. 1908-1929, 1935-41, presiding justice, 1915-23, 1939-41, reelected, 1941-47. Chmn. State Industrial Commn., 1929-35; pres. State Parks Assn.; pres. State Hist. Soc. Home: 134 N.W. 18th St. Address: State Capitol, Oklahoma City OK

DRACH, EDMUND L., chem. exec.; b. Chgo., Jan. 5, 1887; s. Edmund A. and Emilie (Diecke) D.; LL.B., Chgo. Kent Coll. Law, 1912; m. Agnes Mabel Johnson, Jan. 29, 1919; children—Aurie Jane (Mrs. Lester Hornbrook), Lois Marjorie (Mrs. Wilbur Warner); m. 2d, Vesta Tudor, Oct. 29, 1955. Joined Purch, Abbott Labs., North Chicago, 1910, v.p., 1947-53, dir. 1930-71. Mem. Nat. Assn. Purchasing Agts., Chgo. Perfumery, Soap & Extract Assn., Inc., Chgo. Drug and Chem. Assn. (pres. 1933-34), Phi Delta Phi. Republican. Methodist. Mason. Clubs: Chicago Athletic; Evanston Golf; Lauderdale Yacht. Home: Fort Lauderdale FL Died Sept. 10, 1971; buried Memorial Park Mausoleum, Wilmette IL

DRAEMEL, MILO FREDERICK, naval officer; b. Fremont, Neb., May 30, 1884; s. Frederick William and Johanna (Nilson) D.; B.S., U.S. Naval Acad., 1906; degrees from Villanova, Temple U., Univ. of Pa.; m. Marguerite Clise, Oct. 25, 1911; children—Frederick Clise, Eleanor Clise. Commd. ensign, U.S. Navy, 1906, and advanced through the grades to rear adm., 1938; during World War I served as flag lt. on staff comdr. Battleship Force, U.S. Fleet until Sept. 1918, then officer in charge Code and Signal Sect., Navy Dept., until end of war; became comdt. midshipmen, U.S. Naval Acad., 1937-39; comdr. Destroyer Flotilla, 1940; chief of staff and aide to comdr.-in-chief, Pacific Fleet, 1941-42; task force comdr. Eastern Sea Frontier, comdt. Fourth Naval Dist., 1942-46; inactive list Aug. 1946. Vice pres. Temple Univ., Phila.; sec. Dept. Forests and Waters, Commonwealth of Pa. as mem. of Gov. James H. Duff's Cabinet, 1947-52. Decorated: D.S.M. (Navy), Legion of Merit, Am. Defense, Victory Medals, Pacific and Am. Theatre Medals; French Legion of Honor; Venezuelan Order of Bolivar; Grand Officer of Southern Cross (Brazil); Grand Officer Order of Orange-Nassau (Netherlands). Episcopalian. Clubs: Chevy Chase, The Philadelphia, New York Yacht. Gulph Mills. Home: Wynnewood PA Died Mar. 25, 1971; buried Mount Pleasant Cemetery, Seattle WA

DRAKE, RUSSELL PAYSON, pvt. cons.; b. Moline, Ill., Feb. 27, 1901; s. John Payson and Hattie (Krum) D.; B.S., Kan. State Tchrs. Coll., Emporia, 1923; M.P.A., Syracuse U., 1930; student Sch. Mil. Govt., Charlottesville, Va., 1943; m. Helen Buckner, June 18, 1930; children—Barbara A. (Mrs. Wallace Fulton), Helen Elizabeth (Mrs. John Mosedale). Mem. Cin. Bur. Govtl. Research, 1930-35; fiscal cons. N.Y. State Govt., 1935; pub. adminstrn. service cons., 1935-39; dir. social planning and research Mpls. Council Social Agencies, 1939-40; asst. dir. Minn. Divs. Social Welfare, 1940-43, 45-46; asst. dir. Am. Pub. Welfare Assn., 1947-48; spl. cons. Council State Govts., 1948; dir. civil govt. Spl. Econ. Coop. Mission to Greece, 1948-53, dep. chief of mission, 1953-54, dir., 1954-56; evaluation staff ICA, 1956-58; dir. U.S. Operations Mission to Nepal,

1958-60; research and planning officer pub. adminstrn. ICA, Washington, 1960-62; consultant, from 1962. Mem. Am. Soc. Pub. Adminstrn., Sigma Tau Gamma. Home: Silver Spring MD Died Dec. 10, 1971.

DRANSFIELD, JANE, playwright; b. Rochester, N.Y., Dec. 9, 1875; d. Thomas and Elizabeth (Bell) Dransfield; educated Vassar Coll., 1895-98; m. Clarence DeLano Stone, of N.Y. City, 1899; children—DeLano, Catherine Dransfield, Janet (dec.). Lecturer on drama, Inst. of Arts and Sciences, Columbia, 1918-21; play reader for Stuart Walker, 1924-28; acted in The Dybbuk, 1927; dir. course in play writing, Theatre Workshop of the Surry Playhouse, Me., summer 1929. Chmn. of drama com. Poetry Soc. of America. Author (plays prod. and pub.); The Lost Pleiad (in Treasury of Plays for Women), 1918; Blood O'King's (pub. in A Treasury of Plays for Men), 1924; Joe—a Hudson Valley play (in Twenty-five Short Plays—International), 1923; also other plays (produced), The Romance of Melrose Hall, The White Window. Contbr. to mags.*‡

DRAPER, DOROTHY (TUCKERMAN), interior decorator; b. N.Y.C., Nov. 22 1889; d. Paul and Susan (Minturn) Tuckerman; m. Dr. George Draper, 1912 (div.). Decorator, real estate stylist; redesigned, furnished Hampshire House, Terrace Club of World's Fair, Hotel Carlyle, Hollywood's Arrowhead Springs Hotel, Camillia House at Drake Hotel in Chgo., Delnor Hosp., St. Charles, Ill., also Mayflower Hotel, Washington, Greenbrier Hotel; restyled and rejuveniated tenement bldgs.; decorated homes of society leaders; dir. Studio of Architecture Bldg. and Furnishing, Good Housekeeping magazine, 1941; chairman of Dorothy Draper/Gary Pizarelli Enterprises, Incorporated, N.Y. City, N.Y.; nationally syndicated columnist Ask Dorothy Draper; designer Dorothy Draper Dream House for N.Y. World's Fair 1964-65. Named to Hall of Fame, 1933; named sole rep. in decoration Nat. Fedn. Bus. and Profl. Women, 1934. Clubs: River, Tuxedo (N.Y.C.). Author: Decorating is Fun, How to be Your Own Decorator, 1939, rev. edit., 1962; Entertaining is Fun, How to be a Popular Hostess, 1941; Shortcuts to Home Decorating, 1965. Home: New York City NY Died Mar. 1969.

DRAPER, WARREN FALES, executive medical officer; b. Cambridge, Mass., Aug. 9, 1883; s. William Burgess and Carrie Maria (Drew) D.; prep. edn. Waban (Mass.) Sch. for Boys, 1900-02; A.B. Amherst Coll., 1906, D.Sc., 1945; M.D., Harvard, 1910; m. Margaret Gansevoort Maxon, Apr. 6, 1910; children—Warren Fales, Anne Gansevoort. Commd. asst. surgeon, U.S. Pub. Health Service, 1910, surgeon, 1920, asst. surgeon gen. in charge div. domestic quarantine, 1922-31; health commr. of Va., 1931-34; in charge extra cantonment sanitation, Camp Lee, Petersburg, Va., 1917-18, Newport News, Va., Aug.-Sept. 1918; asst. surgeon gen. in charge div. personnel and accounts, 1934-39; dep. surgeon gen., 1939-47, ret.; maj. gen. charge pub. health br. Supreme Hdqrs. Allied Expdnry. Force, 1944-45; asst. to v.p. for health services Am., Nat. Red Cross, 1946-48; exec. med. officer United Mine Workers of America Welfare and Retirement Fund, 1948-69. Alternate mem. Civilian Health and Medical Adv. Council, Office Assistant Secretary of Def., 1956-69; cons. Dept. Occupational Health, United Mine Workers Am., 1969-70. Decorations: Distinguished Service Medal (U.S.); Companion of the Bath (Brit.); Officer Legion of Honor, Croix de Guerre with Palm, Officer Order of Public Health (France); Officer Order of Leopold II (Belgium); Grand Officer Order of Orange-Nassau (Netherlands). Former professorial lectr. on pub. health adminstrn. George Washington U., Jefferson Med. Coll., Phila.; lectr. pub. health U. Mich., Johns Hopkins U. Mem. Nat. Bd. of Med. Examiners, 1940-48. Mem. pub. health adv. com. Commonwealth Fund, 1925-46. Diplomate Am. Bd. Preventive Medicine. Member A.M.A. (house of delegates, 1942-46; former chairman sect. on preventive and industrial medicine and public health; charter member and former member Council on Industrial Health, Com. on Coordination of Medical Activities), mem. American Public Health Association (former mem. governing counsel; former chmn. health officer sect.); hon. life mem. Internat. Soc. of Med. Health Officers, Conf. State and Provincial Health Authorities of N.A., Assn. Mil. Surgeons (pres. 1946-47); mem. Smith-Reed-Russell (hon. med. soc. George Washington U.), Sigma Xi, Alpha Omega Aplha. Club: Cosmos (Washington). Episcopalian. Author many published articles on pub. health adminstrn. and preventive medicine. Home: Arlington VA Died Mar. 19, 1970; buried Columbia Gardens Cemetery, Arlington VA

DRAUGHON RALPH BROWN, sch. adminstr.; b. Hartford, Ala., Sept. 1, 1899; s. John William and Vashti (Roney) D.; B.S., Ala. Poly. Inst., 1922, M.S., 1929; student U. Chicago, summers 1923, 39; LL.D. (hon.), Birmingham So. Coll., 1948; L.H.D., Samford U., 1962; LL.D. (hon.), U. Ala., 1963, Auburn U., 1966; m. Caroline Marshall, June 9, 1931; children—Ann Caroline, Ralph Brown. High sch. teacher, Choctaw Country, 1922-23; principal Sumter County, 1925-27, Louisville (Ala.) High School, 1927-28, Orrville High School, 1928-31; asst. professor of history and polit. sci. Auburn (Ala.) U., 1931-37, exec. sec. and sec. bd. trustees, 1937-44, dir. instrn., 1944-47, acting pres., 1947-48, pres., 1948-65, pres. emeritus, 1965-68, also prof. history and polit. science. Director State Survey Rural Tax Delinquency, 1934; regional supervisor Bur. Agrl. Econ., 1936; dir. survey farm mortgates and sales for 5 S.E. states, 1936; dir. Govs. Emergency Com. Higher Edn., 1946. Commd. 2d lt., Inf. Res., 1922. Trustee Auburn Research Found. Chairman Council of presidents Association Land-Grant Colleges and Universities, 1954-55. Mem. Southern Regional Edn. Bd. Control, 1957-60. Member American Academy of Political and Social Sci., Exec. Council Commn. Higher Edn., So. Assn. Colls. and Secondary Schs., Joint Commn. Assn. Ala. Colls. and High Schools (past pres.), Ala. Edn. Assn. (mem. com. on ethics, mem. legislative com.), N.E.A., Southwest Conf. Athletics (exec. com.), Ala. Hist. Assn. (exec. com.; past pres.), Ala. Acad. Scis. (exec. com.), Omicron Delta Kappa, Kappa Delta Pi, Phi Kappa Phi, Tau Kappa Alpha. Baptist. Mason. Clubs: Kiwanis, Auburn Inter Club Council. Hon. farmer, 1948. Home: Auburn AL Died Aug. 13, 1968; buried Pine Hill Cemetery, Auburn AL

DREHER, MONROE FRANKLIN, advt. exec.; b. Newark, 1899; s. Ernest Alvin and Minnie (Sheller) D.; B.S., Lafayette Coll., Easton, Pa., 1922; m. Elizabeth K. Sterling, Apr. 5, 1926; 1 dau., Joan (Mrs. Robert W. Hopkins). Founder, 1926, owner Monroe F. Dreher, Inc., Advt., N.Y.C., 1926-69; chmn bd. Variety Store Merchandiser, World-Wide Publ. Trustee Lafayette Coll., Antiquarian and Landmark Soc. Conn. Christian Scientist, Mason. Clubs: Lyford Cay (Nassau); Woodway Country, Tokeneke (Darien), Pine Valley Country (Clemton, N.J.); University (N.Y.C.). Pioneer cellophane window in packages, cordless permanent wave machine design. Home: Darien CT Died Dec. 23, 1970.

DREIKURS, RUDOLPH, psychiatrist; b. Vienna; s. Sigmund and Fanny (Cohn) D.; M.D., U. of Vienna, 1923; m. Sadie Garland; children—Eric, Eva. Came to U.S., 1937, naturalized citizen. Began practice of medicine in Vienna, organizing mental hygiene and psychiat. social work; dir. clinics for child guidance, alcoholics and psychopathics, asst. and collaborator Alfred Adler from 1923; prof. psychiatry Chicago Med. Sch., 1942-66, emeritus, 1966-72; with Tex. Tech. Coll., from 1966; vis. prof. U. Vt., from 1968; dir. Alfred Adler Inst., Chgo.; cons. psychiatrist Hull House, 1940-43; vis. prof. U. of Rio de Janeiro, 1946, Northwestern U. Sch. Edn., 1947-51, U. Ore., 1957, Bar Ilan University, Ramat Gan, Israel; lecturer in edn. Ind. U. Gary extension, 1951-54, Loyola U., from 1959; lecturer in psychology Roosevelt U., 1954-56. Medical dir. Community Child Guidance Centers of Chgo. Fellow Am. Psychiat. Assn., Am. Soc. Group Therapy and Psychodrama (pres. 1954-55)); mem. Am. Soc. Adlerian Psychology (pres. 1954-56), Internat. Assn. Individual Psychology (vice chmn. from 1954), American Humanist Association (vice president 1950-56), Ill. Soc. for Personality Study (pres. 1954-56), Sociedade de Psychologia Individual of Rio de Janeiro (hon. pres.) Author: Introduction to Individual Psychology (pub. in English, German, Dutch, Czech, French), Psychic Impotence (German), The Nervous Symptom (German), Education Without Coercion (Dutch); The Challenge of Marriage, 1946; The Challenge of Parenthood, 1947; Character Education and Spiritual Values in an Anxious Age, 1952; Fundamentals of Adlerian Psychology, 1950; Psychology in the Classroom, 1957; (with Dr. Donald Dinkmeyer) Encouraging Children to Learn, 1962; (with Vicki Solts) Children: The Challenge; (with Loren Grey) Logical Consequences, a New Approach to Discipline, 1968; (with Loren Grey) A Parent's Guide to Child Discipline, 1970; (with Berniece Grunwald and Floy Pepper) Maintaining Sanity in the Classroom, 1971; Social Equality: Training-A Parent's Guide, 1972; Coping with Children's Misbehaviour, 1972; (with Pearl Cassel) Discipline without Tears, 1972. Developed Alfred Adler's system of individual psychology into techniques for understanding purposes of disturbing behavior in children and for stimulating coop. behavior without punishment or reward; founded Alfred Adler Inst. of Chgo. and Tel Aviv; inspired internat. movement of family edn. centers, parent study groups. Home: Chicago IL Died May 25, 1972; buried Chicago IL

DRELLER, LOUIS, naval officer; b. Portsmouth, N.H., Mar. 6, 1897; s. Abram and Eva Celia (Polimer) D.; B.S. in E.E., U. of N.H., 1918; LL.D., 1947; student Post Grad. Sch., U.S. Naval Acad., 1920-21; M.S. Columbia, 1925; m. Edythe Molly Maharam, May 22, 1924; children—Selma Dreller Kerr, Doris M. Commd. ensign (engring. duty), U.S. Navy, 1918, and advanced through the grades to rear adm. (engineering duty), 1946; service included sea duty on battleships, destroyers, aircraft carriers; two tours of duty, Elec. Design Sect., Bureau of Engring. and Bureau of Ships; at outbreak of World War II was engr. officer attached to Scouting Force Staff; design supt., planning officer and prodn. officer, Philadelphia Navy Yard, 1942-46; comdr. Pearl Harbor Naval Shipyard, Hawaii, 1946-48; chief office Indsl. Survey for Secretary Navy, 1948-49; Assistant Chief of Naval Material, 1950-51. Decorated Legion of Merit, Asiatic-Pacific Campaign with 2 stars, American Theater, Defense with 1 star, World War I and World War II ribbons (U.S.) Order of Southern Cross (Brazil), Order of Orange-Nassau (Netherlands). Mem. Soc. Naval Architects and Marine Engrs., Am. Soc. Naval Engrs., Naval Order of U.S. (gen. commandery). Mason. Club: Army-Navy Country (Washington); Rotary (hon.); Propeller. Home: Alexandria VA Died May, 1970.

DRESBACH, GLENN WARD, author; b. Lanark, Ill., Sept. 9, 1889; s. William Henry and Belle M. (Weidman) D.; spl. course, U. of Wis., 1908-11; m. Mary Angela Boyle, Jan. 29, 1921 (died 1943); m. 2d, Beverley Githens, April 9, 1944. Agency accountant Panama Canal, 1911-15. In charge med. supply depots Camp Mead, Md., and Med. Supply O.T.S., U.S. Army, rank of capt., 1917-19. Joint recipient with wife of gold medal for Outstanding Lit. Couple from former Pres. of Philippines. Life fellow Internat. Inst. Arts Letters; member United Poets Laureate International, Society of Midland Authors, Bookfellows, also mem. Am. Legion, Authors' Club (London). Episcopalian. Author: The Road to Everywhere, 1916; In the Paths of the Wind, 1918; Morning, Noon and Night, 1920; In Colors of the West, 1922; Enchanted Mesa, 1924; Cliff Dwellings and Other Poems, 1926; Star-Dust and Stone (winner Poetry Society of Texas award), 1928; This Side of Avalon, 1929; The Wind in the Cedars, 1930; Selected Poems, 1931; Collected Poems (1914-1948), 1949; and also represented in anthologies, textbooks for high schs. and colls. Contbr. verse to Poetry, Sat. Even. Post, Am. Mercury, Atlantic Monthly, Virginia Quarterly Review, McCall's, The Ladies' Home Journal, New York Times, The Yale Review, etc. Winner George Sterling memorial prize, 1929; Grace D. Sperling sonnet prize, 1928, 30; Am. Literary Assn. prize, 1928; Star-Dust prize, 1929; Gypsy sonnet prize, 1930; Poetry World prize, 1930; Talaria prize, 1937; Lily Reed Zortman sonnet prize, 1937. Winner Ruth Baldwin Pierson award, 1939; George Sterling memorial prize, 1939; Hamlin Garland memorial prize, 1940; Beulah May Sea Poem Prize, 1940; recipient Karta of Award and laurel wreath with bronze medallion United Poets Laureate Internat., 1964. Selected to give poetry program at Ill. Host House Auditorium Century of Progress Expn., 1933; selected as one of five internat. speakers at Lions Internat. Conv., 1937. Prin. speaker Nat. Poetry Day, State of Ark., 1950. Has given his poetry programs for The League of Am. Pen Women. Society of Midland Authors, Order of Bookfellows, Junior League, D.A.R., Friends of Am. Writers, etc., and for many schools, colls., and women's clubs. Featured in radio programs; works translated into German and Ukrainian; display Internat. Outdoor Poetry Show, New Orleans, 1954. Works appear in anthologies and compilations. Judge Nat. Fedn. State Poetry Socs., 1960. Hon. chancellor Nat. Fedn. State Poetry Socs., 1963. Home: Eureka Springs AR Died June 27, 1968; buried Fayetteville Nat. Cemetery.

DRESLER, EARL LOUIS, banker; b. Harrisonville, Ill., Sept. 23, 1918; s. Theo A. and Elizabeth (Illert) D.; student Seattle U., 1945-47; m. Jean Frances Karney, Aug. 28, 1946; children—Steven Michael, Peter, Teresa Ann. With Lindell Trust Co., St. Louis, 1938-41, Pacific Nat. Bank, Seattle, 1946-48; mem. comptroller of currency office, then nat. bank examiner Treasury Dept., 1948-59; with U.S. Nat. Bank Ore., Portland, 1959-72, cashier, 1964-72, sr. v.p., 1966-68, exec. v.p., 1968-71, pres., 1971-72, also dir. Bd. dirs. Portland Area council Campfire Girls. Served with USAAF, 1941-45. Mem. Bank Adminstrn. Inst., Financial Execs. Inst., Am. Mgmt. Assn., Portland C. of C., Assn. Res. City Bankers. Republican. Roman Catholic. Elk. Clubs: Multnomah Athletic (Portland); Waverly Country, Arlington. Home: Portland OR Died Sept. 8, 1972.

DRESSER, RAYMOND H., lawyer; b. Litchfield, Mich., Jan. 28, 1901; s. Niles E. and Lou (Sherk) D.; L.B., U. Mich., 1924; m. Lola Juckette, May 13, 1923. Admitted to Mich. bar, 1924, practiced in Sturgis, mem. Dresser & Dresser; city atty., Sturgis, 1928-47, 57-62. Dir. Kirsch Co. Fellow Am. Coll. Trial Lawyers, Am. Bar Found.; mem. Am. Bar Assn., State Bar Mich. (pres. 1958-59), Am. Judicature Soc. (dir. 1960-63), Gamma Eta Gamma. Presbyn. (elder). Mason (K.T., Shriner), Elk, Rotarian (dist. gov. 1935-36). Home: Sturgis MI Died Apr. 3, 1967; buried Oaklawn Cemetery, Sturgis MI

DRESSLAR, FRANK A., SR., communications exec., born Ionia, Kan., 1896; son of John Bascom and Flora Belle (Pound) Dresslar; student University of Kansas, 1916-17; married Helen A. Dryer, June 4, 1921;children—Frank A., Forrest Hugh. Vice pres., general manager Pacific Telephone and Telegraph Co., Portland, 1941-44, S.F., 1944-49, Portland, 1949-59, president, chairman of board, director, 1959—. Director Standard Insurance Co., Director Portland Rose Festival Association, 1951; gen. chairman Portland Community Chest Campaign, 1951, v.p., dir. since 1951; 1st v.p., dir. Portland United Fund; v. chmn. Portland U.S.O. City Com. Served as pvt. to 1st lt., U.S. Army, 1917-19. Mem. Portland C. of C. (dir., v.p. since 1949), Profl. Engrs. Soc. Cal. Republican. Clubs:

Arlington, Aero, Waverly Country (Portland); Transportation (San Francisco). Home: Portland OR

DREW, ALFRED STANISLAUS, educator; b. Milw., Mar. 12, 1921; s. Antoni F. and Albina (Budzinski) Drobiszewski; B.S., Wis. State Coll., Milw., 1943; M.Ed., Marquette U., 1952; Ph.D., U. Wis., 1962; m. 2d, Ethel Anna Timper, May 9, 1953; children—Alfred Gregory, Sharon Lynn (Mrs. J. Raymond Hrezo), Philip John, Teresa Ann. Tchr. indsl. sci. and math. Sch. Vocational and Adult Edn., West Allis, Wis., 1946-54, adminstrv. supr. Evening Sch., trade and indsl. coordinator, 1955-58; prof. indsl. edn. Purdue U., West Lafayette, Ind., 1958-72, chmn. vocational-tech. edn. 1967-70. Served to 1st lt. USAAF, 1943-46. Mem. A.A.A.S., Am. Assn. U. Profs., Am. Ednl. Research Assn., Am. Soc. Engring. Edn., Am. Tech. Edn. Assn., Am., Ind. vocational assns., Comparative and Internat. Edn. Soc., Nat. Assn. Indsl. Tech. Tchr.-Educators, Internat. Platform Assn., Nat. Soc. for Study Edn., Phi Delta Kappa. Author: (with others) Educational and Training Adjustments in Selected Apprenticeable Trades, 1969. Contbr. articles to profl. jours. Home: West Lafayette IN Died May 24, 1972.

DREW, GEORGE ALEXANDER, Canadian govt. ofcl.; b. Guelph, Ont., Can., May, 1894; s. John J. and Annie (Gibbs) D.; student Upper Can. Coll., U. Toronto, Osgoode Hall; m. Florenza D'Arneiro Johnson, Sept. 12, 1936; children—Edward, Sandra. Engaged in practice of law. Served as alderman, Guelph, Ont., 1922-24, mayor, 1925; elected to Ont. Legislature, 1939, 1943, 1945; premier of Ont., 1948-56; Canadian high commr., London, Eng., 1957-64; elected to Canadian Ho. of Commons, 1948, 1949. Served with 16th Arty. Battery, Canadian Expeditionary Force, World War I. Mem. Progressive Conservative Party (elected leader, 1948). Address: Ottawa ON Canada Died Jan. 15, 1973.

DREW, GERALD AUGUSTIN, ret. fgn. service officer; b. San Francisco, Cal., June 20, 1903; s. John S. and Theresa M. (Fredricks) D.; B.S., U. of Calif., 1924; student U. of Grenoble (France), 1924-25, U. of Madrid (Spain), 1926-26; m. Doris Hunter, June 20, 1931; children—Deirdre Elizabeth (Mrs. Robert DuBose), Judith (Mrs. James B. Wilkinson), Joan (Mrs. Norman Sweet); m. 2d, Helene Clinton McDill, Feb. 18, 1967. Vice consul, Para, Brazil, 1928-30, 3d. sec. Am. legation, Port au Prince, Haiti, 1930-34, San Jose, Costa Rica, 1934-36; sec. of legation, Guatemala, 1936, (temporarily) Managua, Nicaragua, Nov. 1936, (temporarily) Tegucigalpa, Honduras, Apr. 1937, (temporarily) San Salvador, May 1937; at Dept. of State, Washington, D.C., 1937-40; 2d sec. and consul, Quito, Ecuador, 1940-42, Guatemala, 1942-44; sec. of embassy and consul, Paris, 1944, first secretary, 1945; protocol officer, Internat. Secretariat, United Nations Conf. on Internat. Organization, San Francisco, April-May 1945; political adviser, U.S. Delegation, Assembly of the United Nations, London, Jan.-Feb. 1946; counselor of legation, Budapest, 1947; dep. U.S. Rep. U.N. spl. com. on Balkans, 1947; adviser U.S. delegation, 3d session Gen. Assembly U.N. Paris, 1948; U.S. rep. with personal rank of minister to United Nations Spl. com. on the Balkans, 1949; envoy extraordinary and minister plenipotentiary to Hashemite Kingdom of the Jordan, 1950; career minister, 1952; dir. gen. of the Fgn. Service, 1952-54; U.S. ambassador to Bolivia, 1954-57, to Haiti, 1957-60; insp. gen., fgn. service inspection corps, Dept. State, 1960-62, ret. 1962. Mem. Phi Kappa Tau. Clubs: Rehoboth Beach (Del.) Country; Chevy Chase, Army and Navy (Washington). Home: Rehoboth Beach DE Died Sept. 27, 1970; buried Rock Creek Cemetery, Washington DC

DREW, IRA WALTON, ex-congressman; b. Hardwick, Vt., Aug. 31, 1878; s. John Herring and Fannie A. (Walton) D.; student Hardwick Acad.; D.O., Phila. Coll. of Osteopathy, 1911, LL.D., 1937; m. Margaret Spencer, Oct. 28, 1911; children—John Walton, Hubert Spencer. Learned printing trade, becoming journeyman, 1899; reporter Burlington (Vt.) Free Press, 1899; reporter and news editor, Boston, 1906-08; began practice osteopathy, Phila., Pa., 1911; prof. diseases of children, Phila. Coll. of Osteopathy for 20 yrs. Exec. com. bd. trustees Phila. Coll. Osteopathy. Mem. 75th Congress (1937-39), 7th Pa. Dist. Mem. Iota Tau Sigma. Democrat. Episcopalian. Mason. Elk. Club: Elks (Phila.). Address: Philadelphia PA Died Feb. 1972.

DREW, JAMES BYRON, judge; b. Pittsburgh, Pa., Apr. 27, 1877; s. John and Martha (Rorke) D.; A.M., LL.B., Columbia University, 1900; honorary L.L.D. Duquesne U., U. of Pittsburgh, U. of Pa., St. Francis College, Dickinson College, Columbia University; m. Rhoda Stanley Sproule, Aug. 20, 1903 (died 1916); children—Stanley T., Rhoda (Mrs. O. Parker McComas), John; m. 2d, Mary Black Snyder, July 12, 1918; 1 dau., Barbara (Mrs. H.P. Hoffstot). Admtd. N.Y. bar, 1900, Pa. bar, 1902; in practice at Pittsburgh, 1902-06; city solicitor Pittsburgh, 1906-11; judge Co. Court, 1912-18; judge Common Pleas Court, 1918-29; judge Superior Court of Pa., 1930; justice Supreme Court of Pa. since 1931, became chief justice, March 20,

1950. Served as captain U.S. Army, World War. Republican. Catholic. Clubs: Everglades; Bath and Tennis (Palm Beach); Union Interalliee (Paris); Duquesne, Allegheny Country, Rolling Rock (Pittsburgh). Home: 625 Morewood Av. Address: City-County Bldg., Pittsburgh 19 PA‡

DREWES, ALFRED H(ERMAN), corp. exec.; b. Jersey City, Oct. 24, 1913; s. Henry F. and Anna E. (Ahrens) D.; A.B., Columbia, 1934; m. Marjorie E. Puppo, Sept. 7, 1946; children—Jane Elizabeth, Anne Evelyn, Alfred Herman Ahrens, Jr. Began career with National Lead Company, N.Y.C., 1935, asst. to pres., 1947-50, dir., mem. exec. com. since 1950, v.p., 1951-63, executive vice president, 1963-65, president, 1965-67; director of Titanium Metals Corporation of America; director of the Baker Castor Oil Company, The Chas. Taylor's Sons Co., Master Metals, Inc., Pioneer Aluminum, Inc., Barber Die Casting Company, Ltd., Mineral Deposits Pty., Ltd., Am. Re-Ins. Co., Nat. Starch & Chem. Corp.; mem. adv. com. Bankers Trust Co.; mem. bd. dirs., sec. Baroid de Venezuela, S.A. Clubs: Bankers, Economic (N.Y.C.). Home: Englewood NJ Died June 6, 1967.

DREYFUSS, HENRY, indsl. designer; b. N.Y.C., Mar. 2, 1904; s. Louis and Elsie (Gorge) D.; D.Sc., Occidental Coll., 1953; A.F.D., Pratt Inst., 1963; m. Doris Marks, 1930; children—John Alan, Gail (Mrs. George Campbell Wilson, Jr.), Ann. Opened indsl. design office, 1929; now corporate cons. Faculty Cal. Inst. Tech. Bd. dirs. Ford Found. Ednl. Facilities Labs.; trustee Cal. Inst. Tech.; mem. bd. govs. performing arts council Los Angeles Music Center; trustee People to People, Los Angeles County Art Mus. Decorated Order Orange-Nassau (Netherlands); recipient Archtl. League Gold medal, 1951; Benjamin Franklin fellow Royal Soc. Arts; Distinguished Contbn. award Am. Soc. Indsl. Designers, 1960; design award Phila. Mus. Coll. Art, 1962; design in steel award Am. Iron and Steel Inst., 1965, Ambassador award for achievement, Eng., 1965; Distinguished Contbns. award Nat. Assn. Schs. Art. Fellow Indsl. Designers Soc. Am. (bd. dirs.) Author: Designing for People, 1955, 2d edit., 1967; The Measure of Man, 1960, rev. edit., 1967; Henry Dreyfuss Symbol Sourcebook, 1972. Home: South Pasadena CA Died Oct. 5, 1972.

DREYFUSS, LEONARD, advt. exec.; b. Brooklyn, Nov. 6, 1886; s. Henry and Fannie (Young) D.; grad. Brooklyn Boys' High Sch.; LL.D. (honorary), Seton Hall University, 1950, Fairleigh Dickinson University, 1954; married Alice Ransom; 1 dau., Mrs. William Y. Dear, Jr. Vice pres. John Matthews Co., N.Y. City, 1910-12; sales mgr. Charles E. Hires Co., Phila., 1912-14, Newark Sign Co., 1914-17; v.p., gen. mgr. United Advt. Corp., N.Y. City, 1917-20; pres. United Advt. Corp., Newark, 1920-69; pres., dir. Am. Advt. Co., Long Branch, N.J., 1931-69, Canterbury Realty Co. 1933-69, Lehigh Advt. Co., Allentown, since 1931, Highway Realty Co., South Jersey Advt. Co., 1950-69, United Advt. Corp., Newark, Am. Advt. Co., Long Branch, N.J., Art Sign Co., New Haven, Belpark Realty Co., Canterbury Sign Co., Newark, Cowl Signs, Inc., Meriden, Conn., Hwy. Advt. Co., Newark, Johnston Advt. Co., Reading, Pa., Lehigh Sign Co., Allentown, Pa., Roadside Realty Co., Glassboro, N.J., South Jersey Sign Co., Glassboro, United Advt. Corp. (Me.), South Brewer, Me., Van Wagner Advt. Corp., Jamaica, N.J.; chmn. Camden Sign Co., Newark, United Sign Co., Newark, Empire Advt., Inc., Newark, United Hwy. Sign Co., Meriden, Hamlet Realty Co., Newark; dir. Laird & Co. (Scobeyville, N.J.), Bank of Commerce (Newark), Outdoor Advt., Inc. (N.Y., N.J.). Dir. Civil Def., State N.J., 1942-55. Trustee Newark Mus., Rutgers University, Fairleigh Dickinson U.; dir. St. Barnabas Hosp. Recipient Award as outstanding citizen New Jersey by Advertising Club of New Jersey, 1941. Dir. Junior Achievement, Inc. Mem. A.R.C. (dir. Newark chpt.), Nat. Assn. of State Civil Def. Dirs. (an organizer, chmn. 1941-69), N.J. State Chamber of Commerce (director), N.J. State Com. French Gratitude Train (chmn.), Govs. Conservation Commission (chmn.), Newark Community Chest (dir.) Episcopalian. Clubs: Downtown, Newark Athletic (Newark), Essex Fells (New Jersey) Country; New York Advertising, Church, Uptown, University (New York City, New York); Capital Hill (Washington); Seaview Country (Absecon, Essex Fells NJ Died Dec. 29, 1969; buried New Vernon Cemetery, New Vernon NJ

DRIGGS, FRANK HOWARD, corp. exec.; b. Clinton, Mo., Oct. 25, 1895; s. Augustus LeRoy and Martha (Ogden) D.; A.B., Baker U., 1917, LL.D., 1958; M.S., U. Ill., 1921, Ph.D., 1924; m. Carroll Horton; children—Shirley, Christianna, Martha. Instructor at the University of Illinois, 1924-27; research Westinghouse Lamp Company, Bloomfield, N.J., 1927-34 with Fansteel Metall. Corp., North Chgo., 1934-63; pres., 1952-61, chmn. bd., chief exec. officer, 1961-63; dir. Webster Electric Co. (Racine, Wis.). Mem. bd. of trustees Baker University, Baldwin, Kan. Served as cpl. 110th C.E., U.S. Army AEF, 1917-18. Mem. Ill. Mfrs. Assn. (dir. 1960—). Sigma Xi, Gamma Alpha, Phi Lambda Upsilon, Alpha Chi Sigma, Epsilon Chi. Republican. Methodist. Mason. Club: Exmoor Country. Home: Lake Bluff IL Died Apr. 1969.

DRIGGS, FRANK MILTON, educator; b. Pleasant Grove, Utah, Nov. 20, 1870; s. Benjamin Woodbury and Rosalie Ellen (Cox) D.; educated Brigham Young U., Univ. of Utah and Gallaudet Coll., Washington, D.C.; hon. A.M., Gallaudet Coll., 1911, hon. L.H.D., 1939; M. Maude Elise Short, Sept. 10, 1898; children—Nellie Clarice, Milton Short (dec.). Teacher, Utah Sch. for the Deaf, Salt Lake City and Ogden, 1889-97 and 1899-1901, Ill. Sch. for Deaf, 1898-99; supt. Utah School for Deaf & Blind, Ogden, 1901-41; retired, 1941. President Utah Development League, 1911-12, Utah Chautauqua Association, 1911. Member Am. Conv. of Instructors of Deaf (pres. 1928-29), Utah Ednl. Assn. (ex-pres.), Ogden Chamber Commerce (ex-pres.). Pres. Conf. of execs. of Am. Schools for the Deaf, 1936-39; dist. gov. Rotary International, 1931-32. Republican. Mormon. Clubs: Weber (ex-pres.), Rotary (ex-pres.), Ben Lomond (ex-pres.). Address: 218 Ogden Canyon, Ogden UT‡

DRILL, LEWIS L., lawyer; b. Browerville, Minn., May 9, 1877; s. Charles Warren and Saphrona Ellen (Sheets) D.; student Hamline U., 1897-1900; LL.B., Georgetown U., 1903; unmarried. Began practice, St. Paul, 1904; became U.S. dist. atty., Minn., 1928; now mem. firm Drill & Drill. Republican. Protestant. Home: 149 W. Summit Av. Office: Commerce Bldg., St Paul MN‡

DRINKER, PHILIP, prof. industrial hygiene; b. Haverford, Pa., Dec. 12, 1894; s. Henry Sturgis and Ernesta (Beaux) D.; B.S., Princeton U., 1915; Chem.E., Lehigh University, 1917; D.Sc., Norwich University, Northfield, Vt., 1940; LL.D., Hahnemann Medical College, 1942; m. Suzanne Aldrich, June 17, 1925; children—Suzanne Greene, Mary Eliza, Philip Aldrich. Lt., Air Service, U.S. Army, 1917-19; chem. engr. Buffalo Foundry and Machine Co., 1920-21; instr. Harvard Med. Sch., 1922; instr. ventilation and illumination, Harvard Sch. Pub. Health, 1922-26, asst. prof., 1926-31, asso. prof. industrial hygiene, 1931-36, prof. 1936-60. Awarded John Scott medal by City of Phila., 1931. Harben lectr. Royal Inst. of Pub. Health and Hygiene, 1957. Fellow Royal Society Health; mem. Am. Pub. Health Assn., Am. Chem. Soc., American Assn. Indsl. Hygienists. Republican. Presbyterian. Author: Industrial Medicine (with W. I. Clark), 1935; Industrial Dust (with T. Hatch), 1936. Home: Cambridge MA Died Oct. 1972. Fitzwilliam NH Died Oct. 19, 1972, buried Fitzwilliam NH

DRISCOLL, DANIEL ANGELUS, congressman; b. Buffalo, N.Y., Mar. 6, 1875; s. Timothy and Catherine Blanche D.; high sch. edn. Mem. 61st and 62d Congresses (1909-13), 35th N.Y. Dist., and 63d and 64th Congresses 1913-17), 42d Dist.; Democrat. Address: 373 N. Division St., Buffalo‡

DRIVER, WILLIAM J., ex-congressman; b. Osceola, Ark., Mar. 2, 1873; s. John B. and Margarett (Bowen) D.; ed. common schs.; m. Clara Haynes, Memphis, Tenn., June 2, 1897. Admitted to Ark. bar, 1894, and practiced at Osceola; mem. Ark. Ho. of Rep., 1897, 99; judge 2d Jud. Circuit, Ark., 1911-18; mem. Constl. Conv., Ark., 1918; mem. 67th to 75th Congresses (1921-39), 1st Ark. Dist. Democrat. Mason, Elk. Home: Osceola AR‡

DROEGE, JOHN ALBERT, ry. official; b. Deer Park, Md.; s. Emil Frederick and Emily P. (Reinhart) D.; ed. common schs. of Md.; m. Eleanor Harriet Johnson, of Atlanta, Ga., Aug. 8, 1889; children—John Albert, Sara Elizabeth, Bertha Josephine, Joseph Emil. In ry. service since 1880; successively telegrapher, stenographer, train dispatcher, yardmaster; chief train dispatcher and trainmaster consecutively with B. & O., Chesapeake & O., Norfolk & Western, E. Tenn., Va. and Ga., and Southern rys.; trainmaster Lehigh Valley Ry., 1899-1900; supt. Pa. and New York div. same rd., Sayre, Pa., 1900-04; supt. Providence div. N.Y., N.H. & H. R.R., 1904-12; supt. Shore Line div. same ry., 1912-13, gen. supt. same rd., New Haven, Conn., 1913-17, New York, 1917-25, gen. mgr. since June 1, 1925, also v.p., 1929-31, retired. Clubs: New England Railroad, New York Railroad, New Haven Railroad, Quinnipiack. Author: Yards and Terminals, 1906; Freight Terminals and Trains, 1912, 1925; Passenger Terminals and Trains, 1916. Home: Hudson View Gardens, New York NY‡

DROUGHT, ARTHUR BERNARD, acad. dean.; b. Racine County, Wis., Oct. 24, 1914; s. Arthur Benjamin and Anna M. (Morley) D.; B.Ed., Milw. State Tchrs. Coll., 1935; M.A., Northwestern U., 1942; M.S., Harvard, 1949, S.D., 1950; m. Ruth H. Spink, Dec. 27, 1939; children—Richard M., Michael H., Arthur Bernard II. Engring. draftsman Harnischfeger Corp., Milw., 1935-37; tchr. Milw. pub. schs., 1937-42; teaching fellow elec. engring. Harvard, 1946-47, instr., 1947-48, Henry Weidemar Locke fellow 1948-49; faculty Marquette U., 1949-63, asso. prof. elec. engring., 1953-63, dean Coll. Engring., 1956-63; academic dean United States Naval Academy, 1963-70. Cons. electronics dept. investigative med. VA Hosp., Wood, Wis.; mem. Wis. Adv. Com. Sci., Engring. and Specialized Personnel; asst. to bd. registration for architects and engrs., Wis. Served to lt. (j.g.) USNR, 1942-46. Registered prof. engr., Wis. Mem. Am. Inst.

E.E., Engrs. Council Profl. Development (chmn. guidance com. region VI), Nat. Soc. Profl. Engrs. (pres. Milw. chpt. 1960-61), Am. Soc. Engring. Edn. (gen. council 1956-60), engring. faculty devel. com. 1960-61, chmn. 1961-62), Engrs. Soc. Milw., Am. Interprofl. Inst., Sigma Xi, Eta Kappa Nu, Tau Beta Pi. Conglist. (moderator). Author articles profl. jours. Home: Annapolis MD Died Sept. 18, 1970.

DRUKKER, DOW HENRY, congressman; b. at Sneek, The Netherlands, Feb. 7, 1872; s. Henry and Winifred (Terpsma) D.; brought to America in infancy; ed. pub. schs., Grand Rapids, Mich.; m. Helena M. Denhower, of Grand Rapids, Aug. 31, 1893. Contractor at Passaic, N.J., since 1897; pres. Union Bldg. & Constrn. Co., Union Bldg. & Investment Co.; dir. Hobart Trust Co., 1st Mortgage Title & Ins. Co. of N.J. Mem. Passaic Co. Bd. Chosen Freeholders, 8 yrs.; elected mem. 63d Congress (1913-15), 7th N.J. Dist., to fill vacancy; reelected to 64th and 65th Congresses (1915-19); Republican. Mem. Dutch Reformed Ch. Clubs: Acquackanonk (Passaic), Hamilton (Paterson, N.J.), Commercial (Washington). Home: 202 Lafayette Av. Office: Hobart Trust Bldg., Passaic NJ‡

DRUKKER, RICHARD, newspaper exec.; b. Passaic, N.J., Mar. 30, 1906; s. Dow H. and Helena M. (Denhouwer) D.; A.B., Amherst Coll., 1929; LL.B., Rutgers U., 1943; m. Caroline Cleveland Crane, Sept. 16, 1930; children—Richard Austin. Messenger, Dominick & Dominick, N.Y.C., 1929; treas., dir. Union Bldg. & Investment Co. 1933; exec. v.p., 1953-63., pres., 1963-73; dir. Herald-News, Passaic, 1934-73, treas., 1943, v.p. treas., 1954-56, pres., 1956-73, pub., 1963-73; pub. Daily Advance. Dover, N.J., 1962-73; dir. Bank of Passaic & Clifton, Passaic. Pres., Talking Newspapers for Blind, Herald-News-Drukker Found. Bd. dirs. Def. Orientation Conf. Assn.; trustee YMCA, Passaic, Passaic Gen. Hosp. Mem. Passaic Area C. of C. (dir.), N.J. Press Assn. (past pres.), Psi Upsilon, Delta Theta Pi. Episcopalian Kiwanian Clubs: Metropolitan (N.Y.C.); Seaview Golf (Absecon, N.J.); Pennington (Passiac); Upper Montclair Country (Clifton, N.J.); Montclair (N.J.) Golf; National Press (Washington). Home: Clifton NJ Died Apr. 1973.

DRUM, JOHN SYLVESTER, banker; b. Oakland, Calif., Apr. 16, 1872; s. John Sylvester and Sarah Jane (Gass) D.; A.B., St. Ignatius Coll., San Francisco, 1891; Hastings Coll. of Law (U. of Calif.), 1894; m. Georgie A. Spieker, of San Francisco, Apr. 22, 1908; 1 son, John. Admitted to Calif. bar, 1894, and practiced in San Francisco, until 1909; pres. Savings Union Bank & Trust Co., 1910-20, Mercantile Trust Co. of Calif. (name after merger with Union Bank & Trust Co.), 1920-27, Am. Trust Co. (name after merger with Mercantile Turst Co.), 1927—; also officer or dir. of many other corporations. Apptd. by Sec. McAdoo, Nov. 1917, as state dir. for war savings in Northern Calif.; apptd. by Pres. Wilson mem. Capital Issues Com. under the War Finance Corpn. Act of Apr. 5, 1918. Pres. Am. Bankers' Assn., 1920-21. Democrat. Catholic. Clubs: Pacific Union, University, Olympic, Bohemian, Burlingame Country. Office: Am. Trust Co., San Francisco CA*‡

DRUMHELLER, JOSEPH, chem. engr.; b. Spokane, Sept. 25, 1900; s. Daniel Montgomery and Eleanor (Powell) D.; B.S. in Chem. Engring., U. Wash., 1924; m. Helen Elizabeth Chamberlain, Dec. 14, 1956; children—Mrs. William J. McAllister, Frederick Corbin. Owner, Drumheller Labs., Spokane, 1924—; pres. Densow Drugs Inc., Richland, Wash., 1952—, Idaho Lakeview Mines, Inc., Fern Gold Mining Co., Drumheller Estates, Inc.; dir. West Coast Airlines, Pacific N.W. Bell Telephone Co., Sunshine Mining Co., First Nat. Bank Spokane, Union Iron Works, Spokane. Chmn. Gonzaga U. Great Tchrs. Program, 1955-58; incorporator, dir. Pacific Sci. Center, Seattle. Member Wash. State Senate from Spokane County, 1934-42; mem. city council, Spokane, 1960-64. Bd. regents U. Wash., 1945-50, 55-69, Gonzaga U., 1958-70. Mem. Am. Assn. Cereal Chemists, Spokane C. of C. (pres. 1948-49), Sigma Nu. Spokane WA Died Apr. 28, 1970.

DRUMMOND, HARRISON IRWIN, capitalist; b. Alton, Ill., Dec. 4, 1869; s. James T. and Bethia (Randall) D.; B.Ph., Sheffield Scientific Sch. (Yale), 1890; m. Mary W. Prickett, of St. Louis, Nov. 22, 1892. Began with Drummond Tobacco Co. (founded by father) and became pres. same upon death of father; was 1st v.p. Continental Tobacco Co. (into which Drummond Tobacco Co. was merged); dir. Merchants-Laclede Nat. Bank and Miss. Valley Trust Co. for a number of years; was mem. exec. bd. La. Purchase Expn. removed to Pasadena, Cal., 1906; an organizer of Security Nat. Bank, Pasadena; prominently identified with the Pasadena Rose Tournament Assn. now pres. Drummond Realty & Trust Co., St. Louis. Was mem. staff of Gov. Lon M. Stevens of Mo. and served as q.m. gen. Mo. N.G. 4 yrs. Clubs: Pasadena Country, Midwick Country (Pasadena); St. Louis (St. Louis); University (New York); New York Yacht, Larchmont Yacht. Home: Pasadena CA‡

DRUMMOND, THOMAS RUSSELL, mining engr.; b. Colombo, Ceylon, Aug. 27, 1873; s. Russell and Charlotte Hawtrey (Thwaites) D.; ed. George Watson's Coll. and Herriott-Watt Tech. Coll., Edinburgh (Scotland), School of Mines (London); m. Harriet Blake, of Chariton, Lucas Co., Ia., May 1900; children—Charlotte Blake, George Russell, Thomas Arthur, Ronald Blake. Engr. and assayer for Clarkson-Stanfield Concentration Co., London, 1896-97; mill man and constrn. engr. Prussian Mine, Boulder, Colo., 1897; with Utah Consolidated Mine, Bingham, Utah, 1897-1905; mgr. Dominion Copper Co., B.C., 1905-07, Nipissing Mining Co., Cobalt, Ont., Can., 1907-08, Cactus Copper Co., Newhouse, Utah, 1908-09, Inspiration Copper Co., 1909-12; supt. mines Inspiration Consolidated Copper Co., 1913; pvt. practice, Philippines, China, etc., 1913-18; sec. and treas. Zenda Gold Mining Co.; mgr. Zenda Leadville Mfg. Co. Mem. Am. Inst. Mining and Metall. Engrs. (life). Naturalized citizen of U.S. Republican. Presbyn. Mason. Home: 1627 N. Genesee St., Hollywood, Calif. Office: I.W. Hellman Bldg., Los Angeles CA‡

DRUMMOND, WILBERT IVANHOE, business exec., publisher; b. Sigourney, Ia., Oct. 10, 1874; s. Isaac S. and Rebecca (White) D.; ed. pub. schs. and pvt. courses in agriculture, journalism, polit. economy and pub. relations; m. Mary E. Peckham, at Beaver, Okla., 1897 (died 1914); children—Donald I., Bessie E., Maribel J., Wilbert N.; m. 2d, Anne Ione (King) Bigham, of Kansas City, Mo., May 2, 1920. Owner and editor Beaver (Okla.) Herald, 1896-98; gen. printing business, Enid, Okla., 1898-1914; founder, 1900, and editor Enid Daily Eagle until 1912; engaged in farming and land development. Was a founder of American Farm Congress, 1913, editor of its publications, 1916-28, chmn. and mng. dir., 1914-28. Active in development of Okla.; mng. dir. Internat. Soil-Products Expn., Denver, Colo., 1915, El Paso, 1916, Peoria, 1917, Kansas City, Mo., 1918-19. Republican. Presbyn. Home: 6447 Baltimore Av. Office: 101 W. 11th St., Kansas City MO‡

DRURY, JOHN, journalist, author; b. Chicago, Aug. 9, 1898; s. Michael and Mary (Sullivan) D.; ed. St. Andrew's Parochial Sch., Senn High Sch., and Lane Tech. High Sch., Chicago; m. Marion Neville, 1929. Newspaper reporter Los Angeles (Calif.) Record, 1920-21; reporter City News Bureau, Chicago, 1924; feature writer and columnist The Chicago Daily News, 1926-44; made voyage to South America in Am. Merchant Marine, 1923, to London, 1925; covered Century of Progress Internat. Expn., Chicago, 1933-34; traveled in Can., 1930, Bermuda, British West Indies and British Guiana, 1934. Served with 11th Regt., Ill. Res. Militia, 1918-20; attended Inst. of Mil. Studies, U. of Chicago, 1941-42; served at intervals with Am. Merchant Marine. Mem. Ill. State, Ind. hist. socs., Am. Assn. for State and Local History, Nat. Trust for Historic Preservation in U.S., Soc. Architectural Historians, Chicago Press Vets. Assn., Am. Newspaper Guild (Chicago local), Soc. Midland Authors, Duneland-Chesterton (Ind.) Hist. Soc. (hon. pres.). Club: The Cliff Dwellers (Chicago). Recipient U. of Minn. Regional Writing Fellowship (for preparation of book on famous old Midwest houses), 1944; awarded Distinguished Serv. to Lit. Scroll, Friends of Literature, Chicago, 1946. Author: Arclight Dusks (poems), 1925; Chicago in Seven Days, 1928; Forensic Ballistics (booklet), 1929; Dining in Chicago, 1931; Guide to Chicago, 1933; Old Chicago Houses, 1941; A. C. McClurg Centennial (booklet), 1944; Historic Midwest Houses, 1947; Midwest Heritage, 1948; Old Illinois Houses, 1948; Crossroads of a Metropolis, 1949; Where Chicago Eats, 1953; The American Aerial County History Series, from 1954. Contbr. to mags. Lectr. on hist. subjects before Chicago Historical society and various lit. and hist. assns., also weekly radio program, Chicago a la Carte, on WMAQ, 1945-47; contbr. weekly column to Chicago community newspapers, 1949-54; columnist Townsfolk mag., Chgo., 1951-53; contbr. weekly hist. column on old Chgo. neighborhoods to Chgo. Daily News, from 1957. Hawthornden. Chesterton IN Died Jan. 10, 1972; buried Chesterton Cemetery, Chesterton IN

DUBILIER, WILLIAM, inventor, engr.; b. New York, July 25, 1888; s. Abe and Anna D.; Geo. DeWitt Clinton High Sch., Tech. Inst., Cooper Inst., New York; m. Florence Don. Inventor several systems of wireless telephony and telegraphy, also med. apparatus; has obtained over 300 patents; wireless telephone and telegraph apparatus used by U.S., French, English and Russian govts.; originated, developed and patented the mica condenser now universally used in all broadcasting stations and for high frequency equipment; invented means for locating, obtaining speed and direction of submarines, used by France and England. Supplied first aeroplane wireless communication installations for U.S. Govt., 1914-15, pioneer X-ray equipment for dental surgery, 1910, chief electrician, Continental Wireless Telegraph & Telephone Co., 1908; pres. and tech. dir. Commercial Wireless Telegraph & Telephone Co., Seattle, Wash., 1910; organized Dubilier Condenser Co., Ltd., London, 1910, Dubilier Electric Co., N.Y., 1913, Dubilier Condenser Corp., N.Y., 1916, Radio Patents Corp., N.Y., 1917, Deutsche Dubilier Kondensator Gesellschaft, Berlin, 1922, Cornell-Dubilier Electric Corp., 1933; at present officer or dir. in above orgns.; member board of directors Seagrave Corporation. Patents licensed to Radio Corporation of America, General Electric Company, Westinghouse Electric and Manufacturing Company, Canadian Gen. Electric Co., Gen. Electric Co., England, German Gen. Electric Co. (Hydra), Berlin, Siemens & Halske, A.G., Berlin, etc. Decorated Order Academic Palms, 1949, Chevalier Legion of Honor, 1950; Gano Dunn Medal, Cooper Union, 1955. Fellow Am. Inst. E.E., Inst. Radio Engrs.; mem. Franklin Inst., etc. Co-author articles, books on wireless telegraphy, etc. Home: New Rochelle NY Died July 1969.

DUBLE, LU, sculptor; b. Oxford, Eng., Jan. 21, 1896; d. John Walter and Marianne (Mogridge) Davies; brought to U.S., 1903; student Sacred Heart Acad., 1905-10, Cooper Union Art Sch., 1913-16, Art Students League, 1916-18, Atelier Archipenko, 1929-31, Atelier Hans Hofmann, 1931-32; m. Jesse Clyde Duble, November 26, 1917; m. 2d, Alfred Geiffert, Jr., June 9, 1944. Teacher of sculpture, Bennett Jr. College, Millbrook, N.Y., 1917-70, Brearly Sch., N.Y. City, 1928-30, Dalton Schs., Inc., N.Y. City, 1932-35, Montclair (N.J.) Museum of Art, 1928-30, 39-70. Awarded Guggenheim fellowship, 1937 and 38; Anna H. Huntington prize, 1937; Albert T. Reid medal, 1948; Gold Medal, Audubon Artists, 1948; awarded fellowship of Inst. of Internat. Education for 2 years. Study of Mexican legends for creative sculpture, 1943, A.N.A., 1942; mem. N.Y. Soc. Women Artists, Audubon Artists (v.p. 1948-49), Sculptors Guild, Nat. Sculpture Soc., Architectural League (v.p. 1948) (N.Y. City). Republican. Roman Catholic. Home: New York City NY Died Aug. 10, 1970.

DUBOC, FRANK WINDSOR, ins. co. exec.; b. East St. Louis, Ill., July 22, 1894; s. A.M. and Julia (Denison) D.; student pub. schs.; m. Ruth Green, July 6, 1922; children—William T., Helen Anne (Mrs. Rex D. Johnson). With Western Fire Ins. Co., 1927-68, dir., 1934-68, v.p., 1944-68; with Western Casualty & Surety Co., Ft. Scott, Kan., 1927-68, v.p., 1944-68, dir., 1958-68; dir. Western Ins. Securities, 1945-68. Home: Ft Scott KS Died Dec. 28, 1968; buried Evergreen Cemetery, Ft. Scott KS

DUBORD, RICHARD JOSEPH, lawyer, Democratic nat. committeeman; b. Waterville, Me., Nov. 17, 1921; s. F. Harold and Blanche (Letourneau) D.; B.S. cum laude, Holy Cross Coll., 1943; LL.B., cum laude, Boston U., 1948; m. Evelyn P. Parnell, Sept. 4, 1943; children—Stephen F., William P., Susan P. Admitted to Me. bar, 1948, practiced in Waterville as partner Marden, Dubord, Bernier & Chandler; atty. gen. State Me. Mayor, City of Waterville, 1952-56; mem. Dem. Nat. Com. Served as capt. USAAF, 1942-46. Mem. Am., Me., Kennebec Co. (pres.) Waterville (pres. 1953) bar assns., Am. Legion, Vets. Fgn. Wars. Club: Kiwanis, Elks. Home: Waterville ME Died Jan. 1970.

DUBOSE, FRANCIS GOODWIN, M.D., surgeon; b. Maplesville, Ala., Sept. 27, 1873; s. Franklin Davis and Anna M. (Goodwin) DuB.; prep. edn., Orrville (Ala.) Acad. and Marion (Ala.) Mil. Inst.; student U. of Va.; M.D., Tulane U., 1893; grad. study N.Y. City, Baltimore, Phila. and Chicago, 1893-99, London, Berlin, Vienna, 1900, London and Paris, 1902, Paris, 1924; m. Aimee Nelson, of Selma, Ala., June 11, 1902. Began practice at Selma, 1893; founder, 1911, later mgr. and chief of staff Vaughan Memorial Hosp.; retired, 1931. Mem. Ala. State Com. Nat. Defense, World War. Mem. State Bd. Examiners for Nurses, Ala. Fellow Am. Coll. Surgeons (a founder), Southern Surg. Assn.; mem. A.M.A., Med. Assn., State of Ala., Dallas Co. Med. Soc., Southern Med. Assn. (ex-chmn. sect. on surgery), Ala. State Hosp. Assn. (ex-pres.), Pi Gamma Mu. Presbyterian. Club: Town and Country. Wrote: Episodes in Black and White, 1932. Writer over 30 monographs on surg. subjects. Discoverer of muscle in female perineum; research in gall bladder and pelvic inflammatory disease; devised original technique in many surg. operations; originated and first used Maplesville AL‡

DUBRAY, CHARLES ALBERT, clergyman, educator; b. Villaines-sous-Luce, Dept. of Sarthe, France, Nov. 2, 1875; s. Pierre Michel and Mathilde (Guimier) D.; ed. Petit-Seminaire, Sees, France, St. Mary's Hill, Paignton, Devon, Eng., Marist Coll., Washington, D.C.; S.T.B. Catholic U. of America, Washington, D.C., 1899, Ph.D., 1903. Came to U.S., 1894, naturalized citizen, 1908. Ordained priest, R.C. Ch., 1899; joined faculty, Marist Coll., 1899, pres., 1915-22; prof. Philosophy, Trinity Coll., Washington, 1913-23, Catholic U., 1914-23; pres. Notre Dame, Sem., New Orleans, also prof. philosophy, 1923-34; now prof. philosophy, Marist Coll. Address: Marist College, Brookland Sta., Washington DC‡

DUCASSE, CURT JOHN, philosopher; b. Angouleme, France, July 7, 1881; s. Jean Louis and Clementine Theoda (Grolig) D.; prep. edn., Lycee of Bordeaux, France, and Abbotsholme Sch., Eng.; A.B. magna cum laude, U. Wash., 1908, A.M., 1909; univ. scholar Harvard, 1910-11, Ph.D., 1912; M.A. ad eundem, Brown U., 1943, D.Litt., 1960; m. Agnes Righton, Oct. 22, 1904; m. 2d, Mabel Lisle, June 22, 1921. Came to U.S., 1900, naturalized, 1910. Instr. in philosophy and psychology U. Wash., 1912-16, asst. prof. philosophy, 1916-24, asso. prof., 1924-26; asso. prof. Brown U., 1926-29, prof., 1929-58, prof. emeritus, 1958-69, chmn. dept. philosophy, 1930-51, acting dean Grad. Sch., 1947-49; lectr. summers at Calif., Mich., Chgo., Cornell, Columbia univs.; Howison lectr. U. Cal., 1944; Foerster lectr. U. Cal., 1947; Prall Meml. lectr., 1947; Paul Carus lectr. Am. Philos. Assn. 1949; J.W. Graham lectr. Swarthmore Coll., 1951; Walker-Ames vis. prof. U. Wash., 1946, Flint vis. prof., 1946; Flint vis. prof., U. Cal. at Los Angeles, spring 1947. Pres. Association for Symbolic Logic, 1936-37; mem. exec. com. Am. Council Learned Socs., 1939-41; mem. Am. Philos. Assn. (chmn. orgn. com. Pacific Div. and sec. of Div., 1924-26; vice-pres. Eastern Div., 1933; pres., 1939; del. to Am. Council Learned Soc., 1936-48; mem. Assns.' Commn. on Function of Philosophy in Liberal Edn. Fellow A.A.A.S., Am. Acad. Arts and Sciences; mem. Am. Soc. Aesthetics (pres. 1945-46, trustee 1946-49), Am. Soc. Psychical Research (trustee), Phi Beta Kappa. Club: Faculty. Author: Causation and the Types of Necessity, 1924; The Philosophy of Art, 1930; Philosophy as a Science, 1941; Art, the Critics, and You, 1944; Nature, Mind, and Death, 1951; A Philosophical Scrutiny of Relgion, 1953; A Critical Examination of the Belief in Life after Death, 1961; Knowledge, Truth and Causation, 1969. Contbr. to Contemporary American Philosophy (2 vols.), 1930; The Philosophy of G. E. Moore, 1943, Philosophy in American Edn., 1945, and other publs.; mem. editorial bd. Journal: Philosophy and Phenomenological Research. The East Providence RI Died Sept. 3, 1969; cremated.

DUCKWORTH, GEORGE ECKEL, educator; b. Little York, N.J., Feb. 13, 1903; s. Edwin James and Eva (Eckel) D.; A.B., Princeton, 1924, A.M., 1926, Ph.D., 1931; m. Dorothy Elwood Atkin, July 8, 1929; children—Dorothy Ann (Mrs. Donald L. Brown), Thomas Atkin. Instructor in field of classics Princeton, 1924-25, U. of Neb., 1926-28; mem. faculty Princeton from 1929, acting chmn. classics dept., 1943-46, Giger prof. classics since 1946; dir. summer session, sch. classical studies Am. Acad. in Rome 1952-55; vis. prof. classics Harvard, 1955-56. Trustee Am. Acad. in Rome, 1948-59. Guggenheim fellow, 1957-58. Mem. Archaeol. Inst. Am., Classical Assn. Atlantic States, Am. Philol. Assn. (pres. 1956), Phi Beta Kappa. Author: Foreshadowing and Suspense in the Epics of Homer, Apollonius, and Vergil, 1933; T. Macci Plauti Epidicus, 1940; The Complete Roman Drama, 1942; The Nature of Roman Comedy, 1952; Structural Patterns and Proportions in Vergil's Aeneid, 1962; Vergil and Classical Hexameter Poetry, 1969. Contbr. to ednl. jours. Home: Princeton NJ Died Apr. 5, 1972; buried Mount Pleasant NJ

DUCKWORTH, WILLIAM HENRY, judge; b. Blairsville, Ga., Oct. 21, 1894; s. John Frank and Laura Jane (Noblet) D.; ed. Young Harris (Ga.) Coll., 1915-17; studied law in law office; m. Willibel Pilcher, July 2, 1922; children—Mary (Mrs. L.L. Gellerstedt), Dorothy (Mrs. W.N. Todd), William Henry. Admitted to Ga. bar, 1919, gen. practice law, Cairo, 1919-37; assistant attorney general of Georgia, 1937-38; asso. justice Supreme Court of Ga., 1938-48, chief justice, 1948-69. Served in U.S. Naval Reserve, 1918. Mem. Am. and Ga. State bar associations, Am. Legion. Baptist. Mason. Elk. Clubs: Capital City, Atlanta Athletic (Atlanta). Home: Decatur GA Died Aug. 9, 1969; buried Decatur Cemetery.

DUDLEY, A. DEAN, business exec.; born Concord, N.H. 1878; s. George W. and Sarah Elizabeth (Locke) D.; Ph.B., Brown U., 1902; m. Gertrude Bingham Woodhull, 1911; children—Cynthia D. Post, Jane Grey. Asst. to v.p. United Gas Improvement Co., Phila., 1902-07; comml. mgr., sec., treasurer Syracuse Lighting Co., 1907-29, president, 1929-37; v.p., dir. Central N.Y. Power Corp., 1937-47; pres. Bank Realty Co., 1930-40; director Concord (N.H.) Gas Co.; honorary chairman board Lincoln Nat. Bank & Trust Co., 1930-70. Trustee of the Everon Mus. Arts, 1950-70; mem. Syracuse Cultural and Civic Center Com., 1956-70. Clubs: Century, Onondaga Golf and Country. Home: Syracuse NY Died Sept. 1970.

DUDLEY, JOSEPH GRASSIE, lawyer; b. Winona, Minn., Jan. 19, 1869; s. Joseph Francis and Jessie Duncan (Grassie) D.; A.B., Beloit Coll., 1892; student Harvard Law Sch., 1892-93; m. Angeline Moon, Oct. 8, 1896; children—Dorothy (Mrs. Daniel J. Kenefick, Jr.), Joseph Delos. Admitted to New York bar, 1895, and practiced at Buffalo, N.Y., since 1895; sr. partner Dudley, Stowe & Sawyer, Buffalo, N.Y., since 1917; dir. Mfrs. & Traders Trust Co., Keystone Warehouse Co. Received Beloit Coll. Distinguished Service Citation, 1947. Mem. Am., N.Y. State, Erie Co. bar assns., Newcomen Soc. of Eng., Sigma Chi. Rep. Episcopalian. Clubs: Buffalo (pres. 1939), Saturn (dean, 1906), Country of Buffalo. Home: 715 Delaware Av., Office: Manufacturers and Traders Bldg., Buffalo 2 NY‡

DUDYCHA, GEORGE J(OHN), educator, psychologist; b. Cedar Rapids, Ia., June 26, 1903; s. Charles and Blanche K. (Buresh) D.; B.A., Coe Coll., 1925; M.A., State U. Ia., 1926; Ph.D., Columbia, 1936; m. Martha Malek, Aug. 25, 1927; children—Carol Ann (Mrs. Milton E. Peters), Arthur Lynn. From instr. to prof. psychology Ripon (Wis.) Coll., 1926-50, registrar, 1936-40, dir. student personnel, 1944-50; professor of psychology Wittenberg University, 1950-70, prof. emeritus, 1970-71; chmn. dept. psychology, 1950-66. Mem. Am., Midwest psychol. assns., Am. Assn. U. Profs., A.A.A.S., Soc. Psychol. Study Social Issues, Sigma Xi, Pi Gamma Mu. Author: Psychology for Law Enforcement Officers, 1955; Learn More With Less Effort, 1957; Applied Psychology, 1963. Home: Springfield OH Died Apr. 23, 1971; buried Ferncliff Cemetery, Springfield OH

DUELL, CHARLES HALLIWELL, pub. cons.; b. New Rochelle, N.Y., July 20, 1905; s. Holland S. and Mabel (Halliwell) D.; grad. Hotchkiss School, Lakeville, Connecticut, 1923; A.B., Yale, 1927; student St. John's Coll., Cambridge, Eng., 1927-28; m. Josephine Scott Smith, Oct. 21, 1933 (div. 1944); children—Hemingham Anne, Josephine Scott, Charles Halliwell Pringle; m. 2d, Ruth Potter La Farge, July 14, 1945; children—Roderick Potter, Ruth Evelyn. Condr. advt. research for mag., Crowell Publishing Co., 1928; book advt. mgr. Doubleday Doran & Co., 1929-32; vice pres. William Morrow & Co., 1932-39; pres. Duell, Sloan and Pearce, Inc., 1939-66; mng. dir., chmn. editorial bd. Meredith Press div. Meredith Pub. Co., 1962-66, pub. cons., 1967-70. Served with 101st Cav., N.Y. Nat. Guard, 1929-32; with 51st Inf.; N.Y. Nat. Guard, 1943-45. Am. Book Pubs. Council, 1944-46; dir. Grand Jury Assn. of N.Y. Co., 1947-51; mem. exec. com. Council on Books in Wartime, 1943-45. Presbyn. Clubs: Century Assn., Yale, Coffee House (N.Y.C.). Home: Sherman CT Died July 10, 1970.

DUFF, JAMES H., ex-U.S. senator; b. Mansfield (now Carnegie), Pa., Jan. 21, 1883; s. Joseph Miller and Margaret (Morgan) D.; A.B., Princeton, 1904; grad. student U. Pa. Law Sch., 1904-06; LL.B., U. Pitts., 1907; LL.D., Duquesne U., Albright Coll., Pa. Mil. Coll., Lafayette Coll., Franklin and Marshall Coll., Washington and Jefferson Coll., U. Pa., Temple U., St. Francis Coll., Geneva Coll., Lincoln U., Villanova Coll., Jefferson Med. Coll., Elizabethtown Coll., Lebanon Valley Coll., Drexel Inst., Lehigh U., Rollins Coll., U. Pitts., D.C.L., Hahnemann Med. Coll. and Hosp.; Litt.D., Waynesburg Coll.; D.Sc., Phila. Col. Osteopathy; m. Jean Taylor, Oct. 26, 1909. Practiced law, 1907-43, partner Duff, Scott & Smith, Pitts.; atty. gen. of Pa., 1943-47; gov. of Pa., 1947-51; U.S. senator from State of Pennsylvania, 1950-57; now member law firm Davies, Richberg, Tydings, Landa & Duff, Washington. Pres. Virginia Manor Co. Nat. elector, Pa., 1912; del. Rep. Nat. Conv., 1932, 36, 40, 48, 52. Life trustee Carnegie Library, Carnegie, Pa. Mem. Allegheny County Bar Assn. Republican. Mason. Elk, Rotarian. Washington DC Died Dec. 20, 1969.

DUFFEE, WARREN S(ADLER), journalist; b. Mobile, Ala., May 15, 1917; s. Louis Warren and Susie (Sadler) D.; A.B., Emory U., 1938, postgrad., 1938-39. Grad. asst. journalism dept., acting dir. news bur. Emory U., Atlanta, 1938-39, acting editor Emory Alumnus, 1939; news editor Marietta (Ga.) Times, 1939-40; with U.P.I., 1940-42, 46-67, Congl. and polit. corr., Washington, 1947-67; sometime White House corr. Mem. standing com. corrs. Daily Congl. Press Galleries, 1963-65, chmn., 1964-65. Ex officio mem. 64. Served from ensign to lt., USNR, 1942-46, PTO. Member White House Corr. Association, Sigma Delta Chi, Pi Kappa Alpha, Omicron Delta Kappa. Presbyterian. Clubs: National Press (bd. govs. 1961-66, vice chmn. bd. 1964-66), Touchdown (Washington); Officers (Bethesda, Md.). Home: Washington DC Died Dec. 12, 1967; buried Lake Park Cemetery, Laurel MS

DUFFIELD, MARCUS MCCAMPBELL, newspaperman; b. Ottumwa, Ia., Oct. 4, 1908; s. Marcus Pearl and Jennie (McCampbell) D.; A.B., Pomona Coll., 1925; M.S., Columbia, 1926; m. Margaret Doty, June 6, 1931; children—Timothy, Katherine. With Evening Tribune, San Diego, 1925; with New York Herald Tribune since 1926, successively copy reader, mem. London staff, rotogravure editor and day news editor, author weekly news summary, History in the Making, 1942-62; instr. Columbia U. Sch. Journalism, 1930. Clubs: Century (N.Y.C.); Sachem's Head Yacht (Conn.). Author: King Legion, 1932. Contbr. mags. Home: Guilford CT Died Jan. 11, 1973.

DUFFUS, ROBERT LUTHER, author; b. Waterbury, Vt., July 10, 1888; s. John McGlashan and Helen (Graves) D.; A.B., Stanford, 1910, A.M., 1911; hon. LL.D., Middlebury (Vt.) College, 1938; m. Leah Louise Deane, Feb. 23, 1914; children—Nairne Louise, Marjorie Rose. Reporter, San Francisco Bulletin, 1911-13, editorial writer, 1913-18; editorial writer, San Francisco Call, 1918-19, New York Globe, 1912-23; member of the editorial staff New York Times, 1937-62; Decorated Chevalier Legion of Honor (France). Mem. Phi Beta Kappa. Club: Century (N.Y.C.). Author books including: The Innocents at Cedro, 1944; The Valley and Its People, 1944, 2d edit., 1972; Non-Scheduled Flight, 1950; Williamstown Branch (Memoirs), 1959; The Waterbury Record (Memoirs), 1960; The Tower of Jewels (Memoirs), 1961; Nostalgia, 1963; Santa Fe Trail, 1930, 2d edit., 1972. Home: Palo Alto CA Died Nov. 28, 1972.

DUFFY, BERNARD CORNELIUS, advertising exec.; b. New York, N.Y., Jan. 21, 1902; s. Bernard and Margaret (Connelly) D.; ed. parochial schs. of New York City; LL.D., St. Joseph's Coll., 1956; m. Marion Edna Brutton, Apr. 26, 1930; children—David Edward, Miriam (Mrs. Arthur L. Hawkins). With Batten, Barton, Durstine & Osborn, Inc., 1919-72, v.p., 1936-43, exec. v.p., 1943-45, gen. mgr., 1945, president, 1946-57, vice chairman board of directors, 1957-62, hon. vice chairman of bd., 1962-72. Former director Audit Bur. Circulations. Vice chairman advt. committee Cardinal's Com. Laity; chmn. spl. gifts com. Westchester Heart Assn. Mem. bd. development, N.Y.U.; mem. exec. com., former chmn. president's com. Greater N.Y., U. of Notre Dame. Recipient Good Scout award, 1963; Ben Franklin 50 award Alpha Delta Sigma, 1963. Mem. Am. Assn. Advt. Agys. (former dir. at large), Alpha Delta Sigma, Knight of Malta. Roman Catholic (member Soc. of Friendly Sons of St. Patrick). Clubs: Advertising, Manhattan, New York Athletic (New York); Boulder Brook; Westchester Country. Author: Advertising Media and Markets, 1939; 99 Days, 1933; Profitable Advertising in Today's Media and Markets, 1951. Contbr. articles advt. and selling to trade jours. Home: Rye NY Died Sept. 1, 1972; buried Gate of Heaven Cemetery.

DUFFY, CHARLES, educator; b. Dubuque, Ia., June 16, 1903; s. Thomas Henry and Mary Elizabeth (Murphy) D.; Ph.B., U. Wis., 1926; M.A., U. Mich., 1927; postgrad. U. Vienna (Austria), 1930; Ph.D., Cornell U., 1939; m. Martha Sabeva, June 23, 1935; children—Julia (Mrs. Roscoe Ward), Elizabeth (Mrs. John Woodford). Instr. English, U. Detroit, 1927-29, De Paul U., 1936-37, Cornell U., 1937-42; asst. prof. La. State U., 1942-44; distinguished prof. English Lit. U. Akron, 1945-72; vis. prof. Fordham U., 1945, U. Colo., 1961; staff Am. legation, Sofia, Bulgaria, 1933-36. Fulbright lectr. U. Tubingen, 1954-56. Mem. Modern Humanities Research Assn., Northeastern Ohio Coll. English Assn. (past pres.), Am. Assn. U. Profs., Modern Lang. Assn., Nat. Council Tchrs. English, Omicron Delta Kappa. Roman Catholic. Club: Franklin (Akron). Author: Correspondence of Taylor and Hayne, 1945; Hayne's Letters to Julia Dorr, 1950; (with Henry J. Pettit) Dictionary of Literary Terms, 1950; also articles. Book revs. for N.Y. Times, Cleve. Plain Dealer. Contbr. to encys. Home: Peninsula OH Died May 10, 1972.

DUFFY, JAMES ALBERT, bishop; b. St. Paul, Minn., Sept. 13, 1873; s. James and Joanna (Shiely) D.; ed. St. Thomas Coll. and St. Paul Sem., both of St. Paul. Ordained priest R.C. Ch., 1899; asst. pastor Immaculate Conception Ch., Minneapolis, 1899-1902; pastor St. Ann's Ch., Le Sueur, Minn.; resigned on account of ill health and became pastor Cathedral, Cheyenne, Wyo., and chancellor of the diocese; consecrated bishop of diocese of Kearney, Neb. (now Diocese of Grand Island), Apr. 16, 1913; resigned on account of ill health, 1931. Home: Grand Island NB‡

DUFFY, JOSEPH ALEXANDER, book industry exec.; b. Jersey City, Nov. 9, 1903; s. Joseph Alexander and Mary (Hetherington) D.; grad. Newman Sch., Lakewood, N.J.; student Columbia, 1922-24; m. 2d, Marguerite Rooney O'Brien, Nov. 24, 1949; 1 son, Mark Joseph; 1 dau. by previous marriage, Diana (Mrs. James Thomson). With Harper & Bros., 1924-29; sales mgr. Jonathan Cape & Harrison Smith, 1929-30, Longmans, Green & Co., 1930-32, Columbia U. Press, 1932-45; dir. sales, advt., promotion Henry Holt & Co., 1945-48; research dir. Am. Book Pubs. Council, in charge Ohio Book Project, 1948-49; book pub. cons., gen. mgr. Christophers Lit. Prize Contests, 1949-50; pub. dir. P.J. Kenedy & Sons, 1950-53; instr. English, editing, pub. Columbia, 1950-54; exec. dir. Am. Booksellers Assn., Inc., N.Y.C., 1953-72. Mem. White House Library Com.; mem. steering com. Nat. Book Awards, 1964-72, Nat. Library Week, 1964-72. Del., White House Conf. on Internat. Cooperation, 1965. Mem. Psi Upsilon. Democrat. Roman Catholic. Clubs: Dutch Treat Columbia Univ. (N.Y.C.); Pelham Country. Contbr. poetry, articles to profl. jours., popular mags. contbr. to Americana Ann., 1954-72. Home: Pelham Manor NY Died June 7, 1972.

DUFOUR, FRANK OLIVER, civil engr.; b. at Washington, Jan. 1, 1873; s. John Francis Ruter and Florida E. (Everett) D.; C.E., Lehigh U., Pa., 1896; m. Sarah Breisch, of S. Bethlehem, Pa., Sept. 2, 1901; 1 son, Robert Seton. Asst. engr. Lehigh Valley R.R., 1896-98; instr. civil engring., Lehigh U., 1898-1902; prof. civ. engring., U. of Cincinnati, 1902-04; acting prof. bridge engring., U. of Wis., 1904-05; asst. prof. structural engring., U. of Ill., 1905-13; prin. asst. engr. with D.A. Keefe, 1913; consulting engr., Athens, Pa., 1913-14; sr. structural engr., central dist. Div. of Valuation, Interstate Commerce Commn., Chicago, 1914-15; structural engr. with Stone & Webster, Boston, 1915-21; prof. civ. engring. and dir. Materials Testing Labs., Lafayette Coll., Easton, Pa., 1921-28; now cons. engr., United Engrs. & Constructors, Inc., Philadelphia, Pa. Mem. Am. Soc. C.E., Am. Ry. Engring. Assn., Sigma Xi, Theta Delta Chi. Clubs: Explorers (New York); Penn Athletic, Phila. Cricket, Engineers', Midday, Business Men's Art, Tredyffrin Country (Philadelphia); Camp Fire Club of America (New York). Author:

Bridge Engineering, 1908, revised edit., 1931; Roof Trusses, 1908; Structural Drafting, 1911. Contbr. to various tech. mags. Home: Narberth, Pa. Office: 1401 Arch St., Philadelphia PA‡

DUFOUR, WILLIAM CYPRIEN, lawyer; b. New Orleans, Oct. 31, 1871; s. Elmore and Blanche (Generes) D.; ed. Tulane High Sch., New Orleans; m. Helen McLeary, Sept. 1, 1898; children—Helen, Elmore. Admitted to bar, 1892, since in practice, New Orleans; mem. Dufour, St. Paul & Levy. Mem. La. Ho. of Rep., 1896; counsel for Bd. Liquidation, New Orleans since 1905; v. chmn. Spanish-Am. War Claims Commn. of La. since 1908; mem. Inter-Am. High Commn.; counsel Bd. of Assessors, New Orleans; gen. counsel La. Flood Com. Lt. col. 2d La. Vol. Inf. Spanish-Am. War, 1898. V.p., gen. counsel Federal Land Bank of New Orleans, 1917-18. Dir. Marquette U. Democrat. Catholic. Clubs: Boston, Pickwick (New Orleans); Metropolitan, Chevy Chase (Washington, D.C.). Office: Canal Bldg., New Orleans LA‡

DUGAN, CARO ATHERTON, teacher; b. in Brewster, Cape Cod, Mass.; d. James Atherton and Helen (Cobb) D.; has had normal and kindergarten training; unmarried. Teacher by profession. Author: The King's Jester, 1899; Other Short Plays for Small Stages. Also short stories and verse, mostly in mags. for young people, and also songs for children. Address: Brookline MA‡

DUGAN, LARRY HULL, business exec.; b. Perry, Ia., Nov. 21, 1911; s. Harry Silas and Mary Emaline (Hull) D.; grad., Toledo (Ia.) High Sch., 1929; LL.B., Drake U., Des Moines, Ia., 1935; m. Leas Montgomery, May 23, 1936; children—Larry Montgomery, George Montgomery. Private practice of law, Perry, Ia., 1935-39; chief clerk law dept., C., M., St. P. & P. R.R., Chicago, 1939-41, asst. gen. solicitor, 1941-48, v.p., Seattle, 1948-50, v.p., and western counsel, Seattle, 1951-68; v.p. Milw. Land Co. WI & MRy. Co., Bremerton Freight Car Ferry, Inc.; dir. Puget Sound Mut. Savs. Bank. Mem. Wash., Seattle bar assns., Chi Delta, Phi Alpha Delta. Clubs: Washington Athletic, Seattle Rotary, Rainier, Seattle Yacht, Broadmoor Golf. Home: Bainbridge Island WA Died July 1968.

DUGARDIN, HERVE, opera dir.; b. 1910; ed. Schola Cantorum, Paris. Artistic dir. Theatre des Champs-Elysees, 1948-52; dir. Theatre Nat. de l'Opera Comique, Paris, France, 1962-65. Dir. French br. Ricordi, music pubs. Address: Paris France Deceased.

DUGMORE, ARTHUR RADCLYFFE, author, artist; b. England, Dec. 25, 1870; s. Capt. F.S. and Hon. Emily Evelyn (Brougham) D.; ed. Elizabeth Coll., Guernsey, and Turrell's Sch., Smyrna (Asia Minor); studied painting at Belle Arti, Naples; came to U.S., 1889, from Naples; studied ornithology and continued drawing, painting and illustrating by photography; m. Henrietta Louise Watkins, Jan. 17, 1901. Mem. Am. Ornithologists' Union, Linnaean Soc.; fellow Royal Geog. Soc. (Eng.), Royal Photographic Soc.; hon. life mem. Am. Mus. Natural History, New York Zool. Soc. Clubs: Royal Societies, Shikar (London), Players, Explorers, Camp Fire of America (New York). Author: Bird Homes, 1899; Nature and the Camera, 1902; Camera Adventures in the African Wilds (pub. in English, French and German); Wild Life and the Camera; The Romance of the Newfoundland Caribou. Also writer and lecturer on nature subjects in periodicals. Address: Royal Societies Club, St. James St., London SW England‡

DU HAMEL, WILLIAM, editor of Church Bells since 1888; b. Newark, Del., grad. Del. Coll., 1886, also Univ. of Pa., 1889 (A.M., Del., 1889); deacon, 1887; priest, 1890; asst. in various P. E. chs.; since 1893 asst. St. Augustine's Chapel, Trinity parish, New York. Author: First Millennial Faith. Address: Rehoboth DE‡

DUKE, JAMES THOMAS, army officer; b. California, Md., June 10, 1893; s. John and Lilly (Jarboe) D.; B.S., U. of Md., 1916; grad. Cav. Sch. 1923, Equitation Course, 1924, Ecole d'Application de Cavalrie, Saumur, France, 1928, Command and Gen. Staff Sch., 1934, Chem. Warfare Sch., 1934, Army Indsl. Coll., 1940; m. Lupe O'Neill, May 15, 1919; children—James Thomas, Mary Dolores, Ralph Leonard. Commd. 2d lt., Cav., U.S. Army, 1917, and advanced through the grades to brig. gen., 1943; instr. of equitation, U.S. Cav. Sch., Fort Riley, 1924-27, 1928-32; gen. staff, 1st Cav., Ft. Bliss, Tex., 1937-39; exec. officer, Office Chief of Cav., Washington, D.C., 1941-42; gen. staff, Army Ground Forces, Army War Coll., 1942; comdg. gen., Charleston Port of Embarkation, Charleston, S.C., 1942-50; comdg. officer Ft. Myer, 1950-53; ret. 1953. Decorated D.S.M., Victory, Mexican Service, Mexican Border Service, Am. Defense Service medals. Mem. advisory com. Community Development Council, Charleston, S.C. Mem. Am. Legion, Am. Horse Show Assn., Kappa Alpha Southern. Clubs: Propeller; Army and Navy (Washington, D.C.). Author: U.S. Cavalry R.O.T.C. Manual, 1940, 1941. Mem. U.S. Olympic Equestrian Squad, 1932; U.S. Cav. rep. for equestrian events, inter-Am. Fedn. of Sports, and Olympic Games, 1941-42, Capt., Ft. Myer Horse Show Team, 1932; mem. Ft. Riley Horse Show Team, 1924-27, 1928-32. Participated in engagement with Mexicans, Nogales, Ariz., Aug. 1918. Home: Morganza MD Died Dec. 9, 1970; buried Arlington Nat. Cemetery, Washington DC

DUKE, VERNON, composer (used his name, Vladimir Dukelsky, for serious music only); b. Pskoff, Russia, October 10, 1903; son of Alexander and Anna (Kopyloff) D.; student Kiev (Russia) Conservatory; married Kay McCracken, October 30, 1957. Has spent entire career composing for ballet, symphony, musical shows, films, etc. Named chevalier Order of Sainte Bridgette. Founder and pres. Soc. for Forgotten Music, 1948. Mem. A.S.C.A.P., Russian Nobility Assn. in Am., Music Union. Mem. Greek Orthodox Ch. Wrote music for Zephyr and Flora, ballet produced by Sergei Diaghilev, 1925; two symphonies, played by Boston Symphony Orchestra, London Philharmonic, Warsaw Philharmonic, etc., 1927-28; The End of St. Petersburg, oratorio, 1938; Dedicaces, piano concerto, 1939; Violin Concerto, 1942; Cello Concerto, 1942; Dushenka, duet for women's voices, 1926; Piano Sonata, 1927; Trio for flute, bassoon, piano, 1930; 2 Piano Suites and Victorian Songs, 1942; (ballets) Jardin Public, 1936-37; Entr'acte, 1938; (musical shows) Yvonne, 1926, Yellow Mask, 1928, Open Your Eyes, 1930; Garrick Gaieties, 1930; Walk a Little Faster, 1932; Ziegfeld Follies (2 edits.), 1934, 35; Shoot the Works, 1933; Thumbs Up, 1934; The Show Is On, 1936; Cabin in the Sky, 1940; Ray Bolger's ballet, Raffles, In Keep Off the Grass, 1940; Banjo Eyes, 1941; Lady Comes Across, 1942; Dancing in the Streets, 1943; Cabin in the Sky (film version), 1943; Jackpot, 1943; Tars and Spars (U.S. Coast Guard Revue), 1944; Sadie Thompson, 1944; also music for war film, Battle Stations, 1944; score for musical film, Goldwyn Follies, 1937; incidental music for 11 Paramount films, 1930; (popular songs) This Is Romance, April in Paris, Autumn in New York, What Is There To Say, I Can't Get Started with You, Taking a Chance with Love, Cabin in the Sky; U.S. Coast Guard Fighting Song, The Silver Shield," 1943; Ode to the Milky Way, 1945; Third Symphony, 1946; Ogden Nash's Musical Zoo, 1946, The Littlest Revue, 1956, numerous others; Le Bal des Blanchisseuses (ballet), produced in Paris, Dec. 1946; Violin Sonata, 1948-49; Paris Aller et Retour (Cantata, produced Paris, 1948); Sonata for Harpsichord, 1949; music for Warner Bros. pictures: She's Working Her Way Through College; April in Paris; music for Time Remembered, 1957; Emporor Norton (ballet); Mistress into Maid (opera) (premier), 1958. Author: Passport to Paris, (autobiography), 1955; Epistles (Russian poetry), 1962; Listen Here (a study in music depreciation), published 1963. Recorded album of own music, 1953. Contributor to Stage Mag., Theatre Arts Monthly, Music Publishing Jour. etc. Enlisted as coxswain, U.S. Coast Guard, Aug. 1942; leader Brooklyn Barracks Band, Brooklyn, N.Y.; hon. disch. 1943; comd. lt. (temp. Res.) Mar. 1944. Home: Pacific Palisades CA Died Jan. 16, 1969; buried Santa Monica CA

DULLES, ALLEN WELSH, lawyer; born Watertown, N.Y., Apr. 7, 1893; s. Allen Macy and Edith (Foster) D.B.A., Princeton, 1914, M.A., 1916; LL.B., George Washington U., 1926, LL.D., 1959; LL.D., Brown University, 1947, Temple University, 1952, Columbia, 1955, Princeton, 1957, Boston U., 1961, U. S.C., 1962, Williams Coll., 1965; m. Clover Todd, Oct. 16, 1920; children—Clover Todd, Joan, Allen Macy. Teacher English, Allahabad, India, 1 yr.; entered U.S. Diplomatic Service, 1916; apptd. sec. of Legation, May 17, 1916, and assigned to Vienna, Austria; trans. to Berne, Switzerland, 1917; with Am. Commn. to Negotiate Peace, Paris, Dec. 1918; trans. to Berlin, Germany, Oct. 29, 1919; assigned to Dept. of State, 1920; with Am. Commn., Constantinople, Turkey, Oct. 1920; chief. Div. of Near Eastern Affairs, Dept. of State, Washington, D.C., Apr. 14, 1922 to Apr. 14, 1926; delegate of United States to Internat. Conf. on Arms Traffic, Geneva, Switzerland, May 4-June 17, 1925; mem. Am. Delegation to Preparatory Disarmament Commn., Geneva, Switzerland, June-July 1926; legal adviser to Am. Delegation Three Power Naval Conf., Geneva, June 20-Aug. 5, 1927; legal adviser to Am. Delegation, Gen. Disarmament Conf., Geneva, 1932-33; resigned October 15, 1926, to practice law, with Sullivan & Cromwell, N.Y.C.; dep. dir. Central Intelligence Agy., 1951-53, director, 1953-61; of counsel, Sullivan & Cromwell, 1962-69. Mem. Pres.'s Commn. on Assassination of Pres. Kennedy, 1963-64. Trustee Princeton Univ., 1961. Served during World War II with O.S.S. Decorations: Medal for Merit, also Medal of Freedom, 1946; Officer Legion Honor (France), 1947; Order of S.S. Maurizio e Lazzaro, Italy, 1946; Belgian Cross of Officer of Order of Leopold, 1948; National Security Medal, 1961. Recipient of the ann. citation Salvation Army, 1960; Golden Rule award St. George Assn.; Bernard Baruch gold medal Vets. Fgn. Wars. Mem. Council Fgn. Relations (dir.), Phi Beta Kappa. Presbyn. Clubs: Century Assn., Piping Rock (N.Y.C.); Alibi, Metropolitan (Washington). Author: (with Hamilton Fish Armstrong) Can We Be Neutral?, 1935, Can America Stay Neutral? 1939; Germany's Underground, 1947; The Craft of Intelligence, 1963; The Secret Surrender, 1966. Editor: Great True Spy Stories, 1968; Great Spy Stories from Fiction, 1969. Home: Washington DC Died Jan. 29, 1969; buried Baltimore MD

DUMM, BENJAMIN ALFRED, clergyman; b. Salisbury, Md., Aug. 31, 1867; s. Rev. William Thomas and Anna (Bates) Dumm, sister of Daniel Webster Bates, D.D., and Laurence Webster Bates, D.D.; ancestry (both sides) asso. with Declaration of Independence and U.S. Constn.; A.B., Western Md. Coll., Westminster, 1886, A.M., 1889; Hebrew certificate, Am. Inst. Sacred Lit., student Boston School Expression, and Yale Div. Sch., 1893-94; Ph.D., George Washington U., 1900; A.M., Harvard, 1912; m. Nelle Jamison, 1889; children—Helen Minerva (dec.), Paul Jamison. Prin. Fawn Grove Acad., 1886-88; ordained Ministry Meth. Protestant Ch., 1891; pastor Meth. Prot. Chs., 1891-98; asst. pastor 1st Congl. Ch., Washington, D.C., 1898-1900; prof. philosophy, George Washington U., 1889-1900; pastor various chs., Mass., New Hampshire, 1901-36. Asso. sec. World Conf. on Faith and Order, 1926-27 (wrote on the theological aspect, in symposium by writers of several countries); moderator Merrimack Assn. Congl. Christian Chs.; moderator Hopkinton Town Sch. Meeting, 1934, 35. Mem. N.H. Academy of Science, A.A.A.S.; adjutant general's Emergency Committee, local, 1940. Speaker, N.H. Committee on Public Safety, 4-minute man, World War I. Formerly scoutmaster and special field scout commissioner, Boy Scouts America. Member of Academy of Political Science. President Weare Rifle Club. Republican. Clubs: Pilgrim, Boston City, Harvard Philosophical (president). Author: An Inductive Creed, 1906; The Old Puritanism and the New Age (with C. S. Macfarland, Thomas Sims, S.A. Norton); paper read before N.H. Acad. Sci., Apr. 18, 1952, Cosmology as Affected by Nucleonics (Proceedings 1953) included in A Philosophy of Immediacy, copyright 1952; sermons reported at length in press and many constitutional and civic controversial articles and speeches. Translator (in verse) of Stabat Mater. Lecturer on the Holy Grail, Freedom of the Will, Philosophy of Henri Bergson, Reciprocal Problems of Theology and Philosophy Today. Writer and producer of The Pageant of Civic Weare," 1937. Founder and dir. of North Weare Seminar on the Constitution and the Philosophy of Govt. Platform reader and impersonator Shakespeare and other dramatists. Home: North Weare NH

DU MOUCHEL, LEANDRE ARTHUR, organist, composer; b. Rigaud nr. Montreal, Canada, s. Ignace and Marie Antoinette (Fournier) D.; grad. Rigaud Coll. 1859; studied piano and organ under an aunt who was organist at Rigaud; spent 3 yrs. in Europe, studying piano under Prof. Ignace Moscheles, organ under Dr. B.R. Papperitz and Robert Hopner, harmony and composition under Ernest F. Richter and Dr. Oscar Paul, instrumentation under Dr. Louis Maas and Carl Reinecke; unmarried. Organist, St. Paul's Ch., Oswego, N.Y., 1872-5; organist and choirmaster, Cathedral of the Immaculate Conception, Albany, Apr. 24, 1876—. Composer masses, vespers, offertories, pieces for orchestra, etc. Address: Albany NY‡

DUN, ANGUS, bishop; b. New York, N.Y., May 4, 1892; s. Henry Walke and Sarah Robinson (Hazard) D.; grad. Albany (N.Y.) Acad., 1910; A.B., Yale Univ., 1914; graduate Episcopal Theological School, Cambridge, Mass., 1917; (hon.) D.D., P.E. Theol. Sem. Va., 1935; D.D., Yale, 1941, U. of South, 1945, Harvard 1948, Princeton 1953; S.T.D., Kenyon College, 1942, General Theological Seminary, 1958; LL.D., Am. U.; married Catherine Whipple Pew, June 22, 1916; children—Angus, Junior, Alan Andrews. Ordained to ministry of Protestent Episcopal Ch.; vicar St. Andrews' Ch., Ayer, Mass., 1917-18; sec. of the Com. on the War and the Religious Outlook; student at univs. of Oxford and Edinburgh, 1919-20; instr. asst. prof. and prof. theology, Episcoapl Theol. School, Cambridge, Mass., 1920-40, dean, 1940-44; Bishop fo Washington, 1944-62. Chmn. Commn. of Fed. Council of Chs. on the Christian conscience and weapons of mass destruction, 1950. Hon. Commander of Order of the British Empire records and papers established Episcopal Theol. Sch. Library, Cambridge, Mass. Member Theol. Soc., Elihu Club of Yale, Phi Beta Kappa, American Academy of Arts and Sciences. Author: The Kings Cross, 1926; We Believe, 1934; Not by Bread Alone, 1942; Prospecting for a United Church; The Saving Person, 1957. Home: Washington DC Died Aug. 12, 1971; buried Washington Cathedral, Washington DC

DUNAWAY, JOHN ALLDER, economist; b. Stockton, Mo., Oct. 10, 1886; s. William F. and Lucy J. (Allder) D.; A.B., Park Coll., Parkville, Mo., 1910, A.M., 1912; married May C. Ferguson, July 20, 1916 (died July 10, 1917); m. 2d, Rosa Shayeb, Aug. 22, 1920; children—Allder, William, Sylvia. Prof. economics, King Coll., Bristol, Tenn., 1912-13; grad. student and instr. in industry, Wharton Sch., U. of Pa., 1914-16; chautauqua lecturer, 1916-18; treas. Near East Relief, Aleppo dist., Syria, 1919; chautauqua lecturer, 1920; asst. chief, later chief research div., Bur. Foreign and Domestic Commerce, Washington, District of Columbia, 1921-22; statistician and provincial director of finances Am. Finance Commn., to Persia, 1922-28; economist, later sr. marketing specialist, dairy sect. Agrl. Adjustment Administration, 1933-35; supervisor revenues Republic of Liberia, 1935-38, became financial adviser, 1938; acting dir. TCA, Saudi Arabia, and chief Public Adminstrn. Div., ret. 1953. Del. of Liberia to UN

Conf. on Internat. Trade, Havana, 1947-48. Decorated Comdr. Star of Africa (Republic of Liberia). Mem. Phi Eta. Democrat. Presbyn. Mason. Club: Monrovia. Home: Phoenix AZ Died June 20, 1969; buried East Resthaven Park Cemetery, Phoenix AZ

DUNBAR, ARTHUR WHITE, naval officer; b. Sept. 7, 1869. Entered U.S. Navy, Oct. 25, 1894; promoted through grades to rear adm., Dec. 7, 1926; retired Dec. 1, 1934. Address: 3229 Klingle Rd. N.W., Washington, D.C. Home: Westchester Apartments, 4000 Cathedral Av. N.W., Washington 16 DC*‡

DUNBAR, DUKE WELLINGTON, lawyer; b. Mt. Sterling, Ill., Sept. 3, 1894; s. Homer J. and Mary (Tebo) D.; LL.B., U. Mich., 1920; m. Eva Hillyard, June 5, 1922. Admitted to Ill. bar, 1920, Colo. bar, 1922; practiced in Quincy, Ill., Denver, 1922-41; first asst. atty. gen., State Colo., 1941-44, dep. atty. gen., 1944-48, atty. gen., 1951-72; asst. city atty., Denver, 1948-50. Chmn. Nat. and Colo. Hwy. Safety Council. Served with U.S. Navy, World War I. Recipient Wyman award, 1969-70. Mem. Gamma Eta Gamma. Mason (Shriner), Elk. Home: Denver CO Died Dec. 8, 1972; buried Fairmount Mausoleum, Denver CO

DUNBAUGH, HARRY JOY, lawyer; b. Humboldt, Kan., Nov. 24, 1877; s. Edward Payson and Emma A. (Joy) D.; A.B., Ill. College, Jacksonville, 1899; LL.B., Harvard, 1903; m. Katherine Shortall, Apr. 5, 1923; 1 son, Franklin Perkins (killed in action in Korea, Dec., 1952). Admitted to the Ill. bar, 1903; began as clk. in office of Isham, Lincoln & Beale, 1903, mem. firm, 1914-58, counsel, 1958-69. Commr. Winnetka Park Dist., 1929-35; 1938-39. Student Plattsburgh Mil. Training Camp, 1916. Four-minute man, Chicago, during World War. Trustee Ill. Coll., 1913-23 and 1932-69, chmn. bd. trustees, 1932-55. Mem. bd. mgrs. YMCA, 1924-38; chmn. Y.M.C.A. Hotel, 1925-38, and 1942-45, bd. dirs., 1916-69; mem. exec. com. Legislative Voters' League, 1923-34. Mem. Am., (chmn. sect. of pub. utility law, 1934-35), Ill. Chicago Bar Assn. (mem. bd. mgrs., 1940-41). Republican. Episcopalian. Clubs: Chicago, University, Indian Hill, Huron Mountain. Home: Hubbard Woods IL Died Jan. 3, 1969; buried Graceland Cemetery, Chicago IL

DUNCAN, ALEXANDER EDWARD, ret. comml. banker; b. nr. Louisville, May 27, 1878; s. John Thomas and Ida (Smith) D.; ed. Louisville Male High Sch.; m. Flora Ross, Apr. 11, 1900 (died June 20, 1936); 1 dau., Elizabeth Duncan Yaggy; m. 2d, Mrs. E. Everett Gibbs (Anne Ranson), Mar. 16, 1940. Began as bank clk. at Louisville, 1896; clerk Jungbluth & Rauterberg, Louisville, 1897-99; mem. Ross & Duncan, Crestwood, Ky., 1900-02; spl. and gen. agt. Ocean Accident & Guaranty Corp., Cincinnati, 1903-06; gen. agent at Baltimore for Am. Credit-Indemnity Co., 1907-09; organized, 1909, and pres., dir. until 1912, Manufacturers' Finance Co., Balt., Md. Organized, 1912, and pres., dir. Comml. Credit Co., Balt., chmn. bd., 1916-54, founder chairman, 1954-64, ret.; member. Robert Garrett & Sons, investments, 18 mos., 1916-17; reorganized Humpherys Mfg. Co., Mansfield O., 1917, merged 1956 into and dir. Borg Warner Corp., Chicago; director Am. Credit Indemnity Co. N.Y., Mercantile Safe Deposit & Trust Co. (both Baltimore, Md.). Gen. chmn. YMCA War Work campaign (Baltimore), 1917, and for United War Work campaign, 1918; pres. Community Fund of Baltimore, 1929-31; gen. chmn. Balt. Red Cross War Fund, 1943. Adv. bd. Women's Hosp., Children's Hosp., Inc., Keswich-Home for Incurables. Republican. Episcopalian. Clubs: Bachelors Cotillon, Maryland, Elkridge, Merchants, Center (Balt.). Home: Baltimore MD Died Feb. 7, 1972; buried Crestwood, nr. Louisville KY

DUNCAN, FRANCES (MRS. JOHN L. MANNING), author; b. Brooklyn, 1877; d. Capt. Charles C. and Hannah (Leech) D.; m. John Leroy Manning, May 1914; children—John, Charles Duncan, Margery. Asst. editor Country Calendar, 1904-05; editor garden dept. Ladies' Home Journal, 1907-10; partner in The Kingston Gardeners, 1910-11. Invented gardencraft" for children and other play material in use by Montessori and other educators; lectured on horticultural and children's gardens. Dir. gardening in Sch. of Ethical Culture, Brooklyn, 1923-25; garden editor The Delineator, 1924-25; editor Garden Page for Farm & Orchard, Los Angeles Times, 1926-30; dir. gardening, Girls' Collegiate Sch., Glendora, Calif.; designed playgrounds of Ethical Culture School, Montessori School; gardens of Webb Country Day Sch., Claremont, Calif.; supt. parks, Glendora, 1932; became dir. Sch. of Garden-Craft, Pasedena, 1933; now exec. sec. Southern Calif. Hort. Soc. Author: Mary's Garden and How It Grew, 1904; When Mother Lets Us Garden, 1909; My Garden Doctor, 1914; Roberta of Roseberry Gardens, 1915; The Joyous Art of Gardening, 1917; Pasadena CA‡

DUNCAN, GERALD, city official; b. Baltimore, Dec. 19, 1903; s. Frank K. and Lillian (Hook) D.; student pub. schs., Balt.; m. Betty Gilman; 1 dau., Alison Clare. Newspaper reporter, Balt., Savannah, Ga. dau., Alison Clare. Newspaper reporter, Balt., Savannah, Ga. and Phila., 1921-29, N.Y. Jour., 1929-35, N.Y. Daily News, 1935-44; staff writer Am. Weekly, 1944-46, Los Angeles Examiner, 1947; news editor Bakersfield (Cal.) Press, 1949-50; mng. editor Los Angeles Daily News, 1954; staff writer N.Y. Mirror, 1955-63; editorial page editor, chief editorial writer N.Y. Jour.-Am., N.Y.C., 1963-66, N.Y. World Jour. Tribune, N.Y.C., 1966-67; chief pub. information Cal. Office Civil Def., Sacramento, 1950-53; dir. bus. communication N.Y.C. Dept. Commerce and Industrial Devel., 1967-70. Contbr. nat. mags. Home: New York City NY Died Jan. 12, 1970.

DUNCAN, JAMES FLOYD, prof. education; b. Logan Co., Ill., Apr. 14, 1809; s. Zechariah and Sarah Ann (Killebrew) D.; student Neb. Wesleyan U., 1897-1900; A.B., U. of Nebraska, 1903; A.M. from same university, 1926; m. Susie M. Tyler, of Carleton, Neb., May 31, 1899; children—Lola Lee, Ruth Genevieve, Carl Z., Rex Virgil, Eula, Raymond, Carol. Teacher rural schs., 1893-95; supt. schs., Nelson, Neb., 1904-05; bank cashier, 1905-11; supt. schs. Bartley, Neb., 1911-15, Osceola, 1915-18; normal training insp. Dept. Pub. Instrn., Neb., 1918-20; head dept. edn., Cotner Coll., 1920-1927; dean, 1922-26, acting exec., 1925-26. Mem. N.E.A., Nat. Assn. Supts. and Principals, Neb. State Teachers' Assn., Neb. Coll. Assn., Phi Delta Kappa. Republican. Mem. Christian (Disciples) Ch. Mason, Woodman. Home: 1214 N. 65th St., Lincoln NE‡

DUNCAN, LEWIS JOHNSTON, Independent Liberal minister; b. St. Louis, May 4, 1875; s. Edwin and Emma (Francis) D.; ed. in common schools and Hanover (Ind.) Coll.; m. Oct. 26, 1882, Kate Keath, Quincy, Ill. Admitted to Ill. bar, 1879; bookkeeper, 1882-9; Unitarian minister, Sheffield, Ill., March 1, 1889; sec. Ill. Unitarian conf., 1891-3; minister Ch. of Good Will (Independent), 1893-97; lecturer Milwaukee Ethical Soc., 1897-1900. Advertising mgr. since March 1, 1900, for local firm. Residence: 388 Brady St. Office: 61 New Insurance Bldg., Milwaukee WI‡

DUNCAN, RUTH HENLEY (MRS. ISAAC GREENWOOD DUNCAN), club woman; b. Maury City, Tenn., Dec. 13, 1908; d. Milton Robertson and Lucy Feild (Gibobns) Henley; student Jackson, Tenn., Sch. Bus. Adminstrn., 1927-28; certificate Am. U. Geneal. Inst., 1951; m. William Joseph Godwin, July 20, 1929 (dec. Nov. 1950); 1 dau., Betty Jo (Mrs. William Heiskell Mitchell, Jr.); m. 2d Isaac Greenwood Duncan, Dec. 14, 1952 (dec. July 1955). Partner, So. Wholesale Florists Memphis, 1932-55. Mem. Tenn. adv. council Civil War Centennial Commn., 1961-65. Mem. Tenn. (corr. sec. 1957-58, v.p. 1959-60, v.p. West Tenn. 1961), East Tenn., West Tenn. (life, mem. exec. com.), Tenn. (life, v.p. state at large 1959-60, v.p. W. Tenn. 1961-65) hist. socs., Assn. Preservation Tenn. Antiquities, Memphis Geneal. Soc. (charter mem.) (pres. 1951-53, dir. research 1954-55, 60-61), D.A.R., Daus. Am. Colonists (vice regent 1947-48), Tenn. Soc. Dames Ct. Honor, Huguenots of Manakin in Colony of Va. (life, pres. Tenn. 1957-58, nat. trustee 1963-69), Kings Daus. Magna Charta Dames, Sovereign Colonial Soc., Ams. Royal Descent, Soc. Descs. Knight of Most Noble Order of Garter, Colonial Order of Crown. Episcopalian. Author: The Captain and Submarine CSS H. L. Hunley, 1965. Contbr. articles and chpts. to geneal. publs. Home: Winston-Salem NC Died Nov. 20, 1969.

DUNCAN SAMUEL EDWARD, coll. pres.; b. Madisonville, Ky., Apr. 27, 1904; s. Samuel Edward and Lena (Jordan) D.; A.B., Livingstone Coll., Salisbury, Ky., 1927; Ph.D., Cornell U., 1949; m. Ida Hauser, May 16, 1933. Sci. tchr., athletic coach Washington High Sch., Reidsville, N.C., 1927-30, 38-46; prin. Dunbar High Sch., E. Spencer, N.C., 1931-37; pres. Livingstone Coll., 1958-68; summer vis. instr. A. and T. Coll., Greensboro, Tuskegee Inst., N.C. Coll., U. Miami (Fla.). Vice pres. Piedmont Univ. Center, 1964-68; mem. N.C. Fund Bd., 1963-68, N.C. Bd. Pub. Welfare, 1963-68, N.C. adv. com. U.S. Civil Rights Com., 1962-68. Vice pres. N.C. Council Chs., 1958-67, pres., 1967. Life mem. N.E.A., N.A.A.C.P.; mem. N.C. Tchrs. Assn. (pres. 1964). Home: Salisbury NC Died July 10, 1968; buried Salisbury NC

DUNCANSON, THOMAS SHERRIFF, corp. exec.; b. Edinburgh, Scotland, Nov. 15, 1896; s. James and Alice (Ronaldson) D.; student Toronto Tech. Sch.; m. Jean McGill, Sept. 3, 1922; 1 dau., Dorothy Jean (Mrs. Charles L. Walker). With Moore Corp., Ltd. (and predecessor firm), Toronto, Can., from 1913, sec., 1929-48, dir., from 1948, exec. v.p., 1953-55, pres., 1955-62, chmn. bd. corp. and all subsidiaries, 1962-67, mem. policy com. corp. and all subsidiaries; comptroller Can. William A. Rogers Silverware, Toronto, 1923-25; gen. mgr. F. N. Burt Co., Inc., Buffalo, 1935, v.p., gen. mgr., 1946-55, president, 1952-62, chairman of board, from 1962; chairman board Moore Bus. Forms, Inc., Niagara Falls; director of Can. Life Assurance Company, also National Trust Company. Presbyn. Clubs: National York, York Downs Golf (Toronto); Buffalo, Buffalo Country; Niagara Buffalo NY Died Sept. 18, 1971; buried Buffalo NY

DUNDEY, CHARLES L., lawyer; b. Nauvoo, Ill., Mar. 20, 1872; s. Warren A. and Elizabeth S. (Hodges) D.; ed. pub. and high schs., Nauvoo, Ill., and law sch., Univ. of Mich., LL.B., 1891; m. Omaha, Neb., Mar. 20, 1899, Mae Le Vue Bartlett. Has been employed as atty. by Union Pacific R. R. Co. and its predecessors since 1894, also in gen. pvt. practice since admission to bar, June, 1891. Del. Universal Congress Lawyers and Jurists, St. Louis, 1904. Republican. Residence: 3114 Poppleton Av. Office: Union Pacific Headquarters, Omaha‡

DUNFORD, RALPH EMERSON, coll. dean; b. Amanda, O., Dec. 17, 1896; s. William Michael and Alice Ardella (Rockey) D.; B.A., with Dist., Ohio State U., 1923, M.A., 1924, Ph.D., 1929; m. Mary Ann Dingess, June 5, 1926; children—William Dingess, James Scott. Grad. asst., part time instr. Ohio State U., 1923-26; formerly with U. Tenn., successively asst. prof., asso. prof., prof., dean of students, 1945; head employment officer TVA, 1940-44. Pres. University Concerts, Inc., 1938-73. Mem. com. on Air Force ROTC curriculum Air Univ. Mem. Nat. Assn. Personnel Adminstrs., Am. Psychol. Assn., Phi Kappa Phi, Phi Delta Kappa, Phi Eta Sigma, Omicron Delta Kappa. Home: Knoxville TN Died Apr. 4, 1973.

DUNLAP, DAVID RICHARDSON, company exec.; b. Mobile, Ala., June 19, 1879; s. David R. and Virginia V. (Wheeler) D.; B.S., U. Ala., 1897; m. Tallulah Gordon Sage, Nov. 12, 1918. Sec.-treas. Ala. Iron Works, 1899-1900, pres., gen. mgr., 1903-16; cashier Mchts. Bank, 1900-03; pres. Ala. Dry Dock & Shipbuilding Co., 1916-44, chmn. bd., dir., 1944-56, 63-68; dir. Mchts. Nat. Bank, Mobile Towing &Wrecking Co. Mem. Lloyds Register of Shipping, Am. Bur. Shipping. Club: Athelstan, Alabana. Home: Mobile AL Died Nov. 20, 1968.

DUNLAP, ELBERT, surgeon and gynecologist; b. Miami, Mo., Oct. 2, 1872; s. Dr. John North and Maria A. (Mitchell) D.; Ph.G., St. Louis Coll. of Pharmacy, 1892; M.D., Beaumont Hosp. Med. Coll., St. Louis, 1896; m. Hallie Hudson, June 6, 1901; children—Hallie M. (Mrs. Carl C. Weichsel), James Hudson (M.D.; maj. U.S. Army), John Elbert (M.D.). Specializes in gynecology; prof. gynecology and head dept. Baylor U. Coll. Med. until 1943; now prof. emeritus of gynecol. Southwestern Med. Coll. Fellow Am. Coll. Surgeons, A.M.A.; mem. Central Assn. Obstetricians and Gynecologists. Southern Med. Assn., Tex. State Med. Soc., Texas Surg. Soc. (past pres.), Texas Assn. Obstetricians and Gynecologists (past pres.), Theta Kappa Psi. Democrat. Methodist. Contbr. to mags. Home: 5339 Nakoma Dr. Office: Medical Arts Bldg., Dallas TX‡

DUNLAP, FREDERICK LEVY, consulting chemist; b. Chillicothe, O., May 16, 1870; s. Joseph Levy and Ann Marie (Clingman) Dunlap; student Ohio State University, 1888-89; B.Sc., University of Mich., 1892; D.Sc., Harvard, 1895; studied Yale, 1895-96; m. Eleanor Baldwin, of Worcester, Mass., Aug. 26, 1901; children—Rosalie (Mrs. Paul E. Boyle), Stanton Baldwin. Instr. industrial chemistry, Worcester Poly. Inst., 1896-1900; instr. chemistry, 1900-05, asst. prof. 1905-07, U. of Mich.; asso. chemist, Bur. Chemistry, Dept. Agr. 1907-12, and mem. Bd. of Food and Drug Inspection; consulting chemist, Victor Chem. Works, 1912-15. Mem. Am. Chem. Soc., A.A.A.S., Am. Inst. of Chem. Engineers, Am. Assn. Cereal Chemists, Sigma Xi, Chi Phi; foreign mem. Masaryk Acad. of Work, Czechoslovakia. Republican. Mem. Disciples of Christ Church. Club: Quadrangle (Chicago). Translator: Dr. Hugo Erdmann's Introduction to Chemical Preparations (from the German), 1900. Contbr. in organic chemistry, cereal chemistry, etc. Home: 5527 University Av., Chicago IL‡

DUNLAP, ORRIN ELMER, JR., radio exec., author; b. Niagara Falls, N.Y., Aug. 23, 1896; s. Orrin E. and Agnes Catherine (Stevenson) D.; B.S., Colgate U., 1920; student Harvard Grad. Sch. of Business Adminstrn., 1920-21; m. Louise M. Leggett, Aug. 2, 1924. Began as wireless operator on S.S. Octorora, 1917; with Hanff-Metzger Advertising Agency, 1921 to 1922; radio editor N.Y. Times, 1922-40; with RCA, 1940-61, v.p., chmn. advt. and publicity com., mem. edn. com.; dir. RCA Insts., Inc. Served as radio operator U.S.N., World War I; grad. U.S. Naval Radio Sch., Gt. Lakes Training Camp, and U.S. Naval Radio Sch., Harvard U.; operated Navy Radio Sta., Bar Harbor, Me. Mem. I.E.E.E. (life), Vet. Wireless Operator's Assn. (life mem.); mem. Armed Forces Communication Assn., Nat. Assn. Sci. Writers, Newcomen Soc., Sigma Nu. Republican. Club: Harvard. Author: Dunlap's Radio Manual, 1924; The Story of Radio, 1927; Advertising by Radio, 1929; Radio in Advertising, 1931; The Outlook for Television, 1932; Talking on the Radio, 1936; Marconi—his Life and his Wireless, 1937; The Future of Television, 1942; Radio's 100 Men of Science, 1944; Radar—What Radar Is and How It Works, 1946; Understanding Television, 1948; Dunlap's Radio and Television Almanac, 1951; Communications in Space, 1962. Corresponding editor in charge radio, Scientific Am., 1925-28, also Boy's Life, 1926-33. Home: Great Neck NY Died Feb. 1, 1970; buried Niagara Falls NY

DUNLAP, ROBERT HENRY, lawyer; b. Kankakee, Ill., Nov. 29, 1896; s. Hiram J. and Elizabeth (Frith) D.; Ph.B., U. Chgo., 1917; LL.B., Harvard, 1922; m. Dorothy Miller, Sept. 17, 1921; children—Elizabeth H. (Mrs. U. Grant Buchanan III), Robert B. Admitted to Cal. bar, 1927; mem. firm Dunlap, Holmes, Ross & Woodson, 1947-62; counsel to Holmes, Ross, Woodson, Millard & Ryburn, attys., Pasadena, 1962-69. Sec., dir. Hastings Found. Served from pvt. to 1st lt., U.S. Army, 1917-19. Mem. State Bar Cal., Los Angeles County (dir. 1947-49), Pasadena (pres. 1943) bar assns., Chancery Club. Episcopalian. Clubs: Annandale Golf (dir., v.p. 1949-51) (Pasadena). Home: Pasadena CA Died Jan. 31, 1969.

DUNLAP, ROY JOHN, JR., editor; b. St. Paul, Minnesota, July 18, 1918; s. Roy John and Lulu Marie (Trunkee) D.; student U. Minn., 1937-39; m. Frances Lillico, June 4, 1942; children—Michele Ann (Mrs. Joseph Grantham), Roy John II, Patricia Lynn (Mrs. James C. Shaffer), William Pierce, Dana Kathryn, Elizabeth. Mem. staff St. Paul Pioneer Dispatch, 1938-68, author column, Paul Light, 1951-62, mng. editor, 1962-68; exec. editor publ. services Webb Pub. Co., St. Paul, 1968-70, exec. editor, 1970-72; editor TWA Ambassador mags., 1968-72; lectr., 1950-72; cinematographer, 1947-72. Mem. aviation com. St. Paul area C. of C., 1954-72. Bd. dirs. St. Paul Rehab. Center, St. Paul Indianhead council Boy Scouts Am., St. Paul Winter Carnival Assn., 1970. Served with AUS, 1942-45; PTO. Named Outstanding Aviator, Minn. Aviation Assn., 1962; recipient merit citation Gavel Club, St. Paul, 1970. Presbyn. Clubs: Kiwanis (pres. 1969, dir.), St. Paul Athletic (dir.). Home: St Paul MN Died Sept. 27, 1972; buried Acacia Park Cemetery, Mendota, St Paul MN

DUNLAVY, EDWIN WESLEY, clergyman, educator; b. near Greencastle, Indiana, June 25, 1874; s. Howard Houston and Hannah Elizabeth (Oliver) Dunlavy; A.B., DePauw University, 1900, D.D., from same univ., 1920; state and interstate orator of Western colleges, 1900; spl. research work in sociology. Chicago Training Sch.; student Boston U. Sch. of Theology 2 yrs., spl. work in science, Mass. Inst. Tech. during same period; m. Edna Augustine, June 15, 1905 (died Oct. 27, 1942). Associated with Men and Religion Movement in the Colleges. Licensed Methodist Episcopal ministry, 1897; pastor Trinity Church, Crawfordsville, Ind., 1903-06, 1st Ch., Danville, 1906-09, 1st Ch., Terre Haute, 1909-11, Trinity Ch., Lafayette, 1911-16, 1st Ch., Frankfort, 1916-21—all in Ind.; pres. Iliff Sch. of Theology, Denver, 1921-24; pastor Roberts Park Ch., Indianapolis, known as Mother of Churches," 1924-30, Woodlawn Park Ch., Chicago, 1930-33; on sabbatical leave of absence, 1933; pastor 1st Ch., Freeport, Ill., 1934-37; resigned to devote time to writing and lecturing. Lecturer ednl. and hist. subjects; special writer various papers. Mem. Sigma Nu (editor quarterly 5 yrs.; nat. exec. sec. 5 yrs.) S.A.R. Mason (K.T., 32deg). Clubs: Knife and Fork, South Bend, Lions. Home: New Carlisle IN‡

DUNN, BALLARD, editor, pub.; b. Indianapolis, Sept. 16, 1877; s. William and Amy (Talbot) D.; prep. edn. high sch., St. Louis, Mo.; LL.B., St. Louis Law Sch. (Washington U.), 1898; m. Eleanor Reese, of Chicago, July 27, 1907. Began on St. Louis Chronicle, 1899; with The Gazette, Colorado Springs, Colo., 1900-01; with Chicago Inter-Ocean, Daily News, later city editor Daily Evening Journal, until 1912; pres. Cook County (Ill.) Civil Service Commn., 1912; western sales mgr. Thos. Cusack Co., 1913; pres. Posterette Corpn., 1914-15; in charge pub. relations, U.P.R.R., 1916-18; chief of Bur. for Suggestions and Complaints, U.S.S.R. Administration, Washington, D.C., 1918-19; asst. chief Ins. Div. Bur. War Risk Ins., 1919; in charge group ins. service, Equitable Life Assurance Soc., 1920-24; editor in chief Omaha Bee-News, 1924-29; became editor and pub. Omaha Journal, 1930; then editor and publisher The Keynoter. Served as private Co. B. 1st Mo. Vols., 1898. Republican. Christian Scientist. Mason. Office: Chamber of Commerce Bldg., Los Angeles CA‡

DUNN, BEVERLY CHARLES, army officer; b. Fort Monroe, Va., July 16, 1888; s. Beverly Wyly and Stella (Kilshaw) D.; B.A., U.S. Military Acad., 1910, Engr. Sch., U.S. Army, 1911-12, Army Indsl. Coll., 1927-28, Army War Coll., 1937-38; m. Helen Ward Fay, Nov. 22, 1916; children—Beverly Charles, William Wyly. Commd. 2d lt., engring. corps, 1910 and advanced through grades to brig. gen.; served with engr. installations doing flood control and river and harbor improvement work at Rock Island, Illinois, Memphis, Tenn., Pittsburgh, Pa., New Orleans, La., 1st N.Y. District, Seattle, Wash., Jacksonville, Fla. (intercoastal canal from Jacksonville to Miami); Isthmian Canal Commn. in Panama, supt. 13th Lighthouse District; military aide to the President; chief of finance div., Office Chief of Engrs.; dir., procurement branch, office of Asst. Sec. War, mem. Budget Adv. Bd.; troop duty with 1st battalion engrs., Washington Barracks, Washington, D.C., 3rd engrs., Philippines, 10th engrs. (forestry), Washington, D.C., 5th engrs. training regiment and 33d engrs., Ft. Hunphreys, Va., 209th engrs. Camp Sheridan, Ala., 28th engr. regiment (aviation), Marsh Field, Calif., commd. 6th engrs., Ft. Lawton, Wash.; chief engr. Supreme Hdqrs., Allied Expeditionary Force. Decorated D.S.M. with oak leaf cluster; comdr. Order Brit. Empire; Croix de Guerre, Legion d'Honneur (France and Belgium. Mem. Soc. Am. Military Engrs., Am. Soc. Civil Engrs. Clubs: Army and Navy, Chevy Chase (Washington, D.C.); University (N.Y.C.), N.Y. Athletic. Home: New York City NY Died Aug. 14, 1970; buried U.S. Mil. Academy, West Point NY

DUNN, HARRY THATCHER, mfr.; b. Gardner, Mass., May 10, 1875; s. Thatcher B. and Mary (Dickerman) D.; ed. high sch., Gardner, and Cushing Acad., Ashburnham, Mass.; m. Daisy McCoy, V.p. Willys Overland Co., Toledo, O., 1915-17; pres. Fisk Rubber Co. and Federal Rubber Co., 1917-32; partner J. R. Timmins & Co. Chief of rubber sect. War Industries Bd., Washington, D.C., World War. Republican. Protestant: Club: Creek. Home: Glen Cove, L.I., N.Y. Office: Broadway, New York NY*‡

DUNN, HENRY WESLEY, dean law sch.; b. Waterville, Me., Jan. 27, 1877; s. Reuben Wesley and Sarah Martha (Baker) D.; grad. Coburn Classical Inst., Waterville, 1892; A.B., Colby Coll., 1896; L.L.B., Harvard, 1902; m. Nelly Agnes Houghton, of Auburn, Me., Apr. 19, 1906. Principal Monson Acad., Me., 1896-7; sub-master Worcester Classical High Sch., Mass., 1897-8, Hotchkiss Sch., Conn., 1898-9; practiced law in Boston, 1902-12; dean Coll. of Law, State U. of Ia., Sept., 1912-—. Trustee Coburn Classical Inst., 1910-13. Republican. Member Am. Bar Assn., Ia. State Bar Assn., Am. Judicature Soc. (council), Am. Acad. Polit. and Social Science, Phi Beta Kappa (Colby), Zeta Psi, Phi Delta Phi. Home: 226 S. Johnson St., Iowa City IA‡

DUNN, WALDO HILARY, educator; b. Rutland, O., Oct. 4, 1882; s. Arthur Marion and Isabel (Fowler) D.; B.A., Yale, 1906, M.A., 1909; traveled and studied in Great Britain, 1905, 1914-16, 1925; Litt. D., U. Glasgow, 1916; LL.D., Coll. of Wooster, 1950; m. Fern D. Greenwald, June 11, 1907; children—Dorothy, Lorna, Arthur, Mary. Teacher, pub. schs. of Ohio, 1900-02; prof. English, Davis and Elkins Coll., W.Va., 1906-07; asst. prof. English Coll. of Wooster, 1907-13; prof. rhetoric and English composition, 1913-16, prof. English, head of dept., 1916-34, acting dean, 1924-25; prof. English, Scripps Coll., Claremont, Cal., 1934-52, acting pres., 1940; vis. prof. English, Grad. Sch. Western Reserve U., 1930-31, Scripps Coll., 1931-32. Named life pres. Richard Doddridge Blackmore Soc. London, 1969. Republican. Presbyn. Life mem. Modern Lang. Assn. America, English Assn. Gt. Britain, Facsimilie Text Soc., Conf. British Studies. Club: Rowfant Club (honorary life membership) (Cleveland, Ohio). Author: English Biography, 1916; Life of Donald G. Mitchell (Ik Marvel), 1922; Froude and Carlyle, 1930; Three Eminent Victorians, 1932; George Washington (with N.W. Stephenson), 1940; R.D. Blackmore, 1956; (with Ivor L.M. Richardson) Sir Robert Stout, 1961; James Anthony Froude, vol. 1, 1961, vol. 2, 1963. Editor: (with James Holly Hanford) Milton's De Doctrina Christiana, 1933-34; (with H.F. Lowry and Karl Young) Matthew Arnold's Note-Books, 1952; Carlyle's Last Letters to J.A. Froude, 1956. Lecturer; writer. Editor Wooster Quarterly (now Wooster Alumni Bulletin). 1907-21. Made tour of World, 1932-33 by way of New Zealand, Australia, India, Suez Canal and England; engaged in research in Alexander Turnbull Library, Wellington, New Zealand, Sept. 1932-Mar. 1933. Home: Wooster OH Died May 5, 1969; cremated.

DUNN, WILLIAM FRANK, newspaper man; b. Sedalia, Mo., June 30, 1872; s. Joseph P. and Fannie Helen (Mathis) D.; ed. pub. schs.; m. Mabelle V. Hutchings, of St. Louis, Mo., June 28, 1897; children—Alice Frances (Mrs. Maxwell R. Hott), Mabel Helen (Mrs. Harold E. Peterson). In newspaper business at Sedalia; with St. Louis Chronicle, also Post-Dispatch, 1893-97; moved to Chicago, Jan. 1897, and has since been identified with the Chicago Daily Journal except for 7 yrs. with another Chicago paper; vice pres. Chicago Daily Journal Co., 1910-25. then pres. and publisher, now retired. Democrat. Presbyn. Clubs: Chicago Athletic Assn., Chicago Yacht, Oak Park Country. Home: 643 N. East Av., Oak Park IL‡

DUNNING, HARRY WESTBROOK, author; b. Boston, Dec. 7, 1871; s. Albert Elijah (q.v.) and Harriet W. (Westbrook) D.; B.A., Yale, 1894, Ph.D., 1897; m. Mary Bates Parker, of Everett, Mass., Sept. 23, 1908. Instr. Oriental langs., Yale, 1896-9; mgr. foreign tours, since 1899. Mem. Am. Oriental Soc., Nat. Geog. Soc., Arctic Club. Clubs: Yale (Boston and New York), City (Boston). Authors' (London). Author: To-day on the Nile, 1905; To-day in Palestine, 1907. Translator (from the Arabic): Life of Muhammad, 1894. Home: Brookline, Mass. Office: 14 Beacon St., Boston MA‡

DUNNING, JAMES EDMUND, banker; b. Bangor, Me., Oct. 2, 1873; s. William Henry and Harriet (Pearson) D.; m. Isabel Backus, of Rochester, N.Y., Jan. 28, 1904. Newspaper editor and proprietor in Maine to 1905; consul at Milan, Italy, 1905-09; promoted to Havre, France, 1909-12; promoted consul-gen.-at-large with supervision over dist. of Europe, 1912-14; continental rep. of Nat. City Bank of New York since Mar. 1914, European rep. since Jan. 1916. Commd. temporary capt. U.S.R., Aug. 13, 1917; promoted maj., Nov. 5, 1917; apptd. purchasing agt. in Eng. for A.E.F., Sept. 24, 1917; promoted lt. col. but resigned commn. Mar. 15, 1919. Awarded D.S.O., 1919. Represented U.S. at sessions of Permanent Committee Internat. Congress of Chambers of Commerce, Brussels, 1909, London, 1910, at Congress of Navigation, Phila., 1912; apptd. 1909, second Am. mem. of Perm. Com. of Internat. Chambers of Commerce, Dir. U.S. Trust Corpn., Ltd., Enamelled Metal Products Corpn. Ltd. Clubs: St. James's, Carlton, Royal Societies, Gresham, Devonshire, Ranelagh, Sunningdale. Author: The Vital Decade of Our Commercial History, 1911; American Securities in Europe, 1911. Address: 34 Nicholas Lane, Lombard St., London England‡

DUNNING, JOHN SULLIVAN, newspaper man; b. Lowville, N.Y., Aug. 15, 1869; s. Henry P. and Mary (Sullivan) D.; ed. pub. sch. and Lowville (N.Y.) Acad.; learned printer's trade; m. San Francisco, Sept. 21, 1905, Mary C. Johnston. Worked on various newspapers; sp'l writer on labor, unionism and industrial economics; connected with W.R. Hearst's newspapers since 1890; Washington corr. same since 1902. Residence: San Francisco. Office: Hearst Bureau, Washington‡

DUNNING, MORTON DEXTER, missionary; b. Boston, Mass., Dec. 14, 1872; s. Albert Elijah and Harriet (Wood) Westbrook D.; A.B., cum laude, Amherst, 1896, A.M., 1905; grad. Hartford Theol. Sem., 1899; m. Mary Kingsbury Ward, of Newton Centre, Mass., July 26, 1899. Ordained Congl. ministry, 1899; pastor Forest Grove, Ore., 1899-01; prof. English, Doshisha Acad., Kyoto, Japan, 1902-—. Instr. English, Imperial U., Kyoto, Japan, 1909-10; editor Mission News, 1906-8; treas. Japan Mission, A.B.C.F.M., 1910-15; trustee and treas. Kobe Girls' Coll. Mem. Japan Peace Soc., Asiatic Society of Japan (life), Psi Upsilon. Address: Doshisha Univ., Kyoto Japan‡

DUNNING, PHILIP, playwright producer; b. Meriden, Conn., Dec. 11, 1892; s. John Michael and Mary Ellen (Hart) D.; student pub. and high schs., Meriden, Conn.; m. Frances Elizabeth Fox, Apr. 26, 1919; 1dau., Virginia Fox. Screenwriter for 20th Century-Fox Film Corp., 1948. Served in U.S. Navy, 1917-19. Mem. Dramatists Guild Authors' League Am., Actors Equity Assn., Screen Writers Guild; mem. panel of Am. Arbitration Assn. Roman Catholic. Clubs: Dutch Treat, Artists and Writers Golf. Author (plays): Dollar Bill, 1915; Faint Heart, 1919; Broadway (with George Abbott), 1926; The Understudy (with Jack Donohue), 1927; Night Hostess, 1927; Sweet Land of Liberty, 1929; Lily Turner, 1931; Happy Homes, 1938; Palm Beach (with N. C. Hunter), 1938. Co-producer of 20th Century" (1932), The Drums Begin" (1933), Heat Lightening" (1933), Kill that Story" (1933); co-author and co-producer of Page Miss Glory" (1934); co-author and producer of Remember the Day" (1935); producer of Schoolhouse on the Lot," 1938. Address: Westport CT Died July 20, 1969.

DUNNING, ROBERT M(ACKENZIE), business exec.; b. Boston, Mass., Apr. 24, 1900; s. Henry and Maud (Mackenzie) D.; student Boston (Mass.) Pub. Latin Sch., 1912-16; A.B., Harvard, 1920; m. Phyllis Kraft, July 3, 1924 (div. Nov. 1936); 1 dau., Patricia Currier (Mrs. Richard Bushnell Spear); m. 2d, K. Jean Henry, Dec. 2, 1939; 1 dau., Deborah Roberts Dunning. With export dept. Carpenter Morton Co., Boston, 1920-23; asst. advt. mgr. U.S. Rubber Export Co., Ltd., New York, 1923-26; asst. export mgr. Richardson Merrell, Inc. (formerly Vick Chem. Co.), N.Y.C., 1926-35, export mgr., 1935-40, v.p., 1940-57, sr. v.p., 1957-63, bd. dirs. 1943-69, chmn. drug industry export com. from 1943; adv. com. export-import sect. of O.P.A., 1943-45, drug and chem. sect. bd. econ. warfare, 1945-46. Mem. Proprietary Assn. (chmn. fgn. trade sect. 1942-48). Club: Export Managers of New York (dir. 1941-44, 2d v.p. 1944). Home: Hillsdale NY Died May 28, 1969.

DUNNINGTON, WALTER GREY, lawyer; b. Farmville, Va., Dec. 15, 1891; s. Walter Grey and India W. (Knight) D.; B.A., Hampden Sydney Coll., 1911; B.L., U. Va., 1914; married Alice Bennett. Admitted to New York bar, 1916; counsel Dunnington, Bartholow & Miller, N.Y.C. Served as 2d lt., 10th F.A. AUS, 1917-19. Awarded Distinguished Service Cross, 1918. Trustee Seth Sprague Found., Max C. Fleischmann Found. of Nev. Clubs: Church, Southampton, Brook, Links, Racquet, National Golf Links of Am., River. Home: New York City NY Died May 1971.

DUNSMORE, PHILO CORDON, supt. schs.; b. nr. Milan, Mich., Dec. 14, 1895; s. Hiram Burley and Melvina (Townsend) D.; B.A., Eastern Mich. Coll. Edn., 1921; M.A., U. Toledo, 1923; m. Clara Mabel Polsdorfer, Dec. 28, 1917; children—Philo H., Lois Jean (Mrs. John Myer). Tchr. history, Toledo, O., 1919-23; part-time tchr. social studies, in charge jr. and sr. boys Woodward High Sch., Toledo, 1923-24; supr. social studies, Toledo, 1933-44, asst. supt. schs., edn.,

1945-57, supt. schs., from 1958. Asso. Council Social Agys.; ofcl. bd. Toledo Zool. Soc., Boy Scouts Am., Boys Club of Toledo. Mem. Am., Ohio assns. sch. adminstrs., N.E.A., Nat. Soc. Study Edn., Ohio Edn. Assn., Nat. Council Social Studies, Phi Delta Kappa. Conglist. (ofcl. bd.). Home: Toledo OH Died May 29, 1967.

DUNSTAN, ARTHUR ST. CHARLES, educator; b. Fredricksburg, Va., Mar. 25, 1871; s. John H. and Medora L. (Hall) D.; B.S., Ala. Poly. Inst., 1889, E.M., 1890, C.E., 1892; grad. work Johns Hopkins, 1891-92, U. of Chicago, 1898-99; m. Loula Persons, Sept. 8, 1897; 1 son, Arthur Mell. Asso. prof. elec. engring. U. of Kan., 1894-99; head prof. elec. engring. Ala. Poly. Inst. since 1899. Mem. Tau Beta Pi, Eta Kappa Nu, Phi Kappa Phi. Home: 117 N. Gay St., Auburn AL‡

DUNSTAN, EDMUND FLEETWOOD, banker; b. Elizabeth City, N.C., June 25, 1896; s. William Edward and Emma (Sawyer) D.; A.B., Duke U., 1919; m. Anita Buckley, 1920; 1 son, Edmund F. With Bankers Trust Co., N.Y.C., 1921-61, v.p., 1939-61; dir. marketing Internat. Bank for Reconstruction and Devel., 1947-48; dir. Gen. Security Assurance Corp. of N.Y., Paribas Corp. U.S. rep. Boy Scouts World Bureau. Member Investment Bankers Assn. Am. (chmn. municipal securities com., 1932-34, mem. bd. governors, 1934-36). Chmn. N.Y. City Draft Bd. No. 48, 1940-41, asst. dir. banking and investment div. N.Y. State War Finance Com., 1943. Served as 1st lt. U.S. Army, 1917-19. Mem. Sigma Chi. Episcopalian. Clubs: N.Y. Municipal Bond (pres., 1936-37), Bond (N.Y.C.). Home: New York City NY Died Apr. 21, 1969; buried Elizabeth City NC

DUPEE, JOHN, broker; b. Bangor, Me.; s. John and Eleanor Winslow (Pratt) D.; grad. Park Latin Sch., Boston; m. Evelyn M. Walker. Employed in wholesale grocery house; in 1883 joined Charles Schwartz in organizing firm of Schwartz & Dupee, grain and stock brokers, of which, since 1893, he has been senior partner. Clubs: Chicago, Chicago Athletic, Washington Park. Office: 2 Board of Trade, Chicago‡

DU PONT, ALFRED RHETT, investment banker, broker; b. Wilmington, Del., Dec. 10, 1907; s. Francis Irenee and Marianna (Rhett) Du P.; grad. St. George's Sch., 1926; grad. U. Pa., 1931; grad. student Va. Law Sch., 1932-33; m. Gertrude Murrell, May 4, 1935 (div. 1962); children—Alfred Rhett, Thomas Murrell, Francis Irenee; m. 2d, Dea Johnston, June 1962; 1 adopted son, Peter James Kipp. Partner Francis I. Du Pont & Co. since 1934; mem. N.Y., Midwest stock exchanges, Chicago Bd. Trade. Trustee U. Pa. Mem. Phi Kappa Sigma. Clubs: Luncheon, Union of N.Y. Home: Sullivan's Island SC Died Jan. 1972.

DUPONT, HENRY B., business executive; born at Wilmington, Delaware, July 23, 1898; the son of Henry Behn and Eleuthera (Bradford) DuP.; student Yale U., 1916-20, Mass. Inst. Tech., 1920-23; m. Margaret Wilson Lewis, Oct. 24, 1928 (div. 1948); children—Margaret, Henry, Edward; m. 2d, Emily duPont Smith, Feb. 24, 1949. In engring. dept. Gen. Motors Corp., 1924-27; with E. I. duPont de Nemours & Co., 1927-70, vice president, 1939-63, member finance committee, 1963-70, also dir.; pres., dir. Christiana Securities Co.; trustee Eleutherian Mills; member board directors North Am. Aviation Corp., Wilmington Trust Co., Winterthur Corp. Pres. Longwood Found.; trustee Hagley Found., Episcopal Church School Foundation, Pomfret School, Pomfret, Connecticut, also University of Delaware, Newark. Clubs: Yale, University, N.Y. Yacht (N.Y.C.); Wilmington, Wilmington Country. Home: Greenville DE Died Apr. 13, 1970.

DUPONT, HENRY FRANCIS, chem. exec.; b. Winterthur, Del., May 27, 1880; s. Henry Algernon and Mary Pauline (Foster) du P.; grad. Groton Sch., 1899; A.B., Harvard, 1903; m. Ruth Wales, June 24, 1916; children—Pauline Louise (Mrs. Alfred C. Harrison), Ruth Ellen (Mrs. George deForest Lord, Jr.). Dir. E.I. du Pont de Nemours & Co., Wilmington, Del., 1915-69, mem. finance com., 1916-43, bonus com., 1944-58; dir. Wilmington Trust Company, 1919-69, Gen. Motors Corp., 1918-44, mem. finance com., 1918-37; owner Winterthur Farms. Founder Henry Francis du Pont Winterthur Mus., 1951; life trustee U. Del.; mem. bd. mgrs. N.Y. Bot. Garden; mem. mus. com. Phila. Mus. Art, Whitney Mus., N.Y.C., Pacific Tropical Botanical Garden (mem. bd. trustees). Mem. Horticultural Soc. N.Y. (dir. 1929, v.p. 1934, since 47, pres. 1935-46), Nat. Trust Hist. Preservation, Hist. Soc. Del. (v.p.), Cooper Union Advancement Sci. and Art (bd. dirs.). Home: Winterthur DE Died Apr. 11, 1969; buried Du Pont de Nemours Cemetery.

DUPONT, IRENEE, corporation executive; born near Wilmington, Del., Dec. 21, 1876; s. Lammot and Mary (Belin) du P.; B.S. in Chem. Engring. Mass Inst. Tech., 1897, M.S., 1898; m. Irene Sophie du Pont, Feb. 1900; children—Irene Sophie (Mrs. Ernest N. May), Margaretta L. (Mrs. Crawford H. Greenewalt), Constance S. (Mrs. Colgate W. Darden, Jr.), Eleanor F. (Mrs. Philip G. Rust), Doris Elise (dec. 1930), Mariana (Mrs. Henry H. Silliman), Octavia M. (Mrs. John Bruce Bredin), Lucile E. (Mrs. Robert R. Flint), Irenee. Pres. E.I. du Pont de Nemours & Co., 1919-26, vice chmn. bd. 1926-40, dir., hon. chmn. bd., 1954—. Home: Granogue, Del. Office: DuPont Bldg., Wilmington DE‡

DUPONT, JESSIE BALL (MRS. ALFRED IRENEE DUPONT), business exec., b. Hardings, Va.; d. Thomas and Lalla (Gresham) Ball; student Wytheville (Va.) Sem., and Longwood Coll., Farmville, Va.; D.C.L., U. of South, 1945; L.H.D., Washington and Lee U., 1947, Centre Coll. Ky., 1954; H.H.D., Stetson U., 1952; LL.D., Rollins College, 1953, University of Delaware, 1954, College of William and Mary, 1954; D.H.L. (honorary), Hollins (Va.) College, 1959; married Alfred Irenee duPont, Jan. 22, 1921 (died Apr. 29, 1935). Dir. Fla. Nat. Bank, Jacksonville; chmn. bd. St. Joe Paper Co., Jacksonville; pres. Nemours Found.; v.p. Alfred I. duPont Found.; pres. Alfred I. duPont Radio Awards Found.; former treas. R.E. Lee Memorial Found., Inc.; trustee Estate of Alfred I. duPont; vice pres. Va. Museum of Fine Arts. Mem. D.A.R., Soc. Colonial Dames. Clubs: Florida Yacht, Timuquana (Jacksonville); Wilmington (Del.) Country; Year Round (Miami, Fla.); N.Y. Yacht; Cedar Creek, Inc. (Locust Valley, N.Y.); Ponte Vedra (Jacksonville Beach, Fla.); Sulgrave (Washington); Mt. Vernon (Baltimore). Home: Jacksonville FL Died Sept. 26, 1970.

DUPRE, MARCEL, organist, composer; b. Rouen, France, May 3, 1886; ed. Nat. Conservatoire de Musique, Paris. Made 1st pub. appearance at Elbeuf Ch., 1894; became organist Ch. of St. Vivien, Rouen, 1898 (aged 12); temporary organist Notre Dame, 1916-20; asst. at St. Sulpice, Paris, 1920, organist, 1934-71; prof. organ and improvisation Nat. Conservatoire, 1926-54, dir. conservatoire, 1954-56; became gen. dir. Am. Conservatory in Fontainbleau, 1947; tours of Eng., from 1920, U.S., from 1922, world tour, 1939. Recipient Grand Prix de Rome, 1914; decorated Legion d'Honneur; hon. dr. Pontifical Inst. Rome. Composer works including 2 organ symphonies, many other organ works, 2 symphonies and concerto for organ and orch., works for piano and organ, De Profundis for Voices, organ and orch. Author: Traite d'improvisation a l'orgue, 1925; Methode d'orgue. Address: Meudon (Seine-et-Oise) France Died 1971.*

DUPUIS, RAYMOND, lawyer, business exec.; b. Montreal, Can., Aug. 2, 1907; s. Albert (K.S.G.) and Henriette (Beullac) D.; student Mont-Saint-Louis Coll., Montreal, 1917-24; U. Montreal, 1927-30; LL.D. (honorary), 1959; m. Helene Saint-Pierre, Apr. 24, 1937 (deceased 1961); children—Albert, Claire, Nicole; m. second. Francoise Demezieres, 1962. Read law with Godin, Dussault & Cadotte, Montreal, 1927-30; called to Bar of Prov. of Que. 1930, created K.C., 1945; elected dir. Dupuis Freres, Ltd., department store mail order house, Montreal, 1933, asst. sec.-treas., 1937-42, sec., 1942, treas., 1943-45, 2d v.p., 1945, president and managing director, 1945-61; dir. The Royal Bank of Canada, Domtar Co. Ltd., Burns Foods, Ltd., The Canada Life Ins. Co., Globe Indemnity Co. of Canada, Hudson Bay Ins. Co., Cie d'Assurance du Quebec, Western Assurance Co., Brit. Am. Assurance Co.; Canadian adv. bd. Royal Ins. Co., Ltd., Liverpool & London & Globe Ins. Co. Ltd. Mem. Sales Tax Com., 1955. Bd. of Research Traffic and Transportation Problem, City of Montreal. Past pres. District of Montreal C. of Co., Canadian C. of C.; mem. Montreal Bd. of Trade, Dollar Sterling Trade Adv. Council (Canadian sect.), Centre d'Etudes du Commerce de Paris. Past pres., member exec. com. of Federation of French Catholic Charities; director Canadian Welfare Council; P.Q. Society for Crippled Children; gov. Soc. des Concerts Symphoniques de Montreal, The Canadian Mental Health Assn., Notre Dame and Ste Justine hosps. Mem. French C. of C. in Canada (past v.p.). Roman Catholic. Clubs: Laval-sur-le-Lac, St. Denis, Cercle Universitaire de Montreal, Montreal Badminton and Squash, also Mount Royal, Palestre Nationale, Mount Bruno Country, Montreal, Canadian. Home: St Hilaire Quebec Canada Died 1972.

DUPUY, PIERRE, govt. ofcl.; b. Montreal, Que., Can., July 9, 1896; s. Louis and Anna (Brien) D.; B.A., St. Mary's Coll., Montreal, 1917; LL.L., U. Montreal, 1920; L.Litt., U. Paris, 1933; LL.D. (hon.), Laval U., Quebec, 1960, U. Sherbrooke, 1966, Sir. Geo. Williams U., 1967; m. Therese Ferron, June 8, 1921; children—Jacqueline, Michel. Sec. to commr. gen. Dept. External Affairs, Paris, 1922-28; 2d sec. Canadian Legation, Paris, 1928-40; charge d'affairs to Belgian and Netherlands Govts., London, 1940, French Govt. Vichy, 1940-43, Norwegian, Polish, Belgium, Dutch, Yugoslav, Czechoslovak govts., London, 1943-45; minister, ambassador to Netherlands, 1945-52; ambassador to Italy, 1952-58; ambassador to France, 1958-63; commr. gen. Expo 67, Montreal, 1963-67; spl. missions between London and Vichy, 1940-42, mission to French N.Africa and Dakar, 1943. Decorated companion Order St. Michael and St. George. Author: Andre Laurence, 1927. Home: Montreal Que Canada Died May 21, 1969.

DUQUE, HENRY O'MELVENY, lawyer; b. Los Angeles, July 4, 1904; s. Thomas L. and Elita (Galdos) D.; A.B., U. Cal. at Berkeley, 1927; LL.B., Harvard, 1931; m. Elizabeth McArthur, July 24, 1929; children—Henry M., Elizabeth (Mrs. Richard Anson Hotaling), Mary Delia. Admitted to Cal. bar, 1932, since practiced in Los Angeles; sr. partner Adams, Duque & Hazeltine, 1946-71. Dir. Union Bank, Sequoia Forest Industries, Inc., Charles Luckman Associates. President Board Police Commrs. City of Los Angeles, 1945-51; pres., chmn. Greater Los Angeles Plans, Inc., 1946-71; dir., sec. Civic Auditorium and Music Center Assn. of Los Angeles, 1955-58; pres., chmn. L.A., Civic Light Opera Assn., 1944-47; pres. So. Cal. Symphony Assn., 1945-55, chmn. bd., 1955-62; dir. San Francisco Opera Assn., 1955-71. Dir. No. Cal. sector U.S. Office Civilian Def., San Francisco, 1942-44. Trustee Harvey Mudd Coll. Mem. Am., Los Angeles bar assns., State Bar of Cal., C. of C. (dir. 1953-56). Clubs: California, Bohemian (San Francisco); The Links (N.Y.C.). Home: Los Angeles CA Died May 3, 1971.

DURAND, DAVID, mem. research staff Nat. Bureau of Econ. Research. Address: 1819 Broadway, NY City 23*‡

DURAND, E(DWARD) DANA, statistician; b. Romeo, Mich., Oct. 18, 1871; s. Cyrus Y. and Celia (Day) D.; A.B., Oberlin, 1893; Ph.D., Cornell, 1896; m. Mary Elizabeth Bennett, July 15, 1903; children—Dana Bennett, Bennett, Mary Cecelia, Eric. Legislative librarian N.Y. State Library, 1895-97; asst. prof. adminstrn. and finance, Leland Stanford Jr. U., 1898-99; sec. U.S. Industrial Commn., 1900-02; instr. economics, Harvard, 1902; spl. expert agt. U.S. Census Office on street rys. and elec. light plants, 1902; spl. examiner Bur. of Corps., 1903-07; deputy commr. of corps., 1907-09; dir. of the U.S. Census, 1909-13; prof. statistics agrl. economics Univ. of Minn., Sept. 1913-17; employed by U.S. Food Adminstrn., chiefly in Europe, 1917-19; adviser to food minister of Poland, 1919-21; chief Eastern European Div. U.S. Bur. Foreign and Domestic Commerce, 1921; chief of Div. of Statis. Research, Dept. of Commerce, 1924-29; statis. asst. to U.S. sec. commerce, 1929; chief economist U.S. Tariff Commn., 1930-35, mem. of commn. since Dec. 1935. Mem. Com. of Experts under Internat. Treaty on Econ. Statistics and United States Central Statistics Bd.; mem. joint U.S.-Canada econ. com. Member International Inst. Statistics, Inter-American Inst. Statistics, Am. Econ. Assn., Am. Statis. Assn. Author: Finances of New York City, 1898; The Trust Problem, 1915; Industry and Commerce of the United States, 1930. Contbr. on econ. and polit. subjects. Home: 3613 Norton Pl., Washington DC‡

DURAND, G(EORGE) HARRISON, prof. English; b. Romeo, Mich., Dec. 31, 1868; s. Cyrus Yale and Celia (Day) D.; student Yankton (S.D.) Coll., 1885-87; Ph.B., Oberlin (Ohio) Coll., 1898; A.B., Harvard, 1899, A.M., 1901; grad. study univs. of Munich and Oxford, 1908-09; Litt.D., Yankton Coll., 1927; m. Lillian Mabel Fisher, June 26, 1901; 1 son, Harrison Fisher. Instr. English, Oberlin Coll., 1899-1900, asso. prof., 1911-12; prof. English, Yankton Coll., 1901-11, v.p. and head dept. of English, 1912-45, prof. emeritus since 1945. Trustee Yankton Carnegie Library, 1907-43. Mem. Modern Lang. Assn., Am. Assn. University Profs., Phi Beta Kappa. Conglist. Mason. Author: Joseph Ward of Dakota, 1913. Co-author: (with Joseph Mills Hanson) Pageant of Dakotaland (produced at Garden Terrace Theater), 1936. Originator Garden Terrace Theater, Yankton Coll., 1914. Condr. European travel parties, summers, 1923-30. Co-founder and promoter (with Mrs. Lillian M. Durand) since 1909 of Yankton Coll. Art Collection, officially renamed, 1945, Durand Collection of Art. Home: 816 Pine St., Yankton SD‡

DURAND, LOYAL, JR., former educator; b. Milw., July 12, 1902 s. Loyal and Lucia Relf (Kemper) D.; A.B., U. Wis., 1924, A.M., 1925, Ph.D., 1930; m. Dorothy Lillian Lee, Dec. 25, 1929; children—Loyal, Philip, Lee Mcv., Kemper B. Asst., Wis. Geol. Survey, summer 1926; instr. U. Wis., 1928-30, asst. prof., 1930-44; faculty U. Tenn., 1944, prof. geography, 1946-70. Vis. summer prof. Mankato (Minn.) Tchrs. Coll., 1929, Pa. State Coll., 1938, 40, 53, U. Utah, 1943, U. Wis., 1945, U. Colo., 1946, U. Cal. at Los Angeles, 1947, U. Neb., 1948,52, Central Coll. Edn., Ellensburg, Wash., 1950, 60, U. Wash., 1954, U. Ore., 1956, U. Mich., 1957, 61, 66, U. Hawaii, 1957-58, U. Mont., 1959, U. Minn., 1962; land planning cons. Nat. Resources Bd., 1934-35, spl. land planning cons., 1941; research and analysis div. O.S.S., Washington, 1944. Mem. Nat. Acad. Scis. (nat. research council com., adv. to Office Naval Research 1951-54), Am. Assn. U. Profs., Assn. Am. Geographers (v.p. 1951), Nat. Council Geography Tchrs. (exec. bd. 1947, v.p. 1949, pres. 1950), Wis. Acad. Scis., Arts and Letters (sec.-treas., editor 1935-44), Tenn. Acad. Sci., Phi Beta Kappa Assos., Phi Beta Kappa, Sigma Xi, Sigma Chi. Episcopalian. Author books including: World Economic Geography (with George T. Renner, C. Langdon White), 1951; World Geography, 1954; World Geography Today, 1960; Economic Geography, 1961. Geography editor: Macmillan social studies series; contbg. editor Economic Geography, 1947. Contbr. articles to geog. mags. Home: Knoxville TN Died Oct. 14, 1970.

DUREY, JOHN C., lawyer; born Saybrook, O., Oct. 12, 1880; s. Thomas H. and M. Julissa (Jenks) D.; grad. from Geneva (O.) Normal Sch., 1899; LL.B. cum laude, Yale U., 1906; m. Kathryn Talbot St. John, Oct. 20, 1921; children—John C. Forbes, Patricia Talbot (Mrs. Theodore Haviland III), Jane Sheldon (Mrs. Robert A. Skidmore). Admitted to Conn. bar, 1907, practicing at Stamford; associated with John E. Keeler until 1913; mem. Keeler & Durey, 1913-18, Taylor, Durey & Pierson, 1919-28, Durey, Pierson & Comley, 1929-45; mem. firm Durey & Pierson, 1946-—; vice president dir. Citizens Savs. Bank Stamford, hon. dir. Stamford Water Company, State National Bank of Connecticut. Trustee, Stamford Home for Aged (president 1933-47); member senior council and former dir. Stamford Hosp. Fellow of American Bar Foundation; member American, Connecticut State bar assns., Am. Judicature Soc., Corbey Court. Phi Delta Phi. Republican. St. John's P.E. Ch. (hon. warden). Clubs: Woodway Country; Yale (N.Y.C.). Editor, Yale Law Jour., 1904-06. Home: Stamford CT Died Aug. 16, 1969.

DURHAM, HENRY WELLES, civil engr.; b. Chicago, Sept. 15, 1874; s. Caleb Wheeler and Clarissa Safford (Welles) D.; father inventor of Durham system of house drainage now universally employed in large bldgs.; C.E., Sch. of Mines (Columbia), 1895; m. Josephine Belden Trowbridge, Oct. 1, 1903; 1 dau., Elisabeth Trowbridge. Asst. on surveys for N.Y. Rapid Transit Commn. and with U.S. Geol. Survey, 1895-98, Nicaragua Canal Surveys 1898-1900; asst. engr. in charge of constrn., New York Subway, 1900-04; resident engr. in charge of design and constrn. of all municipal improvements in City of Panama for U.S. Isthmian Canal Commn., 1904-07; resident engr. in charge of surveys and constrn. of Cape Cod Canal, 1907-12; chief engr. of highways Manhattan Borough, 1912-15; engineer, Bergeon Co., N.J., 1916. Mem. Co. I, 7th Inf., N.G.N.Y., 1900-17; Mexican border service, 1916; commd. capt., Engr. R.C., 1917; promoted maj., Engrs. U.S. Army, Dec. 10, 1917, assigned command 41st Engrs.; took battn. overseas, Feb. 25, 1918; in charge forestry operations near St. Dizier, France, advance section, A.E.F., till July, then on staff Brig. Gen. Jadwin, Tours, France, in chg. road maintenance in A.E.F. till July 1919; discharged Oct. 17, 1919; in Peru on studies and plans for sanitation of Lima, Cuzco and other cities, 1920-22; designs, etc., N.Y., Mass. and N.C., 1923-24; engaged in sanitation and paving for govt. of Nicaragua, 1925-30; highway studies in Guatemala, 1931-32; municipal improvements in Barranquilla, Colombia, 1933-34; mine valuation in El Salvador, 1935; paving engr., New York World's Fair 1939, 1936-39; building first highway in Paraguay, 1939-42; C.E., research, Mil. Intelligence, Office Chief of Engrs., U.S. Army, 1943-45. Del. to Third Internat. Road Congress, London, 1913; studied European street paving for President McAneny and Mayor Gaynor; mem. Am. Soc. C.E., Boston Soc. C.E., Permanent Internat. Assn. Road Congresses, A.A.A.S., Am. Road Builders Assn., Am. Public Works Assn., Municipal Engrs. of N.Y., Internat. Engring. Congress, San Francisco, 1915, Soc. Am. Mil. Engrs., Reserve Officers' Assn. of U.S. Mil. Order World Wars, New York Soc. Mil. and Naval Officers of World Wars, Sociedad de Ingenieros del Peru; fellow Am. Geog. Soc. Officier du Merite Agricole, Sept. 1919, for work on restoration of French highways; Conspicuous Service Cross, N.Y. State, also 7th Regt. Cross (15 yrs. service). Col., Army of the U.S. Hon. Res. (ret.). Clubs: Columbia University, Beta Theta Pi. Author: Street Paving and Maintenance in European Cities, 1915; various monographs and articles. Home: Halfway House Sandwich MA

DURHAM, HOBART NOBLE, lawyer; b. Hamilton, Kan., Oct. 30, 1901; s. Edward Alvah and Elma Anne (Corning) D.; B.S., Boston U., 1923; grad. student Harvard, 1923-24, Georgetown U. Law Sch., 1925-28; LL.B., Fordham U., 1929; m. Hortense Rhodes, Dec. 28, 1925; children—Dorothy Anne (Mrs. Thomas M. Fraser, Jr.), Hobart Noble. Asst. examiner U.S. Patent Office, 1924-28; admitted to N.Y. bar, 1930; asso. John D. Morgan, N.Y.C., 1926-36; partner firm Morgan, Finnegan, Durham & Pine, N.Y.C., 1936-69. Mem. Am., Internat. bar assns., Internat. Patent and Trade Mark Assn., Am., N.Y. patent law assns., Assn. Bar City N.Y., N.Y. Law Inst. Copyright Soc., Royal Photog. Soc. (asso.), Soc. Photog. Scientists and Engrs. (past pres. N.Y. chpt.). Clubs: Harvard, Bankers (N.Y.C.). Editor, author: World Patent Litigation, 1967. Author numerous articles on graphic arts. Manhasset NY Died Dec. 25, 1969.

DURHAM, JAMES WARE, clergyman, b. Hawertons, Va., Feb. 20, 1875; s. William Franklin and Mary Adeline D.; A.B., Richmond (Va.) Coll., 1900; B.D., U. of Chicago, 1904; m. Janet Stuart Oldershaw, of Chicago, June 29, 1904. Ordained Bapt. ministry, 1902; pastor Pontiac, Ill., 1904-07, Bainbridge St. Ch., Richmond, Va., 1908-12, First Ch., Roanoke, Va., 1913-14, Calvary Ch., Erie, Pa., since Feb. 1, 1915. Dir. Foreign Mission Bd. of Southern Bapt. Conv.; trustee Woman's Coll., Richmond, Va. Address: 524 W. 10th St., Erie PA‡

DURKEE, J(AMES) STANLEY, clergyman, educator; b. Carleton, Yarmouth County, N.S., Nov. 21, 1866; s. James and Elizabeth (Dennis) D.; came to U.S., 1885; A.B., Bates Coll., Lewiston, Me., 1897, A.M., 1905, D.D., 1920; Ph.D., Boston U., 1906; LL.D., Howard Univ., 1926; D.D., Keuka College, Penn Yan, N.Y., 1940; m. Florence Marion Robbins, August 4, 1897; children—Wanda M., Stanley R. Ordained Free Bapt. ministry, 1898; pastor Auburn, Me., 1898-1901, Roxbury, Boston, 1901-09, South Congl. Ch., Brockton, Mass., 1909-18; pres. Howard U., Washington, D.C., 1918-26; pastor of Plymouth Congregational Church (church of Henry Ward Beecher), Brooklyn, N.Y., 1926-41; now retired. Past pres. Sch. of Expression, now named Curry Coll. (Boston); trustee Am. Tract Soc., Seamen's Friend Soc.; ex-pres. Nat. Temperance Soc. Mem. Clergy Club of New York, Sigma Chi, Alpha Kappa Alpha, Delta Sigma Rho, Phi Beta Kappa, Quill Club. Mason (32deg, K.T.). Author: God Translated, 1915; In the Footsteps of a Friend, 1918; In the Meadows of Memory, 1920; Friendly Chats of the Friendly Hour, 1929; The Pull of the Invisible, 1931; Winds Off Shore (poems), 1932; Where Are They Marching?, 1942. Home: 6725 44th Av., University Park MD‡

DURYEA, DAN(IEL) (EDWIN), actor; b. White Plains, N.Y., Jan. 23, 1907; s. Richard Hewlett and Mable (Hoffman) D.; A.B., Cornell U., 1928; m. Helen Edith Bryan, Apr. 15, 1931 (dec. 1967); children—Peter Lane, Richard William. Appeared on stage, N.Y. City, in Dead End, 1934-35; Many Mansions, 1936-37; Missouri Legend, 1938; The Little Foxes, 1939-40; in motion pictures, 1941-68, among the latest are: Chicago Calling, 1951; Thunder Bay, 1952, Battle Hymn, 1956; Night Passage, 1956; Kathy O', 1958; Taggart, 1964; Incident at Phantom Hill, 1965; Flight of the Phoenix, 1965; also has appeared in numerous television roles, including China Smith series, continuing role series Peyton Place; TV guest appearances various shows. Republican. Home: Hollywood CA Died June 7, 1968; buried Forest Lawn Meml. Park.

DUTTON, RICHARD KING, mfg. co. exec.; b. Pitts., June 18, 1919; s. Clarence Benjamin and Lillian Mary (King) D.; B.S. in Bus. Adminstrn., Ind. U., 1941; J.D., Stanford, 1947; m. Juliann Hoover, Mar. 14, 1942; 1 dau., Kathy Elaine. Admitted to Cal. bar, 1947, Ohio bar, 1960; asso., partner firm of Breed, Robinson & Stewart, Oakland, Cal., 1947-55; staff atty., asst. sec., gen. atty. Glidden Co., Cleve., 1955-63, sec., gen. counsel, 1963-67, dir., 1967-72; v.p., gen. counsel Glidden-Durkee div. SCM Corp., 1967-72; asst. sec. SCM Corp., 1967-72. Mem. Citizens League Cleve., Greater Cleve. Growth Bd., Lake Erie Girl Scout Council, Lakewood Little Theater. Served to maj. USMCR, 1941-46. Mem. Am., Cal., Ohio, Cleve. (corp. counsel com.) bar assns., Am. Judicature Soc., Def. Law Inst., Chgo. Bd. Trade, Am. Soc. Corp. Secs., Am. Legal Execs., Ill., Ohio chambers commerce, Am. Mgmt. Assn., Edible Oils Inst., Ohio Corp. Counsel Inst., Nat. Paint, Varnish and Lacquer Assn., Grocer Mfrs. Assn., Beta Gamma Sigma, Phi Alpha Delta. Conglist. Clubs: Ponte Vedre; Cleveland Athletic, Lakewood Country; Ambassador, Admiral, 100,000 Miler. Research Lakeview Country; Sharon Golf; Briarwood Country; asst., writer Sutherland Statutory Construction, 3d edit., 1943. Home: Rocky River OH Died July 6, 1972.

DUVAL, CHARLES WARREN, pathologist; b. Annapolis, Md., Nov. 28, 1876; s. George W. and Madelaine J. (Stump) D.; A.B., St. John's Coll., Annapolis, 1897; M.D., U. of Pa., 1903; m. Hilda von Stuckradt, Mar. 19, 1906. Rockefeller fellow, U. of Pa., 1902; 1st asst. pathologist, Boston City Hosp., 1905; dir. pathology, Montreal Gen. Hosp., 1908; lecturer on pathology, McGill U., 1906; prof. pathology and bacteriology, Tulane U., since 1909; dir. pathol. labs. of Charity and Presbyn. hosps., New Orleans. Mem. Am. Coll. Physicians. Soc. Experimental Biology and Medicine, Am. Acad. Science, Soc. Am. Pathologists, Soc. Am. Bacteriologists, Am. Federation Allied Sciences, Soc. Experimental Pathology, A.M.A., Nu Sigma Nu, Phi Delta Theta. Mason (32deg). Contbr. research articles on dysentery, tuberculosis, leprosy, scarlet fever. Home: 8 Richmond Pl. Office: 1430 Tulane Av., New Orleans LA*‡

DUVALIER, FRANCOIS, pres. Republic of Haiti; b. Port-au-Prince, Apr. 14, 1907; Dr. Faculty of Medicine, Haiti. Doctor, St. Francois de Sales Hosp.; cons. Emilie Sigueneau Clinic; dir. rural clinic, Anti-Yaws Tng. Center, Am. Health Mission, head malaria control sect., later dir. anti-yams campaign; asst. to Maj. James W. Dwinell, U.S. Army Med. Corps; med. cons. Pub. Health Coop. Service; head preventive medicine div. Inter-Am. Pub. Health Coop. Service; dir. Nat. Pub. Health Service; under-sec. labor, then state sec. labor and pub. health; pres. Republic of Haiti, 1957-70. Hon. dir. Ethonology Bur., Republic of Haiti. Decorated Order Carlos Manuel de Cespedes (Cuba); Most Venerable Order Knighthood of the Pioneers (Liberia); Order Military Merit Jean-Jacques Dessalines the Great, Order of Civil Merit Toussaint-Louverture, Nat. Order Honor and Merit, Order of Petion and Bolivar (Haiti). Mem. Internat. Inst. Am. Ideals (Cuban Group), Internat. Soc. Afro-Cuban Studies (Mexico), Internat. Inst. Anthropology of Paris, Paris Ethnographic Soc., Haitian Soc. History, Geography and Geology, Haitian Med. Assn., Haitian Assn. Pub. Hygiene, Am. Pub. Health Assn., Royal Soc. Tropical Medicine and Hygiene of London. Co-dir. Les Griots, mag., co-founder weekly. Contbr. articles numerous Haitian and fgn. publs. Home: Port-Au-Prince Haiti Died Apr. 21, 1971.

DUVALL, DONALD CHAUNCEY, steel exec.; b. Monessen, Pa., July 26, 1915; s. Chauncey S. and Agnes (Gregg) D.; student Pa. State U., 1933-34, U. Pitts., 1939; B.S., Cal. State Tchrs. Coll., 1938; m. Minnie Nelson, Jan. 5, 1939; children—Mrs. D. R. Koehler, Donna Lee. Tchr. pub. schs., 1938-41; indsl. engr. Pitts. Steel Co., 1941-48, chief indsl. engr., 1949-54, works mgr. Monessen plant, 1954-55, vice president industrial relations, 1956-58, executive v.p., from 1958, also dir.; pres., chief operating officer Wheeling Steel Corp., until 1970. Dir. Charleroi-Monessen Hosp. Mem. Am. Iron and Steel Inst., Soc. Advancement Mgmt., Monessen C. of C. Home: Monessen PA Died Jan. 1970.

DUWE, GEORGE E., ret. food mfg. exec.; b. Chgo., May 1, 1897; s. August and Amelia (Schmidt) D.; student pub. sch.; m. Dora Risch, Mar. 15, 1919; children—Dorothy, Betty. With Scholl Mfg. Co., 1919-21, Calumet Baking Powder Co., 1921-29; with Mickelberry's Food Products Co., 1929-70, pres., dir., 1935-56, chmn. bd., 1956-70, sec.-treas., 1965-70. Home: Hinsdale IL Died Dec. 26, 1972.

DWAN, RALPH HUBERT, lawyer; b. Two Harbors, Minn., Aug. 4, 1901; s. John and Helen R. (Stockdale) D.; B.A., U. Minn., 1922, LL.B., 1925; S.J.D., Harvard, 1926; m. Mary Cochrane, June 28, 1927;children—Susan (Mrs. Lawrence Slaughter), Ralph Hubert, Mary Ann (Mrs. Samuel Ellsworth), Ursula (Mrs. Robert A. Jaeger). Admitted to Minn. bar, 1925; faculty mem. Law School, University Minn. 1926-36, prof. law, 1930-36; acting prof. law Columbia Law Sch., summer 1930, Northwestern Law Sch., summer 1931; lectr. Law Sch., Cath. U. Am., 1942-45; with Gen. Counsel's Office, U.S. Treasury Dept., 1936-39, chief counsel Bur. Customs, 1939-41, asst. chief counsel Internal Revenue Service, 1941-54; pvt. practice, Washington, 1954-69. Adj. prof. Georgetown U. Law Center, 1961-66. Dir. Minn. Mining and Mfg. Co. Del. to negotiate tax treaties with various European countries, 1948, 52. Mem. Am., Minn., Fed. bar assn., Bar Assn. of D.C., Am. Law Inst., Am. Soc. Internat. Law, Order of Coif, Phi Beta Kappa, Phi Delta Phi (province pres. 1948-61). Catholic. Author articles legal journals. Home: Washington DC Died Aug. 27, 1969.

DWIGHT, MABEL, artist; b. Cincinnati, O., Jan. 29, 1876; d. Paul and Adelaide Dwight (Jaques) Williamson; ed. high sch., San Francisco, Calif., and by pvt. tutors; also student Mark Hopkins Art Sch., San Francisco, 1896-97; worked and studied in Paris, 1926-27. Known chiefly for her lithography and water color work; represented in Met. Mus. of Art, Whitney Mus. of Art, N.Y. City; Fogg Art Mus., Cambridge, Mass.; Boston Mus. of Art; Chicago Art Inst.; Cleveland Mus. of Art; Detroit Mus. of Art; Buffalo Mus. of Art; Bibliotheque Nationale, Paris; Albert and Victoria Mus., London; Kupferstich Kabinett, Berlin. Mem. Am. Artists' Congress. Democrat. Home: 55 E. 10th St., New York NY‡

DWIGHT, OGDEN GRAHAM, newspaper editor; b. Burlington, Ia., July 10, 1915; s. Louis Theodore and Elizabeth (Graham) D.; student Burlington Jr. Coll., 1933; B.A. in Journalism, U. Mich., 1937; m. Iris Wilding, Nov. 4, 1938; 1 dau., Elisabeth. With Des Moines Register and Tribune, 1937-70, Sunday Recordings reviewer, 1946-70, Ia. TV mag. supplement editor, 1956-70, TV, drama, music columnist-critic, 1956-70, TV and music editor, 1964-70. Des Moines Adult Edn. Adv. Council, 1961-64, pres., 1962-63; mem. ednl. TV sta. adv. council, 1961-70; mem. Des Moines Retng. council, 1964-66. Mem. Friends of Deaf, Music Critic Assn. Am., Sigma Nu. Democrat. Episcopalian. Club: Des Moines Press and Radio. Home: Des Moines IA Died Sept. 23, 1970.

DYER, FRANK, clergyman; b. Cornwall, Eng., July 29, 1875; s. Charles Barrett and Rebecca (Braven) D.; came to U.S., 1893, naturalized citizen, 1900; ed. Wheaton (Ill.) Coll., Moody Bible Inst., Chicago; student Chicago Theol. Sem.; D.D., Pacific U.; m. Mabel Puckey, of Chicago, Aug. 2, 1897. Ordained Congl. ministry, 1902; pastor Lake View Ch., Chicago, 1902-05, Waveland Av. Ch., Chicago, 1905-08; founder and gen. sec. Congl. Brotherhood America, 1908-12; pastor 1st Ch., Tacoma, Wash., 1913-21, Wilshire Boul. Ch., Los Angeles, 1921-28; brother-pres. The Preaching Friars since 1929; instr. in homiletics, Western Theol. Sem., 1931. Mem. Pacific International Theological Conf. (hon. pres.), Pacific Southwest Theol. Conf. Del. Internat. Congl. Conf., Edinburgh, 1908; del. World Missionary Conf., Edinburgh, 1910; del. Congl. Union Eng. and Wales, 1923. In France with A.E.F. 6 mos. Club: City (Los Angeles). Home: 460 Sycamore Rd., Santa Monica, Calif. Address: 600 Haven St., Evanston IL‡

DYER, JAMES EDWARD, petroleum exec.; b. Crete Neb., Nov. 7, 1894; s. James and Mary (Glancy) D.;

student St. Benedict's Coll., Atchison, Kan. 1912; Kansas City Sch. Law, 1917; m. Monica Ryan June 10, 1931 (dec. 1950); children—Monica, James E., Jr., Mary Ellen. With Sinclair Oil Corp., N.Y. 1916-62, v.p. dir. Sinclair Refining Co., 1944-54; pres., dir., 1954-58; v.p., dir. Sinclair Oil Corp., 1951-58, vice chmn. bd., 1958-62. Hon. life dir. Am. Petroleum Inst. Served with USN, World War I. Home: New Rochelle NY Died May 7, 1970; buried Holy Mount Cemetery, Tuckahoe NY

DYER, JESSE FARLEY, marine corps officer; b. Dec. 2, 1877; entered U.S. Marine Corps, 1903, and advanced through the grades to brig. gen., 1932; retired, 1937. Decorated Medal of Honor. Address: care Marine Corps Headquarters, Navy Department, Washington 25 DC*‡

DYER, JOHN LEWIS, physician; b. New Orleans, Mar. 10, 1914; s. Isadore and Mercedes (Percival) D.; M.D., Tulane U., 1939; m. Margaret Goland, Dec. 25, 1942; children—John Lewis, Thomas B., Nancy B. (Mrs. Richard F. Muller III), Joseph M., Peter, Robert A. Intern, Touro Infirmary, New Orleans, 1939-40, resident in medicine, 1940-41, sr. med. and active staff, untill 1969; postgrad. in cardiovascular renal disease Mayo Found., Rochester, Minn., 1942. Served with M.C., AUS, 1941-46. Diplomate Am. Bd. Internal Medicine. Mem. A.M.A., Am. Heart Assn. Home: New Orleans LA Died Dec. 22, 1969; buried Metairie Cemetery, Metairie LA

DYETT, HERBERT THOMAS, chmn. bd. Rome Cable Corp.; b. Rome, N.Y., Feb. 13, 1875; s. James Stringham and Susan (Hathaway) D.; M.E., Cornell, 1897; m. Blanche Stevens, Oct. 10, 1901 (dec.); children—James Stevens (dec.), Charlotte Van Arman (Mrs. Dyett White), John Hathaway. Clerk Carpenter & Dyett, Rome, N.Y., 1897-98; plant mgr. and later sales mgr. Rome Steel Co., 1899-1901; partner Electric Wire Works, Rome, N.Y., 1901-05; pres. and treas. Rome Wire Co., 1905-27; v.p. and pres. Gen. Cable Corp., 1927-33; chmn. bd. Rome Co., Inc., 1933-35; pres. Rome Cable Corp., mfr. elec. wires and cables, Rome, N.Y., 1936-44, chmn. bd. since 1944. Dir. Rome Community Chest. Chmn. Adv. Com. Ft. Stanwix Council, Boy Scouts Am. Mem. Theta Delta Chi. Republican. Episcopalian. Clubs: Wall St., University (N.Y.C.); Adirondack League; Rome, Teugega Country (Rome, N.Y.); Seminole Golf (Fla.). Home: 1206 N. George St. Office: Rome Cable Corp., Rome NY‡

DYKE, CHARLES BARTLETT, educator; b. at Berea, O., Feb. 2, 1870; s. Henry and Harriet Elizabeth (Bartlett) D.; student Baldwin U., Ohio, 1891-3; A.B., Stanford U., 1897; A.M., Columbia, 1899; Higher Diploma, Teachers Coll. (Columbia), 1899; m. Estelle Darrah, of St. Paul, 1898. Prof. history and civics, State Normal Sch., Mankato, Minn., 1897-8; dir. Normal Dept. and prof. edn., Hampton Inst., Va., 1899-1900; pres. Kamehameha Schs., Honolulu, H.I., 1900-4; instr. edn., U. of Colo., 1906-12, and head master Colo. State Prep. Sch., 1907-12; supt. Vocational High Sch., Youngstown, O., 1912-15; supt. of schs., Millburn, N.J., 1915—. Mem. Nat. Soc. Study of Edn., N.E.A., N.J. State Teachers' Assn. (sec.). Republican. Conglist. Clubs: Short Hills, New Jersey Schoolmasters', New York Schoolmasters'. Author: Economic Aspect of Teachers' Salaries. Home: Millburn NJ‡

DYKEMA, KARL W(ASHBURN), coll. dean; b. Yonkers, N.Y., Jan. 31, 1906; s. Peter William and Jessie Margaret (Dunning) D.; student Antioch Coll., 1923-25; A.B., Columbia, 1928, A.M., 1932; student Alliance Francaise, Paris, France 1930, U. of Berlin, 1931; m. Christine Lillian Rhoades, June 16, 1931; children—Nicholas Edmund, Patricia Caroline (Mrs. Rolf Geisler), Christopher Rhoades. Tchr. music, Towson High Sch., Md., 1928-29, Chateau de Bures Sch. for Boys, par Orgeval, Seine et Oise, France, 1929-30; instr. English and German, Ironwood (now Gogebic) Jr. Coll., Ironwood, Mich., 1932-36; asst. professor, asso. prof., prof. English, and dir. div. lang. and lit. Youngstown State U., 1937-70, dean College Arts and Sciences, 1963-70. Mem. Modern Language Assn., Linguistic Society, American Dialect Society, College English Association, National Council Teachers of English, International Association U. Profs. English, Am. Name Soc., English Assn. Ohio (pres. 1962-63), Am. Assn. Univ. Profs. Author of articles and reviews. Author: (with others) Perrin Writer's Guide and Index to English, rev. edit. 1965. Home: Canfield OH Died July 16, 1970; cremated.

DYKEMA, RAYMOND K., lawyer; b. Grand Rapids, Mich., Feb. 17, 1889; s. Kryn and Mary (Openeer) D.; LL.B., U. Mich., 1911; m. Margery Russel, Aug. 1917; children—John Russel, Mary (wife of Dr. Laurie C. Dickson, Jr.), Raymond K., Jere Hutchins. Admitted to Mich. bar, 1911; with Bundy, Travis & Marrick, Grand Rapids, 1911-12, Angell, Boynton, McMillan, Bodman & Turner, 1912-16, Mich. Central R.R., 1917; pvt. practice law, 1919-23; partner Dykema and Wheat, 1923-26, now Dykema, Wheat, Spencer, Goodnow & Trigg. Member of the advisory board United Foundation. Served as capt. AUS, 1917-19. Mem. Am., Mich., Detroit bar assns., Psi Upsilon. Clubs: Detroit, Country (Detroit); Grosse Pointe; Huron Mountain. Home: Grosse Pointe Farms MI Died 1972.

DYKHUIZEN, HAROLD DANIEL, surgeon, urologist; b. Chgo., Mar. 29, 1908; s. Garret and Nell (Dimnent) D.; A.B., Hope Coll., Holland, Mich., 1930; M.D., U. Chgo., 1935; m. Lucille Walvoord, Aug. 20, 1935; children—Daniel Edward, Ann Marie (Mrs. Brenner), Jane Nell. Asso. of Dr. V.J. O'Conor, Chgo., 1936-39; instr. urology U. Ill. Med. Sch., 1936-39; head dept. urology Mercy Hosp.; head dept. urology Hackley Hosp., Muskegon, Mich., also chief surgery, 1951-54. Dir. Northwestern Oil & Terminal Co., St. Ignace, Mich., Muskegon Northfield, Ltd., Lancashire, Eng.; dir., mem. exec. com. Muskegon Tool Industries. Pres. Mona Shores Bd. Edn.; mem. exec. com., mem. Muskegon County Library Merger Com.; dir., mem. exec. com., chmn. subcom. scope and objectives Hackley Pub. Library. Mem. Muskegon County Republican Finance Com., 1961-67. Bd. dirs., past v.p. bd. Muskegon Children's Home; trustee, exec. com. bd. trustees Hope Coll.; bd. dirs. Mich. Med. Service (Blue Shield), 1966-69. Diplomate Am. Bd. Urology. Fellow Am., Internat. colls. surgeons, Acad. Internat. Medicine, Am. Geriatrics Soc., Am., Internat. colls. angiology; mem. World Med. Com., A.A.A.S., Am. Urol. Assn., Am. Pan Am. med. assns., Muskegon County (dir., past pres.), Mich. med. socs., Pan Pacific Surg. Assn., Mich. Assn. Professions, Nat. Hope Coll. Alumni Assn. (past pres., dir.), Alpha Omega Alpha, Nu Sigma Nu. Mem. Ref. Ch. Am. Rotarian. Clubs: West State Press (charter); Muskegon Country, The Club (Muskegon); University (Chgo.); Century; Otsego (Gaylord, Mich.). Contbr. articles med. jours. Home: Muskegon MI Died Nov. 25, 1967.

DYKSTRA, GERALD OSCAR, educator, lawyer, author; b. Allegan, Mich., May 13, 1906; s. Garrit and Martha Clara (Knuth) D.; student Albion Coll., 1925-26; A.B., U. Mich., 1927, J.D., 1930, M.B.A. cum laude, 1936; m. Lillian May Green, Sept. 4, 1935. Admitted to Ohio bar, 1930; partner Shaver & Dykstra, Cleveland, 1930-35; instr. bus. law Coll. Commerce, Ohio U., 1936-38, asst. prof., 1938-41, asso. prof., 1941-43, prof., 1943-50; prof. bus. law Grad. Sch. Bus. Adminstrn. U. Mich., from 1950, Sch. Banking, from 1952. Recipient Distinguished Teaching award U. Mich. Grad. Sch. Bus. Adminstrn., 1968. Mem. Am. Bus. Law Assn. (pres., 1947-48), Ohio, Mich. bar assns., Rotary internat., Delta Sigma Rho, Beta Gamma Sigma. Republican. Lutheran. Author (with Lillian Green Dykstra): Selected Cases on Government and Business, 2d edit., 1948; Text on Government and Business, 1939; Business Law of Aviation, 1946; Business Law, Text and Cases, 3d edit., 1969; Business Law of Real Estate, 1956; contbr. to profl. jours. Home: Ann Arbor MI Died Apr. 24, 1970; buried Oakwood Cemetery, Allegan MI

DYKSTRA, JOHN, indsl. exec.; b. nr. Stiens, Netherlands, Apr. 16, 1898; s. Theodore and Nellie (DeVries) D.; came to U.S., 1902, naturalized, 1919; mech. engring. course, Cass Tech. Sch., nights, 1915-17; corr. course, LaSalle Extension U., 1921-26; m. Marion S. Hyde, Mar. 2, 1918; children—Betty H. (Mrs. John Steele), John O. Diemaker, later mgr. body plant, Hudson Motor Co., Detroit, 1919-34; with Oldsmobile Corp., Lansing, Mich., 1934-47, works mgr., 1942-47; asst. to v.p. charge mfg., Ford Motor Co., 1947, gen. mgr. plants in Detroit, Canton (O.), and Cincinnati, 1947-49, v.p. aircraft engine, tractor and machined products group 1950-53, vice pres. and group executive, Dearborn, 1953-56, group v.p., Dearborn, 1957-58, v.p. mfg., v.p. def. products group 1958-61, pres., 1961-63, dir., from 1958; dir. Philco Corp. Mem. Society Automotive Engrs. Clubs: Detroit Athletic, Recess, Detroit Golf. Home: Birmingham MI Died Mar. 2, 1972; buried Oakview Cemetery, Royal Oak MI

DYMOND, FLORENCE, orgn. exec.; b. N.Y. City, Aug. 17, 1873; d. John and Nancy E. (Cassidy) Dymond; ed. pvt. schs. and Newcomb Coll. of Tulane U. Sec.-treas., also part owner, American Printing Co., New Orleans, La., since 1922. Mem. bd. dirs. New Orleans Women's Hosp. (pres. bd. 20 yrs.). Mem. Louisiana Hist. Soc., Tulane and Newcomb alumnae assns. Club: Orleans (charter mem.). Home: 839 Pine St. Office: 424 Camp St., New Orleans LA‡

DYNES, OWEN WILLIAM, lawyer; b. Columbus, Wis., May 31, 1869; s. Valentine and Ellen (Komiski) D.; ed. Oshkosh State Normal Sch.; Cornell U.; m. Lucile M. Crosby, Sept. 5, 1900. Admitted to bar, 1895, and began practice at Chicago; asst. gen. solicitor C.,M. & St.P. Ry., 1908-12, commerce counsel, 1912-17, gen. atty., 1917-22, gen. solicitor, 1922-31. gen. counsel C.M.St.P. & P. R.R., 1931-39; retired Jan. 1, 1947. Mem. Assn. Bar, City of N.Y., Am., Ill. State and Chicago bar assns. Clubs: Union League, Hinsdale Golf. Home: 313 N. Madison St., Hinsdale IL‡

EAGAN, EDWARD PATRICK FRANCIS, lawyer; b. Denver, Colo., Apr. 26, 1897; s. John William and Clara (Bartholomew) E.; Ph.B., Yale, 1921; student Harvard Law Sch., 1921-22; A.B., Jurisprudence, Oxford U., Rhodes scholarship, 1924, M.A., 1928; m. Margaret Colgate, Oct. 1, 1927; children—Sidney, Caroline. Toured world with Marquis of Clydesdale, 1926-27; admitted to N.Y. bar, 1932, and since practiced in that state; asst. U.S. Atty., 1933-38; private practice with Daily News legal firm, New York City, 1938-42; now mem. firm Fennelly, Douglas, Eagan, Nager & Voorhees; chmn. N.Y. State Athletic Commn., appointment of Gov. Thomas E. Dewey, 1945-51. Chairman U.S. Olympic Fund Raising Com., 1956, Internat. Sports Com., People-to-People Sports Committee, United States Olympic Finance Com. Served as 2d lt., F.A., U.S. Army, 1918-19; capt. to lt. col., Air Transport Command, A.U.S., 1942-45. Pres. Boys' Athletic League of New York, 1937-38. Member board of trustees of People-to-People. Awarded ribbons in World War I, all three theatre ribbons in World War II; Olympic champion, light-heavyweight, Antwerp, Belgium, 1920; Am. Olympic heavyweight 1924. Mem. Bar Assn. City of N.Y., American Legion, Beta Theta Pi. Republican. Clubs: Book and Snake, Yale (mem. council), Circumnavigators (New York); Am. Yacht, Apawamis (Rye, N.Y.); Author: Fighting for Fun, 1933; 10 Days to a Successful Memory (with Dr. Joyce Brothers). Contbr. articles Sat. Eve. Post. Chmn. People-to-People Sports Com., Inc. Home: Rye NY Died June 14, 1967; buried Greenwood Union Cemetery, Rye NY

EAGER, HENRY GOSSETT, lawyer; b. Kansas City, Mo., Oct. 14, 1923; s. Henry I. and Claudine (Gossett) E.; A.B., U. Mo., 1943; J.D., U. Mich., 1948; m. Ruth Jule Riche, Apr. 2, 1948; children—Julianne, Caroline Riche, Henry Gossett. Admitted to Mo. bar. 1948; practiced in Kansas City, 1948-72; partner firm Swanson, Midgley, Eager, Gangwere, and Thurlo, and predecessors, 1948-72. Active Kansas City Philharmonic Assn., Friends of Art, Civil War Roundtable, Jackson County Hist. Soc., Soc. Fellows Nelson Art Gallery. Served to capt. USMCR, 1943-46, 50-52. Mem. Mo. Bar (bd. govs. 1955-56), Am., Kansas City bar assns., Lawyers Assn. Kansas City (pres. jr. sect. 1952-53), Bar Assn. St. Louis, Am. Judicature Soc., Phi Delta Phi, Phi Delta Theta. Democrat. Conglist. Mason, Rotarian. Clubs: Mission Hills (Kan.) Country; Kansas City (Kansas City, Mo.). Home: Kansas MO Died Nov. 28, 1972.

EAGLE, JOE HENRY, congressman; b. Tompkinsville, Ky., Jan. 23, 1870; A.B., Burritt Coll., Spencer, Tenn., 1887; m. Mary Hamman, of Houston, Tex., 1900. Admitted to Texas bar, 1893; mem. 63d to 66th Congresses (1913-21), and unexpired term 72d Congress, of Daniel E. Garrett, also full term 73d and 74th Congresses (1933-37), 8th Tex. Dist. Democrat. Home: Houston TX‡

EAGLESON, FREEMAN THOMAS, lawyer; b. near Old Washington, Guernsey County, Ohio, Oct. 4, 1876; s. Thomas and Jennie Rebecca (Spence) E.; attended Muskingum Coll., New Concord, O., and Ohio State U. Law Sch.; m. Jessie L. Neely, June 25, 1913; children—Thomas Neely, Freeman Thomas, Jr., David Alexander. Admitted to Ohio bar, 1906; private practice in Cambridge, 1906-13, Columbus, since 1913. Served 3 terms in Ohio House of Rep., floor leader in 1906. Republican speaker of House in 1908. Trustee, The Ohio State Archaeol. and Hist. Soc.; past dir. and past pres., Columbus Acad. Mem. Am., O. State bar assns., Ohio Soc. N.Y., Am. Gas Assn., Ohio Oil Men's Assn., Delta Chi. Clubs: Faculty, Athletic, Country, Columbus, Buckeye Republican (Columbus, Ohio), Castalia Trout (Castalia, O.), Bras Coupe Hunting and Fishing (Quebec). Mem. official bd. Bexley Meth. Ch., Bexley, O. Mason (32 deg., Scottish Rite). Home: 152 N. Drexel Av., Bexley, O. Office: 16 E. Broad St., Columbus 15 OH‡

EARDLEY, ARMAND JOHN, educator; b. Salt Lake City, Oct. 25, 1901; s. John Alma and Elizabeth Emma (Brown) E.; A.B., U. Utah, 1927, D.Sc. (hon.), 1970; Ph.D., Princeton U., 1930; m. Norma Ashton, May 6, 1930; 1 son, Michael John. Mem. faculty U. Mich., 1930-51, prof., dir. geology field work, 1943-49; mem. faculty U. Utah, 1951-72, chmn. Div. of Earth Scis., Coll. Mines and Mineral Industries, 1951-54, prof. geology, prof. emeritus, 1965-72, dean coll. of mines and mineral industries, 1954-65. Distinguished lectr. Am. Assn. Petroleum Geologists, 1951; Reynolds lectr. U. Utah, 1955; nat. lectr. Sigma Xi, 1957. Recipient Distinguished award in sci. Utah Acad. Sci., Arts and Letters, 1956; Distinguished Achievement award Am. Fedn. Mineral Soc., 1968. Fellow Geol. Soc. Am.; mem. Am. Assn. Petroleum Geologists, Geophys. Union of Am., Nat. Assn. Geology Tchrs. (pres. 1962-63), Am. Geol. Inst. (pres. 1964-65). Author: Aerial Photographys; Their Use and Interpretation, 1942; Structural Geology of North America, 1951, 2d edit., 1962; General College Geology, 1965. Contbr. articles tech. lit. Specialist in continental tectonics; structural geology (Utah, Wyo., Mont.), sedimentation, petroleum geology. Home: Salt Lake City UT Died Nov. 7, 1972.

EARHART, ROBERT FRANCIS, physicist; b. Toledo, Ia., Feb. 2, 1873; s. Robert N. and Frances (Fidlar) E.; B.S., Northwestern U., 1893; Ph.D., U. of Chicago, 1900; m. Darline Scofield, of Columbus, O., Aug. 1906; children—Daniel S., Robt. N., Edwin W., Frances, Warren S. Formerly in engring. practice at Moline, Ill.; with Ohio State U. since 1903; prof. physics same, since 1912. Mem. Am. Physical Soc., Sigma Xi. Methodist. Original researches in discharge of electricity through gases. Home: 342 W. 9th Av., Columbus OH‡

EARHART, WILL, music edn.; b. Franklin, Ohio, Apr. 1, 1871; s. Martin Washington and Hanna Jane (Corwin) E.; ed. pub. schs.; music edn. pvtly.; Mus.D., U. of Pittsburgh, 1920; m. Birdelle M. Darling, Dec. 29, 1897; 1 son, William Corwin. Supervisor music pub. schs., Greenville, O., 1896-98, Richmond, Ind., 1898-1912 (condr. festival chorus and symphony orchestra); dir. music pub. schs., Pittsburgh, Pa., 1912-40; lecturer in music, Sch. of Edn., U. of Pittsburgh, 1913-18, prof., 1918-21; lecturer Carnegie Inst. Tech., Pittsburgh, 1916-18, 1921-40. Mem. Pittsburgh Municipal Band Concert Com., 1925-30, Nat. Advisory Com. of Federal Music Project under Works Progress Adminstrn., 1935-36. Mem. Music Educators Nat. Conf. (ex-pres.), Am. Soc. Composers, Authors and Publishers, Am. Soc. Aesthetics, Am. Musicol. Soc., Phi Mu Alpha, Phi Delta Kappa. Republican. Clubs. Musicians, Unity. Author: The Eloquent Baton, 1931; Music the Listening Ear, 1932; The Meaning and Teaching of Music, 1935; Choral Technics, 1937; also several bulls. Co-editor mus. instrn. books. Contbr. to music jours. Home: San Diego 3 CA‡

EARL, HARLEY J., v.p. Gen. Motors Corp.; b. Los Angeles, Calif., Nov. 22, 1893; s. Jacob W. and Abbie (Taft) E.; student Stanford U.; m. Sue F. Carpenter, June 19, 1917; children—J(ames) Milton, J(erome) Courtney. Designer Earl Carriage Works, Los Angeles, Calif., 1918-19; gen. mgr. Don Lee Coach & Body Corp., Los Angeles, 1918-26; dir. styling sect. Gen. Motors Corp., Detroit, Mich., 1926-40, vice president, 1940-58, retired, became consultant; organized Harley Earl Corporation, Detroit, 1945, pres. until 1958; chmn. bd. Harley Earl Assos., Inc., 1958-69; dir. Briggs Mfg. Co. (Warren, Mich.). Methodist. Clubs: Country (Los Angeles); Country, Recess, Yondotega, Question (Detroit); Grosse Pointe (Mich.); St. Clair Flats Shooting Company (Wallaceburg, Ont.). Home: Palm Beach FL Died Mar. 10, 1969.

EARL, N. CLARK, JR., bus. exec.; b. Boston, Dec. 16, 1900; s. N. Clark and Alice (Drake) E.; ed. Berkley Prep. Sch., Boston; m. Consuelo Vanderbilt Smith; 4 children by previous marriage. N.E. mgr. Owens Bottle Co., Boston, 1920-28; owner Earl & Co., Boston, 1928-39; sales mgr. Howard Johnsons, Inc., N.Y. City, 1945-49; pres. Childs Co., 1950, exec. v.p. and dir. since 1950, pres. and dir. all subsidiary cos. since 1950; pres. and dir. Louis Sherry, Inc., N.Y. City, since 1950. Entered U.S. Army as maj., 1939, operations officer, post exchanges; post exchange officer, E.T.O., 1942-44; ret. as col., 1945. Clubs: Retired Officers (Washington); Silver Springs Country (Ridgefield, Conn.); Leash, Metropolitan (N.Y. City); Skye Terrior of America (v.p. and dir.), American Kennel, Afghan Hound, Am. Boxer, N.Y. Boxer. Breeder of dogs, Iradell Kennels since 1943. Ridgefield CT Died Feb. 1969.

EARLE, WALTER KEESE, lawyer; b. St. Louis Park, Minn., Aug. 15, 1886; s. Oliver and Emma (Laycock) E.; A.B., Harvard University, 1910; m. Charlotte Fellowes Harding, June 9, 1914 (deceased on October 27th, 1964); children—Anne French (Mrs. Roy R. B. Attride, dec.), Morris, Margaret Wood, Louise Harding (Mrs. A. Worthington Loomis). Admitted to N.Y. bar, 1913; asso. Cary & Carroll, N.Y.C., 1914-18, partner, 1918; partner Shearman & Sterling, from 1919; N.Y.C. Mgr. N.Y. Inst. Edn. of Blind, from 1934; curator, v.p. Whaling Mus. Soc., Cold Spring Harbor, N.Y., from 1944; chmn. Zoning Bd. of Appeals, Village Oyster Bay Cove. Mem. Assn. Bar City N.Y., Am., N.Y. bar assns. Democrat. Episcopalian (sr. warden). Mason. Clubs: Century, Union, Down Town Assn. (N.Y.C.); Cold Spring Harbor Beach. Author articles whales, whaling, legal and hist. subjects; History of Shearman & Sterling. Home: Oyster Bay NY Died Feb. 10, 1969.

EARLING, HERMAN B., ry. official; b. Wis., Oct. 30, 1862; ed. pub. schs.; married; children—Roy Brown, Everett Allan. Began with C.M. & St.P.Ry., 1879; agt. and operator, 1879-83; asst. and chief train dispatcher, 1883-93; trainmaster, 1893-97; supt. terminals, 1897-98; div. supt., at Marion, Ia., 1898-1903; asst. gen. supt. Middle dist., Milwaukee, 1903-06; Northern dist., Minneapolis, 1906-07; gen. supt. Chicago, Milwaukee & Puget Sound Ry., at Miles City and Butte, Mont., 1907-09; gen. supt. C.M. & St.P.Ry., at Chicago, 1909-12; asst. gen. mgr., 1912-13; v.p. same rd., 1913-28; v.p. C.M. & St.P.Ry., 1928-41, retired. Home: 941 11th Av., N. Office: White Bldg., Seattle WA‡

EARLY, ELEANOR, author; b. Newton, Mass.; d. James A. and Sarah (Dolan) Early; ed. Miss Wheelock's Sch., Boston; unmarried. Washington and Paris correspondent for International News Service. Roman Catholic. Author several books, latest are: New Orleans Holiday, 1946; New York Holiday, 1950; Washington Holiday, 1954; Cape Cod Summer, 1949; New England Cookbook, published 1954; Caribbean Holiday, published 1960; Caribbean Holiday, 1960. Edited Constance Letters of Charles Chapin, 1933. Radio commentator. Mem. Soc. Am. Travel Writers. Clubs: Overseas Press (N.Y.C.); Boston Authors. Contbr. articles to various publs. Home: New York City NY Died Sept. 1969.*

EARNEST, HERBERT LUDWELL, ret. army officer; b. Richmond, Va., Nov. 11, 1895; s. James Alfred and Mary Elizabeth (Talley) E.; student Fork Union Mil. Acad., Va., 1911-14, Med. Coll. of Va., 1915-16; grad. Cav. Sch., 1924, Ecole d'Application de Cavalerie, Saumur, France, 1926. Command and Gen. Staff Sch., 1934, Chem. Warfare Sch., 1936, Army Indsl. Coll., 1939; m. Frances Alexander Campbell, Oct. 20, 1920; children—Clyde Tener, Frances Elizabeth. Commd. 1d lt. U.S. Army, Oct. 26, 1917, and advanced through the grades to maj. gen.; during World War II, comd. Task Force A, 3d Army Britany Peninsula; comd. combat command A, 4th Armored Div., Dec.-Jan. 1944, Jan. 1945; 90th Inf., Mar.-Dec. 1945, assistant chief staff G-3, Army Ground Forces, Ft. Monroe, Va. 1945-47, retired October 1, 1947. Decorated: Bronze Star Medal with Two Oak Leaf Clusters; Silver Star Medal; D.S.M.; Legion of Merit; Hon. Companion British Distinguished Service Order; Chevalier Legion d'Honneir, Croix de Guerre with Palm (French); Czechoslovakian War Cross. Club: Army-Navy (Washington); Commonwealth (Richmond, Va.); Chesapeake (Irvington, Va.); Indian Creek Yacht and Country (Kilmarnock, Va.). Home: White Stone VA Died June 11, 1970; buried Old Christ Ch., Irvington VA

EASBY-SMITH, JAMES S., lawyer, author; b. Tuskaloosa, Ala., May 17, 1870; s. William Russell Smith (mem. U.S. and Confederate congresses—pres. Univ. of Ala., etc.) and Wilhelmine Maria (Easby) Smith; grad. Georgetown Coll., 1891; A.M., 1892, law dept., 1893, LL. M., 1894; m. Washington, June 5, 1894, Lilian Louise Strong. Asso. editor, 1888-90, editor-in-chief, 1891, Georgetown College Journal. Admitted to bar, Washington, 1894; law examiner Dept. of Justice, 1893-9; sp'l asst. U.S. atty., E. dist. La. 1896; pardon atty. Dept. of Justice, 1899-1904; asst. U.S. atty., D.C., 1904-1906; quiz master Georgetown Univ. Law Sch., since 1904; lecturer on constl. history, Georgetown Coll., 1905. Author: The Songs of Sappho (original text Sappho, with life and original verse translation), 1891-01; The Songs of Alcaeus (original text Alcaeus, with life, critical notes and original verse translation), 1901 L25; The Law of Pardons (a digest of the laws and decisions relating to pardons and other acts of executive clemency under the U.S. and the several States), 1903 W8; The Department of Justice; Its History and Functions, 1904 L25; History of Georgetown University, D.C., 1789-1907. Contb'r lit. articles, stories and poems to various periodicals since 1887. Residence: 1358 Kenyon St. Office: Century Bldg., Washington DC‡

EASLEY, KATHERINE, dean of women, univ. prof.; b. New Albany, Ind., May 28, 1877; d. Elihu Parks and Virginia Arisbie (Morrison) Easley; A.B., Ind. Univ., 1912, M.A., 1913. Instr. in English, Ind. Univ., 1913-19; prof. English and dean of women U. of Toledo (O.), 1919-47. Mem. League of Women Voters, Am. Assn. Univ. Women (pres. Toledo branch 1925-28), Phi Beta Kappa (sec. Northwestern Ohio since 1940). Republican. Episcopalian. Home: 1805 Waite Av., Toledo 6 OH‡

EASTER, CHARLES WHITTLESEY, investment banker; b. Seattle, June 15, 1906; s. Frank K. and Sadie Ellen (Whittlesey) E.; B.A., U. Wash., 1929; m. Josephine Elizabeth Brown, July 15, 1933; children—Alison (Mrs. David Clements), Ann (Mrs. James O'Keefe), Charles Whittlesey, Sara Jo. With Dean Witter & Co., Seattle, 1929-42, Merrill Lynch, Pierce, Fenner & Smith, Seattle, 1942; with Blyth & Co., Inc., Seattle, from 1942, v.p., from 1954. Mem. exec. bd. Chief Seattle council Boy Scouts Am.; chmn. exec. com. Wash. Heart Assn. 1949-51; chmn. finance com. Northwest Meml. Hosp., from 1960. Trustee United Good Neighbors King County. Mem. Investment Bankers Assn. Am. (chmn. Pacific N.W. group 1958-59, nat. bd. govs. from 1961), Phi Gamma Delta. Clubs: Seattle Golf (pres., trustee), Rainier (trustee), University, Wash. Athletic (Seattle). Home: Seattle WA Deceased.

EASTIN, BERTRAND P., oil co. exec.; b. Indpls., Apr. 27, 1911; s. Paul and Minnie (Elzea) E.; B.S., U. Cal. at Berkeley, 1937, M.S., 1939; m. Margaret I. Sandeman, Dec. 26, 1941; 1 son, Gary Brian. With Shell Oil Co., 1938-68, dir. prodn. research, exploration and prodn. research div. Shell Devel. Co., 1958-61, v.p. prodn. parent co., 1961-68. Mem. Am. Petroleum Inst., Am. Inst. Mining and Metall. Engrs., Sigma Xi. Home: Darien CT Died July 28, 1968.

EASTMAN, LEROY EMERSON, lawyer; b. Ottawa, O., June 23, 1888; s. Ephriam Richard and Elizabeth Ellen (Parrett) E.; Litt.B., Berea Coll., 1908; student law Yale, 1908-09, Ohio State U., 1910; m. Angela Ann Vocke, June 5, 1913; 1 dau., Susanne Marie (Mrs. Walter Eberhardt Schmitt, Jr.). Admitted to Ohio bar, 1910; partner with father Eastman & Eastman, Ottawa, O., 1910-16; asso. Smith, Baker, Effler & Allen, Toledo, 1917, partner since 1918, name changed to Effler, Eastman, Stichter & Smith, 1945, Eastman, Stichter & Smith, 1955, Eastman, Stichter, Smith & Bergman, 1963; dir. Sheller Globe Corp., Scott Properties Corporation; trustee Edw. Drummond Libbey Estate. Trustee of Toledo Museum of Art and its Endowment Fund. Mem. Toledo C. of C. (pres. 1951), Am., Ohio State, Lucas Co., Toledo bar assns., Beta Theta Pi, Phi Alpha Delta. Mason (33 deg.). Clubs: Toledo, Country (Toledo). Home: Toledo OH Died July 4, 1969.

EASTMAN, MAX (FORRESTER), author, editor; b. Canandaigua, N.Y., Jan. 4, 1883; s. Samuel Elijah and Annis Bertha (Ford) E.; A.B., Williams, 1905; studied Columbia, 1907-10; m. Ida Rauh, 1911; divorced, 1922, 1 son, Daniel (dec. 1969); m. 2d, Eliena Krylenko, 1924 (deceased October 1956); m. 3d, Yvette Szekely, Mar. 22, 1958. Asst. in philosophy, Columbia, 1907-10, associate 1911; engaged in lecturing; editor The Masses, 1913-17, The Liberator, 1918-22. Organized first Men's League for Woman Suffrage in U.S., 1910, roving editor for Reader's Digest 1941-69. Member Delta Psi. Translator: The Real Situation in Russia, by Leon Trotsky, 1928; Gabriel, by Pushkin, 1929; The History of the Russian Revolution, by Leon Trotsky, 1932; The Revolution Betrayed, by Leon Trotsky, 1937; The Young Lenin, by Leon Trotsky, 1972. Author: Child of the Amazons and Other Poems, 1913; Enjoyment of Poetry, 1913 (23d enlarged edit., 1948); Journalism Versus Art, 1916; Understanding Germany, 1916; Colors of Life (verse), 1918; The Sense of Humor, 1921; Since Lenin Died, 1925; Leon Trotsky, 1925; Marx and Lenin, the Science of Revolution, 1926; Venture, 1927; Kinds of Love (verse), 1931; The Literary Mind, Its Place in an Age of Science, 1931; Artists in Uniform, 1934; Art and the Life of Action, 1934; Enjoyment of Laughter, 1936; The End of Socialism in Russia, 1937; Stalin's Russia and the Crisis in Socialism, 1939; Marxism, Is It Science?, 1940; Heroes I Have Known, 1942; Lot's Wife, a Dramatic Poem, 1942; Enjoyment of Living, 1948; The Road to Abundance (with Jacob Rosin), 1953; Poems of Five Decades, 1954; Reflections on the Failure of Socialism, 1955; Great Companions—Critical Memoirs of Some Famous Friends, 1959; Love and Revolution, My Journey Through an Epoch, 1965; Seven Kinds of Goodness, 1967. Editor: Capital and Other Writings (by Karl Marx), 1932. Compiler and narrator: From Czar to Lenin, a motion picture history of the Russian revolution, 1937. Compiler: Anthology for Enjoyment of Poetry, 1939. Home: Chilmark MA Died Mar. 26, 1969; buried Martha's Vineyard MA

EASTMAN, REBECCA LANE HOOPER (MRS. WILLIAM FRANKLIN EASTMAN), author; b. Walpole, N.H., Mar. 22, 1877; d. Franklin William (Ph.D.) and Martha Smart (Holden) Hooper; grad. Adelphi Acad., Brooklyn; A.B., Radcliffe, 1900; post-grad. work, Columbia; m. William F. Eastman, of N.Y. City, July 27, 1912. Producer of plays for 6 yrs.; dir. dept. philology, Brooklyn Inst. Arts and Sciences. Mem. Authors' League America. Republican. Unitarian. Clubs: Women's Univ. (ex-pres.), Radcliffe (ex-pres.), Meridian, MacDowell, Civitas. Author: The Big Little Person, 1918. Wrote Miss Muffett's Birthday Party, for opening of Toy Theatre, Boston, 1915. Contbr. short stories to mags. Home: 96 Columbia Heights, Brooklyn NY‡

EASTWOOD, EVERETT OWEN, prof. emeritus mechanical engineering; born at Portsmouth, Virginia, on February 5, 1876; son of Matthew D. and Mary Anne (Thornton) E.; A.B., University of Virginia, 1899, B.S., 1897, A.M., 1899, C.E., 1896; B.S. in naval architecture, Mass. Institute of Tech., 1902; fellow in astronomy, U. of Va., 1897-1900; m. Nelle Dorothy Halliwall, Dec. 20, 1905; children—Emily Louise (Mrs. R. S. Bunker, Jr.), Mary Elizabeth (Mrs. Oliver Ashford). Draftsman Navy Dept., 1902-03, office of the chief constructor, 1903-04; with Fore River Shipbuilding Co., Quincy, Mass., 1904; instr. mech. engring. and naval architecture, Lehigh U., 1904-05; asst. prof. mech. engring, U. of Wash., Seattle, 1905, asso. prof., prof. and head of dept., 1905-29, dir. aeronautical engring., 1929-46, chmn. com. on Campus Planning, 1938-43, mem. U. Senate. Pres. board of trustees Univ. Congl. Ch., 1913-27; chmn. bd. dirs. Univ. Nat. Bank, Seattle, 1913, 1929. Charge of training course for engr. officers, U.S. Merchant Marine, U. of Wash., during World War I; in charge aviation training courses, Naval cadet classes, U. of Wash. Mem. Am. Soc. Heating and Ventilating Engrs. (v.p. 1941, pres. 1942), Am. Soc. Mech. Engrs. (mem. council, v.p. 1923-29), Am. Arbitration Assn., Am. Engring. Council (mem. council 1929-32), Sigma Alpha Epsilon, Tau Beta Pi, Sigma Xi. Conglist. Clubs: Faculty (U. of Wash.); Seattle Municipal League. Contbr. to tech. jours. Home: 4702 12th Av. N.E., Seattle WA‡

EATON, HORACE AINSWORTH, prof. English; b. Quincy, Mass., Oct. 13, 1871; s. Horace and Rebecca Phipps (Baxter) E.; A.B., Harvard, 1893, A.M., 1897, Ph.D., 1900; m. Emily Russell Lovett, of Brookline, Mass., 1902; children—Rebecca Baxter, Sidney Lovett, Robert Endicott, Elizabeth Russell. Instr. English and German, U. of Vt., 1901-03, prof. English, Syracuse U., since 1903, head of dept. since 1917. Visiting prof. U. of Ore., summer, 1921, 23, Columbia, 1924, 27, 31, U. of Ill., 2d semester 1930-31. Mem. Am. Assn. Univ. Profs., Modern Lang. Assn. America, Phi Beta Kappa, Phi Kappa Phi. Unitarian. Clubs: Faculty, Harvard (Syracuse). Editor of Diary of Thomas De Quincey for 1803. Address: Syracuse University, Syracuse NY‡

EATON, JAMES TUCKER, chem. co. exec.; b. Bonne Terre, Mo., Feb. 24, 1907; s. James A. and Nannie (Tucker) E.; A.B., Central Coll., Fayette, Mo., 1928; M.A., U. Ill., 1931, Ph.D., 1934; m. Margaret B. Alexander, Dec. 24, 1933; children—Shirley, Patricia (Mrs. Thomas M. Scott), and Barbra. Instructor of chemistry Central Coll., Fayette, Mo., 1928-29; asst. instr. U. Ill., Urbana, 1929-33; research chemist Ill. Geol. Survey, Urbana, 1934, Nat. Aniline div. Allied Chem. and Dye Corp., Buffalo, 1934-37; research chemist, E. F. Houghton & Co., Phila., 1938-41, asst. to v.p., 1941-46, mgr. research, 1946-50, dir. research, 1950-68, asst. dir. plants, 1951-54, v.p. prodn., 1955-68; dir., exec. v.p. E. F. Houghton and Co. of Can., Ltd., Toronto, 1955-68; dir. Houghton, S.A. in Buenos Aires. Mem. Hatboro-Horsham Joint Authority, Hatboro, Pa., 1950-53, chmn., 1950-52; mem. Hatboro School Board, 1952-61, president, 1952-55; mayor of Hatboro, 1962-68; Chairman Hatboro committee for Community Advance, 1957-60. Trustee Houghton-Carpenter Found. Dir. Mary Bailey Found.; trustee Presbyn. Hosp. of Phila., 1959-61. Pres. Elder's Assn. of Phila., 1947-49; mem. Presbyn. Social Union of Phila., 1943-68, (pres., 1957-58). Recipient Distinguished Alumnus citation Central College, Fayette, Missouri, in 1963. Mem. Am. Chem. Soc. (councilor 1951-54), A.A.A.S., Am. Leather Chemists Assn., Montgomery County Mayor's Assn. (pres. 1967-68), Alpha Chi Sigma, Sigma Xi. Presbyn. (elder). Home: Hatboro PA Died Mar. 21, 1968; cremated.

EATON, RUSSELL, college president; b. at Bridgewater, Massachusetts, July 6, 1873; s. George and Lucy (Washburn) E.; student Bridgewater State Teachers College, 1892-96, New Church Theological School, Cambridge, Massachusetts, 1897-1900; A.B., Urbana (O.) Univ., 1902; m. Frances Hepburn James, July 2, 1916; children—George, Harriet James, Margaret James, Russell, Lucy Washburn. Ordained ministry New Jerusalem Ch., 1900; pastor and teacher Urbana, 1900-17; pastor Brockton, Mass., 1917-29, Kitchener, Ont., Can., 1929-32; pres. Urbana Jr. Coll. since 1932. Active with Boy Scouts of America, Brockton, 10 yrs.; trustee New Ch. Theol. Sch. Home: 436 S. High St., Urbana OH‡

EAVES, LUCILE, sociologist; b. at Leavenworth, Kan., Jan. 9, 1869; d. David William and Anna C. (Weir) E.; A.B., Stanford U., 1894; U. of Chicago, 1898-9; Columbia, 1905-6; Flood fellow U. of Cal., 1907-9, M.Sc., 1909; Columbia, summer, 1909, Ph.D., 1910; unmarried. Head of history dept., San Diego (Cal.) High Sch., 1894-8; univ. extension lecturer in sociology, U. of Chicago, 1898-9; instr. in history, Stanford U., 1899-1901; head worker, South Park Settlement, San Francisco, 1901-05; dir. Industrial Bur., San Francisco Relief, 1906-07; asso. prof. practical sociology, U. of Neb., 1909-15; lecturer in economics, U. of Cal., 1913-14; dir. economic research, Women's Ednl. and Industrial Union and Simmons Coll., and lecturer at Simmons Coll., Boston, since 1915. Investigator of Carnegie Inst. Mem. Am. Econ. Assn., Am. Assn. for Labor Legislation, Am. Sociol. Soc., Phi Beta Kappa, etc. Club: Collegiate Alumnae. Author: History of the California Labor Legislation, 1910; The Food of Working Women in Boston, 1917. Address: 264 Boylston St., Boston MA‡

EBAUGH, FRANKLIN GESSFORD, psychiatrist; b. Reistertown, Md., May 14, 1895; s. Zachariah Charles and Elizabeth Bell (Gessford) E.; A.B., Johns Hopkins, 1915, M.D., 1919; m. Dorothy Reese, Apr. 9, 1921; children—Franklin G., David C., Donald R., Nancy Haines. Res. med. officer, Henry Phipps Clinic, 1919-20; asst. physician, New Jersey State Hospital., 1920-21; director neuro-psychiatric dept., Philadelphia Gen. Hosp., 1920-24; instr. in psychiatry, U. of Pa., 1922-24; dir. Colo. Psychopathic Hosp., Denver, since 1924; clin. prof. psychiatry University of Colorado, Denver, 1924-53, prof. emeritus 1953-72; pvt. practice psychiatry, 1953. Served as col. M.C., AUS, neuropsychiat. consultant Eighth Service Command, Dallas, Texas, 1942-45, served in Pacific area. Office of Chief Surgeon, June 1945-46. Director Division of Psychiatric Edn., Nat. Com. for Mental Hygiene, 1933-42; mem. Am. Bd. of Psychiatric Examiners, 1933-41; chmn. sect. nervous and mental diseases, Am. Med. Assn., 1931-32; pres. Colo. Soc. for Mental Hygiene; chmn. Gov's. Com. Mental Health, Colo., 1960-61; mem. Ft. Logan Mental Health Center Adv. Com., 1964-65; mem. Am. Bd. of Psychiatry and Neurology, 1934-42; cons.-at-large U.S.P.H.S.; cons. office of Surgeon Gen.; mem. editorial bd. Am. Jour. of Psychiatry, Current Med. Digest, Post-Grad. Medicine, Am. Practitioner, Diseases of Nervous System; contbg. editor Am. Jour. of Med. Sciences; mem. advisory bd. Med. Specialties, 1934-42, Council on Mental Health, Colorado, from 1957. Recipient Distinguished Service award American Psychiatric Association, 1966. Fellow of the American Psychiatric Association (council 1931-34); mem. A.M.A., Colo. Med. Soc. (past chmn. com. mental health), Am. Neurol. Assn., Canadian Neuropsychiatric Assn. (hon.), Nat. Research Council (com. on neuropsychiatry), Am. Psychiatric Association (Colorado District branch president 1960-61, chmn. com. on psychiatry in med. edn.), Assn. Research Nervous and Mental Disease (pres. 1944). Central Psych. Assn. (pres. 1930), Grad. Med. Edn. (mem. commn. 1936-41), Alpha Kappa Kappa, Sigma Xi, Alpha Omega Alpha; corr. mem. Royal Medico-Psychol. Assn. since 1929. Rep. Episcopalian. Mason. Clubs: Mile High, Cactus, Denver Country. Co-author: Practical Clinical Psychiatry (with E. A. Strecher), 1925, 8th edit., 1946; Psychiatry in Medical Education (with Charles A. Rymer), 1942. Contbr. to Am. Jour. Psychiatry, Am. Jour. Med. Sciences, Archives Neurology and Psychiatry, Am. Practitioner, Jour. Nervous and Mental Diseases, Postgrad. Medicine. Home: Denver CO Died Jan. 4, 1972.

EBEL, WILLIAM K., engring. exec.; b. Orangeville, Ill., Jan. 2, 1899; s. William H. and Nora A. (Rubendall) E.; B.A., Heidelberg Coll., 1921, Sc.D., 1942; B.S. in mech. engring. Case Inst. Tech., 1923, Eng.D., 1942; flying cadet U.S. Army A.C. Flying Sch., 1923-24; m. Florence E. Sherck, Oct. 29, 1929; children—William K., Lydia L. Engr. Douglas Co., 1925, Glenn L. Martin Co., Balt., 1924-25, successively asst. chief engr., chief engr., v.p. engring., 1926-48, dir., 1942-48; dir. engring., airplane div. Curtiss-Wright Corp., Columbus, O., 1948-49; v.p. engring. Canadair, Ltd., Montreal, Can., 1949-60; staff exec. engring. Gen. Dynamics Corp., Washington, 1960-63. Fellow Inst. Aero. Sciences, Canadian Aeronautical Institute; member Soc. Automotive Engrs., Sigma Xi, Kappa Sigma. Home: Montreal PQ Canada. Died July 1972.

EBERHARDT, CHARLES CHRISTOPHER, diplomat; b. Salina, Kan., July 27, 1871; s. Christopher and Anna Catharine (Lampert) E.; ed. Kan. Wesleyan U., Salina, LL.D., 1929; unmarried. In lumber business, Salina, 1891-93; with Mass. Mut. Life Ins. Co., Springfield, Mass., 1894-1902, gen. agent in Kan., 1902-03; with Waters-Pierce Oil Co., Mexico City, 1903-04; entered office of Am. consulate-gen. at Mexico City, 1903, consul at Iquitos, Peru, 1906-08; Barranquilla, Colombia, 1908-10; consul-gen.-at-large, for South and Central America, W.I., and Curacao, Jan. 12, 1910; instr. of consuls, Dept. of State, 1919; consul-gen.-at-large for Eastern Asia, 1919-22, consul-gen. Eastern Europe, 1922-24; chmn. exec. com. Personnel Bd. Foreign Service, Washington, D.C., 1924-25; minister to Nicaragua, 1925-30, to Costa Rica, 1930-33, retired. Republican. Methodist. Mason (K.T., Shriner). Clubs: Chevy Chase, Metropolitan, Racquet, Washington Golf and Country (Washington); Buccanneers (Berlin). Home: Salina KS‡

EBERLY, GEORGE AGLER, judge; b. Ft. Wayne, Ind., Feb. 9, 1871; s. John and Mary (Agler) E.; LL.B., U. of Mich., 1892, LL.M., 1893; m. Rose Psotta, Aug. 2, 1899; children—Lloyd A. (dec.), Lola A. (Mrs. John A. Negley), George D. Resident of Neb. since 1873; admitted to bar, 1893; county atty., Stanton County, 1899-1903, 1905-09; apptd. asso. justice Supreme Ct. of Neb. for term, 1925-31, elected for terms, 1931-37 and 1937-43; retired from Supreme Court Bench, January 7, 1943. Sergeant Spanish-Am. War, May 15-Sept. 11, 1898; successively capt., maj. and col. Neb. Nat. Guard, 1902-17; comdr. 4th Neb. Inf., Mexican border service, 1916-17; apptd. col. Inf., U.S.R.C., Feb., 1917; ordered to active duty, O.T.C., May 5, 1917; served as col. inf., O.R.C. and maj. N.A. until Dec. 3, 1918. Recipient Lincoln (Neb.) Kiwanis International Medal, 1948. Mem. Am., Neb., State and 9th Neb. Dist. bar assns., Neb. State Hist. Society, Sons of Union Veterans Civil War (past state comdr.), Naval and mil. order Spanish-Am. War Vets. (comdr.-in-chief, 1949, United Spanish War Veterans (comdr.-in-chief), Am. Legion, 40 and 8, Mil. Order World War. Republican. Conglist. Mason (32 deg., K.T.); mem. Woodmen, Sons of Hermann, Ben Hur. Clubs: Kiwanis, Hiram (internat.), Interprofessional Inst. Sojourners: Apptd. Judge Advocate Gen. United Spanish War Vets. Home: Stanton, NE Address: 900 S. 18th St., Lincoln NE‡

EBERSOLE, J(ACOB) SCOTT, clergyman; b. Springfield, O., Jan. 9, 1869; s. Peter and Hannah (Frantz) E.; student prep. dept. Wittenberg Coll., Springfield, O., 1887-89; Ohio Normal U., Ada, O., summers, 1890-92; Doan Acad., Granville, O., 1893; A.B., Denison U., 1897, D.D., 1926; grad. Rochester Theol. Sem., 1900; m. Maude Detrick, June 17, 1897. Teacher country schs., Ohio, 1889-92; ordained Bapt. ministry, 1900; pastor successively Coshocton, O., Canandaigua, N.Y., Immanuel Ch., Omaha, Neb., North Shore Ch., Chicago, Lafayette Av. Ch., Buffalo, N.Y., term of 8 years, until 1926, erecting new 2-unit ch. bldg. at cost of 25,000; pastor Carbondale, Ill., 1926-30, Champaign, Ill., 1930-35; acting pastor Hildreth Ch., Columbus, O., 1936; First Ch., DeKalb, Ill., and Judson Ch., Oak Park, Ill., 1937, First Ch. Centralia, Ill., 1938; First Ch., Decatur, Ill., 1939; acting pastor First Ch., E. St. Louis, Ill., 1940; acting pastor Herald of Hope Ch., Urbana, 1941; acting pastor Hildreth Ch., Columbus, O., 1942-43, Greenville, 1944, Mt. Vernon, 1945, Robinson (all Ill.), 1946-47. Prof., Old Testament hist., University of Omaha, 1910-11. Y.M.C.A. religious work secretary, United States Naval Air Station, Hmapton Roads, Va., Dec. 1918-Mar., 1919. Trustee Northern Bapt. Theol. Sem. (Chicago), Grand Island (Neb.) Coll. Moderator, Alton (Ill.) Bapt. Assn., 1929-30; dir. Ill. Bapt. State Conv., v.p. and mem. exec. com., 1932-36; moderator Champaign-Urbana Bapt. Assn., 1933-34. Republican. Mason. Home: 707 W. Church St., Champaign IL

EBERSTADT, FERDINAND, investment banker; b. New York, N.Y., June 19, 1890; s. Edward F. and Elenita (Lembcke) E.; A.B., Princeton, 1913; LL.B., Columbia, 1917; D.C.S. honoris causa, New York University; married Mary Van Arsdale Tongue, Dec. 31, 1919; children—Frances Stuart, Mary Van Arsdale, Frederick, Ann Van Arsdale. Began as law clerk with McAdoo, Cotton & Franklin, 1919; partner Cotton & Franklin, 1923-25; partner Dillon, Read & Co., 1925-29; asst. to Owen D. Young, Reparations Conf., 1929; Co., 1925-29; asst. to Owen D. Young, Reparations Conf., 1929; partner F. Eberstadt & Co., investment bankers; dir. F. Eberstadt & Co., Managers and Distributors, Inc.; chairman of The Eberstadt Fund, Inc.; chmn. Chem. Fund, Inc. Hon. dir. Beekman Downtown Hosp. Squadron A, New York Cavalry, 1916-17; with 304th F.A., 77th Division, U.S.A., with AEF, 1917-19; with Army of Occupation, 1919. Chairman Army and Navy Munitions Bd., 1942; v. chmn. War Prodn. Bd., 1942-43; prepared Eberstadt Report" for sec. Navy, 1945; asst. to B.M. Baruch, U.N. Atomic Energy Commn., 1946; prepared report on operations of Nat. Security Resources Bd., 1948; chmn. com. on Nat. Security Orgn. of the Hoover Commn. (Commn. on Orgn. of Exec. Br. of the Govt.). Bd. advisers, Indsl. Coll. of the Armed Forces. Mem. U.S.N. Civilian Adv. Com., A.U.S. Adv. Com.; mem. bd. Presbyn. Hosp. Corp.; mem. bd. visitors U.S. Naval Acad., 1946; mem. Army Ordnance Assn.; mem. (hon.) Navy Indsl. Assn., Navy League of the U.S., U.S. Naval Inst., Naval Hist. Found., Phi Beta Kappa. Presbyn. Clubs: University, Princeton, Squadron A Assn., Downtown Assn., River, Piping Rock (N.Y.C.); Huntington (N.Y.) Country; Seawanhaka-Corinthian Yacht; Lyford Cay (Nassau, Bahamas). Home: Huntington LI NY Died Nov. 11, 1969; buried Huntington.

EBERT, EDMUND FRANCIS, banker; b. N.Y.C., Aug. 11, 1911; s. Samuel Harvey and Emily Grace (Cash) E.; student N.Y.U., 1930-32, 41; m. Lathelia Marie Keesey, Oct. 22, 1938; children—Beth Lynn (dec.), Douglas Edmund, Joan Marie. Began as messenger Bankers Trust Co. of N.Y., 1928, dept. head, 1934-39, field rep., 1939-42, asst. treas., 1942-46, asst. v.p., 1946-48, v.p., 1948-61, sr. v.p., 1961-70, exec. v.p., 1970-72; v.p., dir. Interstate Color Co., Inc., 1936-51. Councilman Town of New Castle, N.Y., 1959-63, chmn. bd. ethics, 1970-72). Commd. lt. (j.g.) S.C., USN, 1944, apptd. dep. fiscal dir., 1945; disch. as lt., 1946; lt. res., 1945-52. Bd. dirs., treas. Ednl. Found. for Fashion Industries. Mem. Am. Bankers Assn. (chmn. credit policy com.), Acad. Polit. Sci., Downtown Lower Manhattan Assn. (dir.). Conglist. Clubs: Union League (N.Y.C.); Mt. Kisco Country (pres. 1956, 57), Bankers of N.Y. Inc.; Seaview Country; Economic; Board Room. Home: Chappaqua NY Died May 7, 1972; buried Kensico Cemetery, Valhalla NY

EBERT, ROBERT EDWIN, business exec.; b. Wilmington, N.C., Feb. 15, 1893; s. R.A. and Lula (Croom) E.; student pub. schs. Wilmington, N.C., Bus. Coll., Columbia, S.C.; m. Rubye Taft Williamson, Sept. 23, 1932; children—Robert Edwin, William Southworth, Michael Preston. Co-owner Central Chevrolet Co. since 1930; Ebert Realty Co., Columbia, S.C., since 1940; pres. Dixie-Home Stores, Greenville, S.C., from 1936; dir., chmn. bd. Charlotte (N.C.) br. Fed. Res. Bd.; dir. S.C. Nat. Bank, First Nat. Bank (both Greenville). Methodist. Home: Greenvile SC Died Aug. 15, 1968; interred Woodlawn Mausoleum, Greenville SC

EBY, FREDERICK, univ. prof.; b. Berlin, Ont., Can., Oct. 26, 1874; s. Aaron (M.D.) and Matilde Croft (Bowers) E.; student Stratford (Can.) Collegiate Inst., 1888-91; A.B., McMaster U., 1895, LL.D., 1921; grad. study U. of Chicago, 1895-97; Ph.D., Clark U., 1900; grad. study U. of Berlin, 1905-06; L.H.D., Baylor U., 1945; m. Elizabeth Nuckolls Newman, Dec. 26, 1900; children—Mary Newman (Mrs. R. F. Howard), Albert Newman, Elizabeth Bowers (Mrs. Byron Vestal), Frederick, Helen (Mrs. Elwin Craig). Came to U.S., 1895, naturalized citizen, 1921. Instr., Morgan Park Acad., 1897-98; prof. philosophy and education, Baylor U., 1900-09; instr. and prof. history and philosophy of edn., U. of Tex., since 1909, also dir. summer session, 1917-31; vis. prof. summer sessions various univs. Democrat. Baptist. Author several books on edn. including: The Development of Modern Education, 1934, revised 1952. Home: 2612 San Pedro St., Austin TX‡

ECHOLS, LEONARD SIDNEY, ex-congressman; b. Madison, W.Va., Oct. 30, 1871; s. George A. and Cartha Grace (Atkins) E.; grad. Commercial Coll. of Ky. U., Lexington, Ky., 1894, Concord Normal Sch., Athens, W. Va., 1898; LL.B., Southern Normal U., Huntingdon, Tenn., 1900; m. Anne Campbell De Pue, of Spencer, W.Va., Mar. 27, 1913; 1 son, Leonard Sidney. Began practice at Point Pleasant, W. Va., 1903; pros. atty. Mason Co., W.Va., 1904-09; asst. state tax commr., W.Va., 1909-19; mem. firm Echols, Lively & Stambaugh; mem. 66th and 67th Congresses (1919-23), 6th W. Va. Dist. Mem. Comm. on Appeals and Review, Treasury Dept., May 1, 1923-Sept. 22, 1924; postmaster Charleston, W.Va., 1925-29; in practice of law and referee in bankruptcy since 1929. Republican. Mason (32 deg.). Home: Charleston WV‡

ECKARD, ELISABETH ELLEN GILLILAND, journalist; b. Des Moines, July 10, 1919; d. Charles Homer and Abbie (Welles) Gilliland; B.A., U. Ia., 1941; m. Vyrle Leo Eckard, Apr. 11, 1945 (div. Nov. 1962); children—Lucille Elisabeth, William Charles. Reporter, Jefferson (Ia.) Bee & Herald, 1941-46, publicity work, 1939-59; feature writer, gen. reporter Carroll (Ia.) Daily Times Herald, 1959-68. Mem. adv. bd. Antonian Sch. Practical Nursing. Mem. D.A.R., Theta Sigma Phi, Am. Legion Aux. Trinity Guild (pres. 1963-64), Ia. Alumni Assn. (sec.-treas. 1959). Republican. Episcopalian. Mem. Order Eastern Star. Home: Carroll IA Died Dec. 16, 1968.

ECKART, E. ALBERT, paint mfr.; b. New Rochelle, N.Y., Sept. 5, 1902; s. Edmund and Emily (Gietl) E.; grad. Yale, 1923; m. Ruth C. Brumley, Oct. 15, 1926 (dec. Aug. 1971); children—Judith B., E. Albert. With Sapolin Paints, Inc., N.Y.C., 1923-71, chmn. bd. Mem. Berzelius Soc. Republican. Clubs: Yale, N.Y. Athletic (N.Y.C.). Home: Westport CT Died Oct. 8, 1971.

ECKEL, CLARENCE LEWIS, univ. dean; b. Buffalo, Ill., Mar. 2, 1892; s. John Louis and Ida Francis (Jack) E.; B.S., U. of Colo., 1914, C.E., 1921; m. Florence Robinson, June 12, 1917; children—Patricia Fairchild (Mrs. Carroll Wilson Griffin), Robert Bruce. Concrete detailer and designer, H. S. Crocker, cons. engr., Denver, 1914, engr., 1926 and 1929; constrn. supt. M. S. Ketchum, Cons. Engr., Longmont, Colo., 1915; detailer, Am. Bridge Co., Pencoyd, Pa., 1922-23; chief constrn. engr., Crocker & Ryan, architect-engr., Air Support Command Base, Colorado Springs, Colo., 1942; instr. in civil engring., U. of Colo., 1914; asst. prof. U. of Pa., 1919-23; prof. U. of Colo., 1923-26, also engr., constrn. dept., 1925, head dept. of civil engring., 1926-43, cons. engr. constrn. dept. since 1936, dean coll. of engring. and prof. civil engring. from 1943; vis. lectr. Coll. Engring., San Diego State Coll., 1960-62. Served as 1st lt., Co. B, Engrs., Colo. Nat. Guard; capt., Co. A, 115th Engrs., AEF, 1917-19, part-time; commander 1st Bn., 115th Engrs. Technical editor civil engring. class, Lefax, Phila., 1920-25. Recipient Faculty Appreciation award Asso. Engring. Student Faculty, 1960; Distinguished Engring. Alumnus award U. Colo., 1966; All Conf. Center Football U. Colo. Hall Honor award, 1972. Mem. Colo. Bd. Examiners for Engrs. and Land Surveyors, from 1942; dir. Western Zone, Nat. Council State Bds. Engring. Examiners, 1946-48; v.p. Nat. Council State Bds. Engring. Examiners, 1948-49 (pres. 1949-50). Mem. Am. Soc. C.E. (pres. Colo. sect. 1932, nat. dist. dir. 1955-58; rep. Engrs. Council for Profl. Development subcom. from 1936), Colo. Engring. Council (pres. 1956), A.I.A. (hon. asso. Colo. chpt. 1956), Am. Society of Engineering Education (member council 1934-37, v.p. 1957), American Concrete Inst., Colo. Soc. Engrs. (Gold Medal award, hon. life), Am. Soc. Mech. Engrs., Colo. Sch. Masters Club, Nat., Colo. edn. assns., Acacia, Alpha Sigma Phi, Tau Beta Pi, Sigma Tau, Sigma Xi, Chi Epsilon (pres. 1950-52). Licensed profl. engr. Pa. and Colo. Mason (Shriner). Club: Boulder CO Died July 31, 1972; cremated.

ECKERT, WALLACE J., astronomer; b. Pittsburgh; June 19, 1902; s. John and Anna (Heil) E.; A.B., Oberlin Coll., 1925, D. Sc., 1968; M.A., Amherst Coll., 1926, U. of Chicago, 1925, Columbia U., 1928, Ph.D., Yale, 1931; m. Dorothy Applegate, May 14, 1932; children—Alice Applegate, John Wallace, Penelope D. Asst., dept. of astronomy, Columbia, 1926-27, instr., 1927-31, asst. prof. 1931-40 and prof., 1940; dir. U.S. Nautical Almanac, U.S. Naval Observatory, 1940-45, dir. dept. pure science, Internat. Business Machines Corp., 1945-52; dir. Watson Scientific Computing Lab., 1945-67; prof. celestial mechanics, Columbia U. Councillor Am. Astronomical Soc. Recipient James Craig Watson medal Nat. Acad. Sci., 1966; IBM award, 1969, IBM fellow, 1967, Fellow A.A.A.S. Mem. Internat. Astron. Union, Am. Astron. Soc., Washington Acad. Science, Am. Math. Society. Author: Punched Card Methods in Scientific Computation, 1940; Coordinates of the Five Outer Planets 1653-2060, 1951; Construction of the Improved Lunar Ephemeris, 1954; Faster, Faster, 1954. Home: Leonia NJ Died Aug. 24, 1971.

ECKERT, WILLIAM D(OLE), retired air force officer, business executive; born Freeport, Illinois, on January 20, 1909; the son of Frank Lloyd and Harriet Julia (Rudy) E.; B.S., U.S. Mil. Acad., 1930; grad. (with pilot's rating), Air Force Flying Sch., 1931; M.B.A., Harvard, 1940, student Army-Navy Staff Sch., 1944; m. Catharine Douglas Givens, June 15, 1940; children—Catharine Julia, William Douglas. Commd. 2d lt. U.S. Army, 1930; advanced through grades to lt. general; transferred to U.S.A.A.F., 1931; served at Albrook Field, Panama Canal Zone, 1935-57, Randolph Field, Tex., 1937-38; budget officer and exec. to comdg. gen., Air Materiel Command, Wright Field, Dayton, O., 1940-44; group comdr., later chief of supply, 9th AFSC, Europe, 1944; executive to Deputy Chief of Staff, Materiel, 1945, chief of readjustment and procurement div., 1946; exec. to Under Sec. of Air Force, 1947-49; comptroller Air Materiel Command, Wright-Patterson Air Force Base, Ohio, 1949-51, asst. dep. comdg. gen., 1951-52; asst. dep. chief of staff Materiel, Hdqrs. USAF, 1952-56; vice comdr. Tactical Air Command, 1956-61; comptroller USAF, Feb.-Mar. 1961, ret. as lt. gen., 1961; major league baseball commr., 1965-69. Chmn. retirement council Air Force. Bd. Advisers Tantallon Community, Air Force Assn. Mem. exec. council of Harvard Bus. Sch., from 1961; trustee Little League Found., Logistic Management Inst.; member board of directors Baseball Hall of Fame, 1966-69. Decorated D.S.M. with oak leaf cluster, Legion of Merit with 2 oak leaf clusters, D.F.C., Bronze Star, Air medal (U.S.); Croix de Guerre with palm (France and Luxembourg). Mem. Air Force Assn., Am. Soc. Mil. Comptrollers (past pres.), Am. Legion, Air Force Assn., Baseball Writers Assn. Am. Episcopalian. Clubs: Army-Navy Country (past pres., Nat. Rocket (dir.), Harvard of Dayton (O.) (past pres.), Air Force Acad. Parents, Lambs, Aviation, Harvard Busines of N.Y., Gate. Home: Clearwater FL Died Apr. 16, 1971.

ECKHART, PERCY BERNARD, lawyer; b. Chicago, Ill., Jan. 20, 1877; s. Bernard A. and Katie L. (Johnston) E.; Ph.B., U. of Chicago, 1899; LL.B., Harvard U., 1902; Doctor of Laws, Northwestern University, 1950; m. Charlotte Briggs Capen, June 6, 1903 (dec.); children—Eleanor (Mrs. Kenneth B. Murdock), Charlotte (Mrs. Thomas Roswell Coyne), Marion (Mrs. A. Eugene Bailey), Elizabeth (Mrs. Darwin P. Kingsley); m. second, Helen Kaiper Van Cleave, Dec. 28, 1955. Admitted Ill. bar, 1902, began practice Chgo., West & Eckhart, 1902-43; mem. Eckhart, McSwain, Hassell & Silliman; pres., dir. DeSoto Securities trustee Ravinia Festival Assn.; lectr. pub. service corps., U. Chgo. Law Sch., 1903-15. Trustee Art Inst., Chgo.; mem. Chgo. Symphony Orchestral Assn. Recipient Centennial award Northwestern U., 1951, citation as sr. counselor Ill. State Bar Assn., 1952. Mem. Am., Ill., Chgo. bar assns., Legal Club, Law Club, Delta Kappa Epsilon, Phi Delta Phi. Republican. Presbyn. Clubs: Chicago, Union League, Commercial, Cliff Dwellers, Mid-day, Indian Hill Country, Executives, University (Chgo.); Lake Placid (N.Y.). Home: Chicago IL Died July 15, 1969; buried Rosehill Cemetery, Chicago IL

ECKLES, ISABEL LANCASTER, educator; b. Wilmington, Del., September 8, 1877; d. Samuel Holedger and Mary Jane (White) E.; A.B., State Teachers Coll., Silver City, N.M., 1914; hon. M.A., 1923; unmarried. Teacher pub. schs., 16 yrs.; county supt. schs., Grant Co., N.M., 1912-19; served as registrar and acting pres. State Teachers Coll.; state supt. pub. instrn., N.M., 2 terms, 1923-27; supt. schs., Santa Fe, N.M., 1927-36. Mem. N.M. State Bd. Edn., term 1927-31. Active in war drives and Red Cross work. Dir. Professional and Service Div., Work Projects Administration, for N.M. Mem. State Girls' Welfare Bd.; dir. Santa Fe Fiesta Assn. Mem. N.M. Ednl. Assn. (pres. 1918-20), Nat. Illiteracy Commn., Nat. Council of Administrative Women in Edn. of N.E.A. (pres. 1931-33). Democrat. Episcopalian. Clubs: Woman's (Santa Fe). Home: Casitas de Analco, 126 E. De Vargas St., Santa Fe NM‡

EDDY, HENRY BREVOORT, artist; b. New York, Sept. 16, 1872; s. Ulysses D. and Jane (Brevoort) E.; prep. ed'n St. Paul's Sch., Concord, N. H., 1884-90; grad. Harvard, 1894; unmarried. Engaged as newspaper artist since 1898; on staff New York Journal. Clubs: Calumet, Harvard. Residence: 501 5th Av. Office: 15 Spruce St., New York‡

EDDY, NATHAN BROWNE, pharmacologist; b. Glens Falls, N.Y., Aug. 4, 1890; s. Charles Appleton and Aletta Amelia (Norcross) E.; M.D., Cornell U., 1911; D.Sc., U. Mich., 1963; m. Wilhelmina Marie Ahrens, Sept. 7, 1913; 1 son, Charles Ernest. Began practice of medicine, N.Y.C., 1911; instr. physiology McGill U., 1916-20; asst. prof. physiology and pharmacology U. Alta., 1920-28, asso. prof., 1928-30; research prof. pharmacology U. Mich., 1930-39; formerly cons. biologist in alkaloids, USPHS, prin. pharmacologist, 1939-48, med. officer, 1948-60, cons. on narcotics, 1960-73. Co-recipient 1st annual award Am. Pharm. Mfrs. Assn., 1939. Profl. asso. NRC, 1960-67, chmn. com. on drug dependence, 1970-71; exec. sec. com. on drug addiction and narcotics, 1947-67; mem. Expert Com. on Narcotic Drugs, WHO, chmn., 1949-51, 57, 63, 67, 68; chmn. adv. com. to Bur. Narcotics under Narcotics Mfg. Act. of 1960; cons. Bur. Narcotics and Dangerous Drugs, 1968-73. Recipient citation Dept. Health and Welfare; Sixth Lister Meml. Lect., Edinburg, 1960; William Freeman Snow award Am. Social Health Assn., 1967; Hillebrand prize Chem. Soc. Washington, 1968; Meml. award WHO, 1968; gold medal Eastern Psychiat. Research Assn., 1970. Fellow A.A.A.S.; mem. Soc. Pharmacol. and Exptl. Therapeutics (mem. council 1944). Soc. Exptl. Biology and Medicine, Coll. Clin. Pharmacology, Coll. Neuro-psychopharmacology, Internat. Narcotics Enforcement Officers Assn., Sigma Xi. Republican. Methodist. Club: Cosmos. Co-author: Pharmacology of Opium Alkaloids; Synthetic Drugs with Morphine-Like Effect; Codeine and Its Alternates for Pain and Cough Relief. Contbr. to med., sci. jours. Address: Bethesda MD Died 1973.

EDELMAN, JOHN W., labor rep.; b. Belleville, N.J., June 27, 1893; s. John Hermann and Rachelle (Krimont) E.; m. Kate Van Eaton, April, 26, 1920; children—Alison (Mrs. Joseph Carter), Arnold, Anne (Mrs. Ben Stephansky). Music and dramatic critic, Springfield Republican, Mass., 1915-18; publicity and research dir., Am. Fedn. Hosiery Workers, 1926-37; regional CIO dir. eastern Pennsylvania, 1937-39; asst. dir. information U.S. Housing Authority, 1939-1940; labor cons. Nat. Defense Adv. Council Consumer div., 1940-42; CIO liaison officer, OPA Labor Office, 1941-42; Washington rep. Textile Workers Union of America, CIO, since 1943. Private U.S. Army, 1918-19. Mem. Nat. CIO Legislative Com., Nat. Policy Com. (exec. com.), Am. Labor Edn. Service (bd. dirs.), OPA Labor Policy Com., Commn. on Children in War Time, U.S. Children's Bureau, Newspaper Guild (charter mem.), Nat. Labor Housing Conf. (sec., 1934-37), Juniata Park Housing Corp. (bd. dirs.), Old Dominion Housing Corp. (pres.), Nat. Housing Conf. (dir.), Com. on Nations Health (dir.). Pioneered in field of pub. relations for labor orgns.; del. to ILO conf., Geneva, 1936. Home: Arlington VA Died Dec. 27, 1971.

EDELMAN, NATHAN, educator; b. Paris, France, Mar. 29, 1911; s. Abel and Sarah (Podvidz) E.; brought to U.S., 1922, naturalized, 1927; student Sorbonne, 1930-31; A.B., Coll. City N.Y., 1932, M.S., 1934; Ph.D., Columbia, 1945; m. Lily J. Podvidz, May 30, 1936; 1 dau., Jean L. (dec.). Instr. French, Coll. City N.Y., 1932-43, Hamilton Coll., 1943-44; instr. French, Columbia, 1944-48, asst. prof., 1948-54, asso. prof., 1954-56; prof., chmn. Romance langs. Johns Hopkins, 1956-66; prof. French, Columbia U., 1966-71, chmn. dept. French and Romance philology, 1968-71. Recipient Columbia U. fellowship, 1937-38, Guggenheim fellowship, 1954-55, sr. fellowship Nat. Endowment for the Humanities. Mem. Modern Lang. Assn. Am., Am. Assn. Tchrs. French, Societe d'Etude du Dix-Septieme Siecle, Phi Beta Kappa. Author: Attitudes of 17th Century France Toward the Middle Ages, 1946. Mng. editor The Romanic Rev., 1948-52; editor Vol. 3, A Critical Bibliography of French Lit., 1961; gen. editor Modern Lang. Notes, 1957-60. Contbr. articles in field. Home: New York City NY Died Nov. 14, 1971; buried Cedar Park Cemetery, Emerson NJ

EDENS, ARTHUR HOLLIS, found. exec.; b. Willow Grove, Tenn., Feb. 14, 1901; s. Everett C. and Barbara Ellen (Jolly) E.; student Cumberland Mountain Sch., Crossville, Tenn., 1921-24; Ph.B., Emory U., 1930, A.M., 1938; student U. of Chicago, 1941; M.P.A., Harvard, 1944, Ph.D., 1949; LL.D., Emory U., Davidson Coll., 1949, University N.C., Wake Forest Coll., 1951, Roanoke Coll., 1953, Am. U., 1956, Northwestern University, 1958, University of Chattanooga, 1959; married Mary Kathleen Bussell, Dec. 24, 1930; 1 dau., Mary Ann. Tchr. Cumberland Mountain School, 1926-27, asst. prin. 1929-30, prin., 1930-37; div. exec. and asso. dean Emory Jr. Coll., Valdosta, Ga., 1937-42, asso. dean undergrad. divs., Emory U., 1942-44, asso. prof. polit. sci., 1944-47, dean adminstrn., 1946; v. chancellor Univ. System State of Ga., 1947; asso. dir. Gen. Edn. Bd., Rockefeller Found., 1948; pres. Duke U., 1949-60; exec. dir. Mary Reynolds Babcock Found., Inc., 1961-66; cons., dir. scholarship program Anne Stouffer Found., 1966-68. Adv. bd. Air Tng. Command, 1954-56; mem. Com. Canadian-Am. Affairs, 1957-60; mem. U.S. Adv. Commn. on Ednl. Exchange, 1954-60; mem. President's Com. on Edn. beyond High Sch., 1956-57; pres. Nat. Commn. on Accrediting, 1954-56, So. U. Conf., 1958-59. Mem. bd. dirs. The North Carolina Fund, 1963-68; bd. trustees Emory University, 1964-68. Member Nat. Assn. Schs. and Colls. Meth. Ch. (pres. 1954), So. Assn. Colls. and Secondary Schs. (exec. com. 1949-53, 57-60), Am. Acad. Polit. and Social Sci., Acad. Polit. Sci., Am. Polit. Sci. Assn., Phi Beta Kappa, Omicron Delta Kappa, Sigma Chi. Democrat. Methodist. Mason, Rotarian. Club: Century (N.Y.C.). Address: Decatur GA Died Aug. 7, 1968; buried Decatur Cemetery, Decatur GA

EDENS, JAMES BENJAMIN, lumber exec.; b. Saron, Tex., Oct. 13, 1913; s. William Frederick and Cordelia (Hooks) E.; student Stephen Austin Coll., Nacogdoches, Tex., 1932; m. Etheldred Devereaux, May 26, 1931; children—James Benjamin II, William D.; m. 2d, Rosa Reiser, Jan. 16, 1955; 1 dau., Cathy. With Edens-Birch Lumber Co., Corrigan, Tex., 1933-52, beginning in sales office, successively sales mgr., gen. mgr., pres., 1946-52; pres. Southwest Lumber Mills, Inc., Phoenix, 1952-72, corp. named Southwest Forest Industries, Inc., 1960, now chmn. bd., chief exec. officer; former dir. Gt. Western Corp., Tucson, adv. dir. Gt. Western Bank, Tucson; pres., dir. Apache Railway Co. Mem. Forest Industries Com. on Timber Valuation and Taxation. Bd. dirs. Phoenix Symphony Assn.; trustee Phoenix Country Day Sch. Mem. S.W. Pine Assn. (past pres., past dir.), Western Wood Products Assn. (dir., past pres.), Nat. Forest Products Assn. (past pres., chmn.), N.A.M. (past dir.), Econ. Council Forest Products Industry (past chmn.), Newcomen Soc. N. Am., Am. Paper Inst. Methodist. Mason (Shriner). Clubs: Executives, Phoenix Country, Cloud, White Mountain Country, Internat. of Houston; Pinetop Country; Plimsoll; Tres Vidas, Paradise Valley Country, Arizona Press. Home: Scottsdale AZ Died Oct. 16, 1972; buried Greenwood Meml. Park.

EDER, PHANOR JAMES, lawyer; b. Palmira, Republic of Colombia, S.A., Dec. 11, 1880; s. James Martin and Lizzie (Benjamin) E.; spl. student U. Liege (Belgium), 1897-98; A.B., Coll. City N.Y., 1900; LL.B., Harvard, 1903; m. Violet Lindo, Apr. 21, 1900; children—Linda Jamieson (Mrs. Storrow), James. Practice in N.Y.C., 1903-—, specializing corp. law, Latin-Am. matters; counsel Hardin, Hess & Eder. Formerly vice consul of Colombia in N.Y.C.; ofcl. del. Colombia to 4th Pan-Am. Congress, Washington, 1916; adj. prof. N.Y. U. Law Sch., 1947-59. Sec., v.p. Merc. Bank of Americas, 1917-22; hon. chmn. Internat. Mining Co.; dir. Colombian Investment Co., Pan-Am. Trade Devel. Co., others. Mem. Colombian Am. C. of C. (dir.), Pan Am. Soc. (dir.), Am., N.Y. State bar assns., Assn. Bar City N.Y., N.Y. County Lawyers Assn., Internat. Law Assn. (council), Am. Assn. Comparative Study of Law Inc., Am. Fgn. Law Assn. (hon. pres.), Soc. Comparative Legislation, Acad. Polit. Sci., Soc. Med. Jurisprudence, Societe de Legislation Comparee, Phi Sigma Kappa; hon. mem. Colombian Acad. Jurisprudence, Colombian Acad. History. Republican. Clubs: Lawyers, Harvard, Explorers; University (Washington); Authors (London). Author: Colombia, 1913; Principles of the Common Law (in Spanish), 1948, 60; A Comparative Survey of Anglo-American and Latin-American Law, 1950; American-Colombian Private International Law, 1956; The Trust in Comparative Law (in Spanish), 1954; El Fundador James M. Eder, 1959; Principles of the Common Law and of Latin American Law. 1960: Law Books in Spanish Translation, 1967; the Colombian Penal Code Translated, 1967. Contbr. articles law jours. Home: New City NY Deceased.

EDGERTON, HENRY WHITE, judge; b. Rush Center, Kan., Oct. 20, 1888; s. Charles Eugene and Annie Benedict (White) E.; student U. of Wis., 1905-07; A.B., Cornell U., 1910; student Law Sch., U. of Paris, 1910-11; LL.B., Harvard, 1914; LL.D., Yale, 1956, Howard U., 1963, George Washington U., 1970; m. Alice Durand, June 28, 1913; children—John Durand, Ann (dec.). Special agent U.S. Bureau of Corps., 1908. With firms of Davis, Kellogg & Severance, St. Paul, 1914, Warner, Warner & Stackpole, Boston, 1915-16, Ropes, Gray, Boyden & Perkins, Boston, 1918-21; mem. law faculty George Washington U., 1921-29, U. of Chicago, 1928-29, Cornell U., 1916-18 and 1929-38; special asst. to U.S. atty. gen., 1934-35; judge U.S. Ct. of Appeals for D.C. Circuit, Washington, 1938-70, chief judge, 1955-58, senior judge, 1963-69. Mem. Phi Beta Kappa. Club: Cosmos (Washington). Contbr. articles legal periodicals; civil liberties opinions pub. as Freedom in the Balance, edited by Eleanor Bontecou, 1960. Home: Washington DC Died Feb. 23, 1970; buried Ft. Lincoln Cemetery, Washington DC

EDGERTON, HERBERT OLIVER, ins. exec.; b. Conway, Mass., Mar. 24, 1862; s. Gurdon and Eleanor (Gunn) E.; student Brimfield Acad., 1878-80; m. Emma T. Houghton, Dec. 21, 1887; children—Gurdon Irving (dec.), Herbert Houghton (dec.). Bank clk., 1880-95; founded Greenfield Life Assn. and connected with same, 1895-1901; gen. agt. Boston Mut. Life Ins. Co., 1901-04, sec., later v.p., 1904-10, pres., 1910-37, gen. adviser since 1937. Conglist. Club: Boston City. Home: 142 Goden St., Belmont, Mass. Office: 160 Congress St., Boston MA‡

EDGERTON, JUSTIN LINCOLN, judge; born Cold Spring, N.Y., Sept. 2, 1908; s. James Arthur and Blanche (Edgerton) E.; A.B., George Washington U., 1929; J.D., 1931; married Catherine Adams Griffith; children—Justin Richard, Margaret Elizabeth. Admitted to D.C. bar, 1930, since practiced in D.C.; mem. firm Pledger, Edgerton & Richardson, 1951-60, Pledger & Edgerton, 1960-64, Pledger, Edgerton & Mahoney, 1964-66; asso. judge D.C. Ct. of Gen. Sessions, from 1966-—. Mem. faculty George Washington U. Law Sch., 1936-70, professorial lectr. law, 1936-70. Recipient Distinguished Service award Washington Bd. Trade, others; named Laymen of Year Methodist Union, 1967. Fellow Am. Bar Found.; mem. Am. Bar Assn., Bar Assn. D.C. (past pres.), Am. Coll. Trial Lawyers, Barristers Club, Lawyers Club, Delta Theta Phi, Order of Coif. Club: Metropolitan, Vinson (Washington). Home: Bethesda MD Died Aug. 28, 1970; buried Parklawn Cemetery, Rockville MD

EDGERTON, WILLIAM FRANKLIN, Egyptologist; b. Binghamton, N.Y., Sept. 30, 1893; s. Charles Eugene and Annie Benedict (White) E.; A.B., Cornell U., 1915; Ph.D., U. of Chicago, 1922; student U. of Pa., 1919, Columbia, 1923-24, U. of Munich, 1927; m. Jean Daniel Modell, May 22, 1918 (div. 1956); m. 2d. Lenetta Margaret Cooper, Feb. 16, 1957. Archeol. survey in Mesopotamia and Syria for Oriental Inst., U. of Chicago, 1920; asst. Oriental Inst., same, 1922-23; asst. prof. ancient history, U. of Louisville, 1924-25; asso. prof. history, Vassar Coll., 1925-26; epigrapher, Epigraphic and Archtl. Survey of Oriental Inst., U. of Chicago, Luxor, Upper Egypt, 1926-29; asso. prof. Egyptology, U. Chgo., 1929-37, prof., 1937-59, emeritus. 1959-70, chmn. dept. Oriental langs. and lit., 1948-54; Fulbright research scholar King's College and University of Cambridge (England), 1951-52; visiting professor U. Cal. at Berkeley, 1964-66; collected demotic and other graffiti at Medinet Habu (near Luxor, Egypt) for Oriental Institute, U. of Chicago 1931-33. Sergt. Medical Dept., U.S. Army, 1918-19. Served as captain, Signal Corps, United States Army, 1942-43, major, 1943-45. Mem. Am. Assn. U. Profs. (council 1953-55), Am. Hist. Assn., Am. Oriental Soc. (president 1944-45), Linguistic Soc. of America, Egypt Exploration Society, Phi Beta Kappa fraternity (member of senate 1952-58). Clubs: University (Chicago); Cliff Dwellers, Quadrangel. Author: Medinet Habu, Vol. I, Earlier Historical Records of Ramses III (with H. H. Nelson, J. A. Wilson and others), 1930; Notes on Egyptian Marriage, Chiefly in the Ptolemaic Period, 1931; The Thutmosid Succession, 1933; Historical Records of Ramses III. The Texts in Medinet Habu (with J. A. Wilson), Vols. I and II, 1936; Medinet Habu Graffiti Facsimiles, 1937; (with E. M. Husselman and A. E. R. Boak) Michigan Papyri from Tebtunis, Part II, 1944. Consulting editor Journal of Near Eastern Studies. 1942-49. Contbr. to scholarly jours. Home: Chicago IL Died Mar., 1970.

EDISON, CHARLES, ex-governor; b. Llewellyn Park, West Orange, N.J., Aug. 3, 1890; s. Thomas Alva and Mina (Miller) E.; prep. edn., Carteret Acad. (Orange, N.J.), Hotchkiss Sch. (Lakeville, Conn.); Mass. Inst. Tech., 1909-13; LL.D., John Marshall Coll., 1940, Newark Univ., 1941, Rutgers, 1941, Upsala Coll., 1943, Hobart and William Smith Coll., Geneva, N.Y., 1944, Lafayette Coll., Easton, Pa., 1945; D.Eng. (hon.), Stevens Inst. of Technology, 1949; D.C.S. (hon.), N.Y.U., 1950; H.H.D. (hon.), Ind. Tech. Coll., 1956; m. Carolyn Hawkins, Mar. 27, 1918 (deceased on June 28, 1963). Former chairman of the board McGraw-Edison Company, ret., 1916; former dir. Nat. Recovery Adminstrn. for N.J. Nat. Emergency Council; former reg. dir. Fed. Housing Adminstrn. for region No. 3; asst. sec. of U.S. Navy, 1937-39, Sec. of Navy, 1939-40; gov. N.J., 1941-44. During World War I directed mfg. of war materials; chmn. West Orange Liberty Loan Orgn. Mem. N.J. Welfare Council; trustee emeritus Newark Mus.; hon. nat. chmn. hon. dir. United Service to China, Inc., N.Y.C.; chmn. bd. of trustees Town Hall, Inc., May 1944-May 1947, later life mem.; pres. National Municipal League, 1947-50. Trustee N. Am. Wildlife Found., Washington; past trustee Stevens Inst. Tech., Hoboken, N.J.; Mem. Navy League of U.S., N.J. Soc. S.A.R., Alumni Assn. Mass. Inst. Tech., Nat. Geog. Soc., Newcomen Soc., N.J. Hist. Society, John Ericsson Society, also Delta Psi. Clubs: Canadian, Marco Polo, The Brook (N.Y.C.); 1925 F St. (Washington); St. Anthony (Boston); Lake Placid (N.Y.). Address: New York City NY Died Aug. 1969.

EDISON, CHARLES B., retail shoe co. exec.; b. 1921; married. With Edison Bros. Stores Inc., 1941-71, exec. v.p., 1968-71, vice chmn. bd., 1968-71. also dir. Served as officer USAAF, 1943-45. Address: St Louis MO Died July 3, 1971.

EDISON, SAMUEL BERNARD, shoe store chain exec.; b. Lithuania, Dec. 25, 1888; s. Abraham and Sarah (Halle) E.; brought to U.S., 1890; m. Sadye Goldman, Oct. 20, 1915; children—Natalie (Mrs. Henry L. Freund), Charles (dec.). With Edison Brothers Stores, Inc. (and predecessors), St. Louis, 1929-71, v.p., treas., 1951-58, exec. v.p., 1958-71, dir., 1929-71. Mason (Shriner). Home: St Louis MO Died Aug. 4, 1971; buried Mt. Sinai Cemetery, St Louis MO

EDMISTON, WILLIAM SHERMAN, pub. Western Farm Life; b. Belvidere, Neb., Apr. 9, 1876; s. Tilmon Gill and Emma (Lackey) E.; student U. of Neb., 1898-99; m. Adelaide J. Swanson, Aug. 11, 1904. Began as news reporter on Hebron (Neb.) Journal, 1896; circulation dept. Omaha Bee, 1890-95, business office of Bee, 1895-96, advt. dept., 1896-1908; pub. Cheyenne (Wyo.), Daily State Leader, 1908-14; with The Western Farm Life, Denver, since 1914, as mgr., 1914-17, owner and pub. since 1917; pres. Farm Life Pub. Co. Home: 831 Cherry St. Office: 1520 Court Place, Denver CO‡

EDMONDS, DEAN STOCKETT, lawyer; b. Washington, Dec. 20, 1879; s. Howard and Mary Elizabeth (Owen) E.; LL.B., Georgetown U., 1899, M.L., 1900; LL.D., Middlebury Coll., 1952; m. Mary Watkins Arms, Dec. 11, 1911; 1 son, Dean Stockett; m. 2d, Marie C. Moore, Aug. 24, 1967. Admitted to D.C. bar, 1900, N.Y. bar, 1910; mem. firm Pennie, Edmonds, Morton, Taylor and Adams. Chmn. bd. U.S. Radium Corp.; dir. Machelett X-Ray Tubes (Gt. Britain), Farrand Optical Co., Mem. Am., N.Y. patent law assns., Am., N.Y. County bar assns., Bar City N.Y., Loyal Legion. Republican. Episcopalian. Clubs: Racquet and Tennis, University, Union League, Grolier, Church, Pilgrims Society, Newcomen Soc., Union (all N.Y.), Pequot Yacht, Fairfield County Hunt, Fairfield Country (Conn.); Royal Palm Yacht and Country. Home: CT Died Sept. 18, 1972.

EDMONDSON, CATHRINE ELIZABETH, lawyer; b. nr. Clarksville, Tenn., Sept. 19, 1903; d. Robin B. and Mary (Ussery) Edmondson; LL.B., Nat. U. Sch. Law, 1936. Tchr., Montgomery County, Tenn., 1920-25, Enid Bus. Coll., 1926-28; tng. instr. nat. office Internal Revenue Service, 1928-36; admitted to Tenn. bar, 1936; atty. Internal Revenue Service, Washington, 1937-63; pvt. practice, 1963-68. Bd. dirs. Clarksville United Givers Fund, 1965-66; v.p., dir. Montgomery County Sr. Citizens Assn., 1964-66. Mem. Clarksville Bus. and Profl. Women's Club, Am. Association of University Women, George Washington Univ. Alumnae Assn. (dir.), Am., Fed., Tenn. bar assns., Nat. Assn. Women Lawyers (dir. 1957-60, recording sec. 1960-62, v.p. 1962-63, pres. elect 1963-64, pres. 1964-65), Montgomery County Bar Assn. (sec.-treas. 1965), Phi Delta Delta (v.p. 1956-58). Club: Altrusa. Home: Clarksville TN Died Feb. 8, 1968; buried Antioch Cemetery, Clarksville TN

EDMONDSON, JAMES HOWARD, ex-U.S. senator; b. Muskogee, Okla., Sept. 27, 1925; s. Edmond Augustus and Esther (Pullen) E.; LL.B., U. Okla., 1948; m. Jeannette Bartleson; children—James Howard, Jeanne, Patricia Lynn. Admitted to Okla. bar, 1948; pvt. practice of law, Muskogee, 1948-53; chief pros., Office Tulsa Coanty Atty., 1953, county atty., 1954-58; gov. Okla., 1959-63; U.S. senator from Okla., 1963-65, mem. Senate coms. on aero. and space science, agriculture and forestry. Counsel to firm Fellers, Snider, Baggett & McLane, Oklahoma City, Oklahoma. Named one of the 10 Outstanding Young Men of nation, 1959; named to Okla. Hall of Fame. Mem. Am. Legion, 40 and 8, Okla. Bar Assn., Air Force Assn., U. Okla. Alumni Assn., Phi Gamma Delta. Presbyn. Mason (32 deg.), Rotarian. Home: Edmond OK Died Nov. 17, 1971; buried Meml. Park Cemetery, Oklahoma City OK

EDMONDSON, WILLIAM JOHN, artist; b. Norwalk, O., Aug. 22, 1868; s. George William and Mary Jane (Mountain) E.; ed. Aman Jean Acad. and Julian Acad., Paris, France; Acad. Fine Arts, Phila., Pa.; m. Florence L. Holloway, 1906. Portrait and figure painter. Exhibited at Corcoran Gallery of Art, Washington, D.C.; Pa. Acad. Fine Arts, Phila.; Cleveland Museum Art; Detroit Inst. Arts; Art Inst. Chicago; San Francisco Expn.; Art Museums in Cincinnati, St. Louis, Indianapolis. Awarded traveling scholarship by Pa. Acad. Fine Arts, 1893; 2d Toppan prize, by same, 1889; Penton medal, Cleveland Museum Art, 1919; 1st prize, figure painting, same, 1919; popular vote prize, 1919, and 1st prize mural and decorative painting, same, 1923; popular vote award, Nelson Gallery of Art, Kansas City, Mo., 1941. Works on permanent exhbn. at Delgado Museum Art, New Orleans; Cleveland Museum Art; Western Reserve U.; Fed. Res. Bank of Cleveland; City Hall, Cleveland; Central Nat. Bank of Cleveland; permanent collection of Fellowship Pa. Acad. Fine Arts; etc. Mem. Fellowship Pa. Acad. Fine Arts, Cleveland Soc. Artists. Unitarian. Home: 2812 Scarborough Rd., Cleveland Heights, O. Studio: 2258 Euclid Av., Cleveland OH‡

EDROP, PERCY T., clergyman; b. Birmingham, Eng., Oct. 18, 1883; s. George Thomas and Annie (Lane) E.; came to U.S., 1895; studied for the ministry P.E.Ch., later under Ref. Episcopal Ch., New York and Phila. Synod; D.D., Ref. Episcopal Sem., at Phila., Pa., 1918; m. Marion Lothrop Stafford, of Brooklyn, N.Y., Mar. 16, 1912. Reporter and mem. editorial staff, New York American, 1905-16; ordained ministry, R.E.Ch., 1907; pastor Ch. of the Reconciliation, Brooklyn, 1910-15, serving without salary; mem. editorial staff New York Tribune, 1919; rector First Ref. Episcopal Ch., New York, since 1919. Chaplain N.G.N.Y., 1916, later chaplain 47th N.Y. Inf., and of 53rd Pioneer Inf.; relieved of regtl. duties by order of Sec. of War Baker, to direct 39 military camp publs. during latter part of World War. Was sec. Gen. Wartime Commn. R.E.Ch., and chmn. of Synod Commn.; mem. S.S.Bd. of R.E.Ch. and of gen. com. of gen. council; v.p. Bd. of Home Missions R.E.Ch. Clubs: Hamilton, Rotary (Brooklyn); Clergy, Old Guard, Columbia Yacht (New York). Wrote larger part of Marching into the Dawn" (war editorials), also brochures, distributed among soldiers; edited Going Over," etc. Home: 194 Clinton St., Brooklyn NY‡

EDSALL, PRESTON WILLIAM, educator; b. Roxbury, N.Y., Mar. 29, 1902; s. Arthur Joseph and Nellie (Preston) E.; B.S., N.Y.U., 1923; A.M., Princeton (Class of 1883 fellowship politics), 1927, Ph.D., 1937; m. Katherine Crichton Alston, June 12, 1928; 1 son, Hugh Crichton. Asst. English, Lehigh U., 1923; instr. history, govt. Emory U., 1924-26; instr. politics Princeton, 1928-31; asst. prof. polit. sci. Rutgers U., 1931-32; research legal and jud. history of N.J., 1932-35; acting asst. prof. polit. sci. N.Y.U., 1933-34; spl. atty. Dept. of Justice, 1935-37; successively spl. examiner, asso. editor-writer, research expert Nat. Archives, 1937-42; sr. negotiator war transfers U.S. Civil Service Commn., 1942-43; prof. polit. sci. East Carolina Tchrs. Coll., 1945; instr. English N.C. State Coll., 1923-24, mem. war tng. faculty, 1943-44, asso. prof. history, polit. sci., 1945-46, prof. from 1946, head dept. history, polit. sci. 1948-65, head department of politics from 1965; also adminstrv. council Consol. U. N.C., 1950-54; organizer, moderator ednl. TV program Report to the People, WUNC-TV, 1955, Legislative Rev., 1957, 59, 61, Legislative Report, 1965; vis. prof. polit. sci. Duke, 1960-61. Assisted in survey of govt. of Trenton, N.J., 1929; chmn. Wake County Bd. Elections, 1956-60. Del. N.C. Dem. State Conv., 1946, 48, 50, 52, 54, 56, 58. Recipient Social Sci. Council award to study legislative politics in N.C. in 1950's, 59. Mem. Am., So. (exec. council 1956-59, pres. 1966-67) political sci. assns., Am. Acad. Polit. and Social Sci., Am. Soc. Pub. Adminstrn., Nat. Municipal League, Am., So. hist. assns., Am. Assn. U. Profs., Phi Kappa Phi. Clubs: History (Raleigh N.C.). Author: Journal of Courts of Common Right and Chancery of East New Jersey, 1683-1702, 1937; also book revs., articles; contbr. to Presidential Nominating Politics, 1952; chpts. to The Politics of Reapportionment (ed. M.E. Jewell), 1962; the Changing Politics of the South (William C. Havard), 1972. Home: Raleigh NC Died May 17, 1972; buried Warrenton NC

EDSON, HOWARD AUSTIN, plant pathologist; b. Randolph, Vt., Aug. 14, 1875; s. Franklin Howard and May Eunice (Bell) E.; grad. Vt. State Normal Sch., 1892; B.S. in Chemistry, U. of Vt., 1906; M.S. in Biology, 1910; Ph.D., U. of Wis., 1913; m. Lillian Sarah Buck, June 21, 1906; children—Thelma Cecilia (dec.), Ralph Howard, Margaret May. Asst. botanist and instr. bacteriology, U. of Vt. and Vt. Agr. Expt. Sta., 1906-09; bacteriologist and asst. prof. bacteriology, same, 1909-10; plant pathologist U.S. Dept. Agr., 1910-27, sr. pathologist in charge cotton, truck, and forage crop disease investigations, 1924-27; chief examiner of U.S. Civil Service Commn., 1927-33, and prin. examiner same, 1933-34; prin. pathologist in charge mycology and plant disease survey, U.S. Dept. of Agr., 1934-45; retired, 1945. Made plant disease survey of Philippines, 1916, and study of sugar beet and Irish potato diseases in Europe, 1914; service for Joint Congl. Commission on Reclassification of Salaries, 1919-20, on staff of Personnel Classification Bd., 1923-24. Fellow A.A.A.S.; mem. Am. Phytopathol. Soc. (treas. and business mgr. Phytopathology, 1935-43). Bot. Soc., America Bot. Soc., Washington, Washington Acad. Sciences, Sigma Xi, Phi Beta Kappa, Phi Delta Theta. Republican. Presbyn. Clubs: Cosmos, Federal (pres. 1932). Home: 3810 4th St. N.W., Washington 11 DC‡

EDSON, STEPHEN REUBEN, ret. naval officer; b. Mpls., Nov. 12, 1895; s. James Richards and Mary Barbara (Strauss) E.; ed. pub. schs.; various Naval courses of instruction; m. Mary Bridget McWilliams, June 10, 1925; children—Stephen R., James, Peter, Charles, Mary, Alice. Enlisted, U.S. Navy, 1917, commd. ensign, 1919, and advanced through grades to vice admiral; assigned to patrol craft, Pacific, World War I; various assignments ashore and afloat, 1919-43; served on staff of Admiral Hewitt, comdr. of Amphibious Forces, Atlantic Fleet, during invasion of N. Africa, 1943-45; served on staff of Admiral Hewitt, comdr. Eight Fleet during invasions of Sicily, Italy and Southern France, 1945; executive officer Naval Supply Depot, Mechanicsburg, Pa., 1945-47; supply officer, Naval Gun Factory, Washington, 1947-49; clothing supply officer of the Navy and comdg. officer, Naval Clothing Depot, Brooklyn, 1949-51, dir. procurement div., office naval material, 1951-53; vice chief of naval material, 1953-54; commanding Naval Supply Depot, Mechanicsburg, Pa., 1954-57. Decorated Legion of Merit with combat device; Gold star in lieu of 2d Leg. of Merit; Commendation ribbon with combat device; Croix de Guerre with silver star; World War I and II Victory medals; Am. Defense service with star; American Area, European-African-Middle Eastern area with star. Republican. Roman Catholic. Elk (life). Home: Chevy Chase MD Died Aug. 28, 1969; buried Arlington National Cemetery, Arlington VA

EDWARDS, ALBA M., statistician; b. Savannah, Mo., Sept. 21, 1872; s. Phineas and Mary (Osborn) E.; A.B., U. of Okla., 1903; A.M., Yale, 1905, Ph.D., 1906; m. Edith Winifred Schurr, Aug. 2, 1910; children—Earl Lester, John Bruce, Lloyd Grant. Special agent Carnegie Instn., of Washington, 1906-07; acting professor Bowdoin Coll., 1907-09; statistician for occupations, Bureau of the Census, 1909-43. Member Am. Statis. Assn. Author: Labor Legislation of Connecticut, 1907; also census reports and articles on statis. subjects. Address: 2522 12th St. N.W., Washington DC‡

EDWARDS, CHARLES VERNON, clergyman; b. Franklin, Ky., Apr. 1, 1870; s. J. W. and Malvenia Elenor Starks Edwards; B.A., Bethel Coll., Ky., 1896, M.A., 1899, D.D., 1908; m. Ilda Crumpton, of Birmingham, Ala., Nov. 21, 1900. Ordained Bapt. ministry, 1894; pastor Middletown, Ky., 1894-6, Lebanon and Springfield, Tenn., 1896-7, Central City, Ky., 1897, Livermore, Ky., 1897-8, First Bapt. Ch., New Orleans, 1899-09, First Ch., Greenwood, Miss., 1909-13, College Av. Bapt. Ch., Ft. Worth, Tex., since Sept., 1913. Home: 1401 Washington Av., Ft Worth TX‡

EDWARDS, CHAUNCEY THEODORE, clergyman; b. Phila.; s. Jonathan (D.D., LL.D.) and Eliza (Rice) E.; A.B., Hanover Coll., Ind., 1879, A.M., 1884; A.B., Central U., Danville, Ky., 1879; Western Theol. Sem., Pittsburgh; grad. Princeton Theol. Sem., 1884; (D.D., Hanover, 1900); m. Annie E. McLean, of Paterson, N.J., 1888. Ordained Presbyn. ministry, 1884. pastor Toms River, N.J., 1884-8, Coudersport, Pa., 1888-96, 1st Ch., Peoria, Ill., 1897-03; stated supply, Portville, N.Y., 1904-6; pastor 1st Ch., Beloit, Wis., 1907-10; head Bible extension work, Beloit Coll., 1910-12; pastor Bay Ridge Ch., Brooklyn, since Jan., 1912. Del. Gen. Assembly Presbyn. Ch. U.S.A., Washington, 1893, Phila., 1901; del. Gen. Council Ref. Chs., Liverpool, Eng., 1904. Home: 225 81st St., Brooklyn‡

EDWARDS, CLEMENT STANISLAUS, consular service; b. N.Y. City, Mar. 4, 1869; s. Clement and Anna (Cameron) E.; prep. edn., pvt. sch., St. Michael's Acad., Chatham, N.B., Can., and high sch., Albert Lea, Minn.; student Parker Coll., Winnebago City, Minn., and Hillsdale (Mich.) Coll.; m. Marguerite Auld, of Burlington, Vt., Mar. 2, 1922. Admitted to Minn. bar, 1894, and began practice at Albert Lea; city atty., Albert Lea, 1896-1900; owner and editor Albert Lea Times-Enterprise, 1904-10; Am. consul, Acapulco, Mexico, 1911-16; service with Citizenship bur., U.S. Dept. State, Washington, D.C., 1916-17; consul in charge legation part of time, Santo Domingo, 1917-19; consul-Paris, France, 1919-21; attached to Am. Commn., Berlin, detailed to Frankfurt am Main, later to Hamburg, Paris and Kovno, Lithuania, 1921-24; consul, Valencia, Spain, 1924-30, Bradford, England, since 1930. Served as capt., inf., Minn. Vols., Spanish-Am. War. Mem. Albert Lea Charter Commn., 1896-1904. Mem. Phi Delta Theta. Mason, K.P. Home: Waylands," Harrogate, Eng. Office: American Consulate, Bradford England‡

EDWARDS, DELTUS MALIN, writer; b. Washington, D.C., Aug. 31, 1874; s. Vedantus Bosby and Mary (Morrison) E.; grad. Washington High Sch., 1893; m. Catherine C. Down. Staff Washington Post, 1893; mem. original staff that started Washington Times, 1894; joined Associated Press, 1896, and removed to New York, with same, 1898; on editorial staff, New York American, 1901-5, New York Herald, Nov. 20, 1905—. Spl. writer on Arctic matters; wrote full page prediction of discovery of North pole printed in Herald Aug. 29, 1909, 4 days before word was received from Comdr. Peary announcing his achievement; was sent North to Battle Harbor, Labrador, by the Herald to meet Peary on the Roosevelt on his return from the Pole. Went as corr. in World War to British and Belgian fronts and Zeebrugge, and was with Am. Squadron of the Grand Fleet in the North Sea at the surrender of the German High Seas Fleet. Methodist. Author: The Toll of the Artic Seas, 1910; also many short stories and spl. articles for leading mags.*‡

EDWARDS, FREDERICK, clergyman; b. Cornwall, Eng.; s. John and Mary (Commins) E.; Ph.B., Dickinson Coll., 1888, M.A., 1891; B.D., Episcopal Theol. Sch., Cambridge, Mass., 1893; m. Emma L. Satterthwait, of Cream Ridge, N.J., July 28, 1891; children—Frederick T. (dec.), Agnes Commins (dec.). Deacon, 1893, priest 1894, P.E. Ch.; rector Trinity Ch., Bridgewater, Mass., 1893-96, St. Paul's Ch., Malden, 1896-1905, St. James Ch., Milwaukee, Wis., 1905-12, Grace Ch., New York, 1912-15; dean St. Paul's Cathedral, Detroit, 1915. Retired 1920. Pres. Am. Soc. for Psychical Research, 1923-26. Author: Sonnets of North and South, 1925; The Natural Year (verse), 6 vols., completed, 1931. Home: 1000 N. Boul., De Land, Fla.; (summer) R.R. 1, St George NB Canada‡

EDWARDS, GEORGE LANE, banker; b. Kirkwood, Mo., Sept., 1869; s. Albert G. and Mary (Jenckes) E.; pub. sch. edn.; m. Florence N. Evans, of Kirkwood, 1892. Pres. A. G. Edwards & Sons Brokerage Co., since 1892; pres. Bank of Kirkwood, Mo.; dir. St. Louis Transit Co., United Ry. Co. Mem. St. Louis Stock Exchange (ex-pres.). Home: Kirkwood, Mo. Office: 410 Pine St., St Louis‡

EDWARDS, HARRISON GRIFFITH, architect; b. Columbia, S.C., Aug. 21, 1907; s. William Augustus and Pearl (Brown) E.; B.S. Ga. Inst. Tech., 1930; m. Betty Grace Fountain, Feb. 22, 1936; children—Margaret Fountain, Alice Landru. Draftsman, Edwards & Sayward, architects, Atlanta 1930-36, Henry J. Toombs, architect, Atlanta, 1937-40; partner Edwards & Goodwyne, pvt. practice, Atlanta, 1940-55. Edwards & Portman, architects, engrs., Atlanta, 1956—; successively asst. prof., asso. prof., prof. Sch. Architecture Ga. Inst. Tech., 1946, mem. alumni adv. bd. 1956. Mem. Men's Council Atlanta League Women Voters, 1942; chmn. Atlanta Merchandise Mart Bldg., 1964; chmn. architects, engrs. div. United Appeal Fund Drive, 1965. Trustee, mem. exec. com. Theatre Atlanta, Inc. Fellow Constrn. Specifications Inst. (past v.p., pres. dir. Atlanta chpt.; President's award for service 1961), A.I.A. (past pres., dir. Ga. chpt., Service to Inst. award 1962); mem. Atlanta C. of C. Ga. Engring. Soc., Assn. Collegiate Schs. Architecture, Sigma Chi. Episcopalian. Club: Ansley Golf. Author: Specifications, rev. edit., 1961. Prin. works include Atlanta Merchandise Mart, Peachtree Center Office Bldg., Greenbriar Shopping Center, Atlanta Decorative Arts Center, Regency Hotel, Infirmary Bldg. Ga. Inst. Tech., Oglethorpe, C.W. Hill, Hendon Schs. (all Atlanta), Dana Fine Arts Bldg. Agnes Scott Coll. (Decatur), Midway, Sequoyah, Hawthorne, Carey Reynolds Schs. (DeKalb County), Spalding Dr. Sch. (Fulton County). Episcopalian (vestryman 1964-66, jr. warden 1966). Home: Atlanta GA Died Feb. 7, 1972.

EDWARDS, JOSEPH LEE, railway service; b. Cuthbert, Ga., Nov. 11, 1870; s. Joseph Asbury and Emma (Miller) E.; ed. high sch., Marshallville, Ga.; unmarried. With Southern Ry. in various capacities, 1892-1912; mgr. Atlanta, Ga., br. of Bonnyman-Norman Coal & Iron Co., Feb.-Oct. 1912; traffic mgr. Atlanta, Birmingham & Atlantic Ry., 1912-18, also Ga. R.R., Atlanta & West Point R.R., Western Ry., Frisco lines east of Miss. river and Charleston & Western Caroline R.R., June-July 1918; mgr. agrl. sect. of traffic div. U.S. Railroad Administration, 1918-20; v.p. Atlanta, Birmingham &Coast R. R. and predecessor co. since 1920. Democrat. Clubs: Capital City, Piedmont Driving, Civitan, Atlanta Traffic (Atlanta, Ga.). Home: 1428 Peachtree St. N.E. Office: 26 Cain St. N.W., Atlanta GA‡

EDWARDS, LINDEN FOREST, univ. prof.; b. Lewisville, O., Nov. 25, 1899; s. Albert Ross and Mary Eliza (Hare) E.; A.B., Ohio State U., 1922, M.S., 1923, Ph.D., 1928; grad. study Franz Theodore Stone Biol. Lab., summer, 1922-24, Univ. of Mich., summer, 1925, Grad. Sch. Univ. of Ill., 1926-27; m. Elizabeth Smith, Sept. 2, 1925; 1 dau., Linda Jane. Grad. asst. in zoology Ohio State U., 1922-23, instr., 1923-25; instr. in anatomy Univ. of Ill., 1925-29; asst. prof. in anatomy Coll. of Medicine and Dentistry, Ohio State Univ., 1929-35, asso. prof., 1935-40, prof. from 1940, chmn. dept., 1957-61. Member Am. Assn. Anatomists, Am. Assn. History Medicine, Ohio Hist. Soc., Ohio Acad. Sci. (v.p.), Ohio Acad. Med. History, Columbus Dental Soc., Gamma Alpha, Sigma Xi, Psi Omega, Omicron Kappa Upsilon. Mason. Clubs: Faculty, Optimist. Author several books on anatomy. Home: Columbus OH Died Apr. 8, 1970; cremated.

EDWARDS, MYRTLE SASSMAN (MRS. HARLAN H. EDWARDS), govt. ofcl.; b. Chgo., Oct. 6, 1894; tchrs. certificate in piano Ill. Coll. Music, 1916; tchrs. certificate in voice Am. Conservatory, 1918; student U. Ill., 1920-21; B.A., U. Wash., 1949; m. Harlan H. Edwards, July 2, 1918; children—Virginia E. (Mrs. Bruce L. Till), Dale Hammond. Mem. Seattle City Council, 1955-69, chmn. parks and pub. grounds commn., 1956-68, pres., 1968-69; mem. council Municipality Met. Seattle, 1958-69; trustee Horizon House Retirement Residence, also sec. corp. Mem. League Women Voters (pres. Seattle 1949-51, pres. Wash. State 1951-55), Am. Assn. for UN, Am. Assn. Univ. Women, Bus. and Profl. Women's Club. Club: Women's University. Conglist. Home: Seattle WA Died Aug. 18, 1969; buried Acacia Cemetery Seattle WA

EDWARDS, PERCY NOYES, communications exec., banker; b. Batchellerville, N.Y., 1889; ed. Princeton, 1912; m. Nancy Brooks; children—Brooks N., John. Former secretary and treasurer New York Telephone Company, ret, 1953; secretary and treasurer Empire City Subway Co.; dir. Pub. Nat. Bank & Trust Co. Home: Garden City LI NY Died Nov. 11, 1968; buried Westhampton Cemetery, Westhampton Beach NY

EDWARDS, RAY GWYTHER, musician; b. Kenosha, Wis., July 16, 1872; s. Alfred Shenstone and Eudora Bird (Henry) E.; ed. in music under pvt. tutors and at Chicago Conservatory of Music; A.B., Ruskin (Fla.) Coll., 1915 (D.Mus., 1917); m. Aurora Leigh Miller, of Ruskin College, Mar. 4, 1914. Mem. Ruskin Colony, Tenn., 1895-9; teacher violin, Chicago and Boston, unitl 1912; founder, and editor The Violinist, Chicago, 1901-04; dir. Ruskin (Fla.) Sch. of Music since 1914. Author: Key to Study of Harmony, 1902. Composer: First Violin Lessons, 1904; also songs, pieces for violin and piano, etc. Writer on community music. Address: Ruskin FL‡

EDWARDS, ROBERT ERNEST, educator; b. Spokane, Wash., Nov. 6, 1923; s. Eber Ernest and Nelle (Isbell) E.; student Willamette U., 1943-45; B.S., U. Ore., 1946, M.S., 1949; Ph.D., U. Wash., 1952; m. Theodora Nelson, Aug. 13, 1944; children—Sandra Lee, Eric Alan. Asst. prof. psychology Rensselaer Poly. Inst., 1953-57; asso. mem. Sterling-Winthrop Research Inst., Rensselaer, N.Y., 1956-62; lectr. pharmacology Albany Med. Coll., Union U., 1957-62; psychologist Psychopharmacology Service Center NIMH, Bethesda, 1962-66, exec. sec. com. on preclin. psychopharmacology, 1962-66; prof., chmn. dept. psychology Cal. State U. at Fullerton, 1966-69. University fellow U. Washington, 1948-51; USPHS fellow Psychiatric Inst. and Hosp., Columbia, 1952-53. Served with USNR, 1942-44. Mem. Am. Psychol. Assn., A.A.A.S., Behavioral Pharmacology Soc., N.Y. Acad. Sci., Royal Soc. Fullerton CA Died Nov. 1, 1969; interred Pacific View Meml. Park Newport Beach CA

EDWARDS, ROBERT WILKINSON, microbiologist; b. Portland, Ore., Apr. 6, 1914; s. William Dresser and Lucy (Wilkinson) E.; B.S., Memphis State Coll., 1948; M.S., U. Tenn., 1949; m. Ruth Mae Rawlins, Apr. 19, 1941; 1son, Robert Wilkinson. Civilian pilot, 1930-40; pres. Edwards Aircraft Corp., Memphis, 1938-40; asst. traffic mgr. Chgo. & So. Airlines, Houston, 1945-46; asst. prof. Tenn. Poly. Inst., Cookville, 1949-51; chief bacteriologist Cook County Hosp., Chgo., 1951-53; microbiologist U.S. Army, 1956-66; tech. staff scientist

Airtronics, Inc., Washington, 1966-69; cons. applied microbiology. Served to maj. USAAF, 1940-45; USAF, 1953-56. Decorated Bronze Star medal, Air medal. Mem. N.Y. Acad. Scis., Am. Soc. Microbiologists, Soc. Indsl. Microbiologists, Nat. Assn. Corrosion Engrs., Marine Tech. Soc., Am. Assn. Contamination Control, Quiet Birdmen. Club: OX-5 of America Braddock Heights MD Died Sept. 24, 1969.

EDWARDS, VELMA GREEN (MRS. LOWELL WAYNE EDWARDS), speech therapist; b. Wake Forest, N.C., Dec. 13, 1914; d. Robert White and Ada (Joyner) Green; student Western Carolina Coll., 1933-35; B.A., Blue Mountain Coll., 1937; M.Ed., U. N.C. at Chapel Hill, 1967; m. Lowell Wayne Edwards, Feb. 14, 1940; children—Robert Wayne, Lawrence Lowell. Tchr. Nash County, (N.C.) schs., Nashville, 1937-44, tchr. 4th and 5th grades, 1949-65, speech therapist, 1965-69. Mem. exec. com. Wren Tb Assn., 1966-68, also bd. dirs. Bd. dirs. Am. Cancer Soc., Rocky Mount, Nash County chpt., 1962-67. Mem. N.C. Edn. Assn. (chpt. v.p. 1954-55), Nash County (v.p. 1964-65, pres. 1965-66), Northeastern Dist. (resolutions chmn. 1966-68) classroom tchrs. assns., Delta Kappa Gamma (2d v.p. 1961-62, 2d v.p. Beta Theta chpt. 1967-69). Baptist (Sunday sch. tchr.). Home: Spring Hope NC Died July 11, 1969.

EDWARDS, WILLIAM HANFORD, b. Lisle, N. Y., Feb. 23, 1876; s. A.B., Princeton, 1900. In ins. business, N.Y. City, until 1907; apptd. street cleaning commr. by Mayor McClellan, 1907, reapptd. by Mayor Gaynor; served as collector internal revenue, N.Y., by apptmt. of President Wilson. Democrat. Office: 80 Maiden Lane, New York NY‡

EELLS, HASTINGS, prof. history; b. Absecon, N.J., June 9, 1895; s. Edward and Annie Eliza (Auchmoody) E.; A.B., Clark U., Worcester, Mass., 1916; A.M., Princeton, 1918, B.D., 1919; Ph.D., Yale, 1921; grad. work U. of Brussels and U. of Ghent, 1921-22 and 1928-29; m. Amy Wright Titus, Aug. 18, 1921; 1 son, William Hastings. Ordained Presbyn. ministry, 1922; pastor First Ch., Paoli, Pa., 1922-25; asst. prof. history, Ohio Wesleyan U., Delaware, O., 1925-27, asso. prof., 1927-31, prof. from 1931, chmn. dept., 1952-56; visiting prof. Duke U., summers 1927, 30, 35, 37, Pa. State Coll., summers, 1939, 40. Gelstron-Winthrop fellow, 1919; fellow of Commission for Relief in Belgium Educational Foundation 1921, 28. Member Clark Scholarship Soc., Am. Hist. Assn., Am. Soc. Reformation Research, O. Acad. of History (pres. 1947), Societe de l'histoire du protestantisme francais, Alpha Sigma Phi, Omicron Delta Kappa. Clubs: Friar, Whig (Princeton); Princeton of N.Y. Author: Attitude of Martin Bucer Toward the Bigamy of Philip of Hesse, 1924; Martin Bucer, 1931; Europe Since 1500, 1933; Learning to Study, 1948; Writing aThesis, 1947. Co-author: Post War World, 1944. Home: Delaware OH Died May 1, 1970; buried Oak Grove Cemetery, Delaware, O.

EGBERT, DONALD DREW, educator, color photographer; b. Norwalk, Conn., May 12, 1902; s. George Drew and Kate Estelle (Powers) E.; A.B., Princeton 1924, M.F.A., 1927; m. Virginia Grace Wylie, Aug. 9, 1946. Mem. faculty Princeton 1929-73, prof. art, archaeology, architecture, 1946-70, Butler prof. history architecture, 1968-70, prof. emeritus, 1970-73, Am. Civilization Program, 1942-70, acting chmn., 1943-44; lectr. Bryn Mawr Coll., 1930; one-man shows Princeton Univ. Library, George Eastman House, Rochester, N.Y., 1958. Fellow (life) Met. Mus. Art. Recipient Haskins medal, Mediaeval. Acad., 1943. Fellow International Inst. Arts and Letters; mem. Soc. Am. Studies, Mediaeval Acad., Soc. Archtl. Historians, Societe Francaise d'Archeologie, Am. Acad. Polit. and Social Sci., Am. Soc. for Aesthetics, Coll. Art Assn., Am. Hist. Assn., Acad. Polit. Sci., Renaissance Soc. Am., Phi Beta Kappa. Author: The Tickhill Psalter and Related MSS., 1940; Princeton Portraits, 1947; Socialism and American Art, 1968; Social Radicalism and the Arts, Western Europe, 1970. Contbr. to Symposia; Foreign Influences in American Life (D. Bowers, editor), 1944; The Modern Princeton, 1947; Evolutionary Thought in America (S. Persons, editor), 1950; Religion in American Life (Smith and Jamison), 1961. Editor (with S. Persons) and co-author: Socialism and American Life, 1952. Home: Princeton NJ Died Jan. 3, 1973.

EGBERT, PERCY T., locomotive mfg. exec.; b. Ithaca, N.Y., 1894; grad. Cornell, 1915. Pres., dir. Montreal Locomotive Works, Ltd., Am. Locomotive Co., now named Alco Products, Inc., then chmn. bd., from 1958; chmn., dir., Montreal Locomotive Works, Ltd. Home: New York City NY Died Aug. 1970.

EGBERT, SHERWOOD HARRY, management and investment consultant; born at Seattle, July 24, 1920; the son of Harry and C. and Charlotte (Brown) E.; student Wash. State Coll., 1937-38, 39-40; m. Doris Ruth McKay, Mar. 1, 1940; children—Sherwood James, Nancy Lee; m. 2d, Diana Nell Johnson, June 4, 1958; children—David Gregory, Robert, Warren, Sherana. With Austin Co., Seattle, 1940-41; asst. to supt. gen. constrn. Boeing Airplane Co., Seattle, 1941-42; with McCulloch Corp., Los Angeles, 1946-61, dir., 1951-61, exec. v.p. all divs., mem. exec. com., 1956-61, also v.p., dir. several divs.; pres., chief exec. officer Studebaker Packard Corporation (name now Studebaker Corporation), South Bend, Ind., 1961-64; chmn. bd. U.S. Filter; pres., dir. Sherwood Prodn. Co., Cascade, Inc.; v.p., dir. Valor Prodn. Co.; dir. Emett & Chandler, Aeronca, Inc., Ind. Gen. Corp., Western Air Lines. Served to maj. USMCR, 1942-46; PTO. Decorated Bronze Star medal. Clubs: Bel Air Country, Eldorado Country. Address: Los Angeles CA Died July 31, 1969; buried Holy Cross Cemetery, Los Angeles CA

EGE, HATTIE B., educator; B.L.; head Dept. of Mathematics, Mills Coll., 1895-16, dean and acting pres. since 1914. Absent on leave in Europe, 1912-13. Address: Mills College P.O., CA‡

EGGERS, OTTO R., architect; b. N.Y.C., Aug. 4, 1882; ed. Cooper Union, 1900-02, Hornbostel Atelier, 1902-12, LeBrun scholar, 1912. Designer, John Russell Pope, 1909-22, mem. firm, 1922-37; partner Eggers & Higgins, N.Y.C., from 1937. Registered architect, N.Y. Fellow A.I.A.; mem. N.A.D., Brit. Royal Soc. Arts. Prin. works include: Marshall Field Estate, Huntington, L.I., 1925; First Presbyn. Ch., New Rochelle, N.Y., 1929; Nat. Gallery, 1941; Jefferson Meml. (award of Merit Washington Bd. Trade), 1943; Nat. Fire Ins. Co., Hartford, Conn., 1948; Stepinac High Sch., White Plains, N.Y. (certificate of Merit, N.Y. State Assn. Architects), 1948; Archtl. Center, N.Y. U. Author: Sketches of Early American Architecture, Home: New York City NY

EGGERSS, H. A.;, b. Persia, Ia., 1890; ed. Univ. of Wis. Pres., Container Co., Van Wert, Ohio; president and dir., Continental Can Co., Inc.; pres. Gould Paper Co., Lyons Falls, N.Y., Continental Can Corp.; dir. Van Wert (Ohio) Nat. Bank, Cameron Can Machinery Co., Chicago, Continental Can Co. of Canada, Ltd., Montreal Que., Continental Can Corp., Havana, Cuba, Continental Overseas Corp., New York City. Home: New York City NY

EGGERT, HARRY T., baking co. exec.; b. Chgo., Aug. 2, 1897; s. Henry F. and Johanna (Croak) E.; student pub. schs.; m. Natalie Davis, Apr. 8, 1935; 1 dau., Millicent G. With Nat. Biscuit Co., 1916-62, beginning in ins. dept. Chgo. office, successively, asst. sec., mgr. ins. dept., v.p. in charge personnel, and labor relations, 1945-62. Mem. board trustees Econs. of Distbn. Found., Inc., B & C Union and Industry National Pension Fund. Served with U.S. C Union and Industry National Pension Fund. Served with U.S. Army, World War I. Mem. Asso. Industries N.Y. State, Inc. (dir., mem. exec. com.), C. of C. State N.Y. (exec. com., chmn. com. indsl. problems and relations), C. of C. U.S., West Side Assn. Commerce, Inc., N.Y.C. (pres. chmn. legislative com.), N.A.M., Am. Bakers Assn. Clubs: Nat. Republican (N.Y.C.); Washington (gov.), Washington (Conn.) Golf. Home: New York City NY Died June 1969.

EGGLESTON, CARY, physician; b. Brooklyn, N.Y., Aug. 18, 1884; s. George Cary and Marion (Craggs) E.; grad. Berkeley School, New York, 1902; studied U. of Jena, Germany, 1903; M.D., Cornell U. Med. Coll., 1907; m. May Appleton Parker, June 3, 1916; children—Nancy May (Mrs. Edward Holcomb), Forrest Cary. Intern New York Hosp., Sloane Hosp. for Women, 1907-09; phys. Spence Sch. Soc. for Crippled Children, 1910-12; mem. Asso. Tuberculosis Clinics, N.Y., 1910-12; chief clinic Children's Dept., Demilt Dispensary, 1911-12; sr. asst. phys. N.Y. Hosp., out-patient dept., 1910-12; asst. phys. Bellevue Hosp. Dispensary, tuberculosis div., 1910-12; instr. pharmacology, 1911-18; asst. prof., 1918-23, Cornell U. Med. Sch., asst. prof. clin. medicine, July 1923-39; asso. prof. clin. medicine since 1939; asst. attending phys., City Hosp., 1915-18; adj. asst. visiting physician Bellevue Hospital, 1919-23; assistant visiting physician, 1923-33, visiting physician, 1933-50, consulting physician from 1950; associate attending physician New York Hospital, 1932-44, attending physician from 1944, cons. phys. from 1951; cons. phys. N.Y. Infirmary for Women and Children since 1934; cons. cardiologist Willard Parker Hosp. since 1932; cons. cardiologist, 1938, Hosp. Special Surgery, Manhattan Eye, Ear and Throat Hosp. from 1945. Fellow (founder) Am. Acad. Compensation Med., 1948. Fellow N.Y. Acad. Med., A.M.A., Assn. Am. Phys., Am. Soc. Clin. Investigation; mem. N.Y. State and N.Y. Co. med. socs., A.A.A.S., Alpha Omega Alpha, Phi Alpha Sigma Dem. Clubs: Quill, West Side Tennis, Univ. Author: Essentials of Prescription Writing, 1913. Contbr. to textbooks. Asso. editor New York Medical Journal, 1911-19; editor in charge dept. of therapeutics, Am. Jour. of Med. Sciences. Second v.p. U.S. Pharmacopoeial Conv. (XII Revision), 1940, pres., 1941-50. Home: New York City NY Died Nov. 15, 1966; buried Eggleston Cemetery, Brooklyn NY

EGGLETON, FRANK E(GBERT), univ. prof.; b. Rutland Center, N.Y., Sept. 24, 1893; s. Lewis Edmund and Eleanor Rickett (Bennett) E.; A.B., Hillsdale Coll., 1922; M.A., U. of Mich., 1923, Ph.D., 1930; m. Gladys Jane Vary, Aug. 6, 1919; children—Reginald Charles, Phylis Roberta, Richard Elton. Asst. biology, Hillsdale Coll., 1919-22; asst. zoology, U. of Mich., 1922-23; instr. zoology, Syracuse Univ., 1923-26; instr. Zoology, U. of Mich., 1926-30, asst. prof., 1930-37, asso. prof., 1937-51, prof. from 1952. Asst. limnology, U. of Mich. biol. sta., 1927-30, mem. station staff since 1931. Served U.S. Army, 1917-19. Received Russel award, Mich., 1937; distinguished alumni award Hillsdale Coll., 1958. Fellow A.A.A.S. (council 1946-52); mem. Am. Micros. Society (v.p. 1938, sec. 1946-51, editor 1946-51, president 1952), Am. Soc. Zoology, Ecol. Soc. Am., Am. Soc. Limnol and Oceanog., American Fish Society, Wilderness Society, Michigan Academy Science, Wis. Academy Science, American Association University Professors, American Soc. Systematic Zoology, Sigma Xi, Phi Kappa Phi, Phi. Sigma. Epsilon Delta Alpha. Delta Sigma Phi. Baptist. Club: University. Co-author: Problems of Lake Biology; Plant and Animal Communities. Contbr. research articles to scientific jours. Editor of Transactions, Am. Micros. Soc., 1946-51, mem. editorial board, 1952-60, mem. exec. com., 1938, and from 1960. Home: Ann Arbor MI Died May 3, 1970; buried Washtenong Meml. Park, Ann Arbor MI

EHRENREICH, JOSEPH, optical co. exec.; b. 1907; m. Amelia Komanoff; children—Robert, Jonathan. Founder, chmn. bd., pres., chief exec. officer Ehrenreich Photo-Optical Industries, Inc., Garden City, N.Y. Address: Garden City NY Died Feb. 7, 1973.

EHRICH, WILLIAM E(RNST) (HERMANN HEINRICH), physician; b. Dahmen, Germany, Nov. 29, 1900; s. William Maria and Hedwig Clara (Menzell) E.; student Freiburg U., U. Munich, Rostock U., 1919-24; M.D., U. Rostock, 1924; M.D. (honorary), University of Freiburg, 1957; m. Marie Louise Goldschmidt, Sept. 7, 1926; children—William G., Anna Louise (wife of Dr. Peter Batson), Helen (Mrs. Andre Armbruster). Came to United States in 1926, naturalized, 1942. Pathologist Rockefeller Inst. Hosp., N.Y.C., 1926-30; privatdozent in pathology U. Rostock, 1930-35; instr. pathology U. Pa., 1936-38, asso., 1938-44, asst. prof., 1944-46. prof., 1946-67, chmn. dept. pathology grad. div. sch. medicine, 1948-67; chief div. pathology Phila. Gen. Hosp., 1942-67. Recipient William W. Gerhard medal Phila. Path. Soc., 1963. Diplomate Am. Bd. Pathology, Fellow Phila. Coll. Physicians; mem. Am. Assn. Pathologists and Bacteriologists, Am. Soc. Exptl. Pathologists, Soc. Exptl. Biol. and Med., Harvey Soc. N.Y., German Pathologists Soc., Sydenham Coterie, German Acad. Sci., German Soc. Internal Medicine (corr.). Author textbook on dental pathology, articles, monographs in field. Home: Philadelphia PA Died Dec. 25, 1967.

EHRLICH, JACOB W., lawyer; b. nr. Rockville, Md., Oct. 15, 1900; legal edn. Georgetown U., San Francisco Law School; LL.D., The George Washington University; m. Marjorie Mercer; children—Jacob, Dora Jane (Mrs. Guy Cherney). Formerly employed as drayman for Wells Fargo; boxed professionally; sec. to v.p. Western Pacific R.R.; admitted to Cal. bar, 1922; spectacular record of acquittals, defense murder trials, also civil practice; well known as The Master. Lectr. Am. Trial Lawyers Assn., Practicing Law Inst., also seminars. Mem. Scribes, Nat. Law Writers Assn., Lawyers Lit. Club (bd. editorial advisers), Author's League Am., Dramatists Guild, Am. Soc. Legal History. Author: Ehrlich's Blackstone; Ehrlich's Criminal Evidence; What is Wrong with the Jury System; The Lost Art of Cross-Examination; The Educated Lawyer; The Contested Divorce Case; Howl of the Censor; The Holy Bible and the Law; A Reasonable Doubt; A Life in my Hands. Contbr. author: U. Cal. Continuing Edn. of Bar Series, Am. Jurisprudence Trial Series. Home: San Francisco CA Died Dec. 1971.

EHRLICHMAN, BEN B., investment banker; b. Mpls., Aug. 20, 1895; grad. pub. schs., Tacoma and Seattle; m. Genevieve Ament Grout, 1920; 1 dau., Mrs. Nancy Ehrlichman Sobek. Office boy, Carstens & Earles, Inc., 1912-15; asst. cashier, mgr. bond dept. Guardian Trust & Savs. Bank, Seattle, 1915-17; mgr. bond dept. Nat. City Bank, Seattle, 1919-20, Puget Sound Nat. Bank, Tacoma, 1920-21; organized Drumheller, Ehrlichman Co., Seattle, pres., 1921-45, name changed to Pacific N.W. Co., 1945; dir. emeritus United Pacific Ins. Co., VWR United Corp. Vice chmn. Seattle Civilian war Commn., 1942-46; chmn. King County Aviation Council, 1948-58; pres. Municipal League Seattle and King County, 1950-53, trustee; regional v.p. Nat. Municipal League, N.Y.; dir. emeritus Seattle Symphony; adv. com., past pres. Central Assn. Seattle; trustee U. Puget Sound, Principia Corp., St. Louis; adv. council Chief Seattle council Boy Scouts Am. Served as 2d lt. AS, U.S. Army, 1918-19. Recipient distinguished citizen award Nat. Municipal League, 1955; 1st Citizen of Seattle award, 1962; Silver Beaver, Boy Scouts of Am., 1968. Mem. Investment Bankers Assn. Am. (past gov.), Seattle C. of C. (sr. council). Christian Scientist. Mason (32, K.T.), Rotarian. Clubs: Harbor (1st pres.), Seattle Tennis, Rainier. Home: Carmel CA Died Oct. 14, 1971.

EHRMAN, SIDNEY M(YER), lawyer; b. San Francisco, Calif., Aug. 23, 1873; s. Myer and Fredericka (Rider) E.; student U. of Munich (Germany), 1892-93;

B.L., U. of Calif., 1896; LL.B., Hastings Coll. Law, 1898; m. Florence Hellman, June 30, 1904; children—Sidney Hellman (dec.), Mrs. Esther Ehrman Lazard. Began practice of law in office of W. S. Goodfellow and Garret W. McEnerney, San Francisco, 1898-1905; mem. Heller, Powers & Ehrman, 1906-21, Heller, White & McAuliffe since 1921. Regent U. Calif.; past Calif. State Chamber of Commerce; director San Francisco Opera Co., San Francisco Musical Assn.; trustee Hastings College Law, San Francisco Law Library, San Francisco War Memorial, Calif. Hist. Soc. Republican. Jewish religion. Clubs: Family, San Francisco Stock Exchange Lunch, St. Francis Yacht. Home: 2970 Broadway. Office: Nevada Bank Bldg., San Francisco‡

EHRMANN, MAX, author; b. Terre Haute, Ind., Sept. 26, 1872; s. Max and Margaret von E.; Ph.B., De Pauw U., 1894. Litt.D., 1938; 2 yrs. postgrad. work in philosophy, Harvard; unmarried. Author: A Farrago, 1898; The Mystery of Madeline LeBlanc, 1899; A Fearsome Riddle, 1901; A Prayer, 1903; Breaking Home Ties, 1904; A Prayer and Selections, 1906; Poems, 1906; Who Entereth Here, 1907; The Poems of Max Ehrmann, 1910; The Wife of Marobius, 1911; Jesus—A Passion Play, 1915; The Seasons, 1917; David and Bathsheba, 1918; A Virgin's Dream, 1922; Life of Paul Dresser, 1924; Be Quiet, I'm Talking, 1926; Love from Many Angles, 1927; Desiderata, 1927; Farces, Bank Robbery and Plumber, 1928; Worldly Wisdom, 1934; also booklets in Scarlet Women Series, The Gay Life, Scarlet Sketches, A Goose with a Rose in Her Mouth, His Beautiful Wife, Her Dream, 1925; De Pauw University Centennial Ode, 1937. Formerly editor The Rainbow of Delta Tau Delta. Home: Terre Haute IN‡

EICHELBERGER, WILLIAM SNYDER, astronomer; b. Baltimore, Sept. 18, 1865; s. Albert G. and Martha (Snyder) E.; A.B., Johns Hopkins, 1886, Ph.D., 1891; m. Vola McCrea, Mar. 21, 1894; children—Emily Louise (dec.), Donald McCrea (dec.), Adele Marie (Mrs. Bernard Tallman). Asst. Nautical Almanac Office, 1889-90, 1896-98; instr. mathematics and astronomy, Wesleyan U., Conn., 1890-96; computer in U.S. Naval Observatory, 1898-1900; prof. mathematics U.S. Navy since 1900; was head of div. meridian instruments, 1902-07; in charge dept. of astron. observations, U.S. Naval Obs., 1907-08; in charge cataloguing Washington Zone Observations of 1846-52, 1908-11; in charge reducing and cataloguing meridian circle observations of 1903-11, 1908-19, dir. Nautical Almanac, 1910-29, U.S. Naval Obs.; with Eastman Kodak Co., Rochester, N.Y., since 1929. Mem. U.S. eclipse expdn., Pinehurst, N.C., 1900; in charge U.S. eclipse stas. at Fort de Kock, Sumatra, 1901, Daroca, Spain, 1905. Asso. Royal Astron. Society; fgn. corr. Bureau des Longitudes; fellow A.A.A.S.; mem. Am. Astron. Soc. Astronomische Gesellschaft, Washington Acad. Sciences, Philos. Soc. Washington (pres. 1915), Phi Beta Kappa. Wrote: Positions and Proper Motions of 1504 Standard Stars," in Astron. Papers of Am. Ephemeris, 1925; (with Arthur Newton) The Orbit of Neptune's Satellite and the Pole of Neptune's Equator," in Astron. Papers of Am. Ephemeris, 1926; contbr. papers to Govt. pubs. and Astron. Jour.; etc. Address: 1447 St. Paul St., Rochester NY‡

EIDEM, OLAF, lawyer; b. Elk Point, S.Dak., May 23, 1875; s. Thomas and Randi (Hoffstad) E.; ed. Augustana Acad., Canton, S.Dak., and U. of S. Dak.; LL.B., U. of Neb., 1899; m. Gertrude Jerde, of Brookings, S.Dak., Aug. 25, 1904; children—Ruth Beatrice, Orpha Gertrude, Dorothy Agnes. Admitted to S.Dak. bar, 1900, and began practice at Brookings; state's atty. Brookings County, 1906-10; del. Rep. Nat. Conv., 1924; became U.S. dist. atty., Dist. of South Dakota, 1926; member law firm of Hall & Eidem. Mem. State Council of Defense, World War, also capt. four-minute men. Lutheran. Home: Brookings SD*‡

EIESLAND, JOHN (ARNDT), mathematician; b. Ny Hellesund, nr. Christianssand, Norway, Jan. 27, 1867; s. Andreas and Angnete (Abrahamsen) E.; Normal Sch. and Gymnasium, Christianssand; Ph.B., U. of S.Dak., 1891; Ph.D., Johns Hopkins, 1898; Johns Hopkins Scholar, 1897-98; m. Clara June Snyder, Sept. 15, 1904. Came to U.S., 1888; teacher Lutheran Acad., Albert Lea, Minn., 1891-92; prof. mathematics, Thiel Coll., Greenville, Pa., 1895-1903; instr. mathematics, U.S. Naval Acad., 1903-07; prof. mathematics and head of dept., W.Va. U., 1907-38, prof. emeritus since 1938. Sec. W.Va. Acad. Science, 1905-06, pres., 1906-07. Fellow A.A.A.S.; mem. Am. Math. Soc., Math. Assn. America, Circolo Matematico di Palermo (Italy), Deutsche Mathematiker Vereinigung, Phi Beta Kappa. Democrat. Lutheran. Author: Advanced Algebra for Technical Schools and Colleges, 1910; also numerous memoirs in math. jours. Home: Morgantown WV‡

EISENBERG, IRWIN WEINMAN, mfr.; researcher; b. Biltmore, N.C., Dec. 1, 1906; s. William S. and Matilda (Krebs) E.; m. to Christine Lucero, May 16, 1964. Engr. Lee Deforest, 1927-29, Jackson Bell, 1929-31; pres. Viking Radio, 1931-33; partner Advance Amusement, 1935-37; founder, 1937, also pres. Phaostron Instrument & Electronic Co., South Pasadena, Cal. Home: Pasadena CA Died May 26, 1970.

EISENBERG, MAURICE, concert cellist; b. Koenigsberg, Germany, Feb. 24, 1902; s. Samuel J. and Fannie (Berlin) E.; brought to U.S., 1903, naturalized, 1905; student Peabody Conservatory of Music, Balt., also with Julius Klengel, Leipzig, Hugh Becker, Berlin Diran Alexanian, Paris, and Pablo Casals in Spain; student harmony with Nadia Boulanger, Paris; m. Paula M. Halpert, June 6, 1921; children—Pablo, Maruta Nadia (Mrs. John P. Friedler). Soloist, Royal Philharmonic, London Symphony in London, Pasdeloup Orch., Paris; soloist, Boston, Phila., Los Angeles, San Antonio orchs.; recitalist, lectr. Assn. Am. Colls., also at Harvard, Princeton, Mass. Inst. Tech., Oxford and Cambridge univs., Royal Acad. Music, London, McGill U., Montreal, others; head cello dept. Longy Sch. Music, Cambridge, Mass.; yearly master classes Internat. Summer Courses, Estoril, Portugal; prof. violoncello and chamber music Juilliard Sch. Music, 1964-72; vis. prof. U. So. Cal.; dir. Internat. Cello Centre, London, Eng. U.S. rep. internat. juries Pablo Casals cello competition, Paris, Mexico, Israel and Budapest. Recipient award N.J. Symphony Arts, 1966. Mem. Bohemians, Violoncello Soc. N.Y. (v.p.). Jewish religion. Author: Violoncello Playing of Today, 1957, now in 2d edit. Contbr. articles to profl. jours. Home: Millburn NJ Died Dec. 13, 1972.

EISENHARDT, RAYMOND F., banker. Sr. v.p. Buffalo Savs. Bank. Home: Buffalo NY

EISENHOWER, DWIGHT DAVID, 34th Pres. of U.S.; b. Denison, Tex., Oct. 14, 1890; s. David J. and Ida E. (Stover) E.; B.S., U.S. Military Acad., 1915; married Mamie Geneva Doud, July 1, 1916; children—Dwight Doud (dec.), John Sheldon Doud. Commissioned 2d lieutenant infantry, United States Army, 1915, and advanced through grades to gen. of the army, Dec. 1944; became Allied Comdr. in Chief, North Africa, Nov. 8, 1942; apptd. comdg. gen. Allied Powers, E.T.O., Dec. 31, 1943; comdr. U.S. occupation forces in Germany, 1945; chief of staff, U.S. Army, Nov. 1945-48; pres. Columbia U., 1948-52; apptd. Supreme Comdr. Allied Powers Europe, Dec. 1950; resigned from U.S. Army, July 1952; inaugurated President of U.S., Jan. 20, 1953, and Jan. 21, 1957. Recipient hon. degrees from instns. in U.S. and abroad; fgn. and U.S. orders, decorations and medals; Gen. Sylvanus Thayer gold medal and scroll West Point, 1961; 1st Am. Patriot's medal Freedom's Found., 1961. Mem. English-Speaking Union U.S. (chmn. nat. bd. dirs.;. Author: Mandate for Change, 1963; Waging Peace: The White House Years, 1956-61, 1965. Chmn. Gettysburg PA Died Mar. 29, 1969; buried Abilene KS

EISENHOWER, EDGAR NUTON, lawyer; b. Hope, Kan., 1889; s. David J. and Ida Elizabeth (Stover) E.; grad. U. Mich., 1914. Partner Eisenhower, Carlson, &Newlands, Riha & Sinnitt; dir. Puget Sound Nat. Bank, F.S. Harmon Co., St. Regis Paper Co., E.L. Bruce Co. Trustee Ams. for Constl. Action. Elk. Home: Tacoma WA Died July 12, 1971.

ELAN, MEIR, bus. exec.; b. Lublin, Nov. 20, 1918; student grad. courses arty. Brit. Army; m. Miriam Mintz, 1942. Maj., Israel Def. Forces, 1948-50, co-founder Arty. Corps, advanced through grades to brig. gen.; chief arty., 1951-54, chief logistics Def. Forces, 1954-60, ret., 1960; gen. mgr. Kiryath Haplada, Ltd., 1961-65; mng. dir. Chems. & Phosphates, Ltd., Haifa, Israel, 1965-71; Dead Sea Works Ltd., 1969-71; dir. gen. inorganic div. Israel Chems. Ltd., 1969-71. Address: Haifa Israel Died Feb. 24, 1971; buried Tel Aviv Israel

EL AZHARI, ISMAIL, pres. of The Sudan; b. Omdurman, The Sudan, 1900; s. Ismail el Azhari; B.A., Am. U. Beirut (Lebanon), 1930; LL.D. (hon.), U. Khartoum, 1967; m. Sit Miaiam Salama, 1943; children—Amal, Samia, Sanaa, Mohammad, Sumayyia, Galaa. Sec.-gen. Sudanese Grads. Club, 1934; sec.-gen. Congress in The Sudan, 1938-40, then pres., 1940; prime minister First Nat. Govt., 1954; pres. Supreme Council of State of Republic of The Sudan, 1965-69. Pres. Ashiga Party, 1943, then Nat. Unionist Party, 1953. Chancellor U. Khartoum, Islamic U. Khartoum. Author: The Way to Parliament. Home: Omdurman The Sudan Died Aug. 1969.

ELDER, ROBERT HENRY;, b. Marlon, Kentucky, Sept. 7, 1877; s. James Tilford and Mary Elizabeth (Dowell) E.; grad. U. of Kan.; m. Martha Jane Noble, of Kansas City, Mo., June 21, 1903; children—Constance Elizabeth, Mary Margaret, Robert Noble. Admitted to Kan. bar, later to Ida. bar; practiced in Coeur d'Alene since Dec. 1903; mem. Dem. Nat. Com. for Ida., 1912-28. Presbyn. Mason. Home: 1136 4th St., Coeur d'Alene ID‡

ELDRIDGE, EDWARD HENRY, educator; b. Phila., Feb. 8, 1870; s. David and Elizabeth P. (Henry) E.; ed. Temple U., Phila., and Amherst Coll.; special studies psychology, U. of Chicago, U. of Pa., Clark U.; Ph.D., Temple U., 1907; m. Florence Beery Heisser, Dec. 27, 1923. Teacher since 1895; dir. Secretarial Sch., Simmons Coll., 1902-36, now emeritus. Pres. Eastern Commercial Teachers' Assn., 1912-13; treas. Nat. Shorthand Reporters' Assn., 1912-14, v.p., 1926-27; mem. bd. regents Am. Inst. for Secretaries. Mem. Nat. Office Management Orgn., Nat. Assn. Commercial Teacher Training Instns.; hon. mem. Mass., N.Y. and Pa. shorthand reports assns. Author: Hypnotism, 1902; Shorthand Dictation Exercises, 1910; Expert Typewriting (with Miss Rose L. Fritz), 1911; Business Speller and Vocabulary, 1913; Essentials of Expert Typewriting (with Rose L. Fritz and Gertrude W. Craig), 1919; New Shorthand Dictation Exercises, 1922; New Expert Typewriting (with Rose L. Fritz and Gertrude W. Craig), 1929; A First Course in Expert Typewriting, 1935; Shorthand Reading and Dictation Exercises (Gregg and Pitman editions), 1939; Standardized Pitmanic Shorthand, 1941; Standardized Pitman Shorthand Supplement, 1941. Home: Marlboro MA*‡

ELDRIDGE, MAURICE OWEN, road expert; b. Lenoir, Tenn., July 3, 1873; s. Simeon G. and Mary S. E.; ed. pvt. sch., 1880-90, Univ. of Tenn., 1890-3; B. S., Columbian Univ., 1898; m. Oct. 14, 1897, Bertha G. Stier (died June 3, 1902). As a boy worked on farm, later work in gen. store; pursued eng'ring course at Univ. of Tenn., teaching sch. and working for local architect during vacations. Became expert draftsman under Gen. Roy Stone, 1893, in office of Pub. Road Inquiries, U.S. Dept. Agr., of which he is now asst. chief. Platform lecturer—notably on Highways of Europe and America; contb'r to mags. Republican. Author: Construction of Country Roads, 1895 U8; Progress of Road Building in the United States, 1899 U8; Good Roads for Farmers, 1900 U8; Earth Roads, 1902 U8; etc. Residence: 1828 9th St. N. W. Office: Agr'l Dept., Washington DC‡

ELGHAMMER, H. WILLIAM, pediatrician, educator; b. Stockholm, Sweden, Mar. 13, 1894; s. William Thure and Emma Sophia (Johnson) E.; S.B., Royal Sci. Coll., 1912; M.D., Loyola U., 1920; m. Stena A. Peterson, Feb. 16, 1921; children—William Robert, Richard Mason. Came to U.S., 1913, naturalized, 1918. Intern St. Anne's Hosp., South Shore Hosp., Chicago, 1920-21; practicing pediatrician, Chicago since 1921; instr. pediatrics Loyola U., 1921-23, asso., 1923-28, asst. prof., 1928-32, asso. prof., 1932-37, prof., chmn. dept. pediatrics, from 1937, prof. dept. pediatrics Stritch Sch. Medicine, 1960; lectr., prof. pediatrics Univ. Ill., 1961; cons. pediatrician Presbyn.-St. Luke's Hosp., Chgo.; chief pediatric staff Mercy Hosp.; attending pediatrician La Rabida Inst.; pediatric cons. Med. adv. bd. Municipal Contagious Disease Hosp., Ill. Central Hosp., St. Bernard Hospital. Former director Klingberg's Children's Home. Served R.O.T.C., 1918. Diplomate Am. Bd. Pediatrics, Fellow A.C.P., Am. Acad. Pediatrics; mem. A.M.A., Ill. State, Chicago med. socs., Chicago Pediatric Soc. (pres. 1947-48), Chgo. Inst. Medicine, Am., Chgo. (gov.) heart assns. Republican. Presbyn. Mason (32 deg.). Author articles med., sci. jours. Home: Chicago IL Died Jan. 25, 1972; buried Oak Hill Cemetery, Chicago IL

ELIAS, ALBERT BARNES, telephone official; b. Spring Brook, Pa., Oct. 25, 1875; s. David Price and Margaret (Brooks) E.; ed. pub. schs.; unmarried. Began with New York Telephone Co., 1900; chmn. bd., dir. and mem. exec. com. Southwestern Bell Telephone Co.; dir. Mississippi Valley Trust Co. Dir. Municipal Theatre Assn. of St. Louis, Central Inst. for the Deaf. Vice pres., dir. and mem. exec. com. St. Louis Chamber of Commerce. Presbyn. Clubs: Noonday, Racquet, Bogey Golf, Glen Echo Country (St. Louis). Home: 275 N. Union Av. Office: Telephone Bldg., St Louis MO‡

ELIASBERG, WLADIMIR G., psychiatrist, neurologist, psychologist, author; b. Wiesbaden, Germany, Dec. 10, 1887; s. Samuel and Rachel E.; student med. colls., univs. Berlin and Heidelberg, M.D., 1912; Ph.D., U. Munich, 1924; m. Esther Talbot; four children. Intern Prof. Kraepelin Hosp., Munich, 1912; voyage as ship's Dr., Far East, 1913; physician Hosp. for Brain Diseases, Munich, 1919-23; founder, sec. gen. German Congress for Psychotherapy, 1926; editor Allg. Aerztl. Ztschrft. f. Psychother.; attending physician and supt. Hosp. for Nervous and Mental Diseases, Munich-Thalkirchen, 1928-30; mem. delegation 7th Internat. Congress for Psychotechnics, 1931; lectr. forensic psychiatry Munich Bar Assn., 1932; chmn. div. indsl. pathology 8th Internat. Congress for Psychotechnics, Prague, 1934; vis. prof. Academie des Sciences Politiques, Prague, 1937; chmn. sci com. for Advancement of Psychotherapy, 1940; Psychiatrist, O.P.D., Mt. Sinai Hosp., 1941-44; lectr. psychology Rutgers U., 1946; psychiat. cons. Bulova Watch Co., 1946; med. dir. Bklyn. treatment unit Citizens Com., N.Y., 1952, Convent Av. and Neighborhood guidance clinics, N.Y., 1953. Certified psychiatrist N.Y. State Bd. Mental Hygiene, 1940; certified examiner State N.Y., 1940. Served as capt. Ger. Army Med. Corps, 1915-18. Diplomate Am. Bds. Neurology and Psychiatry. Fellow Am. Psyhciat. Assn., N.Y. Acad. Medicine, Am. Sociol, Assn.; mem. A.M.A. (life), Rudolf Virchow Med. Soc., Am. Soc. Criminology, Assn. for Psychiat. Treatment Offenders (hon. mem.), Am. Soc. Psychoanalytic Physicians (pres. 1958), N.Y. Soc. Clin Psychiatry, Am. Psychol. Assn., Pirquet Society Clin. Medicine, N.Y. State Assn. Psychology, N.Y. Assn. for History of Medicine, Allg. Aerztl. Ges. f Psychotherapie Vienna (hon.), 1952, Prague Inst. of Psychotechnics (hon.),

1937, Am. Mental Health Found., (v.p.), Acad. Polit. and Social Sci. Phila. Author med. and other books, also numerous articles concerned with psychiatry, psychology, sociology, criminology, child psychology, propaganda, indsl. psychology, grapho-diagnostics, history of medicine. Contbr.: Handbook of Child Guidance, 1940; Handbook of Scientific Proof and Relations of Law and Medicine (Harvard Law Sch.), 1946; Handbook of Correctional Psychology, 1947; Encyclopedia of Criminology, 1948; Handboak of Therapeutic Abortion, 1954; Speaking and Thinking (symposium), 1954; Handbuch d. Neurosenlehre u. Psychotherapy, 1957. Present-Day Psychology, 1955; Psychotherapy and Soc., 1959. Address: NYC NY Died June 1969.

ELIOT, DOUGLAS FITCH GUILFORD, business consultant; born New York City, New York; May 2, 1887; son of Henry Hill and Mary Leavenworth (Fitch) E.; A.B., Yale U., 1909; m. Helen Willard Kelley, June 1, 1921 (dec.); children—Elizabeth W. (Mrs. Harley LeRoy Moore), Henry H. Am. Locomotive Co., Schenectady and Pittsburgh, 1909-10; Western Electric Co., N.Y., 1911-17; Nippon Electric Co., Ltd., Tokyo, Japan, 1917-18; Internat. Western Electric Co., New York, 1919-21; Nippon Electric Co., Tokyo, and Sumitomo Electric Wire and Cable Works, Ltd., Osaka, Japan, 1922-25; Euorpean gen. mgr. Western Electric Co., London, 1926; Western Electric Co., N.Y., 1926-52, vice president, 1946-52; director Mfrs. Junction Ry. Co., Cicero, Ill., 1941-52, president, 1945-52; business consultant since 1952. Member Squadron A, New York State Nat. Guard, 1915-16; pvt., U.S. Army, 1918. Mem. Social Service Fedn. of Englewood (past pres.); mem. Alumni bd., Yale U., 1937-52; past pres., Yale Alumni Assn., Bergen Co., N.J.; bd. trustees Englewood Sch. for Boys, 1943-52 (pres. 1944-47); trustee Eagle Brook Sch., Deerfield, Mass., from 1953, treas., from 1954; mem. bd. dirs. Northern Valley chpt. A.R.C., 1942-45. Mem. Telephone Pioneers of Am., Psi Epsilon. Episcopalian (vestryman 1925-31, warden 1944-46, sr. warden, 1956; mem. finance and adv. bd. Diocese of Newark 1948-50). Republican. Clubs: Yale (N.Y.C.); Englewood (bd. govs., 1950-51, pres. 1951, 52); Knickerbocker Country (Tenafly, N.J.). Home: Englewood NJ Died Oct. 1971.

ELIOT, GEORGE FIELDING, author, journalist; b. Brooklyn, N.Y., June 22, 1894; s. Philip Park and Rena (King) E.; B.A., Melbourne U., Australia, 1914; m. Sara Elaine Hodges, Dec. 23, 1933 (divorced 1942); m. 2d. June Cawley Hynd. Jan. 1, 1943. Accountant Haskins & Sells, Kansas City, Mo., 1922-27; began writing for fiction mags., 1926; writer, especially on mil. and internat. affairs, national security, 1928-71; asso. Center Strategic Studies, Georgetown U., 1967-71. Served Australian Imperial Force, Dardanelles and Western Front, 1914-18; capt., later maj., Mil. Intelligence Reserve, U.S. Army, 1922-30. Recipient Honor medal for distinguished service in journalism U. of Mo., 1962, Alfred Thayer Mahan award for lit. accomplishment Navy League U.S., 1964. Mem. Council on Foreign Relations, Army Ordnance Assn., U.S. Naval Inst., Fgn. Policy Assn., Acad. Polit. Science, American Political Science Association. President Committee Nat. Morale, 1942-45; pres. Assn. of Radio News Analysts, 1943, re-elected, 1951. Episcopalian. Clubs: Century (New York); National Press (Washington, D.C.). Author: If War Comes (with R. E. Dupuy), 1937; The Ramparts We Watch, 1938; Bombs Bursting in Air, 1939; Hour of Triumph, 1944; The Strength We Need, 1946; Hate, Hope and High Explosive, 1948; If Russia Strikes, 1949; Caleb Pettengill, USN (novel), 1956; Victory Without War, 1958; Sylvanus Thayer of West Point, 1959; Reserve Forces and the Kennedy Strategy, 1962; Franklin Buchanan, 1962; articles and fiction mags., newspapers; lectr. internat. relations, mil. affairs. Mil. and naval corr. N.Y. Herald-Tribune, 1939-46; mil. analyst Columbia Broadcasting System, 1939-47, M.B.S., 1950-53; columnist N.Y. Post Home News, 1947-49; Gen. Features Syndicate, 1950-67. Mil. editor Collier's Ency. Home: Litchfield CT Died Apr. 21, 1971; cremated.

ELIOTT, VAN COURTLANDT, editor, assn. exec.; b. Rochester, N.H., July 24, 1904; A.B., Bowdoin Coll., 1928; A.M., U. N.C., 1929, Ph.D., 1933; m. Kathleen Overmyer, June 4, 1938. Instr. Classics, U. N.C., 1930-35; master Latin and Greek, Roxburg Latin Sch., Boston, 1939-64; asso. sec. Mediaeval Acad. Am., 1952-64; exec. sec., 1964—; asst. editor Speculum, 1962-64, editor, 1965—. Mem. Am. Philol. Assn., New Eng. Classical Assn. Mediaeval Acad. Am., Renaissance Soc. Am. Home: Cambridge MA Died Aug. 20, 1970.

ELISOFON, ELIOT, photographer, painter; b. N.Y.C., Apr. 17, 1911; s. Samuel and Sarah (Narazimski) E.; B.S., Fordham U., 1933; m. Mavis Lyons, July 1, 1941 (div. 1946); m. 2d, Joan Baker Spear, July 15, 1950 (div. 1965); children—Elin, Jill. Staff photographer Life mag., 1942, engaged on nat. and internat. assignments Mexico, C.A., S.Am., Africa, South Seas, Japan, Europe; research fellow primitive art Peabody Mus., Harvard; color cons. motion picture Moulin Rouge, 1952, Bell, Book and Candle, 1958, Warlord, 1964; dir. prologue film Khartoum, 1965; dir. Egypt portion Man Builds (Nat. Ednl. TV), 1965; still photographer Dr. Doolittle, 1966; creative dir. ABC-TV Africa Project, 1966-67; visual cons. stage prodn., Baylor U., Of Time and the River; exhibited one-man shows Durlacher Bros., 1958, 60, watercolors Gekkoso Gallery, Tokyo, 1969; rep. permanent collection Mus. Modern Art, N.Y.C., Phila. Mus. Art, Pa. Acad. Fine Arts, Colby Coll. of Me., Fogg Art Mus., Cambridge, Dallas Mus. Contemporary Art, Hononlulu Acad. Art, Nat. Mus. Western Art, Tokyo; lectr. Dallas Theater Center, Yale, Syracuse U., Radcliffe Coll., Wellesley Coll., Sarah Lawrence Coll., Mus. Modern Art, Chgo. Art Inst., R.I. Sch. Design, U. Wis. Mem. Harvard Peabody Mus. New Guinea expdn., 1961. Mem. Royal Anthrop. Soc. Clubs: Overseas, Explorers (N.Y.C.). Author: Food is a Four Letter Word, 1948; Color Photography, 1961; The Nile, 1964; Java Diary, 1969. Illustrator: The Art of Indian Asia, 1955. Illustrator, editor; The sculpture of Africa, 1958; Hollywood Style (Arthur Knight), 1969; Indian Cookbook, 1969. Collector Am. folk art, Pre-Columbian, Pacific, African sculpture in U.S. Contbr. to Nat. Geog., Smithsonian mag. Address: New York City NY Died Apr. 7, 1973.

ELIZALDE, RAFAEL HECTOR, diplomat; b. Guayaquil, Ecuador, S. America, May 31, 1873; s. Juan Bautista and Rosario (Gomez) Elizalde y Pareja; Ph.B., Nat. Coll. of San Vicente del Guayas, 1889; LL.B., U. of Guayas, 1894, LL.D., 1895; m. Teresa MacClure, of Santiago, Chile, Jan. 1906 (died 1909); children—Anita, Rafael; m. 2d, Irene Bernales Lazcano, of Santiago, May 14, 1911; children—Hector, Mercedes, Alicia, Irene, Benjamin. Mem. Congress of Ecuador 3 terms, 1901-05, 1909-11; apptd. 1st sec. of Legation of Ecuador, in Chile, 1902, in Brazil, 1904; res. minister, later E.E. and M.P. to Chile, 1906-12; minister of foreign affairs, Ecuador, 1914-16; E.E. and M.P. to U.S. and Cuba, 1916-24; M.P. to Chile since 1925; on spl. mission to U.S., 1925. Assisted in settlement of boundary line between Ecuador and Colombia. Mem. Sociedad Juridico Literaria (Quito); hon. mem. Sociedad Artes Graficas (Santiago). Decorated 1st Class Order of Al Merito, of Chile; 2d Class Order of Libertador, of Venezuela; 1st Class Order Al Merito, Ecuador. Clubs: Metropolitan (hon.), Chevy Chase of Washington, D.C. (hon.), Club de Union (Guayaquil), Pichincha (Quito). Author: Labores Diplomaticas, 1912; Organizacion de Partidos Politicos, 1913; Requeza Obliga, 1914. Address: 1536 Alonso Ovalle, Santiago Chile‡

ELKINS, JAMES ANDERSON, banker, lawyer b. Huntsville, Tex., Sept. 25, 1879; LL.B., U. Tex., 1901; m. Isabel Mitchell (dec.); children—W.S., James Anderson. Partner firm Vinson, Elkins, Searls & Connally, Houston; sr. chmn. bd. First City Nat. Bank, Houston. Mem. Am. Tex., Houston bar assns. Home: Houston TX Died 1973.

ELLEFSON, BENNETT STANLEY, engring. adminstr.; b. Canby, Minn., Jan. 10, 1911; s. Halvor S. and Sarah (Lewison) E.; A.B., St. Olaf Coll., 1932; M.S., U. Minn., 1933; student N.Y.U. 1933-34; Ph.D., Pa. State U., 1937; m. Dorothea Kinter, Nov. 25, 1948; children—Dana, Kristi Gayle. Teaching fellow N.Y.U., 1933-34; research asst. Pa. State U., 1934-37; with Sylvania Electric Products, Inc., Bayside, N.Y., 1937-60, successively research chemist, asst. to v.p. engring., dir. central engring. labs., dir. research, 1937-56, v.p. engring and research, 1956-59, v.p. tech. planning, 1959-60; v.p. Gen. Telephone and Electronics Labs., Inc., 1960-73. Fellow I.E.E.E., A.A.A.S.; mem. Am. Chem. Soc., Am. Ceramic Soc. Home: Bayside NY Died 1973.

ELLENDER, ALLEN JOSEPH, U.S. senator; b. Montegut, Terrebonne Parish, La., Sept. 24, 1890; son Wallace Richard and Victoria (Javaux) E.; hon. A.M., St. Aloysius Coll., New Orleans; LL.B., Tulane U., 1913; m. Helen Calhoun Donnelly, Mar. 19, 1917 (dec. 1949); 1 son, Allen Joseph. Admitted to La. bar, 1913; city atty., Houma, La., 1913-15; dist. atty. Terrebonne Parish, 1915-16, del. Constl. Conv. of La., 1921; mem. La. State Ho. of Rep., 1924-36 (floor leader, 1928-32, speaker 1932-36); U.S. senator from La., 1937-72, chmn. agr. and forestry com., until 1971, chmn. com. on appropriations, 1971—; pres. pro tempore, 1971. Dem. Nat. committeeman from La., 1939-40. Named Man of Year in So. Agr., Progressive Farmer Mag., 1971; recipient Watchdog of Treasury award, 1971. Home: Houma LA Died July 27, 1972.

ELLENDER, RAPHAEL THEODORE, artist; b. N.Y.C., Feb. 22, 1906; s. Theodore and Ada (Miller) E.; B.A. (N.Y. State Regents Scholar), Columbia, 1926, student Tchrs. Coll., also Sch. Architecture, 1924-26; student Academie Colerossie, Paris, France, 1929, N.A.D., 1938, Art Students League (Saltus Scholar), 1926-27, 37-43. Advt. art dir. for N.Y.C. dept. stores, advt. agys., 1926-46; cons. art dir., 1947-57; instr. drawing and painting Workshop Sch. of Art, N.Y.C., 1947-49, Am. Art Sch., N.Y.C., 1950, Art Students League, 1950, 61, N.Y.U., 1958-64. Exhibited one-man show at Pietrantonio Galleries, N.Y.C., 1970; group exhbns. include Milch Gallery, 1941-47, Kraushaar Gallery, 1940-42, Portraits, Inc., 1940-45, Asso. Am. Artists, 1938-40; jury shows include N.A.D., 1960, Met. Mus. Art, 1943, Bklyn. Mus. Art. 1943, Am. Water Color Soc., 1925, 39-44, Corcoran Gallery Art 1939, Pa. Acad. Fine Arts, 1938, Chgo. Art Inst., 1939 Allied Artists, 1961, 63, 70; portrait commns. include Bernard F. Gimbel, Dr. John H. Garlock, Harold Rome William Kamm. Recipient Benjamin Altman prize for landscape N.A.D., 1960. Life mem. Art Students League, Allied Artists Am. (Famous Artists Sch. prize 1964, honorable mention 1970). Clubs: Salmagundi Manhattan Chess (N.Y.C.). Author: Basic Drawing 1964. Address: New York City NY Died Aug. 24, 1972

ELLERBE, ALMA MARTIN, author; b. Greenfield Ind., Apr. 7, 1871; d. Samuel Marsh (M.D.) and Florence (Howard) Martin; ed. Oxford Female Coll. O.; m. William Chester Estabrook, of Indianapolis, June 30, 1896 (deceased); 2d, Paul Lee Ellerbe, of Denver Oct. 2, 1915. Author: The Rule of Three, 1909. Contbr novelettes and short stories to mags. Address: 500 Sugar Bldg., Denver CO‡

ELLERY, EDWARD, educator, chemist; b. Albany N.Y., July 24, 1868; s. Edward and Abbie Maria (Bellows) E.; A.B., Colgate, 1890, A.M., 1893, Sc.D. 1912; S.C., U. of Pittsburgh, 1931; Univ. of Berlin, 1894 1909; Ph.D., Univ. of Heidelberg, 1896; LL.D. from George Washington U., 1937; m. Adelaide F. True, Feb. 20, 1909. With Union Coll. since 1904, prof. chemistry 1904-40, dean of faculty, 1918-40, acting pres. 1933-35, chmn. of faculty, 1935-40, emeritus prof. chemistry since 1940. Expert chemist for various industrial concerns; chemist for Schenectady Bureau of Health. Member Schenectady Board of Education. Made tour of American Universities, 1914-15, for Union College. Phi Beta Kappa lecturer, Univ. of N.D. and U. of Wash., 1923; lecturer Univs. of London and Belfast, 1925, St. Andrew's Aberdeen, Glasgow and Durham, 1926; Sigma Xi lecturer U. of Fla., 1938, W.Va U., 1939, U. of Ala. 1939; visiting lecturer Univ. of Hawaii, 1941. Mem. Nat. Research Council. Fellow A.A.A.S.; mem. Am. Chem. Soc., Sigma Xi, (exec. com., chmn. research fellowship com., nat. sec., nat. pres.), Phi Beta Kappa (pres. Upper Hudson Assn., also N.Y. State Assn.), Beta Theta Pi. Baptist. Clubs. Forthnightly, Mohawk (Schenectady). Author: The Half Century Record and History of Sigma Xi, 1937, also articles on training of chemists; corr. editor Scientific American, 1921. Address: Union College, Schenectady, N.Y.; and South Paris ME‡

ELLERY, ELOISE, prof. history; b. Rochester, N.Y. June 8, 1874; d. Frank M. and Alida (Alling) E.; A.B., Vassar, 1897; fellow Assn. Collegiate Alumnae, 1899-1900; Ph.D., Cornell, 1902. Asst. in dept. of history, Vassar, 1900, prof. history, 1916-39, prof. emeritus since 1939. Mem. Am. Hist. Assn., Am. Assn. Univ. Women, Phi Beta Kappa. Author: Brissot de Warville, 1915. Address: Vassar College, Poughkeepsie NY‡

ELLIFF, EDGAR ALONZO, physician; b. Milford, Mo., Dec. 7, 1893; s. John Ebenezer and Clara Bessie (Robbins) E.; M.D., Eclectic Med. Coll. Cin., 1919, postgrad. Washington U., 1925-26, U. Vienna, 1926; m. Minnie Mae Bunker, Aug. 18, 1925; children—John Edgar, James Henry. Intern Christ Hosp., Cin., 1919-20; resident West Side Hosp., Chgo., 1919-20; mem. staffs Good Samaritan Hosp., St. Benedict Hosp. Pres., founder Sterling Indsl. Bank, Elliff Land Co. Mem. Med. Adv. Bd., SSS. Mem. Sterling (Colo.) City Council, 1934-44, mayor Sterling, 1944-46; pres. city charter com., 1950; mem. Colo. senate, 1950-58; chmn. Colo. Republican Com., 1955-59. Served with U.S. Army, 1917-18. Diplomate Am. Bd. Otolaryngology. Fellow Am. Acad. Ophthalmology and Otolaryngology; mem. A.M.A., Northeast Colo. Med. Soc. (pres. 1932), Colo. Otolaryn. (pres. 1950-51). Home: Sterling CO Died Oct. 30, 1966; buried Sterling CO

ELLIFF, JOSEPH DOLIVER, coll. prof.; b. Council Grove, Kan., Dec. 1863; s. Constant Powell and Mary (Potter) E.; grad. State Normal Sch., Warrensburg, Mo., 1893; A.B., U. of Mo., 1903, A.M., 1906; grad. student U. of Chicago and Columbia U.; LL.D., St. Louis University, 1933; m. Jean Scott Cumming. Dec. 1893; children—Joseph Cumming, Mary Agnes. Teacher in rural and village schs., 1882-92; prin. high sch. and supt. schs., Joplin, Mo., 1892-1903; supt. pub. schs., St. Joseph, Mo., 1903-04; high sch. visitor and prof. high sch. adminstrn., Univ. of Mo., 1904, until retirement. Director of vocational edn. Mo. (on leave of absence from Univ. of Mo.), 1918. Dir. summer session U. of Mo.; mem. Nat. Assn. High Sch. Inspectors (pres. 1917-18), Mo. State Teachers' Assn. (pres. 1908). Am. Assn. Univ. Profs., Nat. Soc. for Vocational Edn., Coll. Profs. of Edn. Democrat. Bapt. Mason. Clubs: University, Commercial (Columbia, Mo.). Author: A Geography of Missouri, 1911; A Unit in Agriculture, 1911; Laboratory Manual in Vocational Agriculture (with H. J. Waters), 1919. Credited with having done more than any other person for development of secondary edn. in Mo. and for standardization of secondary schs. in the Middle West; served as pres. N. Central Assn. Colls. and Secondary Sch., 1927. Home: Columbia MO‡

ELLIMAN, DOUGLAS LUDLOW, real estate broker; b. Flushing, N.Y., May 24, 1882; s. William and Mary

Lawrence (Bogert) E.; student Berkeley Sch., N.Y., 1897-98, Cutler Sch., N.Y., 1898-99; m. Theodora Trowbridge, Oct. 20, 1900; children—Douglas Trowbridge (dec. Mar. 1972), George Trowbridge, Ludlow; m. 2d, Katherine Scales Moon, Dec. 9, 1929; children—Mary Lawrence, Edward Scales. Clk. Vermilye & Co., bankers, 1899-1903; broker and officer Pease & Elliman, 1903-11; organized Douglas L. Elliman & Co., Inc., 1911, later chmn. bd., dir.; organizer, pres., dir. Douglas L. Elliman Brokerage Corp.; v.p., dir. Midtown Underwriters, Inc., Underhill Soc., 58th and Park Av., Incorporated; member board of trustees Greenwich Savs. Bank and numerous bldg. projects, N.Y.; ex-pres. Real Estate Bd. of N.Y., Inc. Served as ensign U.S.N.R.F., 1918. Member St. Nicholas Society, St. George Soc., Commerce and Industry Assn. Mem. Real Estate Bd. N.Y.; adv. com. Ladies Christian Union. Mem. N.Y. Bldg. Congress (life), Nat. Assn. Real Estate Bds., Pilgrims U.S., Mil. Order World Wars, USNR Officers Assn., Am. Legion, Navy Leagues U.S. (dir.). Methodist. Clubs: Racquet and Tennis, Piping Rock. Home: New York City NY Died Feb. 13, 1972; buried Woodlawn Cemetery, New York City NY

ELLINGTON, BUFORD, gov. Tenn.; b. Holmes County, Miss., June 27, 1907; s. Abner E. and Cora (Grantham) E.; m. Catherine Cheek, Dec. 20, 1929; children—John Earl, Ann. Mgr. Tenn. Farm Bur. Ins. Service, 1949-51; commr. agr., Tenn., 1953-58; gov. Tenn., 1959-63, 67-72; v.p. Louisville & Nashville R.R., 1963-64; dir. Office Emergency Planning, 1965-66. Chmn. So. Regional Edn. Bd., 1961. Chmn. So. Gov.'s Conf., 1961-62; mem. exec. com. Nat. Gov.'s Conf., 1961-62, now chmn.; pres. Council State Govts.; chmn. Cordell Hull Found.; mem. Nat. Adv. Council Econ. Planning. Bd. dirs. Bill Wilkerson Speech and Hearing Center. Trustee George Peabody Coll. for Tchrs., U. Tenn., Rust Coll.; nat. council Boy Scouts Am. Mem. Millsaps Coll. Alumni Assn. (dir., Alpha Zeta (hon.), Alpha Gamma Rho, Lambda Chi Alpha, Delta Kappa. Methodist. Mason (33 deg., Shriner). Home: TN Died Apr. 3, 1972.

ELLINGTON, JESSE THOMPSON, advt. exec.; b. nr. Smithfield, N.C., Dec. 15, 1899; s. John O. and Corrina (Young) E.; student U. N.C., 1916-18, U. Va., 1918-19; m. Elizabeth Turner, Nov. 17, 1927; children—Keren Elizabeth, Jesse Thompson, William D. Turner, Writer, N.W. Ayer & Son, Phila., 1924-33; v.p., dir. J.M. Mathes, Inc., N.Y. City, 1933-38; co-founder Ivey & Ellington, advt. agy., Phila., N.Y., 1938-42; chairman board of Ellington & Co., N.Y.C. Trustee N.Y. Postgrad. Center for Psychotherapy, U. Va. Engring. Board. Mem. Kappa Alpha. Republican. Presbyn. Clubs: Canadian, Siwanoy Golf, New York Southern Society, Indian Harbor Yacht. Author bus. and advt. articles. Home: Greenwich CT Died Mar. 18, 1968; buried at sea, St. Peter Island, Brit. Virgin Islands

ELLIOTT, ALFRED J., ex-congressman; b. Guinda, Yolo Co., Calif., June 1, 1895; m. Jessie June Soults, Aug. 1, 1914; children—Esther, I. J. Engaged as farmer and live stock raiser; mem. 75th to 80th Congresses (1937-49), 10th Calif. Dist. Sec.-mgr. Tulare County Fairgounds, 1929-73; pres. Tulare Daily News. Democrat. Home: Tulare CA Died Jan. 1973.

ELLIOTT, CURTIS MILLER, educator, economist; b. Centralia, Ill., Apr. 10, 1911; s. Curtis Allen and Martha Anne (Miller) E.; A.B., U. Ill., 1934, A.M., 1935, Ph.D., 1940; m. J. Aileen Conner, Dec. 20, 1930; children—Phyllis Jean, Roy William. Instr. econs. Ore. State Coll., 1940-41; prof. econs. and ins. U. Neb., 1941-68, Bert Rodgers Distinguished prof. econs. and ins. 1962-68; cons. ins. companies Neb. Ins. Dept., Interagy. Com. on Civil Disorders, Washington. Dir. Capital Mut. Ins. Co., Nat. Investors Life Ins. Co. Named by student body as Outstanding Prof. U. Neb., 1968. Mem. Am. Risk and Ins. Assn., Delta Sigma Pi, Phi Gamma Delta. Author: Property and Casualty Insurance, 1960; also articles. Home: Lincoln NB Died Jan. 9, 1968; buried Wyuko Cemetery, Lincoln NE

ELLIOTT, JAMES LEWIS, clergyman; b. Erath County, Tex., Sept. 1863; s. James Midleton and Sarah Elizabeth (Clardy) E.; student Trinity U., Tehuacana, Tex., 3-1/2 yrs. (obliged to leave on account of ill health); m. Rosa B. Atchison, June 14, 1887 (died in 1934); children—Ruth L. (Mrs. S. A. Martin), Norma Leigh (wife of Rev. A. L. Faw), Lewis B., Luella (now Mrs. Herman Brock), Rosabel (Mrs. C. M. Mizell); m. 2d, Mrs. I. V. Stine, April 1935. Joined the Cumberland Presbyterian Ch. at 17 and at 18 became a candidate for the ministry; preached in country churches; admitted to ministry, 1888, and served a group of chs. in Tex., also stated clk. of Presbytery many yrs.; settled at Denton, 1925; pastor First Ch., Ft. Worth, beginning in 1929 (resigned); pastor Cumberland Presbyn. Ch., Denton, 1929-36 (built church and secured location for Orphans' Home in Denton), retired; organized 12 chs.; built 5 chs. and 3 manses. Pres. Bd. of Sunday Schools and Young Peoples Work of Texas Synod 6 yrs.; supt. Orphans' Home, Denton, Tex.; elected moderator Gen. Assembly Cumberland Presbyn. Ch., May 1931. Denton TX‡

ELLIOTT, JOHN BARNWELL, M.D.; b. at Greensboro, Ga., Oct. 30, 1870; s. John Barnwell and Lucy Pickney (Huger) E.; B.Litt., U. of the South, Sewanee, Tenn., 1891, M.A., 1891; M.D., Tulane, 1894, LL.D., 1937; m. Noel L. Forsyth, of Nydrie," Albermarle Co., Va., Feb. 8, 1900. Began practice at New Orleans, La., 1894; prof. medicine, Tulane U. of La., 1910-21; consultant medicine Tours Infirmary, 1921-39. Commd. maj. Med. Corps, U.S.A., Apr. 11, 1917; lt. col., June 6, 1918. With A.E.F. in France, Mar. 4, 1918-Feb. 16, 1919; was dir. Base Hosp. 24; group consultant Gen. Med. Bazoilles, Vittel Centre, Aug. 15, 1918-Jan. 20, 1919. Home: 1323 1st St. Office: Audubon Bldg., New Orleans LA*‡

ELLIOTT, JOHN WESLEY, clergyman; b. South Boston, Va., Aug. 19, 1891; s. John Wesley and Sallie Henry (Jeffress) E.; A.B., U. of Richmond, 1913; B.D., Colgate, 1916; M.A., U. of Chicago, 1917; D.D., Kalamazoo Coll., 1935, U. of Richmond, 1936; m. Grace Aline Young, September 25, 1916 (died September 30, 1961); children—Grace Elizabeth (Mrs. Humphrey A. Olsen), Martha Jeffress (Mrs. W. Edgar Diechler), John Young; m. second, Winifred Mills Beckstead, October 14, 1962 (dec. Apr. 1967). Ordained ministry Bapt. Ch., 1917; pastor First Bapt. Ch., Canton, N.Y., 1917-18; acting pastor Haddonfield, N.J., 1918-19; pastor Central Bapt. Ch., Wayne, Pa., 1919-23; gen. sec. Edn. Bd. Pa. Bapt. Gen. Conv., 1923-25; dir. social edn., Am. Bapt. Publ. Soc., 1925-33, sec. of Christian Edn., 1933-39; pres. Alderson-Broaddus College, 1939-50; pastor Central Ch., Westerly, 1950-56, Millers Mills (N.Y.) Community Ch., 1956-67. Mem. Phi Delta Theta. Democrat. Mason. Home: West Winfield NY Died Jan. 23, 1967; buried Baptist Ch. Cemetery, Millers Mills NY

ELLIOTT, RICHARD HAMMOND, newspaper editor; b. Annapolis, Md., Oct. 3, 1893; s. Richard Goodwin and Julia Virginia (Hammond) E.; Class of 1917, St. John's Coll., Annapolis, Md.; student Johns Hopkins, 1923; unmarried. Mem. staff Baltimore (Md.) American, 1922-26, Baltimore (Md.) Evening Sun, 1926-33; editor, Annapolis (Md.) bureau, Associated Press, 1933-38; mem. staff, The Capital-Gazette Press (including The Evening Capital and The Maryland Gazette), Annapolis, Md., 1938-40, editor from 1941, also assistant manager from 1945. Commissioned second lieut., inf., U.S. Army, 1917, promoted 1st lt., and capt., 1918; retired for disability in line of duty, 1920. Past comdr. G. C. Parlett Post, Am. Legion; past pres. Annapolis Civitan Club; disaster chmn., Red Cross, Anne Arundel Co., 1940-47; past mem. bd. U.S.O. Mgt., Annapolis; past mem. dist. com. Anne Arundel Co. Boy Scouts; mem. Annapolis Salvation Army Adv. Bd.; past mem. bd. Annapolis YMCA. Awarded Mexican Border and Victory medals; award of merit U.S. Navy Recruiting Service, certificate recognition patriotic effort, WPB. Mem. Md. Press Assn. (dir.), C. of C., Military Order World Wars Republican. Clubs: Annapolitan (Annapolis). Home: Annapolis MD Died May 3, 1971; buried St. Anne's Cemetery, Annapolis MD

ELLIOTT, SHELDEN DOUGLASS, coll. prof., lawyer; b. Hollywood, Calif., June 2, 1906; s. Edwin Windsor and Therissa Irene (Gilbert) E.; A.B., Yale, 1927, law, 1927-28; J.D., U. So. Calif., 1931, LL.M., 1932; LL.D., Temple Univ., Willamette University, 1954; m. Hilda Elizabeth Johnston, Dec. 29, 1929; children—Shelden Douglass, Mary Therissa. Admitted to California bar, 1931, New York bar, 1957; served as assistant counsel, California State Legislative Counsel Bur., 1932-33; sec. Com. Bar Examiners, Calif., 1933-34; asst. prof., dir. Legal Aid Clinic, U. So. Calif., 1934-37, asst. prof., 1937-38, asso. prof., 1938-39, prof. law 1939-52 dean 1947-52; prof. law N.Y.U., dir. Inst. Judicial Admnstrn. since 1952, vis. prof. law U. Mich., summer 1948, N.Y.U., fall, 1950, Rutgers University, summer 1953, U. of Utah, 1956, Hastings Coll. Law, summer, 1958; cons. Indian Law Inst., New Delhi, 1960. Mem. adv. com. Fed. Civil Rules; mem. Regional Loyal Bd., U.S. Civil Service Commn.; Adv. Bd. Contract Appeals, A.E.C.; Airframe Com. W.S.B. Mem. Calif. State Constl. Revision Com., 1948; Los Angeles Commn. Reorgn. City Govt., 1951. Mem. bd. dirs. National Legal Aid Soc. Served as capt. to lt. col., hdqrs. 7th U.S. Army, 103d Inf. Div., 1943-46; brig. gen. res. Decorated Croix de Guerre. Mem. Am., New York State, Cal. State and Los Angeles bar assns., Am. Arbitration Assn. (mem. labor panel), Nat. Acad. Arbitrators, Assn. Am. Law Schs. (pres. 1954), Order of Coif, Phi Beta Kappa, Phi Kappa Phi, Phi Delta Phi. Episcopalian. Author: California Administrative Law, 1947; Cases and Materials on Legislation (with Nutting), 1950; Improving Our Courts, 1959; Cases and Materials on Pleading and Procedure (with Karlen), 1961; also articles legal jours. Home: New York City NY Died Mar. 1972.

ELLIOTT, STUART RHETT, mining; b. Apr. 26, 1874; s. Middleton Stuart and Ann Stuart (Rhett) E.; B.S., in Metallurgy, Lehigh, 1897, E.M., 1902; m. Bessie G. Reid, Dec. 1, 1919. Asst. engr. The Cleveland Cliffs Iron Co., 1898-1902; supt. Crosby Mine, 1902-04, supt. Negaunee Dist., 1904-06; gen. supt. mines, Bethlehem Steel (Cuba), 1906; again supt. Negaunee Dist., The Cleveland Cliffs Iron Co., 1907-16, mgr. of co. since 1927; v.p. The Cliffs Power & Light Co. Lt. col. Engr. Corps, A.E.F., 1917-19. Pres. Lake Superior Mining Inst. Mem. Am. Inst. Mining and Metall. Engrs. (dir.), Sigma Phi. Republican. Episcopalian. Mason. Home: Ishpeming MI‡

ELLIS, FRANK BURTON, U.S. dist. judge; b. Covington, La., Feb. 10, 1907; s. Harvey E. and Margaret (Whiteside) E.; grad. Gulf Coast Mil. Acad., 1924; student U. Va., 1924-26; LL.B., La. State U., 1929; m. Marjorie Wheatley, Nov. 18, 1965; children—Lilian Emerson, Stephen Grima, Frank Burton. Admitted La. bar, 1930, practiced in New Orleans; sr. mem. Ellis, Lancaster & King; gen. counsel Greater New Orleans Expressway; spl. asst. atty. gen. La.; atty. Interstate Oil Compact; U.S. judge, Eastern Dist. of La., New Orleans, from 1962. Dir. New Orleans TV Corp., Magnolia Wirebound Box Co., Nat. dir. Office Emergency Planning, 1961; mem. NSC 1961; past v.p. Aviation Bd., New Orleans. Active Greek War Relief, A.R.C., United Fund, Community Chest. Mem. La. Senate, 1940-44, pres. pro tempore, 1940-44; del. Democratic Nat. Conv., 1952, 56, mem. Dem. Nat. Conv., 1952-54, Dem. State Chmn. La., 1960-61. Mem. La. State U. Found.; founder Greater New Orleans Opera Found Mem. Internat., Am. (conv. del. London and Paris 1957), La., New Orleans, 22d Jud. Dist. bar assns., Newcomen Soc., New Orleans C. of C., Zeta Psi. Clubs: New Orleans Country, Southern Yacht, Young Men's Business, Athletic, Petroleum (New Orleans); New York Athletic (N.Y.C.); Reading Room, York Country (York Harbor, Me.); Bal Harbour, Racquet (Miami, Fla.); The Racquet, Canyon Country (Plam Springs, Cal.); Covington (La.) Country; Boston, Plimsol (New Orleans); Bel-Air Country (Los Angeles); Beverly Hills (Cal.). Home: Metairie LA Died Nov. 1969.

ELLIS, GEORGE WILLIAM, author; b. Albany, N. Y., Dec., 1870; s. George and Janet (McEwan) E.; grad. Trinity Coll., 1894; m. Hartford, Conn., 1897, Aimee F. Corson. Writer on ins., econ. and hist. subjects. Mem. Conn. Hist. Soc., Conn. Soc. Mayflower Descendants (sec.) Author: (with John E. Morris) King Philip's War, G13. Address: 820 Prospect Av., Hartford CT‡

ELLIS, HAYNE, naval officer (ret.); b. Macon, Ga., Aug. 26, 1877; s. Hayne and Ida Louise (Lamar) E.; B.S., U.S. Naval Acad., 1900; hon. LL.D., Lake Forest (Ill.) Coll., 1939; m. Sally America Long, Dec. 17, 1904; children—Martha Lamar (Mrs. John D. Leland), Hayne, Robert A. Long, Lucia Long (Mrs. Edgar J. Uihlein), Long. Commissioned ensign U.S. Navy, 1902, and advnaced through grades to rear adm., 1933; comdr. patrol force, Atlantic fleet, 1939-40; mem. Gen. Bd. of Navy, 1941; ret. from active service upon reaching statutory age, Sept. 1, 1941; v.p. and dir., Long Bell Lumber Corp., Kan. City, Mo., since 1941. Decorated Comdr. and Grand Officer, Crown of Italy; Order of Naval Merit (Spain); Grand Officer, and Grand Cross Order of Duarte (Republic of San Domingo); Grand Cross, Order of Merit (Haiti). Episcopalian. Clubs: Chevy Chase (Md.), Army Navy, Army Navy Country (Washington), Kansas City (Mo.) Country. Home: 1905 Lombardy Rd., San Marino 9, Calif. Office: R. A. Long Bldg., Kansas City 6 MO‡

ELLIS, HOWARD, lawyer; b. Washington Court House, O., Jan. 15, 1892; s. Daniel Webster and Sarah Alice (Rowe) E.; LL.B., U. Chicago, 1914, J.D., 1915; m. Maude Martin Evers, June 26, 1920. (deceased April 1953). Admitted to Ill. bar, 1915; asso. Kirkland, Ellis, Hodson, Chaffetz & Masters, Chicago, Illinois, partner from 1919. Served as pvt., French Fgn. Legion, 1918. Mem. Am., Ill. State, Chicago bar assns., Chicago Law Inst., Mil. Order World Wars, Phi Beta Kappa. Mason. Clubs: Law, Golf, Tavern, Mid-America (Chicago, Ill.). Home: Chicago IL Died Feb. 18, 1968; buried Washington Court House OH

ELLISON, JOSEPH ROY, lyceum mgr.; b. at Friend, Neb., Aug. 9, 1875; s. George Wilmot and Mary Agnes (Reynolds) E.; Doane Coll., Neb., 1892-7; m. Mary Elizabeth Howell, of Dorchester, Neb., June 18, 1901. Began in lyceum work at Lincoln, Neb., 1897; advance agt. Central Lyceum Bur., 1898-1900; dist. mgr. Redpath Bur., 1900-10; organized Ellison-White Lyceum & Chautauqua Bur., Boise, Ida., 1910, removed to Portland, Ore., 1912; operating 1,033 Chautauquas in 1921; now treas., gen. mgr. Ellison-White Lyceum and Chautauqua Assn.; partner Ellison-White Conservatory of Music; pres. Elwyn Concert Bur., Sunnyside Improvement Co. (Ida.). Trustee Willamette U. Mem. Lyceum and Chautauqua Managers' Assn., Internat. Lyceum and Chautauqua Assn., Phi Kappa Delta. Republican. Methodist. Clubs: Rotary, Portland Golf. Home: 1035 E. Davis St. Office: Broadway Bldg., Portland OR‡

ELLISON, ROBERT S(PURRIER), b. Rush County, Ind., Nov. 6, 1875; s. Franklin and Mary A. (Krammes) E.; A.B., Ind. U., 1900; m. Vida F. Gregory, Aug. 20, 1907. Admitted to Colo. bar, 1903, and began practice at Colorado Springs; atty. Cripple Creek Railroads, 1906-16; atty. Midwest Refining Co., 1916-19, vice-pres., 1919-30; pres. Wyo. Trust Co., Casper, Wyo., 1926-30; pres. Stanolind Pipe Line Co. since 1930. Stanolind Crude Oil Purchasing Co., 1930-38, Stanolind Oil Purchasing Co. since 1938; retired Nov. 5, 1940; pres. Bank of Manitou, since Jan. 1944. Member Colorado House of Rep., 1911-12. Pres. Casper Chamber Commerce, 1924-25; pres. Casper Council Boy Scouts of America, 1926-27, mem. exec. com. Region 8, Boy Scouts of America, 1927-30, mem. Tulsa County Council since 1931 (pres. 1933-40. 2d v.p. Pike's Peak Council, 1944 and mem. Region A. Com.) also mem. Nat. Council. Trustee of town of Manitou Springs, Colo., 1942 and 1943; elected mayor 1944 (2 yrs.). Appointed director Colorado Historical Society, Apr. 1942, 2d vice president since Dec. 1943. Founder Historical Landmark Commission of Wyoming. Honorary life mem. Okla.-Kan. div. of Midcontinent Oil and Gas Assn.; mem. Am. Inst. Mining and Metall. Engrs., Sigma Nu. Republican. Mason (32 deg., K.T., Shriner). Club: Rowfant (Cleveland, O.). Author of monographs on Independence Rock, Short History of Old Fort Bridger, Red Buttes Indian Fight, William H. Jackson—Pioneer of Yellowstone, etc. Given title Wyo-La-Shar by Pawnee Indian Supreme Council for work in preservation Indian history, 1932. Home: Briarhurst, Manitou Springs CO‡

ELLSWORTH, JOHN JAY, co. exec.; b. Somerville, Mass., Sept. 12, 1894; s. Albert E. and Alice (Upham) E.; student Boston U., 1916; m. Anna I. MacEachern, June 6, 1925; children—Anne E. (Mrs. Lumbert), John J., Joan E. (Mrs. Kelwick), Donald U., Jane E. (Mrs. Frye). Internal revenue agt. U.S. Treasury, Washington, 1919-23; pub. accountant, Boston, 1923-43; v.p., treas., dir. United-Carr, Inc., Boston, 1943-59; trustee Estate Tax Cons., Boston; pres., treas., dir. Bankers Service Co., Boston, also H. K. Porter, Inc., Somerville. Bd. dirs. Mass. Heart Assn., Boston. Served with U.S. Army, 1917-19. Republican. Conglist. Mason. Home: Friendship ME

ELLSWORTH, OLIVER B., banker; b. Portland, Conn., July 17, 1897; s. Herbert E. and Emma (Lincoln) E.; student pub. schs.; m. Bessie Miller, Sept. 22, 1937; 1 dau., Lenore (Mrs. Preble). Dir. United Bank & Trust Co., Hartford, pres., 1932-60, chmn. bd., from 1960; Trust Co., Hartford, pres., 1932-60, chmn. bd., from 1960; chmn. bd. The Hanson-Whitney Co., 1960-69; Pres. Portland Trust Co., 1935-50 (merged with Riverside Trust Co. 1950); dir. Fuller Brush Co. (Hartford). Adv. bd. St. Joseph Coll., West Hartford, Conn.; member of finance com. Met. Dist. of Hartford. Corporator Hartford (Conn.) Hosp. Mem. C. of C. (dir.), Conn. Bankers Assn., Newcomen Soc. N.A. Mason (Shriner). Clubs: Hartford, Hartford Golf. Home: Groton CT Died July 1969.

ELMENDORF, FRANCIS LITTLETON, bus. cons.; b. Indpls., July 16, 1902; s. William Horris and Ada May (Littleton) E.; student Ind. U., 1919-20, Butler U., 1921-22; m. Dorothy Amantha Fulton, Mar. 3, 1928; children—William Wood, Judith Ann (Mrs. Dennis T. Fratianne). Mgr. mail order sales, The Higbee Co., Cleve., 1923, 24, various exec. positions, 1926-30; self-employed, sales promotion and advt., 1925, ins., Cleveland 1931-33; with Robert Heller & Assos., engrs. and consultants, 1933-62, pres., 1958-62; pres. Elmendorf & Co., 1962-68. Cons. to sec. of state, chmn. FTC, 1953-54; cons. to postmaster gen., 1953-59, gov. Ind., 1955-56; mem. Pres.'s Ann. Assay Commn., 1953. task force leader, Post Office Dept. Project, Hoover Commn., 1948; cons. Sec. Def., dir. mgmt. adv. group Dept. Defense, 1949-51. Bd. dirs. Am. Cancer Soc. Mem. Cleve. C. of C., Am. Numis. Assn., Holland Soc. of N.Y., Soc. Colonial Wars, S.A.R., Sigma Chi. Republican. Episcopalian. Mason. Clubs: Mayfield, Mid-Day, Union (Cleve.); Chicago. Home: Shaker Heights OH Died Apr. 3, 1972.

ELMER, S(AMUEL) LEWIS, organist; b. Bridgeton, N.J., Mar. 23, 1877; s. Newton and Lucia Rowe (Richmond) E.; fellow honoris causa, Trinity Coll. Music, London, Eng., 1947; L.H.D. (hon.), Ill. Wesleyan U., 1956; m. Helen Shoemaker, Aug. 3, 1904 (dec. July 1936);children—Lucia (Mrs. George E. Johnson), Mary Erety (Mrs. Bruno Vassel), Samuel Lewis, Horace Newton (dec.), Helen Elizabeth (Mrs. Donald S. Jackson); m. 2d, Louise Jones, July 20, 1939. Organist Central Meth. Ch., Bridgeton, N.J., 1895-1903, Central Presbyn. Ch., Phila., 1903-04, St. Mary's Episcopal Ch., Tuxedo Park, N.Y., 1904-07, Meml. Presbyn. Ch., Bklyn., 1907-37; head dept. music James Madison High Sch., N.Y.C., 1925-47. Mem. exec. com., dir. Internat. Music Found. Mem. Am. Guild Organists (warden 1907-49, nat. pres. 1949—), Nat. Music Council (exec. com.), Internat. Congress Organists of London (v.p. 1957). Republican. Presbyn. Mason (past master, past grand organist N.J.). Clubs: The Bohemians (v.p.), St. Wilfrid (N.Y.C.). Home: 22 E. 89th St., N.Y.C. 28. Office: 630 Fifth Av., NYC 20 NY‡

ELSER, WILLIAM JAMES, pathologist, bacteriologist; b. Milwaukee, Wis., Nov. 28, 1872; s. John and Frances (Auer) E.; M.D., Bellevue Hosp. Med. Coll., 1895; post-grad. study, univs. of Berlin, Vienna and Gratz; m. Saturnina Beatrice Rodriquez, Sept. 8, 1911; children—Frances (Mrs. John Pehle), John (dec.), Ramona. Interne Bellevue Hosp. Med. Coll., 1895-97; instr. pathology, Cornell U. Med. Coll., 1901-06, asst. prof. bacteriology and immunology, 1906-09, prof., 1909-32, prof. applied pathology and bacteriology, 1932-38, professor emeritus since 1938; asst. pathologist New York Hosp., 1902-05, director Div. of Labs., 1905-32, dir. Central Labs., 1932-38, retired; consulting bacteriologist Grasslands Hosp., Valhalla, N.Y., since 1920. Served as pathologist and bacteriologist Base Hosp. No. 9, A.E.F., 1917; asst. dir. Div. of Labs. and Infectious Diseases, A.E.F., 1917-18; col. O.R.C. since 1919. Fellow A.A.A.S.; mem. Am. Assn. Pathologists and Bacteriologists, Assn. Mil. Surgeons of U.S., New York Acad. Medicine, Soc. for Exptl. Biology and Medicine, N.Y. City br. of Soc. Am. Bacteriologists, Harvey Soc., New York Bacteriol. Club, Phi Alpha Sigma. Contbr. to publs. dealing with epidemic cerebral meningitis and methods of preserving immune sera. Home: Kent, Conn. Address: New York Hosp., 525 E. 68th St., New York NY‡

ELSTON, DOROTHY ANDREWS (MRS. WALTER L. KABIS), govt. ofcl.; b. Wilkes-Barre, Pa., Mar. 22, 1917; d. Reginald Hastings and Mabel (Aston) Andrews; student Maryville (Tenn.) Coll., 1936; m. Russell Ransom Elston, Sept. 30, 1936 (div. 1960); m. 2d, Walter Lawrence Kabis, 1970. With legal dept. Du Pont Co., Wilmington, Del.; propr. nursery farm, Middletown, 1946-71; treas. of U.S., 1969-71. trustee Kruse Sch., state correctional instn., Marshallton, Del., 1954-57; state adviser Farmer's Home Adminstrn., 1956-59; mem. of the board New York World's Fair. Board of dirs. Nat. Fedn. Republican Women, 1954-71, mem. exec. com., 1956-71, 4th v.p, 1958-60, 1st v.p., 1961-62, pres., 1963-68, name Rep. Woman of Year 1967; mem. National Rep. Finance Committee; member Rep. Senatorial and Congressional Campaign Committees; past pres. Del. Fedn. Rep. Women, now mem. exec. com.; past pres. New Castle County Republican Women. Delaware delegate to Republican National Convention, 1956, 60, alternate from Del., mem. rules com., 1956, mem. platform com. state convs., 1956-68; mem. Del. Central Rep. Com., 1954-58, 63-71; nat. adviser of Teen Age Republicans; founder nat. orgn. Sub-Teen Age Republicans. Named Del. Woman of Achievement, Gen. Fedn. Women's Club, 1966; one of six Rep. women to receive Nat. award World's Fair 1965, League Women Voters; Gold Good Citizenship medal Nat. Soc. S.A.R., 1968. Mem. D.A.R. (past state chmn. conservation, past chpt. regent, past nat. vice chmn. good citizens com.), Grange (state health chmn., lectr.; exec. com. New Castle County-Pomona). Methodist (steward, trustee, chmn. pastoral relations). Club: Odessa Women's (2d v.p.); Newspaper Women's. Home: Odessa DE Died July 1971.

ELTING, WINSTON, architect; b. Winnetka, Ill., Feb. 11, 1907; s. Victor and Marie (Winston) E.; grad. Hotchkiss Sch., 1924; A.B., Princeton, 1929; grad. student Ecoles des Beaux Arts, Paris, 1929-32, Am. Acad., Fontainbleau, 1931; m. Marjorie Horton, May 13, 1933; children—Elizabeth Dudley (Mrs. Bernard Rogers III), Audrey Horton, John Winston; m. 2d, Onnolee Laabs Conway, Feb. 3, 1962; 1 s., Winston Lachlan. With housing div. Pub. Works Adminstrn., Wash., 1935-36; pvt. practice. Chgo., 1937-41, 56-60, 61-68; partner Schweikher & Elting, architects, Roselle, Ill., 1945-53, Elting & Bennett, 1953-56, Elting, Deknatel & Assos., Inc., 1960-61; asst. prof. architecture Univ. Ill., Chgo., 1961-62, asso. prof. 1963-64, prof., 1965-68; works include Fine Arts Center, Chapel and Theatre, dormitory bldgs. Maryville (Tenn.) Coll., 1950-58, Lang. Center, Vassar Coll., 1957, Unitarian Ch., Evanston, Ill., 1958, D. E. Daggitt House, Benton Harbor, Mich., 1958, Earl H. Closser House, Marquette, Mich., 1960, others. Board of directors Adult Edn. Council of Chgo. Served to lt. comdr. USNR, 1942-45. Recipient design award Progressive Architecture, 1954, 56, award Chgo. chpt. A.I.A. and Chgo. Assn. Commerce and Industry, 1955, 59, 60, award Ch. Archtl. Guild Am., 1953, award House and Home mag., 1957; award merit A.I.A., 1965; Archtl. Record award excellence, 1965. Fellow A.I.A. (director Chicago chapter); member Mich. Soc. Architects, Soc. Contemporary Am. Art (past pres.), Art Inst. Chgo. (gov. life mem.), Chgo. Mus. Natural History (life asso.). Clubs: Cap and Gown, Princeton (Princeton); Arts (dir.), (Chgo.); Cliff Dwellers; Rolling Rock (Pa.). Author: (with Talbot Wegg) Ubran Housing, 1936; also articles. Home: Chicago IL Died Jan. 25, 1968; buried Elting Meml. Burying Ground, New Paltz NY

ELVEY, CHRISTIAN THOMAS, astronomer, physicist; b. Phoenix, Ariz., Apr. 1, 1899; s. John A. and Lizzie Christena (Miller) E.; A.B., U. of Kansas, 1921, A.M., 1923; Ph.D., University of Chicago, 1930; m. Marjorie Purdy, Sept. 1, 1934; children—Thomas Christian, Christena Vivian. Instructor in astronomy, University of Kansas, 1921-25, fellow in astronomy, U. of Chicago, 1925-26; instr. in astronomy, Northwestern U., 1926-28; instr. in astro-physics, Yerkes Observatory, U. of Chicago, 1928-32, asst. prof., 1932-35; astronomer and asst. to dir. McDonald Observatory, Fort Davis, Tex., 1935-42, on leave of absence to work with Office of Sci. Research and Development, 1942-45; head, interior ballistics sect. Naval Ordnance Test Station, Inyokern, Calif., Apr.-Nov. 1945, head, applied research div., 1945-47, head research dept., 1947-49, sr. research scientist, 1949-51, head of staff, 1951; head dept. geophysics, and dir. geophys. inst. U. Alaska, 1952-63, vice president research and advanced study, 1961-63, University research professor and spl. asst. to the pres., 1963-67, director emeritus geophysical institute, from 1967. Mem. sci. adv. bd. USAF, 1956-63. Fellow Arctic Inst. of North Am., A.A.A.S., Am. Physics Soc.; mem. Internat. Astron. Union, American Astron. Soc., Am. Geophys. Union (pres. sect. geomagnetism and aeronomy), Internat. Com. Geophysics, Internat. Assn. Geomagnetism and Aeronomy (chmn. com. number 2 aurora and airglow 1957-62), Sigma Xi. Rotarian (pres. 1954-55). Home: Tucson AZ Died Mar. 25, 1970.

ELY, ELIZABETH L., educator; d. George B. and Caroline E. (Boies) E.; student Mt. Holyoke Coll. Associated with sisters in founding the Ely Sch., for girls and young women, Brooklyn, N.Y., 1886; now head mistress Ely Sch., which was moved to Riverside Drive, New York, 1890, and to Ely Court, Conn., 1906; teacher of higher English, history and the Bible. Conglist. Home: Ely Court, Greenwich CT‡

ELY, RICHARD R(OYAL), govt. official; b. Greene Co., Pa., Mar. 23, 1892; s. Jonas and Nancy (Scott) E.; A.B., Washington and Jefferson Coll., Washington, Pa., 1915; m. Mary E. Howell, Feb. 8, 1918;children—Louise H., Nancy S. Teacher, Irwin (Pa.) High Sch., 1915-17; teacher and prin., Philippine public schs., 1917-25; asst. sec. to gov-gen., P.I., 1925-35; mem. staff U.S. High Commr. to P.I., 1935-39; supervisor, Philippine Affairs, Div. of Territories and Island Possessions, U.S. Dept. of Interior, 1939-42; War Manpower Commn., 1942-44; exec. asst. to U.S. high commr. to P.I., 1944-46; asst. chief, Div. of Philippine affairs, U.S. Dept. of State, 1946-47, chief, from 1947. Mem. Phi Gamma Delta. Club: Kenwood Golf and Country (Washington). Home: Sarasota FL Died Aug. 26, 1972.

ELY, SUMNER BOYER, educator; b. Watertown, N.Y., Nov. 5, 1869; s. Frederick Gustavus and Matilda Caroline (Boyer) E.; S.B., Mass. Inst. Tech., 1892; m. Mary Rodman Updike, Jan. 25, 1899; children—Esther Stockton, Frederick Sumner. Asst. supt. Pressed Steel Car Co., McKees Rocks, Pa., 1900; chief engr. Am. Sheet Steel Co., Pittsburgh, 1901; chief engr. Am. Sheet & Tin Plate Co., Pittsburgh, 1903-06; v.p. Chester B. Albree Iron Works, Pittsburgh, 1906-16; prof. comml. engring., Carnegie Inst. of Tech., 1920-40, emeritus; now supt. Bureau of Smoke Prevention, Pittsburgh. Consulting engr. Pa. Giant Power Survey, 1923-24. Sec. Internat. Conf. on Bituminous Coal held under the auspices of Carnegie Inst. Tech., Pittsburgh, 1926, 28; consultant to director of World's Power Conf., Washington, D.C., 1936; technical mem. Pittsburgh Smoke Abatement Commn., 1941. Ex-pres. Univ. Extension Soc., Pittsburgh; mem. Am. Soc. Mech. Engrs., Engrs.' Soc. Western Pa., A.A.A.S. Presbyterian. Home: 520 Roslyn Pl., Pittsburgh PA‡

EMCH, ARNOLD, mathematician; b. Hessigkofen, Switzerland, Mar. 24, 1871; s. Albrecht and Maria (Zurbuchen) E.; Cantonal Coll. of Solothurn, 1886-90; Eidgenossische Technische Hochschule, Zurich, 1890-93; came to U.S., 1893; Ph.D., U. of Kan., 1895; m. Hilda Walters, of Lawrence, Kan., Aug. 31, 1895; children—Walter, Arnold Frederick, Karl. Asst. prof. graphics, U. of Kan., 1895-97; prof. graphics and mathematics, Technikum Biel, Switzerland, 1897-98, Kan. State Agrl. Coll., 1898-1900, U. of Colo., 1900-05, Cantonal Colls. of Solothurn and Basel, 1905-11, U. of Ill., 1911-27; prof. mathematics, U. of Ill. since 1927. Mem. Am. Math. Soc., Sigma Xi, Swiss Math. Soc., Swiss Naturforschende Gesellschaft, Swiss Alpine Club. Author: An Introduction to Projective Geometry, 1905; also writer in various languages on math. subjects. Home: Urbana IL‡

EMERSON, EDWIN, JR., war corr.; b. Dresden, Saxony; s. Edwin and Marie Louise (Ingham) E.; A.B., Cornell, 1890; A.B., Harvard, 1891; unmarried. Was foreign corr. Boston Post, later in editorial work New York Evening Post, Sun and Harper's Weekly; then sec. Teachers Coll., (Columbia) until 1898. Went to front in Spanish-Am. War as corr. Leslie's Weekly; engaged in successful exploration of Porto Rico under direction of Lt. H.H. Whitney, secret agt. U.S. Mil. Information Bur.; joined Roosevelt's Rough Riders, serving in engagement at San Juan and in the trenches before Santiago. Warr corr. Collier's Weekly and Illustrirte Zeitung in S. America; took part in Colombian-Venezuelan war, 1901, as Venezuelan col. vols.; decorated by President Castro with order of Bolivar for gallantry in action. War corr. New York World, Chicago News, Westminster Gazette, Black and White, in Russian-Japanese War. Mem. N.Y. Hist. Soc., Franklin Inst., Japanese Congress (1875-7); resigned from 44th Congress, Dec. 12, 1876; major of New York, Jan. 1, 1877, to Dec. 31, 1878; presdl. elector, 1880; Central Park commr., 1897-8. Democrat. Mem. S.R., Soc. Colonial Wars, Soc. War 1812. Clubs: Century, Manhattan, Democratic. Presbyterian. Home: 47 W. 57th St. Office: 103 Gold St., New York‡

EMERSON, EVALYN (STAGE NAME, EVALYN EARLE), actress, author; b. Sherman, Tex.; d. Dr. Nathaniel W. and Anna E. S. E.; ed. pvt. sch. of Miss Heloise E. Hersey, Burnham, Northampton, Mass.; grad. Am. Sch. Dramatic Arts, New York, 1902. Author: Sylvia The Story of an American Countess, 1901 S9. Address: 78 Powell St., Brookline MA‡

EMERSON, FRANK NELSON, architect; b. Peoria, Ill., Sept. 18, 1876; s. George Francis and Harriet (Woodruff) E.; A.B., Princeton, 1898; B.S., Mass. Inst. Tech.; 1901; student Ecole des Beaux Arts, Paris, 1903-05; unmarried. Practiced at Peoria since 1909; mem. Hewitt, Emerson & Gregg since 1927; architect for Proctor Recreational Center, Barker Memorial, Peoria Life Bldg., Peoria Country Club, Commercial Nat. Bank, Scottish Rite Cathedral, etc. Fellow Am. Inst. Architects; mem. Ill. Soc. Architects. Republican. Mason (32 deg.). Clubs: University, Cleve Coeur, Country (Peoria); Princeton (New York). Home: 400 Parkside Drive. Office: Alliance Life Bldg., Peoria IL‡

EMERSON, GEORGE H., railway official; ed. pub. schs. Began as water boy, G.N. Ry., 1880; apprentice, St. Paul shops, same rd., 1882-7, boiler maker, 1887-90; fireman and engr., Dak. division, 1890-5; locomotive foreman, Glasgow, Mont.; 1895-7; gen. shop foreman and master mechanic, Dak. and Northern divs., 1897-1900, gen. master mechanic, Western dist., 1900-3, supt. motive power, 1903-10, asst. gen. mgr., 1910-12, gen. mgr., since Oct. 1, 1912, G.N. Ry. Office: Great Northern Ry., St Paul MN‡

EMERSON, GUY, found. art dir.; b. N.Y.C., Jan. 28, 1886; s. Nathaniel Waldo and Anna Elvira (Smith) E.; A.B., Harvard, 1908, LL.B., 1911; Litt. D. (honorary), Univ. of Arizona, 1960; m. Margaret Cotton Smith, Jan. 28, 1913; m. 2d Ruth Van Cleve, Aug. 18, 1934. With Treasury Dept., Washington, 1911-13, in business, Dallas, 1913-14; asso. editor Economic World, N.Y.C., 1914-16; mgr. Church Pension Fund (Episcopal), 1916-17; v.p. Nat. Bank of Commerce, N.Y.C., 1917-23; v.p. Bankers Trust Co., 1923-47; became trustee and vice president Samuel H. Kress Foundation, 1949, later art dir. emeritus. Sec. of Theodore Roosevelt League, 1916; director publicity Liberty Loan campaigns, 2d Federal Reserve District, 1917-19, director War Savings, 1919; director National Hoover League, 1920; executive manager Am. Bankers Assn. Conv., 1922 (mem. exec. council 1934-38); chmn. Rep. Nat. Contributors Com. 1924; sec. exec. com. Emergency Employment Com., 1930-33; mem. adv. com. on research in finance Nat. Bur. Econ. Research; hon. trustee Community Service Soc. of N.Y.; chmn. exec. com. Treas. Dept. Def. Bond Com. for N.Y. State, 1941; mem. exec. com. N.Y. State War Finance Com., 1941-46; vice chmn. Nat. Red Cross War Fund, 1941-43; pres. Nat. Audubon Soc., 1940-44, dir. 1936-54, hon. pres., 1954; fellow J. Pierpont Morgan Library; hon. fellow Met. Museum Art; honorary trustee Allentown (Pa.) Art Museum; president Association Reserve City Bankers, 1930; trustee Am. Hist. Assn., 1928-37. Decorated Knight Order of Crown (Italy), Chevalier Legion of Honor (France), Knight 1st Class, Royal Order of St. Olav (Norway). Republican. Mem. Phi Beta Kappa. Club: Harvard. Author: The New Frontier, 1920; The Psalms: A Selection, 1955; (with Ludlow Griscom) The Birds of Martha's Vineyard, 1959. Address: New York City NY Died Jan. 10, 1969.

EMERSON, JABEZ OSCAR, lawyer; b. Lyon County, Kan., Feb. 2, 1875; s. Joseph Jay and Mary Elizabeth (Norman) E.; ed. Kansas Teachers' Coll., Emporia, Kan., 1893-96; m. Carrie E. Doak, Jan. 1, 1902; children—Jean (Mrs. Chester L. Hudson), Paul Lowell, Dorothy Alice, Ralph Waldo. Admitted to Kan. bar, 1898, and began practice at Emporia; moved to Kansas City, Kan. Mem. Kan. Ho. of Rep. 1911; atty. for Bd. of Edn., Kansas City, Kan., 1922-36; mayor of Kansas City, Kan., 1926-27. Mem. Am. and Kan. State bar assns. Republican. Episcopalian. Mason (32 deg.). Home: Kansas City KS Died Oct. 6, 1968.

EMERSON, KENDALL, surgeon; b. Northampton, Mass., June 27, 1875; s. Benjamin Kendall and Mary Annette (Hopkins) E.; A.B., Amherst Coll., 1897, M.A. (honorary), 1922, Doctor of Science, 1950; M.D., Harvard University, 1901; married Josephine Devereux Sewall, Oct. 1, 1903; children—Sewall, Kendall. Intern, Mass. Gen. Hosp., Boston, 1901-02; began practice orthopedic and gen. surgery, Worcester, Mass., 1902; asst. surgeon, Memorial Hosp., Worcester, 1903-10, orthopedic surgeon, 1910-28, cons. surgeon since 1928; mng. dir. Nat. Tuberculosis Assn. 1928-48, retired, 1948, consultant since 1948; president of New York Tuberculosis and Health Association, 1948-49; exec. sec., Am. Pub. Health Assn., 1931-35. Maj., Royal Army Med. Corps (Brit.), 1916-18; maj., Med. Corps, U.S.A., 1918-19, instr., surgeon general's office, Washington, D.C., 1918-19, detailed as spl. Red Cross commr. to Siberia; dir. Am. Hosp. in Paris, 1920; consultant U.S. Pub. Health Serv.; counselor Med. Council of Vets. Adminstrn. Mem. permanent bd. hon. consultants to Army Med. Library. Trustee Smith Coll., Potts Memorial Hosp. Mem. exec. com. Internat. Union Against Tuberculosis; mem. U.S. Commn. to Meeting of

Pan-Am. Sanitary Union, Buenos Aires, 1934. Awarded Trudeau Medal for tuberculosis work, 1947. Fellow Am. Coll. Surgs.; mem. A.M.A., N.Y. Acad. Medicine, New York County Med. Soc., Mass. Med. Soc., New England Surg. Soc., Phi Beta Kappa, Alpha Delta Phi. Decorated Order St. Sava, 1st Class (Rumania). Republican. Episcopalian. Clubs: Century (New York); Cosmos (Washington). Contbr. articles to med. jours. Home: 1070 Beacon St., Brookline, MA Office: 1790 Broadway NY 19‡

EMERSON, LINN, oculist; b. McDonough, N.Y., Sept. 4, 1873; s. Herbert and Amelia (Puffer) E.; prep. edn. Oxford (N.Y.) Acad.; M.D., Jefferson Med. Coll., Phila., 1897; m. Daisy V. Brewster, 1898 (died 1913); children—Gerald Brewster, Dorothy Brewster; m. 2d, Marie D. S. Franklin, 1914; children—Marie Franklin, Barbara Jane. Began practice, Orange, N.J., 1901; attending oculist, Manhattan Eye, Ear and Throat Hosp. (New York), 1901-18, Orange Memorial Hosp., Dover Gen. Hosp., N.J. Orthopedic Hosp., Orphans' Home and House of the Good Shepherd (Orange, N.J.). Oculist to Medical Advisory Board, World Wars I and II. Fellow Am. College Surgeons; mem. Am. Laryngol., Rhinol. and Otol. Soc., Am. Acad. Ophthalmology and Oto-Laryngology, Soc. Surgeons State of N.J., A.M.A., Med. Soc. of N.J., N.Y. Acad. Medicine, Alumni Assn. Jefferson Med. Coll. Methodist. Royal Arch Mason. Author: Michael Emerson and Some of His Descendants, 1912; also about 50 monographs and papers on med. topics. Home: 303 Park Av., Orange NJ‡

EMERSON, SUMMER BROOKS, business exec.; b. Milford, N.H., Jan. 3, 1895; s. Charles Summer and Estella (Abbott) E.; B.S. magna cum laude, Dartmouth, 1917; m. Charlotte Cushman, July 2, 1918; children—Richard P., Charlotte (Mrs. Frederick A. Blount). Mgr. Frontier Employment Record Bur., Buffalo, 1919-22; with Guaranty Co. of N.Y., Buffalo, 1922-28, mgr., Montreal, 1928-30, Phila., 1930-34; financial v.p. dir. Fire Assn. of Phila., Lumbermen's Ins. Co., Reliance Ins. Co., Phila. Nat. Ins. Co., 1934-36; v.p., dir. Morgan Stanley & Co., Inc., 1936-41, partner, 1941-60, ltd. partner, 1960-69. Trustee, v.p. United Hosp. Fund N.Y., 1956-59. Trustee Rutgers U.; mem. Alumni Council Dartmouth, 1934-40, overseer Amos Tuck Sch., 1954-60. Mem. Phi Beta Kappa, Chi Phi, Delta Sigma Rho. Republican. Episcopalian. Clubs: Bond (pres., 1957-58), University (N.Y.C.); Short Hills; Sarasota Field, Sarasota Yacht, Dartmouth of Sarasota (pres.). Home: Sarasota FL Died Apr. 3, 1969; buried Sarasota FL

EMISON, JOHN C., smelting and refining exec.; b. Bruceville, Ind., Mar. 9, 1890; s. John W. and Mary D. (Simpson) E.; B.A., DePauw U., 1911; M.B.A., Harvard Sch. of Bus. Adminstrn., 1913; Doctor of Laws, Vincennes University, 1956; married Naomi Gregg, Jan. 20, 1917 (died 1919); m. 2d, Ruth Miller, June 16, 1921; children—Martha E., John C. Asst. mgr. The Nat. City Bank of N.Y., 1917, asst. cashier, 1918; dir. and treas. Am. Smelting & Refining Co., 1920, became dir., vice pres. and treas., 1932, chmn. finance com., 1949-57 (ret.); trustee emeritus, chmn. Finance com. John Simon Guggenheim Meml. Found.; dir. Anglo-Lautaro Nitrate Corp., Fresnillo Co. Mem. Megantic Fish & Game Corp. Rep. Presbyn. Clubs: Sleepy Hollow Country (Scarborough); Bankers (New York). Home: Scarborough NY Died Mar. 16, 1966; buried Vincennes IN

EMKEN, CECIL WHEELER, govt. ofcl.; b. Portland, Ore., Apr. 27, 1897; s. Henry Andrew and Ida May (Hall) E.; student Ore. Inst. Tech., 1920; corr. La Salle Extension U., 1917-20; m. Grace Inez Hill, Dec. 26, 1923; 1 son, Robert Allan. Accountant Union Pacific System 1917-27; examiner of accounts IIC, 1927-36, sect. of accounts Bur. Motor Carriers, 1936-48, chief sect., 1943-48, chief Motor Carriers Accounts, 1948-49, chief field service Bur. Accounts and Cost Finding, 1950, dir., 1950-53, dir. Bur. of Accounts, 1954-62. Republican. Methodist. Mason. Home: Vienna VA Died Nov. 1970.

EMMERICH, F.J., corp. exec.; b. Mar. 16, 1892; student N.Y.U., D. Sc., 1956. Pres. Allied Chem. & Dye Corp., (now Allied Chem. Corp.), 1946-57, chmn. bd. from 1957. Trustee N.Y.U., N.Y.U. Med. Center. Recipient Gold Medal Am. Inst. Chemists, Madden Meml. award, 1952. Mem. Mfg. Chemists Assn. (pres.), Am. Chemists Assn. (chmn. bd.), U.S.C. of C. (trustee), Nat. Indsl. Conf. Bd. (trustee), Com. Econ. Devel. (trustee), Beta Gamma Sigma. Address: New York City NY

EMMERICH, HERBERT, administrator; b. New York, N.Y., Apr. 27, 1897; s. Walter and Cecelia (Jacobs) E.; B.S., U. Pa., 1918, D.C.L., U. So. Cal., 1955; LL.D., Syracuse U., 1962; m. Janet W. Victorius, Feb. 2, 1922; children—Nancy, Lewis, Walter. With U.S. Secret Service, 1917-18; army field clerk Intelligence Div., Hdqrs. Eastern Dept., U.S. Army, 1918-19; mfr. and indsl. management cons., N.Y.C., 1919-24; exec. v.p. City Housing Corp., N.Y. City, 1924-33; exec. officer and deputy gov. Farm Credit Adminstrn., Washington, 1933-37; staff mem. President's Com. on

Administrative Management, Washington, 1936-37; asso. dir. Pub. Adminstrn. Clearing House, Chicago, 1937-41; exec. sec. Office of Production Management, Washington, 1941-42; sec. War Production Bd., 1942; commr. Federal Public Housing Authority, Washington, 1942-44. Adv., U.S. del. London Conf. UNESCO, 1945; mem. President's Adv. Com. on Mgmt., 1949-52; cons. ODM, 1955-56. Dir. Pub. Adminstrn. Clearing House, Chgo., 1945-56; senior cons. in pub. adminstrn. UN, 1957-63; prof. govt. and fgn. affairs, U. Va., 1963-67; former lecturer U. of Chicago. Member vis. com. Harvard Grad. Sch. Pub. Adminstrn., 1954-66. Recipient Merit medal Am. Municipal orgn., 1925. Fellow Nat. Institute for Public Affairs (hon.); mem. Am. Society for Public Adminstration, Am. Political Science Association, Nat. Assn. Housing and Redevelopment Ofcls., Nat. Acad. Pub. Adminstrn. Nat. Municipal League; Pub. Personnel Assn., Internat. Inst. Administrv. Scis. (pres. 1962-68), Internat. Polit. Sci. Assn. Clubs: Cosmos (Washington). Author: Essays on Federal Reorganization, 1950; A Handbook of Public Administration, 1961; Organization and Administrative Management, 1971. Home: Charlottesville VA Died Sept. 7, 1970; buried Mt. Hope Cemetery, Hastings-on-Hudson NY

EMPRINGHAM, JAMES, temperance advocate; b. King's Lynn, Eng., June 12, 1875; s. James and Elizabeth E. (Clarke) E.; St. James Sch., Lynn, Eng.; ed. U. of London and Gen. Theol. Sem. New York; D.D., Syracuse U., 1910; m. Ethel Mable Ruttan, of Wellington, Prince Edward County, Can., Feb. 15, 1899; children—Walter Ruttan, Elfric Ethelbert, Reginald Ruttan, Cyril King, James Oswald. Came to U.S., 1898, naturalized citizen, 1908. Deacon, 1904, priest, 1905, P.E. Ch.; rector St. Paul's Ch., Syracuse, N.Y., 1906-16; resigned rectorship to become supt. Anti-Saloon League of N.Y.; nat. supt. Episcopal Ch. Temperance Soc. since 1916; nat. sec. Health Edn. Soc., Inc.; dir. Jumel Labs., New York. Pres. Ministers' Assn. of Central N.Y., 1908-11; pres. Syracuse br. Am. Inst. Archaeology, 1910-12; v.p. Anti-Saloon League of America, 1917. Editor of Temperance (official organ Episcopal Ch. Temperance Soc.), and of Health Education (organ of Health Edn. Soc.). Author: Dangerous Deceits Exposed, 1913; Intestinal Gardening, 1924, 26. Address: 885 St. Nicholas Av., New York NY‡

EMSWELLER, SAMUEL LEONAR, biologist; b. Tarentum, Pa., Nov. 1, 1898; s. Samuel Peter and Catherine (Waltzinger) E.; B.Sc., W.Va. U., 1920; Ph.D., U. Cal., 1932; m. Frances P. Fitzgerald, June 30, 1920; children—Eugene S., Frances T. Research asst. U. Cal., 1928-32, asst. prof., 1932-35; prin. horticulturist, head floriculture research Dept. Agr., 1935-51, head horticulturist, ornamental plant crops sect., Beltsville, Md., from 1952. Mem. Internat. Hort. Congress, London, 1952, Netherlands, 1955, sectional chmn., 1955-58, Hort. Congress, France, 1958, Internat. Genetic Congress, Montreal, 1960. Recipient achievement award Am. Hort. Council, gold medal N.E. Gladiola Soc., gold medal Mass. Hort Soc., Jackson-Dawson Medal, 1950; citation for research, Mens Gardens Club of Am., 1958; Superior Service award by U.S. Dept. Agr., 1959; Lytel Cup, Royal Hort. Soc., London, 1959; Medal of Honor, Garden Club Am., 1959, George Robert White Medal of Honor, 1964, Norman J. Colman medal, 1964; named to Floriculture Hall of Fame, 1964. Fellow A.A.A.S.; mem. Am. Genetic Soc. (pres.), Am. Soc. Hort. Sci. (past pres.). American Bot. Soc., Genetics Soc. Am. (rep. div. biology and agr. Nat. Research Council, Bot. Soc. Washington (past pres.), Washington Acad. Sci., Sigma Phi Epsilon, Sigma Xi, Alpha Zeta. Clubs: Bohemian (asso.) (San Francisco); Cosmos (Washington). Office: Beltsville MD Died Aug. 22, 1966; buried Arlington National Cemetery, Arlington VA

ENDERS, HOWARD EDWIN, dean emeritus, professor zoology; b. Enders, Pa., June 18, 1877; s. Charles Washington and Phoebe A. (Buffington) E.; B.S., Lebanon Valley Coll., Anville, Pa., 1897, M.S., 1900; B.S., U. of Mich., 1898; post-grad. work 3 summers, U. of Mich. and Harvard Univ., and Johns Hopkins U., 1903-06; Ph.D., Johns Hopkins Univ., 1906, Sc.D. (hon.), Lebanon Valley College, 1946; m. Susie S. Moyer. Oct. 16, 1901; children—Mrs. Katherine Eleanora Flack, Charles M., Sue E (Winston). Science teacher, Hulst High Sch., Iron Mountain, Mich., 1898-1900; with field party Mich. Geol. Survey, summer, 1899; prof. biol. sciences, Lebanon Valley Coll., 1900-03; research in zoology, U.S. Fisheries Lab., Beaufort, N.C., summers, 1903-08; with Purdue U. since 1906, successively instr. in zoology, asst. prof., asso. prof., 1917, prof. zoology, head of gen. biology, head of dept. of biology since 1926, acting dean Sch. of Science, 1931, and dean, February, 1932-46, on leave, 1946-47; retired July 1, 1947; professor of zoology and biology, 10 summers, Ind. U. and Johns Hopkins; research in parasitology at Kartabo Jungle Lab. of Tropical Biology, British Guiana, S.A., summer, 1925, at research lab. of Inst. of Tropical Biology, Gatun Lake, Panama Canal Zone, summer, 1927; tropical research in Lancetilla Expt. Sta.,

Honduras, summer, 1933. Lecturer on physiology, St. Elizabeth Hosp., Lafayette, Ind., 1915-1940. Fellow A.A.A.S. (sec. 1928; chmn. acad. conf. 1929 and 1933), Ind. Acad. Science (sec. 1913-20; pres. 1921); state sponsor Indiana Junior Acad. of Science; member Am. Soc. Zoologists, Phi Beta Kappa (Johns Hopkins), Sigma Xi of Purdue (pres. 1931). Republican. Mem. U.B. Ch. Clubs: Rotary (pres. 1931-32), Town and Gown (pres. 1933-34). Author: Laboratory Directions in General Biology, 1912, 4th edit., 1936. Home: 249 Littleton St., West Layfayette, Ind.; Winter; Venice FL‡

ENDORE, (SAMUEL) GUY, author; b. New York, N.Y., July 4, 1901; s. Isidor and Malka (Halpern) E.; A.B., Columbia, 1924, A.M., 1925; m. Henrietta Portugal, of Russia, Sept. 30, 1927; 1 dau., Marcia Loo. Author: Cassanova-His Known and Unknown Life, 1929; Man from Limbo, 1930; The Sword of God-Jeanne d'Arc, 1931; The Werewolf of Paris, 1933; Babouk, 1934. Home: Far Rockaway LI NY Died Feb. 12, 1970.*

ENFIELD, GERTRUDE DIXON (MRS. JOHN ENFIELD), author; b. Hume, Mo.; d. Thomas Edmond and Frances Jane (Norfleet) Dixon; B.E., U. Cal., Los Angeles, 1931; M.S. in Speech, U. So. Cal., 1941; m. John B. Enfield, Aug. 5, 1903 (dec. July 1962); children—Dorothy Frances (Mrs. Roy Milton Thoroughman), John Broughton, Virginia Louise. Tchr., pub. sch. prin. Los Angeles and Cal. Bd. Edn., 1920-43; prof. edn. U. Cal., Los Angeles, 1924-27; prof. speech U. So. Cal., Los Angeles, 1933-41. Founder verse choir movement in Cal., verse choir dir., 1927-41. Mem. Nat. League Am. Pen Women (regional chmn. Pacific S.W. 1963-65, pres. Laguna Beach chpt. 1964-69), Colonial Dames XVII Century, Internat. Platform Assn., Nat. Ret. Tchrs. Assn. Democrat. Mem. Ch. Religious Sci. Author: Verse Choir Values and Technique, 1937; Holiday Book for Verse Choirs, 1953. Address: Laguna Beach CA Died June 4, 1969.

ENGEL, CARL HENRY, metal products co. exec.; b. Detroit, Mar. 31, 1924; s. Karl and Augusta Mildred (Sarns) E.; B.S. in Engring., U. Mich., 1947; M.B.A., Harvard, 1949; m. Helen Elaine Masson, July 13, 1946; children—Carolyn (Mrs. Richard W. Comfort, Jr.), Richard Masson, Margaret Jane. Indsl. engr. Harris-Intertype Co., Cleve., 1949-53, budget mgr., 1953-56; div. budget dir. W.R. Grace, Cambridge, Mass., 1956-59; asst. treas. Raymond Internat., Inc., N.Y.C., 1959-65; v.p. finance Hunter-Douglas Ltd., N.Y.C., 1965-67; v.p., treas., dir. Ranco, Inc., Columbus, O., 1967-71; dir. Knowledge Communication Fund, Inc., Columbus. Served with USNR, 1943-46. Mem. Financial Execs. Inst. Presbyn. Home: Columbus OH Died Nov. 28, 1971; buried Centerville, Cape Cod MA

ENGEL, MICHAEL MARTIN, hon. coll. chancellor, counsel; born near Bereg-Szacs, Hungary, April 22, 1896; s. Mor and Lena (Prosper) E.; came to U.S., 1899, naturalized, 1903; student Cooper Union Coll. of Sci. and Art; LL.D., Florida Southern College, 1952; married March 23, 1917, one son, Michael; married 2d, Mary Black Diller, September 22, 1939. Specialist in publicity and pub. relations fine arts profession, 1935-66; director Research Labs. of M. Grumbacher, 1935-46; chancellor Fla. Southern Coll., Lakeland, Fla., 1951-52. Citation for public relations work in Art, Fla. So. Coll., 1950. Mem. Nat. Assn. Pub. Relations Counsel, Inc., 1941-56, Am. Pub. Relations Soc., Publicity Club of N.Y. Pub. relations dir. 7th and 8th War Loan Dist., No. 1, Treas. Dept., N.Y. City, with rating of Gen. of Blue Star Brigade. Founder Audubon Artists, Inc., N.Y. City, 1940-41 (chmn. exhibition com., 1945-46); sec. com. of development Artists for Victory, Inc., 1945; organizer, 1st pres., Profl. Artists Group, N.Y. City, 1940; sustaining mem. Allied Artists of Am., Nat. Acad. of Design, Museum of Modern Art. Publicity chmn. Nat. Celebration of Mark Twain Centennial, 1935; adviser and producer full length Kodachrome film de-picting work of Wayman Adams; lectr. on Contemporary Am. Art and on Palettes of Living Artists, hon. life mem. of Art Center of the Islands. Fellow, life mem. Royal Soc. Arts Eng.; mem. Am. Pub. Relations Soc., Am. Assn. Museums. Columnist Art Digest, 1934-36, Western Artists, 1937-38. Design Mag., 1948-64. Editor: Michelangelo Art News Letter, 1967. Episcopalian. Club: Publicity (N.Y.C.). Home: New York City NY Died Apr. 25, 1969; buried Woodward Hill Cemetery, Lancaster PA

ENGELKEMEIR, DONALD WILLIAM, nuclear chemist; b. Nehawka, Neb., June 10, 1919; s. Julius G. and Mathilda (Ploeger) E.; B.A., U. Cal., Los Angeles, 1942; Ph.D., U. Chgo., 1952; m. Antoinette M. Greiner, July 19, 1947; children—Richard, Ann, Gregory, Jean. Asso. chemist Metall. lab., U. Chgo., 1942-45; asso. chemist Los Alamos (N.M.) Sci. Lab., 1945-46; nuclear chemist Argonne (Ill.) Nat. Lab., 1948-69. Mem. Am. Physical Soc., Am. Assn. Variable Star Observers, Sigma Xi. Democrat. Roman Catholic. Home: Hinsdale IL Died Apr. 29, 1969.

ENGLAND, EDWARD THEODORE, lawyer; b. Jackson Co., W.Va., Sept. 29, 1870; s. A.J.S. and Mary E.; grad. Concord Normal Sch., Athens, W.Va., 1892; LL.B., Southern Normal U., Huntingdon, Tenn., 1898, B.S., 1900; m. Huldah L. Lenburg, of Moulton, Ia., Dec. 25, 1901; children—Arline I., Francis M., Marjorie. Admitted to W.Va. bar, 1899, and began practice at Oceana; moved to Logan, 1900; pres. Altizer Coal Land Co.; sec. Union Coal Land Co. Mem. W.Va. Senate, 1908-16 (pres. 1915-16); atty. gen. of W.Va., 1917-25; mem. 70th Congress (1927-29), 6th W.Va. Dist.; now in practice of law. Republican. Methodist. Odd Fellow, K. of P., Elk, Moose. Home: Logan, W.Va. Office: Charleston WV‡

ENGLAND, WILLIAM HENRY, chief economist, Fed. Trade Commn.; b. Edinburgh, Ind., Dec. 21, 1876; s. Joseph Henry and Laura (Drake) E.; B.S., Neb. Wesleyan Univ., 1902; student Univ. Chicago, 1902; Ph.D., Univ. of Neb., 1906; student Georgetown Univ. Law Sch., 1916; m. Norah D. Collins, June 2, 1917; children—William Henry, Collin Byfield. High school principal, 1902-03; instructor Nebraska Wesleyan Academy, 1900-02, Nebraska Wesleyan University, 1906-08; special agent, Bureau of Corps., 1908-16; research economist Hooker Electro-Chem. Co., 1916-17, 1919-20; asst. chief economist Fed. Trade Commn., 1920-40, chief economist, dir. division of accounts, statistics and economic reports, 1941-47; ret. Paper 7, Organization of Private Electric and Gas Utilities, 3d World Power Conference, Washington, 1936; directed inquiries into petroleum, lumber, fertilizers, export grain, farm implements, automobile industry, electric and gas utilities, etc.; econ. consultant War Dept. com. to survey decartelization and deconcentration accomplishments of mil. govt. in Germany, 1948-49. Served in Philippines, 1898-99; commander captain and advanced to major, 1917-19. colonel in Officers Reserve Corps since June 13, 1932. Awarded Philippine Congressional medal. Member American Rose Society, Potomac Rose Soc., Sigma Xi. Club: Takoma Horticultural. Home: 1344 Iris St., N.W. Office: 6th and Pennsylvania Av., Washington DC‡

ENGLE, JOHN SUMMERFIELD, educator; b. Augusta Co., Va., June 26, 1869; s. Rev. Joseph Jackson and Mary B. (Goodwin) E.; A.B., A.M., Roanoke Coll., 1902; Johns Hopkins, 1903-6; m. Anna M. Sencindivar, of Darkesville, W.Va., Apr. 13, 1892. Ordained M.E., S. ministry, 1890; pastor Middletown, Va., 1891-3, Roanoke, 1893-4, Arlington (Baltimore), 1894-8. Front Royal, Va., 1898-1900, Salem, Va., 1900-3, Emmanuel, Baltimore, 1903-5; editor Baltimore Southern Methodist, official organ of Baltimore Conf. M.E. Ch., S., 1905-7; prin. Southern Sem. System of Schs. since 1907. Author: Analytic Interest Psychology and Synthetic Philosophy. Home: Buena Vista VA‡

ENGLE, WILBUR DWIGHT, chemist; b. Portland, Mich., Aug. 31, 1870; s. David and Ann (Guernsey) E.; A.B., Albion (Mich.) Coll., 1893, A.M., 1894; Ph.D., Columbia, 1898; Sc.D. from the University of Denver in 1914; LL.D. from the University of Colorado, 1927; m. Emma G. Agard, of Litchfield, Mich., Aug. 22, 1895; children—Earl Agard, Dorothy Gail. Instr. in chemistry, Albion Coll., 1893-95; prof. chemistry, 1895-1937, dean Summer Sch., vice chancellor, 1917-37, acting chancellor, 1920-22 and 1927-28, dean Sch. of Science and Engineering, 1930-37, and dean of the Graduate School of the U. of Denver, 1933, retired, 1937. Prof. chemistry, Denver and Gross Colleges of Medicine, 1898-1910. Mem. American Chemical Society, The Teknik Club (Denver), also Phi Lambda Upsilon, Omega Upsilon Phi, Alpha Tau Omega. Methodist. Mem. exec. com. 8th Internat. Cong. Applied Chemistry, 1912-13; has done much expert work in chemistry, especially in toxicology, and recognized as an authority in that subject; especially interested in chemistry of uranium and vanadium, and has devised successful methods for the treatment Denver CO‡

ENGLEHARD, CHARLES WILLIAM, precious metals co. exec.; b. N.Y.C., Feb. 15, 1917; s. Charles William and Emy Marie (Canthal) E.; student St. Paul's Sch.; B.A., Princeton, 1939; m. Jane Reis-Brian, Aug. 18, 1947; children—Annette (Mrs. Samuel Pryor Reed), Mary Susan, Sophie, Alexandra, Charlene. Chmn. Engelhard Minerals & Chems. Corp.; chmn. Engelhard Hanovia, Inc., Am.-S. African Investment Co., Ltd., Johannesburg, S.Africa Forest Investments, Ltd., Johannesburg, dir. Anglo Am. Corp. S. Africa (N. Am.), Ltd., Anglo Am. Corp. So. Africa, Ltd. Charter Consol., Ltd., Hudson Bay Mining & Smelting Co., Ltd., Internat. Silver Co., Nat. Newark & Essex Banking Co., Pub. Service Elec. & Gas Co., Rand Selection Corp., Ltd., Thomas Barlow & Sons (S. Africa) Ltd., Prudential Ins. Co. Mem. Community Relations Service, Easco Corp. mem. Pres.'s Spl. Com. to Study East-West Trade, 1965; mem. Citizens Com. Higher Edn. N.J.; commr. Port of N.Y. Authority; chmn. Newark Mus.; mem. Greater Newark Devel. Council. Mem. N.J. Democratic Com. Trustee, v.p. Am. Mus. Immigration; trustee John F. Kennedy Meml. Library, Am. Heritage Found., Bernards Library Assn., Com. Econ. Devel., Seton Hall U., Foxcroft Sch. mem. Eleanor Roosevelt Meml. Found.; bd. dirs. U.S. Com. for Refugees, Atlantic Council U.S., Inc., N.Y. Zool. Soc., Thomas Alva Edison Found., Atlantic Salmon Assn. (dir.) World Wildlife Soc. (dir.). Served as capt. USAAF, 1941-45. Mem. Fgn. Policy Assn. (dir.), N.J. C. of C. (dir.). Clubs: Racquet and Tennis, The Brook, Jockey; Chemist, Economic; Metropolitan (Washington). (N.Y.C.); Ivy (Princeton, N.J.); Rand (Johannesburg); Travelers (Paris, France); Monmouth (N.J.) Jockey. Home: Cragwood Far Hills NJ Died Mar. 2, 1971.

ENGLISH, FRANK CLARE, ex-coll. pres.; b. Felicity, O., Dec. 27, 1869; s. William Fisher and Sophia Ellen (Fletcher) E.; U. of Cincinnati; A.B., Baldwin U., 1897; B.D., Drew Theol. Sem., 1897; A.M., Ohio Wesleyan Univ., 1908; D.D., Moores Hill Coll., Ind., 1904; m. Rosella A. Littleton, Aug. 25, 1891. Ordained ministry M.E. Church, 1894; pastor, Newark, N.J., 1894-95, Columbia M.E. Ch., Cincinnati, 1900-04; pres. Moores Hill Coll., 1904-08; pres. Cincinnati Training Sch., 1909-10; pres. William and Vashti Coll., Aledo, Ill., 1911-14; dir. extension div., U. of N.D., 1915-16; extension sec., St. Luke's Hosp., Cleveland, O., 1916-26; exec. mgr. The Christ Hospital, Cincinnati, 1926-28. Dir. surveys Am. hosps. and homes for Interch. World Movement, 1919; gen. sec. Protestant Hosp. Association America; mgr. hosp. dept. Marts & Lundy, Inc., N.Y. City, 1935. Republican. Mason (32 deg.). Contbr. articles on sociol., econ. and popular subjects. Address: Hyde Park, Cincinnati OH‡

ENGLISH, JOHN FRANCIS, labor union ofcl.; b. Boston, Apr. 14, 1889; s. James Partick and Mary (Holland) E.; student Bently Sch. Accountancy; m. Gertrude Ann Kurvin (dec. Sept. 1930); 1 dau., Gertrude Ann; m. 2d, Katherine E. Noonan, Dec. 8, 1948. Business agt. Local 68, Teamsters Union, 1910-35; 5th v.p. Internat. Brotherhood Teamsters, 1927-36, gen. organizer, auditor, 1936-46, acting gen. sec.-treas., 1946, gen. sec.-treas., 1947-57; later sec. treas. Teamsters, Chauffeurs, Warehousemen and Helpers of Am.; v.p. Union Label Service Trades Dept., 1957-69; dir. Union Labor Life Ins. Co. Chmn. exec. com. Central Atlantic Area YMCA, 1957-62. Mem. Am. Bible Soc. (bd. mgrs.), Am. Legion, K.C. Elk. Home: Bethesda MD Died Feb. 1969.

ENGLISH, SARA JOHN (MRS. HENRY W. ENGLISH), b. Marion, Ala., Nov. 20, 1872; d. Rev. Joseph Francis and Sara (Davis) John; educated Dallas Acad. Misses Young's Home High School (Selma, Ala.), and Marion (Ala.) Sem.; m. Henry W. English, lawyer, of Jacksonville, Ill., Apr. 29, 1905; 1 son, Henry John. Active organizer and speaker for Dem. Party; was mem. 1st Dem. Central Com. of Women in Ill., 1922, and chmn. 20th Dist. Com. of Dem. Women; an organizer Ill. Women's Dem. clubs; speaker in nat. campaigns, 1924-28, also speaker on hist. subjects; has made extensive researches in genealogy. Alternate del. at large, Dem. Nat. Conv., 1928. Hon. mem. Northwest Territory Commn.; del. 10th gen. assembly, Daughters of Am. Colonists, 1931; past state registrar Ill. Daughters of Am. Colonists; del. to Asso. Council of Nat. Conv. of U.S. Daughters of 1812. Mem. speakers bur., Century of Progress Expn., Chicago, 1933; mem. Dem. Nat. Bur. of Speakers, 1932; mem. Ill. Dem. Woman's State Com. (chmn. 20th Congressional Dist. 1932); chmn. Morgan Co. woman's div. N.R.A. vols., 1933. Mem. D.A.R. (mem. various coms. and alternate Continental Congress), Ills. State Hist. Soc. (dir.), Ill. Daughters Am. Revolution (past state librarian), U.S. Daughters of 1812, Morgan County (Ill.) Hist. Soc. (treas. and dir.), etc. Episcopalian. Clubs: Ill. Woman's Democratic, Fine Point, Household Science, Morgan Country, Jacksonville Country. First woman in Ill. to hold office in Dem. State Conv., being asst. sec. Home: 844 W. College Av., Jacksonville IL‡

ENOCHS, HERBERT ALEXANDER, personnel; b. Libertyville, Pa., Sept. 19, 1874; s. Alexander E. and Frances Irwin (Williamson) E.; ed. high sch.; m. Mary Caldwell Otis, Apr. 15, 1895; children—Evelyn K., Dorothy O., Herbert A., Otis Lane, Marjorie D. Served as sec. Eastern Chairmen's Assn., Brotherhood of R.R. Trainmen; then as gen. chmn. Brotherhood of R.R. Trainmen; was sec. Nat. 8-hour Com.; later supt. Labor and Wage Bur., Pa. R.R., now chief of personnel; v.p. Western Allegheny R.R. Co. Mem. Management-Labor Policy Com. of War Manpower Commn. Mem. exec. com. Bur. of Information of Eastern Rys.; chmn. Eastern Carriers' Com.; chmn. Joint Conf. Com.; mem. regional contact com. Nat. R.R. Adjustment Bd.; mem. com. in connection with operation of Selective Act as applied to r.r. employees. Trustee John Edgar Thomson Foundation; mem. transportation com. Nat. Council of Y.M.C.A.'S. Republican. Episcopalian. Mason. Home: Paoli, Pa. Office: Broad St. Station Bldg., Philadelphia PA*‡

ENRIGHT, ELIZABETH, author, illustrator; b. Oak Park, Illinois, daughter Walter J. and Maginel (Wright) Enright; student Art Students League, N.Y.C., 1926, 27, Parsons Sch. Applied Art, Paris, 1928; m. Robert Marty Gillham, Apr. 24, 1930; children—Nicholas Wright, Robert II, Oliver. Author children's books, including Kintu, A Congo Adventure, 1935; Thimble Summer, 1938; The Sea is All Around, 1940; The Saturdays, 1941; The Four-Story Mistake, 1942; Then There Were Five, 1944; The Melandy Family 1947; Spiderweb for Two, 1951; Gone-Away Lake, 1957; Return to Gone-Away, 1961; also collections adult short stories: Borrowed Summer, 1946. The Moment Before the Rain, 1955; The Riddle of the Fly, 1960; Tatsinda, 1963; Zeee, 1965, Doublefields, 1966. Lecturer in English, Barnard College, 1960-62. Recipient Newbery award, 1939; included in O. Henry Meml. award collections, 1946, 49, 51, 55, 58, 60; Best American Short Story collections, 1950, 52, 54; recipient Children's Spring Book Festival award Herald Tribune, 1957. Mem. P.E.N. Club: Cosmopolitan (N.Y.C.). Home: New York City NY Died June 8, 1968; buried Wainscott NY

ENRIGHT, WALTER J(OSEPH), cartoonist; b. Chicago, Ill., July 3, 1879; s. John W. and Mary B. (Croghan) E.; ed. Armour Inst. Tech.; art edn., Art Inst. Chicago; married. Illustrator for Life, Judge, Scribner's Collier's, etc.; drew Once Upon a Time" strip for McClure Newspaper Syndicate; cartoonist, New York World, 1927-30, New York American, 1930-36; later with Miami Herald. Served as 1st lt., A.S., U.S.A., comdg. officer photog. sect., World War. Clubs: Players, New York Athletic. Author: Once Upon a Time Stories (3 vols. fairy tales retold in pictures), 1926. Home: Delray Beach Fl Died Jan. 1969.

ENSEY, LOT, naval officer; b. Panama Canal Zone, Nov. 9, 1908; s. Charles Ridgeley and Nona Alva (Johns) E.; student Marion Inst., Ala.; B.S., U.S. Naval Acad., 1930; grad. Armed Forces Staff Coll., 1948, Naval War Coll., 1951; m. Kathryn Zeiss, July 9, 1938; 1 son, Lot. Commd. ensign USN, 1930, advanced through grades to vice adm., 1964; various assignments battleship and destroyers Pacific Fleet, 1930-38; insp. turrets Naval Gun Factory, 1938-40; gun officer, exec. officer destroyers North Atlantic, 1940-42; comdr. three destroyers, 1942-45; staff Bur. Naval Personnel, 1945-48; comdr. destroyer div. Pacific Fleet, 1948; staff Naval War Coll., 1949-52; operations officer Atlantic Fleet, 1952-54; comdr. amphibious attack transport Atlantic Fleet, 1955; comdr. Destoyer Squadron Two, Atlantic Fleet, 1956; chief staff Sixth Fleet, 1956-58; asst. comptroller, dir. budget and reports, Navy Dept., 1958-60; dep. controller of the Navy, 1960-63; comdr. Cruiser-Destroyer Flotilla 9, 1963-64; dep. chief naval operations (logistics) Navy Dept., Washington, 1964-67; director logistics Directorate for Logistics, Joint Staff, Joint Chiefs of Staff, Washington, 1967-69. Decorated Bronze Star, D.S.M. Club: Army-Navy Country (Washington). Home: Washington DC Died Oct. 26, 1970.

ENSIGN, FOREST CHESTER, prof. education; b. Defiance County, O., Mar. 22, 1867; s. Dwight Pepoon and Charity (Southworth) E.; M.Di., Ia. State Normal Sch., 1895; B.Ph., State U. of Ia., 1897, M.A., 1900; studied Harvard; Ph.D., Teachers Coll. (Columbia), 1921; m. Lucy M. Smith, Dec. 29, 1896; children—Dwight Chester, Elizabeth. Teacher rural sch., 1892; prin. high sch., Iowa City, 1897-1900. Council Bluffs, 1900-05; prof. edn., 1905, also insp. high schs., 1905-11, dean of men, and registrar, 1911-15, prof. history and philosophy of edn. since 1916. State U. of Ia. Exchange prof. in education, Univ. of Bristol. Eng., 1927. Mem. N.E.A., Nat. Soc. Coll. Teachers of Edn. (pres. 1928-29), Ia. State Teachers' Assn. (pres. 1918-19), A.A.A.S., Soc. Mayflower Descendants, Phi Delta Kappa, Phi Beta Kappa, Acacia. Presbyterian. Mason. Clubs: Triangle, Ia. Union. Student and writer on care of insane in Iowa county and city jails and prisons, relations of compulsory edn. and child labor, edn. in Iowa and the middle west. Home: Iowa City IA‡

ENTRATTER, JACK, hotel exec.; b. N.Y.C., Feb. 28, 1914; s. Max and Anna (Stelzer) E.; widower; children—Caryl (Mrs. Michael Palin), Michele. Engaged in show bus. with French Casino, N.Y.C., 1936-38; mgr. Stork Club, N.Y.C., 1938-40; show producer, partner Copacabana Nightclub, N.Y.C., 1940-52; v.p., producer Sands Hotel, Las Vegas, 1952-55, pres., show producer, 1955-65, chairman bd., pres., from 1965; pres. Jack Entratter Prodns., movie and TV film producing co.; personal business manager, adviser to Red Skelton, from 1961. Pres., Found. for Las Vegas Charities. Member of board dirs. Las Vegas chpt. Nat. Conf. Christians and Jews. Recipient Brownsville (N.Y.) Boys Club award, 1948. Mem. Anti-Defamation League. Jewish religion (pres. temple). Club: Variety (Las Vegas). Address: Las Vegas NV Died Sept. 1971.

EPLER, PERCY H(AROLD), clergyman, biographer, b. Jacksonville, Ill., July 19, 1872; s. Judge Cyrus and Cornelia (Nettleton) E.; B.A., Ill. Coll., 1892, D.D., 1918; studied Yale, 1892-93; B.D., Yale Div. Sch., 1896; m. Helen Esther York, Jan. 1, 1903; children—Palmer York, Helen Cornelia. Ordained in Congl. ministry, 1896; asso. pastor Phillips Ch., S. Boston, 1896-1903, First Ch., Detroit, 1903-05; pastor Adams Sq. Ch., Worcester, Mass., 1905-16, 1st Ch., Indianapolis, Ind., 1916-18, 1st Ch., Methuen, Mass., 1918-23; retired. Author: An Experimental Approach to the Atonement, 1899; The Personality of Christ (Yale Lecture), 1907; The Beatitude of Progress, 1907; Master Minds at the Commonwealth's Heart, 1909; Life of Clara Barton, 1915. Home: Highmount Av., Nyack NY‡

EPLEY, LLOYD L., college pres.; b. Cedarville, Ill., Dec. 19, 1872; s. Peter H. and Henrietta E. (Guldin) E.; A.B., York (Neb.) Coll., 1893, A.M., 1910; studied University of Neb., 1914; D.D. from Philomath College, 1920; m. Mina C. Hall (A.B., York Coll., 1915), Jan. 1, 1894. Ordained ministry U.B. Ch., 1891; pastor in Neb. at Amherst, 1896-8, Elba, 1898-9, Broken Bow, 1899-06, Gibbon, 1906-9; traveling sec. U.B. S.S. Bd., 1909; prof. Latin and Greek, York Coll., 1912-14; pres. Philomath (Ore.) C oll. since June 12, 1914. Supt. W. Neb. Conf., 1900-3, 1909-12. Home: Philomath OR‡

EPP, GEORGE EDWARD, church official; b. Sheboygan, Wis., June 15, 1885; s. Christian E. and Anna (Zenke) E.; grad. Evang. Theol. Sem., Naperville, Ill., 1906, D.D., 1928; LL.D., North Central Coll., 1939; m. Cora M. Runkel, Sept. 3, 1907; children—Helen Mae, John George, Ruth Elizabeth. Ordained ministry Evang. Ch., 1906; pastor Menomonee Falls, Wis., 1906-07, Prairie du Chien, 1907-11, Milwaukee, 1911-16, Racine, 1916-19; exec. sec., treas. Bd. of Missions, Evang. Ch., 1919-30, v.p., 1930-34, pres. since 1934, supporting over 1,000 missionaries in U.S., Can., Germany, Switzerland, France, Poland, Latvia, Africa, Japan and China. Elected bishop Evang. Ch., 1930, and given charge of N.W. Episcopal Area, 1930-34, Central Area, 1934-50. Pres. board trustees N. Central Coll. and Evang. Theol. Sem., Naperville, Ill., since 1930; pres. bd. trustees Evang. Deaconess Soc. (Chicago), Old People's Home (New Carlisle, Ind.), Flat Rock Childrens Home (Flat Rock Ohio); sec. Bd. of Bishops. Republican. Author: Life Sketches of Evangelical Missionaries; Oriental Missions of the Evang. Church; co-author: Lay Leadership in the Evangelical Church, 1943. Editor, Missionary Year Book, 1919-34. Address: Naperville IL Died May 1970.

ERB, CARL LEE, JR., civil engr.; b. Lincoln, Neb., Sept. 11, 1913; s. Carl Lee and Clarence Lillian (Larson) E.; B.Sc. in Civil Engring., U. Neb., 1935; m. Phyllis Lenore Richey, Dec. 6, 1936; children—Julann (Mrs. Lauren E. Meyers), Philip Michael. Constrn. engr. C., B. & O. R.R., 1935-37; office engr. Kingsley Dam Western Neb., designer hydropower and irrigation structures Central Neb. Power & Irrigation Dist., 1938-41; with Howard, Needles, Tammen & Bergendoff, cons. engrs., Kansas City, Mo., Cleve., N.Y., 1941-71, partner, 1957-71; dir. Grand Av. Bank, Kansas City, Mo. Recipient Thomas Arkle Clark award Alpha Tau Omega, 1935, Man of Year award, 1971. Registered profl. engr., Conn., Ida., Ind., Ky., La., Mo., Mont., Neb., N.Y., Ohio, Okla., Pa., W.Va., Wis. Mem. Am. Inst. Cons. Engrs. (nat. pres. 1971), Am. Soc. C.E., Nat. Soc. Profl. Engrs., Kansas City Engrs. Club, Engring. Inst. Can., Am. Rd. Builders Assn., Cons. Engrs. Council, Sigma Xi, Alpha Tau Omega, Sigma Tau, Pi Mu Epsilon. Methodist. Rotarian. Clubs: Mission Hills (Kan.) Country; Kansas City (Mo.); Mid-Ocean (Bermuda). Prin. designer, adminstr. maj. bridges and expressways including Del. Meml. Bridge, Pres. Truman Bridge, Kansas City, Mo. Turnpike, Denver-Boulder Turnpike, urban expressways systems in Cleve., Akron (O.), Toledo, other large cities. Home: Mission Hills KS Died Dec. 5, 1971.

ERBES, PHILIP HENRY, chewing gum mfg. exec.; b. Chgo., Dec. 9, 1906; s. Philip Henry and Kathryn (Dickhut) E.; B.S., Northwestern U., 1928; m. Margaret Sweeney, Dec. 22, 1951 (dec. Nov. 1968); m. 2d, Roslyn Rensch, June 9, 1970. Asso. editor Dry Goods Jour., 1928-29; editorial staff Printers' Ink, 1929-37, asso. editor, 1937-44; with William Wrigley Jr. Co., Chgo., 1944-71, asst. to pres., 1953-61, asst. sec., 1957-59, sec., 1959-71, v.p., 1962-71; dir. Santa Catalina Island Co., Catalina Island Sightseeing Lines, Ariz. Biltmore Hotel, Chgo. Nat. League Ball Club, 1957-71, Catalina Rock & Rauch Co. Sec. The Wrigley Fund, 1956-71. Mem. Am. Soc. Corp. Secretaries, Chgo. Hist. Soc., Sigma Delta Chi Clubs: Headline, Economic (Chgo.). Home: Chicago IL Died May 3, 1971; buried Meml. Park Cemetery, Skokie IL

ERDLAND, BERNARD AUGUST, missionary; b. Oelde, Westphalia, Germany, Oct. 11, 1874; s. Gerhard and Maria (Boeckenfoerde) E.; ed. at Oelde, Antwerp (Belgium), Cheal-Benoit (France), 1883-97; Mission Acad. and U. of Muenster, Germany, 1897-1900. Ordained R.C. priest, 1900; superior of mission in Marshall Islands, 1900-5; administrator apostolic of vicarate same, 1905-10; during the 10 yrs. named, studied the native lang. and folk-lore of Marshall Islands, also lang. of Nauru or Pleasant Island; traveling missionary Missionary Soc. of the Sacred Heart. Now on vacation and intends to devote the remainder of his life to linguistic researches. Author: Woerterbuch und Grammatik der Marshall-Sprache, 1906, 14; Leben und Religion eines Sudseevolkes, 1914. Home: Sparta WI

ERDMAN, FREDERICK SEWARD, educator and cons. engr.; b. Sidon, Syria (Lebanon), Oct. 27, 1901 (parents U.S. citizens); s. Paul and Amanda C. (Jessup) E.; B.S., Princeton, 1924; B.S. in M.E., Mass. Inst. Tech., 1927; M.S., in M.E., Cornell, 1937, Ph.D., 1941; m. Mary Nicol, June 15, 1928; children—Barbara Gertrude (Mrs. David E. Blais), Carol Amanda (Mrs. Douglas H. Merkle), Frederick Seward Erdman, Elizabeth Anna (Mrs. Horace J. Mann), Constance Rebecca (Mrs. George F. Feissner). Tchr. Am. U., Beirut, Lebanon, 1924-25; jr. engineer Worthington Pump & Machinery Corp., Cincinnati, 1927-28; asst. prof. mech. engring. Robert Coll., Istanbul, Turkey, 1928-36; grad. student and instr. coll. of engring., Cornell, 1936-41, asst. prof. mech. engring., 1941-44, asso. prof., 1944-49, prof., 1949-67, emeritus prof., 1967-68, asso. dean, 1962-67; vis. engr. Brookhaven Nat. Lab., 1948, cons., 1949-52; cons. engr., 1942-68. Licensed profl. engr. Mem. Am. Assn. U. Profs., A.S.M.E., Am. Soc. Engring. Edn., Phi Kappa Phi, Sigma Xi. Presbyterian (elder). Author: Principles of Food Freezing (with Gortner and Masterman), 1948. Contbr. articles to tech. jours. and Encyclopaedia Britannica. Home: Ithaca NY Died Sept. 22, 1968.

ERHARDT, JOEL BENEDICT, business man; served in Civil war; U. S. marshal, southern dist. N. Y., 1883-4 police comm'r, 1884; collector port of N. Y., 1889-93; now pres. and dir. Lawyers' Surety Co.; dir. Gamewell Fire Alarm Telegraph Co.; trustee Bowery Savings Bank, and State Trust Co. Residence: 764 Madison Av. Office: 32 Liberty St., New York NY‡

ERICKSON, J(ULIUS) L(YMAN) E(DWARD), univ. prof.; b. Lake Charles, La., Oct. 8, 1901; s. Charles Edward and Ella Jessie (Finlayson); B.A., Rice Inst., 1923, M.S., 1926; A.M., Harvard, 1927, Ph.D., 1932; m. Olivia Bradshaw, Aug. 28, 1928; 1 dau., Jane Vincent. Instr. in chemistry La. State U., 1930-32, asst. prof., 1932-37, asso. prof., 1937-44, prof. organic chemistry from 1944. Fellow The Chem. Soc. (London), Am. Inst. of Chemists, A.A.A.S., La. Acad. Sci.; mem. Am. Chem. Soc., Sigma Xi, Phi Lambda Upsilon, Kappa Sigma. Democrat. Presbyterian. Clubs: Harvard of Louisiana (New Orleans); Faculty (La. State U.). Contbr. articles to professional jours. Holder patents on macrocyclic musk compounds, U.S., British and Canadian; research in organic chemistry dealing with synthesis, mechanism of reactions and natural products. Home: Baton Rouge LA Died Feb. 22, 1968; buried Graceland Cemetery, Lake Charles LA

ERLANGER, MILTON S., bus. exec.; b. Baltimore, Feb. 28, 1888; s. Charles and Rebecca (Strauss) E.; A.B., Johns Hopkins U., 1907; m. Alene Stern, June 1, 1914; children—Milton Charles, Alene Bricken, Sally, Jules, Frederick. Joined B.V.D. Co., now Erlanger Mills Corp., 1907, elected v.p., 1909, pres. 1929, chmn. bd. dirs. 1948-69; dir. N.C. Finishing Co., Salisbury, Erlanger Mills, Inc., Lexington, N.C. Trustee Hudson Guild, 1928-37, v.p. dir., Nat. Assn. of Shirt and Pajamas Mfrs. 1945, dir. 1946-48. Jewish religion. Mason (Shriner). Elk. Home: Oakhurst NJ Died July 1969.

ERNST, EDWIN CHARLES, radiologist; b. St. Louis, Mo., June 26, 1885; s. Charles W. and Catherine (Koche) E.; grad. Moravian Coll., Bethlehem, Pa., 1905; student St. Louis U., 1906-09; M.D., Washington U., St. Louis, 1912; m. Mildred V. Vogt, Aug. 2, 1916; children—Edwin C., Roland, Richard. Began practice at St. Louis, 1912. Commd. maj. Med. R.C., Apr. 15, 1917; served in Base Hosp. 21, France, 1917-18; dir. x-ray dept. and radiologist of the De Paul Hosp., St. Louis; radiologist St. Joseph Hospital, Kirkwood, Mo. President board of dirs. of Beaumont Medical Building. Awarded gold medal of Radiol. Soc. of North America for researches in X-ray unit measurement; the highest IX Internat. Congress Radiology Scientific award, 1959; citation German Roentgen Society of Munic, 1959. Mem. A.M.A., A.C.P., Am. Roentgen Ray Soc., Chgo. Roentgen Soc., Radiol. Soc. of N. America (ex-pres.), Am. Coll. of Radiology, (past pres.), Am. Radium Soc. (past pres.), Radiological Research Inst., Inc. (past pres.), Am. College of Radiology (past pres.), Am. Cancer Soc. (past pres. Mo. div.), Southern Medical Association (2d vice president), Phi Beta Pi. Republican. Protestant. Clubs: University, Mo. Athletic (pres. 1956-57), Algonquin Country. Contbr. to Am. Roentgen Ray Jour. Research in cancer, radiology. Home: Kirkwood MO Died Mar. 1969; buried Sunset Burial Park.

ERNSTENE, ARTHUR CARLTON, physician; b. Parker, S.D., Aug. 4, 1901; s. Edwin Carl and Alice (Goddard) E.; A.B., State U. Ia., 1922, M.D., 1925; D.Sc. (hon.), John Carroll U., 1959, Baldwin-Wallace Coll., 1964; m. Beatrice McGarvey, June 25, 1925 (dec. 1925); 1 son, Marshall Paul; m. 2d, Audra N. Miller, Nov. 20, 1954. Intern Henry Ford Hosp., Detroit, 1925-26; asst. resident Thorndike Meml. Lab., Boston City Hosp., 1926-27, resident 1927-28; research asso. Beth Israel Hosp., Boston, 1928-32; asst. in medicine Harvard, 1927-30, instr., 1930-32; head dept. cardiovascular disease Cleve. Clinic, 1932-48, chmn. div. medicine, 1948-66. Served as lt. comdr. M.C., USNR, 1942-44; chief of medicine, hosps. at Auckland, New Zealand, Espiritu Santo, New Hebrides. Bd. lay trustees John Carroll U. Recipient Gold Heart award Am. Heart Assn., 1964. Diplomate Am. Bd. Internal Medicine (mem. sub-specialty bd. on cardiovascular disease 1956-61). Fellow A.C.P. (gov. Ohio 1957-63, regent 1963-69, pres. 1965-66), A.A.A.S.; mem. A.M.A. (sec. sect. internal medicine 1953-56, chmn. 1956-57), Am. Clin. and Climatol. Assn. (v.p. 1950), Am. Soc. for Clin. Investigation, Central Soc. Clin. Research, Assn. Am. Physicians, Am. (dir. 1953-63; chmn. sect. clin. cardiology 1952-54, pres. 1959-60),

Ohio State (founders group, 1st pres. 1950-52) heart assns., Cleve. Area Heart Soc. (founders group, 1st pres. 1949-51), Acad. of Medicine of Cleve. (sec.-treas. 1940-42, dir. 1946-49), Ohio State Med. Assn. (chmn. com. on sci. work 1951-59), Interurban Clin. Club Cleve. Med. Library Assn. (trustee), Phi Beta Kappa, Sigma Xi, Alpha Omega Alpha, Phi Kappa Psi, Nu Sigma Nu. Author: Coronary Heart Disease, 1948; also articles and papers in field. Home: Cleveland OH Died Mar. 3, 1971.

ERPF, ARMAND GROVER, investment banker; b. N.Y. City, Dec. 8, 1897; s. Bartholomew and Cornelia (von Greiner) E.; B.S., Columbia, 1917; L.H.D., Cath. U. Am., LL.D., Manhattan Coll.; m. Sue Stuart Mortimore, Apr. 7, 1965; children—Cornelia, Armand. Asst. sec. Suffern Co. of N.Y., and asst. mgr. Suffern Co. of Brazil, 1917-19; officer and part owner C.E. Erpf & Co., brokers, 1919-23; made survey of textile enterprise in Saxony, Germany, 1923-24; statistician, later officer, dir. and part owner Cornell, Linder & Co., Inc., N.Y. City, 1924-33; dir. statis. and research departments and subsequently, investment adv. department Loeb, Rhoades & Co., 1933-36, gen. partner, from 1936; chmn. exec. com., dir. Crowell Collier & Macmillan, Incorporated; chmn. Aneid Equities; member of bd. dirs. Adela Investment Co., S.A., Gen. Instrument Corp., Adela Investment Co., S.A., Macmillan Co., Jefferson Ins. Co., Chris-Craft Industries, Inc., Dorr-Oliver, Inc., Jersey External Trust, Stein, Roe & Farnham Internat. Fund. Chmn. council Grad. Sch. of Bus., Columbia U.; chmn. bd. dirs. Arkville Erpf Fund; bd. govs. N.Y. Cultural Center; trustee Chamber Music Soc. Lincoln Center. Commd. 1t. col., U.S. Army, 1942; promoted col., 1944; apptd. to Gen. Staff Corps, 1944; assigned Office of Comdg. Gen. hdqrs. A.S.F., Washington, 1942-45; duty with hdqrs. U.S. Army Forces, Western Pacific, and with comdg. gen. USAF, China Theater, 1945-46. Awarded Legion of Merit. Mem. Council on Fgn. Relations, Inc., Affiliated Business Fellows of Columbia U., Whitney Mus. Am. Art (board of trustee), Victorian Soc., Athenaeum Phila. Delta Sigma Phi. Clubs: Art Collectors, Economic, Wall St. Home: New York City NY Died Feb. 2, 1971; buried Arkville NY

ERVINE, ST. JOHN GREER, author; b. Belfast, No. Ireland, Dec. 28, 1883; s. William and Sarah Jane Park (Greer) E.; student Westbourne Nat. Sch., Belfast, 1890-97; LL.D., St. Andrew's U.; Litt.D., Queen's U., Belfast; m. Leonora Mary Davis, July 15, 1911. Clk. ins. office, Belfast, 1897-1900, London, 1900-12; author plays, novels, from 1911; author: (plays) The Magnanimous Lover, Mixed Marriage, Jane Clegg, John Ferguson, Mary, Mary, Quite Contrary, Anthony and Anna, The Lade of Belmont, The First Mrs. Fraser, People of Our Class, Robert's Wife, Boyd's Shop, Esperanza, Friends and Relations, Private Enterprise, My Brother Tom, Charles and Mary, Progress, Old George Comes to Tea, She was No Lady; (books) Mrs. Martin's Man, 1911, Alice and a Family, Changing Winds, The Wayward Man, The First Mrs. Fraser, Sophia, The Mountain and other Stories, If I were Dictator, Some Impressions of My Elders, A Journey to Jerusalem; The Organized Theatre, How to Write a Play, The Theatre in My Time; (biographies) Parnell, God's Soldier, General William Booth; Craigavon, Ulsterman, Bernard Shaw: His Life, Work and Friends; Oscar Wilde, A Present Time Appraisal; The Wonderful Visit. Served as private later officer Royal Dublin Fusilers, World War I. Mem. Society Authors (Britain, America). Home: Seaton Devon Eng Died Feb. 1971.

ERWAY, RICHARD EUGENE, lawyer; born in Newfield, N.Y., Oct. 15, 1907; s. James Daniel and Harriet (Brown) E.; A.B., U. Mich., 1928; LL.B., Harvard, 1937; m. Lucile Storch, Nov. 16, 1930; 1 dau., Elizabeth Bishop (Mrs. Robert R. Cook). Asst. to chmn. dept. math. U. Mich., 1927-28; life ins. actuary, 1928-34; admitted to N.Y. bar, 1938; investment atty. Met. Life Ins. Co., N.Y.C., 1937-39, 40-45; sec. Acacia Mut. Life Ins. Co., Washington, 1939-40; with law firm Wickes, Riddell, Bloomer, Jacobi & McGuire, N.Y.C., 1945-51; with Equitable Life Assurance Soc. U.S., N.Y.C., 1951-71, v.p., asso. gen. solicitor, 1961-67, vice president, general solicitor, 1967-69, sr. v.p., gen. counsel, 1969-71. Chmn. Greater N.Y.C. com. Harvard Law Sch. Fund, 1970-71. Mem. Am. N.Y. State bar assns., Assn. Bar City N.Y. (chmn. com. ins. law 1963-66), Maritime Law Assn. U.S., Am. Soc. Internat. Law Assn. Life Ins. Counsel, Soc. Actuaries, Am. Soc. C.L.U.'s Phi Beta Kappa Assos. (sec., dir.), Am. Arbitration Assn. (dir.), John Burroughs Meml. Assn. (dir. Phi Beta Kappa, Phi Kappa Phi. Clubs: University (N.Y.C.); Manhasset Bay (L.I.) Yacht. Author: New York Law Relating to Investment of Life Insurance Companies, 1962. Home: New York City NY Died June 1, 1971.

ERWIN, CLAUDE MAYO, lawyer; b. Newport, Ark., Aug. 31, 1906; s. Claude Mayo and Elizabeth (Watson) E.; student Hendrix Coll., 1924-25, U. Ark., 1925-27; grad. Ark. Law Sch., 1931; m. Mildred Sloan, June 24, 1936; children—Claude Mayo III, Harold Sloan. Admitted to Ark. bar, 1930; practice in Newport, 1932-72; pros. atty. 3d Jud. Circuit Ark., 1937-40; county and juvenile judge Jackson County, 1944; city atty., Newport, 1961-63. Pres. Erwin, Inc., Ozark Corp.; dir. Zenith Seed Co., Inc. Pres. Newport Pub. Library Assn.; trustee Remmel Playground Park Assn. Mem. Am., Ark., Newport (past pres.), 8th Chancery (past pres.) bar assns., Am. Trial Lawyers Assn., Sigma Nu. Democrat. Methodist. Mason (K.T.). Home: Newport AR Died Aug. 26, 1972; buried Walnut Grove Cemetery, Newport AR

ERWIN, HOWELL COBB, lawyer; b. Athens, Ga., Dec. 19, 1876; s. Alexander Smith and Mary Ann Lamar (Cobb) E.; A.B., U. of Ga., 1897; B.L., U. of Georgia Law Sch., 1898; married Lucy Grattan Yancey, October 24, 1911; children—Lucy Deupree (deceased), Mary Lamar (Mrs. John Q. West, Jr.), Howell Cobb, Goodloe Yancey. Admitted to Georgia bar, 1898; asso. with father in practice of law, 1898-1907; mem. Cobb & Erwin, 1907-16, Erwin, Erwin & Nix, 1917-36; county atty. Clarke County, 1900-06; now retired from active practice. Dir. Southern Mut. Ins. Co.; trustee Oconee Hill Cemetery. Trustee and chmn. Prudential Com., Univ. of Ga., 1924-32; trustee Lucy Cobb Inst.; trustee Athens Y.M.C.A. Chmn. Dem. Exec. Com. of Clarke County, for eight yrs. Mem. Ga. State and Athens bar assns., Soc. of Colonial Wars, Sigma Alpha Epsilon. Democrat. Baptist (deacon Athens Ch.). Mason. Club: Athens Country. Home: 194 Dearing St., Athens GA‡

ESAREY, LOGAN, prof. history; b. Branchville, Ind., Jan. 3, 1873; s. John Clark and Barbara (Ewing) E.; A.B., Ind. U., 1905, A.M., 1908, Ph.D., 1913; m. Laura Pearson, of Danville, Ind., May 20, 1897; children—Mary Logan, Myra, Ralph Emerson, Rosalie, Robin Adair. County supt. schs., Perry Co., Ind., 1897-1903; prin. high sch., Vincennes, 1907-09; dean Winona (Ind.) Coll., 1909-12; mem. faculty, Ind. U., since 1912. Has specialized in history of Ind. and in development of the West; in charge research work in the Hist. Sem. of the Univ.; sec. Ind. Hist. Survey. Mem. Am. Hist. Assn., Miss. Valley Hist. Assn., Ind. Hist. Soc., Acacia. Republican. Methodist. Mason, Odd Fellow. Rotarian. Author: History of Indiana, 1918; Courts and Lawyers of Indiana. Compiler: Letters and Papers of William Henry Harrison; Messages of Indiana Govenors. Home: 340 S. Henderson St., Bloomington IN‡

ESHELMAN, WALTER WITMER, educator; b. Elizabethtown, Pa., Aug. 7, 1908; s. John W. and Amanda F. (Witmer) E.; B.A., Elizabethtown Coll., 1930, Ped.D. (hon.), 1959; Ed.D., N.Y.U., 1941; LL.B., Blackstone Inst., Chgo., 1931; A.M., Columbia, 1933; m. Mary W. Minnich, Dec. 26, 1931; 1 dau., Donna Faye. Tchr., then prin. Shohola (Pa.) Consol. Schs., 1930-36; supervising prin. W. Pottegrove Twp. Schs., Stowe, Pa., 1936-45, Upper Dublin schs., Ft. Washington, Pa., from 1945. Chmn. U.S. delegation World Confedn. Orgns. Teaching Profession, Amsterdam, Holland, 1960. Sec. Pottstown (Pa.) Civil Def. Council, 1940-45. Mem. adv. com. USAF Recruiting Service. Recipient Merit award N.Y.U., 1960. Mem. Nat. (pres. 1959-60, chmn. com. resolutions 1956), Pa. (pres. S.E. dist. 1956-58), Montgomery County (pres. 1945-46) edn. assns., Am. Assn. Sch. Adminstrs. (yearbook com. 1957), Phi Delta Kappa. Republican. Mason. Kiwanian (lt. gov. Pa. 1944-45). Home: Ambler PA Died May 25, 1971.

ESHKOL (SHKOLNIK) LEVI, prime minister, minister of defense Israel; b. 1895; ed. Hebrew Gymnasium Vilna, Poland; m. Miriam Zelikovitz, in 1964. Emigrated to Palestine, 1913. Agrl. worker various settlements; mem. Jewish Legion, 1918-20; agrl. worker a founder Degania B settlement; elected Rep. of Assembly of Palestine Jewry, del. 12th and following Zionist Congress, chmn. settlement com. various congresses; at times sec. Tel-Aviv Jaffa Workers' Council and sec. Mapai (Workers' Party); mem. Exec. Nat. Workers' Fed. (Histadruth); emissary Histadruth to Lithuania, other countries, also to Socialist Internat.; dir. agrl. settlement sect. Palestine Office, Berlin, during Nazi regime; with Hehalutz movement, Germany and Lithuania; participated in adminstrn. transfer German-Jewish property to Palestine, and in founding and directing Nir and Mekoroth Shikun and Amidar cos.; participated Hehalutz and Ihud Olami confs., U.S.; mem. Exec. Jewish Agy., head Agrl. Settlement Dept., acting treas.; active Haganah from its foundation; formerly dir. ministry of security State of Israel; minister agr., 1951-52, minister finance from 1952-63; minister of def. of Israel, 1963-67, prime minister, 1963-69. Address: Jerusalem Israel Died Feb. 26, 1969; buried Jerusalem Israel

ESKEW, SAMUEL W(ILLIAMS), certified pub. acct., lawyer; b. Bardstown, Ky., Jan. 24, 1889; s. Winfield S. and Sallie (Williams) E.; student bus. coll.; m. Diana Yager, Jan. 22, 1925; children—Estill Lewis, Samuel Williams (dec.). Admitted to Ky. bar, 1912; practice of law, Bardstown, Ky., 1912-17; accountancy, Louisville, from 1920; mem. Eskew, Gresham & Diersen from 1949; pub. acct. from 1920. Mem. Am. Inst. Accts. (v.p. 1952-53), Ky. Soc. C.P.A.'s, Ky. State Bar Assn., Nat. Assn. Cost Accts. Presbyn. Clubs: Louisville Country, Pendennis. Home: Louisville KY Died Nov. 10, 1968.

ESPIL, FELIPE A., diplomat; b. Buenos Aires, Argentina, May 12, 1887; LL.B., U. of Buenos Aires, 1910, LL.D., 1914; m. Courtney Letts Borden, July, 1933. Practiced law in Argentina; apptd. 1st sec. of Embassy, Washington, 1919, counselor, 1920; M.P. to Holland, 1928, to Denmark and Norway, 1929; A.E. and P. to U.S. from 1931. Address: Argentine Embassy Washington DC Died Jan. 23, 1972; buried Buenos Aires, Argentina

ESPINOSA Y SAN MARTIN, ANTONIO, Spanish Diplomate; b. Madrid, Spain, Mar. 26, 1908; s. Gabriel E. and Isabel (San Martin) Espinosa; ed. U. Madrid. Tchr. comml. coll., Spain; joined Spanish fgn. service dept., advancing from vice-consul to sec. Spanish embassies Europe and Washington, 1935-53, spl. consul at Los Angeles, 1953-56, 2d chief protocol in fgn. ministry, 1956-58, consul-gen., 1958-68; presently assigned to N.Y.C.; cultural consellor, Washington, 1960-68; minister plenipotentiary, 1961-68. Spl. del. League of Nations, Geneva, Switzerland, 1936; in charge of Spanish negotiations, Caracas, Venezuela, 1945-50; spl. del. conf. UN, 1959; lectr. hist. topics, Madrid schs., N.Y.U. Created comdr. orders of Civil Merit, Cards III, Isabel la Catolica (Spain); Order of the Liberator (Venezuela); other orders Lebanon, Iran. Club: Chevy Chase (Md.). Address: New York City NY Died Oct. 1968.

ESPOSITO, VINCENT JOSEPH, army officer, educator; b. New York, Apr. 29, 1900; B.S., U.S. Mil. Acad., 1925; Engrs. Sch., civil engr. course (B.S. in M.E., Mass. Inst. Tech.), 1939, company officer course, 1930, Command and Gen. Staff Sch., 1939, Armed Forces Staff College; Industrial College of the Armed Forces, National War College, 1943-47; m. Eleanor Vinyard; children—Vincent Joseph, Michael, Curtis. Entered U.S. Army, as pvt., 1918, advanced through the grades to brig. gen., 1945; War Dept. Gen. Staff, 1943-46; mem. faculty Nat. War Coll., 1946-47; prof. mil. art and engring., U.S. Mil. Acad., from 1947, head dept. mil. art and engring., from 1956. Mem. Sec. Army Hist. Adv. Com., from 1956. Trustee Am. Mil. Inst., from 1957. Address: West Point NY Died June 10, 1965.

ESQUIROL, JOHN HENRY, bishop; b. Bklyn., May 18, 1900; s. Joseph Henry and Grace Ella (Alfred) E.; B.S., N.Y.U., 1920, J.D., 1923, D.D., 1960; postgrad. Gen. Theol. Sem., N.Y.C., 1937; S.T.D., Berkeley Div. Sch., New Haven, 1954; D.D., Trinity Coll., Hartford, Conn., 1959; m. Margaret Louise Joost, Apr. 28, 1927; children—John Henry, Howard. Admitted to N.Y. bar, 1924; practice in Bklyn., 1924-37; ordained priest Episcopal Ch., 1937; asst. to dean Cathedral of Incarnation, Garden City, L.I., N.Y., 1937-39; rector Trinity Ch., Southport, Conn., 1939-56; dean Christ Ch. Cathedral, Hartford, 1956-58; suffragan bishop Diocese Conn., Hartford, 1958-68, bishop coadjutor, 1968-69, diocesan bishop, 1969-70; lectr. ecclesiastical polity, canon law Berkeley Div. Sch., 1951-59, trustee, from 1953. Served with U.S. Army, 1918. Recipient Presidential citation N.Y. U., 1959. Mem. Psi Hartford CT Died Dec. 31, 1970; buried Oaklawn Cemetery, Fairfield CT

ESSER, SIGURD EMANUEL, ednl. cons.; born Scandinavia, Wis., July 3, 1903; s. Nels N. and Elida B. (Johnson) E.; B.A., Concordia Coll., 1925; M.S., N.D. U., 1933; grad. student, U. Minn., Stanford; m. Keziah L. Evingson, Dec. 22, 1933; 1 dau., Elisabeth K. Prin. Kindred (N.D.) High Sch., 1925-27, supt. schs., 1927-32; emergency agrl. asst. Dept. Agr., 1933; tchr. Balboa (C.Z.) High Sch., 1933-38, counselor, asst. prin., 1938-41, prin., 1941-47; dir. research C.Z. schs., 1947-48, dir. secondary edn., 1948-53, supt. schs., and chief state sch. officer 1953-64; educational consultant, from 1964. Chairman C.Z. Administration Intern Selection Com.; mem. selection bds. West Point, Annapolis, Air Force Acad. Bd. dirs. C.Z. Tb. Assn., C.Z.A.R.C. Served as 1st lt. Minn. N.G., 1927-33; mem. U.S. Army Res., 1927-41. Recipient Cruz de la Fundacion Internacional Elay Alfaro, 1961; Distinguished Service awards Panama Canal, 1963, Spl. Edn. Assn., 1963; named mem. Esteemed Order Bearers of Master Key to Panama Canal in grade of hon. aide to gov., 1963. Mem. N.E.A., American Assn. School Administrs., Council Chief State Sch. Officers, Mondamin Soc., Phi Delta Kappa, Phi Theta Kappa. Lutheran. Home: Ft Lauderdale FL Died Feb. 11, 1972; buried Kindred ND

ESSIG, BENJAMIN C(LARK), mfg. exec.; b. Elsie, Mich., Feb. 5, 1892; s. Fred William and Mary Ella (Clark) C.; E.M., Colo. Sch. Mines, 1915; m. Ethlyn Willett, June 16, 1915. Engaged in mining operations, 1915-23; with Gardner-Denver Co., Quincy, Ill., from 1923; dir. U.S. Nat. Bank, Argo Oil Co. Mem. Kappa Sigma, Theta Tau, Tau Beta Pi. Home: Denver CO Died Mar. 24, 1972.

ESTABROOK, JOHN D., civ. eng'r; mem. Am. Inst. Mining Eng'rs; grad. Rensselaer Polytechnic Inst., Troy, N. Y., 1856; employed on Western ry., in city eng'rs' office, Boston, and on sea coast defenses of Mass. Bay.; eng'r of public parks and comm'r of highways, Phila.; supt. of parks, St. Paul, Minn.; sec. and eng'r

Union Depot Co., St. Paul, Minn., and sec. and eng'r of C. C. Washburn's Flouring Mills Co., Minneapolis. Address: Westboro MA‡

ESTENSON, LYLE OSBERN, educator, psychologist; b. Galesburg, N.D., Dec. 28, 1915; s. Emil and Esther (Paulson) E.; A.B. magna cum laude, Luther (Ia.) Coll., 1936; M.A., State U. Ia., 1942; Ph.D., U. Minn., 1951; m. Gladys Jo Olsen, Aug. 9, 1943; children—David L., Thomas L., Paul B., Joan E. Mgr. Ben Franklin Store, Estherville, Ia., 1937-38; high sch. tchr., Rosemount, Minn., 1939-40, Mt. Lake, Minn., 1940-41, Winona, Minn., 1941-42; asst. prof. edn. Purdue U., 1948-52; mem. faculty Carleton Coll., Northfield, Minn., 1952—, prof. psychology, from 1957, head tchr. edn., 1952, summer tchr. numerous univs., from 1950, cons. in field, from 1959. Mem. Minn. Adv. Com. Tchr. Edn., 1952, exec. vice chmn., 1957-58. Chmn. Northfield chpt. A.R.C., 1963-66. Mem. Rice County Republican Com., 1966-67. Served with AUS, 1942-45. Mem. Am. Coll. Personnel Assn. (chmn. profl. standards com. 1954-55), Am. Personnel and Guidance Assn., Am., Minn. psychol. assns., Assn. Higher Edn., Nat. Minn. edn. assns., Nat. Soc. Coll. Tchr. Edn., Nat. Vocation Guidance Assn., Student Personnel Assn. Tchr. Edn. Lutheran. Lion. Home: Northfield MN Died Nov. 29, 1969.

ESTEP, PRESTON, ins. co. exec.; b. nr. Branson, Mo., July 16, 1914; s. Dillard J. and Florence (Keithley) E.; LL.B., U. Mo., 1938; student U. Wis.; m. Lucy Maude Berry, Dec. 20, 1936; children—Preston II, David Berry, Stephen Keithley, Philip Dillard, Sallie Anne. Prin. grade sch., Stotts City, Mo., 1934; admitted to Mo. bar, practiced law, 1938-41; asst. to pres. Nat. Rivers and Harbors Congress, Washington, 1938-41; chief counsel Mo. Div. Ins., 1942-45; gen. counsel Transit Casualty Co., St. Louis, 1945-48, v.p., gen. counsel, 1948-51, exec. v.p., 1951-52, pres., from 1952, then chmn., also dir.; pres., dir. Beneficial Fire & Casualty Ins. Co., Selective Ins. Co.; chmn. bd. Comml. Bank of St. Louis County, Gen. Bancshares Corp., Lindbergh Bank, Bank of St. Louis; dir. Beneficial Standard Life Ins. Co., Baden Bank, Comml. & Indsl. Bank, Memphis, Ill. State Bank, Quincy, Gen. Am. Life Ins. Co., Jefferson-Gravois Bank of St. Louis, Northwestern Bank & Trust' Co., St. Louis, St. Louis Nat. Baseball Club; advisory bd. Bank of Benton (Ill.), Bank of Zeigler. Member executive com., treas. United Fund of Greater St. Louis, Urban Redevelopment Corp. of St. Louis. Dir. Jr. Achievement of Mississippi Valley, Inc., St. Louis and St. Louis County chpt. Nat. Found. Infantile Paralysis, Inc. Mem. Nat. Assn. Independent Insurers (dir., gov. Chgo.), St. Louis C. of C., Municipal Theatre Assn., Newcomen Soc. N.Am., St. Louis Advt. Club, Downtown in St. Louis Inc., Am., Mo., St. Louis bar assns. Clubs: Media; Marco Polo (N.Y.C.); Missouri Athletic, Old Warson Country (St. Louis). Home: St Louis County MO Died Feb. 1, 1970.

ESTERLY, HENRY MINOR, retired lawyer; b. Dodgeville, Iowa County, Wis., Oct. 20, 1873; s. Francis Powell and Julia Bacon (Minor) E.; B.L., U. of Wis., 1900, LL.B., 1902; m. Elizabeth Norcross, Dec. 30, 1908; children—Henry Norcross, Louise Jackson. Began practice at Madison, Wis., 1902; removed to Portland, Ore.; dep. dist. atty. Multnomah County, Ore., in charge Juvenile Court prosecutions, 1908; mem. Exec. Bd., City of Portland, 1908-09; apptd. by Gov. West, commr. Port of Portland, 1911 (law later held unconstitutional); spl. prosecutor, State of Ore., 1912; elected mem. Dem. Nat. Com., 1914. Pres. Portland Housing Assn.; dir. Portland Municipal Assn.; chmn. Com. of 21 apptd. by mayor of Portland to revise housing code, 1928. Mem. Music Edn. Assn. (pres.), Peace League of Ore. (pres.), Am. Civil Liberties Union (pres. Oregon Chapter, 1932). Home: Route 8, Box 1224, Portland OR‡

ESTERQUEST, RALPH THEODORE, librarian; b. Chicago, May 6, 1912; s. Frank A. and Julia (Sandberg) E.; B.S., Northwestern, 1933; grad. study Columbia, 1933-34; B.S. in library sci., U. Ill., 1936, M.A., 1940; m. Dorothy Elizabeth Watson, Aug. 15, 1936; children—Shelley, Peter. Field fellowship Lab. Anthropology, Santa Fe, N.M., summer 1934; reference librarian Northwestern, 1936-37; order librarian U. Ill., 1937-40; asst. librarian Inst. Advanced Study, Princeton, 1940-42; sales mgr. A.L.A., 1942-43; dir. Pacific N.W. Bibliographic Center, Seattle, 1943-46; chief preparations div., prof. U. Denver Libraries, 1947-48, asst. dir., 1948-49; dir. Midwest Inter-Library Center, 1949-58, sec., 1954-58; librarian Harvard Med. Library, 1958-65, Francis A. Courtway Library of Medicine (Harvard and Boston Medical Libraries), 1965-67; dir. internat. relations office A.L.A., 1967-68. Fulbright research fellow, Eng., 1953-54. Cons. University of IFE, Nigeria. Mem. jury of award Internat. Archit. Competition for Trinity Coll. Library, Dublin, Ireland, 1961. Member Am. (council 1947-51), Mountain-Plains (pres. 1948-49), Ill. (director), med. library assns., Special Libraries Assn. Club: Harvard (Boston). Contbr. profl. jours. Home: Brookline MA Died Aug. 10, 1968.

ESTES, GEORGE HENSON, army officer (retired); b. Eufaula, Ala., Jan. 30, 1873; s. George H. and Anna (Thornton) E.; student U. of Ga.; grad. U.S. Mil. Acad., 1894, Gen. Staff Sch., 1920, Army War Coll., 1921; m. Frances Farrell, January 4, 1899; children—Henson F., Frances (Mrs. Claude D. Collins). Commd. 2d lt., inf., U.S. Army June 12, 1894, advanced through grades to col., July 1, 1920; insp. gen., U.S. Army, 1921-25, brig. gen., Jan. 2, 1929. Mem. Gen. Staff War Dept., 1921-25; comdt. U.S. Inf. Sch., Ft. Benning, Ga., 1933-37; retired from active duty, Jan. 1, 1937. War Dept. citations for conduct in action. Baptist. Club: Army and Navy (Washington). Address: 124 Bay Haven, Clearwater FL‡

ETHEREDGE, M(AHION) P(ADGETT), chemist; born near Saluda, S.C., Sept. 27, 1897; s. Joseph Wolfe and Julia Ella (Padgett) E.; B.S., Clemson Coll., 1918; M.S., Miss. State Coll., 1940; Ph.D., Mass. Inst. Tech., 1945; m. Lucile Davis, Sept. 30, 1926; children—Sarah, Dot. Asst. chemist Miss. State Chem. Lab., 1918-23, asst. state chemist of Miss., 1923-45, state chemist from 1945; instr. Miss. State College, 1935-45, head, department of chemistry 1945-63, dean of school of arts and sciences, 1951-63, prof. chemistry and state chemist, 1963-67. Member Council of Oak Ridge Institute for Nuclear Studies, 1949-64. Member board dirs. Miss. Agrl. Indsl. Bd., 1945-67. Attended Officers Training Camp, World War I; War Dept. Civilian Gas Sch., World War II. Awarded 6 Cups for Miss. State Chem. Lab. from Am. Oil Chemists Soc., 1926-39, resulting in a grant-in-aid from Gen. Edn. Bd., 1943-45. Recipient Herty Medal, American Chem. Soc., 1956; Honor Scroll, La. chpt. Am. Inst. Chemists, 1962. Fellow A.A.A.S. (council 1952-54). mem. Am. Chem. Soc. (chairman Mississippi section), American Oil Chemists Society, Association Am. Feed Control Ofcls. (past pres.), Assn. Ofcls. Agr. Chemists (pres. 1957), Assn. Am. Fertilizer Control Ofcls. (pres. 1956), Food and Drug Ofcls. U.S.A., So. Assn. Sci., Industry (past pres.), Newcomen Soc., So. Feed and Fertilizer Control Ofcls. (pres. 1956), Food and Drug Ofcls. S. Central States (past pres.), N.E.A., Internat. Platform Assn., Alpha Chi Sigma, Alpha Epsilon Delta, Phi Kappa Phi, Omicron Delta Kappa. Baptist. Mason (32 deg., Shriner). Contbr. articles to profl. jours. Home: Starkville MS Died July 12, 1971; buried Memorial Gardens, Starkville MS

ETHRIDGE, WILLAIM NATHANIEL, JR., judge; b. Columbus, Miss., Aug. 3, 1912; s. William N. and Laura Mae (Ramage) E.; student Miss. State Coll., 1931-32; A.B., U. Miss., 1935, LL.B., 1937; LL.M., U. So. Cal., 1940; m. Lura Elizabeth Clark, Dec. 14, 1946; children—William Nathaniel, 4th, David, Paul, Ruby, Thomas. V.p., sec. Okolona, Houston & Calhoun City Ry. Co., Houston, Miss., 1935-39; admitted to Miss. bar, 1937, practiced in Oxford, 1937-42; asso. Wells, Wells, Newman & Thomas, Jackson, Miss., 1944-48; asst. prof. law U. Miss., 1942-44, prof., 1948-50; commr. Supreme Ct. Miss., 1950-52, associate justice, 1952-65, presiding justice, 1965, chief justice, 1966—; mem. State-Federal Relations adv. com. Fed. Judicial Center, 1969. Mem. Freedoms Found. Awards Jury, 1956; pres. Goodwill Industries of Miss., 1956. Mem. Am. (nat. dir. procedural reform studies 1943-47), Lafayette Co. bar assns., Miss. State Bar (chmn. jr. sect. 1946-47), American Judicature Society, Inst. Jud. Adminstrn., Am. Law Inst., Phi Delta Phi, Omicron Delta Kappa, Presbyn. Author: Modernizing Mississippi's Constitution, 1949. Contbr. articles law, tax jours. Home: Oxford MS Died July 29, 1971; buried Oxford (Miss.) Meml. Cemetery.

ETS-HOKIN, LOUIS, engring. co. exec.; b. Chgo., July 28, 1893;s. Samuel and Esther (Simon) Ets-H.; A.B., Cornell U., 1915, M.E., 1917; m. Rose Hartman, June 19, 1921; children—Jeremy M., Esther Naomi (Mrs. Robert S. Leuter). Pres. Ets-Hokin Corp., and prececessor, San Francisco, 1920-59, chmn. bd., 1959-71; chmn. bd. Murphy-Pacific Co., 1963-71, Tech. Constrn. Co., 1962-71; also Murphy Pacific Marine Salvage Company. Pres. Assn. Boat Industries, 1946-49, San Francisco Marine Exchange, 1954-56, Western Shipbldg. Assn., 1959-61; environmental engineer Civil Defense, 1968-71; chmn. Gov. Cal. Com. Shipbldg., 1953-58; mem. San Francisco Bay Conservation and Development Commn., 1965-71. Member board directors San Francisco Federation Jewish Charities, 1950-53; pres. San Francisco Maritime Mus. 1955-57; adv. bd. San Francisco Bay Transp. Study. Served with U.S. San Francisco CA Died Aug. 10, 1971.

ETTINGER, RICHARD PRENTICE, publisher; b. New York, N.Y., Sept. 26, 1893; s. Joseph and Marion Prentice (McSorley) E.; LL.B., New York Law Sch., 1913; B.C.S., New York University, 1915; LL.D., John Marshall Coll., Oct. 1947; LL.D., Hobart and William Smith Colls., 1966; m. Elsie Davis, June 30, 1915; children—Virginia Prentice (Mrs. Paul Revere Andrews), Elaine Prentice (Mrs. John G. Powers), Richard Prentice. Began as law clk., 1911; admitted to New York bar, 1915; dir. of efficiency bureau, New York U., 1913-15, instr., later asst. prof. finance, 1915-22; co-founder and pres. of Prentice-Hall, Inc., 1913-49, chairman board, 1949-71; chmn. bd. Inst. for Bus. Planning, Inc. Dir. Def. Orientation Conf. Assn. of U.S. Dept. of Def.; bd. trustees N.Y.U. Recipient Horatio Alger award, 1961; hon. award Beta Gamma Sigma, 1963. Mem. N.Y. Execs. Assn. (pres. 1936-39), N.Y.U. Alumni Fedn. (dir. 1956). Gamma Sigma. Episcopalian. Clubs: Shorehaven (South Norwalk, Conn.); La Gorce Country (Miami Beach, Florida). Author: Income and Federal Tax Reports, 1918; Credits and Collections (with David Golieb), 1917; Corporation South Norwalk CT Died Mar. 1971.

EUSDEN, RAY ANDERSON, clergyman; b. Marne, Ia., Aug. 25, 1889; s. Harry John and Anne Spence (Bonner) E.; student Taber (Ia.) Coll., 1908-11; B.A., Grinnell Coll., 1912; B.D., cum laude, Yale, 1915; M.A., U. of Chicago, 1916; studied Kings Coll., London, Eng., 1919; D.D., Grinnell, 1931; m. Marie Anna Dykstra, Jan. 29, 1921; children—John Dykstra, Ray Anderson, Jr., David Bonner. Prof. philosophy, Kingfisher (Okla.) Coll., 1917-18; ordained Congl. ministry, 1920; minister Plymouth Ch., Lawrence, Kan., 1920-26, Eliot Ch., Newton, Mass., 1926-59, minister emeritus, 1960-71; pastor of the International Pulpit Exchange between Montreal and Boston, 1937. Served with United States Dept. of Pub. Information, 1918; with 13th Regt., U.S. Marine Corps in France, 1918-19. Recipient Alumni award Grinnell College, 1967. Member Nat. Council Com. on Missions, 1921-26; mem. bd. dirs. Congl. Conf. of Kan., 1922-26; pres. Newton Minister's Assn., 1936-37. Mem. bd. mgrs. Boston City Missionary Soc.; mem. Suffolk West Assn. of Congl. Chs.; mem. Nat. Commn. on Evangelism and Devotional Life of Congl. and Christian Chs., 1929-39; mem. Soc. for Propagation of Gospel among the Indians and Others in North America; member advisory council Euthanasia Society of America; advisor to Congl. Bd. of Pastoral Supply; mem. bd. of dirs. Mass. Council of Churches; permanent sec. Class of 1915, Yale Div. Sch. Mem. Am. Legion. Mason, Rotarian. Clubs: Congregational, Monday, Iowa (Boston); Eight O'Clock, Hunnewell (Newton). Contbr. to relig. and ch. periodicals. Home: West Newton MA Died Nov. 20, 1971; buried Newton Cemetery.

EUSTIS, AUGUSTUS HEMENWAY, chem. co. exec.; b. Milton, Mass., Oct. 7, 1877; s. W.E.C. and Edith (Hemenway) E.; A.B., Harvard, 1901, A.M., 1902; m. Elizabeth Bowditch, Oct. 30, 1923 (dec. 1957); children—Elizabeth Bowditch (Mrs. Russell Williamson), Margaret Swann (Mrs. E. Peirson Richardson), Frederic Augustus II. Dir. Eustis Mining Co., Sherbrook, Que., Can., 1910-38, pres., 1932-44; v.p., dir. Va. Smelting Co., W. Norfolk, 1909-32, pres., dir., 1932-57, chmn. bd., 1957-61; chmn. bd. Va. Chems. & Smelting Co., (name changed to Virginia Chemicals, Inc., 1965), Boston, 1961-66, honorary chairman board, 1966-69. Member American Institute Mining, Metallurgical and Petroleum Engineers, American Society Refrigeration Engrs. Clubs: Union (Boston); Harvard (Boston and N.Y.C.). Home: Milton MA Died Jan. 8, 1969.

EUSTIS, FREDERIC AUGUSTUS, metallurgical engr.; b. Milton, Mass., Oct. 7, 1877; s. William Ellery Channing and Edith (Hemenway) E.; A.B., Harvard, 1901, A.M., 1902, S.M., 1903, Sc.D., 1915; studied Mass. Inst. Tech.; m. Edith Tileston, Sept. 15, 1908 (died June 28, 1927); m. 2d, Muriel B. Churchill, Sept. 20, 1937. Secretary and treasurer Virginia Smelting Co.; director Penobscott Chemical Fibre Co., Spl. agt. U.S. Shipping Board, from Feb. 1917-Feb. 1919. Republican. Unitarian. Clubs: Union, Brookline Country, Milton-Hoosic-Whesick, Beverly Yacht (all of Mass.); Harvard, Century (New York). Home: 1452 Canton Av., Milton, Mass. Office: 131 State St., Boston, Mass.; and 270 Madison Av., New York NY‡

EUWER, ANTHONY HENDERSON, illustrator; b. Allegheny Pa., Feb. 11, 1877; s. Anthony Henderson and Virginia (Courtney) E.; grad. Shadyside Acad., Pittsburgh, 1894; student, Princton U., class of 1898; Art Students' League, New York, 1899-1901; studied also at New York Sch. of Expression and Am. Acad. Dramatic Arts; m. Ruby Page Ferguson, Oct. 27, 1920 (divorced); 1 son, Anthony; m. 2d, Ida May Strong, 1935. Illustrated and wrote for Harper's Mag., Outing Mag., N.Y. Sun, Herald, World, American, Collier's, Leslie's, and Nat. Sunday Mag., etc.; lecturing and writing in Eng., 1911-12, illustrated articles in English publs. Republican. Presbyterian. Author: Rickety Rimes and Rigmaro, 1902; Christopher Cricket on Cats, 1907, 2d. edit., 1909; Rhymes of Our Valley, 1916, 2d edit., 1917; The Limeratomy (a limerick anatomy), 1917; Wings and Other War Rhymes, 1918; By Scarlet Torch and Blade, 1923; 2d edit., 1926, 3d, 1935; The Friendly Firs, 1931. Entertainer with A.E.F., 1918-19. Contbr. mag. page to Ore. Sunday Jour., 1922-25; lecturing since 1925. Illustrated articles on bookplates, 1926 Year Book of Am. Soc. of Bookplate Collectors and Designers. Broadcaster over radio under title of Philosopher of the Cross Roads," and Bard of the Air." Author of Woodrow Wilson's favorite limerick, My Face," the first line of which is As a beauty I'm not a great star." This was used as a rep. limerick under the word limerick" in the two latest editions of Webster's International Dictionary; has lectured at Hawaii, and Southern California. Club: Authors of Hollywood. Address: 1330 N. Harper Av., Hollywood 46 CA‡

EVANS, ALLAN, govt. official; b. London, Eng., July 2, 1903; s. Percy Charles and Mary Allan (Whitelaw) E.; came to U.S., 1916, naturalized, 1939; student Loomis Sch., 1918-20; A.B., Harvard, 1924, A.M., 1925, Ph.D., 1931; m. Marjorie Murphy, Sept. 17, 1946. Instr. German, Harvard, 1925-28, asst., instr., tutor history, 1927-38, senior tutor, Leverett House, 1931-37; asst. editor, Speculum, 1931-38; mem. permanent research staff, Huntington Library, 1939-42; field rep., exec. officer, chief, London office, Research and Analysis Branch, Office Strategic Services, 1942-46; dir., Office of Coordination and Liaison, State Dept., 1946-47; dir., Office of Intelligence Research, State Dept., 1947-59; spl. asst. to dir. Bur. Intelligence and Research, State Dept., 1959-61, deputy director of research, 1961-70. Awarded Medal for Freedom, 1946; Dept. of State Civil Servant of Yr., 1959, Distinguished Service award, 1964. Club: Cosmos (Washington). Author: Francesco Balducci Pegolotti (1936). Contbr. articles profl. jours. Home: Washington DC Died Aug. 22, 1970; cremated.

EVANS, EDWARD BENJAMIN, lawyer; b. St. Louis, Dec. 7, 1908; s. George Benjamin and Edith Ida (Rose) E.; M.E., U. Cin., 1931; LL.B., Chase Coll. Law, 1935, J.D., 1969; m. Marion Christine Bond, Oct. 28, 1932; children—Richard Henry, Barbara Jean (Mrs. Jerry K. Muir). Admitted to Ohio bar, 1935; since practiced in Cin., mem. firm Herron & Evans, 1941-71. Lectr. patent law U. Cin., 1955-62; trial counsel in patent litigation, 1948-71. Pres. Leland (Mich.) Vol. Fire Dept., 1967-71. Trustee Mercantile Library Assn. Mem. Am. Soc. M.E., Am. Arbitration Assn. (arbitrator 1967-71), Am. Patent Law Assn., Am., Cin. bar assns., Engring. Soc. Cin., Beta Theta Pi. Republican. Clubs: Queen City, Gyro (Cin.); Wyoming (O.) Golf; Leland (Mich.) Yacht (commodore 1958-65), Leland Country. Home: Cincinnati OH Died Sept. 15, 1971.

EVANS, FRED(ERIC) M(AURICE), lawyer; born Sparta, Wis., Jan. 20, 1895; s. John and Edith Ann (Evans) E.; grad. LaCrosse Normal Sch., 1923; A.B., University Wisconsin, 1925, LL.B., 1932; married to Eluned Davies, December 28, 1954; 1 daughter, Beti Sian. Admitted to the Wisconsin bar, 1932; teacher and coach, Williston, N.D., 1919-22; asst. dir. athletics U. Wis., 1925-31; law practice, Madison, Wis., 1932-41 and since 1950; judge Dane Co., 1941-50. Mem. Gov's. Commn. Human Rights, Wis., 1945-50, chmn., 1945-49; local chmn. Rep. Party, 1934-39, sec. Wis. state central com., 1936; dir. Red Cross (Madison), 1942-49; appeal agt. Selective Service U.S., 1942-47; chmn. War Manpower shows, 1944-45. Elected and installed Welsh bard, 1954. Served as supply officer, lt., Inf., U.S. Army, 1916-19. Mem. Madison Humane Soc. (dir. 1946), Family Welfare Assn. (dir. 1935-39), Am. Bar Assn., Am. Judicature Soc., Wis. Hist. Soc., Madison Business Association (bd. directors 1939-45), Disabled Am. Vets., Am. Legion (post comdr. 1937, 1958-61, judge adv., Wis. dept. 1939-41), 40 & 8 (grand adv. Wis., 1941-50), Ancient and Honorable Cymmrodorian Soc. (v.p.), Welsh Assn. of London, Clwb-Y Cymry (London), Wis. Gymanfa Ganu Assn. (dir.), Wisconsin Institute of Nationalities, Alpha Kappa Psi, Phi Alpha Delta, Phi Pi Phi fraternity (national vice president 1928-29). Elk, Mason (Shriner). Author articles on edn., human rights and legal subjects. Home: Madison WI

EVANS, H(ENRY) DAVID, head master; b. Windermere, Eng., Aug. 3, 1872; s. John David and Emily Isabella (Penny) E.; B.A., St. John's Coll. (Cambridge U.), 1894, M.A., 1896. Came to U.S., 1898; started out-door Ranch Sch., at Mesa, Ariz., 1902; moved to mountains 15 miles east of Tucson, 1921. Episcopalian. Address: Evans School, Tucson AZ‡

EVANS, JESSIE BENTON, artist; b. Uniontown, O., Mar. 24, 1866; d. Dr. Jacob and Amanda (Bowers) Steese; student Oberlin Coll., 1882; grad. Art Inst. of Chicago, 1904; married, Aug. 12, 1886; 1 son, Robert Thomas. Artist in painting oils and water colors. Exhibited Art Inst., Akron, O.; Woman's Club, Phoenix; Paris Salon, 1911, 1912; works permanently owned by Phoenix Country Club, Arizona Club and College Club (Chicago), Mesa Pub. Schools, Chicago Schools, Woman's Club, Akron, O., Woman's Club, Phoeniz, Ariz. Mem. D.A.R. Clubs: Phoenix Fine Arts, Salvator Rosa (Naples, Italy). Translated and illustrated Giulietta and Romeo (by Luigi da Porto), 1934. Home: Jokake AZ*‡

EVANS, JOHN FAIRHURST, lawyer; b. Paterson, N.J., Aug. 10, 1891; s. John William and Emily Ann (Wadsworth) E.; A.B. with distinction, Harvard, 1914; LL.B., Columbia, 1916; m. Mayrose Waterman, Sept. 9, 1918; 1 son, John F. Admitted to N.J. state bar, atty. 1916, counsellor-at-law, 1919; law practice, Paterson, 1916-70; mem. Evans, Hand, Evans, Allabogh & Amoresano, dir. Code Authority for Rayon and Silk Dyeing and Printing Industry, 1934; bd. dirs. N.J. Bank & Trust Co. Mem. bd. mgrs. Paterson Gen. Hosp. Police magistrate, Paterson, 1925-27; city counsel, 1940-46. Served as pvt. to 1st lt., U.S. Army, F.A., 1917-18. Mem. C. of C. Am. Bar Assn., Y.M.C.A. (trustee), Psi Upsilon. Republican. Baptist. Mason. Clubs: Hamilton, Arcola Country, Paramus, Harvard (N.Y.). Home: Glen Rock NJ Died Feb. 15, 1970.

EVANS, JOSEPH E(ARLY), journalist; b. Dubuque, Ia., Feb. 5, 1919; s. John D. and Ellen (Early) E.; student Loras Coll., 1935-37, U. So. Cal., 1937-38; A.B., State U. Ia., 1939, M.A., 1941; m. Marie Petrackova, Mar. 11, 1948; children—Christopher, Catherine, Elisabeth. Began as a grad. teaching assistant in English literature State Univ. of Ia., 1940-42; fgn. corr. Wall St. Jour., Berlin and Europe generally, 1946-49, editorial writer 1949-50, fgn. editor, 1950-51, chief Washington bur., 1952-53, asso. editor, 1953-65, sr. asso. editor, 1965-71, editor, editorial page, 1970-71. Served as technical sergeant with U.S. Army, 1942-45. Recipient Irving Babbitt Meml. prize, 1941; Silurian Soc. editorial writing award, 1956, 58, 65, 66, 67; Am. Artists Profl. League award, 1965; Freedoms Found. award, 1953, 65, 66. Mem. Nat. Conference Editorial Writers, Am. Soc. Newspaper Editors. Clubs: Overseas Press, National Press (Washington). Author chapt. in This Is Germany (Arthur Settel), 1950; Through Soviet Windows, 1957. Home: Pelham Manor NY Died Dec. 27, 1971; interred Huguenot Meml. Ch., Pelham Manor NY

EVANS, JOSHUA, JR., business cons.; b. Marblevale, Balt. Co., Md., Feb. 11, 1877; s. Joshua and May Boyle (Hepburn) E.; student George Washington U., 1906-07; grad. Am Inst. Banking; m. Jessie Wharton Fant, May 25, 1914; children—Joshua (dec.), Philip Wharton (capt. U.S.N.), Mariana Mears (Mrs. Robert Calhoun Creel). Entered banking bus. with Riggs National Bank, Washington, D.C., 1895, asst. cashier, 1907-15, cashier 1915-19, v.p., 1919-25; exec. v.p. and dir. Dist. Nat. Bank, Washington, 1925-30, pres. 1930-33; one of organizers of Hamilton Nat. Bank, 1933, v.p., 1933-51, retired, 1951, now business consultant; chairman advisory board of branches National Bank of Washington. In charge Liberty Loan dept. (organizer 5 campaigns) Riggs Nat. Bank, World War I, treas. Instructive Visiting Nurse soc.; mem. Washington Bd. of Trade (chmn. committee municipal finance 1924-34); trustee Better Bus. Bur., 1921-51, chmn. bd., 1924-32; ex-treas. Nat. Parks Association; an organizer Washington Community Chest (chmn. budget com. 1931, 1932 and 1933); past member of Com. of One Hundred on Federal City; mem. Republican State Com., D.C.; chmn. Com. on Legislation, Hoover-Curtis Inaugural Com.; charter mem. Am. Inst. Banking (Washington), and one of the first three national trustees to be chosen from the younger group of its membership (pres. Washington Chapter, 1911-12); mem. Reserve City Bankers Assn., Am. Bankers' Assn., 1919-51 (exec. council, 1924-26; admn. com., 1925-26) D.C. Bankers Assn. (pres. 1922-23); inaugurated D.C. Bankers' Weekly Luncheon, 1923; mem. Advisory Com. of Civic Development Dept. C. of C. of U.S., 1927. Episcopalian. Clubs: Metropolitan, Chevy Chase, Cosmos (Washington). Home: Washington DC Died Dec. 1970.

EVANS, MARSHALL BLAKEMORE, univ. prof.; b. Boston, Sept. 4, 1874; s. Marshall and Letitia (Blakemore) E.; B.A., Boston U., 1896; Ph.D., U. of Bonn, 1902; m. Elizabeth Theodora Grose, Aug. 18, 1910;children—Gwynne Blakemore, Grose. Began teaching U. of Wis., 1903; prof. German, Ohio State U., 1911-45, emeritus, dir. summer session, 1916-1920; visiting prof. Univ. of Chgo., summer, 1929; visiting lecturer Harvard University, 1945-46; visiting lecturer, Capital Univ. since 1946. Member Modern Lang. Assn. America, Am. Assn. Univ. Profs., Phi Beta Kappa, Beta Theta Pi. Episcopalian. Author: The High School Course in German (U. of Wis.), 1907; Der bestrafte Brudermord—Sein Verhaltnis zu Shakespeare's Hamlet, 1910; Ein Charakterbild von Deutschland (with E. Merhaut), 1914. Beginning German (with H. C. Keidel), 1915; College German (with R. O. Roseler), Shorter College German, 1943; Das Rheinland (with R. O. Roseler), 1934; An Historical and Critical Introduction to the Lucerne Passion Play, 1943. Translator: (from manuscripts of L. Bahlsen) Teaching of Modern Languages, 1905. Editor: Hebbel's Agnes Bernauer, 1912. Co-Editor: Hauptmann's Einsame Menschen, 1931. Contbr. to Modern Lang. Rev., Modern Philology, Modern Lang. Notes Padagogische Monatshefte, etc. Home: 45 Crestview Rd., Columbus OH‡

EVANS, PERCY HENRIQUES, actuary, ins. exec.; b. San Diego, Calif., Nov. 9, 1873; s. James Armstrong and Jessie Hunt (Henriques) E.; ed. U. of Mich., 1892-95, Milwaukee Law Class, 1895-96; m. Eugenia Hotchkiss, Nov. 11, 1897 (died Jan. 20, 1922); m. 2d, Edith Margaret Cullen, Dec. 8, 1922. Actuarial clerk Northwestern Mutual Life Ins. Co., Milwaukee, Wis., 1889-92; actuarial student, 1895-96 life ins. agent and editor Insurance Journal, San Francisco, 1896-1901; asst. supt. Agencies Northwestern Mutual Life Ins. Co., 1901-15, actuary, 1915-29, v.p. and actuary, 1929-46. President of the American Institute of Actuaries, 1924-26; Fellow of the Actuarial Society of America. Mem. Phi Kappa Psi. Republican. Episcopalian. Mason (32 deg.). Clubs: University (Milwaukee); Senior Actuaries (New York). Contbr. articles on life ins. to proceedings of actuarial socs. and jours. Retired since 1946. Home: P.O. Box 539, Saratoga CA‡

EVANS, PEYTON RANDOLPH, lawyer; b. Amherst, Va., Oct. 18, 1892; s. Otto Lewis and Mary (Randolph) E.; studied engring. Va. Poly. Inst., Blacksburg, Va., 1909-13; U. of Va. Law Sch., 1913-15; m. Janetta Fitzhugh, Oct. 6, 1917 children—Peyton Randolph, Thomas Fitzhugh. Began as civil engr., 1912, with Va. State Highway Commn., 1912-13; admitted to Va. bar, 1915, and practiced at Amherst; football coach U. of Va., 1916, Lynchburg Coll., 1920-24; asst. counsel Federal Farm Loan Bur., 1927-29, counsel, 1929-31, gen. counsel, 1931-33; asst. Land Bank commr. Farm Credit Adminstrn., 1933, asst. gen. counsel, 1933-34, gen. solicitor, 1934-35, gen. counsel, 1935 to Mar. 1, 1940; gen. counsel Federal Farm Mortgage Corp., 1935-40; acting gen. counsel Federal Home Loan Bank Bd., Aug.-Sept., 1932; one of legal advisers to Pres. Com. on Reorganization of Govt.; gen. sec., counsel Washington Pubs. Assn., Washington, 1941-47, now cons.; mem. Town Council, Amherst, 1915-17, Va. State Ho. of Rep., 1917-19; chmn. Amherst County Sch. Bd., 1924-25; mayor of Amherst, 1919-27. Mem. endowment com. Petersburg, Virginia. With O. T. C., 1916; commd. 1st lt. R.T.C., 1917; at Camp Meade, Md., 1917-18; served in 351st Field Arty., A.E.F., June 1918-Feb. 1919; commd. capt. R.T.C., 1919. Mem. Am., Federal, and Virginia State bar associations, Internat. Platform Assn., Delta Tau Delta. Democrat. Episcopalian. Mason. Club: Chevy Chase. Author of articles on federal corps. and corporate finance. Home: Fredericksburg VA Died Feb. 1972.

EVANS, RICHARD LOUIS, writer, radio commentator, editor, ch. ofcl.; b. Salt Lake City, Utah, Mar. 23, 1906; s. John Alldridge and Florence (Neslen) E.; student U. of Utah, 1924-26, 1929-32; B.A., major English, 1931, M.A., maj. econs., 1932, LL.D., 1956; D.H.L. (hon.), Cal. Coll. Medicine, 1957; Litt.D. (honorary), Eastern Ky. State College, 1964; m. Alice Ruth Thornley, Aug. 9, 1933; children—Richard Louis, John T., Stephen T., William T. British mission, 1926-29; sec. European Mission, Ch. of Jesus Christ Latter-day Saints, Liverpool, 1928-29; staff announcer, radio sta. KSL, Salt Lake City, 1929, script writer, dir. of publicity, production mgr., 1929-36; radio producer, commentator and writer of Music and the Spoken Word nationwide Tabernacle choir and organ broadcast. Temple Square, Salt Lake City, 1930-71; broadcast on NBC, 1930-32, CBS, 1932-71; director special features KSL, 1936-71. Mng. editor Improvement Era, 1936-49, editor since 1950; feature writer King Features Syndicate, 1946-52; dir. David W. Evans Advt. Agy., Radio Service Corp., Utah, Salt Lake Union Stockyards, Bountiful State Bank, Radio Sta. KSL, Inc., 1st Security Corp.; v.p., dir. Bonneville Internat. Corp. Mem. 1st Council of the Seventy, Ch. of Jesus Christ Latter-day Saints, 1938-53, mem. Council of Twelve, 1953-71; mem. bd. regents U. Utah, 1950-69; pres. alumni assn., 1950-53; mem. of bd. of trustees Brigham Young U.; 1953-71; mem. gen. bd. Young Men's Mutual Improvement Assn., 1935-48; member State Bd. Higher Edn., Utah, 1969-71. Recipient David O. McKay Humanities award, Brigham Young University, 1967. Member Salt Lake Chamber of Commerce, Utah Acad. Scis., Arts and Letters, Newcomen Soc., Pi Kappa Alpha. Clubs: Rotary (pres., 1949-50; Dist. 165 governor, 1956-57, counselor 1957-58, internat. pres. 1966-67); Fort Douglas; Ambassador of Atheltic (hon.), Bonneville Knife and Fork (pres. 1953-54). Author: At This Same Hour, 1949; Tonic for Our Times, 1952; From the Crossroads, 1955; The Everlasting Things, 1957; May Peace Be with You, 1961; Faith in the Future, 1963; Thoughts for One Hundred Days, 1966; An Open Road, 1968; other books, compilations, numerous newspaper and mag. articles, Look, Ency. Brit., Readers Digest, Christian Sci. Monitor. Home: Salt Lake City UT Died Nov. 1, 1971; buried Salt Lake City Cemetery.

EVANS, WALTER HARRISON, botanist; b. Delphi, Ind., Jan. 3, 1863; s. Joseph and Catharine (Bricker) E.; A.B., Wabash Coll., 1887, A.M., 1889, Ph.D., 1896; m. Bessie Binford, Oct. 22, 1890; 1 dau., Margaret B. Instr. botany, Wabash Coll., 1888-90; botanist Eli Lilly Co., Indianapolis, 1890-91; spl. agt. Dept. Agr., 1891-92; chief Div. Insular Stas., Dept. Agr., 1902-33; acting chief, Office of Expt. Stas., 1929-32. Associate and bot. editor Experiment Station Record, 1892-1933. Made agrl. reconnaissance of Alaska, 1897-98; rep. U.S. Dept. of Agr. to congresses of Horticulture, Forestry and Expt. Stas., Paris, 1900; gold medal, Paris Expn., 1900; grand prize, St. Louis Expn., 1904. Fellow A.A.A.S.; mem. Biol. and Bot. socs., Washington, Am. Phytopathol. Soc. Wrote chapters on Economic Botany in New Internat. Ency., 1902-03 and 1914-15, Internat. Yearbook, 1902-24, Am. Yearbook, 1910-19. Contbr. to bot. jours. and publs. Dept. Agr. Special editor Webster's Internat. Dictionary, 2d edit. Home: R.F.D. 2, Florence SC‡

EVANS, WILLIAM DENT, JR., newspaper editor; b. Fairmont, W.Va., July 6, 1907; s. William Dent and Ora (Kinsey) E.; student Fairmont State Coll., 1924-25; student W.Va. U., 1927-30. Reporter, Fairmont (W.Va.) Times, 1923, 1938-46, sports editor, 1924-27, 1947-53, mng. editor, 1953-59, editor, 1959-69; reporter Morgantown (W.Va.) Dominion-News, 1928, Morgantown Post, 1929-30, 1931-34, Clarksburg (W.Va.) Exponent, 1930-31, Fairmont West Virginian, 1934-36; editor, Martinsburg (W.Va.) News 1934; pub.

relations cons. Nat. Bituminous Coal Com., Washington, 1936-37; telegraph ed. Wheeling (W.Va.) News-Register, 1946-47. Mem. Mayors Adv. Com., Fairmont, 1948-50, City Fireman's Civil Service Com., Fairmont, 1959-69; mem. Prickett's Fort State Park Commission; Citizens Committee on State Legislature. Alternate del. Dem. Nat. Conv. 1952, 56, 64. Bd. dirs. Greater Fairmont Devel. Assn., 1959-69. Mem. W.Va. United Press Internat. Assn. (president 1960), West Virginia (president 1954) Southern Conference (president 1954) sports writers associations, Football Writers Assn., Am., U.S. Basketball Writers Assn., W.Va. Press Assn., W.Va. U. Athletic Council, S.R., Sigma Delta Chi. Democrat. Presbyn. Elk, Moose. Clubs: Press (Charleston, W.Va.); Montmarte, Mountain, Touchdown (Morgantown). Home: Fairmont WV Died Nov. 7, 1969.

EVARTS, RICHARD CONOVER, lawyer; b. N.Y.C., Mar. 11, 1890; s. Prescott and Emily (Conover) E.; A.B., Harvard University, 1913, LL.B. cum laude, 1916; m. Mary Lillian Bragan, June 18, 1921 (dec. September 1965); children—Nancy (Mrs. Joseph N. Guelich), Emily (Mrs. Richard S. Gordon), Mary (Mrs. David L. Smith), Sarah (Mrs. Paul G. Haskell). Admitted to the Massachusetts bar, 1916, practiced in Boston, 1916-72; mem. firm Lyne, Woodworth & Evarts, 1923-72; city solicitor, Cambridge, 1930, 38-42. Chairman Cambridge Board Appeals, 1960-72. Served with infantry, United States Army, 1917-19. Member American, Mass., Middlesex County, Boston (past mem. council), Cambridge (past pres.) bar assns., Cambridge Hist. Soc. (pres.). Home: Cambridge MA Died Jan. 27, 1972; buried Mt. Auburn Cemetery, Cambridge MA

EVATT, WILLIAM STEINWEDELL, lawyer; b. Quincy, Ill., Oct. 18, 1892; s. Frank Wilbur and Lelia (Steinwedell) E.; LL.B., Cin. Law Sch., 1917; m. Harriet Torrey, Oct. 18, 1924. Admitted to Ohio bar, 1916; atty. examiner, asst. chief div. securities State of Ohio, 1920-21; pvt. law practice, 1921-29; asst. atty. gen. State of Ohio, 1929-33, chief counsel atty. gen., 1933-39, dir. finance, 1939, tax commr., 1939-45; member Bricker, Evatt, Barton & Eckler, Columbus; associate editor W. H. Anderson Co., Cin. Served as ensign USNRF, World War I. Mem. Am., Ohio, Columbus bar assns., Am. Legion, Ohio C. of C. (chmn. taxation and public expenditures com.). Episcopalian. Home: Columbus OH Died June 4, 1970; buried Columbus OH

EVE, HENRY PRONTAUT, lawyer; b. Augusta, Ga., Oct. 17, 1917; s. William Ralford and Helen (Davies) E.; B.S., Davidson Coll., 1936; LL.B., Emory U., 1939; m. Caroline Hull, Jan. 21, 1942; 1 dau., Mary Hull. Admitted to Ga. bar, 1939; practiced in Augusta, 1939-41, 45-69; partner firm Cumming, Nixon, Eve, Waller & Capers, and predecessor, 1945-69. Dir. 1st R.R. & Banking Co. of Ga., Richmond County Bank, 1st Ga. Devel. Corp. Mem. Ga. Ho. of Reps., 1947-49; mem. Ga. Senate, 1949-50. Served to lt. comdr. USNR, 1941-45. Decorated Bronze Star medal. Mem. Am., Augusta (pres. 1967) bar assns., State Bar Ga. (pres. 1965-66), Com. 100, Augusta C. of C. (past dir.), Phi Delta Phi, Sigma Alpha Epsilon. Elk. Clubs: Augusta Country (pres. 1963), Pinnacle (bd. dirs.) (Augusta). Home: Augusta GA Died June 29, 1969.

EVELETH, TRUE BALLENTINE, assn. exec.; b. Portland, Me., Apr. 28, 1904; s. Samuel True and Annie Louise (Bailey) E.; D. O., Kirksville Coll. Osteopathy and Surgery, 1937, Doctor of Science (honorary), in Osteopathy, 1964; D.Sc. in Osteopathy, Chgo. Coll. Osteopathy, 1965; m. Dorothy M. Leland, Oct. 29, 1929. Treas. F. O. Bailey Co., Portland, Me., 1924-32; med. dir. Osteopathic Hosp., Me., 1946-52; exec. asst. Am. Osteopathic Assn., 1952-56, exec. dir., 1956-68, exec. dir. emeritus, 1968-69. Served as lt. col. AUS, 1940-45. Recipient Distinguished Service certificate Am. Osteo. Assn., 1963. Fellow Acad. Applied Osteopathy, Am. Coll. Osteo. Surgeons (hon.); life mem. Ill., Mich., Me. (dir. 1945-52) osteo. assns.; mem. Am. Osteo. Acad. Orthopedics (hon.), Me. Diabetic Soc. (co-founder, treas.), Am. Soc. Assn. Execs. Address: Cape Elizabeth ME Died Dec. 25, 1969.

EVERETT, ROBERT ASHTON, congressman; b. Obion County, Tenn., Feb. 24, 1915; s. Charles Fowlkes and Lelia Belle (Ashton) E.; B.S., Murray State Coll., 1936. Mem. Obion County Ct., 1936, clk. Circuit Ct. of Obion County, 1938; adminstrv. asst. to Sen. Tom Stewart, Washington, 1945-49, to Gov. Gordon Browning, 1950-52; exec. sec. Tenn. County Services Assn., 1954-58; mem. 86th-89th Congresses, 8th District Tenn. (elected 1958 to fill the vacancy following death of Congressman Jere Cooper). Served as sergeant Army of United States, World War II. Mem. Jr. C. of C. (past state pres.), Am. Legion Democrat. Presbyn. Mason (Shriner, K.T.), Moose, Elk. Home: Union City TN Died Jan. 26, 1969; buried Eastview Cemetery, Union City TN

EVERGOOD, PHILIP (HOWARD FRANCIS DIXON), artist; b. N.Y.C., Oct. 26, 1901; s. Miles and Flora Jane (Perry) E.; student Eton Coll., Eng., 1915-19, Trinity Hall Coll., Cambridge U., Eng., 1919-20, Slade Sch. Arts, London, 1921-23, Art Students League N.Y.C., 1923-25, Julien's Acad., Paris, 1925; m. Julia Vincent Cross, Aug. 15, 1931, Painter, lectr., tchr., draftsman 1921-73. Exhibited in group shows Art Students League 1967-68, Gallery Modern Art at Huntington Hartford Mus., 1967, Whitney Mus. Am. Art, 1967, Smithsonian Instn., 1968, represented in maj. U.S. and fgn. collections including: Met. Mus., Mus. Modern Art, Library Congress, Widener Library, Los Angeles Mus., Whitney Mus. Am. Art, Bklyn. Mus., Boston Mus. Fine Arts, Carnegie Inst. Art, Nat. Gallery (Melbourne, Australia), Geelong Gallery Art (Victoria, Australia), Balt. Mus. Coll., Wadsworth Athenaeum, Hartford, Conn., Tel Aviv (Israel) Mus. Art, Fogg Mus., Cambridge, Mass., Mus. Contemporary Art Dallas, Syracuse U., Cornell U., others; murals Richmond Hill (L.I.) Pub. Library, Kalamazoo Coll. Instr. painting, summer sessions U. Minn., 1955, Ia. State Tchrs. Coll., 1957-58, Skowhegan (Me.) Sch. Art, 1963; retrospective exhbn. 1927-60 Whitney Mus. Am. Art, 1960. Recipient several prizes 1935-73, including Carol H. Beck Gold medal, Pa. Acad., Phila., 1949; 2d prize Carnegie Inst. Art. Pitts., 1949; 2d prize, W.A. Clark silver medal Corcoran Gallery Art, 1951; 1st prizes 1st L.I. Art Festival, 1951, Terry Art Inst., Miami, 1952, Balt. Mus., 1955; Joseph E. Temple gold medal Pa. Acad., 1958, spl. drawing prize, 1961; Purchase award Ford Found., 1962; Knight of Mark Twain, Mark Twain Jour., 1967-68; others. Participant U.S. internat. exhbns., Art of the U.S.A., Venice, London, Brussels, Paris, C.Am., S.Am., Fellow Internat. Inst. Arts and Letters; mem. Artists Equity Assn., Nat. Inst. Arts and Letters (grantee 1956), Kappa Pi (hon.). Author: Evergood-Twenty Years of His Work, 1946; illustrations for Short Stories of Gogol, 1951; Evergood Graphics, 1966. Contbr. to art mags. Home: CT

EVERILL, ROYAL BURDETTE, educator; b. Monroe, Wis., Oct. 3, 1904; s. Charles and Laura (Roberts) E.; B.A., State U. Ia., 1931, M.A., 1937; student U. Wis., 1947-49; m. Alice Grenawalt, Aug. 25, 1927; children—Phyllis (Mrs. Albert L. Winegar), Royal B., Charles H. Tchr. Roosevelt Jr. High Sch., Beloit, Wis., 1927-42; prin. Lincoln Jr. High Sch., Beloit, Wis., 1942-49, Meml. High Sch., Beloit, 1949-69. Mem. Wis. com. North Central Assn. Colls. and Secondary Schs., 1959-62. Mem. N.E.A., Nat., Wis. assns. secondary sch. prins., Wis. Edn. Assn. Conglist. Mason. Home: Beloit WI Died Apr. 24, 1969.

EVERIT, EDWARD HOTCHKISS, telephone engr.; b. New Haven, Conn., Aug. 5, 1870; s. Richard Mansfield and Mary Talman (Lawrence) E.; grad. Hillhouse High Sch., New Haven, 1888; spl. studies, Columbia U., 1891-92; m. Cordelia S. Peck, of New Haven, Nov. 26, 1895 (died 1901); children—Elizabeth C. (Mrs. Robert P. Heald), Arthur M., Mary L. (Mrs. Joseph C. Bauer); m. 2d, Marie S. Withmar, nee Bigger, of Richmond, Va., June 1, 1911. Began in employ of Southern N.E. Telephone Co., 1889, supt. of equipment, 1892, engr., 1903, chief engr., 1910, asst. to gen. mgr., 1927-30, now retired. Fellow Am. Inst. E.E.; mem. A.A.A.S., Soc. for Promotion Engring. Edn., Conn. Soc. C.E., New York Elec. Soc., Telephone Pioneers of America, Zeta Psi. Republican. Episcopalian; vestryman Trinity Ch. Clubs: Quinnipiack, Rotary, New Haven Country, Applachian Mountain; Zeta Psi (New York). Home: 25 Edgehill Terrace, New Haven CT‡

EVERWIJN, JAN CHARLES AUGUST, diplomat; b. Noordwijk, Holland, Nov. 15, 1873; s. Dr. Jan and Amalia Augusta (Stricker) E.; LL.D., Leiden U., 1897; m. Sara Bertruda Crommelin, 1897. Lawyer at The Hague, 1897; entered govt. service, Ministry of Public Works, 1898; sec. commn. Commercial Policy, 1901; chief of commercial dept., Ministry Agr., Industry, and Commerce, 1906; v.p. commn. Netherland participation Panama-Pacific Expn., San Francisco, 1913; charged with different economic negotiations, 1914-19; pres. Netherland Industrial Council, 1919; pres. Netherland Orgn. for the Internat. Chamber of Commerce, 1920; govt. del. conf. at Paris for economic relief to countries of Central and Eastern Europe, 1920; Netherland commr. for economic credit to Germany, 1921; E.E. and M.P. from Netherlands to U.S. since Aug. 1, 1921. Decorated Knight of the Netherland Lion; comdr. Crown of Belgium. Clubs: Place Royale (The Hague), Metropolitan, Cosmos, Chevy Chase (Washington); Union, Union League, University (New York); hon. pres. Dutch Club (New York). Address: 15th and Euclid Avs. N.W. Washington DC‡

EVJUE, WILLIAM THEODORE, newspaper editor; b. Merrill, Wis., Oct. 10, 1882; s. Nils Peter and Mary (Erickson) E.; student U. of Wis., 1902-05; m. Zillah Julia Bagley, May 31, 1913. Began as reporter Milwaukee (Wis.) Sentinel, 1905, night editor, 1908-11; mng. editor Wis. State Journal, Madison, 1911-13, business mgr., 1913-17; founder, 1917, since editor, pres. The Capital Times, Madison; pres. Badger Broadcasting Co., Madison Newspapers, Inc. Mem. Wis. Assembly, 1917-19; mem. Rep. State Central Com., Wis., 1920-24; Rep. presdl. elector, 1924; chmn. of conv. at which new Progressive Party was born, Fond du Lac, Wis., May 1934. Decorated Friedens Cors, 1943, Knight of St. Olav, 1959 (Norway). Mem. Phi Gamma Delta, Sigma Delta Chi (fellow). Clubs: University, Madison. Home: Madison WI Died Apr. 23, 1970.

EWBANK, LOUIS B., lawyer; b. Dearborn County, Ind., 1864; s. John William and Betsey (Blaisdel) E.; m. Effie Shoemaker, Oct. 17, 1893 (died Jan. 12, 1900). Admitted to bar, 1891, and began practice at Indianapolis; prof. law Ind. Law Sch., many yrs., from 1897; judge Circuit Court, Indianapolis, 1914-20; justice of the Supreme Court of Ind., 1920-27. Mason. Clubs: Columbia, Literary, Century. Author: Manual of Indiana Appellate Practice, 1900, 2d edit., 1915; Indiana Trial Evidence, 1904; Indiana Criminal Law, 1907, 2d edit., 1929; Indiana Cumulative Digest, 1906-14; (joint author) Modern Business Corporations, 1906. Home: 614 N. East St. Office: State Life Bldg., Indianapolis IN‡

EWELL, ARTHUR WOOLSEY, physicist; b. Bradford, Mass., Oct. 20, 1873; s. John Lewis and Emily Spofford (Hall) E.; A.B., Yale, 1897, Ph.D., 1899; studied Johns Hopkins, 1899-1900, U. of Berlin, 1904, Radium Inst., Paris, 1924; hon. D. Sc., Worcester Polytechnic Inst., 1946; m. Jane Dodge Estabrook, Sept. 6, 1905; children—Milicent, Jane Estabrook, John Woolsey. Asst. in physics, Yale, 1897-99; instr. physics, 1900-04, asst. prof., 1904-10, prof. since 1910, dir. of physics and gen. science depts., 1935 to retirement 1938, Worcester (Mass.) Poly. Inst.; trustee Bancroft School, Worcester, Mass., 1915-18, treasurer, 1918-28, president, 1928-30; lecturer Massachusetts Institute of Technology; member research staff Westinghouse Electric Mfg. Co., Bloomfield, N.J.; cold storage engr. Dir. Worcester Airport, Am. Soc. Refrigeration Engrs. Trustee Worcester County Instn. for Savings; v.p. board of Gov. Dummer Acad. Capt. U.S.R., Dec. 15, 1917; head of bomb unit, Air Service, A.E.F., after armistice, in charge expt. development and tests of bombs, until May 1, 1919; lt. col. O.R.C.; apptd. spl. aerial bomb expert War Dept., Nov. 1919. Fellow Am. Acad. Arts and Sciences, Am. Physical Soc. (hon. life mem.); mem. American Society Refrigeration Engineers (dir.; hon. member 1945), French Physical Soc., Newcomen Soc. of England, Am. Legion (past comdr. Devens Post), Phi Beta Kappa, Sigma Xi. Episcopalian. Democrat. Clubs: Century, Yale (New York); Myopia Hunt, Worcester, Worcester Fire Society, St. Wulstan. Author: Physical Chemistry, 1909; Physical Measurements, 1910, 1913; numerous papers upon artifical rotatory polarization, magnetic double refraction, aerial bombs and bombing, electrolytic electrode potentials, properties of gases and vapors, refrigeration, ozone, ultra-violet light, food preservation, etc. Mem. editorial staff Refrigeration Data Book, 1940, 1945. Home: Rowley, Mass. Address: 55 Jackson St., Worcester 8 MA‡

EWER, BERNARD CAPEN, psychologist; b. Vernon, Conn., Oct. 5, 1877; s. Charles H. and Mary S. (Capen) E.; A.B., Brown U., 1899, A.M., 1900; Ph.D., Harvard, 1904; m. Florence M. Burt, of Providence, R.I., June 25, 1907. Teacher philosophy, Northwestern U., 1905-11, Reed Coll., Portland, Ore., 1911-15, Brown U., 1915-16; prof. psychology, Pomona Coll., since 1916. Mem. Phi Beta Kappa, Delta Tau Delta. Author: College Study and College Life, 1917; Applied Psychology, 1923. Home: Claremont CA‡

EWERS, JOHN RAY, clergyman; born West Unity, O., Nov. 9, 1877; s. Edwin Patterson and Harriet Jane (Bostater) E.; B.S., Hiram Coll., O., 1899; B.D., U. of Chicago, 1905; D.D., U. of Pittsburgh, 1926; m. Mary Alice Canfield, Sept. 26, 1899 (died 1935);children—Dr. Edwin Patterson, John Canfield; m. 2d, Laura La Croix, 1936. Ordained to ministry Christian Disciples Ch., 1899; pastor Blackrock Christian Ch., Buffalo, 1899, Christian Ch., Bowling Green, O., 1900-03, Irving Park Christian Ch., Chicago, 1903-05, First Christian Ch., Youngstown, O., 1905-09, East End Christian Ch., Pittsburgh, 1909-47, Tourist Ch., Daytona Beach, Fla., 1947-48, Community Ch., Babson Park, Fla., since 1948. Mem. Pittsburgh Housing Commn., 1940-47. Contbr. to Christian Century, also to Twentieth Century Quarterly, since 1919. Mason, Rotarian. Condr. Forum, Pittsburgh, since 1923. Operator dairy farm in Ohio since 1909. Home: Hillcrest Heights, Babson Park. Office: Community Church, Babson Park FL‡

EWING, ALONZO B(YRON), business and financial cons.; b. Lawrence, Kan., Oct. 20, 1894; s. Byron A. and Maggie L. (Moore) E.; student La Salle U., 1919; m. Sally M. Winsby, Sept. 25, 1916; children—H. Blossom, Mildred M., Alan R. (dec.), Barbara J., Roger L. Vice pres., dir. Central Coal & Coke Co., 1924-31; treas., dir. Sunshine Biscuits, Inc., 1932-47; pres., dir. Flour Mills of America, Inc., 1953-54; chmn. bd., v.p., treasurer Slater Tile & Mantel Co., Home of Tile, Inc., dir. Kan. Color Press, Inc., Mantel Co., Home of Tile, Inc., dir. Kan. Color Press, Inc., Lawrence, Kan.; pres., chmn. bd. Regal Plastic Co., Kansas City, Mo., 1958-59. C.P.A., Kan., Mo. Mem. Am. Inst. Accountants. Mason (K.T.). Home: Lawrence KS Died Feb. 15, 1971.

EWING, RUSSELL CHARLES, educator; b. Manhattan, Kan., Feb. 16, 1906; s. Charles Edward and Blanche (Russell) E.; B.A., U. Cal. at Berkeley, 1929, M.A., 1931, Ph.D., 1934; m. Susan Sawyer, Nov. 14, 1929; children—David Russell, John Meredith, Russell Charles II. Regional historian region IV Nat. Park Service, 1935-37; mem. faculty U. Ariz., 1937-72, prof.

history, 1948-72, head dept., 1959-69, Liberal Arts Faculty lectr., 1959; vis. lectr. San Francisco State Coll., summer 1948; participant Am. Assembly, 1959. Mem. Fed. Regional Archives Adv. Council region 9, 1971-72. Mem. Tuscon Sch. Bd., 1955-56, 64-66. Dir. Ariz. Palsy Found., 1955-56. Served to lt. comdr. USNR, 1942-46. Recipient Outstanding Male Faculty award U. Ariz., 1952, Faculty Recognition award Tucson Trade Bur., 1967; Smith-Mundt fellow U. Andes, Bogota, Colombia, 1956-57. Mem. Am. Hist. Assn., Western History Assn., Rocky Mountain Council Latin Am. Studies (pres. 1955-56), Com. Fgn. Relations, Phi Kappa Phi, Sigma Phi. Episcopalian. Co-author: The U.S. and Latin America; Arizona: Its Peoples and Resources; co-author, editor Six Faces of Mexico; also author numerous articles and book revs. Home: Tucson AZ Died Oct. 14, 1972; buried Cyprus Lawn Meml. Park, Daly City CA

EWOLDT, HAROLD BOADEN, mining engr.; b. Bennett, Ia., Dec. 12, 1908; s. Henry Hans and Leitha (Boaden) E.; B.S., S.D. Sch. Mines, 1930; m. Florence Thomas Lead, Aug. 14, 1930; children—Betty (Mrs. William F. McKissock, Jr.), Dorothy (Mrs. E. Dennis Posey), Harold Boaden; m. 2d, Millard Curlin, Apr. 4, 1947. Supt., Double Rainbow Mines, Inc., Deadwood, S.D., 1930-33; sr. foreman constrn., maintenance, U.S.F.S., Deadwood, 1933-36; supt. Gregory Bates Mining Co., Black Hawk, Colo., 1936-39; dist. engr. U.S. Bur. Mines, Norris, Tenn., 1939-44; mgr. Calumet & Hecla, Shullsburg, Wis., 1946-50; v.p., gen. mgr. Copper Range Co., Boston, 1950-56; dir. planning Cerro Corp., N.Y.C., 1956-60; chief mining engr. Le Tourneou Westinghouse, Peoria, Ill., 1960-69; sr. mining engr. WABCO, C.E. div., 1967-69. Served to lt. USNR, 1944-46. Registered profl. engr., Colorado, Wisconsin. Mem. Am. Inst. Mining Engrs., Mining and Metall. Soc., Am. Assn. Cost Engrs. Republican. Presbyn. Mason (Shriner), Elk. Home: Peoria IL Died Dec. 20, 1969; buried Ridgecrest Cemetery Jackson TN

EYSMANS, JULIEN L., ry. official; b. Brussels, Belgium, Mar. 18, 1874; s. Charles P. and Josephine E.; brought to U.S., 1875; ed. pub. schs., Baltimore, Md.; m. Mary Emory, of Baltimore, Md., June 6, 1903; children—Julien L., Thomas Lane Emory. Began as messenger, office of div. freight agt., Pa. R.R., Baltimore, 1891; various clerical positions, same r.r., until 1896; freight solicitor Anchor Line, 1896-98; soliciting agt. same, Baltimore, 1898-1900; freight solicitor, Star Union Line, Reading, Pa., 1900-02, Baltimore, 1903-04; eastern supt. same r.r., N.Y. City, 1904-05; gen. freight agt. Cumberland Valley R.R., 1906-11; with Pa. R.R. since 1911, div. freight agt., Pittsburgh, 1911-12, asst. gen. freight agt., 1912-16, gen. freight agt., 1916-20, traffic mgr. Eastern Region, Pa. System, 1920-23, traffic mgr. Central Region, 1923-24, asst. gen. traffic mgr., 1924, gen. traffic mgr., 1925, v.p. since 1925, v.p., asst. to pres., since 1933. Republican. Epsicopalian. Clubs: Racquet, Philadelphia, Duquesne; Cloud, Traffic (New York); Rolling Rock; Traffic (Chicago). Home: 1924 Panama St. Philadelphia PA‡

EYSTER, WILLIAM HENRY, botanist; b. Fishers Ferry, Pa., July 13, 1889; s. Henry and Alice (Star) E.; A.B., Bucknell U., 1914, A.M., 1915; Ph.D., Cornell U., 1920; grad. study Harvard, 1923, U. of Berlin, 1928, Botanisches Institut, Erlangen, Germany, 1928; m. Elmira Snyder, June 18, 1914; children—William Henry, Paul Morris, Helen Elizabeth. Asst. prof. botany, U. of Mo., 1920-24; prof. U. of Me., 1924-27; fellow John Simon Guggenheim Memorial Foundation for Study Abroad, 1927-28; prof. botany Bucknell U., 1928-45; president Eyster Hybrid Seed Co., 1945-46; professor of botany, Baldwin-Wallace College, 1945-46; prof. edn. Moravian Coll., Bethlehem, Pa., 1959; genetic adviser W. Atlee Burpee Co., Phila.; mng. editor Organic Gardening; asso. editor Organic Farmer; soil scientist for National Soil Conservation, Inc., N.Y. City; agrl. cons. Atlantic Organic Company, Williamsport, Md.; Scientific consultant to Wandel Machine Company, Inc., also Zook & Ranck, Inc., Gap, Pennsylvania; scientific adviser Bally Products, Bally, Pa.; v.p. and dir. research Eastern States Soilbuilders, Inc., Sharpsburg, Md.; v.p. Wandel Machine Co., Inc., Dowingtown, Pa.; agrl. dir. Roper Lumber Co., 1951-52; v.p., dir. prodn. Soil-Tone Corp., Plymouth, North Carolina, 1952-55; director of research for Fertilium, Inc., 1956-58; science director Fertilium Co., 1958-61; inventor organic soil conditioner and plant food; dir. Zeolite Chem. Company, N.Y.C. Trustee Soil and Health Foundation. Fellow A.A.A.S.; member Am. Bot. Soc., German Bot. Soc., Am. Genetic Soc., Am. Soc. of Plant Physiologists, Am. Soc. Naturalists, Torrey Botanical Club, Pennsylvania Acad. Sciences; fellow N.Y. Acad. of Sciences, Sigma Xi, Phi Kappa Phi, Phi Sigma, Phi Gamma Delta. Originator of hybrid corns and marigolds. Author: College Botany, 1931; Genetics of Zea Mays, 1934; Biological Science, 1941. Author many articles. Asst. editor Biological Abstracts. Investor Eysterlite soil conditioner 1963. Address: Emmaus PA Died Apr. 16, 1968.

FABER, JOHN LEWIS, corp. exec.; b. Clifton Forge, Va., Apr. 1, 1924; s. Harry Lewis and Anna (Logan) F.; student N.Y. Trade Sch., 1943; B.S., Va. Poly. Inst., 1949; m. Margaret Fay Howerton, June 3, 1944 (div. Apr. 1963); 1 dau., Karen; m. 2d, Frances Freeman Cook, Oct. 29, 1963. Asst. div. engr. Mo. Pub. Service Co., Sedalia, 1949-54; exec. mgr. Sedalia C. of C., 1954-61; exec. v.p. Greater Albuquerque C. of C., 1961-63; dir. N.M. Dept. Devel., 1963-64; exec. dir. Light Industry Council, Sarasota County, Fla., 1964-65; gen. mgr. Hydronics, Inc., 1965-68; dir. research and engring., 1965-68; sec.-treas. KINE-TICS Corp., Sarasota, Fla., 1967-69. Dir. Mo. C. of C. Mem. Nat. Export Expansion Council, 1962-64; mem. adv. commn. Mo. March of Dimes, 1953-54; Mo. Hwy. 50 Assn., 1958-59; pres. Sedalia Symphony, 1958-60; chmn. pub. utilities study group Sarasota County Community Goals Council; mem. S. Fla. Regional Export Expansion Council, U.S. Dept. Commerce. Bd. dirs. Mo. Council Community Improvement. Served with USAAF, World War II. Mem. I.E.E.E., Mo. Jr. C. of C., Jr. C. of C. Internat., Am., N.M. (sec.-treas.) C. of C. execs. assns., Am. Inst. Indsl. Engrs. (sr. mem., pres. local chpt. 1964-66), Am. Indsl. Devel. Council, Sarasota County C. of C., A.A.A.S., Fla. Acad. Scis. Rotarian Home: Sarasota FL Died Oct. 15, 1969.

FABIAN, SIMON H., motion picture exec.; b. Paterson, N.J., Jan. 29, 1899; s. Jacob and Rose (Glascheib) F.; student Harvard, 1915-17; m. Anna Ettelson, June 18, 1918; children—Edward, Robert, Norma (Mrs. Paul Jacobson) Abraham. Pres. Fabian Theatres; chairman Stanley Warner Corporation, New York City, New York. Chairman of the theatre division of war activities com. Motion Picture Industry, 1939-46; cons. Treasury Dept., World War II. Treas. Theatre Owners Am., Will Rogers Meml. Hosp. Home: New York City NY Died Aug. 17, 1970.

FABIANI, AURELIO, opera mgr.; b. Naples, Italy, Apr. 28, 1895; m. Diana Brewster. Joined Chgo. Civic Opera Co. Orch., 1915; gen. mgr., organizer Phila. Lyric Opera Co., 1957-73. Home: Philadelphia PA Died 1973.

FABING, HOWARD DOUGLAS, physician; b. Cin., Feb. 21, 1907; s. Henry Charles and Jessie (Ammann) F.; A.B., U. Cin., 1927, M.D., 1931; m. Esther Clare Marting, Dec. 16, 1939; children—Suzannah Jane, Priscilla Ruth, Howard William. Rotating intern Cin. Gen. Hosp., 1931-32, resident neurology, 1932-33; pvt. practice psychiatry and neurology, 1936-70; faculty physiology and neurology dept. U. Cin., 1936-42. Served from maj. to lt. col. M.C., AUS, 1942-46; neurologist Walter Reed Hosp.; chief neuropsychiatry Finney Gen. Hosp.; dir. sch. and standardized treatment combat fatigue ETO; research cerebral blast concussion; chief neurology div. VA, Washington, 1945-46; cons. Surg. Gen. U.S. Army, Korea, 1950. Decorated Legion of Merit. Mem. Am. League Against Epilepsy (chmn. legislation com.), Nat. Multiple Sclerosis Soc. (med. adv. bd.), Am. Neurological Assn., Am. Psychiat. Assn., Assn. Research Nervous and Mental Disease (member Commission 1957) Electroshock Research Assn., Cin. soc. Neurology and Psychiatry (pres. 1941), Ohio Med. Assn. (chmn. sect. nervous and mental diseases 1942), Am. Acad. Neurology (pres. 1953-55), Soc. Biol. Psychiatry (pres. 1955-56), Cin. Acad. Medicine (pres. 1956-57). Author: Fischerisms (rev. edit.), 1956; Epilepsy and the Law (with Roscoe Barrow), 1956. Author sci. papers. Home: Cincinnati OH Died July 29, 1970.

FACKENTHAL, FRANK DIEHL, univ. adminstr.; b. Hellertown, Pa., Feb. 22, 1883; s. Michael and Mary Jane (Diehl) F.; A.B., Columbia, 1906, Litt.D., 1920; LL.D., Franklin and Marshall, 1929; Syracuse U., 1947, Princeton, 1947, New York U., 1948; LL.D., Rutgers U., 1947, Trinity, 1955; L.H.D., Union Coll., 1948. Chief Clerk, Columbia U., 1906-10, secretary 1910-37, provost, 1937-45, acting president, 1945-48, retired, June, 1948; secretary University council, 1925-45, chairman Univ. com. on Student Orgns., 1914-45, mem. Univ. com. on War Research, 1914-45; consultant Carnegie Corp., 1948-52, mem. Commn. on Financing Higher Edn., 1949-52; pres. Columbia University Press, 1953-58, chmn., from 1958; pres. Associated Universities, Inc. (Brookhaven Nat. Lab.), 1948-50. Trustee Bushwick Savs. Bank, Bklyn., pres., 1952-54. Trustee Franklin and Marshall Coll., Internat. House, French Institute; member board directors Morningside Heights, Inc., Manhattanville Neighborhood Center, Inc., Bklyn. Eye and Ear Hosp.; trustee Columbia U., Barnard Coll. Awarded Chevalier Legion of Honor; Order Orange-Nassau. Mem. Pa. German Soc., N.Y. Soc., S.R. Officer Order of Crown of Italy, 1939. Republican. Conglist. Clubs: University, Columbia University, Century, Salmagundi, Coffee House, Bklyn., Pilgrims, Thursday Evening. Home: Buck Hill Falls PA Died Sept. 1968.

FADDIS, CHARLES I., ex-congressman; b. Loudenville, O., June 13, 1890; s. Samuel C. and Edna (Moredock) F.; student Waynesburg (Pa.) Coll., 1909-11; B.S., Pa. State Coll., 1915; grad. Gen. Staff and Command Sch., Ft. Leavenworth, Kan., 1930; m. Jane Morris, Dec. 1, 1917; children—William George, James M., Edna G., Laura Lucille. In gen. contracting business, Waynesburg, Pa., 1919-26; broker of oil and gas properties, 1926-72. Served as pvt. Pa. Inf., Mexican border, 1916; capt. and lt. col., inf., U.S. Army, World War; in major offensives and occupation of Germany; with O.R.C. since 1924; commd. col., 1930. Citation by Gen. Pershing; awarded Purple Heart. Mem. 73d to 77th Congresses (1933-43), 25th Pa. Dist. Mem. Am. Legion, Vets. of Foreign Wars, B.P.O.E. Democrat. Home: Waynesburg PA Died Apr. 1972.

FAESI, ROBERT, historian, author; b. Zurich, Switzerland, Apr. 10, 1883; s. Friedrich and Anne (Schalthess) F.; ed. U. Zurich, U. Berlin. Prof. German lit. U. Zurich, 1922-53; poet, dramatist, film writer, novelist, essayist, Zurich, 1953-72. Recipient Kepper prize, 1943, Zurich Lit. prize, 1945. Author: Zurcher Idylle, 1908; Die Fassade, 1918; Der Konig von Ste. Pelagie, 1924; Die Stadt der Freheit, 1944; Die Stadt des Friedena, 1952; Die Gedichte, 1955; Die schwarze, Spinne, 1940; Spittelers Weg und Werk, 1933; C.F. Meyer, Thomas Mann, 1955, others. Home: Zollikon-Zurich Switzerland Died Sept. 18, 1972.

FAGERGREN, FRED C., Midwest regional dir. Nat. Park Service. Home: Omaha NB Died Nov. 6, 1970; buried St. George UT

FAGIN, N. BRYLLION, author, univ. prof.; b. Russia, June 15, 1892; s. Nathan Bryllion and Matilda (Neistadt) F.; brought to U.S., 1900, naturalized 1913; student Mich. State Coll., 1912; A.B., George Washington U., 1923, A.M., 1924; student Columbia, summer 1924, Harvard, summer 1925; Ph.D., Johns Hopkins, 1931; m. Mary Berke, June 4, 1916 (dec. 1964); m. Clarissa Pearlman, Apr. 29, 1965. Clk., Bureau of Chemistry, Washington, 1916-21; instr. English, National U., Washington, 1919-23; asst. prof. English, U. of Md., 1924-25; prof. English, U. of Baltimore, 1925-31; asst. prof. English, Johns Hopkins, 1931-47, associate professor of English and drama, 1947-58, lectr., 1959-72; Whitney vis. professor English, LeMoyne College, Memphis, 1958-59, New College, Sarasota, Florida, 1967-72; director of the Johns Hopkins Playhouse, 1931-58; vist. lectr. U. S.D., summer, 1930; U. of Tenn., summer 1934; vis. asso. prof. English N.Y.U., summer 1951; vis. prof. English U. Rochester, 1953-55; with Salzburg Seminar in Am. Studies, summer 1958. Member Modern Lang. Assn., Am. Assn. Univ. Profs., Am. Ednl. Theatre Assn., Am. Nat. Theatre and Acad., Authors League of Am., Edgar Allan Poe Soc. of Baltimore (former pres.). Clubs: Johns Hopkins; Tudor and Stuart. Author books including: The Histrionic Mr. Poe, 1949. Editor: Poe as a Literary Critic, 1946. Co-editor: O'Neill and his Plays, 1961. Contbr. to publs. Died Jan. 5, 1972.

FAHNESTOCK, JAMES MURRAY, editor; b. Pitts., Dec. 16, 1885; s. Thomas Howe and Mary Heron (Thompson) F.; student Carnegie Inst. Tech., 1908-09; U. Pitts., 1912-13; m. Hazel Margaret Alberts, June 6, 1925;children—Lois Kay, Jean Howe, James Murray. Draftsman, Crucible Steel Co., 1909-12; tech. editor, Motor Cycling Mag., 1912-13; asst. service mgr., Pitts. br., Ford Motor Co.; free lance writer, Motor Age, etc., 1914-18; tech. editor, Ford Power Age Mag., 1923-28; editor Ford Field Mag., 1929-56, special writer, Ford Motor Co., 1932-33; dir. engring., Leaf Spring Inst., Detroit, 1943-55, also speaker and writer on automotive spring suspensions; co-ordinator charge series half-hour TV program on Your Car on WQED, Pitts., 1957-58, 59-69. Instr. Army automotive mechanics, lectr. mechanics in Army, U. Pitts., 1918. Mem. Nat. Soc. Automotive Engrs. (councilor, 1939-40, chmn. Pitts. sect. 1933). Presbyn. Author: Know the Ford, 1928; The Model A Ford,, 1930; Secrets of Ford Engineering, 1927; The Service Handbook (5 edits.), 1934; L'Auto Ford Modele A (in French); Automotive Springs, 1946; Tips on Spring Suspensions: Essentials of Model T Service, 1967; The Model T Ford Owner, 1968; lectr. on automobiles. Club: Pittsburgh Figure Skating. Feature articles on early autos in newspapers and mags. Address: Pittsburgh PA Died Apr. 28, 1969; buried Union Dale Cemetery, Pittsburgh PA

FAHNESTOCK, KAROL JAMES, musician; b. Union City, Ind., Sept. 4, 1914; s. Carl Clifford and Mary (Dunkelberger) F.; studied piano with Bauer, Godowsky, Sileti, Liszniewska, 1935-40, orch. with Riegger, 1945-47; m. Rose Rea Carroll, July 9, 1936. Tchr. piano various cities including N.Y.C., Boston, Phila., 1945-50; lectr. Am. music various colls., including U. Phila., Columbia U., Xavier U., Capitol U.; nat. dir. Nat. Assn. for Advancement Native Am. Composers and Musicians, Richmond, Ind.; nat. dir. ann. Am. Music Festival, Loveland, O.; spl. tchr. piano Cin. pub. schs. Mem. recommendations com. Pulitzer music jury Columbia U. Mem. A.S.C.A.P., N.A.A.C.P. Composer: Dialectic, 1960; Jubilant Overture, 1960; Candy's Dance, 1964; Quite Catchy, 1965; The Delta, 1965; and numerous others. Home: Richmond IN Deceased.

FAIGLE, ERIC H., coll. dean; b. Winterdale, Pa., Aug. 16, 1900; s. Charles H. and Mary (Lang) F.; B.S., Syracuse U., 1928, M.S., 1930, LL.D., 1968; Ph.D., U. Mich., 1935; m. Lucy Pelton, Aug. 30 1929; children—Carolyn, Eric, Cynthia. Instr. coll. liberal arts Syracuse (N.Y.) U., 1928, asst. prof., 1935, asso. prof., 1940, prof. geography, 1943, adminstrv. asst., 1938-39, asst. dean, 1942, asso. dean, 1945, dean 1950-68, v.p.,

1960-68, also dean school of speech and dramatic arts, 1954-68, dean emeritus Coll. Liberal Arts, 1968-71, Sch. Speech and Dramatic Art, 1968-71, v.p. univ. emeritus, 1968-71. Trustee Manlius (New York) Sch. Consultant Post War Planning, com. housing, Syracuse, 1934, to geog. research sect. U.S. Army, Washington, 1942, Army Geo. programs in various colls. 2d Corps Area, 1944; mem. Transportation Com. Onondaga Co., 1943. Chmn. subcom. geog. studies, mem. adv. com. tests and aptitudes NRC, 1943. Recipient S.A.R. medal, 1954, George Arents Pioneer award medal for excellence in edn., 1959, Outstanding Civilian Service medal Dept. of Army, 1962, Syracuse Centennial medal, 1968. Mem. Nat. and N.Y. State councils social studies, Am. Soc. Profl. Geographers, Assn. Am. Geographers, A.A.A.S., N.Y. State Geog. Assn. (pres., 1938) Newcomen Society North America, Sigma Xi, Alpha Epsilon Delta (v.p.), Alpha Chi Rho, Phi Kappa Phi, Chi Gamma Phi, Beta Gamma Sigma. Republican. Presbyn. Club: Century (Syrcuse). Author: World Geography, 1944; a Workbook in World Geography, 1944; also articles in profl. jours. Home: Syracuse NY Died May 17, 1971; buried Hillside Cemetery, Middletown NY

FAINSOD, MERLE, professor; born at McKees Rocks, Pa., May 2, 1907; s. Louis and Frieda (Marcus) F.; A.B., Washington U., 1928, M.A., 1930; M.A., Harvard U., 1931, Ph.D., 1932; LL.D., Washington University, 1956; married Elizabeth Stix, Apr. 27, 1933; children—Elizabeth Stix (Mrs. Frederick Fitzpayne), Mary Lewis (Mrs. Peter J. Katzenstein). Instr. in govt., Harvard U., 1933-38, asst. prof., 1938-44, asso. prof., 1944-46, prof., 1946-64, Leroy B. Williams prof. history and polit. sci., 1964, dir. Harvard U. Library and librarian of coll., 1964-72, Carl H. Pforzheimer professor, from 1965, chmn. dept. of government, 1946-49; visiting lecturer, Yale University, 1940; member staff President's Com. on Administrative Management, 1936; consultant Temporary Nat. Economics Com., 1940; price exec. Consumers Durable Goods, Office of Price Adminstrn., 1941-42, dir. Retail Trade and Services Div., 1942-43. Commd. captain, Specialists Reserve, Army United States, May 1943; deputy director, Civil Affairs Training School, Harvard University, 1944-45. Awarded Sheldon traveling fellowship, Harvard, 1932-33. Trustee East European Fund; dir. Russian Research Center. Mem. Am. Phiios. Soc., Am. Council Learned Socs. (dir.), Am. Polit. Sci. Assn. (pres. 1966-67, exec. council, 1948-50), Am. Acad. Arts and Scis. Author: American People and Their Government (with A. J. Lien), 1933; Internat. Socialism and the World War, 1935; Government and the Am. Economy (with A.L. Gordon), 1941, 48; How Russia is Ruled, 1953, rev. 1963; Smolensk Under Soviet Rule, 1958. Contributor to Public Administration Review, Am. Econ. Rev., Yale Law Jour., Jour. of Politics, Am. Polit. Sci. Review (asso. editor 1951). Home: Cambridge MA Died Feb. 11, 1972; buried Mt. Auburn Cemetery, Cambridge MA

FAIR, GORDON MASKEW, prof. engring.; b. Burghersdorp, Union of South Africa, July 27, 1894; s. Charles and Maria (Maskew) F.; grad. Werner Siemens Gymnasium, Berlin, 1913; S.B., Mass. Inst. of Tech., 1916; S.B., Harvard, 1916; hon. M.S., Tufts Coll., 1934; Dr. Ing. Technische Hochschule, Stuttgart, 1951; hon. fellow Imperial Coll. Sci. and Tech., 1951; Dr. honoris causae, Universidad Nacional de Ingenieria, Lima, Peru, 1960; Doctor of Science, Rose Polytechnic Institute, 1963; Doctor of Science, Rutgers, The State Univ., 1965; m. Esther Lansing Mead, December 21, 1918; children—Gordon Maskew, Cornelius Lansing. Began as sanitary engr., 1917; instr. to prof. Harvard Univ., 1918-35, Gordon McKay prof. of sanitary engring. 1935-65, Abbott and James Lawrence prof. of engring. 1938-65, McKay and Lawrence prof. emeritus, from 1965, dean faculty of engring., 1946-49; master of Dunster House, 1948-61; cons. on san. engring. to govt. agencies, industries; and founds., including National Mil. Establishment 1946-53; internat. health div., Rockefeller Found. 1945-48, 1949-54, Commn. on Environmental Hygiene, Army Epidemiological Bd. 1946-54; chmn. environmental health study sect. NIH, 1952-55; mem. NRC committee on sanitary engineering 1942-64; mem. panel on environmental sanitation WHO. Registered profl. engr., Mass. Served C.E.F., World War I. Fellow Am. Soc. Civil Engrs., Am. Acad. Arts and Scis.; mem. Am. Water Works Assn., Am. Pub. Health Assn., A.A.A.S. (v.p, 1947), Sigma Xi, Nat. Acad. engring., other profl. and scientific socs. and assns. Clubs: Cosmos (Washington); Faculty (Harvard). Author books and chpts. on water supply, and waste water disposal. Contbr. scientific articles to jours. Home: Cambridge MA Died Feb. 11, 1970.*

FAIRCHILD, CLARENCE A., coffee mcht.; b. Flushing, N.Y., Sept. 19, 1871; s. Elias A. and Laura Seymour (de Mauriac) F.; ed. Flushing (N.Y.) Inst.; unmarried. Partner F. N. Saunders & Co., 1905-11; organized, 1911, and head firm of C. A. Fairchild & Co., U.S. agt. for exporters of coffee from Santos and Rio de Janeiro, Brazil; retired 1925. Pres. New York Coffee and Sugar Exchange, Inc., 1919-21. Republican. Clubs: Manhasset Bay Yacht, Huntington Yacht. Home: 29 Colden St., Flushing NY‡

FAIRCHILD, SHERMAN M., aviation exec.; b. Oneonta, N.Y., Apr. 7, 1896; ed. U. of Ariz., Harvard and Columbia. Inventor of Fairchild aerial camera; chmn. of the bd. Fairchild Camera and Instrument Co., 1925-71, head, Dynar Corporation; owner of Fairchild Recording Equipment Corp.; chmn. bd. Fairchild Industries; director Conrac. Corp., IBM Corp. Mem. bd. govs. Audio Engring. Soc. Fellow Inst. Aeronautical Scis., Royal Aero. Soc. Home: Huntington LI NY Died Mar. 28, 1971; buried Oneonta NY

FAIRCLOUGH, GEORGE HERBERT, organist, mus. dir.; b. Hamilton, Ont., Can., Jan. 30, 1869; s. James and Elizabeth (Erving) F.; brother of Henry Rushton F. (q.v.); student U. of Toronto, 1887-89; Toronto Conservatory of Music, 1887-89; Royal High Sch. of Music, Berlin, Germany, 1892-95; Paris and London, England; married Helen Maude Freeman, September 22, 1897 (she died November 18, 1946); children—Gordon Freeman, George Herbert, Helen Elizabeth (Mrs. Charles W. Barnett), Edith Scribner (Mrs. Harold Flemming), James Erving. Has been a church organist since age of 11; organist St. Mark's Church, Hamilton, Ont., Canada, 1880, Ch. of Ascension, Hamilton, 1885, Ch. of Redeemer, Toronto, 1887, All Saints' Ch., Toronto, 1889; frequently played at St. George's English Ch., Berlin, 1891-95; organist St. Luke's Epis. Ch., Kalamazoo, Mich., 1895-1900, St. John's Episcopal Church, St. Paul, Minn., 1900-43, retired (emeritus), 1943; also organist Jewish Temple, St. Paul, 1904-22; head of Piano, Organ and Theory depts., Macalester Coll. Sch. of Music; conductor St. Paul Choral Assn., 1903-08. Mus. dir. Brantford (Ont.) Ladies' Coll., 1889-91; dir. Mus. Dept., Kalamazoo (Mich.) Coll., 1895-1909; conductor of large festival choruses in St. Paul at various times; head of organ dept., U. of Minn. School of Music, 1920-37, emeritus since 1937; acting organist and choirmaster Grace (Episcopal) Cathedral, Jan.-Mar. 1946, St. Francis Episcopal Ch., San Francisco, June-Aug. 1948. Fellow Am. Guild of Organists. Life mem. Phi Alpha Mu Sinfonia. Pres. Minn. Music Teachers' Assn., 1909-10, 1919-20; 2d v.p. Nat. Assn. Organists, 1909-10; dean Minn. Chapter Am. Guild of Organists, 1910-11, 1920-21, 1939-41, 1941-42, 1942-43. Composer of many published songs, ch. music, organ and piano pieces. Episcopalian. Mason (32 deg.). Home: 3045 Scott St., San Francisco 23 CA‡

FAIRFAX, ALBERT KIRBY, 12th Baron Fairfax of Cameron in the peerage of Scotland (confirmed by Com. on Privileges of House of Lords, Nov. 17, 1908); b. Prince George Co., Md., June 23, 1870; s. John Contee F., M.D. (11th baron, b. Md., Sept. 13, 1830); died, Sept. 28, 1900) and Mary, Baroness F., d. Col. Edmund Kirby, U.S.A. Clubs: Union (New York), City of London, Bachelors, Sports (London). V.-p. Soc. of Yorkshiremen in London; mem. London exec. com. The Pilgrims; mem. The Am. Soc. in London. A partner firm of Wm. P. Bonbright & Co., of New York, London and Colorado Springs. Address: 22 Upper George St., London England‡

FALCONER, DOUGLAS PLATT, executive secretary; b. Oak Park, Ill., Apr. 21, 1889; s. Cyrus and Martha (Platt) F.; A.B., Haverford College, 1912; married Margery Annesley Hoyt, 1914 (died 1948; children—Douglas (deceased), George H., Margaret A.; m. 2d, Mary Biddle Sinclair (dec. 1963); m. 3d, Judith Atwater. Child health work, Phila., 1912-13; exec. sec. Essex County Children's Air Soc. and Soc. for Prevention of Cruelty to Children, Newark, New Jersey, 1913-17; executive director Erie County Children's Aid Society and Society for Prevention of Cruelty to Children, Buffalo, New York, 1917-31; also executive director Joint Charities and Community Fund of Erie County for 5 years; (on leave) asso. exec. dir. N.Y. State Temporary Emergency Relief Administration, 1931; gen. sec. Brooklyn Bureau of Charities, 1932-38; (on leave) asso. exec. dir. Emergency Relief Bur. of City of N.Y., 1935; exec. dir. Greater N.Y. Fund, 1938-42; nat. exec. dir. United Seamen's Service, Inc. (recreation and relief to seamen in all parts of the world), Sept. 1942-Mar. 1946; became dep. dir. U.N.R.R.A., China, 1946; now exec. dir. Wyo. Valley Community Chest; has taught courses in child welfare, social case work, community organization at U. of Buffalo, Buffalo State Teachers Coll., N.Y. Sch. Social Work, also community courses to clubs, etc. Organizer and 1st pres. Urban League, Buffalo and Erie County; mem. Hoover White House Conf. on Child Health and Welfare; formerly mem. exec. com. Buffalo Council Social Agencies, president Buffalo Forum, etc.; chmn. Local Draft Bd., N.Y. City; charter mem. Am. Assn. Social Workers; mem. N.Y. State and Nat. Confs. of Social Work; member bd. Nat. Assn. for Advancement of Colored People, Field Foundation, National Opinion Research Center (Denver); mem. bd. visitors, N.Y. Training Sch. for Boys, Warwick, N.Y. Home: Wilkes-Barre PA Died Oct. 15, 1969.

FALCONER, JACOB ALEXANDER, congressman; b. Ontario, Can., Jan. 26, 1869; s. Thomas and Jane (Speers) F.; removed with parents to Saugatuck, Mich., at age of 4; grad. Beloit (Wis.) Acad., 1890; m. Mabel Thomson, of Saugatuck, Mich., Feb. 28, 1896. Located in Everett, Wash., 1894; engaged as mfr. shingles, later buying and selling timber lands on own account; mayor of Everett 2 terms, 1897, 1898; mem. Wash. Ho. of Rep., 2 terms, 1904-8 (speaker of House session of 1907), State Senate, 1909-12, inclusive; mem. 63d Congress (1913-15), Wash. at-large; Progressive. Conglist. Pres. Everett Playground Assn. Address: Everett WA‡

FALES, HERBERT PECK, trust co. executive; b. Detroit, Oct. 29, 1904; s. Bingley Russell and Alice May (Peck) F.; student Princeton University, 1923-25; A.B., Pomona (California) College, 1928; A.M., Oxford University, 1937; married Rose Foster Hyde, Oct. 10, 1938; children—Willia Foster, Alice Peck. Asst. cashier, Union Nat. Bank, Pasadena, Calif., 1930-35; mem. U.S. Naval Observatory Eclipse Expdn. to Niuafoou, Tonga, 1930; apptd. U.S. fgn. service officer of career and vice consul, Berlin, 1937; with visa div., Dept. of State, 1938; vice consul, Vienna, 1939-40; with div. Far Eastern Affairs, Dept. of State, 1940-42, financial div., 1942-44; State Dept. rep. in bilateral tax treaty negotiations between U.S. and fgn. countries, 1943-45; sec. of embassy and consul, London, 1945-46 member fiscal com. League of Nations, 1946; assistant chief, div. Brit. Commonwealth Affairs, Dept. of State, 1947-49; chmn. U.S. reps. U.S.-U.K. consular treaty negotiations, 1948; Nat. War Coll., 1949; chief div. econ. affairs, Office U.S. High Commr. for Berlin, acting U.S. economic advisor, Berlin rep. E.C.A. spl. mission to Germany, 1950; office of Dir. of Econ. Affairs, Bonn, 1951; polit. advisor European Command and U.S. Army, Europe, Heidelberg, 1952; dep. chief of mission, counselor of embassy of U.S. Djakarta, Indonesia, 1955; exec. dir. Bd. of Examiners for Fgn. Service, Dept. of State, 1956-57; dep. chief of mission, counselor of Am. Embassy The Hague, 1958-60; member of foreign service selection boards, 1960; counselor of Embassy, Am. consul gen., Paris. 1961-64; mgr. internat. banking dept. Am. Security & Trust Co., Washington, 1964-71. Bd. of dirs. Internat. Student House, Madeira Sch. Corp., Diplomatic and Consular Officers Retired. Member of the Netherlands-America Society (director). Clubs: Metropolitan, Nat. Press (Washington); Chevy Chase (Md); Reform (London); Princeton (N.Y.C.) Travellers (Paris). Home: Washington DC Died Aug. 1971.

FALES, WINNIFRED (SHAW), writer; b. Antrim, N.H., May 3, 1875; d. Rev. E. Melville and Carolyn (Burpee) Shaw; ed. pub. schs. Rockland, Me., pvt. tutors and Pratt Inst., Brooklyn, N.Y.; m. William E. S. Fales, of N.Y. City, Aug. 1902 (died May 16, 1906). Writer of magazine articles and advertising. Author: The Party Book (with Mary H. Northend), 1912; The Household Dictionary, 1920; The Easy Housekeeping Book, 1922; A Simple Course in Home Decorating, 1923; What's New in Home Decorating, 1936; Personality in Home Decoration, 1937. Home: 43 Park St., Rockland ME‡

FALLON, LESTER (RAYMOND), business exec.; born Dorchester, Mass., April 26, 1896; s. Michael and Harriette (Shields) F.; ed. Mechanic Arts High Sch., Boston; m. Edna Henry, June 16, 1934; 1 son, Peter. Entire career with shoe industry; started wholesale house in Boston after high sch. graduation; later worked for planning depts. of factories and as salesman; in retailing as gen. mgr. of mens chain, Melville Shoe Corp., from 1928, v.p., 1947-49, dir., from 1948, exec. v.p., 1948-56, v.p. from 1956; pres. Thom McAn Shoe Co., dir. of Melville Shoe Corp., from 1956. Club: Wykagyl Country (New Rochelle, N.Y.). Home: New Rochelle NY

FALLS, CHARLES BUCKLES, illustrator; b. Ft. Wayne, Ind., Dec. 10, 1874; m. Bedelia Mary Croly, Mar. 16, 1917; 1 daughter, Bedelia Charles (Mrs. John Larry Washburn). Widely known as designer, artist, mural painter and etcher. Member Society of Illustrators (honorary). Clubs: Artists Guild (honorary president), Century, Players (New York). Home: Falls Village CT‡

FANER, ROBERT DUNN, educator; b. Waterford, Pa., July 12, 1906; s. Joseph F. and Gertrude (Dunn) F.; A.B., Allegheny Coll., 1927; M.A., U. Ia., 1928; Ph.D., U. Pa., 1947. Instr. English, U. Ore., 1928-30; mem. faculty So. Ill. U., 1930-67, prof. English, 1952-67, chmn. dept., 1964-67. Fulbright prof. univs. Aix-en-Provence and Grenoble (France), 1959-60; vis. prof. U. Colo., summers 1940, 41, U. Ill., 1961. Pres. Carbondale Community Concert Assn., 1950-67. Served with USAAF, 1942-45. Named Great Tchr., So. Ill. U., 1964. Mem. Phi Kappa Phi (chpt. pres. 1965). Presbyn. (elder). Author: Walt Whitman and Opera, 1951. Home: Carbondale IL Died Dec. 14, 1967; buried Waterford PA

FANNING, LAWRENCE STANLEY, newspaperman; b. Minneapolis, Apr. 14, 1914; s. Thomas Joseph and Margaret (Ruth) F.; student U. of San Francisco, 1933-35; married Phyllis Burnham, 1936 (divorced, 1951); children—Michael Larry, and Judith Noan; m. second, Virginia Mahoney, 1952; m. third, Katherine Woodruff Field, 1966. Copy boy, copy reader, telegraph editor, asst. news editor, news editor, asst. mng. editor San Francisco Chronicle, 1933-45, then mng. editor till 1954; editor Chicago Sun-Times Syndicate, 1955-57;

asst. exec. editor Chgo., Sun-Times, 1957-59, exec. editor, 1959-62; exec. editor Chgo. Daily News, 1962-65, editor Chgo. Daily News, 1965-66; editor, pub. Anchorage News, Anchorage, Alaska, 1967-71; dir. Field Enterprises. Mem. Am. Soc. Newspaper Editors, Internat. Press Inst., Sigma Delta Chi. Home: Anchorage AK Died Feb. 3, 1971.

FANNING, RALPH, prof. fine arts; b. Riverhead, L.I., N.Y., Nov. 29, 1889; s. William Richard and Ella Jane (Hulse) F.; grad. Friends Acad., Locust Valley, L.I., 1908; B. Arch., Cornell U., 1912; M.S. in History, U. of Ill., 1917, M.Arch., 1920; unmarried. Asso. in architecture, U. of Ill., 1920; asst. prof. fine arts, Ohio State U., 1921-25, prof. fine arts since 1925; lecturer history of fine arts, U. of Calif., summers 1924, 25; lecturer Bur. of University, Travel, summers 1926-37. On staff Emergency Housing Bd., U.S. Ship Building Corpn., 1917; emergency housing staff, Am. Red Cross, in France, 1918; housing staff Friends Reconstruction Unit for devastated regions of France, 1918-19. Exhibitor water color painting, Pa. Acad. Fine Arts, 1924, 32; Internat. Exhbn. water color painters, Chicago, 1924. Awarded medal, Beaux Arts Soc., New York, 1912; Francis Sampson prize, 1912; Robert Wolfe water color prize, 1924. Home: Columbus OH Died Apr. 1971.

FARAGHER, DONALD QUALTROUGH, architect; b. Rochester, N.Y., Apr. 11, 1906; s. William Henry and Ella (Qualtrough) F.; B.Arch., Syracuse U., 1930; m. Harriet Miller Thistlethwaite, June 20, 1931; children—Anthony Thistlethwaite, Rachel Qualtrough. Draughtsman, F.R. Scherer, Architect, Rochester, 1926-33; architect engrs. office City of Rochester, 1933-34; pvt. practice, Rochester, 1934-42, 45-71; partner Faragher & Macomber, 1951-71; supervising architect Rochester-Monroe County Civic Center, 1954-71, master plan Rochester Civic Center 1954-71. Mem. Bd. Examiners Architects N.Y. State, 1950-59, pres., 1954-57; chmn. finance com. Nat. Council Architects Registration Bds., 1959-71; adv. com. facilities and planning N.Y. Dept. Edn.; adviser Rochester Bldg. Bd. on N.Y. State Code, 1951-71; mem. Bldg. Research Inst. representing A.I.A. on Nat. Acad. Sci., 1959; mem. sr. thesis juries Syracuse U. Sch. Architecture, 1949-59, coop. com., 1952-71; bd. appeals N.Y. State Bldg. Constrn., 1960-71. Recipient Lillian Fairchild award U. Rochester, 1952; Arents medal Syracuse U., 1960; citation for Ellison Park Apts., Central N.Y. chpt. A.I.A. and N.Y. State Assn. Architects, 1950; certificate of merit for outstanding design of Rochester E. High Sch., N.Y. State Assn. Architects, 1958. Fellow A.I.A. (mem. commn. on edn. and research, dir. N.Y., trustee Found.); member N.Y. State (pres. 1951-52, dir. 1959-61, chmn. edn. com. 1953-60), Assn. Architects, Rochester (pres. 1948-50, chmn. legislative com. 1959-63), Soc. Architects, Rochester Engring. Soc. (pres. 1957-58, dir. 1958-61), Am. Soc. Testing Materials, Rochester C. of C., Rochester Music Assn., Syracuse U. Archtl. Alumni Assn. (pres. 1958), Sigma Alpha Epsilon, Sigma Upsilon Alpha. Republican. Presbyn. Clubs: Lake Placid (N.Y.); Rochester Country, Torch (dir. 1957-59), University (Rochester). Home: Rochester NY Died Feb. 5, 1971.

FARBER, JOHN CLARKE, lawyer; b. Frankfort, Ind., Mar. 6, 1893; s. John C. and Ruth Margaret (Sims) F.; A.B., Wabash Coll., Crawfordsville, Ind., 1915, A.M., 1916; LL.B., Columbia U., 1921; m. Alice Marion Shaw, Sept. 1, 1923. Admitted to N.Y. bar, 1921 and since practiced in N.Y. City; with Simpson, Thacher & Bartlett, 1921-24; partner Walker & Redman, 1925-29, Roosevelt (Franklin D.) & O'Connor, 1929-33, Basil O'Connor, 1933, O'Connor & Farber, since 1934; specializes in ins. and banking law; pres., treas., dir. Aganox, Inc.; v.p., dir. Malvern Hill & Co., Inc., Peck & Mack Company; dir. J. M. Mathes, Inc. 2d lt. S.C., 1918-19. Trustee, gen. counsel, sec. George Duffy Found. Mem. Am. and N.Y. State bar assns., Assn. Bar of City of New York, N.Y. County Lawyers Assn., Phi Beta Kappa, Beta Theta Pi. Republican. Presbyterian. Clubs: Bankers, Downtown Athletic, Lawyers. Author books and articles including: (with Maurice Mound) An Analysis of the new York Law Relating to Fire and Casualty Insurance, 1939. Home: New York City NY Died Feb. 10, 1969; buried Crawfordsville IN

FARBER, SIDNEY, physician; b. Buffalo, Sept. 30, 1903; s. Simon and Matilda (Goldstein) F.; B.S., U. Buffalo, 1923; M.D., Harvard, 1927; post-grad. research, Germany, 1928-29, Belgium, 1935-36; D.Sc., (hon.), Suffolk U., 1960, Boston U., 1961, Providence Coll., 1961, Albert Einstein Coll. Medicine, 1966, N.Y. Med. Coll., 1970; M.D. (hon.), U. Ghent (Belgium), 1962, Cath. U. Louvain (Belgium), 1965, Karolinska Institute, Stockholm, Sweden, 1969; L.H.D. (hon.), Brandeis U., 1963; m. Norma C. Holzman, July 3, 1928; children—Ellen, Stephen Burt, Thomas David, Miriam. Faculty, Harvard Med. Sch. 1927-70, S. Burt Wolbach prof. pathology, 1967-70, prof. emeritus, 1970-73; prof. pathology, Harvard Med. Sch. at Children's Hosp., 1948-67; pathologist-in-chief, chmn. div. labs. and research, Children's Med. Center 1946-70; chmn. staff Children's Hosp. Med. Center, 1964-70, cons. in pathology and oncology, 1970-73. Founder, sci. dir. Children's Cancer Research Found. 1948-73; cons. Armed Forces Inst. Pathology, U.S. Pub. Health Services, Nat. Cancer Inst. Trustee Worcester Found. Exptl. Biology, Southwest Found. Research and Edn., San Antonio; founding trustee United Cerebral Palsy Research and Ednl. Found.; mem. Nat. Adv. Cancer Council; chmn. panel on cancer. Pres.'s Commn. Heart Disease, Cancer and Stroke, 1964. Pres., Am. Assn. Pathologists and Bacteriologists, 1957-58, Soc. Pediatric Research, 1947-48; pres. New Eng. Pathol. Soc., Boston Pathol. Soc.; bd. dirs. Belgian Am. Ednl. Found.; trustee Brandeis U., sec. bd. trustees, 1967; mem. sci. adv. bds. Rosell Park Research Inst., New Eng. Deaconess Hosp. Recipient Gt. medal U. Ghent, 1959; Modern Medicine award, 1962; Albert Lasker award for clinical research, 1966; Boston medal for distinguished achievement, 1967; Jurzykowski award in med. sci., 1970; Papnicolou award, 1971. Diplomate Am. Bd. Pathology. Fellow N.Y. Acad. Scis., Am. Acad. Arts and Scis.; mem. A.M.A., Am. Pediatric Soc., Asso. Cancer Inst. Dirs. (pres. 1963-65), Am. Assn. Cancer Research (hon.), James Ewing Soc. (hon.), Sigma Xi, Phi Beta Kappa, Alpha Omega Alpha. Club: Harvard. Editorial bd. Cancer, Biochem. Pharmacology. Home: Cambridge MA Died Mar. 30, 1973.

FARENHOLT, AMMEN, officer Navy Med. Corps; b. Norfolk, Va., Dec. 9, 1871; s. Rear Adm. Oscar Walter and Ella Mortimer (Ames) E.; M.D., Harvard, 1893; m. Mrs. William H. Whiting, Aug. 11, 1926. Apptd. asst. surgeon, U.S. Navy, July 2, 1894; promoted through grades to rear admiral, Dec. 7, 1926. Served with Dewey at Manila, later in Philippine Insurrection and on China Coast; duty on U.S.S. Baltimore, Oregon, Maryland, Independence, etc.; comdr. hosp. ship Mercy, 1921, later comdr. Naval Hospital, Mare Island, California, Great Lakes, Illinois, and Puget Sound, Washington; inspector Naval Medical Corps activities on East Coast, 1930, also asst. to chief of Bur. of Medicine and Surgery, Washington; apptd. insp. Med. Dept. activities of West Coast, Aug. 24, 1931; retired, Jan. 1, 1936. Fellow Am. Coll. Surgeons; mem. A.M.A. Campaign awards, also citation for services in World War. Presbyterian. Club: New York Yacht. Contbr. to Naval Med. Bulletin and Naval Institute. Address: 3626 Hyacinth Drive, San Diego CA‡

FARIS, PAUL PATTON, editor, writer; b. Clinton, Ill., June 14, 1877; s. Rev. Wm. Wallace (D.D.) and Isabella Hardy (Thomson) F.; grad. Pittsburgh Academy, 1894; student Rollins Coll., Winter Park, Fla.; A.B., Park College., 1901, Litt.D., 1937; graduate McCormick Theological Seminary, Chicago, Illinois, 1905; m. Mary Helena Alexander, May 24, 1905; children—Eunice Thomson (Mrs. Alexander Cowie), Mary Alexander and Margaret Wallace (twins, both dec.), Rosemary Alexa. Formerly printer and teacher; ordained Presbyn. ministry, 1905; sent as missionary to China, 1905; principal McPherson Acad. for Boys, Ichowfu, 1907-14; lit. editor The Continent, Chicago, 1914-26; editor Fleming H. Revell Co., New York, 1926-29; editor-in-chief of Presbyterian Banner, Pittsburgh, 1932-34; publicity dir. Presbyn. Ch., U.S.A., since 1934. Regional director Internat. Y.M.C.A., in France, 1918-19. Mem. Presbyn. Gen. Assembly, Spl. Com. on Religious Radio, Race Relations publicity com. Fed. Council of Chs., publicity com. of Presbyn. Wartime Service Commn. Author: Builders of the Church, 1922; The Child in His World (with Gertrude Hutton), 1923; Modern Builders of the Church, 1924; Adventures in Money Raising (with Cornelius M. Steffens), 1930; also articles in Dictionary of Am. Biography. Contbr. to religious periodicals. Editor: Presbyn. Pastors' News, 1934-35; Presbyn. Plan Book, 1935-40; Monday Morning, 1939-45; General Assembly Daily News, Presbyterian Interdenominational News. Republican. Club: Canterbury Cleric, (Phila). Home: Buck Inn, Old Buck Lane, Haverford, Pa. Office: 518 Witherspoon Bldg., Philadelphia 7 PA‡

FARLEY, RICHARD BLOSSOM, artist; b. Poultney, Vt., Oct. 24, 1875; son Dickinson Harvey and Freberne Lucia (Blossom) F.; ed. N.J. State Model Sch., Trenton, N.J., studied art at Pa. Acad. Fine Arts, Phila; awarded traveling scholarship and studied in Europe under Whistler and at Beaux Arts, Paris; m. Abigail Rosenthal, June 17, 1914 (died 1926); children—Richard Blossom, Abigail Freberne. Has specialized in portraits and in painting sand, sea and sky. Awards: Fellowship prize, Pa. Acad. Fine Arts, 1912; gold medal, Phila. Art. Club, 1913; silver medal, San Francisco Expn., 1915; Fourth Clark prize, Corcoran Gallery, Washington, D.C., 1914. Represented in Corcoran Gallery by Fog"; in Pa. Acad. by Morning Mists." Mural paintings in Phila. Art Alliance, N.J. State Teachers Coll., Am. Theosophical Soc. (Wheaton, Ill.), South Phila. High Sch. for Girls. Marine camoufleur, stationed at N.Y. City and Norfolk, Va., World War. Fellowship Pa. Acad. Fine Arts; mem. Phila. Sketch Club, Art Alliance, Phila., Phila. Botanical Club, Coin Club, Am. Numismatic Assn. Protestant. Address: Sarobia,", PA‡

FARMER, CHESTER JEFFERSON, univ. prof.; b. N. Andover, Mass., July 18, 1886; s. Thomas Jefferson and Mary Elizabeth (Whittier) F.; student Lowell Textile Inst., 1904-07; A.M., Harvard, 1913; m. Mary Grace Pearson, 1914 (deceased); children—Gilbert Jefferson, Mary Frances; m. 2d, Marjorie Blake Owen, 1938. Austin teaching fellow, Harvard, 1910-11; asst. in biochemistry, Harvard Med. Sch., 1911-13; prof. of biochemistry, Marquette U. Med. Sch., 1913-18; asso. prof. chemistry, Northwestern U. Med. Sch., 1918-19, prof., 1919-51, emeritus; vis. prof. biochem. La. State U. Med. Sch., 1951-53, Fellow Institue Medicine, Chicago; mem. A.A.A.S., Am. Soc. Biol. Chemists, Soc. of Exptl. Biology and Medicine, Am. Assn. Univ. Profs., Phi Rho Sigma, Sigma Xi, Phi Lambda Upsilon. Republican. Episcopalian. Mason. Contbr. articles to med. jours. Home: Cedar Lake IN Died May 1969.

FARMER, DONALD FRANCIS, surgeon; b. Chgo., Feb. 12, 1914; s. James Francis and Mary (Keenan) F.; B.S., Loyola U., Chgo., 1936, M.D., 1938; m. Shirley Gardner, Dec. 28, 1940; 1 dau., Madonna Jean. Intern Little Company of Mary Hosp., Chgo., 1937-38; gen. practice medicine, Chgo., 1938-41, 46-60; med. dir. Fisher Body div. Gen. Motors Corp., Willow Springs, Ill., 1960-67; pres., med. dir. Beverly Blood Center, Inc., Chgo., 1954-67. Served to maj., M.C., AUS, 1941-46. Fellow Internat. Coll. Surgeons; mem. A.M.A., Indsl. Med. Assn., Am. Bd. Abdominal Surgery (founder's group), Chgo. Med. Soc., Med. Dirs. Club of Chgo. Author med. publs. Home: Chicago IL Died Mar. 19, 1967.

FARMER, EDWARD MCNEIL, educator; b. Los Angeles, Feb. 23, 1901; s. Edward Lewis and Elizabeth (Lesley) F.; A.B., Stanford U., 1923, M.A., 1926; Art Students League, N.Y. City, 1929; m. Mabel Ferris McKibbin, Sept. 3, 1927; children—Andrew McKibbin, Mark Lesley, Edward Lewis. Acting instr. graphic art, Stanford U., 1923-25, instr., 1925-32, acting asst. prof., 1932-36, asst. prof., 1936-40, asso. prof., 1940-46, prof. art, 1946-64. Active as painter and designer. Mem. Pacific Arts Assn., Western Coll. Arts Assn. Home: Stanford CA Died Aug. 20, 1969.

FARMER, F. MALCOLM, ret. elec., engr.; born Ilion, N.Y., Mar. 28, 1877; s. William Chesterton and Agnes (MacCrum) F.; prep. edn., Ilion Acad.; M.E., Cornell U., 1899; m. Lucy Merriman, June 6, 1906 (died August 20, 1949); one dau.; Alison (Mrs. Paul Wescott). Served as student engr. of General Electric Co., Schenectady, N.Y., 1899-1900; insp. U.S. Navy Dept., Brooklyn, N.Y., 1901-03; lecturer Cooper Union Inst., New York, 1902-06; tech. asst. Elec. Testing Labs., New York, 1903-06, engr., 1906-12, chief engr., 1912-42, cons. engr. since 1942, v.p. 1929-49, pres., 1949-53, dir., hon. chmn. bd., 1953-57. Tech. cons. insp. methods, N.Y. Ordnance Dist., U.S. Army, 1942-45. An authority on elec. measurements, elec. insulating materials, testing engring. materials and high voltage cables. Awarded War Dept. Certificate of Commendation, 1946. Past chmn. standards council Am. Standards Assn., Engring. Found., John Fritz Medal Com. and Hoover Medal Com.; past pres. United Engring. Trustees. Fellow Am. Inst. Elec. Engrs. (pres. 1939-40); mem. A.A.A.S., Am. Soc. Mech. Engrs., Instn. Electrical Engrs. (British), Am. Soc. Testing Materials (pres. 1924-25, hon. member, 1948), Am. Welding Society (pres. 1926-28). Republican. Club: Engineers. Author: Electrical Measurements in Practice, 1917; also numerous tech. papers before Am. Inst. Elec. Engrs., (paper on high tension cables received both first nat. first dist. prizes, 1926), etc. Contbr. to Standard Handbook of Electrical Engineers, 1933; asso. editor American Civil Engineers' Handbook, 1930; Underground Systems Reference Book, 1931. Made investigation and report on high tension cable practice in Europe, 1923. Home: 331 W. Miner St., West Chester PA‡

FARMER, GENE, mag. editor, journalist; b. Dora, Okla., Aug. 20, 1919; s. Hiram C. and Grace E. (Scott) F.; student Ark. Polytech. Coll., 1935-37; B.A., U. Ark., 1939; M.S. in Journalism, Northwestern U., 1940; m. Kay Doering, Sept. 30, 1949 (div.); children—Jeffrey K., Michele M.; m. 2d, Enid P. Colfer, Oct. 21, 1958; children—Thomas Ian, Terence Scott, Tristram Evan. Reporter, state editor, city editor Cedar Rapids (Ia.) Gazette, 1940-45; national affairs corr. Life mag., 1945-46, sports editor, 1947-49, asst. editor nat. affairs, 1949-50, chief London corr., 1950-53, fgn. editor, 1953-72, also sr. editor. Recipient Distinguished Alumnus citation U. Ark., 1954; decorated chevalier Legion of Honor. Mem. Phi Beta Kappa. Club: Overseas Press (N.Y.C.). Republican. Author: Massachusetts: The Anatomy of Quality. Home: Lexington MA Died June 1972.

FARNELL, FREDERIC JAMES, psychiatrist; b. Providence, R.I., Jan. 14, 1885; s. George and M. Elizabeth (Topham) F.; M.D., Cornell U. Med. Coll., 1908; hon. M.B.A., Bryant and Stratton Coll. Business Administration; m. Jessie Worrell, Dec. 23, 1909 (divorced); children—F. Richard, Marjorie E. (dec.); m. 2d, Eva May Edgett, Jan. 25, 1939. Licensed to practice medicine, R.I., 1909, N.Y. State, 1909; settled in Providence, 1911; clin. prof. psychiatry, New York Med. Coll; asst. psychiatrist, Psychiatry Dept., Flower-Fifth Av. Hosp.; asso. attending neuro-psychiatrist, Met. Hosp., N.Y., attending neurologist, historian, from 1944; attending neurologist Murray Hill Hosp., N.Y. City; visiting neuro-psychiatrist, St. Vincent's Hosp., New Brighten,

S.I.; psychiatrist R.I. State Hosp. for Mental Diseases; has served as psychiatrist or neurologist to Providence City Hosp., St. Joseph's Hosp., Newport Hosp., French Hosp. (Pawtucket, R.I.), pub. schs. of Providence, etc.; asst. in research, neuro-pathology, Mt. Sinai Hosp., 1945-47; cons. neuro-psychiat., U.S. Vets. Bur., Dist. 4.; chief neurology and therapist in psychiatry, Jamaica Center for Psychotherapy, 1958; attending staff Gracie Sq. Hosp., N.Y.C.; courtsey staff neuro-psychiatry Medical Arts Center, N.Y.C., Past chmn., R.I. State Public Welfare Commn.; chmn. com. on spl. legislation on prision labor, Nat. Com. on Prisons and Prison Labor; formerly mem. bd. of dirs. Am. Prison Assn. mem. bd. of Nat. Com. on Prisons and Prison Labor. Qualified psychiatrist N.Y. State Bd. Psychol. Examiners, Mental Hygiene. Diplomate in neurology and psychiatry. Mem. Am. advisory council, Euthanasia Soc. of America. Mem. N.Y. Acad. of Medicine, Internat. Psychoanalytic Soc., N.Y. Psychoanalytic Soc. (ex-pres.), Am. Coll. Physicians (gov.), R.I. Soc. for Mental Hygiene (dir. and exec. com.), R.I. Med. Assn., Am. Neurol. Assn., Nat. Com. of Mental Hygiene, New York Acad. Sciences; asso. mem. Medico-Psychol. Soc. of Paris; hon. mem. Young Men's Council of U.S.; hon. mem. Eugene Field Lit. Soc. Patron Smithsonian Institute (science). Republican. Protestant. Co-author (with Dr. Harms) Handbook of Socio-Psychiatry. Contbr. to Sir William Osler's publs., and med. jours.; collaborating editor Am. Jour. Nervous and Mental Diseases; asso. editor The Nervous Child; mem. editorial bd. Jour. Child Psychiatry. Address: New York City NY Died Nov. 4, 1968.

FARNESS, ORIN JOCEVIOUS, physician; b. DeForest, Wis., Jan. 26, 1907; s. Joseph and Slyvia (Hustad) F.; student St. Olaf Coll., Northfield, Minn., 1924-27; B.S., U. Minn., 1929, M.B., 1930, M.D., 1932; m. Kathleen King Flynn, Mar. 7, 1937. Intern Univ. Hosp., Mpls. Gen. Hosp., 1931-32; resident Bellevue Hosp., N.Y.C., 1936, Desert Sanatorium, Tucson, 1936-40; practice medicine, specializing in internal medicine, Tucson, 1941-42, 46-70; chief staff Tucson Med. Center, 1951-70, chief med. service, 1962-70; mem. staff St. Mary's St. Joseph's hosps.; cons. VA Hosp., Tucson. Mem. Ariz. Bd. Med. Examiners, 1953-56. Dir. Ariz. Land Title & Trust Co. Pres. Community Serve, Inc., 1960-61. Bd. dirs. Western Fund. Served to lt. col., M.C., AUS, 1942-46; PTO. Nominee Presidents medal in Sci. Diplomate Am. Bd. Internal Medicine, Fellow A.C.P., Am. Coll. Chest Physicians (bd. regents); mem. A.M.A., Pima County Med. Assn. (past pres.), Nat. TB Assn. (past dir.), U. Minn. Alumni Assn., So. Ariz. Heart Assn. (pres. 1967—), Founder's For Ariz. Med. Edn., Newcomen Soc. N.Am., Sigma Xi. Republican. Rotarian. Club: Old Pueblo. Contbr. articles med. jours., texts. Home: Tucson AZ Died July 18, 1970; buried Norway Grove Ch. Cemetery, DeForest WI

FARNHAM, ROBERT, chief engr.; b. Washington, D.C., Dec. 19, 1877; s. Robert and Emma Jane (Lowry) F.; student Columbian (now George Washington) U., 1894-95; C.E., Lehigh U., 1899; m. Gertrude Hanley, of St. Paul, Minn., Nov. 22, 1911; 1 son, Robert. Asst., engr. corps, engring. dept., D.C., 1899-1902; with J. H. Gray & Co., N.Y. City, 1902-03; with Pa. R.R. Co. since 1903, transitman, engrs. corps, Mar.-Aug. 1903, asst. engr. constrn., in charge constrn. work, Washington, D.C., 1903-10, asst. engr. office of engr. bridges and bldgs., 1910-13, asst. to engr. bridges and bldgs., 1913-16, asst. engr. bridges and bldgs., 1916-23, engr. same, 1923-27, chief engr., Philadelphia improvements, 1927-37, asst. chief engr. Eastern Region of Pa. R.R. since Sept. 1937. Mem. Am. Soc. C.E. (dir. 1924-26), Am. Ry. Engring. Assn., Am. Soc. Testing Materials, Sigma Chi. Republican. Episcopalian. Clubs: Engineers, Pennsylvania Golf. Home: 7126 Cresheim Rd., Mount Airy. Office: Broad St. Station, Philadelphia PA‡

FARNSWORTH, PHILO TAYLOR, research engr.; b. Beaver, Utah, Aug. 19, 1906; s. Louis Edwin and Serena (Bastian) F.; student Rigby (Ida.) High Sch., 1922-23, Brigham Young U., 1923-25); Sc.D. (honorary), Indiana Inst. Tech., 1951; D.Sci. (honorary) Brigham Young Univ., 1968; m. Elma Gardner, May 27, 1926 children—Philo Taylor, Kenneth Gardner (dec.), Russell S., Kent. Associated with Farnsworth Television & Radio Corp., Fort Wayne, Ind., and predecessors, 1926-58; former pres., dir. Farnsworth Research Corporation division Internat. Tel. & Tel. Co.; former v.p., tech. dir. Farnsworth Electronics Co., lab. cons. International Tel. and Tel. Corp.; founder, pres., dir. Philo T. Farnsworth Assos., Inc. Fellow A.A.A.S., Institute of Electric and Electronic Engineers; mem. Franklin Institute, American Physical Society, Sigma Xi, also mem. Eta Kappa Nu. Recipient of the Brigham Young U. Alumnus award, 1937; hon. mention, 1937, Eta Kappa Nu; Morris Leibnan Memorial Prize, Inst. of Radio Engrs. 1941, named one of 10 outstanding young Am. Pioneers, 1940, 1st medal Television Broadcasters Assn., 1944, Distinguished Alumnus award Brigham Young U., 1953. Mem. Ch. of Latter Day Saints. Holder over 300 Am. and fgn. patents, television, radar, electronics; now directing nuclear research. Home: Salt Lake City UT Died Mar. 11, 1971; buried Provo UT

FARNSWORTH, SIDNEY WOODS, former mfg. exec.; b. Lancaster, Mass., Oct. 23, 1886; s. John Edward and Alice Peck (Woods) F.; B.S., Worcester Poly. Inst., 1906, E.E., 1908. D.Eng., 1967; m. Louise Stevenson, 1916; children—Emillie (Mrs. William Frick), Anne (Mrs. Arthur Huggler), Sidney Woods. Elec. engr. Westinghouse Electric Co., 1908-14; chief engr. U.S. Post Office Dept., Washington, 1922-25; v.p. Case Pomeroy & Co., N.Y.C., 1925-35; with Torrington Mfg. Co. (co. name changed to Torin Co.), 1945-65, pres., 1946-52, chmn. bd., 1952-65. Trustee and mem. exec. com. Worcester Poly. Inst., 1953-63. Asso. sci. attach Am. Embassy, London, World War I; mem. Navy Price Adjustment Bd., World War II. Awarded Civilian Merit (USN). Mem. Sigma Xi, Alpha Tau Omega. Republican. Conglist. Clubs: Upper Montclair (N.J.) Upper Montclair NJ Died Dec. 5, 1972.

FARNUM, GEORGE ROSSITER, lawyer; b. Melrose, Mass., May 30, 1885; s. George Peterson and Mary E. (Rossiter) F.; grad. high sch., Melrose, 1904; LL.B., summa cum laude, Boston U., 1907, LL.M., 1908; hon. Litt.D., Calvin Coolidge Coll., liberal arts, 1942; m. Ida Mae Demers, June 19, 1912. Admitted to Mass. bar, 1907, began practice at Boston; asst. U.S. atty., Mass., 1925-26, acting U.S. atty., 1926; asst. U.S. atty. general, 1927-30; former prof. law Suffolk U. Law Sch.; former lectr. on admiralty law, fed. jurisdiction and practice at Boston University Law Sch., former lectr. law Boston College Law School. Special counsel Finance Commission for City of Boston to conduct investigation into municipal adminstrn., 1934-35; special corp. counsel City of Boston in charge continuance said investigation, 1935; special counsel Finance Commn., City of Boston, to conduct further investigations into municipal adminstrn., 1937. Pres. New England Anti-Vivisection Society. Member of the Massachusetts Law Society, also mem. Phi Delta Phi. Republican. Club: Cosmos (Washington). Writer of numerous monographs and articles on legal, philos. and biog. subjects in law jours., periodicals and newspapers. Home: Boston MA

FARQUHAR, THOMAS LIPPINCOTT, insurance; b. Phila., Pa., Dec. 22, 1875; s. Benjamin Hallowell and Martha D. (Lippincott) F.; ed. pub. schs. and York (Pa.) Collegiate Inst.; m. Mary E. Chapman, of Phila., June 6, 1905; 1 dau., Ellenor Hallowell. Began in ins. business with Spring Garden Ins. Co., 1893; pres. Newark (N.J.) Fire Ins. Co., 1925-30, retired. Protestant. Home: 7 Woodland Rd., Maplewood NJ‡

FARR, CLIFFORD BAILEY, M.D.; b. Landis Twp., N.J., Apr. 17, 1872; s. Lincoln Dow and Hannah (Bailey) F.; A.B., Haverford, 1894, A.M., 1909; M.D., U. of Pa., 1898; m. Katharine Elliott, of Phila., Pa., Nov. 22, 1904; children—Robert Lincoln, Frank Winslow Elliott, James Bailey, Anne Bailey Foot. Began practice, Phila., 1901; teaching staff of med. dept. U. of Pa., 1901-19, advancing to prof. in Grad. Sch.; phys. or asst. to various hosps.; with med. research dept. B.F. Goodrich Co., Akron, O., 1920-22; dir. labs., dept. mental and nervous diseases, Pa. Hosp., 1922-37; psychiatrist, Inst. of Pa. Hospital since 1937. Served as lieut., capt. and maj. Med. Corps, U.S. Army, June 1917-Jan. 1919; with A.E.F. in France 1 yr. Certified by American Board of Psychiatry. Fellow A.M.A.; mem. Pathol. Soc. of Phila., Am. Psychiatric Assn., Coll. Physicians Phila., Phi Beta Kappa. Republican. Epsicopalian. Author: Outlines of Internal Medicine, 5th edit., 1929. Contbr. to Da Costa's Handbook of Med. Treatment, and Craig's Diseases of Middle Life. Home: Bryn Mawr, Pa. Office: 111 N. 49th St., Philadelphia PA‡

FARR, HILDA BUTLER, poet, lecturer, composer; b. Rochester, Kent, England, Jan. 6, 1894; dau. Alfred Charles and Helen Frances (Ward) Butler; student Trinity Coll. of Music, London, England, (two scholarships), 1909-10; m. Earl Edward Farr, Apr. 23, 1917; children—Elsie Muriel, Gordon Butler. Came to U.S. 1915, naturalized, 1917. Composer: (for piano) Roller Skating, 1929; A Waterfall, 1929; A Merry Chase, 1929; (operetta) Top O' The World, 1940; Red Candles, 1946. Author annual book of poems, Songs of the Heart, Dickens' Christmas Carol in verse, 1948, in dramatic form, 1948. Writer of verse for the Wake of the News column, Chicago Tribune, since 1937 (a founder of Wake of the News contributors banquet, 1942, and served annually as chmn.). Contbr. poems, nat. magazines and newspaper columns. Winner of Obermeier piano, open competition, Rochester, England, Dec. 1908; nat. prize, Trinity Coll. Music, 1910; recipient awards from Nat. League American Pen Women. Mem. Dickens' Fellowship, Eugene Field Soc. (hon. mem.), Nat. League Am. Pen Women, Nat. Fedn. Press Women, Ill. Woman's Press Assn., Women's Press Assn., Women's Chicago Beautiful Assn., Mu Phi Epsilon. Methodist. Guest on various radio programs. Lecturer on verse. Condr. contbr. column, Farr Horizons, South End Reporter. Home: Chicago IL Died Aug. 26, 1969; buried Cedar Park Meml. Cemetery, Chicago IL

FARR, MARCUS STULTS, zoologist, paleontologist, geologist; b. Cranbury, N.J., Feb. 19, 1870; s. James and Mary A. (Stults) F.; grad. Princeton Univ., A. B., 1892, M. Sc., 1893; A. M., Univ. of Chicago, 1894; D. Sc., Princeton, 1896; m. Oct. 24, 1894, Luella C. Bergen, Cranbury, N.J. Fellow in biology, Princeton, 1892-3; fellow zoology, Univ. of Chicago, 1893-4; graduate student, Princeton Univ., 1894-6; laboratory asst. paleontology, Princeton, 1896-8; asst. zoologist, N.Y. State Museum, Univ. State N. Y., Albany, 1898-1900; since Oct., 1900, asst. geology and curator dept. vertebrate paleontology, Princeton. Mem. Nat. Geog. Soc. A. A. A. S.; asso. mem. Ornithologists Union; hon. mem. Delaware Valley Ornith. Club. Wrote: Notes on the Osteology of the White River Horses, Proc. Am. Philos. Soc., 1896; Check List of New York Birds, Bull. 33, N. Y. State Museum, 1900. Address: 12 Maple St., Princeton NJ‡

FARRAH, CLARENCE B., psychiatrist; b. Cattaraugus, N.Y., Nov. 27, 1874; s. Thomas Jefferson and Marie (Hawkins) F.; M.D., Johns Hopkins, 1900; D.Sc., McGill U., 1961; LL.D., U. Toronto; m. Joan Jordan. Asst. physician, also dir. lab. Sheppard-Pratt Hosp., Balt., 1900-12; instr., asso. psychiatrist Johns Hopkins, 1906-13; asst. physician N.J. State Hosp., Trenton, 1913-16; chief psychiat. dept. Soldiers Civil Rehab. Center, 1916-23; med. dir. Homewood Sanitarium, 1923-25, Toronto Psychiat. Hosp., 1925-47. Lectr. abnormal psychology Princeton, 1913-16; prof. psychiatry U. Toronto (Ont., Can.), 1925-47, prof. emeritus, 1947-70. Chmn. bd. examiners Hosp. div. Ont. Dept. Health, 1934-47. Decorated Order of Service (Can.). Diplomate Am. Bd. Psychiatry and Neurology. Fellow Royal Coll. Physicians Can. (sec. com. on certification of specialists in neuro-psychiatry 1930-32); mem. Am., Canadian, So. psychiat. assns. Royal Medico Psych. Assn. Asso. editor 100 Years of Am. Psychiatry, 1942-44; editor: Am. Jour. Psychiatry, 1931-65, later editor emeritus. Contbr. articles to med. jours. Home: Toronto Ontario CANADA Died June 3, 1970; buried Cattaragus NY

FARRAR, CLARENCE B., prof. psychiatry; b. Cattaraugus, N.Y., Nov. 27, 1874; s. T. Jefferson and Marie (Hawkins) F.; A.B., Harvard, 1896; M.D., Johns Hopkins, 1900; grad. student, univs. Heidelberg, Paris and London, 1902-04; m. Evelyn Lewis, 1911; children—Aida Evelyn, Clarice Elaine (Mrs. B.E. Middleton); m. 2d, Joan Jordan. Asst. physician, Sheppard-Pratt Hosp., Towson, Md., 1900-02, asst. physician and dir. lab., 1904-12; instr. and associate in psychiatry, Johns Hopkins Med. Sch., 1906-13; lecturer in abnormal psychology, Princeton University, also asst. physician, Trenton (N.J.) State Hosp., 1913-16; chief psychiatrist, Dept. S.C.R., Ottawa, Can., 1916-23; med. dir., Homewood Sanitarium, Guelph, Ontario, 1923-25; director Toronto Psychiatric Hospital, and professor psychiatry, University of Toronto, 1925-47; consultant in psychiatry, Hospital for sick children, Toronto, 1936-70. Served as capt. and major, Canadian Army Med. Corps, 1916-19; med. officer, Queen's Field Ambulance, 1916; seconded Mil. Hosp. Commn., 1916-17; pres. standing med. bd., Cobourg (Ont) Mil. Hosp., 1918; with Dept. Soldiers Civil Reestablishment (Can.), 1919-23. Chmn. bd. examiners Ont. Dept. Health, 1934-47. Diplomate Am. Bd. Psychiatry and Neurology. Fellow Royal Coll. Physicians and Surgeons (Can.); mem. Am. Psychiatric Assn., Acad. Medicine (Toronto), A.A.A.S., History of Science Soc. (mem. council), Royal Canadian Inst., Alpha Omega Alpha. Hon. mem. Verein fur Psychiatric und Neurologie Geseilschatider Aertze (Vienna); corr. member Sociedad Argentina, Sexologia, Biotypologia y Eugenesia (Buenos Aires). Mason (32 deg., Scottish Rite). Clubs: Arts and Letters, Aesculapian, Medical Historical (Toronto). Editor Am. Jour. Psychiatry, 1931-65. Asso. editor: One Hundred Years of American Psychiatry, 1944. Contbr. annual article, Psychiatry" to Funk and Wagnalls New Internat. Year Book, 1940-70. Home: Toronot ON Canada Died June 3, 1970.

FARRAR, FRED, lawyer; b. Evans, Weld County, Colo., Nov. 15, 1877; s. John H. and Agnes I. (Gallaher) F.; ed. Denver High Sch.; LL.B., U. of Denver School Law, 1900; D.Eng., Colorado School of Mines, 1939; m. Mary H. McMenemy, Feb. 12, 1907; children—Frederick M., Elizabeth M. (Mrs. Dixon Wecter). Began practice, Denver, 1900; mem. Bd. of Pardons, State of Colo., 1909-12 inclusive; atty.-gen. of Colo., 2 terms, 1913-16; member firm of Farrar & Martin, 1929-43; general counsel Colo. Fuel & Iron Corp. Pres. Denver Chamber of Commerce, 1927. Mem. bd. trustees Geo. W. Clayton Coll. (Denver), 1924-39; mem. bd. trustees Colo. Sch. of Mines, 1933-38. Democrat. Episcopalian. Clubs: Denver Country, Denver, Mile High. Home: 182 Race St. Office: Security Bldg., Denver*‡

FARRAR, THOMAS JAMES, coll. prof.; b. Oak Springs, Fluvanna County, Va., Apr. 17, 1869; s. Thomas James and Maria Louise (Megginson) F.; B.A., Washington and Lee U., Va., 1895, M.A., 1897, Ph.D., 1901; studied, Gottingen, Germany, 1906, Paris, 1908; m. Margaret Lynn Harris, Dec. 28, 1899. Grad. instr., Washington and Lee U., 1895-99; asso. prin., Donald Fraser Sch., Decatur, Ga., 1899-1901; prin., Presbyterial Inst., Blackshear, Ga., 1901-02; prof. of English, Agnes Scott Coll., Decatur, Ga., 1902-05; prof. modern langs., 1905-10, prof. German, since 1910.

Washington and Lee U. Mem. Modern Lang. Assn. America, Modern Lang. Assn. Va. (pres.), A.A.A.S., Delta Tau Delta (v.p.), Pi Delta Epsilon. Mason (K.T.). Clubs: Rotary (pres.), Square and Compass (pres.), University (Richmond, Va.). Democrat. Presbyterian. Editor La Cigale chez les Fourmis, 1897. Author: The Gerund in Old English, 1901. Home: Lexington VA‡

FARRELL, GABRIEL, clergyman and educator; b. Boston, Mass., Jan. 30, 1886; s. Gabriel and Hannah (Cameron) F.; B.S., Dartmouth Coll., 1911, D.D., 1935; B.D., Episcopal Theol. Sch., Cambridge, 1915, D.D., 1961; m. Elsie C. Comstock, June 14, 1921; children—Gabriel, William, Noami. Ordained to ministry of Protestant Episcopal Ch., 1915; asst. minister, Calvary Ch., Pittsburgh, Pa., 1915-16, Ch. of St. Luke and Epiphany, Philadelphia, Pa., 1916-17, Trinity Church, Boston, Mass., 1917-18; canon missioner for religious education, Diocese of Newark, N.J., 1919-24; rector, Church of the Messiah, Rhinebeck, N.Y., 1924-31; dir. Perkins Instn. and Mass. Sch. for Blind, Watertown, Mass., 1931-51; asst. to dean Episcopal Theol. Sch., Cambridge, 1951-62; lecturer Grad. Sch. of Edn., Harvard U., 1941-52. Served as chaplain, U.S. Army, 1918-19. Director Am. Foundation for Overseas Blind and Found. for Vision, Inc.; dir. Am. Found. for the Blind. Mem. Am. Assn. Workers for the Blind. Mason. Clubs: Harvard Faculty (Cambridge, Massachusetts). Author: The Story of Blindness, 1956; Children of the Silent Night (the deaf-blind), 1956; The Blind in Asia, 1957; also chapters in various publs., also sect. on The Blind" in Social Work Year Book, 1947, and Ency. of Social Welfare. Home: Cambridge MA Died Sept. 18, 1968; buried Glens Falls NY

FARRELL, GLENDA, actress; b. Enid, Okla.; d. Charles and Minnie (Messer) Farrell; m. Henry Ross, Jan. 19, 1940; 1 son, Tommy. Played ingenue leads in Briscoe Stock Co., Morosco Co., Henry Duffy Co., also Monte Carter Co.; N.Y.C. debut in Skiddling, 1929; other Broadway prodns. include Divided Hours, Love, Honor and Betray, Recaptured, On the Spot, Life Begins, Home Is the Hero, The Overtons, Seperate Rooms; motion picture debut in Little Caesar, 1931; other motion pictures include Life Begins, Fugitive From a Chain Gang, Torchy Blaine, Middle of the Night, Kissin Cousin, numerous others; TV appearances include Kraft, Alcoa and U.S. Steel theatres, Play of the Week, Am. Heritage series, The Defenders, Wagon Train, Dr. Kildare, Fugitive, Bonanza, Ben Casey, Directions '65. Recipient Emmy award as best supporting actress, 1963; 1st hon. mayor of North New York City NY Died May 1, 1971; buried Cemetery U.S. Mil. Acad., West Point NY

FARRELL, JOSEPH D., banker. Sr. v.p. Fidelity Union Trust Co., Newark. Office: Newark NJ

FARRELL, PATRICK JOSEPH HOSHIE, b. Calcutta, India, Mar. 18, 1863; s. Gen. G.T. and Louise Helen (Gormanston) F.; ed. in Calcutta, Calif. and Eng.; M.D., U. of Ky., 1892; m. Edna Clare Greatsinger, Sept. 2, 1896; children—Walter Greatsinger (U.S.M.C.), Helen G. (Mrs. Edgar G. Crossman), Jerome G., Louise G. (dec.). Lt., capt. cav., Egyptian, Soudan, & Afendi Wars 1883-86; col. brig gen., Cav., Chilean War, 1889-90; capt. Spanish-Am. and Philippine Wars; commanded first company of U.S. troops that landed in P.I., June 30, 1898. Citation for meritorious service under fire of the enemy; Silver Star medal and medal of Valor for gallantry in action. Major, 1901, col., Cav., 1908. Comdr.-in-chief, Army of the Philippine Vets., 1908-09; comdr.-in-chief, Vets of Foreign Wars of U.S., 1917-18; past comdr. Am. Legion Post. Organized the Boy Scouts of America, 1909; promoted Boy Scouts thousand mile relay race, Washington-Chicago, 1913. Prof. mil. med. hygiene, 1910-16. Fellow Am. Coll. Surgeons. Comdg. officer Advance Sector Hospitals, A.E.F., France, 1918-19. Decorated World War Victory medal, French Medaille Interalliee De La Victoire and Medaille On Ne Passe Pas, Verdun Defense, Surgeon gen. Mil. Order World War, 1925. Col. Res. U.S. Army; brig. gen. Adj. Gen. Calif. Nat. Guard; dir. military and vets. affairs 1939. Clubs: Army and Navy (life mem. ex-pres.); Chicago Athletic, (life mem.); Authors, White Paper, Army and Navy (Washington, D.C.); St. Geroge's (London, England); Los Angeles Athletic, Jonathan (Los Angeles). Home: 2205 W. 6th St., Los Angeles CA‡

FARRINGTON, CARL COLEMAN, v.p. Archer-Daniels Midland Co.; b. Hydro, Okla., Feb. 22, 1905; s. Frank Leslie and Anna Elizabeth (Watson) F.; B.S., Okla. A. and M. Coll., 1928, M.S., 1931; student Am. U., 1930-34; m. Belle Maurine Gayman, July 29, 1928; children—Carl Coleman, Rose Ann, Ruth Maurine; m. 2d Nan Cranna Clark, Oct. 20, 1951. Agricultural economist U.S. Dept. Agr., field service in La. and Tex., 1928-29, Bureau Agrl. Economics, Cotton Div., Washington, 1929-33, Cotton Marketing Sect., A.A.A., 1933-35; chief Ways and Means Sect., Finance Div., A.A.A., 1935-36, asst. to adminstr., Office of Adminstr., 1936-39, asst. dir. Western Div., 1939-40; v.p. Commodity Credit Corp., 1940-47; v.p., mgr. grain dept. Archer-Daniels-Midland Co., 1948-60, dir., 1949-60, mem. exec. com., 1955-59, v.p. agrl. group, 1960-71. Asst. adminstr. Prodn. and Marketing Adminstrn. 1946-47. Mem. Acacia, Alpha Zeta, Phi Kappa Phi. Conglist. Clubs: Minneapolis, Edina Country. Home: Minneapolis MN Died Sept. 1971.

FARRINGTON, EDWARD IRVING, editor, author; b. Manchester, N.H., Nov. 25, 1876; s. Edward T. and Etta E. (Davison) F.; grad. high sch., Manchester, 1893; m. Harriet R. Bachelder, June 12, 1898. Reporter Manchester Mirror, 1895-97; corr. Boston Jour., 1897-98; city editor Salem (Mass.) Gazette, 1898-1900; telegraph editor Rome (N.J.) Sentinel, 1900-03; editor Suburban Mag. (Boston), 1903-05, Suburban Life (N.Y.), 1905-11, Horticulture (Boston), 1919-47; asso. editor Men's Garden Clubs of Am. publs. since 1948; lectr. and publicity rep. Arnold Arboretum, 1913-18. Awarded 2 gold medals for horticultural service. Past sec. Mass. Hort. Soc. and editor of its publications; mem. Am. Rose Soc., Am. Iris Soc., Pa. Horticultural Soc., Men's Garden Clubs of Am. Republican. Club: Horticultural. Author books including: The Garden Almanac, 1939. Contbr. to mags. Home: 65 Church St., Weymouth Heights MA‡

FARRINGTON, ISABELLE SCUDDER (MRS. F. E. FARRINGTON), educator; b. Arni, Madras Presidency, India; d. Ezekiel Carman and Sarah Ruth (Tracy) Scudder; ed. Mt. Holyoke Coll., 1896-98, U. of Calif., 1900-03, The Sorbonne, Paris, 1907-09; m. Frederic Ernest Farrington, of Waltham, Mass., Nov. 23, 1898 (died June 1, 1930). Regent of Chevy Chase Junior Coll. since death of husband, 1930. Mem. Am. Assn. Univ. Women, The Literary Soc. of Washington, League of Republican Women, Alpha Phi. Episcopalian. Clubs: Twentieth Century, The Sulgrave (Washington, D.C.). Actively interested in the drama; has staged many first productions and lectured widely; wrote political plays, Mourning Becomes Election" and Professor's Jambouree, 1934; 1492 And What Have You? Address: Chevy Chase Junior College, Washington DC‡

FARRIS, JOHN WALLACE DE BEQUE, Canadian senator; b. White's Cove, N.B., Can., Dec. 3, 1878; s. Lauchlin P. and Mary Louise (Hay) F.; B.A., Acadia U., N.S., 1899; LL.B., U. Pa., 1920; D.C.L., LL.D.; m. Evelyn F. Kierstead, Aug. 16, 1905; three sons, one dau. Read law with Weldon & McLean, St. John, N.B.; called to B.C. bar, 1903; created King's counsel, 1917; mem. Constituency of Vancouver City, 1916; pres. of council, 1917; atty.-gen., minister of labor, 1917; re-elected for Vancouver, 1921; resigned as atty.-gen., 1922; partner firm Farris, Farris, Vaughn, Taggart, Wills and Murphy, Vancouver, 1922-70; mem. Canadian Senate, 1937-70. Counsel for B.C. Telephone Co.; solicitor Bank of Toronto. Mem. Law Soc. B.C. (treas. 1933-38), Canadian Bar Assn. (pres. 1937-38). Clubs: Vancouver; Capilano Golf and Vancouver BC Canada. Died Feb. 25, 1970; buried Ocean View Burial Park, Burnaby BC Canada

FARRIS, RALPH W., lawyer; b. Rockland, Me., 1886; LL.B., Willamette U.; m. Lillian Essency, 1917; children—Helen, Ralph, Jr., Hubert Edith. Admitted to bar, 1917; atty. gen. State of Maine, 1945-51; formerly state senator and member Ho. of Reps. Mem. Am. and Me. bar assns., Phi Delta Phi. Repubican. Universalist. Mason (Shriner), Elk. Home: Portland ME Died Apr. 1968.

FARROW, MILES, organist, choirmaster; b. Winnsboro, S. C., Oct. 13, 1871; s. Miles Marion and Elizabeth Jane (Caldwell) F.; ed. pvt. schs.; (Mus. B., Univ. of Pa., 1901); unmarried. Organist and choirmaster, St. Paul's P. E. Ch., and Christ P. E. Ch.; organist Baltimore Hebrew Congregation, Madison Av. Temple. Protestant Epsicopalian. Democrat. Mem. Alpha Delta Phi fraternity. Clubs: University, Baltimore Athletic (Baltimore); Alpha Delta Phi (New York). Author: About the Training of Boys' Voices, 1898 Y1. Address: 13 E. Read St., Baltimore‡

FASSETT, WILLIAM M., army officer (ret.); b. Nashau, N.H., Jan. 28, 1876; s. James B. and Elien M. (Morrill) F.; B.S., U.S. Mil. Acad., 1897; unmarried. Commd. 2d lt. U.S. Army, 1897, and advanced through grades to brig. gen. 1918; retired 1924; assigned to inf., Spanish-Am. War; served in Santiago, Cuba; Philippine Insurrection, 1899-1902; various army posts in U.S., World War I; now raises citrus fruit. Decorated, silver star, Spanish-Am. War; D.S.M. (U.S.); Belgian War Cross; Officer the French Legion of Honor. Unitarian. Clubs: Orlando (Fla.), Country; Army and Navy (Washington); Officers' (Orlando Air Base) (hon.). Home: Route 5, Orlando FL‡

FAULCONER, ALBERT, lawyer; b. LaGrange, Mo., Jan. 12, 1874; s. James Coleman and Nancy Jane (Martin) F.; ed. Mo. Pub. Schs., Beetles Normal Coll., 1895-96; studied law privately; m. Grace McMillen, Sept. 24, 1902; children—Ina Elizabeth, Albert, Robert Charles (dec.). School teacher, 1897; admitted to Kan. bar, 1901, and since practiced in Arkansas City; sr. partner Faulconer, Dale and Hickman; city atty., Arkansas City, 1904; apptd. state's atty. Cowley County, 1911. Now judge of Dist. Ct., 19th judicial dist. of Kans. Pres. Chamber Commerce. Treas. Pub. Library. Mem. American Bar Assn. and mem. spl. com. on revision of ethical canons, 1935, member House of Delegates, 1936-41, commissioner to National Conference on Uniform State Law; member Kansas State Bar Assn. (v.p. 1934, pres. 1935); mem. Cowley County Bar Assn. Pres. Arkansas City Rotary Club; dist. gov. Rotary Internat., 1922; mem. Corporate Code Commn. of Kan., 1931-39; mem. Am. Judicature Soc.; state chmn. Am. Bar Assn. Com. on Judicial Reform, 1938-39. Republican. Presbyterian. Chmn. Selective Service Appeal Bd. for S. E. Winfield KS‡

FAULKNER, GEORGENE (THE STORY LADY"), b. Chicago, Ill., Oct. 6, 1873; d. Samuel and Cornelia E. (Smith) F.; grad. Kenwood Inst., Chicago; grad. Nat. Kindergarten Coll. Was the first story teller employed by Chicago Bd. of Edn., 1906; tells stories before library training classes, and in social settlements, schs., etc.; dresses in costumes of various nationalities and gives children's matinees; appeared many times on Chautauqua platform. Mem. Ill. Woman's Press Assn., Am. Pen Women, Central Council of Childhood Education. Presbyn. Clubs: Midland Authors', The Cordon, Chicago Woman's. Author: Story Lady Series; Story Lady's Nursery Tales; Christmas Stories; Red Cross Stories for Children; The Story Lady's Book; Little Peachling; The White Elephant; The Road to Enchantment. Writer under title, Story Lady," in Ladies' Home Journal, 1915-19. Tells stories over radio. Home: 4746 Dorchester Av., Chicago IL‡

FAULKNER, HAROLD UNDERWOOD, historian; born Taylor, Pa., Feb. 25, 1890; s. John Alfred and Helen (Underwood) Faulkner; B.A., Wesleyan Univ., Conn., 1913, L.H.D., 1943; M.A., Columbia Univ., 1915, Doctor of Philosophy, 1916; married Ethel Willard Webb, September 26, 1920; children—Pamela Joyce (Mrs. Frank T. Mansure), Shirley Ann. Assistant in history, Teachers' Coll., Columbia, 1916-17; instr. in history, 1917-18; instr. in history, Dartmouth, 1919; instr. in English and history, Mass. Inst. Tech., 1919-24, asst. prof. history, 1924-25; asso. prof. history, Smith Coll., 1925-31, prof. from 1931, Dwight W. Morrow professor history, 1937-55, professor emeritus of history, 1955-68; visiting prof. Columbia U., summer, 1931; visiting prof. economics (first semester), Amherst College, 1941-42, Mills Coll. (summer), 1946. Pvt. U.S. Army, May-Oct. 1918; F.A. Central O.T.S., Oct.-Nov. 1918. Mem. Am. Hist. Assn., Miss. Valley Hist. Assn., New England History Teachers Assn. (pres., 1942-43), Am. Assn. Univ. Profs., Am. Econ. Assn., Economic History Assn. (trustee, 1942-45), Delta Tau Delta, Pi Gamma Mu. Club: Century (New York City), Author: Chartism and the Churches, 1916; American Economic History, 1924 (German translations, 1929, 57, 58, Spanish translation, 1956, French, 1958), revised editions, 1931, 35, 38, 43, 49, 54, 60; Economic History of the United States, 1928, rev. edit., 1937; Readings in the Social and Economic History of the United States (with Felix Flugel), 1929; The Quest for Social Justice, 1931; America—Its History and People (with T. Kepner), 1934, 5th edit., 1950; American Political and Social History, 1937, 7th edit., 1957 (English edit. A Short History of the American People, 1938; German translation, 1950); The American Way of Life: A History (with Tyler Kepner and Hall Bartlett), 1941, rev. edit., 1945; Spanish translation, 1941); Labor in Am. (with Mark Starr), 1944, rev. edit., 1949 (Japanese trans., 1948); U.S.A. (with Tyler Kepner and Victor Pitkin), 1945 (rev. ed., 1948); History of the American Way (with Tyler Kepner and Edw. H. Merrill), 1950; From Versailles to the New Deal, 1950; The Decline of Laissez Faire, 1951; Politics, Reform and Expansion, published 1959. Contributor to publications including The Social Sciences and Their Interrelations. Essays in Intellectual History, Dictionary of Am. Biography and to encyclopedias and revs. Editor Smith College Studies in History, 1925-41; American Economic History Series; cons. editor Social Science Abstracts, 1928-31. Home: Northampton MA Died June 17, 1968.

FAULKNER, LESTER BRADNER, pres. Olympia Light & Power Co.; b. Rochester, N.Y., Dec. 7, 1868; s. Lester Bradner and Francis Jeanette (Shepard) F.; ed. Phillips Acad., Andover, Mass.; m. Dorothy Sternberg, 1900; children—Donald Ross, Lester Bradner. Purchased from receiver, for bondholders, property of Olympia Light & Power Co., and assumed management, 1897, now pres. and mgr.; sec., trustee Olympia Hotel Bldg. Co. Mem. Northwest Electric Light and Power Assn. (pres.), Olympia Chamber Commerce (twice pres.). Republican. Odd Fellow, Elk. Clubs: Olympia Golf and Country (pres.); Arctic (Seattle). Home: Olympia WA‡

FAULKNER, WILLIAM HARRISON, college prof.; b. Amelia County, Va., June 19, 1874; s. Charles James and Lucy (Harrison) F.; Richmond Coll., Va., 1891-92; A.B., U. of Va., 1895, M.A., 1898, Ph.D., 1902; U. of Berlin, 1906, U. of Leipzing, 1907; m. Eugenie Moore, of University, Va., May 29, 1905 (died Jan. 1, 1906); m. 2d, Sylvia Petrovic, of Ragusa (Dubrovnik), Dalmatia, Dec. 23, 1914; children—William Harrison, Sylvia Petrovic. Instructor modern languages, Univ. of Va., 1894-95; prin. Houston Acad., Halifax Co., Va., 1895-97; Latin and Greek master, Episcopal High Sch.,

Alexandria, Va., 1898-1901; adj. prof. Teutonic langs., 1902-09, asso. prof., 1909-10, prof. Germanic langs., since May 6, 1910, U. of Va. Mem. Modern Lang. Assn. America, Am. Assn. of Univ. Profs., Beta Theta Pi, Phi Beta Kappa. Home: University VA‡

FAUVER, EDWIN, prof. hygiene and physical edn.; b. North Eaton, O., May 7, 1875; s. Alfred and Elizabeth (King) F.; grad. Oberlin Acad., 1895; A.B., Oberlin Coll., 1899, diploma in physical edn., 1906; M.D., Columbia, 1909; m. Anna MacDaniels, Sept. 8, 1908; 1 son, Benjamin Fauver. Instructor in history, and dir. Alma (Mich.) Coll., 1899; tutor in history, and instr. in physical edn., Oberlin Coll., 1900-05; spl. teacher, Columbia, 1905-09; prof. physiology and dir. physical edn., Swarthmore Coll., 1909-11; asso. prof. physical edn., Princeton U., 1911-16; prof. hygiene and physical edn., U. of Rochester, 1916-45; head of Camp Pemigewassett, Inc. (boys' summer camp). Contract surgeon S.A.T.C., 1917. Mem. Am. Physical Edn. Assn., Am. Assn. Univ. Profs., Rochester Med. Soc., County Med. Soc. Presbyn. Home: 920 Highland Av., Brighton NY‡

FAVILLE, DAVID ERNEST, educator; b. Doylestown, Pa., Dec. 8, 1899; s. Ernest E. and Edith B. (Ryan) F.; A.B. magna cum laude, Stanford, 1922; M.B.A., Harvard, 1925; m. Kathryn A. Bailey, Sept. 24, 1932; 1 son, Donald (dec.). Asso. prof. marketing U. Ore., 1925-27, dean sch. bus. adminstrn., dir. bur. bus. research, 1928-32; research supervisor Harvard. Bur. Bus. Research, 1927; instr. in retail store management, Harvard Grad. Sch. Business Adminstrn., 1927-28; asso. prof. marketing. Stanford Graduate School of Business, 1932-37, prof., 1937-65, professor emeritus, from 1965; acting dean fall term, 1949, spring term, 1950; vis. prof. marketing U. Colo., summer 1938. Columbia, 1948, U. Hawaii, 1952, Management Development Institute, U. of Lausanne, Switzerland, 1958-59, Esan, Lima, Peru, summer 1964, 67, University del Valle, Cali, Colombia, summer 1965; mem. adv. com. U.S.N. Ship's Store Office; prin. economic cons., wholesale and retail policy sect. W.P.B., 1942-43, Library bd., Palo Alto, 1941-42, Bd. Pub. Safety, 1944-47, Palo Alto and Allied Area Vets. Employment and Service Council, 1945-47. Mem. bd. dirs. Gantner & Mattern Co., Dallman Co. Mem. Am. Marketing Assn. (dir. 1936-37, 45-46, acad. v.p. 1955-56; recipient Northern California Marketing Achievement award 1962-63), San Francisco Sales Executives Association (director 1938-45), National Federation Sales Executives, Advertising Association, West (chmn. market study com.), Acacia, Phi Beta Kappa, Beta Gamma Sigma, Alpha Kappa Psi, Alpha Delta Sigma, Phi Delta Kappa. Republican. Episcopalian. Club: Bohemian (San Francisco). Author: Merchanidse Availability in Utah (with Dix M. Jones and Richard B. Sonne), 1942; Selected Case Problems in Retailing, 1956; Selected Cases in Marketing Management, 1961. Contributing author, Marketing in the West, 1946; monograph, How Sunset Magazine Subscribers Evaluate the Magazines They Read, 1940; contbr. articles to marketing publs. Home: Palo Alto CA Died Oct. 12, 1970; buried Alta Mesa Cemetery, Palo Alto CA

FAVILLE, FREDERICK F., lawyer; b. Mitchell, Ia., June 5, 1865; s. Amos S. and Esther D. (Crary) F.; B.S., Iowa State College, Ames, Ia., 1887; student University of Md.; LL.B., University of Iowa, 1891; LL.D., Buena Vista College, 1933; m. Cora Thornburg, Dec. 22, 1891 (died Mar. 14, 1919); children—Stanton S., Marion B. Aycock; m. 2d, Josephine Creelman, Jan. 1, 1925. Admitted to Ia. bar, 1891, and began practice at Sioux Rapids, Ia.; county attorney Buena Vista County, Ia., 1895-99; United States attorney Northern District of Iowa, 1907-13; member firm Faville & Whitney, Storm Lake, Iowa, 1907-17, Healy & Faville, Fort Dodge, Iowa, 1918-20; judge Supreme Court of Iowa, 1921-33; resumed law practice, Sioux City, Iowa, 1935-42; code editor and Supreme Court reporter, since 1942. Trustee Buena Vista College, Storm Lake, Iowa. Member American and Iowa State bar assns., Am. Law Inst. (council), Delta Tau Delta, Phi Alpha Delta, Order of Coif. Republican. Presbyterian. Mason (K.T.). Clubs: Kiwanis, Prairie. Home: 4049 Cottage Grove Av. Office: State House, Des Moines IA‡

FAVROT, LEO MORTIMER, b. West Baton Rouge, La. Aug. 31, 1874; s. Henry Mortimer and Celestine (Dubroca) F.; B.S., Tulane Coll., New Orleans, 1894; student Tulane University, 1894-95; A.M., George Peabody Coll. for Teachers, Nashville, Tenn., 1922; LL.D., Tulane University, 1940; m. Rosie Harrison, September 28, 1899; children—Laurence Harrison, Genevieve (Mrs. George A. Peterkin), Agnes (Mrs. E. Denver Morris), Sadie (Mrs. Leo L. Amiss), Leo Mortimer, Yvonne (Mrs. William de B. Bertolette). Teacher, principal high schools and parish superintendent, Louisiana, until 1910; state high sch. supervisor, 1910-12; state agent Negro rural schs., Ark., 1913-16, La., 1916-23; gen. field agent Gen. Edn. Bd. of N.Y. City, 1923-39, retired Aug. 31, 1939; visiting lecturer, La. State Univ., 1940-41; teacher summer schs., La. State U. and George Peabody Coll. for Teachers. Mem. Commn. on Study of Edn. in Haiti, 1930. Mem. N.E.A., N.A.T.C.S., La. State Teachers Assn., New Edn. Fellowship, Kappa Alpha, Phi Delta Kappa. Democrat. Presbyn. Author of numerous reports, bulletins and published addresses Baton Rouge LA‡

FAWCETT, WILFORD HAMILTON, JR., publisher; b. St. Paul, Minn., Aug. 1, 1908; s. Wilford Hamilton and Claire (Meyers) F.; student U. Minn.; m. Mary Blair, Mar. 26, 1932; children—Wilford Hamilton III, William Blair, Michael Blair. Chmn. and dir. Fawcett Publs., Inc.; v.p., dir. C. T. Dearing Printing Co. Home: Norwalk CT Died May 1970.

FAXON, HENRY DARLINGTON, official drug cos.; b. Lawrence, Kan., Jan. 2, 1873; s. Frank Allen and Catherine Lacey (Darlington) F.; student Stanford, 1892-93; m. Sarah Peake Askew, Apr. 7, 1898;children—Sallie Kate (Mrs. Bradley J. Saunders), Lavinia (Mrs. Hugh McMasters Russ). With Faxon Drug Co., 1892-1928, sec., 1908-23, pres. 1923-28; v.p. in charge of McKesson houses in Kansas City, Wichita, Denver; mem. board McKesson & Robbins, New York, since 1929, now regional v. pres. and dir. With Red Cross during World War. Mem. Kansas City Chamber of Commerce, Nat. Assn. Wholesale Druggists (ex-pres.), Zeta Psi. Republican. Unitarian. Club: University. Home: 515 E. 47th St. Office: 708-718 Broadway, Kansas City 10 MO‡

FAXON, WILLIAM OTIS II, engineer; born Stoughton, Mass., Oct. 19, 1910; s. Nathaniel W. and Marie B. (Conant) F.; A.B., Harvard, 1932, M.S., 1933; m. Frances Parker, Sept. 27, 1941; children—David, Susan, Thomas, Roger. Instr. Harvard, 1933-35; comptroller Dorr Co., 1935-42; v.p. Harrison Abrasive Corp., 1946-52, also dir.; v.p. Metals Disintegrating Co., 1952-54; exec. v.p. Tracer Lab., Inc., Boston, 1954-56, dir., 1954-57, pres., 1956-57; pres. Keleket X-Ray Corp., 1956-57, dir., 1954-57, exec. v.p., dir. Comstock & Wescott, Inc., 1957-67, pres., dir., 1967-68. Selectman, Town of Concord. Dir. Manchester (N.H.) Community Chest, 1946-52, Boys Club. Served as lt. comdr. USNR, 1942-46. Registered profl. engr., N.H., Mass. Mem. Harvard Engring. Soc. (sec. 1940-42), Am. Soc. Metals, Am. Soc. Engring. Scis., Am. Metal Powder Inst. Conglist. Home: Concord MA Died Dec. 31, 1968.

FAY, CHARLES W., investment banker; b. San Jose, Cal., Sept. 1, 1903; s. Charles W. and Estelle (Lion) F.; student U. Cal., 1926; m. Dorothy Mein, July 7, 1932; children—Frances (Mrs. John G. Bowes), Dorothy (Mrs. Hamilton Robinson, Jr.), Victoria. Contractor, Fay Improvement Co., 1926-32; real estate broker Buckbee-Thorne & Co., 1932-37; pres., chmn. bd. Hooker & Fay Inc., San Francisco, 1937-63; sr. v.p., mem. exec. com., dir. William R. Staats & Co. (after merger with Hooker & Fay Inc., 1963), 1963-65; sr. v.p., dir. Glore Forgan, Wm. R. Staats Inc. (after merger), 1965-70; sr. v.p. F.I. duPont, Glore Forgan & Co., 1970-72; vice chmn. bd. L. Lion and Sons Co., San Jose, Cal., 1936-67, Roos/Atkins, San Francisco; dir. Clear Lake Water Co., Woodland, Cal., 1939-67. Chmn. mgmt. com. U. Cal. Centennial Fund, 1967; pres. Nob Hill Improvement Assn., 1969-72. Chmn. Bay Area Council A.R.C., 1959-64, now mem.-at-large bd. dirs. Golden Gate chpt.; bd. dirs. United Bay Area Crusade, Nat. Pollution Control Found.; trustee, exec., com. U. Cal. Alumni Found.; trustee Garrison Forest Sch., Balt. Served to lt. comdr. USNR, 1942-45. Mem. U. Cal. Alumni Assn. (alumni council, exec. com.), Delta Kappa Epsilon. Clubs: Bohemian, Pacific Union, Burlingame Country, Golf, Commonwealth of Cal. (San Francisco); California (Los Angeles); Racquet and Tennis (N.Y.C.) Home: San Francisco CA Died June 18, 1972.

FAY, LUCY ELLA, librarian; b. Clinton, La., June 25, 1875; d. Edwin Hedge and Sarah Elizabeth (Shields) Fay; B.A., Newcomb Coll., Tulane U.; M.A., U. of Tex., 1901; B.L.S., New York State Library Sch., 1908, M.L.S., 1926; Doctor of Letters, Russell Sage College, 1948. Head department English, State Coll. for Women, Denton, Tex., 1903-06; asst. in extension div., N.Y. State Library, Albany, 1908-09; librarian, U. of W.Va., 1909-10, U. of Tenn., 1910-18 and 1920-23; instr. and acting dir., Carnegie Library Sch., Pittsburgh, 1918-20; instr. N.Y. State Library Sch., Albany, 1925-26; asst. prof., Sch. of Library Service, Columbia U., 1926-29; asso. prof., 1939-42, asso. prof., retired in 1942; acting librarian, Temple Univ., Philadelphia, 1944-46. Organized sailors' libraries, U.S. Naval Air Station, Pensacola, Ft. Barrancas and Ft. Pickens, Fla., 1918. Pres. Assn. of Am. Library Schs., 1940-41; mem. exec. bd. Am. Library Assn.; mem. Am. Library Inst. since 1942; mem. Bibliog. Soc. of America, Colonial Dames, Phi Beta Kappa. Democrat. Presbyterian. Author: Use of Books and Libraries (with Anne T. Eaton), 3d edit., 1928. Contbr. articles to various library periodicals. Address: 6445 Green St., Philadelphia 19 PA‡

FAY, SIDNEY BRADSHAW, college prof.; b. Washington, Apr. 13, 1876; s. Edward Allen and Mary (Bradshaw) F.; A.B., Harvard, 1896, Ph.D., 1900; Univ. of Paris, 1899; Univ. of Berlin, 1900; L.H.D., Smith, 1929; Litt.D., Columbia, 1940; teaching fellow, Harvard Univ., 1900-02; m. Sarah Proctor, Aug. 17, 1904; children—Mrs. Dwight R. Little, Mrs. William J. Bender (dec.), Mrs. John M. Craig. Prof. history, Dartmouth, 1902-14; prof. European history, Smith Coll., 1914-29; prof. history, Harvard, 1929-46; lecturer, Harvard, 1917-21, Amherst Coll., 1924-25; Columbia, 1926-27, Yale, 1945-46. Round Table leader Williamstown Inst. of Politics, 1924. Pres. N.E. Hist. Teachers Assn., 1914; pres. American Historical Association, 1946; mem. Verein fur Geschichte der Mark Brandenburg, Societe d'Histoire Moderne, Societe de l'Histoire de la Guerre, Am. Hist. Assn., Am. Political Science Association, Mass. Historical Soc., American Philosophical Society, American Academy Arts and Sciences, English Hist. Soc. Author: A History Syllabus for Secondary Schools (edited with com. of New Eng. History Teachers Assn.), 1904, The Records of the Town of Hanover, N.H., 1761-1818, 1905. Editor: Smith College Studies in History, since 1905; Fueter's World History, 1815-1920, 1922; Origins of the World War (2 vols.), 1928, rev. edit., 1930; Guide to Historical Literature, 1931; Rise of Brandenburg-Prussia to 1786, 1937. Contbr. to mags. Home: 194 Brattle St., Cambridge, Mass.; also 21 Lincoln Av., Nantucket MA‡

FAY, WILLIAM PATRICK, Irish diplomat; b. Dublin, Ireland, Apr. 17, 1909; s. Henry Edward and Helene (Browne) F.; B.A., Nat. U. Ireland, 1929, LL.B., 1931; m. Lilian Conolly, July 9, 1940. Called to Irish bar, 1931; practice Dublin Cicuit, 1931-37; with Irish attorney gen.'s dept., 1937-41; joined Irish diplomatic service, 1941; assigned Dublin, London and Brussels, 1941-50; minister plenipotentiary to Sweden and Norway, 1950-51; asst. sec., legal adviser Dept. External Affairs, 1951-54; ambassador to France, also head permanent Irish delegation to OEEC, 1954-60; ambassador to Can., 1960-64, to U.S., 1964-69. Decorated grand cross Legion of Honor (France); grand cross Royal Order of the Phoenix. Member John Carroll Soc. Club: Metropolitan (Washington). Home: Ireland Died Sept. 7, 1969; buried Glasnevin, Dublin, Ireland

FEAGIN, WILLIAM FRANCIS, educator; b. at Midway, Ala., Dec. 26, 1869; s. Daniel and Zilpha Zenobia (Danforth) F.; grad. Midway and James Inst., 1887; B.Sc., Ala. Poly. Inst., 1892, M.E., 1893; (LL.D., University of Alabama, June 1917); m. Elizabeth Chapelle Stuart, of Jonesboro, Ga., Feb. 10, 1897. Prof. mathematics, 7th Dist. Agrl. Sch., Ala., 1893-7, pres., 1897-03; sec. and mem. State Bd. of Examiners of Teachers, Ala., 1903-7; chief clk., Dept. of Edn., Ala., 1907-13; apptd. state supt. edn., Ala., to fill unexpired term, Nov. 20, 1913; elected to same office for term 1915-19; resigned, Oct. 1917; co. supt. schs., Montgomery Co., Ala., 1917-20; state warden gen. of Ala., 1920-Apr. 1, 1923; spl. rep. Guardian Life Ins. Co. of New York since Apr. 1, 1923, with hdqrs. at Montgomery, Ala. Democrat. Mem. M.E. Ch., S. Mem. Phi Delta Theta. Mason, K.P., Odd Fellow. Home: 512 S. Hull St. Address: Bell Bldg., Montgomery AL‡

FEDERBUSH, SIMON, clergyman, Hebrew scholar, orgn. ofcl., author; b. Narol, Austria, Feb. 15, 1892; s. Hersh and Cecylia Czarna (Hirsh) F.; Ph.D., U. Vienna (Austria), 1923; grad. Jewish Theol. Sem., Vienna, 1923; m. Taube Toni Miriam Horowitz, Mar. 25, 1928; children—Uriel, Emanuel. Came to U.S., 1940, naturalized, 1945. Founder, pres. student union Mizrahi, Vienna, 1918; ordained rabbi, 1923; mem. World Zionist Gen. Council, 1923-69; mem. Polish Parliament, 1923-28; pres. Zionist orgn. Mizrahi of Galicia, Poland, 1928-30; adminstrv. com. Jewish Agy. for Palestine, 1929-31; chief rabbi of Finland, 1930-40; rabbi Salanter Congregation, N.Y.C., 1941-69; pres. Zionist orgn. Hapoel Hamizrahi of Am., 1941-45; dir. cultural dept., mem. exec. com. World Jewish Congress, 1945-58; chmn. World Union Hebrew Culture, 1950-69; pres. Hebrew Orgn. Am., 1955-69. Chmn. Com. Reclamation Cultural Property Confiscated by Nazis, 1945-50; exec. com. Am. Jewish Conf., 1946; pres. Hebrew weekly Hadoar, N.Y.C., 1964-69; pres. Jewish Am. Writers Moriah, 1950-69; chmn. Pub. Soc. Moriah, 1952-69; mem. Jewish Welfare Bd. Am.; life mem. World Zionist Action Com. Author (in Hebrew); Yiyunim, 1929; Law and Ethics, 1944; State Law in Israel, 1952; Essays on Talmudical Literature, 1957; Studies in Judaism, 1965; The Hebrew Language in Israel and Among the Nations, 1967; The Evolution of Jewish Law (posthumous). Editor: several vols. of Jewish scholarship, also Jewish Horizon, 1941-45. Author: (in English) Jewish Concept of Labor, 1956; World Jewry Today, 1959; others. Address: Bronx NY Died Aug. 21, 1969; buried Jerusalem Israel

FEE, JEROME JOHN, b. Oct. 13, 1913. Commd. rear adm., U.S. Navy, June 1, 1964, ret., former dir. Queen Mary project, Long Beach, Cal. Home: Long Beach CA Died Mar. 1971.

FEELEY, WILLIAM P., business exec.; b. Eng., 1883; grad. U. Notre Dame, 1906; m. Elsie; children—Mary Grace, William O. Chmn. bd. Great Lakes Dredge & Dock Co., Chgo.; dir. N.Y.C. R.R. Home: Chicago IL Died Dec. 1968.

FEENEY, DANIEL J., bishop; b. Portland, Me., Sept. 12, 1894; ed. Holy Cross Coll., Grand Sem., Montreal,

Que. Ordained priest Roman Cath. Church, 1921; named titular bishop of Sita, and Auxiliary of Portland, 1946, consecrated, 1946; coadjutor bishop; bishop of Portland. Home: Portland ME Died Sept. 15, 1969.

FEENEY, JOSEPH GERALD, transp. co. exec.; b. Scranton, Pa., May 28, 1910; s. John Patrick and Mary Cecil (Saul) F.; B.A., U. Scranton, 1933; LL.D. (hon.), St. John's U., 1951; m. Mary Eileen O'Toole, Nov. 23, 1942; children—Richard J., Michael J., Erin Eileen. Vice pres. Railway Express Agency, Inc., 1961-68; adminstrv. asst. to President Truman, 1949-52; legislative cons. econs. and transp., 1952-68. Served to capt. USNR, World War II. Decorated Navy Cross, Purple Heart. Mem. Nat. Def. Transp. Assn., Am. Transp. Assn., Newcomen Soc. N. Am., Legion of Valor. Club: Army-Navy (Washington). Home: Washington DC Died Oct. 20, 1968; buried Arlington National Cemetery, Arlington VA

FEHR, ARTHUR, architect; b. Austin, Tex., Nov. 18, 1904; B.Arch., U. Tex., 1925; spl. study Columbia, also Beaux Arts Inst. Design, 1926-28. Draftsman, Kenneth M. Murchison, N.Y.C., 1926-28; chief draftsman and designer Harvey P. Smith, San Antonio, 1929-34; archtl. engr. Nat. Park Service, 1934-37; pvt. practice, now with Fehr & Granger, Austin; prin. works include O'Henry Jr. High Sch., Austin, 1953, Jr. High Sch., Victoria, Tex., 1954, Gregg House, Austin, 1955, Albert Sidney Johnson High Sch., Austin, U. Tex. Computation Center, Galveston, 1961. Architect, engr. 8th Service Command, 1942-45; leader inspection team A.I.A., West Republic of Germany, 1953. Recipient Progressive Architecture design award for Terminal Bldg., Municipal Airport, Austin, 1959, numerous other awards. Registered architect, Tex. Fellow A.I.A. (pres. Tex. 1937, exec. bd. 1952-54); mem. Tex. Soc. Architects (dir. 1952, sec.-treas. 1957-60, v.p. 1961). Home: Austin TX Died 1969.*

FEHR, HERMAN, banker; b. Milwaukee, Wis.; s. Jacob and Catherine (Stocker) F.; B.S. and B. Mech. Engring., U. of Wis., 1884, LL.B., 1886; unmarried. In practice of law, 1886-1906; theatrical mgr., 1906-20; engaged in banking since 1920; now chmn. bd. Nat. Bank of Commerce, Milwaukee; chmn. bd. Wis. Shares Corpn. Democrat. Clubs: Wisconsin, Milwaukee, Milwaukee Athletic, Blue Mound. Home: 3014 N. Marietta Av. Office: Brumder Bldg., Milwaukee WI‡

FEIBELMAN, HERBERT U., lawyer; b. Mobile, Ala., Dec. 24, 1889; s. Joseph and Sarah (Frolichstein) F.; Bachelor Arts, University of Alabama, 1911, Bachelor of Laws (cum laude), 1913; m. Yedda Spiro, Oct. 10, 1917; children—Joan (Mrs. Wm. Lehman), Herbert J., Emily (Mrs. Harold Friedman). Admitted to Ala. bar, 1913; practiced Mobile, 1913-25, Fla. bar, 1925, practiced Miami, 1925-67; sr. partner firm Feibelman, Friedman, Hyman & Britton. Commr. on Uniform State Laws, 1933-41. Del. to Fla. Constl. Conv., 1933. Served as 2d lt. to capt., QMC, U.S. Army, 1917-19. Recipient Certificate of Distinction, Commercial Law League Am., editorial contbns., 1958. Member Ala., So. Fla., Am. Jewish hist. socs., Fed., Am., Fla. and Dade Co. bar assns., Am. Judicature Soc., Am. Legion (a founder in Ala., 1919). Founder Temple Israel. Mason. Asso. editor Comml. Law Jour., from 1949; mem. bd. editors Fla. Law and Practice (20 vols.). Contbr. series of biographic sketches in Fla. Law Jours., 1949. Home: Miami Shores FL Died Oct. 21, 1967; buried Mobile AL

FEIERABEND, RAYMOND H., sulphur mfg. exec.; grad. Columbia Sch. Mines. With Freeport Sulphur Co., N.Y.C., from 1942, supt. mine, Grand Ecaille, La., 1953-56, asst. v.p. charge devel., Grand Isle, 1957-61, v.p., from 1961. Mem. Am. Inst. Mining Metall. and Petroleum Engrs. (bd.), Mining and Metall. Soc. Am. Office: New York City NY Died Mar. 18, 1972.

FEIS, HERBERT, historian; b. N.Y.C., June 7, 1893; s. Louis J. and Louisa (Waterman) F.; A.B., Harvard, 1916, Ph.D., 1921; Litt.D., Princeton, 1961; L.H.D., U. Mich., 1966, Cin., 1968; m. Ruth Stanley-Brown, Mar. 25, 1922, Instr. econs. Harvard, 1920-21; asso. prof. U. Kan., 1922-25; head dept. econs. U. Cin., 1926-29; vis. prof. history Harvard 1957; Remsen Bird lectr. Occidental Coll.; Univ. lectr. U. Cal. at Berkeley, U. Tokyo; mem. staff Council on Fgn. Relations, 1930-31; econ. adviser Dept. of State, 1931-37; adviser internat. econ. affairs, 1937-43; spl. cons. to Sec. of War, 1944-46; chief tech. adviser Am. delegation, World Econ. and Monetary Conf., London, 1933; spl. adviser Conf. of Am. Republics, Buenos Aires, 1936, Lima, Peru, 1938, Panama, 1939; adviser on Am. indsl. relations, Internat. Labor Office, League of Nations, various periods, 1922-27. Mem. Inst. for Advanced Study, Princeton, 1948-50, 51, 53, 58-72; hon. research asso. Harvard, 1967; mem. policy planning staff Dept. of State, 1950-51. Served in U.S.N.R.F., World War. Guggenheim fellow., 1926; recipient A.L.A. Liberty and Justice award, 1958; Pulitzer prize for history, 1960. Author books and including: Seen from E.A., 1947; The Spanish Story, 1948; The Road to Pearl Harbor, 1950; The Diplomacy of the Dollar, 1950; The China Tangle, 1953; Churchill-Roosevelt-Stalin, 1957; Between War and Peace: The Potsdam Conference, 1960; Japan Subdued, 1961; Foreign Aid and Foreign Policy, 1964; 1933: Characters in Crisis, 1966; Contest over Japan, 1967; From Trust to Terror, 1970; the Atom Bomb and the End of World War II, 1966; The Birth of Israel, 1969. Contbr. to mags. Home: York ME Died Mar. 2, 1972.

FEIS, HERBERT, historian; born in New York, N.Y., June 7, 1893; s. Louis J. and Louisa (Waterman) F.; A.B., Harvard, 1916, Ph.D., 1921; Doctor of Letters, Princeton University, 1961; L.H.D., U. Mich., 1966, U. of Cincinnati, 1968; m. Ruth Stanley-Brown, Mar. 25, 1922. Instr. economics, Harvard, 1920-21; asso. prof. U. of Kan., 1922-25; head dept. economics, U. Cin., 1926-29; vis. prof. history Harvard 1957; Remsen Bird lectr. Occidental Coll.; Univ. lectr. U. Cal. at Berkeley, U. Tokyo; mem. staff Council on Foreign Relations, 1930-31; econ. adviser Dept. of State, 1931-37; adviser internat. econ. affairs, 1937-43; special consultant to Sec. of War, 1944-46; chief technical adviser American delegation, World Econ. and Monetary Conf., London, 1933; spl. adviser Conf. of Am. Republics, Buenos Aires, 1936, Lima, Peru, 1938, Panama, 1939; adviser on American industrial relations, Internat. Labor Office, League of Nations, various periods, 1922-27. Mem. Inst. for Advanced Study, Princeton, 1948-50, 51, 53, from 1958; honorary research associate Harvard Univ., 1967; mem. policy planning staff. Dept. of State, 1950-51. Served in U.S.N.R.F., World War. Awarded Guggenheim fellowship, 1926; recipient A.L.A. Liberty and Justice award, 1958; Pulitzer Prize award for history, 1960. Author: Settlement of Wage Disputes, 1922; Principles of Wage Settlement, 1924; Europe, The World's Banker, 1931; The Changing Pattern of International Economic Affairs, 1940; The Sinews of Peace, 1944; Seen from E. A., 1947; The Spanish Story, 1948; The Road to Pearl Harbor, 1951; The Diplomacy of the Dollar, 1950; The China Tangle, 1953; Churchill-Roosevelt-Stalin, 1957; Between War and Peace: The Potsdam Conference, 1960; Japan Subdued, 1961; Foreign Aid and Foreign Policy, 1964; Characters in Crisis, 1966; Contest over Japan, 1967; From Trust to Terror: the Onset of the Cold War, 1970. Contbr. to mags. Home: York ME Died Mar. 2, 1972; buried York Cemetery, York ME

FELDBERG, MORRIS, discount chain exec.; m. Anna Marnoy; children—Mrs. David Karp, Mrs. Milton Levy. Co-founder, chmn. Zayre Corp. (name formerly New Eng. Trading Co.), Boston, 1919-69. Fellow, Brandeis U. Address: Natick MA Died Sept. 17, 1969.

FELDMAN, CHARLES K., talent agt., producer; b. N.Y.C., April 27, 1907; student U. Mich., U. Cal.; LL.B., U. So. Cal. Talent agt., 1932-—; pres. Famous Artists Corp., Famous Artists Agy., Inc., Beverly Hills, Cal.; talent chmn., mem. exec. com. Hollywood Victory Com.; 2d v.p. U.S.O.-Camp Shows; prod. Red River, Glass Menagerie, Streetcar Named Desire, Seven Year Itch, What's New Pussycat&?, Casino Royale. Mem. Cal. Bar. Address: Beverly Hills CA Died May 1968.

FELDMANN, LEONARD G., newspaper editor; b. Buffalo, Oct. 27, 1909. With Buffalo Courier-Express, 1926-72, mng. editor, until 1972. Mem. N.Y. State Soc. Newspaper Editors (pres. 1969). Home: Buffalo NY Died Dec. 4, 1972; buried Mt. Olivet Cemetery, Tonawanda NY

FELL, CHARLES ALBERT, newspaperman; b. Helena, Ala., June 19, 1889; s. Richard and Dora (Cobb) F.; student pub. schs. of Birmingham; m. Selina Watkins Perry, Nov. 2, 1927; children—Charles Albert, Henry Perry. Reporter Birmingham (Ala.) Age-Herald, 1907-09; reporter, city editor Montgomery Advertiser, 1910-11; reporter, news editor Birmingham News, 1912-15, mng. editor, 1922-55, editor-in-chief, from 1955; make-up editor Atlanta Georgian, 1915-17; mem. bd. dirs. and exec. com. Birmingham News Co. Served as chief yeoman, USN, 1917-19. Mem. Sigma Delta Chi (pres. Ala. chapter 1956). Author pamphlets on economics, management, editorial content, and other problems of newspaper publication. Clubs: The Club, Downtown. Home: Birmingham AL Died July 23, 1969.

FELLER, WILLIAM, educator; b. Zagreb, Yugoslavia, July 7, 1906; s. Eugene V. and Ida (Perc) F.; M.S., Zagreb Univ., 1925; Ph.D., Gottingen Univ., 1926; m. Clara Mary Nielsen, July 27, 1938. Came to U.S., 1939, naturalized, 1944. In charge of applied math. lab., Univ. of Kiel, 1929-33; research asso., Univ. of Stockholm, 1933-39; asso. prof. and exec. editor, Math. Reviews, Brown Univ., 1939-45; prof. Cornell Univ., 1945-50; Eugene Higgins prof. of math., Princeton Univ., from 1950; consulting and war work; visiting prof. at Rockefeller University. Recipient Nat. medal Science, 1970. Honorary fellow Royal Statistical Society; foreign associate of the Royal Danish Academy; member of National Acad. Scis., Internat. Inst. Statistics American Math. Soc., Am. Acad. Arts Scis., London Math. Soc. (hon.), Inst. Math. Statistics (pres. 1949), Yugoslav Acad. Sciences, Am. Philos. Soc. Former editor Math. Review. Contbr. articles on probability statistics, geometry, differential equations, real variables, etc. Address: Princeton NJ Died Jan. 14, 1970.

FELLINGHAM, JOHN HENRY, secretary Y.M.C.A., b. on farm, nr. Morris, Ill., Feb. 11, 1872; s. Alfred P. and Mary C. (Chapin) F.; M.Di., Ia. State Teachers Coll., Cedar Falls, Ia., 1894; Ph.B., State U. of Ia., 1900; m. L. Lovinia Marsh, of Charles City, Ia., June 5, 1899. Teacher pub. schs., Crawford Co., Ia., 1889-91 teacher science Ft. Dodge (Ia.) High Sch., 1894; gen sec. Y.M.C.A., Ft. Dodge, 1895-7, Ia. U., Iowa City 1897-1900, Ry. Y.M.C.A., Marshalltown, 1900-6, Des Moines, 1906-— (under his administration a modern bldg. completed at Des Moines at a cost of $250,000 Republican. Presbyn. Home: 38th St. and Urbandale Av. Office: Y.M.C.A., Des Moines IA‡

FELTON, SAMUEL MORSE, transportation exec.; b Cincinnati, Feb. 9, 1893; s. Samuel Morse and Dorathea (Hamilton) F.; B.S., Harvard, 1916; m. Louise Merion Garaghty, Oct. 23, 1920; children—Barbara Louise (Mrs. Albert S. Williams, Jr.), Samuel Morse. Engr. J G. White Management Corp., N.Y. City, 1916-17; mgr Oil-Shale div., asst. gen. mgr., Minneapolis, and gen mgr., N.Y. City, Pure Oil Co., 1920-26; dist. mgr. White Motor Truck Co., Phila., 1926-36; gen. sales mgr railway div., Edward G. Budd Mfg. Co., 1936-45; pres. dir. American Ry Car Inst., N.Y.C., 1946-50, pres. chief exec. officer Shippers' Car Line Corp., 1950-55 now dir., mem. exec. com.; pres. Am. Car and Foundry div. ACF Industries, Inc., 1955-57; retired. Mem Transportation Council, Dept. Commerce since 1953 With U.S. Army, 1917-19; executive officer to chief engr., A.E.F.; disch. rank major, C.E. Awarded Purple heart. Meritorious Service citation, Chevalier de l'Etoile Noire. Mem. Mil. Petroleum Adv. Bd. A.S.M.E., Par Am. Ry. Congress Assn. (chmn. indsl. adv. com.), Am Petroleum Inst., Nat. Petroleum Assn., Colonial Soc Pa., S.R., Soc. War 1812. Newcomen Soc. Rep Episcopalian. Clubs: Chicago (Chicago) Railroad-Machinery, Cloud, Harvard Economic Traffic (N.Y.C.); Harvard, Racquet, Phila. Country (Phila.); Duquesne, Rolling Rock, Traffic (Pitts.) Metropolitan (Washington). Home: Delray Beach Fl Died Dec. 1971.

FENN, WALLACE OSGOOD, physiologist; b Lanesboro, Mass., Aug. 27, 1893; s. William Wallace and Faith Huntington (Fisher) F.; A.B., Harvard U. 1914, A.M., 1916, Ph.D., 1919; D.Sc. (hon.), U. Chgo. 1950; Cathedratico Honoraria, U. San Marcos, Peru 1959; Doctor honoris causa, U. Paris, 1960; D.Sc (hon.), U. Rochester, 1965; hon. doctorate, U. Libre de Brussels, Belgium, 1965; m. Clara Bryce Comstock Sept. 9, 1919; children—William Wallace, Ruth Priscilla, David Bryce. Instr. physiology, Harvard Med Sch., 1919-22; traveling fellow Rockefeller Inst. 1922-24, prof., chmn. dept. physiology, School Medicine and Dentistry, U. Rochester, 1924-59, asst dean, 1949-53, asso. dean grad. studies, 1957-58 distinguished univ. prof. physiology, 1961-71; dir. space science center, 1962-66. Pres., 24th Internat. Congress Physiol. Scis., D.C., 1968. Served as 2d lt. Food Division, U.S. Army, and camp nutrition officer, Camp Dodge, 1918-19. Mem.-at-large Div. Biology and Agr. Nat. Research Council 1932-35; mem. com. on med sci., Research and Development Bd., 1949-52; mem biol. adv. com., Nat. Sci. Found., chmn. 1953 Recipient; Gold medal award Rochester Med. Alumni 1958; certificate merit Rochester Acad. Medicine 1961. Daniel and Florence Guggenheim award Internat Acad. Astronautics, 1964; Antonio Feltrinelli internat prize exptl. medicine, Rome, 1964; Distinguished Achievement award Modern Medicine, 1965; Research Achievement award Am. Heart Assn., 1967; Johannes Muller medallion German Physiol. Soc., 1971; Ville de Monaco medal, 1971. Mem. Internat. Union Physiol Scis. (pres. 1968-71), Can. Physiol. Soc. (hon.), Brit Physiol. Soc. (hon.), Nat. Inst. of Health (chmn Physiol. Study Sect. 1947-51), Am. Inst. Biol. Sci. (pres 1957-58), Am. Philos. Soc. (John F. Lewis prize 1949) A.A.A.S., Nat. Acad. Sciences, Am. Physiol. Soc (treas. 1936-40, sec. 1942-46, pres. 1946-47), Soc Experimental Biology and Medicine (pres. 1957-59) British Physiol. Soc., Am. Assn. U. Profs., Internat Acad. Astronautics, Undersea Med. Soc., Italian Soc Exptl. Biology, Rochester Museum and Sci. Centers Am. Acad. Arts and Scis., N.Y. Acad. Scis., Sigma Xi Alpha Omega Alpha, Harvey Soc. (hon.). Corr. mem Sociedad de Biologia, Argentina. Unitarian. Club Cosmos (Washington). Author: Graphical Analysis of Respiratory Gas Exchange, 1955; Handbook of Respiration (2 vols.), 1964. Contbr. numerous articles to sci. jours. Home: Rochester NY Died Sept. 20, 1971 buried Walnut Hill Cemetery, Brookline MA

FENNER, ROBERT COYNER, bus. exec.; b Baltimore, Md., Aug. 28, 1880; s. John Henry and Emma Augusta (Elclip) F.; M.E., Cornell U., 1903; m Sylvia M. Coats, Feb. 12, 1908. Instr. physics, Cornell U., 1903-06; mgr. Boston office, and later Chicago office, Cutler-Hammer Mfg. Co., 1906-16; business counsellor and analyst, Chicago, 1916-30; pres Dixie-Vortex Co., Chicago, 1930-39; chmn. bd Consumers Co.; chmn. bd. Central Scientific Co (Chicago); dir. Butler Brothers (Chicago), Keller Too Co. (Grand Haven, Mich.). Home: Evanston IL Died Oct. 16, 1972.

FENSKE, MERRELL ROBERT, chem. engr.; b. Michigan City, Ind., June 5, 1904; s. William A. and Minna (Glassman) F.; A.B., DePauw U., 1925, D.Sc., 1946; D.Sc., Mass. Inst. Tech., 1928. Research asso. Mass. Inst. Tech., 1928-29; asst. prof. chmn. engring. Pa. State U., 1929-34, asso. prof., 1934-36, prof., 1936-71, in charge Petroleum Refining Lab., 1932, dir. Div. Indsl. Research, 1936-47, head dept. chem. engring., 1959-69; ofcl. investigator and cons. Nat. Def. Research Com., 1941-45; chmn. rev. com. div. chem. engring. Argonne Nat. Lab., 1962-63; cons. NACA, NASA, AEC, Argonne Nat. Lab.; mem. ad hoc com. chem. warfare and biol. warfare programs Dept. Def.; mem. U.S. nat. com. Seventh World Petroleum Congress; mem. air pollution subcom. Nat. Acad. Scis.-Nat. Acad. Engring. Environmental Studies Bd.; dir. Def. Research and Engring., USAF, Baruch Rubber Survey Com., 1942, Metallurgy Lab., U. Chgo., 1944-45. Recipient Naval Ordnance Devel. award, 1945, Certificate of Merit, OSRD, 1945; Nat. award Am. Soc. Lubrication Engrs., 1966; USAF Systems Command certificate of Merit; Mayo D. Hersey award, 1970. Fellow Am. Inst. Chemists, Inst. Petroleum (London) (Redwood medal 1964), Royal Soc. Arts; mem. Soc. Chem. Industry, Am. Soc. M.E., Am. Soc. Lubrication Engrs., A.A.A.S., Nat. Acad. Engring., Am. Assn. U. Profs., Am. Petroleum Inst., Am. Chem. Soc. (past chmn. div. indsl. and engring. chemistry), Am. Soc. Engring. Edn., Soc. Automotive Engrs., Am. Inst. Chem. Engrs., Am. Soc. Testing Materials, Phi Beta Kappa, Tau Beta Pi, Sigma Xi, Phi Lambda Upsilon, Sigma Pi Sigma, Alpha Chi Sigma, Alpha Tau Omega. Club: Chemists (N.Y.). Author chpts., tech. papers and various publs. Home: State College PA Died Sept. 28, 1971; interred Michigan City IN

FENTON, JOSEPH CLIFFORD, clergyman; b. Springfield, Mass., Jan. 16, 1906; s. Michael Francis and Elizabeth (Clifford) F.; A.B., Holy Cross Coll., Worcester, Mass., 1926; J.C.B., U. of Montreal (Can.), S.T.B., S.T.L., 1930; S.T.D., The Angelico, Rome, Italy, 1931. Ordained priest Roman Catholic Ch., 1930; curate, Easthampton, Mass., 1931-33, Leicester, Mass., 1933-34; prof. philos., St. Ambrose Coll., Davenport, Ia. 1934-35; prof. special dogmatic theology, St. Bernard's Sem., Rochester, N.Y., 1935-38; instr. fundamental dogmatic theology, Cath. U. of America, Washington, 1938-40, asst. prof., 1940-43, asso. prof., 1943-52, prof., 1952-64; acting dean faculty of sacred theology, 1941-43, dean, 1943-45. Counsellor of Sacred Congregation of Sems. and Univs., Vatican, 1950; ordinary mem. Pontifical Roman Theol. Academy, 1956-69; pastor, Chicopee, Mass., 1964-69; member Pontifical Theol. Commn. for Preparation 2d Ecumenical Vatican Council, 1960-62; expert for 2d Council and consultor for Doctrinal and Mixed Commissions, 1962-65. Papal Chamberlain, 1951, Domestic Prelate, 1954. Recipient Papal Cross, Pro Ecclesia et Pontifice, 1954. Has served as the editor Am. Ecclesiastical Rev., 1944-64. Cooperated in founding The Catholic Theol. Society of Am., 1946; secretary, 1946-47; cooperated in founding The Mariological Soc., 1949. Author: The Theology of Prayer, 1939; The Concept of Sacred Theology, 1941; We Stand With Christ, 1942; The Calling of a Diocesan Priest, 1944; The Concept of the Diocesan Priesthood, 1951; The Catholic Church and Salvation, 1958; also the co-editor Studies in Praise of Our Blessed Mother, 1952. Address: Chicopee Falls MA Died July 7, 1969; buried St. Thomas' Cemetery, Palmer MA

FENWICK, CHARLES G., polit. scientist; b. Baltimore, Md., May 26, 1880; s. Henry Martin and Gay (Thernan) F.; A.B., Loyola Coll., Balt., 1907; Ph.D., Johns Hopkins U., 1912; hon. LL.D., Marquette Coll., 1930. Holy Cross Coll., 1948; m. Maria Jose Lynch of Rio de Janeiro, July 25, 1942; children—Charles Henry, Francis Edmund. Law clerk div. internat. law, Carnegie Endowment for Internat. Peace, 1911-14; lecturer on internat. law, Washington Coll. of Law, 1912-14; asso. in polit. science, 1914-15, asso. prof., 1915-18, prof., 1918-45, Bryn Mawr College U.S. del. to Inter-American Conf. for Maintenance of Peace, Buenos Aires, 1936; del. to 8th Internat. Conf. of Am. States, Lima, 1938, 9th conference, Bogota, 1948; mem. Inter-American Neutrality Committee, 1940-42, mem. Inter-Am. Juridical Com. 1942-47; dir. dept. international law and organization, Pan-American Union, 1948-62. Mem. American Political Science Assn., American Soc. Internat. Law, Am. Acad. Polit. and Social Science, Internat. Law Assn., Associate editor Internat. Law Journal. Catholic. Author: The Neutrality Laws of the United States (Carnegie Endowment for Internat. Peace), 1913; Political Systems in Transition, 1920; (with W. W. Willoughby) Types of Restricted Sovereignty and of Colonial Autonomy (Govt. Printing Office), 1919; International Law, 1924, 34, 38; Cases on International Law, 1935; Cases on Constitutional Law, 1938, 1942; Am. Neutrality: Trial and Failure, 1940; the Organization of American States: The Inter-American Regional System, 1963. Translator of Vattel's Droit des Gens. 1914; Schucking's Der Staatenverband der Haager Konferenzen, and also of Wehberg's Das Problem eines internationalen Staatengerichtshofes, 1915. Home: Washington DC Died Apr. 24, 1973.

FERBER, EDNA, writer; b. Kalamazoo, Mich.; d. Jacob Charles and Julia (Neumann) Ferber; student pub. schs. Wis.; Litt.D. (hon.), Columbia. Reporter on Appleton Daily Crescent at age of 17; employed on Milw. Jour. Mem. Nat. Inst. Arts and Letters. Author: Dawn O'Hara, 1911; Buttered Side Down, 1912; Roast Beef Medium, 1913; Personality Plus, 1914; Emma McChesney & Co., 1915; Fanny Herself, 1917; Cheerful—By Request, 1918; Half Portions, 1919; The Girls, 1921; Gigolo, 1922; So Big, 1924; Show Boat, 1926; Mother Knows Best, 1927; Cimarron, 1929; American Beauty, 1931; They Brought Their Women, 1933; Come and Get It, 1935; Nobody's in Town, 1937; A Peculiar Treasure, 1939; Saratoga Trunk, 1941; Great Son, 1945; Giant, 1952; Ice Palace, 1958; A Kind of Magic, 1963. Plays: (with George Hobart) Our Mrs. McChesney (with George S. Kaufman) Minick, and the Royal Family; Dinner at Eight; State Door; The Land is Bright; BravoDied Apr. 16, 1968.

FERGUSON, EDWARD, educator; b. Dawson, Ga., Jan. 6, 1907; s. Edward and Lucinda (Perry) F.; A.B., U. Ill., 1929, M.S., 1933, Ph.D., 1942; m. E. Corinne Allen, July 25, 1929; children—Edward III, Lloyd Allen. Instr. biology S.C. State Coll., Orangeburg, 1929-37, prof., head dept., 1951-56; instr. biology So. U. La., Scotlandville, 1937-40; tchr. pub. schs. St. Louis, 1940-46; prof. biology Tenn. A. & I. State U., Nashville, 1946-48; prof. biology Md. State Coll., Princess Anne, 1948-51; prof. biology, chmn. dept. natural scis. and math. Grambling (La.) Coll., 1956-60; prof., head dept. biology, chmn. div. natural scis. and math. Lincoln U. Mo., Jefferson City, 1960-68. Mem. A.A.A.S., Am. Micros. Soc., Am. Soc. Zoologists, Am. Inst. Biol. Scis., Soc. Systematic Zoology, Ecol. Soc. Am., Am. Assn. U. Profs., Marine Biol. Assn. India, Sigma Xi. Contbr. articles to profl. jours. Research on morphology, taxonomy, seasonal life history membs. Crustacean sub-class Ostracoda. Home: Jefferson City MO Died June 12, 1968.

FERGUSON, HARLEY B(ASCOM), army officer; b. Waynesville, N.C., Aug. 14, 1875; s. William Burder and Laura Adelaide (Reeves) F.; grad. U.S. Mil. Acad., 1897, Staff Coll., Fort Leavenworth, Kan., 1904, Army War Coll., 1921; m. Mary Virginia McCormack, of St. Paul, Minn., Jan. 3, 1907; children—Adele, Virginia, Harley B. Commd. add. 2d lt. Corps of Engrs., U.S.A., June 11, 1897, and advanced through grades to col., July 1, 1920. With engr. troops in Cuba, 1898, Philippines, 1899; chief engr. China Relief Expdn., 1900; brig. gen. chief engr. 2d Army Corps, France, World War. Dist. engr., Montgomery, Ala., 1907-09; exec. office in charge raising of Battleship Maine, 1910-11; dist. engr., Milwaukee, Wis., 1913-16, Pittsburgh, Pa., 1920, Cincinnati, O., 1927-29, New Orleans, La., 1927, Norfolk, Va., 1930-31, Vicksburg, Miss., since 1932. In charge orgn. industrial mobilization, office of Asst. Sec. of War (established Army Industrial Coll.), 1921-26. Pres. Miss. River Commn. since 1932; mem. Bd. Rivers and Harbors, 1930; mem. St. Lawrence Waterway Bd. Clubs: Army and Navy, Metropolitan, Vicksburg MS‡

FERGUSON, HILL, real estate; b. Montgomery, Ala., Jan. 6, 1877; s. Frederick Summerfield and Laura (Burr) F.; A.B., U. of Ala., 1896, LL.B., 1897; m. Louise Martin Walker, Dec. 15, 1909; children—Louise (dec.), Hill, Frederick, Virginia. Reporter Birmingham Age-Herald, 1897-99; served as administrative asst., Atlanta zone, Fed. Housing Adminstrn., 1938-39; chmn. Bd. of Equalization of Jefferson County, Birmingham, from 1939. Pres. Birmingham Real Estate Bd., 1914; sec. Nat. Assn. Real Estate Bds., 1916-17; pres. U. of Ala. Alumni Assn., 1904-07, and originator of Greater University" movement; v.p. Am. Inst. of Real Estate Appraisers. Dir. Jefferson County Regional Planning Commission. Trustee U. of Ala. (pres. pro tem. and chmn. exec. com.). Mem. Birmingham Hist. Soc. (pres.); Nat. Assn. Assessing Officers, Ala. Hist. Assn., Newcomen Soc., Omicron Delta Kappa, Phi Beta Kappa, Sigma Nu (v.p.). Dem. Clubs: Rotary, Athletic, Country, Quarterback. Originated the Own Your Home" cooperative campaign idea, 1916. Home: Birmingham AL Died Sept. 18, 1971.

FERGUSON, IRA ALFRED, physician; b. Anniston, Ala., 1896; M.D., Emory U., 1923. Intern Grady Hosp., Atlanta, 1923-25, asst. resident and resident in surgery, 1925-27, chief surgery; resident in surgery Emory U. Hosp., Atlanta, 1927-28, vis. surgeon, until 1970; prof. surgery Emory U. Diplomate Am. Bd. Surgery. Fellow A.C.S.; mem. A.M.A., So. Med. Assn., So. Surg. Assn., Southeastern Surg. Congress. Home: Atlanta GA Died Feb. 26, 1970; buried Atlanta GA

FERGUSON, MELVILLE FOSTER, editor, author; b. Phila., Pa., Sept. 8, 1874; s. John L. and Emma Josephine (Ball) F.; A.B., Central High Sch., Phila., Pennsylvania, 1893; m. Margaret Evelyn Stein, June 28, 1899; children—Dorothy Elizabeth (Mrs. N. Robert Guilbert, Jr.), Marjorie Josephine (wife of Dr. Horace R. Blank), Katharine Murray. Began as reporter with Phila. Record, May 30, 1896, editorial writer, 1903-23, mng. editor, 1923-25, editor, 1926-28; editorial writer Evening Bulletin, 1929-37, editor, 1937-61. Presbyterian. Member Am., Pa. (pres. 1952) socs. newspaper editors. Author: Motor Camping on Western Trails, 1925. Home: Philadelphia PA Died June 15, 1968.

FERGUSON, ROBERT GRACEY, air transp. exec.; b. Pitts., Mar. 6, 1905; s. Huber and Caroline (Kraeer) F.; B.S., Washington and Jefferson Coll. (U. Pa.), 1927; m. Madeleine Campbell, Oct. 14, 1930; children—Robert Gracey, Sally Jayne (Mrs. Sally F. Snyder). With Guaranty Trust Co., N.Y.C., 1928-29; with Pan Am. Airways Corp., 1929-71, sr. v.p. finance, treas., dir., 1965-71. Mem. council financial execs. Nat. Indsl. Conf. Bd. Clubs: Sands Point Golf; Creek, Wings, Treasurers, Sky (N.Y.C.). Home: Locust Valley NY Died Nov. 13, 1972; buried Locust Valley Cemetery.

FERNANDEL (FERDINAND JOSEPH DESIRE CONTANDIN), actor; b. Marseilles, France, May 8, 1903; s. Denis Charles and Desiree (Bedouin) C.; m. Henriette Manse, 1925; 2 daus., 1 son. Theatrical child prodigy; film debut in Black and White; motion pictures include Well-Digger's Daughter, Little World of Don Camillo, Sheep Has Five Logs, Forbidden Fruit, Paris Holiday, Man in Raincoat, Law is Law; role of cabbie in Around the World in 80 Days; Public Enemy No. 1, The Rich Man, The Devil and the 10 Commandments, My Wife's Husband, others; also operettas, stage plays. Decorated officer Legion of Honor, Croix de Devouement, Grand Prix Mondial du Rire, many other awards. Home: Paris France Died Feb. 1971.

FERNBACH, R(OBERT) LIVINGSTON, chemist; b. New York, Sept. 18, 1876; s. Henry and Henriette (Michaelis) F.; B.S., Coll. City of New York, 1896; post-grad. New York U.; m. Gertrude Rich White, of Bangor, Me., Apr. 30, 1906. In chem. work, 1898—; established Fernbach Lab., Paterson, N.J., 1910. Chemist to Broad Silk Mfrs.' Assn. Lecturer industrial chemistry, Brooklyn Poly. Inst., and Brooklyn Inst. Arts and Sciences, 1908-9. Member Soc. Chem. Industry. Republican. Author: Glue and Gelatine, 1907; Chemical Aspects of Silk Manufacture, 1910; Silk Dyeing, 1911. Contbr. to chem. jours. Home: Ridgewood, N.J. Office: Romaine Bldg., Paterson NJ‡

FERNLEY, GEORGE ANDERSON, bus. exec. and adviser; b. Phila., June 13, 1891; s. T. James and Harriet (Adamson) F.; B.S., U. Pa., 1912, grad. work, 1912-14; m. Mildred Bougher, Mar. 15, 1916; children—Lois (Mrs. Henry S. McNeil), Robert Clute, Joan Adamson (Mrs. Stewart McCracken). Partner firm Fernley & Fernley, Phila., 1943-72. Served as capt., ordnance dept., U.S. Army, 1917-18. Received Award of Merit of Hardware Mchts. & Mfrs. Assn., 1946. Mem. Welsh Pony Soc. Am., S.R., Kappa Sigma. Republican. Episcopalian. Clubs: Riomar Bay Yacht, Riomar Country (Vero Beach, Fla.); Philadelphia Cricket, Down Town. Home: Plymouth Meeting PA Died Jan. 26, 1972.

FERRARA, ORESTES, diplomat; b. Naples, Italy, July 8, 1876; s. Vincent and Annunziata (Marino) F.; ed. univs. of Naples, Rome, Geneva and Lausanne; Dr. Jurisprudence, U. of Naples; Dr. Civ. and Pub. Law, U. of Havana, 1902; married Maria Luisa Sanchez y Ramirez, of Havana, Cuba, 1902. Arrived in Cuba, 1896, and enrolled himself in army and took active part in war for independence, advancing to col. gen. staff; prof. law and govt., U. of Havana, since 1904; served as sec. Provincial Govt. of Santa Clara and acting gov. of province during Am. intervention, 1901, speaker Ho. of Rep., Cuban del. to League of Nations and ambassador on spl. mission to Brazil; edited Heraldo de Cuba, and founded La Reforma Social; A.E. and P. to U.S. since 1926. Del. to Cuba to 6th Pan-Am. Conf. Academician of History of Cuba; mem. Nat. Acad. Social Science of Cuba; hon. mem. Hist. Acad. of Mexico; corr. mem. Royal Acad. Moral and Polit. Science of Spain, Internat. Diplomacy Acad., Paris. Awarded Grand Cross Order of Carlos Manuel Cespedes, 1929; Grand Cross Order Crown of Italy, 1930. Clubs: University, New York Athletic, Recess (New York); Union, Tennis, Yacht, Country, Automobile (Havana); Amerique Latin (Paris). Author: Causes and Pretexts of the World War, 1918; Lessons of the War and the Peace Conference, 1919; Vida de Nicolas Maquiavello, 1928; Marti and Eloquence; Jose A. Saco; Interpretacion al Articulo 60 de la Constitucion Cubana; El Panamericanismo y la Opinion Europea, 1930. Editor: The Private Correspondence of Niccolo Machiavelli. Contbr. to La Revue Politique et Parlementaire, Paris. Home: San Miguel y Ronda, Havana, Cuba. Address: 2630 16th St., Washington DC‡

FERRE, NELS FREDRIK SOLOMON, educator; b. Lulea, Sweden, June 8, 1908; s. Frans August and Maria (Wickman) F.; came to U.S., 1921, naturalized, 1931; A.B., Boston U., 1931, Augustus Howe Buck scholar and fellow, 1927-34, Doctor of Divinity, 1956; Bachelor of Divinity, Andover Newton Theol. Sem., 1934; A.M., Harvard, 1936, Ph.D., 1938; student Univs. Upsala and Lund, Sweden, 1936-37; Sheldon traveling fellow, Harvard to Europe, 1936-37; m. Katharine Louise Pond, June 8, 1932; children—Frederick Pond, Mariel Esther, Katharine Kerstin, Faith. Ordained Congl. minister, 1934. Instr. philos. Andover Newton Theol. Sem., 1937-39, Abbot prof. Christian theol., 1939-50;

vis. lecturer, Harvard, 1947-48, Garrett Biblical Inst., summers 1942, 44, 48; prof. philos. theol. Sch. Religion, Vanderbilt University, 1950-57; visiting tutor Hartley Victoria College, Manchester, England, 1956-57; Abbot professor Andover Newton Theological School, 1957-65; scholar: in-residence Parsons College, 1965-68; Ferris prof. philosophy Coll. Wooster (O.), 1968-71; vis. professor Mansfield Coll., Oxford, 1951-52; Fulbright lecturer Oxford University, 1951-52. Co-chmn. Inst. Religious and Social Studies, Boston Sect., 1947-48. Mem. Am. Theol. Soc. (president 1957), Am. Philos. Assn., National Council on Religion in Higher Edn., Conf. on Sci., Philos. and Religion, Phi Beta Kappa, Phi Beta Kappa Assos., Beta Chi Sigma. Author books including: Swedish Contributions, 1939; Faith and Reason, 1946; The Christian Understanding of God, 1951; Sun and the Umbrella, 1953; Christian Faith and Higher Education, 1954; The Living God of Nowhere and Nothing, 1966. Co-author books including: Conflicts of Power in Modern Culture, 1947; Methodism, (W. K. Anderson, editor) 1947; Learning and World Peace, 1948; Fruits of Faith (Richard Spann, editor) 1950; Christ and the Christian, 1958; Searchlights on Contemporary Theology, 1961; Finality of Faith, 1963; Theologians of Our Time, 1966; The Theology of Gustaf Aulen; Essays in Honor of William E. Hopkins, 1966; The Universal Word, 1969. Home: Wooster OH Died Feb. 6, 1971; buried Newton MA

FERREN JOHN (MILLARD), artist; b. Pendleton, Ore., Oct. 17, 1905; s. James William and Verna Zay (Westfall) F.; studied Sorbonne and Academie Colarossi, Paris, Spain and Italy; m. Inez Chatfield (dec.); 1 dau. Gael Chatfield (dec.); married 2d Rae Tonkel, December 1949; 1 son, Bran. Began work as a sculptor and professional stone carver, 1926; painter since 1930; chief of publications, Psychol. Warfare Div., May 1943-July 1945. Algiers, Naples, Rome, London, Paris, New York City; professor of art, Queens College, N.Y.; contributed work in two Alfred Hitchcock films for Paramount Pictures, 1954, 1958. One-man exhbns. including N.Y. 1942, 47, 49, 53, 54, 55, 57, 62, 65, 66, 67, 68, AM Sachs Gallery, 1969. Represented in permanent collections, including Santa Barbara (Cal.) Museum of Art, also Whitney Mus., N.Y., Mus. Modern Art Yale Art Gallery, Wash. U., St. Louis, Cleve. Mus., Solomon Guggenheim Collection, Art of this Century, Museum of Living Art, New York; Hartford (Conn.) Atheneum; San Francisco Museum; Philadelphia Museum, Los Angeles County Mus. Art, Gallery Modern Art, and in many private collections. Awarded Bronze Star for war service. Hon. mention Brooklyn Soc. Artists, 1948; first prize Provincetown Arts Festival, 1958. Am. Specialists Abroad grant U.S. Dept. State, Beirut, Lebanon, 1963-64. Mem. Century Assn. Home: East Hampton LI NY Died July 24, 1970; buried East Hampton NY

FERRIN, AUGUSTIN WILLIAM, b. Little Valley, N.Y., Sept. 1, 1875; s. Augustin William and Flavilla Jane (Van Hoesen) F.; B.A., Yale, 1897; unmarried. Reporter, Buffalo Express, 1898; news editor Am. Press Assn., New York, 1898-1908; pub. and editor Moody's Magazine, 1908-17; asso. editor Nat. Ency. of Am. Biography, 1916-17; pres. Moody Magazine & Book Co. Apptd. trade commr. U.S. Dept. Commerce to investigate investment opportunities in the Far East, Mar. 16, 1917; acting commercial attache, Am. Legation, Peking, China, Jan.-Nov. 1918; commercial attache in Australia, Nov. 1918-Mar. 1919; apptd. Am. trade commr. in Australia and New Zealand, Mar. 1919; reassigned to U.S. Dept. of Commerce, Washington, D.C., Nov. 1, 1921; apptd. foreign service officer, Dept. of State, June 1924; consul at Madrid, Spain, 1924-26, at Tabriz, Persia, 1926-28, at Teheran, Persia, 1928-30, at Malaga, Spain, 1930-35; consul Montevideo, Uraguay, 1935-40; retired Oct. 1, 1940. Mem. Phi Beta Kappa. Sons of the Revolution. Clubs: Salmagundi (New York); University (Washington). Author: Chinese Currency; Australia—a Commercial and Industrial Handbook; Essex County VA‡

FERRIS, CHARLES EDWARD, mech. engr.; b. Napoleon, O., Sept. 23, 1864; s. George Nathaniel and Adelia (Harris) F.; B.S., Mich. Agrl. Coll., 1890; post-grad. work, McGill U., Montreal, Can.; m. Lillian LaCore, 1892; children—George Marvin, Georgia May; m. 2d, Katherine Stollzfus, 1904; children—Mary Elizabeth, Katherine Holly. Instr. engring., 1890-1900, prof. mech. engring., 1900-10; became dean of engring., 1910, U. of Tenn., now dean emeritus. Del. to Am. Engineering Council; mem. Tenn. Highway Commn. Mem. Am. Soc. M.E., Soc. Promotion Engring. Edn.; Am. Soc. M.E. (hon.). Republican. Presbyterian. Mason. Author: Elements of Descriptive Geometry, 1907; Manual for Engineers. Home: Kingston Pike Knoxville TN‡

FERRIS, HELEN (JOSEPHINE), author, editor; b. Hastings, Neb., Nov. 19, 1890; d. Elmer E. and Minnie (Lum) Ferris; A.B., Vassar, 1912; m. Albert B. Tibbets, Feb. 12, 1924. With ednl. dept. John Wanamaker Stores, 1912-18; War Work Council, 1918-19; editorial dept. Camp Fire Girls of America, 1921-23; editor The American Girl, 1923-28; asso. editor The Youth's Companion, 1928-29; editor in chief Junior Literary Guild, 1929-59, member of the editorial board from 1959; trustee North Salem, N.Y. Pub. Library; v.p. Literary Guild of Am. (Doubleday & Co.). Mem. A.L.A., Nat. Council Tchrs. English, Women's Nat. Book Assn., Phi Beta Kappa. Editor (anthologies for girls): Adventure Waits, 1928; Love Comes Riding, 1929; When I Was a Girl, 1930; Five Girls Who Dared, 1931; Here Comes Barnum, 1932; Challenge, 1936; Love's Enchantment, 1944; Writing Books for Boys and Girls, A Young Wings Anthology, 1952; Girs, Girls, Girls, 1956; When Our Town Was Young (with Frances Eichner), 1945; Favorite Poems Old and New, 1957; The Brave and the Fair, 1960; Time of Discovering, 1961; Time of Understanding, 1963. Author or co-author of: Girls' Clubs; Their Organization and Management, 1918; Producing Amateur Entertainments, 1921; Girls Who Did (with Virginia Moore), 1927; This Happened to Me, 1929; Dody and Cap-tin Jinks, 1939; Tommy and His Dog, Hurry, 1944; Watch Me," said the Jeep, 1944; Partners: The United Nations and Youth (with Eleanor Roosevelt), 1950 (recipient Child Study Assn. award, 1951); (with Eleanor Roosevelt) Your Teens and Mine, 1962. Contbr. to mags.; lecturer on children's reading. Home: Brewster NY Died Oct. 1969.

FERRIS, SCOTT, lawyer, ex-congressman; b. Neosho, Mo., November 3, 1877; s. Scott and Annie M. F.; grad. Kansas City Sch. of Law, 1901; m. Grace Hubbert, June 1906. Began practice at Lawton, Okla., 1901; mem. Okla. Ho. of Rep., 1904; mem. 60th and 66th Congresses (1907-21), 6th Okla. Dist.; chmn. Okla. State Highway Commn. since 1935; now practicing in Okla. and Washington, D.C. Formerly mem. Dem. Nat. Com. Home: 2709 N.W. 12th St. Office: Cotton Exchange Bldg., Oklahoma City OK*‡

FERRIS, THEODORE PARKER, clergyman; b. Port Chester, N.Y., Dec. 23, 1908; s. Walter Andrew and Eva (Parker) F.; A.B., Harvard, 1929; B.D., Gen. Theol. Sem., N.Y., 1933, S.T.D., 1961; D.D., Rolins Coll., 1944, Middlesbury Coll., 1955, Boston U., 1958, Harvard Coll., 1969; Mus.D., Westminster Choir Coll., Princeton, N.J., 1967. Ordained to ministry Episcopal Ch., 1933; asst. minister Grace Ch., N.Y.C., 1933-37; fellow tutor Gen. Theol. Sem., 1933-37; rector Emmanuel Ch., Balt., 1937-42, Trinity Ch., Boston, 1942-72; instr. homilectics Episcopal Theol. Sch., Cambridge, 1943-64. Del. gen. conv. P.E. Ch., 1946, 49, 52, 55, 61, 67; alternate del. First Assembly World Council Chs., Amsterdam, 1948. Trustee Boston Symphony Orch. Author: This Created World, 1944; Go Tell The People, 1951; This is the Day, 1951; The Story of Jesus, 1953; Exposition of the Acts of the Apostles in the Interpreter's Bible, 1954; When I Became a Man, 1957; The New Life, 1961; Book of Prayer for Everyman, 1962; What Jesus Did, 1963; The Image of God, 1965. Home: Boston MA

FERRIS, WALTER ROCKWOOD, clergyman; b. N.Y. City, Jan. 22, 1869; s. Frank and Mary A. (Cape) F.; student Coll. of N.J. (Princeton), 1894; Auburn Theol. Sem., 1894-95; B.D., Union Theol. Sem., 1897; B.D., State Bd. of Regents, N.Y., 1897; D.D., Syracuse, 1912; m. Eugenie Viola Hill, of N.Y. City, Nov. 24, 1896; children—Mrs. Henry A. Horstman, Walter Rockwood, Frank Arthur 2d, Muriel. Ordained Presbyn. ministry, 1897; pastor Bay Ridge Ch., Brooklyn, N.Y., 1897-1902, 1st Ch., Middletown, N.Y., 1902-08, Park Central Ch., Syracuse, 1908-28 (emeritus). Moderator N.Y. Synod, 1914; del. Aberdeen (Scotland) World Congress, 1913. Democrat. Mason. Home: By-Peachblossom," Easton MD‡

FERRY, FREDERICK CARLOS, coll. pres.; b. Braintree, Vt., Jan. 22, 1868; s. Amasa W. and Viola H. (Thayer) F.; A.B., Williams, 1891, A.M., 1894; A.M., Harvard, 1895; fellow in mathematics, 1895-98, Ph.D., 1898, Clark U.; studied U. of Christiania, 1898-99, univs. of Berlin, Leipzig and Gottingen, 1899; Sc.D., Colgate Univ., 1909, Knox College, 1936, Clark College, 1937; LL.D., Williams Coll., 1917, George Washington U., 1921, Rutgers U., 1935, Houghton Coll., 1937; J.U.D., Hamilton Coll., 1917; m. Anna Chamberlain, Aug. 2, 1905; children—Evelyn, Chamberlain, Frederick Carlos, Dorothea. Instr. Latin, Greek, and mathematics, 1891-94, asst. prof. mathematics, 1899-1902, prof. and dean, 1902-17, Williams Coll.; pres., trustee and prof. mathematics, Hamilton Coll., 1917-38, pres. emeritus since Aug. 1, 1938. Trustee Teachers Ins. and Annuity Assn. of America, 1919-21; hon. mem. N.E. Assn. of Administrative Officers; mem. Nat. Conf. Com. on Standards of Colls. and Secondary Schs., Assn. of Colls. and Secondary Schs. of Middle States and Md. (pres. 1925), Assn. of Am. Colls. (pres. 1920), Assn. Colls. and Univs. State of N.Y. (pres. 1920, 29), Am. Math. Soc., Math. Assn. America, N.E.A., etc.; fellow A.A.A.S.; trustee, exec. com. Carnegie Foundation for Advancement of Teaching, 1921-39; chmn. 1937; mem. Board of Christian Education of Presbyn. Ch., 1934-38; vice-chmn. College Entrance Examination Bd., 1934-36. Clubs: Williams, Century (New York); University (Washington, D.C.); Green Mountain (Vt.); Shuttle Meadow (New Britain). Author of articles of research in geometry, published in American Journal Mathematics, and abroad. Home: 324 Hart St., New Britain CT‡

FERRY, HUGH J., automotive exec.; b. Grand Rapids, Mich., 1884; student Detroit Tech. Inst. Pres., treas. and dir. Packard Motor Car Co., then chmn. bd.; dir. Grosse Pointe Bank. K.C. Home: Grosse Pointe MI Died Mar. 1970.

FESSENDEN, EDWIN ALLAN, professor mech. engring.; b. Seven Mile, Butler County, O., Aug. 14, 1882; s. Timothy Dwight and Mary Jeannette (Snively) F.; student Washington U. Sch. of Engring.; B.S., U. of Mo. Sch. of Engring., 1904, M.E., 1906; m. Abigail Sayward Roper, Dec. 26, 1906 (died 1916); m. 2d, Louise French Matheny, June 28, 1917; children—Mary Elizabeth (Mrs. Newell R. Washburn), James Dwight, Eleanor Ray (Mrs. James W. Squires). Draftsman various cos., St. Louis and Springfield, until 1906; instr. mech. engring., U. of Mo., 1905-07, asst. prof., 1907-12, asso. prof., 1912-16, also dean Sch. of Engring. and dir. Engring. Expt. Sta. 1 1/2 yrs.; prof. mech. engring. and head of dept., Pa. State Coll., 1916-22; prof. mech. engring., Rensselaer Poly. Inst. from 1922, head of dept. from 1922, professor emeritus also consulting practice. Designed and equipped Mechanical Laboratory Bldg. at Pa. State Coll. Mem. Am. Soc. M.E., Am. Society for Engring. Edn., Soc. Engrs. Eastern N.Y., Sigma Xi, Alpha Tau Omega, Tau Beta Pi, Pi Tau Sigma. Republican. Presbyterian. Mason (K.T.), Rotarian. Author: Problems in Thermodynamics and Steam Power Plant Engineering (with Prof. Thos. G. Estep); The Fessenden Family in America, pub. posthumously. Home: Troy NY Died Nov. 22, 1967; buried Greenwood Cemetery, Hamilton OH

FETZER, WADE, JR., ins. exec.; b. Hinsdale, Ill., Dec. 3, 1903; s. Wade and Margaret (Spilman) F.; B.S., Northwestern U., 1925; m. Florence Otis, Feb. 3, 1934; children—Nancy, Wade III, Peter Otis. With Alexander & Co., Chgo., 1925—, beginning as salesman, successively supr. life dept., asso. mgr. life dept., office mgr., asst. to pres., v.p., treas., 1925-44, pres., 1944-59; chmn. bd., dir. Alexander, Sexton & Carr, ins. brokers, until 1966; dir. LaSalle Nat. Bank, Chgo., Manufacturers Capital Corporation. Chmn. A.R.C. campaign, Chgo., 1947, chmn. Chgo. chpt., 1949, vice chmn. nat. campaign, 1951, 52. Dir. Rehab. Inst. Chgo.; trustee Crusade of Mercy, Am. Inst. Property and Liability Underwriters, Northwestern University. Recipient Woodworth award for conspicuous service to ins., 1943. C.L.U., 1930. Member Newcomen Soc. N.Am., Ill. Assn. Ins. Agts., Nat. Assn. Ins. Agts. (exec. com. 1939-41; chmn. pub. relations com. 1942-43), Chgo. Business Men's Com. (vice chmn.), Phi Kappa Psi. Republican. Clubs: Glenview, Commercial, Commonwealth, Chicago, Economic, Curling (pres. 1955), Attic (Chgo.); Bohemian (San Francisco). Home: Winnetka IL Died July 25, 1968.

FEUER, MORTIMER, lawyer; b. N.Y.C., Nov. 25, 1909; s. William and Gussie (Goldenberg) F.; B.S., Coll. City N.Y., 1928; LL.B., Columbia, 1931; m. Louise Younker Gottschall, July 29, 1937; children—Richard Dennis, Thomas Nelson. Admitted to N.Y. bar, 1932, U.S. Supreme Ct., 1953; practice in N.Y.C., 1932-69, partner firm Hays, Feuer, Porter & Spanier, and predecessors, 1939-69; lectr. corp. law Practising Law Institute, 1954, 58. Dir. Condec Corp., Varifab, Inc. Commr. New York State Commn. to Commemorate War 1812 and Composition Star-Spangled Banner, 1964-69. Del.-at-large Democratic Nat. Conv., 1960, 64; 1st v.p. Amsterdam Dem. Club, N.Y.C., 1958-61, vice chmn. bd. govs., 1959-61. Pres., dir. Dextra Baldwin McGonagle Found., Inc. Mem. N.Y. State Bar Association, Association Bar City N.Y. (mem. corporate law com.), N.Y. County Lawyers Assn. Author: Personal Liabilities of Corporate Officers and Directors, 1961; Handbook for Corporate Directors, 1965; also articles. Editor Columbia Law Rev., 1929-31. Home: New York City NY Died Dec. 17, 1969; buried Beth Olom Cemetery.

FIALA, SIGMUND NICHOLAS, utilities exec., engr.; b. Burstyn, Austria, Dec. 6, 1900; s. Michael Edward and Johanna (Traumer) F.; M.E., Stevens Inst. Tech., 1925; m. Irene Fidrocki, June 23, 1934; children—Barbara Irene (wife Winfield C. Frank, U.S. Army), Janet Ellen (Mrs. Robert W. Gifford), and Howard Sigmund. Began career as power plant engr. N.Y. Edison Co., 1925-27; control engr. Smoot Engring. Corp., 1928-34; engr. Am. Electric Power Service Corp., N.Y.C., from 1934, chief mech. engr., 1945-55, chief engr. all operations, 1955-57, v.p., chief engr., 1957-61, vice president charge engineering, from 1961; vice pres., dir. Beech Bottom Power Company; mem. bd. dirs. American Power Company, Wheeling Electric Company, Ky. Power Co., Ohio Power Co. Fellow Am. Soc. M.E.; member C. of C. of the United States, American Nuclear Soc., Edison Electric Inst., Stevens Alumni Soc., Assn. Edison Illuminating Cos. (chmn. power generation com. 1959-61). Contbr. tech. articles profl. and trade jours. Home: Nutley NJ Died July 2, 1968; interred Immaculate Conception Cemetery, Upper Montclair NJ

FICHTE, HAROLD O., banker; b. Chgo., June 16, 1914; s. Otto F. and Lydia (Hildebrandt) F.; B.A., U. Ill., 1936, LL.B., 1938; m. Veryl Von Almen, Apr. 15, 1939; children—Maxine Marie (Mrs. Leo H.

Bondurant), Bruce H., Royce J. Claim supr., examiner Lumbermen's Mut. Casualty Co., 1938-46, procedures coordinator, 1946-50, mgr. procedures dept., 1951-65, asst. v.p., 1958-65; v.p. Bank of Chgo., 1965-71; admitted to Ill. bar, 1938. Served to lt. col. USAAF, 1941-46. Decorated Bronze Star medal. Mem. Ill. C. of C., Ill. Bar Assn., Am. Inst. Banking, Phi Beta Kappa, Beta Sigma Psi, Sigma Delta Kappa. Lutheran. Home: Prospect Heights IL Died Apr. 8, 1971.

FICKES, ROBERT O., appliance co. exec.; b. Billings, Mont., Nov. 15, 1908; s. Kirke E. and Bertha L. Johnson) B.S., Ia. State U., 1930; m. Sarah V. D. Kilbourn, July 27, 1938 (dec.); children—Sarah E. (Mrs. Raymond P. Drymalski, Jr.), Robert K.; m. 2d, Janet C. Condon, July 27, 1963. Employed General Electric Co., 1930-61, mgr. automatic, blanket and fan dept., 1955-61; pres., chief exec. officer, dir. Elgin Nat. Watch Co., Ill., 1961-62; pres., chief exec. officer Norge Sales Corp., 1962-64; pres., chief exec. officer Philco Corp. Phila., 1964-68, also chmn. bd. dirs. v.p. Ford Motor Co., 1964-68; bus. cons., 1968-69; dir. Penn Mut. Life Ins. Co. Bd. dirs. Univ. Sci. Center, Franklin Inst., Pa. Acad. Fine Arts, Phila. Orch. Assn., Acad. Music, Phila. Mem. National Security Industrial Association (trustee), Greater Phila. C. of C. (exec. com., dir.). Clubs: Racquet, Rittenhouse, Union League (Phila.); Country (Boston); Lyford Cay (Nassau); Chicago. Home: Philadelphia PA Died June 17, 1969; buried Oak Lawn Cemetery, Fairfield CT

FICSHER, MARIO MCCAUGHIN, physician; b. Mpls., May 13, 1899; s. Gustav and Mary (McCaughin) F.; B.S., U. Minn., 1921, B.M., 1924, M.D., 1925; m. Lorraine Koop, May 29, 1931; children—Robert, Richard. Intern St. Mary's Hosp., Duluth, Minn., 1925, mem. staff, 1925-68; pvt. practice medicine, Duluth, 1926-32; dir. pub. health City of Duluth, 1932-65; med. dir. St. Louis County Welfare Bd., 1942-68; dir. pub. health St. Louis County Health Dept., 1944-68; acting dir. IV Rural Health Dist., Minn. Dept. Health, 1944-68; mem. staff St. Luke's Hosp., Duluth; chief staff Miller Meml. Hosp., Duluth, 1941; lectr. St. Mary's and St. Luke's schs. nursing; intermittent mem. faculty U. Minn., extension div., 1935-68. Mem. Gov.'s Tb Facilities Commn., 1953, 54; mem. Gov.'s Commn. on Aging, 1956. Dir. St. Louis County Tb and Health Assn., 1932-50, 51-68, sec., 1933, 35, 36, treas. 1946-50, pres. 1940, 41; dir., mem. exec. com. Minn. Tb and Health Assn., 1938-58; dir. Nat. Tb Assn., 1946-68, v.p., 1953, 54, pres. 1958; founding dir. Duluth Mental Hygiene Assn., 1939-50, 55-64, South St. Louis County chpt. Nat. Found. Infantile Paralysis; founding dir., treas. Minn. Homecrafters, 1939-64; dir. Duluth chpt. Minn. Cancer Soc., 1942-64, St. Louis County Humane Soc., 1932-51, pres. 1939; founding mem. Duluth Vis. Nurse Assn. Served as pvt., inf., U.S. Army, World War I. Mem. St. Louis County Med. Soc. (pres. 1934), Minn. Med. Assn., A.M.A., Am. Pub. Health Assn., Minn. San. Conf. (pres. 1946), Minn. Pub. Health Conf. (1947-68), Minn., Am. thoracic socs., Am. Sch. Health Assn., Am. Assn. Pub. Health Physicians (charter), Phi Kappa Psi, Nu Sigma Nu. Home: Duluth MN Died Jan. 15, 1968.

FIEANDT, RAINER VON, ex-prime minister Finland, banker; b. Turku, Finland, Dec. 26, 1890; s. Alexander and Anna (Karsten) von F.; m. Vera Strahoff, Nov. 7, 1920; children—Berit (Mrs. Eero Kestila), Johan, Otto, Heikki. Vice pres. Nordiska Foreningsbanken, Helsinki, 1924-45, pres., 1945-55; gov. Bank of Finland, 1955-57; prime minister Finland, 1957-58; gov. for Finland, Internat. Bank Reconstruction and Development, from 1958. Address: Helsinki Finland Died Apr. 28, 1972.

FIEKERS, BERNARD ALBERT, clergyman, educator; b. Cambridge, Mass., Jan. 19, 1906; s. Anton and Mary Helen (Schmitt) F.; A.B., Boston Coll., 1927, A.M., 1933, M.S., 1934; student Ignatius Kolleg, Valkenburg, L. Netherlands, 1935-39; Ph.D., Clark U., 1942. Entered Soc. of Jesus, Shadowbrook, Lenox, Mass., 1927; ordained priest Roman Catholic Ch., 1938; philos. and sci. studies Weston (Mass.) Coll., 1930-33; lab. asst. in chemistry, Boston coll., 1933-34, instr. chemistry, 1934-35; student ascetical theology St. Robert's Hall, Pomfret, Conn., 1939-40; instr. chemistry on leave Coll. Holy Cross, Worcester, Mass., and grad. student chemistry Clark U., 1940-42, prof. chemistry Coll. Holy Cross, 1942-73, chmn. chemistry, 1942-62. Mem. A.A.A.S., Am. Chem. Soc. (councilor 1955-63, chem. edn. com. council 1957-59), Am. Inst. Chemists, Am. Assn. Jesuit Scientists (pres. 1947-48), New Eng. Assn. Chemistry Tchrs. (hon.), Albertus Magnus Guild, Sigma Chi. Club: Worcester Chemists (pres. 1946). Editor: Jesuit Science Bull., 1948-50, 1956-60. Address: Worcester MA Died Jan. 9, 1973.

FIELD, ALLAN BERTRAM, engineer; b. New Barnet, Hertfordshire, Eng., Dec. 28, 1875; s. James John and Sarah S. (Dodd) F.; ed. Highgate Grammar Sch., London; Finsbury Tech. Coll., London, 1890-93; B.A., St. John's Coll., Cambridge, 1899, M.A., 1903 (mathematical tripos); B.Sc., London U. (1st Class Honors), 1900; m. Virginia W. Pearne, of Cincinnati, O., Sept. 8, 1911; children—Caroline Pearne, Ellen Kate, Virginia, Allan James Michael. With British Thomson-Houston Co. and Gen. Electric Co. (of U.S.A.), 1900-04; with Bullock Electric Mfg. Co., and Allis-Chalmers Co., 1905-08, and chief asst. on alternating current work to Mr. B.A. Behrend, chief engr. Professionally associated with Mr. Behrend subsequently for several yrs.; engr. with Westinghouse Electric & Mfg. Co., Pittsburgh, 1909-13; cons. engr. and prof. mech. engring., U. of Manchester, Eng. and mem. Univ. Senate, 1914-17; with Messrs. Vickers, Ltd., London, 1917-20; consulting engr. to Metropolitan-Vickers Elec. Co., Ltd., Manchester, since 1920. Temporarily apptd. by British Admiralty 1st tech. dir. of (anti-submarine) Admiralty Expt. Sta., Shandon, N.B., 1918. Fellow Am. Inst. E.E.; mem. Am. Soc. M.E., Instn. Elec. Engrs. London, Inst. Mech. Engrs. London. Home: Marple Cheshire England‡

FIELD, CROSBY, inventor, engr., mfr.; b. Jamestown, N.Y., Mar. 12, 1889; B.S., N. Y. U., 1909; M.E., Cornell U., 1912; M.S. in Elec. Engring., Union Coll., Schenectady, N.Y., 1914; m. Ethel Henriksen, Nov. 23, 1916; children—Margaret Roberta, Dorothy Henrietta, Patricia Crosby. With Gen. Electric Co., 1912-14; in private practice as cons. engr., 1914-15; chief engr., Standard Aniline Products, Inc., 1915-17; engring. mgr., Nat. Aniline & Chem. Co., in charge all engring. including constrn., maintenance, power plant operating, appraisal and engring. research, 1919-23; v.p., dir. and sec., Brillo Mfg. Co., 1923-45; also with FlakIce Corp., 1923-72. Chem. Machinery Corp., 1923-37. Reserve officer. Army Ordnance Dept., Jan., 1917-72; served as 1st lt., capt., maj., U.S. Army, 1917-19, acting chief, explosives and loading sect. Inspection Div.; in active service, col., Army Ordnance Dept., AUS, 1942-45, assigned as asst. dir. Safety Office of Chief of Ordnance. Decorated Legion of Merit. Registered profl. engr. Fellow Am. Soc. M.E. (medalist 1953, hon. mem.), I.E.E.E., A.A.A.S., Am. Soc. Heating, Refrigerating and Air Conditioning Engrs. (past pres., hon. mem.); mem. Am. Chem. Soc., Am. Inst. Chem. Engrs. (past mem. council), Am. Inst. Chemists, Nat., N.Y. socs. profl. engrs., Am. Ordnance Assn., Sigma Xi, Phi Beta Kappa Alumni Assn., Phi Beta Kappa Assos., Pi Kappa Alpha, Tau Beta Pi, Pi Tau Sigma. Mason. Republican. Episcopalian. Clubs: Andiron, Engineers, Chemists (N.Y.C.); Union League (Chgo.). Contbr. numerous papers on engring. specialties to sci. orgns. Inventor of the Oxide Film Lightning Arrestor, 1912, and continuous ice ribbon freezing process, 1916, continuous steel wool mfg. process, 1923; over 140 U.S. patents including elec., chem., mech. and refrigeration processes and equipment. Home: Brooklyn NY Died Sept. 20, 1972.

FIELD, SCOTT, congressman, lawyer; left sch. to enter Confederate army, in which he served as pvt. under Gen. N. B. Forrest in Army of the Tennessee through its Ga. and Tenn. campaigns; after the war resumed studies; finished lit. course Univ. of Va., 1868; taught sch.; read law; admitted to bar, 1872; removed to Texas; m. Lucy Garrett, Calvert, Tex. Has practiced law at Calvert, Tex., since 1872; co. atty., 1875; mem. State Senate, 1888; del. Dem. Nat. Conv., 1892; mem. Congress, 6th Texas dist., 1903-7; Democrat. Address: Calvert TX‡

FIELD, WILLIAM PEREZ, sec. Carnegie Inst. Tech.; b. Geneva, N.Y., Mar. 22, 1873; s. Perez Hastings and Clara Conger (Eddy) F.; A.B., Yale, 1896; unmarried. Employed in finance dept. N.Y.C. & H.R. R.R., New York, 1897-03; sec. Carnegie Inst. Tech., Pittsburgh, since Jan. 1, 1904. Pres. Yale Scholarship Trust. Mem. Am. Assn. for Labor Legislation (gen. administrative council), Am. Acad. Polit. and Social Science, Pa. Soc. for Internat. Arbitration, Pittsburgh Econ. Soc., The Junta. Democrat. Episcopalian. Clubs: University, Pittsburgh Athletic, Yale of Western Pa. Address: University Club, Pittsburgh PA‡

FIELD, WINSTON JOSEPH, former prime minister So. Rhodesia; b. Bromsgrove, Eng., June 6, 1904; ed. Bromsgrove Sch.; m. Barbara Ann Hayward, Feb. 1947; 3 sons, 1 dau. Came to Rhodesia, 1921. Pres. Rhodesia Tobacco Assn., 1938-40; mem. Parliament Fedn. Rhodesia and Nyasaland, leader Opposition, 1957-61; mem. So. Rhodesia Parliament for Marandellas, 1962-65; prime minister, minister pub. service, 1962-64. Pres., Rhodesian Front Party, 1961-64. Decorated mem. Order Brit. Empire, comdr. Order St. Michael and St. George. Clubs: Salisbury, National (Salisbury). Home: Marandellas Rhodesia Died Mar. 17, 1969.

FILER, HARRY LAMBERT, railroad exec.; b. Liberty, Ind., July 3, 1891; s. Aaron Coombs and Charlotte Amelia (Lambert) F.; A.B., DePauw U., 1914; LL.B., Columbia, 1917; m. Ehrma Lee Green, May 22, 1919; children—Harry Lambert, Jr., John Horace. Admitted to N.Y. State bar, 1919, Conn. bar, 1923; mem. legal dept. N.Y., N.H. & H. R.R., New Haven, from 1920, gen. counsel (also subsidiary and affiliated cos. including N.Y. Connecting R.R. Co.) from 1951. Served with U.S. Army, 1917-19. Mem. law com. Assn. Am. Railroads and Am. Transit Assn.; mem. Conn. Bar Assn., Sigma Chi. Republican. Episcopalian. Mason. Clubs: New Haven Country, Quinnipiak, Grads. (New Haven). Home: Cheshire CT Died Nov. 27, 1967.

FILIPOWICZ, TYTUS, diplomat; b. Warsaw, Poland, Nov. 21, 1873; s. Kazimierz and Marja (Samborska) F.; ed. Dombrowa (Poland) Sch. Mines, London Sch. Economics and Polit. Science (U. of London); m. Wanda Krahelska, of Mazurki, Poland, Oct. 3, 1913; 1 son, Michal. Sub-mgr. coal mine, Poland, 1897-99; engaged in mining, Russia, 1906-10; lecturer on history, Cracow (Poland) Sch. Polit. Science, 1912-13; vol., Polish Legions, 1915-17; polit. agt. Vienna, 1917-18; under sec. for foreign affairs, Warsaw, Poland, Nov.-Dec. 1918; mem. Polish delegation to Peace Conf., Paris, 1919; chief of extraordinary mission to Southern Caucasus, 1920; chief of 1st Polish Mission in Moscow, 1921; del. to 3d assembly of League of Nations, Geneva, 1922; Polish minister, Helsingfors, Finland, 1922-27, Brussels, Belgium, 1928-29; ambassador, Washington, D.C., since Mar. 1929. Decorated Double Mil. Cross, Commander Order Polonia Restiuta (Poland); Grand Cordon, Order of White Rose (Finland); Grand Cordon, Order of the Crown (Belgium); Independence Cross (Poland). Catholic. Author: Is the Constituent Assembly in Warsaw Necessary? 1906; Poland and Autonomy, 1907; Political Dreams, 1909; The Problems of Progress, 1910; The Confidential Documents of the British Government Concerning the Insurrection in Poland, 1863, 1914. Address: Polish Embassy, 2640 16th St., Washington DC‡

FILLIS, BEN EARLE, physician; b. Bancfort, Ia., Dec. 4, 1889; s. William Theodore and Eva Mae (Dollman) F.; student Ia. State Coll., 1907-09; M.D., Northwestern U., 1914; m. Pauline Blackledge, May 2, 1915; children—Ben Earle, Yvonne Evelyn (Mrs. Rudolph Pen), Marilyn. Intern, Cook County Hosp., Chgo., 1914-16; gen. practice medicine, Chgo., 1916-19, specializing in urology, Evanston, Ill., 1919-69; mem. staff St. Francis Hosp., Evanston, until 1969, pres. staff, 1931, founder dept. urology, head dept., until 1966; asso. prof. clin. urology Loyola U. Stritch Sch. Medicine, Chgo., 1937-67; former cons. urologist Swedish Covenant Hosp., Chgo. Served to 1st lt., M.C., U.S. Army, 1918-19. Diplomate Am. Bd. Urology. Fellow A.C.S., Internat. Coll. Surgeons; mem. A.M.A., Am. Urol. Assn., Ill., Chgo. med. socs., Inst. Med. Chgo., Am. Legion, Delta Tau, Phi Beta Pi. Republican. Presbyn. Mason, Rotarian. Clubs: University (Evanston); Executives (Chgo.). Home: Evanston IL Died June 21, 1969.

FINCH, HERBERT ISAAC, manufacturer; b. Fort Ann, N.Y., Sept. 12, 1875; s. Isaac Jay and Hannah Maria (Norris) F.; grad. Union Sch., Fort Ann, 1891, Claverack (N.Y.) Coll. and Hudson River Inst., 1892; M.E. in E.E., Cornell U., 1896; m. Sylvia Keith Thomas, of Saratoga Springs, N.Y., Aug. 9, 1906; children—Herbert Isaac, Parker Thomas. Clk. and bookkeeper Finch, Seal & Co., Fort Ann, 1894-96, partner since 1906; teller Lebanon (Kan.) State Bank, 1896-97, pres., 1906-13, v.p., 1913-30; successively draftsman, asst. supt., supt., chief engr., v.p. Emerson Electric Mfg. Co., mfrs. electric, motors and fans, St. Louis, Mo., 1897-1923, pres., 1923-33, chmn. bd., 1933-37; retired; pres. Midwest Savings & Loan Assn., St. Louis, 1923-28, Midwest Agency Co., 1923-28; dir. Kirkpatrick Mortgage Co., Kirkpatrick Finance Co. Mem. Am. Inst. E.E., Nat. Assn. Mfrs. (v.p. 1926-27), New England Soc. St. Louis (pres. 1926). Republican. Conglist. Clubs: Noonday, Bellerive Country, Engineers (v.p. 1913-16), Automobile of Mo. Holder of 15 patents on motors. Home: 6240 McPherson Av., St Louis MO‡

FINCH, JOHN WELLINGTON, geologist, engineer; b. Lebanon, N.Y., Nov. 3, 1873; s. DeLoss S. and Mary Elizabeth (Lillibridge) F.; A.B., Colgate, 1897, A.M., 1898; fellow U. of Chicago, 1898-99, D.Sc., 1913; LL.D., U. of Alabama, 1936; D.Engring., Colorado School of Mines, 1938; m. Ethel Ione Woods, 1901; children—Ione Lillibridge (Mrs. George M. Nye), Nancy Allen. Instr. in geology and physics, Colgate, 1898, in geology, U. of Chicago, 1899; state geologist of Colo., 1901-02; consulting engr. at various times for Guggenheim Exploration Co., Venture Corp. (London, Eng.), Amalgamated and Anaconda copper cos., Hayden, Stone & Co., J. P. Morgan & Co., William Boyce Thompson, Newmont Corp., etc., v.p. and gen. mgr. N.Y. Orient Mines Co., 1916-22; dir. Anglo-Am. Corp. of S. Africa, 1921-22. Exploration in China, Siam and India, 1916-20, Africa, 1921, Turkey and Near East, 1922; v.p. Yunnan Ming Hsing Mining Co., Ltd., since 1920. Industrial adviser to gov. of Yunnan, China, 1922-25. Prof. economic geology, Colo. Sch. of Mines, 1926-30; dean of Sch. of Mines, U. of Ida., 1930-34. Director Ida. State Bureau of Mines and Geology, 1930-34; director United States Anaconda Copper Mining Co., Bureau of Mines, 1934-40; consulting engineer, New York, 1940-45; mem. Assn. of State Geologists, 1930-34, Fellow Geological Society of America; member American Institute Mining and Metallurgical Engineers, Society Economic Geologists, Am. Assn. Petroleum Geologists, Colo. Scientific Soc. (pres. 1929-30), Sigma Xi, Sigma Gamma Epsilon, Sigma Tau, Delta Kappa Epsilon. Author of various scientific articles. Address: 1711 E. Fifth Av., Denver 3 CO‡

FINCH, PEYTON NEWELL, JR., metal and pipe co. exec.; b. Selma, Ala., May 1, 1921; s. Peyton Newell and Lucy (Stounmier) F.; B.S., U. Ala., 1942, LL.B., 1948; m. Betty Stith Rowe, Sept. 10, 1947; children—Elizabeth, Susan, Barbara. Admitted to Ala. bar, 1948; patent atty. Comml. Solvents Corp., 1948-51, Chemstrand Corp., 1952-54; patent counsel, asst. sec. U.S. Pipe & Foundry Co., 1955-64, v.p., sec., 1964-69; dir. Rockwin Prestressed Concrete Corp., Sante Fe Springs, Cal. Mem. Ala. Water Improvement Commn., 1964-69; mem. adv. council Ala. Dept. Indsl. Relations, 1962-69; chmn. water and air resources com. Asso. Industries Ala., 1965-69. Bd. dirs. U. Ala. Law Sch. Found., Gorgas Scholarship Found., Jr. Achievement Jefferson County; adv. bd. Salvation Army City Command; trustee Nat. Trade Relations Council. Served to maj. AUS, 1942-46, 51-52. Mem. Am., Ala., Birmingham bar assns., Birmingham C. of C. (chmn. pub. affairs com.), Phi Alpha Delta, Pi Kappa Alpha. Home: Birmingham AL Died Feb. 29, 1968; buried Elmwood Cemetery, Birmingham AL

FINCH, STANLEY WELLINGTON, editor, publisher, lawyer; b. at Monticello, N.Y., July 20, 1872; s. Phineas (M.D.) and Eleanor (Brown) F.; Baker U., Baldwin, Kan.; Corcoran Scientific Sch., Washington, D.C.; business colls., Albany, N.Y., and Washington; LL.B., Nat. U. Law Sch., Washington, 1908, LL.M., 1909; mem. bar, D.C.; m. Laura Lillian Dyer, of Washington, Dec. 14, 1899; children—Harold Wellington, Lillian Dorothy, Norma Gwendolyn. Entered service Dept. of Justice, 1893, and consecutively clerk, chief bookkeeper, examiner, spl. examiner and chief examiner of U.S. Courts; organizer and chief, Bur. of Investigation of Dept. of Justice, 1909-11; spl. commr. for suppression of white slave traffic," same, 1912-13; pres. Gen. Novelty Mfg. Co., 1914-15; sec. Gen. Welfare League, New York, 1917-19. Editor World's Welfare Magazine, 1918; The World's News, 1918-19; pres. Nat. Novelty Co., 1920-21; spl. asst. to atty. gen., 1922-25; pres. United Factories Corpn. since 1926, Finch Corpn. since 1927. Home: 3060 16th St. N.W. Office: Woodward Bldg., Washington DC‡

FINCHER, EDGAR FRANKLIN, neurosurgeon; b. Stone Mountain, Ga., 1900; s. Edgar Franklin and Grace (Maddox) F.; B.S., Emory U., 1922, M.D., 1925; m. Helen Louise Nichols, Feb. 10, 1934; 1 son, Edgar Franklin. Intern Piedmont Hosp., Atlanta, 1925-26; vol. grad. surgery Peter Bent Brigham Hosp., Boston, 1926; fellow neurol. surgery Washington U., St. Louis, 1926-27; fellow NRC, 1927-28; fellow neurol. surgery Mayo Found., U. Minn., 1928-30; instr. neurosurgery Emory U. Sch. Medicine, 1930-33, asso., 1933-37, asst. prof., 1937-55, asso. prof., 1955-59, prof. neurosurgery, from 1959; sect. head neurosurgery Univ. Clinic; chief neurosurgery service Univ. and Henrietta Egleston hosps.; cons. neurosurgery Grady Meml., VA hosps. Served as maj., M.C., AUS, World War II. Diplomate Am. Bd. Neurol. Surgery (founder mem.; pres. 1957-59). Mem. Harvey Cushing Soc. (founder mem.; pres. 1944), Soc. Neurol. Surgeons (sec.-treas. 1949-53, pres. 1956), So. Neurosurg. Soc. (pres. 1950), So. Surg. Assn., A.M.A., A.C.S., Sigma Xi, Alpha Omega Alpha, Phi Delta Theta, Phi Rho Sigma. Methodist. Clubs: Capital City, Commerce (Atlanta); Highlands (N.C.) Country. Author med. articles. Home: Atlanta GA Died Jan. 12, 1969.

FINCK, EDWARD BERTRAND (BERT FINCK), author; b. Louisville, Ky., Oct. 16, 1870; s. C. Henry and Elisabeth (Jacobs) F.; ed. pvt. schs. in Louisville; LL.B., Louisville, Law Sch., 1906; unmarried. Admitted to the bar, 1906; mem. firm Slattery & Finck. Writer of prose in poetic and philos. vein. Author: Pebbles, 1898; Webs, 1900; Plays, 1902; Musings and Pastels, 1905. Home: 200 E. Gray St. Office: Kenyon Bldg., Louisville KY‡

FINER, HERMAN, educator, author; b. Herta, Roumania, Feb. 24, 1898; s. Max and Fanny (Winer) F.; student Hugh Myddleton Sch., 1910-13, City of London Coll., 1913-16; B.S., London Sch. Economics, 1919, M.S., 1922, D.Sci., 1924; m. Sophie Paul, June 22, 1926; 1 dau., Cherry Paulette. Came to U.S., 1944, naturalized, 1951. dau., Cherry Paulette. Came to U.S., 1944, naturalized, 1951. Lectur. and reader in pub. adminstrn., London Sch. Economics, U. London, 1920-42; dir. research into adminstrn. TVA, 1937-38; spl. cons. Post War Reconstrn. to Internat. Labor Orgn., 1942-44; vis. prof. Harvard, 1944-46; research prof. Yale Inst. Internat. Studies, 1943; prof. polit. sci., U. Chgo., 1946-—; dir. Kellogg Nursing Research project, 1951. Mem. Am. Polit. Sci. Assn., Am. Soc. Pub. Adminstrn., Fabian Soc. (London). Author: Foreign Governments at Work, 1922; Representative Government and a Parliament of Industry, 1924; British Civil Service, 1927, revised and enlarged, 1937; Theory and Practice of Modern Government, 2 vols., 1932 (revised, 1949); English Local Government, 1933; Mussolini's Italy, 1935; Municipal Trading, 1940; Road to Reaction, 1945; The Future of Government, 1946; Chilean Development Corporation, 1946; The United Nations Economic and Social Council, 1946; America's Destiny, 1947; Administration and Nursing Service, 1951; The Presidency: Crisis and Regeneration, 1960; Dulles Over Suez, 1964; Intimate Sketches of My Colleagues. Contbr. articles in Ency. Britannica, also various learned jours. Home: Chicago IL Died Mar. 4, 1969.

FINGER, AARON, lawyer; b. Wilmington, Del., May 25, 1890. Legal, studies, law office of Robert H. Richards; admitted to Del. bar, 1912; mem. firm Richards, Layton & Finger, Wilmington; dep. judge Municipal Ct., Wilmington, 1916-19; asst. atty. gen., Del., 1919-22. Mem. Am., Del. bar assns. Office: Wilmington DE Died June 3, 1969; buried Lombardy Cemetery, Wilmington DE

FINGOLD, SAMUEL, industrialist; b. Lemonville, Ont., Can., Apr. 17, 1911; s. Louis and Jennie (Amsterdam) F.; ed. Claremont (Ont.) Pub. and Continuation Sch.; m. Sidney Rosenberg, Sept. 3, 1933;children—John Paul, David Bruce. Chmn. bd., dir. Slater Steel Industries, Ltd., also chmn. divs.; chmn. bd., dir. Found. Co. of Can., Ltd., Salada Foods, Ltd., Canadian Food Products, Ltd., Coffee Co. Jamaica, Ltd., Salada Foods Jamaica, Ltd., Canadian Found. Ltd.; pres., dir. Salada Realty Ltd.; dir. Found. Co. Ont. Ltd., La Companie Found. Limitee, Found. Maritime Ltd., Found. Devels. Ltd., A.D. Ross & Co., Ltd., Constrn. Equipment Co. Ltd., Found. Can. Engring. Corp., Ltd., Found. Overseas, Ltd., Geocon, Ltd., Coneco Acceptance, Ltd., Frontier Constrn. Co., Ind., Found. Scottish Properties, Ltd., Nat. Materials Handling, Ltd., Erindale Foods, Ltd., Chip-Boy Ltd., Les Produits Salada Ltee, Made-Rite Potato Chips, Ltd., Prior's Foods, Ltd., Salada Sales Co., Ltd., Watson Food Products, Ltd., Salada Foods, Inc., Sarhold Ltd., Jamaica, Shirriff's (Jamaica) Ltd., Salada Holdings, Ltd., U.K. Hon. gov. Canadian Assn. Retarded Children. Jewish religion. Clubs: Canadian (N.Y.C.); York Racquet; Variety, Oakdale Golf and Country, Primrose, Empire, Whist (Toronto). Address: Toronto Ont Canada Died Aug. 2, 1970.

FINK, FRANCIS A., editor; b. Ft. Wayne, Ind., Oct. 12, 1907; s. Francis J. and Loretta Ann (Noll) F.; A.B., Notre Dame, 1930; m. Helen E. Hartman, Feb. 3, 1931; children—John F., William J., James M., Helen Ann, Carol Sue, Thomas M. Reporter Ft. Wayne News-Sentinel, 1928-29; asso. editor Our Sunday Visitor, 1930-35; mng. editor, 1935, trustee and mem. bd., 1954-68, exec. v.p., 1968. Trustee Cath. Ch. Extension Soc., 1955; founded The Family Digest, 1945; bus. mgr. The Priest, 1944-72; v.p., dir. 1st Nat. Bank. 1st pres. Huntington County Community Chest. Awarded Nat. Family Cath. Action Prize, 1948. Mem. Cath. Press Assn. U.S. (pres. 1950-52). K.C., Elk, Moose. Clubs: Lafontaine Country, Rotary (Huntington); Country (Ft. Wayne). Compiler: Church in United States History, 1936. Home: Huntington IN Died Dec. 4, 1971; buried Huntington IN

FINK, OLLIE EDGAR, conservationist; b. Irville, O., July 30, 1898; s. Rodulphus M. and Susannah (Hursey) F.; A.B., Muskingum Coll., New Concord, O., 1922; A.M., Ohio State, 1934, postgrad. College of Education, 1934-41; married Julia B. Leffler, April 10, 1925; children—Ruth Joan, David Edgar. Instructor Nashport (Ohio) High School, 1922-26; supt. Toboso (Ohio) schools, 1926-27; instr. Ohio High Sch., Zanesville, 1927-29, prin. Hancock Jr. High Sch., 1929-38, conservation supervisor, 1938-39; curriculum supervisor conservation edn., State Dept. Edn. of Ohio, 1939-44; dir. Ohio Conservation Lab., Tar Hollow, Leesville, 1940-44; exec. sec. Friends of The Land in charge nat. office, Zanesville, O. (editor Land and Water, official quarterly); nat. lectr. on conservation and ednl. topics, 1944-61; educator Zanesville Pub. Schs., 1959-63. Served S.A.T.C., 1918. Fellow American Geog. Soc., Ohio Acad. Sci.; mem. Nat. Garden Inst. (sec., exec. v.p.), U.S. Jr. C. of C. (chmn. conservation com. 1936-37), Phi Delta Kappa. Methodist. Mason. Author books including: The Teacher Looks at Conservation, 1940; Conservation for Tomorrow's America, 1945; (with Homer Royer) Buckeye Tales, 1945. Co-editor: Soil, Food and Health, 1948; Water and Man, 1949. Home: Zanesville OH Died Feb. 28, 1972; buried Memorial Park, Zanesville OH

FINKE, GEORGE, clergyman; b. Quakenbrueck, Germany, Jan. 2, 1869; s. Rechnungsrat C. and A. (Koehler) F.; grad. gymnasium, Quakenbrueck, 1886; came to U.S., 1889; theol. studies, Luther Sem., St. Paul, 1892; m. Maggie Tamke, Oct. 7, 1892 (died 1902); children—Elsie (dec.), Frieda, Martha, Maria; m. 2d, Della Tamke, June 16, 1903 (died 1915); children—Alma, Carl, George. Ordained Evang. Luth. ministry, 1892; since working in mission fields, Minn., Ida., etc. Justice of the peace, 1904-1914; v.p. Washington Dist. of Ohio Synod, 1909; pres. of the bd. Pacific Luth. Sem., Olympia, Wash., since 1908. Author: Wer hat die funf Bucher Moses verfasst?, 1900, Leipzig; also in Swedish, 1901, Stockholm; Das Schreien der Steine oder Hieroglyphen, Keilinschrift und Bibelwort, 1901; Der Stern aus Jacob, 1901; The Verdict of the Monuments, 1902; Winning the Pacific Northwest, 1936. Contbr. to Evang. Luth. mags., etc. Mem. 12th Ida. Legislature. Home: Southwick Nez Perce County ID‡

FINKE, WALTER WILLIAM, mfg. exec.; b. Mpls., June 16, 1907; s. William and Eva (Schreyer) F.; B.A. cum laude, U. Minn., 1927, LL.B., 1930; m. Lorraine K. Freiberg, July 11, 1932. Exec. v.p. Mpls. C. of C., 1946-51; mgr. ordnance div., asst. to pres. Mpls. Honeywell Regulator Co., 1951-55, v.p. of co., 1958-67, also pres. electronic data processing div., Wellesley, Mass., 1954-67; pres., chief exec. officer Dictaphone Corp., 1967-71, also chmn. exec. com.; dir. Mite. Corp., Barry Wright Corp. Pres. U.S. Jr. C. of C., 1941. Trustee Proctor Acad. Served with USNR, 1942-46; capt. ret. Mem. Bus. Equipment Mfrs. Assn. (past chmn., dir.), Delta Theta Phi, Phi Beta Kappa, Zeta Psi. Mason (Shriner). Clubs: Brae Burn Country (Newton, Mass.); Westchester Country (Harrison, N.Y.), California (Los Angeles); Pinnacle (N.Y.C.). Home: Palm Desert CA Died Feb. 9, 1972.

FINKLER, RITA V. SAPIRO, endocrinology cons.; b. Kherson, Russia, Nov. 1, 1888; d. Woolf and Sara (Hoppner) Sapiro; came to U.S., 1910, naturalized, 1913; B.A., U. Petersburg, Leningrad, U.S.S.R., 1908; M.D., Woman's Med. Coll. Pa., 1915; m. Samuel Finkler, July 6, 1913 (dec. 1941); 1 dau., Sylvia (Mrs. Marvin C. Becker). Intern, Polyclinic Hosp. U. Pa., Phila.; practice medicine specializing in endocrinology Newark, 1919-62, Millburn, N.J., 1962-68; chief endocrine clinic Beth Israel Hosp., Newark, 1934-68, chief dept. endocrinology, 1950-68, chief emeritus, cons., 1960-68. Recipient Woman's Coll. Med. Pa. Gold certificate 50 yrs. in practice, 1965, Achievement award, 1967. Mem. N.J., Woman's Med. Assn. (Woman of Year 1956), Am., N.J., Israel, World med. assns., Am., Internat., N.J. (pres. 1934) woman's med. assns., Endocrine and Sterility-Fertility Assn., Jerusalem Acad. Medicine, UN Am. Assn. Contbr. articles to profl. jours. Home: Short Hills NJ Died Nov. 8, 1968.

FINLAY, GEORGE IRVING, geologist; b. Marlboro, N.Y., July 9, 1876; s. David James and Ella (Peck) F.; A.B., Harvard, 1898; Ph.D., Columbia, 1903; m. Margaret H. Curtin, of New York, July 19, 1905. Asst. geologist, U.S. Geol. Survey, 1901-—; prof. geology, Colo. Coll., Colorado Springs, Colo., 1903-13; asst. prof. geology, New York U., Sept., 1913. Republican. Epsicopalian. Mem. New York Acad. Science, Kappa Sigma. Author: Guide Book to Colorado Springs Rock Formations, 1907; Introduction to the Study of Igneous Rocks, 1913. Address: 134 W. 75th St., New York‡

FINLAY, JAMES RALPH, mining engr.; b. Blenheim, Ont., Can., Sept. 30, 1869; s. Ralph Spence and Anna (Rankin) F.; Colo. Coll., Colo. Springs; A.B., Harvard, 1891; m. Edith D. Adams, of Spokane, Wash., Aug. 10, 1904. Continuously occupied in the management, examination and appraisal of mining properties since 1891. Chief employments: mgr. Portland Gold Mining Co., Cripple Creek, Colo., 1902-03; Goldfield Consolidated Mines Co., 1910; appraisal mining properties of Mich., 1911; appraisal for state of copper mines of Arizona, 1931-32. Lecturer on economics of mining, Harvard and Columbia univs. Mem. Am. Inst. Mining and Metall. Engrs., Mining and Metall. Soc. America (v.p.), Soc. Harvard Engrs. (v.p.). Republican. Clubs: Harvard, University. Author: Cost of Mining, 1909; Appraisal of Mining Properties, 1911; also many brochures and articles on economic mining. Engr. or adviser in many projects of mining, consolidations, etc.; appraised mines of New Mexico for the State. Home: South Av., Redlands, Calif. Address: 20 Exchange Pl., New York NY‡

FINLAY, JOHN JEROME, advt. exec.; b. Galveston, Tex., Nov. 5, 1893; s. Arthur Miller and Stella (Hartnett) F.; student St.L. U. Acad., 1908-11, St. L. U., 1912-13; m. Jane Scriven, Oct. 26, 1928; 1 dau., Barbara Dodd. With Hibbard, Spencer, Bartlett & Co., 1913-15, asst. advt. mgr., 1915; free lance comml. art salesman, 1916-17; mgr. direct by mail dept. Erwin Wasey & Co., 1919; v.p. Arnold Joerns Co., 1920-22; copywriter Charles Daniel Frey, Inc., 1923-24; account exec. Aubrey, Moore & Wallace, Inc., 1925-31; v.p., 1931-52; pres. Aubrey, Finlay, Marley & Hodgson, Inc., Chgo., since 1952; treas. Flexwood Co. of Chgo.; dir. St. L. Drumlummon Mines, Inc. Founder, 1st pres. North Side Boys Club; dir. Off-the-Street Club, Chgo. area project. Served as ensign, U.S. Navy, 1917-19; overseas as watch and communications officer, 1918. Roman Catholic. Clubs: Tavern, Saddle and Cycle, Federated Advt. (Chgo.); Dunham Woods Riding (Wayne, Ill.). Home: Chicago IL Died Apr. 1971.

FINNEGAN, EDWARD ROWAN, circuit ct. judge; b. Chgo., June 5, 1905; s. Patrick and Margaret (Rowan) F.; student Loyola U., Chgo., 1923-24, Northwestern U. Law Sch., 1929; student DePaul U., 1925-29, LL.B., 1930; m. Katherine Coyle, Sept. 14, 1935; children—Sarah (Mrs. L. A. Harris), Moira, Kathleen. Admitted to Ill. bar, 1932; pvt. practice, Chgo., 1931-45, 51-64; asst. states atty. Cook County, 1945-57; asst. corp. counsel City Chgo., 1956-57; mem. 87th Congress 12th Dist. Ill., mem. 88th Congress 9th Illinois District judge Cook County Circuit Ct., 1964-71. Mem. Am., Chgo. bar assns., Phi Alpha Delta. Roman Cath. Elk, K.C. Clubs: Nat. Capital Democratic (Washington); Lake Shore (Chgo.); Dairymen's Country (Boulder Junction, Wis.). Home: Chicago IL

FINNEY, EDWARD CLINGAN, lawyer; b. Milton, Pa., Nov. 12, 1869; s. James Robert and Anne Mary (Clingan) F.; LL.B., U. of Kan., 1891; m. Jean Steele, Aug. 23, 1892; children—Berenice Jean, Edith Elizabeth. Practiced law in Kan., 1891-94; entered Gen. Land Office, Washington, 1894; asst. to sec. of interior, and chief law officer, U.S. Reclamation Service, 1909-10; mem. bd. of appeals, Dept. of Interior, 1914-Mar. 17, 1921; 1st asst. sec. of the interior, 1921-29, solicitor same, 1929-33; member Vogelsang, Brown, Cram, Feely and Finney, Washington, D.C., since 1933. Mem. bar Supreme Courts of U.S., Kan. and D.C. Republican. Presbyterian. Mason. Club: Am. Auto. Home: 3536 Edmunds St., Washington 7‡

FIRESTEIN, ALFRED, cosmetic co. exec.; b. Los Angeles, 1924; legal edn. U. So. Cal. Pres., dir. Max Factor & Co., 1963-73; also chief exec. officer. Home: Beverly Hills CA Died Mar. 1973.

FIRESTONE, HARVEY SAMUEL, JR., rubber co. exec.; b. Chgo., Apr. 20, 1898; s. Harvey Samuel and Idabelle (Smith) F.; grad. Asheville (N.C.) Sch., 1916; A.B., Princeton, 1920; LL.D., U. Akron, Stetson U.; m. Elizabeth Parke, June 25, 1921; children—Elizabeth Chambers (Mrs. Firestone Willis), Martha Parke (Mrs. William C. Ford), Harvey Samuel III (dec.), Anne Idabelle (Mrs. John F. Ball). Actively asso. Firestone Tire and Rubber Co., dir., 1919-69, v.p., 1929-41, pres., 1941-46, pres., chief officer, 1946-48, chmn., chief exec. officer, 1948-63, chmn., 1963-66, hon. chmn., hon. dir. 1966-73; v.p. Firestone Plantations Co. (with rubber plantations in Liberia, West Africa), 1926-32, pres., chmn., 1932-67. Founder Am. Assn. Against Addiction; nat. chmn. U.S.O., mem. internat. com. YMCA; mem. Nat. Com. Washington Cathedral. Mem. nat. council United Negro Coll. Fund; trustee, dir. Episcopal Ch. Found., Asheville Sch., U. Liberia, Ohio Found. Ind. Colls., Inc.; charter trustee Princeton; trustee Thomas Alva Edison Found. (v.p.). Served in Naval Aviation, 1918. Decorated Dept. Def. medal for distinguished pub. service; Officer Legion of Honor (France); Comdr. Order Isabella the Catholic (Spain); Grand Band Order of Star of Africa, also Grand Cordon of the Most Venerable Order Knighthood of Pioneers of Republic of Liberia; Comdr. of the White Rose (Finland); Comdr.'s Cross Order Merit (Germany). Mem. Am. Bible Soc. (v.p.), UN Assn. U.S.A. (dir.), Nat. Conf. Christians and Jews. Republican. Episcopalian. Author: Man on the Move, The Story of Transportation. Home: Akron OH Died June 1, 1973.

FIRESTONE, ROGER STANLEY, mfg. exec.; b. Akron, O., June 25, 1912; s. Harvey S. and Idabelle (Smith) F.; A.B., Princeton 1935; postgrad. Cal. Inst. Tech.; H.H.D., Central Coll., Pella, Ia., 1961; LL.D., Lycoming Coll., 1963, LaSalle Coll., 1966, Allegheny Coll., 1967; m. Mary Davis, Aug. 22, 1936 (dec.); children—Gay (Mrs. P. G. Wray), Peter, John Davis; m. 2d Anne Joers, April 15, 1946; children—Cinda, Susan. Dist. Sales mgr. with Firestone Tire & Rubber Co., Houston, Tex., 1937-38, dir. since 1945, dir. new prdts. dept., 1945-57; pres. Firestone Rubber & Latex Prdts. Co., Fall River, Mass., 1938-42; pres. Firestone Aircraft Co., Akron, 1945-47; pres. Firestone Plastics Co., Pottstown, 1947. Vice chmn. United Cerebral Palsy Assns.; pres. United Cerebral Palsy Research & Ednl. Found.; v.p., nat. exec. bd. Boy Scouts Am. Mem. Nixon for Pres. adv. com., 1968; adviser Pa. Republican financial com. Bd. dirs., trustees Freedoms Found. at Valley Forge; trustee Ind. Coll. Funds. Am., Ind., Lincoln U., Oxford, Pa.; Pa. chmn. Found. for Ind. Colls., Inc. Served as lt. to lt. comdr. USNR, 1942-45; prodn. div. Navy Bur. Aero, Washington, 1942, logistics plans div. Office Chief Naval Operations. 1944-45. Recipient Silver Beaver, Silver Antelope, Silver Buffalo awards Boy Souts of Am. Mem. Sigma Xi. Republican. Episcopalian. Clubs: Chevy Chase, Metropolitan (Washington); River, Brook (N.Y.C.); Crown Colony (Bahamas); Gulph Mills Golf, Union League, Corinthian Yacht, Racquet, Philadelphia (Phila.); Augusta Nat. Golf; Laurel Valley Golf; Rotary (hon. mem.) (Pottstown, Pa.). Home: Bryn Mawr PA Died Jan. 26, 1970; buried Columbiana OH

FIRING, THORALF OTMANN, clergyman, coll. pres.; b. Horten, Norway, Dec. 16, 1890; s. Martinius O. and Maren K. (Madsen) F.; brought to U.S., 1908, naturalized, 1917; B.S., Northwestern, 1921; B.D., Garrett Bibl. Inst., 1921, hon. D.D., 1942; m. Evelyn Thora Thorsen, June 12, 1917; children—Thor Martell, Ethel Dorothy, (Mrs. Leslie Gravesen), Anita Evelyn (Mrs. Robert Lystad), Gene Carol, (Mrs. Charles Paine), Alf Martin, Ruth Ann (Mrs. Charles Williams). Ordained to ministry, Meth. Ch., 1916; pastor Norway, Ill., 1916-19, Portage Park Ch., Chicago, 1919-20; instr. Norwegian-Danish Theol. Sem., Evanston, 1917-19, acting pres., 1919-20, pres., 1920-34; co-founder Evanston Collegiate Inst. (now Kendall Coll.), Evanston, Ill., 1934, pres., 1934-54, pres. emeritus, 1954-71. Officer Rock River Meth. Ch. Conf. Pres. Norweigan-Danish Meth. Hist. Soc.; mem. Am. Edn. Assn., Evanston Hist. Soc., Meth. Ch. Ret. Ministers Assn., Internat. Soc. Norsemen. Republican. Clubs: University, Rotary. Home: Evanston IL Died Feb. 19, 1971; buried Meml. Park Cemetery, Skokie IL

FISCHEL, VICTOR ARNOLD, distillery exec.; b. Montreal, Que., Can., Oct. 11, 1902; s. Gustav and Sara (Green) F.; graduate pub. and high schs.; m. Mollie Bald, Dec. 28, 1926; 1 dau., Gloria (Mrs. Baruh). Came to U.S., 1934. Began advt. career, Montreal, 1923; advt. mgr., provincial sales mgr. Distillers Corp.-Seagrams, Ltd., Montreal, 1928-33. dir. from 1949, Upstate N.Y. mgr. Seagram-Distillers Corp., 1934, Metro, N.Y. mgr., 1935-36, divisional manager, 1936-37, marketing dir., 1937-40, gen. sales mgr., 1940-43, v.p., 1943-48, pres. Seagram-Distillers Co., 1948-55; pres. The House of Seagram, Inc., 1955-62; v.p., dir. Distillers Corp.-Seagrams, Ltd. in Montreal; exec. com. dir. Joseph E. Seagram & Sons, Inc., 1955-69. Vice pres., trustee Samuel Bronfman Found. Club: Fairview Country (Elmsford, N.Y.). Home: Scarsdale NY Died July 1969.

FISCHER, EARL W., banker; b. Victoria, Tex., 1908; ed. Victoria Coll., 1928. Chmn. exec. com., exec. v.p., sr. trust officer, dir. Victoria Bank & Trust Co.; dir. Parkdale Bank; vice chmn., dir. Victoria Fed. Savs. & Loan Assn. Sec., commr. Victoria County Nav. Dist. Lion. Home: Victoria TX Died Mar. 31, 1970.

FISCHER, EDWARD LOUIS, judge; b. Wyandotte City, Kan., Sept. 27, 1870; s. Christian and Margaret (Herget) F.; ed. pub. schs.; LL.B., Kansas U. Law Sch., 1892; m. Minnie M. Hildebrand, Aug. 27, 1901; children—Edward Burell (dec.), Chester Howard. Practiced law, Kansas City, Kan., 1892-97, 1904-09; judge of City Ct., 2d Dist., Kansas City, Kan., 1897-1900; judge Dist. Ct. since 1900, except 1904-09, mem. Judicial Council of Kansas, 1927-43. Member Wyandotte County, Kansas and Am. bar assns. Democrat. Mason (Shriner), I.O.O.F., M.W.A. Clubs: Hi-Twelve, Kiwanis. Home: 2846 Parkwood Blvd. Office: Court House, Kansas City KS‡

FISCHER, JACOB, labor official; b. Osborn, O., Apr. 11, 1871; s. John and Anna (Heiber) F.; ed. pub. sch.; m. Mary M. (Behunan), of Anderson, Ind., Apr. 1900 (died 1923); 1 dau., Barbara A. Gen. pres. or gen. sec.-treas. Journeyman Barbers Internat. Union since 1895; 7th v.p. Am. Federation of Labor. Lutheran. Elk. Home: 426 N. Arsenal Av. Office: 222 E. Michigan St., Indianapolis IN‡

FISCHER, KERMIT, control instrument mfg.; b. Phila., Aug. 1, 1905; s. Adelbert William and Helene (Koerting) F.; certificate mech. engring., Eve. Coll., Drexel Inst. Tech., 1930; m. Janet Elizabeth Piper, Oct. 14, 1960; children—Ralph Lawrence, Elizabeth Josephine (Mrs. Jay Tolson), James Harold. With Atlantic Elevator Co., Phila., 1926-27, Schutte & Koerting Co., Phila., 1927-37; founder, 1937; since chmn. Fischer & Porter Co., Warminster, Pa.; dir. Alloy Steel Casting Co., Warminster Fiberglass Co., Andrews Glass Co., Fischer & Porter Pty. Ltd., Fischer & Porter Ltd., Fischer & Porter Can. Ltd., Otic-Fischer &Porter, Fischer & Porter GmbH, Fischer & Porter de Mexico, Fischer & Porter N.V., Fischer & Porter Italiana S.P.A., Fischer & Porter Iberica, Fischer & Porter de P.R., Fischer & Porter do Brazil, Fisher & Porter Israel Ltd. Mem. Am. Soc. M.E., Am. Inst. Chem. Engrs., Instrument Soc. Am., Franklin Inst. Clubs: Engineers (Phila.); Chemists (N.Y.C.). Home: Furlong PA Died June 6, 1971.

FISCHER, LEO H., sports editor; b. Chgo., Sept. 20, 1897; s. Abraham and Anna (Silverberg) F.; student Northwestern U., 1921-23; m. Margaret MacLean, June 20, 1926; children—Barbara (Mrs. William Swisher), Nancy (Mrs. John W. Gwynne, Jr.). Sports writer Chgo. Examiner, Chicago Herald-Examiner, Chgo. Jour., Chgo. American; sports editor Chgo. Am., 1943-69; sports editor Chicago Today, 1969. Founder, pres. Amateur Softball Assn., 1930-38; pres., Nat. Profl. Basketball League, 1940-44. Trustee Nat. Hemophilia Found.; dir. LaRabida Jackson Park Sanitarium; trustee Ill. Masonic Hosp. Served with USN, 1917-19; editor Great Lakes Bull., 1918; served with Ill. N.G., 1919-20; lt. U.S. Army Res., 1920-27. Recipient U.S.O. citation for vets. recreational services, 1944, citation, Back of Yards Council, 1953; named Press Veteran of the Year, 1963; Chicago Sportsman of the Year, 1968. Member of Editorial Assoc., Chgo. Press Club, Baseball Writers' Assn. Am., Football Writers's Assn. (pres. 1956), other profl. assns., Am. Legion, Sigma Delta Chi. Mason (Shriner). Elk. Clubs: Variety, Ill. Athletic, Headline (president 1951), Sojourners. Author: Winning Softball, 1941; co-author Little Sports Library (10 vols.), 1939. Contbr. articles nat. mags. Home: Chicago IL Died Oct. 1970.

FISCHER, MARY ELLEN SIGSBEE (MARY SIGSBEE FISCHER), illustrator; b. New Orleans, La., Feb. 26, 1876; d. Charles Dwight and Eliza Rogers (Lockwood) Sigsbee; studied Art Students' League, Washington and New York, also in Paris; m. William Balfour Ker; 1 son, David Balfour Ker (dec.); m. 2d, Anton Otto Fischer, of Munich, Germany, Oct. 2, 1912; 1 dau.; Katrina Sigsbee. Illustrator for mags. Home: Woodstock Ulster Co NY‡

FISET, SIR EUGENE (MARIE-JOSEPH), lt. gov. Province of Quebec; b. Rimouski, Que., Mar. 15, 1874; s. Hon. Jean-Baptiste Romuald and Aimee (Plamondon) F.; student Rimouski Sem.; B.A., Laval U., 1894, M.B., 1896, M.D., M.S., 1898, LL.D., 1940, D.C.L., 1941; Dr. honoris causa, U. of Montreal, 1943, McGill U., 1943; m. Stella Taschereau, 1902; 4 daughters. Dir. gen. Canadian Med. Services, 1903-06; apptd. hon. surgeon-gen. to Gov. Gen. of Can., 1905; dep. minister of militia and defense, Can., 1906; prin. med. officer Coronation contingent, 1902; dep. minister nat. defense and v.p. Defense Council, 1923-24; elected mem. Canadian House of Commons. 1924. 25, 26, 30, 35; lt. gov. Prov. of Quebec since Dec. 1939. Served in S. Africa with 2d Batt. Royal Can. Regt., First Can. Contingent, 1899-1900, present at battle of Paardeberg (dispatches thrice); apptd. mag. gen. Can. Med. Service, 1914. Awarded Queen's medal with four clasps, D.S.O. Created Knight, July 1917. Decorated Companion St. Michael and St. George, 1913; Knight of Grace St. John of Jerusalem, 1941; comdr. Legion of Honour, France (Mil.) and Crown of Belgium; Order of St. Sava of Yougoslavia (1st class); Czecho Slovakian Mil. Cross. Hon. col. Fusiliers du St. Laurent (Can. Mil.). Fellow Royal Coll. Surgeons (Can.). Home: Spencerwood. Address: Government House, Quebec Canada‡

FISH, EDWARDS R., mech. engr.; b. Stone Mountain, Ga., Aug. 4, 1870; s. Laurens B. and Amelia R. (Whitman) F.; student St. Louis Manual Training Sch., 1884-87; M.E., Washington U., St. Louis, Mo., 1892; m. Ida M. McBride, Apr. 29, 1902; children—Laurens B., Marjorie, Janet (Mrs. Richard A. Waite), Edwards R. Draughtsman, Lewis Valve Gear Co., 1892; supt. Washington Univ. Testing Lab., 1892-93; asst. engr. Heine Boiler Co., 1893-97, sec. 1897-1914; vice pres. and chief engr., 1914-30; chief engr. boiler div. Hartford Steam Boiler Inspection and Insurance Co., 1930-44; engring. consultant since 1944. Fellow Am. Soc. M.E., Am. Welding Soc. Clubs: Engineers (St. Louis) (sr. mem.); Hartford (Conn.) Engineers. Home: 30 Laurel Av., Windsor CT‡

FISH, FRED ALAN, prof. electrical engring.; b. Milan, Erie Co., Ohio, Feb. 21, 1875; s. Albert M. and Emily Marie (Graves) F.; grad. High Sch., Milan, 1893; science course, Buchtel Coll., Akron, O., 1893-95; M.E. in E.E., Ohio State U., 1898; hon. fellowship in electrical engring., U. of Wis., 1900-01; m. Annie Knower Caulkins (B.S., U. of Wis., 1901), of Troy, N.Y., Aug. 14, 1901; children—Frances Louise, Elizabeth Harriet. Asst. prof. elec. engring., Ohio State U., 1901-05; prof. elec. engring., Ia. State Coll., since 1905. Fellow Am. Inst. Elec. Engrs., 1913; mem. Soc. Promotion Engring. Edn., Nat. Electric Light Assn., Sigma Xi, Tau Beta Pi, Phi Kappa Phi, Phi Delta Theta, Eta Kappa Nu. Home: 503 Ash Av., Ames IA‡

FISH, HERBERT HENRY, b. Oxford, N.Y., Feb. 21, 1870; s. John James and Chloe M. (Bradley) F.; grad. high sch., Neenah, Wis., 1885; student Lake Forest (Ill.) Acad., 1886-87; m. Ella L. Newberry, of Lincoln, Neb., Dec. 5, 1894; children—Herbert Huron, Robert Leon (dec.). With W.C. Ry., 1887-93; mgr., Western Newspaper Union, Lincoln, Neb., 1893-95, auditor, Chicago, Ill., 1895-1900, sec., Omaha, 1903-16, v.p., 1916-18, pres. since 1918; now retired. Republican. Clubs: Scarsdale Golf (Hartsdale, N.Y.); Knollwood Country (White Plains, N.Y.). Home: 40 Olmsted Road, Scarsdale, N.Y. Office: 310 E. 45th St., New York NY‡

FISH, JOHN CHARLES LOUNSBURY, civil engineer; b. Townsend Twp., Huron County, O., June 3, 1870; s. Job and Annie Elizabeth (Peabody) F.; C.E., Cornell U., Ithaca, N.Y., 1892; m. Ethelwyn Rebecca Slaght, July 31, 1894; children—Job (dec.), Lounsbury S., Frances C. (Mrs. Garth L. Young). Asst. to city engr., Sandusky, O., 1886-88; instr. civ. engring., Cornell U., 1892-93; instr. Stanford, 1893-94, asst. prof., 1894-98, asso. professor, 1898-1905; res. engineer L.S.& M.S. Ry., 1905-07; div. engr., same, 1907-09; prof. railroad engring., 1909-25, prof. civil engring., 1925-35, exec. head civil engring. dept., 1928-35, emeritus prof. civil engring, since 1935, Stanford U. Health commr. and mem. Bd. Pub. Safety. Palo Alto, 1909-24. Mem. Am. Soc. C.E., Am. Ry. Engr. Assn., Sigma Xi, Alpha Tau Omega; hon. mem. Sigma Delta Pi. Awarded Fuertes gold medal for original research, Cornell U., 1915. Author: Lettering of Working Drawings, 1894; Linear Drawing & Lettering, 1901; Descriptive Geometry, 1903; Earthwork Haul and Overhaul, 1913; Engineering Economics, 1915, 23. Technic of Surveying Instruments, and Methods, 1917; The Engineering Profession (with T. J. Hoover), 1941. Home: 1336 Emerson St., Palo Alto CA‡

FISH, MILTON ERNEST, seminary dean; born Boston, July 18, 1874; s. William W. and Eliza J. (Gage) F.; A.B., Harvard, 1898; B.D., Andover Newton Theol. Sem., 1901; S.T.M., Boston U., 1926; D.D., Los Angeles Baptist Theological Sem., 1951; m. Daisy G. Earle, Oct. 2, 1902; 1 son, James Bartlett. Pub. sch. teacher, 1897; pastor of Baptist chs. in Mass., Colo., Minn. and Calif., 1901-35; prof. New Testament language and lit. Shelton College, 1935-47; dean Los Angeles Baptist Theol. Sem. since 1947. Trustee Colo. Woman's Coll., Denver, 1908-11. Pres. Western Slope Sunday Sch. Assn., 1905-06; mem. exec. com. Minn. Bapt. Conv., 1912-17, Southern Calif. Bapt. Conv., 1918-24; church surveyor of San Bernardino County, 1920, pres. Southern Calif. Premilen'l Assn., 1922-23; pres. Worcester County Ministerial Conf., 1933; moderator Worcester Bapt. Assn., 1933-34. Republican. Pres. Am. Com. for Evangelization of the Greeks, Inc., 1942-48, pres. emeritus since 1948. Mem. Soc. Bibl. Lit. and Exegesis. Evang. Theol. Soc. Mem. Harvard Club of So. Calif. Home: 715 S. St. Louis St., Los Angeles 23. Office: 560 S. St. Louis St., Los‡

FISHBURNE, EDWARD BELL, educator; b. Charleston, S.C., Dec. 16, 1874; s. Edward Bell and Margaret Gervais (Miller) F.; B.S. in Civ. Engring., The Citadel (Mil. Coll. of S.C.), 1893; M.A., Ill. Wesleyan U., 1898; m. Mary Lou Houston, Dec. 26, 1900; children—Evelyn Houston (Mrs. Frank M. McCraw), Margaret Louise, Edward Bell. Tutor at Kingsford, Fla., 1894-95; prin. grade schs., Summerville, S.C., 1895-96; comdt. and instr. mathematics, Fishburne Mil. Sch., Waynesboro, Va., 1896-1900; supt. Hoge Mil. Acad., Blackstone, Va., 1900-09; prof. mathematics and astronomy, Washington and Tusculum Coll., Washington Co., Tenn., 1909-11; headmaster Tenn. Mil. Inst., Sweetwater, 1911-15; supt. Columbia (Tenn.) Mil. Acad., 1915-23; pres. Ala. Mil. Inst., Anniston, since 1923. Address: Ala. Mil. Inst., Anniston AL‡

FISHER, ANNE B(ENSON), author; b. Denver, Feb. 1, 1898; d. Lorenzo and Annie (Montgomery) Benson; student U. Denver, U. Colo. Med. Sch., 1915-18; R.N., Park Av. Hosp., Denver, 1918; grad. student N.Y. Postgrad Sch., 1919; m. Walter Kenrick Fisher, Sept. 2, 1922 (dec. 1953). Bacteriologist U.S. Bur. Animal Industry, 1918-19; established clin. lab., Salinas, Cal., 1920-22; traveled Europe, 1923, 29, Mexico and Guatemala, 1938; lt. adviser to Beta Sigma Phi. Mem. Authors League. Republican. Episcopalian. Author: No More a Stranger, 1946; Oh, Glittering Promise, 1949; It's a Wise Child, 1949; The Salinas (Rivers of America series); Cathedral In the Sun; The Story of California's Constitution and Laws, 1953; Stories California Indians Told, 1957; Bears, Pirates, and Silver Lace; and other books. Contbr. to jours. Home: Medford OR Died Mar. 5, 1967.

FISHER, ARTHUR WILLIAM, textile mfr.; born Mt. Pleasant, N.C., Jan. 12, 1890; s. William Henry and Margaret (Shimpock) F.; student Mt. Pleasant Collegiate Inst., 1907; A.B., Newberry College, 1909, D.C.S., 1953; m. Loula Belle Schaeffer, June 17, 1925; children—Margaret Elizabeth, Anna Barbara, William Schaeffer. Prin. Watts Mills Grammar Sch., Laurens, S.C., 1909-11; shipping clk., bookkeeper, cotton classer Watts Mills, Laurens, 1911-18; cotton classer Cannon Mills, 1919-20, cotton dept., 1923, mgr. cotton dept., 1928, v.p. from 1928, dir. from 1933; with Williamson, Inman & Stribling, Atlanta, 1920-23. Mem. bd. publs. United Luth. Ch.; bd. trustees Lenoir Rhyne Coll., Luth. Theol. So. Sem., Newberry Coll. Served as corp. U.S. Army, 1918-19. Mem. S.A.R. Lutheran (exec. com. N.C. Synod). Mason. Home: Concord NC Died Feb. 28, 1967; buried Lutheran Cemetery, Mt Pleasant NC

FISHER, EDGAR JACOB, educator; b. Rochester, N.Y., Sept. 28, 1885; s. George and Louisa (Faulden) F.; A.B., U. of Rochester, 1906, A.M., 1907; Ph.D. in History and Polit. Science, Columbia, 1911; m. Elisabeth Marie Fehr, July 31, 1911; 1 son, Edgar Jacob. Prin. high sch., Roselle Park, N.J., 1909-10; head of history dept., high sch., Summit, N.J., 1911-13; asst. prof. history, Robert Coll., Constantinople (Istanbul), Turkey, 1913-15, prof. 1915, dean, 1917-19, and 1922-34; special lecturer, U. of Rochester, and Colgate-Rochester Divinity Sch., 1934-35; asst. dir. Inst. Internat. Edn., 1935-48; exec. sec. Am. Field Service Fellowships for French Univs.; former mem. Adv. Ednl. Com. of the Russian Fund; mem. Adv. Council Nat. Travel Club. Mem. U.S. Com. of International Student Service; member advisory com. on the Adjustment of Foreign Students in U.S.A.; secretary, International Education Assembly; member of Carnegie Endowment Commn. to Study the Organization of Peace from 1930; vis. prof. Div. of Social Studies, Sweet Briar (Va.) College, 1948-49, Carter Glass prof. of govt., 1949-53; director dept. of student affairs American Friends of the Middle East, Inc., 1953-54, dir. So. region Am. Friends of Middle East from 1954, cons., from 1955; Internat. News commentator Chautauqua Instn., 1933-57; professor of social sciences St. Paul's College, Lawrenceville, Virginia, 1959-62; former visiting professor Stanford, Syracuse, Columbia. Former chmn. com. on internat. student exchange Nat. Interfraternity Conf.; mem. exec. com. and treas. World Alliance for Internat. Friendship Through Religion; mem. com. on aid to schs. in Latin Am., Am. Coun. on Edn. Mem. Va. Civil War Centennial Commn., from 1961. Trustee YMCA, N.Y., 1940-49; mem. Internat. Com. also So. Area council YMCA; mem. Nat. Council for Social Studies. Administrative bd. com. on Friendly Relations among Fgn. Students; sponsor World Student Service Fund; U.S. Com. Internat. Student Service; mem. Am. Acad. Polit. and Social Sci., Council on Fgn. Relations, Am. Hist. Assn. Mem. Bd. Corporators, Springfield (Mass.) College. Alpha Delta Phi, Pi Gamma Mu; asso. mem. Fellowship Faiths. Episcopalian. Club: Town Hall (New York). Author: New Jersey as a Royal Province, 1911. Contbr. to mags. Home: Amherst VA Died Nov. 19, 1968; buried Hollywood Cemetery, Richmond VA

FISHER, EDWARD F., business exec.; b. Norwalk, O., 1891. Chairman, dir. Gar Wood Industries, Inc.; v.p., dir. Fisher & Co., Inc., Detroit; dir. Gen. Motors Corp. Home: Brighton MI Died 1972.

FISHER, ELIZABETH FLORETTE, coll. prof.; b. Boston, Mass., Nov. 26, 1873; d. Charles and Sarah Gerrish (Cushing) F.; S.B., Mass. Inst. Tech., 1896; studied Harvard and Radcliffe. Instr. geology and geography, 1894-1906, asso. prof., 1906-08; prof. and head geol. and geog. dept., 1908-26, now prof. emeritus, Wellesley Coll.; lecturer on geography for Commn. on Extension Courses, Boston. Fellow A.A.A.S., Am. Geog. Soc.; mem. Appalachian Mountain Club. Author: Resources and Industries of the United States (text book), 1919. Oil geology expert; lecturer on conservation of natural resources. Home: Wellesley MA‡

FISHER, EMORY DEVILLA, educator, chemist; b. Walker, Ia., May 4, 1908; s. Frank Ray and Clara (Shaffer) F.; B.S., Dakota Wesleyan U., 1931; Ph.D., U. Wis., 1935; m. Marie Elsie Michaelis, Oct. 26, 1935; children—Lawrence Wayne (dec.), Michael Emory, Mary Ellen (Mrs. George Minkevich), Frank Ray. Instr. chemistry Kan. State U., 1935-40, U. Tex., 1940-41; asso. prof. E. Tex. State Coll., 1941-46; prof. U. Mo. at Rolla, 1946-63; prof. chemistry, chmn. dept. U. Wis. Center System, 1963-69. Mem. Am. Chem. Soc., Sigma Xi, Gamma Alpha, Alpha Chi Sigma, Phi Kappa Phi. Home: Madison WI Died Aug. 25, 1969; buried Middleton Junction Cemetery, Dane County WI

FISHER, FRANK CYRIL, lawyer; b. Volga, S.D., July 9, 1893; s. William and Emma M. (Rowe) F.; A.B., Oberlin, 1914; LL.B., Columbia, 1917; m. Julia Anne Potter, Feb. 28, 1924; children—Julian, Peter Rowe. Admitted to N.Y. State bar, 1917, practiced N.Y. City asso. with and mem. Hughes, Schurman & Dwight and predecessor firms, 1920-37; member Royall, Koegel & Rogers, and predecessor firms, 1937-67. Police Justice Bayville, N.Y., 1948-64. Dir. Fownes Bros. & Co., Inc., Gerli & Co., Inc., American-Brazilian Suppliers, Inc., Church & Dwight Co., Inc., Vibro Plus Products, Inc., Parramore Island Corp. Mem. bd. trustees Oberlin College; board visitors Tulane University. Served with USN, 1917-19. Mem. Am., N.Y. State and N.Y.C. (mem. com. on state legisl. 1933-39) bar assns., Republican (mem. N.Y. County com., 1926-30). Clubs: Down Town Assn., Racquet and Tennis, Seawanhaka Corinthian Yacht, Piping Rock. Home: Bayville NY Died Nov. 1967.

FISHER, FRED DOUGLAS, consul general; b. Albany, Oregon, Mar. 13, 1874; s. Ezra Timothy Taft and Hannah Gaylord (Stout) F.; Albany Coll., 1889-91; m. Alameda E. Mason, at Nagasaki, Japan, Jan. 23, 1902; m. 2d, Mary M. Proctor, at Paris, Dec. 19, 1922. Private 2d Ore. Vols., 1898-99; q.m. dept. U.S.A., Manila and Nagasaki, 1899-1901; vice consul and interpreter at Nagasaki, 1901-04; consul at Tamsui, Formosa, 1904-06, at Harbin, 1906-08, at Newchwang, 1908-09; consul-gen. at Mukden, China, 1909-14, Tientsin, 1914-18; consul at Johannesburg, Transvaal, 1918-22, at Nantes, France, 1922-26, Santos, Brazil, 1926-30, Nassau, Bahamas, since Feb. 1930. Home: Salem, Ore. Address: American Consulate, Nassau Bahamas‡

FISHER, FREDERICK CHARLES, judge b. at Plymouth, Eng., July 4, 1875; s. Charles Ponsford and Harriett O. F.; brought to U.S., 1885; ed. grammar sch., Witch Creek, San Diego Co., Cal.; m. Teresa Russell, of Manila, P.I., Sept. 10, 1900. Enlisted in Battery K, 3d U.S. Arty., July 1898, and apptd. sergt.; participated in campaign before Manila and against Philippine Insurrection; recommended by Gen. Merritt for Medal of Honor, and promoted 2d lt.; hon. discharged, July 1899. Sec. to Maj. Gen. MacArthur, mil. gov., of P.I., 1899-1901; clk. Supreme Court of P.I., 1901-04; admitted to Philippine bar, 1903, later to bar Supreme Court of U.S.; practiced in Manila; apptd. asso. justice Supreme Court of P.I., 1917. Mem. bd. dirs. Y.M.C.A. of P.I. Mem. Am. Bar Assn., Cal. Bar Assn. Republican. Unitarian. Mason, Elk. Clubs: Spanish Casino, Manila Gun. Author: Code Pleading and Forms (in Spanish), 1903. Address: Manila PI‡

FISHER, GEOFFREY FRANCIS, archbishop of Canterbury; b. Higham Rectory, Nuneaton, Eng., May 5, 1887; s. Rev. Henry and Katharine (Richmond) F.; student Marlborough Coll., 1901-06; B.A., Exeter Coll., Oxford, 1910, M.A., 1913; D.D. Oxford, 1933, Cambridge, 1946, Princeton, 1946, Edinburgh, 1953, Seabury-Western Theol. Sem., 1954; LL.D., U. of Pa., 1946, Columbia, 1946, U. London, 1948, Manchester Univ., 1950, Yale, 1954, U. British Columbia, 1954; D.S.T., Northwestern U., Evanston, 1954; Th.D. (honorary), General Theol. Sem. N.Y.C., 1957; m. Rosamond C. Forman, April 12, 1917; 6 sons. Ordained to the ministry of the Ch. of Eng., deacon 1912, priest 1913; consecrated bishop, 1932; asst. master Marlborough Coll., 1911-14; headmaster Repton Sch., Derbyshire, Eng., 1914-32; bishop of Chester, 1932-39, bishop of London, 1939-45; dean of Chapels Royal, Prelate of Order of British Empire. Archbishop of Canterbury 1945-72. Privy Councillor, 1939-72. Prelate Order of St. John of Jerusalem. President of World Council Churches, 1946-54. Royal Victorian Chain, 1949. Recipient Grand Cross Order of Redeemer (Greece), Grand Cross of St. Olav (Norway), Order of White Lion, 2d Class (Czechoslovakia); Freeman of Cities of London and Canterbury, 1952; Knight Grand Cross of Royal Victorian Order, 1953. Honorary fellow Exeter Coll. Oxford, 1939. Pres. World Council Chs., 1946. Home: London England Died Sept. 14, 1972.

FISHER, JAMES MAXWELL MCCONNELL, naturalist, writer; b. Clifton, Eng., Sept. 3, 1912; s. Kenneth and Constance Isabel (Boyd) F.; King's scholar Eton Coll., 1926-31; M.A., Magdalen Coll., Oxford U., 1935; m. Margery Lilian Edith Turner, Sept. 16, 1936; children—Edmund Boyd, Crispin James, Selina Toussaint (Mrs. Randal Charlton), Adam J. Kenneth, Anstice Rosina, Clemency Thorne. Asst. master Bishop's Stortford Coll., 1935-36; asst. curator Zool. Soc. London, 1936-39; with Bur. Animal Population, Oxford U., 1940-43, Edward Grey Inst. Field Ornithology, 1944-46; editor William Collins, Sons & Co., 1946-56; dir. Rathbone Books Ltd., 1956-64, Aldus Books Ltd., 1962-64; writer, broadcaster for BBC, 1939—. Dep. chmn. Countryside Commn., 1966—; chmn. Northamptonshire Naturalists Trust; mem. council Royal Soc. Protection of Birds; mem. survival service commn. Internat. Union Conservation Nature and Natural Resources. Recipient Gold medal Royal Soc. Protection Birds; Tucker medal British Trust for Ornithology; Union medal Brit. Ornithologist's Union; Arthur A. Allen award Cornell Laboratory of Ornithology; Silver Medal, Zoological Society of London. Corr. fellow Am. Ornithol. Union; hon. mem. Danish Ornithol. Soc.; mem. Arctic Club (past pres.), Linnean Soc. (past council), British Ornith. Union (past council), British Ornith. Club, British Trust for Ornithology (past hon. sec., treas., vice chmn.), Wildfowl Trust (past council), Nat., Canadian Audubon socs., Cooper, Wilson ornithol. socs., Northeastern Bird Banding Assn., numerous other British and fgn. conservation socs. Author: Birds as Animals, 1939; (with Margaret Shaw) Animals as Friends and How to Keep Them, 1939; (with Julian Huxley) The Living Thoughts of Darwin, 1939; Watching Birds, 1940; The Birds of Britain, 1942; Birds of the Village, 1945; Bird Recognition, 1947—; The Fulmar, 1952; Birds of the Field, 1953; (with others) Fine Bird Books, 1953; (with Peter Scott) A Thousand Geese, 1952; (with R. M. Lockley) Sea-Birds, 1954; A History of Birds, 1954; The Wonderful World, 1954; (with Roger T. Peterson) Wild America, 1955; Rockall, 1956; The Wonderful World of the Sea, 1957, The Wonderful World of the Air, 1958; (with Margery Fisher) Shackleton and the Antarctic, 1958; (with Roger T. Peterson) The World of Birds, 1964; The Migration of Birds, 1966; Shell Nature Lovers' Atlas, 1966; The Shell Bird Book, 1966; Zoos of the World, 1967; Thorburn's Birds, 1967; (with others) Wildlife in Danger, 1969; also numerous articles. Home: Northampton Eng Died Sept. 29, 1970.

FISHER, JOSEPH ANTON, railroad exec.; b. Sayville, L.I., N.Y., Apr. 23, 1895; s. Anton and Barbara (Novotny) F.; B.A., C.E., Lehigh Univ., 1917; grad. Saumur Arty Sch., 1919; m. Fannie Eugenia Raynor, Nov. 27, 1919; children—Robert Joseph, Barbara Gene; m. 2d, Mabel Anderson. Spl. agt. freight traffic dept., Reading Co., Phila., 1921-22, traffic rep., 1922-25, chief clerk to vice pres. freight traffic, 1925-26, fgn. freight agt., 1926-28, asst. gen. freight agt., 1928-35, gen. freight agt., 1935-36, asst. freight traffic mgr., 1936-39, freight traffic mgr., 1939-44, gen. freight traffic mgr., 1944-45, vice pres. freight traffic, 1945-50, exec. v.p. 1950-51, pres., 1951-60, now dir. Perishable Products Terminal Co., Port Reading R.R. Co., Reading Transportation Co., Trenton-Princeton Traction Co., Washington & Franklin Ry. Co., Wilmington & No. R.R. Co.; pres. East Pa. R.R. Co.; vice president, director, member executive com. Ironton R.R. Co.; pres. Eastern Real Estate Co., Phila., Reading & Pottsville Telegraph Co.; v.p., dir., mem. exec. com. Pa.-Reading Seashore Lines; dir. Central-Penn Nat. Bank, Mut. Fire, Marine & Inland Ins. Co., Central R.R. Co. N.J., Plymouth R.R. Co.; dir., mem. exec. com. Lehigh & Hudson River Ry. Co.; dir. Phila. Belt Line R.R. Co.; Phila., Germantown & Norristown R.R. Co., Allentown Terminal Railroad Company; pres. Utility Workers Union Am., until 1960. President United Fund of Philadelphia, Trustee Lehigh University; manager Franklin Institute. Member Am. Soc. Traffic & Transportation, National Freight Traffic Assn., Pa., N.J. and Phila. C.'s of C. Republican. Episcopalian. Clubs: Traffic, Union League, Rittenhouse, Racquet, Downtown, Mfrs. Golf & Country (Phila.); Traffic (N.Y.); Traffic (Reading); Chicago. Home: Flushing NY Died Mar. 9, 1973.

FISHER, (WILLIAM) MARK, artist; b. Boston, of English and Irish parents; ed. pub. schs.; studied art at Lowell Inst.; painted portraits and figures; went to Paris at 20 and studied in Gleyre's atelier; married. Settled first in Boston; later went to England; landscape and animal painter; medals, Paris Expn., 1889, Chicago Expn., 1893; gold medal, St. Louis Expn., 1904. Represented at London, Manchester, Leeds, Bradford, Birmingham, Rochdale, Oldham, Huddersfield, Dudley, Eng., Nat. Gallery, Dublin, at Johannesburg, S.

Africa, and in Australia and New Zealand permanent municipal collections. Asso. Royal Acad., 1911; mem. New English Art Club; pres. Essex Art Club. Address: Hatfield Heath Essex England‡

FISHER, MILES BULL, clergyman; b. St. Helena, Napa Co., Calif., May 3, 1870; s. Galen Merriam and Susan (Talcott) F.; B.L., U. of Calif., 1894; B.D., Yale Div. Sch., 1897; post-grad. work U. of Calif., summer 1912; D.D., Pacific Sch. of Religion, 1916; m. Irene Rhoda Stiles, of Oberlin, O., Aug. 20, 1901; children—May Ellen, Corinna Darling (dec.), Miles Bruce. Ordained Congl. ministry, 1897; asso. pastor Adams, Mass., 1897-1900; pastor Mill Valley, Calif., 1900-02, Plymouth Ch., Oakland, 1902-07; supt. for Northern Calif., Congl. S.S. and Pub. Soc., 1907-10, Pacific Coast sec. Congl. Edn. Soc., 1910-17; sec. Missionary Edn. of Congl. Edn. Soc., Boston, Mass., 1917-19; dir. Dept. of Missionary Edn. Interch. World Movement, N.Y. City, 1919-21; dir. religious edn., Hillside Presbyn. Ch., Orange, N.J., 1921-23; dir. religious edn. and asso. pastor First Congl. Ch., Berkeley, Calif., since 1923. Mem. bd. mgrs. Missionary Edn. Movement, N.Y. City; mem. Berkeley Bd. Religious Edn. (sec. exec. com.). Mem. Beta Theta Pi. Clubs: Outlook, City Commons. Republican. Author: Suggestions to Leaders of Study Classes, 1920; also contbr. chapter, Religious Progress on the Pacific Slope" (in Religious Education), 1917. Home: 1309 Spruce St., Berkeley CA‡

FISHER, SAMUEL HERBERT, lawyer; b. Cincinnati, O., May 26, 1867; s. Samuel Sparks and Aurelia Safford (Crossette) F.; A.B., Yale, 1889, LL.B., 1892, M.A., 1920. LL.D., 1936; LL.D., Colgate University, 1932, Wesleyan University, Conn., 1935, Trinity College, Conn., 1942; student Harvard Law School, several month; m. Margaret Sargent, April 18, 1895; children—Mrs. Margaret Crossette Babbitt, Robert Lewis. Practiced, New Haven, 1892-1916, New York, 1916-31; dir. New York Trust Co., Nazareth Cement Co., New York, and other companies. Fellow of the Corp., Yale, 1920-35. Pres. Litchfield Hist. Soc., 1937; judge adv. gen. on Gov. Baldwin's staff, 1911-15. Chmn Tercentenary Commn. of Conn., 1933-35; chmn. of Conn. Highway Safety Commn., 1936-40; administrator of Defense for State of Conn., 1941-42; member of War Council of Conn., 1943. Member American Bar Association, Association Bar City of N.Y. Democrat. Episcopalian. Clubs: Graduate, New Haven Lawn (New Haven); Hartford (Hartford); Century, University, Links, Yale (New York); Acorn Club of Conn. Compiler of publs. of Thomas Collier, Printer, 1933; Biographical Catalogue of the Litchfield Law School, 1946. Home: North St., Litchfield CT‡

FISHER, THOMAS EDWARD, ry. official; b. at Memphis, Tenn., July 19, 1869; s. Thomas and Jane (Doherty) F.; ed. Christian Bros.' Coll., Memphis, and St. Benedict's Coll., Atchison, Kan.; unmarried. Entered ry. service as clerk U.P. Ry., 1889, becoming city ticket agt. at Denver; chief clerk gen. pass. dept. and asst. gen. pass. agt., U.P., Denver & Gulf Ry., and Denver, Leadville &Gunnison Ry., 1894-9; gen. pass. and ticket agt. C. & S. Ry., Jan., 1899—. Clubs: Denver Athletic, Colo. Traffic. Office: Cooper Bldg., Denver CO‡

FISHER, VARDIS, educator, writer; b. Annis, Ida., Mar. 31, 1895; s. Joseph and Temperance (Thornton) F.; A.B., U. of Utah, 1920; A.M., U. of Chicago, 1922, Ph.D. Magna Cum laude, 1925; m. Leona McMurtrey, Sept. 10, 1918 (dec.); children—Grant, Wayne; m. 2d, Margaret Trusler, Oct. 2, 1928 (divorced); 1 son, Thornton Roberts; m. 3d, Opal Laurel Holmes, Apr. 16, 1940. Instr. in English, U. of Utah, 1925-28; instr. in English, New York U., 1928-31. Served as corpl. U.S. Army, World War I. Author books including: Darkness and the Deep, 1943; The Mothers, 1943; The Golden Rooms, 1944; Intimations of Eve, 1946; Adam and the Serpent, 1947; The Divine Passion, 1948; The Valley of Vision, 1951; The Island of the Innocent, 1952; God or Caesar, 1953; Pemmican, 1956; Jesus Came Again, 1956; A Goat for Azazel, 1956; Peace Like a River, 1957; Tale of Valor, 1958; My Holy Satan, 1958; Love and Death, 1959; Orphans in Gethsemane, 1960; Suicide or Murder?, 1962; The Mothers, 1962; Thomas Wolfe As I Knew Him and Other Essays, 1963; Mountain Man, 1965; (with Opal Laurel Holmes) Gold Rushes and Mining Camps of the Early American West. Home: Hagerman ID Died July 9, 1968; cremated.

FISHER, WILLIAM A(NDREW), mfg. exec.; s. Lawrence and Margaret (Theisen) F.; m. Lura Titus; 1 son, Louis. Founder Fisher Body Corp., chief exec. officer to 1944; vice pres., dir. Citizens Nat. Bank of Norwalk (O.); dir. Detroit Bank and Trust Co. Clubs: Recess, Detroit, Athletic, Golf. Bloomfield. Home: Detroit MI Died Dec. 21, 1969.

FISHER, WILLIAM ORRIS, clergyman; b. New Castle, Pa., Dec. 6, 1875; s. Jacob and Jane (Jones) F.; A.B., Muskingum Coll., New Concord. O., 1898, D.D., 1923; B.D., Pittsburgh Theol. Sem., 1901 (Purdy scholarship); post-grad. work, Edinburgh U. and United Free Coll., Edinburgh, 1905-06; m. Mabelle Thompson, Oct. 10, 1906; children—Frances Thompson (dec.), William Thompson. Ordained ministry, U.P. Ch., 1901; pastor successively New Athens, O., Washington, Ia., Harvard Heights, Los Angeles, Calif., until 1918, First U.P. Ch., San Francisco, 1918-36; stated supply Second U.P. Ch., Los Angeles, 1936-40; supt. of missions, Presbytery of San Francisco; moderator Synod of Calif., 1927-28; denom. rep. San Francisco Ch. Fedn. Home Missions Council of Comity (for Northern Calif.), Calif. State Ch. Fedn. (for Northern Calif.), Anti-Saloon League (for Northern Calif.), Minister's Evang. Fellowship. Republican. Home: 212 S. Crescent Dr., Beverly Hills CA‡

FISHER, WILLIAM VICTOR, business exec.; b. Wapakoneta, O., Apr. 9, 1893; s. William E. and Barbara (Elsass) F.; student Ohio State, 1912-15; m. Marie McFarland, July 10, 1917. Deputy county engr., county engrs. office, Wapakoneta, O., 1915-17; with Hocking Glass Co., Lancaster, O., 1919-37, supt., 1925-37, dir., 1930-37; vice pres. and gen. mgr., Anchor Hocking Glass Corp., Lancaster, O., 1938-44, pres., dir., 1944-61, chmn. bd., from 1961, chief exec. officer, 1961-67; pres., dir. Maywood Glass Co., Los Angeles, Cal., from 1943; dir. Anchor Cap & Closure Corp. of Can., Ltd., Carr-Lowrey Glass Co., Balt. Served in constrn. div., AUS, 1917-19. Home: Lancaster OH

FISK, JESSIE (GLADYS), prof. botany; b. Brookfield, Vt., Mar. 29, 1895; Ph.B., U. of Vt., 1917; S.M., Rutgers U., 1920, D.Sc. (hon.), April 17, 1958. Worked as an assistant seed analyst Agrl. Expt. Sta., 1917-20, state seed analyst, 1920-49; lab. asst. botany N.J. Coll. for Women, 1918, instr., 1918-26, asst. prof., 1927-29, associate prof., 1929, prof., 1930-43, head dept. of botany and zoology, 1943-67. U.S. del. to Internat. Seed Testing Congress, Holland, 1931. Mem. Visiting Nurse Assn. (mem. bd. dirs.), New Brunswik, N.J. Operator summer camp, Brookfield, Vt. Mem. A.A.A.S., Bot. Soc. of Am., Assn. of Ofcl. Seed Analysts, Phi Beta Kappa, Sigma Xi. Republican. Author publs. including: Poison Ivy, 1944; also bulls. Home: Brookfield VT Died Nov. 15, 1967; buried Brookfield VT

FISKE, CHARLES PARKER, finance corp. ofcl.; b. Lynn, Mass., May 21, 1892; s. J(onathan) Parker Bishop and Lucie Adams (Johnson) F.; S.B., Mass. Inst. Tech., 1914; s. Marie Elizabeth Blood, June 16, 1916 (dec. 1964); children—Mrs. Darwin L. Gillett III, Mrs. John M. Thompson III, George Mann; m. 2d, Gladys Dunham Clarke, July 31, 1965. Clk. Kidder, Peabody & Co., Boston, 1914-17; resident mgr. financial sales Gen. Motors Acceptance Corp., N.Y.C., 1920-25, asst. mgr., 1925-28, mgr., 1928-30, v.p., 1930-54, dir., 1941-57, member executive committee, 1941-57, exec. v.p., 1954-57; vice president and dir. Gen. Motors Acceptance Corp. of Can., Ltd., Gen. Motor Acceptance Corp. Continental, Gen. Motors Acceptance Corp., Ltd., Gen. Motors Acceptance Corp. S.A., 1941-57, Gen. Motors Acceptance Corp., Australia, 1956-57; dir., mem. finance com. Gen. Exchange Ins. Corp., 1951-57; trustee, mem. exec. and investment coms. Dry Dock Savs. Bank. Hon. sec. Mass. Inst. Tech. Served as 1st lt. Ordnance, U.S. Army, 1917-20. Mem. Delta Tau Delta, Osiris. Republican. Episcopalian. Clubs: University, Union (N.Y.C.); Cumberland (Portland, Me.). Home: Phippsburg ME Died Aug. 9, 1968; buried Bath ME

FISKE, GEORGE CONVERSE, prof. Latin; b. Roxbury, Mass., Feb. 28, 1872; s. George Alfred and Kate (Washburn) F.; A.B., Harvard, 1894, Ph.D., 1900; studied univs. of Bonn and Halle, Germany; m. Augustine Elleau, of Newark, N.J., Dec. 26, 1908. Teacher Belmont (Mass.) Sch., 1895-97, teacher Greek, Phillips Acad., Andover, Mass., fall of 1900; with U. of Wis. since 1900, asso. prof. Latin since 1910, prof. since 1923. Mem. Am. Philol. Assn., Archaeol. Inst. America, Delta Upsilon. Protestant. Club: University. Wrote: Violation of Neutrality of Belgium (U. of Wis. war pamphlets); Lucilius and Horace (A Study in the Classical Theory of Imitation); Studies in Language and Literature, Number 7. Contbr. articles and revs. to Harvard Studies in Classical Philology, Trans. of Am. Philol. Assn., Classical Philology, etc. Spl. researches in Greek and Roman religion and Roman satire. Address: University Club, Madison WI‡

FISKE, HAROLD BENJAMIN, army officer (ret.); b. Salem, Oregon, Nov. 6, 1871; s. Rufus Eugene and Charlotte (Grubbe) F.; grad. U.S. Mil. Acad., 1897; honor grad. Army Sch. of the Line, 1910; grad. Army Staff Coll., 1911; m. Lucy Brooks Keyes, April 17, 1898; children—Berenice, Virginia. Commd. 2d lt. 18th Inf., Aug. 7, 1897; promoted through grades to maj. gen., Aug. 1, 1933; retired, Nov. 30, 1935. Asst. chief of staff for training, with hdqrs. A.E.F. in France; brig. gen. N.A., June 26, 1918-July 31, 1919; participated in battle at St. Mihiel, Aisne-Marne, Meuse-Argonne. Awarded D.S.M. (U.S.); Comdr. Legion of Honor, Croix de Guerre, with palm (French); Comdr. Crown of Italy; Comdr. Order of Leopold (Belgian). Address: 240 Quince St., San Diego CA‡

FISKE, WILLIAM F., entomologist; b. Webster, N.H., Mar. 20, 1876; s. Friend F. and Jane B. (Smith) F.; spl. course N.H. Coll. Agr. and Mech. Arts; unmarried. Asst. entomologist N.H. Expt. Sta., 1897-1901; asst. entomologist for state of Ga., 1901-3; asst. in forest investigations, 1903-6; in charge Gypsy Moth Lab., Melrose Highlands, Mass., May, 1906-Jan., 1913. U.S. Dept. Agr.; spl. investigator of sleeping sickness in Africa for joint commn. of Royal Soc. and British Colonial Office, 1913—. Mem. A.A.A.S., American Society Economic Entomology, Boston Soc. Natural History, Cambridge Entomol. Soc., Entomol. Soc. Washington, etc. Club: Cosmos (Washington, D.C.). Address: Bur. of Entomology, Dept. of Agr., Washington‡

FISKE, WYMAN P(ARKHURST), consultant; b. Somerville, Mass., Jan. 11, 1900; s. Frederick Augustus Parker and Harriett Lydia (Locke) F.; A.B., Harvard, 1920, Harvard Law Sch., 1920-21; M.B.A., Harvard Grad. Sch. Bus. Adminstrn., 1923; LL.B., Suffolk Law Sch., 1927, hon. Litt.D., 1938; m. Ruth Nichols, July 16, 1927; children—John Wyman, Esther. Instr. accounting, Harvard Grad Bus. Sch., 1923-28; office mgr. in Treas. Office, Amoskeag Mfg. Co., 1928-29; asst. prof. accounting, Mass. Inst. Tech., 1929-34, asso. prof., 1935-39, professor and dir. sponsored fellowship program, 1939-44; sec. Nat. Assn. Cost Accountants, 1944-46; management cons. since 1946. Member American Management Association, Controllers Inst. of America, Nat. Assn. Cost Accountants (pres. Boston chapter, 1932-33, nat. pres. 1942-43). Conglist. Co-author books. Home: Greenwich CT Died July 1972.

FISTELL, HARRY, musician, educator, inventor, bus. exec.; b. Beaver Falls, Pa., Jan. 16, 1907; s. Abraham Isaac and Ella (Pitler) F.; B.A., U. Denver 1930; B.Mus. Edn., Am. Conservatory Music, 1939; m. Marian Leah Wolf, Jan. 13, 1934; 1 son, Ira Jacob. Orch. leader, 1925-33; high sch. tchr., 1931-33; tchr. WPA sch. programs, Chgo., 1933-41; founder, owner pres. Chgo. Music Sales (Ill.). 1941-71, Toneline Mfg. Co., Chgo., 1941-71; pres. Allied Affiliates Inc., Chgo., 1970-71; mgrs. rep. and sales rep., 1941-71, Lowenthal Mfg. Co., Chgo., 1967-71; appraiser, cons. mediator for music industry. Mem. Am. Fedn. Musicians, Fretted Instrument Guild Am.; Nat. Assn. Music Mchts., Ill. Mfg. Assn., U. Denver Alumni Assn., Nat. Band Assn. Mem. B'nai B'rith. Designed and implemented course of music instrn. for individual and class participation (strings, brass and reeds). Home: Chicago IL Died Dec. 28, 1971.

FITCH, JOHN HALL, govt. ofcl.; b. N.Y.C., Mar. 13, 1909; s. Benjamin Homans and Martha Sofia (Johnson) F.; B.S. in Mech. Engring., Rutgers U., 1930; m. Margaret Ridgely, Oct. 27, 1951; children—Lee C., Margo G., John Hall. Various positions prodn. designing, gen. indsl. engring. field, 1930-41; with Fgn. Econ. Adminstrn., 1945; propr. Cladot Trading Corp., 1945-46; gen. mgr. Federal-Huber Co., 1946-47; account exec. Brigg-Stratton Corp., Milw., 1947-48; dir. procurement and prodn. div., staff of asst. sec. def. Dept. Def., 1952-59; dir. budget Air Force and Mil. Assistance Programs, 1959; dep. controller budget Dept. Def., 1959-61; became dep. asst. sec. army for financial mgmt., 1961, later ret.; v.p. for devel. Maremont Corp., Washington, until 1969. Served to col., War Dept. Gen. Staff, AUS, World War II; logistics planner Gen. Hdqrs., Far East Command, Korean War. Clubs: Touchdown; Army-Navy Country (Arlington Va.). Home: Alexandria VA Died Apr. 28, 1969; buried Arlington Nat. Cemetery, Arlington VA

FITCH, TECUMSEH SHERMAN, steel exec.; b. Pitts., Mar. 21, 1908; s. Thomas William and Gray (Emery) F.; B.S., Sheffield Sci. Sch., Yale, 1931; m. Janet McF. Reed, June 24, 1935; children—William T.S., Colin R., Gray M., Mary M., Rosamound T., Thomas E., Madeleine Lem. Laborer, Jessop Steel Co., 1931-33, asst. supt., 1934-36, mgr. composite div., 1937-42; pres. Composite Steels, Inc., Washington, Pa., 1940-69; founder, pres., chmn. bd. Washington Steel Corp. (Pa.), 1945-69; dir. Alan Wood Steel Company. Special assistant steel div. WPB, Washington, 1942-44. Mayor, City of Washington, Pa., 1956-60. Chmn. exec. com. Washington (Pa.) Hosp. Dir. Am. Iron & Steel Inst. Presbyn. Clubs: Duquesne (Pitts.); Pinnacle (N.Y.C.); Laurel Valley Golf (Ligonier, Pa.); Allegheny Country (Sewickley, Pennsylvania); also Pine Valley Golf (Clementon, New Jersey). Author: Carbonarc Welding in Making Composite Steels, 1941. Contbg. author Am. Soc. for Metals Handbook, 1942. Home: Washington PA Died Oct. 7, 1969; buried Washington PA

FITCH, WILLIAM KOUNTZ, mfg. exec.; b. Rockford, Ill., Nov. 2, 1889; s. Dr. William H. and Katherine (Kountz) F.; A.B., Yale, 1910; M.E., U. Wis., 1913; m. Mrs. Natalie Stone Austin, Nov. 1, 1947 (divorced). Sales engr. Dravo Doyle Co., 1913-22, dist. mgr. Cleveland office, 1922-27, v.p., 1926-34, pres., 1934-48, now dir.; v.p. Dravo Corp., 1938-46, dir., chmn. bd., 1946-50, ret.; dir. Dir. Allegheny council Boy Scouts America, 1945-51, member exec. com. 1954; director Allegheny County Community Chest, 1943-45, pres., 1945; dir. Fedn. Social Agencies of Allegheny Co., 1942-48, chmn. interim adjustment com., 1947-51. Pres. Sewickley Valley Hosp, 1954-69; pres. Hosp. Council Western Pa., 1959-62; dir. Hosp.

Assn. Pa., 1962-69, Harmarville Rehab. Center, 1962-69; treas. Hosp. project 1962-69. Mem. Am. Soc. M.E., Soc. Naval Architects and Marine Engrs., Am. Ordnance Assn. (dir. local, 1947-69, pres. 1955-57), Pa. Economy League (finance com. Western div.), Arthritis and Rheumatism Found. (past pres., now dir. W. Pa. chpt.), Newcomen Soc. Served at 1st lt. Ordnance Dept., U.S. Army, 1917-19; capt. Coast Arty. Res. Corps, 1919-25; mem. Ohio National Guard, 1925-27. Clubs: University, Duquesne, Harvard-Yale-Princeton, Allegheny Country, Rolling Rock, Pittsburgh Golf, Fox Chapel Golf, Sewickley Hunt Newcomen (Pitts.); Yale (N.Y.C.). Home: Pittsburgh PA Died June 29, 1969.

FITTS, CHARLES NEWTON, steel construction; b. Norfolk, Va., Aug. 12, 1870; s. Newton and Clymena (Williams) F.; grad. Norfolk Acad., 1887; student Mass. Inst. Tech., 1887-88; m. Onata North, Sept. 16, 1897; children—Doris (Mrs. William Alexander Smith), Lincoln W. With N.E. Structural Co. since 1895, treas. since 1913. Alderman, Newton, Mass., 1915-16. Pres. Am. Inst. Steel Construction, 1928-32, now dir. Republican. Episcopalian. Mason. Contbr. to trade mags. Home: 376 Clinton Rd., Brookline, Mass. Office: Everett MA‡

FITTS, DUDLEY, educator, author; b. Boston, Mass., Apr. 28, 1903; s. Dudley Thomas and Edith Kimball (Eaton) F.; A.B., Harvard Coll., 1925; LL.D., Columbia, 1968; m. Cornelia Butler Hewitt, Sept. 2, 1939; children—Daniel Hewitt, Deborah Whittier. Master in English, Choate School, Wallingford, Connecticut, 1926-41, organist and asso. choirmaster, 1934-41; instructor English, Phillips Acad., Andover, Mass., 1941-68; mem. adv. com. to dept. English, Princeton U., 1951-58; Phi Beta Kappa poet, Harvard, 1961; member of staff Bread Loaf Writer's Conference, 1961; mem. poetry jury Nat. Book Award, 1954, 60; apptd. to Emilie Belden Cochran Foundation, 1948. Awarded grant Am. Acad. Arts and Letters, 1948; fellow Jonathan Edwards Coll., Yale U., 1964-68. Mem. vis. bd. English dept. Harvard Coll., 1966-68. Fellow American Acad. of Arts and Sciences; mem. Academy of Am. Poets (chancellor since 1967), National Institute of Arts and Letters, Modern Language Association, Casa de la Cultura Ecuatoriana (Ecuador), Associacio Protectora de L'Ensenyanca Valenciana (Valencia, Spain). Democrat. Episcopalian. Clubs: Harvard (Boston); P.E.N. (N.Y.C.). Author books including: (with Robert Fitzgerald) Sophocles' King Oedipus, 1949. Editor various publs.; transl. poems; Greek Plays in English Translation (edit.), 1947; Office Hymns and Sequences of the Church (with C. F. Pfatteicher), 1950. Editor: Six Greek Plays, 1955; Yale Series of Younger Poets, 1960-68; An Anthology of Latin American Poetry, 1942. Translator: Aristophanes' Lysistrata, 1954; Frogs, 1955; Birds, 1956; Poems from the Greek Anthology, 1956; Thesmophoriazusae, 1958; Ladies' Day, 1959; Sixty Poems of Martial, 1967. Poet and critic. Home: Andover MA Died July 10, 1968.

FITTZ, AUSTIN HERVEY, b. Westborough, Massachusetts, Dec. 22, 1875; s. Herbert Rogene and Ellen Lavina (Underwood) F.; Ph.B., Brown U., 1900; LL.B., Harvard, 1906; m. Jean Boyd Sharp, June 26, 1907;children—Paul Herbert, Austin Hervey, Ronald Morton. Admitted to Mass. bar, 1906; prin. grammar sch., Keene, N.H., 1900-03; instr. in English, South Boston Evening High Sch., 1903-06; supt. schs., Troy, Fitzwilliam and Rindge, N.H., 1907-09, Norwood, Mass., 1909-19; dir. div. of finance, Babson Inst., Wellesley Hills, 1919-41; pres. Webber Coll., Babson Park, Fla., 1927-29; treas. and clerk Gravity Research Foundation; director Rockwood Sprinkler Co. of Mass., Eagle Signal Corp.; pres., treasurer and trustee, Open Church Association. Mem. Sch. Com., Natick, Mass., 1921-27 (chmn. 1923-27). Mem. Phi Beta Kappa. Republican. Conglist. Home: 82 Bacon St., Natick MA‡

FITZ, HUGH ALEXANDER, wholesale merchant; b. Fredericksburg, Va., July 15, 1876; s. William Henry and Mary Ann (Harrison) F. H.; student Epsicopal High Sch., Alexandria, Va., 1891-94, U. of Va., 1894-95; m. Lena Lea, Oct. 19, 1904; 1 dau., Jeanie L. Dir. Mchts. Nat. Bank, Vicksburg. Served as major Q. M. Corps, U.S. Army, 1917-19; lt. col. Reserve Corps, 1919-33. Mem. Phi Kappa Psi. Home: 1403 Baum St. Office: Levee St., Vicksburg MS‡

FITZGERALD, EDWARD ALOYSLUS, bishop; b. Cresco, Ia., Feb. 13, 1893; s. Edward A. and Emma (Daly) F.; A.B., Loras Coll., 1913; S.T.B., J.C.B., Laval U., 1916; LL.D. honoris causa, Loyola U., 1939; LL.D., Loras Coll., 1958, St. Mary Coll., 1959. Ordained priest, Roman Cath. Ch.; prof. Loras Coll., Dubuque, Ia., 1916-23, registrar, dean studies, 1923-41; pastor Sacred Heart Ch., Osage, Ia., 1941-45, St. Joseph's Ch., Elkader, Ia., 1946; also dean, Clayton Co., Ia.; auxiliary bishop, Dubuque, 1946-49; bishop, Winona, Minn., from 1949. Chmn. Mitchell Co. (Ia.) Price and Rationing Bd., 1944-46. Mem. Nat. Cath. Edn. Assn. (exec. bd. coll. and Univ. dept. 1938-45, chmn. Midwest unit 1938-40), Delta Epsilon Sigma (founder 1939). Home: Winona MN Died Mar. 30, 1972; buried St. Mary's Cemetery.

FITZ GERALD, LESLIE MAURICE, oral surgeon; b. Crecso, Ia., Aug. 18, 1898; s. Edward A. and Emma (Daly) Fitz G.; D.D.S., U. Ia., 1919; D.Sc., Loyola U., 1954, Temple U., 1957; married Marcelle Meis, Oct. 8, 1921; children—Shirley Ann (Mrs. F.D. Gilloon, Jr.), Patricia (Mrs. J.A. O'Brien, III), Jacqueline (Mrs. F. Benjamin Merritt II). Instr. U. Ia., 1919-20; resident oral surgery U. Ia. Hosp., 1919-20; pvt. practice of oral surgery, Dubuque, from 1920; chief oral surgery St. Joseph, Finley, Xavier hosps.; cons. oral surgery Central Office V.A., also Surgeon Gen. U.S.N., v.p. Dubuque Thrift Plan Indsl. Bank, 1931-63, president, from 1963; member board of directors Dubuque Savings & Loan Assn., First National Bank of Dubuque. Chairman of the dental advisory com. to Am.-Korean Foundation, 1954. President Boy's Club, Community Chest, Dubuque, 1931-32; v.p. Centralia Community Fire Dept. from 1947. Served as lt. comdr. Dental Corps, USN. Recipient Arnold K. Maislen Meml. award, N.Y.U., 1958; Thomas P. Hinman award, Atlanta; GIES award, 1972. Honorary col., staff Gov. of New Mexico, Co-founder, and diplomate, sec. Am. Bd. Oral Surgery. Fellow Am. Coll. Dentists (chmn. com. oral surgery), International College of Anesthetists, Acad. Internat. Dentistry, Internat. Coll. Dentists; hon. mem. Alaska, Hawaii, Puerto Rico Dental Socs.; mem. Nat. Inter-Assn. Council on Health, 1954; mem. Am. Dental Assn. (pres. 1953-54, chmn. bur. econ. research and statistics 1943-51; chairman sect. oral surgery 1948, mem. editorial bd. Jour. Oral Surgery 1950-56; chairman council on dental education), Iowa State (president 1942-43, past trustee), Dubuque (pres. 1920-21, 32-33), Chgo. dental socs., Am. Soc. Oral Surgeons (pres. 1941-42, 42-43), Dubuque Co. Med. Soc., Fedn. Dentaire Internat., Jr. C. of C. (pres. 1923-24), Dubuque C. of C. (dir. 1924-30), U. Ia. Coll. Dentistry Alumni Assn. (pres. 1931-32), Am. Legion, 40 et 8, Farm Bur., Guernsey Breeders Assn., Omicron Kappa Upsilon, Xi Psi Phi. Roman Catholic. Elk, Rotarian. (pres. 1930-31). Asso. editor Kruger Textbook of Oral Surgery; Oral Surgery Directory of World. Contbr. articles dental, medical publs. Lectr. in many states and before univs. Home: Peosta IA Died Aug. 28, 1972.

FITZGERALD, THEODORE CLINTON, veterinarian, educator; b. Green Springs, O., Mar. 25, 1903; s. Albert Daniel and Maud (May) F.; student Heidelberg U., Tiffin, O., 1922-23; D.V.M., Ohio State U., 1928, M.S., 1933; m. Frances Clement Bailey, June 27, 1929; children—Robert Theodore, Ivan Dale (dec.). Mem. bur. animal industry Ohio Dept. Agr., also engaged in gen. practice vet. medicine, Ohio, 1928-30; instr. anatomy Ohio State U., 1930-40; prof., head dept. anatomy and histology Auburn U., from 1940. Served with Vet. Corps, AUS, World War II. Grantee NSF, 1961, Mem. Am., Ala., Central Ala. vet. med. assns., Am. Assn. Vet. Anatomists (pres. 1960-61), Animal Disease Research Workers So. States, Ala. Edn. Assn., Phi Zeta, Omicron Delta Kappa, Omega Tau Sigma (Leta award 1958). Author: Anatomy and Histology Coturnix Quail, 1968. Contbr. articles profl. jours. Instituted saliva testing race horses in Ohio. Home: Auburn AL Died Oct. 17, 1967.

FITZHUGH, EDWIN A., editor, writer; b. Phoenix, July 30, 1909; s. Edwin C. and Gustina (Thiesen) F.; grad. Phoenix High Sch., 1925; m. Meryal Meadows, Feb. 13, 1937; children—Lee, Meryal Lee, Reporter. deptl. editor Phoenix Gazette, San Francisco News, Sacramento Bee, Los Angeles Examiner, 1925-31; editor El Centro (Cal.) Imperial Valley Press, 1931-43; owner, pub. El Centro Weekly, 1943-46; pub. El Centro Imperial Valley Press and Morning Post, 1946-51; editor Chgo. Sun-Times Syndicate, 1951-56; editorial writer Indpls. Star, 1956-58; editor Phoenix Gazette, 1958-72. Mem. Am. Soc. Newspaper Editors, Sigma Delta Chi, Ariz. Acad., Newcomen Soc. N.Am., Nat. Conf. Editorial Writers, Internat. Press Inst. Author syndicated newspaper column Close to Home, 1950-60; short stories. Home: Phoenix AZ Died Dec. 3, 1972; cremated.

FITZHUGH, WILLIAM WYVILL, paper co. exec.; b. Bklyn., Aug. 1, 1883; s. William Wyvill and Mary (Keese) F.; ed. pub. schs., Bklyn.; m. Jean Ruskin, Mar. 7, 1945; 1 son, William Wyvill. Founder, 1924, pres., treas. William W. Fitzhugh, Inc., N.Y.C.; vice chmn. bd. New Haven Board & Carbon Co.; trustee City Savs. Bank, Bklyn. Dep. dir. container div. WPB, World War II. Mem. Com. One Hundred, Miami Beach, Fla. Mem. Nat. Assn. Folding Box Mfrs. (past pres.). Mason. Clubs: Stamford Yacht; Key Largo (Fla.). Home: Stamford CT Died Jan. 27, 1966.

FITZPATRICK, DANIEL ROBERT, cartoonist; b. Superior, Wis., Mar. 5, 1891; s. Patrick and Delia Ann (Clark) F.; ed. high sch. Superior and Art Inst. Chicago; Litt.D. (hon.), Washington U., St. Louis, 1949; m. Lee Anna Dressen, May 24, 1913 (deceased on February 26, 1965). Began career on Evening News, Chicago, 1911; cartoonist St. Louis Post-Dispatch, 1913-58. Winner John Frederick Lewis prize for caricature, Pa. Acad. Fine Arts, 1924; Pulitzer cartoon prize, 1926, and 1954; Distinguished Service Journalism Medal, Mo. U., 1958. Home: St Louis MO Died May 18, 1969.

FITZPATRICK, WILLIAM SAMUEL, lawyer; b Shelby County, Ill., Sept. 14, 1866; s. Bird and Jane J (Freeman) F.; ed. pub. schs. and Osage Mission School St. Paul, Kansas; 1 son, Horace C. Admitted to Kansa bar, 1888, and began practice at Sedan; commr. U.S Dist. Court, Kan., at Pawhuska, Indian Ty., 1889-90 same position for Okla., 1890-93; returned to Sedan 1893; became mem. Kan. State Senate, 1900 (pres. pro tem, 1903, 05, 07); gen. counsel Prairie Oil & Gas Co. Independence, Kan., 1908-15, v.p., 1915-23, chmn. bd. 1923-32; company consolidated, 1932, with Sinclai Consol. Oil Corp. and Prairie Pipe Line Co. under th title of Consol. Oil Corp. of which was vice chmn. o exec. com. to 1938, then resigned. Alternate del. to Rep Nat. Conv. from 3d Congressional Dist. of Kan., 1896 del. at large, 1904, del., 1908, 16, del. at large, 1928 Mason (Shriner), Odd Fellow, Elk, Modern Woodman Woodman of World, Internat. Rotary (hon. life) Republican. Home: Los Fresnos, Tex. Office: 310 Firs National Bank Bldg., Brownsville TX‡

FITZROY, HERBERT WILLIAM KEITH adminstr.; born Thompson, Conn., Nov. 4, 1903; s Herbert William and Mary Ogilvie (Keith) F.; A.B., U Pa., 1925, A.M., 1928, LL.B., 1929, Harrison fellow in history, 1930-32; Regents fellow, Trinity Coll. Cambridge U., 1925-26; faculty fellow, law sch. Columbia, 1933-34; LL.D., Virginia Union University 1961. Assistant instructor history U. Pa., 1926-28, instr 1934-36; instr. history Princeton, 1937, asst. dean 1938-42; dir. St. Helena Extension Coll. of William an Mary (a vets. coll.), 1946-48, Marshall-Wythe lectr. Coll. William and Mary, 1948; president U. Center in Virginia (project Gen. Edn. Bd.), 1948-67. Served from 1st lt. to lt. col., USAAF, 1942-46, col. res. Decorated Army Commendation medal, Bronze star. Mem. Am Hist. Assn., Va. Hist. Soc., Va. Acad. Sci., Richmond Pub. Forum (pres.), English Speaking Union (pres. Va br.), Phi Beta Kappa, Omicron Delta Kappa. Democrat Presbyn. Clubs: Appalachian Mountain, Princeto (N.Y.C.). Home: Richmond VA Died Oct. 12, 1967 cremated.

FLAD, EDWARD, civil engr.; b. Arcadia, Mo., Nov 23, 1860; s. Henry and Caroline (Reichard) F.; C.E. Washington U., 1881; m. Emilie E. Speck, Feb. 10, 189 (died 1935); 1 dau., Virginia S. (Mrs. H. Towne Deane). Draftsman and mech. engr. St. Louis Wate Works, 1883-88; Johnson & Flad, consulting engrs 1889-92; gen. consulting engr., 1892-99; water commr City of St. Louis and mem. Bd. Pub. Improvements 1899-1903; consulting engr. since 1903. Mem. Bd. c Freeholders that drafted the charter adopted by the Cit of St. Louis, June 30, 1914. Special master in Pulask Chancery Court on Little Rock, Ark., water works case 1914. Asso. mem. Naval Consulting Bd. of U.S.; mem Pub. Service Commn. of Mo., 1917-21, consulting engr since 1921; mem. Miss. River Commn. since 1924 Republican. Mem. Am. Soc. C.E., Am. Soc. M.E., Loya Legion. Clubs: University, Engineers, Noonday. Home 17 Lenox Pl. Office: 828 U.S. Court House St Loui MO‡

FLAGG, PALUEL JOSEPH, physician; b. Yonkers N.Y., Aug. 22, 1886; s. Howard W. and Lilli (d Marmon) F.; M.D., Fordham U. Med. Sch., 1909; m Stella Robblee, Oct. 8, 1910; 1 dau., Sister Virgini Marie; m. 2d, Dorothy Ritter, Sept. 12, 191 children—Jane Dorita (Mrs. Joseph Richardson) Paluel Venard, Alfred Dante, James Anthony, Doroth Byrne (Mrs. George Webster), Francis Mercier, Pete Guerin, Paul Martin, Mary Ann (Mrs. James Wilson Noel Morrow, Thomas Aquinas; m. 3d, Marcella V Devlin, June 27, 1945. Practiced medicine, 1909-7 cons. pneumatologist, Manhattan Eye and Ear, Nev York City Eye and Ear Hospitals; Queens Hospital, an St. Francis Hospital, Honolulu, Hawaii. Founde Catholic Med. Missions, N.Y.C. Decorated knigh Grand Cross Holy Sepulchre. Fellow Nat. Acad. Scis mem. Soc. for the Prevention of Asphyxial Death, In (founder; pres.), Med. Surgical Soc., Me Jurisprudence, Med. Mission Bd. (founder), Phi Alph Sigma. Author: Patient's Viewpoint, 1923; Art c Anaesthesia, 1916, 1944; Art of Resuscitation, 194 Inventor of apparatus for anaesthesia and resuscitatio Home: Yonkers NY Died Jan. 17, 1970; burie Vinalhaven ME

FLAGLER, HARRY HARKNESS, b. Cleveland, O Dec. 2, 1870; s. late Henry M. and Mary (Harkness) F A.B., Columbia, 1897; hon. Mus.D., New Yor University; married Anne Lamont, April 25, 1894 (die 1939); children—Mary Harkness (Mrs. Melbert B Cary, Jr.), Elizabeth Lamont (Mrs. Flagler Harris), Jea Louise (Mrs. Flagler Matthews). Not a profession musician but for years has devoted time largely promotion of music in New York; a reorganizer Symphony Society of New York and its president man years, assuming its entire financial backing, 1914-2 consol., 1928, with Philharmonic Society and h became pres. of new orgn. (Th Philharmonic-Symphony Soc.) which office h resigned, Oct. 1934. Pres. Millbrook (N.Y.) Fre Library. Decorated Officer French Legion of Hono Mem. France-America Soc., Pilgrims of the U.S Council on Foreign Relations, English-Speaking Unio Phi Beta Kappa, Psi Upsilon. Club: Century. Hom Millbrook, N.Y. Address: 834 Fifth Av., New York NY‡

FLANDERS, RALPH EDWARD, mech. engr., ex.-U.S. senator; born Barnet, Vermont, September 28, 1880; son of Albert W. and Mary L. (Gilfillan) F.; graduate high school Central Falls, Rhode Island; International Corr. Schs.; hon. degrees: M.A., Dartmouth, 1932, LL.D., 1951; M.E. Stevens Inst., 1932; D.Sc., Middlebury (Vermont) College, 1934, Rose Polytechnical Institute, 1935, Univ. of Vermont, 1935; Northwestern U., 1940; LL.D., Harvard University, 1950; also Poly. Inst. Bklyn., 1934, Northeastern University, 1942, Clarkson Inst. Tech., 1949, Marlboro Coll., 1949, Allegheny Coll., 1953, Rollins Coll., 1954, Allegheny Coll., U. R.I.; married Helen E. Hartness, Nov. 1, 1911;children—Helen Elizabeth Ballard, Anna H. Balivet (dec.), James Hartness. Machinist apprentice and draftsman, Providence and Woonsocket, 1897-1901; designer Internat. Paper Box. Mach. Co., Nashua, N.H., 1903; asso. editor Mach., New York, 1905-10; engr. Fellows Gear Shaper Co., Springfield, Vt., 1910; became dir. and mgr. Jones & Lamson Mach. Co., Springfield, 1912, pres., 1933-46; president of Bryant Chucking Grinder Co., 1934-46; dir. Nat. Life Ins. Co.; pres. Fed. Reserve Bank of Bos., 1944-46. Pres. Am. Research & Devel. Corp., 1946, now dir.; U.S. Senator from Vt., 1946-58. Godkin lectr. Harvard, 1949. Trustee St. Johnsbury (Vt.) Academy, Sterling School; member of corp. Mass. Inst. Tech.; mem. bus. adv. and planning council of U.S. Dept. Commerce, 1933; also mem. Indsl. Advisory Bd. of NRA, Advisory Bd. for the Subsistence Homestead Adminstrn.; adminstr. Machine Tool Priorities, Office of Production Management, Washington, D.C., 1941; mem. Economic Stabilization Bd., 1942-44; chmn. Machine Tool Com. of Combined Prodn. and Resources Bd., 1943; chmn. Screw Thread Standardization Bd. of Am. Standards Assn. until 1944; chmn. research com. and trustee Com. for Economic Development. Mem. Nat. Screw Thread Commn., 1920-24; dir. Social Science Research Council, 1932-36; mem. Am. Engrng. Council (v.p. 1937; Hoover medal, 1944). Pres. New England Council, 1941-42; mem. American Society Mechanical Engineers (pres. 1934; Worcester-Warner medal, 1938), Franklin Inst. (Edward Longstreth medal with Ernest V. Flanders), Nat. Machine Tool Builders (pres. 1923), Acad. Polit. and Social Science, Am. Econ. Assn. Hon. mem. M.I.T. Chapter of Tau Beta Pi, Phi Beta Kappa (Dartmouth College, 1948). Republican. Congregationalist. Clubs: Engineers' (New York City, N.Y.); Union (Boston, Mass.); Cosmos (Washington). Author: Gear Cutting Machinery, 1909; Taming Our Machines, 1931; Platform for Am., 1936; The American Century; Letter To A Generation, 1956; Senator from Vermont, 1960.; Models for Living, 1967. Co-author: Toward Full Employment, 1938; also tech. papers. Home: Springfield VT Died Feb. 19, 1970; buried Summer Hill Cemetery, Springfield VT

FLANDERS, RALPH LINDSAY, b. Carroll, Me., Aug. 1, 1869; s. Charles A. and Evelyn Frances (Lindsay) F.; ed. Lee (Me.) Normal Acad.; m. Mary Louise Ayer, of Bangor, Me., Oct. 7, 1896; children—Evelyn H. (Mrs. Snelling S. Robinson), Frances M. (Mrs. Richard F. Howard), Marian L. (Mrs. Josiah P. Huntoon). Began at 19 with L. W. Savage, wholesale tobacconist, Bangor, and later became mem. Savage, Flanders & Co.; asst. mgr. N.E. Conservatory of Music, 1899, general mgr. same since Jan. 1903 (enrollment increased from 1,900 to 3,600); gen. mgr. Boston Opera Co., 1907, 08. Pres. Northport (Me.) Village Corpn. Clubs: Boston Press, Northport Golf (pres.). Home: 737 Washington St., Brookline, MA MA‡

FLANDRAU, CHARLES MACOMB, author; b. St. Paul, Minn., Dec. 9, 1871; s. Charles Eugene and Rebecca Blair (McClure) F.; A.B., Harvard, 1895. Author: Harvard Episodes, 1897; The Diary of a Freshman, 1902; Viva Mexico MN‡

FLANDRAU, GRACE HODGSON, author; b. St. Paul, Minn.; d. Edward John and Mary (Staples) Hodgson; student girls sch. in Paris, France, and Mrs. Backus Sch., St. Paul; Litt.D., Hamline University, St. Paul, Minn.; m. W. Blair Flandrau, Aug. 21, 1909 (dec.). Trustee, Avon Old Farms, secondary sch. for boys, Avon, Conn., Hill Stead Museum, Farmington, Conn., and Minn. Hist. Soc. (exec. council). Mem. Pen and Brush Club, N.Y.C., Nat. Pen Women, Nat. Garden Club. Clubs: Minnesota, Women's City (St. Paul); Colony (N.Y.C.). Author: Cousin Julia; Being Respectable; Entranced; Then I Saw the Congo; Indeed This Flesh; Under the Sun; Viva Mexico. Contbr. novelettes short stories and articles to nat. mags. Home: Farmington CT Died Dec. 27, 1971.

FLATH, EARL HUGO, elec. engr., educator; b. Dayton, O., June 5, 1895; s. Andrew Jackson and Cora Helen (Sigler) F.; E.E., U. of Cincinnati, 1919; M.S., Georgia Sch. of Tech., 1926; m. Ruth Lovertia Riley, June 5, 1920; children—Earl Hugo, Joseph Clarence Andrew. Began as office boy Nat. Cash Register Co., Dayton, 1913; university apprentice same company, 1914-19, asst. elec. engr., 1919; asso. prof. elec. engring., U. of Ala., 1919-20; development and research engr., Bell Telephone Labs., 1920-22; asso. prof. elec. engring. and dir. coop. courses, Georgia Sch. Tech., 1922-25; dean of engring., Southern Methodist University, Dallas, 1925-60, dean emeritus from 1960; prof. elec. engring. Tenn. Poly. Inst., from 1961. Served as 2d lt. inf., U.S. Army, 1918; 1st lt. Ordnance Res. to 1933. Trustee Highland Park Ind. Sch. Dist., 1935-44. Fellow I.E.E.E. (chairman N. Tex. sect., 1944); member Am. Soc. Engring. Edn., Nat. Soc. Profl. Engrs., Am. Legion, Sigma Tau, Phi Kappa Phi, Tau Beta Pi, Eta Kappa Nu, Alpha Tau Omega. Methodist. Club: Dallas Technical. Home: Cookeville TN Deceased.

FLATHER, FREDERICK ARTHUR, textile mfr.; b. Nashua, N.H., Mar. 21, 1867; s. Joseph and Caroline Drusilla (Drake) F.; ed. Bryant & Stratton's Commercial Coll., Boston, and Lowell (Mass.) Textile Inst.; m. Mary Sutherland Prichard, June 1, 1891; 1 dau., Mary Drusilla (Mrs. George Courtenay Riley); m. 2d, Alice Poor Rogers, Apr. 27, 1898; children—John Rogers, Frederick. Apprentice, draftsman, Foreman, Flather & Co., Nashua, 1883-87; supt. Pettee Machine Works, Newton Upper Falls, Mass., 1887-93; asst. to mgr. Lowell (Mass.) Machine Shop, 1893-1900; supt. McCormick Harvesting Machine Co., Chicago, 1901; mgr. of works, Internat. Harvester Co., 1902-05; treas. and dir. Boott Mills, Lowell, since 1905; pres. Proprietors of Locks and Canals on Merrimack River; chmn. Lowell Indsl. Development Co.; v.p. Merrimack River Savings Bank; director Stony Brook Railroad, Merchants National Bank, Boston, American Mutual Liability Insurance Company. Mem. Lowell Division United States War Labor Board, World War. Trustee Lowell Y.M.C.A., Lowell Y.W.C.A. Mem. Am. Soc. Mech. Engineers, Nat. Assn. Cotton Mfrs., Newcomen Soc. of England (Am. Branch). Republican. Conglist. Mason. Clubs: Yorick; University, Down Town, Union (Boston); Union League (New York). Home: 68 Mansur St., Lowell, Massachusetts. Office: 79 Milk St., Boston MA‡

FLEBBE, BEULAH MARIE DIX (MRS. GEORGE H. FLEBBE), author, playwright; b. Kingston, Mass., Dec. 25, 1876; daughter Henry S. and Maria Louise Dix; B.A., Radcliffe College, 1897, M.A., 1898 (Phi Beta Kappa); m. George H. Flebbe, May 5, 1910; 1 daughter Evelyn (Mrs. David Scott). Began literary work in 1895, writing plays, 1896, photoplays, 1916. Author: Hugh Gwyeth, 1899; Soldier Rigdale, 1899; The Making of Christopher Ferringham, 1901; The Beau's Comedy (with Carrie A. Harper), 1902; A Little Captive Lad, 1902; Blount of Breckenhow, 1903; The Fair Maid of Graystones, 1905; Merrylips, 1906; Allison's Lad, 1910; Freinds in the End, 1911; Betty-Bide-at-Home, 1912; Fighting Blade, 1912; Gate of Horn, 1912; Mother's Son, 1913; Little God Ebisu, 1914; Maid Melicent, 1914; Across the Border, 1915; Blithe McBride, 1916; Battle Months of George Daurella, 1916; Kay Danforth's Camp, 1917; The Turned About Girls, 1922; Pity of God, 1932; Life of Jimmie Dolan (with B. Millhauser), 1933; The Wedding Eve Murder, 1941, etc. Plays: Across the Border, 1914; Moloch, 1915; also (with late Evelyn Greenleaf Sutherland) A Rose o'Plymouth Town, 1902; The Road to Yesterday, 1906; The Lilac Room, 1906; Young Fernald, 1906; The Breed of the Treshams, 1903; Boy O'Carroll, 1906; Matt of Merrymount, 1906; The Substitute, 1908; The Arnott Will; also (with B. Millhauser); Ragged Army. Original photoplays and adaptations for the screen: Borderland, (with B. Millhauser) Country Doctory, Silence, Ever in My Heart, College Scandal, etc. Home: 636 Las Casas Av., Pacific Palisades CA‡

FLECK, ALEXANDER, chem. mfg. exec.; b. Glasgow, Nov. 11, 1889; s. Robert and Agnes Hendry (Duncan) F.; S.Sc., Glasgow U., 1916, LL.D., 1953; D.Sc. (hon.), Durham, 1953; m. Isabel M. Kelly, July 11, 1917 (dec. 1955). Mem. Glasgow U. staff, 1911-13, Glasgow Radium Com. staff, 1913-17; chemist Castner-Kellner Alkali Co., Ltd., 1917-19, works mgr., 1919-27; mgr., alkali div. Synthetic Ammonia & Nitrates Co., Ltd., 1927-31, del. dir., 1929-31; mng. dir. Gen. Chemicals div. Imperial Chemical Industries Ltd., 1931-37; chmn. Fertilzer & Synthetic Products, Ltd., Billingham Div., 1937-45; bd. dir. responsible for Billingham & Wilton, Imperial Chem. Industries, Ltd., 1944-51; chmn. Scottish Agrl. Industries. Ltd., 1947-51; dep. chmn. Imperial Chem. Industries, Ltd., 1951-53, chmn., 1953-60; dep. chmn. African Explosives & Chem. Industries, Ltd.; dir. Imperial Chem. Industries (South Africa), Ltd., Cape Explosives Works, Ltd., Imperial Chem. Industries of Australia and New Zealand, Ltd., Canadian Industries, Ltd. Created Knight Order Brit. Empire. Fellow Royal Soc., Geol. Soc. (London); mem. Soc. Chem. London England also Stockton-on-Tees County Durham, Eng. Died Aug. 1968.

FLECK, WILBUR H., educator; b. Tyrone, Pa., Feb. 4, 1874; s. Abram L. and Martha (Cryder) F.; prep. edn., Grove City Acad. and Gettysburg Acad. until 1898; B.A., Gettysburg Coll., 1902; M.A., U. of Pa., 1909; LL.D., Lafayette Coll., Easton, Pa., 1934; L.H.D., Syracuse U., 1940; m. Evelyn Heiney, June 14, 1905. Vice prin. Hazelton (Pa.) High Sch., 1902-07; teacher Latin, William S. Blight Sch. and De Lancey Sch., Phila, 1907-11; with Wyoming Sem., Kingston, Pa., since 1911, successively as teacher, dean, and since Apr. 1936, pres. and teacher of Latin, psychology and Bible. Served as mem. The Sheridan Troop, N.G. Pa. Mem. bd. dirs. Hoyt Library, Nesbitt West Side Hospital, Kislyn Sch. for Boys. Regent and dep. pres. gen. Cum Laude Society; member Phi Beta Kappa. Methodist. Mason. Club: Kiwanis. Address: Wyoming Seminary, Kingston PA‡

FLEESON, DORIS, columnist; born Sterling, Kan.; d. William and Helen (Tebbe) Fleeson; A.B., Univ. of Kansas; L.H.D., Culver-Stockton College, also Russell Sage College; married to John O'Donnell (div.); one daughter, Doris O'Donnell; m. second, Dan A. Kimball, August, 1958. Political reporter, and also Washington correspondent for New York Daily News, 1927-42; war correspondent Woman's Home Companion, 1943-44; Washington columnist United Feature Syndicate (Washington Star, Boston Globe, Kansas City Star, St. Louis Post Dispatch, also the Chicago Daily News), from 1945. Twice awarded New York Newspaperwoman's Club prize for distinguished reporting; recipient Theta Sigma Phi Headliner award, 1951; Mo. Journalism award, 1952; Raymond Clapper award, 1953, 54; Distinguished Alumni citation U. Kan., 1954. Mem. Woman's Nat. Press Club (pres. 1937), Chi Omega. Episcopalian. Clubs: Cosmopolitan (N.Y.C.); 1925 F Street (Washington). Home: Washington DC Died Aug. 1, 1970.

FLEGENHEIMER, ALBERT, sugar industry exec.; b. Schw bisch-Hall, Germany, July 4, 1890 (parents Am. citizens); s. Samuel and Lisette (Rothschild) F.; ed. in Germany; m. Helen Stern, Dec. 21, 1920; children—Ruth (Mrs. Henry H. Herzog), Ernest. Comml. apprentice, Karlsruhe, Germany, 1905-07; various positions sugar industry, Germany, Italy, Rumania, Bulgaria, 1907-37, also mem. mgt. Sueddeutsche Zucker A.G., Mannheim, Germany; organized beet sugar factory, Man., Can., 1939-41; pres. Waverly Sugar Co. (Ia.), 1941-48, Menominee Sugar Co., Green Bay, Wis., 1952-57; dir. Mich. Sugar Co., Saginaw, 1961-72, chmn., 1963-72. Club: Rotary (Waverly, Ia.). Home: New York City NY Died Dec. 1972.

FLEISCHMANN, RAOUL H., publisher; born Ischl, Austria, Aug. 17, 1885; brought to U.S., 1885; s. Louis and Wilhelmine (Herrmann) F.; student Princeton, 1902-03; A.B., Williams Coll., 1906; m. Ruth Gardner Botsford; 1 son, Peter; m. 2d, Dorothy Frowert Munds, November 29, 1939; m. 3d, Patricia Learmonth, Oct. 25, 1965. Office worker in fertilizer plant, 1906; with Fleischmann family bakery, 1907-11; bakery sold to Gen. Baking Co., 1911, dir. and plant mgr., 1911-25; with F-R Pub. Corp. (now The New Yorker Mag., Inc.), from 1925, beginning as v.p., then pres., later chmn. bd. pub. Clubs: Williams, Turf and Field (N.Y.C.). Home: New York City NY Died May 11, 1969.

FLEISHHACKER, MORTIMER, banker; b. San Francisco, Calif., Aug. 22, 1866; s. Aaron and Delia (Stern) F.; ed. pub. schs. of San Francisco; m. Bella Grestle, August 1904; children—Eleanor, Mortimer. Became partner and gen. mgr. A. Fleishhacker & Co., about 1890; organized various cos. and elected pres., Truckee River Gen. Electric Co., 1899, American River Electric Co., 1901. City Electric Co., 1905, Central Calif. Traction Co., 1906, Great Western Power Co., 1908; pres. Fleishhacker Paper Box Co.; dir. many corps. Federal mediator for labor troubles, World War, also head of Exemption Board. Regent U. of Calif. Mem. Golden Bear Soc. (U. of Calif.). Republican. Jewish religion. Clubs: Family, Olympic, Argonant, Concordia, Beresford Country. Home: 2418 Pacific Av., San Francisco, Calif.; (summer) Green Gables. Woodside, Calif. Office: Mills Bldg., San Francisco*‡

FLEMER, JOHN ADOLPH, topographical engr.; b. New York, Apr. 1, 1859; s. Charles H. and Martha (Lindenkohl) F.; ed. Latin sch., 1870-74; grad. Poly. Sch., Cassel, Germany, 1878; course in civ. engring., Royal Tech. High Sch., Berlin, 1878-81; m. Cornelia Chaplin Matthews, Mar. 22, 1887; children—Martchen Lindenkohl (Mrs. James Latane), Ellen Bagby Matthews (dec.), Cornelia Chaplin Matthews (Mrs. Julian Hungerford Griffith). With topog. survey of D.C., 1882-86; asst. U.S. Coast and Geod. Survey, 1886-1900; with F. and F. Nurseries, Springfield, N.J., 1900-03; engr. to commr. for demarcation of Alaskan boundary, 1904-06. Topog. engr. to Commn. on Improvement and Development of Jamaica Bay, N.Y., 1909-10. Fellow A.A.A.S., Am. Geog. Soc.; mem. Washington Soc. Engrs. U.S. Naval Inst.; Soc. of Am. Mil. Engrs., Am. Soc. of Engrs., Va. Acad. of Science; asso. mem. Am. Museum of Natural History, Societe Academique d'Histoire Internationale. Contbr. of articles on photographic surveying to scientific jours., U.S. Coast and Geod. Survey reports, etc. Author: Treatise on Photo-topographic Methods and Instruments, 1906. Oakgrove VA‡

FLEMING, DANIEL JOHNSON, clergyman; b. Xenia, O., 1877; s. Daniel Johnson and Josephine (McClung) F.; B.A., Wooster U., 1898; Union Theol. Seminary, 1901-03; M.A., Columbia, 1903; M.Sc., U. of Chicago, 1904; fellow Punjab University; Ph.D., U. of Chicago, 1914; D.D. from College of Wooster in 1925; m. Elizabeth Cole, Aug. 9, 1904 (dec. 1955);

children—Elizabeth Cole, Edward McClung, Helen Josephine; m. 2d, Helen Mack Howard (dec. 1969). Ordained Presbyn. ministry, 1903; prof. physics and dir., Forman Christian Coll., Lahore, India, 1904-13; organization director department foreign service since 1915, prof. missions, 1918-44, Union Theol. Seminary. Mem. Internat. Commn. on Village Edn. in India, 1919-20; mem. India staff Laymen's Foreign Missions Inquiry, 1930-31, retired July, 1944. Consultant on India, Department of State, 1945-46. Member of Beta Theta Pi, Phi Beta Kappa, Chi Alpha. Author: Social Study, Service and Exhibits, 1913; Devolution in Mission Administration, 1916; Marks of a World Christian, 1919; Village Education in India (with others) 1920; Schools with a Message in India, 1921; Building with India, 1922; Contacts with Non-Christian Cultures, 1923; Whither Bound in Missions, 1925; Attitudes Toward Other Faiths, 1928; Ways of Sharing with Other Faiths, 1929; Helping People Grow, 1931; Ventures in Simpler Living, 1933; Ethical Issues Confronting World Christians, 1935; Heritage of Beauty, 1937; Each With His Own Brush, 1938; Christian Symbols in a World Community, 1940; The World at One in Prayer, 1943; Bringing Our World Together, 1946. Address: New York City NY Died Apr. 1969.

FLEMING, ERNEST JOSEPH, b. North Ridgeville, O., Mar. 27, 1871; s. Albert Eugene and Alice Ellen (Moore) F.; m. Iva Marion Whelpley, Dec. 28, 1897; children—Dorris Lucile (wife of Rev. Stanley Zook), Basil Allen, Justine Alice (wife of Glenn I. Wallace), Wilma-Ruth. Public school teacher, 1889; pastor and evangelist, 1889-1919; gen. church sec., 1919-39; exec. sec. Church of the Nazarene, 1919-39; sec.-treas. and dir. Nazarene Mutual Benevolent Assn., 1919-39; chmn. The Christians Mutual Benevolent Assn., 1939-44. Republican. Address: 615 W. 5th St., Carson City NV‡

FLEMING, JOSEPH BARCLAY, lawyer; b. Scotland, Feb. 4, 1881; B.S., Northern Indiana Normal Sch.; LL.B., John Marshall Law School, 1905; LL.D., Ill. Wesleyan Univ., 1925, Lake Forest (Ill.) Coll.; m. Lily Belland, June 28, 1910 (dec. 1968); children—Charlotte (Mrs. Norman L. Cram), Josephine (Mrs. Thomas M. Thomas), Lily (Mrs. L.F. Holt Maulsby), Jean Alice (Mrs. William C. Phillips). Admitted to bar, 1905; assistant United States atty., Chicago, 1913-17; special assistant to U.S. attorney general in prosecution of war cases, 1917-19; attorney for Illinois Building Commission for investigation of building conditions in Illinois, 1921-23, chief atty. Election Board of Chicago, 4 years; mem. Kirkland, Fleming, Green, Martin & Ellis (now Kirkland Ellis, Hodson, Chaffetz & Masters), 1917-58, counsel, from 1958. Trustee C., R.I. & P. Co., 1933-48. Trustee Lake Forest Coll. (pres.), Ill. Wesleyan U.; former pres. and trustee Chicago Pub. Library, Clubs: Chicago, University, Onwentsia. Home: Lake Forest IL Died Oct. 21, 1970; buried Mt. Hope Cemetery, Chicago IL

FLEMING, WILLARD C., dental educator; b. Sausalito, Cal., Oct. 11, 1899; s. Willard Stephen and Effie (Urquhart) F.; D.D.S., U. Cal., 1923; D.Sc., U. So. Cal., 1947; LL.D., U. Toronto, 1959, U. Cal., 1969; m. Carlotta Heid, Nov. 11, 1924; 1 dau., Gail Allison. Practice of dentistry, Oakland, Cal., 1923-60; mem. faculty, Coll. of Dentistry, U. Cal., 1923-72, instr., 1923-30, asst. clin. prof., 1943-49, prof. operative dentistry 1949-72, vice provost, 1958-64, dean students, 1965-66, chancellor U. Cal. Med. Center, 1966-69, dean Sch. Dentistry, 1939-65. Commr. Western Interstate Commn. Higher Edn., 1956-58; mem. commn. Survey of Dentistry, Am. Council Edn.; mem. Nat. Adv. Dental Research Council, USPHS; mem. dental adv. council W. K. Kellogg Found. Served as pvt. and cpl., A.U.S., World War I. Fellow Am. Coll. Dentists (pres. 1951-52), A.A.A.S (v.p. 1954); mem. Am. Dental Assn., Am. Assn. Dental Schs. (pres., 1946-47), Sigma Xi, Psi Omega, Epsilon Alpha, Omicron Kappa Upsilon. Home: Oakland CA Died Nov. 2, 1972; interred Oakland CA

FLEMINGTON, WILLIAM THOMAS ROSS, govt. ofcl.; b. Britannia, Newfoundland, Oct. 11, 1897; s. Charles and Heartie Melfort Boyce (Bate) F.; B.A. with honours, Mt. Allison, Sackville, New Brunswick, Can., 1922, M.A., 1923, Diploma in Theology, 1926; post-grad. Columbia, 1927; B.Paed., Toronto U., 1930; D.D., Queens, Kingston, 1943, Victoria U., Toronto, 1947, Pine Hill, Halifax, 1960; LL.D., Univ. of New Brunswick, 1950, St. Mary's U., Halifax, 1958, U. of Alberta, 1959, McGill U., 1962, Ricker U., 1962, Mt. Allison, 1964; D.Ped., U. Sacre Coeur, 1960; m. Marjorie Eileen Brownell, June 21, 1924; (dec.); children—Noel Kent. Patricia; m. 2d, Martha Inez Marie Morrison, May 20, 1961. Ordained minister, United Ch. of Can., 1926; instr. Mt. Allison Boys' Acad., 1924-30, headmaster, 1930-45; pres., Mt. Allison U., 1945-62; dir. edn. External Aid Office for Can., from 1962. Trustee Nat. Gallery of Can. Served as pilot, R.A.F., 1917-19, Canadian chaplain, (overseas) 1939-45. Awarded Order of Brit. Empire. Fellow Royal Soc. Arts; mem. Can. Legion, Can. Psychol. Soc., Nat. Conf. Canadian Univs. and Colls. (past pres.), Assn. Univs. Brit. Commonwealth (exec. council). Clubs: Canadian, Rotary; University. Contbr. articles to profl., ednl. and religious jours. Address: Port Elgin NB Canada Died July 10, 1971.

FLETCHER, DANIEL HOWARD, educator; b. Marlborough, Mass., May 20, 1872; s. Lewis Edwin and Lucy (McCracken) F.; grad. Proctor Acad., Andover, N.H., 1895; A.B., Harvard, 1899, A.M., 1913; m. Addie Emerson, of Andover, N.H., Aug. 14, 1899; children—Josephine (dec.), Marion. Teacher in pub. schs. of Mass., 1899-1913; asst. in dept. edn., Harvard, 1913-14; sr. master Loomis Inst., Winsdor, Conn., 1914-16; headmaster Detroit Univ. Sch., 1919-39, retired, also trustee. Mem. sch. com. Marlborough, Mass., 1901-13, Mass. Rep. State Com., 1912. Mem. Nat. Teachers Assn., Mich. Teachers Assn., Harvard Teachers Assn., Headmasters Assn., Phi Beta Kappa, Phi Delta Kappa. Republican. Unitarian. Mason. Club: Harvard of Mich. Home: 678 Lakewood Boul., Detroit, Mich. Address: Cook Rd., Grosse Pointe MI‡

FLETCHER, FRANK JACK, naval officer; b. Marshalltown, Ia., Apr. 29, 1885; s. Thomas Jack and Alice (Glick) F.; B.S., U.S. Naval Acad., 1906; grad. U.S. Naval War Coll., 1930, U.S. Army War Coll., 1931; m. Martha Richards, Feb. 10, 1917. Commd. ensign U.S. Navy, 1908, and advanced through the grades to vice adm., 1942; flag lt. and fleet signal officer, U.S. Atlantic Fleet, 1914-15; comd. U.S.S. Dale, Chauncey, Margaret, Benham, Gridley, Whipple, Sacramento, New Mexico, Cruisers Pacific Fleet; in comd. North Pacific Forces; chmn. Gen. Bd. U.S. Navy; retired as adm., May 1947. Deocrated Medal of Honor for distinguished service at Vera Cruz, 1914; Navy Cross for distinguished service in command of U.S.S. Benham in war zone, 1918; D.S.M. for distinguished service in command of Task Forces at battles of Coral Sea and Midway; Army D.S.M. for duty in comd. N. Pacific Forces, U.S. Pacific Fleet, 1943-45; Purple Heart; Companion Order of the Bath (British); Order of the Green Dragon of Amxam (French). Clubs: New York Yacht; Chevy Chase, Army and Navy (Washington, D.C.) Home: La Plata MD Died Apr. 1973.

FLETCHER, FRED LELAND, banking, mining exec.; b. Virginia City, Nev., Feb. 15, 1911; s. Charles E. and Clara (Collins) F.; B.Engring., U. Nev., 1933; m. Dorothy Ann Edwards, Aug. 6, 1939; children—Douglas C., Bernard J., Charles E. Engr., Nev. Hwy. Dept., 1933-35; engr. Sierra Pacific Power Co., 1935-41, exec. v.p., Reno, 1959-60, pres., 1961-65, now dir.; engr. Central Ill. Electric & Gas Co., Rockford, Ill., 1941-46, gen. sales mgr., 1946-54, v.p., 1954-60; pres. Lands of Sierra, Inc., Reno, 1964-65, Fletcher Engrs., Inc., from 1966, Pan-World Engrs., Inc., from 1966; chmn. bd. Siskon Corp., from 1966. Dir. Pacific Coast Elec. Assn., 1961-65. Mem. Nev.-Cal. Joint Compact Commn., 1964-66. Trustee Lake Tahoe Area Council, 1961-65; nat. trustee Ducks Unlimited. Named to Hall of Fame, U. Nev., 1961; recipient Man of Year award, Reno, 1963-64; nat. trustee Mem. Am. Inst. E.E., A.A.A.S., Am., Pacific Coast (v.p., dir. 1962-63), Midwest (dir. 1947-60) gas assns., Rockford (pres. 1960), Reno (dir., v.p.,). chambers commerce. Republican. Episcopalian. Clubs: Rotary, Prospectors (dir.), Hidden Valley Country (pres. 1966, dir.), Press (Reno). Home: Reno NV

FLETCHER, FREDERICK CHARLES, mfr.; b. Providence, R.I., Sept. 22, 1874; s. Charles and Harriet (Beanland) F.; student Cornell U., 1892-93, Bradford Textile Sch., Bradford, Eng., 1894-95; m. Nina H. Jarvie, of Brooklyn, N.Y., 1902 (died 1903); 1 dau., Nina Fletcher; m. 2d, Alice Ida Benn, of Harrogate, Eng., Apr. 1915. V.p. Lawton Spinning Co. Mem. Psi Upsilon. Republican. Epsicopalian. Clubs: Home Market (v.p.), Country, Eastern Yacht, University (Boston); Union League, Bankers, Cornell Univ., New York Yacht (New York); Larchmont Yacht. Home: 34 Philbrick Rd., Brookline, Mass. Office: 101 Newbury St., Boston MA‡

FLETCHER, INGLIS (MRS. JOHN G. FLETCHER), author; b. Alton, Ill.; d. Maurice William and Flora Deane (Chapman) Clark; student Washington U., St. Louis Sch. of Fine Arts; Litt. D., Woman's Coll., U. of N.C., 1948; m. John George Fletcher; 1 son, John Stuart. Travelled Near East, Africa, Europe, 1928-29; on native safari, Brit. Central Africa, to learn local customs, witchcraft data, 1929. Author: White Leopard, 1931; Red Jasmine, 1932; Realeigh's Eden, 1940; Men of Albermarle, 1942; Lusty Wind for Carolina, 1944; Toil of the Brave, 1946; Roanoke Hundred, 1948; Bennett's Welcome, 1950; Queen's Gift, 1952; The Scotswoman, 1955; The Wind in the Forest, 1956; Pay, Pack, and Follow (autobiography), 1959; Cormorants' Brood, 1959; Wicked Lady (hist. novel); Rogue's Harbor, 1964. Mem. Soc. Am. Historians (Tryon Palace restoration commn.), Colonial Dames of XVII Century, Internat. P.E.N., Cal. Writers Guild, N.C. Lit. and Historic Soc., N.C. Soc. Preservation of Antiquities (v.p.), Garden Club of N. C. (life), Roanoke Island Hist. Assn. (Producing Paul Green's symphonic drama, The Lost Colony), D.A.R., Colonial Dames, Delta Kappa Gamma. Episcopalian. Home: Greenville NC Died May 30, 1969; buried National Cemetery, Wilmington NC

FLETCHER, JAMES DONALD, ins. exec.; b. Buell, Ore., May 2, 1895; s. Archibald William and Mary (Cameron) F.; LL.B., Willamette U., 1918; m. Ona Blanche Walker, Aug. 4, 1924; children—Robert James, John Thomas. With Northwestern Mut. Inc., Co., from 1923, successively salesman, asst. sales mgr., Seattle, sales mgr., dept. mgr. Wash., v.p. and mgr. Western div., 1923-54, exec., v.p., 1954-57, pres., from 1957, dir. Mem. C. of C. Clubs: Washington Athletic, Broadmoor Golf, Rotary. Home: Seattle WA Died Nov. 4, 1970; buried Acacia Meml. Park, Seattle WA

FLETCHER, JOHN, lawyer; b. Scott Co., Ia., Jan. 5, 1876; s. John and Martha F.; student Ia. State Teachers Coll., Cedar Falls, 1894-95, State U. of Ia., 1898-99; m. Marie Schmidt, of Avoca, Ia., June 14, 1905; children—Maurice D., Warren, Margaret Wino. Admitted to Ia. bar, 1899, and began practice at Avoca; city atty., Avoca, 1905-07; mayor of Avoca, 1907-09; asst. atty. gen. of Ia., 1910-25; judge, Dist. Court, Polk Co., Ia., 1925-27; atty. gen. of Iowa, 1927-33; now head of firm of Fletcher and Fletcher, Des Moines, Iowa. Member Delta Theta Phi. Republican. Presbyn. Mason, K.P. Home: 4308 University Av. Office: 405 Crocker Bldg., Des Moines IA‡

FLETCHER, STEVENSON WHITCOMB, horticulturist; b. Littleton, Mass., Sept. 10, 1875; s. Charles Kimball and Anna (Holton) F.; B.Sc., Mass. Agrl. Coll., 1896; M.S., Cornell, 1898, Ph.D., 1900; m. Margaret Rolston, June 28, 1905; children—Robert Holton, Richard Rolston, Stevenson Whitcomb, Peter Whitcomb, John Emmett, Margaret, Emmett Hine. Prof. horticulture and horticulturist, Expt. Sta. of Wash. Agrl. Coll., Pullman, 1900-02; same, W.Va. U., 1902-03; asst. prof. extension teaching in agr., Cornell U., 1903-05; prof. horticulture. Mich. Agrl. Coll., 1905-08; dir. Va. Agrl. Expt. Sta., 1908-16; prof. horticulture, Pa. State Coll., 1917-37; also vice dean and dir. research, 1927-39, dean Sch. Agr., 1939-46, dean emeritus since 1946. Mem. Phi Kappa Phi (Mass. Agricultural College), Alpha Gamma Rho, Alpha Zeta, Sigma Xi. Republican. Baptist. Author: How to Make a Fruit Garden, 1906; Solls-How to Handle and Improve Them. 1907; Strawberry Growing, 1917; The Strawberry in North America, 1917; A History of Fruit Growing in Pennsylvania, 1933; Pennsylvania Agriculture and Country Life (1640-1840), 1950; Pennsylvania Agriculture and Country Life (1840-1940), 1955. Home: State College PA Died Feb. 10, 1971.

FLETCHER, WALTER D., lawyer; b. Heuvelton, N.Y., Apr. 28, 1896; s. Everett H. and Sarah (Wheater) F.; A.B., Columbia, 1918, M.A., 1922, LL.B., 1922, LL.D., 1965; LL.D., Alfred Univ., 1957; m. Eleanor Langley. Admitted to N.Y. bar, 1922, and practiced in N.Y. City 1922-72; mem. firm Davis Polk & Wardwell and predecessor firms; dep. atty. gen. N.Y., 1923; dir., mem. exec. com. City Investing Co.; chmn. bd., dir. Torsion Balance Co.; dir. U.P. R.R., Ore. Short Line R.R. Co., Los Angeles & Salt Lake R.R. Co., Merchant-Sterling Corp., Orama Securities Corp., Ore.-Wash. R.R. & Navigation Co., Sterling Iron & Ry. Co. Volunteer spl. counsel Am. Nat. Red Cross, counsel Greater N.Y. A.R.C. Trustee emeritus Columbia U.; trustee St. John's Guild City of N.Y. (hon.), N.Y. Racing Assn.; gov. Fed. Hall Meml. Assos., Inc.; pres., dir., mem. Dom Mocquereau Found. Served as pilot AC USNRF, World War I. Mem. Am., N.Y. bar assns., N.Y. County Lawyers Assn., Bar Assn. City N.Y. Clubs: Links, Turf and Field, Downtown Assn., Union. Home: New York City NY Died Sept. 20, 1972.

FLEWELLING, RALPH TYLER, clergyman, educator; b. DeWitt, Mich., Nov. 23, 1871; s. Francis Tyler and Mary Cornelia (Whitney) F.; U. of Mich., 1890-92; A.B., Alma (Mich.) Coll., 1895; Garrett Bibl. Inst., 1895; S.T.B., Boston U. Sch. of Theology, 1902; Ph.D., Boston U., 1909, LL.D., 1931; Litt.D., University of Southern California, 1945; married L. Jennie Carlin, Aug. 16, 1893; children—Ralph Carlin, Mrs. Cecil Richardson. Ordained M.E. ministry, 1896; pastor Newton Centre, Mass., 1903-06, Athol, Mass., 1906-09. Harvard Street Ch., Cambridge, Mass., 1909-13. Leominster, Mass., 1913-16, First Ch., Boston, 1916-17; prof. and head dept. of philosophy, U. of Southern Calif., 1917-29; dir. Sch. of Philosophy, same univ., May 16, 1929-45; dir. emeritus, Sch. Philosophy, since 1945; dir. internat. studies, Olive Hill Foundation, 1946-47; visiting professor Calif. in-China Coll. of Chinese Studies, Peiping, lecturer at Yenching U., Peiping, and in various nat. and Christian univs. in China, 1934-35. Lecturer Tully Cleon Knoles Found., Coll. Pacific. At the Sorbonne, 1918; head dept. of philosophy, A.E.F. University, Beaune, France, 1918. Western States rep. for World Congress of Faiths; hon. mem. United Nations Fellowship. Member permanent com. Internat. Congress of Philosophy. Mem. American Philos. Soc. (pres. Pacific Div. 1938-39), British Inst. Philos. Studies, Am. Scientific Assn., Conf. on Science, Philosophy and Religion, Phi Eta Sigma, Phi Beta Kappa, Phi Kappa Phi; founder Pi Epsilon Theta (nat. philosophy honor soc.), 1931. Clubs: University, X Club, Twenty Club. Author: Christ and the Dramas of Doubt, 1913; Personalism and the Problems of Philosophy, 1915. Contbr. to Hastings Ency. of Religion and Ethics, 1917; Philosophy and the War, 1918; Bergson and Personal Realism, 1919; The Reason in Faith, 1924; Creative Personality, 1926; The Basic Ideas of East and West, 1935; The Survival of Western Culture, 1943; Personalism in Theology, 1943; Twentieth Century Philosophy, 1943; The Things That Matter Most, 1946. Founder and editor of the Personalist (quarterly jour. of philosophy, religion, lit.) 1920. Home: 10609 Cushdon Av., Los Angeles 34 CA‡

FLEXNER, MAGDALEN GLASER HUPFEL, fgn. service officer; b. Watervliet, N.Y., July 11, 1907; d. Otto Glaser and Anna Munro (Mott) Hupfel; grad. Emma Willard Sch., Troy, N.Y., 1924; B.A., Bryn Mawr Coll., 1928; LL.B., Cornell U., 1947; m. William W. Flexner, June 16, 1932 (div. 1946). Warden, Bryn Mawr Coll., 1930-32; admitted to N.Y. bar, 1948; law clk. U.S. 5th Circuit Ct. Appeals, 1947-48; legal asst. to chmn. NLRB, 1948-51; atty.-adviser State Dept., 1951-54, asst. pub. affairs adviser, 1954-56; joined U.S. Fgn. Service, 1955; consul, Bordeaux, France, 1956-59; dep. U.S. rep. UNESCO, Paris, France, 1959-62; consul prin. officer, Cardiff, Wales, 1962-65; consul gen., Bordeaux, France, 1965-67. Home: Stuart FL Died Apr. 18, 1972.

FLIEGEL, LESLIE, artist; b. N.Y.C., Jan. 27, 1912; s. John and Mary (Astolascz) F.; student Cooper Union, 1933; m. Jane Constance Russell, May 20, 1950. Numerous one-man shows, 1947-68, including Ward Eggleston Galleries, N.Y.C., 1947-66; Hofstra Coll., 1950; Art Center, Lafayette, Ind., 1965, Brandeis U., 1966; exhibited in numerous group shows; represented in permanent collections U. Miami, Lowe Foundation, Syracuse U., Fla. So. Coll., Howard U., St. Vincent College; tchr. Newark Sch. Fine Arts, 1947-57, Long Island Art League, 1950-55. Recipient many awards and prizes. Mem. Artists Equity, Allied Artists, Audubon Artists, Nat. Soc. Painters in Casein, N.J. Artists Soc., Am. Veterans Soc. Artists. Home: Kew Gardens NY Died July 7, 1968; interred, Maple Grove Cemetery Kew Gardens NY

FLINT, MRS. EDITH FOSTER, prof. English; b. Chicago, Ill., May 13, 1873; d. Richard Norman and Annie (Halsted) Foster; Ph.B., U. of Chicago, 1897; m. Nott Flint, of Chicago, Dec. 22, 1900 (died 1906); children—Richard Foster, Halsted (dec.). Asst. in English, U. of Chicago, 1897-98, head of Kelly House, 1898-1900, instr. in English, 1906-09, asst. prof., 1909-14, asso. prof., 1914-23, prof. 1923-38; now prof. emeritus; dean in Coll. Arts, Literature and Science, 1917-26; chmn. Women's University Council, 1925-31; pres. Chicago br. Am. Assn. of Univ. Women, 1928-30. Epsicopalian. Home: 5631 Kenwood Av., Chicago IL‡

FLINT, JOSEPH MARSHALL, surgeon; b. Chicago, July 8, 1872; s. Francis and Sarah Elizabeth (Dancy) F.; student Princeton U., 1891-93, A.M., 1900; B.S., U. of Chicago, 1895; Johns Hopkins U., 1896-1900, M.D., 1900; U. of Leipzig,1900; Vienna, Bonn, Munich, 1905-07; A.M., Yale, 1907; m. Anne Drusilla Apperson, of Hacienda del Pozo de Verona, Calif., Sept. 15, 1903. Asst. in anatomy, 1897, asso. 1900-01, U. of Chicago; asst. Johns Hopkins Med. Commn. to the Philippines; on spl. plague duty, U.S. Marine Hosp. Service, San Francisco, 1901; prof. anatomy U. of Calif., 1901-07; prof. of surgery, Yale, 1907-21. Chief surgeon New Haven Hosp.; ex-chief surgeon New Haven Disp.; surgeon to Arsakeion Mil. Hosp. during the Graeco-Bulgarian War, summer of 1913; medecin chef. Hopital 32 bis Chateau de Passy, France, July-Dec., 1915; maj. Med. O.R.C., 1917; comdg. officer Base Hosp. No. 39, A.E.F., later Mobile Hosp. No. 39. Mem. med. bd. Council Nat. Defense; liaison officer, chief surgeon's office, A.E.F., to French War Office for mobile sanitary formations; organized first mobile hosp. of A.E.F.; lt.-col. M.C., July 1918; col. Med. R.C. Awarded D.S.M., Mar. 1, 1919; citation for meritorious and conspicuous services, Apr. 19, 1919; Officier de l'Instruction Publique (French), Feb. 17, 1919. Editor Am. Jour. of Anatomy, 1903-07; contbr. on surg. and anat. subjects in med. jours. Fellow Am. Coll. Surgeons, A.A.A.S.; mem. Sigma Xi, Alpha Delta Phi. Clubs: Princeton, University (New York); Graduate (New Haven). Office: 185 Church St., New Haven CT‡

FLIPPEN, EDGAR LUCAS, insurance, banker; born Bryan, Tex., Mar. 7, 1876; s. William Henry and Elizabeth (Lucas) F.; ed. St. Paul's Sch., Garden City, L.I.; m. Minnie May Armstrong, Apr. 5, 1900. In real estate and investment bus. since 1908; partner Flippen-Prather Realty Company, since 1908; pres. Flippen Investment Co., First Nat. Securities Co.; pres. and dir. First Nat. Bank, Dallas, Tex.; pres., dir. Flippen-Prather Stores, Inc.; dir. and mem. exec. com. Southwestern Life Ins. Co.; dir., mem. finance and exec. com., Gulf Ins. Co.; dir., mem. exec. com., Tex. & Pacific Ry. Co.; dir. Hillcrest State Bank, University Park, Am. Nat. Bank, Oak Cliff (both Dallas); dir. Dallas Power & Light Co. Mem. Am. Bankers Assn., Reserve City Bankers Assn. Chmn. bd. governors, Dallas Foundation; dir. and v.p., Dallas C. of C.; dir., v.p., mem. exec. com. and chmn. finance com., State Fair Tex.; dir. Dallas Grand Opera Assn. Trustee, mem. financial com., Dallas Hist. Soc. Mem. Meat Packers and Cotton Seed Products Div. Food Adminstrn., World War I. Pres. Dallas Community Trust. Democrat. Episcopalian. Clubs: Dallas City (dir.), Downtown, Brook Hollow Golf, Northwood Country. Home: 4025 Beverly Dr., Dallas 5. Office: First National Bank, Dallas TX‡

FLIPPIN, PERCY SCOTT, historian, economist; b. Amelia, Va., Sept. 19, 1874; s. George Rush and Susan Booker (Harper) F.; A.B., U. of Richmond (Va.) 1906, (hon. Litt.D., 1941); Ph.D., Johns Hopkins, 1912; m. Laura Arnold Binns, 1921; children—Percy Scott, Laura Arnold. Sec. endowment fund, U. of Richmond, 1909-10; prof. history, Center Coll., Danville, Ky., 1912-16, Hamilton Coll., Clinton, N.Y., 1916-19, Mercer U., Macon, Ga., 1919-27, Coker Coll., Hartsville, S.C., 1927-33; dean Grad. School, Mercer U., 1922-27; research statistician NRA, 1933-34; chief div. of research The Nat. Archives, 1935-38, chief div. independent agencies archives, 1938-43; Economic Research Expert, Economic Warfare Unit, Department of Justice, 1943-44; Statistical Analyst, International Division, Headquarters, Army Service Forces, War Department, 1945-46; historian, Renegotiation Div., War Dept., 1947-48; lecturer in history, University of Texas, summer 1920, University of W.Va., summer 1925, Johns Hopkins U., summer, 1926, U. of N.C., summer, 1927, U. of Va., summer, 1929, 30, Coll. of William and Mary, Williamsburg, Va., summer 1931. Mng. editor Ga. Hist. Quarterly; curator Ga. Hist. Soc. Mem. Am. Hist. Assn., Miss. Valley Hist. Assn., Society Am. Archivists, Am. Assn. of Univ. Profs., Phi Beta Kappa, Pi Gamma Mu. Mem. party of univ. profs. taken to Europe by Carnegie Endowment for Internat. Peace to Study the World Court and the League of Nations, 1926. Awarded Henrico medallion (prize of Colonial Dames of America, Chapter 1) by Johns Hopkins University. Mason. Author: The Financial Administration of the Colony of Virginia, 1915; The Royal Government in Virginia (1624-1775), 1919; The Royal Government in Georgia (1752-1775), 1923; William Gooch—Successful Royal Governor of Virginia, 1925; Herschel V. Johnson of Georgia, State Rights Unionist, 1930; The Archives of the United States Government, A Documentary History (1774-1934), 1938. Contbr. to Dictionary of American Biography, Dictionary of Am. History and to hist. mags. Home: 6139 31st St., N.W., Washington DC‡

FLOERSH, JOHN A., bishop; b. Nashville, Tenn., Oct. 5, 1886; s. John A. Floersh and Minnie O. (Alexander) F.; Ph.D., U. of the Propaganda Fide, Rome, Italy, 1907, D.D., 1911. Ordained priest R.C. Ch., 1911; sec. to Apostolic Delegation, Washington, D.C., 1912-22; consecrated bishop of Lycopolis and coadjutor-bishop of Louisville, Ky., Apr. 8, 1923; became bishop of Louisville, July 26, 1924; archbishop of Louisville, Dec. 9, 1937-Mar. 1, 1967. Home: Louisville KY Died June 11, 1968; buried Calvary Cemetery, Louisville KY

FLOREY, LORD HOWARD WALTER, scientist, college provost; b. Sept. 24, 1898; s. Joseph Florey; ed. St. Peter's Collegiate Sch.; M.D., Adelaide U., Magdalen Coll., Oxford; Rhodes Scholar for S. Australia, 1921; John Lucas Walker student, Cambridge, 1924; Rockefeller Travelling Fellow, U.S., 1925; Freedom Research Fellow, London Hosp., 1926; Fellow Gonville and Caius College, Cambridge, 1926; Fellow, Lincoln College, Oxford; held degrees Bachelor of Medicine, Bachelor of Surgery, M.A., B.Sc., Ph.D.; L.H.D. (hon.), Georgetown University, 1965; D.Sc. (hon.), Harvard Univ., 1967; m. Mary Ethel Reed, 1926 (dec. 1966); 1 son, 1 dau.; m. 2d, Margaret Jennings, 1967. Huddersfield lect. in spl. pathology Cambridge, 1927; Joseph Hunter prof. of pathology, U. of Sheffied, 1931-35; prof. pathology, Oxford, 1935-62; provost Queen's College, Oxford, from 1962. Charles Mickle fellowship, Toronto Univ., 1944. Awarded Cameron Prize, Edinburgh U., 1945; Lister Medal, R.C.S., Eng., 1945; Berzelius Silver Medal, Swedish Med. Soc., 1945; Nobel Prize for Physiol. and Med., 1945; Harmsworth Memorial Award, 1946 Albert Gold Medal, Royal Soc. Arts, 1946; Medal in Therapeutics, Soc. Apothecaries of London, 1946; Gold Medal, Royal Soc. Med., 1947, Royal Medal, 1951; Comdr. Legion d'Honneur, 1948; United States Medal for Merit, 1948; Addingham Gold Medal, 1949; Copley Medal, Royal Society, 1957; Gold medal Brit. Med. Assn., 1964; Lomonossov medal USSR Academy of Sciences, 1964. Fellow of the Royal Soc. (pres. 1960), Royal Coll. Physicians; Am. Acad. Arts and Scis. (fgn. hon. mem.). Pioneered devel. of penicillin for clin. use. Author: Antibiotics (with others), 1949. Editor and part author: General Pathology, 1958. Home: Oxford Eng Died Feb. 21, 1968.

FLORY, ARTHUR LOUIS, artist, tchr.; b. Lima, O., Aug. 14, 1914; s. Louis and Lydia (Badowska) F.; student Phila. Mus. Sch. Art; m. Jane Trescott, Sept. 29, 1941; children—Cynthia, Christine, Erika. Exhibited in nat. exhbns., also Europe, Japan; represented in permanent collections Pa. Acad. Fine Arts, Phila. Mus. Art, New Britain (Conn.) Mus., Albany (N.Y.) Mus., Butler Art Inst., Youngstown, O., William Rockhill Nelson Mus., Kansas City, Mo., Nat. Gallery Art, Washington, Rosenwald collections, Tel Aviv Mus. Israel, Bibliotheque Nationale, Paris, Art Gallery New South Wales, Sydney, Australia, Bridgestone Gallery, Tokyo, Japan; numerous others; instr. paintings, graphics Tyler Sch. Fine Arts, Temple U., 1950-68; adviser lithography Phila. Coll. Art, 1968-70. Served with USCGR, 1942-44. Recipient 1st prize in painting Phila. Regional Art Exhbn., 1951; Purchase prize Albany Print Club, 1952; U.S. Govt. purchase prize, 1940; Eyre medal Pa. Acad. Fine Arts, Phila. Water Color Club. Rockefeller grantee to establish lithography workshop in Tokyo, 1960-61. Mem. Phila. Water Color Soc., Phila. Art Alliance, Artists Equity, Soc. Am. Graphic Artistists, Am. Color Print Soc., Phila. Print Club Rosenwald prize 1961), Print Council Am., Boston Printmakers, Phila. Water Color Club (dir.). Home: Melrose Park PA Died May 9, 1972.

FLOURNOY, WILLIAM WALTON, lawyer; b. Walton Co., Fla., Dec. 5, 1874; s. John and Mary Elizabeth F.; A.B., Florida Agricultural and Mechanical College, 1896; LL.B., Cumberland Univ., Lebanon, Tenn., 1900; m. Marie Alice King, of De Funiak Springs, Fla., June 28, 1900; children—Marie Alice (Mrs. H. L. Pearce), Louise Elizabeth (dec.), Gracie Claude (Mrs. J. P. Ashmore), William W., John Thomas, Willie Louise (Mrs. T. Clyde Beatty), Mary Elizabeth (Mrs. W. Paul Bissett), Eleanor Beatrice. Comdt. cadets and prof. mil. science and tactics, Fla. Agr. and Mech. Coll., 1896-99, inclusive; col. staff, Gov. W. D. Bloxham, 1898. Practiced at De Funiak Springs since 1900; mayor, 1908-11, 1915-21 and 1934-35; mem. Fla. Senate, 1909-11; leading counsel for Gov. S. J. Catts, in Knott-Catts governorship election, 1916. Mem. Bd. of Control of Fla., 1920. Capt. Co. K, 1st Inf. Fla. N.G., at Pensacola, Fla., 1900, at De Funiak Springs, 1904-09. Democrat. Presbyn. Home: De Funiak Springs Fl‡

FLOWER, J(OSEPH JAMES) ROSWELL, clergyman; b. Belleville, Ont., Can., June 17, 1888; s. George Lorenzo and Bethia Adella (Rice) F.; brought to U.S., 1902 naturalized, 1934; LL.D., Bob Jones U., 1946; m. Alice Marie Reynolds, June 1, 1911; children—Joseph Reynolds, Alice Adele (Mrs. Dalton), George Earnest (dec.), Suzanne Grizelle (Mrs. Albert W. Earle), Roswell (dec.), David Warren. Ordained ministry Assemblies of God Ch., 1913; gen. sec., editor publs. Assemblies of God, Springfield, Mo., 1914-19, fgn. missions sec., 1919-25; pastor Pentecostal Ch., Scranton, Pa., 1926-30; dist. supt., 1930-36, gen. sec., 1936-59. Mem. City Council, Springfield, Mo., 1953-61. Mem. adv. bd. Salvation Army, Ozark Empire area council Boy Scouts Am.; director Central Bible Institute. Mem. Springfield C. of C. Club: Commercial. Author articles religious publs. Home: Springfield MO Died July 23, 1970; buried Green Lawn Cemetery, Springfield MO

FLYNN, THOMAS E., labor union ofcl.; b. Chgo., July 1, 1906; s. Patrick P. and Katherine (Nolan) F.; m. Mildred Wanetta Brandeberry, June 16, 1923; children—Robert Thomas, Jerome Patrick, Colleen (Mrs. Robert S. Schwenger) and Maureen (Mrs. John P. Treanor) (twins). Mem. Internat. Brotherhood of Teamsters, 1923-72, internat. dir. Eastern conf., 1953-72, internat. 4th v.p., 1957-72, gen. sec.-treas., 1969-72. Democrat. Catholic. Home: Potomac MD Died Mar. 9, 1972.

FLYNT, HENRY NEEDHAM, lawyer; b. Brooklyn, July 2, 1893; s. George Converse and Helen Pratt (Needham) F.; student Monson (Mass.) Acad., 1908-12; Bachelor of Arts, Williams Coll., 1916. Doctor of Humane Letters, 1958; student Columbia Law Sch., 1916-17, 1919-20; married to Helen Margaret Geier, June 5, 1920;children—Henry Needham, Jr., Juliet Helen (Mrs. Louis Marillonnet), Marjorie (Mrs. James Muir). Admitted to New York Bar, 1921; dir. Cin. Milling Machine Co., 1933-66, Putnam Trust Co., Greenwich, Conn., 1947-70. Chmn. bd. trustees Deerfield Acad.; pres. Pocumtick Valley. Mem. Assn., Bd. Estimate & Taxation, Greenwich, Conn., 1935-45, chmn., 1937-45; pres. Heritage Foundation. Trustee emeritus of Williams College. Served as 1st lieutenant with the United States Army, 1917-19. Mem. Am. Hist. Soc., Am. Antiquarian Soc., Walpole Soc., Nat. Trust Historic Preservations, Antiquarian and Landmarks Soc. Conn. (trustee), Zeta Psi. Author: Heritage Collection of American Silver and New England Silversmiths, 1625-1825. Perpetuating old houses, Deerfield, Mass., as shrines for studies of Am. culture, architl., decoration and 18th century living. Home: Greenwich CT Died Aug. 10, 1970; buried Williams Coll. Cemetery, Williamstown MA

FOELKER, OTTO GODFREY, congressman; b. in Germany, 1875; arrived in America with parents at 13; pub. sch. edn. Admitted to bar, and since in practice at Brooklyn; mem. N.Y. Assembly, 1905-6, Senate, 1907-8; elected to 60th Congress for unexpired term of Charles T. Dunwell, deceased; reelected to 61st Congress (1909-11), 3d N.Y. Dist.; Republican. Address: Brooklyn‡

FOERDERER, PERCIVAL EDWARD, b. Phila., Oct. 25, 1884; s. Robert Hermann and Caroline (Fischer) F.; student William Penn Charter Sch., U. Pa.; LL.D., Jefferson Medical Coll.; m. Ethel Tillyer Brown, June 1,

1910; children—Mignon Estabrook (Mrs. John M. Kelso Davis), Florence Rapelye, Shirley Avril (Mrs. Charles Oakes Ames). Pres. Robert H. Foerderer, Inc., mfrs. of Vici Kid, 1908-46; pres. Robert H. Foerderer Estate, Inc.; Mem. storage com. Council Nat. Def. requirements div., vice chmn. employment mgmt. div. and chief of divisional priorities sect. War Industries Bd., World War I; chmn. Met. Phila. Civilian Aid Com. for AAC, lieutenant col. Army Specialist Corps, World War II. Chmn. Phila. Com. for Econ. Development, 1943-46. Chmn. Tanners Council of America, 1934-36; dir. Found. Tanners Research Lab.; trustee Com. for Econ. Development, Drexel Inst. Tech.; chmn. bd. Jefferson Med. Coll. and Med. Center, 1950-62, trustee 1928-69; vice chmn., dir. Asso. Hosp. Service of Phila. Mem. Numismatic and Antiquarian Soc. of Phila., Newcomen Society, Military Order Foreign Wars of United States, Pannsylvania Commandery, Delta Kappa Epsilon. Clubs: Union League, Gulph Mills Golf, Phila. Country, Poor Richard, Penn, Merion Cricket, Radnor Hunt, Racquet, Rittenhouse (Phila.); Gulf Stream Golf, Everglades, Bath and Tennis (Fla.); Bucks (London, Eng.). Home: Bryn Mawr PA Died Jan. 22, 1969; buried West Laurel Hill Cemetery, Bala-Cynwyd PA

FOKMA, JAN JELLE, lawyer; b. Barradeel, Netherlands, Apr. 2, 1900; s. Frans and Joukje (Fenema) F.; LL.D., Leiden U., 1925; m. Aleida Bosman, Feb. 27, 1934; 4 sons, Frans, Aleidus, Jan, Ruurd. Practice of law, 1925-72; with Drs. v.d. Hoeven, Fokma, Kaulingfreks, Mijs, Korthais, Altes & van Schifgaarde, Rotterdam, 1930-72. Chmn. Holland-Am. Line, United Ropeworks, Rotterdamsch Nieuwsblad (all Rotterdam), Maatschappij van Berkel's Patent N.V., Rotterdam; supervisory dir. Christiani & Nielsen, The Hague, Nehterlands. Decorated officer Order Orange Nassau. Home: Rotterdam Netherlands Died Feb. 9, 1972.

FOLEY, FRANCIS B(ENEDICT), exec. metall. engr.; b. Germantown, Pa., July 7, 1887; s. Dennis J. and Margaret A. (Gribbon) F.; student Girard Coll.; m. Anne M. Flaherty, Apr. 20, 1915 (died 1936); 1 son, Gerard Moylan; m. 2d, Katherine Campbell, Aug. 8, 1938; 1 dau., Frances Campbell. Various positions Midvale Co., 1905-17, dir. research, 1926-49; asst. metallography U. Minn., 1917-19; metallurgist U.S. Bur. Mines, 1919-24, Lucy Mfg. Corp., Chattanooga, 1924-26; cons. metallurgist Internat. Nickel Co., 1950-57; executive metallurgical engineer Pencoyd Steel and Forge Company, Phila., 1957-65; cons., 1965-73. Dollar a year tech. cons. W.P.B.; adviser, research projects Nat. Def. Research Council; com. for investigation prodn. ferromanganese, collaborator Ordnance Dept. on ordnance steels, World War I. Fellow Am. Inst. Chemists; mem. Am. Ordnance Assn., Franklin Inst. (chmn. com. sci. and arts 1956-57). Acid Open Hearth Research Assn. (dir., trustee, pres. 1947), Am. Iron and Steel Inst., Iron and Steel Inst. (London), Alloy Casting Inst. (dir., chmn. tech. com.), Am. Soc. Metals (pres. 1947; Sauveur lectr. 1950), Am. Inst. Mining and Metall. Engrs. (dir.; Howe lectr. 1950), Am. Chem. Soc., Am. Soc. Testing Materials (chmn. joint ASTM-ASME com. on effect of temperature on properties of metals), Girard Coll. Alumni Assn. (pres.), Nat. Acad. Econs. and Polit. Sci. Club: Metals Science (N.Y.C.). Author tech. papers, metallurgy of steel. Home: Philadelphia PA Died Feb. 27, 1973.

FOLEY, MARGARET MARY, educator; b. Lima, W.Va., Feb. 20, 1918; d. Edward S. and Marguerite (Fitzpatrick) Foley; grad. Wheeling Hosp. Sch. Nursing, 1938; B.S. in Nursing Edn., St. Louis U., 1943, Ph.D. in Edn., 1961; M.S. in Nursing Edn., Cath. U., 1947. Gen. staff nursing, Ohio Valley Gen. Hosp., Steubenville, O., 1938-39; instr. Wheeling Hosp. Sch. Nursing, 1941-46, asst. dir., 1947-48; exec. sec. Conf. Cath. Schs. Nursing and cons. in nursing edn. Cath. Hosp. Assn., 1948-68; part-time instr. hosp. adminstrn. grad. sch. St. Louis U., 1961-68; prof. nursing edn., dean sch. nursing Boston Coll., 1969-70. Recipient Alumni Merit award St. Louis U., 1969. Mem. Nat. Council. Cath. Nurses (dir. 1954-64), Am., Mass. (chmn. Mo. com. on legislation 1952-53) nurses assns., Nat. League for Nursing, Sigma Theta Tau. Home: Chestnut Hill MA Died Aug. 1970.

FOLEY, MAX HENRY, engr., architect; b. Norwich, Conn., Nov. 9, 1894; s. Michael James and Ann Elizabeth (Garvey) F.; Ph.B., Yale, 1914; m. Gwendolyn Powell, Feb. 3, 1917 (dec.); 1 son, Max Henry; married second Kathryn McTigue, October 18, 1828; children—Mary Ada (Mrs. William Pedrick), John, Frank, Jean (Mrs. Thomas Rizzo). Associate partner of the firm Voorhees, Gmelin & Walker, 1928-38; partner Voorhees, Walker, Foley & Smith, 1938-54; pvt. practice, 1954-68; cons. N.Y. Housing Commission; mng. partner in Trinidad of Caribbean Architect-Engineer; dir. Fedn. Bank & Trust Co. of N.Y. Mem. engring bd. Port of N.Y. Authority; prin. works include Western Union Hdqrs. Bldg., N.Y.C., Library, Dining halls Coll. New Rochelle, N.Y., N.J. Bell Telephone Bldg., Newark, Gen. Electric Research Lab., Schenectady, N.Y., also Army Air Bases, Trinidad, Antigua, St. Lucia, Brit. Guiana, Dutch Guiana; Loyola Sem., Shrub Oak, N.Y.; AFL hdqrs., Washington; Travelers Insurance Co. office building, Hartford. Trustee American Architectural Found., Inc.; chmn. Architects' Emergency Committee. Chmn. bldg. trades apprenticeship; dir. Greater N.Y. Safety Council; mem. Cardinal's Com. of Laity, N.Y. Chmn. Board of Standards and Appeals, N.Y.C. Profl. engr., N.Y., Ohio, Del. Recipient Sydney Strauss Meml. Award, N.Y. State Soc. Architects, 1961. Fellow A.I.A. (chmn. com. on costs, labor relations, chmn. joint com. A.I.A.-Am. Gen. Contractors Assn.), Am. Soc. C.E., mem. N.Y. Bldg. Congress (past pres., gov.), Liturgical Arts Soc. (treas.), Archtl. League N.Y. (past treas.), Yale Engring. Assn., Nat. Soc. Profl. Engrs., Beaux Arts Inst., Am. Soc. Mil. Engrs., Nat. Sculpture Soc., Am. Inst. Cons. Engrs., Municipal Art Soc., Sigma Xi, Alpha Chi Rho. Clubs: Yale, Canadian (N.Y.C.); Edgartown Yacht. Home: New York City NY Died Dec. 1968.

FOLGER, JAMES A., business exec.; b. Dinard, France (parents Am. citizens), Oct. 5, 1900; s. James Athearn and Clara (Luning) F.; A.B., Yale, 1922; m. Jane Carrigan, Oct. 25, 1924; children—Jane (Mrs. James Carrigan), Sarah Ann (Mrs. Charles Hanger), Claire Dean (Mrs. Bok Reitzel). With Folger Coffee Co., San Francisco, 1923-42, beginning as clerk and becoming pres., 1936; resigned business position and became priorities dist. mgr. War Prodn. Bd., San Francisco, 1942, regional dir., 1943, vice chmn. for field operations, Washington, 1944-45; resigned Nov. 1945; vice chmn. Folger Coffee Co., San Francisco and Kansas City; dir. Wells Fargo Bank & Union Trust Co., Western Pacific R.R. Co. (both San Francisco). Clubs: Pacific Union (San Francisco); Burlingame (Cal.) Country. Home: San Francisco CA Died Dec. 23, 1972; buried Holy Cross Cemetery, San Francisco CA

FOLINSBEE, JOHN FULTON, landscape painter; b. Buffalo, N.Y., Mar. 14, 1892; s. Harrison Davis and Louise (Mauger) F.; ed. Gunnery Sch., Washington, Conn.; studied Art Students' League (New York), Woodstock Sch. of Art, Ulster County, N.Y.; pupil of John Carlson, F. V. Du Mond and Birge Harrison; m. Ruth Baldwin, 1914; children—Elizabeth (Mrs. E.W. Wiggins), Joan Baldwin (Mrs. Peter G. Cook). Awarded third Hallgarten prize, N.A.D., 1916; 2d Hallgarten prize, 1917; Richard S. Greenough prize, Newport, R.I., 1917; hon. mention Art Inst., Chicago, 1918, Com. Acad. Fine Arts, 1919; Isador prize, Salmagundi Club, 1920; Carnegie prize, N.A.D., 1921; J. Francis Murphy prize, 1921; 3d William A. Clark prize, and Corcoran bronze medal, 1921; 3d prize Nat. Arts Club, 1922; hon. mention, Phila. Art Club, 1922; 1st Hallgarten prize, N.A.D., 1923; Phila. Sketch Club medal, 1923; Charles Noel Flagg prize, Conn. Acad. Fine Arts, 1924; Phila Art Club Purchase prize, 1924; Plimpton prize, Salmagundi Club, 1924; Gedney Bunce prize, Conn. Acad. Fine Arts, 1925; Frank A. Thompson prize, Salmagundi Club, 1926; bronze medal, Sesquicentennial Internat. Expn., 1926; Francis Murphy prize, N.A.D., 1926; Vezin prize, Salmagundi Club, 1930; Jennie Sesnan gold medal, Pa. Acad. Fine Arts, 1931; 2d Altman prize, N.A.D., 1936, 1st prize, 1941 and 1950; Century Club medal, 1950; Palmer Marine prize, N.A.D., 1952; Cooper prize Conn. Acad. Fine Arts, 1955; Charles K. Smith prize Woodmere Gallery, Phila., 1961; Oakley Memorial prize Woodmere Gallery, 1961; Century Assn. medal, 1963; Phillips Mill patrons prize, 1963; Pennational prize, 1965; Portrait medal Century Assn., 1966; National Art Club Silver medal, 1969; Kleindienst medal Artists Fellowship, 1970. Represented in Corcoran Gallery (D.C.), Syracuse Mus., Nat. Arts Club, Grand Rapids Art Assn., Phila. Art Club, R.I. Sch. of Design, Reading (Pa.) Museum, Museum Fine Arts (Houston, Tex.), Pa. Academy of Fine Arts, Century Club, N.Y. City, New Britain Mus., Library U. at Beirut; (murals) in postoffice, Freeland, Pa., courthouse, Paducah, Ky. Mem. Nat. Inst. Arts and Letters, Conn. Acad. Arts, A.N.A., 1919, N.A., 1928. Clubs: Nat. Arts, Century (N.Y.C.) Home: New Hope PA Died May 10, 1972.

FOLLANSBEE, GEORGE EDWARD, surgeon; b. 1871; M.D., Western Reserve U. Sch. of Medicine, 1895. Practiced at Cleveland, O., since 1896; visiting surgeon and chief of staff St. Alexis Hosp. Fellow Am. Coll. Surgeons, A.M.A. (chmn. judicial council); mem. Ohio State Med. Assn. Home: 9615 Miles Av. Office: 629 Euclid Av., Cleveland OH‡

FOLLETT, MARY PARKER, author; b. Quincy, Mass., d. Charles Allen and Elizabeth (Curtis) F.; A.B., summa cum laude, Radcliffe Coll., 1898; student Paris and Newnham Coll., Eng. Engaged in public work connected with vocational guidance, civic edn. and community centres, 1900-16; lecturer in America and England, 1924-28. Representative of public on minimum wage bonds. Member Taylor Society, Nat. Community Centre Association (v.p.). Author: The Speaker of the House of Representatives, 1896; The New State, 1918; Creative Experience, 1924. Contbr. to Scientific Foundations of Business Administrations, 1926, Business Management as a Profession, 1927, Psychological Foundations of Management, 1927. Home: 5 Cheyne Pl., London England‡

FOLSOM, SARAH BLANTON (MRS. DOUGLAS LAWRENCE FOLSOM JR.), educator, state ofcl.; b. Notasulga, Ala., Oct. 22, 1915; d. E. E. and Bessie May (Lanier) Blanton; A.B., Judson Coll., 1936, L.H.D. (hon.), 1966; M.S. Auburn U., 1941; LL.D. (hon.), 1966; m. Douglas Lawrence Folsom Jr., Aug. 10, 1940; children—Douglas Lawrence III, James Blanton. Tchr. schs., Ala., 1936-43; supt. schs. Yavapai County, Ariz., 1953-64; supt. pub. instrn. State of Ariz., 1965-69. Named Meth. Woman of Yr., Prescott, Ariz.; recipient Outstanding Citizen award, 1964. Mem. Am. Legion Aux., V.F.W. Aux., Bus. and Profl. Women, Am. Assn. U. Women, N.E.A. Republican, Rebekah, Elks Ladies. Clubs: Federated Women's, Prescott Junior Monday (pres.), Prescott Garden (pres.). Home: Prescott AZ Died June 11, 1969.

FOLTZ, CLARA SHORTRIDGE, lawyer, orator; b. Henry Co., Ind., d. Rev. E. W. and Telitha Cumi (Harwood) Shortridge; went to Pacific coast with parents; m. J. D. Foltz, of Akron, O.; was left a widow, with 5 young children to support; studied law; 1st woman admitted to bar on Pacific Coast; 1st woman trustee State Normal Sch. of Calif.; represented bar of Calif. at World's Columbian Exp'n, Chicago, 1893; addressed Congress of Jurisprudence and Reform on subject, Public Defenders"; drafted bill to create office of Public Defenders and introduced same in legislature of 32 states; organized Portia Law Club (for women), San Francisco; specialty, corporation law. Spoke in campaign of 1900 under auspices Nat. Rep. Com. Atty. for United Bank and Trust Co., San Francisco, and gen. mgr. of its woman's dept. Organized the Woman's Banking Club of San Francisco. Residence: 726 2d Av. Office: Mills Bldg., San Francisco‡

FOLWELL, AMORY PRESCOTT, civil engr.; b. Kingston, N.Y., Jan. 15, 1865; s. Rev. G. W. and Mary P. F.; A.B., Brown U., 1885; studied civil engring. at Mass. Inst. Tech.; Sc.D., Lafayette Coll., Easton, Pa., 1907; m. Helen P. Peck, Dec. 4, 1894. Engaged in practice as cons. municipal engr., asso. prof. municipal engring., 1896-1904, prof. 1904-06, Lafayette Coll.; editor Municipal Journal and Engineer (now Public Works) since 1906. Mem. New Eng. Water Works Assn., American Water Works Assn., Am. Society C.E., Beta Theta Pi, Sigma Xi; ex-pres. Am. Soc. Municipal Improvements. Contbr. to engring. jours. Author: Sewerage, 1897, 11th edit., 1935; Water Supply Engineering, 1900; 3d edit., 1917; Municipal Engineering Practice, 1916; Practical Street Construction, 1916. Home: Montclair, N.J. Office: 310 E. 45th St., New York NY‡

FONTAINE, ARTHUR BENJAMIN, mem. Rep. Nat. Com.; b. Green Bay, Wis., Jan. 31, 1876; s. Benjamin and Desire (Jenquin) F.; LL.B., U. of Wis., 1895; m. Mayme Brehme, of Green Bay, Wis., Dec. 20, 1899; 1 son, Berwyn. Admitted to Wis. bar, 1895, and since in practice at Green Bay. Chmn. Rep. State Com., 1928-29; mem. Rep. Nat. Com. for Wis. since 1933. Mem. Elks. Author: Subterfuge, 1934. Home: 501 Howard St. Office: Minahan Bldg., Green Bay WI‡

FONTANA, LUCIO, sculptor, ceramicist; b. Rosario Santa Fe, Argentina, Feb. 19, 1899; s. Luigi and Lucia (Bottini) F. Founder spaziale" movement, Buenos Aires, Argentina, 1946; exhibited numerous one-man shows, Italy and elsewhere; participated group shows including Venice Biennial, 1954. Recipient numerous prizes including 1st prize in sculpture Buenos Aires, 1943; Grand Internat. prize 9th Triennial of Milan, Italy; (with L. Minguzzi) 1st prize, 5th door Dome de Milan. Home: Milan Italy Died Sept. 7, 1968.

FOOKS, D(ANIEL) W(EBSTER), clergyman; b. nr. Paducah, Ky., Feb. 13, 1874; s. William Franklin and Susan (King) F.; student Cumberland U., Lebanon, Tenn., 1895-98, West Ky. Coll., 1899-1901, Cumberland Sem., 1906; m. Maggie Dale Rudolph, May 2, 1894. Licensed to preach by Mayfield Presbytery, 1898; ordained, 1900; pastor First Ch., Paducah, 1909; supt. construction Mission Bldg., San Francisco, 1914; pastor 1st Cumberland Presbyterian Ch., Nashville, 1915-24; stated clk., gen. traveling sec. Cumberland Ch. since 1915. Supt. transportation and financial agt. and sec-treas. bd. trustees. Gen. Assembly, Cumberland Presbyterian Ch. Made Chinese Survey, 1925, for Women's Bd. Missions; mem. advisory bd. Am. Bible Soc. Mason (Shriner). Home: 1535 Park, Paducah, Ky. Office: 117 8th Av., S., Nashville TN*‡

FOORD, ARCHIBALD SMITH, educator; b. Stamford, Conn., Aug. 13, 1914; s. William Malcolm and Madeleine (Smith) F.; B.A., Yale, 1937, Ph.D., 1942; postgrad. Oxford (Eng.) U., 1937-38; m. Mary Bank Sullivan, June 29, 1940; children—William Malcolm III, Mary Bankhead. Mem. faculty Yale, 1940-42, 46-69, prof. history, 1965-69. Served to lt. comdr. USNR, 1942-46. Mem. Am. Hist. Assn. (Herbert Baxter Adams prize 1964), Conf. British Studies. Author: His Majesty's Opposition, 1714-1830, 1964; (all with T.C. Mendenhall and B.D. Henning): Ideas and Institutions in European History, 800-1715, 1948, The Quest for a Principle of Authority in Europe, 1715—, 1948, Select Problems in Western Civilization, 1956, Foundations of the Modern State, 1952, The Dynamic Force of Liberty in Modern Europe, 1952; (with B.D. Henning and B.L. Mathias) Crises in English History, 1066-1945, Hamden CT Died Mar. 15, 1969.

FOORD, JAMES ALFRED, college prof.; b. Portsmouth, Eng., Oct. 30, 1872; s. James and Elizabeth N. (Knight) F.; came to U.S., 1887; B.S., New Hampshire Coll. of Agr. and Mechanic Arts, 1898; M.S. in Agr., Cornell, 1902; m. Grace M. Law, Nov. 14, 1904; 1 dau., Elizabeth. Asst. in animal husbandry and dairying, Cornell U., 1900-03; prof. agr., Delaware Coll., 1903-06; asso. prof. agronomy, Ohio State U., 1906-07; same, Mass. State Coll., 1907-08, head div. agr., 1908-25 prof. farm management, 1908-33; with Farm Credit, Farm Security and Farmers Home adminstrns., 1933-47; retired. Fellow A.A.A.S.; mem. Sigma Xi, Phi Kappa Phi, Kappa Sigma. Republican. Unitarian. Home: 272 Lincoln Av., Amherst MA‡

FOOTE, PAUL D(ARWIN), physicist; b. Andover, O., Mar. 27, 1888; s. Howard Spencer and Abbie Lottie (Tourgee) F.; A.B., Western Res. U., 1909, D.Sc., 1961; A.M., U. Neb., 1911; Ph.D. U. Minn., 1917; D.Sc., Carnegie Institute of Technology, 1953; m. Berenice C. Foote, Feb. 3, 1913 (died June 10, 1939); children—Mrs. C. Jane Halliwell, William Spencer; m. 2d, Miriam Sage, June 26, 1940; stepchildren—Robert Land, Evan T. Sage. Asst. physicist, U.S. Bureau of Standards, 1911, sr. Physicist, 1924-27; exec. v.p. Gulf Research & Development Co. (Pittsburgh, Pa.); v.p. Gulf Oil Corp., Gulf Refining Co., retired all positions with Gulf, 1954; assistant sec. def., research and engring., Dept. of Def., 1957-58; exec. sec., chmn. Nat. Acad. Sci. Panels adv. to Bur. Standards, 1960-71. Recipient Achievement medal University Minn., 1951; Jr. C. of C. science award, 1953; Pitts. award, 1954; Meritorious Civilian Service medal Dept. Def., 1958. Sr. fellow Mellon Inst. Indsl. Research, 1927-29; fellow Am. Physical Soc. (pres. 1933), A.A.A.S.; mem. Optical Soc. Am., Am. Philos. Soc. (sec. 1956-59), Nat. Acad. Sci., Washington Acad. Scis. (v.p. 1936), Am. Inst. Mining and Metall. Engrs., Am. Geophysical Union, Phi Beta Kappa, Sigma Xi, Sigma Pi Sigma, Sigma Tau, Tau Beta Pi. Club: Cosmos (Washington, D.C.). Author: Pyrometric Practice (with others), pub. 1921; (with Fred Loomis Mohler) The Origin of Spectra, 1922; (with others) Physics in Industry, 1937. Editor in chief Jour. Optical Soc. America, Rev. of Scientific Instruments, 1921-32; asso. editor Jour. Franklin Inst. Home: Washington DC Died Aug. 2, 1971; buried Nat. Meml. Park, Falls Church VA

FORAND, AIME JOSEPH, congressman; b. Fall River, Mass., May 23, 1895; s. Francois Xavier and Meli-Luce (Ruest) F.; student comml. sch., Providence, R.I.; LL.D., Providence Coll., 1951; extension student, Columbia University; m. Gertrude Bedard, November 16, 1931. Newspaper reporter, 1924-30; member Rhode Island House of Rep., 1923-27; sec. to congressman Jeremiah E. O'Connell, 1929-30, to congressman Francis B. Condon, 1930-35; chief R.I. Div. of Soldiers Relief and commandant R.I. Soldiers Home, 1935-36; mem. 75th Congress (1937-39), 77th to 86th Congresses, 1st Rhode Island Dist. Sergt. Motor Transport Corps, U.S. Army, with A.E.F., 1918-19. Mem. Am. Legion, Vets. of Foreign Wars. Democrat. Catholic. Elk, K.C. Clubs: Marquette. Home: Boca Raton FL Died Jan. 1972.

FORBES, EDGAR ALLEN, editor; b. nr. Gainesville, Ga., Sept. 25, 1872; s. Thomas Vanburen and Eliza (Black) F.; ed. Beloit (Kan.) High School; Southern Bapt. Theol. Sem.; Ky. Sch. of Medicine, and Med. Dept., Ky. Univ.; m. Alice Schlueb, June 9, 1916. Mng. editor Mining Mag. and of The Am. Exporter, 1904-05, and of The World's Work, 1906-10, of Leslie's Weekly, 1913-14; sec. Calif. Development Bd., 1914-15; sec. State Commn. Market of Calif., 1915-18, asso. editor of Leslie's Weekly, 1919-20; dir. Oriental and Round the World Tours of Thos. Cook & Son, 1920-23, Around the World Productions, 1923-—. Pvt. 1st Ky. Inf., 1898, Porto Rican campaign. Author: The Land of the White Helmet, 1910; Twice Around the World, 1912; The Voyage of Your Dreams, 1922. Asso. Editor: Photographic History of the Civil War, 10 vols., 1911. Editor: Leslie's Photographic Review of the Great War, 1919.*‡

FORBES, EDWARD WALDO, museum dir.; b. Naushon Island, Mass., July 16, 1873; s. William Hathaway and Edith (Emerson) F.; A.B., Harvard, 1895; spl. student New Coll., Oxford U., 1900-02; spent a great deal of time studying in art galleries of Europe; honorary A.M., Harvard Univ., 1921, Art. D., 1942; LL.D., University of Pittsburgh, 1927; m. Margaret Laighton, January 29, 1907 (dec. Feb. 1966); children—Rosamond (Mrs. Carl E. Pickhardt), John, Mary (dec. 1949), Elliot, Anne. Dir. Fogg Art Museum, Harvard University, emeritus from 1944; lecturer fine arts, Harvard, 1909-35; Martin A. Ryerson lecturer fine arts, Harvard Univ., 1935-41. Hon. dir. and trustee of Wadsworth Atheneum, Hartford, Conn. Trustee of Museum of Fine Arts (Boston), Pub. Reservations of Mass. Unitarian. Clubs: Union, Harvard (Boston); Century, Harvard (New York). Address: Cambridge MA Died Mar. 11, 1969; buried Milton MA

FORBES, HARRYE REBECCA PIPER SMITH (MRS. ARMITAGE S.C. FORBES), author; b. Everett, Pa.; d. William Piper and Rachel Lavinia (Kay) Smith; grad. high sch., Wichita, Kan., 1880; B.A., Episcopal Coll., Wichita, 1883; studied Heatherly Art Sch., London; m. Armitage S. C. Forbes, of Paris and London, Feb. 10, 1886. Originated and established nat. naval memorial ceremony of casting flowers on the sea in memory of naval dead; designed, and was instrumental in placing Mission Bell guidepost on El Camino Real, the historic road joining 21 Franciscan missions of Calif.; induced city officials of Los Angeles to purchase historic site of Campo de Cauenga where articles of capitulation were signed, making Calif. a U.S. province; secured approval of city officials of Los Angeles to dedicate, name and mark with bronze tablets the new bridges over Los Angeles River in memory of early pioneers; placed 110 flags in 1 yr. over pub. bldgs.; state or dist. chmn. 12 yrs. Dept. of Calif. History and Landmarks, for California Federation Women's Clubs; special writer many years for newspapers. Presented with gold badge for patriotic work by Masonic Veterans Association of Pacific Coast, also testimonial by Native Sons of Golden West, and by Calif. History and Landmarks Club. Mem. Hist. Soc. Southern Calif., D.A.R., W.R.C.; hon. mem. Nat. Assn. Ladies of Naval Vets. Republican. Quaker. Clubs: City, Ebell, Friday Morning. Author: California Missions and Landmarks and El Camino Real, 1903; Mission Tales in the Days of the Dons, 1909. Home: 335 W. 31st St., Los Angeles CA‡

FORBES, ROBERT HUMPHREY, agrl. science; b. Cobden, Ill., May 15, 1867; s. Henry Clinton and Laura Jane (Gorham) F.; B.S., U. of Ill., 1892; M.S., 1897; spl. courses in research work, Harvard, 1893-94; Ph.D., U. of Calif., 1916; hon. Sc.D., U. of Ariz., 1925; m. Georgie Hazel Scott, Jan. 16, 1902. Instr., U. of Ill., 1891-93; prof. chemistry, U. of Ariz., and chemist of Ariz. Agrl. Expt. Sta., 1894-99; dir. and chemist, Ariz. Expt. Sta., 1899-1911; dir. Ariz. Expt. Sta., and of agrl. instrn., U. of Ariz., 1912-15; dean and dir. Coll. of Agr. and Agrl. Experiment Sta., U. of Ariz., 1915-18; sec. Ariz. Commn. of Agr. and Hort., 1909-18; agronomist, Societe Sultanienne d'Agriculture, of Egypt, 1918-22; chief engr. Etudes Agronomiques Mission Niger, and counselor tech. Office du Niger, French West Africa, 1922-1939; also dir. expt. stations, Service Technique d'Haiti, 1927-29; rep. Ariz. State Legislature since 1939. Author numerous reports and bulletins on chemistry of soils and water supplies, date palm culture, toxic effects of copper on crops and the agronomy of cotton in Egypt, French West Africa and Haiti; also descriptive articles in mags. Home: 105 Olive Rd., Tucson AZ‡

FORBUSH, GAYLE T., fire insurance; b. Natick, Mass., Mar. 31, 1870; s. James M. and Emilie A. (Whitney) F.; B.S., Mass. Inst. Tech., 1892; m. Helen Grace Walcott, of Natick, June 5, 1895; children—Gayle Walcott, Helen Grace (Mrs. Clarence I. Platt). Began in ins. business, Boston, 1892; pres. Provident Fire Ins. Co. of N.H., 1924-35, still dir.; trustee Ins. Library Assn. Mem. Delta Kappa Epsilon. Republican. Conglist. Clubs: Technology, Framingham Country. Home: Natick, Mass. Office: 111 John St., New York NY‡

FORD, ARTHUR R., editor; b. Point Edward, Ont., Can., Dec. 5, 1880; s. Rev. James E. and Annie (Douglas) F.; B.A., Victoria Coll.; m. May L. Scott, September 1908; children—Gordon, Kenneth, Robert, May; m. 2d, Sophia Woolway, Sept. 10, 1936 (dec.). Reporter, Stratford (Ontario) Herald, Ottawa Journal and New York; successively reporter, city editor, news editor Winnipeg Telegram, 1905-10; news editor Winnipeg Tribune, 1910-11; mem. Press Gallery rep. Winnipeg Telegram. Toronto News, London (Eng.) Times, etc., 1911-19; editor London Free Press since 1921; chancellor, U. of Western Ontario; chmn. Ontario Cancer Treatment and Research Found.; past pres. and dir. Canadian Press; mem. and past chmn. London Pub. Library. Club: Kiwanis (past internat. trustee). Home: London ON Canada Died Apr. 3, 1968.

FORD, CHARLES F., b. St. Louis, 1889. Partner A. G. Edwards & Sons, St. Louis. Home: St Louis MO Died 1971.

FORD, COREY, author; b. New York City, Apr. 29, 1902; s. James Hitchcock and Adelaide C. (Ricketts) F.; educated Columbia, 1919-23; unmarried. Colonel U.S. Air Force. Humorist, magazine writer, playwright, literary parodist under name John Riddell." Special consultant Dartmouth College. Member of Delta Kappa Epsilon. Clubs: Players, Coffee House, Dutch Treat. Author: numerous books including Cloak and Dagger, 1946; The Last Time I Saw Them, 1946; The Horse of Another Color, 1946; A Man of His Saw Them, 1946; The Horse of Another Color, 1946; A Man of His Own, 1949; How to Guess Your Age, 1950; The Office Party, 1951; Every Dog Should Have A Man, 1952; Never Say Diet, 1954; Daughter of the Gold Rush, 1958; You Can Always Tell a Fisherman, 1958; Has Anybody Seen Me Lately?, 1958; The Day Nothing Happened, 1959; Corey Ford's Guide To Thinking, 1961; What Every Bachelor Knows, 1961; Minutes of the Lower Forty, 1962; And How Do We Feel This Morning? 1964; Uncle Perk's Jug, 1964; A Peculiar Service, 1965; Where the Sea Breaks its Back, 1966; The Time of Laughter, 1967. Address: Hanover NH Died July 27, 1969; buried Pine Knolls Cemetery, Hanover NH

FORD, DANIEL, prof. English; b. Cambridge, Mass., Sept. 3, 1876; s. Thomas J. and Mary A. (Toomey) F.; B.L., Dartmouth, 1899; M.A., Harvard, 1905; post-grad. work same univ., 1916-17; m. Amy W. Howell, of Lincoln., Neb., June 5, 1909. Instr. English, Case Sch. Applied Science, Cleveland, O., 1902-04; adj. prof. rhetoric U. of Neb., 1905-10; asst. prof. rhetoric, U. of Minn., 1910-20; prof. English and head of dept., Lake Forest Coll., 1926-31 (resigned), dean of faculty, 1921-22. Mem. Phi Gamma Delta, Phi Beta Kappa. Conglist. Author: Flotsam, 1903. Home: Sarasota FL‡

FORD, EDSEL, poet; b. Eva, Ala., Dec. 30, 1928; s. James Tilden and Nora (Chunn) F.; B.A., U. Ark., 1952; Author poems in numerous publs. including Sat. Rev., McCall's, Ladies' Home Jour., Good Housekeeping, Look, N.Y. Times, Western Humanities Rev., Tex. Quar., also anthologies. Poetry cons., lectr. Kan. U. Writers Conf., 1961-64; recorded poems Library of Congress, 1965. Mem. Ark. Gov's. Adv. Council on Arts and Humanities, 1966-70. Served with AUS, 1952-54; ETO. Recipient Alice Fay di Castagnola award Poetry Soc. Am., 1966; Conrad Aiken prize Poetry Soc. Ga., 1965, 68. Democrat. Methodist. Author: The Manchild From Sunday Creek, 1956; A Thicket of Sky, 1961; Love Is The House It Lives In, 1965; Looking for Shiloh (Devins Meml. award Kansas City Poetry Contest 1968), 1968. Home: Ft Smith AR Died Feb. 19, 1970; buried Benton County Meml. Gardens, Rogers AR

FORD, EMORY M., business exec.; b. Detroit, 1906; Princeton, 1928. Dir., chmn. bd. Wyandotte (Mich.) Chems. Corp., Wyandotte Transptn. Co.; dir. Portland Cement Assn., Difco Labs., Inc., Consol. Coal Co., Cutler-Magner Co., Mfrs. Nat. Bank of Detroit. Pres. bd. trustees Jennings Meml. Hosp.; trustee Mich. Colls. Found., Olivet Coll. Home: Grosse Pointe MI Died June 5, 1971.

FORD, HIRAM CHURCH, judge; b. Scott County, Ky., July 28, 1884; s. John F. and Georgia (Church) F.; A.B., Georgetown (Ky.) Coll., 1905, LL.D., 1937; LL.B., Transylvania College of Law, 1907; LL.D., U. Ky., 1942, Berea Coll., 1963; m. Mary Witherspoon Thomas, November 17, 1913; children—Alice, Katherine. Admitted to Ky. bar, 1907, and practiced in Georgetown; county atty. Scott County, 1910-26; judge 14th Jud. Dist. Ky., 1931-35; U.S. dist. judge Eastern Dist. Ky., 1935-63, senior district judge U.S. Dist. Ct., 1963-69; pres. Georgetown Nat. Bank, 1929-35. Mem. Kappa Alpha. Democrat. Mem. Christian (Disciples) Ch. Mason (past master). Rotarian (ex-pres.). Home: Georgetown KY Died June 8, 1969.

FORD, HUGH, theatrical mgr.; b. Washington, D.C.; s. George and Henrietta (Price) F.; ed. Van der Naillen Sch. of Mines and Engring., San Francisco; m. Jessie Weir Izett, of Denver, Mar. 27, 1898; 1 dau., Jean Henrietta. Began as actor in Lyceum Theatre, New York, 1895; dir. gen. Famous Players Film Co., 1917. Clubs: Lambs, Lotos. Home: 390 West End Av., New York NY*‡

FORD, JULIA ELLSWORTH (MRS. SIMEON FORD), author; b. N.Y. City, Apr. 6, 1859; d. James Edwin and Julia Augusta (Brown) Shaw; ed. Mrs. Williamese's Sch., New York; m. Simeon Ford, 1882; children—Ellsworth, Julia Lauren, Hobart. Author: King Solomon and the Fair Shulamite, 1906; George Frederick Watts (with Thomas W. Lamont), 1908; A.E.—A Note of Appreciation, 1908; The Mist, play prod. Little Theatre, London, Eng., 1913; Imagina, 1914, 2d edit., 1925; Snickerty Nick, play for young people, prod. at Heckscher Theatre, 1919; Pan and Santa Claus, 1925; Consequences (novel); 1929 (later translated in China into Chinese). Established, 1934, Julia Ellsworth Ford Foundation, an annual contest for encouraging literature for the young. Has made a series of 4 motion pictures in technicolor and sound for children called Snickerty Nick Series and uses them in personal showings at schools, hospitals, theatres. Mem. Women Artists of the West, Dramatists Play Service, Studio Guild. Clubs: Cosmopolitan (charter mem.), Women's City (New York); Women's, Am. Yacht, Milton Point, Apawamis (Rye, N.Y.). Home: Rye, N.Y.; also CA*‡

FORD, LEONARD AUGUSTINE, educator; b. Valley Springs, S.D., Oct. 19, 1904; s. John Haqvin and Mary Christine (Ringdahl) F.; A.B., Gustavus Adolphus Coll., 1925; M.S., State U. Ia., 1928, Ph.D., 1931; m. Anne Albertina Swanson, Aug. 14, 1932; children—Barbara Jean (Mrs. Robert E. Olson), Joyce Anne (Mrs. Richard A. Anderson). Instr. sci. high schs. in N.D. and Minn., 1925-29; prin., instr. sci. Roosevelt Mil. Acad., Aledo, Ill., 1931-36; chmn. chemistry dept. Sioux Falls Coll., 1936-39; mem. faculty Mankato (Minn.) State Coll., 1939-67, chmn. div. sci. and math., 1947-64, prof. of chemistry, coordinator spl. programs, 1964-67; chemist Lake Fish Canning Co., Mankato, 1945-48. Mem. Blue Earth County com. Crippled Childrens Soc.; bd. finance Minn. Conf. Augustana Lutheran Ch. Mem. ednl. adv. com. Minn. Republican Party. Mem. alumni bd. Gustavus Adolphus College. Member Am. Chem. Soc., Minn. Acad. of Sci. (councilor 1949-53, pres. 1954-55), A.A.A.S., Phi Lambda Upsilon, Alpha Chi Sigma, Lion.

Author: Chemical Magic, 1959 (translated in Japanese, French, Danish, Spanish). Home: Mankato MN Died Oct. 27, 1967; buried Glenwood Cemetery, Mankato MN

FORD, PAUL CHARLES, elec. co. exec.; b. Flora, Ind., Apr. 15, 1915; s. Charles C. and Eva (Miller) F.; student DePauw U., 1935; B.S., Purdue U., 1937; m. Katherine Farquhar, Aug. 3, 1940. With Wagner Electric Corp., St. Louis, 1937-72, successively transformer engr., supr. unit substa. and dry type transformer engring., asst. mgr. transformer engring. dept., chief elec. engr., exec. engr., 1937-58, v.p. engring., 1958-66, exec. v.p., 1966-72. Mem. Am. Inst. E.E., Soc. Automotive Engrs., Assn. Iron and Steel Engrs., Am. Ordnance Assn., Engrs. Club St. Louis, Beta Theta Pi. Methodist. Home: Ladue MO Died May 27, 1972.

FORD, PEYTON, lawyer, govt. official; b. Sayre, Okla., Feb. 24, 1911; s. Guy and Ethel (Gum) F.; student, Tex. Mil. Coll., 1928-29; A.B., Univ. of Okla., 1934. Bachelor of Laws, 1934; married Helen Hutto, December 29, 1939; children—Patricia (Mrs. Douglas Lynch), Mary (Mrs. Mark Finkeldei). Admitted to Oklahoma State bar, 1934; and practiced in Oklahoma City, 1934-39, 42-43; associated with firm of Chandler, Shelton, Fowler and Swinford, 1939-42; asst. atty. gen. of Okla., 1939-41; spl. asst. to Atty. Gen. of U.S., since 1946, asst. atty. gen. of U.S. in charge of claims div., 1947, The Asst. to Atty. Gen., from 1947, and acting Atty. Gen. in absence of Atty. Gen. and Solicitor General; deputy attorney general 1950-51; mem. of firm Ford, Bergson, Adams & Borkland from 1951, later Ford, Ayer and Horan, until 1971. Served at lt., U.S.N.R. on active duty as gunnery officer in Atlantic, Mediterranean, China, Burma and India, 1943-46. Mem. Am. Law Inst., Am. and Okla. bar assns., Bar Assn. of D.C. Democrat. Clubs: Army-Navy, Metropolitan. Home: Washington DC Died Nov. 22, 1971; buried Rock Creek Cemetery, Washington DC

FORD, RICHARD, physician, educator; b. Cambridge, Mass., Jan. 31, 1915; s. Jeremiah D.M. and Anna (Fearns) F.; A.B., Harvard, 1936, M.D., 1940; m. Hope Cullinan, Jan. 23, 1942; children—Hope, Faith, Cathleen Charity, Lucy Ann. Intern pathology Peter Bent Brigham Hosp., 1940-41, cons. in pathology, 1953—; intern surgery Boston City Hosp., 1941-42; research fellow legal medicine and pathology, med. sch. Harvard, 1945-49, acting head dept. legal medicine, asst. prof. legal medicine, 1949-61, asst. clin. prof. legal medicine, chmn. dept., 1961-65; lectr. legal medicine Harvard, Yale, Tufts, and Boston univs. med. schs.; hon. lectr. forensic medicine U. Southern Cal. School of Medicine, 1953; Rockefeller traveling fellow, 1953. Pathologist to State Police, Commonwealth of Mass., 1949-65; asso. med. examiner Suffolk Co. (Boston), 1946-50, med. examiner, 1950-70; cons. in pathology Peter Bent Brigham Hosp., 1953-70; cons. in forensic pathology Mass. Gen. Hosp., 1959-70, Armed Forces Inst. Path., 1959-70, Fed. Aviation Agy., 1960. Served from 1st lt. to maj. AUS, 1942-45. Certified in Forensic Pathology by Am. Bd. Pathology. Decorated Legion of Merit. Fellow Coll. Am. Pathologists; mem. A.M.A., Am. Assn. Pathologists and Bacteriologists, Am. Acad. Forensic Scis., Am. Assn. Neuropathologists (asso.). Home: Peterborough NH Died Aug. 3, 1970; buried Peterborough NH

FORD, STANLEY MYRON, business exec.; b. N.Y.C., Jan. 14, 1906; s. Percy Myron and Bessie Stanley (Hall) F.; A.B., Colgate U., 1926; m. Madeleine K. Sauer, July 7, 1945; children—Leslie Hall, Katherine Bessie, Robert Stanley. With Gen. Electric Co., 1928-42, mgr. heating device sales, 1937-42; vice pres. Chgo. Electric Mfg. Co., 1945-50, pres., dir. 1950-53; pres., treas., dir. Silex Co., Hartford, Conn., 1953-60; pres. appliance div., treas. Proctor-Silex Corp., Phila., 1960-71, dir. Capt., USMC Res., 1943-45. Mem. Nat. Elec. Mfrs. Assn. (bd. govs. 1952-61), Assn. Home Appliance Mfrs. (mem. exec. com., dir.), National Housewares Mfrs. Assn. (bd. dirs. 1959-66, pres. 1965-66), Clubs: Union League (Chgo.); Phila. Cricket. Home: Philadelphia PA Died Oct. 14, 1971.

FORD, WALTER BURTON, mathematician; b. Oneonta, N.Y., May 18, 1874; s. Sylvester and Emogene (Burton) F.; student Amherst, 1893-95; A.B., Harvard, 1898; Ph.D., 1905; studied in Europe, 1903-04; m. Edith W. Banker, Oct. 20, 1900 (dec. 1959); children—Sylvester (dec.), Clinton B. Instr. math. U. Mich., 1900-03, Williams Coll., 1904-05; again with U. Mich., 1905-39, prof. math., 1917-39. Mem. Am. Math. Soc., Math. Assn. Am. (pres. 1926-28). Societe Mathematique de France, Delta Upsilon. Unitarian. Author: Studies on Divergent Series and Summability, 1916; also various math. texts and research publications. Editor-in-chief Math. Monthly, 1923-27. Home: Ovid NY Died Feb. 24, 1971; buried Ovid NY

FOREMAN, LESTER B., dist. supt. schs., N.Y. Address: Pittsford NY Died June 1969.

FORIO, EDGAR JOSEPH, beverage mfr.; born New Orleans, 1901; grad. Loyola U., 1923, Senior v.p. Coca-Cola Co., Atlanta; chmn. bd., dir. Hickory Publishing Co. Dir. Met. Atlanta Community Service, Inc.; trustee Nutrition Found., Inc., N.Y.C. Mem. Ga. C. of C. (v.p., dir.). Home: Atlanta GA Died Nov. 8, 1971; buried Arlington Cemetery, Atlanta GA

FORNELL, EARL WESLEY, educator; b. Laketown, Wis., Nov. 12, 1915; s. Oscar and Theresa (Larson) F.; B.A., New Sch. Social Research, 1948, M.A., 1949; A.M., Columbia, 1950; Ph.D., Rice U., 1956; student Cambridge (Eng.) U., 1944; m. Martha Steinmetz, Sept. 20, 1947. Documents specialist Columbia, 1947-50; prof. govt. Amarillo Coll., 1950-52; instr. govt. Rice U., 1952-56; prof. polit. sci. Lamar U., Beaumont, Tex., 1956-69. Served with USAAF, with USAAF, World War II; ETO. Decorated Silver Star medal. Fellow Tex. Hist. Assn.; mem. Am., So. polit. sci. assns., Am., So., hist. assns., Am. Assn. U. Profs., Acad. Polit. Sci., Fgn. Policy Assn. Carl Schurz Meml. Found., Am. Philos. Soc., UN Assn. U.S.A., Phi Kappa Phi. Author: Geopolitics of the Gulf Coast, 1956; The Galveston Era, 1961; The Unhappy Medium, 1964. Contbr. to The Handbook of Texas: A Dictionary of Essential Beaumont TX Died Mar. 2, 1969; interred Magnolia

FORNEY, WILLIAM R(UFUS), lawyer and prof.; b. Hudson, Ill., Jan. 11, 1878; s. Henry J. and Melissa (Dull) F.; B.S., Ill. Wesleyan U., 1903; LL.B., Ind. Law Sch., 1908; m. Birdie D. Billman, Nov. 22, 1939. Admitted to Ind. bar, 1908; mem. firm Felt & Forney, Indianapolis, Ind., 1918-26; dean, Benjamin Harrison Law Sch., Indianapolis, 1927-36, Ind. Law Sch., 1936-44; prof. law, U. of Ind. (Indianapolis div.), since 1944; apptd. by Pres. Roosevelt as chmn. U.S. Bd. of Review for Ind.; apptd. by Am. Arbitration Assn. as Ind. mem. Motion Picture Panel of U.S.; aide-de-camp on Ky. Governor's staff with rank of col., 1933-37. Mem. Indianapolis Bar Assn., Phi Gamma Delta, Sigma Delta Kappa. Republican. Methodist. Mason. Club: Columbia (Indianapolis). Home: Indianapolis IN Died Feb. 7, 1971; buried Crown Hill Mausoleum.

FORRESTER, ELIJAH LEWIS, congressman; b. Lee County, Ga., Aug. 16, 1896; s. Richard Alexander and Elizabeth (Kimbrough) F.; student pub. schs. Ga.; m. Thursba Marie Whitaker, June 19, 1929. Admitted to Ga. bar, 1917; practiced law, Leesburg, Ga., 1919-51; solicitor City Ct., Leesburg, Ga., 1920-33; mayor Leesburg, Ga., 1922-31; county atty., 1928-37; solicitor Gen. Superior Cts., S.W. Circuit, 1937-51; mem. 82d-88th Congresses, 3d Georgia District. Served with U.S. Army, World War I. Mem. Am. Legion (comdr. Leesburg post, 1920, Lee County post, 1944), Sigma Delta Kappa (hon. mem.). Democrat. Baptist. Mason. Home: Leesburg GA

FORSTER, E(DWARD) M(ORGAN), writer; b. 1879; s. Edward Morgan Llewellyn and Alice Clara Forster; ed. Tonbridge, King's Coll., Cambridge; hon. fellow Kings Coll., Cambridge; LL.D., Aberdeen, 1931; Litt.D., Liverpool, 1947, Hamilton Coll., 1949, Cambridge, 1950, Nottingham U., 1951, Manchester, 1954, Leyden (Holland), 1954, Leicester, 1958. Rede lectr. Cambridge U., 1941, W. P. Ker lectr., 1944, then fellow. Mem. gen. adv. council BBC Companion of Honor, 1953, decorated Order of Merit (Eng.); recipient Benson medal Royal Soc. Lit., 1937. Hon. corr. mem. Am. Soc. Arts and Letters. Author: A Room With A View; Howards End; Collected Stories; Goldsworthy Lowes Dickinson; Aspects of the Novel; Abinger Harvest; Alexandria: A History and Guide: The Longest Journey; A Passage to India; Two Cheers for Democracy, The Hill of Devi; Eternal Movement, 1964. Librettist (with Eric Crozier) Benjamin Britten's opera Billy Budd; (play) A Passage to India, 1962. Address: Cambridge U ENG Died June 1970.*

FORSTER, JAMES FRANKLIN, mfg. exec.; b. Higginsville, Mo., May 20, 1908; s. James Franklin, Sr. and Emma (Higgins) F.; B.S., U.S. Naval Acad., 1930; M.B.A., Harvard, 1936; Ph.D., Clarkson Coll. Tech., 1969; m. Kathleen Allen, Sept. 18, 1936; children—James Franklin III, Patricia Ann (Mrs. Cameron S. Avery). Staff accountant Arthur Andersen & Co., 1936-39; with Sperry Rand Corp., 1939-72, dir., 1964-72, pres., 1965-72, chmn., chief exec. officer, 1967-72, with Sperry Gyroscope Co., 1939-41, treas., exec. v.p., pres. Vickers, Inc., Detroit, 1941-64, pres. Univac div., N.Y.C., 1964-66; dir. No. Natural Gas, Borden, Inc., Continental Can Co., Inc., NL Industries, Inc. Trustee Conf. Bd., Com. Econ. Devel. Mem. Am. Inst. C.P.A.'s, Am. Soc. M.E. Clubs: Country of Detroit, Burning Tree, Blind Brook, Laurel Valley Golf. Home: New York City NY Died July 1, 1972.

FORSTER, RUDOLPH, asst. sec. to the President; b. Washington, Oct. 30, 1872; s. Herman and Justine F. (Hermann) F.; ed. pub. schs., Washington; LL.B., Columbian (now George Washington) U., 1897; m. Emma Maria Gaisberg, of Washington, Oct. 4, 1889. Entered exec. office of the White House as stenographer, 1897; asst. sec. to the President, Mar. 17, 1903—. Home: 3204 17th St., N.W. Address: The White House Washington DC‡

FORSTER, WEIDMAN WALLACE, editor; b. Mercersburg, Pa., Nov. 27, 1899; s. Carroll and Emma (Mulliken) F.; ed. in schs. of Mercersburg and Phila., A.B. (hon.); m. Lucy Edna McDonald; children—Nancy Carroll (Mrs. Rudolph Hofer, Jr.), Majorie Lee (Mrs. H.A. Wissinger). Editorial work Ladies Home Jour., 1916-17, Pittsburgh Leader, 1917-23; successively reporter, finance-bus. editor, sports editor, news editor and mng. editor Pittsburgh Press, editor, from 1950. Dir. Children's Hosp., Pittsburgh Symphony Soc., Pittsburgh Playhouse, Allegheny Conf. Community Development. Served with U.S. Navy, 1917-19. Mem. C. of C., Swedish Art Soc., Navy Vets. Assn., Inst. of Science, Carnegie Inst. Soc., Am. Soc. Newspaper Editors, Am. Legion, Pa. Soc. Newspaper Editors, Pa. Hosp. Assn., Buhl Planetarium Society, Foreign Policy Association, The Pennsylvania Society,, and Sigma Delta Chi. Politics non-partisan. Presbyn. Mason. Clubs: Duquesne, Pittsburgh Athletic Assn., Chartiers Country, Nat. Press, Pen and Pencil, Chicago Press. Variety, Skytop, Saints and Sinners, Virginia, University. Home: Pittsburgh PA Died Mar. 24, 1969.

FORSYTHE, GEORGE ELMER, educator; b. State College, Pa., Jan. 8, 1917; s. Warren Ellsworth and DeEtta (Brodie) F.; A.B., Swarthmore Coll., 1937; M.S., Brown U., 1938, Ph.D., 1941; m. Alexandra Illmer, June 14, 1941; children—Warren Louis, Diana Elizabeth. Instr. math. Stanford, 1941-42, prof. math., 1957-64, prof., chmn. computer sci., 1961-72; research engr. Boeing Aircraft Co., Seattle, 1946-47; asst. prof. meteorology U. Cal. at Los Angeles, 1947-48, research mathematician, 1954-57; mathematician Nat. Bur. Standards, 1948-54. Fellow A.A.A.S., Brit. Computer Soc.; mem. Am. Math. Soc., Assn. Computing Machinery (pres. 1964-66), Soc. Indsl. and Applied Math. (trustee), Math. Assn. Am., Am. Assn. U. profs. Sierra Club. Home: Stanford CA Died Apr. 9, 1972.

FORTUNE, J(OHN) ROBERT, mechanical engr.; b. Detroit, Aug. 1, 1871; s. Thomas Jenkins and Mary (Buckley) F.; ed. Detroit pub. schs. and by pvt. study. m. Nettie E. Thomas, of Detroit, June 6, 1898. Engr. Murphy Iron Wks., Detroit, 1890-8, Am. Stoker Co. New York, 1898-1900, Automatic Furnace Syndicate London, Eng., 1900-1; chief engr., Underfeed Stoker Co., London, 1901-3; European mgr. Murphy Iron Wks., London, 1903-5; chief engr., Murphy Iron Wks. Detroit, 1905-15; mech. engr. Dodge Bros., Detroit 1915-17; works mgr. Bunting Brass & Bronze Co. Toledo, 1917-18. Mem. Am. Soc. M.E., Engrs. Soc. Western Pa., Detroit Engineering Soc., Ohio Soc. Mech., Elec. and Steam Engrs., Am. Foundrymen's Assn. Inventor and patentee many improvements in mech. stoking apparatus. Club: Ingleside. Home: 3Harold Arms, Toledo OH‡

FORWARD, JOHN F., JR., title insurance, banking; b. Pittsburgh, Pa., Nov. 18, 1876; s. John Ferree and Ella Francis (Dillon) F.; ed. pub. schs. and business coll.; m. Alberta Fairbanks, of Los Angeles, Calif., June 29, 1901 (divorced); 1 dau., Flora Mitchell (Mrs. Leonard H. Brown); m. 2d, Martha Thompson, of San Diego, Calif. June 15, 1920. Searcher of records of title since 1891 pres., Union Title Ins. Co., San Diego, Calif., since 1926 pres. Union Trust Co. since 1926. Mayor of San Diego 1932-35; mem. Republican Central Com. of San Diego County, 1928-32; del. rep. Nat. Conv., Chicago, 1931 mem. bd. dirs. Calif. State Prison Bd.; mem. advisory bd. Automobile Club of Southern Calif. (San Diego County). Mason (32 deg.). Clubs: Cuyamaca, San Diego Press, San Diego Athletic. Home: 4144 Lark St. Office 1028 2d Av., San Diego CA‡

FOSCUE, EDWIN JAY, geographer; b. Camden, Ark. Aug. 26, 1899; son Augustus William and Ida May (Bell) F.; student University of Tex., 1918-20; B.A. Southern Methodist Univ., 1922; M.S., U. of Chicago 1925, Ph.D., Clark Univ., 1931; married Fannie L. Knight, June 2, 1925. Instructor geography, Southern Methodist Univ., 1923-24, asst. professor, 1924-31 asso. prof., 1931-38, prof. from 1938 (on leave of absence, 1943-44), chmn. dept. geography from 1946 vis. prof. geography (summers), U. of Neb., 1937, 38 Western Reserve Univ., 1939, 41, U. Colo., 1940, 42 Univ. Wash., 1946, U. Virginia, 1948, Columbia, 1950 Stanford U., 1951; asst. dir. U.S. Bd. on Geog. Names 1943-44. Del. Internat. Geog. Congress, Lisbon Portugal, 1949, Washington, 1952, Rio de Janeiro 1956, Stockholm, Sweden, 1960, also London, England 1964; Pan-American Consultation on Geography Washington, 1952, Quito, Ecuador, 1959; Department of State delegate to gen. assembly Pan-Am. Inst. Geography and History, Mexico City, 1955. Recipient faculty achievement award Alumni Assn. So. Meth. U. 1960. Fellow A.A.A.S.; mem. Assn. Am. Geographers (councilor 1943-45), S.W. Internat. Devel. Inst. (dir.) Southwestern Social Science Association (president 1950), Phi Beta Kappa, Sigma Xi, Kappa Sigma, Alpha Kappa Psi, Sigma Delta Pi, Blue Key. Author: Gatlinburg—Gateway to the Great Smokies; Taxco Mexico's Silver City; Geographic Regions of the United States, 1958; (with others) Regional Geography of Anglo-America, 1943, rev. edit. 1954, Estes Park Resort in the Rockies, 1949; East Texas: A Timbered Empire, 1960. Contbg. editor Economic Geography. Home: Dallas TX Died Feb. 23, 1972.

FOSDICK, RAYMOND BLAINE, lawyer; b. Buffalo, N.Y., June 9, 1883; s. Frank S. and Amie I. (Weaver) F.; B.A., Princeton, 1905, M.A., 1906; LL.B., N.Y. Law Sch., 1908; LL.D., Colgate and Colo. Coll., 1925, Princeton and Amherst Coll., 1948, Columbia, Wesleyan and U. of Edinburgh, 1949, Swarthmore College, 1950, Dartmouth College, 1951; married Winifred Finlay, December 2, 1910 (died Apr. 3, 1932); children—Susan (dec.), Raymond Blaine (dec.); m. 2d, Elizabeth R. Miner, Apr. 21, 1936. Asst. corp. counsel, N.Y., 1908-10; commr. of accounts, New York in charge investigations of city departments, 1910-13; spent 1913 in Europe in study of police organization, as rep. of Rockefeller Bur. of Social Hygiene. Comptroller Finance Com., Dem. Nat. Com., 1912; mem. N.Y. City Bd. of Edn., 1915-16; spl. rep. of sec. of war on Mexican border, 1916; chmn. Commn. on Training Camp Activities of War and Navy depts., 1917-18; spl. rep. of War Dept. in France, 1918-19; civilian aide to Gen. Pershing in France, 1919; under sec. gen. of League of Nations, 1919-20; mem. Curtis, Fosdick and Belknap, N.Y. City, 1920-36. Mem. Phi Beta Kappa, Am. Philos. Soc., Am. Acad. Arts and Sciences. Trustee Rockefeller Found. and Gen. Edn. Bd., 1921-48, pres. 1936-48. Mem. Joint Army and Navy Com. on Welfare and Recreation, 1941-45. Awarded D.S.M.; Grand Officer Legion of Honor (France); also Woodrow Wilson award Princeton, 1961; award from the Woodrow Wilson Foundation, 1962. Clubs: Century; Union Interalliee (Paris). Author: European Police Systems, 1915; Keeping Our Fighters Fit (with E.F. Allen), 1918; American Police Systems, 1920; The Old Savage in the New Civilization, 1928; Toward Liquor Control (with Albert L. Scott), 1933; Story of the Rockefeller Foundation, 1952; Within Our Power, 1952; John D. Rockefeller, Jr.; A Portrait, 1956, Chronicle of a Generation, 1958; Adventure in Giving; The Story of the General Education Bd., 1962; Letters on the League of Nations, 1966; The League and the United Nations After Fifty Years, 1972. Home: Newtown CT Died July 18, 1972.

FOSS, FEODORE FEODOROVICH, mining and metall. engr.; b. Odessa, Russia, Dec. 29, 1874; s. Feodore A. and Olga A. (Mansfield) F.; grad. Classical Gymnasium. St. Petersburg, 1893; entered through competitive exam. (60 out of 1,000) Imperial Mining Inst. and grad. M.E., cum eximia laude, 1898; m. Zenaida M. Magula, Apr. 28, 1899. Came to U.S., 1917, naturalized citizen 1926. Asst. prof. metallurgy, Mining Inst. of St. Petersburg, 1900-02; as chief engr., later mng. dir. Lyssva Mining Dist., developed iron and steel industry there by introduction of mfr. of tin plate, galvanized sheet iron, hollowware, etc.; developed platinum mining of same district to output of nearly 2 tons per yr.; tinplate produced in the plants under his management was only resource for canning food for Russian armies; during World War built new plants employing 15,000 men to supply Russian armies with shells, fuses, powder boxes, soldiers' canteens and trench instruments; awarded hon. degree in engring. by Imperial Russian Govt.; former pres. and dir. Lyssva Mining Dist., Inc., Russia, Urals, vice chmn. bd. Verch-Issetsk Mining Dist., dir. Bogoslovsk Mining Dist.; col. Russian Mining Corps; came to U.S., 1917, as chmn. industrial commn. to study Am. methods of developing natural resources; severed connection with Russia on account of Bolshevik upheaval; now retired, after 21 years service with Wheeling Steel Corporation as asst. to president, asst. to chairman and director of research and metallurgy. Mem. Am. Inst. Mining and Metall. Engrs., Am. Soc. M.E., Am. Soc. for Metals. Am. Economic Soc., Am. Acad. Polit. Science, Am. Geog. Soc., Army Ordnance Assn., Assn. Iron and Steel Engineers, Am. Polit. Science Assn., Am. Academy Polit. and Social Science. Republican. Unitarian. Home: 1857 E. Las Tunas Rd., Santa Barbara CA‡

FOSS, NOBLE, mfr. cotton goods; b. Boston, Mass., Apr. 8, 1889; s. Eugene N. and Lilla (Sturtevant) F.; student Harvard, 1906-07; m. Katherine Cobb, September 3, 1912 (died October 30, 1960); children—Nancy (Mrs. Richard B. Heath), Constance (Mrs. Edward L. Anthony, II). As aeronautical engineer pioneered design, manufacture airplanes and engines for U.S. Army and Navy; founder and pres., Sturtevant Airplane Co., Boston, 1910-28; v.p. and dir. B. F. Sturtevant Co., mfrs. ventilating, air conditioning apparatus, Boston, 1910-45; pres., dir. Maverick Mills, mfrs. cotton goods, from 1922, White Horse Mill (Greenville, S.C.); pres. and dir. Framingham (Mass) Foundries, Inc., 1919-44. Member corp. Northeastern U. Mem. Soc. Mayflower Descs., Soc. Colonial Wars. Republican. Clubs: Biltmore Forest Country, University, Harvard, Milton, Beverly Yacht. Home: Marion MA Died May 31, 1969.

FOSSEEN, CARRIE S. (MRS. MANLEY L. FOSSEEN), nat. committee woman; b. Fergus Falls, Minn., Jan. 30, 1875; d. Ole and Julia (Hovda) Jorgens; grad. high sch., Minneapolis, Minn., 1895; student Winona (Minn.) State Teachers Coll. and U. of Minn.; m. Judge Manley L. Fosseen, of Minneapolis, Minn., Sept. 15, 1897; children—Freeman F., Rolf. Mem. Rep. Nat. Com. since 1920, Rep. Nat. Exec. Com., 1920-24, 1928-32. Mem. Council of Defense, World War. Chmn. 1st Sane Fourth movement, 1912. Pres. Lymgblomsten Home for Aged, 1906, Fairview Hosp. and Tuberculosis Soc., 1909; chmn. dept. of legislation, Minn. 5th Dist. Fed. Women's Clubs, 1924, 25. Mem. W. C. T. U., Women's Co-operative Alliance, Women's Welfare League (treas. 1914-16), League of Women Voters. Methodist. Clubs: Minneapolis Woman's, Thursday Musical, Civic Music League. Pres. Dome Club of Minn. (orgn. of wives of senators and reps. of Minn.) since 1904. Home: 424 W. Franklin Av., Minneapolis MN

FOSTER, ALBERT DOUGLAS, med. dir., U.S. Pub. Health Service (retired); b. Detroit, Mich., Feb. 13, 1875; s. Edward Dwight and Marian (Langley) F.; M.D., U. of Mich., 1899; m. Hilda Ann Mitcham, Dec. 27, 1911; children—Edith Frances (Mrs. Alfred Leighton Gibson), Albert Douglas, Florence Mitcham (Mrs. Robert Lewis Berg), Theodore Tillinghast. Interne U.S. Marine Hosp., Cleveland, O., 1899; commd. asst. surgeon in U.S. Pub. Health Service, 1902, passed asst. surgeon, 1907, surgeon, 1914, med. dir., 1930; retired from active duty, 1939. Am. vice and dept. consul at Amoy, China, 1909. Fellow Am. Coll. of Physicians; mem. A.M.A., Me. State Med. Soc. Mason (32 deg.). Clubs: Portland Medical, National Sojourner, Torch of Western Maine. Author of monographs, Railway Car Sanitation, School Hygiene, Interstate Migration of Tuberculosis Persons. Home: Bay Shore Dr., Falmouth Foreside ME‡

FOSTER, BERNARD AUGUSTUS, JR., lawyer; b. Spartanburg, S.C., Aug. 30, 1909; s. Bernard A. and Lillie Harris (Veazey) F.; A.B. with distinction, Wofford Coll., 1931; J.D. cum laude, George Washington U., 1937; m. Cecile Bernice Harrington, Sept. 25, 1937; children—Carolyn Cecile (Mrs. Michael A. Meredith), and Bernard Augustus III. Instr. in English, Kershaw (S.C.) Sch.; law clk Petroleum Adminstrn. Bd., 1933-35; admitted S.C. bar, 1936, D.C. bar, 1937, U.S. Supreme Ct. bar 1941, Md. bar, 1954; chief mediation div. Pub. Works Adminstrn., 1936-41; sr. atty. FTC, 1941-42; spl. counsel Fed. Power Commn., 1946-50, asst. gen. counsel, chief natural gas div., 1951-53; gen counsel President's Water Resources Policy Commn., 1950-51; mem. firm Ross, Marsh & Foster, Washington, 1953-68. Lecturer Southwestern Legal Foundation, 1965; public mem. Adminstrv. Conf. U.S., also chmn. com. on personnel, 1968. Trustee Rocky Mountain Mineral Law Found. Served from 2d lt. to lt. col., AUS, 1942-46; chmn. Joint Army-Navy-Air Force Industrial Review Board, 1945-46. Decorated Legion of Merit, Army Commendation medal with oak leaf cluster; recipient Alumni Achievement award George Washington U., 1946. Fellow Am. Bar Found.; mem. Am. (chmn. natural gas com. 1954-55; council 1955-59; chmn. mineral and natural resources law sect. 1961-62; ho. dels. 1962-66, chmn. spl. com. on cts. of spl. jurisdiction, 1963-64, member of the special committee on legal service, 1963-64, mem. spl. com. on code fed. adminstrv. procedure 1968), D.C., Federal Power (executive committee 1955-59, 66-68), Federal bar assns., Am. Judicature Soc., Internat. Relations Club, Res. Officers Assn. U.S. (pres. Va. 1948-49), Mil. Order World Wars, S.A.R., Scabbard and Blade, Blue Key, Phi Delta Phi, Pi Kappa Phi, Pi Kappa Delta, Sigma Upsilon. Democrat. Episcopalian. Clubs: Army-Navy, Lawyers (Washington); Chevy Chase, Edgemoor Tennis, Sherwood Forest, Jefferson Islands (Md.). Editor George Washington Law Rev., 1936-37. Author: (with others) Water Resources Law, 1950. Home: Chevy Chase MD Died June 7, 1968; buried Parkwood Cemetery, Rockville MD

FOSTER, FRANCIS APTHORP, editor; b. Cambridge, Mass., Sept. 21, 1872; s. Francis Charles and Marion (Padelford) F.; Browne and Nichols' Sch., Cambridge; spl. student Lawrence Scientific Sch. (Harvard), 1895; unmarried. Editor Publs. N.E. Hist. Geneal. Soc., 1907-12. Republican. Mem. Am. Hist. Assn., N.E. Hist.-Geneal. Soc., Colonial Soc. of Mass., Me. Hist. Soc., Cambridge Hist. Soc., Bunker Hill Monument Assn. (dir.) Gen. Soc. of The Cincinnati (asst. sec.), Ga. Soc. of the Cincinnati (treas.), Mass. Hist. Soc., Am. Ornithologists' Union, Nuttall Ornithol. Club, Am. Geog. Soc., Am. Soc. of Mammalogists, A.A.A.S., Boston Soc. of Natural History. County Commr. Dukes Co., 1919—. Clubs: Boston City, Club of Odd Volumes. Home: Edgartown MA‡

FOSTER, JEANNE ROBERT (MRS. MATLACK FOSTER), author, editor; b. Johnsburgh, Warren Co., N.Y., Mar. 10, 1884; d. Francis and Lucia (Newell) Oliver; ed. Rochester (N.Y.) Athenaeum and Mechanics Inst., Boston U., and Harvard Extension (spl. courses); grad. Stanhope-Wheatcroft Dramatic Sch., New York; m. Matlack Foster, of N.Y. City, 1901. Began writing for newspapers in childhood; teacher common schs., Adirondack Mountains; writer for Boston newspapers 3 years; lit. editor Review of Reviews, 1910-22; Am. editor Transatlantic Rev. Studied housing and city planning in Europe. Mem. Authors' League America, Poetry Soc. America, Woman's Trade Union League, Acad. Polit. Science, Nat. Civic Fed., English-Speaking Union, League Am. Penwomen. Catholic. Clubs: National Arts, Pen and Brush (New York); Woman's City (Boston); Woman's (Schenectady, N.Y.); Am. Women's (London). Author: Wild Apples (poems), 1916; Neighbors of Yesterday (narrative poems of the Adirondacks), 1916; Rock-Flower (poems), 1922. Contbr. articles and poems to periodicals. Edited John Quinn Letters (2 vols), 1925. Address: New York City NY Died Sept. 1970.*

FOSTER, JOHN MORTON, lawyer, co. dir.; b. Beverly, Mass., Mar. 30, 1888; s. Israel Woodbury and Ella Jane (Tuck) F.; A.B., Harvard, 1911, LL.B., 1913; M. Helen Galloupe Patch, June 20, 1916; children—John Morton, David W. Admitted to Mass. bar, 1913, practiced in Boston; mem. firm Ropes & Gray, and predecessors, from 1930; v.p., dir. Beverly Nat. Bank, dir., member exec. com. Copper Range Co.; dir. Kendall Co., White Pine Copper Co., National Food Products Corporation, Colonial Stores, Incorporated, Geo. E. Belcher Co. Trustee Fisher Charitable Soc., Beverly Fuel Soc.; chmn. finance com. Old Ladies' Home Soc. Beverly. Mem. Am., Boston bar assns. Conglist. (trustee), Clubs: Union, Harvard (Boston); Eastward Ho Beverly MA Died 1971.

FOSTER, JOSHUA HILL, clergyman, educator; b. Tuscaloosa, Ala.; s. Joshua Hill and Frances Cornelia (Bacon) F.; A.B. and A.M., U. of Ala., 1883, LL.D., 1923; grad. Southern Bapt. Theol. Sem., 1888; D.D., Howard Coll., Ala.; m. Eula Sparks, of Cave Spring, Ga., Jan. 15, 1892; children—Edith (Mrs. George R. Boyd), Linton (dec.), Cornelia (Mrs. Henry H. Hale), Joshua (dec.), Ione (Mrs. Howard A. Hanby), Frank, Helen. Teacher pvt. sch., Camden, Ala., 1882-83; prin. Hearne Inst., Cave Spring, Ga., 1883-85; ordained Bapt. ministry, 1888; pastor Union Springs, Ala., 1888-90, Greenville, 1890-92, East Lake Ch., Birmingham, 1892-95, Anniston, 1895-1910, 1st Ch., Wilmington, N.C., 1910-15; pres. Bessie Tift Coll., 1915-22; pres. Central Coll., Tuscaloosa, Ala., since 1922. Actively interested in reform and prohibition movements. Democrat. Author: The Judgment Day, 1910. Home: Tuscaloosa AL‡

FOSTER, LAURENCE, anthropologist; b. Pensacola, Fla., Feb. 3, 1903; s. Frank Lee and Pearl (Hill) F.; A.B., Lincoln U., 1926, S.T.B., 1929; Ph.D., U. Pa., 1931; m. Ella Mae Gibson, June 30, 1936;children—Yvonne Camille, Laurence Foster, Jr. Univ. scholar U. Pa., 1927-29; tchr. history Stowe Tchrs. Coll., St. Louis, Mo., 1929-32; chmn. div. social scis. Lincoln U., Chester Co., Pa.; formerly research asso. U. of Pa. Museum; gen. editor Huxley Publishers, N.Y.C., from 1935; guest lecturer, Museo Nacional de Mexico, 1930; spl. rep. of Pan-Am. Union, Washington, D.C., to Mexico, 1930; dean of instrn. State Tchrs. Coll., Cheyney, Pa., 1933-37; special representative Biol. Abstracts, 1936-37. Field research in Canada, Mexico, and Guatemala, under grant from Columbia U., spring and summer of 1929; grant in aid fellow, Nat. Research Council, 1931-32; exec. dir. Pa. State Temporary Commn. on the Conditions of the Colored Urban Population (wrote preliminary report of Commn., 1941). Formerly pres. the Stevens Housing Corporation; formerly dir. research, National Protestant Council on Higher Edn.; gen. editor The Stackpole Social Sci. Series, Stackpole Co., Harrisburg, Pa., from 1952; chmn. bd. Model Cities Facilities and Services Phila. Republican. Presbyn. Club: Pyramid. Author: The Functions of a Graduate School in a Democratic Society, 1936; also private survey reports of higher ednl. instns. in Ala., Ark., Conn., D.C., Ga., Ill., Ind., Md., Minn., Miss., Mo., N.Y., N.C., O., Pa., S.C., Tenn., Tex., Va. and W.Va. Co-editor: Introduction to Sociology; Selected Readings in Sociology; Introduction to American Government; Readings on the American Way; Analysis of Social Problems. Stockpole series include: Contemporary Social Science, Marriage and Family Relations, Dynamic Urban Sociology, several others. Home: Chester County PA Died Aug. 15, 1969; buried Oxford Cemetery, Oxford PA

FOSTER, MABEL GRACE, author; b. Boston, Sept. 28, 1869; d. Rev. Addison P. and Hariette (Day) F.; ed. Hasbrouck Inst., Jersey City, N.J.; unmarried. Lecturer on art and history, Italian life and literature. Mem. N.E. Woman's Press Assn., Circolo Italo-Americano (Boston). Author: The Heart of the Doctor, 1902. Home: W. Medford, Mass. Office: 8 Beacon St., Boston MA‡

FOSTER, MAXIMILIAN, author; b. San Francisco, Feb. 27, 1872; s. William Hammond and Leila (Love) F.; ed. Drisler Sch., New York, and Andover (Mass.) Acad.; m. Elizabeth Dickson, of Phila., June 25, 1904; 1 dau., Betty. Began as newspaper writer on New York Recorder, dau., Betty. Began as newspaper writer on New York Recorder, 1891; spl. writer, New York newspapers, 1892-99; in mag. work, 1899-1901; with Ellsworth Coal Co., Cleveland, in charge of railroad equipment (pvt. car line), 1901-06. Official corr. for U.S. Govt. with the A.E.F. in France, 1918. Republican. Episcopalian. Club: Players (New York). Author: In the Forest, 1902; Corrie Who? 1908; Keeping Up Appearances, 1911; The Whistling Man, 1913; Shoestrings, 1916; The Trap, 1920; Humdrum House, 1924; I Want to be a Lady, 1926; Crooked, 1927; Bubbles, 1928; (plays) The Whirlpool, 1909; Rich Man, Poor Man, 1916; Smoke (prod. San Francisco, 1919); also various motion picture plays. Contbr. to leading mags. Home: Rangeley ME*‡

FOSTER, MILTON HUGH, surgeon; b. Huntingdon, Pa., Mar. 3, 1873; s. Milton Kirk and Martha (Rodgers) F.; Juniata Normal Sch., 1886-90; B.S., Dickinson Coll., 1894, M.A., 1898; M.D., U. of Pa., 1897; m. Louise Griffiths, Jan. 20, 1901 (died Jan. 19, 1906); children—Houston Griffiths, Robert Foster (dec.); m. 2d, Marion Brown, Dec. 15, 1914. Apptd. asst. surgeon Marine Hosp. Service, Mar. 7, 1898; surgeon U.S.P.H.S., Nov. 12, 1912, med. dir., July 1, 1930. Served as chief quarantine officer at Puget Sound and Porto Rico; later in charge marine hosps., Port Townsend, Baltimore, Chicago and Stapleton; was in charge U.S.P.H.S. hosps. at Biltmore, N.C., and Ft. McHenry, Md.; also chief medical officer U.S. Immigration Station, Ellis Island, N.Y.; now retired. Mem. A.M.A., Am. Hosp. Assn., Phi Beta Kappa. Mason. Club: Richmond County Country. Author: Prevention of Diseases and Care of the Sick (with Dr. W. G. Stimpson), 1919; Manual of Hospital Management for Marine Hospitals, 1930. Contbr. to med. jours. Home: 57 Silver Lake Rd., Brighton Heights, Staten Island NY‡

FOSTER, PAUL F., consultant; b. Wichita, Kan., Mar. 25, 1889; s. Rev. Festus and Lillian (Howe) F.; B.S., U.S. Naval Acad., 1911; m. Isabelle de la V. Lowe, Sept. 8, 1916; 1 son, Paul Lowe (U.S. Navy). Commd. engign, U.S. Navy, 1911, and advanced in regular Navy until resignation as lieut. comdr., 1929; engaged in bus. and engring., New York City, 1929-39; surveyed resources of Galapagos Islands, 1940-41; organizer and pres., Pacific Development Co., 1941; recalled to active naval duty, 1941; conducted naval and mil. inspections for President Roosevelt, 1942-43, asst. naval inspector gen., 1943-46; retired as vice-admiral, U.S.N.R., Oct. 1946. Vice president Mandel Brothers, Inc., Chicago, 1946-50; with Internat. Bank for Reconstrn. and Development, Washington, until 1954; with AEC, 1954-59, asst. gen. mgr. internat. activities, 1954-58, gen. mgr., 1958, dep. gen. mgr., 1959, U.S. rep. to Internat. Atomic Energy Agy., Vienna, 1959-61. Decorated Congl. Medal of Honor, Navy Cross, D.S.M., Legion of Merit. Commendation Ribbon; recipient Distinguished Service medal AEC. Club: Army and Navy, Metropolitan (Washington). Home: Arlington VA Died Jan. 1971; buried Arlington Nat. Cemetery.

FOSTER, PAUL PINKERTON, editor; b. Washington, May 23, 1875; s. Samuel Tufts and Elizabeth (Pinkerton) F.; grad. Pinkerton Acad., Derry, N.H., 1893; has made spl. studies in Spanish, German and French langs.; m. Catherine Spoors, of Boston, Sept. 15, 1903. Organized and developed unique editorial library, containing large classified collection of Am. and foreign periodical lit.; became connected with Youth's Companion, 1894, and in charge Nature and Science Dept. since 1911, asso. editor since 1913. Republican. Conglist. Mem. Special Libraries Assn., El Club Espanol (Boston). Club: Lakewood Tennis, of Newton Highlands. Home: Newton Highlands, Mass. Office: Youth's Companion, Boston‡

FOSTER, ROBERT ARNOLD, mining engr.; b. Sacramento, Calif., Jan. 19, 1877; s. John Curry and Mary Starkweather (Patterson) F.; B.S., Coll. of Mines, U. of Calif., 1898; m. Katherine Lucretia Fairchild, of Canton, O., Aug. 3, 1901; children—Lucretia Mary, Katherine Wilhelmenia. Const. engr., Ariz. Copper Co., Ltd., Clifton, Ariz., 1898-1901; chief engr. and gen. mgr. Mining Corpn., Ltd., Portland, Ore., 1901-03; pres. Alaska-Peninsular Coal & Coke Co., 1903-10; pres. Lewiston-Clarkston Improvement Co., 1913-31; pres. Mexican Coal & Coke Co. Mem. Am. Soc. C.E., Sigma Alpha Epsilon, Sigma Xi. Episcopalian. Mason (33 deg. hon., Shriner). Clubs: University, Mexico City. Home: Las Esperanzas, Coahuila Mexico*‡

FOSTER, THOMAS ARNOLD, pharmacist; b. Camp Hill, Ala., Jan. 26, 1895; s. William Thomas and Eugenia (McLendon) F.; student Howard Coll., Birmingham, Ala., 1911-12; Ph.G., Wilson Sch. Pharmacy, 1916; m. Mary Reeves, Sept. 30, 1919 (dec. Jan. 2, 1942); children—Mary Virginia (Mrs. J. Richard Roberts), Thomas Arnold; m. 2d, Katherine Verschoor, Dec. 8, 1945. Practice pharmacy, Birmingham, Ala., 1917; retail pharmacist, co-owner drug stores, Birmingham, 1919-32; commd. pharmacist USPHS, 1933, advanced through grades to pharmacist dir., 1960; adminstrv. officer, 1933-42, chief supply service hdqrs. Hosp. div., Washington, 1942-44, chief supply officer Office Surgeon Gen., 1944-50, assigned div. civilian requirements, health supplies liaison officer ODM, 1958-60; medical supply cons., Washington, 1960-70; cons. to Office Emergency Planning, Exec. Office Pres., 1964-73. Gen. chmn. convention Assn. Mil. Surgeons, Washington, 1955; Am. Pharm. Assn. del. Conv. Internat. Pharm. Fedn., London, Eng., 1955. Served with U.S. Army, 1917-19. Recipient Founders medal Assn. Mil. Surgeons U.S., 1955, Andrew Craigie award, 1960; medal Swedish Ministry Health, 1959; H.A.K. Whitney award Am. Soc. Hosp. Pharmacists, 1960. Fellow Royal Soc. Health Eng. (life); mem. Am. Pharm. Assn. (chmn. spl. com. Project Hope 1961-62, hon. pres. 1963, chmn. standing com. on disaster preparedness and nat. security 1963, chmn. standing com. govtl. pharm. service 1964, rep. to surgeon gen.'s profl. adv. com. emergency health preparedness, 1963-64), Am. Soc. Hosp. Pharmacists (chmn. com. laws, legislation and regulations 1967-70), assn. Mil. Surgeons U.S., Am. Legion, Commd. Officers Assn. Pub. Health Service, Am. Surg. Trade Assn. Chgo. (hon. life), Med-Surg. Mfrs. Assn. (hon. life). Home: Washington DC Died Jan. 4, 1973; buried Ft. Lincoln Cemetery, Washington DC

FOSTER, VIRGLL ELWOOD, clergyman; b. Onawa, Ia., Sept. 24, 1901; s. John Lewis and Laura Rebecca (Malone) F.; A.B., Tabor Coll., 1923; M.A., U. Chgo., 1926; B.D., Chgo. Theol. Sem., 1926, D.D., 1950; m. Ruth Griffith, Nov. 22, 1927 (died June 30, 1935); m. 2d Imo Ruyle, Feb. 21, 1937. Ordained to ministry Congl. Ch., 1926; minister edn. Bryn Mawr Community Ch., Chgo., 1926-36; asso. minister Pilgrim Ch., St.L., 1936-43, Second Ch. in Newton, West Newton, Mass., 1943-46; instr. Andover Newton Theol. Sem., part-time 1945-46; dir. religious edn. Congl. Christian Conf. Ia., Grinnell, 1946-50; editor Internat. Jour. Religious Edn. (pub. by National Council of Churches of Christ in U.S.A.), N.Y.C., 1950-66; freelance writer and photographer, from 1967. Author: How a Small Church Can Have Good Christian Education, 1956; Close-Up of a Honeybee, 1960; By Deed and Design, 1961; (with Eleanor Shelton Morrison) Creative Teaching in the Church, 1963; Christian Education Where the Learning Is, 1968; also articles religious publs. Home: New York City NY Died July 16, 1970.

FOSTER, W(ALTER) BERT(RAM), author; b. Providence, R.I., Nov. 3, 1869; s. Benjamin Norton and Annie Elizabeth (Dexter) F.; ed. common schs.; m. Clara Louise Read, of Cranston, R.I., July 17, 1893. In lit. work since 1886. Author: The Lost Galleon, 1901; With Washington at Valley Forge, 1902; The Treasure of South Lake Farm, 1902; In Alaskan Waters, 1903; With Ethan Allen at Ticonderoga, 1903; The Eve of War, 1904; The Lost Expedition, 1905; The Quest of the Silver Swan, 1907; Arthur Blaisdell's Choice, 1908; The Heron Nest, 1910; Swept Out to Sea, 1913; The Frozen Ship, 1913; From Sea to Sea, 1913; The Ocean Express, 1913.*‡

FOUGNER, ERNEST HJALMAR, architect; b. Chgo., Aug. 20, 1880; s. Albert Cato and Mathilde (Selmer) F.; grad. Godefroy Prep. Sch. of Architecture, Paris, France, 1906; student Ecole des Beaux Arts, and Ecole des Arts Decoratifs, Paris, France, 1906-09; m. Mildred Bailey, June 3, 1916. Began practice of architecture in Newark, 1910; tchr. architecture Newark Sch. of Fine Arts, 1927; patron Beaux Arts Inst. Design, N.Y.C., 1929; founded Atelier Fougner, prep. sch. of architecture, 1925, discontinued during World War II; practice of architecture, 1953-67. Sec.-dir. N.J. State Bd. Architects, 1953-56, ret. Fellow A.I.A. (life mem., past pres. N.J. chpt.); mem. N.J. (life mem., past pres., dir., chmn. practice com.), Newark (founder, life mem., past pres., trustee) socs. of architects. Home: Lanoka Harbor NJ Died June 17, 1967; buried Good Luck Cemetery, Lanoka Harbor NJ

FOULK, CLAUDE CLAUDE, banker; b. Worthington, Ind., June 17, 1892; s. Frank and Anna (Heaton) F.; A.B., U. Ill., 1916; m. Marie Louise Voigt, Jan. 22, 1921; 1 dau., Elizabeth Carolyn (Mrs. R. G. Kehoe). Accountant Nat. City Bank N.Y., 1916-22; chief accountant Chinese-Am. Bank Commerce, 1922-28; trust adminstr. Bankers Trust Co., 1929; prin. examiner N.Y. State Banking Dept., 1930-35; v.p., comptroller Queens County Savs. Bank, Flushing, N.Y., 1935-57, pres., 1957-61, chmn., 1961-67. Conglist. Mason (32 deg.). Clubs: Fireside; Lake Placid, North Hempstead Country. Home: Manhasset LI NY Died May 27, 1969; buried Flushing Cemetery, Flushing NY

FOULKE, ELIZABETH E., teacher, author; b. Richmond, Ind.; d. William W. and Mary E. F.; ed. city schools, Friend's Acad., Richmond, and partial course at Earlham Coll.; engaged in teaching; unmarried. Author: Twilight Stories, 1895 S6; Braided Straws, 1898 S6; etc. Address: Richmond IN‡

FOULKROD, HARRY ELLSWORTH, mgmt. exec.; b. Williamsport, Pa., Nov. 15, 1903; s. Royden and Mabel (Shultz) F.; A.B., Pa. State Coll., 1925; postgrad. Columbia, Johns Hopkins; m. Margaret Price, Nov. 27, 1925;children—Jay Martin, Daniel Price. Automobile dealer, 1938-52; marketing mgr. Packard Motor Car Co., 1953; gen. sales mgr. Fruehauf Trailer Co., 1958, exec. v.p., 1959, past sr. exec. v.p.; pres. Foulkrod Assos., Mgmt. Cons., Ft. Lauderdale; dir. Dean Research Corp., Kansas City. Chmn. Wray Meml. Found., Ft. Lauderdale; bd. dirs. Nat. Safety Council. Bd. trustees Leelanau Schs. Mem. Nat. Indsl. Conf. Bd., Am. Mgmt. Assn., Am. Ordnance Assn., Sales Execs. Club (dir.), Sales Marketing Internat. (dir., award as marketing exec. 1966), Sales Marketing Detroit (v.p.), Alpha Tau Omega. Rotarian. Clubs: Detroit Athletic, Grosse Pointe Yacht, Detroit Golf; Coral Ridge Country (Ft. Lauderdale). Home: Fort Lauderdale FL Died June 17, 1972.

FOUNTAIN, REGINALD MORTON, ins. and real estate exec.; b. nr. Tarboro, N.C., Oct. 21, 1908; s. Lawrence H. and Sallie (Barnes) F.; student U. N.C., 1926-28; m. Lucille Turner, Oct. 8, 1938; children—Reginald Morton, Theodore Turner. Spl. agt. Jefferson Standard Life Ins. Co., Greensboro, N.C., 1942-69; dir. Coastal Plain Broadcasting Co., Tarboro, 1947-69; dir. Coastal Plain Life Ins. Co., Rocky Mount, N.C., Edgecombe Homestead & Loan Assn., Tarboro; pres., dir. Forest Acres, Inc., Fountain Enterprises, Inc. (both Tarboro). Pres., Edgecombe County Indsl. Devel. Authority, Tarboro; chmn. Edgecombe County Bd. Health, Edgecombe County Bd. Commrs., Tarboro, 1960-69. Mem. N.C. Assn. County Commrs. (pres. 1967-68). Rotarian. Club: Tarboro (pres. 1935). Home: Tarboro NC Died Jan. 4, 1969; interred Greenwood Cemetery Tarboro NC

FOWLE, LUTHER RICHARDSON, treas. Am. Bd. Missions; b. of Am. parents at Talas, Turkey, July 30, 1886; s. James Luther and Carrie Palmer (Farnsworth) F.; prep. edn., Lawrenceville (N.J.) Sch., 1900-03; B.A., Williams, 1908; student Union Theol. Sem., N.Y. City, 1909-11; m. Helen Curtis, Sept. 10, 1912 (dec. 1949); children—Curtis, Wilson Farnsworth, James Warren, Helen Joy, Richardson; m. 2d, Mary Eliza Gleason. Treas. Am. Mission, Aintab, Turkey, 1912-14; asst. treas. Am. Bd. Missions in Turkey, 1914-23; treas. Am. Bd. Missions in Near East from 1923. Am. attache at Swedish Legation, Constantinople, charged with protection of Am. interests in Turkey, 1917-19. Asst. treas. and treas. Am. relief activities in Turkey, 1915-19. Mem. bd. mgrs. Constantinople Am. Hosp.; dir. Am. Chamber Commerce for the Levant, Constantinople Y.M.C.A. Conglist. Home: Stamford CT Died Apr. 5, 1973.

FOWLER, ARTHUR THOMAS, clergyman; b. Oxford, England, Mar. 1, 1868; s. Frederick Storey and Ann (Ayer) F.; came to America, 1883, naturalized citizen of U.S.; ed. Woodstock (Ont.) Coll., 1887, Western University, Ont., 1888; B.A., Des Moines Coll., 1895, M.A., 1896, D.D., 1902; B.A., M.A., Geneva Coll., ad eundem; Ph.D., Wesleyan University, Ill., 1896; grad. study, University of Chicago, also Mansfield College, Oxford University, D.D., Geneva, 1918; m. Jean Bodenham, May 22, 1890 (died December 5, 1934); children—Herbert Carey, Donald Gordon (dec.), Theodore Austen (dec.); m. 2d, Mrs. Frederick Robert Basley, June 20, 1938. Ordained Bapt. ministry, 1889; pastor Muscatine, Ia., Chicago, Minneapolis, Mount Vernon, N.Y., Orange, N.J., Brooklyn, N.Y., and Lawrence, Mass., 1925-34, North Adams, Mass., 1938; summer preacher, Upper Holloway and Bloomsbury Central chs., London, Eng., 1924-36, Adelaide Pl. and Queens Park ch., Glasgow. Pres. Nat. Bapt. Pastors' Conf., 1919-21; pres. Mt. Vernon, (N.Y.) Ministers' Home Soc. (chmn. finance com.); trustee Am. Bible Union; asso. mem. Am. Museum of Natural History; mem. Bapt. Union of Great Britain and Ireland. Fellow Royal Geog. Soc.; charter mem. Am. Micros. Assn.; mem. A.A.A.S., Amateur Astron. Assn., John Burroughs Memorial Assn., Pi Gamma Mu. Repubican. Mason. Clubs: City, Q" Club (N.Y.). Editorial writer and contbr. to mags. and revs. Home: 502 Main St., Waltham 54 MA*‡

FOWLER, C. LEWIS, college pres.; b. Monroe, N.C., Nov. 17, 1877; s. Thomas Lafayette and Margaret Alice (Riggins) F.; A.B., Furman U., Greenville, S.C., 1904; B.D., Newton Theol. Instn., 1907; attended lectures, U. of Oxford, Eng., Aug., 1907; (hon. A.M., Lexington Coll., Mo., 1911; D.D., 1915; LL.D., U. of Southern Minn., 1917); m. Nancie Clarinda Hunter, of Simpsonville, S.C.; Sept. 6, 1904. Began to preach, 1897; pastor country chs. in N.C., 1897-1901, First Bapt. Ch., Georgetown, Mass., 1904-07; traveled and studied in Europe, May-Sept., 1907; pastor First Bapt. Ch., Clinton, S.C., 1907-11; pres. Lexington (Mo.) Coll. for Young Women., 1911-14, Cox Coll., College Park, Ga., 1914-17, Lanier U., Atlanta, Ga., since June 1917. Chautauqua and lyceum lecturer. Democrat. Author: The Baptism of Our Lord, 1909. Address: 614 Peachtree St., Atlanta GA‡

FOWLER, FREDERICK CURTIS, II, clergyman; b. Denver, Dec. 2, 1901; s. Frederick Curtis and Mary Mulvina (McConnell) F.; A.B., Princeton, 1924, M.A., 1927; B.D., Princeton Sem., 1927; Litt.D., Colorado College, 1937; D.D. (honorary), Burton Coll., 1949; married Anna Williams Bucher, March 14, 1928; children—Mary Mulvina (Mrs. James Zitzman), Reverend Frederick Curtis III, Rosalie Ann (Mrs. Gordon Arnold), and Paul Bucher. Ordained to ministry Presbyterian Ch. U.S.A., 1927; stated supply Woodside Ch., Buck Co., Pa., 1925-27, Hopewell (N.J.) Ch., 1927; minister English Ch., Marietta, Pa., 1927-30, First Ch., Mt. Union, Pa., 1930-36, Knoxville Ch., Pittsburgh, 1936-54, First Church, Duluth, Minn., 1954, 68; vis. prof. Ref. Theol. Sem., Jackson, Miss., 1969. Moderator Pitts. Presbytery, 1947, chmn. ministerial relations, Duluth Presbytery, 1956-59, moderator Presbytery of Duluth, 1967; member of the council, chmn., com. social edn. and action Pa. Synod, 1949-52; del. to Holland, to form World's Evang. Fellowship, 1951, 53, 56, mem. internat. relations commn., 1951-62; member World Relief Commission. Vice chmn. All Am. Conf. Combat Communism, 1950-53; chmn. March of Freedom, 1953-54; chmn. of the Billy Graham Crusade for Pitts. Dir. Christian

Freedom Found., Incorporated, also director Christian Research, Inc., 1962-63, Christian Children's Fund, Inc., 1962-69; chmn. bd. dirs. Nat. Right-to-Work Com., 1965-69; dir. Inst. Applied Citizenship, Protestants and Other Ams. United for Separation Ch. and State. Served as chaplain USNR, Okinawa and Pacific, 1944-46, now ret. Recipient spl. award UN Chaplains' Assn., 1954; Christian Crusade award, 1966; named Distinguished Son of Denver, Colorado, 1959. Member of National Assn. Evangs. (exec. pres. 1950-51, pres. 1950-52, chmn. nat. commn. evang. action 1948-60, member board of directors), Protestants Other Americans United (pres. Pitts. chpt., 1950-53). Am. Legion, Regular Vets. Club: Princeton (N.Y.C.). Author articles religious jours. Frequent broadcaster nat. networks, TV. Home: Elk Park NC Died May 24, 1969; buried Knoxville TN

FOWLER, HARRY ATWOOD, surgeon; b. Boston, Sept. 22, 1872; s. Joseph B. and Elizabeth Nancy (Rollins) F.; S.B., U. of Minn., 1895; U. of Chicago, summer, 1897; M.D., John Hopkins, 1901; m. Mary M. Hahn, June 22, 1904. Practiced at Washington, D.C., from 1903. Fellow Am. Coll. Surgeons; mem. A.M.A., Am. Urological Assn. (sec.), Am. Assn. Genito-Urinary Surgeons, D.C. Med. Assn., Phi Gamma Delta. Republican. Methodist. Clubs: University, Cosmos, Chevy Chase Country. Contbr. to med. jours. on surgical subjects. Retired since 1948. Home: The Shoreham Hotel, Washington DC‡

FOWLER, HELEN FRANCES WOSE (MRS. ALBERT VANN FOWLER), editor; b. Syracuse, N.Y., Apr. 20, 1907; d. Alfred Millard and Mabel (Van de Warker) Wose; A.B., Vassar Coll., 1928; M.A., Tchrs. Coll., Columbia U., 1929; M.A., Syracuse U., 1933; postgrad. Syracuse Law Sch., 1935-36; m. Albert Vann Fowler, June 16, 1937; 1 son, Albert Wose. Co-founding editor lit. quarterly Approach, Rosemont, Pa., 1947-68, mng. editor, 1955-67, editor, pub. Ahab Press., 1947-68; law clk. Legislative Index, Albany, N.Y., 1935-36. Sec.-treas. Phila. Center for Older People, 1950-61, Housing Investment Fund, Inc., 1961-68. Mem. Pa. Acad. Fine Arts, Phila. Mus. Art, Vassar of Phila. Author: (narrative poetry) (with Albert Fowler) Scylla The Beautiful, 1939, Lancastle, 1961, Lion of Judah, 1968. Contbr. articles to mags. Address: Rosemont PA Died Dec. 16, 1968.

FOWLER, LAURENCE HALL, architect; b. Baltimore, County, Md., Sept. 5, 1876; s. David and Mary (Brinkley) F.; A.B., Johns Hopkins, 1898; B.S. in architecture, Columbia, 1902; studied Ecole des Beaux Arts, Paris; m. Mary Josephs, Jan. 1926. Practiced at Baltimore since 1906; architect of Calvert Sch. and the War Memorial, Baltimore, Maryland Hall of Records and State Office Building (asso.) Annapolis, Md. and many private residences. Trustee Baltimore Museum of Art, Municipal Museum of Baltimore. Fellow Am. Inst. Architects; mem. art Commn. of Baltimore City; mem. Municipal Art Soc. (dir.), Md. Hist. Soc. (vice pres.), Delta Phi. Democrat. Episcopalian. Club: West Hamilton St. Home: Baltimore MD Died June 12, 1971.

FOWLER, REX H., lawyer; b. Ottawa, Ill., Aug. 27, 1893; grad. Drake U., 1917. Admitted to Ia. bar, 1917; mem. firm Bradshaw, Fowler, Proctor & Fairgrave, Des Moines. Mem. Am., Ia., Polk County bar assns., Internat. Assn. Ins. Counsel. Office: Des Moines IA Died Oct. 14, 1972; buried Resthaven Cemetery, Des Moines IA

FOWLER, RICHARD LABBITT, naval officer; b. May 13, 1913. Commd. ensign U.S. Navy, 1936, advanced through grades to rear adm., 1964.

FOWLER, WILLIAM EDWARD, mfg. exec.; b. Towanda, Pa., July 14, 1888; s. Jewett C. and Ella (Follmer) F.; B.S. in Civil Engring., Pa. State U., 1909; m. Helen Kerr, Oct. 6, 1915; m. 2d, Martha Bailey Walton, Dec. 17, 1950; 1 son, William Edward. Rodman, Pa. R.R., 1909-13; asst. supt., supt. Paxton Brick, 1913-18; resident engr. Montour R.R. Co., 1918-19, chief engr., 1919-28, gen. supt., 1928-29, v.p., dir., 1933-39; gen. mgr., dir. Pittsburgh, Lisbon & Western R.R. Co., Youngstown, O., 1929-34, pres., 1934-39; gen. mgr., dir. Youngstown & Suburban Ry. Co., 1929-34; pres., dir. Chgo. Short Line Ry. Co., from 1942; gen. traffic mgr. Youngstown Sheet & Tube Co., from 1939, v.p. traffic and purchasing, 1955-58. Guggenheim fellow St. Johns College, 1961-62. Mem. Am. Iron and Steel Inst. Republican. Presbyn. Mason. Clubs: Youngstown, Youngstown Country; Chicago; Duquesne (Pitts.) Home: Youngstown OH Died 1967.

FOX, CHARLES JAMES, lawyer, editor; b. Boston, Mass., Dec. 8, 1877; s. James W. and Ella M. (Gray) F.; ed. univs. of Geneva, Paris (Sorbonne), and Heidelberg, Ph.D., 1901; m. Rosette Marston, of England, Nov. 20, 1901; 1 son, James Marston. Newspaper work, N.Y. City and Washington, D.C., 10 yrs.; prof. polit. science, Pei Yang U., Tientsin, China, 1914-21; organizer, 1918, N. China Star Co., pub. N. China Star (daily). Pres. Tientsin Trust Co. President of Am. Chamber Commerce, Tientsin; del. of Chamber to Conf. on Limitation of Armaments, Washington, D.C., 1921. Formerly officer N.G.D.C. Mem. bar Dist. of Columbia. Progressive Rep. Clubs: University, Nat. Press (Washington, D.C.). Address: 78 Rue Pasteur, Tientsin China‡

FOX, FRANCIS MORTON, clergyman; b. Knox County, Bruceville, Ind., Mar. 1, 1866; s. Daniel and Almyra (Ball) F.; student Vincennes (Ind.) U.; A.B., Wabash Coll., Crawfordsville, Ind., 1889, A.M., 1894, D.D., 1908; grad. McCormick Theol. Sem., 1892; m. Manette Wolfe, Sept. 7, 1893 (died Sept. 1905); m. 2d, Grace Curtis Glenn, Dec. 28, 1908 (died Feb. 14, 1943); 1 daughter, Frances Margaret (Mrs. Robert Lincoln Seitz). Ordained ministry Presbyn. Ch. in U.S.A., 1892; missionary and teacher, N.C., 1892-99; pastor Washington Av. Presbyn. Ch., Terre Haute, Ind., 1899-1905, 3d Presbyn. Ch. Fort Wayne, Ind., 1905-10; pastor and grad. student Ia. State U., 1910-13; sec. of men's work, Presbyn. Ch. in U.S.A., 1913-14; pastor Fullerton Av. Presbyn. Ch., Chicago, Ill., 1914-16, 2d Presbyn. Ch., Springfield, O., 1916-20 Summit Presbyn. Ch., Germantown, Phila., Pa., 1920-30, First Presbyn. Ch., West Palm Beach, Florida, 1930-37, now emeritus; moderator Synod of Fla., Presbyn. Ch. in U.S.A., 1937-38. Served as chaplain 2d Regt., Ind. Nat. Guard, 1909-12. Mem. Soc. of the Four Arts, Palm Beach (mem. ednl. com.), Palm Beach Art League, Narten Gallery and School of Art (pres., mem. bd. dirs., 1947-48), West Palm Beach; dir. vocational guidance, Palm Beach High School, 1931-46; is active in youth movements; founder summer sch. for colored children since 1933. Mem. Phi Gamma Delta. Clubs: Huntingdon Valley Country (Phila.); Kiwanis (Daddy" Florida Key Clubs), West Palm Beach Country. Home: Lake Court Apt. Hotel, West Palm Beach FL‡

FOX, FREDERICK S(HARTLE), editor, publisher; b. Reading, Pa., Oct. 23, 1875; s. Cyrus Taylor and Matilda Shenk (Shartle) F.; grad. m. Alma Camillia Mingle, June 15, 1898; children—Lucile, Henrietta, Caroline (Mrs. G. M. Showalter), Jane (Mrs. Charles W. Mullison). Pres., editor Norristown (Pa.) Herald, Inc. (pub. of Norristown Times Herald), from 1944. Awarded Huguenot Cross, Huguenot Soc. of Pa., 1945. Mem. S.A.R., Patriotic Order of Sons of Am. (past pres.), Pa. German Soc. (treas. and dir.). Lutheran. Mason. Home: Norristown PA Died Nov. 8, 1968; buried Riverside Cemetery, Norristown PA

FOX, HENRY, biologist; b. Germantown, Pa., Feb. 18, 1875; s. William and Elizabeth Ellen (Saylor) F.; B.S. in Biology, U. of Pa., 1899, M.A., 1903, Ph.D., 1905; m. Adelaide Townsend Godfrey, June 27, 1906; 1 dau., Emily Elizabeth (Mrs. George Alfred Clark). Instructor biology, U. of Wis., 1902-03; prof. biology, Temple U., Phila., 1903-05; instr. natural science, Manual Training High Sch., Phila., 1905-07; prof. biology, Ursinus Coll., 1907-12; field investigator U.S. Bureau of Entomology, 1912-18; prof. biology, Mercer U., Macon, Ga., 1918-24; asso. entomologist (Japanese Beetle project), U.S. Bureau Entomology, 1925-36; teaching fellow New York U., 1936-39, 1941-43; instr. in entomol., Brooklyn Coll., 1940, retired since 1943. Fellow A.A.A.S.; mem. Am. Entomol. Soc., Phila. Acad. of Natural Science, N.Y. Entomol. Soc., Sigma Xi; pres. Ga. Soc. Biologists, 1923; sec. Ga. Acad. Sciences, 1922-24. Contbr. on professional topics. Address: R. 1, Cape May Court House NJ‡

FOX, JAMES HAROLD, dean of edn.; b. Florence, Ont., Can., Oct. 23, 1900; s. William George and Mary Anne (Beatty) F.; student London (Ont.) Collegiate Inst., 1914-18; first class teacher's certificate, U. of Toronto, 1919; A.B., U. of Western Ont., London, Can., 1925, A.M., 1926; Ed.M., Harvard, 1936, Ed.D., 1937; m. Evelyn Gertrude Joness, Aug. 6, 1927; children—Margaret Helen, James Harold, Jr. Came to U.S., 1936; naturalized, 1942. High sch. tchr., Delaware, Ont., 1919-22; instr., adminstr. 1922-35; instr. in edn., Colgate U., 1936-37; asso. prof. and sec. of exec. com., sch. of edn., George Washington U., 1937-38, dean sch. of edn., 1938-63, prof. edn., 1942-63. President Central Ontario Secondary School Association, 1935; chmn. Nat. Physical Edn. Com., YMCA, 1955-57. Awarded Bd. Governor's Scholarships, U. Western Ont., 1923, 24, Bursary Nat. Research Council of Can., 1925. Mem. N.E.A., Am. Assn. School Adminstrs., Nat. Assn. Supervision and Curriculum Development, Nat. Assn. Secondary Sch. Prins., Am. Assn. Univ. Profs., A.A.A.S., Phi Delta Kappa, Mason. Co-author (with Chas. E. Bush and Ralph W. Ruffner): School Administration. Home: Arlington VA Died June 25, 1972; buried Nat. Meml. Park Fairfax County VA

FOX, JARED COPELAND, III, clothing exec.; b. Atchison, Kan., Apr. 22, 1901; s. Jared Copeland and Ruth Gwendolyn (Parker) F.; student Kan. U., 1919-20; m. Ethel Randlett Carroll, Jan. 27, 1922; children—Jared Copeland, IV, James Carroll. Sec., asst. to pres., dir. Frank Howard Mfg. Co., Atchinson, 1920-29, gen. mgr., 1920-30; buyer J.C. Penny Co., N.Y. City, 1930-36; pres., dir. Blue Bell, Inc., Greensboro, N.C., 1936-48, chmn. bd., treas., from 1948; pres., dir. Globe Superior Corp., 1937, Commerce Nat. Mfg. Co., 1937. Blue Bell, Mid-South Div., Inc., 1947-51. Chmn. work clothing adv. com. O.P.A., World War II. Mem. Phi Gamma Delta. Episcopalian. Club: Greensboro (N.C.) Country. Home: Greensboro NC Died Aug. 29, 1969.

FOX, JOHN PIERCE, municipal consultant; b. Boston, Nov. 5, 1872; s. George William and Mary Susannah (Poor) F.; A.B., Harvard, 1894; m. Esther Taber, Nov. 11, 1908; 1 dau., Katherine T.; m. 2d, Grace Newton Wallace, Aug. 2, 1927; children—Georgia W., John W. Investigated transit conditions in Am. and in European cities, for the Merchants' Assn., the City Club, and the Rapid Transit R.R. Commn. of New York, and other orgns., cos. and cities, 1899-1908; sanitary expert for Met. Sewerage Commn., New York, 1908, 1909, and for N.Y. City in Passaic Valley Sewer case, 1912; investigated Pittsburgh transit conditions, 1908-09; transit expert to City of Pittsburgh, 1909-11; investigated N.Y. City hosp. bldgs., 1912; reported on transit problems of Montreal, Can., 1912, Brookline, Mass., 1914, Reading, Pa., 1916, Springfield, Mass., 1917; transit expert and consultant on city planning to Bd. of Estimate and Apportionment, New York, 1914-18; with Pub. Utilities Commn., Washington, 1918; transit expert, City of Reading, Pa., 1918-19, City of New York, 1919; consultant on zoning to Newton, Fall River, Norwood, Wellesley, Dedham, Winchester, Arlington, Salem, Malden, Weston, Plymouth, Canton, Beacon Hill Assn. (Boston), Maplewood, N.J., Northport, L.I., Keene and Laconia, N.H., North Smithfield, R.I., and to the restoration of Williamsburg, Va., since 1928. Exec. sec., Murray Hill Assn., New York, since 1914. Mem. Am. Transit Assn., A.A.A.S., Am. Assn. Variable Star Observers, Am. Acad. Polit. and Social Science, Am. Meteorol. Soc. Regional Plan Assn., Citizens' Union, Nat. Pub. Housing Conf. Club: City (sec. since Apr. 1943). Home: 440 Richmond Av., Maplewood, N.J. Address: City Club, 55 W. 44th St., New York NY*‡

FOX, SHERWOOD DEAN, educator, sociologist; b. Canton, Mass., Oct. 29, 1917; s. David S. and Jennie (Berkal) F.; A.B., Harvard, 1939, A.M., 1947, Ph.D., 1952; M.A., U. Ill., 1941; student U. Wis., 1941-42; m. Marcia Seidenbond, Dec. 28, 1942; children—Jane, Jonathan Dean, Deborah. Lectr., instr. sociology N.Y.U., 1947-54; asso. prof. Skidmore Coll., 1954-55; cons. Soc. Applied Anthropology, 1955-56; prof. sociology, chmn. dept. sociology and anthropology Union Coll., Schenectady, 1956-71, chmn. div. soc. scis., 1969-71, dir. Social Research Center, 1959-62. Vice chmn. Council World Understanding, 1960-62; mem. Census Tract Com. Schenectady County, from 1961. Bd. dirs. Community Welfare Council of Schenectady County, v.p., 1960-62, 66-67; pres. Community Welfare Council Schenectady, 1968-69; bd. dirs. Schenectady Community Action Program; chmn. adv. com. Schenectady Human Rights Commn., 1963-65; chmn. com. sociology coll. proficiency exam. program N.Y. State Department of Education. Fellow of the American Sociol. Assn.; mem. American Assn. University Professors, Eastern Sociol. Soc., Soc. Study Social Problems, Soc. Psychol. Study Social Issues. Translator: Education and Sociology (Emile Durkheim), 1956. Died Feb. 24, 1971.

FOY, BYRON CECIL, corporation official; born at Dallas, Tex., June 20, 1893; s. Walter F. and Frances (Smith) F.; student U. of Tex., 1912-16; m. Thelma Chrysler, December 3, 1924 (dec. Aug. 1957); children—Joan Chrysler (Mrs. Raymond French), Cynthia (Mrs. Albert Rupp, Jr.); m. 2d, Virginia Peine Reynolds, Apr. 11, 1961, With Ford Motor Co., Dallas, Balt., Boston, 1916-19; pres. Reo Motor Car Co. of Cal., Los Angeles, 1921-25; v.p. J.H. Thompson Co., Chrysler distbrs., Detroit, 1925-27; v.p. Simons, Stewart & Foy, Chrysler distbrs., N.Y. 1927-29; v.p. Chrysler Corp., Detroit, 1929-46; pres. DeSoto Motor Corp., 1931-42; chmn. bd., pres. Jack & Heintz Precision Inds., Inc., Cleve., 1946-47; dir. Dome Mines, Ltd., Mission Development Co., Exec. officer, jr. lt. Naval Aviation, World War I; lt. col. USAAF, 1943—. Mem. Phi Gamma Delta. Clubs: Turf and Field, Racquet and Tennis, The Creek, Piping Rock (N.Y.C.); Country, Detroit, Detroit Athletic, University (Detroit); Bath and Tennis, Everglades, Seminole Golf (Palm Beach). Home: New York City NY Died Aug. 1970.

FOY, MARY EMILY, b. Los Angeles, Calif.; d. Samuel Calvert and Lucinda (Macy) F.; grad. Los Angeles High Sch., 1879; grad. Los Angeles Normal Sch., 1885. Dem. candidate for presdl. elector, 1912; del. Dem. Nat. Conv., St. Louis, 1916; asso. mem. Nat. Com. of Dem. Nat. Com., 1919-20; del. Dem. Nat. Com., San Francisco, 1920; also mem. Com. on Arrangements for Dem. Nat. Conv., San Francisco, 1920. Episcopalian. Home: 400 San Rafael Av., Pasadena CA‡

FRACKER, STANLEY BLACK, entomologist; b. Ashton, Ia., Apr. 8, 1889; s. George H. and Nettie (Black) F.; A.B., Buena Vista Coll., Storm Lake, Ia., 1910; student Lakeside Lab. of U. of Ia., summer 1909, U. of Mich., 1910-11, Cornell U., summer 1911; M.S., Ia. State Coll. Agr. and Mech. Arts, 1912; Ph.D., U. of Ill., 1914; Sc.D., Buena Vista College, Storm Lake, Ia., 1941; m. Grace E. Parker, Sept. 10, 1914; children—Mrs. Doris F. Hoard, Alice Lorraine (Mrs. Philip A. Randall, Jr.), Janet Marie (Mrs. John S.

Watson). Asst. state nursery insp. Ia., 1912-13; asst., acting, and state entomologist Wis., 1915-34; charge plant disease control. Bur. Entomol. and Plant Quarantine, 1934-42; research coordinator, Agr. Research Adminstrn., U.S. Dept. Agr., 1942-51, assistant to the adminstr., 1951-58; asst. to dir. Office Sci. Personnel, Nat. Acad. Sci., 1959—. Agrl. research cons. Research and Development Bd. Department of Def., 1948-54; mem. govt. patents board, 1950-57; mem. National Forest advisory board, 1950-54; U.S. rep. Internat. Phytopathol. Conf., Hague, Netherlands, 1950; mem. U.S. delegation F.A.O. conf., Washington, 1949, Rome, 1953, 57, F.A.O. council, Rome, 1950, 52; chmn. plant protection com. FAO, Rome, 1955; Washington representative Agricultural Research Administration on research in Alaska, 1948-53. United States representative at quarantine conference, Suva, Fiji, 1951. Recipient distinguished service gold medal and award from Dept. of Agriculture, 1957; Verdienstkreuz Ester Klasse, West Germany, 1959; honor award Orgn. Profl. Employees of Dept. of Agr., 1960. Fellow A.A.A.S., Entomol. Soc. Am.; mem. Am. Assn. Econ. Entomol. (chmn. sect. plant quarantine and inspection, 1935), Entomol. Soc. Washington (pres. 1936), Internat. Entomol. Congress, Orgn. of Professional Employes of Department of Agriculture (president 1935-37), American Phytopathol. Society, Wisconsin State Hort. Society, Potomac River Power Squadron, Sigma Xi, Phi Kappa Phi. Presbyn. Clubs: Cosmos, Fossils (Washington). Author: Classification of Lepidopterous Larvae, 1915. Contributor technical and popular articles on entomology and on prevention of spread of plant diseases and bee diseases to profession jours., Bulls. of Wis. State Dept. of Agr. Yearbook of U.S. Dept. Agr., etc. Home: Washington DC Died June 15, 1971; buried Parklawn, Inc., Rockville MD

FRALEIGH, ARNOLD, educator; born in New York on April 14, 1913; A.B., Cornell U., 1934, LL.B., 1936; grad. student, Columbia, 1946. Admitted to N.Y. bar; asst. counsel for trustee in reorgn. ry. firm, 1937-39; asst. legal adviser Dept. State, Washington, 1946-48, atty., adviser, 1948-51, internat. economist, 1951-55; gen. service counsul, sec. Diplomatic Service, 1955; 1st sec., Tokyo, 1956-60; agt. for U.S. Govt., Japanese Property Commn., Tokyo, 1958-60; diplomatic historian Dept. State, 1961-64; asso. professorial lectr. George Washington U., 1963-73. Home: Falls Church VA Died Feb. 13, 1973.

FRANCE, BEULAH SANFORD, editor, health educator; b. Redding, Conn., Oct. 18, 1891; d. George Turney and Florence May (Hill) Sanford; grad. Centenary Collegiate Inst., 1907, St. Luke's Hosp. Sch. of Nursing and Sloane Hosp. for Women, N.Y.C., 1920; grad. work Columbia, 1921-23, George Peabody Coll., 1925-26, Pratt Inst., 1927; Litt.D., Hartwick Coll., 1961; m. Harry C. France, Mar. 26, 1927; 1 dau., Mrs. Winifred Osborn Carriere. Pub. health nurse, Larchmont, N.Y., 1920-21; S. and W. field supervisor pub. health nurses Met. Life Ins. Co., 1921-26; writing, radio broadcasting N.Y. City Dept. Health, 1930-32; health edn. work E.R. Squibb and Sons, 1932-44; free lance advt.-writing, broadcasting, TV, lecturing, 1934-60; child-care editor Curtis Pub. Co. Country Gentleman (later called Better Farming) until publ. ceased; organizer, conductor child care courses The Brides' Sch. of Sci. Housekeeping, N.Y.C., 1932-42. Lectr. on health and child care before student bodies and women's clubs, 1932-46, R.N. Trustee Centenary Coll. Hackettstown, N.J. Fellow Am. Pub. Health Assn., Royal Society of Health (London, England); member of Pub. Health Association N.Y.C., Maternity Center Assn., League of Women Voters (child welfare chmn. 1930-32), St. Luke's Alumnae Assn. (bus. mgr. bulletin 1930-54), American Nurses Assn., Internat. Council of Nurses. Methodist. Club: Nat. Soc. Daus. and Founders Am., Nat. Soc. Colonial Dames Am., Contbr. on health to mags., U.S., Can., Latin Am., England; column Child Care appears in leading papers six days a week with circulation including U.S., Can., P.I.; editorial dir. Am. Baby Mag., 1940-63, editor emeritus, 1963-71; free lance writer. Author: The Expectant Mother; Your Baby from Birth to One Year; How to Have a Happy Child, 1953; The Expectant Mother Month by Month; Ask Beulah France, R.N.; How To Raise A Healthy Happy Baby, 1964. Address: New York City NY Died Dec. 29, 1971; cremated.

FRANCE, HARRY CLINTON, financial writer, lecturer; b. Richmondville, N.Y., July 17, 1890; s. Julius Henry and Ellen Rocelia (Leonard) F.; A.B., Wesleyan U., 1913; grad. student U. of Pa., 1915-17, Columbia, 1923-25; grad. Sch. of Oratory, Northwestern U., 1918; Litt.D. (honorary), Hartwick College, 1958; Doctor of Pedagogy, Houghton College, 1965; m. Beulah Sanford Osborn on March 26, 1927; 1 stepdaughter, Winifred Osborn Carriere. Rural school teacher, Seward, N.Y., 1908-09; head English dept., Banks Business Coll., Phila., 1915-17; dir. Y.M.C.A. public speaking courses, Chicago, 1917-18; public relations successively with Govt. Loan Orgn. of U.S. Treasury, Guaranty Trust Co., Hamilton Nat. Bank, N.Y. City, 1919-26; sec.-treas. Holmes-France Security Corp., Detroit, 1926-30; financial writer, lecturer, adviser from 1931; lecturer at various times at Columbia, New York U., Wayne U. from 1919; lecturer on finance, Rochester Bus. Inst. from 1943; writer of weekly financial column, from 1933, syndicated Gen. Features Corp.; lectr. Town Hall, and socs., bankers groups, etc. Lecturer (rank of 1st lt.), O.T.C., Camp Joseph E. Johnston, Jacksonville, Fla., June-Dec. 1918. Treas. N.Y. Deaconess Assn.; pres., trustee bd. Ch. of St. Paul and St. Andrew, 1945-46; trustee and treas. N.Y. Sch. of Design. Mem. Beta Theta Pi. Clubs: Faculty (Columbia); Quill (pres. 1945-46) (N.Y.C.). Author: The Ethics of Capitalism Careers in Finance; Making Money with Investments, 1957; Your Financial Security, 1960; Dollars That Grow, 1962; Managing Money, 1966. Home: New York City NY Died Jan. 18, 1972; cremated.

FRANCE, MERVIN B., banker; b. Harlem Springs, O., Mar. 31, 1901; s. William A. and Elizabeth Jane (Atwell) F.; student Ohio State U.; m. Berenice Renkert, Oct. 12, 1927; children—William M., Elizabeth Jane (Mrs. Dunn). Banking and investment dept., Union Trust Co., Pittsburgh; successively asst. vice pres., v.p., 1st v.p., pres., dir., chmn. bd., hon. chmn. Society Nat. Bank of Cleveland; dir. Hunkin-Conkey Constrn. Co., Leaseway Transportation Corporation, Consolidated Foods Corporation. Trustee Mount Union Coll., U. Hosp., Ohio State U. Mem. C. of C. (dir.). Clubs: Old Baldy (Saratoga, Wy.); Union Tavern. Country. Pepper Pike, Hunting Valley Gun (Cleveland, O.), Chagrin Valley Hunt (Cleve.); Rolling Rock (Ligonier, Pa.); Pinnacle, Links (N.Y.C.); Bath (Miami, Fla.). Home: Shaker Heights OH Died Feb. 16, 1970; buried Lakeview Cemetery, Cleveland OH

FRANCIS, ARTHUR J., clergyman; b. Oxford, Eng., Nov. 26, 1874; s. William and Matilda (Wilkins) F.; ed. Wesley Coll. (Winnipeg, Can.), Chicago Theol. Sem.; m. May Carroll Chisholm, of Chicago, Oct. 1, 1902. Ordained Congl. ministry, 1893; pastor Beaconsfield, Salem and Tupper circuits, Manitoba, Can., 1895-7, Shiocton, Wis., 1897, Florence, Wis., 1897-9, Douglas Park Ch., Chicago, 1899-1904, Mayflower Ch., Indianapolis, 1904-6, Madison Av. Ch., Chicago, 1906-10, Pilgrim Ch., Chicago, 1910-17; sec. Chicago Community Trust, Sept., 1916-Sept. 1917; with Am. Red Cross, commn. on publicity, 1918-19, raising funds for Salvation Army and other eleemosynary orgns., 1919-20; with Rep. Nat. Com., part of 1920; now engaged in promotion of various enterprises. Mason (32 deg.). Club: Hamilton. Home: 7341 Yates Av., Chicago IL‡

FRANCIS, CHARLES INGE, lawyer; b. Denton, Tex., Sept. 1, 1893; s. William Byrne and Martha Elizabeth (Melugin) F.; B.A., U. of Tex., 1915, LL.B., 1917, LL.M., 1917; student U. of Mich., summer 1915; m. Adelle Adickes, Dec. 28, 1920; children—Martha, Anne. Admitted to The Texas bar, 1917; mem. firm Weeks, Morrow & Francis, Wichita Falls, 1919-34; member firm Vinson, Elkins, Weems & Francis, Houston, Tex., 1934-50; spl. counsel for State of Tex. in important cases involving oil and gas conservation; dir., counsel to pres. Texas Eastern. Transmission Corp., Houston; dir. Nat. Geophysical Co. Served as instr. Aviation Ground Sch., Austin, Tex., 1918; 2d lt., F.A., U.S. Army, 1918. Spl. asst. to atty. gen. of U.S., 1933-34, 1941, counsel for Petroleum Adminstrv. Bd. (1933-34); spl. consultant to sec. of war, 1940. Expert consultant, Dept. of Interior, 1944. Regent, University of Tex. and chmn. land com., 1929-35; founder and president Texas Law School Foundation. Named outstanding alumnus Law Sch. U. of Tex. 1958. Mem. bd. of trustees, Hockaday School, Dallas. Mem. Am. Bar Assn. (chmn. mineral sect., 1934-35), Houston Chamber of Commerce (director), Houston and Texas bar associations, Bar of Supreme Court of the U.S., American Judicature Soc., Am. Law Institute, Am. Legion, Friars, Chancellors, Beta Theta Pi, Phi Delta Phi. Democrat. Presbyn. Mason (32 deg., K.T., Shriner, Scottish Rite). Clubs: Houston, Bayon, Tejas, River Oaks Country (Houston). Author articles on oil and gas law. A founder Texas Law Review, 1922, asso. editor, 1922-24. Spl. lectr. oil and gas law S. Tex. Sch. Home: Houston TX Died Nov. 11, 1969.

FRANCIS, EDWARD, bacteriologist; b. Shandon, O., Mar. 27, 1872; s. Abner and Martha Ann (Vaughan) Francis; B.S., Ohio State U., 1894; hon. D.Sc., 1933; M.D., U. of Cincinnati, 1897; LL.D., Miami U., 1929; unmarried. In U.S. Pub. Health Service since 1900, asst. surgeon, 1900-05, passed asst. surgeon, 1905-13, surgeon, 1913-30, med. dir. since 1930. Member American Medical Association, Assn. Am. Physicians, Association Military Surgeons, Phi Delta Theta and Sigma Xi fraternities. Awarded gold medal by Am. Med. Assn. for contributions to knowledge of tularaemia, 1928. Republican. Conglist. Author: Tularaemia Francis, 1921, a New Disease of Man. (bull.), 1922; also bulls. and papers on yellow fever, pellagra, tetanus, filariasis, rat-bite fever, undulant fever, relapsing fever, athlete's foot and tularaemia. Address: National Institute of Health, Bethesda MD‡

FRANCIS, G. CHURCHILL, pres. Boston Five Cents Savs. Bank. Address: Boston MA

FRANCIS, KAY, actress; b. Oklahoma City, Okla.; d. Joseph Sprague and Katherine Clinton (Franks) Gibbs; ed. various Catholic and Episcopal schs., and the Katherine Gibbs Secretarial Sch., New York; m. 3d, Kenneth MacKenna, Jan. 17, 1931 (divorced). Formerly pvt. sec. to Charles McAlpin and Emerson MacMillian; began stage career with Basil Sidney, later with Stuart Walker's Co., Cincinnati; appeared in Crime, Amateur Anne, Venus, and Elmer the Great; first screen appearance was in Gentlemen of the Press, made more than 50 films, including: Raffles, I Found Stella Parish, Four Jills in a Jeep. Republican. Episcopalian. Home: Hollywood CA Died Aug. 1968.*

FRANCIS, LEE MASTEN, ophthalmologist; b. Sabinsville, Pa., Oct. 8, 1877; s. Walter Robert and Ida Elizabeth (Masten) F.; grad. Norwalk (Conn.) Mil. Inst., 1894; Ph.B., Cornell U., 1898; M.D., Rush Med. Coll. (U. of Chicago), 1901; post-grad. work, U. of Vienna; m. Ethel Waldron, of Pueblo, Colo., Oct. 28, 1903;children—Lee Masten, Ethelwyne. Practiced at Buffalo, N.Y., since 1904; asst. prof. ophthalmology, U. of Buffalo; pres. med. and surg. staff Buffalo Gen. Hosp.; mem. Am. Bd. for Ophthalmic Examinations; head of ophthalmic service, Base Hosp. 115, A.E.F., World War. Fellow Am. Coll. Surgeons; mem. A.M.A., Am. Acad. Ophthalmology and Oto-Laryngology (sec. 1911-18, pres. 1919-20), Am. Ophthal. Soc., Buffalo Ophthal. Soc. (pres. 1925), Internat. Congress of Ophthalmology (chmn. com. on finance), Cornell Alumni Assn. (ex-pres. Western N.Y. br.), Zeta Psi, Nu Sigma Nu. Republican. Episcopalian. Clubs: Saturn, Buffalo Tennis and Squash, Cherry Hill Country. Author numerous tech. articles relating to the eye. Home: 636 Delaware Av., Buffalo NY‡

FRANCIS, RICHARD J., electronics, fiberglass co. exec.; b. Newark, O., June 10, 1910; s. John W. and Ethel (Brill) F.; Chem. E., U. Cin., 1929-34; m. Clara Elzay, Feb. 4, 1953. Engr. Plaskon div. Libbey-Owens-Ford Glass Co., Toledo, 1940-42; Naval Ordnance Lab., Silver Spring, Md., 1942-44. Owens-Corning Fiberglas, Newark, O., 1944-47; pres. Francis Industries, Pataskala, O., 1956-71; mgr. of Richard J. Francis Assos., cons. engrs., Pataskala, O., 1947-71. Cons. Dept. Def., 1959-60; cons. Asso. Tech. Services Internat., Inc. Recipient 2 Naval Ordnance Devel. Awards, World War II. Named Neb. Adm., Ky. Col., Distinguished Engring. Alumnus, U. Cin., Plastics Pioneer, Soc. Plastics Industry. Fellow Am. Inst. Chemists; mem. Soc. Plastics Engrs. (dir. 1950-56), Soc. Plastics Industry (dir. reinforced plastics div. 1947-55), Am. Ordnance Assn., Sigma Xi, Phi Delta Theta. Alpha Chi Sigma. Methodist. Mason (Shriner). Patentee. Author: Drycleaning Text Book (with J.N. Stinson), 1939; Low-Pressure Laminating of Plastics (with Dr. J. S. Hicks), 1947. Contbr. Ency. Americana, articles tech. Pataskala OH Died Nov. 20, 1971.

FRANCIS, THOMAS, JR., physician, coll. prof.; b. Gas City, Ind., July 15, 1900; s. Thomas and Elizabeth Ann (Cadogan) F.; B.S., Allegheny Coll., 1921; M.D., Yale Univ., 1925, honorary M.S., 1941; honorary Sc.D., Allegheny College, 1941. U. Freiburg (Germany), 1968; m. Dorothy Packard Otton, June 29, 1933; children—Mary Jane, Thomas, 3d. Interne in medicine New Haven (Conn.) Hosp., 1925-26, prof. bacteriology, director bacteriol labs., coll. medicine N.Y.U., vis. physician Third med. div. Bellevue Hosp., 1938-41; vis. physician Willard Parker Hosp., 1940-41; Henry Sewall U. prof. epidemiology and chmn. dept. epidemiology, school public health also prof. epidemiology, med. school U. Mich. 41-69. Mem. Armed Forces Epidemiology Bd. 1955-68 (pres., 1958-60), dir. Influenza Commn. 1941-55; cons. Sec. Def., USPHS, Michigan State Department of Health. Mem. Sci. adv. council Am. Cancer Soc.; dir. Poliomyelitis Vaccine Evaluation Program; bd. sci. advisers, bd. dirs. Jane Coffin Childs Meml. Fund for Med. Research. Member of the Lobound Advisory Board, 1958-69. Served as pvt. S.A.T.C., 1918. Awarded Medal of Freedom, AUS, 1946; Lasker Award, Am. Public Health Assn., 1947; Howard Taylor Ricketts award and medal, U. Chgo., 1952; James D. Bruce Meml. medal A.C.P., 1953; Bristol award Infections Disease Soc., 1969; Kovalenka award Nat. Acad. Sci.; Distinguished Service award Japanese Nat. Inst. Health. Fellow A.A.A.S., Am. Pub. Health Assn. (mem. governing council), Am. Acad. Arts and Scis.; mem. Nat. Acad. Scis. (mem. governing council 1958-61), Soc. Am. Bacteriologists (pres. 1947), Am. Society Clin. Investigation (pres. 1945-46), Assn. Am. Physicians, A.M.A., Harvey Society (sec. 1938-40), N.Y. Acad. Medicine, History of Science Society, Am. Soc. Immunologists, Am. Epidemiol. Soc. (pres. 1954-55), Am. Philos. Soc., Constantinian Soc., N.Y. Acad. Sci., Soc. Exptl. Pathology, Soc., for Experimental Biology and Medicine, Phi Delta Theta, Nu Sigma Nu, Sigma Xi, Alpha Omega Alpha, Delta Omega, Phi Kappa Phi. Club: Cosmos (Washington). Home: Ann Arbor MI Died Oct. 1, 1969; buried Forest Hill Cemetery, Ann Arbor MI

FRANCIS, WILLIAM BATES, ex-congressman; b. Updegraff, O.; m. Julia E. Mitchell, of Mt. Pleasant, O. Admitted to bar, 1889, and since in practice at Martin's Ferry, O. Mem. bd. sch. examiners, 6 yrs.; became mem. bd. edn., 1908; city solicitor, 3 yrs.; mem. 62d and 63d Congresses (1911-15), 16th Ohio Dist.; del. Dem. Nat. Conv., St. Louis, 1904. Address: Martin's Ferry OH‡

FRANCK, CHARLES, corp. exec.; b. Berlin, Germany, Nov. 21, 1881; s. Gustav Franck; grad. high sch.; m. 1912; children—Carl G., Ruth (Mrs. H.A. Van Collie). With Holophane Co., Inc., from 1915, successively exec. v.p., chmn. bd. Mem. Illuminating Engring. Soc. Home: Miami FL Died Jan. 21, 1972.

FRANCOIS, SAMSON, pianist; b. Frankfort (Allemagne), May 18, 1924; s. Maurice Francois; m. Josette Bhariset-Ruffin, June 10, 1954; 1 son, Maximillien. Numerous internat. tours including tour Communist China (1st Western musician to appear since 1949); concert composer, prin. interpretation of Chopin, Debussy, Bach, Mozart, Prokojier, others. Recipient grand prize, Lamoureux Concerts, 1941. Home: Paris France Died Oct. 22, 1970.

FRANDSEN, PETER, biologist; b. Vilslev, Denmark, Sept. 27, 1876; s. Soren Johansen and Lena Maria (Buck) F.; A.B., U. of Nev., 1895, LL.D., 1924; A.B., Harvard, 1898, A.M., 1899; studied abroad, 1909-10; m. Alice Sheldon Moreland, June 10, 1902 (died Mar. 19, 1907); 1 dau., Edith; m. 2d, Jane Elliott Higham, Jan. 1, 1913; 1 son, John H. (dec.). Teacher, pub. schs., 1895-96; asst. in zool., Harvard, 1898-1900, Radcliffe Coll., 1899-1900; asst. prof. zool. and bacteriology, U. of Nev., 1900-02, asso. prof., 1902-03, prof., 1903-06, prof. biology since 1906. Republican. Fellow A.A.A.S.; mem. Phi Kappa Phi, etc. Author of Laboratory Manual of General Zoology, Manual for Physiology, Topical Outlines for General and Personal Hygiene, and various bulls. and articles on biol. subjects. Home: 210 Maple St., Reno NV‡

FRANGES, IVAN, counselor; b. Zagreb, Yugoslavia, Nov. 8, 1899; s. Dr. Oton and Stefanie (Hegedic) F.; Dr. of Law, U. of Zagreb, 1923; student economics U. of Berlin, 1922-23; m. Justine Corby, Dec. 7, 1936. Attache, Ministry of Foreign Affairs, Belgrade, Yugoslavia, 1923-26; attache of legation, Athens, Greece, 1926, Vienna, 1927-29; vice consul, New York, N.Y., 1929; acting consul, San Francisco, Calif., 1930; sec. of legation, Washington, D.C., 1931-36; in Foreign Office, Belgrade, Yugoslavia, 1936-40; counselor, Yugoslav Embassy, London, Eng., 1940-42, Washington, D.C., from 1942, charge d'affaires, July 1944-Mây 2, 1945. Served as capt., arty., Yugoslav Army Reserve. Decorated Chevalier Legion of Honor (France). Clubs: St. James (London), Metropolitan (Washington). Home: Wolfeboro NH Died Mar. 1972.

FRANK, EVERETT, business exec.; b. Paris, Tex., Aug. 12, 1893; s. William and Wilhelmina (Fried) F.; grad. Philips Exeter Acad., 1911; A.B., Princeton 1915; m. Ruth Long, Oct. 17, 1921 (dec. Dec. 1963); children—Everett, Ruth Elizabeth (Mrs. Milton Pelovitz); m. 2d, Alice Crabtree, Feb. 24, 1968. With Nat. City Co., 1915-17, Dillon Read and Co., 1919-30; v.p. and pres. Keswick Corp., 1930-45; chmn. bd. Childs Co. 1947-71. Served with U.S. Army, 1917-19. Clubs: Princeton, City Midday (N.Y.C.). Home: Short Hills NJ Died May 1, 1971.

FRANK, GRAHAM, clergyman; b. Cynthiana, Ky., Mar. 19, 1873; s. Joseph Cone and Sarah (Darnall) F.; A.B., Transylvania Coll., Lexington, Ky., 1896, LL.D., 1930; D.D., Texas Christian U., Ft. Worth, Tex., 1935; grad. study Univ. of Pa., 1900-03; m. Emma G. Lucas, March 9, 1899; 1 dau., Evelyn Bronaugh (Mrs. Wingate B. Moorehead). Ordained ministry Christian (Disciples) Ch., 1897; pastor Nicholasville, Ky., 1897-99, Fulton, Mo., 1900, Phila., Pa., 1900-03. Liberty, Mo., 1903-17, Central Christian Ch., Dallas, Tex., since 1918; gen. sec. Internat. Convention of Disciples of Christ, 1913-46. Member continuation com. World Conf. on Faith and Order. Mem. Sherwood Eddy Seminar for European study, 1925; del. to Universal Conf. on Life and Work, Stockholm, 1925. World Conference on Faith and Order, Lausanne, 1927. Director United Charities, Dallas, Gen. Bd. of Edn. Christian Ch. of Tex.; fraternal del. from Internat. Conv. of Disciples of Christ to Annual Conf. of Chs. of Christ of Great Britain and Ireland, Nottingham, England, 1932; mem. Countinuation Com. World Conf. on Faith and Order; mem. advisory council Am. Bible Soc.; rep. Conglists. and Disciples of Christ at conf. in Utrecht, Holland, to draft constitution of World Council of Churches. Mem. Kappa Sigma. Democrat. Mason (32 deg. K.T., Shriner). Home: 3711 University Blvd., Dallas TX‡

FRANK, LAWRENCE KELSO, educator; b. Cin., Dec. 6, 1890; s. August A. and Grace (Kelso) F.; A.B., Columbia University, 1912; LL.D., Wayne University, 1957; m. Alice D. Bryant, Apr. 14, 1917 (dec. May 1928); children—Lawrence B., Alan, Marjorie; m. 2d, Dorothea Davis, Jan. 5, 1929 (dec. Jan. 1934); children—Harley D., Barbara; m. 3d, Mary Hughes, Jan. 27, 1939; children—Colin, Kevin. With N.Y. Telephone Co., 1913-20; research Laura Spelman Rockefeller Meml., 1923-30, Spelman Fund., 1930-31, Gen. Edn. Bd., 1931-36; v.p. Josiah Macy, Jr., Found., 1936-42; sec. sci. com. Nat. Resources Planning Bd. 1942-43; cons., 1944; dir. Caroline Zachry Inst. Human Devel., 1945-50; mem. bd. leaders N.Y. Ethical Soc., 1949-52; vis. prof. Bennington Coll., 1953, Merrill-Palmer Sch., Detroit, 1953; lectr., dept. planning Mass. Inst. Tech., 1955-57; vis. prof. Mass. Inst. Tech., 1959-60, Brandeis U., 1960-61; Burton lectr. Harvard, 1959. Chmn. internat. prep. commn. Internat. Congress on Mental Hygiene, London, Aug. 1948; mem. Inter-Profl. Com. World Fedn. for Mental Health. Trustee Bank St. College Edn., Wheelock Coll., Boston Floating Hosp. Recipient Lasker award in mental health, 1947, Parents mag. award for outstanding book, 1950. Fellow Am. Orthopsychiat. Assn. (past v.p.), Soc. Research Child Devel. (past chmn.), A.A.A.S., American Academy of Pediatrics (honorary), American Academy of Arts and Sciences; member of the Gerontol. Soc. (past pres.), Nat. Council Family Relations (past pres.), Society for General Systemic Research, Am. Psychological Association, Am. Psychosomatic Soc., Assn. Childhood Edn., Nat. Assn. Mental Health, Soc. Gen. Semantics. Clubs: Faculty (Mass. Inst. Tech.); Cosmos (Washington). Author: Projective Methods, 1948; Society as the Patient, 1950; Nature and Human Nature 1951; How to Be a Modern Leader, 1954; The Conduct of Sex, 1961; On the Importance of Infancy, 1966; (with Ruth Hartley, Robert Goldenson) Understanding Children's Play; Personality Development in Adolescent Girls (with others), 1953; (with Mary Hughes Frank) How to Help Your Child in School, 1950, How to Be a Woman, 1954, Your Adolescent at Home and at School, 1956. Contbr. articles profl. jours. Home: Belmont MA Died Sept. 23, 1968.

FRANK, LAWRENCE LOUIS, foods exec.; b. Milw., Mar. 23, 1887; s. Nathan and Bertha (Adler) F.; student pub. schs. of Milw.; m. Henrietta Van de Kamp, June 28, 1913; children—Richard N., Lorraine (Mrs. Raymond Petitfils). Chmn. bd. Van de Kamp's Holland Dutch Bakers, Inc., Los Angeles, 1915—, Tam O'Shanter Inns. Inc., 1922—, Lawry's—The Prime Rib Restaurant, 1938—, Lawry's Products, Inc., (name now Lawry's Foods, Inc.), 1942—. Pres. Crippled Children's Soc. Los Angeles Co., 1926-52. Rotarian. Home: Pasadena CA Died Sept. 21, 1970; buried Forest Lawn, Los Angeles CA

FRANK, LEWIS CROWN, JR., information exec.; b. Detroit, Oct. 11, 1916; s. Lewis Crown and Laura (Perley) F.; B.A., Am. U., 1938; m. Patricia Murphy, Dec. 14, 1940; children—Patricia, Ellen. Chief for radio Foreign Lang. div. OWI, Washington, 1942-43; asso. editor The New Republic, N.Y.C., 1946; managing editor Women's Med. News Service, N.Y.C., 1962-64; exec. dir. Information Center on Population Problems, N.Y.C., 1964-70; asso. seminar on population and social change, Columbia U., 1965-68. Served with AUS, 1941-42. Mem. Am. Vets. Com. (founding bd. mem. 1943), Adult Edn. Assn. U.S., Nat. Assn. Ednl. Broadcasters, Pi Delta Epsilon. Club: Overseas Press. Author: Paintings and People, 1962; Men, Money and Monuments, 1963; Historic Wall Street, 1963; The Population Factor, 1967; Current Methods of Conception Control, 1966. Editor (with R.E. Shikes) Manual of Practical Political Action, 1945. Speaker on population problems, radio and TV, 1964-68. Home: New York City NY Died Nov. 5, 1970.

FRANK, MAUDE MORRISON, author; b. New York; d. Lewis J. and Ada (Myers) F.; A.B., Hunter Coll., New York, 1899; A.M., Columbia University, 1911. Mem. D.A.R. Author of several textbooks on the study of English; also, Short Plays about Famous Authors, 1915; Great Authors in Their Youth, 1915. Contbr. to mags. on lit. topics. Address: care Brown, Shipley & Co., 123 Pall Mall, London England‡

FRANK, WALTER, lawyer; b. N.Y. City, Feb. 10, 1882; s. Philip and Josephine (Louis) F.; prep. edn., Horace Mann; A.B., Columbia, 1903; LL.B., New York Law Sch., 1905; m. Eva F. Auerbach, Nov. 28, 1915 (died 1932); m. 2d, Adelaide Schulkind, April 22, 1944, Admitted to N.Y. bar, 1905; practiced in N.Y.C. until sr. partner firm Kurzman & Frank. Vice chmn. exec. com. Citizens Union. Mem. nat. bd. Am. Civil Liberties Union; mem. Nat. Consumers League (vice chmn.), Citizens League Indsl. Democracy, 1956. Recipient Citizenship award League for Indsl. Democracy, 1956, citation for exceptional civic service Citizens Union, 1966. Mem. N.Y., N.Y. County, N.Y. State bar assns., Bar Assn. City N.Y., Phi Beta Kappa, Pi Gamma Mu. Home: New York City NY Died Dec. 28, 1969.

FRANKEL, BERNARD LOUIS, lawyer; b. Phila., Jan. 17, 1895; s. Perry and Lulu (Rosenau) F.; A.B., U. Pa., 1916, LL.B., 1920; M. Ruth Leipziger, Dec. 11, 1918; children—Robert Perry, Harriet (Mrs. H. Edward Gross), Margaret (Mrs. Richard P. Kahn). Admitted to Pa. bar, 1920, since practiced in Phila.; mem. firm Fox, Rothschild, O'Brien & Frankel, from 1923. Mem. bd. mgrs. Wistar Inst. Anatomy and Biology; asso. trustee U. Pa.; bd. dirs. Phila. Orch. Assn., Phila. Academy of Music; member board directors, exec. com. Fedn. Jewish Agencies Greater Phila.; bd. dirs., mem. publn. com. Jewish Publn. Soc. Am. Served as ensign USNRF, World War I. Mem. Am., Pa., Phila. bar assns., Phi Beta Kappa Assos. Jewish religion (hon. dir. congregation). Home: Philadelphia PA Died Nov. 23, 1970.

FRANKEL, MAX, organic chemist; b. Czechoslovakia, Oct. 31, 1900; s. Siegfried and Rose (Chajes) F.; student tech. U., U. Vienna; Dr.phil., U. Vienna (Austria), 1923; m. Helen Hammermann, 1930. Asst., Inst. Chemistry, also Inst. Chem. Tech., Vienna U., 1920-24; sr. research chemist Verein fuer Chemische und Metallurgische Produktion, Aussig, Czechoslovakia, 1924-25; faculty Hebrew U., Jerusalem, Israel, 1925-71, prof. organic chemistry, dir. dept., 1953-71. Fellow Chem. Soc. London; mem. Am. Chem. Soc., Chem. Soc. Israel. Author numerous books, monographs and articles on topics in chemistry. Research on amino acids, synthesis of polypeptides, polymers and organometallic compounds, sterochemistry. Home: Jerusalem Israel Died Apr. 27, 1971.

FRANKEL, WILLIAM VICTOR, service corp. exec.; b. N.Y.C., Sept. 3, 1903; s. Louis and Julia (Koch) F.; grad. Hamilton Inst., N.Y.C., 1921; extension student Columbia, 1922-23; m. Selma F. Rentner, Apr. 3, 1930; children—Andrew J., Linda (Mrs. Cahill). Salesman, European Chinaware Co., 1924-26; with Nat. Cleaning Contractors, 1926-66, pres., 1950-64, chmn. bd., 1964-66 (merged into Kinney Nat. Service, Inc. 1966), chmn. bd. Kinney Nat. Service, Inc. (name changed to Warner Communications Inc.), 1966-72. Mem. Exec. Assn. Greater N.Y. (pres. 1953-55). Clubs: Harmonie, Manhattan, Governor's (N.Y.C.); Fairview Country (Greenwich, Conn.); Boca Raton Golf, Boca Rio Golf (Boca Raton, Fla.). Home: New York City NY also Boca Raton FL Died June 30, 1972; buried Westchester Hills, Ardsley NY

FRANKENBERG, THEODORE THOMAS, newspaper man; b. Franklin County, Ohio, Sept. 24, 1877; s. Albert H. and Carrie Louise (Allyn) F.; ed. pub. schs., Columbus, Ohio; m. Mary Edith Bell, of Brownsville, O., Feb. 16, 1909. Sub-editor, Columbus Dispatch, 1898-9; dramatic critic, Columbus Citizen, 1899-03; pub. of Caste, 1901-3; dramatic critic, Ohio State Journal, 1903-7; with Toledo Times, Jan.-July, 1908; staff Ohio State Journal, 1908-16; counselor in publicity, Columbus, 1916—. Lecturer on journalism. Pres. Am. Assn. Coll. News Bureaus. Contbg. editor The Week." Independent Republican. Conglist. Clubs: Nat. Press (Washington); Nat. Arts (New York); Athletic (Columbus). Author: Essentials in Journalism, 1912; The Spectacular Career of Rev. Billy Sunday, 1913; Billy Sunday, His Tabernacles and Sawdust Trails, 1917. Home: 1930 Greenway North. Office: 16 E. Broad St., Columbus OH‡

FRANKLIN, ALFRED, judge; b. Kansas City, Mo., Sept. 30, 1869; s. Benjamin Joseph and Anne Barbour (Johnston) F.; studied and traveled 5 yrs. in Europe and Far East; m. Cora Brill, of Phoenix, Ariz., Feb. 19, 1901. Admitted to bar at Los Angeles, Cal., 1892; asst. U.S. atty. for Ariz. during Pres. Cleveland's administration; mem. Constl. Conv., Ariz.; justice Supreme Court of Ariz. since 1911. Democrat. Odd Fellow. Home: Phoenix AZ‡

FRANKLIN, JAMES HENRY, clergyman, educator; b. Pamplin, Va., May 13, 1872; s. Samuel R. and Mary J. (Burruss) F.; ed. Richmond Coll., Va.; Th.M., Southern Bapt. Theol. Sem., 1898; D.D., U. of Denver, 1909, Brown Univ., 1922; LL.D., U. of Richmond, 1925; m. Augusta Terry, Nov. 15, 1900. Ordained Bapt. ministry, 1896; pastor Leadville, Colo., 1898-1901, Cripple Creek, 1901-04; dist. sec. Am. Bapt. Home Mission Soc., 1904-06; pastor 1st Ch., Colorado Springs, Colo., 1906-12; fgn. sec., Am. Bapt. Foreign Mission Soc., 1912-34; pres. Crozer Theol. Seminary, Chester, Pa., 1934-43; now pres. emeritus Crozer Theol. Sem.; mem. Dept. of Religion, U. of Richmond, 1944-46. Pres. Northern Bapt. Conv., 1935-36. Mem. Internat. Missionary Council, 1921-34; chairman Department International Justice and Good Will, Federal Council Churches of Christ in America. Decorated Legion of Honor (France). Mem. Phi Beta Kappa, Kappa Alpha. Author: In the Track of the Storm; The Never Failing Light; Ministers of Mercy. Address: 6430 Roselawn Rd., Richmond 21 VA‡

FRANKLIN, LUCY JENKINS, dean of women; b. Washington Court House, O., Mar. 7, 1877; d. George Coyner and Mary (McLean) Jenkins; A.B., Ohio Wesleyan U., Delaware, O., 1904, A.M., 1907, L.H.D., 1932; L.H.D., Colby College, 1930; LL.D., State University, Bowling Green, Ohio; student Chicago Sch. of Civics and Philanthropy, 1908, Chicago U., summer 1909, Radcliffe Coll., 1912-13, Columbia, 1919; m. Prof. George Bruce Franklin, Sept. 13, 1910; 1son, Robert Bruce. Teacher, oral English, Latin Ohio Wesleyan U., 1904, instr., later asst. prof., oral English, 1904-10; dean of women and prof. English, Evansville (Ind.) Coll., 1919-24; dean of women Boston U., 1924-45. Dir. war job information center, under auspices of War Manpower Commn. and Am. Assn. Univ. Women. Mem. Mass. Com. of 1000. Mem. corporation board Mass. Hosp. for Women and children; mem. coll. com. and asso. bd. for Christian Colls. in China, Yenching Coll. (Peiping); mem. advisory bd. Womens Ednl. and Indsl. Union; mem. bd. dirs. Mass. Soc. for Univ. Education of Women. Trustee, Emerson College, Boston, since 1948. Mem. Am. Assn. Univ. Women (past pres.; mem. state exec. bd. Mass. div.), Nat. Assn. Deans of Women (editor column in Deans' Mag.), Women Press Assn. of Mass. (hon. v.p.), New England Assn. Colls. and Secondary

Schs., Mass. Social Hygiene Assn. (mem. exec. bd), Huguenot Soc., Phi Beta Kappa, Delta Sigma Rho. Club: College (Boston). Home: 45 Dwight St., Brookline 46, Mass. Office: 146 Commonwealth Av., Boston 16 MA‡

FRANKLIN, MARVIN AUGUSTUS, bishop; b. White County, Ga., June 19, 1894; s. Charles Leonard and Eliza (Ledford) F.; A.B., U. of Ga., 1915; D.D., Birmingham-Southern Coll., 1937, Emory U., 1957; LL.D., Millsaps College, 1952; L.H.D., Lambuth College, 1962; m. Ruth Tuck, Nov. 24, 1915 (dec. July 1952); children—Marvin, Jr., Mary Ruth (Mrs. William W. Jeffries), Robert Leonard, Louise (Mrs. Levi Lawson Wade); m. 2d, Mrs. Fae Luster Lane, Dec. 2, 1953; 1 stepdaughter, Carolyn (Mrs. Lee W. Johnson, Jr.). Licensed to preach, October 1910; ordained minister, Methodist Episcopal Church, South, 1917; pastor Center, Ga., 1911-13, Princeton, Ga., 1914-15, Danielsville, 1916-19, Rockmart, 1920-22, Lawrenceville, 1923-24, Barnesville, 1925-26, Park St. Ch., Atlanta, 1927-30; pastor Riverside Park Ch., Jacksonville, Fla., 1931-34, Highlands Ch., Birmingham, Ala., 1935-48; consecrated bishop Methodist Ch., Columbia, S.C., July 1948; apptd. to Jackson, Miss. area; pres. council of Bishops, Methodist Ch., 1959-60. Member General Conf., M.E. Ch. S., 1938; Gen. Conf., Meth. Ch., 1940, 44, 48, Southeastern Jurisdictional Conf. Meth. Ch., 1940, 44, 48; mem. bd. edn., v.p. radio and film commn., bd. publ. Meth. Ch., 1944-48; mem. World Meth. Council. Past pres. Birmingham Protestant Pastors' Union. Dir. Birmingham Community Chest, 1942-44; member national council, Boy Scouts of America. Mem. bd. trustees Millsaps College (chmn.), Rust Coll., Emory U. Recipient Found. award as man of year in religion 1st Fed. Savs. and Loan Assn. of Jackson and U. Miss., 1962. Mem. Phi Beta Kappa, Theta Phi, Delta Tau Delta, Omicron Delta Kappa, Pi Tau Chi. Independent Democrat. Club: Jackson Country. Contbr. articles to secular and ch. periodicals. Home: Jackson MS Died Aug. 23, 1972; buried Lakewood Meml. Park, Jackson MS

FRANKLIN, SIDNEY ARNOLD, motion picture dir. and producer; b. San Francisco, Calif., Mar. 21, 1893; s. Isadore and Mildred (Morris) F.; ed. San Francisco and Burlingame pub. schs.; m. Ann Denitz, Nov. 11, 1921 (divorced 1934); 1 son, Sidney Arnold; m. 2d, Ruth Helms Nagel, Apr. 12, 1937. With brother Chester M. Franklin, wrote, filmed and edited The Baby, purchased by D. W. Griffith, 1914; with brother, directed Let Katie Do It, Going Straight, Jack and Beanstalk, 1916; director films, 1916-38, producer since 1938, later works include: Command Decision, 1949; The Miniver Story, 1950; Young Bess, 1953; Story of Three Loves, 1953. Recipient Irving Thalberg Memorial award from Academy of Motion Picture Arts and Sciences for outstanding production, Mrs. Miniver, 1942. Member Academy Motion Picture Arts and Sciences, American Society of Cinematographers, Screen Producers' Guild Beverly Hills CA Died May 1972.

FRANKLIN, WALTER SIMONDS, ry. official; b. Ashland, Md., May 24, 1884; s. Walter Simonds and Mary Campbell (Small) F.; A.B., Harvard, 1906; LL.D., University of Pennsylvania, 1950; married Cassandra Morris Small, Dec. 6, 1919; children—William Buel II, Cassandra Small (Mrs. Caspar W. Morris, Jr.). Joined Pa. R.R., 1906, advanced to asst. gen. freight agent; became v.p. Am. Trading Co., N.Y., 1919, later pres.; reentered service of Pa. R.R., 1928, apptd. gen. agt. at Det., 1928, gen. supt. Northwestern div., 1929, asst. to v.p. in charge operation, 1931; pres. Det., Toledo & Ironton R.R. Co., 1929-31; became pres. Wabash Ry. Co. and Ann Arbor R.R. Co., 1931, receiver of both Wabash Ry. and Ann Arbor R.R., 1931-33; v.p. traffic, Pa. R.R. Co., 1933-48, exec. v.p., 1948-49, pres., 1949-54; pres. L.I. R.R. Co., 1950-56, resigned Jan. 1, 1956; dir. Curtis Publishing Co., N. & W. Ry. Co., Detroit, Toledo & Ironton R.R. Co., Wabash R.R. Co., Bell Telephone Co. of Pa., Girard Trust Corn Exchange Bank; trustee Western Savs. Fund Soc. Mem. distrbn. com. The Phila. Found. Trustee Presbyterian Hosp. (Phila.) Capt. to lt. col., Transportation Corps, U.S.A. during World War I. Awarded D.S.M. (U.S.); Chevalier Legion of Honor (France); Distinguished Service Order (Gt. Britain). Mem. Pa. Soc. Cin. Presbyn. Clubs: Harvard (N.Y.C.); Gulph Mills Golf, Merion Cricket, Philadelphia, Harvard (Phila.). Home: Ardmore PA Died Aug. 17, 1972; buried St. David's Ch., Devon PA

FRANTZ, ROBERT BENJAMIN, architect; b. Waynesboro, Pa., Mar. 30, 1894; s. Samuel Ryder and Mary Elizabeth (Benson) F.; B.S., U. Mich., 1917, M.S., 1920; married Sarah L'Estrange Stanley, Mar. 1, 1918; children—Peter Benson, Joan Stanley (Mrs. Frederick Meyer). Practice of architecture in Saginaw, Michigan, 1925-71, specializing in schs., hosps., indsl. and comml. bldgs. Mem. Saginaw Planning Commn., 1926-49, pres., 1942-49; pres. Saginaw Mus. Bd. Dirs.; chmn. Commn. Code of Bldg. Ordinances, 1939. Served as 2d lt. 16th F.A., 4th Div. AEF, 1917-19. Mem. Mich. Bd. Registration for Architects, Profl. Engrs., and Land Surveyors, pres., 1951, 57, 64. Registered by National Council Archtl. Registration Bds. Fellow A.I.A. (pres. Saginaw Valley chpt.); mem. Society of Architectural Historians, Architectural League of N.Y., S.A.R. Conglist. Mason (32 deg.). Clubs: Saginaw MI Died June 14, 1971; buried Green Hill Cemetery, Waynesboro PA

FRANZ, ELMER FRANKLIN, mfg. exec.; b. Cin., Aug. 7, 1903; s. John Michael and Clara Maud (White) F.; A.B., U. Cin., 1925; m. Esther Huppertz, June 21, 1926; children—Yvonne (Mrs. Robert Theodore Herz), Nancy Anne (Mrs. Jules Leonard Langert), Elaine (Mrs. Ray M. Witten). Pub. accountant Ernst & Ernst, 1926-33; asst. comptroller Am. Products Co., 1933-36, Hotel Gibson Corp., Cin., 1935-38; financial adviser Pub. Utilities Commn. of Ohio, Columbus, 1939-42; admitted to Ohio bar, 1943, practiced in Cleve., 1943-49; comptroller Weatherhead Co., Cleve., 1942-49; treas. Eaton Yale & Towne Inc., N.Y.C. 1949-68, v.p., 1958-65, v.p., Cleve., 1965-68; dir. F. E. Davenport Co., Stockwell Loc Inspection Co., J. M. Mossman Co., Eaton Yale & Towne Internat. Inc., Eaton Yale & Towne Credit Corp., Yale Banklock Service Co., Rippowan Devel. Co. Mem. City Council, University Heights, O., 1946-49. Chmn. finance com., 1948-49. C.P.A., Ohio Mem. Financial Execs. Inst., Am. Inst. Accountants, Ohio Soc. C.P.A.'s Am. Mgmt. Assn., Machinery and Allied Products Inst. (chmn. Financial sect.; council technol. advancement). Clubs: Clifton (Lakewood, O.); Clevelander (Cleve.); Pinnacle (N.Y.C.). Home: Rocky River OH Died June 18, 1968; buried Lakewood Park Cemetery, Rocky River OH

FRAPS, GEORGE STRONACH, agrl. chemist; b. Raleigh, N.C., Sept. 9, 1876; s. Anton Wenzel and Margaret Elizabeth Lumley (Stonebanks) F.; B.S., N.C. Coll. of Agr. and Mechanic Arts, 1896; fellow Johns Hopkins, 1898-99, Ph.D., 1899; m. Ellen Hale Saunders, June 17, 1903; children—George Saunders, Mary Brandon Tinns, Richard Benbury Saunders (dec.). Asst. chemist, N.C. Expt. Sta., 1899-1903; asst. prof. chemistry, N.C. Coll. of Agr. and Mechanic Arts, 1899-1903; asst. chemist, 1903-04, asso., 1904-05, chemist, 1905-18, chief Div. of Chemistry, 1918-45, collaborating chemist, 1945-47, Texas Agricultural Experiment Station; associate prof. chemistry, 1903-05, acting prof. 1905-06, asso. prof. agrl. chemistry, 1906-12, Tex. Agrl. and Mech. Coll.; state chemist of Tex., 1904-45. Delegate for U.S. to 1st Internat. Congress of Soil Science, 1927. Fellow A.A.A.S.; member American Chemical Society, Am. Society Agronomy, Assn. Official Agrl. Chemists (pres. 1913), Phi Kappa Phi, Phi Beta Kappa. Episcopalian. Author Principles of Dyeing, 1903; Principles of Agricultural Chemistry, 1913; also over 400 bulls. and articles in science jours. Retired since 1947. Address: College Station TX‡

FRARY, IHNA THAYER, author, lecturer; b. Cleveland, O., April 13, 1873; s. George Spencer and Carrie Augusta (Thayer) F.; student Cleveland Sch. of Art; m. Mabel Amanda Guild, June 2, 1904; children—Spencer Guild, Allan Thayer. Designer, Brooks Household Art Co., Cleveland, 1894-1909, Rorimer-Brooks Studios, Cleveland, 1909-14, ind. designer, 1914-18; asso. ednl. dir. Army Y.M.C.A., Southern Dept., 1918-20; membership and publicity sec., Cleveland Mus. of Art, 1921-45; teacher and lecturer, evening classes, Cleveland Sch. of Art; lecturer, Cleveland Sch. of Architecture, Western Reserve Univ.; lecturer John Huntington Poly. Inst., Cleveland. Member Cleveland Society of Artists (hon.), Am. Inst. of Architects (hon.), Cleveland Mus. of Art, (membership sec. emeritus), Am. Assn. Museums (chmn. membership and publicity com. 2 yrs.), Am. Soc. Archtl. Historians, O. State Archaeol. and Hist. Soc., Am. Fedn. of Arts, Va. Hist. Soc., Western Reserve Hist. Soc. (trustee), Oglebay Inst. (hon. trustee). Republican. Conglist. Mason (Shriner). Clubs: Rowfant (Cleveland) (past fellow, past vice pres., past pres.); University (Winter Park, Fla.). Author: Thomas Jefferson, Architect and Builder, 1931, 1939; Early Homes of Ohio, 1936; Early American Doorways, 1938; They Built the Capitol, 1940; Ohio in Homespun and Calico, 1942. Contbr. numerous articles to various periodicals. Home: 188 Sylvan Blvd., Winter Park, Fla; (summer) Bentleyville Rd., Chagrin Falls OH‡

FRASER, ARTHUR MCNUTT, educator; b. Hamiota, Man., Can., Dec. 29, 1915; s. James Moss and Marie (McNutt) F.; B.A., U. Man., 1945; M.A., Columbia, 1947, Ed.D., 1951; m. Ruth Irvine Gordon, Sept. 12, 1942; children—Loran, Bruce, Susan. Came to U.S., 1949, naturalized, 1966. Asst. prof. Whitworth Coll., Spokane, 1951-54; asso. prof. Howard Coll., Birmingham, Ala., 1954-55; prof., dir. Sch. Music, Montevallo (Ala.) State Coll. Liberal Arts, 1955-63; prof. music, head dept. U. S.C., 1963-72; conductor Huntsville (Ala.) Orch., 1955-59, Columbia Philharmonic Orch., 1964-72. Maj. Canadian Armored Corps, 1942-46. Mem. Music Tchrs. Assn., Am. Symphony Orch. League, Southeastern Choral Conductors Conf. (pres.), Columbia Art Museum, S.C. Arts Commn. (exec. com.). Home: Columbia SC Died Apr. 23, 1972; buried Columbia SC

FRASER, BLAIR, magazine editor; b. Sydney, N.S., Can., Apr. 17, 1909; s. John Hugh and Margaret (Blair) F.; B.A., Acadia U., 1928, D.C.L. (hon.), 1953; m. Jean MacLeod, Sept. 28, 1931; children—John MacLeod, Graham Blair. With newspapers in Montreal, 1929-43; asso. editor, book rev. editor Montreal Gazette, 1940-43; Ottawa editor Maclean's mag., 1943-60, editor-in-chief, Toronto, 1960-62, became overseas editor, London, England, 1962, Ottawa editor, until 1968. Occasional correspondent for magazine on international events; contributor of commentaries to Canadian Broadcasting Corp., BBC. Clubs: Rideau, Ski (Ottawa); University (Montreal); Royal Canadian Yacht (Toronto). Address: Ottawa ON Canada Died May 1968.

FRASER, FRANK EDWIN, N.G. officer; b. Tacoma, Mar. 2, 1895; s. Daniel Joseph and Bertha Orienna (Baker) F.; student LaSalle Extension U., 1922, Royal Inst. Fgn. Affairs, London, Eng., 1943; m. Helen Gladys Mitchell, July 5, 1922; children—Frank Edwin (USAF), Mary Elizabeth (wife of Elmer J. Messer, U.S. Army), William H.M. With tax and accounting div. Kennecott Copper Co., 1929-33; revenue adviser Ariz. Legislature in establishment excise revenue div. Ariz. Tax Commn., 1933-40, dir. excise revenue div., comptroller Ariz. Tax Commn., 1933-40; exec. officer Mil. Dept. of Ariz., 1947-52; adj. gen. Ariz., 1952-58; lt. gen. (ret.); director SSS for Ariz., from 1958; mil. adviser to gov. and state legislature; hon. consul of Luxembourg for Ariz. and N.M. Served as sgt., cav., U.S. Army, 1917-19; served from lt. col. to col., AUS, 1940-46; gen. staff officer Allied Forces, 1942, gen. staff Chief Staff Supreme Allied Command, 1943, mil. govt. officer, liaison to Brit. Army, 1944, chief SHAEF Mission to Luxembourg, dep. chief Mission to Belgium, 1944. Decorated Grand Officer Adolphe of Nassau, Order Couronne du Chene, Croix de Guerre with palm and fourragere (Luxembourg); Legion of Honor, Croix de Guerre with palms, Medal of Verdun, Bronze Liberation Plaque of Metz (France); Comdr. Order of Leopold, Croix de Guerre with palm (Belgium); Order Brit. Empire; Legion of Merit with cluster, Bronze Star Medal, Soldier's Medal (U.S.). Mem. Adjutant's Gen. Assn., Nat. Guard Assn. U.S., Assn. U.S. Army, Am. Legion, Vets. Fgn. Wars, Disabled Am. Vets. Roman Catholic. Elk. Clubs: Phoenix Rotary, Arizona. Address: Sun City AZ Died Mar. 24, 1972.

FRASER, HORACE JOHN, mining geologist; b. Girvin, Sask., Can. Nov. 27, 1905; s. Frederick Brisbin and Jennie (Macklin) F.; B.S., U. Manitoba, 1925, M.S., 1927; M.A., Harvard, 1928, Ph.D., 1930; LL.D., Queens U., 1958; m. Catherine W. Cheek, June 4, 1932; children—Ian Bruce, Malcolm Bradley. Travelling fellow sci. U. Manitoba, 1927-28; instr. econ. geology Harvard, 1928-30, research asso. engring sch., 1931-32; fellow geology NRC, 1930-31; geologist Internat. Nickel Co. Can., 1932-35; asst., asso. prof. Cal. Inst. Tech., cons. mining geologist for various cos., 1935-42; asst. divisional chief ferro alloys Fgn. Econ. Adminstrn., Washington, 1942-45; mgr. Falconbridge Nickel Mines, Ltd., 1945-47, gen. mgr., 1948-57, pres., managing director, 1957-69, director of associate and subsidiary companies; member board directors Canadian Imperial Bank of Commerce, Crown Trust Company, United Accumulative Fund Ltd., McIntyre Porcupine Mines Limited. Chairman of the board Laurentian University, Sudbury, Ont., Canada. Fellow Royal Soc. Can., Geol Soc. Am., Mineral. Soc. Am.; mem. Ontario Mining Assn. (pres. 1953), Canadian Metal Mining Assn. (pres. 1954-56), Am. Inst. Mining, Metall. and Petroleum Engrs., Canadian Inst. Mining and Metall. (pres. 1957), Soc. Econ. Geologists, Assn. Profl. Engrs. Ont., Sigma Xi, Gamma Alpha. Clubs: York, Toronto. Home: Palgrave ON Canada Died Feb. 2, 1969; buried Baltimore, Ont., Canada

FRASER, JOHN FALCONER, clergyman; b. Edinburgh, Scotland, Sept. 27, 1875; s. John and Margaret (Falconer) F.; Brandon (Can.) Coll., 1899-1902; Southern Bapt. Theol. Sem., 1905-08; U. of Chicago, 1909-10; D.D., Franklin (Ind.) Coll.; 1917; m. Mina Rowe, Sept. 12, 1906; 1 son, Donald. Ordained ministry Bapt. Ch., 1905; pastor Muncie, Ind., 1913-20, Louisville, Ky., 1920-26, Central Bapt. Ch., N.Y. City, 1926-33, University Bapt. Church, Baltimore, 1933-45; now retired and serving as minister interim, Nat. Baptist Memorial Ch., Washington, D.C. Pres. Ind. Baptist Conv., 1917-20; pres. Southern N.Y. Bapt. Assn., 1927-28; pres. N.Y. Ministers Conf.; chmn. evangelism com. N.Y. City Baptist Mission Soc. Trustee Bibl. Sem. in New York. Mason (K.T.). Clubs: Quill, Clergy. Home: 274 Carroll St., Brooklyn 31*‡

FRAUENHEIM, GEORGE MEYER, malting co. exec.; b. Buffalo, Sept. 27, 1912; s. Edward E. and Mary (Meyer) F.; student Canisius Coll., 1938. LL.D., 1952; m. Grace Yungbluth, Sept. 1939; children—George M., Susan M., Karen G., Rita M., Robert V., Mary Elizabeth, Kathryn A. With George J. Meyer Malt & Grain Corp., 1933-68, asst. treas., dir., 1939-45, pres., treas., dir., 1945-68, pres., treas., dir. The Frauenheim Corp., 1945-68; dir. Merchants Mut. Ins. Co.; trustee Erie County Savs. Bank. Dir. Nat. Grain Trade Council. Vice pres., mem. bd. Bishop's Com. for Retreats. 1949-68; lay chmn. Cath. Charities of Buffalo, Inc., 1954-68; mem. N.Y. State Bd. Social Welfare, 1955-68; pres. Am. Automobile Assn., 1966-68. Bd. dirs. Boland Found.; chmn. bd. regents Canisins Coll.; adv. bd. Rosary Hill Coll., New Canisius High Sch. Founders.

Decorated Knight of Malta. Knight of St. Gregory. Mem. Buffalo C. of C., Corn Exchange of Buffalo, Master Brewers Assn. Am. Home: Eggertsville NY Died Apr. 1968.

FRAWLEY, JOHN MILAN, pediatrist; b. Sudbury, Ont., Nov. 20, 1891; s. Patrick Sinon and Mary Helen (McGinnis) F.; A.B., U. of Toronto, 1914; M.D., C.M., McGill University, Montreal, 1919; m. Brent Dermody, August 8, 1942. Came to United States, 1923, naturalized, 1930. Began practice medicine, 1919; at Wayne, Alberta, 1919-20, Edinburgh Univ., 1921-22; resident phys. Royal Hosp. for Sick Children, Edinburgh, 1922; fellow in pediatrics, Mayo Foundation, 1923-24; engaged in practice of pediatrics, Fresno, Cal., from 1925; mem. staff Fresno County Hosp., Fresno Community Hosp., Valley children's Hosp. Member of A.A.A.S., American Acad. of Pediatrics, Am. Soc. of Anesthesiologists, 1943-48. Roman Catholic. Clubs: Sunnyside Country, Sequoia. Home: Fresno CA Died Apr. 25, 1969.

FRAWLEY, MICHAEL P., chem. co. exec.; b. Worcester, Mass., Aug. 19, 1902; s. Thomas and Ellen (O'Connor) F.; student Holy Cross Coll., 1920-22, Northeastern U., 1922-24; m. Lillian R. Pettengill, July 5, 1929; 1 dau., Christine. Formerly with Colgate Palmolive Co. as gen. sales mgr. until 1958; exec. v.p., dir. B. T. Babbitt, Inc., N.Y.C., 1958-62, pres., dir., 1962-64. Home: Short Hills NJ Died Oct. 1971.

FRAZER, GEORGE ENFIELD, lawyer; b. Amber, Ia., Feb. 1, 1889; s. George Henry and Alzora (Stephens) F.; A.B., State U. of Ia., 1909; J.D., U. of Wis., 1912; LL.D., Rockford (Ill.) Coll., 1938, Washburn Coll., Topeka, Kan., 1940; D.H.L., Kenyon Coll., 1942; m. Helen James, June 9, 1915; children—Edmund James, George (dec.), Richard Symons. Admitted to Wis. bar, 1912, Ill. bar, 1916; prof. pub. accounting and comptroller, U. of Ill., 1913-15; devised Ill. state financial system, 1917; professorial lectr., U. Chgo., 1917-19; asst. dir. finance, U.S. Army, 1918; gen. counsel to gov. and legislature, reorgn. State of Ohio, 1921; sr. partner, Frazer & Torbet, accountants, N.Y.C. and Chgo., 1917-52; chmn. Nat. Transitads, Inc., 1940-54. Trustee Rockford (Ill.) Coll., Kanyon (O.) Coll. C.P.A., Wis. Mason. Clubs: University, Sunset Ridge Country, Chicago (Chgo.); Accountants (N.Y.); Athenaeum Winnetka IL Died Nov. 6, 1972; buried Christ Church Episcopal Church Yard, Winnetka IL

FRAZER, JOSEPH WASHINGTON, corp. official; b. Nashville, Tenn., Mar. 4, 1892; s. James S. and Mary (Washington) F.; ed. Day Sch., Nashville; Boarding Sch., Hotchkiss, Lakeville, Conn.; Sheffield Scientific Sch., Yale; m. Lucille Frost, November 18, 1914; 1 dau., Aerielle (Mrs. Eric Eweson). Mechanic Packard Motor Car Co., 1912; asst. treas. Gen Motors Acceptance Corp., 1920-23; vice pres., Chrysler Sales Div., Chrysler Corp., 1924-39; president and general manager Willys-Overland Motors, Inc., Jan. 1939-Sept. 1943; chmn., pres. Warren City Mfg. Co., Ohio, 1944-46, chmn. Graham-Paige Corp., N.Y.C. since 1944; pres. Kaiser-Frazer Corp., Willow Run, Mich. 1945-49, vice chmn. bd. 1949-54; chmn. Sterling Engine Co. 1951-54; pres. Standard Uranium Co., 1954; pres. Custer Frazier Corp., N.Y.C., from 1958; chmn. bd. Frazer-Walker Aircraft Corp., N.Y.C., Channelair, Inc., N.Y.C.; pres., chief exec. officer Popell (L.F.) Co., Inc. from 1964. Home: Newport RI Died Aug. 8, 1971.

FRAZIER, CHESTER NORTH, prof. dermatology; b. Portland, Ind., Jan. 27, 1892; s. Luther Melanchthon and Etta (North) F.; student Wooster Coll., 1911-13; B.S., Ind. U., 1915, M.D., 1917; Dr. P.H., John Hopkins, 1947; grad. study U. of Paris, 1927, U. of Munich, 1931; A.M. (honorary) Harvard University, 1948; married Sally Harmon, Aug. 3, 1918; 1 son, Philip North. Asst. in dermatology and syphilology, Ind. U., 1919-22, asso. in dermatology, Peiping (China) Union Med. Coll., 1922-26, asso. prof. dermatology and syphilology, 1927-31, professor, 1932-42, librarian, 1937-11, acting dir., 1939-40; head dermatol. service Hosp. of Peiping Union Med. Coll., 1922-42; asst. vis. physician Johns Hopkins Hosp., 1942; prof. dermatology and syphilol., U. of Tex., 1943-48; Edward Wigglesworth prof. dermatol., Harvard U., since 1948; dermatologist-in-chief John Sealy Hospital, 1942-48; consultant in dermatology, M.D. Anderson Hosp. for Cancer Research, 1944-48; cons. Children's Hospital, Boston, 1948; chief dermatol. service Mass. Gen. Hosp. since 1948; cons. Mass. Eye and Ear Infirmary, Army Med. Library (hon.). Served as 1st lt. med. corps, U.S. Army, 1918-19. Chmn. bd. dirs. Peking (China) Am. Sch., 1927-31; vice pres. Internat. Congress Dermatology and Syphilology, Copenhagen, Denmark, 1930; chmn. United China Relief, Galveston, Tex., 1945-46; nat. consultant in dermatology Wartime Post-grad. Meetings, 1945-46; consultant to surgeon gen., U.S. Army, 1945-46. Diplomate, Am. Board of Dermatology and Syphilology. Fellow A.A.A.S., American College of Physicians; member Soc. Exptl. Biology and Medicine, N.Y. Acad. Sci., Hungarian Dermatol. Soc. (corr. mem.), Soc. Investigative Dermatology (dir.), Mass. Soc. for Social Hygiene (president), Swedish Dermatological Society (corr. mem.). Dallas Acad. Ophthalmology (hon.), Human Genetics Soc., Am. Dermatol. Assn. (corr. mem.). Tex. Acad. of Science, Soc. Investigative Dermatology, Assn. Am. Physicians, Am. Assn. History of Med., Am. Acad. Dermatology and Syphilology, N.E. Dermatol. Society, Am. Venereal Disease Assn., Alpha Omega Alpha. Episcopalian. Clubs: Johns Hopkins (Baltimore, Md.); Harvard (Boston); Peking (China). Mem. bd. editors, Jour. Investigative Dermatology; contbr. articles in Am. and Chinese jours. concerning nutritional dermatoses, cutaneous aspects of vitamin deficiency, sex and immunity to syphilis and mode of action of penicillin. Co-author (with H. C. Li): Racial Variation in Immunity to Syphilis; A Formulary for External Therapy of the Skin (with I. H. Blank). Home: Cambridge MA Died Feb. 14, 1973.

FREAS, HOWARD GEORGE, r.r. exec.; b. Fogelsville, Pa., July 13, 1900; s. Oscar Wilson Edmond and Katie Jemina (George) F.; grad. Allentown (Pa.) Bus. Coll., 1916. Mercersburg Acad., 1921; student U. Nev., 1921-22, U. Cal., 1922; law student La Salle U., 1934-36; m. Adelaide Trygstad, July 3, 1924; children—Howard George (dec.), Ann, Jean, William. Employed Merchant Marine, mines, 1921-22; various positions transportation, Pa., Cal., from 1916; asst. rate expert Cal. State Pub. Utilities Commn., 1928-33., examiner, 1933-35, rate expert, 1935-53; mem. Interstate Commerce Commission, 1953-67, chairman, 1958; asst. to pres. Southern Railway System, from 1967; teacher transportation (land, air), Stanford, 1942-45; cons. U.S. Maritime Commn. Mem. U.S. Nat. Commn., Pan Am. Ry. Congress Assn. Mason. Contbr. articles on transportation and regulation Bethesda MD Died Aug. 23, 1971.

FREASE, DONALD WILLIAM, steel co. exec.; b. Canton, O., Oct. 28, 1897; s. Samuel M. and Nancy J. (Meyers) F.; student pub. schs., Canton; m. Evahlyn A. Schneider, Feb. 20, 1919. Supervisory positions Continental Steel Co., Kokomo, Ind., Superior Sheet Steel Co., Canton, O., 1920-30; works mgr. Youngstown plant Sharon Steel Corp., 1930-34; v.p., gen. mgr. Niles Rolling Mill Co. (O.), 1934-37; v.p. Reeves Steel & Mfg. Co., Dover, O., 1937-47, exec. v.p., 1947-57; pres. Empire Steel Corp., 1947-57, Empire-Reeves Steel Corp., Mansfield, O., 1958-62; chmn. Universal-Cyclops Steel Corp., Bridgeville, Pa., 1958-62; pres., chmn. bd., chief exec. officer Sharon Steel Corp. (Pa.), 1962-68. Served with U.S. Army, 1915-18. Mem. N.A.M. (dir. 1956-58), Am. Legion, Ohio C. of C. (dir. 1953-62), Am. Iron and Steel Inst. Meth. Elk, Mason (32 deg. Shriner). Clubs: Congress Lake (Canton, O.); Union (Cleve.); Westbrook Country (Mansfield, O.); Youngstown (O.) Country; Sharon Country. Home: Dover OH Died July 29, 1968; buried Westlawn Cemetery, Canton OH

FRECHETTE, ANNIE HOWELLS, author; b. Hamilton, O.; d. William Cooper and Mary (Dean) Howells; sister William Dean H. (q.v.); ed. common schs.; m. Achille Frechette, chief translator Dominion House of Commons, June 20, 1877. Was for a time lit. editor Chicago Inter Ocean. Author: On Grandfather's Farm; The Farm's Little People (both for children); also (in collaboration with Count de Premio-Real), Popular Sayings from Old Iberia. Address: Ottawa Canada‡

FREDERICK, ROBERT TRYON, army officer; b. San Francisco, Calif., Mar. 14, 1907; s. Marcus White and Pauline Adelaide (McCurdy) F.; student Staunton (Va.) Mil. Acad., 1923-24; B.S., U.S. Mil. Acad., 1928; grad. Coast Arty. Sch., 1938, Command and Gen. Staff Sch., 1939; m. Ruth Adelaide Harloe, June 9, 1928; children—Jane Adelaide, Anne Tryon. Commd. 2d lt., U.S. Army, 1928; served through the grades to col. in Panama, Canal Zone, Hawaii and U.S.; major gen. since 1944; comdr. 45th Inf. Div. Decorated Distinguished Service Cross with Oak Leaf Cluster, Distinguished Service Medal with Oak Leaf Cluster, Silver Star, Legion of Merit with Oak Leaf Cluster, Bronze Star, Air Medal, Purple Heart with 7 Oak Leaf Clusters, Officer of the Legion of Honor, Croix de Guerre with Palm (France), Distinguished Service Order (Great Britain), Grand Officer Order of St. Charles (Monaco), Liberation Cross of Haakon VII (Norway). Home: Palo Alto CA Died Jan. 1971; buried Presidio Cemetery, San Francisco CA

FREDERIK (CHRISTIAN FREDERIK FRANZ MICHAEL CARL VALDEMAR GEORG), IX, King of Denmark; b. Sorgenfri Palace, nr. Copenhagen, Mar. 11, 1899; son Prince Christian and Princess Alexandrine Auguste; student Danish Naval Acad., 1917-21; baccalaureate, U. of Copenhagen; m. Princess Ingrid of Sweden, May 24, 1935; children—Margrethe, Benedikte, Anne-Marie. Commd. sub-lt., Danish Navy, 1921 and advanced to adm., 1947; comdr. in chief Danish Army, 1947, and Danish Air Force, 1951; served as regent during absence or illness of Christian X; became king, Apr. 1947. Address: Copenhagen Denmark Died Jan. 14, 1972.

FREED, ARTHUR, motion picture producer, composer; b. Charleston, S.C., Sept. 9, 1894; s. Max and Rose (Grossman) F.; grad. Phillips Exeter Acad., 1914; m. Renee Klein, Mar. 14, 1923; 1 dau., Barbara (Mrs. Marvin Saltzman). Producer motion pictures, 1938-70, including Meet Me in St. Louis, 1944, Easter Parade, 1948, On the Town, 1949, Annie Get Your Gun, 1950, Show Boat, 1951, An American in Paris, 1951, Singin' in the Rain, 1952, The Band Wagon, 1953, Brigadoon, 1954, It's Always Fair Weather, 1955, Kismet, 1955, Silk Stockings, 1957, Gigi (Acad. award best motion picture SPG award best theatrical film, Photoplay award most popular picture of yr., Hollywood Fgn. Press award best musical, Downbeat award best musical motion picture), 1958, Bells Are Ringing, 1960, Subterreans, 1960, Light in the Piazza, 1962. Decorated chevalier Legion of Honor (France); recipient Acad. award best motion picture of 1951, An American in Paris; Irving Thalberg Meml. award, 1951; award for superlative and distinguished service to the acad. Acad. Motion Picture Arts and Scis., 1968. Mem. Royal Hort. Soc. (Eng.), A.S.C.A.P., Am. Orchid Soc., Acad. Motion Picture Arts and Scis. (pres. 1963-67). Composer: Temptation, Wedding of the Painted Doll, Broadway Melody, Pagan Love Song, Singin' in the Rain, I Cried for You, Fit as a Fiddle, This Heart of Mine, Coffee Time. Home: Los Angeles CA Died Apr. 1973.

FREEDLANDER, A.L., rubber mfr.; b. Wooster, O., June 6, 1889; s. David Lewis and Anna F.; B.S. in chemistry, Case Sch. of Applied Science, Cleveland, O., 1911; D.Sc. (honorary) Ashland College, 1957; unmarried. Rubber chemist and compounder, development engr., B.F. Goodrich Co., Akron, O., 1911-19; factory mgr. and dir. development research, Dayton (O.) Rubber Mfg. Co., 1919-21, vice pres., asst. gen. mgr. and dir. development, 1921-36, became pres. and gen. mgr., 1936; founder, past chmn. bd. and chief exec. officer later chmn. exec. com. and dir. Dayco Corp., Dayton; 1st pres., founder Copolymer Corp., Baton Rouge; mem. rubber adv. com. RFC, from 1951. Mem. bd. directors of the Dayton Art Institute. Served with the 134th F.A., U.S. Army, 1916-17; rubber consultant to Air Force, 1917-18. Recipient John Pottinger World Trade Award, 1952. Deputy chief, rubber branch, W.P.B., 1941; rubber consultant, 1942-43; consultant and chmn. synthetic tire cord and yarn com. Office of Rubber Dir., W.P.B., from 1943; mem. Rubber Industry adv. com. NPA. Active Dayton Philharmonic Orch. Knighted by Norway, Denmark. Mem. Nat. Mgmt. Assn., Rubber Mfrs. Assn. (past dir.) Am. Chem. Soc., Newcomen Soc. Club: Dayton Foremen's (a founder, 1st pres.). Patentee in field. Home: Dayton OH Died Aug. 4, 1971; buried Mayfield Cemetery, Cleveland OH

FREEDLEY, VINTON, producer; b. Philadelphia, Pa., Nov. 5, 1891; s. Angelo Tillinghast and Ida Welles (Vinton) F.; A.B., Harvard Coll., 1914; LL.B., U. of Pa., 1917; m. Mary Middleton Mitchell, June 7, 1917; children—Vinton, Eleanor Mitchell. Appeared in various plays and musical comedies in N.Y. City in support of Grace George, Lou Tellegen, Valli Valli and other stars, 1917-23; produced 1st play, The New Poor, 1923, 1st musical production, Lady Be Good, by Geo. Gershwin, 1924; later prodns. include: Liliom, Cabin in the Sky, Let's Face It; Theatre U.S.A., Showtime U.S.A., 1949-52, (plays) Funny Face, Hold Everything, Girl Crazy, Anything Goes, Red Hot and Blue, Leave It to Me; owned and operated Alvin Theatre, New York City, 1927-33; chairman Entertainment Committee for Army and Navy, Inc., until July 1, 1941. Served with United States Marine Corps, 1918-19. Dir. League of New York Theatres; hon. pres. Nat. Theatre and Acad., Am. Theatre Wing. President and trustee Actors Fund of America; president Episcopal Actors Guild. Clubs: Racquet and Tennis, Harvard, Lambs (New York). Home: Pomfret CT Died June 5, 1969; buried Christ Church, Pomfret CT

FREEDMAN, EMANUEL R(ALPH), editor; b. York, Pa., Dec. 2, 1910; s. Abe and Anna (Liverant) F.; A.B., Columbia, 1931, Litt.B., 1932; m. Eva Magyar, Apr. 10, 1949; children—Eric, Alix. With The N.Y. Times 1934-—, fgn. news editor 1948-64, asst. mng. editor, 1964-71. Mem. Council on Fgn. Relations. Clubs: Overseas Press, Dutch Treat. Home: New York City NY Died Feb. 1971.

FREELING, SARGENT PRENTISS, lawyer; b. McNairy, Tenn., Jan. 25, 1874; s. John William and Rosa (Cantrell) F.; B.S., Southwestern Bapt. U., Jackson, Tenn., 1894; A.B., Harvard, 1899; unmarried. Admitted to Okla. bar, 1900, and practiced in Shawnee; atty. Pottawatomie County 3 terms; atty. gen. of Okla., Jan. 1915, reelected Nov. 1918, terms; atty. gen. of Okla., Jan. 1915, reelected Nov. 1918, term 4 yrs. Democrat. Baptist. Address: Cotton Exchange Bldg., Oklahoma City OK‡

FREEMAN, CHARLES SEYMOUR, naval officer, retired; b. Nov. 19, 1878; s. Henry Anthony and Margaret Anne (Liston) F.; grad. U.S. Naval Academy, 1900; married Alice Nancy Kimball, Aug. 7, 1909 (deceased August 16, 1943); children—Mildred (wife of Col. K. W. Treacy, U.S. Army), Phyllis (wife of Comdr. R. B. Miller, Med. Corps, U.S. Navy), Kenneth Kimball; married 2d Mrs. Fleet Murdaugh Carney, April 19, 1951. Commissioned ensign United States Navy, and advanced through the grades to vice admiral, June 1942; commander U.S.S. Manchuria, U.S.S. Maui, U.S.S.

Orizaba, World War I; supt. Naval Observatory, 1927-30; comd. U.S. Forces in Cuban waters, 1933-34; comdt. Norfolk Navy Yard, Portsmouth, Va., 1935-37; Submarine Force, U.S. Fleet, 1937-39; mem. Gen. Bd. of Navy, 1939-40; successively comdt. Puget Sound Navy Yard, comdt. 13th Naval Dist., comdr. Northwest Sea Frontier, World War II; ret., 1942; vice president National Economic Council, Inc. Decorated Navy Cross, Legion of Merit. Editor: Review of Pre-War Merchant Shipping in Eastern Waters. Clubs: New York Yacht; Army and Navy (Washington); Army-Navy Country (Arlington); The University. Address: Portsmouth VA Died Feb. 22, 1969; buried Arlington National Cemetery, Arlington VA

FREEMAN, CLAYTON E., retail exec.; b. Essex, Vt., Oct. 26, 1872; s. Melvin and Dorcas (Carpenter) F.; student Adams Acad., 1889; m. Winifred Brownell, June 21, 1899; children—Barbara, Brownell, Dorcas. Stock clerk to mgr., Thomas Long Co., Boston, Mass., 1889-1909; pres. and dir. W.T. Grant Co., New York City, 1909-30, retired as pres.; dir. L. Bamberger & Co., Glen Ridge (N.J.) Trust Co., W.T. Grant Co. Trustee Montclair Art Assn.; dir. bd. Chosen Freeholders, Essex Co., N.J. Conglist. Clubs: Union League (New York City); Down Town (Newark, N.J.); Glen Ridge. Home: 83 Ridgewood Av., Glen Ridge, N.J. Office: 157 Washington St., Newark NJ*‡

FREEMAN, ERNEST BIGELOW, mfr. ventilating apparatus; b. Worcester, Mass., July 12, 1877; s. Andrew S. and Sally (Stowe) F.; B.S., Worcester Poly. Inst., 1901; m. Martha Knapp, 1922. Began as engr., B.F. Sturtevant Co., mfrs. ventilating apparatus, etc., Boston, 1903, becoming gen. mgr., 1908, pres., 1932; pres. and dir. Cooling and Air Conditioning Co., Framingham Foundries Co., B.F. Sturtevant Co., Western Div., Inc., B.F. Sturtevant Co of Canada, Ltd.; v.p. B.F. Sturtevant Co. (Calif.); v.p. and dir. Aerofin Corp. Mem. corp. Northeastern U., Boston, Mass. Mem. Phi Gamma Delta. Republican. Mason. Clubs: University, Algonquin, Cohasset Country (Boston); Brae-Burn Country (Newton). Home: Bald Pate Hill Rd., Newton Centre, Mass. Office: Hyde Park, Boston MA‡

FREEMAN, MONROE EDWARD, army officer; b. Washington, Apr. 1, 1906; s. Edward M. and Grace D. (Studeman) F.; B.S., U. Minn., 1928, M.S., 1929, Ph.D., 1931; m. Christina Gray Clinch, Aug. 30, 1929; children—Mary Gray (Mrs. John B. Kelly), Monroe Edward. Instr. chemistry U. Ariz., 1929-30; asst. prof. bio-chemistry U. Me., 1930-36; research prof. chemistry U. Mass., 1936-45; resident prof. research chemistry, 1945-47; chief chem. Walter Reed Army Inst. Research, 1947-53; asst. chief Med. Service Corps, Office Surgeon Gen., 1950-54; research coordinator Army Gen. Staff, 1953-56; comdg. officer European Research Office, U.S. Army, 1956-60; Advanced Project Research Agy. Office Sec. Def., 1960-61; ret., 1961; dir. Sci. Information Exchange, Smithsonian Instn., 1961-71. Served to maj. AUS, 1942-45, to col. U.S. Army, 1947-61. Decorated Army Commendation medal, Legion of Merit. Fellow Am. Assn. Clin. Chemists (pres. 1954), Am. Bd. Clin. Chemists (bd. dirs. 1958-64); mem. A.A.A.S., Soc. Exptl. Biology and Medicine, Internat. Union Pure and Applied Chemistry, Internat. Commn. Clin. Chemistry (sec. 1958-60, pres. 1960-64), Washington Acad. Medicine, Washington Acad. Sci., Internat. Fedn. Clin. Chemists (pres. 1960-64), Sigma Xi, Delta Upsilon. Episcopalian. Club: Cosmos (Washington). Contbr. profl. jours. Home: Washington DC Died Sept. 16, 1972; buried Arlington Nat. Cemetery.

FREEMAN, RALPH EVANS, economist; b. Guelph, Ont., Can., July 23, 1894; s. John Doliver and Clara Belle (Dakin) F.; student Wyggeston Sch., Leicester, Eng., 1907-11; B.A., McMaster U., Can., 1913, M.A., 1914; postgrad. U. Chgo., 1914-16; B.Litt., Balliol Coll., Oxford, 1921; came to U.S., 1929, naturalized, 1940; m. Iline Gertrude Rose, Sept. 10, 1924 (dec.); m. second, Helen Stuart Corcoran, June 23, 1965. Professor of economics at the University of Western Ontario, 1923-29; with the Otis and Co. Investment Bank, 1929-31; prof. econs. Mass. Inst. Tech., 1932-67, head dept. econ. and social scis., 1932-58; staff economist United Business Service, Boston, 1943-65. Served as lt. Royal F.A., 1916-18, Rhodes Scholar. Mem. Am. Acad. Arts and Scis., American Economics Association, Delta Upsilon. Author: Economics for Canadians; Postwar Economic Trends in the Chestnut Hill MA Died May 12, 1967.

FREEMAN, RICHARD D., chem. co. exec.; b. Panama, C.Z., Sept. 28, 1910; s. Floyd C. and Bernice (Hackenberg) F.; B.S., State U. N.Y. Coll. Forestry at Syracuse, 1933, M.S., 1935; m. Florence Tallmadge, June 30, 1936; children—Richard D., Stuart V., Kayleen E. Devel. chemist Dow Chem. Co., Midland, Mich., 1935-43, asst. dir. labor relations, 1943-48, dir. labor relations, 1948-52, mgr. employee relations, 1952-67, dir. corporate labor relations, 1967-68. Pres., Summer Trails Council Boy Scouts Am., Midland, 1946-49, recipient Silver Beaver award, 1948. Mem. Sci. Research Soc. Am., Nat. Field Archery Assn. (past v.p., past pres.), Sigma Xi, Delta Upsilon, Alpha Chi Sigma, Alpha Phi Omega. Rotarian (past pres. Midland). Patentee in field. Home: Midland MI Died Mar. 24, 1968; buried Midland Cemetery Midland MI

FREEMAN, W(ELDON) WINANS, b. Exeter, Ont., Can., June 8, 1872; s. Asahel Davis and Louisa Ann (Winans) F.; ed. grammar and high schs.; m. Ellen Burrows, 1895. Began, 1889, as stenographer, in office general mgr. Edison Electric Illuminating Co. of Brooklyn, and advanced to v.p. and gen. mgr.; resigned, Jan. 1, 1913; v.p. and gen. mgr. Ala. Power Co., Birmingham; identified with Columbia Gas & Electric Co. and allied interests from 1913; was v.p. same; also chmn. bd. Union Gas & Electric Co. (Cincinnati) and officer or dir. various subsidiaries; pres. Intercontinents Power Co., 1930-34; returned to Columbia Gas & Electric Corp., 1934, vice pres., 1934-45, retired since 1945, now director (Columbia Gas & Electric Corp. now Columbia Gas System, Inc.). Former pres. Assn. Edison Illuminating Cos.; mem. N.Y. Elec. Soc. Clubs: Queen City (Cincinnati), Metropolitan Bankers Church (N.Y.), Lawrence Beach, Rockaway Hunting (L.I., N.Y.). Home: 1 E. 60th St., New York 22. Office: 121 E. 41st St., New York 17‡

FREEMAN, WALTER, neurologist; b. Philadelphia, Pa., Nov. 14, 1895; s. Walter Jackson and Corinne (Keen) F.; A.B., Yale, 1916; M.D., U. of Pa., 1920; grad. study in neurology, Paris and Rome, 1923-24; M.S., Georgetown U., 1929, Ph.D., 1931; diplomate Nat. Bd. Med. Examiners and Am. Bd. Psychiatry and Neurology; m. Marjorie Lorne Franklin, Nov. 3, 1924; children—Marjorie Lorne (Mrs. Donald Canter), Walter Jackson III, Franklin, Paul, William Williams Keen (deceased), Robert Fitz Randolph. Med. practice, Washington, 1926; dir. labs. St. Elizabeths Hosp., Washington, 1924-33; prof. neurology George Washington U., 1927-54; specialist neurology, 1926-72; medical practice, Sunnyvale, Cal., 1961-72. Served as private Medical Corps, U.S. Army, Camp Dix, N.J., summer 1918. Fellow A.M.A. (chmn. sect. nervous and mental diseases 1930-31), Am. Neurol. Assn., Am. Bd. of Psychiatry and Neurology (president 1946-47), Santa Clara County Med. Soc., American Association Neuropathologists (president 1944-45), Philadelphia Neurological Society (pres. 1945), Am. Psychiatric Assn., Med. Soc. Dist. Columbia (president, 1949-50), Academia das Ciencas, Lisbon (corr. mem.); mem. Santa Clara-Monterey Counties Psychiatric Soc. (pres. 1958-59), Royal Medico-Psychol. Assn. (corr. mem.), Sigma Xi. Author: Neuropathology, 1933; Psychosurgery (with J. W. Watts), 1942, also 1950; Psychosurgery and the Self (with M. F. Robinson), 1954; The Psychiatrist, 1967. Contbr. to sci. publs. Home: Los Altos CA Died 1972.

FREEMAN, Y(OUNG) F(RANK), motion picture exec.; b. Greenville, Ga., Dec. 14, 1890; grad. Ga. Sch. Tech., 1910; m. Margaret. Vice pres. prodn., dir. Paramount Pictures, Inc., ret., 1959; chmn. bd. Assn. Motion Picture Producers, 1959-64; dep. chmn. Federal Reserve Bank of San Francisco; dir. Hilton Hotel Corp. Trustee U. So. Cal. Home: La Jolla CA Died Feb. 1969; buried Atlanta GA*

FREESE, JOHN HENRY, lawyer, astronomer, writer; b. Bangor, Me., Mar. 4, 1876; s. Andrew Jackson and Harriet (Langdon) F.; ed. Bangor High Sch. and pvtly., Harvard Coll. 1902, Harvard Law Sch. Asst. clerk Supreme Court Me., 1893-6; observer at Harvard Coll. Observatory in 1901; successfully photographed for the first time a spectrum of lightning at the Harvard Coll. Observatory, giving new data about the elements of the atmosphere; (described in Making of the Universe," Century Mag., Dec., 1902). Contb'r to mags. and newspapers. Mem. Am. Social Science Assn., Delta Upsilon, Harvard Union, S. A. R., S. R., Harvard Club, etc. Home: Bangor, Me. Address: 25 W. 42d St., NY‡

FREESTON, WILLIAM D(ENNEY), ins. co. exec.; b. Camden, N.J., Oct. 30, 1910; s. George Denney and Harriet (Harding) F.; B.S. in Engring., Princeton, 1932; C.E., 1933; m. Dorothy Elizabeth Mirtz, Mar. 1, 1941. With Prudential Ins. Co. Am., Newark, 1933-71, sec., 1961-71, v.p., 1962-71. Pres. N.J. Safety Council. Served to lt. (s.g.) USNR, 1943-45. Mem. N.J. Hist. Soc. (trustee). Clubs: Princeton (N.Y.C.); Norwalk (Conn.) Yacht; Edgartown (Mass.) Yacht; Baltusrol Golf (Springfield, N.J.); Essex (Newark). Home: Bernardsville NJ Died Nov. 19, 1971.

FREIBERGER, ISADORE FRED, banker; b. N.Y.C., Dec. 12, 1879; s. Samuel and Esther F.; A.B., Western Res. U., 1901, H.H.D., 1947; LL.B., Baldwin Wallace Coll., 1904; LL.D., Cleve. Marshall Law Sch., 1958; m. Fannie Fertel, June 9, 1903 (dec.); children—Lloyd Stanton, Ruth Mae Gilbert. Chmn. Forest City Publ. Co.; chmn. bd. Cleve. Plain Dealer; dir. Cleve. Trust Co.; dir. Youghiogheny & Ohio Coal Co., Richman Bros. Co. Bd. overseers Case Western Reserve U. Mem. Cleve. C. of C. (treas. 1926, pres. 1927). Jewish religion. Clubs: Mid-day, Oakwood. Home: Cleveland OH Died Apr. 29, 1969; interred Mayfield Mausoleum.

FREIDIN, JESSE, lawyer; b. N.Y.C., July 27, 1909; s. Sidney J. and Jeanette (Cohen) F.; B.Litt., Rutgers U., 1930; LL.B., Harvard, 1933; m. Doris Wechsler, May 19, 1938; children—John Sidney, Ralph Bauman, Leslie Lillian. Admitted to N.Y. bar, 1934; practice to N.Y.C., 1946-68; mem. firm Poletti, Freidin, Prashker, Feldman & Gartner, 1946-68. Gen. counsel NWLB, 1943-45, pub. mem., 1945; Gartner, 1946-68. Gen. counsel NWLB, 1943-45, pub. mem., 1945; gen. counsel Indsl. Relations Research Assn., 1950-68; asso. counsel spl. legislative com. revision and simplification N.Y. State Constn., 1959; mem. Nat. Labor-Mgmt. Panel, 1963-68; asso. Columbia Faculty Labor Seminar, 1950-68. Bd. dirs. N.Y. World's Fair, 1963. Vice chmn., chmn. exec. com. trustees New Sch. Social Research, N.Y.C., 1962-68; trustee Jewish Guild for Blind. Mem. Am., N.Y. State bar assns., Assn. Bar City N.Y. Clubs: Harvard (N.Y.C.); Century Country (Purchase, N.Y.). Author: Multi-Employer Bargaining, 1949; Arbitration and the Courts, 1952; also articles. Home: New York City NY Died July 17, 1968; buried Linden Hill Cemetery, Brooklyn NY

FREIMAN, HENRY DAVID, physician; b. Phila., Nov. 5, 1913; s. Philip and Gussie Freiman; M.D., U. Pa., 1937; m. Rose Specter, Apr. 18, 1943; children—David, Marc, Harriet. Intern, Mercy Hosp., Altoona, Pa., 1937-38; resident in pathology Grad. Hosp., U. Pa., Phila., 1946-47, student basic course in internal medicine Grad. Sch. Med., 1947-48; resident in medicine Albert Einstein Med. Center No. Div., Phila., 1948-49, adj. dept. gastroenterology, until 1970. Served to maj., M.D., AUS, 1943-46. Diplomate Am. Bd. Internal Medicine. Fellow A.C.P.; mem. A.M.A. Home: Philadelphia PA Died Aug. 17, 1970; buried Roosevelt Meml. Park, Philadelphia PA

FREIMANN, FRANK MICHAEL, mfg. exec.; b. Chicago, June 13, 1909; s. Michael and Magdalena (Deffert) F.; ed. pub. schs.; m. Lorraine Gallagher, Nov. 26, 1936 (div.); children—Mary Danielle, Francine. Pres. Electro-Acoustic Products Co., Ft. Wayne, Ind., 1928-38; exec. v.p. The Magnavox Co., Fort Wayne, 1938-Oct. 1950, pres., dir., 1950-68; pres. The Greenville (Tenn.) Cabinet Co., 1950-68. Fellow Soc. Motion Picture Engrs.; mem. Acoustical Soc. Am., Inst. Radio Engrs., Fort Wayne Musical Soc. (Philharmonic Symphony; pres. 1946-47). Roman Catholic. Home: New York City NY Died Mar. 30, 1968; buried Gate of Heaven, Hawthorn NY

FREITAG, JOSEPH KENDALL, civil engr.; b. New York, Sept. 12, 1869; s. F. D. and Annie F. (Kendall) F.; student U. City of New York, 1886; B.S., U. of Mich., 1890, C.E., 1894; married, 1891. Associated as engr. with Burnham & Root, architects, Chicago, 1890-1; asst. gen. supt. Chicago Expn., 1891-3; asst. engr., Met. Elevated Ry., Chicago, 1893-5; civ. engr. and agt. in bldg. constrn. at Boston, 1895-1907; associated with Hecla Iron Works, Brooklyn, to 1907; now sec. and treas. of the Norfolk Iron Co., Norfolk Downs, Mass. Asso. mem. Am. Soc. C.E.; mem. Loyal Legion, Nat. Fire Protection Assn., British Fire Prevention Com. Author: Architectural Engineering, 1895, 2d edit. (revised and extended), 1901; The Fireproofing of Steel Buildings, 1899; Fire Prevention and Fire Protection, 1912. Contbr. to mags. Address: 166 Devonshire St., Boston‡

FRENCH, EDWARD L(IVINGSTONE), found. exec.; b. Scunthorpe, Eng., Dec. 15, 1916; s. William M. and Elizabeth (Picken) F.; A.B., Ursinus Coll., 1938; M.A., U. Pa., 1947, Ph.D., 1950; m. Jean Parker Wingate, June 27, 1942; children—Elizabeth, Jean, Edward Livingstone. Tchr., Chestnut Hill Acad., 1938-43; chief psychologist Vineland Tng. Sch., 1949-50; dir. psychology and edn. Devereux Schs., 1950-57; trustee Devereux Found., Devon, Pa., 1954-69, pres., 1957-69; pres. Inst. Biochem. and Behavioral Research, 1964-69. Served from pvt. to sgt., AUS, 1943-46. Decorated Bronze Star medal. Fellow A.A.A.S., Soc. Research Child Devel., Am. Assn. Mental Deficiency, Orton Soc., Am. Psychol. Assn., N.Y. Acad. Sci.; member American Management Assn. Author: Child in the Shadows, 1960; How to Help Your Retarded Child, 1967; also articles, chpts. tech. books. Home: Wayne PA

FRENCH, EDWARD SANBORN, railway exec.; b. Portland, Me., Dec. 11, 1883; son of James M. and Carrie (Sanborn) French; A.B., Dartmouth Coll. 1906, A.M. 1935; LL.D., Middlebury College, 1947; married Helen Campbell, December 11, 1911; children—Janet E. (Mrs. Robert S. Gillette), Elizabeth S., Helen C. Connected with B.&M. R.R. since 1906, also served in various capacities with subsidiary lines, pres. B.&M. R.R. and subsidiary and leased lines, 1930-52, chmn. bd. dirs. and exec. com., 1952-55; pres. Me. Central R.R. Co. and subsidiary and leased lines, 1932-52, chmn. bd. dirs. and exec. com., 1952-68; dir. Nat. Life Ins. Co., H.P. Hood & Sons, Inc., Oxford Paper Company, Rock of Ages Corporation. Trustee National Foundation; director of Ascutney Fund, Incorporated; life trustee of Dartmouth College. Fellow Am. Acad. Arts and Scis. Clubs: Union, Algonquin (Boston); The Century Association (New York); Cumberland (Portland, Me.). Home: Springfield VT Died June 9, 1968; buried Woodlawn Cemetery, Rochester VT

FRENCH, HARLEY ELLSWORTH, coll. dean; b. Delphi, Ind., Dec. 7, 1873; s. Charles A. and Mina P. (Fischer) F.; B.A., State Coll. of Wash., Pullman, 1902; M.D., Northwestern U., 1907; M.S., U. of Chicago, 1911; m. Mabel Townsley, Sept. 3, 1910 (died Sept. 29, 1945);children—Mary Margaret, Burton Townsley. Teacher, grammar and high schs., 1893-1900, 1902-03; prof. anatomy and physiology, U. of S.D. Sch. of Medicine, 1907-11; prof. anatomy and dean, U. of N.D. Sch. Med., 1911-47, professor and dean emeritus since 1947; assistant professor anatomy (on leave of absence), U. of Pa., 1925-26. Sec. State Bd. of Health, 1921-23. Mem. A.M.A., N.D. Med. Assn. (pres. 1921-22), N.D. Acad. Sciences, Am. Assn. Anatomists. Nu Sigma Nu, Phi Kappa Phi, Alpha Omega Alpha, Sigma Xi, Phi Beta Kappa. Conglist. Mason. Clubs: Lions International, Fortnightly, Franklin. Contbr. to scientific and med. jours. Home: 316 Hamline St., Grand Forks ND‡

FRENCH, JOHN SHAW, school prin.; b. N. Fayette, Me., July 3, 1873; s. Albert Gallatin and Julia Maria (Wing) F.; A.B., Bowdoin, 1895; fellow in mathematics, Clark U., 1896-98, Ph.D., 1898; m. Jessamine L. Davis, of Worcester, Mass., Aug. 1, 1899; children—Albert Harrison, John Burnham. Prof. mathematics, 1898-1908, head hall master, 1902-08, acting dir., 1901, Jacob Tome Inst., Port Deposit, Md.; prin. Morris Heights Sch., Providence, R.I., 1908-18; exec. sec. to the pres. Clark Coll., 1918-20; sec. and chmn. bd. admission Clark U., 1920-21; prin. New Hampton Literary Inst., since 1922. Examiner in math., Coll. Entrance Exam. Bd., 1902; mem. Rhodes Scholarship Com. for R.I., 1909-18. Mem. Am. Math. Soc., A.A.A.S., Circolo Matematico di Palermo, Theta Delta Chi; fellow Am. Geog. Soc.; pres. Clark U. Alumni Assn., 1912-15, Brown U. Teachers' Assn., 1915; mem. Societe Astronomique de France; corporator Gordon Nash Library. Republican. Conglist. Home: Northwood NH‡

FRENCH, JOHN STEWART, clergyman; b. Jonesboro, Tenn., Dec. 31, 1872; s. John Lee McCarty and Mary (Stewart) F.; student Emory and Henry Coll., 1887-91; D.D., Emory U., 1908; m. Janie Preston Collup, Oct. 2, 1895; children—Allen Crockett, Elizabeth Stewart (Mrs. L.C. Buchanan). Ordained Meth. ministry, 1893; pastor Rural Retreat, Va., 1893. Liberty Hill, Va., 1894, Pocahontas, Va., 1894-97, Tazewell, Va., 1897-1900, Abingdon, Va., 1901, Centenary Ch., Chattanooga, Tenn., 1902-06, First Ch., Atlanta, Ga., 1906-10, McKendree Ch., Nashville, Tenn., 1910-14, State Street Ch., Bristol, 1914-16, Church Street Ch., Knoxville, Tenn., 1916-20 (part time on leave in France); pres. of Emory and Henry, and Martha Washington Colleges, 1919-22; pastor Knoxville Dist., 1922-23, State Street, Bristol, 1923-30, First Ch., Memphis, 1930-31, Highlands Ch., Birmingham, Ala., 1931-34, Riverside Park Ch., Jacksonville, Fla., 1934-36, State Street Ch., Bristol, since 1936. Mem. Judicial Council (Supreme Ct.) of Methodist Ch. since 1934. Served as regional sec., Y.M.C.A., Brest, France, 1918-19. Trustee Emory U., Emory and Henry Coll. Mem. Internat. Soc. of Theta Phi, Sigma Alpha Epsilon. Democrat. Mason, K.P. Club: Kiwanis (Bristol, Va.-Tenn.). Contbr. to mags. Home: 1151 Holston Av., Bristol TN*‡

FRENCH, ROY LAVERNE, journalism educator; b. Eureka, Kan., Aug. 6, 1888; s. Albert Lord and Cora Alice (Emmerson) F.; A.B., U. of Wis., 1923, M.A., 1924; Oberlander Trust fellow with study of newspapers in Germany, 1936; m. Una Odetta Meredith, Sept. 22, 1917. Instr. Sch. of Journalism, U. of Wis., 1923-24; organizer and head of dept. of journalism, Univ. of N.D., 1924-27; chmn. and organizer of dept. of journalism, U. of Southern Calif., 1927-33, dir. Sch. Journalism, 1933-53. Served as private, A.E.F. (wounded in action), 1918-19, wearer of the Purple Heart. Major A.C., 1942, on duty with 8th Bomber command hdqrs. in England, as specialist in bomber raid reporting. Intelligence Sect., 1942-43, with hdqrs. of 2d Air Force, as instr. combat intelligence, 1943-44. Vice pres. The Chalfant Press, Inc., printing the only newspapers in eastern Calif.; Inyo Independent, Inyo Register, The Owens Valley Progress-Citizen, Bridgeport Chronicle-Union. Mem. Calif. Newspaper Pubs. Assn., Assn. for Education in Journalism, National Collegiate Players, Live Oaks Tennis Assn., Am. Inst. Journalists (treas.), Assn. Accredited Schs. and Depts. Journalism (v.p.), Sigma Delta Chi (nat. pres., 1926-27), Theta Delta Chi, Phi Kappa Phi. Clubs: Greater Los Angeles Press. Home: Alhambra CA Died Mar. 23, 1968; buried San Gabriel Cemetery, San Gabriel CA

FRENCH, WILLIAM W., JR., business exec.; b. Birmingham, Ala., Oct. 1, 1900; s. William W. and Jane (Van Hoose) F.; B.S., Ala. Poly. Inst., 1920; m. Anna McLester, Oct. 22, 1927; children—Ada, William, Anna, James. With Moore Handley Hardware Co., Inc., Birmingham, from 1922, became v.p., dir., 1941, pres. from 1947, chmn. bd., 1969-70; pres. Pelham Corp.; member of the bd. of directors First National Bank, Birmingham, Jefferson Fed. Bldg. & Loan Co. Served with U.S. Army, 1942-45. Mem. Birmingham Chamber of Commerce, Associated Industries Ala. (mem. exec. com.). Clubs: Mountain Brook, Redstone, Rotary, Birmingham Country, Relay House, The Club. Home: Pelham AL Died Oct. 27, 1970; buried Birmingham AL

FRESEMAN, WILLIAM LANGFITT, engring. exec.; b. Pitts., Dec. 1, 1901; s. William Luther and Irma L. (Gunther) F.; B.S., U.S. Naval Acad., 1922; M.S., Harvard, 1929; certificate, U.S. Naval War Coll., 1935; m. Barbara Rice, Aug. 8, 1947. Enlisted as midshipman, USN, 1918, advancing through ranks to rear adm., 1947; dir. Radar Research Lab., Univ. Miami, 1951-57; dir. Internat. Tel. & Tel. Corp. Projects Group, also v.p. Internat. Standard Engring., Inc., 1957-61; asst. to pres. Radio Engring. Labs., Inc., 1961—; asst. to exec. v.p. Dynamics Corp. Am., 1963—. Decorated Legion of Merit with gold star, Bronze Star; War Medal (Brazil); Croix de Guerre (France). Fellow Radio Club Am.; mem. Navy League of the United States, I.E.E.E., United States Naval Inst., Armed Forces Communication and Electronic Assn. (nat. v.p.), Am. Humane Soc. Clubs: University Yacht (Miami); Army-Navy Country (Arlington, Va.). Author: (with others), Radar Meteorology, 1955. Patentee electronic devices. Home: New York City NY Died Jan. 1971.

FREY, ERWIN MORTIMER, public relations counselor; b. N.Y.C., June 30, 1906; s. Daniel and Deborah (Steinberg) F.; B.A., Dreyton Coll., 1925, M.A., 1926; m. Mary Kraft, Sept. 14, 1954. Writer, King Features, 1926; partner Frey, Rocke, Assos., 1926-29, Erwin M. Frey & Affiliates, 1929-31; exec. v.p. Denson-Frey & Affiliates, 1931-36, pres., 1963-69 (all N.Y.C.). Pres., Better Packaging Adv. Council, 1937-69, Am. Hobby Fedn., 1936-69; chmn. Systems Council, 1959-69; cons. in fields of packaging, food, bldg. supplies, home furnishings, others. Mem. Sales Exec. Club N.Y., Am. Soc. Assn. Execs., N.Y. Soc. Trade Execs. Club: Overseas Press (N.Y.C.). Address: New York City NY Died Apr. 16, 1969; buried Ferncliff Cemetery Hartsdale NY

FREY, JOHN WEAVER, educator; b. Depue, Ill., Mar. 8, 1889; s. Frank and Emily (Griffith) F.; B.S., U. Chgo., 1919; student London (Eng.) Sch. Econs., 1922-23; Ph.D., U. Wis., 1926; m. Quinta E. Jensen, May 30, 1928; 1 dau., Elizabeth Ann (Mrs. Leslie H. Rushton). Faculty geology-geography U. Wis., 1920-28; chief petroleum sect. Bur. Fgn. and Domestic Commerce, 1928-33; marketing adviser NRA, 1933; mem. Petroleum Adminstrv. Bd., 1933-36; asso. dir. petroleum conservation div. Dept. Interior, 1936-41; dir. marketing Petroleum Adminstrn. War. 1941-42, spl. asst. to dep. adminstr., 1942-46; dir. marketing Am. Petroleum Inst., 1947-54; chief oil and gas extraction Bur. Census, 1955-56; chmn. dept. geology and geography Am. U., 1957-61, prof., 1961-62, prof. emeritus, 1962-71. Mem. vol. com. petroleum econs. Fed. Oil Conservation Bd., 1931, chmn., 1932; mem. energy resources com. Nat. Resources Com., 1938-42. Mem. Am. Assn. Geographers, 25 Yr. Club of Petroleum Industry, Sigma Xi, Acacia. Mason. Club: Cosmos (Washington). Contbr. profl. jours. Co-author: World Geography of Petroleum, 1950; Mineral Resources of the World, Atlas of World's Resources, 1952; Economic Geography of Industrial Material, 1956. Co-editor: History of the Petroleum Industry for War, 1946. Home: Washington DC Died Dec. 13, 1971; buried Gettysburg Nat. Cemetery, Gettysburg PA

FRICK, PHILIP LOUIS, clergyman; b. Denver, Colo., Jan. 20, 1874; s. Conrad and Fredericka (Hecken) F.; A.B., U. of Denver, 1897; S.T.B., Boston U. of Sch. of Theology, 1901; studied abroad, 1901-02; Ph.D., Boston U., 1905; D.D., Denver U., 1910; m. Ruth Rishell, of Boston, Oct. 1, 1902; 1 dau., Elizabeth (Mrs. Hugh R. McKean). Ordained ministry M.E. Ch., 1902; pastorates, Westfield, Mass., 1907-1912, Delaware Av. M.E. Ch., Buffalo, 1913-17, First M.E. Ch., Schenectady, N.Y., 1921-29, First M.E. Ch., Cohoes, N.Y., since 1930. Pres. N.Y. State Council of Chs. Del. to M.E. Gen. Conf., 1916, 24, 28. Mem. Beta Theta Pi. Ind. Republican. Mason (Grand Chaplain New York State Grand Lodge). Author: The Resurrection and Paul's Argument, 1912; Flood Tide and Other Verses, 1925; numerous hymns, poems. Contbr. to religious jours.; frequent lecturer of religious, economic and literary subjects. Home: 3 Roosevelt Boul., Cohoes NY‡

FRIED, GEORGE, master mariner; b. Worcester, Mass., Aug. 10, 1877; s. John and Augusta F.; educated pub. schs., Worcester; m. Laura Parmenter, of Cincinnati, O., Mar. 21, 1922. Served in U.S. Army, Spanish-Am. War, 1898; with U.S. Navy, 1900-18; capt. S.S. President Roosevelt; widely known for rescue of crew of British steamer Antinoe in a great storm on the Atlantic, Jan. 1926; rescued entire crew of Italian steamer Florida, Jan. 1929; comdr. S.S. Washington; now supervising insp., Bureau of Navigation and Steamboat Inspection, U.S. Dept. of Commerce. Mem. Neptune Assn., Spanish War Vets., Am. Legion, Lions Club. Protestant. Mason. Home: 516 Caligula Av., Coral Gables, FL Office: 45 Broadway, New York NY‡

FRIEDMAN, MOSES, educator; b. Cincinnati, June 25, 1874; grad. Tech. Sch. of U. of Cincinnati, 1899; studied U. of Cincinnati, U. of Cal.; (hon. M.A., Dickinson Coll., Pa., 1911; Litt.D., Univ. of Pittsburgh, 1913); m. Mary Buford, d. late Gen. Green Clay Smith, of Ky., 1906. Teacher Cincinnati private schs., 1897-1901, Phoenix Indian Sch., Ariz., 1900-4; organized industrial training in Philippines, 1904-6; asst. supt., Haskell Inst., Lawrence, Kan., 1906-8; supt. U.S. Indian Sch., Carlisle, Pa., Apr., 1908-14. An expert in industrial edn.; former editor of the Red Man," official mag. of the Indian Service; author of numerous pamphlets and articles on ednl. subjects. Mem. N.E.A., A.A.A.S., Am. Soc. Promotion Industrial Edn., Am. Civic Assn. (councilor), Internat. Longfellow Soc., etc. Supt. The Anchor Ranch School for Defective Boys, Buckman, N.M., under apptmt. Supreme Court of N.Y., 1915-21; supt. U.S. Vocational Sch., Pocono Pines, Pa., since 1921. Address: Pocono Pines PA‡

FRIEDMAN, SAMUEL, physician; b. Poland, Oct. 3, 1906; s. Maurice and Anna (Litwin) F.; M.D., Boston U., 1931; m. Jane Elizabeth Oltman, Sept. 3, 1937; 1 dau., Judith. Intern. Boston City Hosp., 1931-32, Providence City Hosp., 1933; asst. physician N.H. State Hosp.; asst. physician, sr. physician, clin. dir. Fairfield State Hosp., Newtown, Conn., 1939-42, 46-48, asst. supt., 1948-70; lectr. psychiatry Yale, 1955-70. Served with M.C., AUS, 1942-46. Diplomate Am. Bd. Psychiatry and Neurology. Mem. Am. Psychiat. Assn. Contbr. articles to med. jours. Home: Vienna VA Died May 9, 1970; buried Newtown CT

FRIEDMAN, WILLIAM FREDERICK, cryptologist; b. Kishinev, Russia, Sept. 24, 1891; s. Frederick and Rosa (Trust) F.; brought to U.S. 1893; B.S., Cornell U., 1914, grad. study, 1914-15; m. Elizabeth Smith, May 21, 1917; children—Barbara, John Ramsay. Asst. dept. genetics Cornell U., 1913-15; field asst. Sta. Exptl. Evolution, Carnegie Inst., 1913-14; dir. dept. genetics Riverbank Labs., Geneva, Ill., 1915-18, dir. dept. ciphers, 1917-21; chief cryptanalyst War Dept., Washington, 1921-47; chief Signal Intelligence Service, 1930-40; dir. communications research Army Security Agy., 1942-49; chief tech. div. Armed Forces Security Agy., 1949-50, chief tech. cons. 1950-52; spl. asst. to the dir. Nat. Security Agy. 1953-55; cryptologist Dept. Def., 1947-55, cons., 1955-69; cryptologic cons., lectr. Armed Forces Service Schools and RCA, Washington, D.C.; member sci. 100,000 Congressional award for cryptologic inventions and patents, 1956; Medal for Merit, 1946; National Security medal, 1955; War Dept. Exceptional Service award, 1944; (with wife) Fifth Annual award Am. Shakespeare Festival Theatre and Acad. Served as 1st lt. mil. intelligence, U.S. Army, 1918-19; capt. Signal Corps Res., 1924-26, maj., 1926-36, lt. col., 1936-51. Mem. Sigma Xi. Clubs: Cosmos, Ft. Lesley J. McNair Officers' (Washington). Author War Dept. publs.; (with wife) The Shakespearean Ciphers Examined (May 1958 selection Readers' Subscription; lit. prize Folger Shakespeare Library 1955). Contbr. sci. and lit. jours., encys. Inventor many cryptographic devices and machinery. Home: Washington DC Died Nov. 12, 1969; buried Arlington National Cemetery, Arlington VA

FRIEDMANN, WOLFGANG GASTON, educator; b. Berlin, Germany, Jan. 25, 1907; s. Leonhard and Anna (Kapferer) F.; LL.D., U. London, 1947; Dr. jur., U. Berlin, 1930; LL.M., U. Melbourne, 1948; Barrister-at-law, Middle Temple, London, 1944; m. May Lewis, Jan. 9, 1937; children—Anthony, John Peter, Martin. Reader in law U. London, 1938-47; prof. pub. law U. Melbourne, 1947-50; prof. law U. Toronto, 1950-55; prof. internat. law, dir. internat. legal research Columbia, 1935-72. Vis. prof. U. Paris (France), 1968-69, gen. course, pub. internat. law Hague Acad. Internat. Law, 1969-72; Tagore law profl., Calcutta, 1970; cons. FAO, 1971. Mem. Am. Acad. Arts and Scis., Am. Soc. Internat. Law (bd. editors), Modern Law Rev. (bd. dirs.). Author: Crisis of National State 1943; Allied Military Government of Germany, 1947; Australian Adminstrative Law, 2d edit., 1962; (with D.G. Benjafield) Law and Social Change in Contemporary Britain, 1951; Legal Theory, 5th edit., 1967; Introduction to World Politics, 5th edit., 1965; Law in a Changing Society, 1959, 2d edit., 1971; The Changing Structure of International Law, 1964; Recht und Sozialev Wandel, 1969; De l'Efficacite des Institutions Internationales, 1970; (with Belguin) Joint International Business Ventures With Developing Countries, 1971. Editor: The Pub. Corp., 1954-72, Matrimonial Property, 1955, Anti-trust Laws, 1956, (with R.C. Pugh) Legal Aspects of Foreign Investment, 1959; (with Kalmanoff) Joint International Business Ventures, 1961; (with Kalmanoff and Meagher) International Financial Aid, 1966; (with Garner) Government Enterprises, 1970. 1969. Home: North Salem NY Died Sept. 20, 1972; buried North Salem NY

FRIEL, HENRY CRAIG, r.r. exec., lawyer; b. Dorchester, N.B., Can., Nov. 6, 1901; s. James and Maud Louise (Wetmore) F.; student St. Mary's Coll., Halifax, N.S.,; B.A., St. Francis Xavier U., Antigonish, N.S., 1922; LL.B., Dalhousie U., 1925; m. Margaret Laughton Johnson, Sept. 25, 1947; children—Kenneth James, Marylyn Elizabeth, Sean Johnson. Admitted to N.B. bar, 1925, apptd. Queen's Counsel, 1943; with Messrs. Friel & Friel, Moncton, N.B., 1925-43; regional counsel Canadian Nat. Rys., Moncton, N.B., 1943-45; gen. solicitor, Montreal, Que., 1945-56, gen. counsel, 1956-57, v.p., gen. counsel, 1958-61, vice president for law, 1961-66, tax counsel, from 1967; gen. counsel Air Canada, Montreal, 1958-66. Director St. Mary's Hosp. Mem. Canadian Bar Assn., Barristers' Soc. N.B. K.C. Clubs: St. James (Montreal); Moncton City. Home: Hampstead PQ Canada Died Oct. 3, 1971; buried Cup Pele, NB Canada

FRIELDS, EVA CHRISTINE, school management; b. Tullahoma, Tenn., Apr. 8, 1873; d. Robert Neal and Elizabeth Ann (Wren) Polk; student Ohio Northern U., Ada, O., summers 1893-94; grad. Chicago Training Sch., 1895; m. Prof. Charles Otho Frields, of Ohio Northern U., Dec. 24, 1896 (died Jan. 8, 1899). Teacher pub. schs., Champaign Co., O., 1890-94; superintendent deaconess work, M.E. Ch., Fall River, Mass., 1899-1912; established Girls Industrial Home and Sch. of Domestic Science, Fall River, Mass., Rest Home for Working Girls, Martha's Vineyard, Mass.; supt. Chaddock Boys Sch., Quincy, Ill., since 1912 (25th anniversary celebrated May 1937); also member board trustees. Mem. Alumni Assn. Chicago Training Sch. (pres. 1925-29), Pi Gamma Mu. Republican. Address: Chaddock Boys School, Quincy IL‡

FRIEND, ALBERT WILEY, cons. engr., physicist; b. Morgantown, W.Va., Jan. 24, 1910; s. Lemuel Ellsworth and Louisa Gertrude (Michael) F.; B.S. in Elec. Engring., W.Va. U., 1932, M.S., 1936; S.D., Harvard 1948; m. Evelyn Augusta Hall, Aug. 6, 1931; children—Albert Wiley, Evelyn Joyce (Mrs. William C. Everett), John Robert. Engr., Ohio Power Co., 1933-34; from instr. to asst. prof. physics W.Va. U., 1934-44; instr., research fellow, instr. Harvard (on leave W.Va. U.), 1939-42, 46-47; research asso., staff Radiation Lab., Radar Sch., tech. dir. Heat Research Lab., Mass. Inst. Tech., 1941-44; research staff RCA, 1944-51; dir. engring. Daystrom, Inc., 1951; dir. engring. Magnetic Metals Co., 1951-53; cons. engr., physicist, 1953-72; pres. Amicon Corp., Acoustex, Inc., 1968-72, A.W. Friend Engrs. Lectr., U. Pa., 1965. Cons. controls, electromagnetic isolation, tropoopheric radio echo phenomena; research and devel. electronic color TV system and equipment, also radar, guided missiles, telemetering, electronic computer components, magnetic materials and componenets, weather radar, lunar exploration communications, satellite communications systems, noise abatement, archtl. acoustics, vibration etc. Recipient award for outstanding research RCA Labs., 1950; award for contbns. to advancement electronic art Nat. Electronics Conf., 1955. Fellow I.E.E.E. (chmn. tech. com. recording and reproducing), A.A.A.S., Am. Phys. Soc.; mem. Acoustical Soc. Am., Am. Geophys. Union, Air Force Assn., Am. Inst. Physics, Am. Meteorol. Soc., Am. Ordnance Assn., Harvard Engrs. Soc., Am. Ordnance Assn., Harvard Engrs. Soc. N.Y., Electrochem. Soc., Franklin Inst., Nat., Pa. socs. profl. engrs., Tau Beta Pi, Sigma Xi, Sigma Pi Sigma. Clubs: Engineers (Phila.); Cosmos (Washington). Author numerous tech. papers and reports. Contbg. author: Magnetic Recording in Science and Industry. Holder U.S. and fgn. patents. Home: Bethesda MD Died Sept. 27, 1972; interred Morgantown WV

FRIENDLY, EDWIN SAMSON, newspaper exec.; b. Elmira, N.Y., June 15, 1884; s. Myer and Sarah (Meyerfeld) F.; student Elmira Acad. and graduate The Manlius Sch., Manlius, N.Y.; m. Henrietta S. Steinmeier, Boise, Ida., Dec. 26, 1914; children—Helen (Mrs. Malcolm Foster), Edwin Samson, Jr. Began as clerk in publication office of N.Y. Times, 1909, later fin. adv. mgr. and asst. bus. mgr.; apptd. business mgr. New York Sun and New York Herald, 1922, the latter merged with New York Tribune, 1924; continued as business mgr. of The Sun until Dec. 1941, gen. mgr., 1941-44, vice pres., general mgr. and dir., 1944-50 when the latter was merged with the N.Y. World-Telegram; v.p. New York World-Telegram and Sun 1950-54; v.p. Westchester County Publishers, Inc., 1954-64; chairman committee in charge of Bur. of Advt. of Am. Newspaper Publishers' Assn., 1932-41, treas., 1945-48, mem. board dirs. until 1951, now honorary dir. for life; chmn. com. on advt. agents, Am. Newspaper Pubs. Assn., 1926-31, mem. to 1942; mem. exec. com. on radio, 1932-40; treas., 1943-47, v.p. and dir. Am. Newspaper Pub. Assn., 1947-49, pres., 1949-51, dir. 1951-53; dir. Advt. Council Nat. Chmn. U.S. Victory Waste Paper Campaign, 1943-45; v.p. Better Bus. Bur., N.Y.C., 1945-48, dir., 1945-64. Bd. govs. Hundred Year Assn., N.Y.C., 1932-64; dir. N.Y. Worlds Fair 1964-1965 Corp.; dir. Brand Names Found., 1953-61. Mem. N.Y. Conv. and Visitors Bur. (life dir.). Club: Advertising. Home: New York City NY Died Aug. 1970.

FRIES, AMOS ALFRED, army officer; b. Debello, Vernon County, Wis., Mar. 17, 1873; s. Christian May and Mary Ellen (Shreve) F.; grad. U.S. Mil. Acad., 1898; grad. Engring. Sch., U.S. Army, 1912; m. Elizabeth Christine Wait, Aug. 16, 1899; children—Elizabeth Christine, Stuart Gilbert, Barbara Hyacinth, Carol Stephanie. Commd. 2d lt. engrs., Apr. 26, 1898; promoted through grades to lt. col., May 15, 1917; col. N.A., Aug. 5, 1917; brig. gen. and chief C.W.S., A.E.F., Aug. 16, 1918; brig. gen., July 1, 1920; maj. gen., Feb. 24, 1925; chief C.W.S., U.S. Army, 1920-29; ret. May 16, 1929. Asst. building fortifications mouth of Columbia River, 1898-99; served in Philippines, 1901-03; in charge Los Angeles River and Harbor Dist., 1906-09; laid out complete modern Los Angeles Harbor; dir. mil. engring. in Engring. School, 1911-14; in charge road and bridge constrn., Yellowstone Nat. Park, 1914-17; chief C.W.S., A.E.F., Aug. 22, 1917, to end of war. Awarded D.S.M. (U.S.); Comdr. Legion of Honor (France); Companion St. Michael and St. George (British). Fellow A.A.A.S.; life mem. Am. Soc. C.E., Am. Assn. Engrs., Am. Legion, Veterans of Foreign Wars, Mil. Order World War, National Sojourners (past nat. pres.); hon. life mem. Engrs. and Architects Assn. of Southern Calif. Republican. Episcopalian. Scottish Rite Mason 33 deg. (Shriner). Clubs: Army and Navy, Army and Navy Country; hon. life mem. Chemists Club (New York). Writer on communism and on military subjects. Editor of bulletin Friends of the Public Schools. Home: 3305 Woodley Rd. N.W., Washington 8 DC‡

FRIMI, RUDOLF, composer, pianist; b. Praha, Czechoslovakia, Dec. 7, 1879; s. Frantisek and Maria (Kremenak) F.; came to U.S. 1904, naturalized, 1925; studied piano with Josef Jiranek, composition with Antonin Dvorak at Conservatory of Music, Praha, 1896-99; m. Kay Ling, Apr. 16, 1952. Composed many compositions for piano, violin and cello; (operettas) Firefly, 1912; High Jinks, 1913; The Peasant Girl, 1914; You're in Love, 1916; Katinka, 1916; Sweet Kitty Darling, 1917; Giriana, 1918; Sometime, 1918; Tumble in 1919; Little Whopper, 1919; June Love, 1920; Blue Kitten, 1922; Cinders, 1923; Dew Drop Inn, 1923; Rose Marie, 1923; Ziegfeld Follies, 1921, 23, 24, and 25; Vagabond King, 1925; The Wild Rose, 1926; Palm Beach Girl, 1926; No Foolin', 1926; White Eagle 1927; Three Musketeers, 1928; Bird of Paradise, 1930; The Lottery Bride, 1930; Annina, 1934; (2-piano concerto) Round The World Symphony. Mem. Am. Soc. Composer, Authors and Pubs. Home: Hollywood CA Died Nov. 12, 1972.

FRISBIE, GUY STODDARD, mfg. co. exec.; b. Rochester, N.Y., July 30, 1903; s. Charles Warren and Estella (Lester) F.; B.S., Mass. Inst. Tech., 1926; m. Katherine Menzie, June 16, 1928; children—Patricia (Mrs. Stanley Martin, Jr.); Mary (Mrs. Bond Houser III), Martha (Mrs. William E. Saltzman III). With Hobart Mfg. Co., Troy, O., 1926-68, successively field and home office sales and sales mgmt., corp. sec., v.p., sec.-treas., 1926-56, mem. exec. com., 1954-68, v.p., gen. mgr., 1956-59, exec. v.p., 1959-64, pres., 1964-68, vice chmn. bd., 1968, also dir.; dir. Hobart-Federal Engring. Corp., Mpls., Hobart Mfg. Co., Ltd., Toronto, Can. Mem. bd. edn., Troy, 1940-56. Mem. bd. Stouder Meml. Hosp., Troy. Mem. U.S., Ohio, Troy, Dayton chambers commerce, Newcomen Soc. N.A., Am. Ordnance Assn., Sigma Chi. Presbyn. Rotarian (past pres.). Home: Troy OH Died June 22, 1968; buried Troy OH

FRISCH, RAGNAR ANTON KITTIL, economist; b. Oslo, Mar. 2, 1895; s. Anton and Ragna Fredrikke (Kittilsen) F.; M.A. in Econs., U. Oslo, 1919, Ph.D., 1926; Dr. honoris causa, Handelshogskolan i Stockholm, 1959, Kbenhavns Universitet, 1959, Stockholms Universitet, 1966; D.Sc. (honoris causa), U. Cambridge Queen's Coll., 1967; m. Marie Smedal, Apr. 28, 1920; 1 dau., Ragna. Formerly Jeweller-journeyman; mem. faculty U. Oslo, 1925-65, prof. econs. and statistics, 1931-65, dir. research U. Inst. Econs. Found., 1932-65; vis. prof. Yale, 1930, Sorbonne, Paris, 1933. Chmn. UN Econ. and Employment Commn., 1947; mem. various govt. money and banking cons. Co-recipient Nobel prize in econ. sci., 1969. Fellow Econometric Soc., Inst. Math. Statistics, Royal Statis. Soc. (hon.); corr. fellow British Acad.; hon. mem. Am. Econ. Assn., Am. Acad. Arts and Scis.; corr. mem. Royal Econ. Soc.; mem. Internat. Statis. Inst. Am. Philos. Soc. (fgn.), Det Norske Videnskapakademi i Oslo, Kungl. Humanistiska Vetnkappamfundet i Lund, Kungl, Svenska Vetenskapakademien. Author: New Methods of Measuring Marginal Utility, 1932; Statistical Confluence Analysis by Means of Complete Regression Systems, 1934; Noen Trekk av Konjunkturlderen, 1947. Editor Econometrica, 1933-65. Contbr. papers memoranda and compendia. Researcher regarding nat. income conputations and as result constructed a system describing the econ. circulation, the esocirc system. Interested in genetics, particularly breeding of bees. Address: Oslo Norway Died Jan. 1973.

FRITCH, LOUIS CHARLTON, engineer; b. Springfield, Ill., Aug. 11, 1869; s. Joseph and Margaret (Mather) F.; engring. course U. of Cincinnati; m. Frances Myers Fritch, of Jeffersonville, Ind., Apr. 1904. Div. engr., 1892-99, supt., 1899-1904, B.&O. R.R., at Cincinnati; asst. to gen. mgr., 1904-1906, asst. to pres., 1906-09, consulting engr., 1909, I.C. R.R., at Chicago; chief engr. C.G.W. Ry., Chicago, Nov. 15, 1909-Apr. 1, 1914; asst. to the president Canadian Northern Ry. and gen. mgr. eastern lines, same, Toronto, Can., 1914-17; gen. mgr. S.A.L. Ry., Norfolk, Va., June 15, 1917-Aug. 19, 1918; v.p. C.,R.I. & P. Ry., in charge constrn., maintenance and capital expenditures, 1918-23, v.p. in charge of operation, 1923-36. Mem. Am. Ry. Engring. Assn. (ex-pres.), Am. Soc. C.E., Western Soc. C.E., Sigma Alpha Epsilon. Republican. Methodist. Clubs: Union League, South Shore Country, Rock Island Country. Home: 1648 E. 50th St. Office: 30 N. La Salle St., Chicago IL‡

FRITSCHEL, HERMAN L(AWRENCE), hosp. adminstr.; b. Clayton County, Ia., May 15, 1869; s. Gottfried and Elizabeth (Koeberle) F.; student Wartburg Coll., Mendota, Ill., 1882-86, Wartburg Theol. Sem., Dubuque, Ia., 1886-89, U. of Leipzig, Germany, 1891-92; hon. D.D., Rostock U., Mecklenburg, Germany, 1915; m. Katherine E. Ide, Aug. 23, 1894; children—Herbert E., Margaret E., Roland G., Edgar G., Ruth H. (Mrs. George F. Sullivan). Pastor, Luth. Ch., Superior, Wis., 1893, Brandon, Wis., 1897; gen. dir. all Passavant Instns., 1902-28; rector Luth. Deaconess Mother House, Milwaukee, 1902-28, adminstr. Milwaukee Hosp., 1941-43; pres. emeritus, 1949; mem. editorial staff Hosp. Management since 1930. Commr. European War Relief after World War I. Pres. bd. Milwaukee Hosp., mem. bd. St. Luke's Hosp., Milwaukee, Church-Extension, Iowa Synod. Co-organizer Am. Protestant Hosp. Assn., 1920, pres. bd. dirs., pres., 1928. Co-organizer Am. Coll. of Hosp. Adminstrs. (v.p. 1936), Wis. Hosp. Assn. (pres. 1920-27); co-organizer and mem. bd. dirs. Asso. Hosp. Service of Wis.; Bureau Nursing Edn. of Wis. (president, 1938) Am. Luth. Ch. (pres. bd. trustees, 1930-36; pres. Bd. Edn.); mem. Wis. State Hist. Soc. Republican. Club: Rotary. Home: 6928 W. Wisconsin Av. Office: Milwaukee Hosp., 2200 W. Kilbourn Av., Milwaukee 3 WI‡

FRITTS, CARL EMERSON, highway engr.; b. Hemlock, N.C., Jan 9, 1900; s. Elzie K. and Sevilla E. (Graybeal) F.; student Wash. State Coll., 1918-21; m. Jean Lauder, June 9, 1947; 1 son, Carl Emerson. Various positions constrn., maintenance, traffic engring., planning, adminstrn. Wash. State Hwy. Dept., 1922-42; traffic engr. Hwy. Traffic Adv. Com., War Dept., 1942; hwy. engr. Automotive Safety Found., 1946-49, dir. hwys. div., 1950, v.p. in charge engring., 1951-—. Mem. national advisory com. road test Am. Association of State Highway Ofcls. Mem. hwy. research bd. dept. econs., finance and adminstrn. Served as col. Transportation Corps, AUS, 1942-45. Decorated Legion of Merit. Registered engr., Ida., Ky., D.C., La., Me., Minn. Miss. N.M., N.D., R.I., Ore., Tenn., Va., Wash., W.Va., Montana, D.C., Province of Ontario (Canada), National Bur. of Engring. Registration. Fellow Am. Society C.E. (president of national capital section); member Inst. Traffic Engrs., Sigma Chi. Episcopalian. Club: Cosmos (Washington). Home: Silver Spring MD Died Sept. 1970.

FRITZ, HERBERT DANIEL, pub. adminstrn. cons.; b. Burlington, Ia., Nov. 27, 1908; s. Phillip and Abigail (Flege) F.; B.S. in Civil Engring., Ia. State U., 1930; m. Elizabeth M. Binder, June 6, 1931; children—Elizabeth Joan (Mrs. Donald R. Clark), George Philip. Adminstrv. and tech. positions with various local, state and fed. govts., 1930-45; city mgr., Grand Junction, Colo., 1948, Marshall, Mo., 1948-51, Lexington, Ky., 1941-57, Peoria, Ill., 1958-60; cons. Pub. Adminstrn. Service, Chgo., 1960-66; pub. works engr., municipal mgmt. cons. P & W Engrs., Inc., 1966-69. Registered profl. engr., Ia. Mem. Am. Soc. C.E., Internat. City Mgrs. Assn., Tau Beta Pi. Methodist. Home: LaGrange IL Died Aug. 27, 1969.

FRITZ, LAWRENCE G(EORGE), airline exec.; b. Marine City, Mich., Aug. 7, 1896; s. John Conrad and Sophia (Holstein) F.; student Mich. State Coll., East Lansing, Mich., 1915-17; grad. Air Corps Advanced Flying Sch., 1923, command pilot, 1943; m. Ruth Merritt, Nov. 2, 1929; children—Lawrence George (dec.), James D. (stepson, dec.), John (USAF), Mary, Susan. Transport pilot, 1925; test pilot, Ford Stout Aircraft Co., 1925-27; chief pilot, Maddux Airlines, 1927-29; vice pres. in charge operations, Southwest Air Fast Express, Inc., 1929-30; div. supt. Transcontinental and Western Air, Inc., 1931-32, region supt., 1932-38, vice pres. operations, 1938; v.p. operations dept., Am. Air Lines since Jan. 1946. Served with aviation sect., Signal Corps, U.S. Army during World War I; with U.S. Air Forces, 1942-46, disch. Jan. 1946; brig. gen. since June 1944; asst. chief of staff operations, Air Transport Command, 1942-43, comdg. officer North Atlantic Wing, 1943-44, comdg. gen. North Atlantic Div. June 1944. Decorated Air Medal, Legion of Merit, D.S.M. Mem. Inst. Aeronautical Sciences Nat. Aeronautical Adv. Committee, Quiet Birdmen, American Legion, Air Force Association, Air Force Reserve Officer Association. Mason. Club: Conquistadores del Cielo. Home: Saratoga CA Died Nov. 1970.

FRIZOL, SYLVESTER M., educator; b. Peru, Ill., June 26, 1906; s. Emil John and Dorathea (Hildebrandt) F.; B.S. in Commerce, Loyola U., Chgo., 1931, A.M., 1933; Ph.D., U. So. Cal., 1941; m. Carolyn Miller, Dec. 24, 1934. Asst. prof. Loyola U., Los Angeles, 1934-42; adminstrv. asst. Douglas Aircraft Corp., 1942-45; lectr., then asst. prof. U. So. Cal., 1945-50; prof. Loyola U., Chgo., 1950-72, chmn. dept. finance, 1965-72; cons. in econs., 1962-72. Recipient Outstanding Faculty Mem. award, 1972. Mem. Am., Midwest econ. assns., Am., Midwest Finance assns., Investment Analyst Soc. Chgo., Pub. Utilities Securities Club Chgo., Chartered

Financial Analysts, Blue Key, Artus, Beta Alpha Psi, Delta Sigma Pi, Phi Kappa Phi, Pi Epsilon Theta, Pi Gamma Mu, Beta Gamma Sigma. Home: Chicago IL Died Oct. 3, 1972; buried Peru IL

FRIZZELL, DONALD LESLIE, educator; b. Bellingham, Wash., Oct. 19, 1906; s. Thomas Fisher and Bessie Pearl (Knapp) F.; B.S., U. Wash., 1930, M.S., 1931; Ph.D., Stanford, 1936; m. Harriet Idola Exline, Aug. 29, 1938 (dec. Feb. 1968). Paleontologist Shell Oil Co., Houston, 1936; paleontologist, geologist Internat. Petroleum Co., Peru and Ecuador, 1937-44; asso. prof. geology U. Tex., Austin, 1945-48; asso. prof. geology U. Mo., Rolla, 1948-52, prof., 1952-72. Mem. Geol. Soc. Am., Am. Assn. Petroleum Geologists, Paleontol. Soc., Soc. Econ. Paleontologists and Mineralogists, Soc. Systematic Zoology, Am. Soc. Ichthyologists and Herpetologists. Soc. Vertebrate Paleontology, Sociedad Geologica del Peru (corr.). Research on classification fossil fish otoliths, holcthurians, foraminifera and mollusks. Home: Rolla MO Died Oct. 17, 1972; buried Rolla Cemetery.

FROHLICH, LUDWIG WILLIAM, advt. exec.; b. Germany, July 30, 1913; s. Ludwig and Elsie (Oppeln) F.; B.S., Johann W. Goethe U., Frankfurt, Germany, 1931; student Ecole Dierot, also Inst. des Beaux Arts, France. Came to U.S., 1931, naturalized, 1938. Creative advt., corporate counsel promotional field to 1939; founder L. W. Frohlich & Co., 1939, L. W. Frohlich & Co., Inc., 1943, then chmn.; founder Nat. Sci. Network, Inc., 1964. Dir. Am. Nat. Council for Health Edn. of Public, Inc. Bd. dirs. Royal Soc. Medicine Found. trustee Columbia U. Coll. of Pharmacy, Internat. House Mem. Young Presidents' Orgn. (founding mem.). Clubs: Pharmaceutical Advertising, Art Directors, N.Y. Athletic (N.Y.C.); Maidstone, Devon Yacht (East Hampton, N.Y.). Home: New York City NY Died Sept. 28, 1971; buried Cedar Lawn Cemetery, East Hampton NY

FROHMAN, PHILIP HUBERT, architect; b. N.Y.C., Nov. 16, 1887; s. Gustave and Marie (Hubert) F.; ed. Throop Poly. Inst., Pasadena, Cal., 1899-1903, Throop Coll. Engring. (now Cal. Inst. Tech.), specializing in art, archtl. engring. and civil engring., 1903-07; m. Olivia Avery, July 15, 1922 (dec. Apr. 1955); children—Mary, Alice; m. 2d, Mary Ann Evans, Feb. 27, 1957 (dec. Mar. 1970). Began practice as architect at Pasadena, Cal., 1908; mem. Frohman & Martin, 1909-17; opened office in Boston, 1919; mem. Frohman, Robb & Little, 1920-34; pvt. practice 1934-72; opened office in Washington, 1924, continuing assn. with former partners in Boston and Cal. on certain projects; specializes in church architecture; architects of Nat. Episcopal Cathedral, Washington, Md. Cathedral, Balt., Trinity Coll. Chapel, Hartford, Conn., Catholic Cathedral, Los Angeles, and other monumental churches; cons. architect Kent Sch. Chapel, also various chs.; cons. architect cathedral projects. Served with U.S. Army, 1917-19; assigned to Ordnance Constrn. Sect. and Supply Div.; designed bldgs. at Rock Island Arsenal and Aberdeen Proving Grounds. Decorated Medal Pro Ecclesia et Pontifix (Pope John). Fellow A.I.A. (mem. Washington chpt.); mem. Nat. Cathedral Assn., Guild Religious Architecture, Liturgical Art Soc., The Restorers of Mount Carmel in Md., Am. Ord. Assn. (life). Republican. Catholic. Club: Gibson Island. Specialist in structural engring. as applied to cathedrals, etc. Regarded as an authority on Romanesque and Gothic architecture, stained glass, and also on design and voicing of ch. organs and in field of sci. of mus. sounds. Inventor electric organs and various apparatus for elec. reproduction of mus. sounds. Writer on ecclesiastical art and architecture. Home: Washington DC Died Aug. 7, 1972.

FROMMELT, HENRY JULIUS, chain store exec.; b. N.Y.C., May 18, 1911; s. Alfred J. and Martha (Schoenewerk) F.; student U. Minn., 1933; m. Inez V. Okins, Feb. 15, 1936; children—Roger, Jeffrey, Christine. With Gamble Skogmo, Inc., Mpls., 1934-71, dir. pub. relations, asst. to exec. v.p., 1952-61, v.p. pub. relations, 1961-71; dir. Gambles Holiday Travel Service. Bd. dirs. Mpls. Goodwill Industries, 1955-71, pres. 1965-67, chmn. bd., 1967-71; bd. dirs. Better Bus. Bur. Mpls., 1968-71, Jr. Achievement Greater Mpls., 1963-71. Mem. Mpls. C. of C. (chmn. marketing com. 1958), Mpls. (pres. 1958-59, chmn. adv. com. 1959-60), Nat. (bd. dirs. 1960-61) sales execs. clubs. Mpls. Ad Club, Presbyn. Clubs: Minn. Pres. Interlachen Country (Mpls.). Home: Minneapolis MN Died 1971.

FROST, FREDERICK GEORGE, architect; b. London, Eng., Aug. 22, 1876; s. Thomas Robert and Ellen (Bruce) F.; came to U.S., 1887; naturalized, 1892; student Ecole des Beaux Arts, Paris, 1900-02; m. Bessie Throop Wilcox, Sept. 21, 1904 (dec.); children—Frederick G., Thomas Robert, Barbara (Mrs. Henry Clay Moses, Jr.). Began as archtl. draftsman, 1893; architect successively with Charles D. Wilsey and Merrick & Randall, Syracuse, N.Y., Joseph Freedlander, George A. Freeman, N.Y. City; with Trowbridge & Livingston, N.Y. City, 17 years (designer and mgr. for 10 years); own practice since 1917, partner with son since 1936. Former trustee New Rochelle Library. Fellow Am. Inst. Architects (past pres. N.Y. Chapter); mem. Beaux Arts Architects, Archtl. League of N.Y. Presbyterian. Club: Union League (N.Y. City). Home: 115 Beechmont Drive, New Rochelle, N.Y. Office: 144 E. 30th St., New York NY‡

FROST, LESLIE MISCAMPBELL, former prime minister Province of Ontario, Canada; b. Orillia, Ont., Can., Sept. 20, 1895; s. William Sword and Margaret Jane (Barker) F.; ed. Orillia Collegiate Inst. U. Toronto, Osgoode Hall; LL.D. Queen's U., Kingston, Ont., 1946, Ottawa U., 1948, McMaster U., 1951, U. Toronto, 1952, Assumption Coll. 1954, Royal Mil. Coll., 1960, Laurentian Univ., 1961; D.C.L., U. Western Ont., 1950; m. Gertrude Jane Carew, June 2, 1926 (dec. 1972). Admitted to Ont. bar, 1921; created Kings's Counsel, 1933; mem. Privy Council for Can., 1961-73. Elected mem. Ont. Legislature, 1937, 43, 45, 48, 51, 55, 59; became treas. Ont. and minister of mines, 1943, pres. Provincial Mines Ministers Assn. of Can., 1944; became leader Progressive Conservative Party Ont., 1949-61; prime minister Prov. Ont., and pres. of the Council, 1949-61, treas., 1949-55; mem. law firm Frost, Inrig & Gorwill. Vice pres., dir. Victoria &Grey Trust Co., Bank of Montreal; dir. Can. Life Assurance Co., Massey-Ferguson, Ltd., Radio Station CKLV, and other firms. Chancellor of Trent U., Peterborough. Served from asst. adj. to co. comdr. Simcoe Regt., 1914-18, with 20th Canadian Inf. Bn., France and Belgium, 1917-18. Mem. Canadian Legion (Sir Sam Hughes br. past zone rep.), Bencher Law Soc. Upper Can. (hon.), Phi Delta Phi (hon.). Mem. Progressive Conservative Party. Mem. United Ch. Can. (chmn. mgmt. bd. Lindsay). Mason (Shriner, 33). Clubs: Rotary (past pres.), Lindsay Curling, Albany, Twenty. Garrison, Royal Canadian Mil. Inst., National, Granite. Author: Fighting Men. Home: Lindsay ON Canada Died May 1973.

FROST, THOMAS C., banker; b. San Antonio, Tex., Dec. 22, 1903; s. Thomas C. and Lillie C. (Beall) F.; student San Antonio Acad., U. Tex.; m. Ilse Herff, Aug. 3, 1925; children—Thomas C., Ilse Herff. With Frost Nat. Bank, San Antonio, from 1924, then chmn. bd.; sec. and dir. Elsinore Cattle Co. Trustee Marion Koogler McNay Art Inst. Episcopalian. Home: San Antonio TX

FROTHINGHAM, EUGENIA BROOKS, author; b. Paris, France, Nov. 17, 1874; d. Edward and Eugenia (Mittlin) F.; ed in pvt. schs; unmarried. Clubs: Saturday Morning, McDowell. Author: The Turn of the Road, 1901; The Evasion, 1906; contbr. to mags. Address: Setasti, Reali, Rome Italy‡

FRUEHAUF, HARVEY CHARLES, trailer co. exec., ret.; b. Grosse Pointe Park, Mich., December 15, 1893; s. August C. and Louise (Schuehard) F.; ed. pub. schs.; m. Angela Stewart Peck, Jan. 3, 1920. Started with Allyne Brass Fdry., 1907, later merged with Aluminum Castings Co.; in 1915 became associated with father and founded Fruehauf Trailer Co., Detroit, chmn. bd., ret.; dir. Georgia-Pacific Corp., Portland. Clubs: Detroit, Detroit Athletic, Detroit Country, Bloomfield Hills Country, Grosse Pointe Yacht; Surf, Indian Creek Country (Miami Beach). Home: Detroit MI Died Oct. 14, 1968; buried Woodlawn Cemetery, Detroit MI

FRY, ANSON CLIFTON, mfr. greeting cards; b. Batesville, O., Feb. 28, 1871; s. John Andrew and Ann Elizabeth (Miller) F.; ed. in pub. schs., Caldwell, O.; m. Mary Jane Finley, of Whigville, O., Nov. 24, 1896; 1 son, William Finley. Printer's apprentice, 1884-88; engaged in newspaper work, Caldwell, O., 1888-91, mercantile business, Pittsburgh, Pa., 1891-96, advertising with Scioto Sign Co., Kenton, O., 1896-1902; with Gibson Art Co., mfrs. greeting cards, Cincinnati, since 1902, v.p. and dir. since 1907; established branches in leading cities; dir. Norwood-Hyde Park Bank & Trust Co. (Norwood, O.), Scioto Sign Co. (Kenton, O.), Spray-O-Matic Products Co. (Cincinnati). Charter mem. and dir., Greeting Card Assn.; mem. Nat. Retail Stationers Assn., Nat. Peace Commn. M.E. Ch.; trustee Bethesda Hosp.; trustee M.E. Church. Republican. Methodist. Mason. Clubs: Rotary, Cincinnati, Hyde Park Golf and Country. Contbr. to trade publs. Home: 3523 Paxton Rd. Office: 233 W. 4th St., Cincinnati OH‡

FRY, FRANKLIN CLARK, clergyman; b. Bethlehem, Pa., Aug. 30, 1900; s. Franklin Foster and Minnie Clark (McKeown) F.; A.B., Hamilton Coll., 1921; grad. Phila. Luth. Sem., 1925; grad. work Am. Sch. for Classical Studies, Athens, 1921-22; D.D., Muhlenberg College, 1939, L.H.D., 1952; D.D. Hamilton College, 1946; Th.D., Elizabeth University, Sopron, Hungary, 1947, Goettingen U., Germany, 1956, U. Helsinki, Fin., 1963; LL.D., Thiel Coll., Gettysburg Coll., Wittenberg Coll., 1945, Hartwick Coll., 1946, Waterloo (Can.), 1963, Georgetown U., 1964, Le Moyne U., 1968; D.D., Lafayette and Moravian Colls., 1964; Litt.D., Wagner Meml. Luth. Coll., 1945, U. Alaska, 1958; L.H.D., Roanoke Coll., 1945, S.J.D., 1956; S.T.D., Wycliffe Coll., U. Toronto, 1950; D.D., Yale, 1960; S.T.D., Maryville Coll., 1960; I.R.D., Midland, 1962; D.D., Princeton, 1962, Harvard University, 1962, Luther Sem., 1966, Valparaiso U., 1967; L.H.D., Washington and Jefferson, 1965; J.C.D., Susquehanna, 1966; H.H.D., Lenoir Rhyne Coll., 1966, Augustana Coll., 1968; Litt.D., Akron, 1967; D.C.L., Newberry, 1957; m. Hilda A. Drewes, May 17, 1927; children—Franklin Drewes, Robert Charles, Constance Hilda (Mrs. Richard I. Preis). Ordained to min. of Luth. Ch. synod of New York and N.E., 1925; pastor, Luth. Ch. Redeemer, Yonkers, N.Y., 1925-29, Trinity Luth Ch., Akron, O., 1929-44. Sec. com. on-evangelism United Luth. Ch. of America, 1930-38, mem. bd. Am. missions, 1934-42, mem. exec. bd. United Luth. Ch. Am., 1942-44, pres., 1945-62; pres. of Lutheran Church in America 1962-—; mem. nat. preaching mission and nat. Christian mission dept. evangelism Fed. Council of Chs., 1936, 1941-42; chmn. policy and strategy com. Nat. Council Churches of Christ in U.S.A., 1954-60; president Lutheran World Relief, Incorporated; member exec. com. Luth. World Federation, 1947-69, treas., 1948-52, 1st v.p. 1952, pres. 1957-63; 1st vice chmn. Am. Relief for Korea, 1950-54; dir. Church World Serv., Inc., 1946-50; vice chmn. Central and exec. coms., World Council Chs., 1948-54, chmn. 1954-69. Hon. citizen Korea, 1953. Dir. Wittenberg Coll., 1934-38. Mem. Phi Beta Kappa. Contbr. to publs. Awarded Grosse Verdienst-Kreuz, Fed. Rep. Germany, 1953; Grosses silberne Ehrenzeichen mit stern from Austria, 1955; Grosses Verdienstkreuz mit Stern, 1960; Grosskeruz des Verdienstordens der Bundesrepublik, 1963. Home: New Rochelle NY Died June 6, 1968; buried Trappe PA

FRY, JOHN A.B., clergyman; b. Cathage, N.C., Oct. 23, 1870; s. DeGraffenried and Martha (Redding) F.; ed. Carthage (N.C.) Acad., Trinity Coll. (now Duke U.), Durham, N.C., and Vanderbilt; M.S.T., Pacific Sch. of Religion, Berkeley, Calif., 1918; D.D., Asbury Coll., Wilmore, Ky., 1937; m. Malta Chafin Callahan, May 1, 1895; 1 dau., Annie Ried (Mrs. Royal L. Gardner). Ordained ministry M.E. Ch., S., 1894; pastor chs. in N.C. and Ark. until 1906; pastor Epworth Univ. Ch., Berkeley, Calif., 1906-17 and 1928-34. Presiding elder Los Angeles Dist., Pacific Conf., M.E. Ch., S., 1934-39; later pastor Epworth Meth. Ch., Berkeley, Calif.; now pastor Asbury Meth. Ch., Livermore, Calif. Served as religious worker, Y.M.C.A., Angel Island, Calif., 1917-19. Mem. Gen. Bd. of Sunday Schs., M.E. Ch., S., 1914-22, Gen. Bd. Edn., 1922-26; del. to Gen. Conf. M.E. Ch., S., 1914, 18, 26. Mason (Past Chaplain Grand Lodge of Calif.). Club: Lions. Home: 20 W. Poplar St., Stockton CA‡

FRY, MORTON HARRISON, banker; b. Ephrata, Pa., Jan. 27, 1888; s. Jacob Martin and Margaret (Ruth) F.; prep. edn., Franklin and Marshall Acad., Lancaster, Pa.; A.B., Princeton, 1909; m. Julia Gladys Angell, June 22, 1909; children—Morton Allan Harrison, George Thomas Clark. Partner Scholle Bros., bankers, N.Y. City, 1923-42, Riter & Co., investment bankers, from 1942; president Overseas Securities Co.; dir. and mem. executive committee Alabama Great Southern Railroad; president, director Overseas Securities Co., Inc.; pres., trustee Rembrandt Corporation; dir. Northwest Airlines, Inc. Trustee Hun School, Princeton, New Jersey; trustee of Athens Coll., Greece. Member of American Academy Political Science, Phi Beta Kappa. Democrat. Clubs: University, Princeton, Tiger Inn (Princeton U.), Down Town Assn. Author: Bank Acceptances as an Investment; contbr. numerous articles on Montclair NJ Died Apr. 22, 1971.

FRY; SAMUEL ROEDER, banker, fabric co. exec.; b. Reading, Pa., Nov. 10, 1901; s. Howard Morton and Ella Amanda (Roeder) F.; student N.Y. Mil. Acad., U. Pa.; m. Margaret Thun, June 26, 1924; children—Barbara Ann, Thomas Morton, Howard Morton II, Margaret Victoria. Office mgr. asst. sec. Narrow Fabric Co., Reading, Pa., 1923, v.p., dir., 1931-48, pres., chmn. bd. 1948-71; chmn. bd. Reading Trust Co., 1955-71; treas., dir. Wyomissing Fed. Savs. & Loan Assn., 1933-71. Chmn. supervisory bd. Berks County Boys' Home, 1946-71; mem. board trustees St. Joseph's Hosp., Reading, Pennsylvania. Mem. Theta Delta Chi. Clubs: Union League (N.Y.C.); Radnor Hunt, Racquet (Phila.); Rolling Rock (Ligonier, Pa.); Bath and Tennis (Palm Beach, Fla.). Home: Wyomissing PA Died 1971.

FRYE, BENJAMIN PORTER, finance co. exec.; b. Charleroi, Pa., Sept. 26, 1906; s. Charles Orlando and Lula (Porter) F.; student U. Pa., 1924-25; grad. exec. program bus. adminstrn., Columbia, 1953; m. Margaret Doris Hamilton, Mar. 29, 1930; children—Margaret Jane (Mrs. George Grundy), Meredith Louise (Mrs. Dennis A. Conlan). With Clarence Hodson & Co., N.Y.C., 1927-38; sec., treas. Bankers Nat. Investing Corp., Wilmington, Del., 1938-46, Am. Bus. Credit Corp., N.Y.C., 1946-50; with Beneficial Finance Co.; Wilmington, from 1950, treas., from 1953, v.p., mem. finance com., from 1961, also dir. Club: Newark Country (bd. dirs.). Home: Newark DE Died Apr. 3, 1969.

FRYE, FRANK AUGUSTUS, , lawyer; b. San Diego, Mar. 8, 1904; s. Frank Augustus and Ida (Beck) F.; A.B., Stanford, 1926; LL.B., Harvard, 1929; m. June E. Annable, Sept. 30, 1933; children—Frederick A., Frank Augustus III, Milton. Admitted to Cal. bar, 1929, since practiced in San Diego; partner Gray, Cary, Ames &

Frye, from 1934. Dir. First Fed. Savs. & Loan Assn. San Diego. Past pres. Community Chest of San Diego; harbor commr., San Diego, 1950-54. Mem. Am., San Diego bar asssns., State Bar Cal., Phi Kappa Sigma, Phi Delta Phi. Clubs: Rotary (past pres.), Cuyamaca (past pres.) (San Diego). Home: San Diego CA Died Sept. 3, 1970.

FRYE, LOUISE ALEXANDER (MRS. ROYAL M. FRYE), educator, writer; b. Falmouth, Massachusetts, September 28, 1884; daughter of George and Annie (Salisbury) Alexander; A.B., Boston U., 1913; postgrad. N.E. Conservatory, Simmons Coll. Library Sch.; m. Royal Merrill Frye, June 11, 1915. Tchr. Sea Pines, Brewster, Mass., 1913-15; library worker Mass. Inst. Tech., 1919-21; writer, artist, composer; (plays) Sister Nations, 1922, Forest Interlude, 1928, Nocturne, 1952, Cantata, Pax Mundi, 1954; Peace and the Prophets, 1959; (books illustrated) Graphical Mathematics, 1941, Essentials of Applied Physics, 1947; librarian Coll. Advanced Sci., N.H., 1960-63, Belknap Coll., Center Harbor, N.H., 1963-65. Dir. Credit Union. Chmn. edn. Greater Boston Cooperative Soc., 1943-48; nat. chmn. religious contacts Women's Internat. League for Peace and Freedom. Mem. Am. Assn. Chamber Music Players, Community Orchestras Musical Socs., Zeta Tau Alpha, Phi Beta Kappa. Home: Center Harbor NH Died Apr. 25, 1969; interred Royalston MA

FRYE, THEODORE CHRISTIAN, botanist; b. Washington, Ill., Sept. 15, 1869; s. Joseph and Catherine (Kinzinger) F.; B.S., U. of Ill., 1894; Ph.D., U. of Chicago, 1902; married Else Marie Anthon, June 30, 1908; children—Elizabeth Anthon, Joanne Anthon (dec.). Prin. High Sch., Monticello. Ill., 1894-96; supt. schs., Batavia, 1897-1900; fellow in botany, U. of Chicago, 1901-02; prof. biology, Morningside College, Iowa, 1902-03; professor botany, 1903-46, professor emeritus since 1946; acting dean, College of Science, 1913-15, University of Washington. In charge Puget Sound Biol. Sta., summers, 1905, 07, 08, 09; dir. same, 1913-30; in charge Kelp Expdn. to Southeastern Alaska, for U.S. Bur. of Soils, summer, 1913. Instr. R.O.T.C., U. of Wash., with rank of capt., 1917. Mem. A.A.A.S., Bot. Soc. America. Sigma Xi. Author: (with George B. Rigg) Laboratory Excercises in Elementary Botany, 1910; Northwest Flora, 1912; Elementary Flora of the Northwest (with same), 1913; (with Lois Clark) Liverworts of the Northwest (article), 1929; Ferns of the Northwest. 1934; The Hepaticae of North America (with Lois Seattle 55 WA‡

FRYER, ELI THOMPSON, marine corps officer (ret.); b. Hightstown, N.J., Aug. 22, 1878; s. Samuel and Mary (Shaeffer) F.; student, Brown U., 1895-97; grad. U.S. Mil. Acad., 1899; m. Edna Ella Smith, Jan. 14, 1908. Commd. 2d lt., U.S. M.C., 1900, and advanced through grades to brig. gen., 1934; ret. from active service, Oct. 1, 1934. Awarded Congressional Medal of Honor, 1914. Home: 106 North Vermont Av., Atlantic City NJ‡

FRYER, JANE EAYRE (MRS. JOHN GAYTON FRYER), author; b. Phila., Pa.; d. Mortimer Haines and Isabella (Van der Veer) Eayre; grad. Northfield (Mass.) Sem., 1896; spl. courses in domestic art and domestic science; m. John Gayton Fryer, of Providence, R.I., Jan. 1902. Teacher Latin and English, Mt. Holly (N.J.) Mil. Acad., 1897-98; supervisor domestic sci. and art, Jacob Tome Inst., Port Deposit, Md., 1899-1902. Baptist. Author: The Mary Frances Cook Book, 1912; The Mary Frances Sewing Book, 1913; The Mary Frances Housekeeper, 1914; The Mary Frances Garden Book, 1915; The Mary Frances Dressmaker, 1915; The Mary Frances First Aid Book, 1916; The Mary Frances Knitting and Crocheting Book, 1918; Young American Readers (civic), 1918-1919; The Mary Frances Story Book, 1921; Mrs. Fryer's Loose Leaf Cook Book, 1923; The Bible Story Book for Boys and Girls, 1924. Home: Merchantville NJ

FUGARD, JOHN REED, architect; b. Newton, Ia., Dec. 6, 1886; s. Judson Houston and Ella (Slemmons) F.; B.S. in Architecture, U. Ill., 1910; m. Rowena Owen, June 18, 1910 (dec. 1952); 1 son, John Reed; m. 2d, Roine Russell, June 17, 1953. Sec.-treas. Fugard Orth. & Assos., architects, Chicago, Illinois; designs hosps., hotels, office bldgs.; cons. for Guy's Hosp., London, Eng.; pres. Woodhaven Dairy, Incorporated, Robertsdale, Ala.; dir. Drake Towers, 1965-68. Chmn. Chgo. Housing Authority, 1936-37, 53-54; pres. Met. Housing Council, 1934-35; cons. zoning bd. Chicago Plan Commn. Trustee Chgo. Temple; citizens bd. trustees U. Chgo.; dir. Internat. Coll. Surgeons Hall Fame, 1962-63. Served to capt. Q.M.C., 1917-18. Fellow A.I.A. (dir. 1934-35, treas. 1937-38); mem. Chgo. Dwellings Assn. (pres. 1955), Kappa Sigma. Methodist. Mason (Shriner). Clubs: University, Tavern, Forty, Arts (all of Chicago); Lakewood Golf (Fairhope, Alabama). Home: Chicago IL Died Aug. 17, 1968; buried Memorial Park Cemetery, Evanston IL

FULEIHAN, ANIS, composer, pianist, conductor; b. Cyprus, Apr. 2, 1900; s. Dr. Mulhim and Yasmine (Nassif) F.; student English Sch., Cyprus, also Poly. Sch., Bklyn. Came to U.S., 1915. Debut, Aeolian Hall, N.Y.C., Oct. 1919, since concertized as recitalist and soloist, orchestras U.S. and abroad; prof. music Ind. U., 1947-52; soloist UNESCO Conf., 1948; dir. Nat. Conservatory, Beirut, 1953-60; conductor of Beirut Orchestra, 1955-60, Orchestre Classique de Tunis, 1963-65; visiting lecturer University Illinois, 1967-68; music cons. Baalbek Festival, 1956-60; musical cons. Internat. Cultural Center, Tunis and Tunis Festival, 1962-66; works performed world-wide maj. orchestras U.S., Can., Eng. Guggenheim fellow, 1939; Fulbright research fellow, Egypt, 1952. Orchestral works include: Mediterranean, 1928, Preface Child's Storybook, 1932, Invocation, 1933, Symphony, 1936, Symphony-concertante, 1940, Cyprus Serenades, 1941, Six Etudes, 1943, Comedy Overture, 1943, Concertino, 1957, Greek Suite 1961; Concerti with Orchestra: For Piano Nos. 1 and 2, 1936, Two Pianos, 1941, Violin and Piano, 1944, Theremin, 1945, Violin, 1946, Cello, 1961; Epithalamium, Piano and Strings, 1941, Rhapsody, cello and strings 1945, Duo Concertante, violin, viola and orchestra, 1958, Toccata, piano and orchestra, 1960; Sonatas for flute and piano, 1941, Flute and cello, 1952, violin and piano, 1961, cello and piano, 1962; Five String Quartets, 1940, 49, 57, 60, 65, Quintet horn and strings, clarinet and strings; 14 piano sonatas: Cypriana, 1943, Tributes, 1945, Fugue, 1945, Fifteen Short Pieces, 1946, From the Aegean, 1946; Opera Vasco, 4 acts, 1958; (for oboe and orch.) Pieces Concertantes, 1962; Pour les cordes, string orch., 1962; Concerto Flute and String Orch., 1962; Variations for Piano, 1962, Islands (for orch.), 1962, Symphony No. 2, 1962, Fantasy for viola and orch., 1963, Concerto for viola, 1963, Sonata for viola and piano, 1963, Duo for Viola and Cello, 1963, Concertino for violin and orch., 1964, Concertino for bassoon and orchestra, 1965, Concerto No. 2 FULEIHANfor violin and orchestra, 1965, Concerto No. 3 for violin and orchestra, 1967; Baalbek Festival Overture, 1967; Scene from Hamlet for 2 solo celli and orchestra, 1965; Prelude, Caprice and Epilogue for violin, oboe and orch., 1965, Le Cor Anglais S'amuse, 1969, Bilitis song cycle, 1970, Helen of Troy, 1970. also composer numerous short pieces for piano and other instruments, woodwind quartet, voice, chorus; quintet for piano and string quartet, 1966. Mem. Church of Eng. Home: New York City NY Died Oct. 11, 1970; buried Ferncliff, Hartsdale NY

FULLER, CAROLINE MACOMBER, novelist; b. Bangor, Me., Sept. 10, 1873; d. Henry D. and Julia (Muzzy) F.; B.Litt., Smith Coll., 1895; unmarried. Author: Across the Campus, 1899; The Old Songs (play), 1903; The Alley Cat's Kitten, 1904; The Flight of Puss Pandora, 1906; Brunhilde's Paying Guest (novel), 1907; The Bramble Bush (novel), 1911; Kitten Whiskers, 1927. Contbr. of song-poems to The Magic of Song, 1934, The World of Music, 1936; contbr. Her Christmas Gift" to Christmas Plays for Women, 1936; contbr. poems to mags. Home: Lakewood NJ‡

FULLER, CHARLES E., radio evangelist; b. Los Angeles, Apr. 25, 1887; s. Henry and Helen (Day) F.; B.S., Pomona Coll., 1910; grad. Bible Inst. of Los Angeles, 1919-22; D.D., Los Angeles Bapt. Sem., 1931; D.D., Fuller Theol. Sem., 1961; m. Grace Leone Payton, Oct. 21, 1911 (dec.); 1 son, Daniel Payton. Mgr. So. Cal. Citrus Packing Assn. 1913-19; ordained Baptist minister 1925; founder and pastor, Calvary Ch., Placentia, Cal., 1925-33; instr. theology, Los Angeles Bapt. Sem. 1927-28; chmn. bd. dirs., Bible Inst. of Los Angeles, 1927-31; pres. Fuller Evangelistic Found.; co-founder, hon. chmn. trustees Fuller Theol. Sem., organized 1947; began religious radio broadcasting in 1930 on 1 sta., ministry grew until in 1942 reached virtual world coverage; dir. Gospel Broadcasting Assn. which sponsored Old Fashioned Revival Hour, an internat. broadcast, on which he preached Pasadena CA Died Mar. 19, 1968.

FULLER, CLAUDE A(LBERT), ex-congressman; b. Prophetstown, Ill., Jan. 20, 1876; s. Wilmot P. and Maria (Ocobock) F.; grad. high sch., Eureka Springs, Ark., 1896; student Kent Coll. Law, Chicago, Ill., 1896-97; m. May Obenshain, of Eureka Springs, December 25, 1899; children—Mrs. Ruth Maria Cross, Mrs. Dorothy M. Mathews. Admitted to the Arkansas bar, 1898, and began practice at Eureka Springs. Served as city clerk, Eureka Springs, 1898-1902; mem. Ark. Ho. of Rep., 1903-05; mayor of Eureka Springs, 1906-10, 1920-28; pros. atty., 4th Ark. Dist., 1910-14; was pres. Sch. Bd., Eureka Springs; mem. 71st to 75th Congresses (1929-39), 3d Ark. Dist. Democrat. Baptist. Elk, K.P. Home: Eureka Springs AR‡

FULLER, CLYDE DALE, orgn. exec.; b. Iroquois, S.D., Sept. 24, 1915; s. Clyde DeVere and Hattie Pearl (Stoner) F.; B.A., U. Denver, 1937, M.A., 1939; certificate Russian Inst., Columbia, 1949; m. Ethelyn Goldberg, Dec. 16, 1953; children—Diana Kim, Laurel Jan, Claire Ellen. Instr. social studies Webster (S.D.) High Sch., 1937-38; faculty U. Denver, 1938-42, 46, 53-59, dir. social sci. found., chmn. dept. internat. relations, 1953-59; exec. v.p. Fgn. Policy Assn., N.Y.C., 1959-72; dir. Russian project Nat. Assn. Edn. Broadcasters, 1951-52; mgr. research br. information and reference dept., Radio Free Europe, 1952. Analyst, Journeys Behind the News, weekly radio series, 1938-42, 46; moderator Focus, weekly TV series, 1953-59; narrator 20th Century Revolutions in World Affairs, TV series, 1959. Served with AUS, 1942-46. Mem. Am. Polit. Sci. Assn., Council on Fgn. Relations, Adult Edn. Assn. Author: Training of Specialists in International Relations, 1957; also articles. Home: Mount Vernon NY Died July 11, 1972.

FULLER, GEORGE FREEMAN, mfr. drop forgings; b. Grafton, Mass., Sept. 29, 1869; s. Freeman Loring and Almira Maria (Metcalf) F.; ed. high sch.; m. Sybil Harriet Flagg, Aug. 30, 1893. With the Wyman-Gordon Co., Worcester, Mass., since 1887, successively timekeeper, bookkeeper, draftsman, designer, mgr. of forgings, supt. of shop, mem. of firm, 1905, pres., 1914-43; hon. chmn. bd. of directors Wyman-Gordon Co.; dir. Mechanics National Bank. Member bd. trustees Worcester Poly. Inst., Worcester Boys' Club, Worcester Girls' Club. Republican. Mason (K.T.). Odd Fellow. Home: 15 Massachusetts Av., Worcester MA‡

FULLER, GEORGE GREGG, fgn. service officer (ret.), educator; b. Rochester, N.Y., Oct. 29, 1886; s. George R. and Helen (Gregg) F.; A.B., Yale, 1910; A.M., Queen's U., 1934; grad. study U. Berlin; m. Therese Alson Williams, Feb. 27, 1926 (dec.); children—George Havemeyer, Gregory Alston, Therese Brevoort. Officer various teoephone cos., 1910-13; successively v.p. Standard Automatic Machine Co., Lindsay-Fuller, Inc., and dir. Bjornsen & Co., Oslo and Berlin; vice consul, Oslo and Trondhjem, Norway, 1920, Malmo, Sweden, 1921, Reval, Esthonia, 1922; vice consul, judge Consular Ct., Jerusalem, Palestine, 1923, Bushire and Teheran, Persia (Iran), 1924-25; successively consul Berlin, Niagara Falls, Kingston, Winnipeg, St. John (N.B.), Can.; consul gen., Antwerp, Tunisia, Malta and Tripolitania; assigned Dept. of State, 1922-23, asst. chief div. polit. and econ. information, sec. interdept. econ. liaison com.; Western Europe trade cons. sec. state, 1927; professor internat. econs. Fgn. Service Sch., Georgetown U., Am. U., U. Va.; past pres. Sch. Advanced Study Internat. Understanding, White House Conf. on Aging. Served in Mexican Border campaign, N.Y. Cav.; maj. gen. staff, Washington, World War I; maj. M.I. Res. Mem. Retired Fgn. Service Officers Assn. (founder, exec. dir.), Fgn. Service Assn., Res. Officers Assn., S.A.R., Tunis-Am. C. of C. (hon. pres.), Psi Upsilon, Delta Phi Epsilon. Clubs: St. John Figure Skating (founder); Metropolitan, Washington Figure Skating, Chevy Chase, Dacor (Washington); Yale. Author articles on internat. economics. Home: Washington DC Died Mar. 12, 1973.

FULLER, GEORGE NEWMAN, historian, retired; born Barry County, Michigan, 1873; son of Reuben A. and Delia (Coulter) F.; A.B., U. of Mich., 1905, Ph.D., 1912; A.M. Harvard, 1906 (winner Bowdoin prize 1906, 08, Townshend scholarship, 1906-07); spent summers 1905-09 in Europe; grad. study, Yale, 1909-11; m. Belle Vandervere, 1897 (died 1920); children—Florence, Margaret; m. 2d, Helen Gustine, 1927. Prin. high sch., L'Anse, Mich., 1896-1900, Nashville, Mich., 1900-02; head dept. of history, Mont. State Normal Coll., 1908-09; sec. and editor Mich. Hist. Commn., Lansing, 1913-14 and 1916-46; instructor U. of Mich., 1915-16. Editor of Michigan History Magazine, 1917-46. Member State Hist. Soc. (sec. 1916-46), Mich. Authors Assn. (pres. 1925-26). Republican. Methodist. Club: University. Author: Economic and Social Beginnings of Michigan, 1916; Democracy and the Great War, 1918. Editor: Historic Michigan, 1924; Michigan in the World War, 1924; Messages of the Governors of Michigan, 1925-27; The Centennial History of Michigan and Its People, 1939. Home: Lansing MI‡

FULLER, HELEN, editor; b. Cullman, Ala.; d. Arthur Wright and Lela E. (Thompson) Fuller; A.B., U. Ala., 1933, M.A., 1934, postgrad. Law Sch., 1935. Spl. atty. U.S. Dept. Justice, 1935-39; asst. to adminstr. Nat. Youth Adminstrn., 1939-41; joined New Republic, 1941, asst. editor, 1944-46, Washington editor, 1946-48, polit. editor, 1948-51, mng. editor, 1952-62; polit. columnist Spartanburg Herald and Jour., also other newspapers; contbr. articles to Harper's. Mem. bd. MEDICO, Inc.; bd. dirs. Washington Pub. Welfare Found. Mem. Am. Polit. Sci. Assn., Phi Beta Kappa. Author: Year of Trial, 1962. Home: Rappahannock County VA Died Sept. 15, 1972.

FULLER, J(OHN) DOUGLAS, coll. prof. b. Laurens, S.C., Oct. 30, 1899; s. Claude Stokes and Corinne (Pitts) F.; B.S., The Citadel, 1919; A.M., Johns Hopkins, 1928, Ph.D., 1932; m. Minnie Lawrence Mims, June 1, 1922; children—Minnie Jane, John Douglas. Asso. prof. history Tex. Agr. and Mech. Coll., 1928-35; teaching fellow Johns Hopkins, 1931-32; prof. history Virginia Military Institute from 1935; head departments history and econs., 1952-59, head dept. history econs. and polit. sci., from 1959. Armed Services rep., instructor history and geopolitics, Army Specialized Training Programs, lecturer in geopolitics, R.O.T.C. and O.R.C., 1948-49. Served as 2d lt. U.S. Army, World War I. Member Am. and Southern hist. assns., Am. Polit. Sci. Assn., Am. Assn. Univ. Profs., Nat. Geog. Soc. Democrat. Episcopalian. Author: The Movement for the Acquisition of Mexico, 1846-48, 1936. Co-editor Greenmount: A Virginia Plantation Family During the Civil War, 1962. Home: Lexington VA Died May 30, 1967; buried Stonewall Jackson Cemetery, Lexington VA

FULLER, MYRON LESLIE, geologist; b. Brockton, Mass., Apr. 19, 1873; s. Albert Henry and Phoebe Ann F.; S.B., Mass. Inst. Tech., 1896; m. Lillian A. Gayner, Apr. 26, 1897. Did pvt. field work on pegmatics of N.H., 1895, and in pleistocene deposits of Cape Cod, 1896, field work on copper range, Keweenaw Point, for Mich. Geol. Survey, 1897; asst. in geology, 1897-99, instructor, 1899-1900, Mass. Inst. Tech.; field work in Pa., Ind., Ill., for United States Geol. Survey, 1900-02; organized Eastern sec. of div. of hydrology, Jan. 1, 1903; chief of sect., 1903-06; in charge coastal plain investigations, 1907. U.S. explorations in China, Manchuria and Mongolia, 1913-15; has done much field work in coal, oil and gas fields and on glacial and artesian water problems in U.S. and gen. field work in Alaska, Northern Canada, West Indies, and Brazil. Received Walker prizes of Boston Soc. Natural History, 1897 and 1905; gold medal for govt. exhibit of building stones at Paris Expn., 1900. Extensive contbr. to tech. jours. and to publs. of U.S. Geol. Survey. Mem. Geol. Soc. America, A.A.A.S., Seismological Brockton MA‡

FULLER, OLIVE BEATRICE MUIR, author; b. Kansas City, Nov. 2, 1874; d. John and Libbie (Newbanks) Muir; removed from Portland, Ore., to Brooklyn, N.Y., 1886; ed. pub. sch. and Packer Collegiate Inst., Brooklyn, and Wesleyan Ladies' Sem. to 1892; m. at New York, Dr. David J. Fuller, Jan. 4, 1900. Elocutionist, 1890-1902; has given illustrated lecture on French Revolution. Made trips to Alaska and to Europe; first novel published at 19 yrs. of age; verses in Brooklyn Eagle, 1891-8; short stories in mags. Club: Woman's Press (New York). Author: Thy Name Is Woman, 1894; With Malice Toward None, 1900. Address: 162 Clinton St., Brooklyn‡

FULLER, ROBERT STEVENS, savs. and loan assn. exec.; b. Los Angeles, Mar. 30, 1904; s. Dorwin L. and Fannie (Stevens) F.; B.A., U. Cal. at Berkeley, 1926; m. Marianna Osborne, Oct. 11, 1927; children—Robert O., Ernest L., John S. Appraiser, br. mgr. Bank of Am., 1928-53; with San Fernando Valley Fed. Savs. & Loan Assn., Van Nuys, Cal., 1953-69, pres., 1958-68, chmn. bd., 1961-69, dir. Fed. Home Loan Bank San Francisco, 1963-66; Vice chmn. Los Angeles Mayor's Econ. Devel. Bd., 1963-69. Exec. v.p., bd. dirs. Valley Presbyn. Hosp., 1954-69; vice chmn. adv. com. San Fernando Valley State Coll., 1958-69; bd. dirs., Past pres. San Fernando Valley council Boy Scouts Am.; bd. dirs. Mid-Valley YMCA, 1953-69, also chmn. capital fund com.; council regents Forest Lawn Meml. Parks. Recipient Silver Beaver award Boy Scouts Am., 1963; Golden Book award Met. YMCA, 1966; Fernando award San Fernando Valley, 1964; named Citizen of Year, Van Nuys Coordinating Council, 1959. Mem. Cal. Savs. and Loan League (pres. 1966-67, dir.), Los Angeles (dir.), Van Nuys (past pres.; Man of Year award 1956) chambers commerce. Presbyn. (trustee, past ruling elder). Home: Van Nuys CA Died May 23, 1969; buried Forest Lawn, Hollywood Hills CA

FULLER, TEDDY RAY, artist; b. Gary, Ind., Aug. 15, 1924; s. John Owens and Golda (Hastings) F.; student Capital U., 1943, Ray-Vogue Art Sch., 1946-49, Chgo. Art Inst., 1950; m. Eleanor Victoria Barbier, Dec. 22, 1967. Creative dir. The Bendix Corp., Detroit and So. Bend, Ind., 1951-67; exhibited one-man shows at Merrill Chase Galleries, Chgo., 1969, Calumet City, Ill., 1969, Oak Brook, Ill., 1969, Robertson's, South Bend, Ind., 1969, Grumbacher, Inc. traveling exhibit, 1969, U.S. Dept. of Interior, Washington, 1970. Cons. Bendix Corp., Detroit. Served to 2d lt. USAAF, 1942-45. Address: Rolling Prairie IN Died Jan. 23, 1972.

FULLER, WILLIAM DAVID, supt. schs.; b. Coloma, Wis., Feb. 15, 1873; s. Morgan Henry and Harriet Elmina (Carpenter) F.; grad. Stevens Point (Wis.) Normal Sch., 1902; Ph.B., U. of Wis., 1910; studied U. of Calif., U., of Chicago, Columbia; A.M., U. of Me., 1917; m. Nellie E. Bradlay, of Sparta, Wis., Aug. 29, 1906. Prin. twp. high sch., Eagle River, Wis., 1902-6; headmaster Hillside (Wis.) Home Sch., 1906-9; supt. schs., Sparta, Wis., 1911; instr. high sch., Berkeley, Calif., 1912; supt. schs., Hudson, Wis., 1912-14, Old Town, Orono Me., 1914-18, Portland, Me., 1918—. Lectured on edn., Prince of Wales Coll., summers, 1916-17; asst. prof. edn., summers 1916, 17, prof., 1918, U. of Me. Mem. N.E.A., Me. State Teachers' Assn., Cumberland Co. Teachers' Assn. (pres. 1920.) Democrat. Conglist. Mason (32 deg., K.T.). Club: Kiwanis (pres. 1922). Author: American Industries, 1922. Home: 16 Linden St., Portland ME‡

FULLER, WILLIAM HAYES, lawyer; b. Lenawee Co., Mich., June 19, 1869; s. John C. and Frances (Hayes) F.; grad. high sch., Wellington, O., 1888; LL.B., U. of Mich., 1891; m. Gertrude Lyon, of Wauseon, O., 1892. Began practice at Wauseon, 1891; pros. atty. Fulton Co., O., 1896-1902; moved to McAlester, Okla., 1902, and practiced as mem. firm Fuller & Porter; chief counsel Federal Trade Commn., Washington, D.C., Oct. 1921-Dec. 1925; became mem. Rep. State Exec. Com., Okla., 1920. Presbyn. Mason (33 deg., K.T., Shriner), Elk. Home: McAlester OK*‡

FULLER, WILLIAM PARMER, JR., ret. mfr.; b. San Francisco, May 2, 1888; s. William Parmer and Laura (Pike) F.; A.B., Stanford, 1910; m. Adaline Wright, Feb. 21, 1911; children—William Parmer, III, George Wright, John Malcolm. Resigned as chmn. bd. W. P. Fuller & Company, 1949. Director San Francisco Community Chest, 1928-41, president, 1936-41. Member board trustees Stanford, 1933-58, pres. bd., 1943-48; trustee Mills Coll., 1933-43, pres. bd., 1934-43. Served as lt. USNR, World War I; chief Mission to Poland, Am. Relief Adminstrn., 1919-20. Home: Hillsborough CA Died Aug. 3, 1970.

FULLERTON, ANNA M., physician; d. Rev. Robert Stewart and Martha (White) F.; sister of George Stuart F. (q.v.); M.D., Woman's Med. Coll. of Pa., 1883; post-grad. work abroad, 1884-5; unmarried. Practiced at Phila., 1885-99; clin. prof. gynecology, Woman's Med. Coll. of Pa., 1885-9; phys.-in-charge Woman's Hosp. of Phila., 1886-96; lecturer on surgery and operative midwifery, Med. Sch. for Women, Ludhiana, Punjab, India, 1889-1903; prin. N. India Med. Sch. for Women, 1905-6; in independent med. mission work at Fatehgarh, India, since 1906. Author: Obstetric Nursing; Surgical Nursing. Address: Fatehgarh UP India‡

FULLERTON, HUGH STUART, author; b. Hillsboro, O., Sept. 10, 1873; s. Hugh Stuart and Mary Alice (Miller) F.; prep. edn., high sch., Hillsboro, Ohio; student Ohio State University, 1891-93; Litt.D., Miami University, 1936; m. Edith Zollars, of Fort Wayne, Ind., Aug. 8, 1900; children—Dorothy Zollars (Mrs. Lloyd S. Burns), Hugh Stuart. Began newspaper writing at Hillsboro, 1888; successively with Cincinnati Tribune, Cincinnati Enquirer, baseball writer Chicago Record, 1893-94, sports writer Chicago Tribune, 1894-1917, New York Evening World, 1918-19, New York Mail, 1919-21; with Liberty (weekly), 1923-28, Columbus Dispatch from 1928. Republican. Presbyn. Clubs: Players (New York); Chicago Yacht. Author: Touching Second (with J.J. Evers), 1908; Shasta Boys' Team, 1912; Cascade College, 1912; The Plot for the Pennant, 1912; The Movement of the Tribes, 1916; Tales of the Turf, 1923-24; also articles and short stories in mags. Address: 142 Tullamore Road, Garden City LI NY*‡

FULLERTON, SAMUEL CLYDE, lawyer; b. Lawrence Co., Mo., Sept. 11, 1877; s. Josiah David and Sarah Elizabeth (Gibson) F.; grad. high sch., Sarcoxie, Mo., 1895; m. Minnie L. Beck, of Miami, Okla., Nov. 27, 1901; children—Pauline Florence (Mrs. John C. Newton), Samuel Clyde, Katherine Louise, Gibson Beck, Carrie Belle, Elizabeth Ann, Mary Lou (dec.), Patty Jean. Admitted to Okla. bar, 1897, and began practice at Miami; judge 28th Judicial Dist., Okla., 1919-23; stock raiser of pure bred cattle and hogs. Chmn. Draft Exemption Bd., Ottawa Co., Okla., May-Nov. 1917. Pres. Am. Aberdeen-Angus Breeders Assn. since 1924, Okla. Farm Bur. Federation, 1926-27. Democrat. Presbyn. Mason (32 deg., Shriner). Home: Miami OK*‡

FULP, JAMES DOUGLAS, educator; b. Fort Mill, York Co., S.C., Oct. 13, 1886; s. Richard Amasa and Lucy (Parker) F.; A.B., Presbyn. Coll. of S.C., Clinton, S.C., 1906; studied U. of London, 1919; M.A., U. of S.C., 1925; m. Daisy Wilson, of Ridgeway, S.C., Oct. 14, 1909; children—James D., Jr., John R. Prin. Mt. Zion Inst., S.C., 1906-07; supt. city schs., Ft. Mill and Abbeville, S.C., 1915-17, 1919-23; high sch. insp., S.C., 1923-26; supt. Bailey Mil. Acad., Greenwood, S.C., since 1926. Served as capt. U.S.A., 1917-19; maj. Inf. Res., 1919-25; lt. col. since 1925. Trustee Presbyn. Coll. of S.C. Mem. N.E.A. (life), Nat. Assn. High Sch. Supervisors (pres. 1926), S.C. Teachers Assn. (life; pres. 1926-27), Am. Legion, Pi Kappa Alpha. Democrat. Presbyn. Kiwanian. Home: Greenwood SC‡

FULTON, ALBERT COOLEY, clergyman; b. Indianapolis, Ind., June 2, 1872; s. Harmon Healey and Maria (Newcomb) F.; prep. edn., Mount Hermon (Mass.) Boys Sch.; student Princeton, 1894-97; Hartford Theol. Sem., 1900; S.T.D., Syracuse, 1913; m. Marion Rondthaler, of Chicago, Ill., June 11, 1901; children—Albert Rondthaler, Marion Elizabeth (Mrs. Robert F. Burnham), Frederick Harmon (dec.), Barbara (Mrs. Edward MacNasser), Dorothy Newcomb, Frances Louise. Ordained Congl. ministry, 1900; pastor Second Ch., Kennebunk, Me., and Somersworth, N.H., until 1910; asst. pastor Second Presbyn. Ch., Newark, N.J., 1910-11; pastor First Presbyn. Ch., Syracuse, N.Y., 1911-31; exec. sec. N.Y. State Council of Chs., 1931-32; pastor First Presbyn. Ch., Skaneateles, N.Y., 1933-37; retired. Mem. Co. K, 1st Conn. Vol. Inf., Spanish-Am. War, 1898. Mem. S.A.R., Cliosophic Soc. (Princeton). Republican. Clubs: Citizens, Torch, Rotary. Home: Skaneateles, N.Y.; (summer) Murray Isle, Thousand Islands NY‡

FULTON, CHARLES HERMAN, metallurgist; b. of Am. parents, at Ludwigshafen am Rhein, Germany, July 16, 1874; s. Albert Charles and Bertha Anne (Arzberger) F.; prep edn., Pratt Inst., Brooklyn, N.Y.; E.M., Sch. of Mines (Columbia), 1897; hon. D.Sc., U. of S. Dak., 1911; m. Marion Cunninghame, Sept. 19, 1898; children—Bertha Isabelle, Marion Emily (dec). Asst. in assaying, Columbia, 1898-99; instr. in metallurgy, U. of Wyo., 1899-1900; prof. metallurgy, S. Dak. State Sch. of Mines, Rapid City, S.D., 1900-05, pres., 1905-11; prof. metallurgy, Case Sch. Applied Science, 1911-20; dir. Mo. Sch. of Mines and Metallurgy, U. of Mo., 1920-37, research prof. of metallurgy, 1937-39, acting prof. metallurgy, Montana School of Mines, since 1942; Consulting metallurgical engineer. Member Missouri Academy Science (president 1938-39), American Institute Mining and Metall. Engrs., Theta Delta Chi, Sigma Xi, Tau Manual of Fire Assaying, 1907.‡

FULTON, JAMES GROVE, congressman; b. Allegheny County, Pa., Mar. 1, 1903; s. James Ernest and Emilie (Fetterman) F.; A.B., Pennsylvania State Univ., 1924; LL.D., Harvard, 1927; student Carnegie Inst. Tech. 2 yrs.; unmarried. Admitted to Pa. bar, 1928, in general practice of law, Pittsburgh, Pa., 1928-42; solicitor for Dormont Borough, 1942; state senator 45th Pa. Dist., 1939-40; mem. 79th-82d Congresses, 31st Pa. Dist., mem. 83d-91st Congresses, 27th District Pa.; mem. House Fgn. Affairs committee, chmn. sub-com. for Europe, chmn. spl. sub-com. to investigate Displaced Persons and Internat. Refugee Orgn., mem. Sci. and Astronautics com., mem. vets. affairs com. 87th; U.S. del. UN Internat. Trade Orgn. Conf., Havana, 1947-48, U.S., del. 14th Gen. Assembly UN, 1959. Co-author, Definitive study on Internat. Trade Orgn.; owner, publisher Mt. Lebanon (Pa.) News, The Boro News, and The News (Allegheny County), Chartiers Valley Times Progress, The Tribune, also The News Progress, Dormont News (both Pitts.). Chmn. Pa. Heart Fund, 1970. Bd. dirs. Pitt Sch. Engring.; bd. visitors U.S. Naval Acad., Annapolis, Md. Served as lt. USNR, 1942-45; service Pacific combat area; ret. capt. Mem. bd. dirs. Pittsburgh Playhouse, Pitts. Opera Bd. Mem. Allegheny Bd. Law Examiners, 1934-42. Rep. for President U.S. at Uruguay inauguration, 1954. Decorated by Republic of Italy, 1956; named Distinguished Grad. Pa. State U., 1970; recipient Silver Quill award, 1970; mem. Young Republican Nat. Hall of Fame; life mem. Allegheny County Young Rep. Hall of Fame. Mem. Am., Pa., Allegheny County bar assns., Vets. Fgn. Wars, Am. Legion, Phi Delta Theta. Republican. Elk, Eagle. Clubs: Civic of Allegheny County, Harvard of Western Pennsylvania, Harvard-Yale-Princeton, Duquesne, St. Clair Country, Chartiers Country, Law (Pitts.). Home: Dormont PA Died Oct. 6, 1971; buried Mt. Lebanon Cemetery.

FULTON, MAURICE GARLAND, college prof.; b. Oxford, Miss., Dec. 3, 1877; s. Robert Burwell and Annie (Garland) F.; Ph.B., U. of Miss., 1898, A.M. 1901; U. of Mich., 1901-03. Instr. rhetoric, U. of Miss., 1900-01; asst. in rhetoric, U. of Mich., 1901-03; instr. rhetoric, U. of Ill., 1903-04, U. of Mich., 1904-05; prof. English, Centre Coll. of Central U., Ky., 1905-09; same Davidson Coll., 1909-18; asst. prof. Indiana U., 1919-22; prof. English, Junior College New Mexico Military Institution, 1922-48, prof. emeritus since 1948. Supt. Old Lincoln County Museum, Lincoln, New Mexico, 1948. Mem. Modern Lang. Assn. Am., Nat. Council Eng. Teachers, Delta Psi. Democrat. Presbyterian. Author: Manual of Exercises in Composition (with R.A. Abbott), 1905; Questions on Readings in English Literature (with R.G. Bressler and G.H. Mullin), 1915; Talking Well (with W.L. Harrington), 1926; Questions on Readings in English Literature (with R.G. Bressler), 1928. Compiler and Editor; Expository Writing, 1912; College Life, 1914; Southern Life in Southern Literature, 1917; Writing Craftsmanship—Models and Readings, 1926; New Mexico's Own Chronicle (with Paul Horgan), 1937. Editor: Christmas Night in the Quarters and Other Poems by Irwin Russell, 1918; National Ideals and Problems, 1918; Bryce on American Democracy, 1919; Selections from Roosevelt's Writings, 1920; Pat Garrett's The Authentic Life of Billy the Kid, 1927; Charles Lamb in Essays and Letters, 1930; The College Shakespeare, 1931; The Death of Billy the Kid (John W. Poe's account), 1933; Diary and Letters of Joshiah Gregg, Vol. I, (Southwestern Enterprises, 1840-46), 1941; Vol. II, (Excursions in Mexico and California, 1847-1850), 1944. Home: Roswell NM‡

FUNK, ERWIN CHARLES, editor, pub.; b. Deep River, Ia., Jan. 5, 1877; s. Emanuel M. and Addie (Walters) F.; grad. high sch., Carroll, Ia., 1893; m. Mintie Michael, Nov. 18, 1903. Began as editor Manning (Ia.) Monitor, 1894; editor Springdale (Ark.) Democrat, 1896; editor and pub. Rogers Democrat, 1897-1930; mng. editor Fayetteville (Ark.) Leader, 1931; Washington legislative rep. Nat. Editorial Assn., 1935; Red Cross and Welfare Director, Rogers, Ark., 1936-49. Publicity dir. Ark. Y.M.C.A., 1918; editor Trench & Camp, Camp Pike, 1918; Y.M.C.A. athletic dir., A.E.F., 1918-19. Newspaper code adminstr. for Ark. under NRA. Mem. Nat. Editorial Assn. (v.p., Ark., 10 yrs.; nat. pres. 1928), Ark. Press Assn. (sec. 5 yrs.; pres. 1925-26). Democrat. Presbyterian. Club: Rotary (pres. 1930; sec. 7 yrs.). Home: 612 S. 6th St., Rogers AR‡

FUNK, MILES CONRAD, utilities exec.; b. Summerfield, Grayson Co., Va., Mar. 10, 1887; s. Steven Mckinley and Mollie (Cornett) F.; student pub. schs., Va.; m. Nora Long, Dec. 25, 1912 (dec.); children—Evelyn Merrill, Helen Marie (Mrs. Eugene

Clifford Flannery), Della Mae (Mrs. Lawrence Gardner Dougan), Robert Steven, Betty Jo (Mrs. Betty F. Wilmore). Vice president, director Appalachian Power Co., Roanoke, Virginia from 1943; v.p., dir. Ky. Power Co., Inc. 1943-52; v.p. gen. mgr. Appalachian Power Co., 1943-52; dir. Kingsport Utilities, Inc., Central Appalachian Coal Co., Central Coal Co., Central Operating Co., Am. Electric Power Service Corp., Radford Limestone Co., W.Va. Power Co., First Nat. Exchange Bank (Roanoke, Va.). Mem. Pub. Utilities Assn. of the Vas. (Roanoke), Southeastern Electric Exchange (Atlanta), N.A.M. Clubs: Roanoke Country, Shenandoah (Roanoke, Va.). Home: Salem VA Died Aug. 8, 1968; buried Sherwood Memorial Park Abbey, Salem VA

FUNSTEN, BENJAMIN REED, merchant; b. St. Louis, Nov. 3, 1887; s. James Johnston and Amelia (Moore) F.; ed. pub. schs. of Mo.; m. Gladys Little, Dec. 7, 1921. With Rice Stix Dry Goods Co., St. Louis, 1904, Ralston Purina Co., 1905, Moore Watson Dry Goods Co., 1906, dept. head, 1915-17; 2d v.p. Walton N. Moore Dry Goods Co., San Francisco, 1917-21, 1st v.p., 1921-26, pres. 1926-57; pres. B. F. Schlesinger & Sons, 1932-33; pres. City of Paris Dry Goods Co., 1932; pres., dir. B. R. Funsten & Co., Smith & Lang, Inc.; dir. Baker & Hamilton, Standard Realty and Development Company; director Wells Fargo Bank, Laurentide Financial Corp., Payne Bolt Works, Cal. Trustee, Children's Hosp. Clubs: Bohemian, San Francisco Golf, Pacific Union. Home: San Francisco Died Mar. 15, 1969.

FURAY, JOHN BAPTIST, educator; priest; b. Omaha, Neb., Mar. 25, 1873; s. John B. and Catherine (McShane) F.; A.B., St. Mary's Coll., Kan., 1890; LL.D., Loyola U., 1926, Creighton U., 1928; S.T.D., Gregorian U., Rome; post-grad. philosophy, St. Louis U., 1894-97; student in theology, same, 1902-07. Joined Soc. of Jesus, 1891; ordained R.C. priest, 1905; instr. St. Louis U., 1897-98; asst. prof. classics, St. Ignatius Coll., Chicago, 1898-1902; prof. classics, St. Stanislaus Sem., Florissant, Mo., 1907-08; v.p., dean St. John's U., Toledo, O., 1908-10; pres. St. Ignatius Coll., Cleveland, 1910-15, Loyola U., Chicago, 1915-21; dir. of studies U. of St. Mary of the Lake since Sept. 1921, dean of the theol. faculty. Vice-pres. Nat. Catholic Ednl. Assn. Address: St. Mary of the Lake, Mundelein IL*‡

FURMAN, BESS (MRS. ROBERT B. ARMSTRONG, JR.), govt. ofcl.; b. Danbury, Neb., Dec. 2, 1894; d. Archie Charles and Mattie Ann (Van Pelt) Furman; student Missouri State Tchrs. Coll., Kirksville; grad. Neb. State Tchrs. Coll., Kearney, 1918; student Columbia, 1922; m. Robert B. Armstrong, Jr., Mar. 18, 1932 (dec. Apr. 1955); children—Ruth Eleanor and Robert Furman (twins). Various positions, family weekly Danbury (Neb.) News; with Kearney (Neb.) Hub, 1917-19, Omaha Bee-News, 1919-29; staff Washington bur. Asso. Press, 1929-37; with sister Lucile, writing firm Furman Features, 1937-41; asst. chief mag. div. O.W.I., 1941-43; corr. Washington bur. N.Y. Times, 1943-61; asst. to sec. Health, Edn. and Welfare, Pub. Affairs, 1961-63; historian Public Health Service, 1963-66. Specialist White House history, biographies of wives of the Presidents. Recipient Headliners award Theta Sigma Phi, 1949. Clubs: Omaha Women's Press (past pres.); Women's Nat. Press (past pres.) (Washington). Author: Washington By-line, 1949; White House Profile, 1951. Author mag. articles, book reviews. Home: Washington DC Died May 12, 1969.

FURNAS, CLIFFORD COOK, univ. pres., author; b. Sheridan, Ind., Oct. 24, 1900; s. Thomas Chalmers and Clara Evana (Spray) F.; B.S., Purdue U., 1922, D.Eng. (hon.), 1946; graduate work Carleton College, 1923-24; Ph.D., U. Mich., 1926, D.Eng., 1957; LL.D., Alfred U., 1958; D.Sc., Theil Coll., 1960; Dr. Honoris Causa, University de Paraguay, 1963; m. Sparkle Moore, Apr. 12, 1925; 1 daughter, Beatrice Louise. Teacher of mathematics, Shattuck School, 1922-24; research chemist with U.S. Steel Corp., 1924-25; phys. chemist with U.S. Bur. of Mines, 1926-31; asso. prof. of chem. engring., Yale U., 1931-42; tech. aide, Nat. Defense Research Com., 1941-43; director research, Curtiss-Wright Airplane Div. 1943-46; exec. v.p., Cornell Aeronautical Lab., 1946-54; now dir.; industrial cons.; chancellor University Buffalo, 1954-62, pres. State Univ. of New York at Buffalo, 1962-66, pres. emeritus, 1966-69; pres. Western N.Y. Nuclear Research Center; research asso. Bur. Ednl. Research in Science, summer, 1938; lectr. Bur. of Ednl. Research in Science for Tchrs. Coll., Columbia, summer, 1939. Research chem. engring. and metallurgy; chmn. guided missile com., Research and Development Bd., 1952-53; NACA, 1955-57; chmn. Air Navigation Devel. Bd., 1956-57; chmn. advisory panel on aeros. Dept. of Defense, 1954-55; asst. sec. of def. for research and devel. 1955-57; member of the science advisory panel of the United States Army; chairman New York Adv. Council Industrial Research and Devel., 1961-69; member Defense Science Board, 1957-69, chmn., 1961-65; mem. Naval Res. Adv. Com., 1958-69. Mem. board of directors of Carborundum Hooker Hooker Chem. Co., Mfrs. & Traders Trust Co., Aerospace Corp. Awarded Big 10 Conf. medal for best combined scholastic and athletic record, 1922; mem. 1920 Am. Olympic Team. Decorated gold cross Order of Phoenix (Greece); recipient Vincent Bendix award Am. Soc. Engring. Edn., 1956; Western N.Y. honor scroll Am. Inst. Chemists; gold medal Buffalo Club. Charles M. Schwab Meml. lectr., 1958; Schoellkopf medal, 1962; Fairchild award Arnold Air Soc., 1963; citation Nat. Conf. Christians and Jews, 1965; Chancellor's medal U. Buffalo, 1968. Fellow A.A.A.S., Inst. Aero. Scis. (hon. v.p.); mem. Am. Inst. Chem. Engrs., Nat. Acad. Engring., Am. Chem. Soc., Newcomen Soc., Sigma XI, Phi Beta Kappa, Tau Beta Pi, Phi Lambda Upsilon, Theta Chi. Clubs: Fort Orange (Albany, N.Y.); Chemists (New York); Buffalo, Buffalo Country, Saturn, Aero, Thursday, (Buffalo); Cosmos (Washington). Author: America's Tomorrow, 1932; The-Next Hundred Years, 1936; Man, Bread and Destiny, 1937; section on metallurgy in Technological Trends and National Policy, 1937; The Storehouse of Civilization, 1939; The Engineer, 1966; also author sects. on sci. in various publs. Editor: Roger's Manual of Industrial Chemistry, 1941; Industrial Research: Organization and Management, 1948. Contbr. sect. on sci. and technology Modern World Politics, 1953. Home: Buffalo NY Died Apr. 27, 1969; interred Memorial Chapel, Forest Lawn Cemetery, Buffalo NY

FURNESS, JAMES WILSON, mining engr.; b. Phila., Pa., June 5, 1874; s. Frank and Fannie (Fassitt) F.; prep. edn., William Penn Charter Ch., Phila., 1883-91; B.S., Pa. Mil. Coll. 1895, B.M.S., 1927; m. Adeline E. Brown, Oct. 25, 1899; 1 dau., Adeline Fassitt. Assayer and metallurgist in Colo., 1895-1900; asst. to D.M. Barringer, mining engr., Phila., in examining mining properties in Can., western U.S. and Mexico, 1904-08; operator of mines, 1908-09; asso. with O.A. Robertson in chge. mining properties in Can., Calif., Colo. and Nevada, also visited mines in Belgium, 1910-18; operated mines in Colo. and Ariz., 1919-22; investigated manganese situation in Georgia, Russia, 1920; with U.S. Bur. of Mines, 1922-26; chief of mineral div. U.S. Bur. Foreign and Domestic Commerce. Dept. of Commerce, 1927-34; chief of economics br. Bur. of Mines, 1934-40; retired. Served as officer Ordance Dept., U.S. Army, Aug. 1918-Jan. 15, 1919; lieut. colonel Special Res., U.S. Army, 1937; member Minerals Advisory Com. to War Dept.; mem. Mineral Policy Committee, 1935. Mem. Washington Geol. Soc. Dem. Unitarian. Clubs: Civitan, Down Town (Asheville). Author of many government publications on mineral economics. Home: 76 North Griffing Boulevard, Asheville NC‡

FURNISS, EDGAR STEPHENSON, univ. exec.; b. Hunter, N.D., Apr. 15, 1890; s. George and Anne Jane (Stephenson) F.; B.A., Coe Coll., Cedar Rapids, Ia., 1911; Ph.D., Yale, 1917; LL.D., Coe Coll., 1931, Lehigh University, 1936, Litt. D., Princeton University, 1947; married Beryl Frances Gates, May 15, 1917; children—Edgar Stephenson, Norman Francis. Began teaching at Syrian Protestant Coll., Beirut, Syria, 1911; prof. polit. and social sci. Yale, since 1923, provost from 1936. Mem. Am. Econ. Assn., Am. Polit. Sci. Assn., Am. Acad. Arts and Sciences, Zeta Psi. Presbyterian. Clubs: Century, Graduate. Author: Position of Laborer in a System of Nationalism, 1920; Foreign Exchange, 1922; Labor Problems (with L. R. Guild), 1925; Elementary Economics, 1926; Economics, 1937. Mem. editorial bd. Yale Review. Address: New CT Died July 17, 1972; buried New Haven CT

FURRY, WILLIAM DAVIS, educator; b. Cumberland, Md., June 21, 1873; s. Fred S. and Elizabeth (Davis) F.; B.A., U. of Notre Dame, Ind., 1900, M.A., 1904; Ph.D., Johns Hopkins, 1907; m. Nina K. Smith, of Sharpsburg, Md., Dec. 1896. Pres. Ashland (O.) Coll., 1911-19; head of dept. of philosophy and edn., 1919-21, dean, 1921, acting pres., 1922, pres., since 1925, Shorter Coll., also prof. philosophy and edn. Mem. Am. Philos. Assn., Southern Soc. for Philosophy and Psychology, Huxley Soc. of Johns Hopkins, A.A.A.S., Phi Beta Kappa. Democrat. Mason. Rotarian. Author: The Aesthetic Experience, 1909. Home: Rome GA‡

FURST, SIDNEY DALE, , lawyer; b. Lock Haven, Pa., Sept. 5, 1904; s. Sidney Dale and Aida (Dunn) F.; grad. Hill Sch., 1922; A.B., Princeton, 1926; LL.B., Harvard, 1929; m. Ruth Evelyn Kober, Dec. 28, 1950; children—Carolyn McCormick (Mrs. Carlson), Barbara Lloyd (Mrs. Johnstone), Margaretta McCormick (Mrs. Stewart), Susan Elizabeth Lloyd (Mrs. Maiolo), and Sidney Dale Furst III. Admitted to Pa. bar, 1929, since practiced in Williamsport; with Seth T. McCormick, Jr., atty., 1929-36; partner firm Furst, McCormick, Lynn, Reeder & Nichols, and predecessors, 1936—. Vice pres., dir. Sprout, Waldron & Co., Inc., Muncy, Pa., Williamsport Hotels Co.; sec. Loyalsock Mgmt., Inc.; dir. No. Central Bank & Trust Co., Axeman-Anderson Co., Williamsport, Pa., Darling Valve & Mfg. Co., Syntex Fabrics, Inc., Lyco Systems, Inc., Joseph R. Maiolo, Inc., Dice Drug Co., Inc., Williamsport, Pa., Atelier Bouvier, Grenoble, France. Past chmn. nat. budget com. Community Chests and Councils Am.; mem. 3d Circuit Jud. Conf., Pa. Civil Procedural Rules Com., Governor's Com. on Aging, Gov.'s Come to Consider Merger Depts. of Pub. Assistance and Pub. Welfare; past pres. Pa. United Fund, Inc.; dir., membership chmn. Council on Founds.; past pres., mem. exec. com. Lycoming United Fund, Inc. Bd. dirs. Lycoming College, Williamsport, Pa.; bd. dirs. Horace B. Packer Found., Wellsboro, Pa., Williamsport Found.; trustee State Indsl. Home for Women, Muncy, Pa. Recipient Presl. citation, 1955; Red Feather award Lycoming County Community Chest, 1956. Fellow Am. Coll. Trial Lawyers; mem. Am. Law Inst., Am., Pa., Lycoming County bar assns., Nat. Probation and Parol Assn., Atlantic Salmon Association, American Fisheries Society, National Wild Life Federation, Princeton Alumni Assn., Harvard Law Sch. Assn., Lycoming County Hist. Soc., Am. Social Health Assn. (pres.). Republican. Presbyn. Mason. Clubs: Anglers (N.Y.C. and Phila.); Fly Fishers (London, Eng.); Quadrangle (Princeton); Big Bear, Grays Run, Otter Run, Young Men's Republican, Williamsport Country, Oaks, Ross, Wheel (Williamsport). Home: Williamsport PA Died July 9, 1969.

FURSTENBERG, ALBERT CARL, physician, dean med. sch.; b. Saginaw, Mich., May 27, 1890; s. William C. and Emma Jane (Kerr) F.; B.S., U. of Mich., 1913, M.D., 1915; m. Elizabeth Nancy Maloy, June 18, 1923; children—Nancy, Julie, William Lou. Intern U. of Mich. Hosp., 1915-16; instr. otolaryngology, U. of Mich. Med. Sch., 1918-24, asst. prof., 1924-29, asso. prof., 1929-32, prof., from 1932, dean, 1935-60. Dir. Ann Arbor Trust Co., Ann Arbor Bank. Served as 1st lt. Med. R.C., during World War; consultant, surgeon gen. U.S. Army; hon. cons. Army Med. Library. Diplomate Am. Bd. Otolaryngology. Fellow A.C.S. (2d v.p.; bd. govs., 1943-46); mem. Washtenaw Co., Mich. State med. socs., A.M.A., Am. Acad. Ophthal. and Otolaryngology (pres. 1956), Detroit Otol. Soc., Southwestern Mich. Triological Soc., Am. Laryngol., Rhinol. and Otol. Soc., Inc. (pres., 1946), Am. Otol. Soc. (pres., 1952-53), Am. Laryngol. Soc., Assn. Am. Med. Colleges (past pres.). Clubs: University of Michigan, Ann Arbor, Barton Hills (Ann Arbor); Detroit (Mich.) Athletic; Cosmos (Washington). Contbr. sci. articles to jours. Home: Ann Arbor MI Died Oct. 23, 1969.

FUTRELLE, MAY, author; b. Atlanta, Ga., May 26, 1876; d. David Gabriel and Mary Ellen (Thompson) Peel; grad. Immaculate Conception Acad., Atlanta, Ga., 1894; m. Jacques Futrelle, July 17, 1895 (deceased); children—Virginia Heath (Mrs. Charles Raymond), Jacques, Jr. Writer since 1906. Charter and life mem. Authors League; mem. Nat. League Am. Pen Women (mem. nat. bd.). Republican. Catholic. Author: Secretary of Frivolous Affairs, 1911; Lieutenant, What's His Name?, 1914. Contbr. fiction to mags.; writer and broadcaster of program, Do You Want to Be A Writer?" on Sta. WEEI, Boston. Home: Stepping Stones, Scituate MA‡

GABALDON, ISAURO, Philippine commr.; b. San Isidro, P.I., Dec. 8, 1875; s. Jose and Maria (Gonzalez) G.; B.A., Provincial Inst. of Cuenea, Spain, 1893; LL.B., U. of Santo Tomas, Manila, 1900; m. Bernarda Tinio Diaz, of Aliaga, P.I., Jan. 21, 1900. Provincial gov. of Nueva Elija, P.I., 1906-07; mem. 1st and 2d Philippine Assembly, 1907-12, Senate, 1916-19; res. commr. of P.I., to U.S., Feb. 1920-Mar. 1928, resigned. Address: House Office Bldg., Washington DC‡

GAFFNEY, JOHN MARSHALL, steamship co. exec.; b. Boston, Aug. 18, 1907; s. Peter Joseph and Sarah (Marshall) G.; A.B., Harvard, 1931, student Bus. Sch., 1932-33; m. Marion Mary Russell, Sept. 21, 1936 (dec. Dec. 1968); children—Sarah Jane (Mrs. Jeremy Bull), John Marshall. With U.S. Lines Co., 1933-42, 46-67, European gen. mgr., 1961, dep. European gen. mgr., 1961, v.p. Europe, 1961-67; regional dir., European gen. operations mgr. War Shipping Adminstrn., 1945-46; dir. Soc. Maritime Anversoise, Antwerp, Atlantic Transp. Co., Ltd., London, Rosskai, G.m.b.H., Hamburg, Service de Consignation Atlantique, Paris. Vice chmn. Internat. Chamber Shipping, 1966-67. Served to col., Transp. Corps, AUS, 1942-45. Decorated Legion of Merit; Legion of Honor, Croix de Guerre with palm (France). Mem. Am. C. of C. in London (dir.), Nat. Def. Transp. Assn. (life), Royal Instn. Naval Architects, Harvard Bus. Sch. Assn. Clubs: Propeller (pres.), Harvard, Royal Thames Yacht, Royal Ocean Racing, American (bd. govs.) (London); Sunningdale Golf (Berks., Eng.); Royal Corinthian Yacht (Essex, Eng). Home: London Eng Died Oct. 7, 1967; buried City of Westminster Cemetery, Mill Hill, Eng (Alekseyevich),

GAFFNEY, LEO VINCENT, judge; b. New Britain, Conn., Apr. 14, 1903; s. Bernard Francis and Alice (Sherlock) G.; A.B., Yale, 1925, LL.B., 1928; m. Ruth Boylan, Oct. 21, 1930; children—Patricia Ann (Mrs. Hewes), Judith Lee, Brenda. Admitted to Conn. bar, 1928, since practiced in New Britain; asst. atty. gen. Conn., 1935-44; asst. U.S. dist. atty., 1944; judge Superior Court, State of Conn., 1964-69. Chmn. bd. adjustment City of New Britain, 1938-47, New Britain Redevel. Commn., 1958-61. Fellow Am. Coll. Trial Lawyers; mem. Am. Bar Assn. (ho. of dels. from 1963), State Bar Assn. Conn. (pres. 1962-63), Fedn. Ins. Counsel (bd. govs. 1961-63). Home: New Britain CT Died Sept. 24, 1969.

GAGARIN, YURI (ALEKSEYEVICH), First cosmonaut; b. nr. Gzhatsk, Smolenskaya, Russia, Mar. 9, 1934; s. Alexei and Anna Gagarin; grad. Lyubertsy Vocational Sch., 1951; grad. with honors Indsl. Coll. of Saratov, 1955; grad. with high honors Soviet Air Force Cadet Tng. Center, Orenburg, 1957; m. Valentina Ivanovna; children—Elena, Galyna. Joined Soviet Air Force, 1957; test pilot, cosmonaut trainee; col., Soviet Air Force; manned rocket-propelled space satellite Vostok in earth orbit, Apr. 12, 1961. Elected to Supreme Soviet. Decorated Hero of the Soviet Union; Master of Radio Sport of the Soviet Union; Gold medal British Interplanetary Soc., 1961; diploma and Gold medal Internat. Aero. Fedn., 1961; Galabert International Astronautical prize, 1963. Member of the Young Communist League, also International Academy Astronautics (honorary), Soviet-Cuban Friendship Society (chmn.). Mem. Communist Party. Address: Moscow USSR Died Mar. 29, 1968; ashes interred in Kremlin wall, Moscow, USSR

GAGE, CHARLES AMON, clergyman; b. Winslow, Ill., Nov. 11, 1872; s. Isaac Vail and Arabella Bradford (Sweeley) G.; grad. high sch., Winslow, 1890; student Beloit (Wis.) Acad. and Coll., 1897-1900; grad. Codding Musical Coll., Boston, Mass., 1903; m. Harriet Theresa Wright, of Winslow, Feb. 19, 1893; children—Lueva Vivian, Louella Harriet (Mrs. James Walmsley), Harlan Wright (dec.), Nevin Isaac, Charles Amon, Arthur Willard. Ordained ministry M.E. Ch., 1896; pastorates (all in Ill.) East Dubuque, 1893-95, Orangeville, 1895-97, Durand, 1897-1900, Milledgeville, 1900-03, Rock Falls, 1903-06, Chicago, 1906-08, Oak Park, 1908-09, Elgin, 1909-13, Chicago, 1913-18, Rockford, 1918-23, Hyde Park M.E. Ch., Chicago, 1923-27, Broadway M.E. Ch., Chicago, since 1928; apptd. exec. head of Youths' Service Bur., 1929. Pres. Bd. of Pensions and Relief, Rock River Conf., M.E. Ch., since 1913, mem. Nat. Council Boy Scouts of America. Head of musical dept. of ednl. and recreational work of U.S. Army, Fosdick Commn.; also instr. in music recruit ednl. center, Camp Grant, Ill., 1918-20. Mem. bd. dirs. Chicago Law and Order League, Ill. Vigilance Assn.; chmn. internat. music com. for U.S. and Canada, Kiwanis International, since 1921. On lecture platform with Coit Alber Chautauqua Co. since 1905. Republican. Mason (K.T., 33 deg., Shriner). Clubs: Hamilton, High Noon, Kiwanis. Compiler and editor: Songs of the Jubilee (Methodist), 1909; New and Old Evangelistic Songs, 1910; Songs of Kiwanis, 1921. Musical editor of Kiwanis International; composer of gospel songs, club songs, etc. Author: Why Lincoln Came, 1923. Home: 718 Cornelia Av., Chicago IL‡

GAGE, ELBERT MAUNEY, investment banker; b. El Paso, Tex., Feb. 19, 1912; s. Fred Mauney and Louise (Delauze) G.; B.S. in Mech. and Indsl. Engring., U. Mich., 1933; m. Jean C. Clarke, Sept. 2, 1939; children—John C., William D. Engaged in ins. and real estate bus., 1933-41; with Sparton Co., 1942; pres. Teer. Wickwire Co., auto parts mfrs., Jackson, Mich., 1942-57; with Pacific Industries, Inc., San Francisco, 1958-72, exec. v.p., 1961-72; partner McIntyre and Gage, San Francisco, 1964-70; mgr. corporate finance dept. Hambrecht & Quist, investment bankers, San Francisco, 1970-72. Clubs: World Trade, Bankers (San Francisco). Home: Tiburon CA Died Dec. 24, 1972.

GAGE, JOHN BAILEY, lawyer; born Kansas City, Mo., Feb. 24, 1887; s. John Cutter and Ida (Bailey) G.; A.B., U. of Kan., 1907; LL.B., Kansas City Sch. Law, 1909; m. Marjorie Hires; children—Betty (Mrs. H. W. Jensen), John C., Frank H., Anne (Mrs. Revis C. Lewis). Admitted to Mo. bar, 1909; mem. Gage, Hodges, Park & Kreamer, Kansas City; lecturer on law Kansas City Sch. of Law, 1915-38; dir. Traders National Bank, also Gas Service Company, Safety Federal Savings and Loan Association. Mayor of Kansas City, 1940-46. Chmn bd. of adv. bond trustees of Kansas City, Mo.; regional vice president Nat. Municipal League. Trustee U. Kansas City. Mem. Am. (chmn. adminstrv. law sect.), Mo. State, Kansas City bar assns., Am. Royal Assn. (pres.), Midwest Research Inst. (v.p.), C. of C., Lawyers Assn. of Kansas City, Sigma Alpha Epsilon, Phi Alpha Delta. Democrat. Episcopalian. Clubs: Kansas City, Kansas City Country, Saddle and Sirloin, Rotary. Editor and compiler: Kelly's Missouri Probate Law. Home: Kansas City MO Died Jan. 15, 1970; buried Mount Washington Cemetery, Kansas City MO

GAGE, WALTER BOUTWELL, educator; b. Nashua, N.H., Apr. 21, 1872; s. Minot Gardner and Ellena (Boutwell) G.; grad. Phillips Exeter Acad., 1890, A.B., Harvard, 1894; m. Florence Davis, of Syracuse, N.Y., June 28, 1900; 1 son, Bradford. Instr., 1900-08, head master, since 1908, Hackley Sch. Republican. Unitarian. Home: Tarrytown NY‡

GAGNON, J-ROMEO, bishop; b. St. Cyrille, Que., Can., Feb. 24, 1903; s. Simon and Marie-Anne (Lebeau) G.; B.A., Laval U., 1924; D.Canon Law, Pontifical Angelicum U., Rome, 1935, Ph.L., 1936. Ordained priest Roman Cath. Ch., 1928; parish asst., 1928-29; tchr. Sem. Nicolet, Que., 1929-32, 36-46; vicar gen. Diocese Nicolet, 1946-49; prof. canon law Laval U., 1939-44; bishop of Edmundston, N.B., Can., 1949-70. Home: Edmundston NB Can Died Feb. 18, 1970; buried Crypt of the Cathedral Immaculate Conception, Edmundston, N.B., Can

GAILLARD, FELIX, former prime minister France; b. Paris, France, Nov. 5, 1919; ed. Ecole des Sciences Politiques; holder degree Dr. en Droit. Became insp. of finance, 1943; mem. Delegation Generale de la Resistance, 1943-44; dir. the Cabinet, 1945-46; under sec. of state for econ. affairs, 1947-48; del. to Assembly of Europe, Strasbourg, 1948; dep. for Charente, Nat. Assembly; sec. of state for finances, 1953-54; prime minister of France, Nov. 1957-58. Mem. Radical Party. Home: Paris France Died July, 1970.*

GAINES, JOHN WILLIAM, college pres.; b. Townville, S.C., June 1, 1870; s. John Asbury and Susan Jane (Cox) G.; A.M., Furman U., Greenville, S.C., 1891; studied U. of Va., U. of N.C., U. of Chicago; m. Cora Mathewson, of Westminster, S.C., Oct. 25, 1892; children—Carl, Harold M., Marion. Began as teacher at Williamstown, S.C., 1891; pres. Cox Coll., College Park, Ga., 1907-10; dean Shorter Coll., Rome, Ga., 1910-18; pres. Bethel Woman's Coll., Hopkinsville, Ky., since 1919. Chmn. Y.M.C.A. overseas training confs., New York and Paris, 1918-19, training more than 10,000 secretaries for service with the A.E.F. Moderator Gen. Assn. Ky. Bapts. Mem. Ky. Bapt. Ednl. Soc. (pres. 1922-29), Chi Psi. Democrat. Baptist. Club: Rotary (pres.). Home: Hopkinsville KY‡

GAINEY, PERCY LEIGH, bacteriologist; b. Fayetteville, N.C., March 9, 1887; s. Abraham and Amelia (McNab) G.; B.S., N.C. State Coll., 1908, M.S., 1910; A.M., Washington Univ., 1911, Ph.D., 1926; m. Grace Trueman Deaton, Dec. 25, 1913; children—Janis Leigh, Phillip McNab. Teacher U. of Mo., 1911-14; teacher, Kan. State Coll., Manhattan, head dept. bacteriology 1946-57, soil bacteriologist, Kan. Agrl. Expt. Sta., 1914-57. Received Chilean Nitrate Ednl. award for research in soil sci., 1929. Mem. Kan. Acad. of Sci., Soc. Am. Bacteriologists, Phi Kappa Phi, Sigma Xi, Gamma Alpha, Gamma Sigma Delta, Alpha Zeta. Author books, latest: Biology in Relation to Man (with H.H. Haymaker, E. J. Wimmer, M. J. Harbaugh), 1945; Microbiology of Water and Sewage (with Thomas H. Lord), 1952; Laboratory Manual for Microbiology of Water and Sewage (with Thomas H. Lord), 1952; Fundamentals of Biology (with others), 1953; Basic Bacteriology Laboratory Manual (with Thomas H. Lord and W. A. Miller), 1953; also sci. and tech. papers. Address: Manhattan KA Died Oct. 1972.

GAITHER, P(ERRY) STOKES, life ins. co. exec.; b. Brookline, Mass., Sept. 3, 1907; s. Charles P. and Mary W. (Stokes) G.; grad. Milton (Mass.) Acad., 1925; Ph.B., Yale, 1929; student Am. Inst. Banking, 1928-33; m. Elizabeth Hamlin, Nov. 4, 1938; children—Anne M., John S. Chief investment clk. First Nat. Bank & Trust Co., New Haven, 1929-35; asst. to trust officer Second Nat. Bank, New Haven, 1935-37; asst. trust officer Merchants Nat. Bank, Boston, 1937-43; with New Eng. Mut. Life Ins. Co., Boston, 1946-67, 2d v.p., 1951-57, v.p., 1957-66, sr. v.p., 1966-67; trustee Wm. Underwood Company, Watertown, Mass.; dir. Reichhold Chemicals, Inc., North White Plains, N.Y., Baystate Corporation (Boston), McGregor-Doniger, Inc. Bd. dirs. Fed. Dorchester Neighborhood Houses, Inc.; trustee Yale Scholarship Trust of Boston, 1942-65, chmn., 1953-65. Served as lt. col. Transp. Corps, AUS, 1943-45. Mem. Nat. Inst. Social Scis. Clubs: Dedham (Mass.) Country and Polo (gov. 1957-63; pres. 1961-62); Yale of Boston (pres.), Union, Economic (Boston); Yale (N.Y.C.); Norfolk Hunt (treas.) (Dover, Mass.); The Country (Brookline, Mass.). Home: Dedham MA Died Aug. 4, 1967.

GALARNEAULT, JOHN TOAN, judge; b. Aitkin, Minn., Sept. 23, 1899; s. John B. and Susie (Toan) G.; student St. Thomas Coll., St. Paul, 1914-18; U. Minn., 1918-22; LL.B., U. Mich., 1924; m. Dorothy Kuechenmeister, Aug. 6, 1938; children—John K., Edward T., Robert J., Thomas R. Admitted to Minn. bar, 1924; gen. practice law in Aitkin, Minn., 1924-58; village atty., Aitkin, 1923-30; county atty. Aitkin County, Minn., 1930-54; judge dist. ct., state Minn., 9th dist. USO county drive chmn., 1942-44. County chmn. Dem. Farmer-Labor Party, Aitkin County, 1949-58. Dir. Aitkin Community Hosp., Inc., pres. bd., 1954-58. Served in WWI. Mem. Fifteenth Judicial Bar Assn. (twice dist. pres.), Minn. Bar Assn. Home: Aitken MN Died Dec. Dec. 27, 1967; buried 1967; buried St. Thomas Cemetery Aitken MN

GALBRAITH, ARCHIBALD VICTOR, headmaster; b. Boxford, Massachusetts, September 22, 1877; s. Colonel Frederic William and Abbie Clark (Sayward) G.; A.B., Harvard, 1899, post-grad. work, Harvard, summer 1903, University of Munich, 1905-06; L.H.D., Amherst, 1944; m. Helen Ecob McIntosh, June 29, 1905; children—Frederic McIntosh, Margaret (dec.), Douglas. Teacher mathematics and coached athletics, Milton (Mass.) Acad., 1899-1900, William Penn Charter Sch., Phila., 1900-03; headcoach Harvard baseball team, 1902; teacher mathematics and German, coached athletics and in charge dormitory, Middlesex Sch., Concord, Mass., 1903-19; headmaster Williston Acad., 1919-49. Trustee Clarke School for the Deaf. Mem. Assn. Math. Teachers of N.E. (ex-pres.), Headmasters' Assn. of U.S (ex-pres.), Phi Beta Kappa, Delta Upsilon. Republican. Unitarian. Club: Rotary. Home: 6 Round Hill, Northampton MA‡

GALE, ARTHUR SULLIVAN, mathematician; b. Appleton, Wis., June 26, 1877; s. Rev. Sullivan French and Elizabeth Taylor (Felt) G.; B.A., Yale, 1899, Ph.D., 1901; m. Mary Cotton-Walker Tuke, June 29, 1901; children—Marland, Arthur, Polly Anne; m. 2d, Katharine Bowen, June 26, 1939. Instructor mathematics, Yale, 1901-05; asst. prof. of mathematics, 1905-06, Fayerweather prof., 1906-45, freshman dean, 1921-36, dean Coll. for Men, 1936-39, Univ. of Rochester. Member Nat. Institute Social Sciences, Am. Math. Society, Am. Math. Assn., A.A.A.S., Phi Beta Kappa, Sigma Xi. Author: (Smith and Gale) Elements of Analytic Geometry, 1905; (same) Introduction to Analytic Geometry, 1905; (Gale and Watkeys) Elementary Functions, 1920. Home: 93 Bellevue Drive, Rochester 7 NY‡

GALE, EDWARD JUSTUS, coll. pres.; b. Elmore, Vt., Mar. 18, 1872; s. Lyman A. and Almira (Wells) G.; grad. Montpelier (Vt.) Sem., 1891; A.B., Wesleyan U., Middletown, Conn., 1895; grad. study Boston U., 1895-96; D.D., Mo. Wesleyan Coll., 1914; m. Anna M. Morrison, of Chester, Ill., May 26, 1898; children—Herbert Morrison, Katherine Mabel. Ordained ministry M.E. Ch., 1896; successively pastor Canaan and Island Pond, Vt., Mexico, Macon, Memphis, Trenton, St. Louis, and Cameron, Mo., until 1924; dist. supt. Brookfield Dist., 1924-27; pres. Mo. Wesleyan Coll., 1927-30; now pastor, Perryville, Mo. Four-minute man, St. Louis, World War. Mem. Chi Psi. Republican. Home: Perryville MO‡

GALE, JOSEPH WASSON, physician; b. Milton, Ia., Jan. 21, 1900; s. William and May (Rhoades) G.; M.D., Washington U., St. Louis, 1924; m. Marion Sutherland Reed, Oct. 20, 1928; children—Christina May (Mrs. Michael McPhee), Margaret Reed (Mrs. David Mayer). Intern, Barnes Hosp., St. Louis, 1924-25, asst. resident in surgery, 1925-26, resident, 1926-27; asso. surgeon Wis. State Gen. Hosp.; asst. in surgery U. Wis., Madison, 1927-30, asso. in surgery, 1930-41, prof., 1941-68. Served with U.S. Army, World War I; to col., M.C., AUS, 1942-44. Diplomate Am. Bd. Surgery (founder), Am. Bd. Thoracic Surgery (founder). Fellow A.C.S.; mem. A.M.A., Wis., Dane County med. socs., Am., Central, Western surg. assns., Am. Assn. for Thoracic Surgery, Madison WI Died Oct. 26, 1968.

GALE, MINNA K., actress; b. in N.J.; ed. Frankfort, Germany, and New York; took part in amateur theatricals; joined co. of Lawrence Barrett, 1885; soon became his leading lady. After Mr. Barrett's death, became a star and has since played in tragedy roles.‡

GALE, OLIVER MARBLE, author; b. Chicago, Apr. 2, 1877; s. Edwin Oscar and Julia Esther (Hart) G.; Throop Poly. Inst., Pasadena, Cal.; U. of Cal., 1900-1; m. Permelia Newby, of Ventura, Cal., June 30, 1903. In business and newspaper work until 1908, since writer of hist. novels and juveniles. Mem. Beta Theta Pi. Club: Cliff Dwellers. Author: Princess and Cavalier, 1909; On Savage Shores, 1909; The Red Frontier, 1909; A Rescued Destiny, 1909; Duelling for Empire, 1909; The Knight of the Wilderness, 1909; The Stars and Stripes, 1910; Valor and Victory, 1910; The Great Republic, 1910. Home: 218 N. Kenilworth Av., Oak Park, Ill., and Ventura, Cal. Office: Mallers Bldg., Chicago‡

GALLAGHER, HOWARD WILLIAM, publisher; b. Retsof, N.Y., Nov. 30, 1903; s. William and Alice (Mead) G.; student Union Coll., Albany Law Sch., 1925-27; m. Mary O'Connor, July 23, 1932; children—Nancy (Mrs. Robert Monahan), William. Trust officer Gen. Valley Nat. Bank, Geneseo, N.Y., 1927-31; pres. Williamson Law Book Co., Rochester, N.Y., 1940-70. Mem. A.I.M. (mem. pres. council), Phi Sigma Kappa. Club: Rochester (mem. bd.). Home: NY Died Nov. 2, 1970.

GALLAGHER, HUGH, steamship transportation exec.; b. Ft. Lewis, Colo., Oct. 22, 1888; s. Hugh J. (Capt. U.S. Army, retired) and Amelia (Paschel) G.; student Academy Richmond Co. Mil., Augusta, Ga., 1899-1900; m. Ethel May Scaiefe, August 5, 1915. With Standard Oil Co., Manila, P.I., 1906-09; r.r. constrn. contractor Twohy Bros., 1909-14; agt., operations mgr., dist. mgr. Pacific S.S. Co., 1914-25; operating mgr., v.p., dir. Oceanic S.S. Co., 1925-26, Matson Nav. Co., from 1926. Foreman grand jury, San Francisco, 1934, mem. park commn., 1948-49, mem. bd. freeholders which drew up city charter San Francisco 1930, chmn. San Francisco Mayor's Com. for Shipping, Shipbuilding and Ship Repair; chmn. bd. govs. Cal. Maritime Acad.; trustee San Francisco Maritime Museum. Named man of year, City Coll. N.Y., 1952; Hugh Gallagher Library, Vallejo, Cal., dedicated 1971. Mem. Soc. Naval Architects, Navy League of U.S. Clubs: Pacific Union (San Francisco); Propeller (nat. pres. 1951-53, nat. v.p., 1953-56); Press and Union League. Home: San Francisco CA Died Dec. 31, 1968; buried Holy Cross Cemetery.

GALLAGHER, JOHN JAMES, confectionery exec.; b. Peekskill, N.Y., Sept. 25, 1891; s. William Gilmartin and Ann (Nolan) G.; student N.Y. Univ., 1910; m. Lillian Goodliffe, Nov. 16, 1914; 1 dau., Lillian B. Joined Hershey Chocolate Corp., 1911, became gen.

sales mgr., 1945, dir., 1946, chmn. of bd., dir. of corporation sales, 1956-61; dir. Hershey Trust Co. Mem. bd. mgrs. Hershey Indsl. Sch., Hershey Found. Home: Hershey PA Died July 1968.

GALLAGHER, LOUIS JOSEPH, clergyman, educator; b. Boston, Mass., July 22, 1885; s. James and Sarah (Dempsey) G.; A.B., Woodstock (Md.) Coll., 1911, A.M., 1912; studied theology, same college, 1917-21; LL.D., Georgetown Univ., 1933. Joined The Society of Jesus (Jesuits), 1905; ordained priest R.C. Ch., 1920; prof. classical langs., Fordham U., 1912-17; headmaster Xavier High Sch., N.Y. City, 1921-22; asst. dir. Papal Relief Mission to Russia, 1922-23, also mem. Am. Relief Administration in Russia and supervisor Orenburg div. of Papal Relief; dean Coll. of Arts and Sciences, Georgetown Coll., 1924-26, also mem. bd. dirs., regent and sec.; dir. general of studies of the N.E. Jesuit Province, 1926-31; pres. Boston Coll., 1932-37; asst. dir. Inst. of Social Order since Nov. 1940. Diplomatic courier to transport relics of Andrew Bobola, Polish Jesuit martyr, from Moscow to Rome; mem. State Adv. Com. on U. Extension (Mass.), 1933-36. Author: The China That Was; Episode on Beacon Hill, others. Address: Pomfret Center CT Died Aug. 1972.

GALLAHER, ERNEST YALE, telegraph official; b. N.Y. City, June 3, 1875; s. Samuel Capp and Julia Anna (Beach) G.; student Sch. of Arts, Columbia, 1yr.; LL.M., New York U., 1898; admitted to N.Y. bar, 1899; C.P.A., N.Y. State, 1901; m. Isabelle S. Moore, Feb., 1911. Commr. of accounts, N.Y. City; retired vice president Western Union Telegraph Co. Member Teachers' Retirement Bd., N.Y. City, 1917; asso. with Priorities Com., Washington, D.C., 1917-18. Republican. Episcopalian. Clubs: Arkwright, St. Andrews Golf, Shenorock, Scarsdale Golf, Union League (N.Y.), Forest Lake (Pa.). Home: 28 Greenacre Av., Scarsdale NY*‡

GALLAHUE, DUDLEY RICHARD, ret. business exec.; b. Richmond, Ind., Feb. 24, 1898; s. Philip M. and Pearl Marie (Teague) G. Ins. examiner Ind., 1918-19; with bro. E. F. Gallahue organized Am. States Ins. Co., 1929, chmn. bd., treas., 1947-63; past dir. Mchts. Nat. Bank & Trust Co., Pub. Service Co. Ind.; chmn. bd., treas. Am. Economy Life Ins. Co., 1959-63, Am. States Life Ins. Co., 1957-63; ret., 1963; engaged in investments. Hon. bd. dirs. Boys Club Indpls.; hon. mem. Girl Scouts U.S.A. Recipient Wisdom award. Mem. Indpls. Bd. Trade, C. of C., Children's Mus., Art Assn. Indpls., S.A.R., Ind. Soc. Chgo., Council of Sagamores of Wabash, Newcomen Soc. N.Am. Mason (32 deg., Shriner). Clubs: University, Indpls. Athletic, Columbia, Dramatic Players, Lambs, Woodstock (Indpls.); Athenaeum; Traders Point Hunt. Home: Indianapolis IN Died Sept. 23, 1972.

GALLAHUE, EDWARD FRANCIS, former ins. exec.; b. Indpls., May 12, 1902; s. Philip M. and Pearl Marie (Teague) G.; ed. pub. schs., Indpls.; L.H.D., Boston U., 1956, Earlham Coll., 1957; LL.D., De Pauw U., 1961; m. Dorothy V. Fitzpatrick, Oct. 31, 1943; 1 dau., Gloria Ann. Organized with Dudley Richard Gallahue, Am. States Ins. Co., Indpls., 1929, pres., 1947-63; pres. Am. States Life Ins. Co., Am. Economy Ins. Co., until 1963. Trustee, chmn. gifts and bequests com. Butler U.; pres. Indpls. Hosp. Devel. Assn., 1950-61, dir., mem. exec. com., 1950-71; pres. Ind. Assn. Mental Health, 1948-50; bd. dirs. Yokefellow Assos., 1954-61; trustee Meth. Hosp., Ind. Found. of Meth. Ch., Menninger Found., Topeka; sponsor Edward Gallahue Confs. on Religion and Psychiatry at Menninger Found., Edward F. Gallahue World Religions Conf. at Princeton Theol. Sem. Recipient citations Ind. Assn. Mental Health, Indpls. Med. Soc., Indpls. Hosp. Devel. Assn.; Ind. U. Hall Fame in philanthropy. Mem. S.A.R., Soc. Cincinnati. Methodist. Mason (32 deg.). Clubs: Indianapolis Athletic, Columbia, University, Dramatic, Lambs, Woodstock, Meridian Hills Country, Traders Point Hunt, Crooked Stick Country. Author: Edward's Odyssey (autobiography), 1970. Home: Indianapolis IN Died July 16, 1971; buried Crown Hill Cemetery, Indianapolis IN

GALLO, FORTUNE, impresario; b. Torremaggiore, Italy, May 9, 1878; s. Tommaso and Zelinda (Accetturo) G.; ed. in Italy; m. Cofia Charlebois, 1913 (died Oct. 13, 1948). Came to U.S., 1895, naturalized, 1900. Owner, mgr. opera companies since 1901; now pres. and treas. San Carlo Grand Opera Co. 37th (trans-continental tour). Manager U.S. Tours for Eleanore Duse, Ruggiero Leoncevello; tour dir. Roman Choir of Vatican Churches, 1947-48. Producer summer operetta seasons Jones Beach, L.I., N.Y., Municipal Stadium, N.Y. City, Louisville, Ky., Cleveland O.; grand opera Water Gate, Washington, D.C. Directed tours Anna Pavlowa and Ballet, Original Ballet Russe, Massine Ballet Russe Highlights. Producer, 10 years of grand opera, Center Theatre, Rockefeller Center, N.Y. Knighted three times by Italian Govt.; awarded Chevalier, Commendatore, Crown of Italy. Clubs: New York Athletic, Kiwanis, Lotus, Grand Street Boys. Home: New York City NY Died Mar. 28, 1970; buried Kensico Cemetery, Valhalla NY

GALLOWAY, CHARLES HENRY, organist; b. St. Louis, Dec. 21, 1871; s. William and Phoebe (Lidbury) G.; ed. Smith Acad., St. Louis; m. Garfielda Miller, of St. Louis, June 1, 1905. Was ch. organist when only 7 yrs. of age; when young man was known as the boy organist." yrs. of age; when young man was known as the boy organist." For 4 yrs. studied organ and theory with Alex. Guilmant, Paris; while there was organist Am. Ch. of the Holy Trinity; on return apptd. organist and dir. music, St. Peter's Episcopal Ch., St. Louis; organist and dir. music, Scottish Rite Cathedral, St. Louis, and mus. dir. St. Louis Apollo Club. Official organist, La. Purchase Expn. Episcopalian. Teacher of organ and theory; has given recitals throughout U.S. Address: 3667 Botanical Av., St Louis MO‡

GALLOWAY, CHARLES MILLS, b. Pender County, N.C., Aug. 15, 1875; s. Charles Mills and Ellen (Register) G.; LL.B., U. of S.C., 1907; m. Lyda McNulty. Oct. 23, 1903. News editor The State," Columbia, S.C., 1904-09; member United States Civil Service Commn. by apptmt. of Pres. Wilson, June 20, 1913-Sept. 7, 1919; resigned to practice law at Washington, D.C.; counsel to comptroller gen. U.S., 1929-45; resumed practice of law, 1945. Member Sigma Alpha Epsilon. Democrat. Home: 2900 Connecticut Av., Washington 8‡

GALLUP, EDWARD HATTON, JR., transp. exec.; b. Boston, Jan. 16, 1898; s. Edward Hatton and Marion (Ramsey) G.; A.B., Harvard, 1920, postgrad., 1929; N.Y. U., 1930-31; m. Claire Louise Lenfestey, Dec. 18, 1924; children—Edward Hatton III, Marion Elizabeth (Mrs. Robert H. Drummond). Sales, Bird & Son, Boston, 1923-28, Ginn & Co., Boston, 1928-41; sec. Pitts. Hotels Assn., 1946-53; asst. gen. mgr. Penn-Sheraton Hotel, Pitts., 1953-59; asst. exec. dir. Port Authority Allegheny County, Pitts., 1960-69. Lectr. U. Pitts., 1946-57; cons. Pa. Dept. Labor and Industry, 1966-69. Pres. South Hills Child Guidance Assn., 1957-58; treas. Pitts. Chamber Music Soc., 1962-68; pres. Pitts. chpt. Pa. Assn. for the Blind, 1966-69, trustee, 1959. Served as lt. col. AUS, 1941-46. Mem. Mil. Order World Wars (chpt. trustee 1952-69), Sigma Alpha Epsilon. Presbyn. (trustee). Clubs: University, Longue Vue Country, Harvard-Yale-Princeton (dir. pres. Western Pa. 1951). Home: Pittsburgh PA Died Dec. 7, 1969; interred Boston MA

GALT, HOWARD SPILMAN, missionary; b. Shenandoah, Ia., Sept. 15, 1872; s. Martin Happer and Clara S. (Spilman) G.; B.S., Tabor Coll., Ia., 1895, D.D., 1915; Ph.B., U. of Chicago, 1896; Div. Sch. U. of Chicago, 2 yrs.; B.D., Hartford Theol. Sem., 1899; Ed.M., Harvard University, 1926, Ed.D., 1927; m. Louise Alberta West, of Tabor, Ia., Oct. 5, 1899; children—Mable M., Lawrence L., Dorothy G., Wendell W., Sheffield S. Pastor's asst., 4th Congl. Ch., Hartford, June-Sept. 1899; appointed missionary A.B.C.F.M. to North China, 1899; ordained Congl. ministry, 1899; besieged in British Legation, Peking, June-Aug. 1900; teacher, 1902-11; acting pres., 1909-11, pres., 1911-17, N. China Union Coll.; lecturer on Henry D. Porter foundation, Pomona Coll., Calif., 1917-18; prof. dept. of edn., Yenching Univ., Peiping, China, since 1918, head of dept., 1918-35, chmn. graduate div., 1931-34, acting pres., 1923-24, 1927-28 and 1929-30. Author: The Development of Chinese Educational Theory, 1930; Galt Family Genealogies, 1938. Address: Yenching Univ., Peiping China‡

GALUSHA, HUGH DUNCAN, JR., banker; b. Helena, Mont., Mar. 3, 1919; s. Hugh Duncan and Winifred (Whitaker) G.; student U. Mont., Carroll Coll.; B.S., U. Pa., 1941; m. Jean Shumate, Sept. 20, 1944; children—Duncan, Emily, Hope, Molly. Partner firm Galusha, Higgins & Galusha, C.P.A.'s, Helena, 1941-65, Galusha & Melloy, lawyers, Helena, 1950-65; dir. 9th dist. Fed. Res. Bank, Mpls., 1963-65, pres., 1965-71; past dir. Mountain State Telephone Co. (Denver), Union Bank & Trust Co., Eddy Bakeries Co., Inc., Capri, Inc. (all Helena), Yellowstone Park Co., Haynes, Inc. (both Yellowstone Nat. Park). Chmn. Rhodes Scholarship Selection Com. for Midwest; v.p., chmn. research com. Upper Midwest Research and Devel. Council; bd. dirs. N. Star Research and Devel. Inst.; mem. adv. council Mont. Bd. Equalization; lectr. tax schs. Bd. dirs. Mpls. YMCA; trustee Mayo Found., Rochester, Minn., U. Mont., Carroll Coll. Found., Yellowstone Library and Museum Assn., Greater Mont. Found., Holter Research Found., Nat. Parks Trust Fund; chmn. bd. trustees Carleton Coll., Northfield, Minn. Mem. Am., Mont. bar assns., Am., Mont. insts. C.P.A.'s, Council on Fgn. Relations, Beta Gamma Sigma, Pi Gamma Mu, Phi Delta Theta. Clubs: Minneapolis; Montana (Helena). Home: Deephaven MN Died Jan. 31, 1971.

GAMACHE, GEORGE PAUL, air force officer; b. Fall River, Mass., Sept. 26, 1929; s. Louis Philippe and Rose (Montplaisir) G.; student Assumption Coll., Worcester, Mass., 1947-49; B.S., Okla. State U., 1962, M.S., 1963; m. Pauline Alice Masse, June 4, 1955; children—Monique Marie, Janine Renee, Murielle Ellen, Daniel Charles. Commd. 2d lt. USAF, 1952, advanced through grades to lt. col., 1969; navigator B-29 and RB-47 in Okinawa, North Africa, O., 1952-60; student Air Force Inst. Tech., 1960-63; electronics engr., system analysis div. Hdqrs. Air Force Eastern Test Range, Patrick AFB, Fla., 1963-65; prof. aerospace studies, head dept. Mass. Inst. Tech., 1965-69; chief, sensor monitor control Task Force Alpha, Thailand, 1969-70. Decorated Air Force Commendation medal. Registered profl. engr., Fla. Mem. I.E.E.E., Phi Kappa Phi, Eta Kappa Nu. Roman Catholic. Home: FL Died Mar. 31, 1972.

GAMBLE, DONALD PHELPS, wholesale food co. exec.; b. Mpls., Mar. 24, 1899; s. David Franklin and Jessie (Farmer) G.; A.B., Williams Coll., 1920; m. Edith Schibsby, Jan. 23, 1922; children—Donald Phelps, Douglas Schibsby, Cynthia (Mrs. Harold H. Tearse, Jr.), David Franklin II; m. 2d, Eleanor Robinson, Sept. 9, 1941. With Pacific Gamble Robinson Co., 1921-68, exec. v.p., 1959-68, also mem. exec. com., dir. Mem. Psi Upsilon. Clubs: Minneapolis, Woodhill Country (Mpls.); Seattle Golf; Eldorado Country (Palm Desert, Cal.). Home: Seattle WA Died Oct. 1968.

GAMBLE, SIDNEY DAVID, b. Cincinnati, O., July 12, 1890; s. David Berry and Mary (Huggins) G.; Litt.B., Princeton, 1912; A.M. U. of Calif., 1916; LL.D., Hanover Coll., 1932; L.H.D., Susquehanna University, 1964; LL.D., Lake Erie College, 1965; m. to Elizabeth Pritchard Lowe, January 18th, 1924; children—Catherine (Mrs. J. A. Curran, Jr.), Louise (Mrs. Harper), David L., Anne Van N. (Mrs. Paul S. Symchych). Mercantile bus., 1913-15; Preston School of Industry, Ione, California, 1915-16; asst. dept. of economics, U. of Calif., 1916-17; sec. Internat. Com. (now Nat. Council) YMCA in China, 1918-19, 24-27, recording secretary, 1944-—; chmn. Church World Service, 1960-64. Hon. chmn. Princeton in Asia. Director Josiah Macy, Junior, Foundation. Member American Geographical Society, Royal Geo. Soc. (London), Phi Beta Kappa. Presbyn. Author: Peking—A Social Survey (the first social survey of an Oriental city), 1921; How Chinese Families Live in Peiping, 1933; Ting Hsien: A North China Rural Community, 1953; North China Villages, Social, Political, Economic Activities before 1933, 1963. Home: New York City NY Died Mar. 29, 1968; buried Cincinnati OH

GAMBLE, THEODORE ROBERT, food products mfr.; b. St. Louis, Sept. 22, 1924; s. Merritt C. and Irma A. (Latzer) G.; B.S. in Mech. Engring., Purdue U., 1945; M.B.A., Harvard, 1949; Sc.D. (hon.), Tri-State Coll., Angola, Ind.; LL.D., MacMurray Coll., Jacksonville, Ill., St. Joseph's Coll., Phila.; D.Bus. Adminstrn., Catawba Coll.; m. Rispah A. Dowse, Jan. 20, 1951; 1 son, Theodore Robert. Accountant Pet Milk Co. (co. name changed to Pet, Inc. 1966), 1949-51, asst. to gen. mgr., 1951-54, v.p., asst. to pres., dir., 1954-58, exec. v.p., 1958-59, pres., chief exec. officer, 1959-66, chmn. bd., chief exec. officer, 1966-68, chmn., pres., chief exec. officer, 1968-69; dir. Eatern Air Lines, Inc., Pet-Denia Milk Products, Inc., P.R., Matuano y Petmilk, S.A., Barcelona, Spain, A.B. Estrella, Gothenburg, Sweden, Congeladora y Empacadora Nacional S.A., Mexico City, Mex., St. Louis Union Trust Co., 1st Nat. Bank St. Louis, Helvetia Leasing Co. Mem. Nat. Indsl. Conf. Bd., Bus. Council; mem. adv. bd. Nat. Alliance Businessmen, St. Louis; mem. Civic Progress, Inc. Trustee Food Law Inst., Pet Milk Found.; vis. com. Harvard Grad. Sch. Bus. Adminstrn., 1962-69; bd. govs. Acad. Food Marketing, St. Joseph's Coll.; v.p., exec. com. of nat. bd. Boy Scouts Am., also pres., mem. exec. bd. St. Louis Area council; mem. pres.'s council St. Louis U.; bd. dirs. United Fund St. Louis, Municipal Theatre Assn., St. Louis Symphony Soc., Conv. Bd. Greater St. Louis, Work Opportunities Unlimited, St. Louis; trustee Nutrition Found., Inc. Served as lt. (j.g.) USNR, 1943-46. Named Distinguished Engring. Alumnus, Purdue U., Distinguished Alumnus, Harvard Grad. Sch. Bus. Adminstrn. Mem. Grocery Mfrs. Am. (mem. bd.), Harvard, Purdue U. alumni assns., Newcomen Soc. N.Am., Sigma Phi Epsilon. Republican. Episcopalian. Mason. Clubs: Harvard Business School, Mo. Athletic, University, Noonday, St. Louis (St. Louis); Bogey, Inc.; Bellerive Country (Ladue, Mo.); Media, Links, Round Table, Stadium, Delray Beach Yacht. Home: St Louis MO Died Mar. 13, 1969; buried family plot, Highland IL

GAMEL, W. WARREN, oil co. exec.; b. Loomis, Neb., Jan. 28, 1906; s. William E. and Helen (Potter) G.; B.S., Denver U., 1926; student, U. Cal. at Los Angeles, 1937, Southwestern U., Los Angeles, 1938-39; m. Jessie M. Wurtz, Aug. 30, 1926; 1 dau., Shirley (Mrs. J. D. Dingman). With Producers & Refiners Corp., Sinclair, Wyoming, 1926-30; employed with Richfield division of Atlantic Richfield Company, Los Angeles, 1930-66, comptroller, 1962-66. Mem. Financial Execs. Inst., Am. Petroleum Inst., Los Angeles Petroleum Accountants Soc. Mason. Home: Glendale CA Died Oct. 28, 1966 inurnment at Garden of Honor, Forest Lawn Meml. Park, Glendale CA

GAMMACK, ARTHUR JAMES, clergyman; b. Drumlithie, Soctland, Mar. 29, 1871; s. James (q.v.) and Jane Ann (Wilson) G.; came to America, 1889; B.A., Trinity Coll., Toronto, Can., 1891, M.A., 1892; grad.

Berkeley Div. Sch., 1894; post-grad. studies at Columbia and Yale; m. Mary Thompson Bridgman, of Stamford, Conn., June 6, 1899. Deacon, 1894, priest, 1895, P.E. Ch.; pastor St. Gabriel's Mission, E. Berlin, Conn., 1893 and 1896; curate St. John's, Stamford, 1894, Christ Ch., West Haven, 1898, rector same, 1900-9; rector Trinity Ch., Lenox, Mass., since May 1, 1909. Republican. Author: Simple Counsels, 1897; Good Friday; The Seven Last Words. Address: Lenox MA‡

GAMON, WYLENA CLARISSA, educator; b. Colbert, Wash.; d. Max Antone and Bertha (Harrison) Gamon; B.A., Eastern Wash. State Coll., 1937; postgrad. U. Wash., Seattle Pacific Coll. Tchr. pub. schs., Peach, Wash., 1929-30, Half Moon Elementary Sch., Colbert, 1930-36; tchr. Grand Coulee, 1936-38, prin., 1938-47; tchr. Kent (Wash.) Pub. Schs., 1947-52, prin., 1952-55; dir. spl. edn. Intermediate Dist. IX, Seattle, 1955-68. Named Woman of Achievement in Wash. State, Bus. and Profl. Womens Club, 1967. Mem. Wash. Edn. Assn. (past pres. King County), Council for Exceptional Children (pres. state fedn. 1962-63), Beta Sigma Phi, Delta Kappa Gamma. Presbyn. (elder). Club: Soroptimist. Co-editor: Careers in Special Education. Home: Seattle WA Died June 26, 1968.

GAMOW, GEORGE, author, educator; b. Odessa, Russia, Mar. 4, 1904; s. Anthony and Alexandra (Lebedinzeva) G.; student Normal Sch., Odessa, 1914-20, U. Leningrad, 1922-26 (Ph.D., 1928); m. Loubov Wochminzewa, Nov. 1, 1931 (div.); 1 son, Igor; m. 2d, Barbara Perkins, Oct. 11, 1958. Fellow U. Gottingen, Germany, summer, 1928, U. Copenhagen, Denmark, 1928-29; Rockefeller fellow, Cambridge, Eng., 1929-30; asst. U. Copenhagen, 1930-31; master in research Acad. Scis., Leningrad, 1931-33; lectr. U. Paris and London, 1933-34, U. Mich., 1934; prof. physics George Washington U., 1934-56, U. Colo., 1956-68; lectr. Stanford, 1936; vis. lectr. Venezuelian Assn. for Advancement Sci., 1956. Participated Convegnio Fisica Nucleare, Rome, 1931; Solvay Congress, Brussels, 1933; Internat. Phys. Congress, London, 1934, Warsaw, 1938. Recipient Kalinga Price award UNESCO, 1956. Mem. Am. Phys. Soc., Washington Philos. Soc., Internat. Astron. Union, Am. Astron. Soc., Nat., Royal Danish acads. scis. Author numerous books, latest being: Atomic Energy in Cosmic and Human Life, 1946; One, Two Three.. . Infinity, 1947; Creation of the Universe, 1952; Mr. Tompkins Learns the Facts of Life, 1953; The Moon, 1953; Puzzle-Math, 1958; Matter, Earth and Sky, 1958; (with J. Cleveland) Physics: Foundations and Frontiers, 1960; Biography of Physics, 1961; Gravity, 1962; A Planet Called Earth, 1963; A Star Called the Sun, 1964; Thirty Years That Shook Physics, 1965; Mr. Tompkins in Paperback, 1965; Mr. Tompkins Inside Himself, 1967; articles. Research in problems of nuclear physics. Home: Boulder CO Died Aug. 20, 1968; buried Green Mountain Cemetery Boulder CO

GANDY, JOHN MANUEL, educator; b. Starkville, Miss., Oct. 31, 1870; s. Horace and Mary Ann (Goodin) G.; grad. normal course, Jackson (Miss.) Coll., 1891; A.B., Fisk U., 1898; A.M., 1901; student summer sch. Columbia Univ., 1902-17, Cornell Univ., 1933; Ped.D., Morgan Coll., Baltimore, 1920; LL.D., Howard U., 1937; m. Carrie Senora Brown, July 17, 1901; children—Theodore Irving, Horace (dec.), Marion Elizabeth, John Manuel, Jr. Prof. Latin and Greek, Va. Normal and Collegiate Inst., 1898-1902; prof. pedagogy, 1902-14, pres., 1914-42, Virginia State College for Negroes; retired July 1, 1942. Camp community service, for colored soliders, during war period, at Columbia and Greenville, S.C., and elsewhere. Member committee on employment planning of State Advisory Council of Va. State Employment Service; mem. exec. com. Assn. for Study of Negro Life and History; consultant ex-officio Ednl. Policies Commn. of N.E.A. Mem. State Teachers Assn. of Va., Negro Orgn. Soc. Va. Inter-racial Commn., Advisory Com. on Negro Education, Southern Assn. of Negro High Schools and Colleges, Conf. of Negro Land Grant Coll. Presidents, Inter-racial Cooperative Commn., Nat. Com. for Secondary Edn., Nat. Council Y.M.C.A., Va. Div. of Com. on Illiteracy, Better Homes Assn. Received Harmon award for distinguished service in edn., 1929. Baptist. Home: Etrick VA*‡

GANDY, JOSEPH EDWARD, former lawyer; b. Spokane, Wash., Oct. 9, 1904; s. Lloyd E. and Helen D. (George) G.; B.A., U. Mich., 1926; LL.B., U. Wash., 1929; m. Laurene Tatlow, Aug. 11, 1937; 1 dau., Marilyn L. Admitted to Wash. bar, 1929; practiced law, Seattle, 1929-71; mem. LeSourd, Patton, Fleming & Hartung, 1968-71. Chief, dep. regional dir. WPB, 1942-46; automobile dealer Smith-Gandy, Inc., 1946-71; consul of Ceylon, 1967-71. Chmn. bd. United Good Neighbors, 1953; bd. dirs., v.p. Seattle Urban League, 1954-57, Seattle Art Mus. Vice pres. Seattle Municipal League, 1958; pres. Seattle Symphony Orch. Assn., 1948-50, Seattle World's Fair 1959-62; Neptune Rex X of Seattle Seafair, 1959; v.p. Arboretum Found., 1958-60. Mem. Seattle C. of C. (past pres.), Central Assn. Seattle (past pres.), Nat., Wash. (dir.), Seattle (dir.) auto dealers assns., Phi Gamma Delta, Phi Delta Phi, Phi Kappa Psi. Episcopalian. Clubs: Rainier, Tennis (Seattle). Home: Seattle WA Died June 13, 1971.

GANEY, J. CULLEN, b. Bethlehem, Pa., April 22, 1899; s. Thomas and Catherine (Cullen) G.; A.B., Lehigh U., 1920, LL.D., 1960; LL.B., Harvard, 1923; LL.D., St. Joseph's Coll., 1952; m. Evelyn Gorman, Nov. 19, 1933; 1 dau., Jean Mary. Admitted to Pa. bar, 1923, and practiced in Bethlehem; U.S. attorney for Eastern Dist. of Pa., 1937-40; U.S. federal judge for the Eastern Dist. of Pa., 1940-60; chief judge U.S. Dist. Ct. for Eastern Dist. Pa., 1960-61; judge U.S. Ct. Appeals for 3d Circuit, 1961-66, senior United States circuit judge, 1966-72. Rep. District Judges N.J., Pa., Del. Jud. Conf. U.S. Mem. Am. Bar Assn., Pa. State Bar Assn. Democrat. Home: Philadelphia PA Died Feb. 2, 1972.

GANNON, ANNA, author; b. Phila., June 6, 1876; d. Thomas G.; studied Girls' High School and Acad. Notre Dame, Phila., 1892; visited Europe, 1896, 1898, and 1899. Contb'r to mags. Mem. Browning Soc. Clubs: Civic, Authors. Author: The Song of Stradella, and Other Songs, 1899 L5; A Dream of Shakespeare's Women; etc. Address: 245 W. 39th St., NY‡

GANNON, JOHN MARK, bishop; b. Erie, Pa., June 12, 1877; s. Thomas Patrick and Julia (Dunlavey) G.; A.B., St. Bonaventure's Coll., Allegany, N.Y., 1899; S.T.B., Catholic U., 1900, S.T.L., 1901; D.D. and D.C.L., Appolinare U., Rome, Italy, 1903; spl. studies, U. of Munich, 1902; LL.D., Duquesne U., 1914, Notre Dame U., 1927, St. Bonaventure's Coll., 1933, St. Vincent's Coll., 1935; Litt.D., Catholic Univ. of Am., 1962. Pastor St. Anthony's Ch., Cambridge Springs, Pa., 1904-15, St. Brigid's Ch., Meadville, later St. Andrew's Ch., Erie; supt. Catholic edn., Diocese of Erie, 1911-19; consecrated auxiliary bishop of Erie, Feb. 6, 1918, bishop of Erie, 1920; assistant at the Pontificial Throne, November, 1944; appointed Archbishop, Ad Personam, November, 1953. Episcopal chmn. Catholic Press Assn. Nat. Cath. Welfare Conf., Washington, 1937-44; also Episcopal chmn. Am. Bishops on Mex. Affairs, Washington, 1944-50. Planned Villa Maria Coll. & Mercyhurst Coll., Erie, Pa.; founder Montezuma Sem., Montezuma, N.M., 1937; founder Gannon Coll., Erie, Pa.; treas. Nat. Cath. Welfare Conf., 1944-50; founder Noticias Catolicas, a news service for all Spanish and Portuguese speaking countries; founder Sisters of Congregation of Divine Spirit, an Am. Found., 1956; supreme chaplain Ladies Cath. Benevolent Assn.; state chaplain Cath. Daus. Am. Home: Erie PA Died Sept. 5, 1968; interred crypt, St. Peter Cathedral, Erie PA

GANO, ROY A., retired naval officer, steamship lines executive; born Pipestone, Minnesota, December 3, 1902; s. Harry and Myrtle (Hitchcox) G.; B.S., U.S. Naval Acad., 1926, postgrad. student, 1934; m. Harriet Howard, July 18, 1929; children—Myrtle Eugenia, James A. Commd. ensign USN, 1926, advanced through grades to vice adm., 1954; assigned U.S. ships Tennessee, 1926-29, John D. Edwards, 1929-30, Edsall, 1930-31, MacLeish, 1931-32; engr. U.S.S. Dewey, 1934-37; spl. engr. Naval Research Lab., Bellevue, D.C., 1937-39; material officer comdr. Destroyer Battle Force, 1941; material officer comdr. Task Force 8, Alaska, 1941-42; comdr. U.S.S. Dyson, 1942-44; asst. dir. naval communications for adminstrn., Office Chief Naval Operations, Washington, 1944-46; comdr. Destroyer Squadron 5, also Destroyer Div. 51, Japan-Korea area, 1946-48; dir. recruiting Bur. Naval Personnel, 1948-50, dir. enlisted personnel div., 1950-51; comdr. U.S.S. St. Paul, Korea, 1951-52; chief staff, aide comdr. Service Force U.S. Pacific Fleet, 1952-54; comdr. Service Squadron 3, evacuation refugees from No. Indo-China, 1954; asst. chief staff for logistics, 1954-55; dep. chief staff operations and adminstrn. Far East, UN Commands, 1955-56; dep. comdr. Mil. Sea Transportation Service, 1956-58; commander of Amphibious Group Two, 1958-59, Mil. Sea Transp. Service, 1959-64, ret. USN, 1964; v.p. Moore-McCormack Lines, Washington, 1964-71. Decorated Bronze Star Medal with gold star, Navy Cross with gold star, Legion of Merit with Gold Star, D.S.M. Home: Falls Church VA Died Jan. 20, 1971; buried Arlington Nat. Cemetery, Washington DC

GANOE, WILLIAM ADDLEMAN, b. Mifflintown, Pa., May 14, 1881; s. Rev. William Van Devender and Cynthia Constance (Addleman) G.; grad. Dickinson Sem., Williamsport, Pa., 1898; A.B., Dickinson Coll., 1902, A.M., 1913, Litt.D., 1952; B.S. U.S. Mil. Acad., 1907; grad. Staff and Command Sch., 1925, Army War Coll., 1930; m. Honora Patton Russell; children—Constance, Mary, Honora, Rebecca; m. 2d, Rose Laeh Shelnitt. Commissioned 2d lieutenant, infantry, U.S. Army, June 14, 1907; promoted through grades to major July 1, 1920; lt. col. (temporary), World War; lt. col. (permanent), January 1931; promoted to rank of colonel, Feb. 1, 1936. Has served in Cuba and Hawaii; instr. U.S. Mil. Acad., 1911-12, asst. prof. English, 1916-18, adj., 1918-21; head bd. to edit inf. drill regulation, 1923, history sect. U.S. Inf. Sch., 1923-24; General Staff eligible list, 1925; prof. mil science and tactics, Boston U., 1930-36; comdg. Fort Screven, Ga. and Dist. F, Civilian Conservation Corps, 1936; apptd. chief of staff, 2d Mil. Area, 3d Corps Area, and all reserve units of Western Pa., 1938; dir. Public Relations Div., First Army, 1941; later comdt., U.S. Army forces, Univ. of Mich., Theater Historian, European Theater Operations, U.S. Army, 1943-46; lectr. Brit. officers' schs. including Sandhurst and Oxford. Mem. British-American Liaison Bd., London, Eng. Mem. American Legion and Phi Delta Theta. Methodist. Mason. Author: The English of Military Communications, 1918; The History of the United States Army, 1924; Ruggs—R.O.T.C., 1917 (first story to be reprinted in pamphlet form by Atlantic Monthly); also stories and articles in mags. and Atlantic Narratives. Contributor to American Year Book, 1925-29, Dictionary American Biography, 1929-33, Encyclopedia Britannica, 1925; U.S. Army editor Encyclopedia Britannica, 1929. Radio speaker Yankee Network, 1934-35. Author: Soldiers Unmasked, 1935; History of the United States Army, 1942; My Heart Remembers, 1950; MacArthur Close-Up, published 1962. Decorated Bronze Star, also Medal Legion of Merit (U.S.), Order of British Empire (Gt. Sarasota FL Died Sept. 5, 1966.

GANT, SAMUEL GOODWIN, surgeon; b. Knoxville, Mo., May 9, 1869; s. Jackson D. and Sarah A. (Creason) G.; ed. Carrollton (Mo.) high sch.; M.D., Mo. Med. Coll., 1889; LL.D., William Jewell Coll., Liberty, Mo., 1899; m. Susan Rankin Barret, of Henderson, Ky., Apr. 20, 1898. Splty., diseases of the colon, rectum and anus; formerly prof. diseases of the colon, rectum and anus, N.Y. Post Grad. Med. Sch. Mem. A.M.A., Miss. Valley Med. Soc., N.Y. Acad. Med., etc. Clubs: Westchester Country (N.Y.); Los Angeles Country. Author: Diseases of the Rectum and Anus; Constipation and Intestinal Obstructions; Diarrheal, Catarrhal and Parasitic Diseases of the Gastro-Intestinal Tract. Address: 501 Madison Av., New York NY‡

GANTZ, HALLIE GEORGE, univ. pres.; b. Durham, Okla., May 13, 1910; s. John Gottfred and Letatia Paine (Thomas) G.; A.A., Randolph Jr. Coll., Cisco, Tex., 1929; B.A., Phillips U., Enid, Okla., 1931, M.A., 1932, B.D., 1933, L.H.D., 1956; B.D., Yale, 1937; D.D. (hon.), Tex. Christian U., 1946; m. Sylvia Lee Baker, Nov. 7, 1933; children—Charles Baker, Gwendolyn (Martin), Kaye (Gates). Ordained to ministry Christian Ch., 1933; minister in Ft. Worth, 1933-36, Ft. Trumbull, Conn., 1936-37, Lubbock, Tex., 1938-48, Tulsa, 1948-61; pres. Phillips U., 1961-72. Pres. Tex. Conv. Christian Chs., 1945-46, Tulsa Council Chs., 1950; chmn. com. ministry Disciples of Christ Ch., 1950; chmn. program and arrangements com. St. Louis Assembly Internat. Conv. Christian Chs., 1958. Pres. trustees Okla. Christian Missionary Soc., 1954-55; bd. dirs. Nat. Benevolent Assn. Disciples of Christ, 1952-56; trustee United Christian Missionary Soc., 1957-60, Hillcrest Med. Center, Tulsa, 1956-61; mem. commn. restructure of Christian Ch., mem. commn. Christian Unity Christian Ch., Disciples of Christ, chmn. bd. higher edn., 1968-72; trustee Christian Board of Pub., 1967-72. Pres. Okla. Assn. Ind. Colls. and Univs., 1972. Recipient Pawnee Dist. Conservationist award, 1954, Okla. Lay Conservationist award, 1955. Mason (Shriner). Rotarian. Home: Enid OK Died July 21, 1972; buried Enid Cemetery Enid OK

GANZ, RUDOLPH, pianist, condr., educator; b. Zurich, Switzerland, Feb. 24, 1877; s. Rudolph and Sophia (Bartenfeld) G.; studied in Conservatories of Music, Zurich, Lausanne and Strassburg, later with Busoni, Berlin; composition with Blanchet, Lausanne, and Urban, Berlin; hon. D.Mus., U. of Rochester, Grinnell Coll., De Paul U., Cincinnati Conservatory of Music; Dr. Humane Letters (hon.), Roosevelt University; m. Mary Forrest, concert singer, July 12, 1900 (dec. 1956); 1 son, Anton Roy; m. 2d, Esther La Berge Ganz, December 23, 1959; 1 dau., Jeanne Colette. Debut at Zurich, Switzerland, at the age of twelve; later he made extended concert tours in Europe; came to U.S., 1900; teacher in Chicago, 1901-05; played with leading orchestras and musical organizations, U.S. and Can., 1905-21; condr. St. Louis Symphony Orchestra, 1921-27; pres. Chicago Musical College of Roosevelt U., 1933-54, later president emeritus. Apptd. condr. New York Philharmonic and San Francisco Young People's concerts, 1939-49. Conducted children—concerts of Chicago Symphony Orchestra. Composer of symphony, concerto for piano and orchestra, symphonic sketches, variations on a theme by Brahms, many other pieces for piano, and over 200 songs. Officer French Legion of Honor; chevalier French Order of Arts and Letters; recipient Northwestern Univ. Centennial award; award for performing arts Lincoln Acad. of Ill., 1965. Corr. mem. Royal Acad. in Florence. Clubs: Arts, Tavern. Home: Chicago IL Died Aug. 2, 1972.

GARBER, J(AMES) OTIS, educator; b. Roanoke, Va., Dec. 18, 1902; s. Samuel C. and Mary E. (Garber) G.; student Goshen (Ind.) Coll., 1920-22; A.B. U. Mich. 1924, M.A., 1927; m. Esther A. Gillham, Aug. 28, 1926; children—Bruce Daniel, James Otis, Lynn. Tchr., Royal Oak (Mich.) High Sch., 1924-25; asst. polit. sci. U. Mich., 1925-26; instr., then asst. prof. polit. sci. U. Toledo 1926-28; sec. commn. publicity and efficiency, Toledo, also editor city charter, Toledo, 1928; sec. bur. civic affairs Toledo C. of C., 1929-30; sr. staff St. Louis Bur. Municipal Research, 1930-33; asst. dir. com. relief and employment, St. Louis, 1933-34; chief examiner Fed. Emergency Relief Adminstrn., 1934-35, dep. adminstr., then acting adminstr. Ohio, 1935-38; chief examiner WPA, 1935, dep. adminstr., Ohio, 1935-39, exec. asst. to asst. adminstr., 1939-40; dir. selection Civilian Conservation Corps, Ohio, 1936-38; chief budget examiner U.S. Bur. Budget, 1940-43, chief field service, 1943-51; prof. pub. adminstrn. George Washington U., 1944, Fla. State U., 1950-51; asst. dir. field operations OPS, 1951-53; real estate salesman, 1953; cons. commn. fiscal affairs, N.Y. State, 1954; asst. dir. finance, City Phila., 1955; chief Burma-Thailand div. ICA, Washington, 1956-58; asst. dir. tech. services U.S. mission to Thailand, ICA, 1958-60; chief tech. services div. USOM, Tunis, Tunisia, 1960-62; chief human resources div. USAID, Tunis, 1962-64; asst. chief mgmt. support div. AID, 1964-66; lectr. adminstrn. mgmt., dir. Inst. Mgmt. of Devel. Projects, Grad. Sch. Pub. and Internat. Affairs, U. Pitts., 1966; mgmt. cons., staff cons. Govtl. Affairs Inst., Washington, 1967-69. Mem. Am. Society Public Administration, American Foreign Service Association. Author: Toledo-Our Community (with H. T. Shenefield), 1932. Editor Toledo City Jour., 1928. Home: Washington DC Died Mar. 12, 1969; cremated.

GARBER, PAUL NEFF, bishop; b. New Market, Va., July 27, 1899; s. Samuel and Ida Alice (Neff) G.; A.B., Bridgewater (Va.) Coll., 1919; student Crozer Theol. Sem., Chester, Pa., 1919-21; A.M., U. Pa., 1921, Harrison fellow, 1922-23, Ph.D., 1923; L.H.D., Simpson Coll.; D.D., Duke, Emory U.; LL.D., Randolph-Macon Coll., Bridgewater Coll.; Litt.D., Lycoming Coll., 1965; m. Orina Winifred Kidd, Aug. 21, 1927 (dec. July 1959); m. 2d, Nina Fontana, Apr. 27, 1963. Asst. instr. history U. Pa., 1921-22; instr. in history Brown U., 1923-24; asst. prof. history Duke, 1924-26, prof. ch. history Div. Sch., 1926-72, registrar of sch., 1928-41, dean, 1941-44; dir. Junaluska Summer Sch. (affiliated with Duke), 1934-40. Thirkield lectr. Gammon Theol. Sch., 1941; Southwestern lectr. Southwestern U., 1948; Jarrell lectr. Emory U., 1951; Brown lectr. Randolph-Macon Coll., 1955; chmn. Meth. Commn. on Higher Edn., Meth. Commn. on Camp Activities; v.p. Meth. Bd. Edn., Meth. Commn. of Chaplains; chmn. Bd. Edn., Meth. Ch., 1960-64, mem. Commn. on Promotion and Cultivation, 1960-68, chmn. Bicentennial Hist. Commn., 1965-66; mem. World Meth. Council; Lamar lectures Wesleyan Coll., 1962. Ordained to the ministry Meth. Episcopal Ch., South, 1926; bishop of The Meth. Ch., 1944, assigned to Geneva (Switzerland) Area, 1944-52, Richmond area 1952-64, Raleigh 1964-68; active orgnl. affairs ch., confs., mem. coms. and commns. on internal orgn. and interdenominational relations; mem. Meth. Commn. on Chaplains; pres. Assn. of Meth. hist. socs., 1940-42; Pres. Internat. Meth. Hist. Soc. Trustee Randolph-Macon Coll., Randolph-Macon Women's Coll.; High Point Coll., Westminster Theol. Sem., Pfeiffer Coll., Louisburg Coll., Ferrum Jr. Coll., Randolph-Macon Acad., Am. U., Wesley Theol. Seminary. Member Am. Soc. Ch. History, Am. Hist. Assn., Wesley Hist. Society, Phi Beta Kappa, Delta Sigma Phi, Tau Kappa Alpha, Theta Pi. Author several books, latest being: The Methodists of Continental Europe, 1949. Contbr. to Dict. Am. Biography. Home: Geneva Switzerland Died Dec. 19, 1972; buried Bridgewater Va

GARCIA, CARLOS P., past pres. P.I.; b. Talibon, Bohol, P.I., Nov. 4, 1896; s. Policronio and Ambrosia (Polestico) G.; student Silliman U., 1918-19; LL.B., Philippine Law Sch., 1923; LL.D., Feati Inst. Tech., 1957, Fordham U., 1958, Ariz. State Coll. at Tempe 1958; L.H.D., U. Hawaii, 1958, Xavier University 1958; LL.D., U. Phillippines, 1959; LL.D., Univ. Saigon, 1959; Litt.D., Toyo U., 1959; married Leonila Dimataga, May 24, 1933; 1 dau., Linda D. (Mrs. Fernando Campos). Teacher pub. schs., 1914-17; rep. 3d Dist. of Bohol, 1925-31; gov. of Bohol, 1933-41; senator, 1941-53, minority floor leader, 1945-51, also chmn. fgn. relations com., com. on govt. reorgn., others; v.p., sec. fgn. affairs Philippines, 1953-57, president of the Philippines, 1957-61. Member of Washington for P.I. Rehabilitation and War Damage Claims, 1945; del. World Conf. to Draft Charter of UN, San Francisco, 1945; del. Interparliamentary Union Conf., Dublin, Ireland, 1950; del. Southeast Asia Baguio Conf., 1950; chmn. P.I. delegation Geneva Conf. Korean Unification, 1954; pres. SEATO Conf., Manila, 1954, chmn. P.I. delegation SEATO Conf., Bangkok, 1955. Mem. Nacionalista Party (v.p. nat. directorate 1947-53. Home: Quezon City PI Died June 14, 1971.

GARDNER, ADDISON LEMAN, pres. Chicago Rapid Transit Co.; b. Walworth, N.Y., May 10, 1866; s. Leman and Eliza A. (Knapp) G.; desc. George Gardiner, who came to Mass. in 1637 and settled in R.I. in 1638; ed. Walworth (N.Y.) Acad., Genesee Wesleyan Sem., Lima, N.Y., Columbia, New York; LL.B., Columbia, 1887; m. Jeanie A. Black, Oct. 4, 1893; children—Addison Leman, Isabel B. (Mrs. John N. Shillestad). Admitted to bar, 1887, and began practice at New York; with Jenkins & Harkness, Chicago, 1887-93; asst. atty., South Side Rapid Transit R.R. Co., Chicago, 1890-93; became atty., Met. West Side Elevated Ry. Co., 1893; gen. atty., 1912-24, of Met. West Side Elev. Ry. Co., Northwestern Elev. R.R. Co., South Side Elevated R.R. Co., and Chicago and Oak Park Elevated R.R. Co.; gen. atty. Chicago, North Shore & Milwaukee R.R. since 1916, also of Chicago Rapid Transit Co. since 1924; mem. Gardner, Morrow, Fowler and Merrick; pres. Chicago Rapid Transit Co. since 1938. Mem. Am., Ill. State and Chicago bar assns., Am. Hist. Assn., S.A.R. Republican. Presbyterian. Clubs: Union League, University. Contbr. to legal jours. Home: 308 N. Kenilworth Av., Oak Park, Ill. Office: 231 S. La Salle St., Chicago IL‡

GARDNER, BERTIE CHARLES, banker; b. Bristol, Eng., May 31, 1884; s. Frank Smith and Susannah Moreland (Willis) G.; student Bristol Grammar Sch.; D.C.L., Bishops U., 1952; LL.D., McGill U., 1952; m. Jean E. Milley, Aug. 15, 1922; children—John Milley, Ann Moreland. With Stuckey's Banking Co. Ltd., Eng., 1901-1906; entered service of the Bank of British N.A., Montreal, 1906, appointed mgr., Trail, B.C., 1910, mgr., Rossland, 1911, asst. mgr., Vancouver, 1913, asst. insp. Winnipeg, 1914; asst. mgr. Bank of Montreal, St. John's, Newfoundland, 1920, mgr., 1928, mgr. St. John, N.B., 1930, supt. foreign officers, Montreal, 1931, 2d agt., N.Y., 1932, 1st agt. 1934, asst. gen. mgr. Montreal, 1935, gen. mgr., 1942, dir. vice pres., gen. mgr., 1944, exec. vice pres., 1947, pres. and chief exec. officer, 1948-52, chmn. bd., 1952-54, exec. com., 1952-59; dir. Brit. Newfoundland Corp.; v.p., mem. exec. com. Royal Trust Co.; dir. Anglo-Newfoundland Development Company, Limited, Scudder Fund of Canada Limited; president, director Canafund Co. Ltd.; chancellor McGill University, Montreal, 1952-57, then gov. emeritus. Served from lieutenant to maj. Cameron Highlanders of Can.; France with 43d bn., 1916-19. Decorated Mil. Cross, 1917. Home: Montreal PQ Canada Died Dec. 1972.

GARDNER, EARL WENTWORTH, fund-raising counsel exec.; b. Plymouth, Mass., Feb. 21, 1914; s. Percy Wentworth and Ethel M. (Mooney) G.; B.A., William Jewell Coll., 1940; B.D., Gordon Divinity Sch., 1942; postgrad. Boston U., 1954; m. Phyllis LeBaron, June 13, 1933; children—Arlene LeBaron (Mrs. Donald L. Foulds), Nancy Mae (Mrs. T. A. F. Kerkhoff III), Earl W., Judith Frances (Mrs. W. Gordon). Ordained to ministry Bapt. Ch., 1941; minister 1st Bapt. Ch., Hanson, Mass., 1937-40, Bridgewater, Mass., 1940-42, North Schuate (R.I.) Bapt. Ch., 1942-43; asso. exec. Providence YMCA, 1943-52; with Ketchum, Inc., 1952-70, v.p., N.Y.C., 1962-70, dir., 1962-70. Mem. Am. Assn. Fund-Raising Counsel. Republican. Club: Union League (N.Y.C.). Home: West New York NJ Died Mar. 10, 1970; buried Plymouth MA

GARDNER, GRANDISON, air force; b. Pine Valley, Utah, Sept. 18, 1892; s. John Alexander and Celestia (Snow) G.; B.S., Utah State Coll., 1914; student U. of Calif., 1915-17; M.S., Mass. Inst. Tech., 1928; m. Edith McMurrin, March 25, 1918; children—Joseph Mather, Edith Rose. Commd. 2d lt., U.S. Army, Nov. 27, 1917, and advanced through the grades to maj. gen.; commd. A.F. Proving Ground Comd., World War II; assigned to Strategic Bombing Survey, Berlin, Guam and Tokyo, 1945; assigned Headquarters U.S.A.F., 1946; dir. Joint Air Defense Board, Colo. Springs, Colo., 1951-54; ret., 1954. Awarded Legion of Merit, Distinguished Service Medal, Order of British Empire. Home: Phoenix AZ Died Jan. 19, 1973.

GARDNER, HAROLD WARD, legal and engring. consultant; b. Brodhead, Wis., Nov. 29, 1877; s. John W. and Dorothea Elizabeth (Springstead) G.; student Beloit (Wis.) Acad., 1895-98; B.S., U. of Wis., 1905; studied U. of Ill., 1905-06; M.S., U. of Kan., 1911; grad. study, Art Students' League, New York, Art Inst. Chicago; LL.B., Westminster Law Sch., Denver, 1928; m. Ella Waterbury, Aug. 31, 1909. City engineer, Golden, and town attorney, Lakeside. State Senator, 8th Dist., Colo. Served as pvt. Co. E, 1st Wis. Vol. Inf., Spanish-Am. War. Mem. Am. Assn. Engrs., Colo. Bar, Colo. Soc. of Engrs., Phi Delta Theta, Sigma Nu Phi, Alpha Chi Sigma, Theta Tau; registered civ. engr. in Colo. Republican. Mason, Oddfellow. Contbr. to scientific jours.; author of scientific articles on the new hydraulics; developer of complete gradient diagram. Home: Golden CO‡

GARDNER, HARRY WENTWORTH, architect; b. Dover, N.H., Jan. 8, 1873; student English High Sch., 3 yrs.; B.S., Mass. Inst. Tech. Prof. architectural design Mass. Inst. Tech., 1920-43, emeritus prof. since 1943. Fellow Am. Inst. Architects since 1926. Address: 213 Hunnewell Terrace, Newton 58 MA‡

GARDNER, HORACE TILLMAN, physician; b. Albuquerque, N.M., Aug. 29, 1913; s. Horace T. and Hanna (Costello) G.; B.A., U. N.M., 1935; M.D., Yale, 1941. Instr. medicine and preventive medicine Cornell U. Med. Coll., 1946-47; instr. preventive medicine Yale, 1947-50; sr. physician Brookhaven Nat. Lab., 1950-51; chief dept. medicine Iran Found., Shiraz, Iran, 1953-58; cons. med. edn., preventive medicine, ICA, Lima, Peru, 1958-60; pvt. practice medicine, N.Y.C., Washington, 1960-70; asst. prof. clinical medicine Cornell Univ.; association. vis. physician Bellevue Hospital; assistant attending physician The New York Hospital. Diplomate Am. Bd. Internat. Medicine. Mem. A.M.A., N.Y. Acad. Sci. Club: Yale (N.Y.C.). Home: New York City NY Died Dec. 15, 1970; buried Sunset Memorial Park, Albuquerque NM

GARDNER, IRVINE C(LIFTON), optics physicist; b. Idaville, Ind., Sept. 19, 1889; s. James Wilson and Sarah Jane (Irvine) G.; A.B., DuPauw U., 1910, Sc.D. (hon.), 1938; A.M., Harvard, 1912, Ph.D. (Whiting fellow and Tyndall fellow), 1915; m. Merriel Pratt Maslin, June 30, 1927. Cutting research fellow Harvard, 1916, instr., 1915-17; chief optical instruments sect. Nat. Bur. Standards, 1921-50, chief div. optics and metrology, 1950-59; leader National Geog. Soc.-Nat. Bur. Standards Eclipse Expdn., Ak Bulaak, Russia, 1936, Patos, Brazil, 1940; mem. eclipse U.S.N.-Nat. Geog. Soc., Canton Island, 1937, A.A.F.-Nat. Geog. Soc., Bocaiuva, Brazil, 1947. Del. to Internat. Commn. Optics, London, Eng., 1950, Madrid, Spain, 1953, Boston Massachusetts, 1956. Served with Ordnance Dept., U.S. Army, mil. optical fire control instrument design and development, 1917-21; Ordnance Dept. rep. to visit German optical plants, 1945. Awarded Abrams award, Am. Soc. Photogrammetry, 1950. Fellow Am. Phys. Soc., Soc. Photog. Engrs.; mem. Optical Soc. of America (president 1958; council 1930-31; Frederic Ives Medal 1954), American Soc. Photogrammetry (dir. 1948-50, v.p. 1951, hon. mem.), A.A.A.S., Washington Academy Sci., Washington Philos. Society, Am. Soc. Optics (exec. v.p. 1955-56, president 1958), Sigma Xi, Phi Beta Kappa, Delta Kappa Epsilon. Clubs: Explorers, Harvard, Cosmos (Washington). Author articles in sci. jours. Holder patents. Home: Gaithersburg MD Died Dec. 29, 1972.

GARDNER, JOHN, clergyman, author; b. Dalton-in-Furness, Eng., May 27, 1868; s. William and Elizabeth (Ashworth) G.; ed. Hackney Coll. U. of London; D.D., Fargo, 1913, Carleton, 1923; m. Agnes Annie Baker, Dec. 1, 1892; children—Agnes (Mrs. George Buttrick), Annie (Mrs. Carl A. Glover (she died July 2, 1934), Evelyn, Gladys (Mrs. Richard L. Jenkins), John Ashworth. Ordained to ministry of the Congregational Church, 1893; pastor at Redhill, 1893-1904, Horton Lane, Bradford, 1904-08, Albion Hull, 1908-12; came to U.S., 1912, naturalized citizen, 1918; pastor New Eng. Ch., Chicago, 1912-20, Riverside, Calif., 1921-31, Garden City, New York, 1931-45. Author: The Unrecognized Christ, 1917; Letters to a Soldier on Religion, 1918; An Interpreters' Note Book, 1919-23; The Religious Appeal to the Modern Mind; Evolution and Redemption, 1925; Letters to Bill on Faith and Prayer, 1943. Contbr. to newspapers and mags. Home: 19 E. 95th St., New York NY‡

GARDNER, MARY SEWELL, public health nursing adminstr.; b. Newton, Mass., 1871; d. William Sewall and Mary (Thorton) Gardner; ed. private day schs., Miss Porter's Sch., Farmington, Conn.; grad. Newport (R.I.) Hosp. Training Sch. for Nurses, 1905; hon. A.M., Brown U., 1918; unmarried. Dir. Providence Dist. Nursing Assn., 1905-31; chmn. standing com. on publ. health nursing, Internat. Council of Nurses, 1925-33. Awarded Saunders gold medal for distinguished service in nursing", 1933. Fellow Am. Pub. Health Assn. Mem. bd. and exec. com., Am. Soc. Hygiene Assn., Am. Red Cross (dir. bureau pub. health nursing, 1919; chief nursing sect., Am. Red Cross Tuberculosis Commn. to Italy, 1918-19; advisor on fgn. pub. health nursing in Europe, 1921), Nat. Organization for Pub. Health Nursing (pres., 1913-15). Episcopalian. Independent. Author: Public Health Nursing, 1916-24-33; So Build We, 1942; Katharine Kent, 1946. Home: 302 Angell St., Providence RI‡

GARDNER, MRS. O. MAX (FAY WEBB GARDNER), found. exec.; b. Shelby, N.C., Sept. 7, 1885; d. James Landrum and Kansas (Andrews) Webb; student pub. and pvt. schs.; H.H.D., U. N.C., Greensboro, 1961; m. O. Max Gardner, Nov. 6, 1970; children—Margaret Love (Mrs. N. E. Burgess), James Webb (dec.), Ralph Webb, O. Max (dec.). Mem. exec. staff, cons. stylist Cleveland Cloth Mills, Shelby, N.C., 1937-46; dir. Gardner Land Co., 1947-69; dir. O. Max Gardner Found., Inc., 1942-69, pres. 1947-69. Life mem. N.C. Symphony; pres. Civic League, 1918-19; trustee N.C. Orthopedic Hosp., Gastonia, 1957-69; Tryon Palace Commn., 1954-69, Children's Home Soc., Greensboro, N.C., 1952, Gardner Webb Coll., 1955-65, Harry S. Truman Library and Friends of Library, U. N.C. at Greensboro. Life mem., hon. v.p. Women's Nat. Democratic Club, Washington. Recipient Charles A. Cannon cup, 1953, Woman's Nat. Dem. Club award, 1959; citation as world citizen N.C. Soc. Washington, 1959; citation for service as citizen Gardner-Webb Coll., 1960; named woman of yr., Bus. and Profl. Women, 1961; Distinguished Service award for Women, U. N.C. chapter Chi Omega Fraternity, 1963. Member N.C. Hist. Soc., (life), N.C. Antiquities Soc. (life), N.C. Art Soc. (life), Roanoke Island Assn. (chmn. 1960-62; life mem.) D.A.R. (Benjamin Cleveland organizing chpt. regent 1924-26), U.D.C., Colonial Dames Am., Am. Assn. U. Woman, Bus. and Profl. Women, English-Speaking Union, Nat. (life), N.C. fedns. music clubs, Delta Kappa Gamma (hon.). Baptist (decorating cons.). Clubs: Colonial Dames, 1925 F Street (Washington), Cleveland Country, North Lake (Shelby); 20th Century Book, Cecelia Music, Shelby Women's. Home: Shelby NC Died Jan. 16, 1969.

GARDNER, VERNON O(RACE), labor official; b. Goshen, Ind., Mar. 8, 1877; s. Charles F. and Mary E. (Mock) G.; ed. public schools, Goshen, Ind., and student U. of Valparaiso, Ind., 1898; m. May Laura Matthews, Sept. 12, 1906; children—Everett Maurice, Ruth Frances. Began as railroad agent and telegrapher, 1900; gen. sec. and treas. Order of Railroad Telegraphers, 1924-28, gen. chmn., 1928-35, v.p., 1935-39, pres., May 1939-46; retired. Democrat. Contbr. to Telegraphers Journal. Home: 5830 Neosho St., St Louis MO‡

GARDNER, WILLIAM EDWARD, clergyman; b. Sherborn, Mass., Mar. 22, 1872; s. William Brown and Harriet (Eaton) G.; Ph.B., Brown U., 1895, D.D., 1915; B.D., Episcopal Theol. Sch., 1898; m. Mary Tracy, of Nantucket, Mass., Sept. 14, 1898. Deacon, 1898, priest, 1898, P.E. Ch.; rector Ch. of the Holy Name, Swampscott, Mass., 1898-1903, Christ Ch., Quincy, Mass., 1903-08, St. James Ch., Cambridge, Mass., 1908-10; N.E. sec. Bd. Foreign and Domestic Missions, P.E. Ch., Boston, 1910-12; gen. sec. Gen. Bd. Religious Edn. of P.E. Ch., New York, Nov., 1912-20, exec. sec. nat. dept. of religious edn., 1920-26; now asst. minister Trinity Church, Boston, Mass. Mem. Theta Delta Chi. Club: University. Author: History of Christianity, 1903; Winners of the World (with wife), 1909; Children's Challenge to the Church, 1913. Address: Trinity Church, Boston MA‡

GARLAND, CECIL RAYMOND, foundry exec.; b. Orient, Pa., Dec. 6, 1907; s. Cecil B. and Elizabeth O. (Walters) G.; A.B. in Accounting, Washington and Jefferson Coll., 1929; m. Ruby Gene Haught, Mar. 3, 1929; children—Cecil W., Wibur L. Accountant, Uniontown, Pa., 1929-40, Bender Body Co., Cleve., 1940-41, Welsh & Beard, C.P.A.'s, Cleve., 1941-42; with Larson Consol. Inc. (formerly W.O. Larson Foundry Co.), Grafton, O., 1942-72, sec., 1945-72, treas., 1960-72, v.p., 1961-72; v.p., treas., dir. subsidiary co.; asst. sec. subsidiary Larson Steel Castings, Inc. Treas. Gray Iron Founders Soc., 1957-60, v.p., 1960-61, bd. dirs., 1960-72, pres., 1961-62. Mem. Nat. Assn. Accountants, Am. Foundrymens Soc., Nat. Castings Council. Mason (Jester). Club: Cleveland Athletic. Home: Elyria OH Died Nov. 1, 1972.

GARLAND, CHARLES STEDMAN;, investment banking; b. Pittsburgh, Pa., Oct. 29, 1898; s. Charles and Lillian (Chisholm) G.; B.A., Yale University, 1920; LL.D. (honorary) Johns Hopkins University, 1969; married Aurelia Stoner, May 28, 1925; children—Charles S. Courtney (Mrs. Iredell W. Iglehart), Aurelia (Mrs. Perry J. Bolton). Salesman with Hickman, Williams and Company, Incorporated, iron and steel brokers, 1920, district manager, N.Y., 1924-28, asso. with Brown Bros. & Co., private banking, New York, 1928, mgr. Chicago office, 1929; partner Brown Bros. Harriman & Co., 1933-34, then vice-president, and director; Brown Harriman & Co.; partner Alex, Brown & Sons, Balt.; director Mercantile Trust Co., Merc. Safe Deposit and Trust Co.; chmn. bd. Merck & Co., Inc., 1962-71. Pres. Baltimore Assn. Commerce, 1948-50; trustee Johns Hopkins University, chmn. bd. trustees, 1958-68; trustee Johns Hopkins Hospital; director of Johns Hopkins Fund; campaign chairman 1944, Baltimore War and Community Fund; state chairman War Finance Div. 7th War Loan; chief, financial sect., Office Prodn. Mngt., 1940-41. Served as 2d lt. F.A., 1918. Pres. Investment Bankers Association of America, 1945-46. Mem. Psi Upsilon, Wolf's Head Soc. Pres. Bond Club, Chicago, 1934. Clubs: Yale, Lunch (New York City); Merchants, Md., Elkridge (Baltimore). Member of U.S. Davis Cup Team, 1920; with R. Norris Williams II as partner, won the doubles championship of the world at Wimbledon, Eng., 1920; capt. U.S. Davis Cup Team in 1927. Home: Baltimore MD Died Jan. 28, 1971.

GARLAND JUDY, actress; b. Grand Rapids, Minn., June 10, 1922; d. Frank Avent and Ethel Marian (Milne) Gumm; student, Lawier's Professional Sch., 1929-31, Bancroft Jr. High Sch., 1936-37, Univ. High Sch., 1938-40; m. David Rose, July 8, 1941 (div.); married second Vincente Minnelli, June 15, 1945 (divorced, 1951); one daughter, Liza; m. 3d, M.S. Luft, June 28, 1952 (div.); children—Lorna, Joseph; m. 5th, Mickey Deans. Singer in father's theater, Grand Rapids, Minn., 1926; on the stage until 1935; toured throughout the United States in vaudeville; with Metro-Goldwyn-Mayer, 1935-50; on concert tour of Europe, 1950; played Las Vegas, 1956, Palace, 1956; 2 CBS spectaculars, 1955, 56; in pictures, on radio, in concert with Philadelphia Symphony. Received Academy award, 1939. Motion pictures include: Ziegfeld Girl; Life Begins for Andy Hardy; Babes on Broadway, 1941; For Me and My Gal, 1942; Presenting Lily Mars, 1943; Girl Crazy, Thousands Cheer (1943); Meet Me in St. Louis, Ziegfeld Follies, The Clock 1944; Wizard of Oz, 1939; Summer Stock, 1950; A Star is Born, 1954; A Child Is Waiting, 1963. Beverly Hills CA Died June 1969.

GARMAN, RAYMOND LEROY, corp. ofcl.; b. Schoeneck, Pa., July 21, 1907; s. Albert and Amelia (Wagner) G.; B.S., Franklin and Marshall Coll., 1929; M.Sc., N.Y.U., 1931, Ph.D., 1932; m. Grace Ross, July 1933; children—Elizabeth, Robert. Instr. N.Y.U., 1932, asst. prof. chemistry, 1932-34; instr. Washington Sq. Coll., 1934-41, asst. prof., 1941-42; research group leader Mass. Inst. Tech., 1943-45 v.p. charge research Gen. Precision Lab., Inc., Pleasantville, N.Y., 1945-52, v.p., mng. dir., 1952-56, exec. vice pres., tech. dir., N.Y.C., 1956-57, chmn. bd. and tech. dir. in charge of research and development, 1957-59; v.p. engring. and research General Precision Equipment Corp., 1958-66, senior vice pres. for technology, 1966-68; v.p. chief scientist Gen. Precision, Inc., 1959-68; v.p. charge advanced tech. Singer Co., 1968-70. Cons. sci. adv. bd. USAF. Mem. bd. trustees Franklin and Marshall College. Recipient Presidential Certificate Merit, 1946; Alumni citation Franklin and Marshall Coll., 1963, Alumni medal, 1970. Fellow Soc. Motion Picture & Television Engineers, Institute of Electrical and Electronic Engineers, New York Academy of Sciences; mem. Am. Chem. Soc., Am. Phys. Soc., Optical Soc. Am., Acoustical Soc. Am., Instrument Soc. Am., Inst. Navigation. Author: (with Muller, Droz) Experimental Electronics, 1940. Contbr. articles profl. jours. Home: Hastings-on-Hudson NY Died Jan. 20, 1970; buried Kensico Cemetery, Valhalla NY

GARMHAUSEN, ERWIN JOHN, lawyer; b. Washington, Oct. 13, 1913; s. Erwin John and Hazel (Karshner) G.; LL.B., Ohio State U., 1937; m. Marjorie Marshall Best, Dec. 23, 1938; children—Linda (Mrs. Thomas J. Orlow), John Marshall. Admitted to Ohio bar, 1937; with firm Spencer, Hardman & Fehr, Dayton, 1937-38; practice in Sidney, 1938-72; partner firm Garmhausen, Kerrigan & Elsass, 1960-72. Sec., dir. Am. Budget Co., Caravanner Ins., Inc., Everyday Mfg. Co., Airstream, Inc., Peerless Bread Machine Co.; dir., v.p. Scott Port-A-Fold, Inc.; asst. sec. Sidney Pattern Works Co.; dir. Sidney Electric Co., First Nat. Bank, New Bremen, O., Piqua Engring, Inc., Port Clinton News Herald Pub. Co.; pres., dir. Coldway Food Express, Inc.; partner C J Investment Co. Solicitor, City of Sidney, 1941-48. Trustee, sec. Sidney Community Found. Served to lt. USNR, 1944-46. Mem. Am., Ohio Sidney OH Died Sept. 28, 1972.

GARNER, ALFRED BUCKWALTER, congressman; b. Ashland, Pa., Mar. 4, 1873; ed. pub. schs.; married. Admitted to bar and engaged in practice at Ashland. Mem. Pa. Ho. of Rep., 1900-8; mem. 61st Congress (1909-11), 12 Pa. Dist.; Republican. Address: Ashland PA‡

GARNER, JAMES BERT, chem. engr.; b. Lebanon, Ind., Sept. 2, 1870; s. James Washington and Orrah Jane (Shepard) G.; B.Sc., Wabash Coll., Crawfordsville, Ind., 1893, M.Sc., 1895, D.Sc., 1950; Ph.D., magna cum laude, University of Chicago, 1897; married Glenna May Greene, December 31, 1900 (died Dec. 7, 1918); children—Mrs. Lura Faulkinbury (died October 15, 1946), Mrs. Marjorie Schmeltz, James Herbert, Mrs. Eleanor Shannon, Mrs. Mildred Beckwith, Mason (dec.), Jean Hale, Harry F., Mrs. Glenna MacGregor, Mrs. Ruth Kindelin; m. 2d, Margaret Martin, June 30, 1923 (died Sept. 19, 1932); 1 son, William Jenkins; m. 3d, Sarah Elizabeth Harold, May 12, 1934; 1 dau., Sarah Elizabeth. Teacher chemistry, Bradley Poly. Inst., and Wabash Coll., 1897-1914; fellow and professor Mellon Inst. (U. of Pittsburgh), since 1914, administrative fellow since 1950, director natural gas investigations same, since 1915; dir. research Chem. Storage Fellowship in Mellon Inst. for Pitts.-Des Moines Steel Co. Inventor of gas mask Apr. 1915. Metall. research. Fellow Am. Assn. Advancement of Science, mem. Am. Chem. Soc., Phi Delta Theta, Phi Beta Kappa, Alpha Chi Sigma, Phi Sigma, Sigma Xi. Mem. United Presbyn. Ch. Mason (32 deg.). Home: 54 Lebanon Hills Drive, Mt. Lebanon, Pitts 28‡

GARNER, WIGHTMAN WELLS, chemist, plant physiologist; b. Timmonsville, S.C., July 15, 1875; s. James Nathaniel and Joanna (Wright) G.; S.C. Mil. Acad., 1892-93; A.B., U. of S.C., 1896; Ph.D., Johns Hopkins, 1900; Sc.D., Clemson Coll., and N.C. State Coll., 1937; m. Judith Goode, Nov. 8, 1905. Instr. chemistry, and pvt. asst. to Prof. A. Michael, Tufts Coll., Mass., 1900-03; scientific asst. Bur. Chemistry, Dept. Agr., 1904; scientific asst. in tobacco investigations, 1905-08, physiologist in charge, tobacco and plant nutrition investigations, 1909-40, principal physiol. in charge, tobacco investigations, Bureau of Plant Industry, Dept. of Agriculture, 1941-45; retired. Fellow A.A.A.S.; member American Chemical Society, Am. Genetic Assn., Bot. Soc. America, Am. Soc. Naturalists, Washington Acad. Sciences, Am. Soc. Plant Physiologists (Stephen Hale's award 1930), Am. Soc. Agronomy, Sigma Alpha Epsilon, Phi Beta Kappa. Episcopalian. Author scientific papers in American and foreign jours., and bulls., particularly on photoperiodism in plants, mineral nutrition of plants and tobacco production; The Production of Washington 10‡

GARRETSON, CORNELIUS DAVID, mfg. exec.; b. York, Pa., Feb. 12, 1882; s. Cornelius R. and Sallie V. (Ginter) G.; student Girard Coll., Phila.; m. Katherine B. Miller, Feb. 17, 1904. Asst. treas., sales mgr. Electric Hose & Rubber Co., 1904-23, pres., 1923-53, chmn. bd., 1958-68. Mason. Clubs: Rotary, Wilmington Country (Wilmington, Del.); Union League (Phila.). Home: Wilmington DE Died Jan. 12, 1968; buried Mt. Vernon Cemetery, Philadelphia PA

GARRETT, DONALD WALLACE, banker; b. New Braunfels, Tex., Nov. 6, 1928; s. William W. and Thelma (Crossley) G.; B.A., Tex. A. and M. U. 1950; postgrad. Northwestern U., 1960, So. Meth. U., 1967; m. Ilse Frost, Dec. 27, 1949; children—Ilse Frost, Kathleen Crossley. With Lone Star Brewing Co., San Antonio, 1950-57; asst. v.p. Frost Nat. Bank, San Antonio, 1957-59, v.p., 1959-65, mem. exec. com., 1962-73, sr. v.p., 1965-68, exec. v.p., 1968-73, also dir.; v.p. Frost Realty Co., 1969-73. Past pres., bd. dirs. United Fund San Antonio, also campaign chmn., 1969; past pres., bd. dirs. Fiesta San Antonio Commn.; bd. dirs. Jersig Speech and Hearing Center, 1965-68, Downtown, Inc., 1966-69, Tex. Cavaliers, 1966-70; adv. trustee S.W. Found. for Research and Edn.; trustee San Antonio Acad. Tex.; bd. dirs., v.p. Former Students Assn. Tex. A and M U.; mem. Council of San Antonio TX Died Feb. 3, 1973.

GARRETT, EILEEN JEANETTE, writer, publisher; b. Beau Park, County Meath, Ireland Mar. 17, 1893; d. Anthony and Ann Brownell-Vancho; after death of parents was adopted by William and Martha Lyttle; ed. in Nat. Sch. and private schools, Ireland and England; m. Clive Barry, 1909; 1 dau.; m. 2d, J. W. Garrett, 1918. Various commercial interests, and drama and politics; owner of publishing firm of Garrett Publications; pres. The Parapsychology Foundation, Inc., New York City. Member English Speaking Union, Lyceum, (London) Liberal. Mem. Church of England. Author: (under pen name Jean Lyttle) Today the Sun Rises, 1942; You Are France; Lisette; Sheila Lacey; Threads of Destiny, 1961; (under own name) My Life, As a Search for the Meaning of Mediumship, 1939; Telepathy, in Search of a Lost Faculty, 1941; Awareneess; Man the Maker, 1946; Adventures in the Supernormal, 1949; The Sense and Nonsense of Prophecy; Life is the Healer, 1958; Many Voices, 1968. Home: New York City NY Died Sept. 15, 1970; buried Marseilles, France.

GARRETT, GEORGE ANGUS, ex-ambassador; born La Crosse, Wis., Aug. 5, 1888; s. John Willis and Anna (Laughlan) G.; student Cornell, 1906-07, U. of Chicago; 1907-10; LL.D., Trinity College, Dublin, Ireland, 1950; L.H.D., Clarkson College of Technology, 1956; married Ethel Shields Darlington, Apr. 11, 1935; 1 dau. (by former marriage), Margot (Mrs. Luis Mariano de Zuberbuhler); step-children—Harry Darlington III, McCullough Darlington, Elaine Darlington (Mrs. Anderson Fowler). Began with Harris Trust and Savings Bank, Chicago, 1910; v.p. Dupont National Bank of Washington, D.C., 1913-17; general partner of Merrill, Lynch, Pierce, Fenner & Smith, investment bankers, 1939-60; dir. of the Nat. Savs. & Trust Company, Merchants Transfer and Storage Company. Appointed by President Truman, member of the Redevelopment Land Agency, Washington, D.C., Jan. 1947; appointed U.S. minister to Ireland, April 1947; apptd. U.S. ambassador to Republic of Ireland, 1950. President Federal City Council, 1954-58, then chmn. Owner, Washington Senators. Served as 1st lt. U.S. Army, World War I; OSS, World War II. Pres. Emergency Hosp., Washington, 1943-51; v.p., dir. Nat. Symphony Orch., 1930-51; chmn. ARC Fund Raising Campaign, D.C., 1952; apptd. special assistant to chairman and pres. Am. Nat. Red Cross, 1952; mem. bldg. com. Washington Cathedral; active Navy Relief Soc. Clubs: Metropolitan (pres. 1939-42), Alibi, Chevy Chase (Washington), Brook, Racquet and Tennis, Turf and Field, United Hunts, Jockey (N.Y.C.); Whites (London); The Travelers (Paris). Home: Washington DC Died Sept. 29, 1971; buried Washington Cathedral.

GARRETT, HARRY FREELAND, state justice; b. Corydon, Ia., Dec. 24, 1887; s. John S. and Carrie (Freeland) G.; LL.B., U. Ia., 1911; m. Louie Oneall, June 27, 1927. Admitted to Ia. bar, 1911, since practiced in Corydon; county atty. Wayne County, 1914-18, 28-29; asst. atty. gen. Ia., 1933-37; justice Ia. Supreme Ct., 1958-61; pvt. practice law, 1961-71. Mem. Ia. Ho. of Reps., 1931-32; del. Democratic Nat. Conv., 1948. Served with U.S. Army, 1918-19. Mem. Am., Wayne County (pres. 1950-58) bar assns., Am. Legion. Phi Alpha Delta. Methodist. Mason. Rotarian (pres. Corydon 1955, del. internat. meeting Licerne, Switzerland 1957). Home: Corydon IA Died Aug. 10, 1971; buried Corydon IA

GARRETT, JAMES MADISON, JR., ret. army officer, ret. ofcl.; b. Montgomery, Ala., Nov. 12, 1892; s. James Madison and Lucy (Tankersley) G.; B.A., U. Va., 1913; m. Helen DeLloyd Foster, July 12, 1921; children—James Madison, Elwood, Carolyn. Employed by C.E., U.S. Army, 1913; commd. 2d. lt. F.A., Regular Army, 1917, advanced through grades to col., 1941; comd. 2d Bn., 16th F.A., 1918-20, 186th F.A. Regt., N.Y. N.G., 1941-43; mem. 4th Div. participating in campaigns of Aisne-Marne, St. Mihiel, Meuse-Argonne, Defensive Sector, World War I; exec. officer XX Corps Arty., participating in campaigns of Normandy, No. France, Rhineland, Ardennes-Alsace of World War II; ret. because of physical disability in September 1947; dir. of Civil Def., State Ala., 1951-55. Member of Sigma Alpha Epsilon. Episcopalian. Home: Montgomery AL Died Apr. 14, 1971; buried Greenwood Cemetery, Montgomery AL

GARRETT, JAMES WILLIAM, newspaperman; born Detroit, July 28, 1925; s. James G. and Martha E. (Salsinger) G.; student U. Mich., 1943, B.A., 1951; student Evansville (Ind.) Coll., 1946-48; m. Nancy Ann Notnagel, Aug. 18, 1951; 1 dau., Ann Denise. With Cleve. Press, 1952-70, editor Showtime mag., 1962-70, editor Tv Showtime, 1964-70, book editor, 1965-70. Served with inf. AUS, 1943-46; ETO. Mem. Authors Guild Am., Sigma Delta Chi. Author: (novel) And Save Them for Pallbearers, 1958; also short stories. Home: Shaker Heights OH Died May 2, 1970; buried Acacia Cemetery, Birmingham MI

GARRETT, RAY, lawyer; b. Murphysboro, Ill., Sept. 17, 1889; s. Anderson Barker and Georgia (Williams) G.; student U. Ill., 1906-08; LL.B., Ill. Wesleyan U., 1916; student Northwestern U., 1924-25; m. Mabel Marian May, Aug. 1, 1916; children—Glenn May, Ray, Martha Ann. Ofcl. stenographer Supreme Ct. Ill., Springfield, 1910-17; admitted to Ill. bar, 1916; law asso. A. M. Fitzgerald, Springfield, 1916-17; atty. Chgo. Mill & Lumber Co., 1919-21; counsel A. W. Swayne & Co., 1921-23; asso., partner Cooke Sullivan & Ricks, Chgo., 1923-34; partner Lawyer & Garrett, 1934-39; pvt. practice, 1939-42; asso., partner Garrett, 1934-39; pvt. practice, 1939-42; asso., partner Sidley, Austin, Burgess & Smith, Chgo., from 1942. Pres. Midland Subsidiary Corp., 1937-39, Chgo., South Shore & South Bend R.R., 1938-39; pres., trustee Indiana R.R., 1941-51; counsel to bd. D. & R.G.W., R.R. Co., from 1970; dir. Denver and Rio Grande Western R.R. Served from lieutenant to major, infantry, U.S. Army, 1917-19; AEF. Fellow American Bar Foundation; member American Law Inst., Am. Bar Assn. (former chmn. corp. banking and bus. law), Ill., Chgo. bar assns., Newcomen Soc., Phi Delta Phi. Methodist. Clubs: Mid-Day, Univ., Law (Chgo.); Mich. Shores (Wilmette, Ill.). Co-author: Illinois. Business Corporation Act, Model Business Corporation and Non-Profit Corporation Acts. Contbr. articles legal jours. Home: Evanston IL

GARRETT, WILLIAM ADELOR, journalist; b. Troy, N.Y., Sept. 23, 1910; s. Joseph Adelor and Della Rose (Fassett) G.; student Trinity Coll., Hartford, Conn.; m. Calista C. McEnany; children—Evelyn (Mrs. Victor H. Long, Jr.), William J., Mary L. (Mrs. Mark U. P. Zolly), Margaret (Mrs. Verner Hugh King, Jr.). Reporter, New Britain (Conn.) Herald, 1929-35, Hartford Times, 1935-41, 47-49; editor weekly, Bristol, Conn.; asst. pub. relations dir., news mag. writer, editor New Departure div. Gen. Motors, Bristol, 1942-47; Washington corr. Gannett Newspapers, 1949-72; broadcast interviewer congl. members. Founder, past pres., sec. Eastern Profl. Basketball League. Mem. bd. edn., Bristol, also justice of peace, mem. Housing Authority. Trustee St. Vincent de Paul Soc. Camp St. Florence. Recipient several citations for journalistic achievement. Mem. Bus. Editors South New Eng. (past pres.), White House Corrs. Assn., Senate and House Press Galleries, Sigma Delta Chi. Roman Catholic. K.C. Clubs: Crocodile (Conn.); Nat. Press (Washington); Bristol Exchange (past pres.), Press (past pres.) (Bristol); Nat. Exchange (past dist. gov.). Author: The Frank Wheaton Story. Co-editor: Passionist mag., Retreat Forward, 1948-49. Home: Wheaton MD Died July 20, 1972; buried Gate of Heaven Cemetery, Silver Spring MD

GARRIGA, MARIANO SIMON, bishop; b. Port Isabel, Tex., May 30, 1886; s. Frank and Elizabeth (Baker) G.; student St. Mary's (Kan.) Coll., St. Francis Sem., Wis.; LL.D., St. Edward's U., Austin, Tex., 1936. Ordained priest, R.C. Ch., 1911; asst. to chancellor, San Antonio, 1911-12; asst. pastor, Marfa and missions, 1912-15; vice-rector, St. John's Sem., 1915-16; chaplain, Tex. N.G., 1916; pastor, St. Cecelia's Parish, 1919-36; named domestic prelate, 1935, coadjutor bishop of Corpus Christi, 1936, consecrated coadjutor bishop, 1926; bishop of Corpus Christi. Trained with 144th Infantry, 36th Division, United States Army, Camp Bowie, and A.E.F.; resigned from U.S. Army, 1919. Apptd. Vicar Delegate for Army and Navy, Tex. and La., 1941-42. Pastor St. Peter's Church. Mem. Am. Legion, Vets. of Fgn. Wars, Tex. Hist. Commn., Order of Alhambra. K.C. (3d and 4th degree). Home: Corpus Christi TX Died 1965.

GARRIGUE, JEAN, poet; b. Evansville, Ind., Dec. 8, 1914; d. Allan Colfax and Gertrude Louise (Heath) G.; B.A., U. Chgo., 1937; M.A., U. Ia., 1943. Free-lance writer and editor, 1938-72; intermittent instr. U. Ia., Bard Coll., Queens Coll., New Sch., U. Colo., U. Conn.; lectr. poetry Smith Coll., 1965-66, U. Pa., 1967; vis. prof. English, U. Wash., 1970, U. Cal. at Riverside, 1972. Rockefeller fellow, 1954; Hudson River fellow poetry, 1957 Guggenheim fellow, 1960; recipient grant in lit. Nat. Acad. Arts and Letters, 1952; Radcliffe Inst. fellowship, 1967-68. Mem. P.E.N. Democrat. Author: Thirty-Six Poems and a Few Songs (in Five Young American Poets), 1944; The Ego and the Centaur, 1947; The Monument Rose 1953; A Water Walk by Villa d'Este, 1959; Country Without Maps, 1964; The Animal Hotel, 1966; New and Selected Poems, 1967; Studies for an Actress and Other New York City NY Died Dec. 27, 1972; buried Cambridge MA

GARRISON, CARL LOUISE, educator; b. Chicago, of English parents. Mem. Statist., Audubon, and Nat. Geog. socs. Asso. editor Nat. Geographic Mag. Prin. Thomas P. Morgan School. Author of Key to Metcalf's Grammar. Co-author: Commercial Geography (Gannett and Garrison), 1905 A1. Address: 1304 Yale St., Washington‡

GARRISON, F(RANK) LYNWOOD, mining engr.; b. Philadelphia, Pa., Jan. 12, 1862; s. David Rea and Maria Morgan (Pleiss) G.; ed. Rittenhouse and Rugby acads., Phila.; B.S., U. of Pa., mining and civ. engring. metallurgy, chemistry and geology, 1883; Royal School of Mines of London, England, 1884-85; m. Adele Mary Dwight, Nov. 21, 1894 (died Sept. 1929); children—Dwight, Elizabeth D., Laura D.; m. 2d, Mrs. Edith Brinton McKenna, Oct. 17, 1931. Was in Russia investigating methods of making iron during years, 1887-88; commr. Paris Expn., 1889; practiced profession U.S., Alaska and Canada, 1890-99, in China, 1900; chief engr. Empire Lumber and Mining Co., Johnson County, Tenn., 1902-04; in cons. practice S. America, S. Africa and U.S. since 1904. Mem. Soc. Economic Geologists, Am. Inst. Mining and Metall. Engineers, Franklin Institution, Academy Natural Sciences Philadelphia, Instn. Mining and Metallurgy (London), Newcomen Soc., The Champlain Soc. of Canada, Zeta Psi. Chmn. Nat. Manganese Commn., 1917. Episcopalian. Mason. Club: Union League. Author Kerl's Assaying, 1889; also many tech. papers. Home: 1019 Philadelphia PA‡

GARRISON, HARRELL EDMOND, coll. pres.; b. Hugo, Okla., Nov. 4, 1908; s. James Henry and Cynthia (Adams) G.; A.B., Bethany-Peniel Coll., 1932; M.S., Northwestern U., 1936; Ph.D., George Peabody Coll., 1949; m. Virginia Clarice Taylor, Mar. 5, 1933; children—Linda Clarice, Sandra Sue Rahe. Tchr. pub. schs., Swink, Ft. Towson and Durant, Okla., 1932-45; diagnostician child study George Peabody Coll., 1945-48; dir. Demonstration Sch., North Tex. Tchrs. Coll., 1949, U. Okla., 1950-51; pres. Northeastern State Coll., Tahlequah, Okla., from 1951. Past exec. com. Okla. Congress P.T.A. Mem. Nat., Okla. edn. assns., Am. Assn. U. Profs., Phi Delta Kappa, Kappa Delta, Pi. Kiwanian (past dist. lt. gov.). Co-author: Phonetic Keys to Reading. Home: Tahlequah OK Died Feb. 25, 1972; buried Highland Cemetery, Durant OK

GARRISON, HOMER, JR., police adminstr.; b. Kickapoo, Tex., July 21, 1901; s. Homer and Mattie Bridges (Milam) G.; student pub. schs.; m. Mary Nell Kilgo, June 21, 1931; 1 son, Homer Trey. License, weight insp. Tex. Highway Patrol, 1929, instr. tng. sch., 1930-31, sr. capt. 1932-33, insp. patrol, 1933-35, sr. insp., 1935-68; assistant dir. Dept. Pub. Safety, 1935-38, dir. 1938-68; exec. com. So. Safety Conf., 1943, state dir. 1950; instr. F.B.I. Nat. Police Acad., 1943-48; state mileage adminstr. 1943; state coordinator Tex. Civil Defense and Disaster Relief; dir. Governor's Highway Safety Commission. Chmn. health and safety Boy Scouts of Am., 1941-68, president, Capitol area council, 1957-58. Mem., past mem. or officer, numerous state and nat. coms. or adv. groups in field of policing or pub. safety traffic laws, highway safety, uniform laws and related activities. Has served as mem. examining bds. for chiefs of police various cities. Recipient of Paul G. Hoffman award, Automotive Safety Foundation, 1962. Member of Texas Sheriff's Association, Tex. Police Assn. (pres. 1942), Nat. Safety Council, Internat. Assn. Chief Police (pres. 1948), Am. Soc. Pub. Adminstrn., Pacific Coast Internat. Assn. Law Enforcement Ofcls., Tex. Safety Assn., Am. Assn. Motor Vehicle Adminstrs., Indsl. Plant Protection Assn. Tex. K.P. Clubs: Town and Gown, Rotary (pres.). Home: Austin TX Died May 7, 1968; buried State Cemetery, Austin TX

GARRISON, LEMUEL ADDISON, college pres.; b. Blakesburg, Ia., Aug. 19, 1871; s. Alonzo and Eliza Margaret (Cross) G.; A.B., Central Coll., 1896; grad. Rochester Theol. Sem., 1899; (D.D., Shurtleff Coll., 1904); A.M., Harvard, 1910; m. Mary Firth, of Pella, Ia., Sept. 17, 1894. Taught in pub. schs.; entered Bapt. ministry, 1893; pastor, Lovilia, Ia., 1893-5, Blakesburg, Ia., 1893-6, Keota, Ia., 1895-6, Greece, N.Y., 1897-9, Olathe, Kan., 1899-1900; prof. mental and moral science, Central Coll., Pella, Ia., 1899-1909, v.-p. 1900-3, pres., June 15, 1903-9; pres. Grand Island Coll., 1911—. Chmn. exec. com. Ia. Bapt. Edn. Soc., 1907; chmn. bd. of edn. Neb. Bapt. State Conv., 1910-11, Republican. Address: Grand Island NE‡

GARRISON, WILLIAM HART, printing co. exec.; b. Silver Point, Tenn., Sept. 12, 1920; s. William Claud and Beatrice (Hart) G.; B.S., Wayne U., 1943; M.A., U. Mich., 1950; m. Carrie Wallach, Feb. 10, 1951; children—Roger, Bruce. Tech. writer Gen. Prec. Lab., Pleasantville, N.Y., 1952; saleman Osborne Co. div. Am. Colortype, Clifton, N.J., 1953; founder, dir., pres. Garrison House, Inc., N.Y.C., 1953-68; pres., dir. Polygraphic Co. Am., Inc., 1959-68, chmn. bd., 1962-68; pres., dir. Garrison Color Corp., Dumont, N.J., 1960-68; treas., dir. Olympic Sales Club, Inc., Windsor Locks, Conn., Friendly Card Co., Inc., North Bennington, Vt., 1965-70; v.p., dir. Brook-Parker Co., Montclair, N.Y., 1954-70; chmn., pres., chief exec. officer Garrison Corporation, 1968-70; Garrison Printing Division, Incorporated, 1968—. vice pres., dir Brook-Parker Co., Montclair, 1954-70. Pres. Ossining (N.Y.) Young Republican Club, 1958. Served from pvt. to capt., USAAF, 1942-51; PTO and Korea. Decorated D.F.C., 5 Air Medals. Mem. N.Y. Union League, Ossining C. of C. (pres. 1960-61). Conglist. Clubs: Mt. Anthony Country (Bennington, Vt.); Sleepy Hollow Country, Shattemuc Yacht (Ossining, N.Y.). Home: Ossining NY Died Jan. 13, 1970.

GARRISON, WINFRED ERNEST, educator; b. St. Louis, Mo., Oct. 1, 1874; s. James Harvey and Judith Elizabeth (Garrett) G.; A.B., Eureka Coll., 1892, Litt.D., 1935; A.B., Yale, 1894; B.D., Ph.D., U. of Chgo., 1897; LL.D., Bethany College, 1949; D.D., Butler University, 1955, Yale University, 1964; married Annie Gaines Dye, October 1, 1900; children—Frederic Garrett, Elisabeth Jean Crawford. Assistant in history, U. of Chicago, and instr. in Disiples' Divinity House, 1897-98; prof. church history and Hebrew, Butler College, 1898-1900; asst. editor Christian-Evangelist, 1900-04; pres. Butler College, Indianapolis, 1904-06; pres. N.M. Normal U., 1907-08; pres. N.M. Coll. of Agr. and Mechanic Arts, 1908-13. Founder and head master Claremont (Calif.) Sch. for Boys, 1913-21; dean of Disciples' Div. House, 1921-28; asso. prof. ch. history, Disciples' Divinity House and U. of Chicago, 1921-35, prof., 1935-43; emeritus 1943-69; prof. philosophy and religion U. Houston, 1951-64, chmn. dept., 1955-59, M.D. Anderson prof., 1957-64, professor emeritus of philosophy, 1964-69; Ainslie lecturer Rhodes University, Grahamstown, S. Africa, 1961; Garrison lectr. Yale Univ., 1961. Mem. Constl. Convention 1910, which framed constitution under which N.M. was admitted to Union. Asso. at Oxford Conf. on Life and Work; del. for Disciples of Christ at Edinburgh Conf. on Faith and Order, 1937. Cons. World Council of Churches, Amsterdam, 1948, Third World Conf. on Faith and Order, London, 1952; 2d Assembly, World Council of Churches, Evanston, Illinois, 1954. Winfred Ernest Garrison lectureship established at the Yale Divinity School, 1959. Member Beta Theta Pi, Phi Beta Kappa. Author several books; later ones being: An American Religious Movement (Spanish edition), 1950; A Protestant Manifesto, 1952; Christian Unity and Disciples of Christ, 1955; The Quest and Charter of a United Church, 1957; Twenty Centuries of Christianity, 1959; Heritage and Destiny, 1961; Variations on a Theme, 1964. Editor: 100 Poems of Peace (with T.C. Clark), 1934; 100 Poems of Immortality (with T.C. Clark), 1935; Faith of the Free, 1940. Contributor to dictionaries and encys.; literary editor Christian Century 1923-55. Clubs: Quadrangle, Cliff Dwellers (pres. 1944-46). Sculptor in bronze works in various churches and colleges in Chicago, St. Louis, Houston TX Died Feb. 1969.

GARRY, HAROLD BERNARD, supt. schs.; b. Howard, S.D., Jan. 14, 1923; s. Leo Thomas and Eunice Anne (Gildea) G.; certificate Dakota State Coll., 1941; B.S., S.D. State U., 1948, M.S. in Edn., 1958 specialist in edn. U.S.D., 1970; m. G. Yvonne Luttrell, Sept. 16, 1946; children—J. Michael, Sandra, Gregory, Mary. Tchr. vocational agr., Rutland, S.D., 1948-49; tchr. Partston (S.D.) Pub. Schs., 1949-56, prin., 1956-59, supt. 1959-73. Bd. dirs. Mitchell Area (S.D.) Vocational Tech. Sch. Served with USNR, 1942-46. Inst. for Devel. Edn. Act Fellow, 1970. Mem. N.E.A., S.D. Edn. Assn., Am. Assn. Sch. Administrs., S.D. Sch. Adminstrs., Am. Legion, Tchr. Edn. and Profl. Standards, K.C., Lion (local pres. 1962, state dep. gov. 1964). Home: Parkston SD Died Jan. 15, 1973.

GARTLEY, HAROLD MCKINLEY, pub. relations exec.; b. Newark, Jan. 19, 1899; s. William Henry and Violet (Sendell) G.; M.B.A., N.Y.U., 1920; m. Jeanette Kaye, Aug. 1, 1952. Propr., H. M. Gartley, Incorporated, 1934-42; with Gartley and Mathieu, Incorporated (formerly Gartley & Assos., Inc., N.Y.C., 1942-72, chmn. bd.; dir. Nat. Securities & Research Corp. Served with U.S. Army, 1917-20. Mem. Pub. Relations Soc. Am. (past nat. treas.). N.Y. Soc. Security Analysts, Lawyers Club. Republican. Mason. Author: Profits In The Stock Market, 1934. Home: Menlo Park NJ Died 1972.

GARVER, CHAUNCEY BREWSTER, lawyer; b. N.Y.C., Apr. 4, 1886; s. John A. and Rebecca (Brewster) G.; grad. Phillips Acad., Andover, Mass., 1904; A.B., Yale, 1908; LL.B., Harvard, 1911; m. Alice Pine, June 27, 1917; children—Edith P. (Mrs. F. Y. Larkin), Allison (Mrs. H. A. Caesar II); m. 2d, Virginia Rook, May 7, 1938; children—Joan B., Maud D. (Mrs. Donald Greer), John A. Admitted to N.Y. bar, 1911, since practiced in N.Y.C.; asso. Sherman & Sterling, 1911-17, partner, 1917-73; dir. Stora Kopparberg Corp., N.Y.C. Mayor of Village of Oyster Bay Cove, 1948-59. Bd. dirs. Legal Aid Society of N.Y.; bd. trustees Miriam Osborn Meml. Home, Harrison, N.Y.; hon. trustee, St. Luke's Hosp., N.Y.C. Served as 2d lt., Signal Corps, U.S. Army, 1917-19. Mem. Am., N.Y. State bar assns., Assn. Bar City N.Y. (treas. 1944-52). Clubs: Century Assn., University, Down Town Assn. (N.Y.C.); Capital Oyster Bay NY Died Feb. 21, 1973.

GARVER, EARL S., coll. dean; b. Youngstown, O., Feb. 5, 1911; s. David N. and Martha (Longanecker) G.; A.B., Manchester Coll., 1933; Ph.D., Yale, 1943; grad. study Harvard, summer 1946, U. Chicago, 1951; m. Winifred S. Greene, Dec. 22, 1941; children—David., Carolyn, Daniel. Tchr. Am. history Boardman Sch., Youngstown, 1933-38; instr. econs. Trinity Coll., Hartford, Conn., 1941-42; asso. prof. econs. Manchester Coll., North Manchester, Ind., 1946-50, dean, 1950-68. Dir. Vienna (Austria) Internat. Seminar, summer 1950. Mem. Am. Econ. Assn., Ind. Acad. Social Scis., The Am. Conference of Academic Deans. Author: Puerto Rico: Unsolved Problem (with E. B. Fincher), 1945; chapters in An Introduction to Modern Economics, 1952. Home: North Manchester IN Died Mar. 13, 1968.

GARVER, FRANCIS MARION, coll. prof.; b. on farm near Cleone, Ill., Sept. 29, 1875; s. Abraham Jerome and Nancy Melinda (Morrell) G.; grad. Ind. State Normal Sch., Terre Haute, 1900; A.B., Ind. Univ., 1906; A.M., Columbia, 1912; Ph.D., U. of Pa., 1920; m. Della Viola Hisey, Aug. 18, 1903; 1 dau., Margaret Elizabeth (Mrs. William Sellers). Principal of schools, Ogden, Illinois, 1900-01; principal of high school, Brazil, Indiana, 1901-05, Gallipolis, Ohio, 1906-07, Ithaca, N.Y., 1907-08, Binghamton, 1908-13; supt. schs., Leonia, N.J., 1913-17; head master Oak Lane Country Day Sch., 1917-21; prof. elementary edn., U. of N.Dak., 1921-23; asst. prof. elementary edn., U. of Pa., 1923-26, prof. edn., 1926-46 (ret.); participated in sch. surveys, E. Mauch Chunk, Harrisburg, Wyomissing, Bethlehem, Phila., etc. Mem. N.E.A., Nat. Soc. Coll. Teachers of Edn., Nat. Soc. for Study of Edn., Supervisors and Directors of Instrn., Am. Ednl. Research Assn., Phi Delta Kappa. Democrat. Presbyterian. Mason. Author and editor of language art books for schools. Home: Ivyland PA‡

GARVEY, HELEN MARIE, bus. exec.; b. St. Joseph, Mo.; d. Richard J. and Mary Theresa (Dienger) Garvey; A.B., U. Ill., 1929; M.A., Columbia, 1947; m. Charles Mills, June 1929 (div. Nov. 1936). Investment analyst Glore, Forgan & Co., Chgo., 1929-47; pub. utility analyst Tri-Continental Corp., N.Y.C., 1947-57; financial cons. Am. & Fgn. Power Co., Inc., N.Y.C., 1957-60; pub. utility analyst Wertheim & Co., N.Y.C., 1960-68. Mem. Women's Bond Club N.Y., Nat. Assn. Bus. Execs., N.Y. Soc. Security Analysts, Chartered Financial Analysts. Home: Forest Hills NY Died 1968.

GARVEY, JAMES ALLEN, ex-govt. ofcl.; b. Alexandria, Va., Aug. 29, 1912; s. James Joseph and Emma Rebecca (Allen) G.; student U. Va., 1930-32. George Washington U., 1932-33; LLB., Am. U., 1937; m. Gloria Newton, Sept. 3, 1938. Admitted to D.C. bar, 1937; exec. asst. Office of Plans and Policies, War Assets Adminstrn., 1947, asst. dep. adminstr. Office of Mgmt., 1948-49; dep. dir. for mgmt. Gen. Services Adminstrn., 1949-53, dep. dir. Office of Mgmt., 1955-56, asst. to commr. Fed. Supply Service, 1956-59, asst. commr. Office Utilization and Sales, Fed. Supply Service, 1959-62; dir. div. mgmt. services Peace Corps, 1962-66. Regional pub. adminstrn. adviser ICA, Montevideo. Uruguay, 1953-55. Served to lt., Supply Corps, USNR., 1943-46. Mem. Sigma Phi Epsilon. Club: University Virginia (Washington). Author articles on public administration. Home: McLean VA Died May 25, 1971; buried Bethel Cemetery, Alexandria VA

GARVIN, GEORGE KINNE, broker; b. Monroe, N.Y., July 28, 1897; s. George Kinne and Ella (Conkling) G.; student N.Y.U.; m. Ruth Miller Mitchell, June 26, 1950; children—Margaret Ella (Mrs. John K. Clarke, Jr.), George Kinne, Muriel Alice (Mrs. Harold G. Williams, Jr.). Partner Farber, Garvin & Co., mems. N.Y. Stock Exchange, 1922-31, Garvin, Bantel & Co., mems. N.Y. and other stock exchanges, 1931-70. Served with Am. Field Service. World War I. Died Mar. 1970.

GARVIN, GEORGE KINNE, broker; b. Monroe, N.Y., July 28, 1897; s. George Kinne and Ella (Conkling) G.; student N.Y.U.; m. Ruth Miller Mitchell, June 26, 1950; children—Margaret Ella (Mrs. John K. Clarke, Jr.), George Kinne, Muriel Alice (Mrs. Harold G. Williams, Jr.). Partner Farber, Garvin & Co., mems. N.Y. Stock Exchange, 1922-31, Garvin, Bantel & Co., mems. N.Y. and other stock exchanges, 1931-71. Served with Am. Field Service, World War I. Office: New York City NY Died Apr. 1971.

GASCOYNE, JOHN J., probation officer; b. in Ireland, Mar. 6, 1872; s. Peter and Frances (Carroll) G.; ed. nat. sch., Ireland; m. Delia Marie Callery, of Navan, County Meath, Ireland, Apr. 27, 1892. Apprenticed to pawnbroker at 11 and served 4 yrs.; came to U.S. at 16; connected with dry goods business at East Orange, N.J., until 1889; carpenter and painter, 1889-93; entered employ Associated Charities, Orange, N.J., 1893, and became asst. sec.; chief probation officer, Essex Co., N.J., since Jan. 22, 1903. Mem. Nat. Probation Assn. (pres., 1914), Safe and Sane Fourth of July Com., Orange, 4 yrs.; mem. Vacant Lot Cultivation Com.; mem. advisory bd. Girls' Club, Orange; mem. Orange Bd. of Edn., Home and Sch. Assn., Com. of 50 for Better Management of Saloons, Catholic Children's Aid Assn.; chmn. Jr. Dept. of Essex Co. Pub. Welfare Com. State treas. A.O.H. of America. Democrat. Roman Catholic. Home: 3 Bradford St., Orange NJ‡

GASTON, EVERETT THAYER, educator; b. Woodward, Okla., July 4, 1901; s. Bentley Larn and Jennie Smith (Clyde) G.; A.B., Sterling Coll., 1923, B.M., 1935; A.M., U. Kan., 1938, Ph.D., 1940; postgrad. Bethany Coll., 1925, Colo. State Coll., 1935; m. Ardis May Waite, Aug. 11, 1924; 1 son, Lamont Waite. Tchr. music pub. schs., 1923-34; asst. prof., music edn. U. Kan., 1940-43, asso. prof., 1943-45, prof., chmn. dept. music edn., 1945-62, prof. music edn., dir. music therapy, 1962-70, Univ. prof., 1968-70, first class music therapy, 1946, 1st grad. deg. course, 1948; lectr. music therapy, influence of music on behavior; cons. music therapy Topeka V.A. Hosp., 1948-70, Topeka State Hosp., 1951, Menninger Clinic, 1953-65, Osawatomie St. Hospital, Parsons St. Hospital and Training School. Recipient 1st grant authorized by Nat. Inst. Mental Health in discipline of music therapy. Fellow A.A.A.S.; member Nat. Assn. Music Therapy (pres. 1952, research and edn. coms., liaison appointee A.M.A., hon. life), Am. Psychol. Assn., Music Tchrs. Nat. Assn. Music Educators Nat. Conf., Nat. Fedn. Music Clubs, Pi Kappa Lambda, Phi Delta Kappa, Phi Mu Alpha. Author: Mjsic in Therapy, 1968; also articles in profl. publs. Editor: Music Therapy, 1954, 55, 56, 57; Music in Therapy, 1968. Home: Lawrence KS Died June 3, 1970; buried Lawrence KS

GASTON, GEORGE ALBERT, b. East Liverpool, O., Aug. 23, 1875; s. George and Rachel (Montgomery) G.; student Washington and Jefferson Coll.; LL.B., Western Reserve U., 1901; m. Ethel Ellis. Pres. Gaston & Co., Inc., New York; dir. Am. Transportation Co., Central Vt. Ry., Grand Trunk Western Ry. Mem. Japan Soc., Council on Foreign Relations, Met. Mus. of Art, English-Speaking Union. Republican. Presbyn. Clubs: Bankers, Cherry Valley, Oakland, Garden City; Huddersfield Fish & Game (Can.); American, Royal Automobile, Mid-Surrey Golf (London). Address: 165 Broadway, New York NY*‡

GASTON, JOHN MONTGOMERY, b. E. Liverpool, O., Sept. 12, 1868; s. George and Rachel G.; student Wooster U., D.D., 1918; B.A., Princeton, 1892, M.A., 1895; S.T.D., Princeton Theol. Sem., 1895; LL.D., Johnson C. Smith U., Charlotte, N.C., 1925; m. Harriet Cramp, Dec. 31, 1895 (died Nov. 5, 1922); children—Mrs. Marion Gaston Ballard, John Montgomery; m. 2d, Eva A. Montgomery, Dec. 5, 1925. Ordained Presbyn. ministry, 1895; pastor chs. at Pittsburgh, Pa., 1895-1911; gen. sec. and treas. Bd. of Missions for Freedmen of Presbyn. Ch. of U.S.A. since 1911; sec. Unit of Work for Colored People; gen. sec. and treas. Johnson C. Smith Univ., Charlotte, N.C. Pres. bd. dirs., Presbyn. Book Store, Pittsburgh. Mem. Phi Delta Theta. Republican. Home: 305 Pasadena Drive, Aspinwall, Pa. Office: 510 Bessemer Bldg., Pittsburgh PA‡

GATCH, LEE, artist; b. Balt., Sept. 10, 1902; s. Harry Lee and Martha (Barry) G.; student Md. Inst. Art, 1922-26, Am. Sch., Fontainebleau (France), Academie Moderne (Paris); studied with Andre L'Hote, Moise Kisling; m. Elsie Driggs, Dec. 14, 1935; 1 dau., Merryman. Exhibited paintings, from 1927; group exhbns. include Whitney Mus., Pa. Acad. Fine Arts, Corcoran Gallery City Art Mus. of St. Louis, Syracuse Mus. Fine Arts; one-man shows at Willard Gallery, N.Y.C., 1943, Staempfli Gallery, New York, 1963, 65, 67; works in pvt. collections, museums U.S.; executed murals in pub. bldgs. Recipient 1st prize and gold medal Corcoran Bienniel Exhbn., 1961; award Am. Acad. Arts and Letters and Nat. Inst. Arts and Letters, 1965. Mem. Nat. Inst. Arts and Letters. Roman Catholic. Home: Lambertville NJ Died Nov. 10, 1968; buried Woodlawn Cemetery.

GATELY, JAMES HAYES, mcht.; b. Chgo., Nov. 12, 1882; s. William and Alice (Hayes) G.; student pub. schs., Orr Bus. Coll.; m. Gertrude A. Crane, June 11, 1912; children—John, Dorothy Squyres, Alice Ryan, Rita Kelly. Pres. Peoples Store, Chgo., 1917-55, chmn., 1955-72, also treas. Chmn. Bd. of Zoning Appeals, Chgo., 1935-45; pres. Chgo. Park Dist., 1945-72. Clubs: South Shore Country, Chicago Athletic (Chgo.). Home: Chicago IL Died Feb. 19, 1972.

GATES, ALBERT R., lawyer; b. Wyanet, Bureau County, Ill., Nov. 29, 1869; s. Frances E. and Polly M. Gates; ed. pub. schs. and Lake Forest U. Law Sch.; m. Elizabeth H. Young, June 10, 1911 (died Nov. 12, 1930); 1 son, William A. Admitted to Ill. bar, 1895; to Supreme Court of U.S., 1898; head law firm Gates & Farwell, Chicago, 1897-1903; then in practice alone in Chicago to 1936, largely corp. and banking law. Mem. Ill. State and Chicago bar assns. Pres. Western Golf Assn., 1907-08 and 1921-22; adminstr. Professional Golfers Assn. of America, 1930-35. Removed to Plymouth, Ind., 1936. Retired. Republican. Home: 217 N. Plum St., Plymouth IN*‡

GATES, ARTHUR IRVING, educator; b. Red Wing, Minn., Sept. 22, 1890; s. William P. and Lenore (Gaylord) G.; B.L., University of Calif., 1914, M.A., 1915; Ph.D., Columbia, 1917; m. Georgina Stickland, Aug. 14, 1920; children—Robert Gaylord, Katharine Blair. With Tchrs. Coll. Columbia, 1917-72, successively instr., asst. prof., asso. prof., 1917-24, prof. ednl. psychology, 1924-56, professor emeritus, 1956-72; dir. Inst. Ednl. Research, Sect. D, 1921-30, head dept. ednl. research in Advanced Sch. Edn., 1933-37, asso. dir., 1937-42; exec. office Dept. Psychology and Research Methods, 1933-56, dir. Div. Foundations Edn., 1948-56; supr. of research, Inst. of the Language Arts, from 1956. Mem. com. on research Am. Council Edn., 1942-45. Fellow A.A.S. (vice pres. and chairman sect. Q); mem. Am. Assn. Ednl. Research (v.p. 1941, pres. 1942), Am. Assn. Applied Psychology (chmn. edn. sect. 1940-42), American Assn. School of Adminstrs., Am. Assn. Univ. Profs., N.E.A., etc. American Psychology Association (council, pres., educational section 1948-49), Sigma Xi, Alpha Sigma Phi, Phi Delta Kappa. Club: Century. Author: Psychology of Disability in Reading and Spelling, 1922; Psychology for Students of Education, 1923; Elementary Psychology, 1925; Improvement of Reading, 1927; New Methods in Primary Reading, 1928; Principles of Education (with E. L. Thorndike), 1929; Interest and Ability in Reading, 1930; Reading for School Administrators, 1931; Generalization in Spelling, 1935; Improvement of Reading, 1936; Diagnosis of Disabilities in Spelling (with D. E. Russell), 1937; Spelling Difficulties, 1937; Educational Psychology (with A.T. Jersild, T.R. McConnell and R.C. Challman), 1942; Teaching Reading to Slow Learning Pupils, 1943; also, various ednl. tests, tech. materials, sch. books and articles giving results of research in education and ednl. psychology. Home: Montrose NY Died Aug. 24, 1972.

GATES, CASSIUS EMERSON, lawyer; b. Alma City, Minn., Apr. 26, 1886; s. Emerson and Emma Jane (Grey) G.; LL.B., U. Minn., 1908; m. Clara M. Shaughnessy, Feb. 25, 1911 (dec.); m. 2nd, Mabel Rankin June 29, 1918 (dec.); m. 3d, Rosella M. Paulson, Jan. 14, 1939; 1 adopted son, Robert Emerson; stepchildren children—Chester R. Paulson, Kathryn Paulson (Mrs. Floyd K. McCroskey). Admitted to Minn. bar, 1908; practiced in Mankato, 1909, in Seattle, 1909-72; mem. Bogle, Bogle & Gates (firm now Bogle, Gates, Dobrin, Wakefield and Long), 1926-72; chmn. bd., dir. Citizens Fed. Savs. & Loan Assn., KXA, Inc. Trustee, v.p. Pacific N.W. Research Found.; past trustee Seattle Symphony Orch., former trustee Automobile Club of Wash. Asso. mem. Assn. Bar City of New York; mem. Seattle C. of C. (chmn. mem. council 1923-24, pres. 1933-34), Am. (v.p. 9th circuit, 1935-36; mem. gen. council 1932-35), Internat., Wash. Seattle bar assns., Internat. Assn. Ins. Council (v.p. 1936), Am. Soc. Internat. Law, Am. Judicature Soc., Am. Bar Found., Seattle Hist. Soc. (trustee), World Affairs Council (trustee), English-Speaking Union (past trustee), Am. Coll. Probate Counsel, Nat. Fraternal Congress Am., Delta Theta Phi. Clubs: Seattle Press, Ranier (past pres.), Seattle Golf and Country, Broadmoor Golf and Country, Rotary (pres. 1953-54) (Seattle); Bohemian (San Francisco); Lawyers (N.Y.C.). Home: Seattle WA Died Jan. 14, 1972.

GATES, CLIFFORD ELWOOD, educator; b. Canastota, N.Y., Dec. 31, 1893; s. Roscoe Conklin and Minnie (Clifford) G.; A.B., Colgate U., 1915, A.M., 1917; Ph.D., Cornell U., 1925; student U. Berlin (Germany), 1925, 32, U. Innsbruck (Austria), summers 1958-59, 61; m. Florence Mae Wentzel, Aug. 14, 1918; children—Florence Mae (Mrs. Charles G. Rickard) Elizabeth Anita, Kathryn Patricia; m. 2d, Dorothy Bernice Parcels, June 22, 1962. Mem. faculty Colgate U., 1915-18, 20-64, prof. German lang. and lit., 1919-34, chmn. dept., 1934-42, head dept., 1942-64, nat. dir. univ. alumni service for vets., 1946-62; master German and Spanish, Blair Acad., 1918-20; lectr. on modern Germany; lectr. Kan. State Tchrs. Coll., Emporia, 1964-68. Served to lt. col. USAAF, World War II. Recipient Colgate U. Alumni Corp. award, 1948. Mem. Phi Beta Kappa, Theta Chi (pres. Iota chpt. 1925-57), Delta Sigma Rho. Clubs: Torch; Colgate U. Alumni (N.Y.C.). Republican. Baptist. Author: Im Herzen Europas, 1935. Editor: Tantchen Mohnhaupt, 1927; die Kapitalistinnen, 1928; Herrn Schmidt sein Dackel Haidjer, 1935. Home: Emporia KS Died July 1968.

GATES, EDMUND O., physician; b. Howard City, Mich., 1905; M.D., Northwestern U., 1933. Intern U. Chgo. Hosp., 1932; intern Cook County Hosp., Chgo., 1933-34, resident in ears, nose and throat, 1937-38; resident in eye Presbyn Hosp., Chgo., 1938; mem. staff Grace Hosp., Welch, W.Va., until 1966. Served to col., M.C., AUS 1941-45. Diplomate Am. Bd. Ophthalmology. Mem. A.M.A. Home: Welch WV Died Mar. 17, 1966; buried Woodlawn Cemetery Mausoleum, Bluefield WV

GATES, ERRETT, clergyman, educator; b. Cortland, O., Mar. 2, 1870; s. Orrin and Rachel Louisa (King) G.; A.B., Ohio Normal U., 1887; Union Theol. Sem., 1891-4; A.B., U. of Chicago, 1899, D.B., 1900, Ph.D., 1902; m. Nell Seass, of Arthur, Ill., Mar. 5, 1905. Minister, Disciples of Christ; pastor, Grand Rapids, Mich., 1894-7, Hyde Park Ch., Chicago, 1897-1900; sec. Disciples Div. House, 1900-10; student, U. of

Berlin, 1910-11; asst. prof. ch. history, Disciples Div. House, 1910-—; instr. history, U. of Chicago, 1911-—. Mem. Phi Beta Kappa. Author: Early Relation and Separation of Baptists and Disciples, 1904; History of the Disciples of Christ, 1905. Address: 5616 Kenwood Av., Chicago‡

GATES, ROBERT MOORES, newspaper man; b. Jackson, Tenn., Jan. 5, 1871; s. Robert and Cll (Jester) G.; ed. Jackson public school and (old Southwestern Bapt. University, Jackson; m. Sallie Belle Harrison, of Medon, Tenn., Oct. 27, 1897; one dau.; m. 2d, Mrs. Roberta Chase Harding, of Nashville, Tenn., Aug. 18, 1926. Began newspaper work on Jackson Blade, 1894; later on Jackson Daily Whig; editorial writer, Nashville American, 1898-99; editor, Paducah (Ky.) Daily News, 1899-1901; reporter, Memphis Scimitar, 1901-03, later Washington corr. Memphis Commercial Appeal, 25 years; later Washington corr. Florida Times Union, Jacksonville, and other Southern papers; mem. publicity staff Dem. Exec. Com.; now dir. of pub. relations Dept. of Justice. Democrat. Episcopalian. Club: Nat. Press. Home: Woodley Park Towers. Office: Dept. of Justice, Washington DC‡

GATES, ROBERT S., coll. adminstr.; b. Toledo, Ia., 1909; grad. Coe Coll., 1931; m. Mildred P. Gates; children—Robert P., Mary Anne. Vice pres. for devel. Coe Coll., Cedar Rapids, Ia.; dir. 1st Fed. Savs. & Loan Association, United Fire and Casualty Company, Peoples Bank & Trust Company. Member of Nat. Assn. Accountants C. of C. Club: Union League (Chgo.). Home: Cedar Rapids IA Died Oct. 14, 1968.

GATEWOOD, ARTHUR RANDOLPH, marine engr.; b. Phila., Nov. 6, 1899; s. William and Mary Edwin (Hartzell) G.; B.S. in Civil Engring., Va. Mil. Inst., 1918; S.B. in Naval Architecture and Marine Engring., Mass. Inst. Tech., 1921. Apprentice to chief engr. Merchant Marine, 1921-29; surveyor Am. Bur. Shipping, N.Y.C., 1929-47, chief engr. surveyor, 1947-57, vice president, 1957-62, president, 1963, chairman of the board 1964-66. Engring. spokesman U.S. delegation Safety of Life at Sea Conf., London, 1948, U.S. del., chmn. conf. com. on safety of nuclear ships, 1960, mem. U.S. adv. com. Safety of Life at Sea, 1960-64; U.S. del. Internat. Electrotechnical Commn., 1948-60, Internat. Inst. Welding, 1956-62, Internat. Standards Orgn., 1959-64; mem. U.S. sec. of treas. Com. on Tanker Hazards, 1962-63. Served as 2d lt., inf., U.S. Army, 1918. Recipient David W. Taylor gold medal Society of Naval Architects and Marine Engineers, 1963. Fellow Am. Inst. Elec. Engrs.; mem. Am. Soc. M.E., Am. Soc. Refrigerating Engrs., Soc. Naval Architects and Marine Engrs., Am. Standards Assn., Am. Nuclear Soc., Am. Welding Soc., Inst. Mech. Engrs. (London), Inst. Elec. Engrs. (London), Inst. Marine Engrs. (v.p.; London), Soc. Naval Architects and Marine Engrs. N.Y. (v.p.), Soc. Marine Port Engrs. N.Y., Kappa Sigma, Theta Tau. Episcopalian. Clubs: Whitehall, Engineers, India House (N.Y.C.). Author and composer: Noel, Noel, Our Saviour is Born. Home: New York City NY Died Jan. 15, 1970.

GAULIN, ALPHONSE, JR., consul-general; b. Woonsocket, R.I., May 24, 1874; s. Alphonse and Marcoux (Elmire) G.; B.A., St. Mary's Coll., Laval U., Montreal, 1893; LL.B., Harvard, 1896; admitted to R.I. bar, 1896; post-grad. studies the Sorbonne, Paris, 1898; m. Marguerite H. Steele, of Montreal, Sept. 12, 1905. Mayor Woonsocket, R.I., 1902-05; consul at Havre, France, 1905-09; consul gen. at Marseilles, France, Aug. 1, 1909; now consul gen. at Paris, France. Del. at large Rep. Nat. Conv., 1904. Home: Woonsocket, R.I. Address: American Consulate General, Paris France‡

GAULT, MARK R., treas. Parker-Hannifin Corp. Address: Cleveland OH Died June 9, 1969; cremated.

GAULT, NORMAN COX, lawyer; b. St. Peter, Minn., Aug. 13, 1892; s. Andrew Kelsey and Lillien Mayhew (Cox) G.; LL.B., U. of Neb., 1916. Admitted to Minn. bar, 1930, practiced Omaha, Neb., 1916-30, St. Peter, Minn. since 1930; city atty. St. Peter, 1930-36; legal adviser, appeal agt. Nicollet Co. Draft Bd. since 1950. Alderman of the City of St. Peter, 1959-62. Served on draft bd. Omaha World War I. Nicollet Co. chmn. W.P.B., Salvage Div., World War II. Mem. Minn. State, Dist. and Am. bar assns., S.A.R., St. Peter Civic & Commerce Assn., Minn. State Hist. Soc. (life), Neb. Alumni Assn. (life). Episcopalian (warden, vestryman past 20 yrs.). Elk, Odd Fellow. Club: Lions. Home: St Peter MN Died Oct. 27, 1968.

GAUSE, FRANK ALES, educator; b. Westfield, Ind., Mar. 1, 1874; s. Amos W. and Margaret (Morrow) G.; grad. Friends' Acad., Westfield, Ind., 1891; A.B., Ind. U., 1904, M.A., 1905; post-grad. work, U. of Chicago, 2 yrs. Dist. sch. teacher, 1892-4; asst. prin. Friends' Acad., 1894-05; supt. schs., Cicero, Ind., 1897-03, Salem, 1905-9; supt. U.S. Govt. Schs., Panama, 1909-13; supt. Bay City (Mich.) Schs., since 1914. Mason. Author: Story of Panama, 1912; An Isthmian Idyl, 1913; Business Methods Applied in School Administration, 1918. Address: Bay City MI‡

GAVAGAN, JOSEPH ANDREW, judge; b. New York City, Aug. 20, 1892; s. John and Mary A. (Lyons) G.; LL.B., cum laude, Fordham U., 1920; m. Dorothy Whitehead, Nov. 1933; children—Joseph Andrew, Mrs. Thomas Gorman. Admitted to N.Y. bar, 1920; practiced in N.Y. City. Served as 1st lt., U.S. Army, World War. Mem. N.Y. Assembly, 1923-29; mem. 71st to 78th Congresses (1929-43), 21st N.Y. Dist.; Supreme Court Justice, State of N.Y. Mem. N.Y. State Bar Assn., Bar Assn. of the City of N.Y. Democrat. Clubs: Fordham University, Manhattan, Lawyers. Catholic. Home: New York City NY Died Oct. 18, 1968; buried Gate of Heaven, Pleasantsville NY

GAVIT, JOSEPH, librarian; b. Albany, N.Y., Oct. 10, 1876; s. Joseph and Fanny Breese (Palmer) G.; ed. Albany H.S. and N.Y. State Library Sch.; m. Katherine Hulst, Sept. 17, 1903; children—Frances Cornell (Mrs. John F. Cornell), Henry Hulst. With N.Y. State Library since Feb. 24, 1896, beginning as jr. clerk and advancing through grades to asso. librarian, Jan. 16, 1930, acting dir., 1938-39, 1944-45. Served in N.Y. Nat. Guard, 1897-1911. Mem. A.L.A., N.Y. Library Assn., Am. Antiquarian Soc., New England Hist. Geneal. Soc., N.Y. Geneal. and Biog. Soc., Biblog. Soc. of America, Albany Inst., N.Y. State Hist. Assn. Presbyterian. Author of geneal. booklets. Home: 7 Darroch Rd., Delmar, N.Y. Office: New York State Library, Albany NY‡

GAY, CARL WARREN, univ. prof.; b. Waverly, N.Y., Mar. 14, 1877; s. Charles Warren and Lucy (Lemon) G.; D.V.M., Cornell U., 1899, and post-grad. (fellowship), 1899-1900; B.S.A., Ia. State Coll., 1905; m. Catherine Andrews Gay, Dec. 17, 1906; children—Hayward Andrews, Lucy Satterlee; m. 2d, Flora Dean Latham, June 6, 1932. Veterinarian N.Y. State Bd. of Health, 1900; asst. prof. in Vet. Dept., Iowa State Coll., 1901, 1902; asst. prof. animal husbandry, Agrl. Div., Ia. State Coll., 1904-05; asst. and asso. prof. animal husbandry, Agrl. Coll. of Ohio State U., 1905, 1906; prof. animal industry, U. of Pa., 1907-16; prof. animal husbandry and chmn. animal industry group, U. of Minn., 1916-20; prof. and chmn. animal husbandry, Ohio State U., 1920-40,prof., 1940-47, prof. emeritus since 1947. Presbyterian. Author: Productive Horse Husbandry, 1914; Principles and Practice of Judging Live-Stock, 1915. Editor of The Breeds of Live-Stock, 1915. Home: Worthington OH‡

GEARY, GEORGE REGINALD, retired; b. Strathroy, Ont., Aug. 12, 1874; s. Theophilus Jones and Mary (Goodson) G.; student, Upper-Can. Coll., 1889; Osgoode Hall, 1894, Barrister-at-law U. Toronto, 1896; m. Jessy Beatrice Caverhill, Mar. 23, 1927; children—Mary Rosalind, Richard Reginald Caverhill. Mayor, Toronto, 1910-12; mem. Can. Parliament, 1925-35, privy council, 1935; Minister of Justice, Atty. Gen. of Can., 1935; King's counsel; counsel Corp. Toronto, 1912-27. Served as lt. to maj., C.E.F., 1915-19. Awarded Order of British Empire, Mil. Cross, Legion of Honor, Mentioned in dispatches. Mem. Alpha Delta Phi, Phi Delta Phi. Clubs: York, University, Golf, Cricket (Toronto). Home: 124 Park Rd., Toronto 5 ON Canada‡

GEBHARDT, GEORGE FREDERIC, cons. mech. engr.; b. Salt Lake City, Utah, Mar. 1, 1874; s. Henry Andrew and Wilhelmina (Schuster) G.; A.B., Knox Coll., 1895, M.S., 1897; M.E., Cornell, 1897; m. Edith M. Jensen, Sept. 1, 1914. Professor mech. engring. Armour Inst. Technology, 1902-34, prof. emeritus since 1934; consulting practice. Mem. Am. Society M.E., Western Soc. Engrs., Nat. Assn. Power Engrs., Phi Delta Theta, Tau Beta Pi, Pi Tau Sigma. Republican. Presbyterian. Club: University (Chicago). Author: Combustion, 1925; Steam Power Plant Engineering, 1927. Home: 469 N.E. 69th St., Miami FL‡

GEDDES, ALICE SPENCER, writer; b. Athol, Mass., Nov. 13, 1876; d. William Edwin and Ella Mary (Bowker) G.; grad. Chauncy Hall Sch., Boston, 1894; spl. student Radcliffe Coll. until 1898; unmarried. Lectured on lit. throughout U.S., 1901-4; owner, editor and pub. Cambridge Press, 1902-5, the only newspaper in N.E. edited and printed solely by women; editor Wakefield Citizen and Banner, 1905-6; now spl. writer for Boston Sunday Globe, etc. Club: N.E. Woman's Press. Address: Park Av., Wakefield MA‡

GEDYE, GEORGE ERIC ROWE, author, journalist; b. Clevedon (Somerset), Eng., May 27, 1890; s. George Edward and Lillie (Rowe) G.; ed. Clarence Sch., Weston super Mare, 1899-1901, Queens Coll., Taunton, 1902-07, London Univ., 1907; married Liesel Bremer, 1922 (dec.); m. 2d, Alice Lepper (nee Mehler), 1948; one son, Robin. Began as insurance clerk, England, 1908; ins. and banking, training for management with Brit. Am. Tobacco Co., also fiction writing and free lance journalism to 1914; special corr. for London Times, Rhineland and Ruhr areas, 1922-25, Central Europe, stationed in Vienna, 1926; Central Europe corr. for Daily Express, 1927-29; Daily Telegraph, 1929-38; corr. for New York Times, 1929-43, Central and Southeastern Europe, 1929-39, Moscow, 1939-40, Turkey, 1940-41; apptd. corr. for Central and Southeastern Europe, of London Daily Herald to 1950, for The Observer, London, 1950-52; Central European corr. Overseas News Agency 1951, Manchester Guardian, 1953-54; head evaluation sect., Radio Free Europe, Munich, from 1954; Vienna correspondent Radio Free Europe, 1956-60; special correspondent Manchester Guardian, from 1956. Served British Army, 1914-18; spl. duties Middle East, 1941-45. Decorated British war medals, Allied medal, Victory medal, 1915 Star; decorated M.B.E., 1946. Fellow Inst. Journalists (London); mem. Nat. Union Journalists, Newspaper Guild. Club: Special Forces (London). Author: A Wayfarer in Austria, 1928, rev., 1938; The Revolver Republic, 1930; Heirs to the Hapsburgs, 1932; Betrayal in Central Europe, 1939; Introducing Austria, 1955; Translator: Red Russia After Ten Years (by George London), 1928; The Book of Austria (English text), 1950; Austria in 1953 (Fodor's Modern Guides), 1953. Contbr. to N.Y. Times Sunday Magazine, New Statesman and Contemporary Review, London, Expelled from Austria, 1938, and Czechoslovakia, 1939, on invasion by Nazi Germany. Address: Bath (Som.) England Died Mar. 21, 1970.

GEHLKE, CHARLES ELMER, prof. sociology; b. Cleveland, O., Dec. 11, 1884; s. Charles Henry and Mary Barbara (Herr) G.; A.B., Western Reserve U., 1906; Ph.D., Columbia, 1914; m. Helen J. Hopkins, Aug. 5, 1933. Instructor Rayen Sch., Youngstown, O., 1906-08; successively instr., asst. prof. and asso. prof. sociology, Western Reserve U., Cleveland, 1911-24, prof., 1924-55, emeritus, 1955-68; Whitney prof. Sociology, Fisk Univ., 1956-57; ednl. dir. A.R.C., southwestern div., 1919-20; statistician Cleveland Foundation, 1920-21, also of Criminal Justice in Cleveland, 1922, Mo. Crime Survey, 1926, Crime Commn. State of N.Y., 1927, Ill. Crime Survey, 1929, Judicial System of Ohio, 1936; mem. staff Columbia Law Sch. Survey for an Inst. of Criminology, 1929-30, studying crime conditions in Europe, asst. and asso. director of Wage Stabilization, Regional War Labor Board, Cleveland, 1943-45. Member bd. Brush Foundation, Cleveland. Mem. Am. Sociol. Society, American Statistical Association, American Prison Association, American Assn. University Profs., Acacia, Phi Beta Kappa. Protestant. Author: Emile Durkheim's Contributions to Sociological Theory, 1915, reprinted 1968; Criminal Actions in Ohio, 1936. Collaborator (with W.L. Hotchkiss) Uniform Classification for Judicial Criminal Statistics, 1931. Co-author chapter on Crime and Punishment in Recent Social Trends, 1933. Contbr. to professional jours. Home: Cleveland OH Died Nov. 3, 1968.

GEIGER, WILLIAM FREDERICK, supt. schs.; b. Peoria, Ill., Jan. 23, 1870; s. Frederick and Lena (Hofer) G.; A.B., Dartmouth College, 1892; hon. A.M., 1922; m. Laura Margaret Meyer, of Quincy, Ill., July 1, 1897; children—Frederick Meyer, Jeanne (Mrs. C. H. Shons), Helen Margaret, William Alfred. Teacher high sch., Peoria, Ill., 1892-95; prin. high sch., Quincy, Ill., 1895-1901, East Aurora, Ill., 1901-04, Broadway High Sch., Seattle, Wash., 1904-11, Stadium High Sch., Tacoma, 1911-12; supt. pub. schs., Tacoma, 1912-31; prof. dept. of edn., Dartmouth Coll., since 1931. Dir. Tacoma Pub. Library. Mem. N.E.A., Washington Ednl. Assn., Phi Beta Kappa, Tri Kappa, Kappa Phi Kappa, Casque and Gauntlet (Dartmouth). Democrat. Conglist. Mason, Elk. Clubs: Commercial, Rotary. Home: Hanover NH‡

GEIJSBEEK, JOHN BART, accountant; b. Lemele, Holland, Apr. 24, 1872; s. Dirk and Johanna Wilhelmina Diderika G.; Univ. of Leyden; came to America, 1893; LL.B., U. of Denver, 1907 (M.C.S., 1910); Colo. State degree C.P.A., 1907, Ohio C.P.A., 1908, Cal. C.P.A., 1917; m. M. Lillie Schmidt, of Cincinnati, Oct. 15, 1901. Ex-dean Sch. Commerce, Accounts and Finance, U. of Denver. Consul of The Netherlands for Colo., N.M. and Utah, 1916-—. Christian Scientist. Mem. Colo. Soc. Certified Pub. Accountants (dir.), Denver Civic and Commercial Assn., Phi Delta Phi, etc. Clubs: Denver Country, Rotary, Author: Ancient Double Entry Bookkeeping, 1914. Also many leaflets on commercial edn. Home: 1116 E. 13th Av. Office: Foster Bldg., Denver CO‡

GEIS, GEORGE (SHERMAN), soldier, printer by trade; b. Grand Island, Neb., 1875; s. Col. J. and Eleanor F. G.; early life on plains and Western frontier; worked in hotels of Denver, Chicago and New York while completing ed'n. Served in Astor Battery during Spanish War, and with Gen. Merritt, 1st mil. gov. to Philippines; took part in capture of Manila, Aug. 13, 1898, and Philippine campaign; tour around world, 1902-3; war corr., 1st expd'n into Mindanao. In newspaper work since 1901; contb'r to Success and other mags. on Orient and Far East. Past comdr. Lincoln Camp, No. 7, Sons of Veterans, New York, 1901; maj. and a.-d.-c., gen. staff Sons of Veterans Reserve, 1904-7; del. at large, Calif. Div., Nat. Encampments, Sons of Veterans, 1903-4, senior vice-comdr., 1904-5. Mem. U.S. Revolver Assn., Nat. Soc. Army of Philippines, Am. Geog. Soc., New Thought Federation, United Spanish War Veterans, etc.; sec. Astor Battery Vet. Assn., New York, 1905; Nat. del. from Calif. to United Spanish War Veterans and Army of the Philippine encampments, 1905. Author: History of the Famous Astor Battery, 1905. Address: 345 Golden San Francisco‡

GELEERD, ELISABETH ROZETTA (MRS. RUDOLPH M. LOEWENSTEIN), psychoanalyst; b. Rotterdam, Netherlands, Mar. 20, 1909; d. Moses and Bertha (Haas) Geleerd; M.D., U. Leyden, 1936; grad. study U. Vienna, 1936-38, Psychoanalytic Inst., Vienna, 1936-38, Maudsley Hosp., London, 1938-40; grad. Inst. Psychoanalysis, London, 1940; m. Rudolph M. Loewenstein, July 13, 1946; 1 son, Richard. Came to U.S., 1940, naturalized, 1946. Staff mem. Menninger Clinic, 1940-45; pvt. practice, 1946-69; member faculty of the New York Psychoanalytic Inst., since 1947. Fellow Am. Orthopsychiat. Association, American Psychiat. Assn.; mem. A.A.A.S., A.M.A., Am. Acad. Child Psychiatry, Am. Psychoanalytic Assn., N.Y. Psychoanalytic Soc., N.Y. County Med. Soc., N.Y. Acad. Sci., Am. Assn. for Child Psychoanalysis. Author articles in field. Editor: The Child Analyst at Work, 1967. Address: New York City NY Died May 25, 1969.

GELLATLY, JOHN ARTHUR, investments; b. Grass Valley, Calif., July 6, 1869; s. Andrew and Isabella (Lyle) G.; student Philomath (Ore.) Coll., 1881-85, Ore. Agrl. Coll., 1886-87; m. Laura J. McDonald, of Philomath, Ore., July 10, 1892 (died Dec. 1913); children—Florence Evelyne (Mrs. Frank H. Means), Lester Lyle, Bernice Isabella (Mrs. James M. Greene), Marjorie Gail; m. 2d, Bertha S. Skinner, of Spokane, Wash., May 31, 1916; children—John Arthur, Robert Neil. Engaged in farming in Ore., 1889-1900; pres. and mgr. Gellatly Loan & Investment Co. since 1920. Recorder, Benton Co., Ore., 1895-99; mem. city council, Wenatchee, Wash., 1901, 1906-12; mayor of Wenatchee, 1902-03; auditor, Chelan Co., Wash., 1904-05; mem. Wash. Ho. of Rep., 1919-20; lt. gov. of Wash., 1928-32; Rep. candidate for gov. of Wash., 1932. Chmn. Chelan Co. Council of Defense, World War. Presbyn. Mason, Elk. Club: Wenatchee Golf and Country. Address: Wenatchee WA‡

GELLHORN, ERNST, prof. physiology; b. Breslau, Germany, Jan. 7, 1893; s. Moritz and Hulda (Stein) G.; student Univ. of Berlin, 1910-14; Ph.D., Univ. of Muenster, 1919; M.D., Univ. of Heidelberg, 1919; m. Hilde Obermeier, Aug. 1, 1925; children—Irene Florence (deceased), Helen, Ernest Albert Eugene, Joyce Geraldine. Came to U.S., 1929, naturalized, 1935. Began as instr. physiology, Halle Univ., 1919; asso. prof. physiology, Univ. of Halle, 1925-29; asso. prof. physiology, Univ. of Oregon, 1929-31, prof., 1931-32; prof. physiology, Univ. of Ill. Coll. of Medicine, 1932-43; prof. neurophysiology, U. of Minn. from Sept. 1943. Mem. Am. Physiol. Soc., Soc. Exptl. Biology and Medicine, Central Soc. Electroencephalographers, A.A.A.S., N.Y. Acad. Scis., Sigma Xi. Awarded A Cressy Morrison prize by New York Acad. Sciences, 1930, Alvarenga prize, Coll. of Physicians, Phila., 1934. Author several books and papers, including: Physiological Foundations of Neurology and Psychiatry, 1953; Autonomic Imbalance and the Hypothalmus, 1957. Co-editor Acta Neurovegetativa. Address: VA Died Apr. 13, 1973.

GELMAN, SAMUEL JOSEPH, physician, hosp. adminstr.; b. Phila., Mar. 28, 1914; s. Jacob and Nellie (Manishal) G.; B.A., N.Y.U., 1936; M.D., Anderson Coll. Medicine, Glasgow, Scotland, 1945; m. Judith Fabian, June 17, 1950; children—Sheila, Leonard, Joyce. Admitting physician Harlem Hosp., N.Y.C., 1945; intern Morrisania City Hosp., N.Y.C., 1946-47, admitting physician, 1947, dir. out-patient dept., 1947-52, dep. med. supt., 1949-52; asst. dir. Hosp. Joint Diseases, N.Y.C., 1952-58, asso. dir., 1958-61; exec. dir. Jewish Hosp. and Med. Center, Bklyn., 1961-71. Mem. Workmen's Compensation Bd. for Hosps. Heart, Stroke and Cancer Com. Greater N.Y.; mem. hosp. rev. planning council So. Dist. N.Y., perinatal com. Greater N.Y. Fund, Bklyn. div.; mem. Health Adv. Com. N.Y.C. and Bklyn., Mayor N.Y.C. Com. Mental Retardation. Mem. adv. com. Pride Judea; chmn. homes and hosps. div. United Jewish Appeal, 1958-67; chmn. Greater N.Y. hosp. div. United Fund, 1969. Recipient pub. service civilian def. N.Y. State, citation Fedn. Jewish Philanthropies, N.Y.C., 1963. Licentiate Royal Coll. Phys. and Surg., Edinburgh, Scotland. Fellow Am. Coll. Hosp. Adminstrs., Am. Coll. Geriatrics; member New York State (member board trustees 1968-71), Greater N.Y. (chmn. profl. affairs com. 1964-71, bd. govs. 1964-71, pres. 1968), Am. hosp. assns., British Med. Assn., N.Y.C. Pub. Health Assn., Royal Soc. Health (London), Am. Pub. Health Assn. Jewish religion. Mason. Author articles. Home: Scarsdale NY Died Aug. 1, 1971.

GENET, ARTHUR SAMUEL, corp. exec.; b. N.Y.C. Oct. 7, 1909; s. Samuel J. T. and Jennie Maude (Welde) G.; student U.S. Naval Acad., 1927-29; m. Louise Margaret Scheider, June 3, 1933; children—Barbara Ann, Richard Paul. Asso. Bank of Manhattan, N.Y.C., 1928-39; comptroller Central Coal Co. and affiliated divs., N.Y.C., 1939-41; treas. Met. Coal Co., Boston, 1941-42, v.p., 1942-43; v.p., controller Nat. Carloading Co., N.Y.C., 1943-44, pres. 1944-46; asst. v.p. freight traffic, C. & O. and Pere Marquette Rys., 1946-47, v.p. traffic, 1947; v.p. Covington & Cin. Elevated R.R., Transfer and Bridge Co., 1947-56, Cin. Inter-Terminal R.R. Co. 1947-56; pres. Grayhound Corp., 1956; pres. Brink's, Inc., Chgo., 1959-68; executive v.p., director Pittston Company. Member of various leading freight traffic clubs and orgns. throughout U.S. Presbyn. Clubs: Chicago, Union League (Chgo.); Country, Inc., Pepper Pike Country, Union (Cleve.); Barrington Hills Country (Barrington, Ill.); Pinnacle (N.Y.). Home: Barrington IL Died Sept. 19, 1968.

GENTELE, C. GORAN H.A., opera dir.; b. Stockholm, Sweden, Sept. 20, 1917; s. Marit Bergson. With Dramatic Theatre Tng. Sch., Stockholm, 1941-44; actor Dramatic Theatre, 1944-46, stage mgr., 1946-52; staff Royal Theater, 1952-72, dir., 1963-72; apptd. gen. mgr. Met. Opera Co., N.Y., 1972; vis. stage mgr., Brussels, Belgium, London, Eng.; film writer and producer. Address: Stockholm Sweden Died July 18, 1972; buried Ingaro, Stockholm Sweden

GENTHE, KARL WILHELM, college prof.; b. Leipzig, Germany, June 5, 1871; s. Karl Louis and Anna Emilie (Sohnel) G.; ed. pub. schs., Leipzig, and Realschule, to 1882; grad. Thomasschule, Leipzig, 1891; U. of Leipzig, 1891-8, Ph.D. (summa cum laude), 1897, major, zoology; arrived in America, 1898; m. at New York, Martha Krug (Ph.D., Heidelberg), of Chemnitz, Germany, Jan. 6, 1901. Pvt. tutor, Boston, 1898-9; instr. zoology, U. of Mich., 1899-1901; instr. natural history, 1901-3, asst. prof., 1903-7, prof. since 1907, Trinity Coll., Conn. Fellow A.A.A.S.; mem. Am. Soc. Zoologists, Am. Nature Study Soc. Lutheran. Contbr. to scientific periodicals. Address: Trinity College, Hartford CT‡

GENTILE, EDWARD, designer, illuminator; b. Chicago, Ill., July 20, 1890; s. Joseph and Mary (Tise) G.; student Art Inst., Chicago, 1911-12; m. Ruth R. Running, Dec. 16, 1919; children—Amadeus Edward, Urania Ruth. Commercial artist North American Newspaper, Phila., Pa., 1914; with Studio of Design and Lettering, N.Y. City, 1914-17; free lance artist, 1919-30; manuscript illuminator from 1930. Served as panoramic draftsman Balloon Corps, A.E.F., 1918-19. Paintings extensively displayed in Chicago by U.S. Treasury Dept. in war bond sales. Designs reproduced by The Inland Printer, 1925. Exhibitor at Art Inst. Chicago, Marshall Field Galleries, All-Ill. Soc., one-man show Chicago Galleries, one man exhibit, Town Club. Address: Oak Park IL Died Aug. 4, 1968.

GEORG, WALTER FERDINAND, college pres.; b. Accident, Md., Feb. 11, 1874; s. Henry and Christina (Sperline) G.; student Concordia College. Springfield, Ill., 1892-9; grad. Concordia Theol. Sem., 1899; m. Bertha Fleckenstein, of Saratoga Springs, N.Y., Sept. 7, 1900. Ordained Luth. ministry, 1899; pastor Rockwell City, Ia., 1899-04, Webster City, 1904-12; pres. Bethany Ladies' Coll., Mankato, Minn., since Oct., 1912. Home: Mankato MN‡

GEORGE, JENNINGS BURTON, ednl. exec.; b. Red Bay, Ala., Aug. 20, 1893; s. Abe and Cammiel (Crowell) G.; B.S., Miss. Southern Coll., Hattiesburg, Miss., 1923; M.A., George Peabody Coll. 1925. Ph.D., 1932; student U. of Chicago, 1929-30; m. Wilma Boswell, June 1925; children—Cammiel, Billie. Teacher in rural sch., 1915-21; with Mississippi Southern College, Hattisburg, 1925-29, 32-45, successively instr., asso. prof., prof., v.p., 1932-33, pres., 1933-45; mem. faculty Blue Mountain College, 1930-31; assistant director Goodwin Inst., Memphis, June 1945-46; dir. Goodwyn Inst. June 1946-71; exec. sec., treas., Memphis Bldg. Owners; Mgrs. Assn., 1957-70, v.p., 1959-60, pres., 1960-61. State adminstr. Nat. Youth Adminstrn.; dir. Hattiesburg C. of C.; mem. bd. trustees Bapt. Meml. Hosp., 1948-70, 1st vice president, 1961-70, vice chmn. executive com., building com., 1954-70. Served with 30th Div., U.S. Army, with A.E.F., 1917-18. Mem. Miss. Edn. Assn. Democrat. Baptist (mem. bd. deacons, Bellevue Baptist Ch.). Mason (Shriner). Club: Kiwanis (dir. past pres.). Author: The Influence of Court Decisions in Shaping School Policies in Mississippi, 1932. Contbr. to ednl. jours. Home: Memphis TN Died Mar. 12, 1971; buried Memphis Memorial Park.

GEORGE, JOSEPH WARREN, lawyer; b. Cotesworth, Miss., Aug. 23, 1869; s. James Zachariah and Elizabeth Brooks (Young) G.; student Georgetown U., Washington, D.C., 1886-7; lit. dept., 1887-90, LL.B., 1893, U. of Miss.; m. Kate Hammond George, of Yazoo City, Miss., Apr. 18, 1895. Began practice in Yazoo City, 1893; mem. Miss. Ho. of Rep., 1900-6; co. atty., Yazoo Co., Miss., 1910-11; spl. asst. to U.S. atty. for Southern Dist. of Miss., 1913-14, regular asst., 1914-15; U.S. atty. same dist., by appmt. of President Wilson, July 20, 1915; resigned Jan. 1, 1919, to engage in farming. Democrat. Presbyn. Trustee U. of Miss., 1904-10. Mem. Miss. Bar Assn. Mason, K.P., Elk. Home: Greenwood MS‡

GEPPERT, OTTO EMIL, ednl. pub., sch. map and globe cons.; b. Chgo., July 17, 1889; s. Julius and Wilhelmina (Simmons) G.; student Lewis Inst., 1906-07, YMCA Coll., 1908-09, Northwestern U., 1915-16; m. Margaret Masley, Apr. 28, 1920; children—David Frederick, Robert Roundsville. Clk. law office Dent, Whitman & Eaton, Chgo., 1903; with A. J. Nystrom & Co., ednl. publishers, 1905-16; sec.-treas. Denoyer-Geppert Co., Chgo., 1916-64, pres., 1964-68, chairman of the board, 1968-70, general manager, 1947-70. Director of Chicago YMCA; exec. com. Chgo. Auditorium Restoration; trustee Roosevelt U. Served with intelligence div., U.S. Army, 1918-19; AEF in France. Mem. A. Assn. Sch. Adminstrs., Assn. Am. Geographers (life), National Education Association (life), Institute Internat. Edn. Northwestern Univ. Alumni Assn. (life), Eleanor Assn. (dir.), Acad. Polit. Sci. (life), Am. Civil Liberties Union, Am. Hist. Assn. Mason (Shriner). Rotarian. Home: Wilmette IL Died Apr. 14, 1970; buried Memorial Park Cemetery, Skokie IL

GERASIMOV, MIKHALL MIKHAYLOVICH, anthropologist, archeologist, sculptor; b. 1907. Discovered relic Upper Paleolithic period, Malta settlement, Irkutsk, 1927; worked on facial reconstrn. on basis skull formation; sculptor, 1927-70; works include Pithecanthropos and Sinanthropos, also reprodns. anthrop. types of USSR from Paleolithic times; created portraits hist. figures on basis skull formations including Yaroslav the Wise, Andrey Bogolyubsky, Timur, Shakhrukh, Ulug-bek, Adm. Ushakov. Recipient Stalin prize, 1950. Author: The Principles of Facial Reconstruction on the Basis of Skull Formation, 1949; Facial Reconstruction on the Basis of Skull Formation, Modern and Fossil Man, 1955; The Malta Paleolithic Settlement and its Place Among the Paleolithic Relics of Siberia, 1961. Home: Moscow USSR Died July, 1970.

GERBERDING, RICHARD HENRY, clergyman; b. Fargo, N.D., Dec. 4, 1889; s. George Henry and Anna (Danver) G.; A.B., Thiel Coll., 1912, D.D., 1931; student Chgo. Luth. Theol. Sem., 1912-15; m. Mary Mildred Hamilton, June 17, 1915; children—James Hamilton (USNR), Rev. George Henry, Rev. David Richard, Rev. Milo William, Philip Mortimer, Marianne (Mrs. Thomas Guinn), Charles Danver. Ordained to ministry Luth. Ch., 1915; pastor St. John's Ch., Anderson, Ind., 1915-17, Emmaus Ch., Cleve., 1917-21; field missionary for Minn., 1922-27; pres. English Evang. Luth. Synod of N.W., 1927-48; exec. sec. Bd. Am. Missions, United Luth. Ch. in Am., 1949-57; mem. bd. Lutheran Brotherhood Ins. Soc., 1955-72; consultant on ch. relationships and ednl. program for Luth. Brotherhood Ins. Soc., Mpls., from 1958. Guest prof. Pacific Theol. Sem., 1958. Bd. social missions 1942-48. Mem. Nat. Luth. Council, Nat. Council Chs. (vice chmn. div. home missions 1952-53). Home: Mound MN Died Jan. 12, 1972; buried Lakewood Cemetery, Minneapolis MN

GERDEMANN, HERBERT EDMUND, govt. publ. editor; b. Wright City, Mo., Sept. 29, 1910; s. Robert William and Carrie Charlotte (Nieburg) G.; student Central Wesleyan Coll. (Warrenton, Mo.), 1928-30; B.J., U. Mo., 1933; student So. Ill. U., 1967-69; m. Helen Lucille Mason, May 2, 1942; 1 dau., Lynn Louise (Mrs. David Meinhardt). Pub., Hermann (Mo.) Independent, 1935-56; mng. editor Herald-Tribune, Chester, Ill., 1956-61; city editor So. Illinoisan, Carbondale, Ill., 1961-63; vocational instr., pub. Menard Time, Ill. State Penitentiary, Menard, Ill., 1963-72. Served with AUS, 1943-45; PTO. Recipient Sweepstakes award Am. Penal Press Contest, 1965, 69, 70. Mem. Ill. Press. Assn., So. Ill. Editorial Assn., Chester C. of C., Sigma Delta Chi (bd. dirs. So. Ill. profl. chpt. 1970). Lion (pres. Chester club 1967-68), Elk. Republican. Presbyn. Home: Chester IL Died Mar. 24, 1972.

GEREN, PAUL FRANCIS, diplomat, univ. president; b. El Dorado, Arkansas, Dec. 5, 1913; s. Rev. Hiram Marian and Julia (Goodwin) G.; A.B., Baylor U., 1936; M.A., La. State U., 1937; M.A., Harvard, 1940, Ph.D., 1941; LL.D., St. Mary's U., San Antonio, 1962; married Elizabeth Powers, Apr. 5, 1946; children—Natasha, Juliana, Nancy Magdalene. Lectr. economics Judson Coll., U. Rangoon, Burma, 1941; vol. ambulance driver Chinese Army, Burma, 1942; escaped from Burma in Stilwell March; lectr. economics Forman Christian Coll., Lahore, 1942-43; prof. economics Berea Coll., 1946-47; apptd. v. consul career, sec. Diplomatic Service, 1947; v. consul, Bombay, India, 1948-50; internat. trade economist South Asia sect. Office of Internat. Trade, Dept. of Commerce, 1950-51; consul, 2d sec. Am. Legation, Damascus, Syria, 1951, 1st sec., 1952-54; counselor Am. Embassy, Amman, Jordan, 1954-56; exec. v.p., Baylor Univ., Waco, Texas, 1956-58; executive dir. Dallas Council on World Affairs, 1959-61; dep. dir. Office Internat. and Devel. Affairs, Department State, 1961-62; deputy director Peace Corps., 1961-62; consul gen. with rank of minister Fedn. Rhodesia and Nyasaland, Salisbury, 1962-64; dir. Office Telecommunications and Maritime Affairs, Dept. State, 1964-65; counselor econ. affairs Am. embassy, Tripoli, Libya, 1965-67; president Stetson University, DeLand, Fla., 1967-69. Candidate for U.S. Congress, 1946. Served as combat med., later intelligence officer AUS, CBI, 1943-46; disch. as 1st lt. Decorated Bronze Star Medal. Fellow Soc. for Religion Higher Edn. Baptist. Author: Burma Diary, 1943; The Pilgrimage of Peter Strong, 1948; New Voices, Old Worlds, 1958; Christians Confront Communism, 1962; also econ., religious articles profl. jours. Home: ElDorado AR Died June 22, 1969; buried Lexington Cemetery, Lexington KY

GERHARD, GERHARD RUSSELL, lawyer; b. Eureka Springs, Ark., Aug. 12, 1906; s. Albert W. Rhein and Emme C. Gerhard; A.B., Amherst Coll., 1927; J.D., Harvard, 1930; m. Jean Anne Opdyke, Apr. 7, 1947; children—Geoffrey, Gina. Admitted to Mo. bar, 1930, N.Y. bar, 1931, N.H. bar, 1969; practiced in N.Y.C., 1931-68; of counsel Appleton, Rice & Perrin, 1969-72. Past dir. Cin. Chem. Works. Mem. Sutton Planning Bd., Sutton Bd. Adjustment. Bd. dirs. Kearsage Valley Nurse Assn. Served to lt. comdr. USNR, 1942-45. Mem. Am., N.H. bar assns., Assn. Bar City N.Y., Phi Beta Kappa, Beta Theta Pi. Rotarian. Clubs: Harvard (N.Y.C.); Manhasset Bay (N.Y.) Yacht (past trustee). Home: North Sutton NH Died Aug. 20, 1972.

GERKEN, WALTER DIEDRICK, educator; b. at Plainfield, N.J., Nov. 2, 1875; s. Diedrick and Anna Catherine Harriet (Gerken) G.; B.S., Cornell, 1899; A.M., Columbia, 1902; m. Frances Elizabeth Rowe, of Brooklyn, N.Y., July 2, 1908. Teacher, Prospect Heights Sch., Brooklyn, 1902-3; head of dept. of drawing, Lawrenceville (N.J.) School, 1903-8; headmaster, George H. Thurston Sch., Pittsburgh, 1908-10; headmaster, Junior Sch. of Peekskill (N.Y.) Mil. Acad., 1910-17; owner and prin., Stamford (Conn.) Mil. Acad., since 1917. Also dir. Camp Mowana, Readfield, Me., since 1917. Democrat. Episcopalian. Mason. Mem. Phi Gamma Delta. Home: Ossining NY‡

GERLACH, ARCH C., geographer; b. Tacoma, May 12, 1911; s. William Henry and Kate Alice (Cooper) G.; A.B., San Diego State Coll., 1933, M.A., U. Cal. at Los Angeles, 1935; Ph.D., U. Wash., 1943; m. Arlene M. Schmiedeman, 1935. Geographer Los Angeles City Coll., 1939-42; acting chief map div. Dept. State, 1945-46; asso. prof. geography U. Wis., 1946-50; chief geography and map division, also incumbent chair of geography Library of Congress, Washington, 1950-67; vis. prof. in geography U. Mich., 1957-58. U.S. rep. directing council Pan-Am. Inst. Geography and History, from 1958, v.p., 1965-69; chief National Atlas project United States Geological Survey, 1962-63, staff geographer, 1963-67, chief geographer U.S. Geol. Survey, from 1967. Vice president, U.S. member commn. on nat. atlasas Internat. Geog. Union, 1964-68. Served as lieutenant, cartographer and map intelligence officer, OSS, USNR, 1942-45. Chmn. NRC adv. com. geography Dept. State, 1956-62; Co-ordinator Geographie Applications Program for Remote Sensor Data from Aircraft and Spacecraft, 1967-72. Fellow American Geographic Society (honorary); member American Congress on Surveying and Mapping, Association of American Geographers (pres. 1962-63), Nat. Council Geography Teachers, Special Libraries Association (nat. chmn., geog. and map div., 1953-55, mem. exec. board, 1956-59), Am. Soc. Photogrammetry, Pan Am. Inst. Geography and History (president 1969). Editor of The Professional Geographer, 1951-54. Home: Washington DC Died May 20, 1972; buried Gettysburg Nat. Cemetery.

GERMANY, EUGENE BENJAMIN, petroleum producer; b. Sweetwater, Tex., Sept. 18, 1892; s. John Wesley and Arona (Lea) G.; student Southwestern U., Georgetown, Tex., 1910-12, LL.D., 1947; student So. Meth. U., Dallas, 1915; m. Maggie Lee Wilson, June 8, 1915; children—Eugene Wilson, Annette Myra (Mrs. Jack S. Wilkes), Norman Garvin. Tchr. Grand Saline (Tex.) High Sch., 1915-20; cons. geologist, 1921-27; sr. partner E.B. Germany & Sons, from 1927; past chmn. Preston Bank, Dallas; pres. Lone Star Steel Co., 1947-62, chmn. bd. 1962-63, Columnist The Way I See It. Pres. Dallas Co. Park Cities Water Control and Development; mayor, Highland Park, 1934-42. Pres. Tex. State Parks Development Assn., 1957; chmn. Texas Indsl. Commn., 1958. Exec. com. Meth. Hosp., Dallas; mem. bd. Scottish Rite Crippled Children's Hospital, Dallas, Sabine River Development Board; member board trustees Southwestern U.; trustee Tex. Found. Voluntarily Supported Colls. and Univs. Mem. Tex. Employers' Ins. Assn. (bd.), Red River Valley Assn. (v.p. Tex. 1953), East Tex., Dallas chambers commerce, Philosophical Society of Texas (president 1962), Y.M.C.A. (bd.), Tex. Police Assn., Tex. Alcoholics Anonymous Assn., Petroleum Inst., Am. Foundrymen's Soc., Am. Assn. Petroleum Geologists, Am. Iron and Steel Institute (member of board of directors), American Institute Mining and Metallurgical Engrs., Tex. Acad. Sci., Nat. Assn. Mfrs., Nat. Indsl. Conf. Bd., Nat. Assn. Churches. Democrat (chmn. state exec. com. 1938-41). Methodist. Mason (past potentate), Elk. Clubs: Petroleum, Country (Dallas). Author: Pioneer of the Future, 1938; And Passing Through the Valley of Bacca He Made it a Well, 1941; Birds of a Feather, 1943; Honesty and Integrity in Methodist Church Politics, 1943; Democrary in Acting, 1944; Integrity As I Have Seen It, 1958. Home: Grand Saline TX Died July 12, 1971; buried Grand Saline TX

GERMER, LESTER HALBERT, physicist; b. Chgo., Oct. 10, 1896; s. Dr. Hermann G. and Marcia (Halbert) G.; A.B., Cornell U., 1917; M.A., Columbia, 1922, Ph.D., 1927; m. Ruth Woodard, Oct. 2, 1919; children—Emily (Mrs. V. W. Samms), John Halbert G. Engring. dept. Western Electric Co., 1917-25, research physicist, 1925-53; tech. staff, research physicist Bell Telephone Laboratories, 1925-61, Cornell University, New York, 1961-71. Served as second lt. 139th aero squadron, A.E.F., 1918. Received Elliot Cresson medal, 1931. Fellow A.A.A.S., N.Y. Acad. Sci., Am. Phys. Soc. (chmn. N.Y. sect. 1944); mem. Soc. X-Ray and Electron Diffraction (v.p. 1943, president 1944), American Crystallographic Society, also Sigma Xi. Republican. Club: Appalachian Mountain of Boston (chmn. N.Y. chpt. 1951-52). Author sci. articles. Discoverer (with Dr. C. J. Davisson) of Millington NJ Died Oct. 3, 1971.

GEROW, LEONARD TOWNSEND, army officer; b. Petersburg, Va., July 13, 1888; s. Leonard Rodgers and Eloise (Saunders) G.; B.S., Virginia Military Inst., 1911; m. Mary Louise Kennedy, July 28, 1939. Commd. 2d lt. Inf., U.S. Army, 1911; advanced through grades to lt. gen., Jan. 1945; served as chief of staff, War Plans Div. to Feb. 1942; comdg. gen. 29th Div., Ft. George Meade, 1942-43; comdg. gen. V Corps, European Theater, July 1943-Jan. 1945; comdg. gen. 15th Army, Jan.-Oct. 1945; comdg. gen. Ft. Leavenworth; comdt. Comd. and Gen. Staff Coll. 1945-48; commanding general 2d Army, hdqrs. Fort George G. Meade, Maryland, Jan. 15, 1948 to July 31, 1950. Decorated D.S.M. with Oak Leaf Cluster, Legion of Merit with Cluster, Silver Star, Bronze Star (U.S.); Legion d' Honneur Commander, Croix de Guerre with Palm (France); Order of Bath (Great Britain); Order of Suvorov, 2d Class (Russia); Order of Crown of Luxembourg; Order of Leopold II, Grand Officer with Palm; Croix de Guerre 1940, with Palm (Belgium) Order Military Merit (Brazil); D.S.M. (Va.), D.S.M. (Pa.). Episcopalian. Address: Fort George G Meade MD Died Oct. 1972.

GERRISH, WILLARD PEABODY, engineer, astronomer; b. Roxbury, Mass., Aug. 31, 1866; s. William Hamilton and Eliza Ann (Willoby) G.; ed. Roxbury Latin Sch. and Mass. Inst. Tech.; m. Mary M. Wylie, Oct. 24, 1896. Opened Blue Hill Meteorol. Obs., Milton, Mass., as observer in charge, 1885; joined staff of the Obs. of Harvard U., 1886; asst. in Obs. Harvard, 1892-1913; asst. prof. mech. engring., Harvard U., 1913-38, emeritus, 1938; consulting engr. since 1902. Mem. Amherst Eclipse Expedn. to Japan, 1896. Designer of large telescopes at Harvard U., Amherst Coll. and elsewhere. Author of the Telegraphic Cipher Code in internat. use for dissemination of astron. information. Address: Frankland Rd., Ashland MA‡

GERRY, MARGARITA SPALDING, author; b. Washington, D.C., July 28, 1870; d. Harvey and Sophia (Hutchinson) Spalding; B.S., Wellesley, 1891; m. Philip Fusting Gerry, of Catonsville, Md., and Washington, D.C., July 11, 1898 (died May 1908); children—Harvey Spalding, Marjorie Spofford (Mrs. Waldemar J. Gallman), Philippa Fusting (Mrs. Frederick Allen Whiting, Jr.). Teacher in high schs., Washington, D.C., 1892-98; member Sch. Bd., Washington, D.C., 1915-20; ednl. work for foreign-born in U.S. Bur. of Naturalization, 1918-20; active in local work for new citizens, 1918—. Mem. The Literary," Wellesley Alumnae Assn., Woman's Alliance, District League of Women Voters. Unitarian. Club: Twentieth Century. Author: The Toy Shop, 1908; The Flowers, 1910; Heart and Chart, 1911; As Caesar's Wife, 1912; The Masks of Love, 1914; The Sound of Water, 1914; Philippa's Fortune, 1921; Philippa at the Chateau, 1922; Philippa's Experiments, 1923. Contbr. to mags. Home: 2944 Macomb St., Washington DC‡

GERSBACHER, EVA NINA OXFORD (MRS. W.M. GERSBACHER), educator; b. Cave-in-Rock, Ill.; d. Ernest and Nora (Brownfield) Oxford; B.Ed., So. Ill. U., 1938; M.A., Oberlin Coll., 1939; postgrad (NSF fellow) U. Wis., 1960, (NSF fellow) Ind. U., 1961, (NSF fellow) Lock Haven Coll., 1964, (Nat. Def. Edn. Act fellow) Kan. State Coll., 1962, (Newspaper Fund scholar, Nat. Def. Edn. Act fellow) So. Ill. U., 1963, 64; m. W.M. Gersbacher, July 29, 1938; children—Mary, Jane, Willard, Elizabeth Joan. Tchr. pub. schs., Hardin County, Ill., 1930-37; lab. asst. So. Ill. U., 1937-38; researcher Reelfoot Lake Biol. Sta., Tenn., 1938, 63; tchr. biology, guidance dir. Sesser (Ill.) Community Unit High Sch., 1959-64; head biology dept. Southeastern Ill. Coll., Harrisburg, 1964-73. Active various local youth groups; v.p. City P.T.A. Council, 1956. Democratic precinct com. woman, 1932-35. Recipient awards for youth work, also flower show awards; named Ill. State Mother of Year, Future Homemakers Am., 1957-58. Mem. A.A.A.S., Am. Inst. Biol. Scis., Assn. Midwest Biology Tchrs., Nat. Assn. Biology Tchrs., Ill. Edn. Assn. (biology chmn. So. div. 1963-65, sec. 1961-63), Ill. Assn. Higher Edn., Am. Personnel and Guidance Assn. (life), Am. Sch. Counselors Assn., Council Garden Clubs (flower show judge 1940-60, local pres. 1956, state historian 1956), So. Ill. U. Alumni Assn. (life), Nat. Wildlife Fedn., Saline County Hist. Soc., Southeastern Ill. Faculty Orgn. (v.p. 1969-70), Am. Assn. U. Women, Alpha Delta Kappa (pres. chpt.). Methodist (supt. kindergarten dept. 1943-48, sec. missionary edn. 1954-55). Home: Harrisburg IL Died Jan. 6, 1973.

GERSHON-COHEN, JACOB, radiologist, educator; b. Phila., Jan. 9, 1899; s. Abraham and Dora (Starkman) Cohen; M.D., U. Pa., 1924, D.Sc. in Medicine, 1936; m. Sara Eskin, Mar. 26, 1921. Intern Jewish Hosp., Phila, 1924-25; resident X-ray dept. U. Pa. Hosp., 1926-28 practice medicine specializing in radiology, Phila 1929-71; asst. prof. radiology U. Pa. Grad. Med. Sch 1941-68; dir. div. radiology Albert Einstein Mec Center, Phila., 1949-65; prof. radiology Hahneman Med. Coll., 1952-59; prof. research radiology Temple U Med. Sch., 1965-71; cons. various area hosps., 1929-71 Served to comdr., M.C., USNR, 1942-46. Recipien Alvarenga prize Internat. Coll. Radiology, Gold meda award, 1937; Clement Cleveland award Am. Cance Soc., 1968. Diplomate Am. Bd. Radiology. Fellow An Coll. Radiology, Gerontol. Soc.; mem. Am. Roentge Ray Soc., Radiol. Soc. N.Am., Inter-Am. Col Radiology, Soc. Nuclear Medicine, Fedn. Am. Soc Exptl. Biology, A.M.A., Med. Soc. Pa., Am. Cance Soc., N.Y. Acad. Sci., Coll. Physicians Phila., Phila County Med. Soc., Laennec Soc., Pa. Radiol. Soc Phila. Roentgen Ray Soc. (v.p. 1964-65, pres. 1965-66 Author numerous articles in field. Home: Philadelph PA Died Feb. 1971.

GERSON, OSCAR, high sch. prof.; b. Phila., June 1874; s. Aaron and Eva (Goldsmith) G.; brother of Feli Napoleon G. (q.v.); grad. Sch. of Pedagogy, Phila 1892; Ph.D., U. of Pa., 1898; m. Katharine Bowers, Phila., Oct. 17, 1900. Prin. 3 pub. schs. of Phila., sinc 1893; prof. literature, Central Manual Training Hig Sch. and prof. pedagogy, Temple U., Phila., 1905-1 prof. pub. speaking, West Phila. Boys' High Sch 1913—. Mem. Phila. Teachers' Assn; pre Schoolmen's Club of Phila. Co-author: A Brief Topica Survey of U.S. History (with Oliver P. Cornman), 190 Physiology Primer (with same), 1902; Geograph Primer, 1905; History Primer, 1906; Our Coloni History; Instruction in the Grades. Home: 773 Norwood St., Philadelphia‡

GERSON, THEODORE PERCEVAL, physician; Philadelphia, Pa., May 27, 1872; s. Isidor I. and Ell Hemenway (Woodruff) G.; grad. Central High Sch Phila., 1891; M.D., U. of Pa., 1895; grad. study John Hopkins, 1896; m. Harriet Anna Thompson, Jan. 1899; children—Lowell Woodruff, Gerald Perceva Cecil Alice; m. 2d, Vera Madeline Daniels, Nov. 1923; 1 son, Cedric. Interne, Episcopal, Presbyn. ar Phila. Gen. hosps., 1896-98; in gen. practice at Chicag 1898-99, Lansdowne, Pa., 1899-1903, Los Angele Calif., since 1903. Mem. Pa. Nat. Guard 3 yr Municipal newspaper commr., Los Angeles, 1912-1 Member Municipal League of Los Angeles; physicia California State Personnel Board. Founder, 191 former v.p., sec., now life mem. Hollywood Bowl Assn dir. Hollywood Bowl Opera Assn.; Inc.; mem. adv. b Yenching U. (Peiping, China); dir., pres. Planne Parenthood Center of Los Angeles, Inc.; mem. Na Com. for Planned Parenthood; pres. Severance Clu Fellow Hollywood Acad. Med. (honorary life member member Friends University of California at Los Angel Library, A.M.A., Cal. State Med. Soc., Los Angeles C Medical Soc., Chicago Pathol. Soc., Philadelphi Pathol. Soc., American Academy of Political and Soci Science, Phila. Acad. Natural Scis., Alpha Mu Omega. Home: 1001 N. Sierra Bonita Av., Hollywoo 46 CA‡

GERST, FRANCIS JOSEPH, prof. mathematics; Cincinnati, O., June 29, 1882; s. Frank Joseph ar Caroline (Goessling) G. A.B., Xavier U., Cincinna 1902; A.M., St. Louis U., 1909, M.S., 1911; post gra work, St. Louis U., 1906-09, 1910-11, 1914-18, U. Mich., 1920-21; Ph.D., Johns Hopkins, 1923. Ordaine priest R.C. Ch., 1917; instr. mathematics, U. of Detro 1909-10, John Carroll U., Cleveland, O., 1911-14; ass prof. mathematics, Loyola U., Chicago, 1918-19, pro 1931-62, emeritus, dean graduate sch., 1933-46; pro mathematics, St. Louis Univ., 1924-31. Mem. Ar Math. Soc., Math. Assn. of America. Mem. Soc. Jesus. Address: Chicago IL Died Sept. 30, 1968; buri All Saints Cemetery, Desplaines IL

GERSTELL, ROBERT SINCLAIR, business exe born Wheeling, W.Va., Oct. 31, 1893; s. Arno Frederick and Fannie Brown (Davis) G.; gra Lawrenceville Sch., 1913, Princeton, 1917; m. Ali Augusta Roeth, Jan. 10, 1931; children—Mary Alic Roberta, Arnold Frederick. Vice pres. and dir. Alp Portland Cement Co., Easton, Pa., 1923-56, exec. vi pres., 1956-57, pres., 1957-63, chmn. bd., 1963-73; v. dir. Hotel Easton, 1932-50, pres., dir., 1950-66; v.p., d Gen. Supply Co.; dir. Easton Nat. Bank & Trust C Trustee Lawrenceville Sch. Mem. Easton Area C. of (pres.). Republican. Presbyn. Clubs: Princeto Pinnacle, Union League (N.Y.C.); Northampt County Country, Kiwanis (Easton). Home: Easton F Died May 1973.

GERSTEN, E. CHESTER, pres. Public Nat. Bank Trust Co.; b. July 3, 1889; m. Annette Gerste children—Sarah, Helen. Began as messenger with N Bank of Commerce of N.Y., 1909, appointed officer 1919 and advanced to v.p.; pres. Public Nat. Bank Trust Co., 1929-55; exec. v.p. Bankers Trust, 1955-5 vice chairman of the board, 1956-71; dir. Consol. Cig Corporation, American Broadcasting-Paramou Theatres. Pres. N.Y. State Bankers Assn., 1943. Clu Bankers, New York Athletic, Sea View Golf, Upp Montclair Country. Home: Montclair NJ Died May 2 1971.

GERSTENFELD, NORMAN, clergyman; b. Eng., Sept. 1, 1904; s. Samuel and Bronwyn (Pachman) G.; M.H.L. and Rabbi, Hebrew Union Coll., Cin. 1933, fellow philosophy, 1933-34, L.H.D., 1946, D.D., 1958; L.H.D., U. Tampa, 1946; Litt.D., Am. U., 1955; m. Louise Mundheim, Mar. 22, 1934; children—John, Lynn (wife of Doctor Bernard Kapilof), Roger William, and Norma. Rabbi with Washington Hebrew Congregation, 1935-68; broadcast preacher on Message of Israel, ABC, Canadian Broadcasting System, Church of the Air, CBS, also radio sta. WMAL. Chmn. Com. on Religious Life in Nation's Capital, 1946-47; mem. Bd. Pub. Welfare D.C. Mem. adv. com. Nat. Cultural Center Center, Washington. Mem. Central Conf. Am. Rabbis (former chmn. com. interfaith policy and program), Am. Jewish Com. (mem. nat. bd. govs., hon. chmn. Washington chpt.). Club: Cosmos. Home: Washington DC Died Jan. 27, 1968; buried Washington Hebrew Congregation Cemetery.

GERSTER, JACK ALAN, engring. educator; b. Pitts., Apr. 26, 1919; s. William V. and Myrtle (Heer) G.; B.Chem. Engring., Ohio State U., 1939, M. Chem. Engring., 1940, Ph.D., 1943; m. Bernita Lenore Short, Sept. 5, 1948; children—John William, Catherine Ann. With E.I. duPont de Nemours & Co., Inc., 1944-46; mem. faculty U. Del., 1946-70, Allan P. Colburn prof., chmn. dept. chem. engring., 1966-70; prof. chem. engring. Tulane U., 1943. Mem. Am. Inst. Chem. Engrs. (Profl. Progress award 1964), Am. Chem. Soc., Am. Soc. Engring. Edn., Sigma Xi, Tau Beta Pi. Author articles in field. Home: Newark DE Died Jan. 20, 1971.

GERSTLE, MARK LEWIS, corp. official; b. San Francisco, Calif., May 28, 1866; s. Lewis and Hannah (Greenebaum) G.; student Harvard, 1889, Harvard Law Sch., 1892; m. Genevieve Mills Bennett, Aug. 16, 1936; children—(by previous marriage to Hilda Hecht) Dr. Mark L. Jr., Louise Alice Stahl. Practiced law until 1910; pres. Arroyo Seco Gold Dredging Co., Gen. Metals Recovery Corp.; vice pres. and dir. The Emporium, San Francisco, Met. Laundry Co.; pres. Townsend Co.; dir. Yreka Dredging Co. Attended Mil. Training Camp, Monterey, Calif., in 1916; served during World War I as major. Awarded Distinguished Service Medal by U.S. Govt., 1928. Military aide to Sec. of War, IX Corps Area, since 1929. Clubs: Family; Harvard of New York. Home: 545 Powell St. Office: 310 Sansome St., San Francisco CA*‡

GESNER, BERTRAM MELVIN, physician; b. N.Y.C., Aug. 15, 1931; s. Harry and Mae (Friedman) G.; A.B., Hamilton Coll., 1953; M.D., N.Y. U., 1957; m. Susan Rubin, Aug. 15, 1954; children—Lawrence Henry, Matthew Joseph, Mark Lewis. Intern, Bellevue Hosp., N.Y.C., 1957-58, resident, 1958-60; fellow Sir William Dunn Sch. Pathology, Oxford U., Eng., 1960-61; clin. asso. Nat. Inst. Arthritis and Metabolic Disease, NIH, Bethesda, Md. 1961-63, sr. investigator, 1963-64; practice medicine, specializing in internal medicine, N.Y.C.; mem. staff N.Y. U. Hosp. Center, Bellevue Hosp.; instr., dept. medicine N.Y. U., 1964-66, asst. prof., 1966-68. Diplomate Am. Bd. Internal Medicine. Mem. Harvey Soc., Am. Rheumatism Assn. Contbr. articles to profl. jours. Home: Great Neck NY Died Aug. 21, 1968.

GESSLER, A(LBERT) E(DWARD), chemist; b. Metzingen, Wurtt, Germany, May 8, 1885; s. Edward Albert and Marie Louise (Leuze) G.; B.S., U. of Stuttgart, 1905; Ph.D., U. of Berlin, 1907; m. Mildred B. Murray, Feb. 2, 1915; children—Isolde (Mrs. Craig P. Smith), Albert; married 2d, Helen Yarnall, Mar. 31, 1932; 1 daughter Sally (Mrs. F. G. Appleton). Came to United States, 1908, became naturalized, 1922. Chemist, G. Siegle Co., Rosebank, N.Y., 1908, vice pres. and mem. bd., 1914-18; partner and vice pres. Ultro Chem. Corp., 1918, firm consol. with Zinsser & Co., 1926; chief chemist, mem. bd. and exec. com. Zinsser & Co., 1926-34; dir. research Interchem. Corp., N.Y. City, 1934-44, vice pres. and dir. research, 1944-52, director emeritus of research from 1952; engaged in private practice as chemical cons. Recipient certificate awarded for effective research in connection with atomic bomb, 1945; certificate awarded for effective service in work on camouflage organized through Nat. Defense Research Council, Mar. 1, 1945; recipient grant for cancer research from Lillia Babbitt Hyde Found., 1944-53; Ault Award. National Assn. Printing Ink Makers. Fellow N.Y. Acad. Sci.; mem. Am. Chem. Soc. (councilor), Am. Assn. Cancer Research, A.A.A.S., Electron Microscope Society, Assn. Research Dirs. Rep. Luth. Club: University (Winter Park, Florida). Contributor of papers to chemical and to medicial publications. Holder chemical patents. Full family name—Gessler von Braunegg with hereditary rank of Knight decreed by Emperor Charles VI of Austria, 1726. Home: Sarasota FL Died Dec. 3, 1969; buried Saint Boniface Columbarium, Sarasota FL

GESSNER, ROBERT, author, educator; b. Escanaba, Mich., Oct. 23, 1907; s. Herman and Anna (Silverman) G.; A.B., U. of Mich., 1929; A.M., Columbia, 1930; m. Doris Lindeman, May 27, 1938; children—Peter, Stephen. Instr. English, N.Y. Univ., 1930; screen playwright Warner Bros., 1933; asst. prof. motion pictures N.Y. Univ., 1941-43; asso. prof. chmn. dept. motion pictures N.Y. Univ. 1943-45, prof. since 1945; vis. prof., U. of So. Calif., 1947, Hebrew U., 1949, London U., 1957; Vanderbilt lectr. Smith College, 1961; film adviser Lincoln Center, 1962; cinema Critic Theatre Arts Magazine, 1962; State Dept. rep. Mexican Film Festival, 1963-65. Board directors Motion Picture Foundation for Colls. and Univs., Inc.; chmn. Rosenthal Found. awards in Cinema, 1962-64; chmn. jury Cork Internat. Film Festival, Ireland, 1964; Award New Republic poetry prize, 1934; Peabody Radio Writing Award, 1944. Ford Found. traveling fellow Polish, Yugoslavia cinema acads., 1962; visiting scholar (Ford Found. grant) Harvard, 1962-63; lectr. IDHEC, Paris, 1963. Member Society of Cinematologists (founding president 1959-61, senior councilman 1961-62; 65). Club: Harvard University Faculty. Author of several books, 1931-—, including: Teaching Techniques U.S.A.F., 1953; Irovy Tower, 1957; Behind the Ivy, 1959; The Art of the Moving Image, 1958. Editor: The Democratic Man, 1956. Special cons., also script writer U.S.A.F., 1952-53. Contbr. periodicals on motion pictures and television. Pioneer education in motion pictures as an art form. Home: New York City NY Died June 16, 1968.

GETCHELL, NOBLE HAMILTON, mem. Rep. Nat. Com.; b. Oakland, Calif., Feb. 9, 1875; s. Lysander Waterman and Elizabeth (Farnsworth) G., student U. of Wash., 1893; m. Louise Margaret Meyer, Jan. 1, 1906. Mine surveyor, Wash., 1889; engaged in mining Alaska, 1894, Silver City, Ida., 1895, Colo., 1897, Ida., 1898, Tonopah, Nev., 1900, Calif., 1904, Tonopah, 1906, Goldyke, Nev., 1909, Ariz. 1909, 12, 18 and Nev. since 1920, developing Betty O'Neal and Gold Circle Consolidated mines; vice-president and gen. manager, Getchell Mine, Incorporated, since 1934. Member Arizona State Senate, 1917-18, Nevada State Senate since 1922 (president protem 1927); mem. Nev. State Fact Finding Commn., 1928; chmn. Rep. State Central Com., 3 terms; mem. Rep. Nat. Com., Nev. since 1940; chmn. State Fish and Game Commn. since 1939; dist. chmn. Am. Mining Congress, 1940. Mem. exec. bd. Boy Scouts of America; mem. finance com. Y.M.C.A. Mem. Am. Inst. Mining and Metall. Engrs. Republican. Mason (32 deg., K.T., Shriner), Elk. Home: 305 Belmont Rd. Office 206 N. Virginia St., Reno NV*‡

GETHRO, FRED WILLIAM, dentist; b. Dedham, Mass., May 28, 1873; s. Alexander and Margaret (Denning) G.; ed. pub. schs. and Rice Training Sch., Boston; D.D.S., Northwestern U. Dental Sch., 1899. Practiced, Chicago, since 1899; now prof. operative dentistry and dental anatomy, Northwestern U. Dental Sch. Republican. Mem. Chicago Dental Soc., Ill. State Dental Soc., Nat. Dental Assn., Delta Sigma Delta. Mason, K.T. Clubs: Chicago Automobile, Chicago Yacht, South Shore Country, Chicago Athletic, Flossmoor Country. Home: 1140 E. 46th St. Office: Peoples Gas Bldg., Chicago IL‡

GETSCHOW, ROY MARTIN, corp. exec.; b. Chgo., June 22, 1894; s. George M. and Lillian (Burns) G.; engr. Notre Dame U., 1915; m. LaVerne M. Pinocci, May 1, 1930; children—George J., Roy Martin, Robert E., Lee E., Grace L. (Mrs. Terrill). With Phillips-Getschow Co., Chgo., 1915-68, steam fitter apprentice, cost clk., estimater, draftsman, supt., 1915-25, sec., mgr., 1925-35, dir., 1925-55, pres., 1935-55, chmn. bd., 1955-68; v.p., dir. Sloan Valve Corp., 1940-68; dir., pres. Tower Restaurant, 1952-63. Active in Republican Party. Mem. Nat. Assn. Heating, Piping and Air Conditioning and Contractors (pres. 1946-47). Lutheran. Mason. Home: Kenilworth IL Died Aug. 4, 1968.

GETTY, ROBERT, educator; b. Cin., Nov. 10, 1916; s. Robert and Elsa (Muehe) G.; D.V.M., Ohio State U., 1940; M.S., Ia. State U., 1945, Ph.D., 1949; m. Roberta B. Musgrave, Dec. 28, 1944;children—Rita Ann (Mrs. Charles Hammerberg), Rikel Kent. Practice vet. medicine, Norwood, O., 1940-41; instr. vet. anatomy Ia. State U., 1941-42, asst. prof. vet. bacteriology, 1943-45, asst. prof. vet. anatomy, 1943-49, asso. prof. vet. anatomy, 1949-51, prof., head vet. anatomy, 1951-71, mem. com. biomed. electronics, 1957-71, chmn. 1963-65. Mem. vet. medicine rev. com. N.I.H., 1970-71; exec. bd. Council on Med. TV, 1969-71; exec. bd. Audiovisual Conf. Med. and Allied Scis., 1962-71, co-chmn., 1962-63, v.p., 1963-67, pres., 1967-69. Mem. governing com. Ia. State U. Research Found., 1962-71, trustee, 1964-71, v.p., 1964-66, pres., 1966-68. Recipient Distinguished Alumnus award Ohio State U., 1970, Distinguished prof. vet. medicine award Ia. State U., 1970. Fellow Gerontol. Soc., A.A.A.S.,; mem. N.Y. Acad. Scis., Assn. for Advancement Aging Research (council advisers), World Assn. Vet. Anatomists (v.p. 1960-63, mem. internat. vet. anat. nomenclature com. 1959-71, chmn. sect. organa Sensuum 1959-68), Am. Vet. Med. Assn. (sec. nat. research council 1952-56, chmn. 1956-59), Am. Assn. Vet. Anatomists (pres. 1961-62), Am. Assn. Human Anatomists, Am. Pub. Health Assn. Ia. State U. Alumni Assn. (faculty citation 1968), Sigma Xi, Phi Zeta, Phi Kappa Psi, Gamma Sigma Delta, Alpha Zeta. Author: Veterinary Anatomy, 1962; Veterinary Histology and Embroyology, 1964; Atlas for Applied Veterinary Anatomy, 1964; Atlas and Dissection Guide for the Study of the Anatomy of Domestic Animals, 1960; rev. and updated edit. Sisson and Grossman's Anatomy of Domestic Animals, 1971; also numerous articles, chpts. in books vet. anat. films. Home: Ames IA Died Feb. 18, 1971.

GEYER, BERTRAM BIRCH, advt. exec.; b. Dayton, O., Mar. 16, 1891; s. Charles J. and Clara M. (Birch) G.; student pub. schs. of Dayton; m. Beulah West DeLong, Apr. 22, 1919; children—Robert Charles (dec.), John Rockwell, Richard DeLong, James Birch; m. 2d, Esther Burger, May 10, 1956. Fgn. advt. mgr., Dayton (O.) Herald, 1909-10; established, then pres., Geyer Co., 1912; established, Geyer Advt., Inc., N.Y.C., 1956, chmn. bd., 1956-59; chmn. executive com. Geyer, Morey, Ballard, Inc., 1959-66; pres. River House Realty Co. Rep. Presbyn. Clubs: Metropolitan, Whist (v. pres.), The River (N.Y.C.); Blooming Grove Hunting and Fishing (Hawley, Pa.); Bath and Tennis, The Everglades (Palm Beach, Fla.). Home: New York City NY Died Oct. 31, 1970; buried Ferncliffe, Scarsdale NY

GHALI, PAUL, newspaperman; b. Avignon, France, June 24, 1905; s. Sobhi and Jeanne (de Baroncelli-Javon) G.; B.Litt., Magdalen Coll., Oxford (Eng.) U., 1929-31; m. Bernadette Beaune, June 7, 1961. Admitted to Egyptian bar, 1932; lawyer Mixed Ct. Appeal, Egypt, 1932-38; prof. French law in Egypt, 1936-38; mem. staff Chgo. Daily News, 1939-70, assigned Middle East, 1948-51, chief Paris bur., 1952-70. Named hon. citizen of New Orleans, 1961; decorated chevalier Legion of Honor (France), 1948. Mem. French Hist. Bldg. Assn., French Automobile Club. Club: Anglo-Am. Press (v.p. 1955) (Paris). Author: The Nationalities Detached from the Ottman Empire, 1932. Home: Paris France Died June 3, 1970; buried Avignon France

GHORMLEY, JOHN WALLACE, physician; b. Patridge, Kan., June 5, 1899; s. David Elmer and Elizabeth Read (Wallace) G.; M.D., Johns Hopkins U., 1923; m. Mildred Valentine Harper, Sept. 16, 1929; children—Judith Hale (Mrs. Charles Wing, Jr.), Wallace Brewster; m. 2d, Helen Elizabeth Nordell, Dec. 1, 1965. Resident house officer in surgery Johns Hopkins U. Hosp., Balt., 1923-24; resident in surgery Albany (N.Y.) Hosp., 1924-25, attending orthopedic surgeon, until 1970; co-founder phys. therapy dept. Albany Med. Center Hosp., 1944, med. dir. Phys. Therapy Sch., 1944-55, med. dir. Cerebral Palsy Center, 1945-55; cons. surgeon Eastern N.Y. Orthpedic Hosp., Schenectady; asso. clin. prof. orthopedic surgery Albany Med. Coll., until 1970. Chmn. med. adv. com. Nat. Found., 1941-60; cons. orthopedic surgeon div. med. rehab. N.Y. State Dept. Health; sr. med. cons. vocational rehab. N.Y. State Dept. Edn.; chmn. med. adv. com. Workshop Inc., 1954-60, hon. bd. dirs., 1960. Recipient Service regognition plaque Workshop Inc., 1967. Diplomate Am. Bd. Orthopaedic Surgery. Fellow A.C.S.; mem. A.M.A., N.Y. State Med. Soc. (life), Am. Acad. Orthopaedic Surgeons (emeritus). Presbyn. Author: Outline of Orthopedics for Students, 1944. Contbr. articles to med. jours. Home: Albany NY Died Nov. 19, 1970; buried Partridge KS

GIBB, FREDERICK WILLIAM, army officer; b. N.Y.C., July 24, 1908; s. Frederick Innes and Jessie Anna (Leake) G.; B.S., U.S. Mil. Acad., 1933; grad. Inf. Sch., 1938. Command and Gen. Staff Coll., 1946. Nat. War Coll., 1949; m. Delana Elizabeth Skeldon, June 13, 1933 (dec. Sept. 1959); children—Frederick William II, Jean Innes (Mrs. Fred B. Phillips), m. 2d, Ruth Gidley, Nov. 29, 1960. Commd. 2d lt. U.S. Army, 1933, advanced through grades to maj. gen., 1959; various assignments with inf. units, 1933-42; battalion comdr. 3d Bn., 16th Inf., 1st Inf. Div., 1942-43; asst. chief staff G-3, 1st Inf. Div., 1943-44; regtl. comdr. 16th Inf., 1st Inf. Div., 1944-45; chmn. attack com. Inf. Sch., Ft. Benning, Ga., 1946-48; staff mem. advanced study group dept. of army and joint staff, Joint Strategic Plans Group, Office Joint Chiefs Staff, 1949-52; dep. chief staff plans and operations, Allied Land Forces, S.E. Europe, Izmar, Turkey, 1952-54; chief army war plans br., plans div. Office Asst., Chief Staff G-3, Dept. of Army, 1954-55, asst. chief, then dir. orgn. and tng. div., Office Dep. Chief Staff Operations, 1955-56; comdg. gen. U.S. Army Combat Devel. Expt. Center, Ft. Cid, Cal., 1956-60; comdg. gen. 2d Inf. Div., Ft. Benning, from 1960. Decorated Silver Star, Legion of Merit with oak leaf cluster, Bronze Star with V device with 2 oak leaf clusters. Combat Inf. badge (U.S.); Mil. Cross, 3d class, Order of Lion (Czechoslovakia); Legion of Honor, Fourragere, Croix de Guerre with palm (France); Order of Leopold, Croix de Guerre, Forragere (Belgium). Home: Camp Springs MD Died Sept. 1968.

GIBB, HAMILTON ALEXANDER ROSSKEEN, educator; b. Alexandria, Egypt, Jan. 2, 1895; s. Alexander Crawford and Jane Ann (Gardner) G.; M.A., Edinburgh U., 1919, LL.D., 1952; M.A., London U., 1921, Oxford, 1937; Hon. Dr., U. Algiers, 1943; A.M., Harvard University, 1955, D.Litt. (honorary), 1963; married Helen Jessie Stark, July 12, 1922; children—John A.C., Dorothy S. (Mrs. Edward J. Greenslade). Lectr. Sch. Oriental Studies, 1921-30; prof. Arabic, U. London, 1930-37; Laudian prof. Arabic, U. Oxford, 1937-55; Haskins lectr. U. Chgo., 1945; U. prof., James Richard Jewett prof. Arabic, Harvard,

1955-64. Served as capt., Royal Arty., Brit. Army, 1914-18. Decorated Knight Bachelor (United Kingdom); Comdr. Orange-Nassau (Netherlands); Legion of Honor (France). Fellow Brit. Acad.; corr. fellow Medieval Acad. Am.; hon. fgn. member of the American Acad. Arts and Sciences, American Philosophical Society. Author: The Damascus Chronicle of the Crusades, 1932; Modern Trends in Islam, 1947; (with H. Bowen) Islamic Society and the West, 1950, 57. Died Oct. 22, 1971.

GIBBON, JOHN HEYSHAM, JR., surgeon; b. Phila., Sept. 29, 1903; s. John Heysham and Marjorie (Young) G.; A.B., Princeton, 1923; M.D., Jefferson Med. Coll., 1927, Ph.D.; fellow surgery Harvard, 1930-31, 33-34; fellow surg. research U. Pa., 1936-42; Sc.D., U. Buffalo, Princeton, Dickinson Coll.; m. Mary Hopkinson, Mar. 14, 1931; children—Mary, John, Alice, Marjorie. Intern, Pa. Hosp., 1927-29, cons. surgeon, 1950-73; chief surg. service Mayo Gen. Hosp., 1945; asst. prof. surgery U. Pa., 1945-46; prof. surgery, dir. surg. research Jefferson Med. Coll., 1946-56, Samuel D. Gross prof., head dept. surgery, 1956-67, emeritus prof. surgery, 1967-73. Served as lt. col. M.C., AUS, 1943-46. Recipient Albert Lasker Med. Research award, 1968. Diplomate Am. Bd. Surgery, Am. Bd. Thoracic Surgery. Fellow A.C.S., Royal Coll. Surgeons (Eng.); mem. Am. Surg. Assn. (past pres.), Am. Assn. Thoracic Surgery (past pres.), Soc. Clin. Surgery (past pres.), Phila. Acad. Surgery (past pres.), Heart Assn. Southeastern Pa. (past pres.), Coll. Physicians Phila. (past pres.), Soc. Vascular Surgery (past pres.), A.M.A. Democrat. Contbr. articles to surg. jours. Home: Media PA Died Feb. 5, 1973.

GIBBONS, CHARLES DAVID, transportation exec.; b. Washington, Apr. 18, 1895; s. Charles P. and Caroline B. (Hollingsworth) G.; B.S.C., Benjamin Franklin U., 1930; m. Carolyn B. Gridley, May 17, 1918;children—John David, Janet Carol. Draftsman, USN Dept., bur. of constrn. and repair, Washington, 1913-20; asst. to v.p., budget officer, U.S.S.B. Merchant Fleet Corp., 1921-37, asst. treas., 1932-33, treas., 1933-37; asst. treas. U.S. Lines Co., N.Y.C., 1938-42, treas., dir. 1943-53, v.p., treas., dir., 1953-59, exec. v.p., 1959-60, pres., 1960-61, chmn. finance com., dir., 1961-66, vice chmn. bd., 1966-69. Chmn., director Am. S.S. Owners Mutual Protection and Indemnity Association, New York City, N.Y. Clubs: Propellor (N.Y.C.); India House (N.Y.C.); Maplewood (N.J.) Country. Home: Maplewood NJ Died Aug. 1, 1969.

GIBBONS, EDMUND F., bishop; b. White Plains, N.Y., Sept. 16, 1868; s. James and Joanna (Ray) G.; grad. Niagara U., 1887; study Am. Coll., Rome, Italy, 1887-93. Ordained priest R.C. Ch., 1893; sec. to Bishop Ryan, 1893-96; supt. parish schs., Diocese of Buffalo, 1900-16; pastor St. Teresa's Ch., Buffalo, 1916-19; bishop of Albany, 1919-54. Home: Mater Christi Seminary, 1134 New Scotland Rd., Albany NY‡

GIBBONS, WALTER BERNARD, lawyer; b. Coatsville, Pa., Dec. 19, 1894; s. Patrick Henry and Mary Jane (Bowen) G.; LL.B., Temple U., 1917, LL.D., 1945, J.D., 1968; spl. course U. Pa., St. Joseph Coll.; LL.D., Villanova U., 1960; m. Helen Eustace, Dec. 26, 1918; 1 son, Walter Bernard (dec.). Admitted to Pa. bar 1917, since practiced in Phila.; propr. Donoghue & Gibbons, 1939 (now Gibbons & Obert). Spl. counsel Pa. Turnpike Commn. 1941-51 Chmn., pub. interest dir. Fed. Home Loan Bank Pitts., 1941-65. Chmn. bd. mgrs. House of Detention, 1938-58; mem. Phila. Councilmanic Commn. Commitments and Detentions; commonwealth mem. Southeastern Pa. Transp. Authority, 1964-67; chief standing master bd. governance Supreme Ct. Pa.; permanent mem. Conf. 3d Jud. Dist. U.S. Mem. bd. dirs. Nazareth Hosp., Mercy Catholic Med. Center, Sacred Heart Free Home for Incurable Cancer; trustee Holy Family Coll., Phila. Served as ensign, U.S. Navy, World War I. Mem. Am. Law Inst., Mil. Order Fgn. Wars, Am. Legion, Am. (ho. dels. 1942-44, spl. com. on legal assistance to armed forces 1943-51), Pa., Phila., N.Y. bar assns., Phi Delta Phi. Republican. Roman Catholic. Clubs: Lawyers, Midday, Catholic Philopatrian Literary Inst., Overbrook Farms (past pres.). Author articles legal publs. Home: Philadelphia PA Died Nov. 6, 1972.

GIBBS, CAREY A., clergyman; b. Madison, Fla., Mar. 20, 1892; s. Jack and Lila (Davis) G.; ed. Edward Waters Coll., 1917; B.D., Payne Theol. Sem., 1923; student Wilberforce U.; m. Pennie Simmons; m. 2d, Allthia B. Frazier, Feb. 12, 1962. Ordained to ministry African Meth. Episcopal Ch., 1923; pastor in Fla., 1924-30; pres. Edward Waters Coll., 1930-32; pastor, 1932-48; bishop, from 1948, serving at various times in West Africa, Miss., La., Fla., Ala., West Indies, S. Am., S.C.; past bishop 13th Ky.-Tenn. Episcopal Dist. Former chmn. bd. edn. A.M.E. Ch., past mem. bd. incorporators. Former chmn. bd. trustees Edward Waters Coll., Allen J., Campbell Coll., Daniel Payne Coll. Mem. World Meth. Council, Nat. Council Chs. Mason, Elk. Home: Jacksonville FL

GIBBS, JEANNETTE PHILLIPS, author, lawyer; b. Lynn, Mass., Dec. 23, 1892; d. Benjamin and Clara Elizabeth (Clark) Phillips; A.B., Smith Coll., 1913; LL.B., Boston U., 1917; m. Maj. A. Hamilton Gibbs, Apr. 12, 1919. Practiced law in Boston, 1918-21, later in N.Y. City; mem. Round Table on Internat. Law, Williamstown Inst. of Politics, 1925, 26. Author: Portia Marries, 1926; Humdrum House, 1928; French Leave, 1930; Copy for Mother, 1934. Contbr. to Life, Vogue, New York Times, etc. One of first Am. women who having lost citizenship by marriage, regained it under Cable Act, 1923. Home: Middleboro MA Died Apr. 16, 1969.

GIBSON, CABLE MORGAN, lawyer; b. Nelsonville, O., Aug. 23, 1902; s. William W. and Emma Jane (Morgan) G.; LL.B., Ohio State U., 1924; m. Sally L. Redecker, Nov. 17, 1937. Admitted to Ohio bar, 1925, to U.S. Supreme Ct., 1933; practiced in Columbus, O., 1925-67; sole owner Calbe M. Gibson & Assos..; atty. City Nat. Bank and Trust Co., Columbus, O., 1932-67. Dir., Carl B. King Drilling Co., Midland, Tex., W. W. Investment Co., Cin., Court Investment Co., Cin., Gem. Coal Co., Nelsonville, O., Chevrolet agys. in Columbus, Cin., Cleve., Chgo. Mem. Am., Ohio, Columbus bar assns., Phi Alpha Delta, Delta Chi. Clubs: Columbus Country, Athletic (Columbus); Delaware (O.) Country. Home: Columbus OH Died Dec. 22, 1967.

GIBSON, ERNEST WILLIAM, judge; b. Brattleboro, Vt., Mar. 6, 1901; s. Ernest Willard and Grace Fullerton (Hadley) G.; A.B., Norwich U., 1923; student George Washington Law Sch., 1924-27; m. Dorothy P. Switzer, Oct. 9, 1926 (dec. Aug. 1958); children—Ernest Willard III, Grace, Robert Hadley, David Alan; m. 2d, Ann H. Haag, Jan. 21, 1961. Teacher and track coach N.Y. Mil. Acad., Cornwall-on-Hudson, N.Y., 1923-24; mathematician Coast and Geodetic Survey, 1924-27; admitted to Vt. bar, 1926, practiced law, Brattleboro, Vt., from 1927; sr. partner Gibson, Gibson & Crispe. Elected States' Atty. of Windham Co., Vt., 1928, 30; asst. sec. Vt. State Senate, 1931-33; sec., 1933-40; resigned to serve appointment in U.S. Senate on death of father; mem. Railroad Tax Commn. of Vermont, 1939-40; governor of Vt. 1947-50, resigned to accept appointment as Fed. Dist. Judge for Dist. of Vt., 1950. Elected national chairman of Com. to Defend America by Aiding the Allies, Jan. 9, 1941, succeeding William Allen White. Entered Army as captain, May 19, 1941, served overseas with combat div., September 1942 to January 1944; col., G.S.C., duty War Dept.; disch. Dec. 25, 1945. Decorated Silver Star, Legion of Merit, Purple Heart, War Dept. Citation medals. Mem. Vt. Bar Assn., Phi Delta Phi, Theta Chi. Republican. Episcopalian. Mason, Odd Fellow, Elk. Home: Brattleboro VT Died Nov. 4, 1969.

GIBSON, FINLEY F., clergyman; b. at Hope, Ark., Aug. 29, 1876; s. Arthur Alexander and Mattie R. (Powell) G.; A.B., Quachita Bapt. Coll., 1897, D.D., 1912; Th.M., Southern Bapt. Theol. Sem., 1900; m. Lucille L. Foreman, Apr. 18, 1901; children—Finley Forman, William Oscar. Ordained Bapt. ministry, 1900; pastor Malvern, Ark., 1900-02, 1st Ch., Ft. Smith, Ark., 1902-16, 1st Ch., Bowling Green Ky., 1916-18, Grace St. Ch., Richmond, Va., 1918-19, Walnut St. Church, Louisville, Ky., October 1, 1919-Sept. 30, 1941, pastor emeritus since Oct. 1, 1941. Trustee Foreign Mission Bd. Southern Bapist Conv.; former Trustee Southwestern Theol. Sem., Southern Bapt. Theol. Sem., Home Mission Bd., Ouachita Bapt. Coll. Mason. Preacher annual sermon before Southern Bapt. Conv., 1924. Home: Spring Hill Farm, R. 1, Anchorage KY‡

GIBSON, J(OHN) J(OSEPH), business exec.; b. Brentwood, N.Y., June 16, 1910; s. John James and Lavonne Jeannette (Cushman) G.; A.B., Williams Coll., 1931; LL.B., Harvard, 1934; m. Cornelia Vanderveer, Apr. 14, 1934; 1 son, John Vanderveer. Admitted to N.Y. bar, 1935, practiced as asso. Greene & Hurd, and its successor, Hurd, Hamlin & Hubbell, N.Y.C., 1934-41; sec. Johnson & Johnson, New Brunswick, N.J., 1943-58, v.p., 1958-70, dir., 1945-70, exec. com., 1968-70, general counsel, 1954-67, treasurer, 1967-69; member board of directors State Bank of Suffolk, Bay Shore, N.Y., 1934-57, pres., 1943-56, chmn. bd., 1956-57; director Franklin National Bank of Long Island. Chairman of Islip Town Planning Bd., 1954-57. Mem. N.Y. State Bar Assn., Assn. Bar City of N.Y., Am. Bar Assn., Assn. Gen. Counsel. Home: Bay NY Died June 7, 1971; buried Greenwood Cemetery.

GIBSON, TRUMAN KELLA, life ins. co. exec.; b. Macon, Ga., Aug. 5, 1882; A.B., Atlanta U.; A.B., Harvard; D.Bus. Adminstrn. (hon.), Central State Coll.; L.H.D., Atlanta U.; m. Alberta Dickerson (dec.); children—Truman Kella, Harry H.C., Alberta Marshall. Organizer Fireside Mut. of Ohio, Supreme Life & Casualty of Ohio; hon. chmn. bd. Supreme Life Ins. Co. Am., Chgo.; ins. cons. Pres. Moton Meml. Found., Gloucester, Va.; v.p. Chgo. Burr Oak Cemetery Assn. Recipient Harmon award. Mem. Chgo. Assn. Commerce and Industry, Sigma Pi Phi, Alpha Phi Alpha. Club: City (Chgo.). Home: Chicago IL Died Sept. 19, 1972.

GIEDION, SIEGFRIED, b. Longran, Switzerland, Apr. 14, 1893; s. John and Bertha (Jacobs) G.; Dr. phil., U. Munich; m. Carola Welcher; children—Verena (Mrs. Paffard Keating Clay) Andreas. Charles Elliot Norton prof. Harvard, 1938-39; prof. Fed. Inst. Tech., 1947-58; Mellon lectr. Washington Nat. Gallery, 1957. Author: Space and Time, 1941; Mechanization Takes Command, 1948; The Eternal Present; The Beginning of Art, 1962; The Beginnings of Architecture, 1964. Home: Zurich Switzerland Died Apr. 1968.

GIELNIAK, JOZEF, graphic artist; b. Denain, France, Feb. 18, 1932; s. Stanislaw and Anna (Tejsar) G.; B., U. Paris, 1949; m. Daniela Grazyna Manke, Sept. 12, 1956; 1 son, Jozef-Mirostaw. Works exhibited pub., pvt. collections, Europe, Mus. Modern Art, Library of Congress. U.S.A., 1959-72. Awarded II class State medal, 1964; Thousand Year medal, 1966; knight Cross Revival of Poland, 1968. Mem. Xylon. Works include cycles of lino-engravings. Home: Kowary Poland Died May 28, 1972.

GIESE, HERMAN ROBERT, hardware mfg. co. exec.; b. Denver, Oct. 13, 1904; s. Herman August and Louise (Schlacks) G.; B.S. in Mech. Engring., U. Colo., 1925; M.B.A., Harvard, 1927; m. Margaret Reimers, Oct. 3, 1936; 1 dau., Joan (Mrs. Frank Kenna, Jr.). Prodn. mgr. Stewart-Warner Corp., Chgo., 1932-36; works mgr. Wurlitzer Corp., DeKalb, Ill., 1936-38, Hoosier Cardinal Corp., Evansville, Ind., 1938-42; with Sargent & Co., New Haven, 1942-68, exec. v.p., 1958-62, pres 1962-68, also dir.; dir. First New Haven National Bank; mem. bd. trustees Conn. Savs. Bank. Bd. dirs. Grace New Haven Community Hosp. Mem. Conn. Mfg. Assn. (past dir.), New Haven C. of C. (past pres.), Phi Delta Theta, Sigma Tau. Home: Madison CT Died Nov. 2, 1968; buried New Haven CT

GIESECKE, FREDERICK ERNEST, engineer; b. Washington County, Tex., Jan. 28, 1869; s. Julius and Wilhelmine (Groos) G.; M.E., Tex. A. and M., Coll., 1890; student Cornell, 1893-94; S.B. Architecture, Mass. Inst. Tech., 1904; student Tech. Hochschule, Charlottenburg, 1906-07; Ph.D., Univ. of Ill., 1924, C.E., 1943; m. Hulda C. Gruene, Mar. 5, 1891; children—Bertram E., Alma (Mrs. McCloud B. Hodges,) Linda (Mrs. Preston M. Geren), Minnie (Mrs. Edward A. Wight). Instr. in shop work and drawing, Tex. A. and M. Coll., 1886-88, prof. of drawing 1888-1906, prof. of archtl. engring., 1906-12; prof. archtl. engring., head div. engr. research, Univ. of Tex., 1912-27; dir. expt. sta. and coll. architect, Tex. A and M. Coll., 1927-39, prof. emeritus, 1939-45; cons. engr., New Braunfels, Tex., since 1945. Served as maj. engr. reserves, U.S., 1926-42. Awarded the F. Paul Anderson medal by Am. Soc. Heating and Ventilating Engrs., 1942. Mem. Am. Soc. E.E. (charter and life mem.), Am. Soc. C.E. (life mem., past pres. Tex. sect.), Am. Soc. Heating and Ventilating Engrs. (life mem., past pres. Tex. chapter, nat. pres. 1940), Am. Soc. M.E., A.A.A.S., Am. Soc. Engring. Edn., (past pres. Tex. chapter), Tau Beta Pi, Sigma Xi. Mason (32 deg.). Author: Gravity-Circulation Hot-Water Heating Systems, 1926; Descriptive Geometry and Descriptive Geometry Problems (with A. Mitchell), 1921; Technical Drawing and Technical Drawing Problems (with A. Mitchell and H. C. Spencer), 1933; Hot-Water Heating, Radiant Heating, and Radiant Cooling, 1947. Contbr. about 75 tech. articles in engring. pubs. and bulls. Home: New Braunfels TX*‡

GIESECKE, FRIEDERICH ERNST, educator; b. Washington Co., Tex., Jan. 28, 1869; s. Julius and Wilhelmine (Groos) G.; ed. New Braunfels (Tex.) Acad., San Antonio German-English Sch., Agr'l & Mech. Coll., of Texas, grad., 1886, post-grad., M. E., 1890; Cornell Univ., summers, 1893, 1894, Mass. Inst. Technology, summer, 1898, and grad. dept. architecture, B. S., 1904; m. New Braunfels, Tex., Mar. 5, 1891, Hulda C. Gruene. Prof. drawing, in charge Dept. of Drawing, in Agr'l and Mech. Coll. of Texas since 1888. Mem. Soc. Promotion Eng'ring Ed'n, Texas Acad. Science. Author: Mechanical Drawing, Part I, 1903; Part II, 1904 A7. Address: College Station TX‡

GIFFORD, L. C., newspaper pub.; b. Russiaville, Ind., Aug. 5, 1886; s. John T. and Clara Belle (Francis) G.; A.B., Ind. U., 1910; L.H.D., Lenoir Rhyne Coll., 1966; m. Mildred R. Johnson, Dec. 30, 1915; children—Suzanne (Mrs. Kenneth K. Millholland), Sara Lee (dec.). Instr. U. Cin., 1909-10; tchr. Champaign (Ill.) High Sch., 1910-12; editor Western Newspaper Union, Mpls., 1912-15; editor, pub. Seymour (Ind.) Daily Democrat, 1915-19, Kokomo (Ind.) Dispatch, 1919-29, Daily Record, Hickory, N.C., 1929-69; pres., dir. Hickory Engraving Co.; dir. Hyalyn Porcelain Inc., Hickory Devel. Corp.; v.p., dir. Catawba Valley Radio Corp. Vice pres. N.C. Symphony Soc., mem. Gov.'s Higher Edn. Commn., N.C. Ret. Commn. Mem. Afternoon Dailies N.C., N.C. Press Assn. (past pres.), Am., So. newspaper pubs. assn., Nat. Screen Council, Am. Soc. Newspaper Editors, Delta Tau Delta Sigma Hickory NC Died July 7, 1969.

GIFFORD, WILLIAM LOGAN RODMAN, librarian b. New Bedford, Mass., Nov. 5, 1862; s. Humphrey Almy and Alice Peckham (Francis) G.; A.B., Harvard 1884; m. Eleanor Richardson Dexter (dec.), June 6 1888; children—Catherine (dec.), Humphrey Almy (dec.). Asst. librarian, New Bedford Free Public Library, 1884-95; librarian, Cambridge (Mass.) Pub Library, 1895-1904; librarian St. Louis Mercantile Library, 1904-41, librarian emeritus since May 1, 1941 Home: 411 N. Newstead Av., St Louis MO‡

GIGNILLIAT, LEIGH R(OBINSON), JR., banker; b. Culver, Ind., May 13, 1899; s. Leigh R. and Mary Seddon (Fleet) G.; grad. Culver Mil. Acad., 1917; B.S., Princeton, 1922; m. Charlotte H. Ditt, June 20, 1927; children—Leigh Robinson III, Paul Charles, Charlotte Susan. Trainee, asst. to mgr. mortgage loan dept. Depositors Trust & Savs. Bank, Akron, O., 1923-26; asst. editor, then editor Porter Langtry Corp., Chgo., 1926-34; dept. adminstr. FHA, Washington, 1934-37; sales exec. Comml. Investment Trust, Inc., N.Y.C., 1937-39; asst. v.p. Am. Nat. Bank & Trust Company, Chgo., 1939-41, vice president, 1961-62, sr. vice president, 1962-64; v.p. Glore Forgan, Wm. R. Staats, Inc., Chgo., 1965-72; dir. Martin Marietta Corp., N.Y.C., Nat. Home Corp., Lafayette, Ind., Home Owner Insurance Co., Chgo. Bd. dirs. Culver Ednl. Found., Chgo. Boys Clubs. Mem. Indiana Soc. Chgo. (pres.), Culver Alumni Assn. (pres.), Chgo. Assn. Commerce and Industry (dir. 1949-57). Clubs: Chicago, University (Chgo.); Westmorland Country (Wilmette, Ill.). Author: Bank Loans on Life Insurance Policies; Term Loans and Revolving Credits. Home: Chicago IL Died May 1972.

GIGNILLIAT, LEIGH ROBINSON, educator; b. Savannah, Ga., July 4, 1875; s. William Robert and Harriet (Heyward) G.; grad. Emerson Inst., Washington, 1891, Va. Mil. Inst., Lexington, Va., 1895; M.A., Trinity Coll., 1915; Sc.D. from Colgate U., 1931; LL.D., Kenyon Coll., Gambier, O., 1935; m. Mary Seddon Fleet, Aug. 2, 1898;children—Leigh Robinson, Frederick Fleet, Henry Culver. Asst. engr. boundary line location Yellowstone Nat. Park, 1896. Comdt. Cadets, Culver Mil. Acad., 1897-1910, supt. 1910-39; pres. The Culver Ednl. Foundation 1939-42, now pres. emeritus. Coordinator, Fort Worth, Tex., area for engring. science and management War Training, 1942-45. Apptd. consultant to Secretary of War, 1941. Commd. major R.C., 1916; lt. col. 1st O.T.C., Ft. Benjamin Harrison, Aug. 1917; sr. instr. 2nd O.T.C.; apptd. Gen. Staff, A.E.F., Sept. 1918; commd. col. Feb. 1919, brig.-gen. organized reserves, Nov. 24, 1911; comdg. 168th Inf. Brigade, Reserves, 1921-39. Am. rep. Interallied Mil. Commn., Hq. Army Occupation, Coblenz, Germany, Mar.-July 1919. Pres. Private Sch. Assn. of Central States, 1913-14. Mem. Nat. Council Boy Scouts America; in comd. 300 Am. reps. at Internat. Council Boy Scouts Jamboree, London, 1920. Comdr. Dept. Ind. Am. Legion, 1920-21; mem. Am. delegation Interallied Vets'. Congress, New Orleans, 1922, Brussels, 1923, London, 1924; chmn. Am. delegation to Congress Interallied Veterans, Rome, Italy, 1925, Warsaw, 1926, Paris, 1927, Bucharest, 1929, Washington, D.C., 1930. Mem. Soc. Colonial Wars, Huguenot Society, S.C., Mil. Order World War, Mil. Order Foreign Wars, Association Military Colleges and Schools (president 1927-28), St. Fidac (vice-pres. 1927-28). Awarded D.S.M. (U.S.); Comdr. Legion of Honor (French); Knight Comdr. Order of Nicham Iftikar (Tunis); Comdr. Order of the Star (Rumania); Comdr. Order of Polonia Restituta (Poland), Order of the Crown (Italy). Clubs: Army and Navy (Washington, D.C.); Fort Worth (Fort Worth, Tex.). Author: Arms and the Boy. Home: Blackstone Hotel, Fort Worth TX*‡

GIHON, ALBERT DAKIN, artist; b. Portsmouth, N.H., Feb. 16, 1876; s. Med. Dir. A. L. (U.S.N.) and Clara de Montfort (Campfield) G. pupil of Thomas Eakins, Phila., Benjamin Constant, Jean-Paul Laurens, Gerome, A.T.G. Motley an Ecole des Arts Decoratifs. Awarded Diplome d'Honneur, Expn. Internationale, Bordeaux, France, 1927. For details see Vol. 13 (1924-25). Studio: 59 Av. de Saxe, Paris France‡

GILBER, JAMES HENRY, prof. economics; b. Erwin, Tenn., Mar. 9, 1878; s. Isaac Wilson and Nancy (Clouse) G.; A.B., U. of Ore., 1903; Ph.D., Columbia, 1907; m. Isolene Shaver, June 28, 1911; children—Madeleine, Robert Wilson (dec.), Walter M. With U. of Ore., 1907-47, prof. economics, 1945-47, acting dean Coll. of Literature, Sciences and the Arts, 1925-27, dean, 1927-32, dean Coll. of Social Sci., 1932-42; dean of Liberal Arts Coll., 1942-47. Economic adviser Ore. Tax Investigating Com., 1922-23; mem. Spl. Legis. Com. on Taxation of Municipal Utilities, 1932-33; mem. State advisory com. on Public Works Administrn., 1933-34; spl. rep. U.S. Employment Service, Merit Exam, Ore., 1935; mem. Legislative Interim Commn. on Taxation and Industry, 1941-42. Mem. Pacific Coast Economic Assn., Phi Beta Kappa, Baptist. Clubs: Rotary, Round Table. Author: Trade and Currency in Early Oregon, 1907; Tax Systems of Australasia, 1943. Home: Eugene OR Died Sept. 13, 1972.

GILBERT, ARTHUR HILL, artist; b. Mt. Vernon, Ill., June 10, 1894; s. Tilmon Irving and Mae (Hill) G.; graduate Evanston (Ill.) Acad., 1913; student Northwestern University, 1914-15, Sch. of Commerce, 1916, University of California, 1942-44; grad. Res. Officers Sch., U.S. Naval Acad., 1917; art education, Otis Art Inst., Los Angeles, Paris, London, N.Y. City; m. Audine Abbott, Oct. 18, 1932. Awarded hon. mention, Painters of the West, 1926; Jules Hallgarten prize, Nat. Acad. Design, N.Y. City, 1928, J. Francis Murphy Memorial prize, 1929, Henry Ward Ranger Bequest 1,000 prize and purchase, 1930. Pictures in collections of Wm. Randolph Hearst (Los Angeles), F.N. Southam (Montreal, Can.), Edmond Coblentz (New York), Nat. Acad., New York, etc. Served as lt. j.g. U.S. Navy, overseas service, 1917-19. Coordinator Monterey County Civilian Defense Council, 1942, 43. Mem. Nat. Acad. Design, Carmel (Calif.) Art Assn. (past pres.), Sigma Chi. Club: Bohemian (San Francisco). Home: Stockton CA Died Apr. 28, 1970; buried Casa Bonita Mausoleum, Stockton CA

GILBERT, EDWARD MARTINIUS, prof. botany; b. Blair, Wis., Sept. 20, 1875; s. Thomas J. and Julia (Jahr) G.; grad. Normal Sch., Stevens Point, Wis., 1901; Ph.B., U. of Wis., 1907, Ph.D., 1914; m. Esther Montogomery Lowry, June 15, 1910; children—Jane, Thomas Lowry, Edward Everett. Teacher biology, State Normal Sch., Superior, Wis., 1907-10; with U. of Wis. since 1912 as asst. prof. botany to 1917, prof. botany, 1923-46, emeritus, 1946. Mem. Botanical Society of America, American Phytopathol. Society, American Microscopical Society, Wisconsin, Academy Science, Am. Mycol. Soc., Am. Society Taxonomists, Sigma Xi, Gamma Alpha, Phi Sigma. Club: University. Joint Author: Text-book of Botany for High Schools (with C.E. Allen), 1915; Text-book of General Botany (with Allen, Bryan, Duggar, Evans and Smith), 1924, new edit., 1943. Home: 2120 Chamberlain St., Madison WI‡

GILBERT, FREDERICK SPOFFORD, publisher; b. N.Y.C., May 29, 1912; s. James S. and Grace (Hodson) G.; grad. Lawrenceville (N.J.) Sch., 1930; A.B., Williams College, Williamstown, Mass., 1934; m. Annis Burnham Stearns, November 26, 1937 (dec. July 20, 1957); children—Frederick Spofford, Timothy A., J. Malcolm, Annis Kendall; m. 2d, Clara Locke Warren, Sept. 10, 1960. With Time, Inc., N.Y.C., 1935-70, March of Time (movie), 1935-37, advt. salesman, Time mag., Life, Cleve., 1939-41, br., mgr., Life, Cleve. br., 1941-46, advt. mgr., internat. edition, Life, 1946-48, asst. pub. Time, 1948-53, gen. mgr., 1953-60, gen. mgr. broadcasting div., 1960-70; member board directors Time Life Broadcast, Inc.; mem. bd. Selling Areas-Marketing, Inc. Clubs: Burning Tree Country (Washington); Williams (N.Y.C.); New Canaan Country. Home: New Canaan CT Died July 17, 1970.

GILBERT, JOSEPH OSCAR, newspaper editor, publisher; b. Ste. Anne de Beaupre, P.Q., Can., Nov. 22, 1888; s. Joseph Ludger and Malvina (Lappe) G.; B.A., Laval U., 1908, Master in Polit. Economy; D.S.C.; m. Alice Lamonde, May 17, 1915; 3 sons, Andre, Gabriel, Guy; 5 daus., now mesdames Euclide Bisson Jacques Waquant, Eric Morisette, John Brochu, Pierre Barry. Pres. Le Soleil and L'Evenement-Journal, dailies, 1948-71; pres. Hotel St. Roch, Incorporated; director Banque de Quebec; gov. faculty commerce Laval U. Mem. Nat. Battlefields Commn. Hon. comdr. La Salle contingent, affiliated Royal 22d Regt. Mem. The Canadian Press Quebec Safety League, Bd. of Trade, Retail Mchts. Assn. Clubs: Quebec Automobile (dir.), Garrison. Home: Quebec CAN Died Apr. 1971.

GILBERT, L(OUIS) WOLFE, author, song writer; b. Odessa, Russia, Aug. 31, 1886 s. Alfred and Mar (Palma) G.; brought to U.S., 1886, derivative citizen; student pub. schs., Phila.; m. Rose Hirshfield, Mar. 7, 1939; children—Ethel (Mrs. Philip Bakerman), Ruth (Mrs. Tony Pereira), Doris, Robert W., Ellen. Columnist for N.Y. Clipper, theatrical paper, 1908-10; vaudeville headliner, 1912-35; writer of songs including: Waiting for the Robert E. Lee, Ramona, The Peanut Vender, Jeannine, I Dream of Lilac Time, Down Yonder, Lucky Lindy, others. Mem. A.S.C.A.P. (dir.). Home: Beverly Hills CA Died July 12, 1970; buried Hillside Memorial Park and Mausoleum.

GILBERT, ROBERT RANDLE, banking; b. Paducah, Ky., Aug. 10, 1888; s. Frank and Alice (Wilhelm) G.; ed. pub. schs., Paducah and Dallas, Tex.; m. Grace Gray, Apr. 5, 1910; children—Robert Randle, Mitch Gray. Began with John Deere Plow Co., Dallas, 1903; in employ Gaston Nat. Bank, Dallas, 1905-08; with Guaranty State Bank & Trust Co., Dallas, 1908-14, advancing to asst. cashier; with Federal Reserve Bank of Dallas, 1914-53, served in various ofcl. capacities and was elected pres. 1939; chmn. bd. Nat. City Bank of Dallas, 1953-54 (bank consol. with Republic Nat. Bank of Dallas); vice chmn. bd. Republic Nat. Bank of Dallas, 1954-62; dir. mem. exec. and investment coms. United Fidelity Life Insurance Co., Dallas. Member Federal Open Market Com., 1942-43, 45-46, 48-49, 51-52; vice chmn. Conf. of Presidents of Fed. Res. Banks. 1952-53; mem. bd. trustees Retirement System of Fed. Res. Banks, 14 yrs., chmn. bd., 1950-51. Hon. life dir. Dallas Community Chest, pres. 1944; dir. Dallas chpt. A.R.C., 1954-57; board directors, v.p. Dallas Legal Aid Soc. Mem. exec. com. bd. of development, So. Meth. U.; v.p., mem. executive com. Southwestern Legal Found.; trustee Southwest Bus. Found., Ft. Worth. Mem. Dallas C. of C. (dir. 1954-56), Dallas Hist. Soc. (trustee, chmn. exec. com.), Tex. Bur. for Econ. Understanding (trustee, v.p.), Philos. Soc. Tex. Methodist. Mason (32 degree, Shriner). Clubs: Dallas, Dallas Country (dir. 1935-37, pres. 1937), Town & Gown (Dallas). Home: Dallas TX Died July 7, 1971.

GILBERT, VEDDER MORRIS, educator; b. Amsterdam, N.Y., May 12, 1914; s. Archibald M. and Anna E. (Morris) G.; A.B., Union Coll., N.Y., 1936; postgrad. Montpellier U. (France). 1936-37; M.A., Cornell U., 1938, Ph.D., 1952; m. Gertrude Gile Hosford, Feb. 12, 1944; children—Lindley Anne, Abigail Morris. Instr., U. Mo., 1938-44; grad. asst. Cornell U., 1944-46; asst. prof. U. Toledo, 1946-51; asst. prof. U. Mont., Missoula, 1952-55, Danforth asso., 1954-59, asso. prof., 1955-58, prof., 1958-73, chmn. dept. English, 1957-62, fgn. student adviser, 1957-73, coordinator humanities, 1966-67. Actor, summer stock, 1958-73. Participant, Nat. Assn. Fgn. Student Affairs Seminar, France, 1964; active Peace Corps liaison, 1960-65; co-founder Glastonbury Assn.; del Missoula County Ednl. Council, 1957-60. Past pres. P.T.A. unit. Pres. bd. dirs. Missoula-Mineral County chpt. A.R.C. Mem. Rocky Mountain Modern Lang. Assn. (past pres.), Mont. English Council, Modern Lang. Assn., Council Tchrs. English, Coll. English Assn., Buckinghamshire Arhchaeol. Soc., Johnson Soc. N.W., Psi Upsilon, Phi Delta Phi (asso. charter). Episcopalian (vestryman). Kiwanian. Contbr. articles to profl. jours. Home: Missoula MT Died Jan. 25, 1973.

GILBREATH, SIDNEY GORDON, president normal school; b. Monroe Co., Tenn., Apr. 13, 1869; s. James Asbury and Elizabeth (Brunner) G.; B.S., Hiwassee Coll., 1891; m. Norma Lavinia Henley, Feb. 9, 1893. Co. supt. schs., 1891-5; pres. Hiwassee Coll., 1893-5; state supt. schs., Tenn., 1895-7; pres. Hiwassee Coll., 1897-9; prof. physiology and sch. hygiene, Peabody Normal Coll., 1899-1902; prof. sch. administration, Peabody Coll. for Teachers (U. of Nashville), 1902-3; supt. city schs., Chattanooga, Tenn., 1903-10; pres. E. Tenn. State Normal Sch., 1910—. Mem. Tenn. State Bd. Edn., 1895-99; state inst. conductor, 1899-1907. Pres. Tenn. State Teachers' Assn., 1897-8. Pub. Sch. Officers' Assn., 1910, Southern Conf. for Edn. and Industry, 1916-17. Address: Johnson City TN‡

GILBREATH, W(ILLIAM) SYDNOR, JR., investment banker; b. Chgo., May 9, 1895; s. William Sydnor and Minnie (Schaff) G.; A.B., U. Wis., 1918; m. Marian Dickens, Apr. 29, 1922; children—Marion Dickens (Mrs. Robt. T. Skinner), Nan (Mrs. James M. Chandler), William S. III. With Nat. City Co., New York City, Chicago, 1920-21, Security Trust Company, and Detroit Trust Company, First of Michigan Corp., (predecessor firm First Detroit Co.), Detroit, 1930-72, pres., dir., 1943-63, chmn. bd., 1963-72; director of the Schaff Piano String Company. Member of New York Stock Exchange; associate member of the American Stock Exchange, Vice chairman Mich. War Finance Com., World War II. Mem. Wayne County Republican Finance Com., 1955-60. Bd. dirs. Cranbrook Sch., Bloomfield Hills, Mich., 1948-57; trustee Cranbrook Found., James and Lynelle Holden Fund, The Mary Louise Johnson Found. Member of Investment Bankers Assn. Am. (gov. 1945-48), Nat. Assn. Securities Dealers (gov. 1942-43), Newcomen Soc., Sigma Chi. P.E. Ch. (trustee of Diocese Mich.). Clubs: Yondotega, Analysts, Economic, Bond, Detroit (dir. 1956-61, pres. 1960-61) (Detroit); Orchard Lake (Mich.) Country (treas. 1940); Bloomfield Hills (Mich.) Country. Home: Birmingham MI Died Dec. 24, 1969; buried Greenwood Cemetery, Birmingham MI

GILBRETH, LILLIAN MOLLER, cons. engr.; b. Oakland, Calif., May 24, 1878; d. William and Annie (Delger) Moller; B.Litt., U. of Calif., 1900, M.Litt., 1902, LL.D., 1933; Ph.D., Brown, 1915, Sc.D., 1931; M. Engring., U. Mich., 1928; Dr. Engring., Rutgers Coll., 1929, Stevens Inst. Tech., 1950, Syracuse U., 1952; Sc.D., Russell Sage Coll., 1931, Colby Coll., 1951, Lafayette Coll., 1952; LL.D., Smith Coll., 1945, Mills Coll., 1952; Dr. Humane Letters, Temple U., 1949, Alfred U., 1948; Dr. Indsl. Psychol., Purdue U., 1948, hon. degrees from Milw. Downer, Washington Univ., Princeton, Skidmore Coll., U. Wis., Pratt Inst., U. Mass., Western Coll. Women; Doctor of Laws, Arizona State Univ., 1964; m. Frank Bunker Gilbreth, October 19, 1904; children—Anne Moller (Mrs. Robert E. Barney), Mary Elizabeth (dec.), Ernestine Moller (Mrs. Charles E. Carey), Martha Bunker (Mrs. Richard E. Tallman) (dec.), Frank Bunker, William Moller, Lillian Moller (Mrs. Donald D. Johnson), Frederick Moller, Daniel Bunker, John Moller, Robert Moller, Jane Moller (Mrs. G. Paul Heppes, Jr.). Pres. of Gilbreth, Inc., cons. engrs. in mgmt., Montclair, N.J., from 1924; dir. courses in motion study, 1925-32; prof. mgmt. Purdue U., 1935-48; chmn. dept. of personnel relations Newark Coll. Engring., 1941-43; univ. teaching P.I., Formosa, 1953-54; prof. mgmt. U. Wis., 1955; lectr. on tech. and human relations problems in mgmt. in Asia, Australia, Can., Europe, Mexico, U.S.A., from 1955. Mem. U.S. Govt. coms. on civil def., also state and local coms. Trustee Russell Sage Coll., 1943-45, Montclair Library, 1944-54; mem. Essex County Vocational Bd. Recipient Henry Lawrence Gantt medal (with Frank Gilbreth), Nat. Inst. Social Scis., Wallace Clark International award, gold medal Comite Internat. de l'Orgn. Scientifique, Washington award; Allan R. Cullimore medal, 1959; Hoover medal American Society Civil Engrs., 1966. Mem. Housing Com., 20th Century Fund; mem. N.J. State Bd. Regents, 1929-33; mem. Essex Co. Vocational Bd. Hon. fellow British

Institute of Management, 1951; member American Association University Women, American Management Assn. (hon.), Institute of Management, Soc. for Advancement of Management (hon.), Acad. Masaryk, Am. Psychol. Assn., A.S.M.E. (hon. mem. 1950), Engring. Inst. Can. (hon. mem. 1949), Am. Home Econs. Assn. (honorary member 1952), Soc. Indsl. Engrs. (hon.), Inst. for Scientific Management of Poland, Women's Engring. Soc. of London. Nat. Acad. Engring., Internat. Acad. of Mgmt., Phi Beta Kappa. Author: (with Frank B. Gilbreth) Fatigue Study, 1911. Applied Motion Study, 1917, Motion Study for the Handicapped, 1919; The Psychology of Management, 1921; Living with Our Children, 1928; Normal Lives for the Disabled (with Edna Yost), 1945; The Foreman and Manpower Management (with Alice Rice Cook), 1947; Management in the Home (with O.M. Thomas, Eleanor C. Clymer), 1954, 59. Contbr. Indsl. Engring. Handbook. Home: Upper Montclair NJ also Nantucket MA Died Jan. 2, 1972.

GILCHRIST, JACK CECIL, educator; b. Birmingham, Ala., June 7, 1918; s. James Cecil and Ellen (Norton) G.; B.S., U. Cal. at Los Angeles, 1945, Ph.D., 1950; m. Breta Nissen, Nov. 8, 1941; children—James Carl, McKay, John Henry. Asst. prof. psychology U. Ark., 1948-50; faculty U. Wis., 1950-68, prof. psychology, 1959-68, chmn. dept., 1959-62. Served to capt. AUS, 1940-45. Fellow Am. Psychol. Assn.; mem. Psychonomic Soc., Sigma Xi. Home: Madison WI Died Aug. 12, 1968.

GILCHRIST, JOHN RAYMOND, former air force officer, financial mgmt. exec.; b. Woonsocket, R.I., May 18, 1906; s. John S. and Alice (Talbot) G.; B.S., U.S. Mil. Acad., 1928; grad. Indsl. Coll. Armed Forces, 1948; m. Mabel Moran, Nov. 7, 1930; children—Carole Jean (Mrs. Kimbrough S. Bassett), John Raymond, Robert Michael. Commd. 2d lt. U.S. Army, 1928, advanced through grades to maj. gen., 1952; chief operations Office Chief Finance, 1941-42; chief fgn. fiscal affairs War Dept., 1942-43; chief finance div. German country unit Hdqrs. SHAEF, 1944; dep. dir. econs. div. U.S. Group Control Coun. for Germany, 1944-45; alternate U.S. mem. econ. div. Allied Control Council for Germany, 1945; rep. Sec. War, Reparations Mission to Japan, 1945; chief econs. and supply br. Civil Affairs Div., War Dept. Spl. staff, 1945-47; chief projects Logistics Div., Army Gen. Staff, 1948; dep. dir. finance USAF, 1948-52; comdg. gen. AF Finance Center, 1950-52; dir. finance USAF, 1952-56, asst. comptroller USAF, comdg. gen. Air Force Finance Center, Denver, 1957, ret.; adminstrv. v.p. for orgn. planning and devel. Tidewater Oil Co., 1957-58; adminstrv. v.p., dir. Financial Indsl. Fund Mgmt. Corp., Denver, FIF Assos., Inc.; exec. v.p., dir. Financial Programs, Inc.; dir. Financial Assurance, Inc., Financial Trust Co.; v.p. Financial Indsl. Fund, Financial Indsl. Income Fund, Financial Dynamics Fund, Financial Venture Fund. Decorated D.S.M., Legion of Merit. Clubs: Army and Navy Country (Washington); Denver; Columbine Country (Littleton, Colo.). Home: Littleton CO

GILKEY, CHARLES WHITNEY, clergyman; b. Watertown, Mass., July 3, 1882; s. James Henry and Mary Lottie (Johnson) G.; A.B., Harvard, 1903, A.M., 1904; student sec., Internat. Com. Y.M.C.A., 1903-05; B.D., Union Theol. Sem., 1908; univs. of Berlin and Marburg, 1908-09; United Free Ch. Coll., Glasgow, New College, Edinburg, and Oxford University 1909-10; D.D. from Williams College, 1925, Hillsdale College, 1925, Yale, 1927, Brown, 1928, Harvard, 1929, Colby College, 1930, Oberlin, 1946; L.H.D., Beloit Coll., 1944; m. Geraldine Gunsaulus Brown, July 26, 1915; children—Mary Jane, Langdon Brown. Ordained Bapt. ministry 1910; pastor Hyde Park Baptist Ch., Chicago, 1910-28; prof. preaching U. of Chicago Div. Sch., 1926-47; dean of the chapel, Univ. of Chicago, 1928-47; associate dean, Univ. of Chicago Div. School, 1938-47. Lecturer on homiletics, Andover Newton Theol. Sch., since 1948. Univ. preacher at Harvard, Yale, Princeton, Cornell, Chicago, Toronto, Wellesley, Stanford, Purdue, Etc. Apptd. by U. of Chicago Barrows lecturer to university centres of India, 1924-25. Trustee U. of Chicago, 1919-29, George Williams Coll., 1929-68, Union Theol. Sem. 1945-68; Harvard Bd. Overseers, 1946-48. Member Phi Beta Kappa. Author: Barrows lectures—Jesus and Our Generation, 1925; New Frontiers for Faith, 1926; Cole lectures at Vanderbilt U.—Present-Day Dilemmas in Religion, 1927; Perspectives, 1933. Home: South Yarmouth MA Died Mar. 24, 1968.

GILKYSON, (THOMAS) WALTER, writer; b. Phoenixville, Pa., Dec. 18, 1880; s. Hamilton Henry and Eleanor (Trego) G.; A.B., Swarthmore (Pa.) Coll., 1901, A.M., 1904; LL.B., U. of Pa., 1908; m. Bernice Kenyon, June 11, 1927. In civ. service, Philippine Islands, 1901-03; admitted to Pa. bar, 1908, and practiced at Philadelphia until 1924; mem. Johnson & Gilkyson, 1912-19, Johnson, Gilkyson & Freeman, 1919-24. Served as 1st lt., Ordnance Dept., U.S. Army, Dec. 1917-May 1918, capt., May 1918-Feb. 1919, maj. Feb.-May 1919. Arbitrator, wages and working conditions of employees, Lehigh Valley Transit Co., Pa., 1941, 1944, 1946. Trenton (N.J.) Transit Co., 1941; mem. Nat. Railway Labor Panel, Nat. Mediation Bd., Washington, D.C., from Dec. 1944. Am. sec. Internat. Mil. Tribunal, Nuremberg, Germany, 1946. Mem. Delta Upsilon, Order of the Coif, Book and Key ((Swarthmore). Club: Coffee House (New York). Author: Oil, 1924; The Lost Adventurer, 1927; Lights of Fame, 1930; Tomorrow Never Comes, 1933; Toward What Bright Land, 1947. Contbr. to mags. and Best Short Stories of America (O'Brien Collections), 1925, 1930, 1936. Home: New Hartford CT Died Nov. 7, 1969; cremated.

GILL, KERMODE FREDERIC, builder; b. Cleveland, O., Apr. 12, 1866; s. John and Margaret (Kermode) G.; m. Dorothea A. Ambos, Aug. 21, 1894. Contractor and builder since 1885; president The John Gill & Sons Company; director Buckley Building Company. Bulkley Building Company. Erected Washington (District Columbia) Post Office: Missouri State Capitol; Baltimore Court House; Cleveland Post Office (interior); Hudson County (N.J.) Court House (interior); U.S. Naval Training Sta., Hampton Roads, Va.; Williamson Bldg., Hanna Bldg., Hanna Annex and Theatre, Bulkley Bldg., Allen Theatre, Notre Dame Acad., Masonic Auditorium, Cowell-Hubbard Bldg., Leader-News Bldg., Guardian Trust Co. Bldg., Cleveland Trust Co. Bldg., Federal Reserve Bank, Wade Park Manor, Tifereth-Israel Temple, Fenway Hall, Catholic Charities Parmadale Group," Notre Dame Coll. Building, Cleveland Union Terminal Tower, Lake Shore Hotel, Lake Side Hosp. Group, Huron Road Hosp. (all Cleveland); Benjamin Franklin Hotel (Phila.); Liberty Bank, Shea's Theatre, Buffalo Gen. Electric Bldg. (all Buffalo); Am. Ins. Union Building (Columbus, O.). Formerly mem. Troop A Ohio N.G. Mem. Nat. Inst. Social Sciences, Cleveland Engring. Soc. Republican. Episcopalian. Clubs Union, Kirtland (Cleveland, O.). Home: 2178 Harcourt Drive. Office: Bulkley Bldg., Cleveland OH‡

GILL, THOMAS HARVEY, author, found. exec.; b. Phila., Jan. 21, 1891; s. John Alexander and Clara (Lex) G.; B.A., U. Pa., 1913; M.F., Yale, 1915; Dr. honoris causa, U. Andes, Venezuela, 1953; m. Vivian Perry, Dec. 31, 1918. Asst. instr. forest mensuration Yale Forest Sch., 1914; timber estimator Kaul Lumber Co., 1915; asst. ranger U.S. Forest Service, 1915, forest ranger, 1916-17, dep. forest supr., 1920-21, forest supr., 1922, in charge forest service ednl. activities, 1922-25; asso. editor Am. Forests and Forest Life Mag., 1925; exec. dir. Charles Lathrop Pack Forestry Found., 1952-60, sec. Forestry Found., 1926-60; adviser on forest policy for Philippines, 1959. U.S. del., mem. organizing com. 5th World Forestry Congress, Seattle, 1960, del. 6th Congress, Madrid, 1966 (vice chmn. U.S. nat. com.); mem. U.S. nat. com. 7th Congress, Buenos Aires, 1972; mem. Timber Conservation Bd. (adv. com.); fellow Oberlaender Trust, 1936; mem. Wm. Alanson White Psychiat. Found., 1937-45; mem. publs. com. for psychiatry Jour. Biology and Pathology of Interpersonal Relations, 1937-45; mem. interim com. mgrs. Washington Sch. Psychiatry, 1937-45; spl. adviser on forestry UN Com. on Food and Agr., Copenhagen, Denmark, 1946, adviser Am. delegation, Washington, 1948-49, Rome, 1955; adviser on forest policy for Japan, 1951, Formosa, 1952, 56; del. U.S. Govt. 3d World Forestry Congress, Helsinki, 1949, Inter-Am. Conservation Conf., Denver, 1948; exec. dir. Internat. Union Socs. Foresters, 1966-70; chmn. FAO Com. Unexploited Forests, 1947, chmn. Am. delegation FAO Conf. Land Utilization Far East, 1951, Far East Forestry Commn. meeting, 1952; chmn. FAO com on forestry devel. in tropics, 1967-69; mem. Nat. Acad. Scis. adv. com. on research to Nat. Park Service, 1962-65. Made 1st forest survey, party aerial, tropical forests in Carribean region, penetrating undiscovered sects.; 1st mosaic aerial map U.S., 1919. Served as 1st lt. AS, U.S. Army, World War I. Decorated D.S.C., Germany; Merito Civico Forestal (Mexico), chevalier Merite Agricole (France); Recipient diploma honor Mexican Inst. Renewable Resources, 1966; Fernow award Am. Forestry Assn. and German Forestry Soc., 1967. Fellow Soc. Am. Foresters (Schlich medal 1954) mem. Pacific Sci. Assn. (sec. for com. 1948), Soc. Filipino Foresters (hon.), Internat. Soc. Tropical Foresters (pres.), Am. Forestry Assn. (past v.p.), Soc. Mexican Foresters (hon.), Yale Forest Sch. Alumni Assn. (past v.p.), Nat. Acad. Scis. (chmn. internat. com. tropical forestry), La Sociedad Mexicana de Historia Natural (hon.), La Asociacion Mexicana de Proteccion a la Naturaleza (hon.). Clubs: Explorers (N.Y.C.); Army-Navy, Cosmos, International (Washington). Author books including: Land Hunger in Mexico, 1951; Tropical Forests of the Carribean, 1955; compiler (with E.C. Dowling) The Forestry Directory, 1943, 49. Contbr. articles to publs. Home: Washington DC Died May 21, 1972.

GILLEM, ALVAN CULLOM, JR., army officer; b. Nashville, Tenn., Aug. 8, 1888; s. Alvan Cullom and Lillian Courts (Cummins) G.; student U. of Ariz., 1908, U. of the South, 1908-09, Army Staff Sch., 1922-23, Army War Coll., 1925-26; m. Virginia Lucille Harrison, June 14, 1916; children—Alvan Cullom, II, Mary Virginia, Richard Douglas. Enlisted, Regular Army, Jan. 19, 1910; commd. 2d lt. U.S. Army, Feb. 11, 1911, advanced through grades to maj. gen., Inf., July 12, 1941, and assigned to command III Armored Div.; activated and took command II Armored Corps, Jan. 17, 1942; commanded Desert Training Center, Aug.-Oct. 1942, directing first U.S. Army maneuvers held solely for armored and mechanized troops; appointed comdg. gen., Armored Force, May 14, 1943, and comdg. gen., Armored Command, July 2, 1943, promoted lt. gen., 1945; comdr. XIII Corps, European Theater of Operations; Am. commr. exec. hdqrs., Peiping, China, Oct. 1946-Apr. 1947; comdg. gen. 3d Army, June 15, 1947-50. Mem. Sigma Alpha Epsilon, Omicron Delta Kappa. Episcopalian. Writer of Army notes for instructional purposes in service schs. Home: Atlanta GA Died Feb. 13, 1973.

GILLEN, WILFRED DONNELL, business exec.; b. Houlton, Me. July 28, 1900; s. P. F. and Anna (O'Donnell) G.; student U. of Me., 1919-21; B.S., U. of Pa., 1923; LL.D., Pa. Military College; hon. degrees U. Pa., 1965, Temple U., 1965; m. Frances Wilson, Aug. 9, 1930;children—Nancy Gillen Williams, Helen Gillen Beeson, Wilfred Donnell. Mem. comml. dept. The Bell Telephone Co. of Pa., Phila., 1923-29, gen. sales mgr., 1929-36, div. mgr., 1936-38, gen. comml. mgr. 1938, asst. vice pres. operations 1938-41, v.p. and gen. mgr. Central area, Harrisburg, 1941-47, dir. and v.p. operations, 1947-49, pres., 1949-65; pres. and dir. Diamond State Telephone Co., Wilmington, Del., 1949-67; dir. Phila. Nat. Bank, Acme Markets, Inc., Atlas Chem. Industries, Inc., Reliance Ins. Co., Alan Wood Steel Co. (Conshohocken, Pa.); trustee Penn Mut. Life Ins. Co. Mem. board mgrs. U. of Pa. Hospital, Western Saving Fund Society of Phila.; director Academy Music Phila., Asso. Hosp. Serv., Phila. Orchestra Assn.; chairman board trustees U. of Pennsylvania. Mem. Philadelphia Chamber of Commerce (governing com.). Republican. Roman Catholic. Clubs: Rittenhouse, Philadelphia Country, Racquet, Midday (Phila.); Duquesne, (Pitts.); Rolling Rock. (Ligonier); Union League (Phila.); Skytop. Home: Bryn Mawr PA Died May 1, 1968.

GILLESPIE, LOUIS FRANK, lawyer; b. Vienna, Ill., Jan. 20, 1900; s. George B. and Mary (Oliver) G.; student Cornell U., 1918-21; Ph.B., U. Chgo., 1922, J.D., 1924; m. Frances McGregor, Dec. 31, 1927; children—George B. II, Mary Ellis, Robert E. Admitted to Ill. bar, 1924, mem. Gillespie, Burke & Gillespie, from 1925; gen. counsel Franklin Life Ins. Co., Springfield, 1944-65, sr. counsel, 1965, chmn. bd., 1953-70, also dir. Mem. exec. com. Meml. Hosp., Springfield, Ill., 1960-69. Fellow Am. Coll. Trial Lawyers; mem. Soc. Trial Lawyers, Am. Bar Assn., Assn. Life Ins. Counsel, Phi Delta Phi, Delta Kappa Epsilon. Clubs: Sangamo, Illini Country (Springfield); University (Chgo.). Home: Springfield IL

GILLET, CHARLES, industrialist; b. Lyons, France, Nov. 26, 1879; s. Joseph louis and Marie Mathilde (Perrin) G.; m. Juliette Garin, Mar. 19, 1906; children—Denise (Mrs. Francois Brossette), Michel, Robert, Renaud, Bernard. Past pres. Compagnie Industrielle des Textiles Artificiels, also Textil, Soprina; past dir. Rhone-Poulenc, S.A., Princel. Decorated chevalier Legion Honor. Address: Paris France Died June 1972.

GILLET, GUY MARK, senator; born Cherokee, Ia. Feb. 3, 1879; s. Mark Dennis and Mary (Hull) G. LL.B., Drake U., 1900; LL.D., Drake University, St. Ambrose Coll.; m. Rose Freeman, June 17, 1907; 1 son, Mark Freeman. Admitted to Ia. bar, 1900, and began practice at Cherokee; city atty., Cherokee, 1906-07; county atty., Cherokee County, 1907-09. Served as sergt. U.S. Vol. Inf. Spanish-Am. War; capt. inf., U.S. Army, 1917-19. Mem. Ia. State Senate, 1912-16; mem. 73d and 74th Congresses (1933-37), 9th Ia. Dist.; elected U.S. Senate to fill unexpired term of Louis Murphy, 1936, term expiring, 1939; reelected to Senate of U.S. for term, 1939-45; re-elected Nov. 1948, for 6-yr. term; chairman Surplus Property Board, 1945. President Am. League for Free Palestine, 1945. Member Spanish War Vets., Vets Fgn. Wars, Am. Legion. Democrat. Presbyterian. Mason, K.P. Home: Cherokee IA Died Mar. 1973.

GILLET, PAUL, industrialist; b. Lyon, Rhone, France, Oct. 21, 1874; s. Joseph Louis and Marie Mathilde (Perrin) G.; m. Marguerite Blanchet (dec.). Past dir. Compagnie Pechiney; now hon. pres. Socete Progil, establissements Jacquemaire. Decorated officer Legion of Honor. Home: Lyon France Died 1971.

GILLICK, LAURANCE HENRY, heating co. exec.; b. Mpls., Aug. 25, 1898; s. James Thomas and Elizabeth (Feltus) G.; student Northwestern U., 1915; m. Dorothy Hart, Sept. 1, 1920; children—Dorothy (Mrs. John Drish), Dorice (Mrs. Dino Santoro). With Vapor Corp., and predecessor, Chgo., 1916-66, v.p., 1941-63, vice chmn., 1963-66; pres. AAA Insulaire, Inc., Ft. Lauderdale, Fla., 1966-71. Mem. Am. Soc. M.E., Soc. Automotive Engrs., Soc. Naval Architects. Clubs: Coral Ridge Yacht, Chgo. Athletic. Home: Wilmette IL Died Mar. 3, 1971; buried Calvary Cemetery, Evanston IL

GILLINGHAM, CLINTON HANCOCK, coll. pres.; b. Phila., Pa., Sept. 29, 1877; s. Jonathan and Henrietta

Smith) G.; B.A., Maryville (Tenn.) Coll., 1905, M.A., 1907, D.D., 1919; student Princeton Theol. Sem., 1905-06; B.D., Presbyn. Theol. Sem. of Ky., 1908; spl. studies in Palestine, Jerusalem, 1923; m. Nancy Virginia Gardner, Nov. 2, 1903 (dec.); children—George Gardner, Alice Armitage (Mrs. John C. McDowell), Samuel Wilson, Mary (Mrs. J. M. Padgette) and Jonathan (twins), Edward Clinton; m. 2d, Helen Lewis, July 14, 1935. Ordained Presbyterian ministry, September 29, 1907; with Y.M.C.A., Philadelphia, 1890-93; with Pa. Railroad Company, 1893-1901; with Maryville Coll., 1907-29, registrar, 1907-26, prof. O.T. history and lit., 1907-11, prof. English Bible and head of dept. of Bible and religious edn., 1911-29; pres. Tennent Coll. of Christian Edn., 1929-43; pres. emeritus since 1943; vis. prof. English Bible. Maryville Coll., 1945-46. Served as major inf. 4th Tenn. Regt. 1918-19; reserve officer Tenn. Nat. Guard, 1919-29. Moderator of Presbytery of Union, 1910. Mem. bd. dirs. Presbyn. Theol. Sem. of Ky., 1923-32; mem. bd. trustees Tennent Coll. of Christian Edn. since 1929; pres. 1929-44; sec.-treas. Tenn. Coll. Assn., 1924-29. Club: Kiwanis (past pres.). Home: Maryville TN‡

GILLMOR, HORATIO GONZALO, rear admiral; b. Menomonie, Wis., Jan. 7, 1870; s. Daniel Webster and Jane (Shipman) G.; grad. U.S. Naval Acad., 1891; student Royal Naval Coll., Greenwich, Eng., 1891-94; m. Mary S. Grandy, Apr. 16, 1912 (died 1917); children—Wiley Grandy (dec.), Daniel Shipman; m. 2d, Grace V. Estes, Aug. 31, 1922. Commd. asst. naval constructor, lt. j.g., U.S. Navy, July 1, 1893, and advanced through grades to capt., July 1, 1917; rear admiral, Oct. 1, 1932. Asst. to constrn. officer Navy Yard, N.Y. City, 1894-95; served on U.S.S. New York, 1895-96; superintending constructor Herreshoff Mfg. Co., Bristol, R.I., 1896-98; with Bur. Constrn. and Repair, Navy Dept., 1898; superintending constructor Elswick Shipyard, Newcastle-on-Tyne, Eng., 1898-1900; again with Bur. Constrn. and Repair, 1900-02; superintending constructor Bath (Me.) Iron Works, 1902-07; same, Fore River Shipbuilding Corp., Quincy, Mass., 1907-10; constrn. officer Navy Yard, Norfolk, 1910-15; mem. Bd. of Inspection and Survey, Navy Dept., 1915-27, 1931-32; with Dept. of Justice (assisting defense suits), 1927-31; naval operations, Navy Department, 1932-34; retired; recalled to active duty as member Compensation Board, U.S. Navy Department, July 14, 1941. Member Society Naval Architects and Marine Engrs. Awarded Spanish War, World War and National Defense medals. Episcopalian. Clubs: Army and Navy, Army-Navy Country, Chevy Chase. Home: 1720 N St. N.W., Washington 6 DC‡

GILMAN, HARRY A., investment banking; b. Boston, Mass., Dec. 13, 1876; s. Charles A. and Ella O. (Harrington) G.; ed. George Putnam Grammar Sch., Boston; m. Mabel L. Langille, Apr. 25, 1900;children—Dr. Ralph L., Richard I., Robert A. Entered employ of Brewster, Cobb & Estabrook (now Estabrook & Co.), Boston, June 25, 1891; registered salesman, since 1910; vice pres. and dir. Bernitz Furnace Appliance, Boston, since 1900; dir. Suffolk 1st Federal Savings Loan Assn. Republican. Baptist. Mem. Am. Baptist Home Mission Soc. (past pres., mem. bd. mgrs.), Boston Baptist Social Union (past pres., sec. 25 years), Mass. Baptist Conv. (dir., mem. finance com.), Baptist Home of Mass. (clerk, trustee). Mason. Home: 195 Gibbs St., Newton Center 59, Mass. Office: 15 State St., Boston 9*‡

GILMAN, JAMES HENRY, banker; b. New Hartford, Conn., June 26, 1883; s. Henry P. and Katherine (Crowe) G.; ed. pub. schs., New Hartford; m. Gladys Moore, of Brookline, Mass., Apr. 11, 1916; children—James H., Gloria Moore, George Claflin. Began as office boy and clk., Bank of Bay Biscayne, Miami, Fla., 1902, 1922. City commr., Miami, 1921-27. Republican. Conglist. Mason, Elk. Clubs: Bath, Country. Home: Washington DC Died Mar. 1972.

GILMAN, ROGER, architect; b. Cambridge, Mass., Aug. 21, 1874; s. Francis Brown and Susan Ann (Hood) G.; prep. edn., Cambridge Latin Sch.; B.A., Harvard, 1895, M.A., 1920; studied Ecole des Beaux Arts, 1899-1902; m. Jane Taylor Bowler, June 6, 1918; children—Barbara, Alison (daughter), Susan. With Post & Sons, architects, N.Y. City, 1902-08; practiced alone, Kansas City, Mo., 1908-16; with Y.M.C.A. overseas, in French Army, 1918; dean R.I. Sch. of Design, 1919-29; editor for Fogg Art Museum, Harvard U., 1931-39. Awarded Medaille de reconnaisance (France). Republican. Episcopalian. Author: The Great Periods of Interior Architecture, 1926. Address: 19 Ash St., Cambridge MA

GILMAN, STELLA SCOTT (MRS. MARION VAUGHN), author; b. in Ala.; d. David and Stella (Houghton) Scott; m. Arthur Gilman, July 11, 1876. With him was originator of the Society for Collegiate Instruction of Women, which became Radcliffe Coll., Cambridge, the woman's side of Harvard U. Author: A Mother's Record; Mothers in Council. Home: Cambridge MA‡

GILMER, ELIZABETH MERIWETHER (DOROTHY DIX), journalist; b. Montgomery County, Tenn., Nov. 18, 1870; m. George O. Gilmer, Nov. 21, 1888. Editor woman's dept. New Orleans Picayune, 1896-1901; contributed to that paper series of papers called Dorothy Dix Talks; joined New York Journal staff as writer on spl. topics, April 8, 1901; joined Wheeler Syndicate staff. Jan. 1917; joined staff of Ledger Syndicate, Jan. 15, 1923; joined Bell Syndicate staff, Jan. 1933. Author: Mirandy; Mirandy Exhorts; Fables in Slang; Hearts a la Mode; A Joy Ride Around the World; Dorothy Dix, Her Book; How to Win and Hold a Husband. Home: 6334 Prytania St., New Orleans LA*‡

GILMORE, EUGENE ALLEN, JR., ex-fgn. service ofcr.; b. Madison, Wis., Dec. 27, 1902; s. Eugene Allen and Blanche (Basye) G.; A.B., U. Wis., 1924, Ph.D., 1935; M.B.A., Harvard, 1926; m. Helen Downs, June 17, 1938. Comml. banking, N.Y. City, 1926-27; teaching asst. in economics, U. Wis., 1928-30; instr. U. So. Calif., 1930-32, asst. prof., 1932-35; asst. prof. U. Neb., 1935-39, asso. prof., 1939-41; economic analyst American Embassy, Montevideo, Uruguay, 1941-44; polit. economist Dept. of State, Washington, 1944-47; fgn. service officer since 1947; consul, Calcutta, India, 1947-49, 1st sec. and consul, New Delhi, India, 1949-50, Teheran, Iran, 1950-51; office charge econ. programs For. Service Inst. Dept. State, 1951-52; econ. counselor embassy Peru, 1952-55, counselor embassy, La Paz, Bolivia, 1955-57; econ. counselor embassy, Havana, Cuba, 1957-61, country dir. ICA Tech. Assistance Program, Cuba, 1958-61; dir. Office of W. Coast Affairs, Bur. Inter-Am. Affairs, Dept. State, 1961; lectr. Am. U., Washington, 1965; prof. econs. Baylor U., Waco, Tex., 1965-69. Mem. Am. Econ. Assn., Chi Psi, Delta Sigma Pi. Author: The Monetary Theories of Hawtrey, Hayek, Keynes and Robertson, 1936; Adequacy of Deposit Banking Facilities in Nebraska, 1937. Home: Silver Spring MD Died Jan. 8, 1971.

GILPIN, C. MONTEITH, lawyer; b. Philadelphia, Pa., Oct. 31, 1872; s. Thomas and Sarah Elizabeth (Rowand) G.; student Villanova (Pa.) Coll., 1890-91; A.B., St. Johns Coll., Annapolis, Md., 1894; LL.B., Columbia, 1897; m. Gertrude May Chase, of N.Y. City, Jan. 16, 1901; 1 dau., Georgia Gilpin (dec.). Admitted to N.Y. bar, 1897, and began practice at N.Y. City; dir., sec. and counsel Ansonia Clock Co.; sec. treas. and dir. Nat. Paper Process Corpn.; sec. and dir. N.E. Motor Sales Co., Lenox Corpn., Hayden Automobile Co., Metals Trading Corpn. Served as q.m., U.S. Vols., Spanish-Am. War. Pres. U.S. Hist. Soc.; mem. Am. and N.Y. State bar assns., Soc. of Tammany, Phi Gamma Delta. Democrat. Catholic. Clubs: University, Columbia University. Office: 512 5th Av., New York NY‡

GIMBEL, ADAM LONG, merchant; b. Vincennes, Wis., Dec. 21, 1893; s. Charles and Ella (Long) G.; student Yale, class of 1916; m. Mrs. Sophie Haas Rossbach, Aug. 1931; 1 stepson, Jay Rossbach. Pres. Saks Fifth Avenue; director Gimbel Bros., Tishman Realty & Construction Company, Inc., Twentieth Century-Fox Film Corporation. Served as lieutenant during World War. Decorated Legion of Honor (French). Pres. Uptown Retail Guild; dir. Fifth Avenue Assn., French Chamber of Commerce. Clubs: Yale (N.Y. City); Hollywood Golf (Elberon, N.J.). Home: New York City NY Died Sept. 9, 1969.

GIMBEL, BENEDICT, JR., broadcasting exec.; b. Phila.; s. Benedict and Birdie (Loeb) G.; student U. Pa., 1918-21; L.H.D., Lincoln U., 1952; m. J. Jessie Kane, May 31, 1950; 1 son, Edward Nathanson. With Gimbel Brothers, 1921-31; pres., gen. mgr. radio sta. WIP, 1930-60; v.p., dir. Metromedia, Incorporated, 1960-71. Director Child Welfare Adv. Bd., Robin Hood Dell Concerts, Incorporated. Member of the Crime Prevention Assn. Phila. Dir. Elder Craftsmen Phila.; bd. mgrs. Grad. Hosp., Phila.; asso. trustee U. Pa. Mem. Fire Prevention Assn. Phila. Clubs: Midday, Locust, Variety, Poor Richard ((Phila.); Lambs (N.Y.C.). Home: Philadelphia PA Died Feb. 1971.

GINDER, PHILIP DEWITT, army officer; b. Plainfield, N.J., Sept. 19, 1905; s. Grant D. and Emma Edith (Troxell) G.; B.S., U.S. Mil. Acad., 1927; m. Martha Calvert, 1933 (div. 1945); children—Jean Calvert, Louise Calvert; m. 2d, Jean Dalrymple, Nov. 1, 1951. Commd. 2d lt., AUS, 1927, advanced through grades to maj. gen., 1953; various mil. assignments, 1927-45; sr. mil. attache at Prague, Czechoslovakia, 1949-51; comd. 6th Inf. Regt., 1951-52; asst. chief of staff Intelligence of Army Field Forces, 1952; comd. 45th inf. div., Korea, 1953; comd. 37th inf. div., 1954; comdg. gen. Fifth Army, Chgo., 1955; spl. asst. to chief of staff for Res. Components, 1955-57; dep. comdg. gen. for Res. Forces, 1958-63, ret., 1963; pres. Brazilia-Am. Import Co., 1963-68. Decorated Distinguished Service Cross, Distinguished Service Medal, Silver Star, Legion of Merit, Bronze Star with 2 oak leaf clusters, Purple Heart, Legion of Honor and Croix de Guerre with palm (France), Order of Mil. Merit (Czechoslovakia), Mil. Order of Patriotic Fight (Russia), Fourragere (Belgium), Legion of Merit (Philippines), Order of New York City NY also Danbury CTDied Nov. 1968.

GINTER, RIBERT MCNIEL, b. Delmont, Pa., Apr. 14, 1877; s. Gideon and Emily (Lose) G.; Indiana (Pa.) Normal Sch., Wooster (O.) U.; m. Marguerite E. Sellers, of Waynesburg, Pa., Oct. 5, 1909; 1 dau., Mary Emily Ginter Young. Learned printer's trade on Indiana Times; reporter, telegraph editor, Sunday editor, night editor and mng. editor Pittsburgh Gazette-Times, and Washington corr. for paper, 1911-27, except 3 yrs. as mng. editor. Vice chmn. Pa. Aeronautics Commn. by apptmt. of Gov. John S. Fisher, until July 31, 1931. Republican. Presbyn. Mason. Club: Gridiron (Washington, D.C.). Home: 5759 Howe St., Pittsburgh PA‡

GIRARD, ANDRE, artist; b. Chinon, France, May 25, 1901; s. Marcel and Eva (Neveu) G.; student Ecole Nationale des Arts Decoratif, 1917-18, Ecole Nationale des Beaux Arts, Paris, 1918-21; studied with George Rouault, Pierre Bonnard; Litt.D., Marquette U., 1957; m. Andree Jouan, Apr. 5, 1924; children—Eve Marie (Mrs. Jean Casadesus), Daniele (Mrs. Yves Robert), Mari Therese (Mrs. Raymond Griere), Marguerite. Came to U.S., 1937. Designed sets for Lugne-Poe, Pitoeff, Theatre de l'Oeuvre, 1921-38; exhbt. one man shows Theatre de l'Oeuvre, Art et Action Theatre, Paris, 1921, Galerie de l'Elysse, 1936, Musee de l'Athenee, 1938, Galerie Macght, Cannes, 1942, Bignou Gallery, N.Y.C., 1944, Paris, 1948, Carstairs Gallery, N.Y.C., 1948-58, Art Alliance, Phila., 1951-52; artistic dir. French Pavillion, San Francisco World's Fair, 1939; art cons. Societe Francaise Duco, 20th Century Fox., Coll. St. Mary (Notre Dame); prof. Coll. Notre Dame of Md. at Balt., 1948-49, Coll. City N.Y., 1959-60; full decoration Blessed Sacramento Ch., Stowe, Vt., 1948, Windows, Way of the Cross (meml. to dau. of Clare Booth Luce), St. Ann's Chapel, Palo Alto, 1951; rare books hand printed in Nat. Library Paris, Metropolitan Mus., N.Y.C., Phila. Mus. Arts, Mus. Modern Art, N.Y.C.; lectr. Princeton, Marquette U., N.Y.U., Lycee Technique Estienne (Paris), others. Painted on film in new technic a complete life of Jesus, portions shown on NBC, CBS, ABC; mem. art jury Marymount Coll., Tarrytown N.Y. Served with French Mil. Resistance, 1940-45, chief staff 1942; mem. mission in Am., 1943-44. Decorated officer Legion of Merit. Mem. Assn. des Anciens Eleves de Condorcet, Alumni Assn. Marquette U. Author: Bataille Secrete en France, 1944; Heraclitus Sayings, 1948; Verlaine, 1950; l'Autre Monde, 1935; Ces gens qu passent, 1964. Contbr. articles profl. jours. Home: Nyack NY Died Sept. 2, 1968; buried Nyack NY

GIRARDIN, RAY, chief of police of Detroit, 4 yrs. Died Nov. 1971.

GITHENS, ALFRED MORTON, architect; b. Phila., Pa., Aug. 25, 1876; s. William Henry Harrison and Frances Adele (Stotesbury) G.; B.S., U. of Pa., 1896; John Stewardson scholar, Am. Acad. at Rome, 1901, Ecole Nationale des Beaux Arts, Paris, 1903-05; m. Charlotte Sandys Foulke Sands, June 20, 1906; children—Alfred Sands, Elizabeth (Mrs. James E. Snyder), Frances (Mrs. John W. Minter). Worked under Cope and Stewardson, architects of Philadelphia, and Cass Gilbert and Charles F. McKim, of New York, on univ. and expn. bldgs. and the plan for development of Washington, D.C.; teacher of archtl. design, Columbia, 1918-21, 1925-26, Princeton U., 1927-28; partner Charles C. Haight, New York, 1906-17, Edward L. Tilton, 1917-32, Francis Keally, 1937-42; bldgs. included Currier and Springfield Museum of Fine Arts, Balt. and Brooklyn Public Libraries; since the practicing alone as architect or consultant in planning libraries. Fellow A.I.A.; mem. Am. Library Assn., Century Assn. Asso. Nat. Acad. Design. Rep. Episcopalian. Author: (with Dr. J. L. Wheeler) The American Public Library Building, 1941; (with Ralph Munn) Program for the Public Libraries of New York City, 1945. Contbr. to Collier's Nat. Ency., Hamlin's Twentieth Century Architecture, and to tech. mags. Address: 439 Center St., Laguna Beach CA‡

GITT, CHARLES MOUL, editor; b. Hanover, Pa., Mar. 12, 1915; s. Josiah W. and Elizabeth (Moul) G.; grad. Gunnery Sch., 1934; A.B., Harvard, 1938; m. LaVerne Garland, July 7, 1945; children—Cynthia, Peggy Ann, Stephen. With Gazette & Daily, York, Pa., 1938-70, pres., exec. editor, 1943-70, cons. York Daily Record, 1970-72; dir. Color Systems/York, Inc., also mem. editorial bd. subsidiary Am. History Publs., 1971-72. Club: Lancaster (Pa.) Country. Home: York PA Died Sept. 4, 1972.

GITTINS, ROBERT HENRY, congressman; b. Oswego, N.Y., Dec. 14, 1869; LL.B., U. of Mich., 1900. Practiced, Niagara Falls, N.Y., since 1901; mem. N.Y. State Senate, 1911-13; del. Dem. Nat. Conv., Baltimore, 1912; mem. 63d Congress (1913-15), 40th Dist., N.Y. Home: Niagara Falls NY‡

GIVEN, WILLIAM BARNS, JR., manufacturing executive; born Columbia, Pa., December 7, 1886; son William Barns and Mary (Bruner) G.; student Hill Sch., Pottstown, Pa., 1899-1904, Mass. Inst. Tech., 1904-07; Ph.B., Sheffield Scientific Sch. (Yale), 1908; D.C.S. (honorary), New York University, 1950; LL.D., Franklin and Marshall Coll. (Lancaster, Pa.), 1951; D.Eng. (hon.), Mo. Sch. of Mines, 1951; L.H.D., Hobart and William Smith Colls., 1957; married Dorothy

Weiman, Oct. 8, 1917; children—The Reverend Davis Given, and Dorothy (Mrs. John L. Kee, Jr.). With Am. Brake Shoe Co. (company name changed to Abex Corporation), 1911-68, secretary to president, 1911-16, asst. to pres., 1916-17, asst. v.p., 1919-20, v.p., 1920-29, president, 1929-50, chmn. bd., 1950-63, honorary chairman, board of directors, 1963-68; mem. Uptown adv. com. Bankers Trust Company; director Lloyds-Brake Shoe, Ltd. (England); hon. director Mellon Nat. Bank & Trust Co. (Pitts.); trustee Dry Dock Savs. Bank. Served as 1st lt., later capt., 42d Div., AUS, WW I. Republican. Episcopalian (vestryman); dir. Episcopal Church Found., N.Y.C.; alumni trustee General Theological Sem. Clubs: Racquet and Tennis, Links, Rolling Rock, Chicago, Piping Rock, Brook (N.Y.C.). Author: Bottom Up Management, 1949, Reaching Out in Management, 1953. Home: New York City NY Died Jan. 30, 1968.

GIVENS, RAYMOND L., lawyer; b. Salem, Ore., Feb. 9, 1884; student Colo. Coll.; LL.B., U. Denver, 1909, J.D. (hon.), U. Ida., 1954. Admitted to Ida. bar, 1909, Colo. Bar, 1909; U.S. Supreme Ct. bar, 1939; mem. firm Givens and Givens, Boise, Ida.; pros. atty. Ada County, Ida., 1912-16; state rep. Ida. Legislature, 1919; asst. atty. gen. Ida., 1920; judge 4th Jud. Dist. Ida., 1921-24; justice Ida. Supreme Ct., 1925-54, chief justice 8 terms. Lectr. workmen's compensation Coll. Law U. Ida., 1938-51; mem. conf. Chief Justices, 1949-54; chmn. Constl. Revision Commn. State of Ida., 1965-72. Mem. Ida. State Bar, 4th Jud. Dist. Bar Assn., Phi Delta Phi. Home: Boise ID Died July 22, 1972.

GIVENS, SPENCER HOLLINGSWORTH, state ofcl.; b. Gallatin, Mo., Dec. 29, 1904; s. Nathaniel S. and Martha (Hollingsworth) G.; B.J., U. Mo., 1928. News editor Boonville (Mo.) Advertiser, 1928-33; sec. Mo. Workmen's Compensation Commn., Jefferson City, 1934-42, dir. Mo. div. Workmen's Compensation since 1945. Mem. Internat. Assn. Indsl. Accident Bds. and Commn. (pres. 1948-49). Methodist. Home: Jefferson City MO Died Oct. 21, 1968.

GIVENS, WILLARD EARL, association executive; born in Anderson, Indiana, Dec. 10, 1886; son John Luther and Amanda Elizabeth (Hersberger) G.; student Butler Coll., Indianapolis, 1908-09; A.B., Indiana Univ., 1913, LL.D., 1938; A.M., Columbia U., 1915; diploma Union Theol. Sem., 1916; grad. student in sociology, Columbia, 1915-17; grad. student (part-time) in edn., U. of California, 1925-33; Ed.D., Miami University, Oxford, O., 1941; fellow, Educational Inst. of Scotland, 1947; H.H.D., Coll. Ida., 1950, U. of Pacific, 1951; married Neva Lillian Galbreath, December 10, 1917; children—Willard Earl, Stuart Ray. Rural and high school teacher, elementary and secondary sch. prin., in Indiana, T.H., and California, 1906-23; supt. pub. instrn., T.H., 1923-25; asst. supt. schs., Oakland, Calif., 1925-27; supt. schs., San Diego, Calif., 1927-28; supt. schs., Oakland, Calif., 1928-35; exec. sec. Nat. Edn. Assn., 1935-52. Vis. prof. of education Brigham Young University, two terms, Claremont Graduate School, two terms. Chmn. bd. of trustees, Sr. Citizens of Am., 1954-69; ednl. cons. for U.S. to Philippines, 1953; chmn. U.S. Nat. Commn. for UNESCO 1956; ednl. adv. to U.S. del. to World UNESCO Conf. in New Delhi, 1956. Instructor Naval Officers' Training School, Mare Is., World War I. Campaign chmn. Oakland Community Chest, 1930-32. Pres. Calif. Teachers Assn., 1932-35; mem. Am. Youth Commn. of Am. Council on Edn. Life mem. N.E.A. (state dir. for Calif. 2 yrs., Hawaii 2 yrs.); mem. Ednl. Policies Commn., Am. Acad. Political and Social Science, A.A.A.S. Conglist. Mason (Shriner, 33 deg; dir. of education The Supreme Council 33 deg. Scottish Rite Mason, So. Jurisdiction 1958-69. Author numerous articles in ednl. and lay mags. Mem. U.S. Education Mission to Japan, 1946. Mem. Bd. visitors Air Univ., 1946-50; member com. Armed Forces Edn. Program, 1949-53; chmn. National Conf. for Mobilization of Edn., 1950; educational rep. World Town Hall Seminar, 1949; chmn. 2d U.S. Education Mission to Japan, 1950. Author: People to People, 1949; The Association of Nations, 1954; co-author Our Public Schools, The Road to Freedom, Our U.S.A., Communism Menaces Freedom, Private Enterprise. Home: Bloomfield Hills MI Died May 20, 1971.

GJELSNESS, RUDOLPH H., professor; b. Reynolds, N.D., Oct. 18, 1894; s. Marius and Caroline Lie (Olsen) G.; A.B., U. N.D., 1916, LL.D., 1958; B.L.S., U. of Ill., 1920; student U. of Oslo, Norway, 1924-25; Litt.D., Luther College, 1953; married Ruth Elizabeth Weaver, July 18, 1930; children—Elizabeth (Mrs. Donelson Dulany, Jr.), Barent, AEF University, Reference librarian, Beaune, France, 1919. Order librarian, University of Oregon, 1920-22; senior bibliographer, University of California, 1922-24; asst. librarian and chief classifier, U. of Mich. Library, 1925-28; chief preparation div., N.Y. Pub. Library, 1929-32; librarian, U. of Ariz., 1932-37; prof. library sci. U. Mich., 1937-64, emeritus, 1965-68; chmn. dept., 1940-64; chief spl. collections, prof. library science, University of Arizona, from 1964; lecturer in library science, Columbia, 1930-32, U. of Mich., 1927-28, summer, 1932, U. of Ill., summer, 1935; fellow Am. Scandinavian Foundation to Norway, 1924-25; co.-dir. summer library sch., Bogota, Colombia, 1942. Visiting prof., National School of Anthropology, Mexico, D.F., Feb.-July 1944; director, Benjamin Franklin Library, Mexico, D.F., July 1943--Oct. 1944, and Union Catalog project, Mar. 1943-Oct. 1944; library cons. to pres. U. Baghdad (Iraq), 1962-63. Served Air Service, AUS, with A.E.F., 1917-19. Recipient Beta Phi Mu Award, 1954. Mem. A.L.A. (treas. 1941-47), chmn. committee on cataloging and classification 1930-33, catalog sect. 1934-36, agrl. libraries sect. 1936-37, serial section 1940-41; com. on revision Anglo-Am. catalog rules and editor in chief of revision 1935-41; editor in chief of A.L.A. catalog rules 1941; com. on library cooperation with Latin-America, 1942-46, Assn. of American Library Schools (president 1948-49), Arizona Library Association, American Library Institute, Bibliographical Soc. of Am., Mich. Acad of Arts, Sciences and Letters, Phi Beta Kappa, Sigma Alpha Epsilon, Phi Kappa Phi. Episcopalian. Translator from Norwegian of (novel) Lisbeth of Jarnfjeld by Johan Falkberget, 1930; also short stories from Norwegian; Catalogo colectivo de publicaciones periodicas, 1949; The American Book in Mexico, 1957. Contbr. to library jours. Home: Ann Arbor MI Died Aug. 1968.

GLADSON, GUY ALLEN, lawyer; b. Mason, Ill., Feb. 11, 1892; s. John A. and Eva (Baker) G.; student So. Ill. U., 1906-10; Ph.B., U. Chgo., 1916, J.D., 1918; M. Martha Gertrude Huffman, Feb. 28, 1921; children—Guy Allen, Martha, John, Caroline, Richard. Admitted to Ill. bar, 1918; partner Winston, Strawn, Black & Towner, Chgo.; gen. counsel dir. C.G.W. R.R., 1949-51; dir., counsel Union Stock Yard & Transit Co., Chgo., 1948-51; counsel Toledo, Peoria & Western R.R., from 1927, chmn. bd., from 1952; dir. Live Stock Nat. Bank of Chgo., Produce Terminal Corp., Mercury Manufacturing Company, R.E. Jones Paper Co. Dir. Internat. Kennel Club. Mem. Am., Ill. State, Chgo. bar assns. Episcopalian. Clubs: Mid-Day, Michigan Shores (Wilmette, Ill.); Lawyers (Ann Arbor). Home: Chicago IL Died Apr. 1968.

GLARNER, FRITZ, artist; b. Zurich, Switzerland, July 20, 1899; s. Joseph and Donata (Ahignente) G.; student Regio Instituto di Belle Arti, Naples, Italy; m. Louise Powell, July 12, 1928. Came to U.S., 1936, naturalized, 1944. Exhibited abstract painting in Mus. Modern Art, N.Y.C., 1951, 1st biennial of Sao Paulo, Brazil, 1951, Carnegie Internat., Pitts., 1952, 58, 25th biennial Corcoran Gallery, Washington, 1957, also Tokyo, Japan, Kassel, Germany, Zurich, Switzerland, Venice, Italy; works represented in collections Yale U. Art Gallery, Phila. Mus. Art, Mus. Modern Art, N.Y.C., Balt. Mus. Fine Art, Whitney Mus. Am. Art, Walker Art Center, Mpls., others; Mural Painting, main lobby Dag Hammerskjold Library, UN, N.Y.C., Time-Life Bldg., N.Y.C. Home: Locarno Switzerland Died Sept. 18, 1972.

GLASGOW, FRANK LAWSON, investment banker; b. Hamiota, Man., Can., June 9, 1906; s. Frank William and Edith (Beaton) G. m. Evelyn Helen Davidson, June 16, 1928; children—Beverly Edith (Mrs. William McK. Baird), David Lawson, Gail Evelyn (Mrs. W. Bradley Horwood). With Royal Securities Corp. Ltd., 1926-70, exec. v.p., 1959-70, also chmn. exec. com.; partner Royal Securities Co., 1954-70; v.p. Royal Secutities, Inc., New York, 1961-70; dir. Westeel-Rosco Ltd., Reveistoke Bldg. Materials Ltd., Fed. Grain Ltd. Past pres. Investment Dealers Assn. Can. Mem. Anglican Ch. Clubs: Manitoba (Can.); Vancouver (B.C., Can.); St. James', Royal Montreal Golf, Montreal (Montreal); Chapleau Fish and Game (La Minerve, Que., Can.). Home: Montreal PQ Can Died Jan. 5, 1970.

GLASIER, GILSON GARDNER, lawyer; librarian; b. Muscoda, Wis., May 28, 1873; s. Henry Warren and Jane (Bosworth) G.; student business coll. (Austin) and lit. dept., U. of Wis.; LL.B., U. of Wis. Law Sch., 1900; m. Marybelle Kellogg, June 29, 1899; children—Marshall Willis, Franklin Kellogg, John Strong. Pvt. sec. to Justice R. D. Marshall, of Supreme Court of Wis., 1896-1904; practiced law, Milwaukee, 1904-05; state librarian of Wis. since 1906. Mem. Am. Assn. Law Libraries (ex-pres.), Nat. Assn. State Libraries, A.L.A., Am. Bar Assn., Wis. State Bar Assn. (life mem., editor of bull., 1927-48, sec.-treas., 1920-48, sec. 1948—), Hist. Society of Wisconsin (life member), Phi Delta Phi. Republican. Presbyterian. Mason. Club: Capitol Mutual (ex-pres.). Editor: Callaghan's Wisconsin Digest, 1909-20; Autobiography of Justice Roujet D. Marshall, 2 vols., 1923, 31. Mng. editor Index to Legal Periodicals and Law Library Journal, 1908-11. Spl. honors at 50th anniversary, Am. Assn. Law Libraries Phila., 1956. Home: 1919 Rowley Av., Madison 5. Address: State Library, Madison 2 WI‡

GLASOE, PAUL MAURICE, educator; b. Lanesboro, Minn., Aug. 24, 1873; s. Nias Edward and Anne Kjestline (Hjelde) G.; B.A., from U. of Minn., 1897, N.S., 1898, Ph.D., 1902; LL.D. (hon.) Wittenberg Coll., Springfield, O., 1949; traveled and studied in Eng., Norway, Sweden and Denmark, 1928-29; m. Gena Annette Kirkwold, June 28, 1899 (died 1927); children—Gynther Norris, Alf Melius I (dec.), Alf Melius II. Paul Kirkwold; m. 2d, Agnes Skartvedt, 1929 (died 1931); m. 3d, Hannah Fjeldstad, 1932. Instr. in chemistry, U. of Minn., 1898-1901; instr. in physics and chemistry, St. Olaf Coll., Northfield, Minn., 1901, prof., 1902-07; pres. Spokane Coll., Wash., 1907-10; prof. chemistry, St. Olaf Coll., 1910-16; pres. Augustana Coll., Canton, S.D., 1916-18; v.p. and prof. chemistry, St. Olaf Coll., since 1918, acting pres., 1927-28. Pres. Choral Union of Norwegian Luth. Ch., 1911-47; mem. Bd. of Elementary Christian Edn. So. Minn. Dist., 1920-45; vice pres. United Temperance Movement, 1940. pres. Minn. Anti-Saloon League; mem. Minn. Leif Erickson Monument Assn. Served as capt. Minn. Nat. Guard, 1903-05. Decorated Comdr. Order of St. Olaf, by King Haakon VII, Norway. Fellow A.A.A.S.; mem. Chem. Soc., Minn. Ednl. Assn., Sigma Xi. Republican. Lutheran. Author: General Chemistry, 1913; Introduction to the Periodic System (monograph), 1925; Foundations of General Chemistry, 1927; also numerous articles on teaching of chemistry. Home: 804 St. Olaf Av., Northfield MN‡

GLASSMAN, OSCAR, physician; b. Evanova, Sept. 9, 1901; s. Moss and Anna Glassman; M.D., N.Y.U., 1925; m. Jeanette Bitterbaum, June 5, 1926; 1 son, George. Intern, Bellevue Hosp., N.Y.C., 1925-27, resident in obstetrics, 1927; resident in obstetrics Berwind Maternity Clinic, 1926-27; resident in gynecology Mt. Sinai Hosp., N.Y.C., 1928-29, courtesy staff, until 1970; cons. obstetrician and gynecologist Sydenham Hosp.; attending obstetrician and gynecologist N.Y. Hosp., N.Y. Lying-In Hosp.; courtesy staff Doctors Hosp.; asso. prof. obstetrics and gynecology Cornell U. Med. Sch., N.Y.C. Served from maj. to lt. col., M.C., AUS, 1942-46. Diplomate Am. Bd. Obstetrics and Gynecology. Fellow A.C.S., Internat. Coll. Surgeons, Am. Coll. Obstetricians and gynecologists; mem. A.M.A., A.A.A.S., Am. Geriatrics Soc., Assn. Mil. Surgeons U.S. Home: New York City NY Died Oct. 10, 1970; buried Kensico Cemetery.

GLAVIN, CHARLES C., investment banker; b. Milw., Jan. 15, 1911; s. Charles F. and Lillian E. (Clarke) G.; A.B., Harvard, 1933, M.B.A., 1935; m. Elizabeth G. Lauerman, June 15, 1935; children—Kathryn (Mrs. Joseph F. Gagliardi, Jr.), Jane, Carol (Mrs. William K. Warren). With First Boston Corp., N.Y.C., 1935-71, successively trainee, asst. v.p., 1935-44, v.p., 1944-71, dir., 1950-71, mem. exec. com., 1956-63, chmn. exec. com., 1963-71; dir. Xerox Corp. Mem. Delta Upsilon. Roman Catholic. Clubs: Harvard, Wall Street (N.Y.C.); Laurel Valley Golf (Ligonier, Pa.); Winged Foot Golf (Mamaroneck, N.Y.). Home: Greenwich CT Died Jan. 30, 1971.

GLAVIS, LOUIS RUSSELL, lawyer; b. Eastern Shore, Md., June 10, 1883; s. George Oscar and Loucette Estelle (Smith) G.; student Lawrenceville (N.Y.) Sch., 1897-99. Began as spl. agent Gen. Land Office, Dept. Interior, 1904; admitted to Calif. Bar 1914, and practiced, San Francisco and Washington D.C.; formerly atty. and spl. investigator for U.S. Senate Com. on Indian Affairs; dir. investigations Dept Interior, 1933-36; chief investigator Senate Campaign Expenditures Com., July 1936-Jan. 1937; returned to private law practice. Mason. Clubs: Yarmouth (Nova Scotia) Golf; Arctic (Seattle); Columbia Country (Washington, D.C.); Gibson Island Yacht (Gibson Island, Md.); Missouri Athletic (St. Louis, Mo.) Contbr. series of articles to mags. on Tea Pot Dome oil scandal, Ku Klux Klan, prohibition law, etc. Home Pinehurst NC Died Nov. 30, 1971.

GLENDINNING, MALCOLM, editor; born Salmon Ida., Mar. 12, 1875; s. James and Margaret (Shoup) G. grad. St. Pauls Sch., Concord, N.H., 1893, Yale, 1898 m. Vedah Fairful Morton, Sept. 24, 1908 children—Eleanore (Mrs. T. J. Price), Robert Donald Margaret (Mrs. Richard Paulson). With Salt Lake (Utah) Herald, 1898; Bell Telephone Co., Salt Lake City, 1899-1901; placer mining Anvil Creek, Nome Alaska, 1901; Spokesman Review, Spokane, Wash. 1902-09; pub. Daily (Wallace) Idaho Press, 1909-11 Spokesman-Review, Spokane, Wash., since 1911 as city editor, and news editor, and mng. editor since 1942 Mem. Spokane C. of C., Sigma Delta Chi. Republican Episcopalian. Club: University. Home: South 1518 Madison. Office: Spokesman-Review, Spokane WA*‡

GLENN, CHARLES BOWLES, supt. schs.; b. Auburn Ala., Dec. 1, 1871; s. Emory Thomas and Elizabeth Hunter (Ross) G.; B.S., Ala. Poly. Inst., 1891, M.S. 1892; A.B., Harvard, 1896; LL.D., U. of Alabama, 1918 Litt.D., Birmingham Southern Coll., 1931; m. Elizabeth Roberts Douglass, June 25, 1902; 1 dau., Mari Augustine. Instr. S.W. Agrl. Sch., Evergreen, Ala. 1893-95, 1896-98; prin. Paul Hayne Sch., Birmingham Ala., 1899-1909; asst. supt. schs., Birmingham, 1909-21 superintendent of schools, Birmingham, 1921-42 superintendent emeritus since 1942. Mem. State Tex Book Commn., Ala., 1908-13. Mem. N.E.A. (v.p., mem commn. on character edn., 1931-32, chmn. commn social studies curriculum 1935-36), Ednl. Policie Commn., Am. Assn. of Sch. Adminstrs. (pres. 1937-38) Ala. Ednl. Assn. (ex-pres.), Alpha Tau Omega. Mason (33 deg.). Democrat. Methodist. Clubs: Rotary Country. Home: 2840 Hastings Road. Office: 2015 7th Av., Birmingham AL‡

GLICK, CARL, author, play dir.; b. Marshalltown, Ia., Sept. 11, 1890; s. Charles Glick and Myra (Cannon) G.; B.S., Northwestern U., 1915; m. Sue Ann Wilson, June 27, 1936. Actor with Donald Robertson Players, Chicago Art Inst., 1909-10; tour in Shakespearian repertoire, 1910-11; instr. in drama, Fairmount Coll., Wichita, Kan., 1915-17; dir. Community Theater, Waterloo, Ia., 1917-20; writer, New York, 1920-23; instr. in English and dir. Players Club, U. of Colo., 1923-25; asst. prof. of English and dir. Mont. Masquers, U. of Mont., 1925-27; dir. Little Theater, San Antonio, Tex., 1927-31; writer, New York, 1931-33; dir. Players Club, Sarasota, Fla., 1933-34; dir. Little Theater, York, Pa., 1934-35; writer, New York, 1935-38; columnist on community theaters for Springfield (Mass.) Republican, 1931-40. Dir. Town Theatre, Columbia, S.C., 1938-40; chmn. Inst. of the Theatre, Mohawk Drama Festival, Schenectady, N.Y., 1940; instr. playwriting, div. gen. edn., New York Univ., 1943-55; instr. in drama Cal. Western U., San Diego, 1955, ret. asst. prof., 1961, dir. writers conf., 1958-60; chmn. Com. of Community Theatres for National Drama Week, Drama League of America, from 1940. Mem. Chinese Athletic Club, Phi Kappa Psi. Active in having built the San Pedro Playhouse, city built and city owned, San Antonio, 1930. Served in U.S. Army, 1918-19. Mason (R.A.M.). Author: (plays) The Fourth Mrs. Phillips, Outclassed, Ten Days Later, Sun-Cold, It Isn't Done, 1928; The Devil's Host, 1934; The Unconquered, 1937; (novel) The Laughing Buddha, 1937; (text) Curtain's Going Up (with Albert McCleery), 1939; Shake Hands With the Dragon, 1941; Three Times I Bow, 1943; Oswald's Pet Dragon (juvenile), 1943; Double Ten, Captain O'Banion's Story of the Chinese Revolution, 1945; Mickey—The Horse That Volunteered (juvenile), 1945; Swords of Silence. The Secret Societies of China (with Hong Sheng-Hwa), 1947; The Secret of Serenity, 1951; A Treasury of Masonic Thought, 1953; Death Sits In, 1954; Everyman (adaptation with Kent Wilson), 1956 (with Ollie Rogers) The Story of Our Flag, 1964. Contbr. fiction and articles to mags. Home: San Diego CA Died Mar. 8, 1971; buried Rosecrans Nat. Cemetery, San Diego CA

GLICKMAN, IRVING, educator, periodontist; b. N.Y.C., Jan. 17, 1914; s. Nathan and Rose (Gurland) G.; B.S., Bklyn. Coll., 1933; D.M.D., Tufts U., 1938, postgrad. dept. pathology Med. Sch., 1939-40; m. Violeta Arboleda, Mar. 13, 1954; children—Alan, Denise. Faculty, Tufts U. Sch. Dental Medicine, Boston, 1938-72, prof. oral pathology, 1948-72, research prof. oral pathology, 1960-72, prof. periodontology, 1948-72, chmn. dept., 1960-72, dir. div. grad. and postgrad. studies, 1951-60. Mem. Army Med. Service Adv. Com. on Preventive Dentistry; mem. adv. group Cambridge (Mass.) Health Dept.; lectr. dental pathology Boston U. Sch. Medicine; cons. in periodontology Forsyth Dental Center, Boston, VA Hosp., Boston; cons. Armed Forces Inst. Pathology; dental cons. U.S. Naval Hosp., Chelsea, Mass.; asso. staff New Eng. Center Hosp.; staff Brookline Hosp.; cons. in oral pathology Grove Manor Hosp.; periodontist Boston City Hosp.; dir. Berkshire Conf. on Periodontology and Oral Pathology, 1950-72. Chmn. alumni council Tufts U., 1963-64. Trustee, Combined Jewish Philanthropies, Boston. Recipient numerous awards including Samuel Charles Miller Meml. award in oral medicine, 1965, award for basic research in periodontology Internat. Assn. for Dental Research, 1966. Diplomate Am. Bd. Periodontology, Am. Bd. Oral Medicine, Am. Bd. Oral Pathology. Fellow Am. Acad. Dental Sci., A.A.A.S., Am., Internat. colls. dentists; mem. Am. Acad. Periodontology (Gold Medal award 1972), Am. Acad. Dental Medicine, Am. Assn. Dental Schs., Am. Assn. Anatomists, New Eng. Soc. Pathologists, Internat. Assn. for Dental Research, Internat. Acad. Oral Pathology, Tissue Culture Assn., Am. Dental Assn., Mass. Dental Soc., Tufts U. Dental Alumni Assn. (pres. 1966-67), Sigma Xi, Omicron Kappa Upsilon; also hon. mem. fgn. socs. Jewish religion (trustee temple). Author: Clinical Periodontology, 4th edit., 1972; Periodontal Disease, 1972. Guest editor Symposium on Preventive Dentistry, 1972. Contbr. numerous articles to profl. jours., also chpts. to books. Home: Newton Center MA Died Oct. 2, 1972.

GLOVER, GEORGE HENRY, veterinarian; b. Eagle Grove, Ia., Apr. 2, 1864; s. Russel Bliss and Emily Cook (Garland) G.; B.S., State Agrl. Coll., Ft. Collins, Colo., 1884, M.S., 1903; D.V.M., Ia. State Coll., 1885; m. Margaret J. Glover, Nov. 19, 1887 (dec.); 1 son, George Grout; m. 2d, Lenore Herbert Talty. Practiced in Denver, 1887-91; insp. on Nation Cattle Trail, 1891-1900; head of div. of vet. medicine (Coll. of Vet. Medicine), Colo. Agrl. Coll., 1900-34, retired as dean vet. div. City food insp., Ft. Collins, since 1907. Recipient Honor Trophy conferred by alumni of Colo. State Coll. of A. & M. Arts, 1938; also Alumni Merit award conferred by Chicago Alumni Assn. of Iowa State Coll., 1940. Unitarian. Mem. Am. Vet. Med. Assn. (pres. 1911), Colo. Vet. Med. Assn. (pres. 1909), Am. Vet. Assn. of Coll. Faculties and State Examining Bds. (pres. 1911), Alpha Psi. Mason. Author of various bulls. Home: Ft Collins CO‡

GLOVER, JOHN GEORGE, educator; b. Carlow, Ireland, Jan. 6, 1895; s. John George and Annie Glover; student McGill U., U. Newark; B.C.S., N.Y.U., 1926, M.C.S., 1927, B.S., 1929, A.M., 1930, Ph.D., 1932; m. Augusta M. Behrens, July 10, 1924. Chief accountant T. A. Edison Storage Battery Co., 1920-26; member faculty N.Y.U., 1926-65, research prof. emeritus, 1965-70. Served as colonel USAF 1940-45. Mem. Acad. Mgmt., Operations Research Soc. Am., Ret. Officers Assn. (p.pres. No. N.J. chpt.), Author: Business Operations Research and Reports, 1949; Fundamentals of Professional Mgmt., rev. 1958. Home: West Orange NJ Died Sept. 23, 1970; inurned Fresh Pond Crematory, Middle Village LI NY

GLUECK, BERNARD, psychiatrist; b. Poland, Dec. 10, 1884; M.D., Georgetown U., 1909; studied univs. of Munich and Berlin, 1911; m. Betty J.; children—Bernard, Ruth (Mrs. Addison). Mem. staff Govt. Hosp. for Insane, 1909-16; mental examiner of immigrants, Port of New York, 1913; dir. psychiatric clinic, Sing Sing Prison, 1915-18; dir. of mental hygiene dept., N.Y. Sch. of Social Work, and Bur. of Child Guidance, 1918-23; mem. faculty U. N.C., Chapel Hill, 1956-64; sr. psychiat. cons. John Umstead Hosp., Butner, N.C., 1956-64. Capt. Medical Corps. U.S. Army. 1918; chief of staff Stony Lodge Foundation, Ossining-on-Hudson. Mem. A.M.A., Am. Psychiatric Assn., Am. Psychopathol. Assn., Am. Psychoanalytic Assn., N.Y. Soc. Psychopathology and Psychotherapy (ex-pres.). Author: Studies in Forensic Psychiatry, 1916. Translator: (with John E. Lind) Neurotic Constitution (by Alfred Adler), 1917; Introduction to a Psychoanalytic Psychiatry (by Paul Schilder), 1927; (with Bertram D. Lewin) Psychoanalysis of the Total Personality (by Franz Alexander), 1930. Lecturer New School for Social Butner NC Died Oct. 5, 1972; buried Arlington Nat. Cemetery.

GLUECK, ELEANOR TOUROFF, (MRS. SHELDON GLUECK), criminologist; b. N.Y.C., Apr. 12, 1898; d. Bernard Leo and Anna (Wodzislawski) Touroff; A.B., Barnard Coll., 1920; diploma N.Y. Sch. Social Work, 1921; Ed.M., Harvard, 1923, Ed.D., 1925, Sc.D., 1958; m. Sheldon Glueck, Apr. 16, 1922; 1 dau., Mrs. Joyce Glueck Rosberg (dec.). Engaged in criminology research dept. social ethics Harvard U., 1925-28, research asst. Law Sch. Crime Survey, 1928-30, research asst. criminology Law Sch., 1930-53, research asso. criminology, 1953-72, spl. studies in delinquency, co-dir. program research into the causes, treatment and prevention of juvenile delinquency, 1925-72. Trustee, exec. com. Judge Baker Guidance Center. Recipient (with husband) August Vollmer award Am. Soc. Criminology, 1961; Beccaria Gold medal German Criminological Soc., 1924; Gold medal Inst. of Criminal Anthropology, U. Rome (Italy), 1964. Fellow Am. Acad. Arts and Scis., A.A.A.S.; mem. Am. Soc. Criminology, Nat. Assn. Social Workers, Mass. Conf. Social Welfare, Am. Assn. U. Women, Asso. Alumnae Barnard Coll. (Distinguished Alumna award 1969), Internat. Soc. Criminology, League Women Voters (Cambridge), Assn. N.Y. Sch. Social Work. Author: Community Use of Schools, 1927; Adventure in Japan, 1962; (with Sheldon Glueck) books including: One Thousand Juvenile Delinquents, 1934, After-Conduct of Discharged Offenders, 1945; Unraveling Juvenile Delinquency, 1950; Delinquents in the Making, 1952; Physique and Delinquency, 1956; Delinquents and Nondelinquents in Perspective, 1968. Co-editor: Preventing Crime, 1936; Predicting Delinquency and Crime, 1959; Family Environment and Delinquency, 1962; Ventures in Criminology, 1964; Delinquents and Nondelinquents in Perspective, 1968; Toward a Typology of Juvenile Offenders, 1970; Identification of Predelinquents, 1972. Mem. editorial board Internat. Jour. Social Psychiatry; editorial cons. bd. jours. Address: Cambridge MA Died Sept. 25, 1972.

GLUECK, NELSON, coll. pres.; b. Cincinnati, June 4, 1900; s. Morris and Anna (Rubin) G.; A.B., U. Cincinnati, 1920; B.H.L., Hebrew Union Coll., 1918, Rabbi, 1923; student U. of Berlin and Heidelberg U., 1923-25; Ph.D., U. of Jena, Germany, 1927; LL.D., U. of Cincinnati, 1936, Xavier U., 1969, Miami U., 1962; D.H.L., Jewish Theol. Sem., 1947, Jewish Inst. of Religion, 1947; L.H.D., Brandeis U., 1961, Wayne State U., 1962, N.Y.U., 1963; S.T.D. U. So. Cal., 1964, Ripon Coll., 1969; Litt.D., Dropsie Coll., 1951, U. Pa., 1960, Thomas More Coll., 1968; D.S.L., Kenyon Coll., O., 1955; D.D., Drake U., Ia., 1956, Pacific Sch. Religion, 1966; D.Sc., Lincoln (Ill.) Coll., 1965, Del. Valley Co. Sci. and Agr., Coll. of Holy Cross, 1965, Instituti Divi Thomoe, 1968; m. Helen Ransohoff Iglauer, Mar. 26, 1931; 1 son, Charles Jonathan. Instr. Hebrew Union Coll., 1928, asst. prof., 1931, became associate prof., 1934, professor Bible and Biblican archaeology, 1936-71, pres., 1947-50; pres. Jewish Inst. of Religion, 1949-50; pres. combined Hebrew Union Coll.-Jewish Inst. of Religion, Cin., N.Y., Los Angeles, Jerusalem, 1950-71; lecturer Biblical literature U. Cin., 1935-36; annual prof. Am. Sch. of Oriental Research, Baghdad, 1933-34; dir. Am. School Oriental Research, Jerusalem, Palestine, 1932-33, 1936-40, 42-47; field dir. Baghdad, 1942-47; excavations and important archaeological discoveries in Palestine and Transjordan, 1932-47; archaeol. explorations in the Negev, 1952-—. Dir. Union Central Life Ins. Co. Trustee John F. Kennedy Memorial Library, Cin. Art Mus., trustee American School of Oriental Research. Recipient of Cin. Fine Arts Ward, 1939; Ohioana Career medal, 1956; Ohioana non-fiction book award, 1960. Benediction at inauguration of Pres. U.S., 1961, Pvt. R.O.T.C., 1918; with OSS, 1942-47. Henry S. Morgenthau Traveling fellow, 1925-28. Fellow Am. Acad. Arts and Scis.; mem. of the American Philos. Soc., Central Conf. Am. Rabbis, Archaeol. Inst. Am., Am. Oriental Soc., Israel Exploration Soc., Am. Sch. Oriental Research, Phi Beta Kappa. Democrat. Jewish religion. Clubs: Explores, Pen. (N.Y.C.); Literary, University, Commercial (Cincinnati, O.); Cosmos (Washington); Harvard (Boston). Author: Das Wort Hesed im alttetamentlichen Sprachgebrauche, 1927, 61; Explorations in Eastern Palestine, Vo. 1, 1934, 2, 1935, 3, 1939, 4, 1951, 66; The Other Side of the Jordan, 1940, 69; The River Jordan, 1946, 68; Rivers in the Desert: A History of the Negev, 1959, 60, 68; Deities and Dolphins, 1965, 66; Hesed in the Bible, 1967; Dateline: Jerusalem, 1968. Contbr. articles on archaeology and Bible to mags., books, encys. Home: Cincinnati OH Died Feb. 12, 1971.

GOBER, WILLIAM MATHIS, lawyer; b. Commerce, Ga., July 29, 1875; s. William J. and Clarisa (Embry) G.; ed. high sch., Commerce (non-grad.); m. Gussie E. Jackson, of Commerce, Nov. 21, 1899; children—William A., Maurine. Began practice at Ocala, Fla., 1910; Rep. candidate for Congress, 1st Fla. Dist., 1916, 22; for atty. gen. of Fla., 1920; U.S. dist. atty., Southern Dist. of Fla., 1921-29. Candidate for justice Supreme Court of Fla., 1924. Episcopalian. Republican. Past Chancellor K.P. of Grand Domain of Fla. Home: 3203 Hawthorn Rd. Office: Tampa Theatre Bldg., Tampa FL‡

GODBEY, JOHN CAMPBELL, educator; b. nr. Perry, Mo., July 4, 1882; s. Josiah P. and Nora (Bates) G.; student Woodson (Mo.) Acad., 1898-99, Woodson Inst., 1899-1901; A.B., Central Coll. of Mo., 1904, A.M., 1905; student U. of Mo., 1906, Vanderbilt U., 1908-10, Leipzig U., 1911-12; Sc.D. (hon.), McMurray Coll., 1943; m. Ethel Kring Rush, Sept. 20, 1911; children—John C. (dec.), Mary (dec.), William, Rosalee, Margaret Lee Charles. High sch. teacher New Haven, Mo., 1905-06; asst. supt., coach, football, baseball and track Paris, Mo., 1906-08; mem. faculty Central College, 1910-13; head of the science dept. So. Univ., Greensboro, Ala., 1913-17; head dept. chemistry Southwestern U., Georgetown, Tex., 1917-61, prof. chemistry, from 1917, director phys. sci. dept. from 1939, chmn. div. natural and applied sci. 1942; v.p. Ce-Tex Wool Mohair Co. since 1939. Commr. water and light Georgetown Tex., 1919-42; mayor-pro-tem, Georgetown, 1922-42; commr. Tex. Centennial of Statehood, 1946. Served R.O.T.C., 1918. Fellow A.A.A.S., Am. Inst. Chemists, Tex. Acad. Sci. (past pres.; hon. life fellow); mem. Southwestern Sci. Soc., C. of C. Democrat. Methodist. Clubs: Georgetown Country, Lions, Scholia. Author: General Chemical and Laboratory (manual), 1930; Water Gas Residue, 1912; Organic Chemistry Laboratory (manual), 1935. Home: Georgetown TX Died June 14, 1970.

GODFREY, ALFRED LAURANCE, lawyer; b. Lima, Wis., Jan. 8, 1888; s. Thomas G. and Mary (Dickson) G.; A.B., U. of Wis., 1914; J.D., 1919; m. Helen Humphrey, Apr. 24, 1918; children—Thomas Grant, Richard Laurance. Prin. Westby (Wis.) High Sch., 1910-12, Stevens Point High Sch., 1914-15; admitted to Wis. bar, 1919, engaging in practice of law at Milwaukee, at Elkhorn, 1921-70; on legal staff Soo Line Ry., 1919-21; dir. and gen. counsel State Long Distance Telephone Co.; dist. atty., Walworth County, Wis., 1922-26; chmn. Walworth County Rep. Com., 1926-29; chmn. Rep. Congressional Com., 1st Dist. of Wis., 1931; sec. State Rep. Com. of Wis., 1932-34. Commd. 1st lt. 1917, resigned, 1919; later commd. capt. and maj., Reserve Corps. Chmn. Central Walworth Co. chpt. Am. Red Cross; mem. bd. govs. Wis. State Bar, 1948-51, pres. 1951-52. Fellow American Bar Found.; mem. American (house of delegates 1952-60, Wis. (past president), Walworth County (pres.) bar assns., Phi Delta Phi, Am. Legion. Republican. Conglist. Mason. Club: Kiwanis, Big Foot Country. Home: Elkhorn WI Died Apr. 11, 1970.

GODSHALL, LINCOLN DERSTINE, mining engr., metallurgist; b. Lansdale Pa., Nov. 26, 1865; s. Abraham C. and Anna (Derstine) G.; B.S., Lafayette Coll., Pa., 1887, M.S., Ph.D., 1890; m. Estelle B. Hall, Mar. 30, 1889 (died Feb. 10, 1920); children—Clarence Hall, Leon Deane, William Arthur, Harold Lincoln; m. 2d, Mrs. Laura Chambers Smith, Oct. 8, 1923. Supt. and metallurgist, Colo., 1888-93; sulpt. Puget Sound Reduction Works, Wash., 1894-99; supt. Boston-Wyo. Smelting, Power & Light Co., 1900-02; v.p. and mng. dir. Ariz.-Mexican Mining & Smelting Co., 1904-10; v.p. and mgr. Cocopah Copper Co.; mgr. Needles Mining & Smelting Co. (a subsidiary of U.S. Smelting, Refining & Mining Co.), Nov. 1909-Jan. 1911; v.p. in charge Tecopa (Calif.) Consol. Mining Co., and Tecopa R.R. Co., 1912-28, pres. Ivanpah Copper Co., Los Angeles. Regent U. of Wash., 6 yrs. Republican. Club: Los Angeles Country. Contbr. to engrng. and mining jours. Home: 722 S. Oxford Av. Office: Standard Oil Bldg., 605 W. Olympic Blvd., Los Angeles CA‡

GODWIN, HANNIBAL LA FAYETTE, ex-congressman; b. Harnett Co., N.C., Nov. 3, 1873; s. Archibald B. and Rebecca Eliza (Reeves) G.; ed. Trinity Coll., and U. of N.C., LL.B., 1896; m. Mattie B. Barnes, of Dunn, N.C., Dec. 23, 1896. Admitted to bar, 1896; mayor Dunn, N.C., 1897; mem. N.C. Senate, 1903; mem. State Central Com., 1903-05; presdl. elector, 1904; mem. 60th to 66th Congresses (1907-21), 6th N.C. Dist. Democrat. Home: Dunn NC‡

GODWIN, HERBERT, retired cotton exporter; b. on Woodbine Plantation nr. Memphis, Tenn., Nov. 7, 1869; s. David George (M.D.) and Elizabeth (Douglas) G.; A.B., Emory Coll. (now Univ.), Oxford, Ga., 1889; m. Lila Ward Humphreys, Nov. 9, 1896 (died 1926); children—Elizabeth Douglas (Mrs. DeWitt McLaurine Gordon), Ann Humphreys (Mrs. Charles Ingoldsby McLean), Lila Humphreys (Mrs. Thomas Wm. Moore), Virginia Carrington. Prof. Latin, Bolton Coll., 4 yrs.; sec. Tenn. Dept. of Agriculture, 3 yrs.; entered cotton seed products business at Memphis, 1898; built and operated cotton oil mill at West, Tex., 1899, Houston, 1900; president Godwin-Humphreys Co., cotton exporters, Houston, Tex., and other corporations until 1924; formerly director S. Tex. Commercial National Bank and other corporations. Formerly capt. Taylor Light Guards of Tenn. Nat. Guard; organizer, 1st pres., Houston chapter A.R.C., 1917; 1st asst. food administrator, Tex., 1917-18. Former chmn. Houston Park Board, Houston Civil Service Board; former vice chmn. Houston City Planning Commn.; former pres. of Houston Museum of Fine Arts, Green Mask Players (little theatre). First chmn. Houston Housing Authority (Federal slum clearance). Formerly trustee Ripley Memorial Foundation. Mem. Nat. Econ. League, Virginia Hist. Soc., Houston Philos. Soc., Open Forum, Garden Club of Am., Alpha Tau Omega. Democrat. Episcopalian. Clubs: Thalian, Houston, University, Town and Gown, Houston Country, Eagle Lake Rod and Gun, Camp Sterett, Bayou. Established Godwin Lectureship on Pub. Affairs, Rice Inst. (University). Address: care Lamar Hotel, Houston TX‡

GOERTZ, RAYMOND C., engr.; b. Clearwater, Kan., Mar. 12, 1915; s. Norman E. and Flora (Saint) G.; B.S., Mont. State Coll., 1940; grad. study, Poly. Institute of Brooklyn, 1942-46, Illinois Institute of Technology, 1947-49; m. Helen Boula, September 2, 1950;children—Alan, Jean, and Linda. Jr. engr., project engr. Servomechanisms Lab., Sperry Gyroscope Co., 1940-47; formerly group leader Argonne Nat. Lab., Lemont, Ill., sr. engr. remote control engring. div. U.S. del. 1st and 2d Internat. Confs. on Peaceful Uses of Atomic Energy, Geneva, Switzerland, 1955, 58. Recipient Edward Longstreth medal Franklin Inst., Phila., 1967; Radiation Industry award Am. Nuclear Soc., 1969. Mem. Am. Nuclear Soc., Research Soc. Am., Am. Inst. Chem. Engrs., I.E.E.E., Am. Nuclear Soc., Research Soc. Am. Contbr. articles to profl. jours. Patentee in field. Home: Downers Grove IL Died June 4, 1970; buried Clarendon Hills Cemetery, Clarendon Mills IL

GOETZ, NORMAN S., lawyer; b. New York, N.Y., Mar. 7, 1887; s. Samuel and Julia (Marx) G.; A.B. Columbia U., 1906, LL.B., 1909; m. Mildred Blout, Feb. 12, 1925 (dec. 1953); m. 2d, Beatrice J. Lane. Jan. 12, 1956. Law practice, partner of Leventritt, Riegelman, Carns & Goetz 1912-24; partner Proskauer, Rose, Goetz & Mendelsohn and predecessor firms, from 1925. Dir. Greater N.Y. Fund, 1942-64, v.p., 1945-48, pres., 1956-59, chmn. bd., 1950-51, 55-56; pres. Fedn. Jewish Philanthropies N.Y., 1945-48, chmn. bd., 1961-63, trustee-at-large, 1940-48, hon. trustee from 1948, chmn. lawyers div., 1937-38, chmn. citywide campaign, 1942-43, chmn. com. communal planning, 1951-57; former chmn. legacy com.; dir. Hosp. Council Greater N.Y., 1944-64, pres., 1948-55; trustee State U. N.Y., 1948-58, chmn. com. on med. edn., 1952-57; dir. United Hosp. Fund, 1948-57, mem.-at-large, 1961-64; director of New York Adult Edn. Council, 1941-65, Hillside Hosp., 1941-48; former dir. Welfare Council City N.Y., Council Jewish Fedn. and Welfare Funds; former mem. exec., adminstrv. coms. Am. Jewish Com. Served from pvt. to capt., non-flying AS, 1917-19. Mem. Assn. Bar City of N.Y. (v.p., 1950-52, exec. com. 1943-47), N.Y. County Lawyers Assn. (past chmn. bankruptcy com.). Internat., Am., N.Y. bar assns. Democrat. Jewish religion. Club: Ocean Beach. Home: New York City NY Died Mar. 5, 1972.

GOETZ, WILLIAM, motion picture exec.; b. New York, N.Y., March 24, 1903; s. Theodore and Fanny (Aronsohn) G.; m. Edith Mayer, March 19, 1930; children—Judith Mayer, Barbara. Became asso. producer Fox Films, later 20th Century-Fox, 1930, v.p., 1935, mem. of bd. of dirs. 1942, in charge of prodn., 1942-43; formed Internat. Pictures, Inc., 1943; prodn. exec. for Universal-International Studio, 1945-53; pres. William Goetz Prodns., Inc., 1954-64; v.p. prodn. Seven Arts Asso. Corp., Beverly Hills, Cal., 1964-67; produced movie, Man From Laramie, 1955, also produced movie Sayonara, 1957; as asso. producer for 20th Century, produced, The House of Rothschild, The Bowery, Gallant Lady, Les Miserables, Cardinal Richelieu, The Call of the Wild, 1933-34; also produced for Internat. Pictures, Inc.; chmn. bd. dirs. Westland Capital Corp.; dir. City National Bank of Beverly Hills (California). Trustee, Reed Coll. Mem. Motion Picture Acad. Arts and Scis. Home: Los Angeles CA Died Aug. 1969.

GOETZE, ALBRECHT, educator; b. Leipzig, Germany, Jan. 11, 1897; s. Rudolf and Elsa (Roemmler) G.; Ph.D., Heidelberg, 1920; A.M. (hon.), Yale, 1936; m. Frida Schirbel, Nov. 11, 1922; children—Dieter, Marianne (Mrs. Andrew Pfeiffer), Gabriele Lee. Came to U.S., 1934, naturalized 1940. Docent, Heidelberg, 1923-30; prof. Marburg, 1930-33, dismissed by Hitler govt., 1933; vis. prof., Yale, 1934-36, William M. Laffan prof. Assyriology, 1936-56, Sterling prof., 1956-65, prof. emeritus, 1965-71, chmn. dept. Near East langs., 1958-66; mem. Inst. for Comparative Research in Human Culture, Oslo, Norway; dir. Am. Sch. for Oriental Research, Baghdad, 1948-56. Mem. Am. Oriental Soc., Am. Sch. of Oriental Research, Linguistic Soc. of Am., Archaeol. Inst. Am., Soc. Bibl. Lit., Am. Philos. Soc. (life), Acad. des Inscriptions et Belles Lettres (corr.), Royal Danish Acad. (fgn.), Societe Asiatique de Paris (hon. life), Inst. for Comparative Research in Human Culture (life), German Archaeol. Inst. (life). Author books including: Old Babylonian Omen Texts, 1947; Laws of Eshnunna, 1956; Kuiturgeschichte Kleinasiens, 2d edit., 1957. Contbr. articles to profl. jours. Home: New Haven CT Died Aug. 15, 1971; cremated.

GOGGIN, CATHARINE, teacher; b. in Adirondacks, N.Y.; d. Patrick and Margaret (Kenny) G.; grad. Chicago High Sch., 1872; unmarried. Teacher in pub. schs. from Oct., 1872. With Margaret Haley inaugurated, Jan., 1900, movement for equitable taxation which had, up to Oct., 1902, added $1,250,000 to revenue of Chicago, through legal proceedings brought in the name of Miss Goggin. Mem. Chicago Teachers' Federation, Teachers' Club, Catholic Women's Nat. League, Federation Forum of Ill., Nat. Federation of Women. Residence: 537 La Salle Av. Office: 444 Unity Bldg., Chicago IL‡

GOHEN, CHARLES MARSH, banker; b. Aurora, Ind., Sept. 18, 1875; s. James Alfred and Malvina Fenton (Marsh) G.; ed. pub. schs., Huntington, W.Va.; m. Mary Elizabeth Emmons, June 14, 1906. Began with Commercial Bank, Huntington, 1890; pres. 1st Huntington Nat. Bank 1924-48, ret. treasurer, dir. Fesenmeier Brewing Co., Collins & Mayo Collieries Co.; v.p., trustee Huntington Indsl. Corp. dir. Chesapeake & Potomac Telephone Co., of W.Va., Banks Miller Supply Co. County chmn. War Savings Com. Cabell County, W.Va. Democrat. Episcopalian. Clubs. Guyandot, Guyan Country. Home: 1515 5th Av. Office: 1515 5th Av., Huntington WV‡

GOING, CHARLES BUXTON, writer; b. Westchester, N.Y., Apr. 5, 1863; s. Charles Henry and Eliza (Buxton) G.; Ph.B., Columbia, 1882, hon. M.Sc., 1910; m. Mary Evelyn Thompson, June 1, 1887 (died 1896); m. 2d, Marie Overton Corbin, Dec. 18, 1912 (died 1925); m. 3d, Mathilde Marie Sylvie Roux, Feb. 14, 1929. Asso. editor, New York and London, 1896-98, mng. editor, 1898-1912, editor and v.p., 1912-15, Engineering Magazine; editor Works Management Library, 1915-16 (retired); spl. lecturer, Columbia and Harvard, 1909-15; a leader in organizing Soc. Indsl. Engrs., continuing as chmn. until permanent Officers were elected, 1917. Commd. maj., Ordnance Dept., U.S.R., and on spl. duty, Washington, 1917; spl. asst. to chief ordnance officer, A.E.F., 1918; recommended for lieut. col.; disch., Apr. 1919. Cited for specially conspicuous and meritorious service" in Ordnance Dept., A.E.F. Mem. Poetry Soc. America; corr. mem. Canadian Mining Inst. Auth: Summer-Fallow, 1892; (with Marie Overton Corbin) Urchins of the Sea, 1900, and Urchins at the Pole, 1901; Star-Glow and Song, 1909; Methods of the Santa Fe, 1909; Principles of Industrial Engineering, 1911; David Wilmot, Free-Soiler, 1924; Folklore and Fairy Plays, 1927; Precarious Paradise and other Plays, 1904; On Provencial Roads, 1936 (serial); Adventures in Statecraft, 1940 (serial). Author many songs set to music. Contbr. to mags. Home: Lei Tres Mario, Cassels-sur-Mer, B. du Rh. France‡

GOLAY, JOHN FORD, univ. dean; b. Warrensburg, Mo., July 29, 1917; s. Ned and Martha Aurora (Ford) G.; B.A., U. So. Cal., 1938; B.A. (Rhodes scholar), Oxford U., 1940, M.A., 1941, D.Phil., 1955; m. Leland Theodora Bailey, Mar. 7, 1950; 1 son, John Edward. Asst. to Lord Beveridge, various projects including revision Brit. social ins. system, war-time manpower survey, 1940-42; tchr. polit. sci. Pomona Coll., Claremont, Cal., 1946-48; dep. Am. sec. Allied Secretariat to Allied Mil. Govs. and High Commrs., Berlin and Bonn, Germany, 1948-52, chief Am. sect. Allied Gen. Secretariat, also sec.-gen. Allied High Commn., Bonn; exec. sec. Office U.S. High Commr. for Germany, Bonn, 1952-53; dean faculties, prof. history Roosevelt U., Chgo., 1956-60; provost, grad. dean, prof. history W.Va. U., 1961-69. Served as flight lt., Brit. R.A.F., 1942-46; air navigator. Mem. Am. Hist. Assn., Phi Beta Kappa. Author: The Founding of the Federal Republic of Germany, 1958; also textbook. Contbr. The New Republic, 1953-69. Home: Morgantown WV Died Jan. 27, 1969.

GOLD, HARRY, pharmacologist, cardiologist; b. Russia, Dec. 25, 1899; s Samuel and Naomi (Katz) G.; A.B., Cornell, 1919, M.D., 1922; m. Bertha Goldman, 1926; children—Naomi, Stanley, Muriel. Came to U.S., 1903, naturalized, 1910. Instr. pharmacology Cornell, 1922-29, asst. prof., 1929-44, asso. prof., 1944-47, prof. clin. pharmacology, 1947-65, emeritus, 1965-72; attending-in-charge cardiovascular research unit, Beth Israel Hosp., 1931-65, cons. cardiology, 1965-72; attending cardiologist, chmn. med. adv. bd. hosp. Joint Diseases, 1933-65, cons. cardiologist, 1965-72; mem. med. bd. Doctors Hosp., 1950-63, honorary member of attending staff, 1963-72; consulting cardiologist at St. Vincent's hosps. S.I., Army Med. Center Richmond Meml. Hosp., S.I.; civilian instr. and cons. U.S. Naval Hosp., St. Albans; lectr. therapeutics Post Grad. Extension div. Rutgers U. Mem. revision com. U.S. Pharmacopoeia, 1940-57. Recipient award of distinction as father clin. pharmacology Cornell U. Med. Coll., 1971. Fellow N.Y. Acad. Scis., N.Y. Acad Medicine, A.A.A.S.; mem. A.M.A., Am. Heart Assn. (sci. council), Am. Soc. Pharmacology and Exptl. Therapeutics, mem. N.Y. Heart Assn. (bd. dirs.), Harvey Soc., Am. Coll. Clin. Pharmacology and Chemotherapy (charter mem. bd. regents), Poison Control Center N.Y.C., Alpha Omega Alpha, Phi Beta Kappa; honorary member of Argentine Med. Assn., Cardiological Soc. Brazil. Democrat. Jewish religion. Mng. editor Cornell Confs. on Therapy, 1949-55; asso. editor Am. Jour. Medicine, 1947-57, Am. Jour. Medical Sci., 1944-72; editorial bd. Jour. Clin. Pharmacology, 1963-72. Author: Quinidine in Disorders of the Heart, 1950. Asso. editorial bd. N.Y. State Jour. of Medicine. Contbr. sci. articles Am., European med. jours. Home: New York City NY Died Apr. 21, 1972.

GOLD, NATHAN JULES, retail merchant; b. Hampton, Ia., May 28, 1894; s. William and Pauline (Mayer) G.; student U. Neb.; Dr. Humane Letters (hon.), Neb. Wesleyan U., 1959; m. Evelyn Baum, May 25, 1922; children—William II, Louise (Mrs. Aaron Levitt). With Gold & Co., Lincoln, Neb., from 1911, pres., 1936-55, chairman of the board of directors, from 1955. Head Neb. Famine Relief Drive, 1940; head retail div. Neb. orgn. War Bond Campaign, 1943; co-founder Lincoln Better Bus. Bur., Lincoln Community Chest, Lincoln City Planning Commn.; mem. Neb. Resources Com. Chmn. Neb. Resources Found., 1949-61. Served as 1st lt., U.S. Army, World War I. Recipient distinguished service award U. Neb., 1946. Jewish Welfare Found., 1956. Kiwanis Club, 1959, Lincoln Exchange Club, 1956; gold medal award National Retail Merchants Assn., 1965. Mem. Neb. Hist. Soc. (treas. 1950-54), Lincoln C. of C. (life, v.p., dir.), Nat. Retail Mchts. Assn. (mem. bd., exec. com., pres. 1959). Neb. Alumni Assn. (director); honorary member Beta Gamma Sigma, 4-H Clubs Am., Future Farmers Am., Future Homemakers Am., Soc. of Innocents of U. Neb., Internat. Farm Youth Exchange Program. Home: Lincoln NB Died Feb. 23, 1970.

GOLD, PLEASANT DANIEL, JR., b. Wilson, N.C., May 15, 1876; s. Pleasant Daniel (sr.) and Julia (Pipkin) G.; A.B., U. of N.C., 1898; studied law, Richmond Coll., Va. (never practiced); m. Elizabeth Faust Balsley, of Greensboro, N.C., May 15, 1901. Gen. agt., life ins., 1902-7; organizer, 1907, 1st v.p. and gen. mgr., Jefferson Standard Life Ins. Co. of Raleigh, N.C.; resigned, 1912; mem. P. D. Gold, Jr., & Co., southern investments. Moved to New York City, 1912, engaged in mortgage loan and gen. investments. Pres. Am. Life Conv., 1911-12. Mem. alumni council, U. of N.C.; dir. N.C. Children's Home Soc.; sec., mem. exec. com. N.C. Audubon Soc. for Game Protection; exec. com. N.C. Good Roads Assn.; mem. Kappa Sigma. Mem. Woodrow Wilson Inaugural Reception Com., Mar. 4, 1913; gen. sec. Edward E. McCall Assn., New York mayoralty campaign, 1913; Democrat. Mason (32 deg.). Clubs: Elks, Merchants', Manufacturers' (Greensboro, N.C.), Capital, Raleigh Country (Raleigh), N.Y. Southern Soc., N.C. Soc. of N.Y., Colonia (N.J.) Country. Author of addresses. Home: 3 Riverside Drive. Office: 150 New York NY‡

GOLDBERG, LEO, banker; b. Poland, Dec. 12, 1913; s. Peter and Mary (Pincus) G.; came to U.S., 1929, naturalized citizen; ed. pub. schs., Cleve.; m. Charlotte Gross, Aug. 22, 1937; children—Robert, Gerald, David, Jackaline, Bonnie Ann. Engaged in retail bus., 1932-46, real estate, 1946-55, then bldg. residential and comml. bldgs., 1955-60; with Ohio Savs. Assn., Cleve., 1958-71, pres., 1962-71, pres., dir. family owned corps. in real estate, also co-partner other bus. ventures. Participating, hon. mem. United Jewish Appeal, Jewish Community Fedn.; chmn. Israel Bonds; life mem. Brandies U. Mem. U.S. Savs. and Loan League, Homebuilders Assn. Republican. Jewish religion. Club: Cleve. Commerce. Home: Shaker Heights OH Died Feb. 28, 1971.

GOLDBERGER, ISIDORE HARRY, physician, educator, author; b. N.Y.C., Aug. 24, 1888; s. Herman and Rose (Weiss) G.; grad. N.Y.U. Med. Coll., 1910; m. Minnie Snow, Feb. 12, 1913; children—Eleanor (Mrs. Robert S. Frank), Marjorie (Mrs. Edmund Grasheim). Clin. prof. pediatrics N.Y.U. Med. Coll., 1911-41, spl. lectr. Sch. Edn., also Columbia U. Sch. Pub. Health, Coll. City N.Y.; dir. health edn. Bd. Edn., N.Y.C.,

1914-58; dir. emeritus, 1958-67; co-founder Sch. Oral Hygiene, Columbia U. Coll. Phys. and Surg., mem. faculty, 1915-45; vis. pediatrician Willard Parker Hosp., 1915-48; v.p. med. bd., 1934-40; co-founder Morrisania City Hosp., 1929, dir. pediatrics, 1929-41, now consulting dir.; college medical consultant Bronx Community, Board of Higher Education, City of New York; with Dr. William H. Park; introduced diphteria toxoid, 1917; collaborated in discovery process to incorporate Vitamin D in milk for prevention and cure of rickets; originator School Health Day program for health care of children; founder Let's See Movement, project to furnish free eyeglasses to needy children, 1924. Board of directors N.Y.C. unit Am. Cancer Soc.; past mem. Nat. Com. Child Health and Protection; mem. bd. trustees Lavelle School for the Blind. Recipient award for services to children N.Y. State Assn. Health, Phys. Edn. and Recreation, 1958; trophy for promotion mutual goodwill and understanding Interfaith Movement, 1958; plaque for years distinguished and exceptional pub. service, City N.Y.; Dr. William G. Anderson award, Am. Assn. Health, Physical Education and Recreation, 1963. Diplomate Am. Bd. Pediatrics Fallon N.Y. Acad. Medicine, A.M.A., Am. Pub. Health Assn., Royal Soc. Promotion of Health (Eng.); mem. Am. Health, Phys. Edn. and Recreation (Dr. William G. Anderson award 1963), Medical Society State N.Y., Bronx County Med. Soc. (past v.p.), Bronx Pediatric Soc. (founder, mem. governing council), Am. Sch. Health Assn., N.Y. Acad. Pub. Edn. Rotarian (pres. Bronx 1933-34). Co-author: Health for Life, 1962; textbooks on child health; also articles profl., Bronx NY Died May 9, 1967; buried Ferncliff, Ardsley NY

GOLDEN, BEN HALE, newspaper exec.; b. Barbarville, Ky., Dec. 16, 1910 s. J. Lynn and Blanche & (Hale) G.; B.A., U. Ky., 1935; m. Ruth Rachel Sulzberger, June 1, 1946; children—Stephen Arthur Ochs, Michael Davis, Lynn Iphigene, Arthur Sulzberger. With TVA, 1936-42; pub. Chattanooga Times, 1957-65; pres. Times Printing Co., 1957-65. Served as first lt. USAAF, 1942-46. Mem. So. Newspaper Publishers Assn. treas. 1959-63, pres. 1964). Home: Jacksonville FL Died Mar. 14, 1970; buried Barbarville KY

GOLDEN, GRACE, actress; b. New Harmony, Ind.; studied Coll. Music, Cincinnati and in New York under Mmes. Maretzek and Fursch-Madi; appeared in minor parts, Abbey's Italian Opera Co.; debut in comic operas as Cerise in Erminie, New York Casino, Dec. 8, 1889; has since taken leading roles in DeWolf Hopper's and other comic opera companies. Address: 7 Rue Scribe Paris‡

GOLDEN, JAMES S., congressman; b. Barbourville, Ky., Sept. 20, 1891; s. Ben. B. and Elizabeth (Davis) G.; A.B., U. of Ky., 1912; LL.B., U. of Mich., 1916; m. Ruth Decker, Sept. 29, 1915; children—Richard Davis, James S. (M.D.). Admitted to Ky. bar, 1915, and practiced in Barbourville, Ky., 1916-48, Pineville, Ky., 1948-71; mem. firm Golden & Lay. Mem. 81st and 82d Congresses, 9th Ky. Dist., also 83d Congress, 8th Ky. Dist. Mem. Ky. Bar Assn. Republican. Methodist. Mason. Elk. Home: Pineville KY Died Sept. 6, 1971.

GOLDENBERG, MORRIS, percussionist, composer, b. Holyoke, Mass., July 28, 1911; s. Joseph and Minnie (Daivs) G.; grad. Julliard Sch. Music, 1932; m. Isabella Leon, June 27, 1934; children—William, Lucille (Mrs. H. Mark Goldshag). Appeared with Chautauqua Symphony and Opera Co., 1934-37, Russian Opera Co., 1936, Russian Ballet, 1937, Met. Opera WOR Staff Orch., 1937-52, also appeared with numerous Cinerama Orchs.; performer, composer, mus. dir. NBC, N.Y.C.; mem. faculty Juilliard Sch. Music, 1940-69, Nat. Orchestral Assn., 1950-69, Manhattan Sch. Music, 1959-69. Mem. A.S.C.A.P. Composer: Modern School for Xylophone, 1948; Modern School for Snare Drum, 1955; Marching Drumsticks, 1958; Little Suite for Snare Drum, 1958; Sticks and Skins, 1959; Classic Overtures for Tympani, 1961; March for Two Snare Drums, 1963; Classic Symphonies for Tympani, 1963; 5/8 Etude and 7/8 Etude for Snare Drum, 1963; Simple Simon March, 1963; Soldiers March, 1963; Ramble Rumble, 1963; Romantic Symphonies for Tympani, 1964; Studies in Solo Percussion, 1968; Farfel's Gavotte, 1966; 5/8 Romp, 1966; Graduation Etude, 1966; Left Light March, 1966; No Roll Etude, 1966; 7/8 Romp, 1966; Simple Minuet, 1966; Rim Shot March, 1964; 6/8 Etude, 1965; Lucy's Riff for percussion ensemble, 1968; Snare Drum for Beginners, 1969. Home: Bayside NY Died Aug. 17, 1969; buried PineLawn, Long Island NY

GOLDESBERRY, JOHN MILFORD, lawyer; b. nr. Osceola, Mo., Mar. 13, 1876; s. Joseph Alexander and Easter Ann (Cooley) G.; ed. pub. schs.; m. Fannie M. Stevens, May 30, 1900; children—Oliver Burton, Jesse Milford. Worked as carpenter and studied law, 1898-1903; admitted to Indian Ty. bar, 1903, and began practice at Bartlesville; assistant county atty., Tulsa County, Okla., 1921-22, county atty., 1922-25; U.S. dist. atty., Northern Dist., Oklahoma, 1925-33; now in private practice. Del. to convs. advocating admission of Indian Ty. and Okla. as single state; formerly mem. Rep. State Central Comm., Okla. Republican. Mem. Christian (Disciples) Ch. Mason, K.P. Home: 2623 E. 10th St. Office: Wright Bldg., Tulsa OK*‡

GOLDING, SAMUEL H., chmn. bd. Sterling Nat. Bank & Trust Co., N.Y. City; pres. Sterling Mortgage Co.; dir. Arnold Constable & Co. Home: New York City NY Died Mar. 29, 1970.

GOLDMAN, HETTY, archaeologist; b. N.Y.C., Dec. 19, 1881; d. Julius and Sarah (Adler) Goldman; A.B., Bryn Mawr Coll., 1903; student Columbia, 1903-04, 06-07; A.M., Radcliff Coll., 1910, Ph.D., 1916; Norton fellow of Harvard, Am. Sch. Classical Studies, Athens, 1910-12. Manuscript reader Macmillan Co., 1903-04; excavator, Halae in Greece, 1911-14, 21, 31; dir. of excavations for Fogg Mus. of Harvard at Colophon, Asia Minor, 1922, 25, Eutresis, Greece, 1924-27; vis. lectr. archaeology Johns Hopkins, 1928; mem. representing Fogg Museum of Harvard Archaeological Expdn. to Yugoslavia, 1932; archaeol. reconnaissance for Bryn Mawr Coll. in ancient Cilicia, Turkey, 1934; excavator at Tarsus, Turkey, for Bryn Mawr Coll., Harvard and Archaeol. Inst. of Am., 1935-38, 47, 48; prof., Sch. of Humanistic Studies of Inst. for Advanced Study, Princeton, N.J., 1936-47, emeritus professor, 1948-72. Trustee Archaeol. Inst. Am. Served with Am. Red Cross in Greece, 1918-19; visited Balkan States for Jewish Joint Distribution Com., 1918-19, Paris office, 1920. Recipient Distinguished Achievement medal, Grad. chpt. Radcliffe Alumnae Soc., 1953. Mem. Am. Acad. Arts and Scis., Archaeol. Soc. Am. Am. Numismatic Soc., Am. Assn. U. Women (mem. com. on fellowship award 1936-41), Phi Beta Kappa; corresponding member German Archaeol. Inst. Club: Cosmopolitan (N.Y.C.). Author: Excavations at Eutresis in Beotia, 1931. Editor and co-author: Excavations at Gozlu Kule Tarsus, Vol. I., Vol. II, 1956. Contbr. articles on archaeology to profl. jours.; revised sect. on archaeology of Turkey for Ency. Brit. Home: Princeton NJ Died May 4, 1972.

GOLDMAN, SAMUEL P., lawyer; b. Troy, N.Y., Mar. 13, 1877; s. Charles Jonathan and Anne (Blatt) G.; Ph.B., St. Francis Xavier Coll., N.Y. City, 1895; LL.B., New York U. Law Sch., 1898; m. Josephine Rosenbaum, of N.Y. City, June 5, 1907. Admitted to N.Y. bar, 1898, and since practiced in N.Y. City; mem. Goldman, Heide & Unger. Mem. Am. Bar Assn. (v.-p.), N.Y. State Bar Assn. (chmn. admissions com.), Assn. Bar City of New York, Lawyers' Assn. New York County, Asso. editor Medico-Legal Jour. Mason (32 deg.). Clubs: Bankers', Rocky Mountain. Author: Handbook Stock Exchange Laws, 1914. Home: 771 West End Av. Office: 120 Broadway, New York NY‡

GOLDMANN, FRANZ, physician, educator; b. Elberfeld, Germany, Jan. 2, 1895; s. Felix and Wally (Warschauer) G.; M.D. cum laude, Friedrich-Wilhelms U., Berlin, Germany, 1920; m. Elizabeth A. Warburg, June 10, 1939 (dec. June 1959); m. 2d, Gladys Jacoby Wilson, Apr. 18, 1960. Came to U.S., 1937, naturalized, 1943. Intern various univ. hosps., Berlin, 1920-21; with Berlin Central Health Dept., 1922-29; with div. health services German Ministry Interior, 1929-33; gen. practice medicine, Germany, 1933-37; fellow dept. pub. health Yale Sch. Medicine, New Haven, 1937-39, asso. clin. prof., 1939-46, clin. prof., 1946-47, lectr., 1947-49; asso. prof. Harvard Sch. Pub. Health, 1947-58, emeritus prof., 1958-70; dir. health study Council Jewish Fedns. and Welfare Funds, N.Y.C., 1958-60. Lectr., vis. lectr. numerous instns.; cons. to numerous pub. and pvt. agys. Recipient Ernst P. Boas award for advancement social medicine, 1959. Diplomate Am. Bd. Preventive Medicine. Fellow Am. Pub. Health Assn., Am. Coll. Preventive Medicine; mem. Assn. Tchrs. Preventive Medicine, Group Health Assn. Am., Physicians Forum, Mass. Pub. Health Assn. (pres. 1958-59), Delta Omega (nat. pres. 1958-59). Conglist. Author: Public Medical Care, 1945; Voluntary Medical Care Insurance in the United States, 1948, also others. Co-editor: Readings in Medical Care, 1958. Contbr. numerous articles to sci. publs., also monographs in textbooks. Home: Clinton CT Died Mar. 4, 1970; buried Ferncliff Cemetery, Hartsdale NY

GOLDMARK, PAULINE DOROTHEA, welfare worker; b. N.Y. City; d. Joseph Goldmark and Regina (Wehle) G.; A.B., Bryn Mawr, 1896; post-grad. work, Barnard Coll., 1896-97, Columbia, 1897-98; unmarried. Asst. sec., 1899-1904, exec. sec., 1905-09, chmn. legislative com., 1908-11, Consumers' League of N.Y. City; mem. legislative com., 1904-05, dir. since 1905, N.Y. Child Labor Com.; asso. dir. New York Sch. of Philanthropy and supervisor research bureau Russell Sage Foundation, 1910-12; mem. Industrial Bd. New York State Labor Dept., 1913-15; research sec. Nat. Consumers' League, 1915-18; mgr. women's service section, U.S.R.R. Administration, 1918-20; with Am. Telephone & Telegraph Co., 1921-29. Mem. Taylor Soc., League of Women Voters. Alumnae dir. Bryn Mawr Coll., 1922-25. Clubs: Bryn Mawr, Women's City. Supervisor of investigation and editor of West Side Studies, and The Longshoreman (both pub. by Russell Sage Foundation); compiler (with Mary D. Hopkins) of The Gypsy Trail. Sec. Nat. Com. on Women in Industry under Council Nat. Defense, May 1917-19. Home: Hartsdale, N.Y. Office: Am. Telephone & New York NY‡

GOLDNER, JACOB HENRY, clergyman; b. Bridgewater, Pa., Aug. 8, 1871; s. George and Caroline (Vogt) G.; A.B., Hiram Coll., 1896; student Western Reserve U., 1897, U. of Chicago, 1898-1900, 03, Harvard Univ., 1902; D.D., Hiram College, 1939; m. Harriet Marks, Aug. 10, 1904 (dec.); children—Jacob Henry, Gerould Russell. Ordained ministry Christian (Disciples) Ch., 1896; pastor Chagrin Falls, O., 1896-98; pastor Euclid Av. Christian Ch., Cleveland, 1900-45, now pastor emeritus. Pres. Fed. Chs. Cleveland, 1921; pres. Internat. Conv. of Disciples Christ, 1925; mem. Federal Council of Chs. of Christ of America. Trustee Hiram Coll., Associated Charities, Cleveland, Good Will Industries of Cleveland. Republican. Home: 2528 Edgehill Rd., Cleveland Heights OH‡

GOLDSBERRY, LOUISE DUNHAM, author; b. Antioch, O.; d. Samuel Swinney, M.D., and Jennie (Strickle) Dunham; B.S., Wesleyan Female Coll. (now defunct), Cincinnati, O.; m. James B. Goldsberry, atty., of Cincinnati, 1887 (died 1888). Contbr. since girlhood of poems, short stories, etc., to newspapers and religious jours., including Cincinnati Enquirer, Cincinnati Commercial Gazette, Detroit Free Press, St. Louis Globe-Democrat, The Independent, etc. Author: Ted and Some Other Stories, 1918. Home: 427 4th St. N.W., Washington DC‡

GOLDSBOROUGH, WASHINGTON LAIRD, Philippine Govt. official; b. 1869; s. Washington Elwell and Martha Pearce (Laird) G.; bro. of Winder Elwell G. (q.v.); ed. Wright's Univ. School, and U. of Md., LL.B., 1890; M. Katharine, d. Gen. Harry Clay Egbert, Oct. 3, 1903. Has lived in Far East (China, and the P.I.) 17 yrs. (1879-85, and 1899-1911) and traveled 4 times around the world; admitted to Md. bar, 1890, N.Y. bar, 1892, P.I. bar, 1902, Colo. bar, 1911; capt. 71st N.Y. Vols., 1898; capt. 43d U.S.V., 1899-1901; recommended for bvt. for gallantry in action at Santiago, Cuba, 1898, and at Hilongas, P.I., 1900; pub. prosecutor of Manila, 1901; asst. chief, Philippines constabulary, 1901-02; city atty. of Manila, 1902-3; asst. atty.-gen., P.I., 1903-5; asso. judge, Philippines Ct. of Land Registration, 1905-10; mem. Philippine compilation com., 1907-8; mem. Philippine code com., since 1909; mem. Faculty, College of Law, U. of Philippines, 1911—; commr. from P.I. on uniform state laws, 1911—. Mem. S.R., U.C.V., Mil. Order Foreign Wars, Assn. Bar City of New York, United Spanish War Vets., Mil. Order Carabao. Clubs: Manila PI‡

GOLDSMITH, BROOKS P., textile co. exec.; b. Greenbriar, S.C.; s. A.C. and Lula B. Goldsmith; m. Margaret Elaine Ussery; children—Mrs. S. L. Thompson, Brooks P., J. Patrick. Started as sec. to supt. Columbia div. So. Ry. Co.; later field auditor income tax div. S.C. Tax Commn.; with Springs Mills, Inc., 1938-69, sec., dir., 1961-69; dir. Lancaster & Chester Ry., Lancaster Trust Co., Ft. Mill Trust Co., Kanawha Ins. Co., Leroy Springs & Co. Bd. dirs., mem. exec. com. Elliott White Springs Found. Home: Lancaster SC Died Jan. 9, 1969; buried Lancaster Meml. Park, Lancaster SC

GOLDSMITH, CLIFFORD, author; b. East Aurora, N.Y., Mar. 29, 1899; s. Charles and Edith (Henshaw) G.; student Moses Brown Sch., Providence, R.I., 1914-17; student Univ. of Pa., 1917-18; student Am. Acad. Dramatic Art, 1918-19; m. Kathryn Allen, Dec. 26, 1933;children—Peter White, Thayer White, Barclay, Kathryn, and Timothy. Actor, playing small parts stage, screen, and chautauquas, 1919-22; publicity work for Nat. Dairy Council, Chicago, and Phila. Dairy Council, Phila., 1922-38. Author radio program, The Aldrich Family 1938-45; free lance with stage prodns. Pres. bd. trustees Ariz. Desert Sch., Tucson. Author: What A Life, April, 1938. Mem. Author's League of Am. (vice pres., 1945-47), Episcopalian. Clubs: Franklin Inn (Phila., Pa.); Coffee House (New York, N.Y.); Old Pueblo (Tucson, Ariz.). Home: Tucson AZ Died July 1971.

GOLDSMITH, GOLDWIN, architect; born Paterson, N.J., June 12, 1871; s. James Charlton and Alice Evelyn (Westervelt) G.; Ph.B. in Architecture, Columbia, 1896; studied Atelier Duray, Paris, 1896-97; m. Gertrude Relief Sumner, d. Arnold Burges Johnson, June 12, 1896. Draftsman McKim, Mead & White, 1889-90; traveled in France, Switzerland, Italy, Germany, Belgium, Holland and England, 1896-97; member Van Vleck & Goldsmith of New York, 1897-1913; prof. architecture and first head of department of architecture U. Kan., 1913-28; prof. architecture U. Tex., 1928-55, prof. emeritus, 1955—, U. of Tex., since 1928; chairman of department, 1928-35; mem. graduate faculty since 1930. Special lecturer in Southwest for A.I.A., 1931-36. Inspector Office of Q.M. of Construction, Camp Funston, 1917. Pres. Soc. of Columbia Univ. Architects, 1909-11; v.p. Assn. of Collegiate Schs. of Architecture, 1925-27, pres., 1927-29, exec. com., 1929-31, sec.-treas., 1936-40. Mem. com. to survey schs. of architecture, 1939-40; vice pres., dir. Family Service Soc., 1936-45; dir. Maternal Health Clinic 1939-47; member Pres. Hoover's Conf. on Home Building and Home Ownership; 1931-32; advisory counsellor to Constrn. Specifications Inst. Mem. Am. Institute Architects,

1911, Fellow, 1930, Jury of Fellows, 1941-43 (pres. Kan. chapter 1923-25; v.p. South Tex. chapter 1929-30; president Central Texas chapter 1938-39); mem. Texas Society Architects, Constrn. Specification Institute, Columbia Alumni Association, Delta Upsilon (convention secretary 5 years; ex-pres. exec. council; editor Delta Upsilon Quarterly, 7 years; conv. historian, 1913); Scarab, Sigma Tau, Tau Sigma Delta, Kings Crown, Forty-Niners, Scholia, Die-No-Sir. Conglist. Mason (Blue Lodge). Author: Architects' Specifications—How to Write Them, 1935, 2d ed., 1948. Compiler and pub.: Gertrude Goldsmith, Her Book, 1953. Contbr. Carolyn Wells' Sense of Nonsense. Home: 1902 San Gabriel St., Austin 5 TX‡

GOLDSTEIN, IRVING, judge; b. Chgo., Feb. 3, 1897; s. Samuel and Bertha (Nathan) G.; LL.B., John Marshall Law Sch., 1919; m. Grace Baron, June 20, 1922; children—Paul E., Lois Beth, Bernadine (dec.). Admitted to Ill. bar, 1919, and since in practice at Chicago; with Eisendrath & Solomon, 1919-21, Blum, Wolfsohn & Blum, 1922-23, Peden, Graydon, Kahn and Murphy, 1923-24; mem. firm Cohon & Goldstein 1924-54; dean Lawyers Post-Grad. Clinics, Chgo.; judge Village Court of Skokie (Illinois), 1960-63; associate judge of the Circuit Court of Cook County; professorial lecturer on trial technique Sch. Law, Northwestern University, 1949-64; lecturer law, lecturer med. jurisprudence Sch. of Medicine, 1944-51; instr. in trial technique Raymond Foundn. since 1934. Served with U.S. Army, 1918-19; community comdr. Civilian Defense, Chicago, 1941-43; pub. panel mem. War Labor Bd., 1943-45. Asst. state's atty. Cook County, 1926-28. Mem. Chicago, Ill. State and Am. bar assns., Decalogue Soc. of Lawyers, Am. Acad. Forensic Sciences, Jewish War Vets. of U.S. (Natl. Judge Advocate; 1955-56, past department commander), American Legion (past commander post 124), Am. Jewish Congress, Tau Epsilon Rho. Director and past president Congregation B'nai Shalom, Albany Park, Chgo., dir. Congregation B'nai Emunah, Skokie. Mason (past master, 32 degree, Shriner); mem. B'nai B'rith (past president North Shore lodge). Club: Jewish Men's (Chgo.). Author: Trial Technique, 1935. Coauthor: Medical Trial Technique, 1942; Trial Practice Cases, 1949. Co-editor Med. Trial Technique Quarterly; editor Trial Lawyers Guide (quar.), 1957-62. Home: Skokie IL

GOLDSTEIN, MOLSE HERBERT, architect; b. New Orleans, La., Sept. 17, 1882; s. Julius and Julie (Schwartz) G.; B.E., Tulane U., 1902; M.S., Mass. Inst. Tech., 1905; student Am. Acad. Rome, 1906-07; m. Lois Goetter, Aug. 27, 1924; children—Louis Allan, Molse Herbert, Jr., Nathalie (Mrs. Aaron Stern). Practiced as architect with firm Molse H. Goldstein & Assos., 1914-47, Goldstein, Parham & Labouisse, 1947-63, Molse H. Goldstein & Louis A. Goldstein, 1963-72; prin. archtl. works include Civic Center, New Orleans, 1956-58, Moisant Internat. Airport, New Orleans, 1957-59, Dillard U., 1933-63. Mem. Nat. Archtl. Accrediting Bd., 1941-44. Fellow A.I.A. (bd. dirs. 1936-39). Home: New Orleans LA Died Dec. 28, 1972.

GOLDTHWAIT, JOEL ERNEST, surgeon; b. Marblehead, Mass., June 18, 1866; s. William Johnson and Mary L. (Pitman) G.; S.B., Mass. State Coll., 1885; M.D., Harvard, 1890, and since in practice at Boston; served as house surgeon, Boston Children's and Boston City hosps.; m. Jessie S. Rand, May 16, 1894; m. 2d, Mrs. Philip Leverett Saltonstall, Apr. 30, 1936. Was formerly chief of orthopedic service, Mass. Gen. Hosp., Carney Hosp.; mem. Staff Boston Children's Hosp.; formerly asst. in orthopedic surgery, Harvard Med. Sch.; now instr. orthopedic surgery, Grad. Sch. of same. Ex-pres. Am. Orthopedic Assn.; fellow Am. Coll. Surgeons; mem. British Orthopedic Assn., A.M.A., Mass. Med. Soc. Republican. Conglist. Author numerous monographs; frequent contbr. on orthopedic surgery. Col. Med. Corps, serving 2 yrs. with A.E.F.; now brig. gen. M.R.C. Awarded D.S.M. (U.S.); Companion St. Michael and St. George (Great Britain). Home: Medfield Mass Address: 372 Marlborough St., Boston MA*‡

GOLDTHWAITE, VERE, lawyer; b. Evansville, Wis., June 9, 1870; s. S. Vale and Loma (Armour) G.; student Boston Univ. Sch. of Law, 3 yrs. course; m. Boston, Mar. 21, 1907, Ellen Beach Yaw. Clubs: Boston, Boston City. Editor and Compiler: Philosophy of Ingersoll, 1906 L11; contb'r to mags. Residence: 4 Concord Square. Office: 717 Old South Bldg., Boston MA‡

GOLDWATER, RICHARD M., lawyer; b. Los Angeles, Dec. 10, 1904; A.B., Stanford, 1926, J.D., 1928; student Harvard Law Sch. Admitted to Cal. bar, 1928, mem. firm Wright, Rodi, Wright, Tolton & Van Zyl, Los Angeles. Mem. Am., Los Angeles bar assns., State Bar of Cal. Address: Los Angeles CA Died Mar. 15, 1971.

GOLDWATER, ROBERT, educator; b. N.Y.C., Nov. 23, 1907; s. S.S. and Clara (Aub) G.; B.A., Columbia, 1929; M.A., Harvard, 1931; Ph.D., N.Y.U., 1937; m. Louise Bourgeois, Sept. 12, 1938; children—Michael, Jean-Louis, Alain. Instr. fine arts N.Y.U., 1934-39; from asst. prof. art to prof. Queens Coll., 1939-57; prof. fine arts N.Y.U. Grad. Sch., 1957-73; dir. Mus. Primitive Art, N.Y.C., 1957-63, chmn. adminstrv. com., 1963-73; editor Mag. of Art, 1947-53. Carnegie fellow, 1930-31; Guggenheim fellow, 1944-45; Fulbright scholar, 1950-51. Mem. Coll. Art Assn. (dir. 1956-59), Soc. Aesthetics, Internat. Assn. Art Critics. Author: Primitivism in Modern Painting, 1938; Rufino Tamayo, 1947; Modern Art in Your Life, 1949; Jacques Lipchitz, 1954; Gauguin, 1957; The Sculpture of the Bambara, 1960; Senufo Sculpture, 1964; Primitivism in Modern Art, 1967; Space and Dream, 1967; New York City NY Died Mar. 27, 1973.

GOLOVIN, NICHOLAS ERASMUS, govt. exec.; b. Odessa, Russia, Mar. 18, 1912; s. Erasm N. and Galina A. (Kharchenko) G.; A.B., Columbia, 1933, M.A., 1936; Ph.D., George Washington University, 1955; m. Anne Castrodale, December 30, 1966; children by former marriages—Paul Nicholas, Karl Nicholas, Theresa (Mrs. William J. B. Trittipoe Jr.), Natalie (Mrs. King Nelson). Began as a research statistical analyst for R. H. Macy & Company, 1934-38, dept. mgr., 1938-43; chief prodn. and requirements analysis sect. tool div., WPB, 1943-43; asso. supt. electricity div. Naval Research Lab., 1946-48; head mgmt. div. staff Naval Ordnance Test Sta., Cal., 1948-49; cons. to dir. Nat. Bur. Standards, 1949, exec. asst. to dir., 1949, asso. dir. adminstrn., 1953-55, asso. dir. planning, 1955-58; became chief scientist White Sands Missile Range, N.M., 1958; dir. tech. operators div. Advanced Research Projects Agy., Dept. of Def., 1959; dep. asso. adminstr. NASA, 1960, tech. asst. to asso. adminstr. NASA and dir. NASA-DOD large launch vehicle planning group 1961-62; tech. adviser Office of the Spl. Asst. to Pres. for Sci. and Tech., 1962-69; v.p., gen. mgr. Rabinow Engring. Co., Inc., 1960-61. Mem. Am. Inst. Aeros. and Astronautics, Inst. Elec. and Electronic Engrs., Am. Phys. Soc., Am. Nuclear Soc., A.A.A.S., Philos. Soc. Wash., Am. Ordnance Assn., Phi Beta Kappa, Sigma Xi. Home: Washington DC Died Apr. 27, 1969.

GOLSCHMANN, VLADIMIR, musical conductor; b. Paris, France, Dec. 16, 1893; s. Leon and Marie (Rasumny) G.; Mus. D. (hon.), Wesleyan University, Bloomington, Ill., Columbia University, Missouri, 1956; Litt. D. (hon.), Washington U., St. Louis; m. Odette le Cointe. Founder and conductor Concerts Golschmann, Paris, 1919-24; conductor of the Russian Ballet of Diaghilev, ballets of Anna Pavlova, Serge de Mare; musical director Theatre Beriza, Paris; in Europe has conducted in Paris and all major cities in France; conducted in Brussels, Liege, Madrid, Bilbao, Lisbon, Oslo; conductor of Scottish Orchestra, 1928-31; first appearance in U.S. as guest condr. N.Y. Symphony, 1924; also guest conductor NBC Orchestra, N.Y. Philharmonic, Stokowski's Am. Orch., Tulsa, Atlanta, Louisville, Boston, Chicago, Phila., Mexico, Montreal, Rochester, Detroit, Cleveland, Cincinnati, Minneapolis, San Francisco, Baltimore, Los Angeles, Houston symphony orchestras; also conducted in London, Rome; in Israel, Caracas, Rio de Janeiro, Sao Paulo, Montevideo, Montreux and Lucerne festivals; also summer appearances with the New York Philharmonic at Lewisohn Stadium, Hollywood Bowl, Robin Hood Dell in Phila., Ravinia Park with Chgo. orchestra; condr. St. Louis Symphony Orchestra, 1931-57; now condr. Denver Symphony Orch. Decorated Officer French Legion of Honor, comdr. French Order Arts and Letters. Home: New York City NY Died Mar. 1, 1972.

GOMBROWICZ, WITOLD, author: b. Maloszyee, Poland, 1904; ed. Lwow, U. Warsaw. Author: Memorial, 1933; Ferdydurke, 1937; Twona, 1937; Slub, 1947; Trans-Atlantyk, 1950; Diary, 1957; Pornografia, 1960. Address: Buenos Aires Argentina Died July 1969.*

GOMEZ-MORENO MARTINEZ, MANUEL, educator; b. Granada, Spain, Feb. 21, 1870; s. Manuel and Dolores G. M.G.; Dr. Phil. and Letters; m. Elena Rodriguez-Bolivar Lopez, 1903. Former prof., U. Madrid, dir.-gen. Fine Arts. Mem. Acad. History and Fine Arts. Recipient grand cross Alfonso X el Sabio, and others. Author: Iglesias mozarabes (Arte espanol de los siglos IX al XI); El Arte romanico espanol hasta los almohades; Las Aguilas del Renacimiento Espanol; La novela de Espana, others. Home: Madrid Spain Died June 7, 1970.

GONDELMAN, SIDNEY, lawyer, pipe and fittings manufacturing company executive; born on July 28, 1897; s. Meyer and Rachael (Krisoff) G.; LL.B., St. Lawrence U., 1921; m. Rae Schonfeld, Sept. 9, 1923; children—Herbert L., George I. Admitted to N.Y. bar, 1923; practice of law, Bklyn., 1925-29, 32-40; with Mutual Factors, Inc. (merged into Herbert Lee Corp. 1968) N.Y.C., 1939-70, pres., chmn. bd., 1940-70; with Herbert Lee Corp., real estate and comml. finance, N.Y.C., 1945-70; pres., chmn., 1946-70; with Central Foundry Company, cast iron pipe and fittings, 1959-70, pres. chmn. 1966-70, pres. and chairman bd. Essex Foundry, 1959-70, Cross-Country Leasing Co., Tuscalossa, Ala., 1964-70, Buffalo Foundry, Buffalo, N.Y., 1968-70. Krupp Foundry, Quakertown, Pa., 1968-70. Chairman Federation of Jewish Philanthropies. Past chmn. Pineland College; chmn. bd. trustees Edwards Mil. Acad. Dir., United Jewish Appeal, Jewish Chronic Disease Hosp.; trustee William and Mary Coll.; bd. dirs. Isaac Albert Research Inst.; bd. dirs., mem. exec. com. Kingsbrooke Jewish Med. Center; founder Kingsbrooke Med. Center, Peninsula Hosp. Named La. col.; recipient meritorious service award William & Mary Coll. Mem. Assn. Comml. Finance Cos. of N.Y. (past dir.), N.A.M., Cast Iron Soil Pipe Institute (past pres., director), U.S. C. of C., A.I.M. (mem. presidents' council), Am. Ord. Assn., Am. Foundrymen's Soc., N.J. C. of C., Founders Soc. of Albert Eistein Coll. Medicine (vice chmn.). Mason (32, Shriner). Clubs: Lake Success Golf (Great Neck); Excelsior (bd. dirs.). Home: Great Neck NY Died Dec. 2, 1970.

GONGWER, LILLIAN MAY, author; b. Nimisilla, O., Aug. 3, 1871; d. Samuel and Caroline (Hoy) G.; grad. Irvington (Ind.) High Sch., 1888, Akron (O.) High Sch., 1892; unmarried. Stenographer since 1895. Mem. Disciples' Ch. Author: Animal Life in Rhymes and Jingles, 1902; My A B C Book, 1904; Baby's Friends, 1904; Animal Book, 1904; Tiny Tot's A B C, 1904; Baby's Doings, 1904; Baby's A B C Book, 1904; Flower Babies, 1905. Address: Lagro IN‡

GOOD, EDWIN STANTON, animal husbandman; b. Clarence Center, N.Y., Mar. 16, 1871; s. John and Esther (Hummel) G.; B.S., Mich. Agrl. Coll., 1903; M.S., U. of Ill., 1906; m. Louise A. Millikan, June 24, 1908; children—John Wolcott, Edwin Millikan. Sec. to pres. Mich. State Agrl. Coll., East Lansing, Mich., 1897-99; instr. and investigator in animal husbandry, U. of Ill., 1903-06; head dept. animal husbandry, Ky. Agrl. Expt. Sta., since 1906; prof. animal husbandry, University of Kentucky, since 1912; also chairman of animal industry group and leader in animal husbandry extension, 1919-43, professor emeritus since 1943. Investigated live stock conditions in Eng., Scotland, Holland, France and Belgium, 1905. Isolated and named the bacillus causing infectious abortion in mares, and perfected a vaccine which immunizes mares against this disease. Mem. Ky. Live Stock Sanitary Bd. Mem. A.A.A.S., Am. Soc. Animal Production, Assn. Southern Agrl. Workers, Ky. Acad. Science, Am. Assn. Univ. Profs., Alpha Zeta, Sigma Alpha Epsilon, Sigma Xi. Presbyterian. Club: Kiwanis. Author of animal husbandry section in Hallegan's Fundamentals of Agriculture, 1911; also numerous articles in agrl. periodicals, scientific journals, and bulletins Ky. Agrl. Expt. Sta. Home: 238 Tahoma Rd. Address: Ky. Experiment Sta., Lexington KY‡

GOOD, FREDRICK HOPKINS, physician; b. Holdrege, Neb., May 13, 1911; s. Winfred P. and Nova (McQueen) G.; A.B. (biochemistry fellow 1931-33), Colo. State Coll., 1933; B.S., U. Neb., 1936; M.D., U. Colo., 1938; m. Winifred Kinney, Sept. 1, 1935; children—Stephen F., Sherril Ann (Mrs. M. Timothy Bray). Intern Colo. Gen. Hosp., 1939-40, surg. resident, 1940-43; pvt. practice, Denver, 1945-72, mem. active staff St. Joseph's, Mercy, Children's, St. Anthony's, Rose Meml. hosps., Craig Sanitarium; asso. clin. prof. surgery U. Colo. Med. Sch., 1955-71, prof., 1971-72; chmn. med. edn. com. Mercy Hosp., 1955-72. Trustee Colo. Hosp. Service, 1946-47, pres., 1949-60, commr. dist. IX, 1952-54; chmn. exec. com., dir. Med. Indemnity Am., 1958-61. Commr.-at-large Nat. Assn. Blue Shield Plans, 1956-60, chmn. exec. com., 1956-60, mem. joint exec. com., 1956-60, chmn. physicians relations com. Blue Shield Commn., also nat. v.p., 1964-65, nat. commr. at large, 1964-66, nat. pres., 1965-66; trustee Colo. div. Am. Cancer Soc., 1950-52. Dir. First Trust Corp., Denver. Trustee Sands House, Isaac Walton League, Goodwill Industries. Recipient Distinguished Service award U. Colo. Med. Sch., 1963, Med. Alumni award, 1964. Fellow A.C.S.; mem. Am. Assn. Med. Colls., Am. Assn. U. Profs., A.M.A., Internat. Coll. Surgeons, Southwestern Surg. Congress, Pan-Pacific Surg. Assn., Colo. (speaker ho. of dels. 1961-62, chmn. indoctrination com. 1957-59, chmn. med. services com. 1955; certificate of service 1959), Denver County (pres. 1949-50) med. socs. Presbyn. (deacon, elder). Author articles in field. Home: Denver CO Died May 22, 1972; buried Denver CO

GOOD, PAUL FRANCIS, lawyer; b. Wahoo, Neb., Mar. 16, 1893; s. Benjamin Franklin and Jennie (Jessen) G.; B.A., Amherst, 1913; law-study, U. of Neb., 1913-14; Rhodes scholar from Neb., Oxford U., 1914-17, B.A., in Jurisprudence, 1917, M.A., 1921; m. Dorothy Frances Collins, Sept. 1, 1917; children—John Paul, Robert James, David Martin, Anthony Jessen. Admitted to Neb. bar, 1919, and began practice at Lincoln; mem. bd. dirs. First Nat. Bank, Wahoo; atty. gen. of Neb., for term 1933-35; now mem. Monsky, Grodinsky, Good & Cohen. Ensign, U.S.N.R., on staff Adm. Sims, later on staff Adm. Wilson, Aug. 1917-Jan. 1919. Chancellor, Diocese of Neb., P.E. Ch., 1936-56. Mem. Am., Neb. State (pres. 1946), Omaha bar assns., Am. Law Inst., Phi Beta Kappa, Phi Delta Phi. Democrat. Episcopalian. Mason. Clubs: Lincoln University, Omaha Club. Asst. editor 2d edit. White's Annotated Omaha NB Died June 4, 1971; buried Nebraska City NE

GOODALE, JOSEPH LINCOLN, physician; b. Saco, Me., Jan. 22, 1868; s. George Lincoln and Henrietta Juel (Hobson) G.; A.B., Harvard, 1889, A.M., M.D., 1893; m. Adelaide M. Evans, 1893; children—Robert L., Geoffrey D., Edward E. Began practice in Boston, 1894; asst. physician diseases of throat, Mass. Gen. Hosp., 1895-1913; asst. surgeon throat dept., Boston Children's Hosp., 1895-1907; instr. in laryngology, Harvard Med. Sch., 1908-30. Mem. Am. Laryngol. Assn. (pres. 1917), A.M.A., Mass. Med. Soc., Boston Soc. Med. Science, Boston Soc. Med. Improvement, Am. Acad. of Arts and Sciences; fellow Am. Coll. of Surgeons. Club: St. Botolph. Contbr. to med. jours. Address: Ipswich MA‡

GOODALL, CHARLES EDWARD, clergyman; b. Drighlington, Yorkshire, Eng., May 25, 1876; s. Thomas and Hannah (Ayer) G.; brought by parents to U.S. at early age; grad. South Jersey Inst., Bridgeton, N.J., 1898; Ph.B., Bucknell U., 1902, M.A., 1904, D.D., 1922; B.D., Crozer Theol. Sem., Chester, Pa., 1905; grad. study, Oxford U., 1905-06; m. Sara Mickel, June 19, 1907. Ordained ministry Bapt. Ch., 1906; student pastor Westmont, N.J., 1902-04; asso. pastor Linden Bapt. Ch., Camden, N.J., 1906-07; pastor Huntington, Pa., 1907-09, First Bapt. Ch., Roselle, N.J., 1909-22; exec. sec. N.J. Bapt. Conv. 1922-43; now retired. Trustee Internat. Bapt. Sem., Crozer Theol. Sem. Mem. Phi Gamma Delta, Theta Delta Tau. Republican. Mason. Clubs: Newark Athletic, Locust Grove Golf, Roselle Golf. Editor N.J. Bapt. Bulletin. Home: 2343 Pine Crest Dr., Altadena CA‡

GOODE, GEORGE WILLIAM, osteopathic physician; b. Boston, Mass., Mar. 5, 1870; s. George and Jane (Beamish) G.; ed. Boston U. Law Sch., Northeastern Coll. Sch. of Law; grad. Am. Sch. Osteopathy, Kirksville, Mo., 1905, Los Angeles Coll. of Osteopathy, 1910, Chicago Coll. of Osteopathy, 1919; M.D., Middlesex Coll. of Medicine and Surgery, Boston, 1920; unmarried. Practiced at Boston since 1905. President Mass. College of Osteopathy. Mem. Co. D, 1st Regt., Mass. V.M., 3 yrs. comdr. Roxbury City Guard Vet. Assn. Ex-pres. Mass. Osteopathic Hosp. Assn. Mem. Boston Chamber of Commerce, Brookline Board of Trade, Brookline Municipal League, mem. Am. Osteopathic Assn. (pres. 1922-23), N.E. Osteopathic Assn. (ex-pres.), Mass. Osteopathic Assn. (ex-pres.), Boston Osteopathic Assn. (ex-pres.), Sons of Vets., Roxbury Hist. Soc., Brookline Bird Club, St. Anthony's Guild, Brookline Taxpayers Assn., N.E. Assn. Fire Ghiefs, Fire Chiefs Club of Mass.; sec. Internat. Soc. for Lymphatic Research; sec.-treas. Internat. Soc. Sacroiliac Technicians; mem. Bostonian Society, Audubon Society; nat. dir. Am. Automobile Assn.; dir. Norfolk County Dem. League. Democrat. Elk. Clubs: Boston City, Economic, Boston Autobile (ex-pres.), Field and Forest, 101 Year Club (sec.). Home: 8 Colbourne Crescent, Brookline, Mass. Office: 587 Boylston St., Boston MA*‡

GOODE, WILLIAM ATHELSTANE MEREDITH, newspaper man; b. Newfoundland, June 10, 1875; s. Rev. T. A. G.; ed. Foyle Coll., Ireland; m. Cecilia, d. C. A. Sippi, of London, Ont. Served as purser in British merchant marine; pvt. 4th U.S. Cav., 1 yr. 5 months, serving through railroad riots at Sacramento, Cal.; purchased discharge, Dec., 1894; asst. night city editor New York Recorder, 1895; city editor Mercury; with Associated Press, 1896-1905, chiefly as foreign corr.; represented it on flagship New York during Spanish-Am. War; news editor London Standard since 1904. Author: With Sampson Through the War. Contbr. to mags. Address: The Standard, London England‡

GOODHUE, WILLIAM JOSEPH, physician; b. Athabaskaville, P.Q., Can., Oct. 4, 1869; s. James and Mariam Miranda (Emerson) G.; bro. of E. S. Goodhue; High Sch., Rochester, N.Y., 1882-4; M.D., Rush Med. Coll., Chicago, 1897; (D.Sc., from Milton U., Baltimore, 1913); m. Christina Meyer, of Kalae, Molokai, H.I., Oct. 23, 1905. Surgeon to McBryde Sugar Co., Koloa, H.I., 1902-4; chief surgeon Eleele Hosp., 1902-4; surgeon Molokai Leper Clinic, 1904—; med. supt. Molokai Leper Settlement; mem. Govt. exec. staff segregation of lepers. Author of reports on phases of leprosy, 1906, 8, 10, 12, Hawaiian Bd. of Health, Honolulu. Author section on leprosy in the Sajous Analytic Cyclopaedia of Practical Medicine, 1914. Republican. Unitarian. Address: Kataupapa, Molokai HI‡

GOODIER, JAMES NORMAN, educator; b. Preston, Eng., Oct. 17, 1905; s. James and Martha (Grimshaw) G.; came to U.S., 1929, naturalized, 1946; B.A., Cambridge Univ., 1927; Sc.D., U. of Mich., 1931; m. Marina Timoshenko, July 17, 1931; 1 son, Peter. Research fellow Ontario Research Found., Toronto, Ont., Can., 1931-38; prof. mechanics, Cornell, 1938-47, Stanford U., from 1947. Mem. Am. Soc. M.E., Am. Math. Soc., AM. Soc. Engring. Edn., Am. Inst. Aero. Sci. Author numerous sci. and tech. articles in publs. Home: Palo Alto CA Died Nov. 5, 1969; buried Palo Alto CA

GOODMAN, DAVID, author; b. N.Y.C., Sept. 14, 1894; s. Herman and Cecelia (Edelman) G.; A.B. (Pulitzer scholar), Columbia, 1917, A.M., 1918, Ed.D., 1951; m. Malvina Peterson, Dec. 8, 1924; children—Lawrence, Eric, Prin., Rhodes Prep. Sch., N.Y.C., 1929-55; columnist nat. syndicated column Marriage, Children and You with Bell Syndicate, N.Y.C., 1952-71, profl. marriage counselor, 1970-71. Mem. adv. council Parents Without Partners. Mem. Am. Assn. Marriage Counselors, Soc. for Sci. Study of Sex. Author: A Parent's Guide to the Emotional Needs of Children, 1959; Guidelines for a Healthy Marriage, 1967; What's Best For Your Child and You, 1966; Living From Within, 1968. Contbr. articles profl. jours. Address: Teaneck NJ Died Nov. 5, 1971.

GOODMAN, GEORGE HILL, newspaper pub.; b. Grayson County, Ky., Mar. 28, 1876; s. James Samuel and Martha Ellen (Hill) G.; ed. pub. schs.; m. Margery L. Crumbaugh, June 16, 1910; children—Evelyn Lockett, Martha (dec.), Mary Jane. In liquor business as George H. Goodman Co., 1900-18; pub. Paducah News-Democrat, 1922-29; also pres. and owner News-Democrat Pub. Co. until 1929, when sold his interest. Chmn. McCracken County Council of Defense, Liberty Loan and Am. Red Cross drives, World War. Adminstr. Ky. Emergency Relief Administrn. since 1934, Works Progress Adminstrn., 1935-June 1939; Works Projects administrator, July 1, 1939-June 30, 1943; apptd. state dir. Office of Price Adminstrn. for Ky., June 1943. Democrat. Elk. Clubs: Paducah Country, Big Spring Golf. Home: 2100 Jefferson St., Paducah KY‡

GOODMAN, JESS DEE, hotel exec.; b. in Kan., Dec. 6, 1917; s. William Jess and Blanche (Bradshaw) G.; student Southwestern U., U. Cal.; m. Berenice W. Andrews, Sept. 3, 1940; children—Donald Dee, Richard Allan, James Edward. Successively with Belmont Hotel, Los Angeles, Benson Hotel, Portland, Ore., Mayfair Hotel, Los Angeles, Miramar Hotel, San Diego, Arrowhead Springs Hotel, Lake Arrowhead; then comptroller Hollywood-Roosevelt Hotel (Cal.); pres. Riviera Hotel, Las Vegas, Nev., 1964-68, also. dir. Pres. United Fund Clark County, 1966, also trustee, member exec. com. Served with inf., AUS, World War II; with U.S. Army, Korean War. Recipient Outstanding Citizeship award United Fund, 1963. Mem. Nat. Assn. Hotel Accountants (past pres.), Las Vegas C. of C. (past dir., treas., v.p.). Clubs: Paradise Valley Country (pres.); Skal (pres. Las Vegas chpt.). Home: Las Vegas NV Died July 21, 1968.

GOODMAN, MARY ELLEN, educator, anthropologist; b. Los Angeles, Aug. 8, 1911; d. August and Grace (Gould) Hoheisel; B.Ed., U. Cal. at Los Angeles, 1932; M.A., Radcliffe Coll., 1943, Ph.D., 1946; m. Clark Goodman, Aug. 8, 1933; children—Gaye Ellen, Alan Clark. Instr., then asst. prof. sociology and anthropology Wellesley Coll., 1946-54; social sci. analyst PHA, 1957-58; coordinator studies 1960 White House Conf. Children and Youth, 1958-59; intergroup relations cons. Anti-Defamation League, 1959-60; dir. honors programs U. Houston, 1964-65; mem. faculty Rice U., 1963-69, prof. anthropology and sociology, 1965-69. Mem. exec. com., bd. dirs. Houston Council Human Relations, 1962-66, chmn. Battaglia-VISTA project adv. com., 1962-66; gen. chmn. health and welfare week Community Council Houston and Harris County, 1962; cons. mem. civic affairs com. Houston C. of C., 1963-69. Bd. dirs. Child Guidance Center Houston and Harris County, Houston Planned Parenthood Assn., Am. Social Health Assn., Am. Parents Com. Fulbright research scholar, Japan 1954-55; named Woman of Year, Delta Zeta, 1963; recipient Matrix award Theta Sigma Phi, 1962. Fellow Am. Anthrop. Assn., Am. Sociol. Assn., Soc. Research Child Devel.; mem. N.Y. Acad. Scis., Phi Beta Kappa, Sigma Xi, Delta Kappa Gamma. Author: Race Awareness in Young Children, rev. edit., 1964; Individual and Culture, 1967; Culture of Childhood, 1969; also numerous articles, monographs. Author weekly column Houston Post, 1964-68. Home: Houston TX Died Aug. 24, 1969.

GOODMAN, PAUL, author, educator; b. N.Y.C., Sept. 9, 1911; B.A., Coll. City N.Y.; Ph.D., U. Chgo.; 1 dau. by 1st marriage, Susan; children by 2d marriage—Mathew R. (dec.), Daisy J. Tchr., U. Chgo., N.Y. U., Black Mountain Coll., Sarah Lawrence Coll., U. Hawaii, also Inst. Gestalt Therapy, N.Y.C. and Cleve.; Knapp prof. U. Wis., 1964. Author: (criticism) Growing Up Absurd, Kafka's Prayer, 1947, The Structure of Literature, 1954; The Community of Scholars; Speaking and Language, 1971; (creative writing) The Facts of Life, 1946, The Break-up of Our Camp, 1950, Parents' Day, 1952, Stop-Light, 1942, The Empire City, 1959, Making Do, 1963; Compulsory Mis-Education, 1964; People or Personnel, 1965; Three Plays, 1965; Five Years (autobiographical), 1966; Like a Conquered Province, 1967; Adam and His Works, 1968; New Reformation: Notes of a Neolithic Conservative, 1970; Little Prayers and Finite Experience, 1972; (plays) Stop-Light; Tragedy and Comedy, 1970; (poems) Hawksweed, 1967, Homespun of Oatmeal Gray, 1970. Co-author: Communitas, 1947, Gestalt Therapy, 1951. Editor: Liberation, 1962-69. Contbr. Commentary, Partisan Rev., Keyon Rev., N.Y. Rev. Books. Address: New York City NY Died Aug. 2, 1972.

GOODNIGHT, SCOTT HOLLAND, college prof.; b. Holton, Jackson County, Kan., Jan. 16, 1875; s. Rev. Thomas Henry and Susan Mary (Pittman) G.; B.S., Eureka (Ill.) Coll., 1898, M.A., 1901; studied in Europe, 1898-99; student, summer, U. of Chicago, 1901; Ph.D., U. of Wis., 1905; U. of Leipzig (leave of absence), 1906-07; LL.D. from Eureka College, 1927; m. Gertrude Hamilton, Sept. 3, 1901; children—Mrs. Eleanor Constance Morrison, Scott Hamilton. Prof. modern langs., Eureka Coll., 1899-1901; instr., 1901-07, asst. prof., 1907-12, asso. prof. of German since 1912, dean summer session, 1911-43, dean of men, 1916-45, emeritus since 1945, Univ. of Wis. Director Wisconsin Life Insurance Co.; vice pres. and member board of directors Bank of Madison. Congregationalist. Mem. Assn. Deans and Advisers of Men (exec. com); co-founder and past mem. Summer Session Dirs. Assn.; mem. Kappa Sigma, Phi Kappa Phi, Phi Eta Sigma (nat. pres. 1933-39). Club: University. Author: German Literature in American Magazines Prior to 1846, 1905; The Good(k)night (Gutknecht) Family in America, 1935. Home: Winter Park FL Died Aug. 9, 1972.

GOODNO, WILLIAM COLBY, M. D.; b. Kenosha, Wis.; grad. Hahnemann Med. Coll., Phila., 1870; engaged in practice in Phila. Since then in Hahnemann Med. Coll. as consecutively, demonstrator of surgery; lecturer on microscopy, histology and pathol. anatomy; since 1885 prof. pathology and practice of medicine. Contributor to med. literature; mem. several nomoeopathic socs. Address: 1603 Walnut St., Philadelphia PA‡

GOODNOW, MINNIE, author; b. Albion, N.Y., July 10, 1871; d. Franklin and Elizabeth Jane (Arnold) G.; grad. E. Denver (Colo.) High Sch., 1891; studied art 2 yrs., pvtly.; studied Denver U., 1 1/2 yrs.; studied architecture in office 5 yrs.; grad. Las Vegas Hot Springs Sanitarium, N.M., 1899; grad. Gen. Memorial Hosp., New York, 1900, New York Infant Asylum, 1901; unmarried. Supt. Woman's Hosp., Denver, 1903-6; dir. of nurses, Milwaukee (Wis.) Co. Hosp., 1907; supt. of nurses, Park Av. Hosp., Denver, 1908, supt. Bronson Hosp., Kalamazoo, Mich., 1908-11; war nurse in France, serving with Harvard unit. etc., 1915-17; reconstruction aide in U.S.A., 1919; now supt. nurses, Children's Hosp., Washington, D.C. Episcopalian. Mem. Am. Hosp. Assn. Author: Ten Lessons in Chemistry for Nurses, 1911; First Year Nursing, 1912; Outlines of Nursing History, 1916; War Nursing, 1917; Practical Physics for Nurses, 1919. Office: 9 Park St., Boston MA‡

GOODPASTURE, WENDELL WILLIAMSON, bookseller; b. Springfield, Ill., Jan. 17, 1899; s. Andrew Ward and Claudia Llewellen (Williamson) G.; grad. Springfield High Sch.; m. Lois Adele Powers, Dec. 9, 1920. With J. W. Diller, bookseller, Springfield, 1915-17, Marshall Field & Co., 1918-19; head fiction dept. A. C. McClurg & Co., retail, 1920-23; book buyer Brentano's, Chgo., 1924-33, mgr., 1930-33; Kroch's Bookstores, Inc., Chgo., acquired Brentano's, Inc., 1933, v.p., gen. mgr. three controlled corps., Kroch's & Brentano's, Wabash Av., Kroch's & Brentano's, Randolph St. and Booksellers Catalog Service (Chgo.), 1933-69, Kroch's & Brentano's, Old Orchard and Skokie, Ill. Mason. Club: Union League (Chgo.). Author: Flowers to Paint, 1950. Gen. editor Rinehart's Garden Library, 1952-69. Home: Sikeston MO Died Aug. 11, 1970; buried Meml. Gardens, Sikeston MO

GOODRICH, EDGAR JENNINGS, lawyer; b. Anoka, Minn., Nov. 15, 1896; s. George Herbert and Mary Anne (Funk) G.; spl. course for Am. soldiers, U. of Nancy, France, 1919; LL.B., State U. of Ia., 1922; m. Beulah E. Lenfest, Sept. 30, 1922; children—George Herbert, Mary Alice, Charles Lenfest. Admitted to bar, Ia. and Minn., 1922, W.Va., 1923, to District of Columbia bar, 1935; asst. county atty., Anoka County, Minn., 1922-23; removed to Charleston, W.Va., 1923, and asso. in practice with Price, Smith & Spilman, specialized in federal and state taxation; apptd. mem. U.S. Bd. of Tax Appeals, 1931; reentered law practice, charge Washington, D.C., office Guggenheimer & Untermeyer of New York, 1935, now Washington partner; lecturer, Practicing Law Institute, Federal Taxation. Mem. nat. panel arbitrators, Am. Arbitration Assn. Served with 3d Minn. Inf. on Mexican border, 1916; with 1st Officers Training Camp, Ft. Snelling, Minn., 1917; duty with troops, 34th Div., later staff duty; in France with 59th Field Arty. Brigade; assigned to Air Service as arty. observer 1st Aero Squadron, and served in Army of Occupation; commd. 1st lt. Mem. Am. Bar Assn. (taxation, adminstrv. law sects.), Am. Law Inst., D.C. Bar Assn., Phi Kappa Psi. Republican. Conglist. Mason Clubs: Metropolitan, Chevy Chase, National Press (Washington, D.C.); also Bohemian (San Francisco). Co-author: Procedure Before The Bureau of Internal Revenue, 1951. Contbr. numerous articles on taxation. Home: Washington DC Died Apr. 10, 1969; buried St. George's Cemetery, Lewes DE

GOODRICH, FOSTER EDWARD, mfg. co. exec.; b. Cambridge, N.Y., Aug. 12, 1908; s. Edward and Bertha (Allen) G.; A.B., Colgate U., 1933; m. Dorothy Ada Morgan, Aug. 12, 1937 (dec.); children—Foster Allen, Ann Morgan, Donald William, Jon Edward, Pamela

Jeanne, Trili. Dealer, Stanley Home Products, Inc., Utica, N.Y., 1932, successively coll. mgr. Hamilton, unit mgr. Schenectady, br. mgr. Watertown, dist. mgr. Syracuse, region mgr., asst. sales mgr., promotional sales mgr., gen. sales mgr., 1953-57, v.p. charge sales, 1957, 1st v.p., dir. sales, 1958, pres. Stanley Home Products, Inc., Westfield, Mass., 1960-72, also dir.; dir. Third Nat. Bank Hampden Co. Dir. Frank Stanley Beveridge Found., Inc., Stanley Park of Westfield, Inc. Mem. alumni bd. Colgate U. Served with USNR, 1944-45. Mem. N.Y. Sales Exec. Club, Newcomen Soc., Explorers Club. Republican. Methodist. Westfield MA Died Dec. 12, 1972.

GOODRICH, FRANCIS LEE DEWEY, librarian; b. Manchester, Mich., Jan. 17, 1877; s. Edward Payson and Mary Isabelle (Hall) G.; Mich. State Normal Coll., Ypsilanti, 1893-97; A.B., U. of Mich., 1903, M.A., 1916; B.L.S., N.Y. State Library Sch., 1906; hon. M.Ed., Mich. State Normal Coll., 1936; unmarried. Asst. librarian State Normal Coll. Library, Ypsilanti, 1900-04; asst., N.Y. State Library, Albany, 1905-06; asst. reference librarian John Crerar Library, Chicago, 1906-07; asst., later asso. librarian U. of Mich., 1907-30; asso. prof. and librarian, Coll. City of N.Y., 1930-36, prof. 1937-45, retired; curator of printed books, William L. Clements Library, University of Mich., 1945-46, cons. Bibliography, Clements Library, 1946-53. Instr. Ind. Pub. Libr. Commn. Instr. Summer School for Librarians, 1908, University of Michigan Summer School for Library Methods, 1909-18, 1922; spl. lecturer, dept. library science U. of Mich., 1927-30, summers 1931, 33-36, 39, 41, 45, 47-51. Grad. Library Sch. U. of Chgo., summer 1932, Columbia U. Sch. of Libr. Serv., spring 1933. Served in A.L.A. war serv., Camp Greene, N.C., Key West, Fla., Charleston, S.C., Beaune and Paris, France, 1917-19. Mem. American Library Assn., Washtenaw Hist. Soc., Bibliographical Soc. Am. Historical Soc. Mich., Mich. Library Assn., S.A.R. Phi Gamma Delta. Republican. Presbyterian. Mason. Club: Grolier. Author: Principles of College Library Administration (with W. M. Randall), 1936, 2d edit., 1941; three genealogical pamphlets on Goodrich, Dickinson, Hall families. Contbr. to library periodicals. Home: 14 Geddes Heights, Ann Arbor MI‡

GOODRICH, HALE CALDWELL, civil engr.; b. Upper Sandusky, O., May 19, 1904; s. George E. and Carrie C. (Hale) G.; B.C.E., Ohio State U., 1926; B.B.A., So. Meth. U., 1946; m. Flora Virginia Forehand, Mar. 26, 1933; children—Roy Gordon, Gary Wayne. Rodman, levelman N.Y.C. R.R. and Hocking Valley Ry. Co., asst. erector Western Gas Constrn. Co., Ft. Wayne, Ind., engr. Miss. River bridge constrn., Cape Girardeau, Mo., 1926-28; draftsman Cleve. Union Terminals Co., 1928-31; engr. United Gas Pipe Line Co., Houston, dist. engr., Dallas, gen. office Shreveport, La., 1931-68; noise cons. Active Boy Scouts Am. Registered profl. engr., Tex., La., Miss., Ala. Mem. Am. Gas Assn., Soc. for Exptl. Stress Analysis. Democrat. Methodist. Home: Shreveport LA Died Jan. 15, 1968; buried Centuries Meml. Park Cemetery Park Cemetery Shreveport

GOODRICH, L(AWRENCE) KEITH, publishing exec.; b. Grand Rapids, Mich., June 4, 1906; s. Grant and Emma A. (Knapp) G.; A.B., U. Mich., 1928; grad. Advanced Mgmt. Program, Harvard, 1954; m. Margaret F. Gillan, Oct. 27, 1934; 1 son, John Keith. Accountant, then travelling auditor Gen. Electric Co., 1928-35, plant accountant, 1941-45; asst. treas. Gen. Electric X-Ray Corp., 1935-41; asst. treas. McCraw-Hill Pub. Co., Inc., 1945-49, asst. v.p., asst. treas., 1949-54, v.p., asst. treas., 1954-57, vice pres., treas., 1957-61, executive vice president and treas., 1961-63, exec. v.p., 1963-68, chmn. finance com., 1961-68; dir. Standard & Poor's Corp., Milo Electronic Corp., also McGraw-Hill, Inc., Newton Falls Paper Mill, Inc. Trustee Financial Execs. Research Found. Mem. Financial Execs. Inst. (nat. dir., regional v.p., pres. 1962-64, chmn. bd. 1964-65, dir.-at-large 1965-68), Phi Gamma Delta. Clubs: Seaview Country: Scrasdale Golf (gov. 1956-59). Home: Scarsdale NY Died Apr. 18, 1968.

GOODRICH, ROBERT EUGENE, clergyman; b. Spring Creek, Tenn., Nov. 27, 1876; s. Harvey Edward and Nancy Rebecca (Rollins) G.; Ph.B., Southwestern U., Georgetown, Tex., 1903; D.D., Centenary Coll., Shreveport, La., 1924; m. Moye Aileen Wilson, Oct. 18, 1905; children—Robert E. Lewella Jean, Baxter Dee, Jerome Duncan, Harvey Wilson, Moye Aileen. Ordained ministry M.E. Ch., S., 1903; pastor Alvarado, Tex., 1903-07, Stamford, Tex., 1907-11, St. Luke's Ch., Oklahoma City, Okla., 1911-15, Francis Street Ch., St. Joseph, Mo., 1915-18, Austin Av. Ch., Waco, Tex., 1918-23, First Ch., Shreveport, La., 1923-30, First Ch., Birmingham, Ala., 1930-32, First Ch., Houston, Tex., 1932-36, Laurel Heights Ch., San Antonio, Tex., 1936-41, Methodist Temple Ch., Port Arthur, Texas, since 1941. Appointed on commn. to establish Korean Methodist Ch., 1930. Represented college three times in state inter-collegiate debate and oratory; college delegate to World's Student Conv., Toronto, Can., 1902; del. Ecumenical Conf. of Methodism, London, Eng., 1921. District Supt. of Tyler Dist. Methodist Church, since 1944. Mem. Kappa Alpha (Southern). Mason. Platform lecturer; writer of verse. Address: 210 Mockingbird Lane, Tyler TX‡

GOODSELL, WILLYSTINE, teacher, author; b. Wallingford, Conn., Jan. 8, 1870; d. Willys Jacob and Jennie (Clark) G.; grad. New Haven High Sch., 1888, Welch Training Sch., 1892; B.S., Teachers Coll. (Columbia), 1906, M.A., 1907, Ph.D., 1910. Teacher Welch Training Sch., 1890-92, Penn Charter Sch., Phila., 1892-98, Springfield (Mass.) Grammar Sch., 1898-1902; instr. Teachers College (Columbia), 1905-10, asst. prof., 1910-27, asso. prof., 1927-36; retired 1936. Dir. Am. Eugenics Soc., Euthanasia Soc. America; mem. Fgn. Policy Assn., Am. Assn. Univ. Women. Club: Women's Faculty (Columbia U.). Author: History of the Family as aSocial and Educational Institution, 1915; Education of Women, 1923; Problems of the Family, 1928; History of Marriage and the Family, 1934. Editor: Pioneers of Women's Education in the U.S., 1931. Contbr. of articles on edn. Home: 509 W. 121st St., New York NY‡

GOODSPEED, WALTER STUART, box board mfr.; b. Grand Rapids, Mich., Nov. 17 1902; s. John W. and Agnes (Walter) G.; A.B., U. Mich., 1924; student Harvard Law Sch.; m. Edith Crampton, Feb. 7, 1930; children—Priscilla, David, Robert C., Bennett W. Dir. Am. Box Board Co., Grand Rapids, 1930-71, sec., 1933-36, 1st v.p., asst. gen. mgr., 1936-45, treas., 1937-45, v.p., gen. mgr., 1945-46, pres., 1946-60; pres. Packaging Corp. Am., 1962-63, vice chmn. bd. 1963-71. Home: Grand Rapids MI Died May 1971.

GOODWIN, GRACE DUFFIELD (MRS. FRANK J. GOODWIN), writer; b. Adrian, Mich., Oct. 2, 1869; d. Rev. Samuel Willoughby and Harriet (Hayward) Duffield; grad. Bishopthorpe Sch. (Episcopal sch. for girls), Bethlehem, Pa., 1888; m. Rev. Frank J. Goodwin, of Glen Ridge, N.J., Nov. 11, 1891. Lecturer for Nat. Assn. Opposed to Woman Suffrage. Conglist. Club: Short Story (Providence, R.I.). Author: The Valley of Troubling, 1906; Anti-Suffrage—Ten Good Reasons, 1912; Horizon Songs, 1913. Home: Litchfield CT‡

GOODWIN, KATHRYN DICKINSON, social worker, govt. ofcl.; b. Heartwell, Neb., June 27, 1899; d. James Tomson and Luna Elizabeth (Sanford) Kellie; B.A., U. Cal., 1923; M.A., U. Wis., 1926. Social worker various agencies, 1926-30; field rep. U.S. Children's Bur., 1930-34; dir. social service Wis. Emergency Relief Adminstrn., Madison, 1934-37; regional pub. assistance rep. Social Security Bd., Mpls., 1937-38; asst. dir. Wis. Pub. Welfare Dept., Madison, 1938-39; asst. chief field div. bur. pub. assistance, Social Security Bd., 1940-45; asst. dir. bur. pub. assistance FSA, 1946-53; dep. dir. bur. pub. assistance Dept. Health, Edn. and Welfare, Washington, 1953-59, dir. 1959-62, dir. bur. family services, 1962-63, S.W. cons., from 1963. Member Internat., Nat. assns. social workers, Am. Pub. Welfare Assn., Nat. Conf. Social Welfare. Home: Washington DC

GOODWIN, LEO, SR., ins. exec.; b. Lowndes, Mo., Dec. 30, 1886; s. Dr. Edward E. and Mary Ann (Smith) G.; ed. public schools, Mo. State Normal, home study accounting course; married Lottie Z. Evelsizer, Oct. 15, 1911 (dec.); 1 son, Leo; m. 2d, Lillian E. Sargent Wilson, Jan. 5, 1936 (dec.). Underwriter, office mgr. United States Automobile Assn. San Antonio, 1925-35; one of founders Govt. Employees Ins. Co., exec. v.p., 1936-48, pres., 1948-58, chmn., 1956-57; pres. Govt. Employees Corp., 1949-58; founder chmn., mem. exec. com., dir. Govt. Employees Ins. Co., Govt. Employees Life Ins. Co., Govt. Employees Corp., 1958-71; (all Washington); dir. Riggs Nat. Bank, Washington, past pres. Nat. Assn. Independent Insurers, Chgo.; mem. adv. bd. Washington Mut. Investors Fund. Mem. Washington Bd. Trade, Clubs: Congressional Country (Washington); Coral Ridge Country, Phillips 66 (Ft. Lauderdale, Fla.). Home: Ft Lauderdale FL Died May 28, 1971.

GOODWIN, MARK LONDON, newspaper writer; b. Sedalia, Mo., Oct. 4, 1871; s. J. West and Martha (Hunt) G.; student Scaritt Coll., Neosho, Mo., 1890-92; m. Lillian Crawford, Dec. 30, 1902. Newspaper reporter in St. Louis and Kansas City, Mo., and Houston, Galveston, El Paso, Ft. Worth, Austin and Dallas, Tex., beginning 1892; mgr. Austin Statesman, 1902-06; charge news service in Oklahoma, of Dallas and Galveston News; Washington corr. Dallas News and Dallas Evening Journal, 1914-39. First sergt. Co. K, 3d Tex. Vol. Inf., Spanish-Am. War. Democrat. Episcopalian. Clubs: Nat. Press, Gridiron. Address: Box 1193, Austin TX‡

GORBACH, ALFONS, chancellor of Austria; b. Imst, Tirol, Austria, Sept. 2, 1898; LL.D., Graz U., 1922; m. Maria Gorbach, 1924; 1 dau., Alfonsa. Entered Austrian Civil Service, 1922, with Disabled Soldiers Indemnification Commn. in Graz; Christian Socialist candidate for Graz Municipal Council, 1928; municipal sch. supr. Graz, 1929-33; elected mem. Diet, Province of Styria, later mem. provincial govt. Styria in charge school matters; leader Fatherland Front in Styria, an alliance opposing Nazism in Austria, 1934-38; arrested, polit. prisoner of Nazis in Dachau concentration camp, 1938-43, 44-55; chmn. Austrian com. for repatriation of Austrian prisoners in Germany, 1945; acting chmn. Austrian People's Party in Styria, 1945-60, chmn. 1960; mem. lower house Austrian Parliament, 1945 speaker, 1945-61; chancellor of Austria, 1961-72. Vol 7th Inf. Regt., Imperial Austro-Hungarian Army, Worlc War I; ret. as res. lt. Address: Vienna Austria Died July 1972.

GORBY, PAUL FORD, educator; b. Tucson, Dec. 3 1904; s. John William and Lucia (Ford) G.; B.A. Northwestern U., 1926; postgrad. Kent Coll. Law 1934-36; m. Emeline Joy Tibbetts, Nov. 27, 1929 children—Robert Ford, William Chauncey, Emily Lucia. In exec. offices Marshall Field & Co., Chgo. 1926-30, credit dept. 1930, credit man, 1932 employment mgr., 1937-41, asst. to personnel mgr. 1941-47, mgr. central personnel services, 1947-59; lectr marketing Roosevelt U., 1959-65; lectr. De Paul U. 1939-41, Central YMCA Coll., 1941-44, Northwesterr U., 1944-57. Bd. advisers Unemployment Benefi Advisers, Washington, 1943; mem. Ill. Adv. Com. or Vets. Reemployment, 1948-56; mem. Mayor's Commn Sr. Citizens; chmn. Sr. Citizen Week, 1961; Ill. del White House Conf. on Aging, 1961. Mem. Evanstor Library Bd., 1965-73, pres. N. Suburban Library System, 1966-70. Alderman-at-large Evanston (Ill. City Council, 1953-65; chmn. Council com. to select 1s city mgr., 1953. Pres. Evanston Centennial Com., Inc. 1962-63. Served on faculty E.S.M.W.T.P.; mem regional mgmt. Labor Appeals Panel, War Manpowe Commn., World War II. Mem. Am. Library Truste Assn. (dir., mem. nominating com.), Ill. Library Assn (mem. manpower com. 1969-71, Nat. Library Weel com. 1970-71), Chgo. Indsl. Relations Assn. (chmn study groups 1939-41, exec. com. 1941-42), Nat. Retai Drygoods Assn. (chmn. employe testing com. 1947-49) Ill. C. of C. (chmn. social security com. 1950, 51, 52) Ill. Retail Merchants Assn. (chmn. social security com 1957-63), Indsl. Relations Research Assn., Evansto Hist. Soc. (dir., pres. 1962-64), Alpha Kappa Psi, Ph Gamma Delta. Methodist. Contbr. articles on mgmt. personnel, various aspects govt. Home: Evanston II Died Jan. 16, 1973.

GORDON, ALFRED, neurologist; b. Paris, France Nov. 2, 1874; s. Michael and Esther G.; M.D., U. c Paris, 1895; m. Victorine Lyon, of Bellefonte, Pa., Jul 20, 1898. Came to America, 1896; asso. in nervous an mental diseases, Jefferson Med. Coll., Phila. 1899-1908; examiner of the insane, Phila. Gen. Hosp 1904-08; has served as neurologist Mt. Sina Northwestern Gen., and Douglas Memorial hosps Mem. A.M.A., Am. Neurol. Assn., Coll. Physicians o Phila. Neurol. and Pathol. socs., Omega Upsilon Ph (Rho Chapter). Author: Diseases of the Nervou System, 1908. Address: 1812 Spruce St., Philadelphi PA‡

GORDON, CLARENCE MCCHEYNE, physicist; b Fannettsburg, Pa., Apr. 14, 1870; s. Rev. Jeremia Smith and Margaret Beatty (Kyle) G.; A.B., Princetor 1891, A.M., 1893; Ph.D., Gottingen, 1897; m. Ami Baker Lanier, July 17, 1909; 1 dau., Margaret Lanie Math. fellow Princeton, 1891-92; instr. physic Williams Coll., 1893-95; instr. physical chemistry Harvard, 1897-98; prof. physics, Centre Coll., Ky 1898-1909, Lafayette College, 1909-47, emeritus sinc 1947; prof. physics, Davis and Elkins Coll., since 1948 Optical engr., Wollensak Optical Company, Rocheste New York, 1918-19; electrical engineer Wester Electric Company, New York, 1920; prof. physic Temple U., summer 1923, Muhlenberg Coll., summe 1924, 27. Fellow A.A.A.S., Am. Physical Soc Republican. Presbyterian. Author: Experiments i General Physics, 1922; also articles in Physical Rev Jour. Am. Chem. Soc., etc. Address: Davis and Elkin Coll., Elkins WV‡

GORDON, DONALD, corp. exec.; b. Oldmeldrum Scotland, Dec. 11, 1901; s. John and Margaret L.(Wat G.; LL.D., Queen's U., 1947, U. Western Ont., 195 McGill U., 1965; U. Waterloo, 1966; D.C.L., Bishop U., 1958; D.Sc. Com., U. Moncton, 1966; m. Mais Barter, 1926 (dec. March 1950); children—Donal Ramsay, Michael Huntley; m. 2d, Norma Hobbs, 195 1 son, Campbell. Entered Bank of N.S., Toronto, 191 attached to head office and inspection staff, 1920, ass chief accountant, 1926, asst. mgr. Toronto br., 193 apptd. sec. Bank of Canada, 1935, dep. gov. 193 alternate chmn. Fgn. Exchange Control Bd., 1939, o loan as chmn. Wartime Prices and Trade Bd., 1941-4 dir. Indsl. Development Bank, 1944; exec. dir. Interna Bank for Reconstruction and Devel., 1948; chmn. b and pres. Canadian Nat. Rys., 1950-66; pres., chi exec. officer, dir. Brit. Newfoundland Corp. Ltd chmn., dir. Churchill Falls (Labrador) Corp. Ltd Montreal; dir. Bank of Montreal, Canadian Enterpris Devel. Corp. Ltd., Canadian Investment Fund Ltd Canadian Fund Inc., Hudson's Bay Co. Decorate Companion, Order St. Michael and St. George, 194 Knight of Grace, Order St. John of Jerusalem. Presby Clubs: Mt. Royal, St. James (Montreal); Toront Home: Westmont PQ Can. Died May 3, 1969; burie Mt. Royal Cemetery, Montreal, Que., Can

GORDON, DOROTHY, radio and TV artist; b Odessa, Russia, Apr. 4; d. Leo and Rose (Schwar Lerned; student pvt. tutors, U.S. and abroad; LL.

(hon.), Fairleigh Dickenson Univ., 1959; m. Bernard Gordon, June 28, 1910; children—Frank Harmon, Lincoln. Pioneer children's programs, stage and radio; began career as concert singer, 1925; dir. music programs Am. Sch. of the Air, CBS, 1931-38, condr. Children's Corner, 1936-38; staff MBS, 1938-39; cons. children's programs NBC, also dir. and actor Yesterday's Children, 1939-40; news program for children WQXR, 1940-42; moderator N.Y. Times Youth Forum, 1944-70, Forum on WQXR, 1945-70, Youth Forum on Dumont TV, 1952-58, Dorothy Gordon Youth Forums, NBC-TV, 1958-70; consultant youth activities The New York Times. Dir. children's radio programs OWI, 1942-44. Recipient award Nat. Conf. Christians and Jews, 1948-55, Sch. Broadcast Conf., 1949, Inst. Edn. by Radio, 1949-51, McCall's Gold Mike award, 1951, George Foster Peabody award, 1951, Fedn. Jewish Women's Orgns., 1952, Town Hall, 1953. Columbia U. Scholarship Press gold key, 1954, Ohio State U. award for edn. radio and TV, 1955. Gen. Fedn. Women's Clubs, 1955, Thomas Alva Edison award for sci. information to youth through mass media, Williamsburg Settlement award for developing youth interest in world affairs; Peabody award, 1964, 66; Gov.'s award Acad. TV Arts and Scis., 1965. Mem. Overseas Press Club Am. Author: Sing It Yourself, 1929; Around the World in Song, 1929; Treasure Bag of Game Songs, 1939; Come to France, 1939; Come to the Netherlands, 1940; All Children Listen, 1941; You and Democracy, 1951; Who Has the Answer?, 1965. Home: New York City NY Died May 11, 1970.

GORDON, ERNEST (BARRON), writer; b. Boston, Mass., Mar. 2, 1867; s. Rev. A. J. and Maria (Hale) G.; ed. Boston Latin School, Harvard U., 1888, and in Europe, where he lived many years. Active in anti-alcohol movement; news editor and staff writer on Sunday School Times. Author: The Anti-Alcohol Movement in Europe; Russian Prohibition; Two Footnotes to the History of the Anti-Alcohol Movement; The Maine Law; The Breakdown of the Gothenburg System; When the Brewer Had the Stranglehold; The Dry Fight in Europe; The Leaven of the Sadducees; A Book of Protestant Saints; The Wrecking of the 18th Amendment, 1943; Notes from a Layman's Greek Testament, Ecclesiastical Octopus, Alcohol Reaction at Yale, etc. Editor of Immanuel Hymnal. Address: Francestown NH‡

GORDON, HIRSCH LOEB, neuropsychiatrist; b. Wilno, Lithuania, Nov. 26, 1896; s. Rabbi Elijah and Malcah (Katzenellenbogen) G.; prep. edn. Wolozhin Yeshivah Gymnasium, Odessa, Russia, 1911-14; Ph.D., in Semitic Langs., Yale, 1922; L.H.D. in Egyptology, Cath. U., 1923; A.M. in Diplomacy, American U., 1924; A.M., in Edn., Teachers Coll., Columbia, 1926; D.H.L., Jewish Theol. Sem. of Am., 1928; A.M. in Fine Arts, N.Y.U., 1928; U. Berlin, 1931; Litt.D. in Classical Archaeology, Royal U. Rome, Italy, 1931, M.D., Sc.D., Diplomate Royal Inst. of Legal Medicine, Rome, 1934; m. Tamara L. Liebowitz. Came to U.S., 1915, naturalized, 1922. Lectr. in instructor, tchrs. colls., 1920-27; with neurol. clinic of Mt. Sinai Hosp., N.Y.C., 1935, Maimonides Hosp., Bklyn., 1935-37, physician skin and syphilis clinic, Mt. Sinai Hospital, 1937-40, surgery, 1940-41; member of psychiatric staff of Pilgrim State Hosp., Brentwood, N.Y., 1941-42; Cornell Div. Neurology, Bellevue Hospital, N.Y.C.; Kings County Psychiatric Hospital, Bklyn., 1934-44; Bellevue Psychiatric Hospital, 1944; qualified psychiat., State of New York, 1944; chief, shock therapy, U.S. Vets. Hosp., Northport, N.Y., 1944-46; chief neuropsychiat., U.S. Vets. Adminstrn., Jacksonville, Fla., 1947; neuropsychiat. consultant Div. U.S. Surgeon Gen., U.S. Army, Washington, 1947-48; sr. surgeon (comdr.) USPHS, also chief neuropsychiatry div. U.S. Marine Hosp., S.I., 1948-50; with neuropsychiat. div. Met. Hosp., N.Y.C., 1951-69, now asso. psychiatrist; asso. vis. psychiatrist Bird S. Coler Meml. Hosp., Met. Hosp.; adjunct in neuropsychiatry Beth Israel Hosp.; asso. in psychiatry, N.Y. Med. Coll.; lectr. N.Y.C. Cancer Com., 1935-69, N.Y.C. Dept. Health, 1937-69, L.I. Inst. 1951-53. Member board of appeal New York State SSS, 1951-69. Sgt. Royal Fusiliers, B.E.F., Palestine front, 39th R.F., 1918-19; maj., M.C., AUS, 1944-46. Recipient Maimonides award Michael Reese Med. Center, 1967, Am. Univ. Alumni Recognition award, 1968. Fellow Am. Geriatric Soc., Am. Psychiatric Assn., A.C.P.; mem. numerous medical, psychiatric, other orgns. Mason. Author several books, 1926-69, including Objectors to Electric Shock, 1946; Fractures in Electric Shock, 1946, 50; Shock Therapy Theories, 1946; The Maggid of Caro; Psychiatric Concepts in the Bible, Talmud and Zohar; contbr. literary and scientific monographs in Amer. and foreign reviews. Address: New York City NY Died Jan. 19, 1969; buried Cedar Park NJ

GORDON, RAY P(ERCIVAL), Rep. nat. committeeman; b. Saint Thomas, Virgin Islands, U.S., May 28, 1904; s. Edwin and Elineta Valencia Gordon; student Frederiksted High Sch., 1914-18; m. Grace Urania Wheatley, Apr. 16, 1937; 1 son, Rex. Mem. Municipal Council of St. Thomas and St. John, 1940-72 chmn. 1946-72; chmn. Legislative Assembly of Virgin Islands since 1946; chmn. St. Thomas Development Authority, St. Thomas Tourist Development. Republican Nat. committeeman from Virgin Islands. Mem. St. Thomas C. of C., Virgin Islands Progressive Guide. Roman Catholic. Home: Saint Thomas Virgin Islands Died May 1972.

GORDON, RICHARD SAMMONS, pub. utility economist; b. Oakland, Cal., Jan. 17, 1931; s. Conrad E. and Evelyn (Sammons) G.; B.S., Ore. State U., 1955; M.A. in Econs., Stanford, 1956; m. Carol Ann Braden, Nov. 10, 1951; children—Mark R., Bruce B., Eric R., Scott E. Accountant, Pacific Telephone Co., San Francisco, 1957-61, statistician market research, 1961-63, staff supr. advt., 1963-67, economist, 1969-73; statistician market research Am. Tel. & Tel. Co., N.Y.C., 1967-69. Tchr., cons. in field. Mem. Am., Western econ. assns., Am. Statis. Assn., Nat. Assn. Bus. Economists, Western Govtl. Research Assn. Home: Danville CA Died Jan. 15, 1973.

GORDON, WILLIAM LAWRENCE SANFORD, b. Alexandria, Louisiana, September 8, 1870; s. Jefferson Wells and Eleanor Compton (Sanford) G.; ed. under pvt. tutors and Leesburg (Va.) Acad.; m. Ruth Dowty, of New Orleans, La., July 18, 1894; children—Ruth Louise (Mrs. J. J. Washington), William Thomas Lawrence. Began with H. Haller Mfg. Co., New Orleans, 1889; with Stauffer Eshleman & Co., 1892-1913; vice pres. Gibbens & Gordon, Inc., hardware, New Orleans, since 1913. Postmaster of New Orleans, 1925-1933. Mem. New Orleans Assn. Commerce. Episcopalian. Mason. Club: New Orleans Chess. Home: 1653 Robert St. Office: 532 Canal St., New Orleans LA*‡

GORDON-DAVIS, ALFRED BURWELL (DAVIS BRINTON), lawyer, author; b. Phila., Dec. 29, 1872; s. Alfred Burwell and Eliza M. (Gordon) D.; grad. Univ. of Pa., 1896; admitted to bar, 1896. Mem. Phila. Acad. Natural Sciences, Pa. Hist. Soc., Browning Soc., Phila., Phi Gamma Delta, Southern Club. Republican. Episcopalian. Author: Pen Scratches, 1899 A7; Trusia, 1906 J5. Contb'r short stories to mags. Residence: 4710 Kingsessing Av. Office: 414 Walnut St., Philadelphia PA‡

GORE, HERBERT CHARLES, chemist, inventor, consultant; b. N.Y. City, June 19, 1877; s. Charles Willard and Anna Isabella (Guild) G.; B.S., U. of Mich., 1899; M.S., Ohio State U., 1901; m. Mella Taylor, July 7, 1903; children—Harriet Willard Looney, Richard Taylor, Winifred Loewen, William Robert. Asst. chemist, Ohio State U., 1900-01; teacher of science, high sch., Freeport, Ill., 1901-02; scientific asst., 1902-12, chemist, fruit and vegetable utilization, 1912, Bureau of Chemistry, Dept. of Agr., Washington; research chemist, Fleishmann Labs., New York, until 1942. Inventor of maltose sugar process. Member Am. Chem. Soc. Republican. Congregationalist. Author of numerous papers on chem. technology of fruits, vegetables, cereals and their products. Address: 5301 27th Av., St Petersburg, FL‡

GORMAN, THOMAS J., pres. Farm Bur. Coop. Assn., Inc. Address: Columbus OH Died July 29, 1972; buried Trenton, O

GOROSTIZA, JOSE, diplomat; b. Villahermosa, Tabasco, Mexico, Nov. 10, 1901; s. Celestino and Elvira (Alcala) G.; B.A., Nat. Prep. Sch., 1920; student sch. law, Nat. U., 1921-23; m. Josefina Ortega, Feb. 26, 1938; children—Luis, Marta, Jose. Diplomatic posts, London, 1927-28; prof. lit. Nat. U., Mexico, 1928-36; prof. history Nat. Tchrs. Sch., 1932-36; chief dept. publicity, Ministry Fgn. Affiars, 1936; diplomatic posts, Copenhagen, 1937, Rome, 1939-40, Guatemala, 1940, Havana, 1941-43, The Hague, Athens, 1950-51; dir.-gen. diplomatic service, 1943-49; ambassador, dep. permanent rep. of Mexico to UN, 1951; undersecretary for fgn. relations, 1953-64, sec. for fgn. relations, 1964; pres. Mexican Nat. Nuclear Energy Com., 1965-71; counsellor Dept. Nat. Patrimony, 1971-73; rep. internat. conf., Chapultepec, 1944, San Francisco, 1945, UNESCO, 1945, 1950, 1951, Rio de Janeiro, 1947, Bogota, 1948, Gen. Assembly UN, 1949, 1952, ECOSOG, 1951. Decorated Orden del Libertador (Argentina), Orden Carlos Manuel de Cespedes (Cuba), Orden de la Estrella Brillante (China), Orden Al Merito (Ecuador), Orden Yasco Nunez de Balboa (Panama), Orden del Libertador (Venezuela, Orden del Quetzal (Guatemala), Estrella de Etiopia (Ethiopia), A Merito Bennardo O'Higgins (Chile), Al Merito (Fed. Republic of Germany), Al Merito por Servicios Distinguidos (Peru), Honor of Merito (Haiti), Orden de la Bandero (Yugoslavia), Orden del Merito (U.A.R.), Al Merito (Italy), Orden de Leopoldo II (Belgium), Orden del Tesoro Sagrado (Japan), Orden de la Liberacion de la Republica Espanola (Spanish Republic), Orden de Polonia Restituta (Poland), Orden Nacional del Cedro (Lebanon), Orden del Crucero del Sur (Brazil); recipient Mazatlan Lit. award, 1965; Mexican Nat. award for Lit., 1968. Mem. Mexican Acad. of the Lang. Author: Canciones para Cantor en las Barcas. 1925; sin Fin, 1939, 52, (English translation Death Without End, 1969; Poesia, 1964; Prosa, 1969. Home: Mexico City Mexico Died Mar. 16, 1973.

GOSE, THOMAS PHELPS, lawyer; b. Walla Walla Wash., Dec. 25, 1901; s. Thomas Phelps and Clara (Crowe) G.; LL.B., U. Wash., Seattle, 1925; m. Jane Ankeny, June 29, 1928 (dec.),; children—John Ankeny, Phelps Ridpath, Jane Beclen; m. 2d, Margaret Jane Sell, June 11, 1964. Admitted to Wash. bar, 1925; practiced in Walla Walla, 1925-42, 45-70; mem. firm Gose & Gose, and predecessors, 1925-70; atty. City of Walla Walla, 1932-41. Pres., dir. Ridpath Hotel, Inc., Spokane, Wash., 1951-70; v.p., dir. Walla Walla Canning Co., 1951; mem. adv. bd. for Spokane, Seattle First Nat. Bank, 1958-70; pres., dir. Hotel Spokane, Ltd., 1961-63. Mem. jud. council State of Wash., 1941-42. Bd. regents Wash. State U., 1959-65, pres., 1963-64; dist. dir. Assn. Bds. Univs. and Colls., 1963-65; regent Gonzaga U. Spokane; trustee St. Paul's Sch. Girls, Walla Walla, 1948-68. Served to maj. AUS, 1942-45; ETO. Decorated Bronze Star. Fellow Am. Bar Found.; mem. Am., Wash. (pres. 1967-68) bar assns., Am. Judicature Soc., Eastern Wash. Hist. Soc. (trustee). Episcopalian. Home: Walla Walla WA Died Sept. 9, 1970.

GOSNELL, JOHN ANSLEY, lawyer; b. Little Rock, Ark., July 26, 1901; s. John Absolom and Snow (Ansley) G.; LL.B., Vanderbilt U., 1925; m. Relda Mayfield, Dec. 27, 1933; children—Anne (Mrs. Michael H. Styles), Susan (Mrs. Larry P. Ball), John Ansley. Admitted to Ark. bar, 1925, Ga. bar, 1945, D.C. bar, 1955; legal dept. RFC, Washington, 1933-35; with Nims, Verdi & Martin, N.Y.C., lawyers, 1935-40; staff Defense Supplies Corp., Washington, 1940-44; asst. counsel Coca-Cola Co., Atlanta and N.Y.C., 1944-50; with NPA, Washington, 1950-52; staff counsel Mfg. Chemists Assn., 1952-55; practice of law Gosnell, Durkin & Cappello, and predessor firm, Washington, 1955-69; gen. counsel, exec. sec. Nat. Small Bus. Assn., Washington, 1956-69; mem. firm Am., Fed., Ark., N.Y. State bar assns. Assn. Bar D.C. Conglist. Home: Arlington VA Died July 23, 1969; buried Arlington Cemetery, Eldorado AR

GOSS, BERT CRAWFORD, pub. relations exec.; b. Springfield, Mo., Jan. 21, 1907; s. Oscar L. and Lucy (Longacre) G.; A.B., Drury Coll., 1928; A.M., U. Chgo., 1929; D.C.S., N.Y.U., 1933; m. Ruth R. McCarthy, 1933. Sec. grad. sch. business adminstrn., assistant prof. finance, N.Y.U., 1930-34; associate editor New York Journal of Commerce, 1934-38; bus. editor Newsweek, 1938-42; Inst. Pub. Relations, N.Y.C., 1942-44; v.p. Hill and Knowlton, Inc., 1944-51, exec. v.p., 1951-55, pres., 1955-66, chmn. bd., 1966-71. Recipient Achievement Award, N.Y., Univ., 1956. Mem. Am. Econ. Assn., Kappa Alpha, Pi Gamma Mu. Clubs: University, Overseas Press, Nat. Press. Contbr. financial jours. Home: Bronxville NY Died Apr. 1971.

GOSS, ROBERT WHITMORE, educator; b. Fall River, Mass., May 28, 1891; s. John and Margaret (Murray) G.; B.S., Mich. State Coll., 1914, M.S., 1915; Ph.D., U. of Wis., 1923; m. Betty Walker, Sept. 7, 1921. Asst. prof. plant pathology, U. of Del., 1917-18; asst. plant pathologist, U.S. Dept. Agr., 1919-20; asst. plant pathologist, U. of Neb. Agrl. Expt. Station, 1920-23, asso. plant pathologist, 1923-37, plant pathologist, 1937-70; assistant professor plant pathology, University of Neb., 1920-23, associate professor, 1923-30, prof., 1930-70, dean graduate college, 1941-56, chmn. dept. plant pathology, 1937-49. Served in U.S. Army, 1918-19. Fellow A.A.A.S., Am. Phytopathol. Soc. (v.p. 1938); mem. Phi Beta Kappa, Sigma Xi. Writer of research bulls. and sci. papers on plant pathology. Home: Lincoln NE Died Jan. 10, 1970; buried Geneva NE

GOSSETT, ROBERT KENNETH, sales exec.; b. Indianapolis, Sept. 19, 1921; s. Paull Leland and Leila (Hornberger) G.; B.S., Purdue, 1942; m. Kathryn Moore Bertsch, January 22, 1943 (div.); children—Carolyn (Mrs. Frank L. Sibr, Jr.), Robert Kenneth, Paull; m. 2d, Ann Harrington Bertram, Dec. 16, 1966. Sr. mfg. development engr. R.C.A. Victor Div., Indianapolis, 1942-43; mfrs. sales engring. rep., pres., Gossett-Hill Co., 1946-67; v.p., dir. Zenter Enterprises, Inc., Albion, Mich., 1966-67. Bd. dirs. Vols. America. Served as captain U.S.A.A.F., 1943-46. Mem. Soc. Plastics Engrs. Inc. (nat. pres. 1958), American Management Association, A.I.M., Ind. Soc. Chgo., Phi Gamma Delta. Club: 49'ers Country (Tucson). Home: Des Plaines IL Died Sept. 13, 1967.

GOTSCH, ARTHUR EDWARD, automobile mfg. exec.; b. Forest Park, Ill., Dec. 27, 1900; s. Martin L. and Caroline (Haushalter) G.; grad. Walton Sch. Commerce, Chgo., 1924; m. Gertrude Scheel, Oct. 1, 1924; children—Donald A., James E. Engaged in banking bus., Chgo., 1915-28; with Studebaker-Packard Corp. (formerly Studebaker Corp., South Bend, Ind.), from 1928, beginning as mgr. export credits and financing, successively asst. treas., 1928-56, treas., from 1956; treas. Studebaker-Packard of Can., Ltd., also dir.; treasurer Mercedes-Benz Sales, Inc. Member of administrative com. Foreign Credit Interchange Bur., Nat. Assn. Credit Men. Home: South Bend IN Died Nov. 15, 1966.

GOTSHAL, SYLVAN, lawyer; b. Memphis, Mar. 21, 1897; s. Leopold and Julia G.; A.B., Vanderbilt U., 1917, A.M., 1918; LL.B., Columbia, 1920; m. Violet Kleeman, September 3, 1918; 1 dau., Sue Ann (Mrs. John Weinberg). Admitted to the New York State bar, 1920, practiced law, N.Y. City, mem. firm Rose & Paskus Proskauer, Rose & Paskus, 1920-32, Weil, Gotshal, Manges, and predecessor cos. Chmn. Soc. Nat. Shrine of Bill of Rights; co-chmn. lawyers' div. Nat. Conf. Christians and Jews; member board vice chmn. American Council Nationalities Service, chmn. N.Y. chpt. Nat. Found. Infantile Paralysis; former pres., chmn. bd. United Jewish Appeal Greater N.Y., hon. chmn., trustee; dir. Fed. Bill of Rights Soc.; former treas., now dir. Council Jewish Fedns. and Welfare Funds, Inc.; dir. City of Hope (Los Angeles Sanitorium); chmn. N.Y. A.R.C.; adv. bd. Salvation Army. Dir. Lafayette Fellowship Found., Inc. Fellow Brandeis U. Served as 2d lt., U.S. Army, 1918. Decorated French Legion of Honour; Italian Order Solidarite, Vatican Medal; merit award Government of Israel, Am. Arbitration Association award 1963, Jewish Welfare Board award, 1963. Mem. French Chamber of Commerce of U.S. (councillor), Nigerian-American C. of C. (director), African-American Chamber of Commerce (director) American, N.Y. City, N.Y. State, N.Y. Co. bar assns., Am. Arbitration Assn. (past pres. and chmn.; dir., chmn. world arbitration com. Nat. Urban League, Phi Beta Kappa, Tau Kappa Alpha, Sigma Upsilon. Clubs: City, Uptown, Bankers, Harmonie, Empire State (N.Y.C.); Sunningdale Country (Scardsale). Author: The Pirates Will Get You, 1945; Together We Stand, 1960; The European Common Market, 1961; Today's Fight for Design Protection, 1957. Home: Scarsdale NY

GOTTFRIED, LOUIS ELIO, juvenile furniture mfg. exec.; b. Buczacz, Austria, June 1, 1892; s. Adolf and Sabine (Herman) G.; student in engring. U. Lwow, Austria 1913-14; student Comml. Acad., Vienna, Austria, 1920; postgrad. U. World Commerce, Vienna, 1921; m. Friederike Spitzman, Aug. 29, 1921; children—Helen (Mrs. Henry Curtis), Margaret (Mrs. Eric Suran). Came to U.S., 1940, naturalized, 1945. Pres. LUMAG, wheel good mfrs., Vienna, Austria, 1923-38; pres., mem. bd. dirs. Rex Baby Carriage Mfg. Co., Inc., N.Y.C., 1940-70, Stroll-O-Chair Corp., N.Y.C., 1940-70, Abbott Industries, Incorporated, 1964-70. Served from pvt. to 2d lt., inf., Austrian Army, 1914-18. Inventor convertible line of juvenile furniture. Patentee in field of wheel goods and juvenile furniture. Home: NYC NY Died May 16,1970; buried Westchester Hills Cemetery Ardsley NY

GOTTSCHALL, MORTON, educator; b. N.Y. City, Oct. 16, 1894; s. Edward and Miriam (Spillenger) G.; A.B., Coll. City of N.Y., 1913; J.D., New York University, 1917; married Frances Greenfield, October 16, 1947 (dec. Sept. 1968). Connected with College City of New York since 1913, successivley assistant tutor and tutor, instr. in history, 1918-23, asst. prof., 1923-29, asso. prof., 1928-33, prof., 1933-64, dean Coll. of Liberal Arts and Sci., 1934-64; served as recorder, 1919-34, also taught classes in business law and legal philosophy; pres. Student Houses at City Coll., Inc., 1936-55; named v.p. City Coll. Press, 1949, sec. of City College Fund, 1953. Member of Academy Political Science, American Academy Political and Social Science, Am. Assn. Univ. Profs., City Coll. Alumni Assn. (pres. 1955-57), Phi Beta Kappa. Club: City College Club. Home: New York City NY Died July 30, 1968.

GOUGH, ROBERT E., newspaper exec. Gen. mgr. New Orleans Times-Picayune and States Item, Times-Picayune Pub. Corp. Address: New Orleans LA Died Feb. 1973.

GOULD, ANNA LAURA, teacher; b. Bedford, O., May 8, 1875; d. Otis Harrison and Margaret (Whiteside) G.; grad. high sch., Bedford, 1891; A.B., Hiram (O.) Coll., 1898; Columbia U., 1911-12; S.B., U. of Calif., 1923. Teacher high sch., Bedford, 1898-1903, Toronto, O., 1904-07; prof. history and dean of women, Hiram Coll., O., 1907-21; dean of women, Calif. Sch. of Christianity, 1921-22. Republican. Mem. Ch. of Christ (Disciples). Home: Glendale CA‡

GOULD, CLARENCE PEMBROKE, educator; b. Church Hill, Md., Nov. 1, 1884; s. William Dunbar and Josephine Trenchard (Faithful) G.; A.B., Johns Hopkins, 1907, Ph.D., 1911; LL.D. (hon.), Washington Coll., 1956; m. Gertrude Ruth Schill, June 16, 1933; 1 dau., Mary F. (Mrs. E. L. Currence). Prof. history Coll. of Wooster (Ohio), 1911-18, Kent (O.) State U., summer 1939; pres. Washington Coll., Chestertown, Md., 1919-23; asso. prof. history Western Res. U., 1924-33; prof. history, dean Kenyon Coll., Gambier, O., 1933-39; head dept. history Youngstown (O.) Univ., from 1939; research abroad, 1923-24. Served as lt. jr. grade, U.S.N., 1918-19. Mem. Am. Hist. Assn., Miss. Valley Hist. Soc., Ohio Acad. History, Econ. History Soc., Societe d'Histoire Moderne, Phi Beta Kappa. Author: Money and Transportation in Maryland, 1720-1765, 1915; The Land System in Maryland, 1720-1765, 1912; articles and reviews hist. jours. Home: Maryville TN Died Dec. 13, 1971.

GOULD, HARRY EDWARD, industrialist; born N.Y.City, July 12, 1898; s. John and Julia (Asch) G.; ed. pub. schs. N.Y. City; m. Lucille Quartucy, Sept. 23, 1937; children—Harry E., Peter John, Robert Jay. Pres., Aldine Paper Co., N.Y.C., from 1924; chmn. bd. Gould Paper Corp.; chmn. bd., dir., mem. exec. com. Universal Am. Corp., N.Y.C.; dir., exec. com. PepsiCo, Inc.; dir. Amron Corp. (Wis.), Universal Am. Realty Corp. (Fla.), Young Spring & Wire Corp. (Mich.), Daybrook-Ottawa Corp. (Ohio), Gulf & Western Industries, Inc., Brown Co., 795 Fifth Av. Corp., member board directors of the Livingston Rock & Gravel Company, Inc., Pepsi-Cola International. Member Mayor's Reception Com. N.Y.C.; mem. Citizens Com. for Internat. Devel., Washington, Citizens' Adv. Com. to Office Cultural Affairs, Washington; dir. United Epilepsy Assn., Inc., dir. Boys Clubs Am. Pres. Pepsi-Cola Found., Inc. Mem. Actors' Fund of America, Lucullus Circle, Navy League; also mem. Found. Motion Picture Pioneers. Clubs: Rockrimmon Country (stamford, Conn.); Lambs. Paper. Printing House Craftsmen (gov.), Graphic Arts Square, N.Y. Athletic, Penn Plaza (N.Y.C.); Federal City (Washington); Variety. Home: New York City NY Died Mar. 8, 1971.

GOULD, KENNETH MILLER, editor; b. Cleve.; May 13, 1895; s. Rev. Frederic A. and Alice D. (Miller) G.; A.B., U. Pitts., 1916; A.M., Columbia, 1921; m. Helen V. Rue, Apr. 12, 1919; children—Richard Gordon, David Huntington, Geoffrey Stuart, Elizabeth Beer (Mrs. John P. Sylva, foster dau.). Served as editorial secretary of the Missionary Education Movement, U.S. and Can., 1916-18; asst. editor Jour. Social Hygiene, 1919-21; mng. editor. Am. Jour. Pub. Health, 1921-22; staff Rockefeller Found., 1922-23; contbg. editor Time mag., 1923-24; editor U. Pitts., 1924-25; mng. editor Scholastic mags., 1926-39, editor-in-chief, 1940-60. Adv. com. Scarsdale (N.Y.) Adult Sch.; director Workshop for Cultural Democracy. Mem. Nat. Council Social Studies, Authors League Am., Adult Edn. Assn. U.S.A., Omicron Delta Kappa, Sigma Delta Chi. Democrat. Unitarian. Club: Town (Scarsdale, N.Y). Author: Windows on the World, 1938. Contbr. articles mags., jours. Home: Scarsdale NY Died Mar. 12, 1969.

GOULD, NORMAN JUDD, ex-congressman; b. Seneca Falls, N.Y., Mar. 15, 1877; s. Seabury S. and Mary Mitchell (Judd) G.; M.E., Cornell U., 1899; m. Anna B. Mullin, July 2, 1921. Began with Goulds Pumps, Inc., Seneca Falls, 1899, pres. since 1908. Alternate del. at large Rep. Nat. Conv., Chicago, 1908, and del., 1916; chmn. Rep. Co. Com., Seneca Co., N.Y., 1912-22; mem. Rep. State Com., N.Y., 1914-22; mem. 64th to 67th Congresses (1915-23), 36th N.Y. Dist. 32 deg. Mason, Knight Templar, Shrine (Damascus Temple). Presbyn. Home: Seneca Falls NY‡

GOVE, PHILIP BABCOCK, editor; b. Concord, N.Y., June 27, 1902; s. John McClure and Florence Amy (Babcock) G.; A.B., Dartmouth, 1922, Litt.D., 1963; A.M., harvard, 1925; Ph.D., Columbia, 1941; m. Grace Edna Potter, Aug. 17, 1929; children—Norwood B., Susan (Mrs. Rosser A. Rudolph, Jr.), Doris. Instr. English, Rice Inst., 1924-27, N.Y.U., 1927-42; William Bayard Cutting traveling fellow Columbia, 1939-40; asst. editor Merriam-Webster dictionaries, Springfield, Mass., 1946-51, mng. editor, 1951-52, gen. editor, 1952-61, editor in chief, 1961-72. Mem. editorial bd. Ency. Brit.; mem. adv. bd. Center for Documentation, Communication Research, Western Res. U. Served as lt. comdr. USNR, 1942-46. Mem. Linguistic Soc. Am., Am. Dialect Soc., Nat. Council Tchrs. English, Modern Lang. Assn., Internat. Soc. Gen. Semantics, Coll. English Assn., English Grad. Union (Columbia), Johnson Soc. of London, Nat. Soc. for Study Communications, Phi Gamma Delta. Author: The Imaginary Voyage in Prose Fiction, 1941. Editor: The Role of the Dictionary, 1967. Contbr. articles to learned jours. Home: Warren MA Died Nov. 16, 1972; buried Tewksbury MA

GOW, CHARLES R(ICE), engineering; b. Medford, Mass., Dec. 5, 1872; s. Robert M. and Cordelia (Flynn) G.; B.S., Tufts Coll., 1893, D.Sc., 1919; hon. Dr. Engring., Northeastern Univ., 1932; same, Worcester Poly. Inst., 1935; m. Jeannette A. Weaving, June 12, 1900; children—Ralph F., Arthur R., Jeannette (dec.), Charles R., Grace A. Asst. supt. water dept., Medford, 1893; asst. city engr., Medford, 1895; supt. for contractor in sewer and subway constrn., 1895; asst. engr. Boston Transit Commn., 1895-98; contractor, pub. works and engring. constrn., 1899-1922; cons. engr., Boston, 1922-30; pres. Warren Bros. Co. since 1930; chairman of the board since November 30, 1942. Lecturer on foundations, Mass. Inst. of Tech., 1912-18, prof. of humanics, 1928-30. Postmaster Boston Postal Dist. (25 cities and towns), 1929-30. Served as pvt., advancing to lt. col. engrs., Mass. Nat. Guard, 1889-1908; sergt. maj., later 2d lt. and 1st lt., 5th Mass. Vols., Spanish-Am. War; maj., later lt. col., Constrn. Div., U.S. Army, World War. Mem. commn. on water needs of cities and towns of Ipswich River Valley, 1911-12; chmn. Boston Licensing Bd., 1915-16, Joint N.E. Commn. on St. Lawrence Waterway, 1924-25, Met. Water Supply Investigating Commn., 1924-25, Met. Planning Div., 1928-34. Mem. Am. Soc. C.E., Boston Soc. C.E. (pres. 1915); pres. Associated Industries of Mass., 1921-23. Republican. Conglist. Author: Fundamental Principles of Economics, 1922; Foundations for Human Engineering, 1930; Elements of Human Engineering, 1931. Home: 1751 Beacon St., Brookline, Mass. Office: 38 Memorial Drive, Cambridge MA‡

GOW, JAMES STEELE, ret. found. exec.; b. Pitts., Jan. 3, 1895; s. Harry Campbell and Elizabeth Gray (Steele) G.; ed. Pitts. Acad., 1909-12; A.B. cum laude, U. Pitts., 1916, LL.D., 1938; Ed.M., Harvard, 1927; m. Hazel Evelyn Steele, May 10, 1917; children—James Steele, Don Wallace, Robert Campbell. With U. Pitts., 1916-30, head dept. pub. relations until 1918, financial sec., 1918-20, asst. to pres., 1920-24, exec. sec. of Univ., 1924-29, dean adminstrn., 1929; exec. dir. Falk-Found., Pitts., 1930-65. Austin fellow in edn., Harvard, 1924-25; lectr. ednl. sociology U. Pitts., 1925-35. Instr. O.T.S., U.S. Army, 1918; sec. Bd. Hospitalization for War Vets (U.S. Treasury Dept.), 1920. Trustee Children's Hosp.; mem. bd. Leon Falk Family Trust. Recipient Alan M. Scaife award for leadership in edn., 1964. Mem. Phi Beta Kappa, Omicron Delta Kappa, Pi Tau Alpha, Delta Mu Delta, Sigma Alpha Epsilon. Republican. Baptist. Clubs: Duquesne (Pitts.); Williams Country (Weirton, W.Va.). Home: Pittsburgh PA Died Mar. 13, 1973.

GOWEN, HERBERT HENRY, clergyman; b. Great Yarmouth, Eng., May 29, 1864; s. Henry Cobb and Mary (Fuller) G.; A.B., St. Augustine's Coll., Canterbury, Eng., 1886; 1st class Oxford and Cambridge Preliminary; D.D., Whitman Coll., 1912; m. Annie Kate Green, Jan. 7, 1892; children—Vincent Herbert, Lancelot Edward, Felicia Joyce, Rupert George, Sylvia Mary. Deacon, 1886, priest, 1889, P.E. Ch.; in charge of Chinese Mission, Honolulu, H.I., 1886-90; curate, St. Nicholas Ch., Great Yarmouth, Eng., 1890-92; rector St. Barnabas, New Westminster, B.C., 1892-96, Trinity Parish, Seattle, Wash., 1897-1914; now in charge of St. Barnabas' Chapel, of Seattle; in charge Japanese Missions, Seattle, etc. Prof. Oriental languages and literature, University of Washington, 1900-45, professor emeritus since 1945. President Wash. State Philol. Soc.; fellow Royal Geog. Soc. (London), Royal Asiatic Soc.; hon. fellow St. Augustine's College, Canterbury; member Royal Society Arts, American Oriental Society, Phi Beta Kappa. Clubs: Rainier, University Faculty, University, Monday, China Club (Seattle); Authors' (London). Author: Temperantia, 1891; Paradise of the Pacific, 1892; The Kingdom of Man, 1893; Pioneer Work in British Columbia, 1899 and 1909; Hawaiian Idylls of Love and Death, 1908; The Day of His Coming, 1907; The Revelation of the Things That Are, 1909; An Analytical Transcription of the Revelation of St. John the Divine, 1910; Meditations on the Seven Last Words, 1911; Stella Duce, 1911; An Outline History of China, 1913, Vol. II, 1914, new and revised edit. in 1 vol., 1916; Sonnets for the Sundays, 1917; The Book of the Seven Blessings, 1919; The Napoleon of the Pacific, 1919; Sonnet Stories from the Chinese, 1920; Christ and Colosse, 1922; Asia—A Short History, 1926; An Outline History of China (with J. W. Hall), 1926; The Universal Faith, 1926, 27; An Outline History of Japan, 1927; The Journal of Kenko (U. of Wash. Chap Bk.), 1927; APrecursor of Perry, 1928; The Little Grey Lamb and Other Poems, 1928; The Psalms, or Book of Praises, 1929; A History of Indian Literature, 1931; A History of Religion, 1934; Five Foreigners in Japan, 1937. Home: R. 1, Cobble Hill, British Columbia, Can.; also Port Blakely WA‡

GOWEN, JAMES EMMET, company dir.; b. Phila., Apr. 22, 1895; s. Francis Innes and Alice (Robinson) G.; grad. St. Paul's Sch., 1913; A.B., Princeton, 1917; LL.B., U. Pa., 1921; m. Sally Drexel Henry, June 25, 1925; children—Francis I., Howard H. Admitted to Pa. bar, 1921; with legal dept. Pa. R.R. Co., 1921-30, dir., 1942-71; v.p. Phila. Sav. Fund Soc., 1930-33; pres. dir. Western Sav. Fund Soc., 1933-39; pres., chmn. bd. Girard Trust Bank, Phila., 1939-60; dir. of the Camden Fire Ins. Association, Pennsylvania Gen. Ins. Co., Potomac Ins. Co., Phila., Balt. & Washington Railroad Co., Pitts., Youngstown & Ashtabula Ry. Co., Manor Real Estate Co., Mut. Assurances Co., Pennsylvania General Fire Insurance Company. Served with U.S. Navy, 1917-21. Democrat. Clubs: Philadelphia, Rabbit (Phila.); Schuykill (Pa.). Home: Chestnut Hill, Phila. 18Office: Philadelphia PA Died 1971.

GRABAU, AMADEUS WILLIAM, palaeontologist; b. Cedarburg, Wis., Jan. 9, 1870; s. Prof. William and Maria (von Rohr) G.; S.B., Mass. Inst. Tech., 1896; S.M., Harvard, 1898, S.D., 1900; m. Mary Antin, of Boston, Oct. 6, 1901; children—Josephine, Esther. Prof. geology, Rensselaer Poly. Inst., Troy, N.Y., 1899-1901; adj. prof. palaeontology, 1905-19, Columbia U.; consulting geologist, New York, 1919-20; prof. palaeontology Nat. U., Peking, China, and chief palaeontologist Chinese Geological Survey, 1920—; dean Peking Lab. of Natural History since 1925. Research asso. in palaeontology, 3d Asiatic Expdn. of Am. Mus. Natural History. Fellow Geol. Soc. America, Palaeontol. Soc. America, New York Acad. Science, A.A.A.S., Geol. Soc. China (v.p. 1925-26; 1st award Grabau gold medal), Peking Soc. Natural History; hon. mem. China Inst. Mining and Metallurgy, Science Soc.

of China. Author: North American Index Fossils (with H. W. Shimer), 2 vols., 1909-10); Principles of Stratigraphy, 1913, 2d edit., 1921; Geology of the Non-Metallic Minerals Other than Silicates, Vol. I, 1920, Vol. II, 1922; Text Book of Geology, Vol. I, 1920, Vol. II, 1921; Palaeogoeic Corals of China, 1921, 28; Silurian Fossils of Yunnan, 1926; also many other contbns. on Am., European and Chinese Geology and Palaeontology; Ordovician Fossils of North China, 1921; Evolution of the Earth and Its Inhabitants (in Chinese trans.), 1921; Stratigraphy of China, Vol. I, 1924-25. Address: Geological Survey of China, Peiping China*‡

GRABILL, ETHELBERT VINCENT, lawyer; b. Greenville, Mich., Oct. 6, 1874; s. Elliott Finley and Anna Sutton (Jenney) G.; A.B., Oberlin Coll., Oberlin, O., 1896, LL.D., from same, 1941; LL.B., Harvard, 1899; m. Annie Elizabeth Ziegler, June 7, 1906; children—Olive (wife of Robert K. Carr, asst. prof. Dartmouth), Elliott Vincent, Elizabeth Anna (Mrs. Jarvis Farley). Admitted to Mass. Bar, 1899; practiced with Whipple, Sears & Ogden, 1899-1903; mem. Flye, Grabill, Buttrick & James, 1916-33; now asso. with son, Elliott, Douglas L. Ley, and Harrison D. Mason, as Grabill, Ley & Mason. Mem. American Bar Association, Massachusetts Bar Association, Bar Association of City of Boston, Harvard Law Sch. Assn. (life), Bostonia Society (life), Phi Beta Kappa (Zeta chapter of Oberlin Coll.). V.p. Am. Congregational Assn.; moderator, Mass. Congl. Conference and Missionary Society, 1938-39. Trustee and sec. of Eliot School. Mason (hon. 33 deg., S.R.; dep. Mass. Grand Master, 1949). Clubs: Appalachian Mountain (life), Boston City, Boston Congregational (pres. 1915); Eliot (Jamaica Plain) (pres. 1927-29). Asso. editor Mass. Reports, 1907-20. Reporter of decisions of the Supreme Court of Mass., 1920-35, and since 1939. Author: Sacco and Vanzetti in the Scales of Justice, 1927; (pageant) The Influence of Masonry in the History of Our Nation, 1945; (monograph) Prevention of Industrial Disputes, 1946. Home: 16 Aldworth St., Jamaica Plain, Mass. Office: 10 State St., Boston MA‡

GRABLE, BETTY (ELIZABETH RUTH), actress; b. St. Louis, Mo., Dec. 18, 1916; d. Conn and Lillian (Hofmann) Grable; ed. Mary Inst., St. Louis, Children's Professional Sch., Hollywood, and by private tutors; studied dancing in Los Angeles; m. Jackie Coogan, Nov. 20, 1937 (div.); m. 2d, Harry Haag James, July 5, 1943 (div.); children—Victoria Elizabeth, Jessica. Appeared first in Whoopee and Kiki; tour with Wheeler and Woolsey, 1935; appeared in What Price Innocence, 1933; The Nit Wits; Old Man Rhythm, 1935; Follow the Fleet, Don't Turn 'Em Loose; Pigskin Parade, 1936; This Way Please; Thrill of a Lifetime; College Swing; Give Me a Sailor, 1938; Man About Town; Million Dollar Legs; The Day the Bookies Wept, 1939, Du Barry Was a Lady (N.Y. stage), 1940; Yank in the R.A.F. 1941; Footlight Serenade, 1942; Spring Time in the Rockies, 1942; Down Argentine Way; Tin Pan Alley; Moon Over Miami; Pin-Up Girl; Mother Wore Tights; Lady in Ermine; My Blue Heaven, The Farmer Takes a Wife; Three for the Show, and others; currently appearing on TV, in motion pictures, and on records. Home: Beverly Hills CA Died July 2, 1973.

GRACE, ATONZO G., educator; b. Morris, Minn., Aug. 14, 1896; s. Richard H. and Sarah Elizabeth (Murphy) G.; A.B., U. of Minn., 1917, A.M., 1921; Ph.D., Western Reserve University, 1932; Sc.D., Boston University, 1946; L.H.D., Springfield College, 1951; graduate American Musicians School, Chaumont, France, 1919; mar. Jeanette Meland, June 18, 1921; children—Alonzo Gaskell, Richard Simmons, David Harlan. Instr. U. Minn., 1920-22; professor State Tchrs. Coll., S.D., 1923-25; asst. supr., asst. dir., dir. and chmn. dept. adult edn. Cleve. Bd. Edn., 1925-30; mem. faculty, U. Rochester, 1930-38; commissioner of education, Connecticut, 1938-48; dir. edn. and cultural relations Office Mil. Govt. in Germany and Office High Commr., 1948-50; prof. edn., also chmn. dept. edn. Univ. of Chicago, 1950; prof. education and dir. Div. Advanced Studies, Sch. of Edn., N.Y.U., 1951-60, asso. dean 1952-60; dean College Edn., U. Ill., 1960-64, dean emeritus, 1964-71; instr. Yale, 1940-48; lecturer Western Reserve U., Columbia, Harvard, New York U.; dir. of school surveys, N.Y., Washington, New Orleans, etc. Served as private, corpl., sergt., 2d lt. 135th and 76th F.A., 1917-19; dir. of field operations, Pre-Induction Training Branch, U.S. Army, 1943; dir. study Armed Service Edn. and Training Program since 1946. Mem. Monroe Co. (N.Y.) Charter Commn. Trustee Rochester Sch. for Deaf. Decorated Cross of Merit (Germany Fed. Republic). Mem. A.A.A.S., Am. Soc. Pub. Adminstrn., Am. Assn. Univ. Profs., Phi Kappa Sigma. Clubs: Hartford, Yale, Faculty. Author books including: Educational Lessons from Armed Services, 1948. Home: Andover CT Died Oct. 19, 1971; buried Nathan Hale Cemetery, Coventry CT

GRACE, CARL GUY, mfg. exec.; b. Albany, Mo., May 18, 1907; s. O.L. and Myrtle (Bender) G.; B.S. in Commerce, Northwestern U., 1929; m. Dorothy M. Johnson, Feb. 4, 1933; children—Philip, Joan. With Colgate-Palmolive Co., N.Y.C., 1929-66, gen. mgr. subsidiary, Jamaica, B.W.I., 1939-48, subsidiary, Columbia, S.A., 1948-54, exec. v.p., gen. mgr. subsidiary, Can., 1954-55, pres., gen. mgr., 1955-57, v.p., gen. mgr. toilet article div. parent co., 1957-66, dir. Clubs: Granite (Toronto); Canadian (N.Y.C.). Home: Winter Park FL Died Aug. 12, 1970.

GRACE, JAMES THOMAS, JR., physician, surgeon; b. Troy, Ala., July 16, 1923; s. James Thomas and Anna (Salter) G.; B.S., Yale, 1945; M.D., Harvard, 1948; m. Betty Bryant Thornton, Nov. 21, 1951 (dec.); children—Elizabeth Anne, Mary Day, John Bryant, Patricia Merrill. Practiced medicine, specializing in surgery, Huntsville, Ala., 1950-51; asst. resident surgery Vanderbilt-VA Hosp., Nashville, 1953-56, resident surgeon, 1956-57; mem. staff Roswell Park Meml. Inst., Buffalo, 1957-70, asst. dir., 1959-67, dir. viral oncology sect., 1963-70, dir. inst., 1967-70; faculty Vanderbilt U., 1956-57; faculty U. Buffalo Sch. Medicine, 1958-70, asso. research prof. surgery, 1962-70; research prof. microbiology State U. N.Y., Buffalo, 1964-70. Mem. cancer virology panel NIH, 1961-62; mem. human cancer virus task force USPHS, 1962-64. Recipient Billings medal A.M.A., 1961. Diplomate Am. Bd. Surgery. Mem. A.M.A., Soc. U. Surgeons, A.C.S., Halsted Soc., N.Y. Acad. Scis., Am. Fedn. Clin. Research (councillor Eastern sect. 1960-62), Soc. Exptl. Biology and Medicine (councillor Western N.Y. sect. 1959-64), A.A.A.S., Am. Assn. Cancer Research (dir. 1966-70), Am. Soc. Mammalogists, Surg. Investigators Exchange, Am. Cancer Soc. (pres. Erie County div. 1965-70), Nat. Inst. Gen. Med. Scis. (clin. research tng. com. 1965-70), Sigma Xi, Editor surg. sect. Yearbook of Cancer, 1960-70; editorial bd. Rev. Surgery, 1964-70. Contbr. articles surg. jours. Studies of host defense factors in cancer; immunology of cancer; relationship of viruses to malignancy; surg. physiology; devel. of surg. techniques for management of cancer. Established immunological relationship between cancer and coexisting dermatomysoitis. Home: Clarence NY Died Aug. 13, 1971; buried Huntsville AL

GRACE, JOHN JOSEPH, social welfare adminstr.; b. Jersey City, May 26, 1902; s. Joseph J. and Elizabeth (Mitchell) G.; grad. Salvation Army Sch. Officers Tng., N.Y.C., 1922; m. Alice Owen, Apr. 18, 1930. Commd. officer Salvation Army, 1922, various field adminstrn. appointments, 1922-45; territorial pub. relations dir., N.Y.C., 1945-47; divisional comdr., Buffalo, 1947-50, Phila., 1950-61; nat. chief sec., adminstrv. asst. to nat. comdr., N.Y.C., 1961-70; dir. social adminstrn. team AID, Vietnam, 1969-71. Home: Philadelphia PA Died July 23, 1972; buried Kensico NY

GRACE, LOUISE CAROL, advt. exec.; b. Detroit; d. Edward and Hattie Martin (Rood) Grace; grad. U. Wis. Library Sch., 1914. City librarian, Marshfield, Wis., 1914-15; br. librarian Detroit Pub. Library, 1915-20; research librarian William N. Albee Co., Detroit, 1920-24; advt. mgr. Edmunds & Jones Corp., Detroit, 1924-25; dir. Grace & Holliday, 1925-35; v.p. Grace & Bement, 1935-45; dir. research and media Grant Advt., Inc., Detroit, 1945-55; co-owner, v.p., treas. Cox & Grace, Inc., Detroit, Mich., 1956-66, president, treasurer, 1966-67. Mem. adv. bd. Volunteers of Am., Detroit, from 1950; founder, hon. pres. Women's Auxiliary, from 1952; mem. bd. edn., Detroit, from 1949, pres., 1959-60, 66-67. Pres. Family Service Soc., Met. Detroit, 1958-60; mem. bd. Woman's Hosp.; bd. govs. Wayne State U., 1956-59. Named one of 50 outstanding Mich. women, Women's Expn., Detroit, 1934; named woman of the year Soroptimist Club, Detroit, 1944, woman of achievement, 1951; recipient Headliner award Theta Sigma Phi, 1944; named advt. woman of the year, Detroit, 1949; recipient distinguished service medal Wayne State U., 1956; Ruth Huston Whipple award for exceptional contbn. community and govtl. services Mich. State Fedn. Bus. and Profl. Women's Clubs, 1957. Mem. Am. Marketing Assn., Advt. Fedn. Am. (1st woman sec. 1936), Spl. Libraries Assn. Mich. (pres. 1945-47), Inter-Group Council for Women as Pub Policy Makers (chmn. 1943-46), Detroit Historical Society, Nat. Forensic League, World Study Council (exec. bd. Detroit, 1943-47), Wayne State U. Alumni Assn., D.A.R., Delta Kappa Gamma, Alpha Gamma Delta. Republican. Presbyn. Clubs: Zonta Internat. (nat. pres. 1946-48; pres. Detroit chpt. 1927-28); Women's Advertising (pres. 1934-36), Women's City (dir. 1938-39), Business Woman's, Women Principals, Native Born Detroiters, Native Detroit Women's (Detroit); Edna Chaffee Noble Alumni and Speech; University of Wisconsin Women's. Contbr. articles profl. publs. Home: Detroit MI Died May 1968.

GRACE, THOMAS L., airlines exec.; b. Neb., June 28, 1911; married; 1 dau. Supt. flight and space control Slick Airways, 1946, supt. operation, 1946-49, v.p. operation, 1949-50, v.p. operation, gen. mgr., 1950, pres., 1950-54, following consolidation with Flying Tiger Line, Inc., 1954, became exec. v.p. of new corp., then v.p. operations N.E. Airlines. pres. Ozark Air Lines, Inc., St. Louis, 1964-71. Served as pilot USAAF, 1942-46. Home: St Louis MO Died July 21, 1971; buried Rose Hills Cemetery, Whittier CA

GRACEY, WILBUR TIRRELL, consul; b. at E. Weymouth, Mass., Feb. 26, 1877; s. Samuel Levis and Leonora (Thompson) Gracey; pub. sch. edn.; m. Enid Yale, of Oakland, Cal., July 22, 1906. Apptd. marshal, Apr. 1, 1899, vice-consul, July 31, 1899; vice and deputy consul, May 2, 1902, at Foochow, and several times in charge; served till 1904; vice and deputy consul at Nanking, 1904-5 (in charge consulate Oct., 1904-Aug., 1905); marshal and vice deputy consul at Foochow, Aug.-Nov., 1905; vice and deputy consul-gen. in charge of the consultate-gen. at Hongkong, 1905-6; consul at Tsingtau, 1906-10, at Nanking, China, Apr. 15, 1910-Mar. 13, 1912, at Progreso, Yucatan, Mex., Mar. 13, 1912-14; apptd. consul at Guadalajara, Mex., 1913 (unconfirmed); withdrawn from Mexico upon the occupation of Vera Cruz; consul at Seville, Spain, June 23, 1914-Apr. 1918, at Monterey, Mex., Oct. 1918-Apr. 1919, at Birmingham, Eng., Apr. 1919-—. Contbr. of various articles on China to Am. mags. Home: 287 Euclid Av., Oakland, Calif. Address: Am. Consulate, Birmingham Eng‡

GRADY, ELEANOR HUNDSON, coll. dean; b. N.Y. City, Mar. 18, 1886; d. Seth Charles and Rose (Ogden) Hundson; A.B., Barnard Coll., 1908; A.M., Columbia, 1911, Ph.D., 1930; m. Franklin Grady, Apr. 28, 1917; children—Olivia Hamilton (Mrs. Paul Rousseau), Franklin Ogden. Teacher, Mt. Holyoke Coll., 1911-14; teacher Hunter Coll., 1915-53, dean of faculty, 1941-50, professor of economics, 1943-53, acting president 1950-51. Member American Econ. Assn., Acad. Political Sciences, Nat. Educational Assn., Kappa Kappa Gamma. Author: Epigraphic Sources of the Delphic Amphictyony, 1930. Articles on economics and education. Home: New York City NY Died Jan. 1970.

GRAEFFE, EDWIN O(TTO), coll. dean; b. Brussels, Belgium, May 1, 1900; s. Otto Robert and Constance Marianne (Ellis) G.; LL.M., U. Goettingen, 1920; J.D., U. Tuebingen, 1923; m. Catherine Lawrence, May 4, 1930; 1 dau., Catherine Constance. Came to U.S., 1926, naturalized, 1935. China import, export bus., 1923-26; export dept. Kelvinator Corp., 1926-28; prof. social sci. U. Detroit, 1928-32; prof. social sci. Lawrence Inst. Tech., 1932-40, head dept. bus. adminstrn., 1940-51, dean, from 1951, dir. Sch. Indsl. Mgmt., from 1964. Home: Pleasant Ridge MI Died Jan. 25, 1972.

GRAESSER, ROY FRENCH, educator; b. Creighton, Neb., Oct. 31, 1892; s. Henry Lee and Ida (French) G.; student U. of Ia., 1913-16; A.B., U. of Ill., 1919, A.M., 1922, Ph.D., 1926; m. Lois Mizpah MacClement, Aug. 24, 1921. Teacher math. Sullivan (Ill.) Township High Sch., 1919-20; asst. math. U. of Ill., 1920-22, 1924-26, statistician, 1922-23; asst. prof. math. U. of Ariz., 1926-32, asso. prof. math., 1932-38, prof. math., head dept., 1938-58, prof. math emeritus, 1958-72. U.S. Army Ambulance Service with Italian Army, 1917-19. Mem. Central Assn. Sci. and Math. Tchrs., Math. Assn. Am., Assn. for Teaching Aids in Math., Sigma Xi, Gamm Alpha, Phi Kappa Phi, Pi Mu Epsilon, Sigma Pi Sigma. Home: Tucson AZ Died July 23, 1972.

GRAF, HERBERT, stage dir.; b. Vienna, Austria, Apr. 10, 1903; s. Max and Olga (Hoenig) G.; grad. State Acad. Music; Doctor Phil. et Mus., U. Vienna, 1925; m. Liselotte Austerlitz, Feb. 28, 1927; 1 son, Werner. Came to U.S., 1934, naturalized, 1943. Formerly stage dir. Municipal Theatre Muenster; former chief stage dir. opera houses of Breslau and Frankfurt/Main, Germany; stage dir. Met. Opera Co., 1936-49; head opera dept. Curtis Inst., Phila., 1949-60; gen. mgr. Municipal Opera House, Zurich, Switzerland, 1960-63. Author: The Opera and Its Future in America, 1941; Opera for the People, 1951; Producing Opera for America, 1961. Home: Bedford NY 10506 Died Apr. 1973.

GRAF, HOMER WILLIAM, naval officer; b. Chicago, Ill., Feb. 16, 1894; grad. U.S. Naval Acad., 1915. Commd. ensign, U.S. Navy, 1915, and advanced through the grades to commodore, 1944; served in U.S.S. Florida with British Grand Fleet, during World War I; exec. officer U.S.S. Helena, Asiatic Station, 1921, U.S.S. New Orleans (Vladivostok, Siberia, and Kobe, Japan), 1921-22, U.S. ships Borie, Peary, Penguin and Canopus, 1924-27; exec. officer, U.S.S. Tennessee, 1940; commd. U.S.S. Cincinnati, 1941-42; aide, and officer in charge building and grounds, U.S. Naval Acad., 1942-43; chief of staff to comdr. Seventh Fleet, Southwest Pacific Area, 1943; comdr. transport squadron, transport division; participated Iowa Jima, Luzon campaigns, also occupation of Japan. Supervisor Harbor of New York, 1946-48. Decorated Legion of Merit, Victory Medal with Grand Fleet clasp, Navy Expeditionary Medal with bronze star, Am. Defense Service Medal with fleet clasp, Asiatic-Pacific Area Campaign Medal Philippine Liberation Medal, Japanese Occupation Medal, unit citation medal. Home: Sarasota FL Died Mar. 1970.

GRAF, OSKAR MARIA, author; b. Berg am Starnberger Sec, Upper Bavaria, Germany, July 22, 1894; s. Max and Therese (Heimrath) G.; student village sch., Germany; Ph.D. (hon.), Wayne State U.; m. 2d, Mary Sachs, Oct. 1938 (dec. 1958); m. 3d, Gisela Blauner, June 1962; 1 dau. (by first marriage), Annamaria. Began by learning baking business; at age

16 ran away to Munich and worked at various odd jobs; also was writing stories and books; tramped through South Switzerland and Italy as hobo, 1913; served with German Army on Russian front, 1914-17, but as conscientious objector was interned; witnessed Munich revolution, 1918, German inflation, Hitler putsch, 1923, and beginnings of Nat. Socialism, which he immediately began opposing openly; when Hitler seized power, 1933, voluntarily exiled self to Austria; published protest against burning of books of German authors, 1933; his books then banned in Germany and he was deprived of citizenship; emigrated to Czechoslovakia, 1934, remaining to 1938 and writing three novels; in U.S., 1938-67. Mem. German-Am. Writers Assn. (past pres.), Preussische Akademie der Kuenste (West Berlin); corr. mem. Deutsche Akademie der Keunste (East Berlin). Roman Catholic. Author books including: Wir sind Gefangene (English title Prisoners All), 1927, 46, 59; Das Leben meiner Mutter (The Life of My Mother), 1940-46; Unruhe um einen Friedfertigen, 1947; Eroboerung der Welt, 1948; Mitmenschen (short stories), 1949; Einer Gegen Alle (English title The Wolf), 1950; Kalendergeschichten, 1950; Der Ewige Kalender (poems), 1954; Flucht ins Mittelmaessige, 1959; An manchen Tagen (essays), 1961; Der Grosse Bauernspiegal (stories), 1962; Groesstenteils schimpflich (biog. stories), 1963; Gelaechter von Aussen (autobiography, 2d part), 1966; numerous other books in German (some translated into several langs.), also short stories, poems, essays and articles. Address: New York City NY Died June 28, 1967; buried Bogenhausen Cemetery, Munich, Germany

GRAFF, ELLIS U., supt. schs.; b. Red Oak, Ia., Mar. 9, 1875; s. David W. and Lucy Merton (White) G.; A.B., Lake Forest (Ill.) Coll., 1897, A.M., 1915; post-grad. work, U. of Chicago, summer 1897; m. Adelaide Margaret Conger, of Clinton, Ia., Aug. 18, 1897. Teacher Latin and Greek, high sch., Clinton, Ia., 1897-98; prin. high sch., Red Oak, Ia., 1898-1901, Marshalltown, 1901-04, Rockford, Ill., 1904-07, Omaha, Neb., 1907-11; supt. schs., Omaha, 1911-17, Indianapolis since Sept. 1, 1917. President of National Textbook Company. Mem. ednl. com. Ind. State Council of Defense; delivered many addresses through the state on Education and the War". Mem. Ind. State Bd. of Edn. Trustee John Herron Art Inst. (Indianapolis), Normal and Industrial Inst. (Braxton, Miss.). Pres. dept. of superintendence N.E.A., 1919-20; mem. Nat. Soc. for Scientific Study of Edn., Assn. Coll. Teachers of Edn., S.R. Republican. Presbyn. Mason. Club: Columbia. Author: New Barnes Readers, 1917; Indiana War Service Text, 1918; Wheeler's Graded Arithmetics, 1919; Essentials in Education; The Young American Indianapolis IN‡

GRAHAM, B.A., pres. Sunbeam Corp., Chgo., 1944-50. Home: Paradise Valley AZ Died Apr. 1970.

GRAHAM, BALUS JOSEPH WINDSOR, clergyman, editor; b. Hickory Flat, Cherokee County Ga., July 6, 1862; s. Joseph and Elenah (Day) G.; A.B., Mercer U., 1894, D.D., 1906; m. Nancy Ann Samantha Thompson, Dec. 8, 1878; children—Edward Jackson, James Martin (dec.), Reuben, Jewell (Mrs. Matthews), Jeddie Pearl (Mrs. Albert B. Mobley), Lorena (dec.), Lynette, Mattie (dec.), John (dec.), Edward Jackson (dec.). Mercantile business to 1888; ordained ministry Missionary Bapt. Ch., 1887; pastor in Ga., including Locust Grove, Cochran, Conyers, Social Circle and Hogansville, until 1923, First Ch., Hapeville, 1923-31; financial sec. Ga. Bapt. Home, Atlanta, 1931-33. Pres., gen. mgr. Index Printing Co., Atlanta, Ga., since 1907; pres. Bapt. Song Book Co.; editor and pub. Christian Index (state Bapt. publn.), 1900-20; founder, 1927, and since pres. Co-operative Ednl. Soc.; moderator Atlanta Bapt. Assn.; moderator Carrollton Assn.; pastor Stone Mountain, Temple and Abilene Bapt. Churches, 1939. Founder Locust Grove Inst. Mem. Sigma Nu. Mason. Author: Regeneration in Relation To Other Doctrines, 1912; Baptist Biography (3 vols.), 1916; A Ministry of Fifty Years, 1938. Editor Gospel Songs and Hymns of Praise, 1918. Extensive traveler in Europe, the Orient and America. Home: 570 St. Charles Av. N.E., Atlanta GA*‡

GRAHAM, CLARENCE HENRY, psychophysiologist; b. Worcester, Mass., Jan. 6, 1906; s. Robert Samuel and Ann Jane (Gillespie) G.; A.B., Clark Univ., Worcester, 1927, A.M., 1928, Ph.D., 1930; M.A. (ad eund.), Brown U., 1943, D.Sc., 1958; Guggenheim fellow, Imperial College, London, England, 1959; m. Elaine R. Hammer, September 6, 1949. Instructor, psychol., Temple U., 1930-31; National research fellow, Johnson Foundation for Medical Physics, U. of Pa., 1931-32; asst. prof., Clark U., 1932-36; asst. professor psychol., Brown U., 1936-37, asso. prof. 1937-41, prof., 1941-45; prof., Columbia U., since 1945; on leave as sci. liaison officer, Office Naval Research, London, 1952-53; member of the Applied Psychology Panel of National Defense Research Com., 1942-46; mem. Physiological Psychology Panel, Office of Naval Research, 1947-55; participant Kyoto Seminars in Am. studies, Kyoto, Japan, summer 1952; survey Japanese psychology labs. under State Dept. and Nat. Sci. Found. grants, summer 1960; v.p. section of Exptl. Psychology and Animal Behavior, Internat. Union Biological Scis., 1956-60; mem. Armed Forces, NRC Vision Com., 1946-58, exec. council, 1956-58, U.S. Nat. Com. of Internat. Commn. on Optics, 1957-59. Awarded Howard Crosby Warren medal by Soc. Exptl. Psychologists, 1941; Presdl. Certificate of Merit, 1948; Tillyer medal Optical Soc. Am., 1963; award for distinguished sci. contribution Am. Psychol. Assn., 1966. Mem. American Psychological Assn. (director, 1946-49; policy and planning bd., 1946-49), Am. Physiol. Society, Optical Soc. America, Society Exptl. Psychologists, Am. Acad. Arts and Sciences, A.A.A.S., (vice president, chmn. section I, 1956), Nat. Acad. Scis., Am. Philos. Soc., Nat. Acad. Scis. (sect. chmn. 1953-56), Sigma Xi. Editor, contbr. Vision and Visual Perception, 1965, cons. editor profl. jours. Home: New York City NY Died July 25, 1971.

GRAHAM, DONALD GOODNOW, lawyer; b. Ft. Worth, Tex., Dec. 9, 1894; s. Theodore F. and Carrie (Knight) G.; B.S., Coe Coll., 1916; LL.B., Harvard, 1921; m. Juanita Fisher, Sept. 2, 1919; children—Richard Fisher, Donald Goodnow. Admitted to Wash. bar, 1921; also U.S. Supreme Ct., U.S. Fed. Cts., Wash. State Cts., U.S. Tax Ct.; practice in Seattle, 1921—; asst. U.S. atty., 1924-25; pvt. practice, 1925-73; sr. mem. Graham, Dunn, Johnston & Rosenquist, 1930-73. Dir. Fisher Flouring Mills Co., Fisher's Blend Sta., Inc., San Juan Fishing & Packing Co., West Coast Airlines, Inc., Columbia River Packers. Chmn. advance gift sect. United Good Neighbor Fund, 1936. Treas. Republican Primary campaign U.S. Senate, Janet Tourtellotte, 1950. Pres., bd. dirs. U. Wash. Arboretum Found.; bd. dirs. O.D. Fisher Charitable Found; former gov. for Wash. Nat. Aero. Assn. Served to 1st lt. USAAF, 1917-19, to col., 1942-45. Mem. Am., Wash., Seattle bar assns., Seattle C. of C. (past sect. chmn.), Order Daedalians, Am. Judicature Soc. Episcopalian. Clubs: Rainier, Sea Tennis, Sea Golf, Quiet Birdmen. Home: Seattle WA

GRAHAM, FRANK PORTER, UN ofcl.; b. Fayetteville, N.C., Oct. 14, 1886; s. Alexander and Katherine Bryan (Sloan) G.; A.B., U. of N.C., 1909; A.M., Columbia, 1916; LL.D., D.C.L., Ed.D., D.Litt. (all hon.) numerous colls. and univs.; m. Marian Drane, July 1932. Former prof. history U. of N.C., pres.; pres. Consol. U. of N.C., 1930-49; UN mediator. Chmn. Nat. Adv. Council on Social Security; pres. N.C. conf. for Social Service; former mem. nat. bd. A.R.C.; mem. com. on Civil Rights. Pub. mem. Nat. War Labor Bd.; Adminstr. Def. Manpower U.S. Dept. Labor; UN rep. for India and Pakistan Dispute; mem. UN com. Good Offices Dutch-Indonesian Dispute; apptd. U.S. senator for interim period. First pres. Oak Ridge Inst. of Nuclear Studies. Chmn. National Sharecroppers Fund. Member North Carolina Hist. Literary Soc. (pres.), Phi Beta Kappa. Presbyn. Home: Chapel Hill NC Died Feb. 1972.

GRAHAM, JAMES B., banking; b. Clearfield, Pa., May 21, 1872; s. Edward W. and Frances G. (Moore) G.; ed. high sch., Clearfield; m. Mary S. Emery, of Williamsport, Pa., Oct. 15, 1907. Began with County Nat. Bank, Clearfield, 1890; cashier Nat. Bank of Jersey Shore, Pa., 1902-09; pres. Northern Central Trust Co., Williamsport, 1911-27; pres. Lycoming Mfg. Co., Williamsport, 1917-27; pres. Crescent Refractories Co., Curwensville, Pa., 1920-29; pres. Lycoming Trust Co., 1927-33; dir. N. Am. Refractories Co., Cleveland, O. Republican. Presbyn. Home: 4105 49th St. N.W., Washington DC‡

GRAHAM, JOHN MEREDITH, banker; b. Pinewood, Tenn., Nov. 9, 1873; s. John Meredith, Sr., and Anna (Wright) G.; prep. edn., Montgomery Bell Acad., Nashville, Tenn.; student U. of Ky., 1888-89; Washington and Lee U., 1889-90; m. Maybeth Sullivan, Nov. 5, 1902; children—Laura Weller, Maybeth, John Meredith, Ann Bolling. Settled in Rome, 1896; in grocery business, later wholesale and retail hardware business until 1913; organizer, 1913, and since pres. Nat. City Bank; pres. City Land Co., Nat. City Securities Co., Citizens Fed. Savings & Loan Assn., Unit Bankers of Ga.; v.p. Eagle Stove Works; dir. Georgia Power Co. Chmn. Red Cross and Liberty Loan Drives, World War; mem. Assay Commn., apptd. by President Wilson, 1921. Trustee Darlington Sch. for Boys. Mem. Ga. Bankers Assn. (pres. 1930-31), Kappa Alpha. Mem. Christian (Disciples) Ch. Club: Coosa Country (ex-pres.). Home: Rome, Ga.; (country) Higlands, Ont., Can., and Lake Taccoa, Blue Ridge GA‡

GRAHAM, LENA FORNEY REINHARDT (MRS. JOSEPH GRAHAM), historian; b. nr. Lincolnton, N.C., June 22, 1886; d. Robert Smith and Laura (Pegram) Reinhardt; student Presbyn. Coll., 1902-05, Fairmont Coll. 1905-06; m. George Albert Brown, July 17, 1912 (dec. Oct. 1944); children—Georgette Wheelock (Mrs. Kenneth David Heavner), Roberta Ann (Mrs. Troy Chatham); m. 2d, Joseph Graham, June 10, 1948 (dec. Oct. 1957). Lincoln County hist. agt., Lincolnton, 1940-70. Trustee Confederate Meml. Hall. Mem. D.A.R., U.D.C. Presbyn. (pianist primary dept.). Clubs: Booklovers Book, Lincolnton Music. Contbr. articles in hist. field to profl. jours. Home: Lincolnton NC Died June 9, 1970; buried Machpelah Presbyn. Ch. Cemetery.

GRAHAM, MARY OWEN, educator; b. Wilmington, N.C.; d. Archibald and Eliza Owen (Barry) G.; grad. Queen's Coll., Charlotte, N.C., 18?0; A.B., Teachers' Coll. (Columbia), 1907; studied summers, U. of N.C., and U. of Tenn. Teacher graded schs., Charlotte, N.C., 1892-1907; lecturer on teacher training, County Insts., N.C., N.C. State Coll. Summer Sch., and on primary methods, at Sch. of Methods, Fredericksburg, Va., 1908; teacher N.C. Coll. for Women, 1908-12; teacher primary methods, U. of N.C., summers, 1908-12; asst. supt. schs., Mecklenburg Co., N.C., 1912-16; pres. Peace Inst. (jr. coll. and prep. sch. for girls), Raleigh, 1916-24. Organizer Community Week" for Mecklenburg Co., because of its success the gov. by proclamation made Community Week state-wide. Trustee State Sch. for the Blind; first woman on State Text Book Commn., also on State Bd. of Examiners. Mem. Com. of 100 for State Pub. Welfare. Mem. N.E.A., N.C. Teachers' Assn. (only woman pres. up to 1923), Primary Teachers' Assn. (state pres.), State Literary and Hist. Assn., Federation of Women's Clubs, League of Women Voters, Y.W.C.A. (S. Atlantic field com., speaker war work com.), D.A.R. (chmn. patriotic edn. com.), U.D.C. Pres. Albemarle Presbyterian. Committeewoman Dem. Nat. Com. from N.C., 1918-27. Clubs: Women's, Business and Professional Woman's, Bessie Dewey Book Club. Address: 315 Hawthorne Lane Charlotte NC‡

GRAHAM, ROBERT HENRY, justice Supreme Court of Nova Scotia; b. New Glasgow, N.S., Nov. 30, 1871; s. John George and Jane (Marshall) G.; B.A., Dalhousie U., Halifax, 1892, LL.B., 1894; m. Maude Mary Johnston, Dec. 4, 1901; children—Dorothy (Mrs. Cyril E. Mackenzie), Jane Maude (Mrs. George McG. Mitchell). Barrister, 1894; King's counsel, 1913; practiced law, New Glasgow, 1894-1925; mayor of New Glasgow, 1898-1900, stipendiary magistrate, 1904-08; mem. Assembly of N.S., 1916-25; justice Supreme Court of N.S. since May 1925; also judge in equity since Aug. 1925. Presbyterian. Author: Notes and Digest of Nova Scotia Decisions, 1938. Home: 150 Coburg Road. Office: The Law Courts, Spring Garden Rd., Halifax NS Canada‡

GRAHAM, STEPHEN VICTOR, naval officer; b. Mich., Mar. 4, 1874; s. Lester and Margaret (Smith) G.; grad. U.S. Naval Acad., 1894; m. Viola Jurgens, July 8, 1927. Commd. ensign, U.S. Navy, 1896, retired as capt., 1929; commd. rear adm., retired, 1931; served as naval attache, Vienna, Austria, 1914-17; gov. of Am. Samoa, 1927-29. Decorated Distinguished Service Medal, World War I; special commendation Navy Dept. Home: 2227 Observatory Av., Hollywood CA‡

GRAHAM, STERLING EDWARD, newspaper pub.; b. Cleve., May 16, 1892; s. Thomas C. and Jennie (Wright) G.; A.B., Columbia, 1915; m. Jane Peterson, Feb. 26, 1921; (dec. 1965); children—Thomas R., Sterling Edward, Jane E. (Mrs. Joseph H. Champ); m. 2d, Dorothy Pratt, July 14th, 1966. Display advt. salesman Cleve. Plain Dealer, 1924-28, local advt. mgr., 1928-31, advt. dir., 1931-43, gen. mgr., 1943-53; pres., dir. Forest City Pub. Co., pub. Cleve. Plain Dealer, 1953-63, ret. Served as captain of infantry, U.S. Army, 1917-19. Member Ohio (director), Cleveland (pres. 1950-51, dir.), chambers of commerce, American Legion. Clubs: Union, Madison Country, Automobile (dir.), Advertising, Rotary, City, Cleveland Skating (Cleve.). Home: Shaker Heights OH Died May 24, 1971.

GRAHAM, THOMAS WESLEY, clergyman, educator; b. Carlsbad, Ont., Can., Oct. 12, 1882; s. John and Margaret Marion (Snyder) G.; grad. Ottawa Collegiate Inst., 1889; A.B., U. of Toronto, 1903; student McCormick Theol. Sem., 1904-07; Free Ch. Coll., Glasgow, Scotland, 1907-08; D.D., Macalester Coll., 1920; m. Kate Fullerton, June 16, 1910 (dec. Jan. 1958); m. 2d, Beatrice B. Smith, Oct. 1, 1959. Came to U.S., 1904, naturalized citizen, 1920. Sec. Univ. Y.M.C.A., Toronto, 1903-04, Univ. Y.M.C.A., U. of Minn., 1909-12; ordained Presbyn ministry, 1908; pastor Andrew Ch., Minneapolis, 1912-20; prof. homiletics, Oberlin Grad Sch., 1920-48, dean Grad. Sch. of Theology, 1923-48; counsellor on religious work YMCA, N.Y.C., 1948-59; asst. minister First Presbyn. Ch., Greenwich, Conn., 1959-68, minister emeritus 1st Presbyn. Ch., 1968-71. Represented The Bd. for Christian Colleges in China, Taipei, Formosa, 1953-54. College preacher at many colleges and universities; lecturer at many student confs. in U.S. and Can., also for World's Student Christian Fed. Awarded Alumni Medal for distinguished service to Oberlin Coll., 1949. Mem. Nat. Bd. YMCA chmn. Centennial Com. Nat. Council YMCA; counselor on religion, Y.M.C.A. of New York City. mem. Nat. Com. Student Y.M.C.A.; mem. internat. Com. Y.M.C.A. Army Y.M.C.A. sec., Ft. Snelling, Minn., and Paris, France, 1917-19; bd. dirs. Greenwich (Connecticut) Community Chest, Mem. Fgn. Policy Association. Clubs: Quill, Shanghai Tiffin, Canadican Soc. (N.Y.C.); The Belle Haven (Greenwich, Conn.). Editor: The Story of Jesus,. 1925. Author religious articles. Home: Greenwich CT Died June 4, 1971; buried Oberlin OH

GRAHAM, WILLIAM TATE, orthopedist; M.D., U. of Va. Rept. of Medicine, 1896; prof. orthopedics, Med. Coll. of Va.; pres State Bd. of Health, Va. Home: John Marshall Hotel. Office: Medical Arts Bldg., Richmond VA‡

GRAMBLING, ALLEN ROWELL, lawyer; b. Tyler, Tex., Oct. 26, 1891; s. Allen M. and Ella (Rowell) G.; LL.B., U. Tex., 1912; m. Marion Hogan, June 24, 1919; children—John Allen, Patricia (Mrs. E. R. Harvey). Admitted to Tex. bar, 1913; now mem. firm Hardie, Grambling, Sims & Galatzan; dir., gen. atty. El Paso (Tex.) Natural Gas Co. 1946-73; dir., v.p. Lea Co. Gas Co. 1941-73; dir. First State Bank El Paso. Pres. Sch. Bd., C. of C., Community Chest, El Paso. Bd. dir., v.p. Providence Meml. Hosp. Fellow Am. Bar Found. Mem. Am., Tex. State, Fed. Power Commn., El Paso bar assns. Kiwanian (pres.). Home: El Paso TX Died Jan. 26, 1973.

GRAMMER, ALLEN L(UTHER), pubs. cons.; b. Altonna, Pa., June 4, 1889; s. Allen Jefferson and Clara (Brinkerhoff) G.; ed. pub. schs., Newark, N.J.; spl. courses in engring.; m. Malvina A. Halstead, Oct. 26, 1916; children—Allen Halstead, Ruth Isabel. Staff employee standardization div. Curtis Pub. Co., Phila., 1916-27, asst. treas. and bus. dept. mgr., 1927-37, also asst. sec., 1932-34, sec. and dir., 1934-37; pres. Street & Smith Publications, Inc., N.Y. City, 1938-48, chmn. bd., 1948-49, dir. 1938-50; sec., dir. Grammer, Dempsey & Hudson, Inc., Newark, 1940-59; v.p., dir. Passaic Co. Steel Service, Inc., Paterson, N.J., 1944-59; v.p., director Bridgeport Steel Company, Bridgeport, Connecticut, 1947-59; vice president Art News, 1955-56; v.p., dir. Poanal Corp., Alpo Corp., Milford Corp., 1959-64; pvt. bus. as pubs. cons. Mem. Nat. Assn. Mag. Pubs., Inc. (hon.), Newcomen Soc. Republican. Presbyn. Mason. Inventor Grammer wax spraying process, electromech. selector. Home: Montclair NJ Died Aug. 10, 1969; buried Restland Meml. Park, Hanover NJ

GRAND, GORDON, JR., chem. ofcl.; b. Orange, N.J., Mar. 14, 1917; s. Gordon and Emma (Dill) G.; grad. The Hill Sch., 1934; B.A., Yale, 1938; LL.D., Harvard, 1941; m. Ruth Young, Feb. 27, 1943; children—Minétte, Gordon, III, Lorna, Diana, Timothy. Teacher at the Millbrook (New York) School, from 1938-39; admitted to the N.Y. bar, 1943, to practice before U.S. Supreme Ct.; lawyer Spence, Hotchkiss, Parker & Duryee, N.Y.C., 1946-48; Counsel Rep. mems. Ways and Means Com., U.S. Congress, 1948-52; clk. Ways and Means Com., 83d Congress, 1953; asst. to pres. Olin Industries, Inc., N.Y.C., 1954; sec. Olin Mathieson Chem. Corp., N.Y.C., 1954-55, corporate v.p., 1955-63, vice chmn. bd., exec. v.p., 1964-65, pres., chief exec. officer, from 1965, chmn. 1966-67; dir. Nat. Starch & Chem. Co., 1st Nat. City Bank, Prudential Ins. Co. America, Squibb Beechnut. Gov. Young Rep. Club N.Y.C., 1947-48. Trustee, vice chairman Tax Foundation, Incorporated. Served to Maj., U.S. Army Res., ret. Decorated B.S.M.; 2 croix de Guerre (France). Clubs: Metropolitan (Washington); Links, Yale (N.Y.C.). Author: Federal Legislative Process, 1951; Proposals for Revising the Tax System, 1954. Home: Greenwich CT Died Jan. 16, 1972; buried Millbrook NY

GRANGER, ARMOUR TOWNSEND, engring. educator, b. Austin, Tex., Mar. 21, 1898; s. John and Jane Rebecca (Baker) G.; B.S., U. of Tex., 1918, C.E., 1921; m. Willoughby Crawford, June 15, 1920; children—Amy Jane (Mrs. William A. Haldeman), Charlotte Emily (Mrs. William B. Hinman). Detailer and structural designer, Harrington, Howard & Ash, consulting engrs., Kansas City, Mo., 1919-20; instr., adjunct prof., asso. prof. civil engring., U. of Tex., 1920-28; asst. engr., Ash-Howard-Needles & Tammen, consulting engrs., Kansas City-N.Y. City, 1928-39; asso. prof., U. of Tenn., 1939-40, prof. and head of the department of civil engineering, 1940-56, dean engring., 1956-66; consulting services on unusual or complicated structures, 1940-66. Mem. Tenn. Bd. Archtl. and Engring. Examiners, 1957-63. Registered profl. engr., Tenn. and N.Y. State. Mem. Am. Soc. C.E. (pres. Tenn. Valley sect. 1951), Am. Railway Engr. Assn., Soc. Profl. Engrs., Soc. Am. Mil. Engrs., Am. Soc. for Engring. Edn., Tenn. (pres. 1955), Nat. socs. profl. engrs., Tenn. Acad. Sci., Tenn. Education Association, Knoxville Tech. Soc. (pres., 1946), International Association of Bridge and Structural Engineers, Omicron Delta Kappa, Sigma Xi, Phi Kappa Phi, Tau Beta Pi, Chi Epsilon. Presbyn. Contbr. articles in field to jours. Designer portions of the athletic stadiums of U. of Tex. and U. of Tenn. Home: Knoxville TN Died Sept. 16, 1966; buried Highland Meml. Cemetery, Knoxville TN

GRANGER, SHERMAN MOORHEAD, lawyer; b. Zanesville, O., June 16, 1870; s. Moses Moorhead and Mary Hoyt (Reese) G.; A.B., Kenyon Coll., Gambier, O., 1890, A.M., 1893; m. Wanda Dawson Follett, of Cincinnati, Feb. 7, 1900. Admitted to practice in Ohio, 1892, U.S. cts., 1893, cts. of N.Y. State, 1899; mem. firm of Granger & Granger, 1892-98 and 1900—; practiced in New York, 1899. Mem. City Council, Zanesville, 1896-98; mem. Ohio Rep. State Central Com., 1912-14, Muskingum Co. Rep. Exec. Com., Zanesville Rep. Exec. Com.; mem. Rep. Nat. Com., 1912-16. Episcopalian. Mem. Assn. Bar City of New York, Ohio Soc. New York, Delta Kappa Epsilon, Theta Nu Epsilon. Address: Zanesville OH ‡

GRANIK, THEODORE, lawyer, founder and dir. Am. Forum of the Air; b. N.Y. City; s. Charles and Minnie G.; student Coll. City of N.Y.; LL.B., St. John's University, Law Sch., 1929, LL.D. (hon.), 1943; honorary doctorate, New York Law Sch.; m. Hannah Hayne, June 1931; children—William, Marian. Admitted to N.Y. bar, 1931; asst. dist. atty., N.Y., 1933-37; counsel U.S. Housing Authority, 1937-41. Served as civilian advisor to Brig. Gen. Lewis B. Hershey. Dir. of Selective Service, 1941; chairman bd. CATV Enterprises, Incorporated. Founder, producer Am. Forum Air for weekly radio and TV discussion of nat. problems, 1928, Youth Wants to Know, 1950, radio and television program; producer All America Wants to Know television and radio documentaries for Readers Digest. Mem. White Conf. Children and Youth, 1960. Mem. of the board of trustees New York Law Sch.; mem. Mayor's Policy Commission, New York City. Received Cross of Order of Crown (Belgium), 1946. Michael Award, Acad. Radio & TV Arts & Scis., 1951; awards for TV and radio production, 1953; Sylvania. Ohio State, Nat. Assn. for Better Radio and TV. Freedoms Found., Fame Mag., N.J. State Fair; George Foster Peabody award, 1957. Home: New York City NY Died Sept. 21, 1970.

GRANNAN, CHARLES P., theologian; b. Kenosha Co., Wis.; s. Charles P. and Mary (Conning) G.; student philosophy and theology, Urban Coll. of the Propaganda, Rome, 1870-8, Ph.D., 1875, D.D., 1880. Prof. Sacred Scripture, Mt. Saint Mary's Coll., Emmitsburg, Md., 1880-88; traveled in Egypt, Palestine, Syria, Asia Minor and Greece, and studied langs. and Sacred Scripture at univs. of Paris and Bonn until 1892. Prof. Sacred Scripture, Catholic U. of America, since 1892; vice-rector same, 1905-6. Apptd., Aug. 30, 1901, Am. mem. Internat. Pontifical Bibl. Commn. on Biblical Studies, by Pope Leo XIII; made domestic prelate by Pope Pius X, 1911. Author: Questions d'Ecriture Sainte, 1903; Complete General Introduction to the Bible, 4 vols., 1921. Address: Pensacola Hospital, Pensacola FL‡

GRANNIS, ROBERT MAITLAND, govt. ofcl.; b. Bklyn., July 28, 1903; George Baker and Mable L. (Curtis) G.; student Bklyn. pub. schs.; m. Marvel Lee Neumarker, Jan. 31, 1925; 1 son, John Lee. Reporter, drama critic, 1921-35; asst. city editor Bklyn. Eagle, 1935-37, news editor, 1938-46, city editor, 1946-48, mng. editor, 1948-51 (Pulitzer prize for meritorious pub. service 1951), asso. exec. editor from 1951, author column One Man Says, from 1942. Air tour inspection NATO countries, Dept. Def., 1951; asst. dir. pub. information Dept. of Justice, 1955-58; cons. Dept. Def., 1958-60; spl. and confidential asst. to Asst. Sec. Def. Pub. Affairs, 1960; pub. relations aide Rep. Nat. Com., 1960-73. Recipient Am. Legion Americanism award. Episcopalian. Editor The Republican. Home: Falls Church VA Died Jan. 6, 1973; buried Green Wood Cemetery, Brooklyn NY

GRANT, BISHOP F(RANKLIN), forester; b. Walhalla, S.C., Oct. 30, 1897; s. Thomas Asbury and Ella (Robertson) G.; B.S.F., U. of Ga., 1925, M.S.F., 1933; m. Virginia Shockley, Apr. 12, 1922; children—Mary Virginia (Mrs. Frank Phillips), Frances Eleanor (Mrs. Kenneth Kay). Industrial forester, 1925-29; asst. prof. forestry U. of Ga., 1929-32, asso. prof., 1932-36, prof. forest utilization and dir. summer camp from 1936; consulting forester. Served with A.E.F., 1917-19. Sr. mem. Soc. Am. Foresters; mem. Forest Products Research Soc., Am. Legion, Alpha Zeta, Phi Kappa Phi, Xi Sigma Pi. Democrat. Methodist. Club: Rotary. Home: Athens GA Died Nov. 28, 1970; buried Oconee Hill Cemetery, Athens GA

GRANT, CARROLL WALTER, educator; b. Kalamo, Mich., Nov. 14, 1900; s. Walter Merwin and Sara Eliza (Wilson) G.; B.A., Olivet Coll., 1924, D.Sc., 1960; M.A., Battle Creek (Mich.) Coll., 1927; student Marine Biol. Lab., summer 1926; Ph.D., Yale, 1931; m. Sara Ann Cline, Sept. 1, 1928; children—Linda Lee (Mrs. Robert W. Clark), David Carroll. Asso. prof. biology Battle Creek Coll., 1931; mem. faculty Bklyn. Coll., 1833-63, professor of biology, chairman of the department, 1956-63, prof. emeritus biology, 1963-69; research asso. Scripps Instn. Oceanography, La Jolla, Cal., 1941-42. Served to lt. comdr. USNR, 1942-46. Mem. Soc. Am. Bacteriologists, Acad. Microbiology, A.A.A.S., Sigma Xi. Home: Boca Raton FL Died May 15, 1969; buried Boca Raton Cemetery, Boca Raton FL

GRANT, DAVID ELIAS, lawyer; b. Abiquiu, Rio Arriba County, N.M., May 17, 1893; s. Henry and Sarah (Spiro) G.; A.B., Coll of City of N.Y., 1913; LL.B., Columbia U. Law Sch., 1920; m. Pauline M. Greenberg, May 17, 1921; children—Robert Lewis, Edward H. Sec. to mil. attache, Am. embassy Madrid, Spain, 1917-19; admitted to N.Y and N.M. bars, 1920, and in practice at Santa Fe, N.M., 1920-23; spl. asst. atty. Gen. State of N.M., 1921-22; col. governor's staff, State of N.M.; asst. counsel Gen. Sugar Co., Havana, Cuba, 1923-25; specialist Latin-Am. law, N.Y. City, 1925-30; mem. Schuster & Feuille, N.Y. City, 1930-32; fgn. counsel, Pan-Am. World Airways System, 1932-68; sr. mem. Grant, Hermann & Schwartz; adj. prof., lectr. Latim Am. comml. law, N.Y. Univ. Law Sch., 1932-68, aviation law, Guggenheim Sch. Aeronautics, N.Y. Univ., 1938-42, Latin-Am. civilization, College City of N.Y., 1937-38; moderator, NBC Spanish short-wave program Preguntas y Respuestas, 1943-47. Decorated Commr. Order So. Cross (Brazil), 1952. Mem. commn. legal experts Pan-Am. Union, Washington, 1934-38; mem. Inter-am. Comml. Arbitration Commn., 1939-60. Mem. Am. Bar Assn. (chmn. internat. and comparative law sect. 1941-42), Bolivarian Soc. of U.S., Inc. (v.p., dir.), Columbian Am. C. of C. (pres. 1953-55); Am. Brizilian Assn. (pres. 1950-52), Pan Am. Soc. U.S. (dir. 1950-61), Am. Fgn. Law Assn. (dir.), Omega Pi Alpha, Sigma Delta Pi (hon.). Author, lectr. on Latin-Am. law, Inter-Am. relations. Home: New York City NY Died June 11, 1968; buried New York City NY

GRANT, DEFOREST, mfr. terra cotta; b. N.Y. City, May 13, 1869; s. Gabriel and Caroline (Manice) G.; prep. edn. in pvt. schs. in Germany; B.A., Yale, 1891; m. Mrs. Emilia Brinton Thompson, 1916. With N.Y.C. R.R. until 1895; organizer and pres. Atlantic Terra Cotta Co., 1898, Consol. Atlantic Terra Cotta Co., 1906; pres. and gen. mgr. Federal Terra Cotta Co., 1909; chmn. bd. Federal Seaboard Terra Cotta Corp.; pres. Laredof Corporation; pres. Glenmoriston Corp. Member National Industrial Conference Board since 1922. Member Society Colonial Wars, Soc. War of 1812, Save the Redwoods League (council mem.), Mil. Order of Loyal Legion, New York Zool. Soc. (exec. com and trustee), St. Nicholas Soc. Republican. Clubs: Union, Boone and Crockett, Ends of the Earth, Racquet and Tennis, Riding, Piping Rock, Bar Harbor. Traveler and big game hunter. Home: 962 Park Av., N.Y. City and Bar Harbor, Me. Office: 101 Park Av., New York NY*‡

GRANT, ELLIOTT MANSFIELD, educator; b. Boston, Sept. 6, 1895; s. Ernest and Kate (Mansfield) G.; A.B., Harvard, 1916, Ph.D., 1923; m. Evelyn Nay, Sept. 19, 1922; children—Richard, William, James. Instr., asst. prof., prof. French lang. and lit. Smith Coll., 1922-37; professor Romance languages Williams College, 1937-60. Author: French Poetry of the Nineteenth Century, 1932; The Career of Victor Hugo, 1945; Four French Plays of the XXth Century, 1949; Zola's Germinal, 1962; Emile Zola, 1966. Home: Lyme NY Died Feb. 11, 1969; buried Gardiner ME

GRANT, HENRY WILLIAM, business exec.; b. 1870. Comdr. Navigation Sch., Portsmouth, 1910-12; comd. H.M.S. Hampshire, China and Grand Fleet, 1914-15; asst. dir., later dep. dir. Operations Div. Naval Staff, 1915-18; former dir. Cable and Wireless, Ltd.; mng. dir. Eastern Telegraph Co.; former chmn. and mng. dir. Marconi International Communications Co. Ltd. since 1941. Address: Electra House, Victoria Embankments, London WC 2 England‡

GRANT, LESTER STRICKLAND, mining engr.; b. New Haven, Conn., Oct. 31, 1877; s. Charles Alfred and Mary J. (Strickland) G.; E.M., Colo. Sch. of Mines, 1899; m. Chloe Ella Thornton, 1900; children—Robert Waltman, Richard Thornton. Engr. Isabella Gold Mining Co., Cripple Creek, Colo., 1899-1901, Isabella Mines Co., 1901-03; supt. Isabella Lease, 1904; engr. and assayer, Findley Consol. Mining Co., Cripple Creek, 1905-06; metallurgist and engr. Inca Mining Co., Peru, S.A., 1906-09; asst. supt. Roosevelt Drainage Tunnel, Cripple Creek, 1909-10; supt. Isabella Mines Co., 1910-13; gen. mgr. Jumper, Calif., Gold Mines. Co., Stent, Calif., and v.p. and gen. mgr. Contention Mining Co., Knight Creek, Tuolumne Co., Calif., 1913-19; treas. Ajax Mine Lease Co., Victor, Colo., 1921-22; mgr. and vice president McElroy Ranch Co., Crane, Tex., 1927-49 (ret.); v.p., dir. Franco Wyoming Oil Co., McElroy Royalty Corp. Professor mining, 1919-28, dean, 1921-28, Colo. Sch. of Mines. Served as captain, engineer, Officer Reserve Corps (now retired). Distinguished Achievement Medal, Colo. Sch. of Mines, 1949. Mem. Inst. Mining and Metall. Engrs., Am. Petroleum Inst., Theta Tau, Tau Beta Pi. Republican. Episcopalian. Mason. Clubs: Teknik (Denver); Rotary (Midland, Tex.). Home: 1613 Palmer Park Blvd., Colorado Springs, Colo. Address: P.O. Box 912, Midland TX‡

GRANT, ULYSSES S., III, ret. army officer; b. July 4, 1881; s. Frederick D. (Maj. Gen., U.S. Army) and Ida (Honore) G.; g.s. Pres. U. S. Grant; ed. Theresianum, Vienna, 4 yrs., and Cutler Sch., N.Y. City, 4 1/2 yrs.; student Columbia, 1898; B.S., U.S. Military Academy, 1903; graduate, U.S. Engineer School, 1908, Army War College, 1934, married Edith Root, dau. Hon. Ehihu Root, Nov. 27, 1907; children—Edith, Clara Frances, Julia. Commd. 2d lt., U.S. Army, 1903; advanced through the grades to col., Corps of Engrs., 1934; col. N.A., 1917-20; maj. gen. (temp.) 1943; various assignments U.S. and abroad 1903-42, including Cuban pacification, 1906, Vera Cruz expdn., 1914, Mex., 1916, World War I, II; chief of protection branch, Office Civilian Def., 1942-44; chmn. Nat. Capital Park and Planning Commn., 1942-49; v.p. George Washington

U., 1946-51. Pres. Am. Planning and Civic Assn., 1947-49, Govt. Service, Inc.; chmn. Civil War Centennial Commn., 1957-61; comdr.-in-chief Mil. Order Loyal Legion, 1957-61; trustee Nat. Trust Historic Preservation. Decorated Distinguished Service Medal, Legion of Merit (United States) also decorations from 6 foreign countries. Mem. several vets. orgns., military service organizations, also prof. and engring socs., Columbia Hist. Soc. (pres.). Clubs: Union League, Century (N.Y.C.); Cosmos, Army and Navy, Metropolitan (Washington). Address: Washington DC Died Aug. 29, 1968; buried Hamilton Coll. Cemetery, Clinton NY

GRANT, WILLIAM THOMAS, merchant; b. Stevensville, Pa., June 27, 1876; s. William T. and Amanda Louise (Bird) G.; educated high sch., Malden, Mass.; LL.D., Bates Coll., 1947; L.H.D., U. Miami, 1960; m. Lena Blanche Brownell, Oct. 5, 1907 (dec.); children—Helen (Mrs. Francis Allchin), Marian (Mrs. John R. Henry); m. 2d, Beth Bradshaw, Sept. 3, 1930 (dec.); 1 dau., Shirley (Mrs. Harrington E. Drake Jr.). Founder, 1906, hon. chmn. bd. W.T. Grant Co., chain of dept. stores. Founder, 1936, hon. chmn. bd. The Grant Found., Inc. Mem. N.E. Historic Genealogical Soc. Home: Greenwich CT Died Aug. 6, 1972; buried Oak Grove Cemetery, Fall River MA

GRASSELLI, THOMAS FRIES, business exec.; b. Cleve., Jan. 21, 1903; s. Thomas Saxton and Emilie (Smith) G.; student Cleve. U., 1922; m. Mary Allen, June 24, 1929. With Grasselli Chem. Co., Cleve., 1923-29; with E. I. duPont Co., Wilmington, Del., 1929-70, successively mfg., sales, mgmt. Dir., sec. Boys Club of Wilmington, 1948-70; nat. asso. State of Del. Boys Club of Am. Served from capt. to lt. col., AUS, 1942-46. Mem. Cleve. Mus. Art. Clubs: Wilmington Country; Concord Country. Home: Wilmington DE Died Mar. 23, 1970.

GRAUDAN, NIKOLAI, cellist; b. Libau, Russia; ed. St. Petersburg Conservatory; m. Joanna Freduberg. Formerly prof. St. Petersburg Conservatory, 1st cellist Berlin Philharmonic Orch.; concert tours; later mem. Goldberg and Graudan Trio, Festival Quartet. Address: Pacific Palisades CA Died Aug. 9, 1964; buried Westwood CA

GRAU SAN MARTIN, RAMON, Pres. of Cuba, physician, educator; b. Consolacion del Norte, Pinar del Rio, Cuba, Sept. 13, 1882; ed. Provincial Inst. of Havana; Dr. Medicine and Sciences, U. of Havana, 1905; grad. study in Europe and U.S. Following graduation, became interne Hosp. Nuestra Senora de las Mercedes, a post held in great honor as being reserved exclusively for distinguished professionals; beginning of career devoted to surgery, later, specialist in internal medicine and student of diseases of digestive tract and metabolic upsets; titular prof. physiology U. of Havana from 1921. Mem. Cuban Revolutionary Com., New York City, 1933; mem. bd. dirs. Provincial Govt., Sept. 1933; pres. of Cuba, Sept. 1933-Jan. 1934, and since 1944; during his presidency, govt. has promulgated a system of social, polit., econ. and cultural laws, among them: creation Office of Sec. of Labor, also Sch. of Forestry and Silviculture, laws relating to maximum daily work for labor, minimum salary, protection of working mothers, improvement in rural housing, patriotism of worker (so that 50 per cent of workers should be natives of Cuba). Mem. Sociedad ed Estudios Clinicos de la Havana, Academia de Ciencias Medicas, Sociedad Economica de Amigos del Pais, also to many fgn. sci. assns. Author: Curso de fisiologia, 1925; Las Secresiones internas, 1929; La revolucion Cubana ante America, 1936; also numerous other sci. writings on med. subjects. Address: Havana Cuba Died July 28, 1969.*

GRAUSTEIN, ARCHIBALD R(OBERTSON), lawyer; b. Cambridge, Mass., Aug. 29, 1885; s. Adolf H. and Julia (Caspar) G.; A.B., Harvard, 1905, LL.B., 1907; m. Margaret M. Bertwell, Feb. 19, 1909; 1 son, Archibald Robertson; m. 2d, Claire Patton, Mar. 13, 1929; m. 3d, Hallie Hubbard, June 3, 1944; 1 son, William Chandler. Admitted to Massachusetts bar, 1907, New York bar, 1936; began practice of law in Boston, Mass; partner Ropes, Gray, Boyden & Perkins, 1911-24; pres. Internat. Paper Co. 1924-36; chmn. exec. com. N.E. Power Association (Boston), 1926-35; pres., dir. D.W. Rich &Co., Inc., Synfoam, Yarns, Inc.; dir. Aubrey G. Lanston & Co., Inc., Agency of Can. Car & Foundry Co., Ltd., St. Raymond Paper Co., Ltd. Home: New York City NY Died Sept. 1969.

GRAVEN, HENRY NORMAN, judge; b. St. James, Minn., June 1, 1893; s. Endre Norman and Elise (Thompson) G.; A.B., U. of Minnesota, 1921, LLB., 1921; LL.D., Capital University Columbis, O., 1942; L.H.D. (hon.), Wartburg College, 1962; married Helen T. Davis, Mar. 20, 1926; children—David L., Stanley N., Lloyd. Admitted to Iowa bar, 1921; special asst. atty. gen. and counsel to Iowa State Highway Commn., 1936-37; state district judge, 12th Judicial Dist. of Ia., 1937-44; U.S. dist. judge, No. Dist. of Ia., 1944-61, senior United States dist. judge, 1961-70. Past chmn. bd. pensions Am. Lutheran Ch., mem. bd. adjudication and appeals, 1964-70, chmn. bd. adjudication and appeals, 1966-70. Trustee, Sch. Religion, Ia. State U., 1955-67, chmn. bd. trustees, 1963, 64. Served with combat engrs., World War I. Recipient merit award Ia. Bar Assn., 1957. Mem. Order of Coif. Greene IA Died Feb. 1, 1970; buried Greene IA

GRAVES, GRANT OSTRANDER, educator, physician; b. Columbus, O., Jan. 21, 1905; s. Henry and Kathleen (Ostrander) G.; B.A., Ohio State U., 1926, M.A. in Anatomy, 1929, M.D., 1932; m. Helen Louise Pierson, July 18, 1940; children—Scott, Heather, Holly. Intern Duke U. Hosp., 1932-33; resident Univ. Hosp., Columbus, 1933-34; mem. faculty Ohio State U., from 1935, prof. anatomy, from 1959, chmn. dept., from 1962, asst. clin. prof. medicine, from 1947, asst. prof. radiology, from 1947, med. sci. bldg. named Grant O. Graves Hall in his honor, 1968. Mem. exec. bd. Central Ohio Blue Cross, 1960-65. Diplomate Am. Bd. Internal Medicine. Life fellow A.C.P.; mem. A.M.A., Ohio Med. Assn., Columbus Acad. Medicine (pres. 1951), Alpha Omega Alpha (bldg. named in his honor 1972). Home: Columbus OH Died Feb. 7, 1972.

GRAVES, IRELAND, lawyer; b. Seguin, Tex., July 23, 1885; s. John William and Mary Frances (Ireland) G.; B.S., Southwestern U., 1905; LL.B., U. Tex., 1908; m. Mary Willis Stedman (dec. Mar., 1965); children—Elizabeth Stedman (dec.), Mary Ireland (Mrs. J.Chrys Dougherty). Admitted to Tex. bar, 1908, practiced in Austin; mem. Graves, Dougherty, Gee, Hearon, Moody & Garwood; dist. judge, 1916-21; lecturer law school, University of Texas, 1921-23; Pres. Statesman Pub. Co., 1921-25; dir. Austin Nat. Bank, 1924-66, chmn., 1946-58; director Austin Savings & Loan Association, 1950-67. Treasurer Tex. Law Review, 1922-66, member bd. editors 1937-66. Food Adminstr. Travis County, 1918; mem. Austin Sch. Bd., 1922-24. Honorary member Order of the Coif; fellow Am. Bar Found. Member Am., Tex. and Travis County bar assns., American Law Institute, Chamber of Commerce (v.p. 1921), English Speaking Union, Tex. Philosophical Soc., Phi Delta Theta. Methodist Clubs: Town and Gown, Kiwanis (pres. 1924). Contbr. articles in law publs. Home: Austin TX Died Sept. 26, 1969; buried Oakwood Cemetery, Austin TX

GRAVES, MARY WHEAT (MRS. BILLY Z. GRAVES), educator; b. Marshalltown, Ia., Apr. 24, 1911; d. Clark W. and Lena May (Hill) Wheat; B.A., U. No. Ia., 1931; M.A., State U. Ia., Ph.D., 1935, grad. study, 1941-42; m. Murvie H. Hanawalt, June 2, 1934 (dec. Oct. 13, 1948); children—Patricia, David; m. 2d, Billy Z. Graves, June 24, 1960. Tchr. pub. schs. Ia. and Kan., 1931-39; instr. State U. Ia., 1942-43, dir. extension div., 1943-45; prof. English, Wayne (Neb.) State Tchrs. Coll., 1945-48, chmn. dept. English, 1948-49; prof. English U. No. Ia., 1949-68. Mem. Am. Assn. U. Profs., Ia. Coll. Conf. on English, Am. Assn. U. Women, Modern Lang. Assn. Am., Kappa Delta Pi, Pi Omega Pi, Sigma Tau Delta. Contbr. articles, poems, Ednl. Forum, 1942; poem in A Book of Verse, an anthology, 1937; also several articles on edn. Home: Cedar Falls IA Died Oct. 18, 1968.

GRAVETT, JOSHUA, clergyman; b. Worthing, Sussex, England, Aug. 10, 1863; s. Thomas and Rebecca (Dinnage) G.; grad. Mt. Hermon (Mass.) Sch., 1889; D.D. (honorary) Denver Bible College, 1946; married Charlotte Mary Harrison, Nov. 5, 1890; children—Ruth Amelia (Mrs. Paul T. Cullen), Grace Lucy (Mrs. George Emerson Hook), Hope Frances (Mrs. Donald Sham), Dwight Hamilton. Came to U.S., 1886, naturalized citizen, 1918. Pastor Faith Ch., Springfield, Mass., 1888-90; ordained Baptist Ministry, 1891; pastor Galilee Ch., Denver, Colo., since May 1, 1891. Pres. Colo. Bapt. State Conv., 1926-27, historian since 1917; v.p. Am. Bapt. Home Mission Soc.; trustee Colo. Woman's Coll.; Denver Bible Coll.; dir. Denver Hebrew Mission. Fellow Am. Bapt. Hist. Soc. Republican. Contbg. editor: Grace and Truth and Christian Victory mags.; author of tracts and contbr. to religious papers. Home: 3144 Humboldt St., Denver 5 CO‡

GRAY, ALBERT F(REDERICK), coll. pres.; b. St. Thomas, N.D., Mar. 18, 1886; s. George Alexander and Mary (Baldwin) G.; D.D. (hon.), Anderson (Ind.) Coll., 1932; m. Rosa Lee Brannon, June 17, 1909; children—Lawrence Albert (dec.), Lois Aletha (Mrs. John L. Grover), Dorothy Marian (Mrs. John Paul Howell), Harold Frederick. Evangelist, 1905-15; pastor, Clarkston, Wash., 1915-20; prin. Pacific Bible Inst., 1920-23; pastor, Walla Walla, Wash., 1923-24, Yakima, 1925-26, Anderson, Ind., 1926-33, Seattle, 1933-38; pres. Warner Pacific Coll. (formerly Pacific Bible Coll.), 1937-60, pres. emeritus, 1960-69; chmn. Gen. Assembly Ministerial Ch. of God, 1935-36, 1940-54; mem. Missionary Bd., Church of God; missionary tour, British E. Africa, Middle East, and Europe, 1952-53. Author: Menace or Mormanism, 1926; Christian Theology, 1944; How to Study the Bible, 1949; The Nature of the Church, 1960; Time and Tides on the Western Shore (autobiography), 1966. Home: Portland OR Died May 2, 1969; buried Lincoln Meml. Park, Portland OR

GRAY, BOWMAN, tobacco co. exec.; b. Baltimore, Jan. 15, 1907; s. Bowman and Nathalie Fontaine (Lyons) G.; student Woodberry Forest (Va.) Sch., 1921-25; A.B., U. N.C., 1929; m. Elizabeth Palmer Christian, Nov. 28, 1936; children—Bowman, Frank Christian, Robert Daniel, Lyons, Peyton Randolph. Salesman, R.J. Reynolds Tobacco Co., Winston-Salem, N.C., 1930-39, asst. sales mgr., 1939-49, vice president 1949-55, sales manager 1952-55, executive v.p. 1955-57, pres., 1957-59, chmn. bd., 1959-69, dir., 1947-69; dir. Wachovia Bank & Trust Co., Piedmont Aviation, Inc. Served U.S.N.R., 1942-45. Sr. mem. Nat. Indsl. Conf. Bd. Mem. Delta Kappa Epsilon. Methodist. Clubs: Rotary, Old Town, Twin City, Forsyth (Winston-Salem); Chevy Chase, Metropolitan (Washington); The Links (N.Y.C.). Home: Winston-Salem NC Died Apr. 11, 1969.

GRAY, CLARENCE TRUMAN, teaching; b. Russell, Kan., Nov. 22, 1877; s. Bingham and Evangeline (Anderson) G.; grad. Ind. State Normal Sch., 1902; A.B., Ind. U., 1904; A.M., U. of Chicago, 1911, Ph.D., 1916; m. Bessie Lee Stretcher, July 19, 1905; children—Truman Stretcher, Margaret Elnora. Teacher and supt. schs. Ind. until 1910; instr. ednl. psychology, 1911-15, adj. prof., 1915-18, asso. prof., 1918-25, prof. since 1925, U. of Tex. Teacher summer schs., U. of Chicago, U. of Kan., Northwestern U., U. of Pa., Cornell U., U. of Calif., U. of Southern Calif., Duke U. Mem. Am. Assn. Ednl. Research, Am. Assn. Univ. Profs., A.A.A.S., Am. Psychol. Assn., Texas State Art League (dir.), Sigma Xi, Science Club (Univ. of Texas), Phi Delta Kappa. Methodist. Mason. Clubs: University, Scholia, Fortnightly. Author: Variations in Grades of High School Pupils, 1915; Types of Reading Ability, 1917; Deficiencies in Reading Ability, 1922; Workaday Readers, 1929; Statistics Applied to Education and Psychology (with D. F. Votaw), 1939; contbr. to ednl. jours. Mem. bd. editors Educational Abstracts. Home: 3201 West Av., TX‡

GRAY, DAVID, writer diplomat; b. Buffalo, Aug. 8, 1870; s. David and Martha (Guthrie) G.; A.B., Harvard, 1892; Litt.D., Bowdoin Coll. 1925; m. Mrs. Maude Livingston Hall Waterbury, Oct. 13, 1914. Reporter, editorial writer Rochester Union and Advertiser, 1893; editorial writer Buffalo Times, 1894; sub-editor New York World, 1896; mng. editor Buffalo Courier, 1897; editorial writer Buffalo Enquirer, 1898-99; admitted to bar, 1899; U.S. minister to Ireland, 1940-47. Author: The Sphinx (Harvard Hasty Pudding Club Play), 1892; Gallops I and II (play produced), 1906; The Recantation of an Anit-Imperialist (in Outlook); Mr. Carteret and Others; Smith (with W. Somerset Maugham); Ensign Russell; The Bommerand (novel, based on play by V. Mapes and W. Smith); (play) The Best People (with Avery Hopwood) prod. 1923. Commd. capt., aviation sect., Signal Corps; with AEF in France; charge photographic div. Signal Corps, 1917-18; liaison officer with French 7th and 2d Corps and 10th French Army to 1919. Decorated Corix de Guerre, chevalier Legion d'Honneur, chevalier de la Sarasota FL Died Apr. 1968.

GRAY, EARLE, physician, educator; b. Wabash County, Ill., Nov. 20, 1898; s. George Washington and Martha Jane (Hancock) G.; B.S., U. of Chicago, 1925, M.D., 1929; m. Susan Eleanor Heaney, Apr. 28, 1943; 1 dau., Deborah Floy. Began practice of medicine, 1932; asst. attending physician Presbyterian Hosp., Chicago, 1932-41; asst. in medicine, Rush Med. Coll., 1932-33, instr., 1933-37, asst. clin. prof. medicine, 1937-41, acting dean, 1939-June 1942, on which date Rush Med. Coll. became part of U. of Ill. Med Sch.; asst. clin. prof. medicine, U. of Ill. Med. Sch.; clin. prof. medicine U. Ill. Med. Sch., 1953-67; clinical professor medicine, acting chief med. service Presbyn. Hosp. Served as maj. M.C. Army of the United States, 1942; promoted lt. colonel, 1943, col., 1946; col., Med. Corps Res., 1946-55, ret. Fellow A.C.P.; mem. Am. Assn. Med. Colls., A.M.A., Central Interurban Clin. Club, Am. Heart Assn., Am. Soc. Tropical Medicine, Chgo. Lit. Soc., Lambda Chi Alpha, Nu Sigma Nu. Democrat. Episcopalian. Clubs: University, Caxton. Home: Chicago IL Died Aug. 4, 1967.

GRAY, EARLE, physician, educator; b. Wabash County, Ill., Nov. 20, 1898; s. George Washington and Martha Jane (Hancock) G.; B.S., U. of Chicago, 1925, M.D., 1929; m. Susan Eleanor Heaney, Apr. 28, 1943; 1 dau., Deborah Floy. Began practice of medicine, 1932; asst. attending physician Presbyterian Hosp., Chicago, 1932-41; asst. in medicine, Rush Med. Coll., 1932-33, instr., 1933-37, asst. clin. prof. medicine, 1937-41, acting dean, 1939-June 1942, on which date Rush Med. Coll. became part of U. of Ill. Med. Sch.; asst. clin. prof. medicine, U. of Ill. Med. Sch.; clin. prof. medicine U. Ill. Med. Sch., from 1953; clinical professor medicine, acting chief med. service Presbyn. Hosp. Served as maj. M.C. Army of the United States, 1942; promoted lt. colonel, 1943, col., 1946; col., Med. Corps Res., 1946-55, ret. Fellow A.C.P.; mem. Am. Assn. Med. Colls., A.M.A., Central Interurban Clin. Club, Am. Heart Assn., Am. Soc. Tropical Medicine, Lambda Chi Alpha, Nu Sigma Nu. Democrat. Episcopalian. Clubs: University, Caxton, Chicago Literary. Home: Chicago IL Died Aug. 4, 1967.

GRAY, GILES WILKESON, univ. prof.; b. Shelbyville, Ind., Dec. 11, 1889; s. Isaac Redding and

Lucy Abigail (White) G.; A.B., De Pauw U., 1914; A.M., U. of Wis., 1923; Ph.D., U. of Ia., 1926; student U. of Ill., 1921-24; m. Helen Harris Clark, Aug. 30, 1924; children—Helen Clark (Mrs. Frank C. Crawford, Mary Lucy (Mrs. Wyeth A. Read), Edmund Wright. Assistant in speech, University of Illinois, 1921-24; associate, speech, University of Ia., 1924-26, asst. prof. 1926-32; asst. prof. Speech, La. State U., 1932-34, asso. prof. 1934-37, prof. since 1937; U. of Ga., summer 1929, St. Louis U., summer 1946, University of California (Berkeley), summer 1949. Mem. Speech Assn. of Am. (editor, Quarterly Jour. of Speech, 1939-41), So. Speech Assn. (pres. 1937), Acoustic Soc. of Am., International Phonetic Assn., Sigma Xi, Pi Kappa Delta, Tau Kappa Alpha, Delta Upsilon. Mem. Meth. Episcopal Ch. Author: The Bases of Speech (with C. M. Wise), 1934, 1946, 1959; Public Speaking; Principles and Practice (with W. W. Braden) 1951; editor: Studies in Experimental Phonetics, 1936. Home: Baton Rounge LA Died Aug. 27, 1972; buried Magnolia Cemetery, Baton Rouge LA

GRAY, HAROLD (LINCOLN), newspaper artist; b. Kankakee, Ill., Jan. 20, 1894; s. Ira Lincoln and Estella M. (Rosencrans) G.; B.S., Purdue, 1917; m. Doris C. Platt, Oct. 22, 1921 (died Nov. 22, 1925); m. 2d, Winifred Frost, July 17, 1929. Joined staff of Chicago Tribune as artist, 1917; entered U.S. Army, May 1918, at Camp Zachary Taylor, Louisville, Ky.; at Officers' Camp, Camp Gordon, Ga., Sept.-Nov., 1918; hon. disch. as 2d lt., inf., returned to Tribune, Dec. 1918; left Tribune and started studio, doing commercial art work, Jan. 1920, also asst. to Sidney Smith on The Gumps"; started comic strip, Little Orphan Annie," 1924, in New York News and Chicago Tribune, this strip now appearing in numerous papers. Mem. Purdue Alumni Assn., Am. Legion, Sigma Delta Chi. Republican. Conglist. Mason. Home: Green Farms CT Died May 9, 1968.

GRAY, HAROLD EDWIN, former airline exec.; b. Guttenberg, Ia., Apr. 15, 1906; s. Otis Elmer and Bertha (Hagensick) G.; student State U. Ia., 1922-25, U. Detroit, 1926-28, M. Engring. (hon.), 1939, D.Sc., 1970; m. ExaBell Sublett, Sept. 12, 1929; children—Harold (dec.), Frank. Pilot, Ford Motor Co., 1928; with Pan Am. World Airways, 1929-70, div. mgr. Pacific-Alaska div., 1947-49, v.p., 1949-52, v.p. Atlantic div., 1952-53, exec. v.p. Atlantic div., 1953-60, exec. v.p. overseas div., 1960-64, pres., 1964-68, chmn., chief exec. officer, 1968-70, dir. emeritus, 1970-72. Mem. steering com. N.Y. Gov.'s Commn. on Social Problems. Fellow Am. Inst. Aeros. and Astronautics. Clubs: Sky, Stanwich, Cotton Bay, Round Hill, Blind Brook, Economic of N.Y. Home: New York City NY Died Dec. 23, 1972; buried Greenwich CT

GRAY, HENRY DAVID, univ. prof.; b. Plainfield, N.J., Nov. 6, 1873; s. William MacLean and Henrietta A. (Perry) G.; Ph.B., Colgate U., 1897; Litt.D., 1919; A.M., Columbia, 1898, Ph.D., 1904; m. Emily Hough Tarr, of Baltimore, Oct. 11, 1905; children—Dorothy Sewall, Sydney MacLean. Instr. English and dramatic lit., Am. Acad. of Dramatic Arts, 1900-02; instr. English, U. of Tex., 1902-05; lecturer in English, Columbia Univ., summer session, 1905, Univ. of London (Michaelmas term), 1922; instr. English, 1905-06, asst. prof., 1906-15, asso. prof., 1915-26, prof. since 1926, Stanford U. Prof. of English and dean of the Faculty, Floating Univ., 1928-29; dir. Am. Univ. Union, Brit. Division, 1929-30; nominated honorary corresponding member Institut Litteraire et Artistique de France, 1937. Member Nat. Council of Better Films Com. of Nat. Board of Review of Motion Pictures. Mem. Modern Lang. Assn. America, Am. Philol. Assn. of the Pacific Coast, Phi Beta Kappa. Author: Emerson, a Statement of New England Transcendentalism as Expressed in the Philosophy of its Chief Exponent, 1917; The Original Version of Love's Labour's Lost," with a conjecture as to Love's Labour's Won," 1918. Translator: Pathelin, 1900. Editor: Carlyle's Hero and Hero Worship, 1906; Parallel Passage Shakespeare-—Much Ado About Nothing (with A. G. Newcomer), 1928; Selections from Old Testament Literature, 1929. Contbr. to philol. and other periodicals, chiefly in Shakespearean criticism. Home: Stanford University CA‡

GRAY, HOB, univ. prof.; b. Pleasant Valley, Tex., Apr. 10, 1889; s. Richard and Blanche (McDaniel) G.; student Southwest Tex. Teachers Coll., 1914; A.B., Daniel Baker Coll., 1918; A.M., Columbia, 1925; Ph.D., U. of Tex., 1930; LL.D., Southwestern U., 1948; m. Mary Douglas Tanner, Aug. 29, 1929; children—Margaret Alison, Robert Winston. Rural sch. teacher near Rising Star, Tex., 1909-12; asso. prof. edn. U. of Tex., 1933-48, prof. secondary edn. and dir. teacher placement service, 1948-73. Instr. navigation V-5 program, Tex., 1941-42. Awarded Peabody scholarship, 1927-28. Mem. com. to survey curricula women's colls. in Am., 1932; coordinator Tex. Study Secondary Edn., 1945-46; dir. teachers appointment com. State of Tex. Mem. N.E.A., Am. Assn. Sch. Administrs., Am. Soc. Coll. Teachers Edn., Texas State Teachers Association, Texas Association Sch. Adminstrs. (dir. research), Southern Assn. Secondary Schs. and Colls. (mem. exec. com.; chmn. evaluation criteria com.), Am. Soc. Coll. Deans, Phi Delta Kappa. Democrat. Methodist. Mason (32 deg., Shriner). Author: The Gray-Votaw-Rogers Achievement Test, Advanced, Elementary and Primary, 1949. Home: Austin TX Died Jan. 13, 1973.

GRAY, J. S., editor, writer, pub.; b. Clio, Mich., Feb. 20, 1890; s. John Wesley and Ida Caroline (Smith) G.; A.B., Adrian Coll., 1910, LL.D., 1938; m. Harriett Taylor, Sept. 10, 1912;children—Thorne (Mrs. David C. Hawley), Grattan, Whitmore. Reporter, editorial writer Adrian (Mich.) Telegram, 1911-17, mng. editor, 1919-27, v.p., 1927-72; pres. and editor Monroe (Mich.) Evening News, 1927-72. Trustee Adrian Coll. Served as arty. officer, A.E.F., U.S. Army, 1917-19. Recipient Bronze medal journalism U. Minn., 1949; Inland Press citation for pub. service, 1946. Mem. adv. com. WPB and Civilian Prodn. Adminstrn., 1942-45; mem. nat. adv. council journalism Sch. Adminstrs. Mem. Am. Newspaper Pubs. Assn. (dir. chmn. freedom of press com. 1950-57), Mich. Hist. Soc. (dir.), Am. Soc. Newspaper Editors, Inland Daily (past pres.), Mich. (past pres.), Inter Am. press assn., Mich. Asso. Press Editorial Assn. (past pres.), Internat. Press Inst., Am. Legion (life). Mason (life). Clubs: Detroit Press, U. Mich. Press (past pres.), Washington Press. Collector, annotator hist. maps of southeast Mich. A sponsor of Mich. law under which penal fines are devoted to establishment and maintenance of township libraries. Home: Monroe MI Died Nov. 1, 1972.

GRAY, JOSLYN, author; b. Brattleboro, Vt.; d. Charles Adams (M.D.) and Nellie Ann (Joslin) G.; A.B., Boston U., 1898, A.M., 1901. Club: Boston Authors'. Author: Kathleen's Probation, 1918; Elsie Marley, Honey, 1918; Rusty Miller, 1919; Rosemary Greenaway, 1919; Fireweed, 1920; The January Girl, 1920; Bouncing Bet, 1921; The Other Miller Girl, 1922; The Old Mary Metcalf Place, 1923; Black-Eyed Susan, 1924. Home: Boston, Mass.; (summer) Hinsdale NH‡

GRAY, LEON FOWLER, physician; born in Eastland, Tex., June 4, 1901; s. Andrew Jackson and Cannie Lynch (Fowler) G.; student John Tarleton Agrl. Coll., 1918; A.B., U. Tex., 1925; M.D., Tulane U., 1930; m. Jennie Elizabeth Thomason, Sept. 16, 1942. Intern New Orleans Charity Hosp., 1930-31; resident ophthalmology Bklyn. Eye and Ear Hosp., 1931-33; postgrad. student Royal London Ophthalmic Hosp., London, Eng., 1938-39; hon. ophthalmic surgeon T. E. Schumpert Meml. Hosp., Willis Knighton Meml. Hosp.; ophthalmic surgeon Highland Sanitarium; ophthalmic surgeon Physicians and Surgeons Hosp., 1933-69; practicing ophthalmologist, 1933-69, Bossier General Hosp., Bossier City, La. ophthalmologist-in-chief Shreveport Charity Hosp., 1933-40; sr. cons. ophthalmologist VA Hosp., Shreveport, 1948-69; chmn. dept. ophthalmology Confederate Meml. Med. Center, Shreveport; asso. clin. prof. Shreveport Med. Sch., La. State U. Diplomate Nat. Bd. Med. Examiners, Am. Bd. Ophthalmology, Pan Am. Med. Assn. Fellow Am. Coll. Angiology, Internat. Coll. Surgeons, A.C.S., Am. Acad. Ophthalmology and Otolaryngology; hon. mem. Dr. Barraquer's Inst., Barcelona, Spain; mem. Assn. Research Ophthalmology, Inc., Am., So. med. assns., La., Shreveport med. socs., Ark.-La.-Tex. Acad. Med., Ark.-La.-Tex. Ophthalmic and Otolaryngol. Soc., Pan-Am. Congress Ophthalmology, Internat. Congress Ophthalmology, Pan.-Am. Assn. Ophthalmology, C. of C., Square and Compass, Omega Beta Pi, Phi Beta Pi. Methodist (steward). Mason. Clubs: Shreveport, Lion (hon. pres.). Home: Shreveport LA Died May 27, 1969.

GRAY, MAT, ret. newspaper exec.; b. Ida Grove, Ia., Aug. 4, 1876; s. Mathew Marion and Anna (Page) G.; student pub. schs. Sioux City, Ia.; m. Victoria Gillespie, Aug. 28, 1899; children—Mat, Anna Victoria (Mrs. Carroll B. Annis). Conducted weekly newspapers, Ellisville, Miss., 1897-1904; joined New Orleans Times-Democrat (now New Orleans Times-Picayune), 1904, asso. editor, 1906-52, sr., chief editorial writer, 1914-52, in charge editorial page, 1943-52, ret., 1952. Served as 1st sgt., MCo., 1st Miss. Vol. Inf., 1898; admitted to Miss. bar circa, 1902, capt., adj. Miss. N.G., 1900. Mem. Am. Soc. Newspaper Editors. Home: 1122 Eleonore St., New Orleans 15‡

GRAY, ROLAND, lawyer; b. Boston, Mass., Apr. 1, 1874; s. John Chipman and Anna S. L. (Mason) G.; Hopkinson Sch., Boston; A.B., Harvard, 1895, LL.B., 1898; m. Mary Tudor, Sept. 25, 1907; children—John Chipman, Mary Whitwell, Roland, Christopher. Practiced in Boston since 1899; mem. Ropes, Gray, Best, Coolidge & Rugg. Clubs: Union (Boston); Harvard (Boston); Faculty (Cambridge). Home: 36 Larch Rd., Cambridge. Office: 50 Federal St., Boston MA‡

GRAYDON, JOSEPH SPENCER, lawyer; b. Cincinnati, O., Oct. 19, 1876; s. Thomas William and Anne (Hetherington) G.; A.B., Harvard U., 1898; legal edn., Cincinnati and Harvard law schs., and in office of Maxwell & Ramsey; m. Marjorie Maxwell, Apr. 8, 1901. Sr. mem. Graydon, Head & Ritchey (successors of Maxwell & Ramsey); pres. Ozark Coal Co., Excelsior Coal Co.; dir. Fifth-Third Union Trust Co., Globe-Wernicke Realty Co. Chmn. exec. com. Cincinnati Inst. of Fine Arts; dir. Cincinnati Art Museum; pres. Cincinnati Musical Festival Assn. Mem. Am. Bar Assn., Ohio Bar Assn., Cincinnati Bar Assn. (past president), Modern Language Association of America, Mediaeval Soc. America, English Speaking Union (dir.; pres. Cincinnati Chapter), Ohio Hist. and Philos. Soc., Early English Text Soc., Newcomen Soc. Clubs: Harvard (New York); Rowfant (Cleveland); Rolling Rock (Ligonier, Pa.); Queen City, Country, Literary, Camargo, Print and Drawing Circle, Commercial, Commonwealth (Cincinnati). Republican. Episcopalian. Collector of Chaucer and Early English chronicles. Home: Drake and Brill Rds., Indian Hill. Office: Cincinnati OH‡

GREBE, MARGUERITE LUCKETT, co. exec.; b. Washington; d. Joseph E. and Florence (Balderston) Luckett; ed. high sch.; m. H.C. Grebe, July 11, 1921 (dec. June 1, 1952). With H.C. Grebe & Co., Inc., Chgo., 1952-72, pres., 1952-72. Clubs: Yacht, Lake Shore (Chgo.). Home: Chicago IL Died Nov. 15, 1972.

GREELEY, SAMUEL ARNOLD, cons. engr.; b. Chicago, Ill., Aug. 20, 1882; s. Frederick and Florence Morehouse (Arnold) G.; A.B., Harvard, 1903; B.S. in Sanitary Engring., Mass. Inst. Tech., 1906; m. Dorothy Coffin, Oct. 4, 1913; children—Samuel Sewall, Frederick, Lois, Dorothy. Assistant engineer Hering & Fuller of N.Y. City, 1904-09; was resident engr. in charge construction and supt. in charge operation Milwaukee Refuse Disposal Plant, 1909-11; investigation and report on water supply and sewage treatment, Caracas, Venzuela, 1911; engr. with Sanitary Dist. of Chicago, 1912-15; supervising engr. Camp Custer, Mich., 1917-18, also sanitary engr. U.S. Shipping Bd., operations on Pacific Coast, N.E. Coast and Great Lakes; cons. engr. on sanitary engring. projects for New York, Los Angeles County, Buffalo, Hampton Roads, Minneapolis-St. Paul, Milwaukee, Madison (Wis.), Dallas, Chicago, Phila., Boston, Washington, Toronto, Toledo, Miami, New Bedford, Kansas City, Grand Rapids, Worcester, Peoria, Rockford, and over 200 other cities; mem. Greeley and Hansen, cons. engrs. Chicago. Served as spl. cons. constrn. Div., and Corps Engrs.; gen. charge layout and constrn. camp Forest, Tenn.; World War II. Recipient Brown medal, Franklin Inst., 1951, Charles Alvin Emerson medal, Water Pollution Control Fedn., 1961. Mem. Am. Soc, C.E. (hon. mem.; dir. 1947-50), Am. Water Works Assn., Am. Pub. Health Assn., Am. Assn. Engrs., N.E. Water Works Assn., Am. Pub. Works Assn. (honorary member), Ill. Soc. Engrs., Western Soc. Engrs., etc. Mem. Council and Bd. Local Improvements, Winnetka, Ill., 1916-18. Episcopalian. Clubs: Univ., Engrs., Cosmos. Author: (with Rudolph Hering) Collection and Disposal of Municipal Refuse, 1921. Home: Winnetka IL Died Feb. 3, 1968.

GREEN, ADWIN WIGFALL, univ. prof.; b. Virginia, Sept. 21, 1900; s. Adwin Wigfall and Lillie May (Gray) G.; A.B., Coll. of William and Mary, 1925; LL.B., Georgetown U., 1921; A.M., U. of Va., 1927, Ph.D., 1930; m. Mary Moore (Dooley). Admitted to bar, 1921; in practice law, Washington, 1921-24; asst. prof. English, Gettysburg Coll., 1926-27; prof. English U. of Miss. 1930-66, dean of grad. sch. 1940-46; visiting prof., University of Virginia, 1938, University of Puerto Rico, 1947, Fulbright prof. University of Philippines, 1949-50. Served as chief petty officer, U.S.N.R., 1917-18; colonel, Judge Advocate Gen.'s Dept., World War II; active duty European Theater of Operations, 1942-44, head of Internat. Law Div., Philippines, Korea, and Japan. Member of bar of Supreme Court and Court of Appeals, Dist. of Columbia, bar Supreme Ct. of Miss. Mem. Mod. Lang. Assn., Phi Beta Kappa. Author: Beowulf, A Literal Translation, 1935; Complete College Composition, 1940; The Will of Alfred, King of West Saxons, 1944; Sir Francis Bacon, 1952, 66; The Epic of Korea, 1950; The Man Bilbo, 1963. Co-editor: Prose of the English Renaissance, 1952; Tudor Poetry and Prose, 1953; William Faulkner of Oxford, 1965; The Inns of Court, 1931, 65. Home: Lauderdale by the Sea FL Died June 15, 1966; buried Popano Beach FL

GREEN, CHARLES BODEN, educator; b. Lynn, Mass., Mar. 13, 1875; s. Charles Edwin Lewis and Ruth Ann (Alley) G.; A.B., Tufts Coll., 1897; A.M., Harvard, 1901; m. Margaret F. Lyman, of Pasadena, Calif., July 24, 1918. Teacher of mathematics, Clinton Liberal Inst., Fort Plain, N.Y., 1898-1900, Rugby Sch., Kenilworth, Ill., 1901-02, Hackley Sch., Tarrytown, N.Y., 1902-03; headmaster Northside Sch., Williamstown, Mass., since 1923. Mem. Delta Tau Delta. Address: Northside School, Williamstown MA‡

GREEN, HARRY JOSEPH, lawyer; b. N.Y., Feb. 12, 1906; s. Harry H. and Rose (Achtsam) G.; student Balt. City Coll., 1918-20, Fishburne Mil. Sch., Waynesboro, Va., 1920-22; A.B., Johns Hopkins, 1926, Ph.D., 1929; LL.B., U. Md., 1927; M. Dorothy Eser; children—Mae (Mrs. Louis Sinsheimer), Harrie Ellin (Mrs. Phillip George), Deborah Lynne. Admitted to Md. bar, 1927, D.C. bar, 1930; partner firm Weinberg & Green, Balt., 1932-64; asst. atty. gen. of Md., 1931-35. Bd. dirs. Consol. Foods, Chgo., Food Mfrs., Inc (N.J.). Chmn. Md. Commn. to Study Edn. and Finance, 1951-57, Md. Commn. on State Programs; secretary Baltimore County Advisory Commission; chairman Baltimore Financial Commission; del. President's Conf. on

Education, Washington, 1956. Bd. Asso. Jewish Charities, Sinai Hosp.; past pres. Mt. Pleasant Sanitarium. Served from lt. comdr. to comdr., USCGR, 1942-47. Mem. Jewish Ednl. Alliance (past pres.), Inter-Am., Internat., Am., Md., Balt. bar assns., Am. Polit. Sci. Assn., Am.-Internat. Law Assn., Nat. Tax Assn., U.S. Power Squadron, Phi Alpha. Clubs: Suburban; Md. Yacht; Cambridge Yacht; Kent Island (Md.) Yacht; University, Harmonie (N.Y.C.), Center (Balt.). Home: Baltimore MD Died Oct. 18, 1964.

GREEN, JAMES BENJAMIN, clergyman, educator; b. Lexington, Ala., May 10, 1871; s. Curtis and Sarah (Hammond) G.; Licentiate of Instruction degree, Peabody Normal Coll., Nashville, Tenn., 1893; A.B., U. of Nashville, 1893; grad. Union Theol. Sem., Richmond, Va., 1901; D.D., Presbyn. Coll. of S.C., 1914; LL.D., Southwestern, Memphis, Tenn., 1940; m. Mayme Barnett, May 10, 1904 (died 1919); children—James Benjamin, Mary Gordon; m. 2d, Lillian Clinkscales, June 29, 1922; children—Curtis Vance, Dorothy. Ordained Presbyterian ministry, 1901; pastor Columbia, Tenn., 1901-03, Fayetteville, 1903-07, Greenwood, S.C., 1908-21; prof. systematic theology, Presbyn. Theol. Sem., Columbia, S.C., since 1921; Seminary moved to Decatur, Ga., 1927. Upon retiring as prof. Systematic Theology his chair was endowed by alumni Bd. of Dirs., named J. B. Green Chair of Theology. Elected moderator Gen. Assembly, Presbyn. Ch., U.S., May 1946. Lecturer and leader in Bible study at summer assemblies. Trustee Presbyn. Coll. of S.C., 1911-23. Mem. of Com. on Revision of Westminster Standards, 1935-43. Author: Studies in the Holy Decatur GA‡

GREEN, ROLLAND LESTER, ex-pres. Ill. State Med. Soc.; b. Walnut Ridge, Ark., Sept. 15, 1875; s. James B. and Lizzie (Leary) G.; grad. Little Rock (Ark.) High Sch., 1895; M.D., St. Louis Coll. Phys. and Surg., 1898; m. Florence Prendergast, of Peoria, June 19, 1923. Practiced in Peoria, Ill., since 1898; mem. staff St. Francis Hosp. since 1900. Mem. A.M.A. (del. each yr. since 1922), Ill. State Med. Soc. (pres. 1936-37), Tri State Med. Soc. (past pres.; councilor). Democrat. Mason. Clubs: Creve Coeur, Peoria Country. Home: 1609 N. Glen Oak St. Office: Central Nat. Bank Bldg., Peoria IL‡

GREEN, THEODORE MEYER, professor of philosophy, author; b. Constantinople, Turkey, Jan. 25, 1897; s. Joseph Kingsbury and Mathilde Hermine (Meyer) G.; parents U.S. citizens; A.B., Amherst Coll., 1918; Ph.D., U. of Edinburgh, 1924; LL.D., Davidson (N.C.) Coll., 1941, Hobart Coll., 1942, University of Pittsburgh, 1945, Rockford College, 1947; D.D., Amherst, 1942; L.H.D., Ripon, 1952; D.Litt., Colby, 1953; m. Faith Nelson, Mar. 18, 1920; children—Janey Elmore (Mrs. Harvey H. Meeker), Caroline Irma (Mrs. David Riefler); m. 2d, Elizabeth R. Harris, June 8, 1946. Instr., Forman Christian Coll., U. of Panjab, India, 1919-21; instr. in philosophy Princeton, 1923-25, asst. prof., 1925-28, asso. prof., 1928-38, prof., 1938-45, McCosh prof. philosophy, 1941-45, chmn. div. program in humanities, 1941-45; visiting professor in humanities, Leland Stanford U., 1945-46; prof. philosophy Yale, 1946-55; M. D. Anderson vis. prof. in humanities Rice Inst., Houston, 1955; Henry Burr Alexander prof. in humanities, Scripps Coll., Claremont, Cal., 1955-61; visiting professor American U., Beirut, Lebanon, 1961-62, New Asia College, Hong Kong, 1962-63, Emory University and Agnes Scott College, 1964-67, Bowdoin College, Brunswick, Maine, 1967-68. Master of Silliman Coll., Yale, 1947-53. Served as Y.M.C.A. war sec., Mesopotamia, 1918-19. Traveling fellow Am. Council Learned Socs., 1932-33; Ford grant for study in India, 1958-59. Fellow of American Acad. Arts and Scis.; mem. Am. Philos. Assn., Am. Theol. Soc., American Society for Aesthetics, Am. Assn. Univ. Profs. (pres. Princeton chapter 1941-42), Delta Upsilon, Delta Sigma Rho, Phi Beta Kappa. Author books, latest being: Our Cultural Heritage, 1956; Liberalism, 1957; Moral Aesthetic and Religion Insight, 1958. Editor Liberal Education Re-examined (with others), 1943. Contbr. to books and jours. Home: New Haven CT Died Aug. 13, 1969.

GREENBAUM, EDWARD S., army officer, lawyer; b. New York City, N.Y., Apr. 13, 1890; s. Samuel and Selina G.; grad. Horace Mann Sch., 1907, Williams Coll., Williamstown, Mass., 1910, Columbia Law Sch., 1913; LL.D., Williams Coll., 1946; research asso. Johns Hopkins Univ.; m. Dorothea R. Schwarez, Oct. 21, 1920; children—David S., Daniel W. In practice of law, N.Y. City, 1913-17, 1919-40, 46-70; mem. firm Greenbaum, Wolff & Ernst, 1915-70; D.C., 1933; special asst. to atty. gen., 1938, counsel, Long Island Railroad Commn., 1952-53. Mem. N.Y. Judicial Conf., 1st dept., 1956-67; mem. United States delegation to UN 1956-57. Mem. N.J. Commn. on Dept. Instns. and Agys., 1958. Served in U.S. Army, 1917-19 and, 1940-46; commd. lt. col., 1940, col. 1941, brig. gen., 1943-46. Awarded Distinguished Service Medal, 1945. Mem. American Academy of Arts and Letters, American, City of New York and N.Y. State bar assns., N.Y. County Lawyers Assn. Clubs: Army and Navy (Washington); Williams. Democrat. Jewish religion. Author: The King's Bench Masters (with Leslie I. Reade), 1932; A Lawyer's Job, 1968. Home: Princeton NJ Died June 12, 1970.

GREENBLATT, LOUIS, lawyer; b. Austria, Sept. 24, 1905; LL.B., N.Y. U., 1926. Admitted to N.Y. State bar, 1928, U.S. Supreme Ct. bar, 1964; mem. firm Tenzer, Greenblatt, Fallon and Kaplan; lectr. Practising Law Inst., 1956-72. Mem. Assn. Bar City N.Y. (mem. real property com. 1957-60), N.Y. County Lawyers Assn. Contbr. articles to profl. jours. Address: New York City NY Died July 15, 1972.

GREENE, ARTHUR MAURICE, JR., mech. engr., educator; b. Phila., Pa., Feb. 4, 1872; s. Arthur Maurice and Eleanor J. (Lowry) G.; B.S., U. of Pa., 1893; M.E., 1894, Sc.D., 1917; D.Eng., Rensselaer Polytech. Inst., 1922; studied in Germany, summers, 1896 and 1905; LL.D., U. of Mo., 1940; m. Mary Elizabeth Lewis, June 12, 1906. In charge of apprentice sch., Franklin Sugar Refinery, Phila., 1892-94; instr., Drexel Inst., 1894-95, U. of Pa., 1895-1902; prof. mech. engring., U. of Mo., 1902-07, and jr. dean Sch. of Engring., 1906-07; prof. mech. engring., Rensselaer Poly. Inst., 1907-22; dean Sch. of Engring., prof. mech. engring., Princeton U., 1922-40, dean emeritus since 1940. Consultant engr. for power plants and mfg.; expert in patent causes; consultant Coordinator of Inter-American Affairs; consultant to chmn. War Production Board, February-June 1942. Expert cons. Army Specialized Training Div., U.S. Army. Member World Power Conferences, 1930 and 1936. Former member Board of Education, Princeton, New Jersey. Member National Research Council (engineering division); chairman power plant committtee United States Fuel Adminstrn. for Rensselaer County, N.Y.; Four Minute Man"; mem. War Service League of Troy; mem. engring. council, war com. of tech. socs. Trustee Princeton Hosp.; formerly trustee Troy Public Library and v.p. Troy Y.M.C.A. Mem. Govs. Highway Safety Council of N.J.; mem. N.J. State Board of Professional Engrs. and Land Surveyors. Member War Price and Rationing Board, Princeton, N.J.; mem. Belgian American Ednl. Foundation. Fellow A.A.A.S.; life member Am. Ordnance Assn.; honorary mem. Am. Soc. M.E. (former mgr. and v.p.; chmn. research com.; mem. boiler code com.; chmn. com. on awards); member American Society for Engineering Education (pres. 1919-20), Soc. Engrs. Eastern N.Y. (ex-pres.), Am. Engring. Council, Princeton Engring. Assn. (hon.), Newcomen Soc., Guild of Brackett Lectures of Princeton Univ., Kappa Sigma, Sigma Xi, Phi Beta Kappa, Tau Beta Pi, Mu Phi Alpha. Awarded silver medal by Jugo-Slovakian Red Cross Soc. Republican. Baptist. Mason. Clubs: Nassau (Princeton); University (Columbia, Mo., life); Princeton (N.Y.). Author: Elements of Steam Engineering (with H. W. Spangler and S. M. Marshall), 1902; Pumping Machinery, 1911; Elements of Heating and Ventilation, 1912; Heat Engineering, 1914; Elements of Refrigeration, 1916; Elements of Power Generation, 1933; Elements of Hydraulic Power Generation, 1934; Principles of Heating, Ventilating and Air Conditioning, 1936; Principles of Thermodynamics, Part I, 1938, Part II, 1939. Contbr. to Mech. Engineering American Year Books, 1941. Has traveled widely in America and Europe. Home: 19 Maple St., Princeton NJ‡

GREENE, CHARLES ARTHUR, ednl. dir.; b. Triplett, Mo., Jan. 10, 1875; s. Austin Orlander and Maria Theresa (Elliott) G.; Ph.B., Central Coll., Fayette, Mo., 1897; A.B., U. of Mo., 1900, A.M., 1901; student summers U. of Minn., 1914, Columbia, 1916, U. of Colo., 1919; LL.D., Central Wesleyan Coll., Warrenton, 1941; m. Cordelia Hamer, June 28, 1905; 1 dau., Grace Elizabeth (Mrs. Milton Chamberlin). Prin. Brunswick (Mo.) High Sch., 1894-96; teacher Carrollton (Mo.) High Sch., 1897-99; supt. of schs. (Mo.), Armstrong, 1901-03, Bethany, 1903-06, Trenton, 1906-11, Webb City, 1912-20, Sedalia, 1920-24, St. Joseph, 1924-28; high school inspector for Mo., 1911-12; supt. extension colls., Mo., 1934-35; rep. John C. Winston Co., Mo., 1931-33; pres. Central Wesleyan Coll., Warrenton, Mo., 1939-42; State Ins. Dept., 1942-45; supt. schs., Simmons, Mo., 1945-47; dir. employment and personnel, Chillicothe (Mo.) Business Coll., since 1947. Mem. Missouri Constitutional Convention, 1923. Pres. Mo. School Supts. Assn., 1925, Jasper County Teachers Assn., 1919. Mem. Mo. State Teachers' Assn. Republican. Methodist. Mason (K.T.). Clubs: Rotary (Sedalia); Country, Rotary (St. Joseph). Author: Civil Government of Missouri, 1927. Compiler and editor of register and record books. Home: Chillicothe MO*‡

GREENE, GEORGE LOUIS, clergyman; b. Weybridge, Vt., Jan. 27, 1917; s. Louis and Alice (Castallo) G.; student Middlebury Coll., 1935-36; A.B., Marietta Coll., 1939; B.D., Yale, 1942; D.D., Piedmont Coll., 1957; m. Margaret Elsie Chindahl, June 2, 1942; children—Douglas George, David Louis, Paul Eric. Ordained to ministry Congl. Ch., 1942; pastor 1st Ch. of Christ, Old Saybrook, Conn., 1942-48, Community Ch., Park Ridge, Ill., 1948-57, Pass-a-Grille Beach Community Ch., St. Petersburg Beach, Fla., 1957-68; newspaper columnist. Del. World Council Chs., 1952; dean summer confs., v.p. United Chs. St. Petersburg; chaplain St. Petersburg Beach Fire Dept.; moderator Fla. W. Central Assn. United Ch. of Christ, 1964-65; del. Gen. Synod representing Fla., United Ch. of Christ, 1965; exchange minister to Cambridge, Eng., 1964, 68. Bd. corporator: All children's Hosp.. St. Petersburg. Recipient award for outstanding civic service St. Petersburg Beach City Council, 1962. Mem. St. Petersburg Ministers Assn. (pres. 1966), St. Petersburg C. of C. (dir.). Republican. Mason, Rotarian, Kiwanian, Lion. Author: Think on These Things, 1971. Contbr. buried Winter Park FL

GREENE, HARRY SYLVESTRE NUTTING, pathologist; b. Woonsocket, R.I., Sept. 22, 1904; s. George Wellington and Gertrude (Earl) G.; student Wilbraham (Mass.) Acad., 1917-21; student Brown U., 1921-25; M.D., C.M., McGill U., 1930; A.M. (hon.), Yale, 1943; m. Helen May Davis, Sept. 27, 1930; 1 dau., Judith Ann; m. 2d, Jean Barnes, Dec. 18, 1954; 2 daus., Susan, Melissa. Instr. pathology, Path. Inst., McGill U., 1930-31; asst. in pathology, Rockefeller Inst. for Med. Research, N.Y. City, 1931-35; asso. in pathology, Rockeffer Inst., Princeton, N.J., 1935-41; asso. prof. of pathology and surgery, Yale U. Sch. of Medicine, 1941-43, prof. of pathology, 1943-50, Anthony N. Brady prof. of pathology, 1950-69. Recipient Borden award, 1956. Mem. Am. Assn. Advancement Sci., Am. Assn. Pathologists and Bacteriologists, Am. Genetic Assn., Soc. for Exptl. Biology and Medicine, Soc. for Study of Growth and Development, Am. Assn. for Cancer Research, Harvey Soc. of N.Y., Am. Acad. of Arts and Scis., N.E., Cancer Soc., Sigma Xi, Theta Delta Chi, Alpha Kappa Kappa, Alpha Omega Alpha. Clubs: Interurban Pathological, Faculty, Graduates (Yale). Home: Guilford CT Died Feb. 14, 1969; buried North Smithfield RI

GREENE, JAMES E(DWARD), psychologist; born Donaldson, Ark., Aug. 14, 1900; s. Andrew Watson and Almedia (Anderson) G.; A.B., Henderson State Teachers Coll., Arkadelphia, Ark., 1922; A.M., Vanderbilt U., 1924; Ph.D., Peabody Coll. for Teachers Nashville, Tenn., 1931; Social Sci. Research Council fellow, 1930-31; Am. Council Edn. fellow, 1940-41; m. Sarah Ruth Abernathy, June 8, 1927;children—James Edward, George Robert, Sarah Ruth, William Andrew. Instr. psychology and sociology, Logan College, Ky., 1922-23; instr. English, Hot Springs (Ark.) High Sch., 1924-25; psychologist Tenn. Indsl. Sch., 1926-27; asso. prof. psychology and sociology University of Georgia, 1927-36, prof. edn. from 1937, chmn. div. grad. studies Coll. Edn. 1950, U. Ga. Alumni Found. Distinguished prof., from 1967. Ednl. specialist O.P.A., 1942-43; research specialist, edn. panel, Ga. Agrl. and Indsl. Development Bd., 1944-45; dir. U. of Ga. Guidance Center, 1945-46; dep. dir. of research, ednl. adv. staff, Air Univ., 1946-47; cons. Atlanta Board Edn., from 1946; mem. firm Cons. Psychologists, Inc., Atlanta. Diplomate clin. psychologist, American Board of Examiners in Professional Psychology. Fellow Am. Psychol Assn. (ednl. and clin. secs.), Southern Soc. Psychology and Philosophy; mem. Ga. Psychol. Assn., A.A.A.S., Ga. Acad. Sci., Am. Ednl. Research Assn. Author: Reliability and Validity of Rational Learning Tests, 1931. Contbr. articles to prof. jours. Home: Athens GA Died Nov. 3, 1971; buried Oconee Hill Cemetery, Athens GA

GREENE, JAMES NICHOLAS, mfg. and retailing co. exec.; b. Danbury, Conn., Dec. 29, 1906; s. Michael W. and Catherine (Brennan) G.; student Yale, 1926, Columbia, 1927; m. Jane Allen, Apr. 18, 1938; children—James N., Catherine (Mrs. William Hellauer), Michael, Peter. Vice pres. F.H. Lee Co Danbury, 1926-54; treas., asst. to pres. Montecatini Soc., Milan, Italy and N.Y.C., 1955-63; v.p., sec. Botany Industries, Inc., N.Y.C., 1963-71; dir. Fashion Park, Botany Products, Broadstreets Inc., Weber Heilbroner Inc., Harris Frank, Levensohn Bros. & Co. Mem. Conn. Bd. Edn., 1954-66; chmn. speakers bur. A.R.C., from 1941; mem. President's Com. Edn., 1960. Mem. Conn. Democratic Central Com., from 1950; candidate for Conn. Gen. Assembly, 1956. Mem. Conn. N.G., 1936-41. Recipient citation A.R.C., 1950. Mem. Am. Mgmt. Assn. Elk, Rotarian (past pres. Newtown, Conn.), K.C. (4 Newtown CT Died June 2, 1971; buried St. Peters Cemetery, Danbury CT

GREENE, JOSEPH NATHANIEL, utilities exec.; b. Ft. Logan, Colo., Feb. 1, 1893; s. Lewis Douglass and Lillian Taft (Adams) G.; B.S., U. Ill., 1915; m. Nanine W. Pond, 1917 (div. 1931); children—Joseph Nathaniel, Nicholas Misplee; m. 2d, Margaret Mordock Wright, 1938; children—William Mordock, Elizabeth Kimberly. With Astoria Importing & Mfg. Co., Long Island City, N.Y., 1922-29; officer, dir. Fed. Water Service Corp. or subsidiary firms, 1929-52; pres., dir. Ala. Gas Corp., 1940-52, chmn. bd., 1953-67. Trustee Pelham Manor, N.Y., 1925-27, mayor, 1928-29; coordinator Jefferson County Civilian Def., 1941-46; chmn. local chpt. ARC, 1949-52, chmn. com. on resolutions 1957 conv. Am. Nat. Red Cross, mem. bd. govs., 1960-66; chmn. Alabama Hall of Fame Bd., 1952-69; co-chairman Birmingham Committee of 100, 1954, chairman 1955-57. Served as captain U.S. Army, 1916-19. Member Birmigham Symphony Assn. (pres. 1958-62, chmn. bd. 1961-65, trustee), Sigma Nu. Mason. Club: Birmingham Country. Home: Birmingham AL Died June 20, 1969.

GREENE, M(ARIA) LOUISE, social worker; b. Providence, R.I.; d. Welcome Arnold and Caroline

(Austin) G.; A.B., Vassar, 1891; student Teachers Coll., 1891-92; Ph.D., Yale, specializing in Am. history, 1895; M.Pd., New York University, 1909; unmarried. Specializing in school garden work; investigator for Russell Sage Foundation, New York, 1909. Mem. Sch. Garden Assn. America (v.p. 1912-15), D.A.R., Mayflower Soc. Author: Development of Religious Liberty in Connecticut, 1905; Among School Gardens (for Russell Sage Foundation), 1910, 2d edit., 1911; also popular articles in mags. relating to N.E. history and school gardening. Home: 37 Forest St., Providence RI‡

GREENE, PATTERSON, newspaperman, playwright; b. Superior, Wis., Sept. 20, 1898; s. Peter William and Katherine (Drisoll) G.; A.B., Harvard, 1922; m. Mary Amanda Watson, Sept. 23, 1940; 1 dau., Mary Katherine. Asso. prof. English, U, Philippines, Manila, 1922-24; asso. drama-music editor Los Angeles Examiner (later Los Angeles Herald-Examiner), 1925-32, music editor, 1944-68; free lance writer, 1932-44. Served with M.C., U.S. Army, 1918. Author: Papa is All, 1942; The Closed Room, 1934; Music in the Distance, 1960 (plays); also short stories. Home: Los Angeles CA Died January 27, 1968; buried Holy Cross Cemetery, Los Angeles CA

GREENE, SAMUEL WEBB, Christian Science lecturer; b. Mt. Sterling, Ky., Apr. 15, 1876; s. Lucien Butler and Sarah Frances (Johnson) G.; grad. Ky. Mil. Inst., 1893; spl. work in mathematics, U. of Chicago, 1899; LL.B., U. of Louisville, 1903; m. Blanche Grey Jordan, June 28, 1906 (died 1909); 1 dau., Blanche Jordan; m. 2d, Anna Woolfolk Gault, Mar. 27, 1911 (divorced, 1948); 1 dau., Adelaide Brown; m. 3d Viola Miller Pryor, 1949. Teacher, Kentucky Military Institute, 7 yrs.; practiced law, Louisville, 1903-14; mem. City Council, Louisville, 1910-13 (pres. 1910-12); judge County and Juvenile Court, Jefferson County, Ky., 1914-18; Christian Science lecturer, 1918-26 and since 1929; 1st reader First Ch. of Christ Scientist, 1926-29. Republican. Mason. Home: 999 Lake Shore Drive. Address: 8 S. Michigan Av., Chicago‡

GREENEBAUM, LEON CHARLES, business exec.; b. N.Y.C., Dec. 30, 1907; s. Charles L. and Estelle (Schoeps) G.; B.S., Dartmouth, 1927; m. Myra Cole, May 21, 1948; 1 son, Charles L. Chmn., pres. Met., Distbrs., Inc., N.Y.C., 1936-54; dir., vice chmn. Hertz Corp., N.Y.C., 1955-56, chmn. 1956-68, chief exec. officer, 1960-67; pres. Ryma Corp., 1950-68; dir. Halero Truck Sales Corp., Motorways, Inc. Pres. Charles and Estelle Greenebaum Found., Inc. Clubs: Dartmouth College, Harmonie; Hollywood Golf (Deal, N.J.). Home: New York City NY Died Mar. 25, 1968.

GREENER, JOHN HUNTER, radiologist; b. Bklyn., July 11, 1906; s. John Henry and Ida (Courter) G.; M.D., Rochester U., 1930; m. Claire Cecelia Greaves, June 25, 1932; children—Ann Hunter (Mrs. John Augustus Otaviano), Alan Laurie, Betty Jane (Mrs. James Edward Henry), Jay Henry. Intern St. John Hosp., St. Giles Hosp., Bklyn., 1930-32; radiologist Bay Ridge Hosp., Shore Rd. Hosp. Diplomate Am. Bd. Radiology. Mem. Radiol. Soc. N.Am., Am. Coll. Radiology, Bay Ridge Med. Soc. (chmn. vis. com.), Univeristy Glee Club, Alpha Kappa Kappa. Episcopalian. Home: Huntington NY Died June 18, 1969; buried Rosedale Cemetery, Montclair NJ

GREENING, HARRY CORNELL, cartoonist, comic artist; b. Titusville, Pa., May 30, 1876; s. Samuel Harper and Margaret Jane (Hurst) G.; pub. sch; edn.; attended night class Art Students' League, New York. First work appeared in New York Herald, 1896, and sold drawings to Truth" and Life" same year; on staff New York Journal comic supplement, 1898; subsequently connected with Judge, Puck, Life, Harper's, Scribner's, etc.; originator of various comic series, includine Prince Red Feather" series for St. Nicholas; drew Percy" page series for New York Herald; Fritz von Blitz" comic page in New York Herald; during the war was officially sanctioned by the U.S. Govt. and was used abroad for the A.E.F.; made cartoons for the govt.; running comic series for newspaper syndicate; inventor and mfr. Sporty Sam" novelty; inventor Funnyfishes" toys for children; The Wishbone Man," for newspaper syndicate, and toy entitled The Wishbone Man Game"; also devoted to gen. illustration. Author: The Wishbone Man. Club: Friars. Address: Illustrated Daily News Los Angeles CA‡

GREENLAW, LOWELL M., corp. counsel; 1 dau., Mrs. Robert T. Baker. Successively gen. atty., gen. counsel and v.p. Pullman Co., retired 1947; v.p. and gen. counsel, Pullman, Inc., 1947-50, retired 1950. Home: Chicago IL Died Nov. 15, 1968; buried Morrisonville IL

GREENQUIST, KENNETH LLOYD, lawyer, univ. regent; b. Florence, Wis., Apr. 3, 1910; s. Edwin E. and Ida (Johnson) G.; student U. Ky., 1929-31; LL.B., U. Wis., 1936; m. Hilda Winger, Aug. 24, 1940; children—Katherine, Nancy. Admitted to Wis. bar, 1936, since practiced in Racine; partner firm LaFrance, Thompson, Greenquist, Evans & Dye, 1957-68; city atty., Racine, 1946-49. Co-chmn. Wis. chpt. Am. Cancer Soc., 1967-68. Bd. regents U. of Wisconsin, 1962-68, pres., 1967-68. Partner K & K Investment Co., Greater N. Bay Land Co., MEG Investment Co., Rapds Dr. Shopping Center. Mem. Wis. Senate from Racine County, 1939-42. Served to lt. (s.g.) USNR, 1943-46. Mem. Am., Wis., Racine County (pres. 1965) bar assns., Am. Judicature Soc., Am. Legion (state comdr. 1951-52, mem. nat. exec. com. 1952-54), Benchers Soc. U. Wis. Law Sch., V.F.W. Elk. Home: Racine WI Died Apr. 5, 1968; buried Graceland Cemetery, Racine WI

GREENWAY, JAMES COWAN, M.D.; b. Huntsville, Ala., Jan. 28, 1877; s. Gilbert Christian (M.D.) and Alice (White) G.; B.A., Yale, 1900, M.A., 1916; M.D., Columbia, 1904; m. Harriet Lauder, of Pittsburgh, Pa., May 29, 1902; children—James C., George Lauder, Gilbert C., Anna L. Asso. attending physician, New York Hosp., 1908-16; moved to New Haven, 1916; dir. Dept. of Univ. Health, Yale U. Maj. Med. C., 1917-19. Clubs: Century, Yale (New York). Home: 400 Prospect St., New Haven CT‡

GREENWOOD, JOHN JOSEPH, owner printing co.; b. Charles City, Ia., Nov. 25, 1917; s. Albert Thomas and Kathryn Frances (Dunn) G.; grad. high sch.; m. Arlene A. Kobliska, Aug. 10, 1946; children—Alice (Mrs. Walter Russell), Nancy Ann. With Gen. Electric Co., Pittsfield, Mass., 1935-37, Berkshire Evening News, 1937-39, Winchester Daily News, Winchester, Ind., 1939-41, Charles City (Ia.) Daily Press, 1946-50; owner Tri-County News, Zearing, Ia., 1950-55; owner, operator Greenwood Printing Co., Ames, 1955-71. Served with AUS, 1941-45. Mem. V.F.W., Am. Legion (service officer 1967). Democrat. Roman Catholic. K.C. (past grand knight), Lion (pres. 1964-65), Elk, Moose. Club: Ames Golf and Country. Author: Community History-Zearing, Iowa, 1954; At the Squaw and Skunk, 1955; 1864-1964 Ames Centennial, 1964. Home: Ames IA Died Sept. 14, 1971.

GREENWOOD, MARION, artist; b. Bklyn., Apr. 6, 1909 d. Walter J. and Kathryn (Boylan) G.; student Art Students League N.Y., Academie Collarosi, Paris. Prof. fine arts U. Tenn., 1954-55; one-man shows Asso. Am. Artists Galleries, N.Y.C., 1944, 47, Chgo., 1948, Knoxville, Tenn., 1955, Milch Galleries, N.Y.C., 1959, Mint Mus., Charlotte, N.C., Art Inst., New Britain, Conn., 1960; murals U. San Nicolas Hidalgo Morelia, Michoacan, Mexico, Civic Center, Mexico City, U. Tenn.; represented in collections Met. Mus. Art, Pa. Acad. Fine Arts, Library Congress, Yale U., Am. Acad. Fine Arts, New Britian Art Inst., Mint Mus., various others; executed mural in Syracuse U., 1965; visiting professor fine arts Syracuse University, 1965. Recipient 2d Carnegie prize, 1944, John Herron Art Inst. lithograph prize, 1946; Lippincot award Pa. Acad. Fine Arts, 1951, 1st Altman prize Nat. Acad., 1952; purchase prize, Butler Art Inst., 1956; Grumbacher prize, oil, 1958; Lillian Cotton Meml. award Audubon Artists Ann., 1964; Kleinert award, 1968; Kuniyoshi award, 1969. Academician N.A.D. Home: Woodstock NY Died Feb. 20, 1970.

GREET, WILLIAM CABELL, educator; b. El Paso, Tex., Jan. 28, 1901; s. William Dement and Eleanor Love (Martin) G.; A.B., U. of South, 1920, D.Litt., 1959; postgrad. Harvard Law, 1920-21; A.M., Columbia, 1924, Ph.D., 1926; m. Katherine Hyde, Sept. 11, 1926; 1 dau., Anne Hyde (Mrs. John E. Cushing). Tutor in English, U. Tex., 1921-22; instr. U. of South, 1922, U. Colo., 1924, U. Cal., 1925; lectr. Barnard Coll., Columbia, 1926-27, instr. 1927-29, asst. prof., 1929-38, asso. prof., 1938-46, prof., English, 1946-53, McIntosh prof., 1953-66, emeritus, spl. lectr., 1966-69; lectr. Bryn Mawr Coll., 1937-41, 45; vis. prof. U. Montpellier and U. Aix-en-Provence, France, 1950-51, U. Ariz., 1969, U. Zagreb and U. Ljubljana (both Yugoslavia), 1969-70. Guggenheim fellow, 1952; dir. recordings Am. speech and modern poets; editor Am. Speech mag., 1933-52; speech cons. CBS, 1937-39, 40-70; chmn. editorial adv. com. Funk and Wagnalls Coll. Standard Dictionary, 1942-48; adv. editor Am. Coll. Dictionary, 1942-68; chmn. adv. com. Century Cyclopedia of Names, 1948-72; chmn. adv. com. Thorndike-Barnhart dictionaries, 1949-72; adviser Walt Disney Prodns., 1947; linguistic adviser Scott, Foresman Basic Reading Program, 1956-72. Mem. Modern Lang. Assn. Am., Am. Dialect Soc., Nat. Council Tchrs. English, Linguistic Soc. Am., Internat. Assn. U. Profs. English, Phi Gamma Delta. Democrat. Episcopalian. Clubs: Century, Columbia Faculty. Editor. Author: World Words, 1944, 1948; (with others) Listen, Speak, and Write (a series), 1960-72; My Little Pictionary (child's dictionary), 1962; My Second Pictionary, 1964; In Other Words, a Beginning Thesaurus, 1968; In Other Words, a Jr. Thesaurus, 1969. Contbr. to mags. Home: Santa Barbara CA Died Dec. 19, 1972.

GREGERSEN, MAGNUS INGSTRUP, prof. of physiology; b. Kimballton, Ia., Jan. 27, 1903; s. Rev. Jens Moller and Sofie (Madsen) G.; A.B., Stanford U., 1923; A.M., 1924; student Mass. Inst. Tech., 1925-26; Ph.D. in Physiology (division medical sciences), Harvard, 1930; m. Charlotte Kennedy, May 30, 1931 (divorced); children—Kirsten, Sofia, Charlotta; m. 2d Georgiane Schenck, Nov. 27, 1948; son, Peter. Austin teaching fellow in physiology, Harvard Med. Sch., 1925-27; instr. physiology, 1927-35; professor physiology, University of Maryland Med. Sch., 1935-37, head dept., 1935-37; prof. physiology and exec. officer dept., Coll. Phys. and Surg., Columbia, 1937-61, Dalton prof. physiology, 1945-69; pres. Am. Bureau Medical Aid to China, 1947-56, (honorary president, 1956-69); medical teaching mission, Poland, 1946, China, 1948; special consultant E.C.A., Taiwan, 1951; trustee China Internat. Found., 1952, pres., 1954-69; chmn. bd. Ingalls-Taiwan Shipbuilding & Drydock Co., 1956-62; vice chmn. Am. Emergency Com. for Tibetan Refugees; exec. com. Aid to Refugee Chinese Intellectuals; nat. adv. council Thomas A. Dooley Found.; trustee Mannes College of Music. Member subcommittee on shock, Division Medical Scis. of the Nat. Research Council, World War II. Recipient Special Cravat of the Order of Brilliant Star, Republic of China, 1956. Fellow New York Academy of Sciences, asso. fellow New York Acad. Med., mem. Am. Physiological Society, A.A.A.S., Soc. Exptl. Biology and Medicine, Soc. Rheology, Harvey Soc., Phi Beta Kappa, Sigma Xi. Clubs: 14 W. Hamilton Street (Balt.); Englewood, Englewood Field; University (N.Y.C.). Home: Englewood NJ Died Aug. 26, 1969; buried Solvang CA

GREGG, FRANCIS WHITLOCK, clergyman; b. Florence, S.C., Dec. 1, 1873; s. David Brainerd and Mary Henrietta (Mayes) G.; grad. S.C. Mil. Coll., 1894; B.D., Columbia (S.C.) Theol. Sem., 1899; D.D., Presbyn. Coll. of S.C., 1920; m. Elizabeth Cole Guy, Nov. 21, 1900; children—Frances Wardlaw, Alva Mayes, Margaret Henrietta, David Brainerd, Samuel Guy. Teacher, high sch., York, S.C., 1894-96; ordained ministry Presbyn. Ch. in U.S., 1899; pastor successively Lowrys, Manning, Pendleton, Clemson Coll., Upper Long Cane and Gaffney (all S.C.) until 1910, Rock Hill since 1910. Mem. Gen. Assembly Presbyn. Ch. in U.S., 1909, 1916, 1925; moderator Synod of S.C., 1927. Democrat. Mason, K.P. Kiwanian. Home: 311 E. Main St., Rock Hill SC‡

GREGORY, MARTIN LEROY, food co. exec.; b. Jackson, Tenn., Nov. 30, 1916; s. Charles and Alvena (Magenheimer) G.; B.S. in Mech. Engring., Purdue U., 1939; m. Dorothy Jean Curtis, July 26, 1941; children—Martina Louise, Philip Lowell. With Gen. Foods Corp., 1939-67, gen. mgr. Post div., 1962-64, v.p. corp., 1962-67, gen. mgr. Jell-O div., 1966-67. Home: Greenwich CT Died July 30, 1967; buried Battle Creek MI

GREGORY, NOBLE JONES, congressman; b. Mayfield, Ky., Aug. 30, 1897; s. William Jones and Rosa A. (Boyd) G.; grad. Mayfield (Ky.) High Sch., 1915; spl. work in private schs. and bus. coll.; m. Marion Hale, June 22, 1925; 1 dau., Marion Hale. With 1st Nat. Bank, Mayfield, advancing from bookkeeper to cashier, trust officer, 1917-36; director First Nat. Bank, Mayfield, Ky. & Tenn. Clay Co.; mem. 75th-85th Congresses, 1st Kentucky District; mem. Ways and Means Committee of House; subcommittee on Internal Revenue Taxation, joint com. on Internal Revenue Taxation; mem. Dem. Nat. congl. campaign com. Democrat. Presbyterian. Elk, Odd Fellow, Modern Woodman, Woodman of the World. Club: Filson, (Louisville). Home: Mayfield KY Died Sept. 26, 1971; buried Mayfield KY

GREGORY, WILLIAM K(ING), palentologist, morphologist; b. N.Y.C., May 19, 18976; s. George and Jane (King) G.; student Sch. of Mines, Columbia, 1894-96; A.B., Columbia, 1900, A.M., 1905; Ph.D., 1910; D.Sc., Witwatersrand, 1938; m. Laura Grace Foote, Dec. 4, 1899; m. 2d, Angela DuBois, 1938. Research asst. to Henry Fairfield Osborn, 1899-1913; asst. curator dept. vertebrate paleontology Am. Museum Natural History, 1911-14, asso. in paneontology, 1914-26, curator department comparative anatomy, 1921-44, emeritus, 1944-70, curator dept. ichthyology, 1925-44, emeritus, 1944-70; lecturer, asst. and asso. prof., prof. vertebrate paleontol., Da Costa prof., Columbia, 1943-45, emeritus, 1945-70. Fellow N.Y. Acad. Sciences (pres. 1932-33), N.Y. Zool. Soc., A.A.A.S. (v.p. sect. H, 1931); mem. Am. Soc. Naturalists (v.p. 1936). Am. Assn. Anatomists, Geol. Soc. America, Paleontol. Soc. America, Am. Soc. Mammalogists, Am. Philos. Society, Nat. Acad. Sciences, Am. Acad. Arts and Sciences, Am. Assn. Physical Anthropology (pres. 1941-42), Am. Soc. Ichthyology and Herpetology (pres. 1936-38); fgn. fellow London Zool. Soc.; fgn. fellow Geol. Soc. London, Linnean Society London, Royal Soc. of Queensland, Royal Soc. Science of Upsala, State Russian Paleontological Soc. of Leningrad, Acad. Hon., Museo de la Plata. Clubs: Explorers, Boone and Crockett, Faculty of Columbia Univ. Author: The Orders of Mammals, 1910; On the Structure and Relations of Notharctus, an American Eocene Primate, 1920; The Origin and Evolution of the Human Dentition, 1922; Our Face from Fish to Man, 1929; Fish Skulls—A Study of the Evolution of Natural Mechanisns, 1933; A Half Century of Trituberculy—The Cope-Osborn Theory of Dental Evolution, 1934; In Quest of Gorillas, 1937; Studies on the Origin and Early Evolution of Paired Fins and Limbs, Parts I-IV (with H.C. Raven) 1941; The Monotromes and the Palimpest Theory, 1947; Evolution Emerging also numerous revs. and tech. papers. Home: Kingston NY Died Dec. 1970.

GREGORY, WILLIAM MUMFORD, educator; b. Jonesville, Mich., Jan. 18, 1876; s. Edgar Bartlett and Sarah (Mumford) G.; grad. Mich. State Normal Coll., Ypsilanti, 1894; B.S., Harvard, 1904; m. Julia Emery, of East Tawas, Mich., June 25, 1904; children—Elizabeth, William, Edgar. Supt. schs., East Tawas, 1895-1902; teacher of science, Central High Sch., Cleveland, O., 1904-09; head of geography dept., Teachers' Coll., Cleveland, 1909-28; dir. Ednl. Museum of Cleveland pub. schs. since 1914; lecturer on econ. geography, Cleveland Coll., 1925-29; asso. prof. Western Reserve Grad. Sch., 1925-37; sometime lecturer in summer sessions of U. of Wis., Columbia, George Peabody Coll., U. of Pa., U. of Washington, Clark U. Mem. Mich. Geol. Survey, 1896-1902; hydrographer U.S. Geol. Survey, 1902-05; spl. investigator, water supply of Lower Mich., 1904. Mem. Am. Geog. Soc., Western Reserve Hist. Soc., Am. Assn. of Museums, Nat. Acad. of Visual Instruction (pres.), Nat. Council of Geography Teachers. Republican. Episcopalian. Clubs: Harvard, City Club, Pine Ridge Country. Author: Water Supply of Lower Michigan, 1906; Geological Report of Arenac County, Mich., 1909; Geography and History of Ohio (with W. B. Guitteau), 1921; Visual Aids in the School (monograph), 1925; Work Book in Geography, 1926; Visual Education in Europe (monograph), 1930. Contbr. to Orth's Cleveland, also 40 articles in ednl. mags. Home: 2458 Queenston St., Cleveland OH‡

GRESS, ERNEST MILTON, botanist; b. Fulton County, Pa., Aug. 1, 1876; s. George B. and Rebecca (De Shong) G.; M.E., Shippensburg (Pa.) Normal Sch., 1896; Ph.B., Bucknell U., Lewisburg, Pa., 1907; M.A., U. of Pittsburgh, 1912, Ph.D., 1920; m. Nora Booth Gress, May 16, 1901; children—LaRue Ernestine (Mrs. George Lehman), Margaret Rebecca (Mrs. Thomas R. Tatnall), Dorothy Evelyn (Mrs. Russel Dougherty). Teacher pub. and high schs., Pa., 1893-1920; state botanist of Pa. since 1920. Mem. Bot. Soc. America, A.A.A.S., Pa. Acad. Science. Methodist. Mason. Author: Grasses of Pennsylvania, 1924; Common Wild Flowers of Pennsylvania, 1928; Poisonous Plants of Pennsylvania, 1934; also bulls. and mag. articles. Home: Camp Hill, Pa. Address: 2000 Hight St., Camp Hill PA‡

GRIERSON, JOHN, motion picture producer; b. Kilmadock, Scotland, April 26, 1898; s. Robert Morrison and Jane (Anthony) G.; educated Glasgow and Durham Universities (philosophy); LL.D. (hon.) Glasgow University, 1948; Rockefeller fellow Political Science, U. of Chicago; m. Margaret Taylor, Jan. 1930. Founder Empire Marketing Bd. and Gen. Post Office film units for British Govt., 1929-35; producer and asso. in prodn. more than 1000 documentary films, including Drifters, Song of Ceylon, Night Mail; founder, Film Centre, London, 1939; film adviser to Australian and N. Z. govts., 1939; film commr. Can., gen. mgr. War Information Bd., Canada, 1939-45; director mass communications and public information for UNESCO, 1947-48; film adivser to South African government, 1949; controller of films for Brit. Govt., 1949; exec. producer Group 3, Ltd., 1950. vis. prof. McGill U., 1969-71. Member Commission Freedom of the Press, United States, 1944-46. Author: Grierson on Documentary (book, edited by Forsyth Hardy, Collins, London), 1946; articles on the arts and film edn. for Brit. and Am. jours. Home: Bath England Died Feb. 19, 1972.

GRIFFIN, ANGUS MACIVOR, univ. dean; b. Franklin, N.H., Feb. 4, 1910; s. Chester A. and Maude (Scribner) G.; Ph.B., Brown U., 1931, A.M., 1933, Ph.D., 1938; m. Ruth Clark, Oct. 22, 1938. Instr. Brown U., 1938-40; asst. prof. George Washington U., 1940-44, asso. prof. bacteriology, 1944-49, prof. bacteriology, 1949-70, asst. dean, 1955-57, associate dean, 1957-70. Fellow Am. Pub. Health Assn.; mem. Soc. Am. Bacteriologists, Am. Assn. Immunologists, Soc. Exptl. Biology and Medicine; Washington Acad. Medicine, A.A.A.S., Sigma Xi. Club: Cosmos (Washington). Contbr. articles profl. publs. Home: Falls Church VA Died June 24, 1970; buried Franklin NH

GRIFFIN, BULKLEY SOUTHWORTH, newspaperman; b. Springfield, Mass., Aug. 16, 1893; s. Solomon Bulkley and Ida (Southworth) G.; ed. Springfield Central High Sch., 1909-12; B.A., Williams College, 1916; married Isabel Kinnear, July 8, 1926; 1 daughter, Charmain (Mrs. John Clark, Jr.). Reporter, city editor and Washington coorespondent, Springfield (Mass.) Republican, 1916-17, 1919-22; founder, owner Griffin-Larrabee News Bur., Washington, serving a group of daily newspapers, from 1922. Served in U.S. Navy and U.S. Army during World War; disch. 2d lt. Army Air Service (pilot), 1919. War corr. with 3d Army, Europe, Jan.-June 1945. Clubs: National Press, Overseas Writers, Internat. (Washington). Author: Offbeat History. Donated collection of Mark Twain books, including many in fgn. langs., to Buffalo and Erie County (N.Y.) Library. Home: Washington Died May 15, 1967; buried Timber Ridge Cemetery, nr. Lexington VA

GRIFFIN, FRANK LOXLEY, college pres.; b. Topeka, Kan., Aug. 19, 1881; s. James Franklin and Hetty Rhess (Parsons) G.; B.S., U. of Chicago, 1903, M.S., 1904, fellow in astronomy, 1904-06, Ph.D., magna cum laude, 1906; biomathematic, econometric study in Europe, 1931; LL.D. (honorary), Reed College, 1956; married Mary Louisa Chambers, August 7, 1905; children—Helen Chambers, Ruth Hardy, Frank Loxley, Alice Rhees. On staff Yerkes Obs., Williams Bay, Wis., summer, 1905; instr. mathematics, 1906-09, asst. prof., 1909-11, Williams Coll., prof. mathematics, Reed Coll., Portland, Ore., 1911-52, mem. adminstrn. com. 1920-21, 24, president 1954-56; dir. Mathematics Teaching Seminar, Reed Coll., 1939-40; lectr. U. So. Cal., summer 1937; vis. prof. Weselyan U., 1952-53; vis. prof. Newcomb Coll., 1953-54; lectr. confs. on mathematics, U. of N.C. and Univ. Wash., 1954; member commn. on Place of Mathematics in Secondary Schs.; mem. bd. regents Multnomah Coll., v.p., 1952. Citation for public service, U. Chgo., 1949; citation for service to sci., Oregon Academy Science, 1949. Fellow A.A.A.S.; mem. Am. Math. Soc., Mathematic Assn. Am. (govs. 1940-42, v.p. 1952-53), Nat. Council Teachers of Math., Circolo Matermatico di Palermo, Northwest Sci. Assn., Am. Assn. Univ. Profs. (v.p. 1944-45), Econometric Society, Oregon Academy Sci. (pres. 1950), Sons of Am. Revolution, Sigma Xi, Phi Beta Kappa. Republican. Baptist. Club: City (board govs. 1941-44). Author: Introduction to Mathematical Analysis, 1921, enlarged edit., 1936; Periodic Orbits (with F. R. Moulton, et al.), 1920; Mathematical Analyiss—Higher Course, 1926; Introduction to Spherical Trigonometry (pamphlet), 1943. Contbr. scientific papers and articles on mathematics, astronomy, and population. Foreign corr. Comitati Italiano per lo studio dei problemi delle popolazione. Home: Portland OR Died Nov. 9, 1969.

GRIFFIN, FREDERICK ROBERTSON, clergyman; b. Zanesville, O., May 3, 1876; s. Richard Andrew and Tabitha Folks (Taylor) Griffin; B.A., Bates College, Lewiston, Maine, 1898, D.D., 1923; S.T.B., Harvard, 1901, D.D., 1936; D.D., Amherst, 1943; married Edith Josephine Bell, October 9, 1901 (died November 30, 1939); children—Cynthia, Frederick Robertson. Ordained Unitarian ministry, 1901; pastor All Souls Church, Braintree, Massachusetts, 1901-09, Church of the Messiah, Montreal, Canada, 1909-17, 1st Church, Philadelphia, 1917-47. Mem. Academy Political Science of New York (life), Indian Rights Assn. (dir.), Pub. Edn. and Child Labor Assn. (dir.), Community Health and Civic Assn. (dir.), Joseph Priestley Conf. of Unitarian Chs. (pres. 1933-34), N.E. Soc. of Pa. (pres. 1934-36), Am. Unitarian Assn. (dir.). Mem. bd. of preachers, Harvard, 1934-36, 1938-42; v.p. Seaman's Ch. Inst. Clubs: Union League, Contemporary (pres. 1929-31), Harvard. Home: 523 Oakley Road, Haverford, Pa. Office: 2125 Chestnut St., Philadelphia 3 PA‡

GRIFFIN, LAWRENCE EDMONDS, zoologist; b. Dalton, N.Y., Sept. 10, 1874; s. Milton Joseph and Dona (Edmonds) G.; B.A., Ph.B., Hamline U., 1895; post-grad. study, U. of Minn., 1895-98; Ph.D., Johns Hopkins, 1900; m. Estelle Edwards, of Hamline, Minn., Jan. 1, 1901; children—Curtis Edwards, Lawrence Milton, Richard Edmonds. Instr. in biology, Western Reserve U., 1900-02; prof. biology, Mo. Valley Coll., Marshall, Mo., 1902-08; research asst., Carnegie Inst., 1904-05; asst. and asso. prof. zoology, U. of Philippines, 1908-13, also dean Coll. of Liberal Arts, 1910-13; prof. zoology, U. of Pittsburgh, 1914-20; prof. biology, Reed Coll., Portland, Ore., since 1920; custodian Dept. of Herpetology, Carnegie Mus. Fellow A.A.A.S.; mem. Soc. Am. Zoologists, Am. Micros. Soc. (pres.), Am. Ecol. Soc., Am. Soc. Herpetology, Phi Beta Kappa, Sigma Xi, Omicron Delta Kappa. Republican. Unitarian. Author of numerous papers on zool. subjects. Home: 1325 E. 31st St., Portland OR‡

GRIFFIN, LEE HENRY, sch. and coll. textbook pub.; b. Richland Center, Wis., Apr. 2, 1891; s. Warren Irvin and Cynthia (Shuckhart) G.; student Lawrence Coll., LaCrosse State Coll.; Ph.B., U. Chgo., 1915; student U. London, Columbia; married Janet McQuiston, 1918 (deceased); m. 2d, Helen Osborn, 1929. High sch. prin., Cashton, Wis.; supt. Ontario and Bangor, Wis.; with Ginn & Co., Chgo. and Boston, 1915-61, successively rep., Midwestern mgr., partner, 1933, dir., 1940-63, v.p., 1953-58, chmn., 1958-61, ret. Served from pvt. to 1st lt., U.S. Army, 1918-21; AEF in France. Mem. Am. Assn. Sch. Adminstrs., Nat. Soc. Secondary Edn., Am. Textbook Pubs. Inst., Beta Theta Pi. Methodist. Mason (Shriner). Clubs: Chicago Athletic. Olympia Country Club. South Shore Country. Home: Chicago IL Died Mar. 29, 1963; interred Mt. Moriah Mausoleum, Kansas City MO

GRIFFIN, MARK ALEXANDER, physician; b. Wingate, N.C., Aug. 26, 1883; s. William Powell and Susannah Ellen (Hamilton) G.; student U. of N.C., 1911-14; M.D., Jefferson Med. Coll., Philadelphia, Pa., 1917; m. Penelope Clary Brothers, Oct. 8, 1919; children—Mark Alexander, Richard Hamilton, James Arthur. Mem. staff State Hosp. for Nervous and Mental Diseases, Morgantown, N.C., 1917-20; president and medical director Applachian Hall, Asheville, N.C., 1920-68; president Asheville Holding Company. Member of Medical Advisory Board, 4th N.C. District, World War. Fellow Am. Coll. Physicians; mem. A.M.A., State Med. Soc. of N.C., Southern Med. Assn., Tri-State Med. Assn., Am. Psychiatric Assn., Buncombe County Med. Soc., N.C. Neuro-Psychiatric Assn., Neuro-Psychiatric Assn. (past pres.). Democrat. Episcopalian. Mason (Shriner); mem. Rotary Internat. Asheville NC Died May 20, 1968; buried Calvary Episcopal Cemetery, Arden NC

GRIFFITH, FRANK LESLIE, business exec.; b. Sheldon, Ill., Mar. 24, 1897; s. Alvin Dorsey and Anna Belle (Floyd) G.; A.B., Lake Forest (Ill.) Coll., 1918; m. Anne L. Nylen, Oct. 4, 1918 (divorced July 22, 1936); children—Jane (Mrs. John Sebastian II), Lesley Anne (Mrs. Elmer C. Sproul), Frank Leslie. Began as statistical clerk The Peoples Gas Light and Coke Co., Chicago, 1919, executive office assistant, 1925, v.p. and comptroller, 1934-57, sr. v.p., from 1957; sr. v.p., dir. Chicago Dist. Pipeline Co.; dir. Union Hill Gas Storage Co., Natural Gas Pipeline Co. of Am., Chicago and Illinois Western R.R., Peoples Production Company. Director, treasurer Junior Achievement of Chgo., Inc. Mem. Am. Gas Assn. Republican. Club: Illinois Athletic (Chgo.). Home: Zion IL Died Jan. 1969.

GRIFFITH, FREDERIC RICHARDSON, surgeon; b. Phila., Sept. 17, 1873; s. David R. and Sarah Jane (Richardson) G.; ed. Friends, schs., Phila., and Camden, N.J., grad., 1892, Pa. Nautical Sch., Phila., 1892; M.D., U. of Pa., 1897; m. Lucile Andrews Menken, of New York, Dec. 12, 1900. Surgeon since 1897; surgeon Bellevue Dispensary, 1899-1904; pub. lecturer, on practical surgery, under direction New York City Bd. Edn., 1904-5; examiner First Aid to the Injured Soc., New York, since 1904; lecturer and examiner on first aid to New York City police and fire depts. since 1905. Acting asst. surgeon, 3d Regt. Inf. N.G., Pa., 1897-8. Fellow N.Y. Acad. Medicine; mem. N.Y. Hist. Soc. Sculptor since 1905; studied France, Italy; served in studio C. Daal Magelssen; executed 4 groups. Mem. Friends Meeting. Inventor; chloroform inhaler; eyed grooved dir.; modern enclosed ambulance; instruments to increase safety of anaesthetics, to increase scope of cocaine surgery, and to diagnosticate hydrocele; combination gas and liquid anaesthetizing inhaler; new surg. mallet, chisel, operating table bed, med. chart, and various other devices. Del. 13th Internat. Peace Congress, Lucerne, 1905. Author: Wounds (pamphlet), 1902; Handbook of Surgery, 1904; revised edit. Stoney's Bacteriology and Surgical Technic for Nurses, 1905. Contbr. in surgery to Internat. Clinics, and more than 150 articles in professional and scientific jours. Address: 49 E. 64th St., New York NY‡

GRIFFITH, HARRY MELVIN, M.D.; b. Clinton, Ill., Apr. 14, 1873; s. Isaac and Elsie (Griffith) G.; M.D., Washington U. Med. Sch., 1905; m. Mabel Ware, June 3, 1911. Consulting oto-laryngologist and rhinologist, La Vina (Calif.) Hosp.; attending surgeon ear, nose and throat dept., Pasadena Hosp. Awarded Congressional Medal of Honor, for serving beyond the term of enlistment to help suppress the Philippine Insurrection. Fellow Am. Coll. Surgeons; mem. Am. Med. Assn., etc. Clubs: Kiwanis, University. Home: Twentynine Palms CA‡

GRIFFITH, HEBER EMLYN, lawyer; b. Utica, N.Y., Mar. 11, 1887; s. John D. and Mary (Lewis) G.; A.B., Cornell U., 1911, LL.B., 1914; m. Emily Wilcox, June 27, 1917 (dec. May 1924); 1 son, Hadley Woodward; m. 2d, Lyra Field, June 28, 1932 (dec. Apr. 1949); 1 dau., Nancy G. (Mrs. John True Bergeson); m. 3d, Leila Evans, May 11, 1950. Tchr. dist. sch., Ohio, Herkimer County, N.Y., 1905-06; admitted to N.Y. bar, 1914; practice law Utica, N.Y., 1915-69; mem. firm Griffith, Tibbits & Crego and predecessor firms, 1915-69; dir. atty. 1st Fed. Savs. and Loan Assn. Utica, 1942-69, Utica Duxbak Corp., Utica, 1942-69. First pres. Boys' Club Utica, 1928-43; 1st pres. Cosmopolitan Center Utica, 1938-43; mem. Recreation Commn. City of Utica, 1927-48. Trustee St. Luke's Meml. Hosp. Center, Lee N. Vedder and Grace Q. Vedder Found., Mabel W. Bishop Found. Appeal agt. Draft Bd. 3, Utica, 1943-69. Mem. Utica C. of C., Am., N.Y. State, Oneida County bar assns., Phi Beta Kappa, Acacia. Mason (33 degree, Shriner), Rotarian (past pres. Utica). Clubs: Yahnundasis Golf and Country, Ft. Schuyler, Cedar Lake. Home: Utica NY Died Oct. 7, 1969.

GRIFFITH, JOHN, actor; b. Hamilton, Ont., Dec. 18, 1869; s. John and Agnes G.; common school ed'n, Springfield, Ill.; m. July 2, 1899, Kathryn Purnell, Buffalo, N.Y. Worked 4 yrs. in steel mills, Springfield, Ill.; page in Ill. legislature, 1880-1; played Damon, Hamlet, Richard III, and Virginius at 17; 1st professional debut with Mrs. D. P. Bowers in Queen Elizabeth, 1888; 1st appearance as star, 1893; plays tragic characters; Mephisto in Faust; Richard III; Virginius; leading roles in Fool's Revenge; The Bells; The Avenger, has also played Enemy To The King; Don Caesar De Bazan; The Gladiator. Now starring in Macbeth and Richard III. Address: Springfield IL‡

GRIFFITH, RICHARD, motion picture critic; born Winchester, Va., Oct. 6, 1912; s. Richard Edward and Annie Douglas (Williams) G.; student Va. Episcopal Sch., Lynchburg, 1930-31; A.B., Haverford College, 1935; Rockefeller Found. fellowship (research film history), 1937-38; m. Ann Gilman Warren, Nov. 26,

1947. Motion picture critic Northern Va. Daily, Winchester, 1935-37; theatre mgr. N.Y. World's Fair, 1939-40; asst. to curator Mus. Modern Art Film Library, 1940-42, asst. to dir. 1949-51, curator Mus. of Modern Art Film Library, 1951-65; lectr. on motion pictures Weselyan University, Middletown, Conn., 1967; engaged as film editor, photographic center, signal corps U.S. Army, 1942-46; exec. dir. Nat. Bd. review of Motion Pictures, N.Y. City, 1946-49; N.Y. film corr. Los Angeles Times from 1949. Former member Nat. Bd. Rev. Motion Pictures (mem. com. exceptional films). Author: The Film Till Now: A Survey of World Cinema (with Paul Rotha), 1950; Documentary Film (with Paul Rotha and Sinclair Reed), 1952; The World of Robert Flaherty, 1953; Anatomy of a Motion Picture, 1959; also articles on films in nat. publs. Editor Am. edit., Grierson on Documentary 1947. Co-author: The Movies, 1957. Address: Middletown CT Died Oct. 17, 1969; buried Mt. Hebron Cemetery, Winchester VA

GRIFFITH, SAMUEL HENDERSON, surgeon U. S. N.; apptd. from Pa. asst. surgeon, Dec. 15, 1877; passed asst. surgeon, Dec. 15, 1880; surgeon, March 30, 1895; served at Museum of Hygiene, Washington, 1893-8; was assigned to U. S. S. Mayflower, March, 1898, serving in war against Spain. Rank of lt.-comdr. U. S. N. Mem. Am. Chem. Soc.; m. Ellen Coxe. Address: 1308 N. H. Av., Washington‡

GRIFFITH, VIRGIL A., judge; b. Lawrence County, Miss., Aug. 10, 1874; s. Milton A. and Margaret (Neal) G.; A.B., U. of Miss., 1897; m. Florence Neville, July 16, 1903; children—Margaret (Mrs. R. G. Gillespie), Susan H. (Mrs. V. D. Hagaman), James Neville. Admitted to Miss. bar, 1898, and began practice at Ellisville; chancellor, 8th Chancery Dist., Miss., 1920-28; asso. justice, Supreme Court, Miss., since 1929. Mem. Miss. Code Commn., 1928-30. Mem. Phi Kappa Psi, Phi Delta Phi. Democrat. Presbyterian. Author: Mississippi Chancery Practice. 1925. Home: Edwards Hotel. Office: New Capitol Bldg., Jackson MS*‡

GRIFFITH, WENDELL HORACE, scientist; b. Churdan, Ia., Nov. 7, 1895; s. George William and May Elizabeth (Fowler) G.; B.S., Greenville (Ill.) Coll., 1917; M.S., U. of Ill., 1919, Ph.D., 1923; m. Harriet Isabel Leas, Aug. 31, 1922; 1 son, Wendell Horace. Instr., Cooper Coll., Sterling, Kan., 1919-20, U. of Mich., 1922-23; dept. of biol. chemistry, St. Louis U., 1923-48, prof., 1940-48; chmn., prof. dept. biochem. and nutrition, U. Tex. Med. Sch., 1948-51; chmn., prof. dept. physiol. chemistry U. Cal., 1951-63, prof. emeritus, 1963-68; Gen. Edn. Bd. fellow, Oxford Eng., 1936-37; mil. leave absence, 1941-45; leave absence as FAO nutrition advisor in India, 1959-60, as dir. Life Scis. Research Office, Fedn. Am. Socs. for Experimental Biology, 1962-68; consultant Office Surgeon Gen., Army, 1946-68; cons. Office Surgeon Gen., USPHS, 1949-53, 55-68. Mem. Food and Nutrition board, NRC, 1950-61. Served with U.S.A., 1918-19; col. Sanitary Corps. U.S.A., 1941-46; nutrition officer, chief nutrition br., European Theater Operations, 1942-45. Decorated Legion of Merit, Bronze Star (World War II); recipient Outstanding Civilian Service award Dept. Army, 1966. Fellow Am. Public Health Assn., A.A.A.S., N.Y. Acad. Sci.; mem. Am. Soc. Biol. Chemists, Am. Inst. Nutrition (pres. 1950-51), Am. Chemical Soc., Soc. for Exptl. Biol. and Medicine. A.M.A. (council on Foods and Nutrition, 1953-59), Inst. Food Technologists, Sigma Xi, Alpha Omega Alpha, Phi Lambda Upsilon. Club: Cosmos, Asst. editor: Nutrition Reviews, 1946-50, editorial com., 1952-68. Editorial bd., Jour. Biol. Chemistry, 1949-59. Home: Bethesda MD Died Feb. 5, 1968; buried Oak Hill Cemetery, Kirkwood MO

GRIGGS, THOMAS NEWELL, lawyer; b. Bellevue, Pa., May 20, 1903; s. Thomas Campbell and Christine (Newell) G.; B.S., Carnegie Inst. Tech., 1924; J.D., U. Pitts., 1928; m. Anne Hathaway Kiskaddon, July 13, 1928; 1 dau., Eleanor Christine (Mrs. Francis B. Nimick, Jr.). Admitted to Pa. bar, 1928; partner Griggs, Moreland, Blair & Douglass, Pitts. Pres., dir. Island Properties, Inc.; dir. mem. exec. com. G.C. Murphy Co.; dir. Washington Oil Co., Morgan & Lindsey, Inc., Terry Farris Stores, Inc., M & L Equipment Co., M & L Realty Co., Morris Stores Corp. Chmn. adv. com. U.S. Dist. Ct., Western Dist. of Pa. Recipient Alumni Award of Merit, Carnegie Inst. Tech. Mem. bd. govs. Amen Corner; mem. bd. dir. D.T. Watson Home for Crippled Children. Mem. Am. (mem. first bd. Jr. Bar Conf.), Allegheny Co. (pres., chmn. exec. com.), Pa. (gov.) bar assns., Am. Judiciary Soc., Am. Law Institute, Engineers Soc. of Western Penn., U. of Pitts. Sch. Law Alumni Assn. (past pres.), Phi Kappa Psi, Theta Tau, Delta Theta Phi. Clubs: Allegheny Country, Duquesne, Harvard-Yale-Princeton, Law, Tax (Pitts.), Edgeworth. Home: Sewickley PA Died Jan. 23, 1972; buried Allegheny Cemetery, Pittsburgh PA

GRIMES, DONALD ROBERT, retail food store exec.; b. Chgo., Aug. 12, 1906; s. J. Frank and Barbara (Adam) G.; A.B., U. Ill., 1928; m. Edythe Homan, Nov. 2, 1929; children—Elaine, Diane. Clk. Atlantic & Pacific Tea Co. store, 1928; warehouseman, Sprague Warner & Co., 1928; store engr. Ind. Grocers Alliance, 1929-33, supervision dept. rep., 1933-38, director supervision, 1938-40, assistant to president, 1940-52, pres., from 1952; pres., dir. Ind. Grocers' Alliance Distbg. Co. Trustee U. Ill. Served as capt. signal corps, AUS, 1943-46. Christian Scientist. Home: Evanston IL Died Mar. 26, 1972; cremated.

GRIMES, WILLIAM HENRY, editor; b. Bellevue, O., March 7, 1892; s. Samuel L. and Lucy (Bush) G.; student, Western Reserve U., Cleveland, 1910-13; m. Iva Mae McCormick, Aug. 5, 1915; children—Jane (Mrs. R. B. Benton, dec.), William Henry (killed in action), John Alan. Reporter for Ohio newspapers, 1913-20; mgr. Washington office, United Press, 1920, New York office, 1921; with Washington office, Wall Street Jour., 1923-24, mng. editor New York office, 1934-41, editor since 1941. Awarded Pulitzer Prize for distinguished editorial writing, 1946. Mem. Am. Soc. of Newspaper Editors. Home: Delray Beach FL Died Jan 1972.

GRIMM, JOHN CRAWFORD MILTON, educator; b. Columbus, O., Feb. 1, 1891; s. Willard Conard Preston and Lucy Ann (Crawford) G.; A.B., Ohio State U., 1911, A.M., 1912; Ph.D., U. of Pa. (Harrison Fellowship, 1914-16), 1916; student Sorbonne, U. of Paris, 1919; m. Margaret Moore Craver, June 15, 1929; children—John Russell, Forrest Craver, Lucy Emily. High sch. teacher, Plain City, O., 1912-13; prof. Latin and Greek, Bridgewater (Va.) Coll., 1913-14, Juniata (Pa.) Coll., 1916-17; asst. prof. Latin and French, Ohio Wesleyan U., 1919-22; asso. prof. Romance langs. Dickinson Coll., Carlisle, Pa., 1922-35, prof. Romance langs. from 1935, chmn. dept. modern langs, from 1944, sec. faculty 1944-57, marshall from 1957. Pvt. U.S. Army, 1917-19; instr. in French, Carlisle Barracks, 1949-50. Mem. Pa. State Modern Lang. Assn., V.O.A. Methodist. Author: The Construction APO KOINOU in the Works of Horace, 1916. Cons. Brittanica World Lang. Dictionary, 1954. Stamp collector. Home: Carlisle PA Died Nov. 20, 1970; buried Westminster Cemetery, Carlisle PA

GRIMM, JOHN MURCHISON, lawyer; b. Henry County, Ill., Dec. 21, 1866; s. Charles Henry and Catherine (McLennan) G.; B.S., State U. of Ia., 1888, LL.B., 1890; m. Orphea Bealer, Dec. 27, 1894; 1 son, Donald Stephen. Admitted to Ia. bar, 1890, and practiced at Cedar Rapids until 1929; county atty. Linn County, Ia., 1893-98; gen. counsel Order Ry. Condrs. America, 1900-29; apptd. judge Supreme Court of Ia., 1929, and elected to same office, Nov. 1930, for term expiring 1936; resigned, 1932, to reenter practice of law; president Colo. Consol. Mining & Milling Co., Greater Cedar Rapids Co., Pawnee Land & Improvement Co.; v.p. and sec. Cereal City Realty Co.; dir. Cedar Rapids Food Products Co. In charge 9 counties, Ia., for Liberty Loan drives, World War. Former pres. Ia. Memorial Union (State U. of Ia). Mem. Am. Bar Assn., Greater Ia. Assn., Ia. State Chamber Commerce, Cedar Rapids Chamber Commerce, Delta Tau Delta, Phi Delta Phi, Order of Coif. Republican. Mason (32 deg., K.T., Shriner), K.P., Elk. Clubs: Kiwanis, Cedar Rapids Country (Cedar Rapids). Home: 852 4th Av. E. Office: Merchants Nat. Cedar Rapids IA*‡

GRIMMELSMAN, HENRY JOSEPH, bishop; b. Cincinnati, O., Dec. 22, 1890; s. G(erhard) Henry and Frances Elizabeth (Ronnebaum) G.; ed. Holy Family Sch. and St. Gregory Sem., Cincinnati, O.; student St. Joseph Coll., Collegeville, Ind., 1907-09, Mount St. Mary Sem., Mount Washington, Cincinnati, O., 1909-11; U. of Innsbruck, Austria, 1911-15, S.T.D., 1928. Ordained priest Roman Catholic Ch., consecrated bishop, 1944; bishop of Evansville, Ind., from Jan. 1945. Author of commentaries: Book of Exodus, 1927; Book of Ruth, 1930. Address: Evansville IN Died June 26, 1972.

GRINNELL, HAROLD C., educator; b. Broadalbin, N.Y., July 7, 1895; s. William Manning and Helen L. (Ovitt) G.; B.S., Cornell U., 1921, M.S., 1930, Ph.D., 1941; m. Alice Mary Hopkins, Nov. 8, 1922;children—Helen Alicia (Mrs. George O. Lewis), Barbara Jean (Mrs. Vail K. Haak). Federal Farm Bd. field agt., Burlington, Vt., 1930-31; acting head, dept. agrl. economics, U. of Vt., 1931-32; asst. prof. of agrl. economics, Univ. of N.H., 1932-40, asso. prof., 1940-47, prof., 1947-50, dean Coll. of Agr. and dir. of agrl. experiment sta. 1950-58, dean, coordinator of instrn., research, extension, 1958-61, prof. agrl. econs. and economist expt. sta., 1962-65, professor emeritus of resource econs., 1965-70. Active civic affairs, mem. sch. bd., zoning bd., budget com., etc. Delegate New Hampshire Constl. Conv., 1964. Served as lt., Coast Arty. Corps, World War I. Mem. Am. Assn. Univ. Profs. (asso. mem.), Phi Kappa Phi, Alpha Zeta, Helios, Sigma Phi Sigma. Mason (past master). Conglist. Author 6 publs. of agrl. expt. stas. Home: Durham NH Died Aug. 8, 1970.

GRISCOM, LLOYD CARPENTER, b. Riverton, N.J., Nov. 4, 1872; s. Clement Acton and Frances Canby (Biddle) G.; Ph.B., U. of Pa., 1891, LL.D., 1906; studied U. of Pa. Law Sch., 1891-93, New York Law Sch., 1895; sec. to Mr. Bayard, 1st ambassador to England, 1893-94; admitted to N.Y. bar, 1896; m. Elisabeth Duer, d. Frederic Bronson, of New York (dec.); children—Bronson Winthrop, Lloyd Preston; m. 2d, Audrey Margaret Elisabeth, d. Marlborough Crosse, of South Sea, Eng. Deputy dist. atty. New York, 1897; volunteer in Spanish-Am. War; commd. capt. and asst. q.-m; served 4 months in Cuba as a.-d.-c. to Maj.-Gen. James F. Wade; recommended for promotion, but resigned to reenter diplomacy apptd. sec. legation, Constantinople, July 1899; charge d'affaires, Constantinople, 1899-1901; E.E. and M.P. to Persia, 1901-02, to Japan, 1902-06 (during Russo-Japanese War); A.E. and P. to Brazil, Jan. 29, 1906-Mar. 3, 1907, to Italy, Mar. 6, 1907-June 14, 1909. Pres. N.Y. County Rep. Com., 1910-11 and former mem. Rep. State Com., N.Y.; del. Rep. Nat. Conv., Chicago, 1912. Hon. v.p., Community Service Soc. of New York; hon. pres. Am. Asiatic Assn. Mem. Italy America Soc., Am. Soc. of Royal Italian Orders, New York Water Color Club. Clubs: Knickerbocker, Century, Republican, Piping Rock. Contbr. to Phila. Sunday Press on travels in Central America. Apptd. maj., adj. gen.'s dept., 1917; ordered on active duty, June 26, as a.-a.-g., Eastern Dept.; made a.-a.-g. 77th Div., Nat. Army, at Camp Upton, N.Y., Aug. 1, 1917; with 77th Div. in France; later liaison officer staff of Gen. Pershing; promoted lt. col. Awarded D.S.M.; Knight Comdr. St. Michael and St. George (Brit.), 1919. Author: Tenth Avenue (stage melodrama and moving picture); Diplomatically Speaking (autobiography). Home: Luna Plantation, Tallahassee, Fla.; also Syosset, LI NY‡

GRISSOM, IRENE WELCH (MRS. CHARLES MEIGS GRISSOM), author; b. Greeley, Colo., Dec. 3, 1873; d. William Pringle and Theresa (Crittenden) Welch; Pd.B., Colo. State Teachers' Coll., Greeley, 1894, post-grad. work, 1927, also summer sch. student at Univ. of Montana, 1934, Univ. of Colorado, 1937; m. Charles Meigs Grissom, of Idaho Falls, Ida., September 2, 1903 (died March 1, 1935). Member Northwest Poetry Soc. Author: The Superintendent, 1910; A Daughter of the Northwest, 1918; The Passing of the Desert (verse), 1924; Verse of the New West, 1931; Under Desert Skies, 1936. Apptd. poet laureate of Ida. by Gov. C. C. Moore, 1923. Contbr. to mags. Democrat. Unitarian. Home: Idaho Falls ID‡

GRISWOLD, CLAYTON TRACY, exec.; b. Elmira, N.Y., May 12, 1901; s. Tracy Beadle and Mary Lovina (Carrier) G.; A.B., Amherst Coll., 1923; student U. of Paris, 1925-26; S.T.B., Biblical Sem. in N.Y., 1927; D.D. (hon.), Huron Coll., 1949; m. Miriam Rittenhouse Mayne, June 1, 1925; children—David, Lincoln, Maud Mary, Katharine. Ordained to ministry of Presbyn. Ch., 1927; asst. pastor, First Ch., Cortland, N.Y., 1927-30; pastor, Hobart, N.Y., 1930-34, Watkins Glen, N.Y., 1934-39; sec. youth work Presbyn. Gen. Council, N.Y.C., 1939-48; exec. dir. radio and television Presbyn. Ch., U.S.A., 1948-58; exec. sec. Mayne Ednl. Fund, from 1944. Served as sergt., N.Y. N.G., 1918-19. Trustee Bibl. Sem. in N.Y., 1941-50, Mayne Ednl. Fund (Newark). Mem. gen. bd. Nat. Council Chs.; chmn. Broadcasting and Film Committee, 1953-55; North American representative World Com. for Christian Broadcasting, Hon. life mem. Westminster Fellowship, 1948. Mem. Phi Delta Theta. Clubs: Lake Mohawk Golf, Sparta Chess. Author: The Youth Budget Plan, 1942; Youth Budget Program Guide, 1948; Religious Radio Expediters, 1949. Co-author: Broadcasting Religion, 1954. Home: Sparta NJ Died June 10, 1971; buried Ocean View Cemetery, Staten Island NY

GRISWOLD, RETTIG ARNOLD, surgeon; b. Peru, Ind., Apr. 17, 1898; s. Edward Harvey and Georgine (Rettig) G.; A.B., Harvard Coll., 1921; M.D., U. Louisville, 1925; m. Bonita Bligh, Aug. 8, 1923; children—Rettig Arnold, Bonita, Georgine, Annalee. Grad. tng. in pathology Louisville City Hosp. and U. Louisville, 1925-27; grad. tng. in surgery Western Res. U. and Lakeside Hosp., Cleve., 1927-32; asso. prof. surgery U. Louisville Med. Sch., 1932-37, prof. and head dept. surgery, 1938-52, prof. surgery, 1952-72. Cons. surgeon St. Joseph Infirmary, Ky. Bapt., Meth. and Evang., St. Anthony hosps., Kosair Crippled Children Hosp., John W. Norton Meml. Infirmary. Served as lt. j.g., Flying Corps USN, 1917-21; naval aviator, overseas service, 10 mos.; served to col., M.C., AUS, 1942-44; cons. in surgery 4th Service Command; chief Surg. Service Walter Reed Gen. Hosp., Washington, 1943. Decorated Legion of Merit (U.S.); Mil. Order of Ayacucha (Peru); recipient Citation Navy Dept.; Surgeon's award for distinguished service to safety Nat. Safety Council, 1963. Fellow A.C.S. (2d v.p. 1957-58), Am., Central surg. assns., mem. Societe Internationale de Chirurgie, Am. Assn. for Surgery of Trauma (founder; pres. 1951-52), Am. Bd. Surgery (founders' group), Soc. Surgery Alimentary Tract (a founder), Southeastern Surg. Congress (1st v.p. 1963-64), Western, So. surg. assns., A.M.A., So. Med. Assn. Alpha Kappa Kappa, Alpha Omega Alpha. Republican. Episcopalian. Club: Pendennis. Home: Louisville KY Died May 1, 1972; buried Cave Hill Cemetery, Louisville KY

GRISWOLD, THOMAS, JR., civil engr., cons. engr.; b. Ashtabula, O., Sept. 29, 1870; s. Thomas and Ruth Coleman (Hubbard) G.; B.S. in C.E., Case Sch. Applied

Science, 1896, C.E., 1908; m. Helen Josephine Dow, of Cleveland, O., Nov. 25, 1897 (died 1918); children—Josephine (Mrs. Louis Henry Ashmun), Nelson Dow, Lelia Ruth (Mrs. E. Rex Edick); m. 2d, Vera Ann Hadsall, of Midland, Mich., Oct. 17, 1918; children—Catherine Ann, Grant Hadsall. Chief engr. Dow Chem. Co., Midland, Michigan, 1897-1926, chief of patent department, 1927-37; cons. engineer since 1937; dir. Chem. State Savings Bank. Mem. Am. Inst. Chem. Engrs., Am. Chem. Soc., Am. Soc. Mech. Engrs., Phi Delta Theta, Tau Beta Pi, Sigma Xi. Episcopalian. Clubs: Saginaw Valley Torch, Midland Country. Home: Midland MI‡

GROCHOWSKI, LEON M., bishop; b. Skupie, Poland, Oct. 11, 1886; s. Albert and Victoria (Pienkowski) G.; student Rotwand and Wawelberg Poly., Warsaw, Poland, also Savonarola Theol. Sem., Scranton, Pa.; D.D. (hon.), Nashota (Wis.) House, 1952, Va. Theol. Sem., 1957; m. Bernice B. Baron; 1 son, Mitchell Leon. Ordained to ministry Polish National Cath. Ch., 1910; formerly pastor St. Adalberts Ch., Dickson City, Pa.; bishop of synod, 1924; 1st prime bishop of synod, 1953-69, also bishop of the central diocese; rector Savonarola Theological Sem. Decorated Cross of Polish Legions, Medal of Independence (Poland). Author 2 prayer books, also brochures. Editor: Straz, Polish Nat. Union Weekly, Rola Boza (God's Field), ch. weekly. Address: Scranton PA Died July 17, 1969; interred Polish Nat. Catholic Masoleum, Minooka PA

GROFE, FERDE (FERDINAND RUDOLPH VON GROFE), composer, conductor; b. N.Y.C., Mar. 27, 1892; s. Emil and Elsa Johanna (Bierlich) von G.; ed. primary school, Los Angeles; private school in Germany; St. Vincents, Los Angeles; early musical training by his mother, his grandfather, Bernhardt Bierlich (1st cellist Los Angeles Symphony Orchestra), and by his uncle, Julius Bierlich (concertmaster of same orchestra); studied harmony and counterpoint with C. E. Pemberton at U. of Southern Calif.; studied piano with Homer Grunn, Los Angeles, and Herman Wasserman, N.Y. City; orchestra scores with Maestro Pietro Floridia of N.Y. City; Mus.D., Illinois Wesleyan University, 1946; m. Ruth Harriet MacGloan, May 11, 1929; children—Ferdinand Rudolf, Jr., Anne Carlin; m. 2d, Anna May Lempton, January 12, 1952. Orchestra conductor on radio programs; made personal appearances as conductor at Hollywood Bowl, Lewisohn Stadium, Gershwin Memorial Program, Robin Hood Dell (Phila.), Carnegie Hall Concerts (1937-38), New York World's Fair (Ford Exhibit, Novachord Ensemble, 1939-40). Mem. Am. Soc. of Composers. Authors and Publishers, Phi Mu Alpha. Clubs: Nat. Travel, N.Y. Athletic; Bohemian, (San Francisco). Mason (K.T., 32 deg., Shriner). Compositions: Tabloid Suite, Mississippi Suite, March for Americans, Grand Canyon Suite, Kentucky Derby, Knute Rochne, Three Shades of Blue Suite, Christmas Eve, An American Biography (based on the life of Henry Ford), Ode to the Star Spangled Banner, Cafe Society Ballet, Ode to Freedom, Trylon and Perisphere, Symphony in Steel, Wheels Suite, Hollywood Suite, Blue Flame, Ruby" from Jewel Tones, Miss Mischief, Free Air, Templed Hills, 1941; Daybreak, 1942; Uncle Sam Stands Up, Skylines, 1943; Broadway at Night, 1945; Aviation Suite, 1946; Deep Nocturne, 1947 and some twenty others, 1948-72. Address: Los Angeles CA Died Apr. 3, 1972.

GROMAIRE, MARCEL, painter, engraver; b. Noyelles sur Bambre, Nord, France, July 24, 1892; s. Georges and Marie (Bisiaux) G.; student Lycee de Douai (Nord), Lycee Buffon (Paris); m. Helene Madelin; 1 son, Francois. Pioneer in revival of tapestry; painted pictures and watercolors of N.Y.C. and Paris: numerous exhibitions in Paris and abroad, noteably L. Carre's Gallery, Paris; paintings included in Paris and foreign museums and private collections. Juryman Carnegie Institute, 1950. Recipient 2d prize Carnegie Inst., 1952, Nat. Guggenheim prize (France), 1956); Grand Prix National des Arts, 1959. Served with French Army, 1913-19. Home: Paris France Died Apr. 11, 1971.

GRONER, DUNCAN LAWRENCE, judge; b. at Norfolk, Va., Sept. 6, 1873; s. Gen. Virginius D. and Katharine (Campbell) G.; mother d. late John A. Campbell, justice Sup. Ct. of the U.S.; student Washington and Lee Univ., 1888-92, LL.D., 1933; student Univ. of Va., 1893-94; LL.D., Nat. Univ., Washington, D.C., 1932; m. Anne Vaughan, Apr. 11, 1898 (died Feb. 13, 1930); children—John Vaughan, Duncan Lawrence, Duncan Goldthwaite; m. 2d, Marian Edwards Shouse, July 28, 1934. In practice at Norfolk, 1894-1921; del. Republican Nat. Conv. 5 times, 1904-20; U.S. atty. Eastern Dist. of Va., 1910-13; U.S. dist. judge, Eastern Dist. of Va., by apptmt. of President Harding, 1921-31; judge U.S. Court of Appeals, Washington, D.C., since Mar. 3, 1931, chief judge, 1938-48, retired Feb. 1, 1948. Mem. bd. Washington Nat. Monument Soc., Woodrow Wilson Birthplace Foundn. Mem. Phi Delta Theta, Phi Beta Kappa. Home: 2101 Conn. Av., Washington DC‡

GRONER, JOHN VAUGHAN, lawyer; b. Norfolk, Va., Sept. 21, 1901; s. Duncan Lawrence and Anne (Vaughan) G.; student U. Va., 1922; m. Dorothy Teter, Dec. 29, 1954; children—Barbara (Mrs. E. Sheldon Spicer, Jr.), Sally Anne (Mrs. William B. Terry, Jr.), Anne Vaughan (Mrs. Walter G. Spilsbury), Beverly Jane. Admitted to Va. bar, 1921, D.C. bar, 1926, N.Y. State bar, 1931; practiced in Norfolk, 1922-26; spl. asst. atty. gen., Washington, 1926-29; mem. firm Fish & Neave, N.Y.C., 1929-72. Home: Greenwich CT Died June 1, 1972.

GROPIUS, WALTER ADOLF, architect; b. Berlin, Germany, May 18, 1883; s. Walter and Manon (Schwarnweber) G.; ed. Humanistisches Gymnasium, Berlin, 1903; Technische Hochschule, Munchen, 1903-04, archtl. office of Prof. Solf and Wichards, Berlin, 1904, Technische Hochschule, Berlin, 1905-07; hon. Dr. Engring., Technische Hochschule, Hannover, 1929; M.A. (hon.), Harvard, 1942; D.Sc., Western Reserve U., 1951; Arts.D. (hon.) Harvard, 1953; Dr. Architecture (honorary) North Carolina State College, 1953; D.Sc. (honorary) University Sydney (Australia, 1954; Doctor Honoris Causa, U. Brazil, 1955; L.H.D. (honorary), Columbia University, 1961, Williams College, 1963; A.F.D. (honorary), Pratt Institute, 1961; Dr. Philosophy honoris causa Freie Universitat Berlin, 1963; m. Alma (Schindler) Mahler, 1916; 1 dau., Alma Manon; m. 2d, Ise Frank, 1923; 1 daughter, Beate Eveline. Came to U.S., 1937, Assistant to Professor Peter Behrens, Berlin, Germany, 1908-10; archtl. practice, own office, Berlin, 1910-14; united two art schools under name of Staatliches Bauhaus, Weimar, Germany, 1918 and served as dir.; moved Bauhaus to Dessau, 1925; pvt. practice, Berlin, 1928-34; partner with Maxwell Fry, architect, London, 1935-37; sr. prof. architecture, chmn. Sch. Architecture Harvard, 1938, later prof. emeritus. Formed The Architects, Collaborative, 1946. Cons. Container Corp. of Am., Michael Reese Hosp., Chgo. Vice pres. General Panel Corp., 1942-52; mem. Vis. Com. Sch. Architecture and Planning, Mass. Inst. Tech., 1953-55. Served in German Hussar Regt., No. 15, 1904-05, 1914-18. Decorated Iron Cross. Recipient Grand Prix Internat. d'Architecture, Matarazzo Found., San Paulo, Brazil, 1953; Royal Gold Medal, The Royal institute of British Architects, London, 1956; Hanseatic Goethe prize, U. Hamburg, Germany, 1956; Ernst Reuter medal, City of Berlin, 1957; Grand Cross of Merit with Star, Fed. Rep. Germany, 1958; Gold medal, A.I.A., 1959; Grand State prize Architecture, Germany, 1960, Gold Albert Medal, Royal Soc. of Arts (London), 1961, Goethe Preis, Frankfurt Am. Main, 1961, Kaufmann Internat. Design award, 1961; Cornelius Gurlitt medal German Acad. City and Regional Planning; Presdl. medal Art Directors Club N.Y., 1964. Hon. senator Hochschule furbildende Kunste Berlin. Hon. prof. Escuela Nacional de Ingenieros, Lima, Peru, 1953; Benjamin Franklin fellow Royal Society Arts, London. A.N.A.; hon. academican Royal Acad. Arts, London. Fellow A.A.A.S., A.I.A.; v.p. Internat. Congress Modern Architecture; mem. Am. Soc. Planners and Architects, Inst. Sociology, Royal Society Arts (honorary royal designer for industry) (both London), Nat. Inst. Arts and Letters, Phi Beta Kappa (1942); honorary mem. Royal Institute Brit. Architects, Honorary and corresponding member several foreign professional archtl. associations and socs. Club: Harvard (N.Y.). Author: The New Architecture and the Bauhaus (translated from German by T.M. Shand), 1935; The Bauhaus (1919-1928) 1938; Rebuilding Our Communities, 1946; Scope of Total Architecture, 1955; Apollo in the Democracy, 1969; also other books published in Germany. Editor: Bauhaus 1919-28 (with others), 1938. Contbr. to jours. Home: Lincoln MA Died July 5, 1969.

GROSE, GEORGE RICHMOND, clergyman; b. Nicholas County, W.Va., July 14, 1869; s. Andrew Dixon and Mary Estaline (Harrah) G.; A.B., Ohio Wesleyan U., 1894, A.M., 1896, D.D., 1908, LL.D., 1916; S.T.B., Boston U. Sch. of Theology, 1896; m. Lucy Dickerson, June 28, 1894; children—Mrs. Mary Frances Witman, Wilbur Dickerson, Helen, Virginia, William Edwin. Ordained M.E. ministry, 1896; pastor Cherry Valley Ch., Leicester, Mass., 1894-97, 1st Ch., Jamaica Plain, Boston, 1897-1900, 1st Ch., Newton, Mass., 1900-05, 1st Ch., Lynn, Mass., 1905-08, Grace Ch., Baltimore, 1908-12; pres. De Pauw U., Oct. 1912-24; bishop M.E. Church, assigned to Peking, China, 1924-32 (resigned as bishop). Mem. Ind. State Bd. Edn., 1913-24. Mem. Gen. Conf. M.E. Ch., 1916, 20, 24; pres. Ednl. Assn. M.E. Ch., 1917; mem. Univ. Senate; formerly mem. N. Indiana Conf. Mem. Sigma Alpha Epsilon. Clubs: Twentieth Century (Boston); Eclectic, City (Baltimore); Columbia (Indianapolis); University (Pasadena). Religion editor; Pasadena Star-News, Press-Telegram (Long Beach). Author: The Outlook for Religion, 1913; Religion and the Mind, 1915; Life of James W. Bashford, 1922; The New Soul in China, 1927; Edward Rector—A Story of the Middle West, 1928; The Man from Missouri, 1943. Contbr. to various periodicals. Home: 1420 Morada Pl., Altadena CA‡

GROSS, ALFRED OTTO, biologist; b. Atwood, Ill., Apr. 8, 1883; s. Henry and Sophia (Gross) G.; A.B., U. of Ill., 1908; research scholarship, Bermuda Biol. Sta., 1910-11; Edward Austin research fellow, Harvard, 1911-12, Ph.D., 1912; D.Sc. (honorary), Bowdoin College, 1952; married Edna Grace Gross, July 2, 1913; children—William Albert, Thomas Alfred, Edna Louise (Mrs. Otis N. Minot). Ornithologist, Illinois Natural History Survey, 1906-08; instructor in biology, Bowdoin College, 1912-13, asst. prof. biology, 1913-22, prof., 1922-53, emeritus, 1953; Joshiah Little prof. natural sci. Bowdoin, 1950. Ornithologist, Roosevelt Wild Life Experiment Sta., 1924; in charge Heath Hen Investigation, 1923-27; in charge N.E. Ruffled Grouse Investigation, 1925-35; research at Barro Colorado Island, Panama, 1925, Ecuador and Costa Rica, 1927-28; in charge Prairie Chicken Investigation, Research Bureau, State of Wisconsin, 1929-30; dir. Ornithol. Expdn. to Labrador, 1931; orinthologist in charge Bowdoin-MacMillan Artic Expdn., 1934; mem. Ornithol. Expdn., Cuba, 1947, Panama, 1949, Alaska, 1951; ornithol. investigation around the world, 1953, 56, 58, Africa, 1959, Hawaiian Islands, 1960; official U.S. delegate Internat. Ornighol. Congress, Sweden, 1950, Switzerland, 1954; dir. Bowdoin Biol. Station, 1935; biologist, U.S. Fish and Wildlife Service, 1944; councilor Fedn. of Bird Clubs of New England, Inc.; Me. state adviser National Association of Audubon Societies; advisor to State of Maine dept. of fish and game. Trustee Am. Wild Life Inst. Fellow Am. Zoologists, Am. Ornithologists' Union (council), A.A.A.S., Am. Geog. Soc.; mem. N.E. Bird Banding Assn., (pres.) Boston Soc. Nat. Hist., British Ecol. Soc., Me. Audubon Soc. (pres.), Am. Wildlife Soc., Sigma Xi, Alpha Tau Omega, Gamma Alpha. Republican. Congregationalist. Club: Harvard Travellers. Editor, Maine Audubon Society Bulletin, 1945. Author: The Heath Hen, 1928. Contributor 150 papers on birds and biology to Auk, Jour. Exptl. Zoology, Bull. U.S. Nat. Museum, Wilson Bull., Condor. Brunswick ME Died May 9, 1970; buried Pine Grove Cemetery, Brunswick, Brunswick ME

GROSS, SIDNEY, artist; b. N.Y.C., Feb. 9, 1921; s. Morris and Esther (Alpern) G.; student Art Students' League, N.Y.C. (high sch. scholarship 1939, Schnackenberg scholar 1941, Tiffany fellow 1949); m. Katherine Kranther, Mar. 10, 1944; m. 2d, Juliana Penn, August 6, 1966; m. 3d, Elaine August, Mar. 12, 1969. One man shows Contemporary Arts Gallery, 1945, 46, Tirca Karlis Gallery, Provincetown, Mass., 1960, 61, Frank Rehn Gallery, N.Y.C., 1949, 50, 51, 53, 54, 56, 58, 59, 61, 63, 67, 69; group shows Met. Mus., Whitney Mus., N.A.D., Pa. Acad., Corcoran Galleries, Va. Biennial. Toledo Mus., Albright Gallery, Carnegie Inst., U. Neb., Ill. Wesleyan, U. Ill., Hallmark Art Award show, Pepsi-Cola Gallery, U.Ga., Butler Art Inst., Mpls. Art Inst., N.Y. Armory Show, Brklyn. Mus., Mus. Modern Art, N.Y.C., Inst. Contemporary Art, Boston, W.R. Nelson Gallery, Va. Mus. Fine Arts, Detroit Inst. Art, Joslyn Art Mus., Art U.S.A., Washington Gallery Modern Art, Des Moines Art Center, Isaac Delgado Mus., Fedn. Modern Painters and Sculptors Am., Audubon Artists, Am. Acad. Arts and Letters, Nat. Inst. Arts and Letters, Riverside Mus., Am. Fedn. Artists Nat. Tour, Hallmark European Tour; works in permanent collection Whitney Mus. Am. Art, Lempert Inst., Brandeis, Cornell univs., U. Omaha, Mt. Holyoke Coll., U. Ga., Butler Art Inst., Am. Acad. Arts and Letters, Riverside Mus., Corcoran Gallery, Balt. Mus., Chrysler Museum, Columbia U., Colby Coll., Univ. of Illinois, Morgan State College, Washington Gallery of Modern Art, Syracuse U., Allentown Mus., U. of Rochester, Norfolk Mus., Israel Mus. Jerusalem, U. Md., Mich. State U., Standard Financial Corp., James Michener Coll. of U. Tex., Okla. Art Center; works also pvt. collections; profiles, reprodns. of work in nat. mags., newspapers; tchr. Columbia U., also Art Students League; asso. prof. art Coll. Arts and Scis., U. Md., 1967-69. Recipient grand prize Art U.S.A., 1958; Childe Hassem Fund Purchase prize, 1950, 51, Hallmark Art award, 1949. Mem. Fedn. Modern Painters and Sculptors, Internat. Assn. Plastic New York City NY Died Nov. 17, 1969; buried Mount Ararat Cemetery, Farmingdale NY

GROSSINGER, JENNIE, hotel exec.; b. Vienna, Austria, June 16, 1892; d. Asher Selig and Malke (Grumet) Grossinger; H.H.D., Wilberforce U., New Eng. Coll.; m. Harry, May 25, 1912; children—Paul, Elaine Grossinger (Mrs. David Etess). Came to U.S., 1900, naturalized, 1919. Co-founder Grossinger Country Club, 1914, co-owner, 1914—. Co-chmn. Catskill region, Albert Einstein Coll. Medicine, Yeshiva U. Fellow Brandeis U., 1958; recipient Lafayette Baton award Rotary Internat., citation achievement Golden Slipper Square Club, Phila., Distinguished Service award Advt. Club of Washington, named Woman of Year, 52 Assn., 1957, Key Woman, Fedn. Jewish Philanthropies; citations Nat. Found. Muscular Dystrophy, City of Hope, Father Duffy Canteen, Council, Nat. Council To Combat Blindness, Zionist Orgn. Am., Music and Arts League of Miami Beach, United Jewish Appeal. Grossinger NY Died Nov. 20, 1972; buried Ferndale NY

GROSSMAN, MARC JUSTIN, lawyer; b. Cleve., Sept. 1, 1892; s. Louis J. and Lillie (Meyers) G.; A.B., Harvard, 1913, student Harvard Law Sch., 1914-15; m.

Carolyn Kahn, June 5, 1916; children—Marcia (Mrs. Leslie Goodfriend), Carole (Mrs. Robert Honigsfeld). Admitted to Ohio bar, 1916, practiced Cleve.; sr. partner Grossman, Familo, Cavitch, Kempf & Durkin; chmn. Cuyahoga County Relief Adminstrn., 1933-34, Cleve. Met. Housing Authority, 1933-43. Former chmn. Cuyahoga County Civilian Defense Council, Mayor's Vets. Emergency Housing Committee, Red Cross Home Service. Former trustee Citizens League, Family Welfare Association of America; past president Council Ednl. Alliance, Jewish Family Service Assn.; trustee Mt. Sinai Hosp. (Cleve.). Served as lt. col., A.U.S., 1943-45, M.T.O.U.S.A., 18 mos. Recipient European-African-Middle Eastern Medal, 2 bronze stars. Distinguished Service award, Cleve. Community Chest, 1938. Fellow Am. Bar Found., Ohio Bar Association; member Cleveland (pres., 1950-51), Am. (member ho. of dels.), Cuyahoga County bar Associ8tions, Am. Judicature Soc. (past dir.). Club: City Cleveland (past pres.). Home: Shaker Heights OH Deceased.Heights OH

GROTE, IRVINE WALTER, ret. educator; b. Chattanooga, July 25, 1899; s. Henry John and Elizabeth (Ernst) G.; B.S., U. Chattanooga, 1922; A.M., Columbia, 1923; Ph.D. in Chemistry, U. Cin., 1925, Sc.D., 1967; m. Nita Marie Tansey, Oct. 10, 1926. Research bio-chemist William S. Merrell Co. Cin., 1926, research chemistry, Parke-Davis & Co., 1926; faculty U. Chattanooga, 1931-72, prof. chemistry, 1941-68, prof. emeritus, 1969-72; research advisor dir. Chattem Drug & Chem. Co.; with Oliver Kamm made separation of hormones of posterior lobe of pituitary gland. Mem. Am. Chem. Soc., A.A.A.S., Am. Pharm. Assn., N.Y. Acad. Sci., Am. Assn. U. Prof., Sigma Xi, Kappa Sigma. Club: Mountain City (Chattanooga). Contbr. articles profl. jours. Home: Chattanooga TN Died Aug. 6, 1972; buried Forest Hills Cemetery, Chattanooga TN

GROTH, ARNOLD WILLIAM, banker; b. Davenport, Ia., Apr. 11, 1891; s. William F. and Amelia (Kruse) G.; ed. pub. schs. of Davenport, Ia.; m. Violet M. Bode, Apr. 24, 1915; children—June G. (Mrs. Hubert F. Leonard), Arnold H. Supervising accountant Whitfield, Whitcomb & Co., C.P.A., Portland, Ore., 1917-1920; asst. cashier 1st Nat. Bank, Portland, Ore., 1921-27, v.p. 1927-53, exec. v.p., from 1954, dir., 1953-66; chmn. bd. U. Wash. summer sch. banking. Mem. adv. bd. CCC, Washington, D.C. Life member Portland-Multnomah Co. chapter A.R.C.; mem. bd. govs. (term expires 1950) Am. Nat. Red Cross. Mem. The Robert Morris Asso. (past nat. pres.), Nat. Assn. Credit Men (past nat. dir.), Portland Assn. Credit Men (past pres. and dir.). Presbyterian. Club: Waverly Country (past pres., dir.). Arlington. Home: Portland OR Died Jan. 12, 1972.

GROUITCH, SLAVKO Y., diplomat; b. Belgrade, Serbia, Feb. 15, 1871; s. Yevrem and Helene (Yovanovitch) G.; father was Serbian minister to Constantinople, London and Paris; grad. Lycee of Versailles, France, 1889; LL.D., U. of Paris, 1897; m. Mabel Gordon Dunlap, of Clarksburg, W.Va., Aug. 12, 1902. Began as attache of Ministry of Foreign Affairs, Belgrade, 1898; sec. of Legation, at Constantinople, Turkey, 1898-1900; charge d'affaires, Athens, 1900-2; chief of polit. sect. of Ministry of Foreign Affairs, Belgrade, 1902-4; charge d'affaires, Petrograd, 1904-7, London, Eng., 1907-14; asst. sec. of State, at Belgrade, 1914-17; minister at Berne, Switzerland, 1917-18. E.E. and M.P. from the Kingdom of the Serbs, Croats and Slovenes to U.S. since Jan. 1919. Capt. of cav. of Reserve, in army of the Serbs, Croats and Slovens. Decorated Serbian White Eagle; Knight Comdr. British Empire, etc. Mem. Greek Orthodox Ch. Club: Metropolitan (Washington, D.C.). Address: 1339 Connecticut Av., Washington DC‡

GROVER, EULALIE OSGOOD, author; b. Mantorville, Minn., June 22, 1873; d. Rev. Nahum Wesley and Frances (Osgood) G.; grad. St. Johnsbury (Vt.) Acad., 1891; studied in Germany, later at Sorbonne and College de France, Paris. Conglist. Author: The Sunbonnet Babies' Primer, 1902; Folk-Lore Readers, 1904; The Overall Boys, 1905; Kittens and Cats, 1911; Sunbonnet Babies in Holland, 1915; Overall Boys in Switzerland, 1916; Sunbonnet Babies in Italy, 1921; The Outdoor Primer; The Art Literature Primer and First Reader; The Sunbonnet Babies in Mother Goose Land, 1927; Old Testament Stories, 1927; The Sunbonnet Babies A B C Book, 1929. Editor: Volland Mother Goose, 1915; My Caravan—Poems for Boys and Girls in Search of Adventure, 1931; Robert Louis Stevenson—Teller of Tales, 1940. Home: 569 Osceola Av., Winter Park FL‡

GROVER, FREDERICK WARREN, coll. prof.; b. Lynn, Mass., Sept. 3, 1876; s. Charles Shreve and Mary Otheman (Rogers) G.; S.B., Mass. Inst. Tech., 1899; M.S., Wesleyan U., Conn., 1901; Ph.D., George Washington U., 1907; Ph.D., Ludwig-Maximilians U., Munich, Germany, 1908; m. Bessie Warren Tebbetts, Aug. 14, 1901. Vol. observer, Harvard Coll. Obs., 1899; asst. in physics, 1899-1900, in physics and astronomy, 1900-01, Wesleyan U., Conn.; instr. elec. engring., Lafayette Coll., 1901-02; lab. asst. and asst. and asso. physicist, Nat. Bur. Standards, Washington, 1902-07 and 1908-11; prof. physics, Colby Coll., 1911-20; asst. prof. elec. engring., 1920-22, asso. prof., 1922-32, prof., 1932-46, emeritus since 1946; co-chmn., Div. Engring., 1941-42, Union Coll.; cons. physicist, Bur. of Standards, 1918-38. War work Bur. of Standards, Washington, July-Oct. 1917 and July-Oct. 1918 for the Signal Corps. Republican. Episcopalian. Fellow Am. Physical Soc., A.A.A.S.; mem. Am. Inst. Elec. Engrs. (fellow), Inst. Radio Engrs. (mem. bd. of editors), trustee Dudley Observatory, Sigma Xi, Eta Kappa Nu, Lambda Chi Alpha (hon.). Author: The Pageant of the Heavens, 1937; Inductance Calculations, 1946; also various scientific articles and bulls. Co-author: Principles Underlying Radio Communication (Signal Corps), 1919. Home: 1036 University Pl., Schenectady NY‡

GROVER, JAMES HAMILTON, chmn., St. Louis Union Trust Co.; b. St. Louis, Mo., Oct. 24, 1873; s. Hiram Justus and Charlotte Taylor (Blow) G.; LL.B., Washington U., 1896; m. Ethel Allen, Oct. 17, 1899; children—Allen, Loraine (Mrs. Grover La Farge). Practiced law in St. Louis, 1896-1910; bond dept., Mississippi Valley Trust Co., St. Louis, 1910-12; vice pres. Mortgage Trust Co., 1912-17; v.p. St. Louis Union Trust Co., 1917-31, dir., pres., 1931-46, chmn. of bd. since 1946; dir. Wagner Elec. Mfg. Co., First Nat. Bank, St. Joseph Lead Co. Clubs: Racquet, St. Louis Country, Log Cabin, Noonday, Cuivre (St. Louis, Mo.). Home: 410 N. Newstead Av. Office: 323 N. Broadway, St Louis MO‡

GROVER, WAYNE C(LAYTON), U.S. archivist; born Garland, Utah, Sept. 16, 1906; s. George Frederick and Mary (Clayton) G.; A.B., Univ. of Utah, 1930; A.M., Am. Univ., 1937, Ph.D. (in polit. sci. and pub. adminstrn.), 1946; LL.D., Brown U., 1956, Bucknell U., 1960, Belmont Abbey Coll., 1964; m. Esther Thomas, Nov. 8, 1935;children—Ann (Mrs. John N. Richardson), Mary Esther (Mrs. Alan H. Blumenthal), Jane (Mrs. Steve Brown), Eleanor. Archivist, Nat. Archives staff, 1935-41; technical asst. to bd. of analysts, research and analysis br. Office of Strategic Services, 1941-42; chief, records management br., Adj. Gen. Office, U.S. War Dept., 1943-47; apptd. asst. archivist of U.S., July 31, 1947, archivist, June 5, 1948-65. Consultant on Fed. records management problems, Commn. on Orgn. of Exec. Br. of Govt., 1948; cons. L.B. Johnson Library, 1965-70; member U.S. National Commn. for UNESCO, 1961-70; cons. Canadian Royal Commn. on Government Orgn. Served in AUS, advancing from capt. to lt. col., 1943-46; v.p. western hemisphere Internat. Council on Archives, mem. exec. bd., 1953-70; Awarded Legion of Merit; recipient Distinguished Service award General Services Administration, 1959, Career Service award National Civil Service League, 1961. Mem. American Polit. Sci. Assn., Am. Mil. Inst., Am. Soc. for Public Adminstrn., Soc. of Am. Archivists (president, 1953-54), Am. Hist. Assn., Pi Kappa Alpha. Club: Cosmos. Author: Records Administration Program of War Department, 1948. Contbr. articles in field. Home: Silver Spring MD Died June 8, 1970; buried Rock Creek Cemetery, Washington DC

GROVES, FRANK MALVON, contractor; b. Butler, Mo., Jan. 22, 1887; s. Stephen Jasper and Mary Ann (Frederickson) G.; student pub. schs. and pvt. studies; m. Hazel Olive Nelson, Sept. 25, 1915; children—Frances Mary, Franklin Nelson. With S.J. Groves & Sons Co., Mpls., 1905, pres., 1918, chmn. bd., 1950; pres. and/or dir. subsidiary and affiliated cos. Recipient co. Army citations. Mem. U.S. C. of C., N.A.M., Asso. Gen. Contractors Am., Moles. Club: Athletic (Mpls.). Home: Minneapolis MN

GROVES, LESLIE RICHARD, retired army officer, business consultant; born at Albany, New York, August 17, 1896; son of Leslie Richard and Gwen (Griffith) G.; student U. of Wash., 1913-14, Mass. Inst. of Tech., 1914-16; B.S., U.S. Mil. Acad., 1918; grad. Army Engr. Sch., 1921, Command and Gen. Staff School, 1936, Army War College, 1939; LL.D. (honorary) U. Cal., Hamilton Coll., St. Ambrose; D.S.C., Lafayette, Williams, Hobart, Ripon and Pa. Military Colleges; m. Grace Hulbert Wilson, February 10, 1922; children—Richard Hulbert, Gwen (Mrs. John A. Robinson). Commd. 2d lt. U.S. Army, 1918, advanced through grades to lt. gen., 1948, retired 1948; various assignments U.S., Hawaii, Europe, Nicaragua, dep. chief construction, Corps Engrs. 1941; headed Manhattan Atomic Devel. Project, 1942-47, in responsible charge all phases of project; v.p. Remington div. Sperry Rand Corporation, 1948-61. Decorated Distinguished Service medal, Legion of Merit (U.S.); Presdl. Medal of Merit (Nicaragua); Comdr. Order of the Crown (Belgium); Hon. Companion Most Honourable Order of the Bath (British). Professional engr., D.C. Mem. Am. Soc. C.E., Am. Soc. M.E. Clubs: Army, Navy, Chevy Chase; Univ. (N.Y.). Author: Now it can be Told, The Story of the Manhattan Project. Home: Washington DC Died July 13, 1970; buried Arlington National Cemetery, Arlington VA

GROVES, OWEN GRIFFITH, educator; b. Albany, N.Y., May 11, 1893; s. Leslie Richard and Gwen (Griffith) G.; A.B., Hamilton Coll., 1916; A.M., Columbia, 1917; L.H.D., Adelphi Coll., 1953; m. Marion Louise Nash, Dec. 16, 1922; 1 dau., Charlotte Griffith (Mrs. Stanley W. Larmee). Part-time instr. English, Columbia, 1919-20; instr. English, Hamilton Coll., 1919-20; asso. prof. English, Bucknell U., 1921-24; asst. prof. English, Adelphi Coll., 1924-29, asso. prof., 1929-39, prof., 1939-72, chmn. dept., 1940-63, dir. Inst. Humanities, 1962-72, coll. archivist, 1964-72. Instr. English with U.S. Army, Shrivenham Am. U. Eng., 1945-46, assoc. dir. Garden City Civil Def., from 1950. Served with U.S. Army, 1917-19. Mem. Modern Lang. Assn., Nat. Council Tchrs. English, Am. Assn. U. Profs. Home: Garden City NY Died Feb. 12, 1972; buried L.I. Nat. Cemetery, Farmingdale LI NY

GROVES, ROBERT WALKER, shipping exec.; b. Atlanta, May 16, 1883; s. John Henry and Julia Mann (Walker) G.; student pub. schs. Ga.; m. Evelyn Ragland, Apr. 12, 1915; children—Robert Walker, Julia (Mrs. Robert V. Martin). Clk. Strachan & Co., Savannah, Ga., 1899-1914, inc. as Strachan Shipping Co., 1914, sec.-treas., dir., 1914-23, v.p., 1923-32, pres., 1932-40; corp. succeeded by co-partnership operating under trade names Strachan Shipping Co.-South Atlantic S.S. Line, 1940, served as partner, chmn. bd., dir.; chmn. bd., dir. Savannah Bank & Trust Co.; president and director Atlantic Towing Co.; director Savannah Electric & Power Co., Central of Georgia Railway Company, Union Bag-Camp Paper Corp. President of Savannah Port Authority, 1925-48, dir. of successor, Savannah Dist. Authority, from 1951. Decorated Commander, Order of Orange Nassau. Member Society Colonial Wars (governor general 1960-63), Sons Revolution, Union Soc., N.Y. So. Soc. Episcopalian. Mason (Shriner). Clubs: Oglethorpe (Savannah); Bankers, Metropolitan (N.Y. City); Capital City (Atlanta). Home: Savannah GA Died Apr. 22, 1971.

GRUBER, LEWIS, tobacco exec.; b. N.Y.C., Nov. 14, 1895; s. Bernard and Bertha (Mittler) G.; Cumberland U., Lebanon, Tenn., 1914; student Columbia, 1917-18; LL.D., Cumberland U., 1959; D.C.S., Suffolk U., 1960; m. Stella Neuwirth, June 10, 1926 (dec.); 1 dau., Geraldine (Mrs. Jerome Wolf); m. 2d, Mrs. Lois Greif, Dec. 29, 1961. Admitted to Tex. bar, 1915, practice of law, Dallas, 1915-17; with P. Lorillard Co., from N.Y. dist. mgr., 1925-30, mgr. combination dept., 1930-35, dept. head N.Y. hdqrs., 1935-42, asst. sales mgr., 1942-47, gen. sales mgr., 1947-52, dir. sales since 1952, vice president, 1952-56, dir., pres., 1956-58, then hon. chmn., dir.; dir. Loew's Theatres & Hotels Corporation. Elected to Hall of Fame, Boston Conf. on Distbn., 1954. Decorated Royal Order Phoenix, King Paul of Greece, 1959. Served in Ordnance Corps, U.S. Army, 1918-20. Contbr. articles on sales management, sales techniques, merchandising. Home: New York City NY Died Apr. 1971.

GRUENER, HIPPOLYTE, chemist; b. New Haven, Conn., Feb. 23, 1869; s. Leopold and Katharine (Kern) G.; A.B., Yale, 1891, Ph.D., 1893; post-grad. studies, univs. of Munich and Berlin; m. May Cole, of Cleveland, June 21, 1899; children—Theodore, Katharine Lange, James Cole. Instr. chemistry, 1895-1903, asst. prof., 1903-07, Adelbert Coll.; asso. prof. chemistry, 1898-1907, prof., 1907-39, emeritus prof. since 1939, Mather College, Western Reserve U. Republican. Protestant. Fellow A.A.A.S., Am. Pub. Health Assn.; mem. Am. Chem. Soc., Deutsche Chemische Gesellschaft. Club: University. Contbr. tech. papers to scientific publs. Author: Organic Chemistry (with H. P. Lankelma); also vol. on chemistry in Popular Science series. Home: 2324 Coventry Rd., Cleveland Heights, Cleveland OH‡

GRUGER, FREDERIC RODRIGO, artist, illustrator; b. Phila., Pa., 1871; s. John P. and Rebecca R. G.; ed. high sch., Lancaster Pa., and Acad. Fine Arts, Phila.; m. Florence Felton Gray; children—Elizabeth Rodrigo, Frederic Rodrigo, Dorothy Gray. Home: Foxchase Rd., Chester Township, Morris Co. (PO Gladstone) NJ‡

GRUITCH, JERRY M., business exec.; b. Beckerek, Serbia, Aug. 16, 1904; s. Peter and Helen (Marich) G.; B.S. in Mech. Engring., U. Mich., 1933; M.M.E., M.S. Automotive Engring., Chrysler Inst. Engring., 1940; m. Ruth Storrs Lovejoy, Dec. 4, 1933; 1 dau., Judith Ellen. Successively toolmaker apprentice, labor and personnel supt. Ford Motor Co., 1921-29; chief engr., research and devel., heating and refrigeration airtemp div. Chrysler Corp., 1934-41, asst. chief engr. Dodge Div., 1946-47; v.p. engring. O. A. Sutton Corp., Wichita, Kan., 1947-48; dir. research and devel. Am. Car & Foundry div. ACF Industries, Inc., N.Y.C., 1948-57, dir. def. products, 1957-58; dir. govt. products, marketing, ACF Industries, Inc., 1959-62, corporate project mgr. Minuteman Program, 1961-62; dir. govt. products O. M. Edwards Co., Inc., Syracuse, N.Y., Excel. Corp., Elkhart, Ind., 1962-64; v.p. devel. Stanray Corp., Chgo., 1964-69. Cons. to Office Asst. Sec. Def., 1958-69; mem. steering group, adv. panel on ordnance Office Dir. Def. Research and Engring., 1959-69. Mem. tech. adv. group Air Force Armament Center, USAF Research and Devel. Command; mem. tech. adv. com. on ordnance Office Asst. Sec. Def., Research and Devel.; Nat. Strategy Seminar, Nat. War Coll., 1962.

Col. USAF, 1941-46; Nat. Mil. Establishment research and devel. com. on ordnance, 1948. Awarded Commendation Ribbon with 2 Oak Leaf Clusters, Bronze Star, Legion of Merit; recipient Distinguished Alumnus citation U. Mich., 1957, sesquicentennial award, 1967; Bronze medallion Am. Ordnance Assn., 1967. Registered profl. engr., N.Y.; registered Nat. Bur. of Profl. Engrs. Fellow Am. Soc. M.E., Am. Inst. Aeronautics and Astronautics (asso.); mem. Soc. Automotive Engrs., Am. Soc. Heating, Refrigerating and Air Conditioning Engrs., Am. Ordnance Assn. (chmn. emeritus, prodn. techniques div., dir. Syracuse post, dir. N.Y. post, mem. nat. council), Assn. U.S. Army, Inst. Metals (London), Scabbard and Blade, Triangles, mem. Sigma Xi, Phi Kappa, Tau Beta Pi. Clubs: Engineers, Union League (N.Y.C.); Army-Navy (Washington); Los Alamos Civic; Century (Syracuse); Military Order of the Carabao. Contbr. to engring. jours. Home: Lake Forest IL Died Mar. 1969.

GRUNEWALD, MAX EUGENE, cement mfg. co. exec.; b. Mainz, Germany, May 28, 1904; Ph. D., U. Frankfurt (Germany); m. Edith R. Burlin; 1 dau., Eva R. Came to U.S., 1927, naturalized, 1933. With Coplay Cement Mfg. Co. (Pa.), 1927-71, pres., 1942-71, chmn. bd., 1958-71. Fellow Am. Inst. Chemists; mem. Am. Chem. Soc., Am. Soc. Testing Materials. Clubs: Chemists (N.Y.C.) Home: New York City NY Died Mar. 5, 1971.

GRUNITZKY, NICHOLAS, pres. Rupublic of Togo; b. 1915; ed. Lycee Millet,Aix-en-Provence, also Pub. Works Sch., Paris. Civil servant pub. works dept., Dahomey, later Togo; head Combat Movement, 1940; founder, later gen. sec. Togolese Progress Party; dep. Togolese Territorial Assembly, 1951, 56; mem. French Nat. Assembly, 1951, 56; prime minister, Togo, 1958-60, pres., 1963-67, minister fgn. affairs, interior and nat. def., 1963-67. Formed Union Democratique des Populations, Togalaises, 1959. Decorated grand cross Legion of Honor. Address: Lome Togo West Africa Died Oct. 1969.*

GRUSKIN, ALAN DANIEL, dir. art gallery; b. Manorville, Pa., Dec. 28, 1904; s. Arthur S. and Jennie (Pollock) G.; student Harvard; m. Mary Bovio, July 16, 1940; children—Richard B., Robert A. Organizer, 1932, then director of the Midtown Galleries, N.Y.C.; arranger exhbns. of contemporary Am. art circuited to museums, art assns., univs.; writer radio series Story Behind the Picture, Sta. WOR. Art Appreciation for All, NBC. Mem. adv. com. National Art Mus. of Sport. Board directors Art Dealers Assn. of Am. Author: Painting in the U.S.A., 1946; The Watercolors of Dong Kingman, 1958; The Painter and His Techniques-William Thon, 1964; also forewords for various publs. Home: Stockton NJ Died Oct. 7, 1970; buried Jewish Community Center Cemetery, Flemington NJ

GRUVER, HARVEY SNYDER, supt. schs.; b. Reliance, Va., Nov. 29, 1874; s. Benjamin Franklin and Margaret (Snyder) G.; grad. Shenandoah Normal Coll., 1894; A.B., Otterbein Coll., 1902; A.M., Harvard, 1910; m. Mary Aden Kemp, Dec. 26, 1901; 1 dau., Edith Eleanor. Prin. high sch., Worthington, O., 1899-1900, supt. schs., Worthington, 1900-08, Walpole, Mass. (part time), 1909-10, Methuen, 1910-12; asst. supt. chs., Indianapolis, Ind., 1912-18; supt. schs., Worcester, Mass., 1918-23; supt. of schools, Lynn, Mass., 1923-45, emeritus since 1945; teacher summers University of Indiana, 1917, State Teachers Coll., Colo., 1919, 20, 21, State Normal Sch., Flagstaff, Ariz., 1921, 23, Clark U., Worcester, Mass., 1922, Harvard, 1924, 25, U. of Vt., 1932, 33, Boston Univ. Summer School, 1936. Mem. exec. com. Boy Scouts America; mem. bd. Lynn Chapter of Am. Red Cross (ex-chmn. bd.); dir. Lynn Chamber of Commerce; ex-pres. Alumni Assn. of Harvard Grad. Sch. of Edn. Mem. N.E.A., Am. Assn. Sch. Adminstrs., N.E. Assn. Sch. Supts. (ex-pres.), Harvard Teachers Assn., Massachusetts Assn. School Supts. (ex-pres.), Mass. Schoolmasters' Club (ex-pres.), Phi Delta Kappa. Republican. Conglist. Mason, K.P., Moose. Club: Kiwanis (ex-pres.). Home: Buchanan Circle, Lynn MA‡

GUARD, SAMUEL R., editor, writer; b. Elizabethtown, O., Dec. 25, 1889; s. Bailey and Abba (McKinney) G.; B.S. Agr., Ohio State, 1912; m. Kathryn Darnell, Oct. 8, 1915 (died Mar. 18, 1940); children—Georgia Darnell (dec.), Bailey III, Samuel Roderick; m. 2d, Evelyn McGowin Spencer, July 27, 1943. Associate editor Breeder's Gazette, 1912-20; dir. information, Am. Farm Bur. Fed., 1920-24; dir. Sears-Roebuck Agrl. Foundation and mgr. radio station WLS, 1924-27; editor Breeder's Gazette, 1927-62; bought Roycroft Shops, East Aurora, N.Y., from Elbert Hubbard II, 1939; farm columnist Louisville Courier-Jour.; contbg. editor Ky. Farm Bur. News; pres. Guard Pub. Co., Inc., Vice pres. Friends Ky. Libararies, Inc. Mem. Commn. Jud. Congl. Salaries. Mem. Ky. Council Chs. (pres.), Sigma Delta Chi. Episcopalian. Rep. Clubs: Saddle and Sirloin, Union League (Chgo.); Rotary, Owl Creek Country (Louisville). Author: The Farmer Gives Thanks. Home: Anchorage KY Died Sept. 15, 1966; buried Maine Twp. Cemetery, Park Ridge IL

GUARESCHI, GIOVANNI, author, journalist; b. Fontanelle, Parma, Italy, May 1, 1908; s. Augusto and Lina (Maghenzani) G.; Licenta Maturita Classica, U. Parma, 1927; m. Ennia Pallini, Feb. 12, 1940; children—Alberto, Carlotta. Artist, caricaturist from 1929; author radio scripts; dir. Candido from 1945. Author: La Scoperta di Milano, 1940; Il Destino si Chiama Clotilde, 1942; Il Marito in Collegio, 1943; Favola di Natale, 1945; Italia Provisoria, 1947; Don Camillo, 1948; Lo Zibaldtino, 1949; Diario Clandestino, 1950; Don Camillo and the Prodigal Son, 1952; Don Camillo and his flock, 1954; Don Camillo and the Devil, 1957; House that Nino Built; Little World of Don Camillo; My Secret Diary; Comrade for Camillo, 1963; My Home, Sweet Home, 1966. Address: Parma Italy Died July 22, 1968.

GUCKER, FRANK THOMSON, chemist; b. Phila., Apr. 8, 1900; s. Frank Thomson and Louise Dliphant (Fulton) G.; B.A., Haverford Coll., 1920, A.M., 1921, LL.D., 1966; Ph.D., Harvard U., 1925; m. Eleonore Dubois Harris, 1925; children—Frank Fulton, Katharine Harris (Mrs. Herbert H. Hand). Research asst. Harvard U., 1924-25; nat. research fellow, Cal. Inst. Tech., 1925-27; research fellow, Harvard U., 1927-28; research chemist, duPont Co., 1928-29; asst. prof. Northwestern U., 1929-36, asso. prof., 1936-42, prof. 1942-47; prof. and chmn. dept. of chemistry Ind. U., 1947-51, dean Coll. Arts and Scis., 1951-65, research prof. chemistry, 1965-70, research prof. emeritus chemistry, 1970-73, dir. research on phys. chemistry aerosols, 1970-73. Chief tech. aide Nat. Def. Research Com., 1941-42; mem. com. phys. Chemistry NRC, 1951-54; regional councilor Office Ordnance Research, 1951-54, mem. com. on awards in Chemistry under the Fulbright Act, 1954, chmn., 1955-59. Cons. Nat. Sci. Found. (mem. adv. panel chemistry div. math., phys., engring. scis., 1957-60, chmn. 1958-59); cons. Ford Found. Latin Am. Program, 1965; exec. com. Inter-Univ. Com. Travel Grants, 1966-69. Mem. Oak Ridge Nat. Lab. Adv. Com., Reactor Chemistry, 1961-63. Mem. exec. com. Am. Council Academic Deans, 1961-65; mem. commn. on liberal learning Assn. Am. Colls., 1966-68, chmn. 1968, exec. com. spl. com. liberal studies, 1968. Mem. alumni council Haverford Coll., 1957-60. Fellow Carnegie Instn., 1940-50. Fellow A.A.A.S., Ind. Acad. Sci.; Am. Soc. Testing Materials (instrumentation subcom. com. methods atmospheric sampling and analysis), Am. Assn. U. Profs., Am. Chem. Soc. (asso. editor Chem. Revs. 1950-53; sec.-treas. 1952-53, chmn. elect 1953-54, chmn. div. phys. and inorganic chemistry 1954-55; councilor, chmn. council policy com. 1959-61, mem. com. nominations and elections 1963-68, sec. 1964-66, chmn. 1967-68), Phi Beta Kappa (chpt. pres. 1965-66), Alpha Chi Sigma, Sigma Xi, Phi Lambda Upsilon. Presbyn. Club: Faculty Men's (Ind. U.). Author: (with Ralph L. Seifert) Physical Chemistry, 1966; textbooks; also Bloomington IN Died Mar. 6, 1973.

GUDDE, ERWIN GUSTAV,, author; b. Schippenbeil, Germany, Feb. 23, 1889; s. Franz Gustav and Bertha (Sobke) G.; student Horticulture Coll., Koestritz, 1905-07, U. Berlin, 1910-11; Ph.D., U. of California, 1922; m. to Elisabeth Karpenstein, August 12th, 1941. Came to the United States, 1911, naturalized, 1919. Horticulturist, 1907-10; newspaper writer, Berlin, N.Y.C., San Francisco, 1910-17; faculty U. Cal., 1920-55; exec. sec. Am. Name Soc., 1952-56, founder, editor Names, 1953-56. Mem. Modern Lang. Assn., Pacific Philo. Assn., Cal. Hist. Soc., Am. Philatelic Soc., Am. Assn. U. Profs., Am. Dialect Soc., Am. Name Soc. Club: Sierra (San Francisco). Author: Social Conflicts in Medieval Poetry, 1934; Sutter's Own Story, 1936; 1000 California Place Names, 1947; California Place Names: A Geographical Dictionary, 1949, 60, 67; Bigler's Chronicle of the West, 1962. Editor: Memoirs of Theodore Cordua, 1933; Poems of Lupold Hornburg, 1943; Vischer's First Visit to California, 1944, Neu-Helvetien, 1934; Exploring with Fremont, 1958; From St. Louis to Sutter's Fort 1846, 1961. Home: Orinda CA Died May 7, 1969.

GUDEBROD, LOUIS ALBERT, sculptor; b. Middletown, Conn., Sept. 20, 1872; s. David F. and Marie Steimetz) G.; ed. pub. sch., Middletown, Conn.; 1 term Yale Art Sch., Art Students' League under Mary Lawrence and Augustus St. Gaudens, and in Paris, 1898-1900, under Jean Dampt and Augustus St. Gaudens; unmarried. Dir. sculpture, Charleston Expn., 1901-02; group, The Aztecs, received silver medal. Won competition for Jefferson Davis Arch, Richmond, to cost $75,000, 1902; executed portrait statue of Sieur de la Salle, for St. Louis Expn., 1903-04; monument on site of Andersonville Prison, for State of N.Y., 1910; portrait tablet in bronze of Alfred E. Smith for state office bldg., Albany, New York. Silver design, Spirit of the West," awarded gold medal Panama, P.I., Expn., 1915. Mem. Nat. Sculpture Soc., Architectural League, New York. Baptist. Republican. Home: 46 Silver St., Meriden CT‡

GUENTHER, AUGUST ERNEST, physiologist, educator; b. Sandusky, O., Jan. 20, 1874; s. August and Sophie (Kolbe) G.; grad. Sandusky High Sch., 1892, Univ. of Mich., S. B., 1898; unmarried. Asst. in Univ. of Mich. Mus., 1894-7; asst. in physiology, med. dept. Univ. of Mich., 1897-1901; fellow in physiology, 1903-4, asst. in physiology since 1904, Johns Hopkins Univ. Author: (with Dr. T. C. Guenther) volume on Physiology (in Epitome of Medicine), 1903 L12. Residence: 1818 N. Broadway, Baltimore‡

GUGGENHEIM, EDMOND ALFRED, business exec.; b. St. Gall, Switzerland, Jan. 19, 1888; s. Murry and Leonie (Bernheim) G.; ed. Dr. Sach's Collegiate Inst., Columbia U., and Sheffield Scientific Sch., Yale; m. Marron Price, June 12, 1910 (divorced 1936); 1 dau., Natalie Price (Mrs. Frederick Talbert); m. 2d, Dorothy Russell McGuire (div. 1952); m. 3d, Marlon F. Kaufman, 1955. Admitted to firm of Guggenheim Bros., as jr. partner, 1916, serving as head of mining exploration dept. and a vice pres. in charge of operations of Chile Exploration Co., Braden Copper Co., during early part of World War I; vice pres. Guggenheim Nitrate Corp., 1944-61; dir. 1944-51; dir. Kennecott Copper Corp., 1916-61, mem. exec. com. 1940-61; dir. Braden Copper Co., 1914-61. President Murry and Leonie Guggenheim Foundation, Murry and Leonie Guggenheim Dental Clinic. Special dep. police commr., N.Y. City, in charge Borough of Bronx, also chmn. police pension and relief coms., and mem. crime prevention com., of Police Dept., 1919-25. Mem. Vets. Meml. Assn. Saranac Lake. Clubs: Yale, Elk, Saranac Lake, Saranac Lake Golf, Cloud. Home: Phoenix AZ Died Mar. 1972.

GUGGENHEIM, OLGA H. (MRS. SIMON GUGGENHEIM), orgn. exec.; b. Cincinnati, Sept. 23, 1877; d. Henry and Barbara (Steiner) Hirsh; ed. pvt. schs. in U.S. and Europe; m. Simon Guggenheim, Nov. 24, 1898; children—John Simon (dec.), George Denver (dec.). Founded, with husband, The John Simon Guggenheim Memorial Foundation, 1925 (in memory of son who died 1922), succeeded husband as pres. of the Foundation in 1942; trustee, Museum of Modern Art, N.Y.C. Republican. Episcopalian. Home: New York City NY Died Feb. 14, 1970.

GUILD, JOSEPHUS CONN, utilities exec. b. Chattanooga, Tenn., Dec. 15, 1887; s. Josephus Conn and Mary (Orr) G.; student Baylor Sch. (Chattanooga), 1897-1905, U. of Va., 1905-07, Vanderbilt U. (Nashville, Tenn.), 1907-09; m. Sarah Lamb Nichols, November 14, 1912 (divorced 1940); 1 daughter, Virginia Dale (Mrs. Rupert M. Colmore, Jr.); m. 2d, May Bondurant Young, May 12, 1942. Began as rodman Chattanooga & Tennessee River Power Company and advanced through power sales department to general manager, 1915; on consolidation of co. with The Tenn. Electric Power Co., elected v.p. of latter, 1922, apptd. gen. mgr. 1927, pres. until the Tenn. Electric Power Co. was purchased by Tenn. Valley Authority; past pres. So. Coach Lines, Inc.; past chmn. bd. United Transit Co., now dir.; dir. Provident Life & Accident Insurance Co., Am. Trust & Banking Co., Interstate Life & Accident Co., Coca-Cola Bottling Co. Served as pvt. in F.A., Camp Taylor, Louisville, Ky., World War. Chmn. bd. of trustees Baylor Sch. Mem. Am. Soc. of Civil Engrs., Sigma Alpha Epsilon. Episcopalian. Clubs: Mountain City, Chattanooga Golf Chattanooga TN

GUILFOILE, FRANCIS PATRICK, lawyer; b. Waterbury, Conn., Feb. 4, 1875; s. Michael and Catherine (Lawlor) G.; grad. Waterbury High Sch.; A.B., A.M., Mt. St. Mary's Coll., Emmitsburg, Md., 1895, LL.D., 1908; LL.D., Cath. U. of America, Washington, D.C., 1898; m. Margaret Mary McDonald, of Waterbury, Conn., June 29, 1908; children—Margaret Frances, Mary Catherine. Admitted to Conn. bar, 1899, and since practiced in Waterbury; mem. firm of Cowell & Guilfoile and was sr. partner Guilfoile & McEvoy (dissolved upon appmt. of latter as judge Superior Ct.); mem. Conn. Ho. of Rep., 1901-02; Conn. Constitutional Conv., 1902; corpn. counsel, City of Waterbury, 1909-17; mayor of Waterbury, 1921-29. Nominated as Dem. candidate for lt. gov. of Conn., 1916. Mem. Waterbury City Planning Bd., Bronson Library Bd. Sec. 3d Draft Bd. and mem. legal com. State Council of Defense, World War. Mem. Am., Conn. State, New Haven Co. and Waterbury bar assns. Democrat. Catholic. Home: 182 Robbins St. Office: 192 Grand St., Waterbury CT*‡

GUILLE, PETER, museum dir.; b. N.Y.C., May 20, 1911; s. Raymond and Beatrice (Tucker) G.; student Friends Acad., Locust Valley, L.I., N.Y.; mem. Helen Rockefeller Bowler, 1943; children—Peter, Helen Tucker; m. 2d, Constance E. Blackwood, 1954. Apprentice silversmith, 1930; specialist Old English silver, 1930-53; v.p. Chrichton & Co., Ltd., N.Y.C., 1935; pres. Peter Guille, Ltd. N.Y.C., 1936-53; v.p. Burgil Co., N.Y.C., 1951-70 pres. Peter Guille Assos., 1953-66; ret., 1966. Dir., trustee Sterling & Francine Clark Inst., Williamstown, Mass.; v.p. R. Sterling Clark Found., N.Y.C. Served with AUS, World War II. Mem. Assn. Art Mus. Dirs. Home: Centerport NY Died Oct. 3, 1970; buried Wading River Cemetery, Wading River NY

GUION, CONNIE M., physician; b. Lincolnton, N.C., Aug. 29, 1882; d. Benjamin Simmons and Catherine (Caldwell) Guion; student Kate Ship Sch., Lincolnton,

Northfield (Mass.) Sem.; A.B., Wellesley Coll., 1906, D.Sc. (hon.), 1950; A.M., Cornell, 1913, M.D., 1917, D.Sc. (hon.), Women's Medical Coll. of Pa., 1953; D.Sc. (honorary), Queen's College, Charlotte, N.C., 1957; Doctor of Laws, Univ. of North Carolina, 1965. Successively instr. of chemistry, Vassar Coll., prof. of chemistry and head dept., Sweet Briar (Va.) Coll., asst. attdg. physician, Bellevue Hosp., Cornell U. div. and N.Y. Infirmary for Women and Children; chief med. clinic, Cornell U. Med. Coll., 1929-32; clinic became part of New York Hosp., 1932, and since served as chief med. clinic; asst. prof. medicine, Cornell U. Med. Coll., 1929-36, asso. prof., 1936-46, prof. of clinical medicine, 1946-52, professor of clinical medicine emeritus, 1952-71; asst. attending physician, N.Y. Hosp., 1932-42, asso. attending physician, 1942-43, attending physician, 1943-50, cons. pvt. practice med. N.Y.C. specialist in internal medicine. Recipient Elizabeth Blackwell citation, N.Y. Infirmary for Women and Children, Jan. 1949. Mem. bd. dir., 1956, Sweet Briar Coll. Served as mem. indsl. council, Dept. of Labor of State of N.Y. Formerly chmn. Med. Appeals Unit. Mem. adv. com., Nat. Health and Safety Council of Girl Scouts. Recipient, Award of Distinction, Cornell U. Medical College, 1951, Northfield Award for distinguished service, 1951, Jane Addams medal for distinguished service Rockford Coll., 1963. Diplomate American Bd. Internal Medicine. Member New York Academy of Medicine, New York State Medical Assn., Med. Women's Assn., Shakespeares Soc., Phi Beta Kappa, Sigma Xi, Alpha Omega Alpha. Club: Wellesley (N.Y. City), Cosmopolitan. Contbr. numerous papers on med. subjects. Home: New York City NY Died Apr. 30, 1971; buried Charlotte NC

GULLETTE, GEORGE ALBERT, educator; b. Minneapolis, Jan. 12, 1909; s. Albert Martin and Kate Elden (MacKnight) G.; A.B., Harvard, 1933; A.M., Vanderbilt U., 1934; Ph.D., U. of Mich., 1944; m. Florence Chamney Murrell, June 10, 1933; children—Sara Chamney, David George, Robert Lincoln. Instr. in English, U. of Toledo, 1935-39; asst. prof., 1939-44, asso. prof., 1944-46, asst. dean, arts coll., 1946; dean and prof. of English, Lincoln (Ill.) Coll., 1946-47; head of dept. and prof. of social studies, N.C. State Coll., Raleigh, 1947-69. Mem. Am. Soc. Eng. Edn. (dir. humanistic-social research project, 1954-55), Am. Assn. University Profs., Raleigh Inst. of Religion (chmn. 1951), Phi Kappa Phi. Author: Writing Effectively (with James M. McCrimmon), 1941. Contbr. to profl. jours. Home: Raleigh NC Died Nov. 30, 1969.

GUM, WALTER CLARKE, bishop; b. Monterey, Va., July 4, 1897; s. William Early and Salie Maude (Taylor) G.; grad. Monterey (Va.) High Sch., 1914; student Emory U., 1918-19; student Randolph-Macon Coll., Ashland, Virginia, 1916-18; D.D., 1940; LL.D., Kentucky Wesleyan College. 1961; m. Mary Lucille Hendrick, Oct. 31, 1919; 1 dau., Mary Russell (Mrs. John Wiley Mason, Jr.). Ordained to ministry Meth. Ch., 1919; pastor, 1919-40; district supt. Norfolk Dist., 1940-45; Centenary Ch., Richmond, Va., 1945-50; district supt. Richmond District 1950-56; pastor Park Place Meth. Ch., 1956-60; elected to Episcopacy, 1960, bishop Louisville Area, 1960-64, Richmond Area, 1964-68; with Bd. Evangelism, 1968-69; conf. missionary sec., 1935-37; chmn. conf. commn. on evangelism, 1937-40; All European Conf. Meth. Ch., Copenhagen Denmark, 1939; delegate to Ecumenical Meth. Conf. since 1946; member Crusade for Christ committee of 200; chairman conference Crusade for Christ Council. Member general conference, jurisdictional conference, 1944; mem. jurisdictional council of Southeastern Jurisdiction, vice chmn., 1956-60, chairman bd. missions. Mem. Norfolk Community Council, 1944-45. Chmn. gen. and jurisdictional conf. delegations, 1948, 52, 56, 60; vice chmn. Southeastern Jurisdictional, 1956-60, chmn. bd. missions; chmn. Va. Conf. Bd. of Missions, 1956-60; chmn. Va. Conf. Commn. on local ch. emphasis. 1956-60; pres. Southeastern Jurisdiction Coll. of Bishops, 1962; vice chmn. gen. commn. chaplains, Meth. Ch., mem. gen. bd. missions, vice chmn. nat. div. of bd. missions, chmn. ch. extension sect. Mem. Va. Council Chs. Chmn. of the bd. trustees of Randolph-Macon Acad., also Randolph-Macon Coll.; trustee Va. Wesleyan Coll., Norfolk; dir. Interdenominational Work Found.; chmn. Magee Christian Edn. Found. Mem. Omicron Delta Kappa, Theta Phi. Mason. (grand chaplain, Va. 1946-60; Shriner). Home: Norfolk VA Died May 31, 1969; buried Forrest Lawn Cemetery, Norfolk VA

GUMMEY, HENRY RILEY, JR., theologian; b. Phila., Jan. 12, 1870; s. Henry Riley and Mary (McFarland) G.; B.A., U. of Pa., 1890, M.A., 1893, B.D., 1895; grad. Gen. Theol. Sem., New York, 1893; D.D. in course, Philadelphia Divinity School, 1905; D.C.L., Univ. of the South, 1931; m. Margaret Upjohn, of Phila., June 30, 1897; children—Henry Riley, Margaret McFarland. Deacon, 1893, priest, 1894, P.E. Ch.; curate St. Luke's Ch., Germantown, Phila., 1893-95; rector St. John's Ch., Germantown, 1897-1906, Grace Ch., Haddonfield, N.J., 1907-12; examining chaplain to bishop of N.J., 1908-14; prof. ecclesiastical history and polity, 1912-13, dogmatic theology and polity, 1913-14, U. of the South, Sewanee,

Tenn.; rector St. James' Ch., Downingtown, Pa., 1914-29; prof. of liturgics, ch. polity and canon law, Phila. Div. Sch., since 1929. Examining chaplain to bishop of Pa., 1914-30. Mem. Hist. Soc. Pa. Author: The Consecration of the Eucharist, 1908; also articles and reviews in theol. periodicals. Home: 115 Bethlehem Pike, Chestnut Hill, Philadelphia PA‡

GUMP, LOUIS FRANKLIN, govt. ofcl.; b. Mansfield, O., Jan. 4, 1913; s. Harry Smith and Gladys (Mengert) G.; B.A., Ohio State U., 1934; m. Jeanne Hemphill Richardson, 1936; children—G. Dick (killed in action), Jerry L., Barry H., Judy J. (Mrs. J. T. Ellis). Salesman with Ohio Labs., Inc., 1938-36, sales mgr., 1938-46, dir.; gen. mgr. Bingman Labs., 1947-50; sales mgr. Forest Lawn Meml. Park, Columbus, O., 1950-56, Oakland Hills Meml. Park, Detroit, 1953-54; owner Floral Hills Memory Gardens, 1955-69, trustee, 1955-69; city urban renewal dir., Chillicothe, O., 1963-64; city cons. on urban renewal, Middletown, O., 1965-69, urban renewal dir., 1965-69; pres. Mgmt. Consultants, Inc., Chillicothe, 1954-69. Chmn., Civic Affairs Commn., 1963-64. Bd. dirs. Ross County unit Am. Cancer Soc. Mem. Nat. Assn. Housing and Redevel. Ofcls., Urban Renewal Assn. Ohio (dir. 1966-69), Middletown City Employees Assn. (president 1966-69), Ross County C. of C., Delta Beta Xi, (hon.). Republican. Presbyn. Mason (32 deg., Shriner), Lion. Home: Middletown OH Died June 6, 1969.

GUNDERSON, B. HARRY, educator; b. Stoughton, Wis., Dec. 31, 1906; s. Gabriel Edward and Olena (Tonstad) G.; Diploma, Wis. State Coll., Oshkosh, 1929; B.S., Ohio State U., 1932; M.S., Ind. U., 1940, Ed.D., 1949; m. Florence A. Nipko, Aug. 29, 1930; children—Leanne Marie, Gayne Edward. Instr. indsl. arts School City, Richmond, Ind., 1929-41; dir. tng. Heavy Metal Div., Pressed Steel Car Co., Chgo., 1941-45; grad. asst. Ind. U., 1945, instr. in edn., critic tchr. in indsl. arts, 1945-48, mem. instrn. staff Corr. Study Bur., Div. Adult Edn., 1947-70; asst. prof. indsl. arts Eastern Ill. U., Charleston, Ill., 1948-49, asso. prof., 1949-56; prof., chmn. div. indsl. arts Northern State Coll., Aberdeen, S.D., 1956-70; vis. prof. Colo. Agr. and Mech. U. (name later changed to Colo. State U.) summer, 1954. Toolmaker Sarkes Tarzian, Inc., Bloomington, Ind., vis. prof., Indsl. Arts Inst., U. N.D., summer 1966. Past mem. adv. council as rep. State of S.D. for Ford Indsl. Arts Awards. Mem. S.D. Tchrs. Assn., N.E.A., S.D. Indsl. Edn. Assn., Am. Vocational Assn., Mississippi Valley Indsl. Arts Conference, Am. Indsl. Arts Assn. (chairman national membership committee), Am. Council for Indsl. Art Tchr. Edn., (life), Phi Delta Kappa, Epsilon Pi Tau, Iota Lambda Sigma, Phi Sigma Epsilon, chmn. Dakotas Indsl. Arts Tchr. Edn. Conference (chmn. 1957). Luth. Rotarian. Contbr. civic and profl. publs. Home: Aberdeen SD Died Nov. 25, 1970.

GUNN, JOHN W., lawyer, judge; b. Butte, Mont., June 4, 1920; s. Nelson T. and Jane (Gracey) G.; ed. Pomona Coll.; LL.B., U. Ida., 1948; m. Jean V. Gray, Nov. 7, 1943; children—John W., Laura Jean, George N. Practice law, Boise, Ida., 1949-63, Weiser, Ida., 1963-65, Caldwell, Ida., 1965-70; asst. atty. gen. State of Ida., 1949-60; chief counsel Ida. Employment Security Agy., 1949-63; city atty. Weiser, 1963, Cambridge, 1963-64; justice of peace Canyon County, Ida., 1965-70. Sub-chmn. United Fund Dr., Boise, 1955; chmn. Ida. Anti Sales Tax Com., Weiser, 1964. Served with Inf., AUS, 1943-46; maj. Res. Mem. Ida. Bar Assn., Am. Legion, Phi Alpha Delta, Sigma Chi. Episcopalian (sr. warden 1964, lay reader 1964-65). Mason, Elk, Toastmaster. Home: Caldwell ID Died May 1970

GUNNISON, RAYMOND M., pub. exec.; b. Brooklyn, Apr. 14, 1887; s. Herbert F. and Alice (May) G.; B.S., St. Lawrence U., 1909; m. Olive Mason, Oct. 19, 1912. On staff N.Y. World, 1909; v.p. Brooklyn Daily Eagle, 1929; pres. and dir. R.H. Donnelley Corp., N.Y. City office, 1929-51, chmn. bd. since 1951. Trustee St. Lawrence U. Clubs: University, Municipal, Bankers, Scarsdale Golf, Quaker Hill Country. Home: Menlo Park CA Died Jan. 1972.

GUNSETT, HELEN TOSSEY, mem. Democrat. Nat. Com.; b. Van Wert, O., Oct. 5, 1909; d. Ira and Lucy (Stuckey) Tossey; student Ohio State U., 1927-29; m. Luther Gunsett, Feb. 2, 1936. Mem. Ohio Dem. Exec. Com., 1950-71; charter mem. Ohio Young Dem. Exec. Com.; mem. Ohio Dem. Central Com. from 5th Dist., 1950-71; trustee Federated Dem. Women Ohio, 1955-57; vice chmn. Van Wert County Dem. Exec. Com., 1956-58; mem. Dem. Nat. Com. from Ohio 1956-68; alternate at large Dem. Nat. Conv., 1956, del. at large, 1960, 64, co-chmn. credentials com., 1964, 68. Mem. Van Wert Bd. Health, 1956-71; mem. Presdl. bd. advisers Fed. Reformatory For Women; vice chmn. Van Wert Civic Planning Com. Incorporator Van Wert County Hist. Soc.; mem. twig group van Wert Hosp.; dir. women's aux. Ohio br. Starr Commonwealth Sch. Boys, local A.R.C., YWCA and Am. Heart Assn. Mem. League Women Voters, D.A.R., Columbus Urban League, UN Assn., Federated Dem. Women of Ohio (life), Kappa Delta. Clubs: Van Wert Country Democratic Women's (pres.), Van Wert Woman's (pres. 1954-56). Address: Columbus OH Died Dec. 17, 1971.

GUNTER, FELIX EUGENE, banker; b. Lagrange, Miss., Jan. 20, 1876; s. Andrew Jackson and Sarah Elizabeth (Givens) G.; A.B., Millsaps Coll., Jackson, Miss., 1903; m. Beatrice Davis, of Camden, N.J., Apr. 16, 1908; children—William Davis, Charlton Albert, Andrew Charles, John Burrows. Mgr. Penn Mut. Life Ins. Co., Jackson, 1903-14; vice pres. Merchants Bank & Trust Co., Jackson, 1914-18; exec. v.p. Canal Bank & Trust Co., New Orleans, La., 1918-25; pres. Liberty Central Trust Co., St. Louis, Mo. (merged with 1st Nat. Bank, 1929), 1925-29; vice chmn. bd. 1st Nat. Bank since 1929; also director of many corporations. State director War Savings Stamp Committee, Miss., 1918, La., 1918-19. Mem. City Plan Commn. Mem. Kappa Sigma. Republican. Methodist. Clubs: University, Racquet, Noonday, Bellerive Country. Home: Chesterfield, Mo. Office: 1st Nat. Bank, St Louis MO‡

GUNTON, REBECCA DOUGLAS (MRS. GEORGE GUNTON), pres. Gen. Federation of Women's Clubs, 1898-9; b. La Grange, Ga.; d. John and Frances Berfoot (Mosley) Douglas; ed. at La Grange, Ga.; m. 1st, 1868, William Bell Lowe (deceased); 2d, Feb., 1904, George Gunton. Founder club movement in South; pres. Atlanta Woman's Club, 1896; pres. Ga. State Federation of Women's Clubs, 1897; mem. D.A.R. Since expiration of office, lives at her country home; active in work for improved conditions among women wage earners. Address: Hot Springs VA‡

GUPTON, WILLIAM, postmaster; b. Bowling Green, Ky., Sept. 17, 1870; s. Alexander and Florence D. (McNeal) G.; ed. pub. schs. and bus. coll.; m. Daisie Dean Mason, Feb. 12, 1890; children—Annie Lee, Mrs. Pearl Dean Loser, Will Edwin, Henry A. Began at 16 as driver delivery wagon, retail grocery, Nashville, Tenn.; bookkeeper and shipping clk., mixed feed business, 1889-96; bought out the business, 1896; now propr. Am. Steam Feed Co.; pres. Broadway Nat. Bank, 1930-34; real estate business; mayor Nashville, 1917-21; postmaster of Nashville since 1933. Pres. City Bd. of Edn., Nashville, 1924-30; pres. of the Chamber of Commerce, 1934-35. Pres. Tenn. Mfrs. Assn.; pres. bd. mgrs. Tenn. Bapt. Orphans' Home. Democrat. Baptist. Mason, Shriner, K. of P. Clubs: Kiwanis (pres. 1938), Commercial. Home: Franklin Pike. Office: Post Office, Nashville TN‡

GURKOFF, EUGENE, mfg. exec.; b. Harrisburg, Pa., Nov. 7, 1921; s. Joseph and Anna (Kamin) G.; student pub. schs.; m. Louise B. Buch, Apr. 13, 1948; children—Joseph, Jon, Jeff. Chairman also pres., dir. Capitol Products Corp., Mechanicsburg, Pa. Served with USAAF, 1942-45. Home: Harrisburg PA Died 1972.

GURNEY, DELOSS BUTLER (D. B.), seedsman; b. Monticello, Ia., May 6, 1870; s. Charles Walter and Eliza (Butler) G.; ed. pub. schs.; m. Henrietta Bell Klopping, Feb. 20, 1894; children—Pansy (Mrs. Ralph Mishler), John Chandler, Charles Henry, Henrietta (Mrs. Harold Clark). Mgr. Yankton (S.D.) br. of Gurney Seed Co., 1892-1908 (Yankton became main office 1898), pres. Gurney Seed & Nursery Co. (now The House of Gurney), 1908-39; pres. Meridian Highway Bridge Co. (concrete bridge over Missouri River at Yankton); formerly pres. Fair Price Petroleum Co. Formerly sec. Mount Rushmore Nat. Memorial Commn. in the Black Hills. Republican. Protestant. Mason (32 deg.). Club: Rotary (ex-pres.). Ex-pres. WNAX Broadcasting Co. Address: The House of Gurney, Inc., Yankton SD‡

GURNEY, JAMES PAUL, rose cons.; b. Lansdowne, Pa., Mar. 22, 1915; s. Henry Brandon and Lillie (Crossland) G.; student N.Y. Tech. and Agrl. Inst., 1941; B.S., U. Md., 1950; m. Elizabeth Gessford Ebaugh, Dec. 21, 1945; children—Helen Jessie, Katharine Elizabeth. Exec. sec. Am. Rose Soc., Columbus, O., 1953-61; sec. Am. Rose Found.; rose cons. O.M. Scott & Sons Co., Marysville, O., 1961-62; lectr. on roses to radio, TV, other groups. Mem. Christian Sci. Com. on Publs. for Ohio; sec. City of Columbus Park of Roses Commn. Mem. Clintonville Bus. Men's Assn., Harrisburg Rose Soc. (pres. 1952), Pi Alpha Xi. Home: Columbus OH Died Nov. 17, 1972.

GUSTAFSON, AIRIK, educator, author; b. Sioux City, Ia., Apr. 23, 1903; s. Anders and Elizabeth (Peterson) G.; Ph.B., U. Chgo.; 1925, Ph.D. (fellow English, 1926-27, fellow comparative lit., 1933-34), 1935; Am.-Scandinavian Found. fellow, Upsala (Sweden) U., 1927-28; research resident, Lunds (Sweden) U., 1934; LL.D. (hon.), Uppsala U. (Sweden), 1970; m. Cleyonne Trafford, Oct. 23, 1936. Prof. English, comparative lit., Augustana Coll., Rock Island, Ill., 1929-33, mem. faculty Cornell U., 1933-39; prof. Scandinavian lit. U. Minn. 1939-70, dir. program Scandinavian Area Studies 1948-70, director of the Northwest Europe Center, 1965-70; visiting prof. U. Wis., summers, 1951, 53, 57. Decorated comdr. Royal Order of Polar Star (Sweden). Guggenheim fellow, 1945-46, 46; Fulbright Research Scholar, U. Stockholm, Sorbonne, 1961-62; Fulbright-Hayes research fellow, Sweden, 1966-67. Recipient Henrik Schuck Prize, Swedish Acad., 1961. Fellow Vetenskapssocieteten i Lund, 1948; life mem. Strindbergssaalskapet; mem. Modern Lang. Assn. Am.

(asso. bibliographer ann. bibliography 1958-63), Am.-Scandinavian Found., Am. Nat. Theatre and Acad., Selma Lagerif-sallskapet, Svenska Litteratur-sallskapet i Uppsala (Sweden,) Svenska Litteratur-sallskapet i Finland Varmlands Nation i Uppsala (hon.), Svenska Kulturforbundet i Amerika (hon.). Club: Campus (Mpls.). Author: Six Scandinavian Novelists, published in 1940, revised edition published 1968; A History of Swedish Literature, 1961; Den svenska litteraturens historia, 1962; (with others) A History of Modern Drama, 1947. Editor: Scandinavian Plays of the 20th Century, 1944, 51. Adv. bd. Studies in Romanticism, 1964-70; contbr. Columbia Dictionary of Modern European Literature, 1946, to Am., Swedish publs. Home: Minneapolis MN Died Mar. 24, 1970; buried Lakewood Cemetery, Minneapolis MN

GUSTAFSON, CARL HENRY, marketing organizer; b. Rockford, Ill., Apr. 1, 1869; s. Christopher and Hilda (Malmstrom) G.; ed. pub. schs. and bus. coll.; m. Anna Mathilda Matson, May 20, 1893; children—Esther Florence, Roy Henry, Reuben Roosevelt, Nancy Virginia, Ralph Eric. Taken in infancy by parents to farm in Neb., organized cooperative elevator, Mead, Neb., 1914; mem. Neb. Ho. of Rep., 1911-14; pres. Farmers' Union of Neb., 1913-21, also editor Neb. Union Farmer; pres. Farmers' Union State Exchange, 1915-18, Farmers' Union Live Stock Commn. Co., 1917-21, Farmers' Union Coop. Ins. Co., 1918-21; pres. All-Am. Coop. Congress, 1918; pres. U.S. Grain Growers, Inc. (Chicago), 1921-22, Nat. Coop. Co. (Omaha), 1920-22; v.p. Neb. Farm Bur. Fedn., 1921; dir. Coop. Marketing Dept., Am. Farm Bur. Federation (Chicago), 1921; dir. Neb. State Bd. Agr., 1911-32; orgn. expert Federal Farm Bd. since 1930; chmn. Farmers' Marketing Com. of 17 which investigated grain marketing conditions, resulting in formation of U.S. Grain Growers, Inc., also Farmers' Live Stock Marketing Com. of 15 which investigated live stock marketing conditions, resulting in formation of the Nat. Livestock Producers Assn.; elected pres. Eastern Neb., Public Power District, 1938. Address: R.F.D. 1, Mead NB*

GUSTAFSON, FRANK AUGUST, clergyman; b. Aurora, Ill., Sept. 17, 1871; s. John Gustaf and Mathilda (Sorensen) G.; M.D., Northwestern U., 1892; m. Dora M. Domber, of Aurora, Mar. 28, 1891; children—Harold Ross, Donald Charles, Frances Gertrude. Was prof. materia medica and philosophy of medicine, Denver Coll. Phys. and Surg., later at Hering Med. Coll., Chicago; ordained ministry Ch. of the New Jerusalem, 1899; pastor successively at Olney (Ill.), Buffalo (N.Y.), Urbana (O.), Denver (Colo.), La Porte (Ind.), Detroit (Mich.), St. Louis (Mo.), again at Detroit, 1923; consecrated as gen. pastor May 16, 1926. Editor and pub. Kansas Sunday Sermon Service. Author of The Forward Christianity. Democrat. Mason (32 deg.). Address: Pretty Prairie KS‡

GUSTAFSON, G(USTAF) JOSEPH, clergyman, educator; b. Memphis, Dec. 1, 1910; s. Gustaf William and Nora Margaret (Bourke) G.; student St. Patrick Major Sem., Menlo Park, Cal., 1930-32; M.A., Cath. U. Am., 1936, M.A., 1941, Ph.D., 1944. Ordained priest Roman Catholic Ch., 1936; joined Soc. Sulpicians, 1938; prof. philosophy St. Thomas Sem., Kenmore, Wash., 1946-70; columnist Register, 1950-70, Cath. N.W. Progress, 1961-70. Mem. Am. Cath. Philos. Assn., Nat. Cath. Conf. Interracial Justice. K.C. Editor, Priest mag., 1945-70. Address: Kenmore WA Died Sept. 15, 1970.

GUTHRIE, JAMES ALAN, newspaper publisher, editor; b. San Bernardino, Calif., Sept. 14, 1888; s. William J. and Anna (Lawson) B.; ed. pub. schs., Cal.; L.H.D. (hon.), U. Redlands, 1961; m. Grace E. Kelley, Jan. 8, 1913; children—James K., Kathleen E. (Mrs. John B. Lonergan) (dec.). Reporter, news editor, mng. editor, San Bernardino Daily Sun, 1905-37; editor San Bernardino Sun-Telegram, 1937-66; pres. The Sun Co.; mem. bd. dirs. Riverside Press Co., Acme Colorprint Co., U.S. Nat. Bank of San Diego. Chmn. pub. information com. San Bernardino Co. and City Def. councils; chmn. Cancer Soc. campaign, 1949; chmn. pub. relations San Bernardino War Chest, San Bernardino Red Cross and U.S.O.; dir. Nat. Orange Show, v.p. 1953. Recipient several awards for community service; Laymen's Citation award, U. Redlands, 1952; fellow of U. Redlands. Mem. adv. bd. Automobile Club So. Cal.; bd. dirs. (pres. 1946) San Bernardino C. of C.; mem. San Bernardino County War Savs. Com.; mem. Cal. Hawy. Commn.; treasury Patton State Hosp., 1919-23; mem. Am. Soc. Newspaper Editors, Cal. C. of C., Native Sons Golden West, Sigma Delta Chi. Presbyn. Clubs: California (Los Angeles); Sutter (Sacramento) Elk. Home: San Bernardino CA Died Aug. 23, 1966.

GUTHRIE, ROBERT R., banking executive; b. Paducah, Ky., Jan. 22, 1890; s. Elbridge and Mary (McElroy) G.; ed. Paducah High Sch.; student Centre Coll., 1910; m. Betty MacKenzie, 1938; children—Demia, Robert R., Mary. Owned and operated E. Guthrie Co., dept. store, Paducah, 1910-38; mem. N.Y. Exchange, firm, 1930-36; mem. N.Y. Cotton Exchange N.Y. Coffee and Sugar Exchange, N.Y. Commodity Exchange, 1934-36; mem. bd. dirs. Inter-state Dept. Stores, 1935-38, Phoenix Securities Corp., 1937-42; dir., mem. exec. and finance coms. Allied Stores Corp., N.Y.C., 1938-62; pres. Guthrie Investment Co., Paducah, from 1919; pres., dir. Tampa Bay Bank; dir. First Nat. Bank, St. Petersburg. First Park Bank, Pinellas Park, Fla., American Pioneer Life Ins. Co., Fla. Gas Company (Houston Corporation). Chief Textile, Leather and Clothing Div., OPM and WPB, Washington, 1941-42; asst. chief. Bur. of Industry Branches, WPB, having charge of foods, rubber and clothing, 1942; expert cons. to sec. of war, 1941-42. Mem. Fla. Indsl. Development Council; chairman Florida Nuclear and Space Commission. National vice chairman A.R.C. fund drive, 1952-55, mem. S.E. area council, 1953-54; pres. Children's Service Bureau, 1952-53; bd. dir. Salvation Army; trustee Am. Legion Crippled Children's Hospital; vice chairman United Givers, 1956, member Citizens Advisory Committee for Study Higher Edn. in Florida. President of Florida West Coast Educational Television station, WEDU. Mem. Orange Bowl Com. Mem. Am. Hearing Society (past director), Delta Kappa Epsilon, all Masonic bodies. Democrat. Clubs: Yale (N.Y.C.); Rolling Hills Country (Paducah); St. Petersburg Yacht. Address: St Petersburg FL Died May 1968.

GUTHRIE, S(EYMOUR) ASHLEY, lawyer; b. Chgo., June 20, 1889; s. Seymour and Martha G. (Greene) G.; student Mass. Inst. Tech., 1907-11; LL.B., Northwestern 1915; m. Annie Laurie Rainey, Aug. 22, 1917. Admitted to Ill. bar, 1915, since practiced in Chgo.; with Dent, Dobyns & Freeman, 1919-21; with Tenney, Harding & Sherman and successor firms, Tenney, Bentley, Guthrie, Askow & Howell, 1922-71, partner, 1928-71. Village atty., Riverside. Served as 1st lt. 346th Machine Gun Bn., U.S. Army, 1917-19. Mem. Am., Ill. State, Chgo. bar assns., Chgo. Law Inst., Phi Alpha Delta, Order of Coif. Republican. Presbyn. Clubs: Law, Univ., Legal (Chgo.); Riverside Golf. Home: Riverside IL Died Feb. 13, 1971.

GUTHRIE, THOMAS JOSEPH, lawyer; b. Elkhart, Ia., Apr. 19, 1877; s. John and Mary Ellen (Markham) G.; ed. Drake U., Des Moines, Ia., 1896-98; LL.B., 1903; m. Agnes Hogan, Aug. 26, 1913. Admitted to Iowa bar, 1903; gen. practice of law, 1903 and since 1920; county atty., Polk County, Ia., 1909-15; judge District Court of Ia., 1916-20; mem. Parrish, Guthrie, Colflesh & O'Brien since 1920, senior mem. since 1934. Mem. Am. Bar Assn., Ia. State Bar Assn. (past pres.). Chmn. Draft Bd., Polk County, 1917. Del. Nat. Rep. Conv., Phila., 1940. Republican. Catholic. Clubs: Des Moines, University (Des Moines, Ia.). Home: 3403 Crocker St. Office: Register and Tribune Bldg., Des Moines IA‡

GUTHRIE, WILLIAM TYRONE, theatrical dir., author; b. Tunbridge Wells, Kent, Eng., July 2, 1900; s. Dr. Thomas Clement and Norah (Power) G.; Wellington Coll., Berkshire, Eng., 1918; M.A., St. John's Coll., Oxford, 1923; LL.D., St. Andrews U., U. Western Ontario, Can.; m. Judith Bretherton, August 30, 1930. Adminstr. Old Vic, Sadler's Wells theatres, London, 1939-45, director Old Vic, 1951-52, then governor; director plays, 1924-71, including Gideon (by Paddy Chayesfsky), 1961. Director Shakesperian Festival, Stratford, Ontario, 1953-55. Chancellor Queens U., Belfast. Fellow Royal Soc. Arts. Author plays: Follow Me, 1931; Top of the Ladder, 1950; Life in the Theatre, 1960; A New Theatre, 1964; In Various Directions, 1965. Contbr. of essays, articles theatrical subjects in profl. publs. Guthrie Theatre, County Monaghan Eire Died May 15, 1971.

GUTMANN, ADDIS, savings and loan exec.; b. Victoria B.C., Can., Jan. 6, 1901; s. Moritz and Adelaid (Hyams) G.; grad. U. Wash., 1923; m. Estelle Schlesinger, June 15, 1927; children—Addis, Alene (Mrs. Ralph Nofield). Sec. Alaska Fur Co., Seattle, 1923-40, mgr., 1940-47, pres., 1947-56; pres. Alaska Jewelry Co., 1956-60; pres., dir. Franklin Savings & Loan Assn., Seattle, 1960-71; dir. Plaza Devel. Co. Pres. Jewish Community Center, 1960. Bd. dirs. Arthritis Found.; pres. Seattle chpt. Am. Cancer Soc., 1969-71. Served to col. AUS, 1941-46; PTO, ETO. Decorated Bronze Star with cluster. Mem. Retired Officers Assn. (nat. dir. 1970-71), Am. Legion (comdr. Seattle 1959). Nat. Sojourners, D.A.V. Mason (Shriner), Elk. Clubs: Wash. Athletic, Forty Nine (Seattle); Army and Navy (Washington). Home: Seattle WA Died Oct. 29, 1971.

GUTSCH, MILTON RIETOW, univ. prof.; b. Sheboygan, Wis., Mar. 7, 1885; s. Louis and Laura (Rietow) G.; A.B., U. of Wisconsin, 1908, A.M., 1909, Ph.D., 1916; m. Mary Mayfield, Aug. 29, 1918. Asst. inst. and fellow in history, U. of Wis., 1909-12; reporter, Sheboygan (Wis.) Press, 1909; instr. history, U. of Texas, 1912-16, adjunct prof., 1917-22, asso. prof., 1923-26, prof., 1927-51, chmn. dept. of history, 1927-51, sec. gen. faculty, 1928-51, secretary faculty council, 1944-51, honorary life sec. gen. faculty ıd faculty council, professor emeritus, 1951-71; director Texas War Records, 1918-19. Member American and Texas hist. socs., Medieval Acad. America, Wis. Acad. Scis. and Arts. Democrat. Editor: Texas History Teachers' Bulletin, 1912-21. Contbr. articles and book reviews. Home: Austin TX Died Jan. 1, 1967.

GUTT, CAMILLE, business exec.; b. Brussels, Belgium, Nov. 14, 1884; s. Max and Pauline (Sweizer) G.; grad. Burssels U., 1904, LL.D., 1906; m. Claire Frick, Aug. 26, 1906 (died 1948); children—Etienne, Jean, Max (dec.), Francois (dec.) (both killed in action). Barrister and journalist, 1906; sec.-gen. Belgian War Material Purchasing Commn., London, 1916; sec.-gen. Belgian Delegation to Reparations Commn., 1919; chief sec. to Belgium to Belgian Minister of Finance, 1920; asst. del. for Belgium to Reparations Commn., 1924; deputy to M. Francqui, Chancellor of Exchequer, 1926; Belgian mem. Young Com., 1929; plenipotentiary for Belgium in discussions leading to agreement by Germany to reimburse Marks of Occupation, 1929; plenipotentiary for Belgium in negotions of Hoover Moratorium, 1931; sent on official mission to U.S., 1934; minister of finance, Theunis Cabinet, 1934-35, Pierlot Cabinet, 1939-45; minister of nat. defense, 1940-42; minister of communications, 1940-42; minister of econ. affairs, 1940-45; mng. dir. and chmn. bd. Internat. Monetary Foundn. from 1946. Vice pres. Ford Motors, Belgium. Mng. dir. La Societe Generale des Mineriax and other corps. Served with Belgian Army, 1914-18. Decorated Grand Cordon de l'Ordre de Leopold, Grand Cordon de l'Ordre d'Orange Nassau, Grand Cordon de l'Ordre de la Couronne de Chene, Grand Officer de l'Ordre de la Legion d'Honneur, Grand Cordon de l'Ordre pour le Merite, and many others, including war medals. Club: Metropolitan (Washington). Home: Brussels Belgium Died June 1971.

GUTTRIDGE, G(EORGE) H(ERBERT), univ. prof.; b. Hull, Eng., Aug. 6, 1898; s. Rev. Frederick William Hamilton and Eleanor Cowley (Peace) G.; B.A., Cambridge, Eng., 1920, M.A., 1924; m. Eleanor Mann, Dec. 27, 1928. Came to U.S., 1922. Scholar, St. John's Coll., Cambridge, 1919-21, Prince Consort Prizeman (Cambridge), 1922; lecturer in Brit. Empire history for Bd. of Mil. Studies, 1921-22, for economics tripos (Cambridge), 1923-24; Choate fellow, Harvard, 1922-23; asst. prof. history U. of Calif., 1925-31, asso. prof., 1931-42, prof. English history, 1942-58, Sather professor of history, 1958-64, emeritus, 1965-69. Served as 2d lt., later lt. Royal Garrison Arty., 1917-18. Fellow Royal Hist. Soc., Royal Commonwealth Soc.; mem. Hist. Assn. (London). Author books: (latest) English Whiggism and the American Revolution, 1942; Early Career of Lord Rockingham, 1952. Contbr. articles hist. jours. and Ency. Brit. (14th ed.). Editor: Burke Correspondence Vol. 3. Home: Carmel CA Died Jan. 7, 1969; buried Malvern Wells, Worcs England

GUY, WILLIAM GEORGE, educator; b. Carbonear, Newfoundland, Mar. 17, 1899; s. James P. and Elizabeth (Smith) G.; B.Sc., Mt. Allison U., 1919, A.B., 1920; B.A. (Rhodes scholar), Oxford U., 1922; Ph.D. (du Pont fellow), U. Chgo., 1925; Sc.D., Coll. William and Mary, 1969; m. Gladys E. Bennett, July 29, 1926. Came to U.S., 1923, naturalized, 1938. Asst. prof. chemistry Coll. William and Mary, 1925-27, asso. prof., 1927-30, prof. 1930-68, head dept., 1946-68. Fellow A.A.A.S.; mem. Am. Chem. Soc. (chmn. Va. sect. 1951-52), Virginia Academy of Science (president 1957-58), Sigma Xi, Phi Beta Kappa, Omicron Delta Kappa. Home: Williamsburg VA Died June 14, 1969; buried Williamsburg VA

GUYER, MICHAEL FREDERIC, zoologist; b. Plattsburg, Mo., Nov. 17, 1874; s. Michael and Sarah J. (Thomas) G.; U. of Mo., 1890-92; B.S., U. of Chicago, 1894; A.M., U. of Neb., 1897; Ph.D., U. of Chicago, 1900; LL.D., U. of Mo., 1924; Paris and Naples, 1908-09 (Smithsonian table, at Naples); m. Helen M. Stuaffer, Dec. 21, 1899 (died Nov. 4, 1948); 1 son, Edwin Michael Cooley. Asst. in zoology, U. of Neb., 1895-96; teacher biology, Lincoln (Neb.) High Sch., 1896-97; fellow zoology, U. of Chicago, 1897-1900; head dept. biology, U. of Cincinnati, 1900-11; professor zoology, University of Wisconsin, 1911-45; professor emeritus since 1945. Member National Committee on Medical Education, 1928-32. Fellow A.A.A.S. (vice-pres. sec. F 28); mem. Am. Soc. Naturalists, Assn. American Anatomists, Soc. American Zoologists (pres. 1923), Ohio Acad. Sciences, Wis. Acad. Sciences, Am. Micros. Soc. (pres. 1916-18), Soc. Exptl. Biology and Medicine, Wis. Basic Science Board, Acad. Natural Science of Phila, Sigma Xi, Phi Kappa Phi, Phi Beta Pi; corr. mem. Peiping Soc. of Natural History. Clubs: University, Chaos. Author: Animal Micrology, 1906, revised edits., 1917, 30, 36; Being Well Born, 1915, revised edit., 1927; Animal Biology, 1931 (rev. edit. 1948); Speaking of Man, 1942. Also various tech. biol. researches. Address: 138 N. Prospect Av., Madison 5 WI‡

GUZE, HENRY, educator, psychotherapist; b. Newark, June 7, 1919; s. Julius and Celia (Huberman) G.; B.A., Rutgers U., 1943; Ph.D., N.Y. U. Grad. Sch. Arts and Scis., 1955; m. Vivian Segerman, June 18, 1945. Instr. to adj. prof. psychology Grad. Sch., L.I. U., Bklyn., 1948-70; individual practice psychotherapy, N.Y.C., 1950-70; vis. prof. anthropology Drew U., Madison, N.J., 1966-70. Research asso. Harry Benjamin Found. Gender Research, 1965-67. Mem. exec. bd. Essex Co. br. Am. Civil Liberties Union, 1966-70. Trustee Aureon Found. Fellow A.A.A.S., Soc. Clin. and Exptl. Hypnosis (Merit award 1955), Soc. Sci. Study

Sex (pres.), Acad. Psychosomatic Medicine; mem. Am. Psychosomatic Soc., Am. Assn. Phys. Anthroplogists, Am. Acad. Psychotherapists (Merit award 1964). Research in maternal and sexual behavior in animals; hypnosis; body image; schizophrenia; transsexualism; menustration; physician-patient relationships; psychosomatics; constl. aspects of disease. Home: Verona NJ Died July 1, 1970.

GWINN, JOSEPH MARR, educator; b. near Warrensburg, Mo., April 23, 1870; s. of John Marr and Minerva Jane (Jaynes) G.; B.Pd., State Normal Sch., Warrensburg, Mo., 1893; A.B., U. of Mo., 1902, LL.D., same univ., 1926; A.M., Columbia Univ., 1907; m. Elise Williams, Feb. 2, 1895; children—Gladys (Mrs. R. A. Brown), Joseph M. Teacher rural sch. nr. Warrensburg, 1890-91; prin. village sch., Ashland, Mo., 1893-95, Nevada (Mo.) High Sch., 1895-97, Joplin (Mo.) High Sch., 1897-1900; supt. pub. schs., Joplin, 1902-03; prof. edn., State Normal Sch., Warrensburg, 1903-06; prof. edn. and dir. Teachers Coll. (Tulane U.), 1907-10; supt. pub. schs., New Orleans, Nov. 16, 1910-23; supt. schs., San Francisco, 1923-33; prof. of education, San Jose State Coll., 1936-40. Dir. College of Education, A.E.F. Univ., Beaune, France, 1919. Mem. N.E.A. (trustee; pres. dept. of superintendence, 1927-28); pres. Nat. Soc. Study of Edn., 1915, Nat. Council of Edn., 1922-25, Calif. State Teachers Assn., 1928-32. Officier de Academie Republique Francaise. Mem. Disciples of Christ Ch. Mason (K.T., Scottish Rite, K.C.C.H., Shriner). Clubs: University, Pasadena, Phi Delta Kappa. Home: 1503 Coolidge Av., Pasadena CA‡

GWYNN, J(OHN) MINOR, univ. prof.; b. Glade Spring, Va., Aug. 13, 1897; s. Price Henderson and Mary Waters (Minor) G.; A.B., U. of N.C., 1918, A.M., 1927; grad. study, U. of Chicago, 1927; Ph.D., Yale, 1935; m. Janie Sue Stacy, June 6, 1925; 1 son, John Minor. Elementary sch. teacher, Leaksville, N.C., 1919; high sch. teacher and prin., Leaksvwlle, 1919-20, Reidsville, 1920-24; instr. in Latin, U. of N.C., 1924-26, asst. prof. edn., 1927-36, also supt. schs., Chapel Hill (part of univ. work), 1932-37, asso. prof. edn. and dir. curiculum lab., 1936-45, prof. edn., dir. cirriculum lab., 1945-54, prof. edn., mem. adminstrv. bd. sch. edn., 1954-68; instructor, Yale, 1933-35. Served as 2d lt., inf., U.S. Army, 1918. Mem. Nat. Soc. Study Edn., Am. Assn. Sch. Adminstrs., Assn. for Supervision and Curriculum Development, Nat. Assn. Secondary Sch. Prins., Nat. Vocational Guidance Assn., Am. Acad. Polit. and Social Sci., Nat. Soc. Advancement Edn., Am. Edn. Fellowship (v.p.), N.E.A., Classical Assn. Middle W. and South, Phi Beta Kappa, Phi Delta Kappa. Presbyterian. Mason (Shriner). Asso. editor The High Sch. Jour. (U. of N.C.), 1929-49, mng. editor, 1930-31. Mem. Del. State Sch. Survey, 1946. Author: Curriculum Principles and Social Trends, 1943, rev. edits., 1950, 60, 69. Editor: (with W. Carson Ryan and A.K. King) Secondary Education in the South, 1946; (with A.J. Atkins) Teaching Alcohol Education in the Schools, 1959; Theory and Practice of Supervision, 1961. Chmn., editor U. (Chapel Hill) instn.-wide Tchr. Edn. Self-Study, 1963-64. Home: Chapel Hill NC Died Jan. 16, 1971; buried

HAANSTRA, JOHN WILSON, mfg. co. exec.; b. San Francisco, May 12, 1926; s. John and Sophie W. (Wilson) H.; B.S. in Elec. Engring., U. Cal. at Berkeley, 1949, M.S. in Elec. Engring., 1950; m. June Claire Hill, June 19, 1949 (dec. Aug. 1969); children—Bruce, Sharon, Glenn (dec.). With IBM Corp., 1950-67, asst. mgr. product devel., 1958-59, asst. gen mgr. gen. products div., 1959-61, pres. systems devel. div., 1961-66, v.p. systems div., Gaithersburg, Md., 1966-67; v.p., gen mgr. information systems equipment div. Gen. Electric Co., Phoenix, 1967-69. Mem. I.E.E.E., Sigma Xi, Eta Kappa Nu, Tau Beta Pi. Home: Scottsdale AZ Died Aug. 16, 1969.

HAAS, SAMUEL, oil co. exec.; b. Tiger Bend Plantation, Avoyelles Parish, La., Apr. 7, 1894; s. Dr. William David and Hattie (Haas) H.; B.S., Tulane U., 1915; student bus. adminstrn., Alexander-Hamilton Inst., 1923; m. Lulu Susan Haupt, July 10, 1920; children—Samuel Douglas, Joseph Marshall. Cotton buyer, bookkeeper W.D. Haas & Co., 1915-27; sec. Alexandria Compress Co., 1920-27; pres. Commercial Bank & Trust Co., 1928-33; postmaster, Alexandria, La., 1934-42; pres., gen. mgr. Avoyelles Who Gro Co., Ltd.; pres. Haas Investment Co., Inc., La. Central Land & Improvement Co., Inc., Haas Land Co., Ltd., Bunkie Lumber and Supply Company, Limited; vice president of Union Texas Natural Gas Corporation, and also Farmers Truck & Produce Co., Foster Gin Co., Coastal Hunting Club, Inc.; dir. Gen. American Oil Co. of Tex., La. & Ark. R.R. Co., Meeker Sugar Coop., Inc. Active A.R.C., Community Fund drives. Chmn civil def., Rapides Parish; commr. Alexandria Housing Authority, from 1940. Served from 2d lt. to 1st lt., F.A., U.S. Army, 1917-19; as maj. F.A., AUS, 1940-54. Decorated Verdun medal (France), 1919; recipient Red Cross of Constantine, Masonic Frat. Mem. Alexandria C. of C. (pres. 1942-43), Vets. Fgn. Wars (dep. comdr. La.-Miss. 1930-31), Am. Legion (comdr. 1923), 40 and 8, Officers Res. Corps (past pres. Alexandria), S.A.R., Wholesale Grocers Assn.(past dir., v.p.), La. Motor Transport Assn. (dir.), Nat. Postmasters Assn. (past pres. La.; nat. dir. 1934), Kappa Sigma. Methodist (steward). Mason (K.T., Shriner). Club: Alexandria Rotary (pres. 1930-31). Home: Alexandria LA Died Jan. 5, 1964; buried Hillcrest Cemetery, Dallas TX

HAAS, WILLIAM H., geographer; b. Bellevue, O., June 20, 1872; s. George and Minnie (Hankamer) H.; student Ohio Northern U. (Ada, O.), Butler Coll. (Indianapolis, Ind.); A.B., U. of Chicago, 1903, Ph.D., 1922; m. Marion Mahon, of Ottumwa, Ia., June 29, 1910. With Northwestern U. since 1914, prof. geography since 1924; spl. expert, U.S. Shipping Bd., 1917, 18; v.p. Samuel Mahon Co., wholesale grocers. Mem. Chicago Acad. Sciences, Chicago Geog. Soc., Ecol. Soc. America, Ill. State Acad., Assn. Am. Geographers. Mason. Conglist. Worked out the geography and geology of the Mesa Verde Nat. Park; made study of influence of glaciation in Ohio and spl. studies on the Mississippi River; writer on Am. Indian and on Geography of Brazil, etc. Home: 1812 Hinman Av., Evanston IL‡

HABERMAN, PHILLIP WILLIAM, JR., lawyer; b. St. Louis, Mar. 30, 1905; s. Phillip William and Blanche (Altheimer) H.; A.B., Princeton, 1926; LL.B., Columbia, 1929; m. Helen Liebman, July 30, 1933; children—Charles, Norma. Admitted to N.Y. bar, 1929; asst. counsel Seabury Investigations, N.Y.C., 1930-32; asst., acting corp. counsel City of N.Y., 1934-37; practice in N.Y.C., from 1929; mem. firm Proskauer, Rose, Goetz & Mendelsohn, from 1945. Chief asst. counsel Rapp-Coudert Legislative Com. to Investigate Communism in N.Y. pub. schs., 1940-42; mem. Temporary State Commn. on Govtl. Activities, N.Y.C., 1960-61; mem. N.Y.C. Charter Revision Commn., 1961; mem., vice chmn. Commn. on State-Local Fiscal Relations, 1962-65. Pres. Mt. Sinai Hosp. Sch. Nursing, 1951-60, now mem. bd. dirs.; v.p., bd. dirs. Legal Aid Soc. N.Y.; treas., trustee, exec. com. Practising Law Inst.; trustee Mt. Sinai Hosp., N.Y.C., Simon's Rock, Great Barrington, Mass. Served with USAAF, 1942-45. Fellow Am. Bar Found., Am. Coll. Trial Lawyers; mem. Assn. Bar City of N.Y. (chmn. exec. com. 1958-59, v.p. 1959-60), Am., N.Y. State bar assns., N.Y. County Lawyers Assn., Am. Arbitration Assn. (dir., mem. exec. com. 1963-69). Clubs: Princeton, Harmonic (N.Y.C.), Campus (Princeton, N.J.); Century Country (Purchase, N.Y.). Home: New York City NY

HABERMAN, SOL, microbiologist, educator; b. Chgo., Jan. 15, 1914; s. Nathan and Eva (Yankovitch) H.; A.S., N. Tex. Agrl. Coll., 1934; So. Meth. U., 1935; A.B., U. Tex., 1936, M.A., 1937; Ph.D., Ohio State U., 1941; m. Carleta Jeanne Rambo, May 14, 1948; 1 son, Hardy Kemp. Bacteriologist, immunologist Baylor U. Hosp., from 1939; instr. Coll. Medicine, Baylor U., 1941-43, prof. Coll. Dentistry, 1947, Grad. Sch., from 1950; asso. prof. Southwestern Med. Coll., 1943-52; lectr. bacteriology So. Meth. U.,1947-50; asst. dir. Wadley Research Inst. and Blood Center, 1952-56; dir. microbiology dept. pathology, Baylor U. Med. Center, now dir. grad. studies Dallas div. Grad. Sch. Coll. Dentistry. Pres. immuno-hematology sect. 5th Congress Internat. Soc. Hematology, Paris, France, 1954; med. adv. bd. Leukemia Soc. Recipient of award of merit Tex. Soc. Pathology. Diplomate Am. Bd. Microbiology. Fellow Am. Acad. Microbiology, Am. Coll, Dentists, Am. Assn. Advancement Sci.; mem. Internat. Soc. Hematology (past sec.-gen. Western Hemisphere), Soc. Am. Bacteriologists, Am. Assn. Immunologists, Am. Assn. U. Profs., Am. Soc. Human Genetics, American Academy of Forensic Science, Sigma Xi, Omicron Kappa Upsilon, also Sigma Pi Sigma, Beta Beta Beta, Phi Delta Epsilon. Author: Laboratory Manual for Dental Bacteriology, 1953. Asso. editor various proc. Internat. Soc. Hematology; editor newsletter Am. Bd. Microbiology. Contbr. profl. publs. Home: Dallas TX Died Apr. 17, 1968.

HACK, GWENDOLYN DUNLEVY KELLEY, artist; b. Columbus, O., Nov. 10, 1877; d. Alfred and Mary Craig (Dunlevy) Kelley; ed. Chicago Art Inst., Art Students' League, New York; in Paris studied under Mesdames Debillement and Gallet; m. at Columbus, Dr. Charles W. Hack, May 10, 1905. Specialties miniatures on ivory, pastels, bas-reliefs, etc.; painted portraits on ivory, Queen of Italy, 1895, and received decoration; exhibited paintings in Paris Salon, Nat. Acad. of Design, Chicago Art Inst., Cincinnati Art Mus. and in other cities; also Nashville and Omaha expns. Mem. Soc. Colonial Dames, D.A.R. Episcopalian. Author: (as Gwendolyn Dunlevy Kelley) Annals of Ulidia and the History of the Dunlevy Family, 1901; Poems, 1901; Remenyi, Musician and Man, 1906. Address: New York‡

HACKETT, ARTHUR, tenor; b. Portland, Me., Apr. 5, 1884; s. Charles A. and Bridget (Welch) H.; ed. high sch., Worcester, Mass.; studied violin with Michael Reidel, voice under Arthur J. Hubbard and Vincent V. Hubbard, Boston, and coached under masters abroad; studied acting with Weinschenk, Paris; m. Constance Freeman, Sept. 19, 1914; 1 dau., Anne Dudley. Made many concert tours in U.S.; 5 tours with Geraldine Farrar; soloist in chs., New York; operatic debut in Rigoletto, Paris Grand Opera, 1924; in Europe, 1924-27, singing under name of Granville; with Melba on farewell tour of Brit. Isles, 1926; soloist with New York Symphony, New York Philharmonic, Boston Symphony Orchestra, etc., and sang at many music festivals; sang leading role on tour with The King's Henchman"; prof. of voice, chmn. vocal dept. Sch. of Music, U. Mich., Ann Arbor, 1930-53. Mem. Phi Mu Wolfeboro NH Died Sept. 30, 1969; buried Lakeview Cemetery, Wolfeboro NH

HACKETT, CHARLES MEGGINSON, newspaper editor; b. Wilmington, Del., Apr. 3, 1909; s. Harry Clifford and Elizabeth (Megginson) H.; student U. Del., 1927-29, U. Pa., 1929-31; m. Dorothy Hartmann, Oct. 10, 1930; children—Charles Michael, Henry Clay; m. 2d, Marjorie Regestein, Apr. 5, 1954; 1 dau., Cynthia. With Wilmington Eve. Jour., 1927-28; reporter Wilmington Every Eve., 1929-30, Phila. Record, 1930-34; reporter, city editor Wilmington Star, 1934-37; press officer E.I. du Pont de Nemours & Co., Inc. 1937-64; v.p., exec. editor News-Jour. Papers, Wilmington, 1964-68; pres. News-Jour. Pub. Co., from 1968; lectr. Boston U., 1950-54, U. Pa., 1952-56. Mem. Del. Planning Commn. Mem. Am. Soc. Newspaper Editors, Am. Newspaper Pubs. Assn., Sigma Delta Chi. Home: Wilmington DE

HACKETT, JAMES DOMINICK, labor consultant, author; b. Kilkenny, Ireland, Apr. 14, 1877; s. John Byrne (M.D.) and Bridget (Doheny) H.; ed. Clongowes Wood Coll., Ireland; m. Jessie, d. John Taylor and Julia (Deming) Sherman, of Brooklyn, N.Y., Nov. 7, 1914;children—John, James, Roger, Edmond. Licentiate of Pharmaceutical Soc. of Ireland, 1900; came to N.Y. City, 1904; labor mgr. Nichols Copper Co., New York, until 1914; investigator and consultant on labor problems; dir. Bur. of Industrial Hygiene, N.Y. State Dept. of Labor, 1929. Lecturer New York U., 1919-26. Mem. Friendly Sons of St. Patrick, Am. Irish Hist. Soc. Author: Health Maintenance in Industry, 1925; Labor Management, 1929. Home: 94 Franklin Pl., Flushing, L.I., N.Y. Office: 132 E. 16th St., New York NY‡

HACKETT, SAMUEL EVERETT, steel exec.; b. Coralville, Ia., July 21, 1877; s. Thomas Ross and Amanda (Crozier) H.; ed. high sch. and business coll.; m. Bessie Bischoff, of Chicago, Ill., Sept. 20, 1906; children—Spencer Ross, David Everett (dec.). Clk. for Am. Tin Plate Co., Chicago, 1898, for Republic Iron & Steel Co., Chicago, 1899; mgr. order dept., and purchasing agt., Jos. T. Ryerson & Son, Chicago, 1899-1916; with Jones & Laughlin Steel Corpn. since 1916, as mgr. branch office and warehouse, Chicago, 1916-19, gen. mgr. of sales, Pittsburgh, 1919-23, v.p., 1923-34, pres., 1934-38, resigned as pres., Feb. 14, 1938. Mem. Am. Iron & Steel Inst. Republican. Presbyn. Clubs: Duquesne, Fox Chapel Golf (Pittsburgh). Home: 204 S. Lexington Av. Office: 1100 Union Trust Bldg., Pittsburgh PA‡

HADAMARD, JACQUES SALOMON, prof. mathematics; b. Versailles, France, Dec. 8, 1865; s. Amedee and Claire (Picard) H.; came to U.S., 1941; student Lycee Louis le Grand, Paris, 1877-84; graduate, Ecole Normale Superieure, Paris, 1887, Docteur es Sciences, mathematiques, 1892; hon. LL.D., Yale, 1901, univs. Oslo, Brussels, Liege, Delhi; m. Louise-Anna Trenel, June 30, 1892; children—Pierre and Etienne (died in World War I), Mathieu Georges (died in North Africa, World War II), Cecile Mariette (Mrs. Rene Picard), Jacqueline Claire Jeanne. Commissariat a l'Energie Atomique, Paris; asso. professor, University Bordeaux, 1893, prof. 1896; prof., Coll. de France, 1909, Ecole Polytechnique, 1912, Ecole Centrale des Arts, 1920, emeritus, 1937; visiting prof., Columbia Univ., New York, 1941. Grand Officier of Legion d'Honneur. Mem. Acad. of Sciences (Paris), Nat. Acad. of Sciences (Washington, D.C.); hon. mem. Am. Acad. Arts and Sciences (Boston). Author mathematical textbooks. Home: 12 rue Emile Faguet, Paris France‡

HADEN, ANNIE BATES (MRS. CHARLES J. HADEN), civic and humanitarian work; d. Milledge Llewellyn and Emma (Allen) Bates; A.B., Wesleyan Coll., Ga., 1888; m. Charles J. Haden, Oct. 16, 1895. Was pres. Atlanta Federation of Women's Clubs (100 clubs, 8,000 members), 1912-14; chmn. Nat. Council of Defense, Atlanta Dist., during World War, originating system of med. examination of infants through voluntary service of physicians; chmn. Student Aid Foundation, 1920-36; trustee Tallulah Falls Sch.; trustee and pres. Nat. Alumni Assn. Wesleyan College, 1930-36; pres. Atlanta Y.W.C.A., 1914-16; chmn. Atlanta town com. of Colonial Dames of America, 1938, United Daughters of Confederacy; hon. life dir. Ga. Fed. Women's Clubs; mem. Women's Advisory Bd. for Ga. of New York World's Fair. Democrat. Home: 1521 Peachtree St., Atlanta GA*

HADEN, CHARLES JONES, lawyer, retired; born Huntsville, Ala., Mar. 17, 1863; s. John Tate and Jane (Pickens) H.; ed. high sch.; hon. Dr. Pub. Service, Oglethorpe U., 1938; m. Annie Llewellyn Bates, Oct. 16, 1895. Actively interested in diversification of farm crops, improvement of roads and creation of home markets. Pres. State Chamber of Commerce, Ga., 1913; dollar-a-year man, World War; dir. War Savings Stamp

Campaign, 1918; pres. Ga. Illiteracy Commn., 1924; mem. Ga. State Bd. of Adult Edn. since 1930. Established homes of about 100 acres each for war veterans on one of his plantations; donor of granite shaft in town of Crawford, Ga., as memorial to William H. Crawford, U.S. senator, twice sec. of U.S. treasury and minister to France; also donor memorial to Stephen C. Foster (author of Suwanee River) at the head waters of the river; a leader in securing the Panorama painting" (Battle of Atlanta) as property of City of Atlanta. Mem. Dem. State Exec. Com., Ga., 1896; chmn. finance com. for state of Ga. of Dem. Nat. Com. in presdl. campaign of 1920. Chmn. Federal Farm Debt Adjustment Commn. for Ga., 1934-35. Mem. Acad. Polit. Science, Ga. Soc. (New York); hon. mem. Ga. Press Assn. Methodist. Clubs: Capital City, City, Piedmont (Atlanta). During boll weevil invasion of cotton brought calcium arsenate into Ga. for pub. use. Address: 1521 Peachtree St. N.E., Atlanta GA‡

HADSALL, HARRY HUGH, engr., contractor; b. Wilmington, Ill., July 9, 1875; s. Kittie (Townsend) H.; B.S. in C.E., U. of Ill., 1897; m. Jean Stewart, of Wilmington, July 1, 1903; children—Harry Stewart (dec.), John McIntyre. With Leonard Constrn. Co., Chicago, builders of ry. structures, mfg. plants, hotels, office bldgs., warehouses, etc., since 1907, v.p. and sec. since 1913. Mem. Am. Soc. C.E., Western Soc. Engrs., Kappa Sigma. Clubs: Chicago Engineers', University, South Shore Country, Flossmoor Country. Home: 1121 E. 49th St. Office: 37 S. Wabash Av., Chicago IL‡

HAEBERLE, ARMINIUS T., consular service; b. St. Louis, Mo., Jan. 23, 1874; educated Washington University, St. Louis. Was instructor St. Charles (Mo.) Coll. and prin. pub. schs., Hermann, Mo.; v.-dir. Inst. Ingles, Santiago, Chile, 1898-1903; head modern lang. dept. McKinley High Sch., St. Louis, 1904-07; consul at Manzanillo, Mexico, 1908-10, Tegucigalpa, Honduras, 1910-13, St. Michael's, Azores, 1913-15, Pernambuco, Brazil, 1915-19; Rio de Janerio, 1919-23; Sao Paulo, 1923-25; consul gen. at Dresden, 1925-36; retired Apr. 1936. Mem. Sons of the Revolution. Author: The Story of Old Pewter. Address: care Dept. of State, Washington DC‡

HAFEN, ANN WOODBURY (MRS. LEROY R. HAFEN), author; b. Salt Lake City, May 31, 1893; d. John T. and Mary (Evans) Woodbury; student Brigham Young U., 1914-15, U. Cal. at Berkeley, 1920-21, U. Denver, 1924-25; m. LeRoy R. Hafen, Sept. 3, 1915; children—Norma (dec.), Karl L. Recipient nat. awards in poetry, stories and articles. Mem. Colo. State (past pres.), Utah State (past pres.) poetry socs., Nat. League Am. Pen Women (past pres. Colo.), Altrusa Internat. (past pres. Provo br.). Author: Quenched Fire and Other Poems, 1937; One More American, 1937; Campfire Frontier, New Stories of the Old West, 1946; (with L. R. Hafen) The Colorado Story, 1943 (rev. 1953, 1966); (with L. R. Hafen) Far West and Rockies Series, 15 vols., 1954-62 including Old Spanish Trail, 1954, Journals of 49ers, 1954, Fremont's Disaster Expedition, 1960, Handcarts to Zion, 1960; Campfire Frontier, Stories and Poems of the Old West, 1969; (with L. R. Hafen) The Joyous Journey of LeRoy R. and Ann W. Hafen, an autobiography, 1973. Editor: Utah Sings, IV, 1964. Died Dec. 13, 1970; interred Fairmount Cemetery Denver CO

HAGAR, STANSBURY, ethnologist; b. San Francisco, Calif., Dec. 9, 1869; s. Thomas Smith and Amy T. H.; A.B., Yale, 1892; LL.B., New York Law Sch., 1897; m. Clara Robinson, Sept. 20, 1900 (dec.); 1 dau., Margery. Student of Am. ethnology and archeology of Am. Indians, and of Mexico and Peru; student symbolic astronomy of the Orient; has visited various Indian tribes and was adopted by the Hopi Indians of Arizona. Emeritus life mem. A.A.A.S.; fellow Am. Ethnol. Soc., Am. Anthrop. Assn.; mem. Nat. Inst. Social Sciences, Congres Internat. des Americanistes, Astron. Soc. of the Pacific, Soc. of Old Brooklynites, Astronomick Historiefaskning I Land Sweden. Club: Explorers of New York (life mem.). Home: Polhemus Pl., Brooklyn NY‡

HAGEMAN, HARRY ANDREW, design engr.; b. Niagara Falls, N.Y., July 25, 1877; s. Henry Charles and Kate (Frambach) H.; M.E., Cornell U., 1899; m. Evelyn Chase, Sept. 11, 1926; 1 son, John Andrew. Rodman and chainman Cataract Construction Co., 1894-95; draftsman and insp., Cornell Univ., 1894-96, 1897-99, Niagara Falls Power & Allied Companies, 1899-1906; asst. hydraulic engr. I. P. Morris Co., Phila., 1906-08; asst. mech. engr. Niagara Falls Power & Allied Cos., 1908-10; hydraulic engr. Stone & Webster Engring. Corp., Seattle, Wash., and Boston, 1910-17; mech. engr. Bethlehem Shipbuilding Corp., 1917-21; chief hydraulic engr. Stone & Webster, Boston, 1921-31, pub. bldg. commr., Newton, Mass., 1931-36; chief hydraulic engr. and chief design engr. Tenn. Valley Authority, 1936-41. Mem. American Soc. Civil Engrs., Boston Soc. Civil Engrs. Conglist. Mason (K.T., Shriner). Club: Knoxville (Tenn.) Technical Society. Home: 137 Allerton Rd., Newton Highlands MA‡

HAGEMANN, HARRY H., lawyer; born Black Hawk County, Ia., Jan. 25, 1900; s. Herman C. and Emma (Paul) H.; student Ia. State Tchrs. Coll., 1920-21, State U., Ia., 1922; LL.B., Georgetown U., 1926; LL.D., Wartburg Coll., 1959; m. Shirley Kilpatrick, 1933; 1 dau., Judith A. Admitted to D.C. bar, 1926, Supreme Ct. of Ia. bar, 1926; county atty., Bremer County, Ia., 1928-32; gen. counsel Luth. Mut. Life Ins. Co., 1946-66, v.p., 1961-65; partner Hagemann & Hagemann, Waverly; chmn. bd. Am. Savs. Bank of Tripoli (Ia.); v.p., dir. State Bank of Waverly. Trustee Rohlf Meml. Found., Waverly Community Found. Mem. Ia. state bd. regents, 1951-63, pres. state bd. regents, 1957-63; mem. bd. regents Wartburg Coll., 1965-70, chmn., 1967-70. Served with USN, World War I. Mem. Am., Ia., Bremer County bar assns., Am. Legion, Order of Coif. Elk, Rotarian. Home: Waverly IA Died Dec. 15, 1970; buried Harlington Cemetery, Waverly IA

HAGEN, JERE, editor; born in Seattle on January 7, 1908; s. Herbert B. and Anna (Lewis) H.; student U. Wash., 1925-27, U. Calif., 1929; m. Reva Hansard, Mar. 4, 1933; 1 son, Jere. Reporter Tacoma (Wash.) Ledger, 1923-24, Seattle Times, 1925, San Francisco Chronicle, 1927-30; sports editor, Shanghai (China) Press, 1926; picture editor Atlanta Georgian, 1930-34; picture editor Chgo. Herald-Am. now Chicago Am., 1937-40, Sunday editor 1944-60; Chgo. editor Am. Weekly, 1945-58; exec. editor Calumet Pub. Co., Lansing, Ill., 1962-64; news editor Economist Newspapers, Inc., Chgo., 1964-69. Mem. of board of trustees, Cancer Research Foundation. Member Alpha Delta Phi, Sigma Delta Chi. Clubs: Chicago Press (past pres.), Illinois Athletic. Home: Lake Villa IL Died 1969.

HAGER, ALBERT RALPH;, b. Chicago, Mar. 9, 1874; s. Albert David and Rosanna Field (Blood) H.; B.S., U. of Wis., 1897; m. Emily Read, of Salt Lake City, Dec. 21, 1904. Teacher and prin. high schs., U.S., 1897-01; apptd. instr. in physics, U. of Cal., 1901; instr. in physics, Philippine Normal Sch., 1901-03; chief of edn., Philippine Expn. Bd., Manila, and St. Louis Expn., 1903-4; head of Technical Supply Co., of China; importer technical publs. and equipment, China, Japan and Philippines, residing in Manila and Shanghai, 1905—. Gen. mgr. for Internat. Corr. Schs. in China, Japan and P.I. Progressive. Conglist. Life mem. Ednl. Assn. of China; mem. S.A.R. Clubs: Phi Gamma Delta (New York), University, Elks (Manila), Golf, American, Shanghai Golf, Columbia Country (Shanghai). Home: 18 Rue Corneille, Shanghai. Address: PO Box 429, Manila, P.I.; also Box 552, Shanghai China‡

HAGER, ALICE ROGERS, author; b. Peoria, Ill.; d. Harry James and Caroline Augusta (Sammis) Rogers; A.B., Leland Stanford U., 1915; postgrad. U. Cal., 1917; m. John Manfred Hager, Aug. 3, 1916 (div.); children—Carolyn Anne, Helen Dinwiddie. Spl. agt. Bur. Labor Statistics, U.S. Dept. Labor, 1918, chief pub. information, Women's Bur., 1927-29; reporter Los Angeles Herald, 1923-24; spl. writer N.Y. Times, Washington Star and other newspapers and mags., 1929-34; reporter on aviation N.Am. Newspaper Alliance, 1934-40; chief pub. information CAB, 1940-42; war corr. CBI theatre Skyways Mag., 1944. Washington editor, 1942-47; pub. affairs officer U.S. Embassy, Brussels, Belgium, 1948-52; area officer USIA, 1952-57. Decorated Order of So. Cross, Silver Medal of Order of Merit Santos Dumont (Brazil). Mem. Acad. Polit. Sci., Children's Book Guild, Delta Delta Delta. Episcopalian. Clubs: Overseas Press, Women's Nat. Press (pres. 1946-47). Author books, including Brazil, Giant to the South, 1945; Wings for the Dragon, 1945; Janice, Air Line Hostess, 1947; The Canvas Castle, 1948; Dateline-Paris, 1954; Wonderful Ice Cream Cart, 1955; Washington Secretary, 1958; Love's Golden Circle, 1961; Cathy Whitney—President's Daughter, 1966. Home: Alexandria VA Died Dec. 5, 1969.

HAGERTY, EDWARD DANIEL, physician; b. Nashua, N.H., Oct. 10, 1909; s. Timothy Patrick and Katherine (McLaughlin) H.; M.D., McGill U., 1936; m. Dorothy E. Gerhard, Oct. 25, 1945. Intern, Lynn (Mass.) Hosp., 1936, Worcester (Mass.) City Hosp., 1937-39; resident in orthopedic surgery Kings County Hosp., Bklyn., 1939-42; orthopedic surgeon Sacred Heart Hosp, Manchester, N.H., until 1970. Served from capt. to lt. col., M.C., AUS, 1942-45. Decorated Bronze Star medal. Diplomate Am. Bd. Orthopaedic Surgery. Fellow A.C.S.; mem. A.M.A., Am. Acad. Orthopaedic Surgeons, Internat. Coll. Surgeons, New Eng. Orthopaedic Soc., Boston Orthopaedic Club. Home: Manchester NH Died Apr. 12, 1970; buried Manchester NH

HAGGARD, SIR GODFREY DIGSBY NAPIER, Brit. consul gen., Chgo., 1928-32, Paris, 1932-38, N.Y.C., 1938-44. Address: Essex England Died Apr. 3, 1969.

HAGGERTY, CORNELIUS J., labor union ofcl.; b. Boston, Jan. 10, 1894. s. Daniel and Nora (Driscoll) H.; m. Margaret Kelleher, June 30, 1920; children—Cornelius J., Donald P. Joined Lathers Union, 1915, bus. mgr. Local 42, Los Angeles, 1928-29; 2d v.p. Internat. Union Wood, Wire and Metal Lathers, 1929-33; sec. Los Angeles Bldg. and Constrn. Trades Council, 1933-36; v.p. Cal. Fedn. Labor, 1936, pres., 1937-43, sec.-treas., AFL-CIO, 1943; 1st v.p. Internat. Union Wood, Wire, and Metal Lathers, 1958; pres. bldg. and constrn. trades dept. AFL-CIO, 1960-71. Mem. fed. adv. council employment security Dept. Labor, farm placement com. bur. employment security; mem. Gov's Adv. Council, Cal. Dept. Employment; AFL mem. Latin Am. Unit, Internat. Confedn. Free Trade Unions; mem. Joint U.S.-Mex. Trade Union Com.; v.p. Internat. Labor Press Assn., AFL-CIO. Trustee San Francisco Maritime Mus.; mem. nat. council Nat. Planning Assn.; dir. Nat. Housing Conf. Bd. regents U. Cal. Mem. Am. Legion. Clubs: Commonwealth of Cal., Union League (San Francisco). Home: Palm Spring CA Died Oct. 10, 1971; buried Holy Cross Cemetery, Los Angeles CA

HAGGERTY, JAMES E., lawyer; b. Rochester, N.Y., July 29, 1898; student U. Mich.; L.B., Detroit Coll. of Law, 1923; 1 son, James E. Admitted to Mich. bar, 1923, also U.S. Dist. Ct. Eastern Dist. of Mich., 6th Circuit U.S. Circuit Ct. of Appeals; mem. firm Vandever, Haggerty, Doelle, Gurzia, Tonkin & Kerr, Detroit. Fellow of the American College of Trial Lawyers; member Am., Detroit (past dir.) bar assns., State Bar Mich. (past commr., v.p. 1956-57, pres. 1957-58). Deceased.

HAHN, ALBERT GEORGE, hosp. adminstr.; b. Evansville, Ind., Oct. 10, 1893; s. Louis and Margaret (Bauer) H.; student George Williams YMCA Coll., 1913; D. Humanities, Evansville Coll., 1949; m. Grace Mae Osborn, June 13, 1917; 1 son, Jack Albert. Sec. YMCA, Evansville, 1914; dir. religious edn. St. Johns U. C. of C. Ch., Evansville, 1920; adminstr. Deaconess Hosp., Evansville, 1922-64, adminstr. emeritus, 1965-69. Dir. Ind. Blue Cross. Vice chmn. Council for Licensing and Regulating Hosps., Ind. State Bd. of Health, 1945-69. Fellow Assn. Protestant Hosp. Chaplains; mem. Am. Hosp. Assn., Am. Protestant Hosp. Assn. (past pres.), Ind. (past exec. sec.), Tri-State hosp. assns. (past exec. sec.). Mem. United Ch. of Christ. Mason (32 degree, Shriner). Home: Evansville IN Died Jan. 27, 1969; interred Oak Hill Cemetery, Evansville IN

HAHN, FREDERIC HALSTED, investment banker; b. N.Y.C., July 7, 1896; s. William Eugene and Caroline (Watkins) H.; B.S., Wesleyan U., 1919; m. Marylee Nally, Oct. 4, 1919; children—Frederic Halsted, William N., Lee Ann (Mrs. Neil W. Head), Marylee (Mrs. Kenneth M. Merritt). Salesman, Printers Ink Pub. Co., 1919-22, Curtis Pub. Co., 1922-25; v.p. Percy Gardner Corp., 1925-27; partner Dewey Bacon & Co., Bacon Stevenson & Co., 1927-34; partner Goodbody & Co., N.Y.C., 1935-70, exec. com., dir. prodn. unit div., 1953-65, spl. partner, 1965-70; dir. Pancake Kitchens, Inc. Treas., bd. dirs. Marcus Goodbody Found., 1952-65; Served as lt. (j.g.), Flying Corps, USN 1917-19. Mem. Dallas Cotton Exchange, Chgo. Bd. Trade, Early and Pioneer Naval Aviators Assn., Psi Upsilon. Episcopalian. Clubs: St. Andrews Golf (Hastings, N.Y.); Am. Yacht (Rye, N.Y.); Bankers of Am., Harbor View (N.Y.C.); Ponte Vedra (Fla.); Gulf Stream Golf, Gulf Stream Bath and Tennis (Delray Beach). Home: Scarsdale NY Died Sept. 21, 1972; buried Sleepy Hollow Cemetery, Tarrytown NY

HAHN, OTTO, scientist; b. Frankfurt on the Main Germany, Mar. 8, 1879; s. Heinrich and Charlotte (Giese) II; student U. Marburg, 1897, U. Munich, 1898, Dr. deg., 1901; U. Coll., London, winter 1904-05, Phys. Lab. McGill U., Montreal, Can., winter 1905-06; m. Edith Junghans, Mar. 22, 1913 (dec. 1968); 1 son, Hanno (dec. 1960). Mem. faculty U. Berlin, 1907, prof. chemistry, 1910-33; mem. Kaiser Wilhelm Inst. Chemistry, 1912-28, dir., 1928-45; pres. Max Planck Soc. for Advancement of Sci. (formerly Kaiser Wilhelm Society), 1946-60, hon. pres., 1960-68. Recipient Nobel prize for chemistry for splitting uranium atom, 1944; Enrico Fermi award Atomic Energy Commn., 1966. Mem. Berlin, Goettingen, Munich, Stockholm, Vienna, Madrid, Helsinki, Lissabon. Mainz, Rome (Vatican). Allahabad, Copenhagen, Boston, Indian, Halle, Bukarest acads. sci. Goettingen Germany Died July 28, 1968; buried Stadtfriedhof, Goettingen West Germany

HAIG, (VERNON LESTER HAGUE), publicist; b. at Libertyville, Iowa, February 23, 1877; s. Albert Gallatin and Harriet (Smiley) H.; desc. of Scottish Clan Haig, and Paul Darlington of Revolutionary fame; A.B., magna cum laude, Princeton, 1900; unmarried. Farm broker, Fairfield, 1900-02; with Lee Livestock Commn. Co., Chicago, 1902-09, advancing to v.p. and mgr., also mem. Live Stock Exchange, Chicago; organized chain of banks in Tex., 1909-10; farm broker, Fairfield, until 1925. Candidate for nomination to U.S. Senate against Senator Brookhart, 1924, withdrew in favor of third candidate. Mem. Inst. of Politics, Williamstown, Mass., 1924, 28; life mem. Am. Red Cross, Whig Hall (Princeton). Mem. U.S. Pub. Service Reserve, World War. Founder men's dormitory fund, Parsons Coll., Fairfield, Ia., 1926. Mem. Phi Beta Kappa. Republican. Episcopalian. Club: Princeton (New York). Has written extensively on polit. subjects and the fine arts. Made world tour, 1928, again 1929. Known as Cowboy Critic of the Seven Arts." Home: Klamath Falls OR‡

HAIGHT, CAMERON, surgeon; b. San Francisco, Calif., Sept. 2, 1901; s. Dr. Louis Montrose and Minnie (Schuler) H.; A.B., U. of Calif., 1923; M.D., Harvard, 1926; m. Isabel Hubbard, Sept. 19, 1936; children—Robert Cameron, and Elizabeth (Mrs. Irvine D. Flinn). Served surgical internship at the Peter Bent Brigham Hosp., 1926-28; asst. in surgery, Yale U. Med. Sch., and asst. resident in surgery, New Haven Hosp., 1928-31; instr. surgery, U. of Mich., 1931-34, asst. prof., 1934-38, asso. prof., 1938-50, prof., 1950-70, surgeon in charge sect. thoracic surgery; cons. Jackson County Sanitarium, VA Hosp., Ann Arbor, St. Joseph Mercy Hosp., Ann Arbor, Mich. Recip. William E. Ladd award, surg. sect. Am. Acad. Pediatrics, 1967. Diplomate Am. Bd. Thoracic Surgery (past chmn.). Fellow A.C.S., mem. Am., Central surgical associations, Society of Thoracic Surgeons, American, Michigan heart assns., Detroit Heart Club, Am. Assn. for Thoracic Surgery (pres. 1956-57), A.M.A., Mich. Trudeau Soc., Washtenaw County Med. Soc., Nat. Tb Assn., Internat. Soc. Surgery, Mich. Soc. Thoracic Surgeons (pres. 1966-68), Sigma Xi, Alpha Omega Alpha, Nu Sigma Nu, Sigma Chi; hon. mem. Am. Brocho-Esophogological Assn., Brit. Assn. Paediatric Surgeons, Soc. de Chirurgie de Lyon, Soc. Ecuatoriana de Tisiologia, Soc. Paraguaya de Tisiologia. Episcopalian. Contbr. research papers on lung and esophagus and heart surgery to med. jours. Mem. editorial bd. Jour. of Thoracic and Cardiovascular Surgery. Home: Ann Arbor MI Died Sept. 25, 1970; buried Forest Hill Cemetery, Ann Arbor MI

HAIGHT, CHARLES S., lawyer; b. Elberon, N.J., 1903; A.B., Yale, 1926; LL.B., Harvard, 1929; m. Margaret Edwards; 1 son, Charles S. Admitted to N.Y. bar, 1930, since practiced in N.Y.C.; mem. firm Haight, Gardner, Poor & Havens; counsel to Swedish-Am. Line in Andrea Doria crash hearings, 1956-57. Home: New York City NY Died Apr. 18, 1968.

HAIGHT, H. W., oil co. exec.; b. Chickasha, Okla., July 21, 1902; s. Alfred Warren and Lulu Blanche (Besse) H.; Geol. Engr., Colo. Sch. Mines, 1927; m. Jean Kirkpatrick, Oct. 12, 1929 (dec.); 1 dau., Barbara Jean (Mrs Francis). Pres., dir. Creole Petroleum Corp., Caracas, Venezuela; dir. Standard Oil Devel. Co.; exec. v.p.; dir. Humble Oil & Refining Co.; dir. Esso Research & Enging. Co. Recipient distinguished achievement medal Colo. Sch. Mines, 1952. Mem. A.I.M. (asso.), Am. Inst. Mining and Metall. Engrs., Am. Assn. Petroleum Geologists, Am. Petroleum Inst., Tau Beta Pi, Sigma Gamma Epsilon, Kappa Kappa Psi, Alpha Tau Omega. Home: Houston TX Died Oct. 14, 1970; buried Fairview Cemetery, Albuquerque NM

HAILPERIN, HERMAN, rabbi, educator; b. Newark, Apr. 6, 1899; s. Baer and Sarah (Gutkin) H.; A.B., New York U., 1919; grad. Jewish Theol. Sem. Am., 1922; A.M., U. of Pittsburgh, 1925. Ph.D., 1933; D.D. (honorary). Jewish Theol. Sem. Am. 1956; m. Harriet Silverman, July 4, 1922 (dec.); children—Cyrus Baer, Sarah; m. 2d, Celia R. Moss, December 4, 1966. Rabbi, 1922; rabbi, Tree of Life Congregation, Pitts., 1922-68, emeritus, 1968-73; instr. hist. U. Pitts., 1926-27 and 1943; lecturer on Jewish history, Duquesne University, 1937-41, adjunct prof. history and theol., 1965-73. Mem. Rabbinical Assembly of Am. (mem. exec. com.) Am. Assn. of University Professors, Phi Beta Kappa (hon. member), Phi Alpha Theta. Author: A Rabbi Teaches, 1939; Nicolas De Lyra and Rashi, 1940; several monographs on The History of Intellectual Relations Between Christians and Jews in Europe; edited magnum opus of J.S. Raisin, Gentile Reactions to Jewish Ideals, 1953; Rashi and the Christian Scholars, 1963; columnist for The Jewish Criterion and American Jewish Outlook. Home: Pittsburgh PA Died Jan. 9, 1973.

HAIN, JACOB L., mgmt. cons.; b. West Camp, N.Y., 1902; s. Andrew S. and Anna (Wiles) H.; A.B., Johns Hopkins, 1923; H.H.D., Albright Coll., 1962; m. Mary L. McQuay, July 4, 1946; children—Andrew, John. Dir., mem. exec. com. Am. Bank Note Co., 1952-72; investment adviser, 1944-68; founder Penn Sq. Mut. Fund, 1957, chmn., 1957-68; dir. N.Y. Dock Co., N.Y.C., 1944-58, A.G. Spalding & Bros., Inc., N.Y.C., 1952-67, Gen. Cigar Co., Inc., N.Y.C., 1959-61, N.J. Zinc Co., N.Y.C., 1961-65, Hamilton Watch Co., Lancaster, Pa., 1961-70; chmn. bd. Bush Terminal Co., N.Y.C., 1964-70. Trustee Johns Hopkins, St. Joseph's Hosp., Muhlenberg Coll., Albright Coll. Clubs: Recess (N.Y.C.); Berkshire Country, Wyomissing (Reading). Home: Wyomissing Hills PA Died Apr. 16, 1972; interred Charles Evans Cemetery, Reading PA

HAINES, HARRY B., newspaper editor; b. Altoona, Pa., Sept. 18, 1892; s. Edward B. and Sarah (Barnette) H.; grad. Paterson (N.J.) High Sch., 1898; m. Helen Brundage, Nov. 12, 1920. Asso. editor The Horseless Age (first English publ. devoted to automobile users), 1901-03; sec. Nat. Premium Advertising Association of New York, president, publisher Paterson Evening News. Member Am. Soc. Newspaper Editors. Clubs: New York Athletic, New York Advertising; Preakness Hills Country, Rotary, Lambs, Lotos, Kiwanis, Optimist. Home: Paterson NJ Died Mar. 30, 1972; buried Cedar Lawn Cemetery, Paterson NJ

HAINES, HELEN, writer; b. New York; d. John Ladd (M. D.) and M. A. Stuart (Tannatt) Colby; ed. N. Y. City and Wilson Coll., Pa., study and travel abroad; m. Bethlehem, Pa., 1890, Charles Owens Haines of Savannah, Ga. Began writing, 1905, The Crimson Rambler Series, pub. in Scribner's Mag., 1906. Address: Norfolk VA‡

HAINES, HELEN ELIZABETH, author, librarian; b. N.Y. City, Feb. 9, 1872; d. Benjamin Reeve and Mary Elizabeth (Hodges) Haines; ed. at home and by private tutors; M.A. (hon.), University of Southern California, 1945; unmarried. Editorial asst. Publishers Weekly and Library Jour., N.Y. City, 1892-95; mng. editor Library Jour., 1895-1908; instr. book selection and other bibliographical courses, Library Sch. of Los Angeles Pub. Library, 1914-26; instr. book selection Library Sch. of U. of Calif. and in univ. extension courses, 1924-36; instr. book selection and contemporary fiction, Columbia U. Sch. of Library Service, summers, since 1937; visiting prof. library science, U. of Southern Calif. Sch. of Library Science, Los Angeles, since 1937; lecturer on books Los Angeles Pub. Library, 1926-36, also for many Calif. libraries, women's clubs and other orgns. since 1914. Mem. Am. Library Assn. (mem. council and editor of Proceedings 1896-1906), Calif. Library Assn., Pasadena Library Club (founder 1921). Democrat. Author: Living with Books; The Art of Book Selection, 1935; What's in a Novel? 1942. Contbr. articles and book reviews to library and other publs. Staff reviewer book page Pasadena Star News since 1922. Home: 1175 N Mentor Av., Pasadena 6 CA‡

HAINES, ROBERT TERREL, actor; b. Muncie, Ind., Feb. 3, 1870; s. Adelbert S. and Emma J. H.; ed. pub. schs., Kansas City, Mo.; LL.B., U. of Mo.; m. Genevieve Greville, of New Orleans, Mar. 14, 1895 (divorced, July 5, 1908); m. 2d, Mrs. William McDowell, Dec. 22, 1910. Began career as actor, 1891; served as leading man with Viola Allen, Mrs. Fiske, Blanche Bates, Henry Miller, James O'Neil, and other stars and combinations; played Prince Kara in the Darling of the Gods," 1902-04, 1905-06; starred in the comedy, Once Upon a Time," season 1904-05; leading man with Grace George, in Clothes," 1907-08, in The Rose of the Rancho," 1908; with Olga Nethersole, in The Writing on the Wall," 1908-09; leading man with Mme. Nazimova, in The Commanding Officer," season 1909-10; featured in The Spendthrift," season 1910-11; mgr. Haines' Stock Co., West End Theatre, New York, seasons 1911-12, 1912-13; starred in vaudeville in The Coward," 1913-14; in The Man in the Dark," in The Hyphen," 1914-15; also starred in vaudeville, seasons 1917-19, and in moving picture plays; played the doctor, in The Lost Leader," 1919-20, Sophus Meyers, in Samson and Delilah," 1920-21; played the sheriff, in The Vagabond," Paulson, in The Garden of Weeds," the doctor, in White Cargo," 1924-25, Peter Rankin, in The Donovan Affair," 1926-27, in revival of Pomander Walk," 1928, Senator Krull in This is New York," 1930-31, Dr. Koppel, in Allure," 1934-35, Father Macklin, in Halloween," 1935-36. Featured on many coast to coast radio broadcasts since 1931. Starred in moving pictures, Does It Pay?" and The Governor's Lady," The Victim," The Heart of New York," The Secret Agent." Mem. Phi Delta Theta, Actors' Order of Friendship, Mo. Soc. of New York, Actors' Equity Assn. (mem. council of equity, 1926; asst. exec. 1938-39); elected mem. bd. trustees Actors' Fund America, 1923. Clubs: Players, Lambs (New York); Masquers (Hollywood, Calif.). Author: (plays) The Grass Orphan"; Ashes"; Two Thieves"; The Coward"; You Can't Win". Address: Lambs Club, 130 W. 44th St., New York NY‡

HAISLIP, WADE HAMPTON, army officer; b. Woodstock, Va., July 9, 1889; s. Reuben Drake and Etta (Heller) H.; B.S., U.S. Mil. Acad., 1912; student Infantry Sch., 1923-24, Command and Gen. Staff Sch., 1924-25, Ecole Superieure de Guerre, 1925-27, Army War Coll., 1931-32; m. Alice Jennings Shepherd, July 14, 1932. Commd. 2 lt., June 12, 1912; promoted through grades to general, 1949; served in Vera Cruz, Mexico, 1914; with A.E.F. and Am. Forces in Germany, 1917-21, successively with Gen. Staff, 5th Corps, Div. Machine Gun Officer, 3d Div., Gen. Staff, Am. Forces in Germany; participated in defensive operations in the Vosges, St. Mihiel and Meuse-Argonne operations; instr. U.S. Mil. Acad., 1921-23; asst. exec. Office of Asst. Sec. of War, 1928-31; instr. Command and Gen. Staff Sch., 1932-36 with 29th Inf., 1936-38; in Budget and Legislative Planning Branch, War Dept. Gen. Staff, 1938-41, asst. chief of staff for personnel, 1941; commanded 85th Inf. Div. Apr. 1942-Feb. 20, 1943; commanded XV Corps throughout campaigns of Normandy, Northern France, Ardennes, Rhineland, Central Europe; comd. 7th Army, June-Aug., 1945. Pres., Sec. of War's Personnel Bd., Sept. 1945-April 1946; sr. mem. Chief of Staff's adv. group, 1946-48; dep. chief of staff for adminstrn., 1948-49, vice chief of staff 1949-51; retired from active service, 1951; gov. U.S. Soldiers Home, 1951-66. Awarded Victory medal with 3 bars, Mexican Service medal, D.S.M. with 3 Oak Leaf Clusters, Legion of Merit, Bronze Star with oak leaf cluster, Legion of Honor (grand officer), Croix de Guerre with Palm. Clubs: Army and Navy (Washington); Army and Navy Country (Va.). Home: Washington DC Died Dec. 23, 1971; buried Arlington Nat. Cemetery, Arlington VA

HALE, FRANK JUDSON, corp. official; b. Newton Upper Falls, Mass., Aug. 14, 1862; s. Amos L. and Tamson (Drake) H.; ed. pub. schs.; m. Grace Ella Herrick, Dec. 29, 1890; children—Roger D., Mrs. Marjorie Hale Gardner. Began with Otis, Pettee & Co. (successivley Pettee Machine Works, Saco & Pettee Machine Shops, Saco-Lowell Shops), mfrs. cotton mfg. machinery, Newton Upper Falls, 1880, dir. and gen. agt., 1897-1922, v.p. since 1922; also officer and dir. various other corps. Mem. Common Council, Newton, 1888-89; mem. Sch. Bd., Newton, 1890-1900. Dir. Stone Inst. and Newton Home for Aged People. Clubs: Algonquin (Boston); Prouts Neck (Maine) Country. Home: 80 Bigelow Road, West Newton, Mass. Office: 60 Batterymarch St., Boston MA‡

HALE, ROBERT LEE, prof. law; b. Albany, N.Y., Mar. 9, 1884; s. Matthew and Mary (Lee) H.; student Albany Acad., Albany, N.Y., 1890-1901, Norwich (Conn.) Free Acad., 1898-99, Neues Gymnasium, Brunswick, Germany, 1901-02; A.B.; Harvard, 1906, A.M., 1907, LL.B., 1909; Ph.D., Columbia U., 1918; m. Dorothea Keep, Dec. 20, 1913; 1 son, Robert Lee. Law clerk Rosenthal & Hammill, Chicago, 1909-1910; in legal dept. Am. Telephone & Telegraph Co., New York, 1910-11 and 1912; lecturer and instr. in economics, Columbia, 1915-22, spl. lecturer in law, 1919-22, lecturer in legal economics, 1922-28, asst. prof. legal economics, 1928-31, asso. prof. economics, 1931-35, prof. law, 1935-49, professor of law emeritus from 1949. Mem. American Economics Association, American Polit. Sci. Assn., Acad. Polit. Sci., Clubs: Harvard, Century Assn. (New York), Author: Valuation and Rate-Making. The Conflicting Theories of the Wisconsin Railroad Commission, 1905-17, 1918; Freedom Through Law, 1952. Editor (with Young B. Smith and Noel T. Dowling); Cases on Public Utilities, Second edition, 1936. Contbr. articles to Polit. Science Quarterly, Columbia, Yale, Ill., Mich. and Harvard law reviews, etc.; also contbr. to symposia in The Trend of Economics,' 1924, and The SocialSciences," 1927. Home: New Canaan CT Died Aug. 30, 1969.

HALEY, JAMES FREDERICK, lawyer, apparel co. exec.; b. Worcester, Mass., Mar. 14, 1926; s. Robert Hutchinson and Amelia S. (Kemena) H.; grad. Phillips Exeter Acad., 1944; A.B., Princeton, 1950; LL.B., Harvard, 1953. Admitted to N.Y. bar, 1954, practiced in N.Y.C., 1954-69; asso. Sullivan & Cromwell, 1953-57; sec. Cluett, Peabody & Co., Inc., 1957-69; dir. Lytton's, Henry C. Lyton & Co., Arrow Inter-Am., Inc. Served with AUS, 1944-45, USAAF, 1945-46. Mem. N.Y. State, N.Y. County bar assns., Assn. Bar City N.Y. Republican. Episcopalian. Clubs: Racquet and Tennis, Harvard (N.Y.C.). Home: New York City NY Died Aug. 24, 1969; buried Rock Creek Cemetery, Washington DC

HALFORD, JOHN HENRY, ret. textile mfg. exec.; b. Great Horton, Bradford, Eng., Sept. 29, 1885; s. Robert and Sarah (Helliwell) H.; A.B., Bowdoin Coll., 1907, M.A. (hon.), 1927; m. Hannah More Kellett, Nov. 25, 1914; children—John Henry, Jane Tetley (Mrs. Charles Ellington Parker). Assistant supt. Limerick Mills (Me.), 1905-11, S. B. and B. W. Fleisher Mills, Phila., 1911-13; v.p. James Lees & Sons Mills, Bridgeport, Pa., 1913-51, retired, director until 1962; mem. adv. bd. Liberty Real Estate Trust Co., 1961-63, Fidelity-Phila. Trust Co., 1963-64. President bd. Montgomery Hosp., Norristown, Pa., 1951-60, 1st vice pres., 1960-66; benefactor Hebron Acad., Bowdoin Coll., Montgomery Hosp. Mem. Wages and Hours Committee, Woolen and Worsted Industry, WPB, 1941, industry advisory com., 1943. Trustee Hebron (Me.) Acad., Bowdoin Coll. Mem. Hist. Soc. Montgomery County. New Eng. Soc. Pa., Zeta Psi. Republican. Presbyn. (elder). Rotarian. Club: Union League (Phila.). Home: Norristown PA Died June 1968.

HALL, ALAISTAIR CAMERON, investment banker; b. Edinburgh, Scotland, Jan. 10, 1903; s. William Thomas and Margaret (Cameron) H.; student George Watson's Coll., Edinburgh; m. Consuelo McMicking, June 20, 1930 (dec. 1945); children—Roderick, Ian, Alaistair, Consuelo. m. 2d. Juanita Sudduth, June 19, 1946. Came to U.S., 1953, naturalized, 1956. Mng. partner A. C. Hall & Co., also Hall, Picornell, Origas of Manila, P.I. 1934-53; with Sutro & Co. San Francisco, 1954-71, sr. partner, 1959-71; mem. N.Y. and the Pacific Coast stock exchanges, 1953-71. Past pres. Manila Stock Exchange. Clubs: Cypress Point Golf (Pebble Beach, Cal.); Merchants Exchange, Pacific Union, San Francisco Golf. Home: San Francisco CA Died Jan. 21, 1971; buried Woodlawn Cemetery, San Francisco CA

HALL, ALVIN WILLIAM, dir. Bur. Engraving and Printing; b. Harleigh, Pa., Aug. 23, 1888; s. Charles Wesley and Jane (Marsland) H.; m. Ruth A. Benner, Nov. 20, 1915; children—Alvin W., Ruth Benner (Mrs. James W. Neighbours). Dir. Bur. of Engraving and Printing, 1924-54. Home: Washington DC Died Feb. 11, 1969; buried Parklawn Cemetery, Rockville MD

HALL, CHAFFEE E(ARL), lawyer; b. Oakland, Cal., Mar. 5, 1888; s. Samuel Pike and Charlotte Whippie (Spear) H.; B.L., U. Cal., 1910; m. Emmy Marie

Lemcke, Apr. 6, 1915; children—Chaffee Earl, Marie Hall (Mrs. Penry Griffiths). Admitted to Cal. bar, 1912, then practiced in San Francisco, partner Hall, Henry & Oliver, from 1944; dir. Pacific Lighting Corporation, San Francisco and Napa Valley Railroad. Mem. Sigma Nu, Phi Delta Phi. Republican. Unitarian. Clubs: Bohemian, Cercle de L'Union (San Francisco); Pacific-Union. Home: Felton CA Died Apr. 8, 1969; buried Felton CA

HALL, CLAUDE CALEB, clergyman; b. Hopkins County, Ky., Apr. 20, 1871; s. Benjamin Davis and Mary Josephine (Goodloe) H.; ed. privately; D.D., McKendree Coll., Lebanon, Ill., 1912; m. Katie Elizabeth Young, Mar. 22, 1896; children—Banjamin Henry, Ruth Lucille (wife of Dr. Clyde McNeill), John Crow. Ordained to ministry Meth. Ch., 1896, pastor, Upper Alton, Ill., 1904-07, Granite City, Ill., 1907-09, Vandalia, Ill., 1909-13, First Ch., Mt. Vernon, Ill., 1913-15; dist. supt. East St. Louis Dist., Ill., Meth. Ch., 1915-21, Mt. Carmel Dist., Ill., 1921-24; supt. Orphanage, Mt. Vernon, 1924-28; pastor First Ch. Lawrenceville, 1928-33; dist. supt., Centralia Dist., Ill., 1933-40; pastor Harrisburg (Ill.) First Ch., 1940; chaplain Holden Hosp., Carbondale, Ill., 1943. State president Illinois Anti-Saloon League, 1935-40. Del. to Gen. Conf. Meth. Ch., 1916, 20, 24, 28, 32 and 36; del. to Uniting Conf. of Methodism, 1939; reserve del. to Gen. Conf., 1940; delegate to First Jurisdictional Conf. of the North Central Jurisdiction, 1940. Mem. bd. of trustees McKendree Coll. since 1915, pres., 1923-41. Mason (32 deg., K.T., Shriner). Rotarian. Home: 511 S. University Av., Carbondale IL‡

HALL, EDWARD BIGELOW, investment banking; b. Ishpeming, Mich., Sept. 13, 1886; s. Edward Robert and Jane (Bigelow) H.; grad. The Hill Sch., Pottstown, Pa., 1905; Ph.B., Sheffield Sci. Sch. (Yale), 1908; m. Marjorie W. Kimball, Nov. 12, 1914; children—Mrs. Marion H. Agnew, Gordon Hall. Reporter Chicago Evening Post and Chicago Examiner, 1908-09; became connected with Harris Trust & Savings Bank, Mar. 1909, sales mgr. bond dept., 1919-29, v.p., 1929-35; organized 1935, and pres. Harris Hall & Co., investment underwriters, 1935-53; inactive ltd. partner Dean Witter & Co., 1953-69; dir. Office of Trade, Investment and Monetary Affairs, FOA, 1954-55; cons. Exec. Office of President, 1956-57; asst. to sec. of treasury in War Finance Div., 1943-45. Served as ensign USN, World War. Mem. Investment Bankers Assn, Am. (pres. 1936-37), Chi Phi. Republican. Conglist. Clubs: Chicago, Winnetka IL Died May 30, 1969.

HALL, FRANK A., newspaperman; b. Ora, Ind., Sept. 30, 1894; s. Dr. S. Jerome Hall and Marie Madeline (Keller) H.; A.B., Wabash Coll., Crawfordsville, Indiana, 1920; student at Catholic Univ. of Am., 1921-22; m. Helen Mary Gainer, Apr. 14, 1925; children—Barbara Jean (Mrs. Edward T. Walford), Janet Gainer (Mrs. Frank Fallowfield). Member staff Indianapolis News, 1920; staff of Washington Post, 1921-24, city editor, 1923-24; with Nat. Catholic Welfare Conf. News Service since 1924, successively staff reporter, feature editor and asst. dir., 1924-32, dir., 1932-64. Directed orgn. of Noticias Catolicas, Catholic News Service in Spanish and Portuguese, 1941. Awarded annual Hoey medal for outstanding contribution to cause of interracial justice, 1942. Served as sgt. 2d Ind. Inf., Mexican Border Campaign, 1916-17; U.S. Army, 1917-19, captain F.A., A.E.F.; dir. incoming orgns. Bordeaux Embarkation Camp, 1919. Rep. of U.S. Cath. Press, World Cath. Press Congs., Vatican City, 1936, Rome, 1950 (v.p.), Vienna, 1957, Santander, Spain, 1960. Decorated knight comdr. Order of St. Gregory the Great by Pope Pius XII, 1944, advanced to Gt. Silver Star by Pope Paul VI; recipient award for outstanding contbn. to Cath. journalism Cath. Press Assn., 1960. Mem. Internat. Fedn. Cath. Press Agys. (pres. 1960-63), Internat. Bur. Cath. Journalists (mem. bd. dirs., 1935-50), Internat. Union of Cath. Press (v.p., 1950-57)., Delta Tau Delta, Pi Delta Epsilon. Roman Catholic. Clubs: Nat. Press, Overseas Writers (Washington, D.C.). Contbr. to Encyclopedia Americana, New Cath. Ency. Home: Washington DC Died Nov. 8, 1972.

HALL, FRANKLIN, Washington Corr. Cleveland Plain Dealer since 1900; b. Lansing, Mich., Oct. 1, 1872; s. Benjamin F. H.; ed. Lansing public schools till 1889; grad. Univ. of Mich. (B. L.), 1894. Entered newspaper work; mem. staff Cleveland Plain Dealer since 1895; legislative and polit. corr., 1897-8. Residence: 1330 New York Av. N. W. Office: 9 Postal Telegraph Bldg., Washington‡

HALL, FRED(ERICK) L., judge, ex-gov.; b. Dodge City, Kan., July 24, 1916; s. Fred L. and Etta (Brewer) H.; A.B., U. So. Cal., 1938, LL.B., 1941; m. Leadell Schneider, Apr. 25, 1942; 1 son, Frederick Lee. Admitted to Cal. bar, 1942, D.C. bar, 1943, Kan. bar, 1945, practiced in Los Angeles, Washington, Topeka, Dodge City; co. atty. Ford Co., Kan., 1946-48; lt. gov. Kan., 1950-54, gov. 1954-57; justice Supreme Court of Kansas, 1957-58; dir. mgmt. control Aerojet-General Corp. (Sacramento, Cal.), 1958-70; lecturer, agent, Columbia Lecture Bureau, New York City. Mem. executive committee National Council of Industrial Peace; chairman Interstate Cooperation Commission, Kan. Legislative Council; mem. Kan. Motor Vehicle Reciprocity Commn., State Finance Council. Chmn. bd. Meth. Hosp. Assn. Mem. Am. Bar Assn., Phi Alpha Delta, Phi Kappa Tau. Republican. Methodist. Sacramento CA Died Apr. 1970.

HALL, FRED SMITH, social worker; b. Washington, D.C., June 2, 1870; s. George A. and Sarah S. (Smith) H.; A.B., Wesleyan U., 1893; Ph.D., Columbia, 1898; m. Jennie E. Orcutt, of Stafford Springs, Conn., July 12, 1906. With U.S. Census Bur., 1899-1902; sec. New York Child Labor Com., 1903; asst. sec. City Club of New York, 1904-05; head worker Newark Neighborhood House, 1906-07; sec. Pa. Child Labor Assn., 1908-11; asso. dir. Charity Orgn. Dept., Russell Sage Foundation, 1911-28; editor Social Work Year Book, 1929-35; chmn. Com. for Social Action (N.J. area) of the Congl. and Christian Chs., 1937-38. Mem. Am. Assn. Social Workers, Nat. Conf. Social Work, Alpha Delta Phi. Conglist. Author: Sympathetic Strikes and Sympathetic Lockouts, 1898; American Marriage Laws (with Elizabeth Brooke), 1919; Medical Certification for Marriage, 1925; Child Marriages (with Mary E. Richmond), 1925; Marriage and the State (with Mary E. Richmond), 1929. Contbr. articles to professional publs. Home: 173 Summit Av., Upper Montclair, N.J; (winter) 637 New York Av., Winter Park FL‡

HALL, G(EORGE) EDWARD, ret. univ. pres.; b. Lindsay, Ont., Can., Oct. 10, 1907; s. George W. and Etta (Brandon) H.; B.S.A., Ontario Agrl. Coll., 1929; M.S.A., U. Toronto, 1931, M.D., 1935; Ph.D., 1936, Doctor of Laws, 1959; Doctor of Science, Laval U., 1951; LL.D., University of Windsor, 1954, Madras U., 1957. Queen's Univ., 1958, U. London, 1963, Sc.D., U. Guelph, 1967; m. Lola Ruth McDonald, June 26, 1937; children—Frances, Burt Ann, Sharon, George Edward II, Elizabeth. Prof. of med. research Banting Institute, Toronto, Ontario, Canada, 1939; director medical research Royal Canadian Air Force, 1939-45; dean faculty of medicine, University of Western Ontario, London, Ontario, 1945-47, president and vice chancellor, 1947-67; chmn. bd., dir. No. Life Assurance Co. of Can.; dir. IBM (Can.). Decorated knight comdr. Order St. Gregory the Gt.; Air Force Cross (Gt. Britain), Legion of Merit (U.S.). Mem. Ont. Research Council, 1947-53; mem. Nat. Cancer Inst., 1947-72, pres. 1950-51; chmn. Canadian Forces Med. Council, 1962-66; mem. Nat. Productivity Council, 1962-64; mem. Ont. Council Health, 1966-72. Fellow Royal Soc. Can.; mem. Assn. Univs. and Colls. Can. (pres. 1956-57), Assn. Commonwealth Univs. (chmn. 1963-65). Mem. Ch. of Eng. Clubs: London Hunt and Country, London, Canadian (London). Home: Orillia ON Canada Died Feb. 11, 1972.

HALL, GROVER CLEVELAND, JR., editor; b. Montgomery Ala., Feb. 10, 1915; s. Grover Cleveland and Claudia (English) H. Asso. editor The Montgomery Advertiser, 1947, editor, 1948-56, editor-in-chief, 1956-71; v.p., mem. bd. The Advertiser Co. 1958-71. Received National Headliner award, 1957. Member Nat. Planning Assn. (nat. council), Am. Soc. Newspaper Editors, Nat. Conf. Editorial Writers, Sigma Delta Chi. Methodist. Author: 1,000 Destroyed: The Life and Times of the Fourth Fighter Group, 1945. Home: Montgomery AL Died Sept. 24, 1971; buried Montgomery AL

HALL, HOMER WILLIAM, lawyer, judge; b. Shelbyville, Ill., July 22, 1870; s. William Wesley and Margaret Catherine (Fouk) H.; ed. Ill. Wesleyan U.; student Bloomington (Ill.) Law Sch., 1892; m. Susan Forman, of Bloomington, June 4, 1892; 1 son, Harry H. Admitted to Ill. bar, 1892, and began practice in Bloomington; became mem. firm Hall, Martin, Hoose & DePew, 1914. County judge, McLean Co., 1909-14; master in chancery, 1916-18; mem. 70th to 72d Congresses (1927-33), 17th Ill. Dist.; now judge County and Juvenile Ct., McLean Co. Mem. McLean Co. Bar Assn. (pres.), Bloomington Assn. Commerce, McLean Co. Farm Bur. Republican. Presbyn. Mason, Odd Fellow, Woodman. Clubs: Bloomington, Bloomington Country. Home: 1202 E. Jefferson St., Bloomington IL‡

HALL, HOWARD, corporation exec.; born Onslow, Ia., Dec. 31, 1895; s. Harry Douglas and Margaret (Lamey) H.; m. Margaret Douglas, June 12, 1924. Pres. Iowa Mfg. Co., Iowa Steel & Iron Works; dir. Iowa Nat. Liability Insurance Company, Mchts. Nat. Bank, Ia. Electric Light & Power Co., Quaker Oats Company, Square D Co.; chmn. City Nat. Bank of Cedar Rapids, Ia. Founder Hallmar, also founder Margaret and Howard Hall Radiation Center. Clubs: Tavern, Chicago Yacht (Chicago); Com. of 100, Surf (Miami Beach, Fla.). Home: Cedar Rapids IA Died May 16, 1971.

HALL, JOHN WILLIAM, teacher; b. Camargo, Ill.; s. William Housen and Sarah Jane (Witzman) H.; grad. Ill. State Normal Sch., 1890; studied Jena, Germany, 1892-95, and 1898; B.S., Teachers Coll. (Columbia), 1901, M.A., 1902; m. Cornelia Thomas, of Falls City, Neb., Aug. 15, 1898 (died Oct. 27, 1904); m. 2d, Alice Cynthia King, of Trumansburg, N.Y., July 8, 1912. Teacher of psychology, N.Y. Training School for Teachers, 1901-05; prof. elementary edn., U. of Cincinnati, 1905-20; dean Sch. of Edn., U. of Nev., 1920-37, now prof. emeritus. Instr. summer sessions, Columbia, University of California and West Virginia University, Mem. National Society Study of Education, American Association Univ. Profs., N.E.A., Phi Kappa Phi. Mason. Author: (with wife) The Question as a Factor in Teaching, 1916. Mem. of com. which produced Am. School Citizenship Course in U.S. History, 1920. Home: 424 University Terrace, Reno NV‡

HALL, LESTER W., banker; b. Kansas City, Mo., Aug. 9, 1876; s. W. Ewing Hall; prep. edn., Hopkins Grammar Sch., New Haven, Conn.; Ph.B., Yale, 1898; LL.B., Columbia, 1901; m. Ruth Austin, of Kansas City, 1901. Admitted to Mo. bar, 1901, and began practice at Kansas City; member firm Bowersock, Hall & Hook; v.p. Fidelity Trust Co., 1916 until it was merged into Fidelity Nat. Bank and Trust Co., of which has been pres. since 1924. Ex-president Kansas City Clearing House Assn. Clubs: University, Bankers, Kansas City Country. Office: 9th and Walnut Sts., Kansas City MO‡

HALL, LLOYD AUGUSTUS, chemist; b. Elgin, Ill., June 20, 1894; s. Elisha A. and Isabel (French) H.; Ph.C., B.S., Northwestern U., 1916; grad. student U. Chgo., 1917; Sc.D., Va. State Coll., 1944, Tuskegee Inst., 1947, Howard U., 1959; m. Myrrhene E. Newsome, Sept. 23, 1919; children—Dorothy Ann (Mrs. Lloyd Powell), Kenneth Lloyd. Chemist, Dept. Health Labs., Chgo., 1916, sr. chemist, 1917; chief chemist John Morrell & Co., Ottumwa, Ia., 1919-21, Boyer Chem. Lab. Co., Chgo., 1921; pres., chem. dir. Chem. Products Corp., Chgo., 1922-25; chem. cons., chief chemist, dir. research The Griffith Labs., Inc., Chgo., 1925-46, tech. dir., 1946-59, tech. cons., from 1959; research adv. bd. Tuesdail Labs., Inc., from 1960; v.p. Pilot Chem. Co., Santa Fe Springs, Cal. Mem. food commn. Ill. Dept. Agr., 1944-49; cons. George Washington Carver Found., 1946-48; mem. food protection ind. liaison com. NRC; mem. Chgo. exec. com. N.A.A.C.P., mayor's commn. on Chgo. House of Correction, 1955; Hyde Park-Kenwood Conservation Community Council, 1956-58; adviser Los Angeles County Air Pollution Control Dist., Los Angeles County Water Resources Com., UN, Am. Food for Peace Council, 1965-71; mem. adv. bd. Los Angeles State Coll.; cons. United Cal. Bank, Los Angeles. Mem. bd. Chgo. Urban League, 1935-36, Wabash Av., Washington Park YMCA's, 1935-55, Kenwood Neighborhood Redevelopment Corp., 1954, S. E. Chgo. Com., 1959. Asst. chief insp. powder and explosives Ordnance Dept., U.S. Army, 1917-19; sci. adv. bd., com. on food research Q.M.C., War Dept., 1943-48. Trustee Adler Planetarium, Hull House Assn. Recipient achievement award Phi Beta Sigma, 1952, honor scroll Chgo. chpt. Am. Inst. Chemists, 1956, Brotherhood award Chgo. Conf. on Brotherhood, 1957. Fellow Am. Inst. Chemists (hon.; chmn. Chgo. 1954-55, chmn. com. on econ. status of chemists 1952-53, nat. councilor-at-large, mem. bd. from 1962), A.A.A.S.; mem. Inst. Food Technologists (councilor Chgo. sect. 1950-52, nat. councilor-at-large 1951-53, nat. exec. bd. 1951-52, 54-55), Am. Pub. Health Assn., N.Y. Acad. Sci., Am. Chem. Soc., Am. Assn. Cereal Chemists, Am. Oil Chemists Soc., Ill. Acad. Sci., Soc. Chem. Industry, Pasadena C. of C., Sigma Xi, Phi Tau Sigma, Beta Kappa Chi, Alpha Phi Alpha. Baptist. Clubs: City, Pobla (pres. 1948), Druids (pres. 1945-47) (Chgo.). Asst. editor Beta Kappa Chi Jour., 1948-49; editor The Vitalizer (Chgo. sect. Inst. Food Tech.), 1948; cons. editor, 1949-50; editorial adv. bd. Food Processing mag., 1952-56; adv. bd. Chem. and Engrng. News, 1957-60. Patentee in field, also lectr. Home: Altadena CA Died Jan. 2, 1971; buried Forest Lawn Cemetery, Glendale CA

HALL, NICHOLS, devel. cons.; b. Evanston, Ill., Oct. 13, 1903; s. Charles Hiland and Grace (Nichols) H.; grad. Hotchkiss Sch., 1921; B.A., Williams Coll., 1926; student Cambridge U., Eng., 1923-24; m. Veronique de Ruiloba, Aug. 1929 (div. 1935, remarried Dec. 28, 1964; 1 dau., Mariana de Ruiloba (Mrs. Conrad Van Hyning); m. 2d, Marion Mead, Sept., 1935 (dec. Oct. 1962); one son, Charles Hiland II. With credit department Chase National Bank, 1927-30; asst. treas., dir. Charles Hall, Incorporated, importers and wholesalers, 1930-38; partner Ruth Copeland Studio, 1938-42; asst. to dir. copper div. WPB, 1942-45; various positions pvt. bus.; with ECA and successor agencies, 1949-63, successively dep. dir. productivity and tech. assistance div., Washington, director productivity and tech. assistance div. U.S. Operations Mission to Austria, 1949-58, technical cooperation division, United States mission to NATO and European Regional Organizations, Paris, 1958-63, ret.; cons. indsl. devel. and devel. instns., from 1963. Mem. Delta Psi. Protestant. Clubs: Williams, St. Anthony (N.Y.C.). Address: Sarasota FL Died June 1965; buried Springfield MA

HALL, ORSON LOFTIN, journalist; b. Putnam County, Ind., July 4, 1877; s. Jonathan T. and Julia (Loftin) H.; student Greer Coll., Hoopeston, Ill., 1895-96, Northwestern U., 1899-1902. Teacher in Douglas Co., Ill., 1896-97; reporter and asst. Sunday editor, 1900-03, Sunday editor, 1903-05, Chicago Inter

Ocean; dramatic critic, 1905-25, co-editor, 1925-27, Chicago Journal; teacher dramatic criticism Medill Sch. of Journalism, 1923-26; in Europe and Orient since 1928.*‡

HALL, ROBERT WILLIAM, biologist; b. Cincinnati, O., Aug. 17, 1872; s. Ephraim Gaylord and Alice Cogswell (Crossette) H.; Ph.B., Yale, 1895; A.B., Harvard, 1897, A.M., 1898, Ph.D., 1901; m. Mary Alice Bowers, of Saco, Me., Aug. 4, 1908; children—Mrs. Roberta Bowers McLean, Marjorie Crossette, Roscoe Bowers. Asst. in zoology, Harvard, 1896-99, Yale, 1899-1901; instr., Yale, 1901-02, Woods Hole, 1899-1901; head of dept. of biology, Lehigh Univ., 1902-37, prof. biology since 1937. Fellow A.A.A.S.; mem. Pa. Forestry Assn. (life), Sigma Xi (Yale Chapter). Home: 37 E. Church St., Bethlehem PA‡

HALL, WILBUR CURTIS, lawyer; b. Mountain Gap, Loudoun County, Va., Feb. 5, 1892; s. John W. and Annie E. (Holliday) H.; student Washington and Lee U., 1910-11, 1913-14; LL.B., Georgetown U., 1915; LL.D., Washington and Lee University, Admitted to Va. bar, 1915, practiced at Leesburg. Chief petty officer U.S. N.R.F., July-Dec. 1918. Mem. Va. Ho. of Dels., 1918-35 (chmn. House Finance com.; chmn. Joint Dem. Caucus); mem. Jud. Council of Va., Commn. of Fisheries; Dem. elector 8th Congl. Dist., Va., 1924; Dem. elector, Va. at large, 1932; chmn. Va. Conservation Commn., 1935-39; mem. exec. com. on Commn. to Reorganize Govt. Va., 1948. Former mem. bd. visitors Coll. William and Mary in Va. Mem. Order Coif, Phi Beta Kappa, Omicorn Delta Kappa, Pi Gammu Mu. Episcopalian. Mason (Shriner), Odd Fellow. Clubs: Rotary (Leesburg); University (Washington). Home: Leesburg VA Died Aug. 21, 1972.

HALL, WILLIAM BALDWIN FLETCHER, financing executive; born at Indpls., Jan. 22, 1905; s. Arthur Fletcher and Una Gladys (Fletcher) H.; grad. Lake Forest Acad., 1922; B.S., Yale, 1926; M.S. in Aero. Engring., U. Mich., 1929; m. Sarah Niezer, Dec. 26, 1932; children—Peter Vincent, Ann, Charles Niezer, Michael William. Spl. agt. Lincoln Nat. Life Ins. Co., 1926-27; aviation tng. Naval Air. Sta., Pensacola, Fla., 1929-30; naval aviator U.S.S. Texas, 1930-31; comml. pilot, 1931-32; staff mortgage loan dept. Lincoln Nat. Life Ins. Co., 1932-42, 2d v.p., mgr. mortgage loan dept., 1932-42, mem. finance com., bd. dirs., 1942-67; pres. Gen. Homes div. Sherbrook Homes, Inc., home prefabrication, Ft. Wayne, Ind., 1962-66; pres. Gen. Equity Investment Corp., 1960-66; pres. Colonial Mortgage Co., Inc., 1945-66, chmn. bd., 1966-69; pres. Industries Bldg. Corp., 1951-66; dir. Kissell Co., Springfield, O., Growth Capital, Inc., Cleve., Fox Realty Corp., Ft. Wayne. Chmn. Ft. Wayne Housing Authority, 1937-50; exec. bd. Anthony Wayne council Boy Scouts. Trustee of St. Francis Coll., Ft. Wayne. Served to comdr. USNR, 1942-45. Mem. Home Mfrs. Assn. (past pres., dir.), Appraisal Inst., Sportsman Pilot Assn., Zeta Psi. Roman Catholic. Home: Ft Wayne IN Died Oct. 22, 1969.

HALL, WILLIAM DICKSON, normal sch. pres.; b. Rockland, Me., Sept. 3, 1876; s. Charles Emery and Margaret Elizabeth (Dickson) H.; grad. Rockland Commercial Coll., 1897, Eastern State Normal Sch., Castine, Me., 1901; B.S., U. of Maine, 1907; m. Letitia Alma Hatch, Nov. 16, 1907. Teacher schs. of Me. 2 yrs.; asst. prin. Aroostook State Normal Sch., Presque Isle, 1907-15; asst. prin. Eastern State Normal Sch., Castine, 1915-20, pres. since 1920. Home: Castine ME‡

HALL, WILLIAM THOMAS, chemist; b. New Bedford, Mass., Aug. 4, 1874; s. Anthony D. and Mary E. (Soule) H.; S.B., Mass. Inst. Tech., 1895; studied U. of Gottingen, 1895-97; m. Agnes D. Allen, Apr. 17, 1901; children—Catharine S., Mary E., Margaret D., William A., Constance D. Asst. in chemistry, 1898-1900, instr., 1900-11, asst. prof., 1911-18, asso. prof., 1918-40, prof. emeritus since 1940, Mass. Inst. Technology; head of science department, Thayer Academy, South Braintree, Mass., 1942-43. Assistant editor Chemical Abstracts. Member American Chemical Soc., Mass. Congregational Laymen's Council (since 1946), A.A.A.S., Sigma Alpha Epsilon. Congregationalist. Republican. Author; The Chemical and Metallographic Examination of Iron, Steel and Brass (with R. S. Williams), 1921; Textbook of Quantitative Analysis, 1930. Editor: Moore's History of Chemistry, 1931; Moore's Organic Chemistry, 1933. Translator from the German: (of F. P. Treadwell) Analytical Chemistry (2 vols.), 1903; (of H. Classen) Beet-sugar Manufacture (with G. W. Rolfe), 1906; (of E. Abderhalden) Text-book of Physiological Chemistry (with George Defren), 1908; (of H. and W. Blitz) Laboratory Methods of Inorganic Chemistry (with A. A. Blanchard), 1909; (of H. Blitz) Introduction to Experimental Inorganic Chemistry (with J. W. Phelan), 1909; (of Wilhelm Ostwald) Introduction to Chemistry (with R. S. Williams), 1910; (of W. Borchers) Metallurgy (with C. R. Hayward), 1910; (of A. Classen) Quantitative Chemical Analysis by Electrolysis, 1913; (of Bauer-Deiss) Sampling and Chemical Analysis of Iron and Steel (with R. S. Williams), 1915. Home: Snipatuit Road, Rochester MA‡

HALLAM, CLEMENT BENNER, editor; b. Wilmington, Del., Aug. 30, 1876; s. Charles and Mary Ann (Benner) H.; grad. Wilmington High Sch., 1893; hon. alumnus U. of Del.; unmarried. Began as a printer, 1894; reporter Wilmington Morning News, 1897-1907; city editor Wilmington Evening Journal, 1907-33; dir. and sec. Evening Journal Co., 1907-12; mng. editor Journal-Every Evening, 1933-36; exec. editor News-Journal papers, 1936-48, ret. Member Del. State Athletic Commn., 1930-36, chmn., 1933-36; mem. bd. govs. Municipal Golf and Tennis Assn., 1922-37, pres., 1927-37; v.p. Wilmington Park, Inc., 1941; former mem. Am. Soc. Newspaper Editors, Alumni Univ. of Delaware (hon. mem.), University Club of Del., Touchdown Club of Wil. (sec.), Republican. Mason. Home: 804 W. 5th St. Office: Orange and Girard Sts., Wilmington DE‡

HALLAUER, CARL S., optics mfg. exec.; b. Rochester, N.Y., Jan. 5, 1894; s. Frank and Hattie Hallauer; ed. Rochester Bus. Inst., Rochester Inst. Tech.; Sc.D., Clarkson Coll. Tech., 1947; LL.D., Alfred U., 1955; m. Florence R. Hallauer, June 22, 1918; 1 dau., Nancy Bausch (Mrs. Arnold L. Johnson). Dir. Bausch & Lomb, Inc., Rochester, N.Y.; dir. Community Savs. Bank Rochester, Lincoln Rochester Trust Co., Rochester Gas & Electric Corp., Garlock, Inc. Dir., past pres. Asso. Industries N.Y. State Commr. Saratoga Springs Commn.; mem. Nat. Com. Electoral Reform, 1961-71. Del. Republican Nat. Conv., 1932-71. Trustee Rochester Bus. Inst., Monroe Community Coll., Rochester Inst. Tech., St. John's Home for Aged, Rochester Fire Benevolent Assn., Rochester Community Chest, Salvation Army, Rochester Community Baseball Club; bd. dirs. Saratoga Performing Arts Center; life trustee Clarkson Coll., Rochester Police Benevolent Assn. Recipient Horatio Alger award, 1960. Mem. Am. Ordnance Assn. (past pres., adv. bd.), Am. Chem. Soc., Soc. Naval Engrs., Photographic Soc. Am., Better Vision Inst. (dir.), Sci. Apparatus Makers Assn. (past chmn. bd.), Rochester C. of C., S.A.R., Soc. Cincinnati, Optical Soc. Am. Baptist (trustee). Mason (Shriner), Kiwanian, Elk, Moose. Clubs: Rochester, Oak Hill Country, Genesee Valley, Country, City (Rochester); Capital Hill (Washington). Home: Rochester NY Died Nov. 6, 1971.

HALLBECK, ELROY CHARLES, labor union ofcl.; b. Chgo., May 15, 1902; s. Charles August and Anna Marie (Hansen) H.; ed. pub. schs., Chgo.; m. Myrtle Elizabeth Montgomery, Aug. 30, 1957; 1 dau. by previous marriage, Anna (Mrs. George William Cobert). Joined U.S. Postal Service as clk., Chgo., 1921; sec. Local 1, Nat. Fedn. Postal Clks., AFL-CIO, 1926-34, pres., 1934-36, nat. v.p., 1940-44, asst. nat. legislative dir., Washington, 1944-46, nat. legislative dir., from 1946, pres., from 1960, merged Nat. Postal Transport Assn., United Nat. Assn. Post Office Craftsmen with Nat. Fedn. Postal Clks. to create United Fedn. Postal Clks. AFL-CIO, 1961. Chmn. Govt. Employees Council AFL-CIO; bd. dirs. Union Labor Life Ins. Co., N.Y.C. Bd. dirs. Washington Arthritis and Rheumatism Found. Recipient awards for work in behalf of vets. in fed. service Am. Legion, Am. Vets. Democrat. Unitarian. Mason (32 deg., Shriner). Clubs: Kenwood Golf and Country (Bethesda, Md.); Nat. Press (Washington). Died Jan. 14, 1969.

HALLDEN, KARL WILLIAM, mfg. exec.; b. Halmstad, Sweden, Feb. 12, 1884; s. Alec Julius and Kristina (Svenson) H.; brought to U.S., 1893; B.S., Trinity College, 1909, M.S. (honorary), 1948, Sc.D. (honorary), 1954; married Margaret Justine Mailgan, July 5, 1931. Assistant mechanical engineer Plume & Atwood Mfg. Co., Thomaston, Conn., 1909-14; mech. engr. Seymour (Conn.) Mfg. Co., 1914-16; founder, pres., treas. Hallden Machine Co., Thomaston since 1917; asso. with W.H.A. Robertson Co., Ltd., Bedford, Eng., Hallden-Okura Co., Tokyo, Japan, Hallden-Robertson Co., Dusseldorf, Germany. Trustee Trinity Coll.; incorporator Waterbury (Conn.) Hosp., Morton Plant Hosp., Clearwater, Fla. Decorated Knight Santa Lucia Soc. Stockholm, Sweden, 1963. Recipient Eigenbrodt Trophy, Trinity College, 1954; Silver medal Technical Museet, Stockholm, Sweden, 1963. Mem. Pi Kappa Alpha, Pi Tau Sigma, Tau Alpha. Episcopalian. Mason. Clubs: Rotary, University, Country City (Waterbury); University (Litchfield Co.); Rod and Gun (Thomaston); University (Hartford); Carlouel (Clearwater, Fla.). Inventor Hallden Flying Shear; patentee. Donor Hallden Engring. Lab., Trinity Coll., 1946. Home: Thomaston CT Died Feb. 9, 1970; buried Canton Southwest Cemetery, Canton CT

HALLE, STANLEY JACQUES, investment exec.; b. Hastings-on-Hudson, N.Y., July 6, 1891; s. Jacques Samuel and Hattie (Sidenberg) H.; grad. Phillips Acad., 1908; B.A., Yale, 1912; m. Helen Bernheimer (div. Jan. 1937); children—Anne (Mrs. Seymour), Helen (Mrs. Knothe); m. 2d, Christiane deMilly, Dec. 15, 1937. Sr. partner Halle & Stieglitz, N.Y.C. Mem. N.Y., Am. stock exchanges, New York Cotton Exchange, Chgo. Bd. Trade, Commodity Exchange Investment Bankers Assn., Nat. Assn. Securities Dealers Home: Chappaqua NY Died July 1972.

HALLE, WALTER MURPHY, merchant; b. s. Samuel H. and Blanche (Murphy) H.; student Princeton, 1927; m. Helen Chisholm, Feb. 2, 1929; children—Helen (Mrs. Foster), Chisholm, Kate C. Pres. Halle Bros. Co., Cleveland, ret. as chmn. bd.; dir. Basic, Inc., Cleveland Trust Co. Trustee Cleve. Clinic, Oberlin Coll. Served to lt. col., USAAF, 1942-45. Home: Waite Hill Willoughby OH Died Jan. 1972.

HALLER, H(ERBERT L(UDWIG JACOB), chemist; b. Cincinnati, Aug. 15, 1894; s. Andreas and Gretchen (Hock) H.; Chem.E., U. Cin., 1918; Ph.D., Columbia, 1926; m. Iva M. Shanabrook, May 11, 1921. Jr. chemist Dept. of Agr., 1919-21, asso. chemist, 1921-23, Rockefeller Inst., 1923-29; sr. chemist, insecticide div. Bur. Chemistry and Bur. Entomology and Plant Quarantine, Dept. of Agr., 1929-40, prin. chemist, 1940-47, asst. chief Bur., 1947-53, asst. director crops research, 1954-57, assistant to administrator farm research, 1957-62, assistant administrator farm research, 1962-64; cons. Nat. Agrl. Chems. Assn., 1964-71. Mem. Am. Chem. Soc., Entomol. Soc. Am., A.A.A.S., Chem. Soc. of Washington (treas. 1935, pres. 1941; awarded Hillebrand prize 1933), Entomol. Soc. Washington, Washington Acad. Arts and Scis., Insecticide Soc. Washington (pres. 1941), Sigma Xi, Alphia Chi Washington DC Died Nov. 1, 1972.

HALLIDAY, RICHARD, theatrical producer; b. Denver, Apr. 3, 1905; s. John Craig and Mary (Hope) Hammond; student Washington and Lee U., 1924; m. Mary Martin, May 5, 1940; 1 dau., Mary Heller. Co-producer Broadway prodns. Peter Pan, 1954, The Sound of Music, 1959, Jennie, 1963; producer Broadway prodn. Daughter of Silence, 1961; producer TV prodns. Peter Pan, 1955, 56, 61, 63, 66, Annie Get Your Gun, 1957, Music with Mary Martin, also Magic with Mary Martin, 1959, Mary Martin at Easter, 1966. Mem. Phi Kappa Psi. Author: Fanfare, 1926. Address: New York City NY Died Mar. 3, 1973.

HALLINAN, PAUL JOHN, archbishop; b. Painesville, Ohio, April 8, 1911; s. Clarence C. and Rose Jane (Laracy) H.; B.A., University of Notre Dame, 1932, LL.D. (honorary), 1962; student Saint Mary's Sem., Cleve., 1932-37; M.A., John Carroll U., 1953; Ph.D., Western Res. U., 1963, L.H.D. (hon.), 1967; LL.D., Duquesne U., 1963, Belmont Coll., 1963, St. Bernard Coll., 1965, Coll. Holy Cross, 1967. Ordained priest Roman Cath. Ch., 1937; parish work St. Aloysius Parish, Cleve., 1937-42, Cathedral of St. John, Cleve., 1945-47; diocesan dir. Newman Clubs, Cleve., 1947-58, nat. chaplain Newman Club Fedn., 1952-54; bishop of Charleston, S.C., 1958-62; archbishop of Atlanta, 1962-68. Mem. Liturgy Commn., II Vatican Council, 1962-63; chmn. Concilium on Liturgy; post-conciliar U.S. Bishops' Conf. on Liturgy. Served as capt. Chaplain's Corps, AUS, 1942-45. Decorated Purple Heart. Mem. Cath., Am., Miss. Valley hist. assns., Atlanta Hist. Soc., Atlanta Symphony Guild, Nat. Assn. Newman Chaplains. K.C. Author: Newman Club Manual, 1954. Home: Atlanta GA Died Mar. 27, 1968; buried Arlington Cemetery, Atlanta GA

HALLOCK, GERARD BENJAMIN FLEET, clergyman, author; b. Holliday's Cove, W.Va., Jan. 28, 1856; s. Homan Benjamin and Adelia (Farnsworth) H.; A.B., Princeton, 1882; grad. Princeton Theol. Sem., 1885; post-grad. work under Pres. McCosh, Princeton; hon. A.M., Princeton, 1901; D.D., Richmond (O.) Coll., 1896; m. Anna Catherine Cobb, May 8, 1888; children—Clarissa Cobb (dec.), Archibald Cobb, Marianna Cobb, and Adelia Cobb (twins). Ordained Presbyn. ministry, 1885; pastor Wheatland Ch., Scottsville, N.Y., 1885-89; one of pastors of the Brick Church, Rochester, since Jan., 1890 (one of the largest in denomination in United States). Stated clerk, Presbytery of Rochester, 1901-43, now stated clerk emeritus; editor The Expositor 3 yrs.; commissioner General Assembly of Presbyterian Churches in U.S.A. 4 times; moderator of Synod of New York, 1929-30. Trustee Elmira College, 1918-41. Life member Am. Bible Soc. Republican. Tours in Europe, Egypt and Holy Land, 1902 and 1929. Mem. Sons of Vets. Author: Upward Steps, 1899; The Model Prayer, 1900; Sermon Seeds, 1900; God's Whispered Secrets, 1901; Beauty in God's Word, 1902; The Homiletic Year, 1903; Journeying in the Land Where Jesus Lived, 1903; Growing Toward God, 1904; Wedding Manual, 1904; The Teaching of Jesus Concerning the Christian Life, 1906; Christ in the Home, 1911. Also numerous booklets, tracts, etc., and many articles in religious and secular mags. and jours.; compiler and editor of One Hundred Best Sermons for Special Occasions, 1921; A Modern Cyclopedia of Illustrations for All Occasions, 1922; The Evangelistic Cyclopedia, 1923; One Hundred Choice Sermons for Children, 1924; Cyclopedia of Commencement Sermons and Baccalaureate Addresses, 1924; Cyclopedia of Pastoral Methods, 1924; Doran's Minister's Manual, 1926-52; Cyclopedia of Funeral Sermons and Sketches, 1926; Five Thousand Best Modern Illustrations, 1927; Three Hundred Five-Minute Sermons for Children, 1928; Holy Communion Cyclopedia, 1928. Co-Author: Behind the Big Hill (vol. children's sermons), 1930. Compiler and editor: Prayers for Special Days and Occasions, 1930; Fraternal Sermons and Addresses, 1931; Minister's

Week-Day Manual, 1934; Best Modern Illustrations, 1935; 99 New Sermons for Children, 1937; Practical Use Cyclopedia of Sermon Suggestions, 1942; 210 More Choice Sermons for Children. Made Rochester 8 NY‡

HALLORAN, EDWARD ROOSEVELT, ret. naval officer, pub. information exec.; b. Washington, Dec. 30, 1895; s. Matthew Francis and Mary Agnes (Beadle) H.; LL.B., Columbus U., Washington, 1932; m. Flavia Griffin, Aug. 15, 1926; 1 dau., Julia Ann (Mrs. Richard H. Rush). Admitted to D.C. bar, 1932; reorganized property and supply dept. Fed. Bd. Vocational Edn., 1921; purchasing agt. Bur. Pub. Roads, 1922-24; bus. mgr. VA Hosp., Jefferson Barracks, Mo., 1924-27; securities counselor Young Bros., St. Louis, 1927-28; pres. Halloran & Thorn, Inc., road building, St. Louis, 1929; spl. agt. Dept. Commerce, 1930-32; information specialist RFC, 1932-33; asst. comptroller, credit mgr. Washington Post, 1933-41; served with Md. N.G. on Mexican Border, 1915-17; served to maj. Signal Corps and inf., U.S. Army Res., 1917-40; commd. lt. (s.g.) USNR, 1941, advanced through grades to rear adm. USN, 1958; coordinator press censorship, officer charge overseas telephone communications censorship 12th Naval Dist., 1942-43; served in M.S. Sommels-Dijk, 1943, U.S.S. Rigel, 1943-44; comdg. officer naval beach parties 7th Amphibious Forces, 1944-45; tng. officer, liaison officer Office Pub. Information, Navy Dept., 1946-49; dist. pub. information officer 15th Naval Dist., 1949-52; officer charge fleet home-town news center, Great Lakes, Ill., 1952-57; asst. dir. civil relations Navy Dept., 1957-58; ret., 1958; counselor Richard H. Rush Enterprises, Washington, from 1958. Decorated Legion of Merit with combat V, others; Order of J. Gabriel Duque (Panama). Mem. Gamma Eta Gamma. Clubs: Washington State Press (Seattle); Army and Navy (Washington). Address: Tucson AZ Died Mar. 22, 1972; buried Arlington Nat. Park, Arlington VA

HALLORAN, PAUL JAMES, naval officer (ret.); b. Norwood, Mass., June 26, 1896; s. John Francis and Nora Frances (Knox) H.; B.S., Dartmouth Coll., 1919, C.E. and M.C.E., 1920; m. Catherine Lenihan, June 25, 1927; children—Richard Colby, David Granger, Joan. Commd. lt. (j.g.), Civil Engr. Corps., U.S. Navy, 1921, and advanced through grades to rear adm., 1942; ret., 1948; service as structural designer, supt. of constrn., civil engr.; overseas, 8 yrs.; commd. in Corps of Engrs., Rep. of Haiti; apptd. high chief Am. Samoa; comd. 6th Brigade (Constrn. Bn., Seabess'); comd. naval constrn. forces, Kyushu. Now vice pres. Foley Bros., Inc., internat. contractors, Pleasantville, N.Y. Decorated Legion of Merit with gold star, Presdl. Citation with one star, Navy Unit Citation with one star (U.S.), Presdl. Citation (Rep. of Haiti). Exhibits in Smithsonian Instn., Bishop and Dartmouth museums. Member Am. Soc. C.E., Am. Concrete Inst. (Wason medalist), Soc. Am. Mil. Engrs., Sigma Phi Epsilon, Gamma Alpha, Moles. Roman Catholic. Clubs: Downtown Athletic (New York). Home: Ossining NY Died Feb. 14, 1971; buried Gate of Heaven, Valhalla NY

HALLOWELL, GEORGE HAWLEY, artist; b. Boston, 1872; s. Lewis Morris and Cordelia (Hawley) H.; studied water color painting under Harold B. Warren, architecture with Prof. Warren of Harvard and Arthur Rotch; painting with Frank W. Benson and Edmund C. Tarbell; studied in England, France, Germany and Italy; stained glass with Ford & Brooks. Received gold medal, La. Purchase Exp'n, W. R. Beal prize, New York Water Color Club. Mem. Boston Soc. Architects, Boston Architectural Club, New York Water Color Club, Boston Water Color Club. Served 9 yrs. Mass. Militia; hon. mem. 1st Corps Cadets, Mass. Clubs: St. Botolph, Union Boat, Longwood Cricket, Pokanoket. Address: 101 Beacon St., Boston MA‡

HALLWORTH, JOSEPH BRYANT, author; b. Chelsea, Mass., Apr. 30, 1872; s. Thomas Leigh and Harriet Anna H.; ed. pub. schs.; m. New York, Oct. 15, 1891, Katie B. Fischer. Ran away from home at 14; traveled all over west as cowboy; became engraver, 1892; now engaged in vaudeville magic, traveling with his family known as Victorina Troupe of Hindoo Wonder Workers." Author: Arline Valerie, P3. Address: 14 Belle Av., Lowell MA‡

HALPERN, JACOB, physician; b. N.Y.C., Sept. 25, 1915; s. William and Frieda Gussie (Bleich) H.; M.D., L.I. Coll. Medicine, 1940; m. Helen Elizabeth Bliss, May 18, 1951; children—David Reed, Philip John, Joseph William, Susan. Intern, Kings County Hosp., Bklyn., 1940-42, resident in medicine, 1942-44, asst. in pathology, 1944-45, asst. vis. physician, 1949-52, vis. physician, 1952-58, chief endocrine and metabolic clinic, 1954-55, mem. combined med. bd., 1952-56; practice medicine specializing in internal medicine, Bklyn., 1944-70; attending physician in medicine L.I. Coll. Hosp., Bklyn., also chief endocrine clinic, clin. dir. steroid chem. lab., cons. to isotope service; cons. in medicine Caledonian Hosp.; cons. in endocrinology Midwood Hosp., Diplomate Am. Bd. Internal Medicine. Mem. A.M.A., A.A.A.S., Am. Fedn. Clin. Research, Am. Soc. Internal Medicine, A.C.P. (asso.), Kings County Med. Soc., N.Y. Acad. Scis. Research in endocrine, metabolic and thyroid disease, Addison's disease. Home: Brooklyn NY Died July 9, 1970; buried New Montefiore Cemetery, Pinelawn NY

HALPERN, JULIUS (JULES), physicist, educator; b. Norfolk, Va., Feb. 4, 1912; s. Jacob and Lena (Kanter) H.; B.S., Carnegie Inst. Tech., 1933, M.S., 1935, Sc.D., 1937; m. Phyllis E. Melnick, Feb. 4, 1940; children—Paul Joseph, Sydney Ann. Nuclear physics research U. Mich., 1937-40, U. Cal., 1940-41; staff Mass. Inst. Tech., 1941-46, asso. dir. Brit. br. Radiation Lab., tech. advisor USAAF, 1944-45, physics research Mass. Inst. Tech. Research Lab. Electronics, 1946-47; asst. prof. U. Pa., 1947, asso. prof., 1948-52, prof. from 1952. Chmn., organizer biennial Internat. Conf. on Exptl. Meson Spectroscopy, Phila., 1968, 70, 72. Sr. postdoctoral fellow Nat. Sci. Found., Paris, France, 1956-57; recipient Alumnus Merit award Carnegie-Mellon U., 1970. Fellow Am. Phys. Soc.; mem. Fedn. Am. Scientists (sec. treas. 1951, chmn. 1952, exec. com. 1953), Sigma Xi, Tau Beta Pi, Pi Delta Epsilon, Beta Sigma Rho. Contbr. profl. publs. Home: Philadelphia PA Died May 13, 1972; buried Shalom Meml. Park, Philadelphia PA

HALPERT, EDITH GREGOR, art gallery dir.; b. Odessa, Russia, Apr. 25, 1900; d. Gregor and Frances (Lucom) Fivoosiovitch; student extension courses Columbia, N.A.D., Art Students League; m. Samuel Halpert, May 25, 1918 (dec. 1930), Came to U.S., 1906, naturalized, 1921. Asst. to advt. mgr. Stern Bros., 1917-18; personnel mgr., systematizer, head correspondence dept. S.W. Straus & Co., 1920-25; reorganizer Galleries Lilloise, Lille, France, summer 1925; founder Downtown Gallery Contemporary Am. Art. N.Y.C., 1926, Am. Folk Art Gallery, N.Y.C., 1929-—; organizer 1st Municipal Art Exhbn., Atlantic City, 1929, N.Y.C., 1934; pres. 32 E 51st St. Corp.; lectr. art bus. mgmt. in museums. Pres. Edith Gregor Halpert Found., 1952-—; trustee Shelburne (Vt.) Museum, 1953-—, Skowhegan (Me.) Sch. Painting and Sculpture. Mem. Municipal Art Soc., Nat. Council for U.S. Art, Inc. Contbr. jours. and periodicals. Compiled various catalogs art collections. Home: New York City NY Died Oct. 1970; buried Washington DC

HALSEY, JOHN TAYLOR, physician; b. Elizabeth, N.J., Nov. 8, 1870; s. William Forrest and Frances Evelyn (Haines) H.; Poly. Inst., Brooklyn; Princeton U.; M.D., Coll. Phys. and Surg. (Columbia), 1893; m. Mildred W. Packard, 1899. Asst. in pharmacology, U. of Marburg, 1898-99; asst. prof. pharmacology, McGill U., 1900-04; prof. pharmacology, therapeutics and clin. medicine, Med. Dept., Tulane U., 1904-24, prof. pharmacology, Sch. of Medicine, 1924-37, emeritus since 1937. Mem. A.M.A., La. State Med. Soc., Am. Soc. Pharmacology, Soc. for Exptl. Biology and Medicine, hon. mem. Phi. Chi. Translator: Experimental Pharmacology (by Gottlieb-Meyer), 1913. Home: 1406 7th St., New Orleans LA‡

HALSTEAD, WARD CAMPBELL, psychologist; born Sciotoville, O., Dec. 31, 1908; s. Ward Beecher and Fannie (Campbell) H.; student Miami U., 1925-27; A.B., Ohio U., 1930; A.M., Ohio State U., 1931: Ph.D., Northwesktern U., 1935; Nat. Research fellow, U. of Chicago, 1935; m. Elizabeth Lee, Dec. 6, 1932; 1 son, Mark Beecher. Instr. in exptl. psychology, dept. of medicine, U. of Chicago, 1936-39; asst. prof. and asso. mem. Otho S.A. Sprague Meml. Inst., U. of Chicago, 1939-43, asso. prof., 1943-46, prof. exptl. psychology, dept. of medicine, 1946-69, dir. psychology sect., chmn. sect. biopsychology, 1953; consultant in neurology and blindness Nat. Insts. of Health, 1953-69; vis. prof. psychology, U. of Calif., Los Angeles, 1947, Berkeley, 1949. Spl. lectureships: Hixon Symposium on Brain Mechanisms, Calif. Inst. Tech., 1948; Nineteenth James Arthur lecture, Am. Museum of Natural History, 1950. Mem. com. on psychiatry, Nat. Research Council, 1947-53; cons. Nat. Inst. Neurol. Diseases & Blindness, 1954-69. Mem. Am. Psychol. Assn., A.A.A.S., Am. Physiol. Soc., Am. Neurol. Assn., Soc. of Biological Psychiatry, Midwestern Psychol. Assn. Chicago Neurol. Assn. Chgo. Inst. of Medicine Author: books include Brain and Intelligence, 1947; The Frontal Lobes (with J. F. Fulton, editor), 1948; Brain Mechanisms and Behavior, 1951. Home: Chicago IL Died Mar. 25, 1969.

HALTOM, WILLIAM LORENZ, physician; b. Jonesboro, Ark., Oct. 22, 1904; s. William Columbus and Zepha (McColl) H.; A.B., Hendrix Coll.; B.S., M.S., U. Ala.; M.D., Duke U., 1932; m. Estelle Armstrong, June 8, 1926; children—Jan (Mrs. Everett Lanson Plyler), Martha (Mrs. William Edgar Warrick). Former curator mineralogy Mus. Natural History, U. Ala.; intern Duke U. Hosp., Durham, N.C., 1932-33, asst. resident in urology, 1933-34, resident in urology, 1935-37; resident in urology Kretschmer service Presbyn. Hosp., Chgo., 1934-35; urologist King's Daus. Hosp., Martinsburg, W.Va., until 1970. Served to maj., M.C., AUS. Diplomate Am. Bd. Urology. Mem. A.M.A. Home: Martinsburg WV Died Feb. 16, 1970; buried Martinsburg WV

HAMANN, ANNA, physician; b. Hamburg, Germany, July 8, 1894; d. Carl Friedrich and Minna Maria Margaretha (Feyck) Hamann; M.D., U. Munich, 1921. Naturalized U.S. citizen. Intern, Univ. Hosps. and Clins, Hamburg, Munich, Germany, 1922; resident Radiation Inst., U. Hamburg, 1922-23, asst., 1929-37, asso. radiologist, 1937-38; resident div. radiol. gynecology and surgery dept. U. Munich, 1923-24; asso. radiologist, Kronach, Germany, 1924-29; asst. radiologist St. George's Hosp., Hamburg, 1929-37, asso., 1937-38; attending radiation therapist Evanston (Ill.) Hosp., 1948-62, cons. radiologist, 1962-69; cons. radiologist Swedish Covenant Hosp., Chgo.; instr. U. Chgo., 1938, asst. prof. med. therapeutic radiology, 1939-48; asso. prof. Northwestern U. Med. Sch., Chgo., 1961, asso. prof. emeritus, 1962-69. Diplomate Am. Bd. Radiology. Mem. A.M.A., Radiol. Soc. N.Am., Am. Med. Womens Assn., Am. Soc. Therapeutic Radiologists, Am. Radium Soc. Home: Chicago IL Died Sept. 7, 1969.

HAMBIDGE, GOVE, writer, editor; b. Kansas City, Mo. Nov. 17, 1890; s. Jay and Cordella Selina (deLorme) H.; A.B., Columbia U., 1913; m. Dorothy Cooke, Aug. 16, 1917; children—Gove, Deborah (Mrs. Arthur Witt Brewer). Began as writer, 1913; engaged as assistant district supervisor Charity Orgn. Soc. of N.Y., 1914-15; spl. agent Carnegie Hero Fund Commn., 1915-16; spl. investigator N.Y. City Fire Dept., 1916-18; asst. editor Robert M. McBride & Co., 1919; managing editor World Tomorrow, 1919-22; asst. editor Cosmopolitan Mag., 1922-27; free-lance writer, 1925-35; sr. information specialist, Agrl. Adjustment Adminstrn., U.S. Dept. of Agr., 1935; prin. research writer and editor Yearbook of Agr., Office of Information, U.S. Dept. of Agr., 1936-42; coordinator. Agrl. Research Adminstrn., 1942-45; exec. sec. United Nations Interim Commn. on Food and Agriculture, 1945; dir. of Information, Food and Agriculture Orgn. of U.N., 1945-48, editorial adviser 1948-51, North American Regional rep., 1951-56; cons., 1956; cons. U.S. govt. and U.N. agencies, 1956-70. Exec. sec. Soc. for International Development, 1957-58. U.S. delegate U.N. conf. on Food and Agriculture, 1943. Served as private, later sergt. and 2d lt., Q.M.C., U.S. Army, 1917-18. Awarded Pulitzer scholarship, 1909-13, Carnegie Found. grant, 1939, Lord & Taylor Am. Design award, 1950. Fellow A.A.A.S.; mem. Am. Acad. Polit. and Social Sci. Club: Cosmos (Washington). Author: Time to Live, 1933; Your Meals and Your Money, 1934; Enchanted Acre, 1935; Six Rooms Make a World, 1938; New Aims in Education, 1940; Prime of Life, 1941; The Story of FAO. 1955. Editor: Internat. Devel. Review, 1958-62; Dynamics of Development, 1964. Home: Kensington MD Died Sept. 25, 1970.

HAMBLEN, ARCHELAUS L., army officer; born Me., July 25, 1894; B.S., U. of Me., 1916; grad. Inf. Sch., Advanced Course, 1928, Command and Gen. Staff Sch., 1934, Army War Coll., 1937. Commd. 2d lt., Inf., Nov. 1916, and advanced through the grades to brig. gen., Dec. 1942; served on Gen. Staff, 1940-41. Died Oct. 8, 1971.

HAMBROOK, RICHARD EDWARD, business exec.; born Phoenix, Ariz., Oct. 29, 1899; s. Richard J. and Stella (Bowers) H.; B.S., Calif. Inst. Tech., 1921; m. Mignon Hamilton, June 2, 1926 (dec.); children—Mignon Elizabeth (Mrs. David Cross), Shirley Lorraine (Mrs. James J. Jones, Jr.); m. 2d, Ramona Searle, Apr. 5, 1952. With Pacific Tel. & Tel. Co., from 1921, beginning as student engineer, became general plant supervisor, 1928, general plant manager, 1930, plant operations engineer. 1942, assistant vice pres. operations, 1943, v.p. and gen. mgr., 1943, v.p. in charge of personnel, 1947, v.p. in charge of operations, 1949-54, exec. vice pres., from 1954, also dir.; director Bell Telephone of Nev. Bank of Cal. Served as pvt. U.S. Army, 1917; officer, Engr. Corps, U.S. Army, 1921-35. Republican. Presbyterian. Clubs: Bohemian, Commonwealth, Transportation, Pacific Union, San Francisco CA Died Mar. 23, 1968.

HAMBURGER, LOUIS PHILIP, physician; b. Baltimore, Md., Sept. 18, 1873; s. Philip and Rachel (Bernei) H.; student Md. Coll. of Pharmacy, 1888-89; A.B., Johns Hopkins, 1893, M.D., 1897; grad. student U. of Berlin, 1898-99; m. Freda Rose Hamburger, September 20, 1903; children—Louis Philip, Frederic. Physician, 1899, asst. prof. medicine emeritus, Johns Hopkins Med. Sch.; consultant Baltimore City Health Department since 1937; physician Johns Hopkins Hospital, Union Memorial Hospital, Hospital for Women of Maryland, Church Home and Infirmary, Bon Secours; consultant Sinai Hospital, West Baltimore General Hospital, South Baltimore General Hospital. Mem. Med. Milk Commn.; mem. com. of revision of U.S. Pharmacopaeia for Edition X, 1926. Mem. bd. dirs. Baltimore Chapter Am. Red Cross, 1939-44. Fellow Am. Coll. Physicians; mem. A.M.A., Southern Med. Soc., Baltimore City Med. Soc. (pres. 1931-32), Johns Hopkins Med. Soc. (pres. 1934-35), Md. Med. and Chirurg. Faculty (chmn. interprofessional relations com. since 1940), Am. Assn. Univ. Prof., A.A.A.S., Phi Beta Kappa. Democrat. Clubs: Johns Hopkins (Baltimore), Pithotomy. Contbr. to The Practitioners Library, 1937; contbr. on internal medicine to jours. Home: 1207 Eutaw Place, Baltimore 17‡

HAMEL, CHARLES DENNIS, lawyer; b. Mpls., Nov. 25, 1881; s. Joseph Lewis and Mary T. (Greenagle) H.; B.A. U. N.D., 1903, postgrad. study law; LL.B., Nat. U. Law Sch., 1907; m. Margaret Baptie, Jan. 31, 1914 (dec. June 1932); m. 2d, Ethel Fay Scott, Dec. 26, 1935; 1 son, Charles Scott. Pvt. sec. U.S. Sen. H. C.

Hansbrough, 1906-09; admitted to Ida. bar, 1909; legal staff Dept. Interior, 1909-14; spl. asst. to atty. gen. U.S., trial of cases in Cal., Wyo., 1915-22; legal work Bur. Internal Revenue, 1922-24, chmn. com. on appeals and review, 1923-24; organizer, chmn. U.S. Bd. of Tax Appeals (became Tax Ct. of U.S.) 1924-25; mem. Hamel, Morgan, Park & Saunders, Washington and Chgo., formerly counsel to Joint Congl. Com. on Internal Revenue Taxation. Past mem. compensation bd. Bd. Econ. Warfare; chmn. excess profits tax council U.S. Bur. Internal Revenue, 1946-47. Fellow Am. Geog. Soc.; mem. Am., D.C., Fed., Cal., Va. bar assns., Am. Acad. Polit. and Social Sci., Acad. Polit. Sci., Sigma Chi, Sigma Nu Phi, Delta Sigma Rho, Pi Gamma Mu. Republican. Episcopalian. Clubs: Metropolitan, Chevy Chase, Nat. Press (Washington); Fairfax Hunt (Fairfax County, Va.). Author: Practice and Evidence—U.S. Board Tax Appeals; Practice and Evidence Before the Tax Court of the U.S. Contbr. articles on taxation to mags. Home: McLean VA Died June 5, 1970; buried National Meml. Park, Falls Church VA

HAMER, EDWARD EVERETT, physician; b. Pike County (P.O. Given), O., Feb. 2, 1877; s. John and Mary Ann (Wood) H.; ed. Southern Ohio Sch. of Pedagogy, 1892-93; Mills Training School (for Nurses), New York, 1898-1900; M.D., Ky. Sch. of Medicine, Louisville, 1906; m. Margie Winterhoff, Apr. 7, 1911 (divorced 1920); children—Edward Everett (dec.), Dorothy Louise; m. 2d, Lucile A. Muldoon, Oct. 17, 1920. Engaged in nursing, 1900-06, began med. practice in Pittsburgh, Pa., 1906; surgeon for Am. Locomotive Works, 1912-17; moved to Carson City, 1919; state med. officer of Nev. since 1927. Enlisted in U.S. Army, October 1, 1917, serving with A.E.F.; hon. disch. Apr. 3, 1919. Mem. Nev. State Med. Assn. (pres. 1934-35). Episcopalian. Mason (32 deg., K.T., Shriner); mem. K.P., Eagles. Home: 314 N. Nevada St. Address: State House, Carson City NV*‡

HAMER, PHILIP MAY, historian; b. Marion, S.C., Nov. 7, 1891; s. Philip Bascomb and Gertrude (Buck) H.; B.A., Wofford Coll., Spartanburg, S.C., 1912; M.A., Trinity Coll. (now Duke Univ.), 1915; Ph.D., U. of Pa., 1918; Litt.D., Wofford College, 1936; L.H.D., Brown U., 1962; LL.D., Clemson U., 1963; m. Marguerite Bartlett, Aug. 30, 1920 (divorced); m. 2d, Elizabeth Edwards, May 10, 1940. Teacher high sch., Greenwood, S.C., 1912-14; asst. in history, U. of Pa., 1916-18; research asst., War Trade Bd., 1918-19; prof. history, U. of Chattanooga, 1919-20; asso. prof. history, U. of Tenn., 1920-26, prof., 1926-35, chmn. Grad. Sch., 1930-34, acting dean Coll. of Liberal Arts, 1933-34; dep. examiner The National Archives, 1935, chief Div. of the Library, 1936-38, chief div. of accessions, 1938, chief div. of reference, 1938-41, director of reference service, 1941-44, and dir. of records control, 1944-51; nat. dir. Survey of Federal Archives, 1936-37; sec. Nat. Hist. Publs. Commn., 1946-51, exec. dir. 1951-61; chief editor Henry Laurens Papers, 1961-71; visiting professor of history, George Peabody Coll. for Tchrs., summer, 1920, Ind. U., summer 1926. Delegate International Congress Archives, 1966. Fellow Soc. of Am. Archivists, 1958-71; member council inst. Early Am. History and Culture, 1956-59; mem. Am. Hist. Assn., Miss Valley Hist. Assn. (mem. exec. com. 1929-32), So. Hist. Assn. (v.p. 1936; pres. 1938), East Tenn. Hist. Soc. (pres. 1926-28; mng. editor publs. 1931-35), Society of Am. Archivists (president 1960-61), Mass. Hist. Society, Kappa Alpha (Southern), Phi Kappa Phi, Tau Kappa Alpha. Club: Cosmos. Author: The Secession Movement in South Carolina, 1847-52, 1918; Tennessee, a History, 1933. Editor and Part Author: The Centennial History of the Tennessee State Medical Association, 1930. Mem. bd. editors Miss. Valley Hist. Review, 1932-35, Journal of Southern Hist., 1935-36. Editor: Guide to Records in the Nat. Archives, 1948; Federal Records of World War II (2 vols.), 1950; A National Program for the Publication of Historical Documents. 1954; Guide to Archives and Manuscripts in U.S., 1961; Papers of Henry Laurens, Vol. 1, 1968, Vol. 2, 1970, Vol. 3, 1971. Contbr. hist. articles and book revs. Home: Bethesda MD Died Apr. 10, 1971.

HAMERSCHLAG, ROBERT JOSEPH, stockbroker; b. N.Y.C., Feb. 6, 1894; s. Joseph and Helen (Strouse) H.; ed. Phillips Acad., Andover, Mass., 1910-11, Williams Coll., 1911-13; m. Eleanor Whitney Lloyd. Partner Hamershlag, Borg & Co., mems. N.Y. Stock Exchange. Bd. govs. N.Y. Stock Exchange, 1939-45, trustee Gratuity Fund. Served with inf., U.S. Army, 1917-19; AEF. Decorated knight Order Etoile Noire (France). Mem. Nat. Audubon Soc. (dir. 1952-61), chmn. bd. 1959-61). Home: Katonah NY Died Mar. 1973.

HAMID, GEORGE ABOU, circus and entertainment exec.; b. Lebanon, Feb. 4, 1896; s. Joseph A. and Zyne (Asfar) H. ed. in Lebanon; m. Elizabeth M. Raab, Mar. 17, 1915; children—George Abou, and Zyne Elizabeth. Came to the United States, 1907, naturalized through father. Tumbler, Buffalo Bill Circus, 1907-13, other circuses, 1913-19; propr. booking and importing office for circuses and thrill acts., 1920-55; owner N.J. State Fair Grounds, 1937-71, Steel Pier, Atlantic City, N.J., 1945-71; operator Hamid Morton Indoor Circus, 1936-71. Bd. trustees Am. Guild Variety Artists Welfare Fund; mem. bd. of govs. Betty Bacharach Home. Recipient 1st annual Horatio Alger award, 1948, also awards for World War II fund raising Mem. Nat. Showmens Assn. (founder, pres. emeritus). Mason (Shriner). Author: (autobiography) Circus, 1951. Home: Atlantic City NJ Died June 13, 1971; buried Laurel Meml. Park, Atlantic City NJ

HAMILBURG, JOSEPH M., rubber co. exec.; b. Boston, 1902. Chmn. bd., treas., dir. Plymouth Rubber Co., Inc., Canton, Mass. Home: Boston MA Died Mar. 1968.

HAMILTON, A. J., treas. ICO Industries, Inc. Home: Dallas TX

HAMILTON, ALEXANDER, association executive; b. N.Y.C., Jan. 25, 1903; s. William Pierson and Juliet Pierpont (Morgan) H.; grad. St. Paul's Sch., 1921, Harvard, 1925; m. Elizabeth Malcolm Peltz, Dec. 26, 1935. Formerly dep. commr. N.Y. City Dept. Markets, formerly asst. to commr. Dept. Sanitation. Dir. Ramapo Land Co., Pothat Water Co. Chairman advisory board national shrines, New York City; secretary-treasurer of American Museum of Immigration. Pres., Tuxedo (N.Y.) Meml. Hosp. Served to maj. USMCR, World War II. Mem. St. Nicholas Soc. (past pres.), St. Andrew's Soc. N.Y. (v.p. 1959-60), Am. Scenic and Historic Preservation Soc. (pres.), N.Y. Young Republican Club (past pres.). Republican, Episcopalian. Clubs: Century Association; Racquet and Tennis; Harvard; Brook; Travellers (Paris, France). Home: Sloatsburg Rockland County NY Died May 29, 1970; buried St. Elizabeth's Meml. Chapel, Sloatsburg, Rockland County NY

HAMILTON, ALICE, M.D.; b. New York City, Feb. 27, 1869; d. Montgomery and Gertrude (Pond) H.; Miss Porter Sch., Farmington, Conn., 1887-89; M.D., U. of Mich., 1893, hon. A.M., 1910; postgrad. work, univs. of Leipzig and Munich, 1895-96; Johns Hopkins, 1896-97; U. of Chicago, 1898-1900; Institut Pasteur, Paris, 1903. Prof. pathology, Woman's Med. Coll. of Northwestern U., Chicago, 1899-1902; bacteriologist, Memorial Inst. for Infectious Diseases, 1902-10; med. investigator, Ill. Commn. Occupational Diseases, 1910; investigating industrial poisons U.S. Dept. Labor, 1910-21; asst. prof. industrial medicine, Harvard Med. Sch., 1919-35. Apptd. mem. Health Orgn. of League of Nations, 1924. Mem. Am. Assn. Pathologists and Bacteriologists, A.M.A., Chicago Inst. Medicine, Am. Assn. for Labor Legislation, League of Women Voters, Woman's Trade Union League. Clubs: Woman's City (Chicago and Boston), Cosmopolitan (New York). Contbr. articles to scientific jours. Home: Boston MA Died Sept. 22, 1970; buried Hadlyne CT

HAMILTON, CHARLES WHITELEY, banker; b. Palestine, Tex., Apr. 19, 1907; s. Wiley Ade and Cora (Whiteley) H.; B.A., Rice U., 1928; grad. Rutgers U., Stonier Grad. Sch. Banking, 1940; m. Mary Alice Stevens, Oct. 3, 1933. With Nat. Bank of Commerce, Houston, 1921-66, trust officer, 1944, v.p., 1947-58, sr. v.p., 1958-61, sr. v.p., sr. trust officer, 1961-66; sr. v.p., sr. trust officer, dir. Houston Nat. Bank, 1966, pres., 1966-68, chmn. bd., dir. Tenneco, Inc., Houston. Instr. trusts Southwestern Grad. Sch. of Banking, 1957-71, Pacific Coast Banking Sch., 1961-62. Gen. campaign chmn. United Fund Houston and Harris County, 1961, pres., 1962, chmn. bd., 1963; chmn. Community Council, Houston, 1957-58. Served with AUS, 1942-43. Mem. Am. (div. pres. 1959-60), Tex. bankers assns., Assn. Rice Alumni (pres. 1966-67). Republican. Episcopalian. Home: Houston TX Died July 5, 1971.

HAMILTON, DONALD ROSS, physicist; b. Hartford, Vt., Sept. 5, 1914; s. Rollo Albert and May Davina (Ross) H.; A.B., Princeton, 1935; Ph.D., Columbia, 1939; m. Eileen Mary Clare-Patton, Aug. 20, 1938;children—Erica Lynn (Mrs. Richard S. Weeder), Eleanor Patton (Mrs. Stanley Sienkiewicz), David Ross. Jr. fellow Soc. of Fellos, Harvard, 1939-42; staff Mass. Inst. Tech. Radiation Lab., 1940-46; project engr. Sperry Gyroscope Co. Research Labs., Garden City, N.Y., 1941-42, research engr., 1942-45; asst. prof. physics Princeton, 1946-48, asso. prof., 1948-55, prof. from 1955, dean of the graduate school, 1958-65; member of the Inst. for Advanced Study, 1952; vis. sr. physicist Brookhaven Nat. Lab., 1953. Fellow Am. Phys. Soc., Fedn. Am. Scientists. Author: Klystrons and Microwave Triodes (with J.B.H. Kuper and J.L. Knipp), 1947. Trustee Princeton U. Press, Princeton NJ Died Jan. 4, 1972; buried Fairview Cemetery, Tyler County WV

HAMILTON, HAROLD LEE, v.p. Gen. Motors; b. Little Shasta, Calif., June 14, 1890; s. Hugh Alexander and Clara Lee (De Long) H.; ed. pub. and private schs.; m. Ethelyn Sherer Wheeler, Dec. 24, 1919; children—Warren Kent, Shirley Clair, Audrey Ann. Held positions in mech. and operating depts. of several railroads, 1905-13; in sales dept. White Motor Co., 1913-22; founded Electro-Motive Co., 1922, pres. until 1942, when company was made a div. of Gen. Motors Corp., later v.p., then ret. Home: Palm DesertCA also San Francisco CA Died May 3, 1969; buried Alta Mesa Cemetery, Palo Alto CA

HAMILTON, JAMES ALEXANDER, actuary; b. Kingston, Ont., Can., Sept. 12, 1906; s. John Rennie and Clara (Howlett) H.; B.S., Queens U., 1927; M.S., U. Chgo.; M.A., Pa. State U.; m. Geraldine Lucy Boyce, June 21, 1930; children—Margaret Lynne, Nancy Lee. Came to U.S., 1927, naturalized, 1940. Instr. math. Pa. State U., 1928-33; research Met. Life Ins. Co., 1933-43; with Wyatt Co., also Wyatt Actuaries, Inc., Washington, 1946-69, pres., chmn. bd., 1961-69; cons. actuary, 1969-73; dir. Fidelity Nat. Bank, Arlington, Va. Served to maj. AUS, 1943-46; actuary, then chief life sect., contract ins. br. Office Chief of Finance. Fellow Soc. Actuaries Conf. Actuaries in Pub. Practice; mem. Fraternal Actuarial Assn., Internat. Assn. Cons. Actuaries (vice chmn.), Internat. Congress Actuaries. Author: (with D.C. Bronson) Pensions. Home: Punta Gorda FL Died Feb. 27, 1973.

HAMILTON, JAMES WALLACE, clergyman; b. Pembroke, Ont., Can., May 4, 1900; s. John Wallace and Elizabeth (Warren) H.; student Moody Bible Inst., Chgo., 1920-24; D.D., Fla. So. Coll., 1940; m. Florence Newlan, June 24, 1930; children—John Wallace, Joan Elizabeth, James Raleigh. Ordained to ministry Methodist Ch., 1932; minister Trinity Meth. Ch., St. Petersburg, Fla., 1927-29, Pasadena Community Ch., St. Petersburg, 1929-68; guest preacher seminaries, colls., univs., ministers confs., also on radio; speaker The Protestant Hour, 3 times. Del. Southeastern Jurisdictional Conf., 1960, 64, 68, Gen. Conf. Meth. Ch., 1960, 64, 66. Bd. dirs. Sunny Shores Villas, St. Petersburg, Goodwill Industries, St. Petersburg, Bethune Cookman Coll.; bd counsellors Fla. Presbyn. Coll. Recipient Outstanding Citizen award St. Petersburg Civitan Club, 1947, Freedom Found. award, 1960. Author: Ride the Wild Horses, 1952; Horns and Halos in Human Nature, 1954; Who Goes There, 1958; How to Become a Christian, 1959; The Thunder of Bar Feet, 1964; Serendipity, 1965; Faith for a Nuclear Age, 1966; Overwhelmed, 1968; Where Now Is thy God? 1969; (posthumous) Still the Trumpet Sounds, 1970; What About Tomorrow, 1972. Home: St Petersburg FL Died Oct. 7, 1968; buried Memorial Park, St. Petersburg FL

HAMILTON, JOHN C., hotel exec.; b. Roswell, N.M., 1903; s. Harry W. and Floy (Richey) H.; student U. Tex., 1921-22, Tex. A. and M. Coll., 1922-23. Exec. asst. mgr. St. Anthony Hotel, San Antonio, 1935-43, 48-58, gen. mgr., 1958-68, also sec.-treas. Bd. dirs. San Antonio Live Stock Exposition. Served with AUS, 1943-46. Mem. San Antonio Hotel Assn., Tex. Cavaliers. Clubs: St. Anthony, German, Rotary (San Antonio). Address: San Antonio TX Died May 8, 1968; buried Mission Burial Park

HAMILTON, JOHN SHERMAN, evangelist; b. Ada, Ohio, Dec. 20, 1870; s. Jonathan and Sarah (Anderson) H.; A.M., Ohio Northern U., 1895; post-grad. work, Wooster U.; studied Princeton Theol. Sem. and McCormick Theol. Sem.; m. Agnes Laughlin, of Ada., O., July 27, 1898. Ordained Presbyn. ministry, 1898; in pastorate 6 yrs.; evangelist since 1904. Pres. Interdenom. Evang. Assn.; mem. Fed. Evang. Com.; mem. Internat. Federation of Christian Workers. Gen. Sec. Missionary Activities, Winona Lake, Ind.; dir. of Winona Lake Christian Assembly, Inc. Author (booklets): Is Jesus Coming Again?; Home, How To Make It Happy, The Christian and Amusements. Home: Winona Lake IN‡

HAMILTON, KATE WATERMAN, author; b. Schenectady, N.Y.; d. Farwell H. and Ruth A. H.; ed. chiefly at Steubenville, O. Author: We Three; Vagabond and Victor, 1879; Rachel's Share of the Road, 1882; Tangles and Corners, 1882; Dr. Lincoln's Children; Wood, Hay and Stubble, 1886; The King's Seal, 1887; The Hand with the Keys, 1890; Parson's Proxy, 1896; The Kinkaid Venture, 1900; How Donald Kept Faith, 1900; etc. Address: Bloomington IL‡

HAMILTON, ROBERT PATRICK, prof. law; b. Petersburg, Va., Nov. 23, 1896; s. Robert P. and Sally Parke (Wellford) H.; B.A., U. of Va., 1917; B.A. in Jurisprudence (1st class honours), Oxford Univ., 1922, B.C.L., 1923, M.A., 1928; LL.B., Columbia Univ., 1924; student Caen Univ., France, 1919; Rhodes Scholar 1920-23; grad. U.S. Army Sch. of Mil. Government, 1943; m. Portia Goulder, June 5, 1926 (divorced, Aug. 29, 1947); 1 dau., Portia Virginia. Admitted to Va. State bar, 1920; associate law firm, Root, Clark, Buckner, Howland & Ballantine, N.Y. City, 1924-29; asso. prof. law, Columbia, 1929-37, prof. law since 1937; mem. Alien Enemy Hearing Bd., South Dist. N.Y., 1941-43; govt. appeal agt., Selective Service System, 1942-43. Served as lt. col., on active service, 1943-45, col. 1945-46, col. SA-Res. U.S. Army; overseas July 1943-Apr. 1946; mem. gen. staff corps with troops, 1944-46; Asst. Chief of Staff, G-5, U.S. Administrative Staff, British 21, Army Group, then Seine Sect., Com. Z., E.T.O., 1944-45; dep. comdg. officer, 176th staff and adminstrn. group, O.R.C., 1946-49; special mission to Germany, 1948; special staff, Department of the Army, 1949. Decorated Legion of Merit, Bronze Star Medal, Purple Heart (with Oak Leaf Cluster), Victory Medal with 3 battle clasps, World War I, Victory Medal, World War II. E.T.O. medal with 2 battle stars, Chevalier,

French Legion of Honor Croix de Guerre with Silver Star (1914-18), Croix de Guerre with 2 Palms (1939-45). Mem. Am. Bar Assn., Assn. Am. Rhodes Scholars, Res. Officers Assn., Phi Beta Kappa, Phi Delta Phi. Democrat. Episcopalian. Club: Men's Faculty of Columbia Univ. Co-author: Cases on Business Organization (2 vols.). Home: New York City NY Died July 1970.

HAMILTON, THOMPSON A., ry. pres.; b. St. Louis, Mo., Jan. 21, 1874; ed. pub. schs. Began in employ of C.P. Ry., at Toronto, Ont., Nov. 1, 1890; with C. & G.T. Ry., 1892-93, M.P. Ry., 1893-1900, I.C. R.R., 1900-04, L. & N. R.R., 1904-11, accounting, traffic, executive and operating depts.; with St. L. & S.F. R.R. and its successor, the St. L.-S.F. Ry., 1911, advancing to v.p. and asst. to pres.; now pres. I.G.N. R.R. Office: Mason Bldg., Houston TX‡

HAMILTON, WILLIAM HENRY, naval officer; b. Chestnut Hill, Phila., Pa., Oct. 21, 1899; s. William Henry and Elizabeth Ada (Young) H.; B.S., U.S. Naval Acad., 1923; student Torpedo Sch., Newport, R.I., 1924; m. Marjorie Elvira Powell, July 24, 1926; children—William Henry, Frank Powell. Commd. ensign, U.S. Navy, 1923, and advanced through the grades to commodore, 1943; served in U.S.S. Utah, 1923-24, U.S.S. Hopkins, 1925; flight instr. Naval Air Sta., Pensacola, Fla., 1925; with torpedo squadron two (VT-2), 1926-29; flight instrn., 1929-31; fighting squadron one, U.S.S. Saratoga, 1931-33; supt. engine overhaul Naval Air Sta., Norfolk, Va., 1933-35; observation squadron three, U.S.S., New Mexico and Idaho, 1935-37; fighting squadron four, U.S.S. Ranger, 1937-38; patrol squadron three (later VP-32), 1938-40; mem. staff comdr. aircraft Atlantic Fleet, 1940-41; Bureau of Aeronautics, Washington, D.C., 1941-43; comdr. Fleet Air Wing Seven, 1943-45; comdr. Naval Air Bases 7th Naval Dist., 1945-46; comdg. offices U.S.S. Antretam, 1946-47; dir. plans and policy bd., office of Sec. of Defense since 1948-49; comdr. Naval Air Bases 5th Naval Dist. since 1949. Decorated Legion of Merit (U.S.); Order Comdr. British Empire, Croix de Guerre. Address: Norfolk VA Died 1969.

HAMLIN, JOHN N(ELLIS), orgn. exec.; b. Roseburg, Ore., Mar. 9, 1895; s. Frank B. and Cressida (Williams) H.; student U. Ore., 1915-18; B.S., Harvard, 1923; student U. Buenos Aires Law Sch., 1930; m. Helen Deyche, July 1, 1935; 1 son, John. Dir. coll. bur. Republican Nat. Com., 1923-24; sec. Am. Legation, Tirana, 1924-26, Embassy, Madrid, Spain, 1926-28, Buenos Aires, 1928-34; consul, Naples, Italy, 1934-37; Italian desk officer Dept. of State, 1937-39; consul, Seville, 1939-47, Singapore, detailed Saigon, 1947-50; consul, 1st sec., counselor, dept. chief of mission embassy, Quito, Ecuador, 1950-52, charge d'affaires ad interim 15 mos; consul, consul gen., Kingston, 1952-55; spl. asst. Absentee Voters Bur., D.C. Republican Hdqrs., Washington, 1955-57, and 1959-60, director, 1963-64; member District of Columbia Republican. Com., from 1959, chmn. subcom. fgn. 1959. Served with U.S. Army, 1918. Mem. Am. Fgn. Service Assn., Diplomatic and Consular Officers Retired (bd. govs., exec. dir.), Alpha Tau Omega. Clubs: Harvard, Metropolitan (Washington). Home: Washington DC Died Feb. 26, 1969; buried Rock Creek Cemetery, Washington DC

HAMM, WILLIAM, JR., brewery exec.; b. St. Paul, Sept. 4, 1893; s. William and Marie (Scheffer) H.; B.A., U. Minn., 1915; m. Marie Hersey, Jan. 1, 1934; children—William Hersey, Edward Hersey. Vice pres. Theo. Hamm Brewing Co., St. Paul, 1916-31, president and treasurer, 1931-60, chairman of the board, 1960-70. president of The Emporium of St. Paul, Inc., 1931-52, chmn. bd., 1952-70; dir. First Nat. Bank. Clubs: Athletic, Minnesota, Somerset, University (St. Paul); Minneapolis; Seminole, Jupiter, Island (Hobe Sound, Fla.); Woodhill Country (Wayzata, Minn.). Home: Wayzata MN Died Aug. 20, 1970.

HAMMAKER, WILBUR EMERY, bishop; b. at Springfield, O., Feb. 17, 1876; s. Oliver Grover and Rebecca (Hahn) H.; A.B., Wittenberg Coll., Springfield, 1898, A.M., 1901; student Wittenberg Theol. Sch., 1898-99; B.D., Drew Theol. Sem., 1901; LL.D., Lincoln U., 1919; D.D., Mt. Union Coll., Alliance, Ohio, 1927, Clark University, 1930; LL.D. Mt. Union College, 1939; University of Denver, 1943; married Willamine Weihrauch, August 15, 1901; children—Paul M., W. Eugene (deceased), Roger Emery, Arthur Wilbur (deceased). Ordained M. E. ministry, 1901; pastor Riverdale Church, Dayton, Ohio, 1901-04, Broadway Ch., Middletown, O., 1904-08, Raper Ch., Dayton, 1908-15, Trinity Ch., Youngstown, O., 1915-36; elected bishop, May 1936; assigned to Nanking Area, M.E. Ch. (China), 1936-39, assigned to Denver Area, May, 1939; reassigned, 1940-48; retired 1948; pres. Methodist Ch. Bd. of Temperance, 1944-48; vice president in charge of counseling and public relations Methodist Church Board Temperance, 1948-52; pres. Nat. Temperance and Prohibition Council, 1948-58, Prohibition Trust Fund Assn., 1960-68, Internat. Fedn. Narcotic Edn., 1953-68; chmn., dir. Notable Presentation of the Case for all Senate and House Bills to Prohibit or Delimit Liquor Advertising, 1947; ad interim editor Progress Mag., 1955-57; ad interim administrator International Reform Federation, 1955-57. Chmn. general cirriculum com. Meth. Ch., 1940-48; trustee Nanking Theological Seminary (member executive committee), Nanking University, Hui Wen School for Girls (Nanking), Peking Theol. Sem. (Peiping), Peking Acad., Hui Wen and Keen Schs. (Tientsin). William Nast and Rulisan Schs. of Kiukiang, Baldwin Sch. and Nanchang Acad. of Nanchang; mem. bd. dirs. China Religious Edn. Soc., Isabella Fisher Hosp. (Tientsin); mem. and chmn. bd. dirs. Wuhu Gen. Hosp.; mem. governing bd. Lichwan Christian Rural Project in Kiangsi Province; life mem. Shanghai University Club. Trustee and mem. executive com. Iliff Sch. of Theology, 1940-48, University of Denver, 1940-48. Mem. Nat. Am. First Com., 1940-42. Mem. Gen. Conf. M.E. Ch. 5 times (chmn. delegation 3 times); mem. Ecumenical Meth. Conf., 1931; chmn. Citizens Unemployment Relief Com., 1931-36, Youngstown; mem. Alpha Tau Omega. Mason (32 deg.). Republican. Contbr. on religious subjects. Home: DC Died Aug. 11, 1968.

HAMMER, KENNETH S., supt. schools; b. Morrison, Ill., Feb. 4, 1915; s. Fred C. and Edna (Forth) H.; B.A., Cornell Coll., Mt. Vernon, Ia., 1937; M.Ed., U. Colo., 1940; M.E., Ore. State Coll., 1944; postgrad. U. Ill., Urbana, 1950-51; m. Boneita Schneider, Jan. 4, 1944; children—Don C., Dawn Anne. Tchr. pub. schs., Royal, Ia. and Gunnison, Colo., 1937-41; supt. schs., Vermont, Ill., 1941-42; prin. Center Sch., Morris, Ill., 1946-50; supt. elementary schs., Morris, Ill., 1950-71. Served to tech. sgt. AUS, 1942-46, ETO. Mem. Nat., Ill. (dir.) edn. assns., Am., Ill., assns. sch. adminstrs., Ill. Council Ednl. Adminstrn. (past pres.), No. Ill. Conf. on Supervision (past pres.), Ill. Elementary Sch. Prins. Assn. (past pres.). Lion (past pres. Morris). Home: Morris IL Died Jan. 29, 1971; buried Evergreen Cemetery, Morris IL

HAMMETT, EDWARD, furniture mfr.; b. Evanston, Ill., May 6, 1877; s. Edward and Mary (Culver) H.; student Northwestern U., 1896-97; m. Viva MacMillan, of Cedar Rapids, Ia., Apr. 8, 1903; children—Edward, Constance Elizabeth. Traveling salesman for ry. supplies, hdqrs. Phila., Pa., 1903-10; settled in Sheboygan, Wis., 1910; v.p. and gen. mgr. Sheboygan Ry. & Electric Co., 1910-16; v.p. and gen. mgr. Northern Furniture Co. since 1916. County dir. sale of war savings stamps, World War. Mem. Phi Delta Theta. Republican. Conglist. Mason, Elk. Home: Sheboygan WI‡

HAMMOND, BRAY, writer; b. Springfield, Mo., Nov. 20, 1886; s. Harry H. and Lucy (Bray) H.; A.B., Standord, 1912; m. Melitta de Kern, Feb. 3, 1939. Asst. cashier State Bank, New Sharon, Ia., 1907-09; asst. prof. State Coll., Pullman, Wash., 1913-16; writing, research, pvt. bus., 1919-30; with Fed. Res. Bd., 1930-50, asst. sec., 1944-50. Served from 2d lt. to capt., U.S. Army, 1916-19. Guggenheim fellow, 1950, 55; recipient Pulitzer prize for history, 1958. Author: Banks and Politics in America from the Revolution to the Civil War, 1957; sovereignty and an Empty Purse, 1970. Contbr. articles hist. subjects to periodicals. Address: Thetford VT Died July 20, 1968.

HAMMOND, CHARLES HERRICK, architect; b. Crown Point, N.Y., Aug. 8, 1882; s. Charles Lyman and Mary Electa (Stevens) H.; ed. pub. schs.; grad. Chicago Manual Training Sch.; B.S. in Architecture, Armour Inst. Tech., 1904; winner Traveling Scholarship, Chicago Architectural Club; studied in Paris; m. Marion Eugenie Rogers, Oct. 4, 1911 (died Apr. 2, 1933); 1 dau., Marion Rogers; m. 2d, Mrs. L. K. Stout, February 22, 1934; 1 stepson, Richard H. Stout, U.S.N.R. Practiced at Chicago since 1907; member Chatten &Hammond, 1907-27, Perkins, Chatten & Hammond, 1927-33, Burham & Hammond since Oct. 28, 1933. Supervising architect, State of Illinois, since 1929. Served as maj. res. mil. aviator, Air Service, World War I, Chief Architect 6th Corps Area U.S. Army World War II. Former trustee Foundation for Architecture and Landscape Architecture; former vice-pres. Chicago Assn. Commerce; U.S. del. Internat. Congress Architects, 1937. Fellow A.I.A. (pres. 1928-30; past pres. Chicago chpt.); mem. Ill. Soc. Architects (past pres.); corr. mem. Royal Inst. of British Architects; U.S. del. Pan-Am. Congress Architects (Havana, Cuba), 1950. Mem. Congl. Ch. Clubs; University, Indian Hill, Country, Arts, Chicago Curling. Home: Winnetka IL Died Jan. 1969.

HAMMOND, EDWARD SANFORD, coll. prof.; b. New Britain, Conn., Apr. 21, 1893; s. Frederick Hobart Lawrence and Bertha Clarissa (Sanford) H.; A.B., Yale, 1913, A.M., 1915; Ph.D., Princeton, 1920; m. Ruth Evelyn Mackrille, June 24, 1916; children—Judith Alison (Mrs. David R. Hirth), Laura Sylvia (Mrs. Walter P. Hollmann), Letitia Jeanne (Mrs. John McAdam). Teacher of mathematics, West Haven (Conn.) High Sch., 1915-17; instr. mathematics, Princeton, 1918-21; instr. mathematics Bowdoin Coll., 1921-22, asst. prof., 1922-25, Wing prof. math., 1925-72, dir. of admissions 1935-48. Dir. Portland Jr. Coll., Portland, Me.; trustee North Yarmouth Acad., Yarmouth, Me. Mem. Math. Assn. of America, American Mathematical Soc., Am. Assn. Advancement of Science, Newcomen Soc., Phi Beta Kappa, Sigma Xi, Alpha Tau Omega. Club: Torch of Western Maine (Portland, Me.). Home: Brunswick ME Died Mar. 21, 1972.

HAMMOND, FRANK CLINCH, M.D.; b. Augusta, Ga., Mar. 7, 1875; s. Thomas and Mary Ann (Harries) H.; Boys' High Sch., Phila., 3 yrs.; M.D., Jefferson Med. Coll., Phila., 1895; hon. Sc.D., Temple U., 1929; unmarried. Interne St. Joseph's Hosp., Phila., 1895-96; instr. gynecology, Jefferson Med. Coll., 1896-1905; prof. gynecology, Med. Dept. of Temple U. since 1923, hon. dean; gynecologist Temple U. Hosp., Phila. Hosp. for Contagious Diseases; obstetrician and gynecologist Phila. Gen. Hosp.; sr. attending obstetrician and gynecologist, Jewish Hosp.; cons. gynecologist, Newcombe Hosp. (Vineland, N.J.), Del. County Hosp., Riverside Hosp., Norristown, Pa. Editor Pa. Med. Jour. Med. aide to gov. of Pa., 1918. Fellow Am. Coll. Surgeons, A.M.A.; mem. Pa. State Med. Soc., Phila. County Med. Soc. (ex-pres.), Obstet. Soc. of Phila. (ex-pres.), Phila. Clin. Assn. (ex-pres.) Republican. Episcopalian. Mason (32 deg.). Clubs: Union League, Phila. Medical. Home: 3311 N. Broad St., Philadelphia PA*‡

HAMMOND, GODFREY, publisher; b. Patchogue, L.I., N.Y. Nov. 16, 1891; s. Charles Smith and Ezma (Godfrey) H.; ed. pub. schs.; m. Irma Varian Gillespie, May 17, 1917; children—Marjorie Varian (Mrs. William Tracy Castimore), Robert Godfrey, Donald Gillespie, Philip Townsend, William Pierson. Asso. with Frank A. Munsey Co., pubs., 1907-13, Hearst Mags., 1914-17, N.Y. Tribune, 1919-22; with Popular Science Pub. Co., 1922-28, 37-69, pres., 1939-55, chmn. bd., 1955-69; publisher of the Christian Herald, 1928-37. Served as private with the U.S. Army, 1918-19. Republican. Clubs: Am. Yacht (Rye, N.Y.); Union League; Scarsdale Golf. Nat. publicity dir. Rep. Nat. Com 1944 campaign. Home: Scarsdale NY Died Aug. 19, 1969; buried Kensico Cemetery, Valhalla NY

HAMMOND, JACK, physician; b. N.Y.C., Aug. 18, 1916; B. Sc., Dalhousie U., 1935, M.D., C.M., 1939; m. Elizabeth Hammond, Sept. 20, 1941; children—Robert E., Susan G., David A. Intern Lincoln Hosp., N.Y.C., 1939-41; practice medicine specializing in psychiatry, 1941-73; pvt. practice N.Y.C., 1946-52; sr. psychiatrist Willard State Hosp., 1952-54, supervising psychiatrist, 1954-59; asst. dir. Rome (N.Y.) State Sch., 1959-64, dir., 1972-73; dir. Willowbrook State Sch., S.I., N.Y., 1964-72; attending psychiatrist St. Vincent's Med. Center, Richmond, N.Y., 1965-73; clin. prof. pediatrics Sch. Medicine, N.Y. U., 1964-73, clin. prof. psychiatry Sch. Psychiatry, 1964-73; dir. Assn. for Retarded Children Diagnostic and Counseling Center, Utica, N.Y., 1963-64; dir. Louis Boehm Diagnostic and Counseling Clinic of Guild for Exceptional Children, Inc., 1966-73; cons. S.I. Mental Health Soc., 1964-73; chief psychiat. service Auburn State Prison, 1957-64; psychiatrist Elmira Psychiat. Clinic, 1957-59, Oneida County Child Guidance Center, 1959-64, Rome Adult Mental Hygiene Clinic, 1960-64; mem. N.Y. Edn. Dept. regional adv. com. for comprehensive planning for vocational rehab. services, 1967-73; mem. categorical council on accreditation residential centers for mentally retarded Joint Commn. on Accreditation of Hosps. Mem. Mayor's Com. Mental Retardation, N.Y.C., 1966-73; mem. N.Y.C. Area Com. on Mental Health and Retardation. Bd. dirs. S.I. Aid retarded Children. Served with M.C., USNR, 1941-46. Recipient Congressional Plaque, 1972. Fellow Am. Assn. Mental Deficiency, Am. Geratric Soc.; mem. Internat. Assn. for Sci. Study Mental Deficiency, World Fedn. Mental Health, A.M.A., N.Y. (chmn. subcom. retardation 1967-73), Richmond County med. socs., Am. Psychiat. Assn. (mem. com. mental retardation 1968-71), Am. Acad. Mental Retardation, Assn. Med. Supts. Mental Hosps. Contbr. articles to profl. jours. Address: Rome NY Died Jan. 2, 1973.

HANCHETT, GEORGE TILDEN, electrical engineer; b. Hyde Park, Mass., Sept. 4, 1871; s. George W. and Augusta L. (Tilden) H.; S.B., Mass. Inst. Tech., 1893; m. Dorothy A. Lewis, of Cleveland, Nov. 29, 1894. Worked in factory Brush Elec. Co., Cleveland, later was with E.P. Roberts & Co., Cleveland, laying out plans, designing switch boards and in other consulting engring. work; later in same work at Providence, R.I.; had charge elec. work for Collyer Machine Co., Pawtucket, R.I. Moved to New York, 1895, and was on editorial staff Electric Railway Gazette; afterward on staff Electrical World and Engineering. Inventor various elec. devices; specialist in improved machine design; consulting engr. for numerous corpns. Fellow Am. Inst. Elec. Engrs.; mem. Illuminating Engring. Soc. Author: Modern Electric Railway Motors; Alternating Currents.*‡

HANCOCK, ARTHUR BOYD, live stock breeder; b. Ellerslie Farm, Charlottesville, Va., June 26, 1875; s. Richard Johnson and Thomasia Overton (Harris) H.; student Johns Hopkins U., 1891-93; A.B., U. of Chicago, 1895; m. Nancy Tucker Clay, June 30, 1908; children—Arthur Boyd, Nancy Clay (Mrs. Austin Osgood). Now pres. Bourbon Lumber Co. (Paris, Ky); owner Claiborne (Paris, Ky.) stud. Member School Board, Paris, 1916-34 (chmn. 1921-34); chmn. Bourbon County Council of Defense World War I. also co. chmn.

Am. Red Cross. Former pres. Horse and Mule Assn. Am.; v.p. Am. Thoroughbred Breeders Assn.; dir. Am. Turf Assn., Am. Remount Assn. Democrat. Presbyterian. Clubs: Rotary (Paris); Lexington, Bourbon Country. Home: Paris KY‡

HANCOCK, W(ALTER) SCOTT, lawyer; b. Franklin County, Va., Nov. 19, 1869; s. Col. Abram Booth and Martha Elizabeth (Walker) H.; grad. Va. Mil. Inst., 1890; student Hampden-Sydney (Va.) Coll., 1892; LL.B., U. of Va., 1896; m. Anna Spencer, Nov. 21, 1899; children—Walker Kirtland, Anne Spencer (Mrs. Alfred R. Watt), Laura Marshall (Mrs. John Gardiner Flint), Elizabeth Dwight (Mrs. Donald W. Buchanan), Deane Spencer (Mrs. Edmund Chenault Rogers). Comdt. Fishburne Mil. Acad., Waynesboro, Va., 1 yr., Cape Fear Acad., Wilmington, N.C., 1 yr., admitted to Va. bar, 1896, to Mo. bar, 1897, since practiced in St. Louis; asst. circuit atty., 1900-04, in charge of grand juries; gen. atty. Mo. P. Ry., 1911-14. Served as adjt. 2d Batt., 6th Mo. Vols., Spanish-Am. War; chmn. Mil. Training Camps Assn.; mem. Draft Bd., World War. Pres. Fed. of Improvement Assn.; mem. Citizens Sch. Bd. Commn., Zoning Com. of Commn. on Civic Needs, St. Louis Pub. Health Service Surveys, St. Louis Council of Boy Scouts of America, St. Louis Safety Commn. (chmn. bd. govs.), Chamber Commerce (chmn. mem. conf. and dir.). Mem. Exec. Com. for Protection of Child, Family, School and Church; mem. Am., Mo. State and St. Louis bar assns., Va. Hist. Soc., Mo. Hist. Soc., Am. Liberty League, Council of Southern Commn. to Uphold the Constitution, S.R., S.A.R., S.C.V. (camp commander 1898-99, comdr. Mo. division 1925-26, judge advocate in chief 1930-31, nat. commander in chief 1935-37); adj. gen. chief of staff, United Confederate Veterans. Democrat. Presbyterian (elder, moderator St. Louis Presbytery). Mason (Past Master, 32 deg.). Clubs: Civitan, Scottish Rite (ex-pres.). Home: 5705 Enright Av., St. Louis. Office: 705 Olive St., St Louis 1 MO‡

HAND, GEORGE TROWBRIDGE, civil engr.; b. Elizabeth, N.J., Dec. 1, 1872; s. James A. and Harriet M. (Trowbridge) H.; ed. pub. schs. and business sch.; m. Margaret Healy, May 10, 1897 (died 1928); children—George Kenneth (died 1936), Margaret Jean, James Donald, Frederick Gordon. Rodman, Nat. Docks Ry. (now Lehigh Valley R.R.) at Jersey City, N.J., 1889; prin. asst. engr. Lehigh Valley's Jersey City terminals at Nat. Docks; asst. engr., terminal engr., div. engr., in charge Morris and Essex divs., D., L. & W. R.R., 1891-97; chief engr. Lehigh Valley R.R., 1917-37, cons. engr., 1937-38, now retired. Mem. Am. Soc. C.E. Home: Denville NJ‡

HAND, HAROLD CURTIS, educator; b. Piper City, Ill., Jan. 5, 1901; s. Curtis Judd and Margaret (Adamson) H.; A.B., Macalester Coll., 1924, LL.D., 1949; A.M., U. of Minn., 1930; Ph.D., Columbia, 1933; grad. work, London (Eng.) Sch. of Economics and Polit. Sci., 1937-38; m. Kathryn Alice Guy, May 18, 1923; 1 son Thomas Guy. Prin., High Sch., Monticello, Minn., 1924-26, Thief River Falls, 1926-30; asst. in secondary edn. Columbia, 1930-31, instr., 1931-33; asst. prof. edn., Stanford 1933-36, asso. prof., 1936-40; prof. edn., U. of Md., 1940-43; prof. edn. University Illinois, 1946-64, University of South Florida, 1964-67; guest lecturer American University of Cairo (Egypt), 1943-44; visiting prof. Northwestern U., 1940; asso. dir. Carnegie Guidance Study, 1931-37; supervisor basic research studies in Ill. Curriculum Program, 1947-64; cons. Ednl. Testing Service, Princeton, N.J., 1956; cons ednl. adminstrn. div. Booz, Allen and Hamilton. Served as edn. and research officer, U.S. Army, Cairo, Manila, Tokyo. 1943-46. Mem. adv. bd. Air Tng. Command, 1954-56. Decorated Legion of Merit. Mem. Air Transport Assn. Am. (educator's adv. com.), Assn. Supervision and Curriculum Devel., Nat. Assn. Secondary Sch. Prins., N.E.A., Nat. Soc. Study of Edn., John Dewey Soc. Author: An Appraisal of the Occupations or Life-Career Course, 1934; Neutrality in Soc. Edn., 1940; The Role of the Public Junior College in Ill., 1947; What People Think About Their Schools. 1948; Principles of Public Secondary Edn., 1958. Co-author: Beyond High School, 1938; Designs for Personality, published in 1938; School and Life, pub. 1935; Appraising Guidance in Secondary Schools, 1941; Mobilizing Educational Resources, 1943; General Education in the American High School, 1942; Living in the Atomic Age, 1947; Democracy in School Administration, 1950; Citizen Cooperation for Better Public Schools, 1954; Guidance and the Curriculum, 1955; editor, author, co-author: The Challenge of Education, 1937; Campus Activities, 1938; The Schools and National Security, 1951; National Educational Assessment: Pro and Con, 1966: Curriculum Innovations, 1966— Issues and Trends, 1967. Mem. editorial adv. bd. Edn. Digest, 1958-60; editorial bd. Ednl. Theory, 1958-64; cons. edn. dept. Reader's Digest. Home: Floral City FL Died June 19, 1967.

HANDBURY, JOHN D., dept. store exec.; b. Chgo.; B.A., U. Ill.; m. Margarette Handbury; children—John D., Mark, Holly. With Carson Pirie Scott & Co., Chgo., from 1934, now exec. v.p. wholesale div., also dir.; dir. Roxbury Carpet Co., Saxonville, Mass., Coleman Distbrs., Atlanta. Vice pres. bd. govs. DePauw U., Greencastle, Ind. Served to 1st lt. AUS, World War II. Mem. Chgo. Floor Covering Assn., Carpet Trade Golf Assn., Alpha Delta Phi. Clubs: Merchant and Manufacturers (Chgo.); Glen Oak Country. Home: Glen Ellyn IL

HANDLEY, HAROLD WILLIS, gov. Ind., advt. agy. exec.; b. LaPorte, Ind., Nov. 27, 1909; s. Harold Lowell and Lottie (Brackbill) H.; A.B., Ind. U., 1932, LL.D., Valparaiso U., 1957, Indiana U., 1957, Tri-State College (Angola, Indiana), 1958; married Barbara Jean Winterble, Feb. 17, 1944; children—Kenneth David, Martha Jean. Sales rep. Unagusta Furniture Corp., Hazelwood, N.C., 1940-53; v.p. Darling Motion Picture Sales, 1949-53; Midwest sales rep. John Sutherland Prodns., Hollywood, Cal, 1952; Ind. State senator, 1941, 49-52; lt. gov., State Ind., 1953-57, gov., 1957-61; chmn. bd. Handley-Miller, Indpls. Served with Armed Forces, 1942-46; lt. col. Inf., O.R.C. Mem. Am. Legion, Delta Tau Delta. Republican. Presbyn. Elk, Mason. Eagle, Moose. Club: Lions. Home: Indianapolis IN Died Aug. 30, 1972.

HANDY, RAY D., cartoonist; b. Minneapolis, Aug. 21, 1877; s. DeWitt C. and Nellie (Seamans) H.; pub. sch. edn., Minneapolis; m. Vera E. Mason, of Excelsior, Minn., Sept. 2, 1902. Cartoonist on Duluth News Tribune and mgr. Duluth Photo Engraving Co. Has published 8 books of cartoons, 1904-12. Republican. Home: 1922 E. Superior books of cartoons, 1904-12. Republican. Home: 1922 E. Superior St. Office: The News Tribune, Duluth MN‡

HANES, JAMES GORDON, mfr. hosiery; b. Winston-Salem, N.C., June 12, 1886; s. John Wesley and Anna (Hodgin) H.; A.B., U. of N.C., 1909; m. Emmie Drewry, Nov. 12, 1911 (dec. 1916); 1 son, James Gordon; m. 2d, Molly Ruffin, Apr. 1, 1924 (dec. 1957) In hosiery business, 1909-54; chmn. bd. Hanes Hosiery Mills Co., 1938-54, dir.; dir. Wachovia Bank & Trust Co., Winston-Salem Southbound Ry. Co., other corps. Mayor of Winston-Salem, 1921-25; chmn. bd. County Commrs. of Forsyth County, N.C., 1927-50. Methodist. Club: Twin City, Forsyth Country. Home: Winston-Salem NC Died July 22, 1972.

HANES, LEIGH (BUCKNER), writer; b. Montvale, Bedford Co., Va., Dec. 24, 1893; s. Ernest Langstor and Lillian Barksdale (Kinnier) H.; A.B., Hampden-Sydney Coll., 1916, Litt.D., 1936; LL.B., Washington and Lee U., 1920, M.A., 1938; M. Lillian Lee Thompson, June 20, 1917; 1 son Leigh Buckner. Began practice law, Roanoke, 1920; editor The Lyric (quarterly mag.), 1929-49. Lectr. English and Am. poetry, formerly Hollins College, Univ. of Virginia Extension. Member Poetry Society America, Va. State, Roanoke (past pres.) bar assns., Va. Writers, Poetry Soc. of Va. (adv. bd.), Theta Chi, Sigma Upsilon and Phi Beta Kappa. Democrat. Presbyterian. Author: Song of the New Hercules and Other Poems, 1930; Green Girdle, 1939; The Star That I See, 1950; Wide the Gate (Poems 1925-57), 1957; also wrote the words of songs including: Mountains,' Love Shall Light the Haven,' Mountains in Twilight." etc. Contributor verse and reviews to mags. Poet Laureate for Va. 1949. Home: Roanoke VA Died Sept. 2, 1967; buried Roanoke VA

HANEY, JOHN LOUIS, educator; b. Phila., July 29, 1877; s. Hiram G. and Flora (Scherer) H.; A.B., Central High Sch., Phila., 1895, A.M., 1900; B.S., U. of Pa., 1898, Ph.D., 1901; LL.D., 1939; Harrison scholar, 1898-99, fellow in English, 1899-1912, U. of Pa.; unmarried. Instr., 1900-04, asst. prof. English and history, 1904-05, prof. English philology, 1905-16, head English dept., 1916-20, pres., 1920-43, Central High Sch., Phila.; retired 1943; dir. Derr-Haney Co.; Phila., 1901-16, sec., treas. 1911-16. Vice pres. Am. Theatre Realty Co.; vice pres. and dir. John Church Co., 1930-46, Oliver Ditson Co.; 1931-46; v.p., dir. Theo. Presser Co., 1924-46, pres., 1946-48, dir. since 1948. Sec. Presser Home for Ret. Music Teachers, since 1920, trustee, sec. Presser Foundation since 1923, pres. Haney Family Assn., 1928-47; asso. trustee, Univ. of Pa. since 1932; dir. Mercantile Library Co., 1943-45; trustee Free Library of Phila. since 1944; member Art Jury of Philadelphia, 1948-52; mem. advisory bd. Barnwell Foundation; chmn. Edwin B. Garrignes Found., 1955—; editor, Barnwell Bulletin, 1922-43. Mem. Am. Philos. Soc., Modern Lang. Assn. America, Am. Dialect Soc., Am. Name Soc. Authors' League Am., Concordance Soc., City Historical Soc. Headmasters' Assn., Hist. Soc. Pa., Musical Fund Soc., Phi Beta Kappa, Alpha Chi Rho, Pi Gamma Mu. Clubs: Union League, Franklin Inn Club, Schoolmen's Club. Author: The German Influence on Coleridge, 1902; Bibliography of S. T. Coleridge, 1903; Early Reviews of English Poets, 1904; The Name of William Shakespeare, 1906; Good English, 1915; English Literature, 1920; The Story of Our Literature, 1923; revised edit., 1939; The Haney Family, 1930; Shakespeare and Philadelphia, 1936; Morton W. Easton—A Memoir, 1938; Half a Century of the Century Class, 1945. Plays: Monsieur D'Or, 1910; Girard, 1919. Editor: Shakespeare's Mid-Summer Night's Dream, 1911; Bok's A Dutch Boy Fifty Years After, 1921, and The Boy Who Followed Ben Franklin, 1924; Barnwell Addresses, 3 vols., 1931, 1937, 43. Contbr. Wordsworth Concordance, 1911; Schelling, Anniversary Papers, 1923; Coleridge Studies, 1934. Home: 6419 Woodbine Av., Phila 31 PA‡

HANEY, LEWIS HENRY, economist; b. Eureka, Ill., Mar. 30, 1882; s. Conrad and Sada (Pavey) H.; student Ill. Wesleyan U., Bloomington, 1899-1901; B.A., Dartmouth, 1903, M.A., 1904, Parker traveling fellowship, 1905; Ph.D., U. of Wis., 1906; m. Anna M. Stephenson, 1906 (died 1944); 1 dau., Hope; m. 2d, Louise L. Thion, 1945. Instr. econs. U. Ia. 1906-08; asst. prof. econs. U. Mich., 1908-10; asso. prof. econs. U. Tex., 1910-12, prof., 1912-16; economist Fed. Trade Commn., 1916-19; in charge cost of marketing div. U.S. Bur. of Markets, 1920-21; dir. New York Univ. Bur. of Business Research, 1920-32, and prof. econs., 1920-52, professor emeritus of econs. and lecturer, 1952-55; lecturer Inst. Internat. Affairs, U. Wyo., 1955; econ. consultant Chicopee Mills, Inc., 1956-64. Special expert in (Federal) Census Bureau, division of methods and results, 1904; spl. examiner for Interstate Commerce Commn., 1909; cons. Nat. Assn. Purchasing Agents, 1930-64. Fellow Am. Statis. Assn.; mem. N.Y. Financial Writers Assn., Chi Phi, Phi Beta Kappa. Club: Manhasset Bay Yacht (Pt. Washington). Author books including: History of Economic Thought, 4th edit. 1949; How You Really Earn Your Living, 1952; Business Organization and Combination, 3d edit., 1934; Value and Distribution, 1939. Chief contbr. to Report on the Price of Gasoline in 1915, 1917; Price Fixing in the U.S. during the War, 1919. Contbr. on econ. and statis. topics; syndicated daily financial column in N.Y. Evening Journal and N.Y. Evening Journal-Am., 1928-57. Home: Port Washington NY Died July 1, 1969; buried Nassau Knolls Meml. Park, Port Washington NY

HANFORD, JAMES HOLLY, educator; born Rochester, N.Y., Mar. 19, 1882; s. Henry Samuel and Florence (Saxe) A.; A.B., U. of Rochester, 1904; A.M., Harvard, 1907, Ph.D., 1909; LL.D., U. N.C., 1947, Western Res. U., 1959; m. Helen Margaret Ellwanger, 1909; children—Margaret E., Barbara E., Grace E., Virginia M.; m. 2d, Ursula Farley, 1944; 1 dau., Elizabeth Holly. Teacher English, East High Sch., Rochester, 1904-06; asst. prof. English, Simmons Coll., Boston, 1909-14; prof. English, Univ. of N.C., 1914-21; prof. English, U. of Mich., 1921-28; dir. of grad. work in English, 1927; prof. English in the Grad. School of Western Reserve U., 1928-52; now prof. emeritus; vis. prof. Antioch Coll., 1947-52, Princeton, 1952-53, vis. bibliographer, Firestone Library, Princeton U., 1954-55, 1957-59; resident fellow Newberry Library, Chgo., 1955-59; consultant to Ford Humanities Project, from 1960; visiting professor comparative lit., Damascus Univ., No. Region, U.A.R., 1959, 60; vis. prof. Tex. Technol. Coll., 1962; Distinguished vis. professor Pa. State University, 1963. Member of Modern Lang. Assn. of Am. (v.p. 1922, exec. council, pres., 1957-60), Psi Upsilon. Club: Rowfant. Author: John Milton, Englishman, 1949; The Poems of John Milton, 1953; A Restoration Reader, 1954; Milton Bibliography, 1966; John Milton: Poet and Humanist, 1966; Milton Handbook, 1969. Editor several publs., 1915-34. Contbr. profl. jours. Address: Princeton NJ Died July 28, 1969.

HANGER, FRANKLIN M(CCUE), physician and educator; b. Staunton, Va., Sept. 5, 1894; s. Frank M. and Martha (McDowell) H.; B.S., U. of Va., 1916; M.D., Johns Hopkins U., Baltimore, Md., 1920; m. Harriet Echols Ewing, Apr. 15, 1942; 1 dau., Harriet Echols. Interne and resident Presbyn. Hosp., New York, N.Y., 1920-26, attending physician since 1945; asso. in medicine Columbia, 1926-27, asst. prof., 1928-31, asso. prof., 1931-47, prof. medicine, 1947-60, emeritus, 1960-71; sr. med. cons. Vets. Kingsbridge Hosp., N.Y.C., 1948-61. Emeritus mem. bd. examiners Am. Bd. Internal Medicine. Fellow of American Coll. Physicians (regent; pres. 1962-63); mem. N.Y. Clin. Soc., Assn. Am. Physicians, Am. Assn. Study Liver Diseases (pres. 1954-55), Am. Soc. Clin. Investigation, Am. Assn. Immunologists, Soc. Exptl. Biol. and Med., Harvey Soc., Phi Beta Kappa, Alpha Omega Alpha, Sigma Xi. Democrat. Episcopalian. Club: Century. Contbr. to Nelson System of Medicine, Oxford loose leaf medicine, Cecil Textbook of Medicine. Originator of Cephalin Floculation Test for disorders of the liver. Home: Staunton VA Died Oct. 10, 1971; buried Thornrose Cemetery, Staunton VA

HANGER, ROBERT KITTRELL, lawyer; b. Fort Worth, Tex., July 30, 1894; s. William A. and Mattie (Scruggs) H.; grad. Culver (Ind.) Mil. Acad., 1914; student U. Tex., 1914-17; m. Vivienne (Mrs. Gary B. Laughlin). Admitted Tex. bar, 1919, since practiced Fort Worth; mem. firm Cantey, Hanger, Gooch, Cravens & Scarborough, from 1926; asst. dist. atty., Tarrant Co., Tex., 1919-21, dist. atty., 1922-26; v.p. and dir. Tex. Electric Service Co., Fort Worth, Tex.; director Community Public Service Company Mid-Continent Supply Co., Beta Devel. Co., Mid-Continent Supply Co. (Alta.), Ltd., Mid-Continent Supply Eastern Hemisphere Co., Mid-Continent Supply Western Hemisphere Co., Mid-Continent Supply Co. Nigeria, Ltd., So. N.M. Oil Corp. Served as capt. F.A., AEF, 1918-19. Mem. American Bar Assn., Tex. State Bar.

Presbyn. Mason. Clubs: Links (N.Y.C.); River Crest Country, Ft. Worth, Ft Worth TX Died Apr. 11, 1969; buried Green Wood Cemetery, Ft. Worth TX

HANKINS, FRANK HAMILTON, educator; b. Wilshire, O., Sept. 27, 1877; s. Timothy and Mary Jane (Lewis) H.; A.B., Baker U., 1901; Ph.D., Columbia, 1908; L.H.D., Clark U., 1964; m. Anna Livingston Keeling, Aug. 23, 1905; children—Frank Hamilton, Robert William (deceased), Margaret Anna (Mrs. James A. Farmer), Orville Lewis. Instructor Clark College and lecturer Clark University, 1906-07; assistant professor political and social science, Clark College, 1908-13, professor 1913-22; also instructor sociology Clark U., 1908-15, asst. professor, 1915-17, and prof., 1917-22; prof. sociology, Smith Coll., 1922-46; visiting prof. sociology, Univ. of Penna., 1946-48. Lecturer L'Ecole Libre des Sciences Politiques, Paris, winter 1921; prof. social science, Amherst Coll., 1923-26; visiting prof. Columbia, summers, 1916, 18 and spring, 1927, Cornell U., summer, 1924, U. of Ore., summer, 1926, Smith College School for Social Work, 1929-38, U. of California, 1939; prof. Univ. of Army, Biarritz, France, 1945-46. Mem. Worcester School Commerce, 1913-16. Pres. Eastern Sociol. Soc., 1930-31. Fellow A.A.A.S., Am. Population Assn.; mem. editorial bd. Birth Control Review. Mem. Am. Sociol. Soc. (pres. 1938), Sociol. Research Association, American Population Assn. (pres. 1945), Internat. Population Union (Am. com.), American Soc. of Naturalists, American Eugenics Society, Assn. for Research in Human Heredity, Am. Assn. Univ. Profs., Euthanasia Soc. of America, National Com. for Planned Parenthood, S.A.R., Am. Humanist Assn., Institut Internat. de Sociologie, Alpha Pi Zeta, Tau Kappa Alpha. Club: Northampton Country. Author: Adolphe Quetelet as Statistician, 1908; The Racial Basis of Civilization, 1926. French transla., 1935; An Introduction to the Study of Society, 1928, rev. edit., 1935; also, with others, History and Prospects of the Social Sciences, Introduction to Sociology, Reading in Sociology, Political Theories. Recent Times, Biology in Human Affairs, Contemporary Social Theory. Contributor on econ. polit. and social science to New Internat. Year Book, 1907-19 inclusive, also to Nelson, New Internat. Social Sciences and Standard Jewish encys., Am. Year Book, Dictionary of Sociology, and professional journals; spl. editor for sociology, Webster's New Internat. Dictionary, rev. edit. Editor: Am Sociol. Review, 1936-37. Home: Northampton MA Died Jan. 23, 1970.

HANKS, BRYAN CAYCE, lawyer; b. Gatesville, Tex., May 23, 1896; s. William Henry and Lillian (Cayce) H.; grad. Wichita Falls (Tex.) High Sch., 1915; student Rice Inst., 1915-16, Southwestern U., 1917; LL.B., U. Colo. 1922; m. Virginia Margaret Wooding, Sept. 20, 1921; children—Nancy, Larry (dec.). Admitted to N.Y. bar, 1924, Fla. bar, 1929; asso. firm Highes, Rounds, Shurman & Dwight, N.Y.C., 1922-24; legal dept. Electric Bond and Share Co., N.Y.C., 1924-25; head legal dept. Fla. Power & Light Co., Miami, 1925-36, now pres., dir.; pres. Miami Water Power Co., 1933-39, Miami Beach Ry. Co. and Consumers Water Co., 1937-39; mem. law firm Hanks & Preston, 1939-42; pres. Southeastern Electric Exchange, 1938-39. Served from pvt. to sgt., U.S. Army, 1917-19. Mem. Am. Bar Assn., Am. Legion, Fla. Hist. Soc., Kappa Alpha, Phi Alpha Delta. Democrat. Methodist. Clubs: Lawyers (N.Y.C.); Committee of 100 (Miami Beach); Knife and Fork (Fort Worth); Kiwanis (Miami). Address: Fort Worth TX Died Dec. 18, 1972.

HANKWITZ, ARTHUR WALTER, physician, surgeon; b. Milw., July 31, 1907; s. Dr. Paul Gustav and Mathilda (Steinbeck) H.; B.S., Marquette U., 1929; M.D., Washington U., St. Louis, 1931; m. Ione Campbell, Feb. 25, 1939; children—Frederick P., Carl A., John E., Helen C., A. Walter, Paul E. Intern, St. Louis City Hosp., 1931-32; postgrad. Berlin, Germany and Vienna, Austria, 1932-33, Milw. Hosp., 1933-34; med. staff City of Milw., 1941-70; med. examiner for FAA, 1960-61; pvt. practice medicine and surgery, Milw., 1931-70. Mem. Med. Specialist Panel, 12th Annual Air Safety Seminar, Nice, France, 1959, 4th European World Congress of Aero. and Space Medicine, Rome, Italy, 1959. Active Boy Scouts Am.; bd. mgrs. Bay View YMCA, bldg. fund campaign capt., 1951, pres. bd. mgmt., 1965; com. mem. United Hosp. Fund; pres. Cerebral Palsy Greater Milw., 1963-65; mem. Milw. World Festival Planning Com., 1963-66; chmn. Gov.'s State Nautical Com., 1957. Mem. steering com. on fund drive St. John's Military Academy. Recipient 1960 Civic award Interorganization Council of Bay View; YMCA Service award, 1962. Diplomate National Bd. Med. Examiners. Mem. Milw. Assn. Commerce, Aircraft Owners and Pilots Assn., Nat. Aero. Assn., Aerospace Med. Assn., Mil. Surgeons of U.S. Army, U.S. Power Squadron (past dist. comdr.; asso. editor orgn.'s nat. publ.), Wis. Mil. Assn. (past pres.), Bay View Bus. Assn. (past pres.), Milw. Power Squadron (past comdr.), Navy League U.S., World Med. Assn., A.M.A., Am. Acad. Gen. Practice, Wis., Milw. Co. med. socs., Flying Physicians Assn., Am. Geriatrics Soc. Am. Med. Writers Assn., Am. Heart Assn., Am. Yachtsmen's Assn., Inst. Navigation. Mason (Shriner). Clubs: Lions (past president Bay View); Milwaukee Press, Milwaukee Civic Alliance (past president). Author articles in field. Article on 3 generations Hankwitz physicians featured Wis. Med. Journal, 1961. Home: Milwaukee WI Died Mar. 9, 1970.

HANLEY, ELIJAH ANDREWS, clergyman; b. at Prairie Creek, Ind., May 26, 1871; s. Calvin and Susie (Piety) H.; A.B., Franklin Coll., Ind., 1895; A.M. from Brown U., 1896; University of Chicago, 1896-1901, fellow, 1898-1900; D.D., Franklin College, 1903; m. Sarah Wallace Foster, of Indianapolis, June 24, 1903 (died January 7, 1926); children—Frances Foster, Ruth Elizabeth; m. 2d, Bessie Barton Tingley, New York, June 20, 1934. Ordained Bapt. ministry, 1901; pastor East End Ch., Cleveland, 1901-07, First Ch., Providence, R.I., 1907-11; pres. Franklin (Ind.) Coll., 1911-17; pastor First Baptist Ch., Rochester, N.Y., 1917-21, First Bapt. Ch., Berkeley, Calif., 1921-29; pastor Park Ch., St. Paul, 1929-36; research student Union Theol. Sem. and Columbia, 1936-38, Univ. of Chicago since 1938. Republican. Home: 5744 S. Drexel Av., Chicago IL‡

HANLEY, HERBERT RUSSELL, professor of metallurgical engineering, metallurgical engineer; born Paxton, Illinois, September 18, 1874; son of John M. and Jennie (Byers) H.; Ph.G., Northwestern Univ. Sch. of Pharmacy, 1895; B.S., Mo. Sch. Mines and Metallurgy, 1901, Metall. Engr., 1918; Doctor Engineering (honoris causa), Nov. 1946; m. Bertha M. Miles, May 1905; 1 son, John Miles. Chem. and mining engr. Bully Hill Copper Mining and Smelting Co., 1901-03, supt. copper smelter and mines, 1903-16 (in charge metall. research on electrolytic zinc, 4 years); development and supt. of process and plant production electrolytic zinc and cadmium, U.S. Smelting, Refining and Mining Co., Calif., 1916-20; cons. engr., San Francisco, 1920-23; asso. professor metallurgical engineering, Missouri School of Mines and Metallurgy, 1923-26; prof. 1926-46; prof. emeritus metall. engring. since Aug. 1946; consulting engineer since 1918. Mem. American Inst. Mining and Metall. Engrs., Mining and Metall. Soc., Electrochem. Soc., Tau Beta Pi. Sigma Xi, Phi Kappa Phi. Developed electrolytic zinc and cadminm process, special alloy anodes for electrolytic zinc, etc.; holds several patents on processes. Contbr. to scientific journals. Home: 606 West Eighth Street, Rolla MO*‡

HANLEY, THOMAS JAMES, JR., air force officer; b. Coshocton, O., Mar. 29, 1893; s. Thomas J. and Mary (O'Connor) H.; stu. U.S. Mil. Acad., 1911-15; grad. Air Corps Tactical Sch., 1921, Command and Gen. Staff Sch., 1930; Dr. Mil. Science, St. Vincent's College, Latrobe, Pa.; B.S., U.S.M.A., West Point, N.Y. LL.D., Duquesne University, Pittsburgh, Pa.; married Cecelia Meilleur, June 12, 1917; children—Thomas J., Dexter Long, Cecile Marie. Commd. 2d lt., U.S. Army, 1915, and advanced through the grades to brig. gen (temp.), May 22, 1942, major gen., June 1943; comdg. gen. S.E. Air Force Training Center, Maxwell Field, Ala., 1943-44; comdg. gen Air Service Comd., India-Burma Theater, 1944-45, Army Air Forces, India-Burma Theater, 1945-46, 11th Air Force 1946-48; chief mil. personnel Procurement Service Div., AGO, 1948-52; Decorated Distinguished Service Medal, Legion of Merit with Oak Leaf Cluster, Air Medal; Hon. Companion of the Bath (Brit.); Spl. Collar Ornament Yun Hui (China). Clubs: Army and Navy (Washington); Army-Navy Country (Va.). Home: Chevy Chase MD Died Mar. 1969.

HANLON, LAWRENCE WILSON, coll. dean, physician; b. Wellsburg, N.Y., Nov. 15, 1914; s. James F. and Lula (Halstead) H.; A.B., Cornell U., 1935, M.D., 1938. Intern, then asst. resident Rochester (N.Y.) Gen. Hosp., 1938-40; asst. resident 2d med. div. Bellevue Hosp., N.Y.C., 1946-49; asst. dean Cornell U. Med. Col., 1949-55, asso. dean, 1955-70, sec. faculty, 1962-70. Served to lt. col., M.C., AUS, 1941-45. Mem. Assn. Am. Med. Colls. (chmn. Northeastern region group student affairs 1959-65), Harvey Soc., A.A.A.S. Club: Griffis Faculty (pres.) (Cornell U. Med. Coll.). Home: New York City NY Died Sept. 1970.

HANMER, LEE FRANKLIN, sociologist; b. Watkins, Schuyler Co., N.Y., Oct. 24, 1871; s. Benjamin Franklin and Christiana (Powell) H.; grad. Oneonta (N.Y.) Normal Sch., 1896; Ph.B., Cornell, 1900; summer course in phys. training, New York U., 1905; lectures on phys. training, med. and summer course, same, 1907; m. Mary Belle Garlick, of Sidney, N.Y., June 27, 1900; children—Stephen R., Julia R. Teacher rural schs., N.Y., 1890-92; gen. sec. Cornell Univ. Y.M.C.A., 1898-1900; dir. welfare work for Phelps, Dodge & Co., Bisbee, Ariz., 1900-03; supervisor phys. training, Co., Bisbee, Ariz., 1900-03; supervisor phys. training, 1903-06, insp. of athletics, 1906-07, pub. schs. of New York City; field sec. Playground Assn. America and sec. playground extension com. Russell Sage Foundation, 1907-09; asso. dir. dept. child hygiene. Russell Sage Foundation, Oct. 1909-12; director department of recreation, Russell Sage Foundation, 1912-37, retired, 1937; dir. Recreation Section of Plan of New York and Environs since 1923; chairman Committee of Public Relations of the Motion Picture Producers and Distributors of America; sec. Com. for Study of Music in Instns. Mem. War and Navy Dept. Commns. on Training Camp Activities. Mem. White House Conf. of Child Health and Protection, President's Conf. on Home Bldg. and Home Ownership. Mem. Visual Instruction Association of America, Amateur Cinema League (dir.), National Park Association, N.Y. Adult Education Council, Social work Publicity Council, National Education Recreation Council, American Business Men's Research Foundation, Nat. Conf. on City Planning, Nat. Conf. of Social Work, Am. Physical Edn. Assn., Am. Sch. Hygiene Assn., Athletic Research Soc., Am. Country Life Assn., Nat. Recreation Assn., Sphinx Head Soc. (Cornell), N.Y. City Baseball Federation (v.p.), Sportsmanship Brotherhood (dir.). Mem. Bd. of Edn. of Centralized Schs. of Wallkill, N.Y.; dir. Central Coop. Assn. of Gardiner, N.Y. Republican. Methodist. Clubs: Town Hall, Cornell. Home: Gardiner NY‡

HANNA, KATHRYN ABBEY, educator, historian; b. Chgo., Nov. 5, 1895; d. Charles Peters and Julia (Trimmer) Abbey; A.B., Northwestern U., 1917, A.M., 1922, Ph.D., 1926; L.H.D., Rollins Coll., 1947; m. Alfred J. Hanna, July 5, 1941. Instr., Lenox Hall, St. Louis, 1918-19; instr. Hood Coll., Frederick, Md., 1919-21, asso. prof., 1922-23, head dept. history, 1923-24; fellow Northwestern U., 1924-26; asso. prof. Fla. State U., 1926-27, prof., 1927-30, head dept. history, geography and polit. sci., 1930-41; prof. history extension div. U. Fla., 1941-42; mem. adv. council Am. Scholar, 1941-44; vice chmn. State Speakers Bur., Def. Council, 1941-44; lectr. Latin Am. program Rollins Coll., 1942-49. Dir. survey Fed. Archives of Fla., 1936-37; mem. State Com. for Chinese Relief, 1939, State Internat. Relations Com., 1939; chmn. div. Pan Am. Relations Fla. Fedn. Women's Clubs, 1948-52. Mem. Industry Com. of 50, U.S. Dept. Labor, 1942; sec. Fla. Citizens Com. on Edn., 1944-46; mem., past chmn. Fla. Bd. Parks and Hist. Memls., 1955-65; mem. Fla. Constn. Adv. Commn.; mem. Fla. Quadricentennial Commn., 1964-66, Decorated Cross Chevalier, Order Palmes Academiques (France); Social Sci. Research Council, Am. Philos. Soc. research grant, France, 1952. Mem. Fla. Acad. Scis. (chmn. social scis. sect. 1941), Am., So. (dir. 1934-35, 39-41, past pres.) hist. assns., Fla. Hist. Soc. (v.p. 1936-39; dir. 1939-41), Nat. Soc. Colonial Dames, League Women Voters, Mortar Board, Phi Beta Kappa (sec. S. Atlantic dist. 1940), Phi Kappa Phi, Phi Alpha Theta (nat. v.p. 1938-40). Author: Florida, Land of Change, 1941; (with A.J. Hanna) Lake Okeechobee (in Am. Lake series), Florida's Golden Sands, Confederate Exiles in Venezuela (Confederate Centennial series), 1960, Napoleon III and Mexico, 1971. Editorial bd. Jour. So. History, 1942-44. Contbr. hist. articles jours., also Dictionary Am. Biography, Atlas American History, Dictionary American History. Home: Winter Park FL Died Apr. 16, 1967.

HANNIKAINEN, TAUNO, conductor; born Jyvaskyla, Finland, February 26, 1896; son of Pekka J. and Alli (Nikander) Hannikainen; student Helsinki University, 1914-16, Sibelius Academy, 1914-17; Doctor Music (hon.) Am. Conservatory Music, 1950; studied cello in Paris, conducting in Vienna, Paris, Milan, and Berlin, 1924-30; m. Arvida Niskanen, 1922. Cellist Helsinki Symphony Orchestra, 1916-17 and 1918-19; condr. Finnish Opera, Helsinki, 1921-27; condr. Turku Symphony, Finland, 1927-40; conductor Helsinki Symphony, 1941; conductor Duluth Symphony Orchestra, 1942-47; guest conductor leading orchestras, Stockholm, 1936, Riga, Latvia, 1936, 37, 39, Berlin, 1937, Leipzig, 1937, Warsaw, 1939, Boston, 1938, 40, Phila., 1940, Detroit, 1940, 1941, 1942, Buffalo, 1945; Minneapolis and Toronto, 1946, 47; guest condr. Chicago Symphony Orchestra, twenty-five concerts, 1946-47; guest condr. Chicago Symphony Orchestra, Ravinia Festivals, 1946, 47; apptd. asso. condr., Chicago Symphony Orchestra, 1948-50; apptd. mus. dir. and condr. Helsinki Symphony 1951; appeared in chamber music concerts with brothers in Scandinavian and other European countries; guest conductor Houston Symphony, Baltimore Symphony National Symphony Washington, 1948, Vienna (Wiener Philharmoniker), Belgrade (Yugoslovia), Gothenburg and Malmo (Sweden), Oslo and Bergen (Norway) 1951-52; London (London Symphony Orchestra) 1952. Awarded 4 music-study scholarships. Decorated by Finnish Govt. Lutheran. Address: Helsinki Finland Died Oct. 1969.

HANSELL, GRANGER, lawyer; b. Cartersville, Ga., Oct. 17, 1901; s. William A. and Sarah (Granger) H.; A.B., Emory U., 1923; LL.B., Columbia, 1924; m. Sarah Belle Brodnax, Sept. 16, 1927 (dec. Aug. 1960); 1 son, C. Edward; m. 2d, Lelia Redman Dugger, Sept. 16, 1961. Admitted to Ga. bar, 1925; sr. partner Hansell, Post Brandon & Dorsey, Atlanta, from 1925; instr. law Emory U., 1929-39. Dir. 1st National Bank Atlanta, Fulton Federal Savings & Loan Association, Georgia Marble Company, also J. M. Tull Metal & Supply Co., Atlanta Transit System, Inc., Southeastern Capital Corp., Phoenix Investment Co., So. Bakeries Co. Mem. of bd. of trustees Emory U., Pitts Foundation, Atlanta Arts Alliance, Incorporated. Member of Atlanta Junior C. of C. (life), Am., Ga., Atlanta bar assns., Atlanta C. of C. (past v.p.), Emory U. Alumni Assn. Clubs: Capital City, Piedmont Driving, Commerce Roswell GA Died July 27, 1968; buried Oakland Cemetery, Atlanta GA

HANSEN, ERIC H., humanitarian; b. Copenhagen, Denmark, May 6, 1903; s. Hans Christian and Mary Fernanda (Giese) H.; came to U.S. 1923, naturalized, 1928; ed. Ostersogades Gymnasium, Copenhagen; credited with 4 yrs. of college work, Univ. of State of New York, Albany, N.Y.; student New York U. extension, 1938-39; Doctor of Humanities, Oglethorpe Univ., 1947; m. Miriam C. Allen, Jan. 4, 1929; 1 son, Donald H. Asst. dist. mgr. Am. Soc. for Prevention of Cruelty to Animals, New York, N.Y., 1924-28, dist. mgr., 1928-31; mng. dir. Humane Soc. of Missouri, St. Louis, Mo., 1931-37; gen. mgr. Am. Humane Assn., Albany, N.Y., 1937-42; exec. vice pres. Mass. S.P.C.A., Boston, Mass., 1942-45, also exec. vice pres. Am. Humane Edn. Soc., Boston, 1942-1945; currently director Midwest Humane Conference. Pres. and dir. Mass. S.P.C.A.-Angell Memorial Animal Hospital; dir. N.E. Livestock Conservation, Inc. Received Nat. Humane Key, 1943. Mem. American Humane Education Soc., (pres., dir.), Am. Humane Assn. (sec. and dir. 1937-52, pres. 1952-53); pres. N.E. Fedn. Humane Soc., 1948-49; mem. tech. adv. com. Mass. Com. on Pub. Safety; trustee Mary Mitchell Humane Fund, N.E. Bapt. Hosp., Oglethorpe U. Recipient Silver Medal Royal Danish S.P.C.A., 1951; numerous awards various sectional S.P.C.A., socs.; decorated Officer Ouissam Alaouite (Morroco). Mem. N.Y. State Nature Assn. (dir.), Am. Fondouk Maintenance Com. Africa (pres.), Internat. Soc. Protection Animals (pres.), Navy League United States, Danish American Society, Newcomen Soc., N.A., U.S. Naval Inst. Mason. Clubs: Hyannisport (Mass.) Yacht; University (Albany, N.Y.). Author pamphlets and articles in field. Home: Wayland MA Died June 10, 1965.

HANSEN, FLORENCE FRONEY, artist; b. Sheboygan, Wis., Jan. 25, 1887; d. George and Rachel (Tilden) Froney; student U. Minn., 1907-10, Northwestern Conservatory Music, Italian Sch. Opera, St. Agathas Coll. Music and Arts, Nat. Acad. of N.Y., Juliene Acad., Paris; m. Dr. Marius Hansen, June 18, 1911; children—Verona Froney, Merrill. Exhibited in group shows at Los Angeles, Paris, London, N.Y., Minn. Beards Gallery and others; appeared as lyric soprano in opera La Scala, Milan, Italy, 1918; actress Business Before Pleasure, N.Y., 1922. Recipient gold medal Societe des Artistes Francais, 1926; silver medal portrait Fine Arts Acad., London, 1927; gold medal miniature portrait Miniature Soc. Great Britain, 1928; and others. Mem. Internat. Platform Assn. Presbyn. Clubs: California Art, Ebell of Los Angeles, Sans Souci Celebrities. Author feature stories on early N.Am. Los Angeles CA Died Jan. 6, 1971; interred Los Angelse CA

HANSEN, GEORGE, merchandising exec.; b. Boston, Jan. 15, 1899; s. Henry and Elizabeth (McGrath) H.; B.C.S., LL.B., Northeastern U., LL.D., 1953; m. Virginia Bain, Apr. 16, 1923; children—Virginia L., George, Norman E. Pres. Conrad & Chandler Inc., Boston. Home: Boston MA Died May 2, 1972.

HANSEN, OSKAR J. W., sculptor; b. Norway, Mar. 12, 1892; prep. edn., Port Arthur (Tex.) Coll. and Evanston (Ill.) Acad.; student Northwestern U., 1914-15; m. Eva Brubaker, 1916; children—Herman (dec.), Homer Richard, Philip Waldemar, Beatrice Mary; m. 2d, Vernie Ethel Connelly, 1926; m. 3d, Mary Beatty, March 12, 1929; children—Oskar Johan Wedel, Alexander Wedel Fitzgerald. Came to U.S., 1910, naturalized, 1917. Went to sea as cabin boy and later, as seaman, traveled around the world 5 times. Works: winged figure in bronze, given by Norwegian people as a wedding present to Crown Prince Olav of Norway and the Princess Martha of Sweden; portrait bust of late Joseph Conrad; busts in bronze of Elijah Parish Lovejoy and Joseph Medill; winged figure in bronze, for Rand Tower, Minneapolis; Masque de Dionysos, bronze, in Art Mus. State of Ill.; bronze busts Wilbur and Orville Wright and many others; represented in permanent collections in U.S. and abroad. Winner in nat. competition, sculpture commn. for Boulder Dam, Ariz.-Calif.-Nev., 1935. Collaborator construction astronomical pavement, Nevada plaza, Boulder Dam. Author: Chien-Mi-Lo, 1928; The Sculptures at Boulder Dam, 1942; also various brochures. Lecturer on art. Studio: Charlottesville VA Died 1971.

HANSON, CHARLES LANE, teacher; b. S. Newmarket (now Newfields), N.H., May 22, 1870; s. John Clinton and Annie (Lane) H.; grad. Phillips Exeter Acad., N.H., 1888; A.B., Harvard, 1892; m. Bertha Winthrop Flint, of Cambridge, Mass., June 25, 1902; children— Paul, Helen Bemis, Carol, Charles Lane, Lincoln Flint. Teacher of English, Worcester (Mass.) Acad., 1892-95, English High School, Worcester, 1895-97, B.M.C. Durfee High Sch., Fall River, Mass., 1897-98, Mechanic Arts High Sch., Boston, since 1898, head of the dept. of English since 1907. Pres. N.E. Assn. of Teachers of English, 1905-07. Author: English Composition, 1908; An Introduction to the English Classics (with Profs. W.P. Trent and W.T. Brewster), 1911; Two Years' Course in English Composition, 1912; Outlines of Composition and Rhetoric (with Prof. J.F. Genung), 1915. Editor: Carlyle's Essay on Burns, 1897; Representative Poems of Robert Burns, with Carlyle's Essay, 1899; Macaulay's Life of Samuel Johnson, 1903; Short Stories of Today (with William J. Gross), 1928; Travel Sketches of Today (with same), 1929. Home: 28 Linnaean St., Cambridge‡

HANSON, EPHRAIM, lawyer; b. Ephraim, Utah, Mar. 10, 1872; s. James Peter and Christina (Jeppson) H.; ed. Snow Coll., Ephraim, 1888-90, U. of Utah, 1890-93; LL.B., U. of Mich., 1898; m. Ella Dorius, June 5, 1901; children—Howard Dorius, Ellen Mildred (Mrs. Lee C. Ward), Harris E., Whitney K. Began practice at Ehpraim, 1898; city atty., Ephraim, 14 yrs.; county atty., Sanpete Co., 1910-11; moved to Salt Lake City, 1912; judge 3d Jud. Dist. of Utah, 1920-28; elected asso. justice Supreme Court of Utah, 1929, and re-elected, 1930, for term ending 1941, became chief justice; resigned and moved to Los Angeles, 1939. Republican. Morman. Address: 1252 S. Orange Grove Av., Los Angeles CA Office: Capitol Bldg., Salt Lake City UT‡

HANSON, KARL P(ETER), educator; b. Wood County, Wis., June 2, 1905; s. Peter Hans and Effie (Simpson) H.; B.S., U. of Wis., 1928, M.S., U. of Mich., 1946; m. Eleanor M. Schanel, Sept. 10, 1930; 1 dau., Meryl Eda. Engineer C.A. Hooper Co., Madison, Wis., 1928-29; F.S. Moulton architects, Madison, 1928-29; instr. in mech. engring. Johns Hopkins, 1929-38, asst. prof., 1938-40; asso. prof. mech. engring. U. of Conn., 1940-43, prof. and head mech. engring., 1943-47; prof. and head mech. engring. dept. North Carolina State U., 1947-58, prof. mechanical engineering, from 1958, dir. Freshman Engring. div., 1963-67; test engineer Pa. Water and Power Co., summer 1930, Consol. Gas Elec. Light & Power Co., Baltimore, summer 1931. Mem. Am. Soc. M.E., Am. Soc. E.E., N.C. Soc. Engrs., Sigma Xi, Pi Tau Sigma, Iota Alpha. Club: Raleigh Engineers. Home: Raleigh NC Died Nov. 15, 1967.

HANSON, MURRAY, lawyer, assn. exec.; b. Balt., Dec. 19, 1904; s. John M. and Maude L. (Rowe) H.; student U. Del., Harvard Law Sch. With Baker, Hostetler & Patterson, Cleve., 1930-42, as sec. and asst. to Newton D. Baker, 1930-34; legal service Nat. Assn. Securities Dealers, 1935-42; gen. counsel Investment Bankers Assn. Am., Washington, 1946-54, managing director, general counsel, 1954-66, consultant, 1966-71. Served from 1st lieutenant to col. AUS, 1942-46, asst. exec. officer Asst. Sec. War for Air, 1943-46. Clubs: Burning Tree, Metropolitan, University (Washington); Lunch (N.Y.C.); Farmington Country (Charlottesville, Va.). Home: Washington DC Died Dec. 5, 1971.

HARBAUGH, CHARLES WILLIAM, assn. exec.; b. Port Huron, Mich., May 9, 1914; s. Clayton Dane and Nellie (Crull) H.; B.S., Purdue, 1936, postgrad., 1937-38; m. Charlotte Cooper, Jan. 25, 1952; 1 son, William S. Tchr. pub. schs., Lafayette, Ind., 1936-41; exec. v.p. Connersville (Ind.) C. of C., 1946-47; sec., mgr. Anderson (Ind.) C. of C., 1947-50; exec. v.p. The Am. Guard Co., Anderson, 1950-52; adminstrv. staff U.S. C. of C., Washington, 1952-72, gen. mgr. communications and marketing, 1964-70, exec. mgr., 1970-72; lectr. in field, 1948-72. Bd. dirs. Nat. Center Vol. Action. Served with USAAF, 1941-45. Decorated Bronze Star; recipient Distinguished Service medal Jr. C. of C., 1951. Mem. Am. C. of C. Execs. Assn., Am. Soc. Assn. Execs. Clubs: Army-Navy (Washington); Kenwood Country (Kenwood, Md.). Home: Washington DC Died Sept. 21, 1972.

HARBESON, WILLIAM PAGE, educator; born Philadelphia, Pa., Nov. 27, 1882; s. James Page and Fredericka (Krautter) H.; B.S., U. of Pa., 1906, LL.B., 1910, Ph.D., 1920; unmarried. Admitted to Pa. bar, 1910, and practiced in Phila. as mem. firm Lamberton & Harbeson, 1910-15; mem. faculty U. of Pa. since 1912, John Welsh Centennial prof. of English history and literature, 1937-47, prof. emeritus, 1947-72. Served with F.A., U.S. Army, 1917-18. Mem. Psi Upsilon. Club: Lenape (Phila.). Author: Study of Literature and The Other Arts in Europe, 19th Century, 1952. Home: Philadelphia PA Died Oct. 19; 1972.

HARBOLD, PETER MONROE, prof. edn.; b. Cumberland Co., Pa., Nov. 17, 1873; s. Peter and Leah J. (Burgard) H.; grad. State Normal Sch., Millersville, Pa., 1898; post-grad. course, same sch., 1899; Ph.B., Franklin and Marshall Coll., 1904, hon. Sc.D., 1914; A.M., Harvard, 1905; m. Helen A. Keiser, of Cornwall, Pa., July 24, 1907; children—Elizabeth Keiser, Mary Leah. Teacher rural schs., 1891-93; teacher and prin. grammar sch., Arentsville, Pa., 1893-96; teacher history and edn., Millersville Normal Sch., 1899-1902; supt. Training Sch., same, 1905-11; supt. schs., Lancaster, Pa., 1911-12; prin. Millersville Normal Sch., 1912-18; ednl. dir. Camp Meade, Pa., World War, 1918-19; prof. edn. and psychology, Franklin and Marshall Coll., since 1919. Mem. N.E.A., Pa. State Ednl. Assn. Lutheran. Club: Fortnightly. Home: 343 College Av., Lancaster PA‡

HARDEMAN, NICHOLAS BRODIE, educator; b. Milledgeville, McNairy Co., Tenn., May 18, 1874; s. John Bellefont (M.D.) and Nannie (Smith) H.; A.B., W. Tenn., Christian Coll., Henderson, Tenn., 1894; A.M., Georgia Robertson Christian Coll., Henderson, 1897; m. Joanna Kendall Tabler, of Henderson, Apr. 21, 1901; children— Dorsey B., Mary Nell, Carrie Neal. Supt. pub. edn., Chester Co., Tenn., 1906-18; ordained ministry Ch. of Christ, 1900; founder, 1907, and v.p. Freed-Hardeman Coll., Henderson; pres. same since 1925. In charge four great meetings, Ch. of Christ, in Ryman Auditorium, Nashville, Tenn., 1922-23; toured Europe and Palestine, 1923; evangelical work throughout U.S., 1924-25. Democrat. Author: Hardeman's Tabernacle Sermons, Vol. 1, 1922, vol. 2, 1923, vol. 3, 1928, vol. 4, 1938; The Bible Searchlight. Home: Henderson TN‡

HARDEN, EDWARD WALKER, broker; b. Aug. 20, 1868; s. James and Mary (Walker) H.; pub. sch. edn.; m. Ruth Vanderlip, Sept. 9, 1903; children—Walker, Richard Vanderlip, Mrs. Rosemary Parker (dec.) Financial editor Chicago Tribune, 1895-98; corr. New York World and Chicago Tribune with Am. fleet at Battle of Manila, 1898; volunteered for service during battle; sent first news of battle received in U.S., dispatch reaching New York 5 hours before arrival of Dewey's dispatch at Washington. As spl. commr. of U.S., studied financial and commercial conditions in P.I., 6 mos., 1898; financial editor New York Commercial, 1899-1904; editor in chief Chicago Journal and vice president of co., 1904-05; stock and bond broker since 1905; now member firm of Baker, Weeks and Harden; president Reynolds Development Co.; v.p. Palos Verdes Corp. Mem. Soc. Manila Bay, Mil. Order Carabao. Clubs: Metropolitan, India House, Sleepy Hollow Country. Author: Financial and Industrial Conditions in the Philippines, 1899. Contbr. to mags. Home: Scarborough, New York. Office: One Wall Street, New York NY‡

HARDGROVE, JOHN GILBERT, lawyer; b. Eden, Wis., Nov. 19, 1877; s. Timothy and Bridget Cecelia (O'Loughlin) H.; LL.B., U. of Wis., 1901; m. Katherine Agnes McMahon, Aug. 7, 1907. Admitted to Wis. bar 1901; practiced law alone, Fond du Lac, Wis., 1901-04, mem. firm of Doyle and Hardgrove, Fond du Lac, 1904-09; asso. Miller, Mack & Fairchild, Milwaukee, Wis., 1909-16, partner since 1916. Court commr., 1904-09; mem. Wis. Bd. of Law Examiners, 1913-17. Mem. Am. Law Inst., Am. Bar Assn., Am. Judicature Soc., Wis. State Bar Assn. (pres. 1930-31), Milwaukee County Bar Assn. (pres. 1921-22), Phi Delta Phi. Democrat. Roman Catholic. K. of C. Clubs: Milwaukee, University, Milwaukee Athletic, Blue Mound Golf and Country (all Milwaukee). Contbr. articles to legal jour. Home: 3375 N. Summit VA Office: 735 N. Water St., Milwaukee WI‡

HARDIN, JOHN RALPH, lawyer; b. Newark, Feb. 8, 1897; s. John R. and Jennie Josephine (Roe) H.; student Newark Acad.; Litt.B., Princeton, 1917; LL.B., Columbia, 1924; m. Elizabeth Cooper, Nov. 29, 1924; children—John Ralph, Frances H., Reid. Banking, 1919-21; admitted to N.J. bar as atty., 1923, as counselor, 1927; partner firm Pitney, Hardin & Kipp, Newark, 1925-68, counsel, 1968-70. Director L.V. Ludlow & Co. Trustee, Newark Mus.; v.p., bd. trustees Marcus L. Ward Home for Aged and Respectable Bachelors and Widowers. Served as 1st lt. USMC, 1917-19. Decorated Purple Heart. Mem. Am., N.J., Essex County bar assns., Newcomen Soc. Democrat. Episcopalian. Clubs: Essex (Newark); Princeton (N.Y.C.); Somerset Hills Country (Bernardsville, N.J.); Nassau (Princeton, N.J.); Essex Fox Hounds (Peapack, N.J.). Home: Chester NJ Died Feb. 13, 1970.

HARDIN, ROBERT ALLEN, educator; b. North Platte, Neb., Dec. 10, 1899; s. George Edwin and Eva McNair (Weedman) H.; A.B., Neb. Wesleyan U., 1924; Ph.D., U. Neb., 1935; m. Gladys Ida Starkey, May 26, 1923; children—Gladys Roberta (Mrs. William A. Sellon), Virginia Dulcie (Mrs. Bruce E. Long), Burton Ervin. Instr. manual arts Neb. Wesleyan U., 1924-36; faculty U. Okla., from 1936, prof. indsl. edn., from 1944-66, prof. emertus, 1966-72, chmn. dept., from 1936. Chmn. adv. com. Indsl. Arts in Okla. Sch., from 1956. Mem. Am., Okla. (past pres.). indsl. arts assns., Am., Okla. councils indsl. arts tchr. edn., Miss. Valley Indsl. Arts Conf., Epsilon Pi Tau. Mason (past master). Author: Thomas and Polly Hardin and Their Descendants, 1968. Sculptor in walnut, mahogany, willow, elm and ebony woods. Home: Norman OK Died Apr. 11, 1972; buried I.O.O.F. Cemetery, Norman OK

HARDING, ALFRED, editor, author; b. Washington, D.C., May 10, 1892; s. Rt. Rev. Alfred and Justine Butler (Prindle) H.; grad. Nat. Cathedral Sch. for Boys, Mount St. Alban, D.C., 1912; B.A., Trinity Coll., Hartford, Conn., 1916; m. Sara Smith, Oct. 5, 1921 (dec.); children—Alfred III (dec.), Alfred IV, Douglas II. With Am. Fgn. Banking Corp. and Sinclair Oil Co., in Cuba, 1920; reporter, dramatic ed., critic Washington Daily News, 1921; reporter N.Y. Morning Telegraph, 1922; in charge editorial work, Actors' Equity Association, N.Y.C., 1923-57, assistant to the president, 1944-57; correspondent Montreal (Can.) Daily Star, 1930-31. Went to Poland on a fellowship from Kosciuszko Foundation, and to Hungary and Czechoslovakia on the invitation of their govs. to make a study of their theatre, 1936-37; delegate from the Am. Theatre to the 9th Internat. Congress of the Theatre, Vienna, 1936; mem. national advisory committee Federal Theatre Project, 1935-39; mem. Code

Enforcement Authority, Theatre Ticket Code, 1939-69; organized N.Y. City School Theatre Program, 1941 (chmn. Central Control Board). Mem. Emergency Council Legit. Theatre since 1942. Mem. adv. commn. on the performing arts, Met. Vocational High Sch., N.Y. City, 1946, exec. com. 1948; employee member of the New York State Minimum Wage Board amusement and recreation industry, 1950, 57-58. Mem. Nat. Council Arts and Government (treas. 1956-62). AUS, advancing to 1st lt., World War. Mem. Mil. Intelligence Reserve Soc. (New York), American Academy of Political and Social Science, Alpha Delta Phi. Ind. Democrat. Episcopalian. Author: Tropical Fruit, 1928; The Revolt of the Actors, 1929; The Pay and Conditions of Work of Radio Performers (Actors' Equity Assn.), 1934; also several articles. Home: New York City NY Died June 1969.

HARDING, EDWIN FORREST, army officer; b. Franklin, O., Sept. 18, 1886; s. Clarence Henry and Lilly (Woodward) H.; B.S., U.S. Military Acad., 1909; grad. The Inf. Sch. (advanced class), 1928, Command and Gen. Staff Sch., 1929, Army War Coll., 1934; m. Eleanor Hood, Sept. 23, 1913; children—Davis Philoon, Elinore Hood (wife Lt. Col. James O'Hara, U.S. Army), Edwin Forrest, Jr., Anne Woodward. Commd 2d lt., Inf., U.S. Army, 1909, advanced through ranks to maj. gen., 1942; instr. English, Hist. and Econs. at U.S. Military Acad., 1919-23; instr. The Infantry Sch., 1929-33; sec. U.S. Inf. Assn and editor of The Inf. Jour., 1934-38; commd 27th Inf. at Schofield Barracks, T.H., 1938-40; asst. to div. comdr., 9th Inf. Div., 1941; comd. 32d Inf. Div., Feb.-Dec. 1942, and during early phases of Buna campaign in New Guinea; comdg. Mobile Force Panama Canal Dept., Mar. 1943-Aug. 1944; comdg. Antilles Department, Aug. 1944-45; dir. hist. div. Office Chief of Staff, U.S. Army, 1945-46; ret., 1946. Awarded Silver Star for gallantry in action, Legion of Honor; Order of Abder Calderon, Ecuador; Gran Official del Order Militar de Ayucucho, Peru; Gran Official de la Orden del Condor de los Andes (Bolivia). Co-author and editor Infantry in Battle, 1934. Home: Franklin OH Died June 5, 1970; buried Franklin OH

HARDING, HARRY ALEXIS, bacteriologist; b. Oconomowoc, Wis., Nov. 28, 1871; s. Joseph and Elizabeth A. (Dean) H.; B.S., U. of Wis., 1896, M.S., 1898; studied in Europe and at Mass. Inst. Tech.; Ph.D., Cornell U., 1910; m. Esther Gordon, of Brodhead, Wis., Aug. 31, 1899; children—Harry Gordon, Esther M., Helen A., Ruth. Fellow U. of Wis., 1897-98; bacteriologist, N.Y. Agrl. Expt. Sta., 1899-1913; prof. dairy bacteriology, U. of Ill., 1913-21; chief of dairy research div. Mathews Industries, Inc. Fellow A.A.A.S., Am. Pub. Health Assn.; mem. Soc. Am. Bacteriologists, Am. Dairy Science Assn., Royal Inst. Pub. Health, Eng. Republican. Conglist. Author and joint author numerous agrl. bulls. and articles on bacteriol. topics. Home: Urbana, Ill. Office: 685 Mullett St., Detroit MI‡

HARDING, HARRY PATRICK, supt. schs.; b. Beaufort County, N.C., Aug. 14, 1874; s. Maj. Henry and Susan Elizabeth (Sugg) H.; A.B., U. of N.C., 1899; A.M., Columbia, 1931; m. Lucia Ella Ives, Dec. 23, 1903; children—Lucia Elizabeth, Harry Patrick (dec.), Prin. New Bern (N.C.) City Sch., 1899-1901, supt., New Bern, 1902-04; prin. Charlotte City Schs., 1904-12, asst. supt., 1912-13, supt., 1913-49; instr. Univ. of N.C. Summer School, 1912-13; as supt. organized Oxford (N.C.) City Schs., 1901-02. Trustee Univ. of N.C., 1925-27; mem. State High Sch. Text Book Commn., 1920. Mem. N.C. State Assn. City Supts. (pres. 1917-19), S. Piedmont Teachers Assn. (pres. 1924, 32), N.C. Edn. Assn. (pres. 1933), Sigma Alpha Epsilon, Phi Beta Kappa. Democrat. Methodist. Rotarian. Club: Executive. Address: 202 Poplar Apts., Charlotte NC‡

HARDING, JOHN EUGENE, congressman; b. nr. Middletown, O., June 27, 1877; ed. Pa. Mil. Acad., Chester, and Univ. of Mich. Was mem. Ohio senate; mem. 60th Congress, 3d Ohio dist., 1907-09; Republican. Address: Middletown OH‡

HARDWICK, CHARLES CHEEVER, JR., investment banker; b. Orange, N.J., Apr. 16, 1904; s. Charles Cheever and Charlotte (Ambrose) H.; student Lawrenceville Sch., 1922, Princeton, 1926; m. Mildred Wharton Atkinson, Aug. 7, 1936; 1 son, Charles Cheever III. With Guaranty Co. N.Y., 1927-34. Edward B. Smith & Co., 1934-38; with Smith, Barney & Co. Inc., and predecessor, 1938-70, exec. v.p., 1964-66, vice chmn. bd., 1966-70. also dir., mem. exec. com. Mem. U.S. C. of C. (past chmn. subcom. securities and debt mgmt., chmn. com. study revenue bond financing), Am. Road Builders Association (pres., dir. chairman of the finance committee), Society Colonial Wars. Clubs: Bond, Municipal Bond, India House, Madison Square Garden (N.Y.C.); Coral Beach and Tennis (Bermuda); Essex Country (New Jersey). Home: New York City NY Died Dec. 18, 1970; buried Fairview Cemetery, Red Bank NJ

HARDWICK CLIFFORD EMERSON, surgeon; b. Winona, Minn., Oct. 9, 1904; s. Francis Tiley and Ada (Marks) H.; student U. Wash., 1925; B.S., U. Ore., 1928, M.D., 1929; m. Mary Agnes Beauchamp, June 21, 1931; children—Mary Jo (Mrs. Wilbur M. Bolton, Jr.), Kathryn (Mrs. Jon Lang). Intern, then resident Multnomah Hosp., Portland, Ore., 1928-31; resident proctology Temple U. Hosp., 1946-47; gen. practice medicine, Hood River, Ore., 1929-46; practice colon and rectal surgery, Portland, Ore., 1947-71; asso. clin. prof. surgery U. Ore. Med. Sch. Hosps. and Clinics, 1947-71; Diplomate Am. Bd. Surgery, Am. Bd. Colon and Rectal Surgery (pres. 1965). Fellow A.C.S., Am. Proctologic Soc.; mem. Ore. Med. Assn., Multnomah County Med. Soc., N. Pacific, Portland surg. socs., Portland Acad. Medicine, N.W. (past pres.), Phila. protologic socs. Home: Portland OR Died July 24, 1971; buried Mt. Calvary Cemetery.

HARDY, EDWARD LAWYER, educator; b. Owosso, Mich., Jan. 15, 1868; s. Albert and Cordelia Ann (Cromer) H.; B.Litt., U. of Wis., 1893; M.A., U. of Chicago, 1922; study of secondary edn. in France and Germany, 1898-99; grad. student, U. of Chicago, 1905; LL.D., La Verne College, 1928; m. Mary Cutler, June 28, 1898; children—Mrs. Anne Davis, Mrs. Mary Hobbs, Mrs. Millison Cutler Doble, Mrs. Esther Pomeroy Winterer. Teacher, La Crosse (Wis.) High Sch., 1893; head dept. of history, Milwaukee South Div. High Sch., 1894-98; asso. head master, Los Angeles Mil. Acad., 1899-1901; prin. high sch., Riverside, Cook County, Ill., 1901-06; prin. San Diego (Calif.) High Sch., 1906-10; pres. State Teachers Coll., San Diego, 1910-35, pres. emeritus since 1936; pres. Calif. Assn. for Adult Education, 1937-40; pres. Board of Education, San Diego, Calif., 1941-42; dir. San Diego Museum, 1935-41. Mem. Calif. State Bd. Edn., 1910-11; mem. State (Calif.) Commn. on school districts. Unitarian. A.A.A.S., Beta Theta Pi, Phi Beta Kappa, etc. Club: University (ex-pres.). Address: 3525 Wilshire Terrace, San Diego CA*‡

HARDY, EWING LLOYD, lawyer; b. Louisville, May 26, 1892; s. William Jarvis and Sallie Ewing (Marshall) H.; LL.B., Jefferson Sch. Law, 1920; m. Elise Rutledge Smith, Apr. 28, 1921; children—Ewing L., Benjamin Bd., Burwell M. With sec. office L. & N. R.R., office, 1915-22, asst. to cashier, paymaster, 1917-22; admitted to Ky. bar, 1920; instr. Jefferson Sch. Law, 1925-29; practiced in Louisville, 1922-33, 38-68; mem. firm E. L. Hardy, 1922-27, Hardy & Hardy, 1950-68; field rep. Fed. Home Loan Bank Bd. for Ky., 1933-38, also for Tenn., 1936-38. Dir. Fireside Bldg. & Loan Assn.; 1st v.p., dir. Eagle Engring. Corp., 1962-68, Eagle Machine Co., 1954-68, Gernert Ct., Inc., 1958-68, Jos. C. Hofgesange Sand Co., Inc. Chmn. Planning and Zoning Commn., Anchorage, Ky., 1938-67; chmn. Bd. of Appeals, 1938-65. Dir. Hofgesang Found. Mem. Am., Ky., Louisville bar assns., Soc. for Preservation of Va. Antiquities. Episcopalian. Club: Filson (Louisville). Home: Anchorage KY Died Aug. 8, 1968.

HARDY, KENNETH BURNHAM, pub. accountant; b. St. Louis, Apr. 15, 1908; s. Albert Alfonso and Kate (Jones) H.; grad. St. Louis U., 1931; m. Arline Frances Ameiss, Apr. 8, 1933; children—Kenneth Burnham, Thomas David. Auditor, Nat. Dairy Products Corp., N.Y.C., 1931-39; supervising accountant Ernst & Ernst, St. Louis, 1939-47; chief accountant Von Hoffmann Press, Inc., St. Louis, Publishers Lithographers, Inc., St. Louis; sec.-treas. Von Hoffman Realty & Mortgage Corp., St. Louis, George Von Hoffmann Found., Inc., St. Louis. Trustee, Village of Warson Woods, Mo., 1952; Von Hoffmann Press, Inc. Profit Sharing Plan and Trust. Mem. Am. Inst. C.P.A.'s, Mo. Soc. C.P.A.'s, Nat. Assn. Accountants. Home: Labadie MO Deceased.

HARDY, MARTHA EUGENIA SIDEBOTTOM (MRS. DONALD HARDY), journalist; b. Canon City, Colo., Aug. 8, 1911; d. Jay D. and Grace (Johnson) Sidebottom; student Lindenwood Coll., St. Charles, Mo., 1928-29, Kansas U., 1932; m. Donald Hardy, Sept. 21, 1938, (dec. June 1966); 1 son, David Hardy. Co-owner, writer Canon City Daily Record, Canon City, Colo., 1966-69. Active A.R.C., Little Theatre and Fine Arts activities. Pres. St. Thomas More Hosp. Aux., 1953. Mem. Kappa Alpha Theta. Republican. Home: Canon City CO Died Oct. 1969.

HARE, ARLEY MUNSON (MRS. JAMES A.), M.D., author; b. Bridgeport, Conn., Nov. 14, 1871; d. Thomas Hamilton and Etta (Hill) M.; student Cornell U., 1899-1900; M.D., Woman's Med. Coll. of Pa., 1902; m. James Alexander Hare, of Passaic, N.J., 1924; step-dau., Mrs. Anne Graham. Supt. Zenana Hosp., Nizam's Dominions, India, 1903-08; lectured in Eng. and America on med., travel and religious subjects; practiced, Red Bank, N.J., 1913-17; instr. in serology, Post-Grad. Med. Sch. and Hosp., N.Y. City, 1917-18; serologist Red Cross Mil. Hosp. 2, Paris, 1918-19; one of chief attending physicians of dispensaries and hosps. for Rockefeller Commn. for Prevention of Tuberculosis, in France, 1919-21; asso. editor Internat. Med. and Surg. Survey (N.Y. City), 1922-23; dir. Lit. Research Dept., Am. Inst. of Medicine, Inc., 1923-24; practiced in N.Y. City since 1935. Traveled around the world, 1930-31. Awarded Medaille d'Honneur (French). Episcopalian. Author: Jungle Days, 1913; Kipling's India, 1915. Home-Office: 4570 Sputyen Duyvil Parkway New York NY‡

HARER, WILLIAM BENSON, physician; b. Williamsport, Pa., Oct. 27, 1896; s. William Lloyd and Ella (Foust) H.; M.D., U. Pa., 1921; m. Letitia Rose Burke, Aug. 27, 1921; children—Marian Ellen (Mrs. Henry H. Fetterman), William Benson. Intern, then resident obstetrics and gynecology U. Pa. Hosp., 1921-24; chief obstetrician and gynecologist St. Agnes Hosp., Phila., from 1926, Fitzgerald Mercy Hosp., Darby Pa., from 1933; mem. faculty obstetrics and gynecology U. Pa. Med. Sch., 1924-63, emeritus prof., 1965; dir. dept. med. affairs Blue Cross Phila., from 1963. Mem. Gov. Pa. Hosp. Study Commn.; mem. Upper Darby Township Bd. Health; a founder Community Y East Delaware County. Served with U.S. Army, World War I. Diplomate Am. Bd. Obstetrics and Gynecology. Life fellow A.C.S.; mem. Pa. (trustee, councillor 2d dist. 1956, vice chmn. trustee 1961, pres. 1963), Delaware County (past pres.) med. socs., A.M.A. (ho. of dels. from 1960), Phila. Obstet. Soc. Club: Union League (Phila.). Author 3 textbooks, numerous articles. Address: Upper Darby PA Died Oct. 11, 1968; buried Arlington Cemetery, Drexel Hill PA

HARGREAVES, RICHARD T(HEODORE), coll. pres.; b. Lancashire, Eng., Mar. 17, 1875; s. Richard and Sarah (Capsey) H.; came with parents to U.S., 1883; grad. Washburn Acad., Topeka, Kan., 1896; A.B., U. of Kan., 1902, grad. study, 1905-06; grad. study, U. of Chicago, summers 1903, 04; m. Edna M. Morrow, of Topeka, Aug. 11, 1908. Teacher Latin and history, high sch., Topeka, 1902-05; instr. in Latin, U. of Kan., 1906-07; with Allyn and Bacon, 1907-08; prin. North Central High School, Spokane, Wash., 1909-18; prin. Central High Sch., Minneapolis, Minn., 1918-26; pres. State Normal Sch., Cheney, Wash., since 1926. Mem. N.E.A., Am. Assn. Teachers Colls., Wash. Edn. Assn., Inland Empire Assn., Phi Beta Kappa. Unitarian. Club: Spokane City. Co-Author: The Self-Directed School (with H.L. Miller), 1925. Home: Cheney WA‡

HARING, DOUGLAS GILBERT, anthropologist; b. Watkins Glen, N.Y., Aug. 6, 1894; s. Leon and Emillie N. (Gilbert) H.; B.S., Colgate U., 1914; B.D., Rochester Theol. Sem., 1923; Diploma, Sch. Japanese Lang. and Culture, Tokyo, 1925; A.M., Columbia, 1923; m. Ann Teasdale Howell, Aug. 8, 1918; children—Frances (dec.), Ruth Ann (Mrs Leonard Lief). Commd. missionary Bapt. ch., 1917; ednl., adminstrv. work, Japan, 1917-22, 24-26, acting prof. history Tokyo Gakuin, 1925-26; lectr. sociology Columbia, 1926-27; mem. faculty Syracuse U., 1927-70, prof. anthropology, 1946-70, chmn. dept. sociology, anthropology, 1957-70; visiting lectr. Harvard, 1944-46, Columbia, summer 1951; field research Ryukyu Islands and Japan, Pacific Sci. Bd. Nat. Research Council, 1951-52; cons. expert asst. sec. Dept. Army, 1949. Fellow Viking Fund, 1947-48. Fellow Am. Anthropol. Assn., A.A.A.S., Am. Sociol Soc.; mem. Am. Folklore Soc. (mem. council), Japanese, Am. ethnol. socs., Assn. for Asian Studies (board dirs.), Asiatic Soc. Japan, Am. Inst. Pacific Relations, Photog. Soc. Am., Society for Applied Anthropology (mem. exec. committee), Asia Society, Society for Ethnomusicology, Japan Soc., Toho Gakkai (Tokyo), Phi Beta Kappa, Sigma Xi. Author: The land of Gods and Earthquakes, 1929; Order and Possibility in Social Life (with M. Johnson), 1940; Blood on the Rising Sun, 1943; The Island of Amami Oshima, 1952; Bibliography of the Ryukyu Research Collection, 1969; Okinawan Customs, Yesterday and Today, 1969. Editor and contbr. Japan's Prospect, 1946; Personal Character and Cultural Milieu, 1948-56. Editorial advisor Sociologus. Contbr. books, pamphlets, articles various publs. Home: Syracuse NY Died Aug. 24, 1970.

HARING, PHILIP ERWIN, fgn. service officer; b. Hatfield, Pa., Nov. 24, 1916; s. Philip Erwin and Mary Edna (Munzinger) H.; A.B., U. Ky., 1938; student Temple U. Sch. Law, 1946-47; m. Adelia Capovani, Oct. 27, 1940; children—Evangeline Maria, Jacqueline, Adrienne, Philip Erwin. Immigration insp. and examiner Dept. of Justice, 1940-47; apptd. vice consul, sec. Diplomatic Service, 1947; assigned Dept. of State, Washington, 1947, 52-56; 3d sec., Ankara, 1947-48, vice consul, Istanbul, 1948-49, Singapore, 1949-51; vice consul, Noumea, 1951, consul and cons., 1951-52; 2d sec., consul, Cairo, 1956-58; consul, Damascus, 1958-61; 1st sec., Benghazi, 1961-62, Tripoli, 1962-64; consul, Kobe-Osaka, Japan, 1965-67. Served to ensign USNR, 1944-46. Rotarian. Home: Lansdale PA Died Aug. 7, 1967.

HARKER, RAY CLARKSON, clergyman; b. Leadmine, Wis., Nov. 1, 1866; s. William and Maria (Clarkson) H.; A.B., Northwestern U., 1891, A.M., 1894; B.D., Garrett Bibl. Inst., Ill., 1893; D.D., Lawrence Coll., Wis., 1902; m. Lulu A. Abernethy, Aug. 24, 1897; children—Bernice, Robert A., Miriam, William C., Rowland R. Ordained M.E. ministry, 1893; pastor 1st Ch., South Chicago, Ill., 1893-98, 1st Ch., Appleton, Wis. 1898-1903, Rogers Park Ch., Chicago, 1903-07, Embury Ch., Freeport, Ill., 1907-12, 1st Ch., Phoenix, Ariz., 1912-18, West Adams Ch., Los Angeles, 1918-24, Grace Ch., Long Beach, 1924-27, First Church, Whittier, Calif., 1927-32, White Temple, Anaheim, 1932-36, Crescent Heights Ch., Hollywood, 1936-June, 1939. Retired. Del. Gen. Conf. M.E. Ch., Minneapolis, 1912; trustee Southern Calif. Conf. Mem.

nat. council of Nat. Econ. League, 1917-22; mem. Delta Upsilon. Mason, K.T. Author: Christian Science, 1908; The Work of the Sunday School, 1911; The Ministry of Nature, Music and Tears, 1912. Dir. Internat. Reform Bur., 1917-21; pres. Union Preachers' Meeting, Los Angeles, 1921. Home: 1246 N. Hayworth Hollywood CA‡

HARKINS, EDWARD FRANCIS, editor; b. Boston, Feb. 27, 1872; s. Timothy A. and Margaret (Hankin) H.; ed. pub. schs. and Boston Coll.; m. Mary Elizabeth Kelly, of Boston, June 26, 1901. Author: Pilgrimages Among Men Who Have Written Famous Books, 1901; Pilgrimages Among Women Who Have Written Famous Books (with C. H. L. Johnston), 1901; The Schemes (novel), 1903; also poems and articles (mostly fiction) in various newspapers and periodicals. Home: 2 Chestnut St. Office: 5 Winthrop Sq., Boston MA‡

HARLAN, CAMPBELL ALLEN, elec. engr.; b. Columbia, Tenn., May 31, 1907; s. Alexander and Ellagreen (Pickard) C.; student coll. engring. U. Tenn., 1926-28; D.Sc. (hon.), U. of Detroit; m. Ivabell Campbell, June 29, 1932; children—John Marshall, Campbell Allen, Joyce Lily, James Gregory, Joseph Duncan, Jay Scott, Jeanne Marie. Engr., estimator Turner Engring. Co., Detroit, 1929-35, mgr., 1935-40; chmn. bd. Harlan Electric Co., v.p., dir. subsidiary and affiliated cos.; dir. Power Piping Co., Pitts., Liberty Mut. Co. City National Bank Detroit, Detroit Mortgage & Realty Co.; pres. Univ. House-Holiday Inn, Morgantown W.Va. Bd. dirs. Community Health Assn., Maryglade Coll.; vice chmn. Detroit com. Nat. Jewish Hosp.; mem. alumni bd. govs. U. Tenn.; v.p. dir. exec. com. United Found.; bd. dirs., past pres. Ednl. TV Found; trustee Burton Mercy Hosp., Bethany Coll., Fisk U., Hampton Inst.; trustee emeritus Mich. State U.; fellow Brandeis U.; hon. trustee Brandeis U. Assos. Served as lt. USNR, 1944-45. Mem. Engring. Soc. Detroit, Navy League U.S. (Detroit Council), Mich. Soc. Architects (hon.), Am. Assn. UN (bd. mem.), Detroit Bd. Commerce, Nat. Elec. Contractors Assn., Detroit Elec. Assn. (past pres.). Met Art Assn., Tau Beta Pi, Eta Kappa Nu. Clubs: Detroit Athletic, Recess, Economic (dir.) (Detroit). Home: Bloomfield Hills MI Died June 23, 1972.

HARLAN, JOHN MARSHALL, asso. justice Supreme Ct. of U.S.; b. Chgo., May 20, 1899; s. John Maynard and Elizabeth Palmer (Flagg) H.; A.B., Princeton, 1920, LL.D., 1955; B.A., M.A. (Rhodes Scholar), Balliol Coll., Oxford U., 1923, hon. fellow, 1955; LL.B., N.Y.L.S., 1924, LL.D., 1955; LL.D., Columbia, Brandeis U., Oberlin Coll., Evansville College; married Ethel Andrews, November 10, 1928; 1 daughter, Eve (Mrs. Frank Dillingham). Admitted to N.Y. bar 1925, Circuit Court Appeals, 1925, U.S. Dist. Ct., 1925, U.S. Supreme Court, 1945; asst. U.S. atty. So. Dist. N.Y., 1925-27; spl. asst. atty. gen., N.Y., 1928-30, 1951-53; mem. firm Root, Ballantine, Harlan, Bushby & Palmer, N.Y. City, 1931-54; judge U.S. Ct. of Appeals, 2d Circuit, 1954-55; associate justice Supreme Court of U.S., 1955-71; chief counsel, gen. counsel N.Y. State Crime Commn., 1951-53. Served as col. USAAF, 1943-45, chief operations analysis section, 8th Air Force, Eng. Decorated Legion Merit, Croix de Guerre (France), Croix de Guerre (Belgium). Mem. Am., N.Y. State bar assns., Assn. Bar City of N.Y., N.Y. Co. Lawyers Assn. Clubs: Century Assn., University (N.Y.C.); Country (Fairchild, Conn.); Ivy (Princeton, N.J.). Home: Washington DC Died Dec. 29, 1971.

HARLAN, ROLVIX, social service; b. Forestville, Md., Mar. 7, 1876; s. Burns and Margaret (Honner) H.; A.B., George Washington University, 1899, A.M., 1901; Ph.D., U. of Chicago, 1906; D.D., Sioux Falls (S.D.) Coll., 1918; m. Margaret Maude Wade, Aug. 10, 1904; children—Mrs. Margaret W. Hilton, Laverne Idema (Mrs. Travis Patterson). Ordained Bapt. ministry, 1900; pastor successively, Evansville, Wis., Dixon, Ill., Kansas City, Mo.; prof. history and economics, Ottawa (Kan.) U., 1909-10; dean of Coll. and prof. sociology, same univ., 1912-15; pres. Sioux Falls Coll., 1915-18; sec. social service and rural community work, Am. Bapt. Home Mission Soc., Jan. 1, 1919-22; prof. sociology Univ. of Richmond, 1922-46 (ret.). Lecturer on ethics of industry, lecturer Baptist World Alliance, Berlin, 1934. Mem. exec. com. World Brotherhood Congress, Prague, 1921; pres. Va. Social Science Assn., 1929-30. Mem. Am. Sociol. Soc., Lambda Chi Alpha, Pi Gamma Mu, Tau Kappa Alpha, Omicron Delta Kappa. Mem. of board Community Fund, Richmond, Virginia (for fourteen years). Progressive Republican. Mason (32 deg.). Club: Cosmos (Washington, D.C.), Rotary International. Author: John Alexander Dowie and the Christian Catholic Apostolic Church, 1906; (booklet) Urbanity as a Personal and Social Ideal; Brotherhood and Civilization (the John Clifford lectures before the British Brotherhoods, delivered in Liverpool), 1921; A New Day for the Country Church. Home: 35 Towana Rd., University of Richmond VA‡

HARLAND, JAMES PENROSE, educator, archaeologist; b. Wenonah, N.J., Feb. 5, 1891; s. James and Catherine (Welsh) H.; student William Penn Charter Sch., 1904-09; A.B., Princeton, 1913; A.M., 1915, Ph.D., 1917; student U. Bonn am Rhein, 1913-14, Am. Sch., Athens, Greece, 1914; m. Agnes Westerlund, Feb. 2, 1924 (dec. Aug. 1959). Instr. Greek, U. Mich., 1921-22; asst. prof. classics U. N.C., 1922-23; asst. prof. archaeology and Greek, U. Cin., 1923-26; asso. prof. archaeology U. N.C. 1927-29, prof. 1929-73; excavated at Nemea, Zygouries and other sites; archaeol. study, Greece, U. Uppsala, Sweden, 1939; visited museums eleven countries, Norway to Turkey, 1939. Mem. Town Planning Bd. Chapel Hill. Mem. mng. com. Am. Sch. at Athens, 1959-73. Served from seaman to ensign, communications officer USN, 1917-19. Fellow Archaeol. Inst., Am. Sch., Athens, Greece, 1920-21; Guggenheim fellow, 1926-27. Mem. Archaeol. Inst. Am. (recorder 1946-47, lectr.; pres. Carolina soc.), Am. Schs. Oriental Research, Am. Philol. Assn., Princeton Alumni Assn. of Eastern N.C. (pres.), Am. Research Center in Egypt, Phi Beta Kappa. Presbyn. Club: Archaeological. Author: Peloponnesos in The Bronze Age, 1923; Prehistoric Algina, 1925; Date of Hellenic Alphabet, 1945; Archaeological Excavations, 1946; Sodom and Gommorah, 1961. Contbr. articles to Biblical Archaeologist, Ency. Brit., Jr., Collier's Ency., Interpreter's Dictionary of the Bible, profl. jours. Home: Chapel Hill NC Died Feb. 7, 1973.

HARLLEE, WILLIAM CURRY, marine corps officer; b. Manatee, Fla., June 13, 1877; s. John Waddell and Mary Ellen (Curry) H.; student S.C. Mil. Acad. (The Citadel), 1891-93, U. of N.C., 1893-94, U.S. Mil. Acad., 1897-99; grad. Army War Coll., 1926, Naval War Coll., 1928; m. Ella Florence Fullmore, July 30, 1903; children—John (officer U.S. Navy), Ella Fulmore. Served as pvt., cpl., sergt. and 1st sergt., Co. F, 33d U.S. Vol. Inf., Philippine Insurrection, 1899-1900; comd. 2d lt., U.S. Marine Corps, 1900, advancing through the grades to brig. gen., 1942, retired since 1935. As senior aide and asst. to Maj. Gen. George F. Elliott, comdt. U.S.M.C., devised and established methods of marksmanship training in Marine Corps, 1908-10; asst. dir. gunnery exercises and engring. performances, Navy Dept., 1914-20; established Marine Corps Inst., for extending ednl. and vocational training throughout Marine Corps, Quantico, Va., and removed it to Marine Barracks, Washington, D.C., 1920; comd. 15th Regt., U.S.M.C., and Eastern Dist. under mil. (naval) govt. of Dominican Republic, 1921-22; exec. officer div. of operations and training Hdqrs. U.S.M.C., 1924-25; brig. gen., chief of staff and asst. comdt. Gendarmerie d'Haiti, 1926-27; Fleet Marine Officer, U.S. Fleet, 1929-30. Decorated Comdr. Order of Honor and Merit (Haiti). Formerly dir. and vice pres. Nat. Rifle Assn.; formerly mem. and recorder Nat. Bd. for Promotion of Rifle Practice. Mason. Clubs: Racquet (Philadelphia); Army and Navy, University, Chevy Chase, National Press (Washington, D.C.); New York (N.Y.) Yacht. Author and publisher: Kinfolks, a geneal. treatise and record of early Am. families and their progeny, Vol. I, 1934, Vol. II, 1935, Vol. III, 1937; also of Marine Corps scorebooks and Rifleman's Instructor (1910), and of manuals of instruction and U.S. Navy Small Arms Firing Regulations, 1914-18. Home: 1753 Lamont St. N.W., Washington 10 DC*‡

HARLOW, S. RALPH, educator; b. Boston, Mass., July 20, 1885; s. Rev. Samuel A. and Caroline (Usher) H.; A.B., Harvard, 1908; grad. Union Theol. Sem., New York, 1912; A.M., Columbia, 1919; Ph.D., Hartford (Conn.) Theol. Sem., 1929; m. Marion Stafford, Feb. 1, 1912; children—John Stafford, Ruth Carol, Elizabeth. Ordained ministry Congl. Ch., 1912; asst. minister Spring St. Presbyn. Ch., N.Y. City, 1909-11, chaplain and head of dept. sociology, Internat. Coll., Smyrna, 1912-22; prof. religion and social ethics. Smith Coll., Northampton, Mass., since 1923. Dir. Student's Internat. Union, Geneva, 1931; prof. Y.M.C.A. Summer Sch., Blue Ridge, N.C.; mem. Nat. Com. of Peaceways, Inc.; dir. Nat. Assn. for Advancement of Colored People; dir. Postwar World Council; mem. executive council Am. Palestine Com.; mem. Academic Council Yiddish Scientific Institute. Mem. Cum Laude Society; trustee Alice Freeman Palmer School, Sedalia, N.C.; interchange minister to Great Britain, 1939. Mem. U.N.R.R.A. Mission Greece, 1945-46; visiting prof. Pierce Coll., Athens, 1945-46; mem. Academic Council Nat. Fedn. Constl. Liberties; dir. Friends Am. Studies, Greece; mem. Nat. Council, League for Ind. Democracy; trustee, Marthas Vineyard Assn.; pres. Harlow Family Assn., 1946-47. Mem. Nat. Assn. Biblical Instructors (pres. 1936), Am. Assn. Univ. Profs., Am. Fedn. of Teachers, Pi Gamma Mu, Harvard Club of Conn. Valley, Harvard Club of Marthas Vineyard. Author, works include: Honest Answers to Honest Questions, 1941; Prayers for Times Like These, 1942. Contbr. to religious publs. Home: Northampton MA Died Aug. 21, 1972.

HARMAN, HARVEY JOHN, found. exec. b. Selingsgrove, Pa., Nov. 5, 1900; s. Henry Elias and Cora (Jarrett) H.; B.A., U. Pitts., 1922; M.A., U. Pa., 1928; m. Wilhelmina Hamilton Eakin, July 5, 1922. Head football coach Haverford (Pa.) Coll., 1922-29, U. South, Sewanee, Tenn., 1930, U. Pa., 1931-37, Rutgers U., 1938-41, 46-55; exec. sec. Nat. Football Found. and Hall of Fame, New Brunswick, N.J., 1956-58, exec. dir., from 1958. Mem. Lambert Cup and Trophy Com., from 1958, Liberty Bowl Selection Com., from 1961. Mem. New Brunswick Recreation Com., 1947-62; treas. Raritan Valley (N.J.) United Fund, 1950-58. Borough councilman, Narbeth, Pa., 1934-38. Served with U.S. Army, 1918, as comdr. USNR, 1942-46. Recipient Stagg award Football Coaches Assn., 1960. Mem. Am. Football Coaches Assn. (pres. 1949), Druid, Phi Gamma Delta, Omicron Delta Kappa, Phi Delta Kappa. Mem. Reformed Ch. Am. (deacon 1956-58, elder from 1960). Mason, Kiwanian. Home: Highland Park NJ Died Dec. 17, 1969; buried Mercer PA

HARMAN, JACOB ANTHONY, civil engr.; b. Randolph County, Mo., Mar. 7, 1866; s. Jacob Madison and Emma (Cox) H.; C.E., Nat. Normal U., Lebanon, O., 1887; m. Emma Flagg, Mar. 4, 1889; children—Harris J., Howard W. County surveyor, Iroquois County, Ill., 1889-93; city engr., Peoria, Ill., 1893-95; cons. engr., Ill. State Bd. of Health, 1899-1903; pres. Jacob A. Harman Inc. (successor to Harman Engring Co., established 1892); cons. engr. hydraulic, municipal and drainage work. Pres. Illinois Engineering Council, 1938-39. Cons. Engr. State of Ill. (1944-45). Member American Society Civil Engineers, Western Soc. Engrs., Ill. Soc. Engrs. (pres. 1912); pres. Nat. Drainage Congress (1923). Republican. Mem. Disciples of Christ, Mason. (32 deg. Shriner). Club: Creve Coeur. Home: 1301 Glendale Av. Office: Apt. A., 144 Fredonia Av., Peoria IL‡

HARMAN, JAMES LEWIE, educator; b. Meador, Allen Co., Ky., June 18, 1874; s. Samuel Lewis and Mary (Hogan) H.; ed. Southern Normal Sch., Bowling Green, Ky., 1893-99, and Bowling Green Business Univ.; LL.D., Kentucky Wesleyan College, 1931; m. Nettie Kimberlin, of Springfield, Ky., Aug. 1, 1900; 1 son, J. Lewie. With Bowling Green Business U. since beginning of active career, 1894, pres. since 1921; dir. Potter-Matlock Trust Co. Mem. Ky. Ednl. Survey Commn., 1920; mem. bd. dirs. Ky. Children's Home Soc., Mammoth Cave Nat. Park Assn.; mem. Ky. Normal Sch. Commn. Mem. Nat. Assn. Accredited Commercial Schs. (bd. govs.) Nat. Federation Commercial Teachers, Ky. Endl. Assn., Southern Commercial Teachers' Assn., Ky. Supts.' Assn. Democrat. Methodist. Clubs: Rotary, Country. Speaker on ednl. subjects. Mem. 2 Gen. Confs. M.E. Ch., South and Uniting Meth. Conf. Home: Bowling Green KY‡

HARMON, CAMERON, clergyman, educator; b. Louisville, Ill., Apr. 17, 1876; s. William Albert and Sarah Cathren (McKnight) H.; A.B., McKendree Coll., Lebanon, Ill., 1903, D.D., 1916, LL.D., 1927; m. Ruby Wilson, Oct. 18,1910; children—Dorothy Elizabeth, Nina May, Marion Jane. Ordained M.E. ministry, 1900; pastor Washington St. Ch., Alton, Ill., 1900-02, 1st Ch., Granite City, Ill., 1902-03, Grayville, 1903-06, McLeansboro, 1906-10, Murphysboro, 1910-14, East St. Louis, 1914-17; pres. Mo. Wesleyan Coll., Cameron, Mo., 1917-23; pres. McKendree Coll., 1923-25; pastor 1st Ch., Carbondale, Ill., 1935-39, 1st Ch., Fairfield, Ill., 1939-43; 1st Ch., Lawrenceville, Ill., 1943-47. Built 3 chs. Served as pvt., Co. L, 4th Ill. Vol. Inf., May 1898; wagonmaster in Cuba, Mar. 1899; hon. disch. after 18 mos.' service. Mason, Odd Fellow, K. of P. Democrat. Del. from 3d Congressional Dist. of Mo. to Dem. Nat. Conv., San Francisco, 1920. Elected leader ministerial delegation So. Ill. M.E. Conf. to Gen. Conf., Springfield, Mass., May 1924; elected del. Southern Ill. M.E. Conf. to Gen. Conf., Kansas City, Mo., 1928. Gov. 45th Dist. Rotary Internat. since June 1928. Address: Penney Farms FL‡

HARMON, LEO CLINTON, banker; b. Grand River, S.Dak., Oct. 31, 1871; s. William and Zoe Lulu (Picotte) H.; A.B., Mt. St. Louis Coll., Montreal, Can., 1889; m. Mary E. Maher, of Fort Dodge, Ia., Dec. 28, 1898. Receiver Stockgrowers Nat. Bank, Miles City, Mont., 1894-96; cashier State Nat. Bank, Miles City, 1895-98, v.p., 1898-1900; dir. Lumbermen's Nat. Bank, Menominee, Mich., 1900-13; organizer, 1917, and pres. State Savings Bank, now retired; was v.p. and gen. mgr. Consolidated Lumber Co.; formerly pres. Menominee Electric Mfg. Co., etc.; now exec., New York Evening Journal. Mem. exec. bd. Nat. Great Lakes-St. Lawrence Tidewater Commn. and chmn. Mich. commn. to further same project. Republican. Home: 24 5th Av. Office: 220 South St., New York NY‡

HARNED, ROBERT ELLSWORTH, librarian; b. New Haven, Conn., Oct. 31, 1877; s. James Henry and Phoebe Jeannette (Bull) H.; A.B., Wesleyan U., Conn., 1899, A.M., 1914; B.D., Drew Theol. Sem., 1903; m. Sadie Belle Whittlesey, of Madison, N.J., May 26, 1903. Asst. librarian, Wesleyan U., 1899-1900; asst. editor and editor M.E. Ch. missionary publs., 1903-12; librarian Drew Theol. Sem., Madison, N.J., since Sept. 1, 1912. Mem. N.E. East Conf. M.E. Ch. Trustee pub. schs., Madison, 1912-15; mem. A.L.A., Psi Upsilon. Address: 68 Prospect St., Madison NJ‡

HAROLD, RAYMOND PAGET, savs. and loan exec.; b. Worcester, Mass., July 12, 1898; s. George S. and Sarah (Whittum) H.; student Mass. Inst. Tech., Carnegie Inst. Tech.; LL.D., Assumption Coll., 1959; D.C.S. (hon), Holy Cross Coll. 1966; m. Mrytle S. Harold Rice, 1921; children—Charlote I. (Mrs. John D. Druce), Dorothy A. (Mrs. Lester C. Conner, Jr.), Ruth L. (Mrs. Robert M. Zollinger, Jr.), Asst. trust officer Pa.

Trust Co., Pitts.; staff fgn. dept. First Nat. Bank of Boston; bank examiner, Mass.; treas. Worcester Coop. Bank, 1928; pres. Mass. Coop. Bank League, 1932; dir., organizer Mass. Coop. Central Bank, Coop. Share Ins. Fund, 1933; pres. Fed. Savs. League of New Eng., 1943-44, Nat. League Insured Savs. Assns., 1946-47; pres. Worcester Fed. Savs. and Loan Assn., 1937-72, chmn., 1958-72; pres. Spruce Point Inn, Boothbay Harbor, Me., Green Pastures Farms, West Boylston, Mass.; dir. Harbor Nat. Bank, Boston, Investors Mortgage Ins. Co. Pres., study housing and capital needs in Peru, ICA, 1959; mem. adv. com. on housing and urban devel. AID, State Dept.; mem. Fed. Home Loan Bank Bd., Boston, 1932-48. Chmn. Worcester Housing Authority, 1946-54, Worcester Redevel. Authority. Bd. dirs. Worcester chpt. A.R.C., Hahnemann Hosp., Mass. Heart Assn.; adv. com. Worcester YWCA; trustee New Eng. Bapt. Hosp., St. Vincent Hosp.; former chmn. com. doctors, dentists and nurses Mass. Scholarship Found. Served with Engrs. Corps, U.S. Army, World War I. Recipient distinguished service award Am. Cancer Soc., 1951, award Worcester Vets. Council, 1951, Freedoms Found. award, 1951, Worcester AmVets, 1955, Am. Heart Assn., 1959; Isaiah Tomas award Worcester Advt. Club; comdr. Order of Merit, Peru, 1960. Mem. Am. Legion, Newcomen Soc. N.Am., Internat. Benjamin Franklin Soc., Royal Soc. Arts (London). Clubs: Economic (past pres.) (Worcester); N.Y. Athletic; Boothbay Harbor Yacht; Jonathan (Los Angeles); Key Biscayne Yacht; Conn. Valley Hereford Cattle, Am. Jersey Cattle. Home: Worcester MA Died Oct. 10, 1972.

HAROUTUNIAN, JOSEPH, educator; b. Marash, Turkey, Sept. 18, 1904; s. Garabed and Zekie (Khayyat) H.; student American U. of Beirut (Lebanon), 1919-23; A.B., Columbia, 1926, Ph.D., 1932; B.D., Union Theol. Sem., 1930; D.D., Lawrence College, 1949, Wabash Coll., 1958; S.T.D., Knox College, 1958; m. Helen Augusta Halsey, June 1942; children—Sophie, Joseph Halsey, Peter Isham. Asst. prof. Biblical history, Wellesley Coll., 1932-40; Cyrus H. McCormick prof. systematic theology McCormick Theol. Sem., Chgo., 1940-62; prof. systematic theology Div. Sch., U. Chgo., 1962-68. Mem. Am. Theol. Soc., Am. Soc. Ch. History. Author: Piety vs. Moralism, 1932; Wisdom and Folly in Religion, 1940; Lust for Power, 1949; Calvin Commentaries, 1958; God with Us, 1965. Home: Chicago IL Died Nov. 15, 1968; buried Southampton NY

HARPER, FLOYD ARTHUR, economist, educator; b. Middleville, Mich., Feb. 7, 1905; s. William Robert and Clara Margaret (Howard) H.; B.S., Mich. State U., 1926; Ph.D., Cornell, 1932; m. Marguerite Ruth Kaechele, June 14, 1930; children—Barbara Jean Keith, Harriet M., Helen Louise, Larry Arthur. Asst. and instr. Cornell, 1928-31, instr., 1931-34, asst. prof., 1934-35, prof. marketing, 1935-46; field agt. in research Fed. Farm Bd., 1930-31; bus. analyst Bank for Coop., Farm Credit Adminstrn., 1934; acting head dept. agrl. econs. U. Puerto Rico, 1937; economist Found. for Econ. Edn., Irvington-on-Hudson, N.Y., 1946-58; research economist William Volker Fund, Burlingame, Cal., 1958-62; vis. lectr. social philosophy Wabash Coll., 1962-63; sec. Institute for Humane Studies, Incorporated, 1963-64, exec. v.p., 1964-65, pres., 1965-73; mem. bd. lecturers Freedoms Found., Valley Forge, Pa. Fellow of A.A.A.S.; mem. Mont Pelerin (Internat.) Soc., Soc. for Freedom in Sci., Centro de Estudios Sobra la Liberta (Argentina; hon. mem. adv. bd.), Am. Econ. Assn., Am. Statis. Assn., Am. Acad. Polit. and Social Scis., Am. Marketing Assn., Acad. Polit. Sci., Phi Kappa Phi, Alpha Zeta, Pi Kappa Delta, Pi Delta Epsilon. Club: Varsity. Author several books including: High Prices, 1948; Inflation, 1951; In Search of Peace, 1951; Sequoyah, Symbol of Free Men, 1952; Morals and The Welfare State, 1951; Gaining the Free Market, 1952; A Just Price, 1953; Why Wages Rise, 1957; La Sociedad y la Libertad, Mexico, 1956; The Greatest Economic Charity, 1958; Para Recuperas La Libertad, 1960; Savings: The Greatest Economic Charity, 1965. Contbr.: Essays on Liberty, vols. I-V; articles profl. jours. Home: Atherton CA Died Apr. 1973.

HARPER, HAROLD, lawyer; b. N.Y.C., Nov. 22, 1885; s. James Alsop and Emma Louise (Hageman) H.; A.B., Columbia, 1905, A.M., LL.B., 1907; m. Elizabeth Roop, June 9, 1923; children—James Albert, Mary (Mrs. Mary Harper Hutchins). Was admitted to New York bar, 1907, United States Supreme Ct., 1910, D.C. bar, 1920; practiced law, N.Y.C., from 1907; asso. Davies, Auerbach & Cornell, 1909-13; mem. Harper & Matthews and predecessors, from 1920; asst. U.S. atty., 1913-20; spl. asst. to U.S. atty. gen., 1920; chmn. com. which drafted unified rules U.S. Dist. Cts., So. and Eastern N.Y., adopted 1952, chmn. standing com. rules So. Dist. N.Y.; lectr. N.Y.U. Sch. Law, 1949-52, Practising Law Inst., 1939-46; pub. mem. Joint Industry Bd., Elec. Contracting Industry. Member Selective Service Board, 1941-45. Fellow American Coll. of Trial Lawyers; member N.Y County Lawyers Association (dir., 1943-48, chmn. com. fed. cts., 1938-53, mem. com. on discipline), Assn. Bar City N.Y. mem. com. municipal affairs, 1949-52), N.Y. Bar Assn., Am. Bar Assn., Seventh Regt. Vets. Association (past mem. bd. mgt.), Alpha Chi Rho (nat. v.p., 1925-26). Democrat. Presbyn. Clubs: Univ., Columbia, Lawyers (N.Y.C.). Author monograph Civil Practice in Federal Courts. Home: New York City NY Died Dec. 31, 1971.

HARPER, JAMES R., judge; b. Jacksboro, Tex., May 28, 1869; s. William Mark and Sarah Elizabeth (Aynes) H.; ed. country schs., Tex.; jr. law course, U. of Tex., 1888-89; m. Clara B. Deason, of Ft. Worth, Tex., June 30, 1909; children—Mary Elizabeth, Frank, James R. Admitted to Tex. bar, 1890; justice of the peace, El Paso, Tex., 1892-94; co. judge, El Paso Co., 1896-1902; dist. atty. 34th Jud. Dist. Tex., 1902-04; dist. judge, same dist., 1904-12; chief justice Ct. of Civil Appeals, 8th Supreme Jud. Dist. Tex., terms 1912-18, 1918-24; now in practice of law. Democrat. Mem. Ch. of Christ. Club: Toltec. Address: 1311 E. Rio Grande, El Paso TX‡

HARPER, MARY MCKIBBIN, physician, med. editor; b. Frankford Springs, Pa.; desc. Scotch pioneers who settled in Washington County, Pa., 1745; d. Samuel and Margaret McKibbin; grad. State Teachers' Coll., Indiana, Pa.; laboratory work, Wiesbaden, Germany, 1895; M.D., U. of Mich., 1899; grad. study, clinics of London, Paris, Berlin, Vienna; student Newnham Coll., Cambridge, Eng., 1925; also extension study in lit., U. of Chicago; m. Samuel Harper, 1903; 1 adopted son, Samuel (dec.). Began as teacher in rural schools, Beaver County, Pa., later in McKeesport, Pa., public schools; physician for women and children, McKeesport, 1899-1903, Chicago, Maywood, River Forest, Ill., 1903-25; med. corr. on around the world trip, 1925-26; inspection Am. Women's Hosps., Greece and Turkey, 1929; editor and mgr. Women in Medicine (jour. of American Medical Women's Association), 1926-38; co-editor Medical Review of Reviews, 1928-34. Lecturer on health to schools, clubs, factory girls, etc., beginning 1899; health officer, Maywood, Illinois, 1912-15; one of five founders Oak Park (Illinois) Art League; established Braille service for needy blind, Chicago, 1927; founded Tiny Tim Bed for Dickens Fellowship in Women's and Children's Hosp., Chicago, 1929; mem. Nat. Com. for Better English, 1920; donor nat. prize for lyric poetry, 1921, 22, 23; v.p. Nat. Bookfellow Library Guild; Nat. Com. Unemployment of Women (invited to White House—apptd. by Hon. Harry Hopkins). Awarded European tour by Puritan Pub. Co., Boston, 1895; Book-fellow award of silver torch, 1925; distinguished service citation for alumnae, U. of Mich. Centenary, 1937; portrait hung by Am. Med. Women's Assn. in Quine Library of U. of Ill. Med. Sch., Chicago, 1939; hon. tablet (friend) Med. Woman's Coll., Pa., 1939. Life mem. Am. Med. Women's Assn., Nat. Order Bookfellows; founder and life pres. Chicago, Berkeley and Pittsburgh branches of Dickens Fellowship; hon. mem. Oak Park and River Forest Physicians' Club; mem. Alpha Epsilon Iota. Author: The Doctor Takes a Holiday," 1941; also travel articles published variously, 1926-41. Republican. Protestant. Home: The Carlton Hotel, Oak Park IL‡

HARPHAM, GERTRUDE TRESSEL RIDER, b. at Alliance, Ohio; d. John Harsh (M.D.) and Susanna Teegarden (Hawkins) Tressel; Mus.B., Mt. Union Coll., Ohio, 1897, A.B., 1898, A.M., 1902; post-grad. work, Bryn Mawr, 1901-02; m. Rev. Harold Miloff Rider, of Baltimore, Md., Oct. 8, 1902 (died 1912); 1 son, Theodore Harold; m. 2d, Fred Murcott Harpham, Sept. 29, 1925 (died 1934). Served as librarian for the blind, with Library of Congress, Washington, D.C., 1912-25; inspected libraries and instns. for the blind in Great Britain, France, Holland, Italy and Japan, 1914, 15; created and established library for war-blind soldiers; directing librarian Red Cross Inst. for the Blind; nat. dir. of Braille, Am. Red Cross, 1923-25, now mem. book selection com., Braille transcribing sect.; mem. of Citizens' Library Committee of Ohio, Women's Hosp. Bd., Akron City Hosp. Member Am. Assn. Univ. Women, Delta Gamma Sorority, etc. Episcopalian. Clubs: Akron Garden, Garden Club of Ohio (dir.), Portage Golf, Bryn Mawr Alumnae. Author of Braille Transcribing. Home: (Jan.-Mar.) 127 E. 4th St., Hinsdale, Ill.; (Apr.-Dec.) Apt. 19, 222 Twin Akron OH‡

HARRELD, JOHN WILLIAM, ex-senator; b. Morgantown, Ky., Jan. 24, 1872; s. Thomas N. and Martha (Helm) H.; ed. Nat. Normal U., Lebanon, O.; m. Laura Ward, of Morgantown, Ky., Oct. 20, 1899 (died 1930); 1 son, Ward; m. 2d, Thurlow Ward, 1931. Practiced law at Morgantown, 11 yrs. Ardmore, Okla., 1906-17; moved to Oklahoma City, 1917; county atty., Butler Co., Ky., 4 yrs.; referee in bankruptcy, Okla., 6 yrs.; elected Nov. 8, 1919, mem. 66th Congress (1919-21), 5th Okla. Dist., to fill unexpired term of Joseph B. Thompson, deceased; elected U.S. senator, term 1921-27; now mgr. Petroleum Office Bldg. Oil producer. Republican. Home: 3233 N. Harvey Parkway. Office: Petroleum Bldg., Oklahoma City OK‡

HARRELL, JOEL ELLIS, communications executive, dir. cos.; b. Marshville, N.C., Oct. 12, 1891; s. Oliver Perry and Mary Adeline (Marsh) H.; student Riverside Mil. Acad.; B.S., U. of Ga., 1913; D.Eng., Worcester Polytechnic Institute, 1951; m. Millicent W. Croke, May 24, 1941. Apprentice Am. Telephone & Telegraph Co., N.Y.C., 1913-15; dist. supt. various cities, 1915-24; div. traffic supt. New England Telephone & Telegraph Co., Springfield, Mass., 1925-27; gen. traffic mgr., Boston, Mass., 1928-29, gen. comml. mgr., 1930-35; asst. to pres., 1935-36, v.p., 1936-44, pres., 1944-56, dir., from 1938, chmn. bd., 1956, ret.; dir., chmn. auditing com. Mass. Mutual Life Ins. Co.; dir. G. F. Wright Steel & Wire Co., Worcester, Mass. Mem. corp. Mass. Meml. Hosp.; hon. mem. exec. com. Asso. Industries of Mass.; trustee Theodore Edson Parker Found. Mem. Bostonian Soc. Clubs: Union (Boston); Wianno (Mass.) Golf; Bird Key Yacht (Sarasota, Fla.). Home: Boston MA Died Apr. 6, 1968; buried Sarasota Memorial Park, Sarasota FL

HARRELL, LINWOOD PARKER, banker; b. Edenton, N.C., Jan. 4, 1908; s. John Franklin and Anne (Coffield) H.; B.S., U. of N.C., 1930; m. Evelyn Glenn, March 5, 1932; children—Anne Lyn, Linwood Parker. Pres., Union Trust Co. D.C., 1948-68, chairman board, chief exec. officer, 1968-70. Episcopalian. Home: Washington DC Died Mar. 16, 1970; buried Rock Creek Cemetery, Washington DC

HARRIMAN, ALONZO JESSE, architect; b. Bath, Me., July 6, 1898; s. Charles Alonzo and Nellie Drummond (Coombs) H.; B.S. in Mech. Engring., U. Me., 1920; M.A., Harvard, 1928; A.F.D., Bates Coll., 1961; m. Pearl Lillian Palmer, Sept. 16, 1922; 1 son, Charles Palmer, Jr. partner Coombs & Harriman, 1928-38; with Alonzo J. Harriman Assos., Inc. and predecessors, Auburn, Me., from 1938, treas., from 1948; architect and engr. for airports, shipyards, govt. bldgs., schools, comml. bldgs. Del. UNESCO Conf. on Sch. Bldgs., London, 1962; chmn. local planning bd., 1958. Mem. board dirs. Building Research Institute. Served with U.S. Army, World War I. Recipient award Pan Am. Congress, 1947, Progressive Architecture, 1949, Am. Assn. Sch. Adminstrs., 1955, centennial award New Eng. Council, 1957. Profl. engr., Me., N.H., Mass. Registered architect, Me., N.H., Mass., R.I., N.Y. Fellow A.I.A. (dir. 1959-61, chmn. com. on schs. and ednl. facilities, 1961-63); mem. Nat. Assn. Profl. Engrs., Am. Assn. Sch. Adminstrs. Clubs: Cumberland (Portland, Me.); Harvard (Boston and N.Y.C.). Contbr. articles profl. jours. Home: Auburn ME Died Sept. 9, 1966.

HARRIMAN, EDWARD AVERY, lawyer (retired); b. Framingham, Mass., Dec. 31, 1869; s. Charles Franklin and Mary White (Conant) H.; A.B., Harvard, 1888; studied U. of Va. and Cincinnati Law Sch.; LL.B., Boston U., 1891; married Bertha Cornwall Ray, Aug. 31, 1897 (died Oct. 1941). Admitted to Mass. bar, 1891; practiced in Kansas, 1891-92; professor law, Northwestern University, 1892-1901, and member Chicago bar; practiced in Conn., 1901-20, Washington, D.C., 1920-39; lecturer, Yale Law Sch., 1906-17, Boston University Law Sch. Mem. S.C.W., Harvard Chapter Phi Beta Kappa (1887-88); 1st president Harvard Club of Connecticut, 1908-09; pres. N.E. Federation Harvard Clubs, 1912-13; v.p. Associated Harvard Clubs, 1915-16; pres. Harvard Club, Washington, D.C., 1936-38; pres. Church Club Diocese of Conn., 1916-18. Trustee of donations and bequests for ch. purposes, 1917-18; pres. Churchmen's League of D.C., 1924-26; pres. Nat. Federation of Ch. Clubs, 1926-27; trustee Episcopal Eye, Ear and Throat Hosp., and House of Mercy; pres. Finance Reserve Officers' Assn., 1924-26; treas. Reserve Officers' Assn of U.S., 1925-29. Maj. judge advocate U.S. Army, and counsel to the dir. of finance, U.S. Army, 1919. Lt. col. Q.M.R.C., 1920-21; lt. col. finance R.C., 1921-25, promoted col., 1925. Spl. counsel Interdepartmental Bd. of Contracts and Adjustments, 1922; counsel Am. Economic Assn., 1923-29, and of R.O.T.C. Assn. of U.S., 1929-39; lecturer internat. law, George Washington U. Law Sch., 1923-27; v.p. Am. Society of Foreign Law, 1937-39. Episcopalian. Republican. Clubs: University (Pasadena); Harvard (New York). Author: Law of Contracts, 1896, 1901. Editor: Greenleaf on Evidence, vols. II and III (16th edit.), 1899; The Constitution at the Crossroads, 1925. Finger-print operator, Office of Civilian Defense, Altadena, 1942. Address: 1226 E. Foothill Blvd., Altadena CA‡

HARRIMAN, JOHN WALTER, economist, educator; b. Providence, July 8, 1898; s. John W. and Mary (Jones) H.; Ph.B., Brown U., 1920; M.B.A., Harvard, 1925, D.C.S., 1932; M.A., Dartmouth, 1938; m. Ingeborg Sophie Rathe, Oct. 13, 1945; children—Mary (Mrs. Robert C. Young), Joan (Mrs. John C. Watson). Mem. faculty Grinnell Coll., also U. Rochester, 1925-28; head research dept. Russell, Berg & Co., Boston, also instr. bank mgmt. Harvard Bus. Sch., 1928-32; prof. finance Dartmouth, 1932-46; prof. bus. adminstrn. Syracuse U., 1946-53, dean Bus. Sch., 1950, Grad. Sch., 1952; prof. finance N.Y.U. Grad. Sch. Bus. Adminstrn., 1953-64, prof. emeritus, 1964-72, vice dean, 1953-72; research cons. J.R. Williston & Co., 1955-57; economist Union Service Corp. (Tri-Continental Corp. and Union Service Funds), 1958-68; dir. Atlantic Bank N.Y., Guardian Park Av. Fund Inc.; cons. Whitney Goadby, Inc. Head priorities specialist OPM and WPB, Washington, 1941-42; fgn.

service officer ECA and Mut. Security Adminstrn., Washington, Paris, London, Belgrade, 1949-52, dep. chief mission to UK., 1950-51. Bd. mgrs. Am. Bible Soc. Served from capt. to col. USAAF, SHAEF, 1942-46. Mem. Am. Finance Assn., Am. Econ. Assn., Nat. Assn. Bus. Economists, Am. Assn. U. Profs., N.Y. Soc. Security Analysts, Phi Beta Kappa, Delta Upsilon, Beta Gamma Sigma. Conglist. Clubs: Lawyers, N.Y. University. Home: New York City NY Died Oct. 21, 1972; buried Bangor ME

HARRIMAN, LEWIS GILDERSLEEVE, banker; b. Windsor, Conn., Mar. 24, 1889; s. Frederick W. and Cora Elizabeth (Jarvis) H.; B.S., Trinity Coll., 1909, M.S., 1917, sr. fellow; spl. courses N.Y.U.; LL.D., Trinity Coll., 1954, Alfred U., 1960; m. Grace Bastline, June 24, 1915; children—Lewis G., William B., John H., Thomas J., Elizabeth; m. 2d, Louise Ely, Oct. 11, 1939; children—Joan B., Ann L. Engr., Am. Creosoting Co., Louisville, 1909-11; engr., elec. Am. Real Estate Co., N.Y.C., 1912-15; with Coggeshell & Hicks, and Merrill, Lynch & Co., both mems. N.Y. Stock Exchange, later asst. trust officer and investment trust officer Guaranty Trust Co., N.Y.C., until 1919; v.p. Fidelity Trust Co. of Buffalo, 1919-23, pres., 1924-25; pres. Mfrs. and Traders Trust Co., 1925-54, chmn. bd., 1954-64, hon. chmn., 1964-73; hon. chmn. M. &T. Discount Corp.; vice chmn. Morgan N.Y. State Corp.; dir. T. Discount Corp.; vice chmn. Morgan N.Y. State Corp.; dir. Buffalo City Cemetery, 1929-64, pres., 1958-64 hon. dir., 1964-73; mem. adv. com. N.Y. Agy. R.F.C., 1932-54. Mem. Victory Fund Com. and War Finance Com., 2d Fed. Res. Dist.; chmn. Victory Fund Com., Group I; co-chmn. War Finance Com., Group I; mem. Buffalo War Council. Mem. 9th C.A., N.Y. N.G., 1917-18. Lectr. on finance N.Y.U. Sch. of Commerce, 1917, 18. Pres. Buffalo Clearing House, 1926, 30, 32, 36, 38, 43, 45, 48, 51, Buffalo C. of C., 1927, 28; a founder, v.p. Nat. Better Bus. Bur., 1926-29, Buffalo Better Bus. Bur., 1923-34; treas. Buffalo chpt. A.R.C., 1924-41, chmn., 1941-45; Buffalo treas. U.S.O.; mem. Buffalo Council on World Affairs; a founder Citizens Appeal Rev. Com., chmn., 1955-58. Republican presdl. elector for N.Y., 1956. Chmn. U. Buffalo Found., 1962-64; mem. citizens bd. U. Miami; trustee Trinity Coll., 1927-31, Buffalo Sem., 1925-27; trustee U. Buffalo, 1943-62, vice chmn., 1955-62; trustee Nichols Sch., 1928-48, Joint Charities and Community Fund; chmn. United War and Community Fund, 1942-44; an original incorporator Community Chest of Buffalo, Erie County; fellow in perpetuating Buffalo Fine Arts Acad.; bd. dirs. Buffalo Hist. Soc., Buffalo Philharmonic Orch., 1943-48, Buffalo Conv. and Tourist Bur. (founder), Niagara Frontier Planning Assn.; governing com. Buffalo Found. Named Man of Year, U. Buffalo Sch. Bus., 1954; recipient 4th Ann. Brotherhood citation Nat. Conf. Christians and Jews, 1956, Walter P. Cooke award U. Buffalo. Mem. Buffalo Soc. Natural Scis. (hon. life), Res. City Bankers Assn., Soc. Mayflower Descs., S.R., Newcomen Soc., Cult of White Buffalo (hon.), Psi Upsilon. Republican. Episcopalian (mem. exec. council Diocese N.Y. 1924-26, 32-34). Mason (33). Clubs: Buffalo (pres. 1933); Buffalo Country Thursday (Buffalo); Cherry Hill Golf, University (N.Y.C.); Riviera Country (Coral Gables). Home: Miami FL Died Jan. 7, 1973.

HARRIMAN, RAYMOND DAVIS, educator; b. Grinnell. Ia., June 6, 1888; s. Augustus Chase and Kate Miles (Davis) H.; A.B., Grinnell Coll., 1909, L.H.D., 1959; A.M., U. Wis., 1914. Ph.D., 1914; fellow Am. Acad. in Rome, 1915-16; m. Mary Ruth Martin, Sept. 11, 1918; children—John Martin, Joan Martin. Tchr., Muscatine (Ia.) High Sch., 1909-12; fellow in Latin, U. Wis., 1913-14, asst. in ancient history, 1914-15; instr. ancient langs. U. Utah, 1917-22, asst. prof., 1922-28, asso. prof., 1926-28, also acting dean men; vis. lectr. ancient history U. Wis., 1926; vis. asso. prof. Latin, U. Chgo., summer 1927; asso. prof. classics Stanford, 1928-34, prof., 1934-53, emeritus, from 1953, exec. head dept., 1937-53, chmn. Sch. Letters, 1940-42, chmn. Sch. Humanities, 1941-42, acting dean, 1947-48; vis. prof. classics U. Wash., 1953-54; civilian edn. adviser, spl. tng. and reclassification Unit 3903, 1943 (also coordinator Army spl. tng. unit 3905); also coordinator mil. programs, 1946. Mem. Am. Philol. Assn., Philol. Assn. Pacific Coast (pres. 1945,), Classical Assn. Pacific Coast (pres. 1931), Am. Assn. U. Profs., Phi Beta Kappa, Phi Kappa Phi, Alpha Kappa Lambda. Home: Los Gatos CA

HARRINGTON, CHARLES A., insurance exec.; b. Worcester, Mass., 1874; s. Francis A. and Roxanna M. (Grout) H.; ed. grade and high schools; Worcester Polytechnic Inst.; m. Luella B. Crook, 1900;children—Mrs. Ruth H. Ellsworth, Mrs. Mildred H. McEvoy, Lt. Francis A.; m. 2d, Ethel Lawton Ford, 1942. Asso. with Mass. Protective Cos., Worcester, Mass., since 1895, pres., 1922-44, now chmn. bd. Home: 123 Harrington Way. Office: 18 Chestnut St., Worcester MA‡

HARRINGTON, JOSEPH, mechanical engr.; b. Reading, Mass., Apr. 28, 1873; s. Edward B. and Helen L. (Montgomery) H.; S.B., Mass. Inst. Tech., 1896; m. Cora A., d. James Dunlap, of Champaign, Ill., Oct. 6, 1904; children—Joseph, Jr., Dunlap. Prospecting and mining in Mexico, 1896-99; designer of special machinery for Stillwell-Bierce & Smith Vaile Co., Dayton, O., 1899-1900; became identified with the Green Engring. Co., 1900, and continued as designer, field supt., gen. supt. and chief engr. and sec. until 1913; consulting combustion engr. since 1913; pres. Joseph Harrington Co. (automatic stokers). Mem. Advisory Board of Engrs., Dept. Smoke Inspection City of Chicago. Mem. Bituminous Coal Code Authority, Div. 2. Inventor and patentee of devices for use in automatic stoking. Mem. Am. Soc. Mech. Engrs., Western Soc. Engrs. Republican. Unitarian. Clubs: Technology, Engineers' (New York). Home: Riverside, Ill. Office: 360 N. Michigan Boul., Chicago IL‡

HARRINGTON, MARK RAYMOND, anthropologist; b. Ann Arbor, Mich., July 6, 1882; s. Mark Walrod and Rose Martha (Smith) H.; student U. of Mich., 1903-05; B.S., Columbia, 1907, A.M., 1908; Doctor of Humanities, Occidental College, 1956; m. Alma V. Cocks, June 20, 1904 (dec.); m. 2d. Anna A. Johns, Sept. 6, 1916 (dec.); 1 son, Johns H.; m. 3d, Edna L. Parker, Dec. 16, 1927 (dec.); married 4th, Marie T. Walsh, on April 23, 1949. Asst. in archeology Am. Mus. Natural Hist., 1899-1903; field instr., Peabody Mus., Harvard, summers, 1903-06; ethnol. work, Heye Mus., 1908-11; asst. curator Am. sect. U. of Pa. Museum, 1911-14; archeologist and ethnologist, Museum of Am. Indian, Heye Foundation, 1915-17, 1919-28; dir. research, Southwest Museum, Los Angeles, 1928-29, curator from 1929; research asso. Carnegie Inst. of Washington from 1930; consultant, Nat. Park Service, 1936-43, collaborator from 1943; consultant, restoration of La Purisima and San Fernando Missions from 1936; research asso. anthropology-sociology U. Calif. at Los Angeles from 1949. Served in Officers Training Sch., U.S. Army, 1918; commissioned 1st lieutenant Specialist Reserve. Fellow A.A.A.S., Society for American Archeology; member American Association of Museums, Academia de Historia de la Habana, Southwestern Anthropological Assn. Author: Sacred Bundles of the Sac and Fox Indians, 1914; Certain Caddo Sites in Arkansas, 1920; Cuba Before Columbus (Vols. 1, 2), 1921; Religion and Ceremonies of the Lenape, 1921; Cherokee and Earlier Remains on Upper Tennessee River, 1922; Lovelock Cave (with L.L. Loud), 1929; Gypsum Cave, Nevada, 1933; Dickon Among the Lenape Indians, 1938; An Ancient Site at Borax Lake, California, 1948; How to Build a California Adobe, 1948; the Iroquois Trail, 1965. Contbr. publs. Discoverer Ozark Bluff Dweller culture in Ark. and Mo.; explored Lost City of Nev., Lovelock Cave, Gypsum Cave (both in Nev.), early site at Borax Lake, Calif., Little Lake, Cal., Tule Springs, Nev. Home: Mission Hills CA Died June 30, 1971; buried San Fernando Mission Cemetery.

HARRINGTON, RUSSELL CHASE, orgn. exec.; born Tauton, Massachusetts, Nov. 9, 1890; son Goerge Stanley, Lydia (Roebuck) H.; student U. Mass., 1913; D.Sc. in Bus. Adminstrn., Bryant College; m. Olive Walker, August 23, 1915; 1 dau., Patricia (Mrs. George R. Urquhart, Jr.). With Ernst & Ernst, C.P.A.'s since 1920, staff accountant, 1920-21, mgr. Providence office, 1921-40, resident partner, 1940-55, 58-60, ret.; U.S. commr. internal revenue, 1955-58; president Tax Institute, Incorporated, 1960-71. Vice pres. R.I. Pub. Expenditure Council; chmn. finance com. Greater Providence YMCA. Recipient Alexander Hamilton award U.S. Treasury. Mem. District of Columbia Society of C.P.A.'s, R.I. Soc. C.P.A.'S (past pres.), Am. Inst. Accountants (mem. com. auditing procedure council trail bd.), R.I. Bd. Accountancy (chmn.), Am. Accounting Assn., Nat. Association Accountants, Providence C. of C. (past pres.), U.S. C. of C. (v.p.; dir.; chmn. com. bus. statistics; exec. com.; finance com. governing bd. nation's bus.; chmn. com. govt. expenditures, treas.), Assn. C.P.A. Examiners (past pres.), R.I. Pub. Expenditure Council (v.p.). Clubs: Hope, Turks Head; R.I. Country; Metacomet Golf; Seignory (Quebec). Home: Washington DC Died Aug. 7, 1971.

HARRINGTON, STUART WILLIAM, surgeon; b. Blossburg, Pa., Apr. 20, 1889; s. John C. and Jeanette (Dunsmore) H.; student Pa. State Coll., 1908-09; M.D., U. of Pa.; 1913; M.S., U. of Minn., 1920; m. Gertrude Jones, Nov. 17, 1922. Fellow in surgery Mayo Clinic, 1915, head of sect. on gen. surgery, 1920, became head sect. on thoracic surgery, 1925, asso. prof. surgery, U. of Minn., 1925-36, prof. surgery, 1936, emeritus prof., Lt. Med. Corps, during World War I. Mem. Minn. and Olmsted County med. socs., A.M.A., Southern Minn. Med. Assn., Am. Coll. of Surgeons, Alumni Association Mayo Clinic, American Association for Thoracic Surgery, Am. Surg. Assn., Western Surg. Assn., Southern Surg. Assn., Internat. Soc. of Surgery, Am. Board of Surgery, Sigma Alpha Epsilon, Sigma Xi, Republican. Presbyterian. Mason. Clubs: University Country, Gun. Home: Rochester MN Died Mar. 8, 1973.

HARRINGTON, WILLIAM WATSON, lawyer; born Farmington, Kent County, Del., June 30, 1874; s. Charles James and Mary Elizabeth (Watson) H.; A.B., Delaware Coll. (now U. of Del.), 1895, LL.D.; studied law in office of Edward Ridgely, Dover, Del., 2 yrs., Harvard Law Sch., 1 yr.; m. Sarah Godwin, Oct. 26, 1909; children—Sarah Godwin Herrick, Mary Elizabeth Watson, Anna Banks. Admitted to Del. bar, 1898, and in practice, Dover; register of wills for Kent County, succeeding father, deceased, by apptmt. of Gov. Tunnell, 1900-01; dep. atty. gen. for Kent County, 1909-13; appointed resident asso. judge Kent County, and mem. Supreme Ct. of Delaware, 1921, re-apptd., 1933, chancellor, 1938-50; pvt. law practice, Dover, since 1950. Editor: W. W. Harrington's Delaware Law Reports, Vols. 24-31 Del. Chancery Reports. Trustee, U. Del. Democrat. Episcopalian. Home: Kings Highway. Office: S. State St., Dover DE‡

HARRIS, ALBERT WADSWORTH, banker; b. Cincinnati, O., Nov. 4, 1867; s. Norman Wait and Jacyntha (Vallandingham) H.; ed. pub. schs. of Cincinnati and Evanston, Ill., graduating 1883, and Gem City Business Coll., Quincy, Ill., 1886; m. Harriet Meikle, Nov. 21, 1889; children—Martha Marie (Mrs. Norman Langley MacLeod), Norman Wadsworth. Entered employ of N. W. Harris & Co., 1888, and worked through all depts.; had general supervision of business as mng. partner until Feb. 1907, when firm incorporated as Harris Trust & Savings Bank, of which was pres., 1913-23, chmn. bd., Jan. 1923-Jan. 1943; now retired. Republican. Methodist. Clubs: Chicago, Midday, Attic (Chicago). Home: 4923 Kimbark Av., Chicago 15. Office: 115 W Monroe St., Chicago 90 IL‡

HARRIS, ALEXANDER, mfg. exec.; b. N.Y.C., Oct. 7, 1885; s. Henry and Sarah Harris; student U. London; m. Hannah Lightenburg, June 23, 1907; children—Theodore Paton (dec.), Jonathan, Leonard. Gen. mgr. Cryder & Co., N.Y.C., 1906-10; sec.-treas. Art Metal Works, Inc., Newark, 1910-40, pres., from 1940; pres. Art Metal Works, Inc., Stroudsburg, Pa., Ronson Art Metal Works, Inc. (Newark), Ronson Art Metal Works (Can.), Ltd. (Toronto), New Process Metals Corp. (Newark); dir. Ronson Products, Ltd. London. Founder Theodore Paton Harris Found., Theodore Paton Harris Scholarship Fund. Mem. bd. trustees Temple B'nai Abraham, Newark; mem. endowment com. Newark Beth Israel Hosp. Mason (Shriner), Elk. Club: Newark Athletic. Home: Colts Neck NJ Died Mar. 11, 1969; buried B'nai Jeshurun Cemetery, Hillside NJ

HARRIS, DUNCAN G., real estate exec.; b. N.Y. City, July 1, 1878; s. Richard Duncan and Annie (Gibert) H.; student Cutler's Sch., N.Y. City; A.B., Harvard, 1900; m. Alice Abell, June 18, 1913. Asso. with Astor Estate, 1901; pres., Harris & Vaughn, 1906, Harris, Vought & Co., 1910; v.p., Brown, Wheelock, Harris, Vought & Co., 1925; chmn. bd. Brown, Harris, Stevens, Inc.; member board of directors Fidelity Phoenix Insurance Co.; mem. adv. board Chemical Bank and Trust Co.; trustee Title Guarantee & Trust Co. Served as major, 305th Infantry, World War I; lt. col., Officers Res. Corps. Awarded D.S.C., Purple Heart (U.S.), Chevalier Legion of Honor, Croix de Guerre (France). Roman Catholic. Clubs: Union, Knickerbocker Racquet and Tennis, Harvard, Brook, Catholic (N.Y.C.). Home: New York City NY Died Dec. 13, 1970.

HARRIS, ELLA ISABEL, teacher; A.B., Waynesburg Coll., Pa., 1890; Ph. D., Yale, 1899. Has taught Latin and English in Indianapolis and, since 1899, has taught in Packer Collegiate Inst., and later at Vassar. Author: Two Tragedies of Seneca (verse), 1898 L2. Address: Vassar Coll., Poughkeepsie NY‡

HARRIS, EUGENE DENNIS, writer; b. Chgo., Jan. 4, 1911; s. Edward and Fay (Carr) H.; B.S., U. Ill., 1937; grad. student U. Chgo., 1938; m. Janet Corinne Sasserath, June 19, 1957; 1 dau., Deirdre Moira; 1 stepdau., Corinne. Asst. to v.p. Scott Radio Labs., 1939-42; commd. pvt. U.S. Army, 1942, advanced through grades to lt. col., 1962; served in campaigns in Africa, Italy, Korea; 1st radio corr., Korea, 1950; chief Armed Forces Korea Network, 1957-58; retired, 1964; asso. editor Nat. News-Research, Washington, 1964-71; treas. Electronic Advt. Corp., 1966-71. Decorated Purple Heart, Army Commendation medal; recipient certificate appreciation Boys' Nation, 1956; certificate commendation A.R.C., 1957; commendation Republic Korea, 1952. Member Institute of Electrical and Electronic Engineers, Retired Officers Assn., Pi Kappa Phi, Gamma Theta Phi. Club: Nat. Press (Washington). Author: Non-Commissioned Officers' Guide, 1962; Company Administration and the Army Personnel System, 1963; Interviewing Guide and Rating System for WAC Applicants, 1963; A Handbook on Questionnaire Preparation; A Handbook on Questionnaire Administration; (in Japanese) A Primer of Television Production, 1953. Home: Chevy Chase MD Died June 4, 1971; buried Arlington Nat. Cemetery.

HARRIS, FREDERICK BROWN, clergyman; b. Worcester, England; son of George T. and Ellen (Griffiths) H.; graduate Pennington (N.J.) Seminary, 1905; A.B., Dickinson Coll., Carlisle, Pa., 1909, A.M., 1912, D.D., 1923 B.D., Drew Theol. Sem., Madison, N.J., 1912; Litt.D., Lincoln Memorial Univ., Tenn., 1937, U. Tampa, 1952; LL.D., U. So. Cal., Seoul National University, Korea, 1956, University of

Wyoming, 1965; L.H.D., Ohio Wesleyan University; Dr. of Humanities, Ohio Wesleyan University, 1949; Litt.D. (hon.), Am. U., 1962; Dr. Sacred Lit. (hon.), Technical Coll., Ft. Wayne, Ind., 1962; m. Helen Louise Streeter, June 4, 1914; children—Barbara Louise, Constance Streeter. Ordained ministry, M.E. Ch., 1912; pastor Greenwood Av. Ch., Trenton, N.J., 1912-14, St. Luke's M.E. Ch., Long Branch, N.J., 1914-18, Grace M.E. Ch., N.Y. City, 1918-24, Foundry Meth. Ch., Washington, D.C., 1924-55; national chaplain Freedoms Foundation; chaplain of the U.S. Senate, 1942-46. 1949-68. Spl. ambassador to Korea, 1956, with ofcl. missions to Taiwan and Philippines. Mem. Phi Beta Kappa, Alpha Chi Rho. Mason. Club: National Press. Author: The Blossoming Bough; The Candle and the Flame; Wings of the Morning: The World Made Flesh; (volume of essays) Spires of the Spirit, 1952; Footprints on the Sand (vol. verse). Author weekly syndicated editorial Spires of the Spirit; also 4 vols. Senate Prayers. Contbr. ch. publs. Home: Washington DC Died Aug. 18, 1970; buried Parklawn Cemetry, Rockville MD

HARRIS, GEORGE BARNES, judge; b. Findlay, O., Oct. 27, 1881; s. Julius and Emma (Wolf) H.; A.B., Ohio Wesleyan U., 1900, hon. A.M., 1903, LL.D.; LL.B., Cleve. Law Sch., 1903; m. Fannie B. Davis, Sept. 22, 1909; children—Lucile Lanning (Mrs. David R. Limbach), Martha Bown (Mrs. Joshua Spencer Miller), David G. Prof. mathematics, Baldwin U., Berea, O., 1901-03; admitted to Ohio bar, 1903, and practiced in Cleveland until 1930; special counsel to Ohio atty. gen., 1915-16; judge Court of Common Pleas, Cuyahoga County, Ohio, 1930-35; resumed general practice of law. Jan. 1, 1935. Mem. Ohio Jud. Council, 1929, 30, 55-57; chmn. Cuyahoga County Selective Service Bd. 31; chmn. exec. com. Cuyahoga County Selective Service Chmn., 1940-46. Del. Rep. Nat. Conv., 1936. Pres. Cleve. Adult Edn. Assn., 1939-44. Mem. Am. (gen. council 1930-32, ho. of dels., 1937-38), Ohio (pres. 1922-23). Cleve. bar assns., Inst. Jud. Adminstrn., Am. Judicature Soc., Am. Law Inst., S.A.R., Beta Theta Pi. Phi Beta Kappa. Meth. Mason. Clubs: Union, City (pres. 1938). Home: Cleveland OH Died Nov. 26, 1970; buried Knowlwood, Cleveland Heights OH

HARRIS, GEORGE UPHAM, partner, Harris, Upham & Co.; b. Lake Forest, Ill., Jan. 31, 1898; s. John F. and Gertrude (Upham) H.; ed. St. Mark's School, Southborough, Mass.; m. Lucile Baldwin, Aug. 16, 1924. Partner, Harris, Winthrop & Co., 1925-29; partner, Harris Upham &Co., 1929-71. Mem. N.Y. Stock Exchange. Club: Racquet and Tennis. Home: New York City NY Died Mar. 1971.

HARRIS, GUY W(ALTER), engineer; b. Neosho Falls, Kan., Mar. 7, 1878; s. A. G. and Hattie (Ricketts) H.; ed. high sch., Kansas City, Mo.; m. Maude Leslie, June 20, 1908. Began as rodman Santa Fe, Pacific R.R., Williams, Ariz., 1898; rodman, A.T.& F. Ry., Las Vegas, N.M., 1899-1900, and continued with same rd. as transitman, Pueblo, Colo., 1900-03, asst. engr., 1903-06; asst. engr. in charge constrn. Pecos & Northern Tex. Ry., and Southern Kan. Ry. of Tex., 1906-09; chief engr. constrn. Pecos & Northern Tex. Ry., 1909-12; chief engr. A.T.& F. Ry. Coast Lines, Los Angeles, Calif., 1912-18; corporate chief engr. same rd. Chicago, 1918-20, asst. chief engr. System, 1920-27, acting chief engr., Dec. 1927-Mar. 1928, chief engr. System since 1928. Mem. Am. Soc. C.E., Western Soc. Engrs., Am. Ry. Engring. Assn. Home: 6922 S. Jeffrey Av. Office: 80 E. Jackson Blvd., Chicago IL‡

HARRIS, HERBERT EUGENE, educator; b. Ottumwa, Ia., Sept. 18, 1875; s. Allen Reese and Delphia (Mayhew) H.; Ph.B., Penn. Coll., 1901; A.M., 1904, LL.D., 1931; grad. student U. of Chicago, 1901, U. of Calif., 1908-09, 1917-18; Litt.D., Whittier Coll., 1938; m. Ruth Trueblood, July 20, 1904; children—Marjory Ruth, Charles Richard. Prof. of English, Whittier (Calif) Coll., 1901-10, and 1920-31, v.p., 1931-33, acting pres., 1933-34. Prof. English, Penn Coll., 1919-20; lecturer Calif. State Teachers Assn., 1936. Y.M.C.A. camp secretary, World War. Dist. Gov. Rotary Internat., 1928-29; organized and dir. internat. relations movement in Rotary Internat., 1928-30. Republican. Mem. Soc. of Friends. Rotarian. Author travel sketches, pageants, short stories. Lecturer on social problems. Home: Whittier CA‡

HARRIS, HUGH HENRY, clergyman, educator; b. Coldwater, Mich., July 26, 1875; s. John Henry and Mary Elizabeth (Rice) H.; student U. of Mich., 1895-96; B.A., Northwestern U., 1904, M.A., 1908; studied Yale; m. Isabel Silverthorn Wright, Dec. 8, 1907 (dec.); m. 2d, Ethel Purcell, Sept. 6, 1935. Ordained ministry M.E. Church, 1895; M.E. Church, South, 1913; pastor Gladstone, Mich., 1906-08; dir. religious edn., First Ch., Evanston, Ill., 1908-12; dir. Wesley Memorial Inst., Atlanta, Ga., 1912-13; prof. religious edn., Candler School of Theology, Emory Univ., 1913-43; prof. sociology, Emory Univ., 1926. Visiting prof. religious edn., Yale, 1924-25. Dir. Corr. Sch. Meth. Ch., Emory Univ., Ga. Mem. Phi Beta Kappa. Author: Leaders of Youth, 1922; Organization and Administration of Intermediate Department, 1924; contbr. Jour. Religious Edn., etc. Home: Emory University GA‡

HARRIS, JOHN HARPER, supt. schs.; b. Peoria, Ill., Oct. 30, 1910; s. Lewis P. and Esther (Yutt) H.; B.S., Bradley U., 1935; M.A., Columbia, 1940, Ed.D., 1948; postgrad. U. Ia., 1935-36, U. Ill., 1941-42, Harvard, 1958, Drake U., 1963; L.H.D., Coll. Medicine and Surgery, Des Moines, 1961; LL.D., Simpson Coll., Dr. Pub. Adminstrn., Parsons Coll., 1964; m. Vera Justus, Aug. 10, 1938; 1son, John J. Tchr., Peoria, 1935-41, elementary prin., 1941-43, asst. supt. schs., 1943-53; supt. schs., Downers Grove, Ill., 1953-57, Des Moines, 1957-64; dir. met. pub. schs. Nashville-Davidson (Tenn.) County, 1964-70; summer lectr. Bradley U., 1949, 50, U. Wyo., 1953, U. Miss., 1954, U. Colo., 1956, Drake U., 1961, 62, E. Carolina State Coll., 1963, 64. Dir. Greater Ia. Ins. Co., Des Moines. Mem. exec. bd. Tall Corn council Boy Scouts Am., 1959-70; mem. Child Welfare Bd., 1961-70; adviser to gov. Ia. Ednl. TV Bd., 1962-70. Bd. dirs. Coll. Osteopathic Medicine and Surgery, Jr. Achievement. Fulbright fellow in France, Finland, 1960. Mem. Am., Tenn. assns. sch. adminstrs., N.E.A., Tenn., Nashville edn. assns., Air Force Assn., Ia. Research Assn. (mem. bd.), Nashville C. of C., Phi Delta Kappa. Rotarian. Home: Nashville TN Died Jan. 2, 1970; buried Peoria IL

HARRIS, JOHN PETER, newspaper editor, pub.; b. Ottawa, Kan., Aug. 26, 1901; s. Ralph A. and Eleanor (Shiras) H.; Ph.B., U. Chgo., 1923; m. Sue Catherine Graham, Dec. 19, 1931 (dec. 1962); 1 son, John Graham; m. 2d, Rosalie Smyth O'Brien, November 21, 1964. Asso. editor Ottawa (Kan.) Herald, 1923-28; editor Chanute (Kan.) Tribune, 1928-33; editor, pub. Hutchinson (Kan.) News-Herald, now Hutchinson News, 1933-66, retired as editor of the editorial page, 1966; pub. Salina (Kansas) Journal, also editor Chanute Tribune, Ottawa Herald, Garden City Telegram, Burlington (Ia.) Hawk-Eye, Olathe (Kan.) News Spencer (Ia.) Reporter; chmn. bd. Pub. Enterprises, Inc.; pres. RB, Inc., Burlington, Ia., RF, Inc., Fairfield, Ia. Maj. AUS World War II. Mem. Am. Soc. Newspaper Editors, Internat. (past dir.), Am. (adv. bd.) press insts., Inland Daily Press Assn. (pres. 1958-59, dir. 1959-60, chmn. bd. 1959). Home: Hutchinson KS Died Apr. 13, 1969.

HARRIS, JULIA COLLIER, author; b. Atlanta, Ga., Nov. 11, 1875; d. Charles Augustus and Susie (Rawson) Collier; grad. Washington Sem., Atlanta; student Miss Chamberlayne's Sch., Boston, 3 yrs., Cowles Art Sch., 2 yrs.; course in sociology, U. of Chicago; m. Julian LaRose Harris; executive editor Chattanooga Times, Oct. 26, 1897. Wrote series of articles for New York Herald Syndicate, 1914; also series from Paris for same synidcate, 1919-20; contbr. articles on art and travel to New York Morning Telegraph, and Am. Magazine of Art. Author: Life and Letters of Joel Chandler Harris, 1919; Joel Chandler Harris—Editor and Essayist, 1931. Translator: The Foundling Prince, 1917. Asso. editor Enquirer-Sun, 1927-29; contributing editor Chattanooga Times. Home: 223 High St., Chattanooga TN‡

HARRIS, MATTIE POWELL, coll. pres.; b. Ga., d. William Anderson and Victoria (Gordon) H.; A.B., Wesleyan Female Inst., Staunton, Va. Pres. Virginia Coll. (founded by her father, 1893), 1895—. Episcopalian. One of lady managers Chicago Expn., 1893. Mem. Va. Assn. Schs. and Colleges, Nat. Economic League, Colonial Dames of Va., U.S. Daughters of 1812. Address: Virginia College Roanoke VA‡

HARRIS, MAY, writer; b. in Ala., Aug. 2, 1873; d. Joseph Archibald and India (Crenshaw) H.; ed. at home and under pvt. tutors; unmarried. Episcopalian. Contbr. short stories, essays and one-act plays to Harper's Mag., Harper's Bazar, the Atlantic, Lippincott's, American, etc. Home: Thornfield," Robinson Springs AL‡

HARRIS, NEWTON MEGRUE, banker; b. Champaign, Ill., July 27, 1872; s. Henry Hickman and Melissa M. (Megrue) H.; prep. edn., Lawrenceville (N.J.) Sch.; student U. of Ill., 1890-91; LL.B., Yale, 1895; m. Miss Burnham, Nov. 17, 1897 (died 1921); children—Bruce B., Barbara B. (Mrs. Ray F. Dobbins), Mary Julia (Mrs. D.C. Dodds); m. 2d, Mary E. Stedman, Oct. 24, 1927. With First Nat. Bank, Champaign, since 1895, pres. since 1921. Largely engaged in farming. Member Ill. Seniors Golf Assn., Kappa Sigma. Republican. Methodist. Mason (32 deg., Shriner). Clubs: Champaign Country; Union League, University (Chicago). Home: 603 W. Church St. Office: First Nat. Bank, Champaign IL*‡

HARRIS, NORMAN DWIGHT, coll. prof.; b. Cincinnati, O., Jan. 25, 1870; s. Norman Wait and Jacynthia (Vallandingham) H.; Ph.B., Sheffield Scientific Sch. (Yale), 1892; studied univs. of Chicago, 1894-95, Berlin and Leipzig, 1896-98; Ph.D., Univ. of Chicago, 1901; research work at Paris, London and Rome, 1901, 1905; m. Jane C., d. Dr. Z. H. Going, June 19, 1901 (dec.); m. 2d, Vera Going, d. Charles A. Going, Sept. 2, 1939. Instr. history, Evanston Acad., 1898-99; prof. history, Lawrence Coll., Appleton, Wis., 1902-06; prof. European diplomatic history, 1906-15; head dept. polit. sci. and prof. diplomacy and internat. law Northwestern U., 1915-29, now prof. emeritus. Mem. Col. House's com. gathering data for Peace Conference, 1917-18. Chairman board Daytona Beach (Fla.) Y.M.C.A. Trustee Chicago Training Sch. for Missionaries, and Wesley Memorial Hosp. Mem. Am. Polit. Science Assn. (exec. council, 1913-16), Am. Soc. Internat. Law, Am. Hist. Assn.; fellow Am. Geog. Soc., American Library Assn.; life mem. Art Inst., Chicago; contributing member of the Field Museum, Chicago. Republican. Methodist. Clubs: University (Evanston and Chicago); Yale (New York and Chicago); Rotary (Daytona Beach); American, Union Interalliee (Paris); Evanston Golf; Glen View (Chicago). Author: History of Negro Servitude in Illinois, 1904; Intervention and Colonization in Africa, 1914, revised edit., 1927; Europe and the East, 1925; Moving On," 1939; also numerous mag. articles. Home: 1134 Forest Av., Evanston, Ill.; and 1350 S. Peninsula Drive, Daytona Beach FL‡

HARRIS, PIERCE, clergyman; b. Rome, Ga., Sept. 21, 1895; s. Samuel A. and Lollie (Terry) H.; ed. Reinhardt Coll., Emory U.; m. Mary Smith, June 30, 1918. Pastor Chickamauga, Ga., Buford, Ga., Delton, Ga., St. Luke Methodist Ch., Columbus, Ga., Riverside Park Methodist Ch., Jacksonville, Fla., 1st Methodist Ch., Atlanta, Ga. Methodist. Columnist for Atlanta Journal, 1944-71. Home: Atlanta GA Died Jan. 14, 1971; buried Arlington Cemetery, Atlanta GA

HARRIS, ROBERT ALFRED, assn. exec.; b. Beloit, Wis., Mar. 28, 1905; s. William L. and Florence (Marlatt) H.; student N.M. Mil. Inst., 1924-26; grad. Engring. Mech., U. Notre Dame, 1926-28; m. Marguarite G. Gleeson, Dec. 28, 1929; children—Marguerite G. (Mrs. George Main), Rose Mary (Mrs. Gerard Gunter), Robert Alfred. Commd. 2d lt. U.S. Cavalry, 1928, advanced through grades to capt., 1933; tranferred to USAAF, 1933, advanced through grades to lt. col., 1946; transferred to USAF, 1947, advanced through grades to col., 1954; ret., 1958; mgr. Lake Worth (Fla.) C. of C., 1961-69. Bd. dirs. Community Fund, Lake Worth, 1964-69. Salvation Army, Lake Worth, 1964-69. Bd. dirs. Rehab. Center, Palm Beach County. Decorated Legion of Merit. Kiwanian (lt. gov. 1963-64). Home: Lake Worth FL Died Apr. 4, 1969; buried Palm Beach Meml. Gardens

HARRIS, RUTH MIRIAM, sch. adminstr.; b. Cin., Aug. 15, 1898; d. Rev. Henry Howell and Zelia M. (Ward) Harris; Ph.B. cum laude, U. Chgo., 1921; A.M., Columbia, 1929, Ph.D. 1940. Tchr. pub. elementary schs., St. Louis 1919-23, pub. high schs., 1924-25, Sumner Normal Sch., 1925-26; instr., dean of women, registrar Stowe Tchrs. Coll., St. Louis, 1926-40, pres., 1940-54; dir. edn. Bd. Edn. St. Louis, 1954; asst. supt. St. Louis pub. schs., 1962-72. Mem. Mayor's Race Commn., St. Louis, 1945-72. Named Woman of Achievement, St. Louis Globe Democrat, 1964. Mem. Alpha Kappa Alpha, Kappa Delta Pi, Pi Lambda Theta (nat. v.p.). Christian Scientist. Author: Teachers' Social Attitudes, 1940; Harriet Beecher Stowe Teachers' College and Her Predecessors, 1968. Home: University City MO Died Aug. 7, 1972; buried St. Peter's Cemetery, St Louis MO

HARRIS, SHERWIN BENTLEY, business exec.; b. N.Y.C., Jan. 17, 1909; s. Sherwin B. and Maude N. (Negley) H.; m. Selma Tilker, Jan. 10, 1948; son, Sherwin B. Successively financial dept., hdqrs. auditor, mdse. mgr. Gt. A & P Tea Co., 1929-40, nat. marketing and mdse., 1940-42; pres. Mary Lee Candies, Inc., 1946-51, chmn. bd., 1951-56; pres. Childs Co., Louis Sherry Co., 1951-54; pres. Holly Corp. and subsidiaries, 1954-60; chmn. Holly Minerals Corp. and subsidiaries, 1955-57, Mount Vernon Co. and subsidiaries, 1957-61, Canadian Holly Minerals Corp., 1956-61; pres., sr. partner Exec. Service Corp., mgmt. consultants, N.Y.C.; owner S.B. Harris Jr. & Assos., N.Y.C.; pres. Harris & Harris, mgmt. cons., N.Y.C., Computor Tutor Corp., New Rochelle, N.Y.; chmn. bd. Caribbean Material Supply Co., Inc., St. Croix. Home: Pelham Manor NY Died Oct. 9, 1970; buried Madison WI

HARRIS, STANLEY G., banking; b. Chicago, July 30, 1890; s. Norman W. and Emma (Gale) H.; B.A., Yale, 1912; m. Muriel Bent, June 1913; children—Charity, Ruth, Stanley G., Cynthia. With Harris Trust & Savings Bank, Chicago, 1912-71, last position director and Savings Bank, Chicago, 1912-71, last position director and chmn. board. Life trustee of Northwestern University. Member board of managers Presbyterian Hospital, also the YMCA. Republican. Mem. Winnetka Community Ch. Clubs: Union League, Chicago, University, Mid-Day, Indian Hill, Old Elm, Glenview (Chicago). Home: Winnetka IL Died May 17, 1971.

HARRIS, TITUS HOLLIDAY, neuropsychiatrist; b. Fulshear, Tex., Nov. 11, 1892; s. Dr. Robert Locke and Sallie Bright (Holliday) H.; A.B., Southwestern U., 1915, Doctor of Science (honorary), 1960; M.D., University of Texas, 1919; m. Laura Hutchings, Dec. 17, 1927; children—Mary Elizabeth, Titus, Ann Hutchings, Edward Randall. Intern John Sealy Hosp., Galveston, Tex., 1919-20; practiced medicine, Galveston, Tex., since 1920; instr. medicine U. of Tex., 1920-25, asso. prof., 1925-26, prof. and head dept. neurology and psychiatry, from 1926; ret. chmn. dept.

neurology and psychiatry U. Tex. Med. Br.; dir. div. psychiatric patients, John Sealy Hosp. since 1935; active in promoting mgmt. psychiatric patients in gen. hosps.; founder and editor nat. med. jour., Diseases of the Nervous System. Recipient Hogg Found. Award, 1955, E. B. Bowis award Am. Coll. Psychiatrists, 1965. Mem. Nat. Com. Alcoholism; dir. Med. Research Found. Tex. Mem. Nat. Multiple Sclerosis Soc. (med. adv. bd.), Am. Psychiatric Assn. (vice pres. 1960-61), Nat. Research Council (mem. of subcom. personnel training 1942-43, psychiatry, 1953-45), A.M.A., Central Neuropsychiatric Assn. (pres. 1936), Tex. State Med. Assn., Tex. Neuropsychiatric Assn. (pres. 1943-44), Tex. Soc. Mental Hygiene (pres. 1943), So. Psychiat. Assn. (president 1961-62), Am. Neurol. Assn. Democrat. Methodist. Asso. editor: Am. Jour. of Psychiatry. Contbr. articles to med. jour. Home: Galveston TX Died Apr. 22, 1969.

HARRIS, VICTOR, composer, conductor; b. New York, Apr. 27, 1869; s. Jacob H.; studied entirely in America; pupil of Fred Schilling in composition, William Courtney in singing, Anton Seidl in conducting; asst. to latter 2 yrs.; m. Catherine L. Richardson, June 20, 1916; children—Victor Stevens, Mary Grace, David Taylor, Cecelia. Conductor and vocal teacher at New York for 35 yrs.; now conductor St. Cecelia Club and Wednesday Morning Singing Club. Mem. Am. Acad. of Teachers of Singing. Composer of many songs heard in concerts, also choruses, etc. Home: 405 Park Av. Studio: 140 W. 57th St., New York NY‡

HARRIS, WADE N., business exec.; b. Buffalo, Feb. 17, 1906; s. Sherwin B. and Maud A. (Negley) H. Sr.; B.S., Cornell University, 1925; m. Hazel M. Meyer, November 29, 1934; children—Patricia Ann (Mrs. Frank T. White), Barbara Gene. Director and manufacturing vice pres. Brunswick-Balke-Collender Co., Chicago, 1942-48; automotive operations mgr., The Murray Corp. of Am., Detroit, 1948-50, v.p. automotive operations, dir., 1950-54; exec. v.p. The Midland Steel Products Co. (name changed to Midland-Ross Corp. 1957), Cleve. 1954-56, pres., dir., 1956-65, chairman of board, 1965-67; director of Cleveland-Cliffs Iron Company. Nat. City Bank of Cleve., Corporate Resources, Inc., Standard Oil Co. (Ohio), N. Am. Coal Corporation, Jones & Laughlin Steel Corporation, Sherwin-Williams Company, Midland-Ross Corporation. Vice pres. United Appeal Greater Cleve., 1963-64, pres., 1965; trustee St. Luke's Hosp., Lutheran Hospital, Fenn. Coll., Case Inst. Tech., Ednl. Research Council, U. Circle Devel. Found.; mem. adv. com. The Stouffer Prize, also Cleveland Plan; trustee, member of the executive board of the Greater Cleveland Council Boy Scouts Am.; mem. bus. adv. council Natural Sci. Mus. Member Cleve. Devel. Foundation, Cleve. C. of C. (dir.). Mason (Shriner). Clubs: Cleveland Athletic, Union, Pepper Pike, Mayfield Country (Cleve.); Detroit Athletic, Detroit Golf, Recess (Detroit); Century (Muskegan, Mich.); City (Oswosso, Mich.); Ottawa Shooting (Fremont, O.). Home: Shaker Heights OH Died Aug. 8, 1967.

HARRIS, WINDER RUSSELL, ex-congressman; b. Raleigh, N.C., Dec. 3, 1888; s. Charlotte Lea Meares, 1915; 4 daughters. Sports editor Raleigh Times, 1908; successively sports editor Charlotte (N.C.) News, news editor Spartanburg (S.C.) Herald, state news editor Charlotte Observer, mng. editor Charlotte Evening Chronicle, telegraph editor Raleigh News and Observer, mgr. United Press Bur., Raleigh, news editor Richmond Virginian, news editor Newport News, Times-Herald, city editor Norfolk Virginian-Pilot; mem. staff Universal Service, Washington, D.C., 1918-25 (rep. with presidential nominees, Cox, 1920, LaFollette, 1924, also with Harding and Coolidge); asst. sec. Am. del. to Internat. Narcotics Congress, Geneva, 1924-25; mng. editor Virginian-Pilot, 1925-41; v.p. Shipbuilders Council Am., 1944-58; editor Alexandria Jour., Arlington Jour., Fairfax County Jour.-Standard, 1958-64. Elected to 77th Congress, Apr. 1941, to fill unexpired term of Colgate Darden, Jr., resigned; mem. 78th Congress (1943-45), 2d Va. Dist. Democrat. Home: Alexandria VA Died Feb. 24, 1973.

HARRISON, ALFRED CRAVEN, JR., explorer; b. Phila., Dec. 14, 1875; s. Alfred C. and Kate De Forest (Sheldon) H.; ed. Episcopal Acad., Phila., and St. Paul's Sch., Concord, N.H.; (hon. B.S., U. of Pa.); m. Marie M. Gibson, of Frankfort, Ky., Jan. 5, 1904. Engaged in scientific research, archaeology, anthropology, geography from 1896; expdn. to Spanish Honduras to ruins of Copan, 1896; explorations in Borneo and from Peking to St. Petersburg, via China, Gobi Desert, Mongolia and Siberia, 1897-9; exploring Naga Hills and trip to India, Afghanistan, Cashmere, Upper and Lower Burma, Cochin China and Japan, and investigating the Veddahs of Ceylon, 1900; exploring in Sumatra, 1901-2, sugar planter in Cuba since Jan., 1903. Mem. Royal Geog. Soc., Anthropol. Inst. of Great Britain, Acad. Natural Sicences, Phila., Societe de Geographie de France, Asiatic Soc. of Japan, Nat. Geog. Soc. Club: Rittenhouse (Phila.). Home: Philadelphia PA‡

HARRISON, BENJAMIN FRANKLIN, state budget officer; b. Indian Ty., Jan. 21, 1875; s. Hilburn and Sarah (Colbert) H.; A.B., Trinity Coll. (now Duke U.), Durham, N.C.; m. Grace Liegerot, of Tonkawa, Okla., Dec. 28, 1911; children—Betty Ann, Benjamin F. Mem. Okla. Ho. of Rep., 1907-08, 09, 15, 19, 21; sec. of state, Okla., 1911-15; state budget officer, Okla., 1923-35. Mem. Phi Alpha Theta. Democrat. Mem. Christian (Disciples) Ch. Mason, Odd Fellow. Home: Atwood OK‡

HARRISON, DESALES, sales exec.; b. Atlanta, July 13, 1899; s. James Lawrence and Kathleen (Mecaslin) H.; student Marist Coll., 1913-16; Oglethorpe U., 1917-18; m. Virginia Wyatt Pegram, June 6, 1923; children—DeSales, Virginia (Mrs. Jack Friling), Robert Pegram, Nancy Knight (Mrs. Keith S. Latimore). Salesman various cos., 1919-20; head advt. dept. The Coca-Cola Co., Atlanta, 1925-30, regional mgr. Southeastern Region, New Orleans, 1930-33, v.p. Central Region, Chgo., 1933-34, v.p. in charge of Fountain Sales Div. U.S., 1934-41; chmn. adv. com., dir. Coca-Cola Bottling Co. (Thomas), Inc.; dir. other cos., The Alabama Gt. So. R.R. Interstate Life & Accident Ins. Co., Am. Nat. Bank & Trust Co. Pres. YMCA Chmn. Bd. dirs. Meml. Hosp., Community Found. Greater Chattanooga, Inc.; trustee Benwood Found., Inc. Served to comdr. USNR, 1942-45, H.I., Okinawa, Mem. Am. Soc. Sales Execs., Newcomen Soc. N. Am., Kappa Alpha. Episcopalian. Clubs: Nine O'Clocks, The Fifty Club, Piedmont Driving (Atlanta); Mountain City, Lookout Mountain-Fairyland. Rotary (Chattanooga). Home: Lookout Mountain TN Died Feb. 21, 1973.

HARRISON, GEORGE BILLINGSLEY, banker; b. Howard Co., Mo., Oct. 23, 1870; s. George B. and Louan (Birch) H.; A.B., Pritchett Coll., Glasgow, Mo., 1888; m. Adelaide Ligon, of Honey Grove, Tex., Mar. 4, 1891; children—E. Birch, Ruth (Mrs. John A. Armstrong). Began with Glasgow Savings Bank, 1888, asst. cashier, 1891-1901; cashier New England Nat. Bank, 1901-10, v.p., 1910-14; moved to Upland, Calif., 1914, Denver, Colo., 1926; became pres. Denver Nat. Bank, 1926, now retired; dir. Los Angeles Branch of Federal Reserve Bank, 1925-26. Pres. Mo. Bankers' Assn. 1900. Mason. Address: 6344 Muirlands Drive, La Jolla CA‡

HARRISON, GEORGE MCGREGOR, labor leader; b. Lois, Maries County, Mo., July 19, 1895; s. Louis Harvey and Mary Logan (Coppedge) H.; ed. pub. schs.; m. Averil Mayo Hughes, Oct. 16, 1912; children—Virginia May, Elynor Alma, Mary Jane. Railway clk., 1909-17; local chmn. Brotherhood of Ry. Clerks (St. Louis), 1917-18; gen chmn. Brotherhood of Ry. Clerks of Mo.P. R.R., 1918-22; v.p. Grand Lodge of Brotherhood of Ry. Clerks, 1922-28, pres., 1928-63, chief executive officer, 1963-65, grand president emeritus, from 1965; vice pres. of the American Federation of Labor; chmn. Ry. Labor Executives Assn., 1935-40; dir. Brotherhood of Ry. Clerks Nat. Bank, 1928-43; mem. editorial com., Labor (weekly newspaper). Served on draft com. U.S. Social Security Act, 1934; mem. of Pres.'s Com. on Indsl. Analysis; participated in drafting R.R. Retirement Act, 1937; mem. Joint R.R. Labor-Management Com. on War Effort; mem. Nat. Defense Mediation Bd., 1945; mem. exec. com. Pres.'s Management-Labor Com., 1945; asst. to dir. of Econ. Stblzn. Adminstrn. and asst. to dir. of O.D.M., 1951-52; mem. President's Adv. Com. on Labor-Mgmt. Policy; chmn. labor div. nat. citizens com. internat. cooperation ICY, 1965-66; mem. exec. bd. ICFTU, from 1966. Former pres. Workers Education Bureau; mem. com. on public debt Twentieth Century Fund, Inc.; mem. Com. on Population Redistribution. U.S. delegate, American National Com., Third World Power Conf.; pres. and dir. Brotherhood of Ry. Clerks Bldg. Co.; Am. Labor delegate Governing Bd. Internat. Labor Orgns., Geneva, 1936; Am. Labor delegate Internat. Labor Orgns., Conf. of American Nations, Havana, Cuba, 1939; mem. Presidents Ry. Investigation Com., 1938-39; U.S. del. 13th Gen. Assembly UN, 1958. Chmn. adv. com. on labor policy Nat. Dem. Adv. Council, 1958. Mem. bd. dirs. Franklin D. Roosevelt Meml. Found.; dir. Arthritis and Rheumatism Found.; trustee Harry S. Truman Library, John F. Kennedy Library Corp. Mem. Am. Assn. for UN (dir. 1958), Am. Arbitration Assn. Home: Cincinnati OH Died Nov. 30, 1968; buried Rest Haven Memorial Park.

HARRISON, HAMLETT, lawyer, ins. exec.; b. Dallas, July 25, 1910; s. Edward Tyler and Jessie May (Board) H.; A.B., Yale, 1932; LL.B., cum laude, So. Meth. U., 1935; m. Martha Davis, Oct. 17, 1935; children—Shannon, Carol. Admitted to Tex. bar, 1935, practiced in Dallas, from 1935; gen. counsel Trinity Universal Ins. Co. since 1939, exec. v.p., dir., 1942-70; exec. v.p., dir. Security Nat. Fire Ins. Co., 1942-70; dir. Republic Nat. Bank of Dallas. Served as lt., U.S.N.R., World War II. Mem. Am., Tex., Dallas bar assns., Phi Alpha Delta. Home: Dallas TX Died Mar. 2, 1970; buried Restland Meml. Park, Dallas TX

HARRISON, HARRY P., lyceum mgr.; b. near Grinnell, Ia., Aug. 1878; s. Daniel B. and Elizabeth (Holland) H.; student Cornell Coll., Ia., 1900-03; student law dept., U. of Chicago, 1903-05; m. Etta Parsons, June 21, 1911. Began with Redpath Lyceum Bur., 1901; purchased Slayton Bur. and consolidated same with Redpath, 1910, later acquired Central Bur.; now treas. and gen. mgr. Redpath Lyceum Bur. Founded Talk of the Hour Clubs, 1942. President Village of Kenilworth, 1933-40. Trustee Cornell College; trustee Union League Foundation for Boys Clubs. Director of Cherry Growers, Incorporated. Chief of division of admission, Century of Progress Expn., 1933, 34. During World War chmn. exec. com. Am. Red Cross Nat. Speakers' Bur., exec. chmn. mil. entertainment council War Dept. Commn. on Training Camp Activities, and exec. chmn. Nat. Smileage Book Campaign. Republican. Conglist. Mason. Clubs: Union League, Press. Co-author: Culture Under Canvass, 1958. Home: Leland MI Died Jan. 1968.

HARRISON, IKE H(ENRY), univ. dean; b. San Marcos, Tex., Dec. 20, 1909; s. Ike Henry and Jessie (O'Bannon) H.; A.B., Southwest Tex. Tchrs. Coll., 1929; B.B.A., U. Tex., 1933, M.B.A., 1934; Ed.D., N.Y.U., 1942; M. Anne Randolph, Aug. 25, 1939; 1 son, Ike Henry III. Asst. prof. bus. East Tex. State Coll., 1935-36; prof. bus. adminstrn. Houston State Tchrs. Coll., 1936-46; dean Sch. Bus. U. Houston, 1946-47, Tex. Christian U., 1955-71; vis. prof. N.Y.U., 1937-38, Harvard Graduate School Bus. Administrn., 1962. Served as colonel USAAF, 1942-46, 47-54. Mem. Am. Mgmt. Assn., Am. Marketing Assn., Am. Statis. Assn., Am., So. econs. assns., So. Case Writers, Am. Soc. Quality Control, Sigma Nu. Co-author: Business Policy Cases with Behavioral Science Implications. Home: Ft Worth TX Died Feb. 15, 1971.

HARRISON, JAMES D., banker. Chmn. exec. com., dir. Central Savings Bank, Balt.; dir. J.S. Young Co., Balt., W.D. Byron & Sons, Hagerstown, Md., Hagerstown Shoe Co.; chmn., dir. First Nat. Bank of Md., Balt. Home: Ruxton MD Died Apr. 1972.

HARRISON, JOHN SMITH, author; b. Orange, N.J., Feb. 3, 1877; s. William Ogden and Lottie Ann (Smith) H.; A.B., Columbia, 1899, A.M., 1900, Ph.D., 1903; m. Elisabeth Shepard Southworth, June 27, 1907; children—William Ogden (dec.), Ada Deane, Thurston, Edward Woodberry, Virginia (dec.), Thomas Southworth. Fellow in comparative lit., Columbia, 1900-01; lecturer in English lit., before Teachers' Assn., of Brooklyn, 1902; substitute teacher in English, New York pub. schs., 1903; instr. English, 1903-07, asst. prof., 1907-16, Kenyon Coll., Gambier, O.; professor English, Butler College, 1916-46. Prof. English, summer session, Columbia U., 1917. Awarded Columbia University medal for distinguished service as man of letters and teacher of English literature," 1940. Mem. Modern Lang. Assn., Woodberry Soc., Phi Beta Kappa (Columbia Chapter). Club: Indianapolis Literary. Author: Platonism in English Poetry of the 16th and 17th Centuries, 1903; The Teachers of Emerson, 1910; The Vital Interpretation of English Literature, 1928; Types of English Poetry, 1941. Home: 347 N. Audubon Rd., Indianapolis IN‡

HARRISON, SHELBY MILLARD, b. Leaf River, Ill., Feb. 15, 1881; s. James Franklin and Mary Ellen (Helman) H.; A.B., Northwestern U., 1906; postgrad. work, Boston U., 1906-07, in economics and sociology, Harvard U., 1907-09, A.M., 1909; LL.D., Northwestern U., 1932; Litt.D., Boston University, 1942; married Patti Rodgers, November 19, 1910; children—James Shelby, Rodger Scott. Staff Pittsburgh Survey, 1908; staff Russell Sage Found., 1912-47, vice gen. dir., 1924-31, gen. dir., 1931-47; member board Child Welfare League of Am., Nat. Social Welfare Assembly; exec. dir., Babe Ruth Found., 1948-49; mem. national com. Midcentury White House Conf. on Children and Youth, 1950; bd. Sirovich Day Center, N.Y., from 1958. Chmn. Central dept. research and survey, Nat. Council Chs. Christ in U.S.A., 1951-54; com. Nat. Emergency Services. Mem. President's Research Com. Recent Social Trends, 1929-33. Recipient Northwestern University Merit award, 1940. Fellow A.A.A.S., American Sociological Soc.; member American Statis. Assn., N.Y. Acad. Pub. Edn., Am. Pub. Health Assn., Nat. Conf. Social Welfare (pres. 1941-42), Social Science Research Council, Y.M.C.A. Research Council, Nat. Budget Com., Family Service Assn. of Am. (mem. bd. 1955-58), National Assn. Social Workers, Beta Theta Pi, Phi Beta Kappa. Methodist. Clubs: Nat. Arts, Gipsy Trail, Harvard, Quill (N.Y.). Author: The Disproportion of Taxation in Pittsburgh, 1914; Social Conditions in an American City, 1920. Joint Author: City and Co. Administration in Springfield, Ill., 1947; Public Employment Offices—Their Purpose, Structure and Methods, 1924; Welfare Problems in New York City (with Allen Eaton), 1926; A Bibliography of Social Surveys (with same), 1930; American Foundations for Social Welfare (with F. Emerson Andrews), 1946. Home: New York City NY Died Aug. 5, 1970.

HARRISON, WARD, consulting engr.; b. East Orange, N.J., May 16, 1888; s. George K. and Abby Augusta (Ward) H.; M.E., Stevens Inst. Tech., 1909; hon. D.I.Eng., Case School Applied Science, 1940; m. Dorothy Fuller, June 12, 1913; children—Dorothy (Mrs. Wm. R. Van Aken), Cornelia (Mrs. Wm. L. Schlesinger), John Ward. Was with General Electric Co., 1909-48, dir. engring., Lamp Dept., 1930-48; chairman of Curtis Lighting, Incorporated, 1955-59; member board of directors Thompson Electric Co.;

inventor and designer many types lighting equipment for industrial, commercial and street lighting. Supervising engr., representing U.S. Fuel Adminstrn. in N.E. Ohio, World War I. Mem. advisory committee fluorescent lighting fixture industry, War Production Bd., World War II. Pres. Internat. Commn. on Illumination (24 countries), 1951-55; vice chmn. Adv. Com. on Fine Arts, Cleve.; mem. Cleve. Met. Service Commission, 1956-59. Gold medalist, Illuminating Engrs. Soc., 1949; Distinguished Service award Cleveland Tech. Socs. Council, 1950; Stevens Inst. Silver Medallion, 1950. Fellow Am. Inst. E.E., Illuminating Engring. Soc. (v.p., 1913-15; pres. 1922-23); mem. British Illuminating Engrs. Society (hon.), Assn. Francaise des Eclairagistes; Cleveland Engring Soc. (v.p. 1937), Sigma Xi, Tau Beta Pi. Rep. Presbyn. Author: Electric Lighting, 1921. Coauthor: Street Lighting Practice, 1929. Contbr. many tech. papers in Elec. World, Procs. Illuminating Engring. Soc., etc. Chmn. com. that prepared Charters on Light (text-book). Address: Shaker Heights OH Died Jan. 24, 1970; buried Lakeview Cemetery, Cleveland OH

HARRISON, WILLIAM GROCE, physician; b. Talladega County, Ala., Apr. 29, 1871; s. John Tinsley and Sarah Simmons (Groce) H.; B.Sc., Ala. Poly. Inst., Auburn, Ala., 1890; student Vanderbilt U., 1890-91; M.D., U. of Md., 1892; post-grad. work, Johns Hopkins, Harvard and Vienna, Austria, Dr. Ophthalmology, U. of Colo., 1916; m. Lula Marcia Bondurant, Aug. 19, 1896; children—Emily Bondurant (dec.), Tinsley Randolph, William Groce, Louise Dabney, Alexander Bondurant (dec.), Sarah Elizabeth. Began practice at Talladega, Ala., 1894; moved to Birmingham, 1905; prof. ear, nose and throat diseases, Birmingham Med. Coll., 1912-15; lecturer on history of medicine, Vanderbilt Univ. School of Medicine, 1929-40; retired 1943. Fellow American College of Surgeons; mem. American Medical Association, Medical Assn. State of Ala. (pres. 1930-31), Am. Acad. Ophthalmol. and Oto-Laryngol., Am. Laryngol., Rhinol. and Otol. Soc., Southern Med. Assn. (v.p. 1930-31), Sigma Alpha Epsilon. Democrat. Methodist. Clubs: Quid Pro Quo, Country. Contbr. on diseases of eye, ear, nose and throat to med. jours. Home: 4142 Cliff Rd., AL‡

HARRON, MARION JANET, judge; b. San Francisco, Sept. 3, 1903; d. Charles Merrill and Minnie Jane (Little) Harron; A.B., U. Cal., 1924, J.D., 1926. Teaching fellow, U. Cal., 1924-26; staff Cal. Minimum Wage Commn., 1925; admitted to Cal. bar, 1926, U.S. Supreme Ct. bar, 1938; dir. Survey of Labor Laws in N.Y. State, Nat. Indsl. Conf. Bd., N.Y.C., 1926-27; mem. faculty Inst. of Law, Johns Hopkins, 1928; gen. practice of law, 1929-33; asst. counsel NRA, Washington, 1933-35; regional custodian of rehab. corps. Resettlement Adminstrn., Berkeley, Cal., 1936; judge U.S. Tax Ct., 1936-70. Mem. Fed. Bar Assn., Bar Assn. San Francisco, Internat. Fedn. Women Lawyers, Nat. Lawyers Club, Am. Assn. U. Women, Nat. Assn. Women Lawyers, Woman's Nat. Dem. Club, Phi Beta Kappa, Delta Sigma Tho, Phi Delta Delta. Democrat. Conglist. Author: Current Research in Law (1928-29), 1929. Washington DC Died Sept. 26, 1972.

HARROW, BENJAMIN, chemist; b. London, Eng., Aug. 25, 1888; s. Emil and Erna H.; student Finsbury Coll., London, 1904-06; B.S. (chem.), Columbia, 1911, A.M., 1912, Ph.D., 1913; m Carolyn Solis, July 1917; 1 dau., Margaret. Came to U.S., 1907, naturalized, 1913. Was assistant in organic chemistry, Clark U.; asst. physiol. chemistry, Columbia, 1912-13; asst. prof. biochemistry, Fordham Med. Sch., 1913-14, asso. in physiol. chemistry, Coll. Physicians and Surgeons (Columbia), 1914-28; asst. prof. chemistry, Coll. City of New York, 1928-33, asso. prof. of chemistry, 1933-39, professor since 1939, chairman of department since 1944. Instructor O.T.C., 1917-18. Mem. Am. Chemical Society, Am. Assn. Advancement of Science, Harvey Soc., Soc. for Exptl. Biol. and Med. N.Y. Acad. Med., Am. Society Biol. Chemists, Biochem. Society, Royal Society Arts (Eng.), Sigma Xi. Author books including: Laboratory Manual of Biochemistry (with Drs. G.C.H. Stone, H. Wagreich, E. Borek, A. Mazur), 1940, 2d edit., 1944; also research publs. Editor of Contemporary Sci. in Modern Library, 1921; A Text-Book of Biochemistry (with Dr. C.P. Sherwin), 1935; Casimir Funk, 1955. Home: New York City NY

HARSH, DAVID NEWBY, lawyer, banker, statesman; b. Gallatin, Tenn., Sept. 30, 1897; s. George and Thankful (Barry) H.; LL.B., Cumberland U., 1917; m. Helen Russ Westervelt, Oct. 15, 1919; children—Jane (Mrs. Edward Vieh, Jr.), David Newby, George Westervelt, Ruth (Mrs. Lukin Taylor Gilliland). Admitted to Tenn. bar, 1917; practice in Memphis, 1917-56; partner firm Harsh & Harsh, 1917-27; partner Harsh, Harsh & Harsh, 1927-43; partner Harsh, Pierce, Cochran, Rickey & Carey, 1943-56; chmn., commr. finance, purchases, personnel Shelby County (Tenn.) Commn., 1956-62, ret., 1962; partner Harsh, Harsh & Crawford, Memphis. Co-owner, v.p., dir. Nat. Mfg. Co., Georgian Woods, Inc., Desoto Land Co.; dir. First Nat. Bank of Upper Keyes, Barrow-Agee Co., Barrow-Agee Labs.; asso., atty. Stewart Bros. Hardware Co. Mem. Tenn. Defense Commn., 1940-42; chmn. Memphis Bd. Adjustment, 1939-55; mem. Memphis Planning Commn., 1939-55; chmn. Shelby County Planning Commn., 1939-55; chmn. Shelby County Bd. Adjustment, from 1965. Vice pres. Heart Assn. Upper Keys (Miami). Served to 2d lt., F.A., U.S. Army, 1918. Mem. Am. Legion (past mem. exec. com. from Tenn.), National Association of Real Estate Boards, S.A.R., Isaac Walton League. Democrat. Conglist. Mason (Shriner). Clubs: Rivermont (Memphis), Islamorada Fishing (pres., dir.). Author: Private Acts of Shelby County, 1960. Initiated before U.S. Supreme Ct. case requiring all states to reapportion their legislatures. Home: Islamorada FL also Memphis TN Died Jan. 12, 1972; buried Memphis Meml. Park, Memphis TN

HART, HARRIS, educator; A.B., Richmond College; post-grad. work, University of Chicago and Harvard. Began as teacher elementary sch.; teacher and prin. high sch., Roanoke, Va., 1900-09; supt. schs., Roanoke, 1909-18; state supt. instrn., Va., 1918-31; v.p. Johnson Pub. Co., Richmond, 1931-38; pres. The Baughman Stationery Co., since 1938. Formerly mem. of State Bd. Examiners of Teachers, Va. Address: 1101 E. Main St., Richmond VA‡

HART, HENRY HERSCH;, b. San Francisco, Calif., Sept. 27, 1886; s. Henry and Etta (Harris) H.; A.B., U. of Calif., 1907, J.D., 1909; studied Chinese and Japanese under native teachers; m. Alice Patek Stern, 1912 (deceased, September 18, 1936); children—Peggy H. (deceased April 7, 1952), and Alice Virginia (Mrs. Virginia H. Page, dec.); m. 2d, Helen K. Ach, Aug. 21, 1941. Practiced law in San Francisco, Calif., 1909-19; asst. city attorney, San Francisco, 1911-18; collected Oriental art for collectors, 1922-37; lecturer on Chinese and allied subjects and on comparative religion and literature since 1915, at San Francisco State College, since 1960; lectr. on Chinese art and culture U. Cal., 1933-36; lectr. U. Cal. Extension Div., 1932-60; U. Cal., 1960-68; lectr. on circuit W. Colston Leigh, Inc. since 1950; radio and TV; vis. lectr. numerous orgns., clubs, and univs. on oriental fields, traveled extensively in Far East; mem. executive board Temple of Religion, Golden Gate Internat. Exposition, 1940-41. With U.S. Postal Censorship, 1942; on active duty maj. corps Military Police, A.U.S., service in U.S.A., Africa and India, 1943; special adviser, Office War Information, 1944. Recipient several decorations, 1923, including: Chevalier Order White Elephant of Cambodia (France), 1923; collar and gold medal of mem. Instituto de Coimbra (Portugal), 1941. Licenciate in pharmacy, Cal. Fellow Royal Geog. Society, London, Royal Asiatic Soc.; mem. Hispanic Soc. Am. (corr.), profl. sci. and cultural socs. and assns., U.S., several fgn. countries including Linschoten Vereeniging (Amsterdam), Friends of the Library, San Francisco (pres. 1951-58). Clubs: Faculty (University of Calif.); Commonwealth, Roxburgh (San Francisco); Calif. Writers. Author and translator numerous works relating to China and Portugal, latest being: Sea Road to the Indies (voyages of the Portuguese), 1950. English edit. 1952, German and Polish transls., 1960; Poems of the Hundred Names, 1954; Venetian Adventurer (Marco Polo) in Bantam Biographies, 1956, Spanish, German and Polish transls., 1960; Luis De Camoens and the Epic of the Lusiads, 1962. Joint author: Tamalpais—Enchanted Mountain, 1946. Contbr. articles to Asia, Japan. Home: San Francisco CA Died Dec. 18, 1968.

HART, HENRY MELVIN, JR., lawyer, educator; b. Butte, Mont., Dec. 25, 1904; s. Henry Melvin and Mary (Tyson) H.; A.B. summa cum laude, Harvard, 1926, LL.B. magna cum laude, 1930, S.J.D., 1931; LL.D., Columbia, 1954; m. Mary Jane White, Dec. 3, 1932; 1 dau., Elizabeth Tyson. Admitted to D.C. bar, 1939; law clk. to Justice Brandeis, U.S. Supreme Ct., 1931-32; asst. prof. Harvard Law Sch., 1932-37, professor, 1937-69, Dane professor of law, 1960-69; head attorney with Office U.S. Solictor Gen., 1937-38; spl. asst. assigned to immigration and naturalization service, U.S. Atty. Gen., 1940-41; asso. gen. counsel OPA, 1942-45; gen. counsel, Office Econ. Stblzn., 1945-46; Julius Stone visiting professor at the Ohio State University, 1954-55. Recipient Presdl. Certificate of Merit, 1947. Author: (with Herbert Wechsler) The Federal Courts and The Federal System, Cambridge MA Died Mar. 24, 1969.

HART, JOHN MARION, lawyer; b. Prince Edward County, Va., Jan. 2, 1867; s. John Marion and Fanny Sanford (Smith) H.; student Hampden-Sidney Coll., Va., 1882-86; B.L., U. of Va., 1890; m. Carrie Overton Harris, May 9, 1895; children—Marion Sanford, Margaret Lynn, Lewis. Began practice at Roanoke, Va., 1890; associated in practice with bro. as Hart & Hart, 1896-1922; mem. Bd. of Aldermen, Roanoke, 1903-08; mem. Va. Senate 2 terms, 1908-14; del. Dem. Nat. Conv., Baltimore, 1912; collector internal revenue Western Dist. of Va. by appmt. of President Wilson, 1914-18; apptd. judge of Corp. Court of Roanoke City, by gov. of Va., 1922; elected to same office by legislature 1923, for term ending Feb. 1, 1925, and reelected for term of 8 yrs., ending Jan. 1933; again in practice of law, 1933; revenue commr., Roanoke, since Nov. 1933. Mem. Kappa Sigma. Presbyterian. Home: 1202 2d St., S.W. Office: Municipal Bldg., Roanoke VA‡

HART, JOHN NATHANIEL, indsl. mfg. exec.; b. Chesterhill, O., Nov. 30, 1909; s. Hiram and Lucy (Hambleton) H.; B.S., Ohio State U., 1931, M.A., 1932; m. Gertrude Fox, Oct. 21, 1933; children—Benson, Hannah, Sarah, John. Instr. Ohio State U., 1933-43; dir. research Ohio Dept. Taxation, 1933-43; economist B.F. Goodrich Co., Akron, O., 1945-52, dir. personnel Akron operations, 1952-53, dir. employee relations, 1953-57, controller, 1957-71, vice president, 1960-71; member board directors B.F. Goodrich Canada, Limited, Goodrich Company, Ltd., Ameripol, Inc., B.F. Goodrich Internat. Finance Co. Trustee of Akron Art Inst. Served to lt. USNR, 1943-45. Mem. Financial Execs. Inst., Am. Econ. Assn., Am. Statis. Assn., Child Welfare League Am. (trustee), Delta Tau Delta. Clubs: Akron City, Portage Country (Akron). Home: Hudson OH Died Dec. 8, 1971.

HART, PERCIE (WILLIAM EDWARD), author; b. Halifax, N.S., Jan. 27, 1870; s. A.W. and Maria Wylde (Cunningham) H.; high sch. edn.; m. Annie Louise Stimis, of Newark, N.J., Aug. 11, 1891. Author: The Ludovic Zam Affair, 1901; Hart's Yarns (2 vols.) 1903; Jason—Nova Scotia, 1904; Pleasures Passed Along, 1906; The Plespasalongos Organized, 1907; Ease of Body, 1908. Contbr. short stories, etc., to mags. Club: Press. Editor Ease," mag., and propr. Ease House (sanitorium). Pub. lecturer upon ease." Address: Worcester, Mass., and Crystal Springs FL‡

HART, SIMEON THOMPSON, prof. adminstrn. engring.; b. Farmington, Conn., Feb. 3, 1878; s. John Hooker and Mary Ann (Thompson) H.; student U. of Wis.; B.S., Purdue; M.E., 1911; m. Maude Lee Clark, June 26, 1910; children—Jascah S., S. Willard, Margaret M., Nancy K., Frederick W.; m. 2d, Lenore Zerch, Dec. 26, 1938. Asst. supt., Morgan Machine Co., Rochester, N.Y., 1909-11; supt., Hartford Special Machinery Co., Hartford, Conn., 1911-15; asst. prof., W.Va. U., 1915-20; prof., adminstrn. engring., Syracuse U., head of dept., 1940-70. Mem. A.S.M.E. (chmn.). S.A.M., Phi Kappa Phi, Sigma Iota Epsilon, Alpha Phi Omega. Republican. Conglist. Club: Technology (pres.). Home: Syracuse NY Died June 14, 1970; buried Syracuse NY

HART, THOMAS CHARLES, naval officer; b. at Davidson, Mich., June 12, 1877; s. John Mansfield and Isabella (Ramsay) H.; grad. U.S. Naval Acad., 1897, Navy War Coll., 1923, Army War Coll., 1924; m. Caroline Brownson, Mar. 30, 1910; children—Isabella, Roswell Roberts, Thomas Comins (died 1945), Caroline Brownson, Harriet Taft. Commd. ensign U.S. Navy, 1899, and advanced to captain, Apr. 1, 1918; rear admiral, Sept. 1929. Served in Cuban waters, Spanish-Am. War; comdr. submarines, waters of British Isles and Azores, World War; in Office of Operations, Navy Dept., 1919-20; comdr. U.S.S. Beaver and Asiatic Submarine Flotilla, 1920-22; capt. U.S.S. Mississippi, 1925-27; supervisor N.Y. Harbor and comdr. Torpedo Sta., Newport, R.I., 1927-29; comdr. submarines, Atlantic and Pacific, 1929-31; supt. U.S. Naval Acad., 1931-34, comdr. cruisers Scouting Force, 1934-36; mem. Gen. Bd., 1936-39; comdr. in chief Asiatic Fleet, July 1939-June 1942; comd. allied naval forces in Far East, Jan.-Feb. 1942; retired for age, being 1 yr. overtime, June 30, 1942, and recalled to active service Gen. Bd., July 1942; on inactive list, Feb. 1945. Apptd. U.S. senator from Conn.; served until Dec. 1946, did not stand for election. Awarded Distinguished Service Medal (U.S.), 1918 and again 1942. An Act of Congress, June 1942, provided for retention of rank of adm. when retired. Clubs: University, Adirondack League, New York Yacht (New York); Sharon (Conn.) Country; Army and Navy (Washington); Chevy Chase (Md.). Home: Sharon CT Died July 4, 1971; buried Arlington Nat. Cemetery, Arlington VA

HART, THOMAS PATRICK, editor; b. Cincinnati, O.; s. Thomas and Bridget (Craven) H.; A.B., St. Xavier Coll., Cincinnati, 1886, A.M., 1890, Ph.D., 1891; M.D., Med. Coll. of Ohio (now dept. of U. of Cincinnati), 1887 (class orator); m. Mary Byrne, of Cincinnati, Aug. 16, 1888. Began practice in Cincinnati, 1887; mng. editor The Catholic Telegraph, and pres. The Catholic Telegraph Pub. Co., 1898-1937, now editor emeritus. Charter mem., Catholic Press Assn. of U.S. (pres. 1917-20). Mem. Cincinnati Acad. Medicine. Democrat. K. C., Elk. Club: Duckworth. Home: 446 E. 5th St., Cincinnati OH‡

HART, WALTER MORRIS, prof. English; b. Phila., Pa., Nov. 23, 1872; s. William Robards and Harriet Newell (Willcox) H.; A.B., Haverford Coll., 1892, A.M., 1893, LL.D., 1931; LL.D., University of California, 1944; studied in Europe, 1893-95; A.M., Harvard, 1901, Ph.D., 1903; m. Agnes Borland, Dec. 28, 1898 (died April 30, 1945), Inst. English philol., 1895-1900, 1903-04, asst. prof., 1904, asso. prof., 1910, prof., 1918-43, U. of Calif.; dean summer session, 1916-23; dean of the university, 1923-30, and v.p., 1925-30, professor emeritus since 1943. Member Modern Language Association of America, Philological Assn. of Pacific Coast (ex-pres.), Calif. Branch English-Speaking Union (pres. 1932-38), Phi Kappa Sigma, Phi Beta Kappa. Clubs: University, Harvard Chit Chat (San Francisco); Berkeley, Faculty (pres

1918-30 and 1931-34); Century (New York). Author: Ballad and Epic—A Study in the Development of the Narrative Art, 1907; Kipling, the Story Writer, 1918. Editor: Shakespeare's Twelfth Night, 1912; English Popular Ballads, 1916. Contbr. papers on Chaucer, mediaeval literature, etc. Home: 1401 Le Roy Av., CA‡

HART, WILLIAM LINCOLN, judge; b. Salineville, O., Feb. 5, 1867; s. Benjamin F. and Ariel (Dreghorn) H.; A.B., Mt. Union Coll., 1896, LL.D., 1929; LL.B., University of Mich., 1897; m. Ida B. Caskey, Sept. 15, 1897 (died Dec. 27, 1947); children—Ian Bruce, Wm. Lincoln, Jr.; married 2d Nova E. Westfall. Admitted to Ohio bar, 1897, and since practiced at Alliance; elected judge Supreme Court of Ohio (short term), 1934; reelected, 1938, 1944, 1950, lecturer on international law and internat. relations, Mt. Union Coll., also trustee. Recipient Distinguished Alumni Service Award, U. Mich., 1948. Mem. Am. Law Institute, Am. Bar Assn., Ohio Bar Assn. (pres. 1923-24), Stark Co. Bar Assn., Mich., Union, Soc. Mayflower Descendants (counsellor Ohio soc.), Sons Union Vets. of Civil War. Republican. Mem. Alpha Tau Omega; Delta Theta Phil Methodist. Mason. Clubs: Rotary, Wranglers. Author: Silas Hart and His-Descendants, 1942. Home: 135 Overlook Dr., Alliance, O. Office: Judiciary Bldg., Columbus OH‡

HARTE, EMMET FORREST, writer; b. East View, Ky., Nov. 17, 1876; s. Doctor Mosby and Lillian Belle (Franklin) H.; Central Christian Coll., Albany, Mo., 1895, 96; m. Bertha Alma Henshaw, of Albany, Mo., July 2, 1899; children—Kathleen Elaine, Phyllis Jacqueline. Began as writer of fiction, 1907; has contributed about 300 short stories, and two serials, to 20 Am. mags.; contributed 75 stories to Railroad Man's Magazine, 1908-17; later work devoted to serious psychol. and philos. themes in fiction field; mng. editor, Ill. Central Magazine, 1925-27. Mason. Christian Scientist. Author: Honk and Horace, 1913. Home: Thorntown IN‡

HARTE, HOUSTON, newspaper pub.; b. Knobnoster, Mo., Jan. 12, 1893; s. Edward Stettinius and Elizabeth (Houston) H.; student U. of Southern Calif., 1912-13; B.J., U. Mo., 1915; LL.D., Austin Coll., 1950, Tex. Technol. Coll., 1958; m. Caroline Isabel McCutcheon, Mar. 26, 1921; children—Edward Holmead, Houston Harriman. Reporter Los Angeles (Calif.) Examiner, 1912-13; pub. Knobnoster Gem, 1914; business mgr. Mo. Republican, Boonville, 1915, editor and pub., 1916-20; pub. San Angelo (Tex.) Evening Standard, 1920-62, San Angelo Standard-Times, 1928-62; mem. Harte, Hanks & Co. (pubs. San Angelo Standard (Morning), San Angelo Standard-Times (Evening), Abilene Reporter-News, Corpus Christi Times, Corpus Christi Caller, Paris Evening News, Big Spring Herald, Marshall News-Messenger), Denison Herald, Greenville Herald-Banner, San Antonio Express and Evening News; dir. Times Pub. Co., Wichita Falls, Bryan Daily Eagle, Corsicana Daily Sun, Commerce Jour., Huntsville Item. Mem. Texas Industrial Commission. Pres. Concho Valley Council Boy Scouts Am., 1932-35; mem. Tex. Relief Commn., 1933-35; v.p. Asso. Press, 1935-36, dir. 1937-43, 1st v.p., 1943-46; pres. Texas Pubs. Assn., Inc. Served as 2d lt., later 1st lieutenant and discharged as captain inf., U.S. Army, 1918-19. Dir. Texas Tech. Coll., 1926-33. Mem. West Tex. C. of C. (pres. 1931), Alpha Delta Sigma, Sigma Delta Chi, Delta Upsilon. Awarded medal of honor, Sch. of Journalism, U. of Mo., 1931. Democrat. Presbyn. Clubs: San Angelo Country, San Angelo, River. Editor: In Our Image. Home: San Angelo TX Died Mar. 13, 1972.

HARTE, RICHARD, mfg. exec.; b. Phila., Feb. 1, 1894; s. Dr. Richard H. and Marie (Ames) H.; A.B., Harvard, 1917; LL.D., Bethany College, 1939; m. Mabel Webster, Aug. 16, 1917 (dec.); children—Jane (Mrs. Thomas Hyde Choate), Richard, Nancy (Mrs. Wm. R. W. Fitz), Oliver Ames. Vice pres. Stone & Webster, Inc., 1926-31; pres., dir. Ames Shovel & Tool Co., 1934-70; dir. Nat. Steel Corp., B. & O. R.R. Served as 1st lt., U.S. Army, World War I. Trustee Marietta Coll., Retina Found.; dir. Nat. Indsl. Conf. Bd., So. States Indsl. Council. Mem. bd. aldermen, Newton, Mass., 1928-32; pres. Parkersburg (W.Va.) Community Chest, 1932. Mem. Am. Hardware Mfrs. Assn. (pres. 1940-42), Harvard Alumni Assn. (dir.), W.Va. C. of C. (pres. 1937-41). Republican (chmn. nat. finance com. for W. Va. 1936-52, mem. nat. program com. 1938). Home: Brookline MA Died Mar. 16, 1970.

HARTER, DOW W(ATTERS), ex-congressman; b. Akron, O., Jan. 2, 1885; s. Josiah J. and Anna Lillian (Watters) H.; LL.B., U. of Mich., 1907; m. Winifred Marie Cole, 1911; children—Harry Allan, John David. Began law practice at Akron, O., later practiced at Washington, D.C.; member 73d to 77th Congresses (1933-43), 14th Ohio Dist. Mem. Ohio State Bar Assn., Am. Bar Assn., D.C. Bar Assn. Democrat. Episcopalian. Mason. Clubs: Akron City, Univ., National Press, The Metropolitan (Washington), Portage Country. Home: Washington DC Died Sept. 4, 1971.

HARTHORN, DREW THOMPSON, educator; b. N. Livermore, Me., June 1, 1871; s. William M. and Martha E. (Wyman) H.; A.B., Colby Coll., Waterville, Me., 1894, A.M. from same coll., 1897, L.H.D., 1926; m. Edith S. Vaughan, of Wilton, Me., July 7, 1897; children—Ruth Emily, Mary Wyman (dec.), Clara Martha. Prin. Wilton (Me.) Acad., 1894-1905, Rumford Falls High Sch., 1905-07; again prin. Wilton Acad., 1907-12; prin. Coburn Classical Inst., 1912—. Mem. Legal Advisory Com., World War; four minute speaker. Mem. N.E. Assn. Colls. and Prep. Schs., N.E.A., Me. Teachers' Assn., Delta Kappa Epsilon. Republican. Baptist. Mason. Rotarian. Lecturer on ednl. topics. Home: Waterville ME‡

HARTIGAN, RAYMOND HARVEY, chemist; b. Rensselaer, N.Y., Sept. 2, 1915; s. Raymond A. and Nettie M. (Green) H.; B.S., Rensselaer Poly. Inst., 1937, M.S., 1939, Ph.D., 1941; m. Kathryn P. Comerford, Nov. 29, 1941; children—M. Janice, Donna M., Rana Rae. Asst. instr. chemistry Rensselaer Poly. Inst., 1937-41; indsl. fellow Mellon Inst., Pitts., 1941-47, sr. fellow, 1947-50, adminstrv. fellow, 1951-52, asst. dir. research, 1952-55, dir. research, 1955-58; vice president research and development Foster Grant Co., Inc., Leominster, Mass., 1958-61; dir. research div. Rensselaer Poly. Inst., 1961-65; v.p. research and devel. div. Nat. Dairy Products Corp., 1965, pres. of research and development division, 1965-71; v.p. Kraftco Corp., 1971; pres. Rensselaer Research Corp., 1964-65; instr. Pa. State U. Extension, evenings 1942-44, Carnegie Inst. Tech., evenings 1946-48; asst. mgr., mgr. lab. sect., research dept. Koppers Co., 1950. Alumni trustee Rensselaer Poly. Institute, 1958-61; mem. plastics engrng. adv. com. Lowell Tech. Inst., 1958-61; food industries adv. com. Nutrition Found. Fellow N.Y. Acad. Sci.; mem. Am. Dairy Sci. Assn., Am. Chem. Soc., A.A.A.S., Rensselaer Alumni Assn. (past dir.), Soc. Chem. Ind., Inst. Food Tech., Ind. Research Inst., Nat. Conf. Adminstrn. Research, Sigma Xi, Phi Lambda Upsilon. Methodist. Clubs: Sunset Ridge Country (Winnetka, Ill.); Chemists, Engineers' (N.Y.C.). Home: Lake Forest IL Died July 28, 1971; buried Lake Forest Cemetery, Lake Forest IL

HARTINGER, WILLIAM CALVERT, clergyman; b. Middleport, O., Mar. 26, 1875; s. William Merrill and Mary Mildred (Covert) H.; student Ohio Wesleyan U., 1894-97; Boston U. Sch. of Theology, 1898-1900; Drew Theol. Sem., Jan.-May 1900; D.D., W.Va. Wesleyan Coll., 1917, Ohio Wesleyan U., 1922; m. Lulu May White, May 1, 1900; children—Mildred May (dec.), Helen. Ordained M.E. ministry, 1900; pastor Glenwood, Columbus, O., 1900-03, 1st Ch., Pataskala, O., 1903-06, Trinity Ch., Portsmouth, O., 1906-12 (100,000 ch. built and 1,000 members added), Thomson Ch., Wheeling, W.Va., 1912-16 (125,000 ch. built), 1st Ch., Charleston, W.Va., 1916-21, 1st ch., Columbus, O., 1921-24; supt. Columbus Dist. Ohio Conf. M.E. Ch., 1924-30; pastor Boradway M.E. Ch., Indianapolis, 1930-32; supt. Indianapolis Dist., Ind. Conf. M.E. Ch., 1932-40; hospital minister and field secretary, Indianapolis Methodist Hospital, Oct. 1940-47; retired, June 22, 1947-January 25, 1949; asso. pastor N. Meth. Ch., Indianapolis, since Jan. 1949. Mem. Gen. Conf. M.E. Church as del. from West Virginia Conf., 1920, reserve del. from Ohio Conf., 1924, chmn. delegation from Ohio Conf., 1928, del. from Ind. Conf., 1936 (chmn. itinerancy com. of gen. conf.); del. from Ind. Conf. to Uniting Conf. Meth. Ch., 1939 (vice chmn. on membership and temporal economy, chmn. sub-com. on membership); del. to Gen. Conf. Meth. Ch., 1940; to North Central Jurisdictional Conf., Methodist Ch., 1940; del. to Gen. Conference of Methodist Church, 1944; delegate to North Central Jurisdictional Conf., Meth. Ch., 1944; mem. bd. mgrs. Bd. of Foreign Missions M.E. Ch., 1928-32; mem. Bd. Home Missions and Ch. Extension M.E. Ch., 1936-40; mem. bd. mgrs. Bd. of Missions and Ch. Extension of Methodist Ch. (mem. exec. com. Gen. Bd., also mem. exec. and finance coms. of the Foreign Division); chmn. bd. of ministerial training, Indiana Conf.; dean Indiana Conf. Summer School of Ministerial Training; dean Indianapolis Area Meth. Sch. of the Prophets. Del. to Foreign Missions Conf. Chs. and World Peace, 1929; del. Delaware Conf. on Christian Basis of World Order, 1943; mem. Hdqrs. Com. of Ohio Anti-Saloon League, 1924-30; trustee Ohio Wesleyan U., Ohio Ann. Conf. M.E. Ch., White Cross Hosp (Columbus)—all 1924-30; chmn. bd. control South Side Settlement House, 1924-30; dean Epworth League Inst. O. Conf., Lancaster Camp Ground, 1927-29; trustee Indianapolis Methodist Hosp., Evansville Coll.; dir. City Council and Ch. Extension Soc., Goodwill Industries, Preachers' Aid Soc., Ind. Conf. of Meth. Ch. Lecturer on ednl. and social topics. Home: 36 W. Hampton Drive, Indianapolis 8 IN‡

HARTLEY, CHARLES PINCKNEY, corn expert; b. Ripley Co., Ind., July 7, 1870; s. William Lynn and Lucy Jane (Vines) H.; B.Sc., Kan. State Agrl. Coll., 1892, M.Sc., 1899; m. Anna Gano Brigham, of Watkins, N.Y., July 25, 1905. Taught sch. in Ida., 1892-7; asst. in horticulture and instr. mathematics, Kan. State Agrl. Coll., 1897-9; in charge of investigations regarding corn improvement, Bur. Plant Industry, U.S. Dept. of Agr., since 1899. Fellow A.A.A.S.; charter mem. Am. Breeders' Assn.; mem. Bot. Soc. Washington. Congregationalist. Author: Injurious Effects of Premature Pollination, 1902; Broom Corn, 1903; Corn Growing, 1904; Production of Seed Corn, 1905; Harvesting and Storing Corn, 1907; Cross Breeding Corn, 1911; Popcorn, 1913. Also articles and repts. Home: 3420 Center St., N.W. Address: U.S. Dept. Agr., Washington‡

HARTLEY, FRED ALLAN, JR., congressman; b. Harrison, N.J., Feb. 22, 1903; s. Fred Allan and Frances Alice H.; ed. high sch., Kearney, N.J., and Rutgers U.; m. Hazel Lorraine Roemer, Jan. 30, 1921; children—Henry Allan, Frances Lorraine, Fred Jack. Library commr., Kearny, 1923-25, police and fire commr., 1925-29; mem. 71st and 72d Congresses (1929-33), 8th N.J. Dist., and 73d to 80th Congresses (1933-49), 10th N.J. District. Republican. Protestant. Mason, Elk, Eagle. Home: Kearney NJ Died May 1969.*

HARTLEY, LESLIE POLES, novelist; b. Whittlesea, Eng., Dec. 30, 1895; s. Harry Bark and Mary (Thompson) H.; student Harrow Sch., 1910-15, Balliol Coll., 1919-22; B.A., Oxon, 1922. Author: Night Fears (short stories), 1924; Simonetta Perkins, 1925; The Killing Bottle (short stories), 1932; The Shrimp and the Anemone, 1944; The Sixth Heaven, 1946; Eustace and Hilda, 1947; The Boat, 1949; The Travelling Grave (short stories), 1951; My Fellow Devils, 1951; The Go-Between, 1953; The White Wand (short stories), 1954; A Perfect Woman, 1955; The Hireling, 1958; Facial Justice, 1960; Two for the River, 1961; The Brickfiled, 1964; The Betrayal, 1966; Poor Clare, 1968; The Collected Short Stories of L.P. Hartley, 1968; The Love-Adept, 1969; My Sister's Keeper, 1969; Mrs. Cataret Receives, 1970; The Harness Room, 1971; The Collections, 1971. Served in Brit. Army; 1916-18. Decorated comdr. Order Brit. Empire. Recipient James Tait Black Meml. prize, 1948; W. H. Heineman Found. award Royal Soc. Lit., 1954. Fellow Royal Soc. Lit. Clubs: Athenaeum; Beefsteak. Home: Bath England Died Dec. 13, 1972.

HARTLEY, LOWRIE C., civil engr.; b. Masontown, W.Va., Dec. 29, 1871; s. S. W. and Wilhelmina (Menear) H.; Ohio State U., 2 yrs., spl. course in engring.; m. Eva Grimes, of Uniontown, Ohio, 1900; children—Lois, Margaret, Wilma. Signalman, 1898-1900, asst. on engring. corps, 1900-04, asst. engr. maintenance of way, 1904-07, Pittsburgh, Cincinnati, Chicago & St. Louis Ry.; signal engr., 1907-10, engr. maintenance of way, 1910-11, chief engr., since July 1911, Chicago & Eastern Ill. R.R. Presbyn. Clubs: Chicago Engineers', Ridge Country. Home: 6731 Clyde Av. Office: 6600 So. Union Av., Chicago IL‡

HARTLEY, ROBERT WILLARD, research adminstr.; b. Dayton, O., Mar. 24, 1911; s. Robert Groves and Lillian (White) H.; student U. Cin., 1929-30; B. Archtl. Engring., Ohio State U., 1933; grad. student Am. U., 1937-38; m. Virginia Fox, Jan. 25, 1941. With City Dayton and Montgomery County, Ohio, 1933-34; mem. Ohio Relief Commn., 1934-35; chief fed. program sect. Nat. Resources Planning Bd., 1935-43; budget examiner Bur. Budget, 1943-44; exec. asst. to spl. asst.. to sec. state, 1944-46; sr. staff mem. Brookings Instn., 1946-55, dir. internat. studies, 1955-57, v.p., 1957—. Tech. expert U.S. delegation UN Conf. Internat. Orgn., San Francisco, 1945, adviser gen. problems U.S. delegation 1st Gen. Assembly, London, Eng., 1946. Bd. trustees, exec. com. Fed. Woman's Award, 1960—. Mem. Council Fgn. Relations, Am. Polit. Sch. Assn., Washington Institute Foreign Affairs, also Delta Chi, Tau Beta Pi. Episcopalian. Clubs: University (Washington and N.Y.C.); Metropolitan (Washington). Contributor of articles to professional jours. Editor: Current Developments in U.S. Foreign Policy, 1948-51; asso. editor: America's Needs and Resources, rev. edit., 1955. Home: Washington DC Died Mar. 27, 1971; buried Riverview Cemetery, Portland OR

HARTMAN, CHARLES WILLIAM, univ. dean, pharmacist; b. Shawmutt, Ala., May 8, 1924; s. Andrew Nelson and Sadie (Lee) H.; B.S. in Pharmacy, U. Ga., 1950, M.S. in Pharm. Chemistry, 1953; Ph.D. in Pharmacy, U. Fla., 1956; m. Ruby Haralson, June 23, 1946; children—Charles William, Janice Lee. Mem. faculty U. Ga., 1949-60, asso. prof. pharmacy, 1956-60, chmn. div. pharmacy and pharmacy adminstrn., 1960; dean Sch. Pharmacy, U. Miss., from 1961. Dir. research Inst. Pharm. Scis., from 1961; dir. Bur. Pharm. Services, from 1962. Bd. dirs. Miss. Assn. mental Health. Served with USNR, 1943-45. Mem. Am., Miss. (exec. com.) pharm. assns., Am. Soc. Hosp. Pharmacists, Sigma Xi, Kappa Psi, Phi Kappa Phi, Gamma Sigma, Gamma Phi, Rho Chi. Home: University MS Died Apr. 17, 1970.

HARTMAN, ERNEST HERMAN, county ofcl.; b. Oshkosh, Neb., Feb. 15, 1893; s. Herman S. and Katherine (Cornish) H.; student pub. schs.; m. Martha Wattenbarger, Oct. 15, 1916; s. Raymond S., Hazel (Mrs. Jame W. Spriggs), Henry L., Verda (Mrs. James Hoyt), Vera (Mrs. Elliott Buckman), (twins). Dep. county assessor Freemont County, Wyo., 1924-28, assessor, 1928-67. Democrat. K.P. (trustee). Home: Lander WY Died Aug. 26, 1967.

HARTMAN, FRANK ALEXANDER, prof. physiology; b. Gibbon, Neb., Dec. 4, 1883; s. George

Washington and Flora (Sprague) H.; A.B., U. of Kan., 1905, A.M., 1909; Ph.D., U. of Wash., 1914; m. Anna Caroline Botsford, Feb. 10, 1906; children—William Brewster, Warren Elmer, Donald George, Flora Lilian (Mrs. Milton Victor Jones), Mary Louise (Mrs. Merrill H. Barnebey). Teacher in high school, Beardstown, Illinois, 1906, Wichita, Kansas., 1906-08, Seattle, Wash., 1908-14; Austin teaching fellow, Harvard Med. Sch., 1914-15; lecturer in physiology, Toronto Univ., 1915-18, asst. prof., 1918-19; prof. physiology and head dept., U. of Buffalo, 1919-34; research professor, Ohio State Univ., from 1948. Awarded Chancellor's medal, U. of Buffalo, 1932; gold medal by A.M.A., 1932; Schoellkopf medal by Western N.Y. Sect. of Am. Chem. Soc. Fellow A.A.A.S.; mem. Am. Physiol. Soc. Soc. Exptl. Biology, Am. Soc. Zoologists, Am. Chem. Soc., Assn. for Study Internal Secretions (pres. 1935), A.M.A., Ohio Acad. Science, Sigma Xi, Phi Lambda Upsilon, Phi Beta Kappa, Alpha Omega Alpha. Unitarian. Co-author (book) The Adrenal Gland. Contbr. to scientific jours. Home: Columbus OH Died Mar. 21, 1971.

HARTMAN, JOHN A., steel co. exec.; b. Detroit, 1907. Treas., Detroit Steel Corp. Home: Detroit MI Died June 20, 1967; buried Holy Sepulchre Cemetery.

HARTMAN, LOUIS FRANCIS, educator; N.Y.C., Jan. 17, 1901; s. Louis Francis and Josephine (Grennan) H.; student Mt. St. Alphonsus Sem., Esopus, N.Y., 1922-28; Licentiate Sacred Scripture, Pontifical Bibl. Inst., Rome, Italy, 1932, Licentiate Oriental Langs., 1936. Entered Congregation Most Holy Redeemer, 1922; prof. sacred scripture Redemptorist Sem., Esopus, N.Y., 1932-34, 1936-48; asst. prof. semitics Cath. Univ., 1948-52, asso. prof., 1952-62, prof., 1962-70, head Semitic dept., 1965-67; exec. sec. Cath. Bibl. Assn. Am., 1948-70; annual professor American Schools of Oriental Research in Jerusalem, Jordan, 1959-60. Chmn. editorial board new translation Cath. Bible in English, 1948-70; chmn. com. for nat. observance 500th anniversary Gutenberg Bible, 1952. Mem. American Oriental Society, American Schools Oriental Research, Society Biblical Literature. Author: Encyclopedic Dictionary of the Bible, 1963. Staff editor New Cath. Ency., 1962-66. Contbr. articles profl. jours. Home: Washington DC Died Aug. 22, 1970; buried Mt. St. Alphonsus Sem. Cemetery, Esopus NY

HARTMAN, SARA, journalist; b. Niagara Falls, Can., 1872; d. J. J. and Sara H.; grad. St. Catharines, Ont., Collegiate Inst.; unmarried. Editor and publisher Gulf Messenger, illustrated monthly, San Antonio, Tex., and New Orleans, 1890-5; edited and published Fad, a bibelot, 1895-7; edited dept. of San Francisco Post, devoted specially to women's clubs and general literary matters, 1897-9; left San Francisco May, 1899, to accompany Marie Robinson Wright, as her sec., to S. America, to write a series of S. Am. books. Address: Care G. Barrie & Sons, 1313 Walnut St., Philadelphia‡

HARTMANN, (CARL) SADAKICHI, author; b. Nagasaki, Japan, Nov. 8, 1869; s. Oskar and Osadda H.; ed. Hamburg and Kiel, Germany, 1873-81; studied Spring Garden Inst., Phila., 1882-83; N.Y. Sch. of Artist-Artisans, 1891; m. Elizabeth Blanche Walsh, of New York, 1891; children—Atma Dorothy (Mrs. Otis Hurst), Nurva (Mrs. William J. Gallagher), Paul Walter, Marion (dec.), Edgar Allan. Came to U.S., 1882; naturalized, 1894. First European corr. for S. S. McClure Syndicate, 1893-07; writer for N.Y. Staats Zeitung, 1897-1903; with Carnegie Art Inst., 1907-08; asso. with late Elbert Hubbard, 1912-14, Douglas Fairbanks, 1923, Republican. German Lutheran. Author: (dramas) Christ, 1893; Buddha, 1897; Confucius, 1923; Moses, 1934; (art books) Shakespeare in Art, 1900-1936; Japanese Art, 1901-1920; History of Am. Art, 1935; Am. Sculpture, 1904 (poetry) Drifting Flowers of the Sea, 1906; My Rubaiyat, 1926; Tanka and Haikai, 1926; (miscellaneous) Passport to Immortality, 1927; Seven Short Stories, 1930; My Crucifixion, 40 Years of Asthma, 1931. Home: Banning CA‡

HARTMANN, WILLIAM V., oil exec.; b. Cincinnati, O., Sept. 12, 1871; s. Philip H. and Louise (Jaup) H.; ed. Franklin School, Cincinnati, O.; m. Elizabeth Hopkins, Oct. 24, 1894. Clerk, Alexander McDonald & Co., Cincinnati, O., 1888-92, merged with Standard Oil Co., 1892, asst. agt. of latter, Evansville, Ind., 1893-1903; salesman Gulf Refining Co., New York, 1903-05, asst. gen. sales mgr., Pittsburgh, 1905-12, gen. mgr., 1912-29, v.p. in charge of sales since 1929; dir. Gulf Oil Corp., Gulf Refining Co., Gulf Exploration Co., Gulf Research & Development Co. Mem. Am. Petroleum Inst. (dir.). Dir. Homewood Cemetery, Pittsburgh. Republican. Episcopalian. Clubs: Duquesne, Pittsburgh Athletic Assn. (Pittsburgh); Fox Chapel Golf (Pittsburgh). Home: Schenley Apts. Office: Gulf Bldg., Pittsburgh PA*‡

HARTSFIELD, WILLIAM BERRY, lawyer, cons.; b. Atlanta, Mar. 1, 1890; s. Charles Green and Victoria (Dagnall) H.; educated in public schools and business college, Atlanta; studied law in law office; married Pearl Williams, August 2, 1913; children—William Berry, Mildred; m. 2d, Mrs. Tollie Tolan, July 11, 1962; one adopted son, Carl Hartsfield. Admitted to Georgia State bar, 1917, practice in Atlanta 1917-71; cons. Ford Foundation, also various Atlanta corporations. Member of City Council, Atlanta, 1923-28, State Legislature, Georgia, 1933-36; mayor Atlanta, 1937-61; mem. Am. (past pres.), Ga. (past pres.) municipal assns., U.S. Conf. Mayors, Ga. State Bar Assn., Atlanta Lawyers Club, S.E. Fair Assn. (pres.). Mason. Baptist. Club: Capital City. Home: Atlanta GA Died Feb. 22, 1971; buried West View Cemetery, Atlanta GA

HARTT, MARY BRONSON, writer; b. Ithaca, N.Y., Mar. 23, 1873; d. Prof. Charles Frederick (of Cornell U.) and Lucy Cornelia (Lynde) H.; grad. Buffalo Sem., 1890. Contbr. World's Work, Outlook, Scribner's, Everybody's, Century, etc. Editor Museum News, and acting editor Museum Work, 1924-26. Club: Pen and Brush. Address: 607 W. 137th St., New York NY‡

HARTZ, WILLIAM HOMER, mfr.; b. Tarrytown, N.Y., Dec. 11, 1887; s. Irving Thomas and Lillian Ione (Terhune) H.; B.S., Purdue U., 1907; married Bertha Blanchard Mead, April 25, 1917; children—William Homer, Jr., Betty Mead (Mrs. R. W. Allen). With Morden Frog and Crossing Works, manufacturers of railway track materials, 1911-48, vice president, 1927-30, pres., 1930-48, ret.; pres. Cooke Electric Refrigerator Co., 1930-44; mem. Ill. adv. bd. Am. Mutual Liability Ins. Co., 1940-45, dir. 1945-70; director American Mutual Ins. Co. of Boston. Chmn. ind. com. Ill. Indsl. Progress Commn.; 1941-42; dist. coordinator, defense contract and priorities division Chgo. area OPM, 1941; mem. exec. com. Chgo. Com. of Nat. Def., 1942-45; vice chmn. ind. mem. 6th Regional War Labor Bd., 1941-46; employer mem. Chgo. area War Manpower Commn., 1941-46; mem. Regional Labor Mgmt. Adv. Com. VI, 1946-47; mem. adv. bd. Greater Chgo. Safety Council, 1942-48; treas. Am. Action, 1946-48. Director Ill. Mfrs. Assn., 1930-41, pres., 1939-40, chairman, 1941; dir. C. of C. of U.S., 1942-50; past pres. Chicago Heights (Illinois) Manufacturers Assn., Nat. Ry. Appliances Assn.; past chmn. Manganese Track Soc. Mem. bd. govs. Henrotin Hosp., 1943-53; v.p. Chgo. Bd. Edn., 1948-53. Mem. Delta Upsilon. Republican. Episcopalian. Club: White Lake Golf (dir. 1950—). Home: Ponte Vedra Beach FL Died Nov. 16, 1970; buried Warren Smith Cemetery, Jacksonville Beach FL

HARTZELL, THOMAS B., oral surgeon; b. Beloit, O., June 8, 1866; s. John C. and Louisa A. (Thompson) H.; student Mount Union (O.) Coll.; D.M.D., U. of Minn., 1893, M.D., 1894; m. Maud Berry, Jan. 18, 1899; children—John Berry, Elizabeth Mary. Practiced, Minneapolis, Minn., since 1895; prof. mouth infections, Coll. of Medicine and Surgery, and prof. oral surgery, Coll. of Dentistry, U. of Minn. Chmn. Research Commission of Am. Dental Assn. Pres. Am. Acad. of Periodontology, 1940; mem. com. on legislation and enrollment of dental committee, Gen. Med. Bd. of Council Nat. Defense, 1917. Mem. medical sect. Nat. Research Council; dir. of research in Minnesota for Am. Dental Assn. since 1914; research consultant, Dental Dept., U.S. Bur. Pub. Health, Washington, D.C. Mem. of Nat. Dental Assn. (pres. 1921-22), Minn. State Med. Assn., Phi Delta Theta, Delta Sigma Delta, Sigma Xi. Mason. Clubs: Minneapolis, Minikahda, Lafayette, Minneapolis Athletic, Automobile of Minneapolis. Home: 2508 Pillsbury Av. Office: Physicians and Surgeons Bldg., Minneapolis MN*‡

HARVEY, HOLMAN, writer; b. Washington, Aug. 5, 1894; s. Frederick L. and Pamela D. (Holman) H.; Jr.; student George Washington U., 1912; m. Marie Baylor 1917 (dec.); 1 dau., Barbara H. (Mrs. Morgan Greenwood); m. 2d, Dorothy Hoffman, 1920 (dec.); children—Frederick H., Dean H. (dec.); m. 3d, Phoebe A. Guthrie, Nov. 15, 1941. Reporter, Washington Times, 1913-15; Washington corr. United Press, 1915-18; dir. information FTC, 1919; U.S. editor in chief Cross-Atlantic Newspaper Service 1920; reporter Phila. Enquirer, 1922; roving reporter N.Y. Evening Mail, 1922-23; nat. dir. publicity Hearst mags., N.Y.C., 1925-30; publishers rep., N.Y.C., 1931-34; nat. dir. Mark Twain Centennial Com., 1935; nat. mag. writer, 1936-44; staff writer Readers Digest, 1944-73; assignments to Africa, Mediterranean, Europe, 1951-52, to Italy, 1964-65. Mem. Acad. Polit. Sci. Episcopalian. Clubs: Nat. Press (Washington); Overseas Press (N.Y.C.); Press (London, Eng.). Contbr. articles mags. Address: Charleston SC Died Mar. 10, 1973.

HARVEY, JEAN CHARLES, writer, journalist; b. Murray Bay, Que., Can., Nov. 10, 1891; s. John and Mina (Trudell) H.; student Chicoutimi Coll., 1905-08, Jesuit's Coll., Montreal, 1908-14; B.A., Laval U., Montreal, 1914; m. Eve Pelland; children—Carmen, Claire (Mrs. F. M. Trentham), Jeanne (Mrs. Thola Theilhaber), Charles M., Claude E., Marcel, F. Axel. Reporter La Patrie, daily, Montreal, Que., 1915, La Press, daily, 1916-18; publicity mgr. Nat. Farming Machinery, Montmagny 1919-21; reporter, asst. chief editor, parliamentary corr., le Soleil, Quebec City, 1922-27, chief, 1928-34; chief statistician, P.Q., 1934-37; founder, editor Le Jour, solit. and lit. weekly Montreal, 1937-46; radio producer, commentator, Canadian Broadcasting Corp., CKAC, Montreal, 1946-53; editor Le Petit Jour. Photo-Jour., weeklies, Montreal, 1953-66. Decorated Officier d'Academie (France). Clubs: Twenty, Men's Press. Author: Marcel Faure, 1922; Pages de Critque, 1926; L'Homme qui Va..., 1929; Les Demi-Civilises, 1934; Sebastian Pierre, 1935; Art et Combat, 1938; Eternal Struggle, 1943; Les Paradis de Sabie, 1953; La Fille du Silence (poems), 1958, Pourquoi je suis antisparatiste, 1962; Visages du Quebec, 1965; Des Champs, des bois, des bettes, 1965. Home: Montreal Quebec Canada Died Jan. 1967.

HARVEY, JOHN (LACEY), lawyer; b. Pittsylvania County, Virginia, October 19, 1899; s. Walter Cabbell and Julia Katherine (Brumfield) H.; student William and Mary Coll., 1915-17, U. Richmond, part time 1919-20, Va. Poly. Inst., 1920-21, Tulane U., 1921-23; m. Diana Maria Hewlett, Feb. 2, 1922 (deceased, 1931); married second, Laurene Lillian Russell, May 20, 1937; children—Richard R., Susan L. Insp. Va. State Bd. Health and U.S.P.H.S., 1919-20; food and drug insp. U.S. Bur. Chemistry, 1925; insp. U.S. Food and Drug Adminstrn., 1927-30, asst. dist. chief western dist., 1930-34, dist. chief 1937-48, chief Seattle sta., 1934-37, dir. litigation, Washington, 1948-49, dir. regulatory management, 1949-51, asso. commr. food and drugs 1951-54, dep. commr., 1954-65; counsel law firm Counihan, Casey & Loomis, Washington, 1966-71; mem. adv. panel, Food Additives WHO, UN, Geneva, Switzerland. U.S. Pres. Codex Alimentarius Commn. of WHO-FAO, Rome-Geneva. Chmn. Real Estate and Govt. Space Com., San Francisco Bay Area. World War II. Served in U.S. Army, France, World War I; res. officer, ret. Mem. Food and Drug Ofcls. U.S., Res. Officers Assn., Seattle Acad. Sci. Club: Nat. Lawyers (Washington). Home: Arlington VA Died Mar. 29, 1971.

HARVEY, KENNETH G., bank executive; born Wauneta, Neb., Apr. 2, 1900; s. George C. and Cora (McCallum) H.; grad. Creighton U. Law Coll., Omaha, Neb., 1926; m. Marguerite Martin, Jan. 29, 1927; children—Meroe Lou, Julia Ann, Jack Kenneth. Banker, credit mgr., lawyer, pres. of finance co., pres. of bank, cattle feeder, farmer; pres. Douglas Co. Bank, Omaha, Neb. since 1942; chmn. Douglas County Savs. Bonds Com. Mem. C. of C. (past pres.), Neb. Children's Home Soc. (past pres.). Methodist. Clubs: Athletic, Country, Happy Hollow, Plaza (Omaha). Home: Omaha NE Died Mar. 11, 1967.

HARVEY, LILLIAN A. (MRS. RAYMOND F. HARVEY), dean nursing; b. Holland, Va.; d. John Henry and Clara (Boone) Holland; grad. Lincoln Sch. for Nurses, N.Y.C., 1939; B.S., Columbia, 1944, M.A., 1948; m. Raymond F. Harvey, May 24, 1946; children—Linda Kathleen, Paul, Peter. Formerly asst. instr. anatomy and physiology Lincoln Sch. for Nurses, N.Y.C., then head nurse Welfare Island Dispensary; dir. nursing service Sch. Nursing, Tuskegee Inst., 1949-54, dean Sch. Nursing, from 1954. Mem. nursing adv. com. Kellogg Found. Mem. Nat. League Nursing, Am. Nurses Assn., Alpha Kappa Alpha, Chi Eta Phi. Home: Tuskegee Institute AL Died July 27, 1968.

HARVEY, RAY FORREST, univ. exec.; b. Caney, Okla., Jan. 10, 1905; s. John and Lula (Marshall) H.; student W. Tex. State Tchrs. Coll., 1923-25, N.M. State Teachers Coll., summer 1926; Colo. State Teachers Coll., summer 1927; A.B., U. of Okla., 1929, A.M., 1930; Ph.D., N.Y. Univ., 1934; m. Edrena Fincher, Sept. 2, 1932; 1 dau., Ann Elizabeth (Mrs. Frederick W. Dau). High sch. tchr. and prin., 1925-28; asst. instr. govt. U. Tex., 1930-31; instr., asst. prof., asso. prof., prof. dept. govt., N.Y.U., 1934-63, prof. pub. adminstrn., 1964-68, administrv. asst., div. gen. edn., 1943-46, exec. sec. program for tng. personnel spls., 1943-46, asst. to provost, 1946-52, chmn. dept. govt. Washington Sq. Coll., 1950-53, head grad. dept., govt., 1952-55, dir. office of budget, 1953-58, director, office of educational services, 1958-59, dean of the university summer sessions, 1959-60, dean of grad. school of public adminstrn., 1960-68. Chief research and planning div. N.Y. Vets. Commn., 1944-45, N.Y. Div. Vets. Affairs, 1945-46; dir. in charge reviewers, exec. bd. of review, N.Y. State Div. Vets. Affairs, 1946; mem. com. on within-service tng., coll.-fed. agency council 1947-52. Impartial chairman War Manpower Commission, New York Region, 1944. Mem. Am. Soc. Pub. Adminstrn., Civil Service Assembly for U.S., Can., Am. Polit. Sci. Assn., (mem. exec. council 1950-52), Am. Acad. Polit., Social Sci., Soc. for Personnel Adminstrn., N.E.A., Citizens Union N.Y. Author books including: Final Report, N.Y. State Vets. Commn., 1945. Editor: The Politics of This War, 1943. Contbr. to numerous learned jours. Home: Manhasset NY Died Feb. 2, 1968; buried Nassau Knolls Port Washington NY

HARVEY, W(ILLIAM) W(EST), judge; b. Madison County, Ky., Nov. 21, 1869; s. James Davidson and Rebecca (Sparks) H.; grad. State Normal Sch., Emporia, Kan., 1896; m. Mamie A. Conley, Sept. 5, 1894;children—Howard Sparks, Helen. Admitted to Kan. bar, 1898, and began practice at Topeka; practiced with brother A.M., 3 yrs., then alone; moved to Ashland, Kan., 1906, and associated in practice with H J. Bone; county atty. Clark County, 1907-09; mem. Kan

Ho. of Rep., 1917-21 (speaker of House, 1921); asst. U.S. atty., Dist. of Kan., 1921-23; justice Supreme Court of Kan. since 1923. Became chief justice, 1945. Chmn. Kan. Judicial Council, 1927-41. Mem. Am. Law Institute, 1936-41; dir. Am. Judicature Soc., 1939-43. Formerly lecturer Washburn College of Law, Topeka; actively identified with farming. Republican. Mason. Home: Ashland, Kan. Address: State Capitol, Topeka KS*‡

HASELDEN, KYLE EMERSON, editor, clergyman; b. Latta, S.C., Feb. 12, 1913; s. Hampton Berry and Mary Beulah (Allen) H.; B.A., Furman U., 1934; B.D., Colgate Rochester Div. Sch., 1937; D.D., Morris Harvey Coll., Charleston, W.Va., 1956; LL.D., Keuka Coll., Keuka Park, N.Y., 1960; Litt.D., Chicago (Ill.) Theological Seminary, 1964; m. Elizabeth Denmark Lee, Sept. 8, 1936;children—Kyle Emerson, Alice, Thomas. Ordained to ministry Bapt. Ch., 1937; minister Warburton Av. Bapt. Ch., Yonkers, N.Y., 1937-41, Trinity Bapt. Ch., Mpls., 1941-50, Bapt. Temple, Rochester, N.Y., 1950-54, Charleston, W.Va., 1954-60; mng. editor Christian Century, 1960-64, editor, 1964-68; editor The Pulpit, 1960-68; professional lectr. Divinity School Faculty, U. Chgo., 1960-68; lectr. Rauschenbusch series Colgate-Rochester Div. Sch., Chautauqua, N.Y., Duke Div. Sch. Seminar for Ministers. Garrett Bibl. Inst., Am. Bapt. Assembly; John M. English lectr. Andover Newton Theol. Sch., 1962; Garnett-Nabrit lectr. Am. Bapt. Theol. Sem., Nashville, 1965; lectr. Union Theol. Sem., Richmond, Va., 1965; Samuel Robinson lectr. Wake Forest U., 1967; Alumni lectr. Eden Theol. Sem., Webster Groves, Mo.; bd. trustees Carlton Coll., Northfield, Minn., 1948-50, Colgate-Rochester Div. Sch., 1952-68. Recipient certificate of merit W.Va. Council Chs., 1960; ann. brotherhood award Nat. Conf. Christians and Jews, 1960; co-recipient Edwin T. Dahlberg Peace award Am. Bapt. Conv., 1968. Author: The Racial Problem in Christian Perspective; The Urgency of Preaching, 1963; Death of a Myth, 1964; Mandate for White Christians, 1966; Flux and Fidelity, 1968; Morality and the Mass Media, 1968. Editor: (with Marty) What's Ahead for the Churches, 1964; (with Hefner) The Threat and the Promise, 1968. Home: Evanston IL Died Oct. 2, 1968; buried Florence SC

HASELTINE, NATHAN STONE, newspaperman; b. Edgewood, Pa., July 19, 1911; s. Nathan S. and Mary Anna (Pilgram) H.; student University of Pa., 1932-33, Biarritz (France) Army U., 1945-46; married Emily Harrison Clevenger, June 26, 1937; children—Barbara Ann (Mrs. Robert W. Walker), Lawrence Stone (deceased), Holly Marie, Robert Pilgram. With Phila. Evening Pub. Ledger, 1931-42; news corr., Atlantic City, 1942-43; rewrite-reporter Washington Post, 1946-49, med., sci. writer, 1949-59, med. writer, 1959-70. Incorporator, Council for Advancement Sci. Writing, 1960, mem. bd., 1960-69. Served with AUS, 1943-46. Recipient Howard W. Blakeslee award Am. Heart Assn., 1956, Am. Osteo. Assn. award, 1959; James T. Grady medal (1,000), Am. Chem. Soc., 1964. Fellow A.A.A.S. (George Westinghouse award 1953); member National Assn. Science Writers (editor newsletter), Washington Acad. Scis., Am. Newspaper Guild, Nat., Atlantic City press clubs, Soc. Va., Sigma Delta Chi. Home: Arlington VA Died Aug. 16, 1970; buried Rock Spring United Ch. of Christ, Arlington VA

HASELTON, PAGE SMITH, patent lawyer; b. Hudson, N.H., May 7, 1896; s. Arthur W. and Mary E. (McCoy) H.; B.S., Worcester Poly. Inst., 1919; postgrad. George Washington U., 1920-21; LL.B., Nat. U., 1923; m. Marjorie Scudder, June 19, 1920; children—Jeanne (Mrs. Wilson C. Rich, Jr.), George. Asst. examiner U.S. Patent Office, 1920-22; admitted to Ill. bar, 1924, N.Y. bar, 1926; practiced in Chgo., 1924-25, N.Y.C., 1925-67; sr. mem. Ward, Haselton, McElhannon, Orme, Brooks & Fitzpatrick. Mem. Am. Bar Assn., Assn. Bar City N.Y., N.Y. Patent Law Assn., Lawyers Club, Alpha Tau Omega. Republican. Presbyn. Club: Montclair Golf. Pioneer teleregister broker's bd. system. Home: Upper Montclair NJ Died Apr. 28, 1967; buried Mt. Hebron Cemetery, Upper Montclair NJ

HASKELL, FREDA REW (MRS. GEORGE S. HASKELL), club woman; b. Evanston, Ill., Nov. 9, 1900; d. Alfred H. and Anna F. (Rew) Gross; student Westover Coll., 1917-19, Chgo. Mus. Coll., 1920-21; m. George S. Haskell, Dec. 20, 1925;children—Anne Irwin (Mrs. Allen Worthington Casady), Joan Claflin (Mrs. Fred Philips Naber). Mem. Ill. Children's Home and Aid Soc., 1932-67. Mem. Chgo. Jr. League, Art Inst. Chgo., Los Angeles Philharmonic Society, Laguna Beach Art Association Affiliates. Republican. Episcopalian. Clubs: Contemporary, Saddle and Cycle (Chgo.); Irvine Coast Country (Newport Beach, Cal.). Home: Evanston IL Died Aug. 22, 1967.

HASKELL, GLENN LEACH, chem. co. exec.; b. Chgo., Sept. 9, 1883; s. Walter Hosmer and Jennie (Leach) H.; ed. grammar and high schools; m. Florence Utz, June 20, 1908. With Am. Distilling Co. from 1900 to 1920, starting as clerk and salesman, becoming mgr. Chicago Branch in 1910; sales mgr., 1914-20; asso. with U.S. Indsl. Alcohol Co., N.Y.C., from 1920, first as Western sales mgr., then gen. sales mgr., 1921, vice-pres. and gen. sales mgr., 1925, first vice-pres. from 1930. Pres. U.S. Industrial Chems., Inc., 1943-48, vice chmn. bd., 1948-49. Clubs: Uptown, Union League, Cloud (N.Y. City); Apawamis (Rye, N.Y.). Home: Laguna Beach CA Died Jan. 21, 1972.

HASKELL, HELEN EGGLESTON, author; b. Fairwater, Wis., 1871; d. Julian Alonzo and Helen Elizabeth (Johnson) Eggleston; B.A., Ripon (Wisconsin) College, 1891; Litt.D., (hon.), 1948; student Univ. of Chicago, 1915-16, Columbia, 1920; married William Edwin Haskell, January 26, 1903 (died May 2, 1933). Author: Billy's Princess, 1907; O-Heart-San, 1908; Holding a Throne, 1913 (translated into Spanish); Katrinka, 1915 (50 edits., dramatized; translated into Swedish); Katrinka Grows Up, 1932; Peter, Katrinka's Brother, 1933; Peggy Keeps House, 1935; Nadya Makes Her Bow, 1938; long hist. novel in preparation. Has Written many serials and short stories for mags. Home: 610 W. 110th St., NYC 25‡

HASKELL, HORACE BRAY, clergyman; b. N. Vassalboro, Me., Sept. 5, 1869; s. of Conforth Ladd and Carrie Augusta (Jones) H.; grad. E. Me. Conf. Sem., Bucksport, 1892, Garrett Bibl. Inst., 1899; Ph.B., Taylor U., 1900; M.A., U. of Maine, 1906; D.D., Ia. Wesleyan. 1917; m. Bessie Gott Thurlow, of Stonington, Me., Apr. 16, 1900;children—Marian Elizabeth, Ralph Everett, Margaret Augusta. Entered M.E. ministry, taken into conf. and ordained deacon, 1896, elder, 1900; pastor Dexter and Ripley, Me., 1900-03, Orono and Stillwater, Me., 1904-05; supt. Bucksport Dist., E. Me. Conf., 1906-12; dir. Newman Inst., Jerusalem, Palestine, 1912-17; pres. Beaver (Pa.) Coll., 1917-19; field mgr. Am. City Bureau, New York, 1919-20; financial sec. Montpelier (Vt.) Sem., 1920-21; pastor Gardiner, Me., 1922-29; pastor McKinley Ch., Winona, Minn., 1929-1935; lyceum and chautauqua lecturer; now retired. Mem. Gen. Conf., 1912; pres. 1st Gen. Conf. Dist. Epworth League, 1910-12; pres. N.E. Supts'. Assn., 1911; mem. Bd. of Control, Gen. Conf. Epworth League, 1912-16. Trustee E. Me. Conf. Sem., 1906-17; promoter girls camp, 1927. Contbr. to Stonington ME‡

HASLER, FREDERICK EDWARD, former banker; b. Wethersfield, Essex, Eng., Feb. 27, 1882; s. Thomas and Jane Chatterson (Banyard) H.; ed. pvt. schs., Eng.; M.A. (hon.), Bowdoin Coll., 1943; LL.D., Columbia, 1955, Trinity Coll., Conn., 1957; m Marguerite Isabel Messent, Sept. 5, 1912; children—Audrey, Shirley, Marjory. Came to U.S., 1901, naturalized, 1919. Began as clk., London, 1899; chartering clk. J.H. Winchester & Co., N.Y.C., 1903-06 mgr. Am. Smelters S.S. Co., 1906-08; asst. to pres. Chesapeake & Ohio Coal & Coke Co., 1908-09; sr. partner Hasler Bros., 1909-23; v.p. Bank of Am., 1923-36; pres. Internat. Trust Co., 1929-31; chmn. exec. com. Continental Bank & Trust Co., 1931, chmn. bd., 1941-48; chmn. U.S. bd. N. Brit. & Merc. Ins. Co. Ltd. and subsidiaries, 1946-61; cons., former mem. adv. com. of bd., mem. Lower Manhattan adv. bd. Chem. Bank N.Y. Trust Co., ret.; chmn. Haytian Am. Sugar Co., S.A., 1938-67, dir.; chmn., dir. Signet Fund (Bermuda) Ltd., 1957-68, Hermes Enterprises, Ltd. (Bermuda); dir. La Plantation Dauphin, S.A., Haiti West Indies Co., ECL Industries, Ltd., Haitian Am. Devel. Corp., S.A.; incorporator Litchfield Savs. Soc. Trustee Sch. Indsl. Relations, Cornell U., 1943-45, Leake and Watts Children's Home, St. Margaret's Sch. and others; hon. dir. Americas Found.; bd. dirs. Inter-Am. Literacy Found. others. Decorated Honneur et Merite (Haiti); Orden Nacional del Merito de Carlos Manuel de Cespedes, Orden del Merito Comercial (Cuba); Orden del Libertador Bolivar (Venezuela); Orden Nacional do Cruzeiro do Sul (Brazil); Sul Orden Mexicana del Aguila Azteca (Mexico); Orden al Merito (Ecuador); Orden del Condor de los Andes (Bolivia); Orden de Cristobal Colon, Orden del Merito Juan Pablo Duarte (Dominican Republic); Orden de Vasco Nunex de Balboa (Panama); Orden de Ruben Dario (Nicaragua), others. Mem. N.Y. C. of C. (pres. 1942-44, hon. life mem.), Pan Am. Soc. U.S. (pres. 1940-46, now hon. pres., dir.). Episcopalian. Clubs: Pilgrims, University (N.Y.C.) Home: Washington Depot CT Died Mar. 12, 1973.

HASSELBRING, HEINRICH, botanist; b. at Flint, Mich., Jan. 12, 1875; s. Bernhardt and Augusta (Lange) H.; S.B., in Agr., Cornell U., 1899; Ph.D., U. of Chicago, 1905; unmarried. Asst. in botany, Cornell U., 1899-1900; asst. horticulturist, N.Y. Expt. Sta., 1900-1; plant pathologist, U. of Ill., 1901-3; asst. in botany, U. of Chicago, 1903-7; chief dept. of botany, Estacion Central Agronomica, Santiago de las Vegas, Cuba, 1907-9; with Bur. Plant Industry, U.S. Dept. of Agr., since Apr. 12, 1909. Mem. A.A.A.S., Sigma Xi. Author various articles in Bailey's Cyclopedia American Horticulture, scientific papers on plant physiology and pathology, mag. articles, etc. Address: Bureau of Plant Industry, Dept. of Agr., Washington‡

HASSELTINE, HERMON ERWIN, USPHS ofcl.; b. Bristol, Vt., Aug. 13, 1881; s. Erwin Amos and Jennie (Searles) H.; student Middlebury (Vt.) Coll., 1898-99, U. of Kan., 1899-1900; M.D., Baltimore Med. Coll., 1904; student U.S. Army Med. Sch., 1905-06; D.Sc., Middlebury Coll., 1937; m. Bertha M. Mohl, June 6, 1905; children—Lee Luther, Catherine Luther Jennie, Margery Searles; married 2d, Gertrude A. Kendall, Dec. 26, 1948. Interne Manhattan State Hosp., N.Y., 1904-05; contract surgeon, U.S. Army, 1905-08, lt. Med. Res. Corps, 1908-09; commd. asst. surgeon U.S.P.H.S., 1909, passed asst. surgeon, 1913, surgeon, 1920, sr. surgeon, 1930, med. dir., 1935, dir. U.S. Leprosy Investigation Sta., Honolulu, 1921-24; in charge Psittacosis Research Lab., Pasadena, 1932-35, U.S. Leprosarium, Carville, La., 1935-40; in charge stream pollution investigations, Cincinnati, O., 1940-42, U.S. Quarantine Sta., Boston, Mass., 1942-45; Mem. A.M.A., Am. Pub. Health Assn., Assn. Mil. Surgeons, Am. Soc. Tropical Medicine, Internat. Leprosy Assn., Phi Chi. Republican. Episcopalian. Mason. Nat. Sojourner. Contbr. to jours. Address: Bristol VT Died June 8, 1968; buried Bristol VT

HASSLER, RUSSELL HERMAN, electric company executive; b. Connersville, Indiana, October 24, 1906; the son of Frank J. and Margaret (Schweikle) H.; A.B., Depauw University, 1927; M.A., U. of Ia., 1928; M.A. (hon.), Harvard, 1951; D.Bus. Adminstrn. (hon.), Suffolk U., 1958; m. Edith Beecroft, May 8, 1937; 1 dau., Judy (Mrs. James Wilbert). Began his career with Edward Gore & Company, C.P.A.'s, Chgo., 1929-43; controller Stant Mfg. Co., Connersville, 1943-46; faculty Harvard Grad. Sch. Bus. Adminstrn., 1946-62, prof. bus. adminstrn., 1951-62, asso. dean ednl. programs, 1957-62; v.p. Hawaiian Electric Company, Inc., 1962-63, financial v.p., dir., 1963-66, pres., dir., 1966-69; dir. Aloha Airlines, First Hawaiian Bank, Hawaii Corp., Maui Electric Co. Mem. Hawaii Gov.'s Adv. Com. Finance and Taxes, Gov.'s Adv. Com. Sci. and Tech. Bd. dirs. Aloha United Fund, vice chmn. campaign, 1969; bd. dirs. Downtown Improvement Assn., Honolulu Symphony, Jr. Achievement of Hawaii, Inc., Oahu Devel. Conf., Hawaii Sch. for Girls; bd. govs. Pacific and Asian Affairs Council, pres., 1968; bd. govs. Hawaii Employers Council; trustee Hawaii Joint Council Econ. Edn.; chmn. adv. council advanced mgmt. program U. Hawaii, mem. bus. adv. council Coll. Bus. Adminstrn. C.P.A., Mass., Ill. Mem. Am. Accounting Assn. (pres. 1953), Am. Inst. C.P.A.'s, Financial Execs. Inst., Investment Soc. Hawaii, Pacific Coast Elec. Assn. (v.p., dir.), Investment Soc. Hawaii, Nat. Indsl. Conf. Bd., Hawaii C. of C. (v.p., dir.), Nat. Alliance Businessmen, Social Sci. Assn., Newcomen Soc. N. Am., Phi Beta Kappa, Beta Alpha Psi, Phi Delta Theta, Order of Artus. Clubs: Harvard (N.Y.C., Hawaii and Boston); Outrigger Canoe, Pacific (gov. 1969), Oahu Country. Author: (with Neil Harlan) Cases in Controllership, 1958. Home: Honolulu HI Died May 17, 1969.

HASTINGS, CHARLES HARRIS, librarian; b. Bethel, Me., 1867; s. John and Elizabeth Carter (Atherton) H.; A.B., Bowdoin, 1891; student Johns Hopkins, 1891-93, U. of Chicago, 1893-95 inclusive; m. Alice Duncan Otis, 1895; children—George Sands, Atherton, Helen, Elizabeth. Began library work at U. of Chicago, 1895; chief of card div., Library of Congress, 1901-38; organized and developed card distribution work of the Library; retired, Dec. 1938. Mem. A.L.A., Bibliog. Soc. America. Theta Delta Chi, Phi Beta Kappa. Author: Handbook of Card Distribution, 1925; Library of Congress, Printed Cards, How to Order and Use Them, 1925. Home: 3600 Ordway St. N.W., Washington DC‡

HASTINGS, EDWIN GEORGE, bacteriologist; b. Austinburg, O., Aug. 11, 1872; s. of Oramel Pierce and Susan Elizabeth (Rose) H.; B.S., Ohio State U., 1898; M.S., U. of Wis., 1899; Royal Vet. Sch., Munich, Germany; m. Elvira J. Waters, of Austinburg, O., Sept. 16, 1902. Began as teacher and researcher, U. of Wis., 1899, prof. agrl. bacteriology, 1913; bacteriologist, Expt. Sta. Mem. Wis. State Live Stock Sanitary Bd. Conglist. Fellow A.A.A.S.; mem. Soc. Am. Bacteriologists, Sigma Xi, Sigma Alpha Epsilon. Club: University. Author: Agricultural Bacteriology, 1909; Experimental Dairy Bacteriology, 1909; Dairy Bacteriology, 1910. Contbr. to microbiology, 1911. Home: 1906 West Lawn Av., Madison WI‡

HASTINGS, THOMAS WOOD, M.D., retired; b. St. Louis, Mo., Sept. 29, 1873; s. Samuel Weston and Frances (Wood) H.; ed. pub. schs. and Morris Acad., Morristown, N.J.; A.B., Johns Hopkins, 1894, M.D., 1898; m. Athenia Agnes Belknap, of Yonkers, N.Y., Oct.6, 1909; children—Thomas Wood, John Frazee. House officer Johns Hopkins Hosp., 1898-99; apptd. lt. surgeon Hosp. Ship Maine, 1899; with British Expeditionary Forces, S. African War, 1899-1900, British China Expdn., Boxer Rebellion, 1900-01; instr. in clin. pathology, Cornell U. Med. Coll., 1901-06, prof., 1906-18; substitute clin. pathologist Presbyn. Hosp., 1902-04; asst. visiting phys. Cornell Med. Coll. Dispensary, 1901-07, Bellevue Hosp., 1908-17, acting visiting phys., 1917-21; mem. cons. staff Nassau County Hosp., 1919-22; cons. staff St. Bartholomew's Clinic and Hosp., 1920-21. Lt. Med. R.C., U.S.A., 1910-17; maj., 1917-18; retired as maj., June 6, 1928. Fellow A.A.A.S.; mem. Mil. Order World War, Phi Kappa Psi, Sigma Chi, Alpha Omega Alpha; formerly mem. A.M.A. and many other socs. Republican. Presbyn. Extensive contbr. on med. subjects. Home: Kinderhook NY‡

HASWELL, KANAH ELIZABETH MARCUM (MRS. HAROLD ALANSON HASWELL), civic worker; b. Washburn, Mo.; d. Granville Pillar and Mary Elizabeth (Park) Marcum; student pub. schs.; m. Harold Alanson Haswell, Aug. 27, 1908 (dec. 1948); children—Robert Marcum, Harold Alanson, John Daniel. Tchr. pub. schs., Mo. 1906-08. Vol. worker A.R.C., 1930-69, grey lady and chmn. Canteen Corp., 1940-69. Republican committee-woman, Joplin, Mo., 1935-69. Mem. Mo. State Writers Guild (treas. 1965-69), U.D.C. (pres. 1966-68). Baptist (tchr.). Woodman of World (past pres.). Writer books, short stories. Home: Joplin MO Died Sept. 16, 1969.

HATCH, LOUIS CLINTON, hist. writer; b. Bangor, Me., Sept. 1, 1872; s. Silas Clinton and Sarah Frances (Williams) H.; ed. Bangor pub. schs., Bowdoin Coll., 1891-5, A.B., 1895; Harvard Graduate Sch., 1895-9, Ph.D., 1899; unmarried. Since graduation in hist. work at Cambridge, Mass. Unitarian. Republican. Author: The Administration of the American Revolutionary Army, 1904 L4. Address: 22 Felton Hall, Cambridge MA‡

HATCH, ROBERT SEYMOUR, marine corps exec., lawyer; b. Jamestown, N.Y., July 6, 1907; s. Frank Delos and Aura (Lowell) H.; B.A., Ohio U., 1929; LL.B., Ohio State U., 1931; LL.M., George Washington U., 1943; m. Zetta Collins, Dec. 22, 1928; children—Robert Neil, Margaret Ann. Admitted to Ohio bar, 1931; practice in New Philadelphia, O., 1932-41; sec. to Congressman Thom, 1941-42; atty. Bituminous coal div. Dept. Interior, 1942-43; asst. gen. counsel Solid Fuels Adminstrn. War, 1943-46; asst. counsel Coal Mines Adminstrn., 1946-47; counsel Bur. Naval Personnel, 1947-53, Navy Purchasing office, Los Angeles, 1953-55; counsel for comdt. USMC, from 1955. Mem. Fed. Bar Assn., Phi Alpha Delta. Methodist. Mason (Shriner). Home: Chevy Chase MD Died Sept. 10, 1968; interred Park Lawn Meml. Park.

HATCHER, JOHN HENRY, judge; b. Bland, Va., June 29, 1875; s. Wilson Cary and Anne (Bulman) H.; student Emory and Henry Coll., 3 yrs., W.Va. U., 1 yr.; m. Leona Lyle Bowman, Apr. 12, 1900; children—Lois (Mrs. Frederick M. Simpson), Lyle (Mrs. Herman L. Bennett), John H. Admitted to W.Va. bar, 1899, and began practice at Beckley; mayor of Beckley, 1903; associated in practice with Judge W. H. McGinnis, title of McGinnis & Hatcher, 1907-20, inclusive; judge 10th Judicial Circuit of W.Va., 1921-24 inclusive; judge Supreme Court of Appeals, term 1925-28 inclusive. reelected for term 1929-41. Republican. Methodist. Mason. Home: 1020 Oakmont Road, Charleston WV*‡

HATHAWAY, EVANGELINE, b. Jackson, Me., Jan. 21, 1869; d. James Winslow and Nancy Jane (Durgin) H.; B.A., Wellesley, 1890; postgrad., Oxford U., Eng., 1895-6; unmarried. Was teacher 7 yrs.; head woman mgr. Fisk Teachers' Agency, Boston, 1900-17; Christian Science practitioner since 1917. Mem. Collegiate Alumnae, Field and Forest Club, Coll. Equal Suffrage League. Home: 15 Norway St., Boston‡

HATHAWAY, FONS A., b. Holmes Co., Fla., Apr. 8, 1875; s. James Wilburn and Sarah Jane (Register) H.; A.B., Fla. State Coll., 1902; A.B., U. of Fla., 1911 (LL.D., 1918); m. Annie Elizabeth Van Brunt, of Tallahassee, Fla., June 9, 1903. Prin. Orlando (Fla.) High Sch., 1902-09; prin. Duval High Sch., Jacksonville, Fla., 1909-14; supt. schs., Jacksonville, 1914; now chmn. Fla. State Road Dept. Reconstructed sch. system of Jacksonville and carried through a building program requiring outlay of more than $1,500,000. Democrat. Presbyn.; pres. men's Bible class 1st Presbyn. Ch. Mem. Phi Kappa Phi. Mason (32 deg.), K.P. Address: Tallahassee FL‡

HATHAWAY, JOSEPH HENRY, physician; b. Grinnell, Ia., Mar. 4, 1875; s. Edward M. and Mary E. (Smith) H.; A.B., Ia. (now Grinnell) Coll., 1894; A.B., Harvard, 1896, A.M., 1897; M.D., Johns Hopkins, 1901; m. Ethel H. S. Baird, of Toronto, Can., Jan. 25, 1905. Practiced in Highland Park, Mich., since 1916; prof. anatomy, histology and embryology, Detroit Coll. Medicine and Surgery, 1913-18. Health officer Highland Park, 1917-18. Mem. Am. Assn. Anatomists, Phi Beta Kappa, Sigma Xi, Nu Sigma Mu. Republican. Conglist. Mason. Home: 70 Puritan Av. Office: 2978 Woodward Av., Highland Park MI‡

HATHWAY, GEORGE W., utility exec.; b. Waukesha, Wis., Mar. 6, 1906; s. Clifford W. and Maude A. (Birkenheier) H.; student mech. engring., Marquette U., 1926-28; m. Dorothy L. Counsell, Aug. 15, 1928; children—Charles, Ann, James, Robert. With Central Ill. Light Co., Peoria, 1932-68, pres. 1961-66, chairman board, president, 1966-68, also director; director Jefferson Trust & Savings Bank Peoria. Trustee Meth. Hosp. Central Ill, pres. bd., 1966-68; trustee of Greater Peoria Sanitary District. Member Peoria Assn. Commerce. Methodist (trustee). Club: Creve Coeur. Home: Peoria IL Died Feb. 7, 1968; buried Prairie Home Cemetery, Waukesha WI

HATT, WILLIAM KENDRICK, cons. engr.; b. Fredericton, Can., Oct. 10, 1868; s. George and Sarah Elizabeth (Clark) H.; B.A., Univ. of N.B., 1887, M.A., 1898, Ph.D., 1901; C.E., Cornell U., 1891; m. Josephine Appleby, 1897 (died Nov. 18, 1910); children—Kendrick Appleby, Elise, Robert Torrens, Wilhelmina (dec.). Prof. civ. engring., Univ. of N.B., 1891-92; instr. civ. engring., Cornell U., 1892-93; asso. prof. civ. engring., 1893-95, asso. prof. applied mechanics, 1896-1901, prof., 1902-06, prof. civ. engring. and dir. Material Testing Lab., 1907-38, research prof., 1938-39, emeritus since 1939, Purdue. Fuertes Gold Medalist, Cornell Univ., 1903; Turner Medalist, American Concrete Institute, 1929. Mem. Am. Soc. for Testing Materials, Am. Ry. Engring. Assn., Am. Soc. Civil Engrs., Alpha Tau Omega, Chi Epsilon, Sigma Xi and Tau Beta Pi fraternities; pres. Ind. Engring. Soc., 1907-08; pres. Am. Concrete Inst., 1917-19; dir. Advisory Bd. on Highway Research of Nat. Research Council, 1921-23; state engr., Ind. Conservation Dept., 1921-39; mem. Com. on Building Codes Dept. of Commerce, Washington, D.C., 1921-27, chmn., 1928-32. Episcopalian. Author: Manual of Testing Materials (with H. H. Scofield), 1908; Concrete Work (with W. C. Voss), 1921; also about 100 scientific papers on engring. and structural materials. Home: 402 Observatory Lodge, Ann Arbor MI‡

HAUHART, WILLIAM FREDERIC, educator; b. Valley Park, Mo., June 24, 1873; s. Herman and Mary (Schlueter) H.; A.B., U. of Mo., 1901, A.M., 1902; Ph.D., Columbia, 1909; m. Hertha Londershaus, Aug. 22, 1929. Instr. U. of Mich., 1906-14, asst. prof., 1914-21; dir. Sch. of Commerce, Southern Methodist U., Dallas, Tex., since 1921, dean School of Business Adminstrn., 1941-45, dean emeritus since 1945; now prof. finance, St. Louis U., St. Louis, Mo. Mem. Economists Nat. Com. on Monetary Policy. Mem. Am. Econ. Assn., Kappa Sigma. Methodist. Mason. Home: 9463 Brenda Av., St Louis 23 MO‡

HAUN, BURTON OLIVER, dentist; b. Tuscarawas County, O., Aug. 21, 1877; s. John J. and Mary (Lewis) H.; D.D.S., St. Louis U. Dental Coll., 1907; m. Anna Lorenzen, Dec. 26, 1911; children—Burton Oliver, Ceola Isabel. Acting prof. prosthetics, St. Louis U. Dental Coll., 1917-18; practice limited to dentures since 1931. Pres. St. Louis Dental Soc., 1928; mem. Am. Dental Assn., Mo. State Dental Assn., St. Louis Soc. Dental Science (pres. Gavel Club), Omicron Kappa Upsilon. Republican. Presbyn. (elder 1st Presbyn. Ch., St. Louis, Mo.). Contbr. many arts, on denture prosthesis. Home: 1209 A Big Bend, Richmond Heights, Mo. Office: Missouri Theatre Bldg., St Louis MO‡

HAUPERT, RAYMOND SAMUEL, clergyman, bank cons.; b. Watertown, Wis., Mar. 9, 1902; s. Albert Peter and Maria Louise (Moehrke) H.; A.B., Moravian Coll., 1922; B.D., Moravian Theol. Sem., 1924; M.A., U. Pa., 1926, Ph.D., 1931; D.Sc. in Edn., Lafayette Coll., 1950; LL.D., Lehigh U., 1951; L.H.D., Seton Hill Coll., Greensburg, Pa., 1965, Allentown Coll. of St. Francis, 1971; m. Estelle Hege McCanless, July 30, 1932; children—Albert Peter, William Hege (dec.), Thomas John, Stephen Andrew. Ordained to ministry Moravian Ch. in Am., 1924; instr. Bible, Lafayette Coll., 1924-26; asst. prof. Bibl. lit. and langs. Moravian Coll. and Theol. Sem., 1924-31, prof. 1931-44, pres., 1944-69, pres. emeritus, 1969-72, also pres. Moravian Sem. and Coll. for Women, 1953-54, following merger of two schs. became pres. merged corp. Moravian Coll., 1954-69, pres. emeritus, 1969-72; dir. First Valley Bank and Trust Co., Bethlehem; tng. cons. First Valley Bank, 1969-71. Chmn. Christian edn. bd., Moravian Ch. in Am., No. Province, 1936-41; Joseph Henry Thayer fellow Am. Sch. Oriental Research, Jerusalem, Palestine, 1930-31. Vice chmn. bd. dirs. Hosp. Service Plan of Lehigh Valley; past chmn. bd. trustees St. Luke's Hosp., Bethlehem, Pa.; past dir. Bethlehem Library; past pres., dir. Historic Bethlehem, Inc. Trustee Moravian Music Found. Mem. Pa. Assn. Colls. and Univs. (pres. 1960-61, past chmn. commn. ind. colls. and univs.), Am. Oriental Soc., Archaeol. Inst. Am., Soc. Bibl. Lit. and Exegesis (asso. in council, treas. 1938-41). Nat. Assn. Bibl. Instrs., Assn. Am. Colls. (commn. on religion higher edn.), Council Protestant Colls. and Univs. (past dir., treas.), Fgn. Policy Assn. (Lehigh Valley br., past pres.), Newcomen Soc., Phi Beta Kappa. Clubs: Oriental (pres. 1944-45) (Phila.); Torch (pres. 1946-47) (Lehigh Valley, Pa.); Rotary (pres. 1947-48) (Bethlehem, Pa.). Author: The Lachish Letters, 1938; The Relation of Codex Vaticanus and the Lucianic Text in the Books of the Kings from the Viewpoint of the Old Latin and the Ethiopic Versions, 1931; Pioneers in Moravian Education, 1954. Bethlehem PA Died Dec. 15, 1972.

HAUPT, SARAH MINERVA, physical edn.; b. Hartleton, Union County, Pa., Dec. 12, 1874; d. Philip Steriger and Susan (Whitmer) H.; ed. Bucknell Coll. (Lewisburg, Pa.) and State Normal Sch. (West Chester); grad. New Haven Normal Sch. of Gymnastics, 1899; M.S. in Physical Edn., Arnold College, 1928. Teacher of physical training, St. Margaret's Sch., Waterbury, Conn., 1900-03, Waterbury Inst. of Craft and Industry, 1903-11; with New Haven Normal Sch. of Gymnastics since 1911; dean of women and treas. Arnold Coll. for Hygiene and Physical Edn., New Haven, since 1921, also trustee; pres., treas. Anderson Gymnasium Co. Mem. Am. Physical Edn. Assn. Home: Morgan Terrace, East Haven CT‡

HAUSDORFER, WALTER, librarian; b. Indianapolis, Ind., Apr., 30, 1898; s. Paul Bernhard and Meta (Gausepohl) H.; A.B. cum laude, Temple U., 1925; B.S., Columbia U., 1927, M.S., 1930; m. Abigail E. Fisher, Sept. 6, 1927. Asst. librarian, Temple U. Library, 1925-26; reference asst., N.Y. Public Library, 1927-30; librarian, School of Business, Columbia University, 1930-46; librarian, Temple University, 1946-61, professor of bibliography, 1961-63; library cons. Personnel Department, City of Philadelphia. In Students Army Training Corps, 1918. Mem. Grand Jury, N.Y. County. Chmn. Phila. Metropolitan Library Council, 1947-48. Mem. Middle States Assn. Colls. and Secondary Schs., Am. Library Assn. (mem. bd. personnel adminstration), Special Library Association (president N.Y. chapter, 1933-34; 2d vice pres. 1942-43, vice pres. 1943-44, pres. 1944-45; chmn. finance com.), Am. Assn. for State and Local History, Soc. of Am. Archivists (chmn. com. on institutional archives). Bibliog. Soc. Am., Econ. Hist. Assn., Internat. Inst. Conserv. Historic, Artistic Works, Alpha Kappa Psi. Council of Nat. Library Assns. (sec., treas. 1945-47). Metropolitan Library Council (Phila.). Phila Art Alliance Mem. exec. com. Union Library Cataloge (Phila.); mem. A.L.A. Conf. Program Commn. Author Professional School and Departmental Libraries, 1939 Handbook of Commercial Financial and Information Services. 1944, 56. Editor: Temple U. Library Bull. 1946-63. Contbr. articles and reviews to Library Jour. Spl. Libraries, A.L.A. Bull., Library Quar., Econ History, Library Trends. Home: Philadelphia PA Died June 8, 1970; buried Whitemarsh Meml. Park Prospectville PA

HAUSER, CHARLES R(OY), educator; b. Cal., Mar 8, 1900; s. Charles and Elizabeth (Rogan) H.; B.S., U Fla., 1923, M.S., 1925; Ph.D., U. Ia., 1928; m. Madge L. Baltimore, June 30, 1929; children—Betty L. Frances M., Charles F. Instr. Lehigh U., 1928-29; instr Duke, 1929-35, asst. prof., 1935-41, asso. prof. 1941-46, prof. chemistry, 1946-61, James B. Duke professor of chemistry, 1961-70; cons. Union Carbide Chemicals Co., 1946-61; vis. lectr. Ohio State U. summer 1956; research organic chemistry on mechanisms and syntheses. Recipient certificate of merit OSRD; award Fla. sect. Am. Chem. Soc. 1957 Am. Chem. Soc. award, 1962; Herty medal, 1962 medal Synthetic Organic Chem. Mfrs. Assn., 1967 Member of Nat. Acad. Scis., Am. Chem. Soc. A.A.A.S., Am. Assn. U. Profs., Sigma Xi, Phi Bet Kappa, Phi Kappa Phi, Phi Lambda Upsilon, Gamm Sigma Epsilon. Contbr. Durham NC Died Jan. 6, 1970

HAUSER, HARRY, physician, educator; b. Galveston Tex., Dec. 28, 1904; s. Isaac and Caroline (Klein) H B.A., U. Tex., 1926, M.D., 1929; m. Martha Iren Johnson, Sept. 6, 1936 (dec. Sept. 1967) children—David, Daniel; m. 2d, Miriam Solvit Applesmith, June 1, 1969. Intern, Cleve. City Hosp 1929-30, resident radiology, 1930-32, dir. dep radiology, 1934-71; fellow N.Y. Meml. Hosp., 1932-34 practice medicine, specializing in radiology, Cleve radiologist Grace Hosp., 1939-71; dir. radiology U Hosps., 1942-46; dir. dept. radiology Cleve. Met. Ger Hosp., 1958; clin. prof. Sch. Medicine Case Wester Res. U., 1955-71; emeritus clin. prof., 1971-—; cons radiologist Sunny Acres Sanatorium, 1944-71, Fores City Hosp., 1950-71, Marymount Hosp., 1950-60 Lutheran Hosp., 1963-71; hon. radiologist Marymour Hosp., 1960-71, Diplomate Am. Bd. Radiology. Mem Cleve. Med. Library Assn., Am. Radium Soc. (v.p. A.M.A., Cleve. Radiol. Soc. (past pres.), James Ewin Soc., Med. Arts Club (past pres.), Cleve. Clin. Club, Ph Delta Epsilon, Phi Mu Alpha. Jewish religion. Ass editor: Am. Jour. Roentgenology, 1950-71. Contb profl. jours. Home: Cleveland Heights OH Died Ap 27, 1971.

HAUSERMAN, FREDRIC MARTIN, mfg. exec.; Cleve., Aug. 11, 1909; s. Earl Fredric and Mar (Martin) H.; M.E., Cornell U., 1931; student Harva Bus. Sch., 1931-32; m. Margaret Kenny, Sept. 9, 193 children—Rinda Kenny (Mrs. Lewis A. Burleigh III Jane Kenny (Mrs. William M. Hogan III), Mark Kenny Engr. E.F. Hauserman Co., Cleve., 1932-39, sec 1939-43, pres., 1943-69, chmn., 1969-70; dir. Centr Nat. Bank, Cleve., Ohio Bell Telephone Co. Pre Catholic Charities, 1956-59, Welfare Fedn. Cleve 1962-63; v.p. Community Action for Youth, 196 Decorated Knight of St. Gregory, 1963, Knight Malt 1971; recipient Outstanding Service award Welfa Fedn., 1963; Distinguished Service award Unite Appeal, 1964; U. Sch. Grad. award, 1969. Mer Producers' Council, Inc. (pres. 1957-58), Bld Research Inst. (pres. 1954-55), Young Presidents Org (chmn. Cleve. chpt. 1953, area v.p. 1955). Offic Cleveland OH Died Feb. 5, 1972.

HAUSKENS, PETER BERT, architect; b. Mpls., No 16, 1919; s. Rasmus Soren and Gunheld (Petersen) H B.A. in Architecture, Ariz. State U., 1941, M.A. Architecture, 1953; postgrad. U. Cal. at Berkele 1953-54; m. Alberta Margie Nichols, June 28, 194 children—Nancy Arlene, Ned Albert, Mark For Marcia Karen, Peter Allan. Sr. planning engr. Goodye Aircraft Corp., Litchfield Park, Ariz., 1941-53; arch designer Skidmore, Owings & Merrill, San Francisc

1956-60; individual practice architecture, Oakland, Cal., 1961-72; prof. architecture, Laney Coll., 1967-72. Mem. A.I.A., Am. Assn. Engrs., Soc. Coll. and University Planning, Christian Bus. Men's Assn. Mem. Covenant Ch. (deacon). Mason (Shriner). Home: Lafayette CA Died June 19, 1972.

HAUSMAN, LOUIS, physician, educator; born N.Y.C., Apr. 30, 1891; s. Joseph and Fannie (Dalmatz) H.; M.D., Cornell U., 1916; m. Esther May Hausman, Jan. 14, 1925. Intern Mt. Sinai Hosp., 1916-18, Manhattan State Hosp. Ward's Island, 1920; asst. psychiatrist Phipps Psychiatric Clinic, Johns Hopkins Hosp., Balt., 1921-22; asso. neuroanatomist Cornell, 1922-39, prof. clin. medicine (neurology) med. sch., 1945-58, prof. clin. medicine (neurology) emeritus, 1959-72; dir. neurological service 2d (Cornell) Med. Div. Bellevue Hosp., 1950-56; asso. attending physician N.Y. Hosp., 1945-56; clinical prof. neurpsy med. coll. N.Y.U. since 1945. Mem. Assn. Research Nervous and Mental Disease, Am. Assn. Anatomists, Harvey Soc., Am. Psychiat. Assn., New York Neurological Society (pres. 1961-62), A.M.A., Am. Neurological Assn. Author: Clinical Neuroanatomy, Neurophysiology and Neurology with a Method of Brain Reconstruction, 1958; Atlas III: Illustrations of the Nervous System, 1961. Home: New York City NY Died Dec. 7, 1972.

HAUT, IRVIN CHARLES, scientist; b. Mitchell, S.D., June 7, 1906; s. Adolph and Adeline (Sieg) H.; B.S., U. Ida., 1928; M.S., State Coll. Wash., 1930; Ph.D., U. Md., 1933; m. Marie K. Mahlandt, Dec. 26, 1935 (div. 1961); 1 son, William Frederick; m. 2d, Mary Jane Hurt Noonan, Apr. 16, 1966; step-children—Richard, Thomas, Douglas. Asst. prof., asst. horticulturist Okla. A. & M. Coll., 1933-36; asso. prof., asso. horticulturist Agrl. Expt. Sta., U. Md., 1936-46, prof., head dept. horticulture, horticulturist Agrl. Expt. Sta., U. Md., 1946-72, asst. dir. Expt. Sta., 1950-51, dir., 1951-72, state horticulturist, Md., 1954-72. Mem. A.A.A.S., Am. Soc. Hort. Sci., Wash. Acad. Scis., Sigma Xi, Alpha Zeta, Pi Alpha Xi, Phi Sigma, Phi Kappa Phi (past pres. Md.). Lutheran. Home: Silver Spring MD Died Aug. 21, 1972; buried Montgomery PA

HAVEMEYER, LOOMIS, educator, author; b. Rye, N.Y., June 7, 1886; s. Charles William and Julia Ida (Loomis) H.; Ph.B., Sheffield Scientific Sch. (Yale), 1910; M.A., Yale, 1912, Ph.D., 1915; unmarried. Mem. faculty, Yale, from 1912; registrar Sheffield Scientific Sch. (Yale University), 1920-29, asst. dean, 1929-41, asso. dean, 1941-45; registrar School of Engring. since 1932; dir. undergraduate registration, 1945; asso. dean undergrad. activities, 1948-51, associate dean undergraduate registration, 1951-71; lecturer (with Rank of associate professor) from 1941. Fellow Timothy Dwight College; mem. Am. Anthropol. Assn., Am. Assn. Social Hygiene, A.A.A.S., Sigma Xi Fraternity, Aurelian Honor Soc., and Book and Snake (both Yale), Soc. Colonial Wars. Republican. Clubs: Graduate, Elizabethan (New Haven); Yale (N.Y.). Author books. Editor: Conservation of Our Natural Resources, by Charles R. Van Hise, 1930. Established Julia and Loomis Havemeyer Music Trusts, Yale, 1969. Home: New Haven CT Died Aug. 14, 1971; buried Loomis Chapel, New London CT

HAVENNER, GEORGE CLEMENT, statistician; b. Md., Sept. 23, 1866; s. Walter Samuel and Elizabeth Ann (Thompson) H.; M.D., Howard U. Med. Sch., 1888; m. Mary Elizabeth Linger, Aug. 13, 1889; children—Albert Barnum, George Clement. With Govt. Printing Office, 1887-1901, Bur. of Statistics, Treasury Dept., 1901-03; chief Div. of Publs., Dept. of Commerce and Labor, 1903-13; chief clk. and supt. Dept. of Commerce, 1913-18; investigator U.S. Bur. of Efficiency, 1919-33; liaison officer Govt. Printing Office, 1933-38; retired Sept. 1938. Investigated Govt. Printing Office for President Roosevelt, 1909; rep. Dept. of Commerce at San Francisco Expn., 1915; investigated foreign trade promotion activities for federal govt., 1920; investigated statis. activities of federal govt., 1922; elected mem. first Citizens' Advisory Council to Commrs. of D.C., 1925 (highest vote of any candidate), twice reelected. Pres. Anacostia Bldg. Assn., 1925-32; Anacostia Citizens' Assn.; pres. Fedn. of Citizens' Assns., 1929-32; mem. bd. dirs. Washington Chamber Commerce; mem. Hoover-Curtis Inaugural Com., 1929; trustee Washington Community Chest; mem. Dist. Commrs. Employment Com.; mem. Board of Appeal for the Dist. of Columbia; exec. v.p. D.C. George Washington Bicentennial Commn.; v.p. D.C. Chapter George Washington Memorial Parkway Assn.; mem. bd. trustees Washington Public Library since 1930; vice chmn. Roosevelt-Garner Inaugural Parade Com., 1933 and 1937; hon. life mem. Anacostia, Congress Heights, Washington Highlands and Hillcrest Citizens' assns., The Washingtonians and of Lodges 149 and 189 of the American Federation of Government Employees. Presbyterian. Mason. Wrote bulls.: Foreign Trade Promotion Work, 1920; Statistical Work of the United States Government, 1922; Photostat Recording, 1928; Upsets in the Government Service, 1934. Contbr. to mags. and newspapers. Home: 2912 Albemarle St. N.W., Washington DC‡

HAVIGHURST, FREEMAN ALFRED, clergyman; b. Pekin, Ill., Apr. 8, 1869; s. Rudolph and Sophia (Westenkuler) H.; A.B., Ia. Wesleyan U., Mt. Pleasant, 1889, A.M., 1892 (D.D., 1912); S.T.B., Boston U. Sch. of Theology, 1894; U. of Berlin, Germany, 2 yrs.; m. Winifred Aurelia Weter, of De Pere, Wis., Aug. 29, 1899; children—Robert J., Walter E., Alfred F., James W., Miriam C. Prof. Greek and German, Mo. Wesleyan Coll., Cameron, 1889-91; ordained M.E. ministry, 1892; pastor Virden, Ill., 1892-93, Carlinville, 1895-96, 1st Ch., Springfield, 1896-97; prof. history, Lawrence Coll., Appleton, Wis., 1897-1905 and 1907-09; pastor Lincoln, Ill., 1905-07, Rantoul, 1909-10, Tuscola, 1910-12, 1st Ch., Bloomington, 1912-16, 1st Ch., Decatur, 1916-20, 1st Ch., Springfield, 1920-24; dist. supt. Bloomington Dist., Ill. Conf. M.E. Ch., 1924-30; pastor Grace Meth. Ch., Jacksonville, Ill., 1930-36; lecturer since 1936. Mem. Phi Delta Theta. Home: Bloomington IL‡

HAW, GEORGE EDWIN, lawyer; b. Dundee, Va., Jan. 19, 1881; s. George Pitman and Elizabeth Winston (Price) H.; student McCabe's U. Sch., Richmond, Va.; LL.B., Washington and Lee U., 1904; m. Warfield Crenshaw, Sept. 21, 1918; 1 son, George Edwin. Admitted to Va. bar, 1904, practiced in Richmond, 1904-71; sec. P. L. Farmer Oil Co., Inc.; dir., counsel Savs. Bank & Trust Co., Tri-County Bank. Dir. Richmond Eye Hosp. Mem. Antiquarian Soc. Richmond (pres.), Am. Judicature Soc., Am., Va. State (pres. 1942-43), Richmond bar assns. Presbyn. (ruling elder). Contbr. articles legal journals. Home: Richmond VA Died Aug. 1971.

HAWES, ELIZABETH, author, dress designer; b. Ridgewood, N.J., Dec. 16, 1903; d. John and Henrietta (Houston) Hawes; A.B., Vassar Coll., 1925; m. Ralph Jester, 1931 (div. 1933); m. 2d, Joseph Losey, 1937 (div. 1944); 1 child, Gavrik. Began designing commercially for children's shop, Phila., age 12; apprentice, Bergdorf Goodman, N.Y. City, 1924 designer for the custom-made dress shop, Hawes Inc., N.Y. City, 1929-40; mass-produced designs nationally distributed, 1932-40; first American woman designer to exhibit clothes in Paris, 1930, Moscow, 1935; editor consumer depts., feature writer, newspaper PM, 1940-42; designer blue grey uniforms Am. Red Cross; machine shop operator Wright Aeronautical Corp., 1943; pres. Elizabeth Hawes, Inc., 1948-51; designer women's clothes firm Tillett-Haws, N.Y., 1953. Mem. U.A.W., C.I.O. (internat. rep. attached to edn. dept., 1944); editorial advisor on Labor Book Club, Reynal and Hitchcock, 1945. Author books including: Fashion Is Spinach, 1938; Anything But Love, 1948; But Say It Very Politely, 1951; It's Still Spinach, 1954. Sketches of original designs and collection of models in Bklyn. Mus. Contbr. to mags. Home: Ridgewood NJ Died Sept. 1971.

HAWES, STEWART S(TARKS), banker; b. Troy, N.Y., Dec. 31, 1898; s. William S. and Christine (MacCormack) H.; B.A., Williams Coll., 1920; m. Elizabeth Heald, Oct. 20, 1934; 1 dau., Barbara (Mrs. Meredith Wood, Jr.). With Guaranty Trust Co. of N.Y., N.Y.C., 1920-22; with Blyth & Co., Inc., 1922-67, vice president, 1934-58, pres., 1958-65, chmn. bd., 1966-67; dir. Georgia Pacific Corp. Mem. Phi Beta Kappa, Beta Theta Pi. Clubs: Apawamis (Rye, N.Y.); Recess (N.Y.C.); Scarsdale (N.Y.) Golf. Home: Scarsdale NY Died Nov. 10, 1967; buried Sleepy Hollow Cemetery, Tarrytown NY

HAWKES, ELDEN EARL, newspaper pub.; b. Preston, Ida., Jan. 8, 1908; s. Earl and Margaret (Geddes) H.; B.S., Utah State U., 1929; m. Editha Emiline Rich, Nov. 16, 1930; 1 son, Earl Rich. With Burroughs Adding Machine Co., 1929-30; with Gen. Motors Acceptance Corp., 1930-32; with Farm Credit Adminstrn., 1932-36; with Hearst Newspapers, 1936-64, gen. mgr. Boston Record Am.-Sunday Advertiser, 1960-64; exec. v.p., gen. mgr., pub. Deseret News Pub. Co., Salt Lake City, 1964-67, exec. vice pres., publisher, 1967-71; v.p., sec., dir. Newspaper Agy. Corp.; dir. Prudential Fed. Savs. & Loan Co. Mem. Downtown Planning Assn., Salt Lake City, 1964-71. Bd. dirs. Utah Assn. Mental Health, Utah Symphony, Salt Lake City dist. Boy Scouts Am., Radio Free Europe; mem. exec. com. Pro-Utah Orgn. Served to 1st lt. AUS, 1943-45. Mem. Salt Lake City C. of C. (bd. govs.), Alpha Kappa Psi, Phi Kappa Phi, Sigma Delta Chi. Mem. Ch. of Jesus Christ of Latter-day Saints. Clubs: Bonneville Knife and Fork, Country, Timpanogas, Rotary, Alta. Home: Salt Lake City UT Died July 1972.

HAWKINS, COLEMAN, saxophonist; b. St. Joseph, Mo., Nov. 21, 1904; attended Washburn Coll., Topeka, Kan.; played with Mamie Smith's Jazz Hounds, 1922-23, Fletcher Henderson, 1923-34; then tours in England and on Continent; formed own 9-piece band, 1939; 16-piece band, 1940; own combos in 1940's; led sextet 1944-45 in Cal.; freelanced in East; toured with Jazz at the Philharmonic; European tours in 1967, 68; appeared at Newport Jazz Festival; again toured with Jazz at Philharmonic; appeared Village Vanguard, 1960's. Was first successful jazz saxophonist. Recipient Winner Down Beat award, 1939; Esquire Gold award, 1944-47; Metronome award, 1945-47; Down Beat Critics Poll, 1959-60, Hall of Fame, 1961; Playboy Jazz Poll, 1960-61. Numerous recordings, most notably Body and Soul, 1939. Address: New York City NY Died May 19, 1969; buried Woodlawn Cemetery, Bronx NY

HAWKINS, EARLE T(AYLOR), coll. pres.; b. Harford County, Md., Mar. 5, 1903; s. Philip Hopkins and Laura Bell (Taylor) H.; A.B., Western Md. Coll., 1923; A.M., Columbia, 1928; Ph.D., Yale, 1942; LL.D., Western Maryland Coll., 1948, married Juanita Maxine Greer, June 16, 1951. Teacher, Frederick County, Maryland, 1924; supervisor high schools Md. State Dept. of Edn., 1938-45, dir. division of instr., 1945-47; summer instr. U. of Md., 1938, 1943, Johns Hopkins U., 1944; pres. Towson State Coll., Balt., 1947-69. Mem. gen. com. and exec. com. Cooperative Study of Secondary Sch. Standards, 1940-68; chmn. Econ. Edn. Council Md., 1963-69; organizer, dir., state program curriculum revision, 1945-47; chmn. nat. confs. on citizenship, 1947-49; chmn. dept. research and edn. Md. Bd. Natural Resources, 1948-61; adv. com. Automobile Club Md.; mem. state library survey com. Md. Planning Commission; member of the National Commission on Accrediting, 1961-66; bd. of managers Mary and Training School for Boys, 1959-65. Awarded medal for Distinguished Service to Youth by Central Atlantic Area Council of Y.M.C.A., 1946. Mem. Middle States Assn. Colls. and Secondary Schs. (commn. on higher edn. 1950-55, exec. com. 1956-59), Nat. Congress Parents and Tchrs. (hon. life), Am. Assn. State Colls. and Univs. (pres. 1965-66, chmn. legislative com. 1967-69), Council Cooperation in Teacher Edn. (joint com. on teacher recruitment 1943-45), Am. Assn. Colls. for Teacher Edn. (com. on legislation), Y.M.C.A. (chmn. youth and government), Presbyn. Social Union of Md. (pres. 1947-49), Ruling Elders Assn. of Presbytery of Baltimore (pres. 1940-41), N.E.A. (v.p. 1947-49), Nat. Assn. Secondary Sch. Prins. (state coordinator 1941-47; exec. com. 1945-48; chmn. planning com. 1948-49). Nat. Council Teachers of English (com. on supervision since 1944), Nat. Assn. Sch. Adminstrs., Nat. Soc. Study of Edn., Nat. Assn. Supervision and Curriculum Development, Am. Acad. Polit. and Social Sci., Md. State Teachers Assn. (member executive committee 1949-51, president 1951-52), Md. Hist. Soc. (chmn. com. on history in schs.), Md. Library Assn. (planning com.), Ednl. Soc. of Balt. (v.p. 1948-49), Phi Delta Kappa, Presbyn. Clubs: Balt. Music, Rotary. Author: Reliability of Secondary Sch. Evaluations; contbr. to ednl. jours. Mem. team Baltimore MD Died June 3, 1972.

HAWKINS, JACK, actor, producer; b. London, Eng., Sept. 14, 1910; s. Thomas George and Phoebe (Goodman) H.; ed. Trinity County Sch., Middlesex, Eng.; m. Jessica Tandy, 1932 (div. 1940); 1 dau., Susan (Mrs. John Tettemer); m. 2d, Doreen Lawrence, 1947; 3 children. Actor, 1924-73; made debut on legitimate state in St. Joan, London, 1924, films The Lodger, 1932; appeared on stage and in films, London and N.Y.C., 1924-39, 47-73; more recent films include The Cruel Sea, The Intruder, Front Page Story, Bridge on the River Kwai, Ben Hur, League of Gentlemen, The Spinster, Lawrence of Arabia, Judith, Great Catherine, 1967, Shalako, 1968, Battle of Waterloo, 1969. Decorated comdr. Order Brit. Empire. Joined Royal Welch Fusillers, 1940; serviced in India and Burma until 1946. Home: London England Died July 18, 1973.

HAWKINS, THOMAS HAYDEN, surgeon; b. in Ky.; s. Rev. John and Elizabeth (Stodghill) H.; ed. De Pauw U. (hon. A.M., 1889); M.D., Bellevue Hosp. Med. Coll. (New York U.), 1873; (LL.D.); m. Cecile Feickert, of New York, Aug. 9, 1877. Practiced in New York, 1873-80, at Denver, Colo., since 1880; prof. gynecol. and abdominal surgery, dean many yrs. and later pres. bd. trustees, Denver and Gross Med. Coll. (U. of Denver); gynecologist Nat. Jewish Home for Consumptives; attending surgeon, gynecologist and chief of staff, St. Anthony's Hosp.; attending gynecologist City and County hosps.; consulting surgeon Mercy Hosp. Mem. A.M.A., Rocky Mountain Inter State Med. Assn.; ex-pres. State and Co. Med. socs., and Am. Med. Editors' Assn. Founder Denver Medical Times and editor 25 yrs. Home: Junglewood, Morrison, Colo. Address: Denver‡

HAWLEY, CAMERON, writer; b. Howard, S.D., Sept. 19, 1905; s. Clifford and Atheline (Conover) H.; student S.D. State Coll., 1922-24; m. Elaine Gifford, Sept. 1, 1926. With Armstrong Cork Co., Lancaster, Pa., 1927-51, beginning as advt. writer, successively dir. comml. research, dir. retail merchandising, 1927-43, dir. advt. and promotion, 1943-51; writer of short stories and articles appearing in Sat. Eve. Post, Life, Harper's Collier's, Good Housekeeping mags., and others; dramatic writer for motion pictures, TV and radio. Clubs: The Lambs (N.Y.C.); Hamilton (Lancaster). Author: Executive Suite, 1952; Cash McCall, 1955; The Lincoln Lords, 1960; The Hurricane Years, 1968. Home: Lancaster PA Died Feb. 9, 1969.

HAWLEY, HARRY FRANKLIN, foreign service officer; b. Newark, N.J., July 5, 1880; s. Robert and Sarah Jane (Daft) H.; ed. pub. sch. pvt. instr. and extension courses in economics and pub. speaking, U. of Mich.; m. Agnes Sweet, Jan. 22, 1910; children—Charles Franklin, Robert Barrows, Helen Agnes (Mrs. Archibald M. Adam), John Chadwick. Began as clerk, N.Y. City, 1895-1902; Philippine Civil Service, 1902-06, 1907-09; sec. to Am. Delegation to Joint Internat. Opium Conf., Shanghai, 1909; clk. Am. Embassy, Tokyo, 1907, 1909-17; consul, Am. Embassy, Tokyo, 1917-18; consul at Yokkaichi, Nagoya, Japan; Windsor, Ont.; Nantes, France; Glasgow, Scotland; Oporto and Lisbon, Portugal; Gibraltar; Marseille, France; consul gen., Bilbao, Spain. Clubs: Sociedad Bilbaina; Sociedad de Golt, Neguri. Home: Old Saybrook CT Died July 26, 1970; buried Cypress Cemetery, Old Saybrook CT

HAWLEY, RALPH CHIPMAN, univ. prof.; b. Atlanta, Ga., Mar. 5, 1880; s. Chester Warren and Martha (Jaqueth) H.; A.B., Amherst (Mass.) Coll., 1901; M.F., Yale, 1904; m. Mary Minor, Sept. 1910 (died 1945); children—Alfred Minor, Katharine Jacquet; married 2d, Hilda Happe, October, 1945. Forester asst., U.S. Forest Service, 1904-05; asst. state forester, Mass., 1906-07; prof. forestry Sch. of Forestry, Yale, 1907-48, professor emeritus, 1948-71; treas. and sec. North Eastern Forestry Co.; president Connwood, Inc.; forester, New Haven Water Company. Member American Society Foresters, Am. Assn. Univ. Profs., Conn. Forestry Assn., Delta Upsilon. Republican. Conglist. Club: Graduate. Author: Forestry in New England, 1912; A manual of Forestry, 1918; The Practice of Silviculture, 1921 (5th edit. 1946); Forest Protection (with Paul W. Stichel), 1937, 2d edit., 1948. West Cheshire CT Died Jan. 1971.

HAWXHURST, ROBERT, JR., mining engr., geologist; b. San Francisco, Calif., June 19, 1875; s. Robert and Kate (Stephens) H.; both parents of English descent, and of American Colonial ancestry dating from 1636; ed. U. of Calif., Stanford U. Engr., geol. with various mining, oil and ry. cos., in Central and South America, Hawaii, China, Malay States and East Indies, 1894-1905; gen. mgr. Eden Mining Co., Nicaragua, 1916-19; cons. engr. and geologist, San Francisco, since 1919. Fellow A.A.A.S.; mem. Am. Soc. Civil Engineers, Am. Inst. Mining and Metall. Engineers (past chmn. San Francisco Sect.), San Francisco Engring. Council (1938-41), Seismol. Soc. America, California Academy Sciences, Am. Geophysical Union, Society of California Pioneers, Society Geologie de France, Le Conte Geologists Club. Republican. Episcopalian. Mason. Club: Engineers of San Francisco (past pres.). Home: 2 Presidio Terrace. Office: Crocker First National Bank Building San Francisco‡

HAY, CLARENCE LEONARD, archaeologist; b. Cleveland, Dec. 19, 1884; s. John and Clara Louise (Stone) H.; student Westminster Sch., Simsbury, Conn.; A.B., Harvard, 1908, A.M., 1911; m. Alice Appleton, Aug. 5, 1914; children—John, Adele (Mrs. Creekmore Fath). Central Am. research fellow Harvard Univ. on expdn. with R. E. Merwin to Southern Quintana Roo in Yucatan in search of Maya ruins, 1911-12; excavations in Valley of Mexico, Internat. Sch. Archaeology, 1914, research asso. in Mexican and Central Am. Archaeology, Am. Mus. Nat. History, 1921; sec., bd. trustees Am. Mus. Nat. History, N.Y.C., 1931-54, then hon. trustee. Hon. curator, eonservation and gen. ecology, Am. Mus. Nat. History. Mem. Am. Anthropol. Assn., N.Y. Acad. Scis., Horticultural Soc. of N.Y. (dir.). Republican. Christian. Club: Harvard, Century Assn. Horticulturist. Home: New York City NY Died June 4, 1969; buried Ipswich MA

HAY, MALCOLM, lawyer, judge, N.G. officer; b. Pitts., May 19, 1907; s. Southard and Eleanor (Humbird) H.; grad. Phillips Acad., Andover, Mass., 1925; A.B., Yale, 1930; LL.B., U. Pitts., 1933; m. Martha Verner Leggate, June 4, 1931; children—Eleanor Anne (Mrs. Leon Thomson), Malcolm, Thomas Southard; m. 2d, Mary Otis Mather, Dec. 16, 1943; m. 3d, Jessie F., May 1968. Admitted to Pa. bar, 1933, practiced in Pitts.; partner firm Miller, Hay & Entwisle, from 1957; instr. U. Pitts. Sch. Social Work, 1948-52; judge orphans ct. div. Ct. Common Pleas, Allegheny County, 1968-72. Commd. 2d lt. O.R.C., U.S. Army, 1931, advanced through grades to capt., 1941; active duty in ETO, World War II; col. Res., 1946-61; comdt. Pitts. U.S. Army Res. Sch., 1950-61; adj. gen., Pa., maj. gen. N.G., from 1961; maj. gen. AUS, from 1961. Lay dep. Triennial Conv. P.E. Ch. U.S., 1953-61, mem. com. canons, from 1955; mem. Community Chest Allegheny County, from 1959; Pa. Citizens Assn., from 1959. Chancellor P.E. Diocese Pitts., from 1951, trustee from 1937; trustee St. Margaret Meml. Hosp., Pa. Mental Health Inc.; trustee Family and Childrens Service Allegheny County, from 1947, pres., 1956-57; dir. United Mental Health Service Allegheny County, from 1958. Decorated Legion of Merit. Mem. Pitts. C. of C. (dir., gen. counsel from 1959), Res. Officers Assn. U.S. (pres. Pa. 1955-56, nat. judge adv. 1950-51, nat. council 1951-52, nat. v.p. 1956-57) Am. Legion, Mil. Order World Wars, Assn. U.S. Army, S.A.R., Am., Pa., Allegheny County bar assns., Phi Delta Phi. Mason (320, Shriner). Clubs: Fox Chapel, Pittsburgh, Harvard-Yale-Princeton, University (Pitts.). Home: Pittsburgh PA Died Feb. 4, 1972.

HAYCRAFT, JULIUS EVERETTE, judge; b. Blue Earth County, Minn., Aug. 26, 1871; s. Isaac and Sarah (Jolly) H.; ed. pub. schs., commercial college, and study in law office; m. Marie E. Stelzer, Feb. 4, 1903; children—Howard, Anna C. (Mrs. George C. Hellickson). Admitted to Minn. bar, 1898; postmaster, Madelia, Minn., 1899-1911; became village atty. Madelia, 1903; state senator, 1911-15; city atty. City of Fairmont, Minn., 1915-23; judge District Court, 17th Judicial District of Minn., 1925-48. Pres. Dist. Judges Assn. (Minn.), 1929-30, Minn. Hist. Soc., 1944-45, Martin County Hist. Soc. since 1929. Hon. vice pres. Minn. State Soc. S.A.R. since 1928. Hon. mem. Kiwanis and Rotary clubs, Jr. C. of C. (Fairmont, Minn.). Home: 310 Woodland Av., Fairmont MN‡

HAYDEN, CARL (TRUMBULL), former U.S. senator; b. Hayden's Ferry, now Tempe, Ariz., Oct. 2, 1877; s. Charles Trumbull and Sallie Calvert (Davis) H.; grad. Normal Sch. of Ariz., Tempe, 1896; attended Leland Stanford U., 1896-1900; LL.D., U. Ariz., 1948, Ariz. State U., 1959; m. Nan Downing, Feb. 14, 1908 (dec.). Mem. Tempe Town Council, 1902-04; treas. Maricopa County, 1904-06; sheriff Maricopa County, 1907-12; maj. inf., U.S.N.A., 1918; Member of Congress from Arizona, 1912-27; United States Senator from Arizona, 1927-69, (pres. pro tempore 1957-69); during his Congl. serv. specialized on legislation relating to irrigation of arid lands and Federal aid for hwys.; chmn. Senate com. on appropriations; mem. interior and insular affairs com. Democrat. Mason. Home: Tempe AZ Died Jan. 25, 1972; buried Twin Butte Cemetery, Tempe AZ

HAYDEN, JAY G., newspaper writer; b. Cassopolis, Mich., Dec. 8, 1884; s. James Girt and Ruth (Kingsbury) H.; U. of Mich., 1904-06; LL.D. from George Washington U., 1934; m. Marguerite Scholl, June 20, 1910 (died December 26, 1924); 1 son, Martin Scholl; married second Loretta Taylor, June 15, 1926 (deceased, January 29, 1950); m. 3d, Ruth Haberland Felfe, Dec. 19, 1953. On editorial staff Detroit News, 1907-67, Washington corr., from 1915, reporter Peace Conf., Paris, 1918-19, established London news bureau for Detroit News, 1919; columnist North American Newspaper Alliance, from 1940. Sec. Detroit St. Ry. Commn., 1914-15. Officier de l'Instruction Publique, France, 1919. Honorable memtion Pulitzer award, 1936. Baptist. Clubs: Gridiron (pres. 1931), Nat. Press, Overseas Writers, Columbia Country. Home: Kensington MD Died Oct. 24, 1971; buried Cassopolis MI

HAYDOCK, GEORGE SEWELL, investment counsel; b. Cincinnati, O., Apr. 5, 1876; s. Thomas Thompson and Flora (Sewell) H.; B.A., magna cum laude, Yale, 1897; m. Ellen Graham Carmichael, June 16, 1903;children—Thomas Carmichael, Ellen Elizabeth, Atha Graham, Anne Sewell. Pres. T. T. Haydock Carriage Co., 1898-1903, Standard Carbonic Co., 1905-24, Oakley Machine Tool Company, 1915-18; pres. Haydock, Cresler, Lamson & Company (now senior partner Haydock & Company) since 1925. Student Plattsburg (N.Y.) Training Camp, 1915; 1st lt. Cincinnati Home Guards, production mgr. and 1st asst. to dist. chief of ordnance, Cincinnati, 1917-18. Republican. Quaker. Clubs: University, Cincinnati Country, Commonwealth. Home: 3530 Holly Lane, Cincinnati, O.; also Delray Beach, Fla., and Neahtawanta, Mich. Office: First Nat. Bank Bldg., Cincinnati OH‡

HAYES, HARVEY CORNELIUS, research physicist; b. North Fenton, N.Y., Nov. 2, 1878; s. William Henry and Edith Marion (Reynolds) H.; grad. Normal Sch., Oneonta, 1900; A.B., Harvard, 1907, A.M., 1908, Ph.D., 1911; m. Marjorie Dodge Wood, 1909; children—Shirley Wood, Harvey Cornelius, Gordon Brewster, Benjamin Osgood; m. 2d, Katherine Moore. Research fellow, Harvard, 1911-13; prof. physics, Swarthmore (Pa.) Coll., 1913-17; research physicist U.S. Navy, at New London, Conn., 1917-19, Annapolis, Md., 1919-23, Washington, from 1923. In cooperation with others during World War I, developed methods and apparatus for locating submerged submarines. Fellow Am. Physical Soc.; mem. Washington Acad. Sciences, Geophysical Union, Philos. Soc. of Washington, Phi Beta Kappa. Republican. Club: Cosmos. Awarded Levy gold medal and John Scott medal, by Franklin Inst., Phila., for development of method for measuring ocean depths by means of sound waves, also Cullom geog. medal for same, by Am. Geog. Soc.; Distinguished Service Citation, by Sec. of Navy for service in anti-submarine campaign. Home: Peterboro NH Died July 9, 1968; buried Dublin NH

HAYES, JAMES LEO, advt. exec.; b. Chgo., July 25, 1895; s. Thomas S. and Katherine (Covdierre) H.; A.B., St. Mary's (Kan.) Coll., 1917; m. Edna E. Eischen, Oct. 27, 1934; 1 son, James Leo. Advt. rep. Curtis Pub. Co., 1919-25; asst. to pres. Richfield Oil Co., 1925-32; v.p. Minn. Mining & Mfg. Co., 1941-71; pres. Midland Rubber Corp. from 1949, v.p., gen. mgr. Nat. Advt. Co., Waukesha, Wis., 1951-53, pres. from 1953 (latter firms subsidiaries Minn. Mining & Mfg. Co.); dir. First Nat. Bank of Barrington, Midland Rubber, Nat. Advt. Co., Mutual Broadcasting System, Inc., Washington Park Jockey Club. Clubs: Mid-Day, Tavern (Chgo.); Recess (Detroit); Minnesota (St. Paul); Everglades, Bath and Tennis (Palm Beach, Fla.). Home: Palm Beach FL Died Dec. 25, 1971.

HAYES, JOHNSON JAY, judge; b. Purlear, N.C., Jan. 23, 1886; s. John Lee and Sarah J. (McNeill) H.; ed. Whitsett (N.C.) Inst. and Wake Forest Coll.; m. Willa V. Harless, Nov. 22, 1911; children—Hadley, Johnson, Hayden, Willa Jean, Coral Virginia, Sarah Rebecca. Admitted to N.C. bar, 1909, and began practice at Wilkesboro; pros. atty. 17th N.C. Jud. Dist., 1915-26; mem. firm Brooks, Parker & Smith, Greensboro, N.C., 1927-70; judge U.S. Dist. Court, Middle N.C. Dist., 1927-70. Mem. Rep. Nat. Com., 1926-27. Baptist. Home: Wilkesboro NC Died Oct. 22, 1970; buried Mountlawn.

HAYES, JOSEPH P.;, b. San Francisco, Calif., June 20, 1876; s. Thomas and Margaret (MacMonagle) H.; grad. Evening High Sch. of Commerce, San Francisco, 1893; grad. course in Spanish, Lincoln Evening Sch., San Francisco, 1901; m. Sarah Janette Gibbons, of San Francisco, Feb. 14, 1899. Began as messenger Western Union Telegraph Co., San Francisco, 1892, and became clk. to mgr.; later sec. to gen. mgr. Ocean Shore Ry.; returned to Western Union as chief clk., San Francisco office, 1906; apptd. commercial agt. same co., 1917; del. to constl. conv. of Assn. of Western Union Employes, Chicago, July 1918; nat. pres. of the Assn. since July 20, 1918. Republican. Mem. Knights of Columbus, Young Men's Inst., San Francisco. Home: 5737 Kenwood Av. Office: 309 S. LaSalle St., Chicago IL‡

HAYES, MARY SANDERS (MRS. WILLIAM HENRY HAYS);, b. N.Y. City, Nov. 6, 1876; d. Charles W. and Ella A. (Wickwire) Sanders; A.B., Vassar Coll., 1896; m. William Henry Hays, Oct. 19, 1898; children—Ethel Sanders (Mrs. E. Hays Bonner), William Henry, Grace (Mrs. Henry Stehli). Pres. Y.W.C.A. of N.Y. City, 1928-35; pres. Women's Nat. Republican Club, N.Y. City, 1937-43. Republican Baptist. Clubs: Colony, Vassar, Women's National Republican. Address: 399 Park Av., New York 22‡

HAYES, R.S., pres. Zions 1st Nat. Bank, Salt Lake City. Address: Salt Lake City UT Died July 1972.

HAYES, WAYLAND J(ACKSON), prof. sociology; b. Morgantown, W. Va., Nov. 30, 1893; s. Ulysses S. and Mary Etta (Evans) H.; B.S., U. of Va., 1919, M.S., 1921; Ph.D., Columbia, 1930; m. Mary Lula Turner, July 13, 1916; children—Dr. Wayland Jackson, Jr., Mary Virginia, Carolyn Turner (Mrs. Martin L. Ball, Jr.), Sarah Elizabeth (Mrs. Nat Swann, Jr.). Rural sch. teacher, Priddy's Creek, Va., 1914; prin. consol. rural high sch., Alberene, Va., 1915; teacher, Charlottesville (Va.) High Sch., 1916-18, prin., 1918-25; asst. in ednl. sociology teacher's coll., Columbia, 1926-28; teacher edn. Jamaica (L.I., N.Y.) Teacher's Coll., 1927-28; asst. prof. sociology Vanderbilt U., Nashville, Tenn., 1928-38, asso. prof. sociology, 1938-41, professor sociology, from 1941, chmn. dept., from 1953, prof. sch. nursing, from 1935. Mem. So. Sociol. Soc. (chmn. com. on teaching sociology, 1937-44, pres. 1948-49), Am. Sociol. Soc., Am. Statis. Assn. (life membership awarded by Colliers, 1925), N.E.A., Phi Delta Kappa. Independent. Presbyn. Author: Outline for Sociology (Longmans, 1935); Some Factors Influencing Participation in Voluntary School Group Activities (Teachers Coll. Bur. Pub., Columbia, 1930); The Small Community Looks Ahead: Human Relations in Nursing, 1955, 2d edit. 1959. Contbr. to Encyclopedia of Educational Research (Macmillian, 1940), Collier's Encyclopedia (1947), Manual for Southern Regions (U. of N.C. Press, 1937). Home: Nashville TN Died June 18, 1972.

HAYLER, GUY WILFRID, planning engr.; b. Hull, Eng., Feb. 5, 1877; s. Guy and Elizabeth (Harriss) H.; ed. Collegiate House Sch. (Hull) and Rutherford Coll. (Newcastle); trained as municipal engr. and architect; special study city planning, housing, etc., Great Britain and Continental Europe; married Mollie Beddow, December 13, 1913; children—Guy Beddow, Joan Marylyn (Mrs. Curt Demele). Worked on Further Strand Improvement plans, London; municipal engineer, Gateshead, 1908-09; town planning, western Canada, 1912-13; senior designer South Parks Commissioners, Chicago, 1913-19; made city plans for Richmond, California, 1922; chief engr. Regional Plan for San Francisco Bay Counties, 1926-28; regional planning consultant, Golden Gate Bridge, 1930; city plan cons. for Burlingame and Menlo Park; mgr. land program projects U.S. Dept. of Interior, 1934-35. Asst. engr. U.S. Farm Security Adminstrn., 1942-45. Civil Engineer, U.S. Engrs., San Francisco, 1945-47; research engr., joint Army-Navy Bd. on so. crossing of San Francisco Bay, 1947. Exhibited at 1st Inter Town Plan Exhibition, Royal Academy, London, 1910; made first city planning aeroplane flight over an American City, 1920; directed The Pay Roll Dollar" (city planning motion picture), 1926. Connected during World War I with U.S. Hosp., Div., the War Recreation Bd., and made social surveys for Treasury Department; during World War II, with War Prodn. Bd. War Manpower Com. and War Food Adminstrn. Office of Labor. Mem

Am. Soc. C.E., Royal Sanitary Inst., Instn. Municipal Engrs. (London), Am. Statis. Assn. Author of several booklets on city planning; contbr. to Am. Rev. of Revs. Am. City. Am. Architect, British Architect, etc. Home: 453 34th Av., San Francisco CA‡

HAYMOND, FRANK CRUISE, judge; b. Fairmont, W.Va., Apr. 13, 1887; s. William Stanley and Agnes (Cruise) H.; grad. Fairmont State Normal Sch., 1906; A.B. cum laude, Harvard Coll., 1910; student Harvard Law Sch., 1910-12; LL.D., Morris Harvey Coll., W.Va. U., 1963; m. Susan Watson Arnett, Jan. 25, 1922; children—William Stanley II, Thomas Arnett. Admitted to W.Va. bar, 1912; in gen. practice, specializing in corp. and trial work until 1939; apptd. judge 16th Jud. Circuit of W.Va., 1939, elected 1940, 44, resigned 1945; judge Supreme Court of Appeals of W.Va., 1945-72. Mem. Ho. Dels. W.Va. Legislature, 1916-18; mem. W.Va. Commn. on Constl. Revision. Served from pvt. to capt. U.S. Army, 1918, AEF 1918-19. Mem. W.Va. (pres. 1934-35), Marion County (pres.1929) bar assns.; mem.W.Va. Council 1935-60; chmn. 1948-60; pres. W.Va. Supreme Ct. Appeals, 1949, 53, 58, 61, 64; mem. Conf. Chief Justices, 1949, 53, 58, 61, 64; past pres. W.Va. Jud. Assn. Democrat. Roman Catholic. Press; Harvard (Boston). Lectr. on ins. law, W.Va. U., 1935-39. Home: Fairmont WV Died June 10, 1972; buried Fairmont WV

HAYMOND, THOMAS S., mem. Nat. Bituminous Coal Commn.; b. Fairmont, W.Va., July 15, 1869; s. Judge Adpheus F. and Maria (Boggers) H.; ed. pub. schs. Fairmont; grad. Fairmont State Teachers Coll.; m. Agnes Riggins (now dec.); m. 2d, Mrs. Hattie Bell Scoggins, of Hattiesburg, Miss. Formerly mgr. Mineral Fuel Co., Fleming, Ky.; gen. mgr. Elkhorn Coal Corpn., 1917-37; mem. Nat. Bituminous Coal Commn., by appointment of President F. D. Roosevelt, since 1937. Pres. Big Sandy-Elk Horn Coal Operators Assn. Address: National Bituminous Coal Commn., Washington DC‡

HAYNE, COE, author, clergyman; b. Tecumseh, Mich., Feb. 3, 1875; s. Marcus Eldon and Eleanor Currey, (Tenbrook) H.; A.B. Kalamazoo Coll., 1899, Litt.D., 1932; A.B., U. of Chicago, 1900, grad. work, 1900-03; m. Ethel May Shandrew, July 1, 1909; children—Don William, Eleanor Shandrew, John Wrightwood, Mary Barbara. Contributor to religious publs., 1904-07, 1909-16, ordained Bapt. ministry, 1907; pastor Eaton Rapids, Mich., 1907-09, Burlington Bapt. Ch., Salt Lake City, Utah, 1916-18; Y.M.C.A. service as interdivisional games mgr., Le Mans Area, France, 1918-19; asst. sec. lt. and publicity, Am. Bapt. Home Mission Soc., 1919-30, sec. 1930-44; member board of managers Missionary Education Movement 1923-44, hon. life mem. since 1944; member board of managers American Bapt. Hist. Soc. since 1939; v.p. Nat. Religious Publicity Council, 1937-38, pres. 1939-40. Mem. Divinity Alumni Assn., U. of Chicago (pres. 1925-26). Republican. Author: Old Trails and New, 1920; By-Paths to Forgotten Folks, 1921; Race Grit, 1922; For a New America, 1923; Young People and the World's Work (monograph), 1927; The God of Yoto, 1928; Red Man on the Bighorn, 1929; Prisoners of Spirit Mountain, 1930; Vanguard of the Caravans, 1931; They Came Seeking, 1935; Baptist Trail Makers of Michigan, 1936; Cry Dance (novel), 1939; Rock and Lava, 1942; Kiowa Turning, 1944. Collaborator: America Tomorrow, 1923; The Road to Brotherhood, 1924; The Moccasin Trail, 1923; Roads to Christian Democracy (monograph), 1941; Home Mission Digest, 1943. Home: R. 2, Box 219, St Joseph MI‡

HAYNE, JAMES ADAMS, M.D.; b. Baltimore, Md., Mar. 18, 1872; s. Theodore Brevard and Lillah (Adams) H.; S.C. Mil. Acad., Charleston, 1887-88; U. of S.C., 1889-90; U. of Va., 1890-91; M.D., Med. Coll. State of S.C., 1895. Post-grad. work N.Y. Post-Grad. Med. Sch., 1905; m. Fannie Douglass Thorn, Oct. 20, 1897. Began practice, Greenville, S.C., 1895; examining surg. Pension Bureau, Washington, 1904-05; mem. Bd. U.S. Pension Examiners, Greenville, 1905-07; phys. Isthmian Canal Service, 1907-09; state health officer and sec. State Bd. of Health of S.C. since 1911; prof. public health administration, Med. Coll. of State of S.C. Corporal Co. D, 1st S.C. Vol. Inf., Spanish-Am. War, May-Nov. 1898; 1st lt. Med. Reserve Corps, U.S. Army, Apr. 1909-May 1911. Democrat. Episcopalian. Mem. A.M.A. (chmn. pub. health sect. 1921), Am. Pub. Health Association (pres. Southern Branch 1937), Southern Med. Assn., Am. Assn. Tropical Medicine, S.C. Med. Assn. (pres. 1918), Phi Kappa Psi. Pres. State and Provincial Health Authorities of N.A., 1925. Mason (K.T., 32 deg., Shriner). Home: Congaree, S.C. Office: State Office Columbia SC*‡

HAYNES, HARLEY A(RMAND), physician, hosp. dir.; b. St. Albans, Vt., Dec. 21, 1875; s. Charles M. and Zymira (Duell) H.; M.D., U. of Mich., 1902; m. Inez Downing Harvey, Sept. 9, 1903 (died Nov. 17, 1935); 1 son, Harley Armand; m. 2d, Grace Driggs Lyons, July 3, 1937. Prison physician Mich. Reformatory, Ionia, Mich., 1903-07; asst. med. supt. Mich. Home and Training Sch., Lapeer, Mich., 1907-12, med. supt., 1912-24; dir. U. of Mich. Hosp., 1924-45; dir. State Savings Bank, Ann Arbor, 1935-46, chmn. bd. of dirs. since 1946; dir. Mich. Consol. Gas. Co., 1938-46, Mich. Consol. Gas Co., Ann Arbor Dist. since 1935. Mem. bd. of dirs. Cranbrook Sch., Bloomfield Hills, Mich., 1929-43. Served on Lapeer Co. War Bd. during World War I. Pres. Am. Assn. for Study of Feeble-Minded, 1916. Mem. Am. Coll. Hosp. Adminstrs., Am. Hosp. Assn. (treas. 1942-46), Mich. Hosp. Assn. (pres. 1926; trustee 1936-39), Theta Kappa Psi, Phi Gamma Delta, Alpha Omega Alpha, Phi Kappa Phi. Episcopalian. Clubs: Rotary, Ann Arbor, University of Michigan (Ann Arbor). Contbr. to med. jours. Home: 2 Geddes Heights, Ann Arbor MI‡

HAYNES, JOSEPH WALTON, profl. baseball exec.; b. Lincolnton, Ga., Sept. 21, 1917; s. Thomas Clarence and Lou Mae (Walton) H.; ed. pub. schs.; m. Thelma Robertson Griffith, Oct. 11, 1941; 1 son, Bruce Griffith. Profl. baseball player in minor leagues, 1937-38; profl. baseball player in maj. leagues with Washington Senators, 1939-40, 49-53, Chgo. White Sox, 1941-48; coach Washington Senators, 1953-56, exec. v.p., 1957; exec. v.p. Minn. Twins Baseball Team, from 1961. Home: Hopkins MN

HAYNES, JUSTIN O'BRIEN, business exec.; b. Ft. Wayne, Ind., Mar. 10, 1902; s. Clarence L. and Mary V. (O'Brien) H.; B.S., U. of Pa., 1924; m. Virginia Smathers, July 2, 1928 (divorced, 1943); children—Phyllis, Cynthia (step-daus.), Justin O'Brien; married 2d, Evelyn Green, Apr. 26, 1945; 1 daughter, Amanda. Assistant merchandise manager of the Franklin Simon & Co., N.Y. City, 1924-28; asst. cashier Chase Nat. Bank, 1928-34; pres. Justin Haynes & Co., 1934-40; pres. Crookes Labs., Inc., 1944-55, 57th St. East Corp.; former exec. v.p., treas., dir. Abacus Fund; dir. Bristol Myers Co., 57th Street East Corp. Republican. Roman Catholic. Clubs: Piping Rock; University (N.Y.); Maidstone (East Hampton, L.I.); Lyford Cay (Nassau, W.I.). Home: New York City NY Died Nov. 1972

HAYS, HOWARD H., bus. and newspaper exec.; b. Metropolis, Ill., Nov. 23, 1883; s. William Henry and Jennie Agnes (Burden) H.; student U. Ill., 1903-05, U. Chgo. (law), 1905-06; m. Margaret Mauger, Apr. 15, 1916; children—Howard H., Daniel Mauger, William Henry. Traveling passenger agt. Yellowstone Camps Co., 1905, traffic mgr., 1906-16, pres., 1919-24; gen. mgr. U.P. R.R., C. & N.W. Ry. Tourist Bur., Chgo., 1917, Nat. Parks Bur., U.S. R.R. N.W. Ry. Tourist Bur., Chgo., 1917, Nat. Parks Bur., U.S. R.R. Adminstrn., 1918-19; pres. Sequoia and Kings Canyon Nat. Parks Co., 1926-66; past chmn. Glacier Park Transport Co., 1927-55; Rubidoux Printing Co., 1953-69; pres. Press Enterprise Co. (formerly Daily Press & Riverside Enterprise) Instituted the internat. motor tour transp. system between Glacier Nat. Park (Mont.) and Waterton Lake Nat. Park (Alberta, Can.), 1927. Trustee Riverside Municipal Mus. Mem. Am. Planning and Civic Assn. Rep. Presbyn. Mason. Clubs: Victoria, Rotary (Riverside); Cosmos (Washington). Home: Riverside CA Died Jan. 6, 1969.

HAYS, JACK NEWTON, lawyer; b. Pryor, Okla., May 3, 1917; s. Jack N. and Audrey (Moore) H.; B.A. with honors, U. Tulsa, 1938; J.D. with distinction, George Washington U., 1942; m. Yvonne Webb, Sept. 10, 1940; children—Jackson Newton, Richard Henry. Editor-writer NYA, 1938-42; admitted to Okla. and D.C. bars, 1942; law clk. U.S. Dist. Ct., Tulsa, 1946; mem. faculty U. Tulsa, 1946-54, asso. prof. bus. law, head dept., 1950-54; gen. practice, Tulsa, 1946-70; partner firm Gable, Gotwals, Hays, Rubin & Fox, 1951-70. Gen. counsel, dir. Kin-Ark Oil Co., Tulsa, 1963-70. Co-dir. Modern Cts. for Okla., 1962; panel participant confs. jud. improvement and reform, Colo., 1963, Tex., 1964, Mo., 1965, 68, Mont., 1966, Ariz., 1967, Ky., 1968. Co-chmn. prof. div. Tulsa Com. Chest, 1962; exec. bd. Indian Nations council Boy Scouts Am., 1962-70; counsel, dir. Miss Okla. Pag., 1963-70. Trustee Okla. Bar Found.; sec., dir. St. Simeon's Home Aged, Tulsa, 1959-61; bd. dirs. Friends of Library, Tulsa, 1957-70. Served to lt. USNR, 1942-45. Fellow Am. Coll. Trial Lawyers; mem. Am. (ho. dels. 1961-63), Okla. (pres. 1962), Tulsa County (pres. 1958) bar assns., Fedn. Ins. Counsel, Am. Judicature Soc. (dir., mem. exec. com. 1963-70, vice pres. 1966-70, treas. 1968-70), Judicial Council Okla., Oklahoma Bar Foundation (trustee 1962-65), Def. Research Inst., Assn. Alumni U. Tulsa (pres. 1960), Order of Coif, Phi Alpha Delta, Pi Kappa Delta, Pi Gamma Mu, Delta Sigma Pi, Lambda Chi Alpha. Co-chmn. Okla. Lawyers for Johnson-Humphrey, 1964. Democrat. Episcopalian (vestryman). Clubs: Rotary (sec. 1959, director 1964-65), Tulsa, Tulsa Country, Tulsa Petroleum. Contbr. profl. jours. Editor-in-chief George Washington Law Rev., 1941-42. Home: Tulsa OK Died Apr. 24, 1970; buried Trinity Episcopal Ch. Columbarium, Chapel of Good Shepherd, Tulsa OK

HAYWARD, FRED PRESTON, life ins. company official; b. Dorchester, Mass., Dec. 10, 1871; s. Jonathan Newcomb and Margaret (Codman) H.; ed. English High Sch., Boston; m. Alice Brooks, June 11, 1907; 1 dau., Eleanor. Asso. with John Hancock Mutual Life Ins. Co., Boston, continuously since 1890, and advanced through various positions, now dir., v.p. and treas. Home: 63 Windsor Rd., Waban, Mass. Office: 197 Clarendon St., Boston MA‡

HAYWARD, WALTER BROWNELL, newspaperman; b. St. George's, Bermuda, Aug. 3, 1877; s. Joseph Ming and Maria Louisa (Till) H.; ed. pvt. schs., St. George's; m. Geraldine Jean Le Jeune, Nov. 12, 1904 (died Sept. 1, 1916); 1 son, Walter Le Jeune (dec.); m. 2d, Louisa L. Parmly Ward, June 14, 1919 (died Apr. 7, 1947); stepsons, Louis Francis Ward, John Ward. Came to U.S., 1893, naturalized, 1926. Office boy, mercantile house, 1893; on staff N.Y. Evening Post, successively reporter, copyreader, mag. editor, asst. city editor, 1901-15; on Sunday staff New York Times, 1915-17; city editor New York Evening Post, 1917-19, later mag. editor, rotogravure editor and news editor until 1924; on Sunday staff New York Times 1924-48. Democrat. Club: Town Hall. Author: Bermuda, Past and Present, 1910; The Last Continent of Adventure, 1930. Editor: The Commuter's Garden, 1914. Editor, with Wesley Frank Craven: Journal of Richard Norwood, 1945. Contbr. articles to New York Times Mag. Home: George's St George's Bermuda‡

HAYWOOD, JOHN WILFRED, clergyman; b. Maury County, Tenn., July 4, 1881; s. Charles and Jennie (Kennedy) H.; A.B., Lincoln Univ., Pa., 1903, A.M., S.T.B., 1911, S.T.D., 1925, LL.D. (hon.), 1940; D.D. (hon.) Gammon Theol. Sem., Atlanta, Ga., 1926; m. Lottie J. Burnett, Aug. 4, 1904; children—John Wilfred, Rendall Burnett, Violet G. (Mrs. Violet French). Ordained to ministry of Meth. Ch., 1910; pastor Brooklyn, N.Y., 1911-12, Marshall, Tex., 1912-17; dean Wiley Coll., Marshall, Tex., 1917-19; prof. edn., Morgan Coll., Baltimore, Md., 1920-24, dean 1924-36; pres. Morristown Jr. Coll., Morristown, Tenn., 1936-44; pres. Gammon Theol. Sem., Atlanta, Ga., 1944-48; field sec., Meth. Board on World Peace, from 1948. Sec. Meth. Central Jurisdictional Conf., 1940, 44; asst. sec. Meth. Gen. Conf., 1944. Mem. Pi Lambda Psi. Independent (Socialist). Mem. Am. Woodman (treas.). Home: DC Died May 15, 1972; buried Lincoln Cemetery, Washington DC

HAYWOOD, MARSHALL, JR., publisher; b. Lafayette, Ind., July 20, 1912; s. Marshall and Enid (Carothers) H.; grad. Lawrenceville Acad., 1931; student U. Cal., 1931-32, Princeton, 1932-34; m. Alma Elizabeth Wood, May 24, 1937; children—Marshall, Barry Thayer, Mitchell Carothers. Vice pres. printing div. Haywood Pub. Co., Lafayette, Ind. 1934-49, mgr., 1937-42, v.p. pub. div., Chgo., 1946-49, pres., 1949-70, dir., 1937-70; pres. Marshall Oil & Chem. Co., Dallas, 1954-62, sec., 1962-70; dir. devel. MacLean-Hunter Pub. Co.; dir. Bonnie Dunes Ranch, Valley Cable TV, Mountain Home, Ida. Active Boy Scouts Am. Precinct ward, dist. worker Republican Party, 1956-70; treas. 9th Ill. dist. campaign, 1952. Bd. dirs. North Side Boys Clubs; trustee Chgo. Latin Sch., 1954-60; trustee Lawrenceville Acad., 1963-70. Served from lt. to maj., ordnance dept., AUS, 1942-45. Decorated Bronze Star medal. Mem. Nat. Bus. Publs. Inc. (dir. 1948-54, 56-70, chmn. 1961-62). Episcopalian. Home: Chicago IL Died Oct. 1970.

HAZARD, THOMAS PIERREPONT, estate mgr.; b. Peace Dale, R.I., Oct. 26, 1892; s. Rowland Gibson and Mary Pierrepont (Bushnell) H.; prep. edn., St. George's Sch., Newport, R.I.; A.B., Yale, 1915; m. Anne Francis Cope, May 20, 1922; children—Sophia F. Barringer, Thomas Pierrepont, Mary P. Hoyt, Anne H. Richardson, Oliver Cope. With The Solvay Process Co., 1915-23, tech. supervisor in Can. plant, 1919-20, in purchasing dept., 1920, asst. to pres., 1921-23; now partner Sturges, Chaffee & Hazard; pres. R.I. Estate Corp., Am. Fish Culture Co., Peace Dale Offices, Inc.; dir. United Transit Co., R.I. Hosp. Trust Co., Providence, Allied Chemical Corp., N.Y.C. Trustee R.I. Found. Served as chief, issuance sect., div. priorities, field service, W.P.B., regional officer, Boston, 1941-43. Served as private cavalry, National Guard of New York, advanced to 1st lt., 14th U.S. Cav., 1915-19; maj. lt. col., U.S. Army, World War II; served in European Theater of Operations, Member Town Council, South Kingstown, Rhode Island 1924-30, president, 1930-31, member Rhode Island State Senate, 1930-32; Rep. candidate for Congress, 2d R.I. Dist., 1932; gen. treas. State of R.I., 1938-40. Won Rep. primary nomination for U.S. Senator, 1948. Director Narragansett Library Association (president); member Psi Upsilon, Wolf's Head. Conglist. Clubs: Century, Yale (N.Y.); Dunes, Hope (Providence). Home: Peace Dale RI Died Oct. 1968.

HAZELBAKER, NORVAL DENVER, ednl. adminstr.; b. South West City, Mo., Oct. 12, 1915; s. Noah and Gelia (Selby) H.; B.S., Northeast Okla. State Coll., 1937; M.Ed., Mo. U., 1941; Ed.D., Ark. U., 1952; grad. student U. Minn.; m. Mildred Miller, 1939; 1 son, Kim L. Supt. schs. in Mo., successively Pineville, Jane, Mountain Grove, 1940-52; dean Ark. State Coll., Jonesboro, 1952-59, v.p. charge instrn., 1959-70. Served as ensign USNR, World War II. Mem. N.E.A., Ark. Edn. Assn., Phi Delta Kappa, Kappa Delta Pi. Mason, Kiwanian (pres. Jonesboro 1959). Home: Jonesboro AR Died Aug. 18, 1970; buried Noel MO

HAZELTINE, HAROLD DEXTER, prof. law; b. Warren, Pa., Nov. 18, 1871; s. Abram Jones and Harriet Emeline (Davis) H.; A.B., Brown U., 1894; LL.B.,

Harvard, 1898; univs. of Berlin, Paris and London, Dr. Jur., Berlin, 1905; (hon. M.A., Cambridge, 1906); m. Hope, d. Geo. F. Graves, of Bennington, Vt., June 15, 1911. An editor Harvard Law Review, 1896-8; lecturer on law, U. of Chicago, 1906; prof. law, U. of Wis., 1908; lecturer, U. of London, 1910; lecturer in English legal history, Columbia U., 1912; lecturer in law, 1906—; now fellow Emmanuel Coll., Cambridge, Eng.; reader in English law, U. of Cambridge, 1907—; Downing prof. of laws of England. Mem. Internat. Law Assn., Am. Hist. Assn., Delta Kappa Epsilon, etc. Clubs: Albemarle (London), Conewango (Warren, Pa.). Author: Geschicte des Englischen Pfandrechts, 1907; The Law of the Air, 1911; also articles and essays, mostly upon English legal history. Address: West Lodge, Downing College, Cambridge Eng‡

HAZZARD, JESSE CHARLES, college prof.; b. Kingston, N.Y., Oct. 8, 1871; s. William Henry and Mary C. (Mowell) H.; grad. of Kingston Acad., 1888; A.B., Rutgers, 1892, A.M., 1894; Ph.D., Columbia, 1896; travel and study in Europe, 1908-09; studied Univ. of Chicago; m. Frances Catlin, of Portland, Ore., June 17, 1895 (died Aug. 20, 1923); children—John Catlin (dec.), Mary Catherine (Mrs. Robert F. Budrow), Frances Amanda (Mrs. Harry B. White), Charlotte Deady; m. 2d, Jane Vivian Rice, of Richmond, Ky., Sept. 1, 1926. Head Latin dept., Portland (Ore.) Acad., 1894-1912; prof. English, Albion (Ida.) Normal Sch., 1912-15; head of English dept., La. State Normal Sch., Natchitoches, 1915-18, Dakota Wesleyan U., 1918-20, also dir. summer sch., 1920; head of Latin dept., Macalester Coll., 1920-23; head of English dept., La. State Normal Coll., 1923-30; head of dept. ancient langs., Pikeville Coll., since 1930. Ordained Presbyn. ministry, 1920. Mem. Classical Assn. Middle West and South, N.E.A., Shakespearean Soc. of America, Chi Psi, Pi Kappa Delta. Republican. Rotarian. Author or editor various sch. texts; contbr. articles, stories and poems to ednl. and gen. mags. Home: Pikeville KY‡

HEACOX, ARTHUR EDWARD, musical educator, author; b. Baraboo, Wis., July 22, 1867; s. George Henry and Gertrude Elizabeth (Harseim) H.; student Oberlin (O.) Coll., 1887-93, grad. Oberlin Conservatory of Music, 1893, Mus.B., 1906; studied under Schreck and Reinecke, Leipzig Conservatory of Music, 1 yr., 1899-1900; under V. D'Indy, Schola Cantorum, Paris, 1909-10; m. Katherine Marcy, June 22, 1893 (died 1941); m. 2d, Mary Merrill Woodford, Dec. 13, 1942; children—Gertrude (Mrs. Frank H. Stover), Evelyn. Teacher at Oberlin Conservatory of Music, 1893-1935, prof. of theory, 1902-35, now emeritus; guest professor University of Washington, summer 1926, Northwestern U., summer 1927. Mem. Music Teachers Nat. Assn., Music Supervisors' Nat. Conf., Pi Kappa Lambda; hon. mem. Am. Guild Organists. Conglist. Club: Faculty. Author: Ear Training, 1896; Lessons in Harmony (2 parts), 1904; Keyboard Training in Harmony, 1917; Chants de France (with R. P. Jameson), 1920; Harmony for Ear, Eye and Keyboard, 1922; Project Lessons in Orchestration, 1928; Ten Easy Solos for double bass, or cello, with pianoforte accompaniment, 1934; Sonata for cello and pianoforte, 1939. Home: 1131 W Nicolet St., Banning CA‡

HEAD, JAMES MILNE, surgeon; b. Madison, Aug. 4, 1925; s. Jerome Reed and Jean (Milne) H.; student Middlebury Coll., Vt., 1943-44, Northwestern U., Evanston, Ill., 1946-48; B.A., U. Wis., 1949, M.D., 1952; m. Mary Constance North, Aug. 26, 1950; children—James M., Marcus N., Rollin R., Genevieve N. Intern, Denver Gen. Hosp., 1952-56; resident in gen. surgery Univ. Hosps., Madison, Wis., 1953-57, fellow in thoracic surgery, 1957-58; gen. practice thoracic and cardiovascular surgery Chgo. and suburbs, 1959-69; asso. attending staff Chgo. Wesley Meml. Hosp., Chgo., asso. staff St. Francis Hosp., Evanston; active staff Luth. Gen. Hosp., Park Ridge; asso. in surgery Northwestern U. Med. Sch., Chgo., 1959-69. Served to ensign USNR, 1943-46. Diplomate Am. Bd. Surgery, Am. Board Thoracic Surgery. Mem. Ill., Chgo. med. socs., A.M.A., Am. Coll. Chest Glenview IL Died May 27, 1969; buried Evanston IL

HEAD, MABEL, sec. United Council Church Women; b. Quakertown, N.Y., Feb. 13, 1873; d. Collister M. and Olive (Welch) H.; student State Normal Sch., Genesco, N.Y., 1893; N.Y. School Social Work, 1906. Teacher, Warsaw High Sch., 1893-95; Trenton (Ga.) High Sch., 1896-98; principal Female Coll., Dalton, Ga., 1898-1903; teacher La Grange (Ga.) Coll., 1903-06; sec. Home Missions Meth. Ch. South, Nashville, Tenn., 1906-09, ednl. sec., Bd. Missions, 1909-15, foreign sec., 1915-18; sec. Nat. Bd. Young Women's Christian Assn., N.Y., 1918-26; gen. sec. Cleveland Y.W.C.A., 1926-36; sec. Cleveland Peace Com., 1936-46; sec. United Council Church Women; official observer. United Nations, 1946-50. Member Commission for a Just and Durable Peace; active in business and professional women's clubs; mem. Delta Kappa Gamma. Presbyterian. Lecturer, forum and discussion group leader. Contbr. articles to religious periodicals. Address: 135 E. 52d St., NY City 16‡

HEAD, WALTON O., ins. co. exec.; b. Stephenville, Tex., June 5, 1909; s. William Burres and Lulu Rose (O'Hara) H.; B.A. cum laude, Dartmouth, 1929; LL.B. with highest honors, U. Tex., 1932. Admitted to Tex. bar, 1932; asso. Worsham Rollins, Burford, Ryburn & Hincks, Dallas, 1932-36; with Employers Casualty Co., 1936-72, dir. 1938-72, pres., 1962-72, chmn. bd., 1967-72; with Employers Nat. Inc. Co., 1954-72, dir., 1954-72, pres., 1962-72, chmn. bd., 1967-72; dir. Employers Nat. Life Ins. Co., 1961-72, pres., 1962-72, chmn. bd., 1967-72; with Tex. Employers Ins. Assn., 1936-72, dir., 1956-72, pres., 1962-72, chmn. bd., 1967-72. Served to lt. col. USAAF, 1942-46. Decorated Legion of Merit. Mem. Am. Judicature Soc., Am. Inst. Property and Liability Underwirters, Am., Tex., Dallas bar assns., Internat. Assn. Ins. Counsel. Home: Dallas TX Died June 11, 1972; interred Grove Hill Meml. Park, Dallas TX

HEALD, KENNETH CONRAD, geologist; b. Bennington, N.H., Mar. 14, 1888; s. Josiah Heald and Mary Katharine (Pike) H.; U. N.M., 1907-08; B.S. in Engring., Colorado Coll., 1912; studied Yale, 1912-14; D.Sc., U. Pitts., 1928; LL.D., Colo. Coll., 1955; m. Mary Marguerite Drach, Dec. 26, 1914; children—Mary Katherine (dec.), Kenneth Conrad. Field work, summers, U.S. Geol. Survey, until 1914, and full time, 1914-24, except 1918; chief of Sect. of Oil Geology, U.S. Geol. Survey, 1919-24; asso. prof. petroleum geology, Yale, 1924-25; geologist with Gulf Oil Cos. 1925-53, v.p. 1945, dir. 1950; dir. and v.p. various Gulf Oil subsidiaries; now owner Heald & Heald, geology and engring. cons.; petroleum cons Lectured on petroleum geology, U. Chicago and Johns Hopkins, 1923, 24, U. of Pitts. 1926-53; spl. lecturer, Texas Christian University, Director of Texas Christian U. Research Found. Director Goodwill Industries, Ft. Worth. Capt. engrs., U.S. Army, unattached, staff geologist, 1918. Awarded certificate of appreciation by Am. Petroleum Inst., 1952; Sydney Powers Meml. Award by Am. Assn. Petroleum Geologists, 1952; Metcalf award Engrs. Soc. Western Pa., 1966. Member at large Nat. Research Council, 1925-26; member American Assn. Petroleum Geologists hon. mem.; rep. NRC 1925-25), Geol. Soc. Can., Geol. Society Am. (rep. Nat. Research Council 1927), Soc. Economic Geologists, Am. Inst. Min. and Metall. Engrs., Geol. Soc. Washington, Engrs. Soc. Western Pa., American Petroleum Institute; fellow Am. Association Advancement of Sci., Geological Soc. of Fort Worth. Conglist. Clubs: Cosmos, Mid-River (Washington, D.C.); Fort Worth, Petroleum (Ft. Worth). Author: (bulls.) Geologic Structure of the Pawhuska Quadrangle, Okla., 1918; Structure and Oil and Gas Resources of Osage Reservation, Okla., 1922; Healdton Oil Field, Oklahoma, 1915; Eldorado Oil Field, Arkansas, 1925; Geology of Ingomary Anticline, Mont., 1926. Contbr. papers dealing with geology, geophysics and oil field technology. Home: Fort Worth TX Died Oct. 18, 1971; buried Pittsburgh PA

HEALEY, MICHAEL J., retired mcht.; b. Scranton, Pa., Dec. 23, 1869; s. Michael and Mary H.; ed. pub. schs. and business coll., Scranton; spl. courses in law and engring.; m. Hazel Burke; 1 son, Burke. Began as clerk in father's store in Scranton, later worked as bookkeeper, cashier, credit man, foreman and constrn. engr.; salesman and territory mgr. Deere & Webber Co., Minneapolis, Minn., 1900-11; sec., treas. and mgr. John Deere Plow Co., San Francisco, Calif., 1911, v.p. and gen. mgr., same company, Kanas City, Mo., 1915-39; retired. Former dir. Deere & Co., Moline, Ill.; dir. Chicago & Rock Island Ry. Co.; v.p. and dir. of 41 other mercantile corps. Republican. Catholic. Knight of Columbus. Elk. Clubs: Kansas City, Kansas City Country. Home: 1262 Stratford Rd., Kansas City MO‡

HEALY, DANIEL WARD, JR., educator; b. Bklyn., Oct. 9, 1915; s. Daniel W. and Ada (Owen) H.; B.S., Bowdoin Coll., 1937; M.A., Harvard, 1946, M.E.S., 1948, Ph.D., 1951; m. Barbara Reade, Sept. 2, 1939; children—Michael Reade, Sally Claire. Tchr. pvt. sch., 1937-41; asst. prof. physics and elec. engring. USS Naval Postgrad. Sch., 1946-48; asso. prof. elec. engring. Syracuse U., 1951-58; mem. faculty U. Rochester, 1958-69, prof. elec. engring., chmn. dept., 1958-69. Served to lt. comdr. USNR, 1941-45. Mem. I.E.E.E., Am. Soc. Elec. Engring., Am. Assn. U. Profs., Am. Phys. Soc., Sigma Xi. Home: Victor NY Died Oct. 9, 1969.

HEAPS, WILLIAM JAMES, educator; b. Baltimore County, Md., Feb. 17, 1868; s. James Anderson and Margaret (Wright) H.; A.B., Farmington (Ohio) Coll., 1892; A.M., Allegheny Coll., Pa., 1893; Ph.D., Taylor U., Upland, Ind., 1901; LL.B., Baltimore (Md.) Law Sch., 1903; spl. student in chemistry, Johns Hopkins Univ., 1904-08; m. Caroline Erdman, M.D., Sept. 1, 1909. Organizer and pres. Winfield Acad., Carroll County, Md., 1894-1900; pres. Milton Acad., 1900-09; pres. Milton U. since 1909. Rep. candidate for Congress 2d Dist. of Md., 1915. Editor Sons of America, 1903-31; state sec. of Md. P.O.S. of A., 1905-31, Nat. pres., 1917-19; dir. United Patriotic Orphanage. As sec. of Francis Scott Key-birthplace-monument-com. raised funds for monument, dedicated June 12, 1915. Mem. A.A.A.S., Pi Gamma Mu, Sigma Beta Chi, Delta Chi; fellow Am. Geog. Soc. Mason (33 deg., K.T., Shriner). Clubs: Baltimore City, Optimist. Lecturer on patriotic and scientific subjects. Author: The Perfect Man; Autocracy vs. Democracy; The Book of Books; The Crisis; The Milton Quizzer" for Pharmacy Students; Elementals in Religion; Claire Wellington; God in Genesis and Geology; The Slave and Other Poems. Editor of Sons of America for 30 yrs. Home: Northway Apts., Baltimore MD‡

HEARD, BILL JAMES, automobile co. exec.; b. McCurtain, Okla., Oct. 20, 1920; s. James B. and Irene (Neal) H.; grad. high sch.; m. Betty G. Montgomery, Apr. 22, 1939; children—Terry (Mrs. Dennis Rakosik), Gregory Dean, Neal Allen. Works engr. Detroit engine div. Kaiser Industries Corp., 1947-55, operations mgr. Industries Kaiser Argentina S.A., Buenos Aires, 1955-57, exec. v.p., 1959-64; exec. engr. Willys-Overland Export Corp., Toledo, 1957-59; v.p., asst. to pres. automotive div. Kaiser Jeep Corp., Toledo, 1964, v.p. operations, 1964, then exec. v.p. Served with AUS, 1945-46. Home: Toledo OH Died Nov. 18, 1968.

HEARD, GERALD, author; b. London, Eng., Oct. 6, 1889; s. Henry James and Maud (Bannatyne) H.; student Cambridge U., 1908-13 (grad. with honors in history). Came to U.S., 1937. Worked in Ireland with founder of Agrl. Co-op. Movement, 1919-23; in Eng. with same work, 1923-27; author and lectr., 1927-71; radio lectr., 1930-71; commentator on sci. BBC, 1930-34; lectr. South Place Ethical Soc., 1932-34; lectr., Oxford U., London, 1929-31; lectr. New Sch. of Social Research, N.Y.C. Haskell lectr. Oberlin Coll., 1958; Macliesh lectr. Rockford Coll., 1958. Two-year fellowship, Bolingen Found., N.Y.C., 1954. Mem. council Psychol. Research Soc. Eng., 1933-44. Author books: Ayer Found, lecture, The Eternal Gospel, 1946; Dopplegangers, 1947; Is God In History?, 1949; Is Another World Watching, 1951; The Five Ages of Man; The Perennial Praxis; A Journey Into Consciousness; Training for a Life of Growth. Editor of Realist, London, 1929. Home: Santa Monica CA Died Aug. 14, 1971.

HEARD, JAMES DELAVAN, physician; b. Pittsburgh, Jan. 9, 1870; s. James B. and Emilie Lucretia (Delavan) H.; Western U. of Pa. 2 yrs.; M.D., U. of Pa., 1891, Sc.D., 1938, post-graduate work, 1891; universities of Leipzig and Vienna, 1892-93; m. Edith van Rensselaer McIlvaine, Dec. 27, 1910. Intern, German Hosp., Phila., 1891-92; asso. prof. medicine, 1910-12, prof. since 1912, U. of Pittsburgh. During the war was lt. col., M.C. U.S. Army in charge med. service. Base Hosp. 27, A.E.F.; col. M.R.C., gen. Hosp. No. 27, 1924. Episcopalian. Mem. A.M.A., Assn. Am. Physicians, Pittsburgh Acad. Medicine, Med. Soc. State of Pa., Biol. Soc. U. of Pittsburgh. Mason (32 deg.). Clubs: University, Pittsburgh Golf (Pittsburgh); Pot and Kettle (Bar Harbor, Me.). Home: 5720 Aylesboro Av., Pittsburgh, Pa.; (summer Bar Harbor, Me.). Office: 121 University Pl., Pittsburgh PA‡

HEARE, CLAYTON, lawyer; b. Henrietta, Tex., Oct. 14, 1897; s. Lewis Cass and Martha (Karr) H.; B.A., U. Tex., 1918, LL.B., 1922; M. Jean Ragsdale, July 27, 1935; 1 dau., Marnelle (Mrs. John L. Gafford). Admitted to Tex. bar, 1922; gen. practice, Austin, 1922-26, Shamrock, Tex., 1927-43; asso. justice Ct. Civil Appeals, Amarillo, Tex., 1943-45; partner firm Underwood, Wilson, Sutton, Heare and Berry, Amarillo, 1945-73. Dir. Amarillo Savs. Assn., 1954-73. Pres. Am. Bus. Club, 1948, mem. nat. scholarship com., 1963-67. Bd. dirs. Cal Farley's Boys Ranch, Amarillo, 1955; bd. regents Tex. State Sr. Colls., 1963-69. Served with USMC, 1918-19; AEF in France and Germany. Democrat. Presbyn. Mason (32 deg.). Home: Amarillo TX Died Jan. 16, 1973.

HEARNE, JOHN J(OSEPH), diplomat; b. Waterford, Ireland, Nov. 4, 1893; s. Richard and Alice Mary (Power) H.; grad. Nat. U. Ireland, King's Inn; m. Monica Mary Martin, June 1930; children—Maurice, John Justin, David Anselm, Mary Elizabeth. Jr. counsel Irish Bar, 1919, admitted to Sr. Bar, 1939; asst. atty. gen., 1925; Irish del. League of Nations, 1926. Legal adv. Dept. External Affairs, Dublin, 1927; 1st high commr. Ireland to Can., 1939; ambassador extraordinary and plenipotentiary Ireland to U.S., from 1950. Home: Washington DC Died Mar. 1969.

HEARON, CHARLES OSCAR, b. Bristol, Virginia, May 31, 1876; s. Daniel Scott and Cleo (Miles) H.; ed. King Coll. (Bristol, Tenn.), Emory and Henry Coll. (Emory, Va.) and St. Albans Sch. (Radford, Va.); m. Belle McLaughlin, Sept. 21, 1903; children—Fanning Miles, Elizabeth Hart, Charles Oscar, Belle McLaughlin. Began as reporter, Richmond (Va.) Times, 1898; founder and pub. Bristol (Va.) Herald, 1903-06; editor Spartanburg Herald, 1906-32. Sec. and dir. Spartanburg Adv. Co., broadcasting stations WSPA and WORD. Mem. S.C. State Highway Commn., 1917-37, chmn. 1931-37. Trustee Spartanburg Baby Hosp. Mem. S.C. Press Assn. Democrat. Episcopalian. Home: R.F.D., Route 3. Office: 178 W. Main St., Spartanburg SC*‡

HEARST, GEORGE RANDOLPH SR., newspaper exec.; b. Washington, Apr. 23, 1904; s. William Randolph and Millicent (Willson) H.; grad. Manlius

Sch., St. John's Mil. Sch., student U. Cal. at Berkeley; m. Blanche Wilbut, June 19, 1923 (div. 1930); children—George R. and Phoebe M. (twins); m. 2d, Rosalie Wynn, 1960. Pub. San Francisco Examiner, 1924-27; v.p. Los Angeles Examiner, 1929-53, later v.p., dir. of trustees board Hearst Corp., New York City. Chmn. centennial devel. campaign Manlius (N.Y.) Sch., 1968; founder, pres. Palm Springs chpt. Football Hall of Fame. Pres. Hearst Found., bd. dirs. Palm Springs Boys Club. Home: Palm Springs CA Died Jan. 26, 1972; interred Family Vault, Cypress Lawn, San Francisco CA

HEATH, CLYDE J(AMES), business exec.; b. Muskegon, Mich., Aug. 19, 1897; s. James J. and Clara Belle (Herron) H.; B.S., U. of Mich., 1920; student Harvard Sch. Bus. Adminstrn., 1931; m. Betty Maxwel Lowndes, Dec. 27, 1935; engr., Am. Telephone and Telegraph Co., N.Y. City, 1921-24; engr. New Eng. Tel. and Tel. Co., Boston, 1924-31, div. mgr., 1931-35, asst. gen. comml. mgr., 1935-44, gen. comml. mgr., 1944-46, v.p., treas., 1945-62; dir. Naumkeag Steam Cotton Co. Mem. deptl. com. on bus. adminstrn., Colby Coll. Mem. Newcomen Soc. of England, Delta Upsilon. Republican. Episcopalian. Clubs: Union, Union Boat (dir.) (Boston); Lake Placid (N.Y.). Home: Brookline MA Died Dec. 9, 1970; buried Mt. Auburn Cemetery, Cambridge MA

HEATH, WILLIAM WOMACK, lawyer, ambassador; b. Novmangee, Tex., Dec. 7, 1903; s. John Al and Runie (Hill) H.; student Tex. Christian U., U. Tex. Law Sch.; m. Mavis Barnett, July 14, 1927; children—Cynthia (Mrs. D. G. Ray), and Linda (Mrs. Dean Hester). Admitted to the Texas state bar in 1924; practiced in Anderson, Texas, 1924-33, in Austin, 1933-67; county atty. Grimes County, 1925-29; county judge Grimes County, 1931-32; asst. atty. gen. Tex., 1935-37; bd. dirs., gen. counsel of Tex. counsel numerous ins. companies; U.S. ambassador to Sweden, Stockholm, 1967-70; dir. Dillard Dept. Stores, Braniff Airways, Inc., dir. Capital Nat. Bank, Austin; cattle, sheep and goat rancher, 1950-71. Chmn. Tex. Bd. for Hosps. and Spl. Schs., 1957-59; mem. bd. lease U. Tex. lands, 1959-61; member board regents U. of Texas, 1959-67, vice chairman board of regents, 1961-62, chmn., 1962-66; exec. com. gov. bds. Tex. State Supported Colls. and Univs., 1959-62. Gen. chmn. Gov. of Tex. inauguration, 1961, co-chmn., 1965. Del.-at-large Nat. Democratic Conv., 1960, 64. Mem. Tex. Tax Adv. Commn.; past pres. Tex. Law Enforcement Found.; bd. dirs. Meth. Dist. Bd. Hosps. and Homes. Sec. of state, Tex., 1933-35. Mem. Am. Bar Assn., State Bar Tex., Tex. Bar Found., Am. Judicature Soc. Methodist. Home: Austin TX Died June 22, 1971.

HEATON, HERBERT, econ. historian; b. Slisden, Yorkshire, Eng., June 6, 1890; s. Frederick and Eva (Waterhouse) H.; B.A., Leeds U., 1911, M.A., 1912, D. Litt., 1921; student London Sch. Econs., 1911-12; M. Commerce, Birmingham U., 1914; m. Ellen Jane Houghton, Apr. 11, 1914 (dec. Dec. 4, 1956); children—Helen Joyce (Mrs. Harold Ford), Kathleen Leslie (Mrs. Daniel T. McLaughlin), Frederick William; m. 2d, Edith Ronson, Aug. 6, 1959. Came to United States, 1927, Assistant lecturer commerce, Birmingham U., 1912-14; Sir. John A. Macdonald prof. and head dept. of economics and polit. science, queens U., Kingston, Can., 1925-27; prof. of economic history, U. of Minn., 1927-58, chmn. history dept., 1954-58; vis. prof. Princeton U., 1939-40, Johns Hopkins, 1960; distinguished vis. prof. Pa. State U., 1956-60. Fellow Leeds University, 1912-13; Guggenheim fellow 1931-32. Secretary committee on research in economic history 1940-54. Pres. Workers Ednl. Assn. of Australia, 1920-25. Fellow Royal Hist. Soc.; mem. Royal Econ. Soc., Econ. History Soc. (mem. council), Am. Philos. Soc., Econ. Hist. Assn., American Hist. Assn., Royal, Am. Hist. socs., Am. Assn. Univ. Profs. Episcopalian. Clubs: Campus (Minneapolis); Informal (St. Paul), Author books including: Economic History of Europe, 1936, 1948; A Scholar in Action: Edwin F. Gay, 1952. Home: Minneapolis MN Died Jan. 24, 1973.

HEATON, PERCY, actor; b. N.Y.C., Jan. 31, 1894; s. Alfred and Ellen (Bosher) H.; student pvt. schs. and Peekskill Mil. Acad.; m. Edna Eustace, Oct. 24, 1931. Made debut (with father) in Tony Pastor's Theatre, N.Y.C., 1897; appeared on Broadway in Return of Peter Grimm, Young America, To the Ladies, Poor Nut. One Sunday Afternoon; appeared in approximately 200 movies, 1948-71, including Miracle on 34th St., Hazard, Set Up, Crooked Way, Butch Cassidy; appeared on numerous television shows. Served with U.S. Army, World War I. Decorated D.S.C. Clubs: Lambs (N.Y.C.); Masquers (past 2d v.p.) (Hollywood, Cal.). Home: Hollywood CA Died Sept. 11, 1971.

HEBERT, FELIX, ex-senator; b. Can., Dec. 11, 1874; s. Edouard and Catherine (Vandale) H.; brought by parents to U.S., 1880; ed. parochial and pub. schs. and LaSalle Acad., Providence, R.I.; m. Virginia Provost, Sept. 18, 1900; children—Catherine Virginia, Adrien Warner, Marguerite Rosalie, Edouard Felix. Admitted to R.I. bar, 1907, and began practice at Providence; dep. ins. commr., R.I., 1898-1916; justice, Dist. Ct., R.I., 1909-29; sec. Providence County Court House Commn., 1926; dir. Old Colony Co-Operative Bank, Providence; gen. Counsel Associated Factory Mutual Fire Insurance Companies. U.S. senator from R.I., term 1929-35. Mem. Nat. Rep. Com. for Rhode Island. Clubs: University (Boston); University, Turks Head, Flat River. Home: West Warwick RI Died Dec. 1969.

HECHT, HANS H., physician, physiologist, educator; b. Basel, Switzerland, Jan. 23, 1913; s. Hans and Hannah (Meinhold) H.; came to U.S., 1937, naturalized, 1942; M.D., U. Berlin (Germany), 1936, U. Utah, 1946; sr. yr. certificate, U. Mich., 1944; m. Ilse Wagner, Nov. 8, 1937; children—Hannelore (Mrs. David R. Ebel), Frank Thomas, Susan. Intern, then resident Wayne County Gen. Hosp., Detroit, 1942-44; research fellow U. Mich., 1937-44; from instr. to asso. prof. medicine U. Utah Coll. medicine, 1944-58, L.E. Viko prof. cardiology, 1957-65, prof. medicine, 1958-65, chmn. div. cardiology, dept. medicine, 1944-65; dir. heart sta. Salt Lake County Gen. Hosp., 1944-65; cons. VA hosps., Salt Lake City and Grand Junction, Colo., 1946-64; prof. medicine and physiology U. Chgo. Med. Sch., 1964-71, Blum-Riese prof. medicine and physiology, 1968-71, chmn. cardiology dept. med., 1964-71, chmn. dept. medicine, 1966-69. Mem. tng. grant com. USPHS, 1959-62, mem. cardiovascular study sect., 1965-71; pres. Utah Heart Assn., 1957. Diplomate Nat. Bd. Med. Examiners, Am. Bd. Internal Medicine (subspeciality cardiovascular medicine; vice chmn. cardiovascular bd. 1961-66). Fellow A.C.P., Am. Coll. Chest Physicians, Pan-Am. Med. Assn., N.Y. Acad. Sci.; mem. Am. Heart Assn., Western Soc. Clin. Research (past pres., sec.), Am. Fedn. Clin. Research (western chmn. 1946), Assn. Am. Physicians, Am. Physiol. Soc., Am. Soc. Clin. Investigation, Western Assn. Physicians (councilor 1957-60, 64-65), I.R.E., Inst. Advancement Med. Communication. Royal Soc. Medicine, Assn. Univ. Cardiologists. Mem. editorial bd. Circulation, Diseases of Chest, Excerpta Medica: Cardiovascular Disease, Am. Jour. Medicine, Malatti Cardiovasculari. Home: Chicago IL Died Aug. 12, 1971.

HEDENSTROM PAUL HENRY, physician; b. Cambridge, Minn., May 13, 1926; s. Louis Henry and Ebba H. Hedenstrom; M.D., U. Minn., 1953; m. Bette Joyce Lee, Dec. 30, 1950; children—Robert Paul, Mary Lee. Intern, St. Lukes Hosp., Duluth, Minn., 1952-53; resident in surgery Ancker Hosp., St. Paul, 1959-63; med. fellow in surgery U. Minn.; active staff Princeton Community, St. Cloud hosps.; cons. staff Milaca Community, St. Gabriel's, Bethesda hosps. Served with USNR, 1944-46. Diplomate Am. Bd. Surgery. Mem. A.M.A., Minn. Surg. Soc., Phi Rho Sigma. Republican. Lutheran. Mason. Club: Sertoma. Home: Princeton MN Died Oct. 20, 1969; buried Cambridge MN

HEDGE, HENRY ROGERS, insurance exec.; b. Plymouth, Mass., Jan. 13, 1876; s. William and Catherine Elliott (Russell) H.; S.B., Mass. Inst. Tech., 1896; m. Eadith Heath Doliber, Oct. 11, 1904. Entered insurance business with Johnson & Higgins, Boston, Mass., 1897; with Boston Ins. Co. since 1906, becoming vice pres., 1915, pres., 1943-45, chmn. advisory com., 1945-46; v.p., Old Colony Ins. Co., 1918-43, pres., 1943-45, chmn. adv. com., 1945-46; retired from active participation in business, 1946; dir. Boston Ins. Co., Old Colony Ins. Co. Home: 105 Rockwood St., Brookline 46 MA‡

HEDGES, BENJAMIN VAN DOREN, assn. exec.; born Plainfield, N.J., June 8, 1907; s. Dr. Benjamin Van Doren and Adele Cutts (Williams) H.; student Loomis Sch., 1922-26; grad. Princeton, 1930; student N.Y. U.; m. Alice-Marian Hecht, Feb. 22, 1947; children—Ann Sportswood, Benjamin Van Doren. Personnel adminstr. Bankers Trust Co., 1920-48; nat. dir., exec. v.p. Big Bros. of Am., Inc., 1948-69. Mem. quota com., nat. budget com. Community Chests and Councils; mem. atty. general's nat. conf. on citizenship; mem. com. individual agencies, ad hoc com. social security Welfare Council N.Y.C. Dir. Plainfield Y.M.C.A., 1931-32. Served as comdr., air combat intelligence, U.S.N.R., 1942-45. Awarded Presdl. Unit Citation, Aircraft Carriers 13 Battle Stars. Mem. Nat. Welfare Assn. (mem. coms.), Nat. Conf. Social Workers, Nat. Soc. Welfare Assembly, Alumni Assn. Loomis Sch. (trustee, past pres.). Presbyn. Clubs: Princeton Cap and Gown, Princeton. Home: New York City NY Died Dec. 1969.

HEDRICH, KENNETH, photographer; recipient Fine Arts medal A.I.A. Home: Silver Lake WI Died June 1972.

HEDRICK, TUBMAN KEENE, cartoonist, mag. writer; b. Illawara, La., Feb. 15, 1873; s. Cyrus Alan and Ella Augustine (Travis) H.; ed. country schs., La., and pub. schs., Mineola, Tex., until 12 yrs. old, after that self-taught; m. Mary St. Clair McCamish, Mineola, Tex., Dec. 10, 1903. Was newsboy at 12, postal clerk at 14; contb'r Louisville Courier Journal and Louisville Truth, 1890; railroad clerk, Mineola, Tex., 1891; cartoonist Dallas (Tex.) papers, 1892-4, Houston (Tex.) Post, 1895, Globe-Democrat, St. Louis, 1896-1903; since then free lance mag. writer and cartoonist; writer of essays, verse, humorous articles, etc., editor Wetmore's Weekly. Mem. Am. Press Humorists Assn. Sec. St. Louis Single-tax League, 1901, sec. St. Louis Initiative and Referendum League, 1904. Residence: 1374 Union Boul. Office: 520 Holland Bldg., St Louis MO‡

HEDSTROM, CARL OSCAR, inventor; b. Smoland, Sweden, Mar. 12, 1871; s. Andrew P. and Caroline (Danielson) H.; ed. pub. schs., Brooklyn, N.Y.; m. Julia Anderson, of Portland, Conn., Nov. 12, 1898. Early became expert tool maker, later designer and builder of racing bicycles; connected with Hendee Mfg. Co. since 1901; invented the Indian Motorcycle for which was awarded silver medal and high diploma of merit, St. Louis Expn., 1904. Founder mem. Federation Am. Motorcyclists; mem. Soc. Automotive Engrs. K.P. Clubs: New York Athletic; Hartford Gun; Portland; Middletown Yacht. Home: Portland CT‡

HEEKIN, ALBERT EDWARD, JR., can co. exec.; b. Cin., Sept. 22, 1914; s. Albert Edward and Bertha (Ebersole) H.; A.B., Cornell U., 1936; LL.D., Fordham U., 1939; m. Elizabeth C. Kilpatrick, June 8, 1939; children—Albert Edward III, Brian E. Admitted to Ohio bar, 1939, N.Y. bar, 1941; staff law dept. N.Y. Telephone Co., 1941-46; partner Kyte, Conlan, Heekin & Wulsin, Cin., 1946-50; exec. v.p. Heekin Can Co., Cin., 1950-53, pres., 1953-70, chmn. bd., 1970-71, also director; director of Central Trust Co., Cin. & Suburban Bell Telephone Co., Eagle Picher Industries Incorporated, Union Central Life Ins. Co., Central Bancorp. Mem. board directors Can Mfrs. Inst. Mem. Cin. area Community Chest and Council. President's council Xavier U.; mem. adv. bd. Catholic Charities; lay adv. bd. Good Samaritan Hosp. Mem. Beta Theta Pi. Clubs: Commercial, Camargo, Commonwealth, Hyde Park Cincinnati OH Died Feb. 1, 1971; buried Mt. Calvary Cemetery, Cincinnati OH

HEENEY, ARNOLD DANFORD PATRICK, internat. orgn. ofcl.; b. Montreal, Can., April 5, 1902; s. Canon William Bertal and Eva Marjorie Heeney; student St. John's Coll. Sch., Winnipeg; B.A., U. Manitoba, 1921, M.A., 1923; B.A. (Rhodes scholar), St. John's Coll., Oxford, 1925, M.A., 1936; B.C.L., McGill U., 1929; LL.D., U. B.C., 1948, U. Manitoba, 1950, Mich. State Univ., 1955, Franklin and Marshall Coll., 1954, Kenyon Coll., 1955, University of R.I., 1960, McGill U., 1961; Doctor Canon Law, St. John's Coll., U. Manitoba, 1966; Doctor of Laws, University of Alberta, 1967; m. Margaret Yuile, June 27, 1931; children—William Brian Danford, Patricia Jane. Admitted to Que. bar, 1929; practiced in Montreal, 1929-38; sessional lectr. Faculty of Law, McGill U., 1934-38; prin. sec. prime minister of Can., 1938-40; clk. Privy Council, also sec. to Cabinet, 1940-49; under-sec. of state for external affairs, 1949-52; ambassador, permanent rep. Can. to North Atlantic Council, also Orgn. European Econ. Coop., Paris, 1952-53; Canadian ambassador to U.S., 1953-57, 59-62; chmn. Civil Service Commn. Can., 1957-59; chmn. Canadian sect. International Joint Commn., 1962-70; pres. Canadian Inst. Internat. Affairs, 1963-67; chmn. Can. sect. Permanent Joint Bd. on Def., 1967-70. Bd. govs. McGill U. Decorated companion Order of Can. Queens counsel. Clubs: Rideau, Royal Ottawa Golf, Country (Ottawa); University (Montreal). Home: Ottawa Ontario Canada Died Dec. 20, 1970.

HEERMANCE, EDGAR LAING, author; b. White Plains, N.Y., July 14, 1876; s. Edgar L. and Agnes (Woolsey) H.; B.A., Yale University, 1897, M.A., 1899, B.D., 1901; New Coll., Edinburgh, 1 yr.; m. Nora K. Livingston, of Fairmont, Minn., June 9, 1907; children—Edith, Theodore Woolsey, Robert Livingston, Laura Woolsey, Louise. Ordained Congl. ministry, 1902; pastor Mankato, Minn., 1902-13, International Falls, Minn., 1913-18; with Red Cross civilian relief, 1918-19; literary and exec. work since 1919. Supervisor of survey of scenic and historic places in Conn., 1934; chmn. New England Trail Conf., 1935-39; sec. Conn. Forest and Park Assn. since 1936. Clubs: Graduate, Rotary (New Haven, Conn.). Author: Democracy in the Church, 1906; The Unfolding Universe, 1915; Chaos or Cosmos?, 1922; Codes of Ethics, 1924; The Ethics of Business, 1926; Can Business Govern Itself?, 1933; The Connecticut Guide, 1935. Home: 241 Lawrence St. Office: 215 Church St., New Haven CT‡

HEETER, SILVANUS LAURABEE, school supt.; b. N. Manchester, Ind., Sept. 20, 1870; s. Gideon and Mary Jane (Walters) H.; Normal Coll., Manchester; Nat. Business U., Delaware, O.; Winona Assembly, Winona Lake, Ind.; Ph.B., U. of Chicago, 1904; m. Cora M. Parker, of Converse, Ind., 1898. Teacher rural schs., 1889-91; high sch. prin., 1891-5; supt. city schs. various places in Ind., 1895-1902; asst. supt. pub. schs., Minneapolis, 1904-6; supt. schs., St. Paul, 1906-12, Greater" Pittsburgh, Mar. 1, 1912-—. Republican. Presbyn. Mem. bd. dirs. and council N.E.A.; dir. St. Paul Inst., St. Paul Pub. Affairs Com., etc. Frequent lecturer on ednl. subjects. Clubs: City, Commercial, Informal. Address: Fulton Bldg., Pittsburgh PA‡

HEFFELFINGER, GEORGE W. P., corp. exec.; b. Mpls., 1901; Yale, 1924. Exec. v.p., dir. F. H. Peavey & Co., Mpls.; pres., dir. Russell-Miller Co.; dir. First Nat. Bank, Mpls., First Bank Stock Corp.; dir. Mpls. Grain Exchange. Home: Mound MN Died Oct. 1970.

HEFFERAN, THOMAS HUME, lawyer, corp. exec.; b. Grand Rapids, Mich., Nov. 2, 1908; s. George and Ella (Backus) H.; grad. Taft Sch., 1927; A.B., Yale, 1931; LL.B., U. Mich., 1934; m. Constance Howard, Dec. 19, 1942; children—Thomas Howard, Roger Littlefield. Admitted to Mich. bar, 1934; asso. atty. Warner, Norcross & Judd, Grand Rapids, 1934-42; asst. v.p., trust officer Mich. Nat. Bank, Grand Rapids, 1946-51; real estate developer, builder, Spring Lake, Mich., 1952-58; dir. real property mgmt. Dept. Def., Washington, 1958-61; pres. Thomas H. Hefferan & Sons, Inc., Arlington, Va., from 1962; admitted to D.C. bar, 1967. Served from lt. (j.g.) to lt. comdr., USNR, 1942-45. Mem. Am., Mich. bar assns., Zeta Psi, Phi Delta Phi, Episcopalian. Clubs: Yachting of Am., Yale. Home: Alexandria VA Died Mar. 28, 1969.

HEFLIN, VAN, actor; b. Walters, Okla., Dec. 13, 1910; s. Dr. Emmet E. and Fanny (Shippey) H.; A.B., U. Okla., 1931; postgrad. drama student, U. Cal. at Los Angeles, 1948; m. Frances M. Neal, May 16, 1942; children—Vana Gay, Cathleen Carol, Tracy Neal. Actor theatre, radio, films, 1933-71; plays include End of Summer, 1936-37, Philadelphia Story, 1939-41; numerous motion pictures including Tempest, 1959; They Came to Cordura, A Case of Libel, Madame Bovary, The Prowler, Tomahawk, Weekend with Father, My Son, John, Shane, Wings of the Hawk, Golden Mask, Tanganyika, The Raid, Woman's World, Black Widow, Battle Cry, Count Three and Pray, Patterns, 3:10 to Yuma, Gunman's Walk, Five Branded Women, Under Ten Flags, The Greatest Story Ever Told, Once a Thief, The Wastrel. Served as second lt. 9th Air Force, USAAF, 1942-45. Recipient Acad. Award as best supporting actor, Acad. Motion Picture Arts and Scis., 1942. Home: Los Angeles CA Died July 23, 1971.

HEFNER, RALPH A(UBRIE), coll. dean; b. Bluefield, W. Va., Dec. 20, 1902; s. Oscar Vastine and Zelda (Abernethy) H.; S.B., Roanoke Coll., 1925; M.S., Univ. of Chicago, 1927, Ph.D., 1931; m. Addye Pillow Williamson, July 26, 1928; children—Robert James, Oscar Vernon. Instr. in mathematics, Ga. Sch. of Tech., 1929-31, asst. prof., 1932-34, asso. prof., 1935; prof., 1936-44, dean of gen. studies, 1945-48; dean, gen. coll., Ga. Inst. Tech. (formerly Ga. Sch. of Tech.), from 1948. Fellow Ga. Acad. Sci.; mem. Am. Soc. Engring. Edn., Am. Soc. for Quality Control Ga. Ednl. Assn., Soc. Am. Magicians, Atlanta (Ga.) Soc. of Magicians, Phi Kappa Phi, Tau Kappa Alpha, Phi Kappa Phi, Sigma Xi, Presbyn. Club: Civitan (Atlanta). Author: Practical Mathematics—Electricity, 1943. Contbr. tech. notes, Nat. Adv. Com. for Aeronautics. Home: Atlanta GA Died June 30, 1967.

HEGLAND, MARTIN, clergyman, educator; b. Merton Twp., Steele County, Minn., Jan. 20, 1880; s. Tellef A. and Anne Kirstine (Tyvand) H.; B.A., St. Olaf Coll., 1904; M.A., U. of Minn., 1908; grad. Theol. Sem. United Norwegian Luth. Ch., St. Paul, Minn., 1910; Ph.D., Columbia, 1915; m. Georgina E. Dieson, September 7, 1911; 1 daughter, Anna Tonette (Mrs. Josef M. Jauch). Superintendent schools, Fertile, Minn., 1904-07; holder of St. Olaf Coll. alumni scholarship, 1910-11; grad. scholarship, Columbia, 1911-12; foreign research scholarship, Columbia, 1912, studying ednl. systems in Scandinavian countries; ordained Norwegian Luth. ministry, 1913; pastor Zion Ch., Grand Forks, N.D., 1913-14; pres. Waldorf Luth. Coll.; Forest City, Ia., 1915-19, also pastor Forest City, 1915-18; prof. of religion, St. Olaf Coll. since 1919, head of dept., 1919-41, also college pastor, 1925-41. Dir. Radio Sta. WCAL from 1928. Pres. Young People's Luther League of Norwegian Luth. Ch. of America, 1922-23; pres. Ednl. Assn. same ch., 1921-22. Mem. Council of Defense, World War. Mem. Luth. Brotherhood of Am., Norwegian-Am. Hist. Assn. Phi Beta Kappa. Author: The Danish People's High School (including general account of educational system in Denmark), 1915; The Secret of a Happy Life, 1926; Eyes That See, 1928; Walking with God, 1930; Problems of Young Christians, 1932; Aspirations, 1934; Getting Acquainted with the Bible, 1936. Joint Author: (with Georgina Hegland) In the Holy Land, 1938; For His Name's Sake, 1947. Home: Northfield MN Died Dec. 31, 1967.

HEHER, HARRY, judge; b. Trenton, N.J., Mar. 20, 1889; s. John and Anne (Spelman) H.; student Cathedral Sch. and Trenton High Sch.; studied law pvtly.; m. Anne Egan, Aug. 5, 1925; children—Harry, John Robert, Garrett Martin. Admitted to N.J. bar, 1911, and practiced in Trenton until 1932; apptd. asso. justice N.J. Supreme Ct. ad interim, 1932, apptd. successively for 7 yr. terms, 1933, 1940 and 1947; reapptd. 1954 under constn. provision of tenure to age of 70; counsel Smith, Stratton, Wise &Heher, Princeton. Dir. Trenton Trust Co. Mem. N.J. Ins. Law Revision Commission; chairman com. on State-Employee Relations; chmn. com. to investigate N.J. prison and parole system, 1952. President of the board of trustees of Trenton Free Pub. Library, Trenton, New Jersey. Fellow Am. Bar Found.; mem. Am., N.J., Mercer County bar assns., Am. Law Inst., Am. Judicature Soc., N.J. Inst. Practicing Lawyers, Morrow Assn. N.J. (v.p.), N.J. Hist. Soc. Mem. Dem. nat. convs., 1924, 28, 32, chmn. state delegation. Roman Catholic. K.C. Home: Trenton NJ Died Oct. 17, 1972; buried St. Mary's Cemetery, Trenton NJ

HEIDER, RAPHAEL, coll. ofcl.; b. Marysville, Wash., Aug. 15, 1903; s. Anthony E. and Anna (Keppers) H.; B.F.A., U. of Wash., 1932; M.A., Columbia U. Teachers Coll., 1936; unmarried. Teacher, St. Martin's Coll., Olympia, Washington, 1925-43, pres., 1943, pres., 1943-55, chancellor, from 1955. Mem. Order St. Benedict, Am. Benedictine Acad. Office: Olympia WA Died Feb. 12, 1971.

HEIDINGSFIELD, MYRON S(AMUEL), educator; b. N.Y.C., Feb. 3, 1914; s. Benjamin and Elsie (Byk) H.; B.S., Coll. City of N.Y., 1936; M.A., New York University, 1939, Ph.D., 1943; married Jane Cummins, Feb. 17, 1946; 1 son, Michael John. Assistant research director Life Extension Inst., 1938-39; research statistician Am. Statis. Assn., 1939-40; instr. in statistics Columbia and New York U., 1940-42; tech. research consultant Fed. Works Agency, 1940-42; asst. prof. economics Coll. of William and Mary, 1942-43; chief statistician Army Service Forces, Phila. Q.M. Depot, 1943-44; asst. prof. marketing Sch. of Bus. Adminstrn., Temple U., 1944-47, asso. prof. marketing, 1947-49, prof. and chmn. marketing department, 1949-58; market research cons. Reuben H. Donnelley, Inc., 1946-48, 1951-58; asso. dir. A. B. Blankenship and Assos., Phila., 1949, exec. v.p., 1950-51; mgr. market research RCA consumer products div., 1958-60, market research cons. consumer products div., 1961-62; grad. lectr. in marketing Sch. of Bus. and Pub. Adminstrn., Temple U., 1958-60; asso. dean, prof. marketing sch. commerce and finance Villanova U., 1960-63; Food Fair Stores Found. prof. marketing U. Fla., Gainesville, 1963-69; dir. Internat. Marketing Resource Center, 1964-69. Chairman of the education council Phila. C. of C.; marketing research cons. U.S. and Europe; member N.-Central Regional Export Expansion Council; expert witness before Fed. Communications Commn., Fed. Trade Commn., Pub. Utilities Commn. Named Marketing of Yr., Sales and Marketing Execs. Internat. Fellow Am. Association for Advancement Sci.; mem. Am. Marketing Assn. (chmn. com. on teaching market research; chmn. com. on basic research), Am. Statis. Assn., Am. Assn. U. Profs., Am. Econ. Assn., Phi Beta Kappa, Beta Gamma Sigma. Author: Marketing Strategy, 1967. Co-author: Market and Marketing Analysis, 1947 (Spanish), 1958; Marketing, An Introduction, 1953, lated rev. edit., 1966; Marketing and Business Research, 1962; Changing Patterns in Marketing, 1968; also articles in profl. jours. Home: Gainesville FL Died May 29, 1969; buried West Hills Meml. Park, Gainesville FL

HEILBRONNER, LOUIS, business exec.; b. Marshalltown, Ia., 1866. Chmn. bd. Holeproof Hosiery Co., Holeproof Hosiery Co. of Can. Ltd. Home: 800 Fourth St., Jefferson, Wis. Office: 404 Racine St., Milwaukee WI*‡

HEILNER, VAN CAMPEN, editor, author, explorer; b. Phila., July 1, 1899; s. Samuel and Adelaide Lincoln (Breese) H.; studied Phillips Acad., Andover, Mass.; grad. Lake Placid-Florida Sch., 1918; M.S., Trinity Coll., Hartford, Conn., 1927; studied ichthyology under Dr. J. T. Nichols, Am. Mus. Natural History; m. Mary La Vie, June, 1919 (divorced 1951); children—Mary, Samuel; married second, Raquel Romero, February 19, 1950. Asso. editor Field and Stream; field representative in ichthyology of American Mu. of Natural History, ichthyologist expdn. to Peru and Ecuador, 1924-25, Alaska, 1927, Cuba, 1934-35; Peabody Mus. of Yale expdn. to Tiena del Fuego and Straits of Magellan, 1948. First naturalist to make motion pictures successfully of the roseate spoonbill in its nat. haunts; disc. several new species of West Indian fishes. Fellow Royal Geog. Soc., Royal Anthropol. Inst. (London), Am. Geog. Soc.; mem. Am. Mus. Natural History (hon. life), American Soc. of Mammalogists, Am. Soc. Ichthyologists and Herpetologists, Society of Colonial Wars, Sons of Revolution, Huguenot Soc., Bombay Natural History Soc.; asso. Am. Ornithologists' Union; hon. mem. British Sea Anglers Soc. Republican. Presbyn. Mason (32 deg.). Clubs: Explorers (life); Phlia. Gun. Author books. Master smallest motor boat ever to go from Atlantic City to Venezuela, 4000 miles. Decorated Order of Carlos Manuel de Cespedes (Cuba), 1937. Photographer and dir. short and feature subjects for motion picture companies. Home: Hampton Bays LI NY

HEIM, HERBERT E., physician; b. Lewisburg, Pa., Sept. 23, 1906; s. Ephraim and Elizabeth (Eddelman) H.; M.D., Cornell U., 1931; m. Miriam Anna Diehl, July 18, 1932; children—Alexander D., Elizabeth E. (Mrs. John W. Searight). Intern, Grasslands Hosp., Valhalla, N.Y., 1932-33; practice medicine specializing in psychiatry and neurology, Harrisburg, Pa., until 1970; staff mem. Harrisburg State Hosp., until 1970; clin. dir. Allentown (Pa.) State Hosp., until 1970. Diplomate Am. Bd. Psychiatry and Neurology. Fellow Am. Psychiat. Assn.; mem. A.M.A., Pa. Psychiat. Assn., Lehigh County Neuropsychiat. Assn. Lutheran. Home: Allentown PA Died Dec. 7, 1970; buried Allentown PA

HEIMBACH, HOWARD ANDERS, mfg. co. exec.; b. Kane, Pa., Aug. 16, 1909; s. J.M. and Ada (Anders) H.; A.B. Dartmouth, 1930; student Harvard Bus. Sch., 1930-31, Columbia, evenings 1933-34; m. Dorothea Guja, Aug. 27, 1934; 1 dau., Ada (Mrs. Norman C. Logan). Vice pres. indsl. relations Nat. Electric Products Co., Ambridge, Pa., 1957-59; mgmt. cons., Sewickley, Pa., 1959-60; with Rockwell Mfg. Co., Pitts., 1960-70, v.p., exec. asst. to pres., 1963-70. Mem. Pa. Gov.'s Commn. on Charitable Orgns. Dir. Hosp. Planning Assn., Better Business Bureau, Allegheny Housing Rehab. Corp., So. States Industrial Council. Served with USNR, 1944-46. Mem. Pa. C. of C. (board directors), Greater Pittsburgh Chamber of Commerce (bd. dirs., pres. 1969-70), Am. Mgmt. Assn., Nat. Indsl. Conf. Bd., Am. Ordnance Assn., Pa. Soc. Mason. Home: Pittsburgh PA Died June 10, 1970.

HEIMERICH, JOHN JAMES, educator, architect; b. Clay Center, Kan., Oct. 17, 1906; s. George and Mary Cecilia (White) H.; B.S. in Archtl. Engring., Kan. State U., 1933, M.S., 1945; student U. Okla., spring 1942, U. N.M., 1943-44; M. Audrey Argey Tedrow, Aug. 22, 1935; children—Denis Alton, Lynn Raymond. Tchr., Greenleaf (Kan.) High Sch., spring 1934, Scandia (Kan.) Jr. High Sch., 1934-36, Concordia (Kan.) Jr. and Sr. High Sch., 1936-41; mem. faculty U. Okla., 1941-42; mem. faculty U. N.M., 1942-72, prof. architecture, 1951-72, chmn. dept., 1948-66; part-time pvt. practice architecture, 1950-72. Active local United Community Fund drives. Registered profl. engr. and arch., N.M. Mem. A.I.A. (treas. N.M. chpt. 1956-64, treas. Albuquerque 1965). Mem. Christian Ch. (ofcl. bd.). Co-author: Workbook for Engineering Drawing, 1954. Home: Albuquerque NM Died Apr. 11, 1972.

HEINER, MORONI, corp. official; b. Morgan, Utah, Feb. 18, 1877; s. Daniel and Martha (Stevens) H.; student Morgan (Utah) State Acad., 1890-91, Brigham Young Coll., Logan, Utah, 1896-99; m. Eva Purnell, Dec. 14, 1898; children—Glen P., Iona (widow of Frank Smith), Claude P., Verna (Mrs. R. V. Whipple), Keith P., Louise (Mrs. Carrol Hummel), Daniel, Albert. Began as teacher, 1898, state dairy and food commr., 1900-04; v.p. Castle Valley Coal Co., 1909-14; v.p. U.S. Fuel Co., 1914-32; pres. Utah Fuel Co. since 1932; also pres. Calumet Fuel Co., Wasatch Store Co., Utah Fuel Coal Co. Mem. Salt Lake City Bd. Adjustment. Republican. Mem. Church of the Latter Day Saints. Clubs: Alta, Country, Rotary (Salt Lake City). Home: 1407 Laird Circle. Office: Judge Bldg., Salt Lake City UT‡

HEINICKE, ARTHUR JOHN, pomologist; St. Louis, Mo., Oct. 23, 1892; s. Martin Theodore and Magdalena (Beckert) H.; B.S.A., U. of Mo., 1913, M.A., 1914; Ph.D., Cornell U., 1916; m. Marguerite Eva Riemann, Sept. 15, 1917; 1 son, Arthur John. Fellow in horticulture, U. of Mo., 1913-14; with Cornell U. from 1914, instr. in pomology until 1917, asst. prof., 1917-20, prof., 1920-60, head dept., 1921-60, head div. pomology, 1942, dir. N.Y. State (Geneva) Agrl. Expt. Sta., 1942-60, prof. emeritus, from 1960. Fellow A.A.A.S.; mem. Am. Soc. Hort. Science (pres. 1937), Am. Bot. Soc., Am. Soc. of Plant Physiologists, Sigma Xi, Gamma Alpha, Phi Kappa Phi, Gamma Sigma Delta. Ind. Republican. Lutheran. Author of various research bulls. issued by Cornell U. also articles in profl. jours. Home: Ithaca NY

HEINROTH, CHARLES, concert organist; b. N.Y. City, Jan. 2, 1874; s. Theodore and Charlotte Corday (Monsees) H.; ed. pub. schs., New York and Brooklyn; studied music with John White, Max Spicker, Arthur Friedheim, Otto Hieber and Joseph von Rheinberger, Nat. Conservatory of Music, New York, and Royal Acad. Music, Munich; Mus. Doc., U. of Pittsburgh, 1921; m. Blanche Regina Jackson, June 21, 1899. Organist and mus. dir. St. Paul's P.E. Ch., Brooklyn, 1892-96, Ch. of the Ascension, New York, 1896-1907; also organist and dir. Temple Bethel, 1903-07, and instr. organ, harmony and counterpoint, Nat. Conservatory of Music; organist and dir. music Carnegie Inst., Pittsburgh, Pa., 1907-32; head of music dept., Coll. of City of N.Y., 1932-42; now retired. Has appeared at recitals in all the prin. musical centers of U.S. and inaugurated numerous organs. Pres. Nat. Assn. of Organists, 1933-34; mem. Am. Assn. Univ. Profs.; hon. mem. Kansas City Organists' Assn., Royal Philharmonic Acad. (Rome), Am. Organ Players' Club (hon. mem.). Republican. Lutheran. Club: The Bohemians (New York City). Home: Beach Long Island NY‡

HEINSOHN, ALVIN FREDERICK, corp. exec.; born Charleston, S.C., Jan. 17, 1900; s. Claus J. and Emma R. (Martschink) H.; B.S., The Citadel College, 1921, also Doctor of Laws (honorary); m. Marguerite Melchers, Oct. 17, 1923. Pub. accountant, Jacksonville, Fla., 1921-22; v.p., dir. Raybestos-Manhattan, Inc., North Charleston, from 1946; dir. First Nat. Bank of S.C., S.C. Electric & Gas Co. Chmn. sch. bd., park and playground, North Charleston. Democrat. Lutheran. Clubs: Landmark Lodge, Charleston, Citadel Century, Carolina Yacht, Charleston Country. Home: North Charleston SC Died July 13, 1967; buried Bethany Cemetery, Charleston SC

HEINZE, OTTO CHARLES, financier; b. Brooklyn, N.Y., Dec. 12, 1866; s. Otto and Eliza Marsh (Lacey) H.; ed. Poly. Inst., Brooklyn, and in Leipzig, Germany; m. Ada Louise Martin, June 12, 1900; 1 dau., Ada (Mrs. Ira Follett Warner). Began in dry goods business under father, 1884, established as agt. for European mfrs., 1890; became partner Heinze, Lowry & Co., on death of father, 1891, title changed later to Otto Heinze & Co.; began investing in copper mines and a founder of Montana Ore Purchasing Co.; entered banking business in Wall St., as Heinze & Co., 1899; active in organization of United Copper Co. which took over copper interests of the Heinzes in Mont.; also interested in ships and ship building. Republican. Episcopalian. Address: 140 E. 46th St., New York NY‡

HEISEN, AARON JONAH, physician; b. Huntington, W.Va., 1917; M.D., U. Pa., 1942, postgrad., 1951-52. Intern, Fitkin Meml. Hosp., Neptune, N.J., 1942-43, med. resident, 1943-44; fellow cardiology Grad. Hosp. U. Pa.; asso. cardiologist, Mercer Hosp., Trenton, N.J., 1954-70, attending in med., 1960-70, dir. out patient dept. also chmn. internship and ednl. com., 1963-69, pres. med. staff, 1969-70. Served to capt. M.C. AUS, 1944-46. Diplomate Am. Bd. Internal Medicine. Fellow A.M.A., Am. Heart Assn., A.C.P.; mem. Aero. Med. Assn., Flying Physicians Assn., FAA Aviation Med. Examiners. Home: Trenton NJ Died Dec. 24, 1970.

HEISER, VICTOR GEORGE, hygienist; b. Pennsylvania, 1873; s. George and Mathilde H.; M.D., Jefferson Medical College, Philadelphia, 1897, Sc.D., 1911; Sc.D., Rutgers Coll., N.J., 1917; LL.D., Temple U., 1939; Sc.D., Thiel Coll., 1939; m. Marion Phinny, April 20, 1940. Entered U.S. Marine Hosp. Service, 1898; spl. detail to Europe to report upon emigration to U.S., 1899; spl. detail to Egypt to study plague, 1899; del. Internat. Congress on Tuberculosis, Naples, 1900; to Canada with regard to emigration, 1901; del. Internat. Congress on Med., Egypt, 1902; chief quarantine officer, P.I., 1903-15, and dir. of health, 1905-15; asso. dir. Internat. Health Div., Rockefeller Foundation, 1915-34 (retired); formerly mem. adv. council, Nat. Health Adminstrn., China; pres. Internat. Leprosy Assn., 1931-38; consultant in pub. health administration and industrial medicine; chmn. med. advisory com., New York World's Fair of 1939; consultant on Healthful Working Conditions, National Association of Mfrs., since 1938; mem. bd. directors American Museum of Health. Connected with work of stamping out plague, cholera, smallpox, etc., also the building of the Philippine Gen. Hosp., Coll. Medicine and Surgery, and many hosps. throughout the Philippines; served as prof. hygiene, Coll. Medicine and Surgery, P.I. Received Trimble Lecture Medal, 1935; award for distinguished service in public health by Holland Soc. of N.Y., 1939; gold medal of Pa. Soc. Mem. A.M.A., Am. Acad. Tropical Medicine, Am. Pub. Health Assn., Far Eastern Assn. of Tropical Medicine, J. Aitken Meigs Med. Assn., A.A.A.S., Am. Philos. Soc., Pa. Society. Member committee on nutrition of industrial workers, National Research Council. Clubs: Army and Navy (Manila, Philippine Islands, and Washington, D.C.); Century, New York Athletic (New York City). Author: An American Doctor's Odyssey, 1936; You're the Doctor, 1939; Toughen Up, America1941; Industrial Health Practices, 1941; Health on the Production Front, 1943; Vision in Industry, 1947. Sanitary Code, Manila, Manual Bur. Health, Manila. Co-Author: Handbook of Medical Treatment, 1918; Oxford System of Medicine, 1921; Practice of Medicine in the Tropics, 1922; A System of Pediatrics, 1924; A Text-Book of Medicine by American Authors, 1926; Cyclopedia of Medicine, 1932; Encyclopedia Americana, 1943-46. Mem. American Red Cross Commission to Italy, 1917; mem. com. on health and med. relief, U.S.R.R. Administration, 1918-20. Home: Bantam CT‡

HEISKELL, JOHN NETHERLAND, editor; b. Rogersville, Tenn., Nov. 2, 1872; s. Carrick White and Eliza Ayre (Netherland) H.; A.B., U. Tenn., 1893; Litt.D., Little Rock Coll., 1929; LL.D., Ark. Coll., 1934, U. Ark., 1938, Colby Coll., 1958; m. Wilhelmina Mann, June 28, 1910; children—Mrs. George Whitfield Cook, Mrs. Hugh B. Patterson, Jr. In newspaper work; editor Ark. Gazette, 1902-72; chmn. bd. Ark. Gazette Co. U.S. senator from Ark. by appointment of Gov. Donaghey, Jan. 6-Jan. 29, 1913. Pres. bd. trustees Little Rock Pub. Library. Former chmn. Little Rock City Planning Commn.; former mem. State Planning Bd. 2d v.p. A.P., 1926-27. Recipient citation A.L.A., 1957; medal and citation Syracuse U. Sch. Journalism, 1958; ann. award Columbia Sch. Journalism, 1958; Lovejoy award Colby Coll., 1958; U. Mo. Sch. of Journalism Distinguished Service medal, 1962; John Peter Zenger award dept. journalism U. Ariz.; citation and plaque Sigma Delta Chi, 1966. Fellow Sigma Delta Chi; mem. Sigma Alpha Epsilon. Democrat. Clubs: Country of Little Rock, Top of the Rock, Little Rock. Home: Little Rock AR Died Dec. 28, 1972; buried Mt. Holly Cemetery, Little Rock AR

HEISS, GERSON KIRKLAND, govt. ofcl; b. Timmonsville, S.C., Sept. 18, 1896; s. Samuel and Lillie (Welch) H.; grad. Porter Mil. Acad., Charleston, 1912; B.S. Clemson (S.C.) A. and M. College, 1916; grad. Army Indsl. Coll., 1938; m. Anna M. Milchsack, July 14, 1918; children—Gerson Kirkland, Elizabeth Ann. Chem. and ins. with British Ministry of Munitions, U.S.A., 1916-19; supt. Apex Chemical Co., 1919-21; asso. chemist, Piccatinny Arsenal, 1921-22; served with U.S. Army since 1923, beginning as 2d lt., Ordnance dept., promoted through the grades to brigadier general, Jan. 1946. Awarded D.S.M., U.S. Legion of Merit with Oak Leaf Cluster, Commendation ribbon with two Oak Leaf Clusters. Mem. Army Ordnance Assn., Washington, D.C., Clemson Coll. Alumni Assn. (Washington chapter); Clemson Iptay Club. Mason. Home: Largo FL Died Jan. 1971.

HEITSCHMIDT, EARL T., architect; b. Portland, Ore., June 9, 1894; s. Theodore Frederick and Margaret (MacCormack) H.; student U. Ore., 1916-17, Mass. Inst. Tech., 1921-22; m. Mabel Cochran, Sept. 4, 1918; children—Margaret Louise, Earl. Draftsman U.S. Navy Yard, Bremerton, Wash., 1917-19; Pacific Coast mgr. Schultze & Weaver, architects, N.Y.C.; pvt. practice architecture, Los Angeles, 1929-72; prin. works include pub. sch. bldgs., Los Angeles Corona, Riverside; various pub. bldgs., office and indsl. bldgs., including C. of C. offices, Cal. Bank, Equitable Life Ins. bldg., U. Cal. library and organic chemistry bldgs., CBS, Hollywood, Pico Gardens Housing Project, Los Angeles Shipbuilding & Drydock Co., U.S. Naval Hosp. Expansion, Corona, Victor Orsatti Med. Bldg., Beverly Hills, Clayton Mfg. Co., White Meml. Hosp., Loma Linda U. Med. Center, phys. sci. bldgs. San Bernardino State Coll., Los Angeles Furniture Mart, variety of U.S. Naval Missile projects and others. Chmn. adv. com. Dept. of State for Internat. Brussels Expn. Mem. Cal. Bd. Archtl. Examiners (pres. 1952-53); adv. com. Los Angeles Bldg. Code, 1941-60; pres. Constrn. Industries Expn. and Home Show, 1948-50. Fellow A.I.A. (dir. Sierra Nev. dist. 1946-48, 1st v.p. 1954-55)); mem. Cal. Council Architects (dir. 1945-48), C. of C. (dir. 1946-47), chmn. constrn. industries com. 1946-47, constrn. industries achievement award 1951), Phi Gamma Delta, Lambda Alpha. Republican. Presbyn. Mason (32 deg.). Clubs: California, Jonathan. Home: San Marino CA Died Feb. 26, 1972.

HEKKING, WILLIAM MATHEWS, art director; b. Chelsea, Wis., Mar. 10, 1885; s. Adrian Mathews and Adele (Scherenberg) H.; B.P., Syracuse (N.Y.) U., 1908, Dr. of Fine Arts, 1929; student Art Student's League, New York, and pupil Jean Paul Laurens, Academie Julian, Paris; m. Sarah Marion Swayne, June 27, 1913 (died 1931); children—Marion Elnora, Donald Adrian, Charlotte Adele; married 2d, Iola France, April 8, 1942 (died Jan. 17, 1946). Instructor in art, Syracuse University, 1911-12 and since 1942; director School Fine and Applied Arts, James Millikin U., 1912-15; instr. U. of Mo., summers 1913, 14, 15; asso. prof. of drawing, dept. of architecture, U. of Ill., 1915-16; prof. art, U. of Kan., 1916-22; dir. Columbus (O.) Art Sch. and Columbus Gallery of Fine Arts, 1922-25; dir. Albright Art Gallery, Buffalo, 1925-32; curator contemporary painting and sculpture, Los Angeles Museum of History, Science and Art, Jan.-July 1938, dir. div. of art, 1938-39; chmn. Southern Calif. div. contemporary sculpture and painting, Golden Gate Internat. Expn., 1939; chmn. com. on selection, Southern Calif. div., New York World's Fair, 1939. Marine artist; expert restorer of art works. Represented in perm. collec. Buffalo Fine Arts Acad. Mem. of advisory com., Dept. Fine Arts, Sesqui-centennial Expn., Phila., Pa., 1926. Mem. Am. Assn. Mus. Directors, Am. Assn. Museums (exec. council), Buffalo Soc. Artists, Buffalo Ednl. Council (dir.), Wilmington Soc. Fine Arts, Phi Gamma Delta. Awarded Hiram Gee Fellowship for European study, Syracuse U., 1908; Wanamaker prize, black and white, 1912; Gold medal, Kansas City Art Inst., 1922; Huntington first prize, Columbus Art League, 1923, first prize, black and white, 1924; Dupont first prize, Wilmington Soc. Artists, 1926; first fellowship prize, Buffalo Soc. of Artists, 1932. Presbyterian. Clubs: Salmagundi, Phi Gamma Delta (New York), the Syracuse Citizens. Contbr. to Buffalo Evening News (art critic 1934-37). Home: Woolwich ME Died May, 1970.

HELLAND, ANDREAS, theologian; b. Fitjar, Norway, July 10, 1870; s. Anders C. and Bertha Elizabeth (Meling) H.; B.A., U. of Christiania, 1888, M.A., 1889; post grad. work, same univ., 1904-5; B.D., Augsburg Seminary, Minneapolis, Minn., 1893; m. Clara Rockue, 1893 (died 1900); m. 2d, Helen Anderson, 1905 (died 1919). Ordained ministry Luth. Free Ch., 1893; pastor McIntosh, Minn., 1893-4, Minneapolis, 1894-1902; prof. theology, Augsburg Sem., since 1905, treas., 1901-3. Sec. Luth. Bd. of Missions, 1907-19, now dir. and mem. exec. com. Prohibitionist. Translator various works into Norse, and editor Prof. G. Sverdrop's writings (6 vols.), Barnet's Ven, Gasseren (a missionary paper), 1907-16, etc. Home: 711 21st Av. S., Minneapolis MN‡

HELLER, FLORENCE GRUNSFELD, philanthropist; b. Albuquerque, Mar. 2, 1897; d. Ivan and Hannah (Nusbaum) Grunsfeld; student Bradford (Mass.) Coll.; m. Walter E. Heller, Feb. 22, 1917; children—John A., Peter E., Paul W. Mem. Nat. Jewish Welfare Bd., from 1939, vice chmn. 6th Service Command armed forces com., 1942-46, rep. on UN conf. group of nat. orgns., from 1954, chmn. Jewish Community Center Services, 1949-56, v.p. bd., 1948-64, pres., from 1964; chmn. mgmt. com. Central U.S.O. Club, Chgo., 1942-47, mem. bd. dirs., 1942-47; hon. dir. for life Jewish Community Centers Chgo.; vice chmn. nat. women's div. United Jewish Appeal, 1946-47; pres. women's auxiliary Jewish People's Inst. Chgo., 1928-40; mem. corp. UNICEF, from 1959. Trustee Brandels U., Jewish Fedn. Met. Chgo.; endowed Florence Heller Grad. Sch. Advanced Studies Social Welfare, Brandeis U., 1959. Recipient Frank L. Weil award Nat. Jewish Welfare Bd., 1953; Annual award Research Inst. Group Work Social Agencies, 1960; Annual award Nat. Conf. Social Welfare, 1963. Home: Chicago IL

HELLER, FRANK HENRY, corp. exec.; b. Weimar, Tex., Oct. 1, 1907; s. Henry and Magdeline (Seifert) H.; B.B.A., U. Tex., 1930; m. Jacquelyn Morphis, Feb. 14, 1932; children—Sally (Mrs. John Ward III), Susan (Mrs. Tom Stanzel), Mary. With Remington-Rand, 1930-55, successively salesman, dist. mgr., Ft. Worth, br. mgr., Dallas, 1930-40, sr. br. mgr. Systems div. Sperry-Rand Corp., Dallas, 1951-62; chmn. bd. Exchange Savs. & Loan Assn., Dallas; director Landa Oil Company. National director U.S.O.; pres. Dallas County Community Chest Trust Fund, 1962; dir. Goodwill Industries; director and past pres. Cath. Charities; campaign chairman of the Texas United Funds, 1962. Decorated knight comdr. Order Holy Sepulchre (Papal hon.). Mem. Am. Social Health Assn. (pres.), Nat. Council Cath. Men (sec.), Nat. Sales Execs. Inc. (dir. service), Nat. Conf. Christians and Jews (regional dir.). Clubs: Dallas Country, Lions (past pres.), Sales Executives (past pres.) (Dallas). Home: Dallas TX Died 1971.

HELLER, FRANK MORLEY, newspaper editor; b. Napoleon, O., Oct. 3, 1870; s. Milton Eugene and Elizabeth Angela (Cullen) H.; ed. pub. schs., Defiance, O., and Md. Mil. Acad.; m. Gertrude Lawton Brown, of Toledo, O., May 9, 1903. Began newspaper work in Chicago, Ill., 1890; now editor The Toledo News-Bee, of Scripps-Howard chain of newspapers. Mem. Battery D, 1st Ohio Arty., Spanish-Am. War. Theosophist. Mason, Elk. Clubs: Rotary, Inverness Golf. Home: 2481 Glenwood Av. Office: Jackson and Huron Sts., Toledo OH‡

HELLER, JAMES GUTHEIM, composer, rabbi; b. New Orleans, La., Jan. 4, 1892; s. Max and Ida (Marks) H.; A.B., Tulane U., 1912; A.M., U. of Cincinnati, 1914; Rabbi, Hebrew Union Coll., 1916, D.D., 1944; Mus. D., Cincinnati Conservatory of Music, 1935; D.H.L., Jewish Institute Religion, 1948; married Jean Bettmann, August 15, 1917; children—Cecile L., Claire J., Joan H.; married 2d, Helen R. Bettman, Dec. 5, 1952. Asst. rabbi, Keneseth Israel, Phila., 1916-19; chaplain, U.S. Army, with A.E.F., 1918-19; rabbi, Little Rock, Ark., 1919-20, Issac M. Wise Temple, Cincinnati, 1920-52; pres. Labor Zionist Orgn. of Am. 1952-54; chmn. Community relations, Israel Bonds, 1954-71, Program annotator, Cincinnati Symphony Orchestra, 1926-43; lectr. musicology, Cincinnati Conservatory of Music, 1935-52. Member Bd. of Edn., Cincinnati, 1935-39; dir. Hamilton County Bd., Y.M.C.A., 1934-42; mem. bd. dirs. Union of Am. Hebrew Congregations; chmn. United Palestine Appeal, 1941-46; chmn. administrative council, Zionist Orgn. Am., 1941-42; mem. exec. com., v.p. Zionist Organization of America; vice pres. Central Conf. Am. Rabbis, 1934-41; pres., 1941-43; mem. Zionist general council World Zionist Program since 1951; chmn. commn. on ceremonies Central Conf. Am. Rabbis and Union Am. Hebrew Congs. Mem. Phi Beta Kappa. Reform Jewish religion. Author: As Yesterday When It Is Past, 1942. Chmn. editorial board American Judaism. Composer several pieces including: Three Sketches for Orchestra; Little Symphony; From Noon to Dusk, 11 songs to poems by Robert Nathan; Rhapsody for Orchestra; also hymns and anthems for synagogue, songs, chamber music. Home: New York City NY Died Dec. 1971.

HELLER, WALTER E., financing co. exec.; b. Chgo., 1890. Chmn. bd., chief exec. officer Walter E. Heller & Co.; dir. Helene Curtis Industries. Home: Chicago IL Deceased.

HELM, WILBUR, economist, writer; b. Marion, Ind., Aug. 7, 1879; s. Benjamin Abbott and Millicent (Coggeshall) H.; A.B., DePauw Univ., 1899, A.M., 1900; A.M., Princeton Univ., 1901; m. Margaretta Stevenson Nutt, Nov. 7, 1903 (dec. Aug. 1961); children—Virginia, Standiford, Marjorie (Mrs. Verne Swigert). Instr. in Latin Princeton U., 1900-03; Phillips Exeter (N.H.) Acad., 1904-09; prin. Evanston Acad. of Northwestern Univ., 1909-15; sales exec., Hart Schaffner & Marx, 1915-16; asst. to pres. Sprague Warner & Co., 1916-19; supt. correspondence and adj., Montgomery Ward & Co., 1919-20; vice pres. and sec. R.E. Wilsey & Co., investment bankers, Chgo., 1920-38; with Cent. Republic Co., Chicago, as investment advisor, 1938-57, consolidated with Dean Witter & Co., 1957; with sales dept. Chesley & Co., investment securities, 1961-—; bus. mgmt. adviser; econ. consultant, radio and other industries; specialist in personnel and vocational guidance, institutional publicity and promotional depts. Founder, member Patriotic Edn., Inc., 1955, American Constitutional Association, 1958. Member commission to study teaching controversial issues, Chgo. Bd. of Edn., 1952-54; mem. Com. of 100 for Evanston, Ill., World Council of Churches, 1954. Nat. first v.p. of the Friends of the Pub. schs., 1937-51; pres. since 1951; co-founder, sec. Conf. Meth. Laymen, 1935. Mem. Circuit Riders (founder), Chicago. Assn. Commerce, S.A.R. (pres. Ill. soc. 1935-36, trustee nat. soc., 1935-36), Phi Beta Kappa, Phi Kappa Psi. Methodist (ofcl. bd.). Mem. We the People (fdr.), For Am. Mason. Republican. Club: Union League of Chgo. Editor: Cicero's Orations, 1917. Lectr. and writer on educational, economic and patriotic subjects, speaker for Nat. and Ill. State Rep. Coms., 1940, 1944, 1948. Home: Evanston IL Died Dec. 4, 1970; buried Memorial Park Cemetery, Evanston IL

HELSER, ALBERT D., missionary; b. Thornville, O., July 10, 1897; s. David M. and Emma S. (Zartman) H.; B.A., Manchester (Ind.) Coll., 1919, M.A., 1920; grad. work, Teachers Coll. (Columbia), various periods, Ohio State U., 1921, U. of London and Livingstone Coll., London, 1921-22; M.A., Columbia U., 1930, Ph.D., 1934 (Teachers College fellow); m. Lola Bechtel, August 15, 1922; children—Esther May, David Cameron, Gordon Albert. Traveling secretary United Student Vol. Movement, 1919-20, pres., 1920-21; ordained ministry Ch. of the Brethren, 1922; missionary, Garkida, Nigeria, 1922-36; Sudan Interior Mission, Kano, Nigeria, 1936-57; general director Sudan Interior Mission, 1957-62, gen. dir. emeritus, 1963; later active missionary; distbn. mgr. African Challenge and Sudan Interior Mission dist. supt. Eastern and Western region Nigeria and Ghana; sometime principal schs. W. Africa rep. Am. Mission to Lepers various periods. Translator for Brit. and Fgn. Bible Soc. Fellow Royal Geog. Soc. (life mem. since 1943); mem. N.E.A. Clubs: Cosmopolitan (New York). Author: Labar ata Kira Isa (a life of Christ in Bura), 1925; In Sunny Nigeria, 1926; Thlipa ata Kira Lakur Hyel (teaching about the Road of God in Bura), 1929; African Stories, 1930; Education of Primitive People, 1934; Two Hundred Thousand Lepers in Nigeria, 1935; Cent Mille Lepreux au Congo Belge, 1936; Leper Settlements in Northern Nigeria, 1939; The Glory of the Impossible, 1940; The Hand of God in the Sudan, 1946, Africa's Bible, 1951; The Co-translator: Gospels of Matthew and Mark, into Bura, 1933. Home: Wheaton IL Died Dec. 20, 1969; buried Thornville OH

HEMENWAY, CHARLES CLIFTON, editor; b. Springfield, Vt., Oct. 14, 1883; s. Charles Smith and Lucy A. (Wellman) H.; grad. Brattleboro (Vt.) High Sch., 1902; LL.D., Rollins Coll., 1929; m. Eva Parkhurst Maine, June 7, 1909; children—Richard Maine, Allyn Wellman. Reporter New London (Conn.) Day, Telegraph, 1903-07; night editor New London Telegraph, 1907-08; editorial writer and telegraph editor Brockton (Mass.) Times, 1908-10; successively mng. editor, advertising mgr., editor, gen. mgr., Hartford (Conn.) Post, 1910-20; editorial writer, mng. editor, asso. editor, Hartford Times, 1920-29, editor, 1929-51; asst. sec. and dir. Hartford Times, Inc. Mem. Conn. State Senate, 1917-19; dir. Conn. State Reformatory, 1932-37, dir. Good Will Boys Club Hartford, Vets of Fgn. Wars (hon. mem.). Democrat. Club: Hartford. Home: West Hartford CT Died Dec. 28, 1968.

HEMINGWAY, ALLAN, physiologist, biophysicist; B. Leeds, Eng., Jan. 25, 1902; s. Arthur and Eleanor (Eastwood) H.; B.A., U. B.C., 1925; Ph.D., U. Minn., 1929; Sterling fellow, Yale, 1936-37; m. Gayle Shirey, Nov. 9, 1929, (dec.); 1 dau., Eleanor; m. 2d Claire Conklin Carr, July 5, 1951. Instr., asst. prof. physiol. chemistry U. Minn., 1930-36, asst. prof., asso. prof. physiology, 1936-48, prof. physiology 1948-51; prof. physiology Med. Sch., U. Cal. at Los Angeles, 1951-72; chief cardiopulmonary lab. San Fernando VA Hosp. (Cal.). Served as maj. USAAF, 1943-45; chief lab. biophysics Sch. Aviation Med., Randolph Field, Tex., 1942-45. Mem. Am. Physiol. Soc., Am. Phys. Soc., Am. Chem. Soc., Soc. Exptl. Biology and Medicine, Am. Assn. U. Profs., Sigma Xi, Gamma Alpha, Phi Beta Pi. Contbr. articles to physiol. and biochem. jours. Home: Los CA Died Apr. 22, 1972.

HEMLEY, CECIL, writer, editor; b. N.Y.C., July 21, 1914; s. Frederick and Sarah (Gottlieb) H.; B.A., Amherst Coll., 1934; A.M. U. Chgo., 1950; m. Kathryn Witherstine, May 29, 1945; children—Sara, Frederick; m. 2d, Elaine Gottlieb, July 3, 1952; 1 stepdau., Nola; children—Jonathan, Robin. Founder, 1951, Noonday Press, co-dir. until 1960; company purchased by Farrar, Straus and Cudahy, 1960, past editor-in-chief Noonday Press; dir., editor Ohio U. Press, Athens, 1964-66; co-founder, co-dir. Noonday Rev., 1958-60. Fellow McDowell Colony, 1956. Served to 1st lt. AUS, 1942-46. Mem. Poetry Soc. Am. (pres. 1960-62). Club: P.E.N. Author: (verse) Porphyryis Journey, 1951, Twenty Poems, 1956, In The Midnight Wood, 1960; (novel) The Experience, 1960; Young Crankshaw, 1963. Home: Athens OH Died Mar. 1966.

HEMLEY, SAMUEL, educator; b. N.Y.C., Feb. 8, 1898; s. David and Hannah (Brunner) H.; D.D.S., Columbia, 1918; m. Clara Bernstein, Nov. 24, 1920. Asst. oral surgery Vanderbilt Clinic, Columbia, 1919-25; asst. surgeon L.I. Coll. Hosp., 1924-26; instr. orthodontics coll. dentistry, N.Y.U., 1929-33, asst. prof., chmn. dept. orthodontics, 1933-34, asso. prof., 1934-37, prof., chmn. dept., 1947-66. Served with U.S. Army, 1918, as lt. comdr. USNR, 1936-51. Diplomate Am. Bd. Orthodontics. Mem. Northeastern Soc. Orthodontists, Research Soc. Am. Fellow A.A.A.S., American Coll. Dentistry, Am. Assn. Orthodontics, Internat. Assn. Dental Research, N.Y. Acad. Scis.; mem. Am. Dental Assn., Omicron Kappa Upsilon. Author: Fundamentals of Occlusion, 1944; Orthodontic Theory and Practice, 1953; Myths in Science; A Text on Orthodontics. Contbr. articles profl. Lake George NY Died Aug. 29, 1970; buried Mt. Ararat Cemetery, Farmingdale NY

HENDERSON, ALFRED EDWIN;, b. Liverpool, Eng., July 17, 1877; s. Alfred Edwin and Henrietta (Bruce) H.; Teachers' Coll., Liverpool, 1893-8; Chester Diocesan Training Coll., 1898-1900; Oxford Local Exams., 1893 (distinction in Shakespeare). Has specialized in speech and gesture since 1903; lectured in London (Bd. of Edn.), Paris, France, South of Sweden and in Denmark; came to U.S., 1909; mem. editorial staff New Standard Dictionary, 1909-10; founder, 1909, and pres. Henderson Sch. of Oratory, New York; founder and dir. The Henderson Players. Address: 23 W. 42d St., New York‡

HENDERSON, EDWARD, physician; b. Hendersonville, N.C., Dec. 16, 1896; s. Edward Everett and Muriel Lee (Bell) H.; M.B., B.Chir., M.D., Glasgow U., 1922; Ph.D., Oxford U., 1932; postgrad. Yale, 1937-38; diploma tropical medicine, Tulane U., 1944; m. Kathryn Silverthorne, 1944; children—Edward Bell, Susan Lee (Mrs. Catani). Intern Royal Infirmary, 1922-23; med. officer sci. expdns. Malay archipelago, 1927, China, India, 1929, Central Africa, 1935, Amazon region, 1938-39; med. research div. Schering Corp., Bloomfield, N.J., 1939-62, sec., 1940-52, v.p., 1952-62, dir., 1940-43, dir. div. clin. research, 1945-62; cons. tropical medicine Med. Soc. N.J., 1945; research cons. Mound Park Hosp. Found., St. Petersburg, Fla., from 1955; pres. Ellis Bell & Co., Inc., N.Y.C., from 1967, Bansen, Inc., N.Y.C., from 1967, Henderson Safety Closure Co., Inc., N.Y.C., from 1969; chmn. bd. Elbesa Ltd., London, Eng., from 1970. Bd. dirs. Liberian Inst., Am. Found. Tropical Medicine, 1951; trustee Aging Research Inst., Inc., from 1953, pres., from 1953; pres. Pneumonia Research Found., from 1969. Served as lt., inf., U.S. Army, 1917, capt. Intelligence Corps, 1918. Recipient Willard O. Thompson award, 1961; Malford W. Thewlis gold medal award, 1967. Mem. Internat. Soc. Tropical Dermatology, Pan Am. Med. Assn. (pres. sect. geriatrics and gerontology from 1967), A.A.A.S., Am. Soc. Tropical Medicine, Endocrine Soc., Gerontological Soc., Am. Geriatrics Soc. (dir. from 1952, pres. 1955, editor-in-chief jour. from 1954, exec. dir. from 1962), Am., N.J. rheumatism assns., Assn. Med. Dirs. (pres. 1949-50), N.Y. Acad. Scis. Clubs: New York Athletic; Graduates (New Haven); Columbia University (N.Y.C.). Author: Sixteenth Century Literature and Its Influence on Modern Civilization, 1932; Disorders of Calcium Metabolism, 1952; Section on Cholera, Clinical Tropical Medicine, Gradwohl, Benitex Soto, Felsenfeld, 1951. Contbr. articles sci. jours. patentee chemistry, sci. instruments, safety devices. Home: New York City NY Died Jan. 5, 1973; buried Mill Hill, London England

HENDERSON, ELDON HAZELTON, engr., mfg. exec.; b. Memphis, Mich., July 20, 1908; s. Charles W. and Mary (Haselton) H.; student Detroit City Coll., 1927; m. Alene Zimmerman, Aug. 30, 1934; children—Jane S., John E., Lynn L. Mgr. warehouse control Detroit br., Continental Rubber Works, 1927-29, sales engr., 1929-45; founder Yale Rubber Mfg. Co., Sandusky, Mich., 1945, pres., gen. mgr., 1945-65, chairman of the board, from 1965; mem. bd. dirs. Mich. Mutual Liability Co., Yale Auscao Co., Lima Peru, Info Data, Inc., Trustee Manitou Island Assn.; v.p. Wm. R. Angell Found. Mem. Am. Chem. Soc. Mason, Lion, Rotarian. Clubs: Huron Shores Golf, Horton Ranch, Kingston Hunt. Home: Sandusky MI

HENDERSON, GEORGE BUNSEN, hotel exec.; b. Berlin, Germany, June 26, 1894; s. Ernest Flagg and Berta (von Bunsen) H.; brought to U.S., 1894; student Harvard, 1912-14, U. Wis., 1915-17. Partner Henderson Bros. 1922-59; v.p., sec. and dir. Sheraton Corp. of Am.; officer, dir. many subsidiary corps., including different Sheraton hotels and office bldgs.; dir., v.p., sec. Sheraton Russell, Inc., Portland Sheraton Co. dir., v.p., clk. Beaconsfield Bldg., Inc.; dir., v.p. Sheraton Hotel of Phila., Inc., Sheraton Niagara Corp., Sheraton-Cadillac Corp. Sheraton Whitehall Corp.; dir., sec. Baltimore Sheraton Corp., Chgo. Sheraton Corp., Providence Sheraton Corp., Henderson-Moore Corp., Sheraton Service Co. of N.Y., Inc.; dir. Albany Sheraton Corp., Sheraton Kimball Corp., Sheraton Palace Corp.; dir., clk., sec. Sheraton Service Co. of Mass., Inc.; Sheraton Palace Corp. dir., sec. Rochester Sheraon Corp.; director, asst. treas. Sheraton Restaurants, Inc.; pres., dir. Sheraton Assos., Inc.; clk., sec., Sheraton Constn. Co.; asst. clk. Gen. Commonwealth Corp.; dir., clk. The Sheraton, Inc.; v.p. Sheraton McAlpin Corp.; clk. Sheraton Louisiana Corp.; dir. Sheraton Found., Inc.; dir., clk. Sheraton Plaza Co. Trustee The Henderson-Moore Trust, Mayflower Investment Trust; trustee, mem. corp. Boston Mus. Sci. Clubs: Eastern yacht (Marblehead), Union (Boston), Harvard (Boston). Home: Marblehead MA Died Aug. 21, 1972.

HENDERSON, GRACE MILDRED, home economist; b. nr. Superior, Neb., Dec. 11, 1901; d. Grant and Hannah Cooper (Allen) H.; student, Hastings (Neb.) Coll., 1920-23; B.S., U. of Neb., 1924; student, Kan. State Coll., 1928-29, U. of Wis., summer 1929; M.S., U. of Chicago, 1931; Ph.D., Ohio State U., 1944; unmarried. Co. home demonstration agt., Neb., Kan., 1924-29; state extension specialist in home management, Neb., 1925-26, in orgn., Kansas, 1930; housing resrch., Ore. State Coll., 1931; adult homemaking edn. supervisor, W. Va. State Dept. of Edn., Charleston, 1931-33; state extension program specialist in home economics, Coll. of Home Econs., Cornell U., 1933-38; homemaking edn. supervisor, N.Y. State Dept. of Edn., Albany, 1935-36; instructor, later asst. prof. of adult homemaking edn., Coll. of Home Economics, Cornell, 1933-43, Texas Univ., summer 1937; head, Dept. of Home Econs., U. of Ark., 1944-46; dir. dept. of home econs., Pa. State Coll., 1946-48; dean, coll. of home econs., Pa. State U., 1946-61 Mem. Am. Home Econs. Assn., Am. Vocational Assn., John Dewey Soc., N.E.A., Nat. Council Family Relations, Am. Association of University Women, League of Women Voters, Omicron Nu (nat. v.p. 1966-68, pres. 1969-71), Pi Lambda Theta, Phi Upsilon Omicron, Epsilon Sigma Phi, Pi Kappa Delta, Delta Kappa Gamma. Presbyn. Club: Altrusa, Contbr. to fraternal and ednl. mags. and jours. Home: State College PA Died Nov. 3, 1971; buried Lincoln NB

HENDERSON, HELEN WESTON, author; b. Phila., Sept. 23, 1874; d. William Murray and Jane Rebecca (Tagart) H.; grad. pub. schs. of Phila., 1891; studied Pa. Acad. Fine Arts, 1892-97, Academie Colorossi, Paris, 1905-06. Art and music editor Phila. North American, 1900-04; art editor Phila. Inquirer, 1904-09 and Jan. 1, 1911-1919, foreign correspondent, 1919-37. Officier d'Academie (France), 1933. Club: Fellowship of Pennsylvania Academy of Fine Arts (secretary 1897-1909). Author: The Pennsylvania Academy of the Fine Arts, and other Collections of Philadelphia, 1911; The Art Treasures of Washington, 1912; A Loiterer in New York, 1917; A Loiterer in New England, 1919; A Loiterer in Paris, 1921; A Loiterer in London, 1924; Dianne de Poytiers, 1928; Cathedrals of France, 1929. Address: care Lloyd's Bank, 43 Boul. Capucines, Paris France*‡

HENDERSON, KENNETH MANNING, office equipment mfrs.; b. Weedsport, N.Y., June 18, 1893; s. Charles M. and Alida (Page) H.; B.S., Dartmouth, 1916; m. Marie Blanchard, Sept. 3, 1925; children—Marie Ann (Mrs. Yorke H. Bannard), Kenneth Manning. With Ditto, Inc., Chgo., 1919-58, pres., 1946-58. Lectr. in bus. adminstrn. Sch. Bus. Northwestern U., Evanston, Ill., from 1958. Mem. bd. mgrs. YMCA, Chgo.; pres. Village of Winnetka, 1956-60. Mem. Ravinia Festival Assn. (trustee), Council of Alumni Dartmouth Coll. (past pres.). Conglist. Clubs: University, Commercial (Chgo.); Indian Hill (Winnetka). Home: Winnetka IL Died Oct. 14, 1968.

HENDERSON, LELAND JOHN, secretary; b. Harrisburg, Ore., July 1, 1874; s. John Leland and Harriet Elizabeth (Humphrey) H.; ed. Olympia (Wash.) Collegiate Inst.; m. Mary Alberdia Ansley, of Evergreen, Ala., June 1, 1897. Began as civ. engr. and abstracter, Bay St. Louis, Miss., 1895; has organized a number of land cos.; an organizer, 1908, and sec. Miss. to Atlantic Inland Waterway Assn.; sec. Pensacola Commercial Assn., Dec., 1912-13. Dem. presdl. elector, Fla., 1912. Methodist. Address: Pensacola FL‡

HENDERSON, PERONNEAU FINLEY, lawyer; b. Aiken, S.C., Nov. 29, 1877; s. Daniel S. and Lillie (Ripley) H.; grad. Aiken Inst., 1893; A.B., Davidson (N.C.) Coll., 1897; studied summer sch., Harvard; m. Grace Adelaide Powell, June 29, 1904 (died Nov. 1943); children—Adelaide (Mrs. Wm. F. E. Cabaniss), Eleanor (Mrs. Frank Edwards); m. 2d, June Rainsford Butler, Apr. 28, 1945. Admitted to S.C. bar, 1899, began practice at Aiken; sr. mem. Henderson, Salley Cushman & Summerall; past pres. Carolina Light & Power Co.; v.p. Georgia-Carolina Electric Co.; dir. S.C. Power Co.; Powell Hardware Co., Real Estate & Fidelity Co., Graniteville Mfg. Co., Gregg Dyeing Company; receiver Langley Cotton Mills Company; pres. Langley Realty Co. Spl. judge Court of Common Pleas and Gen. Sessions of S.C., acting asso. justice Supreme Court of S.C. Dist. Dir. Liberty Loan Campaigns, World War. Del. to Dem. Nat. Conv., 1924. Pres. S.C. Bar Assn.; moderator Congaree Presbytery, 1926; moderator Synod of South Carolina, 1939; mem. Permanent Com. of Southern Presbyn. Gen. Assembly on Co-operation and Union. Pres. bd., Aiken Inst.; treas. Aiken Hosp. Assn. Mem. Am. Bar Assn., Aiken Bar Assn. (pres.), Aiken Chamber Commerce (pres.). Phi Beta Kappa.

Beta Theta Pi. Democrat. Mason. Grand Chancellor K.P. of S.C., 1921-22. Clubs: Kiwanis (v.p.), Outing (pres.), Highland Park Golf, Fermata. Delivered addresses Pythian Story; The Doctrine of Imputed Knowlege; (religious dissertations) My Spiritual String of Pearls, The Theories of Atonement, Ta Biblia. Author: A Short History of Aiken and Aiken County. Contributor article The Doctrine of Imputed Knowledge, to law publications. Home: Aiken SC Died Apr. 7, 1968.

HENDERSON, THOMAS HOWARD, univ. pres.; born Newport News, Va., Jan. 31, 1910; s. Rev. Hamilton M. and Mamie J. (Hamlette) H.; B.S., Va. Union U., 1928; A.M., U. of Chicago, 1938, Ph.D., 1946; m. Kate R. Gilpin, Feb. 1, 1936; 1 dau., Tommyzee. Chemistry teacher Amstrong High Sch., Richmond, Va., 1928-41; dean of coll. Va. Union U., Richmond, 1941-60, pres., 1960-70. Mem. Richmond Sch. Bd. Mem. Richmond Urban League, Phi Delta Kappa, Alpha Phi Alpha, Sigma Pi Phi, Alpha Kappa Mu. Home: Richmond VA Died Jan. 17, 1970; buried Hollywood Cemetery, Richmond VA

HENDERSON, WILLIAM THOMAS, justice, Court of Appeal of Ont.; b. Stratford, Ont., Sept. 17, 1874; s. Thomas and Catherine (Collins) H.; student Stratford Collegiate Inst., Osgoode Hall, Toronto; m. Victoria White, Jan. 10, 1914. Read law with the Hon. Mr. Justice Idington, Supreme Court of Can.; called to bar, Ont., Nov. 1894; city solicitor, Brantford, 1898-1934; King's counsel, Nov. 1910; appointed to the Bench, Supreme Court of Ontario, 1934; appointed a Justice in Appeal of the Supreme Court of Ontario, 1935. Served with 54th Battery, C.E.F., World War I; became major, Jan. 1916. Clubs: University (Toronto), Toronto Golf (Long Branch, Ont.), Brantford Golf and Country (Brantford, Ont.). Conservative. Home: 127 Brant Av., Brantford, Ont. Address: Osgoode Hall, Toronto OT Canada*‡

HENDRICK, FRANK, lawyer; b. Boston, Aug. 30, 1874; s. Jairus S. and Jane (O'Brien) H.; A.B., Harvard, 1897; student Harvard Grad. Sch., 1898, Harvard Law Sch., 1899; m. Katherine Edson Mumford, of Phila., June 29, 1901. Practiced at Boston, 1899-1900, at New York, since 1900. Republican. Mem. Delta Upsilon. Clubs: Harvard, Republican, Union League. Author: Railway Control by Commission, 1900; The Power to Regulate Corporations and Commerce; also pamphlets. Home: 75 E. 82d St. Office: 120 Broadway, New York‡

HENDRICK, IVES, psychiatrist; b. New Haven, Conn., Mar. 10, 1898; s. Burton J. and Bertha Jane (Ives) H.; student Phillips Andover Acad., 1913-16, Williston Acad., 1916-17; A.B., Yale, 1921, M.D., 1925; grad. student Psychoanalytical Inst., Berlin, 1928-30; m. Martha Marie Crawford McClung, Nov. 14, 1934 (div. 1945); children—Ives, Jr. (dec.), Bertha-Jane (Mrs. James Rumsey), and Martha (Mrs. Robert Rusnak). Served internship Lenox Hill Hospital, New York City, 1925-26; asst. in the dept. of psychiatry, med. sch., Harvard, 1930-34; instr., 1943-47, asso., 1947-48, asst. clin. prof., 1948-51, associate clinical professor, 1951-54, clin. prof., 1954-65, emeritus, 1965-72; clin. dir. emeritus Mass. Mental Health Center, chief Harvard Teaching Unit, Southard Clinic, 1943-64; dir. med. edn., Boston Psychopathic Hosp., 1949-56; consultant McClean and Mass. Gen. Hosps., 1930-33; pvt. practice psychoanalysis and psychiatry from 1930. Fellow Am. Psychiatric Assn.; mem. Am. Psychoanalytic Assn. (pres.-elect. chmn. bd. prof. standards, 1951-53, pres. 1953-55) Boston Soc. Psychiatry and Neurology, Soc. Research in Psychosomatic Problems, Group for Advancement in Psychiatry, Nu Sigma Nu, American Medical Association, Massachusetts Psychiatric Soc., Mass. Med. Assn., Macy Found. Conf. on Infancy, Boston Psychoanalytic Soc. and Inst. (pres. 1944-45). Clubs: Yale (N.Y. City); Harvard, Harvard Music Association (Boston, Mass.); Harvard Faculty (Cambridge, Mass.). Author: Facts and Theories of Psychoanalysis, 1934, revised edition pub., 1958; (Spanish transl., 1951); Psychiatric Education Today, 1965. Author and editor: Birth of an Institute, 1961. Contbr. sci. publs. Contbg. editor Ency. Brit.; editorial bd. Jour. Am. Psychoanalytic Assn., 1952-56. Address: Boston MA Died May 28, 1972; buried Evergreen Cemetery, New Haven CT

HENDRICKS, ALLAN BARRINGER, JR., electrical engr.; b. Red Hook, N.Y., Jan. 28, 1874; s. Allan Barringer and Anna (Rodgers) H.; student Lawrence Scientific Sch. (Harvard), 1897-1900; m. Sallie Fox Acken, Feb. 8, 1908 (dec. Aug. 12, 1947); children—George Bartlett, Dorothea Brooks, Sylvia Acken. With Stanley Electric Mfg. Co., Pittsfield, Mass., 1900; when this company was absorbed by the General Electric Co., continued as employee in the same plant, until retirement, 1944; organized Testing Laboratory, then became asst. engr. Power Transformer Dept. Specialized in invention and design of apparatus for high voltage and current, both alternating and continuous; first to produce 1,000,000 volts above ground, 1,000,000 volts three phase, 2,100,000 volts single phase, and 1,200,000 volts three phase, at commercial frequency; 20 patents granted. Designed high potential equipment for million volt three phase arc exhibit at New York World's Fair, 1939; now independent designing engr. Home: 115 Wendell Av., Pittsfield MA‡

HENDRICKS, IRA KING, educator; born in Richmond, Utah, Sept. 2, 1900; s. James Warren and Elizabeth (Merrill) H.; B.S., Utah State Agrl. Coll., 1923; A.M., Stanford, 1926, Ph.D., 1941; student U. of Berlin, 1929, 1930; m. Hazel B. Hartle, Feb. 16, 1923; 1 dau., Rebecca Barbara (Mrs. Thomas M. Madden). Teacher of English and head of dept. Branch Agrl. Coll., Cedar City, Utah, 1923-25; asst. prof. of English, Utah State University, 1935-38, asso. prof., 1938-44, professor, 1944-66, emeritus professor of English, 1966-70, director libraries, 1946-55, head English department, 1955-66. Mem. Nat. Council Tchrs. English, Rocky Mountain Lang. Assn. Utah Acad. Arts and Scis. (Distinguished Service award 1970). Author: (with W. Sundermeyer), Yankee Stories and Glimpses of America, English readers for German Schools, 1930; (with L. A. Stoddart) Technical Writing, 1948; (with others) Communication Skills, 1958; Creator and Critic, 1961; (with Irving Shepard) Letters from Jack London, 1965, Jack London Reports, 1970. Home: Logan UT Died Apr. 19, 1970; buried Richmond UT

HENDRIX, JIMI, singer; b. Seattle, Nov. 27, 1942; s. James Allen Ross and Lucille (Jetters); ed. pub. schs. Guitarist in U.S.; leader Jimi Hendrix Experience, 1966-70; numerous appearances in U.S. and Europe; composer many of own songs; recording artist for Warner Bros./7 Arts, 1967-70. Recipient Billboard award, 1968; artist of year award, 1968; 3 gold records; named Playboy mag. Artist of Year, 1969. Home: London England Died Sept. 1970.

HENIE, SONJA, actress, skater; b. Oslo, Norway, April 8, 1912; d. Wilhelm and Selma (Nilsen) Henie; m. Daniel Topping (div.); m. 2d, Winthrop Gardiner, Jr., Sept. 15, 1949; m. 3d, Niels Onstad, June 1956. Began skating at age of 8; won figure skating championship of Norway when 11, second place in world championships when 13, world championship when 14; was world figure skating champion ten times, Olympic champion three times; became professional and came to U.S., 1936, later appearing throughout country; entered motion pictures, 1937, later prodns. include Countess of Monte Cristo, 1948; skated in command performances before many rulers. Donated (with husband) Henie-Onstad Art Center, Ho/vikodden, per Oslo, Norway, 1968. Author: Wings in My Feet, 1940. Home: Los Angeles CA Died Oct. 12, 1969; buried Henie-Onstad Art Center, Ho/vikodden, per Oslo, Norway

HENLE, JAMES, editor; born Louisville, Dec. 20, 1891; s. Frederick and Bertha (Flexner) H.; A.B. with highest honors, Columbia Coll., 1912; m. Marjorie Jacobsen, June 11, 1917; children—Peter, Guy. Pres. Vanguard Press, N.Y.C., 1928-52. Phi Beta Kappa. Author: The Book of Marjorie, 1920; Sound and Fury, 1924; Letters from the Corsican, 1940. Home: New York City NY Died Jan. 9, 1973.

HENNESSY, JOHN FRANCIS, mech. engr.; b. N.Y.C. June 14, 1902; s. John J. and Nora (McCarthy) H.; B.S., in Mech. Engring., Mass. Inst. Tech., 1924; D.Eng., Manhattan Coll., 1956; LL.D., Iona Coll., 1958; m. Dorothy A. O'Grady, Apr. 30, 1927; children—John Francis, Paul Kevin. Founder firm Syska, Hennessy, Inc., cons. engrs., N.Y.C., 1928, pres., 1938-67, chmn., chief exec. officer, 1967-73; dir. Security Nat. Bank; trustee N.Y. Savs. Bank. Asst. to sec. navy, 1944-45. Mem. N.Y.C. Bd. Edn., 1961-63. Pres. Lincoln Hall, 1958-73; mem. Manhattan Coll. Council, 1959-73. Served with USAAF, 1942-44. Decorated Legion of Merit; named knight of Malta, 1945, knight of Sepulchure, 1953. Registered profl. engr., N.Y. Mem. N.Y. Cons. Engrs. (pres. 1951-52), N.Y. Bldg. Congress (pres. 1955-58), Am. Inst. Cons. Engrs., Am. Inst. E.E., Nat. Soc. Profl. Engrs. Home: Remsenburg NY Died Apr. 1973.

HENNESSY, ROLAND BURKE, journalist; b. Milford, Mass., Jan. 30, 1870; s. Timothy Burke and Ulila H.; ed. common schools, Milford, Mass., and Providence, R.I. Engaged in journalism, 1890; editor The Stage; dramatic critic New York Daily News and theatrical writer for McClure Newspaper Syndicate. Has written several songs, including The Songs of Long Ago." Author: Tales of the Heart, and Tales of Broadway, 1897 M27. Residence: St. Paul Hotel. Office: 25 Center St., New York NY‡

HENRETTA, JAMES EDWARD, business exec.; b. Conneautville, Pa., Oct. 5, 1874; s. James and Birget (Bradley) H.; student Edinboro Normal Sch., 1891; A.B., Allegheny Coll., 1897; m. Antoinette Frances Wayave, Aug. 15, 1901 (dec. Jan. 1961); children—James Edward, William Terence, Thomas Eugene, Frances May; m. 2d, Helen H. Havens, Mar. 19, 1964. Asst. prin. Waterford (Pa.) Acad., 1897-98; supervising prin. Kane (Pa.) Pub. Sch., 1898-1902; joined Holgate Bros., Kane, 1902, v.p., 1902-34, president and director, 1934-55; dir. Kane Bank & Trust Co., from 1924, v.p. from 1929; dir. Leonardson Co. Trustee Clairon State Tchrs. Coll., 1934-38; mem. McKean Co. Hist. Soc.; dir. McKean Co. TB and Health Soc., Kane Y.M.C.A., Pa. Economy League. Mem. Pa. State Archaeol Soc. (life), Pa. State C. of C., Phi Beta Kappa. Republican. Conglist. Mason. Clubs: Rotary, Country (Kane, Pesnsylvania); University (Winter Park, Florida). Author: Kane and the Upper Allegheny. Home: Kane PA Died Nov. 16, 1971; buried Forest Lawn Cemetery, Kane PA

HENRICKS, COLEMAN BRESEE, physician; b. Portland, Ore,, June 4, 1907; s. Andrew O. and Fawn (Galbraith) H.; M.D., U. So. Cal., 1937; m. Opal Marie Campbell, Feb. 19, 1935; children—Coleman Bresee, Jon Andrew. Intern Los Angeles County Gen. Hosp., 1937, resident in internal medicine, 1937-39, later sr. attending staff; chief teaching resident in internal medicine Los Angeles County Gen. Hosp and U. So. Cal. Sch. Medicine, 1939-40; practiced medicine specializing in internal medicine; vis. staff Hosp. Good Smaritan. Served to maj. M.C., AUS, 1942-46; CBI. Diplomate Am. Bd. Internal Medicine. Mem. A.M.A., Am. Soc. Investigative Medicine, Alpha Omega Alpha. Republican. Home: Los Angeles CA Died Mar. 17, 1969; buried Forest Lawn Cemetery, Glendale CA

HENRIQUEZ-URENA, MAX, ambassador U.N. rep.; b. Santo Domingo (now Ciudad Trujillo), Dominican Rep., Nov. 16, 1885; s. Francisco Henriquez y Carvajal and Salome (Urena) Henriquez; B.A., Santo Domingo, 1906; LL.D., U. of Havana, 1912, Ph.D., 1916; m. Guarina Lora Yero, Dec. 10, 1914; children—Hernan, Leonardo. Editor newspapers and mags., Santo Domingo, Cuba and Mexico, 1903-30; judge Dominican group at permanent Ct. of Arbitration, The Hague, 1932-38; minister plenipotentiary to Argentina, 1934, Gt. Britain, 1935-41, Netherlands, 1940, Portugal, 1941, Mexico, 1941, Cuba, 1942; chief del. to internat. monetary and econ. confs., London, Eng., 1933, consolidation of peace, Buenos Aires, Argentina, 1936, 8th Pan-Am. Conf., Lima, 1938; permanent delegate League of Nations, Geneva, Switzerland, 1935-40, mem. council, 1938-40; rep. Dominican Republic at coronation of King George VI of Gt. Britain, 1937; spl. ambassador to coronation Pope Pius XII, 1939; ambassador to Brazil, 1943, Argentina, 1945, The Holy See, 1952; ambassador, permanent del. to U.N. since 1947; guest lectr. Colo. Coll., Colorado Springs, 1948, Yale, 1948-49; pres. Trusteeship Council of United Nations, 1950-51. Mem. P.E.N. Club, Acad. Dominicana de la Historia, Acad. Dominicana de la Lengua, Acad. Nacional de Artes y Letras (Cuba) (supernumerary), Acad. Espanola de la Lengua, Acad. Argentina de la Historia, Acad. Portugueza da Historia. Author, latest publs. include: Cuentos Insulares, 1947; series Episodios Dominicanos: La Independencia Efimera, 1938. La Conspiracion de los Alcarrizos, 1941, El Arzobispo Valera, 1944. Home: Forest Hills L.I. NY Died Jan. 1968.

HENRY, ARNOLD KAHLE, educator; b. Pa., Feb. 5, 1898; s. Samuel M. and Emma (Kerr) H.; B.S., U. Pa., 1921, M.A., 1925, Ph.D., 1929; m. Lydia Cresse, Aug. 1930. Instr. commerce transportation U. Pa., 1922-30, asst. prof., 1930-37, asso. prof., 1937-47, prof. transportation and pub. utilities since 1947, asst. dir. student personnel, 1922-34, field sec., 1934-35, dir. admissions, 1936-39, dean student affairs 1939-53, vice provost, 1953-56. Served with Students' Army Training Corps, World War I. Mem. Kappa Sigma. Republican. Club: Phila. Cricket. Author: Transportation by Water, Panama Canal and the Intercoastal Trade, Co-author: Traffic and Transportation Management-U.S.; Traffic and Transportation Management-Canada. Home: Philadelphia PA Died Dec. 25, 1971.

HENRY, DOUGLAS SELPH, lawyer; b. Nashville, Dec. 30, 1890; s. Robert Allison and Emily James (Selph) H.; A.B., Vanderbilt U., 1911, LL.B., 1916; m. Kathryn Craig, Apr. 24, 1924; children—Douglas Selph, Margaret Sinclair (Mrs. Harry A. J. Joyce). Admitted to Tenn. bar, 1915, practiced in Nashville, 1916-49; v.p., gen. counsel Nat. Life & Accident Ins. Co., Nashville, from 1950, also dir.; v.p., gen. counsel WSM, from 1950, also dir. Mem. bd. edn. Davidson Co., Tenn., 1939-42; state senator Davidson Co., 1927-28; mayor City Belle Meade, Tenn., 1938-40. Member board of trustees of the Tennessee Teachers Retirement System, 1945-57. Served as capt. F.A., U.S. Army, 1917-19. Mem. Assn. Life Ins. Counsel, Am., Tenn., Nashville bar assns., Phi Delta Theta. Methodist. Clubs: Belle Meade Country, Colemere, Cumberland (Nashville). Home: Nashville TN Died Sept. 3, 1971.

HENRY, GEORGE MCCLELLAN, lawyer, author; b. Newville, Pa., June 16, 1877; s. Alexander and Ellen (Miller) H.; LL.B., U. of Pa., 1904; m. Elise Koronski, Oct. 10, 1907 (died Jan. 10, 1929); 1 son, George McClellan (dec.). Admitted Pa. bar, 1904, also admitted U.S. Supreme Court; practicing, Philadelphia, since 1904. Served as pvt., Co. I, 3d Regt., Pa. Vols., during Spanish-Am. War. Trustee, treas. and gen. counsel Joseph Priestly House, Inc. Mem. Phila. Bar Association, Pa. Bar Association, Art Alliance (Phila.). Trustee Devereux Foundation. Mayor, Narberth, Pa., 1914-18. Republican. Unitarian. Mason. Author several books, latest: Pennsylvania Evidence, 1953. Revised

Sadler's Criminal Procedure in Pa., 1937. Contbr. to legal jours. Home: Leopard Rd., Berwyn, Pa. Office: Finance Bldg., Phila PA‡

HENRY, HOWARD JAMES, engring. exec.; b. Grand Forks, N.D., Nov. 11, 1911; s. John Dan and Olean (Stennes) H.; B.S. in Mech. Engring., U. N.D., 1933; M.S. in Mech. Engring., U. Kan., 1941; M.E., Mass. Inst. Tech., 1951; Ph.D., State U. Ia., 1952; m. Norma A. Higgins, Dec. 28, 1938; children—John George, Lucinda Scott (Mrs. Richard N. Lapp). Instr. mech. engring. U. N.D., 1936-37; design engr. Fairbanks Morse Co., Beloit, Wis., 1937-38; instr. mech. engring. U. Kan., 1938-41, Carnegie Inst. Tech., 1941-43; design engr. Chgo. Pneumatic Tool Co., Franklin, Pa., 1946-47, dir. engring., 1951-60; prof. mech. engring. Ia. State U., 1947-51; dean Sch. Engring., So. Methodist U., Dallas, Texas, 1960-64; v.p. engring. pneumatic equipment division of the Westinghouse Air Brake Company, Sidney, O., 1964-69. Pres. United Fund Franklin, 1958, Franklin C. of C., 1959; chairman Franklin Planning Commn., 1959-60, Franklin Sch. Authority, 1958. Served to lt. (s.g.) USNR, 1943-46; ret. comdr. Recipient Citizenship award Franklin, 1959. Registered profl. engr., Ia. Mem. Am. Soc. M.E. (vice chmn. N. Tex. sect. 1962-63, rep. dir. to Engrs. Council for Profl. Devel. 1968), American Society for Engineering Education, Sigma Tau, Pi Tau Sigma. Methodist (ofcl. bd.). Elk. Home: Sidney OH Died Aug. 13, 1969; buried Franklin Cemetery, Franklin PA

HENRY, J(OHN) PORTER, lawyer; b. Jefferson City, Mo., Mar. 28, 1884; s. Jesse W. and Kate (Davison) H.; LL.B., Washington U.. St. Louis, 1909; m. Imogen Adams, Jan. 5, 1911; children—J. Porter, Jr., Kilbourne A.; m. 2d, Mrs. Clara Ann Bent, Sept. 22, 1959. Admitted to Mo. bar, 1909, sr. partner Green, Hennings, Henry & Arnold; dir. J.H. Miller Co. Mem. Am. Bar Assn., Sigma Chi, Phi Delta Phi. Club: Algonquin Golf. Home: Webster Groves MO Died Nov. 3, 1969.

HENRY, JULES, anthropologist, educator; b. N.Y.C., Nov. 29, 1904; s. Julius and Fannie (Manheim) H.; B.S., Coll. City N.Y., 1928; Ph.D., Columbia, 1936; m. Zunia Lotte Gechtman, Aug. 27, 1934; 1 dau., Phyllis (Mrs. Peter Kingsmill). Research asst. Columbia, 1934-36, 38-39; hon. prof. U. Michoacan, Morelia, Michoacan, Mexico, 1940; prof. Nat. Politecnic Inst., Mexico, D.F., 1940-41; linguist Departamento de Asuntos Indigenas, Mexico, 1940; with Office Interamerican Affairs, Dept. Labor, Dept. Agr., 1942-47; prof. anthropology and sociology Washington U., St. Louis, 1947-69. Cons., Nat. Inst. Mental Health, U.S. Office Edn., WHO, also ednl. instns., psychiat. hosps. Chief analyst U.S. Strategic Bombing Survey Japan, World War II. Fellow Center For Advanced Study in Behavioral Scis., 1966-67. Fellow Am. Anthrop. Assn., A.A.A.S. Author: Jungle People, 1941; Doll Play of Pilaga Indian Children, 1944; L'Observation Naturaliste des Familles D'Enfants Psychotiques, 1961; Culture Against Man, 1963; Pathways to Madness, 1972; Jules Henry on Education, 1972; Sham, Vulnerability and Other Forms of Self-Destruction, 1973; also many articles. Home: St MO Died Sept. 23, 1969; buried Oak Grove Cemetery, St. Louis MO

HENRY, RALPH COOLIDGE, architect; b. Amherst, Mass., Jan. 10, 1875; s. James Stone and Elikabeth Arvilla (Hills) H.; B.S., Mass. Inst. Tech., 1896; M.S., 1897; m. Frances Stanton Cumming, Jan. 29, 1902; children—Beatrice (dec.), Elizabeah, Margaret. Began with McKim, Mead and White, N.Y.C., 1897; joined orgn. of Guy Lowell, Boston, 1902; member firm Henry and Richmond (successors to Guy Lowell), 1927-46. Firm architects for: Grosse Pointe (Mich.) Yacht Club; Grace Ch. and Hamilton Sch., Newton, Mass.; Dana Hall Auditorium, Wellesley, Mass.; Mass. Sch. of Art and N.E. Trust Co. Bldg., Boston, Morse Memorial Sci. Bldg., Phillips Acad., Andover, Mass.; John Wingate Weeks Jr. High Sch., Newton, Mass.; estate of Charles Sprague Sargent, Brookline, Mass.; residences of Mrs. John Lowell, Chestnut Hill; Francis B. Crowninshield, Boca Grande; Russell G. Hemenway, Wolfeboro, N.H.; Stoneham Pumping Station; Braintree Pumping Station; Frank Carr School, Newton, Mass.; Knowles Apts., Newton; Kilburn House, West Newton; Reginald Washburn, North Haven, Me.; Chilton Club, Boston; Library Bldg., swimming pool (latter with Harry Gulesian) of Babson Inst. Wellesley; Willard Rice House, Dennisport, Mass.; pumping stations at Greenfield and Reading, Mass., Keene, N.H., Durham, N.H., Farmington, N.H. and Westerly, R.I.; residences for Henry L. Whitney, Milton, Mass., and Hon. William B. Baker, Newton, Mass.; Fed.-aided housing project for Boston Housing Authority, South Boston; enlargement Boston Mus. Fine Arts; Walton Restaurants (Boston); Eastern Nazarene College (Quincy, Mass.); archtl. consultants Weston and Sampson, sanitary engrs., Boston; condr. research Boston Traffic and Parking, Am. ry. design, Area-Motive transportation, nuclear energy. With Emergency Fleet Corp., architects. Republican. Conglist. Author: (with Walter Squantum, Mass., World War. Member Am. Inst. Ar- C. Voss) Architectural Construction, 1925. Contbr. to Architectural Forum. Home: 303 Beacon St., Boston and R.D. 4, Loconia, N.H. Office: 131 State St., Boston and Laconia NH‡

HENRY, ROBERT LLEWELLYN, JR., judge; b. Chicago, Ill., Nov. 4, 1882; s. Robert Llewellyn and Ada Camille (Badger) H.; Ph.B., U. of Chicago, 1902, J.D., 1907; Rhodes scholar at Worcester Coll., Oxford, Eng., 1904-07, B.C.L., Oxford, 1907, D.C.L., 1926; m. Elaine Goodale Read, June 30, 1908 (dec.); children—Robert L., Alvan Read, McClelland. Prof. law, La. State U., 1907-11; asst. prof. law, U. of Ill., 1911-12; prof. law and dean Coll. of Law, U. of N.D., 1912-14; prof. law, U. of Calif., summer, 1914; prof. law, State U. of Ia., 1914-16. Capt. inf., O.R.C., Nov. 13, 1916; maj., Mar. 8, 1919; instr. officers training camps and schs., Ft. Sheridan, Ill., Camp Grant, Ill., Camp Lee, Va., May 1, 1917-Mar. 8, 1919; mem. constrn. demobilization com., Gen. Staff, Washington, D.C., Mar. 8-Aug. 1, 1919; mem. War Dept. Bd. Contract adjustment, Washington, D.C., 1919-20; lecturer at Oxford U., 1921-22; later judge Mixed Court, Alexandria, Egypt. Democrat. Mem. Chi Psi, Phi Delta Phi. Author: Liens and Pledges, 1913; Consideration in Contracts, 601 A.D. to 1520 A.D. (article), 1917; Anglo-Saxon Contracts (article), 1917; Contracts in the Local Courts of Medieval England, 1926. Home: Louisville KY Died May 1969.

HENRY, ROBERT SELPH, ry. exec.; b. Clifton, Tenn., Oct. 20, 1889; s. Robert Allison and Emily James (Selph) H.; A.B., LL.B., Vanderbilt Univ., 1911; post grad. work Queens' Coll., Cambridge, Eng., 1919; Litt.D., U. Chattanooga, 1950; m. Lura Temple, Oct. 30, 1929; children—Elizabeth Temple (Mrs. N. B. Musselman), Roberta Selph (Mrs. George B. Vest, Jr.). Began career as newspaper reporter, 1907-13; pvt. sec. to gov. of Tenn., 1913-15; admitted to Tenn. bar, 1911, and practiced in Nashville, 1915-21, asst. to v.p. N.C.&St.L. Ry., 1921-34; asst. to pres. Assn. Am. R.R.'s., 1934-37, v.p., 1947-58. Served as capt. F.A., U.S. Army, 1917-19; maj. and lt. col., Field Artillery Res. Chmn. bd. trustees Ladies Hermitage Assn., Nashville, Tenn., 1926-34; trustee Vanderbilt University. Member Am., So. (v.p. 1956, pres. 1957) hist. assns., Soc. Am. Historians, Phi Beta Kappa, Phi Delta Theta, Phi Delta Phi. Presbyterian. Clubs: Army and Navy, National Press Club, Cosmos (Washington, D.C.). Author: The Story of the Confederacy, 1931; Trains, 1934; On the Railroad, 1936; Portraits of the Iron Horse, 1937; The Story of Reconstruction, 1938; This Fascinating Railroad Business, 1942; First With the Most" Forrest, 1944; Headlights and Markers (with Frank P. Donovan, Jr.), 1945; The Story of the Mexican War, 1950; As They Saw Forrest (editor), 1956; The Armed Forces Institute of Pathology: Its First Century, 1862-1962, 1964. Contbr. articles to profl. jours. Home: Alexandria VA Died Aug. 18, 1970; buried Mt. Olivet Cemetery, Nashville TN

HENRY, SAMUEL CLEMENTS, pharmacist, mem. Nat. Recovery Review Bd.; b. Washington, D.C., Oct. 5, 1872; s. James and Rachel Amelia (Clements) H.; ed. pub. schs., Washington; Pharm. M., Phila. Coll. Pharmacy, 1924; m. Mary Elizabeth Young, 1893; 1 dau., Mary Elizabeth (dec.). Apprentice in Pharmacy, and pharmacist, 1886-91; opened retail drug store in West Phila., 1891, later acquired 2 add. stores; pres. Nat. Assn. Retail Druggists, 1914-15, sec., 1917-33; pres. Nat. Drug Trade Conf., 1920-30, Chicago Veteran Druggists Assn., 1933-34; sec. bd. trustees U.S. Pharmacopoeial Conv. (trustee since 1926); became mem. National Recovery Review Bd., Mar. 6, 1934; asso. editor Am. Druggist, 1934-36; asso. ed. and Western mgr. of Drug Store Retailing Mag.; sec. and treas. Rigidtest Products, Inc. Republican. Presbyterian. Home: 412 N. Maple, Oak Park, Ill. Office: 318 W. Randolph St., Chicago IL*‡

HENRY, WILLIAM M (BILL), columnist, war corr., radio analyst; born at San Francisco, August 21, 1890; s. John Quincy Adams and Margaret (Weddell) H.; ed. various schools in U.S. and abroad; grad. Los Angeles High Sch., 1909; student Sydney U., Australia, 1910, A.B., Occidental Coll., Los Angeles, 1911-14, Litt.D., 1947; Litt.D., University of Redlands, 1957; married Corinne Stanton, 1914; children—Margaret (Mrs. Fred Stichweh), Patricia (Mrs. Yeomans), Mary Virginia (Mrs. Blum) (dec.). With Los Angeles Times, 1911-70; Times and CBS war corr. with R.A.F. in France, 1939; war corr., South Pacific, 1942; news analyst on NBC, until 1970. Adminstrv. Aide to V.P. Nixon on round-the-world Goodwill trip, 1956, spl. asst. to Nixon on African tour, 1957; member President's Com. Fitness for Youth, 1956. Pres. Radio Corr. Assn., Washington, 1947. Chmn. Radio-TV Arrangements Com. for Rep.-Dem. polit. convs., 1948, 52, 56, 60, 64. Mem.-at-large U.S. Olympic Com., 1962; pres. So. Cal. Com. for Olympic Games, 1962-66. Recipient Nat. Headliners Award for 1943 as outstanding columnist; received Headliners Award for radio reporting in 1948; Freedoms Found. Spl. Achievement Award, 1951-52; The Olympic Diploma by Internat. Olympic Com., Helsinki, Finland, 1952; Presdl. Medal of Freedom, 1970. Fellow Sigma Delta Chi for outstanding service to journalism, 1954; Printers Devil award, Theta Sigma Phi, 1957; M and M award for outstanding contbn. to pub. understanding of U.S. Econ. and Political System, 1964. Author: An Approved History of the Olympic Games, 1948. Home: Chatsworth CA Died Apr. 13, 1970; buried Oakwood Memorial Park, Chatsworth CA

HENSON, AUBREY EUGENE, bus. mgmt. cons.; b. Atlanta, June 1, 1930; s. Leo and Fay (Beauchamp) H.; LL.B., Jackson Sch. Law, 1968; m. Elizabeth Smith, May 5, 1951; children—Aubrey Eugene, John Leonard. Agt., Liberty Nat. Life Ins. Co., Fairfax, Ala., 1953-56; v.p. Security Savings Life Ins. Co., Montgomery, Ala., 1956-58; sr. v.p. Certified Credit Corp., also v.p. sub.-cos., Jackson, Miss., 1958-60; pres. Profl. Mgmt. Corp., Gen. Mgmt. Corp., Advertisers Diversified Services, Penthouse Distributors, Inc., Miss. Indsl. Land and Timber Corp., Jackson, Miss., 1960-68. Candidate lt. gov. Miss., 1967. Named lifetime mem. Exec. and Profl. Hall of Fame, 1966. Mem. Am. Mgmt. Assn. (pres.'s council), Miss. Forestry Assn. (bd. dirs.), So. Shippers Assn. (adv. bd.), Ala. Agy. Dirs. Assn. (sec., treas. 1957), Jackson Jr. C. of C. (v.p. 1954). Methodist (bd. stewards 1966-67). Mason (32 degree, Shriner), Moose. Author record: The Negative Man, 1967. Clubs: Kiwanis (v.p. 1955), Laymens (pres. 1954-55). Home: Jackson MS Died May 8, 1968.

HENSON, CLARENCE CHERRINGTON, educator; b. Oak Hill, O., Jan. 8, 1875; s. James K. and Altha (Evans) H.; A.B., Ohio U., 1899, A.M., 1901, Ped.D., 1920; A.M., Columbia, 1903, also diploma Teachers Coll.; m. Nell Wilson, Aug. 23, 1905; 1 son, Clarence Crawford. Prin. high sch., Athens, 1899-1902; asst. prin. Isidore Newman Manual Tr. Sch., New Orleans, La., 1904-07; supt. parish schs., Rapides Parish, Alexandria, La., 1907-08; prin. Isidore Newman Manual Tr. Sch., 1908-17; again supt. parish schs., Rapides Parish, 1917-19; again prin. Isidore Newman Manual Training Sch. (now Newman Sch.), 1919-46, dir. emeritus since 1946; instructor in edn. and geography, Tulane U., summers 1918-36; instr. visual aids in edn. La. State U. Summer Sch., 1941. Mem. La. State Board Edn., 1936-40. Vis. lecturer in edn., Tulane U., 1944-46. Dir. La. Edn. Foundn.; exec. cons. Edward G. Schlieder Ednl. Foundn. Chmn. Junior Red Cross. Mem. Acad. of Science, N.E.A., Southern Assn. Colls. and Secondary Schs., La. State Teachers' Assn., Beta Theta Pi. Democrat. Unitarian. Mason (32 deg.). Club: Round Table. Joint author of Our Country's History (Garner and Henson), 1921. Lecturer on ednl. subjects. Home: 1122 Short St., New Orleans LA‡

HENYEY, LOUIS G(EORGE), astronomer; b. McKees Rocks, Pa., Feb. 3, 1910; s. Bela and Mary (Floszmann) H.; B.S., Case Inst. Tech., 1932, M.S., 1933; Ph.D., U. Chgo., 1937; m. Elizabeth Rose Belak, Apr. 29, 1934; children—Thomas Louis, Francis Stephen, Elizabeth Maryrose. From instr. to asst. prof. Yerkes Observatory, U. Chgo., 1937-47; from asst. to asso. prof. U. Cal., Berkeley, 1947-56, prof., 1956-70, dir. Computer Center, 1956-60, chmn. astronomy dept., 1959-64; research asso. Princeton, 1951-52; prin. investigator optical project NDRC. Guggenheim fellow, 1940-41. Mem. Am., Royal astron. socs., National Academy of Sciences, Astron. Society of the Pacific (president 1964-66), Sigma Xi. Home: El Cerrito CA Died Feb. 18, 1970; buried Sunset Cemetery, El Cerrito CA

HEPBURN, CHARLES KEITH, physician; b. Bloomington, Ind., Jan. 31, 1908; s. Charles McGuffey and Julia (Benedict) H.; B.S., Ind. U., 1930, M.D., 1931, M.D. cum laude, 1933; m. Kathryn Holaday, Sept. 15, 1934; children—Janet (Mrs. John Feemster), Charles Keith, David William, Barbara Kathryn. Intern U. Wis., 1931-32; resident Sch. Medicine Ind. U., 1932-34; resident Eloise Hosp., Detroit, 1938-40; practice medicine, specializing in neuropsychiatry, Indpls., 1940-70; asso. prof. Ind. U.; mem. staff Methodist Hosp., St. Francis Hosp., St. Vincent's Hosp.; cons. Marion County Gen. Hosp. Served to 1st lt., M.C., AUS, 1942-43. Diplomate Am. Bd. Neurology and Psychiatry. Mem. A.M.A., Am. Psychiat. Assn., Electroshock Research Assn., Beta Theta Pi, Nu Sigma Nu. Republican. Episcopalian. Home: Indianapolis IN Died Mar. 12, 1970.

HERBEIN, B. WILLIAM, educator; b. Topton, Pa., Nov. 23, 1895; s. Samuel Minker and Ellen Louise (Brintzenhoff) H.; grad. Kutztown State Tchrs. Coll., 1913; Ph.B., Muhlenberg Coll., 1927; M.A., U. Pa., 1933; m. Louise Hannah Smith, Apr. 23, 1916; children—Woodrow, Mary Ellen (Mrs. Arlan W. Long). Tchr., Charming Forge Sch., North Heidelberg Twp., asst. prin. Longswamp (Pa.) High Sch., later prin.; asst. prin. Topton Jr. High Sch.; prin. Fleetwood (Pa.) High Sch.; supervising prin. Topton Schs.; asst. county supt. Berks County Schs., Reading, Pa., 1946-58, supt., 1958-66. Active Boy Scouts Am.; dir. Berks County Tb Assn.; chmn. Berks County div. Heart Fund; chmn. Topton Borough Planning Commn. Dir. Guidance Inst. Berks County; trustee Pa. State Coll., 1959-63. Mem. Am. Assn. Sch. Adminstrs., N.E.A., Pa. Assn, County Supts., Pa. State Edn. Assn. Burgess of Topton, Pa., 1930-54. Mem. C. of C. (past pres.), Berks-Reading Tb Assn., Berks-Reading Dutch Fersommling Council, Pa. Dutch Folk Culture Soc. (dir.), Phi Delta Kappa. Mason, Lion. Home: Topton PA Died May 7, 1969.

HERBERT, SIR A(LAN) PATRICK, author; b. Eng., Sept. 24, 1890; s. P. H. and Beatrice (Selwyn) H.; student Winchester (Eng.) Sch.; grad. (1st Class Jurisprudence) New Coll., Oxford U.; m. Gwendolen

Quilter, 1914; 4 children. Began writing for Punch (mag.), London, 1910, became staff mem., 1924; admitted to bar, 1918, but never practiced; formerly pvt. sec. to Sir Leslie Scott. Mem. of Parliament (Independent) for Oxford U., 1935-50. Introduced into House of Commons a marriage bill, became Matrimonial Causes Act, 1938. Served with British Royal Navy, 1914-17, and in Gallipoli and France. Rep. Punch at 3d Imperial Press Conference, Melbourne, Australia, 1925. With River Emergency Service, from 1939; with Naval Auxiliary Patrol, 1940-45; Thames conservator, 1940. Trustee Nat. Maritime Mus., 1947. Knighted, 1945; decorated Companion of Honour; mentioned in despatches. Member Society of Authors (president, 1967). Clubs: Black Lion Skittles (president), Savage, Beefsteak, and Pratt's. Author poems, revues, comic operas and novels, including The Bomber Gipsy; The Secret Battle; The House-by-the-River; Light Articles Only; The Wherefore and The Why, 1930; Tinker, Tailor, 1930; The Man about Town; The Old Flame, 1925; The Blue Peter; Laughing Ann; She Shanties, 1927; Riverside Nights (with Nigel Playfair); Plain Jane, 1927; Misleading Cases; The Trials of Topsy; Topsy, M.P., 1927; Ballads for Broadbows, 1930; Honeybubble and Co.; La Vie Parisienne (adaptation); The Water Gypsies, 1930; More Misleading Cases; No Boats on the River, 1932; Still More Misleading Cases, 1933; Holy Deadlock, 1934; What a Word, 1935; Uncommon Law, 1935; Mild and Bitter, 1936; The Ayes Have It, 1937; SipMother of Pearl; Streamline (with Ronald Jeans); Home and Beauty; Bring Back the Bells, 1943; Big Ben, 1946; Point of Parliament, 1946; Topsy Turvy, 1947; Bless the Bride, 1947; Leave My Old Morale Alone (pub. U.S.) 1947; Mr. Gay's London, 1948; Southend Pier, 1948; Tough at the Top, 1949; The Topsy Omnibus, 1949; Independent Member, 1950; Number Nine, 1952; Come to the Ball (with R. Arkell), 1951; Full Enjoyment, 1952; Codds Last Case, 1952; Why Waterloo? 1952; Pools Pilot, 1953; Uncommon Law, 1953; The Right to Marry, 1954; No Fine on Fun, 1957; Made for Man, 1958; Look Back and Laugh, 1960; Silver Stream, 1961; Bardot M.P. and Other Modern Misleading Cases, 1964; Watch This Space, 1964; The Thames, 1966; Wigs At Work, 1966; Sundials Old and New, 1967; The Singing Swan, 1968. Address: London England Died Nov. 11, 1971.

HERBERT, F. M., JR., publisher Atlantic mag., Boston. Died May 16, 1968.

HERBERT, JAMES CASSIDY, newspaper editor; b. Sharon, Pa., Apr. 6, 1875; s. George Dixon and Elba (Cassidy) H.; ed. pub. schs. and tutors; unmarried. Began as reporter York (Pa.) Gazette, 1893, mng. editor and editor, 1895-1904; news editor Harrisburg Patriot, 1905-12; city editor Harrisburg Telegraph, 1912-13; editor Lancaster News, 1914-15, The West Virginian, (Fairmont) 1915-21, The Exponent, Clarksburg, 1921-24, Morgantown Post, 1924-26; editor The West Virginian, and news editor Fairmont Times since 1926; dir. Marion Co. Securities Co. Mason, Rotarian. Office: Newspaper Bldg., Fairmont WV*‡

HERBERT, JOHN KINGSTON, magazine exec.; b. Winthrop, Mass., Feb. 10, 1903; s. John William and Mary E. (Brickley) H.; m. Lucretia Reiner, Jan. 27, 1928; children—Sheila, John Kingston. Salesman, Standard Oil Co. of N.Y., Boston, 1921-28; cotton broker Cooper & Brush, New Bedford, Mass., 1928-31, Jones, Gardner & Beal, 1931-32; salesman Esquire mag., N.Y.C., 1932-38; New Eng. Mgr. Good Housekeeping mag., Boston, 1938-43, eastern advt. mgr., N.Y., 1945-47; gen. advt. mgr., v.p. Hearst Mags., Inc., 1947-50; v.p. in charge radio network sales NBC, N.Y.C., 1950-52, v.p. charge radio and TV sales, 1952, v.p. charge radio and television, 1953-54; exec. pub. N.Y. Jour.-American, 1954-55; pub. The Am. Weekly and Puck, The Comic Weekly, 1955-61; pres. Mag. Pubs. Assn., N.Y.C., 1961-69; pres. Microfragrance Div. John B. Lanigan & Assos., Inc., N.Y.C., 1971-72; v.p., marketing dir. Hearst Mags., 1972. Served as capt. aviation br. USMCR, 1943-45; lt. col. Res., ret. Clubs: Fifth Avenue (N.Y.C.); Everglades, Seminole (Palm Beach); Nat. Golf Links Am. Home: Southampton NY Died Sept. 24, 1972.

HERBST, JOSEPHINE FREY, author; b. Sioux City, Ia., Mar. 5, 1897; d. William Benton and Mary Magdalena (Frey) Herbst; student Sioux City High Sch., Morningside Coll. (Sioux City), State U. of Ia.; A.B., U. of Calif., 1918; m. John Herrmann, Oct. 21, 1925. Awarded Guggenheim fellowship, 1936; recipient of the Longview Foundation award, 1960. Mem. P.E.N. Club. Author: latest publs. include: Somewhere the Tempest Fell, 1947; New Green World, 1954; The Watcher with the Horn, 1955. Contbr. fiction and articles to mags. Home: Erwinna PA Died Jan. 28, 1969.

HERFORD, BEATRICE, monologist; b. Manchester, Eng.; d. Dr. Brooke and Hannah (Hankinson) H.; sister of Oliver H. (q.v.); early yrs. in U.S.; in England, 1893-7; since then has lived in U.S.; m. at London, Sidney Willard Hayward, of Wayland, Mass., 1897. Made debut as monologist in London. Author of the monologues which she acts, most notable being The Shop Girl and the Sociable Seamstress. Club: Twelfth Night (New York). Address: Wayland MA‡

HERLANDS, WILLIAM BERNARD, U.S. dist. judge; b. N.Y.C., July 19, 1905; s. Jacob David and Sarah (Sarason) H.; B.S., Coll. of City of New York, 1925; LL.B., Columbia, 1928; m. Gertrude Carol Bendheim, December 12, 1937; children—Barbara Eleanor, James Owen, Jonathan. Admitted N.Y. bar, 1929; asso. with George Z. Medalie, 1928-31; assistant U.S. attorney Southern District of New York, 1931-34; asst. corp. counsel City of New York, 1934-35; chief asst. to Thomas E. Dewey, special prosecutor of New York County, 1935-37; commr. of investigation, City of New York, 1938-44; justice Domestic Relations Court, 1940; special assistant attorney general, in charge of the Election Frauds Bureau, State of New York, 1944-45; U.S. district judge So. District N.Y., 1955-69. Member New York State Bd. of Mediation, 1950-54; spl. prosecutor to investigate criminal law administration in Richmond Co., 1951-54; commr. investigation State N.Y., 1954; spl. counsel N.Y. State Tax Commn., 1953-54; mem. Manhattan council New York State Commn. Against Discrimination. Mem.-at-large nat. council Boy Scouts America, 1951. Awards: Pell medal as highest ranking student College of City of New York, 1925; distinguished service medal of U.S. Jr. Chamber Commerce, Brooklyn, 1939. Mem. Assn. Bar City of N.Y., N.Y. State, Am. bar assns., N.Y. Co. Lawyers Assn., Am. Arbitration Soc. (panel mem.), Am. Acad. Polit. and Social Sci., Jewish Acad. Arts and Scis., Jewish Edn. Com., Jewish Welfare Board, Jewish Statis. Bureau (dir.), Am.-Jewish Com., Synagogue Council Am., Union Orthodox Jewish Congregations Am. (hon. pres.), Columbia Law Sch. Alumni Assn., Phi Beta Kappa Alumni Assn. Ind. Republican. Jewish religion. Mason. Club: National Republican. Author: Administration of Relief, 1940; Administration of Foreign-Trade Zone, 1940; Administration of Municipal Printing, 1940; Administration of Election Law, 1940; Purchase of School Supplies, 1942; Election Law Manual, 1944. Home: New York City NY Died Aug. 1969.

HERLANDS, WILLIAM BERNARD, U.S. dist. judge; b. N.Y.C., July 19, 1905; s. Jacob David and Sarah (Sarason) H.; B.S., Coll. of City of New York 1925; LL.B., Columbia, 1928; m. Gertrude Carol Bendheim, December 12, 1937; children—Barbara Eleanor, James Owen, Jonathan. Admitted N.Y. bar, 1929; asso. with George Z. Medalie, 1928-31; assistant U.S. attorney Southern District of New York, 1931-34; asst. corp. counsel City of New York, 1934-35; chief asst. to Thomas E. Dewey, special prosecutor of New York County, 1935-37; commr. of investigation, City of New York, 1938-44; justice Domestic Relations Court, 1940; special assistant attorney general, in charge of the Election Frauds Bureau, State of New York, 1944-45; U.S. district judge So. District N.Y., 1955-69. Member New York State Bd. of Mediation, 1950-54; spl. prosecutor to investigate criminal law administration in Richmond Co., 1951-54; commr. investigation State N.Y., 1954; spl. counsel N.Y. State Tax Commn., 1953-54; mem. Manhattan council New York State Commn. Against Discrimination. Mem.-at-large nat. council Boy Scouts America, 1951. Awards: Pell medal as highest ranking student College of City of New York, 1925; distinguished service medal of U.S. Jr. Chamber Commerce, Brooklyn, 1939. Mem. Assn. Bar City of N.Y., N.Y. State, Am. bar assns., N.Y. Co. Lawyers Assn., Am. Arbitration Soc. (panel mem.), Am. Acad. Polit. and Social Sci., Jewish Acad. Arts and Scis., Jewish Edn. Com., Jewish Welfare Board, Jewish Statis. Bureau (dir.), Am.-Jewish Com., Synagogue Council Am., Union Orthodox Jewish Congregations Am. (hon. pres.), Columbia Law Sch. Alumni Assn., Phi Beta Kappa Alumni Assn. Ind. Republican. Jewish religion. Mason. Club: National Republican. Author: Administration of Relief, 1940; Administration of Foreign-Trade Zone, 1940; Administration of Municipal Printing, 1940; Adminstration of Election Law, 1940; Purchase of School Supplies, 1942; Election Law Manual, 1944. Home: NYC NY Died Aug. 28, 1969; buried Cypress Hills Cemetery.

HERMSEN, EDWARD HERMAN, oil co. exec., lawyer; b. de Pere, Wis., Feb. 17, 1911; s. Chris and Emily (Herman) H.; LL.B., Marquette U., 1934; m. Janet L. McGaffey, July 13, 1940; children—Edward S., David C. Admitted to Wis. bar, 1934; practiced in Oconto, Wis., 1934-42; admitted to Cal. bar, 1944; with Tidewater Oil Co., Los Angeles, and successor Getty Oil Co., from 1960, sec., from 1971. Mem. Wis., Cal., Los Angeles County bar assns., Am. Soc. Corporate Secs. Home: Los Angeles CA

HERON, JAMES HENRY (JAMIE HERON), public speaker; b. Toronto, Can., Jan. 9, 1877; s. Archibald and Martha (Henry) H.; common sch. edn.; m. Florence Carroll, of Toronto, 1900; children—James Carroll, Florence Adele, Phyllis (dec.), John Henry, Mary Murial, Donald (dec.), Phillip. Began in insurance business, in Can.; moved to Pa. to represent Canadian Ins. Co., 1907; naturalized citizen, 1914; in employ of John Wanamaker, 1908-11; studied pub. speaking, 1911-13; was selected by William A. Brady to play lead in play Bunty Pulls the Strings," because of ability to speak Scotch dialect, also appearing for Klaw & Erlanger, New York; sec. Canadian Club, New York, after opening of World War; speaker in shipyards and for industries mfg. parts for ships, under U.S. Shipping Bd.; lectured throughout U.S. on business and as official speaker, Nat. Safety Council, Chicago; moved to Tex., to grow grapefruit and flowers for perfume, 1925; now mgr. publicity for Lower Rio Grande Chamber of Commerce. Mem. Protective Home Circle, History Soc. of Tex., Poetry Soc. of Tex. Republican. Mason. Clubs: Rotary, Lions, Kiwanis. Author: The Measure of A Man (verse), 1923. Home: Stuart Place, Tex. Address: Harlingen TX‡

HEROY, WILLIAM BAYARD, geologist; b. N.Y. City, Oct. 9, 1883; s. Newman Lounsberry and Mary Louise (Totten) H.; Ph.B., Syracuse, 1909, Sc.D., 1958; LL.D., Southern Methodist University, 1964; m. Jessie M. Page, June 10, 1909; children—John Newman Heroy, Laura Page (Mrs. Jack S. Guyton), Frances Totten (Mrs. C. J. Kirkland, Jr.), William Bayard; m. second, Mrs. Monroe G. Cheney, Dec. 31, 1960. With U.S. Geol. Survey, 1908-19; asst. geologist, 1910-12, geologist and chmn. water power section Land Classification Board, 1912-13; chmn. irrigation section same board, 1913-15; geologist-in-charge, sect. hydrographic classification, same board, 1915-18; chief division of power resources, 1918-19; advisory engr. Bur. of Conservation, U.S. Fuel Administration, 1918-19; asso. editor Elec. World, New York, 1919; geologist, foreign mgr. Sinclair Consol. Oil Corp., Nov. 1919-28, chief geologist, 1929; chief geologist Consolidated Oil Corp., 1933-39; pres. and mem. bd. dirs. Pilgrim Exploration Co., 1939-42; consultant, Bd. of Economic Warfare, 1942; dir. div. of Reserves, Office of Petroleum Adminstrn. for War, 1942-43; dir. Division of Fgn. Production, 1943-46; spl. asst., Sec. of Interior, 1946; mem. firm Beers & Heroy, 1946-56; mem. adv. com. U.S. Geol. Survey, from 1946; member Sec. Interior's Survey Com. Geol. Survey, 1953-54; v.p. The Geotechnical Corp., 1946-52, pres., 1952-61, chmn., 1961-66; dir. Inst. Study of Earth and Man, So. Meth. U., from 1966. Author articles and reports on conservation, devel. and use of fuels and water resources for power, petroleum geol. and engring. Recipient Powers medal Am. Assn. Petroleum Geologists, 1966. Fellow Of Geological Soc. of America, A.A.A.S.; mem. Am. Inst. Mining, Metallurgical and Petroleum Engrs. (v.p. 1939-42, mem. board directors 1935-39, 1942-45, Legion of Honor 1969), American Association Petroleum Geologists (hon. mem.; pres. 1934-35), Soc. Econ. Geologists (treas. 1935-39, pres. 1942), Am. Petroleum Inst., Am. Geophys. Union, Soc. Exploration Geophysicists, Geol. Soc. Washington, Dallas Geol. Soc., Am. Geog. Soc., Am. Geol. Inst. (v.p., 1948, pres. 1949-51), Am. Assn. Petroleum Geol. (hon.), Paleontological Research Instn. (v.p. 1967), Zeta Psi, Methodist. Clubs: Cosmos (Washington); Mining (N.Y.); Petroleum (Dallas). Home: Dallas TX Died Sept. 23, 1971; buried Fantinekill Cemetery, Ellenville NY

HERR, VINCENT V., clergyman, psychologist, author; b. Caraghar, O., July 2, 1901; s. Joseph August and Maryann (Snyder) H.; A.B., St. Louis U., 1925; A.M., 1926; student Vienna U., 1937-38, London U., summer 1938, U. Mich., summers 1935, 36; Ph.D., Bonn U., 1939. Entered Jesuit order, 1919; ordained priest, Roman Cath. Ch., at St. Mary's (Kan.) Coll., 1932; studied Socialism, annexation of Austria, changes in Prague, etc., Europe 1937-39; faculty Loyola U., Chicago, 1939-70, research prof. psychology, 1965-70, chmn. dept. psychology, 1945-65. Chmn. com. on standards for psychologists in Ill. state service, 1950; mem. adv. com. to chief justice of Supreme Court, 1950-59. Lectured on Panic Prevention of Office Civilian Defense, World War II. Mem. N.Y. Acad. Sci., Am. Psychol. Assn., Am. Catholic Psychological Association (pres. 1954), Ill. Psychol. Association. Degree Licentiate in Theology, 1937. Author: How We Influence One Another, 1945; General Psychology, 1946; Individual Experiments in Psychology, 1948; Screening of Candidates for Priesthood, pub. 1963; Religious Psychology, 1965; The Personality of Seminarians, 1968. Co-author: A Screening Program for Seminarians, 1962. Home: Chicago IL Died May 29, 1970; buried All Saints Cemetery, Desplaines IL

HERRICK, CURTIS JAMES, ret. army officer; b. Fordville, N.D., Aug. 12, 1909; s. James O. and Lillian Madeline (Connolly) H.; B.S., U.S. Mil. Acad., 1931; grad. Command and Gen. Staff Coll., 1942, Army-Navy Staff Coll., 1944, Indsl. Coll. Armed Forces, 1949, Fgn. Service Inst., 1963; m. Alice Milnor Reasoner, Mar. 3, 1936; children—Curtis James, Robert M., Alice (Mrs. Larry J. Reynolds), Mary R. (Mrs Robert P. Moltz). Commd. 2d lt. U.S. Army, 1931, advanced through grades to maj. gen., 1961; various inf. and armor assignments, 1931-42; battalion comdr. and staff positions 11th Armored Div., 1942-44; dep. chief logistics U.S. Army Forces, Pacific, 1944-47; rear echelon comdr. Joint Task Force 7, 1947-48; operations staff officer, chief deployments br. operations, gen. staff Dept. Army, 1949-52; regtl. comdr., asst. div. comdr. 11th Airborne Div., 1952-53; regtl. comdr. 223d Inf. Regt., Korea, 1953; sr. adviser III ROK Corps, Korea, 1953-54; dep. comdr., then comdr. 187th Airborne Regtl. Combat Team, 1954-55; chief staff XVIII Airborne Corps, also dep. comdg. gen. XVIII Corps, 1955-57; asst. div. comdr. 25th Inf. Div., 1957-59; dep.

for adminstrs. USARPAC, 1959-60; chief staff 3d U.S. Army, 1960-61; comdg. gen. XI Corps, 1961-63; chief JUSMMAT, 1963-65; comdg. gen. Mil. Dist. Washington, U.S. Army, 1965-67. Decorated D.S.M., Silver Star, Legion of Merit with oak leaf cluster, Bronze Star, Combat Inf. badge, Sr. Parachutist badge; Ulchi Distinguished Service medal with silver star (Korea). Home: Honolulu HI Died Feb. 9, 1971; buried Arlington National Cemetery, Arlington VA

HERRICK, ELIZABETH, writer; b. West Springfield, Mass., May 24, 1874; d. Nelson J. and Eleanor M. (Granger) H.; grad. high sch., West Springfield; A.B., Smith Coll., 1894. First stories pub.in New England Mag.; contbr. to Scribner's, Century, Cosmopolitan, Red Book, etc. Mem. Phi Kappa Psi. Republican. Conglist. Club: Community. Home: East Longmeadow MA‡

HERRICK, GENEVIEVE FORBES (MRS. JOHN ORIGEN HERRICK), magazine writer; b. Chicago, Ill., May 21, 1894; d. Frank G. and Carolyn D. (Gee) Forbes; prep. edn., Lake View High Sch.; B.A., Northwestern U., 1916; M.A., U. of Chicago, 1917; m. John Origen Herrick, Sept. 6, 1924. Began with Chicago Tribune, 1918, sent to Ireland, 1921, to ascertain conditions in U.S. Immigration Service; experiences at Ellis Island resulted in a call to testify, 1921, before the Congressional Com. of Immigration at Washington. Exec. asst. and press relations chief, W.A.C., 1942-43; asst. chief, later chief, Book and Mag. Bur., Office of War Information, 1943-45. Mem. Civilian Adv. Com. to Women's Army Corps; made official visit, 1946, to Germany, Austria, France and England to inspect W.A.C. activities. Recipient Alumni Award of Merit, Northwestern U., 1947; citation from U.S. Treasury for War Bond work. Mem. Alliance of Business and Professional Women, Theta Sigma Phi, Kappa Alpha Theta, Phi Beta Kappa. Episcopalian. Clubs: Women's Nat. Press, University (Washington, D.C.). Home: Dorset VT

HERRICK, GLENN WASHINGTON, entomologist; b. Otto, N.Y., Jan. 5, 1870; s. Stephen M. and Marion (Botsford) H.; Fredonia State Normal Sch.; B.S.A., Cornell U., 1896; post-grad. work, Cornell and Harvard, 1896-97; m. Nannie Young Burke, Aug. 17, 1898; children—Marvin Theodore, Stephen Marion, Ann Bertha (Mrs. John M. Raines). Professor biology, Mississippi Agricultural and Mechanical Coll., 1897-1908; v.dir. Miss Agrl. Expt. Sta., 1906-08; prof. entomology, Tex. Agrl. and Mech. Coll., 1908-09; asst. prof. economic entomology and entomologist to Expt. Sta., Cornell U., 1909-12, prof. and entomologist, 1912-35, prof. emeritus since 1935. Mem. Am. Palestine Com. Fellow Entomol. Society of America, A.A.A.S.; member American Association Econ. Entomologists (pres. 1915). Biol. Soc., Washington. Acad. Polit. Sci., Am. Assn. Univ. Profs., New York Acad. of Scis., Sigma Xi, Alpha Gamma Rho, Pi Gamma Mu; hon. mem. Eugene Field Soc. Republican. Episcopalian. Author: Text-book General Zoology, 1907; Laboratory Exercises in General Zoology, 1907; Insects Injurious to the Household and Annoying to Man, 1914; Insects of Economic Importance, 1915; Manual of Injurious Insects, 1925; Manual for Study of Insects (with J. H. Comstock and A. B. Comstock), 20th edit., 1930; Insect Enemies of Shade-trees, 1935; also numerous papers and bulls. Contbr. to Ency. Britannica Yearbook. Home: 219 Kelvin Place, Ithaca NY‡

HERRICK, JOHN ORIGEN, govt. official; b. Chicago, Ill., Aug. 3, 1898; s. James Bryan and Zellah P. (Davies) H.; student Chicago Latin Sch., 1908-15; A.B., Harvard, 1921, as of Class of 1919; m. Genevieve Forbes, of Evanston, Ill., Sept. 6, 1924. With Chicago Tribune as reporter, editorial writer and corr., Washington staff, 1921-34; asst. to general manager Division of Subsistence Homesteads, Department of the Interior, 1934-35; executive assistant of Federal Emergency Adminstrn. of Public Works, 1935; apptd. asst. to commr., Office of Indian Affairs, Dec. 1935. Served with Red Cross ambulance service with French Army, and later as pvt. and 2d lt., inf. A.E.F., World War. Mem. Alpha Sigma Phi. Clubs: National Press, Harvard (Washington), Harvard (Chicago). Home: Dorset VT

HERRICK, MANUEL, congressman; b. Tuscarawas Co., O., Sept. 20, 1876; s. John and Belinda (Kail) H.; never attended sch.; unmarried. Moved with parents to Greenwood Co., Kan., 1877; settled in Okla., 1893; farmer and cattle raiser. Mem. 67th Congress (1921-23), 8th Okla. Dist. Republican. Deist. Home: Perry OK‡

HERRICK, PAUL MURRAY, clergyman; b. Scandia, Kan., Apr. 3, 1898; s. Philo M. and Alice Mary (McKee) H.; A.B., Kansas City U., 1922; B.D., Union Theol. Sem., 1927; M.A., Philips U., 1935; D.D., York Coll., 1937; LL.D., Otterbein Coll., 1960; m. Ruth Porter, June 7, 1922; children—Bruce O., Philip O., Laura Ruth. Ordained to ministry Evang. U.B. Ch., 1927; dist. supt., Mo., 1927-29; pastor in Mo., Okla., Kan., 1929-41, 1st U.B. Ch., Dayton, O., 1941-58; bishop Central Area, Evang. U.B. Ch., Dayton 1958-68; bishop of Va., 1968-70. Served with U.S. Army, World War I. Mason (33), Kiwanian. Home: Dayton OH Died Nov. 23, 1972.

HERRICK, RAY W., mfg. exec.; b. Muskegon, Mich., July 20, 1890; s. Ben Gilbert and Catherine Ruth H.; ed. pub. schs. Mich.; married Nov. 29, 1911; children—Catherine, Kenneth, Jean Marie. Chmn. bd., dir. Tecumseh (Mich.) Products Co.; dir. Mich. Associated Telephone Co., Nat. Bank Jackson, Mich., Gen. Telephone Co. Mich. Address: Tecumseh MI Died Apr. 14, 1973.

HERRICK, WALTER R., lawyer; b. Albany, N.Y., May 11, 1877; s. Jonathan R. and Charlotte J. (Brown) H.; B.S., Princeton, 1898; LL.B., Union University, Department of Law, 1900; married Mary Douglas Bosworth, July 5, 1916. Admitted to New York State bar, 1900, and since practiced in Albany and New York City; member firm of Herrick, Hoppin & Thorne since 1935; member New York Assembly, 1911, State Senate, 1913-14; commr. N.Y. Dept. Narcotic Drug Control, 1919-21; pres. Park Bd. and park commr., 1927-33. Served as government appeal agent under Selective Service Act. Mem. Troop B, N.Y. Nat. Guard, 1901-05; mem. Cannon Club of Princeton U., Phi Delta Phi. Democrat. Clubs: University (N.Y. City); Nassau (Princeton, N.J.).‡

HERRING, HERBERT JAMES, educator; born at Pender Co., N. Carolina, December 11, 1899; s. Julian Fletcher and Minnie Alice (Johnson) H.; A.B., Trinity Coll. (now Duke U.), 1922; A.M., Columbia University 1929; LL.D., Juniata College 1948; married Virginia Cozart, December 31, 1929; children—Virginia Frank, Herbert James. Teacher of English, Richard J. Reynolds High Sch., Winston-Salem, N.C., 1922-24; asst. dean, Duke U., 1924-35, dean of men, 1935-42; teacher of speech, 1925-43; dean Trinity Coll., Duke U., 1942-56, v.p. Duke U., 1946-65, president emeritus, 1965-66; general consultant Louisburg College, 1965-66. Member bd. directors Security Savs. & Loan Assn., 1st Union Nat. Bank, N.C. Pres. United Fund of Durham and Durham Co., 1959, chmn. campaign, 1958. Mem. ednl. adv. com. to Com. on Edn., House of Reps., 78th Congress, 1944. Bd. trustees Louisburg (N.C.) Coll. President N.C. Assn. Collegiate Registrars, 1939. Chmn. Academic Deans of Southern States, 1946-47. Mem. Com. Internat. Exchange of Persons, 1950-54. Mem. S.A.T.C., Sept.-Dec. 1918. Pres. North Carolina College Conference, 1956-57. Mem. Newcomen Soc., Tau Kappa Alpha, Sigma Upsilon, Phi Eta Sigma, Omicron Delta Kappa, Phi Beta Kappa, Sigma Chi (grandpractor 1937-45). Democrat. Methodist. Rotarian. Home: Durham NC Died Sept. 23, 1966; buried Maplewood Cemetery, Durham NC

HERRING, HUBERT CLINTON, educator, writer; b. Winterset, Ia., Dec. 29, 1889; s. Hubert Clinton and Mary (Woodbridge) H.; A.B., Oberlin, 1911; A.M., Columbia, 1912; grad. Union Theol. Sem., 1913; Doctor of Literature, Claremont College, 1958; m. Atossa Nilsen, Aug. 20, 1913; children—Atossa Nilsen, Constance Whittemore, Virginia Covell; m. 2d, Helen Baldwin, Feb. 16, 1939; children—Mark, Hubert Baldwin. Minister Congl. churches, Wis. and Kan., 1913-24; dir. social action activities Nat. Congl. chs., 1924-39; exec. dir. Com. on Cultural Relations with Latin America, Inc., 1928-67; dir. annual seminars in Mexico since 1926, seminars in Caribbean, Central America, and S.A. since 1931; professor Latin-Am. civilization, Claremont Coll. and Pomona Coll., 1944-67. Author several books, including: Good Neighbors, 1941; America and the Americas, 1944; A History of Latin America, 1955, latest rev. edit., 1967. Contbr. periodicals, press. Home: Claremont CA Died Sept. 29, 1967

HERRINGTON, ARTHUR WILLIAM SIDNEY, tech. adviser U.S. Mission to India; b. Coddenham, Eng., Mar. 30, 1891; s. Arthur and Mary Matilda (Pottinger) H.; brought to U.S., 1896; ed. Stevens Prep. Sch. and Stevens Inst. Technology, hon. M.E., 1943; honorary Engr. Dr., Rose Polytechnic Inst., 1943; m. Nell Ray Clarke, Feb. 12, 1926; 1 son, Arthur Clarke. Served with U.S. Army, Oct. 1917-Sept. 1919; with motorcycle companies, 7th and 4th infs., Tex.; Motor Transport Corps, Washington, D.C., 2d div. supply train, A.E.F., 1st Army hdqrs., G-4; hon. discharged as capt. Motor Transport Corps. Asso. with various motor car companies and cons. engr. U.S. Army and Marine Corps, 1921-31; designed several types of mil. trucks with 4- and 6-wheel drives, also track laying tractors; vice pres. and chief engr., Marmon-Herrington Co., 1931, pres. 1931-42, chmn. bd., 1940-60; member board directors Gabriel Corporation, Cleve.; economic adviser to government of Pakistan, 1949-50. Director, American Medical Center for Burma, Inc., Phila. Appointed technical adviser to Louis Johnson, head of American Mission to India, 1942. Mem. Soc. Automotive Engrs. (nat. pres. 1942), Soc. Am. Mil. Engrs. (dir.), Army Ordnance Assn. (dir.), Newcomen Soc. Episcopalian. Mason (32 deg., Shriner). Clubs: Indianapolis Service, Indianapolis Athletic, Columbia, Woodstock Country (Indianapolis); Bohemian (San Francisco); Gibson Island (Md.) Yacht, Tred Avon (Md.) Yacht; University, Yacht, Metropolitan (N.Y.C.); Automobile Old Timers (pres.); Cruising Am.; Quisset (Mass.) Yacht. Home: Indianapolis IN Died Sept. 6, 1970.

HERRIOTT, JAMES HOMER, educator; b. Lawrence, Kan., June 21, 1895; s. Walter Thomas Buchanan and Ada Evelyn (Oatman) H.; A.B., U. Kan., 1920, A.M., 1924; Ph.D., U. Wis., 1929; student U. Grenoble (France), 1919, U. Madrid, 1924; research fellow in Europe, Am. Council Learned Socs., 1931-32, m. Bernadine Layman, June 5, 1924 (died 1924); m. 2d, Margot McLellan, Aug. 3, 1929;children—Andra James, Margot Bernadine. Grad. asst. in Spanish U. Kan., 1923-24, instr., 1924-25; instr. U. Wis., 1925-29, asst. prof. Spanish, 1930-31, 1932-39, asso. prof., chmn. dept. Spanish and Portuguese, 1939-42, prof. Spanish, chmn. dept., 1942-45, prof., asso. dean Grad. Sch., 1945-63, asso. dean Coll. Letters and Sci., 1947-49; research asso. Princeton, 1929-30; Fulbright research prof., Spain, 1965-66; Distinguished lectr. U. Wis., Milw., 1966-73. Served with Norton-Harjes Ambulance Corps, France, 1917, cadet and 2d lt. (pilot). Signal Corps, AEF, France and Italy, 1917-19. Mem. Mediaeval Acad., Am. Folklore Soc., Modern Lang. Assn., Linguistic Soc. Am., Archaeol. Soc. Am., Wis. Hist. Soc., Delta Tau Delta. Conglist. Clubs: University. Author: Towards A Critical Edition of the Celestine, 1964. Contbr. articles. Home: Milwaukee WI Died Jan. 3, 1973.

HERROLD, GORDON WILLIAM, glass products mfg.; b. Athens, O., Apr. 19, 1902; s. William H. and Mary E. (Phillips) H.; A.B., Ohio U., 1924; M.B.A., Harvard, 1927; m. Lucille W. Nazor, June 19, 1928; children—Joan (Mrs. D. C. Wood), Joyce N. With Anchor Hocking Glass Corp., Lancaster, O., 1927—, successively supt., plant mgr., charge engring., 1927-55, vice president research and engineering, 1955-63, corporate vice president, 1963—; v.p. Zanesville Mould Co.; pres. Gas Transport, Inc. Mem. vis. com. Sch. Arts and Scis., Ohio U.; mem. Symposiare, YMCA; bd. dirs. Alumni Assn. Mem. Beta Theta Pi, Phi Delta Kappa (hon). Presbyn. Mason. Clubs: Lancaster Country; University (Columbus). Home: Lancaster OH Died June 27, 1968; buried Maple Grove Cemetery, Lancaster OH

HERRON, CHARLES DOUGLAS, army officer (ret.); b. Crawfordsville, Ind., Mar. 13, 1877; s. William Park and Ada (Patton) H.; prep. edn., Wabash Coll., Crawfordsville, 1892-96, A.M., 1908; grad. U.S. Mil. Acad., 1899; attended Gen. Service Sch., 1906-08; distinguished grad. Army Sch. of the Line, 1907; grad. Army Staff Coll., 1908; attended Army War Coll., 1919-20, Field Arty. Sch., 1923-24; m. Louise Milligan, Nov. 12, 1912; children—William Milligan, Louise. Entered army, 1899; advanced through grades to maj. gen., 1937; in operation against Philippine Insurgents, 1899-1901; instr. U.S. Mil. Acad., 1908-10; comd. 313th F.A., 1917-18, Gen. Staff Gen. Hdqrs., 1918; chief of staff of 78th Div., Sept. to Dec. 1918; War Dept. Gen. Staff, 1919, 1920-23; chief of Staff Philippine Dept., 1927-29; exec. for Res. Affairs, War Dept., 1930-35; comdg. Hawaiian Dept., 1938-41; retired Mar. 31, 1941. On active duty with War Dept. Gen. Staff since Sept. 1941; ret. 1946. Decorated with medals, Spanish-Am. War, Philippine Islands, Mexican Border; D.S.M.; Officer Legion of Honor (France); La Solidaridad (Panama). Mem. Beta Theta Pi. Presbyn. Club: Army and Navy. Author: War Dep. Gen. Staff Manual, 1923. Home: Bethesda MD‡

HERSHEY, BURNET, dramatist, newspaperman; born Roumania, Dec. 13, 1896; s. Josef and Bertha (Bughici) H.; brought to U.S., 1899; ed. N.Y.C. public schs.; student Columbia Sch. Journalism, 1915, Sorbonne, Paris, 1917; m. Thyrza Putnam Sturges, June 1935. Gen. news staffs N.Y. Sun, N.Y. Tribune; Paris corr. N.Y. Sun, 1917-20; N.Y. Evening Post on Ford Peace Expedition; N.Y. Times with A.E.F. and French and Belgian G.H.Q.; covered Eastern Front, accredited to German Army with Field Marshal Von Mackensen; corr. Phila. Ledger Fgn. Service at London, Berlin, Geneva; Far East and Asia Minor assignments for Ledger and Times; attached to Am. Commn. to Negotiate Peace, Versailles Peace Conf.; press. rep. of Am. Commn. to French Expn. Indsl. Arts, 1925; fgn. news commentator Station WMCA, N.Y.C., accredited by War Dept., spl. corr., N.Y. Post, in Gr. Brit., North Africa, 1942-43; made air tour of U.S. bases in 1943; corr. Liberty Mag. covering S.H.A.E.F., 1944-45; U.S. Naval corr. in channel ports, 1944; corr. occupied Germany 1945; N.Y. and Wash. corr. Tribune de Geneve. Decorated Medaille Interallie, Palmes Academique, Officier de L'Instruction Publique, Legion of Honor (France). Member Authors League of America, Dramatists Guild, Silurians. Clubs: Lambs (N.Y.C.); Overseas Press Club Am. (ex-pres.). Founder, Am. War Corr. Assn. Author: It's a Small World, 1934; World of Midgets, 1935; The Air Future, 1943; Skyways of Tomorrow, 1944; Bloody Record of Nazi Atrocities, 1945; Trial by Fire, 1964; From A Reporters Little Black Book, 1966; You Cant Go To Heaven on a Roller Skate, pub. 1969; The Pyromaniac (London film), 1969; also Odyssey of Henry Ford and His Great Peace Ship, pub. 1967. Plays: Scattered Seed, 1936; Dealers in Death, 1936; The Brown Danube, 1939, was produced at the Lyceum Theatre, N.Y. Compiled and edited A Documentary History of the Versailles Conference, 15 vols., Biography: Dag Hammarskjold, published in 1961; From a Reporter's Little Black Book,

1967. Contbr. articles and fiction to newspapers, Look, Sat. Eve. Post, Liberty, Readers New York City NY Died Dec. 1971.

HERTERICK, VINCENT RICHARD, automotive and electronic components mfg. co. exec.; b. Orange, N.J., Aug. 24, 1922; s. Michael and Helen K. (McGuire) H.; student Newark Coll. Engring., 1940-44; m. M. Claire Carroll, June 7, 1943; children—Jeanne, Eileen, Michael, Leslie. Project engr. Delco Remy and Eastern Aricraft divs. Gen. Motors Corp., 1940-45; chief engr. Wade Electric Producers Co., Sturgis, Mich., 1945-50; with United-Carr Inc., and divs., 1950-71, pres. Carr Fastener Co. div., Cambridge, Mass., 1959-66, exec. v.p. indsl. products parent co., Cambridge, 1966-71, also dir.; dir. Cambridge Gas Co., Cambridge Electric Light Co.; trustee Cambridge Savs. Bank; incorporator Cambridgeport Savs. Bank. Mem. Northeastern U. Corp. Trustee Lesky Coll. Served with USNR, World War II. Registered profl. engr., Mass. Mem. Soc. Automotive Engrs., Mass. Soc. Profl. Lexington MA Died Aug. 1, 1971.

HERTZ, JOHN, JR., advt. exec.; b. Chicago, Feb. 20, 1908; s. John D. and Frances L. (Kesner) H.; student Culver Mil. Acad., Cornell U. Began with Lord & Thomas, Inc., advt. agy., N.Y. City, 1932-36; v.p. William Esty & Co., Inc., advt. agy., 1936-38, Hanff-Metzger & Co., 1936-68; v.p., dir. Successor co. Buchanan &Co., Inc., pres., dir., chmn. bd., 1945-57; dir. Southwest Harbor Boat Co. Chmn. advt. Met. N.Y. March of Dimes campaign, 1951-54; advt. dir. Greek War Relief exploitation, 1942; exploitation and publicity dir. motion picture div. 6th and 7th War Loan drives, World War II. Clubs: Lotos (New York City); Bar Harbor Yacht, Miami Yacht. Home: Miami Beach FL Died May 9, 1968.

HERTZOG, CHARLES D(EMETRIUS), assn. ofcl.; b. Carrolltown, Pa., July 24, 1897; s. Philip and Mary (Yahner) H.; LL.B., Georgetown U., 1922; m. Julia McKelvey, Oct. 17, 1922 (dec. 1943); children—Julia Ann (wife of Dr. A. L. Shinkus), Carl D., Richard I., Barbara May, Eugene E.; m. 2d, Ruth B. Jarvis, May 28, 1945; children—Mary Joan, Beverely Ann, Philip Arthur. Clk. and stenographer Pa. Coal Co., 1916-17; entered U.S. Civil Service Commn., 1917, career employee, 1918-57 (ret.), regional dir. St. Louis, 1930-32, Chgo., 1932-36, Phila., 1936-52, dir. bur. field operations, Washington, 1952-57; admitted to D.C. bar, 1923, practiced law, 1923-30; office mgr., civil service counsel and mgr. ins. division Nat. Assn. Postmasters, 1958-70. Served in World War I. Recipient citation by Treasury Dept. for work in bond drives; citations for work in charity drives, Community Chest, A.R.C. Mem. Fed. Bus. Assn., St. Louis, Chgo., Phila. bar assns., Cath. Order Foresters. Home: Silver Spring MD Died Nov. 8, 1970; buried Holy Cross Cemetery, Yeadon PA

HERTZOG, WALTER SCOTT, educator; b. California, Pa., Sept. 5, 1874; s. George Gans and Emily Caroline (Hertig) H.; grad. Southwestern State Normal Sch., California, Pa., 1891; A.B., Hiram (Ohio) Coll., 1897, A.M., 1900; postgrad. work, U. of Leipzig, Germany, 1901-2; grad. Chautauqua Lit. and Scientific Circle, 1913; studied Teachers Coll. (Columbia), 1919-21; A.M., from Columbia, 1920, Ph.D., 1921; m. Lura Madge Way, of Rutland, Ohio, Dec. 27, 1898. Principal Beaver Falls (Pa.) High School, 1897-1901; prof. science, Bethany (W.Va.) College, 1902-3; prof. mathematics and science, Southwestern State Normal Sch., 1903-7; state high sch. insp., Pa., 1907-12; prin. Southwestern State Normal School, California, Pa., 1912-19. Mem. N.E.A., Pa. State Ednl. Assn., California Civic Soc. (pres. 1905-7). Republican. Member Christian Church. Club: Century (ex-pres.). Joint author of a course of study for elementary schs. of Pa., also of a manual for Pa. high schs. Author of State Maintenance of Teachers in Training. Institute instr. Home: California PA‡

HERVEY, HARCOURT, retired banker; b. Los Angeles, Sept. 2, 1892; s. Edward King Blades and Browning (Clarke) B.; A.B., U. Cal. at Berkeley, 1916; m. Ruth Brown, June 18, 1917; 1 son, Harcourt. Various positions Security 1st Nat. Bank, Los Angeles, 1920-52, v.p., until 1952. Served from 2d lt. to col., U.S. Army, 1917-19; participated all actions of 1st Division, AEF; apptd. lt. col. ORC; apptd. lt. col. Cal. N.G., 1922, advanced through grades to maj. gen., overseas duty, 1942-45; participant all action of 40th Inf. Div. and Korea occupation, ret., 1947. Decorated Silver Star, Legion of Merit, Air Medal, Purple Heart (U.S.); Croix de Guerre, Fouragerye of Croix de Guerre, Verdun medal (France); Comdr. Philippine Legion of Honor; Medal of Merit with oak leaf cluster (State of Cal.); Cal. N.G. service medal with diamond clasp (25 years). Mem. S.R., Soc. Colonial Wars, Am. Legion, Soc. of First Div., U.S.O. (hon. v.p.), Psi Upsilon, Phi Delta Phi. Episcopalian. Mason (32 degree). Home: Pasadena CA Died Dec. 28, 1970.

HERVEY, HARCOURT, JR., banker; b. Los Angeles, May 14, 1920; s. Harcourt and Ruth (Brown) H.; student U. Cal. at Berkeley, 1939-41; m. Constance B. Smith, Jan. 3, 1946; children—Harcourt III, Robert Rhodes, John Kendall. Loan officer The John M. C. Marble Co., Los Angeles, 1946-52, sec., 1952-60; v.p. The Marble Co., Pasadena, Cal., 1952-68, dir., 1950-68; dir. O. K. Earl Constrn. Co., Pasadena, 1961. Served to maj., inf., AUS, 1941-46; to lt. col., 1950-52. Decorated Bronze Star with two oak leaf clusters, Philippine Medal of Merit. Mem. Pasadena C. of C. (mem. Am. enterprise com.), Soc. Colonial Wars, S.R., Psi Upsilon. Republican. Episcopalian. Mason (32 degree). Clubs: Valley Hunt (Pasadena); Balboa Angling (Newport Beach, Cal.); San Pasqual (pres.) (Pasadena, Cal.). Home: Pasadena CA Died Dec. 30, 1968.

HERVEY, JAMES MADISON, lawyer; b. Stephensville, Tex., July 4, 1874; s. Austin Flint and Emily (Davidson) H.; student Goss Mil. Acad., Roswell, N.M., 1892-94, Albion (Mich.) Coll., 1894-96; LL.B., U. of Mich., 1899; m. Nettie J. Hill, Mar. 8, 1900; children—James Andrew, Ruth (Mrs. James W. Lomax), Virginia (Mrs. E. F. Egleston). Admitted to N.M. bar, 1900; dist. atty., 5th Judicial Dist., 1903-07; atty. gen. of N.M., 1907-09; spl. adviser to the gov., 1918; mem. Hervey, Dow, Hill & Hinkle since 1926. First pres. State of N.M. Bd. of Bar Commissioners, 1927. Mem. Am. Bar Assn., N.M. Bar Assn. Home: 2 Park Rd. Office: J. P. White Bldg., Roswell NM*‡

HERZIG, CHARLES SIMON, mining engr.; b. New York, Jan. 28, 1874; s. Simon and Anna (Schanzer) H.; Coll. City N.Y., 1891; E.M., Sch. of Mines (Columbia), 1895; m. Mae Rose Sullivan, May 12, 1903; m. 2d, Florence F. Upmeyer, of Minneapolis, Oct. 13, 1917. Served various capacities in mines and smelting works, U.S. and Mexico; became rep. and local partner, 1903, in eastern Australia for Bewick, Moreing & Co., mining engrs., of London, Eng., at the time when Herbert C. Hoover was a mem. of that firm, and had charge of a number of cos. as mgr. and dir.; in gen. practice London, 1906-15; returned to U.S., 1915. Has visited most of the principal mining districts of the world. Republican. Mem. Instn. Mining and Metallurgy, London, Am. Inst. Mining Engrs., Tau Beta Pi. Author: Mine Sampling and Valuing. Contbr. to tech. magazines and socs. Home: Ansonia Hotel, New York. Office: 27 William St., N.Y. City, and Boston Bldg., Salt Lake City UT‡

HERZSTEIN, JOSEPH, physician; b. N.Y., 1893; M.D., Cornell U., 1924. Intern, Bellevue Hosp., N.Y.C., 1924-25; asso. Cardiovascular Research Clinic, Beth Israel Hosp., N.Y.C.; sr. clin. asst. in metabolism Mt. Sinai Hosp., N.Y.C. Served with M.C., U.S. Army, 1918. Diplomate Am. Bd. Internal Medicine. Mem. A.M.A. Home: New York City NY Died Feb. 1, 1971.

HESCHEL, ABRAHAM JOSHUA, theologian, educator; b. Warsaw, Poland, 1907; ms. Moshe Mordecai and Reisel (Perlow) H.; Ph.D., U. Berlin, 1933; grad. Hochschule fuer die Wissenchaft des Judentums, Berlin, 1934; LL.D., Notre Dame U.; L.H.D., St. Michael's Coll., Park Coll., Upsala Coll., Spartas Coll.; m. Sylvia Straus. Dec. 10, 1941; 1 dau., Hannah Susan. Came to U.S., 1940, naturalized, 1945. Instr., Talmud, Hochschule fuer die Wissenschaft des Judentums, Berlin, 1932-33; lectr. Mittelstelle fuer Juedische Erwachsenenbildung, Frankfurt, Germany, 1937-38; docent philosophy Inst. Judaistic Studies, Warsaw, 1938-39; founder Inst. Jewish Learning, London, 1940; instr. Jewish philosophy and rabbinics Hewbrew Union Coll., 1940-43, asst. prof., 1943-45; prof. Jewish ethics and mysticism Jewish Theol. Sem. Am., 1945-; Raymond Fred West lectr. Stanford U., 1963; vis. prof. theology U. Minn.; vis. prof. U. Ia., 1961; Henry Emerson Fosdick vis. prof. Union Theological Seminary, 1965-66. Co-chmn. Nat. Com. of Clergy Concerned About Viet-Nam. Fellow Am. Acad. Arts and Scis., Am. Acad. Jewish Research; mem. Am. Philos. Soc., Jewish Publ. Soc., Yivo (dir.), Inst. Non-Violent Social Change. Author: Poems, 1933; Maimondides, 1935; Die Prophetie, 1935; Abravanel, 1937; Ibn Gabirol, 1938; A Concise Dictionary of Hebrew Philosophical Terms, 1941; On the Essence of Prayer, 1941; An Analysis of Piety, 1942; The Holy Dimension, 1943; Faith, 1944; The Quest for Certainty in Saadia's Philosophy, 1944; The Earth is The Lord's, 1950; Man is Not Alone, 1951; Space, Time and Reality, 1952; The Sabbath, 1952; The Moment on Sinai, 1953; Symbolism and Jewish Faith, 1954; Man's Quest for God, 1954; God in Search of Man, 1956; Sacred Images of Man, 1958; The Prophets, 1962; Theology of Ancient Judaism Vol. 1, 1963, Vol. 2, 1965; Who Is Man?, 1965; The Insecurity of Freedom, 1966; Israel, An Echo of Eternity, 1969; God—Torah—Israel, 1970; others. Home: New York City NY Died Dec. 23, 1972.

HESS, FINLEY B., glass co. exec.; b. Uniontown, Pa., 1905; ed. U. Pa., 1928. Pres., chief exec. officer, dir. Brockway Glass Co.; dir. Consomer Glass Co., Ltd. Home: Brockway PA Died Jan. 16, 1968.*

HESS, HARRY HAMMOND, geologist; b. N.Y.C., May 24, 1906; s. Julian S. and Elizabeth (Engel) H.; B.S., Yale, 1927; Ph.D., Princeton, 1932; D.Sc. (hon.), Yale, 1969; m. Annette Burns, Aug. 15, 1934; children—George Burns, Frank Deming Mather. Geologist Loangwa Concessions, Ltd., N. Rhodesia, 1928-29; geologist gravity measuring cruises U.S. submarines S-48 and Barracuda, 1931, 36; asst. instr. Rutgers U., 1932-33; research asso. geophys. lab. Carnegie Instn., Washington, 1933-34; instr. Princeton U., 1934-37, asst. prof., 1937-46, asso. prof., 1946-48, prof., 1948-69, Blair prof. geology, 1964-69, chmn. dept., 1950-66; vis. prof. U. Cape Town, 1949-50, Cambridge U., 1965. Chmn. Space Science Bd., 1962-69; mem. U.S. nat. com. geology Internat. Union Geol. Scis., 1961-69, chmn., 1961-62; mem. div. com. math., phys. and engring. scis. NSF, 1960-64; cons. U.S. Navy Oceanographic Office, 1966-69, Nat. Council Marine Resources and Engring. Devel., 1967-69; mem. Pres.'s Com. Nat. Medal Sci., 1967-69; mem. sci. and tech. adv. com. manned space flight NASA, 1964-69, mem. lunar and planetary missions bd., 1967-69, mem. lunar sample analysis planning team, 1967-69. Served comdr. USNR; commanding officer U.S.S. Cape Johnson, 1945; rear adm. USNR. Recipient Penrose medal Geol. Soc. Am., 1966; Feltrinelli prize Accademia Nazionale dei Lincei, 1966; Distinguished Pub. Service medal NASA, 1969. Fellow Geol. Soc. Am. (pres. 1962), Mineral Soc. Am. (pres. 1954-55); mem. Nat. Acad. Sci. (chmn. sect. geology 1960-63), Mineral Soc. London, Geol. Soc. S. Africa, Soc. Econ. Geologists, Am. Geophys. Union (pres. sect. geodesy 1951-53, pres. sect. tectonophysics 1956-58), NRC (chmn. division of earth sciences 1956-58, chmn. committee on disposal radioactive waste 1955-62), Geol. Soc. London, Am. Soc. Oceanography (dir. 1966-69), Sociedad Venezolana de Geologos (hon.), Am. Philos. Soc., Accademia Nazionale dei Lincei, Am. Acad. Arts and Scis. Clubs: Cosmos (Washington); Nassau (Princeton). Author articles in science journals. Discoverer greatest depth in oceans, 1945. Home: NJ Died Aug. 25, 1969; buried Arlington National Cemetery, Arlington VA

HESS, JEROME SAYLES, lawyer; b. N.Y.C., June 17, 1882; s. Charles A. and Ida (Doctor) H.; A.B., Yale, 1903; Columbia Law Sch., 1906; married Harriette Orline Peloubet, June 20, 1947. Admitted to N.Y. State, 1906, and practiced, N.Y. City, 1966-70; counsel to Hardin, Hess, Eder & Rashap, N.Y.C.; atty. for govt. Mex. in formulating agreements relating to its pub. debt, rep. govt. Italy in consular matters. Decorated Aztec Eagle (Mexico); Order of Crown of Italy (Italy). President American Fgn. Law Assn., 1944-47, former mem. com. on internat. law, com. on courts higher jurisdiction, (former mem. com. on admissions); mem. Assn. Bar City of N.Y.; sec. and mem. com. on judiciary N.Y. County Lawyers Assn.; mem. N.Y. State, Am. bar assns., Internat. Law Assn. (Am. br.), Am. Soc. Internat. Law, Council on Fgn. Relations, Fgn. Policy Assn., Phi Beta Kappa, Zeta Psi. Clubs: Yale University (N.Y.C.), Saratoga Golf (gov.), Turf and Field. Home: New York City NY Died Aug. 27, 1970; buried Woodlawn Cemetery.

HESS, MAX, mcht.; b. Phila., Mar. 23, 1911; s. Max and Florence (Rice) H.; student Allentown (Pa.) Prep. Sch., 1923-25, Moravian Prep. Sch., 1925-27, Mercersburg (Pa.) Acad., 1927-29, Muhlenberg (Pa.) Coll., 1933; m. Elizabeth Douglass, Feb. 3, 1939;children—Jean (Mrs. Edward Russoli), Thomas, Elizabeth. With Hess Bros., Allentown, Pa., 1925, pres., 1935-68, hon. chmn., 1968. Served as mem. retail industry adv. com. OPS, from 1951; also active in civic orgns. Chairman Allentown Traffic Commission, 1958-59. Chairman of the U.S. Valentine Council, 1955. Recipient honors and awards, including, Chevalier du Mrite (France), silver medal City of Rome, 1956, citation Man of Year in Retailing (N.Y.U.), 1952, Alumni achievement award Muhlenberg Coll., 1956; Outstanding Retailer of Yr., Linens and Domestic Buyers Am., 1958; New Products Meritorious award Gov. of Tex., 1956; Eastman Sch. Bus. award, 1961; Distinguished Service award Pa. dept. Am. Legion, 1959; citation Nat. Assn. Profl. Baseball Leagues, 1959; Book of Golden Deeds, Nat. Exchange Clubs, 1966; other awards and citations from various orgns. Mem. Nat. Retail Mchts. Assn. (dir. merchandising div. 1957-58), Nat. Planning Assn. (nat. council 1958). Mason. Clubs: Allentown Varsity, Friars, Marco Polo, Lehigh Valley. Author: Every Dollar Counts, 1952; Allentown, 1959; Markets of America, Vol. 23. Collaborator: Aunt Tuddy, 1958. Established Hess Bros. versatility in design and use competition for mfrs., 1951. Address: Allentown PA Died Sept. 1, 1968.

HESTER, CLINTON MONROE, lawyer; b. Des Moines, Ia., Apr. 16, 1895; s. John Kenton and Sarah Hannah (Hamilton) H.; grad. Phillips-Exeter Acad., 1916; A.B., George Washington U., 1920; LL.B., Georgetown U., 1922; m. Margaret Lee Bixby, July 30, 1965; children—Todd McCane, and Jean Hamilton. Admitted to practice before Dist. of Columbia bar, 1922; atty. Dept. of Interior, 1922; asst. counsel U.S. Shipping Bd. and U.S. Shipping Bd. Emergency Fleet Corp., 1922-27; counsel Office U.S. Alien Property Custodian and special assistant to Attorney General of United States, 1927; chief attorney U.S. Dept. of Justice, 1927-34, U.S. Dept. of Treasury, 1934-35; asst. gen. counsel Dept. of Treasury, 1935-38; adminstr. CAA, 1938-40, supervised construction of Washington National Airport; apptd. mem. Nat. Advisory Com. for Aeronautics, Aug. 23, 1938; resumed private practice of law Oct. 1, 1940. Mem. James Madison Meml. Commn., 1960-71; chmn. exec. com. 1961. Served with

301st Engrs., 76th Div., AUS, 1918-19. Mem. American, District of Columbia bar associations, Phi Gamma Delta. Mason. Owns historic estate Bath Alum, Hot Springs, Va. Pioneered survey airplane flights for comml. passenger service across Atlantic and South Pacific. Home: Washington DC Died July 1971.

HESTON, J(OHN) EDGAR, oil co. exec.; b. Stillwater, Okla., May 24, 1910; s. John Adrian and Margaret Catherine (Shumate) H.; B.S., Okla. U., 1931; student advanced mgmt. program Harvard, 1950; m. Maudie C. Grinnell, Nov. 23, 1937; 1 dau., Marguerite (Mrs. John Meaders). Tchr. Westville (Okla.) High Sch., 1931-3; petroleum engr. Empire Oil & Refining Co., Seminole, Okla., 1933-34; staff geologist, engr. Henry L. Doherty & Co., N.Y.C., 1934-36; dist. engr. Cities Service Oil Co., Hobbs, N.M., 1936-38; petroleum geologist, engr. Cities Service Co., N.Y.C., 1938-41, asst. mgr. oil prodn. and oil pipe line, 1946-50, mgr. oil prodn., 1950-53, pres., chief operating officer, 1968-72, dir., 1950-72, also mem. exec. com.; exec. v.p., dir. Cities Service Prodn. Co.; pres., dir. Cities Service Oil Co., 1963-68; v.p., dir. Cities Service Gas Devel. Co., Canada-Cities Service Co., Bartlesville, Okla., 1953-56; pres., dir. Peruvian Pacific Petroleum Co., N.Y.C., 1953-56, Ark. Pipe Line Corp., Shreveport, Orange State Oil Co., Miami, Fla., 1956-72; dir. Columbian Carbon Co., Tenn. Corp. Asst. dir. prodn. Petroleum Adminstrn. for War, Washington, 1941-45; v.p. Internat. Petroleum Expn. Mem. Am. Assn. Petroleum Geologists, Am. Inst. Mining Metall. and Petroleum Engrs., Am. Petroleum Inst. (dir.), Newcomen Soc. Clubs: Shreveport; Bankers, Wall Street. Home: Tulsa OK Died Apr. 12, 1972.

HETERICK, VINCENT RICHARD, automotive and electronic components mfg. co. exec.; b. Orange, N.J., Aug. 24, 1922; s. Michael and Helen K. (McGuire) H.; student Newark Coll. Engring., 1940-44; m. M. Claire Carroll, June 7, 1943; children—Jeanne, Eileen, Michael, Leslie. Project engr. Delco Remy and Eastern Aircraft divs. Gen. Motors Corp., 1940-45; chief engr. Wade Electric Producers Co., Sturgis, Mich., 1945-50; with United-Carr Inc., and divs., 1950-71, pres. Carr Fastener Co. div., Cambridge, Mass., 1959-66, exec. v.p. indsl. products parent co., Cambridge, 1966-71, also dir.; exec. v.p. T.R.W. Inc., Cleve., 1971; dir. Cambridge Gas Co., Cambridge Electric Light Co.; trustee Cambridge Savs. Bank; incorporator Cambridgeport Savs. Bank. Mem. Northeastern U. Corp.; trustee Lesley College, Cambridge, Massachusetts. Served with USNR, World War II. Registered profl. engr., Mass. Mem. Soc. Automotive Engrs., Mass. Soc. Profl. Engrs. Rotarian. Club: Algonquin (Boston). Home: Lexington MA Died Aug. 1, 1971.

HETTRICK, ELWOOD HARRISON, judge; b. Christina, Florida, February 9, 1909; s. George D. and Lucy A. (Bartlett) H.; A.B., Wesleyan University, Middletown, Conn., 1932; LL.B. cum laude, Boston University School of Law, 1938, LL.M., 1940; LL.D., University R.I., 1949; m. Marjorie Lois Gypson, August 12, 1939; children—Susan (Mrs. James J. Griglun), Pamela B. (Mrs. Andrew K. Selden, II), Sara D. (Mrs. Stephen G. Ladd). With Standard Oil Co., N.Y., 1932-34, S. S. Pierce Co., Boston, 1934-35; admitted to Mass. bar, 1938; registrar and instr. in law, Boston U. Sch. of Law, 1938-40, asst. prof. of law, 1940,41, asst. dean and prof. of law, 1941-42, dean and prof., 1942-66; chief judge Land Ct., Commonwealth of Mass., 1966-72; dir. Boston U. Civil Affairs Training Sch. of Mil. Govt. Div., Provost Marshall General's Office, 1943-44. County chairman, Greater Boston Community Fund, 1939-41; vice chairman instns. division, United War Fund, 1944; chairman board Washingtonian Hosp. Member American (member bd. govs.), Mass. and Boston bar assns., Am. Law Inst., N.E. Law Inst. (dir., treas.), Bigelow Assn., Woolsock, Beta Theta Pi, Delta Theta Phi. Mason. Clubs: Boston City; Wesleyan (Boston); Rotary (Wellesley). Contbr. legal jours. Home: Weston MA Died Jan. 15, 1972.

HEUCHLING, FRED G., banker; b. at Chicago, Ill., Mar. 1, 1886; s. Theodore W. (M.D.) and Margaret (Moller) H.; B.S., Armour Institute Tech., Ch.E., 1910; m. Mabel A. Koch (A.B., Smith Coll.), of Chicago, June 29, 1912. Instr. industrial engring., Armour Inst., 1907-09; structural and railroad engr., C.,M.&St.P.Ry., 1909-10; efficiency engr., City of Chicago, 1910-11; supt. employment, West Chicago Park Commn., 1911-19; mem. staff of Arthur Young & Co., pub. accountants, Chicago, 1912 and 1919-20; mem. staff U.S. Congressional Commn. on Reclassification of Federal Employes, 1919; v.p. Northwestern Trust & Savings Bank, Chicago, 1920-70; pres. Financial Advertisements Corp., 1923-70. Mem. Tau Beta Pi. Clubs: City, Union League. Home: Chicago IL Died July 16, 1970.

HEUER, JOHN HARLAND, paper co. exec.; b. Carthage, N.Y., Jan. 24, 1917; s. Harland Robert and Genevieve (Waters) H.; B.S. in Chem. Engring., U. Wash., 1939; D. Adminstrv. Scis., U. Moncton, 1970; m. Catherine M. Foley, Jan. 4, 1946; children—John Harland, Edward Frederick. Trainee, Oxford Paper Co., 1939-41; chemist Diamond Match Co., 1941-42; tech. dir. Newton Falls Paper Co., 1946-48, St. Regis Paper Co., 1948-51; with Great No. Paper Co., Bangor, Me., 1951-72, mgr. mfg., 1957-59, v.p. mfg., 1959-62, v.p. operations 1962-68, also dir., mem. exec. com.; pres., chief exec. officer Fraser Cos., Ltd., 1968-72, also dir., mem. exec. com.; pres., chief exec. officer Fraser Paper Ltd., 1968-72, also dir., mem. exec. com.; chmn. bd., chmn. exec. com., dir. exec. com., dir. Great So. Land and Paper Co., 1963. Sec., treas. Empire State Paper Research Assos. of State U. N.Y. Coll. Forestry, Syracuse, 1949-51, bd. dirs., 1965-71; chmn. exec. com. U. Me. Summer Inst., 1961-64; chmn. scholarship com. U. Me. Pulp and Paper Found., 1965-72. Served to 1st lt., C.E., AUS, 1942-46. Named Man of Year, U. Me., 1969. Fellow T.A.P.P.I. (exec. com. 1959-61); mem. Canadian Pulp and Paper Industry (exec. bd. 1968), N.Y. Paper Trade Golf Assn. Elk, Kiwanian. Clubs: Canadian (N.Y.C.); Winged Foot Golf (Mamaroneck, N.Y.); St. James (Montreal, Que.); Edmundston (N.B.) Golf; Woodlands Country (Ft. Lauderdale, Fla.). Home: Tamarac FL Died Jan. 1, 1972.

HEUSER, GUSTAVE A., machine co. exec.; b. Louisville, Dec. 23, 1879; s. William Henry and Fredericka (Ackerman) H.; student U. Ky.; m. Anna Margaret Vogt, Jan. 14, 1904; children—Evelyn Vogt, Henry Vogt. With Henry Vogt Machine Co., Inc., Louisville, 1904-72, beginning as clk., successively asst. sec., sec.-treas., 1904-37, pres., 1937-57, chmn. bd., 1957-72; pres. Nat. Realty Co., 1937-72. Pres. Masonic Widows and Orphans Home; past pres. Louisville Safety Council. Mem. N.A.M. (past dir.), Nat. Safety Council (past dir.). Republican. Presbyn. Mason (33). Clubs: Rotary, Pendennis, Audubon Country. Home: Louisville KY Died Aug. 10, 1972; buried Cove Hill Cemetery Louisville KY

HEUSNER, WILLIAM SAMUEL, supt. schs.; b. St. Louis, Mo., Dec. 26, 1872; s. Andrew John and Mina (Kleinschmidt) H.; A.B., Ohio Wesleyan U., 1893; studied summers, U. of Chicago and Columbia; m. Sarah Alice Wilder, of Clay Center, Kan., 1901; children—William W., Alfred S. Teacher, asst. prin. and prin. high sch. until 1899; supt. schs., Clay Center, Kan., 1899-1900, Junction City, 1900-12, Salina, since 1912. Kan. Inst. lecturer. Chmn. bd. Kan. Wesleyan U.; dir. Pub. Library, Salina. Mem. N.E.A., Kan. State Teachers' Assn. (pres. bd. dirs.), Kan. Schoolmasters' Club, Kan. Authors' Club, Beta Theta Pi. Club: Rotary. Home: Salina KS‡

HEWES, AMY, coll. prof.; b. Baltimore, Md., Sept. 8, 1877; d. Ewin and Martha Gardner (Gover) Hewes; B.A., Goucher Coll., 1897; studied U. of Berlin; Ph.D., U. of Chicago, 1903. Prof. economics and sociology, Mount Holyoke College, 1907-43, professor emeritus since 1943; executive secretary Massachusetts Minimum Wage Commn., 1913-15; exec. sec. com. on Women in Industry of Council of Nat. Defense, 1917-19; supervisor industrial service sect. Ordnance Dept., U.S. Army, 1918-19; mem. advisory council Massacusetts State-Federal Employment Service. Mem. Spl. Commn. to investigate operation of Mass. Minimun Wage Law. 1931-32; mem. Adv. Council Mass. Unemployment Compensation Commn., 1936-37; visiting lecturer, Sarah Lawrence Coll., 1943-45, Mass. State Coll., 1945-46; visiting prof., Rockford Coll., 1946-47. Fellow Royal Econ. Soc.; mem. Am. Econ. Assn., Am. Sociol. Soc., Am. Assn. for Labor Legislation, Am. Assn. Univ. Profs., Phi Beta Kappa. Clubs: College, Woman's City. Author: Industrial Home Work in Massachusetts, 1915; Women as Munition Workers, 1917; The South Hadley MA Died Mar. 25, 1970.

HEWETSON, H. H., oil co. exec.; b. Jersey City, N.J., 1896; m. Elinor Ross; children—Mrs. Rundlet Blakemore, Mrs. James Plymire. Pres. Imperial Oil, Ltd., 1945-49, chmn. 1949-50; dir. Standard Oil Co. (N.J.) 1950-59, v.p. 1955-59. Home: New York City NY Died Dec. 1971.

HEWETT, DONNEL FOSTER, geologist; b. Irwin, Pa., June 24, 1881; s. George Claude and Hetty Barclay (Foster) H.; student Georgia School of Technology, Atlanta, Ga., 1895-97; Metall. Engr., Lehigh University, 1902; D.Sc. (honorary), 1942; graduate student Yale, 1909-11, Ph.D., in Geology, 1924; m. Mary Amelia Hamilton, Jan. 14, 1909. Asst. in dept. of metallurgy, Lehigh U., 1902-03; mining practice, Pittsburgh, Pa., 1903-09; geologist vanadium at Mina Raqre, Peru, 1906; geologist U.S. Geol. Survey 1911-71, in charge section of metalliferous deposits 1935-44, strategic mineral investigations, 1939-44, geologist rare earths Mt. Pass, Nev., 1946, research geologist, 1963; research asso. Stanford Univ., Stanford, Cal. Recipient D.S.M., Dept. Interior; Penrose medal Soc. Economic Geologists, 1956; award American Acad. of Achievement, 1965. Mem. Geological Soc. Am. (council 1931-33; v.p. 1935, 45, Penrose medal 1964), Nat. Acad. of Scis., Am. Chem. Soc., Mineral. Soc. Am., Am. Inst. of Mining and Metall. Engrs., Am. Assn. Advancement Sci., American Acad. Arts and Sciences, the Society of Economic Geologists (president 1936), also Tau Beta Pi, Sigma Nu, Sigma Xi, Phi Beta Kappa. Conglist. Clubs: Cosmos. Author: Anticlines of the Bighorn Basin, Wyo. (with C. T. Lupton), 1916; Geology, Oil and Coal Resources in the Oregon Basin, Meeteetse, and Grass Creek Basin Quadrangles, Wyo., 1926; Geology and Ore Deposits of the Goodspring Quad., Nevada, 1931; Geology and Ore Deposits of the Ivanpah Quadrangle, Nev.-Calif., 1956; also numerous smaller sci. reports on mineralogy and ore deposits. Home: Palo Alto CA Died Feb. 5, 1971; buried Palo Alto CA

HEWITT, ERASTUS HENRY, lawyer; b. Williamstown, Mass., Oct. 31, 1888; s. John H. and Mary L. (Downing) H.; grad. Hotchkiss Sch., 1907; A.B., Yale, 1911; LL.B., Harvard, 1914; M. Jane Meldrim, Aug. 20, 1921; children—Jane Meldrim (Mrs. Howard S. Tierney, Jr.), Peter Meldrim. Admitted to Mass. bar, 1915; practiced in Boston, 1915-69; mem. firm Stone, Jones, Hewitt, 1947-69. Dir., past pres. Cambridge (Mass.) Homes for Aged People. Served with AUS, 1918. Mem. Am., Boston, Cambridge bar assns., Soc. Colonial Wars, Beta Theta Pi. Republican. Conglist. Club: Union (Boston). Home: Cambridge MA Died Sept. 15, 1969; interred

HEWITT, H. KENT, naval officer (ret.); b. Hackensack, N.J., Feb. 11, 1887; s. Robert Anderson and Mary (Kent) H.; ed. U.S. Naval Acad., 1903-06, (B.S.), Naval War Coll., 1928-29; LL.D., Middlebury Coll., m. Floride Louise Hunt, Aug. 23, 1913; children—Floride Hunt (wife of Capt. Le Roy T. Taylor, U.S.N. ret.), Mary Kent (wife of Capt. Gerald S. Norton, U.S.N. ret.). Commd. ensign U.S.N., 1908, and advanced through grades to adm., 1945; comdr. U.S. 8th Fleet, also U.S. Naval Forces Northwest African Waters, 1943-45; comd. landings Morocco, Nov. 8, 1942, Sicily, July 10, 1943, Salerno, Sept. 9, 1943, South Coast of France, Aug. 15, 1944; comdr. U.S. 12th Fleet and U.S. Naval Forces in Europe, Aug. 1945-Sept. 1946; U.S. rep. U.N. mil. staff com., N.Y.C.; retired from service 1949. Decorated Navy Cross with gold star, D.S.M. with gold star (Navy); D.S.M. with oak leaf cluster (Army) (U.S.), Knight Comdr. of Bath (Great Britain); Order of Kutuzov, First Class (Russia), Legion of Honor, Croix de Guerre with palm (France), Order of Southern Cross (Brazil), Order of Abdon Calderon (Ecuador), Order of Nichan-Iftikar (Tunis); Order of King George I (Greece), Order of SS. Maurice and Lazarus (Italy), Order of Orange-Nassau (Netherlands), Order of Leopold, Croix de Guerre with Palms (Belgium). Mem. U.S. Naval Inst. Episcopalian. Clubs: Army-Navy, Army-Navy Country (Washington), University, Century (New York). Home: Orwell VT Died Sept. 15, 1972; buried U.S. Naval Acad. Cemetery, Annapolis MD

HEWITT, RICHARD MINER, medical editor; b. New London, Conn., Aug. 20, 1892; s. Richard Wheeler and Carie (Miner) H.; A.B., Wesleyan U. (Conn.), 1914; M.A., Princeton U., 1917; M.D., George Washington U., 1924; m. Dr. Edith Lillian Swartwout, Aug. 19, 1925. Teacher English, Sanford Sch., Redding Ridge, Conn., 1914-16; interne, Gorgas Hosp. Canal Zone, 1924-25; asst. editor, Jour. A.M.A., Chicago, 1925-28; asso. editor div. of publs., Mayo Clinic, Rochester, Minn., 1928-33, head of div., 1933-49, senior consultant, 1949-57, member emeritus staff, 1957-70; instructor in medical lit. Mayo Found. Grad. Sch., U. Minn., 1934, assistant professor, 1935-55, associate professor, 1955-57, emeritus, 1957-70; Alfred P. Sloan visiting prof. Menninger Sch. Psychiatry, Topeka, Kan., 1958. Served in U.S. Army, 1917-19, engaged in clin. pathology and writing Med. Dept., Surgeon Gen.'s Office. Fellow Am. Med. Writers Assn. chmn. ednl. com., 1951-54; distinguished service award, 1954, pres. 1955-56; mem. A.M.A. (asso.), Coffman Memorial Union (life), Alumni Assn. of the Mayo Foundation Member com. on information, Div. of Med. Sciences, National Research Council, 1940-44; mem. sub-com. on information, procurement and assignment service for physicians, dentists and veterinarians, Office Defense Health and Welfare, Fed. Security Agency (later under War Manpower Commn.), 1941-44; expert consultant to Preventive Med. Div., Surgeon General's Office, U.S. Army, 1943-44; Minn. State Med. Assn., Delta Tau Delta, Phi Chi, Phi Beta Kappa, and Phi Beta Kappa Associates, Sigma Xi, American Legion. Republican. Baptist. Recipient Alumni Achievement Award. George Washington U., 1944, also from Wesleyan University (Connecticut), 1963. Author: The Physician-Writer's Book, pub. 1957. Joint editor: Collected Papers of the Mayo Clinic and the Mayo Foundation (annual vols.), 1928-57; gen. manuscript editor National Research Council series of 12 Military Surgical Manuals, 6 vols., 1942-43, mem. editorial bd. War Medicine, 1941-42, and its sponsoring com., 1942-44, The Am. Illustrated Med. Dictionary, 22d, 23d edits. Contbr. med. jours. Home: Rochester MN Died June 4, 1970; buried Cedar Grove Cemetery, New London CT

HEXNER, ERVIN PAUL, educator; lawyer; b. Czechoslovakia, Aug. 13, 1893; s. Dr. Julius and Irene (Teltsch) H.; Doctor Polit. Science, Royal State U., Kolozsvar, Hungary, 1918; LL.D., Czechoslovak State U., Bratislava, Czechoslovakia, 1919; m. Gertrud Stern, July 10, 1922; children—Peter Eugen, John Tomas. Came to U.S., 1939, naturalized 1946. Sec. gen. v.p. Slovak Fedn. of Industries, 1920-35; mem. administrv. council Czechoslovak Nat. Soc. Sec. Bd., 1924-37;

member Governmental Committee for Reform of Pub. Adminstrn. of Czechoslovakia, 1932-39; member exec. bd. Czechoslovak State Railways, 1932-36; mem. bd. and mng. dir. Trade Coordinating Corp. of United Czechoslovak Steel Industries, 1936-39. Adviser in internat. labor confs. in Geneva, 1923, 27, 33, Philadelphia, 1944; participated in Monetary and Financial Conf., Bretton Woods, 1944, Internat. Trade Conference of U.N., Geneva, Lake Success, Havana, 1947-48. Lecturer on pub. administration and administrative law State U. of Bratislava, 1931-39; visiting prof. polit. science and economics U. of North Carolina, 1939-41, asso. prof., 1941-45, prof., 1945-46; sr. counsellor, International Monetary Fund, 1946-49, asst. general counsel, 1949-58; prof. polit. sci., econs. Univ. Pa., 1958-64, prof. emeritus, 1964-68. Member Am. Econ. Assn., Am. Polit. Sci. Assn., Am. Assn. International Law. Author numerous publications, latest are: Studies in Legal Terminology, 1941; The International Steel Cartel, 1943 and 1946; Internat. Cartels, 1946; Carteles Internationales (pub. Mexico), 1950; The International Trade Organization and the Monetary Fund, 1950; The General Agreement on Tariffs and the Monetary Fund, 1951; The Constitutional and Legal Structure of the International Monetary Fund (in German), 1959; The Fixed vs. Flexible Exchange Rate" Controversy: Recent Policy Developments, 1964. Contbr. to Law, State, and International Legal Order, 1964; also articles to legal and econs. jours. Address: State College PA Died May 15, 1968.

HEYDLER, CHARLES, musician; b. Cleveland, O., May 20, 1861; s. Gottlieb and Franceska (Goetz) H.; ed. Central High Sch., Cleveland; pupil of J. Hart and Adolph Nuss, violin, Konigloewe and Ernst Jonas, 'cello. Instr. in violin and 'cello playing and 'cello soloist; dir. Cleveland Conservatory of Music. Mem. Philharmonic String Quartette. Home: 2980 E. Overlook Rd., Cleveland Heights. Studio: 2063 E. 4th St., Cleveland OH‡

HEYDRICK, BENJAMIN ALEXANDER, educator; b. Carlton, Mercer Co., Pa., Dec. 17, 1871; s. Charles William and Mary (Ten Broeck) H.; A.B., Allegheny Coll., Meadville, Pa., 1893; A.B., Harvard, 1895; A.M., Columbia, 1907; m. Ada Elizabeth Charles, of Harrisburg, Pa., July 6, 1905. Head of English Dept., State Normal Sch., Millersville, Pa., 1896-1903; head of same dept., High Sch. of Commerce, N.Y., since 1903. Asso. editor, The English Journal, Chicago, 1911-18. Mem. com. on reorganization of secondary edn., N.E.A.; mem. Phi Beta Kappa, Phi Gamma Delta. Democrat. Presbyn. In war camp community service, World War. Author: How to Study Literature, 1901; Short Studies in Composition, 1905; One Year Course in English and American Literature, 1909. Compiler: Selections from Emerson, 1906; Types of the Short Story, 1913; Americans All, 1920; Types of the Essay, 1921; Forum Papers, 1924. Home: 900 Summit Av., New York NY‡

HEYL, PAUL RENNO, physicist; b. Phila., Pa., June 30, 1872; s. Henry Renno and Mary Clarena (Knauff) H.; B.S., U. of Pa., 1894, Ph.D., 1899; grad. study, Harvard; m. Lucy Knight Daugherty, July 26, 1899; children—Marian (dec.), Alice, Dorothy. Teacher of physics, high sch., 1898-1910; physicist with Commercial Research Co., New York, 1910-20; physicist U. S. Bur. Standards, 1920, until retirement. Mem. Am. Physical Soc., A.A.A.S., Philos. Soc. of Washington, Washington Acad. Science. Awarded Boyden premium, Franklin Inst., 1907. Author: The Common Sense of the Theory of Relativity, 1925; Fundamental Concepts of Physics, 1926; The Philosophy of a Scientific Man, 1933. Contbr. to Scientific Monthly. Inventor (with Dr. L. J. Briggs) of Earth Induction compass. Home: 2800 Ontario Road N.W., Washington DC‡

HEYMANN, EDGAR, banker; m. Leonore Heymann; children—Lois (Mrs. Ruekberg), E. Donald. Past pres., vice chmn. bd. Exchange Nat. Bank of Chicago. Home: Palm Springs CA Died Dec. 17, 1969.*

HEYMANS, CORNEILLE (JEAN) (FRANCOIS), educator; b. Ghent, Belgium, Mar. 28, 1892; s. Jean-Francois and Marie-Henriette (Henning) H.; M.D., University of Ghent, 1920; post grad. work, College of France (Paris), Universities of Lausanne and Vienna, University College (London), Western Res. Univ. Med. School; M.D. hon. University of Utrecht, 1938, Univ. of Louvain, 1940, M.D. (hon.), University of Montevideo, 1948, U. of Montpellier, 1953, U. of Torino, 1954, U. Santiago, Univ. Lima, U. of Bogota, 1958, University of Paris, 1959, U. Alger, 1959, U. Munster, U. Toulouse, U. of Bordeaux, U. Rio de Janeiro; m. Bertha May, Jan. 18, 1921; children—Marie-Henriette, Pierre, Jean, Berthe. Lecturer in pharmacology U. of Ghent, 1923-30, prof. pharmacology, 1930-66; emeritus professor of pharmacology, 1966-68; also lecturer in other large univs. throughout world. Served as lieutenant, F.A. Belgian Army, 1914-18. Head of medical department Belgian Relief Com., 1940-44. Awarded Nobel prize for physiology and medicine (for studies on physiology and pharmacology of respiration), 1939; prizes from Royal Acad. Medicine (Belgium), Pontifica Academia Scientarium, Academie medecine de Paris, Institut de France, Acad. of Science (Bologna), U. of Berne, and others. Decorated Comdr. Order of Leopold, Officer Order of Crown, Cross of War. Mem. Royal Acad. of Medicine of Belgium, Pontificia Academia Scientarium, Physiol. Soc. of Gt. Britain, Soc. for Exptl. Biology and Medicine, Societe belge de biologie, Nederlandsche Vereeniging voor Physiologie en Pharmacologie, Vlaamsche Chemische Vereening, Biol. Soc. Paris, French Soc. Endocrinology, Biol. Soc. Barcelona, Biol. Soc. Argentina, Societa Italiana biologia sperimentale, N.Y. Acad. Medicine, Am. Med. Assn., Acad. Medicine of Buenos Aires, Med. Soc. Argentine, Pharmacol. Soc. Argentine, Soc. Biol. Montevideo, Alpha Omega Alpha. Author: Le Sinus Carotidien, 1933. Contbr. articles on physiol. and pharmacol. problems sci. publs. Home: Ghent Belgium Died July 18, 1968.

HEYNE, MAURICE, Belgian diplomat; born Waremme, Belgium, Nov. 20, 1891; s. Francois and Helene (Gerlache) H.; grad. in coml. consular and colonial sciences, Univ. of Liege, Belgium, 1913; m. Camille Flemal, May 25, 1921 (dec.); 1 dau., Myriam. Entered Belgian fgn. service, 1920; mem. of spl. mission of Belgian Congo, 1918-19; vice-consul, Tangier, Frankfurt (Germany), Lisbon (Portugal), 1920-29; charge d'affairs, Lisbon, 1929; attached to Ministry of Fgn. Affairs, Brussels, 1930; vice-consul, Montreal, 1930, in charge of consulate gen., 1932-35; promoted to consul, 1933, consul gen., 1938; counselor, Belgian Legation (later Embassy), Ottawa, 1938-45, also charge d'affaires, 1945; chief, Belgian Econ. Mission, Montreal, 1945-47; E.E. and M.P., Jan. 1, 1945; mem. Belgian delegation to P.I.C.A.O., 1946, and Internat. C.A. Orgn., 1947; Belgian minister, E.E. and M.P., comml. counselor Belgian Embassy, Washington, 1947-57; officer, dir. Wilmotte & Co., Inc., Amerbel Corp., 1957-72. Decorated Officer of Order of Leopold; Chevalier of Order of Lion; Chevalier of Order of Crown; Croix de Guerre; Mil. medal, 2d class; Croix de l'Yser; commemorative medal; Victory medal; Civic medal of 1st class; Centenary medal; Portuguese Croix de Guerre; Officier de 'Ouissam Alaouite; Officer, Order of Christ of Portugal; medal commemorative of coronation of King George VI and Queen Elizabeth. Home: Washington DC Died Mar. 1972.

HEYNS, GARRETT, penologist; b. Allendale, Mich., Sept. 21, 1891; s. William Wynant and Henrietta (Tien) H.; student Calvin Coll., Grand Rapids, Mich., 1909-11; A.B., U. Mich., 1915, A.M., 1916, Ph.D., 1927; m. Rosa Klooster, Dec. 25, 1916; children—Roger William, Jaqueline Joyce. Engaged in educational work, 1916-37; warden Mich. Reformatory, Ionia, 1937-39, 49-57; lectr. penology U. Mich., dir. Mich. Dept. Corrections, Lansing, 1940-48; mem. Mich. Parole Bd., 1948-49; dir. Wash. State Dept. Instns., 1957-67; exec. dir. Joint Commn. on Correctional Manpower and Training, Washington, 1967-69; consultant corrections div. War Dept.; instr. history Mich. Coll. Edn. Marquette, summers 1929-32; mem. Nat. Adv. Council on Correctional Manpower and Tng. Recipient U. Mich. Outstanding Achievement award, 1960. Mem. Am. Prison Assn. (pres. 1944-45), Am. Parole Assn. (pres. 1944-47), Nat. Probation Assn. (trustee), Nat. Correctional Adminstrs. Assn. (pres. 1962-63), Central States Correctional Assn. (pres. 1956-57), Mich. Sociol. Soc., Mich. Probation and Parole Assn., Mich. Welfare League, Western Council Mental Health Tng. and Research (chmn.), Phi Beta Kappa. Mem. Christian Reformed Ch. Clubs: Torch, Rotary. Author several publs. Candidate for Congress, Dem. Party, 5th Dist. of Mich., 1940. Home: Olympia WA Died Nov. 1969.

HEYWOOD, GENE BRYANT, investment banker; b. Hanford, Cal., Feb. 20, 1897; s. W. Scott and Clara (Bryant) H.; B.S., Cal. Inst. Tech., 1918; m. Cecile Hopf, June 4, 1921; 1 dau., Nancy. Civil engr. So. Cal. Edison Co., Los Angeles, 1919-25; rep. underwriters Feather River Power Project, San Francisco, 1925-28; buying dept. Harris Trust & Savs. Bank, Chgo., 1929-34; partner Young, Clarke & Co., Los Angeles, 1934-35; v.p., dir. Harris, Hall & Co., investment bankers, Chgo., 1935-53; mgr. buying dept. Dean Witter & Co. investment bankers, Chgo., 1953-67, limited partner, 1955-67; dir. McGraw Edison Co., Jennings-Heywood Oil Syndicate, Control Data Corp. Served as 2d lt., Engring. Res. Corps, U.S. Army, 1918-19. Mem. Am. Soc. C.E., Tau Beta Pi. Republican. Episcopalian. Club: Mid-Day (Chgo.). Home: Cave Creek AZ Died Sept. 18, 1971; buried Cave Creek AZ

HIBBARD, ALDRO THOMPSON, artist; b. Falmouth, Mass., Aug. 25, 1886; s. James Thompson and Katherine D. (Swift) H.; grad. high sch., Dorchester, Mass., 1906, Mass. Normal Art Sch., 1909, Museum Sch. of Fine Arts Boston, 1913; awarded Paige traveling scholarship, 1913-15; m. Winifred D. Jackman, May 31, 1925; children—Elaine W. and Malcolm J. Instr. Boston U. Art Dept., founder of Rockport Summer Sch. of Drawing and Painting, Rockport, Mass., 1921-48; academic artist Springfield Famous Art Sch., 1964. Has exhibited throughout U.S. Recipient numerous prizes including First prize for The City Beyond, Duxbury, Mass., 1920; hon. mention Art Inst. Chgo., 1921; 1st Hallgarten prize N.A.D., 1921; Jennie Sesnan gold medal Pa. Acad. Fine Arts, 1922; William Stotesbury prize Pa. Acad. Fine Arts, 1927; 2d Altman prize N.A.D., 1927, 1st Altman prize N.A.D., 1931; Albert M. Davis landscape prize Esther M. Groom prize and Mr. and Mrs. Horace Bean prize, North Shore Art Assn., 1931; Best landscape prize Springfield Art League, 1931; New Haven paint and clay prize, 1933; landscape prize Palm Beach Art Center, 1936; Charles Noel Flagg prize Conn. Acad. of Fine Arts, 1937; landscape prize Jordan Marsh Exhbn., Boston, 1938; 1st prize popular vote Internat. Business Machines Corp., San Francisco World's Fair, 1940; Downes Landscape prize New Haven Paint and Clay Club, 1941; layman's prize Salmagundi Club, 1942; Tonsberg prize Rockport Art Assn., 1942; John Henry Hammond prize Allied Artists of Am., Inc., 1943; The Moate Range purchased by Nat. Acad. Design (Ranger fund), and donated to Portland Art Museum, 1928; Ice Harvest, Addison Gallery prize best landscape Rockport Art Assn., 1933, 48, 54, 57, 60, 66, 68, gold medal of honor, 1965, 70; prize best landscape N. Shore Art Assn., 1954, 60, 64, meml., 1969, best picture, 1963; prize best landscape Academic Artists, Springfield, Mass., 1958, meml. award, 1962, Morton Donald Catak meml. award, 1966, 67; award Dr. M.J. Ritchie Meml., 1970; gold medal of honor Hudson Valley Art Assn., 1965. Retrospective exhbn. Hibbard Collection, Ledgendsee Gallery, 1970. Represented Met. Mus. Fine Arts, N.Y., Boston Museum Fine Arts, Addison Gallery, Andover, Mass., New Britian Mus., Conn., Currier Gallery (Manchester, N.H.), Portland Art Mus., Me., Rochester Athenaeum, Chandler Sch. Women, Boston, Avery Meml. Mus., Hartford, Conn., others. National Academician. Mem. Nat. Acad. of Design, Allied Artists of Am., North Shore (v.p.), Hudson Valley art assns., Guild of Boston Artists (pres.), Rockport Art Assn. (pres. 1926, 40, 42), Conn. Acad. Fine Art, Vermont Artists Guild, Inc. Republican. Clubs: Salmagundi (N.Y.C.); New Haven Paint and Clay. Home: Rockport MA Died Nov. 12, 1972.

HIBBARD, RUFUS PERCIVAL, botanist, plant physiologist; b. New Haven, Conn., Apr. 2, 1875; s. Rufus Piercy and Sarah Amelia (Brown) H.; A.B., Williams, 1899; Harvard, summer 1901; University of Chicago, summer of 1902; Woods Hole, Mass., 3 summers; fellow U. of Mich., 1904-06, Ph.D., 1906; married; children—John Sidney, William Thomas. Teacher of science, Kiskiminetas Springs Acad., Saltsburg, Pa., 1900-01; teacher of biology, Blair Academy, Blairstown, N.J., 1901-04; asst. Woods Hole, Marine Biol. Lab., summers 1903, 04; scientific asst. Bureau Plant Industry, U.S. Department Agr., 1906-08; bacteriologist and plant pathologist, Miss. Agrl. Expt. Sta., 1908-11; collaborator plant disease survey, Bur. Plant Industry, Dept. Agr., Washington, 1908-11; research asso. plant physiology, Mich. Agrl. Expt. Sta. and asso. prof., 1911—. Republican. Conglist. Fellow A.A.A.S.; mem. Am. Genetic Assn., Am. Soc. Plant Physiologists (pres. 1925-26), Bot. Soc. America, Am. Chem. Soc., Sigma Xi. Author various articles and bulls. Home: 512 Hillcrest Av., East Lansing MI‡

HIBBEN, SAMUEL GALLOWAY, engr. elec. illumination; b. Hillsboro, O., June 6, 1888; s. Joseph M. and Henriette (Martin) H.; B.Sc., Case Institute Tech., 1910, E.E. (hon.), 1915, D.Eng., 1952; student U. of Paris, Sorbonne, France, 1918; m. Ruth Rittenhouse, April 14, 1923; children—Eleanor Rittenhouse, Stuart Galloway, Barry Cummings, Craig Rittenhouse. Began as electrician, 1906; illuminating engineer Macbeth Evans Glass Company, Pittsburgh, Pennsylvania, 1910-15; consulting engr., Pittsburgh, 1915-16; with Westinghouse Lamp Co. from 1916, dir. of lighting from 1933. Served as 2d and 1st lt. U.S. Army, searchlight design Washington, D.C., and capt. sound ranging, A.E.F., World War I; U.S. Strategic Bombing Survey, Germany, World War II. Mem. Am. Inst. E.E., Soc. Am. Mil. Engrs., Illuminating Engring. Soc. (p. pres), Am. Soc. Agrl. Engrs., Illuminating Engrs. London, Sigma Nu. Republican. Presbyn. Clubs: Engineers, Ohio Soc. of New York. Contbr. tech. articles. Credited with designing 1st mobile anti-aricraft searchlight, 1917; pioneered marine illumination; designed floodlight displays illuminating Washington Monument, Holland Tunnel, Natural Bridge and Endless Caverns in Va., Carlsbad Caverns, N.M., Crystal Cave, Bermuda. Home: Montclair NJ Died June 9, 1972.

HIBBS, HAROLD DICKSON, supt. schs.; b. nr. Trafalgar, Ind., Dec. 13, 1901; s. George and Martha (Deupree) H.; A.B., Franklin Coll., 1928; M.S. in Edn., Ind. U., 1931; m. Ruby Pearl Graves, June 3, 1936; 1 dau., Marilyn Louise (Mrs. George P. Gray). Tchr. elementary schs., Nineveh (Ind.) Twp., 1920-21, 22-23, 24-26, tchr. high schs. 1926-28, prin. high sch., 1928-62; sch. corp. supt. Nineveh-Hensley-Jackson United Sch. Corp., Trafalgar, 1962-68. Mem. Am. Assn. Sch. Adminstrs., N.E.A., Ind. Assn. Pub. Sch. Supts., Ind. Tchrs. Assn., Ind. Sch. Bds. Assn., Ind. Pub. Relations Assn., Ind. Acad. Social Scis. Mem. Disciples of Christ Ch. (elder, trustee). Home: Trafalgar IN Died July 10, 1968; buried Nineveh Cemetery Nineveh IN

HIBBS, LOUIS E., army officer; b. Washington, D.C., Oct. 3, 1893; s. Frank Warren and Janette (Nelson) H.;

student Culver Military Acad., 1909-11; B.S., U.S. Mil. Acad., 1916; m. Margaret Hayes, Feb. 17, 1923; children—Louis Emerson. Commd. 2d lt., 1916 and advanced through the grades to major gen., 1943; combat duty with artillery, 1st Div. and 2d Am. Corps. 1917-18; adj. and aide to Gen. Douglas MacArthur, 1919-22; staff and command duties, 1922-40, at Ft. Sill, Okla., Ft. Leavenworth, Kans., Hawaii, Ft. Bragg, N.C., Washington, D.C., West Point, N.Y.; comdg. 63d Infantry Division, May 1943-46; Comdg. Field Art. Sch., Aug. 1945-June 1946; comdg. 12th Inf. Div., P.I., 1946, ret. from active duty. Decorated Distinguished Service Medal, Silver Star, Purple Heart with Oak Leaf Cluster. Home: Mirror Lake NH Died Apr. 28, 1970; buried Post Cemetery, U.S. Military Acad., West Point NY

HICHBORN, FRANKLIN, author; b. at Eureka, Calif., Oct. 7, 1869; s. John Edwin and Frances (Hunt) H.; Santa Clara (Calif.) Coll.; Stanford U., 1892-94; (hon. M.A., Santa Clara, 1903); m. Mabel Houlton, of Santa Clara, Calif., Dec. 31, 1897; children—Paul Revere, Deborah, Drusilla, also twins, Frances, Mabel (dec.). Pub. San Jose Letter, 1894-97; city editor Fresno (Calif.) Expositor, 1897-98; editor Winnemucca (Nev.) Silver State, 1899; pub. San Jose Spectator, 1900-01; editor San Jose Herald, 1902-04; news editor, Sacramento Union, 1904-06; writer and lecturer on polit. and economic subjects, 1906-39; pub. Legislative Bulletin, Sacramento, 1915-17. Conducted state-wide publicity campaigns; 1912, in which attempt under initiative provisions, state constitution, to restore race-track gambling in Calif. was defeated; 1914, under which redlight" abatement act was ratified; 1916, for prohibition and no-saloon amendments to the state constitution; 1918, for election of a legislature that would ratify Nat. Prohibition Amendment; 1922-26, for pub. ownership under state supervision of water and hydro-electric power. Club: Commonwealth. Author: Story of the California Legislature of 1909, of 1911, of 1913, of 1915, of 1921 (5 vols.), 1909-21; The System as Uncovered by the San Francisco Graft Prosecution, 1913. Home: Santa Clara CA‡

HICKAM, JOHN BAMBER, physician, educator; b. Manila, Philippines, Aug. 10, 1914; s. Horace Meek and Helen J. (Bamber) H.; B.; A.B., Harvard, 1936, M.D., 1940; m. Mary Margaret Kennedy, May 12, 1945; children—Helen Kennedy, Thomas Bamber. Med. intern, asst. resident Peter Bent Brigham Hosp., Boston, 1940-42; chief med. resident Grady Hosp., Atlanta, 1942-43; instr. medicine Emory U. Sch. Medicine, 1946-47; from asso. in medicine to prof. medicine Duke Sch. Medicine, 1947-58; prof. medicine, chmn. dept. Indiana U. Sch. Medicine, 1958-70. Mem. aero-med. panel of sci. adv. bd. to chief of staff USAF, 1952-56, chmn., 1955-56; mem. cardiovascular study sect. Nat. Insts. Health, 1958-63, chmn., 1959-63; chmn. spl. med. adv. group VA, 1966-70. Trustee, Thomas Alva Edison Found.; Mem. Harvard Med. Alumni Council. Served to capt., M.C., AUS, 1943-46. Recipient exceptional service award USAF, 1957. Diplomate Am. Bd. Internal Medicine (mem. bd. 1965-70), Nat. Bd. Med. Examiners (exec. com., vice chmn.). Fellow A.C.P., Am. Coll. Cardiology; mem. A.M.A., Am. Federation Clin. Research, So., Central societies clinical research, American Physiol. Society, American Society Clinical Investigation, American Clin. and Climatological Association, Assn. Am. Physicians (sec. 1966-70), Am. Profs. Medicine (pres. 1969-70), Marion County Med. Soc., Phi Beta Kappa, Alpha Omega Alpha. Author papers cardiopulmonary physiology and disease. Home: Indianapolis IN Died Feb. 9, 1970; buried Indianapolis IN

HICKENLOOPER, BOURKE BLAKEMORE, U.S. Senator; b. Blockton, Ia., July 21, 1896; s. Nathan Oscar and Margaret Amanda (Blakemore) H.; B.S., Ia. State Coll., 1920; J.D., U. of Ia., 1922; LL.D., Parsons Coll., 1942, Lorcas Coll., 1943, Coe Coll.; D.C.L., Elmira Coll.; m. Verna Eileen Bensch, Nov. 24, 1927; children—Jane Carroll (Mrs. Russell Oberlin), David Bourke. Admitted to Ia. bar June, 1922, and since practiced in Cedar Rapids; with Johnson, Donnelly & Lynch, 1922-25; private practice, 1925-35; formed firm Hickenlooper & Mitvalsky, 1935-42; mem. Ia. House of Representatives, 1935-39; lt. gov. of Iowa, 1939-43, gov., 1943-44; U.S. senator from Iowa, 1945-69. Served as 2d lieutenant, 339th F.A., A.E.F., World War I. Mem. Am., Linn County and Ia. State bar assns., Am. Legion, Phi Delta Phi, Sigma Phi Epsilon. Methodist. Mason (Shriner), Odd Fellow, Elk, Moose. Home: Cedar Rapids IA Died Sept. 4, 1971.

HICKEY, JOHN JOSEPH, judge; b. Rawlings, Wyo., Aug. 22, 1911; s. John J. and Bridgid (O'Meara) H; LL.B., U. of Wyo., 1934; m. Winifred Espy, Jan. 14, 1946; children—John David, Paul Joseph. Admitted to Wyo. bar, 1934, practiced in Rawlins, 1934-42, city treas., 1935; co., pros. atty. Carbon Co., Wyo., 1938, 46; U.S. atty., Cheyenne, since 1949; gov. State of Wyo., 1959-61; U.S. senator from State Wyo., 1961-63; judge 10th Circuit Court of Appeals, Cheyenne, Wyo., 1963-70. Member bd. dirs. Carbon Co. Meml. Hosp., 1935-42, dir., treas. hosp. bd., 1936-42. Served as capt. U.S. Army, 1942-45. Mem. Vets. Fgn. Wars (comdr. Wyo. dept. 1949-50), Sigma Alpha Epsilon. Democrat. Roman Catholic. K.C., Elk. Clubs: Lions, Serra (Cheyenne). Home: Cheyenne WY Died Sept. 22, 1970; buried Rawlins WY

HICKEY, LEE COLE, editor; b. Syracuse, N.Y., Apr. 26, 1911; s. Daniel Coveny and Eleanor (Cole) H.; A.B., Rutgers U., 1933; m. Florence Adair, Sept. 10, 1938; children—Janet Adair, Carolyn Lee. Mng. editor Dept. Store Economist, N.Y. City, 1941; tech. writer Sperry Gyroscope Co., Great Neck, N.Y., 1942-46; asso. editor Elks mag., N.Y. City, 1946-49, editor, 1949-62. Mem. Zeta Psi. Home: Tarrytown NY Died Dec. 23, 1970.

HICKEY, MATTHEW (JOSEPH), JR., business exec.; b. Chicago, July 11, 1896; s. Matthew Joseph and Julia (Daly) H.; student St. Ignatius Coll., 1910-14; m. Naomi Todd Pope, May 4, 1922; children—John, Matthew, Thomas, Naomi (dec.), Suzanne, Jerome. Cashier, Kean Taylor and Co., 1914-16; trader Curtis and Sanger, 1916-19; mgr. trading dept. Halsey Stuart and Company, 1919-26; founder of Hickey Doyle and Co., 1927-37; pres. Hickey & Co. from 1937; dir. Motorola, Inc., Chicago Rivet & Machine Co. N.Y., N.H. & H. R.R. Mem. lay bd. trustees Loyola U.; dir. Asso. Cath. Charities, Chgo., St. Francis Hosp., Evanston. Served Alien Property Custodian, U.S. Govt., World War II as officer and director of many corporations. Member Sovereign Mil. Order Knights of Malta. Roman Catholic. Clubs: New York Athletic (New York City); Knollwood (Lake Forest, Ill.); Chicago Athletic Wilmette IL Died Feb. 27, 1969.

HICKEY, TURNER PAUL, educator; b. Marshall, Mich., Aug. 9, 1873; s. George Smith and Henrietta Anne (Turner) H.; A.B., U. of Mich., 1896; student U. of Wis., summers 1906-11, Sorbonne, France, June-Oct. 1913; LL.D., Albion Coll., 1935; m. Gertrude Eagle, Aug. 15, 1899; children—Elizabeth Henrietta (dec.), Jane Elizabeth (Mrs. Nicholas J. Saulnier). Began as asst. prin. Lansing (Mich.) High Sch., 1896; prin. of high schs. at Alpena, Adrian, Battle Creek, Mich., 1898-1910; head of history dept., Western State Teachers Coll., Kalamazoo, Mich., 1910-19; exec. Upjohn Co., Kalamazoo, 1919-20; educational department Ford Motor Co., 1920-21; pres. Detroit Inst. of Tech. since 1921; became dir. of edn., Detroit Coll. of Law, 1921; now retired. Mem. Phi Beta Kappa, Sigma Alpha Epsilon, Phi Sigma Rho. Republican Methodist. Mason, K. of P. Clubs: International Torch, Michigan Schoolmasters, Pine Lake Golf, Detroit Automobile. Mem. Mich. State Council for Defense. Home: 17249 Melrose Av., Detroit 19 MI‡

HICKS, AMI MALI, b. Brooklyn, N.Y.; d. of George Cleveland and Josephine (Mali) H.; ed. in art under Charles Chaplin, Paris, William Chase and John Ward Stimson, New York. A pioneer in arts and crafts movement in America; founder Guild of Arts and Crafts, New York, 1891. Hon. mention for handicraft work, St. Louis Expn., 1904; exhibitor Met. Mus. Art, 1918. Dir. Free Acres Colony, Berkeley Heights, N.J. Mem. Gamut Club, Town Hall Club (New York); Civic Club, Single Tax Service League. Contbr. articles on interior decoration to Woman's Home Companion, Ladies' Home Journal, etc. Home: Berkeley Heights, N.J. Address: 141 E. 17th St., New York NY‡

HICKS, CLIFFORD E(RVING), business exec.; b. Manhassett, N.Y., Sept. 10, 1887; s. Austin and Jennie Louise (Delamater) H.; B.S. in Civil Engring., New York U., m. Bertha Egner, Apr. 29, 1915 (dec.); children—John S., Alan A. Pres. and dir. N.Y. Dock Co., N.Y. Dock Ry., 1949-56, chmn. bd., 1956-58. Licensed professional engr., N.Y. Mem. Delta Phi. Republican. Mason. Clubs: Downtown Athletic (N.Y.C.); Brooklyn, Municipal (Bklyn.); National Republican Hempstead Golf. Home: Great Neck NY Died Nov. 4, 1969.

HICKS, HANNE JOHN, educator; b. Orrick, Mo., Apr. 16, 1910; s. John A. and Martha (Hanne) H.; B.S., Central Mo. State Coll., Warrensburg, 1938; M.A., U. Mo., 1940, Ed.D., 1950; m. Laurie K. Saxer, Dec. 26, 1937; children—John Martin, Hanne Lane. Tchr., prin., Puxico, Mo., 1928-30, Orrick, Mo., 1930-38; supt., Rayville, Mo., 1938-39; supervising prin., Normandy Sch., St. Louis, 1940-45; supr. curriculum devel. Mo. Dept. Edn., 1945-46; dir. labs. schs., prof. edn. Geneseo (N.Y.) State Coll., 1946-50; vis. summer instr. edn. U. Mo., 1942, 46, 50; asso. prof. edn. Ind. U., 1950-55, prof., 1955-66, chmn. dept. elementary edn., 1956-66, dir. div. of instruction and curriculum, 1962-66, acting asso. dean Sch. Edn., 1965-66; specialist elementary education ICA-Ind. U. Tchr. Edn. Contract, Bangkok, Thiland, 1955-56. Mem. N.E.A., Nat., Ind. (adviser) assns. elementary sch. prins., Ind. Tchrs. Assn., Phi Delta Kappa. Mem. Christian Ch. (ofcl. bd.). Author: Administrative Leadership in the Elementary School, 1956; Educational Supervision in Principle and Practice, 1960. Home: Bloomington IN Died Oct. 13, 1966; buried Rosehill Cemetery, Bloomington IN

HICKS, JOHN DONALD, educator; born Pickering, Mo., Jan. 25, 1890; s. Rev. John Kossuth and Harriett Gertrude (Wing) H.; B.A., Northwestern, 1913, M.A., 1914, LL.D., 1956; Ph.D., U. Wis., 1916; M.A., University Cambridge (Eng.), 1950; LL.D., U. San Francisco, 1957, U. Cal., 1960; m. Lucile Harriet Curtis, June 15, 1921; children—Jane (Mrs. F.N. West), Carolyn (Mrs. John A. Pierce), Marjorie (Mrs. Louis K. Krall). Asst. prof. and prof. hist., Hamline U., 1916-22; prof. history, N.C. Coll. for Women, Greensboro, N.C., 1922-23; prof. Am. history, U. of Neb., 1923-32, chmn. dept. of history, 1925-29, dean Coll. of Arts and Sciences, 1929-32; prof. history, U. of Wis., 1932-42, chmn. dept., 1938-42; A.F. and May T. Morrison prof. history, U. of Cal., 1942-57, emeritus, 1957-72, dean grad. div., 1945-47, chairman department of history, 1947-50; Phi Beta Kappa Visiting Scholar, 1958-59. Lecturer on history, Harvard, 1st half year, 1931-32. Walker-Ames Lecturer, Univ. of Washington, Feb., 1944; vis. prof. Am. Hist. and Instns., U. of Cambridge, England (fellow Trinity Hall), 1950-51. Teacher, summers, Northwestern Univ., Syracuse U., U. of Minn., George Washington U., W.Va. U., U. So. Cal., Columbia, U. of Cal. (Los Angeles), U. Hawaii. Mem. Am. Hist. Assn. (exec. council 1932-36, pres. Pacific coast br. 1955) Miss. Valley Hist. Assn. (pres. 1932-33), Agrl. Hist. Soc. (pres. 1948-49), California Historical Society, Delta Upsilon and Phi Beta Kappa (hon.). Author: The Constitutions of the Northwest States, 1923; The Populist Revolt, 1931; The Federal Union, 1937; The American Nation, 1941; A Short History of American Democracy, 1943; (with T. Saloutos) Agrl. Discontent in the Middle West, 1900-1939, 1951; The American Tradition, 1955; Republican Ascendancy, 1921-1933, 1960; Rehearsal for Disaster, 1961. Contbr. hist. publs. Home: Berkeley CA Died Feb. 5, 1972; buried Palm Springs CA

HICKS, JOSEPH EMERSON, clergyman; b. Bluff City, Tenn., May 31, 1874; s. William Cate and Josephine (Meredith) H.; B.A., U. of Richmond, 1899, M.A., 1900, D.D., 1910; B.D., U. of Chicago Div. Sch., 1903; m. Flora May Baker, of Jefferson City, Tenn., Dec. 23, 1901; children—Joseph Emerson, Mary Meredith, Jaynie Elizabeth. Ordained ministry Bapt. Ch., 1892; pastor First Ch., Danville, Va., 1903-20, First Ch., Baltimore, Md., 1920-32; pastor First Church, Bristol, Va., since 1932; built 2 chs. and Averett Coll., Danville. Y.M.C.A. sec. with A.E.F., 1916-18. Mem. Edn. Commn. of Va. that established the Bapt. system of denom. schs. Trustee Southern Bapt. Theol. Sem., Southwestern Bapt. Theol. Sem., Relief and Annuity Board of Southern Bapt. Conv., University of Richmond, Bapt. Hosp. (Lynchburg, Va.). Mem. A.A.A.S., Phi Beta Kappa. Democrat. Mason. Clubs: Inter-Church, Philosophers', Civitan. Writer and lecturer. Home: 420 Pennsylvania Av., Bristol TN‡

HICKS, W. B., , assn. exec.; b. Houston, Apr. 22, 1932; s. W. B. and Bonnie H. (Craig) H.; A.A., Del Mar Coll., 1958; m. Patricia Ann Walker, Dec. 13, 1965; children—James H., Bonnie S., William B. Asst. pub. Human Events, Inc., Washington, 1958-63; exec. sec. Liberty Lobby, Inc., Washington, 1964-69. Served with USAF, 1950-56. Mem. Phi Theta Kappa (nat. 1st v.p. 1957-58). Republican. Home: Washington DC Died Feb. 9, 1969.

HICKS, WILLIAM MINOR, lawyer; b. Oxford, N.C., Oct. 1, 1903; s. Archibald Arrington and Hettie (Minor) H.; student U. N.C., 1922-26; m. Sarah Hall, Dec. 7, 1940; children—William M., Jr., Archibald Arrington II. Admitted to N.C. bar, 1926; partner Hicks & Hicks, attys. 1926-41; pvt. practice W. M. Hicks, atty., 1941-52; partner Hicks & Taylor, Oxford, 1952-69; county atty., 1959-69. Pros. atty. county ct., 1934-45; mayor Oxford, N.C., 1945-59. Mem. Granville County Bar Assn. (pres. 1960-69), Ninth Judicial Bar, N.C. State Bar (pres. 1962-63), Am., N.C. bar assns. Methodist. Mason (Shriner). Clubs: Kiwanis, Thorndale Country (past dir.). Home: Oxford NC Died Aug. 31, 1969.

HICKS, WILSON, editor; b. Sedalia, Mo., Jan. 7, 1897; s. John Wesley and Davanna (Bonker) H.; grad. Sedalia (Mo.) High Sch.; student U. of Mo., 1914-17; m. Ida Elliott Smith, Aug. 19, 1918; 1 son, David La Conia. Reporter Sedalia (Mo.) Capital, 1914; reporter, rewrite man, copyreader, Kansas City (Mo.) Star, 1917-22; motion picture editor Sydney (New South Wales, Australia) Sunday Times, 1922-23; successively asst. Sunday editor, associate editor magazine, rotogravure editor, Kansas City Star, 1923-27; copy editor, news editor, executive editor feature service, Associated Press, 1929-35, also exec. editor news photo service, 1935-37; asso. editor, later becoming exec. editor, Life mag., 1937-50; lectr. photojournalism and director of University publications U. Miami. Served as cpl. with United States Army, Camp Funston, Kan., 1918. Club: The Coffee House. Author: Words and Pictures, An Introduction to Photojournalism. Home: Homestead FL Died July 5, 1970.

HIESTAND, EDGAR WILLARD, ex-congressman; b. Chgo., Dec. 3, 1888; s. Henry and Sarah (Willard) H.; A.B., Dartmouth, 1910; m. Berenice Craft, July 21, 1911; children—Barbara (Mrs. Fred H. Bragassa), Mary (Mrs. D. McCoy), Janet (Mrs. Norman E. Watts). Various positions Filene's, Boston, Hudson's, Detroit, The Broadway, Los Angeles, Pogue's, Cin., 1912-31, as asst. buyer, buyer, div. mdse. mgr., personnel mgr., gen. office mgr., gen. mdse. mgr.; stores mgr. Sears, Roebuck

& Co., Atlanta, 1931-32, Tulsa, 1932-39, Los Angeles, 1939-49; mem. 83d-87th Congress, 21st Dist. Cal. Pres., dir. Better Bus. Bur.; pres. Bd. Edn., San Marino, Cal. Served as mem. Gen. Staff War Coll., World War I. Mem. Delta Kappa Epsilon. Clubs: Rotary (past dist. gov., pres., dir.), California, University (Los Angeles); Wilshire Country (N.Y.C.). Home: Pasadena CA Died Aug. 1970.

HIGGINS, GEORGE THOMAS, automotive mfg.; b. Buffalo, Mar. 6, 1924; s. George Joseph and Marguerite (Snell) H.; A.B., Manhattan Coll., 1947; LL.B., Harvard, 1950; m. Marilyn Joanne Rees, Apr. 26, 1952; children—Julie Marie, Richard Rees, Thomas, James, George Joseph II. Member corporate secretary's staff Chrysler Corporation, Detroit, 1951-54, assistant secretary, 1954-56, secretary, 1956-65, 1965-68, asst. gen. mgr. cars Dodge div., 1965-68, dir. Washington office parent co., 1968-71; v.p. Chrysler Realty Co., 1968-71. Mem. bd., treas. Traffic Safety Assn. of Detroit; mem. bd. Jr. Achievement Southeastern Mich., Citizens Redevelopment Corp., of Detroit, Mich.; pres. bd. dirs. Catholic Social Services Wayne County, 1962. Served as lt. (j.g.) USNR, 1943-46. Mem. State Bar of Mich. Roman Catholic. Home: Bethesda MD Died July 14, 1971; buried Gate of Heaven Cemetery, Silver Spring MD

HIGGINS, JAMES BENNETT, pub. official; b. Water Valley, Miss., Oct. 12, 1872; s. I. J. and Jane (Knight) H.; moved with parents to Phillips Co., Ark., 1873, Faulkner Co., 1881; ed. pub. schs.; worked way through Quitman Coll.; m. Mary Brady, of Faulkner Co., Oct. 6, 1897; children—Mary Fentem (Mrs. Frank H. Winbourne), Horace Brady, Leone (Mrs. Alfred Rose). Teacher in rural schs., later newspaper reporter and for several years editor and mgr. Conway (Ark.) Weekly Times; chief clk. Ark. Ho. of Rep. for ten years; dep. sec. of state, Ark., for four years; sec. of state, Ark., 1924-30; reelected without opposition, 1926, 28; now deputy sec. of state. Democrat. Methodist. Mason (32 deg., Shriner), K.P., Odd Fellow. Clubs: Lions, Kiwanis, Lakeside Country, Gold Lake Fishing. Home: 1826 N. Monroe St., Little Rock AR*‡

HIGGINS, STANLEY CARMEN, JR., lawyer; b. Logan County, W.Va., Oct. 26, 1913; s. Stanley Carmen and Virginia Meridan (Perkins) H.; LL.B., Washington and Lee U., 1937; m. Jean Annette Kent, Dec. 20, 1938; children—Stanley Kent, David Kent. Admitted to W.Va. bar, 1937, later practiced in Fayetteville; senior mem. firm Higgins, Thrift & Mahan, 1946-72; mem. Jud. Council W.Va., 1962-70. Served to lt. (s.g.) USNR, 1942-45. Mem. Am., W.Va. (pres. 1960-61) bar assns., Am. Judicature Soc., W.Va. State Bar, S.A.R., Phi Gamma Delta, Phi Delta Phi. Episcopalian. Home: Fayetteville WV Died Nov. 27, 1972.

HIGGINSON, FRANCIS LEE, banker; b. Boston, Mass., Nov. 29, 1877; s. Francis Lee and Julia (Borland) H.; A.B., Harvard, 1900; m. Hetty A. Sargent, June 7, 1905 (died June 27, 1921); m. 2d, Aileen M. Johnstone, Oct. 9, 1930. Banking and brokerage business, 1901-69; dir. Gauley Coal Land Co. Clubs: Somerset, Myopia, Harvard, Union Boat (Boston), Harvard (N.Y.), Leander (Eng.). Home: Wenham MA Died July 14, 1969.

HIGHTOWER, LOUIS VICTOR, army officer; b. Union Springs, Ala., Aug. 11, 1909; s. Louis Victor and Annie Jean (Pippin) H.; student U. Tex., 1926-27; B.S. in Mech. Engring., U.S. Mil. Acad., 1931; grad. Nat. War Coll., 1952; m. Aug. 16, 1931; children—Gretchen B., Anne Ellen, Julia T., Louis Victor III (U.S. Army); m. 2d, Virginia Lovell, July 28, 1970. Commd. 2d lt., F.A., U.S. Army, 1931, advanced through grades to maj. gen., 1958; various assignments F.A. units and schools, U.S., 1931-41; assigned 1st Armored Div., ETO, 1941-42; comdr. rank battalion 1st Armored Regt., 1942-43, comdr. regt., 1943-44; pres. Armored Bd., Armored Center, Ft. Knox, Ky., 1944-46, Army Ground Forces Bd. 2, 1946-48; armored adviser, asst. chief U.S. Army Mission to Argentina, 1948-51; research and development coordinator Office Chief Staff, Dept. of Army, 1952-53; chief staff 2d Inf. Div., also comdg. officer 9th Inf. Regt., Korea, 1953-54; comdg. officer 40th Inf. Div., 1954; chief orgn. and tng. div. G3, operations, Dept. of Army, 1954-56; dep. comdg. gen. U.S. Army Carribean, Ft. Amador, C.Z., 1956-57; chief staff Hdqrs. Caribbean Command, Quarry Heights, C.Z., 1957-58; sr. army mem. weapons systems evaluation group Office Dir. Def. Research and Engring., 1958-60; chief staff combined mil. planning orgn. Central Treaty Orgn., Ankara, Turkey, 1960-61, dep. comdg. gen. U.S. Army Ryukyus Islands, IX Corps, 1961-62, Continental Army Command, Ft. Monroe, Va., 1962-63; ret. D.S.C., Silver Star with oak leaf cluster, Legion of Merit with oak leaf cluster, Bronze Star medal with oak leaf cluster. Purple Heart with 5 oak leaf clusters. Clubs: University, Army-Navy (Washington). Home: Washington DC Died July 30, 1972; buried Arlington Nat. Cemetery, Arlington VA

HIGLEY, ALBERT MALTBY, bldg. contractor; b. Cleve., Feb. 2, 1895; s. Frank and Carrie (Maltby) H.; B.S., C.E., Case Institute of Technology, 1917; m. Mildred Schuch, September 11, 1926; children—Ann (Mrs. Joseph F. Kelley), Albert Maltby. Employed by contractor, 1920-25; organized, chmn. Albert M. Higley Co., 1925-69; dir. Central Nat. Bank Cleve., Land Title Guarantee & Trust Co. Chmn. Cleve. chpt. A.R.C., 1945-48; bd. govs. Am. Nat. Red Cross, 1951-54; trustee Denison U., 1954-60, Cleveland Development Found., Cast Inst. Tech. Served as 1st lt. AUS, 1917-19. Mem. C. of C. (dir., past chairman of the board). Clubs: Rotary (past pres.), Union, University, Mayfield Country (Cleve.). Home: Shaker Heights OH Died Dec. 30, 1969.

HIGLEY, CYRUS MARTIN, banker; b. Norwich, N.Y., Mar. 9, 1894; s. Homer Harvey and Cornelia (Martin) H.; grad. Phillips Andover Acad.; Ph.B., Yale, 1915; m. Dorothy Lindley; 1 dau., Alice (Mrs. Philip L. Gilbert). With Chenango County Nat. Bank & Trust Co., Norwich, N.Y., 1915-71, cashier, 1929-39, pres., 1939-71, also dir.; mem. bd. directors Chenango & Unadilla Telephone Corp., Victory Chain, Inc., W. H. Dunne Co. Pres. Norwich bd. edn. Trustee Harper Coll. Mem. Nat. Sch. Bds. Assn. Inc. Episcopalian (treas.). Home: Norwich NY Died Sept. 1971.

HIGLEY, HENRY GRANT, biometrician; b. Lima, Peru, June 11, 1903 (parents Am citizens); s. Henry Grant and Rosario (Andrade) H.; student U. Guadalajara, 1920-24, Ratledge Chiropractic Coll., 1934-37, U. So. Cal., 1953-57; M.S., U. Nuevo Leon, 1957; m. Mary Bavin, Aug. 1931; 1 son, Henry. Research dir. Los Angeles Coll. Chiropractic, 1948-69, also chmn. dept. physiology; dir. dept. research, statistics Am. Chiropractic Assn., 1958-69; statis. analyst Ghormley & Assos., Los Angeles, 1952-56; statis. analyst Vitaminerals, Inc., Glendale, Cal., 1956-57. Mem. Am. Inst. Biog. Scis., Inst. Math. Statistics, Biometric Soc., Am. Documentation Inst., Am. Statis. Assn. Author: (with Haynes) General Chemistry, 1938. Contbr. articles to profl. jours. Home: Alhambra CA Died May 18, 1969; interred Resurrection Cemetery South San Gabriel CA

HIGLEY, WALTER MAYDOLE, clergyman; b. Norwich, N.Y., Jan. 23, 1899; s. Homer Harvey and Cornelia Merritt (Martin) H.; student Phillips-Andover Acad., 1916-18; B.S., Columbia, 1922; S.T.D., Gen. Theol. Sem., 1949, Syracuse U., 1964; D.D., Hobart College, 1962; m. Marion Carr Mason, Oct. 18, 1922; children—Constance (Mrs. James D. Hammond), Cornelia (Mrs. Robert B. Seidel), Faith (Mrs. Faith C. Higley), Walter M. Ordained to ministry Episcopal Ch., 1925, missionary charge Christ Ch., Jordan, 1925-29, Emmanuel Ch., Memphis, N.Y., 1925-29; rector All Saints Ch., Johnson City, N.Y., 1929-43; archdeacon and sec. Diocese of Central N.Y., 1943-48; suffragan bishop, 1948-59, bishop coadjutor, 1959, bishop, 1960-69. Mem. Diocesan Council, 1939-43; chmn. Department Christian Edn., 1934-44; dep. to Provincial Synod, N.Y. and N.J., 1929-43, dep. to Gen. Conv., 1943-46. Mem. N.Y. State Council Chs. (pres. 1966-67). Sigma Chi. Rotarian. Home: Syracuse NY Died May 4, 1969; buried Norwich NY

HILBRANT, ROBERT EDWARD, toilet article mfg.; b. Argenta, Ill., Sept. 21, 1900; s. Samuel Oscar and Wilhelmina Louise (Sternberg) H.; student U. Wis., 1921-22; m. Jose Marie Bash, Dec. 17, 1937. With Colgate-Palmolive Co., 1926-61, beginning as staff office in Chgo., successively staff field sales orgn., home office asst. merchandising mgr., gen. sales mgr., gen. sales and merchandising mgr., gen. mgr. toilet article div., 1952-54, v.p. charge toilet article div., 1954-56, dir. marketing, 1956-60, sales v.p., 1960-61, dir., 1956-58. Mem. Theta Delta Chi. Clubs: Sky Top, Baltusrol Golf; Big Foot Country (Lake Geneva, Wis.); University, Coral Casino, Montecito Country, Channel City (Santa Barbara, Cal.). Home: Santa Barbara CA Died Mar. 1970.

HILD, FREDERICK HENRY, librarian Chicago Public Library since 1887; b. Chicago; ed. public schools, Chicago; has been connected with Chicago Public Library since 1874; mem. of, and has held several offices in, Am. Library Assn. Address: Public Library, Chicago‡

HILL, ALFRED GIBSON, newspaper pub.; b. Emporia, Kan., March 14, 1893; s. Joseph Henry and Sarah Frances (Meldrum) H.; student Emporia (Kan.) State Teachers Coll., 1911-13; A.B., U. of Kan., 1917; m. Julia Gontrum, Dec. 16, 1922; children—Frances (Mrs. Raymond Holton); Thomas Alfred. Began career as student reporter for the Emporia Gazette, 1909; reporter Topeka Capital, 1913-15, 1916, 1919, Phila. Pub. Ledger and United Press, Washington, 1920; alumni mgr. and editor Graduate Magazine, U. of Kan., 1920-24; part owner and advtg. mgr. Arkansas City (Kan.) Daily Traveler, 1924-28; pub. Ft. Collins (Colo.) Express-Courier, 1928-37; pub. Cheyenne (Wyo.) State Tribune, 1937-38; established Morning Guide, Fremont, Neb., 1938, and to 1947; pres. Fremont Guide & Tribune; v.p., gen. mgr. Jamestown (N.Y.) Evening Jour., 1940, Jamestown Post-Journal, 1941-42; president Delaware Broadcasting Company Inc. (station WILM), 1945-49. Wilmington, Delaware; pub. and editor Chester (Pa.) Times, 1942-53. Established Oak Ridge (Tennessee) daily Oak Ridger, 1949; pres. co. purchasing New Kensington (Pa.) Daily Dispatch, 1950-53; asso. owner, mgr. Coral Gables (Fla.) Times. Trustee Crozer Theol. Sem., Chester, Pa. Served from pvt. to 1st lt. inf. U.S. Army, World War I. Citation for Distinguished Service, U. Kan., 1946. Home: Swarthmore PA Died Dec. 14, 1971; buried Edgmont Meml. Park, Concordville PA

HILL, ARTHUR MIDDLETON, transportation exec.; b. Charleston, W.Va., Mar. 23, 1892; s. Arthur Edward and Ellen Dickinson (Middleton) H.; ed. Central Mo. State Coll.; Dr. of Engring. (honoris causa), Drexel Inst. Tech., 1948. married Caroline Quarrier Staunton, June 29, 1918; children—Frederick Staunton, Caroline Quarrier; m. 2d, Mary McDowell Ellis, Dec. 4, 1944. Former chmn., mem. exec. com., director The Greyhound Corporation and subsidiaires, retired, 1965; director, member executive committee Internat. Tel. & Tel.; pres., chmn. Charleston Transit Co. (formerly Charleston Interurban R.R. Co.); dir., pres. Kanawha City Co.; dir. Kanawha Banking & Trust Co., Greenbrier Valley Bank, Diamond Ice & Coal Co.; adv. dir. Riggs Nat. Bank, Washington. Mem. Rep. Nat. Finance Com. Served as 2d lt., advancing to capt., asst chief of staff, 77th Div., AUS, WW I; grad. Army Gen. Staff College, Langres, France. Chairman National Association Motor Bus Owners; director U.S. C. of C., 1935-48; member bd. govs. Nat. Highway Users Conf. Chmn. Motor Bus Code Authority, N.R.A., 1933-35; spl. asst. to sec. of navy, 1942-45; chairman Nat. Security Resources Bd., 1947-48; member of the National Security Council. Awarded Medal for Merit World War II. Republican. Episcopalian. Mason (32 deg., Shriner). Clubs: Metropolitan, Burning Tree, Chevy Chase (Washington); Racquet and Tennis, Links (New York City); Seminole Golf, Bath and Tennis, Everglades (Palm Beach, Florida); Royal and Ancient Golf of St. Andrews (Scotland). Home: Washington DC Died Sept. 6, 1972; buried Lewisburg WV

HILL, CARLTON, lawyer; b. Hart, Mich., May 8, 1894; s. John and Margaret E. (Corcoran) H.; B.S., U. Mich., 1917; LL.B., Chicago Kent Coll. of Law, 1922; m. Janet O'Connor, Sept. 6, 1921; 1 dau., Sue Page (Mrs. George R. Keller). Admitted to Ill. bar, 1922, lawyer, specializing in patents, Chicago, from 1919. Served with U.S.M.C. and Res., 1917-49, active duty world wars I and II; retired as lt. col. Mem. Ill. Mfrs. Assn. (tech. adv. patent and trade mark com.), Am. Ill. State, Chicago bar assns., Am., Chicago (past pres.) patent law assns., Soc. Automotive Engrs., Tau Beta Pi, Phi Delta Phi. Home: Chicago IL Died Dec. 28, 1971; buried All Saints Cemetery, Des Plaines IL

HILL, CHESTER JAMES, JR., educator; b. Hazleton, Pa., Nov. 6, 1914; B.A., Lafayette Coll., M.S., Ph.D., Yale. Henry M. Wriston prof. psychology Lawrence U., Appleton, Wis., until 1969. Died Nov. 22, 1969; buried Riverside Cemetery, Appleton WI

HILL, DAVID GARRETT, industrialist; b. Pitts., June 6, 1902; s. William Fulton and Eleanor Patton (Garrett) H.; M.E., Cornell, 1924; m. Eleanor Campbell Musser, Oct. 6, 1928; children—William Fulton, John Howard. Began as indsl. engr. Pitts. Plate Glass Co. (name changed to PPG Industries, Inc. 1968), 1924, asst. to v.p., 1929-40, gen. supt. plate glass factories, 1940-52, v.p., 1952-55, dir., 1954-73, pres., 1955-66, chmn. bd., chief exec. officer, 1966-67, chmn. exec. com., 1962-67, dir. cons., 1967-73, mem. exec. com., 1967-73; dir. Pitts. Corning Corp., Bell Telephone Co. Pa., Brockway Glass Co., Inc. Bd. dirs. Pitts. Symphony Soc.; trustee Presbyterian-U. Hosp. Mem. Sigma Alpha Epsilon. Republican. Presbyn. Mason. Clubs: Duquesne, Fox Chapel Golf (Pitts.); Rolling Rock (Ligonier, Pa.). Home: Pittsburg PA Died Mar. 1973.

HILL, FELIX ROBERTSON, JR., clergyman, educator; b. Nashville, Tenn., Oct. 21, 1869; s. Felix Robertson and Ordalia (Mayes) H.; A.B., Hiawassee Coll., Sweetwater, Tennessee, 1886; Vanderbilt University, 1889; D.D., Southern College, 1935; m. Cora Hall Lindsay, of St. Louis, Mo., Feb. 1892 (died July 1906); 1 dau., Kathryn (wife of W. O. Rawls, U.S.A.); m. 2d, Edith Baumberger, of Niles, Mich., Oct. 1912. Ordained ministry M.E. Ch., S., 1889; pastor Ferguson, Mo., 1889-91, Washington, Mo., 1891-92, Wagoner Pl. Ch., St. Louis, 1892-96, St. Paul's Ch., St. Louis, 1896-98, 1st Ch., Sedalia, 1898-1901, St. Paul's Ch., Parkersburg, W.Va., 1901-05, Scott St. Ch., Covington, Ky., 1905-06, Crawford St. Ch., Vicksburg, Miss., 1906-10, 25th Av. Ch., Gulfport, Miss., 1910-11, Noel Memorial Ch., Shreveport, La., 1910-11, Rayne Memorial Ch., New Orleans, La., 1912-16, Laurel Heights Ch., San Antonio, Tex., 1916-18; presiding elder, San Antonio Dist., 1918-20; pres. Westmoorland Coll., San Antonio, 1920-23; pastor Hyde Park Ch., Tampa, Fla., 1923-24, St. John's Ch., Memphis, Tenn., 1924-25, Union Av. Ch., Memphis, 1925-27; presiding elder Memphis Dist., 1927-31, Jacksonville Dist. 1931-35; pastor Hyde Park Ch., Tampa, Fla., 1935-37, First Ch., Clearwater, Fla., 1937-39; retired, June 10, 1939. Del. Meth. Ecumenical Conf., London 1921, Atlanta, 1931; mem. Gen. Conf. M.E. Ch. S., 1930. Mem. Chi Phi. Democrat. Mason (K.T., Shriner). Home: 935 S. Oregon Av., Tampa FL‡

HILL, (CHARLES) FRANCIS, author; b. Phila., Pa., June 30, 1875; s. William Henry and Fannie (Fithian) H.; ed. pub. schs. and under pvt. tutors. Club: Franklin Inn. Author: The Outlaws of Horseshoe Hole, 1901; Once on the Summer Range, 1918. Co-Author: Genius and the Crowd (comedy produced 1920). Contbr. short stories, plays and verse. Home: 2125 N. 17th St., Philadelphia PA‡

HILL, FRANK ERNEST, writer; b. San Jose, California, August 29, 1888; s. Andrew P. and Florence (Watkins) H.; A.B., Stanford U., 1911, A.M., 1914; m. Elsa Hempl, 1915 (divorced 1936); children—Russell, Anabel; m. 2d, Ruth Arnold Nickel, May 27, 1938. Asst. in English, U. of Ill., 1912-13; instr. English, Stanford U., 1913-16; in Extension Dept., Columbia, 1916-17; editorial writer N.Y. Globe and Commercial Advertiser, 1920-23, N.Y. Sun, 1923-25; lit. editor The Sun, 1925; editor in chief Longmans, Green & Co., 1925-31; writer and research worker, 1931-69. Democrat. Unitarian. Author and editor various books, including: The Winged Horse and Winged Horse Anthology (with J. Auslander) 1927, 29; trans. Chaucer's Canterbury Tales, 1930, 36; To Meet Will Shakespeare, 1949; (with Bob Allison) The Kid Who Batted 1,000, 1951; (with A. Nevins) Ford: the Times, the Man, the Company, 1954, Ford: Expansion and Challenge, 1915-33, 1957; Ford; Decline and Rebirth, 1963; The World of Wood, 1965; Famous Historians, 1966; The Automobile, 1967. Address: NYC NY Died Nov. 2, 1969.

HILL, FREDERICK THAYER, physician; b. Waterville, Me., June 14, 1889; s. James Frederick and Angie (Foster) H.; B.S., Colby Coll., Waterville, Me., 1910, D.Sc., 1936; M.D., Harvard, 1914; D.Sc. (honorary) University of Maine, 1942; m. Ruby Winchester Choate, June 16, 1924; children—Virginia, Barbara, Joan, Marjorie. Resident in otolaryngology, Mass. Eye and Ear Infirmary, Boston, Mass., 1915-16, mem. staff, 1919-20; engaged in pvt. practice as otolaryngologist, Waterville, Me., from 1920; mem. staff Sisters Hosp. (Waterville), 1920-30; mem. staff Thayer Hosp. since 1930; mem. cons. staff Central Maine Gen. Hosp., St. Marie's Hosp. (Lewiston), Augusta (Me.) Gen. Hosp., Gardiner (Me.) Gen. Hosp., Redington Hosp. (Skowhegan), Knox County Hosp. (Rockland), Waldo County Hosp. (Belfast), Miles Memorial Hosp. (Damariscotta), St. Andrews Hosp. (Boothbay Harbor), Central Maine Sanatorium (Tb); v.p. planning and devel. Trayer Hospital; member consulting staff, Bath Memorial Hospital, Franklin Co. Hosp., Farmington, U.S. V.A. Hosp. Togus. Served as lt. Med. Corps, U.S. Army, 1918-19; instr. Army Sch. of Otolaryngology, Gen. Hosp. No. 14. Mem. Council for Health and Welfare, State of Maine; chmn. Me. Adv. Hosp. Commn. Dir. Am. Bd. Otolaryngology (pres., 1953-54); past mem. Federal Hospital Council; past president of Me. Hosp. Assn.; mem. bd. of directors Me. Heart Assn. Former trustee Colby Coll. Recipient Newcomen award American Laryngological Association, 1953, Roaldes award, 1961; received Roselle W. Huddilston award Me. Tb Association. Fellow A.C.S., Am. College of Hospital Administrators (hon.); mem. Am. Laryngol. Assn. (pres. 1948), Internat. Congress Otolaryngology (treas. 1957), Me. Med. Assn. (past pres.), New England Otolaryngol. Soc. (past pres.), Am. Otol. Soc. (pres. 1953), N.E. Hospital Assembly (pres. 1953), Am. Laryngol., Rhinol. and Otol. Soc., Am. Broncho-Esophol. Assn., American Academy of Ophthalmology and Otolaryngology (1st v.p. 1961), Am. Coll. Chest Physicians, Am. Cancer Soc., Zeta Psi, Alpha Kappa Kappa, Mason (33 deg.), Rotarian. Club: Harvard (Boston). Mem. editorial bd. Annals of Otology, Rhinology and Laryngology. Contbr. to Military Surgical Manual, Otolaryngology, 1942; also numerous articles to professional jours. and med. publs. Home: Waterville ME Died April 1969.

HILL, HARRY W., naval officer; b. Oakland, Calif., Apr. 7, 1890; s. John Clayton and Ida Belle (Miller) H.; B.S., U.S. Naval Acad., 1911; grad. Army Chem. Warfare Sch., 1923, Navy War Coll., 1938; m. Margaret Harwood Hall, Oct. 8, 1913; children—Elizabeth Stockett, John Clayton (capt. USN ret.). Commissioned ensign, United States Navy, 1912, and advanced through grades to 4 star admiral, 1952; commanded U.S.S. Wichita, February 1942, serving in North Atlantic, Marmansk convoy, and with British Home Fleet. Commanded naval task force in South Pacific area, November 1942-Sept. 1943. Ordered to command Amphibious Group 2, U.S. Pacific Fleet, Sept. 1943; comd. assault and capture of Tarawa Atoll, Nov. 1943, and occupation of Apamama Atoll, Gilbert Islands, Nov.-Dec. 1943; comd. occupation force at Majuro Atoll, Marshall Islands, Jan. 31, 1944, where first American flag to fly over pre-war Japanese territory was hoisted. Comd. force which assaulted and captured Eniwetok Atoll, Marshall Islands, Feb. 17-22, 1944. Second in command of assault force which captured Saipan, Marianas Islands, June 15-July 9, 1944. In command of assault force which captured Tinian, Marianas Islands, July 24-Aug. 1, 1944. Second in command Assault Force, Iwo Jima, February-March, 1945. Promoted to vice admiral in command Fifth Amphibious Force, April 1945. In comd. Amphibious Force, Okinawa, May 17-July 1, 1945; in occupation of southwestern Japan, September-October 1945. Founder, comdt. National War College, Washington, 1946-49. Member United States Canadian Permanent Joint Bd. on Defense, 1940-42. Superintendent U.S. Naval Academy, 1950-52; gov. Naval Home, 1952-54. Bd. dirs. Hammond-Harwood House. Decorations: Distinguished Service Medal with Gold Stars in lieu of second and third award, Russian Order of Kutozov (2d Class), British Distinguished Service Order, Companion of the Order of the Bath (Great Britain); Legion of Honor (France). Campaign medals: Mexican, First Nicaraguan, American Defense, American Area, European Area, Asiatic-Pacific Area; expert pistol medal; mem. Helms Hall of Fame for basketball. Mem. Historic Annapolis, Potomac Chrysanthemum Soc. Episcopalian. Clubs: Army and Navy (Washington, D.C.); South River, Annapolis Yacht. Author: Maryland's Colonial Charm Portrayed in Silver, 1938. Home: Annapolis MD Died July 19, 1971; buried U.S. Naval Acad. Cemetery.

HILL, IRVING, banker, mfr.; b. Neodesha, Kan., Dec. 23, 1876; s. William and Ellen Clark (Maxwell) H.; A.B., U. of Kan., 1896; m. Hortense MacDonald Bowersock, Oct. 17, 1899; children—Margaret Maxwell (Mrs. Olaf Randal), Mary Gower (dec.), Justin De Witt, Ellen Elspeth (Mrs. Louis W. Coghill), Dorcas (dec.). Began as teacher and oil and gas producer, 1897-98; with J. D. Bowersock, manufacturer, Lawrence, 1899; president Lawrence Electric Co., 1906-15; pres. Lawrence Nat. Bank since 1922; pres. Griffin Ice Co., 1922-28; pres. Lawrence Paper Mfg. Co.; dir. Union Nat. Bank, Kansas City, Mo.; trustee J. D. Bowersock Trust, M. G. Bowersock Trust. Mem. advisory committee of Office of Production Management for all paper converting industries, World War II. Postmaster, Lawrence, 1906-10; pres. Board of Edn., Lawrence, since 1921. Trustee U. of Kan. Physical Edn. Corp., U. of Kan. Endowment Assn., Midwest Research Inst., Kansas City, Mo.; pres. U. of Kan. Memorial Corp. Chmn. County Bond Drives World War I and II. Mem. Beta Theta Pi. Republican. Clubs: Lawrence Country, Old and New Club. Home: W. 8th St. Lawrence KS‡

HILL, JOHN GODFREY, coll. prof.; b. Philipstad, Sweden, Jan. 7, 1870; s. August Stinneus and Carolina (Nyberg) H.; brought to U.S., 1875; A.B., Cornell Coll., Mt. Vernon, Ia., 1900, A.M., 1902; D.D., 1918; S.T.B., Boston U., 1905, Ph.D., 1914; honorary L.H.D., University of Southern Calif., 1943; studied Harvard and U. of Chicago; m. Ellen Clara Meyer, 1889; m. 2d, Jessie Elder Wright, June 1941. Began as grocery clerk, 1888, later live stock raiser and buyer, and real estate agent; professor Biblical literature, University of Southern Calif., since Sept. 1907. Mem. Religious Education Association, Am. School of Oriental Research League of Western Writers, California Writers' Guild, The Authors League of America, Theta Phi, Phi Beta Kappa, Phi Chi Phi, Phi Kappa Phi, Pi Gamma Pi, Pi Epsilon Theta, Theta Phi; member, lecturer of Southern California Academy of Sciences. Methodist, del. to General Conference, 1929; member Board of Sunday Schools. Author: The Prophets in the Light of Today, 1919; Christianity for Today, 1924; An Everyday Christian; series of articles in current issues of The Christian Advocate, Browsing in the Old Testament". Home: 3519 W. Vernon Av., Los Angeles 43 CA‡

HILL, JOSEPH KNOERLE, univ. adminstr.; b. Springfield, Mo., Nov. 6, 1918; s. Clyde Milton and Doris (Knoerle) H.; A.B., Dartmouth, 1941; M.S., Yale, 1942, Ph.D., 1949; D.Sc. (hon.), L.I.U., 1967; m. Jean Lee Lichty, Sept. 12, 1942; children—Laurinda Lee, Joseph Knoerle. Instr. pub. health Yale Sch. Medicine, 1949-51; lectr. edn. and pub. health Yale, 1951-53; asso. prof. So. Conn. State Coll., 1951-52; asst. to dean, asst. prof. pub. health and preventive medicine Coll. Medicine in Syracuse, State U. N.Y., 1953-56; exec. asst. to pres., exec. sec. Downstate Med. Center, State U. N.Y., 1956-63, v.p. adminstrn., asso. prof. adminstrn., 1963-66, pres., dean Coll. Medicine, 1966-71. Served with AUS, 1942-46; PTO. Clubs: Morys Assn. (Yale); Dartmouth, Yale (N.Y.C.); Pine Orchard (Branford, Conn.). Devel. total computor information system for hospitals, computer assisted admission program for med. schs. Home: Brooklyn NY Died Apr. 19, 1971.

HILL, JOSEPH MORRISON, judge; b. Davidson Coll., N.C., Sept. 2, 1864; s. Daniel Harvey and Isabella (Morrison) H.; student U. of Ark., LL.D., 1931; LL.B., Lebanon (Tenn.) Law Sch., 1883; M. Kate Reynolds, Nov. 19, 1890 children—Martha (Mrs. David R. Williams), Isabel Preston (Mrs. John C. Hill). Admitted to bar, 1883; practiced at Eureka Springs and Ft. Smith, Ark., 1883-1904; chief justice Supreme Court of Ark., Nov. 1, 1904-Feb. 1, 1909 (resigned); chief counsel for the state of Ark. In the railroad rate cases" (cases won for state in Supreme Court U.S., June 1913); chief counsel for state of Ark. in Memphis, Southwestern rate investigation before Interstate Commerce Commn., 1921; served as spl. master in case of State of Okla. vs. State of Tex., 1925; spl. counsel for State in litigation over taxation of Railroads in Bankruptcy, won for State in Supreme Court of U.S., 1941. Chmn. Ark. Construction Commn., 1929-34. Pres. trustees State Tuberculosis Sanatorium, 1909-41, and since 1945. Mem. Dist. Exemption Bd., Western Ark., 1918. Chmn. State Dem. Conv., 1920. Presbyn. Democrat. A compiler of Sandels and Hill's Digest of the Statutes of Arkansas, 1894. Office: Merchants Nat. Bank Bldg., Ft Smith AR*‡

HILL, KNUTE, ex-congressman; b. Creston, Ill., July 31, 1876; s. Rev. Rasmus Ole and Martha (Govig) H.; prep. edn., Red Wing (Minn.) Sem., student U. of Minn., 1903-05; LL.B., U. of Wis., 1906; m. Helen Jensen, June 30, 1908 (died Aug. 2, 1936). In practice of law, Milwaukee and Eau Claire, Wis., 1908-10; teacher pub. schs., Benton County, Wash., 1911-28, prin. Jr. and Sr. High Sch., Prosser, Wash., 1912-28; supt. schs., Benton City, Wash., 1921-22; teacher Grandview (Wash.) High Sch., 1929-30. Lecturer, Wash. State Grange, 1922-23, 1931-32. Mem. Wash. Ho. of Rep., 1927-31; mem. 73d to 77th Congresses (1933-43), 4th Wash. Dist.; supt. Uintah-Ouray Indian Agency, Ft. Duchesne, Utah, 1943; now farm commentator, KGA Radio Station, Spokane. Democrat. Mason; mem. O.E.S., Grange. Club: Current Opinion (Prosser). Address: Ft Duchesne UT‡

HILL, MOZELL CLARENCE, educator; b. Anniston, Ala., Mar. 27, 1911; s. Humphrey and Anna (Taylor) H.; A.B., U. Kan., 1933, M.A., 1937; Ph.D., U. Chgo., 1946; postgrad. London Sch. Econs., 1952-53; m. Marnesba Davis, May 5, 1935; children—Suzanne (Mrs. Oliver O. Slocum, Jr.), Marnesba, Patricia, Stephanie. Instr., Langston U., 1937-40, asst. prof., dir. research, 1940-42, chmn. dept. sociology, prof., 1942-46; prof. sociology Atlanta U., 1946-48, chmn. dept. sociology, editor Phylon, 1948-58; prof. sociology of edn. Tchrs. Coll. Columbia, 1958-62; prof. ednl. sociology N.Y. U., 1963-69; U.S. AID adviser U. Nigeria, Nsukka, 1960-62; dir. Planning Grant Project on Juvenile Delinquency Control, St. Louis, 1962-63; cons. sociologist Bd. Edn., Norwalk, Conn., 1964-69; tech. specialist U.S. Office Edn., 1965-69; cons. personnel selection Bd. Edn., Phila., 1965-66. Mem. Am. Sociol. Assn., So. Sociol. Soc. (past v.p.), N.Y. Acad. Sci., Nat. Council Student YM-YWCA's, Nat. Assn. Intergroup Relations Officers, Alpha Kappa Delta, Kappa Alpha Psi. Author: Culture of the Contemporary Community, 1943. Home: NYC NY Died Mar. 26, 1969.

HILL, NORMAN STEWART, investment banker; b. Cin., Aug. 14, 1889; s. Alfred and Madge (Martin) H.; student Miami U., Oxford, O., 1909-10; m. Elizabeth Alexander, Dec. 1, 1921; 1 son, Dr. Norman A. Mem. Hill & Co., investment bankers, Cin. Clubs: Cincinnati Country, Bankers, Coldstream Country (Cin.). Home: Cincinnati OH Died June 4, 1972.

HILL, REESE FRANKLIN, ins. co. exec.; b. Anderson, S.C., Dec. 10, 1908; s. George Roy and Annie L. (Holbrooks) H.; B.S., The Citadel, 1930; m. R. LaVieve Richards, Jan. 22, 1931; children—Reese Franklin, Adrienne LaVieve (Mrs. David H. Umlauf). With Fidelity & Casualty Co. N.Y., 1930-40, br. office asst. mgr., 1938-40; exec. asst. to pres., also v.p. Am. Casualty Co., 1946-49; pres., dir. Carolina Casualty Ins. Co., 1949-51; sr. v.p. charge casualty and bonding operations Crum & Foster Group Ins. Companies, 1951-69, also dir.; sr. v.p., dir. Westchester Fire Ins. Co., 1960-69, Internat. Ins. Co., 1960-69, N. River Ins. Co., 1960-69; sr. v.p. U.S. Fire Ins. Co., 1960-69, also dir.; dir. American Eagle Life Ins. Company. Ins. adv. bd. sec. def., 1950-53; exec. com. Assn. Casualty and Surety Execs., 1959-69. Served to col. AUS, 1940-46. Decorated Legion of Merit. Mem. Short Hills NJ Died Mar. 19, 1969.

HILL, WILLIAM H., ex-congressman; b. Plains, Pa., Mar. 23, 1877; s. Rev. William J. (D.D.) and Elizabeth (Sowden) H.; ed. high sch., Binghamton, N.Y.; LL.D., Syracuse U.; m. Maude Evelyn Johnson, Apr. 23, 1902 (died 1915); children—Richard, Dorothy; m. 2d, Anne Sands. Pres. Johnson City Pub. Co., Inc. Mayor, Lestershire (now Johnson City), 1898-1901; postmaster, 1902-10; mem. N.Y. Senate, 1914-18; mem. 66th Congress (1919-21); 34th N.Y. Dist.; apptd. by Gov. Alfred E. Smith, mem. Central N.Y. State Parks Commn., 1925, chmn., 1933; del. Rep. Nat. Conv., 1924, 28, 40, 44, 48, 52, 56, 60, del-at-large. 1932; chmn. N.Y. Hoover-for-Pres. Com., 1938; vice chmn. Rep. Campaign Com. in East, 1932. Trustee Syracuse Univ. Methodist. Mason, Odd Fellow. Mem. Nat. Republican Club (N.Y.). Home: Johnson City NY Died July 24, 1972.

HILL, WILLIAM SILAS, congressman; b. Kelley, Kan., Jan. 20, 1886; s. Squire C. and Mary Francis (Longley) H.; student Chillicothe (Mo.) Business Coll., 1903-04, Kansas State Normal Sch., summer 1904; spl. course Colo. Agrl. Coll., 1915, 16, 17; m. Rachel Trower, Mar. 25, 1907; children—Alden Trower, Marjorie Anita (Mrs. Louis E. Hunter). Rural sch. teacher, 1905-19; county agent agrl. work, 1919-23; engaged in real estate, 1923-27; owner Standard Mercantile Co. since 1927. Mem. Colo. State Legislature, 1924-28; sec. to Gov. Carr of Colo., 1939; mem. 77th to 85th Congresses, from 2d Colorado Dist.

Mem. Fort Collins Chamber of Commerce (mem. bd. 2 yrs.). Republican. Presbyterian. Elk, I.O.O.F. Club: Rotary. Contbr. to farm mags. and agrl. publs. Home: Fort Collins CO Died Aug. 28, 1972.

HILLEARY, EDGAR D., ry. official; b. Petersville, Md., Sept. 10, 1877; s. John W. and Elizabeth L. H.; student St. John's Coll., Annapolis, Md., 1892-97; m. Miss N. T. Finch, of Newport, R.I., 1903; children—Elizabeth L., Virginia E. Began, 1897, as clk. P. & R. Ry.; agt. Central States Despatch, Phila., 1905-06; again with P. & R. Ry., successively as div. freight agt., at Phila., 1906-10, at Harrisburg, Pa., 1910-18, asst. gen. freight agt., Phila., 1918-20, gen. freight agt., 1920-21, freights traffic mgr., 1921-23, v.p. in charge of freight traffic, 1923-32, v.p. in charge traffic since 1932; also v.p. Central R.R. of N.J., 1933-38 and v.p. in charge traffic Wharton & Northern R.R., 1935-38; retired on account of health, Dec. 31, 1938. Home: Madison CT‡

HILLES, FREDERICK VANTYNE HOLBROOK, ret. naval officer; b. Chgo., Apr. 18, 1908; s. John Adolphus and Grace (Holbrook) H.; B.S. in Elec. Engring., U.S. Naval Acad., 1930; student U.S. Naval Postgrad. Sch., 1937-38, U.S. Naval War Coll., 1948-49; m. Genevieve McKinley Brown, Dec. 19, 1934; 1 dau., Genevieve Diane (Mrs. Jack D. Clay). Commd. ensign U.S. Navy, 1930, advanced through grades to rear adm., 1958; assigned battleship U.S.S. Idaho, 1930-32, destroyers U.S.S. Hamilton, 1932-33, U.S.S. Barry, 1933-34, ammunition ship U.S.S. Nitro, 1934-35, light cruiser U.S.S. Omaha, 1935-37, destroyers U.S.S. Balch, 1939-41, U.S.S. Maury, 1941-42; comdg. officer destroyer U.S.S. Putnam, 1944-45; comdr. Destroyer Div. 132, 1945-46, gunnery officer 2d Fleet, 1949-51; comdg. officer attach transp. U.S.S. Calvert, 1954-55; comdr. Transp. Div. 52, 1955-56, Amphibious Squadron 5, 1956, Destroyer Flotilla 4, 1960-61; dir. strike warfare div. Office Chief Naval Operations, 1958-60; asst. chief Bur. Naval Weapons (astronautics), 1962; chmn. ship, characteristics bd. Office Chief Naval Operations, 1962-64, comdr. mil. sea transp. service Pacific aera, 1964-65, ret., 1965. Mem. exec. bd. San Francisco Bay Area council Boy Scouts Am., also chmn. sea explorer com. Decorated Bronze Star with V, numerous area and unit ribbons; Navy Legion of Merit. Mem. of the Am. Ordnance Assn., U.S. Naval Acad. Alumni Assn. (trustee 1959-62), U.S. Naval Inst., Nat. Geog. Soc. Episcopalian. Clubs: Propeller (Annapolis, Md.); Army-Navy Country (Arlington, Va.); Commonwealth of California (San Francisco). Author naval manual. Home: San Francisco CA Died Apr. 16, 1969; buried Arlington National Cemetery, Arlington VA

HILLIARD, BENJAMIN CLARK, JR., lawyer; b. Denver, Aug. 30, 1898; s. Benjamin Clark and Tida Elizabeth (Zimmerman) H.; student State U. of Ia., 1916-17; LL.B., George Washington U., 1922; m. Dorothy Lee Weichel; children—Melissa Ann, Albert Weichel, Cynthia Jean. Admitted to D.C. bar, 1922, Colo., 1923, private practice law, Denver, 1923-53; member Moffat Tunnel Commn., 1936-37; pub. adminstr. City and County of Denver, 1937-1951; spl. asst. U.S. Atty. Gen., 1940-46; referee in bankruptcy Dist. Colo., 1953-69. Trustee, Westminster Law School Foundation. Served with U.S. Army, World War I. Mem. Denver, Am. Colo. bar assns., Am. Legion (past dept. comdr.; twice mem. nat. executive com.), 40 et 8 (chef de chemin de fer, 1941), S.A.R. (past pres. Colo. sect.). Episcopalian. Mason. Club: Democratic (Denver). Home: Denver CO Died June 18, 1969; inurned All Souls Walk St. John's Episcopal Cathedral Denver CO

HILLIARD, CURTIS MORRISON, prof. biology and pub. health; b. Dorchester, Mass., Aug. 5, 1887; s. Aubrey and Anna G. (Morrison) H.; prep. edn., Chauncey Hall Sch., Boston; A.B., Dartmouth, 1909; grad. study, Mass. Inst. Tech., 1909-10; m. Helen A. Nixon, June 30, 1914; children—Albert N., Elizabeth. Instr. in biology, Coll. City N.Y., 1910-12; asst. prof. sanitary science, Purdue, 1912-14; asso. prof. and head of dept. biology and health, Simmons Coll., Boston, 1914-18, prof. 1918-52; emeritus prof. biol. and pub. health, 1952, Supervisor bds. of health of Wellesley, Needham and Weston, Mass. Director Moseley Health Fund, Newburyport, Mass., since 1937; dir. Boston and Wellesley chapters Am. Red Cross, chmn. Health Edn. Com.; dir. health div. Mass. Com. Pub. Safety, 1941-44; consultant field training Mass. Dept. Pub. Health from 1950; dir. Nat. Tuberculosis Assn. from 1948. Served as first lieutenant Sanitary Corps, United States Army, 1918-19. Member administrative committee Massachusetts Civic League, executive committee Massachusetts Central Health Council (ex-pres.); vice pres., Mass. Tuberculosis League, 1945. Fellow Am. Pub. Health Assn., A.A.A.S.; mem. Soc. Am. Bacteriologist, Mass. Pub. Health Assn. (ex. pres.), Lemuel Shattuck Medal for Outstanding Service Pub. Health, N.E., Sigma Nu, Sigma Psi, Delta Omega. Mem. Governor's Commn. to Study Health Practice, Mass., 1935. Republican. Unitarian. Author: Bacteriology and its Application, 1928; Prevention of Disease in the Community, 1931. Home: Wellesley Hills MA Died May 14, 1969.

HILLIARD, ISAAC, stock and bond broker; b. Louisville, Oct. 10, 1879; s. John James Byron and Maria Louisa (Henning) H.; grad. Lawrenceville Sch., 1898; A.B., Princeton, 1902; m. Helen Cochran Donigan, Nov. 1, 1910 (dec. 1932); children—Helen (Mrs. Peter E. Spalding, Jr.), James Henning; m. 2d, Elizabeth Haldeman Campbell, June 15, 1934 (dec. 1955). With J.J.B. Hilliard & Son (now J.J.B. Hilliard, W.L. Lyons & Company), Louisville, 1901-70, sr. partner, member Midwest Stock Exchange, 1905-70; past dir. Citizens Union Nat. Bank, Louisville Cement Co., Stearns Coal and Lumber Co., Ohio River Sand Co. Commnr., Jefferson County, 1933-35. Served to capt. U.S. Army, World War I. Clubs: Louisville Country, Pendennis, River Valley (Louisville). Home: Louisville KY Died May 16, 1970.

HILLINGER, RAYMOND PETER, clergyman; b. Chgo., May 2, 1904; s. Peter Leonard and Mary (Neuses) H.; grad. Quigley Prep. Sem., Chgo.; St. Mary of the Lake Sem., Mundelein, Ill. Ordained to priesthood, Roman Cath. Ch., 1932; asst., St. Aloysius Parish, Chgo., 1932-35; missionary Chgo. Archdiocesan Mission Band, 1935-50; rector Angel Guardian Orphanage, 1950-53; bishop of Rockford, 1953-56; auxiliary bishop to Cardinal Stritch, 1956, Cardinal Meyer, Cardinal Cody. Home: Chicago IL Died Nov. 12, 1971; buried All Saints Cemetery, Des Plaines IL

HILLMAN, ALEX L., investment exec.; b. Chgo., Sept. 16, 1900; s. Isaac and Essie (Rose) H.; Ph.B., U. Chgo., 1922; LL.D., Pacific U., 1950; m. Rita Kanarek, Aug. 23, 1932; children—Richard A. (dec.), Alex L. (adopted). Consulate, Shanghai, China, 1923; editor Shanghai Press, 1924-25; pres. William Godwin, Inc., book pubs., N.Y.C., 1927-31; founder, pres. Hillman-Curl, Inc., book pubs., N.Y.C. and Los Angeles, 1931-38; pres. Hillman Periodicals, 1938-61; pub. Pageant Mag. 1944-61, People Today Mag. 1951-61; treasurer The Freeman Magazine, 1952; director Title Guaranty & Trust Company, Warner Bros./Seven Arts. Special consultant, senate appropriations com. 80th and 83d U.S. Congresses, U.S. Dept. State, Senate Republican Policy Com., 1948-61; spl. observer Italian elections, 1948. Mem. art adv. group Dartmouth Council on Creative Arts; mem. vis. com. art dept. Fogg Mus., Harvard. Trustee Pacific U., 1947-52, Izaac Hillman Meml. Fellowship (U. Chgo.), Hist. Research Found. Recipient Freedoms Found. award, 1950; Alumni citation U. Chgo., 1964. Home: New York City NY Died Mar. 25, 1968; buried Kensico Cemetery, Valhalla NY

HILLMAN, JAMES FRAZER, business exec.; b. Pitts., Oct. 10, 1888; s. John Hartwell and Sallie Murfree (Frazer) H.; B.S., Yale, 1912; Doctor of Laws, University of Pitts., 1965; m. Marguerite Cabell Wright, Nov. 25, 1914; children—Constance Cabell (Mrs. John Oliver, Jr.), Marguerite (Mrs. Richard Purnell), Audrey (Mrs. Thomas Hilliard, Jr.), Sally Frazer (Mrs. J. Mabon Childs). Pres., dir. Harmon Creek Coal Corp. and affiliates since 1934; trustee Dollar Savs. Bank, Pittsburgh, Pa., director of Pitts. Chmn. Allegheny Conf. Community Development, 1950-52; pres. Pitts. Park and Playground Soc.; trustee Carnegie Inst.; dir. Civic Light Opera Assn.; vice president of Carnegie Library; mem. fine arts com. Carnegie Mus.; mem. adv. com. Home Crippled Children. Served as capt. inf., 82d Div. U.S. Army, 1918-19. Mem. Pitts. C. of C., Chi Phi. Episcopalian (trustee Pitts. diocese). Clubs: Duquesne, Pittsburgh Golf, Rolling Rock, Fox Chapel Golf, Elizabethan. Home: Pittsburgh PA Died May 1972; buried Homewood Cemetery, Pittsburgh PA

HILLMAN, JOHN WILLIAM, orthopaedic surgeon; b. Dante, Va., Jan. 9, 1921; s. Rolfe L. and Edith H.; M.D., Johns Hopkins U., 1945; m. Virginia Swindler, 1949; children—Ellen (Mrs. Horace Moore), Mary (Mrs. Michael Trueblood), Jayne, Nancy. Intern, Johns Hopkins Hosp., Balt., 1945-46, asst. resident and resident orthopaedic surgeon, 1948-51; visiting orthopaedic surgeon Vanderbilt Hosp., Nashville. Instr. orthopaedic surgery Johns Hopkins U., 1951-52, asst. prof Vanderbilt U., Nashville, 1952-54, asso. prof., 1954-58, prof., 1958-70, chmn. dept., 1962-70. Cons. orthopaedic surgeon Tenn. Crippled Children's Service, Nashville, 1952-70, Ft. Campbell Hosp., 1964, Thayer VA Hosp., Nashville, Sewart AFB, Tenn., 1958-64, Alaska Crippled Children's Com., 1963-66, Am. Bd. Prosthetics and Orthotics, 1967-70; chmn. med. adv. com. Medicenter, Nashville; med. adv. Bd. Edn. Film Prodn.; chmn. profl. services program com. United Cerebral Palsy Assns.; mem. Gov.'s Com. On Employment of the Handicapped; pres. med. staff Jr. League Home for Crippled Children, 1962-63; sci. program com. 3rd, 4th Internat. Confs. on Congenital Malformations. Bd. dirs. Bill Wilkerson Hearing and Speech Center, 1962-70, med. staff, 1958-70; exec. com. Tenn. Council for Handicapped Children, 1962-65, Mid-Cumberland Region Health Planning Council, 1968-70. Diplomate Am. Bd. Orthopaedic Surgeons (dir.). Fellow A.M.A. (orthopaedic residency review com., 1963-70), So. Med. Assn., Am. Coll. Surgeons, Am. Acad. Orthopaedic Surgeons (chmn. rehab. com. 1966-68); mem. Am. Orthopaedic Assn., Tenn., Nashville-Davidson County med. assns., Tenn. Orthopaedic Soc., Am. Acad. Cerebral Palsy (pres. 1969), Clin. Orthopaedic Soc., Internat. Soc. Orthopaedic Surgery and Traumatology, Orthopaedic Research Soc., Am. Assn. Rehabilitation Facilities, Soc. Med. Cons. Armed Forces, Internat. Soc. Rehab. of Disabled, A.A.A.S., Nashville Surgical Soc. (pres. 1968), Nat. Acad. Scis., Am. Physical Therapy Assn. (adv. bd.), World Commn. Cerebral Palsy, Volunteer State Rehab. Assn., Johns Hopkins Tenn. Alumni Assn., Sigma Xi; asso. mem. Am. Acad. Neurology. Asso. editor Jour. Bone and Joint Surgery, 1962-64. Home: Nashville TN Died Mar. 7, 1970; buried Emory VA

HILLS, JOSEPH LAWRENCE, univ. dean; b. Boston, Mass., Mar. 2, 1861; s. Thomas and Amelia Ellen (Drew) H.; B.S., Mass. Agrl. Coll. (now Univ. of Mass.), 1881; B.S., Boston U., 1881; post-grad., Mass. Agrl. Coll., 1881-84; D.Sc. (hon.), Rutgers, 1903, Mass. State Coll., 1931; R.I. State Coll. of A. and M. Arts, 1942, Vt., 1943; m. Kate Conover, Sept. 1888 (dec.). Asst. chemist, Mass. Agrl. Expt. Sta., Amherst, 1882-83, N.J. Agrl. Expt. Sta., New Brunswick, 1884-85; chemist Phosphate Mining Co., Ltd., Beaufort, S.C., 1885-88; chemist, 1888-98, dir., Vt. Agrl. Expt. Sta., 1893-42, emeritus since 1942, prof. agronomy, U. of Vt., 1893-1933, dean, Coll. of Agr. same, 1898-42, emeritus since 1942. Mem. Assn. Land-Grant Colleges and Universities (sec.-treas. 1904-27; pres. 1928); fellow A.A.A.S.; mem. Soc. Colonial Wars, Kappa Sigma, Alpha Zeta, Phi Kappa Phi, Sigma Xi. Episcopalian. Republican. Home: Burlington VT‡

HILMER, WILLIAM CHARLES, college prof.; b. Reinbeck, Ia., May 11, 1871; s. Frederick H. and Aletta S. (Werner) H.; A.B., Baldwin-Wallace Coll., Berea, O., 1899, A.M., 1903; Ph.D., U. of Ill., 1910; m. Emma E. Schmidt, of Charles City, Ia., Oct. 3, 1894. Teacher modern langs., Upper Ia. U., 1900-6; asst. same, U. of Ill., 1906-8; instr. German, Oberlin Coll., 1908-10; asso. prof. German, Ohio Wesleyan U., 1910-14; pres. Charles City (Ia.) Coll., 1914, until its amalgamation, same yr., with Morningside Coll., of which is v.-p. and prof. German lit. Mem. Modern Lang. Assn. America. Republican. Methodist. Club: Crucible. Author: The Rime in Schiller's Poems, 1911. Address: Morningside Coll., Sioux City IA‡

HILTON, HUGH GERALD, steel exec.; b. Strathroy, Ont., Can., Mar. 31, 1889; s. James R. and Harriet Emily (Smythe) H.; B.S., Case Sch. Applied Sci., 1910; m. Ethel Carlson, Dec. 14, 1918; children—Harriet (Mrs. Henry Sprague), Charles C. Blast furnace operating dept. Pickands Mather & Co., Cleveland, 1910-19; asst. blast furnace supt. Steel Co. of Can., Ltd., Hamilton, Ont., 1919, successively blast furnace supt., asst. works mgr., works mgr. Hamilton Works, Steel Co. of Can., Ltd., 1934-37, v.p., 1937-43, dir., 1941-66, exec. v.p., 1943-45, pres. 1945-57, chief exec. officer, 1957-60, chmn. bd., 1960-66, chairman exec. com. of board of directors, 1966; dir. Toronto, Hamilton & Buffalo Railway, Canadian Gen. Electric Co. Mem. Am. Iron and Steel Inst., Brit. Iron and Steel Inst., Am. Inst. Mining Metall. and Petroleum Engrs., Kappa Sigma, Sigma Psi. Clubs: Hamilton Ontario Canada Died Nov. 18, 1966.

HIMLER, LEONARD E., neuropsychiatrist; b. Chicago, Ill., Feb. 6, 1904; s. Leonard M. and Ida (Thimming) H.; A.B., Univ. of Mich., 1928, M.D., 1931; m. Ila Branson, Sept. 29, 1934; 1 dau., Susan Eve. Interne and resident, Univ. Hosp., Ann Arbor, Mich., 1931-33; instr. in neurology, Univ. of Mich. Med. Sch., 1933-35; asst. psychiatrist, Mental Hygiene Unit of Univ. of Mich. Health Service, 1935-38, asso. psychiatrist, 1938-44; asso. staff of State Psychopathic Hosp. and other state hospitals in Mich., 1933-39; asst. prof. mental Health, Sch. Pub. Health, U. of Mich., 1941-48, asso. prof. 1949; cons. psychiatry to bur. of psychol. services of Univ. of Mich. and Gen. Motors Corp., Detroit, Mich., 1942-48; mem. Nat. faculty in psychiatry, 1942-45; pvt. and institutional practice of neuropsychiatry, consultant in indl. psychiatry, lecturer and teacher in psychiatry and mental hygiene, from 1938; chief of staff Mercywood Neuropsychiatric Hospital. Diplomate American Bd. of Psychiatry and Neurology. Fellow Am. Psychiatric Assn. (chmn. com. on indsl. psychiatry, 1947-50); mem. American Medical Association, Group for Advancement of Psychiatry, Mich. State Med. Soc., Mich. Soc. Neurology and Psychiatry (pres. 1951-52), Internat. League against Epilepsy (past v.p.), Am. Assn. Indsl. Physicians and Surgs., Mich. Soc. for Mental Hygiene (bd. dirs., 1946-49), Central Neuropsychiatric Assn., Am. Acad. Neurology, Phi Chi, Delta Omega. Editor: Notes on Dr. Camp's Lectures in Neurology, 1934, 1938. Contbr. about 15 articles to professional jours. on neurology, psychiatry and mental hygiene; numerous articles on indsl. psychiatry and psychology. Home: Ann Arbor MI Died Apr. 30, 1967; interred Washtenong Meml. Mausoleum, Ann Arbor MI

HIMSWORTH, WINSTON E., gas co. exec.; b. Astoria, N.Y., 1912; ed. Lehigh U., 1934. Vice pres. Bklyn. Union Gas Co. Home: Staten Island NY Died Dec. 25, 1970.

HINDERLIDER, MICHAEL CREED, civil engr.; b. Medora, Ind., May 19, 1876; s. Daniel Peck and Ann

Eliza (Wilson) H.; B.S. in C.E., Purdue Univ., 1897; m. Caroline Kirk, Oct. 31, 1900, children—Ruth (Mrs. James Thomas Mac Cluskey), Clyde Kirk, Michael Creed (dec.), Daniel Peck (dec.). Civil engineer on public land surveys in Colo., 1897; draftsman Bd. Pub. Works, Denver, 1899-1900; hydrographer state engr.'s office, Denver, 1901-02; dist. engr. U.S. Geol. Survey, in charge of hydrographic work in Colo., and later in seven states, 1902-07; engr. for U.S. Reclamation Service in charge of surveys, designs and estimates of cost for a 60,000 acre project in Southern Colo. and Northern N.M., 1903-04; engr. in charge of surveys, location and constrn. of a 28,000 horsepower hydro-electric installation on Colo. River, near Glenwood Springs, 1906-07; designed and engr. on constrn. of hydro-electric power plants, dams, irrigation projects in Colo., Calif., Wyo., Ariz., N.M., etc., 1907-23; cons. engr. for State of Calif. on San Gabriel and Pine Canyon dams; state engr. of Colo. since 1923, with supervision over all water supplies and construction of all dams and reservoirs; chmn. State Irrigation Dist. Commn.; sec. and treas. State Bd. of Examiners for Engrs. and Land Surveyors, official in charge of negotiation and administration of all interstate river compacts; interstate river commr. since 1932. Mem. State Planning Commn., State Water Conservation Bd. Consulting engr. for U.S. Corps of Engrs. Mem. Am. Soc. C.E., Colo. Soc. Engrs. Democrat. Presbyn. Mason (32 deg.). Author articles on engring. subjects. Home: 4037 E. 17th Av. Office: State Capitol Bldg., Denver CO*‡

HINDMAN, BAKER MICHAEL, educator; b. Lawrence, Ind., Jan. 19, 1902; s. Harry Francis and Myrtle May (Baker) H.; A.B., Ind. U., 1923, M.S., 1938; Ph.D., N.Y. U., 1953; m. Mildred Mary Smith, June 23, 1932; children—Bernard Wilmot, Allen Edward. Tchr. pub. schs., Princeton, Ind., Miami, Fla., 1923-28; prin. Orange Glade sch., 1928-31, Hialeah sch., 1931-38, Homestead high sch. 1938-45 (all Dade County), Miami; sch. supr. Negro schs., 1945-53, all secondary schs., 1953-55, Dade County, 1945-55; prof. U. Miami, 1955-68, prof. emeritus edn., 1968-69. Recipient citation for outstanding service in fields of education and human relations Bethune-Cookman Coll., 1952. Mem. Am. Ednl. Research, Supervision and Curriculum Devel. Assn., Greater Miami Urban League (exec. bd., 1945), Dade County Council on Community Relations (exec. bd. 1955-69). Contbr. numerous articles on Miami FL Died Mar. 11, 1969.

HINDS, WILLIAM LAWYER, company exec.; b. Binghamton, N.Y., June 28, 1874; s. Addison Joseph and Laura Ferris (Smead) H.; student pub. schs. Watertown, N.Y., 1880-97; m. Ella Davidson, June 28, 1898; 1 dau., Charlotte (Mrs. F. M. Truman). Office boy to buyer Davis Sewing Machine Co., Dayton, O., 1891-1903; joined Crouse-Hinds Co., elec. mfrs., Syracuse, 1903, sec., 1908-24, v.p., gen. mgr., 1924-43, pres., 1943-47, chmn. bd., 1947-55, now dir.; dir. First Trust & Deposit Co., Onondaga Pottery Co., Niagara-Mohawk Power Corp. Trustee Syracuse Savs. Bank, Syracuse U.; chmn. bd. trustee Syracuse Y.M.C.A. Mem. S.A.R., Mass. Soc. of Cincinnati. Mason (33 deg.). Clubs: Black River Valley (Watertown, N.Y.); Electrical Manufacturers; Century, Onondago Golf and Country (Syracuse, N.Y.). Home: Marvelle Rd., R.D. 2, Fayetteville. Office: Crouse-Hinds Co., 7th North and Wolf Sts., Syracuse NY‡

HINDUS, MAURICE GERSCHON, writer; b. Bolshoye Bikovo, Russia, Feb. 27, 1891; s. Jacob and Sarah (Gendeliovitch) H.; came with mother to U.S. 1905; B.S., Colgate, 1915, M.S., 1916, D. Litt., 1931; grad. study, Harvard, 1917; m. Frances McClernan, 1957. Free lance writer, from 1917; visited Russia for Century Mag., 1923, later visited annually for other mags. Mem. Phi Beta Kappa, Delta Sigma Rho. Club: Columbia (N.Y.C.). Author: Russian Peasant and Revolution, 1920; Broken Earth, 1926; Humanity Uprooted, 1929; Red Bread, 1931; The Great Offensive, 1933; Moscow Skies, 1936; Green Worlds, 1938; We Shall Live Again, 1939; Sons and Fathers, 1940; To Sing with the Angels, 1941; Hitler Cannot Conquer Russia, 1941; Russia and Japan, 1942; Mother Russia, 1943; The Cossacks, 1945; In Search of a Future, 1949; Magda; Crisis in the Kremlin, 1954; House without a Roof, 1961; The New York City NY Died July 8, 1969; buried Wading River LI NY

HINES, JOHN FORE, naval officer; b. in Ky., Sept. 22, 1870; grad. U.S. Naval Acad., 1892; Naval War Coll., 1910; m. Mary Dudley Breckinridge, Oct. 1898. Promoted ensign, July 1, 1894; lt. jr. grade, Mar. 3, 1899; lt., July 1, 1900; lt. comdr., July 1, 1906; comdr., Dec. 14, 1911; capt., July 1, 1917. Served on Dorothea during Spanish-Am. War, 1898; on Cincinnati, 1905-7; duty U.S. Naval Acad., 1907-10; exec. officer North Carolina, 1910-12; comd. North Carolina, 1912, Petrel, 1912-13; at U.S. Naval Acad., 1913-16; comd. Chattanooga, 1916-17, Cleveland, 1917; apptd. comdr. Minneapolis, Aug. 1917; comd. Charleston, 1917-18; chief of staff to comdr. Newport News div. cruiser and transport service, Sept. 1918, comdr. same, Jan. 1919; comd. Louisiana, Oct. 1919. Awarded D.S.M., 1919. Home: Bowling Green KY‡

HINES, JOHN LEONARD, army officer; b. White Sulphur Springs, W.Va., May 21, 1868; s. Edward and Mary (Leonard) H.; grad. U.S. Mil. Acad., 1891; m. Rita S., d. Gen. William M. Wherry, U.S. Army, Dec. 19, 1898; children—Alice Grammer (wife of J.R.D. Cleland, U.S. Army), John Leonard (col. U.S. Army). Commd. 2d lt. inf., June 12, 1891; promoted through grades to colonel (temp.), Aug. 5, 1917; colonel 16th Inf., Nov. 1, 1917; brig. gen. N.A., Apr. 12, 1918; maj. gen. U.S. Army, Aug. 8, 1918 (temp.); brig. gen. regular army, Nov. 30, 1918; major general, Mar. 5, 1921; general, U.S. Army, ret., June 15, 1940. Served at Ft. Omaha, Neb., 1891-96; acting q.m. 2d Inf., at Tampa. Fla., and Santiago de Cuba, 1898; Cienfuegos, Cuba, 1899, 1900; in Philippines, 1900-01, 1903-05, 1911-12, 1930-32; chief q.m. Camp of U.S. Troops Jamestown Expn. 1907; asst. to chief q.m. Dept. of Mo., 1908-09; Nagasaki, Japan, 1910, 11; adj. Punitive Expedition into Mexico, 1916-17; asst. adj. gen. A.E.F., May-Oct. 1917; arrived in France, June 13, 1917; col. 16th Inf., Nov. 1, 1917, apptd. comdr. 1st. Brig. Infantry, 1st Div., A.E.F., May 4, 1918; assigned to 4th Div., Aug. 25, 1918; apptd. comdr. 3d Army Corps, Oct. 11, 1918; comdr. 4th Div., Nov. 21, 1919; comdr. 5th Div., Sept. 25, 1920; comdr. 2d Div., July 11, 1921; comdr. 8th Corps Area, Oct. 6, 1921; dep. chief of staff, U.S. Army, Dec. 5, 1922; chief of staff, Sept. 13, 1921; apptd. comdr. 9th Corps Area, Dec. 31, 1926; apptd. comdr. Philippine Dept., Oct. 2, 1930; ret. from active service, May 31, 1932. Awarded D.S.M., 1919, for services as regimental, brigade, division and corps comdr."; D.S.C., for service in Soissons drive,"; Silver Star Medal for service in Cuba, 1898; Comdr. Legion of Honor and Croix de Guerre (French), 1918; Comdr. Order of Leopold (Belgian), 1918; Knight Comdr. of St. Michael and St. George (English), 1919; Order of the Crown (Italian), 1919; Medal of the Solidaridad (Panamanian), 1919; Grand Officer Kingdom of Cambodia (France), 1931; Distinguished Service Medal, State of W.Va., 1941. Mem. Soc. Santiago de Cuba. Home: 3740 Military Rd., N.W., Washington‡

HINES, MURRAY ARNOLD, prof. chemistry; b. N. Adams, Mass., Aug. 5, 1876; s. Miranda and Roxy Ann (Phelps) H.; A.B., St. Lawrence U., 1899; A.B., Harvard, 1901, A.M., 1903, Ph.D., 1906; m. Amy Sanders, of Evanston, Ill., Apr. 6, 1918; 1 son, Roger Arnold. Asst. and teaching fellow, Harvard, 1903-06; chemist Mallinckrodt Chem. Works, St. Louis, Mo., 1906-07; asst. prof. chemistry, 1907-16, asso., 1916-19, prof., 1919-—, Northwestern U. Fellow A.A.A.S.; mem. Am. Chem. Soc., Ill. Acad. Science, Beta Theta Pi, Alpha Chi Sigma, Sigma Xi, Phi Beta Kappa. Conglist. Club: University (Evanston). Specialized in inorganic chemistry. Home: 1416 Hinman Av., Evanston IL‡

HINMAN, E(DGAR) HAROLD, physician, educator; born in Wicklow, Ont., Can., Mar. 20, 1904; s. Edward Minor and Edith (Isaac) H.; student Toronto Normal Sch., 1922-23; B.A. (with honors), Queens U., 1927; M.S., Cornell, 1928, Ph.D., 1930; M.B., La. State U. Med. Center, 1937, M.D., 1938; M.P.H., Johns Hopkins (Rockefeller Found. fellow, 1941-42), 1942; m. Katharine Ellen Fradenburgh, Dec. 25, 1929; children—Edward John, Alan Richard. Came to U.S., 1927, naturalized, 1933. Asst. master Annette Street Sch., Toronto, 1923-26; research and teaching asst., Dept. Entomology, Cornell, 1927-30; Nat. Research Council fellow, Dept. Tropical Medicine, Tulane Med. Sch., 1930-32; asst. prof. parasitology and med. entomology, Dept. Tropical Medicine, La. State U. and Med. Center, 1932-37; sr. biologist, malaria control div., Health and Safety Dept., Tenn. Valley Authority, 1937-42, div. chief, 1946-48; head pub. health officer, health and sanitation div., Inst. Inter-Am. Affairs, San Salvador, El Salvador, Central America, 1942-43, and Mexico, 1943-46; dir., Sch. Pub. Health, U. Okla., 1948-52; dean Sch. of Medicine, U. P.R., 1952-59; chief technical resources division Office Public Health, ICA, Washington, 1959-62; prof., head dept. preventive medicine, Jefferson Med. College, Philadelphia, 1962-70. Vice chairman Division Tropical Medicine 6th Internat. Congresses Tropical Medicine and Malaria, 1958; mem. expert advisory panel on malaria WHO. Recipient Eduardo Liceago medal from govt. of Mexico for distinguished contributions to public health in Mexico, May 1946; travel grant from Rockefeller Found. to observe malaria control activities in Caribbean area, 1947. Diplomate Am. Bd. Preventive Medicine. Fellow Coll. Physicians of Phila., A.C.P., also A.A.A.S., Royal Society Tropical Medicine and Hygiene. Am. Pub. Health Assn., International College Surgeons (honorary), Am. Coll. Preventive Medicine; mem. A.M.A. (pres. section on preventive medicine 1966-67), Am. Soc. Tropical Medicine (pres. 1965), Am. Soc. Parasitology, Pa. State, Phila. County med. socs., Indsl. Med. Assn., Am. Mosquito Control Assn. Sigma Xi, Alpha Omega Alpha, Phi Kappa Phi, Phi Sigma, Sigma Delta Pi and Beta Beta Beta. Democrat. Member Presbyterian Church. Club: Cosmos (Washington). Contbr. articles dealing with research on malaria control, parasitic diseases of pub. health importance, etc., in sci. jours., 1928-72. Address: Philadelphia PA Died Dec. 25, 1971.

HINMAN, GEORGE ELIJAH, judge; b. Alford, Mass., May 7, 1870; s. William C. and Mary A. (Gates) H.; grad. high sch., 1888; spl. course, Yale Law Sch., 1897-98; m. Nettie P. Williams, Sept. 26, 1899 (died June 1932); children—Russell W., Virginia Gates. Newspaper work, 1888-95; editor Willimantic Journal, 3 yrs.; admitted to bar, 1899, and began practice in Willimantic; asst. clk., 1899, and clk., 1901, Conn. Ho. of Rep.; asst. clk. Constl. Conv., 1902; clk. Conn. Senate, 1903, of bills, 1905, 07, 11, engrossing clk., 1909; sec. Rep. State Central Com., 1902-14; atty. gen. of Conn., 1915-18; judge of Superior Court of Conn., 1919-26; justice Supreme Court of Conn., 1926-40; state referee since 1940. Mem. Am. and Conn State bar assns. Conglist. Mason (Past Comdr. St. John's Commandery, K.T.). Club: Rotary. Home: Willimantic CT‡

HINRICHSEN, WALTER, music publisher; b. Leipzig, Germany, Sept. 23, 1907; s. Henri and Martha (Bendix) H.; student Leipzig Acad. Music, 1927; m. Evelyn Elizabeth Merrell, Aug. 2, 1946; children—Martha, Henry. Came to U.S., 1936, naturalized, 1943. Apprenticeship experiences music pub. field include Foetisch in Lausanne, Schott Freres in Brussels, 1928, Augener in London, 1929, Peters Edition, in Leipzig, 1930-35; U.S. music officer U.S. Zone in Germany, 1945-47; owner, pres. C. F. Peters Corp., N.Y.C.; pub. N.Y. Pub. Library Music Publs., 1954. Served from pvt. to master sgt. AUS, 1942-45. Recipient Laurel Leaf award for distinguished achievement in fostering and encouraging Am. music Am. Composers Alliance, 1964. Mem. Mus. Pubs. Association of America (member board of directors), Mus. Library Assn., Am. Musicological Soc. Home: NYC NY

HINSHAW, JOSEPH HOWARD, lawyer; b. Stonefort, Ill., Sept. 19, 1890; s. William Riley and Fanny (Neely) H.; A.B., U. Ill., 1913, LL.B., 1916; m. Madeline Heise, Aug. 20, 1925; 1 dau., Joan Madeline. Admitted to Ill. bar, 1916 and since practice in Chicago; partner Hinshaw & Culbertson, 1934-52; Hinshaw, Culbertson, Moelmann & Hoban, 1952-73. Served as 1st lt., inf., U.S. Army, World War I. Fellow Am. Coll. Trial Lawyers; mem. Am., Ill. (pres. 1951-52) and Chicago bar assns., Internat. Assn. Ins. Counsel, Chicago Law Inst., Soc. Trial Lawyers (past pres.), Delta Phi, Delta Sigma Rho, Order of Coif. Republican. Clubs: University, Executives, Chgo. Farmers (Chgo.); Westmoreland Country. Author: Hinshaw's Trial Briefs (accidents), 1934; Young Man—Your Liberty, 1962; Elements of Truth, 1966. Home: Wilmette IL Died Apr. 10, 1973.

HINSHELWOOD, SIR CYRIL (NORMAN), scientist; b. London, Eng., June 19, 1897; s. Norman Macmillan and Ethel (Smith) H.; M.A., Balliol Coll., Oxford U., 1924, D.Sc., 1947, D.C.L., 1960; D.Sc., univs. Dublin, 1936, London, 1947, Leeds, 1952, Sheffield, 1954, Cambridge, 1955, Bristol, 1956, Hull, 1957, Wales, 1958, Ottawa, 1961, Southampton, 1964. Fellow, tutor Trinity Coll., Oxford, 1921-37; Dr. Lees prof. chem. Oxford, 1937-64; sr. research fellow Imperial Coll., London, 1964-67; fellow Exeter Coll., 1937-67. Chmn. Fuel Research Bd., 1950-55; mem. adv. council sci. policy Brit. Govt., 1953-56; hon. adv. sci. com. Natl. Gallery. Created Knight, 1948; recipient Lavoisier medal French Chem. Soc., Guldberg medal Oslo; Davy and Royal Medalist Royal Soc.; Longstaff and Faraday medalist Chem. Soc.; co-winner Nobel prize for chemistry, 1956; Grand Officer Order of Merti (Italy), 1956; Avogadro medal Accad. dei XL, Rome, 1956. Fellow Royal Soc. (past pres.); mem. Nat. Acad. Scis., Pontifical Acad., Chem. Soc. (pres. 1946-48), British Assn. (president 1964-65), French, Belgian, Swiss, Italian chem. socs. Spanish Society Physics and Chemistry; fgn. mem. Accademia dei XL Rome, U.S.S.R. Academy of Scis., Accademia Nazionale dei Liucei (Rome), Real Academia de Ciencias Madrid, A.A.A.S. Author: Kinetics of Chemical Change, 1946; Chemical Kinetics of the Bacterial Cell, 1946; The Structure of Physical Chemistry, 1951; Growth, Function and Regulation in Bacterial Cells, 1966; also papers in sci. jours. Home: Oxford England Died Oct. 9, 1967.

HINSMAN, CARL B., mfr.; b. St. Johnsbury, Vt., Dec. 25, 1873; s. Charles B. and Kate R. (Bagley) H.; ed. pub. schs.; m. Mary Sherman, d. ex-Gov. John A. Mead, of Rutland, Vt., June 25, 1902; 1 son, John Abner. With the Howe Scale Co., since beginning of active career, pres., 1920-27; pres. Central Nat. Bank, Rutland, 1920-36; v.p. State Mut. Fire Ins. Co.; ex-pres. Scale Mfrs. Assn. Mem. Vt. Senate, 1915-16. Republican. Conglist. Clubs: Rotary, Rutland Country. Home: Rutland VT‡

HINTON, JAMES WILLIAM, surgeon; b. Reedville, Va., Mar. 12, 1894; s. John Braxton and Anne Augusta (Crosswell) H.; student Cluster Springs Acad., Va., 1910-13; M.D., U. Va., 1919; LL.D., Hampden Sydney Coll., 1961; m. Jannett Lord, May 19, 1951. Intern surg. service Boston City Hosp., 1917. U. Va. Hosp., 1918-19, N.Y. Post-Grad. Hosp., 1919-21, Sloane's Hosp. for Women, 1921-22; former dir. fourth surg. service, dir. children's surg. service Bellevue Hosp., N.Y.C.; prof., chmn. dept. surgery Post Grad. Med. Sch., N.Y.U., 1949-60; former dir. surg. service Univ. Hosp.; attending surgeon Beekman Downtown Hosp., N.Y.C.,

Gouverneur Hosp.; cons. surgery N.Y. Women's Infirmary, Jersey City Med. Center, Norwalk (Conn.) Gen. Hosp., Southampton (N.Y.) Hosp., Jamaica (N.Y.) Hosp., St. Agnes Hosp., White Plains, N.Y., Good Samaritan Hosp., Suffern, N.Y., United Hosp., Portchester, N.Y., Nassau Hosp., Mineola, N.Y., Central Suffolk Hosp., Riverhead, N.Y., Elizabeth A. Horton Meml. Hosp., Middletown, N.Y., Wyckoff Height Hosp., Bklyn., Bellevue Hosp., University Hosp., Manhattan VA Hosp., Sherbrooke Hosp.; cons. Columbus Hosp., Manhattan State Hosp. Pres., trustee Royal Coll. Surgeons Found., 1967-73. Diplomate, founders group Am. Bd. Surgery. Fellow Royal Coll. Surgeons Eng. (hon.), Royal Coll. Edinburgh (hon.), A.C.S. (chmn. credentials com.), Am. Surg. Assn., Royal Coll. Surgeons in Ireland (hon.), Internat. Surg. Soc., N.Y. Acad. Medicine (v.p. 1944-46); mem. N.Y. (past pres.), Eastern surg. socs., Am. Gastroenterological Soc., Pan Pacific, So. surg. assns., N.Y. Cardiovascular Surgery, James IV Assn. Surgeons (foundeer, sec. 1957-67), Hon. Company Edinburgh Golfers, Alpha Omega Alpha. Club: Links (N.Y.C.). Home: New York City NY Died Apr. 18, 1973.

HIPSLEY, ELMER R., fgn. service officer; b. D.C., May 21, 1913; ed. high sch., Emerson Inst.; married. With Treasury Dept., 1939-46; spl. agt. Dept. of State, 1946-51, investigator, 1951-53, evaluator, 1953; spl. asst., 1959, chief div. phys. security, 1959; later mem. staff NATO, Geneva, Switzerland.

HIRSCH, EDWIN FREDERICK, physician; b. Milw., Aug. 18, 1886; s. John Fred and Maria Louise (Weiland) H.; A.B., Northwestern U., 1910; A.M. in Zoology, U. Ill., 1911; Ph.D. in Pathology, U. Chgo., 1914, M.D., 1916; Sc.D. (hon.), Morningside Coll., 1955; m. Marion Sharp Lane, Aug. 3, 1918 (dec. Aug. 1945); children—Catharine Louise (Mrs. Bruce Haig), Helen Sharp (Mrs. William P. Kent), Jean Lane (Mrs. Robert E. Priest); m. 2d, Helen Kotas, Mar. 19, 1949. Intern Presbyn. Hosp., Chgo., 1916-17; from fellow to asso. prof. pathology U. Chgo., 1912-51, asso. prof. emeritus, 1951-72; dir. Henry Baird Favill Lab., St. Luke's Hosp., Chgo., 1919-59; emeritus pathologist Presbyn.-St. Luke's Hosp., Chgo., 1959-72; dir. labs. Columbus, Cuneo and St. Francis Cabrini hosps., Chgo., 1963-72. Servéd to capt., M.C., U.S. Army, 1917-19. Mem. Phi Beta Kappa, Sigma Xi, Gamma Alpha, Alpha Chicago IL Died Mar. 5, 1972.

HIRSCH, IRENE DOROTHEA, elec. engring. and contracting co. exec.; b. Columbus, O., Jan. 21, 1903; d. Gustav and Aletta (Kremer) Hirsch; B.S. in Edn., Ohio State U., 1926; grad. Columbus Normal Sch., 1927. Elementary sch. tchr., 1927-28; stenographer, sec. Gustav Hirsch Orgn. Inc., Columbus, 1933-70, chmn. bd. 1959-70; Sky Way Broadcasting Co., Columbus, 1960-70. Bd. dirs. Ohio Mental Health Assn., 1960-70, Jr. Theatre of Arts, 1961-70; exec. bd. Columbus Civic Ballet, 1963-70; pres. S. Encore unit Columbus Symphony, 1966-70; treas. Central Ohio Symphony, 1964-66; bd. dirs. Central Ohio Heart Assn., 1963-70, World Neighbors, 1954-70, Center Sci. and Industry, 1968-70. Named Dau. of 308th Signal Battalion, 1963; recipient plaque Ohio Mental Health Assn., 1962. Mem. Womens Assn. Mech. Engrs., Alpha Delta Pi (chmn. house corp. 1963-66). Republican. Mem. Community Ch. (choir and Sunday sch. tchr., (past mem. mission bd., research group). Clubs: Scioto Country, Columbus Athletic (Columbus); Centurian (Otterbein V.); President (Ohio State U.). Author: My Own Book of Verse, 1958. Home: Columbus OH Died May 7, 1970.

HIRSCH, MAX, banker, investor; b. Cin., Nov. 30, 1877, s. Simon and Rosa (Levi) H.; A.B., Harvard, 1900; m. Effie Wyler, Feb. 22, 1905 (dec. June 1956); 1 dau., Katherine H., (Mrs. John S. Wright); m. 2d, Marga Henle, Oct. 2, 1958. With Star Distillery Co. becoming v.p.; pres. Sachs Shoe Mfg. Co.; v.p. Country Distillers Corp.; dir., chmn. trust and investment coms. Lincoln Nat. Bank. U.S. jury commissioner So. Dist. Ohio. Mem. bd. Ohio Citizens Council; v.p. Cin. Bur. Governmental Research. Rep. War Dept. Commn. Cin. dist. World War I; mem. Draft Bd. 9 and mem. Hamilton County Nat. Def. Council, World War II. Chmn. and pres. civic and social work orgns.; mem. bd. Cin. Community Chest; former pres. Cin. Pub. Recreation Commn.; hon. mem. Nat. Recreation Assn. Home: Cincinnati OH Died Apr. 13, 1968.

HIRSCHLER, FREDERIC SALZ, dept. store exec.; b. San Francisco, Feb. 4, 1902; s. David and Linda (Salz) H.; B.S., U. Cal., 1924; m. Marjorie Manheim, Mar. 15, 1931; 1 dau., Carol Manheim (Mrs. Samuel Goldstein, Jr.). With Emporium Capwell Co., 1925-67, beginning as asst. mgr. toiletries, successively buyer toys, sporting goods, luggage, asst. mgr. basement store, asst. to gen. mdse. mgr., buyer street floor jewelry, handbags, silverware, sales promotion mgr., divisional mgr., gen. mdse. mgr., gen. mgr., v.p., 1925-58, pres., 1958-66, chmn. bd., 1966-67, also dir.; chmn. bd. Fed. Res. Bank San Francisco; dir. Asso. Merchandising Corp., Fed. Res. Bank. Mem. Cal. Retailers Assn. (dir.), Nat. Retail Mchts. Assn. (dir.). Home: Oakland CA Died Jan. 8, 1968.

HIRSH, HERBERT WILLIAM, lawyer; b. Davenport, Ia., Oct. 2, 1902; s. Emil and Olga (Teweles) H.; A.B., U. Wis., 1924; LL.B., Harvard, 1927; m. Katherine Friedman, July 29, 1932 (dec. Feb. 1960); m. 2d, Edna Schram, May 1963; children—William, Steven. Admitted to Ill. bar, 1927, practiced Chgo., partner Clausen, Hirsh, Miller & Gorman; dir. Valspar Corp. Mem. Am. Ill., Chgo. bar assns., Chgo. Law Inst., Zeta Beta Tau. Clubs: Standard (Chgo.); Northmoor Country (Ravina, Ill.); Lake-Shore Country (Glencoe, Ill.). Home: Highland Park IL Died Mar. 31, 1971.

HIRSHBERG, LEONARD KEENE, M.D.; b. Baltimore, Md., Jan. 9, 1877; s. Isidore Nathan and Fannie (Thalheimer) H.; A.B., Johns Hopkins, 1898, M.D., 1902; univs. of Berlin and Heidelberg, 1902, 03, Harvard Summer Sch., 1903; hon. A.M., Loyola Coll., Md., 1913; m. Edna Dalsemer, of Baltimore, Nov. 25, 1904; children—Leonard Keene Dalsemer, Gordon Henry Dalsemer. Instr. neuro-pathology and asso. in bacteriology, Coll. Phys. and Surg., Baltimore, 1904; visiting phys., Mercy, Baltimore City, Md. Gen. and St. Agnes hosps.; research worker, Johns Hopkins; lecturer, Loyola Coll., Baltimore; physician in chief Nat. Health Service, 1926. Chmn. com. scientific research Am. Assn. Clinical Research (pres. 1914-15); mem. A.A.A.S., Am. Neurol. Soc., Soc. of Biologists, Am. Acad. Sciences, etc.; pres. Physicians' Civic Club; v.p. Direct Legislation League. Mason (32 deg., Shriner), Elk, K.P., etc. Clubs: Royal Societies Club (London); Johns Hopkins, Charcoal, Press, Lauraville Country, Bohemians. Author: Collected Humor, Poetry and Philosophy, 1898; Practical Bacteriology, 1904; Action of Light, 1904; What You Ought to Know About the Baby, 1909, 26; Researches in Anaphylactic Medicine, 1911; How to Have a Beautiful Complexion, 1918, 26; Secrets of Health, 1926; The Book of Health, 1926. Contbr. Scientific American, Beautiful Motherhood, Physical Health, Brain Power, Harper's Bazar, and over 100 other Am., English, Canadian and Australian mags., also syndicate artilces in over 600 daily newspapers; owner and pub. Popular Medicine; asso. editor Med. Review of Reviews and other mags. Winner of Fisk Fund prize (R.I. Med. Soc.), N.Y. Med. Jour. prize, etc. Home: 422 National Boul., Long Beach, N.Y. Office: 17 W. 60th St., New York NY‡

HISAW, FREDERICK LEE, prof. of zoology; b. Newton County, Mo., Aug. 23, 1891; s. Frederick Louis and Anna Edith (Cummins) H.; A.B., U. of Mo., 1914, B.S., 1915, A.M., 1916, LL.D., 1938; Ph.D., U. of Wis., 1924; m. Minnie Nancy Reynolds, Sept. 1, 1917; children—Lois Lee, Frederick Lee. Student and asst. in zoology, U. of Mo., 1913-16; asso. prof. of zoology, U. of Miss., 1916-17; asst. prof. Kansas Coll., 1919-24; asst. prof. zoology, U. of Wis., 1924-27, asso. prof., 1927-29, prof. zoology, 1929-35; prof. zoology, Harvard, 1935-53, Fisher prof. natural history, 1953-62, emeritus; sci. dir. Yerkes Labs. Primate Biology. Sr. Fellow Harvard Soc. of Fellows. Served as lt. inf., U.S. Army 1917-19. Recipient Ann. Award, Am. Gynecol. Soc., 1952, medal Endocrine Society, 1956. Mem. Am. Assn. Advancement Sci., Soc. Exptl. Biol. and Medicine, Endocrine Soc. (v.p. 1952), American Soc. of Anatomy, Am. Acad. Arts and Sciences, Am. Physiol. Soc., Soc. Zoologists (pres. 1937). Am. Philos. Soc., Nat. Acad. Scis., Gamma Alpha, Phi Sigma, Sigma Xi, Gamma Sigma Delta, Phi Beta Pi, Phi Beta Kappa. Club: Harvard Faculty Cambridge MA Died Dec. 3, 1972.

HITCH, CALVIN MILTON, consular service; b. Morven, Ga., July 28, 1869; s. Robert M. (M.D.) and Martha (Fall) H.; ed. Emory Coll., Oxford, Ga., class of '88; Commercial Coll. of Ky. U., Lexington, Ky., 1889; m. Ida Blanche Parrish, of Adel, Ga., Feb. 19, 1890; 1 son, Guy Harvard. Admitted to Ga. bar, 1890; solicitor, City Ct., Quitman, Ga., 1892-96; mem. Ga. Ho. of Rep., 1896-97; sec. to gov. of Ga., 1898-1902, 1902-05, 1907-10; sec. to U.S. Senator Augustus O. Bacon, 1905-07; sec. Dem. State Exec. Com., Ga., 1910-12; asst. chief, Latin-Am. Div., Dept. of State, Washington, 1913-15; Am. consul at Nottingham, Eng., 1915-23, Basel, Switzerland, 1923-30; consul gen., Wellington, New Zealand, since 1930. Democrat. Methodist. Mason. Odd Fellow. Home: Atlanta, Ga. Address: Am. Consulate General, Wellington New Zealand‡

HITCHCOCK, CHARLES BAKER, geographer; b. Boston, Mar. 16, 1906; s. John and Esther Mary (Baker) H.; A.B., Harvard Univ., 1928; M.A., Columbia, 1933; D.Sc. (honorary), Temple University, 1954; m. Agnes Murchie, Dec. 3, 1931; children—Gail, Suzanne, Esther Lee; married second, Anita Kincaid, January 19, 1957. Joined Am. Geog. Soc., N.Y. City, 1930, chief dept. Hispanic Am. research and assistant director, 1943-48, acting dir., 1949, exec. sec., dir., 1956-66, research asso., 1967-69, chmn. advisory committee Am. cartography, 1948-69, research and devel. bd., 1949; mem. adv. com. Am. Geography Pan Am. Inst. Geog. and History; mem. nat. atlas com. Nat. Research Council; mem. adv. com. census atlases Bur. Census; expdns. Am. Mus. Natural History, So. Venezuela, 1929, Phelps Venezuela, 1947-49, 51-53, U.S. del. to Internat. Geog. Congress, Amsterdam, 1938, Rio de Janeiro, 1956, London, England, 1964. United States delegate Pan American Inst. Geography and History, Lima, 1941, Caracas, 1946, Buenos Aires, 1948, Santiago, Chile, 1950, Dominican Republic, 1952, Mexico, 1955, Ecuador, 1959, Stockholm, Sweden, 1960; alternate U.S. delegate to the Commn. Cartography, from 1957. Mem. Assn. Am. Geographers (treas., 1948-49), Arctic Institute, N.Y. Acad. Scis., Soc. Geog. de Lima (corr. mem.), Soc. Venezolana de Ciencias Naturales (honorary), Scottish Geographical Society (honorary), A.A.A.S., Geol. Soc. Am., Nat. Geog. Soc. (hon.). Editor Map of Hispanic America, 1938-47. Contbr. articles tech. publs. Recipient Morse medal Am. Geog. Soc., 1966; Explorers Club medal, 1967. Home: Pound Ridge NY Died Mar. 26, 1969.

HITCHCOCK, GEORGE COLLIER, lawyer; b. St. Louis, Dec. 28, 1867; s. Henry and Mary (Collier) H.; B.A., Yale, 1890; St. Louis Law Sch., 1890-91, Harvard Law Sch., 1891-93; m. Elizabeth L. Fiske, Feb. 12, 1901 (she died Nov. 27, 1935); children—Anne W., Mary, Henry, Ethan Allen, Elizabeth F. Admitted to Mo. bar, 1894, practiced at St. Louis Mem. Bd. Commrs. on charitable instns., St. Louis, 1896-1900; asst. U.S. atty., 1899-April 1, 1902; mem. City Council, 1905-07; judge Circuit Ct., term 1908-14. Trustee Mo. Bot. Garden (pres. bd. 1902-47), St. Louis Country Day School, 1917-40; member bd. Mercantile Library, 1916-40 (president 1920-21). Bellefontaine Cemetery Assn.; mem. bd. dirs. of Jefferson-National Expansion Memorial Assn. since 1938. Mem. Am., St. Louis and Mo. State bar assns. Republican. Episcopalian. Clubs: University, Noonday. Chancellor Diocese of Mo., 1921-39. Home: 5363 Waterman Av., St. Louis 12. Office: Commerce Bldg., 418 Olive St., St Louis 2 MO‡

HITCHCOCK, LAUREN BLAKELY, cons. chem. engr., educator; b. Paris, France (parents U.S. citizens), Mar. 18, 1900; s. Frank Lauren and Margaret Johnson (Blakely) H.; S.B. in Chem. Engring., Mass. Inst. Tech. 1920, S.M., 1927, Sc. D., 1933; m. Eleanor M. Mulhern, Sept. 22, 1920 (dec. Aug. 1963); children—Eleanor M. (Mrs. John R. Higgins) (dec.), Patricia (Mrs. Peter Malof), Jacquelyn I. (Mrs. K. E. Aamodt), Hope M. (Mrs. J. A. Maurice Cantin), John; m. 2d, Lusyd Wright Smith, Mar. 1, 1966 (dec. Feb. 1971). Chemist, H. P. Hood & Sons, Boston, 1920; prof. chem. engring. U. Va., 1928-35; cons. chem. engr., research exec., mgr. sales devel. Hooker Electro-Chem. Co., Niagara Falls, 1935-44; mgr. chems. dept. Quaker Oats Co., Chgo., 1944-46, v.p. charge, 1946-49; dir. research and devel. Nat. Dairy Products Corp., also pres. Nat. Dairy Research Labs., Inc., N.Y.C., 1949-53; mgmt. cons., N.Y.C., 1953; pres., mng. dir. Air Pollution Found., Los Angeles, 1954-56; cons. chem. engr. Lauren B. Hitchcock Assos., 1957-63; prof. engring. State U. N.Y. at Buffalo, 1963-72; dir. grad. engring. Mgmt. TV Network, 1969-72; dir. devel. Ecology & Environment, Inc., Buffalo, 1972. Served with U.S. Naval Aviation Corps, 1918; officer U.S. Army, 1921-28. Registered profl. engr., Cal., N.Y., Va. Mem. Am. Soc. Engring. Edn., Am. Inst. Chem. Engrs. (Profl. Achievement award Western N.Y. sect. 1971), Am. Chem. Soc., Soc. Chem. Industry (chmn. Am. sect. 1953-54), Air Pollution Control Assn., Comml. Chem. Devel. Assn. (pres. 1947-49), Niagara Frontier Assn. Research and Devel. Dirs. (pres. 1970-71), Sigma Xi, Alpha Chi Sigma. Clubs: Cosmos (Washington); M.I.T., Chemists (N.Y.C.); Saturn (Buffalo). Author numerous sci. articles field chem. technology and research mgmt. Home: Buffalo NY Died Oct. 16, 1972; buried Belmont MA

HITREC, JOSEPH GEORGE, writer; b. Zagreb, Yugoslavia, Feb. 28, 1912; s. Thomas and Gisele (Molnar) H.; degrees in Russian, Croatian, German, Latin and Greek, in Contemporary European Literature, student in logic, psychology, philosophy, all at Royal U. of Zagreb; m. Jeanette Leyla Saygin, Sept. 19, 1946. Copywriter, mgr. D. J. Keymer & Co. Advt. Agency, India, 1932-46; came to U.S. 1946, naturalized 1951. Advt. exec., N.Y.C., from 1946. Recipient Harper Novel Prize of $10,000 for Rulers' Morning, stories of modern India, published, 1948. Member Literary Circle Kitab Khana, Bombay Chamber Music Soc., Bombay Philharmonic Soc., Bombay Presidency. Clubs: Press and Art of India; The Bombay Gymkhana. Author: short stories, poems and articles pub. in Yugoslav, Austrian, Syrian and Indian periodicals; Angel of Gaiety (novel of wartime India), 1951; Terrorists, 1955; stories, articles in U.S., United Kingdom mags. Reviews for N.Y. Times, N.Y. Herald Tribune, Sat. Rev. Lectr. Home: New York City NY Died Aug. 22, 1972.

HITT, ROBERT MELVIN, JR., newspaper editor; b. Bamberg, S.C., June 12, 1914; s. Robert Melvin and Weinona (Strom) H.; B.A., The Citadel, 1935, LL.D., 1962; m. Ann Elizabeth Leonard, Aug. 6, 1938; children—Joan L., Dianne P., Nancy S., Robert Melvin III, John Thomas Leonard. Prin. Smoaks (S.C.) Grammar Sch., 1935; dist. dir. NYA, 1936; reporter Charleston (S.C.) News and Courier, 1936-37, sports editor, 1938-43; news editor Charleston Eve, Post, 1943-45, mng. editor, 1945-53, editor, 1953-68. Mem. S.C. Fiscal Survey Commn., 1955-56. Past dir. Community Chest. Mem. South Carolina Press Assn. (pres. 1965-66), Am. Soc. Newspaper Editors, Asso. Press Mng. Editors Assn. (dir. 1950-53), Charles C. of C. (dir.), Sigma Delta Chi. Clubs: Lions (pres. 1946), Charleston Country (pres. 1947), Carolina Yacht (commo. 1948), Charleston SC Died June 3, 1968; buried St. Philip's Protestant Episcopal Ch. Graveyard.

HIXON, ERNEST HOWARD, educator; b. Karlsruhe, Germany, Dec. 20, 1922; (parents U.S. citizens); s. Ralph Malcomb and Stella (Saddler) H.; student Ia. State Coll., 1940-42; D.D.S., U. Ia., 1945, M.S., 1949; student Hogskolan, Stockholm, 1949-50; m. Margaret Stroud, Oct. 23, 1945 (div. 1964); children—Katherine, Douglas. Cleft palate research cons. U. Toronto, 1950-51; asso. prof. U. Ia., 1951-54, prof., head dept. orthodontics, 1954-60; prof., head dept. orthodontics U. Mexico, 1960-61, U. Ore., 1961-72. Served as lt. (j.g.) USNR, 1945-47. Mem. Am. Dental Assn., Am. Assn. Orthodontists, Am. Assn. Cleft Palate Rehab., Soc. Research Child Devel., Sigma Xi. Address: Portland OR Died Oct. 8, 1972.

HLAVATY, VACLAV, mathematician; b. Louny, Czechoslovakia, Jan. 27, 1894; s. Hlavaty and Laura (Feltl) V.; Ph.D., Prague U., 1922; grad. study Delft, Rome, Paris, Oxford, 1924-30; m. Olga Neumann, Jan. 10, 1931; 1 dau., Olga (Mrs. Yusufzai). Came to U.S., 1948, naturalized, 1956. Prof. math. Prague U., 1930-48; vis. prof. Princeton, also Inst. Advanced Study, 1937-38; exchange prof. Sorbonne, Paris, 1948; prof. Ind. U., 1948-69, Distinguished Service prof., 1962. World lecture tour on math., U.S., Japan, Hongkong, India, Afghanistan, Iran, Israel, Italy, France, Belgium, Eng., Ireland; co-editor Tensor (Japan), Rendiconti Circ. Mat. (Palermo, Italy). Bd. reviewers Math. Rev., Jour. Math. and Mechanics. Bd. trustees Masaryk Fund. Mem. Soc. Roy. des Sci Liege, Ac. Intern. Libre des Sci Paris, Czechoslovak Soc. Art and Sci. of U.S. (past pres.), Ind. Acad. Sci. Sigma Xi, Mu Epsilon. Author numerous books, latest being Geometry of Einstein's Unified Field Theory, 1958. Contbr. numerous articles tech., profl. jours., U.S. and fgn. countries. Home: Bloomington IN Died Jan. 11, 1969.

HO CHI-MINH, pres. North Vietnam; b. 1890. Pub. Paris Weekly; traveled to USSR, 1924; participant Chinese Revolution, 1925-27; imprisoned for polit. activities in Siam, 1928-30; leader struggle for independence in Indo-China; World War II; leader Communist guerrilla forces, 1945-54; pres. North Vietnam, 1954-69. Chmn. Laodong (Revolutionary Workers' Party), 1951-69. Address: Hanoi North Vietnam Died Sept. 3, 1969.*

HOAG, GEORGE GRANT, business executive; born Minneapolis, Kan., Nov. 5, 1872; s. David Durand and Charlotte Hortense (Chisholm) H.; student high sch., Minneapolis, Kan.; m. Grace Simpson, June 24, 1896; children—George Grant II. Began career as clerk, 1888; mgr. clothing store, 1907-09; with J. C. Penney Co., 1909, buyer mdse., New York City, 1915-22, sales mgr., 1922-25, v.p. and dir., 1916-26, resigned, 1926. Pres. Hoag Foundation, San Marino, Calif., since 1940; mem. bd. trustees, Calif. Inst. Tech., since 1939. Republican. Presbytherian. Mason (32 deg., Shriner, K.T.). Clubs: Los Angeles Country, Newport Harbor Yacht, Los Angeles Shrine, Pasadena Shrine, Al Malaikah Shrine (Los Angeles). Home: 589 Winston Av., San Marino; (summer) 2102 East Central Av., Balboa CA*‡

HOAGE, ROBERT J., statistician; b. Ia., Jan. 27, 1877; s. James A. and Lizzie (Stewart) H.; ed. high sch., Silver Creek, Neb.; corr. course in building and contracting; course in trade relations, Am. Univ., Washington, D.C. Identified with various lines of business until 1908; building contractor, 1908-12; mgr. shingle mill, 1912-13; statistician Industrial Ins. Co., Olympia, Wash., 1913-17, Ore. Industries Co., 1918; dep. engr. Associated Lumbermen, Tacoma, Wash., 1919; chief statistician U.S. Employes' Compensation Commn., Washington, D.C., since Jan. 10, 1919. Mem. Am. Soc. Safety Engrs., Casualty Actuarial Soc. Republican. Methodist. Odd Fellow. Home: 2000 H St. N.W. Address: 15th and K Sts., Washington DC‡

HOAGLAND, WARREN EUGENE, lawyer, govt. cons.; b. Kansas City, Mo., Jan. 6, 1904; s. William Louis and Carrie (McDonald) H.; B.A., Yale, 1926; LL.B. cum laude, Harvard, 1929; m. Helen K. Morley. Jan. 24, 1931; children—Edward M., Mary Elizabeth. Admitted to N.Y. bar, 1929; asso. Davis, Polk, Wardwell, Gardiner & Reed, N.Y.C., 1929-41; counsel fgn. and domestic transactions, various banks and financial orgns.; legal counsel Standard Oil Co. (N.J.) and affiliates, from 1941; cons. Dept. State, 1954-55; U.S. govt. rep. surplus property negotiations with Germany, 1954-55; spl. cons. coordinator U.S. Mission to NATO; U.S. govt. rep. other negotiations with various European govts. for U.S. Dept. Def. Mem. Am., N.Y.C. bar assns., Internat. Law Assn. Episcopalian. Clubs: Union Interalliee (Paris); University (N.Y.); Metropolitan (Washington); Country (New Canaan, Conn.). Home: CT Died June 6, 1967; buried Lakeview Cemetery, New Canaan CT

HOARE, ELMER JOSEPH, lawyer; b. Rochester, N.Y., Sept. 13, 1902; s. Richard E. and Anna (Walker) H.; A.B., U. Rochester, 1924; LL.B., Columbia, 1927; m. Bertha H. Eckenroth, Aug. 26, 1932 (dec.); 1 dau., Ann (Mrs. George G. Snowden III); 2d, Elizabeth Compton, Sept. 10, 1964. Admitted to N.Y. bar, 1928, since practiced in N.Y.C.; asso. Taylor Blanc Capron & Marsh., 1927-43; mem. firm Turk, Marsh, Kelly & Hoare, and predecessors, 1943-71. Mem. Am., N.Y. State bar assns., Assn. Bar City N.Y., Am. Judicature Soc. Clubs: University; Down Town Assn. Home: New York City NY Died May 14, 1971.

HOBART, MRS. LOWELL FLETCHER (EDITH LIELA), ex-pres. gen. D.A.R.; b. Cincinnati, Mar. 19, 1869; d. James Taylor and Anna Martin (Reed) Irwin; ed. pub. schs.; m. Lowell Fletcher Hobart, of Cincinnati, Oct. 1, 1890 (died Feb. 19, 1913); 1 son, Lowell Fletcher. Active in civic, hereditary and patriotic socs.; served in Red Cross and training camp work, World War. Mem. Soc. Mayflower Descendants, Daughters of Founders and Patriots, Colonial Dames of America, Daughters of Am. Colonists, Huguenot Soc. of S.C., D.A.R. (pres. gen. term 1929-32), U.S. Daughters of 1812, New England Women (pres. gen.), Am. War Mothers, Am. Legion Auxiliary (1st nat. pres. 1921-22); 1st Am. v.p. Auxiliary to Federation Interalliee des Anciens Combattants. Introduced at private audience to King George and Queen Mary, King Albert and Queen Elizabeth (Belgium), King Victor Emanuel (Italy), Pope Pius XI. Home: 3130 Fairfield Av., Cincinnati OH‡

HOBBLE, DEBORAH SHARP, educator; b. Great Bend, Kan., Oct. 22, 1918; d. Howard D. and Fannie (Rohrbacher) Sharp; B.S., Kan. State U., 1941, M.S., 1963; postgrad. Colo. State U., 1948, U. Wis., 1949; m. Pierce R. Hobble, Sept. 28, 1951 (dec. Oct. 1960); children—Deborah Frances, Sarah Caroline. Tchr. vocational homemaking Holcomb (Kan.) High Sch., 1941-43, Willimantic (Conn.) High Sch., 1945; jr. asst. applied physics lab. Jones Hopkins U., Balt., 1943-45; Morton County extension home economist, Kan., 1946-47, Ford County, Kan., 1947-54; extension specialist family life Kan. State U., Manhattan, 1963-69. Conducted weekly radio program KGNO, Dodge City, Kan., 1949-54. Mem. Gov.'s Com. on Handicapped Children, 1966. Mem. Nat. Council Family Relations, Omicron Nu, Epsilon Sigma Phi. Methodist. Contbr. articles to ednl. circulars, newspapers. Home: Manhattan KS Died Oct. 25, 1969.

HOBBS, CHARLES SERIGHT, educator; b. Innan, Kan., Feb. 2, 1909; s. Charles S. and Ella Mae (Olson) H.; B.S., Okla. A. & M. Coll., 1938; M.S., Ph.D., Cornell, 1938-41; m. Corinne K. Clay, Jan. 6, 1931; children—Charles Seright, Patricia Corinne, Frank Barron, William Clay, Robert Carlton. Prof. animal husbandry, vet. sci. head agrl. research and teaching U. Tenn. 1947-71. Fellow Am. Soc. Animal Sci. (pres. 1965-66; distinguished service award 1966); mem. A.A.A.S. (pres.), Alpha Zeta, Sigma Xi, Block and Bridle, Phi Eta Sigma, Omicron Delta Kappa, Beta Theta Pi, Phi Kappa Phi. Rotarian. Co-author: The Livestock Book. Author articles profl. jours. Home: Louisville TN Died Dec. 25, 1971.

HOBDY, JOHN BUFORD, vocational edn.; b. nr. Downs, Ala., Jan. 16, 1875; s. Robert Long and Mary (Buford) H.; B.S., Ala. Poly. Inst., 1897, M.S., 1898; grad. study U. of Chicago, 1900, Harvard, 1918, Columbia U., 1929; LL.D., U. of Ala., 1925; m. Mary Florence Smith June 3, 1903; 1 son, Robert Buford. Teacher of science and dir. sch. farm, Albertville, Ala., 1898-1901; pres. 7th congressional Dist. Agrl. Sch. of Ala., 1901-11; supervisor secondary edn., Ala., 1912-14; supervisor rural schs., Ala., 1914-18; supervisor agrl. edn., Ala., 1918-21; Ala. state dir. vocational edn. 1921-45, dir. Rehabilitation Service 1926-45; dir. Crippled Children's Service under Nat. Social Service Act 1935-45; ret. June 1945. Mem. faculty, Summer School, Columbia U., 1930. Mem. Ala. State Textbook Commn., 1908-13; spl. agt. United States Gov. jr. extension work, 1911-14. Dir. Ala. Emergency Relief for Teachers, 1933-34; dir. Nat. Defense Training Program for Ala., 1940-44, Mem. N.E.A., Am. Vocational Assn. (v.p. and mem. exec. com. 1925-27, 1938-39), Nat. Assn. State Dirs. Vocational Edn. (ex-pres.), Ala. Edn. Assn. (ex-pres.), Ala. Vocational Assn. (ex-pres.), Phi Delta Theta, Kappa Delta Pi, Iota Lambda Sigma. Democrat. Episcopalian. K.P. Home: 237 E. Magnolia Av., Auburn AL‡

HOBGOOD, FRANK P., lawyer; b. Oxford, N.C., Dec. 17, 1872; s. Frank P. and Mary Anne (Royal) H.; A.B., Wake Forest Coll., Wake Forest, N.C. 1893; LL.B., George Washington U., 1898. Practiced at Greensboro, N.C., since 1903; mem. N.C. Senate, 1911-15; spl. asst. to atty. gen. of U.S. in oil lands litigation, Wyo. and Calif., 1915-17. Col. and insp. gen. Nat. Guard N.C., 1899-1900. President bd. of trustees of Palmer Memorial Inst. Mem. Am. and N.C. State bar assns., Newcomen Society of England, Phi Delta Phi. Democrat. Baptist. Mason; Grand Master Grand Lodge of Masons of N.C., 1915; Odd Fellow. Clubs: Rotary, Penrose Park Country (Reidsville, N.C.). Home: Reidsville, N.C. Office: Reidsville NC‡

HOBSON A(LPHONZO) AUGUSTUS, clergyman; b. Alexandria, Va., June 17, 1877; s. Mathew and Adrienna Columbia (Grantland) H.; A.B., Columbian (now George Washington U.), 1899; Ph.D., U. of Chicago, 1903; m. Mathilda Christman, Jan. 31, 1899; children—Burton Harper (dec.), Dorothy M., Ruth N., Virginia M. Asst. pastor Immanuel Ch., Chicago, 1900, Englewood Ch., Chicago, 1900-04; ordained Bapt. ministry, 1901; pastor Hyattsville, Md., 1904-06, Beth Eden Ch., Pittsburgh, 1906-10; sec. to chancellor U. of Pittsburgh, 1910-11; pastor First Ch., Waltham, Mass., 1912-21, First Ch., Milwaukee, 1921-25, Upper Alton Ch., Alton, Ill., 1925-35; acting pastor First Bapt. Ch. in Williamsburg, Brooklyn, N.Y., 1938-39; pastor Olivet Baptist Church, Valley Stream, N.Y., 1939-41; Chambers Memorial Baptist Ch., New York, 1944; Lefferts Park Baptist Church, Brooklyn, N.Y., 1944-45, 1947-49; spl. lecturer, teacher, Shurtleff Coll., summers 1926, 27, 33, 34. Author: The Diatessaron of Tatian and the Synoptic Problem, 1904; Positive Protestantism, 1917. Contbr. on religious and social subjects. Home: 142 92d St., Brooklyn 9 NY‡

HOBSON, JESSE EDWARD, consultant, university adminstr; b. Marshall, Ind. May 2, 1911; s. Clayton Arthur and Alice N. (Newlin) H.; B.S. in Electrical Engineer, Purdue University, 1932, M.S., 1933, Doctor of Engring., 1957; Ph.D., Cal. Inst. Tech., Pasadena, 1935; m. Anne Warren, July 8, 1934 (div., Dec., 1949); 1 dau., Carolyn Jean; m. 2d, Louise Smith Taylor, June 30, 1950. Assistant prof. mathematics, Earlham Coll., Richmond, Ind., 1935-36; instr. elec. engring., Armour Inst. Tech., Chicago, 1936-37; central station engr., Westinghouse Elec. & Mfg. Co., Pittsburgh, Pa., 1937-41; dir. and prof. elec. engring., Ill. Inst. Tech., Chicago, 1941-44; director of Armour Research Foundation, 1944-48; dir. Stanford Research Inst., 1948-56; v.p. United Fruit Co., Boston, 1957-61, director of research, 1958-61; v.p. So. Meth. U., 1963-65; pres. Heald Hobson & Assos., 1966-70; exec. dir. Tager (Dallas), 1966-67; cons. in research mgmt. and planning; dir. planning and devel. Southwest Research Institute, San Antonio, Tex.; Tau Beta Pi. Research Fellow, 1932-33; Charles Coffin Found. Research Fellow, 1933-34. Exec. chmn. 1st Nat. Electronics Conf., 1944; chmn. bd. Nat. Electronics Conf., Inc., 1945; bd. adv. Purdue Research Found. Recipient Outstanding Young Elec. Engrs. Award, 1940. Fellow I.E.E.E.; mem. Western Soc. Engrs., Am. Soc. Engring. Edn., N.Y. Acad. Scis., Tau Beta Pi, Sigma Xi, Eta Kappa Nu (nat. pres. 1954-55). Episcopalian. Mason. Clubs: University (Chgo.); Engineers (N.Y.C.); California (Los Angeles). Home: Los Angeles CA Died Nov. 5, 1970; buried Popular Grove Cemetery, Marshall IN

HOBSON, ROBERT LOUIS, indsl. psychologist; b. Blountstown, Fla., Aug. 15, 1918; s. Claude C. and Lenna S. (Van Gundy) H.; A.B., Grinnell Coll., 1940; M.S., Purdue U., 1943, Ph.D., 1948; m. Elizabeth A. Maxwell, Aug. 15, 1941; children—Barbara L., James A., Caroline A., Henry C., Linda S., William T. Lab. instr. Grinnell Coll., 1940-41; pvt. practice indsl. psychology cons., 1941-72; purchasing and materials control Nat. Homes Corps., 1942-44; vocational appraiser Purdue U., 1946-47, test editor div. edn. reference, 1947-48; tng. cons., maintenance Am. Airlines, 1955-57; with psychology dept. U. Tulsa, 1946-73, head dept., 1956-70; personnel cons. Skelly Oil Co., 1965-73. Dir. research Nat. Tng. Dirs. Joint Elec. Apprentice Programs. Served with USAAF, 1944-45. Mem. Am., Midwest, S.W. psychol. assns., Grinnell Friars, Tulsa Personnel Group, Tulsa Tng. Group, Sigma Xi, Psi Chi. Mason. Contbr. articles to profl. publs. Inventor flexible gunnery trainer. Home: Tulsa OK Died Jan. 8, 1973.

HOBSON, WILLIAM ANDREW, clergyman; b. Bibb County, Ala., June 5, 1862; s. Rev. Francis Marion and Mary Catherine (Shows) H.; Ala. State U., 1885; A.B., Howard Coll., Ala., 1892, D.D., 1897; Southern Bapt. Theol. Sem., Louisville, Ky., 1893-94; m. Lou Alma Cheek, Oct. 2, 1887; children—Mary Kate (dec.), Tolbert Francis. Ordained Bapt. ministry, 1885; city missionary, Birmingham, 1885-88; founder Avondale Baptist Church, and pastor, 1886-88; student pastor Baptist Church, Coaling, Warrior, Truesville, Dolomite, 1889-92, Litchfield (Ky.) Baptist Church, 1892-94; pastor Woodlawn Church, Birmingham, 1894-96, Ruhama Church (seat of Howard College), Birmingham, 1896-1900, 1st Church Jacksonville, Florida, 1900-23, Baptist Temple, St. Petersburg, Florida, 1924-27; teacher of Bible, Howard College, 1896-1900; editor Florida Baptist Witness, 1902-03; founder, 1932 and pastor Disston Avenue Baptist Church, St. Petersburg, Fla., 1932-46; pastor emeritus, since 1946. Mem. exec. bd. and pres. Fla. Bapt. Conv., Inc., 1911-23; Fla. mem. exec. com. Southern Bapt. Conv., 1927-36, now mem. hist. com.; moderator Tampa Bay Baptist Assn., 1928-31; mem. Bapt. State Bd., 1900-36. Trustee (formerly spl. rep.) John B. Stetson University, DeLand, Fla.; trustee Florida Baptist Orphanage, Arcadia, Florida; dean of Sch. of the Prophets (summer sch. for Bapt. ministers), 1929-31. Democrat. Mason. Air warden during World War II. Home: 2995 First Av. N., St Petersburg 6 FL‡

HOCA, MYRON MYROSLAW, educator; b. Belz, Ukraine, Feb. 4, 1912; s. Vasyl and Apollonia (Sukhyi) H.; student Tchrs. Seminar and Coll. of Social Work Ukraine, 1937; Ph.D., U. Innsbruck (Austria), 1948; m.

Helena A. Scharmer; children—Claudia, Theodore, Renata. Came to U.S., 1949, naturalized, 1954. Psychol. researcist, journalist, tchr., Ukraine, 1937-40; Weaver until 1952; chemist Pratt & Letchworth, Buffalo, 1952-58; asst. prof., E. European and Soviet Inst., Niagara U., Niagara Falla, N.Y., 1958-63, asso. prof. edn., 1963-69. Recipient first prize for research in psychology Polish Ministry of Edn., 1938. Mem. Schvchenko Sci. Soc. (N.Y.C.). Contbr. articles to profl. jours. Home: Kenmore NY Died June 20, 1969.

HOCH, DANIEL K., ex-congressman; b. Oley Twp., Berks County, Pa., Jan. 31, 1866; widower. Served apprenticeship as printer on Reading (Pa.) Eagle; has worked in all depts. of a newspaper as printer, pressman, reporter, editor, advertising and circulation depts.; county controller, Berks County, 1912-16; mem. 78th Congress (1943-45), 14th Pa. Dist. and 79th Congress (1945-47), 13th Pennsylvania Dist. Active in promotion of Applachian Trail; pres. Blue Mountain Eagle Climbing Club; mem. Pa. Legislature, 1899-1901. Democrat. Lutheran. Past state pres. Patriotic Order Sons of America. Home: Reading PA‡

HOCHSTETTER, ROBERT WILLIAM, chemist; b. Cincinnati, Aug., 1873; s. William and Agnes (Hartmann) H.; early edn. Cincinnati pub. schs.; grad. U. of Cincinnati, 1895; postgrad. studies at Federal Polytechnic, Zurich, Switzerland; unmarried. Pres. Am. Chem. Soc., 1902; v.-p. Ault & Wiborg Co. Home: Oak St., Mt. Auburn, O. Office: 7th and Culvert St., Cincinnati OH‡

HOCHWALD, FRITZ G(ABRIEL), chemist; b. Berlin, Germany, July 23, 1897; s. Moritz and Elsa (Stahl) H.; grad. Berlin Inst. Tech., 1923, Dr. Chem. Engring., 1925; patent law exam., Germany, 1928, U.S., 1945; m. Ilse Eva Wolfsberg, Dec. 29, 1943. Came to U.S., 1943, naturalized, 1947. Admitted to patent law practice, 1928; research chemist Bavarian Cyanamid Co., 1923-28; head central patent dept. German Cyanamid Cos., 1928-38; practice before U.S. and Canadian patent offices, 1945-68, before German Patent Office, 1967-68. Served as lt., Signal Corps, German Army, 1915-19. Mem. Am. Chem. Soc., Washington Acad. Scis., Botanical Society of Washington, New York Patent Law Assn., Internat. Patent and Trademark Assn. Contbr. profl. publs., Germany. Patents cyanamid and accumulator fields. Home: Washington DC Died May 6, 1968.

HOCKADAY, ELA, educator; b. Ladonia, Tex., Mar. 12, 1876; d. Thomas Hart Benton and Mary Elizabeth (Kerr) H.; ed. Denton Normal Sch., U. of Chicago, Columbia U.; Litt.D., Austin Coll., Sherman, Tex., 1940. Prin. pub. schs., Sherman, Tex., 1907-10; instr. in science, Durant (Okla.) State Normal Sch., 1910-12; upon invitation of business men of Dallas, Tex., established The Miss Hockaday Sch. for Girls, 1913, of which is pres., and The Hockaday Junior College, 1931, The Music Institute, 1938. Democrat. Presbyterian. Home: Greenville Rd., Dallas TX*‡

HOCKETT, HOMER CAREY, prof. history; b. Martinsville, O., Dec. 11, 1875; s. Francis Lindley and Rachel (Carey) H.; student Earlham Coll. (Richmond, Ind.) and Indiana U.; B. Litt., U. of Wis., 1903, Ph.D., 1917; grad. scholar and fellow, U. of Wis., 1903-05; Harrison research fellow, U. of Pa., 1919-20; m. Amy Francisco, July 11, 1900; children—Francesca, Robert Casad, Virginia, Charles Francis. In offices of various mfg. concerns, 1892-1901; instr. in history, U. of Wis., Feb.-July 1905; prof. history and economics, Central Coll., Fayette, Mo., 1905-08; instr. in history, U. of Wis., 1908-09; asso. prof. Am. history, Ohio State U., 1909-13, prof., 1913-26, prof. history since 1926, now prof. emeritus; lecturer, summers univs. of Ill., Wis., Pa., Chicago, etc. Mem. Am. Hist. Assn., Miss. Valley Hist. Assn. (pres. 1929-30), Phi Beta Kappa. Conglist. Author: Federalism and the West," in Turner Essays in American History, 1910; Western Influences on Political Parties to 1825, 1917; Political and Social Growth of the American People (1492-1865), 3d edit. 1940; Introduction to Research in Am. History, 1931, (revised 1948); Constitutional History of United States, 1776-1876 (2 vols.); 1939; (with Arthur M. Schlesinger) Land of the Free, 1944. Contbr. to Dictionary of Am. Biography, Dictionary of Am. History, and various hist. jours. Home: 202 W. Valerio St., Santa Barbara CA‡

HODDINOTT, MARY LORETTA, home economist; b. White Plains, N.Y., Jan. 17, 1934; d. Alfred H. and Mary C. (Lewis) Hoddinott; B.S. in Home Econs., U. Conn., 1955. Home economist Paris & Peart Advt. Agy., N.Y.C., 1955-58, Gen. Foods Photography Kitchens, N.Y.C., 1958-67, Gen. Foods Corp., White Plains, N.Y., 1967-68. Vol. chmn. White Plains (N.Y.) Woman's Club, Jr. Sect., 1963-64, 1st vice chmn., 1964-65. Mem. Am. Home Econs. Assn., Home Economists in Bus., Cath. Alumni Club, U. Conn. Alumni Assn., A.R.C. Home: White Plains NY Died Oct. 11, 1968.

HODGE, WILLIAM IRVINE, engr.; b. Salt Lake City, Jan. 7, 1905; s. Robert Henderson and Margaret (Irvine) H.; student U. Utah, 1924-26, Columbia, 1928-30; m. Doris Magee, Apr. 16, 1943. Design engr. Gibbs & Hill, cons. engrs., N.Y.C., 1927-28, Amalgamated Sugar Co., Ogden, Utah, 1933-43; v.p. Utah-Ida. Central R.R., Ogden Transit Co., Ogden, 1944-45, bd. dir.; chief engr. Vitorio-minas R.R. project in Brazil, Raymond-Morrison-Knudsen, 1946-47; prin. engr. Bechtel Corp., Los Angeles, 1948-50; West Coast mgr. Bulkley Dunton Processes, Inc., Los Angeles, 1951-53; supr. N. Am. Aviation, Los Angeles, 1953-58; project engr. Gen. Dynamics-Convair, San Diego, 1958-70; dir. Yucca Mut. Irrigation Dist., Fallbrook, Cal. Mem. Nat., Cal., Ida. socs. profl. engrs., Soc. Am. Mil. Engrs., Phi Delta Theta, Nat. Mgmt. Assn., C. of C. Clubs: Kiwanis, Ogden Weber, Ogden San Diego CA Died Mar. 3, 1970.

HODGES, FRANK, born in Boscobel, Wisconsin, September 19, 1863; s. William Wesley and Lydia Ann (Hartsborn) H.; educated high school, Olathe, Kansas, business college, Kansas City, Missouri; married Jessie McKoin, June 14, 1894; children—Frank, Jessie McKoin; m. 2d, Eunice May Daniels, Aug. 22, 1913. Began as teacher, 1885; now head Hodges Bros., investments and building materials, Olathe; editor Johnson County Democrat; chairman of board First National Bank, Olathe, Kansas; dir. Overland Park State Bank. Formerly mgr. R.F.C. Agency, Kansas City, Mo., resigned Feb. 1, 1943. Mem. Hoo Hoo. Democrat. Mason (32 deg., Shriner), K.P. Clubs: Kansas City (Mo.); Boicourt Hunting; Lake View. Writer column, The Iconoclast. Home: 432 S. Water St., Olathe KS‡

HODGES, GILBERT, manager N.Y. Mets Profl. Baseball Team, Oct. from 1967. Address: Flushing NY Died Apr. 2, 1972.

HODGES, JOHN CUNYUS, coll. prof.; b. Cotton Valley, La., Mar. 15, 1892; s. Floyd Crawford and Addie (Reynolds) H.; A.B., Meridian Coll., 1911; M.A., Tulane U., 1912; Ph.D., Harvard, 1918; Litt.D. (hon.), Tenn. Wesleyan College, 1962; m. Lilian Nelson, Jan. 24, 1914 (deceased July 18, 1951); 1 son, John Nelson; married 2d, Cornelia Smartt Hendley, August 15, 1952. Instr. of English, Northwestern University, 1913-16; Christopher Weld Scholar, Harvard, 1917-18; assistant prof. English, Ohio Wesleyan U., 1918-19, asso. prof., 1919-20, prof., 1920-21; prof. English, U. Tenn., 1921-37, chmn. dept., 1937-62, coordinator Library Development Program, from 1959; vis. prof. English summers at O. State, Harvard and Northwestern; vis. scholar Henry E. Huntington Library, 1951, Folger Shakespeare Library, 1952. Bd. visitors Tulane U., past pres. Alumni Assn. Mem. Conf. Coll. Composition and Communication, Modern Lang. Assn. America (sec., chmn. classical period group, 1957-58), Tenn. Philological Assn. (pres. 1957-58), College English Assn., Am. Assn. U. Profs., Nat. Council Tchrs. English (past mem. commn. English curriculum), Modern Humanities Research Assn., So. Atlantic Modern Language Association (past president), Tennessee Council of Teachers of English, Delta Sigma Phi, Phi Kappa Phi. Presbyn. Clubs: Faculty, Smokers. Author: William Congreve, the Man, 1941; Harbrace Handbook of English, 1941, rev. 1963; Harbrace Omnibus (with H. B. Reed, J. N. McCorkle, W. C. Hildreth), 1942; Basic Writing and Reading, 1943; revised edit., 1944; English Manual for Teachers (with the English Teachers of Tenn.), 1946; Harbrace College Handbook, 1946, rev. 1951, 56, 62, 67; Harbrace College Workbook, 1952, Forms 2, 3, 4, 5, 6, 1953, 56, 57, 62, 67; (with J. H. Wise, J. E. Congleton, A. C. Morris) College English the First Year, 1952, revised 1964; Exercise Manual for Coll. English, 1952; Form 2, 1954, rev. 1964; The Library of William Congreve, 1955; William Congreve: Letters and Documents, 1964; (with Sheila Y. Laws) Harbrace Writing Course, 1967. Contbr. to learned mags. Home: Knoxville TN Died 1967.

HODGES, JOHNNY, saxophonist; b. Cambridge, Mass., July 25, 1907. Mem. Duke Ellington's Orch., 1928-51, 55-70; recording team with organist Wild Bill Davis, 1961-70, albums include Blue Hodge, Mess of Blues, Blue Rabbit, Joes' Blues, Wings and Things. ConSoul Sax; other recordings. Home: New York City NY Died May 11, 1970.

HODGES, JOSEPH GILLULY, lawyer; b. Denver, Apr. 30, 1909; s. William Vanderveer and Mabel (Guilluly) H.; grad. Hotchkiss Sch., 1926; A.B., Yale, 1930; LL.B., Harvard, 1933; m. Elaine Chanute, Mar. 31, 1939; children—Elaine M. (Mrs. Duval Edward Harvey), Joseph Gilluly, Ann V. Admitted to Colo. bar, 1933, later practiced in Denver; dep. dist. atty. Denver County, 1933-34; mem. firm Hodges, Wilson & Vidal, 1934-36; partner Hodges, Wilson & Vidal and Hodges, Vidal & Goree, 1936-53; partner Hodges, Silverstein, Hodges & Harrington and Hodges, Silverstein & Harrington, 1953-69, Hodges, Harrington, Kerwin & Otten, also Hodges, Kerwin, Otten & Weeks, 1970-72. Dir. Colo. Nat. Bank Denver, Colo. Nat. Bankshares, Inc. Pres. Denver Water Bd., 1963-64. Bd. dirs. Childrens Hosp. Assn., Denver, 1969-72; trustee Denver Mus. Natural History, Colo. Hosp. Service. Served to maj. USAAF, 1942-45. Fellow Am. Bar Found., Am. Law Inst.; mem. Am. (past del.), Colo. (past pres.), Denver bar assns., Denver C. of C. (past dir.), Alpha Delta Phi. Episcopalian. Rotarian. Home: Denver CO Died Nov. 24, 1972; buried Fairmount Cemetery, Denver CO

HODGES, LOUISE THREETE, b. Atlanta, Ga.; d. James Madison and Frances (McMullan) Collier; ed. pvt. sch. and home study with tutor; m. Gadsden, Ala., Benjamin F. Hodges (now deceased). Since 1889 in lit. work; has written much for Atlanta and other Ga. papers; contb'r poems, essays, etc., to mags. Author: Thought Blossoms from the South, 1895 L11. Address: Atlanta GA‡

HODGINS, ERIC, editor, author; b. Detroit, March. 2, 1899; s. Rev. Frederic Brinkley and Edith Gertrude (Bull) H.; S.B., Mass. Inst. Tech., 1922; student Harvard Grad. Sch., 1923-24; Litt. D., Bates Coll, 1939; m. Catherine Cornforth Carlson, July 5, 1930 (dec. 1933); 1 son, Roderic Carlson; m. 2d, Eleanor Treacy, Oct. 31, 1936; 1 dau. Eleanor Patricia. Mng. editor Tech. Review Mass. Inst. Tech. publ., 1922-27; editor Youth's Companion, 1927-29; asso. editor Redbook, 1929-33; with Time, Inc., N.Y.C., 1933-58, mng. editor Fortune, 1935-37, pub., 1937-41, v.p., 1938-46. Mem. Pres.'s Materials Policy Commn., 1950-52; mem. com. pub. information Am. Heart Assn., 1965. Recipient George Westinghouse award A.A.A.S., 1953. Author: Mr. Blandings Builds His Dream House, 1948; Blandings' Way, 1950; Episode (Blakeslee award Am. Heart Assn. 1964), 1964. Home: New York City NY Died Jan. 7, 1971.

HODGSON, FRANK CORRIN, lawyer; b. Grant Co., Minn., Apr. 11, 1884; s. Thomas Corrin and Eliza (Clague) H.; A.B., U. Minn., 1907; LL.B., Harvard, 1914; LL.D., Hamline U., 1965; m. Edith Eva Burgstahler, Sept. 11, 1920; 1 dau., Ruth Elaine (Mrs. Don E. Cadwell). Admitted to Minn. bar, 1915, since practiced in St. Paul. Pres. bd. trustees, chmn. bd. Hamline U.; trustee Ramsey County Law Library; dir. Goodwill Industries. Mem. Harvard Law Sch. Assn., Phi Beta Kappa. Mem. Methodist church. Mason (K.C.C.H.). Clubs: Saint Paul Association. Rotary (past pres.), Athletic, Town and Country (St. Paul). Home: St Paul MN Died May 8, 1968; buried Sunset Memorial Park, Minneapolis MN

HODGSON, HARRY, mfr.; b. Athens, Ga., Mar. 6, 1874; s. Edward Reginald and Mary V. (Strahan) H.; A.B., U. of Ga., 1893, LL.D., 1922; m. Marie Bishop Lowe, Jan. 6, 1900; children—Hazel Eveleith (Mrs. M. L. McNeel, Jr.), Harry Lowe, Edward R. III, Virginia (Mrs. Fred S. Robbins), Robert Bishop. Reporter, New York Evening Telegram and Atlanta Constitution, 1893-97; mem. firm Hodgson Cotton Co., commercial fertilizers, since 1897; pres. Hodgson Oil Refining Co.; sec., treas. and dir. Empire State Chem. Co., Hodgson's, Inc. Mem. exec. com. Conf. for Edn. in the South, 1908-14; trustee U. of Ga., 1911-31. Pres. Southern Fertilizer Assn., 1914-20; v.p. Interstate Cottonseed Crushers Assn., 1926-28; pres., 1928-29; pres. Nat. Cottonseed Products Assn., 1929-30; pres. Cottonseed and Peanut Crushers Assn. of Ga., 1945-46. Mem. Phi Beta Kappa Alpha. Democrat. Baptist. Home: Athens GA‡

HODGSON, JOSEPH FREDERICK, soil scientist, educator; b. Rochester, N.Y., Mar. 7, 1929; s. Millard Benjamin and Elsie (Gleason) H.; B.S., U. Md., 1951; Ph.D., U. Wis., 1955; m. Jennie Alexander, June 19, 1952; children—Lyle Ann, Lori Jean. Grad. asst. U. Wis., Madison, 1951-55; biol. asso. Fort Detrick, Frederick, Md., 1955-57; soil scientist U.S. Plant Soil and Nutrition Lab., Ithaca, N.Y., 1957-70; asso. prof. agronomy Cornell U., Ithaca, N.Y., 1965-70. Faculty affiliate Colo. State U., Fort Collins, 1964-65. Served with AUS, 1955-57. Mem. Am. Soc. Agronomy, Am. Chem. Soc., Internat. Soc. Soil Sci., Sigma Xi. Fellow A.A.A.S. Research into reactions of trace metals with clays. Home: Ithaca NY Died Oct. 5, 1970.

HODGSON, JOSEPH PARK, mine mgr.; b. Swathrmoor, Lancashire, Eng., Aug. 19, 1869; s. Wilson Park and Jane H.; ed. night schs., Ishpeming, Mich., 2 yrs., and corr. course Alexander Hamilton Inst., New York; married Ellen Jewell, Apr. 19, 1890; married 2d, Clara W. Naylor, July 2, 1932. Came to U.S., 1889, naturalized citizen, 1894. Miner, timberman, foreman, Lake Superior Iron Co., and Oliver Mining Co., Ishpeming, 1889-1907; asst. supt., supt. and gen. supt. Breitung Mines, Negaunee, Mich., 1907-12; supt. mines Copper Queen Consol. Mining Co., Bisbee, Ariz., 1912-16; apptd. cons. engr. mining dept., Phelps Dodge Corp., Ariz. and New York, 1918, also mgr. mines and reduction plants, same corp., Morenci and Bisbee, Ariz.; became cons. mining engr. Phelps Dodge Corp.; now retired. County supervisor Marquette County, Mich., 6 yrs.; formerly regent, U. of Ariz. Mem. Am. Inst. Mining and Metall. Engrs., Lake Superior Mining Inst., Am. Mining Congress. Republican. Presbyn. Mason (32 deg., K.T., Shriner). Contbr. on mining topics to tech. publs. Home: 1228 Selby Av., Los Angeles 24 CA‡

HODGSON, MARSHALL GOODWIN SIMMS, educator, historian; b. Richmond, Ind. Apr. 11, 1922; s. James Goodwin and Gertrude (Simms) H.; B.A., U. Colo., 1943, Earlham Coll., 1943; Ph.D., U. Chgo., 1951; m. Phyllis Eleanor Walker, May 25, 1958; children—Sara Elizabeth, Beverly Ruth, Cynthia Susan. Research asso. U. Chgo., 1953-56, mem. faculty, 1956-68, prof. in com. social thought and history dept.,

1965-—, chmn. com. social thought, 1965-68; gastdozent U. Frankfurt (Germany), 1952-53; vis. lectr. Harvard, 1964-65. Fulbright grantee, India, 1951-52. Mem. Am. Soc. Study Religion, Am. Oriental Soc., Am. Hist. Assn., Middle East Studies Assn. N.Am., Phi Beta Kappa. Mem. Soc. of Friends. Author: The Order of Assassins: The Struggle of the Early Nizari Ismailis against the Islamic World, 1955; Venture of Islam: A Study of Conscience in History, 3 vols., 1973. Home: IL Died June 10, 1968.

HODGSON, THEKLA ROESE, librarian; b. Detroit, May 17, 1901; d. Frederick A. and M. Bertha (Mau) Roese; A.B., U. Mich., 1922; M. Library Sci., Columbia, 1941. Asst. Detroit Pub. Library, 1922-28, sr. asst. 1937-44, br. librarian Butzel, 1944-45, Campbell 1945-48, Duffield, 1948-50, Benjamin Franklin, 1950-57, 63-66, Parkman, 1957-63, Merrill Palmer Motherhood and Home Tng. Sch., 1928-37. Mem. Am., Mich. library assns., Detroit Pub. Library Staff Assn., Phi Beta Kappa, Beta Phi Mu. Mem. United Church of Christ. Club: Women's City. Home: Grosse Pointe MI Died May 23, 1971.

HODUR, FRANCIS, prime bishop; b. Zarkack, County Chrzanowskiem, Poland, April 2, 1866; s. John and Mary (Koszowska) H.; came to U.S., 1892, naturalized 1894; ed. U. of Crakow, Poland, Nowodawskiego (Polish Lyceum), Polish U. Jagielon, St. Vincent Seminary, Betty, Pa. Began career as clergyman, 1893; organized the Polish Nat. Ch., 1897; elected bishop at the 1st Synod, 1904; consecrated bishop, 1907; organized the Polish Nat. Union (frat. and ins. orgn.), 1907; organized central orgns. of all choirs within the church; founded the Savanrola Seminary 1904; ordained many priests and consecrated 9 bishops; organized Home for the Aged an Inst. of the Polish Nat. Ch. Composed the official church song, Through the Years to Thee O Lord," 1912. Edited the Polish weekly paper, The Guard, 1897; editor of God's Field, bi-monthly paper, 1923. Author: Our Religion, 1900; Articles of Faith, 1904; Arise, 1920; Christ and His Church, 1922; Apokalipca, 20th Century, 1930; Thirty-three, 1933; Threshold of Forty, 1940. Address: 529 E. Locust St. Scranton 5 PA*‡

HOECHST, EDWARD JOHN, packaging co. exec.; b. Buffalo, Sept. 22, 1915; s. Jacob and Wilhelmina (Schenk) H.; B.S., in Indsl. Mgmt., N.Y.U., 1943; m. Pearl Hodges, Aug. 26, 1939; 1 son, Alfred. Mgr. labor relations Bell Aircraft Co., Buffalo, 1943-46, personnel dir. Penn Controls, Inc., Goshen, Ind., 1946-48; v.p., dir. indsl. relations Selby Shoe Co., Portsmouth, O., 1948-55; dir. indsl. relations Fieldcrest Mills, Inc., Leaksville, N.C., 1955-56; mgr. employee relations Am. Bosch Arma Corp., Garden City, N.Y., 1956-62; v.p. indsl. relations Standard Packaging Corp., N.Y.C., 1962-68. Chmn. Scioto County (O.) Community Chest drive, 1954, Scioto County fund raising drive Nat. Fedn. Infantile Paralysis, 1953; mem. Portsmouth Bd. Health, 1954-55, Bd. dirs. Portsmouth Gen. Hosp., 1953-54, Scioto County Tb Assn., 1952. Mem. Am. Mgmt. Assn., N.A.M., Nat. Assn. Personnel Huntington NY Died May 24, 1968.

HOEHLER, FRED KENNETH, cons. pub. adminstrn; b. Shenandoah, Pa., June 6, 1892; s. Henry George and Mina (Kimmel) H.; B.S., Pa. State Coll., 1915; grad. student U. Cin., 1916-17 and 1919-21; m. Dorothy Scovil Stevens, Oct. 18, 1917; children—Fred Kenneth, Caroline Ann (Mrs. James B. Kirkpatrick). First lt. F.A., A.U.S., 1917-19; asst. dir. Berry (Ga.) Sch., 1921-24; dir. pub. welfare, Cin. and Hamilton County (O.), 1927-33, dir. safety, Cin., 1933-35; dir. Am. Pub. Welfare Assn., 1936-43; pres. 1932-35; 51-52; exec. dir. Joint Army and Navy Com. on Welfare and Recreation, Washington, 1941-42; dir. Office of Fgn. Relief and Rehabilitation Operations in North Africa, Jan.-July, 1943, dir. European area, London, 1943; dir. Div. on Displaced Persons, U.N. R.R.A., 1944-45; exec. dir. Community Fund, Chgo., Inc., 1946-49; dir. Dept. Pub. Welfare, State of Ill., 1949-53; exec. dir. Citizens of Greater Chgo., Feb. 1953-Aug. 1954; cons. New World Found., 1954-57; spl. cons. to Mayor, City of Chgo., from 1955; v.p., treas. Willadean Nurseries, Inc.; chmn. bd. Internat. Film Bur.; mem. mental health adv. com. Council State Govts. Decorated Comdr. Nishaan el Iftikhar (Tunis), Grand Comdr. Quissan Alaouite (French Morocco); Recipient Rosenberger Medal, U. Chicago, 1953. President Nat. Conf. of Social Work, 1943; v.p. Internat. Conf. Social Work, 1948-56; mem. Fed. Adv. Council on Employment Security, 1948-55; mem. Nat. Citizens Commn. for Pub. Schs., 1949-55; mem. Commn. on Financing of Hosp., Care, 1950-54; chmn. bd. dirs. Midwest Regional Office of CARE, from 1955; member National Committee on Immigration and Citizenship, from 1955; trustee Nat. Citizens Council for Better Schools, 1956-59; pres. Mental Health Soc. Greater Chgo., 1957-58; bd. mem. U.S. com. World Fedn. for Mental Health, from 1958. Mem. Chgo. Council Fgn. Relations (dir.), Am. Acad. Polit. and Social Sci., Am. Soc. Pub. Administrn. (nat. membership chmn. 1957-59), Cin. Assn. Democrat. Conglist. Clubs: Quadrangle, City, University (Chgo.); Metropolitan (Washington). Author: Europe's Homeless Millions; 50 Years of Health and Welfare in U.S. Co-author (with de Huszar); Persistant International Issues. Contbr. profl. articles Ency. Americana, social service and pub. mgmt. publs. Home: Chicago IL Died Jan. 18, 1969.

HOEHN, KENNETH WILLIAM, broadcasting co. exec.; b. N.Y.C., Mar. 30, 1918; s. William August and Catherine (Hefner) H.; B.A., U. Wis., 1941; LL.B., Harvard, 1948; m. Jean Meredith, Nov. 15, 1943;children—W. Michael, Carol Jean. Admitted to N.Y. bar, 1949; with law dept. RCA, 1948-51; with CBS, 1951-72, tax dir., 1956-64, treas., 1964-72, 1971-72. Served to lt., aviator, USNR, 1941-45. Home: Manhasset NY Died June 18, 1972.

HOELSCHER, RANDOLPH PHILIP, educator; b. Evansville, Ind., Dec. 12, 1890; s. Philip Adolph and Marie (Rheinhardt) H.; B.S., Purdue, 1912, C.E., 1929; M.S., U. Ill., 1927; m. Hazel Heeger, Jan. 27, 1914 (dec. 1963); children—Betty Marie (Mrs. Hilmar B. Christianson, Jr.), and William Randolph; m. second, Ruby V. Faucett, June 26, 1965. Structural engr. George L. Mesker & Co., Evansville, 1912-16; instr. physics Baldwin Wallace Coll., Berea, O., 1916-18; instr. gen. engrng. drawing U. of Ill., 1918-21, asso., 1921-24, asst. prof., 1924-27, asso. professor, 1927-31, prof., 1931-59, professor emeritus, 1959-72, associate dean of engineering science Chicago undergraduate div., 1946-49, head department gen. engrng. drawing 1949-53, head department general engineering, 1953-72. Commr. Champaign County Housing Authority. Secretary University Senate 1945-51. Chmn. Am.-Brit.-Canadian Conf. on Unification of Drawing Standards, N.Y.C., 1952, leader Am. delegation, Toronto, 1957. Mem. Am. Standards Association, Am. Soc. C.E. (past president Central Ill. sect.), Am. Soc. M.E. (service award 1959), American Society Engrng. Edn. (mem. nat. council, 1941-43, 1948-50, past pres. Ill.-Ind. sect.), American Standards Assn. (chmn. com. Y-14, 1949-59), Tau Beta Pi. Mason. Club: Champaign-Urbana Kiwanis (p.p.). Author text books including: Graphic Aids in Engineering Computation (with others), 1951. Editor Proceedings of the Summer School for Drawing Tchrs. (with Justus Rising), 1949; Engrng. Drawing and Geometry (with C. H. Springer), 1956, 2d edit., 1961. Home: Champaign IL Died Jan. 5, 1972; buried Evansville IN

HOFFMAN, CHARLES W., judge; b. Glendale, O., July 31, 1870; s. Wesley E. and Elizabeth (Gorman) H.; student Nat. Normal U., 1887-88; LL.B., Cincinnati Law Sch., 1893; m. Clare H. Lippelman, June 29, 1898 (died July 4, 1925); children—Helen Elizabeth (Mrs. Ewart Simpkinson), Harlan Henry (dec.), Charlotte Virginia (Mrs. Edwin Kinsley); m. 2d, Anne Lippelman Anderson, July 11, 1939. Teacher in pub. schs., 1888-92; admitted to Ohio bar, 1893; practiced law in Cincinnati, 1893-1915; mayor of Glendale, 1903-06; solicitor of Glendale, 1912-15; judge of Juvenile Court and Domestic Relations Court, Cincinnati, since 1915. Lecturer on child welfare. Mem. Sub-advisory com. on probation, parole and penal institutions, Wickersham Law Enforcement Com. Mem. Cincinnati Bar Assn., Nat. Probation and Parole Association (honorary vice president), Social Workers' Club, etc. Democrat. Presbyterian. Club: The Cincinnati. Author: Story of a Country Church, 1900. Home: 25 Oliver Rd., Wyoming, OH Address: Court House, Cincinnati OH‡

HOFFMAN, DEAN MECK, newspaperman; b. Millersburg, Pa., Nov. 11, 1880; s. Issac White and Marian (Meek) H.; student Dickinson Prep. School, 1897-98; A.B., Dickinson Coll., 1902; m. Ethel Wilcox Miller, November 24, 1914; 1 son, Dean Meck. Reporter for Harrisburg and Philadelphia newspapers, 1902-10; city editor Harrisburg Patriot, 1911-12, mng. editor, 1912-17; mng. editor Patriot and Evening News, 1917-20, editor-in-chief, 1922-51, retired. Trustee Dickinson College. Member Phi Beta Kappa, Phi Delta Theta (pres. 1936-38), Sigma Delta Chi. Democrat. Presbyn. Mason, Elk. Clubs: Rotary, Pen and Pencil, Philadelphia. Editor: When Yesteryear Comes Back Again, 1932. Author: Electric Mergers, 1927; Smashing the Home Front, 1919; Twenty Years Out, 1922. Home: St Petersburg FL Died June 1968.

HOFFMAN, FREDERICK JOHN, educator; b. Port Washington, Wis., Sept. 21, 1909; s. Henry W. and Christina (Goldammer) H.; B.A., Stanford, 1934; M.A., U. Minn., 1935; Ph.D., Ohio State U., 1942; Litt.D., Carthage Coll., 1966; m. Eleanor Thompson, Oct. 10, 1936; 1 dau., Caroline; m. 2d, Mary Charlotte Holm, Aug. 19, 1967. Asst. prof. Ohio State U., 1945-47; asso. prof. U. Okla., 1947-48; asso. prof., prof. U. Wis., 1948-60; prof. U. Cal. at Riverside, 1960-65, chmn. English dept., 1961-63; distinguished prof. English, U. Wis., Milw., 1965-67; Fulbright prof. Rennes and Grenoble, France and Rome, Italy, 1953-54; vis. prof. Harvard, 1953, U. Wash., summer 1957, Duke, summer 1958, UNESCO, Brest, France, 1953, Sorbonne, Paris, 1954, U. Minn., 1960, U. Cal. at Riverside, 1963, Wash. State U., 1965, U. Cal. at Los Angeles, 1966, U. Notre Dame, 1966. Rockefeller fellow, 1945. Mem. Modern Lang. Assn., Am. Studies Assn., Nat. Council Tchrs. English, Coll. English Assn., Conf. on Modern Lit. Mich. State U. Author or co-author: Freudianism and the Literary Mind, 1945; The Little Magazine, 1946; The Twenties, 1955; Books on William Faulkner, 1962, Conrad Aiken, 1962, F. Scott Fitzgerald, 1962, Samuel Becket, 1962; The Mortal No, 1964; Literature and Religion, 1967; The Art of Southern Fiction, 1967. Home: Milwaukee WI Died Dec. 24, 1967.

HOFFMAN, HEMAN LESLIE, electronics exec.; b. Chgo., Dec. 23, 1905; s. Heman L. and Flora A. (Selfe) H.; B.A., Albion Coll., 1928, LL.D., 1961; LL.D., U. So. Cal., 1966; m. Frances E. Stevely, May 20, 1941; 1 dau., Jane L. Prodn. supt. Sparton Radio Co., 1928-29; sales dept. Firestone Tire & Rubber Co., 1930-36; mfrs. rep. elec. distbg., Portland, Ore., 1937-41; acquired Mission Bell Radio Manufacturing Company, 1941, became Hoffman Electronics Corp., propr.-pres., from 1941, chmn. bd., 1962-71; dir. Norris Industries, Inc., Los Angeles AMFAC, Inc., Honolulu. Trustee U. So. Cal., Albion (Mich.) Coll., Boys' Clubs Found. So. Cal.; nat. asso. Boys' Clubs Am.; founder, mem. Music Center; founding benefactor Los Angeles County Mus. Art; dir. So. Cal. Visitors Council, Huntington Inst. Applied Med. Research; bd. of mgrs. Silver Hill Found., New Canaan, Conn. Mem. Electronic Industries Assn. (pres. 1955-56, dir.), I.E.E.E., (sr.), So. Cal. Symphony-Hollywood Bowl Assn., Beta Gamma Sigma, Alpha Kappa Psi. Episcopalian. Republican (hon. trustee Rep. Assos. Los Angeles County). Clubs: Hollywood Turf (dir.), California, Valley Hunt, San Gabriel Country; Valley (Montecito, Cal.). Home: San Marino CA Died June 23, 1971; buried Rose Hills Meml. Park.

HOFFMAN, JAMES FRANKLIN, clergyman; b. Marietta, O., June 11, 1876; s. Louis and Mary (Brown) H.; B.A., Mount Union Coll., Alliance, O., 1905, M.A., 1907, D.D., 1921; Drew Theol. Sem., 1908; m. Anna Snyder, Sept. 4, 1907; children—Mary Ellen, Helen Elizabeth. Ordained ministry M.E. Ch., 1908; pastor successively Smithfield, O., Bridgeport, Miles Park Ch., Cleveland Heights, now Ch. of the Savior, Central Ch., Springfield, until 1926. Walnut Hills-Avondale, Cincinnati, 1926-32 South Av. Ch., Wilkinsburg, Pa., 1932-39, Bellevue Meth. Ch., Bellevue, Pa., 1939-45. Del. to Gen. Conf. Meth. Ch., 1932; mem. Alpha Tau Omega, Literary Club of Springfield. Republican. Mason. Rotarian. Home: 419 N. Home Av., Bellevue (Pittsburgh) PA‡

HOFFMAN, JOHN WESLEY, agriculturist, educator; b. Charleston, S.C., Aug. 11, 1870; s. Henry and Barbara H.; is a colored man; ed. Avery Normal Sch., Charleston, S.C., Albion Coll., Mich., Mich. Agr'l Coll.; grad. Howard Univ., Washington, 1889, D.Sc., State Univ. of Ky.; sp'l studies in agriculture and biology; prof. agr. and biology, Tuskegee Inst., 1894-6, State A. & M. Coll., Orangeburg, S.C., and Florida State Industrial Coll.; now prof. agriculture, Lincoln Inst., Jefferson City, Mo. Originated a new strawberry called the Hoffman Seedling Strawberry"; demonstrated that a grade of tea can be grown in Florida that would be superior in every way to imported teas; prepared for U.S. Dept. Agr. a dietary study of the kind and quality of food used by the Negro of the Black Belt" of the South, which has been translated into several languages for use by scientists; introduced farmers' insts. among colored people of South. Fellow Royal Micros. Soc. of England, fellow Royal Agr'l Soc., Am. Geog. Soc.; mem. A.A.A.S. At Lagos, West Africa, 1903-4, in service of British Colonial Dept. of Agr., as dir. of the cotton industry, engaged in introducing cotton growing into that country. Home: Charleston, S.C. Address: Lincoln Institute, Jefferson City MO‡

HOFFMAN, LEROY E., univ. dean; b. Millersburg, Ind., Sept. 12, 1893; s. Jacob and Lydia (Miller) H; B.S. in Agr., Purdue U., 1918; m. Romayne Thompson, Apr. 29, 1919; 1 son, Paul Gordon. With U.S. Bur. Plant Industry, 1918-19; county agrl. agt. Jay County, Ind., 1919-21; asst. county agt. leader Purdue U., 1921-41, asso. dir. agr. extension, 1941-58, dir. agr. extension, asso. dean agr., from 1958. Bd. dirs. Agrl. Alumni Seed Assn., 1937-71; chmn. Extension Com. Orgn. Policy, 1946-50; chmn. Hoffman com. Nat. Project Agr. Communication, 1955-71. Recipient Distinguished Service award U.S. Dept. Agr., 1959. Distinguished Service award Purdue Agrl. Alumni Assn., 1957. Mem. Acacia, Epsilon Sigma Phi (grand chief 1953-54). Mason. Home: West Lafayette IN Died May 17, 1971; buried Millersburg IN

HOFFMAN, ROY, lawyer, soldier; b. Neosho County, Kan., June 13, 1869; s. Peter S. and Julia (Hakins) H.; ed. Kan. Normal Coll., Ft. Scott, Kan.; m. Estelle Conklin, Oct. 5, 1898; children—Dorothy (Mrs. Hubert R. Hudson), Margaret (Mrs. Chas. A. Vose), Roy, Edgar Peter. Founded Guthrie Daily Leader, 1889; admitted to Okla. bar, 1892; dist. judge 10th Dist., 1908-12; U.S. atty., Okla., 1903-07; mem. Miley, Hoffman, Williams, France & Johnson, Okla. City. Past pres. Okla. State Press and Bar Assns.; dir. First Nat. Bank & Trust Co. and other banks and oil cos. Enlisted Spanish-Am. War; capt. Co. K. 1st Vol. Inf., 1898; lt. col. 1st Okla. Inf., 1900; col. same, 1901-16; in comd. same. Mexican Border service, 1916-17; brig. gen. U.S. Army, Aug. 5, 1917, and comd. Ft. Sill, Okla., and 61st Depot Brig., Camp Bowie, Tex.; assisted in orgn. 36th Div.; comdr. 93d Div. (colored), Dec. 3, 1917; organized 93d Div., Newport News, Va.; took same verseas, Feb. 1918, and now in continuous front line ervice under commd. French; attached to 1st Div. in attle of Cantigny; comd. Camp Shelby, Miss.; hon. isch., Mar. 1919; brig. gen. O.R.C., U.S. Army, Apr. 920; assigned as comdr. 95th Div.; retired as maj. gen. omdg. 45th Div., Nat. Guard (states Ariz., N.M., 'olo., Okla.). Decorated by Marshall Foch; Comdr. egion of Honor (French); Comdr. Nichan Iftikhar Tunis); Comdr. of the Crown (Italian, Rumanian, elgian). Awarded D.S.M., State of Okla. Nat. charter iem. and organizer Am. Legion (nat. exec. com. 3 erms), also dept. comdr. Am. Legion, and chmn. Nat. Defense Com.; national v.p. American Legion ounders; pres. Nat. Reserve Officers' Assn., 3 terms. hmn. Nat. Will Rogers Memorial Commn. Now and or 18 yrs. continuously, civilian aide to Sec. of War. Mem. Oklahoma's Hall of Fame. Mason (hon. 33deg.), Odd Fellow, K.P. Clubs: Men's Dinner, Oklahoma, Jniversity, Country, Army and Navy. First chmn. and rganizer State Bd. of Affairs. Home: 1414 N. Hudson v. Office: First National Bldg., Oklahoma City OK‡

HOFFZIMMER, ERNEST K(ASPAR), pianist; b. Cologne, Germany, Dec. 14, 1877; s. Peter and Gertrude (Kuerten) H.; student Coll. in Cologne, 895-99; Degree as Concertpianist, Cologne Cons. of Music, 1900; student masterclass of Feruccio Buconi in Weimar and Berlin, 1900-04; m. Sarah Ellen Rough, une 11, 1929; children—Sarah Christine, Willa Catherine. Came to U.S., 1927, naturalized, 1934. Concert pianist, European Countries, 1900-27; teacher, Conservatory of Music, Duesseldorf, 1901-05; head, masterclass, Sterns Conservatory, Berlin, 1905-27; ead, piano dept., sch. of music, Ind. Univ., 1927-48, ow as prof. emeritus; head of piano dept., Southern Calif. Sch. of Music and Arts, Los Angeles, since 1948; xtension work, Indianapolis, 1927-41. Author: Lecture n the Musical Memory, Univ. Study, 1933. Contbr. rticles in German music periodicals. Researcher in pianotechnique, which aims direct at self expression and ontrol. Address: Pacific Art Center, Rivera Beach Club, Redondo Beach CA‡

HOFMANN, HERBERT ANDREW, corp. exec.; b. Queens County, N.Y., Feb. 24, 1917; s. John and Agnes Brutschin) H.; B.B.A., St. John's U., 1937; m. Erna Last, Apr. 13, 1941; children—Herbert Charles, Erna Margaret, Gregory, Marilyn Agnes, Mary Edna. With Price, Waterhouse & Co., C.P.A.'s, N.Y.C., 1939-40, Harris, Kerr, Forster & Co., C.P.A.'s, N.Y.C., 1940-50; with Tisch Hotels, Inc., N.Y.C., 1951-61, treas., 951-61, exec. v.p., 1958-61, also dir.; exec. v.p., treas., dir. Americana Hotel, Inc., 1956-71; sr. v.p. Loew's Theatres, Inc., 1960-71, also dir.; sr. v.p., dir. Loew's Hotels, Inc., 1961-71, pres., 1971. Served with USNR, 943-46, C.P.A., N.Y. Mem. Am. Inst. C.P.A.'s, N.Y. State Soc. C.P.A.'s. Home: Rye NY Died Mar. 9, 1971; uried St. John's Cemetery, Glendale NY

HOFMANN, HUGO, textile mfr.; b. Worms, Hesse, Germany, Oct. 29, 1898; s. Jean Peter and Katharina Brunner) H.; Ph.D., U. Giessen, Hesse, 1922; student Darmstadt U., also Electro Chem. Inst., Wiesbaden; m. Hedwig Oberthurer, Mar. 20, 1926; 1 dau., Lori (Mrs. . Allen Thomas). Came to U.S., 1926, naturalized, 939. Chief chemist J.P. Bemberg, 1922-24, prodn. mgr., 1924-26; plant mgr., chief chemist American Bemberg Corporation (bought by Beaunit Mills, Inc.), rom 1926, gen. manager, from 1954; v.p. Beaunit Mills, nc., tech. dir. rayon div., 1954-59, pres. fibers div., 959-60, chairman co., from 1960. Mem. Am. Chem. oc., Textile Research Inst., C. of C., Tenn. Acad. Sci. Roman Catholic. Elk. Club: Elizabethton Golf. Patentee ayon mfg. processes. Home: Elizabethton TN Died une 13, 1972.

HOFSTADTER, RICHARD, educator; b. Buffalo, Aug. 6, 1916; s. Emil A. and Katherine (Hill) H.; B.A., J. Buffalo, 1937; M.A., Columbia, 1938, Ph.D., 1942; n. Felice Swados, Oct. 3, 1936 (dec. July 1945); 1 son, Dan; m. 2d, Beatrice Kevitt, Jan. 13, 1947; 1 dau., Sarah . Instr. Bklyn. Coll., 1940-41, City Coll, N.Y., 1941; Wm. Bayard Cutting traveling fellow Columbia, 941-42, asst. prof. history, 1946-50, asso. prof., 950-52, prof., 1952-59, DeWitt Clinton Prof. Am. istory, 1959-—; asst. prof. history U. Md., 1942-46; is. prof., Princeton, 1950, Salzburg, 1950; Fulbright Conf. on Am. Studies, U. Coll. Oxford, 1955; Pitt. rofessor of American history and institutions Cambridge University, England, 1958-59; Jefferson Meml. lectr. U. Cal. Berkeley, 1966. Recipient Beveridge award, 1942, Knopf fellowship in history, 945; Pulitzer Prize in History for book. The Age of Reform, 1956; Guggenheim fellow, 1966-67. Mem. American Academy of Arts and Sciences, American Philosophical Soc., Nat. Acad. Edn., Am. Hist. Assn., American Polit. Sci. Assn., American Studies Assn., Phi Beta Kappa. Author: Social Darwinism in American Thought, 1944; The American Political Tradition, 1948; The Development and Scope of Higher Education in the J.S., 1952; The Age of Reform, 1955; The Development of Academic Freedom in the U.S., 1955; The United States, 1957; Great Issues in Am. History, 958; The American Republic, 1959; American Higher Education, 1961; Anti-Intellectualism in American Life Pulitzer prize for gen. nonfiction 1964; Emerson ward, Phi Beta Kappa, 1963; Sidney Hillman award 1963), 1963; The Paranoid Style in American Politics, 1965; The Progressive Historians, 1968; The Idea of a Party System, 1969; American Violence, 1970; America at 1750, 1971. Home: New York City NY Died Oct. 24, 1970.

HOGAN, DENIS PATRICK, banker; b. Dubuque Co., Ia., Aug. 29, 1869; s. Michael and Mary (Collins) H.; grad. high sch., Corning, Ia.; Master of Accounts, St. Benedict's Coll., Atchison, Kan., 1899; m. Dolly Snelson, Oct. 9, 1901. Began in banking business at Wallace, Neb., 1889; organizer, 1897, now pres. Farmers Savings Bank, Massena, Ia.; pres. Federal Land Bank of Omaha (Neb.), 1917-36; pres. Federal Intermediate Credit Bank, Omaha, 1923-34; owner and operator of 5 farms, comprising 1680 acres, in Cass, Adams and Montgomery counties, Ia.; breeder of registered Hereford Cattle. Mem. Ia. Ho. of Reps., 1911-12; mem. Am. Commn. for Study of Rural Credits in Europe, 1913. Trustee St. James Orphanage, Omaha. Republican. Catholic, Clubs: Rotary, Happy Hollow. Home: 1501 N. 51st St., Omaha NB*‡

HOGAN, EDGAR POE, surgeon; born at Bibbville, Bibb County, Ala., Nov. 4, 1872; s. James and Margaret Elizabeth (Marshall) H.; A.B., Howard Coll., Birmingham, Ala., 1893, A.M., 1897; spl. student U. of Chicago and Harvard; M.D., University of Alabama, 1909; unmarried. Was professor chemistry and biology, comdt. cadet corps and chmn. faculty, Howard Coll.; later prof. chemistry, Birmingham Med. Coll., prof. physiology, Birmingham Dental Coll.; supt., resident physician and surgeon, Hillman Hosp., 1911-30; surgeon Hogan clinic; former asso. prof. abdominal surgery and gynecology, Grad. Sch., U. of Ala., also at the Birmingham Med. Coll. Mem. Ala. Ho. of Rep., 1914-18. Mem. Bd. of Edn., Birmingham, 1907-22. Trustee Howard Coll., 1918-40. Mem. founders group and diplomate Am. Bd. Surgery; mem. Am. Coll. of Surgery, A.M.A., Southern Surg. Assn., (former v.p.), Birmingham Surg. Soc., Ala. State Med. Assn., Jefferson County Med. Soc., Phi Chi. Democrat. Baptist. Clubs: Rotary, Executives, Country (Birmingham). Address: 920 S. 20th St., Birmingham AL*‡

HOGAN, GEORGE ARCHIBALD, surgeon; b. Bibb County, Ala., Jan. 24, 1871; s. Rev. James and Margaret Elizabeth (Marshall) H.; B.S., Howard Coll., Birmingham, 1893; M.D., U. of Ala., 1896; post-grad. work, New York, 1900; m. Myra Clark Gaines, Jan. 25, 1904; children—George Archibald, Ann Marshall, James Thomas (deceased). Interne Davis Infirmary, Birmingham, 1896-98; professor chemistry, Birmingham Medical College, 1896-97; surgeon Tennessee Coal & Iron Company, 1899-1907; professor in minor surgery, Birmingham Medical College, 1907-14; member surgical staff, Hillman Hospital, 1907-28; examiner U.S. Marine Service, 1910-19; coroner Jefferson County, Ala., by apptmt., 1916-20; formerly asso. mem. Hogan Clinic; with Tenn. Coal & Iron Co., now retired. Apptd. convict surg., State of Ala., by Gov. Emmett O'Neal, 1912; report on convict camps resulted in end of convict leasing to pvt. industries in Ala. Mem. A.M.A., Ala. Med. Soc., Jefferson County Med. Soc. (v.p. 1905, 06), Phi Chi. Democrat. Baptist. Mason (Shriner), K.P., Elk, Woodmen of the World. Contbr. to Am. Medicine. Address: 1901 Bessemer Rd., AL‡

HOGAN, HENRY MICHAEL, lawyer; b. Torrington, Conn., Mar. 18, 1896; s. Dennis M. and Anna (McLaughlin) H.; A.B. and LL.D., Holy Cross College, Worcester, Massachusetts; LL.B., Fordham University, LL.D.; LL.D., Fairfield University; married to Gertrude Blumer (deceased March 26, 1952); children—Jane Ann, Nancy Winifred, Henry Michael. Admitted to New York bar and Michigan bar; v.p., gen. counsel General Motors Corp., ret. Served in U.S. Navy, World War I. Mem. Assn. Bar City of New York, Am., Mich. and Detroit bar assns. Roman Catholic. Clubs: Detroit Athletic: Bloomfield Hills Country. Home: Birmingham MI Died June 2, 1968; buried Holy Sepulchre Cemetery.

HOGAN, O. T., chmn. United Ins. Co. Home: Chicago IL Died May 1971.*

HOGAN, WILLIAM RANSOM, educator; b. Toledo, Nov. 23, 1908; s. Lemuel Ransom and Irene (Logan) H.; A.B., Trinity U., 1929; A.M., U. Tex., 1932; Ph.D., 1942; m. Mrs. Jane Carpenter Ogg, June 20, 1949; stepchildren—Mary (Mrs. Randolph Farenthold), Thomas, Jon. Tchr. Ranger (Tex.) Jr. Coll. and High Sch., 1929-31; regional historian Southwestern Nat. Park Service, Dept. Interior, 1935-38; asst. archivist La. State U., 1938-41, asso. archivist, 1941-42, head dept. archives, 1946; asso. prof. history U. Okla., 1946-47; asso. prof. history Tulane U., New Orleans, 1947-49, prof., 1949-71, chmn. dept., 1953-68, faculty adminstrv. chmn. Archive New Orleans Jazz, 1958-65. Served from pvt. to capt. M.I., AUS, 1942-45. Recipient Guggenheim fellowship, 1962-63. Fellow Tex. Hist. Assn.; mem. Am., Miss. Valley, So. hist. assns., La. Hist. Assn., Philos. Soc. Tex., Phi Beta Kappa (hon.). Author: The Texas Republic, 1946; The Barber of Natchez (with E. A. Davis), 1954. Editor: Guide to Manuscript Collections in the Department of Archives, Louisiana State University, 1940; William Johnson's Natchez: The Ante-Bellum Diary of a Free Negro (with E.A. Davis), 1951; (with Jane Hogan) Tales from the Manchaca Hills, 1960. Contbr. to hist. and lit. jours. Home: New Orleans LA Died Sept. 26, 1971.

HOGE, JAMES FULTON, lawyer; b. Concord, N.C., Aug. 2, 1901; s. Beverly Lacy and Nettie (Hatcher) H.; LL.B., Wake Forest (N.C.) Coll., 1922, LL.D., (hon.), 1954; m. Virginia McClamroch, Mar. 26, 1932; children—Barbara (Mrs. Robert A. Daine), James Fulton, Warren McClamroch, Virginia Howe. Admitted to N.C. bar, 1922, N.Y. bar, 1931; in practice of law, Greensboro, N.C., 1922-23; with legal dept. Vick Chem. Co., Greensboro, 1923-27, gen. counsel, 1927-35; mem. firm Rogers Hoge & Hills (formerly Rogers, Ramsay &Hoge), N.Y.C., specializing in law of trademarks, unfair competition and trade regulation, 1933; past gen. counsel U.S. Trademark Assn. Hon. mem., gen. counsel Am. Found. Pharm. Edn.; mem. Internat. Patent and Trade-Mark Assn., Am. Patent Law Assn., Acad. Polit. Sci., N.C. Bar Assn., Am. Bar Assn. (mem. trademark div., section of patent, trademark, copyright law, anti-trust sect., sect. on adminstrv. law, corp., banking and mercantile law sect.), N.Y. State Bar Assn. (mem. drug com. sect. on food, drug and cosmetic law, sect. on anti-trust law), Assn. Bar City N.Y., N.C. Soc. N.Y. (past pres.), Commerce and Industry Assn. of N.Y. (dir. chmn. com. on FTC and anti-trust laws), N.Y. So. Soc., Am. Mus. Natural History, Nat. Geog. Soc., Met. Mus. Art, Met. Opera Guild, S.A.R. (N.C. Soc.), Mus. City of New York, Point O'Woods Assn. (dir.), Omicron Delta Kappa (hon. mem.), Kappa Alpha (formerly pres. N.Y. alumni chpt.), Phi Delta Phi (hon.). Mem. bd. trustees, exec. com. Riverside Ch. Mason. Clubs: Pinnacle (N.Y.C.), University (N.Y.); Nat. Lawyers (Washington). Mem. editorial adv. com. Food, Drug, Cosmetic Law Jour. Editor and pub. The Family of Hoge, 1927. Home: New York City NY Died Sept. 22, 1972; buried Forest Lawn Cemetery, Greensboro NC

HOGE, VANE MORGAN, organization executive; b. Waynesburg, Pa., Feb. 17, 1902; s. Samuel Morgan and Margaret (Yeager) H.; B.S., Waynesburg (Pa.) Coll., 1924; M.D., Jefferson Med. Coll., Phila., 1928; M.B.A., U. Chgo., 1936; Sc.D., Waynesburg Coll., 1952; m. Annabelle E. Ott, Sept. 8, 1935. Commd. in pub. health service, 1928, and advanced to grade of asst. surgeon gen., 1949; intern U.S. Marine Hosp., S.I., N.Y., 1928-30, conducted spl. studies and surveys on community hosp. requirements, hdqrs. Bethesda, Md., 1936-41, in charge of surveys of need and approval of all civilian hosps. constructed under wartime restrictions, hdqrs. Washington, D.C., 1941-46; administrator Nat. Hosp. Survey and Construction Act (public law 725, 79th Congress), 1946-49; asso. chief Bureau Medical Services, 1949-58; exec. dir. Hosp. Planning Council Met. Chgo., 1958-59; dir. Pan Am. office Internat. Hosp. Fedn., asst. dir. Washington service bur. Am. Hosp. Assn., from 1959. Trustee Waynesburg Coll. Mem. Am. Bd. Preventive Medicine and Pub. Health. Fellow Am. Coll. Hosp. Adminstrs., Am. Pub. Health Assn.; member Am. Medical Assn., Am. Hosp. Assn., Md.-D.C. Hosp. Assn., Jefferson Med. Coll. Alumni Assn., Theta Kappa Psi. Mason (32 degrees). Clubs: Medical Administrators, Medical Superintendents; Army and Navy. Contbr. to Hospital and Public Health pubs. Home: Kensington MD Died May 22, 1970; buried Caledonia Cemetery, Caledonia OH

HOGG, ASTOR, state ofcl.; b. Roxana, Ky., Nov. 13, 1901; s. George and Mahala (Combs) H.; LL.B., U. Ky., 1924; m. Gertrude Lewis, June 29, 1927; children—Stanley, Janelle Pope. Admitted to Ky. bar, 1924; practice in Whitesburg, 1924-35, Harlan, 1941-51; county atty. Letcher County, Ky., 1930-34; trial atty. FTC, Washington, 1935-37; spl. asst. to atty. gen. U.S. Washington, 1937-39; commonwealth's atty. 26th Jud. Dist. Ky., 1942-45, circuit judge, 1951-55; judge Ct. Appeals of Ky., Frankfort, 1955-57; chief asst. atty. gen. Dept. Hwys., Frankfort, 1957-60; adminstrv. dir. Cts. of Ky., 1960-71. Mayor of Whiteburg, 1927-28; del. Dem. Nat. Conv., 1928. Mem. Am., Ky. bar assns., Am. Judicature Soc., Ky. Hist. Soc., Phi Alpha Delta. Baptist. Clubs: Whitesburg Rotary (pres.); Kiwanis (Harlan); Filson (Louisville). Home: Frankfort KY Died Aug. 5, 1972; buried Lewis Cemetery, Whitesburg KY

HOHF, SILAS MATTHEW, surgeon; b. Hopkins, Mich., Aug. 30, 1872; s. John and Barbara (Katz) H.; student Grand Island (Neb.) Coll.; M.D., Ill. Med. Coll., Chicago, 1897; post-grad. work, and M.D., Northwestern U. Med. Coll., 1903; m. Carrie E. Sniffin, Oct. 12, 1898 (died May 27, 1917); children—Lillian La Pearl, Florence; m. 2d, Alice H. Pihl, Nov. 26, 1919 (died June 12, 1943); children—Robert Pihl, Elizabeth Joice. Practiced at Yankton, South Dakota, since 1897; surgeon to Sacred Heart Hospital; instructor in surgery, Medical Department University of South Dakota. Captain M.R.C., instr. operative surgery and anatomy, Camp Greenleaf, Chickamauga Park, Ga., 1918; now maj. M.C. (Res.). Trustee Yankton Coll. Fellow Am. Coll. Surgeons; mem. Am., Sioux Valley and South Dakota (ex-pres.) med. assns., Yankton Dist. Med. Soc. (ex-pres.), Clin. Congress of Surgeons of North

America, etc. Republican. Congregationalist. Mason (33 deg.). Home: 411 Pine St. Office: Clinic Bldg., Yankton SD‡

HOHMAN, LESLIE B., physician; b. Columbia, O., July 23, 1891; s. Lee and Hennie (Schlesinger) H.; A.B., U. Mo., 1912; M.D., Johns Hopkins, 1917; grad. student U. Vienna, 1924. Psychiat. tng. and residency Phipps Clinic, Johns Hopkins Hosp., 1917-22; instr. psychiatry Johns Hopkins Med. Sch., 1920-22, asso. psychiatry, 1922-43, asst. prof., 1943-46; prof. of psychiatry sch. medicine Duke, 1946-60, prof. psychiatry emeritus, 1960-72, director child guidance clinic, 1946-53; pvt. practice psychiatry, 1924-72; cons. dept. of psychiatry Duke Medical Center, Veterans Administration, U.S. Army, U.S.N. Served as 1st lt. M.C., U.S. Army, 1917-19; comdr. M.C., U.S.N., 1943-46. Mem. Am. Acad. Cerebral Palsy (past pres.), Am. Psychiat. Assn., A.A.A.S., A.M.A., Am. Neurol. Assn., Am. Psychopath. Association (councillor, past president), North Carolina, Southern medical assns., So. Psychiat. Assn. Author: As the Twig is Bent, 1939. Contbr. articles popular mags., profl. jours. Home: Durham NC Died Jan. 28, 1972; buried Druid Ridge Cemetery, Baltimore MD

HOILES, RAYMOND CYRUS, editor, publisher; b. Alliance O., Nov. 24, 1878; s. Samuel and Phoebe Ann (Ladd) H.; grad. Mt. Union Coll., 1902; m. Mabel Crumb, Feb. 16, 1905; children—Clarence Harrison, Raymond Crumb, Harry Howard, Jane (Mrs. Robert Hardie). Sch. tchr., Alliance, O., 1898-99; pub. Lorain (O.) Times-Herald, Mansfield (O.) News, 1921-30; pres. Freedom Newspapers, Inc., which owns or controls 19 newspapers. Contbr. articles to Barrons' Weekly, Christian Advocate, Faith and Freedom, Christian Econs., The Freeman, The Free Trader. Home: Santa Ana CA Died Oct. 30, 1970.

HOIT, HENRY FORD, architect; b. Chicago, Ill., Aug. 4, 1872; s. Jeremiah Parsons and Elizabeth (Starrett) H.; grad. Chicago Manual Training Sch., 1892; spl. course in architecture, Mass. Inst. Tech., 1897; m. Florence Elinor Stinchfield, Dec. 25, 1900; 1 dau., Imogene Elizabeth. In architectural offices, Boston, 1897-1901; entered offices of Van Brunt & Howe, Kansas City, Mo., 1901, to design the Varied Industries Bldg., St. Louis Expn.; admitted to firm, 1903, title changed to Howe, Hoit & Cutler, 1904, Howe & Hoit, 1907, Henry F. Hoit, Jan. 1, 1910, Hoit, Price & Barnes, Jan. 1, 1919. Mem. bd. to revise bldg. laws of Kansas City, 1907; mem. Bd. of Appeals, Kansas City, 1908, 09, 10. Mem. bd. The Thomas H. Swope Settlement, 1910. Designed Kansas City Athletic Club Bldg., Southwestern Bell Telephone Bldg., R. A. Long Bldg., Independence Blvd. Christian Ch., Jewish Temple, Kansas City Power & Light Bldg., Fidelity Bank Bldg., residence and country estate of R. A. Long; cons. architect for Longview, Wash. Mem. City Plan Commn. (1940-43). Fellow Am. Inst. Architects (dir. 1936-39); mem. Fine Arts Inst., Delta Kappa Epsilon. Conglist. Mason. Clubs: City (pres. 1908), Kansas City Club, Presidents' Round Table (chmn. 1921), Mission Hills Country. Home: 838 W. 58th St., Kansas City 2 MO‡

HOLAND, HJALMAR RUED, author; b. at Oslo, Norway, October 20, 1872; s. Johan and Maren (Rued) Olsen; came to America, 1884; A.B., U. of Wis., 1898, A.M., 1899; m. Theresa Ingersoll, of Sparta, Wis., June 13, 1900; children—Swanhild Ingersoll, Johan Harald, Ivar Whitman, Mildred Valborg. Interpreter of the Runic Stone which was discovered near Kensington, Minn., 1898, which tells of a voyage of discovery made to that region by a party of 30 Scandinavians in 1362. Life member Wisconsin State Historical Society; corr. member Minnesota Historical Soc.; founder and pres. Door County Hist. Soc. Author: History of the Norwegians of the United States (4th edit.), 1911; History of Door County, Wis., 1917; Old Peninsula Days, 1925; Coon Prairie, 1927; Coon Valley, 1928; The Last Migration, 1929; The Kensington Stone, 1932; Wisconsin's Belgian Community, 1933; also numerous mag. articles on hist. subjects. Editor Peninsula Hist. Rev. Adopted as hon. chief by Potawatomi Indians, 1927. Home: Ephraim WI‡

HOLBORN, HAJO, educator; b. Berlin, Germany, May 18, 1902; s. Ludwig and Helen (Bussmann) H.; came to U.S., 1934, naturalized citizen, 1940; student Berlin High Sch., 1908-20; Ph.D., U. of Berlin, 1924; M.A. (hon.), Yale, 1940; D.H.L. (hon.), University of Chicago, 1967; m. Anne-Marie Bettmann, Oct. 2, 1926; children—Frederick, Hanna. Engaged as asst. prof. history, U. of Heidelberg, 1926-31; Carnegie prof. of history and internat. relations, Sch. of Politics, Berlin, 1931-34, and simultaneously lecturer history, U. of Berlin, 1931-34, visiting professor history, Yale U., 1934-38, asso. prof., 1938-40, prof. history since 1940, Randolph W. Townsend prof. history 1946-59, Sterling professor of history 1959-69; simultaneously professor of diplomatic history at Fletcher School of Law and Diplomacy, Medford, Massachusetts, 1936-42; on leave for service with the Office of Strategic Services, Washington, D.C., 1943-45; cons. U.S. Dept. of State 1946-48; Fulbright prof. U. Vienna, Austria, summer 1954, U. Bonn, also U. Cologne (Germany), summer 1966. Decorated Comdr.'s Cross of Merit (Fed. Republic Germany). Mem. Acad. Arts and Scis., Am. Hist. Assn. (pres. 1967), Am. Soc. Ch. History, Council on Foreign Relations, Connecticut Academy of Arts and Sciences. Author of books including: American Military Government, 1947; The Political Collapse of Modern Europe, 1951; A History of Modern Germany, 1959, vol. II, 1964, vol. III, 1969. Co-editor Jour. Modern History, 1943-46; Journal of the History of Ideas, 1942-69. Lutheran. Home: Hamden CT Died June 20, 1969.

HOLBROOK, DONALD, financial cons.; b. Newton, Mass., May 27, 1897; s. Walter and Katharine (Thayer) H.; ed. Harvard, 1920; D.Sc., New Eng. College, Henniker, N.H., 1964; m. Barbara Root Hollister, Apr. 25, 1942; children by previous marriage—Katherine (Mrs. James H. Patteson 3d), Jane (Mrs. Robert A. Deevey), Donald. With Coffin & Burr, Inc., investment bankers, Boston, 1919-28, v.p., gen. mgr. Franklin Mgmt. Corp., Boston, 1928-30; founder The Holbrook Co., 1930; pres. Fire Protection Research Internat., Inc.; chmn., trustee Gen. Investors Trust, mut. fund open-end, Boston, 1956-66. Volunteer fire chief Meadowood County Area Fire Dept., Fitzwilliam, N.H., 1953-68. Trustee New Eng. Coll., Henniker, N.H. Served to lt. (j.g.) with USNRF, World War I; to maj. USAAF, World War II. Mem. Internat. Assn. Fire Chiefs, Nat. Fire Protection Assn. Clubs: Country (Brookline, Mass.); Union (Boston); Harvard (N.Y.C.); Royal Bermuda Yacht (Hamilton). Author: The Boston Trustee, 1937; Civilian Mission, 1947; Up the Ladder, 1957; An Unlikely Firemaster, 1968. Home: Boston MA Died Sept. 6, 1970; buried Newton Cemetery, Newton MA

HOLBROOK, JOHN, ins. co. exec.; b. Yonkers, N.Y., May 25, 1909; s. Harry and Eleanore (Williams) H.; B.A., Yale, 1931; m. Alice Doubleday, June 6, 1936; children—John, David D., Phyllis, Peter M. Exec. v.p., dir. Marsh & McLennan, Inc., 1931-63, president, director, 1963-66, chairman executive committee, 1966-67, also dir.; member board trustees Seamen's Bank for Savs. Mem. United Republican Finance Com., State of N.Y., 1954. Trustee No. Westchester Hosp. Served from capt. to lt. col., USAAF, 1942-45. Decorated Legion of Merit. Episcopalian (trustee). Clubs: Downtown Assn., Racquet and Tennis, Links (N.Y.C.); Bedford (N.Y.) Golf and Tennis; Blind Brook (Rye, N.Y.); Stanwich (Stamford, Conn.). Home: Bedford Hills NY Died Dec. 25, 1970.

HOLBROOK, LUCIUS ROY, army officer (ret.); b. Arkansaw, Wis., Apr. 30, 1875; s. Willard Francis and Mary (Ames) H.; grad. U.S. Mil. Acad., 1896; distinguished grad. Inf. and Cav. Sch., 1905; grad. Staff Coll., 1906; m. Henrietta Coffin, June 7, 1899; children—Frank Coffin, John Ames, Lucius Roy. Commd. add. 2d lt. 4th Cav., June 12, 1896; promoted through grades to lt. col., May 15, 1917; brig. gen. (temp.) Aug. 16, 1918; brig. gen. regular army, Oct. 20, 1925; promoted to rank of maj. gen., Dec. 28, 1933. Duty at Boise Barracks, Ida., 1896-98; in Philippines, 1899-1900 and 1901, 03; organized the training sch. for bakers and cooks, Ft. Riley, Kan., 1907, 11; developed the army field bakery and cooking equipment; attended the French Sch. of Supply, Paris, 1911-13; went to France with the 1st F.A. Brig., July 15, 1917; returned from France, May 1919; senior instr. arty. Command and Staff Coll., 1919-20; mem. Gen. Staff, 1920-24, Inspector Gen. Dept., 1925; comdg. gen. Ft. Douglas, Utah, 1925-26; comdg. Camp Stotsenburg, P.I., 1926-29, Ft. Bragg, N.C., 1919-30; comdr. 1st Division; hdqrs. Ft. Hamilton, N.Y., 1930-36, Philippine Dept. and Troops in China, 1936-38; retired, Jan. 31, 1939. Specially cited for bravery in P.I., 1900; also for skillfully handling artillery" in Cantigny operations and during 2d Battle of the Marne; decorated D.S.M.; Legion of Honor, and Croix de Guerre (French); silver medal for bravery and cross of Prince Danilio (Montenegrin). Episcopalian. Home: McCall ID‡

HOLCOMB, OSCAR RAYMOND, lawyer; b. Gibson County, Ind., Dec. 31, 1867; s. Silas Mercer and Mary Anne (Hopkins) H.; grad. Southwestern Ind. Normal Sch., Princeton, 1888; LL.B., Chicago College of Law, 1892; m. Eva Staser, June 12, 1894 (died Jan. 10, 1934);children—Silas Raymond, Maurice Staser, Mrs. Marjorie Reed, Leland Mercer, Miriam Gladys (Mrs. J. Harold Pfeffer), Mary Maxine (Mrs. Geo. Walter Ginder). Admitted to Ind. bar, 1890, practiced at Fort Branch and Evansville; removed to Ritzville, Wash., 1894; prosecuting atty. Adams County, Wash., 1895-98; commr. of arid lands, State of Wash., 1898-1901; judge Superior Court of Washington for Adams, Benton and Franklin counties, 1909-15; asso. justice, Supreme Court of Wash., 1915-38 (chief justice June 1, 1919-Jan. 12, 1921); retired Jan. 8, 1938. Democrat. Episcopalian. Mason. Home: 3311 Capitol Blvd., Olympia WA*‡

HOLCOMBE, AMASA MAYNARD, lawyer; b. Winchester, Mass., Oct. 27, 1882; s. Frank Gibbons and Inez Norman (Maynard) H; B.S., Mass. Inst. Tech., 1904; law student George Washington U., 1908-10; m. Eleanor Pearl Marshall, Sept. 9, 1909 (dec. 1932); children—Priscilla, Marshall Maynard; m. 2d Violet Strong Gillett, March 10, 1934 (divorced 1946); married 3d, Martha Ellicott Ramey, Feb. 19, 1952. Machine designer Waterbury (Conn.) Farrell Foundry & Machine Co., 1904-05; asst. to treas. Pope Mfg. Mfg Co., Hartford, Conn., 1905-07; asst. examiner U.S. Patent Office, Washington, 1907-10; admitted to D.C. bar, 1910, Mo. bar, 1913; practicing lawyer, specializing in patent law, asso. Carr & Carr, St. Louis, 1910-17; mem. Emery, Booth, Janney & Varney, Washington 1919-29, Emery, Booth, Varney & Holcombe, 1929-33; Emery, Holcombe & Miller, 1933-42, Holcombe Wetherill & Brisebois, from 1953; director Kistner Lock & Appliance Co., Power Condenser & Elec. Corp. Spl. asst. to atty. gen., 1920-24; cons. Dept. Justice, 1946-50; chief patent prosecution sect. Office Allen Property Custodian, Washington, 1942-46. Mem. com. of 100 nat. capitol Am. Civic Assn.; del. Fedn. Citizens Assn. 1926-34. Served as maj., U.S. Army, 1917-19; capt. O.R.C. Mem. Am. Bar Assn., Am. Patent Law Assn. Patent Inst. of Can., Assn. Internat. Protection Industrial Property (Am. sect.), Am. Soc. Mil. Engrs. Washington Soc. Engrs., Am. Ordnance Assn., Am. Soc. M.E., Washington Bd. Trade, S.A.R. Republican. Unitarian (past chmn. bd. trustees). Clubs: Rotary University (Washington); Columbia Country (Chevy Chase, Md.); Montgomery Sycamore Island (Glen Echo, Md.). Holder patent. Home: St Petersburg FL Died May 14, 1971.

HOLCOMBE, OSCAR FITZALLEN, mayor; b. Mobile, Ala., Dec. 31, 1888; s. Robert Slough and Sarah King (Harrell) H.; ed. pub. schs., San Antonio, Tex.; m. Mary Grey Miller, May 3, 1912; 1 dau., Elisabeth Adelaide. In lumber and millwork business, later engring. and constrn.; mayor Houston, Tex., 1921-28, 33-36, 39-40, 47-52, 56-57. Democrat. Baptist. K.P. Elk. Club: Country, Houston. Home: Houston TX Died June 18, 1968; buried Forest Park, Houston TX

HOLDEN, JAMES STANSBURY, real estate; b. Detroit, Mich., June 12, 1875; s. Edward G. and Jean M. (Stansbury) H.; grad. high sch., Detroit, 1894; student Mich. Agrl. Coll., East Lansing, 1890-91; LL.B., Detroit Coll. of Law, 1897; m. Lynelle Anderson, June 10, 1916. Bookkeeper, 1893-98; began in real estate business, 1898; pres. and dir. James S. Holden Co. Grand Lawn Cemetery; director of the Detroit Manufacturers Railroad, Autopulse Corp., First Liquidating Corporation. Served as major, General Staff, U.S. Army, 1918. President of the Detroit Board of Estimates, 1905-08; member of Detroit Common Council, 1917-18, City Plan Commn., 1919-20, Detroit Zool. Park Commn. since 1924. Trustee Grace Hosp. Republican. Unitarian. Clubs: Detroit, Yondotega, Detroit Athletic, Country, Grosse Pointe Club, Prismatic, Witenagemote, Bloomfield Hills Country. Home: 320 Washington Rd., Grosse Pointe 30, M. Office: Buhl Bldg., Detroit MI‡

HOLDEN, LOUIS HALSEY, clergyman, educator; b. Newark, N.J., Aug. 7, 1873; s. George III and Mary A. (Coe) H.; grad. high sch., Newark, 1891; A.B., Yale, 1895, Ph.D., 1903; M.A., Columbia, 1897; B.D., Union Theol. Sem., 1898; D.D., Rutgers, 1923; m. Elizabeth F. Sage, of Catskill, N.Y., June 5, 1906. Ordained ministry Presbyn. Ch., 1898; asst. pastor Presbyn. Ch., Oneida, N.Y., 1898-99, Second Congl. Ch., Waterbury, Conn. 1900-04; pastor Christ Ch. (Ref.), Utica, N.Y., 1904-21; Second Reformed Ch., New Brunswick, N.J., 1921-25; instr. in English Bible, New Brunswick Theol. Sem. since 1924. Mem. Soc. Biblical Lit. and Exegesis, Soc. of the Cincinnati, Phi Beta Kappa. Republican. Home: Bishop Pl., New Brunswick NJ‡

HOLLAND, ELMER JOSEPH, congressman; b. Pitts., Jan. 8, 1894; s. Thomas and Margaret (Keelan) H.; student Duquesne U., 1913-14, U. Montpelier, France, 1919; m. Emily Jane Wilson, June 30, 1941; children—Jane, Christine. Dist. sales mgr. Macbeth Evans Glass Co., St. Louis, 1914-17; sales and adv. mgr. Consol. Lamp & Glass Co., Corapolis, Pa. 1921-30; v.p. Neon Sign Co., Pitts., 1930-32; mem. gen. assembly Commonwealth of Pa., 1934-41, senate 1942-56; mem. 77th Congress, and 84th-87th Congresses, 30th Pa., mem. 88th-90th Congresses 20th Pa. Dist. Mem. United Steelworkers Am., AFL-CIO. Served as 1t. F.A., U.S. Army, 1917-20; as maj., AUS World War II; ETO. Mem. Vets. Fgn. Wars (comdr.) Am. Legion. Democrat. Home: Pittsburgh PA Died Aug. 9, 1968; buried Arlington National Cemetery Arlington VA

HOLLAND, MADELINE OXFORD (MRS. JOHN N. MCDONNELL), editor, cons.; b. Bangor, Pa., Aug. 3, 1916;3d. Raymond and Bertha (Oxford) Holland; B.Sc., Phila. Coll. Pharmacy and Sci., 1937, M.Sc. 1938, D.S.C., 1940; m. Dr. John N. McDonnell, Aug. 9, 1941. Instr. pharmacy Phila. Coll. Pharmacy and Sci. 1937-42; chief pharmacist McDonnell's Inc. Jenkintown, Pa., 1937-41; editor Am. Profl. Pharmacist 1937-60; owner Sci. Adv., 1937-68; cons. pharm. marketing, pharmacology, 1937-68; sci. editor Med. Times, 1937-52; editor El Farmaceutico, 1937-52; corr. editor Pharm. Jour., London, 1960-68. Mem. bd. Women's Med. Coll. of Pa. and Hosp. Recipient ann. alumni award Alumni Assn. Phila. Coll. Pharmacy and Sci., 1957. Fellow Am. Inst. Chemists, A.A.A.S.; mem. Am. Pharm. Assn., Am. Soc. Microbiologists, Am. Chem. Soc., Fedn. Internat. Pharm., Am. Soc. Hosp.

Pharmacists, Phila. Club. Advt. Women, Franklin Inst., Bus. and Profl. Women's Club (past pres. Phila.), Pa. Fedn. Bus. and Profl. Women's Clubs (past pres.), Alumni Assn. Phila. Coll. Pharmacy and Sci. (pres. 1956, dir. 1953-68), Women's Club Columbia U. Coll. Pharmacy (v.p. 1962-63), Am. Assn. U. Women, Clubs: Soroptimist (past pres. Phila., past pres. Old York Rd.); Huntingdon Valley Country (Abington, Pa.). Author numerous articles profl. jours.; also editorials in U.S. and fgn. jours. Home: Meadowbrook PA Died Oct. 1, 1968.

HOLLAND, PHILIP, consul general; b. Murray, Ky., Aug. 26, 1877; s. Philip A. and Sarah (Williams) H.; ed. McFerrin Coll., Martin, Tenn., 1895-96; Union U., Jackson, Tenn., 1897-98; LL.B., Union, 1900; m. Corabelle Anderson, May 10, 1904; children—Philip, Isabelle Christian. Practiced law, Jackson, 1902-10; consul at Puerto Plata, Dominican Republic, 1910-11, Saltillo, Mex., 1911-13, Basel, Switzerland, 1913-23, Guatemala City, Guatemala, 1923; consul gen. Guatemala City, Guatemala, 1924-27, Liverpool, Eng., since Sept. 20, 1927. Mem. Sigma Alpha Epsilon. Methodist. Mason. Home: Jackson, Tenn. Address: American Consulate, Liverpool Eng‡

HOLLAND, SPESSARD LINDSEY, senator; b. Bartow, Fla., July 10, 1892; s. Benjamin Franklin and Fannie Virginia (Spessard) H.; Ph.B., Emory Coll. (now Emory U.), 1912, LL.D., 1943; LL.B., U. Fla., 1916, D.C.L., 1953; LL.D., Rollins Coll., Fla. So. Coll., 1941, Fla. State University, 1956, University of Miami, 1962; H.H.D., University Tampa, 1956; m. Mary Agnes Groover, Feb. 8, 1919; children—Spessard Lindsey, Mary Groover, William Benjamin, Ivanhoe. High sch. teacher, Warrenton, Georgia, 1912-14; teacher in sub-Freshman dept. U. of Fla., 1914-16; admitted to bar, 1916, and since in practice at Bartow, Fla. Prosecuting atty., Polk County, Fla., 1919-20, county judge, 1921-29; mem. Fla. State Senate, 1932-40; served as governor of Florida, term 1941-45; apptd. by Gov. of Fla. to succeed the late Charles O. Andrews in U.S. Senate, Sept. 25, 1946; U.S. senator from Fla., from 1946, mem. com. on agr. and forestry, com. on appropriations, com. on aero. and space scis. Served with C.A.C., all grades through capt., U.S. Army, World War I; 24th Squadron Air Corps, in France. Awarded Distinguished Service Cross, 1918. Trustee of Florida Presbyterian Coll., Fla. So. College, Emory U.; bd. visitors U.S. Air Force Acad. Mem. S.A.R., U. of Fla. Alumni Assn. (member exec. council since 1922; pres. 1931), Am. Legion, Vets. of Fgn. Wars, Phi Beta Kappa, Phi Kappa Phi, Alpha Tau Omega, Phi Delta Phi. Democrat. Methodist. Mason (33 deg., Shriner). Elk. Kiwanian. Home: Bartow FL Died Nov. 6, 1971.

HOLLAND, TRAVIS, banking; b. Searcy, Ark., Dec. 22, 1874; s. A. J. and Sarah (Barber) H.; ed. country schs.; m. Minnie Spivey, of Corsicana, Tex. June 24, 1900; 1 dau., Lillie (Mrs. C. W. Redman). Began as asst. cashier Corsicana Nat. Bank, 1893-1900; pres. First Nat. Bank, Kerens, Tex., 1900-10, Athens (Tex.) Nat. Bank, 1906-08, Southern Trust Co., Houston, Tex., 1911-17; pres. Tex. Body & Trailer Co. since 1917; pres. First Nat. Bank, Port Arthur, Tex., First Nat. Bank, Port Neches, Tex. Mem. Jefferson County Bankers Assn. (pres.), Port Arthur Chamber of Commerce. Mason, Odd Fellow. Club: Port Arthur Country. Home: Port Arthur TX‡

HOLLAND, WILLIAM MERIDETH, lawyer; b. Dallas, Tex., Mar. 29, 1875; s. William C. and Sarah (Saffell) H.; student U. of Tex., 2 yrs.; LL.B., Columbian (now George Washington) U., 1898; m. Frances Elnora Beggs, June 24, 1909; children—Mrs. Virginia Holland McRae, Sara Merideth (dec.), Mrs. Katherine Holland Hooks. Admitted to Tex. bar and began the practice of law at Dallas, 1898; asst. county atty. Dallas County 1899; judge County Court, Dallas County, 1907-11 (declined reelection); nominated under commn. form of govt. and elected mayor of Dallas, 1911, on Citizens' Assn. ticket (non-polit.) over 4 opponents, receiving more votes than all the other four, reelected for term 1913-15; resumed practice. Served without compensation, as Spl. Asst. to Atty. Gen. of U.S., for hearing claims of conscientious objectors, during World War II. Mem. Am. and Tex. bar assns. Democrat. Mason (33 deg.; Past Master Dallas Lodge). Home: 3821 Beverly Drive. Office: Republic Bank Bldg., Dallas TX‡

HOLLANDER, SIDNEY, ret. pharm. mfr.; b. Balt., Dec. 29, 1881; s. Edward and Fanny (Koshland) H.; Pharm.D., U. of Md., 1902; Doctor of Humanities (hon.), Morgan Coll., 1961; m. Clara D. Lauer, June 3, 1908; children—Edward D., Edith L. (wife of Dr. Frank Furstenberg), Sidney, Emily D. (Mrs. Frederick Kunreuther). Began as mfg. druggist, 1900; pres. Md. Pharm. Co., The REM Co., 1900-56, ret. Trustee, Md. Dept. of Welfare, 1920-53; pres. Nat. Council Jewish Fedns. and Welfare Funds, 1938-46; v.p. Family Service Assn. of Am. from 1938, Nat. Budget Com. from 1940, Nat. Conf. of Social Work, 1938-54, Nat. Community Relations Adv. Council, 1945-50; exec. com. Community Chests and Councils, Inc., from 1940, Am. Jewish Com. from 1940, United Service for New Americans, from 1940, U.S.O., Am. Jewish Congress (past pres. Balt.), United Community Def. Services, Nat. Conf. Christians and Jews, Council Jewish Fedns. and Welfare Funds; exec. com. National Social Welfare Assembly, 1945-72, pres., 1955-56; exec. bd. Nat. Travelers Aid Assn., 1960-61; v.p. Council on Social Work Edn., 1954-72; mem. bd. Nat. Urban League, 1945-72, Asso. Jewish Charities, 1930-72, Nat. Publicity Council, Nat. Legal Aid Bur., Am. Council on Race Relations, Nat. Health and Welfare Retirement Assn., Fair Employment Practices Com., Child Welfare League Am., United Def. Fund; trustee Nat. War Fund. Recipient Spl. award Phila. Fellowship Commn., 1956; founder Sidney Hollander Award; spl. award Md. Civil Liberties Union, 1957; Stephen Wise award Balt. Jewish Congress, 1960; awards Family Service Assn. Am., Balt. Urban League, Council Jewish Fedns. and Welfare Funds, Nat. Community Relations Adv. Council. Mem. Trail Riders Canadian Rockies (pres.), Trail Hikers Canadian Rockies (pres.). Club: Alpine (Switzerland). Home: Baltimore MD Died Feb. 1972.

HOLLEMAN, WILLARD ROY, educator; b. Alderson, Okla., Nov. 18, 1909; s. Meredith Flurry and Fannie (Breedlove) H.; B.S., Okla. State U., 1929, M.S. in Physics, 1943; M.S. in Library Sci., U. Ill., 1937; m. Marian Patterson, 1961. Tchr. and adminstr. pub. schs., Okla., 1930-37; reference librarian Okla. State U., 1938-42; physics instr. U.S. Army Air Force, Okla. State U., 1942-44; chief librarian Boeing Airplane Co., Wichita, Kan., 1944-48, Mead Corp., Chillicothe, O., 1948-50; librarian Scripps Instn. Oceanography, U. Cal. at La Jolla, 1950-61; asso. prof. Grad. Sch. Library Sci., U. So. Cal., 1961-63, asso. prof., chmn. dept. library science and head librarian College for Women, University San Diego, 1963-69. Mem. A.L.A., Spl. Libraries Assn. (dir. 1959-62, profl. cons. 1959-69), Cal. (president Palomar dist., 1965-66), La Jolla (v.p., trustee 1965-69) library assns., A.A.A.S., Am. Chem. Soc., Am. Geophys. Union, American Association University Professors, Scabbard Blade, Kappa Delta Pi, Phi Kappa Pi. Rotarian. Author: General Science Manual, 1936. Editorial adv. bd. Inst. for Sci. Information, 1960-69.

HOLLIDAY, HOUGHTON, dentist; b. Sanborn, N.D., July 9, 1889; s. William and Marilla (Hancock) H.; A.B., U. of Minn., 1915, D.D.S., 1917; hon. D.D.S., U. Montreal, 1944; grad. work Columbia, U. of Chicago, New York U.; m. Ellen Hope Wells, Dec. 8, 1917 (dec. June 29, 1945); children—Paul Houghton, Robert William; m. 2d Irmgard Oesterreich Menke, Mar. 9, 1950. Fellow Mayo clinic, 1918-19; supt. coll. dentistry, U. of Minn., 1919-22, asst. prof. dental surgery, 1920-25; dental surgeon Earl clinic, Mound Park Sanitarium and Midway Hosp., 1923-25; asso. in surgery Peking Union Med. Coll. (China), 1925-27; exodontia practice, Minneapolis, Minn., 1927-28; supt., Sch. of Dental and Oral Surgery, Columbia, and instr. in x-ray and periodontia, in charge x-ray div., 1928-30, asso. dean, 1936-45, prof. of dentistry, 1936-54; head of the radiology division, Columbia, 1928-54; attending dental surgeon Presbyn. Hospital 1930-54; engaged in private practice, New York City, 1929-54. Served as 1st lieutenant Army dental reserve corps, 1918; lt. comdr. U.S.N.R. since 1932. Mem. bd. dirs. Am. Bur. Med. Aid to China, Inc.; mem. of dental advisory com. of Community Service Soc. of New York; mem. of Dean's Screening Com. for Navy V-12 program; consultant on dental admissions com. of Army Specialized Training Program. Fellow Am. Coll. of Dentists; mem. First District Dental Soc., N.Y. Acad. of Dentistry, N.Y. State Dental Soc., Am. Dental Assn., A.A.A.S., Internat. Assn. of Dental Research, N.Y. Acad. of Science, Am. Acad. Periodontology, Federation Dentaire Internationale, Sigma Xi, Omicron Kappa Upsilon. Protestant. Author: Dental Radiology Handbook, 1935. Contbr. to dental jours. Home: Oakhurst CA Died Nov. 1972.

HOLLOWAY, WILLIAM JAMES, prin. state normal sch.; b. nr. Salisbury, Md., Jan. 29, 1873; s. Daniel James and Gertrude Caroline (Adkins) H.; student Harvard, summer 1899, Johns Hopkins, 1903-06; A.M., Columbia, 1912, Ph.D., 1928; m. Mary Henrietta Weller, of Washington Co., Md., Dec. 27, 1905; children—William Weller, Mary Louisa (dec.), Margaret Elizabeth, Jeanne Gertrude, Robert Marvin, Nancy Ellen, Edward Francis. Railroad telegrapher and train dispatcher, 1890-93; teacher and prin. elementary and high schs., 1893-1903; instr. Md. State Normal Sch., Baltimore, 1903-08; county supt. schs., Wicomico Co., Md., 1908-17; state supervisor rural schs., Md., 1917-22, asst. state supt. schs., 1922-25; prin. Md. State Normal Sch., Salisbury, since 1925; instr. Johns Hopkins, summers 1913, 16, 17, Md. State Normal Sch., Towson, summers 1918, 20, Ind. U., summers 1924-25. Gen. dir. Salisbury (Md.) Bicentennial Celebration, 1932. Pres. Primitive Bapt. Home. Fellow A.A.A.S., Am. Geog. Soc.; mem. N.E.A., Eastern States Assn. of Professional Schs. for Teachers (mem. for Md. of bd. control), Md. State Teachers Assn. (ex-pres.), Soc. for Preservation of Md. Antiquities (chapter mem.), Wicomico Hist. Soc. (organizer), S.A.R., Phi Delta Kappa, Kappa Delta Pi, Pi Gamma Mu. Democrat. Baptist. Mason (K.T., P.M. and P.H.P.); K.P. (past C.C.); Patrons of Husbandry (past W.M.), O.E.S. (past W.P.), Modern Woodman, Rotarian. Contbr. bulls. and articles on ednl. subjects. Home: Salisbury MD‡

HOLLOWAY, WILLIAM JUDSON, ex-gov.; b. Arkadelphia, Ark., Dec. 15, 1888; s. Stephen Lee and Molly (Horne) H.; A.B., Ouachita Coll., Arkadelphia, 1910; LL.B., Cumberland U., Lebanon, Tenn., 1915; m. Amy Arnold, of Texarkana, Ark., June 10, 1917; 1 son, William Judson. Prin. ward sch., Hugo Okla., 1910-11, high sch., 1911-14; admitted to Okla. bar, 1916, and began practice at Hugo; pros. atty. Choctaw County, Okla., 1916-20; mem. Okla. Senate, 1920-26, pres. pro tem., 1925; elected lt. gov. of Okla., 1926, and became gov. on impeachment of Gov. Henry S. Johnston, Mar. 20, 1929, for term expiring Jan. 1, 1931. Mem. Officers' Training Sch., U.S.A., Louisville, Ky., Oct.-Nov. 1918. Mem. Am. Legion, Democrat. Baptist. Mason (32 deg.), Woodman of World. Home: Oklahoma City OK Died Jan. 28, 1970.*

HOLM, HENRY JESSE, business educator; b. Sheldon, Minn., Jan. 4, 1876; s. Jesse Christiansen and Anna (Henningsen) H.; ed. pub. schs. Minn. and Wis.; grad. Wis. Business Univ., La Crosse, 1896; m. Antoinette Haugan, of Waterford, Wis., Apr. 12, 1903 (died Jan. 10, 1929); m. 2d, Jessie Lu Arnold, of Chicago, Apr. 12, 1930. Teacher Stoughton (Wis.) Acad., 1896-99, The Toland Schs., Wis. and Minn., 1899-1902; mgr. Massey Business Colls., Ga. and Ky., 1902-05, Beutel Business College, Washington, 1906, Gregg Coll., Chicago, since 1907. Mem. Nat., Eastern and Central Commercial Teachers federations. Republican. Protestant. Clubs: Executives, Prosperity, Ill. Athletic, Geneva Lake Yacht and Golf. Home: 8020 Drexel Av. Office: 6 N. Michigan Av., Chicago IL‡

HOLMAN, WILLIAM KUNKEL, Bible publisher; b. Phila., Pa., Nov. 2, 1877; s. William Alfonso and Lena Gross (Kunkel) H.; ed. Protestant Episcopal Acad., Phila., 1888-95; LL.D., Muhlenberg Coll., 1945, hon. A.F.D., 1945; m. Sarah Louise Sharp, June 6, 1906; children—Sarah Louise (Mrs. Scott G. Lamb), Elizabeth Pennock (Mrs. Robert Baden Powell), Wilhelmina Kunkel (Mrs. Frederick Stephen Ball), Patience Burr (Mrs. J. M. von Suttka). With A. J. Holman Company, Bible publishers, Philadelphia, since 1897, beginning as stock boy; apprenticed as printer, 2 years, bookbinder, 1 year, leather gold worker, 1 year, gold stamper, 1 year; purchasing and managing, 1902-12, pres. and production mgr., 1912-30; pres. and sole owner since 1930. Mem. Wayne Protective Assn., Home Civic Assn. (pres. 1918-22), Franklin Inst., Phila. Chamber Commerce, Phila. Bourse. Republican. Episcopalian. Clubs: Union League (Phila); Merion Cricket (Haverford, Pa.). Home: St. Davids, Pa. Office: 1224 Arch St., Philadelphia 7 PA‡

HOLMBERG, ADRIAN OTIS, mfr. graphic arts equipment; b. Goshen, Ind., Mar. 10, 1900; s. Nels and Johannah (Munson) H.; m. Ellen Elizabeth Hagadone, Oct. 11, 1922; 1 dau., Joan E. (Mrs. Robert E. Jackson). With Miehle-Goss-Dexter, Inc., and predecessors, Chgo., 1948-65, exec. v.p., 1959-65. Mem. Am. Ordnance Assn., Newcomen Soc. Mason (32 deg., Shriner). Clubs: Lake Shore (Chgo.); Hinsdale (Ill.) Golf. Home: Winter Park FL

HOLMES, DWIGHT OLIVER WENDELL, coll. pres.; b. Lewisburg, W.Va., Nov. 15, 1877; s. John A. and Sarah (Bollin) H.; A.B., Howard U., 1901, M.A., 1912, LL.D., 1938; M.A., Columbia University, 1915, Ph.D., 1934; m. Lucy C. Messer, June 24, 1907; 1 son, Dwight Oliver Wendell. Teacher Sumner High Sch., St Louis, 1902; vice-principal and head dept. of science, Douglass High School, Baltimore, Md., 1902-17; instr. in edn., Miner Normal Sch., Washington, D.C., 1917-19; registrar and prof. edn., Howard U., 1919-20, dean and prof. edn. Coll. of Edn., 1920-34, dean Grad. Sch., 1934-37; pres. Morgan State Coll., Baltimore, since 1937. Pres. Baltimore Ednl. Assn., 1915-17, Gen. Alumni Assn. Howard U., 1912-15. Mem. exec. com. Bd. of Foreign Missions, Meth. Ch. Mem. Am. Assn. Sch. Adminstrs.; Am. Assn. for the Advancement of Science, Am. Acad. Polit. and Social Science, Nat. Soc. Coll. Teachers of Edn., Pi Gamma Mu, Alpha Phi Alpha, Kappa Mu, Sigma Pi Phi. Rosenwald fellow, 1931-32. Methodist. Club: Schoolmasters Club of Baltimore (pres. 1915). Author: The Evolution of the Negro College, 1934. Contbr. to Jour. of Negro Edn., Jour. of Negro History, Phylon. Retired 1948. Home: 2029 Druid Hill Av., Baltimore MD‡

HOLMES, EDWARD MARION, JR., physician, govt. ofcl.; b. Norfolk, Va., Aug. 4, 1907; s. Edward M. and Emma (Ehrmantraut) H.; grad. St. Mary's Male Acad., Norfolk, 1924; A.B., Georgetown U., 1928, M.A., 1929, M.D., 1933; M.P.H. (Rockefeller fellow), John Hopkins, 1936; m. Sarah Daily Walsh, Apr. 27, 1935; children—Edward M. III, Sarah Daily (Mrs. Venable Lane Stern, Jr.). Engaged as asst. state epidemiologist Va. State Dept. Health, 1934-35; med. dir. Fairfax County Health Dept., Fairfax, 1936-39; dir. bur. veneral disease control, 1939-47; asst. dir. pub. health Richmond City Health Dept., 1947-49; dir. pub. health, 1949-57; asso. prof. pub. health Med. Coll. Va., 1947-52, dir. dept. pub. health medicine, 1949-59, prof. head dept. community medicine, 1952-58, vis. prof. preventive and social medicine, cons. med. edn., All India Inst. Med. Sci., New Delhi, 1958-63; cons. in med. edn. AID, Washington, 1963-64; asso. regional rep.

health and med. affairs Vocational Rehab. Adminstrn., Dept. of Health, Education and Welfare, Atlanta, 1964-67; cons. for med. affairs Social and Rehab. Service, Dept. Health, Edn. and Welfare, 1967-69; dir. Rehab. Programs and Research and Tng. Center 19, U. Ala. Med. Center, Birmingham, 1969-71; with dept. phys. med., rehab. N.Y. U. Sch. Med., 1963-71; cons. med. affairs Soc. and Rehab. Service, 1968-69. Past mem. bd., exec. com. Richmond Area Community Council; mem. Richmond Bd. Cath. Charities; mem. Pan-Am. Sanitary Com. U.S.-Mexican Border Veneral Disease Control Commn., 1942-44. Served from captain to lieutenant colonel Medical Corps, USAAF. World War II. Diplomate AM. Bd. Pub. Health and Preventive Medicine (founder). Fellow Am. Public Health Assn., Royal Society Health; mem. Assn. Tchrs. Preventive Medicine (dir.), Am. Assn. Pub. Health Physicians (sec., editor bull.), Acad. Medicine, American Congress of Physical Medicine and Rehabilitation, Southern Medical Association, Am. Heart Assn., Med. Soc. Va., Soc. Va. Creepers, Phi Chi Fraternity. Clubs: The Club (Birmingham); Country of Virginia Commonwealth (Richmond); Delhi Gymkhana (New Delhi, India). Author: (with Ruth Benson Freman) The Administration of Public Health Services, 1960. Editor: Selected Writings of Marvin Pierce Rucker, 1957. Contbr. to Textbook of Preventive Medicine (Leavell and Clark), 1953; articles profl. jours. Home: Birmingham AL Died Feb. 26, 1971; buried Hollywood Cemetery, Richmond VA

HOLMES, EDWARD THOMAS, educator; b. Augusta, Ga., Mar. 21, 1870; s. Thomas Joseph and Florida (Calvin) H.; Gordon Inst., 1887-88; A.B., Mercer U., 1892, A.M., 1894 (LL.D., 1917); post-grad. work, Harvard, 1900-01; m. Elizabeth Jemison, of Birmingham, Ala., June 27, 1906; 1 son, Edward Thomas. Prin. Washington High Sch., Linton, Ga., 1893; head master, Mercer U. Prep. Sch., 1894-97; asst. prof. English, 1897-99, head prof. Latin, 1901-12, Mercer U.; pres. Gordon Inst., Barnesville, Ga., 1912-23; pres. Georgia Military Coll. since 1923. Pres. Georgia Harvard Club; sec., treas. and exec. com. Southern Inter-Collegiate Athletic Assn., 1901-24; mem. bd. trustees Mercer U. Mem. Harvard U. Classical Assn., Classical Assn. of South and Middle West, Kappa Alpha. Democrat. Baptist. Clubs: Log Cabin (Macon, Ga.); Kiwanis (lt. gov. for Ga., 1926-27). Address: Georgia Military College, Milledgeville GA‡

HOLMES, EDWIN SANFORD, JR., statistician; b. Worcester, Mass., July 24, 1862; s. Edwin S. and Sarah Moore (Crane) H.; grad. Washington High Sch., June 1880, Bliss Sch. of Electricity, Washington, 1893; m. Helen Lake, Phil., Aug. 24, 1885. In mercantile business, St. Louis and Washington, 1881-9; clerk and chief of sect. Census Office, 1890-5; apptd. chief of sect., U. S. Dept. of Agr., Apr., 1895, sp'l field agt., 1899, chief sp'l agt., Jan. 1, 1903, asso. statistician since Nov. 16, 1903, U.S. Dept. Agr. Mem. Am. Statist. Assn. Epscopalian. Republican. Club: Cosmos. Author of numerous publs. on agr'l economics, U8. Residence: 1308 Whitney Av. Office: Dept. Agr., Washington DC‡

HOLMES, JACK ALROY, educator; b. Oakland, Cal., Sept. 23, 1911; s. Jack Alroy and Carrie (Bonham) H.; B.A., U. Cal. at Berkeley, 1938, M.A., 1942, Ph.D., 1948; m. Florence C. Chilton, Sept. 20, 1936; children—Jack, Keith, Daniel. Head chemistry depts. Courtland (Cal.) High Sch., 1940-42, Petaluma (Cal.) High Sch., 1942-43; research phys. chemist Manhattan Project, Radiation Lab., U. Cal. at Berkeley, 1943-45, asst. prof. Sch. Edn., 1950-53, asso. prof., 1953-59, prof. edn. psychology, 1959-67, research psychologist Inst. Human Devel., 1959-67; dir. psychol. research, testing facility Benicia (Cal.) Arsenal, 1945-46; asst. prof. psychology Okla. A. and M. Coll., 1947-48; dir. adult reading clinic, Personnel Research Inst., also asso. prof. psychology Western Res. U., 1948-50; research fellow VA Hosp., Long Beach, Cal., 1956-57. Mem. Am., Cal. (past pres.) ednl. research assns., Am. Psychology Assn., A.A.A.S., Psi Chi, Phi Delta Kappa, Pi Gamma Mu. Contbr. articles profl. jours. Recipient research grants for study substrata-factor theory of reading Okla. Research Found., Carnegie Corp. N.Y., U.S. Office Edn. Home: Orinda CA Died Oct. 19, 1967.

HOLMES, JAMES THOMAS, engring.-constrn. co. exec.; b. Kansas City, Mo., Dec. 1, 1890; s. Robert James and Elizabeth (Vacoe) H.; B.S., Mass. Inst. Tech., 1914; m. Ester Roen, Jan. 25, 1922. Jr. engr. D.C. &W.B. Jackson Co., Boston, 1914-16; from sr. elec. engr. to chief elec. engr. Schofield Engring. Co., Phila., and subsidiary, 1916-20; partner Holmes & Sanborn, Los Angeles, 1920-31; fgn. travel, 1931-33; pres. Holmes & Narver, Inc., Los Angeles, 1933-70, chmn. bd., 1970, also dir. Registered profl. engr., Cal., Nev., Ariz. Fellow Am. Soc. C.E.; hon. mem. Am. Soc. M.E.; mem. Am. Soc. Testing and Materials, Atomic Indsl. Forum, U.S., Los Angeles chambers commerce, Def. Orientation Conf. Assn., Beta Theta Pi. Episcopalian. Clubs: Engineer's, California, Wilshire Country (Los Angeles); Mass. Inst. Tech. Southern California. Home: Los Angeles CA Died Dec. 11, 1970.

HOLMES, JOHN SIMCOX, forester; b. Cobourg, Ontario, Canada, May 31, 1868; brought to U.S., 1881; s. George and Georgina Beatrice (Simcox) H.; ed. private schs., Eng. and N.C., 1875-86, U. of N.C., 1886-88; M.F., Yale Sch. of Forestry, 1905; m. Emilie Rose Smedes, Nov. 1, 1909. Farmer, 1888-1902; entered U.S. Bur. of Forestry as student asst., Nov. 1902, forest asst., 1905-06, forest inspector, 1906-07, forest examiner, 1907-09; state forester N.C. Geol. and Econ. Survey (now Dept. of Conservation and Development) since 1909. Fellow Soc. Am. Foresters; mem. N.C. Acad. Science. Episcopalian (supt. of Sunday Sch.). Club: Civitan (Raleigh). Writer of state reports on forestry, etc. Home: 302 Forest Rd. Office: State Office Bldg., Raleigh NC‡

HOLMES, JOSES B. S., M.D.; grad. Atlanta Med. Coll., 1871; Jefferson Med. Coll., Phila., 1877; some yrs. adjunct prof. obstetrics and gynecology Southern Med. Coll. Mem. Am. Med. Assn.; ex-pres. Ga. Med. Soc.; ex-v.-p. Southern Surg. and Gynecol. Assn.; pres. Ga. State bd. med. examiners; prop'r The Halcyon. Address: 17 W. Cain St., Atlanta GA‡

HOLMES, JULIUS CECIL, U.S. ambassador; b. Pleasanton, Kan., Apr. 24, 1899; s. James Reuben and Louella Jane (Trussell) II; student U. of Kan., 1917-22; m. Henrietta Allen, Apr. 26, 1932; children—Henry Allen, Elsie Jane, Richard Peyton. Served in cav. and inf., Nat. Guard and Reserve, 8 years; major, U.S. Army, Feb. 1942, and advanced to brig. gen., July 1943. Began in ins. business, 1923-25; entered foreign service, 1925; vice-pres., New York World's Fair, charged with relations with Fed. Govt., Foreign Govts. and State Govts., 1937-40; president Gen. Mills, do Brasil, 1941-42, director since 1942; served as asst. sec. of State, resigning Aug. 1945; became vice pres. Transcontinental Western Air, Inc., Dec. 1945; president Taca Airways, S.A., Apr. 1946; appointed U.S. fgn. service officer, 1948; minister Am. Embassy, London; with Department of State, 1953; diplomatic agt., minister, Morocco, 1955-56; spl. asst. to sec. of state for NATO affairs, 1956-59; consul gen., Hong Kong, 1959-61; ambassador to Iran, Tehran, 1961-65 chief U.S. delegation to Internat. Telecommunications Conf., Montreux, Switzerland, 1965; head Joint State-Def. Study of Middle East and Mediterranean, 1967. Mem. China adv. panel Dept. of State 1966-67. Decorated D.S.M., Officer Legion of Merit, United States Army; Commander Crown of Yugoslavia; Comdr. Order of the Foenix, Greece; Lebanese Order of Merit; Officer Southern Cross of Brazil; Officer French Legion of Honor, Croix de Guerre with Palm; Comdr. Oussam Alaouite, Morocco; Grand Officer Nishan Iffticar, Tunisia; Comdr. Crown of Rumania; Comdr. Order Brit. Empire; World War I, N. African, European campaign medals. Fellow Am. Geographic Inst.; mem. Am. Foreign Service Assn., Acad. of Polit. Sci. Clubs: Chevy Chase, 1925 F Street, Army and Navy; Metropolitan (Washington); Whites, Travelers London. Home: Washington DC Died July 14, 1968; buried Arlington Nat. Cemetery.

HOLMES, SAMUEL JACKSON, zoologist; b. Henry, Ill., Mar. 7, 1868; s. Joseph and Avis Folger (Taber) H.; B.S., U. of Calif., 1893, M.S., 1894; fellow in zoology, University of Chicago, 1895-97, Ph.D., 1897; LL.D., University of California, 1943; D.Sc. (hon.), University of Michigan, 1948; married Cecelia Warfield Skinner; children—Samuel Jackson, Marion Virginia, Avis Cecelia, John Warfield, Joseph Edward. Assistant in zoology, Univ. of California, 1893-95; teacher San Diego (Calif.) High Sch., 1898; instr. U. of Mich., 1899-1905; asst. prof. zoology, U. of Wis., 1905-12; asso. prof. zoology, U. of Calif., 1912-17, prof. since 1917. Fellow A.A.A.S. (pres. Western div.); mem. Am. Soc. Zoologists (pres.), Wis. Acad. of Sciences, Am. Psychol. Assn., Am. Soc. Naturalists (pres.), Calif. Acad. of Sciences, Soc. Exptl. Biology and Medicine, Am. Genetics Assn., Eugenics Soc. (pres.), Eugenics Research Assn., Population Assn. of America, Am. Acad. of Arts and Sciences. Democrat. Author: Synopsis of California Stalk-eyed Crustacea, 1900; The Biology of the Frog, 1906; The Evolution of Animal Intelligence, 1911; Studies in Animal Behavior, 1916; The Elements of Animal Biology, 1918; The Trend of the Race, 1921; Studies in Evolution and Eugenics, 1923; Louis Pasteur, 1924; A Bibliography of Eugenics, 1924; Life and Evolution, 1926; The Eugenic Predicament, 1933; Human Genetics and Its Social Import, 1936; The Negro's Struggle for Survival, 1937; Organic Form and Related Biological Problems, 1948; Life and Morals, 1948. Home: 2821 Regent St., Berkeley CA‡

HOLMES, URBAN TIGNER, univ. prof.; b. Washington, D.C., July 13, 1900; s. Urban Tigner (Comdr. U.S. Navy) and Florence Fielding (Lawson) H.; U.S. Naval Acad., 1916-17; A.B., U. of Pa., 1920; A.M., Harvard U., 1921, Ph.D., 1923; student U. of Paris, 1922-23; Litt.D., Washington and Lee U., 1948, Western Mich. U., 1965; m. Margaret Gemmell, June 22, 1922; children—Mary (Mrs. L.L. Bernard), Florence Anne (Mrs. H. Hubbard), Urban Tigner. Asst. prof. Romance langs., U. Mo., 1923-25, asso. prof. U. of N.C., 1925-27; prof. Romance philology, 1927-45; Kenan prof. 1945—; with Office Strategic Services, Wash., Jan. 1943-Sept. 1944. Vis. prof. U. Chgo., spring 1929, U. of So. Cal., summer 1939, La. State U., fall 1950; distinguished vis. prof. Mich. State, 1959, cons. professor, 1960-62; Fulbright prof. U. Melbourne, Australia, 1960; lectr., Mediaeval Institute (Notre Dame), 1948, 56; sr. fellow Southeastern Mediaeval and Renaissance Inst., 1966. Del. Gen. Conv. P.E. Ch., 1946, 49; exec. council Diocese, 1946-49. Adv. com. Southern Fellowship Fund, 1960-63. Served in USNRF, 1918. Decorated Chevalier Legion of Honor (France); recipient John Keble award Am. Ch. Union, 1968. Fellow Mediaeval Acad. Am. (clk. 1954-57, 2d v.p. 1964-67), Am. Numis. Soc., Soc. Antiquaries (London), Linguistic Society of America, (director of Linguistic Inst. 1941-42), Royal Archaelogical Institute, Modern Language Association Am. (exec. council 1940-43), S. Atlantic Modern Lang. Assn. (pres. 1941), Societe de linguistique Paris, Delta Phi, Phi Beta Kappa. Dem. Co-editor: Works of Du Bartas, 1938-40; Mediaeval Studies, 1948; French and Provencal Lexicography, pub. 1964. Author: A French Composition, 1925; Guilaume de Salluste, Sieur du Bartas, 1935; (with H. Giduz) Sept. Contes de la Vicille France, 1930; Contes des Dept. Sages, 1936 (with A. H. Schutz) A History of the French Lang., 1933; Source Book for French lang., 1939; History of Old French Lit., 1937, 1962; New Interpretation of Conte del Graal, 1948; Daily Living in Twelfth Century, 1952-66; Samuel Pepys in Paris and other Essays, 1954; (with Sister M. Amelia Klenke) Chretien de Troyes, and the Grail, 1959; (with K. Scholberg) French and Provencal Lexicography, 1964; Mediaeval Studies in Memory of E. B. Ham, published in 1967. Editor: Volume I, Critical Bibliography of French Lit. (Middle Ages), 1947, 52; Berte aus. grans pies, 1946. Ediotr: North Carolina Studies in Romance, 1940-72, Romance Notes, 1960-72. Contbr. articles to mags. and encys.; asso. editor of studies in Philology. Home: Chapel Hill NC Died May 5, 1972.

HOLMQUIST, CLAIRE WALFRED, grain and lumber co. exec.; b. Oakland, Neb., Oct. 4, 1906; s. August Capanious and Ora Dell (Minier) H.; B.S., U. Neb., 1928; m. Mildred Ruth Romberg, June 12, 1935; children—Cynthia (Mrs. Thomas Fitchett), Nancy (Mrs. Robert Diekman), Jean. With Holmquist Grain & Lumber Co., Oakland, Neb., 1928-72, sec.-treas., 1957-72, mgr., 1960-72. Mem. Neb. Legislature, 1964-68, 70-72. Co-chmn. finance com. Oakland Centennial, 1964. Mem. Oakland City Council, 1959-64, chmn., 1960-64. Bd. dirs. Oakland Meml. Hosp. Assn. Mem. Neb. Lumberman's Assn. (pres. 1956, -mem. legislative com. 1954-56), Nat. Retail Lumber Dealers Assn. (mem. exec. bd. 1957-59), Oakland C. of C. (pres. 1946), N.E. Neb. United Chambers Commerce (pres. 1946), Burt County Agrl. Soc. (dir. 1949-71, pres. 1959-71), Phi Gamma Delta. Mason, Elk, Eagle. Club: Oakland Golf (an organizer 1941, pres. 1945-65). Address: Oakland NB Died Apr. 26, 1972.

HOLMSTROM, ANDREW BIRGER, business exec.; b. Worcester, Mass., Apr. 10, 1895; s. Andrew and Emily W. (Olson) H.; B.C.E., Worcester Poly. Inst., 1917; student Harvard Cadet Sch., 1918, Middlebury Summer Sch., 1921; m. Jennie E. Lofgren, June 30, 1921; children—Barbara E. Adams, Nancy E. Oakes, Joan P. Spence, Carol A. Narbeshuber. With plants engineering dept. Norton Company, 1919-25, civil engr. plant constrn., Europe and Am., 1919-34, gen. mgr. Norton Grinding Wheel Co., Ltd., 1934-39, works mgr. abrasive div. Norton Co., Worcester, 1939-40, v.p. in charge mfg., 1940-42, v.p., gen. mgr. abrasive div., 1944-60, also dir.; dir. Norton Co. of Can., Ltd., Indian Hill Co., Behr-Manning Corp.; supt. sewers City of Worcester, 1925-29. Elected first councillor under new city-mgr. govt., 1949, mayor 1950-54, vice mayor, 1954-58, councillor, 1958-70. Nat. vice chmn. A.R.C., 1956-57, chmn. Worcester, 1956-57; pres. Council Internat. Progress Mgmt. (USA), Inc. 1960-70. Mem. board of trustees Fairlawn Hosp. Served with U.S.N., 1917-19. Recipient citation for outstanding contbn. to Hwy. Safety, 1954 decorated Order of Vasa (King of Sweden), 1960. Fellow Am. Soc. M.E.; mem. Nat. Indsl. Conf. Bd., Inc. (bd. mem.), U.S. C. of C. (mem. manufacture and development com.), Mass. Higher Edn. Assistance Corp. (dir.), Am. Soc. C.E., Worcester Engineering Society, Worcester Society C.E., Worcester Swedish Charitable Assn. (pres.), Am. Legion. Republican. Baptist. Mason. Club: Worcester, Econ. (pres. 1956-57), Country (Worcester). Home: Worcester MA Died Jan. 1970.

HOLMSTROM, GUS EDGAR, banker; b. Round Rock, Tex., June 19, 1897; s. Carl Gus and Anna Sofia (Frejd) H.; student Toby's Bus. Coll.; m. Rose Clara Cervenka, Nov. 24, 1921; 1 dau., Mary Louise (Mrs. Charles T. Floyd). Engaged as tchr., 1919-21, banker, 1921-33, bank examiner, 1933-39; v.p. 1st Nat. Bank, Ft. Worth, 1939-60; with Continental Nat. Bank, Ft. Worth, 1960-67, pres., 1961-67, also dir.; dir. United Founders Life Ins. Co., Oklahoma City. Mem. exec. com. Ft. Worth United Fund, Ft. Worth YMCA. Trustee Tex. Christian U. Mem. Ft. Worth C. of C. (bd. dirs.). Methodist. Clubs: Ft. Worth, Shady Oaks, Colonial Country (Ft. Worth). Home: Fort Worth TX Died Nov. 19, 1967; buried Greenwood Cemetery, Fort Worth TX

HOLSCHUH, LOUIS WILLIAM, investment service; b. Beerfelden, Germany, Oct. 30, 1881; s. John Jacob and Elizabeth (Buchner) H.; ed. public schools and private studies; m. Lina Belle Johnston, Oct. 17, 1908 (died 1921); children—Edward Bronson, John Gage, Frank Johnston; m. 2d, Mrs. Carolyn Lina Tubbs, May 17, 1931. In N.Y. office Am. Tube Works, 1896-1901; with Moody's Investors Service, N.Y. City, 1901-59, v.p. and treas., 1914-44, pres., 1944-56, chmn., 1956-59. Republican. Methodist. Clubs: Bankers, Merchants (N.Y.C.); Merriewold Country. Home: Elizabeth NJ Died May 1971.

HOLSMAN, HENRY K., architect; b. Dale, Guthrie County, Ia., July 3, 1866; s. Henry and Louise (Kerchner) H.; A.B., Ia. (now Grinnell) Coll., 1891; m. Elizabeth Tuttle, May 1, 1896; children—Henry T., John T., William T. Bldg. supt. for contractors, Chicago, 1891-93; mem. Brainerd & Holsman, architects, 1893-97; alone since 1897; mech. engr. to Independent Harvester Co., Plano, Ill., 1910-12. Designed Bacteriol. Lab., U. of Chicago, and many structures for colleges, also a number of chs.; specializes in fireproof apts. and hotels. Park commr. of Ridge Park, Ill., 1908-09. Republican. Conglist. Fellow Am. Inst. Architects; mem. Chicago Archtl. Club (dir. and treas.), Ill. Soc. Architects, Western Soc. Engrs., Chicago Assn. Commerce, Assn. of Arts and Industries (dir.), Municipal Art League (dir.). Club: Cliff Dwellers (dir. and treas.). Designed and patented Holsman" automobile, one model of which in continuous operation since 1900; completed run from Los Angeles to New York World's Fair April 29, 1939, then placed in Smithsonian Instrn. as first 2 cylinder automobile of America. Home: 7202 Oak Av., River Chicago 3 IL‡

HOLT, ERWIN ALLEN, retired mfr.; b. Burke County, nr. Morganton, N.C., Nov. 11, 1873; s. Lawrence Shackleford and Margaret Locke (Erwin) H.; ed. Episcopal High Sch., nr. Alexandria, Va., and Ravenscroft School, Asheville, North Carolina; married Mary Warren Davis, June 16, 1903 (died May 28, 1942); m. 2d, Mrs. Laura Ballard Macgill, Apr. 11, 1944 (dec.). Formerly mem. Lawrence S. Holt & Sons, proprs. Aurora Cotton Mills, Burlington, N.C., and Gem Cotton Mills, Gibsonville, N.C.; now retired. Dem. but was an enthusiastic supporter of Theodore Roosevelt; del. Progressive Party Nat. Conv., 1916. Prominent advocate of good roads. Episcopalian (broad). Has unofficially given publicity since 1907 to Battle of Alamance, in order to perpetuate its memory; battle fought 9 miles from Burlington, N.C., May 16, 1771, between Gov. Tryon's forces of 1,100 militia and 2,000 men of the rural population, known as the Regulators; this was the first armed resistance and bloodshed in Am. colonies against the British; a monument unveiled May 29, 1880, marks the spot. Home: Burlington NC‡

HOLT, MARSHALL KEYSER (MRS. LELAND WALLACE HOLT), b. Alexandria, Ky., Feb. 24, 1874; student State Univ. of Ky.; Ohio Mechanics, Inst., Cincinnati; Inst. of Tech., Munich, Bavaria; m. Leland Wallace Holt, Mar. 18, 1903 (died Nov. 10, 1908); adopted, reared and educated 6 orphan children. Was a teacher of chemistry, 1895-1900; chemist West Java Sugar Expt. Station, Island of Java, 1900-02; pres. and mgr. Holt Land and Cattle Co., Colo. and N.M., 1908-12; pres. New Mexico Iron and Coal Mining Co., 1908-12; owner and pub. Orchard and Farm, San Francisco, 1910-13, editor, 1913-14; mining and chemical engr.; actively engaged in farming, mining and land development. Contbr. to agrl., chem. and mining jours. Mem. Yacqui Indian Tribe, Mexico. Home: Holtwood," San Rafael CA

HOLT, ROSA BELLE, author, rug expert; b. Cleveland; d. Alonzo J. and Lucretia Merriam (Hough) H.; ed. pvt. sch., Buffalo and abroad; unmarried. Editorial writer and spl. corr. for newspapers, 1891-1900; in rug business since 1904. Presbyn. Author: Rugs, Oriental and Occidental, 1901, 3d edit., 1927. Editor: Classical Authors, 1896. Address: 12 East 97th St., New York NY‡

HOLTHUSEN, HENRY FRANK, lawyer; b. New York, N.Y., Aug. 3, 1894; s. Henry and Barbara (Schindler) H.; A.B., Columbia Coll., 1915; LL.B., Columbia, 1917; m. Lenore Adeline Sutter, Oct. 10, 1953. Asso. Cadwalader, Wickersham & Taft, 1917; practiced law with offices in New York City and Norfolk, Va., 1920-24; spl. asst. atty. gen. U.S., Washington, 1924-26; partner House & Holthusen & McCloskey practicing gen., Corporate and admiralty law, New York City, 1927-34; apptd. Envoy Extraordinary and Minister Plenipotentiary to Czechoslovakia, 1931; partner House, Holthusen & Pinkham, New York City, 1934-37, partner Holthusen & Pinkham, 1937-51; staff Bur. Municipal Research. Conducted negotiations with Mexican Govt. for Economic Survey of Mexico by joint U.S.-Mexican Econ. Commn., 1944; visited 23 European countries as consultant to Fgn. Relations Sub-committee of U.S. Senate, 1947; chief of Telecommunications Mission to Japan, Turkey and other countries, 1951-52; counsel and cons. Foreign Relations Subcom. on Overseas Information Programs, 1953; chief Communications Mission for Egypt, 1953; general counsel committee on banking and currency U.S. Senate Study of Internat. Bank and Export-Import Bank U.S., 1954; cons. fgn. relations committee Tech. Cooperation Program, 1955; cons. spl. com. U.S. Senate to study Fgn. Aid Program, 1956; cons. fgn. relations com. U.S. Senate, Latin Am. study, 1958; American specialist U.S. State Department, 1959; cons. fgn. relations com. U.S. Senate, 1962-63; pub. mem. insp. U.S. Foreign Service, 1968; insp. Foreign Service of U.S., Portugal, 1968, France, 1969, Senegal and Gambia, 1970, Switzerland, 1971. Served as major U.S. Army, World War I. Del. Judicial Conv., N.Y. State, 1926. Counsel Protestant Unity League, 1932-34. Member Phi Kappa Psi. Protestant, Episcopalian (formerly vestryman Church of the Ascension). Club: National Republican (chmn. bd. govenors, New York Young Republican Club, 1929). Author: James W. Wadsworth, Jr., 1926; Turning the Hour Glass, 1928. Home: New York City NY Died Sept. 19, 1971.

HOLTON, ELIZABETH CURRAN (MRS. WINFRED BYRON HOLTON, JR.), interior designer; b. Denver; d. Hugh Grosvenor and Pearl (Gildersleeve) Curran; student pvt. schs.; m. Winfred Byron Holton, Dec. 4, 1920; children—Nancy Elizabeth (Mrs. Gordon Beverley Moore Walker); Patricia Curran (Mrs. Claud Morris), Winfred Byron III. Gen. practice interior design, 1920, 58-70; in charge restoration Bartow-Pell Mansion Mus., 1960; adminstrv. cons., chmn. decorating com. of the Mus., 1963; window display Scalamandre Silks, Inc., 1965. Founding mem. Mental Hygiene Assn., Westchester County, N.Y.; bd. mem. Westchester County Council of Social Agys.; founding chmn. Pelham Women's Exchange, Pelham, N.Y.; founding mem. bd. Met. Opera Guild; founded Jr. performances of Met. Opera Guild, Westchester County, N.Y.; founding pres. Jr. League of Palham, Inc. Mem. Nat. Soc. Colonial Dames in State of N.Y., Daus. of the Cin., D.A.R., Am. Inst. Interior Designers. Clubs: Decorators. Needle and Bobbin. Home: Rye NY Died Dec. 20, 1970.

HOLTON, GEORGE VAN SYCKEL, lawyer; b. Jersey City, N.J., Mar. 29, 1890; s. John N. and Mary D. (Bonnell) H.; LL.B., Cornell University, 1911; married Frances Osborne, December 30, 1919 (div. 1956); children—Mary (Mrs. Beane), Anne (Mrs. Bushman); m. 2d, Elizabeth Berry Dunn, July 12, 1958. Admitted to N.Y. bar, 1911; practiced, Rochester, until 1923; became asst. counsel Vacuum Oil Co., N.Y. City, 1923; dir. and gen. counsel Vacuum Oil Co., 1930, Socony-Vacuum Oil Co., Inc., 1932, v.p., 1937, chmn. bd., 1948-55, ret., 1955; dir. Perkin-Elmer Corp., Norwalk, Conn. Served as 2d lt. F.A., U.S. Army, 1918. Mem. Commerce and Industry Assn. N.Y., Inc. (dir. 1948-55, pres. 1951-52) Sigma Chi, Phi Delta Phi. Republican. Conglist. Clubs: Round Hill (Greenwich, Conn.); Woodstock Country. Home: Woodstock VT Died Dec. 10, 1972.

HOLTZOFF, ALEXANDER, judge; b. Nov. 7, 1886; s. Lazarus and Mary (Holtzoff) H.; A.B., Columbia, 1908, M.A., 1909, LL.B., 1911; m. Louise Cowan. Admitted to New York state bar, 1911, and practiced in the state, 1911-24; spl. asst. to atty. gen. of U.S., Washington, D.C., 1924-45, exec. asst., 1945; U.S. district judge for D.C., from 1945. Sec. to adv. com. Supreme Ct. on Fed. rules of criminal procedure; mem., sec. War Dept. adv. com. on mil. justice, 1946; lectr. Washington Coll. Law, also Sch. of Law, Cath. U. Served as pvt. A.U.S. 1918. Received Navy Distinguished Pub. Service Award, 1948. Mem. Am. (chmn. sect. jud. adminstrn. 1955-56), Fed. bar assns., Bar Association of D.C., Association Bar of City of N.Y., American Legion (past comdr. dept. justice post; past parliamentarian dept. D.C.), Phi Delta Phi (hon.), Phi Beta Kappa. Club: Nat. Press. Author: New Federal Procedure and the Courts, 1941; (with Allen R. Cozier) Federal Procedural Forms, 1941; (with William W. Barron) Federal Practice and Procedure. Contributor of articles in legal periodicals. Home: Washington DC Died Sept. 6, 1969.

HOLTZWORTH, BERTRAM ARTHUR, army officer; b. Huntington, W.Va., Apr. 3, 1904; s. Arthur Nicholas and Nettie Belle (Hunt) H.; student Va. Poly. Inst., 1921-23; B.S., U.S. Mil. Acad., 1927; m. Caroline Van Duyn Dorwin, June 25, 1932. Commd. 2d lt. F.A., U.S. Army, 1927, advanced through grades to maj. gen., 1952; successively battery officer, battery comdr., bn. comdr. various field arty. regts., 1927-43; gen. staff 12th U.S. Army Group, United Kingdom, France, Germany, 1943-45; chief staff Armor Center, 1945-47; mem. Dept. Army Gen. Staff, 1948-50; faculty Army War Coll., 1950-52; asst. chief staff J-4, Alaskan Command, 1952-54; asst. chief staff G-4, Continental Army Command, 1954-56; dep. chief staff Army Forces Far East, 1956-57; dep. chief staff programs, comptroller U.S. Army Pacific, 1957-59; chief of staff Sixth U.S. Army, 1959-61, deputy commanding general, 1961-63, ret., 1963. Decorated Distinguished Service medal, Legion of Merit, Bronze Star Medal; Order Brit. Empire; Legion of Honor, Croix de Guerre with palm, Croix de Guerre with gold star (France); Croix de Guerre with palm (Belgium). Methodist. Clubs: Army-Navy (Washington); Army and Navy Country (Arlington, Va.). Home: Washington DC Died Oct. 31, 1971; buried Arlington Nat. Cemetery, Arlington VA

HOLZBERG, JULES DONALD, educator; b. N.Y.C., Mar. 5, 1915; s. Samuel and Mary (Lurie) H.; B.S., Coll. City N.Y., 1937, M.S., 1938; Ph.D., N.Y. U., 1949; M. Betty Abrams, Jan. 25, 1942; children—Carol Ruth, Mark Allen, Robert Lincoln. Dir. psychol. labs. Conn. Valley Hosp., 1946-64; dir. research, 1964-68; asst. clin. prof., then asso. clin. prof. psychiatry (psychology) Yale, 1948-68; asst. prof., then asso. prof. psychology U. Conn., 1949-68; cons. Wesleyan U., Middletown, Conn., 1949-53, lectr., 1953-63, prof. psychology, 1963-73. Mem. psychol. com. Com. Internat. Exchange Persons, 1968-73. Served with AUS, 1943-46. Fellow Am. Psychol. Assn., Am. Orthopsychiat. Assn. (v.p. 1954-55), Soc. Projective Techniques (pres. 1955-56); mem. Conn. Psychol. Assn. (pres. 1955-56), Sigma Xi, Editor Jour. Consulting and Clin. Psychology, 1965-73. Contbr. profl. jours. Middletown CT Died Feb. 17, 1973.

HOMAN, FLETCHER, clergyman; b. Carl, Ia., Mar. 25, 1868; s. Isaac Thomas and Nancy Elin (Wilson) H.; A.B., Simpson Coll., Indianola, Iowa, 1895 (A.M.); S.T.B., Garrett Bibl. Inst., Ill., 1902; D.D., Upper Ia. U., 1908, Garrett Bibl. Inst., 1923; LL.D., Kan. Wesleyan, 1923; m. Kate Wilson, of Corning, Apr. 10, 1890; children—Ralph Fletcher, Paul Thomas, Earl Wilson, Merrill Simpson (dec.), Ruth Carrie (dec.), Kathryn Louise. In mercantile business, 1889-92; ordained M.E. ministry, 1898; pastor Des Moines Conf., Ia., until 1905; v.p. Simpson Coll., Indianola, Ia., 1905-08; pres. Williamette U., Salem, Ore., 1908-15; pastor First Ch., Erie, Pa., 1915-18, Trinity Ch., Kansas City, Mo., 1918-24, Central Park Ch., Buffalo, N.Y., 1924-1926. Del. Gen. Conf. M.E. Ch., 1912; pres. Willamette Valley Chautauqua Assn., 1913-15; exec. com. Nat. Anti-Saloon League, 1913-15, Ore. and Ida. State Y.M.C.A. com., 1909-14, Univ. Senate of M.E. Ch., 1912-15, Pacific Internat. Y.M.C.A. com., 1910-14; del. Ecumenical Conf. of Methodism, London, Sept. 1921; pres. Kansas City Council Chs., 1921-23; chmn. Com. of 100, Internat. S.S. Conv., Kansas City, Mo., 1922; del. to Universal Christian Conf., Stockholm, Sweden, Aug. 1925. Mason (32 deg., Shriner). Kiwanian. Lecturer; preacher at army cantonments. Home: 475 Norwood Av., Youngstown OH‡

HOMAN, PAUL THOMAS, economist; b. Indianola, Ia., Apr. 12, 1893; s. Fletcher and Kate (Wilson) H.; A.B., Willamette U., 1914; B.A., Oxford, England, 1919; Ph.D., Brookings Grad. Sch. of Economics and Govt., 1926; m. Christine Chittenden, June 10, 1924. Mgr. credit dept. Commonwealth Nat. Bank, Kansas City, Mo., 1921-23; instr. in economics, Washington U., St. Louis, 1923-25; asst. prof. of economics, U. of Calif., 1926-27; asst. prof. econ., Cornell, 1927-29, prof., 1929-47; staff, Council of Econ. Advisers to the President, 1947-50; prof. econs. U. of Calif., Los Angeles, since 1950; member research staff Brookings Instn., 1933-35 and 1937-38; economic advisor, O.P.M., 1941-42, W.P.B., 1942-44, W.A.A., 1945-46; dir. supply coordination div., U.N.R.R.A., London, 1944-45; member Com. on War Studies, S.S.R.C., since 1943; U.S. Commn. UNESCO, 1946-47. Served with Mesopotamia Expeditionary Forces, 1916-17; 2d lieut. Air Service, United States Army, with A.E.F., 1918-19. Awarded Rhodes scholarship, Oxford, 1914-16, and 1919-20. Mem. Am. Econ. Assn. (mem. exec. com. 1938-41); fellow Royal Econ. Soc. Author: Contemporary Economic Thought, 1928. Co-author: American Masters of Social Science, 1927; The National Recovery Administration, 1935; The Sugar Economy of Puerto Rico, 1938; Government and Economic Life, 1940. Contbr. to Encyclopedia of the Social Sciences and professional jours. Mng. editor Am. Econ. Review since 1941. Address: Los Angeles CA Died July 3, 1969; cremated.

HOMER, ARTHUR BARTLETT, corporation exec.; b. Belmont, Massachusetts, April 14, 1896; son of Eleazer B. and Elizabeth F. (Hough) H.; Ph.B., Brown U., 1917, LL.D., 1947; LL.D., Alfred Univ., 1952, Moravian College, 1958, Lehigh University, 1959; Dr. Bus. Adminstrn., Northeastern Univ., 1959; m. Sara Yocom, Sept. 14, 1922; children—Constance (Mrs. David L. Rawls, Jr.), Richard W., Stephen B. Vice pres. charge shipbldg. div. Bethlehem Steel Corp., 1940-45, pres., 1945-60, chief exec. officer, 1957-64, chmn., 1960-64. Served at lt. USN, 1917-19. Life trustee Brown U.; trustee Lehigh U., St. Lukes Hospital, Rhode Island School of Design. Member Society of Naval Architects and Marine Engineers (v.p., vice Adm. Jerry Land medal), Am. Iron and Steel Inst. (dir., Gary medal), Alpha Delta Phi. Clubs: Cruising of Am. Links, University (N.Y.C.); Saucon Valley Country (Bethlehem); Black Hall (old Lyme, Conn.); Essex (Conn.) Yacht; Ocean Reef (Fla.). Decorated Knight Royal Order Phoenix (Greece). Address: Bethlehem PA Died June 18, 1972; buried Providence RI

HOMER, FRANCIS THEODORE;, b. Baltimore Co., Md., Jan. 6, 1872; s. Charles C. H.; B.A., Loyola Coll., 1892, M.A., 1894; LL.B., U. of Md., 1894; m. Jennie M. Abell, of Baltimore, 1902. Began practice at Baltimore, 1894; moved to New York, 1912; v.p. Bertron Griscom & Co., Inc., pub. utilities, since 1918; dir. United Gas & Co., Inc., pub. utilities, since 1918; dir. United Gas & Electric Engring. Corpn., Houston Gas & Fuel Co., and many other corpns. Office: 40 Wall St., New York NY‡

HOMER, SOLOMAN JONES, sec. of Choctaw Nation, 1897-1902; b. Jackson, I. T., Jan. 17, 1870; grad. Roanoke Coll., Salem, Va., 1893, at head of class (the first Indian elected valedictorian of a class of white pupils); represented Roanoke Coll. in State oratorical contest at Univ. of Va.; won second place; law student at Harvard, 1894-5; Univ. of Kan., 1895-6; practiced law, 1896-9; m. Feb. 26, 1897, Blanche Marx, Salem, Va. Elected political mgr. in the Hunter-McCurtain gubernatorial election, 1902. Address: Caddo Ind. Ty.‡

HONDORP, PETER, ins. co. exec.; b. Grand Rapids, Mich., Dec. 14, 1903; s. Gerrit John and Gertrude (Van Dommelen) H.; A.B., U. Mich., 1926. With Central Life Ins. Co. Ia., 1926-42, asst. actuary, 1936-42; asso. actuary Continental Assurance Co., Chgo., 1945-62, v.p., 1962-68. Served with USAAF, 1942-45. Fellow Soc. Actuaries. Mem. Reformed Ch. Am. Home: Chicago IL Died Oct. 19, 1970; buried Oakhill Cemetery, Grand Rapids MI

HONEYCUTT, JESSE VERNON, steel mfr.; b. Newton, N.C., Sept. 7, 1893; s. James Thomas and Mary Rachel Elizabeth (Carter) H.; D.B.A. (hon.), Catawba Coll., Salisbury, N.C., 1949; LL.D., Moravian Coll., 1958; m. Anna Dorothy Fry, October 11, 1915; (dec. Apr. 5, 1958); children—Josephine (Mrs. John J. Somerville), Elizabeth (Mrs. Nevin L. Hartz). With Bethlehem Steel Co. (Pa.), 1914-58, mgr. of railroad sales, 1931-34, asst. gen. mgr. sales, 1934-36, asst. v.p., 1936-54, v.p., 1954-58; dir. Bethlehem Steel Corp., 1954-58. Asst. dir. charge prodn. steel div., WPB, 1942-44. Trustee Moravian College; member of the board of trustees Catawba College; mem. gen. bd. trustees Moravian Cong. of Bethlehem; trustee Moravian Music Found., Little League Baseball Found., Williamsport, Pa. Mem. Am. Iron and Steel Inst. (certificate of recognition for services to WPB, World War II, Newcomen Soc. Am. Clubs: Bethlehem, Cloud, Metropolitan, Pinnacle, Twenty-Nine (N.Y.C.); Gulf Stream Golf (Delray Beach, Fla.); Racquet (Phila.); Everglades, La Coquille (Palm Beach, Fla.; Saucon Valley Country (gov.; membership com.). Home: Bethlehem PA Died Oct. 31, 1969.

HOO, VICTOR CHI-TSAI, asst. sec. UN; born Washington, Nov. 16, 1894 (father sec. Chinese legation); s. Wei-Teh and Yung-Tsun (Cheng) H.; grad. Annen Schule, St. Petersburg, Russia, 1912, Ecole Libre des Sciences politiques, Paris, 1915; Licencie en Droit, U. of Paris, 1916, Docteur en Droit, Sciences politiques et economiques, 1918; m. Marguerite Chen, June 1, 1927; children—Peter, Mona, Cindy. Assistant secretary Chinese delegation to Paris Peace Conference, 1919; mem. Chinese delegation to Internat. Finance Conf., Brussels, 1920; attended first five assemblies League of Nations as tech. adviser to Chinese delegation; charge d'affaires for China in Berlin, 1924; sec. to ministry of fgn. affairs, China, 1928; sec.-gen. Chinese delegation to all League of Nations meetings on Sino-Japanese conflict; dir. permanent office of Chinese delegation to League of Nations, 1932-40; envoy extraordinary, Berne, 1933-42; vice minister fgn. affairs, China, 1942-45; rank of ambassador, 1946; del. UN confs., Bretton Woods, Dumbarton Oaks, 1944, San Francisco, 1945, London, 1945, 46; asst. sec. gen. UN, 1946, under sec. for conf. services UN, 1955, commr. for tech. co-operation, 1962-71. Recipient decorations, honors from China, Iran, Eqypt, Belgium, Czechoslovakia, France, Greece, Peru, Brazil. Confucianist. Home: Yonkers NY Died June 9, 1972; buried Ferncliff Cemetery, Ardsley NY

HOOD, OLIVER ROLAND, lawyer; b. Ashville, Ala., July 31, 1867; s. Noah A. and Mary I. (Cooper) H.; graduate Ashville Academy; Peabody Normal College (University of Nashville), 1887; m. Julia Riddle, November 13, 1889; 1 daughter, Margaret Bowman. Practiced at Gadsden, Alabama, since 1890; now sr. mem. of Hood, Inzer, Martin & Suttle; pres. Gadsden Loan & Investment Co. Trustee Alabama Tech. Institute (Auburn) for many years. Member City Council, Gadsden, 1901-03; member Constitutional Conv., Ala., 1901 (only surviving mem. of Com. on Suffrage and Election, com. that wrote the Poll Tax Provision into Ala. constitution). Mem. Am. and Ala. state bar assns. Democrat. Baptist. Mason, K.P. Club: Rotary (charter mem. and later pres.) Home: 862 Chestnut St. Office: Am. Nat. Bank Bldg., Gadsden AL*‡

HOOKER, JAMES MURRAY, ex-congressman; b. Buffalo Ridge, Patrick Co., Va., Oct. 29, 1873; s. John Wesley and Margaret D. (Akers) H.; William and Mary Coll., 1891-93; B.L., Washington and Lee U., 1896; m. Annie Dillard, of Henry Co., Va., Apr. 26, 1905; children—Margaret (dec.), John Dillard, Annie Murray. Began practice at Stuart, Va., 1896; now sr. mem. firm Hooker & Hooker; chmn. Dem. State Com., Va.; mem. Constl. Conv., Va., 1901-02; commonwealth's atty. for Patrick Co. 10 yrs.; mem. Bd. Visitors Va. Mil. Inst. 4 yrs.; mem. Fisheries Commn., Va., 8 yrs.; elected mem. 67th and 68th Congresses (1921-25), 5th Va. Dist., to succeed R. A. James, deceased. Democrat. Baptist. Mem. Va. State Bar Assn., Phi Beta Kappa. Mason, Odd Fellow, K.P. Home: Stuart Patrick Co VA‡

HOOKER, JOHN JAY, lawyer; b. Lebanon, Tenn., Sept. 9, 1903; s. Amzi Waddell and Alice (Williamson) H.; grad. Castle Heights Mil. Acad., 1920; A.B., Cumberland U., 1923, LL.B., 1924, LL.D., 1946; m. Darthula Williamson, June 10, 1925; children—Alice Kirby (Mrs. Robertson McDonald), John Jay, Henry Williamson. Admitted to Tenn. bar, 1924; practicing lawyer, Nashville, 1927-71; member firm Hooker, Keeble, Dodson & Harris. Mem. Tenn. Ho. of Reps., 1927. Trustee Cumberland U. Mem. Am. (Ho. of Dels. 1941-42), Tenn. (pres. 1940-41), Nashville bar assns., Am. Judicature Soc. (dir.), Nashville C. of C., Sigma Alpha Epsilon. Presbyn. Elk, Mason (Shriner, K.T.). Clubs: Cumberland, Belle Meade, Colemere. Home: Nashville TN Died Dec. 24, 1971.

HOOKER, MARGARET HUNTINGTON, artist; b. Rochester, N.Y., June 10, 1869; d. Horace B. and Susan (Huntington) H.; A.B., Vassar, 1890; studied in Art Students' League and Met. schs. of New York; also studied in Paris and London; unmarried. Taught art in Normal School, Cortland, N.Y., 1893-4; illustrated for New York Tribune, 1897. Compiled and illustrated Ye Gentlewoman's Housewifery, 1896. Home: 15 Carthage Rd., Rochester NY‡

HOOLEY, ARTHUR, author, editor; b. Newcastle-under-Lyme, Eng., Dec. 29, 1874; s. Samuel J. and Ellen Barlow (Wood) H.; ed. Newcastle High Sch. and U. of London; unmarried. Came to America, 1908; editor The Forum, July, 1910-Oct., 1915. Author: John Ward, M.D., 1913. Editor: Forum Stories, 1913. Home: 776 Lexington Av., New York‡

HOOVER, ARTHUR MCCALL, mfr.; b. Columbus, O., Mar. 27, 1901; s. Jacob B. and Alice R. (McCall) H.; m. Josephine E. Blacksten, Sept. 10, 1931; 1 dau., Ruth Ann (Mrs. Lynn B. Graves). With Ranco, Inc., Columbus, 1920-72, beginning as engr., successively chief engr., factory mgr. and v.p., pres., now chmn., dir. Home: Powell OH Died Apr. 10, 1972; buried Union Cemetery, Columbus OH

HOOVER, BESSIE RAY, author; b. nr. St. Joseph, Mich., Sept. 28, 1874; d. Alphonzo V. and Etta (Mitchell) H.; ed. Jamestown (N.Y.) High Sch., and Benton Harbor (Mich.) Coll. Taught sch. 6 yrs.; writer since 1900; contbr. to leading mags. Author: Pa Flickinger's Folks, 1909; Opal, 1910. Home: Benton Harbor MI‡

HOOVER, DONALD DOUGLAS, advt. and pub. relations exec.; Indpls., Jan. 6, 1904; s. Samuel Carpenter and Martha Belle (Stinson) H.; student pub. schs.; m. Pauline Holmes, May 28, 1927; 1 dau., Cynthia. Began newspaper career, Indpls., 1921; with Asso. Press Bur., Washington, 1926-28; city desk Indpls. News, 1928-33; advt. pub. relations Bozell & Jacobs, Inc., 1933-41, 48-69, pres. N.Y. Corp., 1950-64, chmn. bd., chief exec. officer, 1964-69; associate editor Indpls. Times, 1946-47. Past pres. Pogakon council Boy Scouts Am., mem. committee; president Indpls. Community Relations Council; bd. mem. of Greater New York Safety Council. Mem. of bd. govs., nat. exec. com. U.S.O., 1958-65. Civilian advisory bd. pub. relations U.S. Military Academy. Served from 1st lt. to col. M.I., Gen. Staff Corps, World War II. Decorated Order Brit. Empire; Philippine Liberation Medal with two stars; seven battle stars; Legion of Merit; recipient Pulitzer prize for Indpls. News, 1931. Mem. Bd. Fundamental Edn., Ind. Soc. (past pres. N.Y.C.), Am. Assn. Advt. Agys. (mem. com. on govt. and pub. relations), Soc. Silurians (v.p.), Conn. Society Prevention of Blindness (director), National Soc. Prevention Blindness (bd. 1959-62), Pub. Relations Soc. Am., Sigma Delta Chi (trustee endowment fund; recipient Wells Meml. Key 1961). Conglist. Clubs: Nat. Press (Washington); Society of Silurians, Advertising, Overseas Press (N.Y.C.); Indianapolis Press (past pres.). Author: Copy New York City NY Died Feb. 1969.

HOOVER, HERBERT, JR., consulting engineer; born at London, England, August 4, 1903; son of Herbert (31st President of the United States) and Lou (Henry) H.; B.A., Stanford U., 1925; M.B.A., Harvard, U. 1928; hon. degrees N.Y.U., Rutgers, Temple U., 1956, U. So. California, Claremont Men's Coll., 1957; m. Margaret Watson, June 25, 1925; children—Margaret Ann (Mrs. Richard Tatem Brigham), Herbert, III, Joan Ledlie (Mrs. William Leland Vowles). Mining engineer, 1925; member research staff, Harvard Business School, 1928-29; communications engineer Western Air Express, 1929-31, Transcontinental & Western Air (T.W.A.), Incorporated, 1931-34; teaching fellow, at the California Institute Technology, 1934-35; president of the Consol. Engring. Corporation, 1936-46, consultant to govts. of Venezuela, Iran, Brazil, Peru, etc., 1942-52; pres., gen. mgr. United Geophysical Co., 1935-52, chmn. bd., 1952-53; under sec. of state, 1954-57; cons. engr., Los Angeles, 1957-69; dir. So. Cal. Edison Co., Monsanto Co., Am. Mut. Fund, Investment Co. Am., Hanna Mining Co., Pacific Mutual Life Ins. Co., Automobile Club So. Cal. (pres. 1965-67). Trustee Claremont Men's College, U. So. Cal., Boys Clubs Am., Freedoms Found. Appointed spl. adviser on worldwide petroleum matters to sec. of state, 1953. Decorated by Venezuela, Chile, Peru; Kemp Medalist, Columbia, 1956; Hoover Medalist, Am. Inst. Mining Engrs., Am. Soc. Mech. Engrs., Am. Inst. E.E., Am. Soc. C.E., 1957. Mem. Am. Inst. Mining, Metall. and Petroleum Engrs., Am. Assn. Petroleum Geols., Society Exploration Geophysicists, Am. Radio Relay League (pres. 1962-66). Cal. C. of C. (dir.). Republican. Clubs: Century, University (N.Y.C.); Bohemian (San Francisco); California (Los Angeles); Metropolitan (Washington); Chevy Chase Country; Eldorado (Palm Desert). Home: Pasadena CA Died July 9, 1969.

HOOVER, HUBERT DON, army officer; b. Bedford, Ia., Oct. 15, 1887; s. Oswald and Sarah Keturah (Hardenbrook) H.; B.L., U. of Calif., 1909, J.D., 1911; m. Gertrude Elizabeth Mills, Sept. 15, 1912; children—Holman Don, Hubert Mills. Law practice, Los Angeles, Calif., 1911-17,. Entered Army as res. officer, 1917, commd. capt., regular Army, Judge Adv. General's Dept., 1920, advanced through grades to maj. gen., 1948; served as asst. judge adv. gen. in charge of br. office of judge advocate gen., with N. African and Mediterranean Theaters of Operations, 1943-45; asst. judge adv. gen., Office of the Judge Advocate Gen., Washington, 1945-48. Decorated Belgian Croix de Guerre with Palm; Legion of Merit with Oak Leaf Cluster. Mem. Delta Chi. Republican. Mason Home: Silver Spring MD Died Apr. 9, 1971; buried Arlington National Cemetery, Arlington VA

HOOVER, J(OHN) EDGAR, dir. F.B.I.; b. Washington, D.C., Jan. 1, 1895; son of Dickerson N. and Annie M. (Scheitlin) H.; LL.B., George Washington U., 1916, LL.M., 1917, LL.D., 1935; LL.D., Pa. Mil. Coll., N.Y. U., 1936, Westminster Coll., 1937, Okla. Baptist U., 1938, Georgetown U., 1939, Drake Univ., 1940, Notre Dame Univ. and St. John's Univ. Law Sch., 1942, Rutgers U., Univ. of Ark., 1943, Seton Hall Coll. and Holy Cross Coll., 1944, Marquette U., 1950, Pace Coll., 1954, Morris Harvey Coll., 1959, The Catholic University of America, 1964; D.Sc., Kalamazoo College, 1937; D.C. L., U. of South, 1941. Mem. bars of Dist. Ct. U.S. for D.C., U.S. Court of Claims, U.S. Supreme Ct. Entered Dept. of Justice, 1917; spl. asst. to atty. gen. of U.S., 1919-21; asst. dir. Bur. of Investigation, 1921-24; dir. Federal Bur. of Investigation, U.S. Dept. of Justice, 1924-72. Trustee George Washington U., elected mem. nat. bd. Boys' Clubs of America, 1943. Member National Court of Honor; honorary member of the national council of Boy Scouts of Am.; mem. nat. advisory council Girl Scout of Am. Recipient President's award for Distinguished Fed. Civilian Service, 1958; Great Living Americans award, C. of C. of United States, 1958; Am. Citizenship award Jr. Order United Am. Mechanics, 1959; U.S. Senate resolution of commendation for distinguished service to U.S., 1961; Criss award Mut. of Omaha, 1961; George Washington Honor Medal Freedoms Found., 1962; Gold Medal Merit, Jewish War Vets. U.S., 1962; Pro Deo et Juventute award Nat. Cath. Youth Orgn., 1963; Americanization gold medal award and citation Vets. Fgn. Wars, 1963. Hon. fellow Am. Bar Foundation; life mem. Internat. Assn. of Chiefs of Police and hon. mem. many police, sheriff and other law enforcement assns.; mem. Kappa Alpha, Omicron Delta Kappa, Delta Theta Phi, Alpha Phi Omega, Zeta Sigma Pi; honorary life member International Assn. for Identification, Chief Constables Association of Canada. Presbyn. Mason (33 degree, grand cross honour; K.T., Shriner), Order of De Molay (active mem. grand council). Author: Persons in Hiding, 1938; Masters of Deceit, 1958; A Study in Communism, 1962; J. Edgar Hoover on Communism, 1969; articles in numerous mags., law revs. and police jours. Club: Columbia Country. Office: Washington DC Died May 2, 1972; buried Washington Congressional Cemetery, Washington DC

HOOVER, JOHN HOWARD, naval officer; b. Seville, O., May 15, 1887; s. Benjamin Franklin and Claudia Irene (Crawford) H.; student U.S. Naval Acad., 1903-06; m. Helen Branconier Smith, Dec. 26, 1916; children—Jacqueline, William Howard, Jean. Commd. comdr. U.S. Navy, 1918, and advanced through grades to rear admiral, 1941, vice adm., 1942. Formerly comdr. Caribbean Sea Frontier, Comdr. Forward Area Central Pacific and Comdr. Mariannas; became dep. comdr. in chief, Pacific Fleet, July 1945. Awarded Navy Cross, 1919, Distinguished Service Medal with two stars, 1944-45. Club: N.Y. Yacht (N.Y.C.). Home: Bethesda MD Died Dec. 3, 1970.

HOPE, CLIFFORD RAGSDALE, ex-congressman, business exec.; b. Birmingham, Ia., June 9, 1893; s. Harry M. and Olive Armitta (Ragsdale) H.; LL.B., Washburn Law Sch., Topeka, Kan., 1917; LL.D., Washburn Municipal University, Topeka, Kan., 1951; D.C.L., Sterling (Kan.) Coll., 1952; D.Agr. (hon.), Kan. State Coll., 1956; m. Pauline E. Sanders, January 8, 1921; children—Edward Sanders (dec.), Clifford Ragsdale, Martha (Mrs. Frank West). Admitted to Kansas bar, 1917; began practice with William Easton Hutchinson, Garden City, Kansas, 1919; member Hutchinson, Hope & Fleming, 1921-27, former mem. Hope, Haag, Saffels & Hope, Garden City, Kan.; past pres. Great Plains Wheat, Inc., cons. Mem. Kan. Ho. of Representatives, 1921-27 (speaker of House, 1925-27); member 70th to 77th Congresses (1927-43), 7th Kan. Dist., mem. 78th to 84th Congresses, 5th Kan. Dist.;

chmn. com. on agr. 80th and 83d Congresses; chmn. Rep. Conf. Ho. of Reps. 81st-84th Congresses. Congl. advisor U.S. delegation to FAO, 1945, 46, 48, 49, 51, 55; mem. United States del Inter-parliamentary Union meeting, Stockholm, 1949, Istanbul, 1951; apptd. member Missouri Basin Survey Commission, 1952; member national committee Boys and Girls Club Work; honorary mem. National Council Boy Scouts of America. Entered 1st O.T.C., Ft. Riley, Kan., May 12, 1917; commd. 2d 1t. Aug. 1917; served in 35th and 85th divs., U.S. Army in France; hon. disch. Apr. 24, 1919. Awarded deg. Hon. American Farmer" by Future Farmers of Am., 1952; Hugh Bennett Gold Medal, Friends of Land, 1954; Founders award Izaak Walton League Am., for distinguished service and outstanding achievement toward furthering conservation of Am.'s natural resources, 1957. Mem. Soil Conservation Soc., Am., Kan. State Hist. Soc., Am. Legion. Republican. Presbyn. Mason (Shriner), Elk. Club: Capitol Hill (Washington). Home: Garden City KS Died May 16, 1970; buried Valley View Cemetery, Garden City KS

HOPE, FRANCIS MOFFAT, b. Edinburgh, Scotland, Apr. 22, 1877; s. Thomas and Margaret (Moffat) H.; student Aird House Sch., George Watson's Coll., Edinburgh; m. Daisy Coleman Shere, May 24, 1921 (dec. Oct. 1953). Came to U.S. 1910, naturalized, 1919. Apprentice and actuarial clk. Caledonian Ins. Co., Edinburgh, 1986-1910; asst. actuary Occidental Life Ins. Co. Cal., Los Angeles, 1910-12, actuary, 1912-30, v.p., actuary, 1930-42, emeritus, 1942-68, dir., 1937-58. Fellow Faculty of Actuaries in Scotland, Soc. Actuaries; mem. Acturial Club Pacific States (pres. 1933). Contbr. articles periodicals. Home: Los Angeles CA Died June 13, 1968; buried Forest Lawn Meml. Park Glendale CA

HOPE, JAMES HASKELL, state supt. schs.; b. Hope Station, S.C., Sept. 22, 1874; s. James Christian and Martha Fletcher (Miller) H.; graduated Newberry (S.C.) College, received degrees, A.B., and LL.D.; student Clemson Agricultural College 2 years, Winthrop Normal Coll. 5 summers; 1 son, James Donald; m. 2d, Wilhelmina Grimsley, Mar. 5, 1921; children—Martha Louise, James Haskell, John Christian, Stuart Cromer. Teacher rural schs. 6 yrs., supt. schs. 12 yrs., supt. city schs. 5 yrs.; state supt. edn., S.C., 1923-47, ret. Capt. S.C.N.G. 2 yrs. Mem. County Bd. Edn., Union County, 1900-16; county supt. edn., Union County, 1916-22. Life mem. N.E.A., S.C. State Teachers Assn. Democrat. Baptist. Mason (Shriner), K.P. Jr. Order United Am. Mechanics. Club: Lions. Home: 129 Walker St., Columbia SC‡

HOPE, MINNIE GAZELLE WELBORN (MRS. TOM HOPE), clubwoman; b. McKinney, Tex., Aug. 17, 1872; d. Samuel Newton and Sarah Ann (Chambers) Welborn; student Halsell Coll., Savoy, Tex.; grad. Le Tellier's Pvt. Sch., Sherman, Tex., 1890; Ed.M., Kid-Key Coll., Sherman, Tex., 1891; grad. study, Sam Houston State Teachers Coll., Huntsville, Tex., 1891-92; m. Tom Hope, of Vernon, Tex., Jan. 28, 1895; 1 son, Tom Welborn. Active in lit., civic and philantropic work since 1895; a founder Ednl. Loan Fund for Girls, Okla., 1910; state chmn. Belgian Relief, 1914-17; a founder state Library Commn., Okla., 1916; state chmn. for registration, Nat. Council of Defense, 1917-18, also state chmn. Women's Speakers Bur., 1917-18; mem. Okla. State Council of Defense, 1917-19; commr. of accounting and finance, Ada, Okla., 1921-22; an organizer and 1st v.p. Okla. Assn. for Prevention of Tuberculosis; mem. State Exec. Com., Okla., of Woodrow Wilson Foundation; etc. Dir. for Okla. of Gen. Federation of Women's Clubs, 1916; pres. 1915-17, hon. pres. for life Okla. State Federation of Women's Clubs; mem. United Daughters of Confederacy; mem. Okla. advisory council of League of Nations Assn.; charter mem. Okla. Epsilon Sigma Omicron Sorority. Democrat. Methodist. Clubs: Twentieth Century of Ada (pres. 1900-12); Twentieth Century of Oklahoma City (hon.); Pioneer Members Club of Okla. Named as mem. Okla. Honor Roll (24 women leaders of state), 1930. Home: 107 E. 14th St., Ada OK‡

HOPKINS, ALTIS SKILES, pres. Standard Oil Co. (Kan.); b. Wilson Co., Kan., Nov. 9, 1872; s. James Madison and Ellen (Skiles) H.; student U. of Kan., 1891-92; m. Helen Blakeslee, Feb. 27, 1898; children—Tom Blakeslee, Grace Ellen, Helen Rosemary. Began as laborer with oil refinery, Neodesha, Kan., 1897, and advanced to supt., 1913; v.p. and gen. mgr. Standard Oil Co. (Kan.), 1923-27, pres. since 1927. Republican. Presbyn. Mason (K.T., Shriner). Clubs: Rotary (Neodesha); Country (Independence, Kan.). Home: Neodesha KS‡

HOPKINS, JAMES R., artist; b. Irwin, O., May 17, 1877; s. Asa G. and Nettie (Miller) H.; ed. Art Acad. of Cincinnati; spent 1 yr. in Paris, then traveled around the world, studying art in Japan, China, Ceylon, Egypt, Italy, etc.; LL.D., Ohio State University, 1948; married Edna B. Boies, September 13, 1904. Painted in Paris for 10 yrs., 1904-14; mem. faculty drawing and painting, Art Acad. of Cincinnati, 1914-19; prof. emeritus Fine Arts, O. State U. Portrait and figure painter; awards: Walter Lippincott prize, Pa. Acad. Fine Arts, 1908; bronze medal, Buenos Aires Internat. Expn., 1910; gold medal, San Francisco Expn., 1915; Norman Wait Harris bronze medal, Art Institute, Chicago, 1916; Thomas Clark prize, Nat. Acad. Design, 1920. Represented in Cincinnati Museum Assn., Atlanta Art Assn., Art Inst. Chicago. A.N.A. Dir., chmn. Farmers Bank, Mechanicsburg. Asso. mem. Societe Nationale des Beaux Arts, Paris; mem. Alpha Tau Omega, Phi Beta Mechanicsburg OH Died Jan. 23, 1969; buried Maple Grove Cemetery, Mechanicsburg OH

HOPKINS, JAY PAUL, army officer (ret.); b. Mattawan, Mich., Nov. 2, 1875; s. Josiah and Elvira (Mains) H.; student Hillsdale Coll., 1892-93; B.E., U.S. Military Academy, 1900; married Jeannette Ward, Aug. 7, 1900; 1 daughter; married 2d, Jessie Howell Zook, Nov. 29, 1927. Commander 2d lieutenant, artillery, 1900, advanced through grades to brigadier gen.; retired as col., C.A.C., 1930, brig. gen. (ret.), 1940; instr. Coast Arty. Sch., 1908-12; chief of antiaircraft service, 1918. Now dir. and pres. First Nat. Bank of Cassopolis, Mich. Awarded Distinguished Service Medal (U.S.), Legion of Honor (France). Republican. Presbyterian. Mason. Clubs: Union League (Chicago); Rotary (Dowagiac, Mich.). Home: 530 E. State St., Cassopolis MI‡

HOPKINS, JOHN APPLETON HAVEN, s. John Milton and Augusta DeBlois (Haven) H.; ed. Columbia Mil. Inst., New York; m. Hilda Elizabeth Stone, of N.Y. City, Nov. 14, 1895 (died Mar. 5, 1899); 1 son, John A.H.; m. 2d, Alison Low Turnbull, October 8, 1901 (divorced 1926); children—J. Milton, Marion, Louise, Douglas T.; m. 3d, Melinda Alexander, December 1, 1930. Began in 1888, with Johnson & Higgins, adjusters and ins. brokers, advancing to v.p.; retired 1919. State chmn. Progressive Party, N.J., 1912, later nat. treas.; Prog. candidate for State Senate, N.J., 1918; chmn. N.J. delegation to Prog. Nat. Conv., 1916; supported Woodrow Wilson for pres., 1916, chmn. institutions Com., N.J., 1917, when conducted succesful fight for reform in state prisons and insane asylums; nat. chmn. Com. of 48 which was established to organize a new nat. Progressive party; treas. Greater New York La Follette Campaign Com. (Progressive Party), 1924; mem. Labor Commn. to Russia, 1927; chmn. examining com. Nat. Bur. of Information and Edn. Home: Essex Fells, N.J., Office: 110 Williams St., New York NY‡

HOPKINS, MIRIAM, actress; b. Bainbridge, Ga., Oct. 18, 1902; m. Brandon Peters, 1926; m. 2d, Austin Parker, 1931; m. 3d, Anatole Litvak, 1937; m. 4th, Raymond Brock, 1939 (div. 1951). Appeared in motion pictures All of Me," She Loves Me Not," The Richest Girl in the World," Becky Sharp," Barbary Coast," These Three," Men Are Not Gods," The Woman I Love," Woman Chases Man," Wise Girl," The Old Maid," A Gentleman After Dark," 1942. Old Acquaintance," 1943-44, The Chase, 1966, others. Starred in stage prodn. Laura," Chicago, 1946, The Skin of Our Teeth. Address: Hollywood CA Died Oct. 1972.

HOPKINS, ROBERT HOLBROOK, lawyer; b. Worcester, Mass., Mar. 22, 1902; s. Frederick Sylvanus and Etta (Holbrook) H.; A.B., Harvard, 1922, LL.B., 1925; m. Margaret Hitchcock Sims, Sept. 7, 1929; children—Anne Sims, Stephen. Admitted to Mass. bar, 1926, since practiced in Boston; partner Gaston, Snow, Motley & Holt, and predecessors, 1945-68. Asst. corp. counsel City Boston, 1938-42, corp. counsel, 1942-43; counsel indsl. Readjustment br. Office Procurement and Material Navy Dept., Washington, 1943-44; counsel Navy Compensation Bd., 1944. Trustee, bd. mgrs., mem. exec. com. Mass. Eye and Ear Infirmary. Fellow Am. Bar Found.; mem. Am., Mass. (past v.p.), Boston (past mem. council) bar assns., Am. Law Inst., Am. Judicature Soc. Republican. Episcopalian. Clubs: Harvard, Saint Botolph, Union Boat, Badminton and Tennis (Boston); Harvard (N.Y.C.); Metropolitan Brookline MA Died Jan. 17, 1968.

HOPPER, DAVID CLAUDE, cons. engr.; b. Caddo Gap, Ark., Nov. 2, 1888; s. John Franklin and Martha (Burke) H.; B.S., U. Ark., 1915; student Chgo. Central Sta. Inst., 1915-16, U. Pitts., 1927; m. Ida Middlebrooks, Dec. 4, 1918; children—Mary Jean (Mrs. K. L. Wommack), Martha Doris (Mrs. Courter D. Mills), Engr. Union Switch & Signal Co., Pitts., 1914; engr. Commonwealth Edison Co., Chgo., 1915-18; engr. Am. Internat. Shipbuilding., Phila., 1918; engr. Va. Power Co., Newport News, 1919-20; engr. No. Ohio Power & Light Co., Akron, 1920-23; engr. Duquesne Light Co., Pitts., 1923-54; instr. Pa. State U., 1954-59; cons. prof. engr., 1959-68. Served as cadet lt. F.A., U.S. Army, World War I. Decorated Legion of Honor. Profl. licensed elec. engr., Pa. Mem. I.E.E.E., Tau Beta Pi, Tau Epsilon Chi. Republican. Mem. Christian Ch. Mason (Shriner). Club: Winston-Salem Engineers. Died Apr. 29, 1968; buried Winston-Salem NC

HOPPER, FRANCES PETERS (MRS. EUGENE D. HOPPER), business exec., b. Cleve., Jan. 13, 1889; d. Richard E. and Jennis (Naylor) Peters; B.A., Doan Coll., 1921; m. Eugene D. Hopper, Feb. 21, 1923; 1 dau., Barbara Ann (Mrs. Gary L. Tinkham). Vice pres., Chevrolet Keystone Co., New Castle, Pa., 1934-44, dir., 1938-58; dir. The Buckeye Co., Youngstown, O., 1940-59, Pfau Chevrolet, Sharon, Pa., 1938-60; dir. The Buick Youngstown (O.) Co. Sec., Youngstown P.T.A., 1951. Bd. dirs. Monday Musical Assn., Youngstown. Clubs: Youngstown, Youngstown Country. Home: Youngstown OH Died Sept. 4, 1970; buried Tod Memorial Cemetery Youngstown OH

HORAN, HUBERT JOSEPH, JR., banker; b. Phila., June 30, 1889; s. Hubert Joseph and Elizabeth Cecelia (Gartland) H.; LL.B. cum laude, U. Pa., 1911; LL.D., LaSalle U., 1953; LL.D., Saint Joseph's College, 1963; m. Agnes R. Mack, Sept. 27, 1916; 7 daus., 2 sons. With Continental Bank & Trust Co. (formerly Broad Street Trust Co.), Phila., from 1921, pres., 1938-59, chmn. bd., chief exec. officer, 1959-65, chairman executive committee, 1965-66, dir.; dir. Warner Co., Union Paving Co., Day and Zimmermann, Incorporated. Rep. U.S. Govt. on Intergovernmental Com. for European Migration, Geneva, 1955. Chmn. A.R.C., Southeastern Dist. of Pa., 1946; mem. Mayor's Com. to Reorganize Finances of Phila., 1947-48; dir. City Trusts, 1946-69; mem. Phila. Parking Authority Bd., from 1965. Dir. Misericordia Hosp.; trustee, 1st vice pres. Estate of Stephen Girarb; director of the United Fund. Decorated Cross of Comdr. Order of Phoenix (Greece), 1951; Papal Knight Malta. Republican. Roman Catholic. Clubs: Union League (Phila.); Merion Cricket (Haverford, Pa.). Home: Philadelphia PA Died May 22, 1971.

HORAN, PHILIP EDWARD, ins. co. exec.; b. Ottumwa, Ia., June 24, 1885; s. Philip and Margaret (Sullivan) H.; student St. Ambrose Coll., Davenport, Ia., 1901-02, 03-04; A.B., Creighton U., 1908, LL.B., A.M., 1913; m. Blanche Coffman, June 24, 1916; children—Philip Edward, William Coffman, Kathleen (Mrs. Donald Peabody). Admitted to Neb. bar, 1913; with firm Mahoney & Kennedy, Omaha, 1913-18 Kennedy, Holland, DeLacy & Horan, Omaha, 1918-20, Sears, Horan & Sears, Omaha, 1921-27; mem. legal staff Mut. of Omaha, from 1927, gen. atty., from 1950, v.p., gen. counsel 1952-60, sr. v.p., from 1960; mem. legal staff United Benefit Life Ins. Co., from 1927, gen. atty., from 1950, also dir. Mem. Am., Neb. Omaha bar assns. Home: Omaha NE Died Feb. 9, 1972; buried Holy Sepulchre Cemetery, Omaha NE

HORENSTEIN, JASCHA, conductor-composer; b. Kiev, Russia, May 6, 1899; s. Abraham and Marie (Jekels) H.; student U. Vienna; grad. Acad. music, Vienna; m. Ernestina Diaz Saenz Valiente, Jan. 30, 1958; 1son by previous marriage, Peter. Made debut with Vienna Symphony Orch.; conductor Berlin Symphony, 1925-28; mus. dir. Dusseldorf Municipal Opera, also guest condr. with many leading European orchestras, 1929-33; filled regular engagement as condr. in Russia, France, Belgium and Poland, 1933-37, appearing with Moscow and Leningrad Philharmonic orchs., Orchestre Symphoniquede Paris, Lamoureux Orch. of Paris, Brussels Philharmonic, Warsaw Philharmonic and Warsaw State Opera, also appearing as guest condr. in Stockholm, Helsingfors, Riga and Vienna; toured Australia and New Zealand, 1938; one of four condrs. (with Arturo Toscanini) Palestine Symphony Orch., 1939; made U.S. debut, 1941; appeared as condr. N.Y. Philharmonic Symphony Soc., Montreal, Havana and Brazilian Symphony (Rio de Janeiro), Teatro Colon Orch. (Buenos Aires), 1946-49; made Mexican debut, 1944; condr. for all major European Orchs., also Opera House of West Berlin, Royal Opera House Covent Garden, London, La Scala, Milano, San Francisco Opera House, festivals of Edinburgh, Florence, Vienna; tours of S.Am., S.Africa, Australia; debut Am. Symphony Orch., 1969; recs. with Vienna Symphony Orch., London Symphony Orch., New Philharmonic Orch. London. Recipient Grand Prix du Disque (3). Address: Lausanne-Pully Switzerland

HORINE, JOHN WINEBRENNER, clergyman, educator; b. Smithsburg, Md., May 23, 1869; s. Mahlon Carlton and Emma Frances (Winebrenner) H.; student Muhlenberg Coll., 1886-89, Luth. Theol. Sem., Mt. Airy, Phila., 1889-92; D.D., Newberry (S.C.) College, 1914, LL.D., 1933; D.D., Roanoke Coll., Va., 1914; m. Helena Laurent, Oct. 31, 1893; children—Frederick Laurent, Charles Schaeffer, John Winebrenner, Robert George. Ordained Luth. ministry, 1892; pastor Ch. of the Incarnation, Phila., 1892-97, St. John's Ch., Charleston, S.C., 1897-1907, St. Luke's Ch., Phila., 1907-14; editor Lutheran Ch. Visitor, Columbia, S.C., 1914-19; prof. exegesis, Luth. Theol. Southern Sem., 1919-42. Author: The Catechist's Handbook, 1909; A Home Enterprise, 1925; Inspirational Prose Quotations, 1932; Sacred Song, 1934; Our Liturgy, 1939. Home: 907 Wildwood Av., Columbia SC‡

HORN, CARLTON WILLIAM, clergyman; b. Middleboro, Mass., Oct. 23, 1905; s. William Walter and Catherine (McLean) H.; student Gordon Coll., 1926-27, Temple U., 1927-28, Franklin and Marshall Coll., 1929-34, Eastern Bapt. Sem., 1927-29; m. Loretta Christen, Nov. 4, 1942. Ordained to ministry Meth. Ch., 1930; pastor numerous chs.; pastor St. Pauls United Ch. of Christ, Ohlman, Ill. Served with USAAF, 1941-45. Mem. Soc. Am. Mil. Engrs., V.F.W. (past nat. chaplain). Mason (32 deg.), Lion, Rotarian. Address: Ohlman IL Died Mar. 24, 1969.

HORN, CHARLES J., mortgage banker; b. Irvington, N.J., 1912; m. Marion Coleman; children—Lawrence, Stuart, Marilyn, Nancy. Exec. v.p., dir. Asso. Mortgage Co.'s Inc., Washington; dir. Taylor Internat. Corp. Home: Cherry Hill NJ Died Jan. 14, 1970; buried Union NJ

HORN, CLINTON MORRIS, lawyer; b. Medina, O., Nov. 14, 1885; s. Henry Adam and Ida (Pulsifer) H.; A.B., Western Res. U., 1908, LL.B., 1911; m. Mabel North Reed, Oct. 16, 1912; children—Miriam (Mrs. John A. Greene), Margaret (Mrs. James H. Foster, Jr.), Virginia (Mrs. John T. White), Martha (Mrs. William C. Bradford). Admitted to Ohio bar, 1911, since practiced in Cleve.; partner firm Arter, Hadden, Wykoff & Van Duzer, and predecessors, from 1920. Dir., sec. Ferro Corp., from 1919; legal counsel Holstein Friedian Assn. Am., 1919-60. Mem. Cleve. C. of C., Benchers (Western Res. U. Law Alumni Assn.). Presbyn. (ruling elder). Club: Union (Cleve.). Home: Shaker Heights OH Died Apr. 1, 1970; cremated, interred Lake View Cemetery, Cleveland OH

HORNBECK, VIVIENNE B. (MRS. STANLEY K. HORNBECK), civic worker; b. Denver, Feb. 24, 1896; d. Newton Evans and Leola (Carter) Barkalow; B.A., Sweet Briar Coll., 1918; m. Leland Davis Breckenridge, June 21, 1921 (div. Sept. 1928); m. 2d, Stanley Kuhl Hornbeck, Aug. 24, 1938. Community worker Jr. Leagues, Denver, 1918-21, St. Louis, 1921-23, Miami, Fla., 1923-27; registrar Natchez (Miss.) hdqrs. A.R.C., 1927, dir. Washington County hdqrs., Greenville, Miss., 1927-28, dir. spring planting McGee (Ark.) hdqrs., 1928; alumnae sec. Sweet Briar Coll., 1929-38; dir. dist. Ill. Am. Alumni Council, 1933-35, trustee, 1934-37, pres., 1936, dir. regional confs., chmn. membership com., 1937-38; dean of women Am. U., Washington, 1944-45; historian Barney Neighborhood House, Washington 1939-42; sec. Child Welfare Soc. Bd., Children's Hosp., Washington, 1939-45, 47-70, chmn. com. on gluetamic research, 1947-48, chmn. bulb com., 1959-70; bd. dirs. United China Relief, Washington, 1939-45; vice chmn. Women's Aux. Greek War Relief, 1939-45; bd. dirs. Netherland-Am. Found., 1944-70; hon. pres. Am. Women's Club, The Hague, Netherlands, 1945-47; hon. mem. Netherlands Red Cross, 1946-47; originator, nat. hon. chmn. Sweet Briar Bulbs from Holland Project, 1950-70, recipient recognition from Sweet Briar Alumnae Club for services in connection with this project, by creation of Vivienne Barkalow Hornbeck Scholarship Fund, 1961. Recipient Merit certificate Community War Fund, 1944; citation Sweet Briar Coll. Alumnae Assn. and Coll. Adminstrn., 1955; beauty Asso. Bulb Growers of Holland, 1961. Decorated Order Ching Hsin (China). Mem. Nat. League Am. Pen Women, Washington Jr. League, Am. Newspaper Women's Club, Fgn. Service Women's Assn. (hon.). Author: Research Catalogue Welfare Agencies in Towns in Mo., Ill., Ark., 1922. Editor: Sweet Briar Alumnae News, 1929-38. Home: Washington DC Died May 1970.

HORNE, NELLIE MATHES, painter; b. at Eliot, Me., May 26, 1870; d. John Harrison and Lizzie N. (Young) Mathes; ed. pub. schs., Eliot, and Portsmouth, N.H.; grad. Commercial Coll., Boston; studied art with U. D. Tenney and others; m. at Portsmouth, N.H., William H. Horne, Aug. 5, 1891. Collaborator in studies with Ulysses Dow Tenney on notable portraits; painted Edward Everett Hale, William Dean Howells, Hon. Frank Jones, ex-sec. John D. Long, 10 living ex-mayors of Portsmouth, etc.; premiums at Brockton, Mass., Concord, N.H. Mem. Professional Woman's Club, Copley Soc., 20th Centruy Club, Boston; vice-regent John Paul Jones Chapter D.A.R. Address: The Dewey Washington DC‡

HORNER, BERNARD JUSTINE, newspaper pub.; b. Uvalde, Tex., July 13, 1895; s. Herman and Clara H.; student Draughons Bus. Coll.; La Salle Extension U.; m. Nov. 20, 1920; children—Madelyn, Bernard Gentson. Entire career with Light Pub. Co., San Antonio, Tex.; advt. dir., 1919-Mar. 1942, became pub., Aug. 1946, editor, vice-pres. Board of directors San Antonio Symphony Soc. Military service with 36th inf. div., 1917; disch. capt. inf., 1919; re-entered mil. service as lt. col. with III Corps, Mar. 1942; overseas duty as col., G-2 III Corps; disch., 1946. Awarded Army Legion of Merit, Bronze Star, Commendation ribbon, Cross of War with Palms (Belgium). Mem. Res. Officers Assn., Tex. Pub. Assn., Am. Legion, San Antonio C. of C. (dir.). Independent. Episcopalian. Mason (Scottish Rite). Rotarian. Clubs: Patio; St. Anthony. San Antonio TX Died Sept. 1968.

HORNIBROOKE, ISABEL (ISABEL HORNIBROOK), author; b. in Ireland, of English parents; d. Nicholls Cole-Bowen and Emma Emilia (Bates) H.; ed. under pvt. tutelage; unmarried. First story accepted for an English mag. at 14; came to America in 1892, and subsequently established home in Worcester. Club: Woman's (Worcester), Author: Camp and Trail, 1897; from Keel to Kite, 1908; A Scout of To-day, 1913; Girls of the Morning-Glory Camp-Fire, 1916; Drake of Troop One, 1916; Camp-Fire Girls and Mount Greylock, 1917; Timmy Whoof, 1917; Scout Drake in Wartime, 1918; Camp-Fire Girls in War and Peace, 1919; Coxswain Drake of the Seascouts, 1920; Pemrose Lorry, Camp Fire Girl, 1921; Pemrose Lorry, Sky Sailor, 1924; Ann of Seacrest High, 1927; Romee Ann, Sophomore, 1925; Pemrose Lorry, Torchbearer, 1926; Romee Ann, Junior, 1926; Drake and the Adventurer's Cup. Hon. mem. with diploma and insignia, Academie d'Histoire Internationale (Paris). Home: 23 Hollywood St., Worcester MA‡

HORRELL, GEORGE ROBERT, pharm. exec.; b. Humbird, Wis., Feb. 23, 1905; s. George H. and Carrie (Colburn) H.; B.A., U. Wis., 1927, postgrad., 1933-35; m. Adele Richard, July 16, 1931; children—George, Nancy, Kathleen, Robert, and David; m. 2d, Martha Huebner, July 14, 1967. Parasitologist various fur farms, 1927-30; farmer, nr. Ann Arbor, Mich., 1930-38; then engaged in pharm. sales and research; now v.p. med. affairs Smith, Miller & Patch, Inc., New Brunswick, N.J. Cons. parasitologist, 1930-38, with U. Mich., 1933-35 Mem. Phi Sigma, Phi Chi. Home: Plainfield NJ Died Feb. 6, 1970.

HORSFALL, FRANK LAPPIN, JR., physician; b. Seattle, Dec. 14, 1906; s. Frank L. and Jessie Laura (Ludden) H.; B.A., U. Wash., 1927; M.D., C.M., McGill U., 1932; Ph.D., Uppsala Univ., 1961; LL.D., U. Alberta, 1963; D.Sc., McGill University, 1963; m. to Norma E. Campagnari, July 1, 1937; children—Frank III, Susan, Mary. House officer pathology Peter Bent Brigham Hosp., Boston, 1932-33; resident physician Royal Victoria Hosp., Montreal, 1933-34; resident surgeon Montreal General Hosp., 1934; asst. The Rockefeller Inst., 1934-37, member, 1941-57, mem., prof., 1957-60, v.p. clin. studies, 1955-60, asst. resident physician Hosp. The Rockefeller Inst., 1934-36, resident physician, 1936-37, physician, 1941-55, physician-in-chief, 1955-60; staff mem. Internat. Health Div., The Rockefeller Found., 1937-41; pres., dir., trustee Sloan-Kettering Institute Cancer Research, 1960-71; director research Memorial Sloan-Kettering Cancer Center, 1965-71, Memorial Hospital Cancer and Allied Diseases, 1965-71; professor of medicine Cornell U. Med. Coll., 1960-71, dir., prof. microbiology Sloan-Kettering Div. Grad. Sch. Med. Scis., 1960-71; cons. to Surgeon Gen. U.S. Army, mem. commn. immunization Army Epidemiol. Bd., 1947-55; cons. USPHS, 1948-53; mem. nat. research council com. adv. U.S. Army Chem. Corps, Washington, 1957-59; chmn. research and engring. adv. panel Def. Dept., 1960-61, vice chmn., 1959-60, mem.-at-large Def. Sci. Bd., 1957-62; vice chmn. Biol. and Chem. Def. Planning Bd., 1959-61; mem. U.S. Panel, U.S.-Japan com. Sci. Coop., 1962-63, Human Cancer Virus Task Force, NIH, 1962-64, Pres.' Commn. Heart Disease, Cancer, Stroke, 1964-65. Chmn. vis. com. Med. Dept. Brookhaven Nat. Lab., Upton, L.I., N.Y., 1955-57; mem. sci. adv. comm. Inst. Microbiology Rutgers U., 1955-62; mem. expert adv. panel virus diseases WHO, Geneva, Switzerland, 1956-71; director of Public Health Research Institute City of New York, Incorporated, 1956-71, chairman research council, 1956-57; special cons. N.Y.C., Dept. Health, 1956-71; member nat. adv. com. Okla. Med. Research Found., Oklahoma City, 1957-71; mem. bd. sci. dirs. Roscoe B. Jackson Meml. Lab., Bar Harbor, Me., 1958-61; mem. exec. com. Health Research Council City N.Y., 1958-68, vice chairman, 1962-66; member panel of advisers New York State Committee for Medical Edn., 1962-63; sci. adv. com. Inst. Cancer Research, 1962-71; sci. adv. council N.Y. State Legislature, 1963-71; mem. Commn. Health Services City New York, 1959-71; member committee respiratory diseases, National Tb Association, 1959-60; chairman program committee 5th Internat. Poliomyelitis Conf., Denmark, 1960; gen. chmn. 2d Internat. Conf. Congenital Malformations. N.Y. 1963; mem. com. virus research and epidemiology Nat. Found., 1956-58, com. on research basic scis., vaccine adv. com., 1959-71; adv. com. electronic computers biology and medicine Nat. Acad. Scis.-NRC, 1959-60; com. sci. and pub. policy Nat. Acad. Scis., 1963-66. Trustee Internat. Med. Congress, Ltd., 1959-71, v.p., 1962-71; trustee Internat. Poliomyelitis Congress Ltd., 1959-71, So. Research Inst., 1960-71, Memorial Sloan-Kettering Cancer Center, N.Y., 1960-71, bd. govs. Weltzmann Inst. Sci., Rehovoth, Israel, 1964-71; trustee Med. Library Center N.Y., 1959-71. Served to comdr. M.C., USNR, 1942-46. Recipient Banting research fellow, McGill U. Med. Sch., 1930-32; Holmes gold medal, 1932; Eli Lilly award bacteriology and immunology, 1937; Casgrain and Charbonneau award in medicine McGill U., 1942; John F. Lewis prize Am. Philos. Soc., 1959; Alumnus Summa Laude Dignatus award Alumni Assn. U. Wash., 1962; gold medal award Peter Bent Brigham Hosp., 1963. Fellow Montreal Medico-Chirurgical Soc.; mem. Am. Assn. Immunologists (councillor 1962-66, v.p. 1966-67, pres. 1967-68), A.M.A., Am. Philos. Soc., Am. Pub. Health Assn. (mem. Lasker awards committee 1958-60), Assn. of Am. Cancer Insts. (president 1968-71), Royal Society Medicine (affiliate), National Institutes Health (member virus and rickettsial study section 1948-53), International Board Editors Excerpta Medica (U.S. sect. rep.), American Soc. Clin. Investigation (past v.p.), N.Y. Acad. Medicom. 1957-58, editorial bd. Bull. 1969-71), Nat. Acad. Scis., Assn. Am. Phys., A.A.A.S., Harvey Soc., Practitioners' Soc. (president 1969-71), Am. Assn. Cancer Research, American Assn. Pathologists and Bacteriologists, Am. Soc. Microbiology, Soc. Exptl. Biology and Medicine, Am. Acad. Arts and Scis., Royal Coll. Physicians and Surgeons Can. Mem. bd. editors Jour. Immunology, 1950-62; asso. editor Virology, 1954-60, co-editor, Journal of Experimental Medicine, 1958-60, adv. editor, 1963-71; mem. editorial bd. World Wide Abstracts Gen. Medicine, 1958-71, Am. Jour. Pub. Health, 1958-60; mem. New York City NY Died Feb. 1971.

HORSFALL, I. OWEN, dean extension univ. prof.; b. Oceanside, N.Y., May 20, 1885; s. Charles George and Mary Brower (Pettit) H.; A.B., U. of Utah, 1905-08; A.M., U. of Chicago, 1927-28; Ph.D., Cornell U., 1928-32; travel, Europe, Asia Minor and Egypt, 1908-11; m. Nora C. Pendleton, July 31, 1913; children—Chester Owen, Warren Pendleton, Bruce Pendleton (dec.), Beth Pendleton (dec.), Hope Pendleton. Instr. math., head dept. and dir. Jr. Coll., Latter Day Saints Coll, Salt Lake City, Utah, 1911-27; instr., Cornell, 1928-33; pres., Snow Coll., Ephraim, Utah, 1933-36; dir., dean extension division, University of Utah, 1936-51, professor of mathematics, 1940-51, emeritus from 1951; curator U. Art Mus. from 1951. State chmn., 10 mm. films, war loan drives; vice chmn., U. of Utah War Council; vice chmn. training com., chmn. finance Com., Salt Lake Council Boy Scouts of America; vice president Local Christians and Jews, Incorporated. Curator Utah Museum Fine Arts. Chmn. Utah Council UNESCO. Mem. Utah Academy Science, Arts and Letters (general secretary), National University Extension Association (exec. com., 1938-41), Am. Assn. Univ. Profs., Sigma Xi, Am. Math. Soc., Math. Assn. of America, Utah Ednl. Assn., Phi Delta Kappa. Clubs: Rotary, Bonneville Knife and Fork (Salt Lake City). Author: Transformations Associated with Lines of Cubic Quadratic or Linear Complex, 1933. Home: Salt Lake City UT Died Nov. 20, 1972; buried Wasatch Lawn Cemetery, Salt Lake City UT

HORST, MILES, govt. ofcl., mem. Rep. Nat. Com.; b. Schaefferstown, Pa., May 25, 1891; s. Uriah Brubaker and Emma (Oberholtzer) H.; grad. Millersville State Tchrs. Coll., Pa. State U.; grad. study Columbia; D. Letters, Lebanon Valley Coll., 1947; m. Kathryn Helen Reitz, Nov. 16, 1932; children—Edwin Lewis, Nancy Elizabeth. Asso. editor Pennsylvania Farmer; sec. Pa. Council Farm Orgns.; mem. Pa. Ho. of Reps., 1933-37; sec. agr., Pa.; mem. Pa. Council Edn., Pa. Planning Bd.; dir. Lebanon Nat. Bank; asst. to sec. of agr. U.S. Dept. Agr.; chmn. primary election Gov. Scranton campaign; asst. to Gov. Scranton. Mem. Rep. Nat. Com.; chmn. Pa. Rep. Party, 1954-56; alternate del. Rep. Nat. Conv., 1948, del., 1956. Bd. dirs. Lebanon Community Chest, Good Samaritan Hosp.; trustee Pa. State U., Lebanon Valley Coll. Mem. Pa. C. of C. (dir.), Future Farmers Am., Pa. Grange (sec., editor news 1939-43), Pa. State U. Alumni Assn. (pres. 1940), Alpha Zeta, Phi Kappa Phi. Home: Lebanon PA Died Apr. 5, 1968; buried Schafferstown PA

HORTENSTINE, RALEIGH, civil engineer, consultant; born at Abingdon, Va., July 12, 1887; s. Joel Wilson and Mary Virginia (Campbell) H.; B.S. in C.E., Va. Poly. Inst., 1906; grad. student Cornell U., 1906-07; m. Helen Buchanan Grant, June 26, 1912; 1 son, Raleigh. Engr. and supt. Penn Bridge Co., Beaver Falls, Pa., 1907-12; contracting engr. Va. Bridge & Iron Co., Dallas, Tex., 1912-18, plant mgr. Memphis, Tenn., 1918-23; v.p., gen. mgr. Wyatt Industries, Inc. (formerly Wyatt Metal & Boiler Works), Dallas, 1923-38, pres. 1938-55, chmn. bd., 1955-61, sr. chmn. bd., 1961-68; consultant Wyatt division U.S. Industries, Inc., 1968-69; dir. Lone Star Steel Co., Dallas; dir. Republic Nat. Bank of Dallas. Mem., past chmn. bd. trustees Tex. A and M Research Found. Mem. N.A.M. (past dir.), Am. Soc. C.E., Tau Beta Pi. Presbyn. Clubs: Country, Petroleum. Home: Dallas TX Died Nov. 15, 1969; buried Hillcrest Mausoleum, Dallas TX

HORTON, BENJAMIN JASON, lawyer; b. Lawrence, Kan., Sept. 8, 1873; s. Benjamin Jason and Sarah Virginia (Yeatman) H.; student U. of Kan., 1892-95, law sch. same, 1895-96; LL.B., Washington U., 1897; m. Isabel Locke, Aug. 17, 1905; children—Martha Virginia (Mrs. Donald A. Draughon), Anita Locke (Mrs. Francis Wadhams), Dorothy May (Mrs. Horton Meyer). In practice of law, St. Louis, Mo., 1897; moved to P.R., September 1899; U.S. Commr., Ponce, P.R., 1901; chmn. Board of Elections, Dist. of Ponce, 1902; spl. dist. atty., Mayaguez, P.R. (investigation of municipal affairs), 1903; dist. atty., Mayaguez Dist., 1905-06; atty. gen. of P.R., 1933-35, acting gov. 6 times, 1933-35; apptd. spl. legal advisor P.R. Reconstruction Adminstrn., 1935. Referee in Bankruptcy Mataguez, 1920-26; del. to Democratic Nat. Convs. 8 times since 1912. Nat. Committeeman, Puerto Rico, Mar. 1932-Mar. 1940. Address: 3424 W. Central, Wichita KS‡

HORTON, DOUGLAS, clergyman; b. Brooklyn, N.Y., July 27, 1891; s. Byron and Elizabeth Swaim (Douglas) H.; A.B., Princeton, 1912; grad. study New Coll., Edinburgh, Scotland, Mansfield Coll., Oxford, U. of Tuebingen, Germany, 1912-13; B.D., Hartford (Conn.) Theol. Sem., 1915; D.D., Lawrence Coll., Chicago

Theol. Sem., 1931, Princeton Univ., 1941, Dartmouth College, 1957, Colgate University, 1958; Litt.D., Marietta Coll., 1942; LL.D., Beloit Coll., 1953; M.A., Harvard, 1955, S.T.D., 1959; L.H.D., Rollins Coll., 1959, Ursinus College, 1960; LL.D., Merrimack Coll., 1966; L.H.D., St. Michael's Coll., 1965, S.E. Mass Tech. Inst., 1966; married Carol Scudder Williams, May 9, 1916 (died 1944); children—Margaret Huntington (Mrs. Robert McQueen Grant), Alan Williams, Alice May (Mrs. Norris Lowell Tibbetts, Jr.), Elizabeth Douglas (Mrs. Charles Breunig); m. 2d, Mildred Helen McAfee, August 10, 1945. Ordained to the ministry Congregational Ch., 1915; asst. minister 1st Ch. of Christ, Middletown, Conn., 1915-16, minister, 1916-25; minister Leyden Congl. Ch., Brookline, Mass., 1925-31; minister United Church of Hyde Park, Chicago, 1931-38; minister of the General Council of Congregational Christian Churches, 1938-55; professor practical theology, Newton Theological Instn., 1930-31; lecturer in practical theology, Chicago Theol. Sem., 1933-38; lecturer in Congregational polity. Union Theological Seminary 1943-55; dean Harvard Divinity School, Cambridge, 1955-59; lectr. United Ch. polity, Chgo. Theol. Sem., 1961. Served as chaplain, U.S. Navy, 1918-19. Chairman of commn. faith and order World Council Chs., 1957-63; moderator Internat. Congl. Council, 1949-53; del. observer Internat. Congl. Council Vatican Council II. Dir. Am. U. at Cairo; mem. bd. trustees Princeton U. Mem. Phi Beta Kappa. Author: Out Into Life, 1925; A Legend of the Grail, 1926; Taking a City, 1934; The Art of Living Today, 1935; Congregationalism, a Study in Ch. Policy, 1952; The Meaning of Worship, published in 1959; The United Ch. Christ, 1962; Vatican Diary, 1963, 64, 65, 66; Toward an Undivided Church, 1967. Co-author: Christian Vocation, 1945; Reform and Renewal, 1966. Editor: The Basis Formula for Church Union, published 1937. Translator: (from the German) Barth's The Word of God and The World of Man, 1928; (from the Latin) Norton's Answer, 1958; co-translator (from Latin, Dutch), translator (from German): William Ames, 1965. Home: Randolph NH Died Aug. 21, 1968; buried Randolph NH

HORTON, EDWARD EVERETT, actor; b. Brooklyn, N.Y., Mar. 18, 1886; s. Edward Everett and Isabelle (Diack) H.; ed. Oberlin Coll. and Columbia Univ.; unmarried. First appearance on professional stage with Louis Mann with a walk-on part in The Man Who Stood Still," Circle Theatre, N.Y. City, Oct. 15, 1908; commenced film career, 1918; appeared in The Terror" (2d talking picture made). Played in (stage plays): The Cheater, Elevating a Husband, The Govenor's Lady, The Wild Westcotts; Never Say Die, The Nervous Wreck, Clarence, The Professor's Love Story, Smilin' Through, Beggar on Horseback, The Rear Car, The First Year, The Swan, The Queen's Husband, A Single Man, Arms and the Man, The Command Performance, The Dover Road, Among the Married, Private Lives, The Shaughraun, The Unexpected Husband, Springtime for Henry, Her Cardboard Lover, The Gossipy Sex, On Approval, Spread Eagle; motion pictures: Ruggles of Red Gap, Too Much Business, The Front Page Story, To the Ladies, Beggar on Horseback, Marry Me, Miss Information, Sunny Boy, The Hottentot, the Terror, Six Cylinder Love, The Sap, Wide Open, Good Medicine, The Right Bed, Trusting Wives, The Big Four, The Toast of the Legion, Holiday, Reaching for the Moon, Once a Gentleman, The Front Page, The Age for Love, A Bedtime Story, It's a Boy, The Way to Love, Design for Living, Alice in Wonderland, The Poor Rich, Easy to Love, Success at Any Price, Sing and Like It, Uncertain Lady, Smarty, Kiss and Make Up, Ladies Should Listen, The Merry Widow, The Gay Divorcee, Biography of a Bachelor Girl, All the King's Horses, The Devil is a Woman, Ten Dollar Raise, In Caliente, Going Highbrow, Top Hat, The Little Big Shot, His Night Out, Her Master's Voice, The Private Secretary, Your Uncle Dudley, The Man in the Mirror, Singing Kid, Lost Horizon; College Swing, Hitting a New High, The Great Garrick, Perfect Specimen, Little Tough Guys in Society, Paris Honeymoon, The Gang's All Here. That's Right, You're Wrong, You're the One, Ziegfeld Girl. Sunny, Bachelor Daddies, Here Comes Mr. Jordan, Week End for Three, Black Widow, I Married an Angel, The Magnificent Dope, Springtime in the Rockies, Arsenic and Old Lace, San Diego, I Love You, Brazil, Weekend for Three, Town Went Wild, Summer Storm, Lady on a Train, Faithful in My Fashion, Ghost Goes Wild, Earl Carroll Sketch Book, Down to Earth. Mem. Screen Actors Guild, Am. Fed. of Radio Artists, Actors Equity Assn., Phi Kappa Psi. Clubs: Bohemian (San Francisco); Beverly Hills, Masquers (Los Angeles); Westport Beach (Venice, Calif.); Mermaid (Brooklyn Poly. Inst.); The Players (N.Y. City); Sterling (London, Eng.). Home: Encino CA Died Sept. 29, 1970; buried Forest Lawn.

HORTON, J(OSEPH) WARREN, acoustical engr.; b. Ipswich, Mass., Dec. 18, 1889; s. Benjamin R. and Susan Elizabeth (Tower) H.; B.S. in Electrochemistry, Mass. Inst. Tech., 1914, D.Sc. in Elec. Engring., 1935; m. Adelina C. Doucet, Sept. 4, 1916; 1 son, Peter. Asst. physics and electrochemistry Mass. Inst. Tech., 1914-16, research asso., 1933-37, asso. prof. biol. engring., 1937-45, asso. prof. elec. communication, dept. elec. engring., 1945-49; tech. staff Bell Telephone Labs., N.Y.C., 1916-28; chief engr. Gen. Radio Co., Cambridge, Mass., 1928-33; tech. expert Naval Expt. Sta., Nahant, Mass., also Naval Hdqrs., London, 1917-18; spl. adviser Nat. Def. Research Com., also OSRD, 1941-45; chief research cons. U.S. Navy Underwater Sound Lab., New London, Conn., 1949-59, technical director, from 1959; lecturer in electrical engineering University Conn., from 1950. Trustee, mem. corp. Cable Meml. Hosp., Ipswich, Mass., from 1940. Served as lt. comdr. USNR, inactive, 1936-51. Recipient best research of year award Am. Inst. E.E., 1927, distinguished civilian service award U.S. Navy, 1958. Fellow A.A.A.S., Acoustical Soc., Am. Inst. E.E. (bd. examiners from 1950), Inst. Radio Engrs. (adminstrv. com. profl. group ultrasonics engring. from 1958), Am. Phys. Soc.; mem. N.E. Soc. Anesthetists (hon.), Newcomen Soc., Audio Engring. Soc. (hon.), Sigma Xi, Eta Kappa Nu. Club: Thames (New London). Author: Fundamentals of Sonar, 1957. Contbr. tech. articles profl. jours. Drafted safe practice recommendations operating rooms for Nat. Fire Protection Assn. Holder 56 patents, including submarine detectors, frequency standardizing systems, picture transmission and TV systems, carrier current and radio secrecy systems. Home: New London CT Died May 10, 1967.

HORVITZ, AARON, industry-labor arbitrator; b. Pitts., Sept. 28, 1888; s. Baer and Minnie (Ehrlich) H.; A.B., Harvard, 1910, LL.B., 1913; m. Beatrice Steinert, May 31, 1946; 1 son by previous marriage, Wayne Louis. Investment counsel, 1920-34; spl. mediator or impartial arbitrator in industry-labor disputes, from 1934, panel chmn., spl. mediation officer, nat. and regional war labor bds.; mem. emergency bds. in railroad and aviation industry and labor disputes, 1946-52; mem. presidential commn. to formulate policy for handling labor relations AEC installations, 1949; mem. AEC labor relations panel, 1949-53. Mem. Nat. Acad. Arbitrators (pres. 1955), Am. Acad. Polit. and Social Sci., Indsl. Relations Research Assn., Freedom House, Acad. Polit. Sci. Jewish religion. Address: New York City NY Died Sept. 18, 1968.

HORWITZ, SOLIS, educator; b. Pitts., Nov. 2, 1910; s. Samuel Abe and Lillian Yetta (Goldman) H.; A.B., U. Pitts., 1930, M.A., 1932; LL.B., Harvard, 1936. Admitted to Pa. bar, 1937, D.C. bar, 1953; practice in Pitts., 1937-42; counsel internat. prosecution major criminals, Tokyo, Japan, 1945-48, acting chief counsel, 1948; spl. counsel armed services com. U.S. Ho. Reps., 1949; spl. counsel chmn. Nat. Securities Resources Bd., 1950-51; gen. counsel RFC, 1951-53; counsel com. govt. operations for Army-McCarthy hearings U.S. Senate, 1954; pvt. practice, Pitts. and Washington, 1954-57; counsel majority policy com., also preparedness investigating subcom., armed services com. U.S. Senate, 1957-60; pvt. practice, Washington, 1961; dir. office orgnl. and mgmt. planning studies, Office Sec. Def., Dept. Def., 1961-64, asst. sec. of def. (adminstrn.), 1964-69; prof. pub. policy Univ. of Pitts., 1968-72. Served with AUS, 1942-45. Mem. Am. Fed., Allegheny County bar assns., Harvard Law Sch. Assn., Phi Beta Kappa. Author: Tokyo War Crimes Trial, 1950. Home: Pittsburgh PA Died Apr. 25, 1972; buried Temple Sinai Cemetery, Pittsburgh PA

HOSTETLER, ERWIN CASE, adj. gen. Ohio; b. Alden, Ia., Apr. 1, 1904; s. Christopher R. and Elizabeth Lee (Jones) H.; student Roanoke Coll., Salem, Va., 1922-23; m. Una Ratcliff, Feb. 2, 1945; stepchildren-Helen Virginia (Mrs. Dale E. McMath), Russell McVay, With B.F. Goodrich Co., 1923-63, sr. specification editor aerospace and def. div., 1954-63; enlisted as pvt. Ohio N.G., 1923, advanced through ranks and grades to maj. gen., 1963; active duty World War II, also Korean War; regimental comdr. 145th Inf., Ohio N.G., 1959-63; adj. gen., also dir. civil def. Ohio, 1963-68, also dir. emergency planning. Mem. Adjs. Gen. Assn., Ohio N.G., Assn. (pres. 1962), Assn. U.S. Army (pres. Buckeye chpt. 1962), 37th Div. Assn. (life; pres. Akron chpt. 1948), Sojourners. Mason (32 deg., Shriner). Home: Columbus OH Died May 7, 1968; buried Rose Hill Cemetery, Akron OH

HOSTETLER, LOWELL COY, sch. adminstr.; b. Sugarcreek, O., Apr. 13, 1928; s. Archie Curtis and Thelma (Schott) H.; B.A., Kent State U., 1950; M.A., Fla. State U., 1958; postgrad. U. Colo., 1959, Ariz. State U., 1961-62; m. Clarice Irene Dettor, June 10, 1951; children—Ronald Curt, Alan Craig. Tchr., Boca Raton (Fla.) Elementary Sch., 1954-55. Delray Beach (Fla.) Jr. High Sch., 1955-57; tchr. Seacrest High Sch., Delray Beach, 1957-59, guidance dir., 1959-63, interim prin., 1963-68; prin. Lantana (Fla.) Jr. High Sch., 1964-68. Mem. Erskine Scholarship Bd., Lake Worth 1st Fed. Savs. & Loan Assn., 1959-64; pub. speaker endl. Boynton Beach. Boca Raton, Delray Beach, 1958-63; mem. Christian Edn. Com., 1961-64; mem. com. selection books Pub. Library Delray Beach, 1955-57, mem. com. children's books, 1956. Served with USAF, 1950-54. Mem. Fla. Assn. Deans and Counselors (past mem. state high sch. coll. relations com.), Nat., Fla. edn. assns., Fla. Assn. Supervision and curriculum Devel., Dept. Secondary School Principals Fla., C. of C. (dir. 1967-69), Fla. Ednl. Research Assn., Nat. Council on Measurement in Edn., Nat. Assn. Secondary Sch. Prins., Palm Beach County Prins. Assn., Phi Delta Kappa. Presbyn. (past deacon, past elder). Rotarian (charter mem.). Home: Boynton Beach FL Died Aug. 9, 1968.

HOSTY, THOMAS EDWARD, stock broker; b. Chicago, Jan. 2, 1891; s. Luke and Elizabeth (Sennett) H.; student pub. schs., Chicago; m. Della Nally, Feb. 17, 1917; children—Thomas Edward, Adele, Patricia, William, John. Messenger boy, Shearson Hammill & Co., brokers, Chicago, 1905; with Bart Frazier & Co., 1906-07; with Sincere & Co., stocks, bonds and grain, 1907-71, member firm, 1922-71, sr. partner, 1941-71. Mem. Midwest Stock Exchange (mem. exec. com.), Chgo. Bd. Trade (chmn., dir.), N.Y. Mercantile Exchange, Memphis Merchants Exchange, Mpls. Grain Exchange, N.Y. Stock Exchange, N.Y. Curb (asso.), N.Y Produce Exchange, Phila. Bourse, Winnipeg Grain Exchange, Chicago Mercantile Exchange (gov. Clearing house), Bd. Trade Clearing Assn. (pres. 1952-57). Knight of Columbus. Clubs: Chicago Athletic Association, Butterfield Country, Elmhurst Country, Long Beach River Forest IL Died Jan. 1, 1971.

HOTCHKISS, J. ELIZABETH, metaphysician, author; b. Elmira, N.Y.; d. Hon. Thomas W. and Jeanie Jewell H.; grad. Elmira Coll., 1887; (M.A., same, 1889, Ph.D., 1894); sp'l studies in metaphysics and psychology under Leander Edmund Whipple, Swami Vivekananda and Chas. Brodie Patterson. Literary editor metaphysical Mag., 1895-6. Practicing metaphysician and teacher of metaphysics and psychology. Author: Psycho-Therapeutics (booklet). Extensive writer on metaphysics and psychology in Metaphysical Mag., Mind, and other mags. and newspapers. Address: 699 Madison Av., New York‡

HOTCHKISS, WILLIS R., missionary; b. Doylestown, Wayne Co., O., Oct. 11, 1873; s. Henry Clay and Elizabeth (Eaton) H.; Oberlin (Ohio) Acad.; Friends' Bible Inst., Cleveland; m. Mathilde Caroline Koehler, of Toledo, O., Sept. 20, 1900. Began missionary work in Africa, 1895; partially reduced Kikamba lang. to writing; organized Friends' Africa Industrial Mission, 1900-2; reduced Bantu Kavirondo lang. to writing; traveling sec. Student Vol. Movement for Foreign Missions, among colls. of America, 1902-3; founded Lumbwa Industrial Mission, 1905. Mem. Soc. of Friends (Orthodox), Nat. Geog. Soc. Author: Sketches from the Dark Continent, 1901. Address: Kericho British East Africa*‡

HOTTENROTH, ADOLPH CHRISTIAN, lawyer; b. N.Y. City, May 9, 1869; s. Christian C. and Catherine (Sandrock) H.; B.S., Coll. City of New York, 1888; LL.B., New York U., 1890; m. Mamie A. Schmidt, of N.Y. City, Apr. 28, 1900; children—Adolph C., Viola Emily, Dorothea Marie, Andrew Chas. Admitted to N.Y. bar, 1890, and began practice in N.Y. City; mem. Gumbleton & Hottenroth, 1892-1900; mem. N.Y. Constl. Conv., 1894; prepared minority report at the convention, of Com. on Canals, and the Canal Amendment," later accepted by popular vote; largely instrumental in preserving Niagara Falls, as a state property, also in securing passage and enforcing the five-cent fare" law; mem. first Municipal Council of Greater New York, 1898-1902; pres. Taxpayers' Aliance, 1896-1900, and counsel to various civic orgns.; an organizer Peoples Guaranty & Indemnity Co., 1896; retired from practice, 1911, to devote time to scientific research. Mem. N.Y. State Bar Assn.; Tammany Soc., hon. mem. Bronx Bar Assn. Lutheran. Mason. Club: Nat. Democratic. Home: 435 Riverside Dr. Office: 42 Broadway, New York NY‡

HOTTES, CHARLES FREDERICK, botanist; b. Mascoutah, Ill., July 8, 1870; s. Frederick and Barbara (Dathan) H.; B.S., U. of Ill., 1894, M.S., 1895; M.A., Ph.D., U. of Bonn, 1901; m. Flora Guth, Aug. 25, 1895; 1 dau., Flora Emily. Asst. in botany, U. of Ill., 1895-98, instr., 1901-02, asst. prof., 1902-13, prof. plant physiology, 1913-38, cons. plant psychologist in agronomy, and head of dept. of botany, 1928-38, prof. emeritus since 1938. Unitarian. Fellow A.A.A.S., Bot. Soc. America; mem. Am. Genetic Assn., Ill. Acad. Science, Acacia, Alpha Zeta, Sigma Xi, Gamma Sigma Delta. Mason (K.T., 32 deg., Shriner), Red Cross of Constantine. Clubs: University, Kiwanis, Chaos. Home: 406 W. Iowa St., Urbana IL‡

HOTZ, H(ENRY) G(USTAVE), coll. dean emeritus; b. Scandinavia, Wis., Apr. 13, 1880; s. Herman and Emma (Hartman) H.; grad. Oshkosh State Normal Coll., 1906; Ph.B., U. Wis., 1913, A.M., 1915; Ph.D., Columbia, 1918; m. Stella Palmer, Dec. 22, 1924; children—Henry Palmer, Oscar Hartman. Supt. schs., Spooner, Wis., 1908-11, Hayward, Wis., 1911-12; prof. edn. Coll. of William and Mary, 1918-19; prof. secondary edn. U. Ark., 1919-23, 25-34, dean coll. edn., 1934-45, dir. summer sessions, 1934-45, dean emeritus, 1945-72, research specialist vocational tchr. edn., 1948-72, chmn. univ. com. postwar edn., 1943-45; state high sch. supervisor, Ark., 1923-25. Sec. commn. secondary schs. North Central Assn. Colls. and Secondary Schs., 1930-36. Mem. adv. com. Ark. Program to Improve Instrn. Mem. N.E.A. (life), Ark. Edn. Assn., Phi Beta Kappa (pres.), Phi Delta Kappa, Kappa Delta Pi.

Democrat. Presbyn. Author: First Year Algebra Scales, 1918; Hist. and Development of Institutional On-Farm Training in Arkansas, 1950; Eight Years of Veterans On-Farm Training in Arkansas, 1946-54; also articles, govt. reports. Home: Fayetteville AR Died Jan. 21, 1972.

HOUCK, IRVIN ELMER, insurance exec.; b. Chgo., Apr. 5, 1901; s. Mallery Harrison and Emma (Knudson) H.; A.B., Oberlin Coll., 1924; m. Margaret L. Ratledge, July 30, 1930 children—Richard, Margaret (Mrs. Eric R.C. Smith), Mary (Mrs. Jon Donald Olson). With Marsh & McLennan, Inc., Chgo., 1924-68, mgr. casualty dept., 1937-47, v.p., 1947-59, sr. v.p., 1959-68, director, 1956-68; dir. Oak Park Trust & Savs. Bank, Oak Park, Ill. Mem. Chgo. Crime Commn. Trustee, Oberlin Coll., bd. dirs. Community Chest of Oak Park and River Forest; budget com. Community Fund of Chgo. Mem. Chgo. Planetarium Soc., Chgo. Hist. Soc., Chgo. Natural History Mus., Chgo. City Missionary Soc., Chgo. Assn. Commerce and Industry. Conglist. Clubs: Oak Park (Ill.) Country (past pres.); University, Executives (Chgo.). Home: Oak Park IL Died Apr. 28, 1970.

HOUGH, GEORGE ANTHONY, editor; b. New Bedford, Mass., Nov. 27, 1868; s. George Thomas and Lydia Winslow (Anthony) H.; ed. high sch. under pvt. tutor; m. Abby Louise Beetle, Oct. 10, 1893; children—George Anthony, Henry Beetle. Reporter Morning Mercury, New Bedford, 1885-87; telegraph editor, 1888, city editor, clk. and dir., 1889-1909, mng. editor and v.p. Evening Standard, 1909-31; pres. Falmouth Pub. Co.; v.p. Vineyard Gazette. Home: North Tisbury, Mass. Office: Vineyard Gazette, Edgartown MA‡

HOUGHTON, ALBERT BALCH, lawyer; b. Oshkosh, Wis., Aug. 27, 1882; s. Frank Wilbur and Mary Julia (Balch) H.; Ph.B., U. of Chicago, 1907, J.D., 1909; m. Janet Fox, May 18, 1916; 1 son, Albert F.; m. 2d, Margaret R. Fox, Aug. 8, 1959. Admitted to Wis. bar, 1909 and began corp. and probate practice, Milw.; atty. City of Wauwatosa (Wis.), 1912-34; prof. law Marquette U., 1912-26. Served as spl. asst. to U.S. atty. gen., World War II. Fellow Am. Bar Assn. (ethics com. 1936-47, bd. govs. 1947-49, chmn. traffic ct. committee 1954-65); member of Wisconsin, Milwaukee bar assns., Beta Theta Pi, Phi Delta Phi. Republican. Dir. Legal Aid Soc. Methodist (pres. bd. trustees Meth. Ch. Wis. Conf., 1930-66). Mason. Clubs: University, Athletic. Home: Milwaukee WI Died May 1969.

HOUGHTON, DOROTHY DEEMER (MRS. HIRAM COLE HOUGHTON), former govt. ofcl.; b. Red Oak, Ia., Mar. 11, 1890; d. Horace Emerson and Jeannette (Gibson) Deemer; A.B., Wellesley Coll., 1912; LL.D., Coe Coll., 1942; L.H.D., Tarkio Coll., 1949; Litt.D., Am. U., 1952; D.Sc. in Govt. (hon.), U. Tampa, 1954; m. Hiram Cole Houghton, Dec. 18, 1912 (dec. 1957); children—Horace Deemer, Cole Hayward, Joan (Mrs. John J. Williams), Hiram Clark. Pres., Ia. Fedn. Women's Clubs, 1935-37, Gen. Fedn. Women's Clubs, 1950-52; dep. dir. refugee program and migration ICA, 1953-56; mem. adv. council OCDM, 1957-60. Adviser, alternate del. 5 internat. sessions Intergovtl. Com. European Migration; v.p. Electoral Coll., 1953-57, hon. life chmn.; mem.-at-large nat. commn. UNESCO: mem. bd. UN Internat. Children's Fund; mem. State Bd. Regents Ia., 1939-51. Nat. bd. mem. Women's Med. Coll. Pa.; trustee-at-large Nat. Soc. Crippled Children and Adults; chmn. 1963 project for Internat. Christian U., Tokyo, Japan; mem. adv. com. N.Y. World's Fair, 1964; trustee Washington Pilgrimage; bd. dirs. Library of Red Oak (Ia.), Seminars of Internat. Understanding. Co-chmn. Nat. Citizens for Eisenhower, 1956. Decorated officer Order Orange Nassau (Netherlands); Insignia and Diploma of Gold Cross of Royal Order Beneficence (Greece). Recipient Am. Heritage award Nat. Assn. Home Builders, 1952; Internat. Cup of Goodwill, All Nations Clubs, 1954; Nansen award for most distinguished service to refugees, Geneva, Switzerland, 1956. Mem. Nat. Assn. Parliamentarians (Ia. dir.), Ia. Safety Council (exec. com.), Congl-Christian Conf. Ia. (asst. moderator), Ia. Hist. Soc. (curator), Nat. Planning Assn. (nat. council), Assn. Bus. and Profl. Women, Am. Assn. U. Women, Pen Women Am., Ia. Library Assn. (pres. 1941-42), D.A.R., P.E.O., Delta Kappa Gamma, Zeta Phi Eta., Pi Beta Phi. Republican. Conglist. Home: Red Oak IA Died Mar. 15, 1972.

HOUGHTON, FREDERICK PERCIVAL, church official; s. William Lanyon and Annie Louise (Micklewright) H.; Lehigh U., 1911-12; grad. Gen. Theol. Sem., 1916; D.D., Pa. Mil. Coll., 1937; m. Catherine Edwards, Nov. 22, 1924; children—Frederick Percival, John Robert. Deacon and priest P.E. Ch., 1916; curate St. Luke's Ch., Scranton, Pa., 1916-17; rector Ch. of the Epiphany, Glenburn, Pa., 1919-27, St. John's Ch., Lancaster, 1927-31; gen. sec. Nat. Council P.E. Ch., 1931-37; exec. sec. Diocese of Pa. since 1937. Served as chaplain 103d Engrs., 28th Div., U.S. Army; participated in Chateau Thierry defensive, Champagne-Marne defensive, Aisne-Marne offensive, Fismes sector, Oise-Aisne offensive, Meuse-Argonne offensive, Thiacourt sector; not lt. col.-chaplain Reserve Corps, U.S. Army; senior chaplain Pa. Nat. Guard. Mem. Delta Upsilon. Republican. Kiwanian. Home: 16 Radcliffe Rd., Bala-Cynwyd, Pa. Office: 202 S. 19th St., Philadelphia PA*‡

HOUGHTON, LOUISE PHILLIPS, educator; b. Brooklyn, N.Y., June 11, 1870; d. John Francis and Mary Virtue (Cranford) Phillips; grad. Brooklyn Heights Sem., 1887; A.B., Smith Coll., 1891; studied Columbia, 1897, Havre, France, 1892-93; m. E. Russel Houghton (N.D.), of N.Y. City, Oct. 6, 1891 (died 1905); children—Seymour Phillips, Augustus Sherrill, Russell Le Roux. Contbr. articles and book revs. to New York Evangelist and other periodicals, 1892-1905; asso. prin. Comstock Sch. for Girls, N.Y. City, 1905-11; prin. Knox Sch. for Girls at Briarcliff and Tarrytown since 1911, moved to Cooperstown, N.Y., 1920. Mem. Smith Coll. Alumnae Assn. Episcopalian. Clubs: Women's Univ., Meridian, Smith Coll. Club (New York). Address: Knox School, Cooperstown NY‡

HOUSE, BYRON ORVIL, judge; b. St. Louis, Sept. 27, 1901; s. Harold Henry and Olive (Edwards) H.; LL.B., U. Ill., 1926; m. Mildred Irene Holston, June 9, 1925; children—James B., Marilyn I. (Mrs. George Mitchell), Dorothy Holston. Admitted to Ill. bar, 1926; mem. law firm House & House, Nashville, Illinois, 1926-56. States attorney, Washington County, 1945-46; circuit judge Third Ill. Judicial Circuit, 1956-57; justice Ill. Supreme Ct., 1957-69, chief justice, 1959-60. Mem. Nat. Commn. on Reform Fed. Criminal Laws, 1967-69. Govt. appeal agt. S.S.S., World War II. Mem. Washington County, Ill. State (chmn. sch. law sect. 1952-54), Am.bar assns., Pi Kappa Phi, Phi Alpha Delta. Republican. Presbyn. Elk, Odd Fellow. Home: Nashville IL Died Sept. 27, 1969; buried Greenwood Cemetery, Nashville IL

HOUSE, GARRY CAMPBELL, insurance; b. Hackensack, N.J., Mar. 25, 1871; s. Samuel Boardman and Harriet Myer (Campbell) H.; grad. pub. schs., Hackensack, 1886; m. Fanny M. Hapgood, June 14, 1898; children—Harriet Hapgood (Mrs. Lucius G. Eldridge, Jr.), Charlotte Waldron. Clk., Commercial Mut. Ins. Co., N.Y. City, 1886-91; chief marine clk., Providence Washington Ins. Co., Providence, R.I., 1891-1907, asst. sec. marine dept., 1907-14, marine sec. 1914-18, Marine v.p., 1918-22, v.p., 1922-29, pres. and dir., 1929-45; chmn. bd. dirs., Providence Washington and Anchor insurance cos., since 1945; treas. Beverly Farm Riding School. Home: 248 Hope St. Office: 20 Washington Pl., Providence 1*‡

HOUSE, JAMES ARTHUR, banker; b. Cleveland, O., Oct. 20, 1871; s. James Wells and Melissa (Neal) H.; ed. pub. schs.; m. Maud Mills, of Cleveland, June 14, 1899 (died Aug. 21, 1920); children—Helen E., James A., Leonard D., Eleanor D.; m. 2d, Genevieve B. Dodge, Feb. 17, 1923. Began as clk in office of Nickel Plate" R.R., 1887, later with Pickands, Mather & Co., Cleveland; with Guardian Trust Co. since 1894, pres. since 1917; dir. N.Y.C. & St. L. R.R. Co., Wheeling & L.E. Ry. Co., Cleveland Builders' Supply Company, Guardian Trust Co., Kilby Mfg. Co., Morris Plan Bank of Cleveland, The Mills Co., Goodyear Tire & Rubber Co., Standard Textile Products Co. Member Cleveland Gatling Gun Battery, 1892, O.N.G., 1894-96. Trustee Univ. Sch. (Cleveland), Ohio Wesleyan U., St. Luke's Hosp., Lakeside Hosp. (treas.). Mem. Am. Bankers' Assn. (ex-pres. trust co. div.). Mem. Ohio Soc. of New York. Methodist. Mason. Clubs: Union, Bankers, Mid-Day, Mayfield Country, Country, Kirtland Country, Hermit, Pepper Pike Country Club. Home: 2574 Fairmount Boul. Office: 623 Euclid Av., Cleveland OH‡

HOUSER, GERALD FRED TILLMAN, hosp. cons.; b. Humberstone, Ont., Canada, Feb. 5, 1902; s. John and Esther Elizabeth (Haney) H.; M.D., University of Toronto, 1926; married Helen Louise Gillis, October 15, 1927 (deceased July 1964); 1 son, Donald Franklin; m. 2d, Ruth V. Dempsey, November 1965. Began practice of medicine, 1926; asst. physician Danvers State Hosp., Harborne, Mass., 1926-27; asst. physician Boston State Hosp., 1927-28, sr. physician, 1928-34, asst. supt., 1934-37; instr. in psychiatry, Tufts Coll. Med. Sch., 1929-37; instr. in clin. psychiatry, Boston Univ. Med. Sch., 1930-37; asst. dir. Mass. Gen. Hosp. Boston, 1937-41, 1941-46; dir. Faulkner Hosp., Boston, 1946-55, hospital consultant, New Rochelle, N.Y., 1955-71; instr. in preventive med., Harvard Med. Sch., 1940-41; supt. Am. Red Cross-Harvard Hosp., Eng., 1941. Director Faulkner Hospital. director Washingtonian Hosp., Boston. Diplomate Am. Bd. Psychiatry and Neurol. Mem. Am. Hosp. Assn., Am. Coll. Hosp. Adminstrs., Soc. Med. Adminstrs. Methodist. Contbr. hosp. adminstrn. to profl. jours. Home: New Rochelle NY Died Aug. 23, 1971; buried Mount Pleasant, Toronto Ontario Canada

HOUSSAY, BERNARDO ALBERTO, scientific investigator; b. Buenos Aires, Argentina, Apr. 10, 1887; s. Alberto and Clara (Lafont) H.; Pharmacist, 1904; M.D., Buenos Aires, 1911; Dr. Honoris causa in medicine, universities Paris, 1935, Montreal, 1946, Lyon, 1946, Geneva, 1946, Asuncion, 1943, Catholic (Chile), 1942, Montevideo, 1948, Brussels, Catholique of Louvain, 1949, Strasbourg, 1949, also Duseldorf, Montpellier, Alger, Brazil, Venezuela, also Salamanco, hon. degrees in science, Harvard, 1936, Sao Paulo, 1936, Oxford, 1947, Mexico, Toronto, Columbia, New York, Cambridge (England) University, 1961; L.H.D. (hon.), Georgetown U., Washington; LL.D., (hon.), Glasgow; Dr. honoris causa med. scis. U. Orienta; Dr. honoris causa chemistry U. Nacional del Sud; married Maria Angelica Cata, Dec. 22, 1920; children—Alberto Bernardo, Hector Emilio Jose, Raul Horacio. Prof. physiology Vet. Faculty, Buenos Aires, 1910-19, Faculty Medical Scis., 1919-43, 45-46, 55-57; hon. prof. faculties of med. univs. of Montevideo, Santiago, Bogota, Lima, Brazil, Bahia, Porto Alegre, Recife, La Habana Concepcion (Chile), Venezuela, Minas Gerais, San Carlos, de Guatemala, Veterinary Sch., Buenos Aires and Lima; faculty sci., Lima; Hitchcock prof. U. Cal., 1948; dir. Inst. Bilogy and Exptl. Medicine, was research prof. Physiology Faculty Med. Scis., Buenos Aires. Decorated Order Merit of Chile, grand officer Order Merit (Italy), Belgian Crown Order, grand cross Order Merit of Germany, Isabel la Catolica, comdr. Legion of Honor, Officer Order of Leopold; Order de San Gregorio Magno (Vatican); Gran Cruz al merito con placa de la Orden Militar Soberanade Malta; gran oficial Order Holandesa de Orange y Nassau; Segunda clase Orden Sol Naciente del Japan; also numerous other decorations and awards; recipient Nat. Award Scis., Buenos Aires, 1923; Charles Mickle Fellowship, Toronto, 1945; Banting medal Am. Diabetes Association, 1946; research award Am. Pharm. Mfrs. Assn., 1947; Baly medal Royal Coll. Physicians, London, 1947; Nobel Prize for Physiology and Medicine, 1947; James Cook medal, Sidney, 1948; Dale medal Soc. for Endocrinology, London; Weizmann prize in scis. and humanities. Foreign associates mem. Nat. Acad. Scis. U.S.A., Royal Soc. London, Am. Philos. Soc., Swedish Acad. Scis., Acad. Medicine Paris, Acad. Sciences, Paris, Deutsche Akdemie fur Naturforschung, Royal Acad. Medicine Belgium, Academia Nazionale dei Lincei (Italy), Academia Inst. Egypt, Ciencias Exactas, Fiscias y Naturales, Lima; hon. mem. academies of medicine of Rio de Janeiro, Madrid, Mexico, N.Y., Lombardia, Bogota, Washington; hon. mem. Am. Physiol. Soc., Physiol. Soc. (Gt. Britain), Italian Soc. Physiology, Royal Soc. Edinburgh, Harvey Soc. N.Y., Mus. de la Plata Argentina, Academy Scis. Cordoba, honorary mem. numerous sci. socs.; pres. Argentine Soc. Biology; past pres. Argentine Assn. Advancement Sci., Nat. Acad. Medicine Buenos Aires, Internat. Union Philosophy of Scis., Physiology and Pharmacology Soc. Israel, Weizmann Inst. Scis., Assn. Am. Physiocians. Author numerous sci. papers. Home: Buenos Aires Argentina Died Sept. 21, 1971.

HOUSTON, OSCAR R., lawyer; b. Logan, O., Mar. 18, 1883; s. Adelbert D. and Jessie F. (Nicklaus) H.; A.B., Columbia, 1904, LL.B., 1906; m. Nelly S. Macdonald, Mar. 7, 1912; children—Charles S. Barbara (Mrs. Grose), Janet (Mrs. Beal). Admitted to bar; with firm Shearman & Sterling, 1906-10, Harrington, Bigham & Englar, 1910-14; partner Bigham, Englar, Jones & Houston (and predecessor), N.Y.C., 1915-63, counsel, 1964-69. Mem. titulaire Com. Maritime Internat. Dep. dir. civilian protection Great Neck, N.Y., 1941-45. Mem. Maritime Law Assn. U.S. (pres. 1950-52), Internat. Law Assn. (former council; pres. Am. br. 1931). Home: New York City NY Died Dec. 19, 1969; buried All Saints Church, Great Neck NY

HOUSTON, VICTOR STEUART KALEOALOHA, naval officer; b. San Francisco, Calif., July 22, 1876; s. Edwin Samuel and Caroline Poor Kahikiola (Brickwood) H.; prep. edn. Real Schule, Dresden, Coll. Cantonal, Lausanne, Force Sch., Washington, D.C.; grad. U.S. Naval Acad., 1897; m. Pinao G. Brickwood, July 19, 1910 (died Sept. 27, 1936). Commd. U.S. Navy, July 1, 1919; advanced through grades to comdr., June 30, 1926 (retired); recalled to active duty in U.S. Navy, Dec. 7, 1941. Served as naval cadet, Spanish-Am. War; lt. comdr. later comdr., World War. Del. to Congress from H.Ty., 3 terms, 1927-33. Republican. Mason. Clubs: University, New York Yacht. Home: 448 Lewers St., Honolulu HI‡

HOVANNES, JOHN, sculptor, instr.; b. Smyrna, Turkey, Dec. 31, 1900; s. Artin and Ibraxi (Mgerdichian) Hovannesian; student Rhode Island Sch. of Design, 1922-24; scholarhip award Copley Soc. of Boston, 1925; Beaux Arts Inst. of Design, New York City, 1926; m. Josephine Daminano, 1928; 1 dau., Joan. Came to U.S., 1920, naturalized, 1936. Teacher private classes, 1927-73; instr. Cooper Union for Advancement of Science and Art, N.Y. City, 1944-73, Bennett Jr. Coll., Millbrook, N.Y., 1943-45, Montclair Art Museum, Montclair, N.J., 1943-44, Am. Red Cross Gen. Halloran Hosp., Staten Island, N.Y., 1943-44, instr. Art Students League of N.Y. City, 1945-73, Great Neck Art Assn., Long Island, 1946-73. Exhibitions: Metropolitan Museum, Brooklyn Museum, Whitney Museum of Am. Art, Riverside Museum, Nat. Acad. of Design, The Art Inst. of Chicago, The Pa. Acad. of Fine Arts, Principal works: Mother and Child in George Gershwin collection: Laundry Workers, Newark Mus., Newark, New Jersey. Received Guggenheim

Scholarship, 1940-41, Eugene Meyer award, 1941, Wings for victory Competition Award. Mem. Sculptor's Guild, Audubon Artists Assn., Armenian Students Assn. Contbr. photographs of works to art mags. Home: New York City NY Died Apr. 1973.

HOVEY, CHANDLER, banker; b. Brookline, Mass., Jan. 8, 1880; s. William Alfred and Frances (Goodridge) H.; student Mass. Inst. Tech., 1899; m. Dorothy Allen, Nov. 1, 1906; children—Charles Fox, Elizabeth (Mrs. Sherman Morss), Chandler, Jr. Clk., Kidder, Peabody & Co., Boston, 1900-10, partner, 1931-71; established own investment and brokerage bus. as Chandler Hovey & Co., 1910. Trustee Investment Trust of Boston, 1950-71, Northeastern U. Corp. in charge E Bond drive in Washington, 1945; chmn. Mass. Aeronautical Commn., 1938-43. Trustee Hahnmann Hospital. Member Travelers Aid Society of Boston Incorporated (director). Clubs: New York Yacht, Eastern Yacht (commodore 1937-38), Down Town, City Corporation, Somerset (Boston); Mng. owner America's Cup Defender class yacht Yankee, 1930, 1934; owned and raced Cup Defender class yacht Weetamoe, 1936, raced Cup Defender Rainbow, 1937, Easterner, 1958, 60, 64. Responsible for the buoy shapes now standardized for this country's coastal and internal waterways to make identification by silhouette possible. Home: Chestnut Hill MA Died July 27, 1971; buried Mt. Auburn Cemetery, Cambridge MA

HOVEY, CHESTER RALPH, judge; b. Holyoke, Mass., Jan. 21, 1872; s. George A. and Jennie (Dyer) H.; grad. high sch., Durand, Wis., 1888; studied law in office of Gilliam & Kauffman, Ellensburg, Wash.; m. Grace Painter, July 10, 1895; children—Joseph C. (dec.), Ann Faulkner. Admitted to Wash. bar, 1893; was pros. atty. and city atty., Ellensburg; moved to Olympia, Wash., 1921; justice Supreme Court of Wash., Sept. 7, 1921, by apptmt. of gov., to succeed Justice Wallace Mont, deceased; now in pvt. law practice. Mem. Wash. State Bar Assn. (ex-pres.), Seattle Bar Assn. (ex-pres). Republican. Home: 1404 38th Av. Office: 1001 Lowman Bldg., Seattle WA*‡

HOVEY, HENRIETTE (MRS. RICHARD HOVEY, FORMERLY MRS. RUSSELL), author; d. Edgar and Catharine (Tyler) Knapp; pupil and some time asst. of Gustave Delsarte, Paris; promoter of Delsartean edn. in U.S.; teacher of acting and Delsartean theory of art; m. Richard Hovey, 1893 (died 1900). Author: Yawning, a book of short essays on edn. and art. Editor of The Holy Grail" and other unfinished plays by Richard Hovey. Address: 560 N. Madison Av., Pasadena CA‡

HOVING, JOHANNES, physician; b. Wilborg, Finland, Apr. 17, 1868; s. Walter and Bertha (Boldt) H.; descendant of Swedish and Dutch ancestry; A.M., Univ. of Helsingfors, 1890; Ph.D., Univ. of Berlin, 1890; M.D., U. of Upsala and Lund, Sweden, and Karolinska Med. and Surg. Inst., Stockholm, 1898; m. Helga Adamsen-Rundberg, June 17, 1894; children—Hannes, Walter, Greta (Mrs. Hoving Persson), Helge Wilhelm (dec.). Came to U.S., 1903, naturalized citizen, 1909. Asst. instr. pediatric hosp. and clinics, Stockholm, 1897-98; chief physician, Baths Mariehamn, Aland, summers 1898-1903; proprietor Dr. Hoving's Med. Inst., Helsingfors, 1898-1903; visting physician Sydenham Hosp., N.Y. City, 1908-11; owner of private hosp., N.Y. City, 1911-14; gen. practice since 1914; mem. board of trustees Assn. of Foreign Press Correspondents of New York. Life mem. Med. Soc. of Sweden; mem. Assn. United Vasa Lodges in Greater New York (hon. chmn.), Scandinavian Progressive League (former chmn.), Swedish Hist. Soc. America, John Ericsson Commn., St. Erik Soc. for Advancement of Swedish Arts, Music and Lit. (hon. pres.), Children's Clubs of Order of Vasa (former chmn.); hon. mem. N.Y. State Physio-Therapist Assn., Swedish Gymnastic Soc., New York and Sweden dists. Order of Vasa, Swedish Glee Club of Brooklyn, Swedish-Am. Lit. Assn., Loges, Dellenbygden and Malardrottningen, Sweden. Leader of Vasa children's tours of Sweden, 1924, 1929, and 1933. Decorated Knight Order of Vasa and Royal Order of the North Star (Sweden); gold medal, St. Erik Soc. (New York). Lutheran. Mason. Extensive writer on musical, biog., social, geneal. and polit. subjects. Home: Grevgaten 14, Stockholm Sweden‡

HOWARD, ALVIN HAYWARD, corp. exec.; b. New Orleans, July 30, 1915; s. Alvin Pike and Laura (Hayward) H.; B.A., U. Va., 1939; M.B.A., Babson Inst., 1940; m. Bruce Blakemore, May 1942 (div. Aug. 1962); 1 son, Alvin Pike; m. 2d, Nell Moore Winston, Aug. 28, 1962; children—Ashley Moore, Laura Neil; stepchildren-Jefferson G., James W. Stephen D. Pres., Danica Oil Co., New Orleans, 1938-42; partner Howard, Labouisse, Friedrichs & Co., New Orleans, 1946-50, Howard, Weil, Labouisse, Friedrichs & Co., New Orleans, 1950-69; v.p. D.E. Vasser, Inc., 1952-57; chmn. bd. Delta Offshore Drilling Co., Inc., 1955-57, La. Offshore Drilling Co., 1956-57, LaDelta Offshore Corp. (merger D.E. Vasser, Inc., Delta Offshore Drilling Co., Inc. and La-Delta Offshore Drilling Co., Inc.), 1957-69; partner Warrior Oil & Gas Co., 1958-69; dir. Times Picayune Pub. Corp. (all New Orleans), Zapata Off-Shore Co. Trustee Woodberry Forest Sch.; former mem. bd. dirs. Internat. House; bd. dirs. La. Dept. Commerce and Industry. Served to capt. AUS, 1942-45. Mem. The Bus. Council. Home: New Orleans LA Died Sept. 22, 1969; buried Metairie Cemetery, New Orleans LA

HOWARD, ARTHUR ETHELBERT, JR., lawyer; b. Hartford, Conn., Dec. 28, 1891; s. Arthur Ethelbert and Mary (Bagley) H.; B.A., Yale, 1914, LL.B., 1917; m. Winifred S. Merrill, Sept. 6, 1920 (dec.). Admitted to Conn. bar, 1917; practice of law, Hartford, 1919-72; with firm Howard, Kohn, Sprague and FitzGerald; asst. clk. bills Conn. Legislature, 1923; asso. judge Ct. of Common Pleas, 1925-31; asst. corp. counsel City of West Hartford, Conn., 1931-39. Served with USN, 1917-18. Mem. Am., Conn., Hartford bar assns., Phi Beta Kappa, Phi Delta Phi, Zeta Psi. Clubs: University (past pres.), Choral (past pres.) (Hartford). Home: West Hartford CT Died Nov. 6, 1972; buried Cedar Hill Cemetery, Hartford CT

HOWARD, ARTHUR PLATT, author; b. at New York, Dec. 16, 1869; s. Joseph Platt and Harriet (Andrews) H.; ed. pvt. sch., New York; m. Annie Legg, of New York, Sept. 6, 1893. Became connected with Howard & Co., jewelers, New York, at 15, and continued 21 yrs.; moved to Salem, Mass., 1908, started the Morning Dispatch; elected mayor after residence of 14 mos. Joined staff of McClure's Mag., 1912, Boston Post, 1914; editor Vermont Advance, Burlington, 1915—. Pres. Dispatch Newspaper Co.; dir. Howard Co., jewelers. Prohibition candidate for lt. gov. of Mass., 1914. Episcopalian. Author: Man Who Bucked Up, 1912; Selling Jewels to Multimillionaires, 1915. Address: Burlington VT‡

HOWARD, BEN ODELL, aeronautical cons.; b. Palestine, Tex., Feb. 9, 1904; s. Sam Taylor and Francis (Reeves) H.; ed. pub. schs. San Antonio; m. Olive Maxine Schoen, Dec. 11, 1931. Mechanic Curtiss Aeroplane Co.; engaged in crop-dusting instrn., Houston, 1925-27; air mail pilot, 1927-36; operated aircraft mfg. co., Howard Aircraft Corp., 1936-40; asst. to pres., Douglas Aircraft Co., Santa Monica, Calif., 1940-47; dir., cons. Consol. Vultee Aircraft Co., San Diego, 1947-50; gen. mgr. Aircraft div. Fairchild Engine & Airplane Co., Hagerstown, Md., 1936, cons., also to Consol. Vultee Aircraft Co., San Diego, Cal. test pilot, 1936-70; designer, builder, and pilot racing airplanes. Winner Bendix Transcontinental, 1935. Home: Los Angeles CA Died Dec. 4, 1970.

HOWARD, (ALAN) CAMPBELL PALMER, physician; b. Montreal, Can., Apr. 2, 1877; s. Robert Palmer and Emily (Severs) H.; grad. Montreal Collegiate Inst., 1893; B.A., McGill U., 1897, M.D., C.M., 1901; m. Ottilie Wright, of Ottawa, Ont., Dec. 27, 1911. Asst. in medicine, Johns Hopkins Med. Sch., 1902-6, McGill U., 1907-10; prof. theory and practice of medicine, State U. of Ia., since 1910; phys. to Univ. Hosp. Maj. Canadian Army Med. Corps, C.E.F., Mar. 1915-Jan. 1916. Mem. Assn. Am. Physicians, Am. Assn. Clin. Investigations, Am. Pathol. and Bacteriol. Assn., Zeta Psi, etc. Episcopalian. Clubs: University, Royal Montreal Golf (Montreal, Can.). Address: Iowa City IA‡

HOWARD, EZRA LEE, clergyman, educator; b. Kalamazoo, Mich., Apr. 14, 1869; s. Lyell Marvin and Mary Catherine (Osborne) H.; William Jewell Coll., Liberty, Mo., 1889-92; U. of Chicago, 1900-2; (D.D., Fargo Coll., 1917); m. Alma Marvin Hayes, of Paola, Kan., Dec. 30, 1896. Licensed to preach in Bapt. ch. at 17, ordained 1890; pastor in Mo. and Kan.; resigned at Paola, Kan., 1896, to enter Congl. ministry; pastor Burlington, Kan., Kansas City, Mo., and Morgan Park, Ill.; pastor Plymouth Ch., Columbus, O., 1903-10, 1st Ch., Painesville, O., 1910-15, St. Anthony Park Ch., St. Paul, Minn., 1915-18; pres. Fargo Coll., 1918-21; pastor Congl. Ch., Prescott, Ariz., 1922—. Mem. Phi Gamma Delta. Republican. Mason (32 deg., Shriner), Elk. Clubs: Yavapai, Rotary, Chamber of Commerce (Prescott); Graduate Chapter Phi Gamma Delta (Phoenix). Home: Prescott AZ‡

HOWARD, FREDERIC HOLLIS, prof. physiology; b. Newburyport, Mass., Sept. 3, 1876; s. Eugene and Susan Ella (Nash) H.; M.D., U. of Pa., 1898; m. Mary Malleville McClellan, of Lakewood, N.J., Apr. 9, 1901; children—Edgerton McClellan, Paul Malleville, Caroline. Began teaching at U. of Pa. (med. dept.), 1899; prof. physiology, Williams Coll., since 1900. Mem. A.M.A. Conglist. Mem. M.C.U.S.A., June 1, 1917. maj., Sept. 3, 1918; with A.E.F., Jan. 7, 1918-Apr. 18, 1919; hon. discharged, May 6, 1919; now lt. col., Med. R.C. Address: Williamstown MA‡

HOWARD, JOSEPH WHITNEY, prof. chemistry; b. Dixon, Ill., June 18, 1889; s. John Fleming and Martha Elizabeth (Regan) H.; A.B., Shurtleff Coll., 1912; fellow U. of Ill., 1912-15, A.M., 1913, Ph.D., 1915; m. Guyda Lang, Sept. 4, 1918; children—Robert Randolph, Guyda Leone. Instr. in chemistry, State U. of Mont., 1915-19, asst. prof. chemistry, 1919-24, asso. prof., 1924-27, prof., from 1927. Mem. Am. Chem. Soc., Sigma Xi, Phi Lambda Upsilon, Gamma Alpha. Awarded Osborne scholarship medal, Shurtleff Coll., 1912. Republican. Baptist. Mason. Club: Authors. Contbr. to Jour. Am. Chem. Soc., Jour. Am. Pharm. Soc., Jour. Chem. Edn. Home: Missoula MT Died Sept. 30, 1968.

HOWARD, JULIA PALMER, librarian; b. Atlanta, Aug. 17, 1917; d. Loring Brainard and Rose (Harris) Palmer; A.B., Spelman Coll., 1938; B.S. in L.S., Western Res. U., 1940; grad. student U. Ark., 1959; m. John Miller Howard, Oct. 18, 1941; children—Roslily Lorraine, Marinelle Joneese. Tchr. pub. schs., Thomasville, Ga., 1938-39; head librarian Agrl., Mech. and Normal Coll., Pine Bluff, Ark., from 1940, instr. library workshops, summers, from 1954. Mem. Am., Ark. library assns., Ark. Tchrs. Assn. (library cons.), Ark. Student Library Assn. (co-founder, charter mem., mem. exec. bd.), Jack and Jill Am., Alpha Kappa Alpha. Mem. A.M.E. Ch. Club: Quettes (Pine Bluff). Home: Pine Bluff AR Died June 3, 1971; buried Miller Meml. Cemetery, Pine Bluff AR

HOWARD, PERRY WILBON, lawyer; b. Ebenezer, Miss., June 14, 1877; s. Perry Wilbon and Sallie H.; student Alcorn (Miss.) Agrl. and Mech. Coll., 1891-92; Rust Coll., Holly Springs, Miss., 1892-98, A.B., 1898 in absence; Fisk U., Nashville, 1898-99; U. of Chicago 3 summers; LL.B., Illinois Coll of Law, 1902-05; LL.D., Campbell College, Jackson, Miss., 1914; m. 2d, Wilhelmina Lucas, of Macon, Miss., Aug. 15, 1907; children—Wilhelmina Estelle (dec.), Perry Wilbon, Edward Lucas. Prof. mathematics, Alcorn A. and M. Coll. winters 1901-05; admitted to Miss. bar, 1905, and began practice at Jackson; spl. asst. to atty. gen. of U.S. since May 15, 1921. Del. to Rep. Nat. Conv. 5 times, 1908-24; chmn. Rep. State Com. of Miss. since 1924; mem. Rep. Nat. Com. since 1924. Pres. Nat. Negro Bar Assn. Methodist. Mason, Odd Fellow, K.P., Elk. Clubs: Mu-So-Lit (Washington, D.C.). Home: Jackson, Miss. Address: Dept. of Justice, Washington DC‡

HOWARD, WILLIAM EAGER, JR., ret. naval officer; b. Wash., June 15, 1906; s. William E. and Katherine (Tufts) H.; B.S., U.S. Naval Acad., 1928; M.S., Mass. Inst. Tech., 1933; grad. Naval War Coll., 1952; m. Frances Bacon, May 14, 1930; children—William Eager III, Richard B. Commd. ensign U.S. Navy, 1928, advanced through grades to rear adm., 1956; assigned Phila. Naval Shipyard, 1933-35; with Bur. Constrn. and Repair Navy Dept., 1936-40; material officer on staff comdr. service force Atlantic Fleet, 1940-42; mem. staff comdr. amphibious force S.W. Pacific, also staff comdr. in chief U.S. Fleet, 1942-43; supt. design, ship-bldg. and hulls, also indsl. engr. officer Mare Island Naval Shipyard, 1943-47; indsl. engring. officer, planning and estimating supt., repair supt. Norfolk Naval Shipyard, 1947-51; asst. chief staff logistics, maintenance officer Atlantic Fleet, 1952-55; comdr. Boston Naval Shipyard, 1955-59; asst. chief plans and adminstrn. Bur. Ships, also insp. gen. bur., 1959-60; comdr. Norfolk Naval Shipyard, 1960-63; director of admissions and registration, dir. financial aid Old Dominion Coll., from 1963. Decorated Commendation ribbon with star, numerous others. Mem. Soc. Naval Architects and Marine Engrs., Am. Soc. Naval Engrs. Club: Columbia Country (Chevy Chase, Md.). Author naval tech. bulls. Home: Portsmouth VA Died June 14, 1972; buried Arlington Nat. Cemetery.

HOWARD, WILLIAM SCHLEY, congressman; b. Kirkwood, Ga., June 29, 1875; s. Thomas C. and Susan (Harris) H.; acad. edn. until 12; m. Lucia Augusta du Vinage, of San Antonio, Tex., Oct. 27, 1905. Admitted to bar, 1895, and since in practice at Decatur, Ga. Mem. Ga. Ho. of Rep., 1899; solicitor-gen., Stone Mountain Jud. Circuit, Ga., 1905-10; mem. 62d to 65th Congresses (1911-19), 5th Georgia Dist.; Democrat. Served in 3d Ga. Vol. Inf. during Spanish-Am. War. Address: Kirkwood GA‡

HOWARD, WILLIAM TRAVIS, pathologist; b. Sans Souci, Statesburg, S.C., Mar. 13, 1867; s. John and Mary Catherine (Macleod) H.; student U. of Va., 1885-87; M.D., U. of Md., 1889; grad. student Johns Hopkins, 1889-93; m. Mary Cushing Williams, Aug. 15, 1896. Engaged in teaching and research in pathology since 1892; prof. pathology, Western Reserve U., Cleveland, 1894-1914; asst. commr. of health, Baltimore, 1915-19; lecturer vital statistics and biometry, Sch. Hygiene and Pub. Health, Johns Hopkins, 1919-25, asso. mem. Inst. of Biol. Research, 1926; voluntary asso. in biology, 1930. Former bacteriologist Cleveland Bd. of Health. Pres. Am. Assn. Pathologists and Bacteriologists, 1902; mem. Assn. Am. Physicians. Author numerous papers on pathology, bacteriology and vital statistics, including Public Health Administration and The Natural History of Disease in Baltimore, Md., 1797-1920, 1924. Home: 835 University Parkway, Baltimore MD*‡

HOWE, EDGAR F., creamery exec.; b. Owatonna, Minn., Feb. 3, 1862; s. L. F. and Mary Tisdale H.; m. Emma Miller, Oct. 18, 1886. With the Fairmont Cremery Co., Omaha, Neb., since 1886, starting as supt. buttermaker, sec., later v.p., then pres. now chmn. bd.; pres. Don Lee Furniture Co. Mem. exec. com. Am. Assn. of Creamery Butter Mfrs., Nat. Poultry Inst. Club: Happy Hollow Golf. Home: 204 N. 52nd St. Office: 1202 Jones St., Omaha NE*‡

HOWE, FREDERIC WILLIAM, JR., business exec.; b. Providence, July 8, 1905; s. Frederic William and Ruth Woodcock (Stone) H.; A.B., Williams College, 1926; student Lowell Textile Inst., 1927; m. Mary F. Washburn, June 7, 1927; children—Frederic William, Barbara Rhodes; m. 2d, Winifred E. Bowler, Jan. 2, 1934; 1 dau., Elisabeth S.; m. 3d, Muriel E. Johnstone, Feb. 23, 1950. Sales trainee Crompton & Knowles, Corp., Worcester, 1927-34, office staff. Phila., 1934-35, so. mgr., Charlotte, N.C., 1935-43, v.p., Worcester, 1943-53, dir., from 1941, gen. sales mgr., 1948-53, pres., gen. mgr., 1953-60, chairman of board, 1969-72; director of Compo Industries, Worcester County National Bank, Societa Nebiolo, Italy; trustee Peoples Savings Bank, Worcester. Mem. Worcester Airport Commn., 1953. Director Asso. Industries Mass.; bd. dirs. Mass. Taxpayers Foundation, Central Massachusetts chpt. Nat. Safety Council; trustee Meml. Hosp., also Clark University, Worcester Massachusetts. Mem. Am. Textile Machinery Assn. (pres. 1953-54), Phila. Textile Inst. (corp., trustee), Worcester Area C. of C., American Association of Textile Chemists and Colorists, S.A.R., Alpha Delta Phi. Clubs: Worcester, Tatnuck Country, University (Worcester); Williams, Union League (N.Y.C.); Algonquin (Boston). Home: New Braintree MA also New York City NY Died Mar. 17, 1972; buried Shrewsbury Cemetery, Shrewsbury MA

HOWE, GEORGE, real estate; b. New Orleans, La., Sept. 22, 1881; s. George (M.D.) and Henriette (Lanauze de Banares) H.; B.E., Tulane U. of La., 1901, M.E., 1903. Instr. in charge Phys. Lab., Tulane U., 1901-04, later power engr. New York Edison Co.; gen. mgr. Met. Engring. Co., 1905-06; founder, 1906, and pres. Howe Engring. Co.; real estate business, since 1907, specializing in development of suburban parks and large estates; organizer and pres. Burhoward, Inc., builders of suburban cooperative apts.; pres. Hillsound Corp., George Howe, Inc. Was founder and editor of magazine Progress, in behalf of Progressive Party of Theodore Roosevelt. Member Westchester County Realty Board (ex-president), Southern Soc. of New York, Delta Kappa Epsilon. Episcopalian. Clubs: University, Indian Harbor Yacht, Westchester Country. Author: Mathematics for the Practical Man, 1908; Economics for the Practical Man, 1948; Memoirs of a Westchester Realtor, 1959. Home: Rye NY Deceased.

HOWE, GEORGE MAXWELL, educator; b. San Francisco, Calif., Oct. 4, 1873; s. Brig-Gen. Walter (U.S.A., deceased) and Elizabeth (Dunn) H.; Cornell Coll., Ia., 1889-92; A.B., Ind. U., 1894; U. of Leipzig, 1895-8; Ph.D., Cornell U., 1901; U. of Berlin, 1905-6; m. Frances M. Chamberlin, of Vicksburg, Miss., June 18, 1908. Instr. German, Ind. U., 1893-5, Dartmouth Coll., 1898-9, Cornell U., 1899-06; prof. German lang. and lit., 1907-11, head prof., 1911-1920, Colorado Col.; prof. German, Marietta Coll., 1920-23; on leave at Harvard as lecturer in German, 1922-23; instr. German, Harvard, 1923-—. Conglist. Mem. Modern Lang. Assn. of America, Am. Assn. Univ. Profs., Beta Theta Pi, Phi Beta Kappa. Dir. du Foyer du Soldat, France, 1918-20. Author of articles on German lit. and of text books for study of German. Home: 160 Lake View Av., Cambridge MA‡

HOWE, HAROLD, non ferrous smelting, refining and mining co. exec.; b. Bklyn., Nov. 9, 1913; s. Frederick and Mary (Collins) H.; m. Elsa Peters, Oct. 5, 1940; children—Barbara (Mrs. Walter E. Lewis), Linda (Mrs. Delmont Irving), Richard. With Am. Smelting and Refining Co., 1931-68, sec., 1955-68; sec. So. Peru Copper Corp., Lake Asbestos of Que., Ltd. Mem. Am. Inst. Mining, Metall. and Petroleum Engrs. Clubs: Bankers, Mining, Downtown Athletic (N.Y.C.); Ridgewood (N.J.) Country. Home: Saddle River NJ Died Dec. 18, 1968; buried Ridgewood, NJ

HOWE, HAROLD, non ferrous smelting, refining and mining co. exec.; b. Bklyn., Nov. 9, 1913; s. Frederick and Mary (Collins) H.; m. Elsa Peters, Oct. 5, 1940; children—Barbara (Mrs. Walter E. Lewis), Linda (Mrs. Delmont Irving), Richard. With Am. Smelting and Refining Co., 1931-68, sec., 1955-68; sec. So. Peru Copper Corp., Lake Asbestos of Que., Ltd. Mem. Am. Inst. Mining, Metall. and Petroleum Engrs. Clubs: Bankers, Mining, Downtown Athletic (N.Y.C.); Ridgewood (N.J.) Country. Home: Saddle River NJ Died Dec. 18, 1968; buried Valleau Cemetery, Ridgewood NJ

HOWE, STEWART SAMUEL, publicist, ednl. adminstr.; b. Streator, Ill., Oct. 25, 1905; s. Orion Harrison and Ethel Irene (Elder) H.; A.B., U. Ill., 1928, M.Journalism (hon.), 1937. Reporter, Times-Press, Streator, 1923-27, city editor, 1927-28; advt., promotion L.W. Ramsey Co., 1928-30; established Stewart Howe Alumni Service, Inc., 1930, pres., 1930-73, also pres., treas. affiliated firms; pub. relations officer 9th Naval Dist., Navy Dept., 1942-43; recruiting publicity WAC, Young & Rubicam, Inc., N.Y.C., 1944; account exec. John Price Jones Corp., 1944-49; regional dir. U. Mich. Meml.-Phoenix Project, 1949-52; v.p. Ill. Inst. Tech., Armour Research Found., Chgo., 1952-58; asst. to pres. for devel. Fordham U., N.Y.C., 1958-59; pres. Recorder Pub. Co., Columbus, O., 1951; pres., dir. Frat. Service, Inc., Evanston, Frat. Mags. Assn.; Inc., Stewart Howe Services, Inc., Evanston, 1963-73, Howe Service, Inc., N.Y.C. and Champaign, Ill., 1945-73; pres., dir. Columbia Bus. Service, Inc. (Mo.), 1960-73; pres. Copy & Mailing Services, Inc., O., 1961-73, Ind., 1965-73. Regional rep. Ill. U.S.D. Mem. Nixon-Agnew nat. campaign pub. relations adv. com., 1968. Trustee, chmn. Stewart Howe Found.; governing mem. U. Ill. Found. Life mem. Nat., Ill., Chgo. Evanston hist. socs.; mem. Pub. Relations Soc. Am. (nat. bd. 1957-58), Am. Coll. Pub. Relations Assn. (nat. bd. 1956-58), Chgo. Soc. Fund Raising Execs. (dir.), Nat. Ednl. Devel. Officers Assn. (pres. 1956), Pub. Relations Clinic, Alpha Gamma (trustee), Skull and Crescent, Kappa Sigma, Sigma Delta Chi, Phi Eta Sigma (nat. pres. 1927), Kappa Tau Alpha. Clubs: Press, Executive, Headline, Tavern, University (Chgo.); N.Y. Athletic, University (N.Y.C.). Contbr. articles to ednl. publs. Home: Evanston IL Died Jan. 7, 1973.

HOWELL, HILTON EMORY, lawyer, univ. trustee; b. nr. Lexington, Tex., May 10, 1897; s. Thomas Andrew and Mamie (Griffith) H.; student Baylor U., 1915-18; B.A. University of Texas, 1921, LL.B., 1922; LL.D., Baylor University, 1962; m. Louise Hatchett, Mar. 27, 1926; children—Hilton Hatchett, Donald Lee, James Louis. Admitted to Tex. bar, 1922; partner firm Naman, Howell, Smith && Chase, and predecessors, Waco, Texas, 1926-66, of counsel, 1966-68; special chief justice Supreme Court of Texas, 1932. Chairman of board of directors KWTX Broadcasting Co., Texoma Broadcasters, Inc., 1964-68; dir. Victoria Broadcaster, Inc., Word, Inc., First National Bank of Waco (Tex.), Brazos Broadcasting Co., 1st Nat. Bank of Durant, Okla. Director, past chairman bd. Hillcrest Hosp., 1933-56; dir. Baylor Stadium Corp., 1950-52, Heart-O-Texas Fair, 1956-57, Baylor-Waco Found.; chmn. bd. trustees Cooper Found., 1956-68, Baylor U., 1958-68; sec. Waco Perpetual Growth Found. Mem. Am., Tex. bar assns., Am. Judicature Soc., Tex. Bar Found., Waco C. of C., Delta Theta Phi. Dem. Baptist. Mason (32 deg.). Clubs: City (Waco); Ridgewood Country. Home: Waco TX Died Apr. 6, 1968.

HOWELL, META PAULINE, librarian; b. Dusseldorf, Germany, Nov. 7, 1899; d. Rudolf A. and Maria (Schiffer) Armbruester; came to U.S., 1902, naturalized, 1916; B.S. in L.S., U. Buffalo, 1924; m. Frederick Stanley Howell, Feb. 10, 1934. Br. librarian Chgo. Pub. Library, 1926-27; asst. librarian, Museum Sci. and Industry, Chgo., 1927-40, head librarian, 1941-47; asst. librarian Chgo. Natural History Mus. (name changed to Field Mus. Natural History), 1947-48, head librarian, 1948-68. Mem. A.L.A., Spl. Libraries Assn. Home: Chicago IL Died Aug. 31, 1968; interred Rosehill Cemetery Mausoleum, Chicago IL

HOWELL, ROGER WILLIAM, physician; b. Ann Arbor, Mich., 1911; s. Robert Brown and Martha (Clark) H.; M.D., U. Mich., 1938; m. Gertrude Sawyer, June 17, 1939; children—Marcia (Mrs. William Litzenberg), Ruth, Roger William. Intern, St. Joseph's Mercy Hosp., Ann Arbor, 1938-39; resident Mercy-Wood Neuropsychiat. Hosp., 1939-40; resident in neurology St. Louis City Hosp., 1940-41; chief psychiatrist VA Hosp., Mpls., 1946-48; instr. psychiatry Neuropsychiat. Inst., Ann Arbor, 1941-46; clin. asst. prof. psychiatry U. Minn., Mpls., 1946-48, asso. prof. psychiatry, 1943-51; prof. mental health U. N.C., Sch. Pub. Health, 1952-56; asso. prof. pub. health practice in mental health U. Mich. Sch. Pub. Health, Ann Arbor, 1959-70. Diplomate Am. Bd. Psychiatry and Neurology. Mem. Am. Psychiat. Assn. Home: Ann Arbor MI Died Dec. 30, 1970; cremated.

HOWELLS, MILDRED, artist, writer; b. Cambridge, Mass., Sept. 26, 1872; d. William Dean and Elinor (Mead) H.; ed. pvt. schs. Painter in water colors; exhibited at Paris Salon, New York, Phila., Boston, etc.; made drawings for A Little Girl Among the Old Masters; illustrated The Howells Story Book, The Literary Primer. Contbr. verse and illustrations to Harper's, Scribner's, St. Nicholas, Century and other mags. Republican. Clubs: Women's City (Boston); Cosmopolitan (New York). Editor: Life in Letters of William Dean Howells, 1928. Wrote foreword for centennial edition of The Rise of Silas Lapham." Home: York Harbor ME‡

HOWES, ROYCE B., writer; b. Minneapolis, Jan. 3, 1901; s. George R. and Alice M. (Bucknam) H. ed. pub. schs. Minneapolis; m. Dorothy Jane Chandler, May 17, 1924; children—Geoffrey C., Jane B. (Mrs. Jerry Flint). Mem. staff bus. office Detroit News, 1924-26; with Detroit Steel Products Co. as editor house publs., 1926-27; mem. editorial staff, Detroit Free Press, 1927-65, editorialist, columnist, 1942-55, asso. editor, 1955-62, editorial dir., 1962-65; instr. journalism Wayne State U., 1931-41. Entered United States Army, rank of capt., 1942; served as officer in charge Army News Service, Army Dept. Spl. Staff; released active service rank of lt. col., 1946. Awarded Bronze star; Pulitzer prize for editorial writing, 1955, award for editorial writing, Nat. Headliners Club, 1955. Mem. Am. Soc. Newspaper Editors, Detroit Hist. Soc., Friends of Detroit Pub. Library. Clubs: Nat. Headliners; Detroit Press. Author: Death on the Bridge, 1935; The Callao Clue, 1936; Night of the Garter Murder, 1937; Death Dupes a Lady, 1937; Murder at Maneuvers, 1938; Nasty Names Murders, 1939; Death Rides A Hobby, 1939; Case of the Copy Hook Killing, 1945; Edgar A. Guest, a biography 1953. Address: Highland Park MI Died Mar. 1973.

HOWKINS, ELIZABETH PENROSE, editor; b. Johnson County, Wyo., Apr. 1, 1906; d. James Norman and Julia (Corcoran) P.; ed. Mount St. Joseph, Chestnut Hill, Phila.; m. Lloyd B. Averill, Sept. 29, 1928 (divorced); m. 2d, Walter Ashby Howkins, Aug. 26, 1952. Publicity dept. E. P. Dutton & Co., pub., New York, N.Y., 1926-27; chief copywriter and stylist, James McCreery & Co., New York, N.Y., 1927-31; merchandise editor Am. Vogue, 1931-33, joined staff of British Vogue, London, 1933, editor, 1935-41; editor Glamour, New York, N.Y., 1941-54. Dir. Conde Nast Publs., Inc. Apptd. to New York Woman's Council, 1945. Contributed sect. on Fashion and Dress to Ency. Britannica Book of the Year, 1938. Home: New York City NY Died Jan. 1972.

HOWLAND, JOSEPH BRIGGS, M.D., b. Brockton, Mass., Dec. 26, 1873; s. Edward Payson and Susan (Freeman) H.; M.D., Harvard, 1896; m. May Sheddon Partridge, June 4, 1908; children—Elizabeth, John Partridge. Began practice at Boston, Mass., 1896; asst. supt. Mass. State Hosp., 1901-02; supt. State Colony for Insane, 1902-07; asst. res. physician, Mass. Gen. Hosp., 1907-19; supt. Peter Bent Brigham Hosp., 1919-39, supt. emeritus since 1939; adminstr. Huntington Memorial Hosp., Boston, 1928-42; sec. Harvard Cancer Commn., 1928-42; pres. Hosp. Council of Boston, 1935-38. Fellow A.M.A., Mass. Med. Soc.; mem. Am. Hosp. Assn. (pres. 1919), N.E. Hosp. Assn. (pres. 1921; trustee), Mass. Hosp. Assn., Weymouth Hosp. (vice pres. 1944). Address: 657 Main St., Hingham MA‡

HOWLETT, FREEMAN S(MITH), horticulturist; born Jordanville, N.Y., June 15, 1900; s. William Jacob and Anna Belle (Smith) H.; B.S., Cornell, 1921, Ph.D., 1925; D.Sc. (honorary), Wooster College, 1968; student University London, Nat. Research Council Fgn. fellowship, biol. sci. John Innes Hort. Institute, London, England, 1932-33; Doctor Science, Wooster College, 1968; m. Jean Margaret Waterbury, Sept. 26, 1925. Instr. in agrl. economics, Cornell, 1921, instr. pomology, 1922-24; asst. horticulturist, Ohio Agricultural Research and Development Center, Wooster, 1924-27, asso. horticulturist. 1924-27, professor and chmn. department horticulture, since 1947; asst. prof. horticulture, Ohio State Univ., 1929-37, asso. prof., 1937-42, prof., 1942-71, chmn. dept. horticulture and forestry, 1947-70; guest lectr. horticulture Agr. Colls. Yugoslavia, 1951, Slovak Academy of Sciences, Czechoslovakia, 1966, Bulgarian Acad. of Sciences, 1962; cons. U.S. AID, Punjab Agr. U., India, 1967. Fellow Royal Hort. Soc. London (England), A.A.A.S., Ohio Academy of Science (past vice president), Am. Soc. Hort. Sci. (president 1958-59); mem. American Institute Biol. Sci. (past gov.), Botanical Soc. Am., Am. Soc. Plant Physiol., Genetics Soc. Am., Ohio State Hort. Soc., Ohio Vegetable and Potato Growers Association, Ohio Forestry Assn., Internat. Soc. Horticultural Science, Sigma Xi, Gamma Sigma Delta, Phi Kappa Phi. Independent. Presbyterian. Author: Modern Fruit Production (with Joseph H. Gourley), 1941. Home: Wooster OH Died Nov. 18, 1970; buried Wooster Cemetery.

HOWLETT, JAMES DAVID, educator; b. at Prince Edward Island, Can., Feb. 24, 1874; s. George and Flora Jane (MacNeil) H.; grad. Coburn Classical Inst., Waterville, Me., 1896; A.B., Colgate U., Hamilton, N.Y., 1900, post-graduate work same univ. 2 yrs.; studied in Europe, 1913; m. Agnes Morrill, of Concord, N.H., 1913. Served as prin. high sch., Plymouth, Quincy and Medford, Mass., Hebron (Me.) Acad.; made latter over into sch. for boys; prin. Liberty High Sch., Bethlehem, Pa., since 1922. Served as rep. of N.E. schs. and colls. on Coll. Entrance Examination Bd.; a founder and first pres. associated charities, Quincy, Mass.; mem. Headmasters' Assn., Delta Kappa Epsilon, Phi Beta Kappa, N.E.A., etc. Mason (K.T.). Home: Prospect Av., Bethlehem PA‡

HOWLETT, WALTER MAIN, clergyman, religious educator; b. Elora, Ont., Can., June 14, 1883; s. George and Mary (Main) H.; A.B., Toronto U., 1909; A.M., Yale, 1911; L.H.D., Coll. Idaho, 1940; m. Lal Sinclair, Sept. 19, 1912. Came to U.S., 1909, naturalized, 1917. Student pastor, Onondaga, Ont., Can., 1903-05; ordained to ministry of the Congl. Ch., 1911; pastor Mt. Sinai Congl. Ch., Long Island, N.Y., 1911-14; head worker Columbia House Settlement and pastor Willow Place Chapel, Brooklyn, N.Y., 1914-17; sec. Y.M.C.A., with 90th div. A.E.F., France, 1918; internat. sec. Daily Vacation Bible Schs., 1919-23, sec. met. fedn. Daily Vacation Bible Schs., 1919-44; sec. dept. religious edn., greater N.Y. Fedn. Chs. and dir. religious edn. extension, Columbia U., 1923-44; exec. sec. greater N.Y. coordinating com. on Released Time of Jews, Protestants and Roman Catholics; exec. secretary interdenominational com. Religious Edn. on Released Time, 1941-44; exec. dir. div. Christian educational

Protestant Council of City N.Y., 1944-45. Dir. World's Sunday Sch. Assn.; bus. mgr. 11th World's Sunday Sch. conv., Rio de Janeiro, Brazil, 1932. Mem. fgn. affairs com. Nat. Rep. Club. Mem. Garden City Country Club. Author: Religion the Dynamic of Education (Harpers), 1924. Home: Brooklyn NY Died Feb. 1972.

HOWZE, HENRY RUSSELL, lawyer; b. Marion, Ala., Nov. 12, 1870; s. Augustin Clayton and Valeria (Long) H.; A.B., Ala. U., 1890, LL.B., 1891; m. Minnie Love, 1909. Practiced law in Birmingham, 1892-1942; acting chmn. Com. on Revision of Code, Ala. Legislature, 1923; probate judge, Jefferson County, 1942-45. Mem. firm Howze and Brown, since 1945. Mem. Civil Service Bd., 1928-34, Library Bd., 1936-46, pres. 1946; mem. Y.M.C.A. since 1890 (pres. board trustees since 1936), American Bar Assn., Ala. Bar Assn., Birmingham Bar (former pres.) Assn., Am. Red Cross (former chmn.), Delta Kappa Epsilon. Club: Mountain Brook, Rotary. Democrat. Presbyterian. Home: 2828 Berwick Road, Birmingham AL‡

HOXIE, GEORGE LUKE, engr. b. Leonardsville, Madison County, N.Y., May 14, 1872; s. Luke and Harriet Ellen (Parker) H.; ed. pub. schs., Leonardsville, Ilion and Utica, N.Y.; M.E. Cornell U., 1892, M.M.E., 1897, Ph.D., 1902; m. Mary Coleta Osborn, June 29, 1896; children—Dorothy E., Robert O., Stephen P., Henry L. Instr., U. of Ariz., 1892-93; acting prof. mechanics and industrial drawing, 1893-94, prof. physics and mechanics, 1894-96; instr. in elec. engring., Cornell U., 1898-1901; engr. Westinghouse, Church, Kerr & Co., 1901-04; cons. engr. in independent practice since June 1, 1904. Mem. Am. Soc. Mech. Engrs.; fellow Am. Inst. E.E. Author: (with Profs. Ryan and Norris) Test-book of Electrical Machinery, Vol. I, 1903; Stock Speculation and Business, 1930; Men, Money and Mergers, 1932. Home: 605 S. Lucerne Blvd., Los Angeles CA*‡

HOXIE, HAROLD JENNINGS, physician; b. Vienna, N.Y., May 11, 1908; s. George Elwin and Elizabeth (Jennings) H.; M.D., Coll. Med. Evangelists, 1933; m. Laura Belle Patterson, June 11, 1932; children—Russell Evan, Patricia (Mrs. Gary Lee Tallman). Intern, San Diego County Gen. Hosp., 1932-33; resident in gen. medicine Los Angeles County Hosp., 1936-39; cons. internal medicine Kern County Hosp., 1945-47. Diplomate Am. Bd. Internal Medicine. Mem. A.M.A., A.C.P., Los Angeles Soc. Internal Medicine (pres. 1948), Med. Research Soc. So. Cal. (v.p. 1949). Contbr. articles to profl. jours. Home: Glendale CA Died Aug. 20, 1967; buried Hollywood Hills-Forest Lawn Cemetery, Glendale CA

HOXTON, ARCHIBALD ROBINSON, headmaster; b. Alexandria, Va., June 28, 1875; s. Llewellyn and Fanny (Robinson) H.; B.A., U. of Va., 1901; Litt.D., U. of South, 1929; A.M., Princeton U., 1937, Harvard, 1949; m. Sara P. Taylor, Dec. 16, 1903; children—Mary Earle (Mrs. William W. Mackall), Archibald Robinson, Jr. Began as teacher, Episcopal High Sch., Alexandria, Va., 1897; headmaster, 1914-47, pres. emeritus since 1947. Mem. Delta Kappa Epsilon. Democrat. Episcopalian. Club: Colonade (U. of Va.). Address: 711 Princeton St., Alexandria VA‡

HOY, ALBERT HARRIS, M.D., author; s. Dr. P. R. and Mary E. H.; served in U.S.A. as acting asst. surgeon during Civil war; grad. Med. Coll. of Ohio, 1864; Rush Med. Coll., Chicago, 1866; practice limited to disorders of digestive system and kidneys; Author: Eating and Drinking, 1896 M5. Residence: 461 State St., Chicago‡

HOYT, DERISTHE LAVINTA, lecturer; b. Wentworth, N.H.; d. Dr. Peter Livingston and Elisabeth (Aspinwall) H.; grad. Kimball Union Acad., 1864; unmarried. Taught Appleton Acad., New Ipswich, N.H., 1865-7, Reading (Mass.) High Sch., 1869-70; studied in S. Kensington Art Sch., London, 1872-3; taught Mass. Normal Art Sch., 1874-91; lecturer in same on history of painting, 1891-13. Author: Historic Schools of Painting; The World's Painters and Their Pictures; Barbara's Heritage. Address: Malden MA‡

HOYT, PHILLIS LUCILLE, sch. adminstr.; b. West Edmeston, N.Y., Dec. 22, 1923; d. James Ricardo and Ida Adele (Tyrrell) Hoyt; student Knox Sch., 1941-43; B.A., Cornell U., 1945. Statis. clk. Eastman Kodak Co., Rochester, N.Y., 1945-48; accounting clk. U. Cal., Los Alamos, 1949; accountant Sandia Corp., Albuquerque, 1950-54; asst. sec.-treas. Western Devel. Co., Santa Fe, 1955-61; partner Nambe Plant Farm, Santa Fe, 1959-70, Santa Fe Bus. Coll., 1962-70. Mem. Delta. Gamma. Republican. Episcopalian. Home: Santa Fe NM Died Dec. 3, 1970.

HOYT, ROBERT STUART, educator, historian; b. Mpls., May 20, 1918; s. Samuel Leslie and Jane (Woodruff) H.; A.B., Harvard, 1940, M.A., 1942, Ph.D., 1948; m. Maurine K. Larson, July 20, 1940; children—Stauart C., Jane D., Martha M. Teaching fellow, tutor Harvard, 1942-45, asst. dean, 1944-45; asst. prof., then asso. prof. U. Ia., 1946-55; asso. prof. U. Minn., 1955-57, prof. history, 1957-71, chmn. dept., 1966. Founder, dir. Internat. Medieval Bibliography, 1967-71; co-chmn. Conf. Medieval Bibliography, 1967-71. Served with AUS, 1945-46. Guggenheim fellow, 1949-50; Fulbright fellow, 1949-50; Social Sci. Research Council faculty fellow, 1960-61. Fellow Royal Hist. Soc.; mem. Medieval Acad. Am. (councillor 1964-67), Am. Hist. Assn., Midwest Medieval Conf. (pres. 1966-67). Author: The Royal Demesne in English Constitutional History, 1066-1272, 1950; Euorpe in the Middle Ages, 2d edit., 1966; Feudal Institutions, 1961. Editor: Life and Thought in the Early Middle Ages, 1967. Home: St Paul MN Died Feb. 24, 1971.

HROMADKA, JOSEF LUKI, clergyman, educator; b. Hodslavice, Czechoslovakia, June 8, 1889; s. Josef and Rosine (Palacka) H.; student Protestant Theol. Faculty, Vienna, Austria, 1907-08, 09-11, U. Basel (Switzerland), 1908-09, U. Heidelberg (Germany), 1911, United Free Ch. Coll., Aberdeen, Scotland, 1911-12; Ph.D., U. Prague, 1920; D.D., Wooster Coll., 1946, Bethlehem Sem. and Coll., 1947, Princeton, 1947, Aberdeen U., 1949, U. Debrecen (Hungary), 1953, Humboldt U., Berlin, Germany, 1959; D. History, U. Warsaw (Poland), 1952; m. Nadia Luklova, June 26, 1924; children—Nadia Eunice (wife of Dr. Jaromir Mikulka), Alena (Mrs. Vojtech Zikmund). Pastor in Evang. Ch., Czechoslovakia, 1912-20; prof. Johannes Hus Faculty of Theology, Prague, 1920-39; guest prof. Princeton Theol. Sem., 1939-47; prof. Comenius Faculty of Theology (formerly Johannes Hus Faculty), Prague, 1947-69, dean, 1950-66. Mem. exec. and central coms. World Council Chs.; mem. bur. World Council of Peace; pres. Christian Peace Conf., 1961. Author: Doom and Resurrection (English), 1945; Theology Between Yesterday and Tomorrow, 1957; Evangelium fur Atheisten (German), 1958; The Gospel on the Way to Man (Czech and German), 1958; Sprung Ueber Die Mauer, 1961; Das Evangelium auf dem Wege zum Menschen, 1961; Ander Schwelle des Dialogs, 1964; numerous others. Home: Prague Czechoslovakia Died Dec. 26, 1969; buried Hodslavice, Moravia, Czechoslovakia

HSIA, DAVID YI-YUNG, physician, educator; b. Shanghai, China, Aug. 22, 1925; s. Ching-Lin and Wai-Tsung (New) H.; came to U.S., 1940, naturalized, 1960; A.B., Haverford Coll., 1944; M.D., Harvard, 1948; m. Hsio-Hsuan Shih, July 23, 1949; children—David, Judith Ann, Lisa, and Peter. Intern Charity Hosp., New Orleans, 1948-49; asst. resident pediatrics, Childrens Hosp., Phila., 1949-50; asst. resident pediatrics New York Hosp., 1950-51; research fellow pediatrics Harvard Med. Sch., 1951-53, instr. pediatrics, 1953-56; research asst. Galton Lab., Univ. Coll., London, 1956-57; faculty Northwestern U., 1957-69, prof. pediatrics, 1960-69, now lectr.; prof. and chmn. dept. pediatrics Loyola U.-Stritch Sch. Medicine, 1969-72; chief pediatrics Loyola University Hospital, 1969-72; consultant pediatrics at Children's Meml. Hosp., Chgo.; attending physician Evanston, Cook County hosps. Bd. dirs. Am. Bur. Med. Aid to China, 1965-72; Cook County chpt. Nat. Found., 1959-72, Chgo. Cystic Fibrosis Found., 1961-72. Recipient Mead Johnson award pediatric research, 1965, City of Hope award, 1971. Mem. Soc. Pediatric Research, Central Soc. Clin. Research, Soc. Exptl. Biology and Medicine, Am. Pediatric Soc., Phi Beta Kappa, Alpha Omega Alpha. Author: Inborn Errors of Metabolism, 2d edit., 1966; Human Developmental Genetics, 1968. Home: Evanston IL Died Jan. 27, 1972; buried Ferncliff, Hartsdale NY

HUARD, LEO A(LBERT), lawyer, univ. dean; b. Manchester, N.H., Dec. 29, 1916; s. Francois Arsene and Eva Maria (Lalumiere) H.; B.A., magna cum laude, St. Anselm Coll., Manchester, 1939; postgrad. U. N.H., Durham, 1939-40; LL.B., Georgetown U., Washington, 1946; m. Jeanne Wiegers, June 28, 1947; children—Jeanne, David. Indsl. chemist, 1940-42; control chemist Food & Drug Adminstrn., 1942-45; law clk. Hon. E. Barrett Prettyman, 1945-46; admitted to D.C. bar, 1945, also U.S. Supreme Ct., 1958; cons. practice in Washington, 1951-59; professor law Georgetown U. Law Center, 1947-59; dean, prof. law U. Santa Clara Law Sch., 1959-69; mem. Adminstrv. Conf. U.S., 1961. Dir. World Affairs Council, San Jose, Cal., 1961-63; founding dir., v.p. Legal Aid Soc., Santa Clara County, 1960-67; dir. Childrens Home Soc. Cal., Central Coast Counties br., 1962-64. Mem. Am. Assn. U. Profs., Am., Fed. bar assns., Bar Assn. D.C., Mensa. Democrat. Roman Catholic. Contbr. articles to law reviews. Home: Santa Clara CA Died Dec. 31, 1969; buried Saratoga CA

HUBBARD, FRANCES VIRGINIA, writer of songs, prose, verse; b. Albany, N.Y.; d. William Howell and Sophronia (Palmer) Thomas; ed. Schoharie (N.Y.) Acad.; spl. studies in Frnech, music and the drama, under private teachers; special courses at N.Y. State Coll.; m. Murray Hubbard, February 2, 1875 (deceased); 1 son, Lester Thomas. Writer of many songs, anthems, cantatas, etc., among them Eternal City, Song of Eternity, Song of the Armourer, Love is a Beautiful Story, At the Gate, Land of Nod, When the Angel Comes; Prodigal, and The Star Divine (cantatas); The Witch of Fairy Dell (3-act opera); also pageants, The Sign in the Sky, 1928; There Were Shepherds, 1929; The Dawn of Hope, 1929; Watermillion Time, Mother, Yours and Mine; also several part songs for men's voices, etc. Member Federated Women's Clubs, Gansevoort Chapter D.A.R. (historian), Albany Colony N.E. Women, Pi Gamma Mu. Clubs: City, Woman's, Monday Musical, Alliance Francaise. Presbyn. Contbr. articles Lippincott's Mag., Brooklyn Eagle, Albany Argus, Troy Times, etc. Awarded prize, 1916, for song written in contest, for Alumni Assn. of N.Y. State Coll., Albany, N.Y. (adopted as Alma Mater song, N.Y. State Coll.); awarded prize in lit. contest Nat. Society N.E. Women, 1921; received award for distinguished service" from Nat. Soc. of New England Women, for literary work and social service, 1939. Pageants: The Prince of the House of David, 1929; It Came Upon a Midnight Clear, 1930; Around the Manger, 1931; In the Days of Thy Youth, 1932; Easter Service, Radiant Easter Morn, 1932. Home: 120 Elm St., Albany NY‡

HUBBARD, HAVRAH WILLIAM LINES, music editor; b. Farmersville, N.Y., Mar. 22, 1867; s. William R. and Augusta (Pearson) H.; high sch. edn.; studied music at Dresden with Lamperti, Scholtz and Fahrmann, 1893-98; unmarried. Music editor Chicago Evening Journal, 1888-91; music editor Chicago Tribune for various periods, beginning 1891, ending June 1920; spl. corr. Tribune, at Vienna, Austria, 1900-01. Resided at Los Angeles, Calif., 1910-11, lecturing on music, throughout middle west and on Pacific Coast; spl. work, Oxford U., Eng., 1911-12; publicity mgr. Boston Opera House, Boston, Mass., 1912-15; presenting operalogues (recital presentations of grand opera), 1913-18, in Boston, New York and later throughout U.S.; song leader for Commn. on Training Camp Activities, San Diego, Calif., naval and mil. camps, Feb.-Oct. 1918; capt. Am. Red Cross service, San Diego, Oct. 1918-Jan. 1919. Resumed operalogues, Nov. 1921, in New York and Boston, and toured U.S. for 3 yrs.; mem. bd. dirs. and asst. gen. dir. Am. Inst. Operatic Art, Stony Point, N.Y., Oct. 1924-Nov. 1925; production dir. Yorick Players, The Yorick (Little Theatre), San Diego, Calif., 1926-29; music and drama critic San Diego Union, 1928-32; lecturer on music and internat. affairs, 1931-32; spl. writer for Am. periodicals, on European conditions, 1932-34, 1938; lecturer on music and social conditions, teacher of drama and pub. speaking, player and lecturer over radio since 1934; official music commentator in Ford Bowl, San Diego Expn., summers, 1935, 36. Author: Chats with Color-Kin (children's fairy stories), 1910; The Joyous Child (biography of Anna Held Heinrich), 1938. Editor-in-chief of Am. Ency. and History of Music, 11 vols., 1908-09. Home: San Jacinto CA‡

HUBBARD, RUSSELL STURGIS, bishop; b. Germantown, Pa., Sept. 8, 1902; s. Russell Sturgis and Elizabeth Russell (Perry) H.; student St. George's Sch., R.I., 1915-20; A.B., Harvard, 1924; B.D., Va. Theol. Sem., 1927, D.D., 1949; student Trinity Coll., Cambridge, Eng., 1924-25; LL.D., (hon.), Gonzaga Univ., Spokane; m. Anna Catherine Pratt, Nov. 3, 1928; children—Ann Perry (Mrs. P.T. Austin), Jane Parkinson (Mrs. John Keydell), Judith Bardbury (Mrs. Thomas Osgood), Russell, Catherine Carroll (Mrs. Richard A. Burke). Ordained deacon, Episcopal Ch., 1927, priest 1928; consecrated bishop, 1948; asst. St. John's Ch., Waterbury, Conn., 1927-29; priest in charge St. Paul's Ch., Vermillion, S.D., 1929-32; rector St. Martin's Ch., Providence, 1932-41, St. Saviour's Ch., Bar Harbor, Me., 1942-48; canon missioner Diocese of Me., 1943-48; suffragan bishop Diocese of Mich., 1948-54; bishop of Spokane, 1954-67. Rotarian. Address: Sequim WA Died Dec. 27, 1972.

HUBBELL, HARRY MORTIMER, prof. Greek; b. Belvue, Kan., Aug. 30, 1881; s. Mortimer Barnett and Hannah Virginia (Buzzard) H.; student Hillhouse High Sch., New Haven Conn., 1894-98; B.A., Yale U., 1902, M.A., 1905, Ph.D., 1913; m. Alice Pendleton Clark, April 5, 1916 (deceased); 1 son, Henry; married 2d, Mary Willard Bird, October 30, 1943. Engaged as asst. principal Waterville (N.Y.) High Sch., 1902-03; master Pingry Sch., Elizabeth, N.J., 1904-07; dean Pennington (N.J.) Sch., 1907-10; instr. Latin and Greek, Yale U., 1911-14; asst. prof, 1914-24, asso. prof., 1924-27, prof., 1927-34; Talcott prof. Greek, 1934-50, emeritus, 1950-71; vis. prof. Greek, U. Calif. at Berkeley, 1950; lectr. Am. Acad. in Rome, 1950-51. Member American Philol. Assn., N.E. Classical Association (pres. 1932-33). Republican. Conglist. Club: Elizabethan, Graduates (New Haven). Author: The Influence of Isocrates on Cicero; the Rhetorica of Philodemus; The Orator of Cicero; Cicero's DeIventione and Topica; also numerous articles in philol. jours. Editor, Yale Classical Studies, 1948-71. Home: Branford CT Died Feb. 24, 1971.

HUBBELL, HARVEY, business exec.; b. Bridgeport, Conn., May 23, 1901; s. Harvey and Louie (Edwards) H.; student Choate Sch.; m. 2d, Virginia W. Hood, Feb. 3, 1956: children—(by previous marriage)—Harvey IV, William Ham, Elizabeth Lorraine, With Harvey Hubbell, Inc., Bridgeport, 1921-68, pres., treas., dir., 1927-57, pres., chmn. bd., 1957-63, chmn. bd., 1963-68. Club: Elec. Mfrs., Brooklawn Country, Exchange, Fayerweather Yacht (Bridgeport); Algonquin, Canadian (N.Y.C.); Bath and Tennis, Everglades, Coral Beach, Sailfish, La Coquille (Palm Beach, Fla.); Ocean

Reef (North Key Largo, Fla.); Palm Bay (Miami, Fla.); Chesapeake (Irvington, Va.); Yachting of Am. Home: Southport CT Died July 12, 1968; buried Mountain Grove Cemetery, Bridgeport CT

HUBBELL, HENRY SALEM, painter; b. Paola, Kan., Dec. 25, 1870; s. Willard Orvis and Maria (Gleason) H.; pupil Art Inst., Chicago, and studied in Paris with Jean Paul Laurens, Raphael Collin, and Whistler; also studied some time in Madrid, Spain; m. Rose Strong, of Wyoming, N.Y., July 30, 1895. Began as illustrator; was for some time associated with Woman's Home Companion. As painter made debut at Paris Salon, 1901, with large picture, The Bargain"; other pictures, The Return," The Poet" (bought by Mr. William M. Chase), Chez Grand'mere," The Caress," Morning," The Brasses" (now in Wilstach collection, Memorial Hall Mus., Phila.), Henry and Jack," The Orange Robe," By the Fireside," Child and Cat" (bought by the French Govt.), The Goldfish" (owned by Booth Tarkington), The Samovar" (now in collection of Baron Edmond de Rothschild), The Departure," Black and White" (now in municipal art collection, Grand Rapids, Mich.); Larkspurs" (bought by French Govt.); also has painted various portraits. Hon. mention, Paris Salon, 1901; medal, Paris Salon, 1904; silver medal, St. Louis, 1904; 3d prize, Worcester Art Acad.; Waite bronze medal, Chicago Art Inst. A.N.A.; ex-v.p. Am. Art Association of Paris; mem. Paris Society of American Painters. Societe Internationale de Peinture et de Sculpture, Paris, National Association Portrait Painters, Silvermine Group of Artists, Electric Group of Painters and Sculptors, Allied Artists America. Clubs: Arts (Washington, D.C.), Salmagundi, Nat. Arts of New York (life). Head of School of Painting and Decoration, Carnegie Inst. Tech., Pittsburgh, 1918-21; now engaged in portrait painting. Address: 1 Lexington Av., Gramercy Park, N.Y.; (summer) Norwalk CT‡

HUBER, CHARLES HENRY, educator; b. Nebraska City, Neb., June 7, 1871; s. Prof. Eli (D.D.) and Mary Ellen (Deibert) H.; grad. Gettysburg (Pa.) Acad., 1888; B.A., Gettysburg Coll., 1892, A.M. 1895, Litt.D., 1914; grad. Gettysburg Theol. Sem., 1896; m. Louise Annan, Dec. 18, 1897; children—Elizabeth Annan (Mrs. William M. Welch II), Charles H. Master in Gettysburg Acad., 1892-96, headmaster, 1896-35; director women's division Gettysburg College, 1935-41, director emeritus since 1941; president Gettysburg Ice & Storage Company, Adams County Cold Storage Company; vice-president Gettysburg National Bank. Chmn. Adams County Council of Defense, World War I. Mem. Assn. Colls. and Prep. Schs. of Middle States, Phi Beta Kappa, Kappa Phi Kappa, Phi Gamma Delta. Republican. Luthern. Club: Tubling Run Game. Home: Gettysburg PA‡

HUBER, MIRIAM BLANTON, educator and author; born at Lynchburg, Tennessee; the daughter of George W. and Laura (Sutton) Blanton; student Ward Seminary and Buford College, Nashville, Tennessee, Kidd-Key College, Sherman, Texas; B.S., Columbia University, 1925, A.M., 1926, also Ph.D., 1928; married Victor H. Huber; one daughter, Charlotte. Successively grade teacher, principal, supervising principal, in the public schools of Marion County, Ind., 1912-19; mem. staff State Dept. Pub. Instrn., Ind., 1915-23; teacher of English, pub. schs., Indianapolis, 1920-22; asst. prof. English, Ind. State Teachers Coll., 1923-24; mem. staff Inst. of Ednl. Research, Teachers Coll. (Columbia), 1926-28; editor The Macmillan Co., 1928-29, Am. Book Co., 1929-32; lecturer in edn., New York U., 1932-35; prof. edn., Ariz. State Teachers Coll., 1935-37. Author: (with H. B. Bruner and C. M. Curry) The Poetry Book, 9 vols., 1926; (with same) Children's Interests in Poetry, 1927; The Influence of Intelligence upon Children's Reading Interests, 1928; (with A. I. Gates) The Work-Play Books, 12 vols., 1930, revised edit., 1939; Skags, the Milk Horse, 1931; Cinder. the Cat, 1931; The Uncle Remus Book, 1935; (with F. S. Salisbury and M. O'Donnell) The Primary Wonder-Story Books, 3 vols., 1938, rev. edit., 1962; Story and Verse for Children, 1940, rev. edit., 1965; (with F. S. Salisbury and A. I. Gates) Core-Vocabulary Readers, 4 vols., 1943; (with same) Today's Work-Play Books, 12 vols., 1945-46; (with same) The Macmillan Readers, 27 vols., 1951-53; (with F. S. Salisbury and Charlotte Huber) The Intermediate Wonder-Story Books, 3 vols., 1953, rev. edit., 1962. Contbr. ednl. mags. Home: Los Angeles CA Died Dec. 8, 1969; buried Forest Lawn Memorial Park, Glendale CA

HUBERMAN, LEO, author, editor; b. Newark, Oct. 17, 1903; s. Joseph and Fannie (Kramerman) H.; student London (Eng.) Sch. Econs., 1933-34; B.S., N.Y.U., 1926, M.A., 1937; m. Gertrude Heller, July 3, 1925 (dec. Sept. 1965). Sch. tchr., 1926-33; chmn. dept. social sci. New Coll., Columbia, 1938-39; labor editor PM, 1940; columnist U.S. Week, 1941; dir. edn. Nat. Maritime Union, 1942-45; editor Reynal & Hitchcock, 1945-46; co-editor Monthly Rev., 1949-68. Author: We the People, 1932; Man's Wordly Goods, 1936; The Labor Spy Racket, 1937; America, Incorporated, 1940; The Great Bus Strike, 1941; The Truth About Unions, 1946; The Truth About Socialism, 1950; (with P.M. Sweezy) Cuba: Anatomy of a Revolution, 1960, Socialism in Cuba, 1969; also pamphlets. Editor (with Sweezey): Paul A. Baran: A Collective Portrait, 1965, Fifty Years of Soviet Power, 1968. New York City NY Died Nov. 9, 1968.

HUDDLESTON, GEORGE, JR., ex-congressman; b. Birmingham, Ala., Mar. 19, 1920; s. George and Bertha (Baxley) H.; A.B., magna cum laude Birmingham-Southern Coll., 1941; LL.B., U. of Ala., 1948; married to Alice Jeane Haworth; children—George III, Margaret, Nancy. Admitted to Alabama bar, 1948, D.C. bar, 1965; dep. circuit solicitor 10th Judicial Circuit, 1948-49; asst. U.S. atty. No. Dist. Ala., 1949-52; practice of law, Birmingham, Alabama, 1952-54; member of 84th-87th Congresses, ninth District of Alabama, member 88th Congress at large, Ala.; asst. to v.p. N.Am. Rockwell Corporation, 1964-71. Served comdr. USN, World War II. Mem. Am. Legion (dept. comdr. Ala. 1950-51), Phi Beta Kappa, Phi Delta Phi. Editor: Index to Official Proceedings of Alabama Constitutional Convention of 1901, 1948. Home: Potomac MD Died Sept. 1971.

HUDDY, GEORGE HENRY, JR., lawyer, banker; b. Providence, R.I., June 29, 1872; s. George Henry and Lavinia Butler (Ash) H.; LL.B., Yale, 1893; m. Frances Newell Snow, Oct. 8, 1901; 1 son, Franklin Snow. Admitted to Conn. bar, 1893, R.I. bar, 1895, bars of U.S. Dist. Court, U.S. Circuit Court of Appeals, Board of Tax Appeals, Treasury and U.S. Supreme Court; began practice at Providence; dir. Title Guarantee Co. of R.I., Industrial Trust Co.; dir. R.I. Electric Protective Co. Republican nominee for mayor of Providence, 1907; assistant U.S. attorney, R.I. 1909-14. Former mem. Jud. Council of R.I. Mem. Am. Bar Assn., R.I. State Bar Assn. (ex-pres.), R.I. Bankers Assn. (ex-pres.), Medico-Legal Soc. (ex-pres.). Republican. Unitarian. Mason (32 deg., K.T.). Clubs: Art, Players. Home: 204 Bowen St., Providence 6 RI*‡

HUDSON, PAUL BATEMAN, lawyer, b. Lawrenceburg, Ind., July 14, 1907; s. Howard H. and Maude E. (Wakefield) H., student Butler U., 1926-28; LL.B., Ind. Law Sch., 1931; m. Marie Bischoff, Aug. 31, 1934; children—Jacqueline Lee (Mrs. Walter W. Bond), Richard P. Admitted to Ind. bar, 1940; br. mgr. Bradstreet Co., 1931-33; with legal dept. Am. States Ins. Co., 1933-43; practice in Indpls., 1943-70; mem. Knightlinger, Young, Gray & Hudson, and predecessor firms, 1943-70, partner, 1945-70. Mem. Indpls. Airport Authority (pres. 1968-70). Recipient Sportsmanship trophy Indpls. Aero Club. Mem. Am., Ind., Indpls. bar assns., Indpls. Lawyers Assn., Delta Theta Phi. Mason (Shriner). Home: Indianapolis IN Died Apr. 14, 1970; buried Washington Park East, Indianapolis IN

HUDSON, RALPH, librarian; b. Tulsa, Okla., June 4, 1908; s. Ralph Waldo and Imogene Pauline (Waggner) H.; A.B., U. of Okla., 1932, B.L.S., 1933; m. Katherine Kaufman, Oct. 10, 1934. Head corr. study div., Univ. of Okla. Library, 1933-35, head loan div., 1935-36; state librarian Okla. State Library, 1937-68, state archivist, 1939-68, state records preservation officer, state records adminstr., 1961-68. Mem. Archives and Record Commn. of Okla., 1939-68, vice chmn., 1947-68; mem. bd. dirs. Community Council of Okla. City and County, 1942-52, Okla. Health and Welfare Assn., 1954-57 (mem. legislative com. 1964-68), Okla. City Travelers Aid Soc., 1947-50, Neighborhood Centers, Inc., 1965-68; cons. Okla. Children's Code Commn., 1947-49; vice chmn. Okla Council on Libraries, 1964-68; sec. Okla. Arts and Humanities Council, 1965-68; vice chmn. Council of State Govt.'s Com. on Automation, Technology and Data Processing, 1966-68. Served in U.S. Army, 1943-46. Mem. A.L.A. (chmn. projected books com., 1949-53, mem. council, 1949-57, chmn. com. state legislative action 1954-55, mem. bd. Exhibits Round Table 1960-63, mem. commn. nat. planning library edn. 1962-68), Nat. Assn. State Libraries (pres. 1955-59), Southwestern (pres. 1944-46), Okla. Canadian library assns., Am. Assn. State and Local History, Soc. Am. Archivists, Am. Assn. Law Libraries, Phi Beta Kappa. Episcopalian. Home: Oklahoma City OK Died Aug. 9, 1968.

HUDSPETH, ANDREW H., judge; b. Fannin Co., Tex., Oct. 23, 1874; s. John H. and Emily S. (Ross) H.; ed. pub. schs.; unmarried. Admitted to bar of New Mexico, 1897, and practiced at Carrizozo; became asso. justice Supreme Court of N.M., 1931, served 8 years; retired 1938. Democrat. Address: Carrizozo NM‡

HUDSPETH, ROBERT HILL, prison warden; b. Lenoir, N.C., Mar. 20, 1877; s. Charles McDowell and Laura Luvenia (Bush) H.; graduate high school, Manhattan, Kan., 1896; m. Fanny Margaret Saler, Oct. 23, 1897; children—Josephine Margaret (Mrs. Frank P. Kelly), Elizabeth Anna (Mrs. Don L. Zinn), Robert John. Successively record clerk, superintendent of identification and parole officer, acting warden, deputy warden Kansas State Prison, Lansing, 1913-30; successively assistant deputy warden, deputy warden and warden, U.S. Penitentiary, Ft. Leavenworth, Kan., 1930-37, warden Main Fed. Prison, Leavenworth, Kan., 1937-43, retired Sept. 1943; returned to prison service as warden Kansas State Prison, Lansing, Kan., Feb. 1944. Republican. Methodist. Mason. Club: Kiwanis of Leavenworth. Home: Lansing. Address: Kansas State Prison, Lansing KS‡

HUDTLOFF, MARTIN JOHN, govt. ofcl.; b. Butte, Mont., Nov. 10, 1902; s. Martin David and Julia (Detloff) H.; A.B., U. Mont., 1925; m. Ruth Hewitt, Jan. 10, 1939 (dec. 1965); son, Martin John. Employee Anaconda (Mont.) Copper Mining Co., 1925-32; controller Mont. Relief Commn., Helena, 1932-35, N.M. Relief Adminstrn., Santa Fe, 1935; commr. accounts, accountant in charge field offices Treasury Dept., 1935-42; joined Dept. Agr., 1946, dir. transportation and storage services division Commodity Stabilization Service, 1949-63; deputy director fiscal division Agriculture Stabilization Service, Department Agr., from 1963; controller Commodity Credit Corp., 1947-49. Served as col. Office Fiscal Dir., War Dept., A.U.S., 1942-46. Decorated Am. Theatre ribbon; European, African, Middle East ribbon; Victory medal; Occupation medal; Commendation ribbon. Mem. Alpha Tau Omega. Presbyn. Home: Kensington MD Died Apr. 1969.

HUEBNER, CLARENCE R., army officer; b. Bushton, Kan., Nov. 24, 1888; s. Samuel G. and Martha (Rishel) H.; grad. business coll., Grand Island, Neb., 1909; grad. Inf. Sch., Advanced Course, 1923; honor grad. Command and Gen. Staff Sch., 1925; grad. Army War Coll., 1929; m. Florence Barrett, December 28, 1921; one daughter, Mary Juliette (Mrs. Richard J. Buck); m. 2d, Anna Imelda Matthews, Oct. 19, 1968 Enlisted, 18th Inf., U.S. Army, 1910-16; commd. 2d lt., Inf., November 26, 1916, and advanced through grades to lt. gen., March 1947; served as capt., major and lt. col., A.E.F., World War I; mem. War Dept. Gen. Staffs Corps, 1940-42; became dir. training, Services of Supply, Jan. 1942. Comdg. gen. 1st Inf. Div., Western Front, 1944; later comdr. 5th Army Corps; dep. comdr.-in-chief European Command and comdg. gen., U.S. Army, Europe, 1947; acting Am. Mil. Gov. in Germany and acting comdr. United States Armed Forces in Europe, 1949-50; director N.Y. Civil Def. Commn., Sept. 1951-72; director National Association of State and Territorial Civil Defense, 1957-58, president, 1958-72. Decorations: Distinguished Service Cross with oak leaf cluster. Distinguished Service Medal with two oak leaf clusters, Silver Star; Legion of Merit; Bronze Star Medal; Purple Heart with oak leaf cluster; Victory medal with 5 battle clasps; French Legion of Honor; French Croix de Guerre with palm; Italian War Cross; Comdr. Order Leopold I (Belgium); Order Sivurov 2d class (Russia); Croix de Guerre with palm (Belgium); Order White Lion 2d class (Czechoslovakia), Grand Officer de la Conronne de Chene (Luxembourg); Companion Order of Bath (Eng.). Retired 1950. Home: Washington DC Died Sept. 23, 1972; buried Arlington Nat. Cemetery, Arlington VA

HUFFARD, JAMES HUDSON, furniture store exec.1b. Bluefield Va., Sept. 3, 1899; s. Samuel Nye and Alice Elizabeth (Yost) H.; student Roanoke Coll., 1918, U. of Va., 1919-21; A.B., Johns Hopkins, 1923; m. Anne Helen Meadows, May 20, 1924; 1 d., Lysbeth Anne; m. 2d, Frances Elizabeth Coyner, Nov. 9, 1929 (dec. 1951); children—Alice Coyner (Mrs. Roy Richards), Nancy Valentine (Mrs. Charles W. Glenn), James Hudson; married 3d, Hilda S. Epperly, July 19, 1952. Pres. The Chgo. House Furnishing Co., Bluefield, Va., from 1924; chmn. bd. Financial & Comml. Investment Co. Va.; dir. Bank of Tazewell County. Mem. organization com. Nat. Postwar Conf. Mem. adv. bd. Salvation Army (Bluefield); mem. bd. dirs., Union Mission; past president League of Virginia Municipalities, 1948-49. Chairman Bluefield, West Virginia-Va. Com. Econ. Development; president Bluefield Area Development Corp., 1958-59. Recipient of John Willis, Jr., award 1959. Vice pres. Va. State C. of C., chmn. com. on better roads, 1955-57; bd. mem. National Found. Consumer Credit, pres., 1958-59, chmn. bd., 1959-60. Mem. Nat. Retail Furniture Assn. (chairman of national war dues com.; past pres. and bd. chmn.), U.S. Chamber of Commerce (mem. com. on domestic distribution, chmn. resolutions com. 1943; com. nat. affairs, 1945), Bluefield Chamber of Commerce (past pres.) and nat. councilor, U.S. Kiwanis Internat. (v.p., 1944-45); mem. bd. trustees; mem. exec. com. of bd., chmn. bd. com. on finance) Soc. of Crippled Children (dir.), Southern Retail Furniture Assn. (past pres.), Alpha Delta Phi. Winner Cavalier award as one of ten outstanding furniture merchants in U.S., 1942. Mem. retailers adv. com. Nat. Defence Adv. Commn., 1939, War Savings Staff, Treasury Dept., 1940. Mayor of Bluefield from 1950. Clubs: University, Bluefield Country, Kiwanis (past dist. gov.), Executives of Bluefield (past pres.), Sales Executives (pres. Bluefield 1956-57). Home: Bluefield VA Died Nov. 19, 1971.

HUGGENVIK, THEODORE, author, prof. religion; b. Mandal, Norway, Oct. 22, 1889; s. Ole Eriksen and Caroline (Carlsen) H.; B.A., St. Olaf Coll., Northfield, Minn., 1915; M.A., U. of Chicago, 1916; student Chicago Luth. Theol. Sem., 1916, Luther Theol. Sem., St. Paul, 1917-18; B.Th., S.T.M., Princeton Theol. Sem., 1922; LL.B., (corr.), Hamilton Coll. of Law, Chicago, 1923; Th.D. (hon.), Augustana Coll., Sioux Falls, S.D., 1943; m. Mrs. Dora Nielsen, May 19, 1922; children—Victoria Grace, Rolf Carlyle, Elinor Caroline. Came to U.S., 1906, naturalized, 1916. Instr. St. Olaf Coll., 1918-21; ordained Luth. ministry, 1922;

pastor Westbrook (Minn.) Ch., 1922-26; prof., dept. of religion, St. Olaf Coll., from 1926, chmn. dept., 1941-54. Mem. Phi Beta Kappa. Author: Fourteen Men Who Knew Christ, 1931; The Approach to Jesus, 1934; An Outline of Church History, 1935, revised edition, 1939; Search the Scriptures, 1936; Lessons on the Life of Our Saviour, 1938; Your Key to the Bible, 1944 (11 printings); Martin Luther (narrative poem), 1949; We Believe, 1950; Faith and Conduct, 1952; Victory by the Cross; A God Who Likes Me, 1956. Recipient 5 consecutive awards from Freedoms Found. Contbr. book revs., religious articles. Home: Northfield MN Died Aug. 5, 1971.

HUGGINS, RICHARD EMMETT, interstate moving co. exec.; b. Indpls., July 25, 1910; s. Emmett S. and Florence (Moore) H.; M.S., Butler U., 1931; LL.B., Ind. U., 1935; m. Louise Eickhoff, June 8, 1935;children—Linda Jane, Andrea Louise. Admitted to Ind. bar, 1934; adjuster Ind. Ins. Co., 1932-35; with Aero Mayflower Transit Co., Inc., Indpls., 1935-71, sec., 1962-71, also dir.; dir. Ind. Ins. Co., Hogan Transfer and Storage Corp. Republican. Presbyn. (trustee, deacon, elder). Mason (Shriner), Kiwanian (bd. dirs. Indpls.). Club: Indpls. Athletic. Home: Indianapolis IN Died 1971.

HUGHAN, JESSIE WALLACE, author; b. Brooklyn, N.Y., Dec. 25, 1875; d. Samuel and Margaret Bailiff (West) H.; A.B., Barnard Coll. (Columbia), 1898; A.M., Columbia, 1899, Ph.D., 1911. Teacher English, high schs., N.Y. City, 1910-27; head of 28th St. annex, Textile High Sch., N.Y. City, since 1928. Socialist candidate for lt. gov., N.Y., 1920, for U.S. senator, 1924, for Assembly, 1933, 37. Mem. War Resisters League (founder and sec.), Fellowship of Reconciliation (council), League for Industrial Democracy (dir.), Alpha Omicron Pi (a founder), Phi Beta Kappa. Unitarian. Author: A Study of International Government, 1923; What is Socialism?, 1928; The Challenge of Mars, 1932; The Beginnings of War Resistance, 1934; If We Should Be Invaded, 1939. Home: 171 W. 12th St., New York NY‡

HUGHES, CHARLES HAYNES, naval architect and engr.; b. Boston, Mass., Sept. 3, 1877; s. Richard and Mary H.; educated English High School, Boston, and Mass. Institute of Tech.; m. Grace F. Charles, Dec. 25, 1918; 1 son, Dr. Charles H. Jr. Held responsible positions with Bath Iron Works, N.Y. Shipbuilding Co., and Crescent Shipyard; tech. aid for U.S. Shipping Bd. during World War I; engaged in spl. engring. work and projects relating to ships, World War II. Mem. Soc. Naval Engrs., Mass. Inst. Technology Alumni Assn. Author: Motor Boats, 1915; Hughes' Handbook of Ship Calculations and Construction (3d edition); Standard Details, 1918. Contbr. to New International Year Book. Awarded prizes for papers on welding by Lincoln Electric Co. and Hobart Bros. Home: 2681 Amboy Rd., New Dorp SI NY‡

HUGHES, JAMES MONROE, prof. edn.; b. Sharpsville, Indiana, Oct. 17, 1890; s. Thomas and Laura (Quinn) H.; ed. rural grade schs., Tipton Co., Ind., 1897-04; high sch., Tipton, 1905-09, A.B., Indiana University, 1916; A.M. Columbia University, 1922; Ph.D., University of Minn., 1924; m. Kathleen Pye, August 15, 1942; one son, James Charles. Rural sch. teacher, Ind., 1909-12; supt. village schs., Ind., 1913-18; prin. high sch., Ind., 1919-22; instr. in edn., Hamline U., St. Paul, Minn., 1922-23; lecturer in edn., U. of Minn., 1923-24, and summers, 1928, 1940; same U. of Pa. summer, 1937; asst. prof. edn., Northwestern U., 1924-26, asso. prof., 1926-27, prof. 1927-56; emeritus professor; 1956-70, dean Sch. of Edn. 1941-51. Member N.E.A., A.A.A.S., National Assn. School Adminstrs., Nat. Assn. Secondary Sch. Principals, Delta Pi Epsilon, Phi Delta Kappa. Methodist. Club: University. Author: (with others) Supervision of Instruction in High School; Attitudes and Preferences of High School Teachers Toward Supervision; Administering the Secondary School; Human Relations in Educational Organization, 1957; Education in America, 1960, 3d rev. edit., 1970. Also of educational tests and contributing articles to ednl. mags. Home: Evanston IL Died Oct. 26, 1971.

HUGHES, JOHN CHAMBERS, mfg. exec.; b. Louisville, Oct. 3, 1891; s. John Cowan Hughes; grad. Princeton, 1914; m. Margaret Kelly, July 27, 1923; children—Jamie, Lawrence. Chmn. adv. bd. Chem. Corn Exchange Bank; dir. Graniteville Company; U.S. permanent rep. on N. Atlantic Council, Orgn. for European Econ. Coop., with rank and status of A.E. N.Y.C. Trustee French Inst. U.S. Lycee Francais of N.Y. Chmn. bd. Free Europe Com. Mem. Council Fgn. Relations. Clubs: Merchants, Brook, Union, Piping Rock, River, Colony. Home: New York City NY Died May 1971.

HUGHES, JOHN HENRY, lawyer, state senator; b. Syracuse, N.Y., Apr. 1, 1904; s. Thomas P. and Susan (Eagan) H.; LL.B., Syracuse U., 1928; m. Mary Loraine Porter, Feb. 26, 1938; children—Mary H. (Mrs. Thomas Francis Dolan III), Suzanne (Mrs. Thomas Francis Quinlan), Thomas Porter. Admitted to N.Y. State bar, 1929, Fed. Ct. bar, 1929, U.S. Supreme Ct. bar, 1942; mem. firm Mackenzie, Smith Lewis, Michell & Hughes, and predecessor, Syracuse, 1928-72; mem. N.Y. State Senate, 1947-72, chmn. jud. com.; chmn. N.Y. Legislative Com. Crime. Bd. dirs. Syracuse Transit Corp.; trustee Onondaga County Savs. Banks, Syracuse; dir. P. & F. Industries. Chmn. Onondaga County Republican. Com., 1960-63. Bd. dirs. United Cerebral Palsy Assn. of Syracuse, Inc., Community-Gen. Hosp., Onondaga County chpt. Assn. for Help Retarded Children, Youth Devel. Center, Syracuse U. Fellow Coll. Trial Lawyers; mem. Am., N.Y. State, Onondaga County (past pres.) bar assns., Fedn. Bar Assns. 5th Jud. Dist. (past pres.), Am. Judicature Soc., Am. Bar Found., Internat. Assn. Ins. Counsel, Phi Delta Phi, Sigma Nu. Republican. Clubs: University, Century, Onondaga Golf and Country (Syracuse). Home: Syracuse NY Died Oct. 13, 1972.

HUGHES, JOHN T., lawyer; b. Tucson, Ariz., 1874; s. Gov. Louis C and Josephine (Brawley) H.; prep. edn. Freehold Acad., N.J.; student law dept. U. of Pa., 1894-5. Practiced in Chicago, 1896-7; supt. co. schs., 1898, 99; asso. editor Ariz. Daily Star, Tucson, 4 yrs.; now practicing law at Tucson. Member of first State Senate, Ariz., 1911-15; introduced and secured passage of many bills of spl. importance, including taxation of inheritances, indeterminate sentence law, publicity of campaign expenses, endowment for state ednl. institutions, constl. amendment granting suffrage to women, etc. Mem. exec. com. Dem. State Com. Mem. bd. regents, 1918-—, chancellor, 1918-19, U. of Ariz. Methodist. Home: Tucson AZ‡

HUGHES, MERRITT YERKES, prof. of English; b. Phila., Pa., May 24, 1893; s. Adoniram Judson and Annabelle (Yerkes) H.; A.B., Boston U., 1915, A.M., 1916; Doctor of Letters (honorary), 1954; M.A., University of Edinburgh, 1918, Litt.D., 1950; Ph.D., Harvard, 1921; student U. of Paris, 1921-22; m. Grace J. Dedman, Aug. 10, 1923;children—David Yerkes, Elspeth Baillie. (Mrs. John F. Benton). Instr. English, Boston U., 1919-20; asst. prof. English, U. of Calif., 1922-26; asso. prof., 1926-36; prof. English, U. of Wis., 1936-63, professor emeritus, 1963-71; chairman department English, 1938-41, 42-43, 46-48, 52-55; Taft lecturer, University of Cincinnati, 1962; summer instr. various univs.; vis. fellow Folger Shakespeare Library, Washington; 1964-65; vis. mem. Inst. Advanced Study, Princeton, 1965-66. Awarded fellowship Am. Field Service, 1921-22, fellowship John S. Guggenheim Meml. Found., 1925-26; fellowship Henry E. Huntington Library and Art Gallery, San Marino, Cal., 1941-42, 66-67; Fulbright grantee U. London, Brit. Mus., 1949-50; research grantee Lon., Am. Philos. Soc., 1968-69. Delivered Tudor-Stuart Lecture at Johns Hopkins U., 1943. Served as sgt. inf. Intelligence Corps. U.S. Army, A.E.F., 1918-19; maj. to lt. col., as field historian, G-5, Third U.S. Army, France, Luxembourg, and Bavaria, 1943-46. Fellow American Academy of Arts and Sciences; mem. Modern Lang. Assn. Am. (council 1948-52). Renaissance Soc. America (council 1958-60), Modern Humanities Research Assn., Am. Assn. U. Profs. (council 1954-57, chpt. pres. 1957-58), Wis. Acad. Scis. Arts and Letters (pres. 1960-61), Internat. Assn. Univ. Profs. English (exec. 1956-65). Mem. Soc. of Friends. Clubs: University (Madison, Wis.); Tudor-Stuart. Author: Ten Perspectives on Milton, 1965. Editor: Milton Complete Poems and Major Prose, 1957; vol. III The Complete Prose Works of John Milton, 1962. Contbr. to scholarly jours. Home: Madison WI Died May 12, 1971; buried Lawnview Cemetery, Philadelphia PA

HUGHES, MILDRED B., internat. trade relations exec.; b. Shelby County, Ill.; d. John Adams and Martha (Lockwood) Barding; ed. Sacred Heart Acad., Springfield, Ill., and Northwestern U.; Masters degree, Ariz. State U.; m. James E. Hughes, July 5, 1923 (dec. Jan. 1964); 1 dau., Mary Beth (Mrs. Taber Loree Collins). Asst. sales dir. Hughes & Co., 1921, mng. dir. Richmond (Va.) office, 1922; dir. sales, James H. O'Hara Co., 1926-27; in govtl. relations, Washington, 1929-34; exec. in internat. relations fields, N.Y.C., 1934-62; exec. v.p. Far East Am. Council of Commerce and Industry, Inc., 1943-62, bd. dirs., 1948-63; economist-adviser, specializing Asia-U.S. econ. affairs. Nat. vice chmn. China Emergency Relief Com., 1940, Nat. Com. United China Relief, 1941. Mem. adv. com. U.S. World Trade Fair, 1957-62. Decorated Most Exalted Order White Elephant (Thailand), 1956. Mem. Asia Soc., Japan Soc., Pan Pacific S.E. Asia Women's Assn. Contbr. surveys and articles to Fortune mag., Jour. Commerce, profl. publs. Home: Phoenix AZ Died Jan. 6, 1972.

HUGHES, RUSSELL HOUSTON, government official; b. Decatur, Ala., Apr. 23, 1891; s. Charles Luther and Elizabeth (Glascock) H.; B.S. in E.E., Vanderbilt U., 1913; m. Gladys Fugette, May 7, 1917 (deceased July 1954; m. 2d, Frances B. Harmon, Mar. 23, 1956. Engineer N.Y. Telephone Co., N.Y. City, 1914-27, asst. v.p., 1927-39; v.p. and gen. mgr., 1939-43, v.p., 1949-56; dir. production, communications, mobilization planning Dept. of Defense, Washington, D.C., 1956-57; asst. dir. production, Def. Moblzn., Washington, 1958-70. Fellow Am. Inst. Elec. Engrs.; mem. N.Y. State C. of C., Am. Inst. Management (asso.). Clubs: Sleepy Hollow Country, Scarborough (Scarsboro-on-Hudson, N.Y.); Fort Orange (Albany, N.Y.); University, Economic (N.Y.C.). Home: Irvington on Hudson NY Died Jan. 8, 1970.

HUKILL, RALPH LEROY, mfg. co. exec.; b. Kansas City, Mo., June 16, 1901; s. Lewis Frank and Anna (Hurley) H.; Ph.B., Washburn, Coll., 1933; M.A., U. Kan., 1938; m. Jessie May Higby, Dec. 24, 1928. Mgr. Commerce Hotel, Topeka, Kan., 1923-27; tchr. high sch., Onaga, Kan., 1933-35; state dir. Fed. Writers Project, Kan., 1936-37; fellow, instr. sociology U. Neb., 1938-40; field rep. U. Kan., 1940-42; pres. Quartz Labs., Kansas City, Mo., 1942-46; v.p., gen. mgr. Roto-Sphere, Inc., mfr. gyroscopes, Chicago, 1946-61, president, chairman board dirs., 1961-68. Served with USN, 1919-22. Fellow Am. Sociol. Assn.; mem. Nat. Quill Club, A.A.A.S., Soc. Study of Social Problems, Alpha Kappa Delta. Home: Chicago IL Died Oct. 13, 1968.

HULICK, PETER VAUGHN, radiologist; b. Nanticoke, Pa., 1909; s. Timothy and Julia (David) H.; M.D., Jefferson U., 1936; m. Helen Barno, Apr. 19, 1935; children—Patricia Helen, Timothy Peter, Peter Richard. Intern Harrisburg (Pa.) Polyclin. Hosp., 1936-37; resident in radiology New Rochelle (N.Y.) Hosp., 1940; resident in radiology and radiotherapy Bellevue Hosp., N.Y.C., 1944-45; former mem. staff Phillipsburg State Hosp., Mercy Hosp., Altoona, Pa., Indiana (Pa.) Hosp., Miners Hosp., Spangler, Pa., later St. Mary's Hosp., Sparta, Wis.; founder sch. radiol. tech. St. Francis Hosp., LaCrosse, Wis., also mem. staff. Preceptor in radiology U. Wis. Active Community Chest. Diplomate Am. Bd. Radiology. Fellow Am. Coll. Radiologists; mem. A.M.A., Radiology Soc. N.Am., Flying Physicians Assn., Isaac Walton League. Elk. Home: LaCrosse WI Died Apr. 7, 1971; buried Woodlawn Cemetery.

HULL, ROBERT WILLIAM, educator; b. LaCrosse, Ind., Apr. 3, 1924; s. Frank Hollis and Adah (Bell) H.; student Coll. Engring., U. Kan., 1942-43; B.S. in Chemistry, U. Ill., 1949, Ph.D. in Zoology, 1953; m. Grace Marie Houf, Feb. 24, 1945; children—Bradford, Sandra, Penna. Mem. faculty Northwestern U., 1953-63, asso. prof. biol. sci., 1959-63; prof. biol. scis., chmn. dept. Fla. State U., 1963-70. Part-time research asso. Ill. Natural History Survey, 1951-53; with Woods Hole Marine Biol. Lab., summer 1951; mem. rev. panel NSF grant program, 1960-63, chmn. rev. panel undergrad. instructional sci. equipment program, 1962; chmn. Internat. Congress on Protozoology, Leningrad, 1969. Grantee Tobacco Industry Research Com., 1961-64, NIH, 1956-61, NSF, 1955-58. Served with USAAF, 1943-46. Fellow A.A.A.S.; mem. Am. Inst. Biol. Scis. (bd. govs. 1962-70; lectr. nat. program vis. biologists to colls. 1961-70), Soc. Protozoologists (pres. 1968-69), Am. Soc. Zoologists, Am. Soc. Parasitologists, Am. Microbiology, Soc., Soc. Am. Bacteriologists Soc. Gen. Microbiology, Assn. Tropical Biology, Fla. Acad. Sci., Sigma Xi. Methodist. Club: Torch. Author: Laboratory Studies in Biology, 1962; Laboratory Studies in General Biology, 1953. Home: Tallahassee FL Died July 13, 1970.

HULL, (JAMES) ROGER, life ins. exec.; b. State College, Miss., Nov. 17, 1907; s. David Carlisle and Madge Cook (Wilson) H.; student Miss. State Coll., 1924-25; A.B., Ky. Wesleyan Coll., 1928, L.H.D., 1957; LL.D., Wheaton Coll., 1963, Houghton Coll., 1963; m. Rosalie Paschal, Dec. 31, 1932; children—James Roger, Rosemary (Mrs. David Mace), Elizabeth (Mrs. David E. Hall). With Mut. Life Ins. Co. of New York, 1928-72, beginning in sales office, Meridian, Miss., successively dist. mgr., mgr., Nashville, asst. supt. agencies home office, v.p., mgr. agys., 1941-50, exec. v.p., 1950-59, trustee, 1950-72, pres., 1959-67, chmn., 1967-72; dir. Dun & Bradstreet, Inc., Hart Schaffner & Marx, Centennial Ins. Co.; trustee Atlantic Mut. Ins. Company. Chmn., trustee American Coll. Life Underwriters, C.L.U., 1934. Mem. Nat. Indsl. Conf. Bd. Member of adv. bd. Salvation Army. Presbyn. (trustee United Presbyn. Found.). Clubs: Links, River (N.Y.C.); Wee Burn Country (Darien). Home: Darien CT Died Feb. 6, 1972; buried Spring Grove Cemetery, Darien CT

HULLINGER, EDWIN WARE, author, motion-picture producer, educator; b. Chicago, Ill., Aug. 13, 1893; s. Henry Church and Lucy Ellen (Ware) H.; student Occidental Coll., Los Angeles, Calif., 1911-13; A.B., U. of Kan., 1917; grad. work, Columbia U. Sch. of Journalism, 1917; D.Sc. Oratory (hon.), Curry Coll., 1963; m. Helen Jean Sawyer, Nov. 20, 1933; children—Cynthia Ware, Mary Martha, Diane, Virginia. Began on staff Los Angeles Tribune, 1913; reporter local papers, then with United Press, becoming fgn. corr., 1918-28 mem. faculty, dept. journalism N.Y.U., 1928, U. Kan., 1936-37; mgr. radio news commentator NBC, sta. KFI, 1930; writer, motion-picture producer and lecturer on international subjects. Senior information specialist, United States Department of agriculture, Washington, District of Columbia, 1939-41; liaison officer Office of War Information and U.S. Dept. Agr., Washington D.C., 1942; asst. dir. Foreign Broadcast Intelligence Service, FCC, 1943-45; production manager, pres. Hullinger Prodns., 1945-55; pres., exec. producer Hullinger

Productions, Inc., 1955-58; professor journalism University of Miami, 1958-61; professor journalism Boston U., 1961-64; pres. Hullinger-White Prodns., Brookline, Mass., 1963-65, Hullinger Productions, Boston and Miami, 1965-68; public relations consultant National Headquarters Civil Air Patrol, Washington, 1949-50. Mem. Sigma Delta Chi, Phi Eta. Clubs: Authors, National Press. Republican. Conglist. Mason. Author: The Reforging of Russia, 1925; The New Facist State, 1928; Plowing Through, 1940; (with others) Flesh Alley (novel), 1931. Produced motion picture, The Private Life of Mussolini, 1938, also a series of motion pictures entitled Makers of Destiny, 1946-47; Washington Report series for Television, 1948, A Day in Congress, 1950, Report From Washington, 1951; What Do You Think (TV series), 1955; Drew Pearson's, Washington Merry-Go-Round (TV series), 1956-57; 12 shows on American life for French TV, 1957. Home: Miami FL Died Oct. 26, 1968.

HULME, EDWARD MASLIN, prof. emeritus; b. London, Eng., Sept. 17, 1868; s. Thomas and Annie Louise (Farmer) H.; B.A., Stanford, 1897; grad. study, Harvard, 1900-01; M.A., Cornell U., 1902; m. Gertrude May Jenkins, June 20, 1906; children—Mary Louise, Kenneth Plowden, Gertrude Ellen. Teacher of lit. and history, high sch., Portland, Ore., 1897-1900; prof. history, 1902-21, dean Coll. of Letters and Science, 1917-21, U. of Ida.; actg. prof. European history, Stanford, winter quarter, 1918; prof. European history, summers, U. of Calif., 1918, U. of Chicago, 1919, U. of Ore., 1925, 26, 38, 39, 41, U. of Utah, 1929, 35, 36, U. of Southern Calif., 1931, Duke University, 1933, New York University, 1934; University of Nevada, 1943; professor medieval history, Stanford, 1921-37; emeritus since 1937. Mem. Am. Hist. Assn., Kappa Sigma, Phi Beta Kappa. Author: Renaissance and Reformation, 1914; A History of the British People, 1924; The Middle Ages, 1929 and 38; Wandering in France, 1941; History and Its Neighbors, 1942. Home: 638 Channing Av., Palo Alto CA‡

HULSHIZER, STANFORD, musician, educator; b. Seward, Neb., Nov. 3, 1903; s. Roy Thomas and Blanche (Gribble) H.; student Kan. State U., 1920-22; Mus.B., Ill. Wesleyan University, 1924, Mus.M., 1938; m. to Emily Pearl Frazier, August 24, 1926; children—Stanford, Dale. Tchr., Robideaux High Sch., St. Joseph, Mo., 1924-25, Central High Sch., Tulsa, 1925-29; prof. music Drake U., 1929-67, head dept. music edn., 1933-67, dir. choral activities, 1933-64, dir. ann. Messiah performances, 1929-64, mus. dir. Night of Opera ann., 1943-67. Choirmaster, White Temple Meth. Ch., St. Joseph, Mo., 1924-25; music dir. Bapt. and Meth. chs., Tulsa, Okla., 1925-29; choirmaster University Christian Ch., Des Moines, 1929-47; dir. Za-Ga-Zig Shrine Chanters, Des Moines, 1943-64; condr. inaugural All-State High Sch. Chorus Festival, 1944 Ia. Centennial Chorus; adjudicator high sch. festival music. Mem. Music Educators Nat. Conf., Phi Mu Alpha Sinfonia, Phi Delta Theta, Pi Kappa Lambda, Pi Kappa Phi. Mason (Shriner). Home: Des Moines IA Died May 6, 1967; buried Masonic Cemetery, Des Moines IA

HULTEN, HERMAN H., clergyman; b. Hannibal, Mo., Oct. 7, 1874; s. Jacob and Harriet (Eby) H.; A.B., William Jewell Coll., Liberty, Mo., 1897; grad. Southern Bapt. Theol. Sem., Louisville, Ky., 1900; (D.D., Wake Forest Coll., N.C., 1907); m. Ollie S. Black, of Kansas City, Mo., Dec. 25, 1901. Ordained Bapt. ministry, 1897; pastor Shelbyville, Ind., 1900-4, Kansas City, Mo., 1904-6, Charlotte, N.C., 1906-12, 1st Ch., Oklahoma City, Okla., 1912-18; now oil producer. Address: Oklahoma City OK‡

HULVEY, OTEY CRAWFORD, educator; b. Staunton, Va., Apr. 18, 1873; s. John Christian and Elizabeth Margaret (Houff) H.; Staunton Mil. Acad., 1886-89, Augusta Mil. Acad., Ft. Defiance, Va., 1889-92, U. of Va., 1893-95; m. Geneva Lee Sillings, June 5, 1895; children—Helen Elizabeth (Mrs. Arthur M. Barnes), Otey Crawford (dec.), Lillian Crawford (dec.), Mary Louise, Marjorie Virginia. Mayor of Mt. Crawford, Va., 1895-97; comdt. and prof. chemistry, Ky. Mil. Inst., Lyndon, 1897-98; pres. Hay Long Coll., Mt. Pleasant, Tenn., and editor, Alkahest Magazine, Atlanta, Ga., 1898-99; prin. Everts High Sch., Circleville, O., 1899-1902; founder 1902, pres. until 1915. Tenn. Mil. Inst., Sweetwater; pres. Columbia (Tenn.) Mil. Acad., 1915-19; supt. North Shore Mil. Acad., Evanston, Ill., 1928-30; founder, 1930, and since pres. Harris Mil. Inst., Roanoke, Va. Mem. Tenn. Nat. Guard, 1912-17; engaged in World War welfare work, 1917-18. Sec.-treas. Assn. Mil. Colls. and Schs. of U.S., 1913-18. Presbyn. Mason (32 deg.), Elk. Clubs: Century, Lions. Author of Oil Shales of Colorado, Coastal Salt Domes, The Making of a Great Race (lecture), Contbr. various ednl. articles. Address: Harris Military Institute, Roanoke VA‡

HUMASON, HARRY BYRD, banker; b. Dodge Center, Minn., Feb. 4, 1875; s. Charles James and Caroline Amanda (Tattersall) H.; ed. pub. sch.; m. Mary Emgene Cowles, Oct. 17, 1900; 1 son, Sherman Cowles. Began with Bank of Minn., 1890; with Northern Exch. Bank which merged with Am. Exchange Bank, 1896, now Am. National Bank of St. Paul; successively asst. cashier, 1896-1912, cashier, 1912-25, v.p., 1925-33, exec. v.p., 1933-39, and pres. American National Bank of St. Paul, 1939-48, executive advisor, since 1948, also director; trustee Minneapolis Mutual Life Insurance Co., St. Paul. Director Booth Memorial Hosp., St. Paul Foundation. Republican. Episcopalian. Mason (Shriner). Clubs: St. Paul Athletic, Minnesota, Rotary. Contbr. on banking topics. Office: The American National Bank, St Paul MN‡

HUMASON, M. L., astronomer; b. 1891; Ph.D. (hon.), Lund U., Sweden. Asst. astronomer Mt. Wilson Obs., 1919-48, asst. astronomer, sec. Mt. Wilson and Palomar obs., 1948-54, astronomer and sec., 1954-57. Mem. Am. Astron. Soc., Astron. Soc. Pacific; asso. mem. Royal Astron. Soc. Address: Mendocino CA Died June 18, 1972; interred Mountain View Mausoleum, Altadena CA

HUMBER, ROBERT LEE, lawyer; b. Greenville, N.C., May 30, 1898; s. Robert Lee and Lena Clyde (Davis) H.; A.B., Wake Forest, 1918, LL.B., Rhodes scholar from N.C., Oxford (Eng.) U., 1923; 1921, LL.D., 1949, M.A., Harvard, 1926; B. Litt. Am. field service fellow, U. of Paris, 1926-28; LL.D., U. N.C., 1958; H.H.D., Duke, 1967; m. Lucie Berthier, Oct. 16, 1929; children—Marcel Berthier, John Leslie. Admitted to N.C. bar, 1920; tutor dept. of govt. history and economics Harvard, 1919-20; lawyer and bus. exec., Paris, France, 1930-40. Founded at Davis Island, N.C., Dec. 1940, Movement for World Federation whose principles and objectives were embodied in a resolution, approving World Federation, that has been passed by 16 State Legislatures of U.S. Rep. Southern Council on Internat. Relations, UN Orgnl. Conf., San Francisco 1945. Co-founder, United World Federalists, 1947, v.p., 1947-50, mem. nat. exec. council, 1947-49, mem. exec. council N.C. br., 1949-70, pres. N.C. br., 1960-66; mem. adv. bd. Am. Freedom Assn., 1953-66, bd. dirs., 1966-70 v.p. N.C. Bapt. State Conv., 1947; mem. N.C. Gov.'s Study Com. in Vocational Rehab., 1967-69; state chmn. UN Day, 1969; mem. Pitt County Good Neighbor Council, 1969-70, N.C. Council on Prevention of Crime and Delinquency, 1968-69; trustee, Meredity Coll., 1947-50; trustee Wake Forest Coll., 1951-54, 59-60, pres. bd., chmn. exec. com., 1960, hon. life trustee, 1969-70; chmn. N.C. Art Commn., 1951-60; chmn. N.C. Arts Council, 1964-67; pres. N.C. Mus. Art Found., 1969-70; mem. N.C. Mus. Bldg. Commn., 1967-70; pres. Tar River Basin Assn., 1965-70; bd. dirs. Am. and Fgn. Christian Union, Inc., 1941-70, Pitt County chpt. A.R.C., 1957-70; mem. adv. bd. Raleigh Historic Sites Found., 1966-68; mem. cultural and lit. centennial adv. com. N.C. State Coll., 1961-62; mem. Pitt. County Devel. Commn., 1959-70, N.C. Rhodes Scholarship Com., 1946-60, 63, Greenville Com. of 100, N.C. Commn. on Interstate Cooperation, 1959-60; bd. dirs. Pitt County United Fund, 1965-70, pres., 1964-65; co-chmn. Greenville Citizens Awareness Com., 1970; mem. cultural arts adv. council N.C. Dept. Pub. Instrn., 1970; mem. Sir Walter Raleigh Commn., 1947-70, chmn. exec. com., 1952-60; mem. exec. com. N.C. Council on World Affairs, 1966; mem. adv. com. N.C. State Library-Community Project, 1958-60, Topographic Mapping of N.C., 1963; mem. com. on art, lit. and music N.C. Planning Bd., 1944; mem. Adv. Com. on Hwy. Safety, 1950; past chmn. Prudential Com. Am. Ch. in Paris; mem. Edenton Hist. Commn., chmn., 1962-70; bd. dirs. Coastal Plains Planning and Devel. Commn., 1962-65, 69-70 chmn., 1962-64; chmn. bd. trustees N.C. Mus. Art, 1961-70; mem. N.C. Conservatory Com., 1962-63, N.C. State Capital Planning Commn., 1962-65, Heritage Sq. Commn., 1962-67; trustee N.C. Symphony; 1955-70, mem. exec. com., 1963-65, 67-70; mem. Tryon Palace Commn., 1956-70; trustee Pitt County Indsl. Edn. Center, 1963-64; chmn. bd. Pitt Tech. Inst., 1964-70. Mem. N.C. Senate, 1959-64. as 2d lt., F.A., U.S. Army, 1918. Recipient World Govt. News medal for most outstanding service by an individual to World Fedn., 1948, Am. War Dads prize for greatest single contbn. toward world peace, 1948; certificate of merit Thomas Gilcrease Inst. Am. History and Art, 1955; Citizen of Month award for meritorious service N.C. Joint Council on Health and Citizenship, 1961; Salmagund: Art Achievement medal, 1966; Peace award Am. Freedom Assn., 1967; N.C. award for public service, 1968. Mem. Am., N.C., Pitt County bar assns., Am. Judicature Soc., Am. Soc. Internat. Law, Am. Acad. Polit. and Social Sci., Acad. Polit. Sci. (life), Nat. Forensic League (hon.), N.C. Farm Bur., Internat. Platform Assn., Am. Legion, Greenville C. of C. and Mchts. Assn., N.C. Music Soc., East Carolina U. Alumni Assn. (life), Pitt County Hist. Soc. (pres. 1964-68), East Carolina Art Soc. (dir. 1956-64), N.C. Soc. for Preservation Antiquities (life), Nat. Trust for Historic Preservation, Pitt County Execs. Club (pres. 1961-63), N.C. Art Soc. (dir. 1945-70, exec. com. 1947-61, chmn. 1949-61, pres. 1955-61; certificate of merit and achievement 1956 N.C. Trustees Assn. Community Edn. Instns. (pres. 1968-70), N.C. Lit. and Hist. Assn. (pres. 1950-51), Roanoke Island Hist. Assn. (dir. 1955-61, chmn. 1955-59), Phi Beta Kappa, Omicron Delta Kappa, Sigma Phi Epsilon, Phi Delta Phi, Epsilon Pi Tau, Sigma Pi Alpha. Democrat. Baptist. Clubs: Greenville Music; Rotary; Watauga (Raleigh, N.C.); Harvard, Century Assn., Salmagundi (N.Y.C.); American resolution: The Declaration of Greenville NC Died Nov. 10, 1970; buried Cherry Hill Cemetery, Greenville NC

HUME, DAVID, lawyer; b. Eagle Pass, Tex., Oct. 2, 1915; s. David E. and Lupita (James) H.; B.A., U. Tex., 1937; student Temple U. Sch. Law, 1939-41; LL.B. with honors, So. Meth. U. Sch. Law, 1939-41; LL.B. with honors, So. Meth. U., 1946; m. F. Arlee Eaton, Aug. 28, 1943 (div.); children—David III, Stephen; m. 2d, Margaret Williams, June 19, 1966; 1 dau., Marge Ann. Admitted to Tex. bar, 1946, D.C., Md. bars, 1954, U.S. Supreme Ct., 1948, also Ct. Mil. Justice, FCC, ICC; trial atty. U.S. Dept. Justice, 1947, spl. asst. to atty. gen. U.S., 1948; with firm Steptoe & Johnson, Washington, 1954-58; mem. firm Hume & Stewart, Washington, 1958-65, Hume & Hume, Eagle Pass, Tex., 1965-72. Hon. cons. to Consulate of Republic of Mex., 1970. Rep. Am. Bar Assn., 12th Inter-Am. Bar Assn. conv. Bogota, Colombia, 1961. Mem. Md. Bd. Natural Resources. Chmn. Democratic Party So. Md., 1958, treas., 1958-60; mem. Dem. Nat. Adv. Council, 1958-60; candidate for Gov. Md., 1962. Bd. dirs. Balt. Civic Opera. Served with Submarine Service, USNR, World War II, Korean War; capt. Res. Decorated Bronze Star. Mem. Am., Inter-Am., Md. bar assns., Tex. Trial Lawyers Assn., State Bar Texas, Border Bar Assn. (dir.), Judge Adv. Assn. Am. Vets. Com., Am. Legion, Navy League, S.A.R., Md. Hist. Soc., Izaak Walton League. Clubs: Terrapin (U. Md.); Jefferson Island (St. Mary's County, Md.); Marlboro Hunt (Prince George's County, Md.); Taylor's Landing Rod and Gun (Washington County, Md.); Hawthorne Country (Charles County, Md.). Author numerous articles on conservation, govt. and agrarian reform, Latin Am. Home: Eagle Pass TX Died Oct. 7, 1972.

HUME, H. HAROLD, dean of agr.; b. Russell, Ont., Can., June 13, 1875; s. John and Esther (McIntyre) H.; B.S. in Agr., Iowa State Coll., 1899; M.S.A., 1901; hon. D.Sc., Clemson Coll., S.C., 1937; m. Emily Georgia Norman, Dec. 24, 1900; children—Edward Grisdale, Harold Norman. Came to U.S., 1898, naturalized, 1912. Asst. botanist, Iowa State Coll., 1898-99; head dept. botany and horticulture Fla. Agrl. Coll. and Fla. Expt. Station, 1899-1904; head dept. horticulture, N.C. State Dept. Agr., N.C. State Coll. and Expt. Station, 1904-06; v.p. and sec., Glen Saint Mary Nurseries Co., Glen Saint Mary, Fla., 1906-29, chairman board since 1929; pres. E. O. Painter Fertilizer Co., Jacksonville, Fla., 1918-29; inspector Fla. State Plant Bd., 1929-31; asst. dir. research, Fla. Agr. Expt. Station, and asst. dean Coll. of Agr., U. of Fla., 1931-38; dean Coll. of Agr., University of Florida since 1938. Provost for Agriculture. Awarded Jackson Dawson Memorial medal by Mass. Hort. Society, 1935; Achievement medal, Florida Academy Science, 1936; Arthur Hoyt Scott Garden Award, 1944. President Fla. State Hort. Soc., 1910-22. Mem. Phi Kappa Phi, Alpha Zeta, Phi Gamma Delta, Phi Sigma, Sigma Xi. Presbyterian. Author: Citrus Fruits and Their Culture, 1904; The Pecan and Its Culture, 1906; Cultivation of Citrus Fruits, 1926; Gardening in the Lower South, 1929; Azaleas and Camellias, 1931; Camellias in America, 1946; Azaleas, Kinds and Culture, 1947. Contbr. numerous articles to agrl. jours.; author agrl. bulletins; speaker at hort. meetings. Address: College of Agriculture, Univ. of Florida, Gainesville FL‡

HUMPHREY, CAROLINE LOUISE, b. Cambridge, Mass., Jan. 16, 1875; d. David and Caroline Jackson (Hall) H.; grad. Cambridge Latin Sch., 1894; A.B., Radcliffe Coll., 1898. Acting dean, Radcliffe Coll., 1913-14; asst. pres. Women's Ednl. and Industrial Union, Boston, July 1, 1917-19; exec. sec. Bradford (Mass.) Acad., 1919-23. Trustee Radcliffe Coll. Mem. Assn. Collegiate Alumnae (pres. 1914-17), Radcliffe Alumnae Assn. (pres. 1914-17), Phi Beta Kappa (hon.). Republican. Unitarian. Club: Boston College (pres. 1908-10). Address: Hotel Beaconsfield, Brookline MA‡

HUMPHREY, CHARLES FREDERICK, JR., army officer; b. Washington, D.C., Aug. 11, 1876; s. Charles Frederick and Juanita DaCosta (Foster) H.; ed. in pub. schs.; grad. Sch. of the Line, 1921, Gen. Staff Sch., 1922, Army War Coll., 1923; m. Helen Kingsbury, Sept. 16, 1903; 1 dau., Helen Elizabeth. Entered U.S. Army as 2d lt. inf., July 20, 1898; advanced through grades to brig. gen., Aug. 9, 1935; served as col. inf., Nat. Army, A.E.F., World War. 1917-19; mem. Gen. Staff Corps, 1923-27, and 1929-33; retired Mar. 31, 1940. Episcopalian. Home: San Antonio TX Died Jan. 1968.

HUMPHREY, EVAN H., army officer; b. Calif., Mar. 5, 1875; grad. U.S. Military Acad., 1899; commd. 2d lt. Cavalry, 1899; advanced through grades to brig. gen., Feb. 7, 1935; retired Mar. 31, 1939. Address: 136 Harrigan Court, San Antonio TX‡

HUMPHREY, GEORGE MAGOFFIN, steel corp. executive; b. Cheboygan, Mich., Mar. 8, 1890; s. Watts S. and Caroline (Magoffin) H.; LL.B., U. of Mich., 1912; m. Pamela Stark, Jan. 15, 1913; children—Pamela (Mrs. Royal Firman, Jr.), Gilbert Watts, Caroline (Mrs. John G. Butler), George M. (dec.). Practiced law with Humphrey, Grant & Humphrey, Saginaw, 1911-18; became gen. atty. The M. A. Hanna Co., steel mfrs.,

Cleveland, O., 1918, became pres., 1929, chmn. bd., 1952, hon. chmn. bd., 1957-70, dir. subsidiary affiliated cos.; chmn. 1957-61, mem. executive committee, dir. Nat. Steel Corp., 1957-70, chmn. of the finance committee, 1964-70; dir., mem. exec. com., Consolidation Coal Co.; sec. Treasury of United States, 1953-57. Chmn. indsl. adv. com. Econ. Coop. Adminstrn., 1948-49. Life mem. corp. Mass. Inst. Tech. Republican. Clubs: Union. Tavern, Chagrin Valley Hunt, Kirtland Country, Fifty (Cleveland); Links, The Brook, Pinnacle (N.Y.C.); Duquesne (Pitts.); Detroit; Glen Arven Country (Thomasville, Ga.); Kitchi Gammi (Diluth, Minn.); Rolling Rock (Pa.). Home: Mentor OH Died Jan. 20, 1970.

HUMPHREY, GEORGE THOMAS, mfg. co. exec.; b. Dallas, Dec. 23, 1917; s. George T. and Pearl (Hamilton) H.; student U. Tex., 1936-39, U. Pitts., 1955; m. Jane Wolverton, Apr. 27, 1940; children—Judith (Mrs. James Bailey), George Thomas III, Carolyn (Mrs. William H. Avery), Gretchen, Nancy, and Jill. Began career as sales trainee Timken Roller Bearing Co., Dallas, 1939-40, asst. to br. mgr., then asst. gen. mgr., Canton, O., 1951-57, gen. mgr., 1957-64; exec. asst. to pres. automotive divs. Rockwell-Standard Corp., 1964-65, v.p. marketing, 1965-66, v.p., general mgr. automotive products divs., 1966-67, pres. aircraft div., Pitts., 1967-69; sr. v.p. Beech Aircraft Corp., Wichita, Kan., 1969-73, also dir.; dir. B.C. Bearing Engring. Ltd. Mem. Automotive Service Industry Assn. (bd. dirs. 1964-67), Bearing Distbrs. Assn. (vice chmn. 1963-64), Am. Mining Congress (bd. govs. 1963-64), Soc. Automotive Engrs. Clubs: Detroit Athletic; Orchard Lake (Mich.) Country; Economic (Detroit); Duquesne (Pitts.); Wichita Country (Kan.). Home: Wichita KS Died Jan. 17, 1973.

HUMPHREY, WALTER R., editor; born Trenton, Mo., Mar. 13, 1904; s. Walter Glenn and Pearl Rosamond (Hedges) H.; A.B., Univ. of Colo., 1926; m. Dorothea Griffith, Oct. 26, 1931; children—Carole, Claire, Jane. Reporter, asst. city editor Ft. Worth (Tex.) Press, 1926-29; editor Temple (Tex.) Daily Telegram, 1929-45; editor Ft. Worth Press, 1945-69; pres. Ft. Worth Press Co. Dir. S.W. Expn. and Fat. Stock Show, Brazos River Authority, 1941-69. Pres., Ft. Worth Area Council Chs., 1964-65. Recipient Lambda Chi Alpha Order of Merit; Ft. Worth Salesman of Year, Sales and Marketing Execs., 1963; National Editorial Association award (2) for community service as the editor of Temple Telegram; Tex. State Fair award (3) for gen. excellence of Temple Telegram. Founder, Save the Soil and Save Texas, soil conservation awards program, 1946. Fellow Sigma Delta Chi (nat. pres. 1933-34, chmn. exec. council 1934-35); mem. Soil Conservation Soc. of Am. (exec. council 1948-51), Am. Soc. Newspaper Editors, Tex. Press Assn. (pres. 1946-47), Texas Newspaper Seminars (chmn.), Round Table Internat. (pres. 1955), Tex. U.P.I. Editors Assn. (pres. 1963), Lambda Chi Alpha. Presbyn. (pres. assembly Men's Council Presbyn. Ch., 1955, mem. bd. Christian edn., 1954-57). Club: Lions (dist. gov. 1934-35, temple pres., 1932-35), Fort Worth. Home: Fort Worth TX Died Aug. 24, 1971; buried Temple TX

HUMPHREYS, ALBERT EDMUND, business exec.; b. Duluth, Minn., Oct. 18, 1893; s. Albert Edmund and Alice (Boyd) H.; student Lawrenceville Acad., Yale U. Sci. Sch., 1912-15; m. Ruth Boettcher, May 3, 1919;children—Ruth (Mrs. David R. C. Brown), Charline Boettcher (Mrs. Vic E. Breeden). Began work as a field executive oil industry, 1915-32; v.p., dir. Humphreys Investment Co., 1928-68, Humphreys Engring Co., 1958-68; pres. Humphreys Mining Company, 1958-68; pres. dir. Humphreys Gold Corp., 1932-68; dir. Ideal Cement Company, Denver National Bank, Potash Company of America. Served with flying service USMC, World War I. Decorated D.S.C. Mem. Am. Inst. Mining and Metall. Engrs., C. of C. Clubs: Yale (N.Y.C.); Denver, Denver Athletic, Denver Denver CO Died Apr. 7, 1968; buried Denver CO

HUMPHREYS, RICHARD F(RANKLIN), physicist, college president; born in Greenville, Ohio, May 16, 1911; son of Robert Thomas and Tunia Daisy (Cunningham) H.; A.B., DePauw University, 1933; M.A., Syracuse U., 1936; Ph.D., Yale, 1939. Instr. physics Syracuse (N.Y.) U., 1939-40; instr. Yale, 1940-42, asst. prof., 1942-47, asso. prof., 1947-49, acting dir. Sloan Lab., 1942-45; cons. physicist New Haven Clock Co., 1943-45; physicist in sonar Bur. Ships, 1945; asst. chmn. physics Armour Research Found., Chicago, 1949-51, chmn., 1951-56, asst. dir., 1956-59, v.p. 1959-61; pres. The Cooper Union, 1961-68. Bd. dirs. Washington Sq. Assn., Josiah Macy Jr. Found., Asso. Hosp. Service N.Y.; trustee Mills Coll. Edn. Mem. Am. Phys. Soc., A.A.A.S., Sigma Xi. Author: First Principles of Atomic Physics (with E. R. Beringer), 1950; also sci. papers. Home: New York City NY Died Aug. 1968.

HUMPHREYS, T(HOMAS) HADDEN, judge; b. Upshur Co., Tex., Sept. 20, 1865; s. John Thomas and Belle (Aldridge) H.; lit. course U. of Ark.; student law U. of Va. (non-grad.); m. Beulah C. Bolefuhr, Sept. 10, 1890 (died Apr. 20, 1926). Practiced in Ft. Smith and Fayetteville, Ark.; mem. Ark. Ho. of Rep., 1899-1901 (speaker 1901); chancellor 11th Dist. of Ark., 1903-16; apptd. justice Supreme Court of Ark., Nov. 15, 1916; elected to same for terms, 1918-42; retired under Retirement Act of 1941, on Jan. 1, 1943, after serving on Supreme bench over 26 years. Was member military dept. Univ. of Ark. 4 yrs., advancing to adj. of battalion. Democrat. Presbyterian. Mem. Am. Bar Assn., State Bar Assn. of Ark., Kappa Sigma. Home: 1424 Battery St., Little Rock AR*‡

HUMPHREYS, WALTER, sec.-treas. Nat. Assn. of Wool Mfrs.; b. Dorchester, Boston, Mass., July 14, 1874; s. Dexter and Maria Townsend (Davis) H.; desc. Jonas Humphreys, the colonist, 1634; B.S. in Mech. Engring., Mass. Inst. Tech., 1897; m. Victoire Elizabeth Casgrain, July 18, 1906; children—James, George Casgrain, Marie Van Dyke, Henry Dexter. With various engring. firms until 1899; registrar Mass. Inst. Tech., 1902-22, asso. prof. 1920-22, sec. Society of Arts (Mass. Inst. Tech.), 1916-22, alumni term mem. corp., 1923-28, life mem. and sec. since 1929. Sec.-treas. Nat. Assn. of Wool Mfrs., and editor of its bull. since 1922; treas. Associated Wool Industries, 1935-39. Sec. Code Authority Wool Textile Industry, 1934-35. Chmn. Brookline Sch. Com., 1916-25; trustee Brookline Public Library, 1916-50, sec., 1916-38, chmn. 1941-46; dir., 1917, dir., sec. since 1918, Harvard Co-operative Soc.; trustee Hahnemann Hospital, Boston since 1939 (pres. since 1949), Boston Museum of Fine Arts, 1950. Former pres. Am. Assn. Collegiate Registrars; ex-treas. Assn. Alumni Secretaries; mem. Alumni Assn. Mass. Inst. Tech., (sec.-treas. 1906-23), hon. mem. alumni council, pres. University Club (Boston) 1932-33. Brookline Hist. Soc. Delta Kappa Epsilon. Unitarian. Republican. Clubs: Faculty (Mass. Inst. Tech.); Brookline Thursday, Am. Newcomen, Soc. Home: 249 Clinton Rd., Brookline Mass. Office: 80 Federal St., Boston MA‡

HUMPHRIES (GEORGE) ROLFE, educator, writer; b. Phila., Nov. 20, 1894; s. John Henry and Florence (Yost) H.; student Stanford, 1912-13; A.B., cum laude, Amherst Coll., 1915, M.A. (hon.), 1950; m. Dr. Helen Ward Spencer, June 26, 1925; 1 son, John, III (dec.). Tchr., athletic coach Potter Sch. Boys, San Francisco, 1914-23; tchr. Latin, Woodmere Acad., 1925-57; tchr. Latin, Hunter College, N.Y.C., 1957; lecturer in English Amherst Coll. Mass., 1957-65, professor emeritus, 1965-69; vis. Walker-Ames prof. English, U. Washington, 1966; mem. of summer faculty University New Hampshire Writers' Conf., Ind. U. Writers' Conf., Writers' Conf. Rocky Mountains (U. Colo.), Colo. State Coll. Education. Served as 1st lt., U.S. Army, 1917-18. Guggenheim fellow creative writing, 1938-39; received Shelley Meml. award in poetry, 1946; Borestone Mountain Poetry award, 1956. Recipient $5000 fellowship, Acad. of American Poets, 1955. Mem. Nat. Inst. Arts and Letters, Theta Xi. Author (verse); Europa and Other Poems and Sonnets, 1929; Out of the Jewel, 1942; The Summer Landscape, 1945; Forbid Thy Ravens, 1947; The Wind of Time, 1949; Poems, Collected and New, 1954; Green Armor on Green Ground, 1956; Nine Thorny Thickets, 1969; Coat on a Stick, 1969; Translator: Poet in New York (by Garcia Lorca), 1940; The Aeneid of Virgil, 1951; Gypsy Ballads (Garcia Lorca), 1953; Ovid's Metamorphoses, 1955; Ovid's Art of Love, 1957; Satires of Juvenal, 1958; Selected Epigrams of Martial, 1963; Collected Poems, 1965; Lucretius' The Way Things Are, 1968. Editor: Wolfville Yarns of Alfred Henry Lewis, 1968. Home: Woodside CA Died Apr. 22, 1969; buried Golden Gate National Cemetery, San Bruno CA

HUNDLEY, JOHN ROBINSON, JR., steel co. exec.; b. St. Louis, Jan. 29, 1917; s. John Robinson and Emily (Shewell) H.; B.Sc. in Bus. Adminstrn., Washington U., St. Louis, 1939; m. Shirley Conrad, May 2, 1941; children—John Robinson III, Nancy Conrad (now Mrs. William F. Hecker), Stephen Thomas. Asst. v.p. Stouffer Corp., 1945-47; personnel dir. Owens-Ill. Glass Co., 1939-42; dir. indsl. relations Granite City Steel Co. (Ill.), 1947-63, v.p., 1963-72; dir. Cemrel, Inc. Mem. Ill. Gov.'s Com. on Unemployment, 1961; pub. mem. Ill. Commn. Aged and Aging, 1958-62; adv. com. Mo. Manpower Tng. and Devel. Act, 1962-72; chmn. Civil Service Commn. Met. Sewer Dist. St. Louis and St. Louis County; mem. citizens adv. com. Ill. State Bd. Higher Edn. chmn. Tri Cities United Fund., 1964-65. Bd. dirs. Washington U., 1958-61, Works Opportunities Unltd.; adv. bd. So. Ill. U. Served to col. USAAF, World War II. Decorated Air medal; recipient spl. merit award for outstanding community service St. Louis Indsl. Relations Club, 1959. Mem. Am. Iron and Steel Inst., Indsl. Relations Club St. Louis (past pres.), Ill. C. of C., Newcomen Soc. Presbyn. (elder). Clubs: Mo. Athletic, Old Warson Country. Home: St Louis MO Died Apr. 8, 1972.

HUNGERFORD, CHARLES WILLIAM, plant pathologist; b. Fillmore County, Minn., Feb. 26, 1885; s. Judson Belee and Alice Helen (Moore) H.; B.S., Upper Ia. U., 1910; M.S., U. of Wis., 1915, Ph.D., 1925; m. Ruth Edna Patridge, June 11, 1913; children—Kenneth, Eugene, Doris Olive, Charles Roger. Prin. high. sch., Houston, Minn., 1910-11; supt. schs. same, 1911-13; asst. in botany, U. of Wis., 1913-14, asst. plant pathologist, 1914; scientific asst., cereal investigations, U.S. Dept. Agr., 1915-17, asst. pathologist, 1917-19; prof. plant pathology, U. of Ida., from 1919, asst. dean of Coll. Agr., 1927-35; vice-dir. Agrl. Expt. Station, 1927-47; also dean Graduate School 1931-51. Recipient award for work in hybridization of beans Bean Improvement Coop. Fellow A.A.A.S.; mem. Am. Phytopathol. Soc., Sigma Xi, Alpha Zeta. Republican. Methodist. Kiwanian. Contbr. articles on plant Moscow ID Died Nov. 6, 1971; buried Moscow Cemetery, Moscow ID

HUNKELER, EDWARD J(OSEPH), archibishop; b. Medicine Lodge, Kan., Jan. 1, 1894; s. Anton and Philomena (Durst) H.; grad. Holy Trinity Parochial Sch., 1906; student Dayton (O.) U., 1907; attended Pontifical Coll. Josephinum, Columbus, O., 1907-19; A.B., D.D., LL.D. (honorary), St. Benedict's College, 1953; Doctor of Laws, Creighton University, 1957. Ordained priest Roman Catholic Ch., 1919; served in the Diocese of Omaha as pastor, Sts. Philip and James ch., Wynot P.O., Neb., 1919-27, Blessed Sacrament ch., Omaha, 1927-36, St. Cecillia's Cathedral, Omaha, 1936-45; elevated to rank of Rt. Rev. Monsignor, 1937; bishop of Grand Island, Nebraska, 1945-51; bishop of Kansas City, Kan., 1951-52, archbishop of Kansas City, 1952-70. Served in many diocesan offices; synodal examiner, synodal judge, bd. Cath. charities, moderator of U.S.O., diocesan consultor, vicar Kansas City KS Died Oct. 1, 1970; buried Mt. Calvary Cemetery, Kansas City KS

HUNNICUTT, WARREN TOWERS, clergyman; b. Franklin County, Ga., Sept. 19, 1862; s. Warren Towers and Fannie M. (Ash) H.; ed. Emory U. (non-grad.); D.D., U. of Ga., 1924; m. Beulah Maggie Watkins, Dec. 27, 1893; children—Warren Paul, William Allen, Theodosia (Mrs. J. P. Bowen), Willard Towers. Ordained ministry M.E. Ch., S., 1894; pastor successively Payne Memorial Ch., Atlanta, Sam Jones Memorial Ch., Cartersville, Cedartown First Ch., St. Johns Ch., Atlanta, 1921-23 (all of Ga.); missionary sec. North Ga. Conf., 1924-27; presiding elder South Atlantic dist., 1928-29; became presiding elder Griffin Dist. of N. Ga. Conf., 1931; pastor Inman Park, Atlanta, Ga., 1930-31, First Ch., Elberton, Ga., 1931-32; now pastor Martha Brown Memorial Methodist Ch., Atlanta. Chmn. bd. trustees Wesleyan Christian Advocate; trustee Reinhardt Coll. Democrat. Mason, Odd Fellow, K.P. Home: 307 W. Cleveland Av., Atlanta GA‡

HUNT, EVERT MERLE, investment banker; b. Friend, Neb., Aug. 27, 1907; s. Edgar and Minnie (Moody) H.; A.B., U. Neb., 1928, LL.B., 1930; m. Margery Alter Hunt, Nov. 14, 1931; 1 dau., Margot Alter. With First Trust Co., Lincoln, Neb., 1928-61, v.p., 1950-61; pres. First Neb. Securities, Inc., 1961-68, chmn. bd., 1968-72; dir. Utah Gas Service Co. Served to lt. USNR, 1943-46. Admitted to Neb. bar. Mem. Neb. Bar Assn., N.Y. Stock Exchange, Investment Bankers Assn. Am., Nat. Securities Traders Assn., Neb. Investment Bankers Assn. (past pres.), Am. Legion, Lincoln C. of C. Sigma Nu. Elk. Clubs: Lincoln Univ.; Lincoln Country. Home: Lincoln NE Died 1972.

HUNT, FREDERICK VINTON, prof. applied physics, Harvard; born Barnesville, Ohio, February 15, 1905; s. Fred and Ella (Shipley) H.; B.A., Ohio State U., 1924, B.E.E., 1925, Master of Arts Harvard University, 1928, Ph.D., 1934, S.D. (hon.), 1945; married Katharine Buckingham, November 25, 1932; children—Thomas Kintzing. Graduate assistant physics, Ohio State University, 1924-25; assistant in physics, Harvard, 1927, 1928-29, instr., 1929-34, instr. physics and communication engring., 1934-37; tutor in div. physical sciences, 1931-38, asst. prof. physics and communication engring., 1937-40, asso. prof. 1940-46; Gordon McKay prof. applied physics, 1946-70, also Rumford prof. physics, 1953-70; director Underwater Sound Lab., 1942-46; chmn. Dept. Engring. Sci. and Applied Physics, 1946-49. Awarded Presdl. Medal Merit, 1947; Emile Berliner Award, 1954, Publs. award, 1956, John H. Potts medal, 1965 (all Audio Engring. Soc.); Pioneers Underwater Acoustics medal, 1965, Gold medal, 1969 (all Acoustical Society of America. Fellow of American Academy of Arts and Scis., Acoustical Society Am. (exec. council, 1938-41, editorial bd. 1940-45, pres. 1951-52), American Physical Society, Institute of Radio Engineers; Phi Beta Kappa, Tau Beta Pi, Sigma Xi, Eta Kappa Nu, Sigma Nu. Club: Cosmos (Washington). Author: Electroacoustics; also research papers on acoustics and applied electronics. Home: LaJolla CA Died Apr. 20, 1972.

HUNT, JAMES STONE, land developer; b. Detroit, Dec. 23, 1897; s. Charles F. and Ina F. (Simpson) H.; student Mich. Mil. Acad., 1913-16; Detroit Coll. Law, 1923-24; LL.D. (hon.), U. Miami (Fla.) 1962; m. Bessie C. Bidigare, May 7, 1924; children—James Stone, John Patrick. Automobile dealer, Detroit, 1924-45; chmn. bd. Coral Ridge Properties, developer, Ft. Lauderdale, Fla.; mng. dir. Royal Amsterdam N.V.; chmn. bd. Bank of Commerce, Ft. Lauderdale, 1962-72, Bank. of Fla., Ft. Lauderdale, 1963-72, also Atlantic Bond and Mortgage Co., Financial Life Ins. Co., Intercoastal Dredging Co., Financial Fire & Casualty Co., Royal Continental

Hotels Corp.; dir. Alleghany Corp. (N.Y.C.), N.Y. Worlds Fair 1964-65 Corp., Investors Diversified Services (Mpls.), N.Y. Central R.R., N.Y.C. Commnr. Detroit Street Ry., 1930; price stabilizer for Pacific, 1947; dir. Fla. Devel. Commn. Chmn. Broward dist. Boy Scouts Am. 1954-55; hon. mem. lay adv. bd. Holy Cross Hosp., Ft. Lauderdale. Served with British Flying Corps, 1916-21; as comdr. USCG, 1941-45; rear adm. (ret.) Res., 1959. Decorated Silver Star; Distinguished Flying Cross (Great Britain); Croix de Guerre (France); Order St. Stanislas, Order St. Anne (N. Russian Expdn.); recipient Citizens award Ft. Lauderdale Daily News, 1953. Mem. Fla. C. of C. (dir.), Coast Guard League (comdr. 1948), War Birds of Royal Air Force. Mason (32 deg., Shriner). Clubs: Metropolitan (Washington); Circumnavigators, N.Y. Athletic, Metropolitan (N.Y.C.); Coral Ridge Yacht, Coral Ridge Country (Ft. Lauderdale); Coral Harbour Yacht (dir.) (Nassau, Bahamas); Nautico, Bankers San Juan, P.R.). Home: Fort Lauderdale FL Died 1972.

HUNT, LEVI CLARENCE, clergyman, educator; b. Seitzland, York County, Pa., July 30, 1873; s. Levi Warner and Elizabeth (Nace) H.; A.B., Dickinson Coll., 1897, A.M., 1899 (D.D., 1916); B.D., Drew Theol. Sem., 1904; post-grad. work same, 1904-05, with lecture course, Columbia; m. Anna L. Frey, Sept. 6, 1905; 1 dau. (adopted), Dorothy Mackay Becker Naus. Teacher pub. schs., 1890-92; prof. mathematics, Albright Coll., Myerstown, Pa., 1898-1901; ordained United Evang. ministry, 1899; pastor Columbia, Pa., 1897-98, M.E. Ch., Centerport, L.I., N.Y., 1901-04, Grace Ch., Reading, Pa., 1905-09, Germantown, 1909-13, Bangor, 1913-16; pres. Albright Coll., 1915-23; pastor Bethany United Evangelical Ch., Allentown, Pa., 1923-26, First Ch., Reading, Pa., 1926-31, Kemble Park, Phila., Pa., 1931-34, Grace Ch., Schuylkill Haven, Pa., 1934-39, Lititz, Pa., 1939-45; Boyertown since 1945. Mem. Pa. State Ednl. Assn., Sigma Alpha Epsilon, Phi Beta Kappa. Mason. Address: Boyertown PA‡

HUNT, MABEL LEIGH, author; b. Coatesville, Ind., Nov. 1, 1892; d. Dr. Tighlman and Amanda E. (Harvey) Hunt; student Depauw U.; student Library Sch. Western Reserve U., 1923-24. Children's librarian and Rauh Memorial librarian Indianapolis Pub. Library, 1918-38. Awarded Ind. U. citation best children's book, 1956, 62. Author: Lucinda, 1934; The Boy Who Had No Birthday, 1935; Little Girl with Seven Names, 1936; Susan, Beware, 1937; Benjie's Hat, 1938; Corn-Belt Billy, 1938; Little Grey Gown, 1939; Michel's Island, 1940; Billy Button's Butter'd Biscuit, 1941; John of Pudding Lane, 1941; Have You Seen Tom Thumb?, 1942; Peter Piper's Pickled Peppers, 1942; The Peddler's Clock, 1943; Young Man of the House, 1944; Sibby Botherbox, 1945; Such a Kind World, 1946; Double Birthday Present, 1947; Matilda's Buttons, 1948; The Wonderful Baker, 1950; Better Known as Johnny Appleseed, 1950 (Graphic Arts selection children's books, 1945-50); The 69th Grandchild, 1951; Ladycake Farm, 1952; Singing Among Strangers, 1954; Miss Jellytot's Visit, 1955; Stars for Cristy, 1956; Tomorrow Will Be Bright, 1958; Cristy at Skippinghills, 1958; Cupola House, published 1961; Beggar's Daughter, 1963; others. Contributor of numerous articles, serials, poetry to anthologies, juvenile magazines, professional jours. Mem. Ind. Hist. Soc., Alpha Phi, Western Res. Alumni Assn., Theta Sigma Phi. Republican. Mem. Soc. of Friends. Clubs: Woman's Press of Indiana, Altrusa. Home: Indianapolis IN Died Sept. 3, 1971.

HUNT, MARION PALMER, clergyman; b. nr. Williamsburg, Mo., July 1, 1860; s. William Bearl and Jane Nicholson (Palmer) H.; student William Jewell Coll., Liberty, Mo., 1886; Southern Bapt. Theol. Sem., Louisville, Ky., 1894; D.D., Okla. Bapt. Coll., Blackwell, Okla., 1904; m. Effie Ann Newman, Oct. 26, 1886; children—Lillian Edna (Mrs. Arthur Pierce Bryant), Mary Ruth, Rogers Comer; also 4 died in infancy. Ordained ministry Bapt. Ch., 1885; pastor in Mo. until 1893, 22d and Walnut Street Ch., Louisville, Ky., 1894-1900, 1905-10, 1913-14, First Bapt. Ch., Fort Collins, Colo., 1911-13, First Bapt. Ch., Fayetteville, Ark., 1914-16, West Broadway Bapt. Ch., Louisville, Ky., 1917-21, later of 18th St. Baptist Ch.; now retired. Led movement for building Ky. Bapt. Hosp. ($640,000), of which is trustee and sec. bd.; western sec. Southern Baptist Conv., 1903-05; exec. sec. Churchmen's Fedn. of Louisville, 1922-23, Ky. Anti-Race Track Gambling Commn., 1922-26; mem. hosp. commn. Southern Bapt. Conv. Democrat. Mason, Odd Fellow. Author: Christian Science Versus the Bible, 1914; Paul's Superlative and Other Sermons; Old Time Revival Sermons, 1940; The Story of My Life, 1941. Home: 824 Cecil Av., Louisville KY*‡

HUNT, O(RA) E(LMER), army officer (ret.); b. nr. Napa, Calif., June 26, 1872; s. Frank Martin and Mary Ellen (Southard) H.; B.S., U.S. Mil. Acad., West Point, N.Y., 1894; distinguished grad. Inf. and Cav. Sch. (1906) and Staff Coll. (1907), Ft. Leavenworth, Kan.; m. Eva B. Smith, Jan. 1, 1896 (div. Aug. 18, 1927); children—Ora Leland, Edna Virginia (Mrs. Colin T. Penn), Margaret (Mrs. M. H. Pringle); m. 2d, Josephine W. Guion, Mar. 16, 1929; 1 dau., Katherine Guion. Commd. 2d lt. Inf., U.S. Army, June 12, 1894 and advanced through grades to brig. gen., Apr. 12, 1918; assigned to Vancouver (Wash.) Barracks, 1894-98; served in Philippines during Spanish War and Philippine Insurrection, 1898-1904; instr. dept. English and history, and dept. modern langs, U.S. Mil. Acad., West Point, N.Y., 1908-10, asst. prof. dept. modern langs., 1910-12, asso. prof. dept. modern langs., 1914-17; with troops at Texas City, Tex., enroute to Mex., 1912-14; sr. instr. Inf. tactics Officers Training Camp, Ft. Myer, Va., 1917; col. 320th Inf., 80th Div., Camp Lee, Va. 1917-18; brig. gen. comdg. 165th Brig., 83d Div., 1918; comdg. gen. 6th Brig., 3rd Div., in St. Mihiel and Meuse-Argonne offensives 1918 and in Army of Occupation, Germany, 1918-19; comdg. gen. 3d Div. Camp Pike, Ark., 1919; assigned to Inspector General's Dept., Washington, D.C., 1919-23; ret. 1923; mem. U.S. mission in Nicaragua supervising presidential elections, 1928. Awarded distinguised service medal, 1918, and silver star citation for services against Germany; U.S. Marine Corps medal for service in 2d Nicaraguan campaign. Mem. West Point Alumni Foundn. (New York). Republican. Presbyterian. Editor Vol. V, Photographic History of the Civil War (Review of Reviews Co., 1911); contbr. to this publ. Home: 443 Kentucky Av., Berkeley 7 CA‡

HUNT, RALPH WALDO EMERSON, real estate; b. Portland, Me., Jan. 4, 1884; s. Enoch Warren and Sarah Frances (Neal) H.; grad. Portland High Sch., Westbrook Sem.; student Tufts Coll., 1904; m. Agnes Mildred Snow, of Cornish, Me., Sept. 3, 1907; children—Emerson Snow, Enoch Warren, Wm. Alfred, Priscilla Ruth, Ralph Waldo Emerson. Ex-pres. Trefether-Evergreen Improvement Assn.; appraiser, Federal Home Owners Loan Corpn. Prominent in war work; mem. State Com. Near East Relief, etc. Chmn. Social and Community Welfare Committee. Mem. nat. trade service com. of Music Industries Chamber Commerce; mem. Portland Chamber Commerce (v.p. 1916-18), Nat. Assn. Music Mchts., N.E. Music Trade Assn., etc. Organizer and past nat. pres. Universalist Comrades; mem. Nat. Laymen's Com. of Universalist Ch., Universalist Hist. Soc., Me. Hist. Soc., Ferry Beach Park Assn. (life), Me. Charitable Mechanics Assn. Licensed lay preacher Universalist Ch.; clk. 1st Universalist Ch., Portland; trustee Universalist Pub. House. Trustee Westbrook Sem.; dir. Portland Boys' Club, Y.M.C.A. Mem. Delta Upsilon. Democrat. Odd Fellow, Elk. Clubs: Kotzschmar, Portland Yacht; Delta Upsilon (New York); Cape Shore Community Club. Home: 14 Woodbury St., South Portland, Me.; (winter) 1903 Jetton Av., Tampa FL‡

HUNT, WALTER REID, church official; b. Camden, Me., Nov. 15, 1867; s. Abel and Evelina (Knight) H.; A.B., Bowdoin Coll., 1890; D.D., 1925; S.T.B., Harvard Div. Sch., 1894; m. Alice Winslow, July 25, 1901. Ordained Unitarian ministry, 1894; pastor successively Duxbury, Mass., Ellsworth, Me., and Orange, N.J., until 1922; gen. field sec. Am. Unitarian Assn. since 1924, administrative v.p., 1927-30, sec., 1930-37. Vol. chaplain Camp Upton, N.Y., 1917-18; capt., serving under Am. Red Cross, Debarkation Hosp. No. 1, Ellis Island, N.Y., 1918-19. Pres. Children's Aid Soc., Orange; an organizer and ex-pres. Orange Ministerial Assn.; trustee Duxbury Free Library; member Unitarian Ministerial Assn., N.E. Soc. (Orange), Psi Upsilon, Phi Beta Kappa. Mason (K.T.). Clubs: City, Clergy. Author: Morning Wish. Home: South Duxbury MA‡

HUNTER, CROIL, airlines exec.; born Fargo, N.D., Feb. 18, 1893; s. John Croil and Emma (Schulze) H.; student Yale U., Sheffield Sci. Sch., 1915; m. Helen Floan, Feb. 24, 1923; children—Andrea (Mrs. Jeremiah Milbank, Jr.), John Croil. Treas. Fargo Merc. Co., 1915-28; N.Y. mgr. First Bancredit Corp., 1928-32; traffic mgr. Northwest Airlines, Inc., 1932, v.p., gen. mgr., 1933-37, pres., gen. mgr., 1937-53, chmn. bd., 1953-70. Served as 1st lt. and capt. F.A., U.S. Army, 1917-19, in active service overseas. Clubs: Book and Snake, Cloister, Minnestoa, Somerset (St. Paul); Burning Tree (Washington). Home: St Paul MN Died July 21, 1970.

HUNTER, FRED HEATON, ex-mayor; b. Dexter, Ia., June 7, 1869; s. Dr. Andrew Oliver and Eliza (Heaton) H.; grad. East High Sch., Des Moines, 1887, Capital City Commercial College, 1889; student U. of Calif. and Ia. State Coll.; m. Mary Bonnet Ankeny, of Des Moines, Dec. 24, 1892; children—Leland Ankeny, Josephine (Mrs. Harvey Thomas Ray), Rolin Valentine Ankeny. Began with Des Moines Register, 1887, then in adv. and ry. business; was founder, and mgr. Inter-State Ry. Adv. Co.; was traveling freight and passenger agt. C.G.W. Ry.; was receiver, auditor, gen. mgr. Minneapolis & Northern Interurban Ry. Co.; auditor and mgr. South Des Moines Coal Co., 1916-20; organizer, with others, Old Colony Bldg. Corpn., 1920; v.p. Inter-State Business Men's Accident Co., Des Moines, Ia. Mem. Ia. Ho. of Rep., 1909-10; mem. Bd. of Supervisors, Polk Co., 1922-26; mayor Des Moines, 1926-28. Dir. Des Moines Council Boy Scouts of America; mem. S.A.R., Des Moines Chamber Commerce. Republican. Unitarian. Mason (32 deg., Shriner). Clubs: Kiwanis, Advertising. Home: Ankeny IA*‡

HUNTER, JOEL, business economist; b. Mobile, Ala.; s. Joseph Theophilus and Laura Douglas (Roberts) H.; ed. Barton Coll., Mobile; m. Lethe Bizzell, of Atlanta, Ga., 1898. Pub. accountant since 1895; largely instrumental in securing passage of Certified Pub. Accountant Act by Ga. legislature, 1908; lecturer on accounting and kindred topics at U. of Ga., Emory U., Oglethorpe U. and Ga. Sch. of Tech.; also lectures on business economics, finance, income taxes, etc.; widely known as examiner of disputed handwriting. Mng. dir. Joel Hunter & Co. Mem. Am. Inst. Accountants, Nat. Economic League, Nat. Tax Assn., Ga. Soc. Certified Pub. Accountants (pres.). Democrat. Methodist. Mason (Shriner). Mem. bd. founders Oglethorpe U. Supt. St. Mark's M.E. Ch. Sch. (largest Meth. S.S. in Ga.). Clubs: City, Capital City, Ansley Golf. Author: Thinking in Figures, 1915; How to Pass C.P.A. Examinations, 1916. Home: 1373 Peachtree St. Office: Atlanta Trust Co. Bldg., Atlanta GA‡

HUNTER, LOUIS JAMES, mgmt. cons.; s. Harry and Elizabeth (Maddocks) H.; student pub. schs., Boston; m. Marie Helen Atwater, June 19, 1912; children—Elizabeth (Mrs. F.G. Hicks), Robert Louis, Ruth (Mrs. Johnson). Treas., dir. Carter's Ink Co.; v.p., dir. Sagendorph Investment Co., dir. Putnam Equities, Inc., Preston Moss Fund. Inc., Putnam Investors Fund, Putnam Duofund Inc., Putnam Mayflower Fund, Putnam Vista Fund, Inc., Putnam Voyager Fund, Inc.; trustee Putnam Inccme Fund, George Putnam Fund of Boston, Putnam Growth Fund. Treas., trustee Univ. Hosp., Boston U. Med. Center. Clubs: Union, Down Town, Algonquin (Boston). Home: Boston MA Died Dec. 14, 1972.

HUNTER, THOMAS, educator; Ph.D., Williams Coll., 1877; (hon. M.A., Columbia, 1864; LL.D., New York U., 1896). Pres. 1870-1906, pres. emeritus since 1906, Normal Coll., New York. Address: 2079 5th Av., New York‡

HUNTER, WARREN CLAIR, physician; b. Dustin, Neb., Feb. 14, 1895; s. Joseph E. and Louisa J. Hunter; M.D., U. Ore., 1924; M.A. in Pathology, U. Mich., 1927; m. Martha Dorothy Schreiner, July 3, 1925;children—Ruth Mary (Mrs. Johannes Horst Max Meyer), Warren Clair. Intern, Multnomah Hosp., Portland, Ore., 1924-25; fellow in med. pathology NRC, 1926-27; dir. pathology lab. Portland Adventist Hosp., 1960-70; instr., asst. prof., asso. prof., prof. pathology U. Ore. Med. Sch., Portland, 1925-60, clin. prof., 1960-65, emeritus prof., 1965-70. Coroner's physician Multnomah County, 1924-60; acting dir. Ore. Police Crime Lab.; area counselor VA, 1945-66. Mem. regional com. Boy Scouts Am., 1941-45; mem. exec. com. Ore. div. Am. Cancer Soc., 1945, nat. bd. dirs., 1947-55, nat. v.p., 1952. Trustee, Lewis and Clark Coll., 1937-62, life trustee, 1962-70. Served with USN, 1917-18. Recipient Distinguished Alumnus award Lewis and Clark Coll., 1954, award for outstanding contbn. to control cancer Am. Cancer Soc., 1955. Diplomate Am. Bd. Pathology. Mem. A.M.A., Coll. Am. Pathologists, Am. Assn. Pathologists and Bacteriologists, Pacific N.W. Soc. Pathologists (pres. 1938-39, 62), Am. Soc. Clin. Pathology, Ore. Pathologists Assn., Ore., Multnomah County med. socs., Portland Acad. Medicine, Alpha Omega Alpha, Nu Sigma Nu. Republican. Presbyn. Contbr. numerous articles to med. jours. Research on hypothermia, origins of embolism, coronary arterial disease. Home: Portland OR Died July 6, 1970; buried Mausoleum, Riverview Cemetery, Portland OR

HUNTER, WILLIAM BOYD, lawyer, economist; b. Ponca, Neb., Apr. 1, 1876; s. William Hugh and Annie (Armstrong) H.; B.S., U. of Neb., 1897, A.M., 1898; unmarried. Statistical expert, Bureau of Census, 1900-04, and in charge of div. of methods and results, 1903-04; economist in charge investigations of monopolies, restraint of trade, and unfair methods of competition, Bureau of Corps. (now Federal Trade Commn.), 1904-13; practiced law in Chicago, 1913-14, in San Francisco, 1914-20, chiefly public utility law and the anti-trust acts; atty.-examiner, hearing railroad-rate cases, Interstate Commerce Commn., 1920-26; spl. atty. Bur. of Internal Revenue, 1926-27; practiced law in Washington, D.C., 1927-35; atty. Federal Trade Commn., 1938-40, and since 1947; now in pvt. practice. Republican. Protestant. Address: P.O. Box 1440, Washington DC*‡

HUNTING, WALTER JUDSON, educator; b. Jasper County, Ia., Feb. 11, 1874; s. Ambrose L. and Addie E. (Mason) H.; A.B., U. of Neb., 1901; studied summer sessions U. of Calif., 1914-37; A.M., Stanford Univ., 1928; m. Harriet A. Dinsmore, July 7, 1903; children—Alden Dinsmore, Walter Ambrose, Gordon Mason. Prin. pub. schs., Ohiowa, Neb., 1901-04, North Platte, 1904-06; supt. schs., Carson City, Nev., 1907-18; supt. pub. instrn., State of Nevada, 1919-26; supt. Lovelock (Nev.) Consol. Schools, 1927-30; teacher Montezuma Boys Sch., Los Gatos, 1930-32; with Lindsey (Calif.) High Sch. 1930-44, as teacher 1932-41; vice-principle 1941-44; retired June 1944. 1943 President Tulare County Council, California Teachers Assn. Baptist. Reorganized the basis of sch. finances in Nev.; author of Nev. Sch. apportionment law of 1917. Home: Pasadena 5 CA‡

HUNTINGTON, ARTHUR FRANKLIN, naval officer; b. Brooklyn, N.Y., Feb. 24, 1877; s. Charles Lathrop and Elizabeth Franklin (Bache) H.; student U.S. Naval Acad., 1894-97; m. Mary E. Klink, Jan. 16, 1907; 1 son, Seymour Franklin (dec.). Asst. paymaster (rank of ensign), U.S. Navy, 1898, advanced through grades to rear admiral, S.C., 1938, filing usual assignments afloat and ashore; retired (statutory age) March 1, 1941; remained on active duty to August 1942. Awarded West Indian Campaign medal, 1898; Sampson medal, 1898; Philippine Campaign medal, 1901; Victory medal, 1918. Mem. U.S. Naval Institute, Naval Hist. Foundation, Naval Acad. Alumni Assn., Nat. Sojourners, Mil. Order of the Carabao. Presbyterian. Mason. Clubs: New York Yacht (N.Y. City); Army and Navy (San Francisco); City Commons (Berkeley). Home: 107 Parkside Dr., Berkeley, CA*

HUNTINGTON, DOROTHY PHILLIPS, writer; b. N.Y.C., Jan. 6, 1893; d. John Sanburn and Jennie Beale (Peterson) Phillips; A.B., Vassar Coll., 1914; student Radcliffe Coll., 1914-16; m. Richard T. Huntington, Sept. 5, 1925 (div. 1944); 1 son, Samuel Phillips. Author shorts stories under pseudonym Dorothy Sanburn Phillips appearing in Am. Mag., Good Housekeeping, Cosmopolitan, Woman's Home Companion, This Week, Am. Girl, also Canadian, English and Scandinavian mags.; instr. short story writing Ballard Sch., N.Y.C. Mem. Pen and Brush (pres. 1951-56, 58-62). Address: New York City NY Died June 23, 1972.

HUNTINGTON, FRANCES CARPENTER (MRS. WILLIAM CHAPIN HUNTINGTON), author; b. Washington, Apr. 30, 1890; d. Frank G. and Joanna (Condict) Carpenter; A.B., Smith Coll., 1912; m. William Chapin Huntington, 1920 (dec. 1958); children—Joanna Carpenter (Mrs. Huntington Noel), Edith Chapin (Mrs. David Benton Williams). Traveled and collaborated with Frank G. Carpenter on tours of investigation in China, Japan, Korea, Egypt and Near East, Europe and Alaska. Trustee Smith Coll., 1936-1944. Fellow Royal Geog. Soc. London; mem. Internat. Soc. Woman Geographers (pres., 1939-42), Alumnae Assn. Smith Coll. (pres. 1932-35). Club: Cosmopolitan (N.Y.). Author (under name of Frances Carpenter): (with Frank G. Carpenter) The Foods We Eat, 1925, The Clothes We Wear, 1926, The Houses We Live In, 1926; Ourselves and Our City, 1928; The Ways We Travel, 1929; Tales of a Basque Grandmother, 1930; Our Little Friends of Eskimo Land, 1931; Our Neighbors Near and Far, An Elementary Geography, 1932; Tales of a Russian Grandmother, 1933; Our Little Friends of the Arabian Desert; My Geography Work Book, 1934; Our Little Friends of the Netherlands 1935; Our Little Friends of Norway, 1936; Our Little Friends of China, 1937; Tales of a Chinese Grandmother, 1937; Our Little Neighbors at Work and Play, An Introduction to Geography, 1939; Tales of a Swiss Grandmother, 1940; Our Little Friends of Switzerland, 1941; Our South American Neighbors, 1942; The Pacific-Its Lands and Peoples, 1944; Canada and Her Northern Neighbors, 1945; Tales of a Korean Grandmother, 1947; Children of Our World, An Elementary Geography, 1949; Caribbean Lands: Mexico, Central America and the West Indies, 1949; Wonder Tales of Horses and Heroes, 1952; Wonder Tales of Dogs and Cats, 1955; Our Homes and Our Neighbors, A Home Geography, 1956; Pocahontas and Her World, 1957; Holiday in Washington, 1958; Wonder Tales of Seas and Ships, 1959. Editor: Carp's Washington, 1960; The Elephant's Bath TubAsian Folk Tales, 1962; African Wonder Tales, 1963; The Mouse Palace, 1964; The Story of Korea, 1968; South American Wonder Tales, 1969; People from the Sky; Ainu Tales from Northern Japan, 1971. Home: Washington DC Died Nov. 2, 1972; buried Oak Hill Cemetery, Washington DC

HUNTINGTON, RICHARD LEE, prof. of chem. engring.; b. Blackwell, Okla., March 24, 1896; s. Richard Collier and Corda Ann (Townsend) H.; A.B., U. of Okla., 1917; student U. of Ill., 1920, Mass. Inst. of Tech., 1930-31; M.S., Ph.D., in Chem. Engring., U. of Mich., 1933; m. Ruth Williams, April 30, 1921; children—Helen Louise, Richard Lee. Chem. engr., The Texas Co., Tulsa, Okla., 1919-20, The Skelly Oil Co., 1920-30; consultant for Phillips Petroleum Co., prof. chem. engring., U. of Okla., 1933-43, chmn. sch. chem. engring., 1937-54, research prof. chem. engring., 1954-72, George Lynn Cross research prof., 1968-72. Served in Water Supply Regt. and C.W.S., U.S. Army, 1917-19; with A.E.F. 14 mos. Mem. Am. Inst. Mining Engr., Am. Chem. Soc., Am. Inst. Chem. Engrs., Alpha Chi Sigma, Sigma Xi, Tau Beta Pi, Sigma Chi. Mason. Club: Faculty (U. Okla.). Author: Natural Gas and Natural Gasoline, 1950. Home: Norman OK Died Oct. 9, 1972.

HUNTLEY, VICTORIA HUTSON, artist; b. Hasbrouck Heights, N.J., Oct. 9, 1900; d. Albert Lendon and Grace (Wolf) Ebbels; student Washington Irving High Sch., N.Y. City, 1914-17, N.Y. Sch. of Fine and Applied Art, 1918-19, Art Students League, 1919-21; m. W. K. Hutson, Jan. 3, 1925; 1 dau., Hazel; m. 2d, Ralph Huntley, Sept. 9, 1934. Painter, lithographer and mural painter, 1928-71. Asst. prof. of fine arts, Coll. Industrial Arts, Denton, Tex., 1921-23; resident artist Redding Ridge (Conn.) Sch., 1939-41; teacher of painting and drawing, Birch-Wathen Sch., N.Y. City, 1934-42; resident artist and teacher of art, Pomfret Sch. (Conn.), 1942-46; Awarded grant by Am. Acad. and Nat. Institute Arts and Letters, 1947; Guggenheim fellowship for creative work in graphic art, 1948; Solo Exhbn. award to drawing The Portal, N.Y.C., 1969. One-man shows N.Y.C., Phila., others. Prints and drawings in collections at Oklahoma Museum of Art, Whitney Museum of Art, Metropolitan Museum, Boston Museum of Fine Arts, Chicago Art Inst., Library of Congress, Phila. Mus. of Art, several other mus. Recipient numerous awards since 1930, later ones include 3d National Pennell Fund Competition, Library of Congress, 1945; 1st prize in lithography, 7th Nat. Exhbn. of Prints, Library of Congress, 1949; Saw Grass Country, the Everglades, prize 75th Diamond Jubilee, Art Students League, N.Y.C.; prize N.J. State Ann. Exhbn.; hon. mention Nat. Arts Club, N.Y., 1968, Pen and Brush N.Y., 1968. Asso. N.A. Mem. Art Students League, Audubon Artists (v.p. graphics 1967-68), Pen and Brush N.Y. Address: Chatham Twp NJ Died July 3, 1971.

HUNTOON, GARDNER A., M.D.; b. Atlantic, Cass Co., Ia., Oct. 6, 1874; s. Hermon M. and Hariet E. (Copeland) H.; 7th from John and Priscilla Alden of the Mayflower; grad. E. Des Moines H.S., 1892; M.D., State U. of Ia. Homoe. Med. Dept., 1896; studied Vienna and Berlin; m. Hattie A. Gesberg of Iowa City, Ia., Sept. 2, 1896; children—Eloise H., Royal G., Jane E. Practiced at Des Moines since 1896; mem. Ia. State Bd. of Health, 1911-13; lecturer on obstetrics, Iowa Congl. Hosp., 1917-26; on obstetrics, Ia. Luth. Hosp., 1926-—. Founder and editor Ia. Homoe. Jour., 1907-15. Mem. A.M.A., Am. Inst. Homoepathy, Obstet. Soc. A.I.H. (pres. 1913, sec.-treas. 1915-—), Hahnemann Med. Assn. of Ia. (sec. 1907-15, pres. 1919), Des Moines Homoe. Med. Soc., Polk Co. Med. Soc., Ia. State Med. Soc., Missouri Valley Med. Soc., Phi Alpha Gamma. Republican. Mem. Christian (Disciples) Ch. Mason (32 deg., Shriner). Clubs: Grant, Professional Men's (pres. local chapter No. 1, 1925), Des Moines Golf and Country. Home: 1086 25th St. Office: 515 Southern Surety Bldg., Des Moines IA‡

HURD, CHARLES W.B., author, publicist; b. Tonkawa, Okla., May 11, 1903; s. Arthur A. and Katherine (Bolick) H.; studied under tutors and in pub. high sch., St. Louus; extension student in langs. and history, Washington U. (St. Louis) and Northwestern U.; m. Eleanor Branson, Mar. 17, 1934. Reporter St. Louis Post-Dispatch, 1918, Des Moines Register-Tribune, 1919; with Asso. Press, Chicago and New York, 1920-25; asso. editor Liberty mag., 1926-28; mem. Washington staff, N.Y. Times, 1929-49, except for 1937, which spent in London bureau and on European assignments; mem. Carl Byior & Assos. (pub. relations) 1949-54; founder Charles Hurd Associates, 1954-68; sr. account exec. Hill & Knowlton, Inc., 1954-58. Mem. American Academy of Political and Social Scis. Sigma Delta Chi. Democrat. Clubs: Metropolitan (Washington); Overseas Press of Am. (N.Y.C.). Author: The White House: A Biography, 1940; The Veterans' Program, 1945; Washington Cavalcade, 1947; The Compact History of the American Red Cross, 1959; Treasury of Great American Speeches, 1959; (with Arthur E. Summerfield) Story of the U.S. Postal Service, 1960; (with Lowell Thomas) Cavalcade of Europe, 1960; (with Eleanor Hurd) Treasury of Great American Letters, 1961; A Treasure of Great American Quotations, 1964; When the New Deal Was Young and Gay, 1965; The White House Story, 1966. Contbr. to mags. Home: New York City NY Died May, 1968.

HURD, GEORGE EDWARD, lawyer; b. nr. Whitleysburg, Del., July 11, 1872; s. James Henry and Martha (Godwin) H.; A.B., Amherst, 1896; Harvard Law Sch., 1896-97; m. Mary Evelyn Hargadine, Dec. 20, 1900;children—Robert H., George E. Began practice at Glasgow, Mont., 1900; mayor Glasgow, 1902-06; spl. prosecutor for Mont., 1911-12 (elected by State legislature); moved to Great Falls, 1913. Member Montana State and Cascade County bar assns., Delta Upsilon. Democrat. Home: 1517 Third Av. N. Office: Strain Bldg., Great Falls MT‡

HURD, GUILFORD LANSING, newspaperman; b. Iowa City, Ia., July 7, 1877; s. John Benjamin and Maretta (De Forest) H.; grad. high sch., Sheldon, Ia.; student Notre Dame University; special student in economics, N.D. Agrl. Coll. and Ore. Agricultural Coll.; m. Clara Ella Benbow, of Archer, Ia., November 10, 1897; children—Mildred Grace (Mrs. Eugene J. Keller), Blanche Esther, Ruth Clara (Mrs. G. Winston Wade), John Paul. Founder, 1895, pub. until 1906, Sioux County Bee, Hospers, Ia.; founder and pub. 1907-09, Adams County Record, Hettinger, N.D.; pub. Stanfield (Ore.) Standard, 1910-15; instr. in economics, Ore. State Coll., 1915-17; business mgr. and one of owners Gazette-Times, Corvallis, Ore., 1920-25; pub. Santa Rosa (Calif.) Evening Republican, 1925-27. With U.S. Dept. Agr. during World War, 1917-19. Sec. Sonoma County Fair Assn. Mem. Calif. Assn. Commercial Secretaries (past state pres.), Nat. Editorial Assn., Calif. Press Assn., Santa Rosa Chamber Commerce (sec.-mgr.), Alpha Delta Sigma. Republican. Presbyterian. Mason, Elk. Club: Rotary. Home: 1745 Proctor Drive. Office: Santa Rosa CA‡

HURDLE, JAMES ERNEST, educator; b. Taylor, Miss., May 3, 1913; s. John G. and Jessie (Bunch) H.; student U. Miss., 1932-33; Miss. Synodical Coll., 1933-34; B.S., U. So. Miss., 1936, M.A., 1951; M. Louise McRaney, Aug. 22, 1937; children—James Ernest, Patricia Louise, Margaret Suzanne. Tchr., coach, supt. Oak Grove High Sch., Hattiesburg, Miss., 1936-43; prin. high sch. dept. Pearl River Jr. Coll., Poplarville, Miss., 1943-44; supt. Woodville (Miss.) High Sch., 1946-51; supt. Summit (Miss.) Separate Sch. Dist., 1952-55; supt. Shelby (Miss.) High Sch., 1955-60; supt. Philadelphia (Miss.) City Sch., 1960-70. Served to lt. (j.g.) USNR, 1944-46. Mem. Miss. Edn. Assn., Miss., Am. assns. sch. adminstrs., Miss. Assn. Sch. Supts., Am. Assn. Sch. Adminstrs., Phi Delta Kappa. Home: Philadelphia MS Died Jan. 4, 1970.

HURFF, LINDLEY SCARLETT, banker; b. Sewell, N.J., June 23, 1895; s. George B. and Lillie (Heritage) H.; grad. Evening Sch. Accounts and Finance, U. Pa., 1920; student Grad. Sch. Banking, Rugers U., 1937; m. May Stafford, Oct. 7, 1922; children—Mary Elizabeth (Mrs. Mozayan Aladj), Barbara Ann (Mrs. Frederic L. Reimensnyder). Cashier, dir. Farmers Nat. Bank, Mullica Hill, N.J., 1925-35; sec., treas. Bound Brook Trust Co., N.J., 1935-39; pres., dir. The First Nat. Bank of Milton, from 1939; former dir. Fed. Res. Bank Phila. Past pres. Milton Community Chest, Milton Boro Council. Served with 78th Div. U.S. Army, World War I; AEF in France. Club: Rotary of Milton (past pres.). Home: Milton PA Died Nov. 17, 1968; buried Milton PA

HURLEY, ROBERT AUGUSTINE, engineer, ex-governor; b. Bridgeport, Conn., Aug. 25, 1895; s. Robert Emmett and Sabina (O'Hara) H.; student The Cheshire Acad., 1914-15, Leghih U., 1915-17; m. Evelyn L. Hedberg, Jan. 22, 1925; children—Joan Elizabeth, Robert Emmett, Sally Ann. Began as asst. to father in constrn. business, Bridgeport, Conn., 1919; formed own firm, Leverty & Hurley, contractors and constrn. engrs., Bridgeport, 1921, and partner, 1921-34; dir. WPA, Fairfield County, Conn., 1935; spl. rep. of fed. govt. to co-ordinate relief activities, Hartford, during floods of 1936; state administrator for WPA., 1936-37; commr. State Dept. of Pub. Works, 1937-40, charged with constrn. of 5,000,000 institutional bldg. program, involving 150 bldgs. on 13 locations, which program completed at saving by 1940; elected Governor of Conn., 1940, for 2-yr. term. Served as radio electrician, Submarine Fleet (on fgn. service) and on U.S.S. Pennsylbania, U.S. Navy, during World War I. Mem. Conn. Soc. Professional Engrs., Am. Legion, Delta Fraternity (Lehigh U.). Democrat. Catholic. Club: Hartford. Sponsored pending legislation for Conn. State Labor Relations Bd. and Wages and Hours Law, patterned after fed. laws, and legislation for increased prices of milk to farmers with resultant less cost to consumers. Home: West Hartford CT Died May 4, 1968.

HURLEY, ROY T., industrialist; b. N.Y. City, June 3, 1896; s. Edward and Phoebe (King) H.; ed. pub. schs. of N.Y. City; m. Ruth Applebee, June 3, 1917 (div.); children—Nancy Ann, Patricia Ann; m. 2d, Esther Sarchian, Oct. 3, 1953; children—Susan Lynn, James Scott. Began career as aircraft engine mechanic, B.F. Sturtevant Co., Hyde Park, Mass., 1916; inspector of airplanes and engines, N.Y. City, U.S.A.F., Dist. Office, 1917-18; chief engr., B. G. Aircraft Spark Plug Co., N.Y. City, 1921-27; vice pres. and gen. mgr., Moto-Meter Co., Long Island, 1927-31, Hurley-Townsend Co. at N.Y. City, 1932-35; vice pres. mfg., Bendix Aviation Corp., Detroit, 1935-47; dir. mfg. engring., Ford Motor Co., Dearborn, Mich., 1948-49; Curtiss-Wright Corp., Wood-Ridge, New Jersey, pres., 1949-60, chmn., 1950 60, ret.; dir. Gen. Cable Corp., Manufacturer's Trust Co. Mem. bd. trusteses, New York University, Deputy of branch commanding officers, Chief of Ordnance, Lieutenant Gen. Levin H. Campbell Jr., World War II. Air Power trophy (N.J. Wing), Air Force Assn.; Internat. Aviation Trade Show award, Horatio Alger award; Pa. Meritorious medal; Stevens Inst. Honor Award; French Legion of Honor, 1957. Member of Eberstadt Task committee, Hoover Commn., July 1948; consultant to Wright-Patterson Air Force Base, Major Gen. F. M. Hopkins, Jr., 1948. Mem. Am. Ordnance Assn., Soc. Automotive Engrs., Nat. Indsl. Conf. Bd., N.J. State C. of C. (dir.). Clubs: Economic (pres. 1958-59), Metropolitan, Wings, (N.Y.C.); Athletic, Recess (Detroit); Nat. Aviation (Washington); Pennington Passaic, N.J.). Died Oct. 31, 1971.

HURREY, CLARENCE BARZILLAI, business and govt. consultant; b. Tecumseh, Mich., July 28, 1876; s. Barzillai and Adelle (DuBois) H.; B.L., U. of Mich., 1900; m. Alice Fryer, of Washington, D.C., Apr. 30, 1904; 1 son, Ross Clarence. Adv. agt. N.Y. City, 1905-08; sec.-treas. Udell Mfg. Co., New York, 1908-09; with P.O. Dept., 1911-13, and assisted in orgn. of postal savings and parcel post systems; field sec.

Chamber of Commerce U.S.A., 1915-17; dep. commr. internal revenue, 1919-20; now mem. Julius Klein and Associates. Was dir. govt. publicity in collection of war revenues. Mem. Alpha Tau Omega. Episcopalian. Mason. Clubs: Nat. Press, University. Home: Ashton, Md. Office: Transportation Bldg., Washington DC‡

HURST, HAROLD EMERSON, educator; b. Weld County, Colo., June 20, 1912; s. Frank North and Anna Marguerite (Stubbert) H.; A.B., U. Colo., 1936, LL.B., 1938; M.S. in Govt. Mgmt. (Alfred P. Sloan Found fellow), U. Denver, 1940; m. Esther Carolyn Walter, July 26, 1938; children—Harold Frank, Janet Marie, Pamela Ann. Admitted to Colo. bar, 1938; dir. research Citizens Tax League Ohio, 1940-41; chief staff services Colo. Dept. Revenue, 1941-42; cons. Ark. Pub. Expenditures Council, 1946-47; asso. prof. law U. Denver, 1947-50, prof., 1950—, dean Coll. Law, 1961-65. Served with USNR, 1942-46. Mem. Am., Colo (gov.), Denver bar assns., Am. Judicature Soc., Assn. Am. Law Schs. (chmn. round table council on multiple div. schs.), Phi Alpha Delta. Contbr. articles to profl. jours. Home: Denver CO Died Dec. 18, 1972.

HURST, PETER F(REDERICK), mfg. exec.; b. Bruchsal, Baden, Germany, Aug. 3, 1910; s. Fritz and Anna (Bornschein) H.; Bachelor Degree, Humanistic Gymnasium, Karlsruhe, Baden, Germany, 1928; diploma engrng. Inst. Tech., Karlsruhe, Germany, 1933; m. Elizabeth S. Duncan, June 16, 1942; children—Ronald F., Anthony P. Came to U.S., 1939, naturalized, 1945. Development engr., Eng., 1933-34; gen. mgr., chief engr. Rotadisk Corp., Berlin, 1934-39; became gen. mgr. Aeroquip Corp., Jackson, 1940, exec. v.p., 1943-44, pres., dir., 1945-69, chmn. bd., 1965-69; dir. Aeroquip (Can.) Ltd., Aeroquip A.G., Switzerland, Aeroquip, G.m.b.H., Germany, Clark Equipment Co., Nat. Bank of Jackson, Jackson Nat. Life Ins. Co., Yardman, Inc., Jackson. Mem. Soc. Automotive Engrs., Inst. Aero. Scis., Jackson Mfrs. Assn., Nat. Rifle Assn. America, Tau Beta Pi. Clubs: Aeroclub of Michigan; Town, Country (Jackson). Jackson MI Died Apr. 8, 1969.

HURT, JOHN JETER, coll. pres.; b. Ballsville, Va., Mar. 1, 1873; s. George S. and Laura E. H.; student Richmond Coll., Va., class of 1900; Th.G., Southern Bapt. Theol. Sem., 1903; D.D., Union U., Jackson, Tenn., 1914, Wake Forest (N.C.) Coll., 1921; LL.D., Georgetown (Ky.) College, 1932; m. Ethelyn Lovell, June 30, 1908; children—John Jeter, Thurston, Harrison, James L., Mary Lee (Mrs. Howard C. Bennett). Ordained Bapt. ministry, 1901; pastor 1st Ch., Durham, N.C., 1912-16, 1st Ch., Wilmington, N.C., 1916-23, First Ch., Jackson, Tenn., 1923-32; pres. of Union Univ., 1932-45, pres. emeritus, since 1945; acting pres. New Orleans Bapt. Theol. Sem., 1946. Editor of The Baptist Advance, 1900-03. Pres. bd. trustees Central Coll., Ark., 1906-12; trustee of the Southeastern Baptist Seminary. President Bd. Edn. Bapt. State Conv., N.C., 1914-22; pres. Bapt. Seaside Assembly of N.C., 1916-22; pres. Alumni Assn. Southern Bapt. Theol. Sem., 1923; v.p. Tenn. Bapt. Conv., 1927, Southern Baptist Convention, 1935; pres. Southern Bapt. Edn. Assn., 1937. Mason. Rotarian. Author: Struggles for Religious Liberty in Virginia, 1912; Some Baptist Whys and Wherefores, 1919; A Handbook for the Every-Member Canvass, 1931. Home: 215 Rumson Rd. N.E., Atlanta‡

HUSAIN, ZAKLR, pres. India; b. Feb. 8, 1897; ed. M.A.O. Coll., Aligarh. (India) U., Berlin (Germany) U.; D.Litt. (hon.), Delhi, Calcutta, Aligarh, Allahbad, Cairo univs. Vice-chancellor Jamia Millia Islmia, Delhi, India, 1926-48, Aligarh Muslim U., 1948-56; pres. Hindustani Talimi Sangh, Sevagram, India, 1938-50; gov. Bihar, India, 1957-62; v.p. India, 1962-67, pres., 1967-69. Mem. Univ. Edn. Com., 1948-49, Indian Press Comm., 1952-54; chmn. World Univ. Service, Geneva Switzerland, 1955-57; mem. exec. bd. UNESCO, Paris, France, 1956-58. Author: Capitalism: An Essay in Understanding; Educational Discourses; Shiksha; Princioles of Educational Reconstruction; Scope and Method of Economists; Ethics and the State. Translator into Urdu: Republic (Plato); National System of Economics (List); Elements of Economics (Cannan); The Dynamic University; Abbo Khan ki Bakri and other Stories. Home: New Delhi India Died May 3, 1969; buried New Delhi, India

HUSSON, CHESLEY HAYWARD, coll. pres.; b. Lynn, Mass., Mar. 14, 1903; s. George Edwin Parsons and Lillian (Rendell) H.; B.S., Mass. State Tchrs. Coll., Salem, 1926; M.S., U. Me., 1939; fellowship diploma, Nat. Coll., Ont., Can.; M.B.A. (hon.), Spencerian Coll., Milw., 1965; D.Sc. in Bus. Adminstrn., Drake Coll., Fla., 1968; m. Dorothy Bell, May 30, 1927; children—Chesley Hayward, Roy George, Paul Edwin. Prin., Me. Sch. Commerce, Bangor, 1926-33, pres., 1933-48; pres. Husson Coll., Bangor, from 1948. Mem. Nat. Accrediting Commn. for Bus. Schs., 1955-60, chmn., 1957-59; dir. Bus. Edn. Research Assos. Bd. dirs. Bangor YMCA, Bangor Community Chest; treas. Sch. Children's Fund Com., from 1950; mem. Me. Small Bus. Adv. Council, since from 1967. Mem. United Business Schools Assn. (director 1962-64), Nat. Assn. Bus. Schs., N.E. Bus. Coll. Assn. (pres. 1958), Eastern, Nat. bus. tchrs. assns., Me. Tchrs. Assn., Nat. Assn. Secondary Sch. Prins., Bangor C. of C. (dir.), Bangor Execs. Club (pres. 1956-57), Am. Assn. Specialized Colls., Am. Assn. of Ind. Coll. and Univ. Presidents, Kappa Delta Phi, Kappa Phi Kappa, Pi Rho Zeta (nat. gov. from 1966). Methodist. Mason (Shriner). Clubs: Lions, Triangle (Bangor). Home: Bangor ME Died Feb. 17, 1972; buried Mt. Hope Cemetery, Bangor ME

HUSTED, LADLEY, biologist; b. Wayne County, N.Y., Sept. 30, 1906; s. Don Gordon and Ruth Lucinda (Tuttle) H.; A.B., Oberlin Coll., 1928; student Cornell U., 1928-29; Ph.D., U. Va., 1934; m. Kathryn Funkhouser, Dec. 26, 1934; 1 son, Robert Ladley. Instr. botany Oberlin Coll., 1929-30; gen. edn. bd. fellow U. Mo., 1934-35, Bussey Inst. of Harvard, 1935-36, John Innes Hort. Inst., London, 1936-37, Inst. Animal Genetics of U. Edinburgh, 1937; asst. prof. biology U. Va., 1937-46, asso. prof., 1946-53, prof., 1953-69, sec. Miller Sch. Biology, 1946-48, chmn. dept. biology, 1949-57. Fellow A.A.A.S.; mem. Am. Soc. Naturalists, Genetics Soc. Am., Bot. Soc. Am., Human Genetics Soc., Genetics Assn., Assn. Southeastern Biologists, Virginia Academy Science, American Association U. Prof., So. Applalachian Bot. Club, Sigma Xi, Phi Sigma. Episcopalian. Clubs: Colonnade (Charlottesville); Farmington (Albemarle, Va.). Author sci. articles. Home: Charlottesville VA Died Mar. 26, 1969; buried U. Va. Cemetery, Charlottesville VA

HUSTED, LADLEY, biologist; b. Wayne County, N.Y., Sept. 30, 1906; s. Don Gordon and Ruth Lucinda (Tuttle); H.; A.B., Oberlin Coll., 1928; student Cornell U., 1928-29; Ph.D., U. Va., 1934; m. Kathryn Funkhouser, Dec. 26, 1934; 1 son, Robert Ladley. Instr. botany Oberlin Coll., 1929-30; gen. edn. bd. fellow U. Mo., 1934-35, Bussey Inst. of Harvard, 1935-36, John Innes Hort. Inst., London, 1936-37, Inst. Animal Genetics of U. Edinburgh, 1937; asst. prof. biology U. Va., 1937-46, asso. prof., 1946-53, prof., 1953-69, sec. Miller Sch. Biology, 1946-48, chmn. dept. biology, 1949-57. Fellow A.A.A.S.; mem. Am. Soc. Naturalists, Genetics Soc. Am., Bot. Soc. Am., Human Genetics Soc., Genetics Assn., Assn. Southeastern Biologists, Virginia Academy Science, American Association U. Profs., So. Applalachian Bot. Club, Sigma Xi, Phi Sigma. Conservative. Episcopalian. Clubs: Colonnade (Charlottesville); Farmington (Albemarle, Va.). Author sci. articles. Home: Charlottesville VA Died Mar. 26, 1969; buried University Cemetery, Charlottesville, VA

HUSTON, HENRY AUGUSTUS, chemist; b. Damariscotta, Me., Apr. 20, 1858; s. Albion G. and Sally (Woodward) H.; A.B., Bowdoin, 1879, A.M., 1882; A.C. (analytical chemist), Purdue U., 1882, D.Sc., 1931; m. Alice Brownson Cooke, Nov. 22, 1899 (died Mar. 25, 1940). Asst. chemistry and physics Bowdoin Coll., 1879-80; sci. tchr., prin. Lafayette High Sch., 1880-84; prof. physics Purdue U., 1884-88; dir. Ind. Weather Service 1884-96; asst. state chemist State Ind., 1884-86, state chemist, 1886-1903; chemist Ind. Agrl. Expt. Sta., 1888-1903, dir., 1902-03; prof. agrl. chemistry Purdue, 1888-1903; mgr. soil and crop service of Potash Syndicate (Kalisyndikat), 1903-23; dir., sec., asst. treas. German Kali Works, N.Y.C., defeating attacks in Congress on Potash Syndicate, 1909-22; in Berlin, Germany, July 1919, arranged for resumption of potash shipment to U.S. suspended, Jan. 1915; cons. agrl. chemist since 1923. Fellow A.A.A.S., Ind. Acad. Sci.; mem. Am. Chem. Soc., Am. Soc. Agronomists, Zeta Psi. Mason. Author: Reports of Indiana Weather Service, 1884-96; Reports of Indiana State Chemist, 17 yrs.; also Descendants of James Huston, 9 generations. Has furnished numerous papers on agrl. chemistry, research work in Bulls. of Ind. Agrl. Expt. Sta., Bull. of Chem. Div., U.S. Dept. Agr. and Ind., Mich., Minn. Agrl. and Hort. Reports, etc. Address: Kew Hall, Kew Gardens 15, NY City‡

HUSTON, RALPH ERNEST, educator; b. Huntington, Ind., Sept. 16, 1902; s. William Franklin and Mary E. (Wetter) H.; B.S., U. Chgo., 1923; B.A. (Rhodes scholar), U. Oxford, Eng., 1926; Ph.D., U. Chgo., 1932; m. Antoinette Killen, July 14, 1934; children—Peter, Kenneth, Richard, T. Michael. Asso. prof. modern lang. Southwestern U., Memphis, 1927-29; asst. in math. U. Chgo., 1930-31; acting prof. math. Ia. State Coll., Ames, 1931; with Rensselaer Poly. Inst., Troy, N.Y., 1934-69, prof. math., 1948-67, prof. emeritus, 1967-69. Mem. Am. Math. Soc. Home: Troy NY Died Oct. 8, 1969; buried Huntington IN

HUSTON, S(IMEON) ARTHUR, bishop; b. Cincinnati, O., Dec. 10, 1876; s. Simeon Atchley and Matilda (Bogen) H.; B.A., Kenyon Coll., 1900, D.D., 1925; grad. Bexley Theol. Sem., 1903; studied Johns Hopkins U., 1920-21; LL.D., Coll. of Puget Sound, 1931; m. Dorothea Josephine Brotherton, Oct. 4, 1911 children—Wilber Brotherton, Dorothea (dec.), Ann Langham, John Arthur. Deacon, 1903, priest, 1904, P.E. Ch.; curate Trinity Ch., Columbus, O., 1903-07, St, Paul's Cathedral, Detroit, 1907-13; rector St. Mark's Ch., Cheyenne, Wyo., 1913-19 Christ Ch., Baltimore, Md., 1919-21, St. Mark's Church, San Antonio, Tex., 1921-25; elected bishop of Olympia, Feb. 3, 1925, consecrated May 15, 1925; retired from active service June 1947. Pres. Wyoming State Board of Education, 1917-19. President ex-officio, board trustees Annie Wright Seminary, Tacoma, Washington. Member Beta Theta Pi, Phi Beta Kappa. Democrat. Mason (32 deg.). Home: R.F.D., Winslow WA‡

HUSTON, STEWART, business exec.; b. Coatesville, Pa., May 9, 1898; s. Charles L. and Annie (Stewart) H.; student Nazareth Hall Mil. Acad., 1912-13, Haverford Sch., 1913-15, Haverford Coll., 1915-17; Met.E., Lehigh U., 1923; m. Mrs. Genevieve (McCready) Hussey, 1943 (dec. 1948); m. 2d, Mrs. Harriet (Lawrence) Cann, 1953. Asst. metall. engr. Lukens Steel Co., Coatesville, 1923-25, plant metallurgist, 1926-32, sec., 1928-63, dir., 1941-71; v.p., 1951-71, also member of the executive committee; managing dir. Citizens Hotel Co., 1925-41, operating v.p., 1941-51, pres. 1951-71; pres. Allegheny Ore & Iron Co., 1939-71; chmn. bd. Quartz Mosaic, Inc. Pres. Coatesville Community Indsl. Devel. Corp., 1961-71; mem. bd. Water Resources Assn. Delaware Valley; mem. Sanitary Water Bd., Commonwealth Pa.; mem. Chester County Planning Commn., Delaware River Basin Research, Inc., Chester County Area Airport Authority, (vice. chmn.), Del. Valley Council. Bd. mgrs. Spring Garden Inst.; trustee of the Atkinson Memorial Hospital; trustee of Franklin and Marshall Coll. Served Sect. Sanitaire Units Etats-1-625, Army of the United States, 1917-19. Awarded the Croix de Guerre, Ordre du Regiment (France). Member American Soc. Testing Materials, Am. Inst. Mining and Metall. Engrs., Am. Soc. Metals, Am., Brit. iron and steel insts., Franklin Inst., Delta Phi. Ind. Republican. Presbyn. Clubs: Oglethorpe (Savannah, Georgia): Country (Coatesville); Union League, Racquet (Phila.); Hamilton (Lancaster, Pennsylvania). Author: Rambles by Dictation, 1937. Home: Coatesville PA Died Aug. 27, 1971; buried Bonaventure Cemetery, Savannah GA

HUTCHESON, JOSEPH C., JR., judge; b. Houston, Oct. 19, 1879; s. Joseph Chappell and Mildred (Carrington) H.; ed. Bethel (Va.) Mil. Acad., U. Va.; LL.B., U. Tex., 1900; m. Anne Elizabeth Weeden, Dec. 21, 1905; children—Joseph C. III, Mary Pye. Practiced law, Houston, 1900-18; mem. successively Hutcheson, Campbell & Hutcheson, Hutcheson & Hutcheson, Hutcheson & Bryan; chief legal adviser City of Houston, 1913-17; mayor Houston, 1917-18; U.S. dist. judge, So. Dist. Tex., 1918-30; U.S. circuit judge, Fifth Circuit, Houston, 1931-64, chief judge, 1948-59, U.S. sr. circuit judge, 1964-68. Mem. council Am. Law Inst.; Am. chmn. Anglo-Am. Com. of Inquiry, 1945-46; mem. adv. com. Nat. Assn. Legal Aid Orgns.; State of Tex. chmn. Am. Bar Assn. Spl. Com. on Restoration of Inns of Ct. Mem. Am., Tex., Harris County bar assns., Houston Philos. Soc., Philos. Soc. Tex., Order of Coif, Kappa Sigma. Presbyn. Club: Country (River Oaks). Author: Law Houston TX Died Jan. 18, 1973.

HUTCHESON, MARTHA BROOKES, landscape architect; b. N.Y. City, Oct. 2, 1871; d. Joseph H. and Ellen D. (Brookes) Brown; ed. in landscape architecture, Mass. Inst. Tech., 1901-03; m. William A. Hutcheson, Oct. 12, 1910. Has practiced extensively in Mass., N.Y., L.I., N.J.; lecturer. Fellow Am. Soc. Landscape Architects; mem. Nat. Soc. Colonial Dames, Garden Club of American. Clubs: Cosmopolitan, Colony. Author: The Spirit of the Garden, 1923; also articles on landscape architecture topics in mags. Home: Gladstone, N.J.; also 1211 Park Av., New York NY‡

HUTCHINSON, EDITH STOTESBURY, author; b. Phila., Apr. 3, 1877; d. Edward Townsend and Frances Bergman (Butcher) Stotesbury; pub. sch. edn.; m. Sydney Emlen Hutchinson, of Phila., Dec. 2, 1903. Episcopalian. Club: Acorn (Phila.). Author: A Pair of Little Patent Leather Boots, 1913. Homes: 1718 Walnut St., Philadelphia, and Beverly Farms MA‡

HUTCHINSON, FORNEY, clergyman; b. Center Point, Ark., Sept. 28, 1875; s. Augustus Simpson and Ozella (Hankins) H.; A.B., Hendrix Coll., 1899, D.D., 1916; B.D., Vanderbilt, 1905; LL.D., Oklahoma City U., 1924; m. Bertie Anderson, Dec. 30, 1908; children—John Paul, Forney, Kelsey, Virginia. Ordained ministry M.E. Ch., South, 1900; pastor successively Little Rock, Hot Springs, Texarkana, Ark., until 1918; pastor St. Luke's Ch., Oklahoma City, Okla., 1918-32, Mt. Vernon Place Ch., Washington, D.C., 1932-35, Boston Av. Ch., Tulsa, Okla., 1935-41, St. Paul's Meth. Church, Shawnee, Okla., 1941-43; retired Oct. 1943. Delegate to Gen. Conf. M.E. Ch., S., 5 times; del. to Uniting Conf. of Methodism, Kansas City, Mo., 1939. Served as mem. State Bd. of Edn., Ark. and Okla.; pres. Okla. State S.S. Conv., 1928-29. Trustee Southern Meth. U.‡

HUTCHINSON, MARK EASTWOOD, educator; b. Providence, R.I., June 29, 1889; s. Bennett W. and Ruth Ann (Eastwood) H.; A.B., Ohio Wesleyan College, Delaware, O., 1910; A.M., U. of Neb., 1913; Ph.D., U. of Wis., 1926; m. Mae Peery, Nov. 23, 1922; children—Mark Eastwood, Haynes Bennett. Acting prof. Latin, Neb. Wesleyan U., Lincoln, 1912-13, Park Coll., Parkville, Mo., 1914-15; asst. in Latin, U. of Wis., 1915-16, 1925-26; prof. Latin and Greek, Emory and Henry Coll., 1919-26; prof. Latin, Cornell Coll., Mt. Vernon, Ia., 1926-34, prof. classical langs. and lit., 1934, later Edwin R. and Mary E. Mason prof. of Latin and Hamline prof. of Greek and archaeology; visiting prof. Latin, summers, State U. of Ia., Iowa City, Ia., 1931, U. Southern Calif., 1932, Columbia U., 1935, U. of Colo., 1936, U. of Neb., 1940, U. of Pittsburgh, 1945, U. of Minn., 1947, Miami U., 1948. Served with A.E.F., 1917-19. Member Am. Philol. Assn., Classical Assn., Middle West and South (mem. com. on present status of classical edn., 1935-37, 1943-44; v.p. for Ia., 1934-38), Am. Classical League (chmn. com. on research in teaching Latin, 1935-38), Am. Assn. Univ. Profs., Phi Delta Kappa, Alpha Sigma Phi. Asso. editor: Classical Outlook Grammar, 1926; Hutchinson Latin Grammar Scales, 1928; Course of Study in Latin for Iowa High Schools, 1930; Bibliography and Outline of a Latin Teacher's Course, 1940; Hutchinson Test in Latin Comprehension (privately printed), 1942. Author: Curriculum Investigations in Foreign Languages (with Algernon Coleman), pub. Rev. of Ednl. Research, 1937. Contbr. numerous articles to classical and ednl. mags. Home: Mount Vernon IA Died Jan. 15, 1968.

HUTCHISON, STUART NYE, clergyman; b. Pleasant Plains, N.Y., May 20, 1877; s. Sylvanus Nye and Sarah Matilda (Seeley) H.; A.B., Lafayette College, 1900, A.M., 1903; graduated Princeton Theological Seminary, 1903; D.D., Hampden-Sidney College, 1916; LL.D., Washington and Jefferson College, 1942, Lafayette Coll., 1943; m. Mary Hall Thompson, Dec. 2, 1907; children—Janet (Mrs. David Evans), Stuart Nye, Richard Hall. Ordained Presbyn. ministry, 1903; assistant pastor South Park Church, Newark, N.J., 1903-04; pastor 1st Ch., Steubenville, O., 1904-06, 1st Ref. Ch., Newark, N.J., 1906-10, First Presbyterian Ch., Norfolk, Va., 1910-21, East Liberty Ch., Pittsburgh, 1921-47; pres. ad interim The Western Theological Sem., 1950-51. Moderator of Presbyterian Church, U.S.A., 1942-43; chmn. Presbyn. War-Time-Service Commn., 1942-44. Trustee Princeton Theol. Sem., Western Theol. Sem., Lafayette Coll., Grove City Coll., Maryville Coll. Mem. Presbyn. Bd. Pensions, 1923-47. Mem. Delta Upsilon. Clubs: Dequesne, Cleric. Author: The Soul of a Child, 1916; For the Children's Hour, 1918; Bible Boys and Girls, 1921; The Voice Within Us, 1932; Holy Ground, 1934. Contbr. to many religious publs. Home: 6112 Alder St., Pittsburgh‡

HUTCHMAN, J(OHNSTON) HARPER, clergyman; b. on farm nr. Pittsburgh, Pa.; s. Samuel and Rachel (Huggins) H.; A.B. Monmouth (Ill.) Coll., 1888; student Pittsburgh Theol. Sem., 1888-91; D.D., Muskingum Coll., New Concord, O., 1917; m. Sarah Ellen Lacey, of Monmouth, Ill., June 15, 1892; children—Grace Evelyn (dec.), Ralph Josiah, Ruth Lacey (widow of Rev. David J. Lewis), Paul Eugene. Ordained ministry Presbyn. Ch.; pastor Cochranton, Pa., Zanesville, O., New Castle, Pa., and Irwin, Pa., 1891-1918; pastor U.P. Ch., Pittsburg, Kan., since 1918; moderator synod of Kan., 1922-23. Dir. Sterling Coll.; mem. bd. edn., U.P. Ch. For 8 yrs. has been holding monthly gospel meetings with the mem of K.C.S. Ry. shops on company time. Home: 810 W. Euclid Av., Pittsburg KS

HUTSON, LEANDER C., mfr.; b. Centertown, Mo., Jan. 16, 1876; s. David N. and Martha Hutson; student Chillicothe Normal Coll.; married, 1906; 1dau., Mildred Elizabeth. Dir. Farmers Gin Co., Okla. Nat. Bank of Chickasha; v.p. Chickasha Bldg. & Loan Co.; pres. Chickasha Acala Cotton Seed Co., Cooper Cotton Oil Co. Mem. Okla. State C. of C. (past pres.). Democrat. Mem. M.E. Ch. Home: 1102 S. 8th St. Office: Chickasha OK*‡

HUTTON, COLIN OSBORNE, educator; b. Dunedin, New Zealand, Jan. 10, 1910; s. John and Jessie Alexander (Holms) H.; M.S., U. Otago, 1934; Shirtcliffe fellow, external research student Emmanuel Coll., 1936-38; Ph.D., Cambridge, 1938, Sc.D., 1952; m. Mary Piggot, Dec. 26, 1940. Came to U.S., 1947. Acting lectr. geology U. Otago, 1934-36, sr. lectr., 1946-47; govt. mineralogist, petrologist, Wellington, New Zealand, 1938-46; hon. lectr. petrology Victoria U. Coll., 1943-46; asso. prof. Stanford, 1947-48, prof. mineralogy, 1948-72. Guggenheim fellow, 1953-54. Recipient Hamilton award, 1937; Sir Julius Von Haast prize. 1934: NSF award research, 1961-63, 64-66, 68-70. Fellow Geol. Soc. Am., Geol. Soc. London, Royal Soc. New Zealand, Mineral. Soc. Am., Cal. Acad. Scis.; mem. Mineral. Assn. Can., Mineral. Soc. Great Britain, Cambridge Natural History Soc., New Zealand Assn. Sci. Workers (hon. life), Sigma Xi. Contbr. sci. articles to profl. jours. Former asso. editor Royal Soc. New Zealand. Home: Portola Valley CA Died Dec. 13, 1971; buried Palo Alton CA

HUTTON, JOSIAH LAWSON, banker; b. Bedford County, Tenn., Mar. 11, 1860; s. John P. and Frances M. (Clark) H.; ed. pub. schs., Shelbyville, Tenn.; studied law, Cumberland U. Law Sch., Lebanon, Tenn.; m. Pierre Coleman, May 15, 1900; children—Josephine (Mrs. Beverly Douglas), Pierre Coleman. Organizer Bank of Bell Buckle, Tenn., 1887, and cashier until 1894; organizer Phoenix Bank, Columbia, Tenn., 1894, and cashier until 1905, when the bank was converted into the Phoenix Nat. Bank, of which was pres.; 1st supt. of banks of Tenn., by appmt. of gov. of Tenn., Jan. 1-May 10, 1914; organizer, May 1914, and since pres. The Mercantile Nat. Bank, Memphis, Tenn.; organizer, 1930, since pres. Middle Tenn. Bank; dir. City Nat. Bank (Decatur, Ala.), Jefferson County Bank (Birmingham, Ala.). Democrat. Presbyterian. Clubs: Memphis Country, Chickasaw, Tennessee. Home: Columbia TN‡

HUXMAN, WALTER A., judge; b. Pretty Prairie, Kan., Feb. 16, 1887; s. August A. and Mary (Graber) H.; student Emporia State Teachers Coll., 1909-11; LL.B., Kan. U., 1914; m. Eula E. Biggs, Jan. 21, 1915; 1dau., Ruth. Admitted to Kan. bar, 1915; asst. co. atty., 1915-19; city atty. Hutchinson, Kan., 1919-21; mem. State Tax Commn., Kan., 1931-32; gov. of Kan., 1937-39; mem. U.S. Circuit Court of Appeals, 10th Circuit, 1939-72. Mem. Christian Ch. Mason, Odd Fellow. Home: Topeka KS Died June 1972.

HYATT, CARL BRITT, exec. dir.; b. Micaville, N.C., Mar. 16, 1893; s. James Lee and Margaret Clara (Griffith) H.; A.B., U. N.C., 1917, grad. diploma history, 1917, certificate in law, 1919; m. Laura Belle Berghauser, Dec. 27, 1917 (died July 1, 1947); children—Carl Battle, John Lee (dec.), William Coleman, Lillian E. (Mrs. John G. DeJesus, Jr.); m. 2d, Alice Scott Nutt, Apr. 17, 1949. Admitted to N.C. bar, 1919; prin. elementary and high sch., Burnsville, N.C., 1917; prin. high sch., Fairview, N.C., 1918; asst. prin., head history dept. high sch., Asheville, N.C., 1919-24; tchr. sch. adminstrn. and management State Summer Sch., Asheville, 1920, 21; judge City-Co. Juvenile Ct., Asheville, 1924-32; cons. in charge fed. juvenile offender program U.S. Children's Bur., Washington, 1932-34, spl. atty. Dept. of Justice, 1935-39; ednl. specialist Immigration and Naturalization Service, 1942-44, asst. commr., 1952-55; original proposer North Carolina Probation law, approved 1937, Fed. Juvenile Delinquency Act, passed by Congress, 1938, Citizenship Day Resolution, passed, 1952; dir. Atty. Gen.'s. Citizenship Program, 1944-55; cons. citizenship com. N.E.A., from 1944. Dir. U.S. Atty. Gen.'s Adv. Com. on Citizenship, 1946-53; one of founders, 1946, member exec. com., from 1946, Nat. Conf. Citizenship, and incorporator, congl. charter, 1953, exec. dir., 1953-66; exec. com. D.C. I Am an Am. Day (now Citizenship Day) since 1943, hon. chmn., 1948. Recipient Patriotic Civilian Service award, Sec. of the Army, 1948; award of Merit, D.A.R., 1955; certificate of award, U.S. Dept. Justice, 1955; Meritorious Service Certificate, N.J. Citizenship Council, 1957; award of Appreciation, Boy Scouts America, 1960; Am. Heritage Found. award, 1961, B'nai B'rith award, 1962; Distinguished Citizen award D.C. Constn. Day Com., 1966. Mem. N.C. P.T.A. (life, sec. 1923), Fed. (chmn. citizenship com. 1942-63), American, International; North Carolina bar associations, Nat. Assns. Social Workers, N.C. Conf. Social Service (pres. 1928), Internat. Soc. Crippled Children (dir. 1933-34), D.C. Assn. Crippled Children and Disabled Adults (pres. 1933-34), D.C. Pub. Welfare Assn. (pres. 1933-34). Author: Gateway to Citizenship, 1943, rev., 1948; also articles social, legal, ednl. publs. Home: Rockville MD Died May 30, 1969; buried Lewis Memorial Park, Asheville NC

HYDE, ARTHUR KNOX, architect; b. Detroit, Mich., June 19, 1895; s. Francis and Caroline (Knox) H.; student Coll. Architecture, U. of Mich., 1921-24; m. Florence M. Moore (nee Henderson), Nov. 27, 1940; children—Alexander W. Moore, James H. Moore. Asso. with Varney & Varney, Albert Kahn, Marcus R. Burrowes, Crombie & Stanton, Varney, Albert Kahn, Marcus R. Burrowes, Crombie & Stanton, Hugh T. Keyes, 1914-25; registered architect in Mich., 1925; practice of architecture since 1925 under following firm names: Arthur K. Hyde, 1925-26, Stratton & Hyde, 1926-31, Arthur K. Hyde, 1931-36, Hyde & Williams, 1936-42; architect-cons. Giffels and Vallet, Inc., L. Rosseti, Detroit, 1942-53, v.p., 1953-57; dir. pub. relations Harley, Ellington & Day, Inc., 1957-62; dir. of pub. and client relations Eberle M. Smith Associates, Incorporated, Detroit, 1962-70. With 57th F.A. Brigade Hdqr. 32d Div., U.S. Army, 1918-19. Fellow Am. Inst. Architects (mem. Detroit chpt.) (treas. 1928-30, sec., 1930-33, v.p. 1936-38, pres. 1938-40, dir. 1940-42); mem. Mich. Soc. Architects (dir. 1947), Engring. Soc. Detroit, Detroit Historical Society, Mich. Archtl. Found. (pres. 1957-62), Essex &Kent Scottish Regiment (Windsor, Ont.), Newcomen Soc. in North America, Pub. Relations Soc. Am., Kappa Sigma. Republican. Episcopalian. Clubs: Press (Windsor, Ont.); Rotary. Detroit Club, University (Detroit). Home: Birmingham MI Died May 21, 1970

HYDE, ELIZABETH A(DSHEAD), author; b. Southport, Eng., July 31, 1876; d. John and Emily (Watson) H.; ed. pub. schs. and pvtly.; studied sociol. problems in Europe, 1903-04. Editorial and statis. work, U.S. Immigration Commn., 1909-11, railroad arbitration bds., 1912-13, U.S. Commn. on Industrial Relations, 1913-15, Nat. War Labor Bd., 1918-19, U.S. Bur. Labor Statistics, 1915-18, 1919-20; statistician Women's Bur. U.S. Dept. of Labor, 1920-30, and editor since Mar. 1, 1927. Author: Little Brothers to the Scouts, 1917; Little Sisters to the Camp Fire Girls, 1918; also numerous short stories and poems. Mem. League of Am. Pen Women (pres. 1909-10), Nat. Women's Trade Union League, United Federal Workers of America. Conglist. Pen name E. A. Watson Hyde. Home: 1760 Euclid St. Office: Dept. of Labor, Washington DC‡

HYDE, GRANT MILNOR, educator; b. The Dalles, Ore., Apr. 4, 1889; s. Will Henry and Georgia Mabel (Colvin) H.; student Beloit Coll., 1906-08; B.A., Yale, 1910, M.A., 1913; M.A., U. Wis., 1912; m. Helen M. Patterson, Aug. 29, 1957. Instr. journalism, U. Wis., 1910-15, successively asst. prof., asso. prof., and prof. of journalism, 1924-59, prof. emeritus, 1959-72, also dir. Sch. of Journalism, 1935-49; editor University Press Bur., 1915-27; formerly mng. editor Popular Science Monthly, also on staff N.Y. Evening Mail, Popular Mechanics Mag., Janesville (Wis.) Gazette, Beloit (Wis.) News, New Haven (Conn.) Journal-Courier, and corr. Christian Science Monitor. Mem. Am. Assn. Schs. and Depts. of Journalism (pres. 1936), Nat. Joint Com. on Newspaper Relations (chmn. 1936-40), Am. Assn. Teachers of Journalism (pres. 1928), Am. Assn. Univ. Profs., Wis. Press Assn., S.A.R., Phi Beta Kappa, Sigma Delta Chi, Kappa Tau Alpha (nat. sec., 1935, v.p. 1937). Episcopalian. Mason (32 deg., Shriner). Clubs: University (pres. 1929), Madison Lions. Author: several books on journalism, including Newspaper Handbook, 1941; Newspaper Reporting, 1912. Home: Madison WI Died Sept. 9, 1972.

HYDE, HENRY MORROW, author, journalist; b. Freeport, Ill., Oct. 6, 1866; s. Henry C. and Mary Campbell (Morrow) H.; Ph.B., Beloit Coll., 1888; m. Miss Robert M. Hanson, Jan. 1896; 1 son, Robert Henry. Editor Technical World 6 yrs.; staff of Chicago Tribune, 1913-20, and London corr. for same, 1919; now Washington corr. The Baltimore Evening Sun. Mem. Phi Beta Kappa. Club: National Press (Washington, D.C.). Author: Animal Alphabet, Child's Book of Verse, 1900; One Forty Two, Confessions of the Reformed Messenger Boy, 1901; Through the Stage Door, 1903; The Buccaneers, 1904; The Upstart, 1906. Contbr. to Saturday Evening Post and many other mags. and periodicals. Home: Blenheim, Albermarle County, Va. Address: National Press Bldg., Washington DC‡

HYDE, HOWARD ELMER, contracting engr.; b. Ithaca, N.Y., May 19, 1876; s. Orange Percy and Eloise (Davies) H.; C.E., Cornell U., 1900; m. Evangeline M. Manatt, June 1917. Engr. dept. of sewers, Havana, Cuba, 1900-01; resident engr. in charge constrn. of substructure Toledo Terminal R.R. Bridge over lower Maumee River, 1901-02; asst. and 1st asst., acting city engr. and mem. Municipal Bd., City of Manila, P.I., 1902-06; 1st engr. Dept. of Pub. Wks., U.S. Provisional Govt. of Cuba, 1907-08; designing and prin. asst. engr. Havana Sewerage and Drainage Contracts, 1908-14; asst. engr. Bd. of Water supply, Providence, R.I., 1915-16; mem. Young & Hyde, Inc., contracting engrs., New York, since 1912, pres., 1917-41; with U.S. Navy on construction of dry docks, Brooklyn Navy Yard, 1941-43, on construction of naval torpedo testing range, Montauk, L.I., 1943-44; with Public Works Dept. of Nassau County, N.Y., 1944-48; retired. Mem. Am. Soc. C.E., Cornell Soc. C.E. Home: R. 1, Lincolnville ME‡

HYDE, HOWARD KEMPER, govt. ofcl.; b. Almont, N.D., Sept. 6, 1911; s. Eber Watson and Ida (Lebert) H.; A.B. summa cum laude Fletcher Coll., 1934; A.M., U. Chgo., 1935, Ph.D., 1961; m. Sarah Marie Black, June 5, 1936; children—Anne Taunton, Hunter Black. Asst. to dean U. Chgo. Grad. Sch. Bus., 1935, mem. research staff dept. polit. sci., 1936-39; research analyst, cons. U.S. Temporary Nat. Econ. Com., Washington, 1939-40; asst. dir. research and edn. U.S. Immigration and Naturalization Service, Dept. Justice, Washington, 1940-42; adminstrv. officer Recruitment and Manning Orgn., War Shipping Adminstrn. and Maritime Commn., Washington, 1942-44; dep. dir., 1944-46, dir., 1946-49; mgmt. engr. fiscal mgmt. div. Office Sec. Def. Dept., 1950-52; dep. dir., 1952-54, dir. 1954-59, mgmt. evaluation officer, 1959-61, systems analysis officer, 1961; chief pub. adminstrn. adviser U.S. AID mission to India, New Delhi, 1961-63, chief management adviser, 1963-69, attache American embassy, 1962-69; resident mgmt. adv. Internat. Bank for Reconstrn. and Development (World Bank), New Delhi, India, 1969-70. Cons. on govt. orgn. Hoover Commn., 1948; cons. interdepartmental relationships Dept. State, 1949; cons. indsl. moblzn. Library of Congress, 1950; lectr., prof. Am. U., 1951-70; chmn. Sec. Def. Com. on Mgmt. Information, 1961; examiner Indian Inst. Pub. Adminstrn., New Delhi, 1962-70; adv. council U.S. Retraining and Re-employment Adminstrn., 1946; mem. President's Com. on Employing the Handicapped, 1947-53. Dir. United Seamen's Service, 1946, 52-63, member of the international council, 1963-70. Fellow Soc. Advancement Mgmt. (nat. dir. 1947-51, nat. sec. 1949-51); mem. Armed Forces Mgmt. Assn. (nat. dir. 1957-61, nat. v.p. 1959-61), Am. Soc. Pub. Adminstrn., Internat. Inst. Adminstrv. Scis., Indian Inst. Pub. Adminstrn., India Mgmt. Assn. (member of the national executive council), Am. Polit. Sci. Assn., Internat. Assn. Polit. Sci. Am. Assn. UN, India Internat. Centre, Soc. Internat. Devel., A.A.A.S. Episcopalian. Clubs: Delhi Gymkhana, Delhi Golf, Delhi Polo. Author: Social Control of Business, 1936; (with Marshall E. Dimock) Bureaucracy and

Trusteeship in Large Corporations, 1940; (with W.Y. Elliott, T.D. Perry) Mobilization Planning and the National Security, 1950. Contbg. author: Fifty Years Progress in Management; Management of Public Enterprise; also articles to profl. jours. Home: New Delhi India Died July 1970.

HYDE, HOWARD LINTON, lawyer, business exec.; b. Chillicothe, O., Dec. 15, 1900; s. Wilby G. and Helen (Frizell) H.; A.B., Ohio State U., 1922; LL.B., Harvard Law Sch., 1925; m. Katharine P. Litchfield, Oct. 1, 1927; children—Alan, Paul. Admitted to Ohio bar, 1925; asso., then partner Thompson, Hine & Flory, Cleve., 1925; v.p., gen. counsel Goodyear Tire and Rubber Co., Akron, O., and subsidiaries, 1939-60, exec. v.p. financial and legal affairs, 1960-64, vice chmn. bd., 1964-66. Vice chmn. Ohio Arts Council; trustee Cleve. Council World Affairs; overseer's vis. com. Harvard Law Sch., also asso. gen. counsel. Mem. Internat., Am., Ohio State, Cleve. bar assns., Phi Beta Kappa, Beta Theta Pi. Episcopalian. Clubs: University (N.Y.C.); Union, Kirtland Country, Tavern (Cleve.); Rolling Rock (Ligonier, Pa.); Mill Cleveland OH Died Sept. 10, 1972.

HYDE, JAMES MACDONALD, mining engr.; b. Mystic Bridge, Conn., June 25, 1873; s. William Penn and Seraphine Smith (Carr) H.; A.B., Stanford, 1901; m. Bessie Lorrain Ransom, of North San Juan, Nevada Co., Calif., 1923; 1 dau., Helen Elizabeth. Curator Calif. State Mining Bur. Mus., 1901-02; asst. prof. mining and metallurgy, U. of Ore., 1903-06; metallurgist Guanajuato Cons. Mining & Milling Co., 1906; supt. Manhattan Ore Reduction & Refining Co., 1907; cons. practice and independent operator, 1907-19; field agt. Mexican Syndicate, 1910; prof. metallurgy, Stanford, 1919-26; engaged as mine operator and in oil production since 1926. Vice pres. Bd. Pub. Works, Los Angeles, Calif., 1929-30, mem. City Council 1931-39. Democrat. Conglist. Mason. Contbr. tech. articles and editorials. Inventor Hyde roughing and cleaning flotation process, Hyde pneumatic flotation machine, etc. Home: 2079 Mound St., Hollywood CA‡

HYDE, JEANNETTE ACORD, b. Spring City, Utah; d. Abraham and Nancy (Frost) Acord; student Brigham Young U.; grad. Normal degree U. of Utah, 1883; m. Joseph S. Hyde, of Salt Lake City, July 22, 1887; children—Jay, Mrs. Romania Wooley, Golda V., Orson A., Frank W. Dir. Civic Campaign of Social Welfare, Salt Lake City, under administration of Grover Cleveland; an organizer of Camp Glen, for working girls; active in conservation movement, World War; exec. mem. State Council Defense, City Council Defense; won nat. prize for best war garden; mem. Women's Liberty Loan Com.; exec. mem. Red Cross Chapter; a founder Women's Civic Center, etc. Chmn. Women's Rep. Orgn. of Utah 12 yrs.; regional dir. Nat. Rep. Orgn.; del.-at-large Rep. Nat. Convention, 1920; mem. Rep. Nat. Com.; mem. Bd. of Regents, U. of Utah. Mormon. Collector of Customs, Honolulu, HI. Address: Customs Office, Honolulu HI‡

HYDE, JOHN BACHMAN, ry. ofcl. (ret.); b. St. L., Mo., Apr. 28, 1890; s. Charles R. (clergyman) and Anne Rea (Bachman) H.; A.B., U. of Va., 1912; LL.B., Chattanooga Coll. of Law, 1914; m. Willa Ker Foster, Jan. 5, 1916; 1 dau., Rose Foster (Mrs. Herbert P. Fales). Admitted to Tenn. bar and practicing atty., Chattanooga, Tenn., 1914-26; solicitor law dept. Southern Ry. Co., 1926-30, gen. atty., later gen. solicitor, 1930-32, v.p. in charge finance, corporate relations, purchases, ins., real estate 1932-56 (ret.); engaged in historical research. Enlisted as private in the U.S. Army, promoted through grades to 2d lt., adj., 1st Bn., 308th Inf., 77th Division, A.E.F., 1918. Mem. Washington Society of Investment Analysts, American Legion, American Bar Association, Sigma Alpha Epsilon, Delta Theta Phi. Republican. Episcopalian. Clubs: Metropolitan, Chevy Chase (Washington); Mountain City (Chattanooga). Author: Second Supplement Legal History Southern Railway Company, 1958. Home: Washington DC Died Mar. 30, 1970.

HYDE, MARY BACKUS, educator; b. Yantic, Conn., Dec. 17, 1869; d. George Rodney and Catherine Rhoda (Dickey) H.; grad. Norwich (Conn.) Free Acad., 1889, Norwich Art Sch., 1893; student summer session, Columbia, 1902; grad. Pratt Inst., Brooklyn, 1902. Supervisor drawing, pub. schs., Norwich, 1898-1900; instr. handwork for elementary schs., Sch. of Manual Training, Teachers Coll. (Columbia), 1902-08; instr. arts and crafts, East Tech. High Sch., Cleveland, O., 1908-09; with Pratt Inst., 1909-35, supervisor classes for training of teacher and instr. in design; retired, June 1935. Exhibitor at Am. Water Color Soc., Brooklyn Soc. of Artists, Brooklyn Museum. Mem. Eastern Arts Assn., Am. Artists Professional League; asso. mem. N.Y. Water Color Club; craftsman mem. Soc. of Arts and Crafts, Boston. Conglist. Home: 62 Church St., Norwich CT‡

HYDE, NELSON COLLINGWOOD, newspaperman; born Syracuse, N.Y., Jan. 21, 1888; s. Salem and Ann (Cheney) H.; student, Phillips Exeter Acad., N.H., 1908-09; m. Naomi Andrews, Jan. 20, 1915 (divorced, 1928); children—Patricia (Mrs. Edward B. Fonda), Ann (Mrs. Ralph Gould); m. 2d, Martha Pleasants, May 17, 1930; 1 son, Nelson Collingwood. Reporter Syracuse Herald, 1909-13, city editor, 1913-14; managing editor Watertown (N.Y.) Standard, 1914-15; Washington corr. for upstate N.Y. papers, 1915-17; editor Bankers Trust Co. publs., N.Y. City, 1919-21; v.p. City Bank and Trust Co., Syracuse, 1921-24; columnist Syracuse Herald, 1924-27; editor and pub. The Pilot (weekly), Sandhills Daily News, So. Pines, N.C., 1927-42; Washington corr. Phila. Eve. Bull., 1943-51; editor, pub. The Outlook, Pinehurst, N.C., 1951-71, Moore County News, Cathage, N.C., 1957-71. Served as 1st lt., U.S. Army A.C., 1917-20. Mem. Sigma Delta Chi. Club: Nat. Press (Washington). Address: Pinehurst NC Died Oct. 14, 1971; buried Bethesda Cemetery, Aberdeen NC

HYER, DAVID BURNS, JR., utilities co. exec.; b. Charleston, S.C., June 10, 1904; s. David Burns and Sally (Mazyck) H.; B.S., Ga. Inst. Tech., 1925; m. Selina Wilson, June 29, 1932; 1 son, David Burns III. Comml. mgr. Fla. Power Corp., St. Petersburg, Fla., 1950; exec. v.p. So. Colo. Power Co. div. Central Telephone & Utilities Corp., Pueblo, 1951, pres., dir., 1952-61, pres., 1961-69; exec. v.p., dir. Central Telephone & Utilities Corp., 1962-69; dir. Minnequa Bank of Pueblo, Ry. Bldg. & Loan Assn. Adv. bd. USAF Acad., 1957; bd. dirs. Pueblo Single Fund, 1953, Pueblo chpt. A.R.C., 1953; trustee Parkview Episcopal Hosp., 1959. Mem. Pueblo Engrs. Soc., Rocky Mountain Elec. League (past pres.), Greenhorns (past pres.), Pueblo C. of C. (v.p.). Episcopalian. Elk, Rotarian. Clubs: Pueblo Golf and country; Denver Country. Home: Pueblo CO Died Aug. 20, 1969.

HYLAN, JOHN PERHAM, educator; b. at Fremont, N. H., Aug. 27, 1870; s. Ira and Susan P. (Lyford) H.; grad. Harvard, 1895; post-grad. studies Clark Univ., 1895-7, Ph.D., 1901; unmarried. Instr. psychology, Univ. of Ill., 1897, asst. prof. 1898; student Leipzig and Heidelberg, 1899-1900; post-grad. at Harvard, 1900-1; teaching doctor of philosophy, Harvard, 1901-2; independent investigator, 1901-3. Author: Public Worship, 1901, 03; also various monographs on psychol. topics. Address: Exeter NH‡

HYLAND, FRANCIS E., bishop; b. Phila., Oct. 9, 1901; s. James J. and Sarah R. (McCarron) H.; A.B., St. Charles Sem., Phila., 1923; J.C.D., Cath. U., Washington, 1928. Ordained priest Roman Cath. Ch., 1927, monsignor, 1933, domestic prelate, 1938; sec. Apostolic Delegation, Washington, 1929-38; pastor Ch. of Resurrection, Chester, Pa., 1938-41, Ch. Our Lady of Lourdes, Phila., 1941-49; apptd. Titular Bishop of Gomphi, auxiliary Bishop Diocese of Savannah-Atlanta, 1949; consecrated Bishop, Cathedral of Phila., 1949; 1st Bishop Diocese of Atlanta, 1956. Home: Atlanta GA Died Jan. 31, 1968.

HYMAN, ALBERT SALISBURY, cardiologist; b. Boston, Mass., Apr. 6, 1893; s. John Jacob and Caroline (Greenwood) H.; A.B., Harvard, 1915, M.D., 1918; Med. Sc.D., U. London, 1924; med. deg. cardiology U. Vienna, 1925; m. Lillian Edyth Levenson, Jan. 29, 1967. Resident physician Boston City Hosp., 1919-20; med. supt. Mt. Sinai Hosp., Phila., 1920-23; med. dir. Jewish Maternity Hosp., Phila., 1922-23; med. supt. Beth David Hosp., N.Y.C., 1923-24; cons. cardiologist VA, N.Y. City Hosp. div. Mt. Sinai Hosp., Manhattan Gen. Hosp. div. Beth Israel Hosp., Richmond Meml. Hosp. (S.I.), Hosp. for Aged (Bronx); cons. cardiologist Wolffe Clinic, Phila., U.S. Naval Hosp., St. Albans, N.Y., Valley Forge (Pa.) Heart Inst. and Hosp., Beth David Hosp., Jewish Meml. Hosp., N.Y.C. Hosp. at Elmhurst, Long Beach Meml. Hosp.; attending physician N.Y. City Hosp.; dir. Daitz Cardiovascular Research Fund, N.Y. Dir. Witkin Found. for Study and Prevention Heart Disease, Cordiosonic Research Found. Examiner, Nat. Bd. Med. Examiners, 1948. Founders trustee Am. Coll. Cardiology; pres. Am. Coll. of Sports Medicine. Served from lt. comdr. to capt., USN, 1934-46; PT., and base hosps. Received Presidential Unit Citation (1st Marine Div.), Navy Commendation Ribbon. Diplomate Am. Bd. Internal Medicine. Fellow A.C.P.; mem. numerous nat., state, local profl. socs. and affiliated orgns., former pres. several. Clubs: Harvard (N.Y.C.); Rod and Gun, Outboard (Fairfield, Conn.). Medical editor Greenwood Collegiate Press. Author several books in field of cardiology latest being: Practical Cardiology, 1958; Acute Medical Syndromes, 1959. Co-author: Medical Care of the Athlete. Editor: The Medical Emergencies, 1957; Practical Cardiology, 1958; Functional Capacity of the Heart in Health and Disease, 1959. Editor: Ency. of Sports Medicine. Contbr. articles to sci. publs. Inventor artificial pacemaker for resuscitation of dying heart and other life-saving apparatus. Home: New York City NY Died Dec. 7, 1972; buried L.I. Nat. Cemetery, Farmingdale NY

HYMAN, LIBBIE HENRIETTA, zoologist; b. Des Moines, Ia., Dec. 6, 1888; d. Joseph and Sabina (Neumann) Hyman; S.B., U. Chgo., 1919, Ph.D., 1915, Sc.D., 1941; Sc.D., Goucher College, 1958, Coe Coll., 1959. Research appt. U. of Chicago, 1916-31, research on physiology and morphology of lower invertebrates; research appointment (hon.) Am. Mus. Natural History, N.Y.C., 1937—. Recipient Gold Medal, Linnean Soc. London, 1960. Mem. Am. Soc. Zoologists, Am. Micros. Soc., Am. Soc. Limnology and Oceanography, National Academy of Sciences, American Society of Naturalists, Soc. Systematic Zoology (past pres.), Phi Beta Kappa, Sigma Xi. Author: A Laboratory Manual for Elementary Zoology, 1919; A Laboratory Manual for Comparative Vertebrate Anatomy, 1922; Comparative Vertebrate Anatomy, 1942; The Invertebrates, 6 vols. 1940-67; also articles sci. jours. Recipient Elliot Gold Medal, 1951; gold medal for distinguished achievement in sci. Am. Mus. Natural History, 1969. Home: New York City NY Died Aug. 3, 1969.

HYMAN, MARION LAROCHE STROBEL (MRS. JOHN PATRICK HYMAN), realtor; b. Yonges Island, S.C., Aug. 2, 1909; d. Edmund Gilmore and Julia (McCants) Strobel; student pub. schs.; m. John Patrick Hyman, July 21, 1935 (dec. Nov. 1958). Technician dept. pathology Med. Coll. of S.C., 1927-37; supply dept. supr. U.S. Naval Ship Yard, Charleston, S.C., 1941-46; financial typist, accounting dept. So. Ice Co., Charleston, 1950-52; sec. C. Bissell Jenkins Jr., Ins., 1952-53; spl. rep. Pilot Life Ins. Co., 1958-63; owner Marion S. Hyman, Real Estate Broker, 1959-70; pres. Shell Point Homes, Inc., 1959-70; agt. Am. Mut. Fire Ins. Co., 1965-70, Am. Agy. Life Ins. Co., 1967-70. Mem. Nat. Assn. Real Estate Bds., Charleston Real Estate Bd., C. of C. Episcopalian. Home: Johns Island SC Died Aug. 29, 1970.

HYMAN, STANLEY EDGAR, literary critic; b. N.Y.C., June 11, 1919; s. Moe and Lulu (Marshak) H.; A.B., Syracuse U., 1940; m. Shirley Jackson, Aug. 13, 1940 (deceased Aug. 8, 1965); children—Laurence, Joanne, Sarah, and Barry; m. 2d, Phoebe Pettingell, Dec. 28, 1966; 1 son, Malcolm. Staff writer New Yorker magazine, 1940-70; mem. of literary faculty Bennington Coll., 1945-46, 52-70; lit. critic New Leader mag., 1961-65; research ancient Greek numismatics; vis. prof. State U. N.Y. at Buffalo, 1969-70. Fellow Am. Council Learned Socs., 1959; Guggenheim fellow, 1969. Recipient award in criticism from National Institute of Arts and Letters, 1967. Member of the American Folklore Society, Am. Numismatic Soc. Author: The Armed Vision, 1948; Poetry and Criticism, 1961; The Tangled Bank, 1962; Nathanael West, 1962; The Promised End, 1963; Flannery O'Connor, 1966; Standars, 1966. Editor: The Critical Performance, 1956; Kenneth Burke's Perspectives by Incongruity, 1964; Kenneth Burke's Terms for Order, 1964; Selected Essays of William Troy, 1967; The Magic of Shirley Jackson, 1966; Come Along with Me (Shirley Jackson), 1968; Iago: Some Approaches to the Illision of his Motivation, 1970. Address: Bennington VT Died July 28, 1970.

HYNES, JOHN B., mayor of Boston, 1949-70. Pres. U.S. Conf. of Mayors. Mem. Nat. Com. for Development of Scientists and Engrs. Address: Boston MA Died Jan. 1970.

HYRE, SARAH EMMA CADWALLADER, b. in Summitt Co., O.; d. Thomas Mifiin and Nancy (Carlisle) Cadwallader; Buchtel Coll., Akron, O. (hon. A.M., 1905); m. Alonzo Eugene Hyre, of Cleveland, Apr. 15, 1886. Taught sch. in and around Akron, O., 5 yrs.; editor The Cuyahogan, 1897-1901; mem. Bd. of Edn., Cleveland, 1905-12, clerk, 1912-1917; has given special attention to use of sch. bldgs. of Cleveland as social centers. Unitarian. Mem. D.A.R., Kappa Kappa Gamma. Club: Woman's. Home: 3325 Archwood Av., S.W., Cleveland‡

HYZER, W. EDWARD, banker; b. Chgo., Jan. 15, 1886; s. William W. and Alice (Crotsenburg) H.; corr. study, U. Wis., 1912-13; m. Edna M. Chase, June 4, 1913. Clk. Rock County Nat. Bank, Janesville, Wis., 1906-17; sec. Rock County Savs. & Trust Co., 1917-23; asst. cashier First Nat. Bank, Janesville, 1923-28, trust officer, 1928-60, v.p., 1937-60, dir., 1945-68; dir. Janesville Bldg. & Loan Assn. Pres. Corporate Fiduciaries Assn. of Wis., 1936-37. Mem. Wis. Bankers Assn., Janesville C. of C. Conglist. Mason; mem. Order Eastern Star. Clubs: Lions; Conservation. Home: Janesville WI Died Dec. 1968.

ICHAILOVITCH, LIOUBOMIR, diplomat; b. Belgrade, Serbia, Aug. 14, 1874; ed. univs. of Belgrade and Paris, France; unmarried. Entered the diplomatic service 1899; represented Serbia in diplomatic affairs with Turkey 1902-12; charge d'affaires and minister at Rome, 1912-15; apptd. minister to Montenegro, 1915, but forced by Austrian invasion to take refuge in France with the Court of Montenegro, 1916; E.E. and M.P. from Serbia to U.S. since Jan. 26, 1917. Home: 1531 New Hampshire Av., Washington DC‡

IGOE, JAMES THOMAS, ex-congressman; b. Chicago, Ill., Oct. 23, 1883; s. Thomas and Helen I.; ed. pub. schs. and business coll., Chicago; m. Katherine Jordan, Oct. 20, 1909; 1 son, James Thomas. Began in printing business as a boy; president of the James T. Igoe Building Corporation. City Clerk, Chicago, 1917-23; mem. 70th to 72d Congresses (1927-33), 6th Ill. Dist. Democrat. Clubs: Lake Shore; Surf, Indian Creek Country (Miami Beach, Fla.). Home: Evanston IL Died 1971.

INGALLS, ROSCOE CUNNINGHAM, corp. exec.; b. Engelwood, N.J., May 3, 1891; s. Roscoe K. and Frances (Hedden) I.; B.S., Columbia, 1912; m. Marjorie Riegel, Apr. 10, 1917; children—Shirley, Roscoe Cunningham. Bond dept. Spencer Trask & Co., 1912-14; partner Struthers & Hiscoe, 1917; sr. partner Ingalls & Snyder, N.Y.C., 1924-69; chmn., dir. Rockwin Oil Corp., Inc.; member bd. dirs. Capital Management Corporation. Governor N.Y. Stock Exchange, 1953-59, chmn. nominating com., 1969. Pres. sch. bd., Pelham, 1945-49. Chmn. Pelham Adult Sch. 1939-41; mem. Columbia Coll. Council; mem. Columbia Assos., chmn. 1955-59; trustee of the Columbia University, 1956-62, Columbia Presbyterian Medical Hospital Fund; trustee Inter-American University, Puerto Rico, director of Columbia Univ. Press. Member board of directors Pelham Community Chest (president, 1934-36), New York Arthritis and Rheumatism Found., Inc.; member Pelham Hose Company No. 2 (deputy chief 1923-25); mem. local bd. 739, Selective Service, 1941-47. Mem. 7th regt. N.Y. N.G. 1911-17; chief petty officer U.S.N.R., 1918-19. Mem. Assn. New York Stock Exchange Firms (pres. 1952-53), U.S., New York chambers of commerce, Columbia Alumni Federation (director), 7th Regiment Veterans Assn. Presbyn. (elder 1929-69). Clubs: Economic, Downtown, Athletic, Bankers, University, Bond (N.Y.C.); Pelham Country, Men's, Rotary (hon.). Lions (hon.) (Pelham); Causeway, Northeast Harbor Yacht (Me.); Blind Brook Golf (Port Chester, N.Y.). Home: Pelham NY Died Nov. 21, 1969.

INGE, WILLIAM, playwright; b. Indepedence, Kan., May 3, 1913; s. Luther Clayton and Maude Sarah (Gibson) I.; A.B., U. Kan., 1935; A.M., Peabody Tchrs. College, 1938. Staff Stephens Coll. for Women, 1938-43; newspaper drama, music critic St. Louis Star-Times, 1943-46; instr. English Washington U., 1946-49. Author plays: Farther Off from Heaven, 1947; Come Back, Little Sheba, 1950; Picnic, 1953 (winner Pulitzer prize, Drama Critics prize, and Donaldson award); Bus Stop, 1955; The Dark at the Top of the Stairs, 1957; A Loss of Roses, 1959; Natural Affection, 1963; Where's Daddy, 1966; author screenplay Splendor in the Grass (winner Acad. Award best original film script), 1961. Home: Hollywood Hills CA Died June 10, 1973.

INGERSOLL, TYRRELL MEYER, lawyer; b. Algona, Ia., Aug. 8, 1902; s. Charles Lawrence and Mathilda (Klamp) I.; A.B., U. Ia., 1925, J.D., 1928; m. Dorothy Denkmann, Apr. 11, 1936. Admitted to Ia. bar, 1928; practiced in Cedar Rapids, 1928-72; partner firm Shuttleworth & Ingersoll, and predecessor, 1932-72; chmn. adv. com. to Ia. Supreme Ct. on rules of practice and procedure. Dir. Diamond V Mills, Inc., Averill Wallace Welch Co., Ky. Midland Co. Inc. Bd. dirs. St. Lukes Methodist Hosp., Cedar Rapids Community Welfare Found., Linn County Humane Soc.; trustee Coe Coll. Fellow Am. Bar Found., Am. Coll. Probate Counsel; mem. Am., Ia. (pres. 1950-51), Linn County (past pres.) bar assns., Nat. Assn. Accountants, Phi Beta Kappa, Order of Coif, Alpha Sigma Phi, Phi Delta Phi. Mason (Shriner, 32 deg.), Elk, Rotarian (past pres.). Clubs: Cedar Rapids Country, Pickwick, Embassy. Cedar Rapids IA Died Jan. 27, 1972.

INGLIS, WILLIAM WALLACE, mfr.; b. Scranton, Pa., Jan. 19, 1871; s. John Scott and Janet Henderson (Lorimer) I.; student Scranton Pub. Schs., 1878-84; m. Gertrude Jayne Kennedy, Oct. 28, 1903 (died Jan. 5, 1937); children—Mary Elizabeth (Mrs. John Dodge Strong), John Scott 2d. Began as office boy Hillside Coal & Iron Co., Dunmore, Pa., 1884-88, chief clerk, 1888-1902; supt. Pa. Coal Co., Dunmore, Pa., 1902-09; gen. supt. Hillside Coal & Iron Co. and Pa. Coal Co., 1909-13, gen. mgr., 1913-16; gen. mgr. coal mining dept., D.L&W. R.R. Co., 1916-17; v.p. and mgr. coal mining dept., 1917-21; pres. Keystone Mining Co., East Brady, Pa., since 1919; pres. Glen Alden Coal Co., Scranton, Pa., since 1921; pres. Shelocta Coal Co., East Brady, Pa, since 1921; chmn. Anthracite Bd. of Concilliation since 1927; dir. First Nat. Bank, Scranton, Pa., First Nat. Bank, Willkes-Barre, Pa., D.L.&W. Coal Co., N.Y., Sprague & Henwood, Inc., Scranton, Pa., Nokomis Water Co., Factorville, Pa., Honey Brook Water Co., Wilkes-Barre, Pa. V.p., sec.-treas. and dir. Moses Taylor Hosp., Scranton, Pa. Mem. Y.M.C.A., Republican. Presbyterian. Mason (Royal Arch, Royal and Select Master, K.T., Consistory, Shriner). Clubs: Scranton, Scranton Country (Scranton, Pa.); Westmoreland (Wilkes-Barre, Pa.). Home: 1025 Vine St. Office: 310 Jefferson Av., Scranton PA*‡

INGRAHAM, EDGAR SHUGERT, college prof.; b. Tidioute, Pa., Aug. 7, 1876; s. Edgar Wilson and Katherine (Shugert) I.; A.B., Colgate U., 1897; univ. scholar, Columbia, 1899-1900, 1901-2; studied U. of Freiburg, 1900, Sorbonne, Paris, 1900-1; Harrison fellow in Romance langs., U. of Pa., 1902-3, Ph.D., 1903; instr. modern langs. Colgate U., 1897-9; asst. prof. Romance langs., 1903-15, prof. since 1915, Ohio State U. Mem. Modern Language Assn. America, Am. Assn. Teachers of Spanish, Am. Assn. Univ. Profs., Assn. Modern Lang. Teachers of Central West and South, Phi Beta Kappa, Delta Upsilon. Conglist. Author: Victoria y otros cuentos, 1905; A Brief Spanish Grammar, 1913; The Sources of Les Amours de Jean Antoine de Baif, 1905. Home: Westerville OH‡

INGRAM, DWIGHT, ins. broker; b. Indpls., Feb. 1, 1894; s. John Carl and Mary (Colby) I.; A.B., Harvard, 1916; m. Dorothy Wilson Fielder, Oct. 16, 1923 (died 1949) children—Fielder Colby, John Dwight, Thomas Edwin. With Chgo. Bd. Underwriters, 1919-21; engr. Moore, Case, Lyman & Hubbard, 1921-26; president Griffin, Ingram & Pfaff, gen. ins., brokers, Chgo., 1926-67; director Huron Press, 1949-67. Trustee John Marshall Law Sch., 1934-67, treas., 1951-54, sec., 1954-67; bd. dirs., pres. Lake County Civic League, 1961-63, v.p., 1963—; trustee Schs. of Shields Twp., 1945-54, pres., 1948-54. Sec. Army YMCA, India, 1916; chief sec. for base area, same, Mesopotamia, 1916-17; served with Tank Corps, U.S. Army, France, 1918-19. Former v.p. trustees Provident Hosp.; mem. exec. com. Fight for Freedom, 1941, Lake Forest Human Relations Council, since 1965; coordinator and chief air raid warden Civilian Def., Shields Twp., 1941-45; controller Lake County Office Civilian Def., 1943-45. Dir. Chgo. Bd. Underwriters, 1932-33, 1955-57, 59-61, Chicago Ins. Agts. Assn., 1932-33, World Mission Assos., 1944-45. Alderman, Lake Forest, 1959-65; mem. finance com. Lake Forest Caucus, 1967. Republican. Presbyn. (commr. to Gen. Assembly, Presbyterian Ch. 1945). Clubs: Onwentsia, Harvard of Chicago (v.p. 1931-32, sec. 1932-34, dir. 1949-51). Author: Property Insurance Salesmanship (corr. course). Home: Lake Forest IL Died June 28, 1967.

INGRAM, LEON JOHN, savings and loan assn. exec.; b. Almont, Mich, June 19, 1899; s. John and Martha Jane (McMorran) I.; LL.B., U. Detroit Sch. Law, 1922; m. Mae Chambers, May 24, 1933; 1 son, John Leon. Investigator Beneficial Loan Corp., Newark, 1918; with Capital Finance Corp., Columbus, O., 1939-65, chmn. bd., chief exec. officer; dir. Local Finance Corp., Marion, Ind.; pres. Economy Savs. & Loan Co., Columbus. Recipient Distinguished Service award Nat. Consumer Finance Assn., 1949. Mem. Nat. Consumer Finance Assn. (dir., exec. com., pres.). Republican. Mason (Shriner). Clubs: Boca Raton (Fla.) Hotel; Athletic (Columbus). Home: Columbus OH Died July 17, 1965.

INGVOLDSTAD, ORLANDO, clergyman; b. Decorah, Ia., May 14, 1885; s. Peter Olson and Josephine (Engebretson) I.; prep. edn. Decorah Inst. and St. Olaf Acad., Northfield, Minn.; A.B., St. Olaf Coll.; grad. study Independent Theol. Sem., Olso, Norway, and U. of Oslo, 1910-11, United Ch. Sem., St. Paul, Minn., 1911-13, U. of Minn., 1913, Bibl. Sem., N.Y. City, 1916-17; B.D., Chicago Luth. Theol. Sem., Maywood, 1918; m. Susanne May Osmon, June 18, 1912 (died April 20, 1946); children—Orlando, Paul Osmon, John Hill, Stephen Philip; m. second Jessie Helen Cole, June 6, 1947 (deceased March 10, 1962); m. third, Sara A. Bumtrock, on August 11th, 1964. Ordained to the ministry United Norwegian Luth. Ch., 1913; pastor Marshalltown, Ia., 1913-16, St. Paul's Ch., Chgo., Ill., 1918-23; founder, 1917, pres. until 1927, Chicago Luth. Bible Sch.; teacher, Northwestern Theol. Sem., Chicago, 1920-21; editor The Bible Student, 1920-27; pastor United Luth. Congregation, Grand Forks, N.D., also at U. of N.Dak. (radio pastor over KFJM), 1927-29; pastor Wicker Park Lutheran Ch., Chicago, 1929-32; pres. Chicago Luth. Bible Sch., 1932-36; Pleasant View Luther Coll., Ottawa, Ill., 1932-37; pastor Immanuel Ch., Chicago, 1933-37, Faith Ch., Chicago, 1937-41. Founder Long Lake Bible Conf., Ingleside, Ill., 1919, Lutheran Open Forum, Chicago, 1922; president Luth. Ministerial Conf., Chicago, 1923; chmn. Luth. Relief Com., Chicago area, 1930-35; pres. Long Lake Bible Conf., from 1931; v.p. and mem. exec. com. and board of Chicago Bible Soc.; Midwest area rep. for Japan Internat. Christian U.; mem. bd. Associated Church Charities of Chicago. Dir. Luth. Boys Camp, 1938; member Christian Unity Com., 1939; president Chicago Circuit Luth. Pastoral Conf., 1939; vice-chmn. Norwegian-American Com., 1939; mem. bd. dirs. Chicago Church Fedn.; mem. bd. govs. Am. Scandinavian Alliance; Ill. state chmn. Norwegian Relief, Inc., 1939, exec. sec. from 1941; mem. Chicago Com. World Council of Churches, 1939; pres. Chicago Bible Soc., 1941-46; speaker for Nat. War Fund, 1944-45; special sec. Am. Bible Soc., 1945-46; pastor United Lutheran Ch., Oak Park, Ill., 1955, Zion Ch., Chgo., from 1955. Decorated Knight of the Order of St. Olaf, 1st class (Norway), 1947. Mem. Am. Scandinavian Found. Norsemen's League. Author: Productive Religion, 1930; Beyond Our Dreams, 1960; Book of Poems, 1961; Second Book of Poems; Boots and Blackie, 1966. Home: Ingleside IL Died Apr. 5, 1969; buried Ridgewood Cemetery, Des Plaines IL

INMAN, HENRY ARTHUR, b. Rome, Ga., Feb. 8, 1869; s. Samuel Martin and Nancy Jane (Dick) I; spl. course, Princeton Univ., class of 1891; m. Roberta Southerland Crew, of Atlanta, Ga., June 6, 1894; 1 son, Arthur Crew. Began in cotton exporting business with father's firm, S.M. Inman & Co., Atlanta, Ga., 1889; partner Inman & Reid, Houston, Tex., later Inman, Nelms & Co., changed to Nelms, Kehoe & Nelms; retired in 1918; officer or dir. numerous corpns. Democrat. Presbyn. Clubs: Capital City, Piedmont Driving. Office: First Nat. Bank Bldg., Atlanta GA‡

INSLEY, WILLIAM HENRY, engineer, mfgr.; b. Terre Haute, Ind., Jan. 16, 1870; s. William Quinn and Celia (Whitmore) I.; student De Pauw U., 1889-92; B.Sc., Rose Poly. Inst., Terre Haute, Ind., 1900, M.S., 1902, C.E., 1910; m. Jane Williams, Jan. 1, 1903 (died Feb. 29, 1948); 1 son, Francis Henry. Founder, 1905, pres., gen. mgr. until retirement, 1940, Insley Mfg. Corp.; engrs. and mfrs. contractors' machinery, and structural iron work, especially concrete distbn. equipment and excavators; patentee of excavating equipment and equipment for distbn. of concrete by gravity; dir. Citizens Gas Co. Cons. engr. for Ind. of U.S. Fuel Adminstrn., World War I, also chmn. Ind. subregion, War Industries Bd. Mem. state com. Indiana Y.M.C.A.; pres. Soc. Ind. Pioneers' past pres. Indianapolis Community Fund; mem. Board Volunteers of America; past pres. Indianapolis Family Welfare Society; mem. Am. Soc. M.E. (organizer and 1st chmn. Ind. sect.), Am. Soc. C.E. (life). Republican. Methodist (trustee). Clubs: Indianapolis Literary, Irvington Dramatic. Home: 445 N. Audubon Rd., Indianapolis 19‡

INSULL, MARTIN JOHN, pub. utilities; b. Reading, Eng., Sept. 18, 1869; s. Samuel, Sr., and Emma (Short) I.; M.E. in Mech. Engring., Cornell U., 1893; m. Virginia Van Vliet, of East Orange, N.J., Dec. 13, 1894; 1 dau., Virginia Cornwell. With Sargent and Lundy, elec. engrs., 1893-98; v.p. and gen. mgr. Gen. Incandescent Arc Light Co., New York, 1898-1904; v.p. Stanley Gen. Incandescent Elec. Co., 1904-06, United Gas & Elec. Co., New Albany, Ind., New Albany Water Works, Louisville & Northern Ry. and Light Co., Louisville & Southern Ind. Traction Co., 1906-12; sr. v.p. Middle West Utilities Co., 1912-24, pres., 1924-32; chmn. Central Power & Light Co., The Great Lakes Power Co., Ltd., Southwestern Gas & Electric Co., Southwestern Light & Power Co., West Tex. Utilities Co.; chmn. bd. Central Me. Power Power Co., West Tex. Utilities Co.; chmn. bd. Central Me. Power Co., Pub. Service Co. of N.H.; vice chmn. Am. Pub. Service Co., Central & Southwest Utilities Co., Nat. Electric Power Co., Nat. Pub. Service Corpn.; vice chmn. bd. New England Pub. Service Co.; pres. Ark.-Mo. Power Co., The Commonwealth Light & Power Co., Inland Power & Light Corpn., Ky. Securities Corpn., Middle West Utilities Co. of Can., Ltd., Miss. Valley Utilities Investment Co., Mo. Gas & Electric Service Co., North West Utilities Co., United Pub. Service Co., United Pub. Utilities Co.; v.p. Am. Central Utilities Co., Pub. Service Co. of Okla. Trustee Cornell Univ. Mem. Nat. Electric Light Assn. (pres. 1921-22), Am. Inst. E.E., Psi Upsilon. Clubs: Chicago, University, Attic, Mid-Day, Exmoor Country (Chicago); Cornell (New York). Home: 428 Sheridan Rd., Highland Park, Ill. Office: 20 N. Wacker Drive, Chicago IL‡

IPATIEFF, VLADIMIR NIKOLAEVICH, prof. chemistry; b. Moscow, Russia, Nov. 9, 1867; s. Nicoay and Anna (Giyky) I.; student Artillery Academy, St. Petersburg, 1889-92; Ch.D., U. of St. Petersburg, 1907; hon. Dr., U. of Munich, Strasbourg, Sofia, Northwestern; m. Barbara Ermakoff, July 26, 1892; children—Nicolay, Vladimir, Anna, Dimitry. Came to U.S., 1931. Prof. of chemistry Artillery Academy, St. Petersburg, 1898-1906; prof. of chemistry, U. of St. Petersburg, 1906-15; mem. Acad. of Science, St. Petersburg since 1915; mem. Am. Nat. Acad. of Science since 1939; prof. chemistry, Northwestern U., 1931-35, prof. emeritus since 1935; dir. chemical research, Universal Oil Products Co. Lieut. gen. Russian Artillery and chmn. Chem. Com. of Russia, 1914-17. Decorated Comdr. Legion d'Honneur (France). Received Berthelot gold medal from French Chem. Soc., 1928, Lavoisier medal, 1939; silver medal from King Boris of Bulgaria, 1939; Palmes d'officier from French Acad. of Sci., 1939; awarded Willard Gibbs medal from Am. Chem. Assn., 1940; title Modern Pioneer" by Am. Nat. Assn. Mfrs., 1940. Recipient Fawcett honor award for work on aviation gasoline, 1943. Mem. Am. Chem. Soc.; hon. mem. Deutsche Chemische Gesellschaft (Berlin), Acad. of Gottingen (Germany). Club: Chicago Chemist's. Author: Text Book Organic Chemistry, 1903-30; Aluminum Oxide as Catalyst, 1929; Catalytic Reactions, at High Pressures and Temperatures, 1936; The Life of One Chemist (memoirs), 1946; also over 300 articles on high pressure catalytic reactions, 1892-1939; holds more than 200 patents. Founded Leningrad. Inst. of High Pressures, 1927; founded Ipatieff Catalytic High Pressure Lab. at Northwestern Univ., 1940. Home: 195 E. Pearson St. Office: Universal Oil Products Co., 310 S. Michigan Av., Chicago IL‡

IREDELL, FRANCIS RAYMOND, educator; b. Titusville, Pa., June 18, 1894; s. Charles Francis and Elizabeth (Hyde) I.; A.B., Pomona College, 1921; A.M., Harvard University, 1922, Ph.D., 1937; Commn. for Relief in Belgium (Belgian-Am.) fellow, U. Brussels, Belgium, 1924-25; m. Ruth Snyder, Aug. 3, 1926; children—Vernon Raymond, William Henry. Instr. philosophy, Pomona Coll., 1925-29, and Claremont Grad. Sch., 1936, asst. prof., 1929-38, asso. prof., 1939-43, prof. philosophy, Robert C. Denison Found., Pomona Coll., Claremont Grad. Sch., 1943-59; sec. faculty, Pomona Coll., 1944-48, dean of faculty, 1948-59, emeritus, 1959-72, head philosophy dept., 1938-54; U.S. Information Agy. grantee serving as dir.

Vietnamese-Am. Assn., Saigon, 1959-63; Fulbright lecturer U. Ceylon, 1954-55; vis. prof. philosophy Portland (Ore.) State Coll., 1965-66; vis. prof. Williamette University, Ore., 1967. Trustee pub. schs., Claremont, Cal., 1942-54. Served as mess sgt., Co. B, 316th Am. Tr., 91st div., U.S. Army, A.E.F., 1917-19. Recipient Distinguished Professorship award, Pomona Coll., 1959; hon. certificate Confucian Studies Assn. of Vietnam, 1960. Mem. Am. Philos. Assn. (mem. exec. com. Pacific Div., 1938-40, vice pres. 1948), Phi Beta Kappa, Cercle des Alumni de la Fond. Universitaire, Belgium, Pacific Conf. on the Teaching of Philosophy (mem. exec. com., 1951, pres. 1952). Author: Viet-Nam, the Country and the People, 1966. Contbr. articles to profl. publs. Address: Claremont CA Died June 9, 1972.

IRELAND, ALLEYNE, author; b. Manchester, Eng., Jan. 19, 1871; s. Alexander I., author of The Booklover's Enchiridion," etc.; ed. at Wrexham, Wales, Ilkley, Yorkshire, Manchester Grammar School and University of Berlin. Certificate as able seaman in sail. Traveled extensively, 1887-97; visited India, Australia, British, French and Spanish W.I. and S.America; lecturer at Cornell U., 1899, U. of Chicago, 1900, Lowell Inst., Boston, 1901-02; spent 1902-04 in Far East as correspondent of the London Times, and as colonial commr. University of Chicago, preparing report on colonial administration Eng., France, Holland and U.S. in that part of the world. Served under Gen. Leonard Wood in Mindanao, against Sultan of Taraca, 1904. Traveled in Europe and Can., 1908-10; one of pvt. secs. of late Joseph Pulitzer, 1911; on editorial staff, New York World, 1912-15. Author: Demerariana—Essays; Georgetown, Demerara, 1897; Tropical Colonization, 1899; The Anglo-Boer Conflict, 1900; China and the Powers, 1901; The Far Eastern Tropics, 1905; The Province of Burma (2 vols.), 1907; Joseph Pulitzer; Reminiscences of a Secretary, 1914; Democracy and the Human Equation, 1921; Can We Save Constitutional Government? 1922; The New Korea, 1927. Contbr. to leading mags. and newspapers. Address: 39 Chestnut St., Albany NY*‡

IRELAND, CHARLES THOMAS, JR., lawyer; b. Boston, Apr. 14, 1921; s. Charles Thomas and Margaret (Keough) I.; A.B. summa cum laude, Bowdoin Coll., 1942; LL.B., Yale, 1948; wife Dorothy; children—Anne, Claire, Stephen, Allan. Admitted to New York bar, associate of White and Case, New York City, 1948-51; sec. N.Y.C. R.R., 1954-59; senior v.p. Internat. Tel. & Tel. Corp.; dir. Investors Diversified Services, Inc., Levitt & Sons, Inc., Sheraton Corp. Am.; dir., mem. Mid-Town adv. bd. Chem. Bank N.Y. Trust Co. Member board overseers Bowdoin Coll.; bd. dirs. Grand Central branch YMCA, New York City. Served as captain USMC, 1942-46. Decorated Silver Star, Bronze Star, Purple Heart. Mem. A.I.M., Am. Bar Assn. Bar City of N.Y., Am. Mgmt. Assn., Phi Beta Kappa, Theta Delta Chi. Home: Chappaqua NY Died June 1972.

IRELAND, LLOYD OWEN, mfg. co. exec:; b. De Kalb, Ill., Apr. 30, 1927; s. George II. and Edith (Nelson) I.; B.S., U. Ill., 1949; m. Frances Valentine, May 9, 1953; children—Paige, Pamela, Randolph. Comml. audit mgr. Arthur Andersen & Co., C.P.A., N.Y.C., 1939-63; controller Colgate-Palmolive Co., N.Y.C., 1963-68; v.p. finance, dir. VIA-TRON Computer Systems Corp., 1968-70; exec. v.p., dir. Kavic House, Inc., 1970-71; v.p., dir. FAIM Information Services, Inc., 1971-73. Mem. Hillsdale (N.J.) Bd. Edn., 1961-66. Served with AUS, 1945-47. C.P.A., N.Y. Mem. Am. Inst. C.P.A.'s, N.Y. State Soc. C.P.A.'s, Financial Execs. Inst. Home: Lloyd Harbor NY Died Jan. 7, 1973.

IRELAND, R.W., air transportation; b. Chicago, July 6, 1892; s. A.D. and Ella May (Strouse) I.; ed. high school Pace Inst., Washington; m. Nell Otis, Nov. 14, 1913; 1 son, James R. Ticket agent Erie Railroad, 1912; civilian chief of div. Office of Chief of Engrs., U.S. Army, 1913-21; sec. War Dept. sub-com. on appropriations U.S. Ho. of Reps., 1921-26; became dist. traffic mgr. and gen. traffic mgr. United Air Lines, and predecessor companies, 1926, vice pres., 1945, v.p. traffic adminstrn., until 1957; dir. Air Cargo Inc.; adminstr. Defense Air Transport Adminstrn., Washington, from 1952. Pres. Air Traffic Conf. of America, 1940, chmn. various commns. on air traffic confs., 1939-42; mem. panel Am. Arbitration Assn. Served as col., U.S.A.A.F., asst. chief of staff and dept. chief of staff Air Transport Command, July 1942-Nov. 1945; brig. gen. U.S.A.F.R. D.S.M., Legion of Merit, O.B.E. Mem. Air Nat. Defense Transportation Assn. (v.p.). Home: Hendersonville NC Died Jan. 26, 1968; buried Hendersonville NC

IRELAND, THOMAS SAXTON, lawyer, author; b. Cleveland, O., Dec. 16, 1895; s. Paul F. and Lucretia (Bailey) I.; A.B., Princeton U., 1918; LL.B., Boston U., 1923, Harvard U., 1927; m. Mildred Locke, Aug. 3, 1932; children—Patricia, Ruth, Tom III, Bill, John, Fred. Admitted to O. bar, 1926; practiced in N.Y. City, later returning to Cleveland; elected judge of Municipal Court of Cleveland, short term, 1937. Grad. Inf. Sch., Ft. Benning, Ga., 1935; on active duty with U.S. Army, Ft. Benjamin Harrison, Ind., 1941-43; capt. inf., reception center, Co. G, comdg. officer, May 1942-June 1943; orientation lecturer, 1942; post defense counsel, courts martial, 1943. Nominated for assembly, 1934, 36; led Cuyahoga County legislative ticket for Rep State Senate nomination, 1938; nominated for State Senate, 1940; led Rep. slate for short term U.S. Senate nomination, Cuyahoga County, 1946; Rep. candidate for mayor of Cleve., 1959. radio news commentator, station WJAY (now WCLE), 1936-38, WTAM, Cleveland, 1938, WACD, Akron, 1941; spl. corr. Cleveland Plain Dealer, Germany, France, 1948. Columbus Dispatch, Europe, Asia, S.A., 1955-58. Mem. Ohio Bar Assn. (member of citizenship committee), Ohio Society New York, Amvets World War II, American Legion. Republican. Mason (32 deg., Shriner), Sojourner. Clubs: Rowfant, Mayfield Country, Ripon, Ocean of Fla. Author: The Greater Lakes—St. Lawrence Deep Waterway to the Sea, 1934; War Clouds in the Skies of the Far East, 1935; Child Labor as a Relic of the Dark Ages, 1937; Ireland Past and Present, 1942; The Great Lakes-St. Lawrence Seaway and Power Project, 1946. Contributing editor: Irish-American Quarterly, 1946-46. Speaks French, German, Spanish, Italian. Reportorial tours Russia, Poland, Czechoslavakia, Yugoslavia, 1955-56. Home: Shaker Heights OH Died Mar. 25, 1969; buried Lakeview Cemetery, Cleveland OH

IRLAND, GEORGE ALLISON, educator; b. Lewisburg, Pa., Jan. 3, 1894; s. Thomas Edwin and Emma P. (McCurdy) I.; B.S., Bucknell U., 1915, E.E., 1922; M.E.E., Johns Hopkins, 1925, Eng. D., 1932; m. Lillian Adelia Sindle, Sept. 16, 1924; children—Ruth M. (Mrs. John H. Morton), Edwin A., Margaret A. (Mrs. J. Landon Short), Barbara E. (Mrs. Kenneth K. Teramoto). Electrical foreman and motor control supervisor, Bethlehem Steel Co., Sparrow Point, Maryland, 1916-Jan. 1918, Jan. 1919-Sept. 1920; mem. faculty, elec. engring. dept., Bucknell U., 1920-—, asst. prof. elec. engring., 1925-38, prof., 1938-62, chmn. dept., 1938-58, chmn. engring. group, 1937-57. Dir. Citizens Electric Co., Lewisburg, 1945-71, pres., 1962-70. Chmn. Union County com. U.S. Savs. Bonds, 1963. Fellow A.A.A.S.; mem. American Institute of Electrical Engineers, Institute of Radio Engineers, Am. Soc. for Engring. Edn., Am. Geophys. Union, Pi Mu Epsilon, Tau Beta Pi, Republican. Presbyn. Author: Construction of Master Oscillator for Testing Seismic Recorders and Other Apparatus (with F.W. Lee), U.S. Bur. of Mines, 1932; A Study of Some Seismometers, U.S. Bur. of Mines, 1934. Home: Lewisburg PA Died June 21, 1971.

IRVIN, REA, artist and art editor; b. San Francisco, Aug. 26, 1881; s. George C. and Mary Jane (Morse) I.; ed. Hopkins Art Inst., San Francisco; m. Dorothy Goodwin, June 12, 1916; children—Virginia, Barbara. Former artist and art editor of The New Yorker. Clubs: The Players (N.Y.C.); Dutch Treat; St. Croix Country. Home: St Croix VI Died May 28, 1972; buried Frederiksted, St. Croix VI

IRVINE, FERGUS ALBERT, business exec.; b. Brisbane, Australia, Oct. 28, 1901; s. Charles Robert and Lucy Flora (Ferguson) I.; student U. of Queensland, 1919-22, B.S., 1922, M.S., 1925; m. Marjorie Lenore Marcy, Dec. 17, 1937; 2 sons, Kenneth, Robert. Came to U.S., 1923, naturalized, 1940. Research chem. engr. E.I. duPont de Nemours & Co., 1923-25; research dept. The Celotex Corp., 1925-32, tech, dir., 1932-40, prodn. exec., 1941-46, v.p., 1947-66, dir., 1954-66. Mem. Am. Chem. Soc., Am. Inst. Chem. Engrs. Clubs: Round Table (New Orleans); University (Chgo.). Home: Glencoe IL Died Feb. 29, 1968; buried New Orleans LA

IRWIN, FREDERICK CHARLES, prof. of chemistry; b. Grass Lake, Sharon, Mich., Feb. 7, 1870; s. John Emery and Amy Ellen (Rice) I.; B.S., U. of Mich., 1895; grad. student, summers 1896-1903; m. Maude Clement, Aug. 4, 1904; children—Charles Clement, Helen Winifred (Mrs. Francis Bennett). Began as teacher, 1895; teacher chemistry and physics, Bay City (Mich.) Central High Sch., 1899-1914; head chemistry dept., Junior Coll., Detroit, Mich., 1914-21, Coll. of City of Detroit, 1921-32; head dept. of chemistry, Wayne U., Detroit, since 1932. Mem. advisory com. City Planning Commn., Detroit. Mem. Am. Chem. Soc., Mich. Schoolmasters Club (since 1895) Detroit Chem. Teachers Assn. (organizer). Republican. Methodist. Mason. Clubs: Men's, Metropolitan, Methodist Church (Detroit). Author: Laboratory Manual in Chemistry, 1901; Elementary and Applied Chemistry, 1914; Chemistry and Its Uses, 1928; General Chemistry for Colleges, 1932; General and Inorganic Chemistry, 1939. Home: 856 Palister Av., Detroit MI‡

IRWIN, INEZ HAYNES, author; b. Rio Janeiro, Brazil, Mar. 2, 1873; d. Gideon and Emma Jane (Hopkins) Haynes; Girls High Sch. and Normal Sch., Boston; spl. student Radcliffe Coll., 1897-1900; m. Rufus Hamilton Gillmore, Aug. 30, 1897; m. 2d, Will Irwin, Feb. 1, 1916. Corr. for various mags. in France, Eng. and Italy, 1916-18; contbr. to Am. and British mags. Founder, with Maud Wood Park, of Nat. Coll. Equal Suffrage League; member nat. advisory council, National Women's Party; pres. Authors' Guild of America, 1929-31; pres. Authors' League of Am., 1931-33; chairman board of dirs. of World Centre for Women's Archives, 1935-40; vice-president New York P.E.N., 1941-44. Club: Query (New York). Author: June Jeopardy, 1908; Maida's Little Shop, 1910; Phoebe and Ernest, 1910; Janey, 1911; Phoebe, Ernest and Cupid, 1912; Angel Island, 1914; The Ollivant Orphans, 1915; The Californiacs, 1916; The Lady of Kingdoms, 1917; The Happy Years, 1919; The Native Son, 1919; The Story of the Woman's Party, 1921; Out of the Air, 1921; Maida's Little House, 1921; Gertrude Haviland's Divorce, 1925; Maida's Little School, 1926; Gideon, 1927; P.D.F.R., 1928; Family Circle, 1931; Confessions of a Business Man's Wife, 1931; Youth Must Laugh, 1932; Angels and Amazons, 1933; Strange Harvest, 1934; Murder Masquerade (in Gt. Britain, Murder in Fancy Dress), 1935; The Poison Cross, 1936; Good Manners for Girls, 1937; A Body Rolled Downstairs, 1938; Maida's Little Island, 1939; Maida's Little Camp, 1940; Many Murders, 1941; Maida's Little Village, 1942; Maida's Little Houseboat, 1943; Maida's Little Theatre, 1946; The Women Swore Revenge, 1946; Maida's Little Cabins, 1947; Maida's Little Zoo, 1949; Maida's Little Lighthouse, 1951. Winner O. Henry memorial prize for best short story of 1924. Home: Scituate MA‡

IRWIN, ROBERT WINFRED, furniture mfr.; b. Harbor Beach, Mich., Apr. 7, 1869; s. Robert W. and Elizabeth (Winsor) I.; ed. pub. schs.; m. Viola Halla, Oct. 18, 1899. Pres. and gen. mgr. Robert W. Irwin Co., Grand Rapids, Mich. Home: 461 E. Fulton St. Office: 23 Summer Av., N.W., Grand Rapids MI*‡

IRWIN, WALTER MCMASTER, clergyman; b. Galesburg, Ill., Nov. 9, 1872; s. John N. and Angie (McMaster) I.; A.B., Knox Coll., Galesburg, 1893; B.D., McCormick Theol. Sem., Chicago, 1897; D.D., Emporia Coll., Kan., 1912; m. Bessie Crane, June 8, 1898; children—Dorothy Helen (Mrs. C.H. Crockett), Margaret Crothers (Mrs. Melvin C. Petersen), Grace Kingsbury (Mrs. F. Ernest Kirk). Ordained Presbyterian ministry, 1897; pastor Deer Creek, Ill., 1897-99, Delavan, 1899-1901, Shelby, Ia., 1901-03, West Side Ch., Wichita, Kan., 1903-13; synodical supt. Presbyn. Ch. for State of Kan., Apr. 15, 1913-Sept. 1, 1919; sec. New Era Movement of Presbyn. Ch. U.S.A., for Northern Pacific District, Portland, Oregon, 1919-21; for Western District, Denver, Colorado, 1921-23, for Rocky Mountain Dist., 1923-24; sec. Gen. Council of Presbyn. Ch. U.S.A., Rocky Mountain Dist., 1924-30; pastor Raton, N.Mex., 1930-31. Address: 4658 Felton St., San Diego CA‡

ISAACS, HART, investment co. exec.; b. Los Angeles, June 9, 1906; s. Louis and Natalie (Hart) I.; student Stanford, 1924-27; m. Senta Vera Chaim; children—Hart, Diane, Steven Michael, Senta Dianne; m. second, Patricia Penetti. Employed with Isaacs Bros. Company, Beverly Hills, California, 1931-—, pres., 1938-—; dir. Hunt Foods & Industries, Inc. Pres. bd. trustees Jewish Big Bros. Assn. Los Angeles, 1936-41; bd. dirs. Cedars of Lebanon Hosp., Los Angeles, 1939-—, pres., 1957-—. Jewish religion (trustee temple). Mason (Shriner). Clubs: Los Angeles Athletic, Hillcrest Country (Los Angeles). Home: Beverly Hills CA

ISAACS, MOSES LEGIS, professor of chemistry; b. Cincinnati, O., June 3, 1899; s. Abraham and Rachel (Friedman) I.; A.B., U. of Cincinnati, 1920, A.M., 1921; Ph.D., 1923; grad. work Columbia, 1924-26; D.Sc. (hon.), Yeshiva U., 1967; m. Elizabeth Klein, May 2, 1926; children—Philip Klein, Nancy Julie (Mrs. Sidney B. Klein). Asst. in chemistry U. of Cincinnati, 1919-21; instr. sanitary sci. Columbia U., 1926-36, asst. prof., Columbia, 1936-42; prof. chemistry Yeshiva Univ., 1942-67, dean 1942-53. Research worker in disinfection process. Mem. Kasruth Bd. N.Y. State Department of Agriculture, 1934-70, vice chairman, 1934-62. Awarded Merrell fellow by U. of Cincinnati, 1921-24, Nat. Research F. at Columbia, 1924-26. Vice pres. Mordecai Ben David Foundation, Pres. N.Y. City br. S.A.B., 1941, f. A.A.A.S., mem. Harvey Soc., Am. Chemical Soc., Society of American Bacteriologists, Societe de Chimie Biologique of France (life mem.), Phi Beta Kappa. Member of the cultural committee Joint; Distbn. Com.; mem. bd. dirs. Union of Orthodox Jewish Congregations. Rep. Jewish religion. Author chpt. on disinfection Agents of Disease by F.B. Gay (Chas. C. Thomas), 1935. Contbr. articles on chemistry and bacteriology to tech. jours. Research in reconstitution of milk. Home: Northport NY Died Feb. 12, 1970; buried Cedar Park and Beth-El Cemetery, Westwood NJ

ISBELL, EGBERT RAYMOND, educator; b. Gaines, Mich., Mar. 17, 1898; s. Walter Newton and Mabel (Brown) I.; student Albion Coll., 1917, Wayne State U., 1919-20; A.B., U. Mich., 1923, LL.B., Ph.D., 1934; exchange student U. Frankfurt Main, 1926-27; m. Florentine Sonnenschmidt, May 21, 1927 (dec. 1957); children—Franziska (Mrs. Robert John Schoenfeld), Melinda (Mrs. Forest Paul Johnson); m. 2d, Mary Duncan Carter, Aug. 15, 1959. Tchr. Detroit Central High Sch., 1927-28, Ann Arbor (Mich.) High Sch., 1928-31; asst. editor, asso. editor Mich. Law Review,

1931-36; head Federal Writers Project for Michigan, 1936-37; associate prof. history Mich. State Normal Coll. (now Eastern Mich. U.), 1937-40, dean of adminstrn., 1940-56, prof. history, 1956-68. Chmn. Ypsilanti Human Relations Commn., 1959. Served with U.S. Army, 1918-19, Mem. Mich. Coll. Assn. (pres. 1946-47), Mich. Assn. for Higher Edn. (pres. 1951-52; N. Central Assn. Academic Deans (v.p. 1955-56), Am. Hist. Assn., Am. Assn. U. Profs. (chpt. pres. 1963-64); Sigma Nu, Kappa Phi Alpha, Phi Delta Phi, Phi Delta Kappa. Democrat. Episcopalian. Rotarian (Ypsilanti, Mich.) (pres. 1947-48). Contbr. articles in field to profl. jours. Home: Ann Arbor MI Died Oct. 8, 1968.

ISELIN, COLUMBUS O'DONNELL, scientist; b. New Rochelle, New York, Sept. 25, 1904; s. Lewis and Marie (de Neufville) I.; A.B., Harvard, 1926, A.M., 1928; D.Sc., Brown U., 1947; m. Eleanor Emmet Lapsley, 1929; children—Eleanor Emmet, Columbus O'Donnell, Marie de Neufville, Victoria David, Thomas Howard. Phys. oceanographer Woods Hole Oceanography Instn., 1932-40, dir., 1940-50, 56-58, senior physical oceanographer, 1950-56, Henry Bryant oceanographer, 1958-70, mem. corp., trustee, 1936-70; professor phys. oceanography Mass. Inst. of Technology, Cambridge, 1959-70, Harvard, 1960-70. Mem. sci. com. ocean research, convenor working group Internat. Indian Ocean Expdn., 1958; mem. subcom. oceanographic research NATO; oceanwide surveys panel NASCO; com. on undersea warfare Nat. Acad. Scis.-NRC. Trustee Bermuda Biol. Sta. for Research, Inc., 1936-70, Marine Biol. Lab., Woods Hole, 1941-52. Recipient Medal for Merit, U.S. Govt., 1948; Henry Bryant Bigelow medal, 1966. Fellow N.Y. Acad. Scis.; mem. Nat. Acad. Scis. (Agassiz medal 1943), Am. Acad. Arts and Letters, Am. Geog. Soc., Am. Geophys. Union, Am. Philos. Soc. Contbr. articles on oceanography to various periodicals. Home: Vineyard Haven MA Died Jan. 5, 1971; buried Lambert's Cove Cemetery, West Tisburg, Martha's Vineyard Island MA

ISERMAN, MICHAEL, physician; b. N.Y.C., Sept. 29, 1898; s. Samuel and Dorothy Iserman; M.D., Cornell U., 1923; m. Marian V. Hayman; 1 dau., Susan (Mrs. Edwin Sunshine). Intern, Montefiore Hosp., N.Y.C., 1923-24, resident in Tb, 1925-26; intern Bklyn. Jewish Hosp., 1924-25; postgrad. in cardiology and internal medicine Columbia Coll. Phys. and Surg., 1936-41; clin. asst. cardiologist Mt. Sinai Hosp., N.Y.C. Served to comdr. M.C., USNR, 1942-46. Diplomate Am. Bd. Internal Medicine. Mem. A.M.A., Am. Heart Assn. Home: New York City NY Died Jan. 4, 1971; buried New York City NY

ISHAM, HENRY PORTER, chmn. Clearing Indsl. Dist. Inc.; dir. Marshall Field and Co.; director First Nat. Bank of Chgo. Trustee Passavant Meml. Hosp., Chgo. Mus. of Natural History, Newberry Library. Home: Lake Forest IL Died Aug. 18, 1969.

ISRAELS, CARLOS LINDNER, lawyer; b. N.Y.C., Nov. 21, 1904; s. Charles Henry and Belle (Lindner) I.; B.A., Amherst Coll., 1925; LL.B., Columbia, 1928; m. Irma Commanday, Sept. 25, 1935 (div. Aug. 1940); children—Charles Henry, Elisabeth Miriam; m. 2d, Ruth L. Goldstein, Dec. 13, 1941; 1 son, Michael Jozef. Admitted to N.Y. bar, 1928; asso. firm White and Case, N.Y.C., 1928-40; asst. gen. counsel Trustees Asso. Gas & Electric Corp., 1940-46; partner firm Berlack, Israels & Liberman, and predecessor, 1946-69; lectr. corp. and financial law Practicing Law Inst., 1937-69; vis. lectr. law Columbia Law Sch., 1946-48, 58, adj. prof., 1962-69; mem. editorial bd., chmn. subcom. on investment securities Sponsors Uniform Comml. Code, 1958-62. Bd. dirs. United Hias Service Inc., and predecessors, 1941-69, pres.,1957-59, 67-69; bd. dirs. Council Jewish Fedns. and Welfare Fund, also treas., v.p.; bd. dirs. Am. Jewish Com., Am. Jewish Dist. Com.; mem. adv. com. 2d Restatement of Contracts, Am. Law Inst. Mem., Am., N.Y. State, New York County, N.Y.C. bar assns., Am. Law Inst. Contbr. articles to profl. jours. Home: New York City NY Died July 24, 1969.

ISSERMAN, FERDINAND MYRON, rabbi; b. Antwerp, Belgium, Mar. 4, 1898; s. Alexander and Bettl (Brodheim) I.; came to U.S., 1906, naturalized, 1918; A.B., U. of Cincinnati, 1919; Rabbi, Hebrew Union Coll., 1922, D.H.L., 1950; A.M., U. of Pa., 1924; postgrad, University of Toronto, 1926-27, U. of Chicago, 1928, LL.D., Douglass University, 1941; D.D., Central College, 1945; m. Ruth J. Frankenstein, June 6, 1923; children—Irma (Mrs. Stanley Gertz), Ferdinand Myron. Asst. rabbi Rodef Shalom Congregation, Phila., 1922-25; rabbi Holy Blossom Congregation, Toronto, Can., 1925-29, Temple Israel, St. Louis, 1929-66, sr. rabbi, 1963-66. Guest rabbi Jewish Community, Hong Kong, 1963-64; Jewish chaplain, assistant professor of religion University of the Seven Seas, 1964-65. Co-founder Social Justice Commn., St. Louis, Mo., 1930-35; member of the Missouri Library Commn. Served with U.S. Army, World War I. Mem. bd. Bible Coll., U. of Mo.; former trustee Hebrew Union Coll.; chmn. Rosalie Tilles Non-Sectarian Fund; chmn. Jewish Welfare Fund Campaign, St.L., 1939; past nat. chmn. combined campaign for support of Hebrew Union Coll.-Jewish Inst. Religion, Union Am. Hebrew Congregations; chmn. Commn. on Social Justice and Internat. Peace of World Union for Prog. Judaism; co-chmn. St. Louis Seminar of Jews and Christians, 1930-34. Pres. Jewish Student Foundn., 1930-48. Chmn. Justice and Peace Commn., 1941-46, Central Conf. of Am. Rabbis; chmn. Am. Inst. on Judaism and a Just and Enduring Peace; past chmn. Am. bd. World Union Progressive Judaism. Served as field dir. A.R.C. in Tunisian campaign; attached to Am. Red Cross Hdqrs. in N. Africa. Recipient citations Met. Ch. Fedn., 1955, St. John's Meth. Ch., 2d Bapt. Ch., 2d Unitarian Church; recipient St. Louis Argus Distinguished Pub. Service award, 1968, Lorenza the Magnificent award, 1970; named Clergy-Man of Year, 1967; honored by resolution of Mo. House of Reps. Mem. bd. Indsl. Aid for the Blind of State of Mo., Urban League, St. Louis; hon. pres. Hillel adv. council U. of Mo.; president St. Louis Rabbinical Assn., 1946, 53-54, 60-61; chmn. Inst. on Judaism and Race Relations, 1945; vice chmn. Nat. Conference Religion and Race, 1963. Member Sigma Alpha Mu. Mason (32 deg.). Author books including: The Jewish Jesus and the Christian Christ, This is Judaism, Rebels and Saints; A Rabbi with the American Red Cross, 1958; Sentenced to Death the Jews in Nazi Germany, 1961; David Friedlander: A Reform Jewish Pioneer. Home: Clayton MO Died Mar. 7, 1972; buried Mt. Sinai Cemetery, St. Louis MO

IVANOWSKI, SIGISMOND DE, artist; b. at Odessa, Russia, Apr. 17, 1875; s. Felix and Amelia (de Vitanowska) I.; ed. acads. in St. Petersburg, Munich, Paris; Coll. in Warsaw; m. London, Eng., Helen Moser, 1900. Served in Russian Army; came to America, 1903. Painted portraits of actresses in their stage characters, including Maude Adams as Peter Pan," Annie Russell as Puck," Blance Bates as Madam Butterfly," Margaret Anglin, The Great Divide." Ethel Barrymore as Captain Jinks," Mme. Modjeska as Lady Macbeth," etc. Clubs: Lambs, Strollers, Players (New York). Address: Westfield NJ‡

IVES, CLARENCE ALBERT, prof. educator; b. Vernon, La., July 17, 1869; s. Christopher and Martha (Bonner) I.; student Ruston (La.) Male and Female Coll., 1886-88; B.S., La. State U., 1893; m. Jessie Bond, July 19, 1898; 1 son, Clarence Albert. Teacher and prin., La., 1888-91, and 1893-1912; instr. La. State U., 1894-95; state instr. condr., 1912-14; state high sch. supervisor, 1914-23; became prof. edn. and dean, Teachers Coll., Louisiana State University, 1923, now emeritus; dir. Baton Rouge Bldg. & Loan Assn. Mem. N.E.A., La. State Teachers Assn., Am. Assn. Univ. Profs., Southern Assn. Colls. and Secondary Schs. (pres. 1936-38), Phi Delta Kappa, Sigma Nu. Democrat. Methodist. Mason, Kiwanian. Ch. City Zoning Com. Member 9 man Com. to make master plan for City of Baton Rouge, La. Home: 940 Park Blvd., Baton Rouge LA‡

IVES, JOHN HIETT, air force officer; b. Delphi, Ind., Aug. 29, 1906; s. George R. and Josephine (Cartwright) I.; A.B., U. Ill., 1928; student Nat. War College, 1946-47; married Katherine Sullivan, January 2, 1936 (deceased, 1955); children—John Hiett, Katherine C.; m. Judith McGowan, Apr. 19, 1958; 1 dau., Laura K. Commissioned second lieutenant, USAF, 1930, and advanced through grades to maj. gen. USAF, 1953; served hdqrs. A.A.C. and PTO, World War II; dep. sec. Joint Chiefs of Staff, 1947-50; chief staff Air Univ., 1950-52; dep. dir. mil. personnel USAF, 1952-53; dir. mil. personnel policy div. Office Asst. Sec. Def. for Manpower and Personnel, 1953-56; chief staff, Continental Air Command, Mitchel Air Force Base, N.Y., 1956-57, comdr. First Air Force, 1957-58; dep. comdr. Third Air Force, 1958-61, comdr., from 1961, also chief Mil. Assistance Adv. Group, United Kingdom. Decorated Legion of Merit (with oak leaf cluster), Bronze Star Medal, D.S.M. Mem. Beta Theta Pi. Home: San Antonio TX Died Mar. 14, 1965; buried Fort Sam Houston Nat. Cemetery, San Antonio TX

IVES, SARAH NOBLE, writer, illustrator; b. Grosse Ile, Mich.; d. William and Sarah Maria (Hyde) I.; adopted d. Mrs. Edna Chaffee Noble; grad. Port Huron (Mich.) High Sch., and Detroit Training Sch. of Elocution and English Lit.; studied art in New York 2 yrs., in Paris 3 yrs. Landscape painter; also contbr. and illustrator McClure Newspaper Syndicate, N.Y. Tribune. Universalist. Author: (also Illustrator) Songs of the Shining Way (verse), 1895; (prose) The Story of a Little Bear, 1908; Key to Betsy's Heart, 1916; Dog Heroes of Many Lands, 1922. Home: Altadena CA‡

IVEY, GEORGE MELVIN, merchant; b. Henrietta, N.C., Aug. 14, 1896; s. Joseph Benjamin and Emma Mahala (Gantt) I.; A.B., Duke U., 1920; m. Lula Groves Campbell, Oct. 10, 1922; children—George Melvin, Jr., Mary Clare (Mrs. T.P. Matthews). Engaged in business as mcht., 1920-68; pres., treas. J.B. Ivey & Co. (Charlotte, N.C.) operator dept. stores in Carolinas and Fla., until 1967, chmn. bd., 1967-68; dir. N.C. adv. bd., dir. Liberty Mut. Ins. Co. Bd. dirs. Lincoln Edn. Found, Meth. Home; trustee Duke U.; mem. nat. council, nat. bd., internat. com. YMCA. Served as 2d lt., F.A., U.S. Army, 1918. Mem. Nat. Retail Mchts. Assn., Newcomen Soc., S.A.R. Methodist. Clubs: Charlotte Country, City, River, Executives. Home: Charlotte NC Died May 3, 1968; buried Elmwood Cemetery, Charlotte NC

IVIE, WILLIAM NOAH, lawyer; b. Huntsville, Ark., Sept. 20, 1873; s. Bacus and Jane (Litterell) L; ed. common schs. and in law office; m. Minnie Vaughan, Dec. 20, 1900; children—Lawrence C., Lillian O. (Mrs. Cecil D. Robinson), Jewell M. (Mrs. Ben C. Henley), Charles N., Naomi R. Editor and newspaper pub. until 1906; admitted to Ark., bar, 1901, and began practice at Huntsville; county and probate judge, Madison Co., Ark., 1908; register U.S. Land Office, Harrison, Ark., 1909-14; U.S. Court commr., 1923-26; asst. U.S. atty., Western Dist. of Ark., 1926-30, U.S. atty., same dist., since 1930. Mem. K.P., Elks. Republican. Home: Ft Smith AR*‡

IVINS, ANTOINE RIDGWAY, clergyman; b. St. George, Utah, May 11, 1881; s. Anthony W. and Elizabeth A. (Snow) I.; student Mexican Sch. Jurisprudence, 1902-05, U. Mich., 1905; A.B., U. Utah, 1909; m. Vilate E. Romney, June 26, 1912. Engaged in agr. and live stock bus., Utah, 1909-21; mgr. sugar plantation, Hawaii, 1921-31; ordained minister Ch. of Jesus Christ of Latter Saints; charge Mexican Mission, 1931-34; mem. First Council of Seventy, 1931-67. Dir. Hotel Utah Co. Past treas. Salt Lake council Boy Scouts Am. Mem. Sigma Chi. Home: Salt Lake City UT Died Oct. 18, 1967.

JACCARD, WALTER M., jeweler; b. St. Louis, Mo., May 10, 1870; s. David Constant and Louise A.J.; grad. Smith Acad., St. Louis, 1886; m. Gertrude E. Hudson, of Kansas City, Mo., Oct. 5, 1896; 1 dau., Gertrude Elizabeth. Began in retail jewelry business at Kansas City, 1888; pres. Jaccard Jewelry Corpn., 1898-1926, chmn. bd. since 1926; pres. Thomas Real Estate Co. since 1915; pres. Waverly Realty Co. since 1920; pres. Hayes Realty Co.; dir. Commerce Trust Co. Trustee Sunset Hill Sch. Assn. Republican. Presbyn. Clubs: Kansas City, Kansas City Athletic, Kansas City Country. Home: 5300 Sunset Drive. Office: 1017 Walnut St., Kansas City MO‡

JACKLIN, EDWARD G., educator; B. Phila., Mar. 23, 1907; s. Harry G. and Anna M. (King) J.; A.B., Woodstock Coll., 1930, M.A., 1931; S.T.L., Gregorian U., 1938; Ph.D., Fordham U., 1950; LL.D., University of Santa Clara (California), 1951; L.H.D. (honorary), Villanova University, 1956. Entered Jesuit order, 1924; instr. Alteno de Manila, Philippine Islands, 1931-34; prof. philosophy, head dept., U. Scranton, 1942-44, dean, 1944-48; prof. philosophy, head dept. coll. arts, scis., Georgetown U., 1948-49, dean, 1949-50; pres. St. Joseph's Coll., 1950-56; professor philosophy, Georgetown U., 1956-61, U. Scranton, 1961-71. Mem. Am. Cath. Philos. Assn., Cath. Hist. Soc., Am. Acad. Polit., Social Scis., Pa., Jesuit Ednl. Assn., Nat. Cath. Ednl. Assn. Home: Scranton PA Died Aug. 3, 1971.

JACKS, LEO VINCENT, writer; b. Grand Island, Neb., Mar. 14, 1896; s. Porter and Margaret Genevieve (McMullen) J.; A.B., St. Mary's Coll., St. Marys, Kan., 1917; A.M., Catholic U., Washington, D.C., 1920, Ph.D., 1922; m. Maxine Frances White, Aug. 2, 1930; children—Marshall Lee, Margaret Marcia Claire. Began writing fiction and biography for Scribner's and other pubs., 1927; lecturer on Greek and Latin langs. and lits., Creighton U., Omaha, from 1929, also dir. depts. of Greek and Latin; dir. ann. writers workshops Cath. U. Served in 34th and 32d combat divs., U.S. Army, 1917-19. Mem. Am. Philol. Assn., Mediaeval Acad. of America, National Rifle Association, L'Association Guillaume Bude, Paris. Author: Service Record by an Artilleryman, 1928; Xenophon, Soldier of Fortune, 1930; La Salle, 1931; Mother Marianne of Molokai, 1935; Claude Dubuis, Bishop of Galveston, 1946; Wires West, 1957; Prairie Venture, 1959; The Turquoise Rosary, 1960. Home: Omaha NE Died Feb. 25, 1972; buried Calvary Cemetery Omaha NE

JACKSON, AMOS WADE, former state justice; b. Versailles, Ind., June 25, 1904; s. Rowland II Georgia W. (Frohliger) J.; A.B., Hanover (Ind.) Coll., 1926; m. Lola M. Raper, Aug. 20, 1927; children—Jeannette (dec.), Ann Louise (Mrs. Richard B. Stanley). Admitted to Ind. bar, 1925, practiced in Versailles, until 1959; pros. atty. Ripley County, 1937-40; asso. atty. C.E., War Dept., 1942-43; asso. justice Ind. Supreme Ct., 1959-71. Pres., Jackson Abstracts, Inc. Mem. Hoosier Hills council Boy Scouts Am., 1928-29. Named Ky. col. Mem. Ind. Judges Assn., Am. Judicature Soc., Ind. Fedn. Art Clubs, Am., Ind., Ripley County, Indpls. bar assns., Southeastern Ind. Park Assn., Lambda Chi Alpha, Phi Alpha Delta, Baptist. Mason (Shriner). Address: Versailles IN Died Sept. 30, 1972.

JACKSON, CHARLES (REGINALD), author; b. 1903; m. Rhoda Booth; children—Sarah Blann, Kate Winthrop. Formerly tchr. N.Y.C., Marlboro Coll., lectured Columbia. Author: The Lost Weekend, 1944; The Fall of Valor, 1946; The Outer Edges, 1948; The Sunnier Side, 1950; Earthly Creatures, 1953; A Second-Hand Life, 1967; also stories in anthologies, radio plays, TV plays, movies; articles and fiction in nat.

mags. Recipient Motion Picture Acad. Award for film of The Lost Weekend. Home: Sandy Hook CT Died Sept. 21, 1968.

JACKSON, CHARLES TENNEY, author; b. St. Louis, Oct. 15, 1874; s. Col. Charles Henry and Eliza (Tenney) J.; ed. Madison (Wis.) High Sch., 1893-96, U. of Wis., 1896-97; left univ. to enter army; pvt. 1st Wis. Vols., 1898; m. Carlotta Weir, 1919. Newspaper corr., Spanish-Am. War; editor Modesto News, 1905-06; on staff San Francisco Chronicle, 1907-1908, Milwaukee (Wis.) Sentinel, 1909. Member of Loyal Legion, Authors' Club of London, England. Author: Loser's Luck, 1905; Day of Souls, 1910; My Brother's Keeper, 1911; The Midlanders, 1912; The Fountain of Youth, 1914; John-the-Fool, 1915; The Call to the Colors, 1918; Jimmy May in the Fighting Line, 1919; Captain Sazarac, 1922. Contbr. to mags. Winner award in O. Henry memorial vol., Best Short Stories of 1921 (Am. Acad. Arts and Sciences), with The Man Who Cursed the Lilies; represented in many collections of best stories.*‡

JACKSON, FRANK LEE, educator, ret.; b. Gastonia, N.C., Aug. 1, 1882; s. John Frank and Mary Isabel (Adams) J.; B.S., Davidson (N.C.) Coll., 1906; grad. Walton Sch. of Commerce, Chicago, Ill., 1917; C.P.A., N.C., 1917; LL.D. (honorary), King College, Bristol, Tenn.; m. Annie M. Chaffin, Sept. 8, 1909; children—Susie McQueen (Mrs. George E. McClenaghan), Frank Lee, Eleanor McGill (Mrs. Thomas V. Northcott), Edward Whitehurst. Prin. high sch., Belmont, N.C., 1906-09; sec., treas. and gen. mgr. Mountain Retreat Assn., Montreat, N.C., 1909-13; treas. and bus. mgr. Davidson Coll. 1913-51, ret., instr. accounting, 1919-26; acting president Montreat College, 1958-59; vice pres., member investment com. Piedmont Bank & Trust Co., from 1940, also dir., dir. Sterling Investment Fund, Inc. Mayor, Davidson, 1951-69. Vice pres. exec. com. Nat. Committee on Standard Reports for Institutions of Higher Edn., 1921-35; mem. financial adv. service Am. Council on Edn., 1935-40. Trustee N.C. Textile Vocational Sch., 1947-51, Mt. Retreat Assn. (dir. 1942-57, acting president 1957-59), Presbyn. Found., Inc., from 1942, president 1956-59. Trustee, member permanent com. of office Gen. Assembly of Presbyn. Church in U.S., 1952-55; chmn. N.C. Synod's Council Presbyn. Ch. in U.S., 1955-57. Mem. Eastern Assn. U. and Coll. Bus. and Offices (exec. com. 1933; v.p. 1937; pres. 1941-42), So. Assn. Coll., Univ. Business Officers (pres. 1935-36), N.C. State Bd. Accountancy, 1928-40 (pres. 1935-40), N.C. Assn. C.P.A. Am. Institute of Accountants, N.C. Citizens Association (director 1943-45), Newcomen Soc., Kappa Alpha, Omicron Delta Kappa (nat. council; nat. pres. 1937-39), Phi Beta Kappa, Scabbard and Blade. Democrat. Presbyn (elder). Mason (32 deg., Shriner). Editorial bd. College and University Business. Home: Davidson NC Died Jan. 19, 1971; buried Davidson College Cemetery, Davidson NC

JACKSON, GEORGE LEROY, coll. prof.; b. Springville, N.Y., May 29, 1875; s. William and Emma (Knowlton) J.; grad. Buffalo State Normal Sch., 1898; A.B., U. of Mich., 1906; A.M., Columbia, 1907, research scholar, 1907-08, fellow in edn., 1908-09, Ph.D., 1909; m. Bessie F. Hazelton, of Bradford, Pa., Nov. 27, 1902. Grammar sch. prin., North Tonawanda, N.Y., 1898-1903; instr. in edn. and asst. prof., 1910-17, asso. prof. history of edn., 1917-24, prof., 1925-36, U. of Mich.; retired, June 1936. Mem. 74th Regiment N.Y.N.G., 1895-98. Fellow A.A.A.S.; mem. Am. Hist. Assn., Society of Coll. Teachers of Education, Mich. Schoolmasters' Club, Phi Delta Kappa. Club: Ann Arbor Golf and Outing. Author: The Development of School Support in Colonial Massachusetts, 1909; Outlines of the History of Education, 1911; The Privilege of Education—a History of Its Extension, 1918; The Development of State Control of Education in Michigan, 1926. Home: 2126 Dorset Rd., Ann Arbor MI‡

JACKSON, JOHN EDWARD, steel exec. Pres., dir. Des Moines Bridge & Iron Works, 1939-71; pres. Pitts. Des Moines Co., 1939-71, dir., 1937-71; mem. firm Pitts. Des Moines Steel Co., 1937-71; pres., dir. Des Moines Bridge & Iron Works, 1939-71; dir. Horton Steel, Ltd., Ft. Erie, Can. Pres., dir. Fox Chapel Water Authority. Trustee Allegheny Coll., Meadville, Pa. Mem. Am. Inst. Steel Constrn. (past pres., dir.), N.A.M. (dir.), Steel Structures Painting Council (past pres., dir.), Steel Plate Fabricators Assn. (regional v.p.). Club: Oakmont Country (past pres., dir.). Home: Pittsburgh PA Died Apr. 1971.

JACKSON, JOHN EDWARD, steel co. exec.; b. Des Moines, Oct. 25, 1898; s. William H. and Minnie (Long) J.; B.S. in Civil Engring., Ia. State Coll., 1924; m. Susie McCutchen, Apr. 17, 1926. With Pitts.-Des Moines Steel Co., 1924-71, pres., 1939-59, chairman board, 1959-71; owner Otwell Dairy Farm, 1958-71. President Steel Structure Painting Council, 1951-59. Pres. Fox Chapel Water Authority, 1951-58. Trustee, chmn. campus planning com. Allegheny Coll., 1939-71. Mem. Am. Inst. Steel Constrn. (pres. 1952-54, chmn. mill relations com. 1961-63), Steel Plate Fabrications Assn. (chmn. mill relations com. 1957-63), N,A.M. (dir. 1954-56), Phi Delta Theta. Mason (Shriner), (Jester). Methodist (past trustee). Clubs: Oakmont (Pa.) Country (pres. 1951-55); Talbot Country (chmn. grounds com. 1962-71) (Easton, Md.). Home: Oxford MD Died Apr. 3, 1971.

JACKSON, JOHN EDWIN, artist; b. Nashville, Tenn., Nov. 7, 1875; s. Travis M. and Nancy (Carlton) J.; student Nat. Acad. Design and Art Students' League, New York; unmarried. Formerly newspaper illustrator on staffs of several New York dailies; more recently illustrator for mags. and books. Has exhibited Nat. Acad., New York, Ia. Acad. Fine Arts, New York Water Color Club, etc. Paintings purchased by New York Pub. Library, Nashville (Tenn.) Art Assn.; makes splty. of New York street scenes. Mem. Soc. Illustrators, Artists' Guild. Club: Salmagundi. Address: 47 5th Av., New York NY‡

JACKSON, JOHN J., lawyer; b. Cicero, N.Y.; s. Elias S. and Mary M. (Baum) J.; A.B., Olivet (Mich.) Coll., 1891, hon. M.A., 1893; m. Clara M. Sweet, of Cicero, N.Y., Oct. 23, 1896; children—Gertrude (Mrs. William D. Bowers), Norma (Mrs. Harold G. Shirk), Andrew. In practice of law at Detroit, Mich., 1896-1909; gen. atty. Westinghouse Electric & Mfg. Co., Pittsburgh, Pa., since 1909; asst. treas. Westinghouse Lamp Co.; dir. Interborough Improvement Co., Turtle Creek & Allegheny River R.R. Co., Electric Bldg. & Loan Assn. Mem. Pa. State Chamber Commerce, Pittsburgh Chamber Commerce. Democrat. Presbyn. Clubs: University, Duquesne, Oakmont, Edgewood, Edgewood Country. Home: 343 Maple Av., Edgewood Park, Pittsburgh, Pa. Office: Westinghouse Electric & Mfg. Co., East Pittsburgh PA*‡

JACKSON, JOSEPH RAYMOND, judge; b. Albany, N.Y., Aug. 30, 1880; s. Michael Joseph and Alice Maud (Birmingham) J.; student Manhattan Prep. Sch., N.Y. City, 1895-96; A.B., Manhattan Coll., N.Y. City, 1900, LL.D., 1930; m. Josephine Kelley, June 30, 1902. Miner, Butte, Mont., 1900-03; teacher and athletic coach high sch., Butte, 1903-04; prin. Industrial Sch., Butte, 1905; admitted to Mont. bar, 1906; county atty. Silver Bow County, Mont., 1917-20; judge 2d Judicial Dist., Mont., 1920-25; commr. of Supreme Court, Mont., 1921-22; private practice of law, N.Y. City, 1926-34; asst. atty. gen. of U.S., customs div., 1934-38; asso. judge U.S. Court of Customs and Patent Appeals, Washington, from 1938; pres. Mont. Bar Assn., 1925. Mem. Am. Bar Assn., Assn. of the Customs Bar. Democrat. Roman Catholic. K.C., Elk. Clubs: Friendly Sons of St. Patrick, Catholic (N.Y. City); Washington DC Died Aug. 29, 1969.

JACKSON, MAHALIA, singer; b. New Orleans, Oct. 26, 1911; d. John Andrew and Charity (Clark) J.; student pub. schs., New Orleans; m. Isaac Hackenbull, 1936. Address: Chicago IL Died Jan. 27, 1972.

JACKSON, MARTHA, art dealer; b. Buffalo; d. Howard and Cyrena (Case) Kellogg; student Smith Coll., 1925-28; D.Art (hon.), Moore Coll. Art, Phila., 1969; m. John Anderson, May 6, 1930; 1 son, David K. Owner, operator Martha Jackson Gallery, N.Y.C., 1953-69; pres. Martha Jackson Gallery Corp., Red Parrot Films. Mem. Mus. Modern Art, Am. Fedn. Art, Met. Mus., Albright Art Gallery, Phoenix Art Mus. Address: New York City NY Died July 4, 1969; buried Forest Lawn Cemetery, Buffalo NY

JACKSON, PAUL RAINEY, clergyman; b. Flandreau, S.D., May 16, 1903; s. Walter Henry and Lillian (Rainey) J.; student Mont. State Coll., 1922-23; B.A., Wheaton Coll., 1926; D.D., Bible Inst. Los Angeles, 1944; m. Stella Chappell, Nov. 16, 1926; children—Mark Evan, Lois Ruth (Mrs. William F. Russell), Donn Paul. Ordained to ministry Independent Ch., 1926, Baptist Ch., 1942; rural evangelism, N.D., 1926-29; pastor, Strathmore, Cal., 1929-34, Ceres, Cal., 1934-45, Grand Rapids, Mich., 1945-46; pres. Bapt. Bible Sem., Johnson City, N.Y., 1946-60; nat. rep. Gen. Assn. Regular Bapt. Chs., Chgo., 1960-69, mem. council of fourteen, 1944-60. Exec. com. Assn. Baptists for World Evangelism; exec. com. Internat. Council Christian Chs., Am. Council Christian Chs. Home: Chicago IL Died May 15, 1969.

JACKSON, PERCIVAL E., lawyer; b. N.Y. City, June 16, 1891; s. Soloman Henry and Belle (Bloch) J.; LL.B., New York U., 1912; m. Irma Weinstock, Oct. 15, 1921 (now deceased); two children—Jean (Mrs. John Von Sternberg), and Muriel (Mrs. Henry Emsheimer). Admitted to the New York state bar, 1912, and practiced in N.Y. City; spl. counsel to McAdoo Senate com. investigating bankruptcy in U.S. Courts, 1936, Dir. United Gas Improvement Company, Long Island Lighting Company, Missouri Public Service Co. Member American N.Y., Nassau County and N.Y.C. bar assns. Clubs: Lawyers, Bankers of Am. Author: Law of Cadavers, 1936; Look at the Law, 1940; What Every Corporation Director Should Know, 1949; Corporate Management, 1955; Justice and the Law, 1958; The Wisdom of the Supreme Court and its Judges, 1961; Dissent in the Supreme Court—A Chronology. Contbr. numerous articles to Brookville NY Died Aug. 22, 1970.

JACKSON, RAYMOND THOMAS,, lawyer; b. Mineral Point, Wis., Apr. 26, 1892; s. John and Alice Mary (Reed) J.; A.B., U. of Wis., 1915, LL.B., 1917; m. Ethel Curry, Sept. 30, 1918. Admitted to Wis. bar, 1919, bar of U.S. Supreme Court, 1926, Ohio bar, 1929; began practice at Milwaukee; moved to Mineral Point, 1920; mem. Fiedler, Jackson and Boardman, 1920-36; also member Baker, Hostetler and Patterson, Cleveland, O., from 1929. Served as enlisted man, later lt. j.g., U.S. Navy, convoy duty on U.S.S. Frederick, 1917-19. Dist. atty., Iowa County, Wis., 1920-24; spl. asst. atty. gen., Wis., and spl. counsel for Minn., Mich., Ohio, Pa. and New York, in lake-level litigation, 1926-29, spl. counsel for Minn., Mich., Wis. and Ohio, 1932-33 and 1934-35; chief trial counsel representing power companies in TVA case, 1937. Mem. Am., Ohio State and Cleveland bar assns., Am. Law Institute, American Society for International Law, Phi Beta Kappa Associates, Phi Beta Kappa, Phi Delta Phi, Omicron Delta Gamma (Artus), Order of Coif. Republican. Methodist. Mason. Clubs: Union, Midday, Country; Nat. Republican (N.Y.). Home: Cleveland OH Died May 20, 1967, buried Lake View Cemetery, Cleveland OH

JACKSON, RICHARD HARRISON, naval officer; b. Tuscumbia, Ala., May 10, 1866; s. George M. and Sarah (Perkins) J.; grad. U.S. Naval Acad., 1887, Naval War Coll., 1920; M.D., U. of Va.; m. Catharine, d. Rear Admiral W.T. Sampson, U.S. Navy, Jan. 6, 1897 (dec. 1924). Hon. discharged from U.S. Navy, June 30, 1889; restored to service, July 1, 1890, by spl. act of Congress for conspicuous gallantry on occasion of wreck of the Trenton, at Apia, Samoa, Mar. 27, 1889"; promoted lt. jr. grade, July 3, 1898; promoted through grades to rear admiral. Served in the Spanish-Am. War, 1898; nagivator Colorado, 1905-07; exec. officer same, 1907-08; in charge naval proving ground, Indian Head, Md., 1908-10, Naval Sta., Cavite, P.I., 1910-11; comd. Albany, 1911-12, Helena, 1912; sr. officer in comd. gunboats on Yangtse River during Chinese Revolution; at U.S. Naval Acad., 1912-13; duty with Gen. Bd., Navy Dept., 1913-15; comd. Virginia, 1915-17; spl. rep. Navy Dept. at Ministry of Marine, Paris, and naval attache, Paris, June 1917-Nov. 1918; commandant Base 24, Bermudas, Jan.-Mar. 1919; comdr. spl. detachment, Azores, and Base 13, Apr.-Oct. 1919; mem. Gen. Bd. Navy Dept., 1921; rear adm. comdg. Battleship Div. 3, 1922; asst. chief naval operations, 1923; vice adm. comdg. Battleship Divs., 1925; admiral, commander-in-chief of Battle Fleet, 1926; mem. General Board, 1927-30; retired. Awarded Navy War Cross (U.S.); Officer Legion of Honor (France); Order of Avis (Portugal); medal for Spanish-Am. War, Philippine Insurrection, Boxer Campaign. Life mem. U.S. Naval Inst. (gold medals essayist). Episcopalian. Clubs: Army and Navy (Washington); Chevy Chase (Md.); New York Yacht. Home: Coronado CA Died Oct. 3, 1971.

JACKSON, THOMAS BROUN, lawyer; b. Charleston, W.Va., Nov. 1, 1892; s. Malcolm and Louise Fontaine (Broun) J.; Litt. B., Princeton, 1916; student U. of Va. Law Sch., 1916-17, 1919-20; student Oxford (Eng.) U., 1919; m. Dorothy Knight Smiley, Dec. 30, 1925; 1 son, William Smiley. Admitted to W.Va bar, 1921; partner Jackson, Kelly, Holt & O'Farrel (formerly Brown, Jackson & Knight 1892-46), Charleston, W. Virginia; director The Kanawha Valley Bank, Slab Fork Coal Company, Eagle Land Co. Served as 2d lt., 148th F.A., 6th F.A., A.E.F., 1918-19. Recipient Bishop's Distinguished Service Cross, Episcopal Diocese of Va., 1965. Former mem. W.Va. Judicial Council. Trustee Woodberry Forest Sch., Orange, Va. Mem. Am. Law Inst., Am. Bar Assn. (bd. govs., Ho. of Dels.), W.Va. Bar Assn. (past pres.), Am. Legion, Soc. of the First Div., A.E.F., Am. Judicature Soc., Sigma Chi, Phi Delta Phi. Republican. Episcopalian. Clubs: Princeton, National Republican (N.Y. City); Cannon (Princeton, N.J.); Edgewood Country, Charleston Tennis (Charleston); Army and Navy; Farmington Country. Address: Charleston WV Died Oct. 13, 1966; buried Spring Hill Cemetery, Charleston WV

JACKSON, THOMAS WRIGHT, army surgeon; b. at Akron O., Aug. 21, 1869; s. Andrew and Lucy Ann (Wright) J.; grad. Akron High Sch., 1887; spl. scientific course, Amherst Coll., 1887-9; M.D., Jefferson Med. Coll., Phila., 1892 (gold medalist); m. Mell V. Odiorne, of Nutley, N.J., Sept. 12, 1894; 2d, M. Louise Odiorne, of Phila., June 1, 1905. Practiced at Akron, O., and Phila., 1892-8; apptd. acting asst. surgeon U.S.A., 1898, and later capt. and asst. surgeon U.S.V., serving in Southern camps, Cuba and P.I.; med. reserve corps U.S. Army since 1908; phys. Bur. of Health for P.I., 1912—. Lecturer on tropical diseases, Jefferson Med. Coll., 1905-7. Mem. Am. Soc. Tropical Medicine, Manila Med. Soc., P.I. Med. Assn. (v.p. 1913-14), Beta Theta Pi. Clubs: Army and Navy (Manila and Washington), Authors' (London). Author: Tropical Medicine, 1907 (used as text-book in U.S.A.). Contbr. to Modern Treatment, Vol. I, 1910. Address: Manila PI‡

JACKSON, WILLIAM H(ARDING), lawyer, investment banker, b. Nashville, Tenn., Mar. 25, 1901;

s. William Harding and Anne Davis (Richardson) J.; grad. St. Mark's Sch., Southborough, Mass., 1920; A.B., Princeton, 1924; LL.B., Harvard, 1928; m. Elisabeth Lyman, Oct. 31, 1929; children—William H., Richard Lee; m. 2d, Mary Leet Pitcairn, Feb. 10, 1951; children—Bruce, Howell; m. 3d, Irma M. Hanly, May, 1970. Began with Cadwallader, Wickersham & Taft; admitted New York bar, 1932; employe Carter, Ledyard & Milburn, 1930, partner, 1934-47; partner J. H. Whitney & Co., investment banking firm, 1947-56. Adv. council Woodrow Wilson Sch. Internat. Affairs. Chairman of President's Com. on Internat. Information Activities, 1953; special assistant to the secretary of state, 1955, to Pres., 1956; mem. bd. cons. Nat. War Coll. Served with U.S. Army, 1942-45; assigned as dep. G-2 on staff Gen. Omar Bradley, E.T.O., 1944; disch. with rank of col. Dep. dir. or Central Intelligence, Washington, 1950-51. Pres. N.Y. Hosp., 1940-49, mem. bd. govs. Mem. Episcopalian. Clubs: Metropolitan (Washington). Home: Tucson AZ Died Sept. 28, 1971; buried Nashville TN

JACKSON, WILLIAM NICHOLS, educator; b. Lyerly, Ga., Dec. 27, 1912; s. William F. and Lavinia (Nichols) J.; B.S., Morehouse Coll., Atlanta, 1933; M.S., Atlanta U., 1938; Ph.D., Ohio State U. 1952; m. Dorwatha C. Watkins, Dec. 22, 1940; children—Gerald W., William N., Bernell R. Tchr. math. and sci., pub. schs. in Chattanooga, Atlanta and Covington, Ky., 1933-54; staff mem. secondary sch. study Assn. Negro Colls. and Schs., 1942-45; mem. faculty Tenn. A. and I. State U., 1954-69, dean faculty, 1963-69. Guest prof. edn. Savanah State Coll., 1949, Tex. So. U., 1952-54; dir. sci. and math. edn. workshops Alcorn Coll., 1944, Atlanta U., 1945-47, Tex. So. U., 1952-53. Fellow Gen. Edn. Bd., 1947-48. Mem. Nat. Council Tchrs. Math., Nat. Sci. Tchrs. Assn., So. Conf. Acad. Deans, Kappa Delta Pi, Phi Delta Kappa, Beta Kappa Chi, Alpha Phi Alpha, Sigma Pi Phi. Baptist. Contbr. articles to profl. jours. Home: Nashville TN 37218 Died Nov. 22, 1969.

JACOB, ROBERT BYRON, mfg. co. exec.; b. Detroit, Oct. 21, 1916; s. Benjamin B. and Nettie (Byron) J.; student U. Detroit, 1935-36; B.S. in Bus. Adminstrn., J.D., U. Miami (Fla.), 1940; m. Reva Goldberg, Sept. 8, 1957; children—Jayne, Robert Benjamin. Founder, pres. Cadillac Plastics & Chem. Co., Detroit, 1945-61; exec. v.p. Dayco Corp., Dayton, O., 1961-62, pres., 1962-68, chairman of the board of directors, 1968-71; also dir.; director of the Philips Industries, Inc. Admitted to Mich. bar, 1940. Member Mich., Detroit bar assns. Clubs: Franklin Hills Country (Franklin, Mich.); Standard, City, One Hundred, Great Lakes (Detroit); Cincinnati; Meadowbrook Country, Dayton, Hundred (Dayton); Brandies Univ. (Waltham, Mass.); Standard (Chgo.). Home: Dayton OH Died Aug. 4, 1971; buried Detroit MI

JACOBI, HERBERT P., educator; b. W. Allis, Wis., Oct. 8, 1916; s. Louis A. and Martha (Draxdorf) J.; B.S., U. Wis., 1937, M.S., 1939, Ph.D., 1941. Became mem. faculty U. Neb. Coll. Medicine, 1941, prof. biochemistry, 1956, chmn. dept., 1953. Mem. Am. Chem. Soc. (chmn. Omaha 1950-51, alternate councilor Omaha), Soc. Exptl. Biology and Medicine, A.A.A.S., Gerontological Soc., Neb. Acad. Sci., Sigma Xi, Nu Sigma Nu (hon.), Phi Lambda Upsilon, Phi Sigma, Gamma Alpha, Alpha Chi Sigma. Author articles enzymes, metabolism, cancer, atherosclerosis. Home: Omaha NE

JACOBS, ELBRIDGE CHURCHILL, univ. prof.; b. Ogunquit, Me., Feb. 15, 1873; s. Benjamin Franklin and Isabella Churchill (Toplis) J.; B.S., Mass. Inst. Tech., 1896; A.M., Columbia U., 1914; m. Mabel Nelson, June 22, 1905 (died July 19, 1913); children—Harold Nelson (dec.), Elbridge Nelson (dec.); m. 2d, Jessie Chapman Noble, Sept. 21, 1918. Asst. instr. mining and metallurgy, Mass. Inst. Tech., 1897-99; instr. analytical chemistry and minerology, U. of Vt., 1899-1901, asst. prof., 1901-03, prof., 1903-24, professor geology and minerology, 1924-44, professor emeritus since July 1, 1944; seismologist, Univ. of Vermont Seismograph Sta.; curator in geology, U. of Vermont Fleming Museum; Vermont state geol., 1933-47; state cons. geol. since 1947. Acting geol. United States Engineer Corps on geology of damsites for Vermont Flood Control, 1929. In charge geog. teaching, U.S. Air Corps Detachment, 1943-44. Fellow Geol. Soc. Am., A.A.A.S.; mem. Am. Assn. U. Profs., Minerol. Soc. America, Seismol. Soc. Am., Geophys. Union, Alpha Tau Omega. Republican. Conglist. Mason. Club: Ethan Allen. Author: Reports of the State Geologist, An Account of Vermont Geology; Geology of the Green Mountains of Northern Vermont; The Great Ice Age in Vermont; The Vermont Geological Survey, 1845-1946; The Physical Features of Vermont, 1948; also various shorter papers on Vt. geology. Home: 146 Williams St., Burlington VT‡

JACOBS, JAY WESLEY, portrait painter; b. Carthage, Mo., Jan. 3, 1898; s. Ernest Biers and Caroline (Farwell) J.; A.B. cum laude, Harvard, 1921; studied in Paris, Madrid, Florence, 1923-29. Exhibited Societe Nationale des Beaux-Arts, Paris, 1925, 26, 27; returned to America, 1929; engaged on commns. as portrait painter, 1929-68; among notables painted: President Truman, Fleet Adm. W.F. Halsey, Vice Adm. H.L. Vickery, Walter S. Carpenter, Mrs. Franklin D. Roosevelt, Jr., Mrs. Lawrence Wood Robert, Jr., Gov. William Scranton of Pa., John G. Searle, L.S. Ayers, Otto Frenzel, S.T. Olin, Louis Schwitzer, F.K. Weyerhaeuser, Anton Hulman, Adm. E.S. Land. Episcopalian. Home: Hobe Sound FL Died May 4, 1968.

JACOBS, JOSEPH EARLE, diplomatic service; b. Johnston, S.C., Oct. 31, 1893; s. Joseph and Nettie (Austin) J.; A.B., Coll. Charleston, 1913, LL.D., 1953; m. Elizabeth McNutt, Aug. 23, 1930. Student interpreter in China and detailed to Peking, Nov. 5, 1915; vice counsul, at Foochow, 1917-18; vice consul and interpreter, Shanghai, 1918; Am. assessor Internat. Mixed Court, Shanghai, 1918-25; judge Consular Court, Dist. of Shanghai, 1919-20; apptd. consul, 1921; reclassified as foreign service officer, 1924; administrative consul at Shanghai, May-Dec. 1925; tech adviser to Am. Commr. on Extra-territorial Jurisdiction in China, 1926; consul at Yunnanfu, China, 1926-28, Shanghai, 1928-30; rep. of Am. minister to China in negotiations with regard to Provisional Court, Shanghai, Dec. 1929-Feb. 1930; duty Far Eastern Div., Dept. of State, 1930-34; foreign service insp., 1935-36; chief Officer of Philippine Affairs, Dept. of State, 1936-40; counselor of Legation, Cairo, 1940-45; attached to polit. sect. Allied Hdqrs., Mediterranean Command Caserta, Italy, Jan. 1945; Am. representative to Albania, May 1945-Nov. 1946; polit. adviser to comdg. gen. Korea, 1947-48; career minister, U.S. foreign service, Nov. 1947; U.S. ambassador to Czechoslavakia, 1948-49, minister to American Embassy, Rome, spl. asssitant for Mutual Defense Assistance Program, 1949-55; United States ambassador to Poland, 1955-57. Member Joint Com. of Experts on Philippine Affairs, 1937; adviser Far Eastern affairs, 3d session Gen. Assembly UN, Paris, 1948. Awarded Patriotic Civilian Service Medal by Dept. of Army, 1949. Home: Washington DC Died Jan. 1971.

JACOBS, MELVILLE, educator; b. N.Y.C., July 3, 1902; s. Alexander and Rose (Blau) J.; A.B., Coll. City N.Y., 1922; A.M., Columbia, 1923, Ph.D., 1931; m. Elizabeth L. Derr, Jan. 3, 1931. Mem. faculty U. Wash., 1928-71, prof. anthropology, 1951-71; vis. prof. U. Wis., 1961-62; summer vis. prof. Columbia, 1931, U. B.C., 1945, U. Ore., 1947, U. Colo., 1962; field research langs., folklores, customs Ore.-Wash. Indians, 1926-39. Mem. Am. Ethnol. Soc., Am. Folklore Soc. (pres. 1963-64), Linguistic Soc. Am., Am. Antrop. Assn. Author: Sketch of Northern Sahaptin Grammar, 1931; Northwest Sahaptin Texts, 1934-37; Coos Texts, 1939-40; Kalapuya Texts, 1945; (with B.J. Stern) General Anthropology, 1947; Clackamas Chinook Texts, 1958-59; The Content and Style of an Oral Literature, 1959; The People Are Coming Soon, 1960; Pattern in Cultural Anthropology, 1964; also numerous articles. Home: Seattle WA Died July 31, 1971; buried Evergreen-Washelli, Seattle WA

JACOBSEN, EINAR A., mfg. co. exec.; b. Racine, Wis., Jan. 21, 1906; s. Knud F. and Ellen S. (Hansen) B.S. in Mech. Engring., U. Wis., 1928; m. Elsa M. Paur, July 20, 1929; children—Mary C. Wellman, Lois J. Watton. With Jacobsen Mfg. Co., Racine, 1928-72, pres., dir., 1958-72; dir. Racine Savs. & Loan Assn., Allegheny Ludium Industries. Mem. Racine Mfg. Assn. (dir., past pres.). Club: Somerset (Racine). Home: Racine WI Died July 18, 1972.

JACOBSEN, ELNAR A., mfg. exec.; b. Racine, Wis., Jan. 21, 1906; s. Knud F. and Ellen S. (Hansen); B.S. in Mech. Engring., U. Wis., 1928; m. Elsa M. Paur, July 29, 1929; children—Mary C. Wellman, Lois J. Medgyesy. With Jacobsen Mfg. Co., Racine, 1928-72, pres., dir., 1958-72, chmn. bd., 1971-72; dir. Racine Savs. & Loan Assn., True Temper Corp., Cleve. Mem. Somerset (Racine). Home: Racine WI Died Aug. 16, 1972.

JACOBSEN, JEROME VINCENT, educator; b. Chgo., 1894; s. James J. and Catherine (Harty) J.; student St. Ignatius Coll., Chicago, 1913-15, St. Stanislaus Sem., Florissant, Mo., 1915-19; B.A. and M.A., Gonzaga U., Spokane, Wash, 1922; student St. Louis (Mo.) Univ. 1925-29; Ph.D., U. of Calif., 1934. Instr. St. Mary's (Kan.) Coll., 1922-25, John Carroll U., Cleveland, 1929-30; instr. history Loyola U., 1931-32, assistant professor, 1934-37, professor, 1938-69, also vice rector, 1955-59; director of the Inst. Jesuit History; editor Mid-America, 1934-70; ordained Roman Catholic priest, 1928; mem. Soc. of Jesus. Mem. Am. Hist. Assn., Orgn. Am. Historians, Inter-Am. Bibliog. and Library Assn. Author: Educational Foundations of the Jesuits in Sixteenth-Century New Spain, 1938. Home: Chicago IL Died Aug. 19, 1970; buried All Saints Cemetery, Desplaines IL

JACOBSON, BELLE ELIZABETH, physician; b. N.Y.C., Mar. 12, 1900; d. Henry and Ida (Cohen) Jacobson; M.D., Boston U., 1926; m. Irving Greenwald, Mar. 25, 1925; 1 son, Edward S. Intern, Montefiore Hosp., N.Y.C., 1927-28, asso. physician cardiovascular service, 1928—; extern Mt. Sinai Hosp., 1926-27; cons. physician New Rochelle Hosp. Diplomate Am. Bd. Internal Medicine. Fellow Am. Coll. Cardiology, A.C.P.; mem. A.M.A. Home: Bronxville NY Died Aug. 25, 1970.

JACOBSON, CARL ALFRED, prof. chemistry; b. Grantsburg, Wis., Jan. 25, 1876; s. Carl John and Anna Britta (Asp) J.; B.S., Carleton Coll., 1903, M.S., 1907; Ph.D., Johns Hopkins, 1908; spl. studies in 3 univs. of Europe, 1911, 12; m. Mary Edna Metzger, June 21, 1906; children—Ernest Howard (dec.), Alfred Marcel (dec.), Carl Metzger, John David, Joseph Edward (Marine pilot, killed in World War II), Samuel Odin, Robert Stanley. Fellow and research chemist, Rockefeller Inst. for Med. Research, New York, 1908-09; prof. agrl. chemistry, U. of Nevada, and chief chemist Nev. Agrl. Expt. Station, 1909-18; fellow Johns Hopkins U., 1919-20; prof. chem., W.Va. U., 1920-26; emeritus since 1946. Fellow A.A.A.S., mem. Am. Chem. Soc., Am. Assn. U. Profs., Phi Beta Kappa, Phi Kappa Phi, Phi Lambda Upsilon. Democrat. Methodist. Author: A Pronouncing Chemical Formula Speller and Contest Guide. Editor-in-chief Ency. of Chem. Reactions (vols. I, II, III). Contbr. on elec. conductivity, phosphatides, chlorophylls, alfalfa constituents, enzymes, poisonous principles, oils, saponins, fluosilicic acid, fluosilicates, silica black and silica fluff, chemical spelling, chemical shorthand, etc. Inventor of various lab. apparatus, a calculating machine, and a new method for determining the solubility of solids at different temperatures; granted U.S. patents on processes for treating powdered coal and on carburized silica." An organizer of Sealco By-Products Co. of W.Va. (by-products of coal), Bluefield (factory of Greer, W.Va.), 1938. Home: 447 Cedar St., Morgantown WV‡

JACOBSON, MOSES ABRAHAM, pathologist; b. Portsmouth, Va., 1896; Ph.D. in Bacteriology, U. Chgo., 1927; M.D., Rush Med. Coll., 1932. Rotating intern Mt. Sinai Hosp., Chgo., 1931-32; chief lab. service VA Hosp., Downey, Ill., 1946-63; Instr. bacteriology Purdue U., Lafayette, Ind., 1916-18; asst. prof. bacteriology and clin. pathology Med. Coll. Va., 1921-22; asso. prof. bacteriology and pub. health U. Tenn., 1922-24; extern instr. bacteriology and pub. health U. Chgo., 1924-27. Served to 2d lt. San. Corps, U.S. Army, 1918-19, to capt. M.C., USNR, 1942-46. Diplomate Am. Bd. Pathology. Mem. A.M.A., Am. Pub. Health Assn., Am. Soc. Bacteriology, Am. Soc. Clin. Pathologists. Home: Waukegan IL Died Aug. 1, 1970; buried Chicago IL

JACOWAY, HENDERSON MADISON, ex-congressman; b. Dardanelle, Ark., Nov. 7, 1870; s. Judge William D. and Elizabeth Davis (Parks) J.; grad. Winchester (Tenn.) Coll., 1892; LL.B., Vanderbilt U., 1898; m. Margaret Helena Cooper, of Beaumont, Tex., Sept. 19, 1907; children—Bronson Cooper, Henderson M. (dec.), Margaret E. In law practice at Dardanelle, 1898-—; pros. atty. 5th Dist. Ark., 2 terms, 1904-08; mem. 62d to 67th Congresses (1911-23), 5th Ark. Dist. (retired voluntarily); now mem. Jacoway & Jacoway; regional atty. Social Security Board, Region IX (Ark., Kan., Mo., Okla.). Was mem. Dawes Indian Commn. Democrat. Home: Little Rock AR‡

JAHN, GUNNAR, economist, statistician; b. Trondheim, Norway, Jan. 10, 1883; s. Christian Fredrik Mikal and Wilhelmina Elisabeth (Wexelsen) J.; grad. law, U. Oslo, 1907, grad. polit. economy, 1909; student Univs. Heidelberg, Berlin, Paris, 1909-12; m. Martha Emily Larsen, Apr. 12, 1911 (dec. 1954). Sec. Norwegian Central Bur. Statistics, 1910-17; tchr. polit. economy, Oslo Bus. Coll., 1913-18; lectr. statistics U. Oslo, 1913-20; dir. Central Rationing Bd., 1918-20, Central Bur. Statistics, 1920-45; minister of finance, 1934-35, 45; governor Bank of Norway, 1946-54, Internat. Bank for Reconstruction and Development, 1946-53, and Internat. Monetary Fund, 1946-54; Norwegian representative economic com., League of Nations, 1928-30, statis. com., 1930-40; statis. com. Internat. Labor Orgn., 1936-40; member of the statistical committee UN, 1946-50; chairman Nobel Peace Prize Committee, 1942-66. Chairman Commn. Internat. Whaling Statistics, 1929-71, Norwegian Whaling Council, 1954-60, Norwegian Joint Com. of Research Councils, 1954-60. Honorary fellow Royal Statistical Society of London; mem. Internat. Statis. Inst. (hon.; v.p., 1947-51), Oslo Acad. Sci., Econometric Soc., Economic Association Norway (past chmn.). Author: Types of Houses in Rural Norway, 1920; statistical Methods, 1937; How to Make Trout Flies, 1938; The Long-Bow, 1938; Miscellany, Articles and Seppeches, 1949; Bank of Norway, 1916-1966. Home: Oslo Norway Died Jan. 31, 1971.

JAHN, WALTER J., corp. exec.; b. Brons, N.Y., Oct. 18, 1918; s. Albert and Rose (Strickler) J.; student N.C. State Coll. Agr. and Engring., 1936-39, Sch. of Marketing, N.Y.U., 1939-40; m. Melissa Del Robbins, Sept. 1, 1951; children—Diane, Hope, Michael. With Gen. Motors Corp., 1941-44; with Schenley Industries, Inc., 1943-70; gen. sales mgr. Tex. Wine & Liquor Co., 1954-57, Miami sales mgr. McKesson & Robbins, div., 1949-54; v.p., dir. marketing parent co., 1957-61; pres. Affiliated Distillers Brands Corp., Erie Liquor Co., Buffalo, Ont. Liquor Co., Rochester, So. Wine & Spirits, Inc., Miami, Fla., Am. Distbg. Co., Jacksonville, Fla., W. Fla. Distbg. Co., Pensacola, Harlan's Merchandising Corp., Worcester, Mass., Walter Jahn Corp., Miami; chmn. bd. David Kay Co., North Hollywood, Long Beach, San Diego and Riverside, Cal.; vice president of

Swedish Internat. Import Co., Miami, Fla.; v.p., gen. mgr. Nat. Distbg. Co., Atlanta, Nat. Wine & Liquor Co., Miami, Bay Distbg. Co., Tampa, Fla. Mem. Commn. Human Relations, Buffalo; mem. joint legislative advisory com. on consumer protection New York State Legislature. Clubs: Beach Point Yacht; Marco Polo, Westwood Country (Williamsville, N.Y.). Montefiore (Buffalo), Buffalo Athletic; Derby (N.Y.C.). Home: Miami FL Died Feb. 14, 1970; buried Lakeside Memorial Park, Miami FL

JAHNCKE, P.F., SR., chmn. Jahnke Service, Inc. Home: New Orleans LA

JAHR, TORSTEIN (KNUTSSON TORSTENSEN), librarian; b. Holmestrand, Norway, Aug. 7, 1871; s. Knut Torstensen and Inger Olea (Olsen) J.; came to America, 1890; A.B., Norwegian Luth. Coll., Decorah, Ia., 1896; B.L.S., U. of Ill., 1900; Columbian (now George Washington) U., 1901-02; m. Gunvor Olsen, of Oakland, Calif., April 18, 1916 (died 1924); 1 son, Olav (dec.). Teacher and lecturer when not attending coll. or univ., 1890-1900; reorganized libraries of Norwegian Luth. Coll., and of Luther Sem., St. Paul, Minn., 1900-01; cataloguer 1901-02, reviser in catalogue div., expert in Scandinavica, 1902-28, Library of Congress. Studied and traveled in Europe. Mem. Royal Norwegian Soc. of Sciences, A.L.A.; pres. Norwegian Lit. Soc., D.C. Knight, first class, Royal Norwegian Order of St. Olav. Club: University. Author: Bibliography of Cooperative Cataloguing (with references to internat. bibliography and the Universal Catalogue), 1902; Oleana, et blad of Ole Bulls og den norske indvandrings historie, 1910. Joint editor Idun (lit. monthly) Chicago, 1908-11, Jul i Amerika, N.Y., 1917-20; contbr. to Illustreret Norsk Konversationsleksikon, 1905-13, and other cyclopedias; also contbr. on hist., lit. and bibliog. subjects to jours. and periodicals. Home: Washington DC‡

JAMERSON, G(EORGE) H., army officer (ret.); b. Martinsville, Va., Nov. 8, 1869; s. Thomas J. and Louisa C. (Salmons) J.; student Ruffner Inst., Martinsville, 1882-87, Va. Agrl. and Mech. Coll., Blacksburg, 1888-89; B.S., U.S. Mil. Acad., 1893, grad. Army War Coll., 1910, 1922; m. Elsie T. Barbour, Oct. 20, 1897; 1 son, Osmond T. Commd. 2d lt., inf., U.S. Army, 1893, and advanced through the grades to maj. gen., 1942; retired, 1933; prof. mil. science and tactics Va. Poly. Inst., 1906-09; with A.E.F., France, 1918-19. Decorated D.S.M., Silver Star, Victory Medal with 4 clasps, Spanish War, Cuban Occupation, Philippine Insurrection and Mexican Border campaign medals. Mem. Va. Hist. Soc. Presbyterian. Clubs: Army and Navy (Washington); Current Events (Richmond). Home: Prestwould Apts., Richmond 20 VA‡

JAMES, APHIE, actress; b. Smith Grove, Ky., Oct. 7, 1869; d. John C. and Susan A. Hendricks; m. at Phila., Louis James (q.v.), Dec. 24, 1892. Joined Frederick Warde and Louis James Co., 1892; starred in all-star cast of Two Orphans, 1903; with Louis James in Shakespearean plays since 1904; starring in Judy O'Hara," 1910-11. Home: Monmouth Beach NJ‡

JAMES, ARTHUR HORACE, ex-gov., Pa.; b. Plymouth, Pa., July 14, 1883; s. James D. and Rachel (Edwards) J.; LL.B., Dickinson Sch. of Law, 1904; LL.D. (hon.), Susquehanna U., 1927, Dickinson Coll., 1938, Temple U., Jefferson Med. Coll., Muhlenberg Coll., Pa. Mil. Coll., Franklin and Marshall Coll., Washington and Jefferson Coll., 1939, U. of Pa., 1940, Moravian Coll., 1941, Lafayette Coll., 1941, Grove City Coll., 1942, Bucknell U., 1942; Gettysburg College, 1942; hon. D.C.L., Hahnemann Med. Coll. and Hospital, 1939; m. Ada Morris, October 23, 1912 (died 1935); children—Dorothy Rachel, Arthur Horace (deceased); m. 2d, Emily R. Case, October 1, 1941. Began as a breaker boy, Nottingham Breaker, Plymouth, Pa., 1896; admitted to Cumberland County (Pa.) bar, 1904, Luzerne County bar, 1905; in practice law, Plymouth and Wilkes-Barre, Pa., 1905-19; dist. atty., Luzerne County, Pa., 1919-26; lt. gov., Pa., 1927-31; judge Pa. Superior Court, 1932-39; gov. Commonwealth of Pa., 1939-43. Mem. bd. of incorporators Dickinson Law Sch. Mem. Pa. Bar Assn. Republican. Methodist (trustee). Home: Plymouth PA Died Apr. 27, 1973.

JAMES, DONALD DENNY, ret. banker; b. Plymouth, Mass., Feb. 5, 1900; s. D. Melancthon and Margaret Virginia (Denny) J.; student Mass. Inst. Tech., 1917-19; Yale Coll., 1919-22; m. Mary Bell Granger, June 7, 1946. Savings teller Alamo Nat. Bank, San Antonio, Tex., 1923-26; credit and field depts. Gen. Motors Acceptance Corp., 1926-27; salesman investment securities W. K. Ewing Co., Inc., later Alamo Nat. Co., 1927-33; mgr. municipal dept. to v.p., W. P. Fitch & Co., 1933-37; pres. Donald D. James Inc., Austin, Tex., 1937-41; asso. E. J. Roe & Co., San Antonio, 1941-44; v.p. Austin Nat. Bank, 1946-65; dir. San Antonio br. Fed. Reserve Bank of Dallas, 1958-63. Mem. investment adv. com. permanent fund U. Tex., 1957-60. Mem. Chi Phi. Methodist. Clubs: Town and Gown, Rotary, Driskill; St. Anthony (San Antonio). Home: Austin TX Died Sept. 1968.

JAMES, EDWARD DAVID, architect; b. Indpls., Oct. 14, 1897; s. David John and Evangeline (Crull) J.; B.Arch., Cornell U., 1923; m. Catharine Lewis, Mar. 26, 1927; children—David Lewis, Stephen Edward. With archtl. offices Price & McLanahan, 1926-29; partner Burns and James, architects, Indpls., 1926-49; pres. Edward D. James Architect, Inc., Indpls., 1949-56; pres., chmn. bd. James Assos., Inc., architects and engrs., Indpls., 1956-69; dir. Brown County Fed. Savs. & Loan Assn.; prin. works include univs., air terminal facilities, elementary and high sch. facilities, hosps., banks, comml. and indsl. installations, residences. Chmn. Ind. Bd. Registration Architects, 1962-64. Pres. Beck Chapel Guild, Ind. U., 1957-69; organizer, fund raiser summer camp Wheeler City Rescue Mission, Indpls., 1958-69. Bd. dirs. Historic Landmarks Found.; adv. bd. Historic Madison (Ind.); ex-mem. Cornell U. Council. Served to 1st lt., Air Corps, U.S. Army, World War I; to lt. col. USAAF, World War II. Recipient award merit from Instns. mag. for design Student Union Bldg., Ind. U. Med. Center, 1946, for Men's Residence Hall, Ind. U., 1952, for Meml. Union Bldg., Ind. U., 1959; hon. mention award Ch. Archtl. Guild Am. for design St. Marks Meth. Ch., Bloomington, Ind., 1958; A.I.A. citation merit for Eastgate Christian Ch., Indpls., 1959. Fellow A.I.A. (past nat. vice chmn. com. preservation historic bldgs., past chmn. com. religious bldgs.), Internat. Inst. Arts and Letters; member Indiana Soc. Architects (past preservation officer Ind.), Ind. C. of C., Newcomen Soc. N.Am., English Nat. Trust, Nat. Trust Historic Preservation, Soc. Archtl. Historians, Art Assn., Gargoyle Archtl. Scholastic Frat., Delta Tau Delta. Clubs: Columbus, Indpls. Service. Author book revs. Home: Indianapolis IN Died Mar. 1969.

JAMES, EDWARD WASHINGTON, coll. dean; b. nr. Piave, Miss., Dec. 2, 1916; s. Edward Washington and Emma (Henderson) J.; B.S., Miss State Coll., 1938; M.A., Miss. So. Coll., 1949; Ed.D., U. Tex., 1953; m. Mexie Bradshaw, Dec. 18, 1937; children—Barbara Faye (Mrs. James Baxter Elliott), Charlotte Ann (Mrs. Keith Dotson), Edward Washington III. Vocational agr. tchr., high sch., Becker, Miss., 1938-41, Ruffin, N.C., 1941-43, Richton, Miss., 1944; supt. Sand Hill Spl. Schs., Richton, 1945-49; supt. high sch., Tylertown, Miss., 1949-51; instr. U. Tex., 1951-53; prof. edn. East Central State Coll., Ada, Okla., 1953-54, dean instrn., 1954-69, dean of Coll., 1970-72. Dir. Okla. State Bank, Ada; mem. Okla. Commn. on Tchr. Edn. and Certification, 1957, v.p., 1958-59, pres., 1959. Mem. Ada City Council, 1962-65. Mem. adv. bd. Salvation Army; drive chmn. Pontotoc County chpt. A.R.C.; mem. Ada Safety Council, Ada Health Council. Mem. Miss. Sch. Adminstrs. Assn. (pres. 1948), Coll. Tchrs. Assn. Okla. (pres. 1956), Okla. Coll. Deans Assn. (pres. 1956), Okla. Council Edn. (v.p. 1955), Okla. Edn. Assn., Nat. Coll. Assn., Ada C. of C., Alpha Tau Alpha, Phi Delta Kappa, Phi Kappa Tau. Baptist (deacon). Kiwanian (pres. 1956, lt. gov. Tex.-Okla. dist. 1957). Home: Ada OK Died Apr. 14, 1972; buried Meml. Park Cemetery, Ada OK

JAMES, EDWIN WARLEY, civ. engr.; b. Ossining, N.Y., Oct. 17, 1877; s. Edwin Thomas and Alice (Warley) J.; grad. Phillips Exeter (N.H.) Acad., 1897; A.B., cum laude, Harvard, 1901; grad. study Mass. Inst. Tech., 1905-07; m. Ethel Townsend, Mar. 4, 1907; 1 dau., Alice. Dist. engr., Bur. Pub. Works, P.I., 1907-09; mem. U.S. Engr. Corps, 1909-10; chief of Inter-American Regional Office, U.S. Public Roads Administration, 1910-39, technical adviser International Diplomatic Conference on Automobile Circulation, Paris, France, 1926; in charge surveys and construction of Inter-American Highway since 1930, as rep. U.S. Bur. Pub. Roads, Dept. of Commerce; mem. Consejo de Vias de Communicacion, Colombia, S.A., 1929; dir. Franklin Manor Beach Co. Recipient Belgian Foundation award, 6th Internat. Road Congress. U.S. del. Pan-Am. Hwy. Congresses, Chile, 1939, Mexico, 1941, 52; staff mem. on U.S. Brazilian Tech. Commn., 1948. Mem. Am. Soc. Civil Engrs., Am. Assn. State Highway Officials (chmn. com. on standards), Washington Soc. Engrs. Baptist. Clubs: Cosmos (Washington); Columbia Country (Chevy Chase, Md.). Author books. Contbr. about 175 tech. articles. Home: 6412 Beechwood Dr., Chevy Chase 15, MD. Office: Bureau of of Public Roads, Dept. of Commerce, Washington DC‡

JAMES, FRANK CYRIL, univ. pres., economist, historian; b. London, Eng., Oct. 8, 1903; s. Frank and Mary Lucy (Brown) J.; student Grocers' Company's Sch., London, 1910-20; B. Commerce, London Sch. of Economics, 1923; A.M., U. of PA., 1924, Ph.D., 1926; hon. D.C.L., Bishops, U. Kansas City; LL.D., U. Brit. Columbia, 1956, Princeton, Queens U., Syracuse U., Ursinus Coll., Cambridge Univ., Glasgow 1953, Rochester, 1954; Toronto U.; New York U.; U. of Saskatchewan, U. of Manitoba, U. of London, U. of Punjab, Lahore, McMaster U., U. of N.B., Northwestern U., 1958, U. of Alberta, 1958, U. Ottawa, 1959; D.Sc., Memorial Univ. of Newfoundland, 1961, Clarkson Coll., U. Punjab (Pakistan), 1962; D.Sc. in economics, Laval U., U. of Pa. (hon.). 1957; Docteur de l'Universite de Montreal; m. Irene L.V. Leeper, Aug. 19, 1926. Lived in U.S., 1923-39. Clerk in Barclay's Bank, London, 1921-23; instr. in finance and trans., U. of Pa., 1924-27, asst. prof. of finance, 1927-33, asso. prof., 1933-35, prof., 1935-39, chmn. graduate faculty in social science, 1936-37, prof. of finance and economic history, 1938-39; prof. of polit. economy, McGill Univ., 1939-63, dir. Sch. of Commerce, Sept.-Dec. 1939, principal and vice-chancellor 1939-63, principal emeritus, 1963-72. Vice chmn. Commn. Econ. Devel. Quebec, 1960-64. Pres. Internat. Assn. Univs., 1960-66. Chmn. exec. com. Oxford Com. Famine Relief, Eng. Has served in a variety of positions in business, primarily in econ. field; has been adv. to numerous organizations and socs. Decorated Chevalier de la Legion d'Honneur. Fellow Royal Econ. Soc. (London). Royal Soc. (Can.). Member several professional assns. Clubs: Atheneum (London); University, McGill Faculty, Royal Montreal Curling (Montreal) University (N.Y.). Author several books, 1926-; including: The Economic Doctrines of John Maynard Keynes (with others), 1938; Economic Problems in a Changing World (with others), 1939; On Understanding Russia, 1960; The Growth of Chicago Banks, 1969. Address: Amersham Bucks England Died May 1972.

JAMES, GEORGE, physician; b. N.Y.C., Nov. 15, 1915; s. Victor and Lillian (Gilman) J.; A.B., Columbia, 1937; M.D. cum laude, Yale, 1941; M.P.H., Johns Hopkins, 1945; m. Beatrice Lucille Kerner, Dec. 16, 1939; 1 dau., Barbara. Intern pediatrics New Haven Hosp., also asst. pediatrics Yale Sch. Medicine, 1941-42; dir. Obion Lake (Tenn.) Health Dist., 1942-44; mem. staff N.Y. State Dept. Health, 1945-55, regional health dir. liaison with N.Y.C., 1951-52, asst. commnr. program devel. and evaluation, also liaison with N.Y.C., 1952-55; lab. asst. biostatistics Johns Hopkins Sch. Hygiene and Pub. Health, 1946; asst. clin. prof. pub. health practice Yale Sch. Medicine, 1947-52; mem. faculty Albany Med. Coll. of Union U., 1949-55, asso. prof. preventive medicine and pub. health, 1949-55; dir. health Akron, (O.) City Dept. Health, 1955-56; mem. staff N.Y.C. Dept. Health, 1956-65, 1st dept. commnr., 1959-62, commnr. health, chmn. bd. health, 1962-65; adj. asso. prof., then adj. prof. Columbia Sch. Adminstrv. Medicine and Pub. Health, 1956-65; exec. v.p. Mt. Sinai Med. Center, 1965-68, pres. 1968-72, prof. dept. community medicine Mt. Sinai School of Medicine, City U. N.Y., 1965-72, dean, 1965-72; professional lecturer preventive medicine St. John's Sch. Edn., 1957-63; vis. lectr. Harvard Sch. Pub. Health, 1962-63. Pres. N.Y. State Conf. County, City and Dist. Health Officers, 1961-62; exec. com. Health Research Council N.Y.C. 1962-72; mem. hosp. Rev. and Planning Council So. N.Y. and N.Y. State, 1962-65; bd. mgrs. State Communities Aid Assn.; subcom. Edn. and supply, Nat. Adv. Com. Health Manpower, 1966-67; mem. N.Y.C. Community Mental Health Bd., 1962-65; Nat. Health Council, Greater N.Y. Safety Council, Nat. Council Alcoholism, N.Y. Blood Center; consultant N.Y. State Joint Legislative Com. Problems Pub. Health and Medicare, 1966-72; ad hoc committee narcotic addiction President's Office Sci. and Tech., 1962-63; White House Conf. Narcotic Addiction, 1963; chmn. Pres.'s Nat. Task Force on Health, 1964; Wooldridge com. evaluation program NIH, 1964, chmn. study sect. regional medicare programs, 1966-72; chmn. nat. conf. pub. health training USPHS, 1967; Lasker Journalism Award Com., 1964-66; cons. USPHS, WHO; Sheckman lectr. Soc. Pub. Health Edn., 1962; Crocker lectr. Roosevelt Hosp., N.Y.C., 1964; sec. Health, Edn. &Welfare's Rev. Com. Prescription Drugs. Chmn. bd. Med. Library Center. Recipient Campbell Gold medal Yale School Medicine, 1941; Bronfman award Am. Pub. Health Assn., 1965; Meritorious Service award National Found. Neuromuscular Diseases, 1966; Herman M. Biggs Meml. award, N.Y. Pub. Health Assn. Diplomate Nat. Bd. of Medical Examiners, American Board Preventive Medicine. Fellow Royal Soc. Health, A.M.A., Am. Pub. Health Assn., N.Y. Acad. Sci.; member of N.Y. Acad. Medicine (anniversary discourse 1964), N.Y.C. Pub. Health Assn. (pres. 1961-62), N.Y. Diabetes Assn. (director 1963-67), American Hospital Association, New York State Acad. Preventive Medicine (exec. bd. 1956-62, pres. 1960-61), N.Y. State, N.Y. County med. socs., N.Y. State Epidemiological Soc. (pres. 1948-49), Hosp. Soc. N.Y., A.A.A.S., Am. Coll. Preventive Medicine (v.p. 1964), Asso. Hosp. Service N.Y. (bd. dirs.), Am. Thoracic Soc., Am. Nat. Council Health Edn. (bd. dirs.), Am. Assn. Pub. Health Physicians, Harvey Soc., Nat. Health Council (pres. 1965-66); Nat. Publicity Council (v.p. 1954-55, exec. bd. 1955-58), Assn. Tchrs. Preventive Medicine, Phi Beta Kappa, Alpha Omega Alpha. Clubs: Columbia Club, Yale Club (N.Y.C.). Presbyterian. Author numerous articles in field. Editorial bd. Med. Opinion & Review, Inc., 1965-72; adv. editor Parents mag. Home: Garden City NY Died Mar. 19, 1972.

JAMES, HERMAN BROOKS, educator; b. nr. Oakboro, N.C., Aug. 27, 1912; s. Martin L. and Carrie Ellen (Brooks) J.; B.S., N.C. State Coll., 1932, M.S., 1940; Ph.D., Duke, 1949; m. Verna Lee Greene, May 31, 1941; children—David Brooks, Sarah Ellen. Tchr. vocational agr., Knightdale, N.C., 1933; county agt., Montgomery County, N.C., 1934-38; farm mgmt. specialist N.C. Agr. Extension Service, Raleigh, N.C., 1939-42; agrl. economist Appalachian and S.E. regions U.S. Dept. Agr., 1943-44, Dept. Agr. adv. com. on agrl.

econs., Raleigh, 1954-73; in charge farm mgmt. extension dept. N.C. State Coll., 1945-46; charge teaching and farm mgmt. research, dept. agrl. econs. as prof. agrl. econs., 1947-49; head dept. agr. econs., N.C. State U., 1949-57, dir. instrn. Sch. Agr., 1958-60, prof., dean agr., 1960-70; v.p. in charge research and pub. service programs Consol. U. N.C., 1970-73. Asst. adminstr. Office War on Hunger, AID, 1968; AID cons. Peru, 1962, Nicaragua, 1964, Laos, 1965, Africa, 1966; mem. Nat. Agr. Research Adv. Com., 1965-69; adv. com. Kellogg Found., 1963-67; chmn. com. agrl. econs. Social Sci. Research Council, 1954-56; mem. adv. bd. Nat. Agrl. Extension Center for Advanced Study, 1961-66; chmn. deans agr. Nat. Assn. State Univs. and Land Grant Colls., 1968. Mem. Am., So. econ. assns., Am. Agr. Econ. Assn. (pres. 1956-57), Nat. Acad. Scis. (agrl. bd. 1956-57), So. Farm Mgmt. Research Com. (chmn. 1949-51), Grange, Farm Bur., Alpha Zeta, Phi Kappa Phi, Kappa Phi Kappa. Author numerous expt. sta. bulls., circulars. Contbr. articles to profl. jours. Home: Raleigh NC Died Mar. 24, 1973.

JAMES, JAMES CHARLES, lawyer; b. Aurora, Ill., Feb. 21, 1882; s. George Albert and Mary (Rooney) J.; A.B., U. of Wis., 1904; student George Washington U. Law Sch.; m. Julia Brady Haring, July 11, 1910; children—Marion, Martha, James Charles, Jr. Admitted to Illinois bar, 1905, Supreme Court U.S., 1926; practiced law at Aurora, Ill., 1905-17; assistant state's attorney Kane County, Illinois, 1907-10; member firm of Alschuler, Putnam & James. Aurora, 1910-17; local atty. C.,B.&Q. R.R. Co., 1914-17; asst. to Ill. dist atty., same road, Chicago, 1917-19, gen. atty., 1919-24, gen. solicitor, 1924-38, gen. counsel, 1938-49, v.-pres. and director, 1939-49, mem. exec. com., 1941, exec. vice president, gen. counsel 1949-52, ret., 1952, dir., mem. exec. com., 1952-69; dir., mem. exec. com. Colo. & So. Ry. Co., 1952-69. Dir. Aurora Found. Mem. adv. bd. St. Joseph Mercy Hosp. Mem. Am. Bar Assn., Phi Kappa Psi. Republican. Clubs: Chicago, Chicago Farmers. Home: Aurora IL Died Oct. 31, 1969; buried Spring Lake, Aurora IL

JAMES, MINNIE KENNEDY (MRS. WM. CAREY JAMES), b. Palestine, Tex., Feb. 1, 1874; d. John Thomas and Anna (Johnson) Kennedy; grad. high sch., Terrell, Tex., 1890; ed. Sam Houston Teachers' Coll., Huntsville, Tex.; m. William Carey James, of Rockport, Aransas Co., Tex., June 20, 1894; 1 dau., Margaret E. Teacher pub. schs., Rockport, 1892-95; mem. examining bd. for teachers, Aransas Co., Tex., 1892-95; mem. exec. bd. Woman's Missionary Union, Bapt. State Conv., Va., many yrs.; pres. Va. W.M.U., 1909-11, 1914-16, now mem. editorial staff W.M.U. magazine, Royal Service"; pres. W.M.U., of Southern Bapt. Conv., 1916-25; presiding chmn. of Woman's Auxiliary, Bapt. World Alliance Meeting, Stockholm, 1923. Home: Richmond VA‡

JAMES, OLLIE MURRAY, newspaperman; b. Kuttawa, Ky., Oct. 16, 1908; s. Edgar Harrison and Mary (Campbell) J.; student U. Louisville, U. Ky.; m. Elizabeth Hazelrigg Hall, Dec. 31, 1931. Reporter, polit. writer, legislative corr. Lexington (Ky.) Herald, 1928-34; reporter, Washington corr., asso. editor Louisville Herald-Post, 1934-36; editorial writer, asst. mng. editor Cin. Enquirer, 1936-44, chief editorial writer, 1944-71; editor Union Central Advocate, nat. policyholders' publ. Union Central Life Ins. Co.; writer column Innocent Bystander; speaker, master ceremonies various radio and TV shows. Trustee voting trust Cin. Enquirer, Inc. Mem. Nat. Conf. Editorial Writers, Sigma Nu, Sigma Delta Chi. Author: Splendid Century. Contbr. articles mags. Home: Covington KY Died Jan. 26, 1972.

JAMESON, JOHN BUTLER, b. Bennington, N.H., Aug. 2, 1873; s. Nathan Cleaves and Idabel (Butler) J.; student Coll. City of N.Y., 1889-91; hon. Sc.D., U. of N.H., 1918; m. Marion Dudley Eidlitz, Nov. 19, 1913; children—John Butler, Robert Dudley, Jane. Dir. First Nat. Bank, Dominion Stores, Ltd. Chmn. Dem. State Com., N.H., 1906-12; del. at large, Dem. Nat. Conv., Baltimore, 1912; Dem. candidate for U.S. Senate, 1918; chmn. N.H. Com. of 100 on Pub. Safety, World War. Presbyterian. Mason. Home: 76 Centre St. Office: 40 N. Main St., Concord NH‡

JAMISON, ALPHA PIERCE, mechanical engr.; b. Lafayette, Ind., Nov. 27, 1875; s. Albert Ringo and Zelina Matilda (Pierce) J.; B.E.E. Purdue U., 1895, M.E., 1897; m. Clara C. Rogers, Lafayette, Ind., July 10, 1901. Prof. in drawing, Purdue U., since 1896. Jr. mem. of Soc. Mech. Engrs.; mem. Kappa Sigma. Republican. Baptist. Author: Elements of Mechanical Drawing, 1901; Advanced Mechanical Drawing, 1905; Isometric Drawing, 1911. Address: Lafayette IN‡

JAMISON, PAUL BAILEY, shoe mfr. and distr.; b. Mondamin, Ia., July 12, 1877; s. Dr. James Watson and Lucretia (Robinson) J.; ed. pub. schs.; m. Ida Boshard, Sept. 4, 1907 (now deceased); children—Elizabeth (Mrs. J. W. Folk), Paul B. Retail clerk, Gamet & Ogden, Mondamin, 1892-1900; traveling salesman, R. P. Smith & Sons Co., Chicago, 1900-04, Roberts Johnson & Rand, St. Louis, 1904-07; supt. factories of Friedman-Shelby br., Internat. Shoe Co., St. Charles, Mo., and Hannibal, Mo., 1907-11; sales mgr., St. Louis, 1911-24, gen. mgr., 1924-47, v.p. and dir. since 1921; ret. as gen. mgr. Friedman Shelby, May 31, 1947. Dir. M.K. & T. R.R., Indsl. Bank, Ill. Nat. Bank of Quincy, Ill. Pres. bd. trustees Westminster Coll., Fulton, Mo. Mem. C. of C., Community Chest, Y.M.C.A. (mem. met. bd.). Presbyterian. Clubs: University, Bogey, Noonday. Home: 6105 Lindell Blvd., St. Louis. Office: 1509 Washington Av., St Louis MO‡

JANES, JOHN VALLE, chem. co. exec.; b. St. Louis, Oct. 31, 1898; s. John M. and Catherine (Valle) J.; student Mass. Inst. Tech., 1923; m. Genevieve Barnickel, May 23, 1927; children—John Valle, Genevieve Brown, William B., Michael V. Vice pres., treas. Gross & Janes Co., St. Louis, 1924-72, Petrolite Corp., St. Louis, 1930-72; pres. Wm. S. Barnickel & Co.; trustee Barnickel Co. Life dir. Boys Club St. Louis; pres. Father Tim Dempsey Charities. Served with U.S. Army, World War I. Decorated Verdun medal, Croix de Guerre (France). Clubs: Metropolitan (N.Y.C.); Petroleum (Dallas and Houston); California (Los Angeles). Home: St Louis MO Died Jan. 6, 1972.

JANNOTTA, ALFRED VERNON, ret. naval officer, corporation exec.; b. Chgo., Dec. 13, 1894; s. Alfredo A. and Stella (Skiff) J.; B.A., Cornell U., 1917; D.Sc., Detroit Institute of Technology, 1961; m. Mary Brokerick Lamm, Aug. 20, 1918; children—Mary Frances, Shirley Skiff (Mrs. Henry C. Nickel), Diane Broderick (Mrs. Wallace B. Mallu). With Jewel Tea Co., Inc., from 1919, mem. salary and profit sharing, stock options and audit coms., from 1934, also dir.; with Lehman Bros., investment bankers, N.Y.C., 1926-27; pres., dir. Motor Inst. Am., Chgo., 1927-32, Tapp, Inc., Chgo., 1932-42; mng. trustee two investment trusts, 1933-42; pres., dir. Consol. Trading Corp., Chgo., 1947-49; cons., dir. Mayfair, Inc., Albany, also Porters, Inc., retail home furnishings, Racine, Wis., from 1949; dir. Western Lithograph Co., Los Angeles, Quality Park Envelope Co., St. Paul, Quality Park Box Co., St. Paul, J. D. Jewell, Inc.; with Standard Packaging Corp., N.Y.C., from 1955, vice chmn. of bd. dirs., also dir., mem. exec. com. Served from seaman to lt. (j.g.) U.S. Navy, 1917-19, from lt. comdr. to comdr., 1942-46; mem. Res., from 1946, rear adm., 1954. Decorated Navy Cross, Silver Star, Bronze Star with V (2), Purple Heart. Mem. Nat. Retail Tea and Coffee Merchants Assn. (dir.), Furniture Mfrs. Assn. (dir.), Navy League, Military Order of Loyal Legion United States, Legion of Valor, Order Lafayette (v.p., dir.), Res. Officers Assn., Soc. Mayflower Descendants, Sigma Nu. Clubs: Savage (Ithaca, N.Y. and London, Eng.); Chicago Athletic Assn.; Bob-O-Link Golf (Highland Park, Ill.); University (Albany, N.Y.); Everglades (Palm Beach, Fla.); Manalapan (Fla.). Home: Lantana FL Died May 31, 1972; buried Arlington Nat. Cemetery, Arlington VA

JANSS, PETER W(ILLIAM), lawyer; b. Atlantic, Ia., Sept. 26, 1904; s. Peter Detlef and Lucy (Lindeman) J.; B.A., State U. Ia., 1926, D.J., 1927; m. Esther Fuller, Oct. 26, 1930; children—Peter Fuller, Mary (Mrs. Lawrence Turner). Admitted to Ia. bar, 1927, and practiced in Des Moines; mem. Janss, Dreher, Wilson & Adams and predecessors, 1930-69. Dir. Walnut Grove Products Co., Great Plains Bag Co., Webster Life Ins. Co.; exec. sec. Nat. Mineral Feeds Assn. Chmn. Polk County Republican Central Com., 1940-46. Dir., pres. Polk County Tb and Health Assn. Ia., 1934; exec. com., dir., pres. Ia. Tb and Health Assn., 1939-46; dir. Nat. Tb Assn., 1945-69, pres.-elect, 1962, pres., 1963-64, v.p., 1967. Mem. Am., Ia., Polk County bar assns., Order Artus, Omicron Delta Kappa, Delta Chi, Phi Alpha Delta. Mason (Shriner, 33 deg.). Clubs: Prairie, Des Moines, Wakonda, Des Moines IA Died July 18, 1969.

JANZEN, ASSAR GOTRIK, educator; b. Goteborg, Sweden, Aug. 22, 1904; s. Anders and Agnes Sofia (Ekeblad) J.; B.A., U. Gothenburg, Sweden, 1929, Ph.D., 1936; m. Saimi Margareta Johansson, Sept. 10, 1936; 1 son, Hans Erik. Came to the United States, 1946, naturalized, 1959. Assistant institute for research in place names, dialects U. Gothenburg, 1929-42, docent U. Gothenburg, 1936-41, research fellow, 1937-38, prof., 1945; faculty Filip Holmguists Handels Inst., Gothenburg, 1930-32; docent U. Lund, Sweden, 1941-46, research fellow, 1942-46; staff Svenska Akademien Lund, Sweden, 1942-45; vis. prof. Scandinavian langs. and lit. U. Cal., 1946-49, prof., 1949-71, chmn. Scandinavian dept., 1951-59. Member American Scandinavian Found. Mem. Modern Lang. Assn. Am., Am. name Soc., Soc. Advancement Scandinavian Study (pres.), Royal Gustaf Adolf Acad. (Stockholm), Royal Society of Humanities (Uppsala, Sweden), Modern Lang. Tchrs. Assn., Vetenskaps Societeten Lund, Royal Soc. Letters, Uppsala, Royal Gustav Adolf Acad., Royal Soc. Letters and Sci., Gothenburg. Knight of Royal Order of the North Star, (Sweden). Author books published in Sweden. Contbr. articles Scandinavian, German, U.S. publs. Home: Berkeley CA Died Dec. 27, 1971.

JANZEN, DANILE H(UGO), govt. ofcl.; b. Mountain Lake, Minn., Mar. 25, 1906; s. Frank and Dina (Risser) J.; B.S., Ore. State Coll., 1929; m. Floyd Foster, 1937; children—Daniel, Katherine. Jr. forester Biol. Survey, Nat. wild-life refuge program U.S. Fish and Wildlife Service, 1929-46, regional dir., Mpls., 1946-57, dir. Bur. of Sport Fisheries, Wildlife, Washington, 1957-64. Recipient Distinguished Service award Interior Dept., 1965. Mem. Wildlife Soc., Soc. Am. Foresters, Am. Fishieries Soc., Phi Kappa Phi, Xi Sigma Pi, Kappa Kappa Psi. Home: Pelzer SC Died Nov 19, 1970.

JAQUA, ERNEST JAMES, educator; born Reinbeck, Ia., Oct. 24, 1882; s. Albert and Mary Jane (Watson) J.; A.B., Grinnell Coll., 1907, LL.D., 1927; grad. study Columbia, 1909-12, M.A., 1910; B.D., Union Theol. Sem., 1912; Ph.D., Harvard, 1919; m. Julia Gwendolyn Evans, Sept. 4, 1912; children—Mary Alice, Eleanor Stark, William Ernest, John Evans, Ernest Lyman. Coll. sec. State Y.M.C.A. of Ind., 1907-09; dean of men, asst. to pres. Grinnell (Ia.) Coll., 1912-17; dean of men, prof. edn. Colo. Coll., 1922-23; dean of faculty, prof. edn. Pomona Coll., Claremont, Cal., 1923-27; pres. Scripps Coll., 1927-42; head employment specialist bur. Tng., War Manpower Commn., 1943; ednl. dir. Baruch Com. on Phys. Medicine, 1944; pres. Multnomah Coll., Portland, Ore., 1951-53. Mem. bd. Community Chest, Portland, Rehabilitation Center, Family Counseling Service (chmn. bd. 1950-52), Ore. Council Chs. Dir. Carmel Found.; bd. dirs. Carmel Valley Manor; adv. com. on ednl. legislation Cal. Legislature; member gen. com. social welfare National Council Chs. Chmn. Mayors Com. on Juvenile Delinquency, Portland, 1950-52; chmn. Govs. Com. on Aging, Ore., 1953-54. Mem. N.E.A., Phi Beta Kappa, Phi Delta Kappa. Republican. Conglist. Club: Harvard (N.Y.C.). Home: Claremont CA Died July 1972.

JAQUES, FRANCIS LEE, artist; b. Genesco, Ill., Sept. 28, 1887; s. Ephriam Parker and Emma Jane (Monninger) J.; student Sch. of Engring., Milwaukee, Wis., 1915-16; m. Florence Sarah Page, May 12, 1917. Began as artist, 1920; with Am. Museum of Natural History, 1924-42, expdns. to Panama, 1925, S.A., 1926, Bahamas, 1926, Arctic, 1928, Eng., 1932, Polynesia, 1934, S.A., 1935; panoramic background paintings and murals in Am. Museum of Natural History, and Minn. Museum of Natural History, Peabody Mus. at Yale, Boston Mus. Sci., others. Private U.S. Army, 1917-19. Mem. Am. Ornithologists Union. Collaborated with Florence Page Jaques on: Canoe Country; The Geese Fly High; Birds Across the Sky; Snowshoe Country; Canadian Spring: Outdoor Life's Gallery of North American Game (book), As Far as the Yukon. Awarded John Burrouhg's medal jointly with wife St Paul MN Died July 24, 1969.

JARDINE, JOHN EARLE, JR., investment exec.; b. Pasadena, Cal., July 31, 1899; s. John Earle and Mary Chater (Peck) J.; student U. Cal. at Berkeley; m. Laura Blair Synder, Oct. 21, 1922 (dec. Sept. 1966);children—John Earle III, Lauris Earle (Mrs. James Albert Phillips III); m. 2d, Alice Ayer Ellis, May 15, 1967. With William R. Staats and Co., Los Angeles, 1922-72, gen. partner charge syndicate buying, 1951-72, sr. v.p., sec.; sr. v.p., dir. Glore Forgan, Wm. R. Staats; v.p. du Part Glore Forgan, Inc. Past chmn. Los Angeles chpt. A.R.C., chmn. fund campaign, 1955, exec. com., dir. Los Angeles chpt., vice chmn. nat. conv., St. Louis, 1956. Bd. dirs., So. Cal. Area Bldg. Fund, AID-United Givers; treas., bd. dirs. Braille Inst. of Am., Inc.; pres., bd. dirs. San Gabriel Cemetary Assn.; bd. govs. Am. Nat. Red Cross. Served as 2d lt. U.S. Army, World War I; as lt. col. AUS, World War II. Mem. Soc. Colonial Wars (gov. for Cal.) S.R., Investment Bankers Assn. Am. (past v.p., past gov.), Assn. Stock Exchange Firms (past gov.), Los Angeles C. of C. (past dir., v.p.), Phi Delta Theta. Clubs: Bond (pres. 1948-49), Municipal Bond (past pres.) (Los Angeles); California; Stock Exchange (dir. past pres.); Valley Hunt. Home: Pasadena CA Died Oct. 16, 1972.

JARRATT, HILL, lawyer; b. Batesville, Miss., Feb. 14, 1906; s. Maury E. and Ethel (Kyle) J.; student Ga. Inst. Tech., U. Ala.; m. Lillian Barnes, Aug. 29, 1947; admitted to Miss. bar, 1935; now gen. practice law, Batesville, Mem. Miss. Ho. of Reps., 1932-36; del. to Nat. Dem. Conv., 1956, 60. Served from pvt. to capt., 1942-46. Mem. Am. Judicature Soc., Miss. State Bar, Am. Bar Assn., Panola County Bar Assn. Democrat. Home: Batesville MS Died Mar. 5, 1969.

JARRELL, ALBERT POLK, supt. schs.; b. Butler, Ga., Aug. 5, 1907; s. Floyd C. and Mary Lee (McCants) J.; student Young Harris Coll., 1927, Mercer U., 1928; A.B., U. Ga., 1933, M.A., 1938; student N.Y.U., 1950; LL.D., John Marshall Law Sch., Atlanta, 1957; m. Carolyn Parham, Dec. 23, 1933; children—Carolyn Parham, Marianne Jackson. Prin., Central Sch., 1927-30; supt. schs., Chattahoochee County, Cusseta, Ga., 1930-39; counselor Div. Vocational Rehab., Albany and Columbus, Ga., 1940-43, asst. dir., 1943-55, dir., 1955-64; asst. state supt. schs. charge rehab. services, Atlanta, from 1964. Bd. dirs. Ga. Soc. Crippled Children and Adults, Inc., 1951-57, Goodwill Industries, from 1952; bd. trustees Atlanta Cerebral Palsy Center, from 1951; adv. bd. Met.-Atlanta Com. for Employment Handicapped, from 1954; mem. cardiac rehab. com. Ga. Heart Assn.; bd. dirs. Ga. chpt. Arthritis and Rheumatism Found., 1964-65. Recipient

H. B. Cummings award; President's award Nat. Rehab. Assn.; Goodwill Industries award of Yr. Mem. Ga. High Sch. Assn. (past regional pres., past v.p.), Nat. Rehab. Assn. (pres. 1964-65, past dir., mem. exec. com.), States Council Vocational Rehab. Adminstrn., Kappa Delta Pi, Kappa Phi Kappa. Methodist (past steward, chmn., vice chmn. bd. dirs., lay leader, Sunday sch. tchr.). Mason (Shriner), Lion. Home: Atlanta GA Died Aug. 1, 1967.

JARRELL, CHARLES CRAWFORD, church official; b. Milledgeville, Ga., Nov. 17, 1874; s. Rev. Anderson Joseph and Elizabeth Anne (Smith) J.; A.B., Emory U., 1894; B.D., Vanderbilt, 1900; grad. study, United Free Ch. Coll., Glasgow, Scotland, 1911-12, U. of Berlin, 1912; D.D., Wofford Coll., Spartanburg, S.C., 1917; m. Margaret Moore, July 2, 1901; 1 dau., Martha Elizabeth (Mrs. Arthur F. Raper); m. 2d, Mrs. Inez Hamrick Foote, June 5, 1942. Ordained ministry M.E. Church, 1894; adjunct prof. ethics and logic, Emory Coll., 1896-99; prof. Latin, Young Harris (Ga.) Coll., 1900-01; pastor N. Ga. Conf. M.E. Ch., S., 1901-16; and 1919-23; commr. and prof. English Bible, Emory U., 1916-20; dir. Corr. Sch., M.E. Ch., S., 1918-20; gen. sec. Gen. Hosp. Bd., M.E. Ch., S., 1923-34. Presiding elder Athens dist. M.E. Ch., S., 1935-36, Atlanta dist. M.E. Ch., S., 1937-38; pastor St. John Meth. Ch., Augusta, Ga., 1939-41, First Meth. Ch., Monroe, Ga., 1941, 42, 43; financial sec. Meth. Children's Home, Decatur, Ga., since 1943. Trustee Paine Coll., Augusta, Ga., Reinhart Coll., Waleska, Ga., Wesleyan Coll., Macon, Ga. Del. to Gen. Conf. M.E. Ch., S., 1918, 22, 24, 26, 30, 34; mem. gen. conf. M.E. Ch., S., 1938; mem. Uniting Conf. of The Meth. Church, 1939; mem. 6th Ecumenical Meth. Conf., Atlanta, Ga., 1932; mem. President's Hosp. Advisory Bd. to Com. on Econ. Security; mem. joint com. of Nat. Hosp. Assns. Founder A. J. Jarrell Lectureship at Emory U. Mem. Hosp. Assn. M.E. Ch., S. (founder, 1st pres.), Am. Protestant Hosp. Assn. (ex-pres.), Alpha Tau Omega, Theta Phi. Democrat. Mason (K.T.). Author: Witnesses to the Word, 1916; Methodism on the March (with others), 1924; Go Thou and Do Likewise, 1929. Contbr. chapters to Wit and Wisdom of W. A. Candler, Christ and the Coming Kingdom; also contbr. to ch. publs. and hosp. mags. Address: 999 Mount Paran Road, Route 6, Atlanta GA‡

JARRETT, CORA HARDY, novelist; b. Norfolk, Va., Feb. 21, 1877; d. Frederick and Charlotte Frances (Graves) Hardy; student Pollock-Stephens Inst., Birmingham, Ala., 1890-94; Miss Baldwin's Sch., Bryn Mawr, Pa., 1894-95; B.A., Bryn Mawr Coll., 1899; post grad. Sorbonne, Coll. de France, and Oxford U., Eng., 1899-1900; m. Edwin Seton Jarrett, June 26, 1906; children—Edwin Seton, William Armistead, Olivia Heather. Teacher English and Greek, Ward-Belmont Sem., Nashville, Tenn., 1902-03, of English, St. Timothy's Sch., Catonsville, Md., 1903-66. Clubs: Womans, Cosmopolitan (New York City). Author: The Cross Goes Westward, 1910; Peccadilloes, 1929; Night Over Fitch's Pond, 1933; Pattern in Black and Red (under pen name of Faraday Keene), 1934; The Ginkgo Tree, 1935; Strange Houses, 1936; I Asked No Other Thing, 1937; The Silver String, 1937. Contbr. fiction to mags. Home: Wild Goose Farm, Shepherdstown, W.Va.; and 144 Mercer St., Princeton NJ*‡

JARVIS, GEORGE TIBBALS, ry. official; b. N.Y. City, Aug. 26, 1869; ed. pub. schs.; spl. student civ. engring., Mass. Inst. Tech. Began as machinist's apprentice, Renovo Shops, Pa. R.R., Jan. 1876, later serving as locomotive fireman; supt.'s clk. Middle div. P. & E. R.R., div. of Pa. R.R., 1882-83; chief clk. transportation dept. Mexican Central Ry., Feb.-Apr. 1883; trainmaster 1st div. same rd., 1883-84; supt. 2d div. same rd., Jan.-Apr. 1884; supt. 1st div. same rd., 1884-88; supt. Duluth, S. Shore & Atlantic Ry., 1888-89; supt. Ohio div. B. & O. R.R., 1890-91; asst. gen. supt. L.E. & W. R.R., 1891-96; receiver Louisville, Evansville & St. Louis R.R., 1896-1901, also New Albany Belt & Terminal Ry.; gen. mgr. W.C. Ry., 1900-01; with Rutland R.R. since 1902, as gen. and federal mgr. v.p. and gen. mgr. during War period. Home: Rutland VT‡

JARVIS, HARRY AYDELOTTE, oil exec.; b. Berlin, Md., May 11, 1909; s. Harry Lee and Maude (Bowen) J.; B.S. in Mech. Engring., U. Md., 1930; grad. advanced mgmt. program, Harvard, 1947; m. Lillian Clarkson, Apr. 14, 1934; children—Henry Aydelotte, Joan Gail. Jr. engr. Compania Nativa de Petroleo, Campana, Argentina, 1931-34, mgr. Bahia Blanca refinery, 1935-36, successively process supt., asst. supt., mgr. Campana refinery, 1937-44, pres., gen. mgr. refining, 1945-46; with Creole Petroleum Corp., Caracas, Venezuela, 1947-64, successively mgr. Amuay refinery, mgr. refining dept., mem. mgmt. com., 1947-54, dir., 1952-64, exec. v.p., 1954-61, pres., 1961-64; pres. Creole Investment Corp., 1961-64; pres., dir. Compania de Petroleo Lago, Caracas. Mem. N. Am. Assn. Venezuela (pres. 1955-56). Mason (32 deg.). Home: Salisbury MD Died Oct. 19, 1972.

JARVIS, ROBERT EDWARD LEE, clergyman; b. Sparta, Tenn., Aug. 6, 1870; s. Sylvester and Maranda (Simril) J.; ed. pub. and pvt. schs. of Tenn. and McCormick Theol. Sem., Chicago, class of 1903; m. Fannie Catron Todd, of Carthage, Mo., Nov. 7, 1894. Ordained Presbyn. ministry, 1898; pastor Mt. Vernon, Mo., 1898-1900, Clay Center, Kan., 1903-8, Winfield, 1908-11, Bethany Collegiate Church (Wanamaker Ch.), Phila., 1911-15, Westminster Ch., Grand Rapids, Mich., 1915-17; apptd. religious dir. for Y.M.C.A., 1917, and assigned to Eagle Rock, Cal. Mason (32 deg.), Author: The Making of a Christian, 1903. Home: Grand Rapids MI‡

JAY, NELSON DEAN, banker; b. Elmwood, Ill., Mar. 7, 1883; s. Fred Dean and Elizabeth (Buchanan) J.; A.B., Knox College, Galesburg, Illinois, 1905, LL.D. (honorary degree), 1960; m. Anne Augustine, June 23, 1910; children—Nelson D., George A. (dec.), Robert Dean. With Milw. Trust Co., 1907-10, mgr., bond dept., 1910; v.p. First Nat. Bank, Milw., 1911-15; mgr. bond dept. Guaranty Trust Co., N.Y.C., 1915-16, v.p., 1916-20; partner Morgan & Cie, Paris, France, 1920-45; chmn. Morgan & Cie, Incorporated, Paris, France, until 1955; member of directors advisory com. Morgan Guaranty Trust Co. Chmn. adminstrv. com. A.R.C., 1943-44; chmn. bd. Am. Hosp. Paris, 1937-57; trustee of Knox Coll. Served from capt. to lt. col., U.S. Army, World War I; asst. gen. purchasing agt. AEF. Decorated D.S.M. (U.S.); Order of Honor with Star (Austria); comdr. Legion d'Honneur (France); officer de l'Ordre de Leopold (Belgium). Clubs: Metropolitan (Washington); Knickerbocker, Century (N.Y.C.); Travellers, Union Interallee (Paris). Address: New York City NY NY also Syosset NY Died June 6, 1972; buried Elmwood IL

JEAN, SISTER ANNE, hosp. adminstr.; b. Montclair, N.J., Dec. 13, 1910; d. Timothy Joseph and Anne (Sharkey) Regan; A.B., Coll. of St. Elizabeth, 1953. Bus. mgr. St. Joseph's Hosp., Paterson, N.J., 1936-42, asst. adminstr., 1942-53, adminstr., 1953-73. Mem. arbitration bd. Province of N.J.; mem. Synod Cath. Diocese of Paterson. Mem. Mayor's Com. on Health, 1960-73. Pres. Mental Health Council; past pres. N.J. Conf. Cath. Hosps.; v.p. Community Home Care Greater Paterson; sec., bd. dirs. Health Edn. Advancement League; bd. dirs. N.J. League Nursing, Community Health Services Council, Passaic Valley Health Facilities Planning Council; trustee St. Mary's Hosp., Passaic, St. Vincent's Hosp., Montclair, Holy Name Hosp., Teaneck, N.J., St. Joseph's Hosp. Fellow Am. Coll. Hosp. Adminstrs. Home: Paterson NJ Died Feb. 13, 1973.

JEAN, SALLY LUCAS, health educator; b. Towson, Md., June 18, 1878; d. George B. and Emilie Watkins (Selby) J.; student Md. State Normal Sch., 1896; grad. Md. Homeo. Hosp. Training Sch. for Nurses, Baltimore, 1898; hon. A.M., Bates Coll., 1924. Nurse, U.S. Army, hosps., Lexington, Ky., and Chickamauga, Georgia, 1898; organizer department of health service, People's Institute, N.Y. City, 1917; lecturer, Sch. for Community Service, N.Y. City, 1917; sec. Com. on Wartime Problems of Childhood, N.Y. Academy Medicine, 1917; director Child Health Organization of America, 1918-1923; dir. health edn. div. Am. Child Health Assn., 1923-24; consultant in health edn. since 1924; consultant to professional and business groups; developed health edn. program for schs.; supervisor health edn. U.S. Indian Service, 1934-35; cons. in health education, U. of Denver summer sch., 1942, Colo. River War Relocation Authority, Poston, Ariz., 1942-43; cons. in Health Edn., Nat. Found. Infantile Paralysis, 1943-51, ret.; dir. edn. service Organizer 1923, exec. sec. health section, World Federation of Educational Assns.; president Association of Women in Public Health, 1937-40; mem. advisory edn. group, Met. Life Ins. Co. Asso. fellow American Academy of Physical Education; fellow and life mem. Am. Pub. Health Assn. (sec. pub. health edn. sect., 1939-41, chmn., 1941-42); life mem. N.E.A., Progressive Edn. Association. Mem. Authors' League Am. until 1943. Awarded medal by L'Oeuvre Nationale de L'Enfance, 1922; 1st class medal, Belgium Red Cross, 1923; State Service Award, N.Y. State Assn. for Health, Phys. Edn. and Recreation, 1948; William A. Howe Award, Am. Sch. Health Assn., 1948. Episcopalian. Co-author: Spending the Day in China, Japan and the Philippines. Address: New York City NY Died July 5, 1971.

JECK, GEORGE G., Dem. nat. committeeman; b. Minonk, Ill., Oct. 5, 1875; s. George and Anna (Robinson) J.; ed. public school, Minonk, Ill.; m. Eda Van Houten, June 28, 1899; children—Roger Simater, George Van Houten. Poultry and egg packer on farm, 1890-91; traveling supt. as mgr. poultry and egg plant (W.F. Priebe), 1891-99; in poultry and egg business, Atlantic, Ia., 1899-1920, continuing with business when taken over by Swift & Co., 1920, retired since 1940; pres. Harlan (Ia.) Produce Co., Inc.; dir. Atlantic (Ia.) State Bank. On Dem. State Com., 1933-44; Dem. nat. committeeman for Iowa since 1944. Mason (32 deg., Shriner), Elk. Home: Atlantic IA*‡

JEFFERSON, BENJAMIN LAFAYETTE, diplomatic service; b. Columbus, Ga., Oct. 26, 1871; s. Rollin and Metta Virginia (Harp) J.; A.B., U. of Md.; M.D., Sch. of Medicine, and D.D.S., Dental Dept., same; m. Clorinte B. Duquette, of Steamboat Springs, Colo., Dec. 21, 1898; m. 2d, Mrs. Virginia L. Kemble, St. Louis, Oct. 24, 1923. Practiced, Littleton, Colo., 1892-95, later in Routt Co., Colo.; mem. Colo. Ho. of Rep. 1898-1900, Senate, 2 terms, 1900-08; register State Bd. of Land Commrs., Colo., 1908-13; served as E.E. and M.P. to Nicaragua, from June 21, 1913; now supt. State Home and Training Sch. for Mental Defectives, Grand Junction, Colo. Dem. presdl. elector, Colo., 1898; Dem. candidate (primary) gov. Colo. (defeated), 1922. Methodist. Mason. Home: State Home Grand Junction CO‡

JEFFERSON, FLOYD WELLMAN, textile merchant; born at Louisville, Ky., Dec. 25, 1878; s. Thomas Lewis and Katherine (Wellman) J.; grad. Abraham Flexners Prep. Sch., 1898; A.B., Yale, 1902; m. Violet Spencer Woodruff, June 14, 1904; children—Janice Townsend (Mrs. William Law Walker), Floyd W.; married 2d, Marjorie Maynard, July 23, 1941. Associated with A.D. Julliard & Co., N.Y. City, 1910, div. mgr., 1910-14; div. mgr. Tatum Pinkham & Greey, N.Y. City, 1914-17; vice pres. and later chmn. exec. and finance com. Hunter Mfg. Co., 1917-27; partner Iselin Jefferson Co., Inc., N.Y. City, 1927-46, pres., dir., 1946-50, chmn. bd., from 1950, ret. dir., co-chmn. bd. 199 Church St. br. Chem. Bank N.Y. Trust Co. dir. Fitzgerald Mills Corp., com.; director Fitzgerald Cotton Mills; treasurer, director Wellman Operating Corp.; dir. textile br. Chemical Corn Exchange Bank; dir., mem. exec. com. Dan River Mills; dir. Iselin-Jefferson Financial Corp., Iselin-Jefferson Found. Past pres., chmn. adv. com. N.Y. Board Trade. Vice pres., mem. exec. com., chmn. endowment com. Met. Opera Assn. Mem. Am. Arbitration Assn. (vice chmn. bd., dir.), English Speaking Union, Society Colonial Wars, S.R., S.A.R., Soc. Am. Historians, Newcomen Soc. Eng. (trustee), Alpha Delta Phi, C. of C. Clubs: Univ., Merchants, Racquet and Tennis, Union (N.Y.C.); Round Hill Golf (Greenwich); New York Southern Society (N.Y.C.); Filson (Louisville); Royal Bermuda Yacht, Mid Ocean, Coral Beach (Bermuda). Author: Arcadian Sunset; Iambic and Dactylic; There Were Giants in the Earth. Contbr. to textile publs. Home: Greenwich CT Died Jan. 1972.

JEFFREY, WALTER ROLAND, civil engr.; b. Ainsworth, Ia., July 25, 1892; s. William Riley, Jr. and Jessie (Brenhoits) J.; student Willamette U., 1912-16; m. Mildred Keith Honey, June 8, 1918 children—Judith Anne (Mrs. Burr E. Lee, Jr.), John Roland. Resident engr., chief estimating engr. Sinclair Refining Co., 1920-24; mgmt. engr. Bus. Research Corp., Chgo., 1924-28; pvt. cons. mgmt. engr., 1929-39; area mgr. Ill. and Ind., U.S. Bur. Census, 1940; exec. accountant OPS, Chgo., 1951-53; supervisory auditor 5th Army Area, Army Audit Agy., 1953-56; bus. adviser to comdr., staff and suppliers Hdqrs. Def. Subsistence Supply Center, Chicago, Illinois, 1957-63, consultant, from 1964; president, chmn. bd. Analytical Tabulating Mgmt., Inc., Chgo., from 1928; v.p. Bills Realty, Inc., Chgo., 1946-47. Dir. Army Emergency Relief, Chgo., 1942; soldiers bonus div. Office Ill. Auditor, 1947-48. Served as pvt. Mexican Border, 1916; to capt. U.S. Army, 1917-19, as col., 1941-45, 49-51. Registered profl. engr., Ill. Recipient certificate outstanding performance Mil. Subsistence Supply Agy., 1961. Mem. Am. Assn. Engrs. (pres., sr. mem.), Soc. Am. Mil. Engrs. (charter mil. mem., past pres. Chgo.), Fed. Govt. Accountants Assn. (past pres. Chgo.), Am. Soc. Mil. Comptrollers (pres. Chgo. 1963), Midwest Joint Small Bus Council (chmn. from 1961), Am. Legion, Res. Officers Assn., Mil. Order World Wars, Retired Officers Assn., Assn. U.S. Army. Def. Supply Assn. (v.p., chmn. membership com., recipient meritorious civilian service award 1963). Republican. Methodist. Club: Union League (Chgo.). Home: Chicago IL Died Jan. 19, 1971.

JENCKES, JOSEPH SHERBURNE, JR., lawyer; b. Phoenix, Oct. 15, 1908; s. Joseph Sherburne and Anne Burbank (Kibbey) J.; student Phoenix Coll., 1926-28; A.B. with high distinction, U. Ariz., 1930; m. Alexandra Karneeva, Aug. 31, 1934; 1 son, Joseph Sherburne V; m. 2d, Mary Louise Ruffalo, May 27, 1949; children—John Kibbey, James Ruffalo. Admitted to Ariz. bar, 1932, since practiced in Phoenix; partner firm Evans, Kitchel & Jenckes, 1947-70. Lawyer del. Jud. Conf. of 9th Circuit 1959-62. Rep. nominee for Congress, at large Ariz., 1942. Trustee, Orme Sch., 1969-70. Served to lt. (j.g.) USNR, 1944-46. Fellow Am. Coll. Trial Lawyers; mem. Am., Maricopa County (pres. 1940) bar assns., State Bar Ariz. (pres. 1963), Navy League U.S., Phoenix Little Theatre (pres. 1941), Internat. Soc. Barristers, Am. Judicature Soc., Ariz. State U. Law Soc. (v.p.), Lawyer Club Phoenix Episcopalian (vestry). Clubs: Phoenix Country (pres. 1959); White Mountain Country. Home: Phoenix AZ Died July 24, 1970.

JENCKES, MARCIEN, lawyer; b. Stamford Conn., Apr. 5, 1900; s. Lawrence Bates and Alice Goddard (Child) J.; grad. St. Paul's Sch., Concord, N.H., 1917; A.B., Yale, 1921; LL.B., Harvard, 1924; m. Mollie Webb Cromwell, June 23, 1932; children—Georgia Cromwell (Mrs. Charles C. Cunningham, Jr.), Marcien C., Lawrence Webb, Mollie Webb (Mrs. Paul E. Shachoy). Admitted to the Massachusetts bar, 1924, United States Supreme Ct., 1929; practice in Boston, 1924-71; mem. firm Choate, Hall & Stewart, 1927-71. Dir. Paine Furniture Co., H.F. Livermore Corp., Am.

Guaranty Corporation. Mem. bd. part commrs., Brookline, Mass., 1942-57, chmn., 1951-56. Vice pres., dir. Childrens Aid Assn., Boston. Served to 2d lt., F.A., U.S. Army, 1918-19. Mem. Phi Beta Kappa, Sigma Chi. Club: The Country (Brookline). Home: Brookline MA Died Oct. 24, 1971.

JENKINS, CHARLES RUSH, clergyman, educator; b. Thomson, Ga., Aug. 25, 1871; s. Daniel and Ann Eliza (Rush) J.; A.B., Emory Coll., Oxford, Ga., 1893; D.D., Birmingham Coll., 1913; m. Beulah Hall, of Midway, Ala., Aug. 18, 1898; 1 son, Alfred Lesesne. High sch. prin. 7 yrs.; ordained ministry M.E. Ch., S., 1900; pastor Richland, Ga., 1901-02; Pelham, 1903-04, Fort Valley, 1909, 1st Ch., Waycross, 1910; presiding elder McRae Dist., South Ga. Conf., spring, 1911; prof. philosophy, Wesleyan Coll., Macon, Ga., 1905-08 (resigned); v.p. same, 1911-12, pres. 1912-20; pastor Fort Valley, 1920-21; presiding elder Thomasville Dist.; pastor St. Luke's Ch., Columbus, 1923-26, Mulberry St. M.E. Ch., Macon, 1927-30, Wesley Monumental M.E. Ch., Savannah, Ga., 1931-34; First Ch., Douglas, Ga., 1935-38; retired, 1939. Mem. Gen. Conf. of M.E. Ch., S. 1914-34. Mem. Phi Delta Theta, Phi Beta Kappa. Mason. Rotarian. Democrat. Home: Baxley GA‡

JENKINS, EDWARD CORBIN, college pres.; b. Syracuse, N.Y., Sept. 11, 1875; s. John Thomas and Mary Cornelia (Corbin) J.; Ph.B., Syracuse University, 1900; M.A., Columbia, 1926; m. Elizabeth Starks, of Montclair, N.J., Dec. 21, 1911. Student sec. N.Y. State Com., Y.M.C.A., 1900-02; sec. to J.R. Mott, Internat. Com. Y.M.C.A., 1902-13; asso. gen. sec. for foreign work, Internat. Com., 1913-25; pres. George Williams Coll., Chicago, 1926-35. Mem. Delta Upsilon. Baptist. Address: 5315 Drexel Av., Chicago IL‡

JENKINS, EDWARD ELMER, realtor; b. Salt Lake City, Utah, Nov. 25, 1873; s. Thomas and Mahala (Elmer) J.; student Latter Day Saints U., Salt Lake City, 1889-91; m. 2d, Edna Talmage, of Salt Lake City, Sept. 14, 1928; children (by 1st marriage) Elmer Cutler, Irving Edward, Harold Cutler, John Cutler. Officer and dir. many corpns. Republican. Mormon. Home: Hotel Utah. Office: First Bank Bldg., Salt Lake City UT‡

JENKINS, FRANCES, college prof.; b. Oswego, N.Y., Nov. 4, 1872; d. Isaac Gray and Rebecca (Congdon) J.; grad. Oswego Normal Training Sch., 1894; critic course, same sch., 1901; B.S., Teachers Coll. (Columbia), 1915. Critic teacher, State Normal Sch., DeKalb, Ill., 1901-5; supervisor Teachers' Training Sch., Baltimore, Md., 1906-8; instr., Howard U., Washington, D.C., 1908-9; supervisor elementary grades, pub. schs., Decatur, Ill., 1909-14; asst. prof. edn., Coll. for Teachers, U. of Cincinnati, since Sept. 1915. Mem. N.E.A., Coll. Teachers of Edn., Ohio State Teachers' Assn., Cincinnati Principals' Association, D.A.R. Presbyterian. Club: Woman's City (Cincinnati). Author: Reading in Primary Grades, 1914; Applied Arithmetics (joint author), 1920. Asst. editor Riverside Readers. Home: 442 Dixmyth Av., Clifton Cincinnati OH‡

JENKINS, HERBERT F(RANKLIN), publisher; b. Rockland, Mass., Oct. 3, 1873; s. Joseph H. and Emily (Clark) J.; grad. high sch., Rockland, 1891; student Harvard, 1891-93; m. Anne H. Bradford, of Abington, Mass., 1897 (died 1914); m. 2d, Bessie Clark Guptill, of Winthrop, Mass., 1921. Reporter Boston Traveler, 1893-96, Boston Herald, 1897-1901; advertising mgr. Little, Brown & Co., 1901-16, editorial dir., 1916-38, v.p., 1927-38. Republican. Clubs: Republican, Boston City (Boston). Home: 129 Dean Road, Brookline, Mass. Office: 34 Beacon St., Boston MA‡

JENKINS HERBERT THEODORE, educator, engr.; b. Detroit, Mich., July 30, 1902; s. Herbert T. and Imogene Belmont (Stone) J., Sr.; B.S. in C.E., U. Mich., 1930, M.S.E., 1932; m. Mary Elizabeth Gill, Dec. 26, 1925; children—Peter VanWyck, Paul Andrew. Pvt. practice civil engring., Ann Arbor and Detroit, 1932-35; mem. faculty, Cornell, 1935-57, prof. civil engring., 1949-57, head civil engring. drawing, 1937-57; cartographer U.S. Geol. Survey, 1950; cons. engr. Bogema, Gifft, & Jenkins, Ithaca, 1948-57; mem. faculty U. Mich., Ann Arbor, prof. civil engring., 1957-70, chairman of the department engineering graphics, 1957-68. Mem. Am. Society C.E., American Soc. for Engring. Edn., mem. Am. Univ. Profits., Seal and Serpent, Chi Epsilon, Tau Beta Pi. Episcopalian (warden, vestryman). Author: Soil Mechanics Laboratory Manual, Physical Properties of Soils, 1947. Home: MI Died Oct. 24, 1970.

JENKINS, HILGER PERRY, surgeon, educator; b. Chgo., Oct. 26, 1902; s. Harry Dodge and Caroline A. (Perry) J.; B.S., U. Chgo., 1923, M.D., 1927; m. Julia Dodge, May 20, 1933; children—Samuel Lincoln, Theodora Neil. Intern Presbyn. Hosp., Chgo., 1926-27; asst. resident surgery Billings Hosp., Chgo., 1927-30, resident, 1930-31; instr. U. Chgo., 1930-33, asst. prof., 1933-38, asso. prof., 1938-46, prof., 1960-68, prof. emeritus, 1968-70; clin. asso. prof. surgery U. Ill. at Chgo., 1947-58, clin. prof. surgery 1958-60, lectr., until 1970. Recipient McClintock award U. Chgo. Sch. Medicine, 1967. Mem. A.C.S. (chmn. motion picture com. 1951-67, Distinguished Service award 1959), Am.,

Central (past pres). surg. assns., Chgo. Surg. Soc. (past pres.), Chgo. Med. Soc. (past pres. Jackson Park br.), Soc. U. Surgeons, Internat. Soc. Surgery, Soc. for Surgery Alimentary Tract. Research on absorption of catgut sutures in surgery, sponge (gelfoam) for control hemorrhage. Patentee rear view automobile mirror; producer films for med. edn. Home: Chicago IL Died Jan. 17, 1970; buried Mt. Auburn Cemetery, Cambridge MA

JENKINS, JAMES ALEXANDER, coll. pres.; b. South Wales, June 23, 1870; s. Rev. Owen Morfab and Miriam Claudia (Jones) J.; brought by parents to U.S. in infancy; A.B., Lebanon Valley Coll., Annville, Pa., 1896, A.M., 1898, Ph.D., 1903, D.D., 1908; B.D., Oberlin (O.) Grad. Sch. Theology, 1901; m. Katherine May Jones, of Iowa City, Ia., May 6, 1894; children—Paul Alexander, James Alan, Miriam Katherine. Ordained ministry Congl. Ch., 1893; pastor successively Welsh Ch., Dundaff, Pa., Mt. Carmel, Pa., Pacific Ch., St. Paul, Minn., Zanesville, O., Immanuel Ch., Brooklyn, N.Y., Cleveland, O., St. Mary's Av. Ch., Omaha, Neb., Warren Av. Ch., Chicago, Ill., until 1920; dean of Union Theol. Coll., Chicago, 1917-20, pres. since 1920; ex-officio dir. Chaplain, Ill. N.G., 1917. Pres. Kymry Soc. (Welsh), Chicago, since 1932; chmn. Welsh festival at Century of Progress Expn., Chicago, 1933. Mason. Club: Apollos. Home: 1106 S. Clinton Av., Oak Park, Ill. Office: 44 N. Ashland Boul., Chicago IL‡

JENKINS, JOHN S., JR., business exec.; b. Portsmouth, Va., Nov. 17, 1895; s. John Summerfield and Mary MacKenzie (Judkins) J.; grad. Woodberry Forest Sch., 1913; A.B., U. of Va., 1916; m. Marjorie Hope Aull, July 26, 1919; children—Marjorie (Mrs. Edward A. Mitchell), Alice H. (Mrs. Stephen P. Mallett), Jean McK. Joined John S. Jenkins & Co., cotton merchants, 1919; organizer and treas. Dixie Jute Corp., Norfolk, Va., 1922-69; dir. and mem. exec. com. Bank of Commerce; dir. Va. Elec. & Power Co., Planters Mfg. Co., Carolinas Ginners Assn. Mem. Norfolk City Sch. Bd., 1932-42, City Recreation Commn., 1944-45, Norfolk Port Authority, 1948; trustee Norfolk Museum of Arts; chmn. Norfolk Community Chest, 1941-43; pres., Norfolk Gen. Hosp., 1946-48; served on Regional War Labor Bd. Panel, adv. draft bds., W.P.B. adv. com., 1941-45. Commd., U.S. Army, 1917, resigned as capt., Coast Arty. A.A., 1918. Mem. Am. Legion. Methodist. Clubs: Norfolk Yacht, Norfolk Country, Rotary. Contbr. articles to trade mags. Home: Norfolk VA Died July 26, 1969.

JENKINS, ROMILLY JAMES HEALD, educator; b. Hitchin, Eng., Feb. 10, 1907; s. James Heald and Theodora (Ingram) J.; B.A., Emmanuel Coll., Cambridge U., 1929; student British Sch., Athens, Greece, 1934; m. Juliette Celine Haegler, Aug. 5, 1932; children—Michael, Romilly, Charles Oliver. Came to U.S., 1960. Lectr. modern Greek, Cambridge U., 1936-46; with British Fgn. Office, 1939-45; prof. modern and Byzantine Greek, King's Coll., London, 1946-60; prof. Byzantine history and literature, also director of studies at the Dumbarton Oaks Research Library and Collection, Washington, 1960-69. Chmn. mng. com. British Sch., Athens, 1951-60. Fellow Soc. Antiquaries. Author: Dedalica, 1936; Dionysius Solomos, 1940; Constantine Porphyrogenitus, de Administrado Imperio (with Gy. Moravcsik), 1949; The Dilessi Murders, 1961; Byzantium; The Imperial Centuries: A.D. 610-1071, 1966. Editor: (Porphyrogenitus) Commentary, 1962; Byzantium and Byzantism, 1963; Byzantium: The Imperial Centuries. 1966. Home: Washington DC Died Sept. 30, 1969.

JENKINS, THOMAS, bishop; b. Shenley, Eng., Jan. 31, 1871; s. John Jenkins and Mary Ann (Boyles) J.; B.D., Kenyon Coll. and Bexley Hall, 1914, D.D., 1924; m. Ruth Mary Prichard, Aug. 15, 1901; 7 children; married 2d, Edith Smith, May 1942. Ordained deacon of the Episcopal Church (Diocese of Southern Ohio), 1900, ordained priest, 1901; member Cincinnati Associate Mission, 1900-02; missionary in Alaska, 1902-10; rector St. Paul's Church, Fremont, Ohio, 1910-15, St. David's Ch., Portland, Ore., 1915-25; gen. missionary and ednl. sec. Diocese of Ore., 1925-29; consecrated bishop of Missionary Dist. of Nev., Jan. 25, 1929, resigned the bishopric, May 1942; assistant bishop, Diocese of L.I., N.Y., 1946-1949. Pres. Standing Com. for Ore., 1919-25; pres. Bd. of Religious Edn., Ore., 1917-25; dep. Gen. Conv., 1907, 16, 19, 22, 25, 28; mem. Pan-Anglican Congress (London), 1908, Lambeth Conf. (London), 1930, 48. Author: The Church in Nevada; The Desert Churchman; The Man of Alaska; Life of Peter Trimble Rowe, Bishop of Alaska, 1895-1942. Address: Shenley House, Port Orford OR‡

JENKINS, WILLIAM ROBERT, insurance exec.; b. Omaha, Neb., July 11, 1902; s. Daniel Edwards and Annie (Finley) J.; A.B., U. Omaha, 1922; Ph.B, U. Chgo., 1924; m. Helen Lindquist, Feb. 4, 1933; children—John Finley, Sarah Burchinal. Mgr. editor DuPont Pub. Co., Chgo., 1925-26; partner, Long & Jenkins, 1927-28; western mgr. Trade-Ways, Inc., N.Y.C., 1929-34; in charge sales research Northwestern Nat. Life Ins. Co., Mpls., 1935-44, v.p. in charge sales, 1944-58, 1st v.pl, dir., 1952-58; president Columbian

Mutual Life Ins. Co., Binghamton, N.Y., 1958-69, also dir.; dir. Marine Midland Trust (Binghamton); lectr. Inst. of Ins. Marketing So. Methodist U., Dallas, Texas, 1958-69, La. State U., 1966-69; chmn. agy. sect. Am. Life Conv., 1954, mem. exec. com., 1968-69; Heubner Foundation lecturer Wharton Sch., 1955. Director Robeson Memorial Center, Binghamton. Member Nat. Fedn. Sales Execs., Life Ins. Agy. Mgmt. Assn. (past dir.), N.Y. State Assn. Life Ins. Cos. (exec. com. 1967-69), Am. Marketing Assn., Chi Psi. Clubs: Binghamton, Binghamton Country. Contbr. articles bus. publs. Home: Vestal NY Died Nov. 22, 1969; buried Forest Lawn Cemetery, Omaha NB

JENNESS, LESLIE GEORGE, chem. engr., exec.; b. Danbury, N.H., Aug. 12, 1898; s. George Burns and Vina (Bean) J.; B.S., N.H. U., 1920; M.S., U. Me., 1924; Ph.D., Columbia, 1930; m. Betty Hooks, June 29, 1926. Tech. dir. Intermetal Corp., 1932-41; div. head Linde Air Products Co., 1941-47; dir. research HumKo Co., 1947-50; asst. to pres. in charge research Kennecott Copper Corp., 1950-51; dir. research 1951-52, v.p., 1952-63; dir. Quebec Iron & Titanium, Quebec, Columbiun Ltd. Civilian with Manhattan dist. AEC, during World War II. Mem. Am. Inst. Mining and Metall. Engrs., Am. Chem. Soc., Inst. Chemists, N.Y. Acad. Scis., Am. Oil Chemists Soc., Sigma Xi, Alpha Chi Sigma. Clubs: Pinnacle Chemists (N.Y.C.). Holder patents. Home: New York City NY Died July 2, 1968.

JENNEY, WILLIAM SHERMAN, lawyer; b. Syracuse, N.Y., Oct., 1867; s. Edwin Sherman and Marie Regula (Saul) J.; A.B., Princeton, 1889, A.M., 1892; studied law, U. of Va. and Cornell; admitted to bar, 1891; m. Nina Bevan, Apr. 16, 1895 (died Sept. 27, 1937). Practiced law, Syracuse, 1891-1905; gen. atty. D.,L.&W. R.R. Co., July 1, 1905-10, v.p. and gen. counsel until Jan. 1, 1939; now retired. Dem. nominee for presdl. elector, N.Y., 1904. Member U.S., N.Y. State and N.Y. City bar assns., Loyal Legion, Sigma Phi. Home: 4 E. 70th St., New York NY E. 70th St., New York NY‡

JENNINGS, B. BREWSTER, trustee; b. New York, N.Y., June 9, 1898; s. Oliver Gould and Mary Dows (Brewster) J.; grad. St. Paul's Sch., Concord, N.H., 1916; A.B., Yale, 1920; m. Kate deForest Prentice, June 18, 1923; children—Mary Brewster (Mrs. Paul J. Chase), Kate de Forest (Mrs. George Seemann), John Prentice. With marine department, Standard Oil Co. of N.Y., 1920-27, purchasing agent, 1927-29, mgr. real estate dept., 1929-35; asst. to pres. Socony Vacuum Oil Co., 1935-39, dir. from 1939, on leave of absence for govt. service, 1942-44, pres. and chmn. exec. com., 1944-55, chmn. Socony-Mobil Oil Co. (co's name changed), 1955-58; trustee of Central Savings Bank, N.Y. Trust Co. Trustee of The Avalon Foundation, director The Greater New York Fund. Served with USNR, 1917-19; commd. ensign, 1917; exec. officer and in command U.S.S.C. 131, overseas. Dir. tanker operations and asst. dep. adminstr. for tanker operations U.S. Maritime Commn. and War Shipping Adminstrn., Washington, D.C., 1942-44. Decorated Navy Cross. Dir. Meml. Hosp., N.Y. Fellow Yale Corp.; mem. Psi Upsilon. Scroll and Key. Clubs: Links, Yale (N.Y.C.); Sewanhaka Yacht (Oyster Bay, N.Y.); Piping Rock (Locust Valley, N.Y.). Address: Glen Head LI NY Died Oct. 2, 1968; buried Oaklawn Cemetery, Fairfield CT

JENNINGS, DEAN SOUTHERN, writer; b. Rochester, N.Y., June 30, 1905; s. Rev. Webster Wardell and Mary (Southern) J.; ed. schools of Munich, Germany, 1911-15, West High Sch., Rochester, N.Y., 1920-23, Lowell High Sch., San Francisco, 1923-24; children by previous marriage—Dorn Webster, David Duffy, Dean Southern, Breslau. D. Melvin and Suzette; married to Mary Elizabeth Foster, April 28, 1953. Reporter San Francisco Jour., 1923; sports writer San Francisco Examiner, San Francisco Herald, 1924; reporter and rewrite man Paris (France) Herald, 1925-27; chief rewrite man San Francisco Call-Bulletin, 1928-34; regional information dir. U.S. Resettlement Adminstrn., Denver, Indpls., 1935-36; regional dir. distbr. promotion, U.S. Govt. films, Chgo., Hollywood, 1936-37; motion picture cons. U.S. Farm Security Adminstrn., N.Y.C., 1937-38; regional information rep. U.S. Social Security Rd., San Francisco, 1937; dir. press Golden Gate Internat. Expn., 1937; Pacific Coast rep. U.S. Film Service, 1939; regional information dir. U.S. Office for Emergency Mgmt., San Francisco, 1941; regional dir. U.S. Office of War Information, San Francisco, 1942-43. Exec. sec. Northern Calif. Newspaper Guild, 1934-35. Mem. Cal. State Recreation Commn., 1966-67. Member Sigma Delta Chi. Democrat. Episcopalian. Clubs: San Francisco Yacht (Belvedere, California); Overseas Press (New York City, N.Y.). Author: The Man Who Killed Hitler, 1939; Leg Man, 1940; The San Quentin Story (with Warden Clinton T. Duffy), 1950; Confessions of a Happy Man (with Art Linkletter), 1960; My First Hundred Years in Hollywood (with Jack L. Warner), 1965; We Only Kill Each Other, 1967. Contributing editor of Coronet, 1944-45; asso. editor Colliers, 1949-50; columnist San Francisco Chronicle, 1951-53. Home: Belvedere CA Died Oct. 1, 1969.

JENNINGS, FRANK E., lawyer; b. Kan., June 9, 1877; s. Theodore and Mary C. (Hawk) J.; student U. Mo. Law Sch., 1900-01; m. Minerva Phelps, June 15, 1907. Admitted to Fla. bar, 1901, since practiced Jacksonville; mem. firm Jennings, Watts, Clarke & Hamilton, Speaker Fla. Ho. of Reps., 1921. Mem. Fla. State Bd. of Control, 1913-17. Mem. Am. and Fla. State bar assns. Mason. Home: 2505 Oak St. Office: Barnett Nat. Bank Bldg., Jacksonville FL‡

JENNINGS, ISAAC, JR., clergyman; A.B., Williams Coll., 1871, A.M., 1874; (D.D., Madison (now Colgate) U., 1889); m. Mary E. Leonard, of Rushville, N.Y., Dec. 13, 1871. Prin. of acad., E. Bloomfield, N.Y., 1871-2; prof., Ingham U., Leroy, N.Y., 1872-5; master, English and Classical Sch., Waterbury, Conn., 1875-80; ordained Presbyn. ministry, 1880; pastor Elmira, N.Y., 1883-1903, later Bennington, Vt. Moderator Synod of N.Y., Syracuse, 1905. Lockport, 1906; trustee, 1883-—, chmn. bd., 1886-—, Union U., Schenectady, N.Y. Home: 332 William St., Elmira NY‡

JENNINGS, JOE LESLIE, textile mfr.; born West Point, Ga., July 26, 1901; s. Reuben William and Sara Frances (Burdette) J.; B.S., Ga. Inst. Tech., 1923; m. Marie Lamar Lanier, May 30, 1935; children—Joseph L., Marie Lanier, Ruth Lamar, Reuben William. With West Point Mfg. Co., from 1924, v.p., 1947-51, exec. v.p., from 1951, also dir.; dir. Wehadkee Yarn Mills, Wellington Sears Co., Cabin Crafts, Inc. Mem. City Council, Lanett, Ala. Trustee Ala. Coll.; mem. regional exec. com., past pres. George H. Lanier council Boy Scouts Am.; past pres. Chattahoochee Valley chpt. A.R.C. Mem. Ala., Ga. textile mfrs. assns., Textile Edn. Found. Inc., Anak Soc. of Ga. Inst. Tech., Ga. Inst. Tech. Alumni Association (past national pres.), Ala. C. of C. (dir.), Phi Delta Theta. Mason. Clubs: Rotary (past pres. West Point); Capitol City, Commerce Riverside Country. Home: Lanett AL

JENNINGS, LESLIE NELSON, writer; b. Ware, Mass., Sept. 6, 1892; s. Roscoe Leslie and Susan Bryant (Dwight) J.; ed. pub. schs.; unmarried. Contributor verse to Smart Set, Nation, New Republic, Poetry, Contemporary Verse, Overland Monthly, Pearson's Mag., etc.; represented in Brqithwaite's Anthology, 1917-18, and Frothingham's Songs of Men. Formerly on editorial staff Current Opinion. Contbr. New Republic. Nation, Bookman, Commonweal, N.Y. Evening Sun, etc., Home: New York City NY Died Mar. 1972.

JENNINGS, STEPHEN RICHARD, coal operator; b. Hillsville, Va., Oct. 18, 1875; s. Charles LaFayette and Eva (Wilkinson) J.; student Emory and Henry Coll., Emory, Va., Eastman Bus. Coll., Poughkeepsie, N.Y.; m. Eva Dickenson, of Castlewood, Va., June 10, 1909; children—Rosalie, Evelyn, Richard, Anne. Buyer, Cranes Nest Coal & Coke Co., Toms Creek, Va., 1900-04; supt. Clinchfield Coal Corpn. and Lick Creek & Lake Erie R.R. Co., 1904-07; gen. supt. Va. Pocahontas Coal Co., 1907-08; pres. Interstate Coal Co., 1908-11; vice pres. Carter Coal Co., 1911-15; pres. Hazard Blue Grass Coal Corpn., Hill Creek Coal Co., Beaver Creek Coal Co., Floyd Elkhorn Consol. Collieries, 1915-26; pres. Wakenva Coal Co. since 1926; pres. Johnson City Hotel Co., Southern Refrigeration Co.; also officer or dir. various other companies. Methodist. Home: 1119 S.W. Av. Office: C.C. & O. Bldg., Johnson City TN*‡

JENNINGS, WESLEY WILLIAM, meat packing co. exec.; b. Bremer County, Ia., Sept. 18, 1903; s. Harry and Alice A. (Crail) J.; student State Coll. Ia., 1923, Ia. State U., 1925-26; m. Ione M. Halaska, May 11, 1935. With Rath Packing Co., Waterloo, Ia., from 1926, v.p. marketing, 1957-62, sr. v.p., 1962-67, exec. v.p., from 1967, also director, member executive com. Mem. Waterloo C. of C. (dir.), Theta Xi. Presbyn. (trustee, elder). Elk. Home: Waterloo IA Died Dec. 18, 1970.

JENSEN, BEN FRANKLIN, congressman; b. Marion, Ia., Dec. 16, 1892; s. Martin and Gertrude Anna (Anderson) J.; attended Exira (Ia.) High Sch.; m. Charlotte Elizabeth Hadden, Dec. 13, 1917; 1 dau., Betty Lorraine (Mrs. Donald G. Fitzpatrick). With Green Bay Lumber Co., Exira, 1914-38, yard manager, 1919-38, member 76th-88th Congresses, 7th Ia. District Commd. 2d lt., U.S. Army, Camp Pike, Ark., 1918. Past 7th Dist. comdr. American Legion, 1936-37. Republican. Lutheran. Mason. Home: Exira IA Died Feb. 5, 1970; buried Exira IA

JENSEN, HOWARD C., magazine art dir.; b. Bellingham, Wash., s. Victor and Ellen (Knutsen) J.; student Western Wash. Coll., 1933-34, Cornish Art Sch., 1934-35; pvt. study with Walt Kuhn, N.Y.C., 1936-46; m. Amy Lee LaFollette, Oct. 1, 1940. With J. Stirling Getchell, Inc., 1938-41, Parade mag., 1941-44, Look mag., 1944-47; with Popular Sci. Pub. Co., Inc., N.Y.C., from 1947, art dir.; dir. The White House Story on TV, 1960. Mem. Soc. Illustrators, Art Dirs. Club N.Y.C. Editor: 39th Annual of Advertising and Editorial Art, 1960. Art editor: The White House and Its Thirty-Two Families (Amy L. Jensen); producer film series America: The Artist's Eye, 1963, also Paintings in the White House. Home: White Plains NY Died July 3, 1972.

JEPSON, IVAR PER, engr., mfg. exec.; b. Onnestad, Sweden, Nov. 2, 1903; s. Per and Maria (Lundgren) Jeppsson; M.E., Hassleholme Tekniska Skola, Sweden, 1922; student U. Berlin (Germany); m. Lillian Borgman, Dec. 21, 1929; children—Brit Marie, Bert. Came to U.S., 1925, naturalized, 1935. Practiced with Swedish, German companies, 1922-24; with Sunbeam Corp. (formerly Chgo. Flexible Shaft Co.), Chgo., 1925-64, beginning as draftsman, successively tool designer, product designer, development engr., mgr. development and research, 1925-52, v.p. charge product design, development and research, 1952-64. Served with Swedish Air Force, 1924-25. Mem. Swedish Engrs. Soc. Chgo. Clubs: Swedish (Chgo.); Oak Park (Ill.) Country. Patentee in field. Home: Oak Park IL Died Nov. 1968.

JERMAN, MRS. CORNELIA PETTY, b. Moore Co., N.C., Dec. 1, 1874; d. William Cary and Emma Virginia (Thagard) Petty; grad. Oxford (N.C.) Coll., 1892; studied N.E. Conservatory of Music, Boston, Mass.; m. Thomas Palmer Jerman, of Raleigh, N.C., Nov. 10, 1898 (dec.);children—Lucy Virginia (dec.), Thomas Palmer. Pres. N.C. Federation of Women's Clubs (chmn. bd. trustees), Raleigh League of Women Voters, Fortnightly Review Club, Woman's Club of Raleigh, St. Cecilia Music Club: trustee Gen. Federation of Women's Clubs; mem. Woman's Nat. Dem. Club (Washington, D.C.). Mem. Dem. Nat. Com., 1928-34; asst. collector of internal revenue, Dist. of N.C., since 1933. Home: 109 E. Lane St., Raleigh NC‡

JERSILD, MARVIN A(MBLE), lawyer; b. Gowen, Mich., July 19, 1897; s. Rev. Thomas N. and Anne (Billie) J.; student Dana Coll., Blair, Neb., U. of Chicago Law Sch. Admitted to Ill. bar, 1922, and since practiced in Chicago; atty. N.Y.C. R.R., 1922-33, asst. gen. counsel, 1933-51, gen. atty. N.Y.C. R.R., 1951-61; gen. counsel Chgo. River & Ind. R.R., 1951-61; Ind. Harbor Belt R.R.; dir. F. W. Means & Co. Served with Tank Corps, AEF, 1918-19. Mem. Chgo. Bar Assn., Am. Judicature Soc., Art Inst. Chgo., Mus. Modern Art N.Y., Alpha Tau Omega. Republican. Lutheran. Club: Chicago. Home: Chicago IL Died Dec. 1967.

JESSE, WILLIAM H(ERMAN), librarian; b. Versailles, Ky., Sept. 16, 1908; s. Watson McIlvain and Helen (Wolfe) J.; student, Transylvania Coll., 1929-31; A.B., Univ. of Ky., 1933; B.S. library sci., Columbia, 1938; A.M., Brown Univ., 1945; m. Edith Miller, Sept. 12, 1938; children—Nan, Alice. Teacher-librarian, Johnson County, Ky., 1933-35, dir. of libraries, Johnson County schs., 1935-38; readers' div. chief, Brown Univ. library, Providence, R.I., 1938-42; asst. dir. of libraries, U. of Neb., 1942; head, reader's and reference div., U.S. Dept. of Agr. library, Washington, 1943; dir. of libraries, and prof. bibliography, U. Tenn., 1943-70; vis. lectr. during summer sessions in library schs., cons. library bldgs., services. Mem. A.L.A. Assn. of Coll. and Reference Libraries Southeastern, Tenn. library assns., So. Assn. Colls and Schools, American Association of University Profs., Pi Kappa Alpha, Beta Phi Mu. Presbyn. Contbr. articles to library, ednl. jours. Home: Knoxville TN Died July 1, 1970; buried Nicholasville KY

JESSUP, EVERETT COLGATE, physician; b. Bklyn., Sept. 11, 1887; s. Benjamin A. and Mary Caroline (Nesmith) J.; B.S. cum laude, Princeton, 1911; M.D., Coll. Physicians and Surgeons, Columbia, 1916; m. Helen Batho Castle, June 2, 1919; children—Mary (Mrs. C. Ogden Amonette), John Batho, Richard Nesmith, Joan (Mrs. John Kean, Jr.). Practiced gen. medicine, internal medicine, Roslyn, L.I., N.Y., 1919-62; instr. medicine Coll. Physicians and Surgeons, 1923-29, asst. prof. clin. medicine, 1929-33; cons. physician North County Community Hosp., Glen Cove, Nassau Hosp., Mineola, South Nassau Hosp., Rockville Centre, North Shore Hosp., Manhasset, Manhasset Med. Centre Hosp., Meadowbrook Hosp. Hempstead; attending physician Green Vale Sch. Mem. exec. council C. W. Post Coll., L.I. U.; dir. Nassau County chpt. A.R.C., Nassau Tb, Heart and Pub. Health Assn.; dir., ex-pres. Soc. Prevention Cruelty to Children; mem. Bd. Health, Nassau County. Entered Plattsburg Tng. Camp 1916; served as lt. and capt., M.C., U.S. Army, AEF, attached to B.E.F., 1917-19; maj. Med. Res. Corps to 1930. Pres. 2d Dist. br. Med. Soc. State N.Y., 1946-47. Diplomate Am. Bd. Internal Medicine. Fellow A.C.P., N.Y. Acad. Medicine; mem. Nassau County Med. Soc. (pres. 1934), A.M.A., Sportsmanship Brotherhood (dir.). Baptist. Clubs: Princeton (N.Y.); Seawonhaka Yacht (Oyster Bay. N.Y.); Lake Placid (N.Y.). Contbr. med. jours. Holds U.S. Interscholastic record for 50 yds., 5-3/5 seconds, made at St. Louis, 1904. Address: Roslyn LI NY Died July 1, 1968; buried Greenwood Cemetery, Brooklyn NY

JESTER, JOHN ROBERTS, clergyman; b. Clay County, Ga., June 8, 1875; s. Thomas P. and Martha Frances (Roberts) J.; student Southwest Ga. Agrl. and Mil. Coll.; B.S., Mercer U., 1899; student Southern Bapt. Theol. Sem., Louisville, Ky., 1904-05; D.D., Okla. State Bapt. Coll., 1909, Bethel (Ky.) Coll., 1910, Mercer U., 1926; m. Annie Allen Perry, Oct. 25, 1900; children—Perry N., Dana E., Harold T., Arthur M. Ordained Bapt. ministry, 1896; pastor in Ga., 1897-1904; corr. sec. Ga. Bapt. Edn. Bd., 1906-08; pres. Okla. State Bapt. Coll., 1908-10; pastor Broadway Ch., Ft. Worth, Texas, 1911-15; field sec. Foreign Mission Bd. and U. of Richmond, 1915-18; pastor First Ch., Greenwood, S.C., 1918-22, First Church, Winston-Salem, N.C., 1922-35; builder First Bapt. Temple of Worship, 1925; general evangelist, 1935-39; pastor First Bapt. Ch., Winchester, Ky., 1940-47. Vice-pres. Okla. Bapt. State Conv., 1909-10, and N.C. Bapt. State Conv., 1930; mem. Mission Bd., Okla., 1909-11; mem. Edn. and Mission boards, Tex., 1912-15, S.C., 1919-22; mem. bd. trustees Southwestern Bapt. Theological Seminary, 1924-27; mem. exec. com. Southern Baptist Conv., 1927-30 and 1942-48; mem. promotion com. Southern Bapt. Conv., 1932-33, v.p. of Conv., 1932; mem. N.C. Inter-racial Com., 1931-35; pres. Gen. Bd. State Bapt. Conv., N.C., 1924-35; mem. exec. bd. Gen. Assn. Bapts. in Ky., 1946-47. Mem. Sigma Nu, Pi Gamma Mu, Kiwanis Club, S.A.R. Independent Democrat. Mason (32 deg., K.T., Shriner). Home: 4431 Pineridge Rd., Columbia SC‡

JETT, ROBERT CARTER, bishop P.E. Ch.; b. King George County, Va., May 10, 1865; s. Dr. William Newton and Virginia (Mitchell) J.; ed. pub. and pvt. schs. and acad.; grad. Theol. Sem. in Va., 1889; D.D., Washington and Lee Univ., 1915; LL.D., Roanoke College, 1936; m. Annie, d. Col. Oliver Ridgeway Funsten, of Va., Oct. 29, 1890; children—Annie Newton (Mrs. Frank W. Rogers), Ethel Fairfax (Mrs. William W. Field). Deacon, 1889, priest, 1890, P.E. Ch.; asst. rector Ch. of the Epiphany, Danville, Va., 1889-90; rector Beckford Parish, Shenandoah County, Va., 1890-93, Emmanuel Ch. (founded under his administration), Staunton, Va., 1893-1913; while rector of Emmanuel Ch., founded St. John's Ch., Waynesboro, Va.; founder, 1913, and rector from opening, 1916 to 1920, then pres. trustees, Virginia Episcopal School, Lynchburg, now hon. trustee; was trustee Va. Theol. Seminary 18 yrs., and for the same period trustee of the Episcopal High School, near Alexandria; trustee Stuart Hall, school for girls, 38 years, pres. trustees for 18 years, now hon. life trustee; dean Southwestern Convocation Diocese of Southern Va. 3 terms; del. to 3d Missionary Dept., and Provincial Synod several times; dep. to Gen. Conv. P.E. Ch., 1907, 10; consecrated first bishop of Southwestern Va., Mar. 24, 1920; pres. Province of Washington, 1930-32; retired, May 17, 1938. Mem. Phi Beta Kappa (hon.). Home: 2802 S. Jefferson St., Roanoke 14 VA†

JEWETT, STEPHEN PERHAM, physician; b. North Waterford, Me., Sept. 1, 1882; s. Stephen Perham and Ella Lucia (Hinman) J.; A.B., Clark U., Worchester, Mass., 1906; M.D., N.Y. Med. Coll. and Flower Hosp., 1910; grad. student Columbia U., 1911-12; D.Sc. (honorary), New York Medical College, 1960, Clark University, 1965; married to Caroline Winterton, June 1, 1910 (died Aug. 1915); 1 son, Stephen Perham; m. 2d, Elizabeth Plunkett, Jan. 25, 1917; children—Mary Rita (Mrs. Jeremiah Donovan), Elizabeth Plunkett (Mrs. Jewett Hayes), Annette Plunkett (Mrs. Jewett Mullen, Jr.), Stephanie Plunkett (Mrs. Richard Byran McCormick). Gen. practice, Buffalo, N.Y., 1912-16; attending physician, psychiatric service, Bellevue and Allied Hosps., New York, 1916-22; with med. examiner's office, N.Y. State Hosp. Commn., 1922-23; psychiatrist Bur. of Children's Guidance and lecturer in mental hygiene and psychiatry, N.Y. School for Social Work, 1922-26; dir. Mental Hygiene Clinic, Hudson Guild Soc. Settlement, 1923-25; cons. psychiatrist Edgehill School, Carmel, N.Y., 1924-32; attending neuro-psychiatrist U.S. Vet. Hosp. No. 81, N.Y. City, 1922-27; cons. psychiatrist and dir. of research, Berkshire Industrial Farm, Canaan, N.Y., 1926-30; cons. psychiatrist and med. dir. mental hygiene dept., Montclair (N.J.) State Teachers' Coll., 1929-33; research consultant in psychiatry and neurology, Dept. of Correction, N.Y. City, 1932-33; attending psychiatrist, Flower-Fifth Av. Hosp., dir. neuropsychiatry, Metropolitan Hosp., Dept. of Hospitals, N.Y.C.; vis. psychiatrist and dir. of psychiatry Bird S. Coler Meml. Hosp. and Home, N.Y.C.; cons. in psychiatry, Paterson General Hospital (N.J.), Riverside Hosp., N.Y.C.; U.S.; consulting psychiatrist of Kings Park (N.Y.) State Hospital, 1958-71; psychiatrist-in-chief of East View Pavilion, New York City, 1958-71. Induction Service for Armed Forces; dir. neuopsychiatric dept., Murray Hill Hosp., N.Y.C.; chmn. deans; com. for neuropsychiatry, Lyons Hosp., N.J.; dean New York Post-Grad. Center psychotherapy; prof. medicine (psychiatry) emeritus N.Y. Med. Coll.; lectr. psychopathology, New York Sch. for Social Work; lectr. Education of the Handicapped, Columbia U. Fellow A.M.A., Am. Psychiatric Assn., Am. Orthopsychiatric Assn.; mem. Nat. Com. for Mental Hygiene, Am. Psychoanalytical Assn. Collaborator, Tices Practice of Medicine and author of many scientific articles and monographs. Clubs: Alpha-Sigma, Physicians. Home: West Falls NY Died Apr. 26, 1971; buried Griffins Mills Cemetery, West Falls NY

JOBES, HARRY C., investment; b. Koseiusko, Miss., Oct. 31, 1877; s. Charles Sumner and Alma Gould (Taylor) J.; student U. of Kan., 1895-98; m. Susan Key Smith, of Macon, Ga., Nov. 1, 1910; 1 dau., Anne Josephine. Engaged in ranching, 1898-1908; in banking business, Kansas City, Mo., 1908-17; in investment business since 1919; mem. C. S. Jobes & Son, 1919-28; organizer, 1928, since v.p. Jobes Investment Co.; treas. Great Western Order Buying Co.; dir. Home Dairy Co. Enlisted in F.A., Mo. N.G., 1917, later in F.A., U.S.A., advancing to capt., World War. Republican. Methodist. Mason. Clubs: University, Kansas City, Kansas City Country. Home: Woodlea Hotel. Office: Live Stock Exchange Bldg., Kansas City MO‡

JOHN FRANCIS, SISTER MARY, coll. pres.; b. Milw., June 25, 1911; d. William John and Eva Mary (Pinter) Schuh; B.A., Mt. Mary Coll., 1933; M.A., DePaul U., 1943; Ph.D., Cath. U. Am., 1953. Mem. Congregation of Sch. Sisters of Notre Dame, Milw., 1936-69; tchr. English, history and journalism St. Michael Central High Sch., Chgo., 1938-47; tchr. English and journalism Mt. Mary Coll., Milw., 1947-49, dean of studies, 1953-54, pres., from 1954. Treas. Wis. Found. Ind. Colls., Inc. Mem. N.E.A., Wis. Assn. Pres.'s and Deans Instns. Higher Learning (exec. com.), Kappa Gamma Pi, Delta Epsilon Sigma, Eta Sigma Phi, Sigma Tau Delta, Alpha Mu Gamma. Address: Milwaukee WI Died July 25, 1969.

JOHNS, CYRUS N., bus. exec.; b. Sedalia, Mo., July 29, 1894; s. William Minton and Alice (Newkirk) J.; student, Univ. of Mo., 1916; m. Helen Steinert, Oct. 8, 1924 (dec. 1937); children—Margery Ann (Mrs. Margery J. Godfrey), Dorothy Helen (Mrs. Richard Coons). Sales engr., Am. Chain & Cable Co., Inc., 1913-14, prodn. mgr., asst. works mgr. and works mgr., 1915-39, v.p. in charge of operations, 1939-46, exec. v.p., 1946, dir., 1939-73, pres., 1951-65, chmn. bd., chief executive officer, 1965-67; dir. Md. Bolt & Nut Company, Dominion Chain Co., Ltd., Bristol Co., Parsons Chain Co., Ltd., Brit. Wire Products, Ltd. (both Eng.). Mem. Am. Iron and Steel Inst., Am. Soc. M.E. Clubs: University (Pitts.); Union, Piping Rock; Rotary (Monessen, Pa.); Cornell (N.Y.C.). Home: Glen Head NY Died Mar. 4, 1973.

JOHNS, FRANK STODDERT, surgeon; b. Buckingham Co., Va., August 16, 1884; s. Reuben B. and Agnes Penultima (Anderson) J.; B.A., Hampden-Sydney Coll., 1908, hon. D.Sc., 1926, LL.D., 1946; M.D., Med. Coll. of Virginia, 1913; married Anne Page, April 30, 1921; children—Thomas Nelson Page, Martha Allen (wife Dr. Herbert Langford), Ruth (Mrs. William Maury Hill), Anne-Rosewell (Mrs. Edwin M. Gaines). Tchr. Blackstone Mil. Acad., 1908-09; surg. service Johnston-Willis Hosp., 1913-17, resident surgeon, 1919-21, associate surgeon, 1921-29, chief surgeon from 1929-65; prof. clin. surgery emeritus Med. Coll. Va. Dir. Va. Trust Co. Served as lt., sr. grade, U.S.N., Med. Division, 1917-19. Pres. Johnston-Willis Hosp., 1946-65; trustee, past pres. bd. visitors Hampden-Sydney Coll. Past pres., Assn. Seaboard Airline Ry. Surgeons. Diplomate Am. Bd. Surgery (founder mem.). Fellow A.C.S. (gov. to 1965); mem. Soc. for Surgery of Alimentary Tract, American Association for Thoracic Surgery, Chesapeake and Ohio R.R. Surgeons Assn. (pres. 1965), Southern Surg. Assn. (pres. 1947), Am. Association for Surgery of Trauma A.M.A., S.E. Surg. Congress, James IV Surg. Association, Frederick A. Coller Surg. Soc. (hon.), Tri-State Medical Assn. of the Carolinas and Va. (past pres.), Richmond Acad. Medicine, Med. Soc. Va., Pan-Pacific Surg. Assn., Internat. Soc. Surgery, Phi Beta Kappa Soc. (hon.), Omicron Delta Kappa, Kappa Alpha. Presbyn. (elder emeritus). Clubs: Westmoreland, Commonwealth, Country of Virginia, Deep Run Hunt, Richmond German. Home: Richmond VA Died Aug. 11, 1971; buried Fork Church, Hanover County VA

JOHNSON, ALBERT HENRY, constrn. co. exec.; b. LaConner, Wash., Aug. 31, 1893; s. John B. and Inga (Erickson) J.; student pub. schs.; m. Beatrice K. Brown, Aug. 27, 1921 (dec. 1958); children—Janet B. (Mrs. Dabney), Allan H., Ervin A.; m. 2d, Helen S. Henderson, December 1960. With Stone & Webster Engring. Corp., 1911-13, Gen. Constrn. Co., 1914-22; supt. Morrion-Knudsen Co., Inc., 1922, project mgr., area mgr., 1929, dir., from 1949, v.p., dist. mgr., 1952-61, cons., from 1961. Served with U.S. Army, 1917-19. Home: Centralia WA Died Aug. 3, 1965.

JOHNSON, ALDEN PORTER, editor, pub.; b. Worcester, Mass., Mar. 24, 1914; s. Charles Warren and Ruby (Allen) J.; student Princeton, 1937; m. Mary Chandler Bullock, Sept. 17, 1938; children—Judith A., Lisa, Peter C. Pres., Johnson-deVou, Inc., Worcester, 1942-46, Barre Gazette, Barre Publ. Co. (Mass.), 1946-72. Trustee Worcester Found. Exptl. Biology; chmn. George I. Alden Trust, 1950-72; trustee Worcester Natural History Soc., Worcester Art Mus., Clark U.; pres. Stetson Home for Boys, Barre, Mass.; bd. dirs. Salisbury Mansion Assos. Mem. Am. Antiquarian Soc. (v.p.), Imprint Soc. (pres.), Mass., Worcester hist. socs., Colonial Soc. Mass. Clubs: Odd Volumes (Boston); Grolier (N.Y.C.). Home: Worcester MA Died Sept. 8, 1972.

JOHNSON, ALVIN SAUNDERS, economist; b. nr. Homer, Neb., Dec. 18, 1874; s. John and Edel Marie (Bille) J.; A.B., U. Neb., 1897, A.M., 1898, LLD., 1940; Ph.D., Columbia, 1902; hon. Dr., Us. of Algiers, Brussels, 1950; Ph.D., Yeshiva U., 1952, Heidelberg, 1955; Litt.D., Brandeis U., 1953; m. Margaret Edith Henry, Apr. 18, 1904; 1 dau., Felicia. Reader in econs. Bryn Mawr Coll., 1901-02; tutor, instr. and adj. prof. econs., Columbia, 1902-06; prof. econs. U. Neb., 1906-08, U. Tex., 1908; acting asso. prof. U. Chgo., summer and fall terms, 1909, asso. prof., 1910-11; prof. econs. Leland Stanford Jr. U., 1911-12, Cornell U., 1912-16; prof. polit. Sci. Stanford U., 1916-18; editor The New Republic, N.Y.C., 1917-23; dir. New School for Social Research, 1923-45, chmn. grad. faculty of polit. sci., 1945; pres. emeritus, 1945-71, also trustee; prof. econs. and dir. gen. studies grad. sch. Yale U., 1938-39. Chmn. N.Y. State Com. on Discrimination in Employment, 1943-45; vice chmn. N.Y. State Commn. Against Discrimination, 1944. Served as pvt. Co. K, 1st Neb. Vols., 1898. Decorated Commander Order of Leopold II (Belgium); Comdr. Legion of Honor (France); Liberation Medal (Denmark); Order of Merit, Fed. Republic Germany. Mem. Am. Econ. Assn. (pres. 1936), Am. Assn. Adult Edn. (chmn. 1936-71, pres. 1939), Phi Beta Kappa. Author: Rent in Modern Economic Theory, 1903; Introduction to Economics, 1909; The Professor and the Petticoat, 1914; John Stuyvesant, Ancestor, 1919; Deliver Us from Dogma, 1934; Spring Storm, 1936; The Public Library; A Peoples University, 1938; The Clock of History, 1946; Pioneer's Progress: An Autobiography, 1952; Essays in Social Economics, 1955; A Touch of Color; The Battle of the Wild Turkey. Asst. editor Polit. Sci. Quarterly, 1902-06; editor econs. new Internat. Ency., 1902-04; editor polit. sci. Am. Edit. Nelson's Ency.; asso. editor Ency. Social Scis., 1927-34; mem. editorial council Yale Rev., 1927-47. Home: Nyack NY Died June 7, 1971.

JOHNSON, CAMPBELL CARRINGTON, army officer, social worker; b. Washington, Sept. 30, 1895; s. Rev. William Henry and Ellen Berry (Lee) J.; B.S., Howard U., 1920, LL.B., 1922; spl. work, Columbia, 1927-28; m. Ruby Etta Murray, Nov. 2, 1918; 1 son, Campbell Carrington. Chief of sect. handling ins. and compensation claims Bureau War Risk Ins., Washington, 1919-23; admitted to N.C. and D.C. bars, 1922; practiced law in Washington as mem. firm Love, Johnson, Mazyck, 1922-26; exec. sec., Y.M.C.A., Washington, 1923-40; instr. in social scis. Howard U., 1932-47; exec. asst. to dir., Selective Service, Washington, 1940-47; exec. asst. to dir. Office Selective Service Records, 1947-48, asst. to dir. Selective Service System since June 1948. Dir. Indsl. Bank of Wash. Mem. D.C. Bd. Parole since 1939, chmn. since 1946. An organizer Washington Community Chest, 1928, trustee 1928-41; an organizer Southeast House, 1929, Southwest Community House, 1929, Northwest Settlement House, 1934, serving as dir. until 1947; organizer Washington Urban League, 1938, dir., 1940-43; organizer Girl and Boy Scouts among Negro children. Lecturer, provisional course, Jr. League of Wash. since 1938. Commd. 1st lt., inf., 1917, and advanced through grades to col., 1943; organized and comd. Battery A., 350th F.A., 1917-18; organized R.O.T.C., Howard U., 1919, served as prof. mil. sci. and tactics, 1919-20; mem. O.R.C., 1920-41, active duty as major, 1941. Decorated D.S.M., Army Commendation ribbon; recipient Howard Univ. 1st alumni award for distinguished post-grad. achievement, 1943; Wash. Fedn. Chs. award for most outstanding layman in City of Washington, 1944; Omega Psi Phi nat. achievement award, 1945; scroll for distinguished and humanitarian service from 48 civic, social welfare, ednl. and religious orgns. of Washington, 1947. Sec. Chesapeake Summer Sch. Assn., 1923-32, pres., 1932-41. Mem. orgn. com. and mem. adv. com. U.S. Employment Service for D.C., 1933-37; mem. com. to reorganize Juvenile Ct. of D.C., 1934-35; mem. steering com. Atty. Gen.'s Juvenile Delinquency Conf., 1947-49; dir. Family Service Assn., 1934-46, Washington Council Social Agencies, 1934-48 (v.p. 1947-48), Washington Housing Assn. since 1935 (v.p. since 1947), Washington Self-Help Exchange since 1938, Bur. Rehabilitation, 1940-47; Wash. Fedn. Chs. (assisted in gaining admission of Negro chs. to fedn.; mem. com. and dirs., 1936-68; v.p. 1947-49). Mem. survey com., reorgn. Pub. Child Welfare Program for D.C., 1938-39. Mem. Nat. Assn. Housing Officials (vice chmn. Potomac chapter, 1945-46, mem. exec. com. 1945-46), Am. Legion, Am. Vets Com. Americans for Dem. Action (award for outstanding contbns. to Washington, 1949), United Community Service (mem. orgn. com. 1948; by-laws and constitution com. 1948-49, exec. com. and trustee since 1948). Citizens Council for Community Planning, Community Chest Fedn. for Nat. Capital Area (trustee since 1946), apptd. by Pres. Truman mem. Nat. Housing Authority, 1950; mem. Nat. Study Commn. Y.M.C.A., 1950-68. Mem. Am. Acad. Polit. and Social Sci., Omega Psi Phi, Sigma Pi Phi. Baptist (trustee). Mason, Elk. Contbd. articles to jours. Home: Washington DC Died Aug. 22, 1968.

JOHNSON, CARL EDWARD, physician; b. Denver, June 20, 1898; s. Swan and Sophia (Johnson) J.; A.B., Leland Stanford U., 1922; M.D., Harvard, 1926; m. Louise Harriet Sharpe, Oct. 16, 1934 (dec. July 1957); children—Carl Edward, William Swan; m. 2d, Ann Ekman Gaines, Jan. 4, 1958. Teaching fellow in comparative anatomy Harvard, 1922-23, instr. histology and embryoyology, 1923-26; intern Yale-New Haven Hosp., 1926-28, asst. resident in surg. obstetrics and gynecology, 1928-30, resident in surgery, 1931-32, resident in gynecology, 1932-33, attending obstetrician and gynecologist, 1932-62; practice medicine specializing in obstetrics and gynecology, New Haven, 1932-70; NRC fellow in physiology Hamburg (Germany) U., 1930-31; chief obstetrician and gynecologist Hosp of St. Raphael, New Haven, 1946-60; cons. Milford (Conn.) Hosp., Griffin Hosp., Derby, Conn. instr. surgery Yale Sch. Medicine, New Haven, 1928-32, instr. obstetrics and gynecology, 1932-34, asst. clin. prof., 1934-49, asso. clin. prof., 1949-56. Surg. cons. to surgeon gen. U.S., Germany, Austria, 1950; mem. Conn. Med. Examining Bd., 1948-60. Served to surgeon USPHS, 1942-47. Diplomate Am. Bd. Obstetrics and Gynecology (chmn. 1952-59). Fellow A.C.S., Am. Coll. Obstetricians and Gynecologists; mem. A.M.A., Am. Soc. for Study Sterility (treas. 1952-59), Internat. Fertility Assn., Conn. Med. Soc., New Haven County, New Haven med. assns., New Eng. Obstet. and Gynecol. Soc., NRC Fellowship, Fedn. State Med. Bds. U.S.A. Contbr. articles to med. jours. Home: Hamden CT Died Nov. 23, 1970; buried Hamden CT

JOHNSON, CHARLES ELLICOTT, educator, univ. dean; b. Worland, Wyo., Sept. 7, 1920; s. Palmer and Rose (Ellicott) J.; B.A., U. Minn., 1942, M.B.A., 1948, Ph.D., 1952; m. Jeanne Seal, Aug. 1, 1942; children—Craig V., Karen E., Kylene D. Pub. accountant Arthur Andersen & Co., C.P.A.'s, Mpls., 1942-43; instr. U. Minn., 1946-51; lectr. U. Cal. at Berkeley, 1951-52; asso. prof. U. Ore., 1952-57, prof., 1958-69, head dept. accounting and bus. statistics Sch. Bus., 1958-69, dean Coll. Liberal Arts, 1963-68, acting pres., 1968-69. Cons. editor McGraw Hill Book Co., 1962-69; cons. U. S. General Accounting Office, 1964-69. Served with AUS, 1943-46. Ford fellow, 1959-60, C.P.A., D.C. Mem. Ore. Soc. C.P.A.'s, Am. Inst. C.P.A.'s, Am. Accounting Assn. (v.p. 1960), Am. Assn. U. Profs. Co-author: Accounting, Introductory, 1962; Accounting, Intermediate, 1963; Accounting, Advanced, 1965. Eugene OR Died June 17, 1969; inurnment at Rest Haven Meml. Park, Eugene OR

JOHNSON, CHARLES PRICE, librarian; b. LaGrange, Mo., Oct. 1, 1914; s. Walter Henry and Margaret E. (Stephenson) J; student Friends U., Wichita, Kan., 1933-34; A.B., U. Ottawa (Kan.) U., 1936; Th.M., Southwestern Baptist Theol. Sem., 1940, M.R.E., 1940, Th.D., 1948; student N. Tex. State U., Denton, 1953-54; m. Lillias Nell Stewart, May 26, 1937; children—Meredith Nell. Stewart Charles. Ordained to ministry Bapt. Ch., 1937; pastor in Kan., Okla., Tex., 1934-42; minister edn. First Bapt. Ch., Ottawa, 1942-43; Christian edn. Kan. Bapt. Conv., 1943-47; reference librarian Southwestern Bapt. Theol. Sem., 1947-57, dir. libraries, 1957-65. United Fund rep. Tex. Bapt. Com. for Deaf. Mem. Am., Tex. library associations, American Theological Library Association (president 1964-65), Academy of Mental Health, So. Bapt. Hist. Soc. (dir.), Tex. Bapt. Library Conv. (pres. 1960-62). Club: Civitan Internat. (chaplain 1958-59). Pub., editor Union List of Baptist Serials, 1960. Circulation mgr. Southwestern Jour. Theology, 1959-65; co-editor J. Howard Williams, Prophet of God, Friend of Man. Contbr. Southwestern Sermons, 1960. Home: Fort Worth TX Died May 22, 1965.

JOHNSON, CRAWFORD TOY, business exec.; b. Chattanooga, Tenn., Oct. 22, 1898; s. Crawford Toy and Anne Caroline (Acree) J.; student Lawrenceville (N.J.) Sch., 1913-17; B.S., Yale, 1920; Yale, 1920; m. Mary-Stuart Snyder, Apr. 30, 1921 (dec. May 1963); children—Crawford Toy, Frederic Stuart; m. 2d Mary Nauman Bartow, Nov. 4, 1965. Clk. Birmingham Coca-Cola Bottling Co. (Ala.), 1920-24, sales mgr., 1924-26; v.p. Crawford Johnson & Co., Inc., 1926-42, pres., 1942-56, chmn. bd., 1956-65, also dir.; pres., chmn. or dir. numerous Coca-Cola Coca-Cola Bottling Cos.; dir. 1st Nat. Bank of Birmingham, Ala. Metal Industries Corp. Served as chief Q.M., Naval Aviation, World War I; lt. col. Fiscal Div., U.S. Army, 1942-45. mem. Book and Snake Soc. Republican. Episcopalian. Clubs: Augusta (Ga.) Nat. Golf; Racquet and Tennis, Links, Leash, River (N.Y.C.); Birmingham Country (pres. 1938), Mountain Brook Country (pres. 1947) (Birmingham); Minneapolis, Woodhill (Mpls.); Louisiana (New Orleans); Rolling Rock (Ligonier, Pa.); Royal and Ancient Golf of St. Andrews (Scotland); Somerset Hills Country, Essex Hunt. Home: Excelsior MN

JOHNSON, E. FRED, banker; b. Cleburne, Tex., Nov. 26, 1896; s. Walter Lee and Della T. (Thompson) J.; m. Faith Hieronymus, Oct. 22, 1935; 1 dau., Judith Patton (Mrs. Fred B. Koontz III). Chmn. bd., chief exec. officer Fourth Nat. Bank of Tulsa, 1943-68. Pres. Tulsa Community Fund, 1932-34. Chmn. Democratic Party Tulsa County, 1923. Pres. YMCA; mem. adv. bd. Salvation Army. Served to 2d lt. U.S. Army, World War I. Hon. col. Okla. Mem. Gilcrease Inst. Am. History and Art (pres.), U.S. Jr. C. of C. (past pres.). Home: Tulsa OK Died Nov. 26, 1968.

JOHNSON, EARL A., coll. dean; b. Petersburg, Ind., Aug. 26, 1899; s. Albert H. and Charlotte (Robling) J.; A.B., Oakland City (Ind.) Coll., 1924; M.A., Ind. U.,

1927, Ph.D., 1929; m. Lennie Hunt, May 11, 1922; children—Patricia E. (Mrs. Charles T. Diebel), Eleanor A. (Mrs. Robert D. Groom), Earl H., Margaret L. (Mrs. Owen R. Thomas). Tchr. elementary pub. schs., Ind., 1918-22; tchr.-prin. high schs. Ind., 1924-27; prin. Burris Lab. Sch., Ball State Tchrs. Coll., Muncie, Ind., 1929-48, head dept. edn. at coll., 1948-61, dean div. edn., from 1961. Mem. Ind. Bd. Edn., from 1957. Served with U.S. Army, World War I. Life mem. N.E.A., Ind. Sch. Mens Assn.; mem. Ind. Tchrs. Assn. (pres. 1959), Phi Delta Kappa. Presbyn. (elder). Kiwanian, Mason. Co-author: Building for Safe Living, 4th edit. 1962; Principles of Teaching, 1958. Home: Muncie IN Died Sept. 14, 1970; buried Odd Fellows Cemetery, Petersburg, IN

JOHNSON, EDGAR AUGUSTUS JEROME, economist; b. Orion, Ill., Jan. 31, 1900; s. Klaes August and Hannah Charlotte (Carlson) J.; B.S., U. of Ill., 1922, A.M., Harvard, 1924, Ph.D., 1929; LL.D., Johns Hopkins, 1972; m. Virginia Gravelle, Aug. 8, 1922; 1 son, Edgar Augustus Jerome. Instr. economics U. of Okla., 1922-23; asst. prof. and asso. prof. various schs., 1924-31; assistant professor economics Cornell, 1931-37, associate professor economic history New York Univ., 1937-41, prof. economic history, 1941-43; vis. prof. of economics U. of Cal., summer 1951, U. Md., U. Pa., 1955-56; prof. internat. econs. Johns Hopkins Sch. Advt. Internat. Studies, 1956-62, professor of economic history, 1962-69; sr. specialist East-West Center, Honolulu, 1968-69. Director of Dept. of Commerce of the S. Korean Interim Govt., 1946, civil adminstr. of the S. Korean Interim Govt., 1946-47, chief adviser to the Govt. of Korea, 1947-48, dir. div. Korea program, E.C.A., Washington, 1948-51; econ. adviser E.C.A. mission to Greece, 1951-52 deputy chief M.S.A. Mission to Yugoslavia 1952-55; cons. Gen. Motors, 1940-41, Govt. India, New Delhi, 1964-65, AID, India, 1966-67. Res. officer (Cavalry), 1922-37; entered active duty, U.S. Army, 1943; served with C.O.S.S.A.C., London, with S.H.A.E.F., London, Allied Land Forces Norway, Oslo, and U.S.F.E.T., Frankfort; disch. rank lt. col., 1946. Decorated: Order of the British Empire, Cross King Haakon the 7th, Bronze star. Mem. Econ. History Assn. (pres. 1960-62). Clubs: Harvard (N.Y. City); Cosmos (Washington, D.C.). Author: American Economic Thought in the Seventeenth Century, 1932; Some Origins of the Modern Economic World, 1935; Predecessors of Adam Smith, 1937; An Economic History of Modern England, 1939; (with Herman Krooss) The American Economy, Its Origin, Development and Transformation, 1960; Market Towns and Spatial Development in India, 1964; The Organization of Space in Developing Countries; American Imperialism in the Image of Peer Gynt; Dimensions of Freedom (pub. posthumously). Translator: Pioneers of American Economic Thought. (Ernst Teilhac), 1935. Editor: The Dimensions of Diplomacy; also 34 vols. of Prentice-Hall Econ. Series; Jour. Econ. History, 1940-43. Interested in Buddhist iconography. Home: Washington DC Died Aug. 17, 1972; buried Arlington Nat. Cemetery, Arlington VA

JOHNSON, EDGAR N(ATHANIEL), educator; b. Chgo., Apr. 4, 1901; s. Frank Emil and Mable Augusta (Walstrom) J.; Ph.B., U. Chgo., 1922, Ph.D., 1931; student U. Munich, Germany, 1927-28; m. Emily Louise Floyd, July 14, 1936; children—John Frans, Thomas Raymond. Instr. history Culver Mil. Acad., 1922-24, U. Chgo., 1928-31; with dept. of history U. Neb. 1931-58, prof., 1941-58; prof., chmn. dept. history Brandeis U., 1958-65; prof. history U. Mass., Amherst, 1965-69; visiting prof. history U. Wis., 1939-40, N.Y.U., 1956-57; lectr. Regis Coll., Weston, Mass., 1968-69; research analyst, research and analysis branch OSS, 1943-45, chief Austrian sect. (Eng., Italy, Austria), 1944-45; spl. asst. to comdg. gen., Office Mil Govt. U.S., Berlin; polit. adviser to comdg. gen. Berlin dist., 1946. Recipient Medal of Freedom. Mem. Am. Hist. Assn., American Academy of Political Science, also Medieval Acad. Am. (mem. council 1946-49), Renissance Soc. Am., Phi Beta Kappa (hon.). Author several books on medieval Europe. Home: Amherst MA Died Dec. 31, 1969.

JOHNSON, EDWARD GILPIN, translator, critic, journalist. Edited: The Private Memoirs of Madame Roland; Best Letters of Lord Chesterfield; Best Letters of Charles Lamb; The Complete Angler; Sir John Reynolds' Discourses on Art (all M5). Address: 3 Waverly Pl., Milwaukee WI‡

JOHNSON, EDWIN CARL, senator; b. Scandia, Kan., Jan. 1, 1884; s. Nels and Anna Belle (Lunn) J.; grad. Lincoln (Neb.) High Sch., 1903; m. Fern Armitage, Feb. 17, 1907; 1 dau., Janet Grace (Mrs. Robert Howsam) and 1 adopted dau., Mrs. Gladys Johnson Arrance. Began as railroad laborer, 1901; successively telegrapher, train dispatcher, homesteader, mgr. farmers coop. assn.; mem. Colo. Legislature, 4 terms, 1923-31; lt. gov. of Colo., 1931-33; gov., 2 terms, 1933-37; mem. U.S. Senate, 1936-48; reelected, 1948, for another 6-yr. term. Democrat. Home: Craig CO Died May 30, 1970.

JOHNSON, FRANCIS ELLIS, educator; b. Leroy, Mich., May 27, 1885; s. John William and Florence Estella (Ellis) J.; A.B., U. of Wis., 1906, E.E., 1909; m. Elizabeth Dale Trousdale, Mar. 8, 1910; children—Ellis Trousdale, Margaret Dale, Florence Whitney, Helen Laurence. Power plant constrn. in Northwest; instr. engring. Rice Inst., Houston, Tex., 1912-15; with U. of Kan., 1915-30, successively instr. engring. until 1916, asst. prof., 1916-18, asso. prof., 1918-21, prof., 1921-30, and head dept. elec. engring., 1928-30; head dept. elec. engring., Ia. State Coll., Ames, Ia., 1930-35; dean Coll. of Engring., U. of Mo., 1935-38; dean Coll. of Engring, U. of Wis., 1938-46; Ednl. dir. Gen. Elec. Co. Nucleonics Project (Hanford), 1946-50, ret. Cons. practice in acceptance tests on power plants, design of transmission lines, valuation of municipal electric systems, etc. Fellow Am. Inst. E.E.; Society for Promotion Engring. Edn., Sigma Xi, Tau Beta Pi, Phi Kappa Phi, Kappa Eta Kappa, Eta Kappa Nu. Republican. Address: Salem OR Died Dec. 2, 1968; buried Forest Hill Cemetery, Madison WI

JOHNSON, FRED G., ex-congressman; b. Saline Co., Neb., Oct. 16, 1876; s. Charles and Jane A. (Johnson) J.; grad. high sch., Dorchester, Neb.; LL.B., U. of Neb., 1903; m. L. Maude Bridgman, of Fairmont, Neb., Nov. 15, 1906. Admitted to Neb. bar, 1903, and practiced at Hastings, also farmer; elected mem. Neb. Ho. of Rep., 1916, State Senate, 1918; lt. gov. of Neb., 1923-25; mem. 71st Congress (1929-31), 5th Neb. Dist. Republican. Home: Hastings NE‡

JOHNSON, FREDERICK, business exec.; b. Southport, Eng., May 4, 1887; s. John and Elizabeth (Fraser) J.; ed. Christ Ch. Schs.; m. Georgina V. Robinson, Aug. 22, 1910. Began as clk. Nat. Telephone Co., Eng., 1904; employed by Bell Telephone Co. of Can., Montreal, Can., since 1910, successively chief accountant, asst. comptroller, comptroller, 1910-35, v.p., in charge accounts and finance 1935-44, became pres., 1944, chmn. bd., 1953-57. Dir. adminstrn. British Purchasing Commn., N.Y.C., 1939-41; pres. N. Am. Telegraph Co.; dir. Northern Electric Co. Ltd., The Steel Co. of Canada, Ltd., Hamilton, Ont., Maritime Telegraph and Telephone Co., Ltd., New Brunswick Telephone Co., Ltd., Sun Life Assurance Co. of Can.; mem. adv. bd., chmn. board of governors, Welfare Federation of Montreal. mem. adv. council Sch. of Commerce, McGill Univ.; mem. adv. bd. Health League of Can., Y.M.C.A. Angelican. Clubs: St. James's, Mount Royal (Montreal); Mount Bruno. Home: Montreal PQ Canada. Died May 14, 1968.

JOHNSON, FREDERICK ERNEST, educator, clergyman; b. Ontario, Can., Oct. 31, 1884; s. Herbert John and Rebecca (Howard) J.; came with parents to U.S., 1889; A.B., Albion (Mich.) Coll., 1906, D.D., 1928; B.D., Union Theol. Sem., 1912; L.H.D., Columbia, 1954; Litt.D., Jewish Theol. Sem. Am., 1961; m. Kate Holmes Crawford, Feb. 20, 1914 (dec. Feb. 14, 1962); children—Catherine (Mrs. A. M. Crawford), Edward. Ordained M.E. ministry, 1908; pastor Holly, Mich., 1906-09; asst. pastor St. Paul's Ch., N.Y.C., 1909-14; pastor Janes Ch., N.Y.C., 1914-16; ednl. work, 1916-18; sec. for research and ednl. work, Fed. Council Chs. of Christ in America, 1918-24, exec. sec., editor Information Service, Dept. of Research and Education, 1924-50; exec. dir., central dept. research and survey Nat. Council of Chs. of Christ in U.S.A. and editor Information Service, 1951-52; ret. 1952; study cons., ch. and econ. life Nat. Council Chs., from 1953; dir. Internat. Survey of YMCA's and YWCA's, 1929-31; prof. edn. Tchrs. Coll., Columbia, 1931-50, emeritus, 1950-69; Rauschenbusch lectr., Colgate-Rochester Divinity Sch., 1939; editor Social Action, 1953-57; chmn. com. on religion and edn., American Council on Edn., 1946-57. Mem. Nat. Child Labor Com. (chmn. 1955-58), Religious Edn. Assn. (pres. 1944-46), Conf. on Sci., Philosophy and Religion (exec. com.), Nat. Commn. UNESCO (3 terms), Delta Sigma Rho, Phi Beta Kappa. Author: Economics and the Good Life, 1934; The Church and Society, 1935; The Social Gospel Re-Examined, 1940; The Church as Employer, Money Raiser and Investor (with J. Emory Ackerman), 1959; A Vital Encounter: Christianity and Communism, 1962. Editor: Social Work of the Churches, 1930; Religion and the World Order, 1944; World Order: Its Intellectual and Cultural Foundations, 1945; Foundations of Democracy, 1947; Wellsprings of the American Spirit, 1949; American Education and Religion, 1952; Religious Symbolism, 1955; Religion and Social Work, 1956; Patterns of Faith in America Today, 1957; Patterns of Ethics in America Today, 1960. Contbr. articles on religious and social subjects. Home: Oak Ridge TN Died July 1969.

JOHNSON, HALLETT, fgn. service officer; b. N.Y. City, Nov. 26, 1888; s. J. Augustus and Fanny V. (Matthews) J.; A.B., Williams Coll., 1908; LL.B., Columbia, 1911; m. Katherine M. Steward, May 20, 1920; children—Katherine Beeckman, Priscilla Livingston, Hallett. Entered diplomatic service, 1912; served as sec. embassies in London, Constantinople, Santiago, and charge d'affairs at Legation in La Paz; acting chief Div. of Latin Am. Affairs, Dept. of State, 1919; 1st sec. Legation, Oslo, 1927-29, embassies at Brussels, 1920-21, Paris, 1924-27; counselor of Legation and charge d'affaires, The Hague, 1929-33, Madrid, 1933-36; in charge of Summer Embassy, Sebastian, Spain, at outbreak of Spanish Civil War, 1936; counselor of Embassy and charge d'affaires, Warsaw, 1936-37; counsel gen. and counselor of Legation, Stockholm, 1937-41; asst. chief, Div. of Controls, Dept. of State, 1941-42; asst. chief, Div. of Defense Materials, 1942-45; ambassador to Costa Rica, 1945-49; retired. Member Co. K, 7th Reg., Nat. Guard of N.Y., 1909-12. Mem. Soc. of Colonial Wars, S.A.R., Delta Psi. Episcopalian. Clubs: Union, St. Anthony (New York); Metropolitan (Washington, D.C.); Travelers (Paris). Home: Princeton NJ Died Aug. 1968.

JOHNSON, HERMAN E., publishing co. exec.; b. 1913; ed. Northwestern U., Marquette U.; married. With Western Pub. Co., Racine, Wis., 1929-72, became asst. mgr., 1955, pres., 1958, then chmn., chief exec. officer, dir. Office: Racine WI Died Feb. 22, 1972.

JOHNSON, HOWARD, restaurant chain exec. Began as operator of drug store, Wollaston, Mass., and specialized in ice cream and soft drinks, expanding to include sales at Wollaston Beach and Nantasket Beach; furnished additional items of food and through gradual expansion operator and supply center for chain of stores throughout most sections of U.S., operated under franchise or directly under own name; former pres., treas., chmn., dir. Howard Johnson Enterprises; ret., 1959. Home: New York City NY Died June 20, 1972.

JOHNSON, J. SIDNEY, merchandising exec.; b. Grand Forks, N.D., May 11, 1890; s. August George and Emma (Mission) J.; student U. Pa., 1909-10, 10-11; A.B., Stanford, 1913; m. Dorothy Ellis, Apr. 14, 1953. Wholesale grocer, Marshalltown, Ia., 1914-34; dir. merchandising I.G.A. Stores, Chgo., 1934-40; merchandising mgr. Nat. Biscuit Co., N.Y.C., 1940-50, asst. v.p. for sales, dir. trade relations, 1950-55, marketing and trade relations counsel, from 1955; dir. Butterick Co., Godfrey Co. Dir. advt. War Food Adminstrn., Washington, 1943-44; dir. trade relations OPA, 1944; trustee Am. Inst. Food Distbn., Inc. Trustee Marshalltown Pub. Library, 1926-34. Served to sgt., C.W.S., U.S. Army, 1918-19. Recipient Albers award Super Market Inst. Mem. Ia. Library Assn. (pres. 1932-33), Ia. Hist. Soc., Associated Advertising Clubs of Iowa (president 1918), Phi Beta Kappa, Alpha Delta Phi. Clubs: University (N.Y.C.); Siwanoy Country (Bronxville); Tavern (Chgo.); Devon Yacht (E. Hampton, N.Y.) Contbr. articles to trade publs. Home: Bronxville, New York City NY

JOHNSON, JOHN BOCKOVER, JR., coll. provost; b. Chicago, Sept. 21, 1912; s. John Bockover and Mary Clyde (Wiltshire) J.; A.B., Williams Coll., 1934; Ph.D., U. Chicago, 1943; LL.D., Ripon (Wis.) College, 1953; married Cloyd Stifler, April 18, 1942; children—David Stifler, Randall Wharton, Lucy Burnley. With Dun & Bradstreet, Inc., Louisville, Ky., 1935-38, credit analyst, 1936-38, Chicago, 1942; mem. faculty Park Coll. Parkville, Mo., 1946-51, chmn. social sci. div., 1947-51, chmn. polit. sci. dept., 1946-51; pres. Milw. Downer Coll., 1951-64; provost Old Dominion Coll., Norfolk Va., 1964-72. Mem. instructional programs adv. com State Council Higher Edn. for Va. Mem. corp. Columbia Hosp., 1951-64; mem. Council United Community Services of Greater Milw., Inc., 1951-64; adv. bd. Gir Scouts U.S.A., 1951-64; cons. bd. World Affairs Council, 1951-64. Exec. com. Wis. Found. Ind. Colls. Inc., 1951-64, also past pres.; joint liaison com. Old Dominion College, Norfolk General Hospital, Norfolk Area Medical Center Authority. Served in Army of United States, 1942-46. Recipient Army Commendation award, 1946 for 2 vol. history. Mem Continuing Conf. on Gen. Edn. and The Social Sci (Carnegie Corp.), 1950-51. Mem. Norfolk Mus. Arts and Scis., Assn. Wis. Presidents and Deans (past pres.) Greater Milw. Assn. Phi Beta Kappa (past pres.), Delta Upsilon. Author: (with Irving Lewis) Registration fo Voting in the United States, 1941; (with Graves T Wilson) History of World War II Research and Development of Medical Field Equipment, 2 vols. 1946. Home: Norfolk VA Died Apr. 6, 1972; buried Norfolk VA

JOHNSON, JOHN EDWARD, mfg. exec.; b. Kansas City, Mo., Aug. 7, 1912; s. John D. and Berth Josephine (Dietrich) J.; student Kansas City Jr. Coll. 1930-31; m. Joan Clark Paton, June 25, 1955 (dec. Jan 1965); children—Geoffrey, Judith, Jill Penelope Jennifer, John Edward; married 2d, Sandra Ann Liakos April 2, 1966. Office machines marketing Burrough Corporation, Detroit, 1935-43; management enginee Ernst & Ernst, Boston, 1946-54; v.p. Datamatic Corp subsidiary Minneapolis Honeywell Regulator Co. an Rayethon Mfg. Co., Newton, Mass., 1955-58; v.p RCA, Camden, N.J., 1959-60, mgr. electronic compute marketing activity, 1958-60; comml. v.p. Itek Corp Waltham, Mass., 1960-61; dir. v.p. RCA, Cherry Hil N.J., 1961-70; pres. John E. Johnson Assos., Lincoln Mass., 1970. Served to lt. (s.g.), Supply Corps, USNR 1944-46. Mem. Am. Mgmt. Assn. Home: MA Die Sept. 17, 1970; buried New Lincoln Cemetery, Lincol MA

JOHNSON, JOSEPH LOWERY, diplomatic servic b. Darke Co., O., Feb. 14, 1874; s. Walter and Lucind Jane (McCown) J.; prep. edn. Union Lit. Inst., Ind

M.D., Howard U., Washington, D.C., 1902; Phar.D., 1905; m. May Belle Williams, of Parkersburg, W.Va., Jan. 18, 1915. Med. clk. U.S. Pension Office, Washington, D.C., 1905-08; practiced at Rendville, O., 1909-14, Columbus, 1914-19; minister resident and consul gen. to Liberia, Aug. 27, 1918-21. Trustee Wilberforce U., 1912-16; now pres. bd. of trustees Wilberforce U. Mem. Ohio State Med. Assn., Columbus Acad. Medicine. Democrat. Methodist. Mason, Elk, Red Man. Home: 1375 E. Long St., Columbus OH‡

JOHNSON, KEEN, ex-gov. of Kentucky; b. Lyon County, Ky., Jan. 12, 1896; s. Robert and Mattie Davis (Holloway) J.; student Central Coll., Fayette, Mo., 1914-17; A.B., U. of Ky., 1922; LL.D., (hon.), University of Kentucky, June 1940; m. Eunice Lee Nichols, June 23, 1917; 1 dau., Judith Keen. Editor Elizabethtown (Ky.) Mirror, 1919-21, Lawrenceburgh (Ky.) News, 1922-25; editor Richmond (Ky.) Daily Register since 1925; pres. Richmond Daily Register Co. With Reynolds Metals Co. asst. to pres.; assigned to Washington office, 1944, vice pres., 1945-46, v.p. for pub. affairs, 1947-70, director, 1949-70. Lt. gov. of Ky., 1935-39, gov. 1939-43; under sec. of labor, 1946-47; president Louisville Safety Council. Bd. regents Eastern Kentucky State Coll. Entered 1st R.O.T.C., Ft. Riley, Kan., May 1917; commd. 2d lt., later 1st lt.; served with 354th Infantry, 89th Div., 1917-19; with A.E.F., 1 year. Mem. Ky. State Press Assn. (former pres.), Public Relations Soc. America, U. of Ky. Alumni Assn. (past pres.), Am. Legion, Vets. Fgn. Wars, 40 et 8, Sigma Alpha Epsilon, Alpha Delta Sigma, Omicron Delta Kappa. Democrat. Methodist. Mason, Elk. Clubs: Metropolitan, National Press (Washington), Pendennis, Rotary (Louisville). Home: Richmond KY Died Feb. 7, 1970; buried Richmond Cemetery, Richmond KY

JOHNSON, LEON H., coll. pres.; b. Hawley, Minn., Mar. 6, 1908; s. Hans L. and Petra (Solum) J.; B.A., Concordia Coll., Moorhead, Minnesota, 1932, Doctor of Humane Letters (hon.), 1966; Ph.D. in Biochemistry (Frasch research fellow 1940-43), U. Minn., 1943; m. Esther Pauline Evenson, June 6, 1936; children—Linda (Mrs. Louis Wendt), Vance (Mrs. Peter Anderson). High Sch. tchr., N.D., 1932-39; instr. agrl. biochemistry U. Minn., 1939-43; asso. prof. chemistry, research biochemist Mont. State Univ., Bozeman, 1943-48, prof. chemistry, 1948-69, dean grad. div. 1955-64, acting president, 1963-64, president, 1964-69, exec. dir. endowment and research found., 1947-65. Mem. Am. Chem. Soc., Sigma Xi, Phi Kappa Phi. Elk, Rotarian (pres. Bozeman 1950). Contbr. articles profl. jours. Home: Bozeman MT Died June 18, 1969; buried Bozeman MT

JOHNSON, LESTER BICKNELL, business exec.; b. Bronxville, N.Y., Jan. 5, 1918; s. Seymour and Carrie (Westfall) J.; B.A., Wesleyan U., Middletown, Conn., 1939; m. Margaret King, Apr. 25, 1942; children—James W., Margaret S. With Standard Oil Co. (N.J.), 1945-65, dep. treas., 1962-63, treas., 1963-65; exec. vice pres. Celanese Corp. of Am., 1965-67, spl. asst. to president 1967-71; dir. Esso Petroleum Co., Ltd., London, Eng., 1961-62. Served with USMCR, 1942-45. Mem. Council Fgn. Relations, Internat. C. of C. (member committee on affairs of U.S. Council); Financial Executives Institute, also member of Delta Tau Delta. Clubs: University (N.Y.C.); American (London). Home: Briarcliff Manor NY Died May 16, 1971.

JOHNSON, LYNDON BAINES, former Pres. of U.S.; b. nr. Stonewall, Tex., Aug. 27, 1908; s. Samuel Ealy and Rebekah (Baines) J.; B.S., Southwest Tex. State Coll., San Marcos, Tex., 1930; postgrad. Georgetown Law Sch., 1935; LL.D., Southwestern U., 1943, Howard Payne U., 1957, Brown U., 1959, Bethany Coll., 1959, U. Hawaii, 1961, U. Philippines, 1961, Gallaudet Coll., 1961, East Ky. State Coll., 1961, William Jewell Coll., 1961, Elon Coll., 1962, S.W. Tex. State Tchrs. Coll., 1962, Wayne State U., 1963, Jacksonville U., 1963, McMurray Coll., 1963, U. Md., 1963, Tufts U., 1963; U. Cal., 1964, U. Tex., 1964, Swarthmore Coll., 1964, Syracuse U., 1964, Georgetown U., 1964; U. Ky., 1965, Baylor U., 1965, Howard U., 1965, Catholic U., 1965; D.C.L., Holy Cross Coll., 1964, U. Mich., 1964; L.H.D., Oklahoma City U., 1960, Yeshiva U., 1961, Fla. Atlantic U., 1964; Litt.D., Glassboro Coll., 1968; D.Litt., St. Mary's Coll. Cal., 1962; D.Polit. Sci., Chulalongkorn U., Thailand, 1966; m. Claudia Alta (Lady Bird) Taylor, Nov. 17, 1934; children—Lynda Bird (Mrs. Charles S. Robb), Luci Baines (Mrs. Patrick J. Nugent). Tchr. Houston pub. schs., 1930-31; sec. Congressman Richard M. Kleberg, Tex., 1931-35; state dir. Nat. Youth Adminstrn. of Tex., 1935-37; elected to 75th Congress (1937-38) to fill unexpired term of Congressman James Buchanan, 10th Tex. Dist.; re-elected to 76th to 80th Congresses (1938-48); U.S. senator, 1949-61, minority leader 83d Congress, majority leader, 84th-86th Congresses; v.p. U.S., 1961-63; 36th pres. U.S. (succeeded to Presidency of U.S. Nov. 22, 1963 on death of Pres. John F. Kennedy), elected Pres., Nov. 3, 1964, took office Jan. 20, 1965. Chmn. Pres.'s Com. on Equal Employment Opportunity; chmn. Nat. Aeronautics and Space Council; chmn. Peace Corps Adv. Council; mem. NSC Council. Comdr. USNR, active duty, 1941-42. Decorated Silver Star. Democrat. Mem. Christian Ch. Author: My Hope for America, 1964; A Time for Action, 1964; This America, 1966; No Retreat from Tomorrow, 1967; To Heal and To Build, 1968; The Choices We Face, 1968; The Vantage Point, 1971. Stonewall TX Died Jan. 22, 1973; buried Family Cemetery, Stonewall TX

JOHNSON, RICHARD NEWHALL, corp. ofcl.; b. Colorado Springs, Colo., Feb. 13, 1900; s. Otis Stafford and Annie (Fisher) J.; A.B., Harvard, 1922, M.B.A., 1923; m. Margaret L. Paisley, July 4, 1924; children—Gordon Otis Fraser, Kathleen Fisher, Margaret Paisley; married 2d Phyllis Rising Walker, Feb. 25, 1950. With Pacific Mills, Boston, 1925-29; pres. and treas. Hillsboro Woolen Mills Co., 1929-36; v.p. Building Products Inc., 1936-39; pub. Boston Eve. Transcript, 1939-42; War Prodn. Bd., 1942-45; asst. treas. Export-Import Bank of Washington, 1945-50; foreign trade policy advisor to the White House staff, 1950-51; assistant director for Mutual Security Executive Office of President, 1951-53; assistant dir. Fgn. Operations Adminstrn., 1953-54; pres. Logetronics, Inc., Springfield, Va., 1955-67, chairman of board from 1968. Served with USN AS, 1918. Home: Annapolis MD Died Nov. 21, 1971; buried Lynn (Mass.) Cemetery.

JOHNSON, ROBERT LIVINGSTON, JR., magazine editor; b. N.Y.C., June 15, 1919; s. Robert Livingston and Anna Talcott (Rathbone) J.; grad. Taft Sch., Watertown, Conn., 1937; A.B., Princeton, 1941; m. Sally Edgerton Schilthuis, June 19, 1943; children—Robert Livingston III, Peter Rathbone, Linda Fitzgerald, Sally Edgerton, Carol Schilthuis. With Promenade mag., N.Y.C., 1941, 46-49, asso. editor, 1946-49; with Sat. Eve. Post, Phila., 1949-69, asso. editor, 1951-62, sr. editor, 1962-69; freelance editor, 1969-70. Served to lt. (s.g.) USNR, 1942-46. Author: mag. articles. Home: Greenwich CT Died Dec. 27, 1970.

JOHNSON, ROBERT WOOD, industrialist; born New Brunswick, New Jersey, Apr. 4, 1893; son Robert Wood and Evangeline (Armstrong) J.; educated at Lawrenceville Sch. and by pvt. tutors; LD.D. (honoris causa), Rockhurst Coll., 1948, Rutgers Univ., 1950, Northwestern, 1952, University of Dallas, 1962; D.Sc. (honorary), Philadelphia College Pharmacy and Sci., 1960; m.; children—Robert W., Sheila; m. 3d Evelyne Vernon, Aug. 1943. Entered family firm Johnson & Johnson, mfrs. of surg. dressings, 1910, v.p., 1918-30, v.p. and gen. mgr., 1930-32, pres., 1932-38, chairman of the board, 1938-63, dir., chmn. finance com., 1963-68. Mem. Borough Coun. of Highland Pk. N.J., 1918-19, mayor, 1920-22. Pres. Middlesex Gen. Hosp., New Brunswich, 1921-27. Entered Ord. Dept., U.S. Army, May 4, 1942, promoted col., May 29, 1942; promoted to rank of brig. gen., May 17, 1943; apptd. chief N.Y. Ordnance Dist., Sept. 14, 1942. Apptd. vice chmn. War Production Board and chmn. Smaller War Plants Corp., 1943. Pub. Interest Award, Pub. Relations Soc. Am., Inc., 1949; Human Relations award, Soc. Advancement Management, 1950; The Charles Parlin Memorial award, 1953, People to People, Inc. award from Pres. Eisenhower, 1957, Brotherwood award Nat. Conf. of Christians and Jews, 1958, N. Am. Industrialist of Year, Soc. Indsl. Realtors, 1959, Gold medal of merit V.F.W., 1959, Distinguished Service award Arthritis and Rheumatism Found., 1964, Gold medal internat. Oceanographic Found., 1964, Exec. of Year award Am. Coll. Hosp. Adminstrs., 1965. Hon. fellow A.C.S., Am. Coll. Hosp. Adminstrs. Patron Am. Mus. Natural History. Episcopalian. Mem. Am. Ord. Assn., Am. Legion. Mason. Clubs: Racquet and Tennis, N.Y. Yacht, Cruising; Surf; Indian Creek County (Surfside, Florida). Author: But, General Johnson (pvtly. pub.); Or Forfeit Freedom (received Franklin D. Roosevelt Memorial Award); Robert Johnson Talks It Over, (Certificate of Merit, 1949 Awards Jury of Freedom Found.); Human Relations in Modern Business (with others). Home: Princeton NJ Died Jan. 30, 1968.

JOHNSON, ROBERT WOOD, JR., marketing exec.; b. New Brunswick, N.J., Sept. 9, 1920; s. Robert Wood and Elizabeth (Ross) J.; grad. Milbrook Sch., 1939; student Hamilton Coll., 1939-41; m. Betty Wold, Oct. 7, 1944; children—Robert Wood IV, Keith W., Elizabeth, Willard, Christopher. With Johnson & Johnson, 1941-42, 46-70, dir. mfg. Ethicon Suture labs., 1948-50, v.p. charge merchandising, advt. Personal Products Corp., 1953-54, exec. com. Johnson & Johnson, 1954-70, exec. v.p. charge marketing, 1955-59, exec. v.p., gen. mgr., 1959-60, president, 1961-70, chmn., also vice chmn. exec. com., 1963-70. Served as staff sgr., AUS, 1942-46. Clubs: New York Yacht; Campfire (N.Y.C.). Home: Princeton NJ Died Dec. 22, 1970.

JOHNSON, WANDA MAE, librarian; b. Hastings, Okla.; d. Edgar Bruce and Magdalene (Farabough) Johnson; B.S., Okla. State U., 1929, M.A., 1932; B.A., U. Okla., 1930; postgrad. Columbia, 1934, 37. Head librarian Stillwater (Okla.) Pub. Library, 1930-36; asst. U.S. Dept. Commerce Library, Washington, 1936-37, dir. library, 1947-70; loan asst. U.S. Dept. Agr. Library, 1937-39; reference and loan asst. U.S. Bur. Agrl. Econs. Library, 1939-41; asst. librarian U.S. Treasury Dept. Library, 1941-43; chief librarian U.S. OPA Library, 1943-47. Mem. Nat. League Am. Pen Women, (past nat. membership chmn., past nat. conv. chmn., past nat. budget chmn.; organizer Capital br. 1960; pres. 1962-64, nat. adv. council 1962-64, D.C. pres. 1964-66), Law Librarians Soc. Washington, D.C. Library Assn., Spl. Libraries Assn. (local chpt. parliamentarian 1957-61), D.A.R. (nat. vice chmn. finance com. 1956; D.C. state printing chmn. 1958-60, regent local chpt. 1961-64), St. Johns Bus. and Profl. Women's Guild (past pres.), Okla. State Soc. (3d v.p. 1960-61), Assn. Preservation Va. Antiquities. Episcopalian. Mem. Order Eastern Star. Club: Washington DC Died Sept. 8, 1969.

JOHNSON, WILLIAM DRISCOLL, lawyer; b. Whitney Point, N.Y., Mar. 29, 1905; s. William H. and Sarah (Driscoll) J.; E.E., Syracuse U., 1925; LL.B., Harvard, 1929; m. Ellen Cregg Johnson, Nov. 26, 1931; s. William C., Edward C., Joanna C., Stephen L., Margaret D. Admitted to N.Y. bar, 1929, since practiced in Syracuse; partner firm Bond, Schoeneck & King, 1946-69. Dir. Engelberg, Inc., Syracuse, 1942-67, Morris Plan Syracuse, 1934-53. Chmn. specialized housing com. Planning Dept. Aging, Community Chest and Council Onondaga County, 1960-69; chmn. Hosp. Rev. and Planning Council Central N.Y., 1955-65. Bd. dirs. Community-Gen. Hosp. Greater Syracuse, 1964-67; trustee Pebble Hill Sch., DeWitt, N.Y., 1950-67, pres., 1955-59; trustee Syracuse Gen. Hosp., 1944-64, pres., 1948-49; bd. dirs. Council Social Agencies, Community Chest and Council Onondaga County, 1946-51, chmn., 1946-51, chmn. legislative com., 1945. Clubs: Century (Syracuse); Skaneateles (N.Y.) Country. Home: Syracuse NY Died June 8, 1969.

JOHNSON, WILLIAM HAROLD, mfg. co. exec., b. Iron Mountain, Mich., Sept. 28, 1920; s. Elmer S. and Emma Catherine (Weidemeyer) J.; B.A., Lake Forest (Ill.) Coll., 1943; student Ill. Tech. Coll., 1945-46, Northwestern U., 1949-51; m. Olga E. Castori, Aug. 16, 1941; children—Paula Karen, Nancy Rae. Office mgr. Hansell Elcock Co., Chgo., 1945-48; controller Chgo. Foundry Co., 1948-51; with White Motor Co., 1951-56, asst. v.p. finance, 1954-56; exec. v.p., White Consol. Industries, Inc., Cleve., 1956-69, pres., 1969-71; dir., v.p. Domestic Sewing Machine Co., Apex Fibre-Glass Products, Inc.; dir. White Sewing Machine, Limited. Elk. Clubs: Cleve. Athletic, Treasurer. (Cleve.); Shaker Heights Country. Home: Cleveland OH Died June 1, 1972.

JOHNSTON, CLARENCE THOMAS, civil engr.; b. Littleton, Colo., Oct. 23, 1872; s. James Albert and Melissa (Drummond) J.; B.S., U. of Mich., 1895, C.E., 1899; m. Bessie Vreeland, Oct. 20, 1897; children—Clarence Nettleton, Franklin Davis. In irrigation work with father, E. S. Nettleton, and Elwood Mead, 1890-1911; in employ state of Wyo., summers, 1891-96; asst. state engr., 1895-99; with U.S. Geol. Survey, 1896-98, and in irrigation and drainage work, U.S. Dept. Agr., 1899-1903 (made trip to Egypt and reported on Egyptian irrigation); state engr. of Wyo., 1903-11; became prof. surveying and geodesy, University of Michigan, 1911, now emeritus. Fellow A.A.A.S.; mem. American Society Civil Engineers (member executive committee div. surveying and mapping, 1926-31; Mich. Engring. Soc., Sigma Xi, Tau Beta Pi, Acacia. Conglist. Author reports, bulls. and papers relating to irrigation and drainage and the principles which should underlie legislation dealing with the use of water from streams and lakes, also contbr. on geodesy and surveying. Home: 1235 Hill St., Ann Arbor MI‡

JOHNSTON, FRANKLIN DAVIS, physician; b. Cheyenne, Wyo., June 23, 1900; s. Clarence Thomas and Bessie (Vreeland) J.; B.S., U. Mich., 1922, M.D.,1929; m. Margaret Newell Woodwell, June 10, 1926;children—Richard W., Robert F., Marjory A. Intern U. Mich. Hosp., 1929-30, resident, 1930-32; practice medicine, specializing in cardiology, Ann Arbor, Mich., 1932-71; with Heart Sta. U. Hosp., 1932-71; sec. Med. Sch. U. Mich., 1943-48, mem. exec. bd. Grad. Sch., 1959-64. Served with U.S. Army, 1918. Recipient Henry Russel award U. Mich., 1937-38; James B. Herrick award Am. Heart Assn., 1969. Mem. Assn. U. Cardiologists (past pres.), Central Soc. Clin. Research, N.Y. Acad. Scis., Am. Heart Assn. (served on research com. many years. Mem. editorial bd. Virculation. Home: Ann Arbor MI Died Apr. 8, 1971; buried Washtenong Meml. Park, Ann Arbor MI

JOHNSTON, HARVEY POLLARD, telephone co. exec.; b. Rossmoyne, O., Jan. 5, 1903; s. John Harvey and Elizabeth (Birrel) J.; ed. pub. schs.; m. Yvonne Henrietta Verney, June 8, 1944. With Cin. & Suburban Bell Telephone Co., from 1920, v.p. charge personnel and pub. relations, 1951-55, v.p. operations, from 1955, also dir.; with Am. T. & T. Co., 1943-44. Div. chmn. Cin. United Appeal, 1953, met. area chmn., 1954. Mem. Armed Forces Communications and Electronics Assn., Engring. Soc. Cin. Mason. Club: Queen City (Cin.). Home: Milford OH Died Nov. 24, 1971.

JOHNSTON, KILBOURNE, forest products company executive; born in Fort Clark, Texas, on April 17th, 1907; the son of Hugh Samuel and Helen (Kilbourne) J.; B.S., U.S. Mil. Acad., 1928; LL.B., Columbia, 1932; m. Dorothy May Ward, June 30, 1928; 1 son, Hugh Samuel. Commd. 2d lt., inf., U.S. Army, 1928, advanced through grades to col., 1942; asst. gen. counsel NRA, 1933-35; asst. adminstr. WPA, N.Y.C., 1935-36; with Judge Adv. Gen. Dept., 1936; mem. gen. staff G-1 Sect., 1939; asst. dir. Nat. Selective Service System, 1940; asst. sec. Army Navy Munitions Bd., 1941; dep. dir. control div. ASF War Dept., 1942-44; base comdr. S.W. Pacific Area, 1944; asst. G-4 Pacific Ocean Areas, 1945; dir. post war planning, legislative liaison div. War Dept. Gen. Staff, 1946; dir. mgmt. div. WDGS, 1947; asst. comptroller U.S. Army, 1948-50; ret., 1950; asst. dir. CIA, 1950-53; mgmt. cons., Washington, 1953-55; chmn. bd. Silverlith Corp., Washington, 1951-65; with Champion Papers, Inc., Hamilton, O., 1955-56, group exec. planning, adminstrv. services, 1961, v.p., group exec. mgmt. services, 1962-65, staff v.p., 1965-66; spl. asst. to chairman U.S. Plywood-Chamipon Papers, Incorporated, 1966-72. Decorated Legion of Merit with oak leaf cluster, Bronze Star medal with combat V. Mem. Tech. Assn. Graphic Arts, Am. Mgmt. Assn., Ret. Officers Assn. Clubs: Army and Navy, Internat. (Washington); Army-Navy Country (Arlington, Va.). Home: Santa Cruz CA Died Jan. 12, 1972.

JOHNSTON, LESLIE MORGAN, business exec.; born Whitesboro, N.Y., Oct. 4, 1876; s. Elliott Waters and Emily Jerusha (Clark) J.; student Mt. Hermon (Mass.) Prep. Sch., 1892-98; A.B., Yale, 1902; m. Rebekah Jane Friend, June 18, 1927. Asst. mgr. A. M. Byers Co., Pittsburgh, 1902-09. gen. mgr., 1909-16, gen. mgr. and treas., 1916-19, vice pres., 1919-30; pres. Keystone Driller Co., Beaver Falls, Pa., 1932-35, Cement Stone Corp., Pittsburgh, 1938-41, Insulmastic Corp. of American, N.Y. City, 1941-44; re., 1944; dir. Excello Corp., Detroit, since 1931. Dir. Pub. Works, in mayor's cabinet, City of Pittsburgh, 1934-36. Served as capt. Inf. Training Bn., Plattsburgh, 1917-18. Mem. Scroll and Key. Alpha Beta Phi. Christian Scientist. Clubs: Duquesne, Pittsburgh Golf, Allegheny Country; Rolling Rock. Professional baseball player in minor leagues, 1896-1901, varsity coach, Yale, 1901-02. Home: 421 Woodland Rd., Sewickley PA‡

JOHNSTON, MARIA ISABELLA, author; b. Fredericksburg, Va.; d. Judge Richards and Julia Miller (Johnston) Barnett; ed. pvt. schs., Vicksburg, Miss., and St. Louis, and pvt. lessons from Dr. J. G. Holland (the poet); studied art in Europe; m. Vicksburg, Charles L. Buck, 1856 (died); 2d, Vicksburg, Dr. William R. Johnston, 1866 (now deceased). Lectures to classes of ladies on history, lit., art and current topics; advocate of and writer for woman suffrage. Reporter and corr. St. Louis Globe-Democrat several yrs., beginning 1879; contbr. New Orleans Times-Democrat and Picayune, 1882-6; editor St. Louis Weekly Spectator, 1891-4. Founder and leader St. Louis Chart Club; mem. D.A.R. Unitarian. Author: The Siege of Vicksburg, 1872; Oh, Come to the West, Love, 1880; Miss Emily's Glove, 1883; Hector, 1904. Address: 5714 Vernon Av., St Louis‡

JOHNSTON, RICHARD HALL, laryngologist; b. Tarboro, N.C., Apr. 6, 1871; s. W. H. and Caroline J.; M.D., U. of Md. Sch. of Medicine, 1894; m. Mary Page Small, of Baltimore, Dec. 21, 1904. Practiced in Baltimore since 1897; clin. prof. largngology, U. of Md. Sch. of Medicine, since 1909; attending laryngologist, U. of Md. Hosp.; laryngologist, St. Joseph's German Hosp.; consulting laryngologist, South Baltimore Eye, Ear, Nose and Throat Hosp., Children's Hosp. Sch., James Lawrence Kernan Hosp.; visiting laryngologist, Havre de Grace Hosp., etc. Fellow Am. Coll. Surgeons; mem. Am. Acad. Ophthalmology and Oto-Laryngology, Am. Laryngol., Rhinol. and Otol. Soc. Democrat. Episcopalian. Address: 807 N. Charles St., Baltimore MD‡

JOHNSTON, ROBERT BORN, banker; b. Rock Falls, Ill., June 21, 1910; s. Robert Ewer and Alda Halderman (Born) J.; S.B., Harvard, 1932, M.B.A., 1934; student Kent Coll. Law. With First Nat. Bank of Chgo., 1934-67, v.p., 1959-67; pres., dir. Johnston Lumber Co., Annawan, Ill., 1944-67; dir. 40-50 W. Schiller St. Corp.; chmn. Midwest Stock Exchange Clearing Corp. Served as pvt. AUS, 1941; to lt. comdr. USNR, 1942-46. Mem. Transportation Association of America (mem. board dirs.). Clubs: Harvard, Harvard Business, Racquet (past pres., gov.), Attic (Chgo.); Shoreacres Lake Bluff, Ill. Home: Chicago IL Died June 5, 1967.

JOHNSTON, SAMUEL M., lawyer; b. Shubuta, Miss., Oct. 13, 1890; s. Arista and Mary (McCoy) J.; student Miss. State Coll., 1906-08; B.S., U. Miss., 1911, LL.B., 1911; m. Ruth Ulmer, Dec. 29, 1912 (deceased October 1963); children—Annie Ruth (Mrs. Sam S. Foshee), William E., J. Sydney, Samuel M.; m. second, Dorothy Addison Parker, Oct. 17, 1964. Admitted to Alabama bar, 1918, practiced in Mobile, special justice, Supreme Ct. of Ala., 1933; special asst. to atty. gen. U.S., 1941-53. Chmn. Mobile Gas Service Corp. Bd. commnrs. Alabama Bar Commn., 1936-45. Mem. Am. Bar Assn. (ho. of delegates, 1941-43), Ala. Bar Assn. (pres. 1940-41). Trustee Ala. Coll., 1931-54. Mem. Democratic party of Ala.; del. from Mobile Co. to State's Rights Conf., Birmingham, Ala., 1948; as chief counsel for States Rights Presdl. Electors and 1948, successfuly defended suits brought in State and Fed. Cts. to force them to vote for Truman and Barkley instead of Thurmond and Wright. Fellow Am. Coll. Trial Lawyers; mem. Newcomen Soc. of Eng. Methodist. Contbr. to law jours. Home: Mobile AL Died Aug. 14, 1969; buried Pincecrest Cemetery, Mobile AL

JOHNSTON, WILLIAM DRUMM, JR., geologist; b. Garrett, Ind., Nov. 3, 1899; s. William Drumm and Jessie Mae (Kane) J.; B.S., U. Chgo., 1921; Ph.D., George Washington U., 1933; m. Madelene A. Thomas, 1931; children—William Drumm Iii, John Thomson, Richard Thomas, Elizabeth Louise. Faculty dept. geology U. Cin., U. Ky., N.M. Sch. Mines, 1922-28; geologist U.S. Geol. Survey, 1928-41, chief sect. fgn. geology, 1945-48, chief Alaskan and fgn. geology br., 1949-51, chief fgn. geology branch, 1951-64, staff geologist, 1965-70; with Bd. Econ. Warfare, Brazil, 1942-45. Del., 3d Pan-Am. Consultation on Cartography, Caracas, 1946; 2d Pan-Am. Congress Mining Engring. and Geology, Rio de Janeiro, 1946; U.S. govt. delegation Internat. Geol. Congress, Eng., 1948, Algiers, 1952, Mexico, 1956, Denmark, 1960, New Delhi, India, 1964, Prague, Czechoslovakia, 1968; del. to 4th Empire Mining and Metall. Congress, Eng., 1949; adv. Joint Brazil-U.S. Tech. Commn., Rio de Janeiro, 1948; chief U.S. Geol. Mission to Thailand, 1949-50; del. Indian Sci. Congress, Bangalore, 1951, centenary of Geol. Survey of India, Calcutta, 1951; adviser coms. on iron and steel and indsl. devel. Econ. Commn. for Asia and Far East, Lahore, 1951, chmn. U.S. delegation 1st Symposium on Devel. Petroleum in Asia, Delhi, 1958, adviser 2d Symposium, Tehran, 1962, 3d Symposium, Tokyo, Japan, 1965, Canberra, Australia, 1969; chmn. U.S. delegation Seminar on Devel. and Use Natural Gas in Asia, Tehran, 1964; del. working party geol. map Asia, ECAFE, Calcutta, 1957, Tokyo, 1960, Manila, 1963, Bangkok, 1966, Terhan, 1968; del. Nat. Acad. Sci., Pacific Sci. Congress, Bangkok, 1958, Tokyo, 1966; observer 4th Inter-Territorial Geol. Conf., Entebbe, 1951; Inter-Guianean Geol. Conf., Georgetown, 1959; adviser conf. on application sci. and tech. for benefit underdeveloped nations UN, Geneva, 1963; del. UNESCO Conf. on Application Sci. and Tech. to Devel. Latin Am., Santiago, Chile, 1965; v.p. for N.A., Internat. Geol. Congress Commn. for Geol. Map of World, 1956-66; mem. U.S. Commn. Geology, 1961-72; pres. sub-com. for Metallogenic Map of World, 1957-72; mem. NAS-NRC com. Inter-Am. Sci. Coop., 1960-62, Latin Am. Sci. Bd., 1963-69. Decorated Cruizeiro de Sul (Brazil), 1952; recipient Distinguished Service medal Dept. Interior, 1959; Jose Bonifacio de Andrade medal Geol. Soc. Brazil, 1959, Leipold von Buch medal German Geol. Soc. 1963; named prof. honoris causa Fed. U. Rio de Janeiro (Brazil), 1970. Fellow Am. Acad. Arts and Scis., Geol. Soc. Am., Mineral. Soc. Am.; mem. Soc. Econ. Geologist (sec. 1938-41, v.p. 1957), Geol. Soc. Washington (pres. 1957), Pan-Am. Inst. Mining, Engring. and Geology (chmn. U.S. sect. 1948-49), Am. Rhododendron Soc., Sigma Xi; corr. mem. geol. socs. Argentina, Brazil, W. Germany, Peru, Brazil Acad. Sci. Clubs: Cosmos (Washington); Engenharia (Rio de Janeiro). Contbr. articles on geology and ore deposits to tech. jours. Home: Washington DC Died Nov. 5, 1972.

JOHNSTON, W(ILLIA)M ALLEN, writer, pub.; b. Palatine Bridge, N.Y., May 12, 1876; s. William Nevins and Elizabeth (Dolson) J.; A.B., Union Coll., N.Y., 1897; post-grad., U. of Mich., 1897-98; m. Anna A. Allaimbie, of Washington, Aug. 26, 1914 (died Oct. 16, 1918); m. 2d, Dorothy Ovens, of San Francisco, Sept. 21, 1921. Adv. and editorial work, Hampton Agency, New York, 1902-04; with Butterick Pub. Co., 1904-05, S. H. Benson, London, Eng., 1905-06; staff writer and contbr. to Hampton's Mag., Delineator, Century, American Mag., Munsey's, Harper's Weekly, New York (Sunday) Herald, 1906-10; writer for Nat. Citizens' League for banking reform, 1911-12; pres. Motion Picture News since 1913. Mem. Phi Beta Kappa, Alpha Delta Phi. Clubs: Alpha Delta Phi, University. Home: Beverly Hills CA‡

JOHNSTONE, ARTHUR EDWARD, composer; b. London, Eng., May 13, 1860; s. Frank E. and Minnie (DeFries) J.; was brought to America, 1868; ed. Coll. City of New York; studied piano with Dr. William Mason, and organ and theory with Samuel Prowse Warren and higher composition with Dr. Leopold Damrosch; m. Clara Archer Butler, June 28, 1885. Has made a specialty of composition including piano methods and music for pub. sch. text books; won medal, 1902, for best original setting of America," offered by Soc. of the Cincinnati. Composer, with Harvey Worthington Loomis, of all the music (6 books) comprising the Foresman System of Pianoforte Instruction," an innovation, utilizing the modern player piano as a means of teaching how to play the piano by hand; also with same, Lyric Music Series, 4 vols. Was exec. editor Art Publication Soc., dir. Progressive Series Teachers Coll. and prof. of harmony and lecturer on music appreciation, Washington U. summer sessions; now teaching harmony, composition and piano. Address: 21 N. Franklin St., Wilkes-Barre PA*‡

JOHNSTONE, BRUCE, lawyer; b. St. Paul, Minn., Sept. 25, 1876; s. Frederick and Wilhelmina (Kaiser) J.; LL.B., Chicago Coll. of Law, 1897; m. Elsie B. Leale, of San Francisco, Calif., Aug. 12, 1905. Admitted to Ill. bar, 1897, and began practice at Chicago; counsel to firm Burry, Johnstone, Peters & Dixon; dir. Standard Oil Co. of Ind. Mem. Am., Ill. State and Chicago bar assns., Phi Delta Phi. Clubs: University, Midday, Law, Quadrangle, Chikaming Country. Home: 5305 Greenwood Av. Office: 105 S. La Salle St., Chicago IL‡

JOHNSTONE, HENRY WEBB, company exec.; b. Mexico City, Mexico (parents U.S. citizens), Oct. 13, 1892; s. Andrew and Minnie S. (Webb) J.; grad. William Penn Charter Sch., 1912; A.B., Yale, 1916; m. Beatrice G. Grieb, June 9, 1917; children—Henry Webb, Barbara Grieb (Mrs. Edward W. Bennett). Instr. Middlesex Sch., Concord, Mass., 1916-17; various positions Colgate & Co., Jersey City, 1919-29; investment counselor Brookmire Econ. Service, N.Y.C., 1929-30; joined Merck & Co., mfg. chemists, Rahway, N.J., 1930, dir. planning, plant mgr., 1931-36, v.p., 1936-50, sr. v.p., May, 1950-57, director, 1945-57; member board dirs. Thomas Y. Crowell Company. Trustee Union Jr. Coll. Served as 1st lt., U.S. Army, 1917-19, with A.E.F., France. Decorated Croix de Guerre (France). Mem. Zeta Psi, Republican. Presbyn. Clubs: Baltusrol Golf; Yale (N.Y.C.). Home: Chesterton MD Died Apr. 5, 1971; buried St. Paul's Churchyard, Chestertown MD

JOLLES, OTTO JOLLE MATTHIJS, educator; b. Berlin, Germany, Mar. 14, 1911; s. Andre and Mathilde (Monckeberg) J.; student U. Leipzig, U. Hamburg; Ph.D., Heidelberg U., 1933; student Sorbonne (Paris), 1934; M.A., U. Coll. Wales, 1938; m. Hermione Reynolds, June 21, 1938; children—Arnold, Martin, Jan, Nicholas. Came to U.S., 1938, naturalized, 1945. Instr. German, U. Coll. Wales, 1935-38; faculty U. Chgo., 1938-62, successively instr., asst. prof., asso. prof., 1938-56, prof., 1956-62, chmn. com. on history of culture, 1958; vis. prof. U. Frankfurt, Germany, 1960; prof. German lit. Cornell University, 1962-68, chmn department of German literature, 1965-68. Mem. Lit Soc. Chgo. (pres. 1954-60), Modern Lang. Assn., Am. Assn. Tchrs. German. Author: Das Deutsche Nationalbewusstein im Zeitalter Napoleons, 1936 Goethes Kunstanschauung, 1957; book on Friedrich Schiller (pub. posthumously). Editor: Deutsche Beitrage zur Geistigen Uberlieferung. Editor, translator: Karl von Clausewitz: On War, 1942. Home: Ithaca NY Died July 15, 1968.

JOLLIFFE, CHARLES BYRON, electronics exec.; b. Mannington, W.Va., Nov. 13, 1894; s. Charles E. and Sallie (Vandervort) J.; B.S., W.Va. University, 1915 M.S., 1920; Ph.D., Cornell University, 1922; LL.D. W.Va. U., 1942; m. Ola Kiser, Sept. 21, 1918 (dec.) children—Jane, Julia (dec.) (twins). Instr. physics W.Va. U., 1917-20, Cornell U., 1920-22; with radio sect Bur. of Standards, Wash., D.C., 1922-30, serving as asst chief and actg. chief; chief engr. Federal Radio Commn and Federal Communications Commn., 1930-35; engr in charge RCA Frequency Bur., Radio Corp. of America, 1935-41; chief engr. RCA Laboratories, 1941 assistant to president, RCA, 1942, vice-president and chief engineer, RCA Manufacturing Co., Inc., 1942 chief engineer, RCA Victor Div., RCA, 1943-45; exec v.p. RCA in charge RCA Labs. Division, 1945-51, vice pres. tech. dir. RCA, 1951-59, also mgr. special systems and development dept.; director of RCA, National Broadcasting Company, Inc., RCA Comunications Inc.; developed frequency standards for measuring operating frequencies of radio stations; mem. 3d and 4th nat. radio confs.; tech. asst. U.S. del. Internat. Radio Conf., Washington, 1927; International Tech. Cons Committee on Radio Meeting, The Hague, 1929; U.S delegate to 2d meeting, Copenhagen, 1931, to Internat Telecommunications Conf., Madrid, 1932; chief tech adviser N. Am. Regional Radio Conf., Mexico City 1933. RCA rep. to internat. radio conferences, Paris 1936, Bucharest, 1937, Inter-Am. Radio Conf., Havana 1937, Internat. Telecommunications Confs., Cairo 1938, Atlantic City, 1947; chief electrical communications div., Nat. Defense Research Com 1940-44; sec. Industry Adv. Com., Bd. of War Communications, 1941-47. Chmn., Allocations Panel Radio Tech. Planning Bd., 1942-46. Profl. engineer New York. Fellow A.A.A.S., American Institute Electric Engineers, Institute Radio Engineers; Radio Club of America; member Sigma Xi, Phi Beta Kappa Presbyterian. Club: Cosmos (Washington). Home Olney MD Died July 16, 1970.

JONAS, CHARLES ANDREW, lawyer; b. Lincoln County, N.C., Aug. 14, 1876; s. Cephus Anderson and Martha Dianna (Scronce) J.; prep. edn., Ridge Acad. and Fallston Inst., both in Cleveland County, N.C. Ph.B., Univ. of N.C., 1902, law course, 1902-05; m. Rosa Petrie, Aug. 23, 1902; children—Lillian Celeste (Mrs. L. T. Gibson), Charles Raper, Donald Roosevelt

Admitted to North Carolina bar, 1906, and began gen. practice at Lincolnton; mem. Jonas & Jonas. Postmaster of Lincolnton, 1907-10; city atty., 1908-12; mem. N.C. Senate, 1915-19, N.C. Ho. of Rep., 1927-29; del. to every Rep. Nat. Conv. since 1916; asst. U.S. atty. Western Dist. of N.C., 1921-25; mem. Rep. Nat. Com. since 1927; mem. 71st Congress (1929-31), 9th N.C. Dist.; U.S. dist. atty., Western Dist. N.C., 1931-32; mem. N.C. Ho. of Reps., 1935-37. Rep. candidate for U.S. senator, 1938. Rep. Nat. committeeman, N.C., since 1927. Mem. bd. trustees Univ. of N.C. since 1917. Mem. Am., N.C. State and Lincoln County bar assns. Methodist. Odd Fellow, Rotarian; mem. Jr. Order United Am. Mechanics. Republican. Home: Lincolnton NC‡

JONAS, JACK HENRY, writer; b. Columbus, O., Nov. 6, 1917; s. Henry Walter and Cecilia (Allen) J.; B.S. in Journalism, Ohio State U., 1940; m. Anne Ellanor McClerkin, Nov. 5, 1952. Reporter, Zonesville (O.) News, 1941-42; reporter, asst. city editor Columbus Citizen, 1942-51; rewrite man Washington Star, 1951-55, daily columnist, 1955-57, travel editor, 1958-61; travel editor Am. Automobile Assn., 1961-68. Cons., Keep Am. Beautiful, Inc. Mem. Soc. Am. Travel Writers (chmn. standing com. on history 1967-68, chmn. S.E. chpt. 1959), Nat. Assn. Travel Orgns., Travel Research Assn., Internat. Assn., Columbus Zool. Soc., Am. Newspaper Guild, Sigma Delta Chi. Club: National Press (Washington). Home: Washington DC Died Aug. 29, 1968.

JONAS, RUSSELL E., coll. pres.; b. Sioux City, Ia., Feb. 9, 1902; s. Charles Edward and Elsie C. (Fry) J.; B.S. in Edn., Northern State Teachers Coll., Aberdeen, S.D., 1931; M.A., Ia. U., 1934, Ph.D., 1936; m. Lorena Sperry, June 28, 1932; 1 son, Maynard Allen. Rural sch. teacher, 1919-26; supt. schs., Meade County, S.D., 1929-32; dep. state supt. pub. instrn. S.D., 1932-33; dir. research, Ia. State Dept. Pub. Instrn., 1936-37, supervisor coll. teacher edn., 1937-42; pres. Black Hills Teachers Coll., Spearfish, S.D., from 1942. Mem. N.E.A., Am. Assn. Sch. Adminstrs., Phi Delta Kappa, Kappa Delta Pi. Republican. Methodist. Home: Spearfish SD Died Dec. 31, 1971; buried Rosehill Cemetery, Spearfish SD

JONES, ALBERT R., oil and gas producer; b. Pekin, Ill., Sept. 14, 1874; s. John Anthony and Ida (Bergstresser) J.; B.S., Northwestern U., 1899; B.L., Ill. Wesleyan Law Sch., Bloomington, 1902; m. Mabel Neer, June 30, 1904; children-Virginia Russel, Laurence. Vice pres. Colo. Interstate Gas Co., South Western Development Co.; pres. Mission Oil Co., West Tex. Gas Co., A. R. Jones Oil and Operating Co., Trojan Oil and Gas Co.; dir. Texoma Gas Co.; president Continental Building Corp., Lotus Oil Co. Trustee U. of Kansas City, Sunset Hill Sch. for Girls, Kansas City Art Inst., Kansas City Museum. Mem. Sigma Alpha Epsilon, Deru. Presbyterian. Clubs: University, Kansas City Athletic. Home: 5701 Mission Drive. Office: Land Bank Bldg., Kansas City MO‡

JONES, ARTHUR JULIUS, prof. edn.; b. Grinnell, Ia., Mar. 21, 1871; s. Publius Vergilius and Lavinia (Burton) J.; A.B., Grinnell (Ia.) Coll., 1893; student U. of Chicago, summer 1894; Ph.D., Teachers Coll. (Columbia), 1907; m. Ethel Louise Rounds, June 26, 1899; children—Burton Wadsworth, Donald Prentiss. Asst. in biology, Grinnell Coll., 1893-95; teacher of biology, Central High Sch., Minneapolis, 1895-98; supt. schs., Redwood Falls, Minn., 1898-1904; teacher Charlton Sch., New York, 1905-06; head Dept. of Edn., R.I. State Normal Sch., Providence, 1907-11; head Dept. of Edn., U. of Me., 1911-15; asst. prof. secondary education, 1915, professor, 1919-42, University of Pennsylvania, professor emeritus, 1942; professor edn., summer sch., U. of Chicago, 1919, Univ. of Wash., 1929, U. of Wis., 1931, U. of Hawaii, 1932, Cornell U., 1933; dir. U. of Pa. field courses in Brazil, 1939; prof. summer sch., U. of So. Calif., 1940, Chico (Calif.) State Coll., 1948, U. Colo., 1949. Member N.E.A., Nat. Soc. Con. Teachers of Edn., Nat. Soc. for Study of Edn., Nat. Vocational Guidance Assn., Phi Beta Kappa, Phi Kappa Phi, Phi Delta Kappa, Kappa Phi Kappa. Presbyterian. Wrote Continuation Schools in the United States (bull. U.S. Bur. Edn.), 1907; Education and the Individual, 1926; Principles of Guidance, 1930, 35, 45; The Education of Youth for Leadership, 1938; Principles of Unit Construction (joint author), 1939; also various articles in ednl. mags. Home: Swarthmore PA‡

JONES, BRIAN, former mem. Rolling Stones. Home: Hartfield England Died July 3, 1969.*

JONES, CHARLES COLCOCK, III, mining and metall. engr.; b. Augusta, Ga., July 28, 1865; s. Joseph and Caroline S. (Davis) J.; student U. of La. (now Tulane U.). New Orleans, 1882, La. State U., Baton Rouge, 1882-84; B.S., Lehigh U., Bethlehem, Pa., 1887; m. Elizabeth Clayton King, May 21, 1898. Asst. supt. blast furnace dept. Pa. Steel Co., Steelton, Pa., 1887-89; supt. and chemist Va. Nail and Iron Works. Reusens, Va., 1889-90; asst. engr., mine surveys corps. Flat Top Coal Land Assn. Pocahontas, 1890-91; mining and civil engr. Cranes Nest Coal and Iron Co. Dunn Coal Land Co., 1891-92; coal operator, Wise County, Va., 1892-96; examining engr. Southern States and Central America, 1896-98; operator of gold mine, Ga., 1897-99; cons. engr. and mine mgr. for Edward N. Breitung, Marquette, Mich. and v.p. and mgr. Mary Charlotte Co., 1899-1902; mining and examining engr., Mountain Copper Co., Keswick, Calif.; rehabilitated Iron Mountain Mine and controlled under ground fire conditions to permit of ore recovery and extraction, 1902-04; discovered and opened inter-mountain phosphate fields of Ida., Wyoming, and Utah, shipped first car of phosphate rock ever mined in west from Cokeville, Wyo., to Los Angeles; cons. engr. Salt Lake City, 1904-06. Moved to Los Angeles, 1906; associated with L.C. Dillman in Copper River, Alaska, properties; pres. and mgr. Compania Mexicana Pacifico de Fierro, iron property, in Michoacan, Mexico, also pres. and mgr. Frances Copper Mining Co., Calif.; owner Vulcan Iron Deposits, Kelso, Calif., until sold to Kaiser interests, June 1942, when its iron ore became initial supply for blast furnace of the Kaiser Co., Inc., Iron and Steel Div., Fontana, Calif. Mem. Am. Inst. Mining and Metall. Engrs., Mining Assn. of Southwest, Soc. Colonial Wars (Calif. chapter), Kappa Alpha (Southern), Sigma Xi. Episcopalian. Author of many articles in tech. publs., including Phosphate Rock in Ida. and Wyo., An Iron Deposit in the Calif. Desert Region, Iron Ores of the Southwest, The Discovery and Opening of a New Phosphate Field in the U.S. and The Pacific Coast Iron Situation; report on Western Phosphate Field, 1903-05, placed in National Archives on request of U.S. Dept. of Interior. Home: University Club of Los Angeles, 614 S. Hope St., Los Angeles 14‡

JONES, CHARLES F., chmn. bd. First Securities Corp., investment bankers. Address: Durham NC Died 1971.

JONES, CHARLES S., oil exec. Dir. Atlantic Richfield Co., Douglas Aircraft Co., Incorporated, Pacific Mutual Life Insurance Co. Home: Pasadena CA Died Dec. 9, 1970.

JONES, CHESTER MORSE, physician; b. Portland, Me., Mar. 29, 1891; s. Harry Lee and Maria Albertina (Morse) J.; B.A., Williams Coll., 1913, D.Sc., 1942; M.D., Harvard, 1919; m. Kathleen Holmes, June 7, 1920; children—Robert H., Elizabeth M. (wife of Dr. Sam L. Clark, Jr.), Anne K. (wife of Dr. Ward Stoops). Intern Mass. Gen. Hosp., 1918-19, various staff positions, 1919-57, bd. consultants, 1957-64, honorary physician, 1964-72; member of the faculty Harvard Med. Sch., 1921-72, clin. prof. medicine, 1940-57, prof. emeritus, 1957-72, also spl. cons. to dean; William O. Moseley Jr. traveling fellow (Harvard) to Strasbourg, France, 1924-25, Henry Pickering Walcott fellow clin. medicine, 1925-28; acting asso. prof. medicine Vanderbilt U., 1940-41; cons. medicine Surg. Gen. U.S. Army, 1944-46; mem. Unitarian Service Com., Med. Missions to Austria, Greece, Italy, 1947-48. Recipient Rogerson cup and medal Williams Coll., 1956; Shattuck lectr. Mass. Med. Soc., 1958. Diplomate Am. Bd. Internal Medicine (chmn. 1955-57), Fellow Royal Coll. Physicians and Surgeons of Can. (hon.); mem. Am. Soc. for Clin. Investigation, Assn. Am. Physicians, Harvard Med. Alumni Assn. (pres.-elect), Am. Gastroenterological Soc. (pres. 1936), Am. Clin. and Climatological Soc. (pres. 1951), A.C.P. (member of board of regents; mastership 1958; pres. 1961-62). Author: Digestive Tract Pain, 1938. Editorial bd. New Eng. Jour. Medicine, Gastroenterology, Annals of Internal Medicine. Author med. articles on digestive tract physiology and disease. Home: Boston MA Died July 1972.

JONES, CYRIL HAMLEN, educator; b. Bournemouth, Eng., Mar. 28, 1893; s. Richard Hamlen and Augusta Marilla (Currier) J.; came to U.S., 1893; A.B., Harvard, 1915; m. Frederica Vanderbilt Webb (Pulitzer), Aug. 12, 1924 (died 1949). Entered U.S.N.R., 1917, commd. ensign, 1918; communications officer, London, 1918, E. M. House Mission and Peace Conf., 1918-19; flag lt. to high commr., Near East, 1919-20; watch officer, U.S.S. Biddle, 1920-21; ret. 1921; instr. Milton (Mass.) Acad., 1923-37, dir. admissions, 1937-41, asso. headmaster, 1941-42, headmaster, 1942-46, ret. 1946, trustee, 1942-48; overseer Browne and Nichols Sch., Cambridge, Mass., 1950-53, pres. bd. overseers, 1953, trustee, 1953-59. Incorporator and nat. v.p. Arthritis and Rheumatism Found., N.Y.C., 1948-56, exec. com., 1948-56, dir., 1956-72, N.E. pres., 1950-54, chmn. Mass. chpt., 1951-53, hon. chmn., 1953-72, hon. chmn. Vt. chpt., 1951-53. Pres. Boston Music Sch., Inc., 1955-59, mgr., 1955-72. Mem. Headmasters Assn. (hon.). Clubs: Union, Harvard (Boston); Century Assn. (N.Y.C.); Wianno. Home: Cotuit MA Died Oct. 8, 1972.

JONES, E(MMETT) MILTON, editor; b. Kingston Springs, Tenn., Oct. 10, 1874; s. Edward Tatun and Florence (Zettiger) J.; ed. Paducah, Ky.; spl. student U. of Ky., and Meadville Theol. Sch.; m. Anna Belle Radant, of Milwaukee, July 31, 1904. Directing editor Ency. of Original Documents (20 vols.), 1896— (Columbia U. Press); mgr. Kable Bros. Co., 1915-18; mgr. Business Science Inst.; exec. sec. Business Science Soc.; pvt. sec. Arthur Frederick Sheldon. Sec. The Civics Soc.; mem. Acad. Polit. Science, Am. Econ. Assn., A.A.A.S. Address: Republic Bldg., Chicago IL‡

JONES, EDWARD PERRY, clergyman; b. Cayuga, Miss., Feb. 21, 1872; s. George Perry and Louvenia M. J.; B.S., Natchez Coll., 1889 (D.D., also D.D., Rust U., 1892); m. Harriet Lee Wynn, of Greenville, Miss., Nov. 19, 1896. Ordained Bapt. ministry, 1894; pastor Mt. Heroden Ch., Vicksburg, Miss., 1902-18, Mt. Zion Ch., Evanston, Ill., 1918—. Pres. Nat. Bapt. Conv., 1915— (purchased Nat. Theol. Sem. and Training Sch., at Nashville, under his administration). Alternate del. Rep. Nat. Conv., 1917; chmn. Rep. State Conv., Miss., 1912. Home: 1104 Ayars Pl., Evanston IL‡

JONES, EDWIN LEE, constrn. exec.; b. Charlotte, N.C., June 10, 1891; s. James Addison and Mary Jane (Hooper) J.; A.B., Trinity Coll. (now Duke Univ.), 1912; LL.D., Wofford College, Spartanburg, South Carolina, 1957, Taylor University, 1963; m. Annabel Lambeth, June 15, 1915; children—Louise Lambeth (Mrs. W. Franklin Brown), Edwin Lee. Entered constrn. business with father, 1912, sec.-treas., J. A. Jones Constrn. Co., 1920-48, gen. manager, 1940-48, president, 1948-60, chairman of board, 1960-71; constructed military air base, Canal Zone, 1930-31, gaseous diffusion plant, Oak Ridge, Tenn., 1942-45; engaged in other constrn. work for Atomic Energy Commn., also constrn. of dams, and fgn. work in Okinawa, Ecuador, El Salvadore, Honduras, Venezuela, Colombia, Panama, Iraq, Canada, Alaska, others; dir. Research Triangle Corp. of North Carolina. Commr., chmn. Charlotte Housing Authority, 1938-68; hon. consul Republic Panama, 1932-48; mem. official observation group, Manhattan District, Bikini, July 1946; member, Spl State Capitol Bldg. Commn. of N.C., 1945-47; mem., Gen. Commn. World Service and Finance, Meth. Ch., 1944-48, 48-52, 52-56, 56-60, 60-64, Meth. Ecumenical Conf., 1947, 51, Gen. Conf., 1948, 52, 56, 60, 64, 66, 68, Jurisdictional Conf., 1948, 52, 56, 60, 64, 68; treas., exec. com. Meth. World Council, 1951-71. Dir., chmn. Charlotte Goodwill Industries, 1964-71; trustee, chmn. Florence Crittenton Home, Charlotte, 1945-48, 1950-51; trustee, Duke U. Lake Junaluska Assembly (chmn. bd. 1948-68), Brevard Jr. Coll. (bd. chmn. 1947-60), Am. U., 1960-64, Methodist Home for Aged, Charlotte, North Carolina Coll., Durham, N.C., 1956-60; director Charlotte Y.M.C.A., 1942-72, pres., 1946-47; N.C. state chmn. Crusade for Freedom, 1950. Mem. North Carolina Atomic Energy Committee. Member Meth. Hall Fame in Philanthropy, 1951. Mem. Asso. Gen. Contractors of Am. (pres. Carolinas br. 1945-46), also mem. Tau Beta Pi. Methodist. Clubs: Engineers (Charlotte, North Carolina); Engineers Alumni (Duke Univ.), Charlotte Kiwanis, City, Charlotte Country Charlotte NC Died Oct. 22, 1971; buried Evergreen Cemetery, Charlotte NC

JONES, ELEANOR LOUISE, librarian; b. West Newton, Mass., Oct. 11, 1875; d. Henry Augustus and Anna Maria (Snow) Jones; student Amherst (Mass.) Summer Library Sch., 1894, Library cataloguer, U.S. and Can. (35 libraries), 1895-1910; asst., Mass. State Library, 1910-12; gen. sec. Mass. Library Commn., 1913-20; library adviser, Mass. Div. Pub. Libraries, since 1920. Pres. Mass. Library Club, 1927; treas. Mass. Library Aid Assn. since 1918. Mem. A.L.A., N.E. Sch. library Assn. Unitarian. Clubs: Women's City, Womans Republican, Western Mass. Library, Old Colony Library, Cape Cod Library, Old Dartmouth Library, Bay Path Library, Charles River Library, Conn. Valley Library. Contbr. to professional mags. Home: 395 Lexington St., Waltham MA‡

JONES, ELI STANLEY, missionary; b. Balt., Jan. 1, 1884; s. Albin Davis and Sarah Alice (Peddicord) J.; A.B., Asbury Coll., 1906, A.M., 1912; D.D., Duke U., 1928; S.T.D., Syracuse U., 1928; m. Mabel Lossing, Feb. 11, 1911; 1 dau., Eunice Treffry (Mrs. J.K. Mathews). Evangelist to high castes of India, 1907-73; elected bishop M.E. Ch., 1928, resigned to continue missionary work; founder two Christian Ashrams at Sat Tal and Lucknow, India, a Psychiatric Center at Lucknow, also active Christian Ashram Movement U.S. and Europe. Chmn. Assn. for United Ch. Am. Author: The Way, 1948; Mahatma Gandhi; An Interpretation, 1948; The Way to Power and Poise, 1950; How to be a Transformed Person, 1951; The Word Became Flesh, 1966; Victory Through Surrender, 1967; A Song of Ascents, 1968; also numerous others. Contbr. articles to Christian Herald Christian Advocate. Address: New York City NY Died Jan. 26, 1973.

JONES, ELIOT, economist; b. Grinnell, Ia., Feb. 12, 1887; s. Richard Davies and Carrie Holmes (Grinnell) J.; A.B., Vanderbilt U., 1906; A.M., Harvard, 1908, Ph.D., 1913; m. Amy Eleanor Jenckes, June 20, 1914 (dec.); 1 son, Eliot; m. 2d, Isabel Charles, June 17, 1929; m. 3d, Mabel Ross. Instr. Harvard, 1912-13, U. of Pa., 1913-14; asso. prof. economics, Ia. State U., 1914-16; prof. economics U. of Tex., 1916-17; asso. prof. economics, Stanford U., 1917-20, prof. from 1920; McKinley prof. economics of public utilities, U. of Ill., 1924-25; prof. economics, U. of Calif., summers 1920, 21, 24, U. of Chicago, summer 1925, U. of Mich., summer 1933, Harvard, summer 1936, U. of N.M., summer 1942, U. of Wash., spring, 1949. With Federal Trade Commn., summer 1917, War Industries Bd., summer and fall, 1918. Fellow Royal Econ. Soc.; mem. Am. Econ. Assn. (v.p. 1925, 31), Pacific Assn. of Schs.

of Business and Depts. of Economics (pres. 1923). Phi Beta Kappa, Sigma Nu. Methodist. Author: The Anthracite Coal Combination in the U.S., 1914; The Trust Problem in the U.S., 1921; Principles of Railway Transportation, 1924; Principles of Public Utilities (with T.C. Bigham). 1931; and articles on economic subjects. Editor: Railroads—Cases and Selections (with H. B. Vanderblue), 1925. Home: Menlo Park CA Died Oct. 17. 1971.

JONES, ELMER ELLSWORTH, ednl. psychology; b. Pennville, Ind., May 31, 1866; s. Edmund Davis and Jennie (Harper) J.; A.B., Monmouth (Ill.) Coll., 1894; A.M., U. of Colo., 1900; Ph.D., Columbia, 1908; univs. of Leipzig and Heidelberg, 1905-07; m. Vera Brown, June 14, 1911; children—Elmer Ellsworth, Dan Brown; married 2d, Mrs. Helena White, July 7, 1946. Professor edn., State Normal School, Farmville, Va., 1902-08; prof. ednl. psychology, Ind. U., 1908-14; head dept. of edn., Northwestern U., Evanston, Ill., 1914-19; dir. Sch. of Edn., same univ., 1919-24, prof. edn., 1924-31; dir. Denver Psychol. Laboratory since 1931. Second lt. in Clendenin's Provisional Regiment from State of Ill., Spanish-Am. War. Progressive Democrat. Methodist. Mem. N.E.A., A.A.A.S., Am. Psychol. Assn., Am. Soc. Coll. Teachers of Edn., Sigma Xi. Clubs: University, Adventurers (Chicago). Author: The Influence of Bodily Posture on Mental Activities, 1908; Principles of Character Education, 1933. Home: 3040 E. Wesley, Denver CO‡

JONES, EVAN J., ex-congressman, lawyer; b. Shamokin, Pa., 1872, grad. Clarion (Pa.) Normal Sch., 1892; LL.B., Dickinson Law Sch., 1898; mem. 66th and 67th Congresses (1919-23), 21st Pa. Dist. Vice pres. and chmn. exec. com. Emporium Lumber Co. and Emporium Forestry Co.; dir. and gen. counsel Grasse River R.R. Corpn. Home: Bradford PA‡

JONES, EVELYN TUBB, bus. exec.; b. McMinnville, Tenn.; d. Monroe Mason and Sallie (Green) Tubb; grad. high sch., McMinnville Bus. Coll., 1943; m. Evelyn Jones (div.); 1 dau., Patricia Ann. Cost accountant Avalon Dairies, Avalon Cheese Co., McMinnville, Tenn., 1945-69, Eagle Pass Cheese Co., Albany, Ky., 1955-69, Avalon Cheese Co., London, Ky., 1964-69, Ardmore, Tenn., 1966-69, bd. dirs., sec.-treas. 1948-69. Club: McMinnville Country. Home: McMinnville TN Died Jan. 1969.

JONES, FLOYD WILLIAM, transportation and radio co. exec.; b. Lebanon, Mo., Jan. 22, 1891; s. John Lewis and Ellen Francis (O'Quinn) J.; grad. high sch.; m. Jessie Gadd, Apr. 21, 1920 (dec. 1949). Dir. Ozark Airlines, Inc., St. Louis, 1950-69, chmn. bd., 1958-68, chmn. emeritus, 1968-69; dir. Ozark Empire Dist. Fair. Served with U.S. Army, 1917-19. Home: Springfield MO Died Feb. 3, 1969; buried Lebanon MO

JONES, FRANKLIN ELMORE, b. Youngsboro, Lee Co., Ala., July 18, 1873; s. Samuel Goode and Aurora Serena (Elmore) J.; ed. U. of the South, Sewanee, Tenn., and Pernin Inst., Detroit, Mich.; m. Elise Marie Sophie Svitzer, of Copenhagen, Denmark, Jan. 19, 1926. Began as paying teller in main post-office, San Francisco, Calif., 1895; served as sec. to paymasters, U.S.N.; San Francisco and New York, and to treasurers and attorneys gen. of Porto Rico until 1922; master, examiner, court reporter, U.S. Court, Porto Rico; court reporter U.S. Court, Virgin Islands, 1923-26; agriculturist, emphasizing production of citrus fruits, tobacco and cotton. Long active in Dem. politics; del. from P.R. to 6 Dem. nat. convs.; mem. Dem. Nat. Com., Virgin Islands. Episcopalian. Odd Fellow, Elk. Clubs: Elks, Spanish Casino (Ponce and San Juan). Home: Calle Los Banos, No. 11, Santurce PR‡

JONES, GEORGE LEWIS, JR., government official; b. Baltimore, Jan. 18, 1907; s. George Lewis and Emma (Little) J.; grad. Boys' Latin Sch., Baltimore, 1925; B.S., Harvard, 1929; student Christ's Coll., Cambridge, Eng., 1929-30, London Sch. Economics, 1930-31; grad. Nat. War Coll., 1950; m. Polly Cooke, Nov. 30, 1935; children—Virginia Lewis, Christopher George Lewis, Andrew Calder Lewis. Began career as clerk to the United States comml. attache, assignments U.S. and abroad 1930-42; Near Eastern Div., Dept. of State, in charge Turkish Affairs, 1942-45; asst. chief Div. Nr. Eastern Affairs, 1945-46; assigned 2d sec., London, 1946, 1st sec., 1947; detailed to Nat. War Coll., 1949-50; mem. policy planning staff Dept. of State, 1950, dir. Office of Near Eastern Affairs 1950-52; consul general Tunis, 1952-53; counselor of embassy, Cairo, Egypt, 1953-55; deputy chief of mission, Tehran, with personal rank of minister, 1955-56; first U.S. ambassador to Tunisia, 1956-59; asst. sec. state, for Near East and South Asian affairs, 1959-61; minister Am. Embassy, London, Eng., 1961-64; coordinator Sr. Seminar in Fgn. Policy, Dept. State, 1964-71; spl. negotiator with personal rank of ambassador, 1964. Clubs: Chevy Chase, Metropolitan (Wash.); Travelers, Garrick, American (London, Eng.). Home: Washington 3DC also Yarmouth Port MA Died Nov. 13, 1971; buried Rock Creek Cemetery, Washington DC

JONES, HARRY BURNELL, lawyer, business exec.; b. Enfield, Ill., July 6, 1888; s. Wesley Livesey and Minda (Nelson) J.; student Howe Mil. Sch., 1904-06; A.B., U. Mich., 1910; student U. Wash., 1910-11; m. Beulah Faye Smith, Dec. 28, 1911 (dec. May 1966); children—Harry Burnell, Wallace, Roger; m. 2d, Mrs. Rena G. Pease, May 16th, 1967. Admitted to Wash. bar. 1911, since practiced in Seattle; partner firm of Jones, Grey, Kehoe, Hooper and Olsen, and predecessor firms, Seattle, Washington, since 1911; pres. Lake Union Drydock & Machine Works, 1942-46, Lake Union Drydock Co., from 1946; vice president of the Crescent Mfg. Co.; dir. Lang & Co., Pacific Textile Co., Seattle Tent & Awning Co., Yakima Tent & Awning Co.; president La Jolla Casa de Manana from 1948; mem. exec. com. Asso. Shipbuilders, 1942-45. Mem. Am. Bar Assn., Phi Delta Phi, Kappa Sigma. Clubs: Rainier, Seattle WA

JONES, I. HOWLAND, architect; b. Boston, Mass., May 22, 1868; s. Henry A. and Mary (Cranston) J.; studied in Europe, 1894-97; m. Edith Katherine Richie, May 17, 1913; 1 dau., Katharine Richie (Mrs. Peter Vosburgh). Associated with Andrews, Jaques & Rantoul, architects, Boston, Mass., 1898-1914; Mem. Andrews, Rantoul & Jones, 1914-45; sr. mem. firm Andrews, Jones, Biscoe & Goodell since 1945. Fellow A.I.A. Home: 10 Tucker St., Marblehead, Mass. Office: 50 Congress St., Boston MA‡

JONES, ILION TINGNAL, clergyman; b. Seymour, Tex., Oct. 28, 1889; s. Walter Albert and Alice Cary (McKeehan) J.; A.B., Trinity U., Waxahachie, Tex., 1913, D.D., 1928; B.D., McCormick Theol. Sem., Chicago, 1916; A.M., Columbia, 1917; m. Kate Salmon Prince, Oct. 15, 1919; children—Virginia Anne, Cary Margaret, Nancy Jane. Ordained ministry Presbyterian Church in U.S.A., 1916; pastor Third Avenue Presbyterian Ch., Corsicana, Tex., 1917-26, Madison Sq. Presbyn. Church, San Antonio, Tex., 1926-35, First Presbyn. Ch., Iowa City, Ia., 1935-45; vice pres. 1945-49, prof. practical theology, San Francisco Theol. Sem., San Anselmo, Cal., from 1945. Author: Is There A God?, 1921; For Times of Crisis, 1931. Home: San Anselmo CA

JONES, JAMES HAZLITT, educator; b. Spring Green, Wis., Dec. 18, 1896; s. Caradog and Mary Albina (Jones) J.; B.S., U. Wis., 1920, M.S., 1921, Ph.D., 1924; m. Charlotte J. Hermes, Dec. 29, 1928. Asst. U. Wis., 1920-24; mem. faculty U., Pa., 1924-71, prof. biochemistry, 1947-68, prof. emeritus, 1968-71, head labs biochemistry Sch. Vet. Medicine, 1957-71, dir. chem. lab. Pa. Hosp., 1942-47. Served to ensign USNR, 1918-19. Recipient Teaching plaque U. Pa. Mem. Am. Chem. Soc. Am. Soc. Biol. Chemists, Am. Inst. Nutrition. Contbr. articles to med. jours. Home: Upper Darby PA 19082

JONES, LAWRENCE CLARK, lawyer; b. Rutland, Vt., Aug. 10, 1893; s. Joseph C. and Alice H. (Long) J.; Worcester Poly. Inst., 1912-15; m. 2d, Clara H. Fitzpatrick, July 29, 1937. Admitted to Vt. bar, 1918, bar of Supreme Court of United States, 1935; practice at Rutland. States atty. Rutland County, Vt., 1925-31; attorney general of Vermont, 5 terms, 1931-41; chief enforcement atty. for Vt., Office of Price Adminstrn., May 26, 1942-Jan. 1, 1945; sec. Civil and Military Affairs, 1945. President National Assn. Attorneys Gen. 1939-40; former dir. Interstate Commn. on Crime; former mem. board mgrs. Council of State Govt., past chmn. Vt. Commn. on Interstate Cooperation; Vt. commr. Nat. Conf. Com. of Uniform Laws. Mem. Am. Judicature Soc., Am., Vt. (pres.) bar assns., Phi Sigma Kappa. Republican. Conglist. Mason (Shriner, past potentate). Home: Rutland VT Died July 9, 1972.

JONES, LEWIS HOWEL, lawyer, judge, b. Brigham, Utah, Feb. 22, 1900; s. Brigham Howel and Melvina (Christensen) J.; student pub. and pvt. schs.; m. Lucille Reeves, May 28, 1929; children—Betty, Ann, Patty, Lewis Howel. Admitted Nev. bar 1922; practiced Brigham, Utah, 1922-36; county atty. Box Elder Co., 1929-36; dist. judge, Utah 1937-69. Served as pvt. inf., U.S. Army, 1918; col., AUS, 1941-48. Mem. Am., Utah, Nev. bar assns. Democrat. Elk. Mem. Ch. Jesus Christ-Latter Day Saints. Rotarian. Home: Brigham UT Died Sept. 11, 1969.

JONES, LOUIS R., ret. marine corps officer; born Philadelphia; s. William F. and Katharine (Reeder) J.; married Rhita Wilmer Thomas, Aug. 8, 1917; children—Virginia Thomas (wife of Lt. Col. Edwin C. Godbold, U.S.M.C.), Robert Alexander (2d lt. U.S.M.C.), Mary Elizabeth. Enlisted U.S.M.C., Dec. 14, 1914, commd. 2d lt., July 5, 1917, and advanced through the grades to maj. gen., ret., 1949; pres. Marine Corps Equipment Board. Decorated Silver Star with oak leaf cluster, Purple Heart, Navy Cross, Legion of Merit with gold star and oak leaf cluster (U.S.), Croix de Guerre (France), Cloud and Banner (China). Mason. Mem. National Sojourners. Club: Army-Navy (Washington). Home: Arlington VA Died Feb. 2, 1973.

JONES, NARD, author; b. Seattle, Apr. 12, 1904; s. Nelson Hawk and Edythe (Benedict) J.; A.B., Whitman Coll., Walla Walla, Wash., 1926; m. Elisabeth Dunphy,

June 21, 1928 (dec.); 1 son, Blair Anthony; m. 2d, Anne Marie Mynar, Nov. 21, 1942; children—Lawrie Anne, Deborah Anne. Reporter, Walla Walla Dally Bull., 1922-26; editor Pacific Motor Boat, 1926-40. Served to lt. comdr. USNR, 1940-44. Mem. Authors League Am., Zeta Phi Epsilon. Clubs: Internat. Flattie Yacht Racing Assn. (N.Y.C.); College (Seattle). Author: Oregon Detour, 1930; The Petlands, 1931; Wheat Women, 1933; All Six Were Lovers, 1934; West, Young Man, 1937; The Case of the Hanging Lady, 1938; Swift Flows the River, 1940; Scarlet Petticoat, 1942; Still to the West, 1946; Evergreen Land, 1947; The Island, 1948; I'll Take What's Mine, 1954; Ride the Dark Storm, 1955; The Great Command, 1959; Pacific Northwest, 1962; Seattle, 1972. Contbr. fiction to mags., indsl. writing on wood cellulose. Home: Bellevue WA Died Sept. 3, 1972.

JONES, NEWELL N., editor; b. Griswold, Ia., Feb. 7, 1905; s. Charles Rutgar and Susan Bates (McKinney) J.; A.B., U. Ia., 1927; m. Mary Kathryn Stephenson, Aug. 9, 1931. Reporter San Diego Sun, 1927-34; reporter Evening Tribune, San Diego, 1934-44, city editor, 1944-51, mng. editor, 1951-52; editorial page editor, 1952-71. Home: San Diego CA Died Mar. 7, 1971.

JONES, NORMAN EDWARD, iron and steel mfg. co. exec.; b. Sydney, Australia, Aug. 2, 1904; s. Edward J. and Eliza Esther (Swain) J.; honours diploma in chemistry, Newcastle (New S. Wales) Tech. Coll., 1925; D.Sc. (hon.), U. New S. Wales., 1955, U. Newcastle, 1966; m. Mabel Elizabeth Swainson, Nov. 17, 1928; 1 son, Ian Edward. With Broken Hill Proprietary Co. Ltd., Melbourne, Australia, 1921-72, chief gen. mgr., 1950-52, mng. dir., 1952-67, dir., 1967-72; dir. Nat. Bank of Australia, Ltd., Australian Paper Mfrs. Ltd., Colonial Mut. Life Assurance Soc., Ltd. Dep. chmn. Australian Adminstrv. Staff Coll.; v.p. Victorian Chamber Mfrs. Mem. council U. Melbourne; bd. dirs. Alfred Hosp., Melbourne. Hon. mem. Am. Iron and Steel Inst.; mem. Am. Inst. Mining, Metall. and Petroleum Engrs., Iron and Steel Inst. London (pres. 1967-68), Australian Inst. Mining and Metallurgy, Toorak Victoria Australia Died Aug. 10, 1972.

JONES, OLIVE M. (OLIVIA MARY), educator; b. New York, N.Y., Dec. 20, 1871; d. Jenkin and Mary (Knowles) Jones; student Hunter Coll., 1886-90, Cornell U., 1892, Teacher's Coll., Columbia, 1892-94, 1899-1902, Harvard, summers, 1890-1903; B.S., New York U., 1928; unmarried. Teacher N.Y. City Schs., 1891-1929, asst. and acting prin., 1903-04, prin., 1905-29; dir. Calvary House, New York, 1928-34; worker for Oxford Group, 1932-41. Formerly mem. N.Y. City Commn. on Teachers' Retirement, Commn. on Teachers' Salaries, Children's Code Commn. of N.Y. State, Friedsom Commn. for Financing Edn.; chmn. com. on pub. edn. Internat. Narcotic Assn., 1926-30; chmn. com. on behavior problems, Nat. Conf. Social Work, 1926-27; dir. Women's City Club of New York, 12 yrs.; chmn. ednl. program for Pro-America, nat. and state of Calif.; lecturer on social and ednl. subjects. Active in Democrat local politics New York until 1929. Hon. life mem. and dir. N.E.A., Acad. of Pub. Edn., New York Prins. Assn.; mem. World Fed. Edn. Assns.; New York U. Alumni Assn., League of Women Voters, Kappa Delta Pi. Episcopalian. Clubs: Friday Morning (Los Angeles); Writers Round Table (Hollywood). Author: Teaching Children to Study, 1907; Inspired Children (trans. into Norwegian, Danish, French, Dutch, Japanese), 1933; Inspired Youth, 1938; also numerous pamphlets on ednl., social and religious subjects. Contbr. to jours. Home: 1127 S. Bedford Dr., Los Angeles 35 CA‡

JONES, PETER SMITH, govt. ofcl.; b. Ehren, Fla., July 1, 1906; s. Aren E. and Eva (Smith) J.; grad. USMC Inst., 1933; m. Mildred M. Osley, Feb. 8, 1946; children—Thomas, Janet, Peter S. II. Served from pvt. to tech. sgt. USMC, 1928-35; with supply div. Treasury Dept., 1936-41; civilian contracts and supply officer U.S. Engrs., 1942-45; liason officer to U.S. Navy for plant conversion War Assets Adminstrn., 1945-46; exec. adminstrn., personnel officer Latin Am. posts, ICA, Dept. State, 1946-59; rep. of ICA to Venezuela, 1959-61; cons. Agy. for Internat. Devel., 1961-62; pub. ofcl. Dekalb County, Ga., from 1962. Decorated Condor de los Andes de Bolivia. Mem. Nat. Assn. Accountants, Nat. Assn. Purchasing Agts. Home: Decatur GA Died Apr. 7, 1972.

JONES, PHILIP HAROLD, physician; b. Jackson, La., Feb. 26, 1896; s. Philip Huff and Annabelle (Smith) J.; B.A., La. State U.; M.D., Tulane U., 1920; Ph.D. in Pathology (Rhodes scholar), Oxford (Eng.) U., 1924. Intern, Charity Hosp. of La., New Orleans, 1920-21, former mem. staff, mem. bd. adminstrs., cons. dept. medicine, until 1970; practice medicine specializing in internal medicine and cardiology, New Orleans, until 1970; mem. staff So. Baptist Hosp., New Orleans, until 1970, former pres. staff. chmn. exec. com., chmn. adv. com.; prof. emeritus Tulane U. Sch. Medicine, New Orleans, until 1970. Served with U.S. Army, 1917, 18. Diplomate Am. Bd. Internal Medicine. Fellow A.C.P. Am. Coll. Cardiology (past gov.); mem. A.M.A. (Ho. of Dels. 1955-70), La. (past pres., editor Jour. 1947-70) Orleans Parish (past pres.) med. socs., New Orleans

Grad. Med. Assembly (past pres.), Am. Soc. Internal Medicine, Am. Med. Writers Assn., So. Med. Assn., New Orleans Acad. Internal Medicine, Alpha Omega Alpha, Nu Sigma Nu. Episcopalian. Contbr. numerous articles to med. jours. Home: New Orleans LA Died Nov. 13, 1970; buried Grace Church Cemetery, St. Francisville LA

JONES, ROBERT FRANKLIN, lawyer, govt. ofcl.; b. Cairo, O., June 25, 1907; s. Jenkin C. and Josephine (DeVine) J.; LL.B., Ohio Northern U., 1929; m. Ida Marie Spreen, June 21, 1930; children—Robert Franklin, Jeraldine Marie. Admitted to Ohio bar, 1929, and began practice at Lima; pros. atty., 1935-39; mem. 76th to 80th Congresses (1939-49), 4th Ohio Dist.; appointed commr. of Fed. Communications Commn. for 7 yr. term, 1947, resigned as mem. Congress, 1947; commr. FCC, 1947-52; practice communications law, Washington, 1952-68; sr. partner Jones, Sells & Baker. Mem. Ohio State and Allen Co. bar assns., Delta Sigma Phi. Republican. Methodist. Mason, Odd Fellow, Eagle, K.P. Author: Who Pays for the New Deal's Propaganda?," Liberty Magazine, Sept. 14, 1940. Home: Silver Spring MD Died June 22, 1968; buried Memorial Cemetery, Lima OH

JONES, ROBERT TYRE, JR. (BOBBY JONES), golf champion; b. Atlanta, Mar. 17, 1902; s. Robert P. and Clara (Thomas) J.; prep. edn., Tech. High Sch., Atlanta; B.S. in M.E., Ga. Sch. of Tech., Atlanta, 1922; B.S., Harvard, 1924; studied law, Emory U., 1926-27; m. Mary Malone, June 17, 1924; children—Clara Malone Black, and Robert Tyre III, Mary Ellen (Mrs. Carl Hood, Junior). Admitted to Georgia bar, 1928, practiced in Atlanta; partner law firm Jones, Bird & Howell; v.p. Spalding Sales Corp., Chicopee, Mass. So. amateur golf champion, 1917, 20, 22; national amateur champion, 1924, 25, 27, 28, 30; British amateur champion, 1930; nat. open champion, 1923, 26, 29, 30; open champion of Gt. Britain, 1926, 27, 30; first official champion in nat. open championships of Gt. Britain and U.S. in the same season, and won both championships same season twice, 1926, 30. Served as lt. col. USAAF, 1944. Clubs: Capital City, Athletic, Piedmont Driving, Royal and Ancient, St. Andrew's; Augusta (Georgia) National Golf (pres.); Peachtree Golf. Author: Down the Fairway (with O. B. Keeler), 1927; Gold is my Game, 1960; Bobby Jones on Golf, 1966; Bobby Jones on the Basic Golf Swing, 1969. Office: Atlanta GA Died Dec. 18, 1971.

JONES, ROBERT VERNON, lawyer; b. Peterson, Ia., Sept. 16, 1901; s. Alonzo W. and Ada Marian (Dunn) J; A.B., Northwestern U., 1923, J.D., 1926; LL.D., Buena Vista Coll., Storm Lake, Ia., 1961; m. Elsie Pierce Brown, 1926 (div. 1963); children—Richard Vernon, Nancy Gwendolyn Green, David Owen, Robert Alonzo; m. 2d, Adelaide Peterson, 1963. Lectr. econ. Northwestern U., 1924-26; admitted to Ill. bar, 1926; law clk. firm Foreman, Bluford, Steele & Schultz, Chgo., 1926-28; partner firm Stearns & Jones, Chgo., 1928-42; practiced law, 1942-45; with U.S. group Control Council for Germany, 1945; past pres. Noble Mfg. Co.; v.p. Sac City State Bank; pres. R.V. Jones & Co., Inc.; prof. bus. and govt. Northwestern U. Sch. Commerce, 1946-48. Governing mem. Orchestral Assn., Chgo. Mem. Am., Ill., Chgo. bar assns., Am. Econ. Assn., Northwestern U. Asso., Order of Coif, Phi Beta Kappa, Alpha Delta Phi, Phi Alpha Delta. Clubs: Law, University (Chgo.); Glen View. Author: The Challenge of Liberty, 1956. Contbr. articles to mags. Home: Mundelein IL Dec. Jan. 29, 1973.

JONES, SAMUEL AUGUSTUS, statistician; b. Genoa, Ohio, Jan. 25, 1874; s. Noah Scarfield and Josephine (Brunner) J.; ed. pub. schs.; M.D., George Washington U. Dept. of Medicine, 1904; m. Ada Ellen Yost, of Toledo, O., Oct. 9, 1901; children—Lincoln Samuel, Bernice Josephine, Katherine Sarah, Ruth Pauline. Accountant Navy Dept., Washington, D.C., 1899-1907; agrl. statistician, Dept. of Agr. since 1907. Presbyn. Home: 2594 Wisconsin Av. Address: Dept. of Agriculture, Washington DC‡

JONES, THOMAS HUDSON, sculptor; b. Buffalo, N.Y., July 24, 1892; s. David and Ann Elizabeth (Hudson) J.; art edn., Albright Art Sch., Buffalo, 1906-11, Museum Sch., Boston, Mass., 1911-13, Carnegie Inst. Tech., 1913-14; fellow Am. Acad. in Rome, 1919-22; m. Mildred Dudley, Oct. 3, 1923; children—Anne Dudley, Kim Hudson, Peter R., June. Instructor Columbia University, 1924-29; prof. fine arts, Am. Acad. in Rome, 1932-33. Prin. works: Portchester (N.Y.) War Memorial; Tomb of the Unknown Soldier, Arlington Nat. Cemetery; bust of U.S. Grant, Hall of Fame, N.Y. City; bronze statue of Christ, St. Matthew Ch., Washington, D.C.; statue of Dr. Moore, Genesee Valley Park, Rochester, N.Y., bronze entrance grille for the Brooklyn Central Library; also Conquest of Yellow Fever" medal, N.Y. Univ. medal of honor, etc. Served with Med. Corps, U.S. Army, World War I. A.N.A., 1932; mem. Archeol. Soc. America, Alumni Am. Acad. in Rome, Nat. Sculpture Soc., Kent Art Assn. Awarded Prix de Rome, 1919. Sculptor for Office of the Quartermaster General. Episcopalian. Home: Hyannis MA Died Nov. 1969.

JONES, VICTOR OWEN, newspaper editor; b. Wallingford, Conn., Sept. 14, 1905; s. Rev. John Owen and Emma (Julbe y Molina) J.; grad. The Choate Sch., 1924; S.B., Harvard, 1928; Dr. Journalism (hon.), Suffolk University, 1960; married Elizabeth S. Weiss, Feb. 18, 1961; stepchildren—Paul S. Weiss, Robert H. Weiss, Louise Weiss. Staff writer The Boston Globe, 1929-33, sports editor, 1933-41, night editor, 1941-55, war corr., ETO, 1944-45, mng. editor, 1955-62, exec. editor, 1962-65. Trustee, mem. grad. bd. Harvard Crimson. Nieman fellow, 1941. Mem. Asso. Press Mng. Editors Assn., Am. Soc. Newspaper Editors, New England Society of Newspaper Editors, also Baseball Writers Assn. Am. (hon.), Charitable Irish Soc. Clubs: Harvard Faculty, Harvard (Boston). Dir. Harvard Alumni Bull. Home: Cambridge MA Died Apr. 21, 1970; buried Green-Wood Cemetery, Brooklyn NY

JONES, MRS. W.J. (MOLLIE ROBERTS JONES), teacher; b. Carbonton, N.C.; d. Bright and Mary A. (Jones) Roberts; grad. Guilford Coll. (N.C.), 1896; attended bus. coll., Baltimore and Columbia; m. G. Frank Edwards, Dec. 18, 1902 (died 1907); children—Lucy Roberts, Louise Osborne; m. 2d, William J. Jones, Nov. 24, 1908; children—Alice Freeman, Emma Smith. Bookkeeper, Baltimore, 1896-97; teacher in various schs. until 1902; with husband established, 1925, since co-pres. Pineland Coll., Salemburg, N.C. Mem. Equalization Fund Commn., 1927-29; del. to Inland Waterway Conv., Richmond, Va., 1928, Forestry Conv., 1929; mem. Dem. Exec. Com., 3d Congl. Dist., N.C., 1927-28. Pres. Farm Woman's Conv. of N.C.; head of home economics dept. N.C. Woman's Federated Clubs: mem. bd. dirs. Penderlea Homesteads. Baptist. Writer and lecturer on country life. Club: Salemburg Woman's (pres.). Home: Salemburg NC‡

JONES, WARREN FRANCIS, ret. univ. president; born Henry County, Ky., Sept. 3, 1896; s. William Henry and Amanda (Washburne) J.; B.S., Georgetown Coll., 1921, LL.D., 1945; student U. of Chicago, summer 1920, Peabody Coll., summer 1925 and by appt., 1945; M.S., U. of Ky., 1937; D. Humanics, Union University, 1963; m. Margaret LeCompte Scott, Aug. 27, 1925 (died 1942); children—Betty Ragland (Mrs. Robert Pearce), Warren Francis II, Billy Maurice, Peggy Frances (Mrs. David Gibson); m. 2d, Dr. Dixie Martin Marcum, Aug. 20, 1946; stepdaughter Jane Marcum (Mrs. Jimmy Matthews). Principal and coach, Pineville (Ky.) High School, 1921-22, principal, 1922-23; superintendent city schools, Pineville, 1923-26; pres. Campbellsville (Ky.) Junior Coll., 1926-30; prin. Winchester (Ky.) High Sch., 1930-36; State rep. in Ky. for Scott, Foresman Co., publishers, Chicago, 1936-41; president Campbellsville (Ky.) Coll., 1941-45, Union Univ., Jackson, Tenn., 1945-63; ret.; acting pres. Belmont Coll., Nashville, 1951-52. Chmn. ednl. commn. So. Bapt. Conv., 1955-56. Served with U.S. Army, 1918-19. Mem. So. Assn. Coll. and Secondary Schs. (mem. higher commission, 1953-59, mem. exec. com., 1955-58), Tennessee College Association (president 1950-51), Ky. Assn. Coll. and Secondary Schs. (mem. commn. 1942-45, chmn. 1945), Ky. Assn. Ch. Related Colls. (sec. 1943-44), Ky. Jr. Coll. Athletic Assn. (sec. 1941-45), Tenn. Endl. Assn., Am. Legion, Kappa Delta Pi, Lambda Chi Alpha. Clubs: Rotary (v.p. 1946-47, pres. 1947-48), Jackson (pres. 1947-48); Winter Park (Fla.) University; Central Fla. Executives. Contbr. articles to ednl. jours. Home: Maitland FL Died June 17, 1971; buried Winter Park FL

JONES, WILLIAM RUSSELL, physician; b. Orange County, Va., Jan. 18, 1870; s. Thomas Scott and Lillie Clark (Coleman) J.; M.D., U. of Va., 1892; Ph.G., Univ. Coll. of Medicine, Richmond, Va., 1894; m. Jane Taylor Fisher, Jan. 5, 1905 (died 1918). Began practice Richmond, 1892; prof. chemistry, toxicology and med. jurisprudence, Univ. Coll. of Medicine, Richmond, 1897-1906, lecturer in clin. medicine and asso. prof. practicing medicine, 1906-12; visiting physician Virginia Hosp., 1897-1912; visiting physician Retreat for the Sick Hosp.; chief med. adviser, chief surgeon Richmond, Fredericksburg & Potomac R.R., Co. In charge med. and surg. relief and suppression of influenza, U.S. Munition Bag Loading Plant, Richmond, World War I; cons. med. officer U.S. War Risk and Veterans' Bur., 1918-22; chief surgeon, maj. Med. Corps, Va. Nat. Guard, 1926. Mem. A.M.A., Med. Soc. Va., Richmond Acad. Medicine and Surgery, Assn. Ry. Chief Surgeons, Chesapeake & Ohio Assn. Ry. Surgeons, Assn. of Mil. Surgeons of U.S. Democrat. Episcopalian. Author: Abstract Lectures on Chemistry, 1899; A Textbook of Chemistry for Students of Medicine, Dentistry and Pharmacy, 1905. Home: 2701 Grove Av., Richmond VA‡

JOPLIN, JANIS, singer; mem. Big Brother and the Holding Company; named most popular female singer Jazz and Pop 3d Ann. Readers Poll. Home: Los Angeles CA Died Oct. 1970.*

JOPP, CHARLES B., banker; b. Winsted, Conn., Aug. 18, 1874; s. Charles S. and Jennie (Bradbury) J.; ed. pub. schs.; m. Harriet Veazie, of Chelsea, Mass., June 8, 1898. Began as messenger with Mercantile Trust Co., Boston, 1891, and became treas., 1899; asst. treas. City Trust Co., 1904-05; pres. Beacon Building Trust, Inc.; v.p. Atlantic Nat. Bank of Boston, F.W. Webb Mfg. Co.; dir. Federal Mutual Automobile Fire Ins. Co.; trustee Charleston Five Cents Savings Bank. Mem. Am. Bankers' Assn., Boston Credit Men's Assn. (dir.). Mason. Office: 31 Milk St., Boston MA‡

JORDAN, CLARENCE LORIN, educator; b. E. New Portland, Me., Jan. 20, 1877; s. John Taylor and Estella (Churchill) J.; A.B., Bates Coll., 1903, A.M., 1907. Taught sch. various places in Me., 1894-1902; traveled in Eng. and France, 1900; jr. sec. Brotherhood of St. Andrew in U.S., 1903; prin. Franklin Mil. Acad., Vt., 1904-6; prof. English and economics, Norwich U., 1906-7; founded Jordan Hall, 1907, mgr. and owner same. Address: St Albans VT‡

JORDAN, FRANK MORRILL, state govt. ofcl.; b. Alameda, Cal., Aug. 6, 1888; s. Frank Chester and Emma Dudley (Morrill) J.; student pub. schs., Cal.; m. Alice Kathryn Crossan, June 10, 1919 (dec. Feb. 1953); 1 dau., Mary Jane (Mrs. Robert E. Law); m. 2d, Alberta Stuzmann, May 28, 1955. Engr., Clara Constrn. Mining Co., Ariz., 1906-11, Auto Club of So. Cal., 1911-17, Western Pipe & Steel Co., San Francisco, 1919-21; partner Jordan-Archer Co., San Jose, Cal., 1922-26; owner Gen. Ins. Agy., Cal., Ore., Wash., 1926-33; dep. sec. state Cal., 1935, sec. state, 1942-70. Served from pvt. to 2d lt., U.S. Army, 1917. Mem. Nat. Assn. Secs. State, Native Sons Golden West, Am. Legion, Vets. Fgn. Wars. Republican. Mason (Shriner), Elk. Club: Jonathan (Los Angeles). Home: Sacramento CA Died Mar. 1970.

JORDAN, HARVEY HERBERT, prof. engring.; b. Waltham, Me., Mar. 7, 1885; s. Roland Herbert and Carrie Frances (Blake) J.; B.S. in C.E., U. of Me., 1910; grad. work U. of Ill., 1912-16; m. Sara M. Slater, Oct. 9, 1919; 1 dau., Donna Elizabeth. Asst. in civ. engring. U. of Me., 1910-11; with U. of Ill. since 1911 as instr., asso. and asst. prof. engring., drawing until 1921, prof. engring., drawing and head of dept. from 1922, asst. dean Coll. of Engineering, 1917-34, asso. dean from 1934. Alderman city of Urbana, Ill., 1921-27. Instr. schs. of Mil. Aeronautics and S.A.T.C., 1917-18. Mem. Am. Soc. C.E., A.A.A.S., American Soc. of Engring. Education (v.p. 1931-32), Ill. Soc. Prof. Engrs., Phi Eta Sigma, Tau Beta Pi, Phi Kappa Phi, Sigma Tau, Chi Epsilon, Triangle. Republican. Mason. Clubs: Kiwanis (Champaign-Urbana); University (Urbana). Author: Engineering Drawing (with R. P. Hoelscher), 1923; Descriptive Geometry (with F. M. Porter), 1929; also bull. The Pipe Orifice as a Means of Measuring the Flow of Water Through a Pipe (with R. E. Davis), 1918. Contbr. on engring. subjects. Home: Urbana IL

JORDAN, HARVIE, cotton planter; b. nr. Monticello, Jasper County, Ga., Jan. 1, 1861; s. William Fleming and Orpah Jane (Goolsby) J..; ed. common schs. of Ga. and Eastman Business Coll., Poughkeepsie, N.Y.; m. Ella Gerdine, Jan. 18, 1893; children—Emma, Clarence L., Evelyn, W. Ervin. Engaged in operating large cotton plantation in Jasper County, Ga.; agrl. editor Atlanta Daily and Semi-Weekly Journal, 1899-1906. Mem. Ga. House of Rep., 1898-1901, 1919-20, Senate, 1902-04 (chmn. com. on gen. agr. of House and Senate during entire period). Pres. Farmers Nat. Congress U.S.A., 1903-04, Southern Cotton Assn., 1905-08, Nat. Cotton Assn., 1909-10; mem. U.S. com. which visited Europe, 1913, to study farm finance, etc.; gen. sec. Am. Cotton Assn. since 1920, mng. dir. boll weevil control campaign. Democrat. Presbyterian. Mason. Home: 69 11th St. N.E., Atlanta GA‡

JORDAN, RICHARD HENRY, army officer; b. Haymarket, Va., Sept. 8, 1877; s. Charles Edward and Alice Melville (Moore) J.; student Va. Poly. Inst., 1893-97, C.E., 1919; student U.S. Mil. Acad., 1897-99; grad. Coast Arty. Sch., Fort Monroe, 1910; m. Frances Bell, Feb. 29, 1920. Commnd. 2d lt. Coast Arty., 1901, and promoted through grades to brig. gen., 1936; had charge of gold star mothers pilgrimage to Am. cemeteries in Europe, 1932-33; mil attache to Brazil, 1919-20; chief of Transportation Div., O.Q.-M.G., 1936-40. Awarded D.S.M. for World War service. Mem. Mil. Order of the World War, Mil. Order of Carabao. Democrat. Episcopalian. Clubs: Army and Navy, Army and Navy Country. Home: Washington DC Died Jan. 30, 1971; buried Arlington National Cemetery, Arlington VA

JORDAN, WEYMOUTH TYREE, educator; b. Hamlet, N.C., Oct. 31, 1912; s. William Daniel and Mary (Utley) J.; B.S., N.C. State Coll., 1933; M.A., Vanderbilt U., 1934, Ph.D., 1937; m. Louise Elizabeth Riggan, Aug. 11, 1935; children—Weymouth Tyree, Elizabeth H. Markowski, William Royster. Fellow history Vanderbilt U., 1934-37; prof. history, head dept. N.C. Indian Coll., 1937-38; from instr. to asso. prof. history, head dept. Judson Coll., 1938-42; asst. prof., then asso. prof., research prof. Auburn U., 1942-49; prof. history Fla. State U., 1949-68, head dept., 1954-64; vis. prof., head dept. history Transylvania Coll., 1936; tchr. summers Blue Mountain Coll., 1938, Stetson U., 1939, U. Okla., 1941, U. Mo., 1958.

Regional asso. Am. Council Learned Societies, 1957-59; adv. bd. Guggenheim Meml. Found., 1959-68; Fulbright-Hays prof. U. Erlangen (Germany), 1964-65. Recipient C.M. McClung award E. Tenn. Hist. Soc., 1939, 41; fellow Social Sci. Research Council, 1940, 41, 47, 50. Gen. Edn. Bd., 1947-48; Guggenheim fellow, 1957-58. Served to lt. comdr. USNR, 1943-45. Mem. Agrl. History Soc. (exec. council 1948-49, 59-67, pres. 1962-63), Fla. Hist. Soc., Am., Miss. Valley So. (chmn. membership com. 1948, program com. 1961, exec. council 1953-55) historical assns., Kappa Sigma, Kappa Phi Kappa, Phi Alpha Theta, Sigma Pi Alpha. Democrat. Episcopalian. Author: Hugh Davis and His Alabama Plantation, 1948; George Washington Campbell of Tenneessee, 1955; Ante Bellum Alabama, Town and Country, 1957; Rebels in the Making, Planters Conventions and Southern Propaganda, 1958; Herbs, Hoecakes and Husbandry, 1960; The United States, 1783-1861: From Revolution to Civil War, 1964; also articles. Editor: The Purchase of Florida (H.B. Fuller), 1964; bd. editors E. Tenn. Hist. Soc. Publs., 1947-52, Ala. Rev., 1948-50, Fla. State U. Studies, 1950-54, Agrl. History, 1957-62, Fla. Hist. Quar., 1959-63, Jour. So. History, 1961-64, So. Humanities Rev., 1966-68; co-editor Fla. State U. Studies, 1950-52, editor, 1952-54. Home: Tallahassee FL Died Nov. 22, 1968; buried Roselawn Cemetery, Tallahassee FL

JOSAPHARE, LIONEL, author; b. St. Louis, May 26, 1876; s. I. C. and Caroline J.; ed. pub. schs., San Francisco, 1886-90; studied law. Was in New York, 1898-1900; returned to San Francisco. Author: The Lion at the Well, 1901; Turquoise and Iron (poems), 1902; The Man Who Wanted a Bungalow, 1907; The World of Suckers, 1909; A Fictitious History of the World (serial), 1910; Modern Poster-painting, 1915. Was asst. editor The Wasp; asst. editor Town Talk, Mar. 1919-—. Address: 936 Leavenworth St., San Francisco CA‡

JOSEPHI, ISAAC A., artist; b. at New York; studied at Art Students' League, New York, and with Leon Bonnat, Paris. Painter of miniatures and landscapes; exhibited at many exhbns.; hon. mention, Paris Expn., 1900; silver medal, Charleston Expn., 1902. Ex-pres. Am. Soc. Miniature Painters; mem. Royal Soc. of Miniature Painters, London, Am. Water Color Soc. Club: Lotos. Home: 140 W. 57th St., New York NY‡

JOSEPHSON, CLARENCE EGBERT, coll. pres.; b. Milan, Minn., Mar. 11, 1897; s. Charles Helmer and Hannah (Johnson) J.; A.B., U. of Wis., 1918; B.D., Union Theol. Sem., 1932, S.T.M., 1933; D.D., Baldwin Wallace Coll., 1937; m. Jean Wallace Dayton, Sept. 9, 1933; children—Robert Arthur, Astrid. Cleveland sales mgr. Aluminum Co. of America, 1919-29; ordained to ministry M.E. Ch., 1931; asso. minister Hitchcock Memorial Ch. (presbyn.), Scarsdale, N.Y., 1932-34; minister First Congl. Ch., Passaic, N.J., 1934-37; pres. Heidelberg Coll., Tiffin, O., 1937-45; head div. ednl. institutions Surplus Property Adminstrn., Washington, D.C., Aug. 1945-Aug. 1946. Chief Ednl. Officer, U.S. Office of Edn., Sept. 1946-July 1947; sec. World Council of Churches, Geneva, 1947-50; asst. to pres. Elmhurst (Ill.) Coll., from 1950. Served as ensign, U.S. Navy, 1918-19. Former pres. Assn. of Prep. Schs., Colls., and Sems. of Evang. and Reformed Chs. Mem. Phi Beta Kappa, Theta Chi. Mem. Evang. and Reformed Ch. Club: University (Cleveland, O.). Address: Elmhurst IL

JOUETT, EDWARD STOCKTON, lawyer; b. Winchester, Ky., Oct. 21, 1863; s. Edward S. and Catherine (Reed) J.; classical course, U. of Va.; B.L., U. of Virginia, 1885; LL.D., Transylvania University; LL.D., Kentucky Wesleyan College; m. Annie Flournoy Ecton, Sept. 28, 1887; children—Sarah (Mrs. F. T. Armstrong), Flournoy J. (deceased), Virginia (Mrs. John S. Winn, Jr.). Admitted to Ky. bar, 1885, and began practice at Winchester; served as city atty. and city judge, Winchester; pros. atty. Clark County, Ky., 1890-93; apptd. gen. atty. L. & N. R.R. Co., 1912, asst. gen. counsel, 1920-21, became v.p. and gen. counsel, April 21, 1921, resigned Oct. 21, 1943, becoming advisory counsel; federal counsel same rd. under Railroad Adminstrn., 1918-20. Formerly pres. Internat. Conv. Disciples of Christ (Christian Ch.), chmn. bd. U. of Louisville; chmn. Frontier Nursing Service. Mem. Am. Bible Soc. (v.p.), Ky. State Y.M.C.A. (v.p.). S.A.R. (ex-pres. for Ky.), English-Speaking Union (ex-pres. Ky. Branch), Delta Psi. Mem. Disciples of Christ. Clubs: Pendennis, Rotary, Salmagundi, Lawyers', Louisville Country, Filson. Home: 1253 Louisville KY‡

JOUETT, JOHN HAMILTON, aviation exec.; b. San Francisco, Calif., May 14, 1892; s. Cavalier Hamilton and Mary Stuart (Hooper) J.; student Pa. Mil. Coll., 1907-10; B.S., U.S. Mil. Acad., 1914; m. Lois Rorebeck, 1915; m. 2d, Fredrika Mason Kellogg, 1919; 1 son, John Kellogg. Commd. 2d lt., Air Corps, U.S. Army, 1914, and advanced to lt. col.; resigned 1930; aviation exec. Standard Oil Co. of N.J., 1930-32, 1935-36; aviation adviser, Republic of China, 1932-35; pres. Fairchild Aircraft Corp., 1936-38; pres. Areonautical Chamber of Commerce and Aeronautical Expositions Corp., 1939-42; exec. vice president Higgins Aircraft, Inc., from 1942; president Blue Star Airlines; vice pres. Higgins Industries, Inc. Pres. Caribbean Corp. from 1945, Jouett Ins. Agy., from 1948. Mem. exec. com. Nat. Aeronautical Assn. Mem. Inst. of Aeronautical Sciences, Beta Zeta Epsilon. Decorated Victory medal with 4 stars (U.S.); Comdr., sr. grade, Order of the Jade (China). Democrat, Episcopalian. Mason (32 deg., Shriner). Clubs: University, Army and Navy (Washington, D.C.); Pickwick, Boston (New Orleans, La.); Shanghai American (Shanghai, China). Home: St Thomas VI Died Oct. 18, 1968; buried at sea.

JOY, RICHARD PICKERING, banker; b. Detroit, Mich., Jan. 25, 1870; s. James F. and Mary (Bourne) J.; Phillips Acad., Andover, Mass., 1890; m. Ella Gertrude Hopkins, of Detroit, Jan. 1, 1896 (died Apr. 10, 1897); 1 dau., Ella Hopkins; m. 2d, at Detroit, Mary Moore, Sept. 9, 1908; children—Richard P., William Moore, Thomas Bourne. Began in engring. dept., Fort Street Union Depot Co.; pres. Nat. Bank of Commerce since June 1, 1907; pres. Detroit Union R.R. Depot and Station Co., LaSalle County Carbon Coal Co.; v.p. Detroit Copper and Brass Rolling Mills; treas. Packard Motor Car Co.; dir. Detroit Trust Co., Grace Harbor Lumber Co., etc. Comptroller of the City of Detroit, Michigan, 1906-07. Mem. Detroit Bd. of Commerce. Republican. Presbyterian. Clubs: Detroit, Country, Old Club. Home: 287 Lakeshore Av. Office: National Bank of Commerce, and 1830 Penobscot Bldg., Detroit MI‡

JOYCE, DWIGHT P., business exec.; b. Memphis, Mich., May 31, 1900; s. Adrian D. and Anna Belle (Page) J.; grad. University School, Cleveland, O., 1918, A.B., University Michigan, 1921; Dr. Bus. Adminstrn., Bowling Green State U., 1953; m. Louise Parker, Mar. 5, 1923 (died Sept. 4, 1932); children—Emily Louise (Mrs. D. R. Webb), Charles, David, Margo (Mrs. James Hardie, Junior); married second to Marion Stephens Brown, May 27, 1944. With Glidden Co., mfrs. paints, foods and chemicals, Cleveland, July 1, 1921-67, successively as varnish maker, foreman, salesman, specialty sales mgr., sales mgr. chem. and pigment div., and dir. merchant sales, became v.p. in charge paint and varnish div., 1934, pres., 1947-64, chief exec. officer, 1955-67, chmn. bd., 1955-67; cons., bd. dirs. Ohio Bell Telephone Co. Mem. bd. trustees Nat. Science Museum, Cleveland, Cleveland (Ohio) Zoo. Organizer and commanding officer Cleveland group, Civil Air Patrol, World War II. Mem. Nat. Pilots Assn., Beta Theta Pi. Unitarian. Club: Union, Mayfield Country, 50 (Cleve.); Wings (N.Y.C.). Home: Lakewood OH Died Aug. 3, 1970.

JOYCE, J(AMES) WALLACE, engr.; b. Cranston, R.I., July 8, 1907; s. James and Annie Josephine (Malkin) J.; B.Eng., Johns Hopkins, 1928, Ph.D., 1931; m. Edith Mae Clagett, June 25, 1932; 1 son, James Wallace. Applied geophysical prospecting U.S. Bur. Mines, 1931-35; observer-in-charge U.S. Coast and Geodetic Survey, Tucson Magnetic Obs., 1935-37, head magnetic sect., 1937-41; elec. engr. U.S. Naval Ordnance Lab., 1941-42; engr. Bur. Areonautics (electronics) U.S. Navy Dept., 1947-51; spl. assignments to Dept. State; mutual def. assistance program, Apr.-June 1949, internat. science policy survey group, 1949-50; deputy science adviser Department of State, 1952-53; asst. dir. electronics and guided missiles Office Sec. Def., 1953-55; head Office for the International Geophysical Year, Nat. Science Foundation, Washington, 1955-58, head Office Special International Programs, 1958-61; spl. asst. to the dir. of foundation, 1961-63; officer in charge general sci. affairs Office Internat. Sci. Affairs, Dept. State, 1963-65, acting dep. dir. internat. sci. and technol. affairs, 1965-67, dep. dir. internat. sci. and technol. affairs, 1967-70. Entered active duty as lt. USNR, 1942; discharged to inactive duty as comdr., 1947. Mem. Internat. Assn. Terrestial Magnetism and Electricity (sec. 1948-51), Am. Geophys. Union (pres. sect. terrestial magnetism and electricity, 1950-53), Seismol. Soc. Am., Washington Academy of Science, Sigma Xi, Tau Beta Pi. Club: Cosmos. Contbr. articles geophysical prospecting (magnetic methods) in pubs. Home: Washington DC Died Jan. 6, 1970.

JOYCE, WALTER EVES, government official, lawyer; b. Scranton, Pa., Sept. 18, 1895; s. Thomas Francis and Ella (Sweeney) J.; LL.B., Nat. U. Law Sch., 1941; m. Alina du Puget, 1919; children—Stanimer (dec.), Ellen Viara (Mrs. Charles Wagoner); m. 2d, Margaret Kyle, 1930. Clerk, Atlantic Refining Co., Scranton, Pa., 1912-13; employed by ICC, Washington, 1913-17; mem. Am. Relief Adminstrn., Paris, France, 1919; sec.-treas. Am. Tech. Adv. Commn. to Poland, Warsaw, 1919-22; mem. firm Drecki & Ska, S.A., Warsaw; mem. Warsaw Grain Exchange, 1922-25; purchasing agt. and rep. Ulen Engring. Co., N.Y. City, 1925-32; employed by RFC, Washington, from 1932, v.p. defense plant corp., 1942-45, dep. dir. office surplus property 1945; asst. to pres. War Assets Corp., from 1946. Served as 2d lt. U.S. Army, 1917-19; with A.E.F. Mem. D.C. Bar Assn., Nat. U. Alumni Assn. Roman Catholic. Clubs: University (Washington, D.C.), Congressional Country. Home: Washington DC Died Mar. 8, 1973.

JOYCE, WALTER FRANK, instrument co. exec.; b. Oshkosh, Wis., Dec. 10, 1905; s. Walter and Theresa (Wolf) J.; B.S., Marquette U., 1932, M.S., 1943; m. Simone Binon, Jan. 4, 1958; 1 son, Jean Pierre; children by previous marriage—Patricia (Mrs. John Kraniak, Jr.), Kathryn S., D. Kevin, Timothy D., Melissa T. Prodn. mgr. Badger Carton Co., Milw., 1935-42; pres., treas. Modern Records Albums, College Point, N.Y., 1946-49; asst. to pres. Arma div. Am. Bosch Co., N.Y.C., 1949; mgr. mfg. Tex. Instruments, Inc., Dallas, 1949-52, v.p., 1952-61, sr. v.p., 1961-68. Served to lt. comdr. USNR, 1942-46. Sr. mem. Am. Rocket Soc., I.E.E.E.; mem. Am. Ordnance Assn. (council, past pres. Lone Star post), Dallas C. of C., Am. Chem. Soc., Air Force Assn., Navy League U.S., Nat. Security Indsl. Assn. (chmn. bd. trustees), Am. Hereford Assn., Am. Quarter Horse Assn. Club: Metropolitan Dallas TX Died July 1968; buried Calvary Hill Cemetery.

JUBE, ALBERT RIORDAN, lawyer; b. N.Y. City, July 26, 1888; s. John H. and Katherine A. (Riordan) J.; B.S., Amherst Coll., 1910; student Columbia Law Sch., 1910-11; LL.B., N.Y. Law Sch., 1913; m. Norma C. Warren, Jan. 20, 1915; m. 2d, Ethel F. Daloia, November 21, 1959. Admitted to N.Y. bar, 1913, N.J., 1917, practiced in N.Y. City and Newark, N.J.; vice chmn. bd. Collins &Aikman Corp.; dir. Firemens Ins. Co., Newark, N.J., also chmn. finance and exec. com., dir. subsidiary cos.; dir. First Nat. State Bank N.J., McGraw-Edison Company, West Orange, N.J., Bush Terminal Bldgs. Co., New York City. Served in U.S Navy, World War I. Member of the American Bar Association, N.Y. Bar Assns., Bar Assn. of City of N.Y. N.Y. County Lawyers Assn., Chi Phi, Phi Delta Phi Clubs: University, Bankers, Union League (N.Y.C.), Downtown (Newark); Baltusrol Golf (Springfield, N.J.) Home: Orange NJ Died Sept. 18, 1970.

JUDD, CLIMENA LYMAN, educator; b. Holyoke Mass., Sept. 18, 1875; d. Charles Clifford and Phebe Jane (Kneeland) J.; grad. high sch., Holyoke, 1893 A.B., Smith Coll., 1897. Began as clk. in insurance office, 1897; asst. registrar Smith Coll., 1904-18, sec. bd of admission, 1918-25; registrar Peking (China) Union Med. Coll., 1925-26; asso. prin. Mary A. Burham Sch. Northampton, Mass., 1926-29, prin., 1929-33; sec. for scholarships, Smith Coll., 1933-—. Mem. N.E. Assn Coll. and Secondary Schs. Republican Congregationalist. Address: Smith College Northhampton MA‡

JUDD, DEANE BREWSTER, color scientist; b. South Hadley Falls, Mass., Nov. 15, 1900; s. Horace and Etta Lois (Gerry) J.; A.B., Ohio State U., 1922, M.A., 1923 Ph.D., Cornell U., 1926; m. Elizabeth Melamed, Aug. 7 1926; children—Dean Burritt, Audrey Lois. Physicis optics Nat. Bur. Standards, Washington, 1927-70, gues worker, 1970-72; pres. Munsell Color Found., 1943-72 Am. rep. Internat. Commn. Illumination, 1931, 35, 48 secretariat dir., 1951; Am. rep. Internat. Commn Optics, 1948; studies color measurement, colo differences, color perception, color blindness; invite prof. Instituto de Optica, Madrid, 1956-57. Recipien Jour. award Soc. Motion Picture Engrs., 1936 Exceptional Service award Gold medal Dep Commerce, 1950; Samuel Wesley Stratton award Na Bur Standards, 1966. Mem. Illuminating Engring. Soc (Gold medal 1961), Optical Soc. Am. (Herbert E. Ive medal 1958, pres. 1953-55, asso. editor jour. 1936-60 editor 1961-63), Inter-Soc. Color Council (Godlov award 1957, chmn. 1940-44). Author: Color i Business, Science and Industry, 1952, (with G Wyszeck) 2d edit., 1963; Home: Chevy Chase MD Die Oct. 15, 1972.

JUDD, GERRIT PARMELE, IV, historian, educator b. Ardmore, Pa., May 15, 1915; s. Gerrit Parmele II and Marguerite (Foulke) J.; grad. Hotchkiss Sch. Lakeville, Conn., 1932; A.B., Yale, 1936, Ph.D., 1947 m. Margaret Stewart, July 5, 1947; 1 son, Gerr Parmele. Mem. Faculty Hofstra Univ., 1950-71, pro hist., 1958-71, chmn. dept., 1950-71. Served to lt comdr. USNR, 1942-46, 50-52. Mem. Am. Hist. Assn Author: Members of Parliament, 1734-1832, 1955 Horace Walpole's Memoirs, 1959; Dr. Judd, Hawaii Friend, 1960; Hawaii, An Informal History, 1961; A History of Civilization, 1966; Readings in the History c Civilization, 1966; A Hawaiian Anthology, 1967 Home: Garden City NY Died Apr. 15, 1971.

JUDD, LAWRENCE MCCULLY, gov. Hawaii; b Honolulu, T.H., Mar. 20, 1887; s. Albert Francis an Agnes Hall (Boyd) J.; ed. Punahou Sch., Honolulu, an Hotchkiss Sch., Lakeville, Conn.; m. Florence Be Hackett, Mar. 6, 1909; children—Helen Florenc Toms, Agnes Elizabeth Du Bois, Sophie Janet Cluf Lawrence McCully; m. 2d, Eva Marie Lillibridge, Au 27, 1938. Salesman, Whiting Paper Co., N.Y.C 1906-09; buyer for Alexander & Baldwin, Ltd Honolulu, 1909-14; dir. Theo. H. Davies & Co 1914-28; mgr. Hawaii Meat Co., 1928-29. Maj. inf. U.S Army, 1917-19; col. in comd. Hawaii N.G., 1920. Mem Senate of Hawaii, 1920-27, pres., 1923; mem. Bd. c Supervisors, Honolulu, 1929; gov. of Hawaii, 1929-3 Pres. Indsl. Assn. of Hawaii; exec. v.p. Bowman Deu Cummings, Inc., from 1938; rent control adminstr., cit and co. of Honolulu, 1944; supt. Kalaupapa Settlemen Molokai, Hawaii, 1947-49; gov. Am. Samoa, 195 Charter member Am. Legion (hon. past comdr., Dep of Hawaii). Hon. mem. C. of C., Honolulu. Republica

Episcopalian. Mason (Shriner). Clubs: Pacific, Commercial. Home: Honolulu HI Died Oct. 4,1968; buried Nuuanu Cemetery, Honolulu HI

JUDGE, WILLIAM JOHN, pres. Nat. Fuel Gas Co., b. Corry, Pa., Apr. 5, 1873; s. William and Joanna (Allen) J.; ed. pub. schs., m. Anna M. Scholl, Oct. 6, 1909; 1 son, Philip Scholl. Pres. Nat. Fuel Gas Co. since 1919; dir. many other pub. utility cos. Home: 36 Glenwood Rd.; Montclair, N.J. Office: 30 Rockefeller Plaza, New York NY*‡

JUDSON, CHARLES WINGFIELD, newspaperman; b. Payette, Ida., Sept. 9, 1909; s. Charles Franklin and Mary E. (Bushnell) J.; student Los Angeles City Coll., 1930-32; m. Alice E. King, Sept. 1, 1937; children—Herbert King, Leona Elizabeth; married 2d, Laurie D. Farley, November 24, 1948; children—Charles Farley, David Dean, Corey Jo. Office boy, librarian, Los Angesles Record, 1932-33, reporter, 1933-34, wire editor, city editor, 1934-35; picture editor Los Angeles Daily News, 1935-36, city editor, 1936-45, mng. editor, 1945-48; exec. editor Los Angeles Independent Pub. Co.; asso. editor Fortnight mag., Los Angeles, 1948-51, Daily Sentenil, Grand Junction, Colo., 1956-58; pub. Pelican Papers, Marin County, Cal., 1951-56; mng. editor Cervi's Rocky Mountain Jour., Denver, 1958-63; city editor, mng. editor. regional editor Telegram - Tribune, San Luis Obispo, Cal., 1963-72. Democrat. Methodist. Home: Cayucos CA Died Jan. 31, 1972.

JUDSON, FLETCHER WESLEY, banker; b. Woodbury, Conn., Mar. 7, 1868; s. John Wesley and Betsy Janet (Tomlinson) J.; grad. Parker Acad., Woodbury, 1885; m. Winnifred L. Hudson, Apr. 3, 1902. Began as broker's clk., 1885; with Waterbury Nat. Bank since 1889; cashier, 1920-29, pres., 1929-39, vice chmn. of bd. since Jan. 1939; dir. Waterbury Bldg. & Loan Assn., Waterbury Second Mortgage Corp. Mem. Watertown (Conn.) Sch. Bd., 1908-37, chmn., 1912-37. Trustee and sec.-treas. Riverside Cemetery Assn. (Waterbury); former trustee Taft Sch. Corp. (Watertown). Republican. Conglist. Mason. Club: Waterbury Club, University (Winter Park). Home: Watertown, Conn. Office: Waterbury CT‡

JULIEN, JULIETTE MARIE, nurse adminstr. b. Troy, N.Y., Aug. 26, 1894; d. Frank and Josephine (Rousseau) Julien; diploma Samaritan Hosp. Sch. Nursing, 1918; B.S. in Nursing, Columbia Tchrs. Coll., 1946. Teaching supr. obstetrics Lying-In Hosp., N.Y.C., 1919-24; pvt. duty, N.Y.C., 1924-26; supr. obstetrics Ellis Hosp., Schenectady, 1926-29; rural pub. health nurse Warren County, N.Y., 1936-38; dir. nursing div. City Niagara Falls, N.Y., 1938-47, county health unit, Rensselaer County, N.Y., 1947-53; SR. nurse officer (comdr.) USPHS, chief nurse adviser Ministry Health of Iran, 1953-58; fgn. service officer, chief nurse adviser ICA mission to India, 1958-63; consultant nurse U.S. AID, 1963-72; lectr. pub. health nursing College Nursing New Delhi U. Fellow Am. Pub. Health Assn.; mem. Am., Iranian nurses assns., League for Nurses, Trained Nurses Assn. India. Club: Washington DC Died June 22, 1972.

JUNG, FRANZ AUGUST RICHARD, physician; b. Suhl, Germany, Oct. 9, 1869; s. Herman and Marie J.; grad. Univ. of Leipzig (M. D.); m. July 23, 1896, Dr. Sofie A. Nordhoff. Is prof. diseases of stomach and intestines, Post-Grad. Med. Sch. of D. C. Mem. Med. Soc. D.C., Med. Assn., D. C., Am. Med. Assn., Washington Acad. Sciences; Knight Order of St. Stanislaus (conferred by Czar of Russia, Apr., 1902), Order of the Crown, conferred by German Emperor, 1905. Extensive contb'r to Am. and German med. jours. Address: 1229 Conn. Av., Washington‡

JUNGE, CARL STEPHEN, artist; b. Stockton, Calif., June 5, 1880; s. Conrad and Mary Barbara (Terre) J.; ed. Hopkins Art Inst. and Partington Sch. of Illustration, San Francisco, London (Eng.) Sch. of Art, Julian Acad., Paris; m. Fannie J. Corbett, Feb. 25, 1908. On art staff San Francisco Examiner, 1897. Exhibited Art Inst. Chicago; Carnegie Inst., Pittsburgh; Toledo Museum of Art; Nat. Arts Club, New York. Awards from Am. Bookplate Soc., 1916, 17, 21, 22, 25, Bookplate Assn. Internat., 1926, 36; Tri Kappa purchase prize, Hoosier Salon, 1941. Works on permanent exhbn. at National Library, Washington, D.C.; British Museum, London, Columbia U. and Metropolitan Museum, New York; Museum Fine Arts, Boston; John H. Vanderpoel Memorial Art Gallery, Chicago. Served with 472d Engrs., U.S. Army, 1918-19. Fellow Royal Society of Arts London, England. Member Chicago Writers' Guild (master 1933-35), Austin, Oak Park and River Forest Art League, Hoosier Salon. Designed ornaments, type faces, and Junge Decorators." Author: Bookplates, 1916; Ex Libris, 1935. Home: Oak Park IL Died Jan. 17, 1972; cremated

JURICA, HILARY STANISLAUS, educator; b. Dvur sv. Juraj, Czechoslovakia, June 19, 1892; son John and Agnes (Kosusnik) J.; brought to U.S., 1893; B.A., St. Procopius Coll., Lisle, Ill., 1917; M.S., U. of Chicago, 1920, Ph.D., 1922. Instr. botany, 1917-22; ordained Roman Catholic priest, 1921; prof. botany, St. Procopius Coll., Lisle, Ill., 1922-70, head dept. of biology; acting head dept. biology, De Paul U., 1938-45, prof. botany, 1938-57. V.p. St. Procopius Coll. Mem. Benedictine Order (v.p.), Botanical Society, Ill. State Acad., Torrey Bot. Club, Am. Soc. Plant Physiologists, Am. Forestry Assn., Am. Genetic Assn., Chgo. Acad. Sci., Ecol. Soc. Am., Sigma Xi; fellow A.A.A.S. Author series of charts, series of outline drawings. Home: Lisle IL Died Feb. 8, 1970.

JUSTIN, MARGARET M., home economist; b. Agra, Kan., June 15, 1889; d. Frank Miner and Jennie (Hillyer) Justin; B.S., Kan. State Agrl. Coll., 1909; M.S., Columbia, 1915; Ph.D., Yale, 1923; unmarried. Settlement worker, Bennett Acad., Mathiston, Miss., 1910-14; home economics specialist, Mich., 1915; leader of home demonstration agts., Northern Peninsula, Mich., 1916-18; in Y.M.C.A. canteen service overseas, 1918-19; dean sch. of home economics, Kan. State Coll., 1923-54, dean emeritus; consultant in administrative home econs., Holland, (Fulbright appt.), 1953-54. Fellow A.A.A.S; mem. Am. Home Economics Association (past president), American Association of University Women, Sigma Xi, Phi Kappa Phi, Iota Sigma Phi, Omicron Nu (ex-pres.), Phi Upsilon Omicron. Author: Your Share in the Home (with L. F. Baxter and L. O. Rust); Home Living (with L. O. Rust), rev. 1953; Foods (with L. Rust and G. Vail), 1956. Contbr. to Jour. Home Economics, Jour. Agr. Research, Proceedings Assn. of Land Grant Colleges, Jour. Am. Assn. Univ. Women, Kansas State Teacher, etc. Home: Manhattan KS Died June 10, 1967; buried Sunset Cemetery, Manhattan KS

KAGAN, HENRY ENOCH, rabbi, psychologist, author; b. Sharpsburg, Pa., Nov. 28, 1906; s. Alexander B. and Sarah Rivlin (Ginsburg) K.; B.A., U. Cin., 1928; rabbi, Hebrew Union Coll., Cin., 1929, D.D., 1956; M.A., W.Va. U., 1934; Ph.D., Columbia, 1949; m. Esther Ruth Miller, July 16, 1939; children—Jonathan Miller, Jeremy Paul. Rabbi, Johnstown, Pa., 1929-30; dir. Hillel Found., W.Va. U., also rabbi, Uniontown, Pa., 1930-34; asso. rabbi, Pitts., 1934-37; rabbi Sinai Temple, Mt. Vernon, N.Y;, 1937-69; vis. instr. psychol. guidance Columbia Tchrs. Coll., 1950; lectr. St. John's Abbey, Collegeville, Minn., 1956, U. Kan. Med. Sch., 1965; dir. research project Cath. U. of Sacred Heart, Milan, Italy, 1966; director Counseling Center, New York Federation of Reform Synagogues, New York City, N.Y., 1967-69. Co-founder Mt. Vernon Round Table Goodwill, 1939; founder, chmn. Mt. Vernon Council Social Agencies, 1940-48; chmn. Mt. Vernon Mental Health Clinics Com., 1950-60; chmn. commn. relations rabbis and social workers N.Y. Fedn. Jewish Philanthropies, 1959-62, chmn. commn. relations psychiatrists and rabbis, 1964-69; pres. Westchester County Rabbis, 1960-62; cons. Judaism to U.S. Joint Commn. Mental Health, also 1960 White House Conf. Children; founder, chmn. com. religion and psychiatry Central Conf. Am. Rabbis, 1945-50, recording sec., conf., 1961-63; mem. nat. bd. Religious Assn. Am., 1963-69. Named Outstanding Rabbi Met. N.Y., N.Y. Fedn. Jewish Philanthropies, 1961. Mem. Am., N.Y. State psychol. assns., Soc. Sci. Study Religion, Internat. Soc. Group Psychotherapy, Central Conf. Am. Rabbis. Author: Changing the Attitude of Christian Toward Jew, 1952; Judaism and Psychiatry, 1956; Six Who Changed the World, 1963; Rabbi as Counselor 1964; also articles. Home: Mt Vernon NY Died Aug. 17, 1969; buried Mt. Hope Cemetery, Hastings-on-Hudson NY

KAGY, ELBERT OSBORN, dean; born Bristolville, O., Jan. 14, 1871; s. John G. and Florilla (Osborn) K.; ed. Farmington Coll., 1890-91, New Lyme Inst., 1894-96, Highland Park Coll., Des Moines, Ia., 1896-99 (Ph.G., Ph.C.); m. Ethel Mae Dodge, Aug. 7, 1900; children—Elberta Marcia (dec.), Virginia Lucie, John Franklin, Edward Dodge (dec.). Pharmacist, Denver, 1899-1908; prof. of pharmacy, Highland Park Coll., 1908-12, dean of pharmacy, 1912-27 (name changed to Des Moines U., 1918); organized and dean Des Moines Coll. of Pharmacy, 1927-39 (college merged with Drake U., 1939); dean, Coll. of Pharmacy, Drake U., Apr. 1939-Sept. 1942, now dean emeritus. Mem. Am. Pharm. Assn., Am. Chem. Soc., Phi Delta Chi. Unitarian. Mason. Club: University. Home: 4139 6th Av., Des Moines IA‡

KAHIN, GEORGE, lawyer; b. nr. city of Peru, Ind., Apr. 23, 1890; s. William and Leone (Hillare) K.; S.B., Harvard, sum laude, 1913; LL.B., Harvard, 1917; m. Helen Andrews, Aug. 20, 1913 (divorced 1938); children—Geroge McTurnan, Margaret (Mrs. O.P. Webb); m. 2d, Hazel M. Britton, Dec. 25, 1939 (dec.). Admitted to Wash. bar, 1919, and since practiced trial law in Seattle; mem. firm Kahin, Horswill, Keller, Rohrback, Waldo and Moren; special assistant attorney gen. Wash. State Legislative Crime Investigating Com., 1951; legal advisor to governor Wash. State, 1957. Served as 1st lt., U.S. Army, 1917-19. Former mem. bd. govs. Nat. Assn. Better Bus. Bureaus. Mem. Am. Legion (comdr., 1921), Am., Wash. and Seattle bar assns., Assn. Life Ins. Counsel, Internat. Assn. Ins. Counsel. Mason. Clubs: Olympic Riding (capt. polo team, 1929-34), University, Washington Athletic. Home: Seattle WA

KAHLER, ERICH GABRIEL, author, lectr.; b. Prague, Czechoslovakia, Oct. 14, 1885; s. Rudolf and Antionette (Schwarz) von K.; student U. Munich, U. Heidelberg; Ph.D., U. Vienna, 1911; hon. degree Princeton, 1969; m. Alice Pick Loewy. Lectr. New Sch. for Social Research, N.Y.C., 1941-42; prof. German lit. Cornell U., Ithaca, N.Y., 1947-55; vis. prof. U. Manchester (Eng.), 1955-56; Mershon vis. prof. Ohio State U., Columbus, 1959; vis. prof. German lit. Princeton, 1960-63; vis. prof. Technisches Hochschule, Munich, 1963-64, mem. Inst. for Advanced Study, Princeton, N.J., 1949; mem. Com. to Frame a World Constn., U. Chgo., 1945-50; fellow Leo Baeck Inst., N.Y.C.; Bolingen Found. fellow, 1948-50, 60-62. Mem. Deutsche Akademie fur Sprache und Dichtung (corr.). Author: Das Geschlecth Habsburgs, 1919; Der Beruf der Wissenschaft, 1920; Der deutsche Charakter in der Geschichite Europaer, 1936; Israel unter den Volkern, 1936; Man the Measure, A New Approach to History, 1943; (with Albert Einstein) The Arabs in Palestine, 1944; Die Verantwortung des Geistes, 1952; The Tower and the Abyss, Inquiry into the Transformation of Man, 1957; Die Philosophie von Hermann Broch, 1962; The Meaning of History, 1964; Stefan George: Grosse und Tragik, 1964; Der Sinn der Geschichte, 1964; Out of the Labyrinth: Essays in Clarification, 1967; The Jews among the Nations, 1967 (Anisfield-Wolf award); The Disintegration of Form in the Arts, 1968; Untergang und Ubergang, 1969; The Orbit of Thomas Mann, 1969; The Inward Turn of Narrative, 1973. Home: Princeton NJ Died June 28, 1970; buried Princeton Cemetery, Princeton NJ

KAHLER, HUGH MACNAIR, writer, editor; b. Phila. Pa., Feb. 25, 1883; s. Frederick A. and Margaret (MacNair) K.; A.B., Princeton, 1904; married Louise Kingsley, October 15, 1907; one daughter, Kingsley (Mrs. F.W. Hubby, III). Fiction editor Ladies Home Journal, 1943-60; contbr. to Saturday Evening Post, Collier's, Country Gentleman, American, etc., Clubs: Cap and Gown, Nassau (Princeton): Coffee House, Players, Dutch Treat (N.Y.C.); Down Town, Franklin Inn (Phila). Author: The Six Best Cellars (with Holworthy Hall), 1919; Babel, 1921; The East Wind, 1922; The Collector's Whatnot (with Booth Tarkington and Kenneth Roberts), 1923; Father Means Well, 1930; Hills Were Higher Then, 1931; The Big Pink, 1932; Bright Danger, 1941. Address: Princeton NJ Died July 10, 1969.

KAHLKE, CHARLES EDWIN, surgeon; b. Rock Island, Ill., Jan. 13, 1870; s. John J. and Louise Elizabeth (Witte) K.; B.S., State U. of Ia., 1891; M.D., Hahnemann Med. Coll., Chicago, 1894; studied U. of Vienna, 1899; 1902; m. Agnes Crawford, June 21, 1902; children—Margaret Louise, Charles E. Intern Cook County Hosp., Chicago, 18 mos., 1894-95; since in surg. practice; ex-consulting surgeon, Cook County Hosp.; attending surgeon Chicago Mem. Hosp. Member American Board of Surgery (founders group), Fellow Am. Coll. Surgeons; ex-pres. Chicago Surg. Soc.; mem. A.A.A.S., Phi Delta Theta. Maj., M.C., U.S. Army, during World War. Republican. Baptist. Home: Benton Harbor, MI. Office: Chicago Memorial Hospital, Chicago IL‡

KAHN, ELY JACQUES, architect; b. N.Y.C., June 1, 1884; s. Jacques and Eugenie (Maximilian) K.; A.B., Columbia, 1903, B.Arch., 1907; grad. Ecole Des Beaux Arts, Paris, 1911; m. Liselotte Hirschmann, Jan. 1964; children—Ely Jacques, Joan, Olivia. Architect, from 1911; prof. architecture Cornell U., 1915; architect for various govt. and state projects and many tall buildings in N.Y.C.; chmn adv. commn. Sch. Indsl. Art. Mem. N.Y. State Adv. Bd. City Planning; former adviser U.S. Housing Authority. Benjamin Franklin fellow Royal Soc. Arts. Fellow A.I.A.; mem. Archtl. League N.Y. (past pres.), Municipal Art Soc. (past pres.), Beaux Arts Inst. Design. (past chmn. bd.). Author: Design in Art and Industry, 1937. Contbr. articles Ency. Brit., other jours. Home: New York City NY Died Sept. 5, 1972.

KAHN, JULIUS BAHR, JR., pharmacologist, educator; b. Chgo., July 7, 1921; s. Julius Bahr and Leona (Kline) K.; B.S., U. Chgo., 1946, M.S., 1947, Ph.D., 1949; m. Carolyn Shadley, Dec. 1, 1948; children—David, Robert, Richard, Deborah. Postdoctoral fellow U. Chgo., 1949; biologist Oak Ridge Nat. Lab., 1949-51; asst. prof., asso. prof. pharmacology U. Cin., 1951-61; vis. prof. Pharmakologisches Institut, U. Berne (Switzerland), 1958-59; asso. prof., prof. pharmacology Northwestern U., Chgo., 1961-68, chmn. pharmacology dept., 1965—; mem. PET-A study sect. USPHS, 1965-68. Mem. bd. United World Federalists, 1966-68. Served with M.C., AUS, 1942-46. John and Mary Markle scholar med. sci., 1954-59. Mem. Am. Soc. Pharmacology and Exptl. Therapeutics, A.A.A.S., N.Y. Acad. Scis., Red Cell Club, Soc. Exptl. Biology and Medicine, Chgo. Med. Soc., Soc. Young Med. Educators (past sec., chmn.), Am. Civil Liberties Union, Com. Sane Nuclear Policy, Sigma Xi. Editor-in-chief Jour. Pharmacology and Exptl. Therapeutics, 1965-68. Home: Winnetka IL Died Oct. 18, 1968.

KAISER, LOUIS ANTHONY, naval officer; b. at Kirkwood, Ill., Apr. 1, 1870; grad. U.S. Naval Acad., 1889. Promoted ensign, July 1, 1891, lt. jr. grade, Dec.

25, 1898; lt., Mar. 3, 1899; lt. comdr., July 1, 1905; comdr., Sept. 22, 1910; capt., Aug. 29, 1916. Served on Concord, Spanish-Am. War, 1898; with Bur. of Equipment, Navy Dept., 1904-6; sr. engr. on the Washington, 1906-8; navigator Colorado, 1908-9; with Bur. of Equipment, 1909-10, Bur. Steam Engring., 1910-12; comd. Montgomery, 1912-14, Boston Navy Yard, 1914-15; at Naval War Coll., 1915-16; comd. New Jersey, June 26, 1916-Aug. 21, 1917. Home: Monmouth, Ill. Address: Navy Dept., Washington DC‡

KAL, NORMAN COLEMAN, advt. exec.; b. Washington, July 12, 1900; s. William Jack and Frances (Levy) K.; student Johns Hopkins, 1914-17; m. Jean Mildred Broun, June 17, 1920; children—Niki (Mrs. Lester C. Haas), Wynn Jack. With Hearst Co., 1921-22, Washington Post, 1922-24, Washington Eve. Star, 1924-26; owner Kal Advt., Washington, 1926-36; chmn. bd. Kal, Ehrlich & Merrick, Inc., Washington, 1961-69.; treas, KEM Investment Co.; dir. Stevenmier. Past pres. Washington Better Bus. Bur.; mem. Washington Bd. Trade. Board directors Washington Hospital Center, Washington Home Retarded Children. Member TV Broadcasters Association Academy TV Arts and Sciences, Washington Advt. Club (past pres.). Clubs: Amity (past pres.), 50 (past pres.), Variety, Circus Saints and Sinners (Washington). Home: Washington DC Died Mar. 2, 1969.

KALKSTEIN, MENNASCH, physician; b. Bklyn., Aug. 24, 1907; s. Joseph and Jennie (Weinberg) K.; M.D., St. Andrews (Scotland) U., 1933; m. Claire Weininger, Dec. 28, 1940; children—Janet (Mrs. Paul L. Plansky), Stephen W., Helen L. Postgrad. instr. Columbia, 1938-40; intern Harlem Hosp., N.Y.C., 1933-34, resident in pneumonia service, 1934; intern, also resident internal medicine Bellevue Hosp., N.Y.C., 1934-37, admitting physician, 1937-38, later asso. vis. physician; phys. pneumonia N.Y.C. Dept. Health, 1938-40, clin. physician Tb, 1938-42; mem. cardiology staff L.I. Jewish Hosp. Asst. clin. prof. medicine N.Y. U. Served to lt. col. M.C., AUS. Diplomate Am. Bd. Internal Medicine. Fellow Am. Heart Assn., A.C.P.; mem. A.M.A., Am. Thoracic Soc., Am. Fedn. Clin. Research, Home: New York City NY Died Mar. 12, 1971; buried Beth-El Cemetery, Westwood NJ

KALLET, ARTHUR, exec. dir. Med. Letter, engr., editor; b. Syracuse, N.Y., Dec. 15, 1902; s. Barnett and Etta (Kaplan) K.; B.S., Mass. Inst. Tech., 1924; m. Opal Boston, Apr. 27, 1927 (dec. 1952); 1 son, Anthony; m. 2d, Mary R. Fitzpatrick, January 28, 1954; children—Cynthia, Lisa. Engaged in editorial work New York Edison Company, 1924-26, then assistant manager editorial bureau 1927; mem. staff Am. Standards Assn. and editor, Industrial Standardization, 1927-34; publicity dept. Regional Plan N.Y., 1929-32; founder, dir. Consumers Union U.S., 1936-57; exec. dir. The Med Letter Drugs and Therapeutics, from 1958; pres. Drug and Therapeutics Information, Inc., from 1958, Buyers Laboratory, Inc., from 1961. Author: 100,000,000 Guinea Pigs (with F.J. Schlink), 1933; Counterfeit, 1935. Home: New Rochelle NY Died Feb. 24, 1972.

KALLGREN, CARL ALFRED, univ. dean; b. New Haven, Conn., Jan. 12, 1894; s. John and Marie Charlotte (Wahlberg) K.; student Suffield (Conn.) Sch., 1910-13; A.B., Colgate University, 1917, A.M., 1925, LL.D., 1962; B.D., Rochester Theological Seminary, 1920; honorary Ph.D., Syracuse U., 1940; m. Marguerite Eleanor Carlson, Oct. 2, 1920; 1 son, Carl Alfred. Ordained to ministry Bapt. Ch., 1918; pastor West Lafayette, Ind., Ch., 1920-21; instr. and asso. prof. public speaking, Colgate U., 1921-27, acting registrar, 1925, asst. dean and dir. admissions, 1926-27; pastor First Congl. Ch., Binghamton, N.Y., 1927-33; dean of students, Colgate U., 1933-42, co-ordinator of the Colgate Unit of the Naval College Training Program V-12, 1943, dean of the college, 1943-70, dean of the univ., 1958-62, dean of the university emeritus, 1962-70, acting pres., 1958-59. Bd. dirs. Mark Twain Library, Redding, Conn. Served as 1st lt., chaplain, U.S. Army, 1918. Trustee Suffield Sch. Recipient alumni award for distinguished service to Colgate, 1956. Mem. Eastern Assn. Deans Men, Nat. Assn. Personnel Administrators. Theta Chi, Delta Sigma Rho, Phi Beta Kappa. Club: Hamilton. Home: Redding CT Died Nov. 19, 1970; buried Umpawang Cemetery, Redding CT

KALLIO, ELMER WILLIAM, accountant; b. Chgo., Sept. 2, 1917; s. William David and Anna (Salenius) K.; student Northwestern U., 1940, C.P. A., Ill., 1945; m. Leona Louise Lauwaert, Sept. 28, 1940; children—William Dean, Robert Frederick. Gen. partner Laventhol Krekstein Horwath & Horwath, Phila., 1939-71, Horwath & Horwath Internat., 1962-71; faculty Brandywine Jr. Coll.; cons., lectr., author on housing, feeding, recreation. Mem. Am., Ill. insts. C.P.A.'s, D.C. C.P.A.'s. Author: (with N. Katz) Annual Restaurant Studies, 1958-64; (with J. Keiser) College Text on Food Service Management, 1973. Home: Berwyn PA Died Jan. 8, 1971.

KAMMER, ALFRED CHARLES, lawyer; b. New Orleans, Dec. 28, 1884; s. Philip J. and Catherine (Meyer) K.; ed. pub. schs., New Orleans; m. Kate Jane McCulloch, June 30, 1909 (dec. July 1940); children—Katherine McCulloch (Mrs. Eugene J. Bergeret), Nolan Charles; m. 2d, Mary Wilmuth Warren, Nov. 15, 1944. Admitted to La. bar, 1912; partner firm Chaffe, McCall, Burke, Phillips, Burke, Toler & Hopkins, and predecessors, New Orleans, from 1956; lectr. Loyola U. Sch. Law, New Orleans, 1925-29. Pres. Orleans Kenner Traction Co., from 1920; sec. New Orleans & Lower Coast R.R. Co.; asst. sec. Island Refining Corp. Presented key to city New Orleans, 1962. Fellow Am. Coll. Trial Lawyers; mem. Am., La., New Orleans (pres. 1948-49) bar assns., Assn. Commerce Greater New Orleans. Club: Boston (New Orleans). Home: New Orleans LA

KAMMERER, WEBB LOUIS, mfg. exec.; b. St. Louis, June 3, 1893; s. William Alexander and Harriet (Webb) K.; B.S. in Civil Engring., Washington U., 1916; m. Else Marie Eyssell, Jan. 18, 1919; children—Marjorie Anne (Mrs. Gary B. Wood), Virginia Else (Mrs. L. W. Bergesch). In melting dept. foundry Warren Steel Casting Co., St. Louis, 1916-18, asst. supt., 1918-20, supt., 1920-23; salesman Midvale Mining & Mfg. Co., 1923-30, v.p., 1930-40, pres., 1940-65, chmn. bd., 1965-71; pres. Midvale Material Handling Equipment Co., St. Louis, 1952-60; dir. McQuay-Norris Mfg. Co., St. Louis, General chmn. Mo. Valley regional tech. conf., Rolla, Mo., 1955; life dir. Washington U.; mem. adv. com. Foundry Edn. Found. (trustee), U. Mo. Sch. Mines and Met.; trustee Training and Research Inst., Chicago. Registered profl. engr., Mo. Served as observer USAC, 1918, 1st lt. res., 1919-24. Mem. Acad. Scis. (St. Louis), Am. Foundrymen's Soc., (nat. dir., 1958-61), C. of C., Mo. Hist. Soc., Ducks Unlimited, Conservation Fedn. Mo., Kappa Alpha. Republican. Methodist. Mason, Rotarian. Clubs: University, Mo. Duck Hunters, Mo. Athletic (St. Louis). Home: St Louis MO Died 1971.

KAMMERT, DONALD MILTON, utilities exec.; b. Chgo., Apr. 1, 1909; s. Christian and Freda (Muench) K.; B.S., U. Ill., 1932; m. Dorothy Hall, Apr. 25, 1934 (dec. Aug. 1957); 1 son, James Lawrence; m. second, Mae Franklin, May 1, 1965. Junior accountant Alexander R. Grant Company, Chgo., 1933-34; accountant Ill. Power Co. subsidiaries and predecessors, Champaign and Decatur, Ill., 1934-42; asst. comptroller Am. Water Works & Electric Co., West Penn Electric Co.; asst. sec. West Penn Power Co., N.Y., 1943-50, comptroller, Pitts., 1951-60, v.p., dir., 1953-61; v.p., dir. Monogahela Power Co., Fairmont, W.Va., 1962-63, pres., 1964-67, 69-71; exec. v.p., dir. Allegheny Power System, Inc., N.Y.C., 1967, pres., chief exec. officer, 1967-71, also dir.; president, dir. West Penn Power Co., 1969-71, Potomac Edison Co., 1969-71. Mem. Edison Electric Inst. (dir. 1968-71), Financial Executives Institute, also mem. Public Utilities Assn. Virginias (pres. 1964-65), Phi Eta Sigma, Beta Gamma Sigma, Beta Alpha Psi. Methodist. Clubs: University, Duquesne (Pitts.); Greensburg (Pa.) Country; Field (Fairmont); Lakeview Country (Morgantown, W.Va.); Rolling Rock (Ligonier, Pa.); Sky, University (N.Y.C.). Home: New York City NY Died Apr. 29, 1971.

KANDER, ALLEN, broker; b. Kansas City, Mo., Aug. 20, 1888; s. Felix Victor and Matilda (Eppstein) K.; student U. Chgo., 1912-14; L.H.D. (honorary), U. of Kentucy, 1962; m. Jennette Unger, Sept. 26, 1916; children—Carol (Mrs. Marcus Smith), Margaret (Mrs. Robert Weisselberg), Kanneth Allen. With Emporia (Kan.) Gazette, 1906-09, Kansas City Star, 1909-11, Chgo. Tribune, 1912-14; various exec. capacities Hearst orgn., 1915-27; negotiator for sale of daily newspaper and broadcasting properties, 1927-70; pres. Allen Kander Assos., Inc., 1961-65. Mem. Washington Bd. of Trade. Member exec. bd. Nat. Conf. Christians and Jews, 1939-40. Recipient spl. award for editorial Twilight of The Kings, following Sarajevo assassination, 1914; Distinguished Service medal U. Mo. Sch. Journalism, 1956. Mem. Sigma Delta Chi. Club: Nat. Press (Washington). Home: Miami Beach FL Died Feb. 24, 1970.

KANE, THOMAS FRANKLIN, educator; b. Westfield, Ind., May 5, 1863; s. John M. (M.D.) and Minerva J. (Conklin) K.; A.B., De Pauw U., 1888, A.M., 1891, LL.D., 1911; Ph.D., Johns Hopkins University, 1895; LL.D. from Univ. of N.D., 1933; m. Dorothy Gammon, Aug. 12, 1896. Prof. Latin and Greek and v.p., 1888-90, acting pres., 1890-91, Lewis Coll.; scholar fellow in Latin, Ph.D., Johns Hopkins, 1895; prof. Latin, 1895-1900, prin. prep. dept., 1897-1900, Olivet Coll.; prof. Latin, 1900-02, acting pres., 1902-03, pres., 1903-14, U. of Wash.; pres. Olivet (Mich.) Coll., 1916-18; pres. Univ. of N.D., 1918-33; dir. seminar in coll. teaching, U. of Wash., summers 1934-37; special lecturer on higher edn., U. of Minn., summer, 19, U. of Wash., summers, 1938, 39 and 40. Mem. N.E.A., Nat. Assn. State Univs. (pres. 1913-14), State Ednl. Assn. (pres. 1925-26), Delta Kappa Epsilon, Phi Beta Kappa, Phi Delta Kappa. Clubs: Grand Forks Commercial, Seattle Municipal League, Rotary, Oval. Address: Malloy Apts., 4337 15th Av., Seattle 5 WA‡

KANNER, SAMUEL JACOB, lawyer; b. Orlando, Fla., Sept. 18, 1912; s. Harry and Rae (Leibowitz) K.; LL.B., U. Miami (Fla.), 1936; m. Patricia Gradwohl, Feb. 18, 1939 (div. June 1950); 1 dau., Susan Gradwohl; m. 2d, Ruth Hirsch, Feb. 6, 1952. Admitted to Fla. bar, 1936, U.S. Supreme Ct., 1958, other fed. cts.; practice in Miami, 1936-67; partner firm Patton & Kanner, 1940-67. Mem. Fla. Bd. Bar Examiners, 1956-62, chmn., 1956-58; bd. mgrs. Nat. Conf. Bar Examiners, 1957-61, chmn., 1961-62. Bd. dirs. Miami Heart Inst. Fellow Am. Bar Found.; mem. Am. (ho. del. 1962), Fla. (bd. govs. 1945-46, chmn. com. strengthen legal edn. 1963-67), Dade County (bd. dirs. 1944-47, chmn. grievance com. 1957-58, chmn. com. continuing legal edn. 1962-63) bar assn., Tau Epsilon Phi Club: Miami (dir. 1962-67, v.p. 1966-67, pres. 1967). Home: Miami Beach FL Died Aug. 9, 1967.

KANSKI, FRANCIS, bishop; b. Chicago, Ill., Jan. 25, 1870; s. John and Frances (Custer) K.; ed. Sacred Heart Acad., Ind. Ty. Ordained priest Old Catholic Ch., 1903; gen. missionary for U.S. and Can.; consecrated abbot O.S.B., M.; consecrated bishop of America by authority of Archbishop J. R. Vilatte, June 22, 1923; official title, Catholic bishop American Catholic Ch. Home: 4417 N. Mulligan Av., Chicago IL‡

KANTER, AARON E., physician, educator; b. Harrisburg, Pa., July 9, 1893; s. Julius and Mary (Rosenberg) K.; B.S., U. Chgo., 1914, M.S., 1915; M.D., Rush Med. Coll., 1917; m. Eleanor Lackritz, Mar. 1, 1925; children—Julian Paul, Alan, Joan (Mrs. Barry Elman). Intern Presbyn. Hosp., Chgo., 1917-19, Cook County Hosp., Chgo., 1919-20; attending obstetrician and gynecologist Mt. Sinai Hosp., Chgo., 1920-67; attending gynecologist Cook Co. Hosp., 1926-67; prof. obstetrics and gynecology Rush Med. Coll., 1937-47, U. Ill., 1944-55; prof. department of obstretics and gynecology Cook County Grad. Sch. Medicine, 1944-65, Chgo. Med. Sch., 1955-67; attending obstetrician and gynecologist Presbyn.-St. Luke's Hosp., Chgo., 1952-67. Served as lt., M.C., USN, 1918-23. Diplomate Am. Bd. Obstetrics and Gynecology, Fellow A.C.S., Internat. Coll. Surgeons; mem. A.M.A., Chgo. Med. Soc., Central Assn. Obstetricians and Gynecologists, Sigma Xi, Phi Delta Epsilon. Home: Chicago IL Died Sept. 26, 1967.

KAPENSTEIN, IRA, bus. exec.; b. N.Y.C., Feb. 12, 1936; s. Joseph and Alice (Asken) K.; B.A. in Journalism and Polit. Sci., U. Ia., 1956; m. Betty Ann Kunik, June 10, 1956; children—Joel, David, James. Engaged as reporter, Washington correspondent with Milwaukee (Wis.) Journal, 1956-63; spl. asst. for pub. information to postmaster gen. U.S., 1963-68; exec. asst. to president McDonnell & Co., Inc., stock brokerage and investment banking firm., N.Y.C., 1969-71; dir. McDonnell Fund, Inc. Special assistant to director Organization Kennedy Campaign. Recipient Benjamin Franklin award postmaster gen., 1965. Mem. U. Ia. Alumni Assn. (nat. council), Sigma Delta Chi, Alpha Epsilon Pi, Omicron Delta Kappa. Jewish religion. Mem. B'nai B'rith. Clubs: Nat. Press (Washington); Milw. Press. Home: Potomac MD Died Mar. 1, 1971.

KAPLAN, BENJAMIN, educator; b. Rechicha, Minsk, Russia, May 10, 1906; s. Joseph and Pesha (Greenman) K.; B.A., Tulane U., 1928, M.A., 1929; student N.Y. Sch. Social Work, also N.Y. U., 1930, Colo. U., 1948; Ph.D., La. State U., 1952; m. Yetive Tatar, May 14, 1933; 1 dau., Barbara Kathleen. Supr., parish dir. La. Dept. Pub. Welfare, 1931-40; faculty U. Southwestern La., 1940-72, prof. sociology, 1954-66, Frank A. Godchaux prof. sociology, 1966-72. Dep. dir. personnel charge tng. Southeastern area A.R.C., 1942-45, chmn. Lafayette Parish chpt., 1946-47; participant White House Conf. Children and Youth, 1960, White House Conf. Aging, 1961, 71; mem. La. Adv. Com. Aging, 1962-64. Mem. exec. com. Evangeline Area council Boy Scouts Am., 1942-55, Bayou council Girl Scouts Am., 1946-56. Fellow Am. Sociol. Assn.; mem. Am. Assn. U. Profs., Theta Xi, Phi Epsilon Pi, Kappa Delta Pi, Phi Kappa Phi. Jewish religion (pres. congregation 1951-52). Rotarian; mem. B'nai B'rith. Author: The Eternal Stranger, A Study of The Small Jewish Community, 1957; Jews and Social Equality, 1963; The Jew and His Family, 1967. Home: Lafayette LA Died July 15, 1972; buried Lafayette Jewish Cemetery.

KAPLAN, HARRY, clergyman; b. Mpls., Oct. 6, 1901; s. Meyer and Rose (Moskowitz) K.; B.A., U. Minn., 1923; M.H.L., Jewish Inst. Religion, 1927; M.A., Ohio State U., 1940, LL.D., 1955; D.D., Hebrew Union Coll., 1953; m. Rebecca Rabinoff, June 10, 1926 (dec.); children—Judith (Mrs. Alvin Mahrer), Ruth Myra (Mrs. Frank Uhlmann), Myron Stephen; m. 2d, Theresa Goode, June 15, 1937; 1 dau., Rosalie Goode (Mrs. Paul Fried). Ordained rabbi in 1927; rabbi Temple Anshe Amonium, Pittsfield, Mass., 1927-35; dir. B'nai B'rith Hillel Found., Ohio State U., 1935-69; Midwest regional dir. and nat. staff B'nai B'rith, 1948-69. Dir. Ohio Citizens Council for Health and Welfare, 1953-69; pres. Pittsfield Council Social Agys., 1933-34. Mem. Nat. Hillel Dirs. Assn. (past pres.), Alumni Assn. Jewish Inst. Religion (past pres.), U. Religious Council (past pres.), Columbus Town Meeting (founder), Central Conf. Am. Rabbis. Mem. B'nai B'rith. Rotarian. Clubs: Crichton, Columbus Torch (past pres.), Ohio State Faculty (Columbus). Contbr. to the National Jewish

Monthly, Religious Education, The Commentator. Home: Columbus OH Died Feb. 7, 1969; interred Greenlawn Cemetery Columbus OH

KAPLAN, MILTON LEWIS, journalist; b. Mpls., May 8, 1920; s. Hyman David and Esther (Codden) K.; B.A., U. Minn., 1943; children by previous marriage—Judith (Mrs. Orlin Silverman), James; m. 2d, Doris Willens, May 26, 1949; children—Jeffrey, Andrew, Dan. Gen. assignment reporter, feature writer, asst. city editor Mpls. Tribune, 1943-48; feature writer I.N.S., 1948-49, fgn. corr., 1950-55, feature editor, 1955-58; editor Hearst Headline Service, 1958-68; chief Washington bur. Hearst Newspapers, 1963-66, nat. editor, 1966-68; exec. v.p. King Features Syndicate, 1968-69, pres., gen. mgr., 1969-72. Clubs: Nat. Press (Washington); Overseas Press (N.Y.C.). Contbr. articles to mags. Home: Yonkers NY Died Dec. 29, 1972; buried Woodstock Cemetery, Woodstock NY

KAPLAN, SAMUEL, radio corp. exec.; b. Chgo., Nov. 25, 1907; s. Abraham and Ida (Slonimsky) K.; diploma in commerce, Northwestern U., 1930; m. June Bockel, Sept. 18, 1937; children—Michael J., Bruce D. With Zenith Radio Corp., Chgo., 1923-70, beginning as office boy, successively asst. treas. and asst. sec., credit mgr., asst. v.p., v.p., controller and v.p., 1923-52, treas., v.p., 1951-59, exec. v.p., treas., dir., 1959-68, pres., 1968-70. Home: Oak Park IL Died Apr. 1, 1970.

KAPPEL, GERTRUDE, soprano; b. Halle, Germany, Sept. 1, 1893; d. Louis and Anna (Dohler) K.; ed. Conservatory of Music, Leipzig; m. Sime Vukas. Debut at 18 in Royal Theatre, Hanover, and returned after 1 yr., continuing there 7 yrs.; sang in State Opera, Vienna, later at Munich, Covent Garden (London), Paris Grand Opera, Amsterdam, Royal Opera, Madrid, etc.; with Metropolitan Opera Co., New York, since 1928; with San Francisco Opera, 1933; also appearing in concerts in Chicago, Cleveland, Minneapolis, Cincinnati, Toronto and other cities. Especially notable in Wagnerlan roles, including Isolde, Sieglinde, Kundry, Brunhilde, Fricka, Elizabeth and Ortrud. Home: Munich Germany Died Apr. 1971.*

KARAVONGSE, PHYA PRABHA, diplomat; b. Bangkok, Siam, Mar., 1873; ed. in Siam, England and France; m. Lamied Purnasiri, of Bangkok, 1900. E.E. and M.P. from Siam, to U.S. since Nov., 1913. Buddhist. Clubs: Metropolitan, Chevy Chase. Address: Siamese Legation, 2300 Kalorama Road N.W., Washington DC‡

KAREL, JOHN CONNELL, lawyer; b. Schuyler, Neb., Feb. 28, 1873; s. John and Elizabeth (Metzner) K.; LL.B., U. of Wis., 1895, Ph.B., 1896; m. Josephine A. Henssler, of La Crosse, Wis., June 11, 1901. Practiced, Chicago, 1895-9, since in Milwaukee; pres. Home Makers' Land Co., Kelling-Karel Co., Chicago; v.p. Union Bank, Milwaukee; sec. State Loan & Finance Co. Mem. Wis. Ho. of Rep., 1901; register of probate, Milwaukee Co., 1903-7; co. judge, 1907—; Dem. candidate for gov. of Wis., 1913. Catholic. Mem. Elks (Exalted Ruler, 1909-13), Equitable Fraternal Union (v.-p.), etc. Clubs: Milwaukee Athletic, Milwaukee Canoe and Yachting, Press, Bohemian-American. Widely known as public speaker. Home: 1302 Lloyd St. Office: Court House, Milwaukee‡

KARLEN, SVEN BERNHARD, broadcasting exec.; b. White Plains, N.Y., May 2, 1914; s. Carl Berhnard and Selma (Nordberg) K.; A.B., Dartmouth, 1935, M.C.S., 1936; m. Catherine Thomasine Booth, June 12, 1941; children—Sven Bernhard, Eric, Kristen, Mark. Sec., treas. Amalgamated Textiles, Ltd., N.Y.C., 1946-58, pres., dir., 1958-69; v.p. Travelers Credit Service, Inc., N.Y.C., 1954-59; controller CBS, N.Y.C., 1959-69; dir. Photometric Corp.; village treas., Bronxville, 1962. Clubs: Apawamis, Bronxville Field. Home: Bronxville NY Died Aug. 23, 1969.

KARLOFF, BORIS, (real name William Henry Pratt), actor; b. Dulwich, England, Nov. 23, 1887; s. Edward and Eliza Sara (Millard) P.; student Merchant Taylor Sch., London, 1897-1902, Uppingham Sch., Rutlandshire, England, 1902-06; m. Dorothy Stine, 1928; 1 daughter, Sara Jane; m. 2d Evelyn Helmore, 1946. Came to the United States, 1909. Actor since 1910; played in stock companies for 10 years; appearances include: Unconquered, Personal Column, Taproots, (Abbot and Costello) Meet the Killers; plays: On Borrowed Time, The Linden Tree, The Shop at Sly Corner, Peter Pan, The Strange Door, Black Castle; stage play, Arsenic and Old Lace (N.Y.C.), The Lark; films: Lost Patrol, You'll Find Out, The Man They Couldn't Hang, The Invisible Ray, Voodoo Island, Dre Monster Dre, Ghost in the Invisible Bikini; TV series Col. March of Scotland Yard; host of television series Thriller 1960-69. Editor: Tales of Terror (anthology), 1943, And the Darkness Falls (anthology), 1946. Clubs: Players, Lambs (N.Y.C.); Masquers (Hollywood, Cal.); Garrick (London). Died Feb. 2, 1969.

KARN, DANIEL EARL, utilities exec.; b. North Peru, Ind., Apr. 29, 1890; s. Jacon Alonzo and Mary Catherine (Zimmerman) K.; B.S. in mec. engring., Purdue, 1915; m. Marie B. Foglesong, June 5, 1915 (dec. 1946); children—Marcia Jean (Mrs. William B. Nichols), James Daniel; married second Vivian Vanderlyn Alter. Joined Consumers Power Co., Jackson, Mich., and asso. cos., 1915, pres. since 1951, dir. since 1933; pres., dir. Mich. Gas Storage Co., 1950-69 director of the Jackson City Bank & Trust Company. Trustee Alma (Mich.) Coll.; dir. Edison Electric Institute. Presbyn. Rotarian. Home: Jackson MI Died June 20, 1969.

KARN, HARRY WENDELL, educator, psychologist; b. Pitts., Feb. 11, 1907; s. Harry Wendell and Emma (Demuth) K.; B.S., Muskingum Coll., 1929; M.A., U. Pitts., 1931; Ph.D., Clark U., 1934; m. Dorothy Lillias Happe, Aug. 10, 1936. Psychologist, Western State Penintentiary, Pitts., 1934-36; asst. prof. U. Pitts., 1936-42, mem. faculty Carnegie Mellon U., 1946-69, prof. psychology, 1952-69; cons. to industry, 1950-69. Served to lt. USNR, 1942-46. Recipient Carnegie Distinguished Teaching award, 1956. Fellow Am. Pa. psychol. assns.; mem. Eastern, Midwestern psychol. assns., Sigma Xi. Author, editor, contbr. 5 books. Contbr. profl. jours. Home: Pittsburgh PA Died Oct. 23, 1969.

KARR, EDMUND JOSEPH, shipping co. exec.; b. N.Y.C., Nov. 3, 1884; s. John and Rosalia (Smith) K.; m. Grace Royer, Nov. 30, 1910; children—Cora E., Dorothy R., Marian L. With Pa. R.R., 1901-07; dir. British Ministry of Shipping, 1917-19; pres. Karr, Ellis & Co., N.Y.C., 1919-21; with Calmar Steamship Corp., 1927-60, pres., 1950-60; also pres. Bethlehem Transportation Corp., Marven Steamship Corp., Ore. Navigation Corp. Former chmn. com. relations with other carriers Intercoastal Steamship Freight Assn.; former chmn. traffic adv. com. and joint steamship and ry. com. Maritime Assn. Port N.Y.; former mem. dirs. com. U.S. Navy for N.Y.; chmn. com. forwarding, port control div. War Shipping Adminstrn., World War II, also liaison officer Office Def. Transportation. Trustee Overlook Hosp. Assn., Summitt, N.J. Decorated Officer British Empire. Mem. N.Y. Produce Exchange Luncheon Club (bd. govs.). Republican. Presbyn. Mason. Home: Chatham NJ Died Nov. 22, 1972.

KARR, ELIZABETH, author; b. Geneva, N.Y.; d. Stephen H. Platt; has lived at North Bend, O., from childhood; m. Gen. Charles W. Karr, who is aCincinnati lawyer and has been adj.-gen. of Ohio. Author: The American Horsewoman, H5. Address: North Bend OH‡

KARR, FRANK, lawyer, ry. official; b. Heyworth, Ill., Feb. 18, 1875; s. Henry Allen and Martha Elizabeth (Storey) K.; ed. Ill. State Normal U. and Stanford U.; m. Dora Van Ordstrand, Oct. 29, 1903; children—Randolph, Dorothy (dec.). Practiced law since 1901; v.p. and dir. Pacific Electric Ry. Co.; atty. Southern Pacific Co., Los Angeles, Calif.; retired, 1945; gen. counsel Am. Transit Assn., Washington, D.C., 1946-47. Home: 443 S. Alexandria Av., Los Angeles 5 CA‡

KARRER, PAUL, educator; b. Moscow, Russia, Apr. 21, 1889; s. Paul and Julie (Lerch) K.; Dr. Philosophy, U. Zurich; m. Helena Froelich, 1914; 2 children. Asst. Chem. Inst., U. Zurich, 1911-12, dir., 1919-50; professor of chemistry University Zurich (Switzerland), 1919-59, prof. emeritus, 1959-71; chemist Georg-Speyer-Haus, Frankfurt-am-Main, 1912-18. Recipient Marcel Benoist prize, Switzerland, Cannizzaro prize, Rome; Nobel prize for chemistry, 1937. Fng. mem. Royal Soc. Author sci. articles. Address: Zurich Switzerland Died June 18, 1971.

KARSNER, HOWARD, pathologist; b. Phila., Pa., Jan. 6, 1879; s. Charles W. (M.D.) and Martha M. (Wright) K.; B.S., Central High Sch., Phila., 1897; Phila. Sch. of Pedagogy, 1899; M.D., Univ. of Pa., 1903; LL.D., Western Reserve University, Cleveland, 1949; m. Audrey W. Stanwood, Dec. 11, 1912 (died 1944); m. 2d Daisy Stanley-Brown, Mar. 12, 1946 (died 1949); married 3d Jessie Spencer Beach, July 5, 1950. Demonstrator pathology, Univ. of Pannsylvania, 1908-11; asst. prof. pathology, Harvard Med. Sch., 1911-14; prof. pathology, Western Reserve U., 1914-49; med. research adviser to Bur. Medicine and Surgry, U.S. Navy, from 1949; dir. Inst. Pathology, 1929-49; dir. Pathology, University Hosps.; div. chief of labs., City Hosp., 1914-49; cons. to Surg. Gen., U.S.A. Mem. sci. adv. bd. Armed Forces Inst. Pathology, adv. med. bd. Leonard Wood Meml. for Eradication Leprosy. Served as capt., Med. R.C., with A.E.F. in France, 1917-Feb. 11, 1918. Awarded W.W. Gerhard Medal, Phila. Path. Soc., Centennial Award, Northwestern U., 1951; Capt. Robert Dexter Conrad award, U.S. Navy, 1961. Fellow Aero. Med. Assn. (hon.), N.Y. Acad. Scis.; mem. Nat. Bd. Med. Examiners (pres. 1951-54), A.M.A., Assn. American Physicians, Am. Coll. Physicians, Am. Soc. Exptl. Pathol., Internat. Soc. Geog. Path. (vice president, Assn. Pathologists and Bacteriologists Society Exptl. Biology and Med., A.A.A.S. (v.p. Sect. N, 1931), Sigma Xi, Alpha Omega Alpha; corr. mem. various orgns. Rep. Club: Army and Navy. Author: Human Pathology, 1926, 55. Editor Year Book of Pathology, 1941-53. Contbr. tech. jours. Chmn. div. med. sciences, Nat. Research Council, 1927-28, chmn. com. on Pathology 1948-58; consultant in pathology, Army Air Forces, Army Med. Mus. and Office Scientific Research and Development, 1943-46; spl. cons. Secretary of War, 1946. Home: Washington DC Died Apr. 8, 1970; buried Beiliel Cemetery, Beiliel MD

KASAVUBU, JOSEPH, ex-pres. Republic Congo; b. Tshela, nr. Leopoldville, Congo, 1910; ed. Cath. missionaries; student seminary at Mbata Kiela, 1928-36; student theology and philosophy, sem. at Kabwe, Kasai Province, 1936-39; married; 8 children. Began career as tchr., 1941-59; clk. Leopoldville govt. offices, also tchr., agronomist, bookkeeper; elected pres. Abako, ethnocultural assns. of Lower Congo, 1955; burgomaster Dendale Commune, 1957; mayor of Leopoldville, 1958-59; imprisioned in Leopoldville, 1959; pres. Republic of the Congo, 1960-65; comdr. in chief Congolese Natl. Army, 1960-69. Author: Manifeste Abako, 1956. Editor: Le Droit du premier occupant. Address: Kinshasa Republic of the Congo Died Mar. 1969.

KASBERG, KARL GARY, poet, educator; b. Duluth, Minn., Mar. 25, 1932; s. Gerhardt and Edith Helen (Nelson) K.; student Concordia Coll., 1950; B.A., U. Minn., 1954; M.A., U. Mich., 1955; postgrad. U. Ind., 1955, U. Ia., 1956-59. Instr. English, U. Ia., 1955-58; instr. humanities Harpur Coll. Vestal, N.Y., 1958-60; fine arts editor Binghamton (N.Y.) Sun-Bull., 1960-61; instr. English, Santa Barbara (Cal.) City Coll., 1962-65; asst. prof., Bogan Coll., Chgo., guest lectr. Athens (Greece) Coll., 1964, various civic and cultural groups, N.Y. State, Cal., from 1958; organizer, dir. Santa Barbara Writers Conf., 1964, 65. Served with USNR, 1950-52. Recipient Edwin Markham award Poetry Soc. Am., 1966. Author: Cain, A Verse Play, Selected Poems, Animal Poems (all pub. posthumously). Contbr. poems in Western Humanities Rev., Etc., Border, Christian Century, Approach. Chicago IL Died Nov. 24, 1971; cremated.

KASTEN, HARRY EDWARD, physician, surgeon; b. Lowell Twp., Wis., Oct. 16, 1888; s. Gustav and Herminia (Stark) K.; student State Normal Sch., 1914-15, U. Wis., 1916-18; M.D., Rush Med. Coll., 1921; postgrad. N.Y. Polyclinic, 1929, U. Vienna, 1931; m. Irene Buckner, Nov. 3, 1925. Tchr. grade schs., Oak Grove, also Burnette, Wis. 1904-14; high sch. prin., Friendship, Wis., 1915; practice medicine, Muncie, Ind., 1922, Beloit, Wis., 1923-68, specializing urology, dermatology, 1931-68. Mem. nat. council Boy Scouts Am., exec. bd. Beloit area, also past pres.; exec. com., dir. Blue Shield Wis. Pres. Beloit City Council, 1940-41. Mem. premanent commn. Museum Med. Progress. Served with U.S. Army, World War I. Diplomate Am. Bd. Urology. Fellow A.C.S., Internat. Coll. Surgeons; mem. U. Wis. Alumni Assn., World Med. Assn., Wis. (pres. 1957-58, councillor 3d dist. 1948-57), Rock County, Mississippi Valley (adv. com.) med. socs., A.M.A. of Vienna (v.p. 1955), North Central Med. Conf. (pres. 1954), Am., Wis. (pres. 1938), Chgo. urol. socs., North Central br. Am. Urol. Assn., C. of C., Am. Legion, Phi Chi, Sigma Sigma. Republican. Rotarian (past pres.). Author articles profl. jours. Home: Beloit WI Died Sept. 28, 1968; buried East Lawn Cemetery, Beloit

KATCHEN, JULIUS, concert pianist; b. Long Branch, N.J., Aug. 15, 1926; s. Ira J. and Lucille (Svet) K.; B.A. in Philosophy and English Lit., Haverford Coll., 1945; m. Arlette Patoux, Apr. 10, 1956; 1 son, Stefan. Debut with Phila. Orch., 1937; then appearances with N.Y. Philharmonic and first UNESCO Festival in Paris with Conservatorie and National orchs., 1946; several world tours, 1946-69; 1st pianist to play complete works of Brahms in 4 recitals. Home: Paris France Died Apr. 29, 1969.

KATEK, CHARLES, fgn. service officer; b. Chgo., Oct. 31, 1910; s. Charles and Josephine Katek; A.B magna cum laude, U. Ill., 1932; A.M. magna cum laude, Northwestern U., 1937, Ph.D., 1942; student U. Cal., 1938; m. Anne Stich, Nov. 29, 1934; 1 dau., Janet. Instr. history Morton High Sch., Chgo., 1932-33; lectr., guidance counsellor Chgo. YMCA, 1933-34; econs. supr. minimum wage div. Ill. Dept. Labor, 1934-38; instr. history and econs. Morton Jr. Coll., Chgo., 1935-41; grad. fellow history Northwestern U., 1941-42; with State Dept., 1947-48; Dept. Army, 1948-60, State Dept., from 1960, assigned embassy, Vienna, Austria. Served to lt. col. AUS, 1942-47; ETO. Decorated Bronze Star. Mem. Am. Hist. Assn., Phi Beta Kappa. Author: Inflation, 1933. Home: Potomac MD Died Nov. 19, 1971.

KATTERLE, ZENO BERNEL, educator; born Sultan, Wash., Mar. 25, 1903; s. Hugo C. and Tillie (Young) K.; student Western Wash. Coll. Edn., 1924-27; M.A., Wash. State Univ., 1929, Ed.D., 1947; postgrad. U. Cal. at Berkeley, summers 1934, 35, 37; m. Kay Fulton, June 10, 1931; children—Zeno, Eleanor Kay, Kristen. Tchr. Chewelah (Wash.) High Sch., 1929, prin., 1930-33; supt. Garfield (Wash.) pub. schs., 1933-38; Toppenish (Wash.) pub. schs., 1938-42; finance supr. State Dept. Edn., Olympia, Wash., 1942; asst. supt. schs., Vancouver, Wash., 1942, 44, Portland, Ore., 1944-46; prof. edn. Wash. State U., Pullman, 1947-69, acting dean Coll. Edn., summer 1951, 52-53, then dean, dir.

summer session; vis. prof. Claremont Grad. Sch. summer, 1952, Tchrs. Coll. Columbia, 1958-59; USSR Education Tour for study edn., 1959, 64. Chmn. policy com., exec. com. N.W. Coop. Project Ednl. Adminstrn. Pres. Educators Life Foundation-State Wash. Recipient Nat. Service Key award Phi Delta Kappa, 1964. Mem. N.E.A., Am. Assn. Sch. Adminstrs., Wash. State Assn. Sch. Business Ofcls., Wash. Edn. Assn., Wash. State Supts. Assn., A.A.A.S., Profs. Ednl. Adminstrn., Am. Acad. Polit. and Social Sci., John Dewey Society, Omicron Delta Kappa, Phi Beta Kappa, Phi Kappa Phi, Phi Delta Kappa, Psi Chi, Tau Kappa Epsilon. Mason. Author: (with R. N. Pike) A Compilation of Laws and Proposals Relation to Federal Aid to Education, 1949; Introduction to Teaching in American Schools; also articles profl. jours. Home: Pullman WA Died Apr. 8, 1969.

KATZ, BENJAMIN SAMUEL, business executive; b. Austria, Apr. 15, 1892; s. Morris and Sadie (Hotez) K.; came to U.S., 1900, naturalized, 1922; ed. in pub. schs. of New York; m. Pearl Markowitz, Dec. 22, 1918 (dec. May 1961); children—Ira Robert, Marilynn; m. 2d, Isabelle Martin, June 15, 1962. Began career as a newsboy; later with John Wanamaker, dept. store; with C.G. Willoughby, camera supplies, New York, 1908-10; prop. of Empire Photo Co., photographic shops, New York, 1910-15; with New Era Mfg. Co., subsidiary of Robt. H. Ingersoll, watches, as salesman, dist. mgr., sales mgr., 1915-17; salesman Dinhofer Bros., mfg. jewelers, New York, 1917-18, v.p. and gen. mgr., 1918-20; organized Katz & Ogush, Inc., mfg. jewelers, New York, 1921, and pres. 1921-35; pres. The Gruen Watch Co., Cincinnati, 1935-53, also treas., 1936-53; chmn. bd. Hartmann Luggage Co., Lebanon, Tenn., 1955. Member exec. com. Hebrew Union Coll., Cin.; mem. bd. trustees Nat. Jewish Hosp., Denver; trustee Cin. Mus. Natural History; nat. chmn. finance com. Am. Jewish Com. Fellow Brandeis U. Mem. Nat. Conf. Christians and Jews, Nat. Council Joint Def. Appeal, Am. Ordnance Assn., Navy League, Am. Watch Assn. (pres. 1949-51). Jewish religion. Club: 24 Karat (N.Y.). Home: Beverly Hills CA Died Nov. 25, 1969; buried United Jewish Cemetery, Cincinnati OH

KATZENBERGER, WILLIAM E., clergyman, educator; b. Baltimore, Md., Nov. 3, 1876; s. John H. and Mary (Bell) K.; coll. and sem. courses, St. Vincent's Sem., Germantown, Pa.; spl. courses, U. of Pa. Joined Lazarist Fathers, 1895; ordained priest R.C. Ch., 1903; prof. mathematics and in charge students, St. John's Coll., Brooklyn, N.Y., 1906-12; dir. seminarians and prof. philosophy, 1912, prefect of studies and prof. mathematics, 1915; v.p. 1915, pres. 1918-27, Niagara U.; prof. theology, St. Vincent's Sem., Germantown, Pa., 1927-29; prof. theology, Niagara U., 1929-35, prof. of Liturgy since 1935. Address: Niagara University, NY‡

KATZ-SUCHY, JULIUSZ, govt. official, diplomate; b. Sanok, Poland, Jan. 28, 1912; s. Stefan and Roma (Ehrlich) K.; degree in law and economics, U. of Cracow (Poland), 1933; student U. of Warsaw, 1936, U. of Prague, Czechoslovakia, 1938; m. Elzbieta Nonkos. Began career as editor and editorial writer for Socialist Press, 1933-39; exile from polit. persecution in Czechoslovakia, 1938-39; escaped to Eng. where worked in war industry as engr., 1940-44; apptd. dep. dir. Polish Press Agency, London, Eng., 1944, press attache and sec., Polish Embassy, London, 1945; acting head Brit. Div., Ministry of Foreign Affairs, Warsaw, Poland; sec.-gen. Polish delegation 1st session U.N., 1946; alternate del. Security Council, 1947, acting rep. of Poland, 1948; E.E. and M.P. to U.N. since 1948; alternate del. 2d session U.N., head of delegation to 8th and 9th session U.N. Econ. and Socil Council, and chmn. delegation to 2d part of 3d session of Gen. Assembly, del. to Paris session. Mem. Polish Inst. to Internat. Affairs. Mem. Polish United Workers Party. Home: New York City NY Died Oct. 28, 1971.

KAUFFMAN, JAMES LEE, lawyer; b. Columbia, Pa., Jan. 18, 1886; s. Christian C. and Margaret (Wilson) K.; B.A., Princeton, 1908; LL.B., cum laude, Harvard, 1911; m. Ethel Cochran, June 7, 1913; children—Peggy Anne, Leesan. Editor of Harvard Law Review, 1909-11; admitted to practice before Pa. Supreme Court, 1911, and began practice at Lancaster; admitted to practice before N.Y. Court of Appeals, 1912; prof. English and Am. law, Imperial Univ., Tokyo, Japan, 1913-19; senior partner McIvor, Kauffman & Christensen, Tokyo. Decorated Order Sacred Treasure 2d class, Order of the Rising Sun 3d class (Japan). Presbyn. Clubs: University, Sleepy Hollow Country. Address: Tokyo Japan Died June 5, 1968; buried Columbia PA

KAUFFMANN, SAMUEL HAY, newspaper exec.; b. Washington, Feb. 24, 1898; s. Victor and Jessie (Christopher) K.; B.S., Princeton, 1920; m. Miriam Hoy, Apr. 6, 1921. Asst. advt. mgr. Evening Star Newspaper Co., Washington, 1926-29, asst. bus. mgr., 1929-44, bus. mgr., 1944-48, dir., 1927-71, asst. sec.-treas., 1936-41, treas., 1941-48, vice pres., 1948-49, pres., 1949-63, chmn. bd., 1963-71; dir. Shenandoah Valley Broadcasting Co., Harrisburg, Va., Evening Star Broadcasting Co. (pres. 1938-54), Washington Hosp. Center; v.p. bd. The Central Dispensary and Emergency Hosp.; dir. Columbia Planograph Company, also The Riggs National Bank, Acacia Mutual Life Ins. Co., Spruce Falls Power and Paper Company, Ltd. Trustee Am. U. Member American Cancer Society, Inc. (dir. D.C. div.). A.R.C. (dir. D.C. chapter; gen. campaign chmn. 1945 for Washington met. area), Washington Nat. Monument Soc. Episcopalian. Clubs: Metropolitan, Chevy Chase, Alfalfa (Washington); Percy (N.H.) Summer (treas.); University Cottage (Princeton, N.J.); Alibi. Home: Washington DC Died Jan. 12, 1971.

KAUFFMANN, VICTOR, newspaper man; b. Washington, Jan. 3, 1868; s. Samuel Hay and Sarah (Fracker) K.; A.B., Princton, 1889, A.M., 1892; m. Jessie Christopher, Nov. 27, 1894; children—Philip Christopher, Samuel Hay. Began as reporter on Washington Star, 1889, became Sunday editor, 1903; treas. and dir. Evening Star Newspaper Co.; dir. Nat. Savings & Trust Co. Episcopalian. Clubs: Chevy Chase, Racquet (Washington); Princeton (New York). Home: 1901 24th St., Washington DC‡

KAUFMAN, DAVID E., lawyer; b. Bradford County, Pa., May 15, 1883; s. Marks and Rachel K.; LL.B., Dickinson Sch. of Law, Carlisle, Pa., 1904; Doctor of Laws, Social Sciences and Political Economy, University of San Simon, Cochabamba, Bolivia, 1928; Dr. Humane Letters, Hebrew Union College, 1957; m. Florence Glass, September 24, 1942. Admitted to Pennsylvania bar, 1904, and began practice with Judge A.C. Fanning, Towanda; E.E. and M.P. to Bolivia, 1928-30; E.E. and M.P. to Siam, July 1930-33; later associated in law practice with Brown & Williams; trustee Philadelphia Rapid Transit Co. First v.p., dir. Pa. Range Boiler Co., Inc., Phila.; spl. master in railroad reorgn. proceedings U.S. Circuit Ct. of Appeals. Mem. adv. bd. So. Pa. Red Cross Membership Fund drive; co-chmn. 1954 campaign, dir. United Jewish Appeal; trustee Council Ref. Synagogues Greater Phila. De. Inter-Am. Bar Assn. Conference, 1954; alternate U.S. deletate Inter-American Conference, 1954. Decorated Grand Cross, Order of Condor of the Andes, Boivia (1st Am. to receive this honor). Clubs: Manfacturers and Bankers Club, Locust, Philmont (Phila.); Palm Beach (Fla.) Country Club; Press Club of Bolivia (organizer; hon. pres.). Apptd. by Pres. Commr. of Soo Locks Centennial Celebration Commn., 1950. Home: Philadelphia PA Died Sept. 5, 1962; buried Har Nebo Cemetery, Philadelphia PA

KAUFMANN, JOHN HEIDEN, economist, govt. ofcl.; b. N.Y.C., May 20, 1919; s. Fritz and Irma (Heiden) K.; B.A. with honors, Swarthmore Coll., 1940; M.P.A., Harvard, 1947, Ph.D. (Littauer scholar 1947-48) in Polit. Economy and Govt., 1953; m. Helen Burrows Reynolds, Aug. 24, 1946; children—Jeffrey Reynolds, Rebecca. Economist, Dept. Labor, 1941-42, 46, Nat. Security Resources Bd., 1948-50, Office of Adminstr. Econ. Stblzn. Agy., 1950-53; econ. cons., Washington, 1953-57; v.p. Boni, Watkins, Jason & Co., 1957-58; econ. adviser Govt. Iran, 1958-61; cons. White House Task Force on Ryuku Islands, 1961; dir. Office of Greece, Turkey, Iran, Cyrpus and CENTO Affairs, AID, Dept. State, 1962-63; mem. sr. seminar in fgn. policy Fgn. Service Inst., 1963-64; asst. dir. devel. planning AID Mission to Brazil, 1964-69; asso. asst. adminstr. Bur. for Program and Policy Coordination, AID, Washington, 1969-72. Served from pvt. to maj., AUS, 1942-46. Mem. Am. Econ. Assn., Soc. Internat. Devel. Home: Hollin Hills VA Died Dec. 31, 1972.

KAUVAR, C(HARLES) E(LIEZER) HILLEL, rabbi; b. Vilna, Russia, Aug. 14, 1879; s. Solomon S. and Rose M. (De Waltoff) K.; came to U.S., 1892; B.A., Coll. City of New York, 1900; M.A., Columbia University, 1901; rabbi Jewish Theological Seminary, 1902, L.H.D., 1909, D.D., honoris causa, 1942; D.D. honoris causa, University of Denver, 1952; m. Belle G. Bluestone, June 25, 1909 (died June 7, 1930);children—Solomon S., Abraham Judah and Golde Fage; m. 2d, Sara Sperber Gross, February 23, 1937. Rabbi Beth ba-Medrosh Hagodol Synagogue, Denver, from 1902, elected for life, 1919; professor Rabbinic literature, Univ. of Denver, 1920-65. Organized Denver Hebrew Sch., 1905; established Belle G. Kauvar Fund for Edn., 1930, Nat. Jewish Edn. Fund, 1933; rabbi C.E. Hillel Kauvar Colony in Israel, established by Denver Jewish Nat. Fund, from 1949; founder Denver Mizrachi, 1911, Denver Zionist Orgn., Jewish Consumptives Relief Soc. Denver, 1904, Intermountain Jewish News, 1913, Jewish Free Loan Soc. Recipient awards and citations Denver Fraternal Order Eagles, 1949, Denver Ministerial Alliance, 1951, Kiwanis Club, 1951, Citizen's Com. Denver, Colo. and Rocky Mountain Region (honoring 50th anniversary in rabbinate), 1952, Denver Area Community Chest, 1954, Cosmopolitan Club, 1954, Am. Jewish Tercentenary Com., 1955, Orthodox Jewish Congregations Am., 1958, Nat. Jewish Welfare Bd., 1959, Jewish War Vets U.S.A., 1959, Kiwanis Club, 1961, Adult Edn. Council Met. Denver, 1962, Nat. Conf. Christians and Jews, 1962, Regis Coll., 1964, Israel Bond Orgn., 1964, State of Colo., 1964, Hadassah, 1965; synagogue built in Ramle, Israel, named in his honor, 1961; Rabbi C.E.H. Kauvar Hebrew Sch. Bldg. named for him by B.M.H. Synagogue, 1952; Kauvar chair in Hebraic studies established at U. Denver, 1966. Fellow Jewish Academy Arts and Sciences, 1950; past president Jewish Welfare Bd., Central Jewish Council, Denver Philos. Soc., Midwest br. Rabbinical Conf.; v.p. United Synagogues America; Colo. del. 1st Am. Jewish Congress, 1917; pres. Rabbinical Council of Rocky Mountain Region. Mem. Denver Morals Commn. Author: Ceremony and Symbol in Judaism, 1914; Pirke Aboth Comments, 1929; What is Judaism (in Hebrew); Religion, the Hope of the World, 1949; The Voice of the Torah, 1952; Faith for Today, 1959; Torah Comments in Hebrew, 1962; Voice of the Prophets, 1965. Home: Denver CO Died Aug. 23, 1971; buried Sanhedria Cemetery, Jerusalem Israel

KAVANAUGH, JOHN MICHAEL, fgn. service officer; b. Clay, La., Mar. 1, 1918; s. Joseph Michael and Mary Ruth (Kendall) K.; B.A., La. Polytech. Inst., 1937; M.A., La. State U., 1937; m. Virginia Ware Gaines, Dec. 30, 1942; children—Michael G., Kathleen V. Asst. prof. English, La. Polytech. Inst., 1937-42; joined U.S. fgn. service, 1946, vice consul, Munich, Germany, 1946-49, Halifax, Can., 1949-50; consul, St. John, N.B., Can., 1950-52; officer charge Australian and New Zealand affairs State Dept., 1952-58; polit. officer Am. embassy, The Hague, Netherlands, from 1958. Served to maj. USAAF, 1942-46; ETO. Decorated Air medal with 6 battle stars. Mem. Sigma Tau Delta, Kappa Delta Phi. Home: Clay LA

KAWABATA, YASUNARI, Japanese writer; b. 1899; B.A., Tokyo U. Mem. editorial staff jour. Bungei Shunju 1925. Bd. dirs. PEN Club. Recipient Bungei Konwa Kai prize, 1937, Goethe medal, 1959, Nobel prize for lit., 1968. Author: Dancers of Izu Province, 1925; Red Group of Asakusa, 1925; Snow Country; Thousand Cranes. Address: Kanagawa Prefecture Japan Died Apr. 16, 1972; buried Kamakura Reien (cemetery park), Japan

KAYAN, CARL F(REDERIC), educator, engineer; born N.Y.C., July 24, 1899; s. John Adam and Johanna (Freund) K.; A.B., Columbia, 1922, M.E., 1924; m. Barbara Helen Sherman, June 24, 1931; children—Cynthia Sherman, Julia Helen. Asst. mech. engring. Columbia, 1924-26, instr., 1926-37, asst. prof., 1937-44, asso. prof., 1944-48, prof., 1948-65, Stevens professor mechanical engineering, 1965-68, Stevens prof. mech. engring. emeritus, 1968-70, exec. officer dept. mech. engring., 1948-55; visiting prof. Royal Sch. Technology, Stockholm, 1955; also cons. engr. Mem. bd. Air Poll. Cont. N.Y.C., 1953-68. Sci. adv. council Refrigeration Research Foundation. Great Tchr. award Soc. Older Grads. of Columbia, 1959. Registered profl. engineer, New York and Cal. Fellow Am. Soc. of Mechanical Engineers, American Society of Heating, Refrigerating and Air Conditioning Engrs. (dr. 1965-68, Outstanding Teacher award 1964, also Distinguished Service award 1968), Instrument Society of American (pres. 1949), A.A.A.S., N.Y. Acad. Scis., Metric Assn. (v.p.), Internat. Inst. Refrigeration (pres. Commn. 2, 1959-67, ancien pres. 1967-70 Paris); mem. Inst. Measurement and Control (London, hon.), United Engring. Center N.Y. (library bd. 1968-70), Institut International du Froid (Paris, hon. member), A.A.A.S., John Ericsson Soc. (hon. v.p.), Am. Soc. Engring. Edn., Deutscher Kaltetechnischer Verein (hon.), Societe d'Encouragement pour la Recherche et l'Invention (comdr.), Sigma Xi, Tau Beta Pi, Pi Tau Sigma, Phi Kappa Psi. Clubs: Cosmos (Washington); Men's Faculty, Columbia U. Contbr. articles on energy-flow analysis, heat transfer, unit systems to sci. jours; contbr. sects. to Kent's Mechanical Handbook, 1948, Perry's Chemical Engineers Handbook, 1962; Marks' Mechanical Engineering Handbook, 1966, Ency. Sci. and Tech., 1968. Inventor, patentee in field. Home: Katonah NY Died July 5, 1970.

KEARNEY, ERICK WILSON, engr.; b. Franklinton, N.C., Feb. 26, 1906; s. Isaac Henry and Ozella (Williams) K.; B.S., N.C. State U., 1928; certificate pub. health U. N.C., 1936; M. Margaret Louise Lewis, Nov. 23, 1932; children—Erick W., William Lewis, Kay (Mrs. Jerry Gilbert), City clk. Town of Franklinton, N.C., 1929; supt. water plant Town of Mt. Airy, N.C., 1929-36; asst. san. engr. State of N.C., 1936-41; gen. engr. U.S. VA, 1946-69. Served to maj. AUS, 1941-46. Registered profl. engr., N.C. Mem. Tau Beta Pi. Democrat. Baptist. Mason. Home: Jackson MS Died Sept. 18, 1969.

KEARNS, WILLIAM MICHAEL, ins. exec.; b. Gardiner, Me., May 1, 1899; s. Peter and Mary (Barron) K.; B.A., U. Me., 1923; LL.B., N.J. Law Sch., 1934; m. Doris Mae Hodgkinson, Aug. 19, 1933; children—William Michael, Joan. Br. mgr. Liberty Mut. Ins. Co., Newark, 1923-33, Am. Lumbermans Mut. Ins. Co., N.Y.C., 1934-35; asst. sec. Sun Indemnity Co. of N.Y., 1936, sec., 1938, v.p., dir., 1948, pres. 1950-55 (merged with Patriotic Ins. Co. Am., Sun Underwriters Ins. Co. N.Y.), pres. Sun Ins. Co. of N.Y., 1955-57, chmn. bd., 1957-64; U.S. gen. atty. Sun. Ins. Office Ltd., 1957-64; past financial sec., dir. Albany Ins. Co., Provident Ins. Co.; past financial sec. Atlas Assurance Co., Ltd., Royal Assurance Co., Ltd. Past mem. U.S. adv. com. Brit. Marine Trust Fund; past mem. exec. com. Nat. Bd. Fire Underwriters. Mem. Beta Theta Pi, Kappa Phi Kappa. Club: Maplewood NJ Died Nov. 28, 1972.

KEATING, F(RANCIS) RAYMOND, JR., physician; b. Phila., May 20, 1911; s. F. Raymond and Metta (Schaaf) K.; A.B., Cornell, 1933, M.D., 1936; M.S., U. Minn., 1942; m. Marion S. Bright, June 17, 1936; children—Priscilla, Peter, Cynthia, Michael. Intern Phila. Gen. Hosp., 1936-38; specializing endocrine and metabolic diseases, 1940-69; cons. medicine Mayo Clinic, 1942-69, prof. medicine Mayo Found. Med. Edn. and Research, grad. sch. U. Minn., 1953-69. Diplomate Am. Bd. Internal Medicine. Fellow A.C.P.; mem. Am., Minn. State med. assns., Minnesota Society of Internal Medicine. Endocrine Soc., Central Soc. Clin. Research, Am. Thyroid Assn. (pres. 1964), Zumbro Valley Med. Soc., Am. Soc. Clin. Investigation, Assn. Am. Physicians, Sigma Xi, Alpha Omega Alpha. Author med. articles. Home: Rochester MN Died Sept. 13, 1969.

KEATING, JOHN, writer, editor; b. N.Y.C., June 8, 1918; s. V. J. and Mary (O'Brien) K.; A.B., Manhattan Coll., 1941; m. Marianne Byer, May 30, 1946. Writer mag. articles, 1946-69; feature editor Cue mag., 1949-52, drama critic, editor, 1952-57; entertainment columnist Cosmopolitan mag., 1956-59; daily television program WOR-TV 1953; entertainment columnist Charm mag., 1951-53. Served as pvt. to 1st lt. U.S.A., 1942-46. Mem. Drama Desk (pres. 1954-56), Critics Circle. Contbr. to N.Y. Times Sunday drama sect. and mag. Home: New York City NY Died Jan. 29, 1968; buried Little Silver NJ

KEATING, LAURENCE FREEMAN, mfg. exec.; b. North Berwick, Me., Sept. 6, 1910; s. Freeman E. and Ora E. (Pitts) K.; M.E., Rensselaer Poly. Inst., 1931; m. Margot J. Henzell, Mar. 5, 1938 (div.); children—Anthony L., John R.; m. 2d, Jeanne Wells, Dec. 17, 1951; children—Patricia, William Harris. Indsl. engr. United Mchts. & Mfrs., Inc., N.Y.C., 1933, also subsidiaries United Rayon Mills, Arkwright Corp., Bristol Supply Co., 1933-35, installed textile mill for subsidiary Sudamtex S.A., Buenos Aires, 1935-39, gen. plant supt. various plants Latin Am., 1939-54, charge parent co. interest in Argentina, Venezuela, Uruguay and Brazil, 1954, then exec. v.p., dir., N.Y.C.; chmn. United Internat. Corp., N.Y.C.; dir. Sudamtex Argentina, Sudamtex de Uruguay, Sudamtex de Venezuela, Sudamtex do Brazil. Home: Buenos Aires Argentina Died Nov. 8, 1968; buried Alfred ME

KEEFE, DAVID ANDREW, consulting engr.; b. Athens, Pa., Jan. 28, 1869; s. Marcus and Mary (Pyne) K.; ed. pub. schs. of Athens and Athens Acad.; m. Clara Angela Wingerter, Sept. 24, 1913; children—Mary Clare, David A. Practiced, Athens, since 1896; pres. Merchants & Mechanics Nat. Bank, Sayre, Pa.; dir. Athens Nat. Bank; cons. engr. for Bradford, Luzerne and Carbon counties, Pa.; designer of reinforced concrete pier at Atlantic City, etc. Del. Rep. State Conv., 1912. Catholic. Mem. Am. Soc. C.E., Engineers' Soc. Pa., etc. Club: Shepard Hills Country. Home: Athens PA‡

KEEFER, CHESTER SCOTT, physician; b. Altoona, Pa., May 3, 1897; s. John Henry and Gertrude (Scott) K.; B.S., Bucknell U., 1918, M.S., 1922, hon. D.Sc., 1944; M.D., Johns Hopkins University, 1922; D.Sc. (honorary), Boston University, 1944, Bates College, 1962; m. Jean Balfour, August 11, 1928 (dec. Apr. 1967); 1 dau, Ishbel McGill; m. 2d, Dorothy Campbell, Mar. 27, 1971. Resident house officer, Johns Hopkins Hosp., 1922-23, asst. resident physician, 1923-26; asst. in medicine, Johns Hopkins U., 1923-25, instr. in medicine, 1925-26; resident physician, Billings Hosp., Univ. Clinics, U. of Chicago, 1926-28; asso. prof. of medicine, Peiping Union Med. Coll., China, 1928-30; asst. prof. of medicine, Harvard Med. Sch., 1930-36, asso. prof., 1936-40; asso. physician, Thorndike Memorial Lab., Boston City Hosp., 1930-40, consulting physician from 1940; jr. visiting physician, Boston City Hosp. from 1937; dir. 2d and 4th Med. Services (Harvard), Boston City Hosp., also chief 4th Med. Service, 1939-40; Wade prof. of medicine, Boston University Sch. of Medicine, 1940-64, Wade professor of medicine emeritus, 1964-72; dir. Robert Dawson Evans Meml. Hosp., 1940-59; physician in chief Mass. Meml. Hosp., 1940-59; dir. Boston U. Sch. Medicine, 1955-59; dir. Boston U.-Mass. Meml. Hosps. Med. Center, 1959-60. Member board directors Merck &Co., Inc. Mem. Exec. com., div. med. sci. NRC, Med. adminstrv. officer Com. Med Research O.S.R.D., 1944, 46, spl. asst. to Sec. of Health, Education & Welfare. Decorated Medal of Merit (U.S.); His Majesty's Medal. Diplomate Am. Bd. Internal Medicine. Fellow A.C.P. (pres. 1960; regent), Am. Acad. Arts and Scis.; mem. Am. Soc. Clinic Investigation Assn. Am. Physicians, Am. Clin. and Climatol. Assn., A.M.A., Am. Phila. Soc., Interurban Clin. Club. Phi Beta Kappa, Phi Gamma Delta, Phi Chi, Alpha Omega Alpha. Repub. Presbyn. Clubs: Harvard, St. Botolph (Boston); Cosmos, Capitol Hill (Washington); Country (Brookline); Harvard (N.Y.); Hunt (London, Ont.). Home: Brookline MA Died Feb. 3, 1972; buried Walnut Hills Cemetery, Brookline MA

KEEGAN, HARRY JOSEPH, physicist; b. Washington, Oct. 11, 1903; s. Harry Michael and Mary C.F. (Turner) K.; B.Mech. Engring., George Washington U., 1940; student U. Cin., 1929-33, U. Mich., 1939; m. Ruth Elizabeth Parker, Dec. 28, 1935; children—Joanne Marie, Rosemary Elizabeth (Mrs. Mark M. Powdermaker). Physicist Nat. Bur. Standards, Washington, 1921-66, coordinator infrared optical measurements program, 1963-66; Sirrine chair textile sci. Sch. Indsl. Mgmt. and Textile Sci., Clemson (S.C.) U., 1966-68. Lectr. mech. engring. machine design George Washington U., Washington, 1942-47; Nat. Bur. Standards rep. to absorption spectroscopy com. Am. Soc. Testing Materials, 1966. Fellow Optical Soc. Am., A.A.A.S., Washington Acad. Sci.; mem. Inter-Soc. Color Council, Nat. Geographic Soc., Am. Chem. Soc., Soc. Applied Spectroscopy, Am. Phys. Soc., Am. Assn. Textile Chemists and Colorists (sr. mem.), Sigma Xi. Contbr. articles to profl. publs. Home: Clemson SC

KEEGAN, JOHN JOSEPH, govt. official; b. Wilmington, Del., July 3, 1872; s. John Augustus and Ann (McCaffrey) K.; ed. public grade and high schs. of Wilmington, Del.; m. Hedwiga Louise Schmidt, Jan. 5, 1917; children—Patricia Mary, Helen Agatha, Theresa Hedwiga. Began as machinist, 1890; v.p. Internat. Assn. Machinists, 1900-06; mem. U.S. Employees Compensation Commn., 1917-25 and since 1937; mem. of Bldg. and Loan Commn., Ind., 1913-15; mem. Ind. Legislature, 1911-13. Democrat. Roman Catholic. Office: Employees Compensation Commission of U.S., Murray Hill Bldg., New York NY*‡

KEEHN, CLARENCE (HECKMAN), business exec.; b. Buckley, Ill., July 5, 1872; s. Hiram William and Katurah Clever (Bertolette) K.; m. Elizabeth Davy, June 1, 1897; children—Hiram Davy, Helen Janet (widow of Dr. Paul M. H. Beard). Temporary employee Bowen Stewart (now Bobbs-Merrill Pub. Co.), Indianapolis, 1883; with Kingan & Co., packers, Indianapolis, 1887-91, cashier, 1891-1900, mgr. fgn. dept., 1900-48, mgr. provision dept. and vice pres., since 1926, bd. drs., 1929-48. Republican. Presbyterian. Mason. Home: 2800 Cold Spring Rd., Indianapolis 22 IN‡

KEEL, ELMO W., 1st nat. comdr., AMVETS; b. Jonesville, Va., Aug. 11, 1914; s. Walter J. and Myrtle (Adkinson) K.; grad. Pennington High Sch., 1929-33, New England Air Craft Sch., 1941-42, Columbia Tech. Inst., 1942; B.S., George Washington U., 1947; m. Polly March, Jan. 27, 1942 (divorced); m. 2d Jessie Howell, June 1950 (dec. 1961); children—Margaret Ann Keel Pollock, Mary Louise; m. 3d, Nora E. Palm Hall, 1963. Public relations work, salesman N. American Cement Corporation. County surveyor in Lee County, Virginia; building inspector 9th Congl. Dist., Va., founder of Am. Vets (Am. Vets of World War II), became nat. exec. committeeman; dist. mgr. Ohio Hoist Mfg. Co., Cleveland; sales engr. Safway Steel Products Co. of Milwaukee. Joined Army Air Corps as private, 1939; became master sergeant; flight engr. in Burma-China Theater; discharged, 1943. Mem. Society for Advancement of Indsl. Management; student mem. Am. Inst. of Electrical Engrs. Awarded Purple Heart Citation, Asiatic-Pacific Theater ribbons. Mem. Goerge Washington U. Veterans Club. Home: Oxon Hill MD Died Jan. 15, 1969; buried Jonesville VA

KEENAN, ALBERT JOSEPH, JR., transportation exec.; b. Bklyn., Apr. 15, 1913; s. Dr. Albert J. and Helen M. (Reichmann) K.; A.B., Dartmouth, 1935; LL.B., Bklyn. Law Sch., 1939; m. Katherine C. Lee, June 20, 1942; children—Albert J. III, Gail Lee, Barbara Lee. Admitted to N.Y. bar, 1939; asso. editor U.S. Code Annotated, 1939-40; with Moore-McCormack Lines, Inc., N.Y.C., 1945-68, gen. passenger traffic mgr., 1954-57, v.p., 1957-68. Mem. travel adv. com. U.S. Travel Service. Served as maj., M.I., AUS, 1941-45. Mem. Defense Orientation Conference Association, Maritime Association of Port of New York, Am. Soc. Travel Agts. (chmn. Western Hemisphere com. 1956-57). Am. Merchant Marine Inst., Vets. 7th Regt. N.Y., S.Am. Travel Orgn. (pres. 1966-68), Inst. Certified Transportation Agts. (founder, trustee), Sigma Nu, Phi Delta Phi. Episcopalian (vestry 1954-60). Clubs: New York Skal, Downtown Athletic, Bon Vivants (N.Y.C.); Propeller U.S. (nat. exec. com. 1957); Travel Executives. Home: New York City NY Died Aug. 14, 1968; buried at sea.

KEENAN, ALEXANDER STANISLAUS, surgeon; b. Lakeville, Calif., Nov. 14, 1872; s. Alexander and Mary (Dougherty) K.; M.D., U. of Calif. Med. Sch., 1898; LL.D., U. of Santa Clara, 1926; m. Laura Maguire, Apr. 16, 1901; children—Mary Jane (Mrs. Wallace Sheehan), Alexander Stanislaus, Olive (wife of Dr. William A. Carroll), Peter. In practice since 1898; visiting surgeon to Mary's Help Hosp. since 1908; commr. Pub. Health, San Francisco, 1927-32. Med. dir. Health Service Systems of San Francisco. Fellow Am. Coll. Surgeons. Democrat. Catholic. K.C., Elk. Club: Olympic. Home: Clift Hotel. Office: Health Service System, Civic Auditorium, San Francisco‡

KEENE, ARTHUR SAMUEL, architect; b. Brighton, Mass., Sept. 21, 1875; s. Samuel and Marianna (Fuller) K.; B.S., Mass. Inst. of Tech., 1898; m. Louisa White Fowler, Sept. 25, 1901; m. 2d, Helen Bangs Clark, March 2, 1935. Began as archtl. draftsman Oct., 1898; partner firm of Keene & Simpson, Architects, since 1909. Chmn. com. to revise Kansas City Bldg. Code. Fellow A.I.A.; mem. Delta Upsilon. Mason (32 deg., Shriner, Scottish Rite). Clubs: Kansas City, Mission Hills Country, Mercury, Hunting and Fishing (Kansas City). Home: 1211 W. 68th Terrace. Address: 15 W. 10th St., Kansas City MO‡

KEENEY, PAUL ALOYSIUS, physician; b. Wilkes Barre, Pa., June 6, 1903; M.D., U. Pitts., 1931; M.P.H., Johns Hopkins, 1940; m. Ann F.W. Keeney; children—Cormac W., Ann F., Sean. Intern, St. Francis Hosp., Pitts., 1931-32, chief resident in medicine, 1932-33; comdg. officer Bermada Base Hosp., Waltham (Mass.) Regional Hosp., Murphy Gen Hosp., Waltham; dir. med. edn. St. Mary and St. Elizabeth Hosp., Louisville; clin. dir. Williamson (W.Va.) Regional Hosp. Served to col. AUS, 1943-55. Diplomate Am. Bd. Preventive Medicine. Fellow A.C.P., Am. Pub. Health Assn., Am. Coll. Preventive Medicine; mem. A.M.A., Alpha Omega Alpha. Home: Louisville KY Died July 17, 1970; buried Arlington Nat. Cemetery.

KEESING, FRANS ARNOLD GEORGE, economist; b. Hilversum, The Netherlands, Aug. 7, 1913; s. Arnold and Francisca (Gunzel) K.; Ph.D. in Econs., U. Amsterdam, 1939; m. Geertruida Kok, Apr. 4, 1939; children—Frans J., Wouter, Hugo A., Joost. With Unilever Bros., London, Eng., 1937-39, Ministry Commerce, The Hague, 1939-45, Ministry Finance, 1945-51; with Internat. Monetary Fund, Washington, 1951-72, dir. fund's inst., 1964-72; prof. money and credit U. Amsterdam, 1946-51. Decorated Lion of Netherlands; Crown of Belgium; Legion of Honor (France). Author books and articles in field. Home: Bethesda MD Died Oct. 1972.

KEEVIL, CHARLES SAMUEL, educator; b. Woodside, L.I., N.Y., Oct. 3, 1899; s. Charles James and Paulina (Harrer) K.; S.B., Mass. Inst. Tech., 1923, S.M., 1927, Sc.D., 1930; m. Charlotte W. Thropp, May 28, 1924 (dec. 1937); 1 son, Charles Samuel; m. 2d, Etta Belle Pence, Sept. 12, 1938. Instr. chem. engring. Mass. Inst. Tech., 1927-30; prof. chem. engring., chmn. dept. Ore. State Coll., 1930-36, Bucknell U., 1936-45; on leave with Nat. Def. Research Com., 1943-45; chem. engr., sr. staff mem. Arthur D. Little, Inc., 1945-59; prof. chem. engring. Northeastern U., from 1960. Recipient Army-Navy certificate of appreciation, 1948. Registered profl. engr., Mass., Cal. Mem. Am. Chem. Soc., Am. Inst. Chem. Engrs., Am. Assn. U. Profs., Sigma Xi, Phi Lambda Upsilon, Theta Delta Chi, Tau Beta Pi, Phi Kappa Phi, Omega Chi Epsilon. Home: Needham MA Died July 19, 1969; buried Urn Garden, Newton (Mass.) Cemetery.

KEFAUVER, CLARENCE EUGENE, savs. and loan assn. exec.; b. Frederick, Md., June 18, 1894; s. William E. and Etta (Koogle) K.; B.C.S., Benjamin Franklin U., Washington, 1922; m. Della Miller, May 16, 1919; 1 son, Clarence Eugene. Teller, Munsey Trust Co., Washington, 1915; stenographer Treasury Dept., 1917-22; auditor Bur. Internal Revenue, 1923-26; engaged as accountant, 1926-28; with Columbia Fed. Savs. and Loan Assn., Washington, 1928-68, pres., 1948-68; dir. Dist., Realty Title Ins. Co. Bd. dirs. Washington Real Estate Bd., 1944-45. Served with U.S. Army, World War I. Mem. Soc. Residential Appraisers (pres. D.C. 1941), U.S. (exec. com. 1951-54), D.C. (pres. 1943-44) savs. and loan leagues. Mason (32 deg., Shriner). Clubs: University (Washington); Columbia Country (Chevy Chase, Md.). Home: Bethesda MD Died Nov. 20, 1968.

KEGEL, ARNOLD HENRY, commr. of health, Chicago; b. Lenox, S.D., Feb. 21, 1894; s. Rev. Arnold and Amelia (Lageman) K.; grad. high sch., Lansing, Ia.; student Dubuque (Ia.) U.; M.D., Loyola U., 1916; spl. student in surgery, Mayo Clinic, Rochester, Minn., 1917-22; m. Marie V. Sahlin, of Chicago, Ill., Aug. 16, 1924; 1 son, Robert Arnold. Began practice at Chicago, Ill., 1922; attending surgeon John B. Murphy Hosp., Ill. Masonic Hosp. and West Suburban Hosp.; commr. of health, Chicago, since 1927. Mem. A.M.A., Chicago Med. Soc., Phi Delta. Mason. Clubs: Lake Shore Athletic, Chicago Yacht, Ridgemoor Country. Home: 2820 Pine Grove Av. Office: City Hall, Chicago IL‡

KEHL, JOHN ELWIN, consul; b. Cincinnati, O., Oct. 10, 1870; s. John and Louise (Buehler) K.; ed. high sch. and business coll.; m. Corine C. Beyer, of Cincinnati, Jan. 10, 1892; children—Willard Driver, Mrs. Naomi Louise Wortham. In printing and pub. business, until 1897; apptd. consul at Stetin, Germany, Oct. 15, 1897; consul at Sydney, N.S., 1908-11, at Saloniki, Turkey, Aug. 19, 1911, at Aarhus, Denmark, 1918-21; attached to Am. Commn., Berlin, Germany, March-Nov. 1921; consul at Breslau, Germany, 1921-24; consul Stuttgart, Germany, 1924-29; consul gen., Hamburg, Germany, since 1929. Episcopalian. Mason (32 deg.). Clubs: Royal C.B. Yacht, Gun and Rod. Address: American Consulate General, Hamburg Germany‡

KEHLENBECK, ALFRED PAUL, educator; b. Omaha, Feb. 24, 1906; s. Hermann and Anna (Stohlmann) K.; B.A., U. Ia., 1927, M.A., 1928; Ph.D., U. Wis., 1934; m. Dorothy Severin, June 27, 1932. Instr. German, Coe Coll., 1928-29, asst. prof., acting head dept., 1930-32; instr. German, Oberlin Coll., 1929-30; asst. prof., acting head dept. German, Ohio Wesleyan U., 1934-35; asst. to prof. modern langs. Ia. State U., 1935-46, prof., head dept., 1950-69; asso. prof. German, U. Va., 1946-50. Editorial cons. Brit. World Dictionary, 1954. Mem. Am. Assn. Tchrs. German (past pres. Ia. chpt.), Modern Lang. Assn., Am. Dialect Soc., Phi Beta Kappa. Mason. Club: Ames Camera (past pres.). Author: (with DeVries) Essentials of Reading German, 1952. Home: Ames IA Died Aug. 4, 1969; buried Ia. State U. Cemetery, Ames IA

KEHOE, ARTHUR HENRY, ret. utilities exec.; b. Bennington, Vt., Feb. 18, 1889; s. Charles S. and Etta M. (Wilkins) K.; B.S., U. of Vt., 1911, D.Eng., 1944; m. Eliza Hart, July 17, 1915; children—Edward Charles (dec.), Hester, Arthur Henry, Charles William. Engring. asst. United Electric Light & Power Co., N.Y. City, 1911-14, dist. engr., 1914-19, supt. transmission and distbn., 1919-21, elec. engr., 1921-32, v.p. United and N.Y. Edison Cos., 1932-36; dir. both cos., 1935-36, v.p. merged co., Consol. Edison Co. of N.Y., Inc., 1936-69, v.p. charge station constrn. and shops, 1936-50, v.p. consultative assignments, 1950-52, v.p. charge of production and operation, 1952-54; dir. New York Steam Company, Consolidated Telegraph & Elec. Subway Co., 1943-54, Yonkers Elec. Light & Power Co., 1943-51. Councilman, mem. bd. edn., Borough of Rutherford. Fellow Am. Inst. E.E., awarded Lamme medal, 1943. Mem. adv. bd. of Edison Electric Inst. (v.p., 1933-40). Dir. Nat. Fire Protection Assn., N.Y. Elec. Soc. (past pres.); bd. dirs., N.Y. Safety Council, Goodwill Industries. Club: Yonticaw Country (pres.). Home: Rutherford NJ Died Jan. 9, 1969; buried Park Lawn Cemetery, Bennington VT

KEHOE, (JAMES) WALTER, congressman; b. Eufaula, Barbour Co., Ala., Apr. 25, 1870; s. John Francis and Anne Virginia (O'Hara) K.; admitted to practice in Fla., at 19, by spl. act of legislature; later admitted to Supreme Court of U.S.; m. Jennie Jenkins, of Geneva, Ala., Sept. 8, 1898. Elected to Fla. Ho. of Rep., 1900, but resigned; was mem. Dem. Congressional Exec. Com.; state's atty., 1st Jud. Circuit of Fla., 1900-9; mem. 65th Congress (1917-19), 3d Fla. Dist.; Democrat. Presbyn. Mason, Elk. Home: Pensacola FL‡

KEILBERTH, JOSEPH, German condr.; b. Apr. 19, 1908; student Karlsruhe Conservatoire. Repetiteur, Karlsruhe State Theater, 1925, gen. mus. dir., 1929; dir. German Philharmonic Orch., Prague, 1940; dir. Dresden State Opera, 1945-50; prin. condr. Berlin State Opera, 1948-50; gen. mus. dir. City of Hamburg and artistic dir. Hamburg Philharmonic State Orch., 1950-59; condr.-in-chief Bamberg Symphony Orch. (successor to German Philharmonic Orch. of Prague), 1950-59; extended concert tours with Bamberg Symphony Orch., concert and operatic engagements in numerous European cities; conducted at Bayreuth Festivals, 1952-56; resident condr. Bavarian State Opera, 1959—; permanent guest condr. Hamberg State Opera. Address: Munich Germany Died July 21, 1968.*

KEISER, LAURENCE BOLLON, army officer; b. Philadelphia, June 1, 1895; s. Elmer Edgar (M.D.) and Jeanie (Deans) K.; B.S., U.S. Mil. Acad., 1917; grad. Inf. Sch., co. officers class, 1923, field officers class, 1933. Command and Gen. Staff Sch., 1939; m. Marion Polk, Mar. 20, 1926. Commd. 2d lt., 6th U.S. Inf., 1917, advancing through the grades to brig. gen., 1944; with 5th U.S. Inf., Div., A.E.F., France, 1918-19; served in Philippine Islands and China, 1920-22; tractical officer Corps of Cadets, U.S. Mil. Acad., 1924-28; comd. 29th Inf., Ft. Benning, 1941-42; chief of staff, 3d Army Corps, Apr. 1942-Sept. 1943; chief of staff, 6th Army Corp., (italy), Sept. 1943-Mar. 1944; dep. chief of staff, 5th Army, Mar.-Apr., 1944; became chief of staff, 4th Army, 1944. Decorated Silver Star, Legion of Merit, Address: Washington DC Died Oct. 1969.*

KEITH, ADELPHUS BARTLETT, retired newspaperman; b. Denison, Ia., Oct. 24, 1877; s. Adelphus Bartlett and Carrie (Bieber) K.; ed. pub. schs., m. Bertha Taft, Aug. 7, 1900; children—Allie Hazelton (Mrs. Theodore F. McFadden), Vernadel Eugenia (Mrs. Winthrop Seelye). Telegraph editor Helena Herald, 1900-01; telegraph editor Butte (Mont.) Miner, 1901-11, city editor, 1911-19, asst. mng. editor, 1926, mng. editor, 1926-28; mng. editor Montana Free Press, 1928-29; staff Spokesman-Review, Spokane, 1929-48; retired. Home: 1402 W. Montgomery Av., Spokane 12‡

KEITHAHN, EDWARD LINNAEUS, museum curator, author; b. Tenino, Wash., May 15, 1900; s. Henry John and Ina Mae (Swift) K.; A.B., U. Wash., 1938; m. Marie Antoinette La Chance, June 15, 1923; children—Yvonne (Mrs. Gale Mueller), Loretta (Mrs. Richard Penrod), Richard Edward. Tchr., Wash. State, 1920-23, Alaska, 1923-41; curator Alaska Hist. Library and Mus., 1941-65. Mem. Alaska adv. com. Bd. Geog. Names, 1948-70; chmn. Alaska Geog. Bd., 1963-70. Served with U.S. Army, 1918. Recipient plaque for distinguished service to Alaska, 1948. Outstanding Citizen award Alaska Press Club, 1964. Certificate of merit State of Alaska, 1965. Fellow A.A.A.S.; mem. Am. Assn. Museums, Soc. Am. Archaeology, Alaska Pioneers, Am. Legion. Democrat. Elk, Rotarian. Author: Igloo Tales, 1944; (with Juliet Morgan) Alaska and Hawaii, 1956; Eskimo Adventure, 1963; Monuments in Cedar, 1963; Native Alaskan Art, 1959; Alaska for the Curious, 1966; also articles. Address: Eugene OR Died Sept. 25, 1970; buried Eugene OR

KEITT, GEORGE WANNAMAKER, plant pathologist; b. Newberry County, S.C., June 11, 1889; s. Thomas Wadlington and Annie Selina (Wannamaker) K.; B.S., Clemson Coll., 1909, Sc.D., 1937; M.S., U. of Wis., 1911, Ph.D., 1914; m. Carol Seaver Keay, Aug. 30, 1927; children—George Wannamaker, Jr., John Keay, Alan Seaver. Asst. in botany and plant pathology, S.C. Agrl. Expt. Station, 1909-10; spl. agt. fruit disease investigations, U.S. Dept. Agr., 1910, and scientific asst., summers; scholar in plant pathology U. of Wis., 1911, lectr., 1912-14, asst. prof., 1914-17, asso. prof., 1917-20, prof., 1920-59, emeritus prof., 1959-69, part-time research professor, 1959-61, chairman dept. plant pathology, 1930-55; lecturer Mycol. Soc. of Am., 1956. Served as 1st lt. and capt. U.S. Army, World War; instr. Sch. of Arms, Camp Lee; asst. div. gas officer, 32d and 37th divs., div. gas officer 36th div., and asst. gas officer 1st Army, in France; maj. C.W.S., O.R.C. Fellow A.A.A.S.; mem. Am. Soc. Naturalists, Am. Phytopathol. Soc. (v.p. 1934, pres. 1937), Bot. Soc. America, Mycol. Soc. of America, Soc. Exptl. Biology and Medicine, Wis. Acad. Sciences, Arts and Letters, American Assn. University Professors (pres. Wis. chapter 1943-44), Indian Phytopathological Society, Nederlandse Plantenziektenkundige Vereniging; 7th Internat. Bot. Cong. (v.p. phytopathol. sect., 1950); guest speaker Brit. Assn. Advancement Sci., Edinburgh, 1951), Phi Sigma (honorary), Sigma Xi (president Wisconsin chapter, 1928-29), Gamma Alpha, Phi Kappa Phi (president Wisconsin chapter 1936-37), Chaos Club. Episcopalian. Club: University. Author of bulletins, contributor to professional journals. Mem. editorial bd. Am. Jour. Botany, 1935-44. Co-discoverer antimycin. Home: Cambridge MA Died Nov. 18, 1969; buried Old St. David's Churchyard, Radnor PA

KELCE, MERL C., ret. coal co. exec.; b. Pittsburg, Kan., 1905. Formerly exec. v.p., later pres., dir. Peabody Coal Co., chmn. exec. com.; past v.p., dir. Broken Aro Coal Co., Key Coal Co., Rogers County Coal Corp., Victoria Coal Corp., Sentry Royalty Co.; past pres., dir. Tecumseh Coal Corp., No. Ill. Coal Co., Sinclair Mines (Can.), Ltd. Home: St Louis MO

KELEHER, WILLIAM ALOYSIUS, lawyer; b. Lawrence, Kan., Nov. 7, 1886; s. David and Mary Ann (Gorry) K.; LL.B., Washington and Lee U., 1915; hon. M.A., U. N.M., 1946, LL.D., 1968; LL.D., U. Albuquerque, 1960; m. Mae J. Kelly, 1918 (dec. 1923); 1 dau., Mary Ann; m. 2d, Loretta Barrett, 1932; children—William Barrett, Michael Lawrence, John Gorry, Thomas Franklin. With Western Union Telegraph Co., Albuquerque, N.M., 1900-06; clk. bd. edn., Albuquerque, 1907-08; reporter, city editor Albuquerque Jour. and Albuquerque Herald, 1908-13; practiced law 1915-72. Chmn. Democratic State Central Com., 1928. Mem. N.M. State Finance Bd., 1932-49; pres. bd. regents N.M. Coll. Agr. and Mech. Arts, 1941-42. Certificate Recognition, Nat. Conf. Christians and Jews, 1966; elected N.M. Hall Fame, 1964. Mem. Am., N.M. bar assns., Phi Beta Kappa, Sigma Chi, Phi Delta Phi. Democrat Roman Catholic. Club: Albuquerque Country. Author: Maxwell Land Grand, a New Mexico Item, 1943; The Fabulous Frontier, 12 New Mexico Items, 1945; Turmoil in New Mexico 1846-1868, 1952; Violence in Lincoln County, a New Mexico Item, 1957; Memoirs 1892-1969, a New Mexico Item, 1969. Home: Albuquerque NM Died Dec. 18, 1972; buried Mt. Calvary Cemetery, Albuquerque NM

KELKER, RUDOLPH FREDERICK, JR., consulting engr.; b. Harrisburg, Pa., Aug. 5, 1875; s. Luther Reily and Agnes Keyes (Pearsol) K.; B.S., Pa. State Coll., 1896, E.E., 1897; m. Georgia Moore, of Rochester, N.Y., May 1911. Engr. with steam and electric rys., Buffalo, Cleveland and N.Y City, 1897-1907; with Bd. of Supervising Engrs. of Chicago, in charge reconstruction of ry. tracks, 1907-14; engr. for Local Transportation Com. of Chicago City Council, 1914—; mem. firm Kelker, DeLeuw & Co., engrs., 1919-29; chief engr. Bur. of Subways, City of Chicago, 1930—. Served in World War as capt., 311th Engrs., 86th Div., U.S.A., and as maj. camp adj., Camp Grant, Ill., and staff duty in France. Mem. Am. Soc. C.E., Western Soc. Engrs., Am. Electric Ry. Assn., Chicago Assn. Commerce, Pa. Soc. S.R. Presbyn. Clubs: Mid-Day, City, University, Westmoreland Country, Mo. Athletic. Author of various reports on traffic and transportation matters for Chicago, New York, Los Angeles, Baltimore, St. Louis and other cities. Home: 999 Michigan Av., Evanston, Ill. Office: 309 W. Jackson Boul., Chicago IL*‡

KELLER, ADOLPH, author, educator; b. Rudlingen, Switzerland, Feb. 7, 1872; s. Johann George and Margarete (Buchter) K.; ed. univs. of Basle, Geneva and Berlin; hon. D.D., univs. of Yale, Geneva, Edinburgh; LL.D., Heidelberg U.; hon. prof., U. of Geneva, Tit. Prof., U. of Zurich; m. Tina Jenny, Jan. 12, 1912; children—Doris, Paul, Marguerite, Esther, Pierre. Mem. scientific expdn. to Mt. Sinai to prepare a new edition of Greek text of the New Testament from which James Moffatt made his English version, 1896-99; pastor John Knox's Chapel, Geneva, until 1909, St. Peters Ch., Zurich, until 1924; dir. European Central Bureau for Relief, until 1945; sec. Swiss Ch. Fedn. until 1941; gen. sec. Internat. Christian Inst. in Geneva until 1930; dir. Ecumenical Seminar in Geneva; European rep. Am. Fed. Council of Churches, 1925-37; cons. mem. World Council of Chs.; mem. Chaplains Commn. for prisoners of war. Nat. Christian Mission in U.S.A. Consultant World Council's Dept. Reconstruction and Inter-church Aid, since 1945. Mem. Reformed Church. Clubs: Swiss Alpine, Psychological. Author: Protestant Europe (with G. Stewart), 1927; Church and State on European Continent, 1937; Religion and Revolution, 1932; Five Minutes to Twelve, 1938; Christian Europe Today, 1942; American Christianity Today, 1945 (pub. in German and French); also serveral books printed in Europe. Contbr. religious articles to Christian Century, etc. Home: 19 Sonnenbergstr, Zurich Switzerland‡

KELLER, AMELIA R. (MRS. EUGENE BUEHLER), physician; b. Cleveland, O., Jan. 12, 1871; d. Frederick and Elizabeth (Ruemmele) Keller; prep. edn. Indianapolis High Sch.; M.D., Central Coll. of Phys. and Surg., Indianapolis, 1893; m. Eugene Buehler (M.D.), of Indianapolis, Dec. 12, 1899. Asso. prof. diseases of children, Ind. U. Sch. of Medicine; lecturer on eugenics and civic subjects. Pres. Woman's Franchise League of Ind., 1910-15; 1st v.-p. Ind. Federation Clubs 1914-16; mem. Indianapolis Hist. Soc. Home: 3515 Bellefontaine St. Office: Pythian Bldg., Indianapolis IN‡

KELLER, HELEN ADAMS, counselor on internat. relations Am. Found. for Blind; b. Tuscumbia, Ala., June 27, 1880; d. Capt. Arthur H. and Katherine (Adams) Keller; deaf and blind since age of 19 mos. as result of illness; ed. under direction of Anne Marshfield Sullivan Macy, her teacher and companion from 1887 until 1936; A.B. cum laude, Radcliffe Coll., 1904; D.H.L., Temple U., 1931; LL.D., U. Glasgow, Scotland, 1932 U. Witwatersrand, Johannesburg, South Africa, 1951; Hon. Fellow Ednl. Inst. of Scotland; Litt.D., U. Delhi, 1955; M.D. (hon.), Free U. Berlin, 1955; LL.D. (honorary), Harvard Univ., 1955. Lectr. in behalf of blind throughout U.S. and in Australia, Can., Egypt, France, Gt. Britain, Greece, Ireland, Israel, Hashemite Kingdom of the Jordan, Lebanon, Syria, Italy, Japan, Yugoslavia, Korea, Manchukuo, New Zealand, Scotland, S. Africa, So. Rhodesia. Now counselor on nat. and internat. relations Am. Found. for Blind, Inc., N.Y.C., also counselor nat. and internat. relations American Found. Overseas Blind, Incorporated. Recipient Achievement prize Pictorial Rev., 1931; Order of St. Sava, Yugoslavia, 1931; Roosevelt medal, 1936; gold key Nat. Edn. Assn., 1938; Scroll of Honor for pioneer work in relief of handicapped Internat. Fedn. Women's Clubs, 1941; W.U.S. Achievement Certificate, 1949; award of dir. gen. Lions Internat., 1951; D.S.M. from Am. Assn. of Workers for the Blind, 1951, Nat. humanitarian award Variety Clubs Internat., 1951, gold medal Nat. Inst. of Social Scis., 1952, meritorious service award Nat. Rehabilitation Assn., 1952, Medal of Merit (Lebanon), 1952, Chevalier Legion of Honor (France), 1952, Southern Cross (Brazil), 1953, award for best feature-length documentary film Nat. Academy Motion Picture Arts and Scis., 1955; Presidential Medal of Freedom, 1964; Golden Plate award American Academy of Achievement, 1965; also recipient many other honors and awards from fgn. govts. and from civic, edn., welfare orgns, throughout U.S., 1951-68; made alumni mem. Phi Beta Kappa, Radcliffe Coll., 1933. Mem. trustees Am. Hall of Fame, Nat. Inst. Arts and Letters. Author: Story of My Life, 1902; Optimism (essay), 1903; The World I Live In, 1908; The Song of the Stone Wall, 1910; Out of the Dark, 1913; My Religion, 1927; Midstream—My Later Life, 1930; Helen Keller's Journal, 1938; Let Us Have Faith, 1941; Teacher, 1955; The Open Door, 1957. Appeared on TV program Wide, Wide World, 1957. Home: Westport CT Died June 1, 1968; buried St Joseph's Chapel in Washington Cathedral, Washington DC

KELLER, HERBERT PAIST, mayor; b. St. Paul, Feb. 7, 1875; s. John M. and Annice Elizabeth (Scott) K.; ed. pub. and high schs., St. Paul; LL.B., U. of Minn., 1896; m. Carrie S. Johnston, of Wabasha, Minn., Dec. 20, 1905. Practiced, St. Paul, 1896—; now mem. firm of Keller & Loomis. City prosecutor, St. Paul, 1902-3; mem. upper br. of City Council, 3 terms, 1904-10; mayor 2 terms, 1910-June, 1914. Republican. Methodist. Mason (K.T.), K.P., Elk. Clubs: Commercial, St. Paul Automobile. Home: 778 University Av. Office: Germania Life Bldg., St Paul MN‡

KELLER, MOLLIE V. EVERETT (MRS. CHARLES C. KELLER), banker; b. Gnadenhutten, O.; d. David W. and Mary (Wakemiller) Everett; student pub. schs.; m. Charles C. Keller, July 14, 1896; (dec.); 1 dau., Mary B. Tchr. pub. schs., Port Washington and Gnadenhutton, O.; dir. 1st Nat. Bank, Dennison, O., 1933-69. Speaker on edn., fraternal and patriotic subjects. Internat. sec. Pythian Sisters, 1924-69; founder

Home for Aged Women, Medina, O., 1914. Trustee Tuscarawas County Childrens Home, 1938-48. Named Hon. Ky. Col. Mem. Daus. Union Veterans, D.A.R., Bus. and Profl. Women's Club. Presbyn. Patentee folding ironing bd. Home: Uhrichsville OH Died Nov. 4, 1969.

KELLEY, CLEMENT EARL, JR., radiologist; b. Clayton, Ind., June 26, 1920; s. Clement Earl and Ruth (Harris) K.; M.D., U. Ind., 1944; m. Ethel Haklitt, Dec. 21, 1946; children—Ross Clement, Joseph Neal. Intern. Indpls. Gen. Hosp., 1944-45; resident radiology Meth. Hosp. Indpls., 1949-52; chmn. radiology dept. Meml. Hosp., Lima, O., 1962; radiologist Bluffton (O.) Community Hosp.; head dept. radiology Lima State Hosp., 1966-69; Mary Rutan Hosp., Bellefontaine, O., 1969-70. Served to capt. M.C., AUS, 1945-47. Diplomate Am. Bd. Radiology. Mem. A.M.A., Radiol. Soc. N.Am., Am. Coll. Radiology, Ohio State Radiol. Soc., Ohio Med. Assn., Lima and Allan County Acad. Medicine, Phi Rho Sigma. Republican. Mason, Elk. Home: Lima OH Died Mar. 24, 1970; buried Shoreham VT

KELLEY, J(AMES) HERBERT, educator; b. Belvidere, Ill., Sept. 10, 1875; s. Loretus M. and Carolyn M. (Pettit) K.; M.Di., Ia. State Teachers' Coll., Cedar Falls, Ia., 1897; B.S., Cornell Coll., Ia., 1900; A.M., Harvard, 1908; D.Litt., U. of Denver, 1916; m. Clara H. Baker (A.B., Cornell, Ia., A.M., U. of Ia.), Aug. 28, 1914. Prin. and supt. pub. schs. in Ia., 1897-1902; pres. Okla. Inst. Tech., 1902-09; exec. sec. U. of Ill., 1909-14; pres. Colo. State Normal Sch., Gunnison, 1914-19; dir. univ. extension and prof. edn., U. of Pittsburgh, 1919-21; exec. sec. Pa. State Edn. Assn. and editor Pennsylvania Sch. Jour., 1921-39; retired. Mason (K.T., Shriner), Acacia. Life member N.E.A. (state dir. for Pa.), Pa. State Edn. Assn., Harvard Glee Club, pres. Western Colo. Teachers' Assn., 1916, Colo. Edn. Assn., 1917; pres. Ednl. Press Assn. of America, 1927. Editor Alumni Record U. of Ill., 1913. Mem. Phi Delta Kappa, Phi Beta Kappa, Kappa Phi Kappa, Phi Sigma Sigma, Kappa Delta Pi. Club: Harvard (New Haven). Awarded distinguished service medal of Pa. State Edn. Assn., 1939. Address: 103 Cottage St., New Haven CT‡

KELLEY, LILLA ELIZABETH, social worker; b. S. Boston, Mass., May 18, 1872; d. Samuel and Mary J. (Fitton) K.; ed. pvt. teachers and Girls' High Sch., Boston, 1887-88; O.B., Emerson Coll. of Oratory, 1890, O.M., 1891; unmarried. Teacher elocution, Tilton (N.H.) Sem., 1895-96, Wesleyan Acad., Wilbraham, Mass., 1896-97; teacher Thompson's Island School for Boys, Boston Harbor, 1908; teacher in Wrentham State Sch. for the Feebleminded, 1910; teacher and matron Lancaster Industrial Sch. for Girls, 1910-17; a parole agent for the Mass. Department of Correction, since 1917. Public reader; contributor stories and poems to mags. Charter mem. Boston Ruskin Club (pres. fifteen yrs.). Author: Three Hundred Things That a Bright Girl Can Do., 1904. Address: Grove Hall P.O., Dorchester MA‡

KELLEY, PEARCE CLEMENT, economist, educator; b. Chicago, Oct. 13, 1895; s. Pearce Clement and Catherine (Morrisey) K.; student U. of Mich., 1913-15; A.B., U. of Calif. at Berkeley, 1922, M.A., 1924, Ph.D., 1930; m. Helen Christine Nelson, July 28, 1935; 1 dau., Kathleen Isabel. Instr. bus. adminstrn. U. of Calif., 1930-31; teaching fellow, 1927-30; asst. prof. U. of Utah, 1931-32; head marketing dept. U. of Ark., 1932-48; asso. prof. U. of Miss., 1948-50; prof. marketing U. of Okla. 1950-65, professor emeritus of marketing, 1965-68, acting chmn. marketing department, summer 1951; guest instr. summer sch. U. of Fla., 1939, Ark. Teachers Coll., 1940, research bur. for retail training U. of Pittsburgh, 1944; mem. panel Inst. Small Bus. Edn., U. of Mich., 1950. Ark. state coordinator distributive edn. and research consultant, 1938-42; dist. supervisor defense training, Ark., 1941-42. Served as pvt. Eighth Aero Squadron, A.E.F., 1917-18. Mem. Am. Marketing Assn., Am. Econ. Assn., Am. Mgmt. Assn., Nat. Council Small Bus. Mgmt. Devel., Am. Nat. Red Cross, Beta Gamma Sigma, Omicron Delta Gamma, Chi Psi. Author: How to Organize and Operate a Small Business, 1949; Cases in Small Business Management, 1952; Consumer Economics, 1952; What Every Business, Ranch and Income Property Buyer Should Know, 1956; Retailing: Basic Principles, 3d edition, 1957; also textbooks; chpt. in Handbook of Business Adminstration, 1931; also articles and reviews in profl. and bus. jours., bulls. Home: Norman OK Died June 27, 1968; buried Calvary Cemetery, Chicago IL

KELLEY, ROBERT MICHAEL, clergyman, educator; b. Manson, Ia., July 24, 1877; s. Michael Bede and Nora M. (Foley) K.; student St. Mary's (Kan.) Coll., 1894-97; joined Soc. of Jesus (Jesuits), 1897; B.A., St. Louis U., 1903, M.A., 1904; studied theology, St. Louis U., 1908-12; LL.D., St. Mary's Coll. (Kan.), 1924. Teacher prep. div., U. of Detroit, 1904-08, prep. div., Creighton U., Omaha, Neb., 1913-14; ordained priest R.C. Ch., 1911; dean Coll. of Liberal Arts, Creighton U., 1914-20; regent Inst. of Law, same univ., 1919-20; pres. Regis Coll., Denver, Colo., 1920-26; asst. to provincial (Mo. Province Soc. of Jesus), 1926-27; pres. Loyola U., 1927-33; became acting pres. St. Mary's (Kan.) Coll., 1933; pres. Regis College, 1935-42; asst. pastor St. Francis Xavier Church, St. Louis, Mo., 1942; acting pres. St. Louis U., 1943; now asst. dir. St. Louis House of Retreats. Mem. Knights of Columbus (4 deg.). Home: Lemay MO‡

KELLEY, WILLIAM ANDREW GRESHAM, lawyer; b. Buffalo, Feb. 4, 1911; s. Harry Joseph and Helen (O'Malley) K.; B.A. cum laude, St. Francis Xavier U., 1930; LL.B., Dalhousie U. (Can.), 1935; postgrad. Harvard, 1935-36; m. Isavel MacKay Ross, Aug. 24, 1937; 1 dau., Mary Jane. Admitted to N.S. bar, 1936, Ont. bar, 1937; later partner firm Borden, Elliot, Kelley & Palmer, Toronto. Mem. Canadian Bar Assn., Phi Delta Phi. Roman Catholic. Clubs: Rosedale Golf; York; Nat.; Briars Golf and Country; Toronto Hunt; Granite; Echo Beach Fishing. Home: Toronto ON Canada Died Canada 9, 1972.

KELLOGG, ARTHUR REMINGTON, biologist; b. Davenport, Ia., Oct. 5, 1892; s. Rolla Remington and Clara Louise (Martin) K.; A.B., U. of Kansas, 1915, M.A., 1916; student U. of Calif., 1916-17, Ph.D., 1928; m. Marguerite Evangel Henrich, Dec. 21, 1920. Taxonomic asst., Mus. of Birds and Mammals, U. of Kan., 1913-16; teaching fellow dept. zoology, U. of Calif., 1916-19; field asst. Bur. Biol. Survey, U.S. Dept. Agr., summers 1915, 16, 17, asst. biologist, 1920-24, asso. biologist, 1924-28; asst. curator, div. of mammals, U.S. Nat. Museum, 1928-40, curator, 1941-48; dir. U.S. Nat. Museum, 1948-62; asst. sec. Smithsonian Instn., Wash., 1958-62, research asso., 1962-69; research asso. Carnegie Instn. of Wash., 1921-43. Member board govs. Crop Protection Inst., 1935-36, Nat. Research Council (div. biology and agr.), Washington, D.C., 1930-54 (vice-chmn. 1945-47). Advisory Committee Chemical-Biological Coordination Center, 1946-52; Pacific Science Board, 1946-52. Am. mem. com. of experts on whaling, League of Nations, Berlin, 1930; apptd. del. Internat. Conf. for Regulation of Whaling, London, 1937, Oslo, Norway, 1938, London, 1938. London, 1944-45 (chmn. Am. delegation), Washington, D.C., 1946 (chmn. Am. delegation and chmn. conf.); London, 1949 (chmn. Am. delegation); U.S. commr. Internat. Whaling Commn., Oslo, Norway, 1950, Capetown, 1951, chmn. of commn. (1952-54), London, 1952, 53, 56-63, Tokyo, 1954, Moscow, 1955, The Hague, 1958, Sandefjord, 1964; del. internat. com. establish Internat. Hylean Amazon Inst., Brazil, 1947. Spl. detail to Brazil, 1943; dir. Canal Zone biol. Area, 1945-46. Arctic Research Lab. Advisory Bd., Navy Dept., 1948-51. Mem. Am. Soc. Mammalogists (past pres.), Paleaobiol. Soc. of Washington (pres. 1935-36), Biol. Soc. Wash., Am. Soc. Naturalists, Am. Assn. Anatomists, Soc. Systematic Zoology, Soc. Study Evolution, Acad. Natural Sciences of Phila. (corr.), Nat. Parks Assn. (trustee, 1931-49), Geol. Soc. Am. (fellow), Nat. Acad. Sci., Zool. Society of London, Am. Philos. Soc., American Academy of Arts and Sciences, Nat. Geog. Soc. (com. research and exploration 1955-69), Sigma Xi. Conglist. Club: Cosmos. Contbr. sci. jours. Home: Washington DC Died May 8, 1969; buried Sunset View Cemetery, Berkeley CA

KELLOGG, BRAINERD, educator; b. at Champlain, N.Y.; s. Lorenzo and Roxanna (Burdick) K.; A.B., Middlebury Coll., 1858, A.M., 1861; (LL.D., Ripon, 1890); m. Julia M. Cutter, Aug. 19, 1862; father of Frederic Rogers K. (q.v.) Teacher in Ky., 1858-9, Macedon Center, N.Y., 1859-60; tutor, 1860-1, prof. rhetoric and English lit., 1861-8, Middlebury Coll.; prof. English lang. and lit. since 1868, dean of faculty since 1899, Poly. Inst. of Brooklyn. Pres. Philol. Dept., Brooklyn Inst. Arts and Sciences; trustee Middlebury Coll. since 1885. Mem. Delta Kappa Epsilon, Phi Beta Kappa. Author: (with Alonzo Reed) Graded Lessons in English; Higher Lessons in English; A One Book Course; A Historical and Scientific Grammar of the English Language. Home: Englewood NJ‡

KELLOGG, CHARLES WETMORE, pub. utility exec.; b. Phila., Pa., Feb. 27, 1880; s. Charles Wetmore and Jane (Henderson) K.; grad. high sch., Brookline, Mass., 1897; B.S., Mass. Inst. Tech., 1902, M.S., 1903; m. Clara Howard Davis, Apr. 6, 1907; children—Jane (Mrs. Herbert H. Corbin), Waters (dec.), Howard, Nancy (Mrs. Robert C. Lea, Jr.). With Stone & Webster, Boston, Mass., 1903; manager Edison Electric Company, Brockton, Mass., 1904-05, El Paso Electric Company, 1905-10, Eastern Tex. Electric Co., 1911-14, Miss. River Power Co., 1914-19; mgr. midwest dist. Stone & Webster, 1916-19; pres. Engineers Pub. Service Co., 1925-33, chmn. bd., 1933-39; pres. Edison Electric Inst. 1936-1946; chief consultant Light, Heat and Power Unit., office of Production Management, Washington, June 1940-June 1941. Dir. Engrs. Public Service Co., Equitable Life Assurance Soc. U.S., Virginia Electric and Power Company. Trustee Teachers Coll., N.Y. City; president, Talbot County (Md.) Free Library; sec. Md. Agrl. Soc.; mem. standing com. Episcopal Diocese of Easton; mem. Md. Gov.'s Com. for Preservation Md. Antiquities; pres. Hist. Soc. Talbot County. Hon. mem. Edison Elec. Inst., mem. Am. Inst. Elec. Engrs., Delta Psi. Republican. Episcopalian (sr. warden). Clubs: Chesapeake Bay Yacht (commodore); St. Anthony, University, (N.Y. City). Home: Queen Anne MD Died Mar. 31, 1969; buried Old Wye Ch., Wye Mills MD

KELLOGG, JAMES H., business exec.; b. Chicago, Ill., 1912; grad. Stanford, 1935; advanced management program Harvard, 1954; m. Jean M. Defrees, 1939; children—Frances D. (Mrs. Wayne E.McConnell Jr.), and James M. Formerly president, dir. Charles T. Brandt, Inc., Balt., 1957; Kellogg Switchboard & Supply Co., Chgo., 1946-56; pres. dir. Harders Engring. Co., Chgo.; treas., dir. Kelran Corp., Harvey, Ill. Episcopalian. Clubs: Casino, University (Chgo.); Glen View. Home: Chicago IL Died Feb. 15, 1967; buried Oak Woods Cemetery, Chicago IL

KELLOGG, LAURA CORNELIUS (MRS. ORRIN JOSEPH KELLOGG), author, lecturer; b. Oneida, Wis., Sept. 10, 1880; d. Adam Poe and Celicia (Bread) Cornelius; grad. Grafton Hall, Fond du Lac, Wis.; studied Stanford U., Barnard Coll., Sch. of Philanthropy of Columbia, U. of Wis., and 2 yrs. abroad; m. Orrin Joseph Kellogg, of St. Paul, Minn., Apr. 22, 1912. Writer and lecturer in behalf of Am. Indian; original researches in Indian langs., social conditions, etc.; originator of Lolomi Policy" of self govt., for Am. Indian, and establishment of model villages for Indians. Mem. League Am. Pen Women. Author: The Lost Empire, 1906; Our Democracy and the American Indian, 1920; (brochure) Indian Reveries; Gehdos of the Lost Empire, 1921. Home: Seymour WI‡

KELLOGG, SCOTT D(OUGLAS), lawyer, banker; b. Chgo., May 18, 1908; s. George W. and Margaret (Cowles) K.; LL.B. cum laude, Nat. U., 1936, LL.M., 1937; m. Marvine Parker, May 19, 1932. Admitted to D.C. bar, 1936; U.S. Supreme Ct., 1940; Cal. bar, 1943; pvt. practice, 1938-68; mem. staff U.S. Reconstrn. Finance Corp., Washington, 1932-34; bd. govs. Fed. Reserve System, Washington, 1934-38; dir. v.p., sec. Druge Brothers, Mfg. Co., 1943-68; dir., sec. Tru-Flate, Inc., 1950-68; pres. dir. Inter-City Service Bur., Inc., 1958-68, Cal. Securities Corp., 1963-68, Cal. Trust Deed Corp., 1964-68; sec. dir. Livermore Dodge, Inc., 1966-68. Mem. Alameda County Instns. Commn., 1961-68. Mem. Am. Ordnance Assn. (life), George Washington Law Assn. (life), Fed. (pres. Oakland Chpt. 1957-58, 1966-68; nat. council 1958-60, 61-68), Am., Alameda County bar assns., State Bar Cal., Bar Assn. D.C., Am. Judicature Soc. Presbyn. Elk, Mason (32 deg., Shriner). Clubs: Democratic Lawyers Alameda County (dir. 1959-68, v.p. 1966-68); National Lawyers (life, founder); Commonwealth (Cal.); Olympic (San Francisco). Home: Oakland CA Died June 26, 1968; inurned Garden of Light West, Chapel of Memories, Oakland CA

KELLOGG, THEODORE H., physician; prep. ed'n Gambier Coll., Ohio; grad. Norwich Univ., Bellevue Hosp. Med. Coll., 1865; unmarried. Began med. practice, 1865; specialist in nervous and mental diseases; supt. New York City Asylum for Insane, 1872-4; supt. Willard State Hosp., N. Y., 1892-5; now conducts, under State license, Dr. Kellogg's House, Riverdale, to treat mental diseases. Fellow New York Acad. Medicine; mem. New York Neurol. Soc., Am. Neurol. Soc., N. Y. Co. Med. Soc. Author: Text-Book of Mental Diseases, 1897 W11. Has publ. numerous monographs on nervous and mental diseases. Address: Riverdale NY‡

KELLY, BRADLEY, editor and syndicate exec.; b. Waterford, N.Y., Oct. 11, 1894; s. James Andrew and Katherine (Bradley) K.; LL.B. Albany Law Sch., Union U., 1916; m. Abigail Adams Johnson, Dec. 2, 1944. Served with A.R.C. in postwar relief activities, Europe, 1919-22, dir. Jr. A.R.C., Albania, 1921-22, established Albania Vocational Sch. in Tirana; asst. to Frank G. Carpenter, traveler, writer, lectr., 1923; feature writer N.Y. Evening World, also writer articles for mags., 1924; with North Am. Newspaper Alliance, 1925; co-propr. Imperial News Service, 1926; editorial staff King Features Syndicate, Inc., N.Y.C., 1927-69, became asso. editor, v.p., 1935, then semi-ret., 1953, cons. Vice pres. George Junior Republic, Freeville, N.Y.; bd. dirs. Boystown of Italy, C.Y.O. Served with U.S. Army, World War I. Knight of Malta. Fellow Royal Soc. Arts; mem. Phi Sigma Kappa. Home: Redding Ridge CT Died Jan. 29, 1969; buried Redding Ridge Cemetery.

KELLY, CHARLES E., banker; b. Chgo., June 6, 1910; s. Thomas L. and Mary (Johnson) K.; student Northwestern U., also Am. Inst. Banking; m. Frances Schlager, Sept. 11, 1937; children—Thomas F., James E. With City Nat. Bank, Chgo., 1927-47; with Lincoln Nat. Bank and Trust Co., Ft. Wayne, Ind., 1947-68, pres., 1964-68; mem. investment com. Lincoln Nat. Life Ins. Co.; dir. Franklin Electric Co., Inc., Bluffton, Ind. Mem., past chmn. Ft. Wayne Bd. Aviation Commnrs. Bd. dirs. St. Joseph Hosp. Mem. Ft. Wayne C. of C., Am. Bankers Assn., Am. Inst. Banking, Robert Morris Assos. Republican. Catholic. Club: Junto (Ft. Wayne). Home: Ft Wayne IN Died June 21, 1968; buried Ft. Wayne IN

KELLY, ELEANOR, music dir.; b. Medina, Mich., Aug. 28, 1879; d. John W. and B. M. (Hogan) K.; grad. high sch., Hudson, Mich.; grad. Thomas Sch. of Music and Art, Detroit, 1902; spl. music study, Ia. Coll., 1908-09, Cornell U., summer 1913; grad. Am. Inst.

Music, Evanston, Ill., 1920; hon. Mus. Doc., U. of Detroit, 1926. Sch. supervisor of Music, Webster City, Ia., 1906-10, Hudson, Mich., 1910-15; prof. pub. sch. music, Hillsdale (Mich.) Coll., 1914-20; dir. Conservatory of Music, same coll., since 1920; in charge pub. sch. music courses, Utah Agrl. Coll., Logan, summer 1927; guest professor Drake U., summers 1928, 29, 30. Dir. choir, Webster City, Ia., 1906-10, Sacred Heart Choir, 1910-14; condr. Soldiers Chorus, Hillsdale County, World War. Mem. Nat. Music Supervisors' Conv. (advisory bd. 1922-23, 23-24), Nat. Federation of Music Clubs, Mich. Music Teachers' Assn., Am. Assn. Univ. Profs., Daughters of Isabella (regent Santa Maria Circle), Sigma Alpha Iota. Republican. Catholic. Club: Federated Woman's. Home: Hillsdale MI‡

KELLY, SIR GERALD, artist; b. 1879; s. Rev. F. F. Kelly; ed. Eton and Trinity Hall, Cambridge U., Eng.; hon. LL.D., Cambridge. Mem. Royal Fine Arts Commn., 1938-43; pres. Royal Acad. of Arts, 1950. Created Knight, 1945. Fellow Royal Inst. Brit. Architects. Works include State Portraits of King and Queen, 1945; rep. in galleries of Marseilles, Brussels, Dublin, Ottawa, Toronto, Sydney, Newport, Tate. Clubs: Athenaeum, Arts, Beefsteak. Address: London England Died Jan. 1972.

KELLY, GEROGE B(RADSHAW), ex-congressman; b. Waterloo, N.Y., Dec. 12, 1900; s. James Peter and Catherine Charlotte (Bradshaw) K.; student St. Peter and St. Paul Sch., 1910-13, and West High Sch., 1913-15; Rochester, N.Y.; m. Catherine Weber, Dec. 10, 1936. Began as clk. Gen. Ry. Signal Co., Rochester, 1915; timekeeper, 1918-19; salesman candy co., 1920; with Fashion Park Clothing Co., 1921-33; mem. N.Y. State Assembly, 1933-34; N.Y. Senate, 1935-36; mem. 75th Congress (1937-38), 38th N.Y. Dist.; now regional dir. Wage and Hour Div., U.S. Dept. of Labor, Democrat. Elk. Clubs: Rochester, Tennis (Rochester, Army and Navy Country (Arlington, Va.). Home: Rochester NY Died Jan. 1972.

KELLY, HARRY FRANCIS, ex-governor; b. Ottawa, Ill., Apr. 19, 1895; s. Henry M. and Mollie (Morissey) K.; LL.B., Notre Dame U., 1917; hon. LL.D., Notre Dame U., Univ. of Detroit, Albion Coll.; m. Anne V. O'Brien, 1929; children—Joanne, Harry and Brian (twins), Lawrence, Roger, Mary. Began law practice after return from World War; state's atty., LaSalle County, Ill., 1920-24, asst. pros. atty., Wayne Co., Mich., 1930-34; mgr. Detroit Office, Mich. Liquor Control Commn., 1935-36; sec. of state, Mich., 1939-42; governor 1943-47; mem. law firm, Kelly, Kelly & Kelly, Detroit, 1924-71; asso. justice Mich. Supreme Ct. Received Croix de Guerre with Palm. Mem. Am. and Mich. bar assns., Canadian Corps Assn. of Mich., Vets. Fgn. Wars, Am. Legion, U. of Notre Dame Alumni Assn. (pres. 1941-43). Catholic. Republican. K.C. Elk. Club. Detroit Athletic. Home: Detroit MI Died Feb. 8, 1971.

KELLY, JOHN WILLIAM, newspaper corr.; b. Portland, Ore., Aug. 27, 1875; s. William James and Harriet (Gleason) K.; ed. Mt. Angel (Ore.) Coll.; m. Mabel M. McHugh, June 1896; children—Mary Alta (Mrs. Malcolm T. McLean), Mary Aileen (Mrs. Robert F. Dwyer), John William, Gleason Sylvester. Newspaper work since 1894; dramatic critic Portland Telegram, 1899-1918, columnist, 1904-07; formerly conductor humor dept. Pacific Monthly; polit. writer Portland Oregonian since 1918, mgr. Washington News Bur. for same paper, 1930-38; Washington mgr. Northwestern News Service, Inc., since 1939; v.p. McLean Lumber Co. Republican. Catholic. Club: National Press. Contbr. articles on pre-historic and early history of the Oregon country. Home: Portland, Ore. Address: Alban Towers, Washington DC*‡

KELLY, MERVIN J., research engr.; b. Princeton, Mo., Feb. 14, 1894; s. Joseph Fenemore and Mary Etta (Evans) K.; B.S., Missouri Sch. of Mines and Metal, 1914; M.S., U. of Ky., 1915, D.Sc. 1946; Ph.D., U. Chgo., 1918; D.Eng., U. Mo., 1936, N.Y.U., 1955, Bklyn. Poly. Inst., 1955, Wayne State U., 1958, Princeton, 1959; LL.D., U. Pa., 1954; Dr. Honoris Causa, U. Lyons, 1957; D.Sc., U. Pitts., 1959, Case Inst. Tech., Stevens Institute Technology, 1959; m. Katharine Milsted, November 11, 1917; children—Mary (Mrs. Robert von Mehren), Robert Milsted. Physicist, research dept. of Western Electric Company, 1918-25; physicist, Bell Telephone Labs., New York, N.Y., 1925-28; dir, vacuum tube development, 1928-34, development dir. Transmission Inst. and electronics, 1934-36, dir. of research, 1936-44, exec. v.p., 1944-51, pres., 1951-58, chmn., 1959, dir., 1944-59, research mgmt. cons. IBM Corp., 1959-65, 68-71; research mgmt. cons., dir. Bausch & Lomb, Inc., 1959-62; dir. Tungsol Electric Incorporated, Prudential Insurance Co. of Am., Bausch & Lomb Optical Co. Chmn. com. Sec. Def. continental def.; spl. cons. Nat. Aeros. and Space Adminstrn.; mem. adv. com. Sci. Manpower; chmn. subcom. role industry coll. N.Y.C. bd. edn.; chmn. com. for Sec. Commerce on Nat. Bur. Standards, chairman of the visiting com., chairman com. evaluaiton of all research and engineering activities; chairman of the task force on research Hoover Commn.; chmn. Dept. of Air Force sci. adv. bd.; v. chmn. Dept. Navy naval research adv. com. Member bd. trustees Stevens Inst. Tech. Awarded Presdl. Certificate of Merit; Indsl. Research Inst. award, 1954; Christopher Columbus Internat. Communication prize, 1955; Air Force Assn. trophy award; James Forrestal medal Nat. Security Indsl. Assn., 1959; John Fritz medal for achievements in electronics, 1959; Mervin J. Kelly award in telecommunication, Am. Inst. E.E., 1960, Am. Inst. E.E. and NEMA Golden Omego Award, 1960, Joint Engrng. Socs. Hoover Medal, 1961. Fellow Rochester Mus. Arts and Scis., 1960; mem. Am. Acad. Arts and Scis., Swedish Royal Acad. Sci., M.I.T. Crop.; chmn. adv. council, dept. elec. engring. Princeton; mem. advisory committee, department of electricity, University Rochester. Fellow Am. Physical Society, I.E.E.E., Institute Radio Engrs., Acoustical Soc. of Am., Am. Philos. Soc., Nat. Acad. Sci., Sigma Xi, Eta Kappa Nu, Sigma Nu, Tau Beta Pi. Rep. Episcopalian. Clubs: Baltusrol Golf (Springfield, N.J.); University (N.Y.C.). Home: Short Hills NJ Died Mar. 18, 1971.

KELLY, MICHAEL D., educator, lawyer executive; b. on farm, Marquette Co., Wis., Apr. 23, 1872; s. John Thomas and Margaret Ellen (Ryan) K.; ed. Milwaukee pub. and high schs.; Wis. State Normal Sch.; U. of Wis.; Milwaukee Law Sch. till 1892; M.A., Litt.D., Muncie Nat. Inst., 1917; m. Carol Louise Alcott, of Milwaukee, Oct. 21, 1896; children—Lenore Marie (Mrs. John Shephard Bartlett), Beatrice Elizabeth (Mrs. James Norman Bird), Daniel Alcott, Paul Ryan. Admitted to practice, Supreme Court of Ind., also U.S. Dist. Court; prin. South Milwaukee High Sch., 1891-92; county supt. schs., Milwaukee Co., 1892-96; justice 4th Jud. Dist., City of Milwaukee, 1908; founder, and pres. Muncie (Ind.) Normal Inst., 1911-17; ednl. dir. Am. Hotel Training Sch., 1912-20; founder Cramer Memorial Inst.; pres. The Franklin Co., Fla. West Coast Ry. Co., Apalachicola Bay Bridge Co. Republican. Catholic. K.P., Elk, Moose. Author of school texts, and treatises on manual, ethical, and vocational education; Technical vs. Vocational Education; The British Empire; Children of the Father; etc. Has traveled throughout N. and S. America, Asia, and Europe and conducted expdns. to Alaska, Mexico and Central America. Lecturer on vocational education and ethics as applied to popular education and citizenship. Home: 2320 E. Bradford Av., Milwaukee, WI (also Butte MT)‡

KELLY, ORIE R., business exec.; b. Butte, Mont., June 5, 1890; s. Daniel and Margaret (Cosgrove) K.; m. Grace Donahue. Mem. adv. com. Bankers Trust Co.; dir. Md. Casualty Co., Starrett Bros. & Eken, Inc., Companion Life Insurance Co. Commr. Westchester Co. Park Commn. College. Trustee Iona Coll. Mem. Army Relief Soc. (treas.), Sovereign Mil. Order of Knights of Malta. Clubs: Athletic, N.Y.; Westchester Country, Empire State (chmn. bd.). Home: White Plains NY Died July 4, 1969.

KELLY, RAYMOND, writer; b. Morgan Park, Chicago, Ill., May 8, 1882; s. Alfred C. and Sarah (Jayne) K.; A.B., U. of Chicago, 1904; m. Bessie Mae Case, of Pekin, Ill., July 26, 1906 (died Oct. 7, 1923); children—Alfred H., Rowland L., Raymond R., David J.; m. 2d, Olga A. Rehner, of La Grange, Ill.; 1 dau., Betsy Anne. Four-minute speaker, World War. Republican. Unitarian. Mason. Author: Gravel Pit Stories, 1923; Adventures of Funny Bunny, 1923; Me and Andy (juvenile novel), 1928; also short stories and poems in mags. and syndicated articles in newspapers. Wrote songs (with Henry P. Eames), Since Thou Art Mine," and Just That I Loved You." Home: 3923 W. 64th St., Chicago IL‡

KELLY, ROBERT JAMES, educator; b. Allen, Copiah County, Miss., June 2, 1877; s. Robert Alpheus and Sarah Catherine (Weeks) K.; student Meridian (Miss.) Male Coll., 1902-04; B.S., Ruskin-Cave Coll., Ruskin, Tenn., 1906; spl. work, Peabody Coll., Univ. of Chicago, Vanderbilt U.; M.A., Vanderbilt, 1927; graduate work, Peabody Coll., 1927-29; m. Claire Frances Sneed, July 20, 1920; 1 son, Robert Sneed. Teacher pub. schs., Miss., until 1902; asst. in science and mathematics, Meridian Male Coll., 1902-04; asst. in science and mathematics, Ruskin-Cave Coll., 1904-06, head dept. science and mathematics, 1906-10, business mgr., v.p. and acting pres., until 1915, active pres., 1915-18; v.p. and head department chemistry and physics, Southern College, Lakeland, Fla., 1918-19; research in economics and sociology, 1919-20; head dept. of science, Centenary Coll. of La., 1920-22; v.p. and head dept. science and mathematics, Trevecca Coll., Nashville, 1922-26, now v.p. financial dir. and head dept. economic research. State publicity agt. Tenn. ry. agrl. train, summer, 1914. Comdt. cadets, Ruskin-Cave Coll.; mem. Draft Bd., World War. Trustee Ruskin-Cave Coll. Fellow Am. Geog. Soc.; mem. A.A.A.S., Tenn. Acad. of Science, Am. Acad. Polit. and Social Science, N.E.A. (life), Omicron Delta Gamma, Pi Gamma Mu, Phi Delta Kappa. Democrat. Nazarene; lay del. Quadrennium, Nazarene Ch., 1928, 32, 36, 40. Club: Artus. Contbr. to newspapers and mags. Home: 204 Spring St., Nashville TN (N.E. Sta. P.O.).‡

KELLY, T(HOMAS) HOWARD, author, editor, pub. relations; b. Fernandina, Fla., June 26, 1895; s. William Redmond and Charlotte Grace (Leddy) K.; ed. St. Joseph's Acad., Fernandina, and Mt. St. Mary's Prep. Sch., Emmittsburg, Md.; student Springhill College, Mobile, Ala., 1911-14, B.Litt., 1917; married Mercedes Siuchninska Peine, Oct. 3, 1936; 1 dau., Patricia (Mrs. Donald W. Morrison). Entered newspaper work, 1915, with United Press, Washington Herald, later mil. corr. Providence Jour., Pawtucket Times and Evening Tribune, Providence; scenario editor and title writer for United Picture Prodn. Corp., 1921; staff corr. and sporting editor, Universal Service, etc.; asso. editor McClure's and Smart Set magazines, 1928-29; on staff of Cosmopolitan Mag., 1930-31; asso. editor Sunday Mirror Mag., 1933; writer and asso. editor Hearst Magazines, 1936; exec. editor, Drug World, American Druggist, 1937; organized Com. on Information for Drug and Cosmetic Industry, 1937, and served as secretary: organized, 1938, and directed United Brewers Industrial Foundations's public relations advertising program in 14 states; consel various industries and companies, 1941; gen. agt. Rahr. Malting Co., Manitowoc, Wisconsin; president The Kelly Company, Chicago, Illinois. Contbr. over 600 stories and articles to magazines from 1922. Enlisted in Battery C, 103d F.A., 26th Div., Aug. 1917; served as non-com. officer in France, Oct. 1917-Apr. 1919; participated in action at Soissons, Toul, Chateau Thierry, St. Mihiel and Verdun; gassed at Chateau Thierry. Mem. U.S. Brewers Found., Amelia Island Hist. Assn., Authors' League Am., Am. Legion. Democrat. Catholic. Clubs: Racquet (St. Louis), Florida Yacht; Sleepy Hollow Country, N.Y. Athletic, Overseas Press, Cork (Houston), Chicago Athletic; Ribault Country & Golf (Florida); St. Anthony (San Antonio); Ponte Vedra (Florida). Author: (books) I Went Doughboy Again, 1941; The Unknown Soldier, 1942; What Outfit Buddy?, 1943; Journey Without End, 1943; plays for motion pictures) His Buddy's Wife: Lovers' Island (with others). Home: Chicago IL Died July 24, 1967; buried Bosque Bello Cemetery, Fernandina Beach FL

KELSEN, HANS, ret. educator; b. Prague, Czechoslovakia, Oct. 11, 1881; s. Adolf and Auguste (Loewy) K.; LL.D., U. Vienna, 1966; Doctor honoris causa, Harvard, U. Utrecht, U. Chgo., Univ. California, Nat. U. Mexico; m. Margarete Bondi, May 25, 1912; children—Anna, Maria. Came to U.S., 1940, naturalized, 1945. Prof. law U. Vienna, 1911-29, U. Cologne, 1929-33, U. Prague, 1936-37; prof. internat. law Grad. Inst. Internat. Studies, Geneva, 1933-40; Oliver Wendell Holmes lectr. Harvard Law Sch., 1940-41; prof. polit. sci. U. Cal., Berkeley, 1942-52, prof. emeritus, 1952-73; hon. prof. Univ. Vienna, U. Rio de Janeiro. Mem. Am. Acad. Arts Scis., Acad. Sci. Austria, Belgium, Netherlands; Academia Nazionale dei Lincei, Rome, Academic delle Sci. di Torino. Author: Law and Peace in International Relations, 1942; Society and Nature, 1943; Peace Through Law, 1944; General Theory of Law and State, 1945; Political Theory of Bolshevism, 1948; The Law of the United Nations, 1950; Principles of International Law, 1952; Communist Theory of Law, 1955; What Is Justice?, 1957. Home: Berkeley CA Died Apr. 1973.

KELSEY, HARLAN PAGE, landscape architect; b. Pomona, Kan., July 9, 1872; s. Samuel T. and Katherine E. (Ricksecker) K.; ed. pub. schs.; pvt. tutors; Sc.D., hon., Univ. of Mass., 1948; m. Florence Low, Nov. 25, 1902; children—Harlan Page, Seth L., Katherine (Mrs. H. Severance Sawyer), Jane (Mrs. John Jerome Hart). Nurseryman, since 1885; prepared city plans for Columbia, Greenville, S.C., 1911-13, plans for Salem, Mass.; pioneer in city planning; organizer, chmn. of pioneer planning bd., Salem, Mass.; chmn., pioneer joint conf. Mass. Planning Bds.; sec.-treas., Am. Joint Com. on hort. nomenclature; collaborator, Nat. Park Service; men. So. Appalachian Nat. Park Commn.; mem. Nat. Arboretum Adv. Council; charge of planning Hampton Rd. Dist., U.S. HousingCorp. Trustee, pub. reservations, Mass. Hort. Soc., dir., Council on Nat. Parks, Forests and Wild Life; consultant to the Mississippi River Parkway Survey. Served in World War I, planning Camp Zachary Taylor, Louisville, Ky., World War II, mission for U.S. Navy to Newfoundland on stabilization of peat hog areas for airport and other uses. Recipient Conservation Award, Trustees of Pub. Reservations, 1947; George Robert White Medal, Mass. Hort. Soc. for distinguished service to horticulture; honored by Am. Inst. of Park Execs., Am. Soc. of Landscape Architects, Am. Forestry Assn., Nat. Gardeners Assn., Am. Assn. of Nurserymen, all for contributions to plant introduction, conservation, park development, plant nomenclature. Mem. Mass. Nurserymen's Assn. (past pres.), New Eng. Nurserymen's Assn. (past pres.), Am. Assn. of Nurserymen (pres., 1923-24), New Eng. Conf. for Protection of Nat. Parks (chmn.), Am. Ornamental Growers Assn., Am. Civic Assn. (past chmn., nuisance com.), Am. Soc. of Park Execs., Salem C. of C., Mass. Forestry Assn., Am. Forestry Assn., Nat. Municipal League, Nat. Conf. on City Planning, Nat. Econ. League (counseller), Salem Civi League (past pres.), Mass. Fedn. of Planning Bds. (past chmn.), Salem Planning Bd. (past chmn.). Clubs: Appalachian Mountain (past pres.), Cosmos, Horticultural (Boston), Economic of Boston (mem. exec. com.). Co-editor: Standardized Plant Names; contbd. articles on hort., city planning, civic, nat. parks. Address: E Boxford MA‡

KELSO, JOHN BOLTON, professor Greek; b. Rawal Pindi, India, Dec. 26, 1875; s. Alexander P. and Louisa Mary (Bolton) K.; A.B., Washington and Jefferson Coll., Pa., 1894; Ph.D., U. of Leipzig, Germany, 1901; post-grad. work, Yale, 1901-02; grad. Western Theol. Sem., Allegheny, Pa., 1904; m. Edith M. Kellogg, of Princeton, N.J., Apr. 25, 1906; m. 2d, Florence K. Root, of Cleveland Heights, O., June 16, 1932. Instr. Western Theol. Sem., 1905-06; ordained Presbyn. ministry, 1906; prof. Greek, Grove City (Pa.) College, 1906-11; prof. of Greek, 1911-32, and dean, 1921-29, Coll. of Wooster; lecturer on art and civilization of Europe, Cleveland Coll., 1932-33; prof. of art history, Macalester Coll., St. Paul, 1933-39; now retired. Mem. Phi Beta Kappa. Author: The Spaniards in Ireland, 1588-1603, 1901. Contbr. to Princeton Review, Bible Magazine, and Proc. Ohio Coll. Assn. Home: 438 Ravina St., La Jolla CA‡

KEMERER, BENJAMIN TIBBITS, bishop; b. Vernon Center, Minn., Dec. 9, 1874; s. Samuel D. and Mary (Tresenriter) K.; ed. Hamline U., 1890-94; D.D., Seabury Theol. Sem., 1931; m. Callie Frederick, Oct. 1, 1896; children—Carol Frederick (wife of H. R. Edwards, M.D.), Elizabeth James (wife of W.J.L. Porcher, M.D.). Began as editor of country newspaper at 16; later proofreader for West Publishing Co., then salesman, manager cutlery dept. and advertising mgr., Simmons Hardware Co., St. Louis; deacon, 1903, priest, 1904, P.E. Ch.; missionary to city instns., St. Louis, 1904-07; rector St. George's Ch., St. Louis, 1907-21; gen. sec. field dept. Nat. Council P.E. Ch., 1921-23; rector St. Clement's Ch., El Paso, Tex., 1923-27, St. Paul's Ch., Duluth, 1927-30; elected bishop coadjutor Diocese of Duluth, June 1930, consecrated Nov. 1930; succeeded as bishop of Duluth on resignation of Bishop Bennett, Nov. 8, 1933. Upon the re-union of the Dioceses of Duluth and Minn., Jan. 1, 1944, became Suffragan Bishop of Minn., ret., 1948. Republican. Mason. Author: Christian Stewardship, 1924; You Can't Take It Minneapolis MN‡

KEMP, (CLARENCE) EVERETT, monologist; b. Shelbyville, Ill., Nov. 2, 1873; s. Isaac and Katharine (Dunn) K.; student McPherson (Kan.) Coll., 1893-95; grad. Columbia Coll. of Expression, Chicago, 1899; post-grad. course 1 yr., same sch.; m. Louise W. Lockwood, Nov. 18, 1905; 1 son, Henry Everett. Teacher in country schs. 4 yrs.; teacher of expression, Lordsburg (Calif.) Coll., 2 yrs.; same, Columbia Coll. of Expression, 1 yr.; lyceum and chautauqua lecturer, 1905-28; radio artist and continuity writer, Midland Broadcasting Co., Kansas City, Mo., since 1928. Democrat. Home: 4711 Grand Av., Kansas City MO‡

KEMP, HAROLD FRANCIS, broadcasting co. exec.; b. Ridgewood, N.J., June 16, 1896; s. Edward and Carrie (Stoddard) K.; ed. pub. schs.; m. Sarah Marguerite Baldwin, Oct. 28, 1923. Booker, Keith Albee Vaudeville Circuit, 1919-28; talent scout, booker Warner Bros., 1928-32; agt. Gen. Artists Corp., 1936-37; radio dir. Roche, Williams & Cleary, 1937-40; with NBC, 1932-36, 50-68, v.p., 1960-68, charge live shows from Cal., 1950-68. Served to 1st lt., inf., U.S. Army, 1917-19. Club: Bell Air (Cal.) Country. Home: Studio City CA Died July 3, 1968.

KEMP, MATTHEW STANLEY, clergyman; b. Tamaqua, Pa.; s. Matthew and Elizabeth Audre (Wartha) K.; B.A., Gettysburg (Pa.) Coll., 1894; M.A., Gettysburg Theol. Sem., 1897; Litt.D., Potomac U., 1910; student U. of Pittsburgh, 1909-12, Temple U., 1921-23; D.D., Susquehanna U., 1920; m. Margaret M. Couch, of Maysville, Pa., June 21, 1911; children—Anna Elizabeth Carolyn, John Stanley Couch. Ordained Luth. ministry, 1897; pastor successively Smicksburg, Avonmore, Turtle Creek and Watsontown, and at Holidaysburg, Pa., since 1920. Served as teacher Smicksburg Normal Sch., Watsontown High Sch. and Altoona Sch. of Religious Edn., also as spl. lecturer various schs. and socs.; now mem. examining bd. Alleghany Synod and mem. bd. dirs. Gettysburg Theol. Sem., etc. Mem. Pittsburgh Hist. Soc., Pittsburgh Cornishmen's Assn. Lecturer for Am. Red Cross, World War; widely known as Chautauqua and summer assembly lecturer. Republican. Mason. Author: Boss Tom, 1905; Ande Trembath, 1906; Lutherans of the Mahonings, 1916; Christmas Poems, 1924; Angels of Christmas (sermons), 1926; also articles in religious Hollidaysburg PA‡

KEMPER, ARTHUR BERNARD, retired educator, chemist; b. Crafton, Pa., Jan. 5, 1912; s. Francis Joseph and Rose Marie (Kreaps) K.; student Grove City (Pa.) Coll., 1928-29; B.S., Carnegie Inst. Tech., 1933; Ph.D., Catholic U. Am. (K.D. fellow, 1933-36), 1936; m. Mary Elizabeth O'Donnell, Apr. 15, 1942; children—Margaret Rose, Mary Frances. Mem. faculty Manhattan Coll., N.Y.C., 1936-69, prof. chemistry, 1945-69, prof. emeritus, 1969-72, head dept. chemistry, 1945-66; chem. cons. (particularly photography), 1942-72. Fellow Am. Inst. Chemists; mem. Am. Chem. Soc., Am. Assn. U. Profs. Home: New York City NY Died Apr. 29, 1972.

KEMPER, JOHN MASON, headmaster; b. Fort D.A. Russel, Wyoming, Sept. 1, 1912; s. James Brown and Mercer (Mason) K.; B.S., U.S. Mil. Acad., 1935; M.A., Columbia, 1942; L.H.D., Williams College, 1948, Colby College, Waterville, Maine, 1958; Litt.D., Tufts College, 1952; LL.D., Harvard University, 1962; m. to Sylvia Mayo Pratt, June 9, 1936 (dec. Sept. 1961); children—Cecily Thomson, Lucy Ord, Rosamond Pratt; m. 2d, Abby Locke Castle, Dec. 27, 1963. Commissioned 2d lt., U.S. Army, 1935 advancing through the grades to col., 1944; chief historical br. War Dept. World War II; headmaster Phillips Acad., Andover, Mass., 1948-71. Decorated Legion of Merit (2). Member Headmasters Assn., Nat. Assn. of Ind. Schools (chairman 1955-57). Clubs: Century Assn., University (N.Y.C.); Tavern (Boston). Home: Andover MA Died Dec. 4, 1971.

KEMPER, WILLIAM MAUZY, educator; b. Warrenton, Va., Feb. 25, 1881; s. Charles Hagar and Susan Hopkins (Gibson) K.; prep. edn., high sch., Warrenton, and Bethel (Va.) Mil. Acad.; A.B., Hampden-Sidney Coll., 1901; m. Lucy Winston Allen, of Woodstock, Va., June 22, 1904; children—Allen Mauzy, Lucy Winston. Supt. Bethel Mil. Acad., 1903-11; pres. Palmer Coll., De Funiak Springs, Fla., 1912-22; supt. Danville Mil. Inst., 1922-38; now exec. asst. to gov. of Va. Mayor De Funiak Springs, 1919-20. Chmn. City Dem. Com.; pres. Citizens Road League of Va. Trustee Columbia (S.C.) Theol. Sem.; dir. Hughes Memorial Sch., Danville Y.M.C.A. Mem. Kappa Sigma, Omicron Delta Kappa. Democrat. Presbyn. Mason. Club: Lions. Home: 301 N. Boulevard, Richmond VA‡

KEMPNER, AUBREY JOHN, prof. mathematics; b. London, Eng., Sept. 22, 1880; s. Nathan and Sophia (Allberry) K.; student U. of Berlin, 1906-07; Ph.D., U. of Gottingen, 1911; m. Kate Henschel, Mar. 29, 1906. Instr. in mathematics, U. of Ill., 1911-14, asso. 1914-19, asst. prof., 1919-25; prof. mathematics, head dept., U. of Colo., 1925-49, ret. past co-editor Am. Math. Monthly; past asso. editor Trans. Am. Math. Soc. Mem. Am. Math. Soc. (mem. council 1925-28). Math. Assn. America (trustee 1924-43; v.p. 1927, 28, 35; pres. 1937-38), Sigma Xi (pres. Colo. sect. 1929-30). Contbr. on math. subjects. Home: 956 13th St., Boulder CO‡

KEMPNER, ISAAC HERBERT, cotton factor, banker; b. Cincinnati, Jan. 14, 1873; s. Harris and Elizabeth (Seinsheimer) K.; student Ball High Sch., Galveston, Tex., to 1886, Bellevue High Sch., Va., 1886-89, Washington and Lee U., 1889-93; m. Hennie Blum, Dec. 17, 1902; children—Harris Leon, Isaac Herbert, Cecile Blum, Lyda, Henrietta Leonora. Called home from coll. by death of father and took charge of cotton factorage business of H. Kempner; with others purchased controlling interest in Island City Savings Bank, 1902, name now U.S. Nat. Bank, of which is chmn. bd.; also pres. Sugarland (Tex.) Industries; chmn. bd. Imperial Sugar Company. Pres. Galveston Cotton Exchange, 1905-19 and 1945; mem. New York cotton exchanges; asso. mem. Liverpool Cotton Exchange. Former mem. administrative com., American Bankers Assn., 1921-25; mem. exec. com. U.S. Cane Sugar Refineries Assn. Mem. American Jewish Committee. One of the originators of commn. form of municipal govt. in America; elected treas. City of Galveston, 1899; commr. of finance and revenue, Galveston, 1901-15; mayor of Galveston, term 1917-19. Mem. Nat. Assn. R.R. Securities (v.p.). Democrat. Clubs: Artillery, Galveston Country. Home: Galveston TX Died July 31, 1967; buried Galveston TX

KEMSLEY, (JAMES GOMER BERRY), Viscount or Dropmore and 1st Baron of Farnham Royal; bus. exec., u. pres.; b. Merthyr-Tydfil, Wales, May 7, 1883; s. John Mathias Berry and Mary Anne (Berry) K.; received honorary LL.D., Manchester U., U. of Wales; m. Mary Lilian Holmes, 1907 (died 1928); children—Lionel, Denis, Neville, Douglas (killed in action, Italy, 1944), Oswald, (dec.), Marchioness of Huntly, Anthony; m. 2d, Edith du Plessis, 1931. Chmn. Kemsley Newspaper Ltd., London, 1937-59; editor-in-chief Sunday Times, 1937-59; Reuters Trustee, 1941-59, chmn., 1951-59; president Univ. Coll. of South Wales and Monmouthshire, 1945-50; justice of peace for Buckinghamshire, 1927; high sheriff for Buckinghamshire, 1929, pres. Merthr Tydfil Gen. Hosp., 1928-1950; chmn. King Edward, VII Hosp. Windsor, 1933-37 Infants Hosp. 1922-37, Master Spectacle Makers Co., 1934-36. Decorated Knight of St. John., Knight Grand Cross Order Brit. Empire; Officer Legion of Honour (France); Grand Cross of George I (Greece); Comdr. Order of the Crown (Belgium). Pres. Football Assn. Wales, 1946-60, Brit. Gliding Assn., 1947-61, Conservative. Clubs: Royal Yacht Squadron, Carlton. Home: London England Died Feb. 6, 1969.

KENDALL, CHARLES HARRY, ins. co. exec.; b. Louisville, Oct. 19, 1902; s. J. Walter and Lillian (Hays) K.; student University Louisville, 1922-24; LL.D., Kentucky Wesleyan Coll., 1963; m. Hazel Marie Newland, Apr. 16, 1942; children—Walter Ross, Linea Laura. With Washington Nat. Ins. Co., Evanston, Ill., 1928-69, successively agt., mgr., div. mgr., 2d v.p., 1928-53, v.p. charge indsl. agy. dept., 1953-56, exec. v.p., 1957-63, co-chmn. bd., 1963-66, chmn. bd., 1966-69, also dir., mem. exec. and finance coms., chmn. exec. com., 1967-69. Mem. Life Insurers Conf. (pres. 1966), Life Ins. Agy. Mgmt. Assn. Mason. Home: Glenview IL Died Dec. 12, 1969; buried Cave Hill Cemetery, Louisville KY

KENDALL, CHARLES HOWARD, lawyer; b. Buffalo, Nov. 9, 1908; s. Charles Adams and Frances Edith (Armstrong) K.; A.B., Union Coll. (N.Y. State scholarship), 1930; Sprague scholarship, U. of Buffalo, 1931-32, LL.B., 1933; m. Irma Roberta Fraser, Sept. 23, 1933. Admitted to N.Y. State bar, Oct. 1933, practiced in Buffalo, 1933-41; lectr. mathematics Millard Fillmore Coll., U. of Buffalo evening session, 1939-40; asst. to John Lord O'Brien, Office Prodn. Management and W.P.B., Washington, 1941-44; gen. counsel Office Fgn. Liquidation Commr., 1947-48; gen. counsel Nat. Security Resources, 1949-51, Def. Prodn. Adminstrn., 1951-52, ODM 1953-58, Office of Civilian and Defense Mobilization, 1958-61, Office Emergency Planning, 1961-65, D.C. Legal Aid Soc., 1965-69, Office Emergency Preparedness, 1969-70. Legal adviser Prosdl. Mission to China and Philippines, 1946. Served in United States Navy, 1944-46; active service on aircraft carrier, P.T.O. Mem. Fed. Bar Assn., Chi Psi, Phi Delta Phi. Republican. Methodist. Clubs: Nat. Lawyers (founder), Bethesda Country. Home: Washington DC Died Nov. 19, 1970.

KENDALL, CHARLES PIERCE, educator; b. Chicago, Ill., Jan. 21, 1873; s. Pierce and Frances Louise (Vosburgh) K.; grad. N.Y. Regents Normal Sch., 1894; grad. Phillips Acad., Exeter, N.Y., 1898; A.B., Harvard, 1902, A.M., 1916; m. Jennie Moss, Sept. 24, 1900; children—George Moss, Lee Gordon, Pauline Lucile, Charles Pierce, Clarence (dec.), Ralph (dec.). Prin. high schs., successively at Vineyard Haven, Wareham and North Easton, Mass.; prin. Wheeler Sch., North Stonington, Conn., 6 yrs.; prin. Howard Sem., West Bridgewater, Mass., 8 yrs.; founder, 1923, and prin. Kendall Hall (sch. for girls), incorporated and moved to Peterboro, N.H., 1935. Chmn. Public Safety Com., West Bridgewater, World War; chmn. World War Memorial Scholarship Fund for Class of 1902, Harvard, and on Scholarship Com. Class of 1898, Phillips Exeter Acad. Mem. Phi Delta Kappa. Conglist. Mason. Clubs: Harvard (Boston); Rotary (pres.; also speaker). Address: Framingham Center MA‡

KENDALL, CHARLES SHILLING, clergyman; b. Fredericksburg, Ind., Apr. 12, 1905; s. Landy Haven and Pearl (Shilling) K.; A.B., DePauw U., 1927, D.D., 1945; S.T.B., Boston U., 1930, S.T.M., 1930-32, Th.D., 1942; student Harvard, 1929-30; D.H., So. Cal. Coll. Osteopathy, 1957; LL.D., Lincoln U., 1965; m. Mary Lous Travis, Jan. 1, 1930; children—Charles Travis, Margaret Ann, Philip Wesley. Ordained to ministry Methodist Ch., 1925; pastor in Maywood, Ind., 1925-28, Gloucester, Mass., 1928-33, Los Angeles, 1933-38, 38-42, Somerville, Mass., 1938, Phoenix, 1942-56, First Meth. Ch., Hollywood, Cal., 1956-70; supt. Tucson dist. So. Cal.-Ariz. Conf., United Meth. Ch., from 1970, trustee, 1954-68. Mem. council world service Meth. Ch., 1952-64; pres. Hollywood Ministerial Assn., 1967, Los Angeles Council Chs., 1964-65, Los Angeles United Ministers Assn., 1968-70. Mem. Ariz. Gov. Com. Youth Prison Reform, 1942-44; mem. Coordinating Council Hollywood, 1958-62. Recipient Goodwill Industries 30 Year award, 1968; Distinguished Alumnus award Boston U., 1964. Mem. Hollywood C. of C., Phi Beta Kappa, Delta Sigma Rho. Optimist, Lion, Mason (32 deg.). Recording artist for Dot, Word records. Home: Tucson AZ

KENDALL, COURTS P., banker; b. Paris, Tenn., Oct. 23, 1869; s. William Devereaux and Ada (Courts) K.; student Md. Acad., Oxford, Md., 1885-87; m. Grace Green, of St. Louis, Mo., Aug. 29, 1908; 1 dau., Elinor. Formerly sec. Atlas Building & Loan Assn., Chattanooga, Tenn.; engaged in cotton oil production; moved to Jacksonville, Fla., 1905, v.p. Fla. Cotton Oil Co., 1905-18; pres. Morris Plan Bank of Jacksonville since 1917; v.p. Barnett Nat. Bank since 1918; dir. Jacksonville Br. Federal Reserve Bank, Victory Nat. Life Ins. Co., Tampa, Fla. Clubs: Seminole, Timuquana. Home: 1824 Donald St. Office: Barnett Nat. Bank, Jacksonville FL‡

KENDALL, EDWARD CALVIN, biochemist; b. South Norwalk, Conn., Mar. 8, 1886; s. George Stanley and Eva Frances (Abbott) K.; B.S., Columbia, 1908, M.S., 1909, Ph.D., 1910, D.Sc., 1951; D.Sc. (hon.), U. Cin., 1922, Yale, Western Res., Williams Coll., Nat. U. Ireland, Columbia, 1951, Gustavus Adolphus Coll., St. Peter, Minn., 1963; m. Rebecca Kennedy, Dec. 30, 1915; children—Hugh, Roy (dec.) Norman (dec.), Elizabeth (Mrs. J.J. Steve). Research chemist Parke, Davis, and Co., Detroit, 1910-11; investigations on thyroid gland St. Luke's Hosp., N.Y. City, 1911-14; head sect. biochemistry Mayo Clinic, 1914, prof. physiologic chemistry Mayo Found., (U. Minn.), 1921-51; visiting prof. chemistry, James Forrestal Research Center, Princeton University, New Jersey, from 1952. Recipient: John Scott prize and Premium awarded by City of Phila., 1921 (researches in thyroxin); Chandler medal, Columbia U., 1925; Squibb award for outstanding research in endocrinology, 1945; Lasker award (jointly with Dr. Hench), Am. Public Health Assn., 1949; Page One award (jointly with Dr. Hench), Newspaper Guild New York, 1950; John Phillips Meml. award, Am. Coll. Phys. in Boston, 1950; Research Corp. award, by Research Corp. of N.Y., 1950; Remsen Meml. award, by Md. sect. Am. Chem. Soc., 1950; Research award, Am. Pharm. Mfrs. Assn., 1950; Passano award for 1950 (with Dr. Hench), Passano Found., San Francisco, 1950; Medal of Honour from Canadian Pharm. Mfrs. Assn., 1950; Nobel Prize in Physiology and Medicine (with Dr. Philip S. Hench and Dr. Tadeus Reichstein), 1950; Dr. C.C. Criss award (jointly with Dr. Hench), 1951, Award of Merit (with Dr. Hench) from Masonic Found. Med. Research and Humane Welfare, 1951; Cameron award (with Prof. Reichstein), U. Edinburgh, 1951; Heberden Soc. award, London, 1951; The Kober award, Association of American Physicians, 1952; Alexander Hamilton medal, Alumni of Columbia Coll., 1961; Sci. Achievement award Am. Med. Assn., 1965. Mem. Am. Philos. Soc., Am. Acad. Arts and Scis., Am. Soc. Biol. Chemists (pres. 1925-26), Am. Physiol. Soc., Am. Soc. Exptl. Pathology, Am. Soc. Exptl. Biology and Medicine, Am. Chem. Soc., Harvey Soc., A.A.A.S., Assn. Am. Physicians, Assn. Study Internal Secretions, Nat. Acad. Scis., New York Academy of Sciences, Swedish Society. Republican. Congregationalist. Contbns. include isolation of thyroxine, crystallization of glutathione and establishment of its chemical structure, separation and identification of a series of compounds from the adrenal cortex; prepared cortisone by partial synthesis (with Merck & Co., Inc.), investigated effects of cortisone and of ACTH on rheumatoid arthritis and in rheumatic fever (with Drs. Hench, Slocumb and Polley). Home: Princeton NJ Died May 4, 1972; buried Oakwood Cemetery, Rochester MN

KENDALL, ELVA ROSCOE, ex-congressman; b. Nicholas Co., Ky., Feb. 14, 1893; s. Preston D. and Luella (Cook) K.; ed. pub. schs. and Y.M.C.A. Sch. of Accountancy, National University; m. Joe Gladys Snapp, of Nicholas County, Aug. 20, 1919; 1 son, Preston Leroy. Public accountant and tax consultant; farmer; field auditor with Treasury Dept. of U.S. 5 yrs.; veteran of World War; mem. 71st Congress (1929-31), 9th Ky. Dist. Mem. Am. Legion, Forty and Eight, Sigma Delta Kappa. Republican. Methodist. Mason (K.T., Shriner). Home: Carlisle KY‡

KENDALL, GEORGE R., insurance exec.; b. Jefferson County, Ky., Mar. 22, 1882; s. Preston B. and Adelia (Scearce) K.; ed. pub. schs., Louisville, Ky.; m. Edna M. Woods, June 19, 1906. With Prudential Ins. Co., 10 yrs., as agent and mgr.; in 1911, organized Washington Life & Accident Ins. Co. which later became Washington Nat. Ins. Co., sec. for 12 years, pres., 1923-51, chairman of the executive committee, 1951-63, hon. chmn. exec. com., 1963-69. Mason. Club: Westmoreland Country, University (Evanston). Home: Kenilworth IL Died June 1, 1969; buried Evanston IL

KENDALL, GEORGE VALENTINE, educator; b. Kirkwood, Mo., Feb. 14, 1891; s. George Johnson and and Eunice (Cole) K.; A.B., Brown U., 1912; A.M., U. Wis., 1913; postgrad. Columbia, 1914-15, U. Besancon, 1919; L.H.D., Wabash Coll., 1942; m. Yvonne Geyer, June 30, 1919. Instr. English, Columbia, 1915-17, 1919-20; prof. English, Wabash Coll., 1920-57, dean, 1923-40, acting pres., 1940-41, dean faculty, 1941-57. Served as 2d lt. Arty., U.S. Army, A.E.F., France, 1917-19; from lt. col. to col. AUS, 1942-44; with Hdqrs. S.W. Pacific Area, U.S. Armed Forces in Far East, Armed Forces in Pacific, 1942-46. Awarded Legion of Merit, 1945. Mem. Delta Phi, Phi Beta Kappa. Home: Duxbury MA Died Sept. 9, 1972; buried Belle Fontaine, St Louis MO

KENDALL, JAMES, chemist; b. Surrey, Eng., July 30, 1889; s. William Henry and Rebecca (Pickering) K.; A.M., B.Sc., Edinburgh U., 1910, Sc.D., 1915; student at Heidelberg, Stockholm and Petrograd; m. Alice Tyldesley, of Victoria, B.C., Sept. 13, 1915; children—James Tyldesley, Isabella Jean, Alice Rebecca. Vans Dunlop scholar in chemistry, Edinburgh U., 1909-12; also 1851 exhibitioner in chemistry, 1912-13; instr. chemistry, 1913-15, asst. prof., 1915-16, asso. prof., 1916-22, prof., 1922-26, Columbia; prof. and chmn. dept. Washington Square Coll. (New York U.), 1926-27, also dean Grad. Sch., New York U., 1927-28; prof., U. of Edinburgh, since 1928. Acting prof. chemistry, Stanford, 1919, 23, U. of Calif., 1923, Pa. State Coll., 1927. Lt. U.S.N.R.F., 1917-19; spl. duty for Bur. of Ordnance as liaison officer with allied navies on Naval Gas Warfare. Lt. comdr. U.S.N.R.F., 1924-26. Fellow Royal Soc., Royal Soc. Edinburgh, A.A.A.S.; mem. Am. Chem. Soc. (chmn. New York sect., 1925), Am. Inst. Chemists (chmn. New York sect. 1926), London Chem. Soc., London Soc. Chem. Industry, Faraday Soc., Phi Beta Kappa, Sigma Xi, Alpha Chi Sigma, Phi Lambda Upsilon. Clubs: Century, Chemists'. Revised and rewrote Smith's Intermediate Chemistry, Smith's College Chemistry, Smith's Elementary Chemistry, Smith's Inorganic Chemistry, and lab. outlines of each, 1922-26. Author: College Chemistry Companion, 1924; Intermediate Chemistry Companion,

1925; General Chemistry and Laboratory Outline, 1927; At Home Among the Atoms, 1929. Home: 14 Mayfield Gardens, Edinburgh Scotland‡

KENDALL, JOHN SMITH, writer, prof. Spanish; b. Ocean Springs, Miss., Apr. 9, 1874; s. John Irwin and Mary Elizabeth (Smith) K.; Tulane U., 1888-91, A.M., 1918; m. Isoline Rodd, July 1, 1903; children—Elisabeth Rodd (Mrs. Frank H. Thompson), Lane Carter. Began as reporter New Orleans Picayune, New Orleans, Louisiana, 1891, and successively lit. critic, war corr. (Spanish-Am. War, Cuban Revolution 1906, Nicaraguan Revolution 1912), editor mag. section until 1914; published articles on leprosy resulting in establishment of State Leprosarium at Indian Camp (now U.S. Leprosarium at Carrville, La.); made several trips as corr. to Europe, Mexico, Central America and W.I.; instr. Spanish, Tulane U., 1914-18, asso. prof., 1918-29, prof., 1929-39, emeritus prof. since 1939. Mem. Tenn. State Commn. for Study of Battle of New Orleans, 1927-34. Mem. Phi Beta Kappa, Sigma Upsilon, Theta Nu fraternities. Literary rep. Rex Carnival Society, 1899-1939. Has written a guide to New Orleans, passing through numerous editions; A History of New Orleans, 1922, also many mag. articles, etc. Mem. editorial bd. La. Hist. Quarterly. Home: 2515 Piedmont Av., Berkeley, Calif. Address: care Tulane U., New Orleans‡

KENDELL, ROBERT LOTHAR, business exec.; b. Ft. Wayne, Ind., Oct. 15, 1900; s. Friedrich August and Magdelena (Brautsch) von Kendall; student Luth. parochial schs., Internat. Coll., Ft. Wayne, U. Chgo.; m. Eulah Esther Byer, May 31, 1931 (dec. 1946); m. 2d Mary Cheavens Easley, Oct. 20, 1947. Tester Cadillac-Lasalle, Chgo., Jordan, Cleve., Auburn, N.Y.C., 1924-25; mgr. theatres Ostrovsky circuit. Chgo. Consol. Amusement Enterprises, N.Y.C., also part owner Flora Theatre, Bklyn., 1926-29; pres. Kendell & Dasserville, Inc., 1930-35; exec. sec. Kendell Co., Am., successor co., 1935-70; owner Kendall Advertising Agency (formerly Continental Advertising Associates), 1936-70, Grapho-Inst., 1946-70, Sivad Press, book publishers, 1947-70. President, treas. American Feline Soc., Inc., cat charity, 1944-70. Home: New York City NY Died July 23, 1970; buried Rosehill Cemetery, Linden NJ

KENDRICK, CHARLES, b. San Francisco, Calif., son of Thomas and Catherine (Marron) K.; educated public schools and private tutors; LL.D. (hon.), University of San Francisco, 1961; married Marie Canepa, Sept. 15, 1905 (died Dec. 2, 1911); children—Marie, Marron; m. 2d, Kathryn Clarke, Apr. 21, 1914; children—Charles, Geraldine, Kathryn, Barbara. Admitted to bar, 1902; chmn. bd. Schlage Lock Co. of Cal. Trustee San Francisco War Memorial, 1920-38; mem. adv. com. San Francisco Water System, 1923-26; mem. San Francisco Planning Commn., 1924-30; member San Francisco Relief Committee, 1932-34; v.p. Golden Gate Internat. Expn., 1938; trustee Phelan Found.; hon. trustee Mills Coll.; mem. adv. bd. Hoover Inst. Stanford U.; chmn. bd. regents U. San Francisco; mem. bd. govs. San Francisco Opera Assn., San Francisco Art Museum; pres. Pan Am Soc., San Francisco; 1942-43; pres. El Buen Vecino, 1944; mem. San Francisco Civilian War Council, 1940-45; member adv. bd. of the San Francisco Ordnance District, 1940-45, member adv. com. War Production Board, World War II. Served as capt. 26th Div., later maj. 5th Army Corps, U.S. Army, World War I. Decorated Silver Star, Order Purple Heart (U.S.); Order of St. Olav (Norway); Officier Legion of Honor (France); Bernardo O'Higgins (Chile); Gold Medal of Pan American Society (New York City); Grand Cross of the Order of Merit (Peru); Papal night of St. Gregroy the Great. Clubs: Bohemian Club, Pacific Union, Press, Menlo Country, Burlingame Country, San Francisco Golf. Home: San Francisco CA Died Aug. 3, 1970; buried Holy Cross Cemetery, San Bruno CA

KENDRICK, NATHANIEL COOPER, educator; b. Rochester, N.Y., Sept. 9, 1900; s. Ryland Morris and May (Cooper) K.; A.B., U. of Rochester, 1921; A.M., Harvard, 1923, Ph.D., 1930; Dr. Humane Letters, Bowdoin Collge, 1966; m. Lucy Hawkins Higgs, July 8, 1927; children—Ann Hawkins, Thomas Ryland. Instr. in history, Bowdoin Coll., 1926-28, asst. prof., 1928-32, asso. prof., 1932-46, prof. of history since 1946, acting dean, 1946-47, dean of coll., 1947-66, emeritus dean, 1966-69. Mem. Am. Hist. Assn., Psi Upsilon. Home: Brunswick ME Died Sept. 2, 1969; buried Brunswick ME

KENIN, HERMAN DAVID, union exec.; b. Vineland, N.J., Oct. 26, 1901; s. Samuel Benjamin and Anna (Gordin) K.; student Reed Coll., Portland, Ore., 1920-21, N.W. Coll. Law, Portland, 1924-26, 30-31; Mus.D. (hon.), Phila. Acad. Music, 1960; m. Maxine Bennett, July 31, 1936; children—Herman David, James Bennett. Profl. musician, 1920-30. Admitted to Ore. bar, 1931; practice of law, 1931-43; mem. Am. Fedn. Musicians, 1920-70, pres. Portland, 1936-56, mem. internat. exec. bd. 1943-58, internat. pres., 1958-70; vice president AFL-CIO, 1963. Representative U.S. workers 1st session adv. com. salaried and profl. workers, ILO, Geneva, Switzerland, 1949; mem. adv. com. Nat. Cultural Center, 1960-70;

mem. Nat. Council Arts, 1965-70. Mem. Am. Arbitration Assn. (dir.), Phi Mu Alpha. Mason (Shriner); mem. B'nai B'rith. Home: Westport CT Died July 22, 1970; buried Portland OR

KENISTON, (RALPH) HAYWARD, college prof.; b. Somerville, Mass., July 5, 1883; s. Charles Edgar and Sarah Elvina (Hayward) K.; A.B., Harvard, 1904, A.M., 1910, Ph.D., 1911; studied in Europe, 1911-13; m. Florence M. Robinson, May 20, 1911; children—Florence, Martha, Allen; m. 2d, Roberta Cannell, June 16, 1928; children—Kenneth, Marjorie. Instr. in Latin, Colby Coll., 1904-05; master Hotchkiss Sch., 1905-07; instr. Romance langs., Harvard, 1908-10; asst. librarian, Hispanic Soc. of America, 1910-11; instr. Romance langs., Harvard, 1913-14; asst. prof. Romance langs., 1914-19, prof., 1919-25, and dean Grad. Sch., 1923-25, Cornell; prof. Spanish lang., University of Chicago, 1925-40; prof. Romance langs., Univ. of Michigan, 1940-53, dean, Coll. of Literature, Science and the Arts, 1945-51; vis. lecturer at Duke University 1952-53; cultural relations attache American Embassy, Buenos Aires, 1942-44; Y.M.C.A. secretary, La Valbonne, France, and Florence, Italy, 1918; speaker for Italian Ministry of Propaganda, in Central Italy, 1918; assistant in office of Military Attache, Am. Embassy, Rome, 1918. Mem. Am. Acad. Arts and Sciences, American Philos. Society, Modern Lang. Assn. America, Phi Beta Kappa, Hispanic Soc. America; Linguistic Society of America (president, 1948). Author: Las Treinta of Juan Boscan, 1911; The Dante Tradition in the Fourteenth and Fifteenth Centuries, 1915; List of Works for the Study of Hispanic-American History, 1920; Garcilaso de la Vega (a critical study of his life and works), 1922; Spanish Idiom List, 1929; The Syntax of Castilian Prose, 1937. Editor: La Barraca por V. Blasco Ibanez, 1910; Maria por Jorge Isaacs, 1918; Fuero de Guadalajara, 1924; Works of Garcilaso de la Vega, 1925. Contbr. to reviews. Home: Ann Arbor MI Died Aug. 1970.

KENNEBECK, GEORGE ROBERT, air force ofcr.; b. Carroll, Ia., June 5, 1892; s. George and Elizabeth (Gleason) K.; D.D.S., State U. of Ia., 1916; m. Elizabeth Scales, June 1, 1927; children—Elizabeth V., George Robert. Commd. 1st lt., Dental Corps, U.S. Army, 1917, and advanced through grades to maj. gen., 1949; chief of dental service, Camp Davis, N.C., 1941-42, chief of dental service U.S. Air Force, Hdqrs. U.S. Air Force, Washington, since 1942; officer U.S. Air Force. Recipient Legion of Merit, Commendation Ribbon, Fellow Am. Coll. Dentists; mem. Am. Dental Assn., Internat. Coll. Dentists. Home: Silver Spring MD Died Apr. 29, 1969; buried Arlington Nat. Cemetery.

KENNEDY, CHARLES A., congressman; b. at Montrose, Ia., Mar. 24, 1869. Mayor of Montrose, 1890-4; mem. Ia. Ho. of Rep., 1903-7; mem. 60th to 66th Congresses (1907-21), 1st Ia. Dist.; Republican. Home: Montrose IA‡

KENNEDY, CHARLES WILLIAM, coll. prof.; b. Port Richmond, S.I., N.Y., Jan. 13, 1882; s. T. Livingstone and Marie Alice (Bush) K.; grad. Phillips Acad., Exeter, N.H., 1899; A.B., Columbia, 1902; New York Law Sch., 1903-04; M.A., Princeton, 1905; Charles Scribner fellowship, 1905-06; Ph.D., Princeton University, 1906; married Lucy Baldwin Walradt, June 3, 1911; 1 daughter, Barbara Cary; married 2d, Elizabeth Deane, March 25, 1940. Instructor in English, 1906-07, Princeton University, Porter Ogden Jacobus fellowship, 1907-08, instructor English, 1908-10, assistant professor, Robert Stockton Pyne Preceptor in English, 1910-19, associate prof., 1919-21, prof. English, 1921-38, Murray prof. of English literature, 1938-44, Murray professor, emeritus, since 1944; visiting prof., Colorado Coll., summer session, 1936, 37, 38; College of Chestnut Hill, spring term, 1938. Commd. 1st lt. Ordnance Res. Corps, May 28, 1917; capt., Ordnance Department N.A., Jan. 22, 1918; on active duty, July 12, 1917, Jan. 10, 1919; service with A.E.F., Sept.-Dec. 1918. Chmn. Princeton Board Athletic Control, 1923-32; pres. Nat. Collegiate Athletic Assn., 1930-32, hon. pres., 1932-69; v.p. Am. Olympic Com., 1928-32. Mem. Modern Lang. Assn. of Am., Huguenot Soc. of Am., Sons of the Am. Revolution, Phi Beta Kappa. Episcopalian. Clubs: Tiger Inn, Key and Seal, Princeton (N.Y.C.). Author The Legend of Juliana, 1906; The Poems of Cynewulf, 1910; The Caedmon Poems, 1916; The Walls of Hamelin, 1922; College Athletics, 1925; Sport and Sportsmanship, 1931; Old English Elegies, 1936; Beowulf, 1940; The Earliest English Poetry, 1943; Early English Christian Poetry, 1952; An Anthology of Old English Poetry, 1960; Early English Christian Poetry, 1963. Home: LaJolla CA Died July 13, 1969; buried Princeton (N.J.) Cemetery.

KENNEDY, CLARENCE, educator; b. Philadelphia, Pa., Sept. 4, 1892; s. Clarence and Jennie May (McClintock) K.; B.S., U. Pa., 1914, M.A., 1915; student Harvard, 1915-16, Ph.D., 1924; studied Am. Sch. Classical Studies, Athens, Greece, 1920-21; m. Ruth Wedgwood Doggett, May 5, 1921; children—Melinda Norris, Robert Lawrence. Prof. art dept. Smith Coll., Northampton, Mass., 1930-60; dir. div. grad. study in Europe, 1925-32; vis. prof. fine arts, N.Y.U., 1932; annual prof., Toledo Museum of Art,

1938-39, Norton fellow, Harvard, 1920-21; Guggenheim fellow, 1930; Research fellow Coll. Art Assn., 1931-32. Cons. Polaroid, Kodak, Meriden Gravure. Mem. Sigma Xi. Baptist. Author: Certain Sculptures of the Dreyfus Collection, 1930; (with F. Hartt and G. Corti) The Chapel of the Cardinal of Portugal, 1964. Editor: Studies in the History and Criticism of Sculpture, 7 vols., 1927-33. Contbr. to art mags. and research in stereophotography and reproduction processes for book illustration; dir. Cantina Press. Home: Northampton MA Died July 29, 1972.

KENNEDY, CLYDE RAYMOND, physician; b. W.Va., Oct. 7, 1894; s. James and Clara Mae (Winfield) K.; M.D., Rush Med. Coll., 1937; M.S., U. Mich., 1941; m. Florence Judith Bondeson, Mar. 20, 1937; children—Candace Dubbs, Kristin, Clyde, Kathleen. Intern, also resident obstetrics and gynecology Henry Ford Hosp., Detroit, 1937-42; sr. staff obstetrics and gynecology Mercy Hosp.; obstet. and gynecol. staff Scripps Meml. Hosp., Donald Sharp Meml. Hosp. Served to ensign U.S. Navy, 1917-18. Diplomate Am. Bd. Obstetrics and Gynecology. Fellow A.C.S.; mem. A.M.A., Am. Coll. Obstetrics and Gynecology. Home: San Diego CA Died Aug. 14, 1970; buried El Camino Meml. Park, San Diego CA

KENNEDY, FRED J(OHNSTON), lawyer; b. Detroit, May 22, 1891; Johnston B. and Jessie (Young) K.; A.B., U. Mich., 1913; J.D., 1915; m. Phyllis Fitzgerald, Dec. 11, 1937. Admitted to Mich. bar, 1915; practice of law, Douglas, Eaman, Barbour, Rogers & Kennedy, Detroit, 1915-25; mem. Butzel, Eaman, Long, Gust & Kennedy from 1925; dir. Kelsey-Hayes Company, Cunningham Drug Stores, Inc., Mueller Brass Co., Murray Corp. of Am., Continental Motors Corp., Continental Aviation & Engring. Corp., Wis. Motor Corp. Served in U.S. Army, 1917-19. Clubs: Detroit, Detroit Athletic, Grosse Pointe. Address: Rancho Santa Fe CA Died Sept. 19, 1969; buried Woodlawn Cemetery, Detroit MI

KENNEDY, GALL, educator, editor; b. Cadott, Wis., Sept. 17, 1900; s. Herbert Daniel and Jessie (Young) K.; B.A., U. Minn., 1922; M.A., Columbia, 1923, Ph.D., 1928; m. Joy E. Peterson, May 28, 1925; children—Miriam Gove (Mrs. Arnold Modell), Margaret Gail (Mrs. Joseph L. Gornick), Jesse Ward. Fellow Columbia, 1923-24, lecturer in philosophy, 1924-25; assistant director New School Social Research, 1925-26; instructor philosophy Amherst Coll., 1926-30, asst. prof., 1930-36, asso. prof., 1936-39, prof., from 1939, on Henry C. Folger Found., from 1953. Price officer Western Mass. office OPA, 1943. Guggenheim fellow, 1929-30. Mem. Am. Philos. Assn., Am. Assn. U. Profs. Editor, author: Education at Amherst: The New Program (with others), 1957. Editor: Bacon, Hobbes, Locke: Selected Writings, 1937; Democracy and the Gospel of Wealth, 1949; Pragmatism and American Culture, 1950; Education for Democracy, 1952; The Classic American Philosphers (with Max H. Fisch and others), 1951; Evolution and Religion, 1957; (with Milton R. Konvitz) The American Pragmatists: Selected Writings, 1960 (with Joseph Epstein) The Process of Philosophy, 1966; Transcendentalist Revolt, 1968. Contbr. to Sidney Hook and The Comtemporary World, 1968, also articles and revs. profl. jours. Home: Amherst MA Died Apr. 18, 1972.

KENNEDY, GILBERT FALCONER, lawyer; b. Kingston, N.Y., Apr. 10, 1871; s. Dr. David and Eliza (Gilbert) K.; Amherst Coll., 1891-93, hon. M.A. Amherst, 1943; B.S., Harvard, 1895; Columbia Law School, 1895-97; m. Helen C. McCormick, Sept. 15, 1900 (died, 1918); 1 dau., Charlotte (Mrs. Giovanni Petrina); m. Florence Boylston, Apr. 24, 1930 (dec. 1959). Admitted to N.Y. bar, 1898; practiced in N.Y. City, 1898-1922; of counsel to Am. Embassy, Consultate, London, 1924-58; U.S. Govt. Service in London, 1922-23; internat. law practice, 1924-58; partner, Breed, Abbott & Morgan, N.Y., Washington and London, 1929-58, retired; arbitrator Ct. Arbitration, Paris, France, 1928; counsel to British Inland Revenue on Am. taxation, 1930-58; officer and mem. gen. exec. com Am. Soc. in London, since 1927; represented U.S. Dept. of Justice in London as special asst. to atty. gen., 1936-42; apptd. mem. Am. Com. for evacuation of Americans from England, 1938-39; organizer and counsel for Am. Ambulance Great Britain, 1940-44. Trustee, Williston Academy, 1916-30; dir., counsel, Am. C. of C., London, since 1931; mem. com. on internat. law N.Y. State Bar Assn.; mem. Am., Internat. bar assns., Fed. Bar Assn. of Washington, Chi Psi. Clubs: American (hon. sec., treas., gov.), St. James, Ranelagh, Pilgrims, Ends of Earth, Monday Luncheon, Am. Soc. (all of London); Broad Street, University, Metropolitan (N.Y.C.). Home: Palisades NY Died Jan. 30, 1971.

KENNEDY, JOHN BRIGHT, editor; b. Quebec, Can., Jan. 16, 1894; s. John James and Georgiana Bright (Delara) K.; came to U.S., 1909; prep. edn. in Can. and Eng.; student St. Louis U., specializing in philosophy, 1913; m. Blanche Gayhart, of Toronto, Can., May 4, 1916; children—Constance, Josephine. Newspaper man in London, Montreal, Toronto, St. Louis, Chicago and New York; corr. in Europe, World War; associated with Herbert Hoover in relief work; founder, 1921, and editor Columbia (representing K. of C.); was mng. editor Collier's Weekly, now asso. editor. Lecturer radio station WJZ. Decorated Officer French Acad.; Star of Morocco (French); Knight of Leopold (Belgian). Republican. Catholic. Author: (with Maurice F. Egan) The Knights of Columbus in Peace and War, 1920. Contbr. to mags. Office: 250 Park Ave., New York NY*‡

KENNEDY, JOHN PENDLETON, editor; b. at Charlestown, Jefferson Co., W.Va., May 17, 1871; s. John Willoughby and Sarah Mark (Rutherford) K.; ed. pub. schs. and by pvt. instrn.; m., Washington, Minnie Haukness, of Albert Lea, Minn., May 9, 1903. Civil engr., 1895-9; asst. librarian, Library of Congress, 1899-1903; state librarian of Va., 1903-7; editorial work for Silver, Burdett & Co., New York, since Sept., 1907. Pres. Nat. Assn. State Librarys, 1906; v.-p. League of Library Commrs., 1907; mem. A.L.A., Am. Hist. Assn., W.Va. Soc. of New York. Republican. Episcopalian. Editor: Calendar of Transcripts, Virginia State Library, 1905; Journals of the House of Burgesses of Virginia, 4 vols., 1905-7; also reports, brochures, etc. Has made spl. vols., 1905-7; also reports, brochures, etc. Has made spl. study of hist. sources and collections. Home: 502 W. 113th St. Address: 231 W. 39th St., New York NY‡

KENNEDY, JOSEPH PATRICK, financier; born at Boston, Mass., Sept. 6, 1888; s. Patrick J. and Mary (Hickey) K.; grad. Boston Latin Sch., 1908; A.B., Harvard, 1912; hon. LL.D., National U. of Dublin, Ireland, 1938, and from universities of Edinburgh, Manchester, Liverpool, Bristol and Cambridge, 1939; hon. LL.D., Catholic U., Washington, Oglethorpe U. (Ga.), U. of Notre Dame, Colby Coll.; m. Rose Fitzgerald, Oct. 1914; children—Joseph (dec.), John Fitzgerald (Pres. of United States 1961-63; dec.), Rosemary, Kathleen (dec.), Eunice (Mrs. Robert Sargent Shriver, Jr.), Patricia (Mrs. Peter Lawford), Robert F. (dec.), Jean (Mrs. Stephen Smith), Edward. Began career as Bank examiner Mass., 1912-14; pres. Columbia Trust Co., Boston, 1914-17; asst. gen. mgr. Fore River (Mass.) plant Bethlehem Shipbldg. Corp., 1917-19; mgr. Hayden-Stone Co., investment bankers, Boston br., 1919-24; pres. and chmn. bd. dirs. Film Booking Offices of America, 1926-29; chmn. bd. dirs. Keith, Albee, Orpheum Theatres Corp., 1928-29; pres. and chmn. bd. dirs. Pathe Exchange, Inc., 1929-30; corporation finance, 1930-34; apptd. to Securities Exchange Commn., July 2, 1934; elected chmn., 1934, reelected, 1935, resigned, Sept. 1935; chmn. U.S. Maritime Commn., 1937; ambassador to Ct. of St. James's, 1937-Nov. 1940; chmn. special commn. relative to establishing Dept. of Commerce in Mass. Founder Joseph P. Kennedy Jr. Foundation, 1945. Mem. Commn. (apptd. by U.S. Senate) on Orgn. Exec. Branches U.S. Govt., 1947, 53. Trustee Notre Dame U. Knight of Malta, Grand Knight of Order of Pius IX; Knight of Equestrian Order of Holy Sepulchre; Grand Cross Order of Leopold II (Belgium). Democrat. Catholic. Author articles in mags. and publs. on econ. and internat. questions. Home: Palm Beach FL Died Nov. 8, 1969.

KENNEDY, OLIN WOOD, newspaperman; b. Feesburg, O., May 9, 1874; s. William H. and Narcissa Delia (Norris) K.; ed. pub. schs., Cincinnati, also under tutors and at Bethel (O.) Normal Sch.; m. Lovetta D. Stoner, of Springfield, O., May 11, 1895. Founder, 1899, and pub. until 1903, Muncie (Ind.) Morning Star; publicity dir. Colo. Democratic State Com., 1912; mng. editor Washington (D.C.) Herald, 1918-20; mng. editor and asst. to pub. Miami (Fla.) Herald, 1920-27. Dem. candidate for Congress, 3d Calif. dist., 1916; chmn. Fla. State Library Bd. 1927-29; referee for Cleveland Newspaper Pubs. Assn., 1927-—, Richmond (Va.) Newspaper Pubs. Assn., 1930-—. Mem. Soc. Am. Newspaper Editors. Democrat. Mem. Christian (Disciples) Ch. Mason. Club: City. Author of newspaper Serials; compiled history of Red Cross Socs. of the World, 1919. Home: 1245 N.W. Third St., Miami, FL Office: Hanna Bldg., Cleveland OH‡

KENNEDY, ROBERT FRANCIS, U.S. senator; born Boston, Nov. 20, 1925; s. Joseph Patrick and Rose (Fitzgerald) K.; B.A., Harvard, 1948; L.B., Va. Law Sch., 1951; LL.D., Assumption Coll., 1957, Mt. St. Mary's Coll., 1958, Tufts U., 1958, Fordham U., 1961, Nihon U., 1962, Manhattan Coll., 1962; hon. degrees U. Phiippines, 1964, Marquette U., 1964, Free U. Berlin, 1964; m. Ethel Skakel, June 17, 1950; children—Kathleen Hartington, Joseph Patrick, Robert Francis, David Anthony, Mary Courtney, Michael L., Mary K., Christopher, Matthew. Admitted to Massachusetts bar, 1951, United States Supreme Court, 1955; attorney criminal division Department of Justice, Washington, 1951-52; asst. counsel U.S. Senate permanent subcom. on investigations, 1953, chief counsel to minority, 1954, chief counsel, staff dir., 1955; asst. counsel Hoover Commn., 1953; chief counsel U.S. Senate select com. on improper activities in labor on mgmt. field, 1957-60; attorney gen. of U.S., 1961-64; U.S. senator from New York, 1965-1968. Presdl. campaign manager for John F. Kennedy, 1960. Member advisory council of University of Notre Dame Law School. Served with USNR, 1944-46. Named one of ten outstanding young men in U.S., U.S. Jr. C. of C., 1954; named outstanding investigator Soc. Profl. Investigations, Inc., 1957; recipient patriotism award U. Notre Dame, 1958, Lantern award Mass. council K.C., 1958. Democrat. Author: The Enemy Within, 1960; Just Friends and Brave Enemies, 1962; Pursuit of Justice, 1964. Home: Glen Cove NY Died June 6, 1968.

KENNEDY, ROBERT MACMILLAN, librarian; b. Camden, S.C., Sept. 24, 1866; s. Robert MacMillan and Margaret (Doby) K.; A.B., U. of S.C., 1885, M.A., 1898; m. Julia Calvert Hunter, Dec. 31, 1902; children—Margaret Stuart, Julia Calvert (dec.), Robert Hunter. Instr. U. of S.C., 1885-87; supt. pub. schs., S.C., 1887-1912; librarian U. of S.C., 1912-40, prof. library service, 1925-40, librarian emeritus since 1940. Head of A.L.A. war campaign in S.C. (for soldier libraries in World War). Mem. A.L.A., S.E. Library Assn., S.C. Library Assn. (ex-pres.), N.E.A., S.C. Supts. Assn. (ex-pres.), Phi Beta Kappa, Kappa Alpha. Democrat. Club: Kosmos. Co-Author: Historic Camden, part 1—Colonial and Revolutionary, 1905, part 2—Nineteenth Century, 1927. Contbr. bulls. and hist. publs. Home: 2301 Lee St., Columbia SC‡

KENNEDY, RUBY JO REEVES, educator; b. Sanger, Tex., Nov. 5, 1908; d. Felix Monroe and Birdie (Saunders) Reeves; A.B., Tex. State Coll. for Women, 1929; A.M., Yale, 1936, Ph.D., 1938; m. Raymond Kennedy, July 20, 1939; 1 dau., Ellen Reeves. Teacher public speaking Grand Prairie (Tex.) High Sch., 1929-31; research asst. Yale Inst. of Human Relations, 1931-36; asst. dir. sampling Urban Study of Consumer Purchases, Bur. Labor Statis., Dept. Labor, Washington, 1936-37; instr. sociology, Tex. State Coll. for Women, 1938-39, asst. prof., 1939-41; instr. sociol. Vassar Coll., 1941-42, asst. prof., 1942-44, asso. prof., 1944-45; prof. sociol. and chmn. dept. Conn. Coll., 1945-70. Mem. Am. and Eastern Sociol. Socs., Am. Assn. Univ. Profs. Author: The Social Adjustment of Morons in a Connecticut City (State of Conn.), 1948. Editor: Modern Marriage and Family Living, 1957; Papers of Maurice R. Davie, 1961; A Connecticut Community Revisited: A Study of the Social Adjustment of a Group of Mentally Deficient Adults in 1948 and 1960. Contbr. various articles to Am. Jour. Sociol. and The Sociol. Rev. Home: Waterford CT Died Jan. 5, 1970; buried Evergreen Cemetery, New Haven CT

KENNEDY, SIDNEY ROBINSON, author; b. at Brooklyn, Nov. 19, 1875; s. Elijah Robinson and Lucy Brace (Pratt) K.; A.B., Yale, 1898; m. Natalie Stanton, of Brooklyn, Nov. 15, 1906. Sec. Fidelity Phenix Fire Ins. Co. of N.Y.; dir. Franklin Safe Deposit Co. Treas. Tenement House Com. of Brooklyn. Steward Soc. Colonial Wars. Clubs: Down Town, Yale, Crescent Athletic. Author: The Lodestar, 1905; White Ashes (with Alden Charles Noble), 1912. Home: 200 Hicks St., Brooklyn. Office: 80 Maiden Lane, New York NY‡

KENNEDY, STANLEY CARMICHAEL, shipping and aviation exec.; b. Honolulu, Hawaii, July 7, 1890; s. James A. and Minnie C. (Kirkland) K.; student Punahou Acad., Honolulu, 1904-08; A.B., Stanford Univ., 1912; m. Martha G. Davenport, Dec. 3, 1919; children—Stanley C., Martha Patricia. With Inter-Island Steam Navigation Co., Ltd., Honolulu, in various depts., 1913-49, pres. and dir., 1932-49; organizer of Hawaiian Airlines, Ltd. in 1929, pres., dir., 1932-56, chmn. bd. 1956-68; pres., dir., Coca-Cola Bottling Co., of Honolulu, Inc., 1937-67, chmn. bd., 1967-68; dir. First Nat. Bank of Hawaii. Mem. Honolulu C. of C. (past pres.). Republican. Club: Pacific. Home: Honolulu HI Died Apr. 21, 1968.

KENNEDY, SYLVESTER MICHAEL, corp. exec.; b. Alton, Ill., Nov. 21, 1894; s. Phillip and Anastasia (Dawson) K.; student Pace and Pace Inst., N.Y. City, 1917-19, Walton Sch. of Commerce, Chicago, 1919-20, DePaul U., 1920-23; m. Leona E. Walter, December 29, 1921; one daughter, Marilyn June (Mrs. Frederick L. Goss, III). Accountant, William W. Thompson & Company, C.P.A.'s, Chgo., 1919-26 and 1937-39; v.p., sec.-treas. Nat. Grocers Co., Ltd., Toronto, Ont., 1926-31; v.p., gen. mgr. Almar Stores Corp., Phila., 1931-34; pres. The Fargason Co., Memphis, 1934-37; v.p., dir. Consol. Foods Corp., Chgo., 1939-47, pres., 1947-62, vice chmn. bd., chmn. finance com., 1962-67, chmn. bd., dir., 1967-73; dir. Nat. Boulevard Bank of Chicago. Roman Catholic. Clubs: Union League (Chgo., Ill.); Michigan Shores (Wilmette, Ill.). Home: Kenilworth IL Died Jan. 16, 1973.

KENNEDY, W. MCNEIL, lawyer; b. Jamestown, N.Y., Jan. 24, 1909; s. Thomas J. and Margaret (Keough) K.; J.D., Ohio No. U., 1930, LL.D., 1970; m. Dot Behan, May 25, 1940; children—Kael, Susan (Mrs. Philip Hackbarth). Admitted to Ill. and Ohio bars, 1930; author, editor: Federal Securities Law Service, also Stock Exchange Service, 1930-35; profl. lectr. finance U. Chgo., 1937-41; regional adminstr. SEC, 1935-42; solicitor U.S. Alien Property Custodian, 1942-44; sr. partner firm Pone, Ballard, Kennedy, Shepard & Fowle, and predecessor, Chgo., 1944-70; dir. Standard Kollsman Industries, Inc., Belden Mfg. Company. Bd.

dirs. Cath. Charities Archdiocese Chicago; trustee Ohio No. Univ.; chairman citizens board Loyola U., Chgo., 1966-68; Catholic co-chmn. Nat. Conf. Christians and Jews. Fellow American Bar Foundation; mem. Am., Chgo. (1st v.p. bd. mgrs. 1958-60, 68-70) bar assns., Phi Kappa, Theta. Clubs: Chicago, Law, Legal (Chgo.); Saddle and Cycle. Home: Evanston IL Died May 5, 1970.

KENNEDY, WILLIAM PARKER, labor leader; born Huttonville, Ont., Can., Apr. 3, 1892; s. William James and Margaret Ann (Parker) K.; ed. pub. schs., Huttonville and Chicago; m. Amy Hannah Berglund, Jan. 21, 1913; children—Phyllis, Rupert Parker, William Harlow, Dean Colbeck. Began as news butcher, Rock Island Lines between Chicago and Des Moines, 1909; freight brakeman Dakota Div., G. N. Ry., Grand Forks, N. D., 1909-11; switchman C. P. Ry., Calgary, Alberta, Can., 1911; switchman C., M., St. P. & P. R. R., Minneapolis, 1912-20, sec. gen. grievance com., 1920, chmn., 1921-35; del. to conventions Brotherhood of Railroad Trainmen, 1917, 19, 22, 25, 28, mem. bd. trustees, 1928-35, v. p. in charge N. W. Territory, 1935-44, in charge Super-Promotion dept., Chicago, 1944-46, gen. sec. and treas., 1946-49, pres. since 1949. Served as nat. reporting officer R.R. Retirement Bd. Lutheran. Mason (Shriner). Author: History of Banking in Minneapolis MN Died May 13, 1968.

KENNEDY, WILLIAM PIERCE, political writer; b. Lake City, Minn., Oct. 8, 1877; s. William Andrew and Mary Eleanor (Quinn) K.; A.B., Holy Cross Coll., 1900; Litt.D., Holy Cross Coll., Worcester, Mass., 1925; m. Cora E. Sweeney, Sept. 2, 1908; children—Mary Augusta Jahn and John Rochford; m. 2d, Nancy E. Hanks, June 15, 1938. Began newspaper work on Springfield (Mass.) Union, 1895 and has since been identified with newspapers of principal cities of Mass., Conn., and other states; settled in Washington, D.C., 1911; polit. writer on Washington Star. Mem. Capitol Press Galleries nearly 35 years. Retired Jan. 1, 1947. Hist. Wash. Soc. Friendly Sons of St. Patrick; curator; Div. Washingtonlana and U.S. Govt. Publs. Library of Holy Cross Coll.; p.p. N. Capital Citizens Assn.; mem. Am.-Irish Hist. Soc. (v.p. for D.C.). Mem. K.C., 4th Degree. Club: Eve. Star. Originated You and Uncle Sam" newspaper articles descriptive of U.S. Govt. activities. Author: History of the National Shrine of the Immaculate Conception, 2 vols., 1917-27; The Mary Book, 1928. Contbr. to The Book of Washington, 1927; U.S. House of Representatives document, Matthew Lyon cast-deciding vote that elected Jefferson, 1942; U.S. Senate document, America's War. Congress, 1943; also author D.C. chapter Friendly Sons of St. Patrick Yearbook since 1929. Contbr. Capitol Sidelights" column to newspapers. Home: 4 Park View Rd., Chevy Chase 15 MD‡

KENNEDY, WRAY DAVID, advt. exec.; b. Bklyn., Feb. 14, 1917; s. Augustus James and Ruth H. (Devlin) K.; B.A., Wesleyan U., Middletown, Conn., 1938; postgrad. student, N.Y.U., 1939-40; m. Lucy C. McCorkle, May 19, 1945; children—David, Jane, Douglas, Lucy, Elizabeth. With J. Walter Thompson Co., 1938-47; with Mogul, Williams & Saylor, Inc., and subsidiaries, N.Y.C., 1947-69, exec. v.p., 1963-66; exec. v.p. Albert Woodley Co., Inc., N.Y.C., 1966-68; president A.J. Wordsmith Co., 1968-69, also dir.; member board directors Design Label Mfg., Inc. Served with USAAF, 1941-45. Mem. Am. Arbitration Soc., Financial Pub. Relations Assn., Am. Assn. Advt. Agencies, N.Y. Financial Advertisers, Delta Upsilon. Clubs: Cornell (N.Y.C.); Mile Creek (Old Lyme, Conn.). Home: Essex CT Died June 12, 1969; buried Parasmus NJ

KENNICOTT, CASS (LANGDON), chemist; b. Chicago, Feb. 25, 1871; s. Ransom (U.S.A.) and Helen M. (Smith) K.; ed. Chicago pub. schs. and Case Sch. of Applied Science, Cleveland; m. Mary E. Barstow, June 6, 1894; children—Ruth Barstow (Mrs. C. R. McEldowney), Marjorie Barstow (Mrs. Robert Mount). Chief chemist Municipal Lab., Chicago, 1893-98; inventor Kennicott water softening machine and numerous other patented devices, and v.p. Kennicott Co., 1899-1916; former pres. Mariner and Hoskins, Inc., cons. chem. engrs., Chicago; later operated under name The Kennicott Co.; now retired. Fellow London (Eng.) Chemical Soc., mem. Chicago Acad. of Sciences. Club: Engineers' (Chicago). Author: Dust Explosions, 1894; Chicago's Milk Supply, 1895; Ice, 1896; Water Analysis, 1891; Food Adulteration, 1898. Home: Donswood," R.F.D. 2, Chesterton IN‡

KENNY, THOMAS JAMES, investment banker; b. West Bend, Wis., Nov. 19, 1921; s. Delbert James and Olive (Kauffung) K.; student St. Norbert Coll., 1940-42; B.S., U.S. Naval Acad., 1945; LL.B., Marquette U., 1950; m. Roberta Therese Morris, Oct. 11, 1947; children—Thomas James (dec.), John P., Kathleen J., Daniel J., Mary J., Colleen F. With underwriting dept. B.C. Ziegler & Co., West Bend, 1950, 52-58, mgr. underwriting dept., v.p., dir., 1958-65, pres., 1965-72, chmn., 1966-72; pres. 1st Ch. Financing Corp., 1965-72; chmn. Security Co.; pres. Ziegler Financing Corp., Ziegler Fund, Ziegler Select Fund, Inc.; dir. Newton Fund. Dir., clk. West Bend Sch. Bd., 1959-65. Trustee St. John's Mil. Acad., Delafield, Wis. Served with USNR, 1945-47, 51-52. Mem. Am. Legion. Rotarian (pres. 1965), K.C. Clubs: West Bend Country; Union League (Chgo); University West Bend WI Died June 15, 1972; buried Holy Angels Cemetery, West Bend WI

KENT, CHARLES STANTON, educator; b. Mpls., Jan. 20, 1914; s. Raymond Asa and Frances Stanton (Morey) K.; B.Mus., U. Louisville, 1936; student Juilliard Grad. Sch., 1933-35; M.Mus., Eastman Sch. Music, 1938, Ph.D., 1951. Tchr. theory, music lit., music history Oberlin Coll., 1938-41, Western Res. U., 1941-42, New Eng. Conservatory Music, 1945-48, U. Miss., 1951-56, Ind. U., 1956-61; dean Peabody Conservatory Music, Balt., 1961-62, acting director, 1962-63, dir., 1963-69. Vice chairman Governor's Council Arts Maryland. Member board Baltimore Symphony Orchestra, Balt., Civic Opera. Served with USAAF, 1942-45. Decorated Bronze Star. Mem. Alpha Sigma Phi, Phi Kappa Lambda. Author: Two-Part 16th Century Counterpoint, 1948. Composer (opera): A Room in Time, 1954. Collaborator: (annotated trans. Descartes) Compendium of Music, 1960. Home: Baltimore MD Died June 2, 1969.

KENT, DONALD PETERSON, educator, gerontologist; b. Phila., June 4, 1916; s. Ralph and Ida (Peterson) K.; B.S., Pa. State Coll., 1940; M.A., Temple U., 1945; Ph.D., U. Pa., 1950; m. Marion H. Clime, Aug. 30, 1941; children—Marion H., Martha H. Instr. sociology U. Pa., 1945-50; asso. prof. sociology U. Conn., 1950-57; dir. Inst. Gerontology, 1957-61; spl. asst. to sec. health, edn. and welfare, Washington, 1961-63; dir. U.S. Office Aging, Washington, 1963-65; prof., head dept. sociology and anthropology Pa. State U., University Park, 1965-72. Chmn., Conn. Commn. on Services for Elderly Persons, 1957-61; vice chmn. Pres.'s Council on Aging, 1961-63. Recipient Distinguished Service award Inst. for Ret. Profls. Fellow Gerontological Soc. (pres. psychol. and social sect. 1966-67), Am. Sociol. Soc. Author: The Refugee Intellectual, 1953. Editor-in-chief: Gerontologist, 1967-70. Contbr. articles profl. jours. Home: State College PA Died Mar. 20, 1972.

KENT, EDWARD MATHER, physician; b. Syracuse, N.Y., May 2, 1907; s. Edward Enos and Eunice (Mather) K.; B.S., Pa. State Coll., 1929; M.D., Syracuse U., 1932; M.Sc. in Surgery, U. Pa., 1940; m. Dorothy Jean Dearborn, June 17, 1935; children—Jean (Mrs. Jean McNutt), Brian Mather, Beth Anne. Intern, St. Mary's Hosp., Rochester, N.Y., 1932-33; postgrad. in gen. surgery Grad. Sch. U. Pa., 1934-37; resident in surgery Abington (Pa.) Meml. Hosp., 1935-37; resident in thoracic surgery Norwich (Conn.) State Tb Sanatorium, 1937-39; fellow in thoracic surgery Washington U., Barnes Hosp., St. Louis, 1939-40; resident Tb Sanatorium, Glendale, Md., 1941-42; attending surgeon Allegheny Gen. Hosp., Pitts., chmn. surg. div. med. staff, 1965-69, pres. staff, 1968; area cons. thoracic surgery VA, Pitts.; cons. staff Columbia, St. Francis, St. Margaret's, South Side hosps., also others; asst. prof. surgery U. Pitts. Sch. Med., 1946-51, asso. prof., 1951-54, clin. prof. surgery, 1954-70; mem. exec. com., 1959. Kellogg Meml lectr. in surgery George Washington U., 1952; Trudeau Meml. lectr. Trudeau Sanatorium, Saranac Lake, N.Y., 1954; mem. med. adv. bd. Heart House. Bd. dirs. Allegheny County unit Am. Cancer Soc., 1956-59. Served to comdr., M.C., USNR, 1942-46. Diplomate Am. Bd. Surgery, Am. Bd. Thoracic Surgery (founder mem., dir. 1955-60). Fellow A.C.S. (past gov.); mem. A.M.A., Pa., Allegheny County med. socs., Am. (council 1963-67, 69-70, pres. 1968-69), Pa. assns. thoracic surgery, Am. Coll. Chest Physicians (v.p. Pa. chpt. 1956), Am., Central surg. assns., Soc. Internationale de Chirurgie (titulaire), Am. Coll. Cardiology, Soc. Thoracic Surgeons, Pitts. Acad. Medicine, Pitts. Surg. Soc. (pres. 1963), Western Pa. Heart Assn. (dir.). Republican. Roman Catholic. Contbr. articles to med. jours., chpts. to books. Home: Wexford PA Died June 6, 1970; buried Syracuse NY

KENT, LOUISE ANDREWS, writer; b. Brookline, Mass., May 25, 1886; d. Walter Edward and Mary Sophronia (Edgerly) Andrews; B.S., Simmons Coll., Boston, Mass., 1909; m. Ira Rich Kent, May 23, 1912; children—Elizabeth Kent Gay, Hollister, Rosamond Mary (Mrs. Arthur C. Sprague). Writer of column, Boston Traveler, under pen name, Theresa Tempest, 1911; editorial contbr. to Boston Herald, 1928-31. Independent. Episcopalian. Clubs: Junior League, Saturday Morning (pres. 1929, 30). Author: Douglas of Porcupine, 1931; Two Children of Tyre, 1932; Jo Ann—Tomboy (with Ellis Parker Butler), 1933; The Red Rajah, 1933; The Terrace, 1934; He Went with Marco Polo, 1935; Het Went with Vasco da Gama, 1938; Paul Revere Square, 1939; He Went with Christopher Columbus, 1940; In Good Old Colony Times (with Elizabeth K. Tarshis), 1941; Mrs. Appleyard's Year, 1941; Mrs. Appleyard's Kitchen, 1942; He Went with Magellan, 1943, Country Mouse 1945; Village Greens of New England, 1948; With Kitchen Privileges, 1953; The Brookline Trunk, 1955; The Summer Kitchen (with Elizabeth Kent Gay), 1956; He Went with John Paul Jones, 1958; He Went with Champlain, 1959; He Went with Drake, 1961; (with Elizabeth Kent Gay) The Winter Kitchen, 1963; He Went with Hannibal (Cadmus award 1967), 1964; The Vermont Year Round Cook Book, 1965; Mrs. Appleyard and I, 1968. Contbr. articles and short stories to mags. Home: Calais VT Died Aug. 5, 1969; buried Robinson Cemetery, Calais VT

KENT, NORMAN, artist; b. Pittsburgh, Oct. 24, 1903; s. Carl Hayes and Nella Louise (Howe) K.; grad. Sch. of Fine and Applied Art, Rochester Inst. Tech., 1925; student, Art Students League of N.Y., 1925-26, studio in Italy, 1933-34; m. Diana Grace Whittinghill, Nov. 9, 1933; children—Mary Argyle, Diana Suzanne Howe. Free-lance illustrator with studio in Buffalo, 1926-28. Rochester, N.Y., 1928-33; Geneva, N.Y., 1934-43; instr. art William Smith Coll., Geneva, N.Y., 1934-36, asst. prof. art Hobart and William Smith colleges, Geneva, N.Y., 1936-43, prof. art, on leave, 1943-45; mng. editor Am. Artist (mag.) 1943-48; art dir. Internat. Editions, The Reader's Digest, 1948-51; art editor of True mag., 1952-55; editor of the American Artist (magazine), 1956. One man shows major cities and mus. both U.S. and fgn., 1930-72; exhibited regional and nat. shows U.S., 1927-72. Represented in many permanent collections, including Balt. and Phila. museums of art, Library of Congress, Carnegie Inst., and others. Recipient numerous awards, including; Lillian Fairchild award (woodcuts), U. of Rochester, 1929, Mildred Boericke prize, Print Club of Philadelphia, 1941, Library of Congress, 1951, Oh'Hara and Osborn prizes Am. Watercolor Soc., 1954-59, gold medal of honor National Arts Club, 1967, and others. Elected Academician, Nat. Acad. Design, 1949. Mem. (life) Art Student League N.Y., Print Club of Rochester, several other profl. organs. Episcopalian. Clubs: Century, Salmagundi (honorary). Author several items in field: Watercolor Methods. 1955; Seascapes and Landscapes in Watercolor, 1956; 100 Watercolor Techniques, 1968; Drawings by American Artists, 1968. Home: Mamroneck NY Died 1972.

KENT, RICHARD T., pres. New Eng. Confectionery Co., Cambridge, Mass.

KENT, ROCKWELL, artist, author; b. Tarrytown Heights, N.Y., 1882; s. Rockwell and Sara (Holgate) K.; ed. Horace Mann Sch., New York and Columbia U.; studied art under William M. Chase, Robert Henri, Hayes Miller, Abbott H. Thayer; m. Kathleen Whiting, 1909; children—Rockwell, Kathleen, Clara, Barbara, Gordon; m. 2d, Frances Lee, 1926; m. 3d, Sally Johnstone, 1940. Landscape and figure painter, wood engraver, lithographer; represented at Metropolitan Museum of New York, Art Inst. of Chicago, Brooklyn Museum and other Am. Museums, Pushkin Mus., Moscow, Hermitage, Leningrad; exhbtd. U.S., S.A. and Europe. Chmn. Nat. Council Am.-Soviet Friendship. Recipient International Lenin prize for strengthening peace among the nations, 1967. Member National Acad., Nat. Inst. Arts and Letters, Acad. Fine Arts USSR (hon.). Author: Wilderness, 1927; Voyaging, 1924; N. by E., 1930; Rockwellkentiana, 1933; Salamina, 1935; This Is My Own, 1940; It's Me O Lord, 1955; Of Men and Mountains, 1959; Greenland Journal, 1963; After Long Years, 1968. Contbr. to mags. Home: Au Sable Forks NY Died Mar. 13, 1971.

KENT, STEPHEN G(IRARD), lawyer, banker; born Brooklyn, Jan. 21, 1890; s. Stephen Waterbury and Carabel (Steele) K.; A.B., Williams Coll., 1911; LL.B., Columbia, 1914; m. Philena Marshall, June 11, 1921; children—Stephen Girard, George Marshall, Thomas Day. Admitted to N.Y. bar, 1914; asso. Shearman & Sterling, N.Y. City, 1914-17, Dorman & Dana, 1917-20; staff lawyer Irving Trust Co. and predecessor, N.Y.C., 1920-55; asst. resident counsel, 1926, resident counsel, 1929, sec., 1939, head legal div., 1931-55, gen. counsel, 1953-55. Mem. bd. mgrs., exec. and finance (chmn.) coms. Broadcasting and Film Commn., Nat. Council Chs. of Christ in U.S.A.; member bd. mgrs. of United Church Men. Served as 2d lt. 323d inf. 81st Div., A.E.F., World War I. Mem. Am. Soc. Corporate Secs., Inc., Am. Bar Assn., N.Y. Co. Lawyers, Assn., N.Y. Law Inst., Phi Beta Kappa, Psi Upsilon. Clubs Williams (N.Y. City); Canoe Brook Country (Summit, N.J.). Home: Summit NJ Died Nov. 29, 1969.

KENT, WILLIAM J., JR., chain food store exec.; b. St. Paul, 1897; ed. Yale Pres., dir. H.C. Bohack Co., Bklyn., 1957-63; dir. Am. Ice Co., U.S. Cold Storage Co.; trustee East N.Y. Savs. Bank; mem. adv. bd. Chase Manhattan Bank. Home: Brooklyn NY Died Nov. 1971.

KENYON, DOROTHY, lawyer; b. New York, N.Y. Feb. 17, 1888; d. William Houston and Maria Wellington (Stanwood) Kenyon; A.B., Smith Coll., 1908; J.D., N.Y.U. Law Sch., 1917; LL.D., Keuka Coll., 1939; LL.D. (hon.) Smith Coll., Wilson College, 1948, Oberlin Coll., 1950; L.H.D., Beaver College, 1949; LL.D., Western College for Women, 1966. Admitted to the New York bar, 1917; in general practice of law, New York, 1919-39; mem. Straus and Kenyon, 1930-39; justice Municipal Court, City of New York, 1939-40; resumed gen. practice, 1940; 1st dep. commr. of licenses, City of New York, 1936-38. Mem. League of Nations Com. on Legal Status of Women, 1938-43; mem. exec. com., Citizens Union of N.Y.;

Womanpower Comm., apptd. by N.Y. State Indsl. Commr. to advise on wartime employment problems of women, 1942; nat. dir. Am. Civil Liberties Union, vice chmn., sec., chmn. equality com.; nat. bd. Am. Middle East Rehab.; v.p. League Mut. Aid; adv. council Urban League, N.Y.C.; bd. dirs. Com. Civil Rights Met. N.Y.; former v.p. Am. Assn. U. Women; dir. Pioneer Youth Am., Assn. for Aid of Crippled Children, Consumers Coop. Services, Inc., Internat. Alliance of Women for Suffrage and Equal Citzenship (past v.p.); mem. com. to draft model state law on consumer cooperative corp., 1937; past pres. Our Cooperative House, 433 W. 21st St., Inc.; past pres. Consumer's League of N.Y.; past v.p. Alumnae Assn. Smith Coll., U.S. del. to United Nations Commn. on the Status of Women, 1946-49; director New York chapter, Member national board Ams. for Dem. Action; mem. nat. bd. YWCA; bd dirs. Lower W. Side Anti-Poverty Bd., Inc. mem. adv. council for Christian Action, Am. Friends of Middle East; adv. com. League for Mut. Aid, Greater N.Y. Urban League; administrv. and exec. com. Intergorup Committee for Integration of N.Y.C. Schools. Exec. com., past chmn. patronage com. New Chelsea Reform Democratic Club; N.Y. County Dem. committeewoman. Mem. American, N.Y. City and N.Y. State bar assns., New York County Lawyers Association, Internat. Law Assn., Am. Med. Women's Assn. (hon.), N.Y. State (hon.), N.Y.C. (hon.) Women's med. assns., Am. Assn. U. Women, League Women Voters, Nat. Assn. Women Lawyers, New York U. Law Sch. Alumni Assn. (mem. bd.), Phi Beta Kappa (senator united chpts. 1940-58). Clubs: Cosmopolitan, Smith College, Women's University, Women's City (N.Y.C.). Contbr. to Equality, 1965. Home: New York City NY Died Feb. 12, 1972.

KENYON, JOHN SAMUEL, educator; b. Medina, O., July 26, 1874; s. Charles Champlin and Lucy (Gouldin) K.; A.B., Hiram (O.) Coll., 1898; A.M., U. Chgo., 1903; Ph.D., Harvard, 1908; Litt.D., Western Res. U., 1954; m. Myra Alice Pow, July 12, 1899 (dec. Jan. 7, 1955); children—Martha Elizabeth, Elizabeth Sheldon (Mrs. A. E. Andress). Tchr. Greek and mathematics, West Ky. Coll., 1898-99; prof. Greek, Christian U., Canton, Mo., 1899-1901; fellow in English; U. Chgo., 1903-04; scholar and asst. in English, Harvard, 1905-06; prof. English and head of dept., Butler Coll., Indpls., 1906-16; prof. English language Hiram Coll., 1916-44, prof. emeritus, 1944-—; prof. of English, summers, U. Ind., 1915, Harvard, 1924, U. Tex., 1928, U. Mich., 1929; lectr. in English language, Western Reserve U. Grad. Sch., 1929-37; research asso. in English, U. Wis., 1940-41. Student of English lang. and phonetics, University Coll., London, 1926-27 (Soames prize for research in phonetics), Hiram Coll. Distinguished Service award, 1943. Member Modern Lang. Assn. Am., American Dialect Soc., Am. Assn. U. Profs., Assn. Phonetique Internationale (adminstrv. council, 1929-—), Linguistic Soc. Am., Phi Beta Kappa (hon. U. Wis.). Mem. com. Am. Council Learned Socs. to plan linguistic atlas of U.S. and Can.; participating del. 2d Internat. Congress of Phonetic Sciences, London, 1935. Mem. Disciples Ch. Club: Indianapolis Literary. Author: The Syntax of the Infinitive in Chaucer, 1909; American Pronunciation—A Textbook of Phonetics, 1924, 10th ed., 1954. Contbr. to Modern Language Notes, Modern Philology, etc. Editor of phonetic terms and consulting editor of pronunciation, and author of A Guide to Pronunciation, Webster's New Internat. Dictionary (2d edit.). Author: (with Thomas A. Knott) A Pronouncing Dictionary of American English, 1944. Asst. editor Garfield of Hiram. 1931. Home: Hiram OH‡

KEPHART, CALVIN IRA, lawyer, historian, author; b. New Britain, Pa., May 27, 1883; s. George Elwood and Anna Catherine (Weisel) K.; B.S. cum Laude, U. Cal., 1913; LL.B., LL.M., M.P.L., Nat. U., 1922, D.C., 1928; B.C.S., Southeastern U., 1923; Ph.D., Am. U., 1933; m. Olga Ahlson von Zweigbergk, Apr. 21, 1917; children—Arnold Ahlson, Robert Drake, George Weisel, Calva (Mrs. William L. Collier). Asst. chief clk., chief clk. United Railways San Francisco, 1906-08, constrn., valuation engr. Utilities and Interstate Commerce Commn., 1913-18; auditor, engr. Pub. Service Commn. Ore., 1918-20; hearing examiner Interstate Commerce Commn., 1920-49; admitted to D.C. bar, 1922, Md. bar, 1950; asso. prof. law Nat. U., Washington, 1927-39. Sec., chmn. Pub. Service Commn., Arlington County, Va., 1930-35. Served to col., World War II. Mem. Md. State Poetry Soc. (1st v.p. 1962-69), Anthrop. Soc. Washington, Huguenot Soc. Pa., Bucks, County Hist. Soc., Mil. Order World Wars, S.A.R., Soc. War 1812, Mil. Order Crusades, Baronial Order Magna Charta, Ret. Officers Assn., Tau Beta Pi, Sigma Xi, Sigma Nu Phi, Chi Psi Omega. Mason (K.T.), Kiwanian, mem. Order Eastern Star. Author: Sanskrit—Its Origin, Composition, and Diffusion, 1949; Origin of Heraldry in Europe, 1953; Races of Mankind-Their Origin and Migration, 1960; Concise History of Freemasonry, 1964. Contbg. editor: Western Destiny Mag. Contbr. articles numerous publs. Home: Shady Side MD Died Aug. 17, 1969; buried Arlington Nat. Cemetery.

KEPPLER, JOSEPH, cartoonist; b. St. Louis, Apr. 4, 1872; s. Joseph and Pauline (Pfau) K.; father was founder of Puck; ed. Gymnasium, Heilbronn, Germany; Columbia Inst., New York; Acad. of Arts, Munich; m. Lulu E. Bechtel, of Stapleton, N.Y., Apr. 4, 1895. Began as cartoonist, 1891. Home: Stapleton, N.Y. Office: 295 Lafayette St., New York‡

KERCHEVILLE, F(RANCIS) M(ONROE), educator; b. Pearsall, Tex., Feb. 18, 1901; s. Richard and Laura (Long) K.; A.B., Abilene Christian Coll., 1924; M.A., U. Wis., 1927, grad. fellow, 1929, Ph.D., 1930; post grad. study or spl. research Nat. U. Mexico, 1924, Sorbonne, U. Paris, 1926, U. Madrid, 1935, U. Chile (Inst. Internat. Edn. fellow), 1941; m. Christina Johnson, Aug. 25, 1927; 1 dau., Francina. Teaching asst. U. Wis., 1924; asso. prof., acting head dept. Spanish, U. S.D., 1930; became prof. modern langs., head dept., U. N.M., 1931; vis. prof. U. Guadalajara (Mexico), 1955, 58, 61; ofcl. cons. Spanish, N.M. Dept. Edn., 1955-64; prof., dept. head fgn. langs. Texas College of Arts and Industries, Kingsville, Tex., 1964-69, adviser, coordinator Inter-Am. Studies, 1966; ednl. dir. fgn. travel N.M. Ednl. Assn., Dept. Edn., 1956-58; dir. Com. Subversive Research, 1955-56. Mem. orgn. com. Inst. do Literatura Ibero-Americano, 1947-49; N.M. chairman of Revolving Student Loan Fund higher edn., 1960-61; civilian advisor 4th Army, 8th Corps Area, 1961-62; Armed Forces Adv. Commn., 1962. Recipient Internat. Sertoma award for citizenship, 1955, state silver citation annual award for Americanism, 1955; Army Civilian Service citation in field of edn., 1962. Served as capt., Mil. Intelligence, U.S. Army, World War II. Mem. Army Adv. Com., 1945-69. Mem. International Council of Inter-American Studies, New Mexico Art League (past pres.), Am. Assn. Tchrs. Spanish and Portuguese (past nat. pres.), Modern Lang. Assn. Am., Rocky Mountain Modern Lang. Assn. (co-founder, co-pres. 1947), Am. Assn. U. Profs., Am. Legion, Phi Kappa Phi, Phi Sigma Iota. Mason (32 deg., K.T., Shriner). Author, co-author or co-editor of books relating to field, 1934-69. Author of poetry vol.: The White Thorn, 1966. Editor, chief cons. Joint Publs. Americanism series, joint com. Am. Legion-N.M. Edn. Assn., 1955; editor: Practical Spoken Spanish, 25th anniversary rev. edit. 1959-60; also syndicated newspaper series Dialogues of Don Placido, 1960-61. Lectr.; writer in fields of interest. Home: Kingsville TX Died Oct. 9, 1969; buried Sandia Gardens, Albuquerque NM

KEREKES, TIBOR, univ. prof.; b. Budapest, Hungary, Feb. 5, 1893; s. Geza and Ilona (Polonyi) K.; student of Univ. of Budapest and Univ. of Vienna; m. Maria Theresa Ardizzone, Sept. 2, 1923; children—Stephanie Elena, Tibor, Richard Karl. Began as tutor in the imperial house of Hapsburg; prof. of history, Georgetown U., 1927-61, prof. emeritus, 1961-69, chmn. dept. history, member executive board, 1950-61; professor St. Joseph's College, 1966-69; professorial lectr. grad. sch. Boston Coll., St. John's U.; Danforth vis. lectr., 1960-61; lectr. Fordham U., Cath. U. Am.; research counselor. Exec. dir., Am. Hungarian Federation; trustee American Military Institute; dir. Ethnic Inst.; coordinator, Am. Hungarian Relief. Decorated comdr. Order of St. Sylvester. Republican. Roman Catholic. Member Am. Historical Association, Hungarian Academy of Arts and Sciences, Phi Alpha Theta. Author: History of Modern Europe, 1939; Hungary: The Problem of the Danubian Basin, 1941; Rejuvenated Italy, 1961. Co-author: Contemporary Europe, 1947; Contemporary Political Idealogies, 1961. Editor: The Arab Middle East and Muslim Africa, 1961. Home: New York City NY Died Oct. 5, 1969; buried Georgetown University, Washington DC

KERENSKY, ALEXANDER FEDOROVITCH, ex-premier Russia; b. Simbirsk, Russia, 1881; ed. Tashkent and St. Petersburg U. Called to St. Petersburg bar, 1904; mem. 4th State Duma (Parliament), 1912-17; minister of justice Provisional Govt., 1917, of war and navy, 1917; minister-president, 1917; comdr.-in-chief, 1917; living in U.S., 1940-70; writer, editor, lectr., vis. prof.; research project on Russian Provisional Govt. of 1917. Author: The Prelude to Bolshevism, Soviet Russia in the Autumn of 1919, 1919; Allied Policy Towards Russia, 1920; The Catastrophe, 1929; The Crucifixion of Liberty, 1934; Russia at History's Turning Point, 1965. Address: New York City NY Died June 11, 1970; buried Putney Vale, London England

KERN, EDITH KINGMAN, b. Harvard, Ill.; d. Adoniram Judson and Sarah Matilda (Cronkhite) Kingman; ed. Valparaiso, Ind., and Chicago Normal schs.; LL.B., Washington (D.C.) Coll. of Law, 1907; m. Ulysses Grant Poyer, 1894 (died); m. 2d, Josiah Quincy Kern, Ph.D., of Washington, 1903 (died 1913). Taught pub. schs. in Ill.; admitted to D.C. bar, 1907, to practice before Supreme Ct. of U.S., 1913; was mem. Bd. of Edn., Washington, 2 terms. Ex-pres. League Am. Pen Women; mem. Authors' League America. Clubs: College Women's, 20th Century. Monday Evening, Archaeological, Arts, City. Author: Little Journey to Alaska, 1897; Little Journey to Australia, 1897. Contbr. to newspapers. Home: 1912 G St. N.W., Washington DC‡

KERN, JOHN WORTH, judge; b. Indpls., July 7, 1900; s. John W. (ex-U.S. senator) and Araminta (Cooper) K.; A.B., Washington and Lee University, Lexington, Va., 1920; LL.B., Harvard, 1923; m. Bernice Winn, Apr. 30, 1927; 1 son, John Worth. Admitted to Indiana bar, 1923, and practiced in Indianapolis until 1931; U.S. commr., 1923-30; judge Superior Court of Marion County, 1931-35; mayor of Indianapolis, 1935-37; professor, Indiana Law School, 1925-35; member United States Board of Tax Appeals, 1937-42; judge, Tax Ct. of the U.S., 1942-61, chief judge, 1949-55, recalled for active service, 1961. Lecturer University Va. Law School, 1948, 1949. Member of the American Law Inst., Phi Gamma Delta. Democrat. Presbyterian. Mason. Clubs: Metropolitan (Washington); Farmington Country (Charlottesville, Va.); Chevy Chase (Chevy Chase, Md.); Lake Placid (Essex Washington DC Died Jan. 29, 1971; buried Crownhill Cemetery, Indianapolis IN

KERNOCHAN, JOSEPH FREDERICK, lawyer; b. New York; s. Joseph and Margaret (Seymour) K.; grad. Yale Coll., 1863, and law school, Columbia Coll., 1865; engaged in practice of law; m. 1869, Mary Stuart Whiting. Address: 44 Pine St., New York‡

KEROUAC, JACK (JEAN-LOUIS KEROUAC), author; b. Lowell, Mass., Mar. 12, 1922; s. Leo-Alcide and Gabrielle (Levesque) K.; student Columbia University, 1940-42, New School of Social Research, 1948-49; m. Stella Sampas, 1966. Author:(novels) The Town and the City, 1950, On the Road, 1957, The Subterraneans, 1958, The Dharma Bums, 1958, Doctor Sax, 1959, Maggie Cassidy, 1959, Visions of Cody, 1960, Tristessa, 1960, Lonesome Traveler, 1960, Book of Dreams, 1961, Big Sur, 1962, Visions of Gerard, 1963; (poetry) Mexico City Blues, 1959; (also sound track narrator film) Pull My Daisy, 1959; (philosophy) The Scripture of the Golden Eternity, 1960; Desolation Angels, 1965; Satori in Paris, 1966, 3 record albums poetry and prose; stories, articles and poems in publications. Served with U.S. Merchant Marine, 1942-44. Mem. Authors Guild Am. Home: St Petersburg FL Died Oct. 1969.

KERR, ALEXANDER TAYLOR, labor union exec.; b. Weaver, Ill., Dec. 11, 1920; s. Robert and Isabella (Lang) K.; student N.Y.U., 1947-48; m. Mildred Agnes Kluber, Oct. 6, 1945; children—Elaine Margaret, Robert Anthony, Susan Amy. Member Seafarers Internat. Union N.Am., AFL-CIO, 1943-72, fiscal officer, 1961-65, sec.-treas. internat. union, 1965-72, sec.-treas. Atlantic, Gulf, Lakes and Inland Waters div., 1962-72; sec.-treas. Seafarers Sea Chest Corp., Seafarers Port O'Call Club, Seafarers Balt. Port O'Call Corp., Seafarers Bldg., Corp., Seafarers Balt. Bldg. Corp., Seafarers Phila. Bldg. Corp., Seafarers La. Bldg. Corp., Seafarers Boston Bldg. Corp., Seafarers Ill. Bldg. Corp., Log Press, Inc., Seafarers Washington Bldg. Corp., Seafarers Mich. Bldg. Corp. chairman Seafarers Welfare Plan, Seafarers Vacation Plan; secretary United Industrial N.Am. Welfare Plan Served with USNR, 1942-44. Decorated Purple Heart. Member American Numismatic Assn. Eagle, Moose. Club: Tough (N.Y.C.). Home: Oradell NJ Died Jan. 26, 1972; buried George Washington Cemetery, Paramus NJ

KERR, EUGENE WYCLIFF, mech. engr.; b. McKinney, Tex., Feb. 16, 1874; s. J.L. and O.J.K.; M.E., Agrl. and Mech. Coll. of Tex., 1899; spl. courses in mech. engring. in Stevens Inst. of Tech., U. of Wis., and Purdue U.; m. Rita Sbisa, Sept. 5, 1900; children—Eugene James, Janet Katherine, William Ray. Asst. prof. mech. engring., Agrl. and Mech. Coll. of Tex., 1896-1903; instr. machine design, Purdue U., 1903-05; prof. mech. engring., La. State U., 1905-16; in charge of investigations in sugar engring., La. State Expt. Stations, 1908-16; engr. Cuba Cane Sugar Corp., 1916-31; cons. mech. engr. since 1931. Mem. Am. Soc. Mech. Engrs. Presbyterian. Mason. Author: Power and Power Transmission, 1902; also various papers and pamphlets on subjects pertaining to sugar engring. Home: 808 Lake Park, Baton Rouge LA‡

KERR, H(ENRY) FARQUHARSON, ocean transportation; b. Jamaica, B.W.I., July 18, 1874; s. John Edward and Margaret Ann (Pengelly) K.; ed. pvt. sch., Eng. Associated for many yrs. with father, firm of J. E. Kerr & Co., shipping fruit from Jamaica to U.S. and Eng.; organized, 1915, and pres. the Kerr Steamship Line, operating steamers to Europe during World War; organized, 1916, and pres. Kerr Steamship Co., Inc., now chmn. bd.; pres. Kerr Steamship Co., London; operates line of steamers to Brazil, and between New Orleans and Mexican ports. Lives in Europe. Office: 46 Beaver St., New York NY‡

KERR, JOHN N., steel co. exec.; b. Niles, O., Sept. 14, 1890; s. James M. and Linnie M. (Cessna) K.; student pub. schs.; m. Jane Foster Smith, Jan. 21, 1966; children—John E., Mrs. Edward F. Better Mgr. sales Mahoning Valley Steel Co., Niles, 1925; pres., treas. Ohio Corrugating Co., Warren; dir. Union Savs. & Trust Co., Warren. Trustee Trumbell Meml. Hosp., Warren Mem. C. of C. (dir.). Mason. Clubs: Trumbull Country (Warren); Youngstown (Ohio) Country, Youngstown; Union (Cleve.); Downtown Athletic (N.Y.C.). Home: Warren OH

KERR, JOHN WALTER, public health officer; b. Grand Rapids, O., Dec. 4, 1871; s. William Barton and Jane (Culbertson) K.; student Westminster Coll., Pa., 1888-90; M.D., Western Reserve U. Med. Coll., 1897; m. Jessie Kerr, July 5, 1905; 1 dau., Helen Pratt (wife of Colonel J.W. Ferris). Apptd. asst. surgeon, U.S. Public Health Service, 1898; passed asst. surgeon, Jan. 12, 1904; surgeon, Mar. 3, 1913; med. dir., July 1, 1930, assistant surgeon general U.S.P.H.S., retired. With service stations at San Francisco, Honolulu, New Orleans, Cincinnati, also at Ellis Island, Quebec and St. Johns, Can.; detailed for duty at Am. Consulate, Hong Kong, China, 1900-03, to prevent spread of plague and cholera to Philippines and ports of U.S.; asst. surg. gen. charge Div. Sci. Research, Washington, D.C., 1905-18; chief med. officer Ellis Island, 1918-21; asst. surgeon gen. in charge of personnel, 1921-28; chief quarantine officer Hampton Roads, Va., 1928-33 (retired); established medical examination of aliens in Gt. Britain, 1925. Sec. sect. on state and municipal control of Internat. Congress on Tuberculosis, Washington, 1908; sec. sect. on hygiene of traffic and transportation of XV Internat. Congress on Hygiene and Demography, Washington, 1912; del. of U.S. to International Congress of Medicine, London, 1913, to International Red Cross Conf., Geneva, 1925, to Internat. Congress on Immigration, Havana, 1928; mem. med. advisory bd. of Am. Red Cross War Council, World War. Dir. Am. Assn. for Study and Prevention of Infant Mortality; mem. Permanent Bur. of Internat. Union for Protection of Infant Life; mem. A.M.A., Am. Pub. Health Assn., Assn. Mil. Surgeons of U.S. (ex-pres.); Am. Assn. Med. Milk Commns. (ex-pres.). Contbr. on med. subjects. Home: 3610 Van Ness St., N.W., Washington DC‡

KERR, LEGRAND, pediatrist; b. at New York, May 11, 1870; s. Charles Hutchinson and Agnes Turnbull (Miller) K.; M.D., Bellevue Hosp. Med. Coll. (New York U.), 1892; m. Edith May Lewis, Nov. 20, 1897. Visiting pediatrist to the Williamsburgh Hosp. since 1899; physician to Swedish Hosp., Brooklyn, since 1905; phys.-in-chief to children's depts. of M.E. and Bushwick hospitals, cons. physician to children's wards of Industrial Home for Children and the Rockaway Beach Hosp. Consulting Pediatrist, Nassau Hospital, Mineola, L.I. Mem. N.Y. and Brooklyn med. socs., Pathol. Soc., etc. Author: Diagnostics of the Diseases of Infants and Children, 1907; Baby, Its Care and Development, 1908; The Care and Training of Children, 1910; Surgical Diseases of Children, 1913. Address: 311 Candee Av., Sayville LI NY‡

KERR, WILLIAM WATT, physician; grad. Univ. of Edinburg, Scotland, 1881; prof. clin. medicine, med. dept. Univ. of Calif.; visiting physician, City and Co. Hospital; also Children's Hosp. Address: 1200 Van Ness Av., San Francisco CA‡

KERR, WINFIELD S., ex-congressman, lawyer; b. Monroe Tp., Richland Co., O.; s. Alexander and Ursula K.; grad. law dept., Univ. of Mich., 1879; m. Susie E. Barr. Mem. Ohio State senate 4 yrs.; practices law, Mansfield, O.; mem. Congress from 14th Ohio dist., 1895-1901; executor and biographer of late Hon. John Sherman. Republican. Address: Mansfield OH‡

KERRICK, HARRISON SUMMERS, army officer; b. Minonk, Woodford Co., Ill., Oct. 13, 1873; s. Josiah and Margaret (Hollenbeck) K.; student Ill. Wesleyan U., 1890-92; B.S., Northern Ill. Normal Sch., Dixon, 1894; grad. Arty. Sch., Ft. Monroe, Va., 1906; m. Lena May Clark of Urbana, Ill., Oct. 21, 1903. Teacher and prin. pub. schs., Ill., 1892-98, div. supt. schs., P.I., 1901, enlisted Co. G, 2d Ill. Vol. Inf., June 18, 1898, and advanced through grades to capt. 30th Vol. Inf., 1899; apptd. 2d lt. arty. corps, regular army, July 1, 1901; promoted through grades to col., Mar. 20, 1926. Served in Cuba, 1898-99; Philippines, 1899-1901, and 1925-27; in France with A.E.F., 1918; comdt. Heavy Arty., 7th French Army (Haute Alsace), Aug.-Oct. 1918; served as supt. Water Transp., Port of New York; pres. Hoboken Shore R.R.; asst. for Water Transp. Embarkation Service, 1919-20; transp. officer of Dept., Chicago, 1921; comdg. officer Columbus (Ohio) Gen. Reserve Depot, 1922-25; instr. Coast Arty. Res. Regiments, N.E. States, 1928; coordinator under chief coordinator and Bur. of the Budget, 6th Area, Kansas City, Mo., Apr. 1, 1929-Feb. 1, 1933; inspector harbor defenses, Manila and Subic Bay, 1933; staff officer Dept. of P.I., July-Oct. 1934; retired Oct. 31, 1934. Fellow Am. Geog. Soc.; mem. Mil. Order Foreign Wars, Mil. and Naval Order Spanish-Am. War, Nat. Sojourners, Sigma Chi, Pi Gamma Mu; mem. nat. exec. com. Am. Legion, Dept. Philippine Islands, 1928-36. Methodist. Mason (32 deg.). Clubs: Army and Navy, Army, Navy and Marine Corps Country (Washington, D.C.); Hamilton Club (Chicago). Author: Military and Naval America, 1916; The Flag of the United States, 1925. Lectures: (illustrated) The Evolution of the United States Flag; Flags Famous in American History. Prize essayist Mil. Service Instn., silver medalist, 1908, gold medalist, 1913. Home: Minonk, IL Address: War Dept., Washington DC‡

KESSLER, BERNARD, retail exec.; b. N.Y.C., Jan. 2, 1922; s. Morris and Kate (Harrison) K.; B.S. in Bus., N.Y. U., 1946; student Amos Tuck Sch., Dartmouth,

1942; m. Debra Dubin, Feb. 14, 1951; children—Peter, Susan, Matthew, David. Founder, pres. Knighthood Shirt Corp., 1947-50; mdsg. v.p. men's haberdashery chain, 1951-56; founder Unishops, Inc., 1957, chmn. bd., chief exec. officer, 1962-72. Pres. Mass Mdsg. Research Found. Mem. pace setters com. United Jewish Appeal, 1968-69. Trustee Daus. Israel, Pleasant Valley Home Aged, Jewish Community Council. Daniel I. Kessler Meml. Found. Served with USMCR, 1941-45. Recipient Mass. Mdsg. Hall of Fame award U. Mass., 1965. Mem. Sales Execs. Club N.Y.C., A.I.M. (pres. council). Clubs: Green Brook Country (N. Caldwell. N.J.); Brentwood Country (Los Angels); City Athletic, Manhattan, Marco Polo (N.Y.C.). Home: Short NJ Died Apr. 21, 1972.

KESTER, REUBEN P., agrl. editor; b. Clearfield County, Pa., Jan. 18, 1869; s. Samuel Lewis and Alice (Wall) K.; ed. normal sch. and business coll.; m. Myrtle May Davis, of Grampian, Pa., Aug. 16, 1894; children—Elisha Howard, Lucretia Mott (Mrs. Albert C. Mammal). Adviser on soil management and farm methods, Pa. Dept. Agr. 1904-14; editor Pennsylvania Farmer since 1914. Served as justice of the peace and mayor of Newtown, Pa. Trustee George Sch., Pa. Mem. Patrons of Husbandry. Republican. Quaker. Odd Fellow. Club: City. Lecturer on agriculture and social questions. Home: Newtown, PA Office: 261·S. Third St., Philadelphia PA‡

KETCHAM, FRANK ATHERTON, mfr.; b. Saginaw, Mich., Oct. 14, 1875; s. Philip H. and Ella (Atherton) K.; ed. U. of Mich., 1897; m. Ruby Moffett, June 11, 1907. Gen. sales mgr. Western Electric Co., 1918-25; exec. v.p. Graybar Electric Co., 1926-28; pres. Graybar Electric Co., Inc., N.Y. 1929-41, chmn. since 1941; dir. Marine Midland Trust Co. of N.Y. Mem. Phi Alumni Assn. of Psi Upsilon. Clubs: Bankers, Union League. Wykagle Country, American Yacht. Home: 166 Valley Rd., New Rochelle. Office: 420 Lexington Av., New York NY‡

KETTERING, EUGENE WILLIAMS, diesel engr.; b. Dayton, O., Apr. 20, 1908; s. Charles Franklin and Olive (Williams) K.; student Cornell U.; D. Sc., Fenn College; H.H.D., University of Dayton; m. Virginia Weiffenbach, Apr. 5, 1930; children—Charles Franklin II, Jane (Mrs. Richard D. Lombard), Susan (Mrs. Peter D. Williamson). With Winton Engine Co., Cleve., 1930-36, Detroit diesel div. Gen. Motors Corp., 1936-37, chief engr. Electro-Motive div., LaGrange, Ill., 1938-56, dir. research 1956-58, research asst. to gen. mgr., 1958-59, cons., 1959-60; chmn. bd. C. F. Kettering, Inc., Winters Nat. Bank; dir. Flexible Co. (Loudonville, O.). Chmn. bd. Air Force Mus. Found., Inc., Aviation Hall of Fame; founder Charles F. Kettering Meml. Hosp., Dayton, Hinsdale Med. Center, including Health Mus., Health Library; pres. Charles F. Kettering Found.; trustee Meml.-Sloan Kettering Cancer Center, Kettering Hosp., Loudonville, O.; v.p.; dir. Thomas Alva Edison Found., Sloan-Kettering Inst.; bd. dirs. Monmouth Coll.; trustee Berea Coll., So. Research Inst. Ala. Recipient Elmer A. Sperry award. Mem. Aircraft Owners and Pilots Assn., A.A.A.S., Cornell Soc. Engrs., Def. Orientation Conf. Assn., Soc. Automotive Engrs., Chi Phi. Clubs: Oakbrook Polo, Moraine Country, Engineers, Buz Fuz, Dayton Bicycle (Dayton, O.); Hinsdale (Ill.) Golf: Cornell U. Home: Dayton OH Died Apr. 19, 1969; buried Dayton

KETTLER, STANTON PETER, broadcasting co. exec.; b. Wheeling, W.Va., Nov. 18, 1907; s. Charles Louis and Mary Ellen (Stanton) K.; B.S., Washington and Jefferson Coll., 1929; m. Virginia Pennington, Jan. 19, 1935; children—Sally Pennington (Mrs. Walter G. Evans), Peter Stanton. Salesman, Dillon Read & Co., Reliance Life Ins. Co., Sun Life Assurance Co., Re-Ly-On Products, 1929-37; with Storer Broadcasting Co., Miami Beach, Fla., 1937-71, v.p. charge operations, 1955-58, exec. v.p. operations, 1958-61, executive vice president, 1961-65, pres., 1965-67, vice chmn. bd., 1967-71, dir., dir. N.E. Airlines, Inc. Mem. Orange Bowl Com. Bd. dirs. Miami Heart Inst., Miami Beach, 1951-71; trustee Washington and Jefferson Coll., Washington, Pa. Mem. Broadcast Pioneers (mem. bd. directors 1966-69), Internat. Radio and TV Soc., Miami Beach, Miami Shores chambers commerce, Kappa Sigma. Elk. Mason, Kiwanian. Mem. Community Ch. Clubs: Indian Creek Country (Indian Creek Village, Fla.); LaGorce Country (Miami Beach); Miami, Beach Colony, Country of Miami, Variety of Greater Miami; Old Baldy (Saratoga, Wyo.); Jockey (Miami). Home: Miami Shores FL Died Aug. 1971.

KETTON-CREMER, ROBERT · WYNDHAM, author; b. Plymouth, Devon, Eng., May 2, 1906; s. Wyndham Cremer and Emily (Bayly) Ketton-Cremer; B.A., Balliol Coll., Oxford, 1928, M.A., 1938; Litt.D. (hon.), University East Anglia, 1969. Author: The Early Life and Diaries of William Windham, 1930; Thomas Gray, 1935; Horace Walpole, 1940; Norfolk Portraits, 1944; A Norfolk Gallery, 1948; Country Neighbourhood, 1951; Thomas Gray, 1955 (recipient James Tait Black Meml. prize, W. H. Heinemann Found. award for best biography of 1955); Norfolk Assembly, 1958; Forty Norfolk Essays, 1961; Felbrigg: The Story of a House, 1962; Norfolk in the Civil War,

published 1969. Rede lecturer at Cambridge University, 1957; Warton lecturer at British Academy, 1959; also Lamont Memorial lectr. Yale, 1960. Justice of the peace, Norfolk, 1935-69, high sheriff, 1951. Trustee Nat. Portrait Gallery, London, 1958-69. Fellow Soc. Antiquaries, Royal Soc. Lit. (London), Brit. Acad. Home: Norwich England Died Dec. 12, 1969.

KEY, JAMES BIGGERS, banker; b. Harris County, Ga., June 21, 1877; s. Howard W. and Ozella (Biggers) K.; prep. edn., Webb Sch., Bellbuckle, Tenn.; student Southwestern Presbyn. U., Clarksville, Tenn.; m. Lydia May Botts, Mar. 3, 1897; children—Jack committee 1943, vice-pres. 1945), American Bar Assn., B. Lydia May (Mrs. Theo. Golden, Jr.), Jamie H. (dec.). Josephine (Mrs. Herbert D. Groover), Dorothy A. Engaged in wholesale grocery business, Columbus, Ga., 1898-1916; later in cotton warehouse business; with Merchants and Mechanics Bank since 1916, now chmn. bd. Chmn. Liberty Loan drives, West Ga., World War. Alderman, Columbus, 1898, police commr., 1901; trustee Bd. of Edn., Columbus; chmn. Muscogee County Commn. Rds. and Revenues; pres. Boy Scouts America, Columbus. Methodist. Club: Rotary (ex-pres.). Home: 1820 Wynnton Rd. Office: Merchants & Mechanics Bank, Columbus GA‡

KEY, JOHN A., congressman; b. Marion, O., Dec. 30, 1871; pub. sch. edn.; m. Cora M. Edwards, 1906. Began as journeyman printer; letter carrier, Marion, 1897-03; county recorder, Marion Co., Ohio. 2 terms; pvt. sec. to late Hon. Carl C. Anderson. 4 yrs.; mem. 63d Congress (1913-15), 13th Ohio Dist., and 64th and 65th Congresses (1915-19). 8th Dist.; Democrat. Home: Marion OH‡

KEYES, FRANCES PARKINSON (MRS. HENRY WILDER KEYES), author, editor; b. Charlottesville, Va., July 21, 1885; d. John Henry and Louise Fuller (Johnson) Wheeler; ed. pvt. sch., Boston, Switzerland and Berlin, Germany; Litt.D., George Washington U., 1921, Bates Coll., Lewiston, Me., 1934, Diploma of Amis de Saumur, 1948; L.H.D., University of New Hampshire, 1951; married Henry Wilder Keyes (formerly governor of New Hampshire, and United States senator), June 8, 1904 (died June 19, 1938); children—Henry W., John P., Francis. Mem. Nat. Society Colonial Dames, National Society Women Geographers. Clubs: National Women's Press, Sulgrave (Washington); Orleans (New Orleans, La.). Author: The Old Gray Homestead, 1919; The Career of David Noble, 1921; Letters from a Senator's Wife, 1924; Queen Anne's Lace, 1930; Silver Seas and Golden Cities, 1931; Lady Blanche Farm. 1931; Senator Marlowe's Daughter, 1933; The Safe Bridge, 1934; The Happy Wanderer, 1935; Honor Bright, 1936; Written in Heaven. 1937; Capital Kaleidoscope, 1937; Parts Unknown, 1938; The Great Tradition, 1939; Along a Little Way, 1940; The Sublime Shepherdess, 1940; Fielding's Folly, 1940; The Grace of Guadalupe, 1941; All That Glitters, 1941; Crescent Carnival, 1942; Also the hills, 1943; The River Road, 1945; Came a Cavalier. 1947; Once on Esplanade, 1947; Dinner at Antoine's, 1948; Therese: Saint of a Little Way, 1950; All This Is Louisiana, 1950; The Cost of a Best-Seller, 1950; Joy Street, 1950; Steamboat Gothic, 1952; Bernadette of Lourdes, 1953; The Royal Box, 1954; Frances Parkinson Keyes Cookbook, 1955; Mother of Our Saviour, 1955; The Blue Camellia, 1957; Land of Stones and Saints, 1957; Victorine, 1958; Station Wagon in Spain. 1959; Mother Cabrini: Missionary to the World, 1959; Frances Parkinson Keyes' Christmas Gift, 1959; The Third Mystic of Avila, 1960; Roses in December, 1960; The Chess Players, 1960; The Rose and the Lily, 1961; Madame Castel's Lodger, 1962; A Treasury of Favorite Poems, 1963; The Restless Lady and Other Stories, 1963; Three Ways of Love, 1963; The Explorer, 1964; I, the King, 1966; Tongues of Fire, 1966; The Heritage, 1968; All Flags Flying, 1972. Past contbg. editor Good Housekeeping traveller magazine: world trip as a representative in 1925-26, also a trip through S. America, 1929-30, also 10 trips to Europe and 1 to Persia, 1931; intermittent contbr. to numerous other publs. On staff Our Lady of the Lake Coll., San Antonio, Tex., 1941. Editor: Nat. Hist. Mag., pub. by D.A.R., 1937-39. Lecturer. Awarded Siena Medal, 1946, as outstanding Catholic woman in U.S. medal Honor Gen. Council Seine, 1950, Silver Medal French Recognition, 1951; Christopher award. 1953; Order Isabella the Cath., 1958; Legion Honour, 1962; Mother Gerard Phelan medal, 1964; Sol de Peru, 1966. Home: North Haverhill NH Died July 3, 1970; buried Newbury VT

KEYSTON, GEORGE NOEL, stock broker; born San Francisco, Calif., Dec. 3, 1890; son James Woods and Leila Ada (Baker) K.; B.S., U. of Calif., 1913; Flood Fellow in Economics, Univ. of Calif., 1914; m. Hazel Jeans Elander, Apr. 12, 1919; children—George Noel, David Hill. Statistician and office mgr. for a N.Y. Stock Exchange firm, 1914-19; mng. partner Keyston & Co., stock brokers, San Francisco, 1919-68; director Pacific Intermountain Express Co., Westates Petroleum Co.; chmn. bd. Anza Pacific Corp. Pres San Francisco Stock Exchange, 1930, 40 and 41. Trustee Cogswell Poly. Coll. Acad. Pol. Sci. Served in U.S. Army, 1918-19. Fellow Royal Hort. Soc.; mem. Am. Hort. Soc., Beta Gamma Sigma. Republican. Clubs: Commonwealth of

California, Stock Exchange (San Francisco). Home: San Mateo CA Died July 30, 1968; buried Cypress Lawn, Colma CA

KEZER, ALVIN, agronomist; b. Bower, Neb., Nov. 7, 1877; s. George E. and Clara E. (Bower) K.; B.S., U. of Neb., 1904, M.A., 1906; m. Harriet M. Mitchell, June 19, 1906; children—Munro, James. With U.S. Dept. Agr., 1904-06; in charge soils, U. of Neb., 1906-09; prof. agronomy, Colo. State Coll. of Agr. and Mechanic Arts, 1909-46; retired July 1, 1946; agrl. cons. in soils, crops and animal nutrition, since 1946. Chairman of seed committee Colorado Council of defense, 1917. Member Colorado State Planning Commn. President State Soil Conservation Board, Jan. 1945. Mem. Am. Chem. Soc., A.A.A.S., Am. Genetic Assn., Soc. Promotion Agr. Science, Am. Soc. Agronomy, Am. Farm Economics Assn., Alpha Zeta, Sigma Xi, Phi Kappa Phi. Mason. Unitarian. Author various bulls. and articles on agrl. subjects. Home: 515 Remington, Ft Collins CO‡

KHRUSHCHEV, NIKITA SERGEYEVICH, polit. figure USSR; b. Apr. 17, 1894 to family of miner, Kursk Region, Center of European Russia; edn.; Workers' Faculty, Indsl. Inst., Donetsk, Ukraine, 1922-25; Indsl. Acad., Moscow, 1929-30. In youth a worker in Donbas (Donets Coal Basin, Ukraine); mem. Communist Party Soviet Union (CPSU), 1918-71; main stages of activity: fighter in the ranks, polit, commissar Civil War USSR, 1918-20; exec. of coms. CPSU, Stalino, Kiev (both Ukraine), 1926-28; sec. Moscow dist. coms. CPSU, 1931; sec. Moscow city and region coms. CPSU, 1932-34; member Central Com. CPSU, 1934-64; sec. Moscow City Com., also Moscow Regional Com. CPSU, 1935-37; sec. Central Com. Communist Party Ukraine, 1938-48; chmn. Council of Ministers of Ukrainian Soviet Socialist Republic, March to December, 1947; member Presidium, Central Com. CPSU, 1939-64; mem. mil. councils several fronts, lt. gen., World War II; sec. Central Com. CPSU, 1949-53; 1st sec. Central Com. CPSU, 1953-64; chmn. Council Ministers USSR, 1958-64. Decorated numerous orders USSR including Hero of Socialist Labour (3), Internat. Lenin Peace Prize Laureate. Author (in Russian): For Durable Peace and Peaceful Coexistence, 1958; For Victory in the Peaceful Competition with Capitalism; Let us Live in Peace and Friendship, 1959; A World Without Arms—a World Without Wars, 2 vols., 1969; Peace and Happiness for the Peoples; For Peace, for Disarmament, for Freedom of the Peoples, 1960; The Foreign Policy of the Soviet Union, 2 vols., 1961. Several vols. of speeches pub. in English, Cross-currents Press, N.Y.C., including Khrushchev in America, Khrushchev in New York, Khrushchev on the German Question. Visited Am.: meetings with President Eisenhower, 1959; attended 15th session Gen. Assembly, 1960. Address: Moscow USSR Died Sept. 11, 1971.

KIANG, CHIPING H. C., Chinese diplomat; b. Shanghai, China, Aug. 19, 1908; s. Mason and Chih-Ching (Yeh) K.; LL.B., Soochow U., 1932; student London Sch. Econs., 1935-38, Berlin U., 1938; m. Min-Hsieh Yang, June 5, 1942; 1 son, Heng-Pin. Admitted to Chinese bar, 1932; practiced in Shanghai, 1932-35; lectr. internat. law Central U. China, 1941-42; exec. asst. to prime minister, Republic of China, 1946-47; alternate rep. Republic of China, UN Security Council, 1953-68, rep. Trusteeship Council, 1956-68, minister plenipotentiary, 1953-68. Recipient numerous Chinese decorations. Mem. Chinese Bar Assn., China Inst. Internat. Affairs, Am. Soc. Internat. Law. Home: Larchmont NY Died Sept. 9, 1968; buried Ferncliff Cemetery, Hartsdale NY

KIBLER, RAYMOND SPIER, physician; b. East Aurora, N.Y., Nov. 8, 1917; s. Michael and Rose (Spier) K.; M.D., U. Buffalo, 1941; M.Sc. in Medicine, U. Ill., 1948; m. Diana Duszynski, Mar. 8, 1943; 1 dau., Jacqueline Louise (Mrs. Byledbal). Intern, Buffalo Gen. Hosp., 1941-42, asst. resident in internal medicine, 1942-43, resident in internal medicine, 1943, jr. clin. med. asst. in hematology and clin. pathology, 1957-69; practice medicine, specializing in nuclear medicine, Buffalo; Med. fellow U. Buffalo, 1946-47, U. Ill., 1947-48; sr. cancer research intern dept. nuclear medicine Roswell Park Meml Inst.; instr. State U. N.Y. at Buffalo. Served from 1st lt. to capt. AUS, 1943-46. Diplomate Am. Bd. Internal Medicine. Mem. A.M.A., Am. Soc. Clin. Pathologists, Soc. Nuclear Medicine, Am. Soc. Hematology. Home: Buffalo NY Died June 4, 1969; buried Mt. Calvary Cemetery, Cheekborough NY

KIDD, ROBERT L(OUIS), oil exec.; b. Brazil, Ind., July 7, 1901; s. John Charles and Nancy (Spear) K.; A.B. in Geology, Ind. U., 1923; m. Jane Carpenter, Aug. 17, 1927 (dec.); children—Louann, Susan (Mrs. F. Terry Diacon), John; m. 2d, Mary Marjorie Quigg, February 22, 1952. Partner Brazil Coal Co., 1923-25; resident geologist Empire Cos., Madison, Kan., 1925-26, prodn. geologist, Oil Hill, Kan., 1926-30; subsurface geologist Cities Service Gas Co., Bartlesville, Okla., 1930-33; with Cities Service Oil Co., successively in Western Kan., and Bartlesville, Okla., as seismograph party chief, chief geophysicist, asst. chief geologist, chief geologist, mgr. exploration, 1933-51, v.p. exploration and prodn., dir., 1951-53; pres., dir. Ark. Fuel Oil Corp., Shreveport, La., 1953-56, Cities Service Oil Co. (Dela), 1956-60, Can-Cities Service Petrol. Corp., from 1961; chmn. bd. Cities Service Co., from 1960; dir. Cities Service Oil Co., N.Y.C., 1st Nat. Bank & Trust Co., Tulsa. Vice pres. prodn., mem. exec. com., dir. Am. Petroleum Inst.; director Indiana University Foundation. Member Am. Assn. Petroleum Geologists. Soc. Exploration Geophysicists, Am. Petroleum Inst., Mid-Continent Oil and Gas Assn (dir.), Newcomen Soc. N.Am., Phi Kappa Psi. Mason. Republican. Clubs: Nat. Rifle Assn., Shreveport Country, Cherokee Yacht; Bankers (N.Y.C.); Southern Hills Country, Tulsa (Tulsa); Hillcrest Country, Bartlesville Rifle and Pistol (Bartlesville). Home: Bartlesville OK Died Feb. 12, 1972.

KIDD, SAMUEL ELBERTS, clergyman; b. Allentown, Pa., Feb. 20, 1914; s. Harvey Samuel and Anna Florence (Kramer) K.; A.B., Muhlenberg Coll., 1935, D.D., 1959; grad. Lutheran Theol. Sem., Phila., 1938; m. Elizabeth Gehman, July 1, 1939; children—Suzanne E. (Mrs. Fred C. Damarin, Jr.), Elizabeth G. (Mrs. Wendell C. Ehinger), Margaret L. (Mrs. Donald R. Jacoby), John S. Ordained to ministry Lutheran Ch., 1938; asst. pastor Lancaster, Pa., 1938-40; pastor Easton, Pa., 1941-43, Norristown, Pa., 1943-53; stewardship sec. Evang. Luth. Ministerium Pa., adjacent states, 1953-61, pres., 1961-62; pres. Eastern Pa. Synod Luth. Ch. Am., 1963-68; exec. dir. Mich. Council Chs., 1969-72. Mem. Exec. council Luth. Ch. Am.; vice chmn. commn. on world missions Luth. World Fedn. Author: Texts for Church School. Contbr. articles to profl. jours. Home: East Lansing MI Died Dec. 25, 1972.

KIDDER, BRADLEY PAIGE, architect; b. Denver, July 22, 1901; s. Frank Eugene and Katherine Emory (Newhall) K.; A.B., Colo. Coll., 1924; student architecture, U. Pa., 1924-26; m. Harriet W. Bumstead, Apr. 5, 1928; children—Katherine Alice, Bradley Paige. Mem. Historic Am. Bldgs. Survey, N.M., 1934; with firm John Gaw Meem & Assos., architects, Santa Fe, 1934-42; pvt. practice, Santa Fe, 1947-57; partner firm McHugh & Hooker, Bradley P. Kidder & Assos., Santa Fe, 1957-65, partner firm McHugh & Kidder Architects; prin. works include Santa Fe Pavilion, 1957, Methodist Ch., Farmington, N.M., 1959, St. James Ch., Taos, N.M., 1960, Immaculate Heart of Mary Sem., Santa Fe, 1961; also pvt. residences. Trustee Am. Archtl. Found., 1957-59; pres. A.I.A. Found., 1960-61; chmn. N.M. Bd. Examiners for Architects, 1951-57; chmn. N.M. Constrn. Industries Commn., 1967-73. Served with USNR. 1942-45. Fellow A.I.A. (pres. N.M. 1950-51, regional dir. 1955-58; Edward C. Kemper award 1959); mem. N.M. Soc. Architects (pres. 1965), Phi Delta Theta, Theta Alpha Phi. Episcopalian. Lion (dist. gov. 1954-55). Home: Santa Fe NM Died Jan. 1973.

KIEFFER, PAUL, lawyer; b. Hagerstown, Md., July 16, 1881; s. Joseph Spangler and Mary Martin (Clarke) K.; A.B., Franklin and Marshall Coll., 1901; Harvard Law Sch., 1903-04; B.C.L. (1st class) Oxford U., England, 1907; hon. LL.D., Franklin and Marshall Coll., 1934; m. Mabel Wallace, Apr. 24, 1937; 1 dau. (by prior marriage) Betty. Admitted to N.Y. bar, 1908, practiced in N.Y.C., 1908-69; mem. firm, Kieffer and Hahn. Pres. bd. trustees, Franklin and Marshall Coll., Lancaster, Pa., 1941-55, hon. president for life, 1955-69; president Assn. Am. Rhodes Scholars. Mem. Am. and N.Y. State bar assns., N.Y. County Lawyers Assn., Internat. Law Assn., Phi Beta Kappa. Clubs: Century, University, Harvard, Players, Bankers, British Schools and Universities (N.Y.C.); Thames (New London, Conn.). Home: New York City NY Died June 8, 1969.

KIEFNER, CHARLES E., ex-congressman; b. Perryville, Mo., Nov. 25, 1869; s. John and Anna Catherine (Lakel) K.; ed. pub. schs.; m. Jettie Catherine Luckey, of Perryville, July 10, 1895; children—Charles Harold, Edwin Luckey, Frank Wilson, John, Kathryn. Began with J. Tlapek Lumber Co., Perryville, 1894, mgr. and principal owner until succeeded by Kiefner Lumber Co., of which is pres.; pres. Home Trust Co.; mem. firm Kiefner & Geile, road builders; ex-mayor of Perryville; mem. Mo. Ho. of Rep. 3 terms; mem. 69th and 71st Congresses (1925-27, 1929-31), 13th Mo. Dist. Mem. South East Mo. Lumbermen's Assn. (pres. 17 terms). Republican. Presbyn. Mason. Home Perryville MO‡

KIEL, EMIL CHARLES, air force officer; b. Manitowoc, Wis., Sept. 25, 1895; s. Henry and Katharine (Reis) K.; student Stout Inst., Menomonie, Wis., 1915-17; m. Elizabeth F. Cass, Nov. 1, 1919; children—Betty Frances, Margaret Anne. Commd. 2d lt. Kelly Field, Tex., 1918; promoted through grades to brig. gen. (temp.), 1943; chief of staff, 4th Air Force, Dec. 1941-June 1944; deputy comdr., 8th Air Force, Nov. 1944-July 1945, chief of staff, July-Oct. 1945; commanding general, 8th Frontier Command, Oct. 1945-Feb. 1946; commander 40th Bomb Wing, Mar.-Dec. 1946; pres. War Crimes Court, Dachau, Germany, Jan.-Aug. 1947. Comdg. gen., Scott Air Force Base, Ill., 1947-49, Sheppard Air Force Base, Wichita Falls, Tex., 1949-50; comdg. gen. Caribbean Air Comd., Albrook AFB, C.Z., from 1950; ret. Decorated Air Medal, 1943, Legion of Merit, 1945; D.S.M., Bronze Star; Comdr. British Empire, Belgian Croix de Guerre. Home: San Francisco CA Died Nov. 1971.

KIERNAN, LOYD JULIAN, ret. r.r. ofcl.; b. Vicksburg, Miss., Sept. 12, 1895; s. Thomas and Margaret Elizabeth (Hartman) K.; Master of Accounts, Holy Cross Coll., New Orleans, 1909; m. Jennie P. Howard, June 29, 1921; children——Loyd J., Frances Margaret (Mrs. Wm. A. Ries). With I.C. R.R., 1911-37; with Equitable Life Assurance Soc., 1938-42, Assn. Am. R.R.'s, Washington, 1942-55; exec. v.p., chief exec. officer B. & M. R.R., 1955; cons. transportation U.S. Govt., other countries, 1956-61, Sec.-gen. 8th Pan-Am. Ry. Congress, Washington, 1953. Served from pvt. to 1st lt., 155th Inf., U.S. Army, 1916-19; capt. O.R.C. ret. Episcopalian, Club: Army and Navy (Washington). Contbr. articles to profl. publs. Home: Miami FL Died Mar. 27, 1972.

KIESEL, FRED WILLIAM, banker; b. Corinne, Utah, Feb. 11, 1874; s. Frederick John and Julia (Schansenbach) K.; ed. Harvard, 1892-93; m. Jane Birdsall, of Sacramento, Calif., Dec. 18, 1901; children—Corinne, Phyllis Jane, Robert Allen, Ogden. Identified with banking business, 1898-1933; pres. Calif. Nat. Bank, Sacramento, 1924-33. Mason, Elk. Club: Sutter. Home: 1236 N St., Sacramento CA‡

KILANDER, H(OLGER) FREDERICK, coll. adminstr.; born St. Peter, Minn., November 24, 1900; s. Karl August and Augusta Louise (Anderson) K.; A.B., Gustavus Adolphus Coll., 1922; A.M., Columbia, 1925, Ph.D., 1930; m. Juanita Claire Miller, Jan. 1, 1930; children—Carole Louise, Holger Frederick. Prof. biology Upsala Coll., 1923-33; dean Panzer Coll., 1933-42; sect. chief War Food Adminstrn., 1942-45; asso. health edn. Nat. Tb Assn., 1945-47; ednl. specialist U.S. Office Edn., 1947-53; prof. edn. N.Y.U., 1952-62; dean Grad. Sch., Wagner Coll., S.I., 1962-66, special assistant to the president, 1966—. Am.-Scandinavian Found. fellow, 1928. Mem. Am. Sch. Health Assn. (pres. 1954-56; Howe award 1960), Luth. Ch. Men Am. (pres. 1957-62). Author: Health Knowledge Test, 1936; Nutrition for Health, 1951; Health for Modern Living, 1957; School Health Education, 1962; (with others) School Health Services, 1953; Youth Grows Into Adulthood, 1954; Sports and Recreation Facilities, 1958. Home: Staten Island NY Died Dec. 7, 1968.

KILDAY, PAUL JOSEPH, judge; born Sabinal, Uvalde County, Tex., Mar. 29, 1900; s. Patrick and Mary (Tallant) K.; grad. high school, San Antonio, Tex., 1918; LL.B., Georgetown U., Washington, 1922; LL.D., St. Mary's U. of San Antonio, Tex., 1963; m. Cecile Newton, Aug. 9, 1932; children—Mary Catherine, Betty Ann. Clerk U.S. Civil Service, Washington, D.C., 1918-21; law clerk U.S. Shipping Bd. Emergency Fleet Corp., 1921-22; admitted to Tex. bar, 1922, and began practice in San Antonio; first asst. dist. atty., Bexar County, 1935-38; mem. 76th-87th Congresses, 20th Tex. Dist., resigned; judge U.S. Ct. Mil. Appeals, 1961-68. Mem. Am., Tex., San Antonio bar assns. Democrat. Roman Catholic. K.C. Address: Washington DC Died Oct. 12, 1968; buried Arlington Nat. Cemetery, Washington DC

KILDUFF, EDWARD JONES, educator, author; b. Waterbury, Conn., Dec. 15, 1889; s. Edward G. and Margaret E. (Jones) K.; A.B., Yale, 1912; A.M., New York University, 1915; m. Ellen M. Steinberg, August 1, 1962. Instructor of business English, New York U. Sch. of Commerce, Accounts and Finance, 1912-15, prof., 1920-55, asst. dean. 1928-44, associate dean, 1944-49, sr. prof., 1950-55, prof. emeritus, 1955-69. Mem. Nat. Assn. Tchrs. of Marketing (pres. 1922), Am. Business Writing Assn. (pres. 1937-39), acting chmn. N.Y. University Alumni Fund 1951-52. National Council Teachers of Eng., English Speaking Union, Phi Beta Kappa, Beta Gamma Sigma, Alpha Kappa Psi, Alpha Phi Sigma, Alpha Delta Sigma. Clubs: Yale (New York), Pomonok Country of Flushing, (vice president), Watertown (Connecticut) Country Club. Author: Handbook of Business English (with G. B. Hotchkiss), 1914, 3d edit., 1945; The Private Secretary, 1916; Credit and Collection Letters, 1916; Business English Folder; Advanced Business Correspondence (with G. B. Hotchkiss), 1921, 4th edit., 1947; The Stenographers Manual, 1921; How to Choose and Get a Better Job, 1921; Vocabulary Builder Notebook, 1923, 2d edit. (with J.H. Janis) 1948; Words the Secretary Must Watch, 1940; How to Write Effective Business Letters, 1940; Words and Human Nature, 1941; Knowing and Using Words, 1948, Practice in Business Writing (with Janis and Manville), 1952; Business English (with Janis and Dressner) 1956; Business Speaking (with Clyne, Dwyer and Zink), 1956. Staff member New Century Dictionary, N.Y.U. Meritorious Service Award, 1947. Home: Harwinton CT Died Jan. 3, 1969.

KILGEN, EUGENE ROBYN, business exec.; b. St. Louis, Oct. 20, 1897; s. Charles C. and Louise (Robyn) K.; student St. Louis Acad., 1912-16, St. Louis U., 1917; m. Marie von Phul Michel, Oct. 29, 1931 (dec. Mar. 1969); children—Marie Michel (Mrs. Charles Michael Drain), Eugene Robyn Kilgen, Junior. Joined Kilgen

Organ Co., St. Louis, 1919, apprentice, 1919-20, installation dept., 1921, engring. and sales, 1922-25, sec., 1925-35, v.p., 1935-39, pres. 1939-67; president Kilgen Aircraft, St. Louis, 1942-45, chmn. bd., 1956-67, dir. research, 1958-67; independent research and consulting, 1959-67. Mem. the bd. of control St. Louis Symphony Orchestra, 1936. Served as cadet pilot, U.S. A.A.F., 1917-18. Mem. Am. Guild Organists, Inst. Aero. Scis., St. Louis C. of C. (air bd.), St. Louis Academy of Sciences, Better Business Bureau (St. Louis). Club: University (St. Louis). Designer, collaborator in design of large organs as one in St. Patrick's Cathedral, Carnegie Hall, N.Y.C., St. Louis Cathedral. Invented Control Master for air traffic, 1953; Lightning Control System for TV studios, 1954. Home: University City MO Died Apr. 5, 1967.

KILGORE, JAMES, educator, clergyman; b. De Witt County, Tex., Jan. 15, 1865; s. James Thomas and Caroline Elizabeth (Bookwalter) K.; B.A., Southwestern U., Georgetown, Tex., 1889; M.A., 1890, D.D., 1910; studied U. of Chicago 5 summers; m. Lucy B. Pritchett, Jan. 27, 1892 (died Apr. 3, 1894); m. 2d, Faerie Blanton, Jan. 29, 1896 (died Apr. 7, 1930); children—John E. Donald G., James A. Ordained ministry M.E. Ch., S., 1892; became prof. philosophy and religion, Southern Meth. U., of Dallas, Tex., 1915, now emeritus. Mem. Gen. Conf. M.E. Ch., S., 7 times; pres. Conf. Bd. of Edn.; mem. Gen. Finance Bd. of M.E. Ch., S. Phi Delta Theta. Democrat. Mason. Home: 3415 University Blvd., Dallas TX*‡

KILLEN, JAMES SINCLAIR, govt. ofcl.; b. Port Townsend, Wash., Jan. 14, 1908; s. Henry Sinclair and Maude (Rose) K.; m. Alice B. Orem, 1933 (dec. 1965); children—J. Richard, Sandra L., Linda R.; m. 2d, Marilyn A. Lerch, 1966. Gen. rep., then 1st v.p. labor union, 1937-52; asst. to dir. bur. WPB, 1944-45; chief labor div. SCAP, 1947-48; with ECA, London, Eng., 1949-50; chief Mut. Security Agy. (later FOA and ICA) Mission to Yugoslavia, 1952-56; evaluation officer ICA, Washington, 1956-57; dir. USOM to Pakistan, 1957-61, with personal rank minister, 1959-61; dir. USOM to Korea, 1961-64, with personal rank minister, 1962-64; dir. with personal rank minister AID Mission to Vietnam, 1964-65; evaluation officer AID, Washington, 1965-67; dir. with personal rank minister AID Mission to Turkey, 1967-70; dir. Operations Appraisal Staff, AID, Washington, 1970-72. Recipient Distinguished Service award ICA, 1955, AID, 1961, 72. Address: Washington DC Died May 3, 1972.

KILLIAN, JOHN CALVIN, church official; b. Reading, Pa., July 6, 1870; s. John D. and Katharine (Helena) K.; ed. Lebanon Valley Coll.; grad. Crozer Theol. Sem., 1894; D.D. Western Bapt. Theol. Sem., Portland, Ore., and Alderson-Broaddus Coll., Philippi, W.Va.; m. Addie E. Smith, Sept. 3, 1899 (died July 31, 1931); m. 2d, Luella E. Adams, May 27, 1934. Ordained ministry Baptist Ch., 1894; pastor Hammonton, N.J., 1894-1898; associate pastor First Ch., Trenton, 1898-1900; pastor successively Alderson, W.Va., New Britain, Pa., Grace Ch., Trenton, until 1910; with Am. Bapt. Publ. Soc., 1910-20; pastor First Ch., Parkersburg, W.Va., 1920-24; field rep. Northern Bapt. Conv., 1924-27; field rep. Am. Bapt. Publ. Soc., 1927-41; retired Apr. 30, 1941; sec. Colporter-Missionary Work of Am. Bapt. Publ. Soc. and Am. Bapt. Home Mission Soc., 1932. Mason. Home: Spencerport NY‡

KILPATRICK, ARMOUR KEMP, corp. exec.; b. Okalona, Miss., Aug. 9, 1898; s. Peter and Nancy (Long) K.; student La. Polytech. Inst., 1915-16; m. Martha Bennett, Nov. 1, 1922; children—Martha Clayton (Mrs. Kellogg), Nancy Jane (Mrs. Wilbert). Pres., owner Standard Office Supply Co., Monroe, La., A.K. Kilpatrick, Inc., Monroe; dir. Gen. Am. Oil Co., Dallas, Nat. Am. Life Ins. Co., Baton Rouge. Former mem. Democratic Nat. Com. from La. Mem. Monroe C. of C. (pres. 1940). Episcopalian. Mason (Shriner). Home: Monroe LA Died 1960.

KIMBALL, DAN A., ex.-sec. navy; b. St. Louis, Mar. 1, 1896; s. John H. and Mary (Able) K.; ed. pub. schs., St. Louis; m. Dorothy Ames, June 22, 1925; married second Doris Fleeson, August 1958. Began Los Angeles manager, General Tire & Rubber Co., 1920, v.p., 1942-69; chmn., president Aerojet-General, El Monte, Cal.; chmn. bd. Bank of Sacramento; director Frontier Airlines. Served with A.A.C., advancing to rank of 1st lt., World War I. Apptd. assistant secretary of navy of air, Mar. 1949, under sec. navy, 1949-51, sec., 1951-53. Named Home Study Man of Year, Internat. Correspondence Schs., 1968. Conglist. Democrat. Clubs: Los Angeles Country, Jonathan (Los Angeles); Metropolitan, Burning Tree (Washington). Home: Washington DC Died July 30, 1970; buried Arlington Nat. Cemetery, Arlington VA

KIMBALL, HERBERT HARVEY, meteorologist; b. Hopkinton, N.H., Feb. 13, 1862; s. Elbridge Gerry and Mary (Butler) K.; B.S., N.H. Coll. Agr. and Mechanic Arts, 1884; M.S., Columbia (now George Washington) U., 1900; Ph.D., George Washington U., 1910; fellow U. of Pittsburgh, 1912-13; hon. LL.D., U. of N.H., 1921; m. Margaret Gertrude Cowling, Nov. 4, 1891; children—Mrs. Dorothy Lingenfelter, Herbert Cowling, Donald Butler. Meteorol. observer, 1884-85, clerk at central office, 1886-1900, asst. editor of Monthly Weather Review, 1901-03, editor same, 1918-19, librarian, 1904-08, in charge of solar radiation investigations, 1908-32, U.S. Meteorol. Service; research asso. Harvard, in charge solar radiation investigations at Blue Hill Obs., 1932-39. Mem. Philos. Soc. Washington, Am. Geophysical Union; fellow A.A.A.S., Am. Meteorol. Soc. (ex-pres.). Baptist. Home: 1819 Monroe St. N.W., Washington DC‡

KIMBLE, JOSEPH CHANSLOR, lawyer; b. Hanford, Cal., Jan. 3, 1910; s. Robert and Laura (Wiley) K.; A.B., U. Cal. at Berkeley, 1931; LL.B., Harvard, 1934; m. Betty Minturn, Mar. 19, 1937 (div. July 1960);children—Ward Minturn, Betsy Kennedy; m. 2d, Sally S. Waldo, July 25, 1961; children—Steven Waldo, Wendy Waldo, Carolyn. Admitted to N.Y. State bar, 1935, Cal. Bar, 1937; practice in Fresno, 1939; partner Kimble MacMichael Jackson & Magarion; lectr. law U. Cal. at Berkeley, 1952. Mng. partner Caldarko Gas Co., 1958-72, K.A.L. Oil Co., 1957-72; v.p., dir. McCarthy Tank &Steel Co., Bakersfield, Cal., 1949-72; mgr., dir. Kennedy Co., 1957-66. Mem. Gov. Cal. Com. Agrl. Labor Resources, 1951. Mem. Fresno County Republican Central Com. 1943-49. Pres. Fresno City and County Children's Hosp. and Guidance Clinic, 1950-51. Mem. Am. Bar Assn., State Bar Cal. (chmn. com. taxation 1946-48, Central Valley Empire Assn. (pres. 1948-49), Fresno City and County C. of C. (pres. 1946-48), Phi Gamma Delta. Conglist. Clubs: Rotary (pres. 1948-49), Harvard (pres. 1959-60), San Joaquin Country; Lincolns Inn (Harvard Law Sch.); Family, Commonwealth (San Francisco). Author articles taxes. Home: Fresno CA Died Apr. 16, 1972.

KIMBROUGH, HERBERT, educator; b. Carthage, Ill., June 13, 1876; s. Thomas Jefferson and Rebecca Susan (Stebbins) K.; student Springield (Mo.) Normal Sch., 1893-95; studied music in Kansas City, Mo., 1895-96, in Berlin, Germany, with Profs. Heinrich Barth and Franz Kullak, and Dr. Ernest Jedliczka, 1898-1900; with Paolo Gallico, New York, summers, 1925, 30; LL.D., State Coll. of Wash., 1938; m. La Verna E. Askin, Aug. 16, 1923. Instr. in music, 1902, prof., 1909, dean since 1917, Sch. of Music and Fine Arts; vice-pres. State College of Washington, 1937-46; vice-president emeritus since 1946. Member Washington State Music Teachers' Assn. (pres. 1919-20). Mason. Mem. Phi Kappa Phi, Phi Mu Alpha (supreme pres. 1937-39), Phi Sigma Kappa. Home: Pullman WA‡

KIMBROUGH, ROBERT ALEXANDER, clergyman; b. Cornersville, Tenn., May 7, 1869; s. Duke Love and Sallie Polk (Bryant) K.; A.M., Southwestern Bapt. U., Jackson, Tenn., 1895; student Southern Bapt. Theol. Sem., Louisville, Ky., 1902; D.D., Union U., Jackson, Tenn., 1912; m. Annie Donaldson, of Brazil, Tenn., 1895 (died 1897); m. 2d, Martha Conn, of Corinth, Miss., Aug. 3, 1898; children—Robert Alexander, Martha (Mrs. Harry L. Yates), Annie Walne (Mrs. Paul Cooper). Ordained to ministry Baptist Church, 1892; pastor country chs., 1892-99; asst. prof. Latin and Greek, Union U., 1895-99; prin. Union Acad., Murfreesboro, Tenn., 1899-1900; pastor successively Shelbyville, Tenn., Tupelo, Miss., and Blue Mountain, Miss., until 1911; pres. Union U., Jackson, Tenn., 1911-13; pastor Abilene, Tex., 1913-15; evangelist, 1915; pastor Shreveport, La., First Ch., Vicksburg, Blue Mountain, Miss., until 1920; enlistment missionary North Miss., 1920-23; pastor Baptist Ch., Charleston, Miss., 1923-32, Baptist Ch., Luxora, Ark., 1932-36; now pastor Middleburg Ch. Trustee Blue Mountain Coll., Simmons Coll., Abilene, Tex. Pres. Miss. Bapt. Conv. Bd., 1923-32; v.p. Miss. Bapt. State Conv., 1927. Mem. Sigma Alpha Epsilon. Mason (K.T.), K.P. Home: Jackson TN‡

KIMMEL, HUSBAND EDWARD, naval officer; b. Henderson, Ky., Feb. 26, 1882; s. Manning Marius and Sibbie (Lambert) K.; student Central U., Richmond Ky., 1899-1900; B.S. in Engring., U.S. Naval Academy, 1904; hon. Doctor of Law, Centre College, 1941; m. Dorothy Kinkaid, January 31, 1912; children—Manning Marius (U.S. Navy), Thomas Kinkaid (U.S. Navy), Edward Ralph. Commd. ensign, U.S. Navy, 1906, and advanced through the grades to rear adm., 1937, admiral, Feb. 1, 1941; comdg. Cruisers Battle Force, U.S. Fleet, 1939-41; command U.S. Pacific Fleet and the combined U.S. Fleet, 1941; retired, 1942. Decorated Cuban Pacification, Mexican, Grand Fleet World War campaign badges. Mem. Sigma Alpha Epsilon. Club: Army and Navy (Washington, D.C.). Address: New London CT Died May 15, 1968.

KIMMELSTIEL, PAUL, physician; b. Hamburg, Germany, Mar. 21, 1900; s. Adolf and Ernestine (August) K.; M.D., Tubingen (Germany) U., 1923; m. Charlotte Rose van Biema, Feb. 22, 1924; children—Ruth (Mrs. Norbert Freinkel), Marion (Mrs. Norman Goldberg). Came to U.S., 1934, naturalized, 1940. Intern, Hosp. of St. George, Hamburg, 1924-25; fellow bacteriology and immunology dept. Allgemeines Krankenhaus Rudolf Eppendorf, Hamburg, 1925, resident dept. pathology, 1929-30, asso. prof., 1930-33; resident dept. pathology Allgemeines Krankenhaus St. George, Hamburg, 1925-27; instr. pathology Harvard, 1934-35; coroner City of Richmond (Va.), 1936-40; pathologist, dir. clin. labs. Charlotte (N.C.) Meml. Hosp., 1940-58; asso. prof. pathology Med. Coll. Va., Richmond, 1935-40; prof., pathology Marquette U. Med. Sch., Milw., 1958-64, research prof., 1964-66; distinguished prof. pathology U. Okla., Oklahoma City, until 1970. NIH grantee. Recipient medal Am. Cancer Soc., 1956, Elliott Proctor Joslin medal New Eng. Diabetes Assn., 1966, medal Japanese Soc. Nephrology, 1968. Diplomate Am. Bd. Pathology. Fellow A.C.P.; mem. A.M.A., Am. Soc. Clin. Pathologists, Coll. Am. Pathologists, Am. Assn. Pathologists and Bacteriologists. Discovered Kimmelstiel-Wilson disease, 1936. Home: Oklahoma City OK Died Oct. 7, 1970; buried Dresher PA

KINCAID, TREVOR, zoologist; b. Peterboro, Ont., Can., Dec. 21, 1872; s. Dr. Robert and Margaret K.; B.S., U. of Wash., 1899, A.M., 1901; m. Louise F. Pennell, Aug. 23, 1917; children—Marjorie Farrar, Dorothy Elizabeth, Barbara Louise, Thomas Farrar, Mary Pennella, Kathleen. Instr. of biology, U. of Wash., 1895-99; asst. Am. Fur Seal Commn., 1897, acting prof. entomology, Ore. Agrl. Coll., 1897-98; entomologist Harriman Alaska expdn., 1899; asst. prof. biology, 1899-1901, prof. zoology, U. of Wash., 1911-47; retired; professor emeritus of zoology, since 1947; Austin scholar, Harvard, 1905-06; special field agt., U.S. Dept. Agr., in Japan, 1908, in Russia, 1909 (investigation of parasites of gypsy moth). Mem. Am. Soc. Econ. Entomologists, Entomol. Soc. Washington. Contbr. to Entomological News and to other publs., various papers and reports relating to the entomology of the Pacific Coast and particularly to Alaska, and papers on the oyster industry of the Pacific Coast. Home: 1904 E. 52d St., Seattle WA‡

KINCER, JOSEPH BURTON, meteorologist; b. Wythe Country, Va., Nov. 15, 1874; s. Alonzo and Margaret (Hilton) K.; ed. in pvt. schs.; m. Cora Helen Lampe, Aug. 26, 1896; children—Lockie Inez (Mrs. J.W. Davies), Alice Ruth (Mrs. W.T. Webb). Pub. sch. teacher, Wythe County, Va., 1894-1901; dep. treas. Wythe County, 1901-04; entered U.S. Weather Bureau as asst. observer, 1904, and promoted successively through various grades to prin. meteorologist and chief division of climate and crop weather, Washington, D.C.; now retired. Fellow A.A.A.S., Am. Meteorol. Soc. (pres. 1936-37); mem. Assn. Am. Geographers, Am. Geophysical Union, Internat. Climatol. Commn., Internat. Commn. Agrl. Meteorology. Lutheran. Mason. Odd Fellow. Wrote sect. on climate in Atlas of American Agriculture, also numerous meteorol. bulletins pub. by U.S. Dept. of Agr. Editor of Weekly Weather and Crop Bulletin. Home: 4112 Fessenden St. N.W., Washington DC‡

KING, ADEN J(ACKSON), prof. chemistry; b. La Fayette, N.Y., Nov. 25, 1897; s. Newton Earl and Orpha Amanda (Hoyt) K.; B.S., Syracuse U., 1921, M.S., 1922, Ph.D., 1927; m. Gladys Susan Nutter, Dec. 6, 1917; 1 dau., Mary E. Kelly. Instr. chem., Syracuse U., 1921-27, U. of Ill., 1927-28; Nat. Research Fellow (chemistry), U. of Ill., 1928-29; prof. chemistry and x-ray crystallography. Syracuse U. from 1929, acting chmn. dept. chemistry 1949-50; sabbatical term study, U. of Manchester, England, 1935; co-founder and pres., King Labs., Inc., 1931. Mem. Am. Chem. Soc., Am. Constallographic Assn., Am. Orchid Soc., Sigma Xi, Phi Beta Kappa, Alpha Chi Sigma, Phi Lambda Upsilon. Club: Men's Garden of America (Syracuse). Inventions and patents on use of alkaline earth metals in electronic industry. Home: Syracuse NY Died Dec. 1971.

KING, ALBION ROY, educator, writer, lecturer; b. Plevna, Kan., Nov. 21, 1895; s. Clarence William and Della (Parker) K.; A.B., Southwestern Coll., Winfield, Kan., 1920; S.T.B., Boston U., 1925; studied at U. Strasbourg and traveled Europe, 1926; Ph.D., U. So. Cal., 1932; m. Fern Creekmore, July 19, 1920 (dec. Apr. 1963); 1 son, James Edgar; m. 2d, Gertrude Shell Miner, June 20, 1964. Ordained to ministry Meth. Ch., 1923, served as minister, Revere, Mass., 1924-27; instr. philosophy and psychology W. Va. Wesleyan Coll., 1927-29; instr. philosophy U. So. Calif., 1929-30; asst. prof. philosophy Cornell Coll., Mount Vernon, Ia., 1932-35, John Edward Johnson prof. religion and ethics, 1935-61, dean men, 1932-49; lectr. Yale Sch. Alcohol Studies, 1954, 55. Meth. Bd. Ministerial Tng. Pastors' Schs. Served as pvt., USMC, 1918. Member of the Inter-collegiate Association for the Study of the Alcohol Problem (nat. pres.), Am. Philos. Assn., Nat. Assn. Bibl. Instrs. (past pres., Western div.), Am. Legion (past comdr.), Phi Beta Kappa. Mem. State Bd. Ia. Temperance League; Ia. Conf., Meth. Ch. Club: Lions (past pres.). Author: The Psychology of Drunkenness, 1943; The Problem of Evil, 1952; Basic Information of Alcohol, 1953, 4th edit., 1964. Contbr. articles to religious and profl. jours. Home: Mount Vernon IA Died May 6, 1972; buried Mt. Vernon Cemetery.

KING, CHARLES BANKS, college pres.; b. Giles Co., Va.; A.B., A.M., D.D., Roanoke Coll., Salem, Va. Ordained Lutheran minister, 1887; pastor, St. John's Ch., Salisbury, N.C., 10 yrs.; resigned to build Elizabeth Coll. for Women, Charlotte, N.C.; Founder, pres. and owner of Elizabeth Coll. Active mem. Southern Soc. of Philosophy and Psychology. Address: Elizabeth College, Charlotte NC‡

KING, CHARLES BURTON, manufacturer; b. Marion Co., O., Jan. 25, 1875; s. George Titus and Margaret (Barnhart) K.; Ohio Wesleyan U., 1891-94; m. Ethel Liggett, of Chicago, Ill., Nov. 30, 1898. Connected with the Marion Steam Shovel Co. since 1895, v.p. since 1914, gen. mgr. since 1917; pres. The New Hotel Co. (operating Hotel Harding, Marion, O.); dir. City Nat. Bank & Trust Co., Sunlight and Ohio Valley coal cos., Wilson Bohannon Lock Co.; partner Marion Stock Yards. Pres. Ohio Manufacturers' Association. Designer of first electrically driven shovel and many other excavating machines. Mem. U.S. Fuel Administration during war period. Trustee Harding Memorial Assn., Washington, D.C. Mem. Am. Soc. M.E., Nat. Assn. Mfrs., Army Ordnance Assn., Am. Acad. Polit. and Social Science. Republican. Methodist. Mason (32 deg., K.T., Shriner). Clubs: Marion, Marion Country, Columbus Athletic (Columbus, O.). Home: 807 S. Windsor Boul., Los Angeles CA‡

KING, DENNIS, actor; b. Coventry, Eng., Nov. 2, 1897; s. John and Mary Elizabeth (King) Pratt; student pub. schs. Birmingham, Eng.; m. Edith Wright, July 17, 1920; children—Dennis, Michael. Began as call-boy Birmingham Repertory Theatre, debut as Dennis in As You Like It, 1916; Am. debut with Ethel and John Barrymore in Clair de Lune, 1921; played Cain in Back to Methuselah, 1922. Mercutio in Romeo and Juliet, 1924, Francois Villon in Vagabond King, 1925, D'Artagnan in Three Musketeers, Ravenal in Show Boat; also played in Richard II, Peter Ibbetson, A Doll's House, He Who Gets Slapped Searching Wind, Blithe Spirit, Pygmalion, Devil's Disciple, Billy Budd, Edward, My Son, Medea, ADay by the Sea; Affair of Honor, 1956; Shangri-La., 1956; Greatest Man, 1957; Hidden River, 1957; The Miracle, 1959; Love and Libel, 1960; Lets Make Love, 1960; Photo-Finish, 1963; Minor Miracle, 1965; Loves of Cass Maguire, 1967; Portrait of a Queen, 1968; Remembering Mr. Maugham, 1969. Home: Brookville LI NY Died May 21, 1971

KING, EDGAR, med. officer U.S. Army; b. Van Buren, Ark., Aug. 1, 1884; s. Lilburn Henderson and Minnie Bauregard (Childress) K.; M.D., U. of Ark., 1906; grad. Army Med. Sch., 1907; m. Susan Nickerson Moody, Jan. 28, 1910; children—Susan Childress (Mrs. Frederick J. Dau), Dorothy Moody (Mrs. Victor B. Geibel). Interne St. Vincent's Infirmary and Parlaski County Hosp., Little Rock, Ark., 1903-04 and 1906; commd. 1st lt., U.S. Army, 1907, and advance through grades to brig. gen., 1942; retired from active service as brig. general, 1948. Special work in mental diseases and their relation to mil. service disciplinary problems. Decorated D.S.M., Legion of Merit. Mem. A.M.A. Address: Reno NV Died Oct. 17, 1970; buried Ft. Leavenworth Nat. Cemetery.

KING, EDNA ELVIRA SWANSON (MRS. EDGAR J. KING), poet; b. Marquette, Kan.; d. John Peter and Ida Sofia (Nelson) Swanson; student U. Kan., 1915-16, U. Denver, 1945-47; m. Edgar Johnson King, May 13, 1918; children—Edna (Mrs. Martin Doyne), Roberta (Mrs. Charles Howe), Beatrice (Mrs. Eugene Gayhart), Yvonne (Mrs. Harvey Garner), Edgar Johnson. Writer poetry, 1945-69; works appeared in N.Y. Times, N.Y. Jour.-Am. Today's Health, Pen Mag., Denver Post, Ave Maria, Manna, Lamp, Rosary, War Cry, Gospel Herald, Teens, Young People, Front Rank, other publs. Mem. Poetry Soc. Colo. (recipient poetry awards, treas. 1962-63, 1st v.p. 1963-65, pres. 1965-67), Nat. League Am. Pen Women. Republican. Episcopalian. Home: Denver CO Died Mar. 26, 1969.

KING, EDWIN BURRUSS, educator; b. Wilmington, N.C., May 24, 1876; s. J. Francis (M.D.) and Susan LeRoy (Neilson) K.; grad. St. Mark's Sch., Southboro, Mass., 1894; B.A., Yale, 1898, M.A., 1908; m. Mary Semmes Forbes, of Warrenton, Va., June 24, 1905; children—Mary Forbes, Edwin Burruss (dec.), Emily North. Master, St. Mark's Sch., 1898-1907; senior master, Ridgefield Sch., 1907-09; head master, Gilman Country Sch., Roland Park, Md., 1909-12, Stuyvesant School, Warrenton, Va., since 1912. Episcopalian. Mem. Alpha Delta Phi. Clubs: Graduate (New Haven, Conn.); University (New York); Warrenton Hunt (chmn., 1923-24, 1926-28), Fauquier (Warrenton, Va.). Home: Warrenton VA‡

KING, ELISHA ALONZO, clergyman; b. Providence, R.I., Dec. 24, 1870; s. Benjamin Peck King and Sophronia Adelaide (Gammons) K.; grad. Internat. Y.M.C.A. Coll., Springfield, Mass., 1894, Bach Humanics, 1900; student Lane Theol. Sem., Cincinnati, O., 1897-99; B.D., Oberlin Grad. Sch. of Theology, 1900; student U. of Washington, summer 1915; grad. Chautauqua Lit. and Scientific Circle, 1904; D.D., Piedmont Coll., 1924; Master of Humanics, Springfield (Mass.) Coll., 1941; m. Frances Elvira Leach, Aug. 25, 1897 (died July 7, 1938); m. 2d, Elizabeth A. Cooley, May 29, 1940. In Y.M.C.A. work until 1897; licensed to preach, 1897, ordained Congl. ministry, 1900; pastor Marysville and Sandusky, O., and Yakima, Wash., until 1914; acting pastor Plymouth Ch., Seattle, 1914-15; pastor San Jose, Calif., 1916-21; instr., Coll. of the Pacific, San Jose, 1920; pastor Community Ch., Miami Beach, Fla., 1921-40, pastor emeritus since 1940; editor church methods dept., The Expositor, Cleveland, O., 1908-25; writer for The Congregationalist since 1897. Y.M.C.A. lecturer on social hygiene at Pacific Coast camps and in France, World War. Trustee Piedmont Coll. (v.p.), Atlanta Theol. Sem. Pres. Fla. Congl. Conf. of Chs.; v.p. Greater Miami Ministerial Assn., Miami Community Chest, Dade County Welfare Bd.; pres. Council of Social Agencies, Miami, Miami Beach Welfare Bd.; pres. Ohio Christian Endeavor Union, 1905-07, Wash. C.E. Union, 1910-14; dir. Isles of Shoals Conf., 1931-32; mem. Broadcasting Commn. and Commn. for Missionary Edn. of Nat. Council of Congl. Chs., mem. of Commn. on the Ministry; mem. Dade County Planning Council; moderator S.E. Coast Assn. Congl. Chs. Hon. corr. member, Institut Litteraire et Artistique de France, Paris; mem. Commn. of 100 for Internat. Peace, Com. of 100 (Miami Beach), Miami Beach Chamber of Commerce (governing bd.), Fla. State Conf. Social Work (dir.), Nat. Conf. of Social Work, Am. Social Hygiene Assn. Republican. Mason (32 deg.); chaplain Ocean Bay Lodge 180. Clubs: Lions, Massachusetts (pres.). Author: Helps to Health and Purity, 1903; Clean and Strong, 1909, 1917; Planting a Church in a National Playground, 1920-40; (brochures) Some Religious Implications of the Theory of Evolution; The Work of the Christian Ministry; series of 5 social hygiene circulars issued by the Health Dept., Yakima, Wash., 1912; Cure for Worry; Fruits of Silence; The Mystery Side of Jesus' Life; The Vision Splendid; St. Paul of Yesterday and the Church of Today; The Lord's Prayer Today; Epic of the Inner Life—the Drama of Job; Morning Visions, The Fascinating Book of Acts; That Grotesque Last Book in the New Testament, Revelation, Contb. editor Christian Sun, editorial writer; columnist Business of Living," in Miami Daily News. Lecturer on religious and travel topics; weekly preacher over station WIOD, 1926-38; also Masonic lecturer. Frequent lecturer on Biblical literature, U. of Miami. Address: 237 N.E. 108th St., Miami 38 FL‡

KING, EVERETT EDGAR, univ. prof., b. Warren, Ind., Jan. 17, 1877; s. John Walter and Margaret Ellen (Foreman) K.; B.S., Rose Poly. Inst., Terre Haute, Ind., 1901; B.A., Indiana U., 1910; M.C.E., Cornell U., 1911; m. Anna May Owen, Oct. 8, 1903. Civil engr. Mexican Central R.R., Mexico City, 1901-02, Cincinnati, Hamilton & Dayton R.R., Cincinnati, 1902-03, C.,R.I.&P. R.R., Chicago, 1903-07; prof. civil engring., Oklahoma. Agrl. and Mech. Coll., 1907-10; grad. student and asst. Cornell U., 1910-11; prof. ry. engring., Ia. State Coll., 1911-18; prof. ry. civil engring., Univ. of Illinois, 1918-45; prof. emeritus, ry. civil engring., 1945-68. Mem. Am. Soc. Civil Engrs., Am. Ry. Engring. Assn., Am. Assn. Railroads (signal sect.), American Soc. for Engring. Edn., Tau Beta Pi, Phi Kappa Phi, Theta Tau, Sigma Xi, Alpha Sigma Phi. Republican. Christian Scientist. Mason, Rotarian. Urbana IL Died July 16, 1960; buried Mt. Hope Cemetery Mausoleum, Champaign IL

KING, FAIN WHITE, archeologist; b. Paducah, Ky., Sept. 3, 1892; s. Charles Henry and Katie Andrews (Burnette) K.; ed. Ky. pub. schs. and U. Chgo; m. 2d, Blanche Black Busey, June 6, 1935. Owner King Mill and Lumber Co., from 1912, also K.R.B. Realty Co.; pres. Paducah Development Co.; treas. Three Rivers Oil Co.; dir. Associated Realty Co., Central Warehouse Co., Paducah Roofing Co. Co-owner, Natural Flourite Optical Co. In charge dist. inspection Constrn. Div., War Dept., 1917-19. Mem. bd. regents Ala. State Mus. Natural History; dir. Collectors and Dealers Nat. Assn. Indian Relics; mem. bd. dirs. Nat. Econ. League for Ky.; research dir. of archeology for Ky. under govs. Chandler and Johnson. Reapptd. state archaeologist for 4th time as dir. archaeology under Gov. Simeon Willis, dept. conservation. Dir., mem. exec. com. Ballard Co. of Ky. Lake Assn. Mem. Mus. Natural History (N.Y.C.), Ill. State Archaeol. Soc., Ky., Tenn. acads. sci., Ky. Ornithol. Soc., Wis. Archeol; Soc., Am. Legion, Col. Gov. Laffoon's staff. Democrat. Episcopalian. Editor, Gems and Minerals dept. Hobbies mag. Contbr. Wis. Archeologist, Ky. mag.; mem. adv. bd. Ky. Nature mag. Discoverer and excavator ancient buried city in Ky., at junction of Ohio and Mississippi rivers; has broadcast from site of excavations over NBC network; also from Radio City, Chgo. Home: San Diego CA Died June 5, 1972; buried Oak Knoll Cemetery, Paducah KY

KING, FRANK LAMAR, fgn. service officer; b. Augusta, Ga., Aug. 22, 1909; s. Robin Oren and Kate (Tarver) K.; student extension, William and Mary Coll., Richmond, Va., 1930-32, Theodore Irvine Sch. of the Theatre, 1932-35; m. Gladys Merritt Carter, Apr. 2, 1934; children—Marian (Mrs. Grant D. Green III), Gail (Mrs. Sidney Seid), Sallie (Mrs. Nigel B. Jones), and Bonnie (Mrs. Donald Macauley). Appeared as an actor at the Roxy Theatre, 1932, Radio City Music Hall, 1933, Tobacco Road, 1933-36, Boy Meets Girl, London, 1936, Brother Rat, 1937; mgmt. exec. R. H. Macy & Co., 1938-42; govt. service, 1942-70; fgn. service officer, 1948-70, assigned successively, London, Eng., Berlin, Germany, Baghdad, Iraq, 1948-57, chief tng. officer U.S. Information Agy., Washington, 1957-60; pub. affairs officer Am. embassy, Freetown, Sierra Leone, W. Africa, from 1960, then newseditor and program coordinator Africa div., Washington, ret., 1970. Served with USNR, 1944-45. Clubs: American (London); Kenwood Country (Washington). Home: Chevy Chase MD Died Oct. 1970.

KING, FRANK O., cartoonist; b. Cashton, Wis., Apr. 9, 1883; s. John J. and Caroline I. (Harris) K.; grad. high sch., Tomah, Wis., 1901; student Chicago Acad. Fine Arts, 1905-06; m. Della Drew, Feb. 7, 1911; 1 son, Robert Drew. Artist and cartoonist, Minneapolis Times, 1901-05, Chicago Examiner, 1906-09, Chicago Tribune and Chicago Tribune-New York News Syndicate, Inc., since 1909. Drew Bobby Make-Believe" and the Rectangle," before starting upon Gasoline Alley" in 1918. Recipient Freedoms Found. awards, 1949, 50; Best Strip Cartoonist, National Cartoonists Society, 1957, named cartoonist of the year for 1958. Member National Cartoonists Society (New York), Society of Illustrators (N.Y.). Clubs: Tavern, Midland Authors, Lake Shore. Author: Skeezix and Uncle Walt, 1924; Skeezix and Pal, 1925; Skeezix at the Circus, 1926; Skeezix Out West, 1928. Winter Park FL Died June 23, 1969; buried Tomah WI

KING, HOWELL ATWATER, life ins.; b. Manchester-by-the-sea, Mass., Sept. 8, 1896; s. Edward Gilbert and Theodora (Atwater) K.; B.C.S., U. of Md., 1925; D.C.S., Chicago Law Sch., 1931; m. Gladys C. Passano, Jan. 15, 1920; children—Charlotte Howell, Mary-Louise Atwater, Gladys Theodora, Arabelle Knight. Principal clerk and asst. to dean U. of Maryland, 1924; exec. sec. and teacher accounting Univ. of Baltimore, 1925, exec. dean, 1925-33, acting president, November 1933-January 1935, also secretary bd. trustees; City Service Commissioner, Baltimore; special rep. U.S. Treasury Department 1936-39; spl. agent, Baltimore agency, Mut. Benefit Life Ins. Co. of Newark, N.J., 1939-42, asst. gen. agent since 1942. Gen. Agent Occidental Life Ins. Co. of Calif., 1944; mem. bd. dir. Security Title Guarantee Corporation of Baltimore, Maryland Mortgage Company, Fed. Savings and Loan Association, Incorporated. Served in World War 3yrs.; 29th divisional citation for bravery, Silver Star medal. Mem. Pi Gamma Mu, Pi Delta Tau, Delta Sigma Pi. Mem. Occidental Leading Producers Club; life mem. Million Dollar Round Table since 1941. Episcopalian. Clubs: Cosmopolitan International of Baltimore, Md., Lions, Advertising (dir., mem. bd. govs.). Home: Towson MD Died Dec. 28, 1971.

KING, IRVING, educator; b. Richmond, Ind., July 17, 1874; s. Edward and Mary Buffington (Evans) K.; A.B., Earlham Coll., Ind., 1896; Ph.D., U. of Chicago, 1904; m. Alta F. Burke, of Tonganoxie, Kan., Sept. 7, 1898. Prin. Tonganoxie Acad., 1896-8, Bloomingdale (Ind.) Acad., 1898-1900; fellow, U. of Chicago, 1901-3; prof. psychology, Oshkosh (Wis.) State Normal Sch., 1903; prof. psychology and history of edn., Pratt Inst., Brooklyn, 1903-6; asst. prof. edn. and insp. secondary schs., U. of Mich., 1906-9; prof. edn., State U. of Ia., 1909-20. Lecturer on edn., U. of Wis., summer, 1911. Progressive Republican. Quaker. In ednl. service under Y.M.C.A., Camp Travis, Camp Logan and Ft. Bliss, Tex., 1918-19; organized demobilization school for soliders, Camp Travis. Poultry fancier and owner of hatchery. Author: Psychology of Child Development, 1903 (transl. into Japanese and Bohemian); The Development of Religion, 1910 (transl. into Japanese); Social Aspects of Education, 1912; Education for Social Efficiency, 1913; The High School Age, 1914; Hygienic Conditions in Iowa Schools, 1915; articles on Australian morality, and inhibition in Hastings' Dictionary of Religion and Ethics. Home: Iowa City IA‡

KING, JAMES WILLIAM, supt. schs.; b. Pueblo, Colo., Dec. 5, 1905; s. Harry M. and Lena (Armstrong) K.; B.A. magna cum laude, Pacific U., 1927; M.A., U. Ore., 1935; m. Bessie N. Hawes, June 18, 1928; children—Lauren Dale, Janice Muriel (Mrs. Stanley McClellan), Michael Craig. Salesman, Buster Brown Shoe Co., Pendleton, Ore., 1927-28; tchr., coach pub. schs., Imbler, Ore., 1928-29, supt. schs., 1929-35; supt. schs., Union, Ore., 1935-39, Lebanon, Ore., 1944-70; prin. high schs., LaGrande, Ore., 1939-44. Bd. dirs. Lebanon Community Hosp., Lebanon United Fund. Mem. Am., Ore. (pres. 1945-46, 59-60) assns. sch. adminstrs., N.E.A., Eastern Ofe. Regional Tchrs. Assn. (past pres.), Lebanon C. of C. (past pres.), Blue Key, Phi Delta Kappa, Phi Alpha Tau. Mason, Elk, Lion (pres. Lebanon 1962-63). Home: Lebanon OR Died July 4, 1970.

KING, LOUISA YEOMANS (MRS. FRANCIS KING), b. at Washington, N.J.; d. Alfred (D.D.) and Elizabeth Blythe (Ramsay) Yeomans; private schools; m. Francis King, Chicago, Ill., June 12, 1890. Pres. Garden Club of Mich., 1912-15; hon. pres. Woman's Nat. Farm and Garden Assn.; mem. Garden Club America (ex.-v.p.), Am. Dahlia Soc., American Rose Society, Am. Gladiolus Soc., Royal Hort. Soc. Great Britain, Royal National Tulip Society of England. Clubs: Women's National Republican Club (New York); Garden (London). Author: The Well-Considered Garden, 1915; Pages from a Garden Note-Book, 1921; The Little Garden, 1921; Variety in the Little Garden,

1923; Chronicles of the Garden, 1925; The Beginner's Garden, 1927; The Flower Garden Day by Day, 1927; The Gardener's Colour Book, 1929; From aNew Garden, 1930. Contbr. to mags. Awarded by trustees of Mass. Hort. Soc., George Robert White medal for eminent service in horticulture," 1921; Garden Club of America Medal of Honor, 1923; Distinguished Service award, Nat. Home Planting Bur., 1931. Home: South Hartford NY‡

KING, MARY PERRY, teacher, lecturer; b. Oswego, N.Y.; d. Hon. Albertus and Eliza (Grant) Perry; grad. Oswego (N.Y.) Normal Coll., 1879; study interpretive motion and diction in spl. schs., Paris, London, Phila., and New York; m. Morris Lee King, M.D., of New York, 1887. Founder Unitrinian School of Personal Harmonizing Interpretive Motion and Speech, New York. Episcopalian. Author: Comfort and Exercise, 1900; The Basis of Beauty, 1901; An Ideal Gymnasium, 1902; The Making of Personality (with Bliss Carman), 1906; Daughters of Dawn (with same), 1913; Earth-Deities; Hymn of Freedom, 1916; War Poems, 1917; Musical Speech, 1926. Contbr. to mags. Lyceum reader and lecturer. Founder and dir. Harmony House. Home: New Canaan CT‡

KING, MAXWELL CLARK, finance co. exec.; b. Greeley, Colo., July 22, 1899; s. Ralph W. and Daisy (Clark) K.; A.B., Stanford U., 1921; student Harvard Grad. Sch. Bus., 1921-22; m. Barbara Miller Loomis, May 12, 1923; children—Maxwell C., Clark L. With Pacific Finance Corp., 1925-64, pres., 1942-64. Pres. Am. Finance Conf., 1945-46, chmn. exec. com. 1947-48. Clubs: University; Wilshire Country; California; Newport Harbor Yacht, Rotary. Home: Los Angeles CA Died Nov. 1969.

KING, RAYMOND THOMAS, lawyer, b. Springfield, Mass., Aug. 15, 1893; s. Thomas Edward and Anna (Davis) K.; A.B., Dartmouth, 1915; LL.B., Harvard, 1919; m. Olive Geran King, Oct. 19, 1918; children—Joan (Mrs. Eugene Loveland), Nancy (Mrs. Hobart Swan), Lucy, Raymond T., Mary (Mrs. Charles Whelan). Admitted to Mass. bar, 1919; pvt. practice law, Springfield, 1921-71; mem. Ely, King, Kingsbury & Corcoran; city solicitor City of Springfield, 1936-37, spl. counsel, 1939-40. Dir. Legal Aid Soc., 1942-71; mem. Cath. Scholarships for Negroes, Inc., 1948-71; dir. Springfield Community Chest, 1936-40; organizer, dir. War Chest, 1941-43, United Fund Greater Springfield, Inc., 1950-51; mem. Mass. White House Conf. on Youth, 1950; area chmn. Easter Seal campaign Bay State Soc., 1956; pres. Concert Association of Springfield, 1933-48; Springfield chmn. Am. Aid for Children to Palestine, 1948, Children's Med. Center, Boston, 1949. Served as capt. inf. U.S. Army, 1917-19. Recipient citation for work among Boys Clubs Am., 1955. Mem. Am., Mass., Hampden County (pres. 1942-43) bar assns., Harvard Law Sch. Assn., Am. Legion. K.C. Clubs: University, Dartmouth (Springfield); Dartmouth (N.Y.C.). Home: Springfield MA Died Feb. 20, 1971.

KING, ROBERT LUTHER, management consultant; b. Crestline, O., Oct. 10, 1912; s. Charles Vinton and Grace Virginia (Deam) K.; A.B., Western Res. U., 1934, student Law Sch., 1923-35; m. Ruth Mann, Oct. 27, 1934; children—Susan Deborah, Geoffrey Mann. Supr. labor relations Swift & Co., Cleve., 1936-40; dir. indsl. relations Fisher Body div. Gen. Motors Corp., Cleve., 1940-43, Flint, Mich., 1946; dir. indsl. relations Inland Container Corp., Indpls., 1946-49, Kansas City Power & Light Co. (Mo.), 1949-56, Theodore Hamm Brewing Co., St. Paul, 1956-58; v.p. indsl. and pub. relations Rexall Drug & Chem. Co., Los Angeles, 1954-64; asso. Heidrick & Struggles Co., Los Angeles, 1964-66; pres. Robert L. King & Associates, 1966-67. Served to lt. comdr. USNR, 1943-46. Clubs: Midday (Cleve.); Union League (Chgo.); Indpls. Athletic; Kansas City (Mo.); St. Paul Athletic; Santa Monica CA Died Nov. 6, 1967.

KING, THOMAS LUTHER, chem. co. exec.; b. Wadley, Ala., May 4, 1908; s. John Thomas and Ida Bell (Murphy) K.; B.S., Emory U., 1929; M.S., U. N.C., 1930, Ph.D., 1932; m. Frances Elizabeth Carraway, Aug. 28, 1943; 1 son, Frederick Richard. Research chemist So. Dyeing Co., 1932, Ideal Mercerizing Co., 1933, chemist Merck & Co., Rahway, N.J., 1929, 33-36, lab. supr., 1937-47, mgr. quality standards, 1948-53, mgr. plant control operations, 1954-64, asst. dir. quality control, 1964-69; pres. Merck Rahway Credit Union, 1939-46, treas., 1947-49. Chmn., Readington Twp. Indsl. Commn., 1961-63; pres. Am. Cheviot Sheep Soc., 1954-56, dir., 1957-66, v.p., 1967, adv. mgr., 1952-63. Trustee Hunterdon County (N.J.) Heart Assn., treas., 1967-69. Mem. White House (N.J.) C. of C. (dir. 1959-63, pub. relations mgr. 1960-63), Am. Soc. Testing and Materials (chmn. filtering materials subcom. 1949-69), Instrument Soc. Am., Sigma Xi, Alpha Chi Sigma. Co-inventor cruciform lab., table; inventor apparatus for measurement of powder flowability. Author: (with Joseph Rosin) Reagent Chemicals and Standards, 1937. Home: White NJ Died Mar. 15, 1969.

KING, WILLIAM REYNOLDS, banker; b. Union Point, Ga., Jan. 3, 1869; s. Ulysses Baldwin and Clifford Celeste (Swinney) K.; student U. of Ga., 1 yr.; m. Elfrieda Wangemann, of Schulenburg, Tex., Jan. 29, 1902. On S.P.R.R., New Orleans to El Paso, Tex., 1899-1900; mgr. San Antonio office of Burwell, King & Co., brokers, 1904-07; elected v.p. City Nat. Bank, San Antonio, 1907, and assisted, 1921, in merger of City Nat. Bank, State Nat. Bank and Central Trust Co.; now pres. City Nat. Bank; also pres. Melvine Land & Irrigation Co. Democrat. Presbyn. Mason (K.T., 32 deg.). Clubs: Alamo, San Antonio Country. Office: City National Bank, San Antonio TX‡

KINGDON, FRANK, columnist, author, lecturer; b. London, England, Feb. 27, 1894; s. John and Matilda (Caunt) K.; A.B., Boston U., 1920; grad. work Harvard, 1920-21, Mich. State Coll., 1926; D.D., Albion (Mich.) Coll., 1927; LL.D., Ohio Northern U., 1931; married Gertrude Littlefield, February 27, 1915; children—John Gilmore, Frank Oliver, David Chariton, Gertrude Matilda, Barrie Knight; m. 2d, Marcella Markham, November 29, 1946; 1 son, Tom. Came to United States, 1912, naturalized, 1918. Ordained Methodist ministry, 1912; member E. Me. Conference, 1912-16, New England Southern Conference, 1916-20, New Eng. Conf., 1920-23, Mich. Conf., 1923-28, Newark Conf., from 1928; pres. Dana Coll., Newark, N.J., 1934-35; pres., U. of Newark, 1936-40. Campaign chmn. Newark Community Chest, 1935, 36, 37; pres. Welfare Fedn., Newark, N.J., 1937-39; chmn. Internat. Rescue and Relief Com.; chmn. N.Y. Chapter Com. to Defend America by Aiding the Allies; chmn. Fight for Freedom Com., 1940-41; spl. asst. to chmn. War Manpower Commn., chmn. War Prodn. Bd.; mem. Civilian Defense Bd. Mem. Phi Beta Kappa. Pi Lambda Phi medal, 1939; Page One Award, N.Y. Newspaper Guild, 1945; King Christian Medal by Danish Govt., 1946. Clubs: Town Hall, Harvard. Author: Humane Religion, 1930; When Half-Gods Go, 1933; Life of John Cotton Dana, 1940; 1776, and Today, 1941; Our Second War of Independence, 1942; Jacob's Ladder, 1943; That Man in the White House, 1944; An Uncommon Man: Or, Henry Wallace and 60 Million Jobs, 1945. Contbr. to Freedom (a symposium), 1940; Architects of the Republic, As FDR Said, 1950. Contributor articles, verse. News analyst. Home: New York City NY Died Feb. 24, 1972.

KINGMAN, A(LICE) SALOME (MRS. WYATT KINGMAN), writer; b. Toledo, Mar. 11, 1895; d. Ernest and Alice Lee (Kloffenstein) Baur; student Davis Bus. Coll., Toledo, summer 1914, Toledo U., 1920-23, San Jose State Coll., 1929-34; m. Carl Holliday, Dec. 21, 1921 (dec. Aug. 1936); 1 son, George Hayes; m. 2d, Wyatt Kingman, Apr. 14, 1945. Sec., Baur Land Co. Baur Collection Agy., Toledo, 1914-21; typist manuscripts for Dr. Carl Holliday, 1921-36; took dictation for Mrs. Fremont Older, Saratoga, Cal., 1933-38; with Housing Project, San Jose, Cal., 1941-43; writer book revs. San Dieguito Citizen, Solana Beach, Cal., Cardiff (Cal.) Star-News, San Luis Rey Bull., Oceanside, Cal.; librarian San Luis Rey Homes; cons. various authors, 1950-70; writer column book revs. Del Mar (Cal.) Surfcomber. Chmn. press, publicity, historian Palomar Handweavers Guild, North San Diego County, 1952-70; v.p. Santa Clara County P.T.A., 1931-32. Mem. P.E.O. (publicity, press chmn.), Nat. League Am. Pen Women (rec. sec., corr. sec., editor Yearbook, press chmn.). Address: San Luis Rey CA Died Mar. 23, 1970.

KINGMAN, HENRY SELDEN, banker; b. Mpls., Dec. 25, 1893; s. Joseph R. and Mabel (Selden) K.; B.A., Amherst Coll., 1915; student sch. bus. administrn., Harvard, 1915-16; m. Josephine M. Woodward, June 4, 1921 (dec. Aug. 1968); children—Henry Selden, Woodward, Helen W. (Mrs. David R. West, Jr.). Dist. sales mgr. Russell Miller Milling Co., Mpls., 1919-26; sec. Farmer's & Mechanics Savs. Bank, Mpls., 1926-32, treas., 1932-39, pres., 1939-57, chairman bd., 1957-68, also trustee; trustee Mut. Life Ins. Co. N.Y.; dir. Gen. Mills, Inc., 1946-66, Soo Line R.R. Trustee Dunwoody Indsl. Inst., Mpls., Amherst Coll.; vice chmn. Internat. Thrift Inst., Netherlands, 1950-60; trustee, pres. Gen. Mills Found., 1954-66; trustee Mpls. Found.; trustee, v.p. Minn. Community Research Council. Mem. Nat. Assn. Mut. Savs. Banks (pres. 1949), Am. Bankers Assn. (pres. savs. div. 1934). Clubs: Minneapolis; Woodhill Country; Am. Alpine; Alpine of Can.; Alpine of London. Home: Wayzata MN Died Dec. 12, 1968.

KINGSFORD, JOAN ELIZABETH,, indsl. editor; b. Meriden, Conn., Feb. 1, 1930; d. Allen R. and Florence (Weisgraber) Kingsford; student pub. schs. Proofreader, Meriden (Conn.) Morning Record, 1947-49, soc. editor, 1949-60; asst. editor Beacon Bulletin, Travelers Ins. Co., Hartford, Conn., 1960-62, editor, 1962-71. Mem. Conn. Indsl. Editors Assn. (recording sec. 1962-63, bd. govs. 1963-64, treas. 1964-65, v.p. memberships 1965-66, v.p. programs 1966-67, pres. 1967-69). Home: Meriden CT Died Apr. 24, 1971.

KINGSLEY, BRUCE GORDON, organist, director; b. London, Eng., June 6, 1875; s. James Bruce and Louise K.; student Univ. Coll., London; Mus. B., Trinity Coll., Cambridge, Eng., 1898; unmarried. Came to America, 1902; lecturer for Bd. of Edn., New York, 1903-5; trans-continental recital tour, 1904; organist and mus. dir., Christ Ch., Rye, N.Y., 1906, Temple Auditorium, Los Angeles, 1906-8; mus. lecturer Ebell and Cosmos clubs, Los Angeles. Musical critic, Los Angeles Examiner; special contbr. to The Musician; European musical tours, 1910, 1911; Am. concert tour, 1913; organist and musical dir. First Presbyn. Ch., Seattle, 1913; spl. engagement for 35 organ recitals, Panama Expn., San Francisco, 1915; organist Trinity Auditorium, Los Angeles, since 1915. Mem. Los Angeles City Club. Pres. Cal. Anti-Vivisection Soc. Author: (glee) To America; (anthem) The Roseate Hues of Early Dawn; (songs) Hail to the Fleet; The Voices of Home Sweet Home; The Sweet Little Doll. Address: Trinity Auditorium, Los Angeles CA‡

KINGSLEY, HIRAM WEBSTER, merchandising exec.; b. Madison, Wis., Aug. 1, 1888; s. Hiram A. and Cora Belle (Webster) K.; A.B., Washburn Coll., 1911; married Eloise Sargent; children—Carol (Mrs. Hoyt S. Pardee), Robert Sargent. Timekeeper, assistant superintendent, asphalt chemist, Kaw Paving Co., Topeka, Kan., 1911-13; with Sears Roebuck and Co. 1913-49, became mgr. billing dept., Chicago mail order plant, 1920, asst. to operating supt. Philadelphia mail order, 1920-25, operating supt. Kansas City mail order, 1925-28, operating supt. Phila. mail order, 1928, dist. mgr. eastern retail stores, 1929, territorial officer Pacific Coast, 1930-31, dist. mgr. Middle West retail stores, 1932-33, gen. mgr. Los Angeles mail order, 1934-42, regional mgr. Pacific Coast territory, 1942-45, vice pres. in charge Pacific Coast territory, 1945-49. Served with U.S. Navy, 1918. Mason (Shriner), Kiwanian. Clubs: Los Angeles Country, Jonathan (Los Angeles). Home: Los Angeles CA Died Mar. 10, 1971.

KINKAID, THOMAS CASSIN, naval officer; b. Hanover, N.H., Apr. 3, 1888; s. Thomas Wright and Virginia Lee (Cassin) K.; grad. U.S. Naval Academy, 1908; m. Helen Sherburne Ross, Apr. 25, 1911. Promoted through grades to admiral. Tech. advisor to Am. del., Gen. Disarmament Conf., Geneva, Switzerland, Jan.-July 1932; naval attache Am. Embassy, Rome (Italy), Nov. 1938-Mar. 1941; additional duty naval attache Belgrade, Yugoslavia, 1939-41; promoted rear adm., 1941; now adm.; comd. cruiser group action off Bougainville, Feb. 20, 1942; Salamaua-Lae raid, Mar. 10, 1942; Battle of Coral Sea, May 4-8, 1942; Battle of Midway, June 3-6, 1942; comd. Enterprise carrier group, Guadalcanal-Tulagi landings, Aug. 7-9, 1942; battle of Eastern Solomons, Aug. 25, 1942, Santa Cruz Islands, Oct. 26, 1942; Guadalcanal, Nov. 15, 1942; comdr. North Pacific Force in Aleutian campaign, Jan.-Oct. 1943; promoted vice adm., June 1943; comdr. 7th Fleet, and comdr. Allied Naval Forces, Southwest Pacific Area, Nov. 1943-Sept. 1945, New Guinea and Philippine campaigns, including battle for Leyte Gulf, Oct. 25, 1944; promoted admiral, Apr. 1945; landed 24th Corps in Korea, Sept. 1945, and with Lt. Gen. Hodge, took surrender of Japanese Army and Navy in Seoul; landed Am. Marines under Maj. Gen. Rockay at Taku and at Tsingtao, China; transported 5 Chinese armies from Haiphong, Kowloon and Ningpo, landed them at Formosa, Chingwantao and Tsingtao; detached 7th Fleet Nov. 19, 1945; took comd. Eastern Sea Frontier and Atlantic Res., Jan. 16, 1946; retired from active duty May 1, 1950. Vice chmn. Am. Battle Monuments Commn. Mem. Nat. Security Training Commn. Decorations; Navy D.S.M. with 3 gold stars, Army Legion of Merit, Army D.S.M. Presidential Citation, Victory Medal, Atlantic Clasp, American Defense Service Medal, Asiatic-Pacific Campaign Medal (10 battle stars), W.W. II Victory Medal; Companion Order of the Bath (British); Grand Officer Order Orange Nassau with Swords (Netherlands); Order Al Merito, Gran Official (Chilean); Grand Officer Order of Leopold with Palm, Croix de Guerre with Palm (Belgian). Mem. Soc. Cincinnatus in State N.H. Clubs: Chevy Chase, Army-Navy, Aibi (Washington), Union (N.Y.). Home: Washington DC Died Nov. 17, 1972; buried Arlington Nat. Cemetery, Arlington VA

KINKEAD, ELIZABETH SHELBY, lecturer on English literature since 1897; b. Fayette Co., Ky.; d. Judge William Bury and Elizabeth de la Fontaine (Shelby) K.; sister of Eleanor Talbot K. (q.v.); ed. State Coll. of Ky., and by her father, a classical scholar; unmarried. Lecturer at Ky. Chautauqua, 1898-9, and at Chautauqua, N.Y., 1900; lecturer on English lit., State Coll., Ky., since 1903. Author: A History of Kentucky, 1896. Address: 423 2d St., Lexington KY‡

KINNARD, LEONARD HUMMEL, telephone official; b. Harrisburg, Pa., Sept. 5, 1869; s. Leonard Hervey and Mary Elizabeth (Hummel) K.; ed. high sch. and business coll.; m. Sarah Elizabeth Peters, Apr. 4, 1893; 1 son, Leonard Richard. Mgr. Pa. Telephone Co. (Bell), Carlisle, Lancaster and Harrisburg, 1891-96; div. supt., Harrisburg, 1896-1902, gen. supt., 1902, gen. mgr., 1902-07; at Phila. with Bell Telephone Co. of Pa. and asso. cos. since 1907, becoming pres., 1919, chmn. bd., 1933-34; retired; dir. Bell Telephone Co., Pa. Co. for Ins. of Lives and Granting Annuities, Pa. Salt Mfg. Co., Barber Oil Corp., Pennsylvania Fire Ins. Co. Mem. Phila. Com. on Nat. Defense Advisory Com. on Purchase of Army Supplies, World War I. Mem. Phila. Telephone Pioneers of America (pres. 1924). Guild of Brackett Lecturers (Princeton Univ.), Newcomen Soc., (life) Franklin Inst. Democrat. Lutheran. Mason. Club: Rittenhouse. Home: Wister Rd., Wynnewood, Montgomery County PA‡

KINNEY, ANSEL MCBRYDE, mfg. exec.; b. Honolulu, Hawaii, Feb. 1, 1898; s. William Ansel and Alice Vaughan (McBryde) K.; A.B., Harvard, 1920, A.M., 1921, Ph.D., 1923; m. Elinor Woodward, Apr. 28, 1928; children—Douglas McBryde, Barbara Woodward, Joan Woodward. Sales engr. Standard Oil Co., 1923-30; sales engr. Internat. Register Co., 1930-37, dir., 1930-69, v.p., 1937-52, pres., 1952-63, chairman of the bd., 1963-69; senior vice president, director Coral Research & Development Co., Miami, Fla. Mem. bd. dirs. Chgo. Commons Assn. Served as pvt. C.W.S., U.S. Army, 1918. Clubs: University (Chgo.); Old Elm (Ft. Sheridan, Ill.); Onwentsia (Lake Forest, Ill.); Gulf Stream Golf (Delray Beach, Fla.). Home: Lake Forest IL Died Feb. 11, 1969; buried Rose Hill Cemetery, Chicago IL

KINNEY, HENRY WALSWORTH, writer; b. Wailuku, Territory of Hawaii; s. Henry A. and Selma S. (Schandorff) K.; M.A., U. of Copenhagen, 1897; post-grad. work in pedagogy, and English, U. of Calif., 1897-98; m. Helen Kalolawahilani, of Honolulu, T.H., Apr. 2, 1904 (dec.); m. 2d, Teru Hirose (painter), of Tokyo, Japan, 1924. Teacher, chemist, reporter, city editor Evening Bulletin of Honolulu; editor of Hilo Tribune, 1909-14; supt. pub. instrn. T.H., from May 1, 1914-Apr. 1, 1919; mng. editor The Trans-Pacific, Tokyo, Japan, 1919; corr. Phila. Pub. Ledger in Peking, 1925; with South Manchuria Railway Company, Dairen, 1925-35; attached to Japanese assessor with Lytton Commn. on Manchuria; with Japanese delegation at League of Nation's session on Manchurian question, 1932. Decorated Order of the Sacred Treasure (Japanese); Order for assistance in establishment of the Empire (Manchoukuo). Democrat. Clubs: University (Honolulu); Dairen Club; Mukden Club. Author: The Island of Hawaii, 1913; The Code of the Karstens, 1923; Broken Butterflies, 1924; Manchuria, 1927; Earthquake, 1928; Manchuria French Oceania‡

KINNEY, LUCIEN BLAIR, educator; b. Hudson, Wis., Jan. 15, 1895; s. Andrew J. and Susan (Pierce) K.; A.B., U. of Minn., 1923, Ph.D., 1931; m. Ida Ormsrud, June 3, 1922 (dec. Sept. 1967); m. 2d, Joye Sherwood Valentine, Dec. 1968; 1 stepdau., Joan S. Valentine. Staff bur. ednl. research, U. of Minn., 1931-32, instr. edn., 1931-37; head dept. mathematics and acting registrar Oswego (N.Y.) State Normal Sch., 1937-40; vis. prof. Colo. State Coll., Fort Collins, summer 1936, sch. edn., Syracuse U. spring 1940; asso. prof. Stanford U., 1940-45, prof. edn., 1945-64, prof. emeritus, 1964-71; vis. prof. U. Cal., 1964. Recipient achievement award U. Minn., 1960. Mem. Am. Ednl. Research Assn., Phi Delta Kappa. Author: High School Curriculum (with Harl Douglass et al.), 1964; (with Rubie and Brown) Holt General Mathematics, Vol I, 1965, Vol. II, 1967; (with Thomas and Coladarie) Perspective on Educaton, 1961; Certification in Education, 1963; (with Marks and Purdy) Teaching Elementary School Mathematics for Understanding, 1965, 70; (with Ruble and Brown) Problem Solving Mathematics, 1971; other math. textbooks. Home: Palo Alto CA Died Dec. 24, 1971.

KINNEY, MARGARET WEST, etcher and decorator; b. Peoria, Ill., June 11, 1872; d. John A. and Margaret (McMillan) West; grad. high school, Peoria, 1890; studied Art Students' League, New York, 1892-93, Julian Acad., Paris, 1893-97; pupil of Fleury, Lefebvre, Collin and Mercon; m. Troy Kinney, June 9, 1900; 1 son, John West. In collaboration with husband illustrations and designs for leading publs. and novels; decorations in Grand Opera House, Chicago; Hotel Baltimore, Kansas City; Ben Greet's production of Midsummer Night's Dream; etchings of heads of Apostles from Great Chalice of Antioch. Home: Wangum, Falls Village CT‡

KINSELL, LAURANCE WILKIE, physician; b. Landsdowne, Pa., Oct. 15, 1908; s. S. Tyson and Clementine Keyser (Lynd) K.; M.D., Hahnemann Medical Coll., Phila., 1932, D.Sc., 1965; D.Sc., Blackburn College, 1960; m. Martha L. Williams, September 15, 1934; children—Laura Anne, Judith Scott, Martha Lynd. Intern, resident, grad. work Hahnemann Hosp., Phila., and instns. affiliated with Columbia U., 1932-35; clin. medicine, 1935-39; research fellow Columbia U., 1939-40; research fellow (med. and pharmacology), Harvard U. and Mass. Gen. Hosp., 1941-43; research asso., U. of Cal., 1943-44; United States Navy, 1944-46; consultant in medicine and endocrinology U. Cal. and other hosps. since 1946; asso. clin. prof. medicine U. Cal. Med. Sch., San Francisco, 1948-50; dir. Inst. for Metablolic Research of Highland General Hosp., Oakland, since 1950. Diplomate Am. Bd. Internal Medicine. Fellow A.C.P.; mem. A.M.A., Cal., Alameda Co. medical assns., Endocrine Soc., Am. Diabetes Assn., Am. Fedn. Clin. Research, Western Soc. Clin. Research. Soc. Exptl. Biology and Medicine, Am. Soc. Clin. Nutrition, Am. Inst. Nutrition, Western Assn. Physicians, Alpha Omega Alpha. Asso. editor American Jour. Clin. Nutrition, Metabolism, Excerpta Medica; editor Hormonal Regulations of Energy Metabolism, 1956; Cardiovascular diseases. Author papers and chpts. on endocrinology and metabolism. Home: Oakland CA Died July 9, 1968; buried Mountain View Cemetery, Oakland CA

KINSELLA, THOMAS JAMES, physician; b. Grand Meadow, Minn., Oct. 9, 1895; s. William Dennis and Anne (Grimes) K.; student Mont. State Coll.; M.D., U. Minn., 1920; m. Sara Monahan, Jan. 28, 1924. Intern, Mpls. Gen. Hosp., 1919-20, later attending thoracic surgeon; fellow in medicine Mayo Found., Rochester, Minn., 1920-22; asst. med. dir. Glen Lake Sanatorium, 1925-28, head, dir. thoracic surgery, 1928-36, cons. thoracic surgeon, 1936-69; practice medicine specializing in thoracic surgery, 1936-65; clin. prof. surgery U. Minn., 1949-64, prof. emeritus, 1965-69; sr. cons. thoracic surgery VA Facility, Ft. Snelling, N.D. State Sanatorium; surgeon Minn. State Sanatorium; surg. staff St. Mary's, Abbott, Northwestern hosps.; cons. staff Mt. Sinai Hosp. Diplomate Am. Bd. Thoracic Surgery (founder). Fellow A.C.S., Internat. Coll. Surgeons; mem. A.M.A., Western Surg. Assn., Am. Assn. Thoracic Surgery, Am. Coll. Chest Physicians, Am. Thoracic Soc., Nat. Tb Assn., Alpha Omega Alpha. Author: Tumors of the Chest. Contbr. numerous articles to med. jours. Pioneer non-Tb chest conditions. Home: Minneapolis MN Died Nov. 12, 1969; buried Resurrection Cemetery, Minneapolis MN

KINSEY, JOHN DE COU, ret. sales exec.; b. Chicago, Jan. 7, 1895; s. Edmund B. and Evalyn (Bennett) K.; attended Lewis Inst., Chicago, 1915-18; m. Constance Lumbard, Oct. 1, 1927; children—Katharine C. (Mrs. Mark H Baxter), John DeCou. Asst. to superintendent Weller Mfg. Company, Chicago, 1919-21, sales engr., 1921-27; dist. mgr., Cleveland Worm & Gear Co., Cleveland, 1927-45; sales exec. and partner Ehret & Kinsey, (representing C.W. & G. and Farval divisions Eaton Manufacturing Company, Cleve., Mechanical Power Transmission Div. Zurn Industries, Inc., Erie, Pa., Lubrication Products Co., Cleve., Chgo., 1945-64; dir. Vulcan Iron Works Fla., West Palm Beach; dir. Vulcan Iron Works, Chattanooga, Tenn. Registered Profl. Engr., Ill. Mem. Western Soc. Engrs., Assn. Iron and Steel Engrs., Am. Soc. Tool Engrs., Am. Soc. Lubrication Engrs. Episcopalian. Clubs: Chicago Yacht, Chicago Athletic Assn., Mackinac Island Yacht. Home: Evanston IL Died Dec. 16, 1967.

KINSLER, JAMES C., lawyer; b. Quincy, Ill., Mar. 17, 1869; s. James T., M.D., and Mary J. (Callan) K.; A.B., Creighton Coll., Omaha, 1891; LL.B., Harvard, 1898; m. Ada Mistrot, of Galveston, Tex., Dec. 20, 1905; children—Mary Jane, James Mistrot, Margaret Ann. Practiced at Omaha since 1898; U.S. atty., Dist. of Neb., 1921-30. Mem. Am., Neb. State and Douglas Co. (Omaha) bar associations. Home: 131 N. 32d Av., Omaha NE‡

KINSLEY, CARL, elec. engr., physicist; b. Lansing, Mich., Nov. 25, 1870; s. William Wirt and Mary (Jewell) K.; A.B., Oberlin, 1893, A.M., 1896; M.E., Cornell U., 1894; scholar, Johns Hopkins, 1898-99; student Cavendish Lab., Cambridge, Eng., 1905; m. Harriet Buchly, June 1, 1901 (died Oct. 19, 1910); m. 2d, Prudence Ellis, June 7, 1913; children—Colony, Stephanie, Penelope, and Roger (dec.). Instr. in physics and elec. engring., Washington U., 1894-99; elec. expert for War Dept., 1899-1901; fellow in physics, 1901, instr., 1902, asst. prof., 1903, asso. prof., 1909-19, U. of Chicago. Served in U.S. Army, as maj. Signal Corps, Dec. 1917-Aug. 1919; detailed to Gen. Staff and made chief of Sect. 10 of Mil. Intelligence Division, for radio, telegraph and telephone operations; cons. engr. elec. research and development since 1919. Republican. Congregationalist. Fellow A.A.A.S., Am. Physical Soc., Am. Inst. Elec. Engrs.; mem. Am. Soc. Testing Materials, Sigma Xi. Club: Cosmos (Washington). Has invented methods and apparatus of printing telegraph systems, storage batteries, radio circuits and method for non-destructive testing of steel. Contbr. engring. jours. and scientific mags. on radio, telegraphy, alternating currents, testing of steel, etc. Address: Box 905, Falls Church, Va., and Cosmos Club, Washington DC‡

KINSMAN, WILLIAM A(BBOT), company exec.; born Salem, Mass., Oct. 17, 1877; s. William Low and Sarah Augusta (Nichols) K.; B.S., Mass. Inst. Tech., 1899; m. Edith Corey, Dec. 19, 1914. Joined Towle Mfg. Co., Newburyport, Mass., 1914, gen. mgr., 1914-47, pres., 1928-50, chmn. bd. since 1950; v.p., trustee Five Cents Savs. Bank. Treas. Mosley Fund for Social Service in Newburyport; director Newburyport Health Center (president 1924-50). Member exec. com. Asso. Industries of Mass. since 1930. Home: 348 High St. Office: 260 Merrimack St., Newburyport MA‡

KINTNER, EDWIN G., naval officer; b. Harrison County, Ind., May 5, 1881; s. James P. and Anna (Montgomery) K.; U.S. Naval Acad., 1898-1902; M.S., Mass. Inst. Tech., 1908; m. Susie Grice, Sept. 6, 1906 (dec.); children—Edwin G., James G., Susan B. Entered U.S. Navy, 1898; advanced to capt., 1925; served on Olympia, Marietta, Prairie, and Atlanta, 1902-05; Norfolk Navy Yard, 1908-11; inspector, Phila., 1911-15; Norfolk, 1915-1919; Panama, 1919-21; Portsmouth, 1921-23; Camden, 1923-28; Navy Dept., 1928-32; mgr. Norfolk Naval Shipbldg. Yard, 1932-36; Navy Dept. 1936-46. Sr. mem. Compensation Bd., U.S. Navy. Mem. Soc. Naval Architects. Home: Washington DC Died Feb. 5, 1971; buried Arlington Nat. Cemetery, Arlington VA

KIOKEMEISTER, FRED LUDWIG, mathematician, educator; b. Chgo., May 5, 1913; s. Bernhard and Marian (MacMillan) K.; B.A., U. Wis., 1935, M.A., 1937, Ph.D., 1940; m. Evelyn Elizabeth Sharp, Aug. 25, 1940;children—Karen, Elizabeth Ann. Instr. U. Wis., 1940-42, Cornell U., 1942-43, Purdue U., 1943-46; asst. prof. Mt. Holyoke Coll., 1946-48, asso. prof. 1948-56, John Stewart Kennedy Found. prof., 1956-69. Univ. of Wis. fellow, 1938-39, Ford Found. fellow, 1951-52. Mem. Math. Assn. Am., Am. Math. Soc., Sigma Xi, Phi Beta Kappa. author: (with R. E. Johnson) Calculus with Analytic Geometry, 1957, Calculus, 1959. Home: South Hadley MA Died May 26, 1969; buried Walworth WI

KIRBY, WILLIAM GERARD, bus. counselors; b. Grand Haven, Mich., June 20, 1916; s. Edward P. and Ruth (Harrison) K.; student Assumption Coll., Winsdor, Ont., 1930-32, in Real Estate, Marquette U., 1941; m. Marion Simmons, Feb. 25, 1939 (div.); children—Diane, Joan, William G., Thomas S. Sec.-treas. Kirby Investment Co., 1943-45; pres. Eastern Cabinet Works, Detroit, 1945-60; pres. Archtl. Spltys., Inc., Detroit 1955-69; partner Fintermann, Kirby & Co., 1962-69, Detroit. Mem. Grosse Pointe Farms (Mich.) city council, 1944-69; mem. bd. suprs. Wayne County, 1950-54. Pres. Mich. Municipal League, 1962-63. Vice chmn bd. County Instns., Wayne County, 1954-61. Recipient Service awards Wayne County Bd. Instns., 1961, Mich. Municipal League, 1963. Roman Catholic. Club: Athelstan. Home: Grosse Pointe Farms MI Died Aug. 4, 1969.

KIRK, DOLLY WILLIAMS, teacher; b. Tuscaloosa, Ala.; d. George Hamilton and Julia Anne (Owen) K.; ed. pub. schs.; grad. New Orleans High Sch. Teacher in Montgomery (Ala.) High Sch., since 1894; winner, with a Shakespearian paper, ann. prize of Ala. State Federation Women's Clubs, 1903; contb'r of poems and stories to mags. Mem. D. A. R. Club: Tintagil Literary. Author: (with Frances Nimmo Greene) With Spurs of Gold, 1905 L6. Address: 216 S. Court St., Montgomery AL‡

KIRK, LESTER KING, ins. exec.; b. Garnett, Kan., May 1, 1899; s. Paul H. and Frances (Myers) K.; A.B., Carleton Coll., 1922; student Harvard, 1924-25; m. Lucille Barnard, Aug. 19, 1926 (dec. 1962); 1 son, Paul; m. 2d, Edith Cobae, Mar. 21, 1964. High sch. tchr., Walnut Grove, Minn., 1922-23; tchr. State Tchrs. Coll., Winona, Minn., 1923-24; prof. U. Detroit, 1925-29; with Standard Accident Ins. Co., Detroit, 1929-64, treas., 1932-42, v.p., treas., 1942-54, pres., 1954-63, chairman of the board of directors, 1963-64, past dir.; chmn., dir. Pilot Ins. Co., Toronto, Canada; dir. Reliance Ins. Co. Phila. Dir. Mich., Wayne County Tb assns. Trustee Detroit Tb Sanitarium, chmn. bd. trustees Olivet Coll. Mem. Mich. Crime and Delinquency Council, Am. Econ. Assn., Am. Statis. Assn., Beta Gamma Sigma (hon.). Club: Detroit. Home: Detroit MI Died Nov. 18, 1970.

KIRKHAM, WILLIAM BARRI, biologist; b. at Springfield, Mass., Feb. 11, 1882; s. James Wilson and Fanny Curtis (Barri) K.; B.A., Yale, 1904, M.A., 1906, Ph.D. 1907; studied Harvard, 1904-05; m. Irma Chapman, June 25, 1910; 1 dau., Marguerite. Archaeol. trip around the world, 1907-08; instr. biology, Sheffield Scientific Sch. (Yale), 1908-16; asst. prof. biology, same, 1916-20; prof. biology, Internat. Y.M.C.A. Coll., Springfield, Mass., 1921-30, also dean freshmen until 1930; cons. dir. Museum Natural History, Springfield, from 1930; v.p. Springfield Library and Mus. Assn., 1934-41, and from 1959, pres., 1941-59. Dir. Springfield Safe Deposit & Trust Co. from 1938. President Oak Grove Cemetery Assn., 1947-51 Lectr. on scientific subjects. Recipient Pynchon medal, Springfield Advt. Club, 1958. Mem. Am. Assn. for the Advancement of Sci., American Assn. Anatomists, Am. Soc. Zoologists, Am. Anthrop. Assn., New York Zool. Soc., Sigma Xi. Beta Theta Pi. Republican. Conglist. Author: You and I and the Universe, 1948. Contbr. result of researches on embryonic development of mice. Home: Springfield MA Died May 14, 1969.

KIRKPATRICK, CLIFFORD, univ. prof.; b. Fitchburg, Mass., Oct. 22, 1898; s. Edwin Asbury and Florence May (Clifford) K.; A.B., Clark Coll., 1920; A.M., Clark U., 1922; Ph.D., U. of Pa., 1925; m. Doris Katherine Upton, June 8, 1927; 1 dau., Judith K.; m. 2d, Marjorie Dietz, June 30, 1939 (dec. May 14, 1957); children—Meredith Kay, Laird Clifford; m. 3d, Mazelle Van Cleave, Apr. 24, 1959. Instr. Andover Academy, 1920-21; fellow and assistant in sociology, Clark U., 1922-23; instr. sociology, Brown U., 1923-24; Harrison fellow, U. of Pa., 1924-25, asst. prof., 1926-30; asso. prof. sociology, U. of Minn., 1930-35, Indiana Univ., 1949-53, professor of sociology, 1953-71. Guggenheim research fellow in Germany, 1936-37. Private A.U.S. Ambulance Service, World War I. Team research dir. U.S. strategic Bombing Survey, Germany, 1945.

Decorated D.S.C., 1918; recipient of the E. W. Burgess award for 1965. Pres. Ohio Valley Sociol. Soc., 1959; mem. Am. Association of Marriage Counselors, Sociological Research Assn., Am. Sociol. Assn. Club: Faculty. Author: Capital Punishment, 1925; Intelligence and Immigration, 1926; Religion in Human Affairs, 1929; Nazi Germany—Its Women and Family Life, 1938; What Science Says About Happiness in Marriage, 1947; The Family as Process and Institution, 1955, rev. 1963; report of Research into Attitudes and Habits of Radio Listeners, 1933. Contbr. to Statistics in Social Studies, 1930; 10 chapters in Man and His World, 1932; articles to Am. Jour. Sociology, Social Forces, Human Biology, Jour. Abnormal Social Psychology Am. Sociol. Review, and other scientific jours. Home: Bloomington IN Died Jan. 11, 1971.

KIRKPATRICK, GEORGE HOLLAND, physician; b. South Thomaston, Me., Dec. 20, 1880; s. George and Emma (Bartlett) K.; student U. of Vt., 1897-98, M.D., 1906; m. Mary Lovejoy, July 30, 1923; 1 step-son, Herbert V. Olds. Intern, Lynn Hosp., 1906, house officer, 1906-07; out-patient surgeon, 1907-15, asst. vis. surgeon, 1915-25, vis. surgeon, 1925-1938, former president of visiting staff, honorary staff since 1938. Served as capt., med. corps 104th inf., 26th Division. U.S. Army, World War I. Decorated Silver Star medal. Mem. bd. governors Lynn Home for Aged Women. Mem. Lynn and Mass. State med. socs., Am. Med. Assn., Lynn Hist. Soc., S.A.R., Am. Legion, Yankee Div. Vets. Orgn., Mass. Audubon Soc. Episcopalian. (vestryman, St. Stephen's Church, Lynn, 20 yrs.). Mason. Clubs: Eastern Yacht (Marblehead, Mass.); Whiting, Harvard (Lynn). Address: Lynn MA Died Aug. 23, 1968.

KIRKPATRICK, SIDNEY DALE, chem. engr., cons.; born Urbana, Ill., Apr. 2, 1894; s. Frederick Dilling and Virginia Mae (Hedges) K.; B.S., U. of Ill., 1916, grad. study, 1916-17; Sc.D., Clarkson Coll. of Tech., 1946; D. Engring., Polytechnic Institute, Brooklyn, 1948; m. Bonnie Jean Hardesty, Aug. 6, 1919; children—Mary (Mrs. A. H. Gable), S. Dale, Chemist and editor Ill. State Water Survey, 1916-17; chem. adviser U.S. Tariff Commn., 1917-18, spl. expert with same, 1919-21; with McGraw-Hill Pub. Co., N.Y.C., 1921-59, as asst. editor Chemical & Metall. Engineering (mag.), 1921-25, asso. editor, 1925-28, editor, 1928-50; editorial dir. Chem. Engring. and Chemical Week, 1950-59; v.p., McGraw-Hill Book Co., ret. 1959; director General Aniline & Film Corp., Mich. Chem. Corp., 1960-61, Carus Chem. Co., Roger Williams Tech. & Econ. Services, Inc.; cons. engr., 1959-73. Served as 2d lt. and 1st lt. S.C., A.E.F., 1918-19; chem. advisor Am. Commn. to Negotiate Peace, 1919; mem. referee bd., Office of Prodn. Research and Development, War Prodn. Bd., 1942-45; cons. on engring., W.M.C., 1942-45; member advisory bd. U.S. C.W.S., 1935-62; consultant on research to U.S.Q.M.C., 1943-45, to tech. indsl. intelligence com. investigating Germany, 1945, to sec. of war, Operations Crossroads, Bikini, 1946; consultant U.S. Atomic Energy Commission, 1950-55; chmn. AEC, adv. com. on information for industry, 1950-55, Recipient Founders award, Am. Inst. Chem. Engrs., 1958; Meml. award, Chem. Market Research Assn., 1959, Fellow Am. Institute Chemists, 1949, hon. member, 1952; mem. Am. Inst. Chem. Engrs. (dir. 1932-39, 1946-49; v.p. 1940-41; pres. 1942), Am. Electrochem. Soc. (dir. 1933-35; v.p. 1931-35; pres. 1944-45), Am. Chem. Soc. (councillor), Society Chemical Industry Great Britain (dir. 1942-44; chmn. 1946-47), A.A.A.S., Am. Soc. Engring. Edn., Sigma Xi, Phi Lambda Upsilon, Alpha Chi Sigma, Sigma Delta Chi, Pi Delta Epsilon, Omega Chi Epsilon, Theta Delta Chi. Awarded silver anniversary medal American Institute Chemical Engineers, 1932; Chemical Industry medalist, 1945. Republican. Methodist. Clubs: Chemists (trustee), Western Universities. Editor: Twenty Five Years of Chemical Engineering Progress. 1933. Co-editor: Perry's Chemical Engineers' Handbook, 1963; cons. editor Chem. Engring. series (36 titles). Contbr. to Chem. Engring. Address: Short Hills NJ Died Feb. 1973.

KIRKPATRICK, WILLIAM HUNTINGTON, judge; b. Easton, Pa., Oct. 2, 1885; s. of Hon. William S. (former atty. gen. of Pa.) and Elizabeth H. (Jones) K.; A.B., Lafayette Coll., 1905, LL.D., 1944; student law dept., U. of Pa., 1905-06, LL.M., 1937; m. Mary Stewart Wells, May 17, 1913; children—William S., Miles. Admitted to Pa. bar, 1908; mem. 67th Congress (1921-23), 26th Pa. Dist.; U.S. dist. judge for Eastern District of Pa., 1927-58, sr. dist. judge, 1958-70. Trustee Lafayette Coll. Lt. col. Judge Adv. Gen.'s Dept., and mem. Bd. of Review of Courts Martial. World War. Republican. Presbyn. Home: Harwood MD Died Nov. 28, 1970.

KIRKWOOD, ARTHUR CARTER, cons. engr.; b. Colorado Springs, Colo., June 17, 1900; s. Thomas Carter and Lillie Marie (Gard) K.; A.B. in Mech. Engring., Stanford U., 1923; M.S. in Elec. Engring., Mass. Inst. Tech., 1924; m. Frances Noble Tucker, June 20, 1925; children—Thomas C., Beverley John, Ann Marie (dec.), Jr. engr., field engr., Wood & Weber, Cons. Engrs., Denver, 1924-29; asso. engr., Burns & McDonnell Engring. Co., Cons. Engrs., Kansas City, Mo., 1930-40, prin. engr., 1940-47; founder, A.C. Kirkwood & Assos., Cons. Engrs., 1947, sr. partner 1951-70, pres., dir. Kirkwood Assos., Inc., Con. Engrs., 1955-70. Bd. Govs., adv. com. Kansas City Citizen's Assn., 1945-70; chmn. Mo. Adv. Com. for Sci. Engring. & Specialized Personnel of Selective Service System, 1955-70. Mem. adv. bd. Kansas City council Boy Scouts Am. Registered profl. engr., Kan., Mo., Colo., Okla., Ark., Ill., Mich., Ore. Mem. I.E.E.E. (life mem.), Engrs. Club Kansas City (pres. 1939, life mem.), Kan. Engring. Soc., Am. Soc. M.E. (life), Am. Inst. Cons. Engrs., Nat. (nat. dir. 1954-57, chmn. bd. Ethical Rev. 1965-66, v.p. 1966-70), Mo. (pres. 1956) socs. profl. engrs., Am. Water Works Assn., Nat. Assn. Housing and Redevel. Ofcls. Rotarian. Home: Kansas City MO Died Oct. 5, 1970; buried Kansas City MO

KIRSTEIN, MAX, corp. exec.; b. Poland, 1897. Chmn. Seagrace Corp., Irving Tanning Co. Home: Swampscott MA Died June 2, 1969.*

KIRTLAND, FRED DURRELL, naval officer; b. Salina, Kan., Nov. 6, 1892; s. Charles Byron and Elizabeth (Dohmyer) K.; S.B., U.S. Naval Acad., 1916; B.S., Columbia, 1922; m. Mary Adikes, Sept. 14, 1921; 1 son, Robert A. Commd. ensign U.S. Navy, 1916, and advanced through grades to rear adm., 1943; served on U.S.S. Wyoming and Brit. Grand Fleet, 1917-18; sea service in battleships, cruisers, destroyers and shore duties, 1919-39; comdg. officer and div. comdr., destroyers, N. Atlantic neutrality patrol, 1939-40; squadron comdr., Atlantic convoy and anti-submarine duty, 1941-42; comdr. U.S.S. Ala., with Brit. Home Fleet, 1943, S. and Central Pacific to Japan, 1943-44; comdt., Naval Operating Base, Okinawa, 1945-46; comdr. Amphibious Training Command, U.S. Atlantic Fleet, with hdqrs. at Little Creek, Va., from 1946. Awarded Legion of Merit, commendation ribbon. Presbyterian. Clubs: Army Navy Country (Washington), Manhasset Bay Yacht (L.I., N.Y.). Home: New Cambria KS Died Oct. 1972.

KIRWAN, ALBERT DENNIS, educator; born Louisville, Dec. 22, 1904; s. Martin John and Margaret (O'Sullivan) K.; A.B., U. Ky., 1926; LL.B., U. Louisville, 1929, M.A., 1945; Ph.D., Duke, 1947; M. Elizabeth Lewis Heil, Aug. 14, 1931; children—Albert Dennis, William English II. Tchr., coach, pub. schs. of Louisville, 1927-37; coach U. Ky., 1938-45, asso. prof. history, dean of men, 1947-49, dean of students, 1949-54, prof. history, 1954-71, president, 1968-69, dean Grad. Sch., 1960-66, Distinguished professor College of Arts and Sciences, 1967. Guggenheim fellow, 1960-61; Fulbright fellow at University of Vienna, 1966-67. Mem. Am., So. (recipient Charles Sydnor Book award 1964), Miss. Valley historical assns., Nat. Collegiate Athletics Assn. (chmn. rules infractions com. 1955-61), Phi Beta Kappa, Phi Alpha Theta, Phi Delta Phi. Author: The Revolt of the Rednecks, 1951; Johnny Green of the Orphan Brigade, 1956; The Confederacy, A Documentary History, 1959; The Life of John Jordan Crittenden, 1962; (with T.D. Clark) The South Since Appomattox, 1966. Editor: The Civilization of the Old South: Writings of Clement Eaton, 1968. Home: Lexington KY Died Nov. 30, 1971; buried Lexington Cemetery, Lexington KY

KIRWAN, MICHAEL JOSEPH, congressman; b. Wilkes-Barre, Pa., Dec. 2, 1886; s. John and Mary (Duddy) K.; m. Alice Kane, Sept. 15, 1920; children—John Joseph, Michael Joseph, Mary Alice. Member Youngstown City Council, 1932-36; mem. 75th to 91st congresses, 19th Ohio District. Asst. Chmn. V.I. and Guam office of territories. Served with 64th Artillery, United States Army, with A.E.F., 1917-19. Mem. Am. Legion, Vets. of Fgn. Wars. Democrat. Home: Youngstown OH Died July 27, 1970

KIVLIN, VINCENT EARL, coll. dean; b. Oregon, Wis., Sept. 15, 1896; s. Michael and Catherine (Glennon) K.; B.S. in Agr., U. Wis., 1918, M.S., 1928; m. Frances Landon, Jan. 1, 1927; children—Sheila (Mrs. Henry J. Reul), Thomas M. Prin. Mukwonago (Wis.) High Sch., 1919-20; tchr. agr. Wis. Bd. Vocational Edn., 1920-24, tchr. trainer, 1924-29; dir. farm short course U. Wis., also asst. prof. agri. edn., 1929-42, asso. prof., 1942-66, emeritus asso. prof., 1966-67, asso. dean Coll. Agr., 1942-66, emeritus dean, 1966-67. Chmn. pre-service and grad. coms. of senate Land Grant Coll. Assn. Mem. Dane County Sch. Com. Served with U.S. Army, 1918-19. Mem. Phi Eta Sigma, Phi Delta Kappa, Alpha Gamma Rho, Alpha Zeta, Phi Kappa Phi. Home: Madison WI Died June 4, 1967.

KJELLGREN, BENGT R. F., beryllium mfr.; b. Dalby, Sweden, July 19, 1894; s. Hugo and Hulda (Johanson) K.; student Swedish pub.; pvt. schs.; Chem.E., Royal Inst. Tech., Stockholm, 1918; grad. student Mass. Inst. Tech., 1923-24; m. Florence M. Gylfe, Oct. 3, 1925; 1son, Bengt Hugo. Asst. plant engr. Bergman Mfg. Co., Trollhattan, Sweden, 1918-20; asst. to chief engr. Hoganas-Billesholm Corp., Hoganas, Sweden, 1920-22; research engr. Uddeholms Corp., Skoghall, Sweden, 1922-23; research engr. Brush Labs. Co., Cleve., 1924-31, v.p., dir., 1931-68; v.p. Brush Beryllium Co., Cleve., 1935-48, pres., 1948-60, chmn. board, mem. exec. com. 1960-68; formerly chief exec. officer, also dir. Recipient Modern Pioneer award, 1940. Mem. Am. Chem. Soc., Electrochem. Soc., Inst. of Metals (London), Cleve. C. of C. Clubs: Mentor Harbor (O.) Yacht; University (Cleve.). Author tech. articles on beryllium and alloys. Holder patents on beryllium and alloys, on crystals prodn. piezoelectric. Home: Chagrin Falls OH Died Nov. 10, 1968; buried N. Rada, Varmland Sweden

KLABER, EUGENE HENRY, architect; b. New York, N.Y., Oct. 1, 1883; s. Maurice and Dora (Frankfeld) K.; B.S. in Arch, Columbia, 1906; Architecte Diplome par le Gouvernement Francaise, Ecole des Beaux Arts, Paris, 1910; m. Doretta Oppenheim, Aug. 31, 1913; children—Joseph Henry (deceased), Susan. Archtl. designer, 1910; practicing architect, New York, 1914-24, Chicago, 1924-33; chief of tech. staff, Housing Div., PWA, Washington, 1933-34; dir. of architecture for rental housing, FHA, Washington, 1934-42; practicing architect, Washington, 1942-44, Dir. Div. Planning and Housing, Sch. of Architecture, Columbia Univ., N.Y., 1944-46; housing and planning consultant since 1946. Served as 1st lt., U.S. Engrs., 1918. Fellow A.I.A. (past pres., Chicago chapter); mem. Am. Inst. Planners, Regional Development Council of America, Am. Soc. Planning Ofcls. Author: Housing Design, 1954, Russian edit., 1960. Lectr. throughout U.S.; contbr. articles to profl. jours. Home: Quakertown PA Died Nov. 6, 1971.

KLAUBER, LAURENCE MONROE, elec. engr.; b. San Diego, Calif., Dec. 21, 1883; s. Abraham and Theresa (Epstein) K.; A.B., Stanford Univ., 1908; honorary LL.D., University of California, 1941; Westinghouse Grad. Apprenticeship Course, 1910; m. Grace Gould, Nov. 29, 1911; children—Alice Gould (Mrs. David M. Miller), Philip Monroe. With San Diego Gas & Electric Co. since 1911, successively salesman, engr., dept. supt., v.p. operation, v.p. gen. mgr., pres., 1946-49, chmn. bd., 1949-53, cons. 1953-65; member board of directors Klauber Wangenheim Co. Chmn. San Diego Pub. Library Commn.; chmn. citizens com. San Diego County Air Pollution Control Bd. Lectr. biology, Stanford U.; cons. curator of reptiles, San Diego Zool. Soc.; cons. curator of herpetology and patron San Diego Soc. Natural History. Fellow I.E.E.E., A.A.A.S., California Acad. Sciences (hon.), Am. Geog. Soc., Acad. Zoology of India (honorary), member American Soc. C.E., Am. Soc. M.E., Am. Chem. Soc., Pacific Coast Elec. Assn. (pres. 1923-24), Am. Gas Assn., Pacific Coast Gas Assn. (pres. 1927-28), Am. Math. Soc., Math. Assn. America, Seismol. Soc. Am., Am. Mus. Natural Hist. (corr. mem.), Am. Soc. Ichthyologists and Herpetologists (pres. 1938-40), San Diego Zool. Soc. (pres. 1949-51), Am. Meteorol. Soc., Am. and Cal. Folklore Socs., Cal. Hist. Soc., Am. Ecological Soc., So. Cal. Acad. Sci., Internat. Society Toxinology, Society Industrial and Applied Mathematics, Southern California Air Pollution Control Council, Western Soc. of Naturalists (pres. 1946), Am. Statist. Assn., Soc. Systematic Zoology, (pres. 1955) Inst. Math. Statistics, Herpetologists League, Am., California library associations, also Biometric Soc., Sigma Xi, Tau Beta Pi. Republican. Rotarian. Author various publs. on elec. distribution, also reptiles, including Rattlesnakes: Their Habits and Life Histories, 2 vols., 1956, rev. edit., 1972. Home: San Diego CA Died May 8, 1968; buried Home of Peace Cemetery, San Diego CA

KLAUS, IRVING GONCER, urologist; b. N.Y.C., Oct. 15, 1900; s. Samuel and Mary (Goncer) K.; M.D., U. Pa., 1924; m. Ruth Mendel, Nov. 11, 1926; children—Robert L., Stephanie (Mrs. L. Roy Newman), Richard L. Intern, also mem. staff Jewish Hosp.; chief attending urologist No. div. Albert Einstein Med. Center; asso. urologist Montgomery Hosp., Norristown, Pa. Served with M.C., AUS, 1943-45. Diplomate Am. Bd. Urology. Mem. A.M.A., Am. Urology Assn., (Mid-Atlantic sect.). Home: Philadelphia PA Died May 17, 1969.

KLAUSMEYER, DAVID MICHAEL, mfg. exec.; b. Norwood, O., Feb. 2, 1902; s. Edward J. and Mary V. (Miller) K.; m. V. Jane Donnellan, Sept. 2, 1931; 1 son, David Michael. Designer Barley Motor Co., 1922-24; engr. Chevrolet Motor Co., 1924-35, plant mgr., 1935-46; pres., dir. Merz Engring. Co., 1946-50; pres. McGregor & Werner, Internat. Inc., 1963-70; pres. Marmon-Herrington Co., Inc., Indpls., 1946-63; chmn. bd. Tung-Set Corp., 1958-62; pres. Ruedas y Otros Productos S.A. de C.V., Mexico, 1964-70; president El Toro Products Company, 1968-70; v.p., dir. Middle East Internat., Inc., 1963-70, McGregor & Werner, Inc., 1964-70. Mem. bd. advisers St. Francis Hosp. Mem. Soc. Automotive Engrs., Soc. Am. Mil. Engrs. Clubs: Indianapolis Athletic, Columbia (Indpls.); Union League (Chgo.). Home: Rockville MD Died Nov. 3, 1970; buried Gate of Heaven Cemetery, Silver Spring MD

KLEEGMAN, SOPHIA JOSEPHINE, physician; b. Kiev, Russia, July 8, 1901; d. Israel and Elka (Siergutz) K.; came to U.S., 1906, naturalized, 1923; M.D., N.Y.U., 1924; m. Dr. John H. Sillman, Dec. 31, 1932; children—Frederick Holden, Anne Marice. Practicing physician obstetrics and gynecology, 1924-71; mem.

teaching staff N.Y.U. Coll. Med., clin. prof. obstetrics and gynecology, 1929-71, 1952-71; attending vis. staff obstetrics and gynecology Bellevue Hosp., 1929-71; med. dir. N.Y. State Planned Parenthood Assn., 1936-61; med. cons. Eastern League Planned Parenthood, 1961-71; director Infertility Clinic New York U.-Bellevue Med. Center, 1958-71. Member board governors N.Y.U. School Medicine Alumni, 1956-71, pres., 1965-66. Mem. bd. National Com. Maternal Health, 1958-71, Sex Information and Edn. Council U.S., 1965-71. Named Med. Woman of Yr., Am. Women's Med. Assn., 1966. Diplomate Am. Bd. Obstetrics and Gynecology. Fellow A.C.S., International College of Surgeons, New York Academy Medicine, Am. Coll. Obstetrics and Gynecology, Am. Assn. Marriage Counselors (charter mem., president 1960); mem. A.M.A., Internat. Society Cytology Council (founder mem.), Society Scientific Study of Sex, Planned Parenthood Federation America (mem. med. adv. com.), American Fertility Soc. (honorary v.p. 1967-68). Internat. Soc. Fertility and Sterility, Women's Medical Association of New York (president 1942-44, chairman exec. bd. 1944-48), Alpha Omega Alpha, League of Women Voters. Author articles on med. subjects. Home: New York City NY Died Sept. 26, 1971.

KLEEGMAN, SOPHIA JOSEPHINE, physician; b. Kiev, Russia, July 8, 1901; d. Israel and Elka (Siergutz) K.; came to U.S., 1906, naturalized, 1923; M.D., N.Y.C, 1924; m. Dr. John H. Sillman, Dec. 31, 1932 (dec.); children—Frederick Holden, Anne Marice. Practicing physician obstetrics and gynecology from 1924; mem. teaching staff N.Y.U. Coll. Med., from 1929, clin. prof. obstetrics and gynecology, from 1952; attending vis. staff obstetrics and gynecology Bellevue Hosp., from 1929; med. dir. N.Y. State Planned Parenthood Assn., 1936-61; med. cons. Eastern League Planned Parenthood, from 1961; director Infertility Clinic New York U.-Bellevue Med. Center, from 1958. Member board governors N.Y.U. School Medicine Alumni, from 1956, pres., 1965-66. Mem. bd. National Com. Maternal Health, Sex Information and Edn. Council U.S. Named Med. Woman of Yr., Am. Women's Med. Assn., 1966. Diplomate Am. Bd. Obstetrics and Gynecology. Fellow A.C.S., International College of Surgeons, New York Academy Medicine, Am. Coll. Obstetrics and Gynecology, Am. Assn. Marriage Counselors (charter mem., president 1960); mem. A.M.A., Internat. Society Cytology Council (founder mem.), Society Scientific Study of Sex, Planned Parenthood Federation America (mem. med. adv. com.), American Fertility Soc. (honorary v.p. 1967-68). Internat. Soc. Fertility and Sterility, Women's Medical Association of New York (president 1942-44, chairman exec. bd. 1944-48), Alpha Omega Alpha, League of Women Voters. Author articles on med. subjects. Home: New York City NY Died Sept. 26, 1971.

KLEIN, FRANCIS JOSEPH, bishop; b. Sedley, Saskatchewan, Aug. 6, 1911; s. Edward and Catherine (Heinrich) K.; student St. Anthony's Coll., Edmonton, Alberta, 1926-29, Campion Coll., Regina, Saskatchewan, 1929-31, St. Joseph's Sem., Edmonton, 1931-32, Regina Cleri, 1932-34, Laval U., Que., 1934-35. Ordained priest Roman Cath. Ch., 1934; priest, Dysart, Saskatchewan, 1935, Qu 'Appelle, Saskatchewan, 1935-36, Mutrie, Saskatchewan, 1936-45, Quinton, 1945-52; bishop of Saskatoon, 1952-67; bishop of Calgary, 1967-68. Address: Calgary Alberta Canada Died Feb. 3, 1968; buried Sedley, Saskatchewan Canada

KLEIN, GERALD BROWN, lawyer; b. North Liberty, O., Nov. 7, 1902; s. William and Ida (Brown) Kleinknecht; student Tulsa U., 1920-21; B.A., Miami U., Ohio, 1924; LL.B., Cumberland U., 1928; m. Marjorie Abbott, Aug. 29, 1927; 1 son, Tomas Abbott. Admitted to Okla. bar, 1928, U.S. Supreme Ct., 1950; practice in Tulsa, 1928-68; mem. firm Houston, Klein & Davidson, 1945-68. Gen. counsel Home Fed. Savs. & Loan Assn., Tulsa; sec., counsel General Television, Inc.; dir. Hanna Lumber Co. Faculty Okla. Sch. Bus., 1936-42, U. Tulsa Law Sch., 1946-58. Active U.S.O., A.R.C., Community Fund. Pres. Okla. Bar Found., 1957-58; trustee Okla. N.G. Armory of Tulsa. Served from capt. to lt. col., USAAF, 1942-45. Fellow American Bar Foundation, American College of Probate Counsel. Winner of dramatic teachings contest Readers Digest, 1941. Mem. Am., Fed., Okla. (pres. 1946, chairman of judicial appointments committee 1965), Inter-Am., Tulsa County (pres. 1940), Tulsa County Jr. (pres. 1932) bar assns., Internat. Assn. Ins. Counsel, Am. Judicature Soc., Tulsa C. of C. (chmn. civic dept. 1947), Phi Kappa Tau, Sigma Delta Kappa, Tau Kappa Alpha, Pi Kappa Delta. Republican. Presbyn. Clubs: The Tulsa (pres. 1957), Southern Hills Country, University (Tulsa); Nat. Lawyers (gov. Washington 1963-68). Home: Tulsa OK Died Sept. 23, 1968; buried Rose Hill Mausoleum.

KLEIN, HARRY MARTIN JOHN, educator; b. Hazelton, Pa., Dec. 9, 1873; s. George and Rebecca (Schaeffer) K.; student Muhlenberg Coll., 1889-91; A.B., Franklin and Marshall Coll., 1893, Ph.D., 1907; Litt.D., Franklin and Marshall College, 1935; studied U. of Berlin, 1899; student Theol. Sem. Ref. Ch., Lancaster, Pa., 1893-96; m. Mary Winifred Shriver, Sept. 14, 1899; children—Richard Henry, Frederic Shriver, Philip Shriver. Ordained ministry Reformed Ch. in U.S., 1896; pastor Grace Ch., York, Pa., 1896-1905, Zion Ch., Allentown, Pa., 1905-10; Audenried prof. history and archaeology, Franklin and Marshall Coll., since 1910, acting pres., 1940. Prof. history, U. of Pittsburgh Summer Sch., 1912. Pres. Eastern Synod of Ref. Ch., 1914-15. Mem. Am. Acad. Polit. and Social Science, Pa. Assn. of Planning Commrs. (pres.), Lancaster Chamber of Commerce (pres. 1931-32), Phi Gamma Delta, Phi Beta Kappa, Tau Kappa Alpha. Pres. Hist. Soc. of Reformed Ch. in U.S. Contbr. articles on history, religion and philosophy to various periodicals. Editor The History of Lancaster County, Pa., 1923. Author: A Century of Education of Mercersburg, 1936; History of the Eastern Synod of the Reformed Church in U.S., 1943; History of St. James' Protestant Episcopal Church, Lancaster; History of Cedar Crest Coll., 1948; History and Customs of the Amish People. History of the Pennsylvania Y.M.C.A., 1950; History of Franklin and Marshall College, 1952. Received Lancaster Citizenship Award, 1947. Home: 828 Buchanan Av., Lancaster PA‡

KLEIN, HENRY WEBER, lawyer; b. N.Y.C., Apr. 14, 1918; s. Isidor William and Natalie (Weber) K.; B.A., with distinction, Cornell U., 1938; LL.B., Harvard, 1941; m. Ruth Feder, Apr. 6, 1942 (dec. 1965); children—Jeffrey D. and Norman R. (twins). Admitted to N.Y. bar, 1942, practiced in N.Y.C., 1942-69; partner firm Wien, Lane & Klein, 1951-69. Mem. president's council Brandeis U., 1959-69; trustee Fedn. Jewish Philanthrophies, 1963-69, mem. exec. com., 1966-69; pres. Lexington Sch. for Deaf, N.Y.C., 1963-69. Served to capt. USAAF, 1941-46. Mem. Am. Bar Assn., N.Y. County Lawyers Assn., Assn. Bar City N.Y., Phi Beta Kappa, Alpha Epsilon Pi. Clubs: Harvard (N.Y.C.); Quaker Ridge Golf (Scarsdale, N.Y.). Home: New York City NY Died Aug. 5, 1969; buried Mt. Ararat Cemetery, Farmingdale NY

KLEIN, MELANIE, author. Author: Contributions to Psychoanalysis, 1921-45; (with others) Developments in Psychoanalysis; Envy and Gratitude, 1957; (with others) Love, Hate and Reparation; (with others) New Directions in Pscycho-analysis, 1955; Psychoanalysis of Children, 3d edit. Address: New York City NY Died Sept. 22, 1960.

KLEIN, SANDOR SIDNEY, newspaper editor; b. Szerencs, Hungary, June 21, 1906; s. Harry and Mary (Wohl) K.; m. Edith I. Miller, July 11, 1949; children by prev. marriage—Robert Laurence, Kathryn Mary (Mrs. Julian Caplan), Brenda Joan (Mrs. Rafi Tofig), Daniel Wohl. Came to U.S., 1909, naturalized, 1916. With N.Y. Times, 1924-26; with U.P.I., 1926-52, chief staff Capitol Hill, 1945-48, mem. UN news staff, 1946-48; adminstrv. asst. to U.S. Senator Dworshak, 1952-54; with Statesman Newspapers, Boise, Ida., 1956-70, mng. editor, 1959-68, executive editor, 1968-70. Member of board Boise Philharmonic Association, Boise Music Week. Recipient U.S. Navy commendation for outstanding performance and service as war corr., 1946; Newsman's Newsman award Ida. Press Club, 1967. Mem. Sigma Delta Chi.; hon. mem. U. Ida. Alumni Assn. Home: Boise ID Died June 4, 1970; buried Morris Hill Cemetery, Boise, Ida

KLEIN, WILLIAM, JR., chocolate co. exec.; b. Elizabethtown, Pa., Jan. 10, 1917; s. William and Ray (Trelchler) K.; student Franklin and Marshall Acad., 1930-31; m. Elizabeth Ann Fisher, Dec. 29, 1951; 1 son, William III. With Klein Chocolate Co., Elizabethtown, from 1933, treas., gen. mgr., from 1954, pres., from 1962; pres. Kleins Kars. antique cars. from 1956; v.p. Strasbury R.R. Co. (Pa.), also dir. Bd. dirs. Elizabethtown Library, Mem. N.A.M., Pa. Assn. Mfrs., Chocolate Mfg. Assn., N.Y. Cocoa Exchange, Antique Auto Club Am., Bentley Drivers Club, Brit. Racing Drivers Club, Rolls Royce Owners Club, Lancaster Aero. Club, Royal Photog. Soc., Classical Car Club Am. Home: Elizabethtown PA

KLEINER, HUGO GUSTAV, clergyman; b. Welland, Ont., Can., Aug. 12, 1897; s. Karl and Rosalie (Bartz) K.; LL.D., Concordia Coll., Ft. Wayne, Ind.; student Concordia Lutheran Sem., St. Louis, 1915-18. Ordained to ministry Luth. Ch., 1918; pastor in Buffalo and Bklyn., 1918-21, Redeemer Luth. Ch., N. Tonawanda, N.Y., 1921-63. Moderator Luth. Ch.-Mo. Synod, 1926-40, sec. mission commn., 1940-46, v.p. English dist., 1946-51, pres. synod, 1951, hon. pres., 1963, chmn. bd. higher edn., 1951-63. Address: Grand Island NY Died Dec. 15, 1963.

KLEMME, EDWARD JULIUS, educator; b. Butler, Ill., Mar. 4, 1875; s. August A. and Susan J. (Hoes) K.; A.B., Central Normal Coll., Danville, Ind., 1895; A.M., Northwestern U., 1906; Ph.D., Ewing (Ill.) Coll., 1908; studied Stanford U. and Teachers Coll. (Columbia); m. Bertha May Lipe, of Irving, Ill., Aug. 8, 1906; 1 son, Leslie Raymond. Prin. and supt. schs., Murphysboro, Ill., until 1905; head of edn., State Normal Sch., Ellensburg, Wash., 1906-15; in charge extension service, State Normal Sch., Bellingham, Wash., 1915-24; pres. Intermountain Union Coll., Helena, Mont., since 1924. Republican. Methodist. Mason (32 deg.), K.P., Rotarian. Home: 309 N. Rodney St., Helena MT‡

KLEMPERER, OTTO, conductor; b. Breslau, Germany, 1885; ed. Frankfurt Conservatory; LL.D., Occidental Coll., also U. Cal. at Los Angeles; widower; children—Werner, Lotte. Condr. various European opera Cos., also guest condr. N.Y. Philharmonic Orch.; later condr. Los Angeles Philharmonic Orch.; prin. condr. for life and hon. pres. New Philharmonia Orch. and Chorus, London; appeared as condr. of concerts and operas Russia, Europe, N.Am., S.Am., Can., Israel, Australia. Composer operas, symphonies, chambers mus. songs. Author: Minor Recollections, 1964. Home: Zurich Switzerland Died July 6, 1973.

KLETZKI, PAUL, condr.; b. Lodz, Poland, Mar. 21, 1900; ed. Warsaw U. and Conservatory, also, Hochschule, Berlin, Germany; m. Celine Hildegard Woodtli. Mem. Lodz Philharmonic, 1914-19; conducting debut, 1927; on tour Europe, Australia, S. Am., Central Am., 1948; U.S. debut, 1958; prof. Lausanne Conservatory, also Milan Superior Sch. Music, 1935-38; regular condr. Lucerne Festival; condr. concerts Israel Philharmonic, 1953; mus. dir. Dallas Symphony, 1958-61, Orch. Suisse Romand, Geneva, 1967-70; numerous guest appearances Composer; 3 Symphonies, Concerti for Violin and Pianoforte; 4 String Quartets, other works. Address: Geneva Switzerland Died Mar. 5, 1973.

KLIBANOW, WILLIAM J., realtor; b. Russia, July 11, 1900; s. Jacob and Eva (Sanders) K.; came to U.S., 1905; m. Eleanor Astrohan, Aug. 23, 1925. Owner, William J. Klibanow & Co., Real Estate, Chgo., 1922-69; dir. Exchange Nat. Bank, Mem. N.W. Territory Celebration Commn. Ill. Dir. Mt. Sinai Hosp. Mem. Real Estate Bd., Chgo. Bd. Underwriters. Mem. Chgo. Assn. Commerce, Nat. Assn. Real Estate Bds. Club: Covenant (dir.) (Chgo.). Home: Chicago IL Died Apr. 16, 1969.

KLINCK, LEONARD SILVANUS, univ. pres.,; b. Victoria Square, Ont., Can., Jan. 20, 1877; s. Thomas William and Catherine (Woodard) K.; B.S.A., U. of Toronto, 1903; M.S.A., Iowa State Coll., 1905; D.Sc., 1920; LL.D., U. of Western Ont., 1924, F.R.S.C., 1942; m. Mary Alice MacDougall, 1904 (died 1939); 1 son, Ronald Woodard; m. 2d, Elizabeth B. Abernethy, 1941. Pub. sch. teacher, 1895-98; lecturer, Iowa State Coll., 1904-05; in charge cereal husbandry dept., Macdonald Coll., 1905-07, prof., 1907-14; prof. agronomy and dean faculty of agr., U. of British Columbia, 1914-19, pres. since 1919. Fellow Can. Soc. Tech. Agrls. (1st pres., 1920-21). Awarded Order of Agricultural Merit, 1928; Officier de l'Instruction Publique, 1931. Mem. United Ch. Home: 2026 West 13th Av. Office: The University of British Columbia, Vancouver BC‡

KLINE, ALLAN BLAIR, farm orgn. ofcl.; b. Waterbury, Neb., Nov. 10, 1895; s. Charles E. and Mame (Allen) K.; B.A., Morningside Coll., 1915, LL.D., 1953; B.S., Ia. State Coll., Sc.D., 1958; Litt.D., Parsons Coll., 1953; LL.D. (honorary), Hillsdale College., 1963; m. Gladys R. Remer, 1920; children—Robert, Charles, Winifred Lois (Mrs. M. G. Smith). Farmer, Grand Rapids, N.D., then Vinton, Ia.; leader Farm Bur., including twp. dir., pres. Benton County Farm Bur., v.p., dir., later pres. Ia. Farm Bur. Fedn.; v.p. Am. Farm Bus. Fedn., 1945-47, pres., 1947-54. Staff U.S. Office War Information-Brit. Ministry Information in Britain, 1944; Farm Bur. del. Internat. Fedn. Agrl. Producers, London, 1946, pres., 1953-54; pub. mem. U.S. team Japanese Trade Negotiations, Geneva, 1955; attended East Asian Rural Reconstruction Conf., Tokyo, Japan, 1955; spl. com. U.S. Senate on mil. and econ. support to Yugoslavia, 1957; bd. directors Federal Reserve Bank of Chgo., 1948-54, J. I. Case Co., Racine, Wis. Mem. of Nat. Service Com. 4-H Club Work. Chairman bd. trustees Farm Found.; member Conf. Nat. Orgns.; trustee Eisenhower Exchange Fellowships, Inc. Mem. bd. dir. Inst. for Am. Strategy. Conglist. Home: Western Springs IL Died June 14, 1968; buried Vinton IA

KLINE, PAUL ROBERT, physician; b. Trenton, N.J., Apr. 1, 1907; s. Abraham and Celia (Budson) K.; M.D., N.Y. Med. Sch., 1930; m. Renee Kusselman, June 29, 1941; children—Victor, Peter. Intern, William McKinley Meml. Hosp., 1930-31; asso. attending in dermatology and syphilis N.Y. Skin & Cancer Unit Postgrad. Hosp., N.Y.C.; cons. dermatologist N.J. Neuropsyhiat. Inst., Skillman, Princeton Hosp., McKinley Meml. Hosp., Trenton; asso. in dermatology and syphilis Univ. Hosp.-Bellevue Med. Center. Served with USNR, 1942-46. Diplomate Am. Bd. Dermatology, Pan Am. Med. Assn. Mem. Am. Acad. Dermatology, A.M.A., Soc. Investigative Dermatology, A.A.A.S., N.Y. Acad. Scis., Argentine Assn. Dermatology and Syphililogy (hon.). Hon. editor Jour. Practica Medica, Barcelona, Spain. Contbr. articles to profl. jours. Home: Princeton NJ Died July 11, 1970; buried People of Truth Cemetery, Trenton NJ

KLINGBIEL, RAY I., judge; b. 1901; student U. Notre Dame and Augustana Coll.; LL.B., U. Ill., LL.D., Chgo. Kent Coll. of Law, 1964; m. Julia Stone;

children—Donna, Tom. Admitted to Ill. bar, 1924; practiced in East Moline, Ill.; city atty., 1925-39; judge Ill. Circuit Ct., 1945-53; became justice Supreme Ct. Ill., 1953, chief justice, 1956-57, 63-66. Mayor, East Moline, 1939-45. Named Citizen of Year East Moline, 1957. Past pres. Ill. Municipal League. Mason (33). Contbr. articles law jours. Home: Moline IL Died Jan. 18, 1973.

KLUBERTANZ, GEORGE PETER, clergyman, coll. dean; b. nr. Columbus, Wis., June 29, 1912; s. Joseph and Clara V. (Belda) K.; student Salvatorian Sem., St. Nazianz, Wis., 1926-31; A.B., St. Louis U., 1935, M.A., 1938; Ph.D., U. Toronto, 1947. Mem. Soc. of Jesus, 1931; ordained priest Roman Catholic Ch., 1944; instr. classics and philosophy Creighton U., 1939-40; instr. philosophy St. Louis U., 1948-51, asst. prof., 1951-54, asso. prof., 1954-59, prof., 1959, acting dean Coll. Philosophy and Letters, 1952-53, dean, 1953-70, chmn. dept. philosophy, 1965-68, acting dean Sch. Div., 1970-72. Mem. Am. Cath. Philos. Assn. (past pres.), Psychologists Interested in Religious Issues, Metaphys. Soc. Am. (pres. 1956-57, exec. council 1958-62). Societe philosophique de Louvain. Author: The Discursive Power, 1952; The Philosophy of Humam Nature, 1953; Introduction to the Philosophy of Being, 1955; St. Thomas Aquinas on Analogy, 1960; (with Maurice R. Holloway) Being and God, 1963; The Habits and Virtues, 1965. Editor: Avicenna' De Anima', 1949; editor The Modern Schoolman, 1937-38, 50-59, 64-72, mem. editorial bd., St. Louis MO Died May 5, 1972.

KLUCKHOLN, FRANK LOUIS, newspaperman; b. St. Paul, Minn., Nov. 24, 1907; s. Frank Louis and Lillian (Dodson) K.; ed. University of Minnesota, 1925, Centro de Estudios Historicos, Madrid, Spain, 1930; m. June Elizabeth Warner, July 7, 1945; children—Michael and Richard. Engaged as a reporter St. Paul Dispatch, 1926-28; foreign reporter Boston Globe, 1929; foreign correspondent New York Times, 1929-33, mem. Washington staff, 1933-36, Spanish War corr., 1936, Mexico City corr., 1937-38, on Washington staff, 1938, presidential correspondent, 1939-42; war corr., London, Aug.-Nov. 1942, North African campaign, 1942-43, Far East, September 1943, chief of Pacific staff, 1945, chief of S.A. staff, 1946; advisor sec. of Defense, 1948; exec. IBM World Trade Corp., 1950-70; publicity Rep. Nat. Com., 1952-70; consultant to Department of State, 1955-61; staff United States Congress, 1961-70. Mem. White House Corrs. Association Episcopalian. Clubs: Overseas Writers, Nat. Press (Washington, D.C.); Ataneo (Madrid); Churubusco Country (Mexico City). Author: The Mexican Challenge, 1939; America Listen, 1961; Naked Rise of Communism, 1962; What's Wrong with U.S. Foreign Policy, 1963; Lyndon's Legacy, 1964; The Inside on LBJ, 1964; The Drew Pearson Story, 1967; The Man Who Kept the Peace (A Study of John Foster Dulles), 1968; The Real Eisenhower, 1969. Contributor to magazines. Home: Shepherdstown WV Died Oct. 2, 1970; buried Chicago IL

KLUGESCHEID, RICHARD CHARLES, lawyer; b. N.Y.C., Nov. 16, 1889; s. Richard and Caroline (Stadinger) K.; A.B., Columbia, 1911, LL.B., 1913; m. Helen Ballard, Sept. 29, 1920; 1 dau., Elizabeth (Mrs. Ralph H. Alexander, Jr.) (dec.). Admitted to N.Y. bar, 1915, since practiced in N.Y.C.; counsel Ocean Accident & Ins. Co., 1915-16; mng. atty. O'Gorman, Battlee Vandiver, 1916-17; spl. rep. sec. war, 1919-20; asst. gen. counsel Guggenheim Bros., 1920-28; sec., gen. counsel, v.p. Kennecott Copper Corp., N.Y.C., 1933-54; dir. subsidiaries; pres., dir. Mesabi Iron Co., N.Y.C., 1957-68; dir. Indsl. Bank of Commerce. Served from lt. to capt., U.S. Army, 1917-19. Mem. Bar Assn. City N.Y., Law Inst., Gen. Counsels Assn. Home: Bronxville NY Died Oct. 30, 1968.

KNAPP, A(RTHUR) BLAIR, educator; b. Duluth, Minn., Apr. 30, 1905; s. Arthur Henry and Alice F. (Peers) K.; A.B., Syracuse U., 1926, A.M., 1928; LL.D., Syracuse U., 1951, L.H.D., Temple U., 1952, Trinity College, 1955, U. of Redlands, 1959; H.H.D., Bowling Green University, 1958; Dr. of Letters, Lincoln Memorial University, 1964; married to Gertrude M. Park, July 26, 1930; children—Susan Park, Richard Blair. Grad. student and instr. in polit. sci., Syracuse U., 1926-29, dean of men, 1935-46; pvt. bus., 1929-35; dean of students, Temple U., 1946-1949, vice pres., 1949-1951; pres. of Denison U., 1951-68. Major, USAF, 1943-46. Mem. exec. com. bd. of trustees Coll. Entrance Exam. Bd., 1956-59; vice chmn. Am. Council Edn., 1958-59; chmn. Ohio Found. of Ind. Coll., 1953-54; member Am. Coll. Personnel Assn. (mem. exec. com.), 1950-52, Nat. Assn. Student Personnel Adminstrs. (pres. 1951-52), Assn. Am. Colls. (mem. commn. faculty and students), Ohio Coll. Assn. (exec. com. 1962-68; pres. 1964-65), Phi Beta Kappa, Phi Kappa Phi, Phi Kappa Alpha, Psi Upsilon. Republican. Baptist. Clubs: Century (N.Y.C.); University (Columbus, O.); Union (Cleve.). Author articles on ednl. personnel. Home: Granville OH Died May 14, 1968; buried Denison U. Coll. Cemetery, Granville OH

KNAPP, FRANCIS ATHERTON, printing co. exec.; b. Mpls., July 2, 1907; s. Albert Henry and Laura Anna (Bean) K.; A.B., Stanford, 1929; student San Diego State Coll., 1925-27; m. Alice Royal McCarthy, Dec. 17, 1933; 1 son, David Atherton. Office mgr. Cal. Art & Engraving Co., 1929-32; prodn. mgr. Lederer, Street & Zeus Co., Berkeley, Cal., 1932-69; pres. Asso. Printing Industries, Oakland, Cal., 1956-69. Commr., Cal. Apprenticeship Council, 1960-69, chmn., 1966-67. Mem. trade adv. com. Peralta Colls., 1946-69; mem. Greater E. Bay Apprenticeship Com., 1946-69. Mem. Alameda-Contra Costa County Com. for Equal Opportunity in Employment and Tng., 1965-69; active Nat. Found.; chmn. Typog. Welfare Trust Fund, 1955-69; mem. com. Cal. Jr. Coll. Assn., 1966-69. Bd. dirs. Printing Industry Pension Fund. Served from lt. to lt. comdr. USNR, 1942-46. Mem. Printing Industries No. Cal. (dir.). Clubs: Commonwealth of Cal. (San Francisco); San Francisco Press; Outlook (Berkeley); Berkeley Breakfast. Home: Berkeley CA Died May 24, 1969.

KNAPP, GEORGE LEONARD, author; b. Dover, Olmsted Co., Minn., Apr. 6, 1872; s. Leonard and Lucretia (Harris) K.; M.D., Dunham Med. Coll., Chicago, 1902; m. Eva B. Loehr, of Bloomington, Ill., Sept. 3, 1907; children—Barbara H., Charles L. Practiced medicine at Chicago, 1902-03, Pueblo, Colo., 1903-06; editorial writer, Rocky Mountain News, 1906-11, Chicago Journal, 1912-25, Labor, Washington, D.C., 1925-1934. Democrat. Author: The Scales of Justice, 1910; The Face of Air, 1912; Brigham Young (with Frank J. Cannon), 1913; Quest of the Golden Cities, 1924; A Young Volunteer with Old Hickory, 1929; Boys Book of Annapolis, 1930; Lone Star of Courage, 1931; Boys Book of West Point, 1931; Uncle Sam's Government at Washington, 1933; The Story of the Constitution. Contbr. to mags. Address: 10th and K Sts., Washington DC‡

KNAPP, GRACE HIGLEY, missionary; b. Bitlis, Turkey, Nov. 21, 1870; d. George Cushing and Alzina Maria (Churchill) K.; parents both Am. missionaries; B.Litt., Mt. Holyoke (Mass.) Coll., 1893. Missionary in Turkey, for Woman's Bd. of Missions, Congl. Ch., 1893-1902. and 1910-15; with Near East Relief in N.Y. City, 1918-22; on editorial staff Am. Board of Commrs. for Foreign Missions, Boston, 1922-40. In Turkey during massacres of 1895-96; in Van, Turkey, during 4 weeks' siege of Turkish Army, 1915, the Americans caring for 6,000 refugees; later obliged to flee to Russia with entire Christian population of Van Province. Author: The Mission at Van, 1915; (with C. D. Ussher) An American Physician in Turkey, 1917; The Tragedy of Bitlis, 1919; Voyage of Adventure (poems). Address: 138 Hancock St., Auburndale MA‡

KNAPP, WALTER I(RVING), engineer; b. Austinburg, O., July 15, 1899; s. William G. and Laura I. (Tallman) K.; student Case Sch. Applied Sci., Cleve., 1919-20; B.S. in Elec. Engring., Ohio No. U., 1923; student design and lighting in architecture Cranbrook Acad. Art, 1935-36; m. Ruth L. Snyder, May 7, 1924; 1 dau., Margaret Louise. Jr. engr., elec. and sales engr. Wilson-Painter Elec. Co., Canton, O., 1923-26; lighting engr. and sales Netting Co., Detroit, 1926-32; pres., design engr. Lighting Corp., Detroit, 1932-34; lighting design engr. Detroit Edison Co., 1934-44; product design, development and Marketing, Detroit, from 1944; work includes sunray finishing machine for stainless steel ware, plastics top fillet, seaming bridge for plastic counter tops, door actuated elevator cabinet, V arm metal secondary electric pole design, vertirail mass. transit system also designed all-purpose assessory light stanchion, Met. Civic Centers; pvt. research, guided missile control and space techniques; collaborator on design of bi-level stabilized rapid transit system, 1971. Registered professional engineer, Mich. Mem. Engring. Soc. Detroit (dir. 1942-45), Delta Sigma Phi. Methodist. Mason. Address: Detroit MI Died Nov. 23, 1971; buried Woodlawn Cemetery, Ada OH

KNATHS, (OTTO) KARL, painter, artist; b. Eau Claire, Wis., Oct. 21, 1891; s. Otto Julius and Theresa (Dietrich) K.; grad. Portage (Wis.) High Sch., 1910; studied Art Inst. Chicago, 5 yrs.; A.F.D. (hon.), Chgo. Art Inst., 1951; m. Helene Weinrich, 1922. Represented Met. Mus. N.Y.C., Phillips Memorial Gallery, Washington, Gallery of Living Art, Phila. Mus. Art, Detroit Mus., Whitney Mus., Art Inst. Chicago, N.Y. Mus. Modern Art, guest artist Phillips Memorial Gallery. Biennial exhbns. Paul Rosenberg Gallery, N.Y.C.; exhibited Fine Arts Mus. Boston, 1960. Recipient Norman Wait Harris silver medal Art Inst. Chgo., 1928; medal of Boston Tercentenary; 1st prize Carnegie Inst., 1946; 1st prize Met. Mus., 1950; Brandeis U. creative art award, 1961; Benjamin Altman 1st prize, N.A.D., 1963; Audubon Art award, 1964, Benjamin Altman award in landscape painting, 1965. Mem. Nat. Inst. Arts and Letters, Am. Fedn. Art., Nat. Acad. Home: Provincetown MA Died Mar. 9, 1971.

KNEASS, GEORGE BRYAN, banker; b. Phila., Oct. 25, 1897; s. Strickland Landis and Mary Stewart (Edwards) K.; A.B., U. Pa., 1918; m. Louise Dudley Hines, June 9, 1923; children—Mary Stewart (Mrs. Emmett E. Kelly), George B.; m. 2d, Clarissa White, Nov. 21, 1951. With Drexel & Co., Phila., 1919-26; asst. mgr., corr. Phila. office Guaranty Trust Co. of N.Y., 1926-35; mgr. investment adv. dept. Phila. Nat. Bank, 1935-42, v.p., head investment division, 1942-59, senior vice president, 1959-62; financial cons. Inter-Am. Devel. Bank, Washington, 1963-65; mgr. instl. dept. Newburger & Co. Phila., from 1965; asst. to sec. of treas., Washington, 1956-57. Served as ensign USN, World War I. Mem. Phi Kappa Sigma. Clubs: Rittenhouse, Merion Cricket (Phila.). Home: Bryn Mawr PA Died June 1, 1971.

KNECHT, KARL KAE, cartoonist; b. Iroquois, S.D., Dec. 4, 1883; s. Harry August and Bridget Marie (Fahey) K.; ed. pub. and high schs., Freeport, Ill., 1889-1902, Art Inst. Chicago, 1903-06; Litt.D. (hon.), Evansville College, 1953; married Jannie Elwood Moore, Aug. 22, 1918. Newspaper reporter, Freeport, later clk., I.C. R.R., Freeport and Chicago, and theatre usher and doorman until 1906; cartoonist Evansville (Ind.) Courier, Inc., 1906-61, retired as v.p., 1961, remained as dir. Organizer, 1925, National Association Circus Fans, pres. 1951; founder The White Tops, monthly magazine; mem. Evansville City Board of Education, 1942-43; formerly commr. Evansville Parks and dir. Mesker Zoo. Dean Am. newspaper editorial cartoonist, 1951. Member of the American Association of Editorial Cartoonists, Modern Woodman, Nat. Circus Fan clubs Britain, France, Holland, Swiss, Italy (honorary). Club: Evansville (Ind.) Country. Author: Surprise Drawing Puzzle Book, 1928; How to Put on Your Own Circus. Contbr. to Billboard, Courier, King Pole, World's Fair (London), others. Illustrator of Child Jingles, by Winifred Sackville Stoner. Home: Evansville IN Died July 28, 1972.

KNEELAND, GEORGE JACKSON, sociological investigator; b. Griggsville, Ill., Sept. 1, 1872; s. Charles W. and Mary L. (Folger) K.; A.B., Ill. Coll., 1901; Yale Div. Sch., 1901-2; m. Adelaide R. Hardy, Nov., 1911. Editorial dept. Cosmopolitan Mag., 1903-4; editorial staff School Journal, New York, 1905-6; office mgr. Industrial Press, New York, 1907-8; dir. investigations for research com. of Com. of Fourteen, New York, 1908-10, for Vice Commn. of Chicago, 1910-11. Assisted in preparation of reports: The Social Evil in New York City, 1910; The Social Evil in Chicago, 1911. Dir. investigations for Bur. of Social Hygiene, New York, 1912-13; dir. Dept. of Investigation, Am. Vigilance Assn., New York, 1912-13, for American Social Hygiene Association, 1914; directed investigations with relation to the social evil for Vice Commn., Phila., and state, municipal and pvt. coms. in other states and cities, 1912-13. Author: Commercialized Prostitution in New York City, 1913 (issued under auspices of Bur. of Social Hygiene). Office: 105 W. 40th St., New York NY‡

KNEELAND, ROBERT SHEPHERD, lawyer; b. Northampton, Mass., Apr. 26, 1883; s. Frederick Newton and Adelaide F. (Dyer) K.; B.A., Amherst Coll., 1905; LL.B., Harvard, 1908; m. Annie Peters, Oct. 4, 1911 (deceased June 14, 1964); m. second, Madeleine E. Aldrich, August 1965. Admitted to the Massachusetts bar, 1908, practiced in Northampton, 1908-09, Springfield, from 1911, pres. Holden Patent Book Cover Co. to 1959; dir. Buxton, Inc.; hon. dir. Third Nat. Bank of Hampden County. Member Longmeadow Park Bd., 1931-39. Director Richard Salter Storrs Library. Member Phi Beta Kappa, Beta Theta Pi. Conglist. Club: University (Springfield). Home: Longmeadow MA Died Sept. 10, 1971.

KNEELAND, YALE, JR., physician; b. Rumson, N.J., July 18, 1901; s. Yale and Anna Ilsley (Ball) K.; A.B., Yale, 1922; M.D., Columbia, 1926; m. Deborah Dyer, Jan. 4, 1930; children—Hopeton Drake, Deborah Van Dyck, Yale, III, Anne Ball. Interne Presbyn. Hosp., New York City, 1926-28; asst. in medicine Coll. of Physicians and Surgeons, Columbia, 1928-31, instr. medicine, 1931-34, asso. in medicine, 1934-39, asst. prof. medicine, 1939-47, asso. prof. 1947-58, professor, 1958-67, professor of medicine, 1967-70; attending physician Presbyn. Hosp., N.Y. City, 1945-70; clin. dir. Columbia service Goldwater Memorial Hosp., N.Y. City; consulting physicians Sharon (Conn.) Hosp., St. Francis Hospital, Poughkeepsie, N.Y.; civilian expert cons. to War Dept. Served as col. med. corps U.S. Army, 1942-45, sr. consultant infectious disease, E.T.O.; cons. in medicine United Kingdom base. Fellow Am. Coll. Physicians; mem. Am. Soc. Clin. Investigation, Assn. Am. Physicians, Phi Beta Kappa, Alpha Omega Alpha. Republican. Protestant Episcopalian. Clubs: Union, Century Association (president 1964-68), Grolier (New York City, N.Y.). Contributor of articles on infectious diseases to med. jours. Home: Millbrook NY Died Dec. 15, 1970.

KNICKERBOCKER, WILLIAM SKINKLE, educator, editor; b. N.Y. City, Jan. 7, 1892; s. Thomas Henry and Lucy Bulson (Skinkle) K.; student Bibl. Sem. of New York, 1911-14; A.B., Columbia, 1917, A.M., 1918, Ph.D., 1925, Proudfit fellow, 1918-20; m. Frances Wentworth Cutler, June 2, 1921; children—Charles H., Richard W. Instr. in English, Dartmouth, 1918-19; asst. prof. English, Syracuse U., 1920-26; prof. English, Univ. of the South, 1926-43; prof. English, Columbia, summer 1928; visiting Carnegie prof. to univs. of Manchester and Aberdeen, Gt. Britain, 1935; master in English, The

Loomis Inst., 1943-46; prof. English, Univ. of Mass., 1946-48; prof. English, Emerson Coll., Boston, 1948-57; professor English Newton Junior Coll., 1957-58. Delegate World Conf. English-Speaking Union, London, 1951; leader Intercollegiate tour, Britain, France, Holland, 1952. Editor Sewanee Review, 1926-42; contbg. editor Institute Current Literature; asso. editor Am. Bookman since 1943. Member Modern Lang. Assn. Am., Am. Assn. U. Profs., Knickerbocker Hist. Soc., Dutch Settlers of Albany, Phi Beta Kappa, Alpha Xi Sigma, Kappa Sigma, Sigma Upsilon (nat. pres.), Alpha Pi Theta. Democrat. Author: Creative Oxford, 1925; Victorian Education and Concept of Culture, 1949. Editor: Culture and Anarchy, by Matthew Arnold, 1925; Classics of Modern Science, 1927; consultant and contbg. editor Dictionary of World Literature, 1943; 20th Century English, 1946. Editor; Victorian Notes. Home: Waban MA Died Jan. 15, 1972; buried Phillips Chapel Cemetery, Andover MA

KNIGHT, CHARLES, architect; b. Poissy, France, Nov. 27, 1877; s. (Daniel) Ridgway (q.v.) and Rebecca Morris (Webster) K.; brother of L(ouis) Aston K. (q.v.); ed. Ecole des Beaux Arts, Paris; m. at Paris, Miss Bouchery, Aug. 11, 1903. Only practicing Am. architect in Paris with diplomas of the French Govt. and Ecole des Beaux Arts; hon. mention, Paris Salon, 1905. Address: 11 Rue Marbeuf, Paris France‡

KNIGHT, EUGENE HERBERT, architect; b. Jacksonville, Fla., Nov. 30, 1884; s. Albion Williamson and Anna (Bishop) K.; student Atelier Hornbostel, Soc. Beaux Arts Architects, N.Y.C.; m. Nellie Rae Reeder, July 10, 1907; children—Marguerite Naomi, Louise Alberta, Albion Williamson; m. 2d, Elizabeth Jane Ward, July 7, 1957. With Harry B. Wheelock, 1902, Clinton & Russel, 1910, later York & Sawyer, William C. Weston; architect Eugene H. Knight, 1914-16, Warren & Knight, 1916-21, Warren, Knight & Davis from 1921. Fellow A.I.A. (past sec., pres. Ala. chpt., chmn. Ala. centennial com. 1957); mem. Birmingham C. of C., Soc. Colonial Wars, Nat., Ala. assns. registered architects, Nat. Inst. Archtl. Edn., Birmingham Art Assn., Y.M.C.A., 365 Crippled Childrens Clinic Club. Awarded gold medal and hon. mention, So. Archtl. Exhbn., 1929; hon. mention, Gulf State regional exhbn., Am. Inst. of Architects, 1954. Presbyterian (elder). Mason. Clubs: Mountain Brook, Engineers, The Club (Birmingham). Home: Birmingham AL Died Nov. 6, 1971; buried Elmwood Cemetery.

KNIGHT, FRANK HYNEMAN, educator; b. White Oak Twp., Ill., Nov. 7, 1885; s. Winton Cyrus and Julia Ann (Hyneman) K.; student Am. U., Harriman, Tenn., 1905-07; Ph.B., Milligan (Tenn.) Coll., 1911; B.S., A.M., U. of Tenn., 1913; Ph.D., Cornell University, 1916; D.Litt. Princeton U., 1946; LL.D., Northwestern U., U. of Glasgow, 1951, University of Rochester; and L.H.D., Columbia U., 1954; H.H.D., U. Ill., 1967; m. Minerva O. Shelburne, May 23, 1911 (div. 1928); children—Laura Eleanor, Alice Louise, Horace Shelburne, Gladys Susan; m. 2d, Ethel Verry, Sept. 30, 1929; children—Frank Bardsley, Charles Alfred. Instr. econs., Cornell U., 1916-17, U. of Chicago, 1917-19; asso. prof. economics, U. of Ia., 1919-22, prof. 1922-28; prof. econs. U. Chicago, 1927-46, Morton D. Hull Distinguished Service prof., 1946-51, emeritus, 1951-72; fellow Center for Behavioral Studies, 1957. Recipient Walker medal, 1957, Great Living American award, U.S. C. of C., 1959. Fellow Am. Academy Arts and Sciences; mem. Am. Econ. Assn. (pres. 1950), Royal Econ. Society, Accademia Nazionale dei Lincei, Rome, Phi Beta Kappa (honorary Upsilon chpt. University Tenn.). Club: Quadrangle. Translator: General Economic History (by Max Weber), 1927. Author: Risk, Uncertainty and Profit, 1921, reprinted London, 1933; The Ethics of Competition and Other Essays, 1935; (with Thornton W. Merriam) The Economic Order and Religion, 1945; Freedom and Reform, 1947; The Economic Organization, 1951; Essays on History and Method of Economics 1956; Intelligence and Democratic Action, 1960. Contbr. to econ. jours. Home: Chicago IL Died Apr. 15, 1972.

KNIGHT, GOODWIN (JESS), former gov.; b. Provo, Utah, Dec. 9, 1896; s. Jesse and Lillie J. (Milner) K.; A.B., Stanford, 1919; student (Telluride scholarship) Cornell U., 1919-20; m. Arvilla Pearl Cooley, 1925 (dec.); children—Marilyn (Mrs. Robert A. Eaton), Carolyn (Mrs. Charles V. Weedman); m. Mrs. Virginia Carlson, 1954. Admitted Cal. bar, 1921; practiced in Los Angeles, 1921-35, 46-53; judge superior ct., Los Angeles co., 1935-46; lt. gov. Cal., 1946-53; gov. 1953-59; former owner, operator Elephant-Eagle Mines, Soledad Mountain, Kern Co., Cal. U.S. Navy, World War I, 1918-19. Comdr. Decorated Star of Italian Solidarity (1st class); Grand Cross Order Star (Ethiopia); Royal Order of Phoenix (Greece). Mem. Am. Legion, Vets. Fgn. Wars, Am. and Cal. State Bar Assns., Alpha Delta Phi Phi Alpha Delta, Sigma Delta Chi, Delta Sigma Rho. Republican. Protestant. Mason, Shriner, Sciots, K.P., Eagles, Moose, 100F, Elks, Ahepa. Club: Jonathan, Wilshire Country, Bel Air (Los Angeles); Sutter, Del Paso Country (Sacramento). Author: Good's Budget of Boys' Stories, 1910. Address: Los Angeles CA Died May 1970.

KNIGHT, HARRY EDWARD, army officer; b. Elizabeth, N.J., July 9, 1876; s. Henry Warren and Tressa (Taylor) K.; grad. Montclair (N.J.) Mil. Acad., 1895; student Lehigh U., 1895-98; grad. Infantry and Calvary Sch., 1904, Army War Coll., 1928; m. Celeste Foote, Dec. 12, 1905. Enlisted as pvt., U.S. Army, 1898; apptd. 2nd lt. inf., 1898; advanced through grades to maj. gen.; retired May 31, 1938. Mem. Mil. Order of World War, Psi Upsilon. Conglist. Club: Army and Navy (Washington). Home: 2126 Connecticut Av., Washington DC*‡

KNIGHT, JAMES ERNEST, editor; b. Lake Crystal, Minn., Dec. 21, 1890; s. George Corbley and Mary Rosella (Patton) K.; B.A., U. Wash., 1915; m. Pearl Fallis, Apr. 23, 1918; 1 daughter, Virginia Lee (Mrs. Tyler Raymond Matthew). Sports editor Tacoma Tribune, 1915-17, wire editor, 1917-18; city editor Tacoma Ledger, 1919-23, news editor, 1923-37, mng. editor, 1937; exec. editor Tacoma News Tribune, 1937-55, editor, 1955-64. Regional vice chmn. bd. overseers Whitman Coll.; regional vice chmn. Pacific N.W. Assn., 1962-63. Mem. Tacoma Planning Commn., 1963-72. Served with AEF in France, 1918-19. Mem. Pacific N.W. Trade Assn. (Puget Sound v.p. 1962-63), Sigma Delta Chi (regional dir. 1960-61). Presbyn. Elk. Home: Tacoma WA Died May 1972.

KNIGHT, MILTON, banker; b. Toledo, Aug. 18, 1906; s. W. W. and Edna S. (Ford) K.; A.B., Yale, 1928, LL.B., 1931; m. Dorothy Gardner, Nov. 7, 1941; children—William G., Barbara Ross, Milton Ford. Admitted to Ohio bar, 1931; with law firm Marshall, Melhorn, Marlar & Martin, Toledo, 1931-36; asst. sec. to v.p. Libbey-Owens-Ford Glass Co., from 1936, sec., v.p. charge Spl. Products div., until 1942, chmn. bd., exec. com., 1965-71, dir., 1940-71; pres., dir. First Nat. Bank of Toledo, 1946-62, chmn. bd., 1962-66, chairman trust investment com., 1966-71; dir. Wyandotte Chemicals Corp., Toledo Scale Corp., until 1968. Pres. Toledo Community Chest, 1949; mem. adv. council Civil Aeros. Authority, 1940. Trustee, Toledo Mus. Art, Toledo council Boy Scouts Am., Jr. Achievement, Boys Clubs Toledo. Served as lt. comdr. USNR, 1942-45; PTO; MTO. Mem. Res. City, Perrysburg OH Died Nov. 10, 1971.

KNOBLOCH, HENRY F(REDERICK) J(ACOB), lawyer, business exec.; b. Jersey City, N.J., Oct. 12, 1877; s. Henry and Sophia Elizabeth (Hanstein) K.; LL.B., N.Y. U., 1897, LL.M., N.Y. Law Sch., 1898; m. Isabelle Stuart Woodruff, Dec. 17, 1906. Admitted to N.Y. State bar, 1899, and practiced in N.Y. City, 1900-47; counsel to William Boyce Thompson and his interests; dir. Bingham Central Mining Co., Mason Valley Mining Co., Inspiration Cooper Co., Magma Copper Co., Zinc Mines Co., Newmont Mining Co., Hendee Mfg. Co., Knox Hat Co., Torrington Co., 1906-18; sec. Tex. Gulf Sulphur Co., 1916-47, v.p., 1918-19, treas., 1919-47, dir. 1916-19 and 1926-52. Mem. Acad. Polit. Sci. Republican. Conglist. Mason (K.T., Shriner). Clubs: Union League (N.Y.C.); St. Petersburg (Fla.) Yacht; Orient (N.Y.), Yacht; Bath (Redington Beach, Fla). Home: 16341 Redington Dr., St Petersburg FL‡

KNOOP, FREDERIC BARNES, pub.; b. Troy, O., Oct. 25, 1908; s. Louis P. and Lucy (Barnes) K.; student Ohio State U., 1926-29; m. Annette Wurlitzer, Sept. 14, 1934; children—Janet, John, Christopher, Richard, Rudolph, Anthony. Advt. dept. Proctor & Gamble, Cin., 1930-35; account exec. Byrne Orgn., Cin., Atlanta, 1935-41; editor Auto Digest Pub. Corp., Cincinnati, since 1942; co-founder, editor Modern Photography, 1949-69; co-founder, and pub. Farm Quar. Mag.; v.p., dir. F&W Pub. Corp. Served as lt. comdr. USNR, 1943-46. Mem. MacDowell Soc., Sigma Alpha Epsilon. Clubs: Coldstream Country; Literary (Cin.). Author: The Good Life; also articles on photography and modern farming in mags. and profl. jours. Home: Cincinnati OH Died Sept. 19, 1969.

KNOPF, BLANCHE (WOLF), publisher; b. N.Y.C., July 30, 1894; d. Julius and Bertha Wolf; grad. Gardner Sch., N.Y.C.; Litt.D., Franklin and Marshall Coll., 1962; Litt.D., Adelphi U., 1966; m. Alfred A. Knopf, Apr. 4, 1916; 1 son, Alfred. Started publishing, 1915; v.p., dir. Alfred A. Knopf, Inc., N.Y.C., 1921-57, pres., dir. 1957-66; dir. Random House, Inc., 1960-66. Cons., AAF Personnel Narratives Office, 1945. Decorated Chevalier de la Legion d'Honneur, 1949, Officier, 1960; Cavaleiro da Ordem Nacional do Cruzeiro do Sul, 1950, Oficial, 1964 (Brazil). Died June 4, 1966.

KNOPF, WILLIAM CLEVELAND, JR., univ. dean; b. Louisville, Dec. 13, 1910; s. William Cleveland and Anne (Flood) K.; B.S., Washington and Lee U., 1932; M.S., Vanderbilt U., 1941; Ph.D., Northwestern U., 1950; m. Mary Gene Herren, Jan. 18, 1941; children—Katherine Herren (Mrs. H. James Stadelman), Gene Miller (Mrs. Randolph N. Jonakait). Asst. dean Northwestern U., 1945-51; asst. dir. research Internat. Minerals and Chem. Corp., Skokie, Ill., 1951-59; dir. research U.S. Industries Tech. Center, Pompano Beach, Fla., 1959-61; prof. elec. engring. U. Fla., 1961-63; prof. elec. engring. and ocean engring. U. Miami (Fla.), 1963-—, dean Sch. Engring., 1965-70; lectr., research asso. Ill. Inst. Tech., 1941-43; cons. to govt. and industry, 1945-70. Chmn. sci. and oceanography Dade County (Fla.) Com. 21, 1966-70; mem. Fla. Tech. Services Program, 1966-70, Fla. Articulation Com. Engring., 1965-70; chmn. oceanography Fla. Space Eta Study Task Force, 1962-63. Mem. A.A.A.S., I.E.E.E., Instrument Soc. Am. (chmn. marine sci. div. 1964-66), Am. Soc. Engring. Edn., Miami-Dade County C. of C., Sigma Xi, Tau Beta Pi, Eta Kappa Nu, Alpha Tau Omega. Rotarian. Club: Riviera Country. Contbr. profl. jours. Home: Coral Gables FL Died Feb. 6, 1970.

KNOTT, VAN BUREN, surgeon; b. Joliet, Ill., Nov. 14, 1871; s. John M. and Caroline (Van Buren) K.; grad. Sioux City (Ia.) High Sch., 1888; M.D., Columbian (now George Washington) U., Dept. of Medicine, 1893; m. Bertha E. Peirce, of Sioux City, Apr. 18, 1895. Practiced in Sioux City since 1894; surgeon 52d Ia. Vol. Inf., Spanish-Am. War; surgeon St. Joseph's Hosp. and others. Mem. A.M.A., Ia. State Med. Soc., Western Surg. Assn., Des Moines Path. Soc., Kappa Sigma, etc. Republican. Presbyn. Mason (32 deg.). Clubs: Hawkeye, Commercial, Country, Sioux City Boat. Commd. maj., Med. R.C., 1917; comdg. Field Hosp. No. 133. Home: 2323 Nebraska St. Office: Security Bldg., Sioux City IA‡

KNOTTS, RAYMOND, editor and author; b. Chatham, Ill., Nov. 27, 1893; s. Albert G. and Minnie A. (Read) K.; student Ill. Wesleyan U., U. Chicago, also tech. schs.; m. Jessie Wetzel, Sept. 1, 1914. Worked on Ill. State Journ., State Register, Springfield, Ill., Times, Post-Dispatch, St. Louis, Mo., before joining Chgo. Am., served as night editor, city editor, columnist, chief editorial writer of Am. Author: The Whispering Drum; And the Deep Blue Sea; Meeting by Moonlight; also short fiction. Home: Berwyn IL Died Feb. 6, 1968.

KNOWLES, ARCHIBALD CAMPBELL, clergyman; b. Phila., Pa., July 11, 1865; s. George Lambert and Matilda Josephine K.; ed. U. of Pa., class of '85; attended lectures at Cambridge and London, England; D.D., Nashotah, 1937; m. Mary Clements Stocker, Apr. 20, 1893; children—Margaretta Lewis (Mrs. M. Thurston Tilton), Mary Clements Stocker (Mrs. Alan Maxwell Palmer, died 1933). Ordained deacon, 1898, priest, 1899, P.E. Church; rector St. Alban's Church, Olney, Phila. Author: The Belief and Worship of the Anglican Church, 1895; Joscelyn Vernon, 1898; Turning Points, 1898; The Triumph of the Cross, 1900; Come Unto Me, 1901; The Holy Christ Child, 1905; The Life of Offering, 1906; The Practice of Religion (over 100 copies sold), 1906; Adventures in the Alps, 1913; Reminiscences of a Parish Priest, 1935; Franklin Delano Roosevelt—The Great Liberal, 1937; A Rendezvous with Destiny (The Life and Career of Franklin Delano Roosevelt) 1946; Lights and Shadows of the Sacred Ministry, 1947. Was engaged in banking and other business enterprises for ten years before entering ministry. Has traveled extensively in Europe, specially interested in ecclesiastical art and architecture; rebuilt St. Alban's Church as a memorial to his parents in the style of French Decorated Gothic of the 13th Century. Home: 555 Pelham Rd., Germantown, Philadelphia PA‡

KNOWLES, EDWARD GILLETT, lawyer; b. Denver, Nov. 13, 1892; s. Charles Nelson and Florence (Reily) K.; A.B., U. Colo., 1914, LL.B., 1916; m. Helen Montgomery Dorsey, Sept. 28, 1920; children—Helen Dorsey (Mrs. Thomas E. Buchanan, Jr.), Clayton Dorsey. Admitted to Colo. bar, since practiced in Denver; now mem. firm Knowles, Hopper & Molen; gen. atty. Colo. Union Pacific R.R. Co., 1937-69. Delegate to International Bar Association conference, Salzburg, 1960, chairman committee scope and corr., 1960; chairman nat. conf. bar presidents Am. Bar Assn., 1960. Served to 1st lt., cav., U.S. Army, 1917-19. Mem. Am. (mem. of house of delegates 1955-63, board of governors 1963-66), Colorado (pres. 1950-51), Denver (pres. 1948-49) bar assns., Beta Theta Phi, Phi Delta Phi. Clubs: Denver, Denver Country, University (Denver). Home: Denver CO Died 1969.

KNOWLES, EDWIN BLACKWELL, educator; b. N.Y.C., May 14, 1903; s. Edwin B. and Grace E. (Western) K.; B.A., Wesleyan Coll., Middletown, Conn., 1924; M.A., N.Y.U., 1929, Ph.D., 1938; m. Lois Beckwith, May 25, 1929; children—Lawrence B., Alison (Mrs. Dick Higgins). Instr. English, U. Ill., 1925-27, N.Y.U., 1927-42; asst. prof. Queens Coll., 1942-48; mem. faculty Pratt Inst., 1948-67, prof. English, 1952-67, chmn. dept., 1954-64, dean div. gen. studies, 1960-62. Vice pres. bd. edn. Reformed Ch. Am., 1962-66. Mem. Modern Lang. Assn., Am. Assn. U. Profs., Coll. English Assn., Nat. Council Tchrs. English, Renaissance Soc. Am. (treas. 1951-67), Hispanic Soc. Am. (corr. mem.), Phi Beta Kappa, Psi Upsilon. Club: Andiron (pres. 1955-58) (N.Y.C.). Author: Influence of Don Quixote on English Literature, 1938; also articles, reviews comparative English-Spanish lit. and history. Brooklyn NY Died May 12, 1967.

KNOWLES, FREDERICK MILTON, newspaper man, playwright; b. Providence, R.I., Mar. 28, 1877; s. Lindley Murray and Cornelia R. (Logee) K.; grad.

grammar sch., Providence, 1892, L.I. Business Coll., Brooklyn, 1894; m. Kate I. McMurray, of Brooklyn, N.Y., Oct. 25, 1904. Reporter, 1894, asst. city editor, 1898, telegraph and dramatic editor since 1902, Brooklyn Times, Republican. Baptist. Author: ACheerful Year Book (with C. F. Lester), 1906; also plays: The Heir of the Wallaboat; Deliver Me From My Friends; The North Shore Boom, etc. Home: 435 Washington Av., Brooklyn‡

KNOWLES, MELITA, educator; b. Cambridge, Mass., Dec. 31, 1875; d. George and Adelaide Viola (Knowles) Spaulding; prep. edn., Cambridge Sch. for Girls, 1888-93; A.B., Radcliffe, 1897, grad. study, 1926-28, A.M., 1929; student Boston Mus. Sch. of Drawing and Painting, 1897-98, Harvard, 5 summers to 1929. Teacher of history, English, and history of art, Abbot Acad., Andover, Mass., 1900-05, Miss Head's Sch., Berkeley, Calif., 1906-08; mgr. food shop and exec. sec. Women's Ednl. Union, Boston, Mass., 1908-10, 1912-14; teacher of history, high sch., Brookline, Mass., 1910-12; teacher of history, Ethical Culture Sch., N.Y. City, 1914; teacher of history, Brearley Sch., N.Y. City, 1916-23; same, Bancroft Sch., Worcester, Mass., 1923-26, academic sec., 1926-28; prin. Goddard Sch. for Girls, Barre, Vt., 1929-1934. Member Foreign Policy Assn. Radcliffe Coll. Alumnae Assn., Am. Assn. Univ. Women, Vt. Council of Y.W.C.A. Republican. Episcopalian. Clubs: College (Boston); Barre Woman's. Address: 40 Commonwealth Av., Boston MA‡

KNOWLES, NATHANIEL, ex-fgn. service officer; b. Chelten Hills, Pa., Aug. 30, 1899; s. Nathaniel and Clive (Ellis) K.; C.E., Princeton, 1921; Ph.D., U. Pa., 1939; m. Isabelle Place Roper, Jan. 26, 1924; children—Isabelle (Mrs. Eberhard Trams), Clive (Mrs. William Hulick), Nathaniel III. Exec. asst. Bell Telephone Co., Pa., 1923-35; research, tchr., 1936-41; staff WPB, 1941-42; asst. to pres. Hanover Shoe Co. (Pa.), 1945-48; dir. office statistics ECA, Washington, 1948-50; dep. adminstr. Def. Prodn. Adminstrn., Washington, 1950-52; vice chmn. munitions bd. Dept. Def., 1952-53; dep. dir. bur. fgn. commerce Dept. of Commerce, 1953-65; assigned econ. sect., London, Eng., ret., 1965; vis. lectr. Lincoln U. (Pa.), 1965-66. Served to col., AUS, 1943-45. Decorated Legion of Merit. Home: Littlestown PA Died Jan. 17, 1972.

KNOWLTON, CHARLES OSMOND, mfg. exec.; b. nr. Baton Rouge, Oct. 30, 1895; s. Charles A. and Florence S. (Osmond) K.; student U. Cin., 1921; m. Isabel I. Taylor, Oct. 18, 1924; children—Carlisle, Penelope T. (Mrs. Phillip M. Pierce). With Am. Laundry Machinery Co., Cin., from 1919, Eastern div. mgr., 1944-50, v.p., gen. sales mgr., 1950-54, exec. v.p., from 1954, dir., from 1951. Served with U.S. Federalized N.G., 1916-17; as 1st lt., 136th F.A., 37th Div., U.S. Army, 1917-19; AEF in France. Mem. Sigma Chi. Republican. Episcopalian. Club: Union League (N.Y.C.). Home: Glendale OH Died Apr. 9, 1962.

KNOWLTON, DANIEL CHAUNCEY, author, educator; b. Cazenovia, N.Y., July 16, 1876; s. Charles M. and Martha Jane (Badley) K.; grad. Cazenovia Sem., 1893; A.B., Cornell, 1898, Ph.D., 1906; student Bonn U., Germany, 1903-04; m. Lou Osburn, Aug. 11, 1898; children—Daniel Chauncey, Donald Blackstone. Asst. in English, Cornell, 1898-99; head dept. of history, high sch., Ithaca, 1900-03; president White traveling fellow, Cornell, 1903-04; head dept. of history, high sch., Montclair, N.J., 1904-07; asst. in history, high sch., N.Y. City, 1907-08; asst. head of dept. and supervisor history and social studies, high schs. of Newark, N.J., 1908-20; in charge history and civics, Lincoln Sch., Teachers Coll., 1920-26; asst. prof. visual instrn., Yale, 1926-28; research asso. (asso. prof. rank) in visual instrn., same, 1928-29; lecturer Harvard and Boston univs., 1929; head of history dept. Fieldston Sch., New York, 1929; asso. prof. edn., New York Univ., 1930-32, prof. of edn. since 1932, chmn. dept. of social studies, 1940-43, professor emeritus since 1943. Assistant editor Illustrated Current News, Educational Service, 1927-30; now associate editor Education; member advisory board Social Studies, True Comics; on staffs summer schs., Harvard, etc. Mem. Am. Hist. Assn., N.E.A., Assn. History Teachers of Middle States and Md. Dept. Visual Instrn. (exec. com.), Nat. Council Social Studies, Phi Beta Kappa, Phi Delta Kappa, Pi Gamma Mu, Kappa Delta Pi. Presbyterian. Club: Graduate. Author: The Government of New Jersey, 1909; (with S.B. Howe) Essentials in Modern European History, 1917; Making History Graphic, 1925; History and the Other Social Studies in Jr. High School, 1926; Motion Pictures in History Teaching, 1929; The Knowlton Workbook in American History, 1930; Our America—Past and Present, 1938; (with Samuel Steinberg) The American Way in Community Life, 1947. Editor: Illustrated Topics in Ancient, Medieval and Modern History, 1920; Wall Maps of European History, 1920; asso. editor Larned History for Ready Reference, also (series) Westward March of Man (4 vols.), 1933-34; Home Study Courses in Ancient, European and American History, etc. Mem. ednl. staff Literary Digest, 1919-26, Pictorial Events since 1940. Home: Cazenovia NY‡

KNOWLTON, FRANK P(ATTENGILL), univ. prof.; b. Holland Patent, N.Y., June 17, 1875; s. Charles Fox and Mary (Patengill) K.; A.B., Hamilton Coll., N.Y., 1896; M.A., U. of Mich., 1897; M.D., Syracuse U., 1900; grad. student, U. of Cambridge, 1911, University Coll. London, 1911-12; m. Clara Avis Roberts, June 25, 1902; 1 dau., Catharine Morilla (Mrs. Lucius Foote). Instr. physiology and embrology Coll. of Medicine, Syracuse U., 1897-00, lecturer in physiology, 1900-06, asso. prof. physiology, 1906-08, prof., 1908-46, emeritus prof. since 1946. Trustee Marine Biology Lab., Woods Hole, Mass., 1923-46, emeritus trustee since 1946. Fellow A.A.A.S., A.M.A., mem. Physiol. Soc. (Gt. Britain), Am. Physiol. Soc., Soc. Exptl. Biology and Med., N.Y. State Med. Soc., Syracuse Acad. Medicine, Delta Upsilon, Nu Sigma Nu, Sigma Xi, Alpha Omega Alpha, Phi Kappa Phi. Republican. Presbyterian. Home: 1356 Westmoreland Av., Syracuse 10 NY‡

KNOX, MRS. FRANK, pres. Union Leader Publishing Co.; b. Alma, Mich., Oct. 13, 1875; d. Darius and Margaret June (Lawrence) Reid; student Alma Coll., Mich. Univ.; m. Frank Knox, Dec. 28, 1898. Wrote editorials, news stories, and shared management of Manchester Union Leader while Major Frank Knox, pub. of newspaper, was on active duty in France, World War I; pres. Union Leader Pub. Co., Manchester, N.H., 1944-48, mem. bd. dirs., 1914-48, retired. Dir. N.H. Tuberculosis Assn. Trustee N.H. State Tuberculosis Sanatarium, Glencliff, N.H. Active interest in Navy Relief Orgn., while living in Washington as wife of Sec. of Navy. Mem. Manchester Coll. Women's Club. Republican. Conglist. Home: 2800 Alhambra Circle, Coral Gables FL‡

KNOX, JESSIE JULIET (DAILY), author; b. at Cleveland, Tenn.; d. Rev. William Clinton and Julia Ann (Godby) Daily; ed. in sch. at Cleveland, Tenn., sem. at New Market, Tenn., and pub. schs., Knoxville, Tenn., grad. 1884; also spl. studies in music; moved to San Jose, Cal., after graduation; m. at San Jose, Charles W. Knox, June 4, 1890. Pres. Pacific Short Story Club of Cal. First contbr. of verse to papers and mags.; since 1900 writer of prose, chiefly on subject of Chinese on the Pacific Coast, with whose home life has had special facilities for intimate knowledge; lecturer on that subject, Oct., 1911—. Author: Little Almond Blossoms, 1904; In the House of the Tiger, 1911; Bunnyville Folk, 1911. Address: 5453 Manila Av., Oakland CA‡

KNOX, RAYMOND COLLYER, clergyman; b. Beacon, N.Y., Apr. 21, 1876; s. Starr Brush and Amy Beckwith (Collyer) K.; grad. Porter Mil. Acad., Charleston, S.C.; student Columbia U., 1902-04; Union Theol. Sem., 1902-05, B.D., 1907; Fellow Union Theol. Sem. in Europe, studied at U. of Berlin and Oxford U., 1905-07; S.T.D., Hobart, 1915; D.D., U. of Kings Coll., 1939; m. Florence Curtis Breed, Dec. 1908; 1 dau., Alexina B. Ordained in ministry of P.E. Ch., 1907; chaplain Columbia U., 1908-42 (now chaplain emeritus), also prof. Bibl. study, Columbia and Barnard colls. Mem. Nat. Assn., Bibl. Instructors, Soc. Bibl. Literature and Exegesis. Author: Knowing the Bible, 1927, revised, 1936; In Lumine Tuo, 1931; Religion and the American Dream, 1934. Home: Sylvan Lane, Old Greenwich CT‡

KNUTSON, KENT SIGUART, ch. ofcl.; b. Goldfield, Ia., Aug. 7, 1924; s. Gunner and Gertrude (Thorsheim) K.; B.A. Ia. State U., 1947; B.Th., Luther Theol. Sem. St. Paul, 1951; Ph.D., Columbia, 1961; m. Norma E. Arnesen, Sept. 5, 1951; children—Kirsten, Kristofer, Kent, Kaia, Kimberly, Karl. Chem. engr. Standard Oil of Ind., 1948; ordained to ministry Lutheran Ch., 1954; pastor Our Saviour Luth. Ch., S.I. N.Y., 1954-58; prof. theology Luth. Sem. St. Paul, 1958-68; pres. Wartburg Theol. Sem., Dubuque, Ia., 1968-70; pres. Am. Luth. Ch., Mpls., 1971-73. Served with USNR, 1944-46. Author: His Only Son Our Lord, 1964; The Struggle for Middle America, 1965; God's Drama-Seven Acts, 1969. Editor: Dialog, A Jour. of Theology, 1965-68. Home: Minneapolis MN Died Mar. 1973.

KOCH, FRED CHASE, engring. exec.; b. Quanah, Tex., Sept. 23, 1900; s. Harry and Margaret (Mixson) K.; student Rice Inst., 1917-19; S.B., Mass. Inst. Tech., 1922; Doctor of Science (honorary), Park College; m. Mary C. Robinson, Oct. 22, 1932; children—Frederick R., Charles deG., David H., William I. Chief engr. Medway Oil & Storage Co., Ltd., Isle of Grain, Eng., 1924-25; v.p. Winkler-Koch Engring. Co., 1925-41; pres. Koch Engring. Co., Inc., Wichita, Kan., 1941-50, chmn. bd., 1950-67; pres. Wood River Oil & Refining Co., Inc., Wichita, 1944-59; pres. Rock Island Oil & Refining Co., Inc., Duncan, Okla., 1947-66, chmn. bd., chief exec. officer, 1966-67; pres. Koch Oil Corp., Inc., Wichita, 1943-67, Matador Cattle Co., 1964-67; director of the Minn. Pipe Line Co., S. Saskatchewan Pipe Line Co., Great No. Oil Co., St. Paul, Minn., also the Coleman Company, Inc.; builder oil refineries in Eng., France, Belgium, Germany, Russia, Rumania, Portugal, Italy, Near East, Burma, S. Africa, Canada. Member of American Petroleum Inst., Am. Chem. Soc., Am. Inst. Chem. Engrs. Clubs: Chicago (Chgo.); University (N.Y.C.); Wichita, Wichita Country, Rotary (Wichita); Bear River (Ogden, Utah). Author: A Business Man Looks at Communism. Home: Wichita KS Died Nov. 17, 1967.

KOCH, GEORGE PRICE, Naval officer; b. Cresson, Pa., June 21, 1910; s. Edward Louis and Mary (Price) K.; B.S., U.S. Naval Acad., 1933; m. Virginia Vredenburgh, June 5, 1937; children—George Price, James Peter, Alexander Richard, Virginia Cabell. Commd. ensign U.S.N., 1934, advanced through grades to rear adm., 1961; designated naval aviator, 1934; various assignments in ships and ashore, 1934-42; comdg. officer Hdqrs. Squadron 5, 1942-43; mem. staff comdr. in chief U.S. Fleet, 1943-44; comdg. officer U.S.S. Humboldt, 1944-45; navigator, operations officer U.S.S. Leyte, 1945-47; grad. Naval War Coll., 1948; exec. officer Naval Air Tech. Tng. Center, Memphis, 1948-50. Naval Sta., Kodiak, Alaska, 1950-52; operations officer, then chief staff on staff comdr. Fleet Air Wings, Atlantic, 1952-53; head, war plans br. Office Chief Naval Operations, 1953-55; comdr. Naval Air Sta., Barbers Point, Hawaii, 1955-57; chief staff to comdr. Fleet Air, Quonset Point, R.I., 1957-58; comdr. Fleet Air Wing 3, 1958-59; comdg. officer Naval Air Sta., Norfolk, Va., 1959-61; comdr. Carrier Div. 18, 1961-62, Fleet Air Wings Atlantic, 1962-63; chief, Naval Air Res. Tng., 1963-65; comdr. Carrier Task Force, Mediterranean, 1965-67; comdr. Naval forces So. Command, comdt. 15th Naval Dist., Canal Zone, 1967-69; comdt. Naval Dist., Washington, 1969-72. Decorated numerous unit, battle and area ribbons. Home: Tingey House Washington DC Died Sept. 17, 1972; buried U.S. Naval Academy, Annapolis MD

KOCHAN, EDWARD JOHN, oral surgeon; b. Bridgeport, Conn., Nov. 24, 1922; s. John and Julia (Fekete) K.; student U. Va., 1942-44; D.D.S., U. Pa., 1948; m. Anna Epifano, Jan. 6, 1949; children—Edward John, Jeffrey, Kenneth. Intern, resident Bellevue Hosp., N.Y.C., 1948-49, clin. visiting, 1950-53; practice oral surgery, Bridgeport, 1949-69; lectr. Fones Sch. Hygiene, St. Vincents Hosp. Sch. Nursing; chief dept. dentistry, oral surgery St. Vincents Hosp.; mem. staff Bridgeport Hosp., Park City Hosp. Served with USNR, 1943-44; to capt. USAF, 1953-54. Diplomate Am. Bd. Oral Surgery. Mem. Am., Conn., Bridgeport (pres.) dental assns., Am., Conn. (past pres.), New Eng. socs. oral surgeons, N.Y. Soc. Oral Surgery, Kappa Sigma, Delta Sigma Delta. Lion. Contbr. articles to profl. jours. Home: Easton CT Died June 16, 1969.

KOCHER, A. LAWRENCE, architect, editor; born San Jose, California, July 24, 1885; s. Rudolph and Anna (Luchsinger) K.; B.A., Stanford University, 1909; student Massachusetts Inst. Tech., 1910-12; M.A., Pa. State Coll., 1916; New York U., 1924-25; m. Amy Agnes Moerder, May 23, 1910; m. 2d, Margaret Mercedes Taylor, 1932; children—Sandra A., Lawrence T. Was instructor in architecture, Pennsylvania State Coll., 1912-14, asst. prof., 1914-16, asso. prof., 1916-18, prof. and head of dept., 1918-26; head of McIntire Sch. of Art and Architecture, U. of Va., 1926-28; spl. lecturer Summer Sch., Pa. Acad. Fine Arts, 1926; mng. editor, editor Archtl. Record, N.Y.C., 1928-38. Visting prof. architecture, Carnegie Inst. Tech., Pittsburgh, 1938-40; prof. architecture, Black Mountain Coll., Black Mountain, N.C. (Carnegie Corp. Grant), 1940-43; lecturer in Fine Arts Coll. of William and Mary, 1944-59; archtl. cons. Nat. Park Service, Jamestown Festival, 1957; supervising architect, restoration of home of Washington Irving, Tarrytown, N.Y. Editor architectural records Colonial Williamsburg, 1944-54. Member State Board of Registration of Architects and Engrs. of Va.; chmn. State Art Commn. of Va., 1926. Mem. Am. Inst. Architects (chmn. com. on preservation historic monuments and scenery), Coll. Art Assn. America, Architectural League of New York, Sigma Phi, Sigma Tau, Alpha Rho Chi, Scarab; mem. Advisory Com. of Architects on Restoration of Williamsburg, Virginia, 1928-69. U.S. del. Internat. Congress, Art and Applied Design, Paris, 1937. Hon. mem. Phi Beta Kappa. Presbyn. Clubs: Salmagundi (N.Y.) Colonnade (U. Virginia). Author: Architecture of Lancaster County (Pa.), 1919; Fireplaces in England (with Guy Rothery), 1926; also Early Architecture of Pennsylvania (15 articles in Architectural Record), 1920-22; Colonial Williamsburg its Buildings, and Gardens (co-author); Shadows in Silver, 1954; Record Houses of the Year, 1956. Home: Williamsburg VA Died June 6, 1969; buried San Jose CA

KOCHIN, LOUIS MORDECAI, physician, rabbi; b. USSR, Oct. 18, 1898; s. Elihu Wolfe (Bessie (Reznik) K.; M.D., Northwestern U., 1926; M.Sc., W. Va. U., 1922; postgrad. Vienna U., Med. Center, Berlin Med. Center; m. Ethel Levine, Apr. 4, 1933; children—Frances Ruth (Mrs. Harvey Gordenker), Carole Joy (Harvey A. Wolsh). Intern, Presbyn. Hosp.-Chgo. Contagious Hosp., 1925-26; mem. staff Montefiore Hosp., Magee Hosp. (both Pitts.); ordained rabbi, 1921. Diplomate Am. Bd. Pediatrics. Mem. Pitts. Pediatric Soc., Zionist Orgn. Am., Pitts. Med. Forum, Jewish Publ. Soc., A.M.A. Jewish religion (pres. synagogue, hon. bd. adviser). Home: Pittsburgh PA Died Mar. 9, 1971; buried Tiphereth Israel Cemetery, Pittsburgh PA

KOCOUREK, ALBERT, lawyer; b. Louisville, Ky., July 9, 1875; Lake Forest (Ill.) Coll., 1895-96; LL.B., U. of Mich., 1897. Practiced, Chicago, 1897—; lecturer on jurisprudence, 1907-14, prof. law, 1914—,

Northwestern U. Law Sch., Chicago; lecturer, John Marshall Law Sch. Mem. editorial com. Assn. Am. Law Schs. (Philosophy of Law Series), 1910-—. Mem. Am. Bar Assn., Am. Judicature Soc., Internationale Voreinigung fur Rechts und Wirtschaftsphilosophie (Berlin), etc. Club: University. Translator: Gareis's Science of Law, 1911. Editor: (with Dr. John H. Wigmore) Evolution of Law Series, Vols. I, II, 1915. Contbr. to legal publs. Home: Lombard, Ill. Office: 31 W. Lake St., Chicago‡

KOEHLER, OTTO A., b. N. Warren, Pa., July 24, 1893; s. Charles C. and Lina (Unverzacht) K.; student Stevens Inst. Tech., Wahl-Henius Inst., Newark, Fermentation Lab., Chgo.; m. Marcia Marriner, Aug. 17, 1921; 1 son, Otto A. Chmn. bd. and president of Pearl Brewing Company, San Antonio, Texas; member board of directors National Bank Commerce, Tex. Transp. Co. (both San Antonio). Founder Otto Koehler Found. for student scholarships, 1959; donor proceeds book, Ku-Winda, to Boys Clubs Tex. Bd. dirs., life mem. San Antonio Zool. Soc.; bd. dirs. San Antonio Livestock Exposition. Served with F.A., U.S. Army, World War I; AEF in France. Mem. Tex. Chevaliers, Sigma Phi Epsilon. Clubs: San Antonio Country, San Antonio. Home: San Antonio TX Died June 1, 1969.

KOEHRING, WILLIAM J., business exec.; b. Kiel, Wis., 1872. Chmn. bd. and dir. Koehring Co., Milwaukee, Wis.; pres. and dir. Badger Brass and Aluminum Foundry Co. Home: 2371 North Sherman Blvd., Milwaukee, WI. Office: 3026 West Concordia Av., Milwaukee WI*‡

KOENIG, JOSEPH PIERRE, French army officer; b. Alsace. Commd. in inf. at age of 19 yrs.; awarded Medaille Militaire for service during World War I; fought in Foreign Legion, Morocco, in Riff campaign; promoted capt., 1939; served in Norway, and promoted major during Narvik operations; returned to France and fought near coast in Brittany; evacuated to England, and with regt. joined Gen. Charles de Gaulle just before French Armistice; sent to help reorganize French troops in French Equitorial Africa, 1940; served in Eritrea and Syria as chief of staff to Gen. Legentilhomme, 1941; became gen. comdg. all resistance forces in France, including underground fighters and French Forces of Interior, June 1944. Home: Paris France Died Sept. 2, 1970.

KOENIG, MYRON L(AW), educator; born Minneapolis, Aug. 1, 1910; s. Alfred E. and Myra (Manning) K.; A.B., Grinnell Coll., 1932; A.M., U. of Ia., 1933, Ph.D., 1938; student, U. of Chicago, 1944-45; L.H.D., Grinnell College, 1968; married to Lou Pate, Dec. 28, 1957. Dean of Junior coll., prof. Am. history George Washington U., 1945-58; cultural attache Am. Embassy, London, 1954-56; asso. dean Sch. Fgn. Affairs, FSI, Dept. State, 1958-62, dean, 1962-65, dean for acad. relations, 1965-71. Mem. Bd. Edn., Cedar Rapids, Ia., 1942-45; trustee. Presbyn. Archives of Presbyn. Ch. of U.S.A. (Philadelphia). Mem. Am. Hist. Assn. Club: University (Washington). Address: Washington DC Died Mar. 19, 1971.

KOERNER, THEODOR, Federal Pres. of Austria; b. Komorn, Austria, Apr. 24, 1873; s. Theodor and Karoline (Fousek) von K.; student Civilian lower coll., Reichenberg and Vienna, mil. upper coll., Mahrisch-Weisskirchen, War Acad. at Vienna; Dr. honoris causa, Mil. Tech. Acad., Vienna; unmarried. Officer in the Austro-Hungarian Army, 1st in Pioneer Corps, then in Gen. Staff, 1894-1918; chief of Gen. Staff of Austrian Republic, then head of office in Ministry for Mil. Affairs, Supt. of Army, 1918 until ret. as gen., 1924. Socialdemocratic mem. Bundesrat (Upper House of Parliament), 1924-34, last chmn. 1934; imprisioned Feb.-Dec. 1934, also in 1944; mayor and governor of Vienna, 1945-51; Federal president of Austria since June 1951. Recipient numerous mil. decorations. Home: Himmelstrasse 26, Vienna XIX, Austria. Office: Hofburg, Vienna I Austria Austria‡

KOHLER, HERBERT VOLLRATH, manufacturer; b. Sheboygan, Wis., 1891; s. John Michael and Wilhelmina (Vollrath) K.; Ph.B., Sheffield Scientific Sch. (Yale), 1914; LL.D., University Wis., Beloit College; Litt. D., Lakeland College, Sheboygan, Wisconsin; m. to Ruth Miriam De Young, 1937 (dec.); children—Herbert Vollrath, Jr., Ruth De Young II, Frederic Cornell. Identified since 1914 with Kohler Co. (founded by father, 1873); chmn. bd., 1940-68, president, 1937-62. Life trustee Beloit College. Sr. mem. National Industrial Conference Board; president of Kohler (Wis.) Found., Inc., Friendship House, Inc (Sheboygan, Wis.); trustee Layton Sch. Art, Milw.; hon. v.p., dir. U. Wis. Found., gen. chmn. centennial fund. Served as capt., F.A., with A.E.F., 1918-19; participated in Haute Alsace defensive, Aisne-Marne, Oise-Aisne and Meuse-Argonne offensives. Recipient Good Citizenship award Sheboygan Rotary Club, 1960. Mem. Wis. Mfrs. Assn., N.A.M. (dir. 1941-45, Man of Year award 1958), Am. Legion, V.F.W. (Distinguished Citizen award local post 1966), Antarctic Assos., Inc. Republican. Episcopalian. Clubs: Yale (N.Y.C.); University, Arts (Chgo.); University, Milwaukee (Milw.). Address: Kohler WI Died July 28, 1968.

KOHLER, WOLFGANG, medical psychologist. Address: Swarthmore PA Died 1967.

KOHLHEPP, CHARLES E., public utilities exec.; b. Baltimore, Md., Sept. 15, 1896; s. George J. and Ida (Pohl) K.; student Baltimore Poly. Inst., Baltimore Sch. of Commerce and Finance, Johns Hopkins (night classes), corr. courses; m. Margaret Gram, Oct. 1918 (dec.); children—Dorothy (Mrs. William Washburn), John G.; m. 2d, Mary Agnes Meagher, December 1953. Began as clerk-acct. Consol. Gas & Electric Light & Power Co., Baltimore; with Wis. Public Service Electric Light & Power Co., Baltimore; with Wis. Public Service Corp. and predecessor cos., Milwaukee, 1920-55, as auditor, treas., v.p. and treas., v.p. and gen. mgr., and pres. to 1955; pres., dir. N.J. Power & Light Co., 1955-72, Jersey Central Power & Light Co., 1955-72; dir. N.Y. & Long Branch R.R. Director Trees for Tomorrow. Member board directors Edison Electric Institute. Served as sergeant, F.A., United States Army, World War I. Dir. program bur., W.P.B.; acting dir. for program Nat. Prodn. Authority. Mem. Greater Milwaukee Com.; mem. N.J. Atomic Energy Commn. Mem. Controllers Inst. Am., N.J. C. of C. (dir.), N.J. Utilities Assn. (dir.). Conglist. Clubs: Seaview Country (Absecon, N.J.); Baltusrol Golf (Milburn, East Orange NJ Died 1972.

KOHLMER, FRED, motion picture producer; b. N.Y.C., Aug. 10, 1905; s. Lee and Minna (Wolferman) K.; ed. pub. schs., N.Y.C.; m. Maxine Sickle, Feb. 14, 1928. Press rep. A. H. Woods, Broadway producer; motion picture agt. William Morris Agy.; prodn. asst. to Samuel Goldwyn; motion picture producer 20th-Century-Fox, Paramount Pictures, Inc., Columbia Pictures; prodn. include Kiss of Death, The Late George Apley, The Ghost and Mrs. Muir, Picnic, Solid Gold Cadillac, Last Angry Man, Bye, Bye Birdie. Home: Beverly Hills CA Died Oct. 12, 1969.

KOHLSTEDT, DONALD WINSTON, library dir.; b. Milwaukee, Apr. 16, 1909; s. Edward Delor and Hannah Carrie (Sandmeir) K.; student Dakota Wesleyan U., 1925-28, LL.D. (hon.) 1953; A.B., U. of Ill., 1929, B.S. in Library Sci., with honors, 1930, A.M., 1935; m. Ethelyn Adelia Dunn, Feb. 22, 1930; children—Roger Winston, Carolyn Sue, Linda Rae. Stack supervisor, Univ. of Ill. Library, 1929-30; 1st asst. St. Louis Municipal Reference Library, 1930-34; instr. in public library adminstrn., U. of Ill. Library Sch., summer 1935; librarian Kansas City (Kan.) Pub. Library, 1935-44; became librarian Grand Rapids (Mich.) Pub. Library, 1941, later library dir.; bus. mgr. Pub. Libraries, a periodical, 1952-54; lectr. Library Sci., U. Mich., extension service, 1956-57, 59-60, 64-65, 67-68. Mem. Kansas State Planning Board, 1939-40; mem. Mich. State Bd. for Libraries, 1949-54, chmn. 1952-54; bd. dirs. Grand Rapids Council on World Affairs, Family Service Assn. (pres. 1955-57); chmn. steering com. Liberal Adult Edn. Program, Grand Rapids; chmn. Grand Rapids com. for rev. lit.; secretary Grand Rapids Historical Society; mem. exec. board Grand Rapid Adult Edn. Council, Friends of Library; mem. Mich. Council Better Libraries, Grand Rapids Cultural Devel. Com.; mem. Governor's Nat. Library Week Com., 1966. Mem. A.L.A. (council, 1949-52; chmn. library radio broadcasts com. 1939-40; chmn. audio-visual com. 1941-43, vice chmn., 1944-46; mem. fin. com. 1942-44, chmn. Constitution, Bylaws Com., 1954-56, exhibits round table exec. bd. 1954-56, chmn. standards com.; exibits cons. since 1969), Kansas Library Assn. (N.E. district chmn. 1935-36), Mich. Library Assn. (legis. com.; chmn. planning com. 1944-45, pres. 1946-47); v.p. U. Ill. Library Sch. Alumni Assn., 1935, 1942. Mem. Y.M.C.A. Edn. Com.; mem. bd. of dirs. Friends of Am. Art (1941-45). Better Films Council (pres. 1945-46), (both of Grand Rapids). Mem. Grand Rapids Furniture Designers Assn., Alpha Kappa Delta, Sigma Tau Delta, Beta Phi Mu. Republican. Methodist (bd. stewards First Ch., Grand Rapids, since 1941). Rotarian. Club: Torch (Grand East Grand Rapids MI Died July 23, 1971; buried Woodlawn Cemetery, Grand Rapids MI

KOHN, JACOB, rabbi; b. Newark, N.J., Sept. 14, 1881; s. Siegfried and Bertha (Kussy) K.; Ph.B., New York U., 1902; studied Jewish Theol. Sem., D.H.L., 1917; m. Augusta Hirsch, of Newark, June 14, 1908; children—Gustav, Hannah, David, Jonathan. Fellow in philosophy, New York U., 1902-03, ordained rabbi, 1907; rabbi Congregation Adath Jeshurum, Syracuse, N.Y., 1907-11, Temple Ausche Chesed, N.Y. City, 1911-68; lecturer dept. relig. edn., Teachers Coll. Visited France, 1918, as mem. commn. of Jewish Welfare Bd.; conducted services at G.H.Q., Chaumont, France, fall of 1918; assisted in mobile hosp. at the front during St. Mihiel drive, v.p. and mem. exec. council United Synagogue America; mem. exec. com. Rabbinical Assembly of Jewish Theol. Sem., also mem. bd. dirs.; mem. exec. com. New York Jewish Community; mem. Am. Jewish Com., Jewish Hist. Soc., Judaeans, Phi Beta Kappa. Democrat. Contbr. to Jewish Year Book, Jewish New York City NY Died Sept. 9, 1968.

KOKERNOT, HERBERT LEE, rancher; b. Gonzales County, Tex., Dec. 28, 1867; grad. Moulton (Tex.) Acad.; student Southwestern U. and U. of Tex.; m. Elizabeth Vanham, Oct. 28, 1891; children—Margaret Josephine (Mrs. Ira C. Ogden), Mary Elizabeth (Mrs. Job Gunter Hardie), Herbert Lee. In mercantile business, Gonzales, 1888-97; rancher, with J.W. Kokernot, in Brewster and Lubbock counties, 1897-1915, with son since 1915, on ranch comprising about 260,000 acres and grazing 15,000 cattle; dir. Frost Nat. Bank (San Antonio). Pres. Tex. Livestock Marketing Assn. (Fort Worth); chmn. bd. Bapt. Foundation of Tex. Democrat. Mason (32 deg.). Club: San Antonio Country. Home: 115 E. Lynwood Av., San Antonio TX*‡

KOLB, ELLSWORTH LEONARDSON, scenic photographer; b. Pittsburgh, Pa., Dec. 27, 1876; s. Edward and Ella (Nelson) K.; ed. pub. schs.; unmarried. In photograph business with brother, Emery C., at Grand Canyon, Ariz., since 1902; made trip with party in boats through canyons of the Green and Colo. rivers, taking numerous motion pictures, time required in the passage, Sept. 8, 1911-Jan. 18, 1912. Author: Through the Grand Canyon from Wyoming to Mexico, 1914. Home: Grand Canyon AZ‡

KOLE, LESSING LAWRENCE, cosmetic mfr.; b. Milw., Aug. 28, 1894; s. Julius and Jennie (Frank) K.; student pub. schs., Milw.; m. Carol Ann Jahn, Oct. 22, 1921; 1 son, Richard L. With Cutler Hammer Mfg. Co., Milw., 1914-15, A. O. Smith Corp., Milw., 1916-19; sales mgr. George J. Meyer Mfg. Co., Milw., 1920-21; with Kolmar Labs., Milw., 1921-69, pres., 1921-55, chmn. bd., 1956-69, also chmn. Port Jervis, N.Y. and Los Angeles; v.p. Kolmar-Internat., Can., Mexico, Paris, London, Offenbach, Germany, Tokyo, India. Mem. Toilet Goods Assn. (dir.), Chemists Club. Clubs: Rotary, Wisconsin (Milw.). Home: Milwaukee WI Died Apr. 3, 1969; buried Wis. Meml. Park.

KOLMAN, BURTON A., tchr., county ofcl. Instr. De Paul U., Chgo.; magistrate Circuit Ct. Cook County. Named Young Man of Yr., Chgo. Jr. C. of C., 1968. Address: Wilmette IL Died Feb. 24, 1967.

KOLSETH, J. HAROLD, mgmt. cons., corp. exec.; b. Schenectady, May 4, 1904; B.A., Union Coll., 1928; student Universite de Dijon (France), 1928; M.A. in Bus. Adminstrn., Harvard, 1931; m. Adele Rouyon Mackey, 1940; children—Sandra (Mrs. David F. Mawicke), Karen (Mrs. James P. Brossard). Faculty, Union Coll., 1928-29; with Atlas Supply Co., 1931-51, dir. research and devel., 1947-51; exec. v.p., dir. Devoe & Raynolds Co., N.Y.C., 1951-55; v.p. Anheuser Busch Inc., St. Louis, 1956-57; parnter, v.p. Barrington Assos., N.Y.C., 1957-58; prin. Kolseth & Partners, Greenwich, Conn., 1958-—; mgmt. cons. Mem. WPB, 1942-43; dir. operations Smaller War Plants Corp., 1944; cons. Dept. of State, Chile, 1957, Cuba, 1958, Ecuador, 1960, Brazil, 1961, Spain, 1961, Jamaica, 1962. V.p. Council Internat. Progress in Mgmt., 1966-67, also bd. directors. Served lt. comdr., USNR, 1944-45. Mem. Phi Beta Kappa; Pi Gamma Mu. Clubs: Indian Harbor Yacht, Harvard, Sky (N.Y.C.); Army and Navy (Washington); Greenwich Country. Contbr. articles to various mags. Home: Greenwich CT Died May 31, 1972.

KOMMERS, WILLIAM JOHN, banker; b. Mt. Calvary, Wis., Jan. 13, 1872; s. Matthias and Margaret (Wolf) K.; ed. St. Lawrence Coll., Mt. Calvary, and Pio Nono Coll., Milwaukee, Wis.; m. Louise M. Klinkert, Sept. 21, 1897; children—William Adolph, Henry Anthony, Margaret Anna, Joseph Adam. Began as messenger Northwestern Nat. Bank, Superior, Wis., 1890, cashier, 1897-1902; asst. cashier Old Nat. Bank, Spokane, Wash., 1902-10; v.p. Union Trust Co., Spokane, 1910-19, pres., 1919-24; v.p. and trust officer Old Nat. Bank & Union Trust Co., 1924-33; pres. First Nat. Trust & Savings Bank (affiliated with Old Nat. Bank), 1933-35; now conducting own business of organizing and managing businesses, properties and estates. Federal lease negotiator, HOLC Homes Use Service. Mem. Spokane Chamber of Commerce, Wash. Bankers Assn. (organizer, first pres. trust div.), Republican. K.C., Elk. Clubs: City, Spokane Country. Recognized as a leader in promotional work of trust cos. in the West through cooperative publicity. Address: E 429 Sharp Av., Spokane 11 WA‡

KONENKOV, SERGEI TIMOPHEEVITCH, sculptor; b. Smolensk, Russia, June 28, 1874; s. Timophei Terentievitch and Anna (Danina) K.; ed. Moscow Sch. of Fine Arts, and Imperial Acad. of Fine Arts, St. Petersburg, Russia; m. Margarita Vorontzova, Sept. 22, 1922. Came to U.S., 1924. Exhibited in Art Center Gallery, Reinhardt Galleries, New York; Art Institute, Chicago; Sesqui-Centennial Expn., Phila. Work permanently exhibited in museums of Moscow, Leningrad and other cities of Russia and in U.S. Works; (portrait busts) Justice Oliver Wendell Holmes, U.S. Supreme Court; Justice Benjamin Cardoza, Harvard; Justice Harlan F. Stone, Columbia U.; Prof. Albert Einstein, Inst. for Advanced Study, Princeton, N.J.; Dr. Adolf Meyer, Johns Hopkins U.; Dr. Hedeyo Noguchi and Dr. Simon Flexner, Rockefeller Inst. for Med. Research, N.Y. City; Dr. William Welch, Johns Hopkins U.; Maxim Gorky, his studio; Sergi New York City NY Died Oct. 1971.*

KONJOVIC, PETAR, composer; b. Curug, Yugoslavia, May 5, 1883; s. Pavle and Katica (Pivnicki) K.; grad. Conservatory of Prague (Czechoslovakia), 1906; m. Milena Stanisic, Oct. 14, 1907; 1 son, Jovan. Tchr. Serbian Sch. Music, Belgrade, 1907-14; composer, Sombor, 1914-16, Zagreb, 1917-18; insp. music Ministry Edn., Belgrade, 1919-21; dir. opera, Zagreb, 1921-26; dir. Nat. Theater, Osijek, 1927-32, Zagreb, 1933-39; prof., dean Acad. Music, Belgrade, 1939-50; founder, dir. Musiciological Inst., Belgrade, 1947-54, retired. Recipient Medal of Merit, 1953, Life-work award, 1946. Fellow Serbian Scis. and Art. Works include operas, folk operas, folk songs for voice and piano, symphonic poem, sonata for violin and piano, concerto for violin and orch., symphony for orch., chamber music works, choirs. Author: Personalties in Theater and Music; Serbian and Slav Music; Miloje Kilojevic, Stevan Mokranjac-a musical portrait, 1956; Essays About Music, 1965. Address: Belgrade Yugoslavia Died Oct. 1, 1970.

KONTA, ANNIE LEMP, author; b. St. Louis, 1867; d. William Jacob and Julia Lemp; m. Alexander Konta (q.v.), of Budapest, 1895. Author: The History of French Literature, 1910. Home: Hempstead LI NY‡

KOONS, CHARLES ALFRED, financier; b. Youngstown, O., Oct. 29, 1908; s. Herman W. and Catherine M. (Ratjen) K.; student Western Res. U., 1927-30; m. Rosemarie C. Gaffney, June 1940; children—Karen M., Charles Alred, Keven J. With Union Paper & Twine Co., Akron, O., 1931-37, Charles F. Hubbs & Co., N.Y.C., 1937-39; sr. partner Charles A. Koons & Co., N.Y.C., from 1940; pres. dir. Charles A. Koons Machines, Inc. from 1945, Charles A. Koons, Inc.; pres. Italit. Inc., from 1955, Diaminter, Inc., from 1955; president International Products Corp., N.Y.C., 1956-61; dir. Tri-Boro Steel Supply Co., Inc. (N.Y. and Ohio). Financial adviser Govt. of Paraguay, 1959. Decorated cavaliere ufficiale of merit Order Republic of Italy, 1956. Mem. Am. C. of C. for Italy, Ohio Soc. N.Y., St. Louis Zool. Soc., Newcomen Soc., Circumnavigators, U.S. C. of C., Navy League (life), Pan Am. Soc., Delta Kappa Epsilon. Mason (32 degree). Clubs: Yale, Netherland (N.Y.C.); Union (Cleve.); Youngstown Co.); Wee Burn Country (Darien). Home: Darien CT Died Feb. 26, 1968 buried Darien CT

KOPP, ARTHUR WILLIAM, congressman; b. at Big Patch, Wis., Feb. 28, 1874; s. William and Elizabeth Jane (Thomas) K.; grad. Platteville (Wis.) State Normal Sch., 1895; LL.B., U. of Wis., 1900; m. Emily Katherine Hutton, of Waukesha, Wis., Nov. 19, 1902. Mem. law firm Kopp & Brunckhorst, since 1907. City atty., Platteville, 1903-4; dist. atty. Grant Co., Wis., 1904-8. Mem. 61st and 62d Congresses (1909-13), 3d Wis. Dist.; Republican. Congregationalist. Address: Platteville WI‡

KOPP, GEORGE A(DAMS), educator; b. Montgomery City, Mo., Feb. 7, 1900; s. Philip R. and Mary E. (Smith) K.; A.B., Monmouth Coll. 1926, M.S., U. Wis., 1930, Ph.D., 1933; m. Julia R. Ball, June 22, 1924 (div. 1948); children—Joseph Blair, Kathleen Louise, Doris Helen; m. 2d Harriet C. Green, June 19, 1948. Chmn. speech dept. Jamestown (N.D.) Coll., 1926-28; instr., later asst. prof. U. Wis., 1928-36; asso. prof. Columbia (on leave Bell Telephone Lab., 1943-46), 1939-46; asso. prof. speech U. Mich., 1946-48; asst. prof. Wayne U., Detroit, 1936-39, prof. speech from 1948. Mem. Nat. Soc. for Crippled Children and Adults, Inc., Nat. Assn. Tchrs. Speech, Am. Speech and Hearing Assn. (sec., treas., pres.), Mich. Speech Correction Assn., Speech Assn. Am., Sigma Xi, Tau Kappa Alpha, Pi Kappa Delta, Delta Sigma Rho, Theta Alpha Phi. Author: Visible Speech (with R.K. Potter Birmingham MI Died Sept. 14, 1968; buried White Chapel, Bloomfield Twp. MI

KORIN, PAVEL DMITRIEVICH, artist; b. Palekh, Russia, July 8, 1892; s. Dimitriy and Nadejda (Talanova) K.; student Moscow Sch. Painting, Sculpture and Architecture, 1916; m. Praskovja T. Korina, Mar. 7, 1926. One man exhbns. include Moscow, 1963, N.Y.C., 1965, also in Italy, Germany, Sweden, France, Eng.; rep. permanent collections Tretyakow Gallery, Moscow, Russian Mus., Leningrad, museums in Riga, Voronezh, Novosibirsk, Astrakhan, Alma-Ata, Irkutsk. Named USSR Peoples' Artist, 1962; recipient Lenin prize, 1963. Mem. USSR Acad. Arts, Union Artists USSR. Decorated Order of Lenin; recipient Gold medal 40th anniversary USSR, 1957, Gold medal Brussels Worlds Fair, 1958; Gold medal Moscow USSR Acad. Arts, 1958. Mem. Orthodox Ch. Had large collection ancient Russian art. Home: Moscow USSR Died Nov. 22, 1967, buried Novo-devichy Monastery

KORN, PETER GEORGE, ins. exec.; b. Kalispell, Mont., Mar. 7, 1903; s. Daniel and Theresa (Calary) K.; Ph.B., U. Chgo.; m. Mary Elizabeth Bulfer, Aug. 14, 1926; 1 dau., Elizabeth A. Chief claim adjuster Continental Casualty Co., 1924-41; exec. v.p. Nat. Casualty Co., 1941-65, pres., 1965-72, also dir. Home: Troy MI Died May 24, 1972.

KORNER, THEODOR, pres. of Austria; b. Komorn, Hungary, Apr. 24, 1873; s. Theodor and Karoline (Fousek) K.; ed. Mil. School, Vienna and Vienna Mil. Acad.; hon. Dr., Vienna Inst. Tech., 1945; unmarried. Entered Austrian army and served as col. and chief of Gen. Staff, World War I; after war, was apptd., with rank of gen. insp., to Ministry of Defense, to reorganize the army; retired from army, 1919, and became affiliated with Social Dem. party; later apptd. mem. Commn. for Mil. Matters; rep. to Bundesrat from Vienna, 1925, later served as pres. to 1934; was then imprisioned for polit. reasons, 11 mos.; re-established Socialist party in Vienna after World War II; mayor of Vienna, 1945-51; pres. of Austria since 1951. Address: Neues Rathaus, Vienna 1 Austria*‡

KORNFELD, MURRAY, exec. dir. Am. Coll. Chest Physicians; married, Julia Hook; 1 son, Leonard Bertram. Founder and managing editor, Diseases of the Chest since 1935, Diseases of the Nervous System, 1940-43, Diseases of the Eye, Ear, Nose and Throat, 1941-43. Exec. dir. Am. Coll. of Chest Physicians, 1935-72. Organized Internat. Congresses on Diseases of Chest. Recipient Am. College of Chest Physicians medal for meritorious achievement, 1959; medal Soviet Acad. Surgery, Moscow, 1966; medal, Nat. Order Merit, Republic Ecuador, 1967. Honorary fellow of American College Chest Physicians; member of Asso. Editors of Tuberculosis Publs. (past pres.; mem. exec. bd.). Med. Soc. Execs. Conf., Pan Am. Council, Council Internat. Affairs, Am. Acad. Polit. and Social Sci. Certificates of merit Argentina, Brazil, Chile, Cuba, Ecuador, Germany, Greece, Italy, Mexico, Panama, Peru, Portugal, Spain, Uruguay, Korea, Japan, Thailand, Phillippines, Hong Kong. Clubs: Horse Shoe (Eng.); Rotary. Home: Chicago IL Died May 1972.

KOSA, EMIL JEAN, JR., artist; b. Paris, France, Nov. 28, 1903; s. Emil Jean and Jeanne (Mares) K.; grad. Acad. of Fine Arts, Prague, 1921; student, L'Ecole des Beaux-Arts, Paris, 1927-28; student, Calif. Art Inst., Los Angeles, 1922; m. Mary Odisho, Aug. 11, 1928; m. 2d, Elizabeth J. Twaddell, Aug. 26, 1952. Brought to U.S., 1907, and 1921, naturalized, 1927. Portrait and landscape painter, 1920-68; art dept. 20th Century-Fox Film Corp., 1932-68; teacher Otis Art Inst., 1940, Chouinard Art Institute, 1947-48, also at Laguna School of Art, fall, 1962. Represented in permanent collections; National Academy Ranger Collection, Mus. of Boston, Springfield (Mass.), Asheville (N.C.) Art Mus., Dayton, Toledo, Los Angeles, San Diego, Santa Barbara, La Jolla, Santa Paula; Cranbrook Art Inst. (Mich.); New Britain Inst., Dover (Del.), Wash. State Coll., Calif. State Library, Phoenix Mus., Cal. Watercolor Soc., Chaffey Jr. Coll. Exhibited Nat. Acad., Am. Water Color Soc., 1936-69; Pa. Acad., 1938-53, Carnegie, 1941-—; Corcoran, 1941-—; Art Inst., Chicago, 1940-48; Metropolitan, 1942; Virginia, 1940-55; Herron Inst., 1944, 1946; Colo. Springs, 1941-47. Had one-man shows: Los Angeles Mus., 1940; San Diego, 1941; Santa Barbara, 1945; Oakland, 1939; Vose Gallery, 1942; Macbeth Gallery, 1940, 1946; Cowie Galleries, 1941-69, Corona del Mar, 1969, Laguna Art Assn., 1970. Recipient Ranger purchase award Nat. Acad. Design, 1941, 1st prize, 1949, Cannon prize, 1951, Child Hassom purchase award, 1952, Adolph and Clara Obrig prize, 1954; Osborn purchase prize Am. Water Color Soc., 1938, Zabriskie purchase prize, 1939, H. S. Stuart purchase award, 1953; bronze medal Panama Pacific Expn., 1928; 1st prize Cal. State Fair, 1939, 54, 1st popular award, 1949, 55; 1st prize Ariz. Fair, 1947; 1st prize Found. of Western Art, 1919-42, Ann. Honor award, 1945; Chouinard-Patrick award Cal. Water Color Soc., 1945; special honorary mention Audubon Artists, 1949, cash award Audubon Artist, 1956; Jarvis House spl. distinction award, 1958; Academy award for special effects for Cleopatra, 1964; Henry Ward Ranger Fund purchase award for Nat. Art Gallery, 1969; and numerous other regional and local show awards. Nat. academician. Mem. Am., Cal. (pres. 1945) water color socs., Audubon Artists. His works are included in several collections of reproductions. Home: Los Angeles CA Died Nov. 4, 1968; buried Los Angeles CA

KOSER, RALPH B., ret. advt. exec. b. Williamsport, Pa., Nov. 27, 1909; s. Ralph S. and Clara (Russell) K.; student Bucknell U., 1927-30; m. Helen Gould, Aug. 11, 1934; 1 dau., Marcie E. (Mrs. Richard Henry Greenwell). With N. W. Aver & Son, 1930-33, J. M. Mathes, Inc., 1933-37; with McCann-Erickson, Inc., 1937-60, v.p., 1949-60; sr. v.p., dir. McCann-Erickson (USA), 1960; exec. v.p., dir. McCann-Marschalk Co., Inc., N.Y.C., 1960-64, ret.; currently engaged free-lance writing. Trustee Scarborough Country Day Sch., 1955-61. Recipient ann. writing awards Freedom Found., Sat. Rev., others. Served to 1st lt., inf., AUS, World War II. Mem. Sigma Alpha Epsilon. Presbyn. Club: Sleepy Hollow Country (Scarborough, N.Y.). Home: Naples FL Died Apr. 28, 1969.

KOSER, STEWART ARMENT, bacteriologist, educator; b. Harrisburg, Pa., Mar. 30, 1894; s. Alexander Stewart and Ella Lucretia (Arment) K.; Ph.B., Yale, 1915, M.A., 1917, Ph.D., 1918; m. Hilda Marion Croll, Aug. 23, 1927; 1 dau., Marion Aimee (Mrs. Armstrong). Asst. in bacteriology, Yale, 1916-18; bacteriologist U.S. Bur. Chemistry, 1919-23; asst. prof. bacteriology, U. Ill., 1923-28; asst. prof. bacteriology U. Chicago, 1928-36, asso. prof., 1936-43, prof. bacteriology, 1943-59, professor of bacteriology, emeritus, 1959-71; mem. adv. com. lab. standards Ill. State Health Dept., 1943-47; chmn. Lilly award com. (bacteriology), 1940-42. Served as sgt., U.S. Army, World War I; adv. to pre-med. students war training program, 1943-44. Awarded Pasteur award by Soc. Ill. Bacteriologists, 1949. Mem. Soc. Am. Bacteriologists (councilor 1934-36, 38-40, dir. local brs. 1936-39), Soc. Ill. Bacteriologists (pres. 1943-44); Soc. Exptl. Biology and Medicine, Am. Pub. Health Assn., A.A.A.S., Internat. Assn. Dental Research, Sigma Xi, Gamma Alpha, Alpha Chi Sigma. Club: Quadrangle (Chicago). Author: Vitamin Requirements of Bacteria and Yeasts, 1968. Mem. editorial bd. Jour. Bacteriology, 1935-51, Jour. Infectious Diseases since 1941. Contbr. sci. jours. Home: Red Bank NJ Died Apr. 15, 1971; buried Womelsdorf PA

KOSZALKA, MICHAEL FRANCIS, physician; b. Bklyn., May, 25, 1911; s. John and Mary (Wojtas) K.; B.S., St. Bonaventure Coll., 1935; M.D., Georgetown U., 1938; m. Helen Charlotte Groniak, Aug. 14, 1942; children—Michele (Mrs. Gustav Massee), Michael Francis, Pamela. Intern, Kings County Hosp., Bklyn., 1938-40; practice medicine specializing in internal medicine, Woodhaven, N.Y., 1940-41; resident in internal medicine Norwalk (Conn.) Gen. Hosps., 1941-42, Mpls., 1949-50; resident in internal medicine VA Hosp., Wood, Wis., 1946-48, chief sect. gastroenterology, 1948-49; chief med. service VA Hosp., Fargo, N.D., 1950-69, chief staff, Hosp., 1969-70; teaching asst. Marquette U. Sch. Medicine, Milw. 1948, clin. instr. med., 1949; clin. asst. dept. medicine U. Minn., Mpls., 1949-50; asso. teaching staff U. N.D. Sch. Medicine, Fargo, 1954-68, asst. clin. prof. medicine, 1969-70, asso. prof. clin. medicine, 1970; adj. prof. pharmacology N.D. State U., 1969. Mem. Fargo-Moorhead Fed. Exec. Council, 1968-70; mem. med. subcom. N.D. Council for Safety, 1961; chmn. bus. sect. Cass County chpt. Am. Cancer Soc., 1963; mem. N.D. Com. on Mental Health with Spl. Interest in Alcoholism, 1969. Bd. dirs. Fargo VA Employees Credit Union, 1962-70, v.p., 1963, pres., 1963-70; trustee United Fund of Fargo, 1963-65. Served to maj., M.C., AUS, 1942-46. Diplomate Am. Bd Internal Medicine. Fellow A.C.P.; mem. A.M.A., Am. Soc. for Gastrointestinal Endoscopy, Am. Gastroscopic Soc., Am. Thoracic Soc., 1st Dist. Med. Soc. N.D. (asso.), Assn. U.S. Army, Res. Officers Assn., Am. Legion, Catholic War Vets. Elk. Contbr. articles to med. jours. Home: Fargo ND Died Nov. 11, 1970; buried Nat. Cemetery Ft Snelling St Paul MN

KOUNTZE, CHARLES THOMAS, banker; b. Omaha, Neb., Sept. 26, 1871; s. Herman and Elizabeth (Davis) K.; grad. St. Paul's Sch., Concord, N.H., 1889; Ph.B., Yale, 1892; m. May Burns, of Omaha, Feb. 5, 1896 (died Oct. 21, 1922); children—Herman Burns (dec.), Denman, Elinor; m. 2d, Maud Borup, of St. Paul, Minn., Jan. 17, 1925. Began as clk., First Nat. Bank, Omaha; pres. same, 1907-14, chmn. bd., 1914-31. Democrat. Episcopalian. Club: Yale (New York). Home: Salisbury CT*‡

KOYRE, ALEXANDRE, educator; b. Taganrog, Aug. 29, 1892; s. Vladimir and Catherine (Liewen) K. student Gottingen U., Ecole Pratique des Hautes Etudes, Paris; Ph.D., U. Paris, 1923, Docteur es lettres, 1919; m. Dora Reyberman, 1922. Prof. Ecole Pratique des Hautes Etudes, Sorbonne, Paris, 1932-64; asso. prof. U. Montpelier, 1930-31; prof. Ecole Libre des Hautes Etudes, N.Y.C., 1941-45; mem. faculty New Sch. Social Research, 1942-45; mem. Inst. Advanced Study, Princeton from 1955; sometime vis. prof. U. Cairo, U. Chgo., Johns Hopkins, U. Wis. Mem. Internat. Acad. History Sci. (sec.), Internat. Inst. Philosophy (v.p.), Societe Philosphique de France, Am. Philos. Assn., Am. History of Sci. Soc., Nat. Acad. Arts and Sci. Author: La Philosophie de S. Anselme, 1923; La Philosophie de Jacob Boehme, 1929; Etudes Galileennes, 1939. Discovering Plato, 1945; Documentary History of the Problem of Fall, 1955; From the Closed World to the Infinite Universe, 1957; La Revolution Astronomique, 1961; Newtonian Studies, 1965; Etudes de La Pensee Philosophique, 1961; Etudes de La Pensee Scientifique, 1966; Metaphysics and Measurement, 1968. Contbr. articles profl. publs. Home: Paris France also Princeton NJ Died 1964; buried Paris, France

KRAFT, JOHN H., food mfg. cons.; m. Odean Waugh. Retired pres. and chmn. bd. Kraft Foods Co., later founder, pres. John Kraft Sesame Corp., Paris, Tex.; founder, chmn. bd. Grenada Farms Inc. (Miss.). Mem. Hoover Commn.; nat. chmn. Future Farmers Am. Bd. dirs. Chgo. Boys Clubs. Baptist. Mason (32 deg., Shriner). Clubs: Sunset Ridge, Chicago Athletic, Tavern; Burning Tree (Washington). Home: Winnetka IL Died Jan. 22, 1972; buried Memorial Park, Skokie IL

KRAL, JOSEF JIRI, commercial economist; b. Louzna, Bohemia, Oct. 15, 1870; s. Josef and Josefa (Hulcova) K.; grad. Gymnasium, Klatovy, Bohemia, 1889; LL.B., U. of Mich., 1892; m. Antonia Krizan, of Chicago, Ill., Sept. 14, 1899; children—Georgina, Victor Hugo, Franklin. Came to U.S., 1889, naturalized citizen. Editor Slavie, Bohemian weekly, Racine, Wis.,

1894-1904, Spraveldlnost, daily, Chicago, 1905-11; with Bur. Foreign and Domestic Commerce, Washington, D.C., 1911—. Socialist candidate for Congress, Chicago, 1906. Freethinker. Author: Americke Pravo, 1899; Vira a Veda (Faith and Science), 1902; German Trade and the War, 1918; Americky Kongres, 1920. Contbr. to Universal Cyclopedia, and to New Internat. Cyclo. Home: 1814 Kilbourne Pl. N.W., Washington DC‡

KRAMER, A. WALTER, composer, music critic; born New York City, September 23, 1890; s. Maximilian and Anna Kramer; student (class of 1910) Coll. City N.Y.; m. Rosalie Virginia Rehling, Dec. 21, 1922 (dec.); 1 dau., Anne; m. 2d, Merle Campbell Montgomery, Nov. 16, 1957. Gen. asst. Musical America, 1910, active in editorial and adv. depts., 1910-22; resigned 1922 to live in Europe until 1925, devoting time to composing at Lausanne, Switzerland, and Asolo and Florence, Italy, also visiting other countries; editor in chief Musical America, 1929-36; gen. music supervisor for Columbia Broadcasting System, 1927 (when it began) to 1928; v.p. and managing dir., Galaxy Music Corp., N.Y., 1936-56. Mem. Am. Soc. Composers, Authors and Pubs. (bd. dirs., 1940-57), Internat. Soc. Contemporary Music (U.S. sect.), Soc. for Pub. Am. Music (pres. 1934-41), Phi Epsilon Pi, Phi Mu Alpha. Club: The Bohemians (New York City); Musicians (president 1958-60) (N.Y.). Works: Two Symphonic Sketches, Op. 37a (N.Y. Philharmonic, 1916); Symphonic Rhapsody in F Monor (for violin and orch.), Op. 34a (N.Y. Philharmonic, 1919); transcription for symphonic orchestra of Bach's Chaconne; In Normandy (cycle for chorus of women's voices and orchestra), Op. 49; many shorter compositions for violin, including Eklog, Op. 41, No. 1a (Fritz Kreisler and others); also piano compositions including, A Fragment: When the Sun's Gone Down (Percy Grainger and others); also some 300 other published compositions, including The Last Hour, Beauty of Earth, Pleading, The Great Awakening, The Faltering Dusk, The Patriot, Green; about 100 songs, many sung by celebrated singers. Contbr. to The Chesterian and The Sackbut (London), The Musical Quarterly; contbg. editor to Internat. Cyclopedia of Music. Address: New York City NY Died Apr. 10, 1969.

KRAMER, ANDREW ANTHONY, mfr., inventor; b. Kansas City, Kan., June 4, 1867; s. Frederick and Margaret (Hartman) K.; ed. pub. schs.; m. Ella Mary Conway, Nov. 27, 1890; children—William Francis, Clarence Anthony (dec.), Walter Andrew, (dec.), Helen Ione, Joseph Michael. Founder, 1893, since pres. Columbian Steel Tank Co., mfrs. sheet steel products and metal specialties, Kansas City; Pres. Steel Mfg. & Warehouse Co. Mem. Am. Soc. M.E. (awarded 5 gold medals for excellence of manufactured products), Kansas City Chamber Commerce, St. Vincent de Paul Soc. Democrat. Mem. Knights of Columbus. Clubs: Kansas City, Blue Hills Country. Inventor of appliances for safe handling, transportation and storage of gasoline and other inflammable liquids; holder of nearly 300 patents. Home: 6700 Elmwood Av. Office: 1509 W. 12th St., Kansas City MO‡

KRAMER, JOHN F., formerly prohibition commr.; b. Butler, Richland Co., O., Feb. 10, 1869; s. Jonathan and Sarah C. (Niman) K.; A.B., Ohio Northern U., 1892; LL.B., Ohio State U., 1902; m. Emma Maglott, of Richland Co., O., July 31, 1895; children—Helen M., John F., Dorothy N. Began practice at Mansfield, 1902; mem. 4th Constl. Conv., Ohio, 1912; mem. Ohio Ho. of Rep., 2 terms, 1913-17 (dem. floor leader, 1913-15); spl. counsel to Joseph McGhee, atty. gen. of Ohio, 1917-19; federal prohibition commr. Nov. 17, 1919-June 1921. Pres. bd. dirs. Wittenberg Coll., Springfield, O.; mem. exec. bd. United Luth. Ch. in America. Active worker in Church and S.S. Lutheran. Mason. Home: Mansfield OH‡

KRAMER, SIMON GAD, clergyman; b. Austria, Jan. 29, 1903; s. Michael and Bella (Surkis) K.; brought to U.S., 1913, naturalized, 1927; A.B., U. Chicago, 1924, M.A., 1926; Rabbi Hebrew Theological College, 1925; Ph.D., New York University, 1962; m. Tirza Nelson, Aug. 14, 1932; 1 son, Jay Michael. Rabbi, Congregation Knesseth Israel, Hammond, Ind., 1925-28; Temple Beth-El, Gary, 1928-31, Hebrew Inst. U. Heights, N.Y. City, since 1931; founder, prin. Akiba Hebrew Acad., N.Y.C., 1947-64; pres. Hebrew Theological College, and Jewish University of America, Chicago, Illinois, 1964-70. President Synagogue Council Am., 1951-52, N.Y. Bd. Rabbis, 1949-50; v.p. Rabbinical Council Am., 1940-48, v. chmn. bd. pension and ins. plan since 1947; mem. chaplaincy bd. N.Y.U. since 1947. Mem. religious panel Commn. Occupied Areas, 1950; member Gov's. Com. of 100 Youth and Edn., 1950; adv. council City N.Y. Office, Civil Def., 1950-70. Bd. dirs. Hebrew Theol. Coll., Chgo., 1926-27, Jewish Edn. Com., N.Y.C., 1947-50; trustee Fedn. Jewish Philanthropies, N.Y.C., 1951-70. Served as Jewish liaison rep. to Am. Mil. Govt., Germany, U.S. Army, 1948-49. Author: God and Man in the Sefer Hasidim. Contbr. articles to various publs. Home: Chicago IL Died Feb. 17, 1970; buried Emerson NJ

KRANNERT, HERMAN C(HARLES), business exec.; b. Chicago, Nov. 5, 1887; s. Charles and Louise (Jacob) K.; B.S. in Mech. Engring., U. of Ill., 1912; LL.D., Ind. U., 1957, Butler U., 1960, Evansville Coll., 1963, DePauw U., 1964, Univ. of Illinois, 1965, Ind. Central Coll., 1967; D. Indsl. Adminstrn., Purdue U., 1962; m. Ellnora D. Decker, Oct. 1, 1919. Founder, chmn. bd., dir. Inland Container Corp., Anderson Box Co.; v.p., dir. Ga. Kraft Co.; member board of directors of Indiana National Bank, Morgan Packing Co., Inc., Austin, Ind. Pres. bd. trustees Indpls.-Marion Bldg. Authority; bd. dirs. Indpls. Civic Progress Assn., Herman Charles and Ellnora Decker Krannert Found., Inland Container Corp. Found., Inc.; trustee Indiana Central College, also Indianapolis, Butler University, Indpls. Recipient Achievement award U. Ill., 1960, Law Day award Appellate Ct. Ind., 1964. Mem. Nat. Assn. Mfrs., Ind. Mfrs. Assn., Am. Soc. M.E., Fibre Box Assn., Nat. Paperboard Assn., U.S., Ind., Indpls. C. of C., Chi Phi. Republican. Methodist. Mason (Shriner, K.T., 33 deg.), Sagamore of the Wabash. Clubs: Columbia, Athletic, University, Country, Indianapolis Athletic (Indpls.); University, Mid-America (Chgo.); Woodstock; Meridian Hills Country. Home: Indianapolis IN Died Feb. 1972.

KRANS, HORATIO SHEAFE, author; b. Boston, Mass., December 9, 1872; s. Rev. Edward H. and Charlotte (Sheafe) K.; A.B., Columbia, 1894, Ph.D., 1903. Engaged in lit. work for mags. and revs. and editorial work since 1900. Lit. adviser to G.P. Putnam's Sons, 1905-08; to Sturgis & Walton Co., 1909-13; asso. editor Internat. Year Book, 1913-15; on contributing staff of New Internat. Encyclopedia, 1913-16; editorial staff Harper's Magazine, 1916; dir. Columbia U. War Service Bureau, Paris, 1918-19; asso. dir. Am. U. Union, Paris, 1919-29, dir., 1930-June 1940 (German occupation of Paris), Officer of Legion of Honor. Club: Columbia U. (N.Y.); Author: Irish Life in Irish Fiction, 1903; William Butler Yeats and the Irish Literary Revival, 1904; Oliver Goldsmith, a Critical Biography (in Vol. I of Turks Head Edition of the Works of Goldsmith), 1907; Handbook for American Students in France, 1926, 2d edit., 1938. Editor: Lincoln Tribute Book, 1909; English Love Poems, 1909; The Lost Art of Conversation, 1911. Asso. editor The World's Wit and Humor (10 vols.), 1906. Address: 116 East Chestnut St., Asheville NC‡

KRATHWOHL, WILLIAM CHARLES, educator; b. Buffalo, N.Y., Oct. 10, 1882; s. Charles Gottlieb and Minnie (Stutzriem) K.; A.B., Harvard, 1907, A.M., Columbia, 1910; Ph.D., U. of Chicago, 1913; married Sarah H. Reading, July 14, 1917 (deceased); one son, David R.; married 2d, Marie A. Reimold, June 3, 1922 (dec.). Instr., Barnard Coll., Columbia U., 1907-11, Washington U., St. Louis, Mo., 1911-12; prof. mathematics, Ripon (Wis.) Coll., 1913-14; asst. prof. of mathematics, Armour Inst. Tech. (now Ill. Inst. Tech.), 1914-19, asso. prof., 1919-31, prof. since 1931, chmn. dept. of mathematics, 1931-34, dir. dept. educational tests and measurements 1938-45, dir. of tests, Inst. for Psychol. Services, 1945-69. Diplomate Am. Bd. Examinations in Professional Psychology; fellow A.A.A.S.; mem. Am. Math. Society, Math. Assn. of America, Am. Soc. for Engring. Edn., Central Assn. of Science and Mathematics Teachers, Nat. Vocational Guidance Assn., Am. Psychol. Assn., Midwest Psychol. Assn., Ill. Psychol. Assn., Chicago Psychol. Club, Phi Delta Kappa, Sigma Chi. Co-author: Analytic Geometry, 1921. Office: Chicago IL Died Apr. 16, 1969; buried Riverview Cemetery, South Bend IN

KRATZ, ALONZO PLUMSTED, educator; b. Champagn, Ill., June 17, 1885; s. Edwin Augustus and Annie Mary (Bradley) K.; B.S., U. of Ill., 1907, M.S., 1909; m. Alma Zella Glanzner, Aug. 10, 1920. Asst. in physics lab., U. of Ill., 1907-10, instr. mech. engring., 1910-12, research asst., 1912-15, research asso., 1915-18, research asst. prof., 1918-21, research prof. mech. engring., 1921-46, research prof. Mech. engring. and acting head of dept., Nov. 1945-Sept. 1946, research prof. mech. engring., emeritus, 1946-70. Author many tech. papers and bulletins. Home: Urbana IL Died Dec. 12, 1970.

KRAUS, EDWARD HENRY, educator, mineralogist; b. Syracuse, N.Y., Dec. 1, 1875; s. John Erhardt and Rosa Kocher (Knobel) K.; B.S., Syracuse U., 1896, M.S., 1897, Sc.D. (hon.), 1920, LL.D., 1934; Ph.D., U. Munich, 1901; Sc.D., U. Mich., 1967; m. Lena Margaret Hoffman, June 24, 1902; children—Margaret Anna (Mrs. Edward T. Ramsdell) (dec.), Edward Hoffman (dec.), John Daniel. Asst. in mineralogy and German, Syracuse U., 1896, instr., 1897-99, 1901-02, asso. prof. mineralogy, 1902, prof. geology and chemistry, summers, 1903, 04; head, dept. sci. Central High Sch., Syracuse, 1902-04; asst. prof. mineralogy U. Mich., 1904-06, jr. prof., 1906-07, mineralogy and petrography, 1907-08, prof. and dir. mineral lab. 1908-19, prof. crystallography and mineralogy, and dir. Mineral Lab., 1919-33, prof. crystallography and mineralogy, 1933-46, sec., 1908-10, acting dean, 1911-15, dean summer session, 1915-33, acting dean, 1920-23, dean Coll. Pharmacy, 1923-33, and Coll. of Lit., Sci. and Arts, 1933-45, dean emeritus 1945-73; Henry Russel lectr. U. Mich., 1945; Orton lectr. Am. Ceramic Soc., 1954. Recipient Roebling medal Mineral. Soc. Am., 1945. Fellow Geol. Soc. Am., A.A.A.S. Mineral Soc. Am. (pres. 1920, hon. pres. 1955-73), Am. Coll. Dentists (hon.), Optical Soc. Am.; mem. Am. Gem Soc. (hon. certified gemologist 1954), German Mineral. Soc. (hon.), Am. Chem. Soc., Mich. Acad. Sci. (pres. 1920), Am. Inst. Mining and Metallurgy Engrs., Am. Pharmacy Assn., Mich. Schoolmasters Club (pres. 1943-44), Gemological Assn. Gt. Britain (hon., v.p. 1956-73), German Gemological (hon.), Gemological Inst. Am. (pres. 1948-70), Phi Beta Kappa, Sigma Xi, Phi Kappa Phi. Author: Essentials of Crystallography, 1906; Descriptive Mineralogy, 1911; Tables for the Determination of Minerals (with W.F. Hunt) 1911; Mineralogy (with W.F. Hunt), 1920; Gems and Gem Materials (with E.F. Holden), 1925, 5th edit. (with C.B. Slawson), 1947; also numerous articles in scientific and ednl. jours., U.S. and abroad. Home: Ann Arbor MI Died Feb. 3, 1973.

KRAUSE, HARRY THEODORE, container co. exec.; b. Lorain, O., Apr. 9, 1894; s. Arthur and Augusta (Kuehn) K.; ed. pub. schs.; m. Methyl Caswell; 5 children. With Greif Bros. Cooperage Corp., Delaware, O., from 1925, pres., from 1956. Served with U.S. Army, World War I. Home: Worthington OH

KRAUSE, LOUISE B., librarian; b. Kalamazoo, Mich.; d. Ustick O. and Mary (King) Krause; student McGill U., Montreal, Can., 1892-96; grad. Ill. State Library Sch., 1898. Library organizer, 1898-1903; asst. librarian and instr. in library methods, Tulane U., 1903-09; librarian, H.M. Byllesby & Co., Chicago, 1909-39; retired. Spl. lecturer, U. of Chicago Sch. of Commerce, 1916-18. Mem. A.L.A. (exec. board 1927-31), Chicago Library Club (ex-pres.). Club: Covington Garden Club (pres. 1941-42). Author: The Business Library, 1921; Better Business Libraries, 1922. Lecturer to library schs. and contbr. to library and tech. periodicals. Home: 724 Boston St., Covington LA

KREISMANN, FREDERICK HERMAN, mayor; b. Quincy, Ill., Aug. 7, 1869; s. Frederick and Frances (Bruner) K.; ed. Central High Sch., St. Louis; m. Pauline Whitman, of St. Louis, Jan. 25, 1902. Civil engr. and surveyor, 1888-90; spl. agt. Aetna Ins. Co. for Neb., 1891-3; sr. mem. Kreismann & Theegarten, ins. agts., St. Louis, since 1893. Clerk Circuit Ct., 1907-9; mayor of St. Louis, 1909-13; Republican. Episcopalian. Mason. Clubs: Mo. Athletic, St. Louis, Mercantile. Home: 4362 McPherson Av. Address: City Hall, St Louis MO‡

KRESS, WALTER JAY, lawyer; born at Johnstown, Pa., May 21, 1893; the son of Jacob Fronheiser and Myrtle L. (Zimmerman) K.; grad. Lawrenceville (N.J.) Sch., 1911; B.S. in Econs., U. Pa., 1920; mem. Princeton, class 1915, Cornell U. Coll. Law, class 1918; student Oxford (Eng.) U., 1919, U. Pa. Law Sch., 1920-23; m. Arline Mae Hill, Oct. 11, 1924. Admitted to Pa. bar, 1924; practiced in Johnstown, 1924-29, Harrisburg, 1937-39; sec. Pa. Bd. Finance and Revenue, 1929-37; head revenue dept. Commonwealth Pa., 1939-42; head Pa. Corp. Taxes, 1945-47; mem. Pa. Tax Equalization Bd., 1947-56; mem. program com. Nat. Tax Assn., 1955, bank tax com., 1951-57, exec. dir. assn., hdqrs. Harrisburg, 1956-66. Chmn. Cambria County (Pa.) Rep. Com., 1926-28; mem. exec. com. Pa. Rep. Com., 1934-36; sec.-treas. Rep. Nat. War Vets., 1940-42. Served from 2d lt. to col. World Wars I and II; brig. gen. (ret.) Pa. N.G. Decorated Army Commendation ribbon with oak leaf cluster; recipient J in Life, Johnstown Jr. Chamber of Commerce, 1942; commd. Kentucky Colonel, 1962. Member of American, Pa., Dauphin County bar assns., Pa., Harrisburg chambers commerce, Am. Legion (comdr. Pa. 1936-37, chmn. nat. rehab. com. 1937-38), Mil. Order World Wars (past Pa. comdr.), Princeton Alumni Assn. Central Pa. (v.p. 1960-64), Nat. Tax Assn. (hon.), Pa. Soc. of N.Y., Harrisburg Execs. Club (past pres.), Sigma Chi, Phi Delta Phi. Lutheran (past Vestry). Rotarian, Mason (Shriner). Clubs: Vesper (Phila.): Officers (various posts). Author numerous articles on taxes. Home: Harrisburg PA Died Apr. 25, 1968; buried Franklin NH

KRESSMAN, MABEL A. GRIDLEY (MRS. FREDERICK W. KRESSMAN), chem. co. exec.; b. Morrison, Ill., Feb. 11, 1887; d. John and Mary Ann (Ward) Gridley; B.S. in Chemistry, U. Ill., 1909; m. Frederick W. Kressman, June 20, 1912 (dec. Oct. 1954); children—Frederick W., Elsa (dec.), John G. Sci. tchr., 1910, 11; chemist Continental Turpentine & Rosin Corp., Laurel, Miss., 1925-35, personnel dir., 1935-44, treas., dir., Shamrock, Fla., 1954-70; dir. Conturps Corp., Shamrock, 1957-70. Mem. Dixie County C. of C., Colonial Dames, D.A.R., U. Ill. Found. Clubs: Cross City Garden, Cross City Womens. Home: Cross City FL Died Jan. 7, 1970.

KRIEGE, OTTO EDWARD, univ. pres.; b. Belleville, Ill., Nov. 20, 1865; s. Eberhard Henry and Mary E. (Lehr) K.; A.B., Central Wesleyan Coll., Mo., 1888, A.M., 1890; post-grad. univs. of Bonn and Berlin, Germany, Chicago and Denver; D.D., Baker, 1906; m. Emma R. Frick, Sept. 16, 1890; children—Edith Helene (Mrs. P.E. Hemke), Herbert Frick. Ordained M.E.

ministry, 1890; pastor Arlington, Neb., 1890-93, Omaha, 1893-98, Sedalia, 1898-99; prof. psychology and ethics, 1899-1910, pres., 1910-25, Central Wesleyan Coll.; pres. New Orleans U., 1925-35. Del. Gen. Conf. M.E. Ch., Baltimore, 1908, Minneapolis, 1912, Saratoga Springs, 1916. Mem. Coll. Presidents' Assn., Am. Geog. Soc., Sigma Tau Delta. Mason. Author: History of West German Conference, 1907; History of Methodism, 1909; A Century of Service, 1940. Home: 5300 St. Charles Av., New Orleans LA‡

KRILL, ALEX EUGENE, ophthalmologist, educator; b. Cleve., Oct. 20, 1928; s. Samuel and Bertha (Rosner) K.; B.S., Western Res. U., 1950; M.D., Ohio State U., 1954; m. Suzanne Altschui, May 31, 1964; 1 dau., Eileen. Intern, Phila. Gen. Hosp., 1954-55; resident ophthalmology U. Ill., 1958-60, USPHS spl. trainee ophthalmology, 1960-61; postgrad. fellow in visual physiology U. Mich., 1961; asst. prof., research asso. in ophthalmology U. Chgo., 1961-65, asso. prof. 1965-68, prof., 1968-72, mem. com. on genetics, 1967-72. Served with USNR, 1955-57. Recipient award of merit Am. Acad. Ophthalmology and Otolaryngology, 1970; certificate of merit A.M.A., 1970. Diplomate Am. Bd. Ophthalmology. Mem. Am. Acad. Ophthalmology and Otolaryngology (sect. chmn.), A.C.S., Am. Ophthal. Soc., Internat. Congress Neuro-ophthalmology (sec. Western Hemisphere), Internat. Soc. Clin. Electroretinography (v.p. Western Hemisphere), Phi Beta Kappa, Sigma Xi, Alpha Omega Alpha. Chief editor Ophthalmology Digest, 1970-72; mem. editorial bd. Am. Jour. of Ophthalmology, 1966-72, Investigative Ophthalmology, 1969-72, Documents Ophthalmologica, 1970-72, Survey of Opthalmology, 1970-72. Contbr. articles to profl. jours. Home: Chicago IL Died Dec. 8, 1972.

KRITZ, KARL, condr. Former condr. Met. Opera Co., N.Y.C., Chgo. Symphony Orch., also other mus. groups; last position as condr. Syracuse Symphony Orch. Home: Syracuse NY Died Dec. 17, 1969.

KROECK, LOUIS SAMUEL, biologist; b. Dayton, Ia., June 13, 1872; s. Louis F. and Charlotte (Veith) K.; B.S., Coll. of the Pacific, 1895, M.S., 1898; A.M., Stanford University, 1897; Sc.D., Coll. of the Pacific, 1931; research work, Hopkins Biol. Lab. (Stanford) 3 summers, Calif. Acad. Sciences, 2 summers; m. Bertha Graff, of San Jose, Calif., June 30, 1904; children—Graf Louis (dec.), Margarethe Etamina, Bertha Louise, Theodora Wilhelmina, Barbara Fourth, Louis Graf. Instr. biology, 1896-99, prof. biology and geology, 1899-1904, prof. biology, 1904-32, Coll. of the Pacific, now emeritus. Fellow A.A.A.S., Calif. Acad. Sciences; mem. Am. Genetic Assn., Save the Redwood League. Methodist. Specilizes in micro-biology. Home: 205 Euclid Av., Stockton CA‡

KROEZE, BAREND HERMAN, college pres.; b. Kampen, Netherlands, Dec. 8, 1868; s. Henry J. and Nellie (DeBrink) K.; brought to America in infancy; A.B., U. of Mich., 1894, post-grad., 1895; grad. McCormick Theol. Sem., 1898; studied U. of Chicago, 1901; M.A., Lenox Coll., Hopkinton, Ia., 1902; D.D., Coe Coll., Ia., 1906; LL.D., Jamestown (N.D.) College; L.H.D., University of North Dakota, 1945; married Nettie Muzetta Gray, Nov. 30, 1904. Ordained Presbyn. ministry, 1898; pastor Lewistown, Minn., and Central Ch., Austin, Minn., 1898-1901; v.p. Lenox Coll., 1902-05; pres. Whitworth Coll., Tacoma, Wash., 1905-09; pres. Jamestown (N.D.) Coll., since orgn., 1909. Appointed by Governor a member of Rent Control Bd. Mem. Commn. on Higher Instns. of North Central Assn. of Colleges and Secondary Schs. Mem. Presbyn. College Union (pres. 1927-28), Assn. Am. Colleges (charter mem.), National Education Association and Pi Kappa Delta. Republican. Mason. Rotarian (pres. 1941). Counselor of Yenching U., Peiping, China. Received award for distinguished service in Christian edn., Gen. Assembly of Presbyn. Ch., 1938. Jamestown ND‡

KROLL, JACK, labor exec.; b. London, Eng., June 10, 1885; s. Mark and Julia Kate (Blumberg) K.; came to U.S. 1886, naturalized 1892; ed. pub. schs., Rochester, N.Y., 1890-1900; m. Sara Sylvia Raben, Jan. 19, 1920; 1 son, Mark Harold. Clothing cutter, Rochester, N.Y., and Chicago, Ill., 1901; vol. labor organizer, 1910-18; organizer Amalgamated Clothing Workers of Am., N.Y. City, 1919-26, mgr. Cincinnati Joint Bd., 1926, vice pres., 1928-66; pres. Ohio C.I.O. Council, 1939-52; co-dir. AFL-CIO com. on Political Education; dir. Political Action Com., from 1946. Dir. Amalgamated Ins. Co., Cincinnati, United Nations Associates, Cincinnati. Home: Cincinnati OH Died May 26, 1971.

KRONE, MAX THOMAS, prof.; b. Clarence, Pa., Aug. 21, 1901; s. Eugene and Anna (Zangler) K.; A.B., Univ. of Ill., 1923, B.S., 1927; M.S., Northwestern, 1930, Ph.D. in Music, 1940; m. Harriet Beach, June 1923; children—Jeanne (Mrs. H. E. Rogers), Robert; m. 2d, Beatrice Perham, November 1936. Instr., Univ. of Ill. Sch. of Music, 1927-29; head music dept., Sch. of Edn., Western Reserve Univ., 1929-32; dir. Arthur Jordon Conservatory, Indianapolis, 1932-35; dir. choral orgns., Northwestern, 1935-39; asso. dir., Sch. of Music, U. of So. Cal., 1939-46, dean of Institute of the Arts, 1946-53, prof., 1953-68, dir. emeritus Idyllwild Sch. Music and Arts, 1968-70. President of the Idyllwild Arts Foundation, 1946-70. Member Phi Beta Kappa, Pi Kappa Lambda, Phi Del. Kappa, Phi Mu Alpha. Meth. Author: Expressive Conducting, 1945; The Chorus and Its Conductor, 1946; (with Melville Smith) Fundamentals of Musicianship, 4 vols., 1933-37; (with Griffith Jones) The A Cappella Chorus, 6 vols., 1931-33; A World in Tune, 19 vols. 1944-54 (with Beatrice Krone); Music Participation in the Elementary School, and Music Participation in the Secondary School (with Beatrice Krone), 1952. Music editor: Together We Sing series, 14 vols., 1954-70, Language Through Song Series, 7 vols., 13 records. Editor and arranger numerous separate choral works and collections. Home: Laguna Hills CA Died June 24, 1970.

KRONSHAGE, THEODORE, JR., lawyer; b. at Boscobel, Wis., Nov. 6, 1869; s. Theodore and Pauline (Hildebrand) K.; A.B., U. of Wis., 1891, LL.B., 1892; m. Maud Barnett, of Boscobel, Sept. 7, 1907. In practice at Milwaukee, Sept. 1, 1892-—; sr. mem. firm Kronshage, McGovern & Hannan; pres. Milwaukee Free Press Co., 1901-—. Pres. bd. regents State Normal Schs. of Wis.; mem. Rep. State and Co. Central coms. Mem. Delta Upsilon. Mem. State Bd. of Edn. Clubs: University (Madison, Wis.), Milwaukee Club. Home: Fox Point, WI Office: Wells Bldg., Milwaukee WI‡

KROYT, BORIS, violinist, violist; b. Odessa, Russia, June 23, 1897; s. Ossip Joseph and Cecilia (Friedman) K.; student Royal Acad. (Odessa), 1906-08; Stern'sches Konservatorium (Berlin), 1908-12; studied with Alex Fiedeman, Dr. Paul Yuon, Wilhelm Klatte, Wladimir Metzl; m. Sophie Blumin, July 27, 1932; 1 dau., Yanna Maria (Mrs. Nathan H. Brandt, Jr.). Came to U.S., 1936, naturalized, 1944. Concert debut Odessa Philharmonic, 1905; soloist, recitals European orchestras; mem. Fiedeman Quartet, 1915-18, Anbruch Quartet, 1921-24, Kroyt Quartet, 1924-26, Guarneri Quartet, 1926-33; mem. Budapest Quartet, 1936-69; in residence Library of Congress, 1938-62, State U. N.Y., Buffalo, 1962-69; concerts U.S., Europe, Japan, Australia, S.Am., P.R., Venezuela, others; prof. violin, viola, chamber music U. Buffalo, 1962-69; mem. Marlboro Music Festival, 1964-69; solo recitals, 1966-67. Recipient Gustav Hollaender gold medal, medal State of Israel; Grammy and Billboard awards; hon. mem. Phila. Orchestra. Mem. Music Library Assn. Home: Washington DC Died Nov. 15, 1969.

KRUG, JULIUS ALBERT, bus. exec.; born Madison, Wis., Nov. 23, 1907; s. Julius John and Emma (Korfmacher) K.; A.B., U. of Wis., 1929, A.M., 1930; D.Eng., Colo. Sch. Mines, 1949, Mont. Sch. Mines; hon. degree Reed Coll.; m. Margaret Catherine Dean, Mar. 22, 1926; children—Marilyn Ann, James Allan. Research statistician Wis. Telephone Co., 1930-31; chief depreciation sect. Wis. Pub. Service Commn., 1932-35; pub. utilities expert Federal Communication Commn., Washington, D.C., 1936-37; tech. dir. Ky. Pub. Service Commn., 1937; chief power engr. Tenn. Valley Authority, 1938-40, mgr. of power, 1940; chief power consultatn O.P.M., 1941; dep. dir. gen. for priorities, War Prodn. Bd., 1942; WPB program vice-chmn. and dir., Office of War Utilities, Feb. 1943-44; chmn. War Production Bd., Aug. 1944-45. Lt. Comdr. U.S.N.R., Apr.-Aug. 1944. Sec. of the Interior, 1946-49; chmn. bd. Brookside Mills, Inc., 1949-70; chmn. bd. Volunteer Asphalt Co., Knoxville, Tenn., 1956-70. Leader UN Flood Control Mission to Pakistan, 1955-56. Home: Washington DC Died Mar. 26, 1970; buried Arlington Nat. Cemetery, Washington DC

KRUTCH, JOSEPH WOOD, author; b. Knoxville, Tenn., Nov. 25, 1893; s. Edward Waldemore and Adelaide (Wood) K.; B.A., U. of Tenn., 1915; M.A., Columbia, 1916, Ph.D., 1923, Litt.D. (hon.), 1955; D.H.L. (hon.) Northwestern University, 1958, University of Arizona, 1960; married to Marcelle Leguia, Feb. 10, 1923. Instr. English, Columbia, 1917-18; traveling fellow, 1919-20; asso. prof. English, Polytechnic Inst. of Brooklyn, 1920-23; dramatic critic and asso. editor The Nation, 1924-32, mem. bd. of editors, 1932-37, dramatic critic 1937-52; spl. lecturer, with rank of prof. Vassar Coll., 1924-25; asso. prof. School of Journalism, Columbia U., 1925-31; lecturer New School for Social Research, 1932-35; prof. English, Columbia U., 1937-43, Brander Mathews prof. dramatic lit., 1943-52; narrator, performer NBC spl. The Voice of the Desert, 1963. Cons. on Am. culture to Library of Congress, 1967-70. Guggenheim fellow, 1930-31. Mem. Psychol. Corps, AUS, 1918. Trustee Ariz.-Sonora Desert Mus., Tucson. Recipient Richard Prentice Ettinger medal, 1964; Emerson-Thoreau medal Am. Acad. Arts and Sci., 1967. Fellow Am. Acad. Arts and Scis.; mem. Am. Philos. Soc., Am. Acad. Arts Letters, Nat. Inst. Arts and Letters; pres. N.Y. Drama Critics Circle, 1940-41; mem. bd. editors, Am. Men. of Letters Series, 1947-70. Author: Comedy and Conscience After the Restoration, 1924; (with others) Our Changing Morals, 1925; Edgar Allan Poe—A Study in Genius, 1926; The Modern Temper, 1929; Five Masters, 1930; (with others) Living Philosophies, 1931; Experience and Art, 1932; Was Europe a Success?, 1934; (with others), America Now, 1938; The American Drama Since 1918, 1939; Samuel Johnson, 1944; Henry David Thoreau, 1948; The Twelve Seasons, 1949; The Desert Year, 1952; The Best of Two Worlds (published), 1953; Modernism in Modern Drama, 1953; The Measure of Man (recipient Nat. Book Award), 1954; The Voice of the Desert, 1954; (with others) Is Common Man Too Common?, 1954; The Great Chain of Life, 1957; Grand Canyon: To-day and All Its Yesterdays, 1958; Human Nature and the Human Condition, 1959; The Forgotten Peninsula, 1961; More Lives Than One, 1962; Herbal, 1965; If You Don't Mind My Saying So, 1964; And Even If You Do, 1967; The Most Wonderful Animals That Never Were, 1969; The Best Nature Writings of Joseph Wood Krutch, 1969; A Krutch Omnibus, 1970. Rec., Bird Songs in English Literature, 1967. Editor: The Plays of William Congreve, 1927; Nine Plays by Eugene O'Neill, 1932; Marcell Proust's Remembrance of Things Past, 1934; Representative Am. Dramas, 1941; Select Letters of Thomas Gray, 1952; Great American Nature Writing, 1950; The Gardener's World, 1959; The World of Animals, 1961; (with P.S. Erikson) Treasury of Birdlore, 1962. Home: Tucson AZ Died May 22, 1970.

KRYL, BOHUMIR, cornet virtuoso; b. Horice, Czecho-Slovakia, May 2, 1875; s. John and Josefa (Klikova) K.; ed. high sch.; m. Marie Jerabek, of Vienna, Austria, May 19, 1896; daughters, Josephine, violin soloist, who studied with Ysaye, and Marie, pianist, who appeared with Chicago Symphony Orchestra at 16. Came to U.S., 1889; began as cornet soloist, New York, under John Philip Sousa, 1900; as bandmaster has toured extensively; organizer army bands, during war period, at Camp Dodge, Ia., Camp Custer, Mich., etc.; largely interested in mfr. of band instruments, Chicago, and in banking business; pres. First Nat. Bank of Berwyn, Ill. Mason. Club: Union League. Art collector. Home: 1900 S. Spaulding Av., Chicago IL‡

KUBAT, JERALD RICHARD, govt. ofcl.; b. Crete, Neb., Jan. 22, 1928; s. Joseph Robert and Ruth E. (Wheeler) K.; B.A., Doane Coll., Crete, Neb., 1952; grad. student Wichita (Kan.) State U., 1953-54; fellow Woodrow Wilson Sch., Princeton, 1966-67; m. Marykathryn Ufford, May 28, 1950; children—Mark Philip, Christine Ann, Carl Jay. With Boeing Co., 1952-64; chief Appollo planning NASA, 1964-66, dir. Appolo program control, 1967-68, dir. Manned Space Flight Program Control, 1968-69; cons. in field, 1952-69. Sec.-treas. St. Anthony Jr. Rifle Club, 1968-69; sr. instr. Acorn Jr. Rifle Club, 1967-69. Served with AUS, 1946-47. Recipient citation for outstanding pub. service Exec. Office President, 1966; Presdl. citation for outstanding service to country, 1969; certificate of appreciation NASA, 1969, Exceptional Service medal, 1969. Home: Falls Church VA Died May 4, 1969; buried National Meml. Park, Falls Church VA

KUETHER, FREDERICK WILLIAM, research physicist; b. Fon du Lac, Wis., June 19, 1922; s. Frederick Charles and Laura (Stoltz) K.; B.S., Miami (O.) U., 1944; M.S., Mich. State U., 1946, Ph.D., 1951; m. Dorothy A. Tyrrell, Sept. 20, 1947; children—Charles W., Richard A., Thomas B. Cottrell fellow, Mich. State U., 1949-50, instr. physics, 1950-51, sr. physicist Honeywell Research Center, Mpls., 1951-55, prin. scientist, 1955-60, sr. prin. scientist, 1960-69. Active Boy Scouts Am. Mem. Am. Phys. Soc., Electro Chem. Soc. Patentee in field. Home: Minneapolis MN Died Mar. 18, 1969.

KUHNS, WILLIAM RODNEY, editor; b. Elwood, Ind., Jan. 21, 1897; s. John Hill and Margaret Darraugh (Nesbit) K.; student Denison U., Granville, O., 1915-17; Litt.B., Columbia, 1921; m. Elinor Chamberlain, Apr. 12, 1927; children—William Chamberlain, Mary Margaret; m. 2d Helen Simmonds, July 8, 1949. Reporter on the Paris Herald, 1921; corr. of United Press in New York, London, Paris, 1921-24; corr. and service rep., United Press, in Far East, 1924-28; financial feature editor Associated Press, New York, 1928-30; asso. editor Am. Bankers Assn. Jour., 1930-33; mng. editor Banking, 1933-37, editor, 1937-62, editorial cons, from 1962, director pub. relations council, 1953-57; sr. dep. mgr. Am. Bankers Assn., 1957-62. Mem. U.S. Treasury Indsl. Adv. Com., 1948. Served with Signal Corps, U.S. Army, 1917-19. Mem. Am. Econ. Assn., Nat. Press Club (Washington), Am. Statis. Assn., Sigma Delta Chi, Phi Delta Theta. Republican. Methodist. Club: Columbia University (New York). Editor Banking's Reference Supplement, 1936; Banking Monthly News Letter since 1941; Present Day Banking (year book), 1947-63, gen. editorial cons., 1963-—; The Return of Opportunity, 1944. Home: Flemington NJ Died July 7, 1972; buried Prospect Hill, Flemington NJ

KULER, FRITZ, TV exec., orgn. ofcl.; b. Temple, Tex., May 18, 1914; s. Oscar Godfred and Effie Lee (Bowling) K.; student pub. schs.; m. Florence Nadine Boren, July 6, 1937; children—Klarice (Mrs. Lloyd Darton Blaylock), Merrily. Program dir. sta. KFDM, Beaumont, Tex., 1933, KFJZ, Ft. Worth, 1935, KTAT, Ft. Worth, 1938; announcer, prod. KRLD, Dallas, 1939-41; chief faculty Inst. Radio Broadcasting, Dallas, 1947-52; prodn. mgr. KRLD-TV, Dallas, 1952-59, program dir., from 1959. Served to lt. (j.g.) U.S. Maritime Service, 1941-45. Recipient Honor Key, Civitan Internat., 1959. Mem. S.W. Assn. Program Dirs. for TV, Am. Fedn. Radio and TV Artists, Golf Execs. Inc. Presbyn. Club: Civitan (pres. Dallas 1956-57, spl. asst. to internat. pres. 1957-58, first internat. dir. membership, 1958-60, internat. pres. 1962-63). Home: Dallas TX Died June 21, 1971.

KULIKOWSKI, ADAM (HYPPOLIT), publisher, editor; b. Vilno, Poland, Aug. 22, 1890; s. Kalkist and Frances (Chevalier) K.; grad. Russian Gymnasium; A.B., Olivet Coll., 1913; grad. study U. Chgo., 1913-14; m. Mary Terrell Sanders, 1918; 1 son, Leon T. Came to U.S., 1910, naturalized, 1927. With Am. Embassy, Petrograd, U.S.S.R., 1915-16; clk. Wilson & Co., Chgo., 1918, European rep., London, Eng., 1919-22; v.p., treas. Food Display Machine Corp., Chgo., 1923-27, pres. from 1927; v.p., treas. Fabrix, Inc., Chgo., from 1934; pub. Opportunity mag. since 1935, editor from 1935. Cons. to dir. O.W.I., Washington, 1943-44. Served as 2d lt. Imperial Russian Guards, 1914-15. Clubs: University, Tavern (Chgo.): Farmington (Charlottesville, Va.). Home: Chicago IL Died 1966.

KUNKEL, A. WILLIAM, librarian; b. Munich, Germany, Oct. 27, 1925; s. Adolf and Mary (Hois) K.; came to U.S., 1929, naturalized, 1946; A.B., Union Coll., 1950; A.M. Western Res. U., 1952, M.L.S., 1953; m. Rose Marie Lavery, June 12, 1949; children—Cynthia Marie, Joan Louise. Student asst. Union Coll. Library, 1948-50; student, circulation asst. Western Res. U. Library, 1951-53; reference librarian Ohio U. Library, 1953-55; Lamont Library asst., asst. circulation supr. Widener Library Harvard, 1955-57; supr. book processing Newton (Mass.) Free Library, 1957-58, chief librarian, 1958-67; adminstr. Eastern regional pub. library system Boston Pub. Library, 1967-72. Sec., Mass. Eastern Regional Adv. Council, 1962-65, vice chmn., 1965-67, chmn., 1967. Served with AUS 1946-47. Mem. A.L.A., Mass. (past pres.), New Eng. library assns., Greater Boston Pub. Library Adminstrs. Newton MA Died Jan. 21, 1972.

KUNKEL, BEVERLY WAUGH, biologist; b. Harrisburg, Pa., Oct. 27, 1881; s. Charles A. and Eliza B. (Waugh) K.; grad. Lawrenceville (N.J.) Sch., 1898; Ph.B., Yale, 1901, Ph.D., 1905; studied U. of Freiburg, 1911-12; studied in London, 1925; m. Caroline T. Jennings, June 24, 1908; children—Mary T., Sarah W. Asst. in biology, 1901-05, instr., 1905-12, Yale; prof. zoology, Beloit (Wis.) Coll., 1912-15; prof. biology, Lafayette Coll., 1915-69. Fellow A.A.A.S.; mem. Am. Soc. Zoologists, Am. Assn. Anatomists, Am. Assn. Univ. Profs., Sigma Xi, Delta Phi. Conglist. Contbr. numerous papers chiefly on vertebrate embryology and the relations of the colleges to intellectual leadership. Home: Easton PA Died Mar. 6, 1969; buried Yelping Hill, West Cornwall CT

KUNKEL, JOHN CRAIN, congressman; b. Harrisburg, Pa., July 21, 1898; s. John C. and Louisa Espy (Sergeant) K.; student Harrisburg (Pa.) Acad.; B.S., Yale, 1919; LL.B., Harvard, 1926; m. Katherine Brawner Smoot; 3 foster children. Admitted to Pa. bar, 1926; mem. 76th to 81st Congresses, 19th Dist. Pa.; 87th Congress, 18th Dist. Pa.; 88th to 89th Congresses, from 16th Congressional District of Pennsylvania. Dir., Commonwealth Nat. Bank, Harrisburg. Pres., Boy's Club, Harrisburg. County commr., Dauphin County, 1952-56. Bd. dirs. Harrisburg Hosp.; trustee Franklin and Marshall Coll., Wilson Coll., Chambersburg, Pa. Served with S.A.T.C., World War I. Mem. Am. Legion. Elk, Odd Fellow. Republican. Home: Harrisburg PA Died July 27, 1970.

KUNO, HISASHI, educator; b. Tokyo, Japan, Jan. 7, 1910; s. Kamenosuke Kuno and Tome Yoshikawa; student U. Tokyo Geol. Inst., 1929-32, D.Sc., 1948; m. Kimiko Kuno, Nov. 26, 1940; children—Takashi, Shizuko. Asst. U. Tokyo, 1933-39, asst. prof., 1939-55, prof., 1955-69; internat. vis. sci. Am. Geol. Inst., 1961; vis. prof. U. Minn., 1964. Recipient Japan Acad. prize, 1954. Fellow (hon.) Geol. Soc. Am.; fellow Am. Geophys. Union, Mineral. Soc. Am.; mem. Internat. Assn. Volcanology (past pres.), Volcanological Soc. Japan (past pres.), Geol. Soc. Japan (pres. 1969), Geol. Soc. London, Nat. Acad. Sci. (fgn. asso.). Spl. study volcanoes of Japan and Hawaii. Home: Tokyo Japan Died Aug. 6, 1969.

KUNZ, ADOLF HENRY, prof. chemistry; b. Leavenworth, Kan.; s. Albert Louis and Bertha Louise (Holbein) K.; A.B., William Jewell Coll., Liberty, Mo., 1923; M.S., U. of Iowa, 1926, Ph.D., 1928; m. Bernice Madeline Bullock, July 26, 1927; 1 son, Alan Adolf. Teacher, high sch. science, Marshall, Mo., 1923-26; asst. lab. instr., U. of Ia., 1926-28; asst. prof. chemistry, U. of Ore., 1930-32, 1934-36, asso. prof., 1936-43, prof., 1943-66, acting head, dept. of chemistry, 1941-42, head of dept., 1942-66; asst. prof. chemistry, Ore. State Coll., 1932-34. Nat. research fellow in chemistry, Calif. Inst. Tech., 1928-29. Member State of Ore. Basic Science Com. since 1941. Mem. Am. Chem. Soc., A.A.A.S., Am. Assn. Univ. Profs., Phi Gamma Delta, Pi Kappa Delta, Pi Mu Epsilon, Sigma Xi, Phi Lambda Upsilon. Home: Eugene OR Died Oct. 14, 1966.

KUNZ, JOSEF L(AURENZ), internat. lawyer; b. Vienna, Austria, Apr. 1, 1890; s. Josef Laurenz and Ida (Zalaudek) K.; LL.D., Univ. Vienna, 1913, Dr. Polit. Sci., 1921; student Univ. Paris, 1911-12, Univ. London, 1913-14; LL.D. honoris causa, National University of Mexico, 1955. Came to U.S., 1932, naturalized, 1940; lecturer in internat. law, Vienna Univ. Law Sch., 1927-32; prof., Hague Acad. of Internat. Law, 1929-32; Rockefeller research fellow in internat. law, in U.S., 1932-34; prof. internat. law, Univ. Toledo since 1934; vis. prof., Nat. Univ. of Mexico, 1948; prof. Inter-Am. Acad. Comparative Internat. Law, Havana, 1950; vis. prof. U. of Calif., 1950-51; visiting prof. National Univ. of Mexico 1952, now hon. prof.; vis. prof. S.M. U. Law School and dir. Law Inst. of Americas, Dallas, 1952-53. Speaker for Carnegie Endowment, 1934-70; lectr. U. Valladolid, Spain, 1954, Hague Acad. Internat. Law, 1955. Jurdical dir. Austrian League of Nations Union, Vienna, 1920-32. Hon. mem. Mexican Bar Assn.; mem. American Society of International Law, American Political Science Assn., A.A.A.S., American Acad. Polit. and Social Sci., Argentine Inst. of Juridical and Social Philosophy, Hellenic Inst. of Internat. Law, Institut de Droit Internationale (asso.). Democrat. Roman Catholic. Author numerous books in German, French, English, Spanish on problems of internat. law.; The Mexican Expropriations, 1940; intro. Latin-Am. Legal Philosophy, by Harvard U. Press, 1948, La Teoria Pura del Derecho, National University of Mexico, 1948; Latin-American Philosophy of Law in the Twentieth Century, 1950; Changes of International Law, 1968. Bd. editors, American Jour. International Law, 1944-70 (collaborator Journals of International Law In United States, Europe and Latin America). Member XXth Century Legal Philosophy Series, Assn. of Am. Law Sch., 1939-70. Co-editor Austrian Journal Public Law. Contributor numerous articles on internat. law and philosophy of law in English, French, German, Italian and Spanish jours. Home: Toledo OH Died Aug. 1970.

KUNZE, WILLIAM FREDERICK, ex-mayor; b. Sleepy Eye, Minn., June 1, 1872; s. Fred and Minnie (Krueger) K.; B.S., U. of Minn., 1897, m. Galena Muedeking, Aug. 12, 1902; children—Florence Myrtle (Mrs. Wilfred L. Husband), Dorothy Lucile (Mrs. C. Howard Mattson), William Frederick, Jr. Instructor in chemistry, U. of Minn., 1897-98; prin. high school, Lake City, Minn., 1898; supt. schs., Hastings, 1899-1901, Red Wing, 1901-07; prin. high sch., St. Paul, 1907; sec. Smith System Heating Co., Minneapolis, 1907-22; v.p. Marquette Nat. Bank since 1922; v.p. and associate trust officer, Marquette Ins. Agency, Bank Shares Corp.; pres. Nevens Co. since 1943; director Murray Institute. Member Minn. Ho. of Rep., 1911-13; member Minneapolis Charter Commn., 1913-15; mem. Minneapolis Bd. Pub. Welfare, 1919-21 and 1924-31; mayor of Minneapolis, 1929-31; chmn. Hennepin County Child Welfare Board, 1922-36; mem. Children's Protective Society (dir. since 1922, pres., 1928-32), Hennepin Co. Pub. Health Assn. (pres. 1924-30); dir. Working Boys' Band; regional dir. for Minn., War Finance Com., Treasury Department. Mem. Sigma Xi. Republican. Methodist. Mason (Scottish Rite), Acacia. Club: Minneapolis Athletic. Author: Outlines of Physical Geography, 1897; Exercises in Arithmetic, 1906; The Economy System of Penmanship. Home: 3123 4th St. S.E. Office: 517 Marquette Av., Minneapolis MN‡

KUNZEL, FRED, judge; b. Buffalo, June 2, 1901 s. Herman and Regina (Schwarz) K.; A.B., Stanford, 1925, J.D., 1927; m. Wana Keesling, Feb. 1, 1928; children—Frederick K., Regina F., Mary K. Admitted to Cal. bar, 1927; partner Luce, Forward, Kunzel & Scripps, San Diego, 1934-59; U.S. Dist. Ct. judge So. Dist. Cal., 1959-68, chief judge, 1968-69. Comdr. USNR. Mem. Am., Cal., San Diego (dir. 1934-37) bar assns., Maritime Law Assn. U.S., Zool. Soc. San Diego (sec. and dir. 1935-69, president 1957-60), Phi Alpha Delta, also Zeta Psi. Club: University (pres. 1937). Home: San Diego CA Died Nov. 19, 1969; buried El Camino Meml. Park, San Diego CA

KUNZMANN, JACOB CHRISTOPH, clergyman, educator; b. Bauscholtt, Baden, Germany, Dec. 31, 1852; s. Christian Jacob and Louisa (Stoehr) K.; came to U.S., 1860; A.B., Thiel Coll., Greenville, Pa., 1875, A.M., 1878; grad. Phila. Theol. Sem., 1878; D.D., Bethany Coll., Kan., 1900; m. Anna Christian Mathay, June 20, 1878; 6 children. Ordained Luth. ministry, 1878; pastor Kittanning, Pa., 1878-81, Greensburg, 1881-92, Grace Ch., Pittsburgh, 1892-99. Pres. Pittsburgh Synod, 1895-98; pres. trustees Thiel Coll. 10 yrs. Supt. English missions of Gen. Council Evang. Luth. Ch. in N. America, 1899-1918; supt. Western Dist. of Home Missions of Ch. Extension Bd., U.L.C.A., 1918-19; president of Pacific Theol. Sem., 1919-24, since emeritus. Author of Lutherans in America," America and World Evangelization," The Power of Pentecost." Address: 4300 E. 45th St., Seattle WA*‡

KUO, PING WEN, Chinese educator; b. 1880 ed. Columbia U. Dean, Nanking Coll., 1915, pres. 1917; pres. Nat. Southeastern 1918-25; chmn. ednl. commn. to Japan and Philippines, 1918; trustee, China Foundn. for Edn. and Culture, 1924-29; vice pres. World Fedn. of Ednl. Assns., 1923-29; dir. China Inst. in America, 1926-31; lecturer, Harris Foundation Inst., Chicago U., 1925; dir. Bur. Foreign Trade, Ministry of Industries and Commerce, 1935-37; mng. dir. Shanghai Trust Co.; dir. Nat. Indsl. Bank, 1933-37. Del. to Congress of Internat. Chambers of Commerce, Amsterdam, 1929, Copenhagen, 1939; mem. Chinese financial mission to Washington, 1936, 38; dir. Chinese Govt. Trading Commn. in Great Britain, 1938-44; financial counsellor Embassy, London, and vice-minister finance, 1938-44; chief del. to U.N. Conf. on food and agr., Hot Springs, Va., 1943; del. U.N. Monteray Conf., Bretton Woods, 1944; dep. dir.-gen. U.N.R.R.A., Washington, D.C., 1944-47; chmn. Com. on Planning and Advising Chinese Students in U.S., 1944-59; exec. dir. Chinese-Am. Inst. Social Sciences, 1948; chmn. Chinese Adv. Com. on Cultural Relations in Am., 1957-69; founder, pres. Sino-Am. Cultural Soc. Author: Chinese System of Public Education; translator Webster's Collegiate Dictionary into Chinese language. Address: Washington DC Died Aug. 29, 1969.

KUPLIC, J. L., mfg. co. exec.; b. Manitowoc, Wis., Sept. 23, 1911; s. James J. and Anna (Peysar) K.; B.A., Beloit Coll., 1934; m. Nancy E. Tyrrell, Feb. 4, 1935; children—Mrs. Donald L. Gehrke, James B., Mrs. Quinten G. Carman, Mrs. Brian Moore, Bradley T. Instr., St. Borbert Coll., De Pere, Wis., 1934-35; engaged in pvt. business, 1935-43; with Kohler Co. (Wis.), 1943-68, pres., until 1968; pres., dir. Kohler de Mexico S.A. de C.V., Mexico City, Kohler Can. Ltd., Toronto; dir. Helvex, S.A., Mexico City, Security First Nat. Bank, Sheboygan, Wis. Vice pres., dir. Friendship House, Sheboygan, bd. dirs. Sheboygan YMCA, 4-H Club Found., Boy Scouts Am.; trustee Beloit Coll. Recipient Distinguished Service citation Beloit Coll., 1964. Mem. Wis. Mfrs. Assn. (bd. dirs.), Tau Kappa Epsilon. Methodist (trustee). Home: Sheboygan Falls WI Died July 22, 1968; buried Sheboygan Falls WI

KURTZ, LOUIS CHARLES, merchant, banker, realtor; b. Des Moines, Ia., Nov. 28, 1867; s. Louis H. and Anna M. (Kula) K.; student St. Benedict's Coll., business coll.; m. Alice McDonnell, June 23, 1896; children—Louise Clarence, Bernard D. Pres. L.H. Kurtz Co. since 1922; pres. Kurtz Realty Co.; chmn. Kurtz Co., Mason City, Ia.; was v.p. German Savings Bank, which bank consol. with Des Moines Nat. Bank, in which served as pres. until consol. of Des Moines Nat. with Ia. Des Moines Nat. Bank, after which was dir. and chmn. bd., still dir.; pres. and dir. Hawley Foundation; pres. of Iowa Des Moines Bldg. Co.; chmn. exec. com. Iowa Des Moines Nat. Bank. Del. Rep. Nat. Conv. from 7th Dist. Ia. that nominated Harding for President. Former member Greater Des Moines Com.; pres. Des Moines Sch. Bd., 1899-1900, 1902; postmaster Des Moines, 1911-15; was chmn. Compliance Bd., N.R.A., Des Moines and vicinity. Former dir. Des Moines C. of C. Elk, K.C. Club: Des Moines. Home: 220 37th St. Office: 312 Walnut St., Des Moines IA‡

KURZ, WALTER CHARLES, newspaper exec.; b. Chgo., May 25, 1908; s. Charles C. and Meta M. (Mueller) K.; B.S., U. Ill., 1929; m. Ethel Hull, Jan. 20, 1934; children—Robert H., Ronald W., Roger and Susan (twins). With Chgo. Tribune, 1933-71, mgr. gen. display advt. dept., 1948-55, advt. mgr., 1955-60, exec. v.p. Tribune Co., 1967-70, gen. mgr., 1968-70, pres., 1970-71; chmn. exec. com. Chgo.'s Am. instr. advt. and mdsg. Medill Sch. Journalism, Northwestern U., evenings 1942-48. Dir. Chicago's Am., KDAL, Inc., Orlando Daily Newspapers, Met. Sunday Newspapers, Inc.; pres. Newspaper I. Successor trustee McCormick-Patterson Trust, Robert R. McCormick Charitable Trust; sec., dir. Passavant Hosp., Chgo.; bd. dirs. Tb Inst. Chgo. and Cook County, Community Fund Chgo., Ill. Inst. Tech.; asso. Nat. Coll Edn.; mem. Northwestern U. Assos.; mem. advisory board Y.M.C.A. of Chicago; member citizens board U. Chgo. Mem. Advt. Research Foundation (bd. dirs.), Am. Newspaper Pubs. Assn. (chmn. bd. Bur. Advt.), Sigma Phi Epsilon. Clubs: Racquet (Chgo.), Mid-America, Chicago, Commonwealth, Commercial (Chgo.); Indian Hill (Winnetka); Old Elm (Ft. Sheridan, Ill.); Tres Vidos, Wayfarer's. Home: Winnetka IL Died Sept. 23, 1971.

KURZMAN, HAROLD PHILLIP, clothing mfr.; b. N.Y. City, Feb. 2, 1902; s. Samuel and Bessie (Strauss) K.; B.S., Mass. Inst. Tech., 1924; m. Eleanor Hess, Apr. 24, 1928; children—Phyllis E., Peter H., Harold P., Paul A. Management engr. Spezesi & Co., 1924-27; mdse. mgr. L. Bamberger & Co., Newark, 1933-38, mdse. buyer B. Altman & Co., 1939; with Lily of France, Inc., N.Y. City, 1939-65, pres. 1942-65, past dir.; pres. Harman Corporation, New York City. Dir. Endl. Found. for Apparel Industry; pres. Found. Garment Inst. of Am.; president Nat. Corset and Brassiere Assn. Mem. industry adv. com. W.P.B. and O.P.A. Home: New York City NY Died Sept. 30, 1972; buried Woodlawn Cemetery.

KUSCHNER, BEATRICE BARBARA KATZ (MRS. JOSEPH P. KUSCHNER), civic worker; b. N.Y.C., May 21, 1913; d. Jacob F. and Rose (Ehrlich) Katz; student U. Cal. at Los Angeles, 1931-34; m. Joseph P. Kuschner, Dec. 1, 1935; children—Liane (Mrs. Richard

Kamola), Nancy (dec.). Pres., Los Angeles Council Pioneer Women, 1949-51, pres. W. Coast region, 1951-54, auditor, 1942-69, mem. nat. bd., 1951-54. Active A.R.C., United Jewish Welfare Fund; mem. Bur. Jewish Edn., Westwood Gardens Civic Assn., Welfare Assos. Jewish religion (chmn. bd. synagogue 1964-66, 68-69). Home: Los Angeles CA Died Feb. 19, 1969.

KUSSY, NATHAN, author, lawyer; b. Newark, N.J., July 13, 1872; s. Gustav and Bella (Bloch) K.; LL.B., New York Law Sch., 1894; m. Tennie Levi, Apr. 25, 1900 (died Dec. 26, 1935); children—Hazel M. (Mrs. Raymond H. Cohn), Bella N. (Mrs. Milton Bernstein), Gustave (died Aug. 11, 1921), Engaged in the practice of law in Newark since 1895; mem. Bd. of Edn., 1898-1902; asst. city atty., 1917-21. Mem. Authors League America, Dramatists' Guild. Democrat. Jewish religion. Author: Grinmar, 1907; The Abyss, 1916; The Victor (pub. in England), 1922; also playlets—The President Speaks; The Diamond Necklace; The Schemers; Crooks (pub. by War Dept., U.S.A., for performance at cantonments, World War I; also included in plays for performance in camps in World War II). Article: Newark, Universal Jewish Encyclopedia. Home: 158 S. Harrison St., East Orange, N.J. Office: 790 Broad St., Newark NJ‡

KUSWORM, SIDNEY GROVER, lawyer; b. Dayton, O., Feb. 28, 1885; s. Moses and Mollie (Witkowsky) K.; LL.B., Cin. Law Sch., 1908; m. Helen Block, Dec. 10, 1910 (dec.); 1 son, Sidney Grover, Jr. Admitted to Ohio bar, 1935, mem. firm Kusworm & Myers and predecessor firm, 1937-69. Mem. of the executive committee of the Jewish Boy Scouts Am.; mem. adv. bd. Nat. Council Naturalization and Citizenship; mem. nat. council Joint Distbn. Com., Boy Scouts Am.; v.p., bd. govs. World Com. for Employment Handicapped. Pres. Jewish Community Council, 1947; mem. bd. sponsors Nat. Arthritis Research Found.; trustee Bellefaire Home for Disturbed Children, Cleve., Nat. Jewish Hosp. for Consumptives, Denver, Leo N. Levi Meml. Hosp., Hot Springs, Ark., Nat. Home for Asthmatic Children, Denver; sole rep. State Ohio at Nat. Citizenship confs., Washington, 1953-56; mem. bd. Nat. Council United Hias Service, Inc.; mem. atty. gen. U.S. citizenship adv. com. Bd. dirs. Nat. Citizenship Conf. Member Ohio Bar Assn., Nat. Conf. Christians and Jews (co-chmn. local chpt.), Am. (standing com. on citizenship; member of the fellows), Dayton bar assns., Jewish religion. Elk (past dist. dep., grand exalted ruler Ohio), B'nai B'rith (mem. youth commn., internat. treas., bd. govs. 1921-69, member of international council 1961-69). Club: Dayton Lawyers. Contbr. articles legal, Jewish publs. Home: Dayton OH Died Oct. 4, 1969; buried Dayton OH

KUTZ, CHARLES WILLAUER, army officer; b. Reading, Pa., Oct. 14, 1870; s. Allen and Emily (Briner) K.; grad. U.S. Mil. Acad., 1893; Engr. Sch. of Application, 1896; m. Elizabeth Randolph Keim, June 25, 1895; children—Mrs. W.G. Bingham, Mrs. L.T. Ross, C.R. Commd. add. 2d lt. engrs., June 12, 1893; 2d lt. Oct. 2, 1895; promoted through grades to col., June 1, 1920; served as col., later brig. gen. N.A., 1917-20. Duty Willets Pt., N.Y., 1893-96; fortification, river and harbor work, Baltimore, Md., 1896-1900, Portland, Me., 1900-01; asst. to chief of engrs., Washington, D.C., 1903-06; instr. mil. engring., U.S. Mil. Acad., 1906-08; fortification, river and harbor work, Seattle, Wash., 1908-11; chief engr. officer, Philippines Dept., 1911-14; engr. commr. Dist. of Columbia, 1914-17; in France, 1 yr., 1917-18; assigned to comd. engr. camp. at Camp Humphreys, Va., Aug. 1918; engr. commr., Dist. of Columbia, 1918-21; div. engr., Central Div., Cincinnati, 1921-28; mem. Mississippi River Commn., 1925-28; dept. engr. Hawaiian Dept., 1928-29; retired with rank of brig. gen., 1929; active as engr. commr., Dist. of Columbia, since May 1941. Mem. Am. Soc. C.E. Universalist. Club: Army and Navy. Home: 2028 Allen Pl. N.Y., Washington DC*‡

KVALE, WALTER FREDERICK, educator, physician; b. Orfordsville, Wis., July 30, 1907; s. O.J. and Ida T. (Simley) K.; student St. Olaf Coll., 1926-28; M.B., Northwestern U., 1929, M.D.; M.S. in Medicine, U. Minn.; m. Mary Loretta Lawler, Feb. 14, 1939; children—Tonette, Jay, Christopher, Katherine, Kevin, Michael. Intern Ancker Hosp., St. Paul, 1933-34; fellow med. Mayo Found., 1934-36, 38; attending physician Ft. Peck (Mont.) Hosp., 1936-37; mem. staff Mayo Clinic; prof. medicine U. Minn. Recipient gold medal for exhb. A.M.A., 1952. Fellow A.C.P.; mem. Sigma Xi, Nu Sigma Nu. Home: Rochester MN Died Nov. 25, 1970.

KYES, ROGER M., corp. exec.; b. E. Palestine, O., Mar. 6, 1906; s. Lafayette and Myra (Rogers) K.; A.B., cum laude, Harvard, 1928; spl. work in business adminstrn. and administrative engring.; m. Helen Jacoby, June 5, 1931; children—Carolyn, Frances, Katharine, Anne. Asst. to pres. Glenn L. Martin Co., Cleveland, and Baltimore, 1928-30; asst. to vice pres. Black & Decker Mfg. Co., Towson, Md., 1930-32; vice pres. Empire Plow Co., Cleveland, 1932-41; exec. cons. Ferguson-Sherman Mfg. Corp. (now Harry Ferguson, Inc.), Detroit, 1939-41, exec. vice pres. and gen. mgr., 1941-43, pres. and gen. mgr., 1943-47; exec. in charge of procurement and schedules staff, Gen. Motors Corp., Detroit, 1948-50, gen. mgr. Truck & Coach Div., Pontiac, Mich., 1950, became v.p. Gen. Motors Corp., 1950, dir., 1954-70, v.p., group executive in charge of Accessory Group, 1959-65, vice president group exec. Automotive Components and Def. Divs. 1965-66, exec. v.p. charge Automotive Components Group and Def. Divs., 1966-67, exec. v.p. charge car, truck, body and assembly, automotive components group, 1967-70, ret., 1970; chmn. bd. Am. Shipping Co., 1970-71; gen. partner Lazard Freres and Co., 1971; deputy secretary of defense United States Department of Defense, 1953-54. Founder and 1st chmn. Detroit Agrl. and Indsl. Found. Elected hon. Am. Farmer, 1941; recipient Medal Freedom, 1954; Exceptional Service Award, USAF, 1956; Distinguished Service Citation, Reserve Officers Association, 1956 Navy Distinguished Public Service Award, 1956: Distinguished Service Citation, U.S. Army, 1957. Member Am. Soc. Agrl. Engineers Soc. Automotive Engrs. Presbyn. (hon. life chmn. of bd. of trustees). Clubs: Detroit, Detroit Athletic, Recess (Detroit); Harvard (Mich., and N.Y.C.); Bloomfield Hills Country. Home: Bloomfield MI Died Feb. 13, 1971; buried White Chapel Cemetery, Bloomfield Hills MI

KYLE, EDWIN DEWEES, ry. official; b. Fayetteville, N. C., 1869; married; children—Rebecca Devereux (Mrs. Duncan McRae), William Emmet, Edwin Dewees. Began with Cape Fear & Yadkin Valley R.R., 1885, occupying various positions in local frt. office, including that of cashier; rate clerk, chief rate clerk and chief clerk in gen. frt. agent's office, same line, 1888-91; gen. frt. and pass. agt., Charleston, Sumter & Northern R.R., 1891-92; soliciting agt., traveling frt. agt., div. frt. agt., asst. gen. frt. agt. and frt. traffic mgr. Seaboard Air Line, 1892-1912; traffic mgr. Norfolk Southern R.R., 1912-20; v.p. in charge traffic, same, since Jan. 1920. Club: Southern Mfrs. (Charlotte, N.C.). Home: 104 Garden Apts. Office: Terminal Station, Norfolk VA‡

KYLE, EDWIN JACKSON, educator; born in Kyle, Hays County, Tex., July 22, 1876; s. Ferg and Anna (Moore) K.; B.S., Agrl. and Mech. Coll. of Texas, 1899; B.S.A., Cornell, 1901, M.S.A., 1902; hon. D.Sc. in Agriculture, U. Arkansas, 1941; m. Alice E. Myers, Dec. 21, 1904; children—Lily Bess, Kyle Baker. Prof. horticulture, 1902-35, dean of agr., 1911-44, dean emeritus since 1947, Sch. of Agriculture, Agrl. and Mech. Coll. of Tex. Pioneer in Tex. in movement for teaching agr. in pub. schs.; organizer of High School Day, Farmers' Short Course, and Smith Hughes Day at A. and M. Coll. Toured Central and South America, 1941 for Coordinator of Inter-Am. Affairs for purpose of studying the agricultural economy, visiting educational institutions, and promoting friendship. Apptd. by Dept. of State and Dept. of Agr. as official delegate to Second Inter-Am. Conf. on Agr., Mexico City, June 1942, Third Conference, Caracas, Venezuela, July 1945, and on Com. of Inter-Am. Coop. in Agricultural Edn., 1943. Mem. adv. com. on Inter-Am. coop. in Agrl. Edn., Dept. of State, 1943; U.S. Commn. Inter-Am. Developments, Coordinator Inter-Am. Affairs, 1944; joint com. on Latin-Am. studies, conf., Bd. Asso. Research Councils, 1944. Ambassador to Guatemala, 1945-48. Awarded Order of Quetzal (Guatemala). Mem. Assn. Land Grant Colls., Am. Soc. Hort. Science, Tex. Pecan Growers' Assn., Nat. Econ. League, Alpha Zeta. Democrat. Methodist. Mason. Rotarian. Author: Fundamentals of Farming and Farm Life, 1912; Pecan Growing, 1925; Agriculture in the Southwest, 1940; also numerous bulls. Sr. educationist (specialist in coll. curriculum on Land Grant Coll. Survey), authorized by Congress, 1927. Dir. Federal Farm Credit Administration, Houston, since Jan. 1934; trustee Luling (Tex.) Foundation. Pioneer in the development of econ. agr. in land grant colls. Home: W. 34th St., Bryan TX‡

KYLE, JOHN WILLIAM, judge, ex-legislator; b. Batesville, Miss., Aug. 21, 1891; s. Albert Sidney and Mary (Heflin) K.; B.A., U. of Miss., 1912, LL.B., 1913; Rhodes scholar, Oxford (England) U., 1913-14. Admitted to Miss. bar, 1913; practiced law, Sardis, 1915-50; atty. for bd. suprs. of Panola County, 1920-50; vice pres. Panola County Bank, Sardis, 1945-56; owner farm lands devoted to cotton prodn. Mem. Miss. State Senate, 1928-50, chmn. Senate Finance Com., 1932-36, 1940-44, 1948-50; mem. Miss. State Bldg. Commn., 1940-50, atty. gen. Miss. 1950; judge Supreme Court of Miss., 1950-65. Mem. Miss. Bar Assn., Am. Legion, 40 and 8, Delta Kappa Epsilon, Phi Delta Phi, Omicron Delta Kappa. Methodist. Democrat. Home: Sardis MS Died May 4, 1965.

KYLE, LAURENCE HARWOOD, physician, educator; b. Huntington, Mass., Apr. 16, 1916; s. Clayton Harwood and Alice Margaret (Millea) K.; B.S. U. Mass., 1937; M.D., Boston U., 1941; m. Margaret Ann Stringer, May 13, 1944; children,Margaret Alice, Patricia Adelaide, Laurence Harwood. Intern Nassau County Pub. Gen. Hosp., Hempstead, N.Y., 1941-42; resident medicine Boston City Hosp., 1946-47; sr. research fellow NIH, 1947-48; William Wade Hinshaw research fellow Georgetown U. Sch. Medicine, 1948-50, mem. faculty, 1948-71, prof. medicine, chmn. dept., 1958-71; dir. dept. medicine Georgetown Univ. Hosp., 1958-71. Cons. medicine Walter Reed Army Med. Center, Bethesda Naval Med. Center, Clin. Center of NIH, Mt. Alto VA Hosp.; cons. metabolism Walter Reed Army Inst. Research. Served with AUS, 1942-45. Recipient Raskob award research Georgetown U. Sch. Medicine, 1959. Diplomate Am. Bd. Internal Medicine. Master A.C.P.; member A.M.A. (del. to house of delegates 1964), Association of Am. Physicians, Am. Soc. Clin. Investigation, Am. Fedn. Clin. Research (chmn. Eastern sect. 1955), So. Soc. Clin. Investigation (counselor 1957-60, pres. 1960), Endocrine Soc., Soc. Exptl. Biology and Washington DC

KYLES, LYNWOOD WESTINGHOUSE, bishop; b. Ivy Depot, Albemarle Co., Va., May 3, 1874; s. Burrell and Mary K.; A.B., Lincoln U., Pa., 1901; grad. theol. dept. same univ., 1904; m. Jenny Smith, of Ridgewood, N.J., 1897 (now deceased); m. 2d, Louella Marie Bryan, of Winston-Salem, N.C., Dec. 18, 1908. Entered ministry A.M.E. Zion Ch., 1896; editor and gen. mgr. A.M.E. Zion Ch. Review, 1908-16, also sec. and treas. Ministerial Brotherhood and Relief Dept.; elected bishop, May 16, 1916. Pres. bd. trustees Walters Inst., Warren, Ark.; trustee Livingstone Coll., Salisbury, N.C; nat. trustee World's Christian Endeavor Soc.; chmn. central com. and gen. dir. Tercentenary Campaign for One Million Dollars; del. 4th Ecumenical Conf., London, 1921. Mason, Odd Fellow, K.P. Home: 1612 E. 14th St., Winston-Salem NC‡

LABRUM, J. HARRY, lawyer; born at Philadelphia, Pennsylvania; s. Thomas Joseph and Mary Theresa (Conlen) LaB.; LL.B., Georgetown U., 1925; postgrad. work, Cambridge U., England; LL.D., St. Josephs College, 1956; HH.D. (honorary), Philathea Coll., London, Ont., 1958; m. Catharine Agatha Foley, June 29, 1921; 1 dau., Agatha Mary (Mrs. Paolo Clemente). Admitted to Pa., D.C. bars, 1925; mem. LaBrum & Doak. Member board dirs. Hemphill Ferguson Company, Inc., John D. Grover & Sons, Inc., Polychrome Corp. Pa., Polychrome Corp., ER & T Sta. WHYY, Georgetown Textile & Manufacturing Co., Inc.; spl. dep. atty. gen. Commonwealth, Pa., 1936-37; mem. Pa. State Welfare Commn., 1954-55; pres. Phila. Bd. Pub. Edn. 1953-65; pres. Phila. council Boy Scouts America 1956-58, hon. pres., 1958-59; pres. Fedn. Ins. Counsel, 1957-58, chmn. bd., 1959; trustee PMS Colls.; pres. Fedn. of Ins. Counsel Found., from 1962. Served as brig. gen. U.S. Army, Signal Corps Res. Decorated Legion of Merit (U.S.); Order of The Crown of Italy; Knight Comdr. Order White Rose (Finland); recipient star and cross acad. honor Am. Internat. Acad., 1958; Distinguished Service Medal, Pa. dept. Am. Legion, 1968; George W. Yancey Meml. award, Internat. Assn. Ins. Counsel, 1968; John Carroll award, Georgetown University Alumni Association, 1968. Fellow Am. Bar Found., Am. Coll. Trial Lawyers; Internat. Acad. Trial Lawyers (dir. 1962-65, from 1967); mem. Am., Pa., Philadelphia bar associations (various coms. of each), Pa. State Chamber of Commerce (dir. 1965-69), Phi Alpha Delta (distinguished service chpt.), and many other nat., state and local profl. and civic orgns. and assns.; has served as officer of several, active in coms. of many; has served as mem. several govtl. coms. Clubs: Nat. Press, The Army and Navy (Washington), India House (N.Y. City); Union League, Racquet, Downtown, Philadelphia Country, Lawyers', Pen and Pencil (Phila.); and others. Contbr. articles in profl. jours. Home: Philadelphia PA

LACEY, RAYMOND HENRY, coll. prof.; b. Laceyville, Pa., Jan. 27, 1876; s. Henry Washington and Olive (Durand) L.; grad. Mansfield (Pa.) State Teachers Coll., 1896; A.B., Syracuse U., 1905, A.M., 1906; A.M., Johns Hopkins U., 1909; Ph.D., Princeton, 1915; m. Rosalind Runyan, Dec. 30, 1910 (died, 1919); children—Douglas Raymond, Jeanette Elizabeth, Margaret Runyan; m. 2d, Rose Elizabeth Rainey, Aug. 21, 1920; children—James Rainey, Louise Durand. Teacher pub. schs., Pa., 1893-94, 1896-99; asst. in Greek, Syracuse U., 1905-06, instr. of Greek, 1906-07; instr. in Greek and Latin, Peekskill Mil. Acad., 1907-08; instr. in Latin, Lafayette Coll., 1909-14, prof., 1915-17; prof. of Greek and Latin, Ill. College, Jacksonville, Ill., since 1917, dean, 1933-38, administrative head, summer 1937. Mem. Am. Philol. Assn., Classical Assn. of Middle West and South, Phi Beta Kappa. Presbyterian. Author: The Equestrian Officials of Trajan and Hadrian, 1917. Home: 831 W. College Av., Jacksonville IL‡

LA CHANCE, LEANDER HANSCOM, mfr.; b. Wausau, Wis., Oct. 28, 1874; s. Leandre and Imogen Florence (Hanscom) L.; ed. high sch., Merrill, Wis., and business coll.; studied law, Columbian (now George Washington) U.; m. Helen Grace Sargent, of Wausau, Wis., Aug. 20, 1901; children—Donald, Virginia, Helen. Stenographer, law office, San Jose, Calif., 1893-95; with U.S. Agrl. Expt. Sta., Tucson, Ariz., 1896-97; clk. Navy Dept., Washington, D.C., 1898-99; mgr. London br. Chicago Flexible Shaft Co., 1900-03; mgr. home office same co., 1903-08, v.p., 1908-18; pres. Stewart Mfg. Corpn. since 1918; pres. Stewart Die Casting Corpn. Republican. Methodist. Clubs: Union League, Chicago Athletic, Westmoreland Country. Home: Belmont Hotel. Office: 4535 Fullerton Av., Chicago IL‡

LACHMAN, ARTHUR, chemist; b. San Francisco, Calif., Dec. 4, 1873; s. Abraham and Marie (Lazarus) L.; B.S., U. of Calif., 1893; Ph.D., summa cum laude, U. of Munich, 1895; m. Bertha Nathan, June 28, 1898; children—Gertrude (Mrs. F. Eberson), Ruth (Mrs. J. Colyer). Asst. in chemistry, U. of Mich., 1896, instr., 1896-97; prof. U. of Ore., 1897-1902; cons. chem. engr., 1902-06; mfr., 1906-18; research asso. U. of Calif., 1920. Fellow A.A.A.S.; mem. Am. Chem. Soc. Author: Spirit of Organic Organic Chemistry, 1899; also numerous papers on pure and applied chemistry. Received various patents in petroleum technology. Address: Hotel Shattuck, Berkeley 4 CA‡

LADA-MOCARSKI, VALERIAN, banker; b. Russia, 1898; M.A., Columbia Library Sch., 1954; m. Laura Klots. Member of board of directors of J. Henry Schroder Banking Corp., N.Y.C., Schroder Trust Co., N.Y.C. Adviser Russian Book Collection, Yale U. Libraries; dir. Internat. Students Center, New Haven; trustee Yale U. Assos.; fellow Pierson Coll., Yale U. Mem. Am. Craftsmen's Council (hon. trustee N.Y.C.). Clubs: Lawn, Mori's, Social Science (New Haven); Coffee House, Yale Grolier (N.Y.C.). Author: Bibliography of Books on Russian Alaska Before 1868, 1969; also articles. Home: New Haven CT Died June 8, 1971; buried Wood Lawn Cemetery, New York City NY

LAETSCH, THEODORE (CARL FERDINAND), prof. of theology; b. Milwaukee, Wis., Feb. 11, 1877; s. Rudolph and Elizabeth (Eissfeldt) L.; ed. Concordia Coll., Milwaukee, 1889-95; Concordia Theol. Sem., St. Louis, 1895-98; D.D., Concordia Coll., Unley, South Australia, 1939; m. Martha Polzin, June 21, 1899 (died Jan. 4, 1919); children—Theodore, Bernard, Harold, Willis; m. 2d, Louise Holling, Feb. 5, 1920. Ordained to ministry of Lutheran Church, Aug. 14, 1898; pastor Chippewa Falls, Wis., 1898-1901, Deer Park, Wis., 1901-04, Epiphany Ch., Eau Claire, Wis., 1904-14, Immanuel Ch., Sheboygan, Wis., 1914-20, Trinity Ch., St. Louis, 1920-27; prof. of practical theology, Concordia Theol. Sem., St. Louis, since 1927. Mem. editorial staff Der Lutheraner and Concordia Theol. Monthly. Home: 5705 Gresham St., St Louis 9 MO‡

LAFFERTY, ABRAHAM WALTER, lawyer; b. in Audrain Co., Mo., June 10, 1875; s. Abraham M. and Helen (Kinney) L.; ed. pub. schs., Mo.; student law dept. U. of Mo., LL.B., 1899; unmarried. Admitted to bar and practiced at Montgomery City, Mo., until 1904, Portland, Ore., 1906-19, New York since 1919. Was pros. atty., Montgomery County, Mo.; mem. 62d and 63d Congresses, from Portland, Ore., 1911-15. Author of bill to authorize each state to manufacture pure beer, wines and liquors for medical purposes without need of physician's prescription, but providing penalties for misuse. Address: 510 Park Av., New York NY‡

LA FOLLETTE, FOLA, actress; b. Madison, Wis.; d. Robert Marion and Belle (Case) L.; B.A., U. of Wis., 1904; m. George Middleton Oct. 29, 1911 (dec. 1967). Played with Ada Rehan, Alice Fisher, Leo Ditrichstein and others; also in The Scarecrow." Clubs: Twelfth Night, Women's City (New York); Three Arts (London, Eng.). Contbr. to magazines on dramatic and social questions. Home: New York City NY Died Feb. 1970.

LAGEN, MARY HUNEKER (MRS.), journalist; b. at Phila.; d. John and Mary Elizabeth (Gibbons) Huneker; grad. St. Joseph's Acad., Emmitsburg, Md.; m. Phila., Oct. 1, 1874, Charles A. Lagen. First woman in Phila. to wear a short skirt for cycling; began series of articles for Phila. Press called Woman Awheel;" remained with Phila. Press until 1895; since then with Phila. Inquirer, under pen-name of Diana on Woman's Sports the World Over," the first of its kind in America, reporting golf tournaments east and west, and Nat. horse shows; since 1899 editor Woman's Page. Mem. League Am. Pen Women, Professional Woman's League, New York, Geog. Soc., Pa., Women's Press Assn. Clubs: New Century, Browning (Phila.); Lyceum (London). Author: (with Cally Ryland), Daphne and Her Lad, 1904 H4. Residence: The Covington, Philadelphia PA‡

LAHEY, EDWIN A., journalist; b. Chgo., Jan. 11, 1902; s. James F. and Alice (Burns) L.; ed. Chicago schs.; student on Nieman fellowship, Harvard U., 1938-39; m. Grace Seidcheck, Aug. 28, 1929;children—Jane, Judith. Chief correspondent Knight Newspapers. Roman Catholic. Clubs: National Press (Washington), Harvard; Gridiron. Home: Washington DC Died July 17, 1969; buried Gate of Heaven Cemetery, Silver Spring MD

LAHM, FRANK PURDY, army officer; b. Ohio, Nov. 17, 1877; grad. U.S. Mil. Acad., 1901; grad. Mounted Service Sch., 1911; m. Gertrude Jenner, Oct. 18, 1911. Commd. 2d lt. 6th Cav., Feb. 18, 1901; capt. Aviation Sect. Signal Corps, Apr. 1, 1916; lt. colonel, July 2, 1920; promoted colonel Air Corps, Oct. 7, 1931. Made many experiments with balloons for war purposes and participated in nat. and internat. races; won James Gordon Bennett cup in Internat. Balloon Race, Paris, France, Sept. 30-Oct. 1, 1906. Organized aviation service in Philippine Islands, 1912, conducting training on airplanes and seaplanes there, 1912-13; sec. Signal Corps Aviation Sch., North Island, San Diego, Calif., 1916-17; ordered to command Balloon Sch., Ft. Omaha, Neb., Apr. 1917, to England, Aug. 1917, thence to France, inspecting balloon services; organized Lighter than Air Service in A.E.F.; on duty Hdqrs. Chief of Air Service to Feb. 1918, Hdqrs. Zone of Advance Air Service to May 1918, Hdqrs. First Army Air Service to July 1918; air officer in G-3, 1st Army, to Oct. 1918; organized and commanded 2d Army Air Service, Oct. 1918; disbanded May, 1919; spl. student Army War Coll., 1919-20; G-3, War Dept. Gen. Staff, 1920-24; 9th Corps Area Air Officer, 1924-26; apptd. brig. gen. for period of 4 yrs., and asst. to chief of Air Corps, to organize and command Air Corps Training Center, 1926-30; air officer 9th Corps Area to July, 1930; apptd. air attache, Am. Embassy, Paris, France, July 1931. Awarded D.S.M. First airship pilot and first balloon pilot in U.S. Army. Address: War Department, Washington DC‡

LAI, CHIA-CHIU, Chinese diplomat; b. Kiangsi, China, May 19, 1922; s. Hsing-Shu and Lien-Cheng (Tseng) L; LL.B., Nat. Chengchi U., Chungking, China, 1945; m. Lingling Du, May 1, 1951; children—Robert, Stanley. Mem. staff treaty dept. Ministry Fgn. Affairs, Chungking, 1946-49; sec. Chinese delegation 48th session Gen. Assembly UN, 1949; chief 1st sect. E. Asian dept., Ministry Fgn. Affairs, Taipei, 1950-52; 1st sec. embassy, Washington, 1952-61, counselor charge polit. affairs, 1961-62; consul gen., Seattle, 1962-69. Dean Counsular Corps Seattle, 1963-69; hon. v.p. China Club Seattle. Club: Rainier (asso.) (Seattle). Died Jan. 1969.

LAIDLER, HARRY WELLINGTON, author, economist; b. Brooklyn, N.Y., Feb. 18, 1884; s. William Ebenezer and Julia (Heary) L.; A.B., Wesleyan U., Middletown, Conn., 1907; hon. A.M., 1933; LL.B., Brooklyn Law Sch., 1910; Ph.D., Columbia, 1914; m. Agnes Fuller Armington, Nov. 5, 1919; children—John Armington, Rosamond. Reporter, staff Brooklyn Daily Eagle, 1907-10; a founder, 1905, sec., 1910-21, Intercollegiate Socialist Society; executive director of the League for Industrial Democracy, 1921-57; emeritus 1957-70; editor Intercollegiate Socialist, 1913-19; editor Socialist Rev., 1919-21. Coll., univ. lectr.; dir. Nat. Bureau Economic Research since 1920, v.p., 1928, pres., 1930-32, 1948-49, chmn. bd. dirs., 1932-34; member Industrial Division, Federal Council Chs., 1924-51; mem. dept. social welfare, National Council Churches, 1951-53. Socialist candidate for gov. of N.Y., 1936; for U.S. senator from N.Y., 1938. Mem. N.Y. City Council from Brooklyn, 1940-41. Mem. program committee Institute for Social Progress, 1936-57; member Public Affairs Committee since 1943; dir. Nat. Housing Conf., 1931-65, hon. dir., 1963—; lectr. economics, N.Y.C. 1942, Brooklyn College, 1943-44, College City of New York, 1942-45. Member New York Bar, Phi Beta Kappa, Phi Delta Phi. Commons. Club: Nat. Arts. Socialist. Author many books in field, including Social-Economic Movements, 1944; History of Socialism, 1968; Boycotts and the Labor Struggle (first edition 1913), 1968; co-author: What Do You Know About Labor, 1956; author economic brochures; latest being: Socialism in U.S., Brief History, 1952. Editor books and brochures in field, latest include: John Dewey at Ninety, 1950; Needed: A Moral Awakening in America, 1952; How Free is Free Enterprise, 1954. Home: Brooklyn NY Died July 14, 1970; buried Swans Point Cemetery, Providence RI

LAIDLEY, ROY RUSSELL, food co. exec.; b. Chgo., Dec. 25, 1904; s. Walter C. and Pearl (Wilbur) L.; student LaSalle Extension U.; m. Doris Groves, Sept. 5, 1931; children—Russell James, Nancy (Mrs. Robert L. Shaski). With Brennan Packing Co., Chgo., 1921-24; asst. mgr., corp. sec. Laidley & Co., investment ins., Chgo., 1924-26; with Mickelberry's Food Products Co., Chgo., 1926-68, pres., 1956-68, also dir.; pres. and/or v.p., dir. 12 subsidiary companies. Mem. Chgo. Assn. Commerce and Industry. Club: Olympia Fields (Ill.) Country. Home: Chicago IL Died Feb. 7, 1968.

LAIPPLY, THOMAS CHARLES, educator, physician; b. Cleve., Apr. 30, 1910; s. Adam Henry and Helena (Gaffney) L.; A.B., Western Res. U., 1933, M.D., 1936; m. Bernice Irma O'Grody, Nov. 29, 1941; 1 son, Thomas Charles. Rotating med. intern Univ. Hosp., Cleve., 1936-38, resident pathology, 1938-41; pathologist Univ. Hosp., Medina (O.) City Hosp., Lakewood Hosp., 1941-46; from instr. to asst. prof. pathology Western Res. U., 1939-46; chmn. dept. pathology Chgo. Wesley Meml. Hosp., 1946-68, founder, dir. Sch. Med. Tech., 1946-68, dir. intern and resident tng. programs, 1950-64; mem. faculty Northwestern U. Medical Sch., 1946-68, prof. pathology, 1956-68; cons. VA Research Hosp., Chgo., 1950-68; cons. med. research program Chgo. Bd. Health, 1962-68. Diplomate Am. Bd. Anatomic and Clin. Pathologists. Mem. Am. Assn. Cancer Research, Am. Assn. Pathologists and Bacteriologists, A.M.A., Am. Soc. Clin. Pathologists (dep. commnr. res. tutorials 1962-64, commnr. continuing edn. 1964-68). Am. Coll. Pathologists, Ill., Chgo. med. socs., Ill., Chgo. pathologists socs., Sigma Xi, Phi Chi. Author numerous articles in field. Home: Glenview IL Died Feb. 9, 1968.

LAIRD, JOHN BAKER, clergyman; b. Lancaster County, Pa., Feb. 14, 1866; s. Clarkson and Anna (O'Neil) L.; A.B., Lafayette Coll., 1892, A.M., 1895 (D.D., 1903); grad. Princeton Theol. Sem., 1895; unmarried. Ordained Presbyn. ministry, 1895; pastor Frankford Ch., Phila., 1895-96; now retired. Served as moderator of Presbytery and Synod of Pa. Trustee Lafayette Coll.; pres. Red Cross auxiliary of 18,000 members; organizer and trustee Frankford Hosp.; pres. trustees Wilson Coll. for Women; dir. and trustee Princeton Theol. Seminary; trustee and former pres. bd. Lincoln Univ.; mem. Bd. of Nat. Missions of Presbyn. Ch. and trustee Bd. of Publication same ch.; many times mem. Gen. Assembly; mem. Council Ref. Chs. and Presbyn. Alliance. Pres. Pa. Scotch-Irish Society, 1912-13; dir. Frankford Hist. Soc. Republican. Clubs: Adelphia, Union League, Country. Contbr. numerous religious and ednl. articles. Dir. of The Presbyterian." Home: 4925 Saul St., Philadelphia 24 PA‡

LAKE, DEVEREUX, ex-pres. Sandusky Foundry & Machine Co.; b. Mobile, Ala., Aug. 29, 1876; s. Thomas Harden and Sarah Elizabeth (Hopkins) L.; student Barton Acad., Mobile, 1886-92; B.S., Vanderbilt U., 1896; m. Jeanette Barrett, Mar. 12, 1906; children—Madeline (Mrs. Scott Elder), Elizabeth. Newspaper reporter, New York and Nashville, 1897-01; saw mill supt., Mexico, 1910-13; salesman for Birmingham mfrs., introducing Ala. coal in Cuba and Ala. cast iron water pipe in Chile and other Latin-Am. countries, 1914-20; with Sandusky Foundry & Machine Co. since 1920, pres. 1935-43. Mem. bd. trustees Vanderbilt U. since 1936. Author: (historical narrative) The Lake Family in America, 1937. Home: 234 E. Washington St., Sandusky OH‡

LAKE, HARRY BEASTON, investment banker; b. Port Norris, N.J., Jan. 24, 1886; s. Henry H. and Emma (Sheppard) L.; Ph.B., Brown Univ., 1909; m. Jane Cooper, Oct. 14, 1921 (dec.); 1 dau., Nona (Mrs. Lloyd P. Tevis, Jr.); m. 2d, Dulce Simoes-Correa. Partner Ladenburg, Thalmann & Co., N.Y.C., 1921-69; dir. Cooperstown Corp. (Md.), Sutton Pl. South Corp. Mem. of American Soc. French Legion of Honor, Inc. (dir.). Republican. Episcopalian. Clubs: City Midday, Metropolitan, N.Y. Yacht, Recess, Knickerbocker (N.Y.C.). Home: New York City NY Died Sept. 25, 1969; buried Ferncliff, Hartsdale, Hartsdale

LAKIN, HERBERT CONRAD, lawyer; b. Worcester, Mass., Mar. 11, 1872; s. George Boyer and Ellena Kimball (Putnam) L.; grad. high sch., Worcester, 1890; A.B., summa cum laude, Harvard, 1894, LL.B., 1898; m. Helen Wardner Beaman, Oct. 8, 1902; children—Hettie Beaman (Mrs. F. Ritter Shumway), Eleanor Putnam (Mrs. David Porter Guest), Charles Beaman, Mary Stacy (Mrs. George G. Hoffman). Admitted to N.Y. bar, 1899, and began as clk. for law firm Evarts, Choate & Beaman, N.Y. City; clk. Lord, Day & Lord, 1901-05; mem. firm 1905-19; pres. The Cuba Co., 1919-30, Compania Cubana, 1919-30, Cuba R.R., 1919-25; dir. and counsel same cos., Cuba Northern Rys. and Consolidated R.R. of Cuba until 1933; pres. Cuban Land Co.; dir. L.I. R.R. Company; v.p. and director J. A. Wigmore Land Co. Trustee Scarsdale Bd. of Edn., 1914-19 (pres. 1917-19); trustee, chmn. finance com. Greenwich (Conn.) Public Library, 1935-41. In Stockbridge; former pres. Laurel Hill Assn.; chmn. Town Planning Bd.; mem. Post War Planning Bd. Mem. law firm of Wing, Lakin & Whedon 1930-May 1, 1940. Mem. N.Y. Nat. Guard, 1903-09. Mem. Am. Bar Assn., Assn. Bar City of N.Y., Phi Beta Kappa, Sigma Alpha Epsilon. Republican. Episcopalian. Clubs: Harvard, Century (N.Y.); Manursing Is. (Rye). Editor Crimson, 1892-94, Harvard Law Rev., 1895-96, Record of Sigma Alpha Epsilon, 1896-1900. Address: Stockbridge MA‡

LA MARR, ESTHER BERNICE RANDALL, govt. ofcl.; b. Balt., May 30, 1916; d. Arthur George and Ada (Bradley) Randall; B.A., Talladega Coll., 1938; M.S.W., U. Mich., 1949; LL.B., U. Detroit, 1953; m. Bernard Howard LaMarr, Nov. 23 (div. Aug. 1946); 1 son, Bernard Howard. Case worker Wayne County Bur. Social Aid, Detroit, 1940-41, Detroit Dept. Pub. Welfare, 1941-42, home service div. A.R.C., Detroit, 1943-56, Wayne County Probate Ct., Detroit, 1956-62; exec. sec. Detroit Commn. on Children and Youth, 1962-64; spl. asst. to adminstr. vets affairs VA, Washington, 1964-67. Mem. Mich. Adv. Com. on Ednl. Needs of Youth, 1963-64, Mich. Ad Hoc Com. on Out of Sch. and Unemployed Youth, 1962-64, Mich. Gov.'s Commn. on Status of Women, 1963, Mich. Welfare League, 1962; tech. adv. com. Spl. Youth Employment Project, 1954; chmn. Friends of Eastern High Sch. Com., 1964; mem. Neighborhood Conservation Program Improvement Com., 1962-64; mem. spl. services to youth com. Neighborhood Service Orgn., 1962-64; now mem. Nat. Women's Com. on Civil Rights, Receiving Hosp. League, Com. Foster Children and Child Care, Trade Union Leadership Council, Chmn., Women's Vol. Assn., 1953, mem. 1st Dist. Vol. Democrats, 1964, Wayne County Dem. Women, 1953. Bd. dirs. Wayne County chpt. Mich. Soc. Mental Health, 1962, Detroit Council for Youth Service, Inc., 1962-64, Dem. Action Com. 1st Dist., 1964, Lewis Bus. Coll., 1963, Community Action for Detroit Youth, 1963-64; exec. bd. Coordinating Council on Human

Relations, Commn. on Community Relations, 1962-64, Detroit Sch.-Community Behavior Project, 1962-64, Detroit council Campfire Girls, 1963-64, Fedn. Community Councils, 1962-64; trustee Emergency Psychiat. Facilities for Children, Inc., 1963; bd. mgmt. Downtown br. YWCA, 1964, chmn. pub. relations com., 1964, chmn. by-laws com. for provisional com., 1963, 1st v.p., 1961-63; adv. council Jr. Red Cross, 1964; adv. com. Detroit Foster Homes Project, 1964. Named Outstanding Citizen of Year, Mich. Chronicle, 1960; Outstanding Civic Achievement award LeMoyne Coll. Alumni, 1962; named Woman of Year, St. John A.M.E. Ch., 1962; Nat. Sojourner Truth award, 1964. Mem. League Women Voters, N.A.A.C.P., Nat. Council Cath. Women (chmn. social legislation com. Detroit archdiocese), Altar Guild, Nat. (edn.) and incentive com.), Detroit (health and welfare com.) urban leagues, Acad. Certified Social Workers, Bus. and Profl. Women's Clubs, Cath. Interracial Council, Delta Sigma Theta (pres. Detroit 1959-61, mem. nat. com. on publs. and pub. relations 1961). Home: Washington DC Died Aug. 20, 1967.

LAMB, JAMES GIBSON, business exec.; b. Balt., Feb. 20, 1889; s. George M. and Annie L. (Roberts) L.; A.B., Swarthmore Coll., 1910; m. Anne H. Bunting, Apr. 15, 1914; children—James Gibson, Susan B., John P. With Scott Paper Co., Chester Pa., 1910-27, v.p., dir., 1910-27; pres. Lamb & Keen, Inc., advt., Phila., 1930-54; partner, chmn. bd. Arndt, Preston, Chapin, Lamb & Keen, Inc., 1954-59, pres. from 1954, chmn. exec. com. advt. agency, from 1959. Republican. Mem. Soc. of Friends. Clubs: Union League, Racquet (Phila.); Rose Tree Fox Hunting (Media, Pa.). Home: Wallingford PA Died Feb. 6, 1929.

LAMBERT, ADRIAN VAN SINDEREN, surgeon; b. New York, N.Y., June 30, 1872; s. Dr. Edward Wilberforce and Martha Melcher (Waldron) L.; A.B., Yale, 1893, M.D., Columbia, 1896; grad. student, Germany and Austria, 1899-1900; m. Mary Shipman Robinson, June 1, 1905; children—Mary Robinson (wife of Dr. George A. Carden, Jr.), Adrian (M.D.), John Trumbull (M.D.), Ruth (wife of Seymour Preston). Med. interne New York Hospital, 1896-98, surgical interne, New York Hospital, 1898-99; attending surgeon, New York Lying-In Hospital, 1901-02, Lincoln Hospital, 1902-09; associated with Roosevelt Hospital, as 2d asst. attending surgeon, 1908-10, 1st asst. attending surgeon, 1910-12; asso. attending surgeon Presbyterian Hosp., 1912-14, attending surgeon, 1915-16, dir. of surgery, 1917-20, cons. surgeon since 1921; attending surgeon Bellevue Hosp., 1920-40, consulting surgeon Bellevue Hospital since 1941; cons. surgeon N.Y. Infirmary for Women, N.Y. Polyclinic, Neurol. Inst., Sea View Hosp., Nyack Hosp., Bellevue Hosp., 1940; with Coll. of Physicians and Surgeons, Columbia U., since 1901, as demonstrator of anatomy, 1901-05, 1901-05, instr. of surgery, 1906-12, asso. prof., 1913-21, acting head of surgery, 1918-19, prof. of clin. surgery, 1922-23, clinical professor of surgery, 1924-46, now clinical professor emeritus since 1946. Fellow Am. Coll. Surgeons; fellow N.Y. Acad. Medicine; mem. N.Y. County Med. Soc., N.Y. State Med. Soc., A.M.A. Am. Soc. Thoracic Surgery (pres. 1939-40), N.Y. Surg. Soc., Delta Kappa Epsilon. Clubs: Century, Union (New York); Graduates, Elizabeth, Lawn (New Haven). Editor: A Terminology of Disease; Textbook of Surgery (by Brewer). Contbr. to med. jours. Home: 242 E. 72d St., New York NY‡

LAMBERT, AVERY ELDORUS, anatomist, educator, author; b. Waldoboro, Me., Oct. 31, 1873; s. Ellison and Angouleme (Lambert) Maddocks (obtained right to use mother's maiden name, 1892); prep. edn., pub. schs., Waldoboro, Me., and Tabor Acad., Marion, Mass.; grad. Bangor (Me.) Theol. Sem., 1896; B.S., Dartmouth, 1902, Ph.D., 1906; grad. study, Harvard, 1917, U. of Chicago, 1920-22; m. Dora L. Hersom, 1896; 1 son. G. Hersom; m. 2d, Irene Lamson Adams; children—Mary Lamson, Adams. Ordained ministry Congl. Ch., 1896; pastor, Lebanon, Me., 1896-98, Thetford, Vt., 1898-1900; instr. zoology, Dartmouth, 1902-04; instr. biology, Framingham (Mass.) Normal Sch., 1904-10; prof. biology, Middlebury (Vt.) Coll., 1911-16, also dean, 1912-14; prof. of anatomy, U. of Vt., 1917-19; prof. anatomy and head of dept., U. of Ala., 1920-25; prof. histology and microscopical anatomy, State University of Iowa, 1925-1944; retired 1944. Fellow A.A.A.S.; member American Assn. Anatomists, Sigma Xi, Phi Beta Pi, Ia. Acad. Sci., Am. Geog. Soc. Clubs: Iowa Authors, Kiwanis, Triangle. Author: A New Trilobite from the Littleton Formation, 1905; History of the Procephalic Lobes of Epeira Cinerea, 1909; Guide to the Study of Histology, 1931; Poems of the Air (broadcast series), 1935; Introduction and Guide to the Study of Histology. Contributor to scientific and other periodicals. Asso. dir. of Morning Chapel, Radio Station, WSUI. Home: 1416 E. College St., Iowa City IA‡

LAMBERT, ROBERT EUGENE, stock and seed farmer; b. Claiborne, Ala., Aug. 29, 1869; s. Robert Amos and Martha Verdelia (Busey) L.; ed. Howard Coll., Birmingham, 1890-91, Richmond (Va.) U., 1891-92; m. Agnes Asenath Hopkins, Feb. 26, 1901; children—Robert Eugene, James Ernest. Stock farmer, cattle breeder, 1897-1910; also production of farm seed, 1910-24; admitted two sons to partnership, forming firm R.E. Lambert & Sons, growers of and dealers in farm seed, breeders of livestock, gen. farming, since 1924. Master Farmer award, by Ala. Polytechnic Inst., 1927. Trustee Howard Coll., Bapt. Foundation of Ala., Farm Foundation; pres. Southern Livestock Assn., 1931-32; mem. Southeastern Council. Democrat. Baptist. Address: Darlington AL*‡

LAMBERTON, CHESS, banker; b. Franklin, Pa., Nov. 1, 1877; s. Robert G. and Louella (Chess) L.; ed. Grove City (Pa.) Coll., 1897-98; grad. Eastman Business Coll., Poughkeepsie, N.Y., 1899; m. Lauretta L. Lamberton, Aug. 11, 1925. In banking business at Franklin since 1898; pres. and trust officer Lamberton Nat. Bank, Franklin; pres. First Nat. Bank (Cochranton, Pa.); v.p. Joy Mfg. Co.; dir. Sylvania Producing Co., Industrial Silica Corp. (Youngstown), Fed. Reserve Bank, Cleveland, 1920-37. Mem. N.G. Pa., 1899-1913, retiring as adj. gen. Republican. Presbyn. Mason (K.T., 32 deg.), Elk, Moose, Eagle. Clubs: Franklin; Wanango (Reno, Pa.). Home: Franklin PA*‡

LAMBLE, JOHN W., ins. exec.; b. England, 1897; student Merchant Taylors Coll., England; Deytheur Sch.; m. Mildred Feemster; children—Charmain, John. With White Star Line, 1920-23; Liverpool and London and Globe Ins. Co., 1923-29; Fidelity & Guaranty Fire Corp., Baltimore, 1929-38, sec. 1938-49, comptroller, 1941-42; U.S. Sec., Car and Gen. Ins. Corp., Ltd., 1942-46; v.p. North Star Reinsurance Corp., N.Y.C., 1946-50, pres., dir. from 1950. Pres. Ins. Accts. Assn., 1948-49. Home: Port Washington NY Died Feb. 1969.

LAMBRIX, JOSEPH H., business exec.; b. Lancaster, N.Y., Sept. 27, 1896; s. Henry V. and Anna (Eiles) L.; student parochial schs.; m. Sophia Emma Reeves, Nov. 11, 1920; children—Lois Jane, Judith Ann. Engring. dept. Gould Storage Battery Co., 1913-18, 19-25; engr. Curtiss Aeroplane & Motor Corp., Buffalo, 1918; engr. USL Battery Corp., 1925-29, asst. purchasing agt., Niagara Falls, N.Y., 1929-35, purchasing agt., 1935-42; asst. purchasing agt. Electric Auto-Life Co., Toledo, 1942-48, asst. dir. purchases, 1948, dir. purchases, since 1948, v.p. from 1950. Home: Toledo OH Died July 22, 1971.

LAMONT, PETER T., oil co. exec.; b. Rotterdam, The Netherlands, Apr. 8, 1900 (parents U.S. citizens); s. John George and Florence Louise (Theobald) L.; grad. The Hill Sch., Pottstown Pa., 1918; B.S. in Petroleum Engring., Mass. Inst. Tech., 1922; m. Dorothy Hogencamp, June 14, 1924; 1 dau., Louise Florence. Tng. in oil prodn., refining and marketing Standard Oil Co. (N.J.), 1922-25, marketing asst. in Germany, 1925-30, mem. various bds. of European affiliates, 1930-41, marketing advisor for Central Europe, 1946-48, transferred to N.Y. as asst. marketing coordinator (world wide), 1948, marketing coordinator (world wide), 1949-54, v.p., dir., 1954-61. Served as comdr., USNR, 1942-45. Decorated Legion of Merit; Croix de Guerre with Gold Star; comdr. Order Merit Republic Italy; comdr.'s cross Order Orange Nassau (Netherlands). Mem. Theta Xi. Clubs: University (N.Y.C.); American (London); Greenwich (Conn.) Country. Home: Greenwich CT Died Nov. 25, 1970; buried Putnam Cemetery, Greenwich CT

LAMORISSE, ALBERT, motion picture prod., dir., writer; b. Paris, France, Jan. 13, 1922; s. Albert Gusman and Elise (Decaux) L.; studied Institut des Hautes Etudes Cinematographiques; m. Claude Jeanne Marie Duparc, Nov. 24, 1947; children—Pascal, Sabine, Fanny. Began career as script writer, photographer, 1945; tech. asst. film Kairouan, Tunisia, 1946; prod. documentary film, Djerba, 1946, Bim, 1949; writer, prod. Crin Blanc, 1952; writer, prod., dir. Le Ballon Rouge, 1955, director of Stowaway in the Sky, 1960, U.S., 1962, Fifi la Plume, 1965, Versailles, 1967, Paris Never Seen, 1968; The Lover's Wind (Iran), 1969; developed process to enable motion pictures to be filmed from a helicopter. Recipient Academy Motion Picture Arts and Sciences award, 1956, Grand Prix for short films, Cannes Festival, 1956, Prix Jean Vigo, internat. prize for youth, also Epi d'Or of Rome; San Gregario prize Internat. Festival Religious Films, Officer Order Arts and Letters, film critics awards West Germany, Mexico, Switzerland, also Tokyo, London, N.Y.C.; numerous prizes Prague, Venice, others. Roman Catholic. Home: Paris France Died June 2, 1970; buried Chateau de Meaulvuar, So. France

LA MOURE, HOWARD ALEXANDER, psychiatrist; b. Albany, N.Y., Dec. 13, 1875; s. Ten Eyck and Janet Josephine (Alexander) L.; grad. Albany Acad., 1893; M.D., Albany Med. Coll. (Union U.), 1900; m. Ina M. Salisbury, Apr. 5, 1904 (died Feb. 25, 1922); m. 2d, Josephine M. Fortier, Apr. 2, 1923. Med. interne, Rochester (N.Y.) State Hosp., 1900-01; asst. physician, Craig Colony for Epileptics, N.Y., 1902-03; asst. physician, Rome (N.Y.) State Custodial Asylum, 1903; 1st asst. physician, Sch. for Feeble Minded, Faribault, Minn., 1903-07; supt. N.D. Sch. for Feeble Minded, Grafton, 1907-10; asst. supt., 1911-12, supt., 1912-28, Colo. State Hosp., Pueblo; supt. and med. dir. Woodcroft Hosp., Pueblo, 1928-32; physician State Hosp. Annex, Pueblo, 1932-35; supt. Colo. State Home and Training Sch. for Mental Defectives, Ridge, Colorado, 1935-50. Member Colo. State Med. Soc., Clear Creek Valley Med. Soc., Am. Psychiatric Assn., Phi Sigma Kappa. Presbyterian. Address: 3871 Estes St., Wheat Ridge CO‡

LAMSON, GUY CALEB, general sec. Am. Bapt. Publ. Soc.; b. Newfane, Vt., June 29, 1875; s. Caleb Blakeslee and Phila Louise (Holden) L.; B.S., Middlebury (Vt.) Coll., 1896 (D.D., 1913); B.D., Rochester Theol. Sem., 1900; m. Ethel Bruce, of Brattleboro, Vt., May 17, 1900. Ordained Bapt. ministry, 1900; missionary pastor Vt. Bapt. Conv., 1900-2; pastor 1st Ch., Montpelier, Vt., 1902-5, Hyde Park Ch., Boston, 1905-11; dist. sec. (N.E.) Am. Bapt. Publ. Soc., 1911-13; missionary and Bible sec., Phila., 1913-15, gen. sec. since Aug. 1916, same soc. Mem. Delta Upsilon. Republican. Home: 531 Pelham Rd., Germantown. Office: 1701 Chestnut St., Philadelphia PA‡

LANCASTER, JOHN HERROLD, librarian; b. Nelsonville, O., Sept. 5, 1898; s. Stephen Henry and Mabel Edna (Gardner) L.; B.S., Ohio Wesleyan U., 1920; M.A., Ohio State U., 1926; Ph.D., B.S. in L.S., Columbia, 1941; m. Florence Stinchcomb, Aug. 10, 1922; children—John Herrold, James Roydon. Tchr. Wauseon (O.) High Sch., 1920-24, Oak Harbor (O.) High Sch., 1924-25; supt. Old Fort (O.) Rural Schs., 1925-27; dir. student teaching Heidelberg Coll., 1927-39, librarian, 1939-43; supr. engring., sci., management War Tng. Program, Toledo Coll. Engring., 1942-43; asst. prof. library sci. and physics U. Ill., 1943-45; librarian, asso. prof. library sci. George Peabody Coll. Tchrs., 1945-49, vis. prof. library sci., summers 1955, 56-57, 59, 61; dir. library Ohio Wesleyan U., 1949-64; head librarian Baldwin-Wallace Coll., Berea, Ohio, from 1964; visiting associate professor of library sci. Syracuse University, in summers 1951, 52; vis. instr. library sci. Kent State U., summer 1965. Mem. Joint Com. on Library Work as Career, 1947-54, Com. on Inter-Library Coop. Ohio Colls. and Univs., 1951-60; staff aquatic sch. A.R.C., Culver, Ind., summers 1942, 1943; scoutmaster, 1928-51; troop committeeman, dist. v.p., dist. chmn. leader tng. Boy Scouts Am., 1952-58, dist. chmn., 1958-59, dist. chmn. orgn. and extension, 1959-64, council exec. bd., 1958-64. Served as 2d lt. inf. U.S. Army, 1918. Mem. A.L.A., Ohio Coll. Assn. (coll. library sect. chmn. 1959-60, teaching aids sect.), N.E.A. (div. audio visual instrn.), Endl. Film Library Assn., Audio Visual Council O., Assn. Coll. and Reference Libraries (tchr. tng. sect. sec. 1947-48, chmn. 1948-49), Assn. Am. Library Schs. (com. on recruiting and personnel 1946-49, chmn. 1947-49), O. Library Assn. (v.p. 1942-45, chmn. librarians sect. 1959-60), Am. Assn. U. Profs., C. of C., Phi Delta Kappa, Kappa Delta Pi. Methodist (curator Ohio Conf. Meth. Hist. Commn.), Mason. Clubs: Kiwanis (pres. 1963), Nashville Library (pres. 1948-49). Mem. editorial staff Lincoln Library Essential Information, 1959—. Contbr. articles profl. jours. Home: Delaware OH Died Oct. 19, 1969.

LAND, EMORY SCOTT, naval officer; b. Jan. 9, 1879; s. Scott E. and Jennie Taylor (Emory) L.; B.S., M.A., U. of Wyo., 1898; grad. U.S. Naval Acad., 1902; M.S., Mass. Inst. Tech., 1907; LL.D., U. of Wyo., 1939, Calif. Maritime Acad., 1940; Dr. Engring., N.Y. U., 1944; LL.D., Columbia, 1947; m. Elizabeth C. Stiles, Apr. 15, 1909. Commd. midshipman, U.S. Navy, 1901; naval constructor since 1904; asst. chief Bur. of Aeronautics, Navy Dept., 1926-28; chief of Bur. of Construction and Repair, 1932-37; commr. United States Maritime Commission, 1937-38, chairman, 1938-46. Appointed administrator, War Shipping Administration, February 9, 1942. Served as member staff Admiral Sims, World War I. Vice-pres. and treas. Daniel Guggenheim Fund for Promotion of Aeronautics, 1928-29. Pres. Air Transport Assn. of America since 1946. Mem. Society Naval Architects and Marine Engrs. (pres. 1940-42), Inst. Aeronautic Sciences, Brit. Inst. Naval Architects, Royal Aero Soc. Decorated Navy Cross (U.S.); Spanish Campaign Badge; Victory Medal, World War I; Army of Occupation of Germany Medal; Arthur Williams Memorial Award; Gold Medal of Bolivar-San Martin of Pan-Am. Soc.; D.S.M., Army, Navy; Knight Comdr., Mil. Div., Order of the British Empire; Grand Officer in the Order of Orange-Nassau (Netherlands); Order of Polonia Restituta (Poland); Comdr. Legion of Honor (France); Cross of Comdr. of the Order of Leopold (Belgium); Commanders Cross with star, Royal Order of St. Olav (Norway), 1948. Clubs: Army and Navy, Metropolitan, Army-Navy Country, Chevy Chase, Alibi (Washington); New York Yacht; Engineers' (Phila.). Home: Washington DC Died Nov. 1971.

LANDAHL, CARL WILLIAM, missionary; b. Sorasen, Boras, Sweden, Jan. 3, 1870; s. Carl Carlson and Anna Catharine (Swensdotter) L.; Red Wing (Minn.) Sem., 1895, D.D. (hon.), Luther Sem., St. Paul, 1930; m. Alice Holmberg, Aug. 2, 1899; children—Catharine Mei-gwei, Lillian Cynthia, Marion Alice Cecelia (Mrs. O.T. Haaland), Margaret Charlotte, Carl Wilfred, Frances Dorothy Christine (Mrs. B.L. Schroder), Herbert Daniel Cervin. Entered U.S., 1888; naturalized, 1895. Missionary to China, 1895 (Hauge Synod Mission Bd.); opened station, Taipingtien,

Hupeh, 1896; supt. Hauge Mission, 1908-17 (comdr. 13,000 militia, protective, during revolution, 1911); supt. Luth. United Mission, 1917-32; chmn. Union Luth. Ch. Council, 1917-20; 1st. pres., Honan-Hupeh Synod Luth. Ch. of China, 1928-32; chmn. 1st Gen. Assembly Luth. Ch. of China; missionary, Francheng, Hupeh, 1932-39; in U.S.A., field (deputation) work for the Board of Foreign Missions of the N.L.C.A., 1939-46; field representative for Lutheran Literature Soc. for China since 1946. Home: 1335 Keston St., St. Paul 8 MN Office: 425 S. Fourth St., MN‡

LANDAU, JACOB, laundry co. exec.; b. Warsaw Poland, May 5, 1900; s. Charles Samuel and Helen Eva (Syten) L.; LL.B., N.Y. Law Sch., 1927; m. Florence Benaghi, Aug. 20, 1931; children—Jacob Charles, Joel Ralph. Admitted to N.Y. bar, 1928, N.J. bar, 1933; practice in N.Y.C., 1928; with Consol. Laundries Corp., N.Y.C., from 1943, legal counsel and atty., 1944-59, exec. v.p., 1959-62, pres., from 1962, chmn., 1962-64, also dir. Home: New Rochelle NY Died Sept. 1966.

LANDAU, LEV DAVIDOVICH, physicist; b. Baku, USSR, Jan. 22, 1908; s. David and Lubov Landau; grad. Leningrad State U., 1927; married in 1939; 1 son. Mem. faculty Leningrad Physico-Tech. Inst., 1928-31; head theoretical div. Phys. and Tech. Inst., Kharkov, 1932-37; prof. theoretical physics Vavilov Inst. of Physical Problems, Moscow, 1937-68; spl. research solid state physics, low temperature physics, nuclear physics, quantum field theory. Recipient Lenin prize for sci., 1962, Nobel prize for physics, 1962. Mem. Acad. Scis. USSR, Royal Soc. London, Nat. Acad. Scis., Am. Acad. Arts and Scis., Royal Danish Acad. Scis., Royal Acad. Scis. Netherlands, Phys. Soc. London. Author: (with E. M. Lifshitz) Course of Theoretical Physics, 7 vols., 1938-62. Address: Moscow USSR Died Apr. 2, 1968.

LANDES, WILLIAM GRANT, b. Lancaster, Pa., May 31, 1865; s. John Shoemaker and Catharine (Wanner) L.; grad. high sch., Lancaster, 1881; hon. C.E.D., Susquehanna U., 1922; m. Bertha N. Lukens, June 18, 1890. Watchmaker and jeweler, Sheldon, Ill., until 1893; inspector Elgin Watch Co., 1894-97; traveling salesman, 1897-1903; gen. sec. Pa. State S.S. Assn., 1904-22; gen. sec. World's S.S. Assn., 1922-27. Attended 6 world's convs., Rome, Washington, D.C., Zurich, Tokyo, Glasgow and Los Angeles; mem. exec. com. Internat. S.S. Assn. 5 yrs.; as statis. sec. World's S.S. Assn., reported membership of 30,296,531 in 1920; was gen. sec. N.Y. State Council of Churches and Religious Edn., 1927-34. Address: Box 65, Park Ridge NJ‡

LANDIS, CHARLES WILLIAM, cons. engineer; b. Sacramento, Calif., Aug. 9, 1877; s. Leonidas Hamilton and Lovica (Smith) L.; B.S. in C.E., U. of Calif., 1902; m. Louise Coan, July 26, 1910; 1 dau., Mary Louise. Associated in practice with A. J. Cleary, San Francisco, since 1921; in analysis of Muscle Shoals project and preparation of bids for its operation, 1921; a designer, with Mr. Cleary, of Rincon Hill-Oakland Bridge across San Francisco Bay, 1926; asso. engr. for Pacific Gas & Electric Co. in underground water supply studies on Mokelumne River in Calif., 1930-31; consulting engr. on water supply problems with Cyril Williams, Jr., San Francisco, 1933-34; pioneer in development of Mokelumne River Water Supply project, American River project, etc. Mem. Am. Soc. Civil Engrs. Republican. Presbyn. Home: 2606 Harrison St., Oakland, Calif. Office: 269 Pine St., San Francisco CA‡

LANDIS, GERALD WAYNE, congressman; b. Bloomfield, Ind., Feb. 23, 1895; s. John Dowell and Netta Criss (Oliphant) L.; B.S., Ind. U., 1923, M.S., 1938; student U. of Ill., summer 1925; m. Vera Helen Wilson, Jan. 2, 1926; 1 dau., Mary Lou. Formerly athletic dir.; mem. 76th to 80th Congresses (1939-49), 7th Ind. Dist. Served as lt., U.S. Army, 1918. Mem. 40 & 8, Am. Legion, Greater Linton Club, Delta Upsilon. Republican. Mem. Disciples of Christ. Ch. Mason (32 deg.), Elk, K.P., L.O.O.M. Home: Linton IN Died Sept. 6, 1971; buried Fairview Cemetery, Linton IN

LANDIS, JESSIE ROYCE, actress; b. Chgo.; d. Paul Bernard and Ella (Gill) Medbury; ed. pub. schs., Chgo. Conservatory Music and Dramatic Art, pvt. coaching; m. Maj. Gen. J.F.R. Seitz, Dec. 2, 1956. Actress appearing in N.Y. and London theatre, motion pictures, TV; stage credits include Highwayman, Merrily We Roll Along, Papa Is All, Wings of Chance, Larger Than Life, Come Live With Me, Kiss and Tell, Richard II, Winter's Tale, the Furies, Command Performance, Solid South, Love from a Stranger, Sing Me No Lullaby, Love's Old Sweet Song, others; motion picture debut in Mr. Belvedere Goes to College, 1949; film credits include It Happens Every Spring, My Foolish Heart, Critics Choice, Tonight at 8:30, To Catch a Thief, The Swan, Bon Voyage, Boys' Night Out, North by Northwest. Recipient award for best performance for Larger Than Life, London, 1950. Home: Ridgefield CT Died Feb. 2, 1972.

LANDIS, PAUL NISSLEY, educator; b. Womelsdorf, Pa., Aug. 8, 1893; s. Frank Theodore and Cora (Nisley) L.; grad. Keystone State Normal Sch., 1910; A.B., Franklin and Marshall Coll., 1913, A.M., 1915; Ph.D., U. of Ill., 1923; m. Agnes Wickfield Vrooman, June 10, 1924; children—Caroline Julia, Martha. Teacher Franklin and Marshall Acad., 1913-16; asst. in English, U. of Ill., 1916-23; prof. of English, Franklin and Marshall Coll., 1924-25; mem. faculty U. Ill., 1925-61, prof. English 1945-61, prof. emeritus, 1961—, acting head of dept., 1947-50. Served as sergt. 56th Pioneer Inf., U.S. Army, 1918-19; in Meuse-Argonne campaign, mem. Army of Occupation. Mem. Modern Lang. Assn., Phi Beta Kappa, Phi Kappa Sigma. Home: Urbana IL Died May 21, 1970.

LANDON, CHARLES RAEBURNE, air force officer; b. Auburn, Ill., May 4, 1900; s. Charles and Margaret Alberta (Wyatt) L.; B.S., U.S. Mil. Acad., 1924; student Inf. Sch., 1927-28, Tank Sch., 1928-29, Command and Gen. Staff Sch., 1935-36; m. M. Elizabeth Shufflebarger, Nov. 19, 1929; children—Frances Elizabeth, Charles Raeburne. Pvt., later corpl. U.S. Marine Corps, 1918-19; Inf., U.S. Army, 1924-35; Adj. Gen. Dept., 1936-49; assigned duty with Air Force, Air Def. Command, 1946; trans. to Air Force, 1949; dir. Statis. Services since 1950; promoted through grades to maj. gen. Decorated Legion of Merit, Bronze Star, Commendation Medal, Marine Corps Good Conduct, Victory Medal (2). Am. Def. with star, Am. Theatre, E.T.O. with five stars, Occupation medal (U.S.); Officer Coronne de Chene, Croix de Guerre (Luxembourg); Officer Order Brit. Empire (Gt. Britian); Legion of Honor, Croix de Guerre with palm (France); Officer Order of Leopold with palm, Croix de Guerre with palm (Belgium); War Cross (Czechoslovakia). Mem. Nat. Sojourners, Am. Legion. Mason. Home: Arlington VA Died Sept. 1970.

LANDRETH, EARL, retired army officer, govt. ofcl.; b. Albany, Ore., Feb. 5, 1893; s. George Albert and Emma Jane (Weiss) L.; grad. Inf. Sch., 1921, Command and Gen. Staff Sch., 1923, Army War Coll., 1933; m. Frances Thomason, Sept. 21, 1919; children—Nancy (wife of Charles Lennhoff, U.S. Army), Margaret (Mrs. William Wesselhoeft). Enlisted in U.S. Army, 1912; commd. 1915, advancing through grades to col., 1942; with 21st Inf., Vancouver Barracks, Wash., 1915, Philippine Scouts, Parang, Mindanao, 1915-17, 15th Inf., Tientsin, China, 1917, prin. in Tientsin Incident, 1919; comdg. Demonstration Bn. 29th Inf., 1921-22; gen. staff ACOFS G-2, 1st Cav. Div., Ft. Bliss, Tex., 1923-27; instr. Command and Gen. Staff Sch., Ft. Leavenworth, Kan., 1927-32; instr., head rifle and gen. coms., pres. bd. testing new inf. div. Inf. Sch., Ft. Benning, Ga., 1935-39; comd. Ft. Missoula (Mont.) and Civilian Conservation Corps Dist., 1939-40; took 1st troops to Ft. Richardson, Alaska, 1940; pres. Exptl. Bd. Cold Weather Equipment, 1941; comdg. 349th Inf., 88th Div., Camp Gruber, Okla., chief staff, command, Fiji Russell Islands, Otaru, Japan, dep. chief staff South Pacific Base Command, 1943-45; mil. observer with 1st Marine Corps, Okinawa, 1945; ret., 1945. Sec. P.R. Hurricane Relief Commn., 1933-35; acting dir. Div. Tys. and Island Possessions, 1934; dir. Civil Def., Ty. Alaska, 1951. Decorated Legion of Merit, Bronze Star with oak leaf cluster. Clubs: Tientsin (China); Army and Navy (Manila, P.I.); Army and Navy Country (Washington). Author Washington Diaries, 1932-35, articles Inf. Jour. and local newspapers; also portions of R.O.T.C. Manual. Home: Seattle WA Died Jan. 14, 1967; buried Arlington Nat. Cemetery.

LANDRY, AUBREY EDWARD, educator; b. Memramcook, N.B., Can., Nov. 24, 1880; s. Tilman Thomas and Elizabeth (McSweeney) L.; brought to U.S., 1893, naturalized, 1913; student Boston Latin Sch., 1894-97; A.B., Harvard, 1900; fellow Johns Hopkins, 1906-07, Ph.D., 1907; m. Margaret Elizabeth O'Neil, June 15, 1908 (dec. Sept. 18, 1923); m. 2d Mary Wynne Collins, June 22, 1927. Teaching fellow mathematics Cath. U. Am., 1902-07, instr., 1907-10, asso. prof., 1910-13, prof., 1913-52, head dept. mathematics, 1913-49; vis. prof. Georgetown U., 1952-59. Mem. Am. Math. Soc., Math. Assn. Am., Phi Beta Kappa. Home: Washington DC Died May 3, 1972; buried Gate of Heaven Cemetery, Washington DC

LANE, SIR ALLEN, pub.; b. Bristol, Eng., Sept. 21, 1902; s. Allen and Camilla (Williams) L.; grad. Bristol Grammar Sch.; M.A. (hon.), Bristol U.; LL.D., Manchester U., Birmingham U.; D.Litt., Oxford, Reading U.; m. Lettice Orr, June 28, 1941; children—Clare, Christine, Anna. With John Lane The Bodley Head, 1919-35; founder, chmn. Penguin Books, Ltd., from 1935; dir. Penguin Books, Inc., Penguin Books Austraila, Ltd.; chmn. Allen Lane The Pengiun Press. Decorated Companion of Honor. Recipient gold Albert medal Royal Soc. Arts. 1969. Hon. fellow Royal Coll. Art. Club: Garrick (London). Office: Harmondsworth Middlesex England Died July 7, 1970.

LANE, CHARLES ELMAAR, lawyer; b. Cheyenne, Wyo., Aug. 11, 1878; s. William Wallace and Ellen (Flaherty) L.; grad. Cheyenne High Sch.; LL.B., Georgetown U., Washington, D.C., 1911, LL.M. and M.P.L., 1912; spl. courses in internat. law and polit. economy, George Washington University and Wyoming University; m. Alma Margaret Brockstedt, June 20, 1917; children—Mary Ellen, Robert B. (petty officer, U.S.N., South Pacific), William Henry (sergt., 85th Mountain Infantry, 10th division, served in Italy). Taught country school; circulator and reporter, Wyoming Department, Denver Rocky News, also Denver Republican; contributor to Cheyenne newspaper; accountant, asst. mgr., Cheyenne Light Co.; sec. to U.S. Senator Francis E. Warren of Wyo., 1905-1912; asst. clerk, U.S. Senate Com. on Mil. Affairs, also Com. on Appropriations. Admitted to bar, Dist. of Columbia, 1912, bar of Wyoming, 1912; bar of U.S. Supreme Court, 1928; practiced law at Cheyenne since 1912; pros. atty., Laramie County, Wyo., 1918-1921. Mem. Wyo. Ho. Rep., 1927-29; state del. Rep. Conv., 1900; chmn. of Wyo. Naturalized Citizens Div., Rep. Nat. Com., 1936-40. Commr. State of Wyoming to National Conference on Uniform State Laws, from 1929, and a mem. of its scope and program sub-com. of exec. com., 1941; mem. of its com. on property, com. on criminal law; chmn. com. on the Constitution of the U.S., Commercial Law League of America from 1925; mem. Hoover com. which drafted uniform mechanic lien act; mem. Comml. Law League of Am. since 1925; chmn. com. on Constn. of U.S.; mem. executive committee Nat. Com. for Protection of Child, Family and Church. Chairman Wyo. Liberty bond and stamp campaign, World War I. Mem. local council Boy Scouts of America, committeeman Troop 104, and chmn. of Sea Scout Ship Coyote" No. 2, Cheyenne. Nat. council mem. Boy Scouts of Am., rep. Long's Peak council, from 1943, elected district com. mem. Long's Park council, 1963. Mem. Am. Bar Assn. (mem. Am. citizenship com., 1929-30; mem. gen. council, 1932-1936; mem. council of sect. on real property, probate and trust law since 1937, vice chmn. and dir. Real Property Division, 1940, assembly delegate, 1950), American Judicature Society, Wyo. State, Laramie County bar assns., Am. Law Inst. (life mem.), mem. nat. com., first nat. conv. Am. War Dads, 1943, Izaak Walton League, Phi Alpha Delta (dist. justice 4th Dist., 1937-39). Mason (K.T.), Elk. Clubs: Cheyenne, Golf, Chamber of Commerce. Writer on Federal Constitution; also, God Save this Honorable Court, Constitutional Democracy, No Despotism for America, The San Francisco Peace Conference; Peace in Our Time. Republican. Presbyterian. Home: Cheyenne WY Died June 15, 1964.

LANE, FRANK HARDY, educator; b. Deer Isle, Me., Jan. 30, 1870; s. Oliver and Mary (Hardy) L.; A.B., Northwestern U., 1895, Ph.M., 1899; m. Eliza Trimble, Sept. 9, 1900. Prof. English and speech, Oberlin Coll., 1896-98, Northwestern Coll., 1900-04, became prof. of English and speech, U. of Pittsburgh, 1912. Mem. Am. Assn. Univ. Profs., Eastern Conf. of Teachers of Speech, Nat. Assn. of Teachers of Speech. Dramatized Charles M. Sheldon's In His Steps," 1910, and directed presentation of play in Dr. Sheldon's Ch.; has presented Shakespeare's Royal Portrait Gallery at various chautauquas. Awarded Am. Poetry Circle prize for poem Washington." 1938. Contbr. prose and verse to mags. Home: 701 Second Av., Chula Vista CA‡

LANE, LORAS T., bishop; born Cascade, Iowa, October 19, 1910; son Thomas James and Josephine (Barrett) L.; Ph.B., U. Notre Dame, 1932; A.B., Loras Coll., 1933, LL.D., 1960; S.T.L., Gregorian University, 1937; graduate study State University Ia., 1941-43; J.C.D., Cath. University America, 1947; LL.D., St. Ambrose College, 1961. Ordained priest Roman Catholic Church, 1937; assistant pastor Ch. of the Nativity, Dubuque, Ia., 1937-40; instr. Spanish and econs. Loras Coll., 1940-44, pres. 1951-56; bishop Rockford, Ill., 1956-68; secretary to Archbishop of Dubuque, Iowa, 1947-49; apptd. domestic prelate, 1949; consecrated titular bishop Benecenna, auxiliary to Archbishop of Dubuque, Aug. 1951. Vice chancellor Archdiocese of Dubuque, 1947-51, v. officialis, 1950-51; Archdiocesan dir. Cana Confs., Legion of Decency, Orgn. for Decent Lit., Bur. Family Life; mem. commn. on sems., univs. and Cath. edn., 2d Vatican Council, 1963; chmn. U.S. Bishops' Com. on Priestly Formation, 1966-68; adminstrv. bd. Nat. Conf. Cath. Bishops, 1966-68. Address: Rockford IL Died July 22, 1968.

LANE, ROSE WILDER, author; b. De Smet, Dak. Ty. (now S.D.), Dec. 5, 1887; d. Almanzo James and Laura Elizabeth (Ingalls) Wilder; grad. Crowley (La.) High Sch., 1904; m. Gillette Lane, Mar. 24, 1909 (divorced 1918). Translator: The Dancer of Shamahka, 1923; Bastiat's The Law, 1947. Author: Henry Ford's Own Story, 1917; Diverging Roads, 1919; (with Frederick O'Brien) White Shadows in the South Seas, 1919; The Making of Herbert Hoover, 1920; The Peaks of Shala, 1923; He Was a Man, 1925; Hill-Billy (novel) 1926; Cindy, 1928; Let the Hurricane Roar, 1933; Old Home Town, 1935; Give Me Liberty, 1936; Free Land, 1938; The Discovery of Freedom, 1943. Editor: Nat. Econ. Council's Review of Books. Contbr. to leading mags. Home: Danbury CT also Harlingen, TX Died Oct. 1968.

LANE, SAMUEL MORSE, lawyer; b. Quincy, Mass., July 9, 1909; s. Carleton Cushing and Susan Godfrey (Morse) L.; A.B., Harvard, 1931, LL.B., 1934; m. Marian Ware Barnum, Oct. 3, 1936; children—Joshua Hubbard, Peter Cushing (dec.), Pamela Barnum, Margarett Currier, Jonathan Cushing. Admitted to

Massachusetts bar, 1934, New York bar, 1935, since practiced in New York City; partner firm Casey, Lane & Mittendorf, from 1952; special assistant to attorney gen. U.S., 1949-50. President Westfield Minerals, Ltd., Toronto; dir. Sperry & Hutchinson Co. Exec. dir., gen. counsel Waterfront Commn. N.Y. Harbour, 1954-55. Bd. dirs. Riverdale Childrens Assn. Fellow Am. Coll. Trial Lawyers; member American, New York State bar associations, Federal Bar Association, Association Bar City N.Y., N.Y. County Lawyers Assn. Unitarian (past sec., v.p., pres. bd. trustees). Home: New York City NY

LANE, WILLIAM THOMAS, advt. and pub. relations exec.; b. Auburn, N.Y., Oct. 8, 1905; s. John W. and Mary Elizabeth (Hayes) L.; student pub. schs., N.Y.; m. Thelma Ruppel, 1925 (div. 1939); 1 son, John W.; m. 2d, Norma Stevens, May 1, 1940; children—Neil Terrence, Sharon Ann. Propr. William T. Lane Advt. Agy., Inc., Syracuse, N.Y., 1937-41; v.p., gen. mgr. radio sta. WAGE, Inc., Syracuse, 1941-51; v.p., gen. mgr. Broadcasting, Inc., WLTV, Atlanta, 1951-53; propr. William T. Lane Co., Syracuse, 1954-59; v.p. Carrier Corp., Syracuse, 1959-72; dir. First Fed. Savs. & Loan Assn., Syracuse. Pres. bd. Community-Gen. Hosp., Syracuse; trustee N.Y. State Coll. of Forestry; bd. regents Le Moyne Coll., Syracuse. Home: Camillus NY Died Mar. 27, 1971; buried St. Mary's Cemetery, Syracuse NY

LANG, ARTHUR H., fgn. service officer; b. N.Y.C., Sept. 17, 1909; s. Louis and Jennie (Huler) L.; B.S. in Mech. Engring., Tri-State Coll., Angola, Ind., 1931; grad. work sch. and pub. adminstrn., Temple U., 1938-41, Yale, 1933-37; m. Sarah Stamm, November 1932 (divorced July 1941); one son, D. Baer; married second, Dorothy A. Hart, September 23, 1949; children—Jennie H., Louis H. With New Haven Bd. Edn., 1932-37, Del. Bd. Edn., 1937-41, U.S. Department Interior, 1941-42, War Manpower Commn., 1942; chief job skills tng., indsl. personnel div., Army Service Forces, Army Dept., 1942-44; regional coordinator Office Chief Ordnance, U.S. Army, 1944-46; chief orgn. and methods div. War Assets Adminstrn., 1947-48; dir. div. adminstrn. NLRB, 1948-58; pub. adminstrn. adviser U.S. Operations Mission to Afghanistan, Kabul, 1959-61; chief pub. services div. U.S. Operations Mission to Korea, Seoul, 1961-63; spl. asst. to chmn. NLRB, Washington, 1963-64; mgmt. cons. to Pres.'s Com. on Equal Employment Opportunity, 1963-64; dir. office mgmt. systems Manpower Adminstrn., U.S. Dept. Labor, Washington, 1964-71; mgmt. adviser Office of Gov. S.C., Columbia, 1971-72. Recipient award Pres. South Korea, 1963; Distinguished Achievement award U.S. Sec. Labor. Mem. Am. Soc. Pub. Adminstrn., Internat. Assn. Machinists, Am. Acad. Polit. and Social Sci. Lion, Elk. Author state and govt. publs. Home: Lexington SC Died July 9, 1972.

LANG, C. THOMPSON, newspaper exec.; b. New Rochelle, N.Y., Jan. 5, 1912; s. Cornelius Leonard and Eleanor Mary (Pepperday) L.; student Ottawa Model Sch., 1925-26; grad. Ottawa Ashbury Coll. Boarding Sch., 1931; m. Margaret Hughes, Dec. 1, 1940; children—Thompson Hughes, William Pepperday. City circulation mgr. Alburquerque (N.M.) Pub. Co., 1933-36; dist. mgr. San Francisco Examiner, 1937-41; dist. sales Albuquerque Broadcasting Co., 1945-48; pres. Jour. Pub. Co., Alburquerque, 1948-71; pres., treas. Albuquerque Pub. Co., 1956-71. Member USNRF. Mem. Ch. of Eng. Home: Albuquerque NM Died Apr. 29, 1971.

LANG, KARL, diplomat; b. Bremerhaven, Germany, July 27, 1871; s. Oswald and Elisabeth Lang; grad. gymnasium, Mannheim, 1889; student univs. of Heidelberg, Leipzig and Berlin, 1889-93; grad. in law, Heidelberg; m. Ilse Swartte-Schring, of Berlin, Nov. 13, 1907. With Foreign Office, Germany, 1897-99; actg. consul, Hongkong, later Canton, China, 1900-02; asst. councillor, Foreign Office, 1902-09; consul gen. at Montreal, Can., 1909-14; again with Foreign Office, 1914-21; charge d'affaires, Washington, 1921; now consul gen. at New York. Protestant. Address: German Consulate General, New York NY‡

LANG, MERLE HOWIE, veterinarian; b. Brooklyn, Ia., Dec. 19, 1921; s. Howie and Stella (Hendrickson) L.; student Ia. State Coll., 1941, U. Miami, 1949-50; D.V.M., Ia. State U., 1954; m. Mary Patricia McGuirt, Feb. 14, 1943; children—Suzanne (Mrs. James Earl Robbins), Rodney Howie. Instr. Embry Riddle Aviation Sch., Miami, Fla., and Sao Paulo, Brazil, 1942-43; salesman Gen. Mills, Miami, 1947-48; mgr. Beacon Dairy Farm, Deland, Fla., 1948; practice vet. medicine, Davenport, Ia., 1954-72; pres., partner Kimberly Crest Vet. Hosp., 1971-72. Dir., pres. Res. Credit Inc., Davenport, Ia., 1970-71. Mem. Scott County Extension Council 1964-68. Served with AUS, 1944-46. Mem. Ia. Acad. Vet. Practice (pres. 1970), Ia (exec. bd. 1965-69), Eastern Ia. (pres. 1969) vet. med. assns., Davenport C. of C., Ia. State U. 4-H Club Found. Mason. Club: Ia. Wesleyan Coll. Davenport IA Died Aug. 31, 1972.

LANGDON, RUSSELL (CREAMER), army officer (ret.); b. Brooklyn, N.Y., June 20, 1872; s. Brig. Gen. Loomis Lyman and Hattie Molleson (Creamer) L.; B.S., U.S. Mil. Acad., West Point, N.Y., 1896; Army Sch. of the Line, Ft. Leavenworth, Kan., 1908, Army Signal Sch., Ft. Leavenworth, 1909, Army War Coll., Washington, D.C., 1922; m. Adria Maude Semple, Apr. 10, 1907 (dec. Oct. 13, 1947); 1 step-son, Comdr. Eduard-Semple Moale; married 2d, Lois Alene Demorest, November 19, 1950. Commd. 2d lt. U.S. Army, 1896, and advanced through grades to col., 1936; served in campaign against Santiago de Cuba, Spanish Am. War, 1898, Philippine Insurrection, 1899-1901; inf. officer, 1st, 2d and 32d divs., World War I; prof. mil. sci. and tactics, N.Y. Univ., 1925-28; assigned to office of adj. gen., Washington, D.C., 1919-21; advanced to brig. gen. by spl. act. of Congress, 1940; liaison between bd. of edn. of city N.Y. and Armed Services, war industries training program for nat. defense, World War II. Awarded commendation for organizing native municipal govt. in Pueblo de Bulacan and for influence with natives during Philippine Insurrection, 1899-1901; distinguished service cross, distinguished service medal, silver star with oak leaf cluster, N.Y. state conspicuous service cross, Officer of the Legion of Honor (France), Croix de Guerre with Palm, Croix de Guerre with Gilt Star. Mem. Am. Legion, United Spanish War Vets., Army and Navy Legion of Valor U.S. Independent. Conglist. Club: Army and Navy (Washington). Author articles in field. Home: 12 W. 95th St., New York City 25‡

LANGE, HALVARD MANTHEY, former minister of foreign affairs of Norway; born at Oslo, Norway, September 16, 1902; s. Christain L. and Bertha (Manthey) L.; M.A., Univ. of Oslo, 1929; student U. of Geneva, 1921-22, 1926-27, London Sch. Econ., 1923-24, 1927; LL.D. (honorary), Birmingham University; married Karen Boe, 1930 (divorced 1938); 1 son, Christian; married 2d, Aase Monsen, September 15, 1939; children—Viggo, Even, Harriet. Assistant sec. International Fellowship of Reconciliation, London, 1923-25; teacher econ. history, Oslo High School of Commerce, 1930-35; sec. Norwegian Workers Ednl. Assn. and lecturer modern history, Univ. Oslo, 1935-36; warden, Norwegian Central Trade Union Coll. and Soermarka Workers High School, 1938-40; exec. Norwegian Labour Party, 1933-39 and 1945-67; arrested by Gestapo Aug. 1940-June 1941, Aug. 1942-May 1945 (Sachsenhausen Feb. 1943-45); minister for Fgn. Affairs, 1946-65; member of Parliament, 1965-69; head of the Norwegian del. to Peace Conf., Paris, July-Oct. 1946, UN Gen. Assembly Oct.-Nov. 1946; later head Norwegian dels. to U.N. Gen. Assemblies. Author: History of Norwegian Trade Unions, 1933; Nazi and Norway, 1934; Political Labour Internationals, 1914-34, 1935; History of World Political Labour Movement 1914-36, 2 vol., 1936-37; History of Norwegian Labour Party 1887-1914, 2 vol., 1937, 1939; Norwegian Foreign Policy since 1945, 1952; From Sect to Party, 1962 (all published in Norwegian). Home: Oslo Norway Died May 19, 1970.

LANGENWALTER, JACOB HERMANN, clergyman, educator; b. Halstead, Kan., Jan. 12, 1877; s. Daniel and Christina (Schmutz) L.; jr. diploma, Bethel Coll., Newton, Kan., 1900; A.B., German Wallace (now Baldwin-Wallace) Coll., Berea, O., 1904, D.D., 1917; B.D., Oberlin Theol. Sem., 1910; Harvard, 1913-14; S.T.M., Hartford Theol. Sem., 1915; m. Jessie Braunlich, Oct. 18, 1905; children—Irma Katherine (dec.), Charles Daniel (dec.), Hermann Jacob (dec.), Ruth Elizabeth, Lois Edith, Richard Braunlich, Robert George. Ordained ministry Mennonite Ch., 1902; student pastor Sterling, O., 1902-05; pastor Halstead, Kan., 1905-09; acting pres. Bethel Coll., 1910-11; dean Bible Dept. same, 1911-14; dean Mennonite Sem., Bluffton, O., 1915-19; again with Bethel Coll., as dean, 1919-21, pres., 1921-25; prof. in Biblical Sch., Friends U., Wichita, Kan., 1925-36; pastor First Mennonite Ch., Reedley, Calif., 1936-43; minister-at-large, Pacific Dist. Conf. of Mennonites 1943-44. Minister-at-large under appointment of the Bd. of Educ. of the Gen. Conf. of the Mennonite Church of N. Amer. 1944-45. Minister Lorraine Av. Mennonite Ch., Wichita, Kan., 1945-50. Member Bd. of Edn., Gen. Conf. of Mennonites 1938-45. Mem. Nat. Assn. Bibl. Instrs., Pi Gamma Mu. Exec. sec. Wichita Council of Chs., 1929-31; mem. Evang. Com. Pacific Dist. Conf., 1936-44; mem. Edn. Com. Western Dist. Conf., Mennonites, 1946-50. Author: Immigration of Mennonites to America, 1919; Christ's Headship of the Church, 1917; The Charge of the Church of Jesus Christ to You, 1923; Watch Your Controls, 1938; For All Mankind, 1943; The Challenge of the Present, 1950. Home: North Newton KS‡

LANGLEY, JAMES MCLELLAN, publisher; b. Hyde Park (Boston), Mass., Oct. 11, 1894; s. Frank Elmer and Mary Bradford (McLellan) L.; grad. high sch., Barre, Vt., 1913; B.S., Dartmouth Coll., 1918; m. Florence May Granger, July 1, 1918; children—James M., Joyce; m. 2d, Lois Hammond, June 29, 1947; children—Jane, Jeremy, Jill. Pub., Concord Monitor, N.H. Patriot, 1923-61, editor, 1961-68; ambassador to Pakistan, 1957-59. Chmn. U.S. delegation Philippine Trade Negotiations, 1954. Chmn. N.H. Planning and Development Commn., 1934-41; pres. Concord Hosp. 1944-50. Served as captain, inf., U.S. Army, World War. Mem. N.H. Constl. Conv., 1930, 38, 41, 56; pres. N.H.-Vt. Hospitalization Service, 1942-57. Independent Republican. Home: Concord NH Died June 23, 1968; cremated.

LANGLEY, WILSON D(AVIS), educator; b. Charleston, S.C., Jan. 7, 1895; s. Philip Gendron and Catherine (Porcher) L.; B.S., Wesleyan Univ., Conn., 1918, M.S., 1919; Ph.D., U. of Ill., 1922; m. Lucie Root, Aug. 12, 1922; children—Leonard R., Sarah C., Martha E., M. Louisa. Instr. physiol. chemistry, U. of Pa., 1922-28; asst. prof. med. sch., U. of Buffalo, 1928-34, asso. prof., 1934-46, prof. biochemistry, 1946-65, head dept., 1952-65. Mem. A.A.A.S., Am. Chem. Soc., Am. Soc. Biol. Chemists, Am. Assn. Clin. Chemists, Sigma Xi, phi Lambda, Upsilon. Home: East Amherst NY Died Feb. 20, 1969; cremated.

LANGSDORF, ALEXANDER SUSS, engineer; b. St. Louis, Mo., Aug. 31, 1877; s. Adolph and Sarah (Suss) L.; B.S. in Mech. Engring., Washington U., 1898; M.M.E., Cornell U., 1901; m. Elsie H. Hirsch, June 26, 1906; children—Helen (Mrs. L. Shiman), Alexander, Jr. Instr. in physics, Washington U., 1898-99, 1899-1900, asst. prof. electric engring. in charge of dept., 1901-04, prof., 1904-20, dean Schs. of Engring. and Architecture, 1910-20; engr. sec. Crunden Martin Mfg. Co., 1920-22; alumni rep., Washington U., 1922-23; v.p. and chief engr., Alvey Mfg. Co., 1923-26; dir. Dept. Industrial Engring. and Research, Washington U., 1926-1944, acting dean Schs. of Engring. and Architecture, Jan. 1928-June 1929, dean, 1929-48, dean emeritus since 1948; prof. of applied mathematics, 1932-38, prof. of elec. engring., 1938-48, prof. emeritus since 1948; lecturer in elec. engineering, Mass. Institute Tech., summer 1927. Mem. Jury of Awards (elec. sect.) St. Louis Exposition, 1904; mem. City Plan Commn., 1915-35 (v. chmn. 1917-35); mem. Mo. State Planning Bd., 1933-35; regional adviser, Region 16, Engineering Science, Management War Training Program, 1940-45. Served as public panel member, Regional War Labor Board (VII). Chmn. bd. dirs. Met. Planning Assn. of St. Louis. Fellow A.A.A.S., American Institute Electrical Engineers (secretary St. Louis section, 1905-08; chmn. St. Louis section 1908-10). Mem. Am. Soc. Mech. Engrs., Am. Inst. Architects (hon.), Am. Soc. Engring Edn., Engineers Club of St. Louis (sec. 1908-10, 1st v.p. 1911, pres. 1912), Acad. Science St. Louis (sec. 1929-32, v.p. 1932-37), Am. Arbitration Assn., Ethical Soc. St. Louis (pres. bd. trustees 1930-37), Am. Ethical Union, Fraternity of Leaders, Mo. Academy Science (1st president 1934-35), Sigma Xi, Tau Beta Pi, Theta Ix (pres. Grand Lodge 1922-28). Club: Town and Gown. Author: Principles of Direct Current Machines, 1915, 5th edit., 1940; Theory of Alternating Current Machinery, 1937; (with G.E.M. Jauncey) M.K.S. Units and Dimensions. Contbr. to tech. jours. Home: 5187 Cabanne Av., St Louis MO‡

LANKFORD, WILLIAM CHESTER, ex-congressman; b. Camp Greek, Ga., December 7, 1877; s. Jesse and Mary A. (Monk) L.; grad. Ga. Normal Coll. and Business Inst., Abbeville, Ga., 1899; B.L., U. of Ga., 1901; m. Mattie Lott, of Douglas, Ga., Oct. 17, 1905; children—Chester Lott, Wm. Cecil, Laura Ava. Practiced at Douglas since 1901; served as mem. sch. bd., mayor, and judge City Court; mem. 66th to 72d Congresses (1919-33), 11th Ga. Dist. Democrat. Methodist. Home: Douglas GA*‡

LANNING, ROBERT LEE, clergyman, editor; b. Cambridge, O., Aug. 5, 1872; s. George and Keziah (Speers) L.; A.B., Ohio Northern U., 1893, A.M., 1895; student Pittsburgh-Xenia Theol. Sem., 1895-98; D.D., Whitworth Coll., Tacoma, Wash., 1909; LL.D., Monmouth (Ill.) Coll., 1938; m. Nellie Fulton, 1900; m. 2d, Belle Edie, 1918; children—Robert Lee, George Edie. Ordained ministry U.P. Ch., 1898; pastor U.P. Ch., Everett, Wash., 1900-12, New Castle, Pa., 1913-18; asso. editor Bd. of Publ. U.P. Ch., 1918-26, editor 1926-44, gen. mgr., 1935-45; retired July 1, 1945. Mem. Internat. S.S. Lesson Com. (now incorporated in Internat. Council of Religious Education), 1918-45 (chmn. home daily Bible readings com. 1922-41; chairman com. for meeting British lesson committee 1937-40). Trustee (sec.-treas. bd.) Gen. Assembly of the U.P. Ch., moderator, 1941. Republican. Home: 7129 Thomas Blvd., Pittsburgh 8 PA‡

LANSDALE, MARIA HORNOR, author; b. Phila., Pa.; d. Philip and Olivia (Luce) L.; ed. pvt. schs. in U.S. and Italy. Author: Paris, Its Sites, Monuments and History, 1899; Scotland, Historic and Romantic, 1901; The Chateaux of Touraine, 1906. Translator: Constantinople, 1895; Morocco, 1896 (both from Italian of Edmondo de Amicis); After the Divorce (by Grazia Deledda), 1905; A Woman at Bay (by Sibilla Alerama), 1909. Editor: Florence (by Charles Yrairte) 1897; Rome (by Francis Wey), 1897; Vienna and the Viennese (by Victor Tissot), 1902. Home: 1011 Pine St., Philadelphia PA‡

LANSING, ELEANOR FOSTER (MRS. ROBERT LANSING), b. Cincinnati; d. John Watson (Sec. of State in President Harrison's Cabinet) and Mary Parke (McFerson) Foster; ed. Mt. Vernon Sem., Washington, D.C., and Smith Coll.; m. Robert Lansing, Sec. of State, Jan. 15, 1890. Mem. bd. dirs. Y.W.C.A., Washington, D.C.; mem. D.A.R. Presbyn. Club: Washington. Home: 1323 18th St., Washington DC‡

LANSING, JOHN BELCHER, educator, economist; b. Geneva, N.Y., July 11, 1919; s. John Ernest and Josephine (Belcher) L.; B.A., Hobart Coll., 1940; student Columbia, 1940-41, U. N.C., 1942; M.A., Harvard, 1947, Ph.D., 1949; m. Marjorie Tillis, Sept. 9, 1945; children—John Stephen, Carol, Philip. Instr. econs. and social sci. Mass. Inst. Tech., 1946-49; mem. faculty U. Mich., 1949-70, program dir. Inst. Social Research, 1956-70, prof. econs., 1962-72, chmn. econs. dept., 1970. Author: Transportation and Economic Policy, 1966; (with G.P. Ginsberg and K. Branten) An Investigation of Response Error, 1961; (with D. Blood) The Changing Travel Market, 1964; (with Eva Mueller and Nancy Barth) Residential Location and Urban Mobility, 1964; (with Nancy Barth) Residential Location and Urban Mobility: A Multivariate Analysis, 1964; Residential Location and Urban Mobility: A Second Wave of Interviews, 1964; Automobile Ownership and Residential Density, 1967; (with Stephen B. Withey) Working Papers on Survey Research in Poverty Areas, 1970; (with Robert W. Marans and Robert B. Zehner) Planned Residential Environments, 1970. Home: Ann Arbor MI Died Sept. 8, 1970.

LANSINGH, VAN RENSSELAER, metal refiner; b. Albany, N.Y., Feb. 2, 1873; s. Killian Van Rensselaer and Orrea W. (Dempster) L.; student Coll. City New York; B.S., U. of Chicago, 1896; B.S. in E.E., Mass. Inst. Tech., 1898; m. Marian L. Minor, Oct. 2, 1900; children—Killian Van Rensselaer, Emily Stuart (Mrs. William H. Muir). Began in engring. dept., Western Electric Co., Chicago, 1899; cons. engr., Chicago, 1900-01; gen. mgr. Holophane Co., 1901-14; pres. By-Lo Store Co., 1914-18; works mgr. Metz Co., airplane bldrs., 1918; pres. York Metal & Alloys Co., refiners of tungsten, molybdenum, etc., 1920-30, merged, 1930, with Molybdenum Corp. America, of which has since been v.p. Served with U.S. Vol. Engrs., Spanish-Am. War. Mem. Council of Nat. Defense, 1917-18; asst. dir. Am. Univ. Union, Europe, 1918. Trustee Mass. Inst. Tech. Mem. Illuminating Engring. Soc. (pres. 1912). Republican. Unitarian. Clubs: Engineers (New York); California (Los Angeles). Author: Practical Illumination, 1907. Home: 1120 Fifth Av., New York. Office: 500 5th Av., New York‡

LANTAFF, WILLIAM C. (BILL), ex-congressman; b. Buffalo, July 31, 1913; s. Walter R. and Charmaine (Brooks) L.; A.B., U. of Fla., 1934, LL.B., 1936; m. Betty Wilcox, May 11, 1938; children—W. Courtland, Kent, Cathy. Admitted to Fla. bar, 1936, and practiced in Miami, 1936-41, and 1945-70; member firm Walton, Lantaff, Schroeder, Carson & Wahl; city judge, Miami Beach, 1938; mem. Fla. State Legislature, 1946-50; mem. 82d-83d Congresses, 4th Dist., Fla.; dir. City National Bank of Miami. Entered Armed Services as 1st lt., Fla. N.G., 1941; service with Gen. Staff Corps; disch. to res. as lt. col., 1945; asst. chief of staff G/2, 51st Inf. Div., Fla. N.G., 1945-50; col. M.I. Div., Dept. Army. Pres. Dade County Community Chest 1957, chmn. drive, 1955-56; president Orange Bowl Committee, 1967; president United Fund, 1962, chmn. bd., 1963; chairman board Dade Foundation, 1967, 68. Delegate Democratic Nat. Conv., 1956, 60; pres. Dade Co. Young Dems., 1947-48. Elected 1 of 5 outstanding citizens Fla. by C. of C., 1948. Mem. Am. Legion, Mil. Order World Wars, Am., Fla., Dade County bar assns., Miami Beach Jr. C. of C. (pres. 1938), Phi Alpha Delta, Phi Kappa Tau. Mason (Shriner, Jester). Clubs: Metropolitan (Washington); Lions, Miami (gov. 1964), Country Miami. Home: Miami Springs FL Died 1970.

LAPHAM, SAMUEL, architect; b. Charleston, S.C., Sept. 23, 1892; s. Samuel and Annie Grey (Souie) L.; A.B., Coll. Charleston, 1913; B.S., Mass. Inst. Tech., 1916; m. Lydia LaRoche Thomas, July 8, 1926; children—Anne Souie Blevins, Samuel Thomas (dec. 1943), Samuel Peyre. Draftsman, Fay, Spofford & Thorndike, Boston, 1916; designer Carmichael Constrn. Co., Akron, O., 1917, C. F. Warner Co., Cleve., 1919; partner Simons, Lapham, Mitchell & Small, architects, Charleston, 1920-72; works of firm include: plantation house Chelsea, for Marshall Field III; Windsor for P.D. Mills; post-office and post exchange, Parris Island; monuments, restorations, residential and ednl. bldgs. Partner, chief architect Housing Architects Asso. and Housing Authority Architects, Charleston, 1935-41, 67-71; acting prof. engring. Coll. of Charleston, 1925-26, 29-30; dist. officer S.C. historic Am. bldgs. survey, Nat. Park Service, U.S. Dept. Interior, 1933-42. Served with U.S. Army, 2d lt., CAC, 61st arty., 33d arty. brigade, 1st Army AEF, France, 1917-19; lt. to lt. col. C.A.C. Res. Corps, 1923-41; lt. col. (C.A.C.), insp. gen. dept., Insp. gen. 4th service command, 1942-45; col. U.S. Army, 1945; col. C.A.C. Res., 1946, ret. 1952. Fellow A.I.A. (past pres. S.C. chpt.); mem. Bldg. Council of S.C., Soc. for Preservation of Old Dwellings (hon.), Alumni Assn. of Coll. Charleston (past pres.), St. Cecilia Soc., S.C. Soc., Soc. Mayflower Descs. In S.C., Soc. Colonial Wars S.C. (dep. gov.-gen.), Charleston Ancient Arty. Soc. Democrat. Episcopalian. Mason Clubs: Charleston, Old Town, Carolina Yacht. Author and editor: (with Albert Simons) Charleston, S.C., Vol. 1 of Octagon Library of Am. Architecture, 1927; The Early Architecture of Charleston, 1970. Editor: (with Editor: (with Albert Simons) Plantations of the Carolina Low Country, 1938, 6th edit., 1970. Contbr. articles to archtl. and hist. publs. Home: Charleston SC Died Oct. 2, 1972; buried Magnolia Cemetery, Charleston SC

LA PIANA, GEORGE, prof. church history; b. Palermo, Italy, Feb. 28, 1879; s. Vincenzo and Josephine (Capaci) La P.; grad. Lyceum of Monreale, Italy, 1895; Licentiate in theology, Theol. Sch., Monreale, 1900, in letters, U. Geneva, Switzerland, 1908; Ph.D., U. Palermo, 1912; unmarried. Came to U.S., 1913, naturalized, 1918. Prof. history Lyceum of Monreale, 1901-04, prof. Latin, 1904-06; prof. history Theol. Sch. of Palermo, 1909-13, also pres. St. Rock Coll., 1909-13; with Harvard U. since 1915, successively instr. in ch. history, asst. professor, and Morison professor of church history, 1926-48, emeritus, 1948-71; lecturer at Lowell Inst., 1922 and 1930. Mem. Bd. of Scholars of Dumbarton Oaks Research Library and Collection, Washington since 1942. Fellow Am. Acad. Arts and Sciences, Mediaeval Acad. America; mem. Am. Acad. Polit. Science; asso. mem. Colonial Soc., Boston. Clubs: Harvard, University (Boston). Author: Chiesa e Stato in Francia nel Sec. XVIII, 1909; Le Rappresentazioni Sacre nella Letteratura Bizantina, 1912; The Church of Rome at the End of the Second Century, 1925; The Immigrant Groups in Rome during the First Three Centuries of the Empire, 1927; What to Do with Italy (in collaboration with Prof. G. Salvemini), 1943. Contbr. hist. studies in various revs. Home: Wellesley MA Died Feb. 18, 1971.

LAPORTE, OTTO, physicist, educator; b. Mainz, Germany, July 23, 1902; s. Wilhelm and Anna Laporte; Ph.D., U. Munich (Germany), 1924; m. Eleanor Anders (dec. 1957); m. 2d, Adele Pond, Oct. 6, 1959; children—Claire, Irene, Marianne. Naturalized United States citizen, 1935. International Edn. Board Fellow National Bureau Standards, 1924-26; mem. faculty U. Mich., 1926-28, 29-71, prof. physics, 1937-71; lectr. Kyoto (Japan) Imperial U., 1928-29, U. Munich, 1937; intelligence analyst U.S. Army, Europe, 1949-50; sci. attache Am. embassy, Tokyo, Japan, 1954-56, 61-63, spl. research fluid dynamics at very high temperatures. Mem. Am. Phys. Soc., Nat. Acad. Scis. (posthumously elected). Author numerous articles in field. Home: Ann Arbor MI Died Mar. 28, 1971.

LAPORTE, RAYMOND, French diplomat; b. Paris, France, Dec. 22, 1911; s. Henry and Lucile (Peronne) L.; grad. Faculte de Droit, Ecole des Sciences Politiques; m. Marie Poliakoff, July 30, 1935; children—Catherine, Elisabeth (Mrs. Antoine Lazerges); m. 2d, Marie-Louise Laparra, June 1952; 1 dau., Ariane. Attache, French embassy, Geneva, Switzerland, 1937-39; sec. French embassy, Warsaw, Poland, 1945-50; chief Eastern European desk, 1950-52; counsellor French embassy, Athens, Greece, 1952-56; 1st asst. sec. state, 1956-58, minister plenipotentiary, 1956; consul gen. of France, N.Y.C., 1959-63. Served to lt. French Army, 1939-45; Prisoner of War, 1940-45. Home: Paris France Died July 9, 1970; buried Keran, Arradon, Morbihan France.

LARCO HERRERA, RAFAEL, Peruvian politician; b. Lima, Peru, July 22, 1872; student San Juan College, Trujillo, Peru, Internat. Institute, Lima; m. Esther Hoyle; 3 sons. Field adminstr. of Chiquitoy Ranch, 1890, of Chiclin Ranch, 1895; treas. of a small local polit. group, 1890; pres. Radical Party, 1896; pres. of the Patriotic Assembly, Chicama Valley, 1897; mgr. Larco Herrera Bros. Sugar Co., 1901; pres. Sanitary Com., Chicama Valley, 1902; pres. of Com. on Sugar, 1928; apptd. minister of fgn. affairs, and of finance, 1931; also became pres. The Chronicle and Variety Pub. Co., Ltd., 1931; pres. Patriotic Union, 1931; apptd. del. Congress of Am. Nations, Paris, 1937; elected first v.p. of Peru. Made elaborate junket tour of U.S., 1941; has been called strongest supporter of United States among Peruvian politicians. Member Geographical Society of Peru, Hist. and Geog. Soc. (Mexico City), Econ. Society of Friends (Madrid), Hist. Am. Instn. of Cultural Relations (Madrid), Alzate Sci. Soc. (Mexico City), Hist. and Archeol. Soc. (Lima), Nat. Geog. Soc. (Washington, D.C.), Forestry Soc. (Mexico City), Chamber of Commerce of Trujillo, Peru, Acad. of Hist. (Bogota), Nat. Acad. of Hist. (Buenos Aires), Insts. of Ital.-Peruvian Culture, and of N. Am.-Peruvian Culture, Franco-Am. Com., and, in Lima, Rotary Club, Nat. Agricultural Soc., Nat. Club, Soc. of Friends of the Pres. Awarded Commander of the Order of the Sun, Peru, Officer of the Legion of Honor, Knight of the Order of Alfonso XII (Spain), Commander of the Order of the Eagle of the Andes (Bolivia). Author: Primer on Hygiene, 1920; 27 Years of Work in Chiclin (memoirs), 1923; Towards the Awakening of the Indian, 1924; The Work of the Goya, 1929; The Work of Velasquez, 1930; Cuzco Archeology, 1933; Mexico, 1933. Contbr. to periodicals, Peruvian and abroad, on agricultural subjects. Address: Pando 758, Lima Peru‡

LARDNER, JAMES LAWRENCE, univ. prof.; b. Mt. Ayr, Indiana, Oct. 17, 1873; s. Alexander and Sarah Ann (Leese) L.; B.S., Wabash Coll., Crawfordsville, Ind., 1896, A.M., 1908; grad. Northwestern U. Sch. of Oratory, 1900; m. Lida Burkhard, June 24, 1903; children—Lynford Alexander, Mary Jean. Prof. English and oratory, Rochester (Ind.) Normal U., 1900-01; same, Dakota Wesleyan U., Mitchell, S.D., 1901-06; prof. reading and pub. speaking, Ind. State Normal School, Terre Haute, Ind., 1907-09; prof. pub. speaking, Northwestern Univ., 1909, literature interpretation, 1920-41, retired, June 1941; prof. speech, Evanston Collegiate Inst., 1943-47. Mem. Nat. Assn. Teachers of Speech (pres. 1916-17), Phi Kappa Psi. Republican. Methodist. Club: University. Home: 810 Milburn St., Evanston IL‡

LARIMER, EDGAR BROWN, naval officer; b. Tipton, Mo., Aug. 12, 1876; s. George and Laura Bennett (Ferguson) L.; grad. U.S. Naval Acad., 1899; m. Mary Bradford Burwell, July 21, 1906; 1 dau., Mary Burwell. Ensign U.S. Navy, Jan. 28, 1901; promoted through grades to rear adm., Oct. 1, 1932. Served on Indiana, Spanish-Am. War, 1898; in Philippine Insurrection, 1902; comd. Paul Jones and Perry, 1907-09, Niagara and New Orleans, 1917-20; comd. Naval Torpedo Station, Alexandria, Va., 1921-23; chief of staff, Scouting Fleet, 1923-24; comd. Naval Torpedo Station, Newport, 1925-27; comd. U.S.S. New Mexico, 1927-29; asst. to chief Bur. of Navigation, 1929-31; chief Bur. of Ordnance, 1931-34, retired, Nov. 1, 1934. Awarded Navy Cross (U.S.); War Cross of Czechoslovakia. Clubs: Chevy Chase, Army and Navy, New York Yacht. Home: 32 Altamont Apts., Charlottesville VA‡

LARIMER, LOYAL HERBERT, clergyman; b. New Cumberland, O., Oct. 27, 1869; s. Hugh Minnis and Mary (Williams) L.; Ph.B., Scio (O.) Coll., 1892; A.B., Wittenberg Coll., 1894, A.M., 1897, LL.D., 1940; B.D., Hamma Div. Sch., 1897; D.D., Susquehanna, 1910; m. Mary Alice Rees, Aug. 14, 1902 (died 1920); children—Elisabeth, Paul Rees, John Minnis, Mary. Began preaching at Shanesville, O., 1897; with Hamma Div. Sch. since 1908; prof. O.T. Lang. and Lit. until 1922, prof. homiletics and practical theology, 1923, 45, dean, 1924-40, retired 1945. Mem. Beta Theta Pi. Republican. Lutheran. Club: Young Men's Literary. Widely known as preacher and platform speaker. Home: 287 W. Cecil St., Springfield OH*‡

LARIMORE, JOSEPH WILLIAM, physician; b. Greenfield, Ind., Apr. 5, 1887; s. James Madison and Florence Clementine (Taylor) L.; A.B. DePauw U., 1908; M.D., Washington U. Med. Sch., St. Louis, Mo., 1913; m. Ruth Evans, Mar. 1, 1928; children—Ann Evans (Mrs. John F. Kolars), and Joseph William, Jr. Served as intern at Washington U. Med. Sch. Hosp., 1913-14; asst. physician, Barnes Hosp., 1915; instr. clin. med., Washington U. Med. Sch., 1915-28; asst. roentgenologist for gastro-enterology, Washington U. Med. Sch. Edward Mallinckrodt Inst. of Radiology, 1925-52; asso. prof. clin. medicine, Washington U. Med. Sch., 1928-52; emeritus associate prof. clinical med.; asst. roentgenologist, St. Louis Children's Hosp., 1930-52; gastro-enterologist staff, Missouri Pacific Hospital, 1928; staff. St. Luke's Hospital, since 1930. Lieutenant, later captain, Med. Corps, U.S. Army, 1917-19; served U.S. Base Hosp. No. 21, British Gen. Hosp. No. 12, and Am. Red Cross Hosp. No. 9, Paris. Diplomate Am. Bd. Internal Med. (gastroenterology), 1937; fellow Am. Coll. Physicians; mem. A.A.A.S., A.M.A., Southern Med. Assn., Am. Gastroenterol. Assn., Am. Roentgen Ray Soc., Radiol. Soc. N. Am., Mo. Hist. Soc., Sigma Xi, Alpha Omega Alpha, Sigma Chi. Mason (Scottish Rite). Club: University (St. Louis, Mo.). Contbr. med. papers on clin. and roentgenological gastroenterology. Home: St Louis MO Died Mar. 22, 1971.

LARKIN, JOSEPH MAURICE, steel mfr.; b. Quincy, Mass., Aug. 30, 1888; s. Richard J. and Annie (Heaney) L.; ed. pub. schs., Mass.; m. Evelyn F. Kelley, Aug. 31, 1918; children—Dorothy (Mrs. W.P. Barrett), Margaret, Pauline (Mrs. W.G. Dillon), Joanne (Mrs. R.E. Brothers). Began with Bethlehem Steel's Quincy Yard, 1904, successively as apprentice supervisor, and supt., labor relations; asst. to pres. Bethlehem Steel Co., 1918, dir., 1924, v.p., 1924, vice pres., 1934-61; retired; director Bethlehem Steel Corp., 1935. Member bd. National Industrial Conf. Bd.; mem. Am. Iron and Steel Inst. Republican. Catholic. Clubs: Metropolitan (New York), N.Y. Athletic Club, Saucon Valley Country (Bethlehem). Home: Bethlehem PA Died Oct. 1970.

LARKIN, OLIVER WATERMAN, educator, writer; born Medford, Mass., Aug. 17, 1896; s. Charles Ernest and Kate Mary (Waterman) L.; A.B., Harvard, 1918, A.M., 1919; m. Ruth Lily McIntire, July 30, 1925; 1 son, Peter Sydney. Asst. fine arts Harvard, 1921-24; asst. prof. art Smith Coll., 1924-25, asso. prof., 1926-30, prof. art, 1931-65, Jessie Wells Post professor of art; instr. Ia. State University, summers, 1925, 26; lectr. Salzburg (Austria) Seminar in Am. Studies, 1950, 55. Served as pvt., 73d Regt., U.S. Army, 1918-19. Recipient Pulitzer prize for 1949 in Am. history. Mem. Am. Assn. U. Profs., Phi Beta Kappa. Author: Art and Life in America, 1949; Samuel F. B. Morse, 1954; articles, revs. in arts, lit. publs. Home: Northampton MA Died Dec. 17, 1971; cremated.

LARKIN, THOMAS B., army officer; b. Louisburg, Wis., Dec. 15, 1890; s. Thomas and Dorothy (Donders) L.; B.A., summa cum laude, Gonzaga U., Spokane,

1910., hon. D.Sc., 1936; B.S., U.S. Mil. Acad., 1915; grad. Engr. Sch., 1916, Army Industrial Coll., 1927, Command and Gen. Staff Sch., 1929, Army War Coll., 1938, Naval War Coll., 1939; m. Mary Regina Irwin, April 16, 1917; children—Thomas B., Elizabeth Barbour, Harrison, Mary Virginia. Commd. 2d lt. Engrs. Corps, 1915; promoted through grades to lt. gen., 1949; on Mexican campaign, 1916-17; overseas, 1917-19; with Office Chief of Engrs., Washington, 1920-21; asst. mil. attache, Tokyo, 1921-23; asst. dist. engr., Pittsburgh, 1923-25; with Office Chief Engrs., 1925-28; asst. dist. engr. and engr., Vicksburg, Miss., 1929-33; in charge Ft. Peck Project, Mont., 1933-37; in charge 3d Locks Project, Panama Canal, 1939-42; chief engr. and chief of staff, Services of Supply, 1942-43; comdg. gen. Services of Supply and Communications Zone, N. Africa, 1943-44; Commd. hdqrs., dep. comdr. and chief of staff, Communications Zone, ETO 1943-44; comdg. gen., 2d Service Comd., Govs. Isl., N.Y., 1945-46; Q.M.G., rank of Major General; dir. logistics div., Gen. Staff, Dept. Army, 1949-52, ret., 1952; made econ. survey Dominican Republic, 1953; asst. in econ. survey West Berlin, 1953; cons. to asst. sec. def. on facilities assistance progress, Europe and Near East, 1953-60; dir. mut. weapons devel. team Dept. Def., 1955-60; project dir. transp. survey Argentine Govt.-World Bank, 1960-62; cons. Blauvelt Engring. Co., N.Y.C., 1962, Colfax Chem. Co., Cal., 1962-68. Decorated Silver Star (three bronze stars), Distinguished Service Medal (two oak leaf clusters), Legion of Merit, Bronze Star, Brazilian Military Order of Merit, Grand Officer, Order of Crown of Italy, Comdr. Honorable Order of the Bath; Grand Officer, Order of Ouissan Alouit Cherifils (Sultan of Morocco, 1945); Grand Officer 1st class, Order of Nichantan Ikhar (Bey of Tunis, 1945); Comdr. French Legion of Honor, Croix de Guerre with Palms (1945). Mem. Am. Soc. Civil Engrs., Soc. Mil. Engrs. Clubs: Chevy Chase; The American (London). Contbr. to engring. jours. Home: Washington DC Died Oct. 17, 1968; buried Arlington Nat. Cemetery, Arlington VA

LARKIN, WILLIAM HARRISON, artist; b. Washington, Dec. 8, 1902; s. William Ashby and Jennie (Peters) L.; student U. Va., 1922-24, 26-27, George Washington U., 1924-25, Art Students League N.Y., 1952-59; m. Lois Stover, June 25, 1941. Exhibited in group shows at Boston Printmakers, Library Congress, Am. Color Print Soc., Soc. Am. Graphic Artists, others; represented in permanent collections at Met. Mus. of Art, Brandeis U., M.H. de Young Meml. Mus. (San Francisco), Seattle Art Mus., Denver Art Mus., Berkshire Mus., Smithsonian Institution, others. Mem. Am. Color Print Soc., Artists Equity, Boston Printmakers. Home: New York City NY Died Oct. 1, 1969.

LARMON, RUSSELL RAYMOND, educator; born Red Oak, Ia., Mar. 6, 1897; s. Peter John and Sophia (Peterson) L.; A.B., Dartmouth., Coll., 1919, M.C.S., 1920, A.M., 1934; Dr. Civil Law, New England Coll., 1963; m. Katharine Graves, December 20, 1938; children—John Russell, Jane Russell. Sec. to pres., Dartmouth Coll., 1919-22, exec. asst. to pres., 1922-26, prof. adminstrn., 1934-63; asst. sec. Dept. Health Edn. and Welfare, 1953-54; cons. orgn. and adminstrn. N.H.; state dir. OPA, 1942-43; dir. No. R.R.; chmn. bd. Rumford Press, 1951-52. Mem. Nat. Adv. Heart Council, 1955-58, Nat. Adv. Health Council, 1959-63. Trustee Mary Hitchcock Meml. Hosp. Served with USN, 1917-18. Mem. Phi Gamma Delta. Republican. Home: Hanover NH Died Jan. 4, 1973; buried Pine Knoll Cemetery, Hanover NH

LARNER, EDWARD ATKINS, ins. exec.; b. Cambridge, Mass., May 15, 1897; s. Marshall and Francws (McMahon) L.; grad. Mass. Inst. Tech.; student Harvard Bus. Sch., 1923; m. Eleanor Chaplin, Feb. 26, 1919; children—Edward Atkins, Marshall P., Priscilla C. (Mrs. William R. McEwen Jr.), Chester C.; m. 2d, Mary Otis Booth, Nov. 15, 1969. With Employers' Fire Ins. Co., from 1926, successively asst. sec., v.p., asst. to mgr., 1926-47, pres., 1947-58, chmn. of bd., from 1959; pres. Am. Employers' Ins. Co., 1947-58, chmn. of the bd., from 1959, Halifax Ins. Co. of Mass., 1954-58, Employers' Group Assos., The Employers' Life Insurance Company of America, Employers' Surplus Lines Company; past chmn. bd. Employers Fire Ins. Co.; United States mgr., atty. Employers Liability Assurance Corp., Ltd., 1947-54, U.S. gen. mgr., atty., 1954-58. Mem. Pilgrims of U.S. Clubs: Algonquin, Down Town, Union, Harvard, Commercial (Boston); Metropolitan (N.Y.C.); Naushua Country. Home: Amherst NH Died Dec. 29, 1970; buried Cambridge MA

LA ROCHELLE, PHILIPPE DE, author; b. Ste. Victoria, Quebec, Can., Feb. 18, 1871; s. Michael de and Jovite (Augers) L.; B.Litt., Coll. of St. Hyacinthe, Quebec, 1892; studied Paris, France, Harvard and Columbia; m. Anna M. Drew, of Boston, Mass., 1899. Came to U.S., 1892; teacher of ancient and modern langs. in Boston, at U. of Pa., in schs. of N.Y. City, at Coll. of New Rochelle, N.Y.; instr. modern langs., Columbia, since 1917. War work service at Camp Sevier, Mineola, L.I., N.Y., 1917-19. Mem. Modern Lang. Assn. America, Societe Nationale des Professeurs de Francais, Alliance Francaise (New York). Roman Catholic. Clubs: Faculty (Columbia), Harvard Law (New York). Author: Guide to French Pronunciation, 1909; New Study of French Verbs, 1909; A Modern French Grammar, 1919; French Composition, 1920. Address: Columbia University, New York‡

LARRICK, GEORGE P., consultant; b. Springfield, O., Nov. 19, 1901; s. Benjamin Franklin and Laura Dye (Simpson) L.; student Wittenberg Coll., Springfield, O., 1919-21, Ohio State U., 1921-23; D.Sc., Drexel Institute Tech., 1955, Phila. Coll. Pharm. & Sci., 1957, Wittenberg Coll., 1958; m. Alice May Gelsanliter, June 18, 1928; children—Ben F., Laura C., Bob D., Don M. Inspector with U.S. Bur. of Chemistry and Food and Drug Adminstrn., enforcing Fed. Pure Food and Drug Law, 1923-30; chief inspector U.S. Food and Drug Adminstrn., Washington, 1930-45, asst. commr., 1945-48, asso. commr., 1948-51, dep. commr., 1951-54, commr., 1954-65; cons. on food and drug law and adminstrn., 1966-68. Pub. mem. bd. trustees Food Law Inst. Recipient Nat. Civil Service League award, 1957. Hon. Mem. of American Pharm. Assn. Member Soc. Cosmetic Chemists. Beta Theta Pi. Phi Chi. Mason (32 deg.) Clubs: Cosmos, National Press, The International (Washington, D.C.). Author articles in field. Home: Arlington VA also Dahlgren, VA Aug. 11, 1968; buried Columbia Gardens, Arlington VA

LARSEN, FINN JACOB, mfg. exec., govt. ofcl.; b. Bergen, Norway, Nov. 16, 1915; s. Alf Andreas and Gerde (Folkestad) L.; brought to U.S., 1921, naturalized, 1923; B.Ed., Mankato State Tchrs. Coll., 1939; M.A., Drake U., 1941; Ph.D., Ia. State Coll., 1948; m. Valerie. Instr. physics Ia. State Coll., 1946-48; research physicist Mpls.-Honeywell Regulator Co., 1948-49, research supr., 1949-51, dir. ordnance engring., 1951-53, dir. research, 1953-59, v.p. research, 1959-61; asst. sec. of army for research and devel., 1961-63; v.p. Honeywell, 1963-66, v.p., gen. mgr. systems and research div., 1965-66; prin. dep. dir. Office Dir. Research and Engineering, Office of the Secretary of Defense, 1965-69; v.p. Toro Mfg. Co., Mpls., 1969-71, gen. mgr. turf products div., 1970-71, also dir. corp.; vice chmn. bd. corporate mem. N. Star Research and Devel. Inst., Mpls.; trustee Research Analysis Corp., Md.; dir. Fabri-Tek, Inc. Sci. adv. council Ballistic Research Labs., Aberdeen (Md.) Proving Ground, 1954-61; company rep., bd. dirs. Indsl. Research Inst., 1960-61; chmn. Aerospace Tech. Council. Bd. dirs. St. Mary's Hosp., Mpls., Assumption Sem., Chaska, Minn. Served from ensign to lt. (s.g.), USNR, 1943-46. Named leader of tomorrow in Mpls., Time mag. and Mpls. C. of C., 1953. Mem. Am. Phys. Soc., I.E.E.E., Sigma Xi, Sigma Zeta, Kappa Mu Epsilon, Phi Mu Epsilon. Home: Hopkins MN Died Oct. 11, 1971; buried Ft. Snelling Nat. Cemetery, Minneapolis MN

LARSEN, HENNING, ednl. adminstr.; b. Decorah, Ia., June 28, 1889; s. Peter Laurentius and Ingeborg (Astrup) L.; A.B., Luther Coll., 1908; A.M., U. of Ia., 1911; student Royal Frederik's Univ., Oslo, Norway, 1912-13, 1923-24; Ph.D., Princeton University, 1915; Litt.D., Luther College, 1949; married Gwendolyn McClain, Aug. 2, 1922. Teacher of English, Decorah (Ia.) High Sch., 1911-12; asst. prof. of English, U. of Ia., 1915-29, prof., 1929-39; prof. of English, U. of Ill., 1939; acting head, Dept. of English, 1945-46; head, 1946-49, dean college of liberal arts, 1947-53, provost, 1953-56, v.p., provost, 1956-57, emeritus, 1957-71; staff dir. Instl. Cooperation com., Council Big Ten Univs. and Chgo. U., 1958—; grad. lecturer Wayne State University, 1958; Fulbright lecturer Oslo U., 1958; acting professor English, U. Chgo., summers, 1928, 30-31, Stanford U., 1929, N.C.U., 1935; visiting prof. of English, U. of Tex., 1936-37. Commd. 2d lt., 1st O.T.C., Ft. Snelling, Aug. 1917, 1st lt., 1918; asst. to military attache, Kristiania, Norway, 1918-19. Served in Office of Strategic Services, 1944. Mem. Modern Lang. Assn. America. Linguistic Soc. America, Medieval Acad. Am., Soc. for Advancement of Scandinavian Study, Norwegian Am. Hist. Soc., Nat. Council Teachers of English, Am. Assn. Academie Deans (chmn.), Assn. Land Grant Colls. and Univs. (chmn. div. arts and scis., 1952), Phi Beta Kappa, Phi Kappa Phi, Phi Gamma Delta. Club: Cosmos (Wash., D.C.). Liberal Republican. Lutheran. Author: An Old Icelandic Medical Miscellany, 1931. Associate editor Philological Quarterly, 1929-39, advisory editor, 1940-41; asso. editor Jour. of English and Germanic Philology, 1941-42, and since 1946, cooperating editor, 1942-46. Mem. editorial com. Publs. Modern Lang. Assn. Co-editor Scandinavian Studies Presented to George T. Flom, Urbana, 1942. Contbr. to professional jours. Home: Urbana IL Died Mar. 10, 1971; ashes interred Decorah IA

LARSEN, WILLIAM, clergyman; b. Racine, Wis., May 19, 1909; s. Martin P. and Margarethe (Andersen) L.; B.A., Dana Coll., Blair, Neb., 1933; B.D., Trinity Theol. Sem., Blair, 1936; M.A., Boston U., 1936-40, grad. student, 1951-52; D.D., Wartburg Theol. Sem., 1957; student Harvard, 1940-43, U. Minn., 1946-47; m. Inga M. Schultz, June 12, 1936; children—William A., Ellen M., Nancy E. Ordained to ministry United Evangel. Lutheran Ch., 1936; pastor Bethany Luth. Ch., Boston, 1936-43; Luth. pastor to students U. Minn., 1946-47, Ohio State U., 1947-48; exec. dir. Luth. Student Found. Minn., 1948-56; pres. United Evangel. Luth. Ch., 1956-61; vice president American Lutheran Ch., executive director for division theological edn., 1967-71; secretary to Luth. Council United States Am. Chmn. Joint Union Com. Served as chaplain USNR, 1943-46; capt. Res. Author: We Believe, 1947. Minneapolis MN Died Aug. 5, 1971.

LARSON, AGNES M(ATHILDA), coll. prof.; b. Preston, Minn., Mar. 15, 1892; d. Hans Olaf and Karen Maria (Nordgaarden) L.; A.B., St. Olaf Coll., 1916; A.M., Columbia, 1922; Ph.D., Radcliffe Coll., 1938; Dorothy Bridgman Atkinson fellow, Am. Assn. U. Women, 1931-32; fellow in regional writing, U. of Minn., 1940. High sch. teacher, 1916-20; instr. history, Mankato (Minn.) State Teachers Coll., 1922-25; asst. prof. history, St. Olaf Coll., Northfield, Minn., 1925-29, asso. prof., 1932-38, prof. from 1938, chmn. dept. of history from 1942. Mem. Am. Hist. Assn., Am. Assn. Univ. Women, Minn. Hist. Soc., Business Hist. Soc., Norwegian-Am. Hist. Soc., Phi Beta Kappa. Author: The History of the White Pine Industry in Minnesota, 1949; John A. Johnson, An Uncommon American, 1969. Lutheran. Home: Northfield MN Died Jan. 24, 1967; buried Oaklawn Cemetery, Northfield MN

LARSON, CHRISTIAN DAA, author; b. Winnebago Co., Ia., Feb. 1, 1874; ed. Ia. State Coll. Author: The Great Within, 1907; The Hidden Secret, 1907; Mastery of Fate, 1907; Mastery of Self, 1907; Poise and Power, 1907; How to Stay Young, 1908; On the Heights, 1908; How Great Men Succeed, 1909; The Ideal Made Real, 1909; The Pathway of Roses, 1910; Perfect Health, 1910; Your Forces and How to Use Them, 1910; Thinking for Results, 1911; Business Psychology, 1912; How to Stay Well, 1912; Just Be Glad, 1912; Mind Cure, 1912; Scientific Training of Children, 1912; How the Mind Works, 1912; What Is Truth? 1912; Brains and How to Get Them, 1913; The Good Side of Christian Science, 1916; In the Light of the Spirit, 1916; My Ideal of Marriage, 1916; Nothing Succeeds Like Success, 1916; Steps in Human Progress, 1916; What Right Thinking Will Do, 1916; Healing Yourself, 1918; Business Inspirations, 1919; Concentration, 1920; Practical Self-Help, 1922; The New Science of Work, 1924; Constructive Child Training, 1929. Home: Los Angeles CA‡

LA RUE, DANIEL WOLFORD, professor psychology; b. Newton Twp., Lackawanna County, Pa., Oct. 9, 1878; s. Daniel Wolford and Abigail Ann (Warren) L.; grad. State Normal Sch., East Stroudsburg, Pa., 1898 (valedictorian); A.B., Dickinson Coll., 1904 (valedictorian), A.M, 1905; A.M., Harvard, 1907, Ph.D., 1911; studied Columbia, 1908, Cold Spring Harbor, N.Y., 1913; m. Mabel Scudder Guinnip, Dec. 24, 1907; 1 son, Daniel Wolford. Teacher and prin. elementary sch., Chinchilla, Pa., 1898-1900; same, Grammar Sch., Boonton, N.J., 1900-01; supervising prin. schs., Milford, Del., 1904-06; supt. schs., Augusta, Me., 1907-10; prof. psychology and edn., head of dept., State Teachers Coll., East Stroudsburg, 1911-49; acting pres., 1939; lecturer Harvard Grad. Sch. of Edn.; mem. ednl. survey, Honesdale, Pa., 1921. Served as capt. Sanitary Corps, U.S. Army, Jan.-Dec. 1918; chief psychol. examiner, Camp Meade, Md. Mem. N.E.A., Am. Eugenics Soc., Inc., Pa. State Ednl. Assn., American Genetic Society, Federal Union, Inc., Phi Beta Kappa, Nat. Com. for Mental Hygiene; research worker, A.A.A.S., on value of a phonetic alphabet, 1919. Fellow A.A.A.S. Unitarian. Author of several books relating to field including: Let's Have a Better World, 1955; also contbr. to professional publs. Awarded prize for the best statement of the principles of Am. democracy as basis for a world govt. in contest sponsored by Federal Union, Inc., 1943. Awarded Medal of Liberation by King Christian X of Denmark, 1946. Address: East Stroudsburg PA Died Jan. 7, 1969; buried Prospect Cemetery, East Stroudsburg PA

LA RUE, MABEL GUINNIP, author; b. near Honesdale, Pa. Feb. 26, 1880; d. William Baker and Florence R. (Scudder) Guinnip; ed. Del. Valley Acad., Damascus, Pa., Pa. State Teachers Coll., East Stroudsburg, Syracuse U.; m. Daniel Wolford La Rue, Dec. 24, 1907; 1 son, Daniel Wolford, 3d. Taught pub. schs., N.Y. and Pa., Pa. State Teachers Coll., East Stroudsburg; writer of juvenile fiction from 1920. Mem. Authors' League of America. Republican. Unitarian. Author: The F-U-N Book, 1923; Under the Story Tree, 1924; In Animal Land, 1924; The Billy Bang Book, 1927; Little Indians, 1930; The Good Time Book, 1931; Zip, The Toy Mule, 1932; Hoot-Owl, 1935; The Tooseys, 1938; Cats for the Tooseys, 1939; A Letter to Popsey, 1942; Dicky and The Indians, 1947; Tiny Toosey's Birthday, 1950; Tiny's Big Umbrella, 1963. Contbr. to Story Parade and other magazines for children. Home: East Stroudsburg PA Died Dec. 12, 1971; buried Prospect Cemetery East Stroudsburg PA

LA RUE, WILLIAM EARL, clergyman; b. Buffalo Prairie, Ill., May 5, 1876; s. Isaac B. and Melissa (Adams) L.; B.D., Rochester Theol. Sem., 1917; M.A., Am. Univ., 1925; m. Cordie C. Short, Mar. 27, 1907; children—Lorraine Short, Irma Jean. Ordained Bapt. ministry, 1913; pastor 1st Ch., Weedsport, N.Y., 1914-17, Lyell Av. Ch., Rochester, N.Y., 1917-21,

Tokoma Park Ch., Washington, 1921-45, now pastor emeritus. Mason. Author: The Foundations of Mormonism, 1919. Address: 1007 Glenwood Rd., Glendale 2 CA‡

LASBY, WILLIAM FREDERICK, dean emeritus; b. Castle Rock, Minn., Oct. 25, 1876; s. Walter and Lavinia (Freeman) L.; B.S., Carleton Coll., Northfield, Minn., 1900; D.D.S., U. of Minn., 1903; m. Genevieve P. Adams, June 9, 1904 (died May 28, 1921); 1 dau., Helen Adams (Mrs. Robert N. Jeffrey); m. 2d, Rachel Mae Griffith, May 22, 1922 (died 1945); married 3d, Irma G. Lowe. Practicing dentist, Fairmont, Minnesota, 1903-08; instructor, University of Minnesota School of Dentistry, 1908-10, asst. prof., 1910-12, asso. prof., 1912-19; prof. and chmn., prosthetic dentistry, 1919-27, dean, 1927-45, now dean emeritus; v.p. and director University Nat. Bank, Minneapolis. Maj. Dental Res., U.S. Army, 1924; lt. col. (inactive) since 1934. Fellow Am. Coll. Dentists (v.p., 1935; regent 1939-1944); mem. Am. Dental Assn., Minn. State and Minneapolis Dist. Dental Socs. (life), Am. Assn. Dental Schs. (ex-pres.), Internat. Assn. for Dental Research, A.A.A.S., Minn. Acad. Science, Phi Beta Kappa, Omicron Kappa Upsilon (past nat. pres.), Xi Psi Phi. Republican. Congregationalist. Mason (32 deg., Shriner), Eastern Star. Clubs: U. of Minn. Campus; Kiwanis; U. of Minn. Golf. Contbr. Papers to dental jours. and professional socs. Home: 425 Walnut St. S.E., Minneapolis MN‡

LASKOSKE, ALOYSIUS WILLIAM, business exec.; b. Michigan City, Ind., July 21, 1901; s. John and Lillian (Zebrowske) L.; m. Mildred Caroline Merritt, May 25, 1926; children—M. James, Nancy Ellen. With N.Y.C. R.R., 1917-66, v.p. operations, 1963-66. Clubs: Union League (Chgo.); Woodmar Country (Hammond, Ind.); Sleepy Hollow Country (Scarborough, N.Y.). Home: Bronxville NY Died June 5, 1969; buried Oakridge Cemetery, Buchanan MI

LASKY, WAYNE EDWARD, chem. engr.; b. Normal, Ill., Nov. 8, 1902; s. Walter E. and Effie (Deal) L.; B.S., Ill. Wesleyan U., 1924; m. Lucille Dickinson, Aug. 4, 1926; 1 dau., Mary Lu (Mrs. Dwight Ostrowski). Tchr. pub. schs., Joy, Ill., 1924-25; engr. Electric Refrigeration, Evanston, Ill., 1925-26, Chgo., 1926-29; pres. Lasky-Jones, Inc., Bloomington, Ill., 1930-34; mgr., owner Lasky Grocery, Normal, 1931-48; chem. engr. Kankakee Ordinance (Ill.), 1942-43; chief chemist Alton R. R. (Ill.), 1943-48; engr. tests G.M.&O. R.R., Bloomington, 1948-68. Trustee Town of Normal, 1929-33. Fellow Am. Inst. Chemists; mem. Am. Soc. Lubrication Engrs. (nat. dir. 1954-57), Soc. Automotive Engrs., Am. Assn. R.R. (chmn. lubrication com. 1964-67), Nat. Assn. R.R. Engrs. of Tests (chmn. 1952-53), Nat. Ry. Lubrication Council (founder, chmn. 1955-58), Am. Soc. Testing Materials, Am. chem. Soc., Tau Kappa Epsilon. Mem. Christian Ch. Clubs: Optimist, Lakeside Country (Bloomington). Contbr. articles to profl. jours. Patentee in field. Home: Bloomington IL Died Aug. 8, 1968.

LA SPISA, JAKE ANTHONY, utility co. exec.; b. Melrose Park, Ill., May 16, 1909; s. Joseph and Maria (Sapenzia) La S.; student Ill. Bus. Coll., 1929; m. Eglantine Mattazza, May 6, 1933; children—James Michael, Joseph Albert. With No. Ill. Gas Co., 1925-72, supr. bldg. and grounds and stores dept. W. Central div., Glen Ellyn, 1962-72. Mayor for Village Melrose Park, Ill. Chmn., Am. Cancer Soc., Melrose Park, 1954, A.R.C. dir., 1954, 63, March of Dimes, 1963-64. Chmn. board dirs. Melrose Park Pub. Library, 1957-72. Mem. Inst. Sanitation Mgrs. (chpt. pres. 1963-65), Ill. Library Assn. Italo Am. Nat. Union (pres. 1965). Kiwanian (pres. 1962). Home: Melrose Park IL Died Nov. 11, 1972.

LASSITER, NEWTON HANCE, lawyer; b. Lexington, Tenn., Sept. 13, 1860; s. Henry and Eliza L.; A.B., Cumberland U., Lebanon, Tenn., 1881; m. Elizabeth Davis, July 9, 1890. Admitted to bar; resident of Ft. Worth since Mar. 1, 1885; v.p. and gen. solicitor, C., R.I.&Gulf Ry. Co., now retired; dir. State Reserve Life Ins. Co. Home: Hotel Texas, Ft Worth TX‡

LASSITER, ROBERT, cotton mfr.; b. Henderson, N.C., Aug. 2, 1877; s. Harrison and Harriet (Thrower) L.; prep. edn., pvt. schs. and Horner Mil. Acad., Oxford, N.C.; student U. of N.C., class of 1898; m. Daisy Hanes, Dec. 14, 1905; children—James Harrison, John Hanes, Robert, Frederic Hanes. Began in wholesale and retail mercantile business, Henderson, 1897; also engaged in cotton business and banking; pres. Henderson Loan & Trust Co., 1903-07; v.p. First Nat. Bank, 1903-07; settled at Charlotte, 1908; served as dir. Fed. Reserve Bank of Richmond for 24 yrs.; chmn. bd. for 10 yrs.; now chmn. bd. Mooresville Mills, Lassiter Press; pres. Hosp. Saving Assn. of N.C.; dir. Seaborad Airline R.R. Co. Home: 1600 E. 4th St. Office: 1143 E. 4th St., Charlotte NC‡

LASTINGER, JOHN WILLIAMS, elec. utility exec.; b. Valdosta, Ga., Sept. 26, 1902; s. Bill Griffin and Mattie Elizabeth (Williams) L.; student Emory U.; m. Marie Beechwood, June 21, 1927; 1 son, John B. Accountant, Ga. Power & Light Co., Valdosta, Ga., 1926-29, asst. auditor, 1929-30, asst. to gen. mgr., 1930-32, dist. mgr., 1932-45, v.p., 1945-51, pres., 1951-57; co. merged with Ga. Power Co., 1957; exec. v.p. Ga. Power Co., Atlanta, 1959-72, also dir.; v.p. Citizens & So. Nat. Bank; dir. So. Electric Generating Co., Birmingham, Ga. Motor Club (Am. Automobile Assn.). Chmn. Ga. Indsl. Devel. Council; chmn. Valdosta State Coll. Found., 1970-71; chmn. Valdosta Indsl. Authority, 1972. Mem. bd. visitors Emory U. Mem. Ga. C. of C. (pres.), Sigma Chi. Rotarian. Clubs: Commerce, Capital City, Atlanta Athletic (Atlanta). Home: Valdosta GA Died June 14, 1972; buried Sunset Hill Cemetery, Valdosta GA

LATHAM, CHARLES LOUIS, consular service; b. Greenville, N.C., Dec. 18, 1877; s. Hon. L. C. and Lavinia Emilia (Monteiro) L.; grad. Bingham Mil. Acad., Asheville, N.C., 1898; LL.B., Georgetown Univ., D.C., 1904; m. Elizabeth Mathews, of Washington, D.C., Feb. 18, 1903. Was employed as clk. in War Dept.; apptd. consul at Cartagena, Colombia, Feb. 17, 1909; consul at Punta Arenas, Chile, 1911-15, at Dundee, Scotland, 1915-17, at Kingston, Jamaica, since July 1917. Address: Am. Consulate, Kingston Jamaica‡

LATHAM, HAROLD STRONG, author and editor; born Marlboro, Conn., Feb. 12, 1887; s. Charles Arthur and Minnie Alice (Strong) L.; A.B., Columbia, 1909. With the Macmillan Co., pubs., since 1909, head trade dept., 1919, dir., 1920, v.p., 1931-52; pres. Universalist Pub. House, 1950-52. Chmn. bd. govs. West Hudson Hosp.; pres. West Hudson Hosp. Association, 1958-61; chmn. adv. bd. Salvation Army, 1960-61; chmn. bd. Kearney Junior Historical Museum, 1966-69. Named Outstanding Citizen of West Hudson by C. of C. Mem. Nat. Assn. Universalist Laymen (founder). Republican. Universalist (pres. Universalist Church of Am., 1947-51; nat. trustee, 1939-47). Clubs; Players, Columbia Univ., Phi Sigma Kappa, Century (N.Y.C.); Onteora, Kiwanis. Author: Under Orders—The Story of Tim and the Club, 1918; Marty Lends a Hand, 1919; Jimmy Quigg, Office Boy, 1920; The Perry Boys; The Making of Larry; The Thirteenth Domino; My Life in Publishing, 1965; also numerous mag. articles. Home: Arlington NJ Died Mar. 1969.

LATSHAW, DAVID GARDNER, clergyman; b. Brookville, Pa., Dec. 7, 1869; s. David and Matilda E. (Gardner) L.; A.B., Allegheny Coll., Pa., 1895, D.D., 1908; S.T.B., Boston U. Sch. of Theology, 1899; m. Lura Lucretia Marvin, Aug. 31, 1898; children—David Marvin, Margaret Elizabeth (Mrs. William L. Hearn, dec.). Ordained M.E. ministry, 1899; minister of Westwood Ch., Cincinnati, 1899-1906, St. Paul's Ch., Dayton, O., 1906-10; acting minister Ch. in the Gardens, Forest Hills, L.I., N.Y., 2 yrs.; sec. Internat. Com. and Nat. Council, Y.M.C.A., 1910-30; with War Work Council, U.S. and Europe, sr. sec. Dept. Ch. Relations, Nat. Council, until 1930. Mem. Sigma Alpha Epsilon. Mason (32 deg.). Author: Money Power, National Survey Relations of Church and Y.M.C.A. Home: Hotel Martinique, 32d St. and Broadway. Office: 347 Madison Av., New York 17 NY‡

LATTIMORE, JOHN AARON CICERO, physician; b. Selby, N.C., June 23, 1876; s. John Carpenter and Marcella (Hambrick) L.; A.B., Bennett Coll. (then co-educational), Greensboro, N.C., 1897; M.D., Meharry Med. Coll., Nashville, Tenn., 1901; post grad. work U. of Chicago; m. Naomi Anthony, Aug. 11, 1928. Engaged in private practice Louisville, Ky., since 1901. Chmn. Negro health com. in charge of venereal disease clinic Louisville Health Center; mem. staff Red Cross Hosp.; mem. Louisville Interracial Como., Louisville Area Development Assn. (mem. hosp. com.); chmn. Negro Health Com. Mem. Nat. Med. Assn. (vice pres. 1920-21; pres. 1947-48), Louisville Urban League (an organizer; mem. bd.), John Andrew Clin. Soc., Nat. Assn. Advancement Colored People (an organizer), Falls City Med. Soc., Blue Grass State Med. Assn. (past pres.; v.p.), Meharry Alumni Assn., Psi Boule, Alpha Phi Alpha (past pres.; awarded trophy for achievements in med. profession). Awarded certificate of merit by U.S. Govt. for medical work with soldiers. Democrat. Methodist. Elk. Home: 1502 W. Walnut St. Office: 1432 W. Walnut St., Louisville 3*‡

LAUBACH, FRANK CHARLES, missionary, educator, preacher; b. Benton, Pa., Sept. 2, 1884; s. John Brittain and Harriet (Derr) L.; M.E., Bloomsburg (Pa.) State Normal Sch., 1901; student Perkiomen Seminary, 1904-05; A.B., Princeton University, 1909, Doctor of Philanthropy, 1952; A.M., Columbia University, Ph.D., 1915; D.H.L., Wooster College, 1950; student Union Theological Seminary, 1911-14; married Effa Seely, May 15, 1912; 1 son, Robert S. Became asso. Spring St. Community House, N.Y. City, 1910; sec. Charity Orgn. Soc., N.Y. City, 1914; evang. missionary, Cagayan, Misamis, P.I., 1915-19; dean, Union Coll., Manila, P.I., 1922-26; dir. Maranaw Folk Schs., Lanao, Philippine Islands, since 1930; conducted literacy tours, India and Near East, 1935, India and Africa, 1937, 39, Mexico, 1941, Central and S.A., 1942-43, Latin Am., 1944, 45, Egypt, Ethiopia, Lebanon, Syria, Irak, Iran, 1947, West and South Africa, 1947-48, Siam, India, New Guinea, Australia, Korea, 1949, Liberia, Angola, Mozambique, Nyassaland, Tanganyika, Uganda, Ruanda Urundi, French Cameroons, 1950, Algiers, Tripoli, India, Pakistan, Afghanistan, Burma, Singapore, Malaya, Indonesia, 1951, India, Pakistan and Nepal, 1952-53. Chairman of the board of trustees of Silliman University, 1939-41. Mason (32 deg.), Conglist. Author: Why There Are Vagrants, 1915; People of the Philippines, 1924; Seven Thousand Emeralds, 1929; Rizal, Man and Martyr, 1936; Letters of Modern Mystic, 1937; Toward a Literate World, 1939; India Shall Be Literate, 1940; You Are My Friends, 1942; The Silent Billion Speak, 1943; Streamlined English Lessons, 1945; Prayer, the Mightiest Force in the World, 1946; Story of Jesus, 1946; Making Everybody's World Safe, 1947; Teaching the World to Read, 1947; Pray for Others, 1948; Wake Up or Blow Up, 1951; The Wise Man, 1951. Editor: English Maranaw Dictionary, 1937; Moro Folklore, 1939; Lanao Progress, 1928-41; Clear Horizons, 1947. Co-author, more than 200 primers for illiterate adults in over 165 langs., in 51 countries. Home: Benton PA Died June 11, 1970; buried Benton PA

LAUBACH, HOWARD L., army officer; b. Allentown, Pa., Aug. 24, 1870; s. Dr. Amandus J. and Wilhelmina (McHose) L.; B.S., U.S. Mil. Acad., 1893; m. Katherine Hague, Dec. 26, 1895. Commd. 2d lt. inf., June 12, 1893; promoted through grades to brig. gen., Apr. 1, 1931; organized and commanded 14th Div., U.S. Army, World War; retired Aug. 31, 1934. Address: 2901 7th Av., St Petersburg FL‡

LAUGHLIN, JOHN EDWARD, JR., lawyer; b. Pittsburgh, June 18, 1908; s. John Edward and Marie Rose (Kelly) L.; student Georgetown Coll. Prep. Sch., 1920-23; A.B., Georgetown U., 1923-27; LL.B., Harvard, 1930, LL.M., 1931; LL.D., St. Vincent College, 1952; married Mercedes Vilsack Maloney, Oct. 14, 1937 (dec.); children—Deborah, Joan, Mercedes; m. 2d, Elizabeth Stewart Coates, Oct. 9, 1952 (deceased); m. third, Kathryn McSwigan, Dec. 31, 1962. Admitted to N.Y. State bar, 1932, practiced, N.Y.C., 1931-34; Pa. bar, 1930, practiced in Pitts., as mem. Thorp, Reed & Armstrong, 1934-70; dir. Majac, Inc., Kennywood Park Corp. Trustee Ohio Valley Improvement Assn. Mem. bd. lay advisors St. Vincent Coll.; bd. Duquesne U.; trustee Mercy Hosp.; pres., dir. St. Vincent Coll. Ednl. Found., Inc. Decorated Knight Hospitaller of St. John of Jerusalem. Mem. Am. Judicature Soc., Am., Pa. Allegheny County bar assns., Am. Law Inst. Republican. Roman Catholic. Clubs: Duquesne, University, Lawyers (Pitts.), Williams Country (Weirton, W. Va.); Harvard (N.Y.C.). Editor: Harvard Law Rev., 1930; Contbr. publs. Home: Pittsburgh PA Died Aug. 5, 1970; buried Calvary Cemetery, Pittsburgh PA

LAUGHLIN, T. COWDEN, educator; b. at Barnesville, O., 1870; s. of Hon. J. W. and Margaret (Cowden) L.; grad. Princeton, A.B., 1892, S. T. B., Princeton, 1897, Ph. D., Princeton, 1902; B.D., Harvard, 1898; won 1st Greek prize, middle yr., and New Testament fellowship upon graduation, 1897, in Princeton Theol. Sem.; won fellowship at Harvard on thesis, 1898; studied Gottingen and Berlin Univs., 1898-1900, and in France, 1900, Princeton, 1901-2. Prof. New Testament literature and exegesis, Pacific Theol. Sem. since Oct., 1902. Address: 2223 Atherton St., Berkeley CA‡

LAURENT, ROBERT, sculptor; b. Concarneau, France, June 29, 1890; s. Louis and Yvonne (Fraval) L.; came to America, 1902; student British Acad. Fine Arts, Rome, Italy; pupil of Hamilton Easter Field and Maurice Sterne; m. Marie Caraes, of Lannilis, France;children—Jean Louis, Paul Robert. Specializes in sculpture wood and direct cutting in plaster, stone and marble. Director Ogunquit Sch. of Painting and Sculpture; prof. art. Ind. U.; sculptor in residence Am. Acad., Rome, 1954-55, Represented in collections of large museums throughout U.S. Recipient of numerous prizes and awards. Served with U.S. Naval Aviation Corps, 1917-19. Fellow Nat. Sculpture Soc.; member Nat. Acad. Arts and Letters, American Soc. Painters, Sculptors and Gravers, Modern Artists of Am., Audubon Artists, Sculptors Guild, Indiana Artists; v.p. Salons of Am.; pres. Hamilton Easter Field Art Found. Contbr. Ency. Brit. La Toilette, selected for Am. Art Exhbn., Moscow, 1959. Home: Cape Neddick ME Died Apr. 20, 1970; buried Cape Neddick ME

LAURIE, JAMES WOODIN, clergyman, univ. pres.; b. Bellingham, Wash., Sept. 10, 1903; s. James Anderson and Mina (Woodin) L.; A.B., Coe Coll., 1924, D.D., 1941; M.A., Princeton, 1927; Th.B., Princeton Theological Seminary, 1927; graduate study Columbia University, summer 1926; LL.D., University of Tulsa, 1960; married Dorothy Augustine, April 15, 1932; children—Dorothy Jean (Mrs. Barry Floyd), Sarah Bradford (Mrs. Wilbur Drake), Mary Woodin (Mrs. Thomas B. Butler), and James Robertson. Ordained to ministry of Presbyn. Ch., 1926; pastor 2d Presbyn. Ch., Rahway, N.J., 1927-36, Wilkinsburg, Pittsburgh, 1936-42, Central Presbyn. Ch., Buffalo, 1942-51; pres. Trinity U., San Antonio, since 1951. Mem. council theol. edn. Presbyn. Ch. in U.S.A., 1943-56, mem. Gen. Council Gen. Assembly 1948-56, vice chmn., 1949-56; moderator Presbytery of Buffalo-Niagara, 1950;

moderator Synod of Texas, 1955. Trustee Southwest Foundation for Research and Education; pres. Council Chs. of Buffalo and Erie County, 1947-49, Ch.-Related Colls. South, 1958, Tex. Council Church-Related Colls., 1961, Texas Fedn. Volunteer Supported Colleges and Universities, 1957-58; vice president Presbyterian Coll. Union, 1962-63. President San Antonio Library Bd., 1961-63. Named outstanding citizen of Buffalo, 1951, outstanding citizen of San Antonio, 1961. Mem. C. of C. (pres. 1959), Pi Kappa Delta. Mason. Clubs: Rotary (pres. 1967-68), San Antonio Country (San Antonio); Princeton (N.Y.C.); Torch (pres. 1966). Home: San Antonio TX Died Sept. 9, 1970.

LAURITSEN, CHARLES CHRISTIAN, educator; b. Holstebro, Denmark, Apr. 4, 1892; grad. Odense Tekniske Skole, Denmark, 1911; Ph.D., Cal. Inst. Tech., 1929; LL.D., U. Cal., 1965; m. Sigrid; 1 son, Thomas. Elec. and radio engring., 1911-26; asst. prof. physics Cal. Inst. Tech., 1930-31, asso. prof., 1931-35, prof., 1935-62, prof. emeritus, 1962-68. Mem. numerous govt. adv. groups, 1940-68, including U.S. Army Sci. Adv. Panel, Army Missile Command Missile Sci. Adv. Group, Army Combat Devel. Command Sci. Adv. Group; bd. visitors USAF Systems Command; cons. Pres.'s Sci. Adv. Com. Served with NDRC, OSRD, 1940-42. Recipient numerous honors and awards including Gold medal Am. Coll. Radiology, 1931; U.S. medal for Merit, 1948; certificates appreciation Dept. Army, 1953, USAF, 1955; Capt. R.D. Conrad award USN, 1958; T.W. Bonner prize Am. Phys. Soc., 1967. Fellow Am. Phys. Soc. (pres. 1951), Coll. Radiology, Royal Soc. Copenhagen, A.A.A.S.; mem. Nat. Acad. Scis., Am. Phil. Soc., Sigma Xi. Contbr. sci. jours. Home: Pasadena CA Died Apr. 13, 1968.

LAURVIK, J(OHN) NILSEN, dramatist and art critic; b. Fredericksvaern, Norway, Nov. 27, 1877; s. Edward August Nilsen and Anne Christine (Olesen) L.; ed. in Norway, Battin High Sch., Elizabeth, N.J., Cooper Inst., New York, and Antwerp (Belgium) Acad. Came to America, 1888; on staff Ethical Record, New York, 1904; editor The Sketch Book, Chicago, 1906; became art editor New York Evening Post, 1907; now dir. San Francisco Art Assn. Translator: Andrea (from the Danish), 1904; The Letters of Henrik Ibsen (from the Norwegian), 1905. Home: 3469 Jackson St. Address: San Francisco Art Assn., California and Mason Sts., San Francisco CA‡

LAUTMANN, HERBERT MOSES, lawyer; b. Hammond, Ind., May 31, 1891; s. Jonas M. and Ida (Schaffner) L.; LL.B., U. Mich., 1913; m. Edith May Shultz, Aug. 30, 1915 (dec. June 6, 1946); children—Robert (dec.), Marilyn, Ralph Ernest, Susan Bright, Sarah May (twins); m. 2d, Margaret Baxter, Aug. 28, 1948 (div. 1952); married third, Babette Boyell, February 27, 1957. Admitted to Michigan bar, 1913, Ill., 1914; law clk. Sonnenschein, Berkson & Fishell, Chgo., 1913, jr. mem. Sonnenschein, Berkson & Lautmann, 1917, mem. firm Sonnenschein, Berkson, Lautmann, Levinston & Morse, 1919-58. Past pres. Chgo. Jewish Welfare Fund, Highland Park (Ill.) Community Chest. Asso. trustee Northwestern U.; trustee Twp. Sch., Deerfield, Ill. Fellow Am. Coll. Trial Lawyers; mem. Am., Ill., Chgo. (pres. 1935-36) bar assns., Law Inst., Art Inst. Chgo., Chgo. Hist. Soc. Mason. Clubs: Standard (pres. 1939-40), Law, Chicago (pres. 1954-55); Tamarisk Country (Palm Springs, Cal.). Address: Cathedral City CA Died Nov. 1970.

LAUTZ, HENRY B(ITZEL), ry. official; b. Pekin, Ill., Aug. 2, 1876; s. George and Barbara (Bitzel) L.; ed. Topeka, Kan., pub. schs.; m. Edith L. Ott, Nov. 14, 1906; children—Philip O., Barbara. With A.,T.&S.F. Ry. Co. since Sept. 8, 1890, began as office boy and held various clerical positions to 1905, asst. to gen. mgr., 1905-16, supt. at Newton, Kan., 1916-28, asst. gen. mgr. at La Junta, Colo., 1928-32, gen. mgr. Western Lines at Amarillo, Tex., 1932-39, gen. manager Eastern Lines at Topeka, July 1, 1939-July 31, 1946, retired. Republican. Methodist. Mason (K.T.). Rotarian. Home: 620 W. 9th St., Topeka KS‡

LAVALLE, JOHN, artist; b. Nahant, Mass., June 24, 1896; s. John and Alice Cornelia (Johnson) L.; student, St. Paul's Sch., Concord, N.H., 1909-14, Boston Mus. Sch., 1919-23, Julian's Acad., Paris, France, 1925; A.B., Harvard, 1918; m. Ellen Tufts, Oct. 4, 1919 (died Jan. 8, 1932); children—Alice (dec.), Mary Dean (dec.), John Edward, Ellen; m. 2d, Virginia Wilson, Sept. 15, 1932; (divorced 1947); 1 dau., Virginia; m. 3d, Martha Nicholson Hoyt, Jan. 3, 1948. Exhibited Pa. Acad., Nat. Acad. of Design (New York); Boston Tercentenary Expn., Art Institute (Chicago); Corcoran Gallery of Art; Carnegie Inst. (Pittsburgh); Salon des Artistes Francais; and others; painted portraits in Europe and America. Represented in Boston Museum and Brooklyn Museum. Mem. Jury of Admission and Awards, Pa. Acad., 1929, Boston Tercentenary Expn., 1930. Mem. R.O.T.C., Plattsburg, N.Y., 1916; enlisted in Aviation Sect., S.O.R.C., 1917; trained overseas with Royal Flying Corps; commd. 1st lt., Mar. 1918; served with 33d Wing, Royal Air Force, as bombing pilot, World War I; hon. disch., Dec. 1918. Commd. Capt., Air Corps, 1942. Served as Camouflage Officer with Air Force Camouflage Sch., Hamilton Field, Calif., Engineer Board, Ft. Belvoir, Va., and Africa-Middle East Wing in preparation for N. African landings. Camouflage Officer for 12th Air Force for Sicily invasion. Maj. 1944, Pub. Relations Officer for 12th Air Force in Italy. Painted over 100 portraits & landscapes for Mediterranean Allied Air Force which were exhibited in London; at National Gallery, Washington, D.C.; and Metropolitan Mus., N.Y. Hon. discharge, Sept., 1945. Recipient hon. mention, Century, 1948, Lynch award, Providence Art Club, 1952, Bronze Medal of Honor, National Arts Club, 1954. Mem. Guild Boston Artists, Boston Soc. Water Color Painters, Copley Soc. of Boston (sec. 1926-28), Grand Central Art Gallery Assn., Rockport Art Assn., North Shore Arts Assn., American Veterans Society of Artists, American Watercolor Soc. Republican. Episcopalian. Clubs: St. Botolph, Badminton and Tennis (Boston); Harvard Century Assn., Coffee House, Knickerbocker, Brook, Southampton, Salmagundi (N.Y.); Providence Art. Contbr. to magazines. Drawings for Bay Window Ballads," Scribner, 1935; Air Force paintings reproduced in Mediterranean Sweep," Duell, Sloan & Pearce, 1945. Home: New York City NY Died Nov. 13, 1971; buried Providence RI

LAVINDER, CLAUDE HERVEY, physician; b. Lynchburg, Va., July 24, 1872; s. Nathan Hervey and Ella Chambers (Hamner) L.; Randolph-Mason Coll., Ashland, Va., 1891, 92; M.D., U. of Va., 1895; m. Frances Moore Fair, 1899. Entered U.S. Pub. Health Service as asst. surgeon, 1897, retired as medical dir., 1938. Engaged in hospital, quarantine, epidemic and spl. work; has devoted much time to investigating pellagra. Lecturer on public health and sanitary science, Post-Grad. Med. Sch., N.Y. City, part of sessions 1914-15, 1915-16; was in charge of Hosp. Div. of P.H.S. and supervising all of P.H.S. work in furnishing medical care and treatment to disabled veterans, World War, 1920-22. Fellow American College Surgeons; mem. A.M.A., Assn. Mil. Surgeons (pres. 1928-29), Nat. Assn. Study Pellagra (pres. 1912), Ga. Med. Soc. (hon.), Phi Beta Kappa, Beta Theta Pi. Episcopalian. Mason. Translated and edited (with Dr. J.W. Babcock), Pellagra (by Marie), 1910. Author: Epidemiologic Studies of Poliomyelitis in New York City and the Northeastern United States during the year 1916 (with A.W. Freeman and W.H. Frost), 1918. Contbr. numerous articles concerning pellagra and other med. topics. Home: 139 St. John's Pl., Brooklyn NY‡

LAVIS, FRED, cons. engineer; b. Torquay Devon, Eng., Jan. 8, 1871; ed. St. Luke's Sch., Torquay; m. Blanche Biddle, Dec. 22, 1902; 1 son, Fred. Came to U.S., 1887, naturalized citizen, 1904. Cons. engr., specialist in transportation, also in ry. and highway economics, location and constrn., N.Y. City, since 1903; pres. Internat. Rys. of Central America, hdqrs. N.Y. City, 1928-31; dir. Chesapeake & Potomac Telephone Cos. of Washington. Trustee Village of Scarsdale, N.Y., 1915-17, mayor, 1931-33; supervisor Town of Scarsdale, 1916-17. Cons. engr. Ministry of Pub. Works, Venezuela, 1938-44. Mem. Highway Research Bd., Am. Soc. C.E., Am. Ry. Engring. Assn.; Pan-Am. Soc. N.Y. (council), Instn. of Civil Engrs. (Great Britain), The Pilgrims. Republican. Club: Union League. Author: Railroad Location Surveys and Estimates, 1906; Building the Rapid Transit System of New York City, 1915; Instructions to Locating Engineers and Field Parties, 1916; Railroad Estimates, 1917. Contbr. papers on ry. constrn. Home: Scarsdale Lodge, Scarsdale, N.Y. Office: 30 Broad St., New York NY‡

LAW, FRANCIS MARION, banker; b. Bryan, Tex., Jan. 3, 1877; s. Francis Marion (M.D.) and Mary Jane (Howell) L.; B.S., Agrl. and Mech. Coll. of Tex., 1895, LL.D.; law student U. Tex., 1896-97; m. Frances Mann, Apr. 20, 1898; children—Francis Marion, Elizabeth Mann (dec.). Teacher rural schs., Tex., 1895-96; bookkeeper, later asst. cashier First Nat. Bank, Beaumont, Tex., 1910-15; v.p. First Nat. Bank, Houston, Tex., 1915-30, pres. 1930-45, chmn. of bd. 1945-53; consultation chmn. First City Nat. Bank of Houston; dir. Burlington, Rock Island Ry., Mound Co. Dir. Meml. Hosp. of Houston, United Fund; pres. bd. dirs. Agrl. and Mech. Coll. of Tex., 1922-44. Mem. Am. (pres. 1933), Tex. (ex-pres.) bankers assns., Sigma Chi. Democrat. Baptist. Mason (Shriner). Home: Houston TX Died June 1970.

LAW, HERBERT EDWARD, financier; b. Sheffield, Eng., Dec. 5, 1864; s. Crossley and Rebecca (Brown) L.; brought to U.S., 1866; ed. pub. schs. and German Am. Inst., Chicago, Ill. Began as instr. German, Am. Inst., at 18; joined brother in selling subscription books in San Francisco, 1884; entered mfr. proprietary medicines, 1889, later incorporating as The Viavi Co.; sold out, 1914; with others built the Crossley Bldg., Rialto Bldg., Monadnock Bldg., etc., in San Francisco; as pres. of Western Steel Corp. negotiated, 1910, the largest coal and steel contract the Chinese Govt. had ever made. Mem. Citizens' Com. which framed present charter of 1921 and County of San Francisco, 1897-98; police commr. City and County of San Francisco, 1906; mem. Com. of 50 which had charge of relief measures following earthquake and fire of 1906; an organizer San Francisco Merchants' Assn. (now Chamber of Commerce); a founder San Francisco Symphony Assn. Fellow Chem. Soc. of London. Republican. Baptist. Author: The Power of Mental Demand and Other Essays, 1913. Translator: (with Charles Lincoln Rhodes) Napoleon in His Own Words, 1916. Clubs: Metropolitan (New York); Royal Societies (London). Home: 1298 Sacramento St., San Francisco; and Lauriston, R.F.D. No. 1, Redwood City, Calif. Office: Monadnock Bldg., 681 Market St., San Francisco 5 CA*‡

LAWALL, CHARLES ELMER, engineer; b. Catasauqua, Pa., Nov. 21, 1891; s. Charles Elmer and Maria (Thomas) L.; E.M., Lehigh U., 1914, M.S., 1921, LL.D., 1939; LL.D., Waynesburg Coll., 1939; Doctor of Science, Morris Harvey College, 1950; m. Marjorie Berger, April 29, 1920; 1 son, Charles Elmer. Testing engr. Pittsburgh Testing Labs., 1914; chemist N.J. Zinc Co., Palmerton, Pa., 1915-16; mining engr. Peal Peacock & Kerr, St. Benedict, Pa., 1916-17; metallurgy dept. Gen. Motors Co., Detroit, 1917; mining engineer Bethlehem Steel Co., 1917-18, research engr., 1919-21; instructor Geology Department, Lehigh University, 1921; became assistant professor West Virginia Univ., School of Mines, 1921, later prof. and dir. to 1938; acting pres. W.Va. U., 1938-39, pres., 1939-45; engr. coal properties, Chesapeake & Ohio Ry. Co., Huntington, 1945-47, asst. v.p., 1947-56, v.p., 1956-58. Chief engineer and vice president Western Pocahontas Corp., Huntington, 1956; coal consultant, 1958-73. Member executive committee Engineers Council for Professional Development, 1949; chairman mining development committee Bituminous Coal Research, Incorporated, 1948-60; regional adviser, Engineering, Science and Management War Training Program: expert cons., Army Specialized Training Program; civilian member Selection Committee of Navy V-12 College Training Program. Served in U.S.A., France, 1918-19. Recipient Bituminous Coal Research award, 1957; Mineral Industry Edn. award, Am. Inst. M.E., 1958; Percy Nicholls Award, 1962. Member Veteran Council, West Virginia Department of Vets. Affairs; trustee Waynesburg Coll. Mem. Am. Inst. Mining and Metall. Engrs. (chmn. coal div., 1940); W.Va. Coal Mining Inst. (sec.-treas. 1930-39; president 1929), Huntington Chamber of Commerce, American Legion (state historian, 1944), Vets. Foreign Wars, Newcomen Soc. (chmn. W.Va. com.), A.I.M.E. (chmn. Appalachian sect., 1948), W.Va. Soc. Profl. Engr. (pres., 1948), Am. Soc. Engring. Edn., Mining and Metal. Soc. America, W. Va. Acad. Sci., Soc. Mining Engrs. (vice president 1958-61), Scabbard and Blade, Phi Beta Kappa, Sigma Gamma Epsilon, Sigma Xi, Tau Beta Pi. Presbyn. Clubs: Mining (N.Y.C.); Engrs., Kiwanis, Guyandotte, Guyan Golf and Country (Huntington). Contbr. numerous articles on coal mining to tech. jours., bulletins, etc. Home: Huntington WV Died Apr. 1973.

LAWLESS, THEODORE KENNETH, dermatologist; b. Thibodeaux, La., Dec. 6, 1893; s. Rev. Alfred and Harriet (Dunn) L.; A.B., Talladega (Ala.) Coll., 1914, D.Sc., 1945; grad. student U. Kan., 1917; M.D., Northwestern U., 1919, M.S., 1920; fellow Vanderbilt Clinic, Columbia, 1920-21, Harvard, Path. Inst. Freiburg, Germany, 1922-23; LL.D., Bethune-Cookman Coll., 1952. Fellow dermatology, syphilology Mass. Gen. Hosp., 1920-21, St. Louis Hosp., Paris, France, 1921-22, Kaiser Joseph Hosp., Vienna, Austria, also clinics Switzerland, other European med. centers; practice of medicine, Chgo., 1924-71; fellow, instr., med. sch. Northwestern U., 1924-41; cons. dermatology, syphilology Geneva Community Hosp.; sr. attending physician dept. dermatology and syphilology Provident Hosp. Chgo.; pres. Service Fed. Saving & Loan Assn., Chgo., 1951, Gentilly Garden Apts., New Orleans, 1950-71, 4213 S. Mich. Corp., 1946. Mem. Prison Welfare Com. Cook Co.; Chgo. Bd. of Health; adv. bd. Chgo. Civil Liberties Com. Chmn. bd. trustees Talladega Coll.; trustee Fisk U., Roosevelt U., Dillard U., Houston-Tillotson Coll. Rocky Mt. Coll., Ada S. McKinely Settlement House, Chgo.; chmn. budget com. Board of Home Missions of the Congregational-Christian Churches. Consultant United States Chemical Warfare Bd., adv. com. venereal diseases, World War II. Recipient Harmon award for outstanding work in medicine, 1929; Am. Mus. Festival award, 1949; award for distinguished service to community Chgo. Negro C. of C., 1952; Spingarn medal N.A.A.C.P., 1954. Diplomate Am. Bd. Dermatology and Syphilology. Mem. A.M.A., Nat., Ill., Chgo. med. socs., Chgo. Acad. Sci., Internat. Congress Dermatology, A.A.A.S., Met. Dermatol. Soc. (1st pres.), Am. Missionary Assn., Alumni Assn. U. Kan., Art Inst. Chgo., Nat. Geog. Soc. Conglist. Home: Chicago IL Died May 1, 1971; buried Mount Olivet Cemetery, New Orleans LA

LAWRENCE, DAVID, editor; b. Phila., Dec. 25, 1888; s. Harris and Dora Lawrence; B.A., Princeton U., 1910; m. Ellanor Campbell Hayes, July 17, 1918 (dec. 1969); children—David, Mark, Nancy (dec.), Etienne. Joined Washington staff Assoc. Press, 1910; Washington corr. N.Y. Evening Post, 1916-1919; writing first Washington dispatch to be syndicated nationally by wire; pres. Consolidated Press Assn., Washington, 1919-33; founder, pres. The U.S. Daily, Washington, 1926-33; pres., editor U.S. News, 1933-48; founder, pres. World Report, 1946-48, pres., editor U.S. News & World Report, 1948-59, chmn. bd., editor, 1959-73. Writer of dispatch on nat. and world affairs syndicated to more than 200 daily newspapers in U.S. Fellow Sigma Delta Chi. Clubs: National Press, Metropolitan, Cosmos, Princeton. Author: True Story of Woodrow Wilson, 1924; The Other Side of Government, 1929; Beyond the New Deal, 1934; Stumbling into Socialism, 1935; Nine Honest Men, 1936; Who Were the Eleven Million, 1937; Diary of a Washington Correspondent, 1942; also various mag. articles. Address: Washington DC Died Feb. 11, 1973.

LAWRENCE, JOHN WILLIAM, univ. dean; b. New Orleans, Oct. 30, 1923; s. William Noel and Theresa (Ormond) L.; B.S. in Arch., Tulane U., 1944; M.S. in Arch., Columbia, 1948; m. Maxine Marie Stiegler, Dec. 16, 1950; children—Mark Francis, John Hilliard, Mary Elisa, Annette Marie, Elizabeth Ann. Faculty Tulane U. Sch. Architecture, 1949-71, prof. architecture, dean sch., 1960-71; pvt. practice specializing residential and religious architecture, New Orleans, 1949-71; lectr. religious and residential architecture, also urban aesthetics; work exhibited Work of Younger Architects at Archtl. League N.Y., 1958, Gold Medal Exhbn. Bldg. Arts, 1959. Mem. Vieux Carre Commn., New Orleans, 1953-54; mem. adv. com. Spaeth Liturgical award. Served to lt. (j.g.) USNR, 1943-46; PTO. Recipient 18 nat. and regional awards for archtl. excellence. Mem. A.I.A., Cath. Art Assn., Assn. Collegiate Sch. Architecture (com. advancement archtl. edn.), So. Regional Edn. Bd. (study com. archtl. edn.), Tau Sigma Delta, Gargoyle. Mem. editorial com. A Guide to New Orleans Architecture, 1699-1959, also author foreward to contemporary sect. Home: Metairie LA Died Apr. 20, 1971.

LAWRENCE, NEWBOLD TROTTER, shipping exec.; b. N.Y. City, Jan. 9, 1893; s. Newbold Trotter and Isabelle (Gillett) L.; B.S., U.S. Naval Acad., 1916; m. Mary Evelyn Cromwell, June 7, 1916 (dec. Nov. 1968); children—Newbold Trotter, Richard Cromwell. Asst. to v.p. in charge freight traffic U.S. Shipping Bd., Washington; gen. mgr. operations U.S. Lines Co., N.Y. City, 1937-49, asst. v.p. operations, 1949-51, v.p. operations from 1951. Dir. Security Bur. Served in U.S. Naval Sub-marine Service, 1916-20. Mem. Soc. Naval Architects and Marine Engrs., U.S. Naval Acad. Alumni Assn., Maritime Assn. Port N.Y. (pres., dir.), N.Y. Shipping Assn. (dir.). Home: Huntington LI NY Died Nov. 1968.

LAWRENCE, RALPH RESTIEAUX, coll. prof.; b. Boston, Mass., Feb. 28, 1873; s. Charles H. and Isabel M. (Restleaux) L.; B.S. in E.E., Mass. Inst. Tech., 1895; m. Reba M. Bush, June 17, 1922. Asst. in physics, Mass. Inst. Tech., 1896-98, instr., 1898-1901, instr. elec. engring., 1901-04, asst. prof., 1904-06, asso. prof. 1906, prof. elec. machinery, 1922, prof. emeritus since 1941. Fellow Am. Inst. Elec. Engrs.; fellow Am. Acad. Arts and Science. Author: Principles of Alternating Current Machinery; Principles of Alternating Currents. Home: 66 Stone Rd., Belmont MA‡

LAWRENCE, ROBERT H., JR., astronaut; b. Chgo., 1935; s. Robert H. and Gwendolyn Lawrence; B.S. in Chemistry, Bradley U., 1956; Ph.D., Ohio State U., 1965; m. Barbara H. Cress, 1957; 1 son, Tracey. Joined USAF, 1956, advanced through grades to maj., 1967; assigned Pilot Instrn. Sch., Craig AFB, Ala., 1957, then USAF base, Furstenfeldbruck, W. Germany; grad. Aerospace Research Pilot Sch., Edwards AFB, Cal., 1967; astronaut Manned Space Program, NASA, 1967. Home: Chicago IL Died Dec. 8, 1967.

LAWRENCE, WILLIAM APPLETON, bishop; b. Cambridge, Mass., May 21, 1889; s. William (bishop) and Julia (Cunningham) L.; A.B., Harvard, 1911; student Union Theol. Sem., 1911-12; B.D., Episcopal Theol. School, 1914; D.D., Lawrence Coll., Appleton, Wisconsin, 1929, Amherst (Mass.) College, 1937; S.T.D., Trinity College, 1938; L.H.D., American International College Springfield, Massachusetts, 1938; m. Hannah W. Cobb, June 1, 1912; children—Susan, William, Charles Kane Cobb, Elizabeth Codman, Sarah, Hannah, Samuel Appleton. Ordained ministry Episcopal Ch., 1914; curate Grace Ch., Lawrence, Mass., 1914-16; rector St. Stephen's Ch., Lynn, Mass., 1916-26, Grace Ch., Providence, R.I., 1926-36; consecrated bishop of the Episcopal Diocese of Western Mass., 1937-57. Mem. Nat. Council P.E. Ch., 1936-42, Mass. Council of Churches (pres. 1943-45); chmn. Episcopal Pacifist Fellowship, 1939-45; chmn. Nat. Commn. of Protestant Episcopal Ch. on Conscientious Objectors, 1943; pres. Province, of New England, 1950-56; exec. dir. personnel information service, from 1957. Trustee Wellesley College, from 1937; trustee Lenox School, Mt. Holyoke Coll., 1941-51; mem. bd. overseers Harvard Coll., 1949-55; trustee Gen. Theol. Sem., N.Y., 1949-55; chmn. nat. chmn. marriage and div. P.E. Ch.; mem. corp. Springfield Coll., 1946-56; vis. com. Harvard Div. Sch., 1949-55; mem. Com. on Stillman Infirmary and Harvard U. Health Services. Author: Christian Marriage, 1929; Parsons, Vestries and Parishes, 1961. Home: Cambridge MA Died Dec. 21, 1968.

LAWRENCE, WILLIAM HEREFORD, horticulturist; b. Lake City, Ia., Feb. 3, 1877; s. George Washington and Vesta (Easton) L.; B.S., S.D. State Coll. Agr. and Mechanic Arts, 1899; B.A., M.S., State Coll. of Wash., Pullman, 1902; Cornell U., 1906-7; m. Edith Florence MacDermott, of Meadville, Pa., June 8, 1908. Asst. in botany and agr., S.D. State Coll., 1897-9; asst. in botany and entomology, 1901, instr., 1902, instr. botany and asst. at Expt. Sta., 1903-6, asst. prof. plant pathology, 1906-7, supt. Western Wash. Expt. Sta. and plant pathologist State Expt. Sta., 1907-11, all State Coll. of Wash.; plant pathologist and horticulturist, Hood River Apple Growers' Assn., 1911-13; prof. horticulture and horticulturist, U. of Ariz., 1913-15; prof. horticulture, U. of Mo., 1915-18; capt., Sn. Corps U.S.A., chief ednl. officer, Reconstruction Sch. U.S.A. Gen. Hosp. 21, Denver, Colo., 1918-—. Mem. Sigma Xi (Alpha Chapter, Cornell). Presbyn. Author: Apple Growing, 1911, also 22 expt. sta. bulls. Address: 1454 Williams St., Denver CO‡

LAWRENCE, WILLIAM HOWARD, radio-TV news reporter; born Lincoln, Nebraska, January 29, 1916; son Edward H. and Daisy (Minner) L.; student University Nebraska, 1933; Dr. Humane Letters (hon.), Grinnell Coll., 1967; married Elizabeth Currie, 1937 (div. 1946);children—William E., Ann E.; m. 2d, Constance Marcy McGregor, 1951 (div. 1958); m. 3d, Mary Jacqueline Eidel, 1971 (div. 1972). Reporter, Lincoln (Neb.) Star, 1932-35, Asso. Press, Lincoln and Omaha, 1935-36, United Press, Chgo., Detroit, Washington, 1936-41; chief corr. N.Y. Times, Moscow, 1943-45, war corr., Pacific, 1945, staff UN Bur., 1946, chief Balkan corr., 1947-48, nat. corr., 1948-61; national political editor and White House corr. ABC, 1961-68, nat. affairs editor, 1968-72. Recipient George Foster Peabody broadcasting award, 1964. Clubs: Nat. Press (pres. 1959-60), Washington. (Washington); Burning Tree (Bethesda, Md.). Home: Washington DC Died Mar. 2, 1972.

LAWSON, HURON WILLIS, M.D.; b. Disco, Mich., Mar. 15, 1873; s. James S. and Paulina T. (Cannon) L.; B.S., Mich. State Coll., 1895; student, U. of Chicago Grad. Sch., 1897-98; M.D., Columbian (now George Washington) U., 1903, M.S., 1904; Vienna and Berlin hosps., 1904; m. Franceska Kaspar, of Washington, Sept. 14, 1910. Mich. State dairy and food insp. and asst. analyst, 1895-96; supt. pub. schs., Lawton, Mich., 1896-97; asso. editor Expt. Sta. Record, and contbr. to publs., U.S. Dept. Agr., 1898-1907; asst. prof. bacteriology and pathology, 1906-09, prof. histology and embryology, 1909-12, asso. prof. obstetrics, 1912-15, prof., 1915-26, prof. obstetrics and gynecology, 1926-32, emeritus prof., 1933-—, George Washington U. Address: 1717 N St., Washington DC‡

LAWSON, WARNER, ednl. adminstr. Dean. Coll. Fine Arts Howard U., Washington. Home: Washington DC

LAWTON, ALEXANDER ROBERT, lawyer; born Savannah, Ga., Aug. 16, 1884; s. Alexander Rudolf and Ella Stanly (Beckwith) L.; ed. St. Paul's Sch., Concord, N.H., 1898-1902; Ph.B., Sheffield Scientific Sch. (Yale), 1905; U. of Ga. Law Sch., 1906; U. of Va. Law Sch., 1908; m. Elizabeth Wallace Shotter, Dec. 5, 1911 (deceased July 8, 1956); children—Alexander Robert III, Spencer. Admitted to Ga. bar, 1909; mem. firm Lawton, O'Donnell, Sipple & Chamlee; chmn. bd. Chatham Savings Bank; dir. Colonial Oil Industries, Lieut. col., National Guard Ga., Mexican border service, 1916; lt. col. 118th F.A., U.S. Army, World War; hon. disch., 1919. Mem. Ga. Gen. Assembly, 1925-26; mem. Alumni Adv. Bd., Yale U., 1927; mem. com. to draft Constn. for State of Ga., 1931. Ex-pres. Telfair Acad. of Arts and Science. Mem. Savannah Bar Assn. (pres. 1941), Union Soc. Savannah (pres. 1937-39), Ga. Hist. Soc., Delta Psi. Dem. Episcopalian. Clubs: St. Anthony (New York); Oglethorpe, Savannah Golf, University (Savannah). Home: Savannah GA Died Sept. 25, 1963.

LAWTON, LOUIS BOWEN, army officer; b. Independence, Iowa, Mar. 13, 1872; s. Albert Wheeler and Mary (Vorhis) L.; prep. ed'n at Owasco and Auburn, N.Y.; grad. West Point, 1893; m. Auburn, N.Y., July 26, 1893, Theresa Emily Kelsey. Apptd. 2d lt. June 12, 1893, 1st lt. Apr. 26, 1898, 9th inf.; capt., Feb. 2, 1901, 26th inf., U.S.A.; maj., Jan., 1903; served in battles of Santiago, Cuba; Guadalupe Ridge, Japote River, Calulut, Bamban and many minor engagements in Philippines; battle of Tientsin, China (wounded), 1900; recommended for promotion in many battles; awarded medal of honor for most distinguished gallantry" at Tientsin, China, July 13, 1900. Commandant Shattuck Sch., 1901. Retired Jan., 1903, wounds. Address: Care War Dept., Washington‡

LAWWILL, STEWART, physician; b. Danville, Ky., May 28, 1892; s. William H. (M.D.) and Lucy Bell (Mefford) L.; M.D., Vanderbilt U., 1915; grad. Army Med. Sch., 1917; special studies, New York Eye and Ear Infirmary, Boston Charity Eye and Ear Infirmary, Roosevelt Hospital (New York), New York Post-graduate Hosp., University of Vienna (Austria) and U. of Pa. Grad. Sch. of Medicine; m. Sue Frierson, Mar. 3, 1925; children—Stewart, Margaret, Nina Elizabeth, Theodore. Began practice of medicine at Chattanooga, 1921; specialized in treatment of eye, ear, nose and throat; chief of staff, Meml. Hosp., Chattanooga, 1952. Served as 1st lt. Med. Corps, U.S. Army, 1917-19; with 307th San. Train, 82d Div., overseas, May 1918-July 1919. Fellow Am. Coll. of Surgeons, Am. Acad. of Ophthalmology and Oto-Laryngology, Am. Laryngol., Rhinol. and Oto-Laryngol. Soc.; mem. A.M.A., Southern Med. Assn., Tenn., and East Tenn. med. socs., Chattanooga and Hamilton County Medical Society (president 1945), Chattanooga Soc. Ophthalmology and Oto-Laryngology (pres.), Phi Kappa Chi, Alpha Omega Alpha, Phi Beta Phi. Presbyterian. Mason (K.T., Shriner). Clubs: Mountain City, Fairyland Golf. Home: Lookout Mountain TN Died Aug. 22, 1967; buried Forest Hill Cemetery, Chattanooga TN

LAY, WILFRID, author; b. Brooklyn, N.Y., Jan. 3, 1872; s. Oliver Ingraham and Hester Marian (Wait) L.; A.B., Columbia, 1893, Ph.D., 1898; studied U. of Bonn; m. Anna R. Melville, of N.Y. City, Apr. 22, 1896; children—Theodore Melville, Dorothea, Sylvia. Teacher since 1898, now with Flushing (N.Y.) High Sch. Mem. Phi Beta Kappa. Democrat. Mem. Religious Soc. of Friends. Author: Man's Unconscious Conflict, 1917; The Child's Unconscious Mind, 1919; Man's Unconscious Passion, 1920; Man's Unconscious Spirit, 1921; A Plea for Monogamy, 1923. Spent 6 months studying analytical psychology in London, 1925. Club: Players. Address: 16 Gramercy Park, New York NY‡

LAZARUS, REUBEN AVIS, lawyer; b. N.Y.C., Feb. 2, 1895; s. Isaac and Fannie (Shapiro) L.; student Coll. City of N.Y., 1928; L.B., Union Coll., Albany, N.Y., 1931; m. Ruth Freedman, Dec. 28, 1921; 1 son, Andrew Joseph. Page, N.Y. State Legislature, 1913; clerk legislative div. (Albany), Office of N.Y.C. Corp. Counsel, 1914, spl. asst. corp. counsel, 1931, asst. in charge legislative matters, 1932-39; spl. legislative rep. of N.Y.C., 1939-46, asso. counsel N.Y.C. Charter Commn., 1935, 62; counsel, N.Y.C. Bd. Statutory Consolidation, 1936-46, 61-62, Charter Revision Commn. City N.Y., 1961; asst. to pres. N.Y.C. City Council, 1938-43; asst. to mayor of N.Y.C., 1944-46; counsel charter-code unit Office of Mayor, N.Y.C. Mem. N.Y.C. Bd. of Higher Edn., 1940-49; mem. N.Y. State Commn. on Municipal Revenues, cons. Municipal Affairs N.Y. State Legislature, 1946-—; legal cons. to coms. on local govt. and home rule, edn., state and local finances of the N.Y. State Constl. Conv., 1967; mem. N.Y. State Commn. on Revision and Simplification of the Constitution. Bd. dirs. Municipal Credit Union. Mem. Am., N.Y. State bar assns., Albany Soc. of N.Y. (pres.), The Players, Phi Sigma Kappa. Codified N.Y. City Laws. Contbr. articles to legal publs. Home: Pawling NY Died July 11, 1971.

LAZARUS, ROBERT, mcht.; b. Columbus, O., Sept. 20, 1890; s. Fred and Rose (Eichberg) L.; student Ohio State U., 1912; m. Hattle Weller, Feb. 1, 1917; children—Charlotte, Babette, Jean Lillian, Robert, Jr. With F. & R. Lazarus & Co. since beginning of career, v.p., sec., 1930-48, pres., 1947-59, chmn. bd., 1959-69, chmn. emeritus, 1969-73; dir., v.p., mem. exec. com. Federated Dept. Stores Inc., Cin. Mem. Columbus Met. Commn.; chmn. bd. Community Fund, 1936; v.p. Children's Hosp., 1917-7 sponsors council palnned Parenthood-World Population Internat. Mem. Ohio Bd. Regents; alumni adv. bd. Ohio State U. Clubs: University, Faculty (Columbus); Winding Hollow Country. Home: Columbus OH Died Feb. 5, 1973.

LEACH, CHARLES NELSON, physician; gov. A.R.C.; b. Burlington, Vt., July 2, 1884; s. Horatio Nelson and Phylinda (Clark) L.; A.B., Stanford, 1909, M.D., 1913; M.P.H., Johns Hopkins, 1921; m. Florence Dixon, Sept. 11, 1922; children—Carolyn Worden (Mrs. William H. Gorman II), Nancy Murchison (Mrs. H.A. Sackett), Charles Nelson. Intern Lane Hosp., San Francisco, 1914; with Rockefeller Found., 1921-49, asst. dir. internat. health div., 1947-49. Nat. bd. govs. A.R.C., 1954-60; trustee U. Vt., 1961-67. Mem. Commn. for Relief in Belgium, 1915-18, Am. Relief Adminstrn., 1919-21. Mem. exec. com. Belgian Am. Ednl. Found. Served as capt., M.C., U.S. Army, World War I. Decorated Order of Crown (Belgium); Polonia Restituta (Poland). Fellow Am. Coll. Preventive Medicine, Am. Soc. Tropical Medicine, Royal Soc. Tropical Medicine and Hygiene; mem. A.A.A.S., Am. Pub. Health Assn., Die Gesellschaft der Aerzte in Wien. Address: Newfane VT Died Apr. 3, 1971.

LEACH, ELLIS, textile mfr.; b. Wigan, Eng., Oct. 5, 1906; s. John W. F. and Fanny (Large) L.; m. Estella I. Tucker, July 28, 1928; 1 son, Robert E. Office boy Sanford Mills., 1921, successively asst. supt., co-supt., gen. exec. mfg. and sales, 1922-43; dir., treas. Woonsocket Falls Mill; gen. mgr. E. F. Timme & Son, 1943-56; treas., dir. Victoria Plush Mill., 1944-52; exec. v.p., treas., dir. Timme Corp., 1952-56; sec., dir. 75 Central Park West Corp., 1951; pres. Collins & Aikman Corp., N.Y.C., 1956-61, chmn., 1961-66. Episcopalian. Mason, Elk. Clubs: Union League; Canadian; Lake Shore (Chgo.); Detroit Athletic; Spring Lake Golf and Country, Spring Lake Bathing and Tennis (Spring Lake, N.J.); Recess. Home: Spring Lake NJ Died Feb. 1971.

LEACH, FRANK ALEAMON, JR., pub. utility official; b. Vallejo, Calif., Oct. 1, 1871; s. Frank Aleamon and Mary Louise (Powell) L.; grad. high sch., Oakland, Calif.; m. Margaret Helen Leach, of Oakland, June 11, 1895; children—Margaret Elizabeth (Mrs. Guy C. Calden, Jr.), Frank Powell. Apprentice, later asst. mgr. Oakland Enquirer Pub. Co., 1886-98; jr. clk., advancing to gen. mgr. Oakland Gas Light and Heat Co. and Pacific Gas and Electric Co., Oakland, 1898-1920; v.p. and gen. mgr. Pacific Gas and Electric Co., San Francisco, 1923-29 (retired). Republican. Mason. Clubs: Bohemian (San Francisco); Athenian-Nile (Oakland). Home: 125 Hillside Av., Piedmont CA‡

LEACH, HENRY GODDARD, author, educator; b. Philadelphia, Pa., July 3, 1880; s. Dr. Alonzo Lemuel and Jennie (Goddard) L.; A.B., Princeton Univ., 1903; A.M., Harvard, 1906, Ph.D., 1908; LL.D., Rollins Coll., 1927; Litt.D., Augustana Coll., 1938; LL.D., Upsala Coll., 1945; Ph.D., U. Upsala (350th Anniversary), 1945, U. Iceland, 1961; m. Agnes Lisle Brown, Feb. 20, 1915; adopted children—Annis Leach (Mrs. Charles W. Young), Jeffery E. Fuller. Master, Groton School, 1903-05; travelling fellow, Harvard U. in Denmark, 1908-10; instr. Eng., Harvard, 1910-12; sec. Am.-Scandinavian Foundation, N.Y., 1912-21, pres., 1926-47; prof. Scandinavian civilization, U. of Kansas City, from 1947; curator Scandinavian history and lit., Harvard, 1921-31; editor The Forum, 1923-40. Secured economic support, 1919, for exchange of 40 students annually between U.S. and Scandinavian countries; former v.p. Am. unit P.E.N.; mem. N.Y. State Jud. Council, 1940-50; trustee Council Religious and Internat. Affairs; pres. Poetry Soc. Am., 1934-37. Lectr. Canadian Inst. Internat. Affairs, 1947; lecturer at universities in Sweden, 1958; president International Auxiliary Language Assn. Comdr. of Vasa Order and Comdr. of North Star (Sweden); Comdr. of the Dannebrog (Denmark); Comdr. of St. Olav (Norway); Comdr. of Falcon with Star (Iceland); Comdr. of the White Rose (Finland). Recipient Gold Medal American-Scandinavian Foundn. Mem. Soc. Mayflower Descendants, Soc. Colonial Wars, S.R. Clubs: Ausable, Century, Church (pres. 1923-26), Harvard, Piping Rock (New York); Faculty (Cambridge); Savile (London). Author: Scandinavia of the Scandinavians, 1915; Angevin Britain and Scandinavia, 1921; Pageant of Old Scandinavia, 1946; The Fire's Center, 1950; My Last Seventy Years, 1956; An Interrupted Courtship, 1963; Echoes of Childhood, 1966. Lectr. and contrbr. to periodicals. Home: New York City NY Died Nov. 11, 1970.

LEACH, HUGH, banker; b. Richmond, Va., Sept. 24, 1894; s. James Archibald and Mary Thomas (Cleaton) L.; grad. McGuires U. Sch., Richmond, 1913; B.A., University of Virginia, 1916, M.A., 1917; married Alice Creath Angel, June 28, 1923 (died June 14, 1941); 1son—Hugh; m. 2d, Mrs. Marian Wood Burgess, Aug. 28, 1952; stepson, John M. Burgess. Clk. Old Dominion Trust Co., Richmond, 1916; bookkeeper, later office manager, A.P. Youngblood, Inc., member New York Produce Exchange, 1917-1918; cadet Air Serv. U.S. Army, 1918; mem. staff, Richmond, of F.W. La Frentz & Co., pub. accountants, N.Y., 1919-20; asst. auditor and auditor Fed. Res. Bank, Richmond, 1921-27; mng. dir. Charlotte, N.C., br. of same, 1927-31, of Baltimore br., 1931-35, except while treas. Reconstruction Finance Corp., Washington, Feb. 2-Sept. 25, 1932; later pres. Federal Reserve Bank of Richmond. C.P.A. (Va.), Chmn. war finance com. 5th Fed. Res. Dist., 1942, 43; bd. trustees Richmond War and Community Fund, 1941-48; bd. counselors Evening Sch. U. of Richmond. Pres. U. of Va., class of 1917. Mem. bd. of visitors, Medical Coll. of Va., 1941-53, pres. University of Va. Alumni Assn., 1944-47. Mem. Pi Kappa Alpha, Phi Beta Kappa, Beta Gamma Sigma. Raven Society. Democrat. Presbyn. Clubs: Country of Va. (pres. 1942-43), Commonwealth (Richmond). Home: Richmond VA Died Oct. 16, 1971.

LEACH, RALPH WALDO EMERSON, mechanical engr.; b. Watertown, Mass., June 6, 1874; s. Charles Henry and Mary Elizabeth (Barrett) L.; M.E., U. of Pa., 1898; m. Avis Spurr Standing, of Boston, Mass., Oct. 20, 1910 (dec.). With U. of Pa. and Schuylkill Elec. Ry. Co., 1895-96; treas. and dir. Phila. Constrn. Co., and Phila. Car Equipment Co., 1897; cashier Norfolk & Ocean View Railway & Hotel Co., 1899; testing engr. Am. Stoker Co., New York, 1900-02; research in manufacture of Portland cement treatment of ores, and dissociation of hydrogen in steam at high temperatures, in cement manufacture, 1902-03; experimental engr. Eldred Process Co., 1904; mgr. stoker dept. Westinghouse Machine Co., Pittsburgh, Pa., 1905-07; mgr. Castalia Portland Cement Co., 1908-09; N.E. mgr. Am. Engring. Co., 1910-19; gen. representative same co., Phila., since 1919. Mem. 1st Pa. Vols., Spanish-Am. War, 1898; with U.S. Fuel Administration, World War. Mem. Am. Soc. Mech. Engrs., Nat. Electric Light Assn., Am. Electric Ry. Assn., Engineers' Club (Boston), Phi Gamma Delta. Republican. Christian Scientist. Mason (32 deg., K.T., Shriner). Clubs: Blue Room, Square & Compass (Boston); Vesper Country (Lynsboro, Mass.); Commercial (Montreal, Can.). Home: 32 Fletcher St., Winchester, Mass. Office: 470 Atlantic Av., Boston MA‡

LEACH, W(ALTER) BARTON, educator; b. Boston, Jan. 6, 1900; s. Walter Barton and Grace Winifred (Wise) L.; A.B., cum laude, Harvard U., 1921; grad. student Universite de Grenoble, summer 1920; LL.B. cum laude, Harvard U. Law Sch., 1924; m. Florence T. Malcolm, June 14, 1924 (divorced 1941); children—Barbara, Richard Malcolm; m. 2d, Jane McIlwraith, Mar. 10, 1944 (dec. 1963); 1 son, David; m. 3d, Blanche C. Bartlett, Jan. 3, 1964. Sec. to Jus. Oliver Wendell Holmes, U.S. Supreme Ct., 1924-25; admitted to Mass. bar, 1925, and engaged in gen. prac. of law at Boston, asso. with firm Warner, Stackpole & Bradlee, 1925-30; instr. law, Harvard U. Law Sch., 1929, asst. prof. law, 1930, prof. law, 1931-69; prof. Harvard grad. sch. pub. adminstrn., 1954; vis. prof. Oxford U., 1952; mem. editorial board, Law Book Dept., Little Brown & Co., from 1938; Cons. to USAF, from 1947. Served as pvt. inf., U.S. Army, 1918; commissioned major, Army of United States, June 1942; lt. col. Air Corps, Jan. 1943; col. Air Corps, Aug. 1944; brig. gen. U.S. Air Force Reserve, 1949. Legion of Merit, 1945; Exceptional Civilian Service award, 1949, Meritorious Civilian Service award, 1966. Mem. Am., Mass. bar assns., Pi Eta Soc., Lincoln's Inn Society, Universalist. Clubs: Harvard, Weston Golf (Boston, Massachusetts). Author of: Cases on Future Interests, 1935; Cases on Mass. Law of Evidence, 1935; Cases on Wills, 1939, revised edition, 1960; Handbook of Massachusetts Evidence, 1940, fourth edition (with Paul J. Liacos), 1968; Cases and Text on Property (with A. James Casner), 2d edit., 1969; The Rule Against Perpetuities (England, with J. H. C. Morris), 1955; The Rule Against Perpetuities (U.S., with Owen Tudor), 1957; (with J.K. Logan; Cases and Text on Future Interests and Estate Planning, 1961; Property Law Indicated, published, 1967; also author articles in legal and other periodicals; co-author of Am. Law of Property, 1952. Home: 295 Meadowbrook Rd., Weston MA Address: Cambridge MA Died Dec. 15, 1971; buried Cambridge MA

LEACH, WILLIAM FILLMORE, chain store exec.; b. Wilmington, Del., June 23, 1894; s. James F. and Susan (Lyons) L.; student pub. schs. of Bayonne, N.J.; m. Doris Fairbrother, Dec. 31, 1919; children—Marian Feaster, Audrey Longacre. With A. & P. Co. since 1915, Atlantic div. pres. 1938-66; mem. bd. A. & P. of America (Maryland Corporation), 1947-—, also v.p. Mem. American Legion. Home: Marlton NJ Died Dec. 29, 1968; buried Clove Cemetery, Sussex NJ

LEADBETTER, CAROLINE PITTOCK, publisher; b. Portland, Ore., 1875; d. Henry Lewis and Georgiana Martin (Burton) Pittock; grad. Anne Wright Sem., Tacoma, Wash.; m. F.W. Leadbetter, Sept. 23, 1893; children—Georgiana, Dorothy, Pittock, Elizabeth. Pres. Oregonian Newspaper, Portland, Ore.; dir. Columbia River Paper Co., Vancouver; Oregon Pulp and Paper Co., Salem, Ore. Republican. Episcopalian. Clubs: Town (Portland, Ore.); Little Town, Garden (Santa Barbara, Calif.). Home: Portland OR‡

LEAHY, FRANK, football columnist; b. O'Neill, Neb., Aug. 27, 1908; s. Frank and Mary (Kane) L.; B.S., U. Notre Dame, 1931; m. Florence Reilly, July 4, 1935; children—Frank, Susan Marie, Florence, Jerry, James Patrick, Frederick John, Mary Patricia, Christopher. Line coach Georgetown U., 1931, Mich. State U., 1932, Fordham U., 1933-38; head coach Boston Coll, 1939-41; head football coach U. Notre Dame, 1941-54; with Merritt-Chapman Scott Co.; exec. v.p. charge sales Exothermic Alloys Sales & Service, Michigan City, Ind.; pres. Leahy-Sullivan, Inc., ins. agy.; exec. v.p. Hamilton Oil & Gas Co., Denver; football columnist Chgo. Daily News; now asst. to pres. Canteen Corp., Millbrae, Cal. Spl. cons. to Mayor Daley on summer youth programs, 1967-68; football broadcaster, CBS, 1967-68. Served to lt. USNR, 1944-45. Named Coach of Year various newspapers, 1941, 46, 47, 48, 49; named Football Man of Year, Football Writers Assn. Am., 1949; recipient Emmy award for Sports Commentator on Big News Nat. Acad. TV Arts and Scis., 1968-69; named Sportsman of Yr., 1969; elected to Coll. Football Hall of Fame, 1970. Roman Catholic. Knight of Malta. Address: Millbrae CA Died June 21, 1973.

LEAKE, JAMES PAYTON, M.D., pub. health officer; b. Sedalia, Mo., June 4, 1881; s. James Payton and Matilda Ann (Love) L.; grad. Smith Acad., St. Louis, Mo., 1900; A.B., Harvard, 1903, M.D., 1907; m. Mary D. Ray Quinn), Alice King (Mrs. Fred S. Lawless). In U.S. Pub. Health Service, 1909-45, retired 1945; in charge serums and vaccines, Hygienic Lab., 1913-22, in charge office indsl. hygiene and sanitation, 1930-33; in charge epidemiological sect., 1933-45. First secretary Basic Science Board, District of Columbia. Mem. A.M.A (vice chmn. council on pharmacy and chemistry), Am. Epidemiol. Soc. (president 1943), Am. Pub. Health Assn. (governing council), Assn. Mil. Surgeons of U.S. (vice president), Soc. Exptl. Biology and Medicine, N.Y. Acad. Medicine, Delta Upsilon. Improved smallpox preventions, and worked toward better controls in epidemiological studies. Washington DC Died Feb. 21, 1973.

LEAKEY, LOUIS SEYMOUR BAZETT, archaeologist; b. 1903; ed. Weymouth Coll., St. John's Coll., Cambridge (Eng.) U.; M.A., Ph.D., D.Sc. (fellow), St. John's Coll., 1930-35; LL.D., U. Cal., 1963, U. of Geuiph (Can.), 1969. Leader, East African archaeol. expdns., 1926-27, 27-28, 29, 31-32, 34, 35; Munroe lectr. Edinburgh (Scotland) U., 1936; with Criminal Investigation Dept., Nairobi, World War II; curator Coryndon Meml. Museum, Nairobi, Kenya, 1945-61, hon. keeper paleontology and prehistory, 1961, 62; dir. Nat. Mus. Centre for Prehistory and Palentology, 1962; prof. at large Cornell U., 1966. Recipient Halle Sellassie award and medal, 1968. Hon. fellow St. John's Coll., Cambridge, 1966. Fellow British Acad. Author: Stone Age Culture of Kenya; Stone Age Races of Kenya; Stone Age Africa; Adam's Ancestors; Olduval Gorge; White African; Kenya Contrasts and Problems; Mau Mau and the Kikuyu; Defeating Mau Mau; (with Yila) Animals of Africa; Some East African Pleistocene Fossil Suidoe; First Lessons in Kikuyu Language; Olduval 1951-1961; The Progress and Evolution of Man in Africa; (with V. Godall) Unveiling Man's Origins, Nairobi Kenya Died Oct. 1, 1972.

LEANDER, HUGO AUSTIN, business exec.; b. Cambridge, Mass., Dec. 2, 1894; s. Carl F. and Clara W. (Carlson) L.; B.S., Harvard, 1916; student grad. sch. bus., N.Y.C., 1921-22; m. Marguerite R. McFarland, Nov. 29, 1917; children—Jeanne, Hugh A. Spl. accountant Union Pacific System, N.Y., 1916-18; auditor Gen. Electric Co., Schenectady, 1918-21; supervisor methods Del. & Hudson Co., N.Y., 1921-24; mgr. Arthur Andersen & Co., N.Y., 1924-26; financial and indsl. cons., dir. Am. Rayon Products Corp., Consol. Laundries Corp., Gen. Laundry Machinery Corp. (all N.Y.C.), 1926-30; v.p. Am. Founders Corp., Am. Gen. Corp., 1930-36; mgr. indsl. dept. Van Alstyne, Noel & Co., 1936-38; vice president dir. Reynolds Metals Co., Richmond Radiator Co.; dir. U.S. Foil Co., Reynolds Corp., Robertshaw Thermostat Corp., Fulton-Sylphon Corp., Reynolds Research Corp., 1938-41; v.p., treas., dir. Tobe Deutschman Corp., 1941-42, Mu-Switch Corp., 1941-43; v.p., dir. W. L. Maxson Corp., N.Y.C., 1944-47, pres., 1947-59, dir. to 1960; dir., chmn. exec. com. Avionics Investing Corp., 1960-61; pres., dir. Avionics Mgmt. Corp.; dir. Leetronics, Incorporated. Mem. N.Y. C. of C., New Eng. Soc., Harvard Engring. Soc. Member Union League Club (N.Y.C.) Conglist. Home: Darien CT Died Apr. 14, 1970; buried Mt. Auburn Cemetery, Cambridge MA

LEARNARD, GEORGE EDWARD, engring.; b. Boston, Mass., July 16, 1874; ed. pub. schs.; m. Elinor Nye, of N.Y. City. Pres. Internat. Combustion Engring. Corpn., Green Engring. Co., Internat. Pulverized Fuel Corpn., Raymond Bros. Impact Pulverizer Co., Coxe Traveling Grate Co., Lopulco Systems, Inc.; chmn. bd. Internat. Combustion Tar & Chem. Co., Internat. Coal Carbonization Co., N.J. Coal & Tar Co., Pa. Coal & Tar Co., Combustion Corpn. America; vice pres. Coshocton Iron Co.; chmn. bd. Heine Boiler Co., Combusion Engring. Corpn.; dir. Internat. Combustion, Ltd., Coal Oil Extraction, Ltd. Dir. Societe Anonyme des Foyers Automatiques, Kohlenscheidungs-Gesellschaft. Home: Beausite," North St., Greenwich, Conn. Office: 200 Madison Av., New York NY‡

LEARY, FRANCIS THOMAS, journalist; b. New London, Conn., Jan. 31, 1914; s. Cornelius Patrick and Elizabeth (Galligan) L.; student Bliss Sch. Elec. Engring., Washington; m. Esther Sharpe, Aug. 16, 1940; children—Edward S., Karen M. With United Press Internat., 1934-68, central div. news mgr., 1948-59, day news mgr. N.Y.C., 1958-60, mng. editor world hdqrs., N.Y.C., 1960-65, vice president and executive editor, 1965-68. Member FCC nat. advisory committee, 1964-68. Served with AUS, 1944-46. Mem. Chgo. Press Vets., Sigma Delta Chi. Clubs: National Press; Chicago Press. Home: New Rochelle NY Died Sept. 1968.

LEARY, MONTGOMERY ELIHU, physician; b. Rochester, N.Y., July 9, 1868; s. Daniel and Caroline W. (Montgomery) L.; A.B., U. of Rochester, 1892; M.D., U. of Pa., 1895; m. Caroline A. Tegg, Aug. 6, 1896 (died Oct. 30, 1936); m. 2d, Norma C. Shaughnessy, May 16, 1941. Coroner's physician, Rochester, 1898-1902; lecturer on physiology and biology, Mechanics' Inst., Rochester, 1898-1904; sec. Rochester Acad. of Science 1898-1904; health officer, Gates, N.Y., 1896-1920; sec. and managing dir. Rochester Pub. Health Assn., 1896-1910, v.p., 1911-18; organized first open air school for pre-tubercular pupils in State of New York, 1908, founder, supt., sec. and treas. Iola Sanatorium (tuberculosis hosp.), 1910-17; sec. Supts. and Mgrs. of Tuberculosis Hosps., 1914-17; trustee and sec. Children's Hosp.; etc. Mem. A.M.A., Medical Society State of New York, Rochester Pathological Society, Monroe County Medical Society, Rochester Medical Assn., Academy of Medicine, Assn. Military Surgeons, Am. Sanatorium Assn., Nat. Tuberculosis Assn., Am. Pub. Health Assn., N.Y. State Sanitary Officers' Assn. (ex-pres.), Delta Kappa Epsilon, Am. Legion (comdr. Memorial Post, 1922-23; v. comdr. Monroe County Legion, 1927-29, 1948-49); comdr. Rochester Chap. Mil. Order World War, 1921-22, 1923-26; pres. Rochester Chapter No. 61, National Sojourners' (mem. com. of 33 since 1934); nat. surgeon of National Sojourners, 1936-47. Commissioned captain Medical R.C., U.S. Army, June

11, 1918; maj. M.C., Oct. 11, 1918; served at Gen. Hosp. No. 16, New Haven, Conn., Gen. Hosp. No. 18, Waynesville, N.C., and Base Hosp., Camp Jackson, S.C.; disch., 1918; col. M.C., O.R.C. Called to active duty, U.S. Army, as med. officer in charge of med. care of personnel in Rochester Area, June 1, 1943-Aug. 1, 1945. Spl. citation for war services, 1947. In charge for Monroe County, N.Y., of Citizens' Mil. Training Camps since 1921. Mem. Rochester Council Boy Scouts America, 1923-29. Republican. Presbyn. Mason (32 deg., K.T., Shriner; mem. service and rehabilitation com. of N.Y. Grand Lodge), K.P. Rotarian. Adopted, Oct. 3, 1915, into Seneca Indian Tribe, Beaver Clan, and given name of Hah-yah-dah-ga-has (Great Benefactor"); adopted, Mar. 29, 1941, by same tribe, Snipe Clan, and given name of Ha-dey-jehs-go-wah (Great Medicine Man"). Home: 827 W. Main Rochester 11 NY‡

LEAVELLE, ROBERT BRYAN, surgeon; b. Los Angeles, Oct. 22, 1916; s. Arnaud B. and Elizabeth (Bryan) L.; A.B., U. Cal. at Los Angeles, 1938; M.D., U. So. Cal., 1943. Intern, Los Angeles County Gen. Hosp., 1943-44; resident in ophthalmology Mass. Eye and Ear Infirmary, Boston, 1951-54, ophthalmic surgeon, 1954; practice medicine specializing in ophthalmology, Los Angeles, 1954-69; asst. clin. prof. ophthalmology surgery U. Cal. at Los Angeles, 1955-69; staff surgeon St. Joseph Hosp., Burbank, Cal., Valley Presbyn. Hosp., Van Nuys, Cal., Jules Stein Eye Inst., Los Angeles; cons. retinal detachment U.S. Vets Hosp., Los Angeles. Diplomate Am. Bd. Ophthalmology. Mem. Am., Los Angeles County med. assns., Los Angeles Soc. Ophthalmology, Pacific Coast Oto-Ophthal. Soc. Club: Lakeside Golf (North Hollywood, Cal.). Home: Encino CA Died May 10, 1969.

LE BLOND, HAROLD R., business exec. Chmn. bd. J. H. Day Co. (formerly Cleve. Automatic Machine Co.); dir. U.S. Shoe Corp., Cin. Gas & Electric Co., Cin. Enquirer, Inc. Home: Indian Hill OH Died June 22, 1968; buried Spring Grove Cemetery, Cincinnati OH

LE BRETON, TOMAS ALBERTO, Argentine diplomat; b. Buenos Aires, 1868; s. Tomas Le Breton and Dolores Ibarguren; ed. Faculty of Law, Buenos Aires (degree of Lawyer, 1885-91); m. Maria Pereyra. Co-founder of Young Peoples' Civic Union, Buenos Aires, 1889; on confidential diplomatic mission (ad honorem) to Europe, in connection with boundary dispute between Argentina and Brazil; del. Congress of Industrial Properties of Berlin, 1904; deputy from Federal Capital, 1914-18, 1918-20; pres. of Buenos Aires committee, Civic Radical Union, 1915-16; ambassador to U.S., 1920-22; minister of agr., 1922-28; ambassador to France, 1930-38; ambassador extraordinary to England for coronation of George VI, 1937; ambassador to Great Britain since 1938; on bd. of dirs. of Belgian-Argentine Bank. Mem. College of Lawyers, Buenos Aires; Academie d'Agriculture, France; scientific and juridical societies, London, Paris, Wash., and Melbourne; Buenos Aires Rowing Club. Author of Patentes de invencion; also contbr. to La Pressa, La Argentina, La Epoca, B.A. Address: Cangallo 466, Buenos Aires Argentina*‡

LECHNER, CARL BERNARD, physician; b. Erie, Pa., Dec. 11, 1908; s. Bernard Joseph and Katherine Mary (Klang) L.; M.D., Western Res. U., 1935; m. Dolores Barbara Tellers, July 22, 1936; children—Carl Bernard, Richard J., Brenda (Mrs. Dana F. Bigelow), Mark D. Intern, St. Vincent's Hosp., Erie, 1935-36, asst. radiologist, until 1970, head radiology, 1965-70; postgrad. in radiology U. Pa., 1939-40, Drs. Putts and Bacon, 1940-42; asst. radiologist Hamot Hosp., Erie. Pres., United Fund Erie County, 1961-62; mem. law adv. bd. Mercyhurst Coll., 1968-70; mem. Erie Arts Council. Served to maj., M.C., AUS, 1942-45. Diplomate Am. Bd. Radiology. Fellow Am. Coll. Radiology, Am. Roentgen Ray Soc., Am. Med. Writers Assn.; mem. A.M.A., Pa. (pres.-elect 1969-70), Erie County (pres. 1956-57) med. socs., Radiol. Soc. N.Am., Alpha Omega Alpha. Roman Catholic. Med. editor: Pa. Medicine, Erie PA Died Oct. 13, 1970; buried Trinity Cemetery, Erie PA

LECLAIR EDWARD E(MILE), JR., educator, anthropologist; b. Southbridge, Mass., Sept. 27, 1922; s. Edward E(mile) and Marguerite (Bosquet) LeC.; student Wesleyan U., Middletown, Conn., 1940-41; A.B., Clark U., 1948, M.A., 1949, Ph.D., 1953; student Northwestern U.,1951-52; m. Doris Marie Girard, July 20, 1945; children—David Alan, Robert Richard. Asst. prof. Norwich U., 1950-51; instr. Middlebury Coll., 1952-55; asst. prof. Cornell U., 1955-58, project field dir. unvi. India project, 1955-56; mem. faculty Rensselaer Poly. Inst., 1958-69, prof. anthropology, chmn. dept., 1964-69; lit. editor Albany (N.Y.) Times-Union, 1961-66. Dir., vice president R.C. Fund for Campers, Inc. Served with USAAF, 1943-46. Research Tng. fellow Social Sci. Research Council, 1951-52. Fellow Am. Anthrop. Assn.; mem. Soc. Applied Anthropology, Am. Ethnol. Soc. Co-editor: Economic Anthropology: A Reader in the Theory and Analysis, 1968. Home: Troy NY Died Sept. 23, 1969; buried St. Mary's Cemetery, Troy NY

LECLAIR, TITUS G., engr. exec.; b. Superior, Wis., Aug. 26, 1899; B.S., Electrical Engineering, University of Idaho, D.Sc., 1951; married; children—Richard D., Hugh G., David V., Diane B. Test engr., General Electric Co., 1922-23; various positions with Commonwealth Edison Co., 1923-32; development engr., 1932-36; supervising development engr., 1936-42; staff asst., 1943-45; chief staff engr., Commonwealth Edison Co., 1945-48, asst. chief elec. engr., 1948-50, chief electrical engr., 1950-52; mgr. engring. Commonwealth Edison Co., 1952-54, engring. assistant to v.p., 1954-56, mgr. research and development, 1956-60; nuclear cons., 1960-64, mgr. nuclear power applications gen. atomic div. Gen. Dynamics (now Gulf Gen. Atomic), San Diego, 1960-68. Fellow I.E.E.E. (dir. 1941-45, v.p. 1946-48, pres. 1950-51); mem. Am. Nuclear Soc. (dir.), Engrs. Joint Council pres. 1952), Am. Soc. Engring. Edn., Ill. Engring. Coun. (dir. and p.p.), Western Soc. Engrs. (p.p.), Ill. and Nat. socs. profl. engineers, Sigma Nu, Eta Kappa Nu. Club: Union League. Author of numerous papers pub. in technical press and given before engring. socs. Inventor pilot wire relay schemes, high current conductors, automatic multicircuit printing ammeters and other devices used in the electrical industry. Home: La Jolla CA Died Mar. 26, 1968.

LECOMPTE, IRVILLE CHARLES, educator; b. Pittston, Pa., July 31, 1872; s. Charles Thomas and Mary Jane (Calkins) L.; B.A., Wesleyan U., Conn., 1897; studied Columbia, 1897-99; Ph.D., U. of Strassburg, 1905; m. Harriet B. MacLachlan, Mar. 26, 1902; 1 son, Philip Medford. Instr. Barnard Sch. for Boys, N.Y. City, 1897-1900; prof. Eng. lang. and lit., Ursinus Coll., Collegeville, Pa., 1900-03; instr. and asst. prof. French, Yale, 1905-17; prof. Romance langs., University of Minnesota, August 1917-June 1941, emeritus since June 1941. Mem. of Modern Language Association of America, Delta Kappa Epsilon, Phi Beta Kappa. Club: Campus. Episcopalian. Contributor articles on Early French and Provincial lang. and lit., in Modern Philology, and the Romanic Rev., The Roman des Romans, Elliott Monographs, 1923. Compiler: (with Colbert Searles) Anthology of Modern French Literature, 1931. Author: Unified French Course (with Myrtle Violet-Sundeen), 1937. Home: 1000 University Av., S.E., Minneapolis MN‡

LECOMPTE, KARL MILES, congressman; b. Corydon, Ia., May 25, 1887; s. Charles Francis and Hannah (Miles) LeC.; A.B., State U. of Ia., 1909; m. Dorothy Tye, Aug. 10, 1927. Pub. Corydon Times-Republican, 1910-72; mem. 76th-85th Congresses, 4th Ia. Dist. Mem. State Senate Ia., 1916-20. Served in U.S. Army, 1918. Mem. Ia. Hist. Soc., Sigma Delta Chi, Sigma Delta Kappa, Phi Theta Pi. Republican. Mason, Elk, K.P. Home: Corydon IA Died 1972.

LEDDY, BERNARD JOSEPH, judge; b. Underhill, Vt., March 18, 1910; s. John Thomas and Anna (Marlow) L.; A.B., St. Michael's Coll., 1931; LL.B., Boston Coll. Law Sch., 1934; m. Johannah Mahoney, July 15, 1939; children—Ann (Mrs. Alan J. Charron), James Patrick, Johannah (Mrs. Thomas J. Donovan), Mary E., John. Admitted to State of Vt. bar, on October 5, 1934; alderman for the City of Burlington 1935-40; Dem. candidate for atty. gen. of Vt., 1938, for Congress, 1940; asst. U.S. atty. for Vt., 1940-54; U.S. district judge, District of Vt., 1966-72; Dem. candidate for governor Vermont, 1958; civilian aide to sec. of army, 1962-66. Associate trustee, St. Michael's College, Winooski Park, Vermont; trustee Med. Center Hospital of Vt., Inc., Burlington, Fanny Allen Hospital, Colchester, Vt. Mem. Am. and Vt. bar assns. Home: Burlington VT Died Jan. 9, 1972; buried Resurrection Park, South Burlington VT

LEDERER, FRANCIS LOEFFLER, surgeon; b. Chgo., Sept. 18, 1898; s. Jacob and Frances (Loeffler) L.; S.B., U. Chgo., 1918; M.D., Rush Med. Coll., 1921; postgrad. U. Berlin and U. Vienna, 1925; m. Anne Pollock, Mar. 4, 1925; 1 son, Francis II. Practiced in Chgo., 1921-73; emeritus prof., former head dept. otolaryngology U. Ill.; mem. sr. staff Michael Reese, Grant, Columbus hosps.; former chief otolaryngol. service Research and Ednl. Hosps., and dir. otolaryngol. service Ill. Eye and Ear Infirmary, Hines Hosp. (sr. cons.); cons. emeritus Presbyn.-St. Luke's Hosp.; cons. otolaryngology VA; nat. cons. surgeon gen. USAF. Served with U.S. Marines, World War I; captain M.C. (S) USNR, World War II; chief eye, ear, nose and throat service, chief aural rehab. U.S. Naval Hosp., Phila., 1942-46. Cons. otolaryngology U.S. Naval Hosp., Great Lakes, Ill. Fellow A.C.S., Internat. Coll. of Surgeons (hon.); mem. A.M.A., Ill., Chgo. med. socs., Inst. Med., Chgo. Lryngol. and Otol. Soc., Am. Otol. Soc. (past pres.), Chgo. Path. Soc., Am. Acad. Ophthalmology and Otolaryngology (past pres.), Am. Otol., Rhinol. and Laryngol. Soc., Am. Laryngological Assn., Am. Bronchoesophagol Assn., Am. Coll. Chest Physicians, Am. Assn. Mil. Surgeons, Sigma Xi, Alpha Omega Alpha, Phi Delta Epsilon, others. Mason (32, Shriner). Jewish religion. Author: Diseases of the Ear, Nose and Throat, 6th edit., 1953. Co-author: Atlas of Otorhinolaryngology and Bronchoesophagology, 1968. Contbr. to jour. and books on subjects pertaining to ear, nose and throat splty. Home: Chicago IL Died Apr 3, 1973.

LEDNICKI, WACLAW, educator; b. Moscow, Russia, Apr. 28, 1891; s. Alexander and Maria (Odlanicka-Poczobutt) L.; student Polish lang. and lit., U. of Cracow, 1910-11; diploma 1st degree in Romance and German philology, U. of Moscow, 1915; Ph.D., U. of Cracow, 1922; m. Baroness Isabella Heydel, Aug. 11, 1920 (marriage annulled, 1938); children—Jan, Maria. Sec. Polish Mission, Moscow, 1918; in Polish Fgn. office, 1919-21; docent history of Russian lit., U. of Wilno, 1926; charge de cours Slavonic langs. and lits., U. of Brussels, 1926-28; prof. agree, 1932, honorary professor, 1947; professor extraordinary history of Russian literature, University of Cracow, 1928-34, ordinary professor, 1935-39; visiting lecturer in Slavic, Harvard Univ., 1940-44; prof. agree Ecole Libre des Hautes Etudes, N.Y. City; vis. prof. Slavic Dept., U. Cal., 1944-45; prof. Slavic languages, U. Cal., from 1945, chmn. Slavic dept., 1949-50, and 1952-58; lectr. Lowell Inst., Boston, 1943. Volunteered I Lancer's Regt., Polish Army, 1918-19, participated in action; released for service in ministry of Fgn. Affairs, 1919; volunteer Bolshevik-Polish War, 1920. Chmn. founder of Polish Soc. for Study of Eastern Europe and the Near East, Cracow; vice pres. Polish Commn. Polish-Belgian Intellectual Exchange, 1936; member of committee Oriental and Slavonic Institute, Brussels; chairman, section literature and arts, mem. board of Polish Inst. of Arts and Scis., 1942; corr. mem. Polish Acad. of Scis. and Letters, 1937, Sch. of Slavonic Studies, Kings Coll., London, 1928; fgn. mem. Slavonic Inst., Praha, 1938; mem. Polish Sci. Council Abroad, 1949, council humanities div. Polish U. Abroad, 1951 (both London); mem. Polish Lit.-Hist. Soc. Paris, 1952; hon. mem. Polish Historical Society London, 1954. Decorated Cross of Valour; commander Belgian Order of Leopold; Grand Officer of Order Polonia Restituta, 1958; received gold medal, high school, Moscow, Medal of Alliance Francaise for knowledge of French; Medal University of Brussels, 1948, 57; Kosciuszko Foundation Medal, 1959; Guggenheim fellowship, 1953, 57. Club: Faculty (U. Cal.). Author several books from 1923, including: Russia, Poland and the West, 1954; Pushkin's Bronze Horseman (The Story of a Masterpiece), 1955; Bits of Table Talk on Pushkin, Mickiewicz, Goethe, Turgenev and Sienkiewicz, 1956. Editor publs. Polish Soc. Study Eastern Europe and the Near East (17 vols.); collective work on Pushkin, 1939, on Mickiewicz, 1956. Contbr. European and Am. revs. Home: Berkeley CA Died Oct. 27, 1967.

LEDVINA, EMMANUEL B., bishop; b. Evansville, Ind., Oct. 28, 1868; s. George E. and Mary (Kiefer) L.; ed. St. Meinrad. (Ind.) Coll. and Sem. Ordained priest R.C. Ch., 1893; asst. pastor Holy Trinity Ch., Evansville, 1893-94; asst. St. John's Church, Indianapolis, 1894-95; pastor St. Joseph's Ch., Princeton, Ind., 1895-1907; 1st gen. sec. Catholic Extension Soc. of Chicago, 1907-21, also v.p.; elevated to rank of domestic prelate by Pope Benedict XV, 1918; hon. canon of the Basilica of Our Lady of Guadalupe of Nat. Shrine of Mexico, 1919; consecrated bishop of Corpus Christi, June 14, 1921, retired; made asst. to the Pontifical Throne, May 30, 1931. Home: 620 Lipan St., Corpus Christi TX‡

LEDYARD, JOSHUA HEARD, cotton mfr.; b. Shubuta, Miss., Sept. 3, 1875; s. Thomas A. and Carrie (Heard) L.; A.B., Agrl. and Mech. Coll. of Miss., 1892; studied Lowell (Mass.) Textile Sch.; m. Anne Robins, June 23, 1901; children—Dabney Allen, Quitman Robins, Caroline Heard, Annie Bell, Frances Heard. Asst. mgr. Meridian (Miss.) Cotton Mills, 1903-05; treas. and gen. mgr. Tupelo Cotton Mills since 1905; dir. Cotton States Life Ins. Co., Southern Art. Corp. Capt. Co. A, Miss. Nat. Guard, 1892; mem. Internat. Jury Textiles, St. Louis Expn., 1903; mem. U.S. Price Fixing Com. for Textiles, 1918-19. Mem. Gen. Bd. M.E. Ch., S.; chmn. Am. Red Cross, Lee County, Miss. Mem. Sigma Alpha Epsilon. Mason, K. of P. Club: Rotary. Home: Tupelo MS‡

LEE, DAVID B., san. engr.; b. Douglasville, Ga., Sept. 23, 1907; s. W. A. and Mollie (Smith) L.; B.S., U. Fla., 1932, D.Sc. (hon.), 1968; M.S., Harvard U., 1937; married Billie Rawls, July 28, 1939; children—David B., and Susan Rawls. With Fla. State Bd. of Health 1932-68, field engr., 1934-35, dist. engr., 1935-37, malaria control engr., 1938-41, dir. Bur. San. Engring., 1941-68; pres. David B. Smith Engrs., Inc., Gainesville, 1968. Loaned by U.S. Army to Inst. of Inter-Am. Affairs specialist in malaria control engring; spl. consultant U.S.P.H.S. on san. engring. problems 1948-68, engring. dir. res.; vis. lectr. U. Fla., 1959-60; permanent chairman Fla. com. on water supply and sewerage edn., U. Fla.; registered prof. engr. State of Fla. Adv. to U.S. World Health Orgn.; mem. delegation 2d World Health Assembly, Rome, 1949; conferred with A.E.C. on radioactive indsl. waste disposal; served on panel of environmental sanitation of the President's Commn. on Health Needs of the Nation, 1952; mem. Nat. Research Council's Commission on san. engineering and environment. Served as maj. San. Corps, Med. Dept., U.S. Army, 1942-45. Received Kenneth Allen award Fedn. Sewage Works Assns., 1948; award Fla. Engring. Soc. for exeptional service to engring. profession State of Fla., 1949; Man of Year award, Am. Soc. San. Engring., 1954; Centennial award

U. Fla., 1953; Fuller award Am. Water Works Assn., 1954; Meritorious award Fla. Pub. Health Assn., 1964. One of Ten Top Men Yr., 1961, Am. Pub. Works Assn.; Gold Merit award notable achievement state govt. service Asso. Industries Fla., 1965; Charles Alvin Emerson medal meritorious service Water Pollution Control Federation, 1966. Fellow of the Fla. Engring. Society (secretary 1946-50, president 1952-53), Am. Pub. Health Association; member Nat. Assn. Sanitation (hon.), Nat. Soc. Profl. Engrs. (dir.), Fedn. Sewage and Indsl. Waste Assns. (pres. 1954-55) Conf. State San. Engrs. (chairman 1948-49), Am. Water Works Assn. (nat. dir. 1948-51; vice chmn. Fla. sect., 1957-58, chmn. 1958-59), Newcomen Soc. N.A. (mem. Fla. com.), Acad. Sanitary Engrs. Council Cons., Nat. Sanitation Found., Harvard Pub. Health Alumni Assn., Fla. Water and Sewage Works Operators Assn. (life), Fla. Pub. Health Assn. (pres. 1950-51), Fla. Anti-Mosquito Assn. (pres. 1946-47), Am. Soc. C.E., Fla. Pollution Assn. (pres. 1941-42, hon. mem. 1956), Nat. Swimming Pool Inst., Water Pollution Control Federation (honorary), Sigma Tau. Episcopalian (sr. warden). Club: Kiwanis (pres. 1953). Home: Jacksonville FL Died Oct. 31, 1968; buried Pensacola FL

LEE, DELIA FOREACRE (MRS. BLEWETT LEE), librarian; b. Atlanta, Ga., 1871; d. Capt. Greenberry Jones (C.S.A.) and Delia (Nicholls) Foreacre; ed. pvt. sch., Atlanta; Pratt Inst. Sch. of Library Science, 1904-6; m. Percival C. Sneed, of Savannah, Ga., Nov. 8, 1892 (died 1900); 2d, Blewett Lee, of Chicago, July 20, 1915. Instr. Atlanta Library Sch., 1906-8, chief instr., 1908-11, prin., 1911-14; librarian Carnegie Library of Atlanta and dir. Library Sch., 1914-15. Episcopalian. Mem. Council A.L.A.; pres. League of Library Commrs., 1908-9; organizer and mem. Georgia Library Commn. since 1906. Home: 716 Rush St., Chicago‡

LEE, FREDERIC PADDOCK, lawyer; b. Lincoln, Neb., Jan. 6, 1893; s. George Sterling and Maud Maria (Paddock) L.; Ph.B., Hamilton Coll., Clinton, N.Y., 1915, LL. D., 1964; M.A., Columbia, 1916, LL.B., 1918; m. Marian A. Armstrong, June 22, 1918; children—Eleanor (Mrs. Frederick R. Ahmuty), Sterling, Barbara (Mrs. Walker B. Blincoe), Richard Curry. Began as assistant legislative counsel United States House of Representatives, 1919-23; legislative counsel, U.S. Senate, 1923-30; mem. law firm of MacCracken & Lee, Washington, 1930-34; spl. counsel Sec. of Agr., 1933; member board and gen. counsel Federal Alcohol Control Adminstrn., 1934-35; mem. law firm Alvord & Alvord, Washington, D.C., 1935-49; mem. law firm Lee, Toomey & Kent 1950-61, ret., 1961; prof. law Georgetown University, 1929-35; dir. Garlock, Inc., 1952-62. Lectr. on law, polit. sci. at various times Williams Coll., Harvard, Brookings Instn., U. Va., Am. U. Columbia U. President County Council for Montgomery County, Md., 1949-50, Montgomery County (Md.) Civic Fed., 1931-33; mem. Maryland Nat. Capital Park and Planning Commn., 1934-35; chmn. Montgomery Co. (Md.) Charter Bd., 1942-44; mem., chmn. adv. council Nat. Arboretum, 1946-68. Trustee Hamilton Coll., 1942-63, emeritus, 1963-68; trustee Schwarzhaupt Found., 1937-68, Washington Center for Met. Studies, 1961-68. Served as private inf., 1918; 2d lt. inf. O.R.C., 1918-23; capt. judge advocate, 1924-29. Mem. Am., D.C. bar assns., Assn. Bar City N.Y., Am. Soc. Internat. Law, Am. Hort. Soc. (dir. 1951-68, 1st v.p. 1947-50, Gold medal 1959), Am. Rhododendron Soc. (gold medal for hort. achievement 1964), N.Am. Lily Soc., Am. Daffodil Soc., Am. Holly Soc., Am. Assn. Bot. Gardens and Arboretums, Internat. Soc. Plant Taxonomy, Royal Hort. Soc. Democrat. Clubs: Cosmos, Columbia Country. (Washington). Author: The Azalea Book, 1958. to profl. jours. Home: Bethesda MD Died Oct. 2, 1968; buried Hamilton College, Clinton NY

LEE, GORDON CANFIELD, educator; b. N.Y.C., Feb. 26, 1916; s. Edwin A. and Edna (Canfield) L.; B.A., U. Cal. at Berkeley, 1937; M.A., Columbia, 1938, Ph.D., 1948; m. Grace Marietta Eaton, June 22, 1940; children—Marshall MacDowell, Gordon Tamalon. Tchr. history, civics and English, Univ. High Sch., Oakland, Cal., 1938-42; tchr. history Beverly Hills (Cal.) High Sch., 1942-43; instr. history edn. Columbia Tchrs. Coll., 1947-48; prof. edn., chmn. dept. edn. Pomona Coll., Claremont, Cal., 1948-58; prof. history and philosophy edn. Columbia Tchrs. Coll., 1958-61, prof., 1967-69, on leave as chief of party U.S. AID team, Kabul, Afghanistan, 1967; dean Coll. Edn., Tex. Tech. U., 1969-72; dean Coll. of Edn., U. Wash., 1961-67. Resident prof. Claremont Grad. Sch., summer 1948-50, 52, 53, 55, Columbia Tchrs. Colls., 1958-61; vis. prof. U. Cal. at Berkeley, summer 1951, U. Cal. at Los Angeles, 1957, Columbia Tchrs. Coll., 1956, U. Alaska, 1960; vis. lectr. Fulbright Conf. Am. Studies, Cambridge (Eng.) U., summer 1952. Hon. adviser British Summer Sch. Program, 1954-58; adviser ednl. policies commn. N.E.A., 1955-72. Served with AUS, 1943-46. Fulbright Research fellow U.K., 1953-54. Mem. Am. Hist. Assn., N.E.A., Nat. Soc. Coll. Tchrs. Edn., Am. Assn. U. Profs., Phi Delta Kappa. Author: The Struggle for Federal Aid: First Phase, 1949; An Introduction to Education in Modern America, rev. edit., 1957; Crusade Against Ignorance: Thomas Jefferson on Education, 1961; Education and Democratic Ideals, 1965. Co-editor: Crucial Issues in Education, An Anthology, 1959, rev., 1964. Home: Lubbock TX Died Nov. 26, 1972.

LEE, GYPSY ROSE (ROSE LOUISE HOVICK), entertainer; b. Wash. state, Jan. 9, 1914; d. John M. and Rose (Thompson) Hovick; m. Arnold R. Mizzy, 1937 (div. 1941); m. 2d, Alexander Kirkland, 1942 (div. 1944); 1 son, Erik; m. 3d, Julio de Deigo, 1948 (div. 1955). Debut as entertainer Knights of Pythias, Seattle, 1917, burlesque dancer Minsky's Theatre; appeared in motion picture My Lucky Star, also Belle of the Yukon; role Broadway musical, Star and Garter, 1942; head nat. company Threepenny Opera, 1961; hostess syndicated TV talk show, 1966. Entertainer war bond drives, U.S. Army camp shows, other benefits. Author: The G-String Murders; Mother Finds A Body; (play) The Naked Genius, 1943; Gypsy, 1957 (Broadway musical 1959). Home: Beverly Hills CA Died Apr. 1970.

LEE, JAMES J., investment banker; b. Newton, Mass., Nov. 22, 1900; s. George C. and Madeline (Jackson) L.; A.B., Harvard, 1924; m. Emily D. Schniewind, Apr. 10, 1926; children—James J., Henry C. With Lee Higginson & Co., 1924-26, 28-32, Higginson & Co., London, Eng., 1926-27; with Lee Higginson Corp., N.Y. City, 1932-51, v.p., dir., resigned 1952; gen. partner W. E. Hutton & Co., investment bankers, 1952-72; dir. Hampton Shirt Co., Kinston, N.C. Bd. govs. Am. Stock Exchange, 1964-69. Mayor Inc. Village of Muttontown (N.Y.). Mem. Investment Bankers Assn: Am. (pres. 1959-60). Episcopalian. Club: The Creek. Home: Syosset NY Died Dec. 1972.

LEE, JOSEPH WILCOX JENKINS, diplomat; b. Oct. 9, 1870; s. Charles O'Donnell and Matilda (Jenkins) L.; ed. U. of Md. Traveled in Brazil, 1884, 1887, 1900 and 3,000 miles up Amazon Valley in connection Acre Rubber Concession and boundary trouble, 1901. Sec. Am. Legation at Panama, 1904-5; consul-gen. to Panama, Mar. to Sept., 1905; E.E. and M.P. to Ecuador, 1905-7, to Guatemala and Honduras, Jan. 10-July 1, 1907, to Guatemala, July 1, 1907-Mar., 1908. Planter at Needwood Forest," Knoxville, Md., since Mar., 1908; m. Mary Kuhn Harris, of Philadelphia, May 18, 1911. Fellow Royal Geog. Soc. of Great Britain; mem. Nat. Geog. Soc. Club: Calumet (New York). Author: Ropes of Sand (poems); Hilos de Arena (published in Guatemala), 1907 Address: Knoxville MD‡

LEE, MANFRED B., (co-writer with Frederic Dannay, under pseud. Ellery Queen and Barnaby Ross); m. Kaye Brinker, July 4, 1942; eight children. Co-author numerous books 1929-71; latest publs.; The Murder Is a Fox, 1945; Rogues' Gallery, 1945; To the Queen's Taste, 1946; Ellery Queen's Awards annually, 1946-71; 20th Century Detective Stories, 1948; Cat of Many Tales, 1949; Double, Double, 1950; The Literature of Crime, 1950; The Origin of Evil, 1951; Calendar of Crime, The King Is Dead, 1952; The Scarlet Letters, 1953; The Glass Village, 1954; Quuen's Bureau of Investigation, 1955; Inspector Queen's Own Case, 1956; In the Queen's Palor, 1957; Ellery Queen's 13th Annual, 1958; The Finishing Stroke, 1958; Ellery Queen's 14th Annual, 1959; Ellery Queen's 15th Mystery Annual, 1960; Ellery Queen's 16th Mystery Annual, 1961; The Quintessence of Queen, 1962; The Player on the Other Side, 1963; To Be Read before Midnight, 1963; And on the Eighth Day, 1964; Ellery Queen's Internat. Case Book, 1964; Ellery Queen's Mystery Mix, 1964; Queens Full, 1965; Ellery Queen's Double Dozen, 1965; The Fourth Side of the Triangle, 1965; Ellery Queen's 20th Anniversary Annual, 1966; Ellery Queen's Crime Carousel, 1966; Face to Face, 1967; Ellery Queen's All-Star Lineup, 1967; Poetic Justice, published in 1967; (author with others) The Adventures of Ellery Queen, The Further Adventures of Ellery Queen, 1958; The House of Brass, 1968; Ellery Queen's Mystery Parade, 1968; Cop Out, 1969; Q.E.D.: Queen's Experiments in Detection, 1969; TV radio program and co-editor Ellery Queen's Mystery Mag. Recipient Edgar Allan Poe awards, Iona Coll. award in Mystery, 1968. Past co-pres., grand master Mystery Writers Am. Address: Roxbury CT Died Apr. 3, 1971; buried Roxbury CT

LEE, MARY CATHERINE (JENKINS), author; b. New Bedford, Mass.; d. Perez and Jane (Taber) Jenkins; ed. New Bodford and New York; m. Roswell Lee, of Springfield, Mass. Author: A Quaker Girl of Nantucket, 1889; In the Cheering-Up Business, 1891; A Soulless Singer, 1893; An Island Plant, 1895; Lois Mallet's Dangerous Gift, 1903; A Little Field of Glory, 1907. Address: Springfield MA‡

LEE, ROBERT CORWIN, shipping company executive; born Central City, Nebraska, Aug. 30, 1888; s. William A. and Molly (Foulks) L.; ed. U.S. Naval Acad.; m. Elsie Calder, June 15, 1918; children—Katherine Calder, Lee Keenan, Mary Anne Foulks, Lee Llerena, Elsie Calder Lee Brothers, Robert Corwin Jr. Officer, USN, 1906-20; captain Destroyer Wainwright, and U.S. Naval Port Officer at Nantes, France, during World War I. Pres. Foreign Shipping Service Co. and R.C. Lee, Inc., 1920; asst. treas. Moore & McCormack Co., Inc., 1921, now dir. and ret. chmn. bd., also ret. chmn. of all asso. cos.; v.p. Am. Scantic Line, Inc., from 1927; pres. Am. Scantic Line in Poland, from 1930, also dir. Served as capt. to commodore, spl. asst. Naval Trans. Service; with Admiral Nimitz staff in Pacific, Adm. Stark and Gen. Eisenhower in Europe; rear adm. USN. Received Cruzeiro do Sul of Brazil (Grande Oficial), Oficial do Merito Naval (Brazil), ship-owners delegate for U.S. to 21st and 22nd Maritime Sessions Internat. Labor Conf. at Geneva; member maritime section International Labor Conf., Geneva, Soc. of Naval Architects and Marine Engrs., Maritime Exchange, Knight Order of Polonia Restituta. Mason. Clubs: Somerset Lake and Game, Army-Navy, India House, Downtown Athletic (Washington); Morristown (N.J.); Nat. Republican. Home: New York City NY Died Sept. 1, 1971; buried Arlington National Cemetery, Arlington VA

LEE, THOMAS FITZHUGH, investment banking; b. Feb. 23, 1877; s. Henry F. and Josephine (Miller) L.; ed. Dennison U., Granville, O., Normal Sch., Ada, O., U. of Mich.; m. Julia Gorby, Sept. 9, 1897;children—Hal F., Robert E.; m. 2d, Peggy G. Wisdom, June 1, 1927. Engaged in civ. engring., on port works, Manzanillo, Mexico, later in ry. constrn. work, Mexico, 1904-07; financial and econ. survey and other financing, behalf of New York and Boston capitalists, 1907-11; engring., financing, developing, Rio Grande Valley, Tex., 1912-17; lecturing, writing, financial work, 1917-19; exec. dir. Nat. Assn. for Protection Am. Rights in Mexico, 1919-22; financial work and investment banking since 1922; organizer, 1928, North Am. Trust Shares; organized Latin Am. Bondholders Assn., Inc.; also devoting time to travel, lecturing, writing. Episcopalian. Mason. Clubs: Lotos, Downtown Athletic, Ends of Earth (New York). Author: Latin American Problems, 1932. Contbr. to Nat. Geographic Mag., World's Work, Outlook, Mentor, Travel, etc. Home: 6 Heathcote Rd., Scarsdale NY‡

LEE, WESLEY T(ERENCE), physician, educator; born Charleston, Mass., Mar. 8, 1872; s. John M. and Ellen M. (Moulton) L.; B. Chir., Boston U., 1897, M.D., 1898, D.Sc. (hon.), 1948; m. Alice H. Bidwell, June 18, 1908. Intern, Mass. Memorial Hosp., Boston, 1898-99; prof. dermatology, sch. medicine Boston U. since 1917. Trustee Boston U. (sec. exec. com.), Mass. Meml. Hosp. Served as maj., Medical Corps, 1919. Mem. Mass. Med. Soc., N.E. Dermatol. Soc., Alpha Sigma. Methodist (trustee). Mason. Home: 295 Beacon St., Boston 16 MA‡

LEEDOM, BOYD STEWART, govt. ofcl.; b. Alvord, Ia., Sept. 28, 1906; s. Chester Nevius and Gertrude Emmaline (Stewart) L.; LL.B., U. S.D., 1929; m. Irene Cecil Robertson, Dec. 29, 1927; children—Chester Boyd, Linda Ann, Mary Catherine. Admitted to S.D. bar, 1929; practiced in Rapid City, 1929-51; became justice Supreme Ct. of S.D., 1951; mem. NLRB, 1955-65, chmn., 1955-61, trial examiner, 1965-69. S.D. state senator 1949-50. Candidate Rep. nomination for gov. of S.D., 1950. Served as lt. USNR, 1943-45. Mem. Phi Delta Phi, Phi Delta Theta. Methodist. Mason. Home: Arlington VA Died Aug. 11, 1969.

LEEK, JOHN HALVOR, educator; b. Batavia, Ill., June 14, 1896; s. John DeWitt and Alice Maud (Button) L.; A.B., Millikin U., 1920; A.M., U. Ill., 1921; Ph.D., U. Pa., 1925. Instr. polit. sci. U. Pa., 1921-25; faculty U. Okla., from 1925, David Ross Boyd prof. govt., from 1949. Served with U.S. Army, 1918-19; AEF in France. Mem. So., Western polit. sci. assns., Southwestern Social Sci. Assn., Miss. Valley Hist. Assn., Am. Assn. U. Profs., Phi Beta Kappa. Author: Legislative Reference Service, 1925; Government and Labor in the United States, 1952. Co-author: Principles and Functions of Government in the United States, 1948. Home: Norman OK Died Feb. 14, 1967; buried I.O.O.F. Cemetery, Norman OK

LEERMAKERS, PETER ANTHONY, educator; b. Rochester, N.Y., Mar. 28, 1937; s. John A. and Jeanne (Olson) L.; B.A., Wesleyan U., Middletown, Conn., 1958; Ph.D., Cal. Inst. Tech., 1961. Postdoctoral fellow Yale, 1961-62; asst. prof. Wesleyan U., 1962-66, asso. prof., 1966-69, prof. chemistry, 1969-71; vis. prof. U. Wis., 1970. Cons. Scott Paper Co., 1966-70; reviewer for jours. and pub. cos. Alfred P. Sloan fellow, 1967-69. Mem. Am. Chem. Soc., Faraday Soc. Co-editor: Energy Transfer and Organic Photochemistry, Technique of Organic Chemistry Vol. XIV, 1969. Contbr. articles profl. jours. Home: Middletown CT Died Aug. 16, 1971; interred Mariposa CA

LEFEVRE, ALBERT, prof. philosophy; b. Baltimore, Oct. 4, 1873; s. Jacob Amos and Catherine Louise (Sauerwein) L.; A.B., U. of Tex., 1894, A.M., 1897; studied Johns Hopkins, 1894-5; Ph.D., Cornell U., 1898; studied U. of Berlin, 1899-1900; (LL.D., U. of S.C., 1905). Lecturer in philosophy, 1898-9, instr., 1900-2; asst. prof., 1902-3, Cornell U.; prof. philosophy, Tulane, 1903-5, U. of Va., since 1905. Presbyn. (Southern). Mem. Am. Philos. Soc., Southern Soc. Philosophy and Psychology (pres. 1909-10), Kappa Alpha, Phi Beta Kappa. Club: Colonnade (Va.). Translator: (with J. E. Creighton) Immanuel Kant—His Life and Doctrine (by Frederick Paulien), 1901. Home: University VA‡

LEFEVRE, FRANK JACOB, ex-congressman; b. New Paltz, N.Y., Nov. 30, 1874; s. Jacob and Ann Amelia (Woolsey) L. (Huguenot ancestry); ed. New Paltz Normal Sch.; m. Elizabeth Anderson, of Port Richmond, S.I., N.Y., Feb. 17, 1908. Pvt. sec. to father, during latter's terms in Congress, 1892-6; traveled for a yr. in West and Mexico; engaged in banking since Jan. 1, 1898; now pres. Huguenot Nat. Bank, to which was elected on death of father. Mem. N.Y. Senate, 1902-4, 25th N.Y. Dist.; supt. N.Y. State Bldg. at St. Louis Expn., 1904; mem. 59th Congress (1905-7), 24th N.Y. Dist. Address: New Paltz NY‡

LEFEVRE, JAY, congressman; b. New Paltz, N.Y., Sept. 6, 1893; s. Abram Philip and Mary Emma (Van Derlyn) LeF.; student Lawrenceville Acad., 1911-14, Dartmouth Coll., 1914-16; m. Mildred Hiltebrant, Jan. 3, 1920; children—Elaine, Jay Abram, John Hiltebrant. Began as coal, lumber and feed merchant, 1916; pres. A.P. LeFevre & Son; partner Clintondale Supply Co.; dir. Huguenot Nat. Bank; trustee New Paltz Savings Bank. Mem. 78th Congress (1943-44) 27th N.Y. Dist., 79th, 80th 81st Congresses (1945-51) 30th N.Y. District. Deputy dir. Civilian Defense. Trustee Village of New Paltz. Served as 2d lt., F.A., World War I. Trustee Memorial Library; sec. bd. of visitors New Paltz State Teachers Coll. Trustee Holland Soc. (N.Y.). Mem. exec. com. Lawrenceville Alumni; mem. Am. Legion, Alpha Delta Phi. Republican. Mem. Dutch Reformed Ch. Clubs: The Paltz, Army and Navy (Washington, D.C.); Twaalfskill (Kingston, N.Y.); Amrita (Poughkeepsie). Home: New Paltz NY Died Apr. 26, 1970.

LEFFINGWELL, FORREST EMMETT, physician; b. Severy, Kan., Apr. 21, 1904; s. Howard Gordon and Etta (Warner) L.; A.B., Union Coll., Lincoln, Neb., 1926; M.D., Loma Linda U., 1933; m. Shirley Nicola, Aug. 3, 1926. Intern, Glendale (Cal.) Sanitarium and Hosp., 1932-33; pvt. practice, Montebello, Cal., 1934-40; resident anesthesiology White Meml. Hosp., Los Angeles, 1940-41, dir. dept. anesthesiology, 1946-68; sr. attending anesthesiologist Los Angeles County Hosp., 1955-69; prof. anesthesiology, chmn. dept. Loma Linda U., 1955-66. Served to lt. col., M.C., AUS, 1941-46; PTO. Diplomate Am. Bd. Anesthesiology (sec.-treas. 1958-69, bd. dirs. 1955-69, pres. 1969). Mem. Am. (speaker ho. dels. 1953-60, bd. dirs. 1950-69, pres. 1961-62), Cal. (pres. 1949), socs. anesthesiologists, Am., Cal., Los Angeles County Med. assns., Internat. Anesthesiology Research Soc., Internat. Coll. Surgeons, Los Angeles Acad. Medicine. Acad. Anesthesiology, Alpha Omega Alpha. Address: Pasadena CA Died Oct. 28, 1919; buried Rose Hills, Whittier CA

LE FORGEE, CHARLES CHAMBERS, lawyer; b. Decatur, Ill., July 7, 1867; s. Jesse and Julia Alizabeth (Smallwood) LeF.; LL.B., Union Coll. of Law (Northwestern U.) Chicago, 1888; m. Isabel P. Vennigerholz, Nov. 20, 1895; children—Charles Granville, Isabel Valette (Mrs. William Barnes II). Practiced at Decatur since 1887; now mem. Le Forgee & Samuels; chief counsel A. E. Staley Mfg. Co. since 1910; chief counsel for trustees of Millikin University and for trustees of Estate of James Millikin; chief counsel for Len Small, governor of Illinois, in trial at Waukegan, Ill., 1921, leading to verdict of not guilty"; chief counsel for I.C. R.R. Co., at St. Paul, Minn., in litigation involving approximately $3,000,000 in personal injury cases, out of which originated doctrine restraining citizens of one state from going into another state to prosecute suit where the local court had jurisdiction. Mem. Am. and Ill. State bar assns., Phi Delta Phi. Democrat. Episcopalian. Clubs: Decatur, Country, Elks (Decatur). Home: 560 Powers Lane, Decatur, Ill., and Mackinac Island MI‡

LEFSCHETZ, SOLOMON, educator, mathematician; b. Moscow, Russia, Sept. 3, 1884; M.E., cole Centrale, Paris, France, 1905; Ph.D., Clark U., 1911; m. Alice Berg Hayes, July 3, 1913. With Westinghouse Electric & Mfg. Co., Pitts., 1907-10; instr. math. U. Neb., 1911-13; instr. math. U. Kan., 1913-16, asst. prof., 1916-19, asso. prof., 1919-23, prof., 1923-25; vis. prof. Princeton, 1924-25, asso. prof., 1925-28, prof., 1928-32, H.B. Fine Research prof., 1934-53, emeritus; prof. Nat. U. Mex., 1954-72; vis. prof. Brown U.; dir. RIAS Math. Center, 1958-72. Decorated associ tranger Order Aztec Eagle; recipient Bordin prize French Acad., for work in algebraic geometry, 1919; Bocher prize Am. Math Soc., 1924; Feltrinelli prize Academia dei Lincel, 1956; Nat. Medal of Sci. for Math., 1965. Mem. Royal Soc. (fgn.), Am. Math. Soc. (pres. 1935-36), Math. Assn. Am., A.A.A.S., Nat. Acad. Scis., Am. Philos. Soc., Societe Math. de France, Sociedad Mat. Mexicana, Academie des Sciences de Paris. Author of L'Analysis Situs et la Geometrie Algebrique, 1924; Topology, 1930; Algebraic Topology, 1942; Introduction to Topology, 1949; Algebraic Geometry, 1952; Differential Equations; Geometric Theary, 1958; (with J. P. Lasalle) Stability Theory by Liepunor's Direct Method; Stability of Nonlinear Control Systems, 1962. Home: Princeton NJ Died Oct. 27, 1972.

LEGGE, LIONEL KENNEDY, justice; b. Charleston, S.C., Dec. 11, 1889; s. Claude Lascelles and Elizabeth Judd (Hutchinson) L.; A.B., Coll. of Charleston, 1909, LL.D., 1955; m. Dorothy Haskell Porcher, Dec. 9, 1920; children—Dorothy Porcher (Mrs. Frederick Deane, Jr.), Elizabeth Lascelles (Mrs. John W. Littlefield). Admitted to S.C. bar, 1913; practicing atty., 1913-54; asso. justice Supreme Ct. S.C., from 1954. Served as capt., inf., AEF, 1917-19. Mem. Am., S.C. bar assns., S.C. Soc., Soc. of Cin. Home: Charleston SC Died July 22, 1970; buried St. Philip's Churchyard, Charleston SC

LEGGE, ROBERT THOMAS, physician, prof.; b. San Francisco, Calif., July 16, 1872; s. Robert and Anna (Stelljes) L.; Ph.G., U. of Calif., 1891, M.D., 1899; diploma, U. of Vienna, 1924; m. Rene Farjeon, Nov. 23, 1903; children—Robert Farjeon, Margery Ann, Herbert William. Interne St. Luke's Hosp., San Francisco, 1899; chief surgeon McCloud River R.R. and Hosp., 1900-14; prof. hygiene and univ. physician, U. of Calif., 1915-42, emeritus. Lecturer on industrial medicine, U. of Calif. Med. Sch.; specialist in industrial hygiene and surgery. Dir. of Ernest V. Cowell Meml. Hosp., U. of Calif., ret. Was capt. Med. Corps, U.S. Army, 1917-18; lt. col. Med. O.R.C. Recipient of William S. Knudsen Award, 1950-51. Member Alameda County Instns. Commn. Mem. permanent Internat. Com. on Indsl. Medicine. Mem. adv. council Calif. State Bd. Vocational Edn. (rehabilitation). Past pres. Western Assn. of Indsl. Physicians and Surgeons. Diplomate Am. Bd. Pub. Health and Preventive Medicine. Fellow Am. Coll. Surgeons; mem. A.M.A., A.A.A.S., Am. College Health Assn. (Pacific dir.), Acad. Occupational Med. (hon.), Pan Am. Med. Assn. (emeritus), Calif. Heart Assn., Calif. Council Agencies for Handicapped, Calif. Academy Med. Calif. State Med. Soc., Alameda Co. Medical Assn., Sigma Xi, Delta Omega, Alpha Kappa Lambda, Nu Sigma Nu, Ramazzini Soc., Scabbard and Blade; hon. mem. Am. Indsl. Physicians, Am. Assn. U. Profs. Republican. Episcopalian. Mason (K.T.). Clubs: Faculty, City Commons (Berkeley); Bohemian (San Francisco). Asso. editor Industrial Medicine and Surgery. Home: 6 Roble Rd., Berkeley 5 CA‡

LEGGETTE, LUBIN POE, educator; b. Fairmont, N.C., Sept. 12, 1912; s. William A. and Elizabeth (Purvis) L.; A.A., Mountain Park Coll., 1930; A.B., U. N.C., 1932, A.M., 1938; Ed.D., Columbia, 1956; m. Jeanne Hester, Sept. 17, 1943 (dec.); children—John McCrea, Thomas Alan, Lyle Poe; m. 2d, Martha Louise Oliver, November 8, 1963. Teacher, Reidsville (N.C.) High Sch., 1934-36; instr. English, speech Sullins Coll., Bristol, Va., 1938-40; instr. speech, drama Marshall Coll., Huntington, W.Va., 1940-42; directional staff Lost Colony, Roanoke Island Hist. Assn., summers 1937-41, 46; asst. prof. speech George Washington U., 1946-47, asso. prof., 1947-52, Depew prof., chmn. speech, drama dept., 1952-68; guest lectr. Naval Intelligence Sch., 1947, 49, Nat. War Coll., 1948-50. Walter Reid Army Med. Sch., 1950, 52; Cons. IBM, 1949-50, 52-53, Internat. Bank and Monetary Fund, 1952-54. Armed Forces Inst. Pathology, 1953-68, Army Engr. Research and Development Lab., 1954-68, Army Med. Service Sch., Ft. Sam Houston, 1957, Army Map Service, 1963-68. Cons. St. Elizabeth Hosp., 1966. President Fairfax County Cultural Association, member profl. advisory bd. Childrens Theatre of Washington, 1966-68; president of the Walnut Hill Citizens Assn., 1952-54; cons., prodn. exec. Faith of Our Fathers, Nat. Capital Sesquicentennial Commn., 1950-51. Served from ensign to lt. (s.g.), USNR, 1942-46. Member of the International Platform Association, Speech Assn. Am., Am. Ednl. Theatre Assn., Am. Assn. U. Profs., Nat. Acad. Polit. and Social Sci., Nat. Collegiate Players, Am. Acad. Polit. and Social Sci., Am. Soc. Tng. Dirs., Washington Drama Soc. (life), Kappa Delta Pi, Alpha Psi Omega, Phi Delta Kappa. Club: Arts (Washington). Home: Falls Church VA Died Feb. 8, 1968.

LEGIER, JOHN, banker; b. New Orleans, July 18, 1878; s. John Robert and Marie (Mason) L.; B.L., Tulane U., 1899; m. Henrietta Buddig, June 14, 1899 (dec. Jan. 1961); children—Henrietta Diga (Mrs. B. Colomb), Gladys (Mrs. Harold E. Clayton). Practice law in Parish of Orleans, Fed. Cts., Eastern dist. La., 1899-12; pres. Cosmopolitan Bank, New Orleans, 1912, (merged with City Bank) became pres. City Bank and Trust Co., 1913, this bank was sold to Whitney Bank, New Orleans, v.p., 1919-24; pres. Am. Bank, 1924-73, became Nat. Am. Bank of New Orleans, 1944, pres., chief exec. officer, 1944-58, chmn. bd., 1958-73, pres. 1963-65, also dir.; dir. WWL Broadcasting Sta. Bd. regents Loyola U. of South, New Orleans. Mem. Blue Key. Clubs: Southern Yacht (life), Boston (New Orleans). Home: New Orleans LA Died Jan. 5, 1973.

LEHMAN, ALCUIN WILLIAMS, advt. media research specialist; b. East Steuben, N.Y., June 13, 1897; s. Fletcher Van Wie and Jennie Alice (Williams) L.; student New York U. Sch. of commerce, 1920-23; m. Adelina Perrotty, May 10, 1944. Specialty selling, New York City, 1921-25; chain store merchandising in New York City, 1925-28; mgr. research and service depts., Association National Advertisers, New York, 1928-41, asst. mng. dir., 1929-41; mgr. Cooperative Analysis of Broadcasting, 1934-44, pres., 1944-46; tech. dir. Advertising Research Foundation, Inc., New York, 1941-44, mng. dir., pres., 1949-66, cons., 1966-70; mng. dir. Traffic Audit Bur., 1943-44, tech. cons., 1944-45. Guest lectr. Am. Press Inst., Columbia, 1946-51. Mem. Am. Statistical Association, Market Research Council, Royal Statistical Society, also member Delta Sigma Pi. Mem. Dutch Reformed Ch. Clubs: Metropolitan Southampton (New York) Beach. Author: (with George H. Allen) How to Conduct Consumer and Opinion Research, 1946; Radio Programs, The New Internat. Year Book, 1943, 44; Ten Years of Network Program Analysis, 1939; Program Popularity in 1938, 1939, 40, 41, 42, 43, Broadcasting Yearbook, 1939-44; The Advertiser Looks at Radio, 1930; Survey of Window Display Installation Services, A Comparison of Local and National Newspaper Rates, 1929; Audience Study of 11 Magazines in Canada, 1949. Home: New York City NY also Southampton NY Died Aug. 23, 1970; buried Gate of Heaven, Hawthorne NY

LEHMAN, EUGENE HEITLER, educator; b. Pueblo, Colo., Sept. 5, 1879; s. Moritz and Rosa (Heitler) L.; B.A., Yale, 1902, M.A., 1910; studied University of Berlin and Columbia; married Madeleine Davidsburg, April 2, 1913 (died December 1, 1931); children—Eugene Herbert, Godfrey, Carol Estelle; married 2d, Elizabeth Novitzky Meyer, Sept. 12, 1938; step son, Rodger Chase Lehman. Director Highland Nature Camp for Girls, South Naples, Me., 1910-72; director Lehman-Leete School for Girls, 1915-19; director Highland Manor (boarding sch. for girls), 1920-72; pres. Highland Manor Sch. and Jr. Coll., West Long Branch, N.J.; a founder, pres. Monmouth Coll., West Long Branch, 1956-72. Member Camp Directors Assn. America (v.p.), Nat. Assn. Directors of Girls' Camps (ex-pres.), School Masters' Assn. Mayor of Tarrytown, 1931-33. Pres. Westchester Council of Utility Rates Committee, Community Chest of the Tarrytowns; mem. Planning Commn. of Tarrytown. Hebrew religion. Rotarian. Author: (also editor) Junior Bible (3 vols.), 1914; Jewish Teacher (3 vols.), 1916. Editor: Camps and Camping, 1921. Asso. editor Camp Life. Contbr. article on camping to Ency. Brit. Home: West Long Branch NJ Died Aug. 21, 1972; buried Sleepy Hollow Cemtery, Tarrytown NY

LEHMAN, FRANK ALFRED, railway exec.; b. Mast Hope, Pa., May 31, 1871; s. Charles Augustus and Mary Clara (Robinson) L.; ed. pub. schs.; m. Matilda Louise Sneed, of El Paso, Ill., June 12, 1900;children—Marion Frances (Mrs. Raymond Joseph Stipek), Stanley Sneed. Began as telegrapher Atchison, Topeka & Santa Fe Ry. Co., 1888, successively train dispatcher, clk. in gen. roadmaster's office, trainmaster's office, vice president's office until 1902, chief clk. to v.p. in charge of operation, 1902-07, supt. of transportation, 1907-09, asst. to v.p. in charge operation, 1909-14, gen. supt. Western Dist. Eastern Lines, Nov. 1914-May 1915, asst. to vice president, 1915-21, gen. mgr. Western Lines, 1921-27, gen. mgr. Eastern Lines since Apr. 1, 1927; pres. and dir. St. Joseph Terminal R.R. Co.; vice president and dir. New Mexico Central Ry. Co. to 1939, retired July 1, 1939. Republican. Presbyn. Mason. Clubs: Rotary, Topeka Country, Chicago Athletic Assn. Home: 1271 Fillmore St. Address: A., T. & S.F. Ry. Co., Topeka KS‡

LEHMAN, GEORGE MUSTIN, consulting engr.; b. Lebanon, Pa., May 13, 1863; s. Benjamin Bringhurst and Susanna (Mustin) L.; ed. Episcopal Acad., Lebanon, Pa.; m. Corinne May Stockton, Nov. 12, 1891 (died Feb. 6, 1933); 1 son, George Stockton (dec.). Aid, asst. and topographer Geol. Survey of Pa., 1882-89; chief asst. engr. surveys for extension Gettysburg & Harrisburg R.R., Gettysburg, Pa., to Washington, D.C., Brooklyn, Bath & West End R.R., N.Y., topographic and geologic survey, Navassa Island, W.I., relief map of same (from this survey U.S. Navy made nautical chart), later, elec. ry. surveys, 1889-90; engr. location and constrn. Great Falls Water Power & Imp. Co.'s canal, dams and location town (now Roanoke Rapids, N.C.), 1890-93; chief asst. engr. charge surveys for ship canal from Delaware River to Raritan Bay, 1894; principal assistant engineer in charge of surveys and estimates for the Lake Erie and Ohio River Canal, from Pittsburgh to Lake Erie, 1895-96; U.S. asst. engr. on improvement Allegheny, Pa., West Fork, W.Va., Youghiogheny, Pa., rivers, etc., assisted in inspection and report for permanent U.S. Army camp sites, Conewago Valley and Somerset, Pa., 1896-1903; constructed large relief map, Pittsburgh and vicinity, for Pittsburgh Chamber of Commerce, 1903-04 (gold medal at St. Louis Expn., 1904); engr. of parks, Pittsburgh, 1905; incorporator, 1905, and since chief engr. Lake Erie and Ohio River Canal Co.; sec.-member Pittsburgh Flood Commn. and engr. in charge investigations, surveys, and plans for flood prevention and protection (suggested commission and reservoir control) since 1908; chief engr. Lake Erie and Ohio River Canal Board to 1917; investigations and report on modes and costs of transportation by canal and river, 1917, 21. Reported to Com. on Inland Waterways of U.S. Railroad Administration on various canals as a war measure; production engr., and claims adjustment, U.S. Ordnance Dept., 1918-19; engr. Dept. of Internal Affairs of Pa., 1920; chief div. of Waterways, same, 1921-23 (resigned and division abolished); cons. practice since 1923, on waterway engring., including transportation methods; engr. River Front Improvement and River-Rail Terminal Plans of Department of Public Works; chief engr. L.E.&O.R.

Canal Bd. Mem. Am. Soc. C.E., Swedish Colonial Soc., Phila., Pa. Forestry Assn. (council), Engineers Soc., Western Pa., Flood Commn. of Pittsburgh, Pittsburgh Chamber Commerce, Rivers and Harbors Congress (Washington), Propeller Club, The Pa. Soc. (N.Y. City). Home: 3937 Cloverlea St., Brentwood. Office: County Office Bldg., Pittsburgh PA‡

LEHMAN, ROBERT, investment banker; b. New York, N.Y., Sept. 29, 1891; s. Philip and Carrie (Lauer) L.; prep. education, Hotchkiss Sch. Lakeville, Conn. 1905-09. A.B., Yale, 1913; married Lee Anz Lynn, July 10, 1952; 1 son by previous marriage, Robert Owen. Partner Lehman Bros., investment bankers, N.Y.; chmn. bd., chief exec. officer Lehman Corp. (investment trust); dir. Asso. Drygoods Corp., So. States Land & Timber Co., Gimble Brothers, United Fruit; dir. and mem. exec. com. 20th Century Fox Films Corp., Pan-Am. World Airways, Inc. Dir. Met. Opera; trustee assos. fine arts, gov. bd. art gallery, Yale U.; adv. com. Inst. Fine Arts, mem. bd., council N.Y.U.; chmn. bd. Met. Mus. Art; mem. vis. com. Fogg Art Mus. Trustee Mt. Sinai Hosp.; chmn. Hertz Found. Amassed one of most important pvt. art collections ever assembled, exhibited at Louvre, 1957, and donated to Met. Mus. Art, 1969. Served as capt. 318th F.A., U.S. Army, AEF, World War I. Mem. Council Fgn. Relations, French Legion of Art, N.Y. Stock Exchange, Delta Kappa Epsilon. Clubs: Yale, Turf and Field. Home: New York City NY Died Aug. 9, 1969.

LEHMANN, EMIL WILHELM, agrl. engring. consultant; born in Oldenburg, Mississippi, Apr. 19, 1887; s. Charles A. and Arminia (Volkhausen) L.; B.S. in E.E., Mississippi State University, 1910; student Cornell U., summer 1910, U. of Wis., summer 1912; E.E., Tex. Agrl. & Mech. Coll., 1913; B.S. in A.E., Ia. State U., 1914, A.E., 1919; m. Stella Spence, Aug. 5, 1915; children—Margaret Louise (Mrs. LeRoy D. Prey), Mary Bain (Mrs. Wm. B. Browder), Josephine (Mrs. Hugh J. Miser), E. Wendel, Stella Jean (Mrs. Alonzo L. Hunter). Instr. physics Tex. Agricultural & Mech. Coll., 1910-13; instr., later asst. prof. agrl. engring., Ia. State U., 1913-16; asso. prof. and head dept., later prof. agrl. engring., U. of Mo., 1916-20; agrl. engring. editor Successful Farming Mag., Des Moines, 1920-21; prof. agrl. engring. and head dept. U. of Ill., 1921-55, emeritus, 1955-72, spl. rep. v.p. farm equipment product planning Internat. Harvester Co., 1955-58, ret.; now cons.; representative Heli Coil Corp., Danbury, Conn.; collaborator Bur. Home Econs., U.S. Dept. of Agr., 1933; coop. agent Soil Erosion Service, U.S. Dept. of the Interior, 1934; collaborator Nat. Resources Bd., 1934. Mem. State Rural Electrification Com. Nat. Safety Council Occupational Advisory Com.; Subcom. on Young Workers in Wartime Agr., Children's Bur., U.S. Dept. of Labor; chmn. State Safety Com., vice chmn. Ill. Farm Electrification council. Chmn. First National Farm Safety Week; governing bd. Agrl. Research Inst. Recipient distinguished service to safety award Nat. Safety Council, 1958; John Deere medal Am. Soc. Agrl. Engrs., 1965. Life fellow Am. Soc. Agrl. Engrs.; member Ill. Soc. of Profl. Engrs. (bd. dirs., p.p. Champaign County chap.), Am. Soc. of Engring. Edn., Am. Assn. Univ. Profs., Am. Farm Bur. Fedn., Am. Forestry Assn., Ill. Fire Prevention Conf. (com. fire prevention edn.), Friends of the Land, Ill. Agrl. Assn., Nat. Fire Protection Assn. (farm fire protection com.), Nat. Soc. Professional Engrs., Nat. Farm Show Committee, Alpha Epsilon, Tau Beta Pi, also mem. Sigma Xi, Phi Kappa Phi, Alpha Zeta, Alpha Tau Alpha, Gamma Sigma Delta, Acacia. Chmn. Bd. of Dirs. U. of I. Y.M.C.A. Presbyn. (mem. session, First Ch., Urbana). Club: Rotary (Urbana). Registered professional engr. in Ill. Author numerous tech. bulls. and leaflets. Co-author: Farm Urbana IL Died 1972.

LEHRMAN, DANIEL SANFORD, educator, psychologist; b. N.Y.C., June 1, 1919; B.S., City Coll., 1947; Ph.D., N.Y.U., 1954; m. 1962; 2 children. Asst. psychologist Haskins Labs., 1945-47; lectr. psychology Coll. City N.Y., 1947-50, N.Y.U., 1950; from asst. prof. to asso. prof. Rutgers U., 1950-58, prof., 1958-72, dir. Inst. Animal Behavior, 1959-72; vis. prof. Yale, 1957-58. Mem. Nat. Acad. Scis., Am. Acad. Arts and Scis., Soc. Zoologists, Ecol. Soc., Psychol. Assn., Ornithol. Union, Animal Behavior Soc., Soc. Neurosci., Soc. Exptl. Psychology. Research on animal instinct; comparative and evolutionary study of animal behavior; hormones and behavior; investigated behavior and physiology of ring-neck dove for explanation of interaction of hormones, experience and external stimuli. Editor: Advances in the Study of Behavior; asso. editor Jour. Comparative and Physiol. Psychology. Home: NJ Died Sept. 1972; buried Vets. Cemetery, Santa Fe NM

LEIBOLD, PAUL FRANCIS, bishop; b. Dayton, O., Dec. 22, 1914; s. Frank A. and Philomena E. (Kirchner) L.; A.B., U. Dayton, 1936; student St. Gregory Sem., Cin., Mt. St. Mary of West, Norwood, O.; J.C.L., Cath. U. Am., 1942; J.C.D., Angelicum U., Rome, Italy, 1949. Ordained priest, Roman Cath. Ch., 1940; asst. chancellor Archdiocese of Cin., 1942-48, chancellor, 1948-58; papal chamberlain, 1948, domestic prelate, 1950; pastor St. Louis Ch., Cin., 1956-66; consecrated titular bishop of Terbenna, aux. bishop of Cin., 1958; vicar gen. Archdiocese of Cin., 1958-66; bishop of Evansville (Ind.), 1966-69; archbishop Cin., 1969-72. Address: Cincinnati OH Died June 1, 1972; buried Gate of Heaven Cemetery, Cincinnati OH

LEIBOWITZ, RENE, composer, conductor; b. Warsaw, Poland, Feb. 17, 1913; s. Max and Nadia (Berman) L.; ed. high sch., also pvt. tutoring; divorced; children—Tamara, Cora. Violinist, 1921-72; conductor, 1938-72. Author: Schoenberg and His School, 1946; Introduction to 12 Tone Music, 1949; History of the Opera, 1959; Thinking for Orchestra, 1961. Composer: Symphony 4, 1940; The Explanation of Metaphors, 1946; 6 Little Pieces for Orchestra, 1952; Piano Concerto, 1954; Violin Concerto, 1960; Les Espagnois A Venise, 1965. Address: Paris France Died Aug. 28, 1972.

LEICHLITER, GOULD A., clergyman, author; b. Rockwood, Pa., Oct. 5, 1891; s. John Lyons and Emma (Gould) L.; student Otterbein U., Westerville, O., 1910-12, Bonebrake Theol. Sem., Dayton, O., 1912-14; Ph.B., Ia. Christian Coll., Oskaloosa, Ia., 1915, B.D., 1916, A.M., 1917, D.D., 1918; Th.B., McMaster U., Hamilton, Ont., 1922, D.D., 1945; m. Clyda Huston, Dec. 28, 1910. Ordained to ministry Bapt. Ch., 1913; pastor Colo. Av. Bapt. Ch., Dayton, 1912-16; gen. evangelistic work, 1916-19; pastor Adelaide St. Bapt. Ch., London, Ont., Can., 1919-23, Prospect Av. Bapt. Ch., Buffalo, 1923-29, Coll. St. Bapt. Ch., Toronto, Can., 1929-45; promotional dir. South Fla. Bapt. Hosp., Plant City, 1946-53; interim pastor Bapt. Chs., Brandon, Fla., 1966-67, Tampa, Fla., 1967-68. Spl. cons. nursing home program Bur. Spl. Health Services, Fla. Bd. Health, 1961-65. Exec. sec. the Fla. Bapt. Found., 1953-60. Trustee Fla. Normal and Indsl. Meml. Coll., So. Bapt. Found., S. Fla. Bapt. Hosp. Recipient Wisdom award honor Wisdom Soc., 1970; citation distinguished service Norman Coll., Norman Park, Ga. Mem. Fla. Bapt. Conv., So. Bapt. Conv. Ednl. Commn., Ont. and P.Q. Bapt. Conv. (v.p. 1943), Toronto Bapt. Assn. (moderator 1936). Mason (32 deg., Shriner). Author (poetry): Songs to Men and Nature, 1938; Other Songs, 1940; Let Me Sing My Song, 1941; also various hymns (words and music). Weekly contbr. Plant City Courier, 1946-71; contbr. Canadian Anthology of Verse and Paebar Anthology; Ency. So. Baptists, 1958; various theol. pubs. Home: Plant City FL Died Nov. 28, 1971.

LEIDESDORF, SAMUEL DAVID, public accountant; b. N.Y.C., Sept. 25, 1881; s. David and Pauline (Baumann) L.; Dr. Humane Letters, N.Y.U., 1949; L.H.D. (hon.), Hebrew Union Coll., 1957; Dr. Comml. Science (honorary), Pace Coll., 1964; m. Elsa Grunwald, Jan. 16, 1916 (dec.); children—Arthur David, Helen L. Banks; married second, Ethel Wormser Skutch, May 11, 1956 (dec. July 1967). Founding partner of S. D. Leidesdorf and Company, C.P.A.'s, N.Y.C., from 1905; president Pershing Sq. Building Corp., from 1920; chmn. bd., dir. Baker Evans & Co.; pres. Murray Hill Operating Co., from 1943; chairman bd. dirs 100 Park Av., Inc., from 1948. Hon. trustee, asso. chmn. bd. trustees Fedn. Jewish Philanthropies (pres. 1935-36); bd. trustees N.Y. Inst. Credit; chmn. bd. trustees, mem. finance com. Inst. for Advanced Study; treas., dir., mem. exec. com. Nat. Fund Med. Edn.; dir., chmn. budget com. Greater N.Y. Fund; treas., mem. exec. com. United Jewish Appeal Greater N.Y.; hon. v.p. Am. Jewish Com.; trustee and chmn. finance com. Nat. Conf. Christians and Jews; life mem. exec. bd., bd. govs. Am. Jewish Joint Distbn.; vice pres. Accountants Foundation; honorary life trustee Community Service Society; member board of trustees Montefiore Hosp.; chmn. bd. Med. Center, N.Y.U., trustee, mem. exec. and finance coms. N.Y.U.; mem. N.Y. State Banking Bd. Trustee Inst. Crippled and Disabled; spl. gifts com. N.Y.C. Cancer Commn.; chmn. accountants division, member special gifts committee Greater New York council Girl Scouts America; member nat. council, chmn. found. gifts com. United Negro Coll. Fund; mem. at large Greater N.Y. council Boy Scouts Am.; vice chmn. N.Y. chpt. A.R.C. Recipient certificate of recognition by Columbia Alumni for work in philanthropy and religion; award of Interfaith Work, from National Conference of Christians and Jews, 1952; gold medal for humanitarian services, Nat. Inst. Social Scis., 1955; Gold Medal award, Hundred Yr. Assn. N.Y., 1958; Silver Beaver award. Boy Scouts of America, 1958; N.Y.C. Citizens Bronze Medallion, 1961; Leahy award National Fund Medical Education, 1961; Protestant Council Distinguished Service award, 1966. C.P.A. Mem. N.Y. Commerce and Industry Assn. (hon. dir., past pres.), Am. Arbitration Assn. (dir.), Accountants Club Am. (advisory committee). Clubs: 60 East, City Athletic, Harmonie, Metropolis Country, Ocean Beach, Pinnacle, Economic. Home: New York City NY Died Sept. 21, 1968.

LEIGHTON, MORRIS MORGAN, geologist; b. Wellman, Ia., Aug. 4, 1887; s. Stephen Tibbetts and Jane (Wellman) L.; B.A., U. Ia., 1912, M.S., 1913 (Frank O. Lowden prize in geology), distinguished alumnus, 1947; Ph.D., U. Chgo., 1916; D.Sc. (honorary), University Southern Ill., 1954; m. Ada Harriette Beach, Aug. 12, 1913; children—Freeman Beach, Morris Wellman, Richard Tibbetts. Apprentice and printer 1901-06; supt. Weber Printing Co., Iowa City, Ia., 1908-09; instr. in geology, U. of Wash., 1915-16; instr. same, summer field course, U. of Chicago and State U. of Ia., 1916; asst. prof. geology, Ia. State Teachers Coll., Cedar Falls, Ia., 1916-17; asst. prof. geology, U. of Wash., 1917-18, also geologist Wash. Geol. Survey; acting prof. geology, Ohio State U., in absentia from U. of Wash., 1918-19; asst. prof. geology, U. of Ill., 1919-23, also geologist Ill. Geol. Survey, 1919-23; chief of Ill. Geol. Survey, 1923-54, chief emeritus, 1954-71; mem. com. on metals and minerals O.P.M., 1941-46; mem. State Mus. Bd., 1937-61, chmn., 1957-61; mem. Ill. Postwar Plan, Commn. (vice chmn. 1945-47); adv. com. U.S. Geol. Survey, 1943-59, cons. on midwest glacial geology, from 1956; dir. Am. Geol. Inst., 1950, pres., 1956; mem. delegation to XXth Internat. Geol. Congress, Mexico City, 1956; mem. coordinating com. on nat. water policy Engrs. Joint Council, N.Y., 1950-51. Instr. S.A.T.C. Ohio State U., 1918. Fellow Chgo. Geog. Soc., Geo. Soc. Am. (councillor 1937-40), A.A.A.S. (v.p. representing geology, 1941), American Ceramic Soc.; mem. American Assn. State Geologists (hon.; pres. 1931-34), Soc. Econ. Geologists (pres. 1950), Chgo. Acad. Sci., (hon.), Am. Assn. Petroleum Geologists (honorary), Am. Inst. Mining and Metall. Engrs. (chairman Indsl. Minerals Div., 1939), Ill. Soc. Engrs. (dir. 1924-27), Ill. State Academy Science (pres. 1930), American Academy of Arts and Sciences, Illinois Mining Inst. (pres. 1941), Western Soc. Engineers, Wash. award commission, 1934-1937, Sigma Xi. Methodist. Clubs: Chaos, Dial, University. Author books relating to field, from 1917, including: Atlas of Illinois Resources (a compilation), 1944; Loess Formations of the Mississippi Valley (sr. author), 1950; also numerous geol. articles. Editor State Geologists Journal, 1949-54; bus. editor Economic Geology, from 1941. Home: Urbana IL Died Jan. 7, 1971.

LEIMBACH, ALFRED T., shoe chain exec.; b. Altenburg, Mo., Nov. 21, 1901; s. Ernst A. and Anna (Holschen) L.; student bus. colls., Nashville and St. Louis; m. Marie Ballhausen, Mar. 15, 1952; children—Gary, Jane (foster children), Carol Ann. Bookkeeper, Lebanon Woolen Mills (Tenn.), 1922-24; cost accountant, Blanke-Wenneker Candy Co., 1924-26; auditor Ernst & Ernst, C.P.A.'s, both St. Louis, 1926-29; with Edison Bros. Stores, Inc., St. Louis, 1929-68, controller, 1933-44, v.p., 1944-66, vice president, treasurer, 1966-68, also dir. until 1968, adv. mem. bd., 1968-71; dir. Concordia Publishing House, St. Louis, 1941-71, chmn. bd., 1956-71. Financial sec. Luth. Laymen's League, 1943-49; dir. Aid Assn. for Lutherans, 1947-52, Luth. Hosp., St. Louis, 1955. Mem. Financial Execs. Inst. Clubs: Mo. Athletic, Sunset Country. Home: St Louis MO Died Aug. 6, 1971; buried Our Redeemer Cemetery, St Louis County MO

LEISEN, (JAMES) MITCHELL, motion picture dir.; b. Menominee, Mich., Oct. 6, 1898; s. Earle B. LeFave), Albert N. Various editorial positions Boston Sunday Post, 1916-20, asst. editor, 1920-41; editor-in-chief McClure Newspaper Syndicate, N.Y.C., 1941-45, contbg. editor, 1945-53; sec. to lt. gov. of Mass., 1947-49; dir. Mass. Republican Information Service, 1949-52; mem. Eisenhower Hdqrs. Com., 1952; asst. to sec. to Pres. of U.S., 1953; dir. pub. information Dept. Commerce, 1953-72, asst. to sec. commerce, 1955-72. Served with U.S. Army, World War I; AEF. Home: Washington DC Died Aug. 1972.

LEISENRING, EDWARD B., JR., coal co. exec.; b. 1926; grad. Yale, 1949. Pres. Va. Coal & Iron Co.; member executive committee, member board directors Whitehall Cement Manufacturing Company; pres., dir. SKF Industries, Inc., Westmoreland Coal Co., Wentz Corporation; chmn. Gen. Coal Company; dir. Fidelity-Phila. Trust Co., Central Supply Co. Va., Southern Ry. Co., Va. Wholesale Co., Clear Creek Water Co., Cumberland Water Co. Trustee Lankenau Hosp. Home: Berwyn PA Died May 23, 1968.

LEISY, ERNEST ERWIN, prof. English; b. Moundridge, Kan., Dec. 22, 1887; s. Emil A. and Lena (Krebill) L.; B.A., U. of Kan., 1913; grad. study, Harvard, 1913-14; M.A., U. of Chicago, 1919; Ph.D., U. of Ill., 1923; m. Elva Krehbiel, Aug. 14, 1917; children—Melvern, Margaret, James. Prof. English, Bethel Coll. (Kan.), 1914-17; instr. in English, U. of Ill., 1918-23; prof. English and head of dept., Ill. Wesleyan U., 1923-27; prof. English, Southern Methodist U., from 1927; chmn. dept., 1940-41; visiting prof. summers, Washington State College, 1934, Duke U., 1935, 36, 39, Colorado U., 1937, 47, U. of Tex., 1938, U. of N.C., 1946, U. of Wash., 1949; exchange prof. U. of Vienna, 1951, U. of Bonn, 1952. Mem. Modern Lang. Assn. American (Mem. exec. com. and editor 1951, pres. 1957, South-Central br.), Am. Assn. U. Profs., college English Assn. (pres., 1951-53), Tex. Inst. of Letters, Tex. Coll. Teachers of English, Phi Kappa Phi. Club: Town and Gown. Author: American Literature, 1929; also author The American Historical Novel, 1950. Editor: Facts and Ideas (with John Beaty and Mary Lamar), 1930, 2d series, 1939; The Scarlet Letter, 1929; Major American Writers (with H.M. Jones), 1935; Horseshoe Robinson, 1937; Voices of England and America (with D.L. Clark and W.B. Gates), 1939; Snodgrass Letters of Mark Twain, 1946; Bibliographer

Am. Lit. group. Modern Lang. Association America, 1927-37, chmn. Anglo-German Group, 1937, chmn. Am. Lit. Group, 1949. Compiler (with J. B. Hubbell) of Doctoral Dissertations in American Literature, 1933. Contbg. editor, Southwest Rev.; asso. editor Am. Lit. Home: Dallas TX Died Mar. 8, 1968; interred Halstead Mausoleum, Halstead KS

LELAND, FRANK BRUCE, banker; b. at Rose, Mich.; A.B., U. of Mich., 1881, LL.B., 1884. Practiced law at Flint, Mich., 1885-90, Detroit, 1890-5; gen. counsel since 1895, later gen. mgr. and sec. Nat. Loan & Investment Co.; organized, 1901, and since pres., Detroit United Bank. Home: 185 Burns Av., Detroit MI‡

LELAND, JOSEPH DANIELS, architect; b. Brookline, Mass., June 16, 1885; s. Joseph Daniels, Jr., and Grace Adams (Rogers) L.; student Harvard, 1905-09, Atelier Chifflot, Paris, 1909-11; grad. Sch. Applied Science, Harvard, 1912; m. Countess Dedons de Pieerefeu (nee Elsa Tudor), Sept. 4, 1916 (div. Feb. 25, 1936); 1 son, Surya Tudor. Draftsman, Peabody & Stearns, architects, Boston, 1910-13; partner, Loring & Leland, Boston, 1913-17; asst. dir. bureau indsl. housing and transportation, also v.p. U.S. Housing Corp., operating for War and Navy depts., Washington, D.C., 1917-19; sr. partner J. D. Leland & Co., architects and engrs., Boston, 1919-35; sr. partner, Leland & Larsen, from 1935. Chmn. Town of Milton (Mass.) Planning Bd. and Bd. of Survey; Fellow Am. Inst. Architects, Boston Soc. of Architects; mem. Mass. State Assn. Architects, Boston Archtl. Center. Clubs: Myopia Hunt, Tennis and Racquet, Hoosic-Whisick, Milton. Awarded 2d prize Boston Contest, 1944. Home: Milton MA Died Apr. 1968.*

LELAND, ORA MINER, univ. dean, civil eng.; b. Grand Haven, Mich., June 28, 1876; s. George Spencer and Harriett Elizabeth (Perkins) L.; B.S. in C.E., U. of Mich., 1900, C.E., 1920; m. Mary Yoeckel, June 28, 1906 (died Oct. 2, 1913); children—Mary Louise (Mrs. Bruce L. Clark), Walter Perkins; m. 2d, Lottie Susan Potts, Aug. 5, 1914; children—Miriam Irene (Mrs. William C. Kahle), Paul Miner. Chief clerk and draftsman, office of surveyor-gen. of Fla., 1898-99; in Gen. Land Office (div. of surveys), Washington, D.C., 1900, 03; aid and computer, U.S. Coast and Geod. Survey, in U.S., Alaska and P.R., 1900-03; mem. faculty Coll. Civ. Engring., Cornell U., 1903-20, head dept. of topographic and geodetic engineering, 1911-20, prof. geodesy and astronomy, 1916-20; engring. supervisor, J.G. White Engring. Corp., 1920; dean colls. of engring., architecture, and chemistry, U. of Minn., 1920-36; dean of adminstrn., University of Minnesota, Inst. of Technology, 1936-44; dean emeritus since 1944. Surveyor and chief of party to United States commissioner for demarcation of boundary between Alaska and Canada, 1904-11; mem. Commn. of Engrs. in Costa Rica-Panama Boundary Arbitration, 1911-13, Demarcation Commn., 1921. In service U.S. Army, as capt., maj. and lt. col. engrs., Apr. 1917-June 1919; with 303d Engrs., 78th Div., A.E.F., until Nov. 1918; with 314th Engrs., 89th Div., A.E.F., Nov. 1918-June 1919; colonel commanding 313th Engr. Regt., 88th Div., 1922-40; colonel inactive since 1940. Fellow A.A.A.S.; mem. Am. Soc. C.E., Am. Assn. Engrs., American Society Engring. Edn. (ex-president). Am. Astron. Soc., Soc. Am. Mil. Engrs. (dir.), Engrs. Club of Minneapolis, Am. Legion, Sigma Xi, Tau Beta Pi, Chi Epsilon (nat. hon.), Scabbard and Blade, Phalanx, Triangle. Author: Practical Least Squares. Home: 911 Fifth St., S.E., Minneapolis 14 MN‡

LEMASS, SEAN FRANCIS, prime minister Ireland; b. Dublin, Ireland, July 15, 1899; s. John and Frances (Phelan) L.; ed. Christian Brothers Schs., Ireland; LL.D., Iona Coll., New Rochelle, N.Y., 1953, U. Villanova, Phila., 1963, U. Dublin, 1965; D.Econ. Sci., Nat. Univ. Ireland, 1954; m. Kathleen Hughes, Aug. 28, 1924;children—Noel, Maureen (Mrs. Charles Haughey), Margaret (Mrs. John O'Brien), Sheila (Mrs. John O'Connor). Participated in Easter Week Rising, Irish Volunteers, 1916, and served with volunteers until 1922; prisoner, 1916, 21, 22; mng. dir. Irish Press, Ltd., 1948-51; minister for industry and commerce, 1932-39, 41-48, 51-54, 57-59; for supplies, 1939-45; dep. prime minister, 1945-48, 51-54, 57-59; teachta dala, Dublin S., 1924-28, Dublin S. (Central), from 1948. prime minister, 1959-66. Decorated grand cross Pian Order; grand cross Order Gregory the Great; grand cross Order of Merit (Federal Republic Germany). Home: Dublin Ireland Died May 1971.

LEMMON, SARA ALLEN PLUMMER, botanist, artist; b. New Gloucester, Me.; d. Micajah S. and Elizabeth (Haskell) Plummer; became a teacher in New York; m. John Gill Lemmon, botanist, 1880 (died Nov. 24, 1908). With her husband has botanically explored the Pacific coast from Mexico to British Columbia; was artist Cal. State Bd. Forestry, 1887-91; has written and illus. books and articles upon various branches of botany; apptd. chmn. on Forestry for Cal. Federation of Women's Clubs, 1900. Chmn. Nat. Floral Soc. for Cal.; mem. exec. bd. Cal. State Red Cross, Cal. Woman's Press Assn., Water and Forest Assn.; hon. mem. Cal. Floral Soc., Ebell Club, Oakland, etc. Author: Marine Algae of the West; Western Ferns; Record of Red Cross Work on the Pacific Slope, 1902; How to Tell the Trees (with J. G. Lemmon), 1902. Address: 5979 Telegraph Av., Oakland CA‡

LENGEL, WILLIAM C(HARLES), editorial exec., author; b. Durango, Colo.; s. William F. and Alice (Wuerz) L.; LL.B., Kansas City Sch. Law; m. Nelle E. McNeff; one son, Hughes McNeff. Admitted to Mo. bar and practiced in Kansas City; admitted to practice U.S. Supreme Ct., 1960; associated with Internat. Mag. Co., N.Y.C., 1920-33, successively as editor Cosmopolitan Book Corp., mng. editor Hearst's Internat. mag., European editorial rep., London; then editor Smart Set and asso. editor Cosmopolitan; asso. editor Liberty, 1933-35; Eastern story editor Columbia Pictures Corp., 1935-37; editor-in-chief Gold Medal Books, Fawcett Publs., Inc., N.Y.C., 1942-54, Fawcett World Library, 1955-65. Publicity dir. employment mgmt. sect. War Industries Bd., 1918; editorial adviser war finance div. Treasury Dept., 1944-45. Mem. Catholic Actors Guild, Soc. Illustrators, Artists and Writers Assn., Dramatists Guild, Authors League Am., Cath. Inst. of Press. Ind. Democrat. Roman Cath. Clubs: Dutch Treat, Lambs, Overseas Press (N.Y.C.); Savage (London, Eng.). Author: (pseud. Warren Spencer) Forever and Ever, 1932, Mad Melody, 1932; (pseud. Charles Grant) Torch Singer, 1933, More Money, 1934; Candles in the Wind, 1937; also numerous short stories, articles nat. mags. Co-author: (plays) Tin Pan Alley, 1921, Twenty Four Hours, 1931; also several produced one-act plays. Home: New York City NY Died Oct. 11, 1965.

LENTINE, JOSEPH, physician; b. Italy, 1906; M.D., Tufts U., 1932; m. Madelene Hallock, June 12, 1943; 1 dau., Marylyn. Intern, Burbank Hosp., Fitchburg, Mass., 1932-33, Boston City Hosp., 1933-34; resident Mass. Eye and Ear Infirmary, 1934-36, surgeon, 1936-—; asst. surg. Boston Dispensary New Eng Med. Center; cons. Evangeline Booth Maternity Hosp. & Home; surgeon Mass. Gen. Hosp.; asso. surgeon Mt. Auburn Hosp., Cambridge, Mass.; jr. vis. surgeon Mass. Meml. Hosp., Boston; vis. surgeon St. Elizabeth's Hosp.; cons. Lemuel Shattuck Hosp. Instr. otolaryngology Harvard; clin prof. otolaryngology Tufts U.; instr. otolaryngology Boston U. Served as maj. M.C., AUS. Diplomate Am. Bd. Opthalmology and Otolaryngology. Mem. Am. Acad. Opthalmology and Otolaryngology, A.M.A., New Eng. Otol. and Layngol. Soc. Home: Belmont MA Died May 2, 1970.

LEON, HARRY JOSHUA, educator; b. Worcester, Mass., Sept. 4, 1896; s. Jacob and Rachel (Hoch) L.; A.B. summa cum laude, Harvard, 1918, M.A., 1919, Ph.D., 1927; m. Ernestine Franklin, July 1, 1924;children—Isabel (Mrs. M. Samfield), Judith (Mrs. Scott M. Smith), Benjamin. Sheldon traveling fellow Harvard, 1920-22; vis. fellow Am. Acad. Rome, 1920-22; instr. Latin, U. Pitts., 1922-23; mem. dept. classical langs. U. Tex., 1923-—, instr., 1923-26, asst. prof., 1926-34, asso. prof., 1934-42, professor, 1942-67, chairman department 1942-62, conductor classical study tour of Italy, 1962. Recipient Fulbright research award to Italy, 1950-51. Member American Philological Assn., Archeol. Inst. America, American Classical League, Classical Assn. (Britain), Classical Assn. Middle West and South (pres. 1957-58), Am. Assn. U. Profs., Tex. Classical Assn., Classical Soc. Am. Acad. Rome (pres. 1960, mem. adv. council School Classical Studies), Texas Foreign Lang. Association (hon. life), Am. Philatelic Soc., Am.-Italy Soc. Dallas Philol. Soc., Kallah Tex. Rabbis, Virgilian Soc. Am., Am. Friends of Greece, Tex. Assn. Coll. Tchrs., Tex. Fine Arts Assn., Phi Beta Kappa (pres. S. Central Dist.). Jewish. Mem. B'nai B'rith. Clubs: Austin Stamp, Fortnightly, Scholia. Author: Tacitus (with Marsh), 1936 (rev.) 1963; The Pastoral Elegy (with Harrison), 1939; The Jews of Ancient Rome, 1960. Member of the editorial bd. The Jewish Apocryphal Lit. Contbr. articles Jews of Ancient Rome, Roman lit. and antiquities, profl. publs. Home: Austin TX Died Dec. 4, 1967.

LEONARD, ARTHUR THOMAS, banker; b. Chicago, May 15, 1894; s. Thomas J. and Mary (Gleason) L.; student Loyola Acad., Chicago, 1909-13; Northwestern, 1913-16; m. Mona Dunne, Oct. 15, 1924. Admitted to Ill. bar, 1916, engaged in practice of law, Chicago, 1916-17; trust officer and sec., Central Trust Co. of Ill., 1919-23, v.p., 1930-32; treas. Dawes Bros., Inc., 1923-30; v.p. City Nat. Bank & Trust Co. of Chicago, 1932-45, sr. v.p. and dir., 1946-51, became pres., 1951, pres. and chief exec. officer, 1956-61; chmn. exec. com. Continental Ill. Nat. Bank & Trust Co., 1961-66. Dir. Cath. Charities. Mem. citizens' bd. U. Chgo.; mem., trustee James S. Kemper Found. Served as lt. USN, 1917-19. Mem. Chgo. Assn. Commerce and Industry (pres. 1953-54; mem. sr. council), American, Ill., Chgo. bar associations, Phi Delta Phi. Republican. Roman Catholic. Clubs: University, Commercial, Glenview, Casino, Economic, Commonwealth, Chicago (Chgo.); Executives, Bankers (pres. 1955), Old Elm. Home: Evanston IL Died Oct. 19, 1968.

LEONARD, JACK E., comedian; b. Chgo., Apr. 24, 1911; married. Frequent TV, night club appearances; recorded by RCA Victor. Elected prior of Friar Club N.Y.C., 1968. Address: New York City NY Died May 11, 1973.

LEONARD, NEIL, lawyer; b. Worcester, Mass., Sept. 8, 1898; s. Patrick and Ann (Connolly) L.; A.B., Colby College, 1921, Doctor of Laws (honorary); LL.B., Yale University, 1924; married Hildegard Drummond, Apr. 28, 1925; children—Neil, Ann (Mrs. George Macomber). Admitted to Mass. bar, 1924, and practiced in Boston; mem. Bingham, Dane & Gould; spl. counsel Mass. Commnr. Back Bay sect., Boston. Member board of directors Boston Globe. Chairman board of trustees Colby Coll.; trustee Newton-Wellesely Hosp., 1942-52; former pres. Newton Community Chest, Douglas A. Thom Clinic for Children; mem. bd. overseers Boys' Clubs of Boston, Inc.; vice pres. Museum of Science, Boston. Member of Massachusetts Bar Assn., Bar Assn. City Boston. Clubs: Union, Union Boat (Boston). Home: Boston MA Died Sept. 15, 1968.

LEONARD, ROBERT WALTON, educator; b. San Diego, Apr. 6, 1910; s. James Walton and Jessie Almira (Norton) L.; B.A., U. Cal. at Berkeley, 1935, M.A., 1936, Ph.D., 1940; m. Viola Groch, Dec. 18, 1936 (div.); children—James Walton, William Curtis, Katherine Marie. Mem. faculty U. Cal. at Los Angeles, 1941-67, prof. physics, 1955-67. Fellow Am. Phys. Soc., Acoustical Soc. Am. (pres. 1962-63). Contbr. sections handbook. Home: Pacific Palisades CA Died Apr. 9, 1967.

LEONARD, WARREN H(ENRY), agronomist; b. New Sharon, Ia., July 5, 1900; s. Edward James and Zilla (Miller) L.; B.S., Colo. A. & M. Coll., 1926; M.S., U. of Neb., 1930; Ph.D., U. of Minn. 1940; m. Editha Todd, June 4, 1930; 1 dau., Kay. Asst. extension agronomist, Colo. A. & M. Coll., 1926-27, asst. editor publs., 1928; grad. asst. U. of Neb., 1928-29; asst. prof. of agronomy Colorado State Univ., 1929-34, asso. prof., 1934-42, prof., 1946-48, since 1949; asst. agronomist, asso., agronomist Colo. Agrl. Experimental Sta., 1929-42, 46-48, 49-66. Survey U. of Peshawar, Pakistan for Fgn. Operations Adminstrn. and Colorado State Univ., 1954; cons. agrl. prodn. Mission to Libya International Bank Reconstruction and Development, 1959. Member adv. bd. Am. Inst. Crop Ecology, Washington, 1952; ofcl. del. 6th Nat. Conf. UNESCO, San Francisco, 1957. Served as first lieut., captain, major C.A.C., U.S. Army, 1942-46; chief (as maj.), Agrl. Div., Natural Resources Sect., G.H.Q., Supreme Comdr. for the Allied Powers, Tokyo, Japan, 1945-46, chief (civilian) 1948-49; 1st. col. United States Army Reserve, retired. Decorated Legion of Merit by Gen. Douglas MacArthur, July 22, 1946; Department of the Army commendation for Meritorious Civilian Service, 1949; fellow Population Reference Bureau, Washington, 1956; profl. achievement award, Colo. State U., 1957. Fellow A.A.A.S., American Society of Agronomy; mem. Bot. Soc. of Am., Am. Genetics Assn., Genetics Soc. of Japan, Genetics Soc. of America, American Statis. Assn., Biometric Soc., Am. Soc. of Sugar Beet Technologists, Japanese Society of Breeding (hon. member), Sigma Xi, Phi Kappa Phi. Author: Civil Affairs Handbook: Japan: Agrl. (War Dept., Army Service Forces Manual No. 354-7A). 1945; Field Plot Technique (with Andrew Clark) 1939; Principles of Field Crop Prodn. (with John H. Martin), 1949; Field Crops in Colorado (with R. S. Whitney), 1950; (with John H. Martin) Cereal Crops, 1963; other technical works on barley genetics, applied statistics, corn breeding, gen. field crops, and Japanese agr. Home: Ft Collins CO Died Aug. 23, 1966; buried Grand View Cemetery, Ft Collins CO

LEONI, RAUL, pres. of Venezuela; b. 1905; ed. Bogota, Colombia; Dr. rer. pol. Founder mem. ORVE polit. movement, 1935; founder mem. Accion Democratica (formerly Nat. Democratic Party), 1937, pres., 1958-—; minister of labour, 1945-48; in exile, 1949-58; pres. of Venezuela, 1964-69. Address: Caracas Venezuela July 5, 1972.

LEPPART, JOHN CULVER, chem. corp. exec.; born Boston, Sept. 25, 1898; s. John H. and Charlotte Blanche Westley) L.; B. Chem., Cornell, 1919; m. Eleanor Jewel Buxton, Oct. 30, 1926; 1 dau., Suzanne Charlotte. Head tech. service dept., Solvay Process, Syracuse, 1919-26; asst. dir. spl. product sales, Solvay Sales Corp., New York, 1926-30; asst. dir. sales, Columbia div. of Pittsburgh Plate Glass Co., 1930-32; dollar-a-year man, Adminstr. W.P.B., Chem. Bur., Washington, 1942-45; asst. to operating v.p., Southern Alkali Corp., Corpus Christi, Tex., 1945-47; v.p. Prior Chem. Corp., New York, 1947-48; exec. vice pres. and director, Olin Mathieson, Chemical Corporation, from 1948. Clubs: University, Cornell, Uptown (N.Y.C.); Baltimore Country. Home: New York City NY Died May 1968.

LE PRINCE, JOSEPH AUGUSTIN, sanitary engr.; b. Leeds, Eng., Aug. 8, 1875; s. Louis Aime Augustin and Sarah Elizabeth (Whitley) L.; brought to U.S. at age of 6; grad. Sach's Collegiate Inst., New York, 1894; C.E., Columbia, 1898, A.M., 1899; m. Julia Mercedes Lluria, July 4, 1902; children—Julia Elizabeth, Marie Ysabel, Joseph Whitley, Alicia Ana, Aimee. Ry. surveys and constrn., W.Va., 1899-1900; engring. design and constrn., Pa., 1900; asst. to chief sanitary officer at Havana, 1901-02 inaugurating first successful campaign in the Western Hemisphere against yellow fever and malaria; res. engr. mine plant constrn., W.Va., 1903; health officer Panama Canal Zone, 1904-14, also of City of Panama, during yellow fever epidemic, 1905; determined the flight range limits of malaria conveying mosquitoes, 1912, and devised traps for making disease bearing mosquitoes trap themselves; sanitary engr. malaria investigating div. U.S.P.H.S., 1915, sr. san. engr., 1917-31; in charge anti-malaria activities at 28 extra-cantonment zones, Army and Navy camps, 1917-19, reducing malaria sick rate to one-half of one per cent of that of Southern camps in Spanish-Am. War. Dir. yellow fever control Mexican Oil Field Area, 1923; dir. Am. Red Cross malarial control activities, Miss. River flood area, 1927; consultant in malaria control to Tenn. Valley Authority since 1935. Mem. Internat. Conf. on Health Problems in Tropical America, Jamaica, British West Indies, 1924; vice chmn. and acting sec. National Malaria Com., 1929, chmn., 1930. Mem. Assn. State Sanitary Engrs., Tenn. Acad. Science, Sigma Chi.; chmn. Commn. on Engring. of Nat. Malaria Com. 12 yrs. Episcopalian. Author: Mosquito Control in Panama, 1916; also many papers before med. and engring. assns. Devised mechanical method of anopheles destruction by dusting. Home: 929 Oakmont Pl. Office: Federal Bldg., Memphis TN*‡

LERNER, JOSEPH S., corp. exec.; b. 1898; married. Pres. Mid-Continent Stores, Inc.; with Nat. Bellas Hess Inc., 1962-71, sr. v.p., gen. mgr. ready to wear operations in U.S., and P.R., 1967-71, also dir. Address: North Kansas City MO. Died Apr. 21, 1971.*

LE ROSSIGNOL, JAMES EDWARD, univ. prof.; b. Quebec, Can., Oct. 24, 1866; s. Peter and Mary (Gillespie) Le R.; A.B., McGill Coll. Montreal, 1888; Ph.D., U. of Leipzig, 1892; fellow psychology, Clark U., 1892; LL.D., U. of Denver, 1911; LL.D., McGill U., Montreal, 1921; m. Jessie Katherine Ross (A.B.), Sept. 2, 1898; children—Edward Ross, Helen, Marian Henderson. Prof. psychology and ethics, Ohio U., 1892-94; prof. economics, U. of Denver, 1894-1911; professor of economics 1911-1944, dir. Sch. of Commerce, 1913-19, dean Coll. of Business Administration, 1919-41, U. of Neb. Spl. lecturer in economics, McGill U., 1900; lecturer in polit. science, U. of Wis., summer session, 1903; investigated economic conditions in New Zealand, Aug.-Dec. 1906; prof. polit. economy, U. of Neb., 1908-09 (on leave absence from U. of Denver). Acting prof. economics, Stanford, summer, 1923, Univ. of Calif., at Los Angeles, summer, 1926. Chairman Lancaster County Fuel Com., 1917-19. Chmn. U. of Neb. Council on Postwar Reconstruction, 1943-45; chmn. Lincoln Com. British War Relief Soc. Mem. Am. Econ. Assn., Am. Acad. Polit. and Social Science, Am. Assn. Collegiate Schs. of Business (pres. 1925-26), Canadian Authors' Assn., Nebraska Writers Guild (pres. 1930-31), and Chi Phi, Beta Gamma Sigma, Alpha Kappa Psi, Phi Beta Kappa. Clubs: Rotary Club, The Club, Round Table (Lincoln, Neb.). Author: Monopolies, Past and Present, 1901; Orthodox Socialism, 1907; Little Stories of Quebec, 1908; State Socialism, in N.Z., 1910; Jean Baptiste, 1915; What is Socialism?, 1921; Economics for Everyman, 1923; First Economics, 1926; The Beauport Road, 1928; The Flying Canoe, 1929; The Habitant-Merchant, 1939; from Marx to Stalin, 1940; Inflation and How to Scotch It, 1943; also writer on econ. subjects, monographs, short stories. Home: 1801 Pepper Av., Lincoln NE‡

LERRIGO, MARION OLIVE, (MRS. WILLIAM J. MCWILLIAMS), author; b. Topeka, Oct. 27, 1898; d. Charles Henry and Annabel (Barry) Lerrigo; A.B., Washburn Coll., 1919; M.A., Columbia, 1921, Ph.D., 1926; m. William John McWilliams, Aug. 10, 1929 (dec. May 1957). Editor joint com. health problems edn. N.E.A. and A.M.A., 1922-24; mem. joint com. 1928-38; staff mem. Am. Child Health Assn., 1927-28, 29-33; instr. Springfield Coll., summer 1929. Mem. White House Conf. Child Health, 1930; nat. phys. edn. com. Nat. Council YMCA, 1952-70; mem. Larchmont Human Rights Commn.; chmn. health edn. com. YWCA, 1945-50, chmn. publs. com. The Woman's Press, 1949-51, chmn. editorial bd. Internat. House Quar., 1945-47. Mem. adv. bd. Guidance Center New Rochelle. Distinguished service award Alumni Assn. Washburn U., 1960. Mem. Am. Pub. Health Assn., League Women Voters, A.A.H.P.E.R., Delta Gamma. Presbyn. Clubs: Woman's (Larchmont); Adirondack Mountain. Author: Health Problem Sources, 1926; (with Thomas D. Wood) Health Behavior, 1928; Teaching How to Get and Use Human Energy, 1928; The Healthy Personality, 1935; (with Jean Broadhurst) Health Horizons, 1931; (with Thomas D. Wood and others) Now We are Growing 1936; Many Ways of Living, 1936; Keeping Fit, 1936; Blazing the Trail, 1936; How we Live, 1936; New Ways for Old, 1938; (with Thomas D. Wood and Thurman B. Rice) Sex Education, a Guide for Teachers and Parents, 1937; Children Can Help Themselves, 1943; (with Toru Matsumoto) A Brother is a Stranger, 1946; (with Helen Southard) A Story About You, What's Happening to Me? Learning About Love, Parents' Privilege, Sex Facts and Attitudes, 1956; (with Benjamin Spock) Caring for Your Disabled Child, 1965; also monthly series Watch Your Child Grow, in Today's Health, 1950-52; numerous articles in field. Home: Larchmont NY Died Sept. 29, 1968.

LESH, ULYSSES SAMUEL, lawyer; b. Wells County, Ind., Aug. 9, 1868; s. Joseph and Sarah L.; LL.B., U. of Mich., 1891; m. Minnie Fulton, June 27, 1894; children—John M., Lex, Joseph F. (dec.), Robert D. (dec.), James E., Samuel T. Began practice at Huntington, Ind., 1891, first as Kenner & Lesh, later with his younger brother; city atty., Huntington, 1902-04; county atty., Huntington County, 1907-09; Rep. candidate for judge of appellate court, 1914 (defeated); asst. atty. gen. of Ind., 1917-21, atty. gen., 1921-24 inclusive. Mem. Ind. State and Marion County bar assns. Presbyterian. Author: A Knight of the Golden Circle, 1911; Three Profiteers, 1924. Address: Lesh Bldg., Huntington IN‡

LESLIE, JOSEPH ALEXANDER, JR., editor; b. Tazewell, Va., Apr. 3, 1894; s. Joseph Alexander and Ella (Bland) L.; A.B., U. Richmond, 1916; m. Nell Combs, June 24, 1919; children—Joseph Alexander, Jean Carter. Staff Richmond Virginian, Newport (Va.) Daily Press, Newport News Times-Herald, Norfolk Virginian-Pilot, Norfolk Ledger-Dispatch, 1934-59, editor 1950-59. Mem. Va. World War II History Commn. Trustee U. Richmond; Fork Union Military Acad. Served 111th F.A., Va. N.G., 1917, 2d lt. U.S. Army, 1918. Mem. Am. Soc. Newspaper Editors, Phi Kappa Sigma, Pi Delta Epsilon. Democrat. Baptist. Mason. Club: Norfolk Yacht and Country. Home: Norfolk VA Died Nov. 1972.

LESOURD, HOWARD MARION, pub. relations exec.; b. Cin., Nov. 18, 1889; s. Marion and Edith May (Thompson) LeS.; A.B., Ohio Weleyan U., 1911, LL.D., 1941; A.M., Columbia, 1913, Ph.D., 1929; grad. Union Theol. Sem., 1915; m. Lucile Leonard, June 3, 1916; children—Leonard Earle, Patricia. Ordained ministry M.E. Ch., 1914; dir. religious edn. Madison Av. M.E. Ch., N.Y.C., 1916-17; with Army YMCA, 1917-18; pastor Ohio State U., 1919-22; pastor Ben Avon M.E. Ch., Pitts., also instr. religious edn. Western Theol. Sem., 1923-26; prof. religious edn. Duke, 1926-29, nat. fellow religion, 1927; prof. religious edn. Boston U. Sch. Religious Edn., 1929-33, dean Grad. Sch., 1933-44, dean Sch. Pub. Relations, 1947-53, emeritus, 1954; asst to Dr. Norman Vincent Peale, 1954-61; pres. Am. Christian Assn. Israel, 1962-72. Bus. mgr. Am. Fedn. Religion and Psychiatry, 1955-69; cons. on devel. Protestant Council N.Y.C., 1960-72; dir. Inst. Democratic Edn., 1943-57 (chmn. bd. govs.), Am. Christian Palestine Com., 1944-47. Fellow Nat. Council Religion Higher Edn.; mem. Pub. Relations Soc. Am., Phi Delta Kappa, Phi Gamma Delta. Republican. Mason. Club: Boston Authors. Home: New York City NY Died Sept. 8, 1972; buried Spring Hill Cemetery, Hamilton OH

LESSING, OTTO EDUARD, prof. German; b. Heimsheim, Wuerttemberg, Germany, Sept. 28, 1875; s. Gustav Adolf and Bertha (Majer) L.; ed. Royal Gymnasium, Stuttgart, 1887-89; theol. seminaries at Maulbronn and Blaubeuren, 1889-93; U. of Tubingen, 1893-94; U. of Mich., 1894-96, A.B., 1895, Ph.D., 1901; studied art and lit., Munich, 1898-1900, 1903-07; m. Maria Wilhelmina Dilg, of Boeblingen, Wuerttemberg, Aug. 9, 1898; children—Marion, Otto. Instr. German, U. of Mich., 1896-98, U. of Wis., 1900-02, Smith Coll., Mass., 1902-03; asso. prof. German, 1907-13, prof., Sept. 1, 1913-22, U. of Ill.; prof. of German, Williams Coll., 1923. Mem. Modern Lang. Assn. America, German Assn. for Culture (New York), Swabian Schiller Soc., Phi Beta Kappa of U. of Mich. Author: Schiller und Grillparzer, 1901; Grillparzer und das Neue Drama, 1905; Rebekka (play), 1905; Die Neue Form, 1910; Masters in Modern German Literature, 1912; Geschichte der deutschen Literatur, 1921; Liebe im Herbst (verse, under pen-name Peter Landgraf"), 1924; Bruecken ueber den Atlantik, 1927. Translator: Whitman's Prosaschriften, 1906; Williamstown MA‡

LESSLER, MONTAGUE, lawyer, congressman; b. New York, Jan. 1, 1869; s. Siegmund and Annie L.; grad. Coll. City of New York, B.S., 1889; law ed'n Columbia Law Sch.; m. Chicago, Dec. 5, 1898, Miss T. Sondheimer. Elected Jan. 7, 1902, mem. Congress to fill vacancy in 7th N.Y. dist. Mem. Naval Com. 57th Congress. Republican Club of City of New York. Residence: 7 Central Av., Tompkinsville, S.I. Office: 31 Nassau St., New York‡

LESTER, ROBERT MACDONALD, educational exec.; b. Center, Ala., Nov. 7, 1889; s. Rev. Samuel Robert and Ann Virginia (Watson) L.; A.B., Birmingham-Southern College, 1908; A.B., Vanderbilt Univ., 1911; Buhl fellow in classics U. of Mich., 1911-12; A.M., Columbia, 1917; Litt.D., Birmingham-Southern Coll., 1931; D.C.L., Acadia U., Can., 1933; LL.D., Univ. of N.M., 1936, Tulane U., 1940, Duke U., 1941, St. Francis Xavier, Canada, 1953, University of North Carolina, 1958, University of Chattanooga, 1960; L.H.D., Southwestern at Memphis, 1954, U. Ala., 1962; D.C.L., U. of South Sewanne, Tenn., 1943; m. Memory Aldridge, Jan. 30, 1915; 1 son, Robert MacDonald. Instr. Greek, Birmingham-Southern Coll., 1907-08; teacher English and dir. athletics, Byars-Hall High Sch., Covington, Tenn., 1912-16, asst. prin., 1912-14, prin., 1914-16; mem. Columbia U. library staff, 1916-17, and 1921; supt. pub. schs. Mayfield, Ky., 1917-18, Covington, Tenn., 1919-21; mem. Columbia U. dept. English, 1921-26; instr. Columbia Coll., 1922-24, administrative officer for men univ. undergrads, 1923-26, asst. to dir. univ. extension, 1924-26; asst. to pres. Carnegie Corp. 1926-34, sec., 1934-54; asso. sec. Carnegie Found. for Advancement of Teaching, 1947; sec., 1949-54; exec. dir. So. Fellowship Fund, 1954-69; dir., v.p. Home Trust Co., 1934-54. Cons. Council of So. Universities, Inc., 1964-69. Trustee Am. U., 1941-65. Served as pvt. U.S. Inf., World War I; served in 7th Regt. N.Y. Guard, through grades to captain, 1942-45. Mem. Assn. Am. Colls. (exec. com. 1935-36), Am. Library Assn. (hon. life), Kappa Sigma, Phi Beta Kappa. Democrat. Methodist. Clubs: Century; Men's Faculty (Columbia); Cosmos (Washington); Rotary. Compiler (with others) The Diffusion of Knowledge, 1935. Author of Forty Years of Carnegie Giving, 1941; A Thirty Year Catalog of Grants, 1942; A Summing Up, 1964; also spl. reports and revs. of Carnegie Corp. activities, pub. under gen. title The Audit of Experience. Home: Chapel Hill NC Died Feb. 21, 1969.

LE TOURNEAU, ROBERT GILMOUR, mfg. exec.; b. Richford, Vt., Nov. 30, 1888; s. Caleb T. and Elizabeth (Lorimer) Le T.; student pub. schs., Duluth, Minn., and Portland, Ore.; Internat. Corr. Schools; hon. Dr. Mech. Engring., John Brown Univ., 1939; hon. Dr. Science, Stetson Univ., 1942; LL.D., Miss. Coll., 1946; m. Mary Evelyn Peterson, August 29, 1917; children—Caleb Thomas (deceased), Louise (Mrs. Gus Dick), Donald (dec.), Richard, Roy, Ted L., Ben W. Various positions, 1902-17; engaged in garage business, 1917-29; contractor and builder land leveling equipment, 1929-69; pres. R. G. Le Tourneau, Inc., 1929-69; pres. Le Tourneau Found., Le Tourneau of Liberia, Ltd., Le Tourneau of Peru, Inc., R. G. Le Tourneau Sales & Service Co., Le Tourneau Off Shore, Inc., RGL Corp. Trustee of the John Brown U.; chmn. Le Tourneau College; mem. Bd. of Reference, Wheaton (Ill.) Coll. Recipient Beaver award, 1958. Decorated Grand Comdr. Order Star Africa. Mem. Soc. Automotive Engrs., Inc., Am. Soc. M.E., Soc. Am. Mil. Engrs., Am. Ordnance Assn., Nat. Def. Transp. Assn., Internat. Gideons Soc., Christian Business Men's Com. Internat. (past pres., vice chmn.), Nat. Laymen Evangelical Assn. (exec. com.). Republican. Mem. Christian and Missionary Alliance Ch. Home: Longview TX Died June 1, 1969; buried Longview TX

LETOURNEAU, SEVERIN, chief justice of the Province of Quebec; b. St. Constant, Quebec, May 23, 1871; s. Hubert and Laurence (Vedney) L.; student Ecole Normale Jacques-Cartier, 1886-91, Universite Laval, 1891-95; Docteur en Droit de l'Universite de Montreal; m. Antonine Lanctot, June 30, 1896; children—Paul Emile, Andrea (Mrs. Adelard Descarries), Severine (Mrs. Robert Lariviere), Marcelle (Mrs. Auguste Descarries), Hubert, Jean, Magdeleine (Mrs. Marc Boyer), Rachel (Mrs. Robert Lee Smith). Began as advocate, July 1895; apptd. King's counsellor, July 1, 1906; apptd. organizer of Liberal Party of Quebec, Feb. 1911; elected mem. Quebec Legislature for Hochelaga Div., May 1912; named to Legislative Council of Quebec, June 1919; head of law firm, Letourneau, Beaulieu, Marin et Mercier; apptd. justice of the Court of King's Bench, appeal div., Jan. 1922; chief justice of the Province of Quebec since Jan. 1942. Clubs: Cercle Universitaire, Chapleau, Liberal Party. Roman Catholic. Home: 421 Argyle Av., Westmount, Montreal. Address: Court House, Montreal PQ Canada‡

LEUTZE, TREVOR WILLIAM, naval officer; b. Santa Barbara, Calif., Oct. 13, 1877; s. Rear Adm. E.H.C. and Julia Jarvis (McAlpine) L.; (grandson of Emanuel Leutze who painted Washington Crossing the Delaware); student Hartford High Sch., Washington High Sch., U.S. Naval Acad., Corcoran Scientific Sch., Washington, D.C.; m. Leobelle S. Wilfert, Apr. 7, 1927. Commd. ensign, Pay Corps, U.S. Navy, advanced through the grades to rear adm., 1928; relieved from active duty, Nov. 1, 1942. Decorated Spanish War, Marine Campaign (Panama) and Mexican Campaign medals, World War I medal with Silver Star, Am. Defense Medal, World War II Medal, Commendatory Ribbons from both Army and Navy, Al Merito 1st class (Chile). Home: 1169 Lakeview Dr., Winter Park FL‡

LEV, RAY, pianist; b. Rostov-Don, Russia; d. Moisse and Debora (Lev) Lev; student Music Sch. Settlement with Rebecca Davidson, later with Alexander Lipsky, Gaston Detheir, Tobias Matthay in London. Debut in Eng. with Sir Landon Ronald, 1931; appeared for BBC with orch., solo concerts in provinces; Am. debut at Carnegie Hall with Nat. Orch. Assn. under Barzin, 1933; toured throughout U.S., Europe, Israel, Near and Far East; thirty three Carnegie Hall solo orch. concerts including several with N.Y. Philharmonic; other appearances with St. Louis, Rochester, Cin., Indpls. symphony orchs.; chamber music concerts with Budapest, Pascal, Guillett, Gordon, Kroll quartets; tchr. piano and chamber music Tokyo U. Arts and Music under auspices Japanese Ministry Edn., 1962-64; soloist with Japan Philharmonic Symphony Orch. at Tokyo, Met. Festival Hall, Bunkio Hall; solo concerts Hibya Hall at Am. embassy, at Nasu Internat. Chamber Music

Festival, also over NHK radio and TV, Fuji Tv and radio; mem. jury several Fulbright competitions; toured Europe, 1962, 63, 65; recording artist for Music-Craft and Concert Hall Soc. Founder War Stamp Concert Assemblies in N.Y. pub. schs.; hon. pres. Assn. Philharmonic Scholarship Com. Winners Assn.; established fund for original composition Greenwich House Music Sch., 1948, also for Internat. Soc. Contemporary Music. Mem. adv. bd. Music Sch. Settlement. Recipient Matthay prize N.Y. Philharmonic Symphony Soc. scholarships; cash and gold medal in open competition, London, 1933; two citations Treasury Dept. for patriotic services, also spl. award distinguished service to N.Y. War Fund, War Savs. Staff and USO; two command performances at 10 Downing Street; played at White House for Pres. and Mrs. Roosevelt. Mem. Am. Guild Mus. Artists (bd. govs.), Nat. Music League, Am. Matthay Assn., Musicians Club Am. (charter). Piano transcription of Vivaldi Bach Concerto Grosso in D Minor; 2 piano transcription of Bach Bist de Bei Mir; 25 songs of Stephen Foster (book of Month Club selection 1946); Centuries of Masterworks for the New York City NY Died May 1968.

LEVANT, OSCAR, composer, pianist b. Pitts., Dec. 27, 1906; s. Max and Annie (Radin) L.; ed. grades and high sch., Pitts., studied music under Sigismund Stojowski; studied composition with Arnold Schoenberg, 1935-37; m. Barbara Smith, Jan. 5, 1932; m. 2d, June Gale, Dec. 1, 1939; children—Marcia Ann, Lorna, Amanda. Composer and asst. to producer of motion pictures; appeared as soloist with New York Philharmonic, Cleve., Pitts., Phila., Rochester, Los Angeles, San Francisco, St. Louis, Cin., Montreal, Detroit, Mpls. and NBC orchs.; conducted original composition with three of above orchs. Composer: (songs) Blame It on My Youth, Lady Play Your Mandolin. Music Expert" on Information Please" radio program. Appeared in pictures, Rhythm on the River, Kiss the Boys Goodbye, Rhapsody in Blue, Humoresque, Barkley's of Broadway, An American in Paris. The Bandwagon, Recorded album of modern piano music and Gershwin Concerto in F with New York Philharmonic Soc. for Columbia, Rhapsody in Blue with Phila. Orch. for Columbia; original compositions played by Boston, Cleve., St. Louis, Rochester, Pitts., Mpls., Bklyn. and NBC symphony orchs. Author: A Smattering of Ignorance, 1940; Memoirs of An Amnesiac, 1965; The Unimportance of Being Oscar, 1968. Contbr. to Good Housekeeping, Harpers, Town and Country, Vogue. Home: Beverly Hills CA Died Aug. 14, 1972; buried Westwood Meml. Park, West Los Angeles CA

LEVENSON, JOSEPH RICHMOND, educator; b. Boston, June 10, 1920; s. Max Lionel and Eva (Richmond) L.; A.B., Harvard, 1941, A.M., 1946, Ph.D., 1949; m. Rosemary Sebag-Montefiore, Oct. 5, 1950; children—Richard Montefiore, Irene Anne, Thomas Montefiore., Leo Montefiore. Teaching fellow Harvard, 1946-48; jr. fellow Soc. Fellows, 1948-51; mem. faculty U. Cal. at Berkeley, 1951-69, prof. history, 1961-69, Sather prof. history, 1965-69, vice chmn. dept., 1964-66, 68-69. Served to lt. USNR, 1942-46. Fulbright fellow, 1954-55; fellow Center Advanced Study Behavorial Scis., 1958-59; Guggenheim fellow, 1962-63; Am. Council Learned Socs. fellow, 1966-67. Mem. Assn. Asian Studies (bd. dirs. 1965-68), Am. Hist. Assn. (prize Pacific Coast br. 1959), Assn. Asian Art, Phi Beta Kappa. Democrat. Jewish religion. Club: Berkeley Tennis. Author: Liang Ch'i-ch'ao and the Mind of Modern China, 4th edit., 1967; Confucian China and Its Modern Fate: The Problem of Intellectual Continuity, Vol. I, 3d edit., 1965, The Problem of Monarchical Decay, Vol. 11, 1964, The Problem of Historical Significance, Vol. 111, 1965, 1st combined edit., 1968; Europe's Expansion and the Counter Example of Asia: 1300-1600, 1967; (with Franz Schurmann) China: An Interpretive History.. ., 1969; Modern China: An Interpretive Anthology, 1971; Revolution and Cosmopolitanism: the Western Stage and the Chinese Stages, 1971 (last 3 posthumous). Bd. editors jour. Asian Studies, Pacific Hist. Rev. Home: Berkeley CA Died Apr. 6, 1969; buried Home of Peace, Oakland CA

LEVERONE, NATHANIEL, food service exec.; b. Wakefield, Mass., June 26, 1884; s. Robert and Rose (Fosser) L.; B.S., Dartmouth Coll., 1906; m. Martha Ericsson, June 25, 1925; 1 child—Meredith. Western mgr. Bates Number Machine Co., 1908-12; sec. and gen. mgrs., Hill Pump Valve Co., 1912-22; pres. Nathaniel Leverone Co. (real estate investments), 1922-29; founder Canteen Corporation (formerly known as Automatic Canteen Company of America), 1929, president, 1929-39, chairman board, 1939-60, then founder chairman; president of Canteen Company, 1946-51, chmn. bd., from 1951, pres. M-M Drilling Corp., from 1948; dir. LaSalle Nat. Bank, Finance Club., Inc., Chicago Federal Savings & Loan Assn., State St. Ins. Agy., Inc. Hon. chmn. Chgo. Heart Assn., from 1963; bd. dirs., exec. com.; pres. Goodwill Industries, 1943-45, dir., from 1940; pres. Chicago Youth Week, 1945-59; life mem. Chgo. Crime Commn.; dir. Rehab. Inst. Chgo.; member citizens bd. U. of Chicago; mem. Council of Laymens Nat. Com.; trustee Hadley Sch. Blind, Curry Coll., Culver-Stockton Coll.; bd. dirs. Am. Found. Religion and Psychiatry; chmn. bd., dir. Kansas City Athletics, Inc., 1954-60; pres. Chgo. chpt. Am. Scandinavian Found., from 1963; co-chmn. Mayor's Com. Cleaner Chgo., from 1954; former mem. and exec. numerous civic coms. and commns. Mem., sometime officer numerous trade and profl. assns. and orgns. Mason. Presby. Clubs: Univ., Union League, Mchts. and Mfrs., Execs., Rotary, Casino, Saddle & Cycle Mid-Am., (Chgo.); Everglades (Palm Beach); Capitol Hill (Washington); Bath and Tennis (Palm Beach, Fla.). Author numerous articles on business and social problems. Home: Chicago IL Died May 1969.

LEVETT, BENJAMIN ARTHUR, lawyer; b. Hartford, Conn., Feb. 16, 1873; s. Morris Henry and Orynthia (Da Costa) L.; ed. pub. schs.; read law in offices of Solicitor Gen. Aldrich and Robert T. Lincoln, of Chicago, 1890-94; m. Cornelia Gulick, June 12, 1902; children—Beatrice Adelaide Barnes, Warren Arthur. Admitted to Illinois bar, 1894, New York bar, 1894; Hawaiian bar, 1906; practiced with firm of Dyer & Seely, patent lawyers, New York, N.Y., 1894-96; law clerk, later asst. counsel Treasury Dept., before board of United States Gen. Appraisers (Customs Court), 1896-1906; mem. com. on customs regulations of Am. section Internat. Chamber Commerce, 1923; proprietor Customs Maze Pub. Co. Mem. 9th Coast Arty., Nat. Guard N.Y., 1917-1919. Republican. Clubs: Circumnavigators, University, Downtown Athletic. Author: Through the Customs Maze, 1923; A Martian Examines Christanity, 1934; Culbertson in Rime, 1934; Selected Poems, 1939; also poems, stories, monographs and mag. articles. Home: 175 Riverside Drive. Office: 8 Bridge St., New York NY‡

LEVEY, MARTIN, educator, chemist; b. Phila., May 18, 1913; s. Joseph and Julia (Brodie) L.; A.B., Temple U., 1934; student U. Pa., 1934-37; Ph.D., Dropsie Coll., 1952; m. Mary A. McGlinchy, Jan. 8, 1944; children—Susan B., Peter A. Chemist, 1942-49; instr. chemistry Pa. State U., 1953-55; instr. math. Temple U., Phila., 1956-59; mem. Inst. Advanced Study, Princeton, 1959-60, 65-66; NSF research fellow College de France, 1960; research asso., prin. investigator Yale, 1960-64; prin. investigator Rockefeller U., 1964-65; prof. history of sci. State U. N.Y., Albany, 1966-70, chmn. dept. history and systematics of sci., 1969-70. Served with U.S. Merchant Marine, 1938-42. Fellow Medieval Acad. Am.; mem. Am. Chem. Soc. History Sci. Soc., Am. Inst. History Pharmacy (Edward Kremers award distinguished writing 1968), Soc. Study Alchemy and Ancient History, Japanese History Sci. Soc., A.A.A.S., Am. Hist. Assn., Am. Chem. Soc. (councillor 1960-64, chmn. history chem. div. 1964-65; Dexter award 1965), Am. Oriental Soc., World Future Soc., Author: Chemistry and Chemical Technology in Ancient Mesopotamia, 1959; Medieval Arabic Bookmaking and Its Relation to Early Chemistry and Pharmacology, 1962; Al-kitan al-jabr wal-muqabala of abu Kamil Shuja ibn Aslam in a Commentary by Mordecai Finzi, 1965; The Medical Formulary of Aqrabadhin of al-Kindi: The Roots of Arabic Medicine and Its Influence on Later Arabic and Latin Literature, 1965; (with M. Petruck) Kushyar ibn Labban, Principles of Hindu Reckoning, 1965; (with N. Al-Khaledy) The Medical Formulary of al-Samarqandi and the Relation of the Early Arabic Simples to Those Found in the Indigenous Medicine of the Near East and India, 1967; Medieval Arabic Toxicology; The Book on Poisons of ibn al-Wahshiya and Its Relation to Early Indian and Greek Texts, 1966; Medical Ethics of Medieval Islam with Special Reference to al-Ruhawi's Practical Ethics of the Physician, 1967; Substitute Drugs in Early Arabic Medicine with Special Reference to the Texts of Masarjawaih, al-Razi, and Pythagoras, 1969; Kitab al-Taswiyah of al-Nasawi: A Theoretical Treatise on Medicine of the Eleventh Century, 1969; Chemical Aspects of Medieval Arabic Minting in a Treatise by Mansur ibn Bara, 1969. Editor: Archeological Chemistry, 1967. Mem. bd. editors Chymia, 1964, Jour. History Chemistry, 1969; corr. editor supplements to Japanese Studies History of Sci., 1969. Contbr. articles profl. jours. Home: Albany NY Died Aug. 22, 1970.

LEVI, HARRY, rabbi; b. Cincinnati, O., Aug. 7, 1875; s. Isaac and Belle (Engelstein) L.; B.A., U. Cincinnati, 1897; rabbi, Hebrew Union Coll., Cincinnati, 1897; D.D., Boston U., 1936; m. Ruth Wolf, Feb. 2, 1908; children—Robert, Harry. Ordained rabbi, 1897; rabbi, Wheeling, W.Va., 1897-1911, Temple Israel, Boston, since 1911. Mem. Central Comn. of Am. Rabbis. Mem. B'nai B'rith. Mason. Clubs: City, Twentieth Century, Elysium, Pine Brook Valley Golf (all hon.). Author: Jewish Characters in English Fiction, 1899; The Great Adventure, 1929; A Rabbi Speaks, 1930. Contbr. to Effective Preaching and Community Addresses, 1929, also to The Field of Social Service, and to Boston Preachers; contbg. editor of World Unity. Home: 84 Salisbury Rd., Brookline MA*‡

LEVI, JULIAN CLARENCE, architect, painter; b. N.Y.C., Dec. 8, 1874; s. Albert Augustus and Henriette Mathilde (Meyer) L.; A.B., Columbia, 1896, postgrad. work Columbia Archtl. Sch; Architecte Diplome, Ecole des Beaux Arts, Paris, 1904; m. Alice Fries, October 3, 1900 (deceased July 20, 1961). Architect in New York City, from 1904; and first asso. with Francis H. Kimball; mem. Taylor & Levi (architects numerous indsl., comml., ednl., meml. bldgs. and churches, also pvt. residences in N.Y.C. and other cities), 1907-62; rep. French Am. Union to establish program for constrn. open air schools Ministry Edn., Paris, 1921; founder, chairman Architects Emergency Committee, 1930-35, later honorary chairman; collaborating architect U.S. Pavilion, International Expn., Paris, 1937; cons. architect Romanian House, N.Y. World's Fair, 1939. Del. internat. archtl. congresses, Paris, Washington, Montevideo, Lima, Havana, Mexico, Lausanne, Morocco, Portugal, 1937-53, London 1961; mem. permanent com. Pan-Am. Congress Architects. Mem. Columbia Assos.; fellow in perpetuity Met. Museum Art. Served as captain American Red Cross, World War I; chief, construction Base Section, France, 1918-19; mem. adv. com. arts and awards U.S. Army Service Forces, World War II. Decorated Chevalier Legion of Honor, 1921, Officer, 1938, Comdr., 1951, Officer de l'Instruction Publique, 1927, Medal of Honor, Assistance Publique (France), Knight Royal Order North Star (Sweden); recipient Medal of Honor, Mexico, 1952; medal Hist. Monuments Architects of France, 1955, City of Lille medal, 1959; bronze trophy, Nat. Inst. Archtl. Edn., 1956; Alumni medal Columbia University, 1962; Bronze Columbia Lion, Columbia Univ., 1969. Fellow A.I.A. (chairman foreign relations 1934-40, 46-50; founder, 1st chmn. travelling fellowships in Am. for French architects; mem., past officer N.Y. chpt.; organizer exhbns. Am. architecture numerous fgn. cities, 1921-40, Washington, 1939); mem. Archtl. League N.Y. (past pres.; received president's medal 1933; citation for 50 yrs. service to profession 1956), Nat. Sculpture Soc. (past v.p.), Nat. Soc. Mural Painters, Soc. Beaux Arts Architects (past pres.), Vets Fgn. Wars, Soc. des Architects Diplomes par le Gouvernement (past pres.), Am. Soc. French Legion of Honor (exec. com.), Nat. Inst. Architectural Education, Fine Arts Federation N.Y., French Inst. in Am., Municipal Art Soc., Iranian Inst. and Sch. Asiatic Studies (mem. bd.), New York Building Congress (honorary life mem.); hon. or corr. mem. numerous similar fgn. orgns. Paintings in exhbns. including Paris Salon, Boston Art Club. Bklyn. Mus. Art, Internat. Water Color Exhbn. (Chgo.), Archtl. League. Recipient awards including hon. mention Paris Salon, 1904, Turin, 1920; gold medal, Santiago, Chile, 1923; silver medal Diplome Soc., Paris, 1925; grand prize internat. Expn., Paris, 1937; medal Soc. Centrale des Architects, France, 1950. Club: Coffee House. Donated Laura Boulton Collection Traditional and Liturgical Music to Columbia U. Home: New York City NY Died Aug. 21, 1971.

LEVIN, JOSEPH JAY, investment banker; b. Chgo., Jan. 7, 1897; s. Hirsh and Toba (Jaffe) L.; Ph.B., U. Chgo., 1917; m. Madeleine Despres, Aug. 19, 1928; children—Alice (Mrs. John Rapisarda), Elizabeth (Mrs. Pier Paolo Bigongiari). Retail mcht., 1918-22; with A.G. Becker & Co., Inc., Chgo., from 1922, executive vice pres., 1959-64, senior vice pres., 1964-66, cons., from 1966; dir. Balmorhea Ranches, Inc., Danly Machine Specialities, Inc., Mansfield Tire & Rubber Co. Mem. exec. com. Am. Jewish Com., from 1946, chmn. Chgo. chpt., 1957; dir. Bur. on Jewish Employment Problems, from 1958, pres., 1960-62; pres. Ill. div. UN Assn., from 1967. Mem. Phi Beta Kappa. Home: Chicago IL Died Mar. 18, 1972.

LEVIN, THEODORE, judge; born Chicago, Illinois, Feb. 18, 1897; s. Joseph and Ida (Rosin) L.; LL.B., U. of Detroit, 1920, LL.M., 1924; Doctor of Laws (hon.), Wayne State U., 1961; D.H.L., Hebrew Union Coll., 1970; m. Rhoda Katzin, May 31, 1925; children—Charles L., Miriam L., Daniel E., Joseph. Admitted to Mich. state bar, 1920; gen. practice of law, Detroit, 1920-46; U.S. dist. judge Eastern Dist. Mich., 1946-70, chief judge, 1959-67. Trustee philanthropic insts. Jewish religion. Home: Detroit MI Died Dec. 31, 1970.

LEVINE, HARRY HARVEY, physician; b. Bklyn., Apr. 6, 1919; s. Philip F. and Henrietta Levine; M.D., Middlesex U., 1943; M.P.H., Columbia, 1958; m. Anita Weintraub, Mar. 4, 1943; children—Gloria, Richard, Amy. Intern, Cumberland Hosp., Bklyn., 1943-44; resident Sea View Hosp, 1944-45, Richmond Boro Contagious Hosp., 1944-45; resident tng. N.Y.C. Dept. Health and Health Ins. Plan Greater N.Y., 1957, 58; v.p. Health Ins. Plan Greater N.Y., until 1969; past pres. med. bd. La Guardia Hosp., Queens, N.Y.; adj. clin. prof. preventive medicine Albert Einstein Coll. Med., Yeshiva U. Served to comdr., M.C., USNR, 1945-46, 55-56. Diplomate Am. Bd. Preventive Medicine. Fellow Am. Pub. Health Assn.; mem. A.M.A., Group Health Assn., Brit. Med. Assn. Home: Brooklyn NY Died Feb. 3, 1969; buried Mt. Ararat, Long Island NY

LEVINE, MARKS, concert mgr.; b. New York, N.Y., Aug. 19, 1890; s. Jacob and Anna (Smelansky) Levitzki-Levine; elementary and high sch. edn. in Russia; B.S. in Civil Engring., Cooper Union, N.Y. City, 1914; m. Emily Schifferdecker, Jan. 1, 1926 (div. 1952); m. 2d, Florence Wolfe, March 7, 1953. Engaged in civil engring., 1914-21; concert mgr., Daniel Mayer, Inc., 1921-30; mgr. concert div. Nat. Broadcasting Co., 1930-41; v.p., dir. concert div. Nat. Concert and Artists

Corp., N.Y.C., 1941-48, pres., 1948-55; gen. cons. Little Orchestra Soc., American Guild Mus. Artists, musical orgns. and individuals. Made three tours of Australasia, with Mischa Levitzki, pianist (a brother), Giannini, Flagstad, also three tours of Europe, one tour of Orient with Levitzki and six trip to Honolulu. Chmn. board, National Concert and Artists Corp.; chmn. bd. and vice pres., Civic Concert Service, Inc. Dir. Rachmaninoff Memorial Fund. Mem. Am. Soc. Composers, Authors, Pub. Author: First Performance, 1957. Composer: (lyrics) When I Love You (Marsden); Spring Came (McArthur); Do You Remember? (Levitzki); We Love and Dream (Luboshutz); I Looked at a Tulip (MacArthur). Home: New York City NY Died May 28, 1971; buried Mt. Lebanon Cemetery, Brooklyn NY

LEVINE, MAURICE, physician; b. Cin., June 10, 1902; s. Louis and Esther Levine; B.A., U. Cin., 1923, M.A. in Psychology, 1924; M.D., Johns Hopkins, 1928; grad. Chgo. Inst. for Psychoanalysis, 1937; m. Diana Bailen, Aug. 12, 1934; children—Ann (Mrs. Philip M. Meyers), Ellen (Mrs. Michael H. Ebert), Martha (Mrs. David M. Dunkelman). Jr. intern in surgery Twillingate, Nfld., Can., 1927; intern in medicine Johns Hopkins Hosp., Balt., 1928-29, resident in psychiatry Phipps Psychiat. Clinic, 1929-32; instr. psychiatry Johns Hopkins, 1929-32; asst. prof. psychiatry U. Cin. Coll. Medicine, 1933-44, asso. prof., 1944-46, lectr. abnormal psychology Evening Coll., 1933-46, lectr. psychiatry Sch. Pub. Adminstrn., 1934-36, prof. psychiatry, dir. dept., 1947-71; dir. psychiatry service Cin. Gen. Hosp., 1947-71, Children's Hosp., Cin., 1947-71; faculty Chgo. Inst. for Psychoanalysis, 1942-71; cons. psychiatrist, mem. dean's com. Cin. VA Hosp.; cons. psychiatrist Jewish, Drake, Dunham, Children's Convalescent hosps., Vis. prof. psychiatry U. Wash. Grad. Sch., summer 1944; dir. Central Psychiat. Clinic of Community Chest, 1947-71; Samuel D. Gross lectr. U. Louisville, 1945; Eli Moschowitz lectr. Mt. Sinai Hosp., N.Y.C., 1952; Frank L. Weil lectr. relgion and humanities Hebrew Union Coll., Cin., 1968-69; cons. to surgeon gen. USPHS, 1950-58, nat. adv. mental health council Nat. Inst. for Mental Health, 1953-57. Bd. dirs. Inst. for Intercultural Studies, N.Y.C., 1965-71. Recipient Dolly Cohen award for distinguished univ. teaching U. Cin., 1970. Diplomate Am. Bd. Psychiatry and Neurology (examiner 1945-50). Fellow Am. Psychiat. Assn. life, exec. council 1953-56), Am. Orthopsychiat, Assn. (life); mem. A.M.A., Group for Advancement Psychiatry, Am., Internat. psychoanalytic assns., Cin. Psychoanalytic Soc. (pres. 1967-68), Assn. for Research in Nervous and Mental Disease, Soc. for Applied Anthropology, Am. Psychosomatic Assn. (council 1948-51), Cin. Soc. for Neurology and Psychiatry (pres. 1946-47), Sigma Xi, Alpha Omega Alpha. Author: Psychotherapy in Medical Practice, 1942 (also Swedish, Spanish and Yugoslav edits.) Co-editor: Psychiatry and Medical Education, 1952; mem. editorial bd. Jour. Am. Psychoanalytic Assn., 1951-53; mem. editorial adv. bd. Jour. Nervous and Mental Disease, 1960-66; mem. internat. editorial bd. Mind and Medicine (monograph series), 1962-71. Contbr. articles to med. jours., chpts. to books. Home: Cincinnati OH Died May 1, 1971; buried Cincinnati OH

LEVINE, MORRIS, dept. chain exec.; b. Chgo., Dec. 22, 1900; s. Michael and Inc.; chmn. bd. Gulfstan Corporation; member of the adv. bd. Chem. Bank N.Y. Trust Co. Lectr. history U. Va., 1968-70. Chmn. bd. Reston Found., 1968-71. Professional engr., Mich., Ohio, Cal., Ontario. Republican. Roman Catholic. Clubs: University, Engineers, Metropolitan (N.Y.C.). Home: Reston VA Died Dec. 28, 1972; buried St. Ignatius of St. Thomas Manor, Port Tobacco MD

LEVINGS, MIRIAM FAIRBANK (MRS. NELSON T. LEVINGS), singer, civic worker; b. San Diego, Cal., Feb. 14, 1900; d. David C. and Maude (Gamble) Patterson; grad. Nat. Cathedral Sch., Washington 1920; student New Eng. Conservatory of Music, Boston, 1920-21; m. Livingston Fairbank, Oct. 14, 1922, (died July 1934); children—Jane Boyce (Mrs. James Oughton), Livingston; m. 2d, Nelson Trimble Levings, Dec. 5, 1941. Singer of German lieder and French songs, recitals include Salle Pleyel, Paris, France, Acad. Rome (Italy), Vienna, Prague, U. Ill., Dante Soc. N.Y.C. Chmn. entertainment com. Citizens Com. for Army and Navy, 1941-46, also various other N.Y.C. coms. Mem. Jr. League Chgo. Home: New York City NY Died June 10, 1969.

LE VINSEN, FLORENZA D'ARONA (FLORENCE ROOSEVELT), singer, vocal teacher; b. Pittsfield, Mass.; d. Alonzo and The Hon. Elizabeth (de Griemly) Roosevelt; ed. Sacre Coeur, Paris; Anne's Sem., Reading Berks, Eng.; studied piano with Sir Steindale Bennett, London; singing with Viadot Garcia, Paris; 8 yrs. with Francisco Lamperti, Milan; was his interpreter and accompanist; m. New York, Sept. 20, 1890, Baron von Brockdorff Le Vinsen. Sang and played at Crystal Palace, London, when 5 yrs. old; debut, Maldran Theatre, Venice; appeared in Italian cities 3 yrs., also in Paris and London; in U.S. with Mapleson; toured Mex. and W.I. with Rosa's Royal Italian Opera Co., Europe with own concert co. Vocal teacher in New York, 14 yrs., Paris, 3 yrs., also Berlin and Rome. Has produced many operatic, concert, oratorio artists and choir soloists. Contb'r to mus. jours. Author: The Siren's Net, 1905 L26; The Vocal Teacher, I2. Residence: Copenhagen Denmark‡

LEVITT, ALBERT, lawyer; born Woodbine, Md., March 14, 1887; son of Thomas Reeve and Ida Alice L.; B.D., Meadville Theol. Sch., 1911; B.A., cum magnis honoribus, Columbia, 1913; LL.B., Harvard, 1920; J.D., Yale, 1923; m. Elsie Mary Hill, Dec. 24, 1921; 1 dau., Leslie Hill-Levitt. Lecturer in philosophy, Columbia, 1913-14; acting prof. philosophy, Colgate, 1915-16; asst. prof. law, George Washington U., 1920-21; prof. law, U. of N.D., 1921-22; lecturer on med. jurisprudence, Johns Hopkins Med. Sch., 1924; prof. law, Washington and Lee U., 1924-27; prof. law, Brooklyn Law Sch. of St. Lawrence U., 1927-30; lecturer law of finance, Sch. of Commerce, New York University, 1939; professor of law, Hastings College of the Law, University of California, 1942-43; special asst. to attorney general of U.S., 1923-24, 1933-35, 1936-37; judge U.S. Dist. Ct. of V.I., 1935-36. Mem. U.S. Assay Commn., 1921; rep. of U.S. Dept. of Justice on committee of Advisors on Codification of Nationality Laws of the U.S.; spl. advisor to Office of Production Management, Priorities Div., 1941. Candidate of Independent Rep. party for gov. of Conn., 1932; Republican candidate U.S. Senator, Cal., 1950. Served as private and sergeant Hospital Corps., U.S. Army, 1904-07, in Philippines, 1906-07; with Am. Ambulance, French Army, at the front, 1915; regtl. sergt. maj. Harvard R.O.T.C., June-Sept. 1917; chaplain U.S. Army, 1917-Jan. 1919, overseas after Apr. 1918; in Baccarat sector, Oise-Aisne and Meuse-Argonne offensives; wounded and gassed. Mem. Am. Inst. Criminal Law and Criminology, Internat. Assn. Penal Law, Phi Beta Kappa, Delta Sigma Rho. Republican. Unitarian. Author: Code of International Criminal Law, 1928; An Outline Digest of the Criminal Law of New York, 1930; The Public Utilities of Connecticut, 1931; Community Property Law of California, 1951. Contbr. numerous articles on legal subjects; associate editor Central Law Journal, St. Louis, 1921-30. Home: Redding CT Died June 1968.

LEVY, CLIFTON HARBY, rabbi, writer; b. New Orleans, La., June 21, 1867; s. Eugene Henry and Almeria Emma (Moses) L.; A.B., U. of Cincinnati, 1887; rabbi, Hebrew Union Coll., 1890; grad. study, Johns Hopkins, 1896; m. Sara Lang, Mar. 8, 1891 (deceased); m. 2d, Cora Bacharach, Apr, 28, 1903. Rabbi, N.Y. City, 1890-91, Lancaster, Pa., 1892-94, Baltimore, 1894-96, Tremont Temple, N.Y. City, 1906-21; editor Jewish Comment, Baltimore, Md., 1894-97; engaged in writing since 1896; organizer, 1909, since mgr. Internat. Copywright Bur. Mem. Central Conf. Am. Rabbis, New York Bd. Jewish Ministers (ex-pres.), Assn. Reform Rabbis; organizer, 1924, Centre of Jewish Science for Spirtual Healing. Democrat. Mason; mem. B'nai B'rith. Author: Life of Guynemer (transl. from French), 1918; Judaism Applied to Life, 1926; The Ant People (transl. from German), 1927. Contbr. Bibl., archeol. and scientific articles to Am. Weekly and various newspaper syndicates; issued Ten Constructive Commandments," 1934; The Bible in Art, 1936. Art editor Universal Jewish Encyclopedia, 1940. Founding mem. and lecturer, Am. Council for Judaism since New York NY‡

LEVY, MATTHEW MALLTZ, judge, civic leader; b. Brest Litovsk, Russia, Mar. 1, 1899; s. Aaron Malitz and Rachel (Gold) L.; brought to U.S., 1904, naturalized, 1920; B.S. (Charbonnier Physics prize), U. Ga., 1919; LL.B., Harvard, 1922; m. Pearl Gold Spivak, May 13, 1922. Admitted to N.Y. bar, 1923, also U.S. Supreme Ct. Dist. Cts., Tax Ct., Circuit Ct., U.S. Bd. Immigration Appeals; law clk. Guggenheimer, Untermyer & Marshall, 1921; Rabenold & Scribner, 1922-24; pvt. practice of law, 1924-37, 39-50; mem. firm Polies & Levy, 1924-28, Panken & Levy, 1928-34; spl. dep. asst. atty. gen. State of N.Y., 1927, spl. asst. atty. gen., 1937; atty. labor unions, housing coops. and tenants assns., 1928-50; judge Municipal Ct. City of N.Y., 1938; justice Supreme Ct. State N.Y., 1951-71. Vice pres. New Leader Pub. Assn., 1935-37, 40-43, pres., 1943-50; former dir. Levy Jewelers, Inc., Ray Jewelers, Inc. (both Savannah, Ga.); dir., trustee Jos. D. Bookstaver Agy., Inc., N.Y.C. Chief counsel Bronx Tenants Emergency League, 1935; bd. legal examiners U.S. Civil Service Commn., N.Y.C., 1942-43; mem. N.Y.C. Council Def. Fire Protection, 1941-45; lectr. Practicing Law Inst., N.Y.C., also Phila., 1944-45; incorporator, presiding judge Jewish Conciliation Bd. Am.; founder United Jewish Appeal of Greater N.Y.; mem. nat. council Am. Jewish Joint Distbn. Com. Candidate Socialist party N.Y. State Supreme Ct., 1932; candidate Am. Labor party for pres. Borough Bronx, 1941, for N.Y. State Supreme Ct., 1943. Trustee Federation Jewish Philanthropies of New York, 1947-71, v.p., 1969-71, chairman committee on religious affairs, 1961-65, honorary chairman, 1965-71, chmn. Bronx div., 1953-63, hon. chmn., 1963-71; mem. com. on communal planning, exec. com., hon. chmn. labor com. bldg. fund campaign, 1962; past mem. Am. Civil Liberties Union, N.Y.C. Com. for Pub. Adult Edn., So. Electoral Reform League, Citizens Non-Partisan Com. for County Reorgn. and a Better City Council, Freedom House, League for Indsl. Democracy. Labor rep. legislative com. Bronx Council Social Agencies; del. Gov. N.Y. State Conf. Crime, Criminal and Society, 1935. Mem. city com. Citizens Union City N.Y., 1939-50; bd. dirs., and vice chairman LaGuardia Memorial Association; chairman of the Upper East Bronx div. Jewish Edn. Com., 1940; chmn. Liberal party Bronx County, 1944-50; mem. Social-Democratic Fedn. State of N.Y., 1936-50. Sponsor, vice chmn. Bronx Symphony Soc., 1941; trustee Lebanon Hosp., N.Y.C., 1945-62, chmn. com. to study future devel., 1961-62; v.p., trustee Bronx Lebanon Hosp. Centre, N.Y.C., 1962-71; former cons. admissions committee University Ga. Served as 2d lt. infantry, U.S. Army, 1918. Patron Internat. Bar Association; member Am. (spl. com. to consider race discrimination 1943), N.Y. State, Bronx County (v.p. 1950, bd. dirs. 1943-50, chmn. Bronx bar informal law conf., mem. director's council 1951-—) bar assns., Bronx County Bar Endowment, Am. Law Inst., Am. Judicature Soc., Inst. Jud. Adminstrn., Assn. Bar City N.Y. (chmn. com. conf. legal topics 1935-37), N.Y. County Lawyers Assn. (bd. dirs. 1939-45), Legal Aid Soc., Council Jewish Fedns. and Welfare Funds (mem. nat. bd. dirs. 1952-59, member executive committee), Workmen's Circle, Jewish War Veterans U.S., Assn. Supreme Ct. Justices State N.Y. (sec. 1968, v.p. 1969-70, pres. elect. 1971, chmn. com. on reform of law 1959-65, hon. chmn. 1966-71), Nat. Conf. State Trial Judges, Harvard Law Sch. Assn. (trustee N.Y.C. 1957-60, v.p. 1965), Alumni Assn. U. Ga., Grand Street Boys Assn., Order of Coif (hon.), Phi Beta Kappa (pres. N.Y. Alumni 1957-58), Phi Beta Kappa Assos., Phi Delta Phi (hon.), Sigma Upsilon. Recorded in Hall Fame, Bd. Edn., Savannah, Chatham County, Ga., 1970; recipient Tzedakah (Charity and Justice) award Commn. on Synagogue Relations, Fedn. Jewish Philanthropies N.Y., 1971. Jewish religion. Editor Harvard Law Rev., 1921-22. Home: New York City NY Died Sept. 4, 1971; buried Bonaventure Cemetery, Savannah GA

LEVY, RAPHAEL, educator; b. Balt., Nov. 4, 1900; s. Max and Dora (Pollack) L.; A.B., Johns Hopkins, 1920, M.A., 1922, Ph.D., 1924; student U. Paris, 1922-23; m. Helen Silverman, June 30, 1929; children—Manford Harold, Jerome Seymour. Instr., U. Wis., 1924-29, U. Balt., 1931-43; asst. prof. La. State U., 1943-46; prof. romance langs. U. Tex., 1946-69. Trustee, Balt. Hebrew Coll., 1940-43, J.S. Geggenheim Found., fellow, 1929. Mem. Modern Lang. Assn., South-Central Modern Lang. Assn., Societe-des Anciens Textes Francais. Club: Fortnightly. Author: The Astrological Works of Abraham ibn Ezra, 1927; Lexicographic Research on the Ancient French Texts from the Original Jewish, 1932; Repertory of Lexicons from the Old French, 1937; An Introduction to Current Affairs, 1939; The Beginning of Wisdom, 1939; Approximative Chronology of French Literature of the Middle Ages, 1957; Contribution to the French Lexicographie according to the Ancient Texts from the Original Jewish; Treasures of the Language of French Jews of the Middle Ages, 1964, others. Contbr. numerous articles profl. jours. Home: Austin TX Died July 18, 1969.

LE WALD, LEON THEODORE, roentgenologist; born 1874; M.D., College Physicians and Surgeons (Columbia), 1895; grad. U.S. Army Med. Sch., 1903; diploma in Radiology, Cambridge, Eng., 1926. Practiced at N.Y. City, 1895-1934 (retired); prof. roentgenology, New York U. Coll. of Medicine, 1917-39; retired. Mem. A.M.A., Am. Assn. for Thoracic Surgery, Am. Coll. Physicians, New York Gastro-Enterol. Assn. (pres.), Am. Roentgen Ray Soc., New York Roentgen Ray Soc., Radiol. Soc. N.A. (v.p.), Am. Coll. Radiology (former chancellor), Med. Assn. of Greater City of N.Y. (pres.), Soc. of Med. Jurisprudence (trustee), Am. Soc. of Plastic and Reconstructive Surgery; hon. mem. Nat. Gastroenterol. Assn. Lt. col. U.S. Army Res. Home: 1200 5th Av., New York 29 NY‡

LEWIS, ARTHUR, artist; b. Mobile, Ala., April 7, 1873; s. Seth Francis and Ida (Clark) L.; studied with Geo. B. Bridgman and Gerome. Exhibited at Paris Exp'n, 1900. Address: Players Club New York‡

LEWIS, D(OMINIC) B(EVAN) WYNDHAM, writer; b. 1891. Author: A London Farrago, 1922; At the Green Goose, 1923; At the Sign of the Blue Moon, 1924; At the Blue Moon Again, 1925; On Straw and Other Conceits, 1927; Francois Villon, 1928; The Anatomy of Dandyism (trans. from Barbey D'Aurevilly), 1928; (with G. C. Heseltine) A Christmas Book, 1928; King Spider: Louis XI of France, 1930; The Stuffed Owl—An Anthology of Bad Verse (with Charles Lee), 1930; The Emperor of the West (Charles V), 1932; Take it to Bed, 1944; Ronsard, 1944; The Hooded Hawk, 1947; Four Favourites, 1948; The Soul of Marshal Gilles de Raiz, 1952; (with Ronald Searle) The Terror of St. Trinian's, published 1954; Doctor Rabelais, published in 1957; A Florentine Portrait, 1959; Moliere: The Comic Mask, 1959; The Shadow of Cerevantes, 1962. Died Nov. 31, 1969; buried Altea, Alicante, Spain

LEWIS, DAVE, actor; b. Louisville, Ky., Dec. 22, 1870; s. Abraham and Amelia (Tobias) Levi; ed. pub. sch., Brooklyn; m. Lillian Frey, of New York, Jan. 18, 1892.

Debut as Mooney," in By the World Forgotten," Havlin's Theatre, Cincinnati, Aug. 28, 1892; has since played in Dore, Davidson Co.; Belle of Bohemia"; The Telephone Girl"; vaudeville, Eng. and America; in Royal Chef"; Don't Lie to Your Wife"; starring in September Morn," 1914-15; with Joe Weber prod. the Only Girl" by Victor Herbert, also The Fallen Idol" by Guy Bolton, 1915-16; wrote and prod. Within the Loop" for Messrs. Shubert, 1916-17; featured in burlesque over Columbia circuit, 1917-18. Life mem. Actors' Fund, Lodge of Elks, No. 4. Club: The Friars. Home: 732 Union Av., New York City‡

LEWIS, EDMUND HARRIS, lawyer; b. Syracuse, N.Y., Aug. 30, 1884; s. Ceylon H. and Jennie M. (Heffron) L.; A.B., Yale U., 1907, LL.D., 1954; LL.B., Syracuse U., 1909, LL.D., 1937; LL.D. Colgate U., 1940, Middlebury Coll., 1948, Hamilton Coll., 1954; m. Laura R. Strong, June 1, 1910; children—Mary Strong (dec.), Janet L. Dickson, Katharine Strong (dec.), Margaret L. Crosman. Admitted to N.Y. bar, 1909, and began practice at Syracuse; dep. atty. gen. of N.Y., 1915-18; corp. counsel Syracuse, 1920-22; elected justice Supreme Ct. of N.Y., 1929; asso. justice Appellate Div., 4th Dept., Oct., 1933-Jan. 3, 1940. Apptd. by gov. asso. judge Ct. of Appeals, Jan. 3, 1940, elected full term, Nov. 1, 1940; chief judge N.Y. Ct. Appeals, 1953-54; with Mackenzie, Smith, Lewis, Mitchell & Hughes, 1955-—. Chmn. mng. bd. Syracuse Community Chest, 1928-29. Mem. bd. trustees Syracuse U. Maj., Judge Adv. Gen.'s Corps, U.S. Army, 1918. Mem. N.Y. State Bar Assn. (pres. 1955), Onondaga County Bar Assn. (pres. 1929), Assn. Bar City New York, Syracuse C. of C. (pres. 1928-29), Delta Kappa Epsilon, Phi Delta Phi. Republican. Presbyn. Clubs: University of Syracuse (pres. 1926-27); Century (Syracuse); Skaneateles Country. Home: Skaneateles NY Died July 30, 1972.

LEWIS, EDWARD GARDNER, publisher; b. Watertown, Conn., Mar. 4, 1869; s. Rev. William Henry and Catherine C. L.; ed. Cheshire (Conn.) Acad. and Trinity Coll., Hartford, to jr. yr.; m. Baltimore, Mabel G. Wellington. Began publication The Woman's Mag., 1900 and has edited it ever since, bought Woman's Farm Journal, 1902, and has since edited it; formed Lewis Publishing Co., which took over publs., and is its pres.; also pres. People's United States Bank of St. Louis, University Heights Realty and Development Co., U.S. Fibre Stopper Co. Episcopalian. Republican. Clubs: St. Louis, Mercantile, Glen Echo. Address: University Heights, St Louis‡

LEWIS, FRED, pub. co. exec.; b. N.Y.C., 1888. Formerly gen. mgr. Hearts Mags., now exec. v.p.; pres., dir. Periodical Publs. Service Bur., Inc.; v.p., dir. Hearst Corp., Popular Mechanics Co.; dir. Nat. Mag. Co., London, Eng., Good Housekeeping, Inc. Home: Forest Hills NY Died Oct. 30, 1970; buried Northport Rural Cemetery, Northport, Suffolk County NY

LEWIS, FREDERICK WHEELER, clergyman, educator; b. Columbus, Miss., July 26, 1873; s. Hiram Wheeler and Lucy (Strong) L.; A.B., with honors, Princeton, 1895; B.D., McCormick Theol. Sem., 1898; D.D., Coll. of Emporia, 1916; m. Grace Howell Lewis, June 22, 1898; children—Katharine Ramsay (Mrs. D.L. Hibbard), Lucy Strong (Mrs. James R. Tolley), F. Howell, Herbert Wheeler, Margaret Williams (Mrs. C.D.L. Mosser). Ordained Presbyn. ministry, 1898; pastor Roseland Ch., Chicago, 1898-1901, Albion, N.Y., 1901-05, First Ch., Saginaw, Mich., 1905-09, Forest Hill Ch., Newark, N.J., 1909-18; pres. Coll. of Emporia, 1918-28, v.p. Bibl. Sem. in New York, 1928-34, pastor Throop Av. Presbyn. Ch., Brooklyn, 1934-43; retired. Mem. S.A.R. Club: Kansas Author. Home: 106 22 St., Pass-a-Grille FL‡

LEWIS, HENRY CARLETON, lawyer; b. Washington, Jan. 16, 1873; s. Edward Napoleon and Anne (Oakshott) L.; ed. pub. schs. and pvt. tutelage; LL.B., Nat. U., Washington, 1896, LL.M., 1897; unmarried. In law office of Judge Joseph K. McCammon, 1889, 1890; with Southern Ry. Co., 1890-1900; with Dept. of Justice, 1900-14; spl. asst. to the Atty.-Gen., 1909-14; resumed law practice at Washington. Episcopalian. Mem. Sigma Nu Phi. Club: University. Contbr. newspapers and mags. Home: 1419 Columbia Rd. Office: Bond Bldg., Washington‡

LEWIS, HERBERT LEFKOVITZ, editor; b. Austin, Minn., Oct. 16, 1898; s. Joseph and Regina (Levy) L.; B.A., U. of Minn., 1920, M.A., 1921; m. Georgiana Ingersoll, Feb. 11, 1930 (dec. 1962); children—Piers Ingersoll, Georgiana Ingersoll, Herbert Finlay; m. 2d, Emily L. Read, July 6, 1963. Reporter Marshall (Minn.) News Messenger, 1915-16; reporter St. Paul Pioneer Press and Dispatch, 1916-21, editorial writer, 1921-26, chief editorial writer, 1926-33, editorial dir. 1933-49, acting managing editor, 1942-45, editor, 1949-64, editorial cons., 1964-71; radio commentator, 1934-40; board directors, Minn. Broadcasting Corp., 1942-46. Served as private U.S. Army, 1918. Awarded Harris political science prize, 1920. Mem. Internat. Press Institute, National Council on Foreign Relations, National Conf. Editorial Writers. Mem. Fgn. Policy Assn. (dir. St. Paul br., chmn. 1940-41; American Society of Newspaper Editors, Phi Beta Kappa, Sigma Delta Chi. Clubs: Minnesota, Athletic Club (St. Paul); National Press (Washington, D.C.). Home: St Paul MN Died May 5, 1971; buried St. Paul MN

LEWIS, IRVING STANTON, fgn. service officer; b. Columbus, O., Dec. 11, 1919; s. William Vermylee and Viola (Nickels) L.; student Ohio State U., 1941-42, 46-47; B.A., Western Res. U., 1948; M.A., Georgetown U., 1950; m. Patricia Jean Claflin, June 7, 1947; children—Patricia H., Paul N., Penelope J., Philip H., Peter M. With Cleve. Council World Affairs, 1947-48; legislative ref. asst. to mem. U.S. Congress, 1949-50; dir. Binational Cultural Center, LaPaz, Bolivia, 1950-54, Guatemala City, Guatemala, 1954-57; joined U.S. Fgn. Service, 1957; cultural affairs officer Am. embassy, San Salvador, El Salvador, 1957-62; desk officer, Mexico, C.Am., Panama, U.S. Information Agy., Washington, 1962-65; pub. affairs officer Am. Embassy, Managua, Nicaragua, 1965-69, Montevideo, Uruguay, 1969-70; with USIA, Washington, 1970-71. Served to 2d lt., Med. Adminstrv. Corps, Silver Spring MD Died Feb. 14, 1971.

LEWIS, J(OSEPH) VOLNEY, geologist; b. Rutherford County, N.C., Sept. 14, 1869; s. Jay Whittington and Mary Catherine (Bennett) L.; B.E., U. of N.C., 1891; S.B. in Geology, Harvard, 1893; grad. student, Harvard, Johns Hopkins, Columbia; m. Margaret Hendon, Dec. 24, 1895 (dec.); children—Eleanor (Mrs. Ellis B. Cook), Lydia (dec.); m. 2d, Mildred Leo Clemens, June 29, 1938. Asst. in biology, U. of N.C., 1889-91; prof. geology, Clemson Coll., 1896-1904; prof. geology and mineralogy, dir. geol. mus., and head of dept., Rutgers U., 1904-26; U.S. Geol. Survey, 1891, 1902, 18, 34; regional geologist, region IV, National Park Service, San Francisco, 1934-42; metals and mineral specialists Dept. of Commerce, Bur. Foreign and Domestic Commerce, Washington, June-Dec. 1942; geologist, mining engineer, section chief, Mining Div., War Production Bd., Washington, D.C., 1942-45; North Carolina Geological Survey, 1891-96, Geological Survey of N.J., 1905-25. Cons. mining and petroleum geologist in U.S., Mexico, Canada, Alaska and South America since 1906; chief staff geologist, foreign operating companies of Gulf Oil Corp. of Pa., 1925-31; in charge of design and construction of earth science exhibits, Century of Progress Exposition, Chicago, 1931-32. Special consulting editor, Engineering and Mining Journal, 1920-23. Fellow Geol. Soc. America; mem. Soc. Economic Geologists (sec. and treas. 1921, treas. 1923-26), Am. Inst. Mining and Metall. Engineers, Mining and Metallurgical Soc. America, Pan American Institute of Mining Engineering and Geology, Phi Gamma Delta, Phi Beta Kappa, Sigma Xi, Mining Club of New York (incorporator and mem. bd. govs., 1930). Author: Determinative Mineralogy (4 edits., 5th in preparation); Geologic Map of New Jersey (with Henry B. Kummel); Geology of New Jersey (with same); numerous reports, scientific papers and monographs on geology, mineralogy, and mining topics; contbr. to annual vols. of The Mineral Industry, 1914-22, to Yearbook and annual review numbers Engineering and Mining Journal, 1924-28. Address: San Francisco CA Died Jan. 1969.

LEWIS, JOHN NEHER, clergyman; b. Annandale, N.Y., Jan. 18, 1869; s. John Neher and Christina Jane (Nelson) L.; A.B., Williams, 1889 (D.D., 1917); grad. Berkeley Div. Sch., 1892; m. Mary Newell Stone, of N.Y. City, June 5, 1894. Deacon 1892, priest, 1893, P.E. Ch.; asst. minister St. George's Ch., N.Y. City, 1892-94; rector Grace Ch., Honesdale, Pa., 1894-97; dean Christ Ch. Cathedral, Lexington, Ky., 1897-1900; rector St. John's Ch., Waterbury, Conn., since 1900; rector St. Margaret's Sch. for Girls, Waterbury, since 1900, Westover Sch. for Girls, Middlebury, since 1909. Chaplain 2d Inf., Ky. N.G., 1898-99, 2d Inf. Conn. N.G., 1907-12; chaplain A.R.C., Mobile Hosp. No. 1, A.E.F., 1918. Commr. Pub. Charities, Waterbury, 1912-13; dir. Conn. State Reformatory and State Bd. of Parole, 1924-31. Commissioner of Public Welfare, 1940-—. Mem. Sigma Phi. Clubs: Williams (New York); Graduates (New Haven). Home: 21 Church St., Waterbury CT‡

LEWIS, JOSEPH, labor exec.; b. Centerville, Calif., Oct. 1, 1906; s. Manuel S. and Mary S. (Francisco), L.; student pub. schs. Centerville; m. Marie Narcizo, Mar. 1929; 1 son, Joseph C.; m. 2d Gladys Florence Goulart, Mar. 28, 1947; 1 dau., Jo-Ann. Internat. v.p. Stove Mounters Union, A.F. of L., 1935, 1938, 1941, became internat. pres., 1944; sec., treas. Union Label and Service Trades Dept. AFL-CIO, from 1956. Moose. Eagle. Home: Silver Spring MD Died Dec. 14, 1970; buried Holy Sepulchre Cemetery, Hayward CA

LEWIS, MARVIN HARRISON;, b. Elizabethtown, Ky., June 16, 1873; s. Rev. John William and Lucy Blain (Donaldson) L.; ed. pub. schs., under pvt. tutors and at S. Ky. Coll. (non-grad.); m. Isabel Rodgers, of Pittsburgh, Pa., Aug. 14, 1903; 1 son, Marvin Arthur. Formerly reporter and editorial writer, Louisville Courier Journal; founder, 1906, and head of Marvin H. Lewis & Company. Former member Board of Public Safety, Louisville; former chairman of the executive committee My Old Kentucky Home" and raised funds establishing the Home nr. Bardstown, Ky., as a state shrine; chmn. Four-Minute Men, Louisville, and of Ky. Speakers' Bur., World War. Former trustee U. of Louisville, Louisville Industrial Sch.; trustee Wakefield Memorial Assn.; mem. bd. councillors Saratoga Battlefield Assn. Mem. Soc. Colonial Wars, Nat. Sec. S.A.R. (pres. gen. 1924-25). Republican. Clubs: Pendennis, Conversation (Louisville), Yorktown (Va.) Country (hon. life). Writer and speaker on economic and hist. subjects. Home: Broadway at Third St. Office: Keller Bldg., Louisville KY‡

LEWIS, MELVIN S(OWLES), coll. prof.; b. Colfax, Wash., Dec. 25, 1881; s. Babour and Jean (Fulton) L.; student Wash. State Coll., 1899-1901, A.B., 1906; student Stanford U., 1902-03, M.A., U. of Calif., 1924; Ed.D., U. of Calif., 1927; m. Josephine Fonner, June 18, 1912. Teacher Bellingham, Wash. High Sch., 1906-07; dept. head, Everett, Wash. High Sch., 1907-08; supt. schs., Kennewick, Wash., 1908-18; supt. schs., Auburn, Wash., 1918-19; state dir. Vocational Edn., Boise, Idaho. 1919-23; research fellow U. of Calif., 1923-25; lecturer in edn., U. of Calif., 1925-27; asso. prof. edn., Indiana U., 1927-29; prof. edn., from 1929, dir. Ind. State Sch. Survey, Ind. Com. on Govtl. Economy, 1934-35. Mem. Am. Vocational Assn., Ind. Vocational Assn., Nat. Vocational Guidance Assn., Nat. Assn. Trade Teachers Trainers, Miss. Valley Indsl. Arts Conf., Ind. Indsl. Edn. Assn., Ind. Teachers Assn., Phi Beta Kappa, Phi Delta Kappa, Phi Kappa Phi, Delta Pi Epsilon. Congregationalist. Author: Trade Course in Lumber Grading, 1922; Trade Course in Log Scaling, 1922; Commerce for Idaho High Schools, 1922; Analysis of the Plasterer's Trade, 1924; Analysis of the Auto-mechanic's Trade, 1925; Business Training in Junior High School (with Alfred Sorensen), 1927; Instruction Sheets for the General Shop (with John H. Dillon), 4 vols., 1932; Orientation in Education (with T. H. Schulte and others), 1932; Indiana State School Survey (with Raleigh Holmstedt), 1935. Home: Bloomington IN Died Aug. 3, 1969.

LEWIS, MERTON HARRY, govt. sales exec.; b. Rochester, N.Y., Mar. 17, 1902; s. Charles Edson and Glenna (Ives) L.; student U. Rochester, 1921-25; m. Mary Leader, Apr. 17, 1933; children—Charles Merton, Robert Leader. Chemist, metallographer N.E. Electric Co., Rochester N.Y., 1921-25; chemist Compania Minera Asanco, Monterrey, Nueve, Leon, Mex., 1926-27; sales rep. sci. equipment and chems. Will Corp., Rochester, N.Y., 1927-36; sales rep., govt. sales exec. Eastman Kodak Co., 1936-69; adminstrv. asst. Govt. Markets Services Dept. Active Boy Scouts Am. Trustee Allendale Sch. for Boys, Rochester, N.Y., 1950-60. Mem. Am. Soc. Photogrammetry, Civic Music Assn. Club: Calvary (Rochester). Episcopalian. Home: Rochester NY Died Dec. 13, 1969.

LEWIS, OSCAR, educator; b. N.Y.C., Dec. 25, 1914; B.S.S., Coll. City N.Y., 1936; Ph.D., Columbia, 1940; married 1937. Research asso. Yale, 1942-43; propaganda analyst U.S. Dept. Justice, 1943; social sci. Dept. Agr., 1944-45; Dept. State vis. prof., Havana, 1945-46; asso. prof. anthropology Washington U., St. Louis, 1946-48; prof. anthropology U. Ill., 1948-70; cons. anthropologist Ford Found., India, 1952-54. Social Sci. Research Council summer seminar fellow, 1952; grant-in-aid behavioral sci. div. Ford Found., 1952. Fellow Am. Acad. Arts and Scis.; mem. Am. Anthrop. Assn. Author: Tepoztlan, Village in Mexico; Life in a Mexican Village; Tepoztlan Restudied; Five Families: Mexican Case Studies in the Culture of Poverty; Children of Sanchez; Pedro Martinez: A Mexican Peasant and His Family; La Vida, A Puerto Rican Family in the Culture of Poverty: San Juan and New York (Nat. Book award for nonfiction 1966; Anisfield-Wolf award 1966; Midland Lit. citation Soc. Midland Authors 1966), 1966; A Study of Slum Culture: Backgrounds for La Vida, 1968; A Death in the Sanchez Family, 1969; Anthropological Essays, 1970. Address: Urbana IL Died Dec. 16, 1970.

LEWIS, TED (THEODORE FRIEDMAN), entertainer; b. Circleville, O., June 6, 1891; m. Ada Baker, 1922. First appearance as entertainer, Circleville, O., 1906; burlesque, vaudeville tours, night club shows; mem. trio N.Y. Hammerstein's Theatre, 1911; singer When My Baby Smiles At Me, Ted Lewis Club: with Eddie Chester sang Me and My Shadow. Club: Friars (herald, N.Y.C.). Home: New York City NY Died Aug. 1971.*

LEWIS, WILLIAM STANLEY, lawyer, writer; b. Hamden, N.Y., July 21, 1876; s. William Abbott and Fannie Bostwick (Shaw) L.; Stanford University, 1894-96; studied law pvtly.; m. Hildegard Fjerd Johannessen, Jan. 11, 1911; children—Hildegard Karen, Frances Charlotte. Admitted to bar, Wash., 1898, Ida., 1899; gen. practice Calif., Ore., Wash., Ida. and Mont., office at Los Angeles; attorney for Indian tribes of Northwest in claims against Government. Former member Co. I, 2d Inf., Wash. N.G.; 1st lt. Co. L, 3d Wash. Inf.; bn. adj. 3d Bn., 3d Regt.; resigned 1919. A founder Spokane Pub. Museum. Mem. Spokane County War Hist. Com. (chmn.), Spokane County Pioneer Soc. (historian), Eastern Wash. State Hist. Soc.

(a founder and sec.), Spokane Nat. Indian Congress (acting sec. and organizer, 1st Congress). Republican. Conglist. Moose, Elk. Author: The Case of Spokane Gardy, 1907; Early Days in the Big Bend Country, 1921. Editor: (with Naojiro Murakami) Ranald MacDonald (narrative of his life), 1923; (with Paul C. Phillips) Journal of John Work, 1923. Contbr. on Indians and early Northwest history; contbr. Dictionary of Am. Biography, Dictionary of Am. History, etc. Tested constitutionality of pocket veto practice before U.S. Supreme Court in case of Okanogan Indians vs. U.S., 1929. Address: Pershing Square Bldg., Los Angeles CA‡

LEY, WILLY, educator, author; b. Berlin, Germany, Oct. 2, 1906; s. Julius Otto and Frida (May) L.; student U. Berlin, 1927; Doctor of Humane Letters, Adelphi Coll., 1959; m. Olga Feldman, Dec. 24, 1941; children—Sandra, Xenia. Came to U.S., 1935, natrualized, 1944. Free lance writer from 1927; sci. editor newspaper PM, N.Y. City, 1940-44; research engr. Washington Inst. Tech. College Park, Md., 1944-47; information specialist office tech. services, Dept. Commerce, Washington, since 1947. Fellow Brit. Interplanetary Soc.; mem. German Rocket Soc. (founding mem. 1927, v.p. 1928-33), Inst. Aeronautical Sci., Am., Pacific rocket socs., Royal Astron. Soc. Can., Soc. Am. Mil. Engrs., A.A.A.S. Author: Die Moglichkei der Weltraumfahrt, 1928; Konrad Gesner, Leban und Werk, 1930; Grundriss einer Geschichte der Rakete, 1931; The Lungfish and the Unicorn, 1940; Bombs and Bombing, 1941; Shells and Shooting, 1942; The Days of Creation, 1942; Rockets, 1944; Rockets and Space Travel, 1947, rev. 1957, 61; Conquest of Space, 1948; Dragons in Amber, 1950; Lands Beyond (with L. S. de Camp), 1952; Engineer's Dreams, 1954; Salamanders and Other Wonders, 1955; The Exploration of Mars (with Wernher von Braun), 1956; Willy Ley's Exotic Zoology, 1959; Watchers of the Skies, 1963; Beyond the Solar System, 1964; The Dawn of Zoology, 1968; On Earth and in the Sky, 1969; Events in Space, 1969; articles mil. publs. and mags. Address: Jackson Heights NY Died June 24, 1969.

LEYDON, JOHN KOEBIG, investment banker; born in the city of Philadelphia, Pennsylvania, Oct. 14, 1916; s. John William and Dorothy (Koebig) L.; B.S., U.S. Naval Acad., 1938; M.S., Cal. Inst. Tech., 1945; m. Elizabeth Martin Rivinus, July 11, 1940;children—John Koebig, Edward Rivinus, Lisa Martin, Christopher Francis. Commd. ensign U.S. Navy, 1938, advanced through grades to rear adm., 1964; designated naval aviator, 1941; engring. assignments, 1945-59; comdr. U.S. Naval served in U.S.S. Ranger, 1941-43; various areo. Air Turbine Test Sta., Trenton, N.J., 1959-61; dep. chief naval material Navy Dept., 1963-64, chief naval research, 1964-67; partner Paine, Webster, Jackson & Crutis, 1967-71. Dir. Access Crop., Laser Diode Labs., Inc. Crutis, 1967-71. Dir. Access Crop., Laser Diode Labs., Inc. Clubs: Army Navy Country (Washington); City Midday (N.Y.). Home: Lahaska PA Died Feb. 2, 1971; buried Arlington Nat. Cemetery, Arlington VA

LEYMAN, HARRY STOLL, banker; b. Crestline, O., Feb. 7, 1873; s. Henry Templeton and Susannah (Fitzsimmons) L.; ed. pub. schools of Columbus, O.; m. Eva Belle Peck, June 14, 1906; children—Grace Templeton (Mrs. Raymon M. Lull), Elizabeth (Mrs. Louis B. von Weise, Jr.), Susannah (Mrs. George R. Atterbury), Harry. Sec.-treas. Internat. Motor Co., 1900-03; gen. sales mgr. Pope Toledo Motor Car Co., Toledo, 1903-09; owned and operated Leyman-Buick Co., Cincinnati (distributed cars to O., Ind., W.Va., Ky.), 1909-30; pres. Gibson Hotel Co., Cincinnati, 1925-34; dir. First Nat. Bank since 1920, chmn. bd. since 1932; pres. and dir. Leyman Corp., Cincinnati. Republican. Clubs: Queen City (gov.), Cincinnati, Country, Camargo (Cincinnati), Bath, Indian Creek (Miami Beach, Fla.). Home: Grandin Rd. Office: First National Bank Bldg., Cincinnati OH‡

LEYS, WAYNE ALBERT RISSER, educator; b. Bloomington, Ill., June 29, 1905; s. John Albert and Stella (Risser) L.; A.B., Ill. Wesleyan U., 1926; Ph.D. (fellow philosophy 1928-30), U. Chgo., 1930; m. Helen Benson, Aug. 26, 1930; children—Portia Leys Sonnenfeld, Carolyn Anne Leys Moyer, Prof. philosophy Central YMCA Coll., Chgo., 1932-45; pub. panel mem. NWLB, 1943-45; dean faculties Roosevelt U., Chgo., 1945-55, prof. philosophy, 1945-63, v.p., 1949-55, dean grad. div., 1955-63; prof. philosophy So. Ill. U., 1964-73; vis. lectr. philosophy Johns Hopkins, summer 1950, Northwestern U., summer 1954, U. Mich., spring 1955; lectr. U. Chgo., 1956-61. Cons. operations research office Johns Hopkins: research dir. ethical standards project Nat. Inst. Labor Edn., 1960-61; Dept. State Cultural Exchange lecture tour, 1962. Mem., sec. bd. trustees Roosevelt U., 1945-50, 53-59; pres. bd. Student Christian Found., 1967-69. Rockefeller Found. grantee, 1950-51. Mem. Am. Assn. U. Profs., Am. Philos. Assn. (sec.-treas. Western div. 1947-49, mem. nat. bd. officers, 1948, 49, chmn. com. to advance original work in philosophy 1958-69, exec. com. Western div. 1965-68, sec. travel grants, mem. com. internat. coop. 1969-72), Am. Soc. Polit. and Legal Philosophy, Am. Arbitration Assn. (panel mem. 1946-73), Nat. Conf. Christians and Jews (nat. commn. on ednl. orgns. 1949-58), Midwest Conf. Grad. Study and Research (exec. com. 1963-64), Am. Civil Liberties Union, Ill. Agl. Assn., Mind Assn., Am. Soc. Pub. Adminstrn. (pres. So. Ill. chpt. 1968-69), Phi Kappa Phi, Pi Kappa Delta. Conglist. Mason. Club: The Cliff Dwellers (v.p. 1950) (Chgo.); University (Carbondale). Author: The Religious Control of Emotion, 1932: Ethics and Social Policy, 1941: Ethics for Policy Decisions, 1952: Philosophy and the Public Interest (with C. M. Perry), 1959; Gandhi and America's Educational Future (with P.S.S. Rama Rao), 1969. Editorial bd. Dewey Publ. Center, 1966-73. Contbr. articles, book revs. various pub.; lectr. various univs. and govtl. agys. Home: Makanda IL Died Mar. 7, 1973.

LIBBY, ARTHUR STEPHEN, educator; b. Corinna, Me., Mar. 9, 1877; s. Clements Coffin and Estelle D. (Allen) L.; Ph.B., Bowdoin Coll., 1902; A.B., U. of Me., 1903; A.M., Sorbonne, Paris, 1903; A.M., Brown, 1904; Ph.D., U. of Paris, 1906; studied law depts. U. of Me. and Columbia; m. Prof. Cora M. Steele, Aug. 20, 1907. Prin. high schs. in Me., several yrs.; instr. French, Brown U., 1903-04; prof. modern langs., Converse Coll., Spartanburg, S.C., 1901-12; pres. of Southern Travel-Study Bur., Spartanburg, since 1911. Lecturer for Dept. of Edn., San Francisco Expn., 1915; traveled extensively in India, South Seas, Siberia, Africa, 1912-14; lyceum and chautauqua lecturer on travel, exploration, history and world politics since 1914; actg. prof. history and polit. science, Wofford Coll., 1917-19; dean Sch. of Commerce and prof. polit. science and internat. law, Oglethorpe U., 1919-30; founder, 1930, and pres. Libby Grad. Sch. of Business Administration and Finance (first grad. professional school of business in Southern States); founder, 1931, and pres. U. of Robert E. Lee (embracing Libby Grad. School as one of its depts.); prof. psychology at Grady Hosp. Training Sch., 1934. Served as dir. language instrn., Army Y.M.C.A., with 27th Division, and ednl. dir. and lecturer Army Camps, World War army interpreter and staff officer, rank of maj.; also speaker for Am. Red Cross and War Loan campaigns. Mem. Am. Hist. Assn.; del. from S.C. to Internat. Congress of Edn., Brussels, Belgium, 1910; founder and dir. Southern Bur. of Business Research. Lecturer economics and law, Am. Inst. of Banking, Mayor N. Atlanta, Ga., since 1924. Mem. N.E. Club, Ga. Soc. Certified Pub. Accountants, Nat. Assn. of Teachers of Marketing and Advertising, Am. Legion, Kappa Alpha, Phi Kappa Delta, Phi Beta Sigma. Democrat. Presbyn. Mason. Home: Mooresville NC. Died Sept. 24, 1948

LIBBY, FREDERICK JOSEPH, exec. sec. Nat. Council for Prevention of War; b. Richmond, Me., Nov. 24, 1874; s. Abial and Susan Hildreth (Lennan) L.; A.B., Bowdoin, 1894; studied Berlin, Heidelberg, Marburg and Oxford; S.T.B., Andover Theol. Sem., Cambridge, Mass., 1902; m. Faith Ward, June 1932. Pastor Union Congl. Ch., Magnolia, Mass., 1905-11; traveled in China, Australia, etc., 1911-12; teacher Phillips Exeter Acad., 1912-20; asso. with Soc. of Friends in reconstruction and relief work in France, 1918-19, as European commr., Apr.-Dec. 1920, in Phila. office, Jan.-Aug. 1921; exec. sec. Nat. Council for Prevention of War 1921-70. Mem. Alpha Delta Phi. Quaker. Mason. Home: Washington DC Died June 26, 1970; buried Richmond ME

LIBBY, SAMUEL HAMMONDS, engr.; b. Limerick, Me., Nov. 20, 1864; s. Hall Jackson and Mary Caroline (Hasty) L.; ed. pub. schs., Mass.; student Lowell (Mass.) Commercial Coll., 1881-82; m. Florence Emeline Price, Feb. 8, 1894; children—Eugene Herbert, Donald Price, Margaret Caroline (Mrs. Chas. P.W. Schmidt). Apprentice in iron molding, Boston, Mass., 1882-86; worker in pattern and model making, 1886-89; mech. draftsman, Thomson-Houston Electric Co., Lynn, Mass., 1889, continuing through formation of Gen. Electric Co., then filling positions in railway engring. dept., as draftsman, exptl. engr. and constrn. engr.; transferred to Schenectady (N.Y.) works, 1894; supervised equipment with electric motors Nantasket Beach branch of New Haven R.R., 1895-96; installation electric equipment South Side Elevated R.R., Chicago, Ill., 1897-98, Brooklyn Elevated R.R., 1898; engineer electric hoist department, Bloomfield (N.J.) works, 1904-23, cons. engr., 1922-26, also editor works paper 1919-26, safety engr., 1926; became supervisor personnel, continuing work with plant paper, safety work, and as mem. com. on adjustment of wages and working conditions, 1928-32; retired 1932. Fellow Am. Soc. M.E. (formerly chmn. metropolitan sect.; com. on relations with colleges; com. on admissions). Formerly active in civic, ednl. and church work in New Jersey. Mem. Kiwanis Club of East Orange since 1922; pres. 1924; lt. gov. N.J. Dist., 1925-26. Co-organizer of Retired Business and Professional Men's Association of the Oranges. Mason. Member First Baptist Church of East Orange (deacon.). Holder of 34 patents covering electrical apparatus. Home: 23 Whittlesey Av., East Orange NJ‡

LIBERMAN, SAMUEL HALPERN, lawyer; b. St. Joseph, Mo., Feb. 4, 1895; s. Samuel and Edith (Halpern) L.; student U. Utah, 1913-14; LL.B., U. Mo., 1918; m. Berenice A. Wise, Oct. 9, 1939; children—Pierce, Samuel Halpern II. Admitted to Mo. bar, 1917; practiced in Kansas City, 1919-21, St. Louis, from 1921; counsel, Bd. of Freeholders, City of St. Louis, 1949-50, city counselor, 1953-56; gen. counsel of Commission on Government Security, 1956-57; partner Lewis, Rice, Tucker, Allen & Chubb. Chmn. Mayor's Com. on Pub. Transit Ownership, 1952; mem. bd. police commrs. City St. Louis, 1937-41; mem. St. Louis Housing and Land Clearance Authorities, 1959-61. Served F.A., U.S. Army, 1918. Mem. Am., Mo. bar assns., Bar Assn. St. Louis (pres. 1936-37), Am. Law Inst., Phi Alpha Delta, Order Coif. Club: Westwood Country. Home: St Louis MO Died Dec. 20, 1966.

LICHTENBERGER, ARTHUR CARL, bishop; b. Oshkosh, Wis., Jan. 8, 1900; s. Adam and Theresa (Heitz) L.; Ph.B., Kenyon Coll., 1923, D.D., 1948; B.D., Episcopal Theol. Sch., 1925, S.T.D., 1967; grad. work Harvard, 1927-28; D.S.T., Gen. Theol. Sem., 1951; D.D., Amherst, Bard. Va. Theol. Sem., U. of South, Princeton, Huron Coll., Wycliffe Coll., Toronto, Ont., Episcopal Theol. Sch., LL.D., Brown University; S.T.D., Trinity, Berkeley Div. Sch., Phila. Div. Sch., Seabury-Western Theol. Sem.; L.H.D., Hobart, St. Augustine's Coll.; LL.D., St. Paul's, Tokyo, Japan; D.C.L., Nashota House; J.C.D., Ch. Div. Sch. of the Pacific; m. to Florence Elizabeth Tate, February 8, 1924; children—Elizabeth Theresa (deceased), Arthur Tate. Ordained ministry Episcopal Church, 1925; prof. of New Testament, St. Paul's Divinity Sch. Wuchang, China, 1925-27; rector Grace Ch. Cincinnati, O., 1928-33; rector St. Paul's Ch., Brookline, Mass., 1933-41; dean Trinity Ch. Cathedral, Newark, N.J. 1941-48. lecturer, Episcopal Theol. Sch., Cambridge, Mass., 1935-41; prof. pastoral theology, Gen. Theol. Sem., N.Y. City, 1948-51; bishop coadjutor diocese of Mo. 1951-52; bishop of Mo., 1952-58; presiding bishop Protestant Episcopal Ch., 1959-64; prof. pastoral theology Episcopal Theol. Sch., Cambridge, Mass., 1965-68. Mem. Sigma Pi. Club: Century (N.Y.). Author: The Day Is At Hand. Home: Cambridge MA Died Sept. 3, 1968; ashes interred Chapel of Christ Church Cathedral, St.Louis MO

LICHTENSTEIN, JOY, retired ins. exec.; b. San Francisco, Oct. 14, 1873; s. Morris and Amelia (Marks) L.; ed. U. of Calif., 1897-1901; m. Anna Wolfe, July 12, 1899; children—Stanley, Joyce (Mrs. Harold Alanson Minkler). Assistant librarian of the San Francisco Public Library, 1894-1906; successively general agent American Bonding Company of Baltimore, secretary Pacific Coast Casualty Co mgr. Globe Indemnity Co.; v.p. Hartford Accident and Indemnity Co., Pacific Dept., 1914-46; mgr. Hartford Fire Ins. Co., Pacific Dept., 1924-46; cons. prof. ins. Stanford U. Former mem. Nat. Automobile Underwriters Assn. (adv. com.; chmn. Pacific Coast Com.); mem. Bd. of Fire Underwriters of the Pacific (chmn. dept. of pub. relations; pres. 1936-37), Fire Underwriters Assn. of the Pacific (pres. 1937), National Automobile Club (director). Member Beta Gamma Sigma. Clubs: San Francisco Commercial (hon.). Author: For the Blue and Gold, 1900. Complied: Bibliography of Louis Agassiz, 1893; In Praise of Walking 1942; Kelly, Burke and Shea, 1945. Home: 775 Post St., San Francisco 9‡

LICHTENWALTER, FRANKLIN H., congressman; b. Palmerton, Pa., Mar. 28, 1910; s. Bert A. and Ellen M. (Ash) L.; ed. in high sch.; m. Marguertie M. Stoneback, Sept. 21, 1931. Elected to Pa. Ho. of Reps., 1938, 40, 42, 44 and 1946; majority leader of the House, 1943, 45, speaker, 1947; mem. 80th and 81st Congresses (1947-51), 8th Pa. dist. Dir. Goschenhoppen Mutual Fire Ins. Co. since 1942. Chmn., Northeast Div. of Problems of Social Welfare and Relief of Council of State Govts.; mem. Nat. Conf. on Child Welfare and Youth; mem. exec. com. Interstate Commn. on Delaware River Basin; sec. Gov's. Adv. Commn. on Flood Control and Navigation Projects under Nat. Flood Control Act; mem. Nat. Com. Rivers and Harbors Congress. Trustee Pa. Assn. for Blind; mem. Pa. Soc. Republican. Mason (Shriner); mem. Macungie Grange. Clubs: Lions (past pres.), American Business. Address: Center Valley PA Died Mar. 1973.

LICHTY, L(ESTER (CLYDE), engr., educator; b. Carleton, Neb., July 5, 1891; s. William Willis and Pauline Marie (Becker) L.; B.S. in mech. engring., Univ. of Neb., 1913; M.S., Univ. of Ill., 1916; research asst., Yale, 1923-24, M.E., 1925; M. Hazel Virginia Kelso, Aug. 5, 1919; children—Jean Lee (Mrs. Joseph K. Hill), Betty Lou (Mrs. James H. Johnson), Patricia Ann (Mrs. Thomas J. Morse). Asst. prof. mech. engring. U. Okla., 1916-21, asso. prof., 1921-24; asst. prof., Yale, 1924-30, asso. prof., 1930-45, prof., 1945-50, Robert Higgin prof. mech. engring.; 1950-72. Served as lt. with U.S. Air Service, 1917-19; contractor, A.A.F., analytical research on engine performance, 1940-43; consultant Socony-Vacuum Labs., 1945-72, U.S. Navy Underwater Ordnance Sta., 1951-72. Mem. Am. Soc. Mech. Engrs., Soc. Automotive Engrs. (v.p., diesel engine sect., 1941), Am. Chem. Soc., Am. Assn. Engring. Edn., Sigma Xi, Tau Beta Pi, Sigma Tau, Beta Theta Pi. Republican. Conglist. Clubs: Faculty, Grad., Mory's (all New Haven). Author: (Natural Gas, 1924; Thermodynamics, 1936, 1948; Internal Combustion Engines (with Streeter), 3d and 4th eds., 1929, 1933;

Internal Combustion Engines, 1939; contbr. sect. on internal combustion engines to Marks' Mech. Engrs. Handbook, 1941, 51, 58. Home: New Haven CT Died Dec. 13, 1972; buried New Haven CT

LIEBEL, MICHAEL, JR., congressman; b. Erie, Pa., Dec. 12, 1870; A.B., Canisius Coll., Buffalo, N.Y. Engaged as mfr., also real estate and construction business; mayor of Erie three terms; mem. 64th Congress (1915-17), 25th N.Y. Dist. Democrat. Home: Erie PA‡

LIEBERMAN, ELIAS, author; b. St. Petersburg, Russia, Oct. 30, 1883; s. Nathan David and Sophia L.; came to U.S., 1891; A.B., cum laude, Coll. City of N.Y., 1903; A.M., New York U., 1906, Ph.D., 1911; m. Rose Kiesler, July 1, 1913; children—Amy, James. Teacher in elementary and high schs., N.Y. City, since 1903, head dept. of English, Bushwick High Sch., N.Y. City, 1918-24; lecturer in poetry writing, Coll. City of New York 1921-38; prin. Thomas Jefferson High School, Brooklyn, N.Y., 1924-40; asso. supt. of schs., N.Y. City, 1940-54; instr. New Sch. of Social Research, 1954; lecturer in poetry appreciation, Hunter Coll. and Bklyn. Coll., 1924-33; Steinman Endowment lectr. on poetry Bethany Coll., 1965; editor Puck," 1917-18. Recipient Gold medallion Nat. Poetry Center for 3d book of verse, 1940; Townsend Harris Medal Alumni Assn. City Coll. N.Y., 1953; James Joyce award Poetry Soc. Am., 1965. Fellow Poetry Soc. Am. (mem. exec. bd.; v.p. 1940-62); member New York Acad. Public Education, Asso. Alumni, Coll. City of N.Y. (bd. dir.; pres. 1941-43), English Teachers' Assn., High School Principals Association of N.Y. City (pres. 1935), Phi Beta Kappa; mem. Vigilantes, World War I. Democrat. Jewish religion. Clubs: The Craftsman Group, Writers', Town Hall. Author since 1912; latest publication being: To My Brothers Everywhere, 1954; also recording for The Spoken Work, Inc. of selected poems from own publs.; recording of poems for Fairleigh-Dickinson U. collection Am. Poetry read by their authors; author lyrics City Coll. alma mater song Lavender. Elias Lieberman Manuscript Collection established at Syracuse U., 1964. Home: Richmond Hill LI NY Died July 13, 1969; buried Old Mt. Carmel Cemetery, Queens NY

LIEBERS, OTTO HUGO, dairy corp. exec.; b. Minden, Neb., June 25, 1887, s. August and Anna (Koehler) L.; grad. Neb. Sch. Agr., 1909; B.S., U. Neb., 1913; m. Ethel L. Kindig, Sept. 3, 1913; children—Lawrence, Harry, Ruth (Mrs. Robert C. Ellis). Agrl. agt., Gage County, Neb., 1913-16; agrl. immigration agt. lines West, C.B.&Q. R.R., 1917-20; mgr. Neb. Dairy Development Soc., 1924-33; founder, pres. Skyline Farms, Inc., Lincoln, Neb., 1924; dir. Nat. Bank of Commerce, Lincoln. Co-chmn. Salt Valley Watershed Assn., 1950-56, chmn., 1957-68, pres. emeritus, 1968; chmn. Neb. Gov.'s Adv. Council on Watershed Protection and Flood Control, 1952-58; chmn. Neb. Beautification Program, from 1960; chmn. com. on regulatory billboard advt. Neb. Interstate Hwy.; mem. Nat. Watershed Devel. Com., 1953; mem. Nat. Rivers and Harbors Commn. Mem. Neb. Unicameral Legislature, from 1951, mem. budget com., from 1951, chmn. tax com., 1952-55, chmn. legislative council, 1957-59. Chmn. Second Presbyn. Ch. Found., Lincoln; pres. Neb. Hall Agrl. Achievement, from 1950; bd. dirs. Westminster Ch. Found., Govtl. Research Inst., Inc., Lincoln, Resources for Future, Ford Found., Washington; mem. state adv. council U. Neb. Recipient nat. merit award Alpha Gamma Sigma, 1955, Distinguished Service award U. Neb., 1955, Distinguished Service award Kiwanis Club of Lincoln, 1956. Hon. mem. Neb. Vet. Med. Assn., Innocents Soc. U. Neb.; mem. U.S. (dir.), Lincoln (dir. 1951-53) chambers commerce, Am. Guernsey Cattle Club (dir. Peterborough, N.H.), Nat. Dairy Shriner, Alpha Zeta. Presbyn. (elder). Mason. Clubs: Rotary (dir. 1952-54), University (Lincoln). Home: Lincoln NB Died Oct. 25, 1968; buried Lincoln Memorial, Lincoln NB

LIEBES, MRS. DOROTHY WRIGHT, textile designer; b. Santa Rosa, Cal., Oct. 1899; d. Frederick L. and Elizabeth (Calderwood) Wright: grad. San Jose State Tchrs. Coll., 1919, U. Cal., 1919-23, Cal. Sch. Fine Arts, 1926, Columbia, 1926-28; hon. LL.D., Mills Coll., 1948; m. Leon Liebes, 1929 (div.); m. 2d, Reiman Morin, 1948. Tchr. art Horace Mann Sch., Columbia, 1925-28; designer Textiles Goodall-Sanford; designer, colorist United Wallpaper Co., 2 Liebes Wallweaves 3; pres. Dorothy Liebes Design, Inc.; designer Quaker Lace Co., Phila., Jantzen Knitting Mills, Portland, Ore., Bates Fabric, Inc., 1956-57; also designer, stylist, colorist Dow Chem. Co., 1958-61; Columbia Mills, Kenwood Mills; design con. Dupont Co., Wilmington, Collins and Alkman, Forstman Woolens, Bigelow-Sanford Carpet, Inc., Flexaium div. Bridgeport Brass Co., Stroheim & Romann, Inc., Eagle Ottawa Leather Co., 1958-59; designer Fairtex Sales, Inc., Charles Bloom, Inc. Jasco Fabrics, Inc., 1964-65, Imperial Wallpaper, Inc., 1965; designer, stylist U.S. Finishing Co., Century Fed. Savs. & Loan Bank, N.Y.C., Nat. Design Center for Interiors, N.Y.C.; work exhibited in 15 mus. shows; mem. bd. R.I. Sch. Design; lectr. textiles, 1938-72; dir. N.Y. World's Fair Corp.; trustee Parson Sch. Design, N.Y.C.; dir. Cal. Sch. Fine Arts; dir. decorative arts exhibit Golden Gate Internat. Expn., 1939; dir. art San Francisco Expn., 1939. Dir. Mus. Modern Art, 1944, San Francisco Mus. and Art Assn., 1930-44, Mus. Contemporary Crafts, N.Y.C., 1958-59; mem. art bd. Scripps Coll.; mem. art jury Lord & Taylor, Robineau Ceramic, Louis Comfort Tiffancy Found., Am. House Inst. Internat. Edn. Com. on Applied Arts; originator, nat. dir. arts and skills unit A.R.C.; dir. San Francisco Housing Commn.; mem. com. Save the Redwoods League. Mem. Pres.'s Com. for the Handicapped, 1965. Awarded: 1st Lord & Taylor 1,000 design prize, 1938; Am. First award Am. Plastics in Textiles, Plastic Assn.; First Honor award, Paris Inst. Expn. for Am. Textiles, Inst. Architects, Am. Inst. Decorators, 1947; Am. Designers League; Nieman Marcus prizes; gold medal, A.I.A., Elsie de Wolfe award, award design textiles (5) Triennale di Milano, 1965: highest award for design influence A.I.D., 1968. Benjamin Franklin fellow of Brit. Royal Soc. of Arts; mem. Am. Arbitration Assn., Phi Beta Kappa, Kappa Alpha Theta, Presbyn. Clubs: Century of Cal. (San Francisco); Cosmopolitan (N.Y.C.); Faculty (U. Cal.). Home: New York City NY Died Sept. 1972.

LIEBMANN, PHILIP, bus. exec.; b. N.Y.C., Feb. 19, 1915; s. Alfred and Alma (Wallach) L.; student Westminister Sch., Simsbury, Conn., 1930-32; B.S., Wharton Sch., U. Pa., 1936; m. Dorothy Walp, 1942 (div. 1953); 1 adopted stepson, Charles Dean Temple (dec.); m. 2d, Monetta Eloise (Linda) Darnell, 1954 (div. 1955); m. 3d, Joan Barry, 1955; 1 dau., Alfreda Ann. With Liebmann Breweries, Inc., Bklyn., 1936-71, v.p., treas., dir., dir. advt. and pub. relations. 1943-50, pres., 1950-71; dir. U.S. Brewers Found. Mem. N.A.M., Assn. Nat. Advertisers, Advt. Fedn. Am. Republican. Roman Catholic. Clubs: Brooklyn; Advertising (N.Y.C.). Home: Rye NY

LIECTY, AUSTIN N., born at Albany, N.Y., Oct. 11, 1866; s. John L. and Jane L. (Spelman) L.; grad. Albany High Sch., 1884; unmarried. Clerk with Fairbanks Co., 1885; pub. Syracuse Courier, 1894-97; pub. Schenectady Gazette, 1899-1944; retired 1944. Charter mem. Associated Press. Mem. Dutch Reformed Ch. Clubs: Mohawk, Mohawk Golf (Schenectady, N.Y.); Mountain Lake (Lake Wales, Fla.). Home: 3 Douglas Rd., Schenectady NY‡

LIES, EUGENE THEODORE, social and civic worker; b. Buffalo, N.Y., May 8, 1876; s. Peter and Caroline (Schorr) L.; B.S., Cornell University, 1900; grad. N.Y. School of Philanthropy, 1901; m. Emily Margaret Smith, July 12, 1900; children—Marjorie S. (Mrs. Ray Gibbons), Paul E. Agt. for Buffalo Charity Organization Soc., 1900-01, Chicago Bur. of Charities, 1901-07; gen. sec. Minneapolis Asso. Charities, 1907-12; gen. supt. Chicago United Charities, 1912-18 (leave of absence, Apr.-Aug. 1917 to aid establishment of family war work, Am. Red Cross, Washington, and Apr.-Aug. 1918 to organize dept. of investigation, U.S. Bur. of War Risk Ins.); gen. mgr. War Camp Community Service and Community Service, Chicago, Sept. 1918-Oct. 1920; spl. rep., lecturer, writer, research worker, and community organizer, Community Service, Inc., and Nat Recreation Assn., 1920-40; forum counselor, S.E. States, U.S. Office of Edn., Dec. 1940-July 1941; sec. Occupational Planning Committee of Cleveland, O., Sept. 1941-June 1944. Mem. American Association for the League of Nations, United World Federalists, Am. Sociol. Soc. Author: The Leisure of a People, 1929; The New Leisure Challenges the Schools, 1933; Larger Leisure for Larger Living, 1934; The Leisure-Time Problem of Cincinnati and Vicinity, 1935; Group Work Study of Cleveland, 1935; How You Can Make Democracy Work, 1942; many reports of community surveys. Home: 1520 Seneca St., Tucson AZ‡

LIGHT, RUDOLPH ALVIN, surgeon; b. Kalamazoo, Sept. 21, 1909; s. Stellar Rudolph and Rachel Winifred (Upjohn) L.; Ph.B., Yale, 1931; B.A. in Physiology, Oxford (Eng.) U., 1934, M.A., 1937; M.D., Vanderbilt U., 1939; m. Ann Bonner Jones, June 8, 1932 (div. 1960); one daughter, Deborah Ann (Mrs. Peter J. Perry); m. second, Helen Ann Rork, Mar. 25, 1960. Began as junior intern, then sr. intern surgery, Lakeside Hosp., Cleve., 1939-41; asst. resident, then resident surgery, Vanderbilt Hosp., 1941-43, 46-47; asst. chief surgery VA Hosp., Nashville, 1947-48, dir. research, 1947-49, acting chief surgery, 1948; asso. prof. surgery Vanderbilt U. Sch. Medicine and Hosp., 1948-57, dir. surg. research, 1949-57, dir. rehab. service, 1956-57; vis. surgeon Nuffield dent. surgery Oxford U., 1958-62. Dir. Upjohn Co., Kalamazoo. Mem. exec. bd. Middle Tenn. council Boy Scouts Am., 1949-58, later member of the National council and member of the national executive board; pres., dir. Nashville Civic Music Assn., 1951-53; pres. Nashville Ednl. Television Found., 1953-57, Light Found., Kalamazoo, from 1958; exec. com. Tenn. Heart Assn., 1955-58, dir., 1956-58, sec., 1956-57; pres., trustee Rudolph A. Light Scholarship Found., from 1966; trustee Nashville Children Mus.; dir. Middle Tenn. Heart Assn., 1950-53, 56-58. Hon. fellow St. Catherine's Coll., Oxford U., Eng.; trustee Vanderbilt U.; Senior Citizens, Inc., Nashville. Served to capt., M.C., AUS, World War II; PTO. Decorated Bronze Star medal; hon. comdr. Most Excellent Order of British Empire; recipient Silver Beaver award Boy Scouts Am. Diplomate Am. Bd. Surgery. Mem. A.C.S., Soc. Univ. Surgeons, So. Surg. Assn., Am. Fedn. Clin. Research, Southeastern Surg. Congress, A.A.A.S., N.Y. Academy Sciences, A.M.A., Tennessee State Medical Society, Sigma Xi, Alpha Chi Rho, Phi Chi. Clubs: Yale (N.Y.C.); University (Chgo.); Belle Meade Country (Nashville); Farmington Country (Charlottesville, Va.); Tryall Country, Half Moon Rose Hall Country (Jamaica, W.I.); Metropolitan (N.Y.C.); Lost Tree, Lost Tree Village (North Palm Beach, Fla.) Cumberland Nashville TN Died Jan. 1970.

LIGHTNER, EZRA WILBERFORCE, Washington and European correspondent-editorial writer Pittsburg Dispatch since 1877; b. Mercer Co., Pa.; began writing for the press, 1865; editor and prop'r Greenville, Pa., Advance, 1871-2; editor Meadville, Pa., Republican, 1873; editorial writer Cleveland Leader, 1874-5; special writer New York dailies, 1876-7. Address: 18 2d St. N.E., Washington‡

LIGHTNER, MILTON C., mfr.; b. Detroit, Mich., 1890; s. Edwin N.L. and Jane (Cass) L.; ed. Univ. of Mich., 1910; grad. Harvard Law Sch., 1913; m. Margaret D. Griffin, Aug. 16, 1917. Began practice of law, New York, 1913; mem. firm VerPlanck, Prince, Burlingame & Lightner; became vice-pres. Singer Sewing Machine Co., Elizabeth, N.J., Mar. 1927, pres., 1949-58, chmn. bd., 1958-61; v.p. and dir. Singer Mfg. Co. 1928-49, pres., 1949-58, chmn. bd., 1958-61; dir. Safe Deposit Co. of N.Y., North Jersey Trust Co. (Ridgewood, N.J.). Mem. N.A.M. (pres. 1958). Home: Ridgewood NJ Died Mar. 1968.

LILJESTRAND, GORAN, educator, scientist; b. Gothenburg, Sweden, Apr. 16, 1886; s. Petter Erik and Tekia (Carlberg) L.; Candidate Medicine, Stockholm, 1909, Licentiate of Medicine, 1915, M.D., 1917, D.Sc. (honorary), 1952; M.D. (honorary), Dorpat, 1932, Ghent, 1955, Paris, 1958; was married to Elsa Margareta Wretlind, Dec. 10, 1910 (dec. 1948); children—Brita (Mrs. Sven Grape), Ake, Margit (Mrs. Kjell Halvarson); m. 2d, Maud von Koch, Oct. 24, 1949; 1 son, Nils Goran. Asst. prof. physiology Caroline Inst., Stockholm, Sweden, 1917-23; asst. prof. physiology and pharmacology, 1923-27, prof. pharmacology, 1927-51. Mem. Nobel Com., 1938-51, sec. for physiology and medicine, 1918-60; sec. 12th Internat. Physiol. Congress, Stockholm, 1926. Recipient Alvarenga prize from Swedish Med. Soc., 1918, 23, 25, Regnell prize, 1946; Bjorken prize U. Uppsala, 1930; Schmioberg Plaquette Deutsche. Pharmakol. Ges., 1962. Honorary member of the American, British, Scandinavian (secretary 1926-31, 35-51) physiological societies, British Pharmacol. Soc., Deutsche Pharmakol. Ges., Swedish Med. Soc., A.M.A., Alpha Omega Alpha; mem. Swedish, Danish, Finnish acads. sci., Akad. of Naturforscher, N.Y. Acad. Medicine, hon. mem, Acad. de Medicine Brussels Soc. Philomatique, Paris. Author: Lehrbuch der Pharmakologie (Leipzig). Contbg. author: Nobel, the Man and His Prizes; Karolinska Institutets historia 1910-60; (with B. Holmstedt) Readings in Pharmacology, 1963. Editor of Acta Physiologica Scandinavica, 1940-67, Les Prix Nobel, 1953, 64. Published over 200 papers mainly on respiration and circulation. Home: Bromma Sweden Died Jan. 16, 1968.

LILLARD, WALTER HUSTON, educator; b. Paris, Ill., Nov. 20, 1881; s. David Irvine and Emma Ada (Huston) L.; B.S., Dartmouth, 1905, A.M., 1910; studied Oxford U., Eng., 1909-10; Litt.D., Hobart College, Geneva, New York, 1935; m. Ethel Augusta Hazen, Sept. 5, 1907; children—Walter Huston, Virginia, Barbara Ann, Jane Hazen. Sec. Dartmouth Coll. Club, also grad. student, Dartmouth, and grad. mgr. athletics, 1905-07; instr., later asst. to headmaster, Phillips Acad., Andover, Mass., 1907-16; was first faculty coach of football at Phillips Acad.; headmaster Tabor Acad., Marion, Mass., since June 1916; developing Tabor Acad. as a prep. sch., with nautical training; coordinator for education in Mass., 1941; chief of personnel sect. (G-1), Mass. State Mil. Staff, 1941; dir. Sch. Munitions Technology, National Fireworks, Inc., West Hanover, Mass., since 1942; Am. Rep. in Germany of Intergovernmental Committee on Refugees, 1945; chief resettlement div., Austria, Internat. Refugee Orgn., 1947. Lecturer 1949; director of Civil Defense from 1950. Member Selective Service State Staff. United States guard, Paris Exposition, 1899-1900; enlisted in Battery D, 1st Mass. Field Artillery, Feb. 1916; commd. lt. Co. L, 8th Mass. Inf., Apr. 1916; served on Mexican border, June-Aug. 1916; capt. Co. D, 17th Regt. Inf., Mass. State Guard, May 26, 1917; apptd. comdt. Camp Cleveland (jr. naval training sch.), Marion, Mass.; field supervisor of development bns., Adj. Gen.'s Dept. U.S. Army, Sept. 1918; commd. capt. and assigned as div. personnel adj., Oct. 1918; lt. col., O.R.C. Acting chief seascout, Boy Scouts of America, 1922. Chmn. Internat. Schoolboy Fellowship; regent dist. 2 Cum Laude Soc. Mem. Headmasters Assn., N.E. Assn. Colls. and Prep. Schs., Delta Kappa Epsilon, Casque and Gauntlet. Republican. Conglist. Home: Cohasset MA Deceased.

LILLIS, DONALD CHACE, investment banker; b. Niagara Falls, N.Y., Sept. 6, 1901; m. Helen Crawford, Aug. 27, 1927. With Bear, Stearns & Co., N.Y.C., 1943-68, partner, 1945-56, ltd. partner, 1956-68; owner, pres., dir. N.Y. Jets football club; dir. Pabst Brewing Co., Bankers Security Life Ins. Co., Bankers Financial Life Ins. Co., Nat. Can Corp., Piasecki Aircraft Corp., Inter-Am. Capital Corp., Quaker City Life Ins. Co.; trustee Postal Life Ins. Co. Mem. N.Y. Stock Exchange. Mem. So. Md. Agrl. Assn. (pres.). Clubs: Winged Foot Golf (Mamaroneck, N.Y.); Pelham (N.Y.) Country; Chicago; Wall Street (N.Y.C.); Misquamicutt (Watch Hill, R.I.). Home: Palham NY Died July 23, 1968; interred Christ Church, Pelham NY

LIMBACH, RUSSELL THEODORE, artist; b. Massillon, O., Nov. 9, 1904; s. Martin and Flora (Bullock) L.; student Cleve. Sch. Art, 1922-25; student lithography, Paris, Vienna, 1929-30; m. Edna D. Gluck, July 2, 1936. Instr. Cleve. Sch. Art, 1927-29; prof. of art Wesleyan University, Middletown, Conn., 1941-71; represented permanent collections Cleve. Mus. Art, Whitney Mus. Am., N.Y. Pub. Library, Met. Mus. Art, Bklyn. Mus., Smithsonian Inst., San Francisco Mus., Library Congress John, Herron Inst., U. Glasgow, Scotland, Massillon Mus., Yale, Lyman Allyn Mus., New London, Connecticut, and Carnegie Institute, Pittsburgh, also colleges and universities. Awarded 1st prize lithography Cleve. Mus. Art, 1926, 28, 31, 33; silver medal Internat. Printmakers Exhbn., Los Angeles, 1928. Mem. Nat. Acad. Graphic Art. Soc. Am. Graphic Artists. Club: Columbiad. Author, illustrator: But Once a Year, American Trees, 1942. Illustrator: Revolt of the Cats in Paradise, 1945; Chico Mico, 1947. Home: Middletown CT Died Jan. 10, 1971.

LIMON, JOSE ARCADIO, concert dancer, choreographer; b. Culiacan, Sinaloa, Mexico, Jan. 12, 1908; s. Florenico and Francisca (Traslavina) L.; brought to U.S., 1915; student U. Cal., 1926-28; studied art, N.Y.C.; studied dance with Doris Humphrey, Charles Weidman, N.Y.C., 1930-40; D.F.A. (hon.), Wesleyan U., 1959, Colby Coll., 1967, U. N.C., 1968; M. Pauline Lawrence, Oct. 3, 1941. With Humphrey-Weidman Co., 1930-40; also dancer, choreographer various Broadway shows, 1933-40; faculty, dance dept. Bennington Coll., Temple U., U. Pitts., Mills Coll., U. Cal. 1935-42, Dance Players Studio, Sarah Lawrence Coll., own co. with Doris Humphrey as artistic dir., made concert tours of U.S., Can.; performed in Paris, 1950; invited by Nat. Inst. Fine Arts of Mexico to perform and choreograph with Nat. Acad. Dance, 1950-51; N.Y. season 1952 sponsored by Rothschild Found.; participated as dancer, choreographer and instr. Am. Dance Festival sponsored by Conn. Coll., summers seasons 1948-69 dancer cultural mission Am. Nat. Theatre and Acad. for State Dept. to S.A., 1954, Europe, 1957, C.Am. and S.A., 1960, Far East and Australia, 1963; adviser on dance inst. internat. Edn., N.Y. State Council Arts, 1963; artistic dir. Am. Drama Theatre; mem. dance faculty Julliard Sch., 1953-72. Dance works include The Moor's Pavane, The Exiles, La Malinche, The Visitation, Chaconne, There is a Time, Emperor Jones, The Traitor, Missa Brevis, Choreographic Offering, The Winged. Home: Stockton NJ Died Dec. 2, 1972.

LIN, PIAO, def. minister People's Republic China; b. Ungkung, Hupeh Province, Central China, 1906; student Whampoa Mil. Acad., Canton; m. Liu Hsi-hing, 1937; 1 son, 1 dau. Mem. Koumintang (Nationalist party), 1922-27; defected to join Chinese People's Liberation Army, 1927; upon defeat joined Mao Tse-Tung and aided in formation Fourth Workers and Peasants Red Army, 1927; comdr. 4th F.A., 1929-32, 1st Army Corps, 1932, Eastern Front Army, 1932-35; pres. Mil. Acad., Yenan, 1936-37, 1941; comdr. 115th Div. 8th Route Army, 1937; seriously wounded at Pinghsing Pass, went to USSR for treatment and remained until 1941; mem. central com. Chinese Communist Party, 1945-72; organizer army in Manchuria which took Peking, 1948; comdr. Chinese force during Korean War; mem. Central People's Govt. Council and People's Revolutionary Mil. Council, 1949-54, chmn. Central S. China Adminstrv. Com., 1953-54; vice premier State Council, also vice chmn. Nat. Def. Council, 1954-59; named marshal, elected to Chinese Communist party's Politburo, 1955; named to central com., 1956, vice chmn. party, mem. Politburo standing com., 1958; minister of nat. def., 1959-72. Author mil. tng. manuals. Address: Peking China Died Sept. 12, 1971.*

LINCOLN, DANIEL WALDO, lawyer, museum trustee; b. Worcester, Mass., Sept. 2, 1882; s. Waldo and Fanny (Chandler) L.; student France and Germany; grad. Pomfret Prep. Sch., 1900; A.B., Harvard, 1904, LL.B., 1907; m. Harriet Brayton Nichols, Dec. 29, 1917; 1 son, Brayton. Admitted to Mass. bar, 1907, practiced in Worcester; also trustee real estate, other trustees, fed. receiverships; referee bankruptcy Worcester Co., 1921-47; mem. Mass. Appellate Tax Bd., 1947-53. Mem. Worcester City Govt., 1913-15, Mass. Ho. Reps., 1916-17. Honorary trustee of Worcester Art Mus.; council, recording sec. Am. Antiquarian Soc., from 1938; adv. trustee Meml. Hosp., Worcester. Served as 1st lt., inf., U.S. Army, 1917-19; AEF in France, 1918-19. Mem. Am., Mass. (past v.p.), Worcester Co. (past president), bar associations, American Judicature Soc., also Worcester Fire Soc., St. Wulstan Soc. Unitarian. Clubs: Harvard (N.Y.C.); Worcester City, Harvard (Worcester); Tatnuck Country. Home: Worcester MA Died Mar. 16, 1971; buried Rural Cemetery, Worcester MA

LINCOLN, FRANCIS CHURCH, mining engr.; b. Boston, Mass., Sept. 8, 1877; s. Charles Thayer and Lena Simmons (Church) L.; grad. English High Sch., Boston, 1895; S.B. in mining engring., Mass. Inst. Tech., 1900; E.M., N.M. School of Mines, 1904; A.M. in geology, Columbia, 1906, Ph.D., 1911; m. Gertrude Whipple Appleton, June 19, 1901 (deceased); children—Leslie Appleton (Mrs. Jean de Berard), Francis Appleton; m. 2d, Florence May Curtis (Hill), Dec. 22, 1923; children—William Theodore, Robert Charles. Was assayer for Butterfly-Terrible Gold Mining Co., Ames, Colo., 1900-01; prof. geology and metallurgy, N.M. Sch. of Mines, 1901-04, asst. supt. Ruby Gold & Copper Co., Batamote, Mex., 1904-05; lessee, Ariz. Gold & Copper Co., Patagonia, Ariz., 1905-06; cons. mining engring. practice, New York, 1906-07, 1910-11; prof. geology, Mont. Sch. of Mines, Butte, 1907-10; asst. prof. mining, U. of Ill., 1911-13; mining engr. Bolivian Development and Exploitation Co., La Paz, Bolivia, 1913-14; state ore sampler for Nev., 1917-20; director Mackay School of Mines (University of Nevada), 1914-23; prof. mining, South Dakota State Sch. of Mines, 1923-44; cons. mining engr. United States Bureau of Mines, 1942-44; project engineer, U.S. Bureau of Mines, Platteville, Wis., 1944-45; State Inspector of Mines for S.D., 1945-46; head mining dept., acting head metall. dept., S.D. Sch. Mines and Technology, 1946-48; cons. mining engr., geologist, Chula Vista, California since 1948. Mem. Am. Inst. Mining and Metall. Engrs., Society Econ. Geologists. Republican. Unitarian. Club: Lions. Author: Coal Washing in Illinois, 1913; Mining Districts and Mineral Resources of Nevada, 1923; The Mining Industry of South Dakota, 1937; U.S. Bur. of Mines Reports of Investigations on Zinc Ore in Wis. and Ill., 1946-48. Contbr. to Economic Geology, Trans. Am. Inst. Mining Engrs., Engring. and Mining Jour., Nelson's Encyclopedia, etc. Home: 326 I St., Chula Vista CA‡

LIND, ETHEL C. (MRS. WALTER C. LIND), accountant, ch. worker; b. Norway, Mich., Aug. 4, 1910; d. John J. and Annie (Johnson) Lof; B.S. in Accounting, Walton Sch. Commerce; m. Walter C. Lind, Aug. 5, 1945. Accountant, mem. internal audit staff Walgreen Co., Chgo., 1938-45; accountant Harry E. Kamins, C.P.A., 1945-50; owner, operator Lind Assos., accountants, Park Ridge, Ill., 1958; treas. Engring. Mgmt., Inc., 1962-70. Dir. Newberry Av. Center, Chgo., 1952-53; v.p., dir. Marcy Center, 1957-58. Mem. Am. Accounting Assn., Park Ridge C. of C. dir. 1959-61. Chmn., Commn. on Missions, Meth. Ch. of Park Ridge, 1954-59, mem. finance commn., 1954-59, mem. bd. social and econ. relations Rock River Conf., 1951-54; pres. Woman's Soc. Christian Service, Park Ridge, Ill., 1949-50, sec. Christian social relations Rock River Conf. of Meth. Ch., 1951-53, v.p., dir. 1953-57; v.p., dir. Ch. Fedn. of Greater Chgo., 1958-61; finance officer United Ch. Women of Greater Chgo., 1957-59. Mem. Order Eastern Star (Park Ridge, Ill.); White Shrine of Jerusalem (Iron Mountain, Mich.). Home: Libertyville IL Died Apr. 30, 1970; buried Norway MI

LINDBECK, JOHN M(ATTHEW) H(ENRY), educator; b. Kikungshan, China, July 8, 1915; s. John Walter and Magda Georgina (Hallquist) L.; student Kikungshan-Redcroft Am. Sch., Kuling, China, 1929-33; B.A., Gustavus Adolphus Coll., 1937; student U. Mich., summer, 1938; B.D., Yale, 1940, Ph.D., 1948; Rockefeller Found. fellow Oriental langs. and history, Harvard-Yenching Inst., 1946-48; m. Nancy Margaret Gantt, Feb. 28, 1943 (dec. June, 1954);children—John Robert, Sarah George; m. 2d, Dorathea Wehrwein, Mar. 10, 1956 (dec. July 1965); children—Dorathea Ann, Katherine Louise; m. third, Anne M. Jackson, September 10, 1966. Lectr., Sch. Mil. Govt., Princeton, 1944-45; asst. Prof. polit. sci. Yale, 1948-49, asst. prof. Far Eastern studies, 1949-52, humanities faculty research fellow, 1951-52, also lectr. Inst. Far Eastern langs., 1948-52, dir. undergrad. Far Eastern area studies, 1950-51; pub. affairs adviser Chinese affairs Dept. State, 1952-58; dep. dir. research project on men and politics in Modern China, Columbia, 1958-59; research fellow Chinese studies Harvard, 1959-67, asso. dir. East Asian Research Center, 1959-67, field research Hong Kong, 1961-62, lectr. govt., 1963-67, mem. com. regional studies Harvard, 1964-67; dir. East Asian Inst., Columbia U., N.Y.C., 1967-71; cons. Rand Corp., 1959-71, Inst. Def. Analysis, 1961-71, Dept. State, 1963-71; bd. dirs. Chinese Materials and Research Aids Service Center, Assn. Asian Studies, Taipai, Taiwan, 1964-71. Mem. joint com. on Contemporary China, Am. Council Learned Socs.-Social Sci. Research Council, 1959-71, sec., 1959-61, chmn., from 1964; chmn. com. on scholarly communication with Mainland China, Nat. Acad. Scis., 1968-71, also mem. Pacific sci. bd., 1968-71; bd. dirs. Nat. Com. on U.S.-China Relations, v.p., 1968-71; mem. Council Fgn. Relations. Mem. bd. dirs. Universities Service Center. Hong Kong, 1965-71. Served to lt. USNR, 1942-46. Conglist. Contbr. articles profl. publs. Home: North Tarrytown NY Died Jan. 9, 1971; buried New Fairfield CT

LINDEMAN, CHARLES BERNARD, pub. exec.; b. Seattle, Wash., Dec. 5, 1891; s. Bernard and Selma (Bushman) L.; ed. Seattle Pub. Schs., Broadway High Sch.; m. Helen Bigelow, June 26, 1919. Copy boy on Seattle Times, 1909; advt. mgr. Carnation Milk Co., 1912-13; reporter, San Francisco Chronicle, 1914-15; western advt. mgr., Firestone, San Francisco, 1915-17; Boston dist. mgr. Firestone Tire Co., 1919-24; promotion-advt. mgr., Seattle Times, 1924-29; associate publisher, Post Intelligencer, 1930-43, pub., 1943-65, pres., 1965-69; dir. Hearst Consol. Publications, Rainier Nat. Park Company, president Mountain Construction Co., v.p. Lake Tapps Development Co., Island Estate Company. Trustee C. of C., Seattle Symphony Orchestra, Community Fund. Driver, Am. Field Service in France for 11 months, World War I. Decorated Croix de Guerre. Mem. Pacific N.W. Trade Assn. (ex-pres.). Clubs: Rainier, Wash. Athletic (ex-pres.), Seattle Golf (ex-pres.), Broadmoor Golf, Seattle Tennis. Home: Seattle WA Died Apr. 30, 1969; cremated.

LINDLEY, HARLOW, historian; b. Sylvania, Parke County, Ind., May 31, 1875; s. Mahlon and Martha (Newlin) L.; B.Litt., Earlham Coll., Richmond, Ind., 1898, A.M., 1899; Litt.D., Hanover Coll., 1923; studied U. of Wis., summer, 1899, U. of Chicago, 1902-04; m. Olive S. Rogers, June 24, 1908; children—Roger M., Eleanor S. Librarian, 1898-1928; instr. history and mathematics, 1899-1901, asst. prof. history, 1901-05, prof. history and polit. science, 1905-28, Earlham Coll. Prof. history, Ind. State U., summer, 1911; dir. dept. of history and archives, Ind. State Library, 1907-23; sec. 1915-23, dir. 1923-24, Ind. Hist. Commn.; actg. asso. prof. polit. science, Stanford, 1918; librarian Hayes Memorial Hist. Library and Museum, Fremont, Ohio, 1928; curator of history, Ohio State Archeol. and Hist. Soc., 1929-34, dept. of history, Ohio State U., 1932. Charter mem. Richmond City Planning Commn. Del. to World Conf. Friends Council of the Midwest Museums Hays),mem. Council of the Am. Assn. for State and Local History; chmn. exec. com. Anthony Wayne Memorial Assn. Mem. Soc. of Am. Archivists, Ohio War History Commn., Am. Hist. Assn., Am. Polit. Science Assn., Miss. Valley Hist. Assn. (pres. 1918-19), Ind. Hist. Soc., Ohio Valley Hist. Assn., Ohio State Archeol. and Hist. Soc. (sec., editor and librarian, 1934-46); Ohio Revolutionary Memorial Commn., 1934-46; Mich.-Ind.-Ohio Museums Assn. (pres.), Pi Gamma Mu. Mem. Ohio State Advisory Commn. on the Northwest Territory Celebration, 1937-38. Mem. Friends Church. Club: Ohio State University Faculty. Author: The Government of Indiana, 1909; The Quakers in the Old Northwest, 1912; Report on the Archives of Indiana (U.S. Govt. publs.), 1912; Indiana as Seen by Early Travelers, 1916; The Indiana Centennial, 1919; A Century of Quakerism in Indiana, 1922; The Ordinance of 1787 and the Old Northwest Territory, 1937; The Quaker Contribution to the Old Northwest, 1938; Ohio in the Twentieth Century, 1942; Captain Cushing in the War of 1812, 1944. Contbr. to Dictionary of American Biography, Grolier Encyclopedia and Dictionary of American History; chmn. Publication Com. of History of Ohio (6 vols.), editor, 1942-44. Home: 121 E. Tulane Rd., Columbus 2 OH‡

LINDSAY, F(RANK) M(ERRILL), publisher; b. Decatur, Ill., Nov. 9, 1879; s. John and Edna (Nicholson) L.; LL.B., U. of Illinois, 1904; LL.D., Millikin U., 1954; m. Vivian Simpson, Oct. 7, 1908 (dec. June, 1919); 1 son, Frank Merrill; m. 2d Marjorie Ruth McKay, Mar. 1921; children—Donald McKay, Marjorie Edith, Shirley Jean. Dir. Lindsay-Schaub Newspapers, Inc. (pubs. of Decatur Daily Rev., Decatur Herald, Decatur Sunday Herald and Rev., from 1931, also Champaign-Urbana (Ill.) Courier, from 1934, pres., from 1947; pres., dir. East Shore Newspapers, Inc. (pubs. of Metro-East Jour., East St. Louis, Illinois), from 1932, Southern Ill. Publications, Inc. (publishers Southern Illinoisan, Carbondale-Herrin-Murphysboro, Ill.), from 1947; dir. Quincy (Ill.) Newspapers, Inc. (pubs. of Quincy Herald-Whig), from 1926, pres., from 1956. Mem. Illinois State Planning Association, 1938-43, Ill. Post War Planning Commn., 1943-47; dir., Am. Planning and Civic Assn., 1939-50, Ill. State Housing Bd., from 1948, Decatur and Macon Co. Hosp., 1921-54; mem. Decatur Planning Commn., from 1940, Urban Renewal Commn., from 1957. Mem. Acad. Polit. Sci., Sigma Delta Chi, Delta Tau Delta. Conglist. Mason. Clubs: Country, Decatur. Author: A Publisher Reports Observations from 46 Years of Newspaper Management, 1960. Home: Decatur IL Died June 11, 1972; buried North Fork Cemetery, Decatur IL

LINDSAY, LYNN GROUT, mfg. exec.; b. St. Paul, Sept. 19, 1893; s. Frederick Francis and Effie (Grout) L.; student pub. schs.; m. Beatrice L. O'Neill, Sept. 30, 1916; children—James F., Lynn G., Mary Patricia (Mrs. James L. Sexton), Barbara Joan (Mrs. H. John Thayer); m. 2d, Helen Hessing, Apr. 3, 1967. Dir. nat. sales, heating div. Crane Co., Chgo., 1936-42; organized, v.p. Fed. Dessicant Co., St. Paul, 1942-45, v.p. chem. div. United Refrigerator Mfg. Co., St. Paul, 1942-45; founder, pres., chmn. bd., dir. The Lindsay Co. (acquired by Union Tank Car Co. Chgo. 1959), St. Paul, 1945-68. Mem. Water Conditioning Found. (past pres.). Methodist. Clubs: Coral Ridge Yacht (Fort Lauderdale, Fla.); Minnesota, White Bear Yacht. Home: St Paul MN Died Apr. 15, 1968.

LINDSAY, THE RT. HON. SIR RONALD, diplomate; b. May 3, 1877; s. of 26th Earl of Crawford; m. Martha, dau. J. Donald Cameron, of Pa., 1909 (died 1918); m. 2d, Elizabeth Sherman, dau. of Colgate Hoyt, of N.Y. City, 1924. Diplomatic service since 1898; at Washington, D.C., 1905-07, and counselor of Embassy, 1919-20; minister plenipotentiary to Paris, 1920-21; undersec. of state at Foreign Office, London, 1921-24, later ambassador at Constantinople and Berlin; permanent undersec. of state for foreign affairs, July 16, 1928; A.E. and P. from Gt. Britain to U.S. since Mar. 1930. Address: British Embassy, Washington DC‡

LINDSEY, EDWARD ALLEN, banker; b. Nashville, Tenn., Aug. 27, 1871; s. Alonzo and Etha (Hagen) L.; ed. pub. schs.; m. Alice Miller Hall, of Nashville, Tenn., Oct. 27, 1896; children—Martha Jane, Alice Hall (Mrs. J. Pembroke Hart). Began as runner First Nat. Bank, Nashville, 1888, asst. cashier, 1898-1901; cashier Merchants Nat. Bank, 1901-06; v.p. First Nat. Bank, 1906-15; pres. Am. Paper Box Mfg. Co., Tri-State Paper Box Mfg. Co., Memphis, Tenn.; pres. McEwen Laundry Co., Nashville, Tenn. Ex-pres. Nashville Bankers' Assn., Nashville Clearing House, Nashville Chamber Commerce, Tenn. Soc. S.A.R., Tenn. Bankers Assn. Pres. bd. of trustees Hermitage Assn. (home of Andrew Jackson). Democrat. Presbyn. Home: 201 24th Av., S. Office: American Paper Box Co., Nashville TN‡

LINDSEY, KENNETH LOVELL, textile mfr.; b. Boston, Mar. 4, 1888; s. William and Anne (Sheen) L.; A.B. cum laude, Harvard, 1910; m. Anne Currier, Oct. 12, 1917; children—Leslie Huntoon, Christopher Francis, Anne Day. With Mills Equipment Co., Ltd., London, Eng., from 1913, chmn., from 1930, also dir.; with Textron, Inc., Providence, from 1924, also dir. Mem. com. A.R.C., World War II; dir. Civilian Relief, Gt. Britain, 1939-41. Served as 1st lt., F.A., U.S. Army, World War I. Clubs: White's, Boodles (London); Somerset, Tennis and Racquet (Boston); Racquet and Tennis, Harvard (N.Y.C.). Home: London England Died May 6, 1969.

LINDSEY, LOUIS, univ. prof., research scholar; b. Hartford, N.Y., Dec. 12, 1877; s. Daniel and Josephine Lindsey; student Cortland (N.Y.) State Normal Sch.; A.B., Syracuse U., 1906, M.A., 1909. Ph.D., 1911; m. Edith L. MacFarran, Aug. 2, 1922; children—Robert L., Jean Francis. Asst., U.S. Naval Observatory, Washington, 1908-12; instr. applied mathematics, Syracuse U., 1911-12; asst. prof., 1912-17, asso. prof., 1917-25, prof. applied mathematics, 1925-47, prof. emeritus since July 1947; research in applied mathematics related to engring. work since 1948. Past mem. Am. Math. Soc., Am. Math. Assn., Sigma Xi, Tau Beta Pi, Phi Beta Kappa, Pi Mu Epsilon, Phi Kappa Phi. Republican Presbyterian. Author: Definitive Orbits of Comet, 1902 and Kress comet (Astron. Jour. and Astronomische Nachrchte). Home: 854 Maryland Av., Syracuse 10 NY‡

LINDSEY, THERESE KAYSER (MRS. S. A. LINDSEY), writer; b. Tyler, Tex., Oct. 2, 1870; d. Albert and Mary Louise (Lawrence) Kayser; grad. high sch., Tyler, 1889, San Marco (Tex.) Normal Sch., 1905; student U. of Chicago, 1907-09, Harvard, 1922; m. Judge S. A. Lindsey, of Tyler, June 1893; children—Samuel Albert (dec.), Louise Elizabeth. Contbr. verse to newspapers and mags. since 1914. Mem. Poetry Soc. America, Tex. Poetry Soc. (organizer), S.C. Poetry Soc. Author: Blue Norther (verse), 1925. Home: Tyler TX‡

LINDSTROM, CARL E.,, retired newspaper editor, professor of journalism; born Wallace, Michigan, Mar. 1, 1896; s. Gustaf and Ida (Stenberg) L.; student Beloit (Wis.) Coll.; m. Ethel Sworsbourne Sept. 28, 1921; 1 son, Walter Swornsbourne L. Reporter Davenport (Ia.) Democrat, Beloit (Wis.) Daily News, 1915-16; telegraph editor Waterbury (Conn.) Republican, 1917; copy editor, music critic Hartford (Conn.) Times, 1917-46, mng. editor, 1946, exec. editor, 1953-59; prof. journalism U. Mich., Ann Arbor, 1959-61. Mem. Pulitzer Prize Screen Jury in Journalism. Distinguished service mem. Am. Soc. Newspaper editors. Mem. Internat. Press Inst. Lutheran. Clubs: Hartford, Twentieth Century. Author: The Fading American Newspaper, 1960. Founder The Am. Editor. Contbr. articles mus. mags. Home: Windsor CT Died Apr. 2, 1969.

LING, CHARLES JOSEPH, coll. prof.; b. Auburn, Cayuga County, N.Y., Dec. 8, 1867; s. Henry and Elizabeth (Hollingworth) L.; B.S., Cornell U., 1890; A.M., Denver U., 1900, Ph.D., 1902; m. Myrtle Rowland Ryan, Nov. 24, 1890; children—Elizabeth Pauline (Mrs. Ronald Reamer), Ernest Fitchard, Ruth (Mrs. W.H. Runk). Science teacher, Carrollton, Ill., 1890; instr. science, State Normal Sch., Natchitoches, La., 1890-92, Pueblo (Colo.) High Sch., 1892-94; instr. physics, Manual Training High Sch., Denver, Colo., 1894-1906; prof. physics and astronomy, Allegheny Coll., Meadville, Pa., 1906-33, prof. emeritus since 1933. Instr. mathematics and astronomy, Denver U., summer, 1903; dir. summer session, Allegheny Coll., 1925, 26, 27. Mem. Am. Assn. Univ. Profs., Sigma Alpha Epsilon, Sigma Xi. Home: Apt. C-7, 1225 Park Av., Rochester 10 NY‡

LINN, HENRY W., univ. pres.; b. St. Louis, Oct. 16, 1904; s. Henry and Catherine (Haberstock) L.; student St. Stanislaus Sem., Florissant, Mo., 1923-27; A.B., St. Louis U., 1929, A.M., 1930, Ph.D., 1934, S.T.L., 1937. Member Society of Jesus. Instructor in classics, Xavier University, Cincinnati, Ohio, 1927-28, St. Louis (Mo.) University, 1937; instructor and associate prof. classics, Creighton U., Omaha, Neb., from 1938, mil. liaison officer, 1943-44, civilian military chaplain, 1943-44, dean Sch. of Journalism, 1944-48, dir. Inst. Indsl. Relations, 1945-48; exec. sec. to pres., 1946-50, exec. asst. pres., 1950-55, v.p. in charge of pub. relations and development, 1955-58, v.p. in charge of University relations, 1958-62, pres., 1962-69. Mem. Neb. Assn. Ch. Colls., Neb. Assn. Colls. and Univs., Assn. Am. Colls., Assn. Urban Univs. Mem. Am. Medieval Acad., Nat. Classical Assn., Am. Philol. Assn., Am. Assn. U. Profs., N.E.A., Nat. Cath. Edn. Assn., Jesuit Ednl. Assn., Am. Coll. Pub. Relations Assn., Am. Alumni Council, Ak-Sar-Ben, Omaha C. of C., Joslyn Liberal Arts Soc., Alpha Kappa Psi, Alpha Sigma Nu. Address: Omaha NB Died Nov. 1, 1969; buried Holy Sepulchre Cemetery, Omaha NB

LINNEMAN, HERBERT F., fgn. service officer; b. Buffalo, Oct. 22, 1914; s. Frederick and Loretta (Reisch) L.; LL.B., Southeastern U., 1940; m. Luisa Coll., Oct. 23, 1943; children—Elena Christina (Mrs. Patrick J. Miliffe), Douglas Luis. Admitted to D.C. bar; radio actor, announcer, 1934-35; adminstrv. asst. Treasury Dept., 1936-40; field examiner U.S. Civil Service Commn., 1940-42; sr. legal cons. U.S. Bd. Vets. Appeals, 1946-49; dep. dir. Office of Security, Dept. State, 1949-53; dep. asst. dir. USIA, 1953-54; attache and exec. officer Am. embassy, New Delhi, India, 1954-56; program and policy officer USIA, 1957-58; 1st sec., dep. pub. affairs officer Am. embassy, Tehran, Iran, 1958-60, counselor for pub. affairs, 1960-63; dir. Am. Cultural Center, Brazzaville, Congo, 1963-65; exec. officer Am. embassy, Karachi, Pakistan, 1966-67; 1st sec. Am. embassy, Tokyo, Japan, 1967-69. Served from ensign to lt. USCGR, 1942-46. Mem. Sigma Delta Kappa. Home: Miami Beach FL Died July 25, 1971; interred Miami FL

LINNEY, ROBERT JOSEPH, mining co. exec.; b. Old Forge, Pa., Jan. 18, 1908; s. Joseph Robert and Elizabeth (Davies) L.; student Yale, 1927-29; m. Jane Moore, Oct. 4, 1952; children—William Joseph, Joseph Robert, Elizabeth Irene (Mrs. William Garfield Hamel), Mary Agnes (Mrs. Ross Ducatte), Nancy Jayne (Mrs. Paul Schendel). Started career as a mining engr. Chateaugay Ore & Iron Co., Lyon Mountain, N.Y., 1929-31, supt. concentrating and sintering, 1931-37, gen. mgr., 1937-39; gen. supt. Republic Steel Corp., Port Henry, N.Y., 1939-46, dist. mgr., 1946-50; mgr. operations Res. Mining Co., Silver Bay, Minn., 1950-56, v.p. operations, 1956-58, exec. v.p., 1958-60, pres., dir., 1960-64; exec. v.p. Hanna Mining Co., Cleve., from 1965; pres., dir. Escanaba & Lake Superior R.R., Hanna Nickel Smelting Co., Wells Randville Co.; v.p., dir. Australian Hanna, Ltd., Compania Minera de Matosa, Hanna Devel. Co., Itasca Pellet Co., Lowphos Ore., Ltd., Matonipi Mines, Ltd., No. Iron Ore Mines, Ltd., Sandore, Inc., Southwestern Metals, Inc., Teal Lake Iron Mining Co., Western Copper & Mining Co.; v.p. operations Iron Ore Co. of Can., Carol Pellet Co.; v.p. Butler Bros., Hanna Coal & Ore Corp., Hanna Iron Ore div. Nat. Steel Corp., Hanna Mines Co., Hanna Ore Mining Co., Morton Ore Co., No. Land Co., Philbin Mining Co., Pilot Knob Pellet Co., South Agnew Mining Co.; dir. Mesaba-Cliffs Mining Co., North Star Co., Inc., Taconite Realty Corp., Hanna Commerce Corp. Recipient William Lawrence Saunders gold medal, 1960. Mem. Am. Inst. Mining, Metall. and Petroleum Engrs., Mining and Metall. Soc. Am. Republican. Presbyn. Mason (Shriner), Elk. Clubs: Cleveland Athletic; Canterbury Golf; Union (Cleve.). Home: Shaker Heights OH Died May 24, 1971; buried Lakeview Cemetery, Cleveland OH

LINSLEY, DUNCAN ROBERTSON, securities; b. New London, Conn., Apr. 22, 1900; s. James Russell and Helen (Robertson) L.; B.A., Mass. Inst. of Tech. 1922; m. Julia Quaintance, Sept. 5, 1925; children—Julia Williams, James Duncan. Started as clerk Harris, Forbes & Co., N.Y. City, 1922-29, dir. 1929-31; v.p. Chase Harris Forbes Corp., N.Y., 1931-33; sr. v.p. First Boston Corp., N.Y.C., 1934-59, dir., 1934-72, chmn. exec. com., 1951-55, vice chmn., 1955-60. Mem. Sigma Alpha Epsilon. Republican, Episcopalian. Clubs: University, Down Town Assn. (N.Y.C.); Church, Country of Fairfield. Home: Fairfield CT Died May 1, 1972.

LINSON, CORWIN KNAPP, artist; b. Brooklyn, N.Y., Feb. 25, 1864; s. William Van Keuren and Maria Louisa (Knapp) L.; studied at Acad. Julian and Ecole des Beaux Arts, Paris (1st prize in composition, also hon. mention in composition and drawing); pupil of Gerome and Lefebvre and Jean Paul Laurens; m. Annie G. Prickitt. d. Hon. William A. Prickitt, U.S. consul, at Reims, France, July 20, 1898; children—Elizabeth Louise, Rosalind Van Keuren. Returned to U.S., 1901; designed 5 memorial windows in Baptist Temple, Brooklyn, memorial window in Presbyn. Ch., Rumson, N.J. Exhbtd. Nat. Acad. Design; New York Water Color Club; New York Water Color Soc.; Art Inst., Chicago; Corcoran Gallery, Washington, D.C.; Pa. Acad. Fine Arts; Buffalo Expn., 1900; St. Louis Exposition, 1904, etc. Portraits: Mark Hopkins, former pres. Williams College; Hon. Edmund Wilson, former atty. gen. State of N.J.; Dr. Hunter McGuire; Col. Charles Jefferson Wright, founder of New York Mil. Acad.; John Willard Raught in Scranton Museum; etc. Mem. of Allied Artists of America, (resigned). Baptist. Contbr. descriptive articles and verse to mags. Awarded bronze medal and diploma by Greek Com. on Athletics, Athens, 1896, as artist corr. for Scribner's mag. Home-studio: 27 Hooper Av., Atlantic Highlands NJ‡

LIPCHITZ, JACQUES, sculptor; b. Druskieniki, Latvia, Aug. 22, 1891; s. Abraham Isaac and Rachel Leah (Krynski) L.; student Ecole des Beaux-Arts, also Academie Julien; L.H.D., Columbia, 1968; m. Berta Kitrossky, May 13, 1925. Citizen of France. Exhibited Leonce Rosenberg Gallery, Paris, 1920; ann. exhbns. Salon des Independents, Salon des Tuilleries, Paris, 1928-35; exhbn. Gallerie la Renaissance, Paris, 1930, Bucholz Gallery, N.Y.C., 1948; Prometheus exhibited Palais de la Decouverte, Internat. Paris Expn., 1936; works represented collections of Musee de L'Art Moderne, Paris, Musee de Genoble, Mus. Modern Art, N.Y.C. Met. Mus. Albright Mus., Buffalo, Phila. Mus. Art, Worcester Mus. Art, also pvt. collections; works include Variation, The Promise, Yara and I, Album Page, Innocent Victim, The Pilgrim, Blossoming, The Prayer, Angel's Struggle with Jacob. Recipient gold medal for sculpture Am. Acad. and Nat. Inst. Arts and Letters, 1966. Mem. Nat. Inst. Arts and Letters (mem. council), Am. Acad. Arts and Letters. Address: New York City NY Died May 26, 1973.

LIPPHARD, WILLIAM BENJAMIN, editor, author; b. Evansville, Ind., Oct. 29, 1886; s. Rev. William Augustus and Martha (Liefield) L.; B.A., Yale, 1908, M.A., 1910; B.D., Colgate-Rochester Div. Sch., 1920; D.D., Franklin Coll., 1932; Litt.D. (hon.) Ottawa (Kansas) University, 1949; m. Helen Stella Dickinson, Oct. 15, 1914; children—Dickinson, Stella D. (Mrs. L.D. Clarke). Asst. sec. Am. Bapt. Foreign Mission Soc., 1913-19, recording sec., 1918-33, asso. sec., 1919-33, asso. editor Missions." 1922-32, editor, 1932-52. retired as editor emeritus for life; secretary program committee American Baptist Convention, 1928-32 Mem bd. mgrs. Am. Baptist Hist. Soc. Relief work Europe in cooperation with and Can. Relief work in Europe in cooperation with Am. Relief Adminstration, 1920-21; del. to Bapt. World Congress, Stockholm, 1923, Toronto, 1928. Berlin (Germany), 1934, Atlanta, 1939, Copenhagen (Denmark), 1947, Cleve., 1950, London, 1955. World Conf. on Ch. and State, Oxford, 1937, World Conf. on Faith and Order, Edinburgh, 1937, World Council Chs., Holland, 1948; Evanston, Ill., 1954; visited Far East, 1925; in the interests of mission work; Eng., 1928, in interest of John Bunyan Tercentenary; Soviet Russia, 1930, Germany, 1933, Mexico, Italy, 1935, Rumania, 1937, Czechoslovakia, 1938, in special study of conditions. Sec. World Relief Com. of American Bapt. Conv., 1940-52. Church press Rep. United Nations Conf., San Francisco, 1945. U.S. War Corr., Germany, 1946 Mem. National Council of Churches Dept. Internat. Affairs; pres. Asso. Ch. Press, 1947-49, exec. sec., 1951-61. Mem. Fgn. Policy Assn., Am. Com. World Council Chs. Received Church Press award, 1951, for eminence in editorial writing. Fellow American Geographical Society; member of New York Baptist City Soc. (life), Alpha Sigma Phi. Am. Baptist Hist. Society (vice president 1948-50), Republican. Clubs: Authors (London); Yale, Quill, Clergy. Author: The Ministry of Healing, 1920. The Second Century, 1926; Communing with Communism, 1931; Out of the Storm in China, 1932; Fifty Years an Editor, 1963; A History of the Associated Church Press, published 1965; Disillusioned World, pub. 1967. Contributor to The Religions of America, 1954, Why I Am a Baptist, 1957, We Believe in Prayer, 1958. Dir. Ch. Press World Council Chs., 1954. Home: Yonkers NY Died Apr. 14, 1971; buried Rochester NY

LIPPITT, CHARLES WARREN, real estate broker; b. Providence, May 15, 1894; s. Charles Warren and Margaret (Farnum) L; S.B., Harvard, 1921; M.B.A., N.Y.U., 1957; m. Frances Pomeroy, June 20, 1920 (div. Jan. 1938); children—Charles Warren III (dec.), Rhoda (Mrs. Elisha Harris Howard III); m. 2d, Louise Davies Greenwood, June 22, 1938. With D.M. Collins & Co., 1931-33, Smith, Graham & Rockwell, 1933-36, Graham & Co., 1936-40; v.p. Morris & Cumings Dredging Co., 1945-48; sec. Sapolio Products Co., N.Y.C., 1949-50; v.p. Joseph P. Day Realty, Inc., 1952-70. Served to colonel F.A., U.S. Army, 1917-66; ETO. Decorated Bronze star (U.S.); Croix de Guerre (France). Mem.

Soc. Real Estate Appraisers, Am. Soc. Appraisers, N.Y. State Soc. Real Estate Appraisers, N.Y. Bd. Trade, Real Estate Bd. N.Y., Assn., U.S. Army, Soc. Cincinnati (pres. gen. 1965-70), Mayflower Soc., Soc. Colonial Wars, S.A.R., Mil. Order Fgn. Wars, Mil. Order World Wars, Order La Fayette, Sprouting Rock Beach Assn., Phi Beta Epsilon. Republican. Clubs: New York Yacht; Newport (R.I.) Reading Room. Home: Wilton CT Died June 22, 1970.

LIPPMANN, ROBERT KORN, physician; b. N.Y.C., Sept. 10, 1898; s. David and Lillie (Korn) L.; B.S., Columbia, 1918; M.D., Johns Hopkins, 1922; student Jubilaeum Spital (Vienna), 1925, Istituto Rizzoli (Bologna), 1926; m. Helen Kaufmann, Oct. 20, 1927; children—Nancy L. (Mrs. Richard Heon), Robert D. Intern Mt. Sinai Hosp., N.Y.C., 1923-25; resident Istituto Rizzoli (Bologna), 1925-26; practice medicine specializing in orthopaedic surgery, N.Y.C., 1926-69; mem. staff Mt. Sinai Hosp., Blythedale Hosp.; prof. emeritus, dept. orthopaedics Mt. Sinai Hosp. and Med. Sch., 1967-69. Fellow N.Y. Acad. Medicine, A.C.S., Am. Acad. Orthopaedic Surgeons, Am. Orthopaedic Assn., Internat. Soc. Orthopaedic Surgery and Traumatology, Orthopaedic Research Soc.; mem. A.M.A. Home: NYC NY Died June 9, 1969; buried Ferncliff Cemetery Hartsdale NY

LIPPS, OSCAR HIRAM, educator; b. Fayette, Ind., July 8, 1872; ed. pub. schs. of Tenn., Powel's Valley Sem. (annex of Grant U., Athens, Tenn.), American U., Harriman, Tenn.; m. Maude Etta Rader, Dec. 19, 1897; children—Homer Hiawatha, Lucile, Unita, Mack, Idaho, Mary Elsie, Milton Edward, Ruth, Helen. Teacher pub. schs., Tenn., 1890; post school teacher, U.S. Army, 1891-93; teacher Evergreen (La.) Coll., 1894; prin. Big Valley Acad., Andersonville, Tenn., 1896-97; entered U.S. Indian Sch. Service as teacher, 1898; supt. Indian Boarding Schs., Utah, Minn., Okla., N.D. and Ida., 1900-09; dist. supervisor Indian Schs., 1909-14; supt. Carlisle (Pa.) Indian Sch., 1914-17; chief supervisor Indian Schs., 1917-20; supt. Nez Perce (Ida.) Indian Agency, 1920-26; dist. supt. of Indian affairs, 1926-31; in charge Chemawa (Ore.) Indian School, 1927-31; supt. Sacramento (Calif.) Indian Agency, 1931-35; field representative U.S. Indian Service, 1935-37; made survey and report of social and econ. conditions of Indians and Eskimos of Alaska, 1936; retired from U.S. Indian Service, July 31, 1937. Author: A Little History of the Navajos, 1909; Daily Lesson Plan Book for Vocational Teachers, 1919; (brochures) The Case of the California Indians, 1932; Our National Indian Problem and the Chief Factors in Its Solution, 1933. Compiler: Laws and Regulations Relating to Indian Affairs, 1913. Home: 38 Park Av., Salem OR‡

LIPSCOMB, GLENARD P., congressman; b. Jackson, Mich., Aug. 19, 1915; s. Paul E. and Eva Marie (Kipp) L.; ed. U. So. Cal.; m. Virginia Sognalian; children—Diane Marie, Joyce Elaine. Pub. accountant Lipscomb, Hahn & Brown, Los Angeles. Served as mem. Cal. Ho. Reps.; elected mem. 83 Congress, 24th Cal. Dist., to fill term of Norris Poulson (resigned), mem. 84th-91st Congresses. Served with finance corps U.S. Army, World War II. Republican. Baptist. Mem. Nat. Soc. Pub. Accountants, Am. Legion. Elk. Club: Kiwanis. Home: Los Angeles CA Died Feb. 1970.

LIPSEY, PLAUTUS IBERUS, JR., newspaperman, educator; b. Mufreesboro, Tenn., Sept. 27, 1893; s. Plautus Iberus and Julia Toy (Johnson) L.; B.A., Miss. Coll., Clinton, 1913; grad. study, Columbia, 1924, Baylor U., 1924-25; Master of Arts, Univ. of Ala., 1951; m. Sue Price, June 14, 1927; children—Jeannie Howe, Ann Crawford and Laura Kate. Was chief of bureau, Asso. Press, Memphis, 1926-27; mem. staff Associated Press, London, 1927-29, corr. and chief of bur., Geneva, Switzerland, 1929-33; congressional corr. Universal Service, Washington, D.C., 1934; foreign editor Universal Service, N.Y. City, 1934-35; head of Journalism Dept. and dir. of publicity, Stetson U., De Land, Fla., 1935-40; special news corr. in Southeast Europe, summer, 1940; pub. relations dir., Tolan Com., Congress, Washington, 1941; asst. coordinator of internat. broadcasting, N.Y. City, 1942; supervisor of shortwave news broadcasts to Latin America from NBC, N.Y. City, for Coordinator Inter-Am. Affairs; later chief of Radio News, C.I.A.A., New York City; then dir. U.S. Information Office, Santiago, Chile. Lectr. in history Miss. Coll., 1951-57, prof. history, 1957-64. prof. emeritus, 1964-70. research in Far East, 1959, Near East, 1960. Lt. inf., U.S. Army, 1917-20. Home: Clinton MS Died Feb. 18, 1970; buried Clinton MS

LIPSKY, LOUIS, editor; b. Rochester, N.Y., Nov. 30, 1876; s. Jacob and Dinah R. (Philipowsky) L.; ed. Rochester Free Acad. and 1 yr. at Columbia University; m. Charlotte Schacht, of Riga, Kurland, Mar. 20, 1907; children—David, Eleazar, Joel. Began as collaborator with Dr. Joseph Jacobs in editorship of the Am. Hebrew, New York, 1899; dramatic critic Morning Telegraph 2 yrs.; then contbr. to Associated Sunday Mags., New York Press, etc., and editor Maccabean Monthly, official organ Federation of Am. Zionists; has devoted much time to speaking, writing and organizing for Zionist movement; v.p. Zionist Congress, Carlsbad, Czechoslovakia, 1923; mem. World Zionist Exec. Com., London, 1923, Prague, 1933; chmn. Zionist Orgn. of America, 1922-24, pres., 1924-30; editor The New Palestine; now pres. Eastern Life Ins. Co. of N.Y. Mem. Soc. of the Genesee. Jewish. Home: 302 W. 86th St. Office: 386 4th Av., New York NY‡

LIST, CARL F., physician; b. Salbke, Germany, Sept. 14, 1902; s. Reinhold and Evelyn (Calmann) L.; m. Eva Neumann, Feb. 24, 1929; children—Suzanne (Mrs. Frank Friedlander), Walter. With Wenzel Haucke Krankenhaus, Breslau, 1927-28; Hufeland Hosp., 1928-31; Peter Bent Brigham Hosp., Boston, 1931-32; 3d Surg. U. Clinic, Berlin, 1932-33; Centre Neurologue, Brussels, 1933; instr. U. Mich. Hosp., 1934-46; practice medicine, specializing in neurosurgery, Grand Rapids, Mich., 1946-68. Contbr. profl. jours. Home: Grand Rapids MI Died Dec. 12, 1968.

LIST, KURT, composer; b. Vienna, Austria, July 21, 1913; s. Karl and Stephanie (von Ehrenfels) L.; diploma in conducting, Conservatory, Vienna, 1934; Ph.D., U. Vienna, 1938; m. Ursula Stenz, Apr. 25, 1961. Editor, Listen, the Guide to Good Music, N.Y.C., 1944-51; musical dir., v.p. Westminster Recording Co., N.Y.C., 1951-63; musical dir. Musical Heritage Soc., Inc., N.Y.C., 1963-70; chief condr. Biedermeier Orch., Vienna, Austria, 1963-70; composer in residence, Burgtheater, Vienna, 1963-70. Composer: String Quartet, 1946, Wind Quintet, 1949, The Wise and the Foolish (opera), 1951, Hochzeitstag (opera), 1959; composer stage music to plays, Saul and Alkestis (by A. Lernet-Holenia, Burgtheater, Vienna), 1964, La Machine Infernale (by J. Cocteau), 1965; Der Triumph des Todes (opera), 1965; Der Thronfolger (opera), 1969. Member of the International Society of Contemporary Music, Am. Composers Alliance, Am. Acad. Recording Arts and Scis. Author: An Introduction to the Instrumental Music from Monteverdi to Mozart, 1965. Contbr. articles profl. publs. Address: Vienna Austria Died Nov. 16, 1970.

LITCHFIELD, EDWARD HAROLD, bus. exec.; b. Detroit, Michigan, Apr. 12, 1914; s. Adelbert Leigh and Ethel Blanche (McKim) L.; A.B., U. of Mich., 1936, Ph.D. (Carl Braun fellow), 1940; D.C.S., Pace Coll., 1956; LL.D., Temple U., 1957; L.H.D., Hahnemann Medical College, 1957; D.Sc. (honorary), West Virginia University, 1959; LL.D., Waynesburg College, 1961, Indiana State University, 1966; Doctor of Adminstrn., Youngstown U., 1962; m. Anne Muir Macintyre, Sept. 11, 1940 (dec.); children—Peter M., Janet M., Anne Roberta; m. 2d, Mary Carolyn Morrill, March 30, 1957; children—Edward Harold, DeForest. Engaged as executive secretary of Michigan Merit System Association, Lansing, 1937-38; instructor political science, Brown University, 1940-41; training specialist, The Panama Canal, 1941; deputy director, Michigan State Civil Service Commission, Lansing, 1942-45; lecturer in public administration, U. of Mich., 1942-45; spl. asst. to U.S. chief of mission to Germany, U.S. Dept. State, 1945-46; dep. dir. of civil adminstrn. div., Office Mil. Govt. for Germany, Berlin, 1946-47, dir., 1947-49; cons. to under sec. of Army, 1949; exec. dir. The American Political Sci. Assn., 1950-53; vis. professor Cornell Univ., 1950, professor adminstrn., 1950-55, dean sch. bus. and pub. adminstrn., 1953-55; chancellor U. Pitts., 1955-65, prof. adminstrn. and political sci., 1955-65. Director of Avco Corp. President Governmental Affairs Institute, Washington, N.Y.C., 1950-55, chmn. bd., from 1955; chairman bd. dirs. SCM Corp., from 1956, Litchfield Assos., Inc., from 1959, Oakland Corp., 1962-65, Corporate Investment Co. (now Capital for Tech. Corp.), from 1966; dir. Nat. Capital Airlines. Mem. U.S. delegation to Moscow and London confs. of the Council of Fgn. Ministers, 1947, and London Tri-partite Conferences, 1948, Atlantic Congress, London, 1959. Chairman of the board of Legal Research Found., 1964-65. Decorated comdr. Order of Dannebrog (Denmark). Mem. Am. Polit. Sci. Assn., Am. Assn. U. Profs., Am. Soc. Pub. Adminstrn., Am. Acad. Polit. and Social Sci., Newcomen Soc., Pa. Soc., Phi Beta Kappa. Clubs: University (D.C., N.Y.C.); Duquesne (Pitts.); Rolling Rock (Ligonier, Pa.). Author: Voting Behavior in a Metropolitan Community. 1940; The State Administrative Board, 1938; (also editor) Governing Post War Germany, 1953. Contbr. articles to profl. jours. Home: Coudersport PA Died Mar. 8, 1968.

LITMAN, SIMON, economist; b. Odessa, Russia, Oct. 13, 1873; s. Jacob and Pauline (Helfman) L.; A.B., Odessa Commercial Coll., 1892 (hon. citizenship for scholarship); grad. Ecole des Sciences Politiques, 1899; research U. of Munich, 1899-1900; Dr. Jur. Pub. et Rer. Cam., U. of Zurich, 1901; m. Rachel Frank, Aug. 14, 1901. Served under Richard Watson Gilder as an insp. and tabulator on New York Tenement House Com., 1894; apptd. lecturer, Ecole Russe des Hautes Etudes Sociales, Paris, 1902; instr. economics, University of California, 1903-08; asso. in commerce, University of Illinois, 1908-10, asst. prof. economics, 1910-19, professor, 1919-42; emeritus since 1942, acting head of department, 1936. Mem. Am. Econ. Assn., Citizens Conf. on Internat. Econ. Union Acad. Polit. Science, Foreign Policy Assn., Am. Polit. Science Assn., Am. Jewish Hist. Soc., Royal Econ. Soc. Gt. Britain, Am. Assn. Univ. Profs., Phi Kappa Phi, Phi Beta Kappa, Pi Gamma Mu, Beta Gamma Sigma, Pan-Xenia (international president 1938-40), Artus, Phi Kappa Epsilon. Clubs: University, Rotary, Export Managers' of Chicago (honorary). Author: Die Moglichkeit der Lohnsteigerungen und die Lohnfondstheorien, 1902; Trade and Commerce, 1911; Price Control in Great Britain and the United States, 1919; Essentials of International Trade, 1923, revised edit., 1927; also numerous articles on commerce, transportation, etc. Home: 1108 S. Lincoln Av., Urbana IL‡

LITSEY, EDWIN CARLILE, author; b. Beechland, Ky., June 3, 1874; s. William Henry and Sarah Elizabeth (Johnston) L.; ed. pub. and pvt. schs.; m. Carrie Rachel Selecman, June 5, 1900 (died Oct. 23, 1910); 1 dau., Sarah Selecman. In banking business from age of 17. Named Poet Laureate of Ky., 1954. Life mem. Acad. Soc. Internat. History (Paris). Clubs: Authors' (London); Nat. Arts (New York); Arts (Washington and Louisville, Ky.). Author: The Princess of Gramfalon, 1898; The Love Story of Abner Stone, 1902; The Race of the Swift, 1905; The Man from Jericho, 1911; A Maid of the Kentucky Hills, 1913; Spindrift, 1915, A Bluegrass Maid of the Kentucky Hills, 1913; Spindrift, 1915, A Bluegrass Cavalier, 1922; Grist, 1927; Shadow Shapes, 1929; The Filled Cup (verse), 1935; The Eternal Flame (novelette), 1937; Stones for Bread. Won first prize in the Black Cat story contest of 1904, over 10,000 competitors. Contbr. to mags. and Lebanon KY Died Feb. 3, 1970.

LITSINGER, EDWARD ROBERT, lawyer; b. Chicago, Ill., Sept. 19, 1874; s. Edward and Julia L.; grad. Holden Sch., Chicago, 1890; LL.B., Kent Coll. of Law, 1898; m. Lady Marion Ford, of Chicago, Oct. 5, 1901; children—Edwina Marion, Lady Eleanore Admitted to Ill. bar, 1898, and since practiced at Chicago; mem. firm Litsinger, Healy & Reid since 1917; pres. Ford Roofing Products Co., Litsinger Motor Co. Asst. state's atty., 1899; alderman, 1901-03; mem. Bd. of Review, Cook Co., 1917-32. Mem. Am., Ill. State and Chicago bar assns. Trustee Ill. Industrial Home for the Blind, 1906-09. Republican. Lutheran. Clubs: Union League, German, Exmoor Country, Knollwood Country, Beverly Country. Home: 1400 N. State Parkway. Office: 111 W. Washington St., Chicago IL‡

LITTLE, ARTHUR MITCHELL, clergyman; b. Ft Wayne, Ind., Apr. 10, 1865; s. George Obadiah (D.D.) and Martha Hart (Mitchell) L.; grad. Phillips Acad. Andover, Mass., 1884; student Amherst Coll., 1884-87 A.B., Yale, 1889, B.D., 1891; grad. study U. of Leipzig 1887-88, 1891-92, Ph.D., Leipzig, 1892; D.D., Knox Coll., Galesburg, Ill., 1912; m. Marion Percival Keene June 2, 1891; children—Edward Norton, Mildred Prince (Mrs. B. F. Groot), Dwight Prince. Ordained ministry Presbyn. Ch., 1892; served and organized Presbyn. churches at Takoma Park, D.C., and Kensington, Md., 1892-93; pastor Takoma Park, D.C. 1892-95, Presbyn. Ch., La Grange, Ill., 1895-1900, 2d Presbyn. Ch., Peoria, Ill., 1900-19, Congl. Ch., Lincoln Mass., 1920-21, Hammond St. Congl. Ch., Bangor, Me. 1921-39, pastor emeritus since 1939. First pres. and charter mem. Peoria University Club; Mem. Bangor Hist. Soc., Phi Beta Kappa, Alpha Delta Phi, Pi Alpha Epsilon. Republican. Clubs: Kiwanis, Twentieth Century. Author: Mendelssohn's Music to the Antigone of Sophocles, 1893. Home: 189 W. Broadway, Bangor ME‡

LITTLE, CLARENCE C(OOK), biologist; b. Brookline, Mass., Oct. 6, 1888; s. James Lovell and Mary Robbins (Revere) L.; grad. Noble and Greenough Sch., Boston, Mass., 1906; A.B., Harvard, 1910; S.M. Grad. Sch. of Applied Science (Harvard), 1912, Sc.D. 1914; LL.D., U. of N.H., 1924, Albion (Mich.) Coll. 1925, U. of N.M., 1929, Colby College, Waterville, Me. 1935; Litt.D., U. Maine, 1932; Sc.D., U. Chgo., 1950 Boston U., 1951; L.H.D., Dickinson Coll., 1951; Ed.D Marietta Coll., 1952; m. Katharine Day Andrews, May 27, 1911 (div. 1929); children—Edward Revere, Louise Robert Andrews; m. 2d, Beatrice W. Johnson, 1930 children—Richard Warren, Laura Revere. Sec. to Corp Harvard Univ., 1910-12; research asst.in genetics 1911-13, research fel. in genetics (cancer commn.) 1913-17, asst. dean College and acting Universit marshal, 1916-17, overseer, 1942-48, 1955-61, all o Harvard U.; associate in comparative pathology Harvard Medical Sch., 1917-18; research associate 1919-21, and 1922-25; asst. dir., 1921-22, Sta. for Expt Evolution, Carnegie Instn., Washington; pres. U. o Me., 1922-25; president University of Michigan 1925-29; director Jackson Meml. Lab., 1929-56 director emeritus, 1956-71. Director Liberty Nationa Bank, Ellsworth, Me. Dir. Am. Cancer Soc., 1929-45 Sci. dir. Tobacco Industry Research Com., from 1954 member scientific adv. bd., Gesell Inst. Chil Development, from 1952. Sec. gen. and chmn. exec com., Second Internat. Congress of Eugenics, New York, 1921; mem. Eugenics Com. of U.S. from 1922 dir. Am. Birth Control League from 1925, pres 1936-38; president International Neo Malthusia League, 1925, American Euthanasia Society, 1938-43 mem. exec. com. First World Population Conference Geneva, 1927; dir. council for Democracy, Euthanasi Soc. pres. 1939-43; pres. Race Betterment Congress 1928, 29; secretary general and chmn. Council 6t

Internat. Congress of Genetics, Ithaca, 1932; mem. Nat. Advisory Cancer Council, 1937-39. Trustee of Mount Desert Island Biol. Lab. (pres. 1931-33). Commissioned capt. Aviation Section R.C., 1917; maj. Adj. Gen.'s Dept., 1918; hon. disch., 1918; lt. col., Specialist Reserves, 1928-39. Vice chmn. Civilian Def. for State Me., 1941. Fellow Nat. Acad. Scis., Am. Acad. Arts and Scis., N.Y. Acad. Medicine, A.A.A.S., Nat. Inst. Social Scis.; honorary mem. St. Louis Medical Society; member American Soc. Naturalists, Am. Soc. Zoologists, Am. Assn. Cancer Research (v.p. 1929; pres. 1930, 40), Soc. Exptl. Biology and Medicine, Eugenic Research Assn., Am. Pub. Health Assn., Population Assn. America (dir.), Am. Eugenics Soc. (pres. 1928), Am. Assn. Anatomists, Am. Soc. Mammalogists, Am. Social Hygiene Assn. (v.p.), Mich. Acad., Pan-Am. Med. Soc., New Eng. Cancer Soc., Phi Beta Kappa, Phi Kappa Phi, Phi Sigma, Sigma Xi, Phi Eta Sigma, Phi Epsilon Kappa, Scabbard and Blade, Galton Soc., Harvey Soc. (hon.). Episcopalian. Mason (Shriner); Odd Fellow. Clubs: Harvard (N.Y.); Harvard (Boston); Pot and Kettle. Author: The Awakening College, 1930; Civilization Against Cancer, 1939; Genetics, Biological Individuality, and Cancer, 1954; Inheritance of Coat Color in Dogs, 1956; also articles on genetics, cancer research, edn. and social problems. Awarded Am. Cancer Soc. medal, 1950; Pioneers Hall of Ellsworth ME Died Dec. 22, 1971; buried Ledgelawn Cemetery, Bar Harbor ME

LITTLE, HERBERT SATTERTHWAITE, lawyer; b. Manchester, Eng., Oct. 6, 1902; s. George Henry and Jessie Milton (Gearing) L.; migrated to U.S. 1914, naturalized, 1920; J.D., U. Wash., 1923, A.M., 1927; m. Katharyn Stubbs, Sept. 30, 1939 (div. 1970); children—Anne Tucker, Nancy Wardell, Gwendolyn Gearing, Kathy Milton. Admitted to Wash. bar, 1923; asso. firm Stratton and Kane, Seattle, 1923-35; mem. firm Stratton, Leader, Little & Stratton, 1935-36, Little & Stratton, 1935-36, Little & Leader, 1936-41, sr. partner successor firms until retirement, 1969. Dir. Sheetwood Products Co., Gosspulp Corp., Am. Pacific Dairy Products, Inc. Vis. lectr. Am. diplomacy and internat. relations, Oriental Summer Coll., Tokyo and Kyoto Imperial univs., Japan, 1931; chmn. Am. Found. World Court Com. for Wash., 1930-34; Am. del. internat. conf. Inst. Pacific Relations, 1936, 47, 50; lectr. internat. law Inst. World Affairs, Riverside, Cal., 1939, 40. Chmn. Seattle chpt. Com. to Defend America by Aiding the Allies, 1941; mem. Wash. br. Commn. to Study Orgn. of Peace, 1941. Bd. dirs. Wash. Assn. Mental Health, Near East Found.; chmn. Northwest br. Am. Council Inst. Pacific Relations, 1946-47, trustee, 1946-49; bd. regents U. Wash., 1960-65, pres., 1964-65; trustee YMCA, Wesley Found., 1930-40, Seattle Symphony Orch. (exec. com.), 1946-50; pres. Japanese Internat. Trade Fair, Seattle, 1951; dir. Internat. Trade Fair, Inc., 1951-60; mem. Nat. Adv. Com. Internat. Jud. Procedure; dir. Am. Com. United Europe, 1950. Maj., Army of U.S., Office Undersec. War, 1942-43, OSS, 1943-46; then lt. col., chief br. Decorated Bronze Star, 1945; recipient Civic award Seattle, 1946. Mem. council sect. internat. and comparative law, Council Fgn. Relations N.Y. mem. Internat., Inter-Am., Fed., Am., Seattle, Wash., bar assns., Am. Soc. Internat. Law (exec. council, v.p.), U. Wash. Alumni Assn. (pres. 1935-36), Japan, China, Philippines Socs. of Seattle (dir.), Phi Alpha Delta, Tau Kappa Alpha, Pi Sigma Alpha. Clubs: Rainier (Seattle); Bohemian (San Francisco). Seattle WA Died Dec. 15, 1972; buried Acacia Meml. Park, Seattle WA

LITTLE, MITCHELL STUART, mfr.; b. Hartford, Conn., Jan. 5, 1885; s. George Henry and Mary Belle (Little) L.; B.A., Yale, 1907; m. Elizabeth Hill Hapgood, Feb. 8, 1919; children—Virginia, Stuart West, Edward Hapgood. Connected with mfg. business since 1907; sec. Whitlock Coil Pipe Co., 1910-12; founder and pres. M.S. Little Mfg. Co., from 1912; chmn., dir. The Little Products Co., Excercycle Corp.; director The Smyth Manufacturing Company, Terry Steam Turbine Co., Hartford Gas Co., The Collins Co., Arrow-Hart & Hegeman Electric Co., Hartford Nat. Bank & Trust Co.; trustee Soc. for Savings. Chmn. bd. Hartford Hosp. Mem. Yale Alumni Assn. Republican. Conglist. Clubs: Hartford, Twentieth Century, Hartford Golf, Yale (N.Y.). Home: West Hartford CT Died Aug. 7, 1969.

LITTLE, SIDNEY WAHL, coll. dean; b. Buffalo, Sept. 10, 1904; s. Charles and Lavinia (Wahl) L.; B.Arch., Cornell U., 1926; M.Arch., Tulane Univ., 1941; diploma, Ecole Beaux Arts, France, 1927; m. Catherine Stark, June 24, 1936. Asst. prof. architecture, Clemson Coll., 1929-37; asso. prof. architecture, Ala. Poly. Inst., 1937-45; prof. architecture, dean Sch. Architecture U. Ore., 1945-58; head dept. architecture, dean Coll. Fine Arts, U. Ariz., 1958-64, dean College of Architecture, 1964-70, dean emeritus, 1970-72. Design consultant to the City of Tucson. Member Oregon Capitol Planning Commission; director So. Ariz. Opera Guild, Tucson Symphony Orchestra, Tucson Festival Soc.; vice president, director Tucson Regional Plan, Inc. Fellow Internat. Inst. Arts and Letters, A.I.A. (vice pres. Southern Arizona chapter, now member national board directors); mem. Ariz. Soc. Architects (pres.), Am. Assn. University Profs., Assn. Collegiate Schs. Architecture. Am. Inst. Interior Designers (asso.), Western Coll. and Pacific (pres.) Arts assns., Western Museum Dirs. Assn., C. of C. (chmn. com. housing). Author: Four-Language Phase Book, 1954. Co-author: The Architect at Mid-Century, 1954. Contbr. to profl. jours. Home: Tucson AZ Died Mar. 26, 1972.

LITTLE, TOM, cartoonist; b. nr. Franklin, Tenn., Sept. 27, 1898; s. John Wallace and Florence (Johnson) L.; student art Watkins Inst., Nashville, 1912-15; student Montgomery Bell Acad., Nashville, 1917-18; pvt. cartooning under Carey Orr, 1913-16; m. Helen Dahnke, Oct. 19, 1926 (dec. Dec. 24, 1938); m. 2d Lillian Hannah, Oct. 20, 1945. Reporter Nashville Tennessean, 1916-23, N.Y. Herald Tribune Syndicate, 1923-24, Nashville Tennessean, 1924-31, city editor, 1931-37, cartoonist from 1937; drew syndicated comic panel Sunflower Steet, King Features Syndicate, N.Y. City, 1934-49; cartoon illustrations New York Times Mag., from 1951. Cartoons in permanent traveling exhibit National Cartoonists Society Winner National Headliners' award for outstanding editorial cartoons, 1947; Christopher Award, 1953; Freedoms Found. medal, 1955, 56; Pulitzer Prize for cartoons, 1957. Mem. Assn. Am. Editorial Cartoonists, Nat. Cartoonists Soc. Mason (32 degree, Shriner). Club: Richland Golf and Country (Nashville). Home: Nashville TN Died June 20, 1972; buried Woodlawn Cemetery, Nashville TN

LIVELY, CHARLES ELSON, univ. prof., sociologist; b. Marshall County, W.Va., Sept. 29, 1890; s. Milton Alexander and Susannah Jane (Riggs) L.; student Peru Teachers Coll., Neb., 1910-13, U. of Mont., summer 1914; A.B., U. of Neb., 1917, M.A., 1918; Ph.D., U. of Minn., 1931; m. Ethel Dell Johnston, Sept. 21, 1918. Country sch. teacher, 1909-10; pub. sch. supt., Shickley, Neb., 1913, Grafton, 1914, Madison, 1918; instr. in sociology U. of Minn., 1919-21, asso. prof. rural sociology, 1930-31; asst. prof. rural sociology Ohio State U., 1921-30, asso. prof., 1931-36, prof., 1936-38, on leave as research analyst Fed. Emergency Relief Adminstrn., Washington, 1934; prof. rural sociology and chmn. dept. U. Mo. 1938-61, professor emeritus of rural sociology, 1961-69, also exec. dir. Inst. for Research in Social Scis. 1951-56; vis. prof., researcher pub. health So. Ill. U., 1962-63; state supr. rural research, W.P.A., Ohio, 1935-38, Mo., 1938-39; collaborator U.S. Forest Service, 1939-45; collaborator Farmers Home Adminstrn. and Bureau of Agrl. Economics, advisor to U.S. Forest Service on problems of human relations, 1939-45; vis. prof. Garrett Biblical Inst., summer, 1956. Asso. editor, Rural Sociology, 1937-42; American del. Internat. Population Congress, Paris, France, 1937; mem. exec. com. Mo. Assn. for Social Welfare, 1939, regional chmn., 1945, mem. health com., 1948-49; tech. adviser Mo. State Nurses Assn., 1947-48; mem. Gov.'s Com. on Aging. Recipient W. Scott Johnson award for service to pub. health, 1961. Fellow A.A.A.S. (sec. adv. council on human relations 1939-45), Am. Sociol. Soc. (exec. com. 1943-46); mem. Rural Sociol. Soc. of Am. (v.p. 1940; pres. 1942), Midwest Sociol. Soc. (v.p. 1941), Population Assn. of Am. (mem. bd. dirs. 1937-42), International Union for Study of Population Problems, l'Institut International De Sociologie, Alpha Kappa Delta, Gamma Sigma Delta, Phi Delta Kappa, Alpha Pi Zeta. Author: (with Taeuber) Rural Migration in the United States, 1939; (with Preiss) Conservation Education in the Colleges and Universities of the United States, 1957; also monographs, articles, chapters in books on population and rural sociology. Compiler: Readings in Rural Sociology, 1933. Contbg. editor Dictionary of Sociology, 1943. Asso. editor: Journal Health & Human Behavior, 1959-63; editorial adviser Focus-Midwest, from 1963. Vocalist Ellison-White Chatauqua, summer 1916, White & Myers, 1918. Home: Columbia MO Died Dec. 1969.

LIVERMORE, NORMAN BANKS, engr.; b. Oakland, Calif., July 20, 1872; s. Horatio P. and Mattie H. (Banks) L.; student U. of Calif.; C.E., Cornell U., 1899; m. Caroline Sealy, Jan. 5, 1910; children—Norman B., George S., John S., Horatio P., Robert. Began as U.S. asst. engr., fortifications and harbors; later engr., water and power works; cons. engr., San Francisco, since 1908; dir. Calif. Packing Corp. since 1915, Pacific Gas & Electric Co. since 1916, Crocker First Nat. Bank since 1930 (also mem. exec. com.), Firemans Fund Indemnity Co. since 1930, Natomas Co. since 1920 and others. Lt. col., U.S. Army, World War I; awarded French Legion of Honor. Pres. bd. trustees Calif. Acad. Sciences. Mem. various engring. and scientific socs. Contbr. to jours. Travel and exploration (agrl. investigation and studies) in Africa and Orient. Home: Ross, Marin County, Calif. Office: 216 Pine St., San Francisco 4‡

LIVINGOOD, CHARLES JACOB;, b. Reading, Pa., Feb. 6, 1866; s. J.S. and L.J. (Shalter) L.; A.B., Harvard, 1888; traveled in Europe; m. Lily B. Foster, Dec. 30, 1896. Surveyor, in Rocky Mountains; with Thomas Emery's Sons, builders of flats, Cincinnati, O., since 1890; mgr. of estate of Mrs. Mary M. Emery since 1906; pres., mgr. T.J. Emery Memorial; pres. and mgr. Mariemont, a national exemplar in town planning." Republican. Episcopalian. Clubs: Harvard, Camargo, Optimist, Commercial, Literary, Queen City (Cincinnati). Home: 2766 Baker Place, E. Walnut Hills. Office: 315 Mercantile Library Bldg., Cincinnati OH‡

LIVINGSTON, DOUGLAS CLERMONT, prof. geology; b. London, Eng., June 12, 1877; s. Clermont and Mary Ellen (Clark) L.; student McGill U., Montreal, Can., 1910-04, B.Sc. in M.E., 1906; student Stanford U., 1905; m. Phoebe Alice Baynes Reed, of Victoria, B.C., June 24, 1908; children—John Clermont (dec.), Carroll Clermont. Connected with Tyee Mine, B.C., 1898-1901; engr. Tigre Mining Co., Sonora, Mexico, 1906-08; supt. North Tigre Mine, 1908-10; pvt. engring. work, Douglas, Ariz., 1910-11; prof. mining, later prof. geology, U. of Ida., 1911-20; prof. geology, Sch. of Mines, Ore. Agrl. Coll., Corvallis, Ore., 1920-29; apptd. supt. Spokane Idaho Copper Co., 1929; became prof. geology, University of Idaho, 1931; now consulting geologist Comox, Vancouver Island, B.C. Naturalized citizen of U.S., 1917. Mem. Zeta Psi, Sigma Xi. Republican. Episcopalian. Author: Tungsten Cinnabar Deposits of Idaho (U. of Ida.), 1919; Copper Deposits of Seven Devils (Ida. Bur. Mines), 1920; Reconnaissance in South Central Idaho (same), 1920. Home: Comox, Vancouver Island BC‡

LIVINGSTON, HOMER J., banker; b. Chicago, Ill., Aug. 30, 1903; s. John C. and Evelyn (Lewis) L.; LL.B., John Marshall Law Sch., Chicago, Ill., 1924; m. Helen G. Henderson, Sept. 29, 1928; 1 son, Homer J. Admitted to Ill. bar, 1925; atty., First Nat. Bank of Chicago, 1930-44, counsel, 1944-45, v.p., 1945-50, pres., 1950-55, chief exec. officer, 1955-69, chairman of the board, 1960-69, chmn. finance com., 1969-70; dir. Continental Casualty and Continental Assurance cos., Armour and Co., Sears, Roebuck & Co., Standard Oil Co. (Ind.), Inland Steel Co. Trustee U. Chgo. Co., Standard Oil Co. (Ind.), Inland Steel Co. Trustee U. Chgo. Mem. Am. Bankers Assn. (past pres.). Clubs: Commercial, Chicago, Union League, Mid-Day, Law, Legal, Chicago Golf (Chgo.); Oak Park (Ill.) Country. Author: Management Policies in American Banks. Home: River Forest IL Died May 9, 1970.

LIZARS, RAWSON GOODSIR, business exec.; b. Chicago, Ill., Jan. 26, 1900; s. Valentine and Sarah Elizabeth (Murphy) L.; student De Paul U., 1919-20, Kent Coll. of Law, 1920-22; m. Frances Underwood, Sept. 6, 1922; children—Henrietta Underwood (Mrs. Lizars Connell), Rawson Goodsir. With Rawson Lizars & Co., 1930-42; chmn. bd., pres., dir. Certain-teed Products Corp., Ardmore, Pa., 1944-69. Episcopalian. Clubs: Canadian (N.Y.C.); Merion Cricket (Haverford, Pa.); Philadelphia Country; Bath and Tennis, Everglades (Palm Beach, Fla.). Home: Bryn Mawr PA Died Dec. 27, 1969; buried All Saints Church Yard, Wynnewood PA

LLEWELLYN, FREDERICK BRITTON, research physicist; b. New Orleans, Sept. 16, 1897; s. Frederick Thomas and Virginia (Britton) L.; student Staunton Mil. Acad., 1917; M.E., Stevens Inst. Tech., 1922; Ph.D., Columbia, 1928; m. Beatrix Gunther, Feb. 25, 1924; 1 daughter, Barbara Elizabeth (Mrs. Joseph Matchette Walters, Jr.). Served intermittently as radio operator at sea, 1915-21; with F. K. Vreeland Laboratory, 1922-23, Western Electric Company, 1923-25; with Bell Telephone Labs., 1925-61, circuit research engr., 1935-44, cons. engr., 1945-53, systems studies engineer, 1953-55, communications cons., 1955-56, asst. to pres., 1956-61; research physicist Inst. Sci. and Tech., U. Mich., 1961-62, sci. adviser, dept. dir., 1962-65; dir. research Polytechnic Inst. Bklyn., 1965-71; expert consultant to Office Sec. of War, 1944, weapons systems evaluation group Joint Chiefs of Staff, 1951-53, exec. sec. sci. adv. com. O.D.M., 1951; member United States national com. internat. electro-tech. com. 1950-54. Alumni rep. on bd. trustees Stevens Inst. Tech., 1957-60. Licensed profl. engr. N.Y. Served in U.S. Navy, World War I. Fellow Am. Phys. Soc., Inst. of Radio Engineers (dir. 1939-45; recipient Morris Liebmann prize, 1935; chmn. papers com., 1942-45; pres. 1946). Mem. U.S. delegataion to Internat. Telecommunications Union, 1947; Internat. Cons. Com. on Radio, Stockholm, 1948. Received Stevens Honor award, 1949; Stevens Alumni award, 1962. Mem. Newcomen Society of North America, A.A.A.S., also Stevens Institute of Technology Alumni Association (pres. 1956-57), Operations Research Soc. Am., Sigma Xi, Tau Beta Pi. Clubs: University (N.Y.C.); Cosmos (Washington). Author: Electron Inertia Effects, 1941. Home: New York City NY Died Dec. 1971.

LLOYD, ELLA STRYKER MAPES, author; b. Binghamton, N.Y., June 2, 1870; d. Alonzo and Elizabeth (St. John) Stryker; ed. The Lady Jane Grey Sch., Binghamton, and lit. courses at Harvard Summer Sch.; twice married; m. 2d, Charles L. Lloyd, of New York, Nov. 14, 1903. Began lit. work in mag. articles, 1898; contbr. to Bookman, Critic, Outlook, Lamp, etc. Presbyn. Republican. Clubs: Unity (Cleveland); Atlantic Union (London). Author: Because of Power, 1903. Address: 97 Croxted Rd., Dulwich England‡

LLOYD, HAROLD (CLAYTON), motion pictures; b. Burchard, Neb., Apr. 20, 1894; s. J. Darsie and Sarah Elizabeth (Fraser) L.; ed. high schs., Denver, Colo., and San Diego, Calif.; m. Mildred Davis, Feb. 10, 1923; children—Mildred Gloria, Marjorie Elizabeth. Harold. Began motion picture career as extra" at age of 19, with the Edison Company, at San Diego, Calif.; later with the Universal and other Hollywood film cos.; joined Hal E. Roach, 1914, starring in one-reel comedies known as Lonesome Lukes"; star in Sailor Made Man, Grandma's Boy, Dr. Jack, Safety Last, Why Worry, etc.; organized Harold Lloyd Corp., 1923, producing Girl Shy, Hot Water, The Freshman, For Heaven's Sake, The Kid Brother, and Speedy; 1st talking picture, Welcome Dangerproducer, Professor Beware; A Girl, a Guy and a Gob (for R.K.O. Radio Pictures). Clubs: Uplifters, Los Angeles Athletic, Writers, Los Angeles Country, Southern Calif. Athletic, Hollywood Athletic, Wilshire Country; Lambs (New York). Mason; Past Potentate Al Malaikah Temple of the Shrine; Imperial Potentate (Shrine) since 1949. Home: Beverly Hills CA Died Mar. 8, 1971.

LLOYD, HENRY DEMAREST, bus. exec.; born Boston, Oct. 18, 1907; s. Henry Demarest and Elizabeth McEwen (Mason) L.; A.B., Harvard, 1929, grad. study, 1930-32; m. Norah Alice Keating, June 23, 1934;children—Dorothy Elizabeth, Shelia Andrea. With Ont. Paper Co., Ltd., Thorold, Ont., 1932-34, dir. since 1947; classified advt. Chicago Tribune, 1934-39; office mgr. and sch. coordinator airport operation Civil Pilot Tng. Program, Civil Air Patrol, Northbrook, Ill., 1939-42; dir. Tribune Co., Chicago Tribune Bldg. Corp., radio stas. WGN, Inc. and WPIX, Inc., Que. North Shore Paper Co., Manicouagan Power Co., News Syndicate Co., Inc., Que. & Ontario Transportation Co., Ltd., Ill. Atlantic Corp., Marlhill Mines Ltd., Chicago Tribune-New York News Syndicate, Inc.; trustee Henry D. Lloyd, Watch House Trust, Elizabeth Mason Lloyd Ins. Trust. Mem. corp. St. Andrews Sch., West Barrington. Served as lt. and lt. comdr., USNR, 1942-46. Mem. Harvard Bus. Sch. Assn., R.I. Audubon Soc. Clubs: Harvard (Boston and R.I.); Turks Head (Providence); R.I. Country, Automobile (R.I.) Died Aug. 26, 1970; buried Forest Chapel Cemetery, Barrington RI

LLOYD, L(AWRENCE) DUNCAN, lawyer; b. Catlin, Ill., Jan. 6, 1899; s. Fred R. and Jennie (Duncan) L.; A.B., U. Ill., 1920; LL.B., Harvard, 1923; m. Olivia Schad, Sept. 10, 1921; children—Katherine Jane, Virginia Ann. Admitted to Ill. bar, 1923, partner Lord, Bissell &Brook, later of counsel; dir. Craft Mfg. Co. Mem. Internat. Assn. Ins. Counsel (exec. com. 1946-49, pres. 1949-50), American, Ill. and Chgo. (bd. mgrs. 1946-48) bar associations, Bar Assn. of Seventh Fed. Circuit (bd. govs.), Lambda Chi Alpha. Republican. Methodist. Mason. Clubs: Skokie Country (Glencoe, Ill.); University, Attic, Law (Chgo.). Home: Glencoe IL Died Jan. 16, 1972.

LLOYD, RALPH IRVING, med. coll. prof.; b. Poughkeepsie, N.Y., Sept. 11, 1875; s. Russell G. and Florence C. (Monell) L.; grad. Poughkeepsie High Sch., 1892; M.D., N.Y. Med. Coll. and Flower Hosp., 1896; post-grad. course N.Y. Ophthalmic Hosp. Coll., 1899; m. Nettie Hesson Limburg, June 30, 1904 (died 1937); married 2d, Carrie O. Fleming, 1942. House physician Brooklyn Homeopathic Hospital, 1896-97; house surgeon Pittsburgh Homeopathic Hospital, 1897-98; lecturer New York Med. Coll., 1899-1907, asst. prof. of anatomy, 1907-11, prof., 1911-16; lecturer on ophthalmology, N.Y. U. Med. Sch., since 1933; cons. ophthalmologist, Long Island Coll. Hosp., Cumberland Hosp., Prospect Heights Hosp., Brooklyn Eye and Ear Hosp., Carson Peck Memorial Hosp. Fellow Am. Coll. Surgeons; mem. Am. Acad. of Ophthalmology and Otolaryngology (pres. 1942), A.M.A., N.Y. State Med. Soc., Kings County Med. Soc., N.Y. Acad. of Medicine. Am. Ophthal. Soc., N.Y. Ophthal. Soc. Address: 14 Eighth Av., Brooklyn NY‡

LLOYD, WOODROW STANLEY, premier of Sask.; b. Webb, Sask., Can., July 16, 1913; s. Allen Edward and Myrtle Belle (Davis) L.; B.A., U. Sask., 1940; m. Victoria Marie Leinan, July 2, 1936; children—Maureen (Mrs. Kenneth Neuman), Dianne (Mrs. John C. Norton), Michael, Evan. Tchr. elementary grades, Swan Lake, Sask., 1932-34; tchr., prin., Stewart Valley, Sask., 1934-36, Vanguard, Sask., 1936-41, Composite Pub. and High Sch., Biggar, Sask., 1941-44; mem. Sask. Legislature from Biggar Dist., 1944-62; minister edn. Sask., 1944-60; treas. Sask., 1960-61; polit. leader Sask. sect. Coop. Commonwealth Fedn. New Democratic Party, premier Sask., 1961-64. Pres. Sask. Tchrs. Fedn., 1941-44; exec. com. Canadian Tchrs. Fedn., 1942-44. Mem. senate U. Sask., 1942-44. Author articles. Home: Regina SK Canada Died Apr. 8, 1972; buried Regina Sask CAN

LOBDELL, EFFIE L(EOLA), M.D., surgeon; b. Washington Island, Wis.; d. Joseph Judson and Elizabeth M. (Napier) L.; grad. Green Bay High Sch., 1886; M.D., Ph.G., U. of Ind., 1891. Practiced at Chicago since 1891; specializes in operative gynecology and obstetrics; chief woman phys., staff of Ill. Eastern Hosp. for Insane, 1893; obstetrician and pediatrician, Cook Co. Hosp., 1900-04; attending gynecologist, Municipal Tuberculosis Sanitarium, 1916; staff surgeon West Side Hosp., Grant Hosp. Fellow American Coll. Surgeons; mem. Ill. State and Chicago med. socs., Ill. Press Assn., Alliance of Business and Professional Women, Nu Sigma Phi, Pi Gamma Mu, Alliance Francais. Clubs: Medical Women's, Medical and Dental Arts, Woman's Republican, The Cordon, etc. Home: Congress Hotel. Office: 310 S. Michigan Av., Chicago IL‡

LOCKE, EUGENE MURPHY, ambassador, lawyer; b. Dallas, Jan. 6, 1918; s. Eugene Perry and Marie (Murphy) L.; B.A., U. Tex., 1937; LL.B., Yale, 1940; m. Adele Neely, Oct. 27, 1941; children—Aimee Marie, John Patrick, Thomas Neely. Admitted to Tex. bar, 1940; with firm Locke, Purnell, Boren, Laney and Neely, and predecessors, 1940-41, sr. partner, from 1946; United States ambassador to Pakistan, 1966-67; deputy ambassador to South Vietnam, from 1967; with OPA, Washington and Dallas, 1941-42. Chmn. exec. com. Lomas and Nettleton Financial Corp., from 1962; dir. Trinity Steel Co., Trammell Crow Realty Trust. Mem. Dallas Com. Econ. Devel., from 1958; pres. Sr. Citizens Found., Dallas, from 1961. Chmn. Tex. Democratic Exec. Com., 1963; del. Dem. Nat. Conv., 1964; campaign mgr. Connally for Gov. Tex., 1962. Bd. dirs. Sam Rayburn Found.; mem. land planning com. Grad. Research Center Southwest. Served to lt. USNR, World War II. Mem. Tex. Ind. Producers and Royalty Assn. (past pres.), Mid-Continent Oil and Gas Assn. (dir.), Am., Dallas bar assns., Yale Law Sch. Alumni Assn. (v.p., exec. com.), Phi Beta Kappa, Order of Coif, Phi Delta Theta. Clubs: Dallas Country, Dallas, City, Idlewild, Petroleum (Dallas); Lawyers (N.Y.C.); Petroleum (Houston); Austin (Tex.). Home: Dallas TX Died Apr. 28, 1972.

LOCKE, HARRY LESLIE FRANKLIN, pediatrician; b. Hudson, Mass., Oct. 30, 1886; s. Frank Daniel and Carrie Louise (Woodward) L.; M.D. cum laude, Tufts Coll., 1912; grad. student Trinity Coll., 1922-24; m. Katherine Elizabeth Entress, Nov. 11, 1914, children—Carolyn Elizabeth de Kanter, John Dustin, Janet Page. Supt., res. physician Hartford Isolation Hosp., 1914-21; in pvt. practice, specializing in pediatrics, from 1921; attending pediatrician McCook Meml. Hosp., 1922-59, chief-of-staff, 1938-48; physician-in-charge Children's Village, Hartford, 1932-50; cons. pediatrician St. Francis Hospital, Manchester Memorial Hospital. President Greater Hartford Tb and Public Health Society, 1932-33; secretary, director Hartford Citizens Com. for Civic Progress, 1935-38; v.p. Greater Hartford Cerebral Palsy Assn., 1955-62; pres., 1962-64. Past chmn. Conn. Commn. for Care and Treatment of Chronically Ill, Aged and Infirm. Served in Med. R.C., U.S. Army, 1918. Diplomate Am. Bd. Pediatrics. Fellow Am. Acad. Pediatrics; mem. A.M.A., Soc. Founders and Patriots (Connecticut governor 1945-46), Psi Upsilon. Republican. Mason (K.T.). Clubs; Civitan (president of Hartford 1940-41, internat. pres. 1942-43). Hampsted Hill. Home: West Hartford CT Died Sept. 5, 1968; buried Hartford CT

LOCKE, ROBERT WYNTER, publishing co. exec.; b. Princeton, N.J., Oct. 10, 1926; s. Bradford B. and Philena (Fine) L.; grad. Kent (Conn.) Sch., 1943; A.B., Harvard, 1948; m. Patricia Fahnestock, Oct. 24, 1953; children—Alison Post, Robert Wynter, Katharine Beekman, Evelyn Fahnestock. With McGraw-Hill Book Co., 1948-71, v.p., 1963-65, sr. v.p., 1965-68; exec. v.p., 1968-71. Mem. N.J. Gov.'s Commn. on Pub. Broadcasting, 1968; mem. edn. com. Nat. Urban League, 1971; mem. bd. edn. Bedminster Pub. Sch., 1966-70; mem. vis. com. Harvard U. Press, 1970; mem. forum on ednl. tech. White House Conf. on Children, 1970; chmn. State Adv. Council on Title III, 1965 Edn. Act, 1971. Trustee Bernardsville (N.J.) Library, 1955-68, pres., 1957-66; trustee Matheny Sch., Peapack, N.J., from 1958; trustee Far Hills (N.J.) Country Day Sch., 1965-71, pres., 1969-71; trustee Somerset Hills chpt. A.R.C., 1960-63; dir. Am. Assn. Publishers, 1967-71. Served with USMCR, 1944-46. Home: Far Hills NJ Died Mar. 28, 1971; buried Princeton NJ

LOCKE, VICTOR MURAT, JR., Indian service; b. Ft. Towson, Okla., Mar. 23, 1876; s. Victor Murat and Susan Priscilla (McKinney) L.; ed. Austin Coll. (Sherman, Tex.) and Drury Coll. (Springfield, Mo.); married; 1 dau., Rose Ba-Nat-ima. Mem. by blood relationship of Choctaw Tribe of Indians; served as pvt. Spanish Am. War; maj. inf. U.S.A., World War. Principal chief Choctaw Tribe, 1911-18; now supt. under U.S. Govt. for Five Civilized Tribes. Mem. S.A.R., Am. Legion. Republican. Catholic. Home: Antlers, Okla. Address: Muskogee OK‡

LOCKERBY, FRANK MCCARTHY, newspaper editor; b. Rockford, Ill., Dec. 28, 1899; s. Samuel McCarthy and Clara (Wells) L.; B.A., U. Wash., 1922; m. Lucile Laura Ramthun, Nov. 9, 1922; children—Lucile (Mrs. Earl Francis Luebker), Joan (Mrs. Wayne Haslett). Editor, Asso. Press, Spokane, Wash., 1922-23; reporter Seattle Times, 1923; city editor Columbian, Vancouver, Wash., 1923-25; with Tacoma News-Tribune, 1925-69, successively copy editor, asst. city editor, city editor, exec. editor, mng. editor, 1925-64, editor, 1964-69. Mem. Wash. bds. edn. and vocational edn., 1948-69. Served with U.S. Army, 1918. Mem. A.P. Mng. Editors Assn., Am. Soc. Newspaper Editors, Alpha Delta Phi, Sigma Delta Chi. Republican. Home: Tacoma WA Died Feb. 24, 1969; buried Mountain View Meml. Park, Tacoma WA

LOCKHART, CAROLINE, author; b. Eagle Point, Ill., 1875; d. Joseph Cameron and Sarah (Woodruff) Lockhart; ed. Bethany Coll. (Topeka, Kan.), Moravian Sem. (Bethlehem, Pa.). Formerly on staff Boston Post, Phila. Bulletin; owner and pub. Cody Enterprise; pres. Cody Stampede (wild west show). Republican. Presbyterian. Author: Me-Smith, 1911; The Lady Doc., 1912; Full of the Moon, 1914; The Man from the Bitter Roots, 1915; The Fighting Shepherdess, 1919; The Dude Wrangler, 1921; Old West and New, 1933. Owner of cattle ranch in Mont. Home: Dryhead Post Office MT‡

LOCKHART, ERNEST RAY, utility exec.; b. Raton, N.M., Dec. 23, 1911; s. Ernest Vilroy and Elizabeth A'rae (Mackie) L.; student Tex. Western U., 1929-31; B.S., Cal. Inst. Tech., 1933, M.S., 1934; m. Alice Vivian Brunner, Mar. 26, 1938; children—George Read, William Mackie. With El Paso Electric Co., 1934-40, 63-71, pres., 1963-71; power sales engr. Brockton Edison Co., 1940-42; with Stone & Webster Service Corp., 1942-63, v.p., 1954-63, dir., 1960-63. Pres. United Fund El Paso, 1966. Mem. El Paso C. of C. (pres.-elect 1966). Home: El Paso TX Died Sept. 30, 1971; buried Rest Lawn Meml. Park, El Paso TX

LOCKHEED, ALLAN HAINES, aircraft engring.; b. Niles, Calif., Jan. 20, 1889; s. John and Flora (Haines) Loughead; ed. elementary schs.; m. Dorothy E. Watts (died 1922); children—Flora Elizabeth, John Allan, m. 2d, Helen M. Kundert, June 5, 1938; 1 son Allan Haines, Jr. Learned to fly, 1910; exhn. flying, 1910-15; designed and built one of first successful tractor seaplanes, 1911-12; flew this seaplane and had passenger carrying concession at World's Fair, San Francisco, 1915; pres. Loughead Aircraft Co., Santa Barbara, Calif., 1916-19; with brother, Malcolm, designed first successful twin-engined 10-passenger seaplane (made sight-seeing trip in this plane with King Albert and Queen Elizabeth of Belgium, 1919); with brother designed a sport plane, first streamlined fuselage, made of plywood moulded under pressure; organized and became vice-pres. Lockheed Aircraft Co., Los Angeles, 1926; supervised design and constrn. of Lockheed Vega, a high-wing cantilever monoplane of plywood constrn. (this Vega model used by Sir Hubert Wilkins in Alaska-to-Spitzenbergen flight, by Wiley Post in 2 flights around the world, and by Amelia Earhart in flight to Ireland and flight, Honolulu to San Francisco; Col. and Mrs. Charles Lindbergh used a later model in flight to China and flight to Europe, via Greenland); resigned from Lockheed Aircraft Co. when it merged with Detroit Aircraft Co., 1929; pres. Lockheed Bros. Aircraft Co., Los Angeles, 1930-34, changed his name from Loughead to Lockheed, legally, Feb. 1934; designed and supervised constrn. Olympic high-wing cantilever, twin-engined monoplane; travel, research, consulting, 1935-36; organized and pres. Alcor Aircraft Corp., San Francisco, 1937-39; designed twin-engined, low-wing cantilever monoplane; travel, research, 1940; vice-pres. and dir. Berkey & Gay Furniture Co., Grand Rapids, Mich., as dir. aircraft engring. and mgr. aviation div., 1941. Apptd. by Jesse Jones mem. Cargo Plane Com. to approve a design for a cargo-carrying plane, Aug. 1941; com. completed its work, Jan. 1942, and planes now being built. General manager, Aircraft Div., Grand Rapids Store Equipment Co., Grand Rapids, Mich., since Nov. 1942. Mem. Early Birds. Republican. Protestant. Home: Sepulveda CA Died May 1969.

LOCKLEY, LAWRENCE CAMPBELL, market analyst, educator; born Salem, Ore., Nov. 21, 1899; s. Fred and Hope (Gans) L.; student Ore. Agrl. Coll., 1917-18; B.A., U. of Calif., 1920, M.A., 1921; M.A., Harvard, 1928, Ph.D., 1931; m. Phyllis Harrington, May 11, 1920;children—Robert Campbell (dec.), Neil Harrington; m. 2d, Naomi M. Hewes, Nov. 19, 1938. Reporter Oregon Journal, Portland, 1917 and 1920; asso. in English, U. of Calif., 1921-27; also cons. work 1921-27; mem. research staff Harvard Grad. Sch. Business Administration, 1929-30; asst. prof. business adminstrn. and head of dept. orgn. and management, Temple U., 1930-32, became prof. of marketing and head of dept. of marketing, 1932. Technical expert U.S. Census of Business, 1935; market analyst with div. of comml. research Curtis Pub. Co., Phila., 1935-42; mgr market research div., E. I. duPont deNemours & Co. 1942-46; Prof. Retailing and dir. Research, Sch. of Reatiling N.Y. Univ. 1947-49, prof. marketing, Grad Sch. Bus. Adminstrn., 1949-51; dean Sch. of Commerce, U. of So. Cal., 1951-59; prof. bus adminstrn., chmn. dept. marketing U. Santa Clara (Cal.), from 1960; vis. prof. marketing Columbia U. N.Y.C., 1959-60. Cons. State Dept. on Latin Am. Mem S.A.T.C., Corvallis, Ore., 1918. Mem. Am. Econ. Assn. Am. Marketing Assn., Fed. Mediation Service (arbitration panel), Am. Arbitration Assn. (arbitration panel), Skull and Dagger, Rho Epsilon, Sigma Delta Pi Phi Kappa Phi, Alpha Kappa Psi, Beta Gamma Sigma (grand vice pres. 1958-61), Phi Sigma Epsilon, also the Sigma Phi Epsilon, Pi Gamma Mu, Alpha Delta Sigma and Eta Mu Pi fraternities. Member Society of Friends Author: Faulty Paragraphs for Composition Classes (with Phyllis H. Lockley), 1923; Making Letters Build Business, 1925; A Road Map to Literature (with P. H Houston), 1926; Principles of Effective Letter Writing

1927, revised edit., 1933; Vertical Cooperative Advertising, 1931; Use of Motivation Research in Marketing, 1960. Co-Author: Advertising Agency Compensation, 1934; How to Conduct Consumer Opinion Research, 1946; Marketing by Manufacturers, 1947, rev. edit. 1950; Cases in Marketing, 1954, 3d edit., 1964; Sales and Marketing Management, 1957; A Guide to Market Data in Central America, 1964; Readings in Marketing, 1964, rev., 1968; A Market Guide To Peru, 1964; co-author: The American Association of Collegiate Schools of Business 1916-1966, 1966. Translator: The Science of Success and the Art of Prudence (Gracian), 1967. Editor: Lessons in California History (Harr Wagner and Mark Keppel), 1924. Member editorial board Jour. Marketing, 1939-47, 56—. Contbr. to Theory in Marketing, 1964. Author Monthly Econ. Letter, 1952-69. Home: San Jose CA Died Oct. 27, 1969.

LOCKWOOD, ALFRED COLLINS, lawyer; b. Ottawa, Ill., July 20, 1875; s. Walter C. and Elizabeth W. (Peers) L.; ed. pub. and high schs.; m. Daisy Maude Lincoln, June 15, 1902; children—Lorina Elizabeth, Alfreda Charlotte, Chester Ralph. Teacher public schools, Maricopa County, Ariz., 1897-1902; admitted to Ariz. bar, 1902, and practiced at Nogales and Douglas; city atty., Douglas, 1905-10; judge Superior Court of Cochise County, 1913-24; asso. justice Supreme Court of Ariz., 3 terms, 1925-43, chief justice, 1929-30 and 1935-36, 1941-42; retired from Supreme Ct. bench Jan., 1943; has since engaged in pvt. practice, Phoenix, Ariz. Pub. mem. 10th region, Nat. War Labor Bd., since 1943. Mem. bd. trustees Arizona Teachers Retirement System. Democrat. Conglist. Mason. Elk. Home: 84 W. Cypress St. Address: Phoenix National Bank Bldg., Phoenix AZ‡

LOCKWOOD, HAROLD PAUL, clergyman; b. Hebron, Neb., Feb. 28, 1902; s. Myron Dayman and Laura (Arle) L.; student Johnson Bible Coll., 1924-27, 33-34; A.B., Tex. Christian U., 1940; m. Doris Harvey, May 15, 1932; children—Harvey M., Richard K.; m. 2d, Bernice M. Witherell. Ordained to the ministry, 1934; minister of the First Christian Ch., Beeville, Tex., 1941-43, First Christian Ch., Sterling Colo., 1943-45, First Christian Ch., Pacific Grove, Cal., 1945-50; minister Vista Grande Av. Christian Ch., Daly City, Cal., 1962-64, Golden Gate Ch., San Francisco, 1964-69. Active Boy Scouts Am., 1949-53. Mem. Cal. Acad. Scis. Mason, Kiwanian. Home: San Jose CA Died Oct. 12, 1969.

LOCKWOOD, HELEN DRUSILLA, educator; b. Clifton Springs, N.Y., May 8, 1891; d. William A. and Mary (Lamson) Lockwood; A.B., Vassar College, 1912; A.M., Columbia, 1913, Ph.D., 1927; student Sorbonne, 1922-23. Tchr. English, librarian Roselle Park (N.J.) High Sch., 1913-14; tchr. English, Latin and history The Elms, Springfield, Mass., 1914-15; tchr. English Baldwin-Sch., Bryn Mawr, Pa., 1916-22; instr. English, Bryn Mawr Summer Sch. for Women Workers, 1921-23; instr. English Wellesley Coll., 1925-27; prof. English Vassar Coll. from 1927; lectr. Vassar Summer Inst., 1940-44. Chmn. program com. Poughkeepsie (N.Y.) Open Forum, 1937-41; mem. exec. com. Poughkeepsie Speaks (radio forum); moderator radio series civil liberties. Mem. exec. com. and pres. bd. trustees Hudson Shore Labor Sch. 1943-53; bd. dirs. Dutchess Co. Philharmonic Soc. Mem. Modern Lang. Assn., Am. Assn. U. Profs., Am. Assn. Tchrs. Journalism. A.A.A.S. Poughkeepsie NY Died Mar. 27, 1971.

LOCKWOOD, STEPHEN TIMOTHY, lawyer; b. Buffalo, N.Y., Jan. 7, 1874; s. Stephen and Oriel A. (Wood) L.; A.B., Princeton, 1894; m. Sada F. Daly, June 1899. Began practice at Buffalo, 1897; U.S. atty. Western Dist. of New York, 1915-22; natural gas utility exec.; pres. British-Am. Utilities Corp. (N.Y.), North East Heat and Light Co. (Pa.), Pine Valley Methane Corp. (N.Y.). Mem. Renegotiation Bd., Rochester Ordnance Dist., U.S.A., 1942. Member Judiciary Committee of Erie County Bar Association. Member American and New York state bar assns., Engring. Soc. of Buffalo, Buffalo Soc. Natural Sciences (bd. mgrs.). Democrat. Presbyterian. Expert in rare metals; awarded silver medal for exhibits of uranium, radium, thorium, vanadium, etc., at St. Louis Expn., 1904. Home: 311 Downing St., Buffalo 20 NY Office: 37 Church St., Buffalo 2 NY‡

LOEB, ARTHUR JOSEPH, paper co. exec.; b. Phila., Apr. 27, 1914; s. Adolf and Hortense (Huntsberry) L.; grad. Mercersburg Acad., 1932; B.A., Yale, 1936; m. Kathleen Vachreau, Nov. 12, 1941; children—Barbara H., Joan M., M. Kathleen. With Olin Mathieson Chem. Corp., and predecessors, 1936-68, v.p., gen. mgr. Ecusta paper div., 1964-68. Chmn. trustees Transylvania Community Hosp., 1963-68. Served to capt. USAAF, 1942-45; PTO. Mem. Writing Papers Mfrs. Assn. (chmn. thin paper group), Soc. Advancement Mgmt. Elk. Club: Yale (N.Y.C.). Home: Brevard NC Died Dec. 5, 1968; buried Brevard NC

LOEB, MILTON B., mfg. exec.; b. Lafayette, Ind., 1889; grad. U. Mich., 1908. Pres. Brillo Mfg. Co.; v.p., dir. S. Loeb & Sons, Loeb & Hene Co., Loeb's, Inc., Loeb Realty Co.; pres. Williams Co., London, O.; mng. dir. Brillo Mfg. Co. of Gt. Britain, Ltd., London; sr. v.p. Purex, Ltd., Lakewood, Cal.; dir. Brillo Mfg. Co. of Ireland, Ltd. Home: New York City NY Died Jan. 27, 1972.

LOEFFLER, CARL AUGUST, elective officer U.S. Senate; b. Washington, D.C., Jan. 12, 1873; s. Charles David Adam and Louisa (Brown) L.; ed. graded schs., Spencerian Business Coll., 1892, Columbia U., 1894-95; m. Minnie Schneider, April 17, 1901; children—Margaret Louise (Mrs. Richard Josephenson), Carleen Elizabeth (Mrs. Clarence C. McClaine), Appointed page U.S. Senate, 1889, served in several appointive positions, elected acting asst. doorkeeper of the Senate, 1913, asst. doorkeeper, 1919-27, asst. sergt. at arms, 1928, sec. for the majority of the Senate, 1929, sec. for minority, 1933-46; sec. of Senate, 1947-48. Life mem. George Washington U. Alumni Assn.; mem. Mil. Order of the Loyal Legion, Am. Polit. Sci. Assn. Republican. Lutheran. Mason. Clubs: Congressional Country; Nat. Press. Home: Washington DC Died Feb. 1968.

LOFTUS, JOHN THOMAS, coll. dean; b. Ivesdale, Ill., Nov. 21, 1908; s. John Walter and Katherine (Foohey) L.; student Mount St. Francis Jr. Coll., St. Frances Coll., Syracuse, St. Anthonly-on-Hudson, St. John's U., Notre Dame U.; A.B., Cath. U., 1932, M.A., 1938. Ordained priest Roman Cath. Ch., 1932; instr. Mount St. Francis Sem., 1933-50, prin., 1938-50; editor The Companion, 1939-57; Superior Immaculate Conception Friary, 1950-57; dean Bellarmine Coll., Louisville, 1953-69. Mem. programming com. Commn. on Human Rights; mem. Mayor's Committee on Accommodations and Facilities, also Louisville Committee for the Handicapped. Bd. dirs. Ky. Mental Health Assn., Ky. Opera Association, Louisville Philharmonic Orchestra, Kentucky Conference Christian Leadership. Served to maj., Chaplains Corps, Army of the United States, 1944-46, Mem. Franciscan Ednl. Conf., Nat. Council Tchrs. English, Am. Assn. Coll. Tchr. Edn., Nat. Cath. Edn. Assn. (chmn. So. region), Am. So. assns. acad. deans, Conf. Coll. Composition and Communication, Ky. Conf. Acad. Deans, N.E.A., Ky. Edn. Assn., History Edn. Soc., Urban League (dir.), English-Speaking Union, Am. Legion. K.C. Mem. adv. com. Jour. of Family Law. Address: Louisville KY Died Jan. 7, 1969; buried Mt. St. Francis Seminary IN

LOGAN, ARCHIE FRANCIS, airplane co. exec.; b. Fresno, Cal., Feb. 28, 1892; s. Lindsey H. and Clara L. (Merritt) L.; m. Jessie F. Johnson, May 27, 1950. Successively prodn. mgr., bus. mgr., gen. mgr. Seattle Times, 1925-37; bus. mgr. Los Angeles Examiner, 1938; v.p. operations Hearst Condol. Publs., 1939-41; successively asst. to pres., dir. indsl. relations, v.p. The Boeing Company, Seattle, from 1942. Home: Seattle WA Died Oct. 31, 1970; buried Evergreen-Washelli Meml. Park, Seattle WA

LOGAN, CHARLES ALEXANDER, missionary; b. Shelbyville, Ky., Nov. 14, 1874; s. George William and Josephine (Bell) L.; B.A., Center Coll., Danville, Ky., 1893; B.D., Ky. Theol. Sem., Louisville, Ky., 1899; D.D., Westminster Coll., Fulton, Mo., 1914; m. Patty Blain Myers, of Lexington, Va., Nov. 22, 1899; children—Josephine Bell (wife of Rev. Hugh C. Hamilton), Mary Nelson, Martha Myers. Ordained ministry Presbyn. Ch. in U.S., 1899; pastor Jackson, Ky., 1899-1901, Wilmore, 1901-02; missionary at Tokushima, Japan, since 1902. Chmn. Federation of Christian Missions of Japan, 1923. Mem. Sigma Nu. Author: Soseiki Jidai" (devotional commentary on Genesis), 1926; Mose No Jidai" (devotional commentary on Exodus), 1928; Shu Iesu no Jiko-Shokai" (Our Lord's Self-Introductions). Address: 171 Terashimamachi, Tokushima Japan‡

LOGAN, JOHN DANIEL, editor; b. Antigonish, N.S., May 2, 1869; s. Charles and Elizabeth (Rankin) L.; ed. Pictou Acad.; grad. Dalhousie Coll., A.B., 1893, A.M., 1894; Harvard, A.B., 1894, A.M., 1895, Ph.D., 1896; m. New York, Oct. 27, 1897, Minerva Shephard Bromer. Asst. to editors The Philosophical Review, 1896; acting prof. of philosophy and psychology, Ursinus Coll., Pa., 1897; asst. philosophy, Harvard, 1897; prin. Hampton Acad., N.H., 1898; head of dept. and prof. English and philosophy, Univ. of S. Dak., 1899-1902; editor on literary staff of Siegel, Cooper & Co., since 1902. Charter member Western Philos. Assn. Author: The Structural Principles of Prose Style, 1900 W14; also numerous articles on philosophy, literature, art and ed'n in mags. Address: Care Siegel, Cooper & Co., New York‡

LOGAN, W(ILLIAM) TURNER, ex-congressman; b. Summerville, S.C., June 21, 1874; s. Roswell Turner and Alice (Plowden) L.; A.B., Charleston Coll., 1895; m. Louise G. Lesesne, Nov. 16, 1909; 1 son, William Turner. Admitted to S.C. bar, 1895, and began practice at Charleston; sr. mem. Logan & Logan. Mem. S.C. Ho. of Rep. 2 terms, 1902-06; chmn. Dem. Exec. Com., Charleston County, 1910-19; corp. counsel, Charleston, 1914-18; mem. 67th and 68th Congresses (1921-25), 1st S.C. Dist. Mem. Hibernian Soc. of Charleston (pres. 3 terms), St. Cecilia Soc. Episcopalian. Mason, K.P., Elk. Club: Charleston Rifle. Home: 38 Murray Blvd. Office: 57 Broad Street, Charleston SC*‡

LOGGINS, VERNON, author and teacher; b. Hempstead, Tex., Jan. 10, 1893; s. John Nimrod and Martha (Williams) L.; A.B., U. of Tex., 1914; A.M., U. of Chicago, 1917; Ph.D., Columbia, 1931; grad. work at U. of Montpellier, France, and the Sorbonne. Teacher English, U. of Chicago, 1916-17, U. of Minn., 1917-18, Ala. Poly. Inst., 1919-20, New York U., 1920-25, Columbia University, 1925-60, prof. emeritus English and comparative lit., 1960-68; lecturer at Manhattan School Music, 1962-64. Sometime lectr. American Lit., Brooklyn Coll. Grad. Sch. and Rand Sch. of Social Science; visiting lecturer in France, University of Lille, Strasbourg, and Aix-en-Provence, 1955-56. Served with A.E.F., 1918-19. Member Soc. of Felibrige of Provence, Sigma Upsilon, Authors League of America, Poetry Soc. of America, MacDowell Colony Assos., Am. Assn. U. Profs., Acad. Polit. Sci., P.E.N., MacDowell Assn. (corporate mem.). Mem. jury of award Elizabeth Marbury Prize, 1938-41. Clubs: Authors, Columbia U. (N.Y.C.). Author: Chansons du Midi, 1924; The Negro Author, 1931; Am. Literature, 1933 (reprinted 1947); I Hear America, 1937; Two Romantics, 1946; The Hawthornes, published 1951; Where the Word Ends, published 1955; Andre Chenier, pub., 1965. Editor: Eggleston's Hoosier Schoolmaster, 1957; Bennett's Much Loved Books, 1960, Three Great French Plays, 1961. Contbr. short stories, verse, critical essays and book revs. to various periodicals. Home: New York City NY Died Oct. 3, 1968.

LOHMAN, JOSEPH D(EAN), univ. dean; b. N.Y.C., Jan. 31, 1910; s. Isaac and Lena (Dean) L.; A.B., U. Denver, 1930; M.A., U. Wis., 1931; grad. study U. Chgo., 1931-32; m. Fern Bernice Campbell, Sept. 14, 1932; 1 dau., Barbara Susan. Research sociologist Behavior Research Fund, Chgo., 1932-33; sr. research sociologist State Ill., 1934-39; instr. sociology U. Chgo., 1939-41, asst. prof., 1941-45, professorial lectr., 1947-59; exec. sec. Nat. Com. on Segregation in the Nation's Capitol, Inc., Chgo., 1946-48; asso. prof., chmn. dept. sociology Am. U., 1945; asso. prof. U. Wis., 1946; vis. prof. U. Mich., U. Wash., U. Denver; chmn. Div. of Corrections, State Ill., 1949-52, chmn. Parole and Pardon Bd., 1952-53; sheriff Cook Co., Ill., 1954-58; state treasurer State of Illinois, 1959-61; prof. criminology, dean Sch. of Criminology, University of California, Berkeley, 1961-68. Mem. adv. bd. W. H. Anderson Publishing Co. Consultant Tennessee Valley Authority, AEC, Dept. of Interior, Ill. Selective Service System; cons. to civil govt. Guam, 1951; cons. police problems; cons. human resources research office George Washington U., 1953-68; cons. UN Command Repatriation Group, 1953-54; consultant to the Ford Foundation. Mem. National Capitol Planning Commn., 1950-57, chmn., 1950-51; mem. Nat. Com. Narcotic Addiction; demonstration panel President's Comm. Delinquency and Youth Crime; research adv. council Cal. State Dept. Corrections; chmn. State Cal. Adv. Com. on Compensatory Edn., 1966-67, State Cal. Adv. Com. on Narcotics Edn.; mem. com. consultants on conseling and testing Fed. Adv. Council Employment Security, U.S. Dept. Labor; cons. Conf. Race Relations and World Perspective, U. Hawaii, 1954; cons., lectr. So. Police Inst., U. Louisville, cons. Lemberg center for Study Violence, Brandeis U., impartial adminstr., seniority system Elec. Joint Arbitration Bd., Chgo., 1951-54; mem. impartial internat. appeals bd. Upholsterers Internat: Union, AFL; arbitration panel Fed. Mediation and Conciliation Service; mem. com. on counseling and testing U.S. Employment Service. Trustee Jud. Research Found., Inc. Recipient Edward Bernays award, 1949; Medal of Freedom, Dept. Army, 1954; NBC Pub. Service award, 1958. Mem. Fed. Mediation Service, Nat. Acad. Arbitration, Am. Correctional Assn., Am. Sociol. Soc., Soc. Sociol. Research, Am. Arbitration Assn., Ill. Acad. Criminology, Am. Social Health Assn. (dir.), Am. Prison Assn. Author: Police and Minority Groups, 1947. Home: Orinda CA Died Apr. 26, 1968; interred Chapel of the Chimes, Oakland CA

LOHR, LENOX RILEY, pres., Mus. of Sci. and Industry; b. Washington, Aug. 15, 1891; s. Gustavus Peter and Margaret (Bean) L., M.E., Cornell, 1916 (honor grad.); grad. Army Gen. Staff Coll., Langres, France, 1918; Clare Coll., Cambridge U., Eng., 1919; D. Eng. (hon.), Ill. Inst. Tech. 1949; LL.D. (hon.), Knox Coll., 1950, Bradley U., 1955, Loyola U., Chgo., 1956, De Paul U., 1958, Northwestern, 1962, C.E., Rensselaer Polytech. Inst., 1952; D.Sc. (honorary), Shurtleff College, 1954; married Florence Josephine Wimsatt (M.A., M.D.), November 18, 1924; children—Margaret Priscilla (Mrs. R.L. Brown), Patricia (Mrs. James K. Rocks), Mary Josepha, Lenox Riley, Donald. Member board directors, exec. secretary Soc. Am. Mil. Engrs. 1922-29, editor The Mil. Engr., awarded its D.S.M., 1930, pres. 1954; mem. Com. on War Memorial to Am. Engrs. at Louvain U., Belgium, 1928; gen. mgr. A Century of Progress Expn. Chicago, 1929-35; pres. N.B.C., Inc., 1935-40; president of the Museum of Science and Industry, Chicago, Illinois, 1940-58, trustee, 1935-68. Bd. mem. Met. Fair and Expn. Authority, chmn., 1952-57. Fellow Inst. Medicine of

Chicago, Pres. Chicago R.R. Fair 1948-49. Dir. Civil Def. State of Ill., 1950-52; pres. Centennial of Engring., 1952, Inc.; chmn. Higher Edn. Commn. of Ill., 1954-59; hon. trustee Mary Thompson Hosp. (pres. 1952-55), Heart Assn., Chgo. La Rabida Jackson Park Sanitarium, Chgo., Thomas Alva Edison Found., N.Y.C., Air Force Mus. Found.; chmn. U. Ill. Citizens Com.; mem. U. Chicago Citizens Bd. and Northwestern U. Assos.; member citizens board Loyola University. Pres. committee Notre Dame. Mem. Sec. of Navy's Civilian Adv. Com., 1946-48. Served as 2d and 1st lt. C.A.C., U.S.A., 1916; capt. to maj. Corps Engrs., 1917-29, resigned 1929; co. comdr. and topog. officer 4th Engrs.; Brigade Adj. 57th Inf. Brigade, 29th Div.; participated in Alsace defensive sector, Meuse Argonne, returned to U.S., July 13, 1919; in Office of Chief Engrs. Decorated Silver Star medal, citation; Navy Distinguished Pub. Service award, 1954 (U.S.); Officer Order Ouissam Alaouite Cherifien of Morocco. Recipient Deutsches Museum citation, 1960; Rosenberger medal; citation U. Ill., 1964. Mem. Am. Soc. C.E., Inst. Am. Strategy (pres. 1958-62, dir.), Soc. Am. Mil. Engrs., Assn. U.S. Army, Navy League U.S., Sigma Phi Sigma (gen. pres. 1916; hon. key 1936), Phi Sigma Kappa, Chi Epsilon. Clubs: Economic, Chicago, Commercial, Antique Auto, Nat. Press. Author: Magazine Publishing, 1932; Television Broadcasting, 1940; Fair Management, 1952; Centennial of Engineering, 1953. Home: Evanston IL Died May 28, 1968.

LOMAX LOUIS EMANUEL, writer; b. Valdosta, Ga., Aug. 16, 1922; s. James and Fannie (Hardon) L.; B.A., Pame Coll., Augusta, Ga., 1942; grad. student Am. U., Yale; m. Betty Bell, Sept. 19, 1961; 1 step-son, Hugh. Engaged in newspaper work, 1941-58; free lance writer, 1958-70; newscaster sta. WNTA-TV, N.Y.C., 1958-60. Author: The Reluctant African (Anisfield-Wolf award, 1961), 1960; The Negro Revolt, 1962; When the Word is Given, 1963; Thailand: The War That Is, The War That Will Be, 1967; also numerous articles. Died July 1970.

LOMBARD, FRANK ALANSON, educator; b. Sutton, Mass., Nov. 21, 1872; s. Henry Faulkner and Nellie (Callahan) L.; grad. Worcester (Mass.) Acad., 1892; A.B., cum laude, Amherst Coll., 1896, A.M., 1899; grad. Hartford Theol. Sem., 1899; fellow in edn., Clark U., 1903-04, 1910-11; visiting student, Harvard, 1918-19; m. Alice Goodrich Ward, of Newton Centre, Mass., June 21, 1911; 1 dau., Margaret (dec.). Ordained to the Christian ministry, 1900; instructor, Doshisha College, Kyoto, Japan, 1900-04, prof. English lit. and dean, 1904-10; prof. English lit., Doshisha U., 1910-26; lecturer in English lit., Imperial U., 1908-26; exchange lecturer Peking (China) U., 1921-22; emeritus missionary, A.B.C.F.M., since 1926; emeritus prof. Doshisha U. since 1926; dir. of Oriental Tours, lecturer on Far East; sec. for academic contacts, Bur. of University Travel, 1929-39; retired, engaged in writing. Republican. Conglist. Author: Pre-Meiji Education in Japan, 1913; Imperial Japanese Poems of the Meiji Era, 1915; An Outline History of the Japanese Drama, 1929. Editor: The Student's Shakespeare, 1919. Home: Crown Wellesley MA‡

LOMBARDI, VINCENT THOMAS, profl. football coach; b. Bklyn., June 11, 1913; s. Henry and Matilda (Izzo) L.; B.S., Fordham University, 1937; LL.D. (honorary), Saint Norbert College; Doctor of Humane Letters, St. Peter's College; m. Marie Planitz, Aug. 31, 1940; children—Vincent, Susan. Tchr. chemistry, coach St. Cecelia High Sch., Englewood, N.J., 1938-48; coach U.S. Mil. Acad., West Point, N.Y., 1948-54, N.Y. Giants, 1954-59; coach Green Bay (Wis.) Packers, 1959-69, gen. mgr., 1959-69; exec. v.p., head coach Washington Redskins, 1969-70. Chmn., City of Hope. Bd. dirs. Cancer Fund, Washington; trustee Fordham University. Named Coach of Year, A.P. and U.P.I., 1959, 61-67; recipient Insignis medal; Senator Bryan MacMahan award; Silver Buffalo award Boy Scouts Am. Mem. American Football Coaches Association, also Alpha Sigma Nu. K.C. (4 deg.), Elk, K.M. Author: Run to Green Bay WI Died Sept. 3, 1970.

LONG, AUGUSTINE J., chain store exec.; b. Macon, Ga., 1903. Vice chmn., mem. exec. com., dir. Colonial Stores Inc. Home: Cincinnati OH Died Sept. 9, 1969; buried Gate of Heaven Cemetery, Montgomery, OH

LONG, CYRIL NORMAN HUGH, biochemist, physiologist; b. Nettleton, England, June 19, 1901; s. John Edward and Rose Fanny (Langdill) L.; came to U.S., 1932, citizen, 1942; B.Sc., U. of Manchester, Eng., 1921, M.Sc., 1923, D.Sc., 1932; M.D.C.M., McGill University, 1928; honorary M.A. degree from Yale U., 1936; M.D. (hon.), U. Venezuela, 1962; honorary D.Sc., Princeton, U., 1946, McGill U., 1961; m. Hilda Gertrude Jarman, July 28, 1928; children—Barbara (Mrs. R. P. Simons), Diana (Mrs. D. D. Hall). Demonstrator physiology, U. Coll., London, 1923-25; lectr. med. research, McGill U., 1925-29, assistant professor, 1929-32; director of George S. Cox Med. Research Inst., and asst. prof. med. U. Pa., 1932-36; professor physiol. chemistry Yale, 1936-38, Sterling prof. physiol. chemistry, 1938-52, chmn. dept., 1936-52, dean sch. Medicine 1947-52, Sterling prof. physiology, 1952-69, Sterling prof. emeritus, 1969-70. Chmn. dept. physiology, 1952-64; fellow John B. Pierce Found. Lab., 1969-70. Mem. Biochem. Society (Great Britain), Brit. Diabetic Assn. (hon. life), Physiological Society (Great Britain), Am. Soc. of Biol. Chemists, Soc. Exptl. Biology and Medicine (pres. 1953-55). Am. Physiol. Soc., Am. Assn. Physicians. Soc. for Clin. Investigation (pres. 1944-45), Nat. Acad. Sciences, The Endocrine Society, (president 1947-48), Am. Diabetes Assn., Argentine Soc. for Biology (hon. mem.), Am. Philosophical Society, Am. Acad. Arts and Scis. Sigma Xi. Alpha Omega Alpha, Nu Sigma Nu. Clubs: Yale (N.Y.C.); Faculty (New Haven). Writer numerous scientific papers reporting researches in biochemistry, physiology and experimental medicine. Home: Hamden CT Died July 6, 1970; buried Grove Street Cemetery, New Haven CT

LONG, EARL ALBERT, chemist; born Altoona, Pa., July 2, 1909; s. Arthur Russell and Grace Emma (Beattie) L.; A.B., Catawba Coll., 1930, D. Sc. (hon.), 1951; M.S., Ohio State U., 1932, Ph.D., 1934; m. Marietta Susan Moss, Feb. 8, 1947; step children George E. Shambaugh, Susan S. (dec.). Nat. Research fellow chemistry U. Calif., 1934-36, instr., 1936-37; fellow Lalor Found., 1937-38, asst. prof. U. Mo., 1938-43, asso. prof., 1943-45, prof. chemistry, 1945; with Los Alamos Lab., 1943-46, asst. dir., 1945; prof. inst. metals and dept. chemistry U. Chgo., 1946-61, dir. Inst. Study of Metals, 1957-61; asst. lab. dir. Gen. Atomic div. Gen. Dynamics Corp., 1960-66; chmn. dept. physics U. Ala., 1966-68. Fellow Am. Phys. Soc.; mem. Sigma Xi, Phi Lambda Upsilon. Home: Tuscaloosa AL Died May 15, 1968; buried Guave Pines Cemetery, Los Alamos NM

LONG, EDWARD VAUGHAN, ex-senator; b. Lincoln County, Mo., July 18, 1908; s. Leslie D. and Lillian (Shields) L.; student U. Mo., 1925-26, Culver-Stockton Coll., 1927-30; LL.D., 1961; L.H.D., Tarkio Coll., 1962; m. Florence Secor, Aug. 11, 1935; 1 dau., Ann Carner. Admitted to Mo. bar, 1932; practiced in Bowling Green, 1935-72; pros. atty., Pike County, Mo., 1937-41; city atty., Bowling Green, 1941-45; mem. Mo. Senate, 1934-58, maj. floor leader, 1949-54, pres. pro tem, 1955-56; lt. gov. of Mo., 1956-60; U.S. senator from Mo., 1960-68. Pres. Canton State Bank (Mo.), Farmers State Bank, Greenfield, Ill., Tower Loan Co., Fed. Loan Co., Pike Loan Co., Long Theatre Co., Bowling Green. Trustee Culver-Stockton Coll. Mem. Mo. Bar Assn., S.A.R. Democrat. Baptist, Elk, Odd Fellow, Mason (33, Shriner); mem. Order Eastern Star. Clubs: Pike County Country; Vandalia Country; Jefferson City Country; Missouri Athletic, Media (St. Louis); Metropolitan, F Street, Columbia Country (Washington); Rotary (past dir.). Home: Clarksville MO Died Nov. 6, 1972.

LONG, ERNEST D., college pres.; b. Andrews, Ind., July 5, 1872; s. Charles Morgan and Ida M. (Cole) L.; student Tri-State Coll. (prep. and jr. coll.), Angola, Ind.; A.B., Hiram (Ohio) Coll., 1896; studied U. of Mich., 1903-04; A.B., Ind. State Normal Sch., 1908; studied U. of Chicago, 1908-09; m. Mina Goff, of Angola, Oct. 30, 1902; 1 son, Robert Goff. V.p. and head dept. of edn., State Normal Sch., La Crosse, Wis., 1912-23; pres. Tri-State Coll. since 1923. Mem. N.E.A. Mem. Ch. of Christ. Home: Angola IN‡

LONG, JAMES PARKER, insurance; b. Rangoon, Burma, of Am. parents; s. Samuel Parker and May (Clark) L.; brought to America in infancy; grad. Phillips Exeter Acad., Exeter, N.H., 1907; A.B., Harvard, 1911; m. Frances Rogers Chadwick, Mar. 18, 1914; children—May Moulton, Helen Chadwick. Began as real estate salesman, 1911; farmed, 1914-27; instr. English, Starkey Sem., Lakemont, N.Y., 1927-35, was acting pres. and trustee, 1935; clerk bd. Lakemont Academy, successors to Starkey Seminary; mem. Yates County Bd. of Supervisors, 1922-24; justice of the peace, Town of Italy, N.Y., 1924-27. Pres. Bd. of Edn., Lakemont Union Free Sch. Dist., 1932-36. Pres. Yates County Econ. Council, 1932-36; director New York State Economic Council, 1932-37; exec. dir. Yates County Def. Council, 1941-42; mem. Naples Youth Corp., 1945-63; councilman N.Y. State Conservation Council, 1948-61. Mem. Naples Valley Fish and Game Assn., Delta Upsilon. Republican. Methodist. Mason, Rotarian. Author of Starkey Naples NY Died Mar. 7, 1970; buried Naples NY

LONG, LEROY DOWNING, surgeon; b. Caddo, Indian Ter., Mar. 15, 1897; s. LeRoy (M.D.) and Martha (Downing) L; student Okla. U., 1915-17; M.D., Harvard, 1921; post grad. work at Vienna and Berlin, 1923; m. Mary Louise Clymer, Sept. 15, 1927; children—LeRoy, III, Margaret Ann. House officer Meth. Hosp., Brooklyn, 1921-23; surgeon in LeRoy Long Clinic, Oklahoma City, since 1924; instr. surgery, U. of Oklahoma Medical School, 1924-29, asst. prof., 1929-31, asso. in surgery, 1936-43, asso. prof. surgery, 1943-49; prof. clin. surgery, 1949-70. Mem. of Oklahoma City Appeals Review Board. Maj. Med. Corps, Oct. 1940-March 1942. Member of Founder's Group American Board of Surgery. Fellow A.C.S. (governor); mem. Am. Okla. County and Okla. State med. assns., Western Surg. Assn. (v.p., 1954), Am. Assn. for Study Goiter, S.W. Surg. Congress (founder member), Oklahoma City Surgical Society (president 1952), Okla. City Acad. of Medicine, Southern Soc. of Clin. Surgeons (pres. 1933-34), Phi Beta Pi, Sigma Alpha Epsilon. Democrat. Methodist. Clubs: University, Oklahoma City Golf and Country, Beacon. Contbr. to med. jours. Home: Oklahoma City OK Died Apr. 24, 1970.

LONG, LUMAN HARRISON, editor; b. Rolla, Mo., Jan. 20, 1907; s. Edwin and Daysie (Harrison) L.; student U. Mo., 1925-27; m. Violet Hoepfner, Sept. 23, 1944; 1 son, Thomas Harrison. Editor, Rolla New Era, 1933-42; city editor Gloversville (N.Y.) Morning Herald, 1942-43; reporter, rewrite man N.Y. Sun, 1943-50; rewrite man, polit. writer N.Y. World-Telegram and Sun, 1950-56; asso. editor World Almanac, 1956-65, editor, 1965-71. Mem. Kappa Sigma. Methodist. Mason. Home: Chatham NJ Died Sept. 12, 1971.

LONG, ROBERT FRANKLIN, physician; b. Lexington, Ky., Apr. 18, 1920; s. James Lynn and Rebecca (Sutton) L.; M.D., Tulane U., 1948; m. Elizabeth Ebbett Ellis, Oct. 17, 1942; children—Robert Franklin, Barbara (Mrs. Kenneth E. Meyer), Nancy Lynn, David Ellis. Intern, Scott and White Clinic, Temple, Tex., 1848-49; radiol. intern Johns Hopkins Hosp., Balt., 1949-50, asst. resident in radiology, 1950-51, sr. asst. resident, 1951-52, Nat. Cancer Inst. fellow, 1951-52; radiologist Somerset (Ky.) City Hosp., until 1970. Served to 1st lt. AUS, 1944. Diplomate Am. Bd. Radiology. Mem. Am. Coll. Radiology, Radiol. Soc. N.Am., Ky. Med. Assn. (trustee 1967-69), Theta Kappa Psi. Democrat. Roman Catholic. Home: Somerset KY Died Dec. 8, 1970; buried Meml. Gardens, Somerset KY

LONG, ROSE MCCONNELL (MRS. HUEY P. LONG), ex-senator; b. Greensburg, Ind.; d. Peter Martin and Sallie Armitage (Billiu) McConnell; ed. pub. schs., Shreveport, La.; m. Huey Pierce Long, Winnfield, La., Apr. 12, 1913; children—Rose Lolita, Russell Billiu, Palmer Reid. Apptd. mem. U.S. Senate by Gov. J.A. Noe, Jan. 31, 1936, to fill the vacancy caused by the death of her husband until the gen. election in Apr.; unanimously nominated by Dem. State Central Com., Feb. 6, for election to complete the term of her husband, expiring Jan. 1, 1937. Baptist. Home: Shreveport LA Died May 1970.*

LONGACRE, LINDSAY BARTHOLOMEW, minister; b. Pottsville, Pa., Jan. 26, 1870; s. Orleans and Rachel (Bartholomew) L.; E.M., Sch. of Mines (Columbia), 1892; B.D., Drew Theol. Sem., 1896; U. of Jena, Germany, 1905-06, 1910; Ph.D., New York U., 1908; m. Arabella Hyland, 1904 (died 1930); m. 2d, Florence Biggart, 1936. Ordained M.E. minister, 1896; held various pastorates in New York Conf., 1896-1910; prof. O.T. lit. and religion, Iliff Sch. of Theology, Denver, 1910-42, retired. Mem. Soc. Bibl. Lit. and Exegesis, Nat. Assn. Biblical Instrs., Hymn Soc. of America, Am. Guild of Organists. Author: A Prophet of the Spirit, 1917, 22; Amos&eProphet of a New Order, 1921, 23; Deuteronomy&eA Prophetic Law Book, 1924; The Old Testament: Its Form and Purpose, 1945. Joint editor of Riverdale Hymn Book, 1912. Home: Hudson View Gardens, New York 33 NY‡

LONGEST, CHRISTOPHER, educator; b. near Pontotoc, Miss., Feb. 23, 1874; s. Ruffin and Sarah (Thompson) L.; student Miss. Coll., 1893-94, 1895-96; A.B., U. of Miss., 1900; student Johns Hopkins University, 1904-08; Ph.D., U. of Chicago, 1915; LL.D., Mississippi College, 1950; married Ann Waller Reins, Sept. 9, 1908. Public sch. teacher, Pontotoc, 1894-95, 1895-96; Englisr teacher Maasin and Barugo, Leyte, Philippine Islands, 1901-04; instr. in English, John Hopkins, 1904-05; asst. prof. Latin, U. of Miss., 1908-10, asso. prof., 1910-20, prof. of Spanish 1920-53, registrar, 1920-30, chmn. Modern lang. dept. since 1945. Pres. First National Bank of Oxford, Miss. Served as chmn. Home Service, Lafayette County, Miss., A.R.C.; Dollar a Year Man, World War I. Mem. Modern Lang. Assn. Am., South Central Modern Lang. Assn., Oxford C. of C. Democrat. Baptist. Home: 1003 S. Lamar St., Oxford MS‡

LONGWELL, DANIEL, editor; born in Omaha, July 11, 1899; s. Alfred Marshall and Alice Charlotte (Haynes) L.; grad. Central High Sch., Omaha, 1918; student Columbia U., 1918-23; m. Mary Douglas Fraser, Dec. 16, 1938. Publishing exec., Doubleday, Page & Co. (Doubleday, Doran & Co.), 1923-34; publishing mgr. book trade depts. Doubleday Doran Co., 1929-34; special asst. to pres. of Time Inc., 1934-36, asso. editor of Time, 1934-36; exec. editor Life, 1936-44, managing editor Life 1944-46; chmn. bd. editors Life, 1947-54; pres. Am. Fedn. of Arts, 1954-56, trustee 1949-68; trustee Nat. Book Com., Inc., 1953-68. Clubs: Columbia University, Coffee House, River, Century (New York City). Home: Neosho MO Died Nov. 20, 1968; buried Neosho MO

LONGYEAR, ROBERT DAVIS, geologist, corp. exec.; b. Petoskey, Mich., July 11, 1892; s. Edmund Joseph and Nevada (Patten) L.; A.B., Williams Coll., 1914; M.A., U. Wis., 1915; postgrad. Stanford, 1915-16, U. Minn., 1933; m. Barbara Elizabeth Lyon, Dec. 3,

1918; children—Roanne Elizabeth (Mrs. B. C. Corbus, Jr.), and Martha P. (Mrs. George R. Stevenson, Jr.) (dec.). Geologist exploration Falcombridge nickel mine, Sudbury, Ont., 1916-17; pres. E. J. Longyear Co., Mpls., 1923-58, chmn., 1958-70; dir. Cascade Corp., Kona Iron Co. Mining machinery adv. com. WPB, 1940-45; mem. Greater Mpls. Citizens League; hon. dir. Pillsbury-Waite Neighborhood Services. Second lieut., C.A.C., U.S. Army, 1918. Mem. Am. Inst. Mining, Metall. and Petroleum Engrs. (past dir. Soc. Mining Engrs.), Can. Inst. Mining and Metallurgy, Mpls. C. of C., Diamond Core Drill Mfrs. Assn. (past president), also fraternity Beta Theta Pi. Episcopalian (past vestryman). Clubs: Minneapolis, Engineers (Mpls.). Home: Minneapolis MN Died May 20, 1970; buried Lakewood Cemetery, Minneapolis MN

LOOMIS, ALFRED F(ULLERTON), (pseudonym Spun Yarn), author; b. Flatbush, New York, on August 23d, 1890; the son of Charles Battell and May Charlotte (Fullerton) L.; ed. pub. schs. and Mt. Pleasant Mil. Acad., Ossining, N.Y., 1906-07 (non-grad.); m. Priscilla Lockwood (Barnard, 1913), June 5, 1922; children—Alfred W., Robert L., Sarah W. (Mrs. Ward C. Campbell). Harvey B. Member of the editorial staff of Country Life (magazine), 1907-12; asso. editor Motor Boating, New York, 1913-17. Enlisted in U.S.N.R.F., May 6, 1917; assigned to Adriatic detachment of 110-foot sub.-chasers; commd. ensign, at Spalato, Dalmatia, December 12, 1918; commd. lieutenant commander, U.S.N.R., Jan. 17, 1941, comdr. Aug. 1942, capt. Nov. 1945. Navigated 28-foot yawl Hippocampus from New York to Panama and Pearl Islands, 1921; navigated 58-foot schooner, Pinta, in Transatlantic race for Queen of Spain's cup, 1928; navigated 61-foot schooner Brilliant to England, 1933, and the J-class cutter Yankee, 1935; known for long distance small-boat cruising and racing; lectr. yachting subjects. Clubs: Royal Ocean Racing, Lloyd's, Royal Thames, Ocean Cruising (England); Off Soundings, Los Angeles Yacht. Transpacific Yacht, Cruising of America, Cold Spring Harbor Beach; Coconut Grove Sailing, Cayman Yacht, The Windjammers; The Coffee House, The Century (New York); Royal Swedish Yacht. Author: The Cruise of the Hippocampus, 1922; Fair Winds in the Far Baltic, 1928; Hotspur's Cruise in the Aegean, 1931; Yachts Under Sail, 1933; Paradise Cove, 1933; Millions for Defense (with Herbert L. Stone), 1934; Ocean Racing, 1936, rev. 1946; Ranging the Maine Coast, 1939; The Hotspur Story, 1954; What Price Dory (with Chon Day), 1955; author (juveniles) The Sea Bird's Quest, 1923; The Bascom Chest, 1926; Walt Henley, D.S.M., 1927; Sea Legs, 1927; Walt Henley Overseas, 1928; Walt Henley, Skipper, 1929; Troubled Waters, 1929; Tracks Across the Sea, 1932; also contbr. mags. asso. editor Yachting, from 1934, Yachts and Yachting (Eng.), 1947-66. Lecturer. Home: New York City NY Died Mar. 26, 1968; buried Litchfield CT

LOOMIS, HAROLD FRANCIS, army officer; b. Rockville, Conn., June 19, 1890; s. Harry Merrifield and Mattie (McLean) L.; B.S., U.S. Mil. Acad., 1914; grad. Coast Arty. Sch., 1925, Command and Gen. Staff Sch., 1928, Ecole Superieure de Guerre, 1934, Army War Coll., 1939; m. Bessie Oler Kimberly, Sept. 8, 1915. Commd. 2d lt. Coast Arty. Corps, U.S. Army, 1914, advanced through grades to brig. gen. (temp.), Oct. 31, 1941; served on War Dept. Gen. Staff, 1939-41; with Allied Force Headquarters and Supreme Headquarters Allied Expeditionary Force. Clubs; Army and Navy (Washington, D.C.). Retired as brig. gen. Address: Washington DC Died Oct. 21, 1970; buried West Point NY

LOOMIS, HELEN AUGUSTA, educator; b. Stamford, N.Y., Aug. 6, 1875; d. Justin R. and Frances (Goodrich) Loomis; ed. Stamford Sem., 1880-92. Berlitz Sch. Languages, 1892-94. Cornell U., 1894-96. With St. Mary's Sch., Memphis, Tenn., since 1897, became prinicipal and propr., 1910. Democrat. Episcopalian. Address: 1257 Poplar Blvd., Memphis TN‡

LOOMIS, HENRY M(EECH), chemist; b. Yokohama, Japan, July 19, 1875; s. Henry and Jane H. (Greene) L.; B.S. in Chemistry, Mass. Inst. Tech., 1897; m. Eleanor W. Wallace, of Harrisburg, Pa., Nov. 10, 1908. Asst. chemist Mathieson Alkali Works, Niagara Falls, N.Y., 1897-1900; asst. supt. bleaching powder plant, Castner Electrolytic Alkali Works, Niagara Falls, 1900-02; chemist Internat. Acheson Graphite Co., Niagara Falls, 1902-04; with U.S. Dept. Agr. since July, 1907, as food and drug inspn. chemist, 1907-13, mem. Bd. of Food and Drug Inspn., 1913-14, chemist in charge of food control, 1914-16; now with Nat. Canners Assn. Mem. Am. Chem. Soc. Conglist. Club: Cosmos. Home: 2115 P St. N.W., Washington DC‡

LOOMIS, JOHN, financial adviser; b. Cleveland, O., Mar. 29, 1875; s. John and Mary Frances (Stranahan) L.; ed. pub. schs.; m. Harriet Bashore, Jan. 1902; 1 dau., Mrs. Cathryn Loomis Wayman. With Bureau of Supplies, Philippine Civ. Service, 1905-15, chief of Div. of Supplies, 1911-15; successively dir. gen. of internal revenue, auditor gen. and treas. gen., Republic of Santo Domingo, 1916-22; with General Sugar Co., Havana, Cuba, 1923-25; mem. Am. Financial Mission to Persia, as dir. gen. finances of East Persia, 1925-28; financial adviser to Republic of Liberia, 1928-32 and 1934-35. Knight Commander of The Star of Africa. Mem. Philippine Soc. (New York). Mason (K.T., Shriner), Rotarian. Home: 543 West Park Av., Tallahassee FL‡

LOOMIS, NOEL MILLER, educator, author; b. Wakita, Okla., Apr. 3, 1905; s. LeRoy Parker and Florida Bess (Miller) L.; student Clarendon (Tex.) Coll., 1921, U. Okla., 1931; m. Dorothy Moore Green, Dec. 7, 1945; children—James LeRoy, Mary (Mrs. Gary Liljenberg). Free-lance writer, 1929-69; free-lance editor, 1930-69; asst. prof. English, San Diego State Coll., 1958-69, founder, dir. Writers' Workshop, from 1961; writing cons. San Diego city schs., 1961-69. Mem. Nat. Postal Com., 1954-58; made nat. survey writers' incomes, 1953, contracts, 1955-56. Pres. Hulburd Grove Improvement Assn., 1960-67. Recipient Silver Spur for best Western novel, 1958, for best Western short story, 1959. Mem. Cal. Writers Guild, P.E.N., Am., Western history assns., Westerners Clubs, Am. Assn. U. Profs., Nat. Council Tchrs. English, Am. Acad. Polit. and Social Sci., Western Writers Am. (pres. 1954, sec.-treas. 1957-61). Author 50 books including: Rim of the Caprock, 1952; The Buscadero, 1953; Man with Absolute Motion, 1953; West to the Sun (Gold medal), 1955; The Twilighters, 1956; Short Cut to Red River, 1958; The Texan-Santa Fe Pioneers, 1958; Time for Violence, 1960; Pedro Vial and the Roads to Santa Fe, 1786-1808, 1967; Illustrated History of Wells Fargo, 1968. Home: Descanso CA Died Sept. 7, 1969; buried Memory Garden, Alpine Cemetery, Alpine CA

LOOSE, KATHARINE RIEGEL (GEORG SCHOCK"), writer; b. Centreport, Pa., June 18, 1877; d. Charles G. (M.D.) and Sarah E. (Riegel) L.; A.B., Bryn Mawr, 1898. Author: Hearts Contending (novel), 1910; The House of Yost, 1923. Contbr. short stories to mags. Home: 221 S. 5th St., Reading PA‡

LOOSE, KATHARINE RIEGEL (GEORG SCHOCK"), writer; b. Centreport, Pa., June 18, 1877; d. Charles G. (M.D.) and Sarah E. (Riegel) L.; A.B., Bryn Mawr, 1898. Author: Hearts Contending (novel), 1910; The House of Yost, 1923. Contbr. short stories to mags. Home: 221 S. 5th St., Reading PA‡

LOPER, DON, fashion designer; b. Toledo, 1906. Profl. dancer, appearing in movies including Lady In the Dark, until 1946; fashion designer, Los Angeles, 1946-72. Address: Los Angeles CA Died Nov. 23, 1972.

LOPEZ-MATEOS, ADOLFO, pres. of Mexico; b. Atizapan de Zaragoza, Mexico, May 26, 1910; s. Dr. Mariano Lopez and Elena Lopez de Mateos; student Sci. and Liberary Inst. of Toluca; B.A., Nat. Autonomous U. of Mexico; law degree, 1934; m. Eva Zamano, 1937; 1dau., Eva Sec. to Carlos Riva Palacio, head Nat. Revolutionary Party, 1931; auditor Workers' Nat. Development Bank, 1934; chmn. editorial commn. Ministry of Edn., asst. dir. Dept. Fine Arts; tchr. Spanish-Am. lit., world history Sci. and Literary Inst. of Toluca, later dir.; founder Sch. of Econs., Nat. Autonomous U.; sec.-gen. Nat. U. of Ednl. Workers; senator, State of Mexico; sec.-gen. Party of Revolutionary Institutions, chmn. Senate Fgn. Relations Com.; chmn. Mexican delegation ECOSOC meeting, Geneva, Switzerland, 1951; campaign mgr. Party of Revolutionary Instns. candidate, mem. Fed. Election Commn., 1952; became minister of labor and social welfare, 1952; pres. of Mexico, 1958-64. Address: Mexico City Mexico Died Sept. 22, 1969.

LORCH, EMIL, prof. architecture; b. Detroit, July 21, 1870; s. Gabriel and Pauline (Schober) L.; student Mass. Inst. Tech., 1890-92; study in Paris, 1898-99; dept. of architecture, Harvard, 1901-02; Harvard Grad. Sch., 1902-03, A.M., 1903; m. Jemina Adam Elmslie, Aug. 22, 1906. Instr. Detroit Museum Art Sch., 1895-98; gen. asst. to dir. Art Inst. Chicago, 1899-1901; sec. Chicago Sch. Architecture, Art Inst. and Armour Inst. (affiliated), 1900-01; teaching asst. in architecture, Harvard, 1901-03; asst. and head dept. architecture, U. of Mich., 1906-31, dir. of coll., 1931-36, mem. exec. com., 1936-40, prof. emeritus since 1940, architect of archtl. bldg., 1927. Archtl. cons., Mackinac Island State Park Commn. since 1946. Practicing and cons. architect; architect and mem. Detroit-Belle Isle Bridge Commn., 1915-18. Mem. Mich. State Bd. for Registration of Architects, 1915-19; mem. Mich. State Bd. Examiners for Architects, Engrs., Surveyors, 1919-33. Fellow A.I.A. (com. on registration laws, 1941-44); mem. Detroit Chaper A.I.A. (pres. 1940-42); Mich. Soc. Architects (chmn. com. on Mich. architecture since 1938), Assn. Coll. Schs. of Architecture (pres. 1921-23), Washtenaw Hist. Soc. (pres. 1942-45), Tau Beta Pi, Alpha Rho Chi, Tau Sigma Delta. Pres. Nat. Council Architectural Registration Bds., 1921. Home: 1023 Forest Av., Ann Arbor, MI*‡

LORD, EDWARD THOMAS SUMNER, publisher; b. Limington, Me., Nov. 18, 1871; s. William Godding and Mary Shepard (Clark) L.; A.B., Dartmouth College, 1891, A.M., 1894; Litt.D., Bates College, 1939; m. Agnes Halladay, Apr. 18, 1905; children—William Shepard, George Alexander, Edward Sumner, Elizabeth Halladay. Instr. English and mathematics, Worcester (Mass.) Acad., 1891-92; N.E. agt. D.C. Heath & Co., pubs., 1892-93; mgr. ednl. dept. Charles Scribner's Sons, 1893-1901; pres. Lothrop Pub. Co., Boston, 1901-02; v.p., dir. and mgr. ednl. dept. Charles Scribner's Sons, 1902-47; retired; chmn. Glen Ridge Trust Co. Mem. Am. Hist. Assn., N.E.A., Phi Beta Kappa, Delta Kappa Epsilon. Democrat, Conglist. Clubs: Dartmouth Coll. of New York, D.K.E., Glen Ridge Country, Glen Ridge. Home: 78 Lincoln St., Glen Ridge NJ‡

LORD, ISABEL ELY, editorial work; b. Saybrook, Conn., Feb. 7, 1871; d. Henry S. and Elizabeth Alice (Ely) L.; grad. Hartford Pub. High Sch., 1887; diploma for French, Sauveur Sch. of Languages, 1891; B.L.S., N.Y. State Library Sch., 1897; grad. student Bryn Mawr, 1897-1900. Librarian Bryn Mawr Coll., 1897-1903, Pratt Inst. Free Library, 1903-10; dir. Pratt Inst. Household Science and Arts, 1910-20. Pres. of The Proxy Shoppers, Inc., 1923-26; editor and consultant since 1927. Episcopalian. Mem. Am. Home Economics Assn., A.L.A., Girls' Friendly Soc. Club: Cosmopolitan. Author: Budgeting Your Income, 1922. Editor: Everybody's Cookbook, 1924, new edit., 1937; The Household Shelf, 1936. Home: 176 Emerson Pl., Brooklyn, N.Y.; also Ely Homestead, Joshuatown, via Old Lyme CT‡

LORD, JOHN FOLEY, govt. ofcl.; b. Foley, Minn., June 6, 1909; s. William H. and Mary (Hall) L.; B.A., Coll. St. Thomas, St. Paul, 1929, LL.B., 1930; m. Lillian M. Busian, Aug. 31, 1932; children—John Foley, Michael Dooley, William Busian, James Hall, Mary Antonia. Asst. county atty. Benton County, Minn., 1928-29; admitted to Minn. bar, 1930; mem. firm Swenson & Lord, Foley and Sauk Rapids, Minn., 1930-31; pvt. practice, St. Paul, 1931-33; sr. atty. 7th dist. FCA, 1933-46; mem. firm Sullivan, Kelsch, Fleck & Lord, Mandan N.D., 1946-51, Lord, Ulmer, Baird and Daner, Mandan and Bismarck, N.D., 1951-61; asst. gen. counsel Fed. Deposit Ins. Corp., 1961-62, gen. counsel, 1962-64, special assistant to chairman, 1964-67; attorney Treasury Department, 1967-70. General counsel N.D. Hospital Association, 1958-61, N.D. Bankers Association, 1960-61. Founder, pres. Bismarck Psycht. Center, 1959. Democratic candidate for gov. N.D., 1958. Bd. dirs. Custer-Ft. Lincoln Found., 1960; pres. lay adv. bd. Sr. Alexius Hosp., Bismarck, 1957-60. Served with AUS, 1945. Mem. Am., Fed., N.D., Morton County bar assns., Nat. Assn. Claiments Compensation Attys. (asso. editor jour. 1954-61, bd. govs. 8th circuit 1958-60), Am. Legion, 40 and 8, Internat. War Vets. Alliance. Kiwanian (lt. gov. 1961), Elk, K.C. (4 deg.). Home: Arlington VA Died Feb. 18, 1970; buried Gettysburg Nat. Cemetery.

LORD, JOHN W(HITAKER), JR., fed. judge; b. Phila., Dec. 19, 1901; s. John W. and Mary (Apprich) L.; LL.B., Temple U., 1928; m. M. Lilias Montgomery, Feb. 19, 1930; 1 son, John Whitaker, III. Admitted to Pa. bar, 1928, since practiced in Phila.; dep. atty. gen., 1939-46; prof. law Temple U., 1938-54; judge U.S. Dist. Ct., Eastern Dist. Pa., 1954-71. State senator, Pa., 1947-51; councilman-at-large, Phila., 1952-54. Home: Philadelphia PA Died May 1972.

LORD, LILLOS MONTGOMERY (MRS. JOHN W. LORD, JR.,), polit. worker, club woman; b. Phila.; d. William Morgan and Elizabeth (Leewright) Montgomery; student U. Pa., 1927-29; m. John Whitaker Lord, Jr., Feb. 19, 1930; 1 son, John Whitaker III. Mem. adv. bd. Salvation Army, 1954-70, co-chmn. gen. gifts, com. Capital Improvement Campaign, 1968; mem. women's com. Phila. Civic Opera Co., 1953; Pa. del. White House Conf. Hwy. Safety, Washington, 1954; campaign vice chmn. women's div. March of Dimes, Phila., 1952-54, vice chmn. women's com., 1968; hon. chmn. The Hannah Penn Aux. St. Christopher's Hosp. Children, 1956; mem. Nat. Com. for Children and Youth, 1965; mem. bd. Phila. Assn. Retarded Children. Pres. Republican Women Pa., 1948-54, 62-70; mem. exec. com. Southeastern dist. Rep. Finance Com. Pa., 1952-70; state publicity chmn. Pa. Council Rep. Women, 1963, state chmn. teenage groups, 1964, mem. bd., 1966-70; exec. mem. nat. council Women's Rep. Club, Inc., 1964; alternate del. Rep. convention, 1968. Mem. Huguenot Soc. Pa., Daus. Am. Colonists, Nat. Soc. Sons and Daus. of Pilgrims, D.A.R. (chpt. regent 1957-60), Nat. Soc. Daus. Colonial Wars. Episcopalian. Mem. Order Eastern Star. Clubs: Germantown Cricket, Regents. Home: Philadelphia PA Died Mar. 23, 1970.

LOREE, JAMES TABER, corp. official; b. Logansport, Ind., Apr. 6, 1888; s. Leonor Fresnol and Jessie (Taber) L.; B.A., Yale, 1909; m. Miriam G. Collins, Mar. 23, 1927. Began as file clerk, K.C.S. Ry., 1909; became traveling auditor and chief travelling auditor, same road; signal department Pa. Lines west of Pittsburgh, 1910-11; head of party on constrn. and location S.P. Lines in Ore., Feb.-June 1911; chief tunnel insp. same rd., June-Sept. 1911; draftsman for construction engr. D.&H., at Colonie, N.Y., Sept.-Nov. 1911; spl. mission studying English railroad practices, Dec. 1911-June 1912; asst. div. engr., S.P. Co., 1912-13; with D.&H. Co. 1913-38, successively as asst. trainmaster, trainmaster to 1914, supt. Susquehanna div., 1914-15, asst. gen. supt. transportation, 1915-16, gen. mgr., 1917-23, became v.p. in charge of operation, 1923; officer or dir. many cos. Served as enlisted man, 2d lt., 1st lt. and capt. N.Y.N.G., 1915-17; maj., lt. col. and col. U.S. Army, 1917-20; served on Mexican border; later with 27th Div. and 80th Div. in France and as chief of staff Am. Mission, Interallied Mil. Mission to Hungary and as dep. U.S. commr. Decorated D.S.M. (U.S.); Legion of Honor and Croix de Guerre (French); Order Crown of Roumania; Order Crown of Italy; Order of Leopold (Belgian); Order of Simon Bolivar; Order of Danilo. Mem. Beta Theta Pi. Republican. Catholic. Clubs: University. Ft. Orange, Albany Country, Schuyler Meadows (Albany); Mohawk Golf (Schenectady); University, Yale (New York). Home: Albany NY Died Apr. 1973.

LORENZ, HENRY WILLIAM FREDERICK, chemist; b. Springfield, O., Apr. 27, 1871; s. Rev. Henry and Margaret L.; grad. Wittenberg Coll., Springfield, O., 1893 (A.M.); studied Univ. of Tubingen, 1893-4, Univ. of Berlin, 1894-8 (A.M., Ph.D., 1897); asst. to Prof. S. Gabriel (Univ. of Berlin), 1898. Instr. organic chemistry Univ. of Pa., 1899-1901. Mem. Deutsche Chemische Gesellschaft. Contb'r to Am. and German jours. Author: Electrolysis and Electro-synthesis of Organic Compounds, 1898 W9; Practical Urinary Analysis, 1903 W9. Address: Fernbank OH‡

LORENZ, MAX OTTO, statistician;b. Burlington, Ia., Sept. 19, 1876; s. Carl Wilhelm Otto and Amalie Marie (Brautigam) L.; A.B., U. of Ia., 1899; Ph.D., U. of Wis., 1906; m. Nellie F. Sheets, Oct. 28, 1911; children—Frederick, Roger, Julian. Teacher high sch., Burlington, Ia., 1899-1901; instr. in economics, U. of Wis., 1901-07; dept. commr. of labor and industrial statistics, Wis., 1907-09; spl. agt. U.S. Bur. of Census, 1909-10; statistician Bur. of Ry. Economics, 1910-11; asso. statistician Interstate Commerce Commn., 1911-16; sec. 8-Hour Commission, 1916-17; dir. statistics, Interstate Commerce Commn., 1917-44, retired since 1944. Home: 253 Oxford Av., Palo Alto CA‡

LORING, HOMER, b. Newton Center, Mass., Oct. 1875; s. Stanton Dunster and Helen (Bird) L.; ed. pub. schs.; m. Mary Bennett; 1 dau., Elizabeth. Was chmn. bd. Boston & Me. R.R., State Finance Commn. of Mass.; pres. United Merchants & Mfrs. Assn. and prominently identified with reorganization of textile industry of New England; dir. Boston Safe Deposit & Trust Co. Home: 468 Beacon St. Office: 31 Milk St., Boston MA‡

LORING, PAULE STETSON, cartoonist, marine artist; born Portland, Maine, March 24, 1899; son of Jacob Gray and Jennie Marie (Bye) L.; educated grammar and high school, Freeport, Me.; m. Eunice May Chase, July 14, 1923 (div.) m. 2d, Virginia Marie Craig, April 4, 1932; 2 sons, Bruce Stetson, Ronnie Craig. Successively ins. man, truckdriver, foundry worker, mechanic, timekeeper; art editor of ho. organ, Graton & Knight, Worcester, Mass., 1917-18; advtg. art dir. Greenfield (Mass.) Tap and Die Co., 1919-21; cartoonist Springfield (Mass.) Union, 1921-26, Providence (R.I.) Evening Bulletin and Sunday Jour., from 1926; drew daily editorial cartoon; war correspondent for the Atlantic and the European Theatres War; pres. Loring Shanty Products. Sponsor art sch. Harbor Art Galleries, Wickford; mem. Nat. Harbors and Rivers Congress. Fellow Royal Soc. Arts London; mem. Fifty Am. Artists, U.S. Naval Inst. (asso.), South County Art Assn., Assn. Am. Editoral Cartoonists, Narragansett Bay Yachting Assn. Republican. Conglist. Clubs: Edgewood (R.I.) Yacht; Barnacle (Wickford); Royal Lymington Yacht (Eng.). Author: Dud Sinker, Lobsterman, 1964; Loring's Marine Sketchbook, 1964; Lancelot, The Swordfish, 1964. Home: North Kingstown RI Died Feb. 1968.

LORNE, MARION, actress; b. Pa., Aug. 12, 1888; d. Dr. William Lorne MacDougall; student Wyoming Sem., Kingston, Pa., also Am. Acad. Dramatic Art; m. Walter Hackett (dec. 1944). First appearance Madison Square Theatre, N.Y.C., 1905; mem. Hunter-Bradford Stock Co., Hartford, Conn., 1909-14; 1st London appearance, Prince of Wales Theatre, 1915; appeared in plays, including Freedom of the Seas, Ambrose Applejohn's Adventure, Other Men's Wives, 77 Park Lane, The Way to Treat a Woman, Gay Adventure, Afterwards, Hyde Park Corner, Espionage, London After Dark; actress Mr. Peepers show on TV, then Gary Moore Show, CBS-TV; played Aunt Clara in TV show Bewitched (Emmy award Best Supporting Actress 1968). Died May 9, 1968.

LORWIN, LEWIS L., economist, author; b. near Kiev, Russia, Dec. 4, 1883; s. Jacob and Anna L.; came to U.S. (with parents), 1887; ed. public schools in New York, prep. schs. in Russia, Switzerland and France; Ph.D., Columbia U., 1912; married Rose Strunsky. Economic expert, N.Y. Dept. of Labor, 1912-16; instr., Columbia, 1914-15; lecturer Wellesley Coll., 1916; instr., asst. prof. and prof. economics, U. of Mont., 1916-19; spl. writer econ. problems, New York World, 1919-20; prof. economics and finance Beloit (Wis.) Coll., 1920-21; corr. in Russia for Chicago Daily News, 1921-22; mem. research staff Inst. of Economics of Brookings Instn., 1925-35; economic adviser of Internat. Labor Office, Geneva, Switzerland, 1935-39; economic consultant Temporary Nat. Economic Com., Nat. Resources Planning Bd. and Bd. of Econ. Warfare, 1939-42; economic adviser Nat. Resources Planning Bd., 1942-43; economic adviser Foreign Economic Administration, 1943-45; economic adviser, Office International Trade, U.S. Department of Commerce, from 1945. Delegate to 3d Institute Pacific Relation, Kyoto, 1929, 5th at Banff, 1933, 6th at Yosemite Nat. Park, 1936. Adviser to U.S. Delegation to 1st Gen. Assembly of U.N., London, Jan.-Feb. 1946. Mem. of Adv. Staff of U.S. Delegation to Econ. and Social Council, 1946-49; mem. of trade mission to Moscow, summer 1946. Mem. American Economic Assn., National Econ. and Social Planning Assn. (founder 1934, chairman board trustees, 1934-38), chmn. bd. trustees and editor World Economics, 1943-46. Club: Cosmos. Author numerous books relating to field since 1912. Home: Washington DC Died June 1970.

LORY, CHARLES ALFRED, educator; b. Sardis, O., Sept. 25, 1872; s. Chris and Ida (Stauffer) L.; attended Sardis Pub. Sch.; family moved to Colo., 1888; assisted father in developing homestead; made own way through coll.; Ped.B., State Normal Sch., Greeley, Colo., 1898; B.S., U. of Colo., 1901, M.S., 1902, LL.D., 1909; D.Sc., Univ. of Denver, 1914; LL.D., Colo. Coll., 1924; Ed.D., Colo. State Coll. of Education, 1934; D.Sc., Colo. State Coll., 1940; m. Carrie Louise Richards, June 8, 1904; children—Marion Richards, Earl Christian, Anna. Asst. in physics., U. of Colo., 1899-1902; prin. Cripple Creek High Sch., 1902-04; acting prof. Physics, U. of Colo., 1904-05; professor of physics, State Agricultural College (now Colorado State Univ.), Fort Collins, Colo., 1905-07, prof. elec. engring, 1907-09, pres., 1909-40, retired as pres. emeritus. Irrigation mgr. for U.S. Dept. Agr., summer, 1907; supt. Big Cut Lateral Reservoir Co., 6 summers; consultant Nat. Resources Planning Board, 1940-43. Director North Colo. Water Conservancy Dist., 1940-54; mem. Merit System Council of Colo., from 1942; Select. Service System Appeal Bd., Colo. Pres. Assn. Western Agrl. Colls., 1915; 1st v.p. Assn. Land Grant Colleges and Universities, 1909, 1917-18, pres. 1919, mem. exec. com., 1926-36 and 1937-40; pres. Assn. Colo. State Instns. of Higher Learning, 1926-40; chmn. U.S. Reclamation Repayment Commn., 1937-38. Mem. Colo. Council Defense, 1917-18. Pres. Colo. Conf. of Social Workers, 1923. Fellow A.A.A.S.; mem. Newcomen Soc., Colo. Ednl. Assn. (pres. 1925), Alpha Chapter Colo. Phi Beta Kappa, Sigma Xi, Phi Kappa Phi, Epsilon Sigma Phi, Delta Tau Delta. Mason (33 deg., K.T.). Clubs: Schoolmaster's, Rotary. Republican. Unitarian. Home: Estes Park CO Died Jan. 1970.

LOTHROP, FANNIE MACK, author; b. Decatur, Wis.; d. late Isaac Foster and Frances Pierpont (Day) Mack; Oberlin Coll., 1869-71; grad. Cook Co. Normal Coll., Chicago; studied music under I. V. Elagler, Severini, Mme. Canissa and others; m. Ivan B. Lothrop, Sept. 26, 1883. Owns the largest collection of portraits in the world comprising over 400,000 pictures of world celebrities. Author of many contributions in prose to mags. and periodicals, particulary on biog. subjects; asso. editor The Searchlight. Address: 106 W. 90th St., New York‡

LOTSPEICH, WILLIAM DOUGLAS, educator; b. Cin., May 30, 1920; s. Claude Meek and Helen Wilson (Gibbons) L.; A.B., Cornell U., 1941; M.D., U. Cin., 1944; m. Sylvia Howard Taft, June 13, 1942; children—Sylvia, Charles, Stephen. Intern N.Y. Hosp., Cornell Med. Center, 1944-45; instr. physiology Cornell U. Med. Coll., 1945-46; instr., asst. prof. Syracuse U., 1946-51, scholar in med. scis. of John and Mary Markle Found. of N.Y., 1948-52; vis. research fellow biochemistry Oxford U., Eng., 1949-51; Joseph Eichberg prof., chmn. dept. physiology U. Cin., 1951-59; prof., chmn. dept. of physiology, Sch. of Medicine and Dentistry, University of Rochester, 1959-67; exec. sec. designate Am. Friends Service Com., 1967-68; vis. prof. U. Lagos (Nigeria) Med. Sch., 1962. Mem. physiol. study sect. Nat. Insts. of Health, U.S. Public Health Service, 1955-60. Member Mayor's Friendly Relations Com., Cin., 1954-59, Am. Friend's Service Com., 1951-68, adv. council Life Ins. Med. Research Fund, 1957-61. Member board trustees Wilmington Coll., 1959-60. Mem. Am., British physiol. socs., Soc. for Exptl. Biology and Medicine, A.A.A.S., Mt. Desert Island Biol. Lab., Delta Upsilon, Alpha Omega Alpha, Sigma Xi. Mem. Soc. Friends. Clubs: Pundit (Rochester); Literary (Cin.). Author: Metabolic Aspects Renal Runction, 1960; How Scientists Find Out, pub. 1966; also author articles on physiology and exptl. medicine. Home: Philadelphia PA Died Nov. 28, 1968.

LOTT, ABRAHAM GRANT, army officer; b. Gettysburg, Pa., June 21, 1871; s. Jacob and Joanna (Houghtlin) L.; grad. high sch., Abilene, Kan., 1889, U.S. Mil. Acad., 1896, Army Sch. of the Line, 1911, Army Staff Coll., 1912, Army War Coll., 1923; m. Clara Buel Mercur, 1897. Commd. additional 2d lt. cav., U.S. Army, June 12, 1896; advanced through grades to brig. gen., Dec. 20, 1927; retired June 30, 1935. Served on the Western plains, in Cuba, the Philippines, Panama, France and Hawaii. Awarded D.S.M. (U.S.). Club: Army and Navy (Washington). Address: 1510 W. Huisache Av., San Antonio 1 TX‡

LOUCHHEIM, WALTER CLINTON, JR., investment cons.; b. Overbrook, Pa., Aug. 20, 1899; s. Walter C. and Francis (Appel) L.; student Princeton, 1916-18; B.A., Harvard, 1921; m. Kathleen Scofield, June 25, 1926;children—Mary (Mrs. Jerome Lieberthal), Judith (Mrs. J. Dudley Haupt). Engaged in investment banking, N.Y.C., 1921-31; with SEC, 1934-53; investment cons., Washington, 1953-73. Vice chmn. Nat. Capital Planning Commn., 1961-73; adviser U.S. delegation Bretton Woods Conf., 1944. Served with USNR, 1917-18. Clubs: Fed. City, City Tavern, Cosmos. Harvard (Washington). Home: Washington DC Died Jan. 31, 1973.

LOUCKS, ELTON CROCKER, found. exec.; b. Council Bluffs, Ia., June 2, 1892; s. Charles A. and Alice (Crocker) L.; student Reed Coll., 1912-13; B.A., U. Ore., 1915; student Harvard Grad. Sch. Bus. Adminstrn., 1917-18; m. Myrne Gilchrist, Mar. 27, 1923;children—John Gilchrist, Mary Jean (Mrs. Arlyn Neiswander), Barbara (Mrs. Alvin Berger), Patricia Myrne. Engaged in pub. accounting, 1923-69; partner firm John M. Gilchrist & Co., C.P.A.'s, Omaha, 1927-33, mng. partner, 1933-61; company merged with Peat, Marwick, Mitchell & Co., 1961, now cons.; pres. Eugene C. Eppley Found., Inc., Omaha, 1958-69, also dir. Chmn. adv. com. Grad. Sch. Hotel, Restaurant and Instl. Mgmt., Mich. State U. C.P.A., Neb. Mem. Am. Inst. C.P.A.'s, Neb. Soc. C.P.A.'s (past pres.), Phi Gamma Delta. Mason (Shriner). Clubs: Omaha (past dir.), Omaha Country (past dir.), Garden of Gods Omaha NE Died Feb. 11, 1969.

LOUD, JOHN HERMANN, organist, composer; b. Weymouth, Mass., Aug. 26, 1873; s. John Jacob and Emily Keith (Vickery) L.; grad. Thayer Acad., S. Braintree, 1893; student N.E. Conservatory of Music, 1889-90; studied in Germany, France and Eng., 1893-95; m. Myrta Elsa Fiske, Apr. 16, 1901; children—John Francis, Richard Fiske. Ch. and concert organist and teacher, Boston, since 1895; has appeared in leading cities of America; repertoire of more than 1,000 compositions; now organist and choirmaster, Park St. Ch., Boston. Fellow Am. Guild Organists (dean N.E. chapter, 1922-26); asso. Royal Coll. Music, London. Republican. Conglist. Home: 5 Strathmore Road, Brookline 46 MA‡

LOUIS, ANDREW, educator; b. Bklyn., July 5, 1907; s. Rudolf and Julia (Jurgens) L.; Ph.B., Wesleyan U., Middletown, Conn., 1929; student U. Marburg (Germany), 1929-30; Ph.D., Cornell U., 1935; m. Virginia O'Dell Gooch, Mar. 23, 1940 (div. May 1965); children—Andrew David, Julia Caroline. Instr. German, Cornell U., 1932-34, Colgate U., 1934-37; from instr. to asst. prof. German, U. Tex., 1937-46; mem. faculty Rice U., 1946-67, prof. German, chmn. dept., 1947-61, dir. modern langs. labs., 1962-66; vis. prof. U. Houston, 1961, 65. Served to capt. USAAF, World War II. Decorated Bronze Star. Mem. Modern Lang. Assn. Am., S. Central Modern Lang. Assn. (exec. sec. 1966-67), Am. Assn. Tchrs. German, Houston Council Tchrs. Fgn. Langs., Houston Philos. Soc., Phi Beta Kappa, Delta Sigma Rho, Delta Phi Alpha, Sigma Nu. Episcopalian. Author: German Grammer: An Houston TX Died Sept. 20, 1967; buried Veteran's Cemetery, Houston TX

LOUTHAN, HATTIE HORNER, author; b. Quincy, Ill., Feb. 5, 1865; d. Dr. John and Charity (White) Horner; grad. State Normal Sch., Emporia, Kan., June 1883; B.Pd. and B.Litt., Univ. of Denver, 1915, Doctor of Letters, College of Journalism, 1943; married Overton Earle Louthan, June 21, 1893 (died June 12, 1906). On staff Denver Republican; lit. editor The Great Southwest, monthly. Prof. of English and head of Dept. of English, U. of Denver, since Sept. 3, 1910, dean of women, 1918-24. Lecturer, English subjects, Law School, U. of Denver, Denver Women's Club and Register College of Journalism. Founder of the John Horner Reference Library, Denver, Dr. and Mrs. John Horner Memorial Essay Contest (annual, endowed; humane education subjects), Eldorado, Kan. Author: Poems, 1885; Some Reasons for Our Choice (ednl.), 1886; Not at Home (travels), 1889; Collection of Kansas Poetry, 1891; Thoughts Adrift, 1902; In Passion's Dragnet, 1904; This Was a ManThe Modern Business Letter, 1917; Business Rhetoric, 1921, 2d edit., 1932; Business Exposition, 1923; Short Story Craftsman, 1930, 2d edit., 1933; The Holy Shadow (novel), 1938; Alone in the Afterglow (poems), 1939; So Small (mostly quatrains), 1947. Contbr. to mags. and newspapers. Editor Western Pen Worker. Home: 3602 Raleigh St., Denver 12 CO‡

LOUTTIT, WILLIAM EASTON, JR., laundry and cleaning co. exec.; b. Cranston, R.I., May 26, 1904; s. William E. and Sophia (Robley) L.; Ph.B. (fellow), Brown U., 1925, L.H.D., 1955; m. Doris May Carpenter, Sept. 8, 1925; children—Zoe (Mrs. Ralph Finkbinder), William Easton III, Lorraine (Mrs. Kenneth D. Pettigrew). Chmn. bd., treas. Louttit

Laundry Co. Swiss Cleansing Co., Baybrink, Inc., Louttit Garage Co., Regal Cleansers, Lolaco Supply Co., Stork Service, E. & R. Co.; exec. v.p. What Cheer Laundry, Louttit Corp.; dir. Indsl. Nat. Bank, Merchants Cold Storage and Warehouse Co., Heat & Process Steam & Piping Co., Farview, Inc. Mem. emeritus bd. fellows Brown U.; bd. dirs. Swan Point Cemetery; bd. mgmt. John Carter Brown Library. Mem. Theta Delta Chi. Clubs: Hope, Turks Head, University (Providence); Odd Volumes (Boston); Grolier (N.Y.C.); Rowfant (Cleve.). Home: West Greenwich RI Died Mar. 2, 1973.

LOUW, ERIC HENDRIK, minister fgn. affairs S. Africa; b. Jacobsdal S. Africa, Nov. 21, 1890; s. J.A. and M.M. (de Villiers) L.; holds degrees: B.A., LL.B., D. Commerce; m. Anna Snyman, July 6, 1918;children—Jan, Martin. Practicing advocate 1916-18; comml. exec., 1918-24; mem. S. African Parliament, 1924-25, 38-68; mem. S. African Trade Commn. in N.Y., 1925-28; high commr., London, 1929; minister plenipotentiary, Washington, 1930-33, Rome, 1934, Paris, 1935-37; minister econ. affairs, 1948-54, minister of finance, 1955-56, minister external affairs, 1954-63. Rep. of S. Africa as mem. internat. confs., including League of Nations (twice), UN (nine times), also also at meetings of Internat. Monetary Fund, and Internat. Bank. Home: Pretoria S Africa Died June 24, 1968.

LOVATT, GEORGE IGNATIUS, architect; b. Phila., Pa., Feb. 13, 1872; s. Thomas Butler and Joanne Elizabeth (Finnegan) L.; ed. privately; m. Elizabeth Joanne Roken, Sept. 20, 1898; children—George Ignatius, Mary Regina (Mrs. J. Marxwell Smith), Edwin J. Student in office of Prichett & Smith, 1888-90; student, draftsman with Adrian Worthington Smith, 1890-96; practice (splty. Ecclesiastical Work), 1896-1900; in private practice 1900-40; entered into partnership with son George L. Lovatt, Jr., in 1940. Awarded Medal of the Phila. Chapter of A.I.A., 1931, for Ecclesiastical Design. Fellow A.I.A. (past pres., Phila. Chapter). Home: 49 W. La Crosse Av., Landsdowne, Pa. Address: 1500 Walnut St., Philadelphia PA

LOVE, ALBERT GALLATIN, med. officer U.S. Army; b. Trezevant, Tenn., July 31, 1877; s. Albert Gallatin and Rosa L. (Patton) L.; A.B., U. of Miss., 1899; M.D., Memphis Hosp. Med. Coll., 1904; hon. grad. and medalist, U.S. Army Med. Sch., Washington, D.C., 1906; grad. Advanced Course, same, 1927; D.P.H., Johns Hopkins U., 1928; grad. Advanced Course, U.S. Army Med. Field Service Sch., Carlisle Barracks, Pa., 1930; m. Alice T. Stone, Dec. 3, 1906; children—Alice Elizabeth, Rosa Margaret, Albert Gallatin. Contract surgeon U.S. Army, Sept. 22, 1905; 1st lt. M.C., June 20, 1906; promoted through grades to col., June 20, 1932; lt. col. (temp.), 1918-20; brigadier general (temp.), October 1940-June 1941; active duty, August 1941-March 1946; promoted to brig. general retired August 16, 1948. Fellow Am. Coll. Surgs.; mem. A.M.A., Assn. Mil. Surgeons, Delta Omega. Democrat. Presbyterian. Mason. Author: Physical Examination First Million Draft Recruits—Methods and Results (with Charles B. Davenport), 1919; Defects Found in Drafted Men (with same), 1920; Army Anthropology (with same), 1921; Medical and Casualty Statistics of the United States Army in the World War, 1925; War Casualties, Their Relation to Medical Service and Replacements, 1931; Physical Measurements—Their Relation to Health, 1932; The Geneva Red Cross Movement, European and American Influence on Its Development, 1942; all Govt. publs. Home: 2709 Wisconsin Av., Washington 7 DC‡

LOVE, ALBERT IRVING, corp. exec.; b. Walterborn, S.C., June 16, 1905; s. A.I. and Tillie (Barth) L.; student The Citadel, 1924; B.A., U.S.C., 1926; m. Julia E. Shiver, Dec. 21, 1935; children—Judith (Mrs. Farris P. Hotchkiss), Diane (Mrs. Gary B. Crocker), Elizabeth. Various positions in pub. field, from 1933; mng. partner Albert Love Enterprises, 1939-61; pres. Albert Love Enterprises, Inc., from 1961; pres. Foote & Davies, Inc., Atlanta, 1944-63, Foote & Davies, 1963-65; v.p. McCall Corp., N.Y., from 1963; exec. v.p. McCall Printing Division, New York City, from 1966; president Tupper & Love, Incorporated, 1951-60, chairman board, from 1960; member board of dirs. Plimpton Press, Norwood, Mass., March Plantation, Inc., U.S. Timber & Land, Inc., Chisholm Plantation, Inc. (all Walterboro, S.C.), Security Fed. Savs. & Loan Assn. Atlanta, Ga. Peoples Life Ins. Co. Trustee Fine Arts Found. of Atlanta, Oglethorpe U.; adv. council Clarke Coll. Mem. People-to-People Sports Committee, Incorporated, Atlanta Traffic and Safety Council, Atlanta Freight Bur., A.I.M. (president's council), Printing Industry Am., Ga., Atlanta chambers commerce, Atlanta Art Assn., Atlanta Hist. Soc., Newcomen Soc. Am. Clubs: Commerce, Standard Town and Country, Shakerag Hounds, Atlanta Hunt (Atlanta); Dogwood Hills Country, March Hunt (Walterboro, S.C.); Daytona Beach (Fla.) Yacht. Home: Atlanta GA Died June 23, 1971; buried Walterboro SC

LOVE, CORNELIUS RUXTON, JR., stock broker; b. Bklyn., Nov. 11, 1903; s. Cornelius R. and Grace Anderson (Smith) L.; B.A. cum laude, Yale, 1925; m. Audrey Josephthal, Sept. 8, 1928; children—Noel Love, Iris. Mem. Diplomatic Service, Peking, China, 1927-28; mem. N.Y. Stock Exchange, 1930-71; partner Josephthal & Co., N.Y.C., 1929-71. Mem. Alpha Delta Phi. Clubs: Racquet and Tennis (N.Y.C.); Elizabethan (New Haven); Coral Reef (Coconut Grove); Surf (Miami Beach); Key Biscayne Yacht Vizcayans (Miami). Home: New York City NY ALSO Greenwich CT and Key Biscayne, FL Died Sept. 4, 1971.

LOVE, EDWARD BAINBRIDGE, lawyer; b. Hattiesburg, Miss., Sept. 11, 1906; s. Elihu Bay Gaston and Elizabeth Arlone (Maddux) L.; A.B., U. Mich., 1931, J.D., 1934; m. Geraldeane Virginia Smith, June 13, 1931;children—Mary (Mrs. Paul D. Brown), John Charles, David Maddux. Admitted to Mich. and Ill. bars; pvt. practice, Oxford, Mich., 1934, Monmouth, Ill., 1934; sr. partner Love, Beal & Pratt Mem. adv. council legal publs. U. Ill. Law Sch., 1950-53; chmn. joint com. for 1970 constitution and merit judge selection Ill. and Chgo. bar assns. Bd. govs. Ill. Rep. Citizens League, 1961-65. Exec. bd. Ill. area council YMCA, 1948-49. Mem. Am. (ho. dels. 1960-62), Ill. (bd. govs.; 1948-51, 53. secr., 1953-59, pres. 1960-61, chmn. retirement benefits for lawyers com.), Minn., N.D., Chgo., Mich., Warren County (pres. 1956-57, 71-72) bar assns., Am. Judicature Soc., Am. Law Inst., Nat. Assn. Bar Assn. Presidents, Am. Trial Lawyers Assn., Internat. Acad. Law and Sci., Monmouth C. of C. Home: Monmouth IL Died July 9, 1972.

LOVE, JAMES SANFORD, JR., hotel and television exec.; b. Hattiesburg, Miss., Apr. 28, 1910; s. James Sanford and Lillie (Bufkin) L.; student U. Miss.; LL.B., Cumberland U.; m. Joe Ellis Buie, Aug. 20, 1932; children—Mrs. R.A. Little, Mrs. Howard McMillan, James Sanford III. Pres., J.S. Love Co., Jackson, Miss.; pres. Lakewood Meml. Park, Jackson; pres. Hotel Buena Vista, Inc., Biloxi, Miss.; pres. WLOX TV Broadcasting Co., Biloxi. Chmn. Biloxi Cancer Drive; chmn. Heart Fund Drive. Bd. dirs. Miss. Childrens Home Soc. Mem. Am. (past dir.), Miss. (past pres.), Miss Coast hotel assns., Hotel Sales Mgrs. Assn., Newcomen Soc., Sigma Chi. Lion. Address: Biloxi MS Died Mar. 1972.

LOVE, JULIAN PRICE, clergyman, educator; b. Lexington, Ky., June 10, 1894; s. John Haviland and Carrie (Price) L.; A.B magna cum laude, Miami U., 1915, D.D., 1933; A.M., U. of Cincinnati, 1917, Ph.D., 1930; B.D., Lane Theol. Sem., 1918; m. Evelyn C. Linder, Aug. 6, 1925; children—Bruce Webster, Paul Linder. Ordained Presbyn. minister, 1918; pastor Fourth Ch., Dayton, O., 1918-21; prof. N.T. lang. and lit., Lane Theol. Sem., 1921-31; prof. English Bible, Louisville Presbyn. Sem., 1931-39, prof. Biblical theology, 1931-64, acting pres., 1964-66. Mem. National Association of Biblical Instrs., Phi Beta Kappa. Author: How to Read the Bible; The Missionary Message of the Bible, The Gospel and the Gospels; The Layman's Bible Commentary, vol. 25; In Quest of a Ministry. Member bd. editors, The Westminster Study Bible. Home: Louisville KY Died May 12, 1969; buried Wesleyan Cemetery, Cincinnati OH

LOVEJOY, JOHN MESTON, petroleum corp. executive; b. N.Y.C., July 1889; s. John F. and Abbie (Babson) L.; E.M., Columbia School of Mines, 1911; hon. D.Sc., Colby Coll., 1937; m. Leslie Mackintosh, Nov. 1920; children—Leslie (Mrs. John Scott Paine), John Stuart. Began business career as mining engineer; in oil business with Standard Oil Company, 1914, as geologist; v.p. and gen. mgr. Amerada Petroleum; was geologist Tex. Oil Co.; chmn. and pres. Seaboard Oil Co, of Del., 1930-54; director Drilling and Exploration Co., Inc. 1st lt., later capt. F.A., United States Army, 1917-19. Director, treasurer Nat. Multiple Sclerosis Society. Member American Inst. Mining and Metall. Engrs. (dir. and past pres.), Am. Petroleum Inst. (dir.), Am. Assn. of Petroleum Geologists, Nat. Petroleum Council. Clubs: University, Mining (New York); Round Hill, Indian Harbor Yacht Greenwich CT Died Nov. 1968.

LOVELL, WALTER RALEIGH, clergyman, editor; b. Pilot Mountain, N.C., June 7, 1890; s. Jesse and Lightford (Pace) L.; student Bennett Coll., 1914-17, U. Ore., 1928-32; B.A., D.D., Livingstone Coll., 1912; m. Hera Drusilla Blakey, Mar. 8, 1963; children by previous marriage Ida Lightford, Constance Barnet (Mrs. Robert Roberts), Walter Raleigh, Jesse Edward. Ordained to ministry A.M.E. Zion Ch., 1914; pastor in N.C. Cal. and Ore., 1914-39; editor Star of Zion, ofcl. ch. publn., 1939-68; tchr. Latin and alegebra Stephens-Lee Jr. High Sch., Asheville, N.C., 1914-22. Presiding elder Cal. Conf. A.M.E. Zion Ch., 1935-39. Mem. Alpha Phi Alpha. Democrat. Author: (poetry) Lyrics of Love. Editor Lovell Series. Home: Charlotte NC Died Nov. 16, 1968; buried Lovell's Chapel Cemetery, Pilot Mountain NC

LOVERIDGE, BLANCHE GROSBEC, educator; b. Watseka, Iroquois Co., Ill., Sept. 26, 1871; d. Eugene Fenwick and Elizabeth (Mather) L.; Ph.B., U. of Chicago, 1903, A.M., 1913. Began as teacher rural schs., Lake Co., Ill., later in pub. schs., Chicago; was prin. high sch., Fargo, N.D., later dean of women, Denison U., and U. of Ala.; founder and pres. Elizabeth Mather Coll., Atlanta, Ga. Lecturer on vocational edn. Clubs: Woman's, College Women's, Writers' and Univ. of Chicago. Address: Elizabeth Mather College, Atlanta GA‡

LOVET-LORSKI, BORIS, sculptor; b. Lithuania, Russia, December 25, 1894; s. Ilyia Brois and Anna (Kournoff) L.; student, Acad. of Art, St. Petersburg, Russia. Came to U.S., naturalized, 1925. Held one-man exhbns. of sculpture in Boston, N.Y., Washington, Chgo., Kansas City, Los Angeles, Santa Barbara, San Francisco, Seattle, etc. Rep. in permanent collections: Brit. Mus., London; Luxembourg and Petit Palais, Metropolitan Mus., N.Y. City; Columbia U.; Boston U.; Museums, Seattle, Wash., Rockford, Ill., San Diego, Los Angeles, etc. Executed: heroic statue of Abraham Lincoln as young lawyer for city of Decatur, Ill., 1946; heroic head in bronze of Franklin D. Roosevelt for city of Paris, France, 1949, monumental busts of Charles DeGaulle, Dwight D. Eisenhower, John Foster Dulles in Paris, 1959; sculpture for U.S. War Meml., Manila, 1954-56; heroic bronze head of John Foster Dulles for Washington Internat. Airport, 1963; heroic bronze bust of John F. Kennedy for Brandeis U., 1965. Decorated Chevalier Legion of Honor. Fellow Nat. Sculpture Soc.; mem. Am. Soc. French Legion of Honor, Nat. Acad. Design. Russian Orthodox. Clubs: Lotos. Author: Lithographs of Lovet-Lorski. 1929; Tribute to Woman (text by John Erskine); Sculpture, Lovet-Lorski; 1930. Home: New York City NY Died Mar. 1973.

LOVETTE, JOYCE METZ, lawyer; b. N.Y.C., Jan. 1, 1924; d. Sigmund and Mimi (Silber) Metz; B.A., Queens Coll., 1945; LL.B., Columbia, 1947; m. Eugene S. Lovette, Jan. 25, 1945; children—Bradford, Spencer, Clifford. Admitted to N.Y. bar, 1948, U.S. Supreme Ct., 1964, U.S. Ct. of Claims, 1964, U.S. Ct. Appeals, 1966; partner Metz & Lovette, N.Y.C., 1949-68. Sec. Mobo Toys, Inc., 1947-68, dir. 1947-68; sec. Token Importers, 1951-68; dir. Commoys of London, Inc. Chmn. Fluoridation Com., Westbury, N.Y., 1952; bd. dirs. Ch. of Advent Nursery Sch., 1959-61; v.p. Westbury Gen. P.T.A., 1959-60; bd. dirs. League Women Voters, Westbury, 1953-57. Mem. Nat. Assn. Women Lawyers (N.Y. state del. 1964-66), Nassau County Women's Bar Assn., Columbia U. Alumni Assn., Queens Coll. Alumni Assn., Internat. Fedn. Women Lawyers, Am. Bar Assn., Upsilon Phi. Mem. Ch. of the Advent. Westbury NY Died Mar. 8, 1968; interred Nassau Knolls Port Washington NY

LOVETTE, LELAND PEARSON, ret. naval officer, author; b. Greeneville, Tenn., Dec. 11, 1897; s. Oscar Byrd and Lillie (Fowler) L.; student Tusculum Coll., 1913-14; B.S., U.S. Naval Acad., 1917; certificate Naval War Coll., 1928; student Georgetown U. Sch. Fgn. Service, 1928-29; student langs. Berlitz and Sanz schs.; LL.D., Tusculum College, 1959; m. Charmian K. Brietson, May 26, 1925. Commissioned ensign USN, 1917, advanced through grades to vice admiral; served on staffs commander mine force, commander battle ship divisions, commander battle force, comdr.-in-chief Asiatic fleet; commander subchasers, mine-sweeper, gunboats, destroyers and battle cruiser, World War II; officer charge pub. relations Navy Dept., 1937-40; comdg. squadron leader and destroyer div., 1940; dir. pub. relations USN, 1942-44; chief of United States Naval Mission to Brazil, 1946-48; ret., 1949; dir. pub. relations Vets. Fgn. Wars, 1949-55, cons. Pres. United Cerebral Palsy chpt. Washington; mem. sr. bd. govs. U.S.O., Washington. Trustee Jackson Meml. Lab. for Cancer Research. Decorated Legion of Merit (2); Order Brit. Empire; grand officer Naval Merit (Brazil); Medal Merite Combattant (France); recipient gold medal U.S. Naval Inst.; nat. citation Veterans of Foreign Wars, United Cerebral Palsy. Member Presbyn. Ch. Clubs: New York Yacht (N.Y.C.); Army-Navy (Manila, P.I.); Army-Navy, Cosmos, Nat. Press (Washington); Friends of Lafayette. Author: Naval Customs, Traditions and Usage, 1934; School of the Sea; Annapolis Tradition in American Life, 1941, also numerous articles. Home: Alexandria, VA Died July 10, 1967; buried Arlington Nat. Cemetery.

LOVRE, HAROLD O., lawyer; born in Toronto, S.D., Jan. 30, 1904; grad. Toronto High Sch., 1922; student St. Olaf, Northfield, Minn., 2 yrs.; LL.B., U. of S.D., 1927; m. Viola Florell, 1928; children—Janice Ann, Carmen Nedra, Sandra Mae, Linda Kay. Practiced law, Hayti, S.D., 1927-44, Watertown, S.D., 1944-54, state senator, 1941-44; mem. 81st to 84th Congresses, 1st S.D. Dist.; practiced law Washington, from 1957. Chmn. Rep. State Central Com., 1946, 47. Mem. Lambda Chi Alpha, Phi Delta Phi. Lutheran (chmn. council). Mason (Shriner, 32 deg.), Elk. Home: Kensington MD Died Jan. 17, 1972; buried Parklawn Cemetery, Silver Spring MD

LOWE, DONALD VAUGHN, paper industry exec.; b. Fitchburg, Mass., Feb. 13, 1891; s. Herbert George and Mary Adelaide (Vaughn) L.; Chem. Eng., Columbia, 1911; post grad. Charlottenburg (Germany) Univ., 1912; extension work, Columbia and Rutgers U.; m. Charlotte Foxwell Werner, Dec. 1, 1917; children—Betsy (Mrs. F. Waring Burke), Patricia (Mrs.

Savage Frieze, Jr.), Nancy (Mrs. Donald McBride, Jr.), Mary Jane (Mrs. William G. Nagle). President of the Lowe Paper Co., Ridgefield, N.J., 1942-63, chairman board, 1964-69, also dir.; dir. N.J. Mfrs. Ins. Cos. Commr., former chmn. Port of New York Authority. Former N.J. chmn. of the Citizens' Com. for the Hoover Report. Chmn. exec. com., Engineering Council of Columbia U., vice chmn. council, 1963-66, chmn., from 1966. Served as 1st lt., nitrate div., Ordance Dept., U.S. Army, World War I. Served on casein industry adv. com., W.P.B., World War II. Pres. Dwight Sch., Englewood, N.J., 1942-50; chmn. Bergen Co. Vocational Adv. Council, 1943. Mem. exec. com., past pres., former dir. Bergen County YMCA. Recipient Egleston medal Columbia, 1962, Alumni medal, 1966. Member of American Pulp and Paper Association (past member bd. of govs.), Palisades Nature Assn., Bergen County C. of C. (exec. com., past pres.), Ridgefield (past pres.), N.J. (trustee) mfrs. assns., N.J. Council on Econ. Edn. (dir.), Pan-Am. Soc. U.S., Tau Beta Pi, Sigma Chi. Republican (conv. del., 1944, 48; com. chmn. Bergen County 1938-48). Presbyn. Clubs: Columbia University, Knickerbocker Country; Norfolk Country, Doolittle Lake; Essex (Newark). Home: Tenafly NJ Died Dec. 10, 1969.

LOWE, ELIAS AVERY, palaeographer; b. Oct. 15, 1879; s. Charles and Sarah (Ragoler) L.; student Coll. of City of New York, 1894-97; A.B., Cornell U., 1902; grad. study at Halle; Ph.D., U. of Munich, 1907; D.Litt. (hon.), Oxford; fellow American School at Rome, 1908-10; hon. LL.D., Univ. of North Carolina, 1946; m. Helen Tracy Porter, Feb. 8, 1911 (dec.); children—Prudence Holcombe (dec.), Frances Beatrice, Patricia Tracy. Lecturer in paleography, Oxford U., Eng., since 1913, reader since 1927; Sandars reader, Cambridge U., 1914; asso. in paleography, Carnegie Instn., Washington, from 1911; prof. paleography, Inst. for Advanced Study, Princeton, since 1936; consultant in paleography, Library of Congress; hon. fellow Corpus Christi Coll.; Chichele lectr. All Souls, Oxford, 1961. Recipient Haskins medal, Medieval Acad. Am.; Gold medal award, Biblog. Soc., London, 1959. Fellow Medieval Acad. Am., Am. Acad. Arts and Sci., Brit. Acad. (corr.); mem. Phi Beta Kappa, Hispanic Soc. Am.; corresponding member Acad. of History of Madrid, Bayerische Akademie der Wissenschaften, Accademia dei Lincei, Rome, Inst. France; hon. mem. Royal Irish Acad., Dublin. Club: Authors. Author: Scriptura Beneventana, English Uncial, and Codices Latini Antiquiores, 12 vols. numerous books since 1908; contributor to learned publications. Address: Oxford England Died Aug. 8, 1969; buried Corpus Christi College, Oxford Eng

LOWE, FRANK E., army officer; b. Springfield, Mass., Sept. 20, 1885; s. George and Mary (Jackson) L.; B.S., Worcester (Mass.) Poly. Inst., 1908; m. Rachel Lowell, Nov. 22, 1911. Veteran of World Wars I and II. Maj. gen Officers Res. Corps. Mem. Reserve Officers Assn. of U.S. Am. Legion, Phi Gamma Delta. Clubs: Cumberland (Portland, Me.); Army and Navy (Washington, D.C.). Address: Harrison ME Died Dec. 27, 1968; buried Hope Cemetery, Worcester MA

LOWE, JOE, food mfr.; b. Syracuse, N.Y., Oct. 18, 1883; s. Sigmund and Bertha (Wiseman) L.; grad. Syracuse High Sch.; m. Emily Lynch, Mar. 17, 1943. Co-founder, pres. Joe Lowe Corp., 1902, 1906—; mem. bd. dirs. Fruit Products Corporation, N.Y.C. Co-donor Lowe Art Center, Syracuse U., Lowe Gallery, U. Miami, 1950; treas. Joe and Emily Lowe Found., N.Y.C.; trustee Lowe Gallery, U. Miami, Coral Gables, Fla., Hudson Guild Settlement House, N.Y.C.; co-owner Emily Lowe Hall at Hofstra University. Member Southern Bakers Assn., Bakers Club. Mason (32 deg., Shriner). Club: Beach Point (Mamaroneck, N.Y.). Home: New York City NY Died Oct. 1969.

LOWE, LOUIS ROBERT, lawyer; b. Greensburg, Ind., Aug. 28, 1906; s. Marsh and Grace (Barlow) L.; B.S. in Civil Engring., Purdue U., 1928; LL.B., Benjamin Harrison Law Sch. (now Ind. U.), 1935; m. Madelyn Markley, Sept. 6, 1929; children—Nancy (Mrs. David Kriplen), Louis Robert. Admitted to Ind. bar, 1934, since practiced in Indpls.; partner Dowden, Denny, Daughran & Lowe, 1954-68; dir., sec., treas. Contrn. Products Corp., Indpls., 1953-68; dir., pres. Irvington Plaza Corp., Indpls., Trustee Purdue U., Long Coll., Hanover, Ind. Mem. Am., Ind., Indpls., 7th Circuit bar assns., English Speaking Union. (dir., sec. 1949-68), Phi Delta Theta. Republican. Presbyn. Mason. Home: Indianapolis IN Died Aug. 1968.

LOWE, LOUISE, physician; b. N.Y.C., Sept. 17, 1905; d. Albert William and Caroline (Rau) Klein; B.C.S., N.Y.U., 1926, A.B., 1937; M.D., State U. N.Y. Coll. Medicine at N.Y.C., 1941; m. Boutelle E. Lowe, June 28, 1926. Intern L.I. Coll. Hosp., Bklyn., 1941-42; intern Hackensack (N.J.) Hosp., 1942-43, attending thoracic surgery, 1946-69, asst. attending surgery, 1947-69; resident surgery Norwegian Luth. Deaconess Home and Hosp., Bklyn., 1943; resident thoracic surgery Bellevue Hosp., N.Y.C., 1944; practice medicine, specializing thoracic surgery and surgery, Hackensack, 1945-69; asst. attending thoracic surgery Queens Gen. Hosp., Jamaica, L.I., 1949-51, Triboro Hosp., Jamaica, L.I., 1949-51; attending surgery Bergen Pines Hosp., Paramus, N.J. Fellow Am. Coll. Chest Physicians; mem. A.M.A., Am. Med. Women's Assn., Trudeau Soc., Phi Beta Kappa. Republican. Hasbrouck Heights NJ Died Aug. 11, 1969; interred George Washington Meml. Park Paramus NJ

LOWE, MALCOLM BRANSON, paper co. exec.; b. Fitchburg, Mass., May 21, 1892; s. Herbert George and Mary (Vaughn) L.; C.E., Princeton, 1913; postgrad. N.Y.U., 1914-15; M. Florence Pruden, May 21, 1921; children—Malcolm Branson, Gordon V., Prudence Ann (Mrs. Harold F. Miller, Jr.). With Lowe Paper Co., Ridgefield, N.J., 1913-71, v.p., dir., 1943-60, dir., chmn. bd., 1960-64, dir. hon. chmn., 1964-71; pres. Ridgefield Nat. Bank, 1934-59, dir., 1921-59; dir., chmn. exec. com. Nat. Community Bank, Rutherford, N.J., 1959-71. Trustee Boxboard Research & Devel., 1958-60. Served as 2d lt. U.S. Army, 1917-19. Mem. Folding Paper Box Mfrs. Assn. (past pres.), Cardboard Mfrs. Assn. (past pres.), Am. Paper and Pulp Assn. (past bd. govs.), Speciality Paper and Board Affiliates (past pres.), Nat. Paperboard Assn. (trustee), N.J. (past mem. exec. com.), Bergen County (past pres.) bankers assns., Princeton U. Alumni Assn. No. N.J. (pres. class 1913). Republican. Presbyn. (deacon, trustee). Mason (Shriner). Clubs: Princeton, University (N.Y.C.); Englewood (N.J.); Nassau, Charter of Princeton University (Princeton, N.J.); Nat. Golf Links Am. (Southampton, N.Y.). Home: Tenafly NJ Died Sept. 6, 1971; buried Brookside Cemetery, Englewood NJ

LOWE, RICHARD BARRETT, former gov.; b. Madison, S.D., July 8, 1902; s. Dr. William and Edna (Beck) L.; B.S. in Edn., Eastern State Tchrs. Coll., S.D., 1929; A.M., U. S.D., 1938; Ed. D., Ottawa U., 1942; student U. Wis., Defiance Coll., Peabody Coll. for Tchrs.; m. Emma Louise Anderson, June 17, 1925; children—Bruce A., Cameron A. Rural and elementary sch. tchr.; managed a store; supt. of schs., Alcester, S.D., Wessington Springs, S.D., Yankton, S.D., 1929-41; lectr. edn. U. S.D.; pres. Sioux Falls Coll., 1941-43. Comdr. U.S.N.R.; commanding officer Navy V-12 Units, Peru State Tchrs. Coll., U. Neb., and Creighton U.; edn. and religion officer of Mil. Govt., Tinian, Marianas Islands; dean Peru State Tchrs. Coll., 1946; dir. sch. and coll. relations for Navy Recruiting Service, 1947-53; gov. of Am. Samoa, 1953-56, Guam, 1956-60; cons. Office Civil and Def. Mobilization, 1960-61; ofcl. UN observer and liaison for N.E.A., 1962-64; cons. Nat. Council for Social Studies, 1964-66. Mem. exec. com. Conf. Group U.S. Nat. Orgn. on UN, 1963. Chmn. Beadle Centennial Com. and represented S.D. at installation Beadle Statue in Nat. Statuary Hall, 1938; pres. S.D. Sunday Sch. Conv., 1940, 41, Trustee Sr. Citizens of Am. Recipient Friend of Year award Filipino Community of Guam, 1958; Presdl. Commendation. Mem. S.D. Edn. Assn. (pres. 1938), N.E.A., S.D. Hist. Soc., S.D. State Soc. Washington (pres. 1966), Beadle Club. Republican. Mason. Club: Army and Navy (Washington). Author: Heroes and Hero Tales, 1931; Twenty Million Acres, 1936; Problems in Paradise-The View from Government House, 1967. Wrote scenario and directed motion picture, Dacotah 1929; Developed U.S. Navy Occupational Handbook for Men, 1948, U.S. Navy Occupational Handbook for Women, 1952. Development Navy Recruiting Policy for Schools, 1947. Home: Alexandria VA Died Apr. 16, 1972; buried Madison SD

LOWE, STANLEY, dir. athletics; b. Appleton, Wis., Aug. 24, 1903; s. John J. and Bridget (Powers) L.; B.S. in Bus. Adminstrn., Marquette U., 1925; m. Hazel Wistron; children—Robert J., Catherine J. (Mrs. James Karolzak), Peter C., Mary A. (Mrs. Gerald Fetherston), Stanley J.; m. 2d, Helen M. Brill, Apr. 19, 1958. With Marquette U., Milw., 1924-69, bus. mgr. athletics, 1947-62, asst. dir. athletics, 1962-64, dir. athletics, 1964-69. Mem. Coll. Athletic Bus. Mgrs. Assn., Nat. Assn. Coll. Dirs. Athletics, Wis. Cath. Interscholastic Athletic Assn. (named Man of Year 1966), Central Collegiate Conf. (sec.-treas. 1937-69). Roman Catholic. Clubs: Milwaukee Athletic, Marquette M. (exec. sec., 1946-69), Marquette University Faculty (pres. 1962), Marquette University Quarter Century (pres. 1964-65) (Milw.). Home: Milwaukee WI Died Aug. 16, 1969.

LOWENSTEIN, MELVYN GORDON, lawyer; b. Cincinati, Mar. 30, 1892; s. David and Jennie (Goldsmith) L.; LL.B., U. Cincinnati, 1914; m. Katherine Goldsmith, Nov. 17, 1925; children—James Gordon, Hugh Price, Peter David. Admitted to Ohio bar, 1913, N.Y. bar, 1920; asst. corp. counsel, Cincinnati, 1914-17; adv. commn. Council Nat. Def., Washington, 1917; general counsel Whitman & Ransom. Dir. Benrus Corporation. The Harman Corporation, Parents' Mag. Enterprises, Inc. Dir. Am. Parents' Com., The Children's Village; trustee Goldsmith Found., Inc. Served as ensign U.S. Navy, 1918. Mem. Am., N.Y. State, bar assns., N.Y. County Lawyers Assn., Assn. Bar City of N.Y., Internat. Law Assn., World Peace Through Law Center. Mason (32 deg.). Clubs: City Mid-Day, Regency, Economic (N.Y.C.); Century Country (Purchase, N.Y.). Home: Greenwich CT Died Sept. 5, 1971.

LOWMAN, HARMON, coll. pres.; b. Staples, Tex., Nov. 30, coll. pres.; b. Staples, Tex., Nov. 30, 1894; s. Quincy Joseph and Mellie (Scott) L.; student Coronal Inst., San Marcos, Tex., 1909-11, Washington and Lee U., 1915-17; A.B., S.W. Tex. State Teachers Coll., 1924; A.M., U. of Tex., 1925; Ph.D., U. of Chicago, 1930; m. Marguerite Hightower, April 6, 1918; children—Harmon L., Bill J. Teacher rural schs., Tex., 1921-25; dir. Demonstration Sch., Stephen Austin State Teachers Coll., Nacogdoches, 1925-27, prof., 1927-36; supt., Livingston Schs., 1936-37; supt., Goose Creek Schs., and pres., Lee Jr. Coll., 1937-40; exec. sec. Southern Meth. U., 1940-41; pres. Sam Houston State Teachers Coll. from 1941. Served as 1st lt., 345th F.A., 90th Div., with A.E.F., 1917-19. Decorated by U.D.C., 1938. Mem. Tex. State Teachers Assn., N.E.A., Phi Delta Kappa, Kappa Delta Phi. Methodist. Club: Rotary (Huntsville, Tex.). Author: History of Teacher Training in the Gulf States. Home: Huntsville TX Deceased.

LOWNDES, CHARLES HENRY TILGHMAN, physician, naval officer (ret.); b. Baltimore, Md., July 7, 1866; s. Dr. Charles and Mary Catherine (Tilghman) L.; student Johns Hopkins U.; M.D., U. of Md.; m. Mary Lucien Baker, Feb. 21, 1900; 1 son, Charles Lucien. Began as physician, 1888; entered in service of Med. Corps, U.S. Navy, as asst. surgeon, 1889, advanced through various grades to appt. as rear adm., Med. Dept., 1919; retired, 1929. Democrat. Catholic. Club: Army and Navy (Washington). Author: Reports on Results of Indian Conditions on Various Reservations; contbr. articles to med. publs. Home: Easton, Md. Office: The Fairfax, Washington DC*‡

LOWNSBERY, CHARLES HATCH, artist; b. Oxford, N.Y., May 24, 1910; s. Benjamin Ferris and Frances (Lakin) L.; grad. Pratt Inst., 1931; m. Anne Elizabeth Grimes, May 22, 1965. Comml. designer pvt. studio, Roslyn Heights, N.Y., 1964-69; exhibited in one man shows at Arts Club Washington, 1954, Burr Galleries, N.Y.C., 1963, Bryant Library, 1967-68, Hempstead, 1968; exhibited in group shows at Am. Artists Profl. League, 1958, 62, Am. Miniature Soc's. Ann. Corcoran Gallery, Washington, 1958. Chmn. East Hills Nonprofl. Art Shows, 1969. Bd. dirs. Burr Artists (N.Y.C.). Sec. treas. Norgate Civic Association. Mem. S.A.R., So. Soc., Composers, Authors and Artists Am. Episcopalian. Address: Roslyn Heights NY Died Dec. 16, 1969.

LOWRIE, WALTER, clergyman; b. Phila., Apr. 26, 1868; s. Samuel Thompson and Elizabeth A. (Dickinson) L.; A.B., Princeton, 1890, A.M., 1893, D.D., 1930; Princeton Theol. Sem., 1890-93, U. of Griefswald, 1893-94, U. of Berlin, 1894; fellow Am. Sch. Classical Studies, Rome, 1895-96, and 1889-1900; m. Barbara Armour, 1918. Deacon, 1895, priest, 1897. Protestant Episcopal Church; rector Trinity, Southwark, Phila., 1903-04, Trinity Ch., Newport, 1905-07, St. Paul's Am. Ch., Rome, 1907-30. Honorary canon of Trinity Cathedral, Trenton. Decorated: Knight of Dannsbrog (Danish Order), 1948. Author: The Doctrine of St. John, 1899; Monuments of the Early Ch., 1901; The Church and Its Organization, 1904; Gaudium Crucis, 1905; Abba, Father, 1908; Problems of Church Unity, 1924; Fifty Years of St. Paul's Church, and The Birth of the Divine Child, 1926; Jesus According to St. Mark, 1929; Religion or Faith, 1930; Our Concern with the Theology of Crisis, Kiekegaard, 1937; SS. Peter and Paul in Rome, 1940; A Short Life of Kierkegaard, 1942; The Short Story of Jesus, The Lord's Supper and the Liturgy, 1943; Gustav Theodor Fechner; Art In the Early Church, 1947; also translations (12 vols. from Kierkegaard's works). Address: 83 Stockton St., Princeton NJ‡

LOWRY, EDITH C., educator; B.A., Mt. Holyoke Coll.; M.A., Radcliffe; Ph.D., Oxford (Eng.) U. Asso. prof. history Sweet Briar (Va.) Coll. Home: Perkinsville VT Died Mar. 11, 1970.

LOWRY, FRANK CLIFFORD, business exec.; born Philadelphia, Oct. 30, 1878; s. Charles Stokes and Millie J. (Server) L.; ed. Adelphia Acad., Phila.; m. Harriett Livingston James, Apr. 14, 1904; children—Harriett Livingston, Charles Stokes. With Smith & Schipper, 1900-04; gen. sales mgr. Federal Sugar Refining Co., 1904-16; partner Smith & Schipper, gen. agents Federal Sugar Refining Co., 1916-21; partner E. Atkins & Co., 1921; pres. Lowry & Co., Inc., N.Y. City, 1926-50; pres. South P.R. Sugar Trading Corp., 1950-54; pres. N.Y. Coffee & Sugar Exch., Inc., 1927-29, mem. bd. mgrs., 1926-29; pres. Warner Sugar Corp. 1930-31, directed affairs for Bondholders and Trust., 1933-45; pres. and dir. Lowry Securities Corp. (Lowry Sugar Corp.), 1929-44, Lowry & Co., Ltd., Havana, 1925-48; dir. South P.R. Sugar Co. (N.J.), from 1928, chmn. exec. com., 1950-55; dir. Hanover Fire Ins. Co., Fulton Ins. Co. Trustee Mountainside Hosp., 1937-52, pres., 1948-52. Mem. budget com. Montclair Community Chest, 1924-31, 1939-42. Clubs: Union League, Down Town, Montclair Golf (past pres.); Point O'Woods Yacht (commodore 1929-33). Home: Montclair NJ Died Nov. 1968.

LOWRY, H(OMER) H(IRAM), govt. ofcl.; b. Peking, China (Am. parents), Oct. 6, 1898; s. George Davis and

Cora (Calhoun) L.; A.B., Ohio Wesleyan U., 1918; du Pont fellow, Princeton U., 1918-20, A.M., 1919, Ph.D., 1920; m. Helen Mary Smith, June 30, 1920 (div. 1939); children—Helen Louise, Barbara; m. Gertrude Hurney Tomlinson, Dec. 16, 1949. Chem. research Western Elec. Co., N.Y.C., 1920-25; phys. chemist Bell Telephone Labs., N.Y.C., 1925-30; dir. coal research lab., Carnegie Inst. Tech., 1930-53; cons. Army AC, 1943, Nat. Def. Research Council, 1941-43, Nat. Inventors Council, 1941-43; assistant research dir. Pitts. Coal Research Center, U.S. Bureau of Mines, Pittsburgh, Pennsylvania, 1960-64; staff research coordinator Office Dir. Coal Research, Bureau of Mines, Washington, from 1964. Chmn. committee on chem. utilization of coal, Div. of Chemistry and Chem. Tech., Nat. Research Council, 1937-45; Editor-sec., com. on chemistry of coal Nat. Academy Sciences-National Research Council, 1957-63. Mem. of tech. indsl. intelligence com. of Combined Intelligence Objectives Subcom. of SHAEF, 1945. Hon. pres. sect. on chem. in relation to fuel, power and transport, XIth Congress on Pure and Applied Chem., London, 1947. Served as pvt. C.W.S., 1918; lt. comdr. USNR, from 1936; cons. C.E. Dept. of the Army, 1948. Recipient Percy Nicholls award, Am. Inst. Mining, Metallurgy and Petroleum Engrs. and Am. Soc. M.E., 1959. Fellow A.A.A.S., Inst. Fuel (London), Royal Soc. Arts; hon. mem. Am. Coke and Coal Chems. Inst.; mem. New York Academy of Science, American Chemical Society, Am. Gas Assn., Am. Inst. Mining, Metall. and Petroleum Engineers, Geo-chemical Society of Am., Engrs. Soc. Western Pa., Eastern States Blast Furnace and Coke Oven Assn., Phi Beta Kappa, Sigma Xi, Phi Kappa Phi, Alpha Sigma Phi. Author numerous papers on gas absorption, coal, carbon, theory of dielectrics, insulating materials. Editor: Chemistry of Coal Utilization, 2 vols., 1945. Corr. editor Fuel (London, England). Home: Wilmerding PA Died May 20, 1971.

LOWRY, HOWARD JAMES, lawyer; b. Colfax, Wis., June 22, 1894; s. George and May (Turner) L.; Ph.B., Lawrence Coll., 1917; LL.B., U. Wis., 1922; J.D., John Marshall Law Sch., 1946; m. Irene L. James, Nov. 9, 1944; 1 dau., Ruth Miriam (Mrs. Raymond Luciano). Admitted to Wis. bar, 1922, Ill. bar, 1946, U.S. Supreme Ct., 1949; practiced in Madison, Wis., 1922-40, Chgo., 1946-49, Washington, 1949-56, Menomonie, Wis., 1956-67; mem. Wylie, Sutherland & Lowry, Madison, 1922-24; partner Lowry, Beggs & Dawson, Madison, 1924-40; associate firm of Peterson, Thedinga & Peterson, Menomonie, 1956-67; assistant district attorney civil Peterson, Menomonie, 1956-67; assistant district attorney civil affairs Dane County, Wisconsin, 1936-38; associate general counsel VA Central Office, Washington, 1946-56. Treas. Nat. Mut. Benefit Life Ins., Madison, 1926-48, dir., 1949-67. Served with Wis. N.G., Mexican border, 1916-17; U.S. Army, France, 1917-19; with AUS, Europe, Africa, Asia, 1940-46. Decorated Purple Heart, French Croix de Guerre, Officer Order of Brit. Empire. Mem. Am., Wis., Dunn-Pepin bar assns., Vets. Fgn. Wars, Am. Legion. Unitarian. Mason, Moose. Home: Colfax WI Died Sept. 15, 1967.

LOWTH, FRANK JAMES, educator, author; b. Lowell, Wis., Jan. 2, 1872; s. James and Jessie (Aimer) L.; grad. Whitewater State Teachers Coll., 1900; studied U. of Chicago, summers 1920, 21; m. Maude D. Francis, June 26, 1901; children—Geneva L. (wife of Dr. C.W. Connell), Lowell J., Jean F. (wife of Frank Byers), (dec.). Teacher rural schs. 4 years, grammar school, 3 years; superintendent and high school principal, Walworth, Clinton and Evansville, Wisconsin, 11 years; principal Normal School, Janesville, 22 yrs.; condr. teachers' insts. in Wis., speaker at teachers' meetings and convs., 30 years. Mem. N.E.A. (life), Wis. Teachers' Assn., Southern Wis. Teachers' Assn. (pres. 1933). Republican. Conglist. Mason. Club: Twilight of Janesville. Author: Everyday Problems of the Country Teacher, 1927, rev. edit., 1936; The Country Teacher at Work, 1930. Editor of Dept. Rural Edn., Wis. Jour. of Edn., 1920-28, and Foundation Classroom Materials, 1934-37. Writer and speaker on ednl. subjects, 30 years. Home: 218 S. Wisconsin St., Janesville WI‡

LUBKE, CARL HEINRICH, president of the Federal Republic of Germany; born at Enkhausen, Germany, Oct. 14, 1894; son of Friedrich-Wilhelm and Karoline (Becker) L.; grad. Gymnasium; student univs. Bonn, Berlin, Munster; Degree in Engring.; hon. Dr. Degree, universities of Bonn, Munich, Lahore, Bangkok, New Delhi (India), Cebu (P.I.), Rio de Janeiro, Addis Ababa; m. Wilhelmine Keuthen, 1929. Entered Prussian Parliament in Berlin, 1931, dismissed when Nazis came to power; minister food, agr. and forestry West German govt., 1953-59; pres. Federal Republic of Germany, 1959-69. Served as lt. German Army, World War I. Decorated Iron Cross Medal (2). Recipient medal Fed. Republic of Germany. Roman Catholic. Address: Bonn Fed. Republic of Germany Died Apr. 6, 1972.

LUCAS, JIM GRIFFING, reporter; b.Checotah, Okla., June 22, 1914; s. Jim Bob, Jr., and Effie Lincoln (Griffing) L.; student U. Mo., 1932-33. Reporter, feature writer Muskogee (Okla.) Daily Phoenix and Times-Democrat, 1934-38; news broadcaster, sta. KBIX, Muskogee, 1936-38; reporter, feature writer Tulsa Tribune, 1938-42; Marine combat corr. battles Guadalcanal, New Georgia, Russell Islands, Tarawa, Saipan, Tinian, Iwo Jima, 1942-45; corr. Scripps-Howard Newspaper Alliance Washington, 1945-70. 1st lt. USMC, World War II. Decorated Bronze Star. Recip. Nat. Headliners award best combat reporting, 1943; George Polk Meml. award, 2 Ernie Pyle awards, Omar Bradley Gold Medal; Pulitzer Prize; Korean Nat. Medal; Marine Corps Res. Officers Assn. award; 1st annual Fourth Estate award Am. Legion, 1958; First Annual Mark Watson award, 1968. Mem. Amvets (charter mem.), White House Corrs. Assn., Assn. U.S. Army, Nat. Headliners, Air Force Association, Sigma Delta Chi. Methodist. Clubs: Nat. Press (Washington); Overseas Press. Author: Combat Correspondent, 1944; Battle for Tarawa (with Capt. Earl J. Wilson, Sgts. Samuel Shaffer, Cyril Peter Zurlinden), 1944; Dateline-Vietnam, 1966. Home: Alexandria VA Died June 1970.

LUCIER, PHILLIP JOSEPH, telephone co. exec.; b. Abilene, Kan., Jan. 11, 1921; s. Ralph F. and Ruby (Norman) L.; B.S., U. Notre Dame, 1942; m. Marcella Fried, Jan. 7, 1946; children—E'Louise, David, Suzanne, Laurence, Therese, Phillip, Charles, Mary Jane, Bernadette, Barbara, Jeanette. Asst. treas. Stromberg-Carlson Corp., Rochester, N.Y., 1946-60; founder pres. Continental Telephone Corp., St. Louis, 1961-70; dir. St. Louis County Nat. Bank. Pres. bd. trustees Fontbonne Coll., St. Louis. Served with USNR, 1942-46. Mem. U.S. Ind. Telephone Assn. (dir. 1965-70), Ind. Telephone Pioneer Assn. Roman Catholic. Club: St. Louis. Home: St Louis MO Died July 24, 1970; buried Calvary Cemetery, St Louis MO

LUCKEY, DAVID FRANKLIN, veterinarian; b. Brazeau, Mo., Sept. 23, 1869; s. Robert Armstrong and Margaret Jane (Wilson) L.; grad. Warrensburg (Mo.) State Normal Sch., 1891, Ontario Veterinary Coll., Toronto, Can., 1896; m. Nan Frances Doherty, June 24, 1908; children—David Franklin, Frances Louise (Mrs. James Pierce Scamman), Samuel Monroe, Supt. pub. schs., Aurora, Mo., 1891-93; engaged in tick fever quarantine work, 1896-1900; Mo. State vet., 1900-12 and 1913-22, in 1900 began campaign against contagious diseases in animals, especially cattle tuberculosis; worked successfully on tick fever eradication in Mo., also eradication of glanders in horses and mules; successful in keeping foot and mouth disease out of Mo. during violent outbreak in neighboring states, 1914-15; stamped out hog cholera in Mo. by 1918; developed intradermal method of testing cattle for tuberculosis, used in Mo. since 1911, and adopted by Fed. govt., 1921. Awarded Internat. Veterinary Congress Prize for work on the development of the Intradermal Tuberculin Test, 1944. Home: 3969 Palm St., St Louis 7 MO‡

LUDDY, MICHAEL G(ABRIEL), lawyer; b. Bridgeport, Conn., Mar. 19, 1893; s. James Peter and Mary (Maloney) L.; LL.B., Catholic U. of America, 1916, LL.D., 1964; M. Anne Teresa Dunn, Feb. 10, 1918; 1 dau., Marybeth. Admitted to Conn. bar, 1916; gen. practice Hartford, 1916-20, Sioux Falls, S.D., 1920-31, Los Angeles 1931-67, specializing in banking and corporate law; mem. Bodkin, Breslin &Luddy; dir. 1st Nat. Bank, Glendale, Oilfields Nat. Bank (Brea, Calif.), Peoples Bank (Lakewood Village, Calif.), Rotary Materials Co., Gremac Oil Corp. (Long Beach), Fibre & Metal Products Inc. Downey, Cal. Recipient award Outstanding Achievement in field of law, Cath. Univ. Am. Alumni Assn., 1964. Fellow Am. Coll. Trial Lawyers; mem. Am., Cal., S.D. and Los Angeles bar assns. Republican. Roman Catholic. K.C. Clubs: Newman, Stock Exchange (Los Angeles), Friendly Sons St. Patrick Glendale CA Died May 17, 1967; buried Holy Cross Cemetery.

LUDOVICI, ALICE EMELIE, artist; b. Dresden, Germany, Nov. 7, 1872; of Italian and English desc.; d. Julius and Emelie (Jones) L.; brought to U.S. in infancy; ed. pvtly.; studied music and art in Europe. Painter of portraits and miniatures. Exhibited at Am. Soc. Miniature Painters, New York; Fine Art Soc., Chicago; Pa. Soc. Miniature Painters; Biltmore Salon, Los Angeles, Calif., etc. Awarded silver medal, Alaska, Yukon, Pacific Expn., 1909; gold medal, Calif. Soc. Miniature Painters, 1914; gold medal, San Diego Expn., 1915. Painted miniature of Gladys and Dorothea Cromwell, of New York. Mem. Calif. Soc. Miniature Painters (pres. 8 yrs.). Republican. Episcopalian. Home: 167 N. Orange Grove Av., Pasadena CA‡

LUDWIG, CHARLES H(EYLER), psychiatrist; b. Blue Canyon, Cal., Feb. 28, 1921; s. Charles Heyler, Sr., and Duri (Erskine) L.; A.B., U. Cal., 1943, M.D., 1946; m. Lydia Marian Engram, Jan. 4, 1942; children—Laurie, Lynn, Louis, Lucy Lila. Resident intern San Francisco City and County Hosp., 1946; resident psychiatrist Langley Porter Clinic, San Francisco, 1947-49; clin. dir. Sonoma State Hosp., 1950-52; clin. instr. psychiatry U. Cal. Med. Sch., 1950-54; supt., med. dir. Porterville State Hosp., 1952-54; practice medicine specializing in psychiatry, Porterville, 1954-56, Fresno, 1956-71; clin. dir. Kings View Psychiat. Hosp., 1956-57; cons. psychiatrist Exeter Meml. Hosp.; med. staff St. Agnes Hosp., Fresno Community Hospital (chairman department of psychiatry 1963), Gen. Hosp. Fresno County. Mem. adv. bd. Fresno Mental Assn. Assn. Diplomate Am. Bd. Psychiatry and Neurology, Pan Am. Med. Assn. Fellow Am. Psychiat. Assn., Am. Assn. Mental Deficiency; mem. A.M.A., Cal. Med. Assn., Fresno County Med. Soc. (bd. govs. 1963-64), A.A.A.S. Address: Fresno CA Died Apr. 30, 1970.

LUETTE, ELEANOR (MRS. PAUL LUETTE, JR.), psychologist; b. Williamstown, Mass.; d. John Jay and Mary (Mahoney) O'Brien; A.B., U. Denver, 1942, M.A., 1943; m. Paul Luette, Jr., Sept. 15, 1936. Mem. faculty Denver U., 1938-67, asso. prof. psychology, 1955-67. Mem. social com. for Denver Symphony Guild, Mt. Airy (Mental) Hosp. Mem. Am. Assn. U. Profs., Am., Colo. psychol. assns., Colo. Mental Health, U.N., Colo. Edn. Assn., Phi Beta Kappa. Home: Denver CO Died July 15, 1970; interment Fairmount Denver CO

LUGG, THOMAS BRANSFORD, corp. exec., clergyman; b. Salem, Wis., Dec. 11, 1889; s. Edward H. and Susan G. (Parrott) L.; B.S., Northwestern, 1912; S.T.B., Garrett Bibl. Inst., 1918; D.D. (hon.), Ill. Wesleyan U., 1933, LL.D., 1949; m. Lucile C. Knox, Sept. 24, 1919; children—Elizabeth Lucile, Susan Louise. Ordained to ministry Meth. Ch., 1918; pastor, Sadorus, Ill., 1919-22, LeRoy, 1922-24, Springfield, 1924-28, Mattoon, 1928-32, Decatur, 1936-44; supt. Quincy-Jacksonville (Ill.) Dist., 1932-36; exec. sec., treas. Gen. Commn. World Service and Finance, Meth. Ch., Chgo., 1944-52; gen. sec., treas. Council on World Service and Finance, 1956-60; president Nat. Mut. Ch. Ins. Co., from 1961; dir. Nat. Mut. Ch. Fire Ins. Co. Chgo. Mem. Gen. Conf. M.E. Ch., 1932, 36, Uniting Conf., 1939, mem. Gen. Conf. Meth. Ch. (com. on rules), 1940, 44, 48, 52, 56, Ecumenical Meth. Conf., 1948; pres. treas. funds Meth. Ch., World Service Funds, Episcopal Funds, Gen. Adminstrn. Funds, Crusade for Christ Funds; mem. bd. Nat. Council Chs. in U.S.A., from 1952; mem. 1954 Assembly National Council of Churches in U.S.A.; consultant 1954 World Council Chs. Pres. bd. trustees MacMurry College, from 1959; member board trustees Northwestern Univ., Wesley Found. of U. Ill., Ill. Wesleyan U. Served as 1st lt., chaplain, U.S. Army, 1917-19. Mem. Council Secs. Meth. Ch. (treas.) Ill. Conf. Meth. Chs. (pres. Preacher's Aid Soc. from 1944), Phi Gamma Delta. Mason. Club: Union League (Chgo.). Home: Evanston IL Died Aug. 30, 1967; buried White Hall (Ill.) Cemetery.

LUKAS, PAUL, actor; b. Budapest, Hungary, May 26, 1895; s. Janos and Maria (Zilahy) L.; m. Daisy Benes, May 26, 1927. Asso. with Comedy Theatre, Budapest, 1918-27; motion picture actor, Hollywood, Calif., and London, Eng.; starred in plays, Watch on the Rhine, The Doll's House (N.Y. City); film plays, Dodsworth, Dinner at the Ritz, The Lady Vanishes, Confessions of a Nazi Spy, Hostages, Address Unknown, Experiment Perilous, Uncertain Glory. Received Motion Picture Academy Award for best acting performance, 1943. Served as aviation officer Hungarian-Austrian Army, World War. Clubs: Racquet (Palm Springs, Calif.); Tennis (Los Angeles). Home: New York City NY Died Aug. 1971.

LUKE, EDMON G., textile mfr.; b. Jersey City, Aug. 20, 1903; s. Edmon Conner and Lilliam M. (Brock) L.; student pub. schs.; m. Gertrude C. Sanial, June 29, 1934; children—John Edmon, Edmon George, Jr., James Philip. Exec. Bates Fabrics, Inc., N.Y.C., 1942-51, synthetics dept. head, 1943-51, pres. Fox-Wells Luke Div., Inc., 1951-53; v.p. Textron, Inc., 1953-56; pres., dir. Amerotron Co. Mem. rayon industry adv. com. OPS; industry adv. com. Quartermaster Assn. Mem. Nat. Fedn. Textiles Inc (v.p., dir.), Am. Cotton Mfrs. Inst., Am. Textile Mfrs. Inst. (past dir.). Clubs: Lambs, Weavers, Princeton (N.Y.C.); Ridgewood (N.J.) Country. Home: Ho-Ho-Kus NJ Died Nov. 1968.

LUKEN, MARTIN GIRARD, surgeon; b. Niles Center, Ill., Sept. 20, 1882; M.D., Univ. of Ill. Coll. Medicine, 1906; m. Amanda Clara Smith, June 28, 1910. Attending surgeon St. Elizabeth's, Cook County and Angel Guardian Orphanage hosps. Served as health officer, City of Chicago, 1906-10. Fellow Am. Coll. Surgeons; mem. A.M.A., Ill. State and Chicago med. socs., Elks. Home: Chicago IL Died July 1968.*

LULEK, RALPH NORBERT, chem. mgr.; b. Graz, Austria, Fort Lauderdale FL chem. mgr.; b. Graz, Austria, Aug. 13, 1901; s. Dr. Fery and Nelly (von Arthold) L.; Ph.D., U. Graz, 1924; m. Noronica R. Beatley, June 24, 1929. Came to U.S., 1925, naturalized, 1935. Group leader E.I. duPont de Nemours & Co., Wilmington, 1925-43; plant mgr. Publicker Industries, Phila., 1943-46; mgr. research Heyden Chem. Corp., N.Y.C., 1946, v.p., 1948-53; plant mgr. Heyden Morgantown Ordnance Works, 1946-47, v.p., dir., 1948-53; pres., dir. Heyden Pharmacal Co., Heyden Labs., Inc., 1948-53; dir. Jamieson Pharmacal Co., Detroit, Nyal Co., 1948-53, Am. Potash & Chem. Co., 1950-52; v.p., dir. St. Maurice Chem., Ltd., Can., 1952-53; v.p., dir. Grace Chem. Co., N.Y.C. 1953-55; cons. Sun Chem. Co., Johnson and Johnson, Nobel-Boyel Co., France, other, 1955-70. Recipient

Modern Pioneer award, N.A.M., award for contbn. to atomic bomb War Dept., award Nat. Geographic Soc. Mem. Am. Inst. Chem. Engrs., Am. Chem. Soc., Am. Assn. Textile Chemists and Colorists, W.Va. Soc. Profl. Engrs., Assn. Research Dirs. of N.Y., Soc. Chem. Industry London, Soc. de Chemie Industrielle, N.Y. Acad. Sci. Elk. Clubs: Wall Street, Chemists; Univ. (N.Y.C.). Author tech. articles. Holder 75 patents. Address: Candlewood CT Died May 3, 1970, buried Mountain Grove Cemetery, Bridgeport CT

LULL, CABOT, physician; b. Wetumpka, Ala., June 21, 1874; s. Cabot and Sarah Graham (Foster) L.; M.D., U. of Mich., 1899; m. Dorothy Eaves, June 25, 1913 (died 1934); children—Dorothy, Mary. Intern, Lakeside Hosp., Cleveland, O., 1899-1901; in private practice at Birmingham, Alabama, since 1901; consulting physician at the Jefferson Sanitorium; visiting phys. St. Vincent's Hospital. Major Medical Corps, U.S. Army, 1917-19, in France, 1918. Mem. A.M.A., Southern Med. Assn., Med. Assn. State of Ala., Jefferson County Med. Soc., Nat. Tuberculosis Assn. Democrat. Presbyn. Club: Birmingham Country. Home: Highland Plaza, 2250 Highland Av., Birmingham AL‡

LULL, GERARD BRAMLEY, forester; b. Chatsworth, N.J., Mar. 4, 1877; s. William Bell and Mary Ann (Le Valley) L.; grad. Delaware Acad., Delhi, N.Y., 1900; grad. Forest Engr., Cornell U., 1904; m. Margaret Elizabeth Young, of E. Palmyra, N.Y., June 29, 1907. Asst. in Forest Service of Cal., 1904-6, asst. forest insp., Jan.-July, 1906, state forester of Cal. since July, 1906. Sec. Cal. State Bd. of Forestry; mem. advisory bd. Forestry Soc. of Cal., Cal. Promotion Com. Mem. Soc. Am. Foresters, Am. Forestry Assn., Commonwealth Club, San Francisco. Republican. Presbyn. Clubs: Sutter, Country, Union Republican (Sacramento), Transportation (San Francisco). Address: 2223 K St., Sacramento CA‡

LULL, HERBERT GALEN, educator; b. Antrim Co., Mich., May 15, 1874; s. Benjamin Franklin and Ella Irene (Davis) L.; life certificate, Mich. State Normal Coll., 1898, M.Pd., 1912; A.B., U. of Mich., 1904; M.A., U. of Wash., 1911; Ph.D., U. of Calif., 1912; m. Mallah Godfrey, of Corona, Calif., Jan. 17, 1901; children—Herbert Orren, Harriett. Supt. schs., Mt. Clemens, Mich., 1904-05; supervisor Training Sch., Wash. State Normal Sch., Bellingham, Wash., 1905-07; asso. prof. edn., 1907-13, prof., 1913-16, U. of Wash.; acting asst. prof. edn., U. of Calif., 1911-12; dir. teacher training Kan. State Teachers Coll., Emporia, Kan., 1916-20; dir. Superior Sch. of Pedagogical Sciences, U. of Tech. Sch., Lima, Peru, 1921; again dir. teacher training, Kan. State Teachers Coll., since 1922, head of dept. of edn. and dir. teacher training, since 1927. Prof. edn., Ohio State U., summer 1931. Dir. Emporia Consumers Cooperative Assn., and Consumers Cooperative Assn. (Wholesale), North Kansas City, Mo. Mem. Nat. Soc. for Study of Edn., Nat. Soc. of Ednl. Research, Kan. State Teachers Assn. (dir.). Conglist. Author: Inherited Tendencies of Secondary Instruction in the United States, 1912; Secondary Education, Orientation and Program, 1932; Principles of Elementary Education, 1935. Co-Author: Redirection of High School Instruction, 1921; Modern Methods of Teaching, 1923. Contbr. more than 100 articles on edn. Home: 1402 West St., Emporia KS‡

LUND, CHARLES CARROLL, surgeon; b. Boston, Apr. 15, 1895; s. Fred Bates and Zoe M. (Griffing) L.; A.B., Harvard, 1916, M.D. cum laude, 1920; m. Alice C. Marden, May 22, 1925. Intern Mass. Gen. Hosp., Boston, 1920-22, resident in surgery, 1922-23; pvt. practice surgery, Boston, 1923-68; mem. faculty, Med. Sch., Harvard, 1923, asst. clin. prof. surgery, 1953-55, clin. prof. surgery, 1955-61, prof. emeritus, 1961-72; asso. with Collis P. Huntington Meml. Hosp., 1924-41, Boston City Hosp., 1924-68 surgeon-in-chief 1951-60, cons. surgery, 1961-66, hon. surgeon, 1966-68; surgeon New Eng. Deaconess Hosp., 1926-68; mem. med. adv. com. Mass. Red Cross Blood Program, 1963-72. Bd. dirs., pres. Blood Research Inst., 1960-69. Fellow A.C.S.; mem. A.M.A., Am. Surg. Soc., Soc. Clin. Surgery, Am. Cancer Soc. (bd. dirs. 1947, pres. 1951-52), Nat. Research Council, N.E. Surg. Soc., N.E. Cancer Soc., Suffolk Dist., Mass. (pres. 1958-59) med. socs., Boston Surg. Soc. (pres. 1960-61), Harvard Med. Alumni Assn. (pres. 1958-59), Aesculapian, Nat. Rowing Found. (dir. 1965), Phi Beta Kappa, Alpha Omega Alpha. Clubs: Country (Brookline); St. Botolph (pres. 1946-46), Harvard (pres. 1953-55) (Boston); Friends of Harvard Rowing (chmn. 1959-69). Contbr. articles to med. jours. Home: Chestnut Hill MA Died July 27, 1972.

LUND, FRED BATES, surgeon; b. Concord, N.H., Jan. 4, 1865; s. Charles C. and Lydia (French) L.; A.B., summa cum laude, Harvard, 1888 (Phi Beta Kappa), A.M., 1892, M.D., 1892; m. Zoe M. Griffing, 1893; children—Charles Carroll, Fred Bates, Edward Griffing, Zoe M. (dec.), Joseph W., Lydia Margaret. Interne Mass. Gen. Hosp., 1890-1903; lecturer on surgery, Harvard Med. Sch.; former surgeon in chief Boston City Hospital; cons. surgeon City Hosp. (Quincy), Burbank Hospital (Fitchburg), Newton Hosp. Fellow Am. Coll. Surgeons; mem. A.M.A., Mass. Med. Soc., Am. Surg. Assn. (ex-pres.), Soc. Clinical Surgery, etc. Republican. Unitarian. Clubs: Harvard, Tavern, Club of Odd Volumes and Harvard of N.Y. Home: 133 Dudley Rd., Newton Centre MA‡

LUNDAY, CHARLES G., railroad exec.; b. New Cambria, Mo., Jan. 5, 1872; s. John W. and Mary A. (Wilson) L.; student pub. schs.; m. Edna B. Van Anglen, Nov. 16, 1893. Clk., operator, agt. Hannibal & St. Joseph Ry. (now C.,B.& Q. R.R.), 1886-1903; traveling auditor St. Louis Southwestern Ry., 1904; agt., yardmaster St. Louis Iron Mountain & So. (now M.P. R.R.), 1904-09; trainmaster La. & Ark. Ry., 1910-11, supt., 1911-16, gen. supt., 1916-20, gen. mgr., 1920-22, v.p., gen. mgr., 1922-30, v.p. since 1930. Mem. Am. Ry. Engring. Assn. Republican. Presbyn. Mason. Home: Caddo Hotel. Office: Central Station Bldg., Shreveport LA‡

LUNDBERG, CLARENCE HARRY, clergyman; b. Milaca, Minn., Apr. 14, 1907; s. John Robert and Anna Dorothea (Lund) L.; grad. Trinity Sem. and Bible Inst., 1935; m. Volga Jensen, Nov. 26, 1937; children—Merrill, Bernadine V. (Mrs. Wayne G. Christiansen), Philip. Ordained to ministry, 1940; pastor Bethel Ch. of Washington Island, 1937-58, First Congl. Ch., Hancock, Minn., 1960-67, 1st Congl. Chs. of Staples and Aldrich (Minn.), 1967-68. Editor weekly news bull., 1947-58. Home: Staples MN Died Jan. 11, 1968; buried Forest Hill Cemetery Milaca MN

LUNDBERG, FRANK A., clergyman, educator; b. Sweden, Apr. 11, 1875; s. Frank A. and Klara L. (Lindgren) L.; came to U.S., 1884; A.B., Ft. Worth (Tex.) U., 1905, A.M., 1906; M.D., Northwestern U. and Fort Worth U., 1909; m. Lydia E. Linstrum, July 25, 1911; 1 daughter, Mrs. Ruth Lindquist. Prof. chemistry, med. dept. Fort Worth U., 1909; prof. psychology and ch. history, Swedish Theol. Sem., Evanston, Ill., 1910-18; pres. same, 1918-24; pres. Tex. Wesleyan Coll., 1924-27, also pastor Meth. Ch., Taylor, Tex.; pastor First Swedish Meth. Ch., Los Angeles, 1927-31, Kingsburg (Calif.) Meth. Ch., 1931-39; retired. Democrat. Address: 1524 20th Av., Kingsburg CA‡

LUNDIE, EDWIN HUGH, architect; b. Cedar Rapids, Ia., Oct. 13, 1886; s. Samuel F. and Emma Lenora (Hitchcock) L.; student Am. Soc. Beaux Arts Architects, St. Paul Sch. Art; m. Grace Holroyd Nash, Oct. 17, 1917; 1 dau., Ellen Louise (Mrs. Charles Edward Thompson). Student, later mem. staff Cass Gilbert, Thomas G. Holyoke, Emanuel L. Masqueray, architects, 1905-16; pvt. practice architecture, St. Paul, 1917, religious architecture, 1917-25, domestic architecture, 1925-72. Mem. City Planning Bd., St. Paul, 1937-72. Fellow A.I.A.; mem. Minn. Soc. Architects. Home: Mahtomedi MN Died Jan. 8, 1972; buried Roselawn Cemetery, St Paul MN

LUNDSTRUM, ALLAN WINSTON, gas co. exec.; b. Joliet, Ill., Mar. 31, 1902; s. Alick and Christine (Herteen) L.; B.S. magna cum laude, U. Wash., 1923; M.S., Mass. Inst. Tech., 1926; m. Delia Bailey Dunbar, Nov. 23, 1926; 1 dau., Christine Fay (Mrs. Herbert William Kochs, Jr.). With Ebasco Services, N.Y.C., 1930-45; dir. research United Gas Pipe Line Co., Shreveport, La., 1945-47; cons. engr. Stewart-Warner Corp., 1948-51; gen. mgr. Ohio Fuel Gas Co., Columbus, 1951-52, pres., from 1952, dir., from 1951, later chmn. bd.; chmn. bd. Columbia Gas of Ohio, Inc., Ohio Valley Gas Co.; dir. Columbia Gas System Service Corp. (N.Y.C.). Registered profl. engr., Ohio. Mem. Nat., Ohio socs. profl. engr., Ohio (dir.), Columbus (dir.) chambers commerce, Sigma Chi. Mem. First Community Ch. Mason, Rotarian. Inventor gas appliances without chimneys. Home: Columbus OH Died May 21, 1972.

LURIE, LOUIS ROBERT, realtor, builder; b. Chgo., Sept. 6, 1888; s. Robert and Lena (Joffee) L.; student pub. schs.; m. Babette Greenebaum, May 21, 1918 (dec. Mar. 1956); 1 son, Robert A. Pres. The Lurie Co., San Francisco, 400 Montgomery Street, Inc., San Francisco, Pioneer Realty Co., San Francisco; chmn. Lurmont Co., San Francisco Bd. dirs. Damon Runyon Meml. Fund, N.Y.C.; pres. A.P. Giannini Scholarship Found., Louis R. Lurie Found. Col., Civil Air Patrol, 1951-72. Clubs: Maimonides of San Francisco; Harmonie, Lambs (N.Y.C.); Friars (Los Angeles); Concordia-Argonaut, Commonwealth, Press (San Francisco). Home: San Francisco CA Died Sept. 6, 1972.

LUSK, GEORGIA L. (MRS.), ex-congresswoman; b. Carlsbad, N.M., May 12, 1893; d. George and Mary Isabel (Gilbreath) Witt; student State Teachers Coll., Highlands U. and Colo. State Tchrs. Coll.; m. Dolph Lusk, Aug. 1915 (dec. 1919); children—Virgil (killed during World War II), Dolph (dec.), Eugene (dec.). Tchr., schs. in N.M., several yrs.; served as county supt. Lea County; state supt. pub. instrn., 1930-34, 1942-46, engaged in ranching more than 20 yrs.; mem. 80th Congress, at-large from N.M. Democrat. Address: Santa Fe NM Died Jan. 5, 1971; buried Carlsbad NM

LUSK, WILLIAM FOSTER, prof. agrl. edn.; b. River Falls, Wis., Aug. 1, 1874; s. David McKinley and Susan Ann (Foster) L.; grad. State Normal Sch., River Falls, Wis., 1896; Ph.B., U. of Wis., 1903; studied Cornell U., 1913; M.S., U. of Minn., 1916; m. Lucy Kimberley Peckham, of Neenah, Wis., June 18, 1905. Prin. of high schs., Wis., 1897-1901, 1903-5; prin. Teachers' Training Sch., St. Croix Falls, Wis., 1905-7; teacher science, Wis. State Normal Sch., 1907-12; asst. prof. agrl. edn., U. of Minn., 1914-17; prof. rural edn., Cornell U., 1917-20; head dept. agrl. and industrial education, Miss. Agricultural and Mechanical College, 1920—. Member N.E.A., Nat. Soc. for Vocational Edn., Am. Assn. for Advancement Agrl. Teaching, Honor Soc. Agr., Gamma Sigma Delta, Acacia. Episcopalian. Mason. Home: 503 Dryden Rd., Ithaca NY‡

LUSTMAN, SEYMOUR LEONARD, physician, educator; b. Chgo., Apr. 23, 1920; s. Irving and Anna (Lee) L.; B.S., Northwestern U., 1941; Ph.D., U. Chgo., 1949; M.D., U. Ill., 1954; m. Katherine L. Ritman, June 1941; children—Jeffrey S., Susan T. Intern U. Ill. Research and Edn. Hosp., 1954-55; resident Yale, 1955-58; practice medicine, specializing in psychiatry, New Haven, 1958-71, asso. prof. psychiatry Child Study Center, Yale, 1958-64, prof. psychiatry, dir. research, 1964-71, master Davenport Coll., 1971; cons. div. research grants Nat. Inst. Mental Health, 1963-67, also adv. com. clin. research br.; chmn. Task Force IV, Joint Commn. on Mental Health of Children. Fellow Center for Advanced Psychoanalytic Studies, Princeton, 1963-71. Dir. Robert Knight Research Fund. Served to capt., adj. gen. dept., AUS, 1942-46. Recipient Chandler prize, 1954, David Papaport prize, 1962; Commonwealth Fund fellow, 1954-57; fellow Davenport Coll., Yale, 1967—. Mem. Am. Psychoanalytic Assn. (sec. bd. profl. standards), Am. Psychiat. Assn., Am. Orthopsychiatric Assn., Western New Eng. Inst. for Psychoanalysis, Pi Epsilon Pi. Editor: The Psychoanalytic Study of the Child, 1968. Contbr. articles profl. jours. Home: New Haven CT Died Aug. 5, 1971.

LUTHER, JOHN CARLYLE, lawyer; b. Piper City, Ill., May 25, 1910; s. Ferd A. and Elisabeth (Stadler) L.; B.S., Monmouth Coll., 1932; J.D., U. Ill., 1941. Admitted to Ill. bar, 1941; gen. law practice, Petersburg, from 1941. Mem. Ill. Bar Assn., Am. Civil Liberties Union, Sangamon County Hist. Soc., Internat. Platform Assn., Am. Judicature Soc., Inst. Am. Democracy (asso.). Presbyn. Address: Petersburg IL

LUTHER, MARK LEE, author; b. at Knowlesville, N.Y., Jan. 5, 1872; s. Ira M. and Jane (Cole) L.; ed. pub. and pvt. schs., and Harvard U.; studied law, Columbia U., and in offices of Hon. Wilson S. Bissell, Buffalo, N.Y.; m. Grace Montagu Richmond, Apr. 8, 1901. Asso. editor of The Smart Set, 1911-14. Author: The Favor of Princes, 1899; The Henchman, 1902; The Mastery, 1904; The Crucible, 1907; The Sovereign Power, 1911; The Woman of It, 1912; The Hope Chest, 1918; Presenting Jane McRae, 1920; The Boosters, 1924; The Clean Up, 1927; It's What You Are, 1931. Co-Author (with Lillian C. Ford): Card 13, 1930; The Saranoff Murder, 1930; The Corcorans, 1931; (with Don Wilkie) American Secret Service Agent, 1934. Clubs: Authors (New York); P.E.N. Home: 601 S. Rampart Blvd., Los Angeles CA‡

LUTTRELL, JOHN E., judge; b. near city of Hillsboro, Tex., Jan. 26, 1889; s. Thomas Jefferson and Martha Sarah (Goodrich) L.; private study of law; m. Mary Dorothy Morter, July 8, 1915; 1 s., John M. County sch. teacher nr. Norman, Okla., 1906-10; admitted to Okla. State bar, 1913, and practiced in Norman, 1913-47; city atty., 1919-23; justice Supreme Court of Okla. from 1947, later vice chief justice. Served as state senator, 1923-27. Chmn. Okla. Employment Security Commn., 1944-47. Mem. Okla. Bar Assn. (pres. 1940), Am. bar Assn., Phi Delta Phi (hon.). Democrat (del. nat. conv., 1928). Methodist. Club: Lions. Home: Norman OK Died Feb. 24, 1969; buried I.O.O.F. Cemetery, Norman OK

LUTZ, E. RUSSELL, internat. lawyer; b. Lancaster, Pa., June 1, 1902; s. Henry F. and Anna (Barr) L.; A.B., George Washington U., 1922; LL.B., Yale, 1926; m. Mildred Estelle Maddox, Aug. 20, 1928; 1 dau., Virginia Davis (Mrs. Townsend M. Belser, Jr.). Admitted to D.C., bar, 1927, U.S. Supreme Ct., 1930; asst. solicitor, asst. legal advisor State Dept., 1926-37; atty., asst. gen. counsel U.S. Maritime Commn., 1937-41; Am. President Lines, 1941-49, dir. and v.p., 1942, exec. v.p., 1943-49; mgr. W. R. Grace & Co., 1949-54, v.p. 1954-68, v.p. Grace Line, Inc., 1950-68. Vice pres., dir. Pacific Am. S.S. Assn., 1941-49, pres., 1944-48; dir. Waterfront Employers Assn. San Francisco, also Pacific Shipowners Assn., 1946-49; mem. Travel Advisory Com., Dept. Commerce, from 1954. Industry rep. or observer at various Inter-Am. confs. Mem. Inter-Am., Fed. bar assns., Maritime Law Assn. U.S., Maritime Adminstrv. Bar Assn., American Society Internat. Law, Am. Bar Assn., Beta Theta Pi, Phi Alpha Delta. Clubs: Yale, Bohemian, Pacific Union (San Francisco, California); Cosmos, Metropolitan (Washington, District of Columbia); Book and Gavel Law (Yale). Collaborator: Convicting the Innocent (with Dr. Edwin M. Borchard), 1932. Home: Washington DC Died Jan. 12, 1970; buried Marshall Cemetery, Marshall VA

LUTZ, RALPH HASWELL, educator; b. Circleville, O., May 18, 1886; s. Harry Elmer and Florence May (Haswell) L.; A.B., Stanford, 1906; studied law same univ.; LL.B., U. of Wash., 1907; Ph.D., Heidelberg, 1910; LL.D., University of Southern California, 1942; m. Margaret Longyear, Sept. 12, 1927; children—Katherine May, Mary Margaret, Elizabeth Longyear. Practiced at Seattle, 1910-11; instr. history, U. of Wash., 1911-15; lecturer history, Stanford, 1915-16; asst. prof. history, U. of Wash., 1916-20; asso. prof. history Stanford University 1920-29, prof., 1929-52, professor emeritus, 1952-68; mem. adv. bd. Hoover Institution, Stanford, 1952-68; mem. Borden Merit Award Committee, 1958-68; vis. professor U. Cal., Los Angeles, 1952-53; dir. Hoover Library on War Revolution and Peace, Stanford U., 1920-44, chmn. dirs., 1925-44, dean of grad. study 1933-47; mem. and dir. Belgian Am. Ednl. Foundation. Student at first Officers Training Corps, Presidio, San Francisco, May-Aug. 1917; commd. 1st lt. inf. and assigned to hdqrs. 40th Div.; arrived in France, Aug. 1918, and assigned hdqrs. First Army, in Argonne; later with Am. Mil. Mission, Berlin, with Supreme Econ. Council, Paris, and spl. mission to Poland; hon. disch., Sept. 6, 1919. Member National Committee Franklin D. Roosevelt Library, 1938. Mem. Am. Hist. Assn. (pres. Pacific coast br., 1941; mem. council 1944-48), American Military Institute (trustee 1941-43), American Political Science Association, Am. Assn. Univ. Profs. (mem. council, 1944-46, pres. 1948-50), Soc. of Am. Archivists, Societe d'Histoire Moderne, Conseil Historique et Heraldique de France, Sons American Revolution. Kappa Sigma, Delta Chi, Phi Beta Kappa, Phi Alpha Theta. Republican. Presbyterian. Clubs: Faculty; Roxburghe (San Francisco). Author: Die Beziehungen zwischen Deutschland und den Vereinigten Staaten wahrend des Sezessionskrieges, 1911; The German Revolution, 1918-19, 1922; Fall of the German Empire (2 vols.), 1932; The Treaty of Saint Germain (with Nina Almond), 1934; Bibliography of the Paris Peace Conference (with same), 1935; Biographical Sketch of Hanssen, 1955. Editor: The Causes of the German Collapse in 1918, 1934; (with Suda Bane) The Blockade of Germany After the Armistice, 1918-19; The Organization of American Relief in Europe (with Suda Bane), 1918-19, 1943; Electoral Map of Reichstag Election March 1933 (with Pearle Quinn Bradley), 1944; H.P. Hanssen in War Time (with Mary Schofield and Oscar Winther); Diary from a Dying Empire: Berlin Home Front, 1914-18; (with Charles B. Burdick) The Political Institutions of the German Revolution, 1918-19, 1966. Mem. bd. editors journal of Central European Affairs. Co-author: Public Opinion and World Politics (Harris Foundation Lectures), 1933; Dictatorship in the Modern World, 1935. Home: Twenty-nine Palms CA Died Apr. 1968; buried Golden Gate Nat. Cemetery, San Bruno CA

LUXFORD, ANSEL F(RANK), lawyer; b. Harian, Ia., July 11, 1911; s. Frank Wallace and Alta Jenny (Newman) L.; student Iowa U., 1929-30, Creighton U., 1930-31; B.S., Catholic U. Am. 1933, LL.B., 1935; m. Angela M. Valenza, Sept. 21, 1935; children—Angela Valenza (Mrs. Henry D. Kerfoot, Jr.), Ansel Frank, Stephen Newman. Admitted to D.C., Ia. bars, 1935; Minn. bar, 1940, also U.S. Supreme Ct. bar; atty. gen. counsel's office, Treasury Dept., Washington, 1935-39; atty., specialist on fgn. funds and econ. warfare, gen. counsel's office, 1940-42; chief counsel, fgn. funds control, 1942-43, asst. gen. counsel, 1943-44; chief legal adviser to Am. delegation United Nations Monetary and Financial Conf., Bretton Woods, 1944; asst. to sec. of treasury, 1944-46; asst., later asso. gen. counsel, Internat. Bank for Reconstruction and Development, 1946-51; partner Pehle, Luxford, Riemer Schlezinger & Naiden, 1951-68, Morgan, Lewis & Bockius, Washington, 1968-71. Pres., dir. Providence Savs. & Loan Assn., Vienna, Va.; dir. EMB, Ltd. Mem. Am., D.C. bar assns. Club: Cosmos (Washington). Home: McLean VA Died Sept. 4, 1971; buried Leibinsville Presbyn. Cemetery, McLean VA

LYALL, TONI OWEN, fashion designer; b. Chgo., July 26, 1911; d. Roy Owen and Pearl (Gebhart) Owen; B.S., U. Wis., 1932; m. Elliott H. Morgan 1938 (div. 1950); m. 2d, William Lord Lyall, Jr., Sept. 18, 1952; children—Lois (Mrs. Arthur B. Pacheco), William Lord, III, David Edward. Pres. Owen-Morgan, Inc., N.Y.C., from 1946, designer ladies' sportswear and separates. Recipient Mademoiselle Award, 1947, Coty Award, 1948, Glamour Magazine Award, 1956. Patron of the Brooklyn Museum. Member of Fashion Group. Club: Morris Country Golf (Morris Town, N.J.). Home: Madison NJ Died Dec. 28, 1968.

LYBARGER, DONALD FISHER, judge; b. Harrisburg, Pa., Dec. 19, 1896; s. Jesse James and Margaret Shuler (Fisher) L.; A.B., Gettysburg Coll., Gettysburg, Pa., 1919; J.D., Western Reserve, 1923; LL.D. (hon.), Cleveland Marshall Law School, 1967; m. Cornelia Marjorie Hartshorne, Sept. 16, 1924 (deceased November 4, 1953); children—Cornelia Marie (Mrs. Henry C. Neuswanger), Virginia Dowler Patterson, Lee Hartshorne, Leonard Fisher; married 2d, Helen Baldwin Dean, August 7, 1956; 1 stepdau., Dianne Dean Keogh. Admitted to Ohio bar, 1923, U.S. Supreme Court, 1926; engaged in practice of law with firm of Horn, Weisell, McLaughlin and Lybarger, Cleveland, 1923-28, 1932-45; county recorder of Cuyahoga County, Cleveland, 1933-50; judge of ct. of common pleas, 1950-70, chief justice, 1967-69. Served USN, World War I. Chmn. Spirit of '76 Commn. 1936. Pres. Woodland Center Neighborhood House, 1942-43. Trustee Woman's Hosp., from 1943, Gt. Lakes Shakespeare Assn., from 1962, Presbytery of Cleveland, 1949; adv. com. Lakewood br. Ohio State Univ.; member board of fellows Gettysburg College, 1967. Member Cleveland Sesquicentennial Commission, 1946. Recipient Distinguished Alumni award from Gettysburg College, in 1968. Member of the Cleveland, American, Cuyahoga, bar associations, Sojourners, Early Settlers Assn. (pres. 1946-59), Western Reserve, Ohio (trustee 1959-62) hist. socs., Ohio Recorders Assn. (pres. 1950), Army and Navy Union, Am. Philatelic Soc., (pres. 1943-49; recipient Gold Service medal 1968), American Legion, Sons of the American Revolution, (historian gen., 1944-46), Richard III Soc. London (v.p.), Theta Kappa Nu (a founder 1924, nat. treas, 1924-28, exec. sec., 1928-32, nat. pres., 1938-39), Lambda Chi Alpha (nat. vice pres., 1939-43), Tau Kappa Alpha, Delta Theta Phi (honorary life mem.). Democrat. Presbyterian. Mason (33 deg.). Club: Garfield-Perry Stamp (pres. 1938). Author: History of the Lybarger Family, (printed pvtly.), 1921, 59; Vir Quisque Vir Est., 1929; English Ancestry of the Belden Family, 1942; History of the Western Reserve (pub. pvtly.), 1933; The U.S. Offset Issue of 1918-20, 1937 (won 1st award Am. Philatelic Congress, 1936); The Light of Other Days, 1962; The Crum Family, 1963; The Family of Cornelius Baldwin, 1965; Shakespeare and the Law, 1965; What Ever Happened to Poetry, 1966; Mental Illiness as a Defense in a Criminal Case, 1966. Home: Lakewood OH Died Nov. 6, 1970; Criminal Case, 1966. Home: Lakewood OH Died Nov. 6, 1970; buried Lakewood Cemetery.

LYDER, JAY W., banker; b. Alliance, O., Oct. 20, 1868; s. John Wesley and Mary (Bedortha) L.; grad. high sch., Akron, O., 1887; student Buchtel Coll., Akron, 1886-87; m. Grace A. Trimble, Sept. 12, 1899; 1 dau., Caroline T. Began with 2d Nat. Bank, Akron, 1887; with City Nat. Bank, 1889-1900, asst. cashier, 1895-1900; sec. Akron Trust Co., 1900-02; moved to Duluth, Minn., 1902; cashier Duluth Savings Bank, 1902-09, and its successor, Northern Nat. Bank, 1909-17, vice-pres. since 1917; pres. First Federal Savings & Loan Assn.; treas. Minn. Arrowhead chapter Am. Red Cross; dir. Duluth Civic Symphony Assn. Episcopalian; treas. Duluth Diocese; Jr. Warden Trinity Cathedral. Mason. Clubs: Kitchi Gammi, Rotary. Home: 2201 E. First St. Office: Lonsdale Bldg., Duluth MN‡

LYLE, CLAY, coll. dean; b. Lux, Miss., Jan. 25, 1894; s.James Madison and Sallie (Hendrix) L.; B.S., Miss A.&M. Coll., 1917, M.S., 1931; Ph.D., Iowa State College, 1937; m. Annie Laurie McKay, July 7, 1930; 1 d., Sarah Ann (Mrs. George Bennett, Jr.). Teacher, Tate County Agricultural High Sch., Senatobia, Miss., 1917-18; farmer, Ralls, Tex., 1919-20; gen. insp. Miss. State Plant Bd., State Univ., Miss., 1921-31, exec. officer 1931-51; asso. prof. entomology and zoology Miss. State Univ., 1928-31, dept. head, 1931-51, entomologist Miss. Expt. Sta., 1931-51, Miss. Extension Service, 1943-45; dean Sch. Sci., 1945-51, dean Sch. of Agr., 1951-61, director Miss. Agr. Expt. Station, 1951-61, Miss. Agr. Extension Service 1951-61, School of Forestry, 1934-61; cons. in entomology AID, Formosa, 1961-63; estate planner Miss. State U. Devel. Found., 1963-68. Charter mem. bd. dirs. First Fed. Savs. & Loan Assn., Starkville, 1934-70. Served in U.S. Army, 1918-19. Named Miss. Farmer of Year, Miss. Farmer paper, 1954; Man of Year in Agr., Progressive Farmer mag., 1959; recipient Distinguished Service award Miss. Entomol. Assn., 1959. Fellow A.A.A.S., Entomol. Soc. Am.; mem. Am. Assn. Econ. Entomologists (pres. 1946), National Plant Board, 1941-51, Southern Plant Bd. (sec. 1937-41), Apiary Inspectors of Am. (sec. 1937-41), Cotton States Entomologists (pres. 1936), Miss. Acad. of Sci. (president, 1953), Assn. Southern Agricultural Workers (vice pres. 1959), Southern Extension Directors (chmn.) 1955-56), Sigma Xi. Beta Beta Beta, Omicron Delta Kappa, Phi Kappa Phi, Alpha Zeta. Jeffersonian Dem. Methodist (chmn. bd. stewards, Sunday Sch. supt.). Address: State College MS Died Dec. 23, 1971; buried Odd Fellows Cemetery, Starkville MS

LYLE, EUGENE P., JR., author; b. Dallas, Tex., Dec. 31, 1873; s. Eugene P. and Mary E. (Angers) L.; moved with parents to Kansas City, Mo., 1879; ed. pub. schs., 1880-92, U. of Mich., 1892-94; married; children—Eugene P., Marjorie Virginia, Ethel; m. 2d, Gwladys Myfanwy Morgan, San Diego, Calif., Apr. 8, 1927. On editorial staff, Kansas City Times, 1894-97, lit. work in Mexico, 1897-1900, 1903-05, 1906-07; staff corr. in Europe, for Everybody's Mag., 1900-02; staff corr. World's Work, 1905-07, Broadway and Hampton's Mag., 1908-10; also farming in Va., 1907-16. Author: The Missourian, 1905; The Lone Star, 1907; Blaze Derringer, 1910; The Transformation of Krag, 1911; D'Artagnan of Kansas, 1912-14, in Everybody's Mag.; A Dash of Irish (with W. F. McCaleb), in Adventure, 1913; The War of 1938, 1918; Castaway's Island, 1925; also stories for motion pictures. Club: The Padres. Home: 4027 3d Av., San Diego CA‡

LYMAN, CHARLES HUNTINGTON, III, naval officer; b. Phila., Nov. 24, 1903; s. Maj. Gen. Charles Huntington and Anne Blaine (Irvine) L.; B.S., U.S. Naval Acad., 1926; grad. student ordnance engring., USN Postgrad. Sch., 1934-37; grad. Nat. War Coll., 1948, Naval War Coll., 1953; m. Marjorie Leigh Young, June 30, 1928; 1 dau., Marjorie Anne (Mrs. Arthur P. Miller, Jr.). Commd. ensign USN, 1926, advanced through grades to rear adm., 1953; comd. destroyers in Pacific, participated amphibious operations for recapture of Philippines, during war; operations officer Operations Crossroads, Bikini atomic tests, 1946, Atlantic Fleet, 1946-48; with Bur. Ordnance, 1949-51; comdr. Destroyer Squadron 24, Pacific, Caribbean and Mediterranean, 1951-52; head dept. strategy and tactics Naval War Coll., 1952-53; USN attache, London, 1953-56; comdr. destroyer Flotilla, U.S. Atlantic Fleet, 1956-57, chief of staff Naval War College, 1957-59, commandant Fourth Naval District, Philadelphia, 1959-61; commander destroyers Atlantic Fleet, 1961; commandant 8th Naval District, 1962-65, ret. 1965; field asst. to Presidents of U.S. Nat. Navy League, Washington, 1966-72. capt. USN Academy tennis team, mem. Navy Leech Cup tennis teams, 1926, 27, 28, 35. Decorated Legion of Merit with gold star; Order of Almirante Padilla (Republic Colombia). Mem. Royal Soc. St. George. Club: Army-Navy Country (Arlington, Va.). Home: Bethesda MD Died Dec. 28, 1972; buried U.S. Naval Acad. Cemetery, Annapolis MD

LYMAN, EDWARD BRANCH, publicity dir.; b. Greenfield, Mass., June 7, 1876; s. Edward E. and Martha L. (Branch) L.; A.B., Yale, 1895; m. Blanche Rodale Chrysler, of Chrysler, Ont., Can., Aug. 1908. Began as reporter Springfield (Mass.) Republican; wire editor Associated Press, New York, 1907; Canadian mgr. Associated Press, 1908-10, N.E. mgr., 1911-14. Mgr. Belgian Relief Fund, which raised first $2,000,000 in U.S. for starving Belgium, 1914-15; raised $75,000 from American children for food sent by steamer to Princess Marie Jose, for Belgian children, 1915; organized Paderewski's Polish Victims' Relief Fund, securing $1,000,000, 1916; active in nat. and internat. publicity; specializing in institutional and public relations publicity, since 1920. Treas. and trustee St. Stephen's Coll. (Columbia U.). Republican. Episcopalian. Clubs: Yale, City, Nat. Arts, Nantucket Yacht. Author: Me'ow Jones, Belgian Refugee Cat, 1918; Baseball Fanthology, 1925; motion picture plays and newspaper verse. Home: 360 E. 55th St. Office: 12 East 41st St., New York NY‡

LYMAN, HARRY WEBSTER, otolaryngolist; b. Cedar Rapids, Ia., Mar. 10, 1873; s. James Edward and Martha Elona (Day) L.; M.D., St. Louis Coll. of Physicians and Surgeons, 1895; m. Sarah Elizabeth Long, Dec. 12, 1900; children—Elizabeth Mary (Mrs. Allan E. Clark), Edward Harry. Interne St. Louis Woman's Hosp., 1895-96; gen. practice of medicine, St. Louis, Mo., 1896-1900, specialist in otolaryngology since 1900; demonstrator and prof. of anatomy, St. Louis Coll. of Phys. and Surgs., 1900-06; volunteer asst. dept. of otolaryngology, Washington Univ., Sch. of Medicine, St. Louis, 1910-14, asst. in otolaryngology, 1914-17, instr., 1917-21, asso. clin. otolaryngology, 1921-24, asso., 1924-26, asst. prof., 1926-34, asso. prof., 1934-40, prof., 1940-43, prof. emeritus since 1943. Consultant in otolaryngology U.S. Vets. Hosp., U.S. Marine Hosp. Served as capt. med. corps, U.S. Army, 1917-19. Mem. A.M.A., Am. Coll. Surgs., Am. Acad. Ophthalmology and Otolaryngology (vice pres.), Am. Laryngological, Rhinological and Otolaryngological Soc. (pres. 1946-47), Am. Laryngological Assn., Am. Otol. Soc., Southern and Mo. State Med. Assns., St. Louis Med. Soc., Phi Beta Pi. Conglist. Mason. Contbr. about 40 articles on otolaryngology to various med. jours. Home: 6224 Washington Av., St. Louis 5 MO Office: 308 N. Sixth St., St Louis 1 MO‡

LYMAN, LAUREN DWIGHT, mfg. exec.; b. Easthampton, Mass., Apr. 24, 1891; s. Henry Lauren and Annie (McMahon) L.; grad. Williston Acad., 1911; Yale, ex 1918; m. Mabel Styring, June 29, 1921 (dec. Dec. 1947); children—Ellen Styring (dec.), Elizabeth Dwight (Mrs. Kendric Packer), Philip Henry, Anne McMahon (Mrs. William H. Dunn), Mary (Mrs. H. Schreiber); m. 2d, Bertha H. Williams, June 11, 1949. Reporter N.Y. Times, 1919-38; with United Aircraft Corp., from 1938, asst. to pres. 1938-43, asst. to chmn., 1943-46, v.p., from 1946. Trustee Williston Acad., Easthampton, Mass., Rectory Sch., Pomfret, Conn.; mem. bd. dirs. Baldwin Sch., Bryn Mawr, Pa., 1940-50. Served U.S. Army, 1917-19. Recipient Pulitzer prize for reporting, 1936. Clubs: include: There's Magic in Music, Major and the Minor, Henry Aldrich Gets Glamour, And the Angels Sing, Out of This World, Our Hearts Were Young and Gay, Ruthless, Texas, Brooklyn and Heaven, My Friend Irma, Bedtime for Bonzo, People Against O'Hara, Meet Me at the Fair, Plunder of the Sun. Mem. Acad. Motion Picture Arts and Sci. Home: Beverly Hills CA Died Dec. 17, 1971.

LYNCH, RAYMOND A., lawyer; b. Dallas, Apr. 15, 1913; LL.B., U. Tex., 1939. Admitted to Tex. bar, 1934; partner firm Lynch, Chappell, Allday & Culp, Midland, Tex. Fellow Am. Coll. Probate Counsel; mem. Am., Midland County bar assns., State Bar Tex., Order of Coif, Chancellors, Phi Delta Phi. Address: Midland TX Deceased.*

LYNCH, THOMAS FRANCIS, lawyer; b. N.Y.C., Jan. 30, 1900; s. Thomas and Elizabeth (Stretton) L.; LL.B., St. John's U., 1931, LL.M., 1932; m. Nonie Elizabeth Tully, June 30, 1923; children—Thomas Philip, John Peter, Richard William. Admitted to N.Y. bar, 1932; with Am. R.R. Assn., 1918-20; joined U.S. Steel Corp., 1920, traffic dept., 1920-32, law dept., 1932-65, asst. to gen. counsel, 1944, asst. gen. counsel, 1945-52, asso. gen. counsel, 1952-65; pvt. law practice, from 1965. Mem. Am., N.Y. bar assns., Assn. ICC Practitioners. Address: Yonkers NY Died Apr. 11, 1968.

LYND, ROBERT STAUGHTON, university prof.; b. New Albany, Ind., Sept. 26, 1892; s. Staughton Browning and Cornelia (Day) L.; A.B., Princeton, 1914; B.D., Union Theol. Sem. 1923; Ph.D., Columbia, 1931; m. Helen Merrell, Sept. 3, 1921; children—Staughton, Andrea Merrell. (Mrs. Joseph Nold). Mng. editor Publishers' Weekly, N.Y.C., 1914-18; dir. small city study, Inst. of Social and Religious Research, N.Y.C., 1923-26; asst. dir. ednl. research div., Commonwealth Fund, N.Y.C., 1926-27; permanent sec., Social Sci. Research Council, N.Y.C., 1927-31; prof. of sociology Columbia U. Grad. Sch. from 1931. Trustee Twentieth Century Fund. Mem. Am. Sociological Society, Am. Econ. Assn. Author: sect. on The People as Consumers in Recent Social Trends, 1933; (with Helen Merrell Lynd) Middletown, 1929 and Middletown in Transition, 1937; Knowledge for What, 1939. New York City NY Died Nov. 1970.

LYNDE, CARLETON JOHN, physics; b. Mitchell, Ont., Can., Sept. 1, 1872; s. Frederich George and Isabella (Aiken) L.; B.A., U. of Toronto, 1895; Ph.D., U. of Chicago, 1905; m. Helen Eldred Storke, June 21, 1905 (died Feb. 11, 1940); 1 son, Carleton John; m. 2d, Katharine Koon Truxell, Mar. 5, 1941. Science teacher, high sch., Auburn, N.Y., 1896-99; physics teacher, University High Sch., Chicago, 1899-1905; prof. physics, Washington and Jefferson Coll., 1906-07, Macdonald Coll., Ste. Anne de Bellevue, P.Q., Can., 1907-24; prof. physics, Teachers College (Columbia), 1924-38, prof. emeritus since 1938. Mem. Am. Phys. Soc. A.A.A.S., Am. Soc. Illuminating Engrs., Zeta Psi, Sigma Xi. Democrat. Club: Faculty. Author: Home Waterworks, 1912; Physics of the Household, 1914; Laboratory Physics of the Household, 1919; Hydraulic and Pneumatic Engineering, 1920; Light Experiments, 1920; Glass Blowing, 1921; Everyday Physics, 1930; A Laboratory Course in Everyday Physics, 1931; Science Experiences with Home Equipment, 1937; Science Experience with Inexpensive Equipment, 1939; Science Experiences with Ten Cent New York NY‡

LYON, ADRIAN, judge; b. Pluckemin, Somerset County, N.J., July 25, 1869; s. William L. and Ursula (Sebring) L.; LL.B., New York Law Sch., 1894; m. Cornelia Post, May 8, 1895; 1 son, Howard S. Admitted to N.J. bar, 1892; supt. schs., Perth Amboy, 1894-05; city atty., 1895-98; pres. Perth Amboy Savings Inst. since 1899; mem. N.J. Legislature, 1900-01; judge Perth Amboy Dist. Court, 1901-09; referee in bankruptcy, 1913-30; judge Middlesex County Court of Common Pleas, 1909-11, and since 1930. Treas. Perth Amboy Gen. Hosp. since 1901; pres. Perth Amboy Y.M.C.A. since 1912; chmn. Gen. Bd. Nat. Council Y.M.C.A., 1925-35; mem. Gen. Council Presbyn. Ch., U.S.A., 1931-37; trustee Princeton Theol. Sem. Mem. Am., N.J. State and Middlesex County bar assns., N.J. State Bankers Assn. (pres., 1914), S.A.R. (pres. 1922, 23). Republican. Clubs: Union League (New York); Rotary, Masonic. Address: 84 Gordon St. Office: 210 Smith St., Perth Amboy NJ*‡

LYON, EDWIN BOWMAN, army officer; b. Las Cruces, N.M., Dec. 8, 1892; s. William Braden and Corie (Bowman) L.; student State Coll., Mesilla Park, N.M., 1904-10; B.S., U.S. Mil. Acad., 1915; grad. Air Service Tactical Sch., 1924; distinguished grad. Command and Gen. Staff Sch., 1927; grad. Army War Coll., 1932; m. Elsa Franzen. Commd. 2d lt. cav., U.S. Army, 1915, and advanced through the grades to major gen.; transferred to Aviation Sect., Signal Corps, 1917, to Air Service, 1920; rated command pilot and combat observer. Comdr. 6th Bomber Command, Moffett Field, Calif., 1941; dir. sect. Air Force Personnel Council. Episcopalian. Home: Washington DC Died Aug. 1971.*

LYON, GEORGE HARRY, editor; b. Binghamton, N.Y., April 2, 1890; s. Harry Fred and Minnie (Lester) L.; A.B., Hamilton Coll., 1913; m. Elizabeth Darrow, Sept. 11, 1919 (died Oct. 6, 1931); m. 2d, Eva Bryan, Jan. 7, 1932; children—Sally Antonia, John Sherwin, Eve. Reporter, 1914-19; editor Binghamton Morning Sun, 1919-21; night city editor, N.Y. Evening Telegram, 1921-27, asst. city editor, 1927-29, later city editor; city editor, New York World-Telegram, 1929-33; editor The Buffalo Times, 1933-40; mng. editor, The Newspaper PM, 1940-41; deputy director U.S. Office of War Information, attached to Supreme Hdqrs. Allied Expeditionary Force, 1944-45. Served in photographic sect., Signal Corps, U.S. Army, 1918-19. Mem. Phi Beta Kappa, Chi Psi. Episcopalian. Home: Washington DC Died 1971.

LYON, HERB, columnist; b. Chgo., Aug. 22, 1918, m. Lyle Hoffenberg; 2 sons. Pub. relations staff Eisenhower presdl. campaign, 1952; now columnist Chgo. Tribune. Home: Chicago IL Died Aug. 6, 1968.*

LYON, J(AMES) ADAIR, coll. prof.; b. York, Pa., May 4, 1876; s. James Adair and Elizabeth (Barringer) L.; M.A., Southwestern (Clarksville, Tenn., since removed to Memphis), 1895; ScD., 1918; grad. U. of Va. in astronomy and natural philosophy, 1900; m. Elizabeth Winston Antrim, 1900, (died 1944), children—Margaret Blair (Mrs. Parks Brinkley Pedrick), Elizabeth Antrim (Mrs. Joseph William Reddoch); m. 2d, Mrs. Claire Hutchinson Kimbrough, July 9, 1946. Teacher, 1895; McCormick fellow in astronomy and instr., U. of Va., 1897-1900; prof. physics, Newcomb Coll. (Tulane), 1900-41, now emeritus; dir. Div. for Teachers, Tulane, 1913-41, dir. Tulane Summer Sch., 1937-41, dir. Thomas F. Cunningham Observatory, 1941-51, prof. astronomy, Tulane, since 1942. Trustee and sec., Monteagle S.S. Assembly, Tenn., 1916-46, chairman committee on Secondary Schools, Southern Association of Colleges, 1927; director and president board, Louise S. McGehee School, New Orleans, 1936-48; director Austin (Tex.) Theol. Sem. (Presbyn.), 1941-47. Fellow A.A.A.S.; mem. State Adv. Com., La. Civil Service League, Am. Physical Soc., Illuminating Engring. Soc., New Orleans Acad. Sciences, New Orleans Astronomical Soc. (pres.). Phi Beta Kappa, Sigma Alpha Epsilon. Presbyterian. Democrat. Mason. Club: Round Table (pres. 1939-41). Co-author: Laboratory Exercises in Physics, 1933. Home: 1210 Broadway, New Orleans 18 LA‡

LYON, MILFORD HALL, clergyman; b. Waukon, Allamakee County, Ia., Feb. 10, 1868; s. Edmond Burke and Harriet (Sisson) L.; youngest of 14 children; A.B., State U. of Ia., 1892; D.D., Wheaton (Ill.) Coll., 1916; m. Effie Cornelia Forest, Nov. 10, 1892; children—Merle Paul, Helen (Mrs. R.E. Beebe), Arthur Eugene, Margaret (Mrs. H.M. Morgan), Ruth. Pres. Ellsworth Coll., Iowa Falls, Ia., 1892-94; ordained Congl. ministry, 1894; pastor Harvey, Ill., 1894-96, Bethel Ch., Chicago, 1896-99; evangelistic work, 1899-1930 (delivered over 8,000 addresses in 36 States, 150,000 professed conversions); pastor Morgan Park Presbyn. Ch., Chicago, 1930, 31, First Presbyn. Ch., Daytona Beach, Fla., 1932-39. Dir. Winona Assembly, 1915-20; pres. Interdenominational Assn. Evangelists, 1917-18; ex-pres. Daytona Beach Ministerial Assn. On staff Y.M.C.A., with A.E.F. in France, 1917-18. Republican. Author: The Lordship of Jesus, 1905; For the Life That Now Is, 1909; The Basis for Brotherhood, 1923. Mem. St. John's Presbytery. Home: 1001 S. Josephine Av., Denver CO‡

LYON, NELSON REED, ins. exec.; b. Gardner, Mass., June 14, 1905; s. James H. and Jennie M. (Moody) L.; student Boston U. Coll. Bus. Adminstrn., 1925-29. With Mass. Bonding & Ins. Co. (merged to form Hanover Ins. Co., 1961), Boston, from 1932, successively accountant, asst. sec., asst. treas., 1932-52, v.p., 1952-58, later treas.; treas. Mass. Bay Ins. Co., Fulton Ins. Co. Mem. Assn. Ins. Accountants. Mason. Home: Wellesley Hills MA Died Jan. 11, 1972.

LYONS, COLEBURKE, accountant; b. Kingston, Ont., Can., July 18, 1899; s. Edward and Mary E. (O'Brien) L.; B.C.S., U. Detroit, 1922; m. Nell Hamilton, July 12, 1927; children—Edward Hamilton, Thomas Francis. Came to U.S., 1918, naturalized, 1932. Pub. accountant, Detroit, 1925-64; partner Lyons, Teetzel, Wyllie & Borland, and predecessors, 1922-59, Lybrand, Ross Bros. & Montgomery, 1959-64. C.P.A., Mich. Mem. Am. Inst. C.P.A.'s (vice president 1952-53, past member of the council), Am. Accounting Assn., Mich. Assn. C.P.A.'s (past president) U.S. Mens Curling Association (past pres.). K.C. (past state treas., dist. dep., grand knight). Clubs: Detroit, Detroit Curling; Paul Bunyan. Home: Detroit MI Died June 13, 1967; buried Detroit MI

LYTTELTON, OLIVER, English govt. ofcl., mem. Parliament; b. Eng., 1893; stu. Eton Coll. and Trinity Coll. Cambridge; m. Lady Moira Godolphin Osborne; 3 sons (1 killed in World War II), 1 dau. Continuous active service in World War I, 1915-18; became mng. dir. Brit. Metal Corp., Ltd.; controller of non-ferrous metals, 1939-40; became pres. Bd. of Trade, 1940; mem. War Cabinet and Minister of State in Middle East, 1941, Minister of Prodn. 1942, co-head (with Donald Nelson) of new combined Prodn. and Resources Bd. aimed at pooling prodn. of U.S. and Britain, 1942-45; Minister of Prodn. and Pres. Bd. of Trade May-July, 1945; Privy Councilor; chmn. Asso. Elec. Industries, Ltd., 1945-51, dir. Alliance Assurance Co., Ltd., 1946-51. Mem. Parliament for Aldershot, Hants, 1940-72; sec. of state for the colonies, 1951-54. Awarded Distinguished Service Order, Mil. Cross. Address: London Eng Died Jan. 21, 1972.

LYTTON, BART, financier; b. New Castle, Pa., Oct. 4, 1912; s. Eliah Kaplan (foster father) and Ina Robins; student Westminister Coll., 1930-32, U. Va., 1932-34; LL.D., Wilberforce U., 1963; m. Beth Golden, July 17, 1936; one daughter, Timothea B. (Mrs. Herbert Edward Stewart, Jr.). Founder, chmn. bd., pres. Metropolitan Mortgage Co., 1948; founder, chmn., pres. Lytton Co., mortgage brokers and bankers; mng. partner Beth-Bart Homes, 1954-56; chmn. bd. First Western Savs. & Loan Assn., Nev., 1954-58; chmn. bd., pres. Silver State Savs. & Loan Assn., Nev., 1957 (merged with First Western); chmn. bd. Canoga Park Savs. & Loan, 1956-58; chmn. bd., pres., mng. officer Lytton Savs. and Loan, Los Angeles, 1958-68; founder, chmn., pres. Lytton Financial Corp., 1959-68; chmn. Home Builders Savs. & Loan Assn., Pomona, 1959 (merged with Lytton Savs. 1959); dir. Home Found. Savs., Palo Alto, 1960-62; chmn. Lytton Savs. & Loan Assn. of No. Cal., 1962; chmn., dir. Beverly Hills Fed. Savs. & Loan Assn., 1961-64, pres., 1962-64; pres. Southland Co., 1961-68; founder, chmn. Lytton Capital Corp., 1961-68; chmn. Title Acceptance Corp., 1959-68. Mem. Gov.'s Adv. Council Bus. Econs., 1959. Chmn. campaign A.R.C., So. Nev., 1957. Del. Democratic Nat. Conv., 1956, 60, 64; finance chmn. Cal. Dem. Central Com., 1958-60, 60-62; chmn. adv. council Los Angeles County Dem. Central Com., from 1960. Pres., founder Muscular Dystrophy Assn., Los Angeles, hon. chmn. Western States, 1957; hon. chmn. Muscular Sclerosis, Los Angeles, 1960; nat. bd. govs. Nat. Med. Center, 1959; bd. govs. Los Angeles County Mus., from 1963; gen. chmn. 1st Internat. Music Festival U. Cal. at Los Angeles, 1961; gen. chmn. for So. Cal., Eleanor Roosevelt Research Inst. Cancer; founder Lytton Center of Visual Arts, Los Angeles, Palo Alto, Pomona. Decorated commendatore II Cancelliere dell, Ordine (Italy); recipient National Man of Year award City of Hope, 1960. Mem. Nat. League Insured Savs. and Loan (gov. 1955-58, dir.), U. Va. Alumni Assn. (bd. mgrs.). Clubs: Friars; Malibu, Beverly Hills; Press (Los Angeles); Nat. Democratic (Washington). Donor (with Mrs. Lytton) Lytton Gallery, Los Angeles County Mus. of Art. Home: Los Angeles CA Died June 1969.

MAAG, WILLIAM FREDERICK, JR., editor; b. Youngstown, O., July 26, 1883; s. William Frederick and Elizabeth (Du Casse) M.; A.B., Harvard University, 1905, A.M., 1915; hon. Litt.D., Youngstown U., 1946; L.H.D., Kenyon Coll., 1948. Editor, pub. Youngstown Vindicator; pres. WFMJ Broadcasting Co. Trustee Youngstown Coll., Youngstown Hosp., Kenyon Coll., pres. Youngstown Public Library, Friends of Youngstown Coll. Library, v.p., Youngstown C. of C. Clubs: Youngstown, Country, Union. Contbr. to Irving Babbitt, Man and Teacher. Home: Youngstown OH Died Feb. 29, 1968.

MAAS, CARLOS J., steel mfr.; b. Eau Claire, Wis., Aug. 21, 1897; s. Theodore J. and Ida (Sutter) M.; grad. Lick Wilmerding Sch., San Francisco, 1915; m. Roberta Clancy, Apr. 18, 1931; children—Millicent R., Carlos J., Diana N. Pres. Judson Steel Corp., San Francisco, from 1923; dir. Bothin Real Estate Co., Security Pacific Nat. Bank, San Francisco. Sec., trustee Bothin Helping Fund; dir. Cal. Sch. Mech. Arts, San Francisco. Home: San Francisco CA Died Apr. 12, 1972.

MABBOTT, THOMAS OLLIVE, educator; b. New York City, July 6, 1898; s. John Milton and Kate (Ollive) M.; A.B., Columbia, 1920, Ph.D., 1923; m. Maureen Cobb, August 30, 1928; 1 dau., Jane (Mrs. Carl J. Austrian, Jr.). Assistant, N.Y. Hist. Society, 1922; assistant, graduate sch., Columbia, 1922-25; asst. prof. English, Northwestern U., 1925-28, Brown U., 1928-29, Hunter Coll., 1929-37, asso. prof. 1937-46, prof., 1946-66; summer schs. U. of Chicago, 1923, Duke U., 1940-41, 1949, U. of So. Calif., 1947. Awarded silver medal of merit, Am. Numismatic Assn., 1949. Fellow Royal Numismatic Society, Am. Numismatic Soc., Metropolitan Museum Art (life); member the New York Historical Society, Modern Lang. Assn. Protestant. Author or editor: Poe's Politian, 1923; Life and Works of E.C. Pinkney (with F.L. Pleadwell), 1926; Walt Whitman's Half-Breed, 1927; Selected Poems of Poe, 1928; Poe's Doings of Gotham, 1929; portions vols. 1, 12, 13, 18, Columbia edit. of Milton, 1931-38; Paste Prints, 1932; Poe's Al Aaraaf, 1933; Vols. 78, 95, 97 and 99, of Heitz Einblattdrucke series (on 15th Century relief prints), 1932-41; Poems of W.W. Lord, 1938; Poe's Tamerlane, 1941; Wilmer's Merlin, 1941; Poe's Raven and other Poems, 1942; Selections from Poe, 1951; Bryant's Embargo, 1955; Poe's Collected Works, Vol. I (poems), pub. posthumously, 1969. Editor: Numismatic Review (periodical), 1943-48. Contbr. to learned jours. Discovered first book publ. of Poe's Raven". Home: New York City NY Died May 15, 1968; buried Greenwood Cemetery.

MABEY, CHARLES R., ex-governor; b. Bountiful, Utah, Oct. 4, 1877; s. Joseph Thomas and Sarah Lucretia (Tolman) M.; U. of Utah, 1893-96, U. of Chicago, 1908-09; m. Afton Rampton, 1905; children—Rendell N., Charles Pace, Robert Burns, Edward Milo. Began in banking business, 1906; was cashier of Bountiful State Bank, 1906-21; pres. and manager Builders Finance Corp.; president and dir. Bountiful State Bank. Was councilman and mayor of Bountiful; mem. Utah Ho. of Rep., 1913-15; gov. of Utah, term 1921-25. Captain Utah Nat. Guard; private, corpl. and sergt. Utah Light Arty., Spanish-Am. War, serving in Philippines; vol. World War and mustered in as capt. 145th F.A.; maj. F.A., U.S. Army, 1918.

Received Silver Star Citation, May 14, 1899. Department comdr. American Legion, Utah, 1932-33, nat. vice-comdr., 1933-34. State Adminstr. War Bond Staff for Utah since 1941. Mem. Poets of the Pacific (pres.), S.A.R. League of U.S. (v.p.), Utah State Hist. Soc. Republican. Mormon. Author: Utah Batteries, a History; The Pony Express; Our Father's House, a Biographical History. Club: Commercial. Home: 6405 Orchard Dr., Salt Lake City UT‡

MACANALLY, JAMES R., railroad exec.; b. Phila., July 23, 1908; s. James C. and Alexandrina (Macleod) MacA.; student pub. schs., N.J.; m. Helen Marie Cornick, Sept. 6, 1930; children—Richard Bruce, Barry James. Stenographer Pa. R.R., 1925-26, U.P. R.R., 1925-28, passenger clk., 1928-30, (both Phila.), asst. chief clk., freight traffic agt., chief clk., Chgo., 1930-41, gen. agt., Milw., 1941, asst. gen. agt. freight dept., Chgo., 1941-44, asst. to gen. freight traffic mgr., Omaha, 1944-46, asst. Freight traffic mgr. 1946-49, gen. freight traffic mgr. 1949-59, traffic v.p., 1959-68, became sr. v.p., 1968. Republican. Presbyn. Clubs: Athletic, Happy Hollow, Omaha Plaza (Omaha); Union League (Chgo.). Home: Omaha NE

MACARTHUR, ROBERT HELMER, educator, biologist; b. Toronto, Can., Apr. 7, 1930; s. John Wood and Olive (Turner) MacA.; came to U.S., 1947; B.A., Marlboro Coll., 1951; D.H.S. (hon.), 1972; M.S., Brown U., 1953; Ph.D., Yale, 1958; m. Elizabeth Bayles Whittemore, June 14, 1952; children—Duncan, Alan, Elizabeth, Donald. From asst. prof. to prof. U. Pa., 1958-65; mem. faculty Princeton, 1965-72, Henry Fairfield Osborn prof. biology, 1968-72; hon. research asso. Smithsonian Tropical Research Inst. Acad. adviser Marlboro Coll. Served with AUS, 1954-56. Recipient Mercer award Ecol. Soc. Am. Fellow Am. Acad. Arts and Scis., Nat. Acad. Scis. Research theory community structure and evolution. Home: Princeton NJ Died Nov. 1, 1972.

MACARTNEY, JOHN W., pres. H.C. Bohack Co., Inc. Address: Brooklyn NY Died 1966.*

MACAULAY, FREDERICK ROBERTSON, economist; b. Montreal, Can., Aug. 12, 1882; s. Thomas Bassett and Henrietta Maria (Bragg) M.; student McGill U., Montreal, 1899-1902, Colo. Coll., 1906-07, U. of Ariz., 1907-08; B.A., U. of Colo., 1909, M.A., 1910, LL.B., 1911; Ph.D., Columbia, 1922; m. Beulah Ines Stearns, 1910; children—Barbara Elizabeth, Marjorie Janet. Came to U.S., 1902, naturalized citizen, 1920. Admitted to Colo. bar, 1911, but did not practice; instr. in economics, U. of Wash., 1915-16; asst. prof. economic theory and theory of statistics, U. of Calif., 1916-20; economist Nat. Bur. Econ. Research, N.Y.C., 1920-38; Nat. Securities and Research Corp.; lecturer New School for Social Research, 1921-26; dir. Central Nat. Corp. Fellow Am. Statis. Assn. Author: Income in the United States—Its Amount and Distribution (with others; 2 vols.), 1922; The Smoothing of Time Series, 1931; Some Theoretical Problems Suggested By the Movements of Interest Rates, Bond Yields and Stock Prices in the United States Since 1856, 1938; Short Selling on the New York Stock Exchange, (with David Durand), 1951. Home: Great Neck NY Died Mar. 27, 1970; crematated.

MACAULEY, CHARLES RAYMOND, author, illustrator, cartoonist; b. Canton, O., Mar. 19, 1871; s. John K. M.; ed. pub. schs., Canton, O.; studied law 2 yrs., Canton; m. New York, Apr. 16, 1897, Emma Worms. Adopted art career quite by accident; won $50, 1st prize, Cleveland Press, 1891; a fortnight later joined staff of Cleveland World; during 10 following yrs. contributed cartoons to leading met. papers and periodicals; Feb., 1901, resigned from staff New York Herald to enter lit. field; now regularly contributing drawings to Life, New York. Author: and Illustrator (collaboration John Kendrick Bangs): Emblemland, 1902 R7. Address: 115 W. 64th St., New York‡

MACBETH, GEORGE DUFF, glass mfr.; b. Pittsburgh, Pa., Aug. 11, 1892; s. George Alexander and Kate (Duff) M.; Ph.B., Yale, 1913; m. Beatrice Holmes, Apr. 29, 1922. Began in glass mfg. business with Macbeth-Evans Glass Co., Charleroi, Pa., 1913, pres. and gen. mgr., 1926-36; v.p., dir. Corning Glass Works, Corning, N.Y., from 1936, controller from 1943; made hon. vice pres., 1957; dir. Pitts. Corning Corp. Dir. The Corning Mus. of Glass. Trustee Corning Glass Works Found. Mem. Phi Gamma Delta. Mason (32 deg., Shriner). Clubs: Duquesne (Pitts.); University (N.Y.). Home: Corning NY also Balholmie, Scotland. Died May 1, 1968; buried Corning NY

MAC CALLUM, JOHN BRUCE, educator, physician; b. Ontario, Can., June 8, 1876; s. Dr. G. A. MacC.; supt. asylum, London, Ont.; grad. Toronto Univ., 1896; med. dept. Johns Hopkins, 1900. Asst. anatomy, Johns Hopkins, 1900-2; asst. physiology, 1903-5, prof. same since 1905, Univ. of Calif. Translated from German and edited: Histology and Microscopic Anatomy (Szymonowicz and MacCallum), 1902 L12. Writer of monographs on physiol. and biol. topics and contb'r to med. jours. Unmarried. Address: Berkeley CA‡

MACCAUD, FRANCIS WILLIAM, P. E. clergyman; b. in Ireland; s. Edward David and Mary (Burrows) M.; ungrad. Trinity Coll., Dublin, 1889-90; grad. with honor St. Andrew's Divinity Sch., Syracuse, N.Y. Ordered deacon, 1895; ordained priest, 1897; in charge Grace Ch., Whitney Point, N.Y., 1895-7; m. 1897, Lucy, d. W. J. Foweraker, London, S.W. In charge St. Paul's Ch., Antwerp, N.Y., 1898; chaplain St. Anna's chapel and The House of the Good Shepherd," Syracuse, N.Y., 1899; rector of Grace Ch., Huron, S.D., 1900-4; missionary of Whatcom Co., Wash., 1904-5. Wrote series of articles, God in Science, 1895 O1. Also philol. letter to The Living Church; etc. Address: Blaine WA‡

MACCHESNEY, CLARA TAGGART, artist; b. Brownsville, Calif.; d. Joseph Burwell and Sarah (Jewett) M.; pupil Virgil Williams, San Francisco; H. S. Mowbray and J. C. Beckwith of New York; Courtois and Girardot at Colarossi School, Paris, France; unmarried. Received 2 medals, Chicago Expn., 1893; Dodge prize, New York, 1894; 3 medals, Colarossi Sch., Paris; gold medal, Phila. Arts Club, 1900; 2d Hallgarten prize, Nat. Acad. Design, New York, 1901 Exhibited Paris Salon, 1896, 1898; St. Louis Expn., 1904. Mem. New York Soc. of Painters, Nat. Arts Club (life), Nat. Assn. Woman Painters and Sculptors, Barnard Club, Lyceum Club (London), Am. Water Color Soc. Represented in Erie (Pa.) Art Club; Union League, Chicago; Nat. Gallery, Washington, D.C.; Nat. Arts Club, Barnard Club, New York; State Capitol, Sacramento, Calif.; Altoona (Pa.) Pub. Library; Boston Art Club; Emigrant Savings Bank, Hill Pub. Co., Aldine Club, all of New York; Palace of Legion of Honor, San Francisco. Club: Woman's City. Home: 15 W. 67th St., New York NY‡

MACCLINTOCK, PAUL, geologist; b. Aurora, N.Y., Feb. 2, 1891; s. William D. and Lucia (Lander) MacC.; B.S., U. of Chicago, 1912, Ph.D., 1920; m. Elizabeth S. Copeland, Sept. 5, 1925; children—Lucia, Copeland. Teacher, Indianapolis (Ind.) Manual Training High Sch., 1913-14; instr. mathematics, U. of Chicago, 1921-28, asst. prof., 1926-27, asso. prof. 1927-28; Knox Taylor prof. of geography, Princeton, 1928-59. Served with Co. A, 29th Engrs., U.S. Army, 1916-18. Mem. A.A.A.S., Geol. Soc. America, Sigma Xi, Alpha Delta Phi. Contbr. to revision of Chamberlin and Salisbury College Geology; contbr. articles on physiography and glacial geology to sci. jours. Home: Princeton NJ Died Mar. 23, 1970.

MACCLINTOCK, SAMUEL, editor, educator; b. Bourbon Co., Ky., June 22, 1872; s. Alexander and C. (Darnall) M.; Ph.B., U. of Chicago, 1896, Ph.D., 1908; m. Helen, d. Charles Allen Marsh, of Chicago, June 2, 1910. Instr. Armour Inst. of Tech., Chicago, 1897-8; div. supt. of schs., P.I., 1902-5; Am. consul, Honduras, 1909-10; ednl. dir. and sec., La Salle Extension U., Chicago, since 1910. Editor Personal Efficiency" (mag.); mng. editor Business Administration Library and Interstate Commerce and Railway Traffic Library. Pres. Assn. of Doctors of Philosophy of U. of Chicago, 1915-17. Clubs: Quadrangle, City, Chickaming Country. Author: Aliens Under the Federal Laws of the United States, 1909; also articles on the Philippines and Central America. Home: 1229 E. 56th St. Office: 4046 Michigan Av., Chicago‡

MACCLOSKEY, JAMES EDWARD, JR., lawyer; b. Pittsburgh, Pa., Dec. 16, 1876; s. James Edward and Catherine Hayes (Houston) MacC.; A.B., Harvard, 1900; LL.B., 1902; m. Helen Irwin, Nov. 1, 1905 (died Jan. 26, 1941); m. 2d, Mrs. Martha Heron Brooks, Feb. 21, 1942; children—Katharine (Mrs. Samuel B. Crocker) and Helen (Mrs. Howard F. Rough). Admitted to Pa. Bar 1902, and since practiced in Pittsburgh; former chmn. bd. Harbison-Walker Refractories Co.; dir. Mellon Nat. Bank and Trust Co., Townsend Co. Vice pres. and trustee Hosp. Service Assn. of Pittsburgh; trustee Shadyside Hospital; sec. and treas. Pittsburgh Park and Playground Soc.; v.p. Pa. Coll. for Women. Republican. Unitarian. Clubs: Duquesne, Allegheny Country, Harvard-Yale-Princeton (Pittsburgh); Rolling Rock. Home: West Drive, Sewickley, Pa. Office: Farmers Bank Bldg., Pittsburgh PA‡

MACCOLL, ALEXANDER, clergyman; b. Glasgow, Scotland, Dec. 27, 1866; s. Hugh and Janet (Roberton) MacC.; ed. Glasgow High Sch. and Univ., and Union Theol. Sem. (non-grad.); D.D., Rutgers, 1914; m. Grant Stuart Hally Craig, June 15, 1892; children—Ailsa Craig Pender, Alexander Meredith (dec.). Came to U.S., 1886, naturalized citizen, 1899. Editor New Bedford (Mass.) Evening Journal 5 yrs.; ordained ministry, 1897; asst., N. Ref. Ch., Newark, N.J., 1896-97; minister Congl. Ch., Briarcliff Manor, N.Y., 1897-1907, South St. Presbyterian Ch., Morristown, N.J., 1907-11, Second Church, Philadelphia, 1911-49, minister emeritus since 1949. Trustee General Assembly Presbyn. Church in U.S.A.; univ. preacher many yrs., Princeton, Harvard, etc. Clubs: Union League, Phi Alpha, Merion Cricket. Author: A Working Theology, 1909; The Sheer Folly of Preaching, 1923; Two Hundred Years of the Evangel, 1945. Address: 6339 Sherwood Rd., Philadelphia 31 PA‡

MACCRACKEN, HENRY NOBLE, educator; b. Toledo, O., Nov. 19, 1880; s. Henry Mitchell and Catherine (Hubbard) MacC.; B.A., New York U., 1900, M.A., 1904; M.A., Harvard, 1905, Ph.D., 1907; LL.D., Smith Coll., 1915, Brown U., 1915; m. Marjorie Dodd, June 12, 1907;children—Maisey, Joy, Calvin, James. Instructor in English Syrian Protestant College, 1900-03; John Harvard fellow, 1907-08, instr. English, 1908-10, asst. prof., 1910-13, Sheffield Scientific Sch. (Yale); prof. English, Smith Coll., 1913-15; pres. Vassar Coll., 1915-46. Pres. Kosciuszki Foundation from 1925; chmn. 1st and 2d Internat. Councils of Christians and Jews, 1946 and 1948; pres. Internat. Inst., N.Y. City, 1946; ednl. cons., Nat. Conf. of Christians and Jews, 1946, gen. sec., 1947-48. Conglist. Mem. Modern Lang. Assn. of Am., Psi Upsilon, Phi Beta Kappa. Author: First Year English, 1903, 2d edit., 1905; English Composition in Theory and Practice (part author), 1909, 2d edit., 1912, 3d edit., 1931; An Introduction to Shakespeare (part author), 1910; Manual of Good English (part author), 1917; John the Common Weal, 1927; The Family on Gramercy Park, 1949. Editor: The Serpent of Division, 1911; Minor Poems of Lydgate, Part I, 1912, Part II, 1934; The College Chaucer, 1913; Shakespeare's Principal Plays, 1914, 23, 35; Ten Plays of Shakespeare, 1927. Home: Poughkeepsie NY Died May 7, 1970.

MACCRACKEN, WILLIAM PATTERSON, JR., lawyer; b. Chicago, Sept. 17, 1888; s. William P. and Mary Elizabeth (Avery) MacC.; prep. edn., Montclair (N.J.) High Sch., South Side Acad. and Univ. High Sch., Chicago; Ph.B., U. of Chicago, 1909, J.D., 1911; LL.D., Norwich U., Northfield, Vt., 1936; m. Sally Lucile Lewis, Sept. 14, 1918; children—Wm. Lewis, Nell Elizabeth. Admitted to Ill. bar, 1911, and began practice in Chicago; asst. atty. gen of Ill., 1923; asst. state's atty. Cook County, 1924; asst. sec. of commerce for aeronautics, U.S., Aug. 11, 1926-Oct. 1, 1929; resigned to enter pvt. practice; now member firm MacCracken, Collins & Hawes; secretary Am. Bar Assn., 1925-36, life mem. house delegates; vice pres., dir. National Aviation Center, Inc. Chairman of Pan-Am. Commercial Aviation Conf., Washington, 1927; v. chmn. Internat. Civil Aeronautics Conf., Washington, 1928; head U.S. delegation to Internat. Conv. for Air Navigation, Paris, 1929. Served in Air Service, U.S., 1917-18; mem. Nat. Advisory Com. for Aeronautics, 1929-38; chmn. Joint Airport Users Conf., Civil Aviation Joint Legislative Com. Decorated Officer Order of Crown of Italy. Alumni Citation Award, University of Chicago; Elder Statesman of Aviation, 1955, Wright Brothers Memorial Trophy, 1959. Fellow of American Bar Found.; mem. Am., Ill., Fed., Chgo., D.C., Can. (hon.) bar assns., Am. Optometric Found. (life), Am. Law Inst., Am. Patent Law Assn., Nat. Aeronautic Assn. (gen. gounsel), Inst. Aeronautical Sciences, American Legion, Psi Upsilon, Phi Delta Phi, Legal Club, Law Club. Republican. Clubs: Nat. Press, Metropolitan, Chevy Chase Capitol Hill (Washington). Asso. editor U.S. Aviation Reports. Home: Washington DC Died Sept. 1969; buried Washington DC

MACDONALD, ANNA ADDAMS, librarian; b. Scottsville, Va., June 6, 1871; d. Abraham Addams and Isabella Plunket (Maclay) M.; prep. edn., St. Louis High Sch., 1889-91; studied pvtly., State Coll., Pa., 1891-1907; Sch. of Library Science, Pratt Inst., Brooklyn, N.Y., 1907-08. With Pa. State Coll. Library, 1895-1907; in charge traveling libraries of Free Library Commn., Pa., 1908; cons. librarian, same, 1910; with library extension div., Pa. State Library, 1910-24; acting dir. Pa. State Library and Mus., 1924, dir., 1926; extension librarian Library Extension Div. of Pa. State Library and Mus., 1927; retired, 1931. War library work for A.L.A., at Gettysburg, Pa., and in France, 1918-19. Mem. A.L.A., Pa. Library Assn., Pa. Library Club. Republican. Presbyn. Clubs: Civic, Business and Professional Women's. Home: Millerstown PA‡

MACDONALD, ARCHIBALD ARNOTT, supt. schs.; b. Hartley, Ia., Feb. 11, 1876; s. Archibald and Mary (Wallace) M.; A.B., Oberlin, 1900; A.M., Columbia, 1916; m. Dorothy W. Connors, of Parker, S.D., June 4, 1903; children—Jean Wallace, Robert Rowe, Dorothy Connors, Archibald Arnott. Began teaching at Pischelville, Knox Co., Neb., 1893; asst. prin. Yankton (S.D.) High Sch., 1900-01; instr. in sciences Sioux Falls High Sch., 1901-02, prin., 1902-07; supt. schs., Sioux Falls, since 1907. Mem. N.E.A. (life), S.D. Ednl. Assn. Conglist. Mason (33 deg., Shriner). Home: 1610 S. Duluth Av. Office: 200 Williams Bldg., Sioux Falls SD‡

MACDONALD, AUGUSTIN SYLVESTER, industrial developer; b. San Francisco, Calif., Apr. 19, 1865; s. J.H. and Catherine E. (Lydeard) M.; grad. Sackett Coll.; m. Maie Tucker, Dec. 31, 1899; 1 dau., Mora (Mrs. Brooks). Industrial developer of land, water, electrical energy, mines and oil; pres. Riverdale Mining Co., Richmond Wharf & Dock Co., Pamure Oil Co., Van Ness Land Co. Founder and 1st pres. Municipal Playgrounds, Oakland, Calif.; also founder Boy Scouts. Oakland. Mem. Calif. State Hist. Assn. (pres.), Alameda County Hist. Soc. (pres.), Oriental Print Soc. (pres.), Richmond Chamber Commerce, San Francisco Art Assn. (life). Republican. Clubs: Pacific Union, Claremont Country, Calif. Book, Garden, Etchers. Author: Californiana, 1902; Little Literary Lights, 1915. Home: 325 Vernon St., Oakland CA‡

MACDONALD, IAN (GIBBS), surgeon; b. Calgary, Can., Apr. 9, 1903; s. Alexander D. and Gertrude (Gibbs) M.; M.D., C.M., McGill U., 1928; m. Esther Case, Sept. 16, 1931; children—Alexander Case, Sharon; m. 2d, Eve March, July 14, 1946; children—Bruce, Katharine; m. 3d, Eleanor G. Clark, March 17, 1963. Came to U.S., 1932, naturalized, 1941. Intern, resident Montreal General Hosp., 1927-30; resident pathology U. Mich. Hosp., 1930-31; resident surgeon Toronto Gen. Hosp., 1931-32; pvt. practice, Los Angeles, from 1943; instr. surgery U. So. Cal., 1932-33, asso. prof., 1943-56, clin. prof. surgery, from 1956; dir. tumor clinic Cornwall Hosp., 1935-38; clin. research Am. Coll. Surgeons, 1938-40; asso. Los Angeles Tumor Inst., 1941-43; sr. attending surgeon tumor surgery Los Angeles County Hosp., Hollywood-Presbyn. Hosp., St. Vincent's Hosp.; cons. radium therapist Children's Hosp., Los Angeles, from 1943. Recipient award for distinguished service in cancer control Am. Cancer Soc., 1951. Diplomate Am. Bd. Radiology, 1938. Fellow A.C.S.; mem. Los Angeles Surg. Soc., Assn. Cancer Research, Am. Radium Soc., A.M.A., A.A.A.S., Pacific Coast Surg. Assn., Am. Coll. Radiology, Ewing Soc., Pacific Coast Roetgen Soc., Soc. Head and Neck Surgeons, Sigma Xi. Author articles on biology and treatment of cancer, contbr. textbooks. Editor bull. Los Angeles County Med. Assn. Office: Los Angeles CA Died Mar. 9, 1968.

MACDONALD, JESSE JUAN, mining engr.; b. in Iowa; s. Samuel Franklin and Amanda Catherine (Roads) M.; ed. Professor Dick's Normal Sch., Denver; spl. student Columbia, 1906, 07; m. Maty E. Gilbert, of Chicago, 1898. Began as assayer, Colo., 1893; one of the first in America to make use of cyanide process in extracting gold and silver from ores; spent many yrs. in Mexico and S.A., in remote places, working out metall. problems; was metall. engr. Utah Copper Co., and oil flotation expert Ray Consolidated Copper Co.; sales engineer Taylor Wharton Iron and Steel Co.; now mgr. Downtown Mines Co., Leadville, Colo. Republican. Baptist. Mem. Am. Inst. Mining Engrs., Am. Geog. Soc., Beta Theta Pi. Mason (32 deg.). Address: Leadville CO‡

MAC DONALD, WILLIAM J., congressman; b. in Grant County, Wis., Nov. 17, 1874; married. Served as pros. atty. Keweenaw County, Wis., 4 yrs., Houghton County 4 yrs.; mem. 63d Congress (1913-15), 12th Mich. Dist.; Progressive. Home: Calumet MI‡

MACEDO SOARES, JOSE CARLOS, economist, educator; b. Sao Paulo, Brazil, Oct. 6, 1883; s. Jose Eduardo and Candida (Sodre) de Macedo Soares; student Faculty Law, Sao Paulo, Brazil, 1905; m. Mathilde Fonseca, Dec. 15, 1910. Prof. adminstrv. and econ. scis. U. Brazil; prof. law Cath. U.; ambassador to Italy; dep, Constituent Assembly, 1933-34; minister fgn. relations, 1934, 56; minister justice, 1937; fed. insp., Sao Paulo, 1945-47; dir. Banco de Sao Paulo, Companhia Paulista de Artefatos de Aluminio, Companhia Campos de Jordao, Companhia Anglo-Brasileira de Tecidos de Juta, Companhia Paulista de Estrada de Ferro, A Sao Paulo, ins. firm. Mem. Brazilian Commn. for Codification Internat. Law; chief Brazilian del. Disarmament Conf., 1932, 16th Internat. Labor Conf., 1932, Roosevelt Peace Conf., Buenos Aires, 1936. Decorated San Mauricio and San Lazaro, Italian Crown (Italy); San Lazaro (Jerusalem); Order Leopold (Belgium); San Gregorio Magno, Holy Sepulcher (Vatican); Legion Honor (France); Mil. Order Christ (Portugal); Sun of Peru; Merit (Chile); Condor of Andes (Bolivia); Red Cross (Germany) Order Boyaca (Colombia); Order Merit (Ecuador; Austria); Oder Brilliant Jade (China). Mem. Brazilian Acad. Letters (pres. 1942-43), Brazilian Geol. and Hist. Inst. (pres.), Brazilian Geog. Soc. (pres.), Acad. Scis. Lisbon, Geography Soc. of Lima, Argentine Acad. Letters, Ecuadorian Acad. Nat. History, Portuguese Hist. Soc., Chilean Acad. History and Geography, Commercial Assn. Sao Paulo (pres.), Assn. Rio de Janeiro (pres.). Author: Brazil and the League of Nations, 1927; The Financial Policy of President Washington Luiz, 1928. Address: Sao Paulo Brazil Died Jan. 1968.

MACELROY, ANDREW JACKSON, author; b. Homeworth, O., Sept. 14, 1875; s. William and Elizabeth (Dennison) M.; B.S., Cornell U., 1898; m. 2d, Mrs. Jeanette Wells, of Rockville Centre, N.Y., Sept. 19, 1925; children—Webster Wells, Hetty Wells (Mrs. F. W. Finn). High sch. prin., 1898-1904; with Ginn & Co., 1905-07; with editorial and sales depts. Appleton Co., 1908-19; leave of absence, 1909, making trip around the world as rep. of New York American, crossing Siberia; with Popular Science Monthly, 1919-20; field director of The Iroquois Pub. Co., 1928-32; president Acorn Pub. Co. Cadet Cornell U., 1894-96; pvt., 2d lt. and 1st lt., 47th N.Y. Inf., 1915-17; capt. Air Service, 1917; maj., 1919; rated as reserve mil. aviator (pilot); was attached to Royal Air Force as U.S. Air Service insp., 1918, and mem. hist. sect. Gen. Staff, U.S. Army, A.E.F., 1919. Mentioned in orders and awarded D.S.O. (British). Mem. Acad. Polit. Science, Sigma Alpha Epsilon, Pi Gamma Mu. Republican. Presbyn. Mason. Clubs: Cornell, Fraternities, Masonic, Adventurers, Army and Navy (New York); Rockville Country (Rockville Centre, N.Y.). Author: Cantonment Manual, 1917; Manual of Military Maps, 1918; Fascinating France, 1921. Home: Rockville Centre, N.Y., and Old Field, East Moriches, L.I. Address: 23 Vassar Pl., Rockville Centre, Long Island NY‡

MACELWANE, JOHN PATRICK, architect; b. Port Clinton, O., May 3, 1896; s. Alexander Joseph and Catharine Agnes (Carr) M.; student Holy Cross Coll., Worcester, Mass., 1915-17; B.S. in Archtl. Engring., Ohio State U., 1922; m. Geraldine Frances Connell, July 23, 1938;children—Mary (Mrs. Stephen J. Pero), Kathleen (Mrs. Anthony A. Wernert). Engaged as constrn. engineer, 1922-27; as supervising architect Toledo Cath. Diocese, 1927-35; devel. and constrn. pub. housing projects in Toledo for U.S. Govt., 1937-39; with Britsch & Munger, 1939-45, associate member firm, 1945-55; senior partner of Britsch, Macelwane, Poseler & Lubeck, Toledo, from 1955; projects include hospitals, college dormitories, public and parochial schools, commerical projects. Member of the Toledo-Lucas County Plan Commn., 1938-45; mem. Ohio Bd. Bldg. Standards, 1954-63; chmn. format cour. Toledo Bldg. Code Revision Com., 1960-63. Served with USMC, 1917-19. Registered architect, Ohio, Mich.; registered profl. engr., Ohio. Fellow A.I.A. (past pres. Toledo); mem. Architects Soc. Ohio (pres. 1956-57), Toledo C. of C. (co-chmn. Toledo met. plan commn. 1944-47), Am. Legion, Phi Kappa Theta. Home: Toledo OH Died Aug. 1, 1970; buried Calvary Cemetery, Toledo OH

MACFARLAND, LANNING, banker, pub.; b. Chicago, Jan. 15, 1898; s. Henry J. and Lina Wheeler (Cook) M.; A.B., Harvard, 1919; m. Elizabeth Stuckslager, Nov. 22, 1923; children—Lanning Willard C., David B., Mary Elizabeth. Clk., No. Trust Co., Chicago, 1921, v.p., 1931-53; vice pres., dir. Law Bulletin Pub. Co., Chicago, pub. Chicago Daily Law Bull.; dir. Intermountain Lumber Co., Missoula, Mont., Bear Brand Hosiery Co., Chgo. Life trustee Chgo. Wesley Meml. Hosp. Served with Am. Ambulance Field Service, France, 1916-17; with Am. Relief Commn. and A.R.C., Balkans, 1918-19; lt. col., A.U.S., World War II. Recipient Order of White Eagle (Serbia), Order of Redeemer (Greece), Legion of Merit (United States). Trustee of Cornell College, Mount Vernon, Ia., Chicago Meml. Hosp., Chicago Child Care Soc. Republican. Episcopalian. Clubs: Chicago, Union League, Harvard (Chicago); Indian Hill Country (Wilmette, Ill.); Bohemian. Home: Winnetka IL Died Oct. 12, 1971.

MACFARLANE, CATHARINE, gynecologist; b. Phila., Pa., Apr. 7, 1877; d. John J. and Nettie Ottinger (Huston) Macfarlane; student U. of Pa., 1893-95, M.D., Woman's Med. Coll. Pa., 1898, D.Sc., 1950; D.Sc., Ursinus Coll., 1948, Jefferson Med. College, 1958; D.M.S. (hon.), Drexel Inst. Tech., 1956; unmarried, Intern Woman's Hosp., Phila., 1898-99; pvt. practice, Phila., from 1889; instr. in obstetrics, Woman's Med. Coll., 1899-1900; prof. of gynecology, 1922-42, research prof. gynecology from 1942; gynecologist Woman's Hosp., Phila., 1908-28; gynecologist in chief Woman's Med. Coll. Hospital, 1922-42; gynecologist and obstetrician Phila. General Hosp., 1922-42; pres. bd. dirs. Phila. div., Am. Cancer Soc., 1943-53; chmn. of Commn. on Cancer, Med. Soc. Pa., 1956, Awarded grant by the Am. Med. Association for research on value of early examination for cancer, 1938, 39; awarded grants by Internat. Cancer Research Foundation for research on value of periodic examination in control of cancer 1940-43; awarded (1940) Gimbel Brothers' award for outstanding service to humanity in Philadelphia during year 1940; Strittmatter award, 1948; joint Lasker award for inspiring application of preventive medicine to cancer control, 1951. Fellow A.C.S., College Physicians of Phila. (1st woman member); president Obstetrical Society of Phila., 1943; mem. A.M.A., Pa. State Medical Society, Philadelphia County Medical Society, Am. Med. Women's Assn., Med. Women's Internat. Assn., Fellow, founder, Am. Academy Obstetrics and Gynecology, Am. Assn. Univ. Women. Republican. Presbyn. Clubs: Women's University, Cosmopolitan (Phila.). Author: Textbook of Gynecology for Nurses, 1908. Home: Philadelphia PA Died May 1969.

MACFARLANE, CHARLES WILLIAM, economist; b. Phila.; s. David and Catherine (Macfarlane) M.; prep. edn. Phila. High Sch.; student Lafayette Coll., 1874; C.E., Lehigh U., 1876, LL.D., 1922, post-grad. work in analytical chemistry; engaged in engring., etc., but retired from business, 1888; student philosophy and economics, U. of Pa., 1888-89; Ph.D., Freiburg, 1893; m. Kathleen, d. William Wilson Selfridge, of Phila., Mar. 8, 1883. Mem. Am. Econ. Assn. (v.p. 1913-15), Am. Acad. Fine Arts, Am. Hist. Assn., Am. Geog. Soc., Hist. Soc. Pa. Clubs: University, Contemporary, Franklin Inn, Philobiblon, Merion Cricket. Author: Pennsylvania Paper Money, 1896; Value and Distribution, 1899; The Three Primary Laws of Social Evolution, 1902; Economic Interpretation of Early Roman History; Place of Economics and Philosophy in the Curriculum of a Modern University, 1913; Economic Interpretation of Early Roman History, 1915; Les Defenses du Sanglier, 1915; The Economic Basis of an Enduring Peace, 1918; also various other monographs on economic, philos. and hist. subjects. Translator: The Ultimate Standard of Value (by Eugene*‡

MACFARLANE, HOWARD PETTINGILL, lawyer; b. Tampa, Fla., May 28, 1888; s. Hugh Campbell and Frances (Pettingill) M.; A.B., Princeton, 1911; LL.B., Washington and Lee U., 1913; m. Carolyn Persis Kenyon, Apr. 17, 1914; children—Jean Fries (Mrs. Colin F. Stanley), Hugh Campbell II, Anne Pettingill (Mrs. Charles F. Clark). Admitted to Fla. bar 1913, practiced in Tampa; city atty. City of West Tampa, 1913-25; mem. Macfarlane & Macfarlane, 1917-25, Macfarlane, Pettingill, Macfarlane & Fowler, 1925-35, McKay, Macfarlane, Jackson & Ferguson, 1935-47, Macfarlane, Ferguson, Allison & Kelly, from 1947; gen. counsel Tampa Morning Tribune, Tampa Daily Times. Bd. dirs. Community Chest of Tampa, 1922-48, pres., 1931-33; chmn. Hillsborough County Def. Council, 1939-45. Served as 2d lt., inf., U.S. Army, World War I. Mem. Am., Tampa, Hillsborough County bar assns., Fla. Bar, Am. Legion (dept. judge adv. 1925-28, dept. comdr. 1928-29), S.A.R., Kappa Alpha (So.), Phi Delta Phi. Clubs: Rotary, Tampa Yacht and Country, University (Tampa). Home: Tampa FL

MACGINLEY, JOHN BERNARD, bishop; b. Tirconaill, Ireland, Aug. 19, 1871; s. Thomas Colin and Margaret Theresa (Sinnott) MacG.; ed. St. Eunan's Sem. and Blackrock Coll., Ireland; D.D., Collegio Americano del Nord, Rome, 1896. Ordained priest R.C. Ch., 1895; came to U.S., 1896, naturalized citizen, 1902; asst. rector Our Lady of Rosary Ch., Phila., Pa., 1896-98; prof. Latin and moral theology, St. Charles Sem., Overbrook, Phila., 1898-1903, rector Seminary, Vigan, P.I., 1903-05; asst. rector St. Charles Ch., Phila., 1905-10; consecrated bishop of Nueva Caceres, P.I., May 10, 1910; bishop of Monterey-Fresno, Calif., since Mar. 27, 1924. Mem. Alumni Am. Coll. of Rome. Home: 2820 Mariposa St., Fresno CA‡

MACGOWAN DAVID BELL, foreign service; b. Memphis, Tenn., June 5, 1870; s. Evander Locke and Mary Jane (Burrow) M.; A.B., Washington and Lee U., 1890; univs. Halle and Berlin 2 yrs.; m. Emma Birkhead Woods, of Memphis, Apr. 5, 1894. Reporter and spl. corr., Chicago Tribune, 1896-98, and corr. in Berlin, 1899-1900; corr. Associated Press, St. Petersburg, 1901-03, Berlin, 1903; corr. London Standard, at St. Petersburg, 1904-08; editor Knoxville (Tenn.) Sentinel, 1908-14; corr. Associated Press in Galicia, Armenia, Persia and the Caucasus, Turkey, 1915, St. Petersburg, 1915. After examination apptd. Am. consul, Oct. 18, 1915; detailed to Moscow, Jan. 1, 1916; consul at Vladivostock, Sept. 1, 1920-22; first sec. of legation, Riga, Reval and Kovno, 1922-32; assigned as consul to Bern, Dec. 22, 1931, as consul gen., Mar. 27, 1935; retired, June 30, 1935. Unitarian. Home: 106 Madison St., Lynchburg VA‡

MACGOWAN, GAULT, journalist, mag. publisher; b. Eng., Feb. 1894; m. Wendy Smith, 1923; 1 son, Corr. Asso. Press for Northwest Frontier of India, 1922-23; editor Times of Mesopotamia, 1924; sub-editor The Times 1925; staff corr. Daily Express, Paris, 1926-27; asst. editor, leader-writer Evening Express, Cardiff, 1927-38; editor Londoner's Diary, Newspaper Features, Ltd., 1928-29; mng. editor Tinidad (W.I.) Guardians, 1929-34; formerly corr. at Trinidad for the Times (London), also for New York Times, other American and European newspapers; joined New York Sun, Oct. 1934; special corr. The Sun at Coronation of King George VI, Spanish Civil War, in Morrocco with French Foreign Legion, 1937; war corr. The Sun in Battle of Britain, Battle of the Atlantic, Dieppe; with Am. Army in North West Africa, 1942-43, France and Germany, 1944-47; del. West Indies 4th Imperial Press Conf., 1930; formerly fgn. corr. North Am. Newspaper Alliance; founder, pub. European Life, monthly mag. for Americans, Heidelberg, West Germany, 1956-70. Served in World War I. Recipient Selfridge prize Company of Newspaper Makers, 1932; Officer de l'Instruction Publique, 1930, Chevalier de la Legion d'Honneur, 1934 (both of France); Officer Mil. Order of Christ (Portugal), 1933; Officier de Quissam Alaouite (Morocco), 1937; Croix de Guerre (Tunisia), 1943; Purple Heart, 1943. Rep. The Sun at the Cairo Conf., 1943. Potsdam Conf., 1945, Paris Peace Conf., 1946. Traveler, notably in Himalayas; discovered new pass Into Little Thibet (received thanks of Survey of India); made first flight over Orinoco Delta and across Venezuelan Llanos, between Trinidad and Maracay; first flight between Trinidad and British Guiana. Clubs: Authors', Press (London). Author: To the End of the World and Beyond; My Desert Dash to Damascus; Elizabeth Stuart: Her Story, 1963. Address: Federal Republic of Heidelberg Germany Died Nov. 30, 1970; buried New Schlierbach Cemetery, Heidelberg.

MACGREGOR, CHARLES PETER, clergyman; b. St. Andrews East, P.Q., Can., July 6, 1871; s. John and Jennie (Mac Arthur) MacG.; B.A., McMaster U., Toronto, 1899; B.D., Union Theol. Sem., 1905; M.A., Columbia, 1908; Th.D., Boston, 1953; m. Mary E. Mercer, 1901 (died April 21, 1943); children—Helen Stuart (Mrs. Frederick G. Wale), Margaret Jean (Mrs. William Ashley Magie, II), Robert Mercer; m. 2d, Mrs.

Sarah Curtis Dow, Apr. 4, 1945. Naturalized citizen of U.S., 1908. Ordained to ministry of Baptist Church, 1895; pastor Calvary Baptist Church, Toronto, Canada, 1894; pastor in British Columbia, 1895-98, Bayonne, N.J., 1900-05; asso. pastor Calvary Ch., New York, 1905-09; pastor 1st Ch., Pittsfield, Mass., 1909-18, 2d Ch., Lawrence, Mass., 1918-21, 1st Ch. Manchester, N.H., 1921-31, 1st Church, Penacook, N.H., 1931-44, since 1948. Trustee Colby Junior College, New London, since 1924, Golden Rule Farm, Tilton, since 1935; chmn. exec. com. Mass. Bapt. Conv., 1914-19, pres., 1920-21; mem. exec. com. N.H. Council of Religious Edn., 1922-46, exec. sec., 1925-46; pres. Mass. S.S. Assn., 1918-20; mem. corp., dir. and recording sec. N.H. Bible Soc.; mem. N.H. Bapt. Bd. of Promotion; mem. hdqrs. com. N.H. Christian Civic League. Republican. Mason (32 deg., grand chaplain Grand Lodge N.H. F.&A.M. since 1926). Retired. Home: 2 Bouton St., Concord, N.H., and New Hampton NH‡

MACGREGOR, DAVID HUTCHISON, economist; born Angus, Scotland, May 10, 1877; s. Robert and Lilias (Hutchison) M.; ed. George Watsons Coll., Edinburgh, Univ. Edinburgh, Trinity Coll., Cambridge; hon. LL.D., Edinburgh, 1948; m. Claire Nelson. Prof. economics, Leeds Univ., 1909-19, Manchester Univ., 1919-21, Oxford Univ., 1922-45. M.C., 1917. Author: Industrial Combination, 1906; Evolution of Industry, 1911; Enterprise Purpose and Profit, 1934; Public Aspects of Finance, 1939; Economic Analysis and Policy, 1949. Home: Three Lucerne Rd., Oxford. Office: All Souls Coll., Oxford England‡

MACGREGOR, FRANK SILVER, publisher; b. Lunenburg, Nova Scotia, Jan. 13, 1897; s. Charles William and Rhoda (Silver) MacG.; A.B., Harvard U., 1918. Asst. purchasing agent, Newport Co., Milwaukee, Wis., 1919-21; entered publishing business as college traveler, 1921-24; head of coll. dept., Harper Brothers, 1924-43, v.p. 1930-42, exec. v.p. 1942-45, sec. 1943-45, president, 1945-55, chairman of the board, 1955-62. Served with the United States Navy, 1918-19. Mem. local bd. Selective Service System, World War II. Mem. Am. Hist. Assn. Clubs: Dutch Treat, Century Association, West Hamilton Street (Baltimore). Home: New York City NY Died Jan. 11, 1971.

MACHROWICZ, THADDEUS M(ICHAEL), judge; born in Gostyn, Poland, August 21, 1899; s. Boniface and Frances (Werbel) M.; came to U.S., 1902, naturalized, 1910; student Alliance Coll., Cambridge Springs, Pa., 1916, U. of Chicago, 1917, DePaul U., 1921; LL.B., Detroit Coll. Law, 1924; m. Sophia Jara, June 5, 1935; children—Tod, Don. Admitted to Mich. bar, 1924, and practiced in Detroit, 1924-34; city atty., Hamtramck, Mich., 1934-36, municipal judge, 1942-50; U.S. district judge Eastern Dist. Mich., 1961-70; legal dir. Mich. Pub. Utilities Commission, 1938. Mem. 82d-87th Congresses from the 1st Mich. Dist. Served as lieut. in Polish Army in France and Poland, 1917-20. Mem. Am. Tech. Adv. Bd. to Poland, 1920-21; pub. mem. War Labor Bd., World War II. Mem. Nat. Advocates Assn., Polish Am. Congress, Am. Legion, Polish Nat. Alliance, Mich. and Detroit bar assns. Democrat. K.C. Home: MI Died Feb. 17, 1970; buried Mt. Olivet Cemetery, Detroit MI

MACINTYRE, ARCHIBALD JAMES, educator, mathematician; b. Sheffield, Eng., July 3, 1908; s. William Ewart Gladstone Archibald and Mary (Askew) M.; Ph.D., U. Cambridge, 1933; m. Sheila Scott, Dec. 30, 1940; children—Alister W., Douglas Scott (dec.), Susan E. Came to U.S., 1958. Asst. lectr. U. Swansea, 1930-31, U. Sheffield, 1931-36; lectr. U. Aberdeen, 1936-58; mem. faculty U. Cin., 1958-69, Charles P. Taft prof. math., 1963-69. Mem. Royal Soc. Edinburgh. Address: Cincinnati OH Died 1969.

MACIVER, ROBERT MORRISON, sociology; b. Stornoway, Scotland, Apr. 17, 1882; s. Donald and Christine (Morrison) MacI.; M.A., Edinburgh U., 1903, D.Ph., 1915, LL.D., 1952; B.A., Oxford U., 1907; Litt.D., Columbia U., 1929, Harvard, 1936. Princeton, 1947; Jewish Theol. Sem. Am., 1950; D.Sc., New Sch., 1950; L.H.D., Yale, 1951; LL.D. (honorary), University of Toronto, 1957; married Ethel Marion Peterkin, Aug. 14, 1911; children—Ian Tennant Morrison, Christine Elizabeth, Donald Gordon. Lecturer on polit. science, Aberdeen U., 1907, on sociology, 1911; prof. polit. science, U. of Toronto, 1915-22, head dept. polit. science, 1922-27; prof. social science, Barnard Coll. (Columbia), 1927-36. Lieber professor political philosophy and sociology, Columbia U., 1929-50; dir. City of N.Y. Juvenile Delinquency Evaluation Project, 1956-61; president of New School for Social Research, 1963-65, chancellor, 1965-66; vice chairman of the Can. War Labor Bd., 1917-18. Fellow Royal Society Can., World, Am. acads. Arts and Scis., Am. Philosophical Society; member of American Sociol. Soc., British Academy (corresponding member), Inst. Internationale de Sociologie, Phi Beta Kappa. Author: Community—A Sociological Study, 1917; Labor in the Changing World, 1919; Elements of Social Science, 1921; The Modern State, 1926; Relation of Sociology to Social Work, 1931; Society— Its Structure and Changes, 1931: Economic Reconstruction, 1934; Society — A Textbook of Sociology, 1937; Leviathan and the People, 1939. Social Causation. 1942, Toward an Abiding Peace, 1943; The Web of Government, 1947; The More Perfect Union, 1949; The Ramparts We Guard. 1950; Democracy and the Economic Challenge, 1952; Academic Freedom in Our Time. 1955; The Pursuit of Happiness, 1955; Life: Its Dimensions and Its Bounds, 1960; The Challenge of the Passing Years, 1962; Power Transforms, 1964; The Prevention and Control of Delinquency, 1966; (autobiography) As aTale that Is Told, 1968. Home: Palisades NY Died June 15, 1970.

MACK, CARL THEODORE, lawyer, elec. engr.; b. Easton, Pa., July 24, 1896; s. George Brinton and Barbara Henrietta (Kilian) M.; E.E., Lafayette Coll., 1917; LL.B., George Washington U., 1924; m. Rose B. Snyder, June 20, 1928 (dec. Apr. 1947); m. 2d, Elizabeth E. Roulette, Oct. 1, 1949. Engr., Henry L. Doherty and Co., 1917-21; asst. in patent lawyers office, 1921-28; mem. patent firm Stone, Boyden & Mack. 1928-56, Stone & Mack, 1956-67. Trustee Lafayette Coll. Research Found. Served with U.S. Army, 1917-19. Mem. Am. Patent Law Assn. (treas. 1944-46, sec. 1946-48, bd. mgrs. 1948-51). Am., D.C. bar assns., All Pa. Coll. Alumni Assn. Washington (pres. 1961-63), Phi Beta Kappa, Tau Beta Pi. Presbyterian. Mason (32, K.T., Shriner). Home: Washington DC Died Dec. 1, 1971.

MACK, GEORGE HERBERT, clergyman, educator; b. Weyauwega, Wis., Apr. 18, 1874; s. John and Helen (Slocum) M.; A.B., Mo. Val. Coll., 1898, LL.D., 1938; B.D., Cumberland U., 1901; m. Margaret Keller, Oct. 14, 1902; children—John Keller, George H., David S. Ordained ministry Presbyn. Ch., 1900; pastor Harris St. Ch., Atlanta, Ga., 1901-07, Garden St. Presbyn. Ch., Columbia, Tenn., 1907-10, Russell St. Presbyn. Ch., Nashville, Tenn., 1910-16; supt. home missions, Presbyn. Synod of Tenn., 1916-22; also stated clk. same synod, 1918-22; dist. sec. nat. missions, St. Louis, Mo., and Chicago, Ill., 1922-27; pres. Mo. Valley Coll., Marshall, Mo., 1927-38; pastor Presbyn. Ch., Butler, Mo., 1938-40; Auburn, Ky., 1940-45; dir. Presbyn. Restoration Fund, 1945-46; stated clerk, Synod of Ky., since 1948; intermin pastor Bowling Green, Ky., 1951-52. Dir. Y.M.C.A., camp religious work, Ft. Oglethorpe, Ga., 1917-18. Mem. Kappa Sigma. Mason. Club: Rotary. Address: 833 Wakefield Av., Bowling Green KY‡

MACK J(AMES) S(TEPHEN), business exec.; born McKeesport, Pa., Feb. 9, 1914; s. John Sephus and Margaret L. (Gordon) M.; B.S., William and Mary Coll., Williamsburg, Va., 1935; M.B.A., Harvard, 1936; m. Barbara Frost Small, Jan. 25, 1936; children—James Sephus, Margaret Elizabeth, and Barbara Ann. Associated with G.C. Murphy Company, since 1936, constrn. supervisor, 1936-38, special assignments in real estate dept., 1938-39, asst. store mgr., 1939-40, store mgr., 1940-42, dist. store mgr., 1942-45, dir. of co., 1940, v.p. real estate and constrn. div., 1945, v.p. finance, real estate and office mgmt., treas., 1946-53, pres., 1953-68, chmn. bd., 1962-68. Dir. Indiana (Pa.) Hosp. Trustee, pres. J.S. Mack Found., Indiana, Pa. Mem. U.S., Pa. chambers commerce, Variety Stores Assn. (dir.), Nat. Nat. Adv. Council, Boston Conf. Distbn., Am. Retail Fedn., Alpha Kappa Psi, Omicron Delta Kappa, Theta Delta Chi. Republican. Presbyn. Clubs: University, Duquesne (Pitts.); Indiana Country; Union League (N.Y.C.). Home: McKeesport PA Died May 21, 1968.

MACKALL, (ALEXANDER) LAWTON, writer, lecturer; b. Chestnut Hill, Pa., May 23, 1888; s. Leonard Covington and Louisa Frederika (Lawton) M.; student Sheffield Scientific Sch. (Yale), 1 yr.; B.A., Yale, 1910, M.A., 1911; M. Virginia Woods, Mar. 15, 1913; 1 son, Robert Lawton (dec.); m. 2d, Ruth Dexter MacMillan, Apr. 22, 1926. Fellow in English, Yale, 1910-11; mem. editorial staff Century Mag., 1912, later staff of Vanity Fair, and asst. editor with G. Schirmer, Inc., music pubs.; mng. editor Judge," also dramatic editor Leslie's until 1920; editorial dir. New Fiction Pub. Corp., 1920-23. Mem. Bd. Higher Edn. of N.Y.C., 1936-54; adminstrv. com. Hunter City, Bklyn. and Queens colls. Mem. Authors' League Am., Wine and Food Soc. N.Y. (exec. council), Confrerie des Chevaliers du Tastevin, Campagnons de Bordeaux (honorary), Les Amis d'Escoffier (past chairman); corr. mem. Portuguese Archaeol. Soc. Decorated Officer Order of Christ (Portuguese). Clubs: Players, Dutch Treat. Author: Scrambled Eggs, 1920; Bizarre, 1923; Poddle Oodle of Doodle Farm (with Ruth Mackall); Portugal for Two, 1931; The Restaurateur's Handbook (with Charles A. Faissole), 1938; Knife and Fork in New York, 1948. Contbr. essays, stories, articles to newspapers and mags. Home: Staten Island NY Died Mar. 1968.

MACKAY, HELEN (MRS. ARCHIBALD MACKAY), author; b. Livingston Co., N.Y., Aug. 10, 1876; d. Alfred L. and Arabella (Magee) Edwards; ed. pub. schs.; m. Archibald Mackay, of Lenox, Mass., Nov. 24, 1896. Author: Houses of Glass, 1909; Half Loaves, 1911; Stories for Pictures, 1912; Cobweb Cloak, 1912; Accidentals, 1915; London One November (poems), 1916; Journal of Small Things, 1917. Decoration: Reconnaissance Francaise for 4 yrs.' service Hopital St. Louis, Paris. Address: 7 Place du Palais Bourbon, Paris France‡

MACKAY, JOHN KEILLER, Canadian govt. ofcl.; b. Plainfield, Pictou County, N.S., July 11, 1888; s. John Duncan and Bessie (Murray) M.; B.A., St. Francis Xavier U., 1912, LL.D., 1951; LL.B., Dalhousie U., 1922, LL.D., 1958; LL.D., U. Ottawa, 1958, U. Western Ont., 1959; D.C.L. (hon.), U. N.B., 1959; m. Katherine Jean MacLeod, July 14, 1943; children—Ian Reay, Donald Alastair, James Keiller. Called to Nova Scotia bar, 1922, Ontario bar, 1923; created King's counsel, 1933; apptd. justice of the Supreme Court of Ont., 1935-50, Ct. Appeal Ont., 1950-57; lt. gov. Province of Ontario, 1957-63; mem. law firm Mackay, Matheson & Martin, Toronto. Dir. Eastern & Chartered Trust Co., Bramalea Consol. Devels. Ltd. Vice patron Oxfam of Can.; hon. pres. Ont. Cancer Soc.; chmn. Ont. Council for Arts. Chancellor U. Windsor; bd. govs. U. Toronto. Served as lt. col. in command 6th brigade Canadian F.A., 1914-18. Awarded D.S.O. and bar; mentioned in dispatches three times. Hon fellow Acad. Medicine Toronto; mem. St. Andrew's Soc. (past pres.), Can. Leg. (hon. life mem., grand pres. Ont.), Clan MacKay Soc. Can. (hon. chieftain), Canadian Bar Assn. (hon. life), Medico-Legal Soc. Toronto (hon. life), Law Soc. Upper Can. (hon. bencher), English-Speaking Union (hon. v.p. Toronto), Shakespeare Soc. Toronto (hon. pres., life mem.). Clubs: Royal Canadian Mil. Inst., Nat., Empire, Canadian, Ashburn Golf and Country. Home: Toronto ON Canada Died June 12, 1970.

MACKAY, MARGARET, author; b. Oxford, Neb., Nov. 19, 1907; d. Thomas Ferdinand and Meta (Meyer) Mackprang; A.B., Univ. of Calif., 1928; student of the late Victorian period (1880-1900) in China and Hawaii, including Boxer Rebellion of China in 1900; m. Alexander H. Mackay, Oct. 25, 1932 (killed in action with British Army, May 2, 1942). Lived in Peiping, China, 1931-35, Tientsin, China, 1935-39, in Peiping, 1939-41, in Honolulu, T.H., 1941-45, England, France and Italy, 1947-50. Johannesburg, So. Africa, 1950-51, in England, since 1951. Author: Like Water Flowing, 1938; Lady with Jade, 1939; Valiant Dust, 1941; For All Men Born, 1943; Homeward the Heart, 1944; Great Lady, 1946; Sharon, 1948; Give Him My Love, 1949; The Flowered Donkey, 1950; The Poetic Parrot, 1951; Summer at the Spa, 1952; I Live in a Suitcase, 1953; The Four Fates, 1955; The Wine Princes, 1958; The Little General, 1963; Lost Island, 1963; Dolphin Boy, 1963; Angry Island, 1964. Contbr. to nat. publications in Am. and Eng. Mem. Alpha Chi Omega, Theta Sigma Phi. Address: London England Died Oct. 14, 1968.

MACKAY, ROBERT, editor; b. Virginia City, Nev., Apr. 22, 1871; s. Duncan C. and Rosa (Augustine) M.; g.g.s. Noah Webster, American lexicographer; ed. public schools, Cordelia, Cal., and San Francisco; m. Lenora Lash, of New York, Mar. 7, 1901. Reporter San Francisco Chronicle, 1886; worked steadily on newspapers as printer, reporter and editor until 1895, when traveled extensivley over the world for Internat. News Syndicate; joined staff of New York World, 1899; mng. editor Success Magazine, 1900-8, The Delineator, 1908; editorial staff the Frank A. Munsey Co., 1909-15, The People's Home Journal, 1917-19; mng. editor Success Magazine since 1919. Contbr. short stories and other prose and verse to mags. Home: 201 W. 108th St. Office: 1133 Broadway, New York NY‡

MACKENZIE, ALASTAIR ST. CLAIR, educator; b. Inverness, Scotland, Feb. 17, 1875; s. Alasta Forbes and Christina Douglas (Macdonald) M.; M.A., Glasgow U., 1892; U. of Edinburgh, 1892-93, Oxford U., 1893-94; LL.B., U. of Ky., 1912; LL.D., Ky. Wesleyan U., 1911; Litt.D., Cumberland, 1913; unmarried. Prof. English and logic, Sept., 1899, prof. English and comparative lit., 1910-16, dean of Grad. Sch., 1912-16, State University of Ky.; pres. Lenox College, Hopkinton, Ia., 1916-17; research work in New York, 1918-28; editorial work since 1928. Institute lecturer since 1905; Ropes Foundation lecturer, University of Cincinnati, 1911-12; lecturer on comparative literature, U. of Tenn., 1912. Sec. Am. Iona Soc., 1926-28; fellow Royal Soc. of Lit.; mem. Royal Asiatic Soc. (London), Am. Philol. Assn., Modern Lang. Assn., N.E.A., Alpha Delta Sigma (pres. 1923); hon. mem. Inst. de Sociol. (Bruxelles). Mason (K.T.). Clubs: University, Masonic, Caledonian and Filson. Author: History of Lexington Lodge (F. and A.M.), 1904; The Evolution of Literature, 1911 (translated into Spanish, 1913); History of English Literature, 1914. Collaborator on Library of Southern Literature (15 vols.), 1910. Contbr. to lit. and other periodicals. Home: 70 2d St., Weehawken NJ‡

MACKENZIE, ARTHUR, freight traffic; b. Leeds, Eng., Oct. 28, 1869; s. James and Nellie (Lee) M.; ed. pub. schs. Toronto, Can.; m. Genevieve Duff, of Chicago, Ill., Jan. 3, 1912; 1 son, Howard Arthur. Vice pres. C., R.I. & P. Ry., in charge freight traffic. Republican. Episcopalian. Clubs: Traffic, Chicago Athletic Assn. Home: 2054 E. 69th St. Office: La Salle St. Station, Chicago IL‡

MACKENZIE, J. GAZZAM, manufacturer; b. Vineland, N.J., Nov. 28, 1870; s. John F. and Emma L. (Gazzam) M.; Lawrenceville (N.J.) Acad.; grad. Pa. Charter Sch., Phila., 1892; U. of Pa., 1893-4; m. Jennie Randolph Dorsey, of Phila., June 13, 1894. Salesman in Phila., 1895, for Ames-Bonner Co., mfrs. brushes and mirrors, Toledo, O., now v.-p., treas., gen. mgr.; pres. Toledo Webb Press Mfg. Co., Kenilworth Land Co., Kenilworth Co., Asheville, N.C. trustee Toledo Expn. Co. Trustee Toledo Univ Republican. Episcopalian. Mem. Toledo Commerce Club (ex-pres.), Bus. Men's Club (ex-pres.), Toledo Credit Men's Club (ex-pres.), Phi Kappa Psi (ex-pres. Ohio and Toledo assns.). Mason. Clubs: Toledo, Toledo Yacht, Toledo Automobile, Inverness Golf, Rotary (Toledo); Phi Kappa Psi (Phila.); Univ. of Pa. (New York). Mem. publicity com. Chamber of Commerce U.S. Address: Toledo OH‡

MACKENZIE, KENNETH GERARD, chem. engr.; b. N.Y.C., Feb. 4, 1887; s. Kenneth and Caroline M. (Weeks) M.; Ph.B., Yale, 1907, M.S., 1909; m. Margerie Mitchill, June 29, 1910 (div. Oct. 1960); children—Neil Mitchill, Kenneth Donald, Jean M. (Mrs. Albert T. Scully). Asst. instr. chemistry Yale, 1907-08; research chemist N.Y. Testing Lab., Maurer, N.J., 1908-10; chief chemist Nairn Linoleum Co., Kearney, N.J., 1910-11; cons. chemist The Texas Co., 1911-33, asst. to v.p., chief technologist, 1933-54; v.p., dir. research Texaco Devel. Corp., 1933-54; pres. Kenneth G. Mackenzie Assos. Cons., 1954-67. Fellow A.A.A.S., Chem. Soc., Am. Inst. Chemists, Inst. Petroleum (Gt. Britain); mem. Am. Soc. Testing Materials (past pres.), Soc. Chem. Industry Soc. Automotive Engrs., Am. Inst. Chem. Engrs., Am. Chem. Soc., Air Pollution Control Assn., Franklin Inst. (mem. com. sci. and arts), Am. Petroleum Inst., Am. Inst. Mining, Metall. and Petroleum Engrs. Republican. Episcopalian. Clubs: The Chemists' of New York (past pres.), Yale, Cloud; Chemists' of Chicago. Address: Chicago IL Died Dec. 8, 1967.

MACKIE, ERNEST LLOYD, univ. prof.; b. Yadkinville, N.C., Nov. 27, 1893; s. E.C. and Anise (Hinshaw) M.; A.B., U. of N.C., 1917; M.A., Harvard, 1920; Ph.D., U. of Chicago, 1927; m. Romagna Gallaway, June 25, 1925; children—William Ernest, Anne Gallaway. Instr. in mathematics, Clemson Coll., 1917-19; part-time instr. Harvard, 1920-21; asst. prof. of mathematics, U. of N.C., 1921-26, asso. prof., 1926-34, prof. from 1934, dean of men, 1944-46; dean studs. and chmn. Div. Stud. Welfare, 1946-48; dean of student awards and distinctions, 1948-59. Fellow A.A.A.S.; mem. Math. Assn. Am., Am. Math. Soc., Elisha Mitchell Sci. Soc. (pres. 1944-45), N.C. Acad. Sci. (v.p. 1950-51), Golden Fleece (U.N.C.), Phi Eta Sigma, Alpha Phi Omega, Sigma Xi, Phi Gamma Delta, Phi Beta Kappa (senator 1958-69, chmn. 1946-49, mem. exec. com. 1952-55, So. Atlantic Dist. United Chpts. Phi Beta Kappa; secretary-treasurer 1955-58). Clubs: Chapel Hill Country (ex-pres.); Harvard of N.C. Presbyn. Author: The Jacobi Condition for a Problem of Mayer with Variable End Points. Co-author: Freshman Mathematics, Elementary Coll. Mathematics. Home: Chapel Hill NC Died Apr. 18, 1972; buried New Garden Cemetery, Guilford College NC

MACKIE, PAULINE BRADFORD (MRS. HERBERT M. HOPKINS), author; b. Fairfield, Conn., July 6, 1874; d. Rev. Andrew and Sarah (Dennistoun) M.; ed. pub. schs., Toledo, O.; m. Rev. Herbert Muller Hopkins, of N.Y., City, Aug. 2, 1899 (died Jan.14, 1911); 1 son, Cecil Mackie. Author: Mademoiselle de Berny, 1898; Ye Lyttle Salem Maide, 1899; The Georgian Actress, 1900; The Washingtonians, 1902; The Flight of Rosy Dawn, 1902; The Voice in the Desert, 1903; The Girl and the Kaiser, 1904; The Story of Kate, 1907; The Moving House, 1918; also plays, Yellow Bird; The Moving House, 1915; The Spell (with Sarah Jefferis Curry), 1916; Whistler, 1920; The Geranium Lady (with Sylvia Chatfield Bates). Contbr. stories to mags. Address: 61 W. 9th St., New York NY‡

MACKIN, JOSEPH HOOVER, geologist; b. Oswego, N.Y., Nov. 16, 1906; s. William David and Catherine (Hoover) M.; B.S., N.Y.U., 1930; M.A., Columbia, 1932, Ph.D., 1937; m. Esther Fisk, Sept. 16, 1930; children—Barbara Catherine, Robert Fisk. Mem. faculty U. Wash., 1934-61, prof. geology, 1946-61; Farish prof. geology, U. Tex., 1961-68; part-time geologist U.S. Geol. Survey, 1943-54. Cons. NASA, 1963; cons. engring. geology to govt., state hwy. depts., bus. firms. Chairman div. of earth scis. NRC, 1965-67. Fellow Geol. Soc. Am. (chmn. cordilleran sec. 1950, councillor 1950-53); mem. Nat. Acad. Scis., Soc. Econ. Geology, Am. Geophys. Union, Am. Assn. Petroleum Geologists (distinguished lectr. 1953), A.A.A.S., Sigma Xi (nat. lectr. 1963). Club: Cosmos (Washington). Home: Austin TX Died Aug. 12, 1968.

MACKINNON, HAROLD ALEXANDER, business exec.; b. Chelsea, Mass., Nov. 26, 1902; s. Alexander and Christine (MacKichan) MacK.; grad. Bentley Coll. Accounting and Finance, Boston, 1922; m. Mary Ethel Costello, Dec. 7, 1925; children—Lois Edith (Mrs. Walter O. Davis), Jean Mary (Mrs. William M. Rogers), Robert Harold, Richard Alexander, William Peter. Chief traveling auditor Gen. Electric Co., 1930-35; asst. gen. auditor, 1935, asst. comptroller, 1936-52, v.p., 1953-67; dir. Lincoln Nat. Corp., Ft. Wayne, Schenectady Trust Co.; dir. emeritus Ft. Wayne Nat. Bank; dir. Lincoln Nat. Life Ins. Co., Ft. Wayne. Past pres. Parkview Meml. Hosp., Ft. Wayne. Dir. Ellis Hosp.; chmn. trustees Elfun Trusts, Elec. Funds, N.Y.C.; trustee Bentley Coll., Waltham, Mass.; adj. trustee Rensselaer Poly. Inst., Troy, N.Y. C.P.A., N.Y. Mem. Financial Execs. Inst. Clubs: Mohawk Golf, Mohawk. Schenectady NY Died Aug. 11, 1972; buried Park View Cemetery, Schenectady NY

MACKINTOSH, KENNETH, judge; b. Seattle, Wash., Oct. 25, 1875; s. Angus and Elizabeth (Peebles) M.; student at U. of Washington, 1891; A.B., Stanford U., 1895; LL.B., Columbia, 1900; m. Francisca Arques, Nov. 18, 1908; 1 son, Angus. Began practice at Seattle, 1900; pros. atty., King County, Wash., 1905-09; judge Superior Court of King County, 1912-18; asso. justice Supreme Court of Wash., Mar. 1918-Jan. 1927, chief justice, 1927-29. Mem. Nat. Commn. on Law Observance and Enforcement, 1929-31. Republican. Clubs: Rainier, College, Seattle Golf. Home: Olympic Hotel. Office: 1725 Exchange Bldg., Seattle 4‡

MACKINTOSH, WILLIAM ARCHIBALD, ret. univ. adminstr.; b. Madoc, Ontario, May 21, 1895; s. William and Agnes (Cowie) M.; ed. St. Andrew's Coll., Toronto; M.A., Queen's U., 1916; Ph.D., Harvard, 1922; m. Jean Isobel Easton, Aug. 11, 1928; 1 dau. Sir John A. MacDonald professor of political and econ. sci. Queen's U., 1927-51, vice-prin., 1947-51, vice chancellor, prin., 1951-61, vice chancellor, 1961-65, dean, Faculty Arts, 1946-51; served in Departments of Finance and Reconstruction, Ottawa; Canadian delegate Bretton Woods Conf., 1944; Economic and Social Council, 1946; mem. Can. Council, 1957-60, Committee on Organization of the Government of Ontario, 1958-60; mem. Royal Commn. on Banking and Finance, 1961-63; director Bank of Can., from 1964. Decorated Companion St. Michael and St. George Fellow Royal Soc. Canada (pres. 1956-57); hon. life mem. Am. Geographic Soc. N.Y. Presbyn. Club: Cataraqui Golf and Country. Editor: Can. Frontiers of Settlement, 9 vols., 1934-36. Contbr.: Pioneer Settlement. Address: Kingston ON Canada. Kingston ON Canada. Died Dec. 29, 1970; buried Cataraqui Cemetery, Kingston.

MACLANE, GERALD ROBINSON, educator, mathematician; b. Ludlow, Mass., June 22, 1919; s. Donald Bradford and Winifred (Saunders) MacL.; B.A., Yale, 1941; M.A., Harvard, 1942; Ph.D., Rice U., 1946; m. Ingeborg Dinkel, Dec. 25, 1946; 1 dau., Alison Saunders. Temporary mem. Inst. Advanced Study, Princeton, 1946-47; B. Peirce instr. Harvard, 1947-48; from asst. prof. to prof. Rice U., 1948-64, chmn. dept. math., 1963-64; prof. math Purdue U., 1964-72, head div. math. scis., 1964-69; vis. mem. Courant Inst. Math. Sci., N.Y. U., spring 1963; cons.-examiner N. Central Assn. Colls. and Secondary Schs. Mem. Am. Math. Soc., Math. Assn. Am., Soc. Indsl. and Applied Math., Phi Beta Kappa, Sigma Xi. Contbr. profl. jours. Home: West Lafayette IN Died Mar. 11, 1972.

MACLEAN, MUNROE DEACON, educator; b. Quincy, Mass., June 1, 1907; s. Daniel J. and Mary Jane (Munroe) MacL.; B.S., West Chester State Coll., 1931; M.A., Columbia, 1934; postgrad. Boston U., 1951; m. Clara Elizabeth Schatz, June 16, 1934; children—Jean Ann, Mary Carol (Mrs. J. Noel Heermance). Tchr. Hazleton (Pa.) High Sch., 1931-34, West Chester (Pa.) State Coll., 1934-36, P.S. duPont High Sch., Wilmington, Del., 1936-37, Quincy (Mass.) High Sch., 1937-51, asst. dir. health, phys. edn., athletics, 1951-59, coach, dir., health, phys. edn., health services, athletics, 1959-69. Participant in President's Phys. Fitness Conf., Washington, 1962; mem. Mass. state basketball tournament com., 1961-69. Bd. dirs. YMCA, 1952-69, chmn., phys. edn. com., 1963-65, v.p.; bd. dirs. A.R.C., 1959-69, chmn. first aid. Served to lt. comdr., USNR, 1943-46. Recipient citations for work with youth, Amvets, 1962, Am. Legion, 1955, Boy Scouts Am., 1958; named Man of Year, Montclair Men's Club, 1962; 1st mem. inducted into Mass. Basketball Coaches Hall of Fame", 1964. Mem. Mass., Quincy tchrs. assns., Mass. Athletic Dirs. Assn., Mass. Coaches Assn., Am. (chmn. city and county dirs. 1965), Mass. assns. health, phys. edn., recreation, Am. Legion, Amvets. Elk, Lion. Author: Curriculum Guide in Health Education, 1961, Curriculum Guide in Physical Education, 1963. Assisted in writing U.S. Navy Phys. Fitness Manual, 1962. Home: Quincy MA Died Jan. 24, 1969.

MACLEAN, PAUL ROBERT, wood mfg. co. exec.; b. New Albany, Ind., Apr. 12, 1902; s. William Archibald and Elizabeth (Krebs) MacL.; Ph.B., Yale, 1925; student Exeter Coll., Oxford (Eng.) U., 1926-27; m. Margaret Shireman, June 3, 1930. With Wood-Mosaic Corp., Louisville, from 1927, 1st. v.p., 1959-63, president, from 1963, also director; president Wood-Mosaic (Canada), Tweed, Ontario. Vice president MacLean Found., from 1964; trustee U. Louisville, 1950-52. Mem. Beta Theta Pi. Republican. Clubs: Pendennis, Louisville Country, Wynn-Stay, Filson (Louisville); United Services (Montreal, Can.); Desert Fish and Game (Maniwaki, Can.), Yale (N.Y.C.). Home: Louisville KY Died Apr. 27, 1971.

MACLEAN, STUART, musical critic and author; b. Yorkville, S.C., Nov. 11, 1872; s. Joseph Adams and Clara Victoria (Dargan) M.; U. of the South, 1894-5; unmarried. Head of English dept., Sewanee Mil. Acad., since 1917. Mem. Delta Tau Delta. Episcopalian. Mason. Author: Alexis (musical novel), 1917. Contbr. nine articles on boy voice training to The Churchman, New York, 1914-15; also articles and stories to mags. Home: University of the South, Sewanee TN‡

MACLEISH, JOHN E., lawyer; b. Glasgow, Scotland, May 13, 1879; s. Samuel L. and Agnes (Frew) MacL.; grad. Lewis Inst., 1901; LL.B., Kent Coll. of Law, 1904; m. Gladys Thrift, August 9, 1905 (deceased August 1953); one daughter, Virginia. Admitted to the Illinois bar, 1904, and practiced in Chicago; sr. mem. MacLeish, Spray, Price & Underwood. Mem. Am., Ill. State, Chicago bar assns., Law Club. Clubs: Chicago, Union League, U. Home: Winnetka IL

MACLELLAN, KENNETH F., chmn., president United Biscuit Co. of America, Chicago; dir. Mfrs. Trust Co., Am. Locomotive Co. Home: Chicago IL Died 1971.

MACLELLAN, ROBERT LLEWELLYN, ins. exec.; b. Chattanooga, Nov. 1, 1906; s. Robert J. and Cora (Llewellyn) M.; A.B., Dartmouth Univ., 1928; LL.D., Maryville Coll., 1968, King Coll., Bristol, Tenn., 1970; m. Kathrina Howze, Sept. 2, 1939; children—Anne Llewellyn, Robert Howze. Agy. sec. Provident Life & Accident Ins. Co., Chattanooga, 1930-32, agy. v.p., 1932-35, v.p., 1935-51, pres., 1952-69, also mem. exec. com., chmn. bd., chief exec. officer, 1969-71; dir. Am. Nat. Bank & Trust Company, Forest Hills Cemetery Association. Mem. executive committee American Life Convention. Vice pres. McCallie Sch., Chattanooga, from 1937. Chmn. Community Chest dr. 1946. Trustee University of Chattanooga; bd. dirs. Bd. Annuities, Presbyn. Ch. U.S., Life Ins. Medical Research Fund; bd. trustees S.S. Huebner Foundation Ins. Education; mem. bd. dirs., exec. com. Greater Chattanooga Devel. Com.; mem. Army Adv. Com. Mem. Inst. Life Ins. (dir. 1962-64), Life Ins. Assn. Am. (dir. 1961-64), Newcomen Soc., Alpha Sigma Phi. Presbyn. (elder). Clubs: Lookout Mount. Golf, Chattanooga Golf and Country, Lookout Mountain, Fairyland, Mountain City (Chattanooga); University (N.Y.C.). Home: Lookout Mountain TN Died Dec. 15, 1971; buried Chattanooga TN

MACLENNAN, SIMON FRASER, coll. prof.; b. Harriston, Ont., Sept. 18, 1870; s. George and Mary (Currie) MacL.; A.B., U. of Toronto, 1893; Ph.D., U. of Chicago, 1896; m. Miss Browne, of Des Moines, Ia., Aug. 23, 1900; children—Janet Fraser, Sarah Browne, Ronald Fraser. Asso. prof. psychology and pedagogy, 1897, prof., 1900, prof. philosophy and psychology, 1903, prof. philosophy, 1909, prof. philosophy and comparative religion since 1912, Oberlin Coll. Mem. Am. Philos. Assn.; mem. Research Com. Oberlin Br. of Nat. Research Council. Conglist. Club: Oberlin Faculty. Author: The Evolution of Morals. Home: Oberlin OH‡

MACLEOD, COLLN MUNRO, educator; b. Nova Scotia, Can., Jan. 28, 1909; s. John Charles and Lillian (Munro) MacL.; M.D., McGill U., 1932; m. Elizabeth Randol, July 2, 1938; 1 dau., Mary. Came to U.S., 1934, naturalized, 1941. Intern Montreal Gen. Hosp., 1932-34; resident in medicine, Rockefeller Inst. Hosp., 1937-38; asst. to asso. in medicine Rockefeller Inst. for Med. Research, 1934-41; prof. microbiology New York University College Medicine, 1941-56; professor research medicine University Pa. School Medicine, 1956-60, prof. medicine N.Y.U. Sch. Medicine, 1960-66; mem. Pres.'s Sci. Adv. Com., 1961-64; chmn. Life Scis. Panel; exec. com. div. med. scis. Nat. Research Council, 1952-56; dir. Commn. on Pneumonia Army Epidemiol. Bd., 1941-46; chief preventive medicine sect. Com. Med. Research Office Scientific Research and Development, 1944-46; pres. Armed Forces Epidemiol. Bd., 1947-55; mem. panel mil. and field medicine Com. Med. Scis. Nat. Mil. Establishment, 1948-52; adv. panel on med. scis. to Asst. Sec. Def. for research and devel., 1952-56; chmn. com. on research in influenza USPHS; member Army Sci. Adv. Panel, 1958-61; chmn. sci. adv. com. Walter Reed Army Inst. Research, 1957-61; chmn. Health Research Council N.Y.C., from 1960; deputy director Office Sci. and Tech., 1963-64; v.p. med. affairs Commonwealth Fund, from 1966; consultant President's Sci. Adv. Com., from 1964; U.S. chmn. U.S.-Japan Coop. Med. Sci. Program, 1965-72; pres., sci. dir. Okla. Med. Research Found., 1970-72; mem. sci. adv. com. Hosp. for Sick Children, Toronto; vis. com. biology Harvard; adv. bd. chemistry Princeton. Dir., Merck & Co.; trustee Merck Co. Found., Sloan-Kettering Inst. for Sci. Research. Recipient Bristol award Infectious Disease Soc., 1971. Mem. Nat. Acad. Scis., Am. Epidemiol. Soc., Am. Assn. Immunologists (pres. 1951-52), Soc. Am. Bacteriologists, Assn. Am. Physicians, Soc. Clin. Investigation, N.Y. Acad. Medicine, Am. Philos. Soc., Am. Acad. Arts and Scis., Harvey Soc. (pres. 1955-56). Club: Century Association. Contbr. articles med. jours. Home: OK Died Feb. 12, 1972.

MACLEOD, IAIN NORMAN, Brit. fovt. ofcl.; b. Yorkshire, Nov. 11, 1913; s. Dr. Norman Macleod; student Fettes Coll.; B.A., Conville and Caius Coll.,

Cambridge U., 1935; student Inner Temple. 1938-39; m. Evelyn Blois, 1941; 2 children. With De La Rue's, 1935-38; joined Conservative Parliamentary Secretariat, 1946; head home affairs research dept. Conservative Party, 1948-50; mem. House of Commons, Parliament, 1950-70; minister of health, 1952-55, minister of labor and nat. services, 1955-59, minister state for colonies, 1959-62; chancellor of exchecquer, 1970; former leader Ho. of Commons, chmn. Conservative Party. From pvt. to maj., Brit. Armed Forces, 1939-46. Clubs: Crockford's, White's. Author: Bridge is an Easy Game, 1952. Bridge editor Sunday Times, 1950. Home: Enfield England Died July 1970.

MACLEOD, ROBERT BRODIE, educator; b. Martintown, Ont., Can., Jan. 31, 1907; s. John B. and Helena Margaret (Brodie) M.; B.A., 1926, M.A., 1927, Ph.D., 1932; m. Beatrice Fullerton Beach, Oct. 17, 1936;children—Ian Fullerton, Alison Stuart. Came to U.S., 1930. Lectr. in psychology, McGill U., 1927-28, chmn. dept. psychology, 1946-48; chmn. dept. psychology and edn., Swarthmore Coll., 1933-46; instr. psychology, Cornell, 1930-33, Susan Linn Sage professor psychology, from 1948, chmn. dept. psychology, 1948-53, 65-66; vis. prof. psychology, U. Michigan, 1953, 64-65; dir. survey of Coll., U. Pennsylvania, 1957. Served with O.S.S., E.T.O., 1944-45. Fellow Belgain American Educational Found., 1939, Guggenheim fellow, 1942. Mem. Am., Can. and Eastern psychol. assns., A.A.A.S., Nat. Council Religion in Higher Edn., Am. Assn. U. Profs., Sigma Xi. Author Ithaca NY Died June 19, 1972.

MACMANUS, SEUMAS, author, lecturer; b. Donegal, Ireland, 1869; ed. Lesterkenny, also Donegal; LL.D., Notre Dame, Ind., 1907; m. Ethna Carbery, 1901 (died 1902); m. 2d, Catalina Violante Paez, of Venezuela, 1911; children—Mariquita, Patricia. First visited U.S., 1899, and has since made tours as lecturer annually. Author: Through the Turf Smoke; The Bewitched Fiddle; In Chimney Corners; Donegal Fairy Tales; 'Twas in Dhroll Donegal; Ballads of a Country Boy; The Leadin' Road to Donegal; The Red Poacher; Irish Nights; The Bend of the Road; Dr. Kilgannon; A Lad of the O'Friels; Yourself and the Neighbors; Lo and Behold Ye; Top o' the Mornin'; Donegal Wonder Tales; Ballads of a Country Boy; Ireland's Case; The Story of the Irish Race; (plays) The Woman of Seven Sorrows; The Hardhearted Man; Orange and Green; The Lad from Largymore; Rory Wins; Bong Tong Come to Balvithery; Mrs. Connolly's Cashmere; Nabby Harren's Matching; The Miracle of Father Peter; Bold Blades of Donegal, Rocky Road to Dublin, Dark Patrick, Well o' the World's End.*‡

MACMILLAN CARGILL, business exec.; b. LaCrosse, Wis., Oct. 10, 1900; s. John Hugh and Edna (Cargill) MacM.; grad. Phillips Acad., Andover, Mass., 1918; B.A., Yale, 1922; m. Pauline Whitney, May 1, 1926; children—Cargill, Whitney, Pauline (Mrs. Keinath). Pres., dir. Cargill, Inc., Mpls. and subsidiary and affiliated firms; dir. Northwestern Nat. Bank of Mpls. Home: Wayzata MN Died Oct. 12, 1968.

MACMILLAN, SIR ERNEST CAMPBELL, organist, conductor, composer, organist, conductor, composer, educator; b. Mimico, Ont., Can., Aug. 18, 1893; s. Rev. Alexander and Wilhelmina (Ross) MacM.; student Rosedale Sch. and Jarvis Collegiate Inst., Toronto, and Viewpark Sch., Edinburgh, Scotland; B.A. with honors in Modern History (in absentia), U. Toronto, 1915; B. Mus., Oxford (Eng.) U., 1911, Mus. D. (in absentia), 1918; Mus.D. (hon.), Laval U., 1947, U. Rochester, 1956; LL.D., U. B.C., 1936, Queen's U., Kingston, 1941, U. Toronto, 1953, Mount Allison U., N.B., 1956; Litt.D. (hon.), McMaster U., 1948, U. Ottawa, 1959; studied under Frederick Niecks, Alfred Hollins and W.B. Ross, Edinburgh; m. Laura Elsie Keith, Dec. 31, 1919; children—Keith Campbell, Ross Alexander. Apptd. organist and choirmaster Knox Ch., Toronto, 1908, later held similar positions in other churches; visited Wagner Festival, Bayreuth, summer 1914; interned in prison camp Ruhleben, Berlin, Germany, for duration World War I, acted as condr. prison mus. prodns.; organist, choirmaster Timothy Eaton Meml. Ch., Toronto, 1919-25, conducted 1st regular ann. performances Bach's St. Matthew Passion; prin. Toronto Conservatory of Music, 1926-42; dean faculty of music U. Toronto, 1927-52; appeared as concert organist throughout U.S. and Can.; condr. Toronto Symphony Orch., 1931-56, Toronto Mendelssohn Choir, 1942-57; conducted choral and orchestral broadcasts in England, 1933-37; guest condr. Hollywood Bowl, 1936, Ford Sunday Evening Hour and with Chgo., Phila., Washington, NBC, Vancouver, Montreal orchs.; toured Australia conducting orchestras of Autralian Broadcasting Commn. in five cities, 1945; conducted series of concerts, Rio de Janeiro, 1946. Knighted by George V for services to music in Canada (1st musician in British Dominions so honored), 1935. Chmn., Canadian Music Council, 1947-66, later hon. pres.; pres. Canadian Music Centre, 1959-70, later hon. pres.; pres. Les Jeunesses Musicales du Canada, 1961-63, later hon. pres. Mem. Can. Council, 1957-63. Fellow Royal Coll. Music (1st Canadian so honored), Royal Coll. Organists (Carte Lafontaine prize 1910, v.p. 1936); mem. Royal Acad. Music (hon.), Composers, Authors and Pubs. Assn. Can. (pres. 1947-69), Royal Canadian Coll. Organists, Royal Canadian Inst. (hon.), Toronto Arts and Letters Club (pres. 1930-32). Presbyn. Composer: String Quartet in C Minor, 1914-21; England Code for solos, chorus and orch., 1917-18; Overture (orch.), 1924; Two Christmas Carols (voice, string trio or piano), 1926; Two Sketches (string quartet or string orch.), 1927; Three Indian Songs of the West Coast, 1928; Six Bergerettes du Bas Canada (voices, oboe, viola, cello, harp), 1928; Three French Canadian Sea Songs (for voice, string orch.), 1930; Sonnet (voice and piano), 1934; Te Deum Laudamus (chorus and orch.), 1944; A Song of Deliverance (chorus and orch.), 1945; Cortege academique (organ), 1953; editor, mus. arranger for several song books, including A Canadian Song Book, 1928, Vingt-et-une chansons candiennes, 1928; author, collaborator, editor several ednl. works. Address: Toronto Ontario Canada Died May 7, 1973.

MACMILLAN, GEORGE WHITFIELD, pres. Richmond Coll. (O.), and pastor Presby'n ch.; b. York Co., Pa.; ed. West Alexander Acad. and Princeton Coll. (Ph. D.); grad. Princeton Theol. Sem., 1857; (D.D., Richmond Coll.); m. 1858, Nancie Josinah MacMillan. Author: Coming Millenium; Creation and Development; Moral Science; etc. Address: Richmond OH‡

MAC MULLAN, RALPH A., state ofcl.; b. Detroit, Sept. 2, 1917; s. A.B. in Zoology, U. Mich., 1939, Ph.D., 1960. Game research biologist Mich. Dept. Natural Resources, Rose Lake Wildlife Sta., 1946, pheasant research, Lansing, 1947-50, head Houghton Lake Wildlife Expt. Sta., 1950-56, head game research, Lansing, 1956-62, asst. chief game div., 1962, dep. dir. in charge of staff, 1963, dir. dept., 1964-72. Mem. Nat. Adv. Com. Oceans and Atmosphere, 1971; liaison and protocol officer Mich. Sister-State Relationship with Shiga Prefecture, Japan, Belize and Dominican Republic; active Mich. Natural Resources Council, Greater Mich. Found. Served to maj. USAAF, World War II. Recipient Nat. Outdoor Life Conservation award, 1969; named Mich. State Conservationist of Year Nat. Wildlife Fedn., 1970. Mem. Internat. Assn. Game, Fish and Conservations Commrs. (pres.), Wildlife Soc. (v.p.), Nat. Assn. State Outdoor Recreation Liaison Officers (past pres.), Mich. Assn. Conservation Ecologists. Author: Life and Times of Michigan Pheasants (Wildlife Soc. award), 1956. Contbr. articles to Lansing MI Died Sept. 1972.

MACNAUGHTON, EDGAR, educator; b. Argyle, N.Y., May 4, 1887; s. James and Emma (Bain) MacN.; M.E., Cornell U., 1911; m. Mary A. Ross, Aug. 31, 1915 (dec. Oct. 1955). With Gen. Electric Co., 1911-14; instr. mech. engring. Tufts Coll., 1911-18, asst. prof., 1919-23, prof. in charge, 1923-71; asso. mech. engring. U. Ill., 1918-19. Registered engr., Mass. Mem. A.S.M.E. (chmn. Boston sect. 1940), Am. Soc. Engring. Edn., Am. Assn. U. Profs., Cornell Soc. Engrs., Mass. Soc. Profl. Engrs. Pi Tau Sigma, Delta Upsilon, Sigma Psi, Tau Beta Pi. Club: Cornell of New Eng. (Boston). Author: Elementary Steam Power Engineering, 1923, rev. edits. 1933, 48. Home: West Medford MA Died Oct. 21, 1971.

MACNAUGHTON, LEWIS WINSLOW, geologist; b. Nueva Gerona, Isla de Pinas, Cuba, Apr. 23, 1902; s. David and Mabelle Asenath (Drisko) M.; brought to United States in 1908; Bachelor of Arts Cornell U., 1925; m. Ina Mantooth, Dec. 6, 1928; children—Bruce Alan, Lewis Eugene. With Humble Oil & Refining Co., 1926-28, Rycade Oil Corp., 1928-30, Amerada Petroleum Corp., 1930-36; petroleum cons., Dallas, 1936-38; partner DeGolyer & MacNaughton, 1939-49, pres., 1949-56, chmn., 1956-62, sr. chmn., 1962-67; ret.; dir. Great Plains Devel. Co. Can., Ltd., Nat. Beryllia Corp., Cities Service Co., Dresser Industries, Inc., Republic National Bank Dallas, Southwestern Public Service Co., Trunkline Gas Co. Trustee S.W. Center Advanced Studies, Ft. Burgwin Research Center, Incorporated. Pres., trustee Sci. Information Inst., Dallas; dir. Greenhill Sch. Fellow A.A.A.S., Am. Geog. Society, Geological Society of London; member Anglo-Texas Society, Asociacion Mexicana de Geologos Petroleros, Dallas Geol. Soc., Am. Assn. Petroleum Geologists, Am. Inst. Mining and Metall. Engrs., N.Y. Mineral. Soc., Tex. Acad. Sci., Alberta Soc. Petroleum Geologists, Soc. Exploration Geophysicists, also member of Dallas Council World Affairs, Am. Geophys. Union, Am. Petroleum Inst., Am. Mgmt. Assn., Am., Tex. philatelic socs., Archeol. Inst. Am., Engrs. Club Dallas, Geochem. Soc., Internat. Oil Scouts Assn., Geologische Vereinigung, Germany, Nat. Indsl. Conf. Bd., Nat. Oil Equipment Mfrs. and Dels. Soc. (hon.), Nat. Oil Scouts and Landmen's Assn. (asso.), Newcomen Soc., Paleontol. Assn., Philos. Soc. Tex., Tex. Soc. Profl. Engrs., Soc. Econ. Paleontologists and Mineralogists, Koninklijk Nederlands Geologisch Mijnbouwkundig Gerootschap, Netherlands, Dallas Hist. Soc. Sigma Gamma Epsilon. Clubs: Brook, Explorers, Cornell (N.Y.C.); University (Mex., D.F.); Petroleum (Los Angeles); Ranchmen's (Calgary); Houston; Petroleum, Dallas, Lancers, Northwood, Chaparral, Texas (Dallas). Contbr. articles profl. jours. Home: Dallas TX Died Feb. 26, 1969.

MACNEIL, CAROL BROOKS, sculptor; b. Chicago, Jan. 15, 1871; d. Alden F. and Ellen W. Brooks; pupil Art Inst. and Lorado Taft, Chicago, and of MacMonnies and Injalbert, Paris; m. Hermon Atkins MacNeil, Dec. 25, 1895. Exhibited Chicago Expn., 1893, Paris Salons, 1894, 95, 1900; hon. mention Paris Expn., 1900; bronze medal, St. Louis Expn., 1904. Mem. Nat. Sculpture Soc., Soc. Women Painters and Sculptors. Has made a specialty of child life in sculpture, portraiture and landscape painting. Home: College Point Long Island NY‡

MACNEIL, NEIL, editor, author; b. Boston, Feb. 6, 1891; s. John A. and Catherine (MacNeil) MacN.; B.A., St. Francis Xavier U., 1912, LL.D., 1947; LL.D., Cath. U. Am., 1955; m. Elizabeth Quinn, June 28, 1920; children—Neil, Mary Rose (Mrs. H. B. Cumbaugh), Ann Elizabeth (Mrs. J.S. Kramer). City editor Daily Mail, Montreal, 1914-16; corr. Gazette, Montreal, 1916-18; nat. editor, fgn. editor, then city editor, asst. mng. editor N.Y. Times, 1918-51; editorial dir. Hoover Commn., 1954-55, asst. to Hon. Herbert Hoover, 1954-58. Dir. Parrish Art Mus. Served as sgt. maj. U.S. Army, World War I. Recipient Cath. Inst. of the Press award, 1949, John O'Hara Cosgrave medal for distinguished service to journalism, 1951. Mem. Clan MacNeil Assn. Am. (pres. emeritus), PAM Players (pres.), International Friends Antigonish Movement (pres.), Soc. Silurians (past pres.), Cath. Inst. Press (founder). Clubs: Dutch Treat (chmn.), New York Athletic (past gov.), Players (N.Y.C.); Southampton. Author: Without Fear or Favor, 1940; How to Be a Newspaperman, 1942; An American Peace, 1944; The Highland Heart in Nova Scotia, 1948; (with Harold W. Metz) The Hoover Report, 1953-55; Chester Dale and His Pictures, 1963; Tales from a Bull Pen, 1964. Home: Southampton NY Died Dec. 30, 1969; buried Southampton NY

MACNICOL, ROY VINCENT, artist; b. New York, N.Y., Nov. 27, 1889; s. Archibald and Consuela MacNicol; early art training at U. of Ill.; later studied at Paris and Toledo, Spain; m. Fay Courtney, singer, Jan. 26, 1920 (died Feb. 14, 1941). Began as an actor, then took up art; 1st recognition in art, 1931, doing decorative screens, murals and panels; later land and sea scapes and character portrait studies; water colorist. Has exhibited at Chicago Art Inst., Nat. Acad., Archtl. League and museums of U.S. and Europe, Palace of Fine Arts. Mexico City, has held 29 one-man exhbns. Represented in museums in Palm Beach Fla., Mexico City Beverly Hills, Calif., Chicago, N.Y. City, Paris, London, China, S. America and Brit. West Indies. Has traveled in many parts of the world to complete his Round the World collection; lived in Mexico from 1942. Died Nov. 1970.*

MACNIDER, HANFORD, mfr.; b. Mason City, Ia., Oct. 2, 1889; s. Charles Henry and May (Hanford) M.; grad. Milton (Mass.) Acad., 1907; A.B., Harvard, 1911; M.M.S., Norwich, 1926; LL.D., Syracuse, U., 1932, Simpson Coll., 1962; m. Margaret McAuley, Feb. 20, 1925; children—Tom, Jack, Angus (dec.). Chmn. bd. Northwestern States Portland Cement Co. State comdr. Am. Legion, 1920-21, nat. commander, 1921-22; asst. sec. war, 1925-28; U.S. minister to Can., 1930-32; mem. Geo. Washington Bicentennial Commn., 1925-30, Del. at large Nat. Republican Conv., 1924, 48; endorsed for presdl. nomination Ia. Rep. Conv., 1940. Trustee, Grinnell Coll., 1929-30; overseer Harvard Coll., 1946-52. Mexican Border service, 2d Inf. Ia. N.G., 1916-17; World War I, 2d lt., lt. col., 9th U.S. Inf., 2d Div., AEF, 1917-19; World War II, col., brig. gen., G.H.Q., S.W.P.A., 32d Div., 1st Cav. Div., 158 R.C.T. (Bushmasters), Jan. 1942-Feb. 1946; maj. gen. 103d Inf. Div. (OR), 1946-51; ret. lt. gen., 1956. Decorated D.S.C. with 2 clusters, D.S.M., Silver Star with 2 clusters, Legion of Merit, Bronze Star with cluster, Air Medal, Purple Heart with cluster, Bronze Arrowhead, Distinguished Unit Badge with 2 clusters (U.S.); Comdr. Legion of Honor, Croix de Guerre, five citations, Fourragere, C. de G. (France); Croce al Merito di Guerra (Italy); comdr. Legion of Honor (P.I.). Mason. Home: Mason City IA Died Feb. 17, 1968.

MACQUEEN, DONALD BRUCE, clergyman; b. Manilla, Ont., Dec. 23, 1876; s. Malcolm and Mary (Campbell) MacQ.; B.D., Rochester (N.Y.) Theol. Sem., 1908; D.D., Rochester U., 1929; m. Bertha M. Coone, Apr. 1, 1902; children—Mary Campbell, Dorothy Grose, Malcolm John. Came to U.S., 1904, naturalized citizen, 1916. Teacher pub. schs. of Province of Ontario, 1894-96; prin. pub. schs., Manilla, Ont., 1896-99; accountant, 1899-1901; traveling salesman for sawmill machinery, 1901-04; ordained ministry Bapt. Ch., 1908; pastor successively at West Henrietta and Batavia, N.Y., and Bridgeport, Conn. until 1922, First Church, Rochester, New York, 1922-42, Morton, New York, since 1943; manager American Baptist Foreign Mission Society; surveyor Northern Bapt. Missions in China, Japan and Philippines, 1926-27; mem. asso. boards for Christian Colleges in China since 1940; member, board of founders, Shanghai University. Pres. Temperance League of New York; trustee Colgate-Rochester Divinity Sch. Camp pastor, Camp Cody, Deming, N.M., 1916-17. Republican. Home: Morton NY‡

MACRAE, HUGH, b. Carbonton, N.C., Mar. 30, 1865; s. Donald and Julia (Norton) MacR.; B.S. in M.E., Mass. Inst. Tech., 1885; m. Rena Nelson, Feb. 4, 1891; children—Nelson, Mrs. Agnes Morton. Founder, 1902, Hugh MacRae & Co., establishing agrl. colonies in Wilmington dist.; dir. N.C. R.R. Co. Gen. chmn. Southern States Asso. Com. on Rural Development, 1927; pres. Southeastern Economic Council, 1931. Democrat. Clubs: Cape Fear (Wilmington); Nat. Arts (New York). Home: Wilmington NC*‡

MACTAVISH, WILLIAM CARUTH, educator; b. N.Y.C., June 13, 1893; s. William Caruth and Ida Gertrude (Koehler) MacT.; B.S., New York U., 1924; M.A., Columbia U., 1926; m. Josephine Munson, Sept. 14, 1928 (dec.); m. 2d, Agnes Marie Heermann, May 30, 1942. Asst. New York U. Coll. of Medicine, 1913-17, instr., 1917-26, asst. prof., 1926-30; instr. chemistry, Washington Square Coll. (New York U.), 1919-24, asst. prof. and chmn., 1924-26, asso. prof. and dir. labs., 1926-29, prof., also lab. dir., 1929-30, prof. chemistry, chmn. dept., 1930-48, prof. chemistry, 1948-58, emeritus prof. A founder N.Y. U. Bellevue Med. Center, 1950; pres. N.Y. U. Coll. of Medicine Alumni 1956-57. Visiting toxicologist Grasslands Hospital, 1932-64, hon. cons. div. pathology, 1965-68; consulting chemist, French Hospital, since 1938; mem. adv. com. on pub. health Worlds Fair, 1938-40; mem. Chandler Centenary com., Columbia U., 1938-39; academic advisor to Italian Consulate, N.Y. City, 1933-39 (passing on records of Am. students applying to Italian Med. Schs.); mem. registrants adv. bd. Selective Service, N.Y., 1941-42; mem. draft bd. No. 15, N.Y. City, 1942-68; selectman of Dennistown Plantation, Sommerset County, Maine, 1953-68, civil defense and pub. safety dir., 1963-68. Enlisted in the First F.A., N.G., 1915, served on Mexican Border, 1916, master hosp. sergt., World War, with U.S. Army Lab. No. 1, Neufchateau, 1918-19. Recipient N.Y. U. Alumni meritorious award, 1958. Fellow London Chem. Soc. (life), A.A.A.S., N.Y. Acad. Medicine; mem. Am. Chem. Soc. (nat. councillor, 1935-37; bd. dirs., 1935-37; chmn., 1937-38; mem. Nichols Medal Jury, 1937-43; chmn., 1942-43; nat. councillor, 1945-46; chmn. and mem. bd. dirs. N.Y. sect.), (asso.) A.M.A., Am. Assn. Univ. Profs., Am. Tree Farm System, Sigma Xi, Phi Lambda Upsilon, Phi Delta Theta. Episcopalian. Home: Jackman ME Died Sept. 14, 1968.

MACVEAGH, EWEN CAMERON, lawyer; b. Santa Barbara, Cal., Mar. 7, 1895; s. Charles and Fanny Davenport (Rogers) MacV.; grad. Groton (Mass.) Sch., 1914; A.B., Harvard, 1918, LL.B., 1923 m. Louise Thoron, June 28, 1923; children—Eileen (Mrs. Vladimir I. Toumanoff), Edith Cameron (Mrs. G. H. Harris Huey), Moria Cameron (Mrs. Daniel McF. Burnham). Began career with the Girard Trust Co., Phila., 1919-20; v.p. Trojan Tool Corp., N.Y.C., 1920; admitted to N.Y. bar, 1924; with firm Covington, Burling & Rublee, Washington. 1924-25; with law firm Davis, Polk and Wardwell, and predecessors, New York City, 1927-71, partner, 1940-71; counsel American banks German Bank Indebtedness confs., 1933-40, 53-57; adviser Am. banks Internat. German Debt Conf., London, Eng., 1952-53. Dir. Tex Instruments Co., Brooks Bros. Ltd. (Eng.). Trustee Davenport Home, Bath, N.Y., 1925-58, pres., 1950-58; hon. chmn. Ira Davenport Meml. Hosp., Bath, 1958-71; trustee Dublin (N.H.) Sch., 1954-66, hon. trustee, 1966-71; mem. bd. dirs., 1st v.p. Doctors Hosp., N.Y.C., 1930-71. Served with U.S. Army, Mexican Border, 1916, AEF in France, 1917-19. Mem. Soc. Mayflower Descendants, New York City Chamber of Commerce. Clubs: Century Association, University, Harvard (N.Y.C.); Harvard (Boston); Metropolitan (Washington). Author: The Yankee in British Zone (with Lee D. Brown), 1920; also articles, pamphlets Home: New York City NY also Dublin, NH Died Feb. 17, 1971.

MACVEAGH, LINCOLN, publisher, diplomat; b. Narragansett Pier, R.I., Oct. 1, 1890; s. Charles and Fanny Davenport (Rogers) MacV.; student Groton Sch., 1903-09; A.B., Harvard, 1913; student at Sorbonne, Paris, 1913-14; Ph.D. (honorary), Athens University; married to Margaret Charlton Lewis, Aug. 17, 1917 (died Sept. 9, 1947); 1 dau., Mrs. Samuel E. Thorne; married 2d, Virginia Ferrante Coats, May 12, 1955; stepchildren—Colin MacVeagh, Mrs. Hugh Reynolds, Gloria MacVeagh, Sec. to dir. Boston Art Mus., 1912-13; with United States Steel Products Company, 1914-15, Henry Holt Company, 1915-17, 1919-23; pres. Dial Press, Inc., 1923-33; E.E. and M.P. to Greece, 1933-41; to Iceland, 1941; to Union of South Africa, 1942; ambassador to Greece and Yugoslavia, 1943, to Greece, 1944, Portugal, 1948, to Spain 1952-53. Served as 1st lieutenant, later capt. and maj., Army Expeditionary Force, World War I; cited by Gen. Pershing for exceptionally meritorious and conspicuous services;" Grand Cross of George the First of Greece, 1954. Decorated Grand Cross Mil. Order Christ (Portugal), 1960. Hon. Citizen Athens; trustee Am. Sch. of Classical Studies; hon. fellow Archaeol. Society of Athens; member Society Mayflower Descendants, Stewart Society of Edinburgh, Council Fgn. Relations, Am. Legion, P.E.N., Phi Beta Kappa. Democrat. Episcopalian. Clubs: Jefferson Islands Country; Century, University (N.Y.C.); Metropolitan (Washington), New Canaan Country. Editor: New Champlin Cyclopedia for Young Folks, 1924, 25, 30, Poetry from the Bible, 1925. Author: (with Margaret MacVeagh) Greek Journey, 1937. Address: Estoril Portugal Died Jan. 15, 1972.

MAC VEY, WILLIAM PITT, college pres.; b. Toledo, O., Mar. 25, 1873; s. Alfred Henry and Anna (Holmes) M.; brother of Frank LeRond M. (q.v.); A.B., Des Moines Coll., 1892; B.D., Drew Theol. Sem., N.J., 1896; U. of Leipzig; (D.D., Iowa Wesleyan U., 1908); m. I. Gertrude Hobson, of E. Orange, N.J., 1896. Entered M.E. ministry, 1892; pastor Cincinnati, 1892-3; missionary Foochow, China, 1896-7; pastor Minneapolis, 1898, Grand Forks, N.D., 1898-1902, Pekin, Ill., 1903-6, Rock Island, 1907; pres. Hedding Coll. since 1907. Prohibitionist. Author: Genius of Methodism, 1903. Address: Abingdon IL‡

MACY, JOSIAH, JR., airline exec.; b. Morristown, N.J., Apr. 20, 1910; s. Josiah and Elizabeth Wyatt (Wise) M.; grad. Taft Sch., 1928; A.B., Princeton, 1932; student U. Munich (Germany), 1930; LL.B., U. Pa., 1935; m. Mary Charlotte Emerson, July 3, 1939; children—Josiah III, Thomas Truxtun, Deborah Wright, Michael Emerson Fitzgerald. Admitted to N.Y. bar, 1936, N.J. bar, 1946; gen. practice of law, N.Y.C., 1935-41; asso. Shanley & Fisher, Newark, 1945-48; sec. Mut. Ins. Adv. Assn., N.Y.C., 1948-51; atty. Daystrom, Inc., Murray Hill, N.J., 1951-52; asst. sec. Pan Am. World Airways, Inc. N.Y.C., 1952-60, sec., 1960-72; sec. Intercontinental Hotels Corp., 1960-72, also sec., dir. affiliated hotel cos. Former adv. mem. Morristown Plan Bd. Candidate N.J. Senate, 1949. Past chmn. Morristown Assn.; trustee New Vernon (N.J.) Cemetery Assn.; past bd. dirs. Morristown chpt. A.R.C.; sec. U.S.-Nigerian Found. Served to maj. AUS, 1941-45; ETO. Decorated Bronze Star. Episcopalian. Clubs: Colonial (Princeton), Shakespeare (past pres.) (Morristown). Home: Morristown NJ Died Aug. 24, 1972.

MACY, VALENTINE E(VERIT) JR., bus. exec., trustee; b. N.Y. City, Apr. 28, 1898; s. V(alentine) Everit and Edith (Wiesman) Carpenter M.; student Browning Sch., N.Y. City, 1907-13, Hotchkiss Sch., Lakeville, Conn., 1913-15; Evans Sch., Mesa, Ariz., 1915-16; A.B., Harvard, 1920; m. Harriet A(yer) Seymour Helm, Oct. 12, 1934. Dir. Deed Realty Corporation, Peerless Photo Products, Incorporated, Westchester Rockland Newspapers, Incorporated, Vision, Incorporated; trustee inter-vivos and testamentary trusts. Commr. Westchester Co. Park Commn., 1933-42, Playland Authority, 1940-42, and Cross County Parkway Authority, 1941-42. Trustee Tchrs. Coll. Columbia, Nat. Information Bur., Inc. Clubs: Devon Yacht, Maidstone, Mill Reef, Harvard, University, Union Died Aug. 4, 1970; buried Sleepy Hollow Cemetery, Tarrytown NY

MADDEN, JAMES LOOMIS, lawyer; b. N.J., July 5, 1892; s. James Thomas and Jane (O'Neill) M.; A.B., Washington Coll., Chestertown, Md., 1911, A.M., 1916, LL.D., 1951; J.D., N.Y. U., 1917; LL.D., Middlebury Coll., 1952; m. Irma Twining, Jan. 12, 1920; children—Mary Carolyn, James E., Richard B., Robert T. Admitted to N.Y. bar, 1917, U.S. Supreme Ct., 1926; 2d v.p. Met. Life Ins. Co., 1927-63; mem. adv. bd. Lumbermans Mut. Casualty Co.; dir. Mueller Corp., Metropolitan Fire Ins. Co. Acting chancellor N.Y. U., 1951-52, vice chmn. trustees, 1952-62, mem. faculty Law School, 1936-47; v.p., dir. Law Center Found., N.Y. U.; fellow Ins. Inst. Am.; trustee Kempner Found., Duke; Brackett lectr. Princeton, 1950; lectr. Mgmt. Inst., Oxford U. (Eng.), 1949; past trustee, treas., chmn. finance com. Nat. Indsl. Conf. Bd., also sr. mem. Pres. North Pond Assn. Capt. ordnance, U.S. Army, World War I; civilian mem. U.S. Army Gen. Staff, Manpower Bd., also mem. adv. bd. to surgeon gen. U.S. Army, and mem. adv. com. representing banking and ins. Management-Labor Bd., War Manpower Commn., World War II. Life mem. Am. Mgmt. Assn. (past treas., chmn. finance com.), Transp. Assn. Am. (past chmn. bd. dirs., chmn. exec. com.); mem. U.S. C. of C. (past dir., chmn. tax com. 1952-56), Marketing Execs. Soc., Newcomen Soc., Phi Delta Phi, Beta Gamma Sigma (hon.), Knight of Malta, Knight Order Holy Sepulchre. Roman Catholic. Author: Wills, Trusts and Estates in Relation to Life Insurance; also various papers. Home: Short Hills NJ Died May 30, 1972.

MADDEN, JOHN, business exec.; b. Chgo., Mar. 12, 1900; s. Patrick James and Katherine Veronica (Garvey) M.; student U. Mich. 1922; m. Margaret C. Finn, June 20, 1923; children—John Finn (dec.), Patricia, (Mrs. R.F. Wright), John. With James B. Clow & Sons, 1922-69, v.p., 1946-52, later pres., then chmn. bd., also dir.; chmn. Yeomans Bros. Co., Ill., Aero-O-Flo Corp., Florence, Ky.; director Seng Co., Borg-Warner Corp., Nuclear-Chicago Corp. (all Chgo.), H. M. Harper and Co., Morton Grove, Illinois; dir., chmn. exec. com. Inland Life Ins. Co., Chgo. Dir. Evanston Hosp. Assn., Chicago Crime Commn., American Red Cross, Peacock Camp for Crippled Children. Mem. lay bd. Loyola U., St. Vincent's Orphanage and Maternity Hospital. Mem. Chgo. Assn. Commerce and Industry (dir.), Cast Iron Pipe Research Assn. Chgo. (chmn.), Phi Gamma Delta. Clubs: Glen View Golf, Winnetka IL Died Sept. 8, 1969.

MADDEN, JOSEPH WARREN, judge; b. Damascus, Stephenson County, Ill., Jan. 17, 1890; s. William James and Elizabeth Dickey (Murdaugh) M.; grad. Northern Ill. State Normal Sch., DeKalb, Ill., 1908; A.B., U. of Ill., 1911; J.D., U. of Chicago, 1914; m. Margaret Bell Liddell, July 16, 1913; children—Mary Esther, Joseph Warren, Robert Liddell, Margaret Elizabeth, Murdaugh Stuart. Prof. law, U. of Okla., 1914-16; practiced law, Rockford, Ill., 1916-17; prof. law, Ohio State U., Columbus, O., 1917-21, also pvt. practice; dean Coll. of Law and prof. law, W.Va. U., 1921-27; prof. of law, U. of Pittsburgh, 1927-38; chmn. Nat. Labor Relations Bd., Washington, D.C., 1935-40; judge, U.S. Court of Claims, Washington, 1941-61, ret. judge 9th Circuit Ct. Appeals, 1961-72; tchr. Hastings Law Sch., San Francisco, from 1961; asso. dir. Legal Division, U.S. Mil. Government of Germany, 1945; dir. Legal Div. and Legal Advisor to U.S. Mil. Governor of Germany, 1946; acting prof. law, Stanford, 1930-31; visiting prof. of law, U. of Chicago, 4 summers to 1948, Cornell U., summer 1930, Stanford U., summer 1933; spl. asst. office atty. gen. U.S., summer 1920; U. N.C., 1941-44, Yale, summer 1947, Vanderbilt U., summer 1951, 53; lectr. German U. Law Schs., summer 1949; assisted West Va. Revision and Codification Commn. in revising property statutes, 1925; adviser on property and torts to Am. Law Inst., 1934-50; past mem. (Pa.) Commn. on Spl. Policing in Industry; exchange legal specialist, Germany, summer, 1953. Awarded Medal of Freedom (for work with mil. govt. Germany), 1947. Mem. Am. Law Institute, Delta Upsilon, Phi Alpha Delta, Order of Coif. Democrat. Club: Cosmos (Washington). Author: Treatise on the Law of Domestic Relations and Persons, 1931. Editor (with W.R. Compton) Cases on Persons and Domestic Relations, including Marriage and Divorce, 1940; (with H.A. Bigelow) Cases on Rights in Land, 1934; Introduction to Real Property (with same), 2d edit., 1934. Home: Falls Church VA Died Feb. 17, 1972; buried Falls Church VA

MADDOCK, CATHARINE YOUNG GLEN, writer; b. Elizabeth, N.J., Aug. 26, 1872; d. Charles T. and Catharine F. Glen; grad. Mt. Holyoke Coll., S. Hadley, Mass., 1894; m. Frederick Richard Maddock, of Newark, N.J., Apr. 24, 1909. Has contributed short stories and poems to Century, St. Nicholas, Harper's, Youth's Companion and other periodicals since 1895. Address: 300 Roseville Av., Newark NJ‡

MADDOCK, WILLIAM ELI, educator; b. St. Joseph, Ill., June 26, 1868; s. David and Jane H. (Mills) M.; B.L., Earlham Coll., Richmond, Ind., 1894; A.B., Harvard, 1904; M.A., Stanford, 1922; m. Lida Margaret Shobe, Aug. 31, 1904; children—Helen Jane, Margaret Ruth (Mrs. H. E. Anderson); m. 2d, Grace Trimble, Aug. 30, 1926. Began as teacher pub. schs., Kingman, Ind., 1889; prin. Damascus (O.) Acad., 1894-95; prin. pub. schs., Ashley, O., 1895-1900; school prin. Superior, Wis., 1900-03, supt. schs., 1905-16; supt. schs., Butte, Mont., 1916-21; prof. edn. Mont. State U., 1922-42, also chmn. bd. of recommendations and dir. extension div., 1922-37, asst. dir. Summer School, 1928-35, dir., 1935-37. Mem. N.E.A., Mont. Edn. Assn., Mont. Soc. for Study of Edn. (dir.), Alpha Sigma Phi, Phi Delta Kappa. Republican. Conglist. Club: Missoula Authors. Contbr. to ednl. periodicals. Home: 426 McLeod Av., Missoula MT‡

MADDOX, ROBERT FOSTER, banker; b. Atlanta, Ga., Apr. 4, 1870; s. Robert F. and Nannie (Reynolds) M.; student U. of Ga. and Harvard; m. Lollie Baxter, June 12, 1895; children—Robert F., Nathaniel Baxter, Laura. Vice-pres. Am. Nat. Bank, 1900-16; pres. Atlanta Nat. Bank, 1916-24; chmn. bd. Atlanta & Lowry Nat. Bank, 1924-29; chmn. exec. com. First Nat. Bank after merger of banks, 1929-33; chmn. bd. First Nat. Bank, Atlanta, 1934; dir. Ga. Power Co., Southern Bell Telephone Co., First National Bank; now retired. Commissioner Roads and Revenue of Fulton County, Georgia, 1906-07; mayor of Atlanta, 1909-10; pres. Ga. State Bd. Health; pres. Atlanta Chamber of Commerce, 1904-05, Atlanta Community Chest; trustee, treas. Berry Schs., Rome, Ga.; chmn. bd. High Museum Art. Mem. com. Am. Bankers' Assn. that presented resolutions concerning monetary system to Congress, 1913; pres. Ga. Bankers Assn., 1911-12, Am. Bankers Assn., 1918-19; chmn. com. to cooperate with export-import banks, Washington, D.C. Mem. of Sigma Alpha Epsilon. Democrat. Methodist. Mason (Shriner), Elk. Clubs: Capital City, Piedmont Atlanta GA‡

MADDOX, WILLIAM PERCY, fgn. service officer; b. Princess Anne, Md., Nov. 21, 1901; s. Robert Franklin and Ella Virginia (Hoblitzell) M.; A.B., St. John's Coll., Md., 1921; B.A., Oxford, Eng., 1925; Ph.D., Harvard, 1933; LL.D. (hon.), Pratt Inst., 1968; m. Louise Shaw Hepburn, June 15, 1945; 1 dau., Alexandra Cortelyou. Reporter on Baltimore Evening Sun, 1921-22; instr. polit. sci. U. of Ore., 1925-27, asst. prof., 1927-28; acting asso. prof. polit. sci. U. of Va., 1928-29; instr. in govt. Harvard U., 1930-36; asst. prof. politics Princeton, 1936-38; asso. prof. polit. sci. U. of Pa., 1938-46 (on leave 1942-46); asst. to pres. Fgn. Policy Assn., 1942;

chief div. of tng. services Dept. of State, 1946-47, dir. Fgn. Service Inst., 1947-49; counselor of embassy at Lisbon, Portugal, 1949-52; consul gen. Port of Spain, Trinidad, 1952-55; Counselor of embassy, Pretoria, Union of South Africa, 1955-59; consul gen., Singapore, 1959-61; staff adviser U.S. Arms Control and Disarmament Agy., 1962-65; dir. Midtown Internat. Center N.Y.C., 1965; v.p. for acad. affairs Pratt Inst. Bklyn., 1965-66, acting pres., 1967-68, cons., 1968-70. Served with Office of Strategic Services, A.U.S., in E.T.O. and M.T.O., 1942-45, advancing to rank of col. Decorated Legion of Merit with oak leaf cluster (U.S.), Hon. Officer Mil. Div. Order Brit. Empire, Chevalier Legion of Honor (France), Polonia Restituta (Poland). Mem. Council Fgn. Relations, Phi Sigma Kappa. Club: Harvard (N.Y.C.). Author: Foreign Relations in British Labor Politics, 1934. Contbr. profl. jours. Home: Rocky Hill NJ Died Sept. 27, 1972; buried St. David's Episcopal Ch. Cemetery, Radnor PA

MADDUX, JARED, lawyer, state govt. ofcl.; b. Buffalo Valley, Tenn., July 20, 1911; s. Solon and Daisy (Jared) M.; B.S., Tenn. Polytech. Inst., 1934; LL.B., E. Tenn. Law Sch., 1938; m. Mary V. Lane, July 6, 1935; children—Virginia L., John Jared, Rachel N. Admitted to Tenn. bar, 1940; mem. firm Maddux, Moore & Moore. Chief clk. Tenn. Ho. of Reps., 1944; comptroller Tenn. Treasury, 1945-49; state senator, speaker Tenn. Senate, also lt. gov. Tenn., 1953-58, 65-66. Young Man of Year award Tenn. Jr. C. of C., 1943; Good Govt. award, U.S. Jr. C. of C., 1948. Mem. Tenn. (pres. 1944-45), Elizabethton (pres. 1941-42) jr. chambers of commerce, Am. Legion (vice chairman national legislative commission). Democrat. Methodist. Mason (Shriner). Club: Lions. Home: Cookeville TN Died May 22, 1971.

MADEIRA, JEAN BROWNING, opera singer; b. Centralia, Ill., Nov. 14, 1924; d. Lee Roy and Noma Jane (Eubanks) Browning; student Leo C. Miller Music Sch., St. Louis, 1936-41, Washington U., 1940-41, Julliard Grad. Sch., 1941-45; Master Arts (honorary), Brown University, 1961; Ph.D. (hon.), Washington U., 1970; m. Francis King Carey Madeira, June 17, 1947. Concert pianist St. Louis Symphony, 1938; leading contralto Chautauqua (N.Y.) Opera Co., 1943-47, San Carlo Opera Co., 1947-48; debut Met. Opera, 1948, roles include Carmen, Amneris in Aida, Azucena in Il Trovatore, Ulrica in Masked Ball, Delilah, Orfeo, Klytemnestra in Elektra, Brussels, from 1965; concert singer radio, TV appearances, from 1950; leading contralto opening Vienna Staatsoper, 1955, Covent Garden, Stockholm Opera, Munich and Salzburg festivals, 1954-55; Bayreuth Festival, 1956-58; Salzburg Festival, 1957; Seville Spain Festival, 1957; Munich Festival, 1962-64; Bilbao Festival, 1963; Teatro Colon, Buenos Aires, 1958; Brussels Worlds Fair, 1958; Debut, LaScala, Milan, 1958; Carmen at Met. Opera, 1956-61; Teatro San Carlo, Naples, Italy, 1959; only American ever to sing Carmen in Aix En Provence Festival, 1957; Paris Opera, 1957, 65; debut as Delilah, Israel Nat. Opera, 1962; soloist opening of Lincoln Center-Met. Opera presentation Altantida, 1962; made debut in Spain as Carmen, 1963; Salome in Paris Opera; Carmen in Germany, Yugoslavia, Switzerland, also Cin. Zoo Opera; Azucena in the Frankfurt (Germany) Opera House, 1965; Dame Quickly in Falstaff, Munich Festival, 1966; Armide (Gluck) in Scwetzingen (Germany) Festival, 1966; Countess Geschwitz in Lulu, Munich, 1967; Klytemnestra in Elektra, Met. Opera, 1968; roles of Circe and Melantho, world premiere, Ulysses, Berlin, 1968, Italian premiere, Milan, 1969, BBC London premiere, 1969; role of Erda, Ring, Munich, 1969. Rept. Woman of Achvmnt. award, St. Louis, 1947, Hon. Alumni citation Washington U., 1962. Mem. Jobs Daughters, Mu Phi Epsilon. Home: Warwick Neck RI Died July 10, 1972.

MAGAW, CHARLES ALBERT, lawyer; b. Fairhaven, O., Aug. 15, 1872; s. John B. and Margaret (Van Dyke) M.; student Washburn Coll., Topeka, Kan., 1890-96; LL.B., U. of Kan., 1897; unmarried. In gen. law practice, Topeka, 1897-1911; asst. gen. atty. law dept. Union Pacific Railroad, 1911-17, asst. gen. atty. for Neb. and Ia., 1917-18, gen. atty. for Neb. and Ia., 1918-33, gen. solicitor U.P.R.R. Co., 1933-36; gen. law practice, Topeka, since 1936; now in farming and livestock bus.; lectr. on constl. law Washburn Coll., 1937-41. Repbulican. Home: Hotel Jayhawk, Office: Nat. Bank of Topeka Bldg., Topeka KS‡

MAGEE, CHARLES LOHR, b. Petersburg, Pa., Apr. 1, 1876; s. John A. and Harriet G. (Miller) M.; ed. high sch. and Columbian U.; m. Gustava L. Herrle, of Washington, June 30, 1903; children—Charles Herrle, Robert Colin, Marion, Helen. Sec. Am. Nat. Red Cross, 1905-17; asst. dir. Civilian Relief, 1917-20; private business, 1920-21; with U.S. Veterans' Bur. since 1921. Served in U.S.N. during Spanish-Am. War. Republican. Home: 116 Tennessee Av., Washington DC‡

MAGEE, CLARE, congressman, lawyer; b. near Livonia, Mo., Mar. 31, 1899; s. James Wallace and Dora Amelia M.; student Kirksville State Normal Sch., summer 1916; U. of Mo., 1917-22; m. Mary Frances Sheets, Sept. 7, 1927; (died. Aug. 1945); 1 daughter, Marjorie Lee; m. 2d, Mrs. Ruth Rixey, Homesteaded in Big Horn Basin, Wyo., 1920-21; laborer U.S. Reclamation Service, Deaver, Wyo., 1920-21; owner and operator farm near Livonia since 1932; admitted to Mo. state bar, 1922, and practiced in Unionville; postmaster, Unionville, 1935-41. Rep. from 1st Mo. Dist., U.S. Congress, 1949-52. Pres. Unionville Park Bd., 1945-46. Served as apprentice seaman to 1/c seaman, U.S. Navy, 1918; pvt. F.A., U.S. Army, 1942; capt., A.A.F., 1942-44. Hon. mem. Vets. Fgn. Wars; mem. Am. Judicature Soc., Am. Legion, Mo. Bar Assn., Mo. Archeol. Soc., C. of C. (past pres.); Phi Delta Phi. Democrat. (chmn. central com. of Putnam County, 1926-32; mem. state speakers bur., and orgn. bur.; del. to state convs., chmn. 1st dist. caucus, 1930-32). Protestant. Odd Fellow. Eagle. Mason (O.E.S., 32 deg., Shriner). Clubs: Quo Vadis (past pres.), Rotary (past pres.), Young Democrats Jefferson (past pres.). Home: Unionville MO Died Aug. 1969.

MAGEE, J(UNIUS) RALPH, bishop; b. Maquoketa, Ia., June 3, 1880; s. John Calvin and Jane Amelia (Cole) M.; B.Di., Ia. State Teachers Coll., Cedar Falls, 1901; Ph.B., Morningside Coll., 1904, LL.D., 1931; S.T.B., Boston U. Sch. of Theology, 1910; D.D., Upper Iowa University, 1921, Boston University School of Theol., 1947; L.H.D., Coll. of Puget Sound, 1932; LL.D., Illinois Wesleyan University, 1945; Litt.D., Hamline U., 1948; m. Harriet A. Keeler, Sept. 10, 1902 (died Oct. 31, 1943); children—John Homer, Dorothy Jean. Principal Public Schools, Nora Springs, Iowa, 1901-02; ordained ministry M.E. Ch., 1902; deacon, 1904, elder, 1906; pastor Rustin Avenue Church, Sioux City, 1902-04, Paullina, Iowa, 1904-07, Falmouth, Massachusetts, 1907-11, Taunton, 1911-14, Daniel Dorchester Memorial Church, Boston, 1914-19, St. Mark's Church, Brookline, 1919-21, First Ch., Seattle, Wash., 1921-29; became supt. Seattle dist. 1929; elected bishop of the Methodist Episcopal Church, May 1932; pres. Hamline U., 1933-34; bishop St. Paul Area Meth. Ch., 1932-39, Des Moines Area Meth. Ch., 1939-44, Chicago Area Meth. Chs., 1944-52. Chairman Methodist Survey Commission, 1948-52; president of the Council of Bishops, 1950. Dir. of the Crusade for Christ of the Methodist Ch. Trustee Northwestern University, Evanston Collegiate Institute, Garrett Biblical Inst., Wesley Memorial Hosp., Illinois Wesleyan U., McKendree College, Lake Bluff Orphanage, Wesley Foundn., U. of Ill. Trustee, Seattle Chamber Commerce, 1925-32. Member Mayor's Commission on Unemployment, Seattle, 1931. Mem. Gen. Conf. M.E. Ch., 1928, 32 (mem. com. on entertainment); pres. Minn. State Pastors Conf., 1939; dir. Crusade for Christ, Meth. Ch., 1944-48. Member Pi Gamma Mu, Pi Kappa Delta. Republican. Mason (K.T., grand orator, Grand Lodge of Wash., 1931-32), K.P. (grand prelate for Mass., 1909-13). Home: Evanston IL Died Dec. 19, 1970; buried Memory Glen, Evergreen Park, Seattle WA

MAGGARD, EDWARD HARRIS, ry. official; b. Meridian, Miss., Aug. 19, 1875; s. David Geary and Marry Louise (Cain) M.; ed. pub. schs.; m. Mabel F., Petaluma, Calif., April 31, 1913; 1 dau., Jane M. Began as call boy with Mo., Kan., Tex. R.R. Co., 1890; now pres. and gen. mgr. Northwestern Pacific R.R. Co., Petaluma & Santa Rosa R.R. Co. Republican. Elk. Clubs: Bohemian, Commercial, Transportation (San Francisco); Meadow Golf (Marin Co.). Home: Ross, Calif. Office: 65 Market St., San Francisco CA‡

MAGIE, DAVID, prof. classics; b. N.Y. City, Jan. 20, 1877; s. David and Margaret (McCosh) M.; A.B., Princeton, 1897, A.M., 1899; Ph.D., U. of Halle, 1904. Instr. Latin, 1899-1905, preceptor classics, 1905-11, prof. since 1911, Princeton. Mem. Am. Philol. Assn., Archaeol. Inst. America. Presbyn. Home: 101 Library Pl., Princeton NJ‡

MAGIL, MARY ELLEN RYAN (MRS. ELIAS MAGIL), psychologist-educator; b. Phila; d. William P. and Mary Anne (Gamble) Ryan; B.A. in Psychology, Temple U., 1957, M.S. in Sch. Psychology, 1959; m. Elias Magil, Feb. 7, 1941; children—Leonard (dec.), Edward Joseph. Intern, Psychol. Clinic, Camden (N.J.) Bd. Edn., 1958-59; tchr. psychology Ogontz Center, Pa. State U., 1960-68, Coatesville (Pa.) Hosp., 1960-68, Easton (Pa.) Hosp., 1960-61, Grandview Hosp. Sellerville, Pa., 1962-68; pvt. practice psychology, Phila., 1959-68. Chmn. entertainment, instrn. and supply N.W. chpt. A.R.C., 1950-52; bd. dirs. Temple U. Liberal Arts Alumni, 1960-68, chmn. luncheon com., 1962-68, chmn. Alumni Forum, 1962-63. Mem. Am., Pa. psychol. assns., Am. Personnel and Guidance Assn., Am. Coll. Personnel Assn., Am. Assn. U. Women, A.A.A.S., Nat. League for Nursing, Guidance Assn. of Greater Phila., Psi Chi, Philadelphia PA Died Nov. 29, 1968.

MAGILL, WILLIAM SEAGROVE, surgeon, pathologist; b. Lynne, Conn., July 7, 1866; s. William Alexander and Mathilda Wakefield (Smith) M.; A.B., Amherst Coll., 1887, A.M., 1892; B.L., B.S., U. of Paris, 1889, M.D., 1894; studied Institut Pasteur, Paris, 1892-97, U. of Burich, 1894; m. Camille Grandclement, Princess of Graves, Russia, 1915 (died 1928); 1 son, William Camille. Prof. pathology and dean Coll. of Medicine, U. of W.Va., 1900-01; research bacteriologist Carnegie Lab., New York, 1901-03; spl. investigator, Paris, Berlin, Vienna, Munich, 1903-08; surgeon New York Nose, Throat and Lung Hosp., 1908-09; dir. labs., N.Y. State Dept. Health, 1909-14; owner and operator Wolfram (tungsten) Mines, Portugal, 1917-22. First lt. U.S. Army Med. Reserve Corps, 1909-15; chief interpreter Internat. Tuberculosis Congress, Washington, D.C., 1909, and Internat. Congress of Hygiene, Washington, 1912. Lt. gen. M.C., Russian Imperial 3d Army, 1914-15. Inventor of processes and products mostly concerning milk in dry form for which over 400 patents have been issued. Fellow Am. Acad. Medicine; mem. Internat. Univ. Com. (founder, Paris, 1896), etc. Extensive contbr. on med. subjects. Home: Amherst MA*‡

MAGILLIGAN, DONALD JAMES, physician; b. Bklyn., Aug. 30, 1903; s. Francis J. and Anna I. M. (Clark) M.; A.B., Coll. Holy Cross, 1924; M.D., L.I. Coll., 1929; m. Eileen J. McLoughlin, Dec. 26, 1935; children—Mary V. (Mrs. Robert J. Wiggers), Eileen J., Donald J., Anne C. (Mrs. Maurice T. Hartigan II), John F. Intern, St. Catherine's Hosp., Bklyn., 1929-31; practice medicine specializing in orthopedic surgery, Bklyn., 1931-68; mem. staffs St. Charles, Long Island Coll., Holy Family, Bklyn., VA hosps.; cons. surgeon St. Mary's Hosp.; clin. prof. orthopedic surgery N.Y. Med. Coll., 1964-68. Diplomate Am. Bd. Orthopedic Surgery. Fellow A.C.S., Am. Acad. Orthopedic Surgeons; mem. Am. Assn. Med. Colls. Home: Brooklyn NY Died Aug. 19, 1968.

MAGNER, JAMES JOSEPH, lawyer; b. Seymour, Conn., Aug. 2, 1897; s. James and Mary (O'Brien) M.; LL.B., U. Chgo., 1923; m. Adelaide B. Casey, June 27, 1923; children—Mary Barbara, Judith Ann (Mrs. Nicholas DePasquale). Admitted to Ill. bar, 1923, since practiced in Chgo.; partner firm Taylor, Miller, Magner, Sprowl & Hotchings, 1927-69. Mem. Am., Ill., Chgo. bar assns. Club: Union League (Chgo.). Home: Winnetka IL Died Sept. 28, 1969; buried All Saints Cemetery, Des Plaines IL

MAGNUSSON, MAGNUS VIGNIR, diplomat; b. Reykjavik, Iceland, Oct. 10, 1910; s. Magnus and Astridur (Stephensen) Sigurdsson; LL.M., U. Iceland, 1936; postgrad. internat. law Sorbonne, Paris, 1936-37; m. Anna Gudrun Sveinsdottir, June 17, 1950; children—Elin, Anna Gudrun. Sec., Ministry Fgn. Affairs Reykjavik, Iceland, 1937-41, sec.-gen., 1951-56; first sec. Legation, London, Eng., 1941-44; counselor Legation, Washington, 1944-50; ambassador to Sweden, Finland, 1956-62; minister to Iran, Israel, Japan, 1957-69; ambassador to Fed. Republic Germany, Switzerland, Greece, 1962-69, to U.S.A., Can., Mexico, Brazil, Argentina, 1969-71. Decorated comdr. first class Icelandic Falcon; Dannebrog (Denmark), White Rose, Lion (Finland), Grand Cross, North Star (Sweden), Order of Merit (Germany), George I (Greece), Homayoun (Iran). Died Apr. 4, 1971.

MAGONIGLE, EDITH MARION, artist; b. Brooklyn, N.Y., May 11, 1877; d. John and Clara Marion Perry (Stafford) Day; ed. pvt. schs.; m. Harold Van Buren Magonigle, Apr. 24, 1900 (died Aug. 29, 1935). Painter and sculptor. Prin. works: frieze, Administration Bldg., Branch Brook Park, Newark, N.J.; murals in Playhouse, Wilmington, Del.; residence of Isaac Guggenheim, Port Washington, L.I., etc.; various works in architectural sculpture; Asia," Victory Way, Park Av., New York. Mem. Women's Roosevelt Memorial Assn. Mem. Nat. Assn. Women Painters and Sculptors (pres. 1920-22), Nat. Soc. Mural Painters. Republican. Clubs: Skating (New York); Lyceum (London). Home: 875 5th Av., New York NY*‡

MAGOUN, JEANNE BARTHOLOW (MRS. FRANCIS P.), author; New York, Oct. 9, 1870; d. John M. C. and Louise (Cassard) Bartholow; ed. pvt. schs.; m. Francis Peabody Magoun, of New York, Oct. 8, 1892. Author: The Light, 1911; The Mission of Victoria Wilhelmina, 1912. Address: 3 Concord Av., Cambridge MA‡

MAGRUDER, CALVERT, judge; b. Annapolis, Md., Dec. 26, 1893; s. Daniel Randall and Rosalie Eugenia Stuart (Webster) M.; A.B., St. John's Coll., 1913; A.M., 1917; LL.B. cum laude, Harvard, 1916; LL.D., Brandeis U., 1956, Northeastern U., 1957; m. Anna Saltonstall Ward, Oct. 8, 1925; children—Calvert, Robert Stuart, Michael. Mem. Md., Mass., N.H., U.S. Supreme Ct. bars; sec. to Mr. Justice Brandeis, Washington, 1916-17; atty. U.S. Shipping Bd., Washington, 1919-20; asst. prof. law Harvard, 1920-25, prof., 1925-39, vice dean, 1930-39, lectr., 1947-59; on leave as gen. counsel Nat. Labor Relations Bd., Washington, 1934-35, as gen. counsel wage and hour div. Dept. Labor, 1938-39; apptd. U.S. circuit judge, 1939, ret., 1959; sat on 9th, 2d, D.C., 6th, 5th circuits, 1st Circuit Ct. of Appeals, also P.R. Dist. Ct.; designated judge U.S. Emergency Ct. Appeals, 1942. Chmn. U.S. Labor Mission to Bolivia, 1943; lectr. law Hastings Coll. Law, San Francisco, 1959-60, Columbia, 1960-61, Ohio State U., 1961, U. P.R., 1962. Served as 1st lt., inf., U.S. Army, 1917-19. Fellow Am. Acad. Arts and Scis.; mem. Am. Bar Assn., Am. Law Inst., Am. Judicature Soc. Democrat. Episcopalian (past jr. warden). Clubs: Country, Harvard

(Boston), Editor: (with J.A. Crane) Cases on the Law of Partnership, 1923. Contbr. legal articles to univ. publs. Home: South Tamworth NH Died May 22, 1968.

MAGUIRE, HAMILTON EWING, army officer; b. Detroit, Mich., Nov. 24, 1891; s. James Herbert and Ann (Ewing) M.; student U. of Michigan, 1910-12; B.S., U.S. Mil. Acad., 1916; grad. F.A. Sch., 1924, Command and Gen. Staff Sch., 1930, Army War Coll., 1938; m. Anne Droop, June 21, 1924; children—Nancy Ewing, Anne Droop, Mary Ewing, Hamilton Ewing, Edward Frederick Droop. Commd. 2d lt., U.S. Army, 1916, and advanced through the grades to brig. gen., 1944; served War Dept. Gen. Staff, 1938-42; chief of staff, XIX Corps, 1944-48. Decorated Distinguished Service Medal, Legion of Merit, Bronze Star, 5 campaign stars (Normandy, Northern France, Rhineland, Ardennes, Germany) (U.S.), Legion of Honor, Croix de Guerre (France). Mem. Delta Kappa Epsilon. Clubs: Chevy Chase, Army and Navy (Washington). Home: Washington DC Died Feb. 20, 1971; buried Arlington Nat. Cemetery, Arlington VA

MAGUIRE, JOHN ARTHUR, congressman; b. Jo Daviess Co., Ill., Nov. 29, 1872; s. Francis and Margaret (Bough) M.; student S.D. Agrl. Coll., 1890-3; B.S., Ia. State Agrl. Coll., 1894; A.M., U. of Neb., 1898, LL.B., 1899; unmarried. Deputy treas. Lancaster Co., Neb., 1900, 1901; in practice at Lincoln, Neb., since 1902; del. Dem. Nat. Conv., St. Louis, 1904; sec. Dem. State Com., Neb., 1905; mem. 61st to 63d Congresses (1909-15), 1st Neb. Dist. Roman Catholic. Address: Burr Blk., Lincoln NE‡

MAHAFFIE, CHARLES DELAHUNT, lawyer; b. Olathe, Kan., Dec. 5, 1884; s. George B. and Mary Frances (Williams); A.B., Kingfisher (Okla.) Coll., 1905; Rhodes scholar from Okla., at Oxford, Eng., 1905-08, mem. St. John's Coll.; B.C.L. (Oxon), 1907; post-grad. work, Oxford U., 1907-08; LL.D., Washington and Lee University, 1934. Amherst (Massachusetts) College, 1952; married Isabel Cooper, August 25, 1928; 1 son, Charles Delahunt. Instr. in jurisprudence, Princeton Univ., 1908-09; practiced, Chickasha, Okla., 1909-11, Portland, Ore., 1911-16; solicitor Dept. of Interior, Washington, 1916-21; atty. U.S.R.R. Administration, 1921-22; dir. of finance, Interstate Commerce Commn., 1922-30; mem. Interstate Commerce Commn., Sept. 2, 1930-54; chmn., 1936, and 1949; mem. U.S. Nat. Commn., Pan-Am. Railway Congress Assn., 1949-56, chmn. adminstrv. division, 1942-54; partner Gardner, Morrison & Rogers, 1954-69. Exec. sec. Conservation Commn. of Ore., 1913-16. Treas. Oregon Bar Assn., 1914-16. Admitted to practice in D.C., Oklahoma, Ore., and before U.S. Supreme Court. Democrat. Club: Cosmos (Wash.). Home: Washington DC Died June 11, 1969; buried Hobart OK

MAHANA, GEORGE SHAW, mfg. exec.; born Des Moines, Ia., Apr. 29, 1870; s. John Oscar and Sarah (Shaw) M.; student pvt. schs. of Des Moines, Ia. and Shattuck Sch., Faribault, Minn.; m. Dorothy Ellis, June 21, 1924; 1 dau., Dorothy S. Treas. Rockford (Ill.) Sugar Refining Co., 1895-97; mgr. Glucose Sugar Refining Co., Chicago, 1897-1900; mng. dir. Corn Products Co., Ltd., London, Eng., 1900-06; mgr. fgn. dept., Corn Products Refining Co., N.Y. City, 1906-18, v.p. since 1918; dir. Lee Rubber & Tire Co., Bloomingdale Rubber Co. Mem. Soc. of Mayflower Descendants, S.A.R., Soc. Colonial Wars. Republican. Episcopalian. Clubs: Creek, Piping Rock, Metropolitan, Church, Seawanhaka (N.Y. City). Home: 960 Fifth Av. Office: 17 Battery Pl., New York City*‡

MAHAR, EDWARD ALBERT, newspaperman; b. Albany, N.Y., July 16, 1900; s. Patrick H. and Elizabeth (Graham) M.; m. Edna Donnelly, Feb. 17, 1931; children—Patricia (Mrs. John M. Webster), Kevin J. Reporter Albany Argus, 1916-20, Albany Times-Union, 1920-29, N.Y. Jour., 1929-33; asst. city editor N.Y. Jour.-Am., 1933-55, city editor, from 1955. Founder, 1946, 1st pres. Cath. Inst. of Press, 1946-48. Served with U.S. Marine Corps, 1917-20. Recipient Americanization award L.I. Council K.C., 1955; co-recipient various award for capture of mad bomber in N.Y.C., 1957. Home: Flushing NY Died Feb. 1973.

MAHENDRA BIR BIKRAM SHAH DEVA, King of Nepal; b. Kathmandu, Nepal, June 11, 1920; s. King Tribbuban Beer Bikram Shah Deva and Queen Kanti Rajya Lakshmi Devi Shah; ed. privately; m. Princess Indra Rajya Lakshmi Devi Shah, May 8, 1940 (died Sept. 4, 1950); m. 2d, Queen Ratna Rajya Lakshmi Devi Shah; children—Princess Shanti Shah, Sharanda Shah, Crown Prince Birendra Beer Bikram Shah Deva, Prince Gnanendra Beer Bikram Shah Deva, Princess Shobha Shah, Prince Dhirendra Beer Bikram Shah Deva. Twice served as mem. Council of State during extended absence of father abroad; regent, Feb. 18-Mar. 13, 1955; enthroned as king, Mar. 14, 1955. Formed interim cabinet, Jan. 1956, which resigned July 15, 1957; formed Council of Ministers, July 26, 1957; cabinet resigned, Nov. 14, 1957; formed new cabinet, May 15, 1958; New Constitution promulgated, Feb. 12, 1959; first gen. elections, Feb. 18, 1959; dissolved Parliament, 1960; introduced Panchayat system of Democracy, 1961; 2d Constn. of Nepal promulgated, 1962; Panchayat elections, 1963; opened 1st Nat. Panchayat, 1963; participant non-aligned Summit Confs., 1961, 64. Chancellor, Tribhuvan U., Royal Nepal Acad. Patron, Rotary Internat., other orgns. Author: A Harvest of Poems, 2 books of poetry. Address: Kathmandu Nepal Died Jan. 31, 1972.

MAHER, CHAUNCEY CARTER, physician; b. Payson, Ill., Oct. 26, 1897; s. Ernest Phillip and Goldie Viola (Culver) M.; B.S., Univ. of Ill., 1921; M.D., Univ. of Ill., 1923; m. Martha Peppers, Sept. 10, 1932; children—Chauncey Carter, Constance, Barbara (by previous marriage), David Willard. Intern Cook County Hosp., 1923-25; began practice in Chicago, 1925; instr. in medicine, Northwestern U., 1928-30, asso., 1930-32, asst. prof. 1932-43, asso. prof. since 1943; attending med. staff Passavant Memorial Hosp. (chief, 1951-52) and Cook County Hosp., 1931-51; chmn. Dept. of Internal Medicine, Cook County Hospital, 1938-47; consulting cardiologist, Illinois Central Railroad; practice limited to heart disease. Enlisted in Am. Field Service with French Army, Apr. 1917; trans. to U.S. Army, Sept. 1917; with U.S.A.A.S., until Apr. 1919; hon. disch. at St. Aignan, France. Divisional citation, 1918; decorated Croix de Guerre (France). Certified by the Am. Bd. (cardiology), 1937. Fellow Am. Coll. Chest Physicians, A.C.P.; mem. A.M.A., Ill. and Chgo. med. socs., Chgo. Soc. Internal Medicine, Inst. of Med., Central Soc. of Clin. Research, Am. Heart Assn., Chgo. Literary Soc. (past pres.), Ill., Chgo. (bd. govs. 1933-57) heart assns., Miss. Valley Med. Soc., Society Med. History of Chicago, Chicago Historical Soc., Nu Sigma Nu, Alpha Omega Alpha. Club: Tavern. Author: Electrocardiography, 1934, 3d edit., 1940. Home: Chicago IL Died July 2, 1970; buried Burlington WI

MAHON, STEPHEN KEITH, business exec.; b. Cincinnati, O., Sept. 17, 1877; s. William and Mary (Darling) M.; grad. Phillips Exeter Acad., 1896; B.L., Ohio Wesleyan Univ., 1900, D.D., 1915; LL.D. (hon.), Univ. of Toledo, 1944; m. Jeannette Nelson, Apr. 1905 (died 1933); children—Jeannette, Frances, Patricia; m. 2d, Helen Ann Wright, 1934; 1 son, Stephen E. Ordained to ministry of Methodist Ch., 1904; pastor Massillon, O., 1900-06, Mansfield, O., 1906-11, Delaware, O., 1911-16, Toledo, O., 1916-30; asst. to pres. and dir. pub. relations, Toledo (O.) Edison Co. since 1930, mem. bd. dirs. Mem. bd. dirs. Univ. of Toledo since 1923 (pres. since 1934), Toledo Foundation, Flower Hosp., Hosp. Service, Chamber of Commerce; mem. bd. trustees O. Wesleyan Univ., Fgn. Missions (Meth. Ch.). Mem. Good Will Commn. to Spain (sent by city of Toledo, O.), May 1934; one of 4 rep. attending fiesta; in Toledo, Spain, as guests of Spanish rep. attending fiesta; in Toledo, Spain, as guests of Spanish govt. Decorated Order of Isabella the Catholic. Mem. Acad. Polit. Sci., Toledo Mus. of Art, Toledo Friends of Music, Nat. Spanish Soc., Alpha Tau Omega. Mason (32 deg.). Club: Toledo. Toledo OH‡

MAHONEY, JEREMIAH T., lawyer; b. New York, N.Y., June 23, 1878; s. Jeremiah and Mary E. (Harron) M.; A.B., Coll. of the City of N.Y., 1895; LL.B., New York U., 1898, LL.M., 1901; A.M., St. Francis Xavier College, New York City, 1903; hon. LL.D., Lincoln Univ. (Tenn.), 1942; married Mollie Cashen, Jan. 17, 1911 (dec. 1939); Admitted to N.Y. bar, 1899; now member of law firm of Mahoney, McNulty, McCarthy and Andrews; engaged as counsel to controller of the City of New York, 1902-10, Aqueduet commn., 1911; commr. of accounts, N.Y. City, 1911; mem. Bd. of Education, 1912; counsel New York State Banking Dept., also mem. State Banking Commn., 1913; jusge Court of Gen. Sessions, N.Y. City, 1912-13; justice Supreme Court of N.Y. State, 1923-29; pres. Federation Bank & Trust Co., 1932; dir. Union Labor Life Ins. Co., Hamlin & Co., also director of the Stettenheim Foundation, Lexington Av. & 42d St. Corp., Amateur Athletic Union U.S. (pres. 1935-36). Comdr. of Grand Ducal Order of Luxembourg. Winner of many athletic championships; mem. Am. Olympic teams, Am. Olympic Com. (exec. com.). Dep. police trial commr. of N.Y.C., 1939; chmn. N.Y. Regional Labor Bd.; mem. Allen Enemy Hearing Bd., 1941-44. Del. to Nat. Dem. Conv., 1920, 32, 36, 40, 44, 48, 52. Drafted many platforms Dem. State Convs., 1922, 30, 32; mem. N.Y. State Dem. Coms. Dem. candidate for mayor of N.Y. City, 1937. Democrat. Catholic. Clubs: Winged Foot Golf (Mamaroneck, N.Y.); Pinehurst Country, Tin Whistles Golf (Pinehurst, N.C.); N.Y. Athletic, Bankers, Manhattan, National Democrat (N.Y. City). Home: New York City NY Died June, 1970.

MAHONEY, JOHN DENNIS, educator; b. Phila., Pa., Aug. 16, 1876; s. Dennis and Sarah Jane (Elliott) M.; B.A., U. of Pa., 1897; grad. work in med. and law schs., 1898-1901; m. Mabel Vickers Kennard of Seneca, Kan., June 10, 1903; children—Mrs. Jean Carroll, Mrs. Sarah Louise Gabriel. Was reporter and editorial writer, Philadelphia Press, 1901-04; special writer for various newspapers till 1908; instr. English, Northeast High Sch., Phila., 1904-12; head dept. of English, West Phila. High Sch. for Boys, since 1912; lit. adviser Fidelity Mut. Life Ins. Co.; lecturer on social and lit. subjects for Y.M.C.A. during World War; lecturer on staff of The Phila. Forum since 1923. Mem. N.E.A., Alpha Chi Rho, English Club. Mason. Clubs: University, Comet, Contemporary, Pen and Pencil. Contbr. to lit. and ednl. jours. Has lectured widely on lit., social, polit. and ednl. topics. Home: 122 S. 43d St., Philadelphia, Pa.; (summer) Six Acres, R.F.D. 1, Sellersville PA‡

MAHONY, THOMAS HARRISON, lawyer; b. Boston, Mass., Feb. 19, 1885; s. Denis W. and Ellen A. (Driscoll) M.; LL.B., Harvard, 1906, Boston Univ. Sch. of Law, 1909; m. Mary C. McSweeney, June 22, 1948; children—Thomas H., Edward F., Moira, Gael. Admitted to Mass. bar, 1909, N.Y. bar, 1922; in gen. practice law, Boston, since 1909; asst. dist. atty. Suffolk Co., Mass., 1921; mem. firm Mahony, Bryer, Coffin and Willis, Boston, from 1938; instr. world law and world orgn. N.E. U. School of Law, Mem. Am., Mass., Boston bar associations, Law Soc. of Mass. (pres.), Cath. Assn. for Internat. Peace (pres.). Contbr. numerous articles on world orgn. and world peace to law jours. Home: Boston MA Died July 1969.

MAINE, MARY TALULAH, educator; b. North Stonington, Conn., Oct. 6, 1869; d. Ephraim Wheeler and Catharine (Thompson) M.; prep. edn., Providence High Sch. (classical dept.); B.A., Wellesley, 1898. Began as teacher English and drawing, pub. schs., Stamford, Conn., 1898; then teacher English and mathematics, Boston; founder Brantwood Hall Sch., South Orange, N.J., 1904; head of Brantwood Hall Sch. (coll. preparatory), Bronxville, N.Y., since 1906. Republican. Mem. Reformed Ch. Club: Women's. Home: 81 Tanglewylde Av., Lawrence Park. Address: Brantwood Hall, S. Woodland Av., Bronxville NY*‡

MAINS, KATHRYN PAULINE, govt. adminstr.; b. Jersey City; d. Louis William and Mabelle (Kopf) Mains; student George Washington U., 1950, Am. U., 1959-60, U.S. Dept. Agr. Grad. Sch. Sec. mil. intelligence USAF, S. Atlantic, 1944-45, U.S. Army, Recife, Brazil, 1946-52; with Nat. Inst. Allergy and Infectious Diseases, NIH, USPHS, Balt., Bethesda, Md., 1952-70, pub. information specialist, 1959-64, information officer div. dental health, 1964-70. Mem. secretariat 8th World Health Assembly, Mexico City, Mexico, 1955. Mem. Am. Med. Writers Assn., Audubon Naturalist Soc. Unitarian. Home: Silver Spring MD Died Dec. 7, 1970.

MAIRS, ELWOOD DONALD, aluminum co. exec.; b. Bridgeport, Pa., Mar. 30, 1905; s. Elwood Herbert Corson and Elizabeth (Patterson) M.; student Mercersberg (Pa.) Acad.; B.S. in Metall. Engring., Pa. State U., 1926; m. Lucille E. Wallace, June 26, 1930 (dec. Sept. 1964); 1 dau., Lesly Elizabeth (Mrs. John M. Senker); m. 2d, Margaret E. Hood, Oct. 1, 1966. With Aluminum Co. Am., 1926-70, gen. mgr. personnel, 1962-63, v.p. charge personnel and indsl. relations, 1963-70. Recipient David F. McFarland award for achievement in metallurgy Pa. State U., 1957. Mem. Alpha Chi Sigma, Tau Beta Pi, Sigma Gamma Epsilon. Episcopalian. Mason. Clubs: University (Pitts.); City (Knoxville). Home: Louisville TN Died Dec. 10, 1972.

MAIRS, THOMAS ISAIAH, retired educator; b. Browning, Mo., Apr. 16, 1871; s. Joseph Watson and Mary Elizabeth (Curtis) M.; B.Agr., U. of Mo., 1896, B.S., and M.S., 1900; grad. student, Mich. State Agrl. Coll. and U. of Ill., 1896-97; m. Charlotte Marie Riley, July 30, 1902 (died July 24, 1929); children—Thomas Isaiah, John Curtis, Edward Shrader; m. 2d, Mary Susanna Lutz, June 26, 1943. Superintendent field experiments, U. of Ill., 1896-97; asst. in agr. and supt. coll. farm, U. of Mo., 1897-1901; prof. agrl. edn. and supt. corr. courses in agr., Pa. State Coll. since 1901. Mem. Am. Genetic Assn., Alpha Zeta, Gamma Sigma Delta. Republican. Presbyterian. Mason. Specialized in pub. sch. agr. and instruction by correspondence. Author: Some Pennsylvania Pioneers in Agricultural Science, 1928; also wrote chapters on edn. and orgn. in Rural Pennsylvania, 1905. Home: State College PA‡

MAJESKI, JOHN F., publisher; b. New York, N.Y., 1892; s. Anton and Anna Barbara (Salzer) M.; m. Augusta Verengel, Apr. 2, 1917; 1 son, John F. With Music Trades Corp., from 1910, owner, from 1929; pres., publisher and dir. The Music Trades, from 1929. Address: New York City NY Died Nov. 19, 1971.

MAJOR, J(AMES) EARL, judge; b. Donnellson, Ill., Jan. 5, 1887; s. Charles R. and Emma (Jones) M.; grad. high school and business college; student Ill. Coll. of Law; m. Ruth Wafer, Aug. 13, 1913. Admitted to Ill. bar, 1910, and began practice at Hillsboro; mem. Miller, Major & Major; state's atty., Montgomery County, Ill., 2 terms, 1912-20; mem. 68th and 70th to 73d Congresses (1923-25 and 1927-35), 21st Ill. Dist.; resigned, upon apptmt. as judge U.S. District Court, for Southern Dist. of Ill., 1933; chief judge U.S. Circuit Court of Appeals for 7th circuit since 1953. Democrat. Presbyn. Mason, Odd Fellow, Moose, Elk. Home: Hillsboro IL Died 1972.

MAKITA, YOLCHIRO, exec. pres. Mitsubishi Heavy Industries, Ltd. Address: Tokyo Japan Died Dec. 7, 1972.

MALCARNEY, ARTHUR LENO, electronics mfr.; b. Ramsaytown, Pa., Feb. 9, 1913; student Air Corps Tech. Sch., 1931-32, Harvard Bus. Sch., 1952; m. Anita Keenan, Jan. 11, 1937; children—Courtney, Arthur, Ronald. Joined RCA, 1933, beginning as radio test and inspector, successively foreman, supt., plant mgr., gen. mfg. mgr., 1933-56, v.p., gen. mgr. comml. electronic products div., 1956-57, exec. v.p. for defence electronic products, from 1957, later group exec. v.p., also dir. Served as pvt. USAC, 1930-33. Mem. Armed Forces Communication and Electronics Assn., Am. Soc. Naval Engrs. K.C. Club: Rotary. Home: Haddonfield NJ Died May 28, 1968.

MALCOLM, RUSSELL LAING, surgeon; b. Ann Arbor, Mich., Oct. 8, 1906; s. John Karl and Clara (Laing) M.; A.B., U. Mich., 1928, M.D., 1931, M.S. in Surgery, 1935; m. Bernice Frances Staebler, Sept. 1, 1928; children—Russell Laing, Marshall Day, Miller Day (twins). Instr. surgery U. Mich., 1934-37; pvt. practice surgery, Richmond, Ind.; sr. surgeon Reid Meml. Hosp. Trustee Earlham Coll., 1962-67. Served from capt. to col., M.C., AUS, 1942-45. Decorated Bronze Star medal; Bronze Plaque award Am. Cancer Soc. Fellow A.C.S.; mem. A.M.A., Wayne County Med. Soc., Central Surg. Assn., F.A. Coller Surg. Soc., Norman Miller Gynecol. Soc., Ind. Cancer Soc. (past pres.). Rotarian (pres. 1947-48). Home: Richmond IN Died Dec. 21, 1967; interred Earlham Cemetery, Richmond IN

MALLETT, DONALD ROGER, univ. ofcl.; b. Guthrie Center, Ia., July 23, 1910; s. Frank Arthur and Eleanor (MacDonald) M.; B.A., Drake U., 1931; M.A., U. Ia., 1934, Ph.D., 1936; m. Catherine L. Doepke, Aug. 19, 1936; children—Donald A., J. Craig. Coach, tchr. sci. and mathematics Belle Plaine (Ia.) High Sch., 1931-32; mgr. housing service State U. Ia., 1936-39, asst. dean of men, 1939-41, asso. dir. student affairs, 1942-45; asst. dir. student affairs Purdue U., 1945-51, acting dir. student affairs, 1952, dean of men, 1952-56, exec. dean, 1956-68, v.p., 1961-71. Edn. adviser National Interfraternity Conference, 1955-57, 59-61, mem. exec., policy coms., 1956-71. Co-chairman Lafayette Community Fund campaign, 1950-54, vice pres. United Fund Drive of Greater Lafayette and Tippecanoe County, 1961; sec.-treas. Assn. NROTC Colls., 1960-66, pres. 1966-71; vice pres. bd. Lafayette Young Men's Christian Association, 1955-56, gov., 1960; council mem.-at-large Boy Scouts America, 1960; chmn. camp development com. Lafayette Girl Scouts, 1947-51; mem. bd. Lafayette Symphony Orch., 1951-54, 60; Adv. Bd. Ednl. Requirements, Sec. Navy, 1964-67; adv. bd. U.S. Naval Postgraduate School. Recipient distinguished alumni award Drake Univ., 1956; Distinguished Service award Navy, 1963, 69; Outstanding Civilian Service award Army, 1965. Member Arnold Air Society, National Association of Student Personnel Adminstrs. (v.p.), Am. Personnel and Guidance Assn., Am. Coll. Personnel Assn., Nat. Vocational Guidance Assn., N.E.A., Ind. Soc. Chgo., Lafayette (Ind.) C. of C. (director 1959-62), Big Ten in Chgo., Phi Delta Kappa, Pi Kappa Delta, Alpha Phi Omega, Phi Eta Sigma, Gamma Alpha, Phi Mu Alpha, Alpha Tau Omega. Mem. Disciples of Christ Ch. Elk, Rotarian (past pres. Lafayette chpt.). Home: West Lafayette IN Died Nov. 26, 1971.

MALLISON, RICHARD SPEIGHT, pub. utility exec.; b. Rocky Mount, N.C., Sept. 8, 1908; s. William H. and Mattie (Barnes) M.; grad. King's Bus. Coll., Raleigh, N.C., 1927; M. Elizabeth Brooks, July 8, 1939. With Carolina Power & Light Co., Raleigh, 1927-71, sec., 1961-71. Home: Raleigh NC Died Feb. 21, 1971; buried Montlawn Meml. Park, Raleigh NC

MALONE, KEMP, philologist; b. Minter, Miss., Mar. 14, 1889; s. John W. and Lilliam (Kemp) M.; A.B., Emory U., 1907, Litt.D., 1936; Ph.D., U. Chgo., 1919, L.H.D., 1953; Litt.D., Yale, 1951; Litt. D., University North Carolina, 1964; L.H.D., Johns Hopkins, 1965; LL.D., Kenyon Coll., 1966, grad. study U. Copenhagen, 1915-16, U. Iceland, 1919-20, Princeton, 1920-21; m. Inez Rene, dau. J. Henry Chatain of Richmond, Va., Apr. 28, 1927. High sch. tchr., 1907-11; exchange tchr. to Prussia, 1911-13; instr. Cornell U., 1916-17; asst. prof. English, U. Minn., 1921-24; with Johns Hopkins, 1924-71, prof., 1926-56, prof. emeritus, 1956-71; vis. prof. English and linguistics Georgetown U., 1956-58, also dir. Georgetown English lang. program, sponsored by Internat. Coop. Adminstrn., Ankara, Turkey, 1956-58; Berg vis. prof., English at N.Y.U., 1961-62; vis. prof. English So. Ill. U., Carbondale, 1963-64; vis. prof. English, Catholic Univ. of Am., 1966-67; vis. prof., lectr. numerous Am. and fgn. univs. Co-founder of American Speech, mng. editor, 1925-32; co-editor of Anglia, 1950-64, Acta Philol. Scand., 1952-—; asso. editor Early English MSS in Facsimile, 1951-71. Rep. U.S. govt. 4th Internat. Congress Linguistics, 1936, 5th Congress, 1939. Served from 1st lt. to capt. U.S. Army, 1917-19. Decorated King Christian X Freedom Medal, Knight of Dannebrog (Denmark), Knight of Falcon (Iceland). Jubilee vol., Philologica, the Malone Anniversary Studies, 1949; recipient of Guggenheim fellowship, 1958-59. Fellow Mediaeval Acad. Am., Soc. Am. Historians; mem. Am. Philos. Soc., Royal Danish Academy, Islenzkt Bokmentafjelag, Linguistic Society of American (past pres.), Am. Dialect Soc. (past pres.), Am. Name Soc. (past pres.), Modern Humanities Research Assn. (president 1958), Modern Lang. Assn. of Am. (president 1962), numerous other Am. and fgn. learned socs. Episcopalian. Clubs: Maryland, Johns Hopkins, Tudor and Stuart; Army and Navy (Washington). Author and editor various works, 1923-45. Author: Chapters on Chaucer, 1951; Studies in Heroic Legend, published, 1959. Co-author: Literary History of England, 1948; Literary Masterpieces of the Western World, 1953. Editor: Thorkelin Transcripts of Beowulf, 1951; Deor, rev. edit., 1966; Widsith, rev. edit. 1962; Nowell codex in facsimile, 1963. Co-editor: Modern Lang. Notes, 1925-56; etymol. editor Am. Coll. Dictionary, 1947; Random House Dictionary English Lang., 1966. Contbr. verse and articles to lit. and philol. jours. Home: Baltimore MD Died Oct. 13, 1971; buried Hollywood Cemetery, Richmond VA

MALONEY, PAUL HERBERT, ex-congressman; b. New Orleans, La., Feb. 14, 1876; s. Patrick Joseph and Margaret Delap (Woods) M.; ed. pub. schs. and Mrs. Ashe Pvt. Sch., Pass Christian, Miss.; m. Adaline Gertrude Lecourt, Dec. 20, 1899; children—Paul Herbert, Margaret Delap (Mrs. Fernand C. Gandolfo, Jr.). Began as printer's devil, Coast Beacon; office boy, Heaslip Drayage Co., 1893, advancing to pres., 1918; organizer and pres. Linen Supply Co., Maloney Trucking & Storage, Incorporated, Maloney Motor Car Company, Gallagher Transfer and Storage Co.; former pres. Linen Supply Assn., Team Owners Bureau of Transportation and Automotive Dealers Assn. of La. Mem. La. N.G., 1895-98. Mem. La. Ho. of Reps., 1914-16; mem. New Orleans Levee Bd., 1917-20, pres. 1919-20; mem. com. pub. utilities, City of New Orleans Common Council, 1920-25; delegate to Democratic Nat. Convs., 1924, 28, 32, 36; mem. 72d to 79th Congresses (1931-41, 1943-47); U.S. Collector of Internal Revenue, State of La., 1941-42; mem. New Orleans Assn. of Commerce. Democrat. Episcopalian. Mason (Past Potentate Jerusalem Temple), Elk. Club: New Orleans Country. Home: 4160 Vendome Pl. Office: 945 Magazine St., New Orleans LA‡

MALONEY, WALTER H., lawyer; b. Glencoe, Wis.; Apr. 6, 1885; s. Patrick and Margaret (Moloney) M.; LL.B., U. Mich., 1907; m. Madaline Juneau Farley, Aug. 12, 1929; children—Walter Henry, Thomas Patrick, James Joseph. Admitted to Mich. bar, 1907, Mo. bar, 1908; practice in Kansas City, 1908-67; mem. Nat. Bituminous Coal Commn. (lectures and speeches on Bituminous Coal Control Act and Regulations); opened law office, Washington, 1940; spl. judge Jackson County (Mo.) Circuit Ct. Former chmn. Speakers Bur., United Charities of Kansas City; mem. Traffic Adv. Com. of Washington; organizer, pres. Nat. Capital Baseball Fedn. Mem. Central Bus. Assn. (v.p., dir.), Mo. State Soc. (past pres. Washington chpt.), Am., Mo., Kansas City, D.C. bar assns. Clubs: Divitan (bd. dirs.); chmn. Americanization com.), U. Michigan (past pres. Kansas City chpt.), Kansas City Athletic Washington DC Died Nov. 14, 1967.

MALONY, HARRY JAMES, army officer; b. Lakemont, N.Y., Aug. 24, 1889; s. Dr. John Montgomery and Josephine (Huson) M.; student Yale, 1907-08; B.S., U.S. Mil. Acad., 1912; grad. Field Arty. Sch., Ft. Sill, 1922, Command and Gen. Staff Sch., 1926, Army War Coll., 1936; m. Fanny Hunter Lockett, July 21, 1913; 1 son, James Lockett; m. 2d, Dorothy Brentnall Fitch, Nov. 30, 1928; step-children—Dorothy Anne Thurman, Barbara Fitch Thurman, Alice Merritt Thurman. Commd. 2d lt. inf., U.S. Army, 1912; transferred to field arty., 1916, and advanced through the grades to maj. gen., August 1942. Served with 10th Inf., Panama Canal Zone, 1912-16; instr. Machine Gun Sch., Tex., and duty in Exptl. Dept., Springfield Armory, 1916-17, armament officer, Air Service, with A.E.F., France, 1917-19; sec. F.A. Sch., Ft. Sill, 1921-24; 7th F.A., 1926; Gen. Staff Corps, Atlanta, Ga., 1927; instr. mil. science U. of Okla., 1931-35; mem. F.A. Bd., 1936; instr. Army War Coll., 1937-40; mem. Army-Navy Bd. for selection of air-naval bases in Brit. transatlantic possessions, 1940; mem. President's Commn. for negotiating lease of air and naval bases, 1941; War Plans Div., War Dept. Gen. Staff, 1941; dep. chief of staff, G.H.Q., 1941-42; Munitions Assignment Bd. Combined Chiefs of Staff; comdg. gen., 94th Inf. Div. 1942-45; U.S. Exec. London Munitions Assignment Bd. 1945; mem. of Presdl. Mission to Observe Greek Elections with rank of U.S. Minister, 1946; chief Hist. Div., War Dept., 1947-48, ret. 1949; retained by United Nations as deputy dir., Khashmir Plebescite, 1949; consultant Department of Defense, Southeast Asia policies, 1950-51; tech. cons. U.S. Ordnance Co., Washington. Decorated D.S.M. with oak leaf cluster, Silver Star, Bronze Star; Officer Legion d'Honneur, Croix de Guerre, Ordre d'Etoile Noire (France). Mem. Arlington Ridge Rd. Divic Assn. (past v.p.), Sigma Chi. Presbyn. Club: Army and Navy (Washington). Author: Machine Guns (with J.S. Hatcher and G.P. Wilhelm), 1916. Home: Arlington VA Died Mar. 23, 1971; buried Arlington Cemetery, Arlington VA

MALSBARY, GEORGE ELMER, physician; b. Hutchinson, Kan., June 3, 1873; s. John S. and Alice (Olden) M.; grad. Med. Coll. Ohio, 1896; m. Madisonville, O., Nov. 7, 1893, Sarah Mahon. Was med. reporter before entering on practice of medicine, 1896; apptd., 1896, asst. to chair of theory and practice of medicine, Med. Coll. Ohio. Mem. Am. Med. Assn., Ohio State Med. Soc., Cincinnati Acad. Medicine, etc. Author: Practice of Medicine, 1899 L12. Contb'r to Wood's Reference Hand-Book Med. Sciences, 1901 W11, etc. Residence: 2202 Auburn Av. Office: 14 E. 7th St., Cincinnati‡

MALTBIE, MILO ROY, public utility expert; b. Hinckley, Ill., Apr. 3, 1871; s. Henry M. and Harriet (Delano) M.; Ph.B., Upper Ia. U., 1892; Ph.M., Northwestern, 1893; Ph.D., Columbia, 1897; Honorary LL.D. conferred by Upper Iowa U., 1942; m. Lucia McCosh, July 11, 1901. Prof. economics and mathematics, Mt. Morris (Ill.) Coll., 1893-95; fellow in administrative law, Columbia, 1895-96; sec. Reform Club Com. on City Affairs, 1897-1902; sec. New York Art Commn., 1902-07; mem. Pub. Service Commn. of N.Y., 1st Dist., 1907-15; mem. advisory board on r.r. valuation, Interstate Commerce Commn., 1915-16; chamberlain of City of N.Y., 1916-18; chmn. Pub. Service Commn. of N.Y. State and head N.Y. State Dept. Pub. Service, Mar. 20, 1930-49, resigned 1949. Cons. and expert pub. utilities since 1915. Editor of Municipal Affairs, 1897-1903; traveled in Europe in summer of 1899, investigating municipal problems for Reform Club, and in 1903 civic art; prize lecturer on municipal govt., Columbia, 1900; conducted investigation in Great Britain into relative merits of municipal and pvt. management of pub. utilities, 1906. War work in War Dept. (ordnance and finance), U.S. Shipping Bd. and War Industries Bd., 1917-18. Mem. Am. Econ. Assn., Am. Political Science Assn. Author: English Local Government of To-day, 1897; Municipal Functions, 1898; Street Railways of Chicago, 1901. Contbr. to econ. jours. Clubs: Downtown Athletic, City (New York); Cosmos (Washington). Home: 580 West End Ave., New York 24 NY‡

MALVERN, VISCOUNT, ex-prime minister Rhodesia; b. Bexley, Eng., July 6, 1883; s. Godfrey H. and Emily (Blest) M.; ed. Malvern Coll., Worcestershire, Eng., also St. Thomas Hosp. Med. Sch.; licentiate Royal Coll. Physicians, St. Thomas' Hosp., London, 1906; D.C.L., Oxford U., 1951, U. London, 1955, U. Rhodes (S. Africa), 1957; LL.D., U. Whits (S. Africa), 1953; m. Blanche E. Slatter, Nov. 27, 1921; children—John G., James M. Former house surgeon St. Thomas Hosp., also supt. Hosp. for Sick Children; migrated to Salisbury, So. Rhodesia, 1911; physician and surgeon, 1911-13; surgeon, from 1913; mem. parliament, So. Rhodesia, 1923-53; prime minister So. Rhodesia, 1933-53, also minister native affairs, 1933-49, minister def., 1948-53; prime minister Fedn. Rhodesia and Nyasaland, 1953-56, also minister def. and external affairs. Dir. British So. Africa Co., Rhodesia br. Standard Bank So. Rhodesia, Scottish Rhodesia Finance Company, Limited, Merchant Bank Central Africa, Rothmans of Pall Mall (Rhodesia). Served with the British Army, 1914-18. Created knight comdr. St. Michael and George, companion of Honour, Privy Councellor, knight St. John. Hon. fellow Royal Coll. of Physicians (Edinburgh); fellow Royal Soc. Arts, Royal Coll. Surgeons. Rotarian. Author: Amputation Stumps, Care and After Treatment, 1918. Address: Salisbury Rhodesia Died May 8, 1971; interred National Bay, Salisbury Cathedral, Salisbury, Rhodesia

MANCE, ROBERT WESTON II, physician, ch. ofcl.; b. Newberry, S.C., Dec. 13, 1903; s. Robert Weston and Elizabeth (Grimes) M.; B.A., Howard U., 1925, M.D., 1929; LL.D. (hon.), Wilberforce U., 1963; m. Pearl Lucile Murph, June 30, 1936; children—Elizabeth Lillian, Robert Weston III. Intern Freedmen's Hosp., Washington, 1929-30; practice medicine in Columbia, S.C., 1931-54; treas. A.M.E. Ch., 1954-68, mem. World Council Chs., 1954-68; del., Evanston (Ill.) conf., 1954, New Delhi (India) conf., 1961; v.p. Nat. Council Chs., 1963-68; del. World Conf. Methodists, Oxford, Eng., 1951, Lake Janaluska, N.C., 1956, Oslo, Norway, 1961. Mem. Columbia City Planning Commn., 1951-54. Trustee Allen U., Columbia, 1932-68, Interdenominational Theol. Sem., Atlanta, 1957-68, Wilberforce U., 1960-68. Recipient Alexander Meiklejohn. award acad. freedom Am. Assn. U. Profs., 1961. Mem. Medico Chirugical Soc., Nat. Med. Assn., Sigma Pi Phi, Alpha Phi Alpha. Home: Washington DC Died July 8, 1968; buried Columbia SC

MANCHEE, ARTHUR LEAVENS, merchandising exec., b. Newark, Oct. 23, 1899; s. Wilfrid Arthur and Annie Bowen (Leavens) M.; grad. Newark Acad., 1918; A.B., Princeton, 1922; m. Elinor Lambert, Mar. 17, 1924 (dec. 1953); children—Marilyn (wife of Dr. Harry C. Wortman), Cynthia (Mrs. James McC. Clark), Sally (Mrs. Richmond W. Bachelder); m. 2d, Katheryn Hail Dorflinger, Sept. 21, 1957; 1 dau., June Dorflinger (Mrs. John A. Hardy, Jr.). With The Tench Studios, mfg. jewelers, Newark, 1922-28; with R. H. Macy & Co., Inc., N.Y.C., from 1928, successively mgmt. exec. Macy's New York, v.p., gen. mgr. L. Bamberger & Co., 1928-49, sr. v.p. operations Macy's N.Y., 1949-58, pres., 1958-62, chmn. bd., chief exec. officer Bamberger's N.J. div., from 1962; dir. R. H. Macy &

Company, Inc., Macy's Bank. N.J. retail chmn. U.S. Savs. Bonds; mem. Newark Mayor's Indsl. Devel. Commn.; mem. Mass Transp. Commn. of Essex County Bd. Freeholders; Member Greater Newark Development Council, Newark Bureau Municipal Research; vice chairman regional executive committee, pres. exec. bd. Robert Treat council Boy Scouts Am.; vice chmn. exec. com. mchts. council N.Y.U. Sch. Retailing; trustee N.J. Safety Council, Newark Acad., Newark Mus.; bd. fellows Fairleigh-Dickinson U. Served as pvt. U.S. Army, 1918. Mem. Commerce and Industry Assn. Newark (dir.), N.J. Regional Plan Assn. Clubs: Essex (Newark); Essex County Country (West Orange, N.J.); Nassau (Princeton, N.J.); Princeton (N.Y.C.). Home: West Orange NJ Died May 17, 1970; buried Cedar Lawn Cemetery, Paterson NJ

MANCUSO, FRANCIS X., judge; b. Cosenza, Italy, Nov. 1, 1888; s. Pasquale and Maria (Milano) M.; came with parents to U.S., 1897; student Fordham Coll.; LL.B., Fordham U., 1911, LL.D., 1927; unmarried. Admitted to N.Y. bar, 1912; spl. dep. asst. atty. gen., N.Y., 1915; dep. asst. dist. atty., N.Y. County, 1916-18; city magistrate, New York, 1918-21; judge Court of Gen. Sessions, 1921-35. Mem. N.Y. State Bar Assn., Assn. Internat. Law, Chevalier and Commendatore of Crown of Italy; Commendatore Order of Constantine. Democrat. Catholic. K.P.; mem. Foresters of America. Clubs: Manhattan, New York Athletic, Siwanoy Golf and Country, North Hills Country. Home: New York City NY Died July 1970.

MANDEL, ROBERT, chmn. bd. Mandel Bros.; b. Chicago, Ill., July 16, 1871; s. Leon and Isabella (Foreman) M.; ed. pubs. schs., New York, 3 years; private sch., 6 yrs.; Paris, France, 1 yr.; business Coll., New York, 1 yr.; m. Stella Kaufman, Feb. 3, 1903. Began as stockboy of Mandel Brothers, 1889, advanced to salesman, asst. buyer and buyer, apptd. foreign buyer, 1891, asst. supt., 1897, gen. mgr. and dir., 1899, now chmn. bd. Home: 1107 S. Sheridan Rd., Highland Park, IL Office: 1 N. State St., Chicago IL*‡

MANEY, RICHARD, press agent; born Chinook, Mont., June 11, 1892; s. John and Elizabeth (Bohen) M.; grad. U. of Wash., 1913; m. Elizabeth Breuil, June 18, 1931. Theatrical press agent in N.Y.C., 1924-68, having publicized numerous plays and musicals, legitimate theatre. Mem. Sigma Delta Chi. Author: Fanfare: Confessions of a Press Agent, 1957. Contbr. to mags., theatre pages of N.Y. dailies, N.Y. Times magazine. Home: Norwalk CT Died June 30, 1968; buried Willowbrook Cemetery, Westport CT

MANGEL, SOL, retail store exec.; chmn., chief exec. officer Mangel Stores Corp. Home: New York City NY Died 1972.

MANGOLD, GEORGE BENJAMIN, sociologist; born Waupeton, Ia., July 7, 1876; s. John and Mary (Datisman) M.; A.B., Cornell Coll., Mt. Vernon, Ia., 1901; student Drew Theol. Sem., 1901-02; A.M., U. of Chicago, 1903; Ph.D., U. of Wis., 1906; m. Edith E. Putnam, Sept. 7, 1905. Began teaching at Pullman, Wash., 1903; dir. Missouri School of Social Economy (under auspices of U. of Mo.), 1912-24; social service sec., St. Louis Ch. Fed., 1924-28; prof. sociology, U. Southern Calif., 1928-46; now professor of sociology, Pepperdine College. Member Am. Sociol. Soc., Am. Economic Assn., Am. Assn. for Labor Legislation, National Conf. Social Work. Presbyn. Mason. Author several books relating to field since 1910. Home: 3764 Olympiad Dr., Los Angeles 43 CA*‡

MANGUM, JOSIAH THOMAS, clergyman; b. Greenville, Ala., Apr. 13, 1876; s. Theophilus Fields and Julia Frances (Perkins) M.; student Southern U., Greensboro, Ala., 1888-89; Ala. Poly. Inst., Auburn, Ala., 1892-96; studied theology, Vanderbilt U., 1909-10; m. Edith Hooper, of Selma, Ala., Apr. 2, 1901; 1 dau., Edith Hooper. Ordained ministry M.E. Ch., S., 1901; pastor Greenville, 1901, Eufaula, 1902, Jackson, 1903, Montgomery, 1904-05, Tallassee, 1906-09, Waynesville, N.C., since 1922. Accompanied Bishop Walter R. Lambuth, as sec., to The Congo, Belge, Africa, 1913-14, and assisted in establishment of the first mission of M.E. Ch., S., in that country. Capt., chaplain 2d Regt., Ala. N.G., 1905-09; gen. sec. Army Y.M.C.A., Camp Greene, N.C., 1918. Trustee Ala. Woman's Coll., 1906-14; trustee Rutherford (N.C.) Coll., Children's Home, Junalusk Summer Sch. Mem. Sigma Nu. Democrat. Mason (K.T., Shriner); Past Grand Prelate Grand Comdry. of Ala., K.T. Home: Waynesville NC‡

MANION, EDWARD J., pres. Order R.R. Telegraphers; b. Derby, Conn., July 21, 1872; s. John and Vrede (Ready) M.; ed. pub. schs. to 13; m. Louise Erspan, of San Francisco, Calif., Aug. 8, 1919. Formerly telegraph operator N.Y., N.H. & H. R.R.; elected local chmn. Order R.R. Telegraphers; later gen. chmn. N.Y., N.H. & H. System, O.R.T.; elected v.p. of the order, 1913, pres., 1919-23; retired, May 23, 1939; pres. Telegraphers Nat. Bank, St. Louis, Mo., 1923-39. Catholic. Home: 4515 Maryland Av., St Louis MO‡

MANION, WILLIAM CECIL, physician; b. Bethel, Conn., July 30, 1916; s. William Stephen and Anna (Flagherty) M.; B.S., Catholic U., 1939; M.D., Georgetown U., 1943; m. Billie Pappas, Aug. 7, 1944; children—William, James, Eugene, Brian. Intern, Garfield Meml. Hosp., Washington, 1943-44; resident Gallinger Municipal Hosp., Washington, 1946-48, cons. in pathology, 1963-70; pathologist Prince Georges Gen. Hosp., Cheverly, Md., 1948-52; postgrad. George Washington U., 1947; instr. pathology U. Md. Med. Sch., Balt., 1948-53; instr. pathology Georgetown U., Washington, 1950-52, asst. prof. medicine, 1960-61, asso. prof. medicine (cardiology), 1962-70; registrar cardiovascular registry Armed Forces Inst. Pathology, Washington, 1953-70, asst. chief cardiovascular pathology and geog. pathology brs., 1952-53, chief cardiovascular br., 1953-70. External examiner in medicine U. Witwatersrand (South Africa), 1963-64; cons. on research on Chagas disease in S. Am. and medicine in Europe to surgeon gen. of army; chmn. study sect. on cardiovascular diseases in animals WHO, 1961; Pauline King Meml. lectr. Vanderbilt U. Served to lt., M.C., USNR, 1944-46. Recipient citation Coll. Am. Pathologists, Am. Coll. Cardiology, Am. Coll. Chest Surgeons, Outstanding Achievement award VA, 1964, Outstanding Achievement award Catholic U., 1963, Meritorious. Civilian Service award Dept. Army, 1965. Diplomate Am. Bd. Pathology. Mem. A.M.A. (Hektoen award), Am. Soc. Clin. Pathologists, Coll. Am. Pathologists, Am. Assn. for Study Neoplastic Diseases, Assos. Clin. Pathology, A.A.A.S., Med. Soc. D.C., Washington Heart Assn., Washington Soc. Pathologists, Internat. Acad. Pathology, Am. Heart Assn., John Carroll Soc.; hon. mem. Acad. Med. Scis. (Barcelona), Nat. Heart Inst. Mexico, Pathology Soc. Venezuela. Roman Catholic. Contbr. articles to med. jours., also chpts. to books. Designed heart model of aortic arch. Home: Kensington MD Died Nov. 5, 1970; buried Gate of Heaven Cemetery Silver Spring MD

MANIS, HUBERT CLYDE, entomologist; born Bozeman, Mont., July 18, 1909; s. James Howell and Sarah C. (Clack) M.; B.S., Mont. State Coll., 1933; M.S., Kans. State Coll., 1936; Ph.D., Ia. State Coll., 1940; m. Marian Mercer, Aug. 12, 1948; children—James Morgan, Jean Marie. Began as assistant entomologist U. of Ida., 1940-42, asso., 1944-46, entomologist and head of dept. from 1946. Mem. Entomological Society of America (past chmn. Pacific br.), Ida. Acad. Sci., A.A.A.S., C. of C., Sigma Xi, Gamma Sigma Delta, Phi Sigma. Elk. Author of articles on biology and control of insects. Home: Moscow ID Died Aug. 26, 1968; buried Moscow, ID

MANLEY, NORMAN WASHINGTON, ex-premier Jamaica; b. Roxburgh, Manchester, Jamaica, July 4, 1893; s. Thomas Albert Samuel and Margaret (Shearer) M.; student Jamaica Coll., 1912; B.A., B.C.L. (Rhodes scholar 1914), Jesus Coll., Oxford, 1921; LL.D. (hon.), Howard U., 1946; m. Edna Swithenbank, June 30, 1921; children—Douglas Ralph, Michael Norman. Called to bar, Gray's Inn, 1921; admitted to practice, Jamaica, 1922; practice civil and criminal law in Jamaica until 1955; founder, 1938, since pres. People's Nat. Party; leader opposition Jamaica Ho. of Reps., 1949-55; chief minister, Jamaica, 1955-59, priemier, 1959-62; founder, 1957, since president of West Indies Federal Labour Party; leader of the opposition, from 1962. Founder Jamaica Social Welfare Commn., 1937. Hon. fellow Jesus Coll. Mem. Hon. Soc. of Gray's Inn. Home: Kingston Jamaica WI Died Sept. 1969.

MANLY, CHESLY, newspaperman; b. Jones County, Tex., Oct. 9, 1905; s. Julius Price and Mittie Ruby (Dyer) M.; student Clarendon (Tex.) Jr. Coll., 1923-25; B.J., U. Mo., 1927; m. Mary Jane Gleiber, Nov. 7, 1936; m. 2d, Elisabeth Hoepp Halasz, June 17, 1969; 1 son, Chesly John. Reporter, Milw. Jour., 1927-29; reporter Chgo. Tribune, 1929, asst. Washington corr., 1934-46, became UN corr., 1946, mem. Chgo. staff, from 1954, mem. editorial bd., 1969-70. Served with USAAF, 1942-45. Decorated Order of Leopold II (Belgium). Mem. Sigma Delta Chi, Kappa Tau Alpha. Republican. Clubs: Chicago Press; Nat. Press (Washington). Author: The Twenty Year Revolution, From Roosevelt to Eisenhower, 1954; The UN Record, Ten Fateful Years for America, 1955. Contbr. mags. Home: Glenview IL Died June 9, 1970.

MANLY, LEWIS FREDERICK, educator; b. Erie, Pa., Apr. 23, 1903; s. William Jared and Harriet (Miller) M.; B.S., Wooster Coll., 1925; M.A., Tufts U., 1927; Ph.D., Harvard, 1951; m. Susie Elizabeth Sandford, June 15, 1929; children—John Sandford, William Michael. Instr. dept. econs. Tufts U., 1927-31, asst. prof., 1931-42, asso. prof., 1942-46, prof., 1946-69, prof. emeritus, 1969-70, chmn. dept., 1942-68. Chmn. regional dispute panels War Labor Bd., 1943-45, chmn. wage stblzn. panel, 1944-45; pub. mem. New Eng. Wage Stblzn. Bd., 1952-53. Mem. research adv. com. Com. of New Eng., 1951-54; mem. Am. Econ. Assn., Am. Statis. Assn., Association, Am. Association of U. Profs., Indsl. Relations Research Assn., Delta Upsilon. Contbr.; Unemployment Benefit Costs in Massachusetts, 1950. Home: Medford MA Died Nov. 2, 1970; buried Calais VT

MANN, ARTHUR ROBERT, architect, engr.; b. Eng., June 28, 1877; s. George and Eliza (Lingard) M.; student Nicker Normal Coll., 1900-01; B.S. in Engring., U. Kan., 1906; m. Ida May Smith, Aug. 24, 1904 (dec. Sept. 1971); children—Dorothy (Mrs. Ralph L. Calvert), Robert E. Came to U.S., 1879, naturalized, 1887. Partner Mann and Gerow, architects, 1909-24; owner Mann and Co., 1924-34; partner (with son) Mann & Co., architects, 1934-65, consulting architect-engineer, 1965-68 (all in Hutchinson, Kansas). Chief architect for Black & Veatch, Ski Cantonment, Camp Hale, Colo., also Hutchison Naval Air Sta. Licensed architect, Okla., Kan.; licensed engr., Kan. Fellow A.I.A.; mem. Am. Soc. Heating and Air Conditioning Engrs., Am. Concrete Inst. Home: Hutchinson KS Died July 7, 1968.

MANN, ERIKA (MRS. WYSTAN HUGH AUDEN), author, actress, b. Germany; d. Thomas and Katja (Pringlsheim) Mann; studied under Max Reinhardt; m. Wystan Hugh Auden (British poet). Played at an early age in Berlin, Munich and Hamburg; traveled extensively in Europe. Author, actor and dir. Peppermill" (produced over 1000 times in 6 countries). Co-author: Escape to Life; The Other Germany, 1940; The Lights Go Down; The Gang of Ten. Died Sept. 1969.

MANN, FRED PARKER, merchant; b. Elgin, Ill., Nov. 6, 1870; s. Frank and Julia (Parker) M.; ed. grade schs., Sauk Center Minn.; m. Jennie Smith, of Sauk Center, June 23, 1894; children— Fred Phillip, J. Adin, Jane. Started as grocer's handy-man 1888; became owner of small grocery on $75 borrowed capital; now owner one of largest retail stores in state of N.D. Mem. Bd. of Review of NRA, 1934. Mem. bd. dirs. Chamber Commerce of U.S., 1929-31. Served on local civic bds. and orgns. Republican. Presbyn. Mason (32 deg., K.T., Shriner). Rotarian. Home: Devils Lake ND‡

MANN, FREDERICK MAYNARD, prof. architecture; b. New York, N.Y., May 1, 1868; s. Samuel Rexford and Georgianna (Teall) M.; B.C.E., U. of Minn., 1892, C.E., 1898; B.S. in architecture, Mass. Inst. Tech., 1894, M.S. in architecture, 1895; m. Grace Hitchcock, July 29, 1902 (died 1937); children—Dorothy Hitchcock, Eleanor Hitchcock, Fred Maynard. Instr. architecture, U. of Pa., 1895-99; practicing architect, Phila., 1898-1902; prof. architecture, Washington U., 1902-10, U. of Ill., 1910-13; became prof. of architecture U. of Minn., 1913, now prof. emeritus; practicing architect, Minneapolis, 1914-26. Ex-pres. Minneapolis City Planning Commn.; mem. State Planning Commn. Trustee Minneapolis Inst. Art. Fellow A.I.A. (regional dir.); mem. Tau Beta Pi, Sigma Xi, Psi Upsilon. Conglist. Home: Healdsburg CA‡

MANN, HENRY, bus. exec.; b. Germany, Feb. 18, 1890; educated Europe; m. Helen Grimes, April 23, 1924; children—Helen Louise (Mrs. Helen M. Wright), William Houston, Mary C. (Mrs. Gerald R. Cummins), Barbara, Michael. Comptroller, Crown Cork and Seal Co., 1917-26; European v.p. Nat. City Co., 1926-34; mng. dir. Brown Harriman and Co., Ltd., London, 1934-40; pres., dir. Henry Mann Securities Corp., E. Leitz, Inc., N.Y.C., Manaca, Inc., Opto-Metric Tools, Inc. Member C. of C. N.Y. State, German-American Chamber of Commerce (dir.). Clubs: Greenwich (Conn.) Country; Maidstone (East Hampton, L.I., N.Y.); Wall Street, Union League (N.Y.C.); American (London), Metropolitan (Washington); National Golf Links of America (Southampton, N.Y.). Home: New York NY Died Aug. 1968.

MANN, MARGARET, librarian; b. Cedar Rapids, Ia.; d. Amasa and Emily Lucy (Devendorf) M.; ed. Armour Inst. Tech., Chicago Asst., Armour Inst. Tech., 1894-95, 1896-97, U. of Wis. Library Sch., summers 1895, 96; cataloguer and asst. librarian U. of Ill. Library, and instr., Library Sch., U. of Ill., 1897-1903; head of catalogue dept. Carnegie Library, Pittsburgh, Pa., and instr., Carnegie Library Sch., 1903-19; instr., Library Sch., Riverside Calif., summer 1911, winter 1918; cataloguer and classifier, Engring. Socs. Library, N.Y. City, 1919-24; instr. in cataloguing, Paris (France) Library Sch., 1924-26; asst. prof. library science, U. of Mich., 1926-27, asso. prof. since 1927. Mem. A.L.A. (1st v.p. 1924; mem. exec. bd. 1921, 24, 30, 31), Bibliog. Soc. America, Mich. Library Assn., Association des Bibliothecaires Francaise. Unitarian. Club: Women's Research. Author: Subject Headings for Use in Dictionary Catalogs of Juvenile Books, 1916; Introduction to Cataloging and the Classification of Books, 1930. Home: 619 E. University Av., Ann Arbor MI‡

MANN, NANCY MURRAY, b. Spencer, W.Va.; d. Rev. P.H. and Sara Frances (Graves) Murray; student Broaddus Coll., Clarksburg, W.Va.; grad. Western Coll. for Women, Oxford, O., 1884; m. Frank N. Mann, of Alderson, W.Va., Sept. 21, 1892; children—Nancy Kavanaugh (Mrs. Garland R. Johnson), Ellsworth Forsythe. A leader in fight for woman suffrage; former pres. 5th Congl. Dist. Fed. of Women's Clubs; mem. advisory bd. Federal Industrial Instn. for Women, Alderson, W.Va.; trustee Greenbrier Coll., Lewisburg,

W.Va. Republican; seconded nomination of President Hoover for Rep. candidate, 1932. Presbyn. Club: Womans. Contbr. verse to mags. Home: 1621 5th Av., Huntington WV‡

MANN, WILLIAM ALFRED, physician, educator; born Chicago, Mar. 21, 1898; s. William Alfred (M.D.) and Anna Damon (Cram) M.; B.S., U. Ill., 1921, M.D., 1923; grad. study, 1924-26; M.S., Northwestern, 1938; grad. study, Vienna, 1926; m. Maud L. Davison, May 30, 1931; children—William Alfred, III, Nancy Davison (Mrs. Germanetti), David Leonard. Interne, Evanston (Ill.) Hosp., 1923-24; specialist in treatment of the eye since 1926, pvt. practice Chicago since 1926; mem. faculty Northwestern U. Med. Sch., 1927-71, prof. ophthalmology, 1949-66, emeritus, 1966-71; chmn. dept. ophthalmology, Wesley Meml. Hosp., emeritus, 1966-71; consultant-in-chief in ophthalmology U.S. Veterans Hosp., Hines, Ill. Sec., treas. Ophthalmic Pub. Co., Revision Com., U.S. Pharmacopeia, 1950-60. Pres. Profl. Interfraternity Conf., 1933-35; chmn. Med. Interfrat. Conf., 1947-49. Trustee, member exec. com. Hadley School for The Blind. Mem. A.M.A., Illinois, Chicago med. socs., Chicago Ophthal. Soc. (pres., 1946-47), Am. Acad. Ophthalmology and Otolarngology, Am. Ophthal. Society, Association for Research in Ophthalmology, Pan American Association Ophthalmology, Oxford Ophthalmological Congress, Lambda Chi Alpha (organizer, pres. Mid-West Conclave, 1921-23), Alpha Kappa Kappa (grand primarius 1949-53, 63-65; past pres.; past grand v.p.; and former grand historian; also former editor in chief of the Centaur, ofcl. mag.), Omega Beta Pi (hon. nat. pres., 1932-35), Sigma Xi, Pi Kappa Epsilon, Chicago Alumni Assn. of Lambda Chi Alpha (pres. 1921). Republican. Conglist. Mason (K.T.). Associate editor, Am. Jour. Ophthalmology. Home: Chicago IL Died May 18, 1971; buried Memorial Park Cemetery, Skokie IL

MANNING, CLARENCE AUGUSTUS, educator; b. N.Y.C., Apr. 1, 1893; s. Dr. Frank Orlando and Nellie Secor (Vail) M.; A.B., Columbia, 1912, A.M., 1913, Ph.D., 1915; Ph.D. (hon.) Ukrainian Free U., Munich, 1948; m. Louise F. Marshall, June 21, 1941; 1 dau., Alice Vail. Lectr. in Slavonic langs. Columbia, 1917-21, instr., 1921-24, asst. prof., 1924-35, asst. prof. East European langs., 1935-47, asst. prof. Slavic langs., 1947-52, asso. prof. Slavic langs., 1952-58, ret.; mem. Sch. Slavonic Studies, U. London. Served as sgt. intelligence police corps, U.S. Army, 1918-19, attached to translation sect., mil. intelligence div. gen. staff. Decorated officer Order White Lion (Czecholsovak), Order Yugoslav Crown, comdr. Order Poland Restored, Order White Star (Estonia), Order 3Stars (Latvia), Order Grand Prince Gediminas (Lithuania), Order Stars (Latvia), Order Grand Prince Gediminas (Lithuania), Order Civil Merit (Bulgaria). Recipient Freedom award Urkanium Congress Com. Am., 1966. Mem. Polish Inst. Arts and Sci. Am., Modern Lang. Assn., Linguistic Soc. Am., Shevchenko Sci. Soc., Slavonic Inst. Prague (fgn. mem.), Am. Mil. Inst., Phi Beta Kappa. Episcopalian. Author: A Study of Archaism in Euripides, 1916; (with O. M. Fuller) Marko The King's Son, Hero of the Serbs, 1932; Ukrainian Literature-Studies of the Leading Authors, 1944; Soldier of Liberty, Casimir Pulaski, 1945; Taras Shevchenko, Poet of Ukraine, 1945; The Story of Ukraine, 1947; Twentieth Century Ukraine, 1950; The Siberian Fiasco, 1952; The Forgotten Republics, 1952; Russian Influence on Early America, 1953; Ukraine Under the Soviets, 1953; Hetman of Ukraine, Ivan Mazeppa, 1957; History of Slavic Studies in the United States, 1957; (with R. Smal-Stocki) The History of Modern Bulgarian Literature, 1960. Translator: Birds of Heaven by V. G. Korolenko, 1919; A Prince of Outlaws by A. K. Tolstoy, 1927, Rays of the Microcosm by Peter II Petrovich Negosh, 1953; Bellerophon by N. J. Spyropoulos, 1955, Moses by Theol. B. Constantino, 1962, and others. Mem. editorial bd. Rev. of Religion; editorial adv. bd. Ukranian Congress Com. Am.; adv. bd. for Slavic archaeology Am. Jour. Archaeology. Contbr. Pleasantville NY Died Oct. 4, 1972.

MANNING, JOSEPH THRUSTON, 3D, yarn broker; b. Phila., Nov. 22, 1917; s. Joseph Thruston and Ruth Stevens (Turner) M.; student Temple U., 1937-40; m. Virginia R. Larzelere, Mar. 16, 1940; children—Carol Stevens, Joseph T., Deborah D. Clk. 1st Pa. Bank & Trust Co., Phila., 1935-40; asst. metallurgist, sales Copperweld Steel Co., Warren, O., 1940-45; yarn sales Dayton Larzelere, Phila., 1945-62; v.p., sec., treas. Pharr Yarn Sales, Inc., N.Y.C., 1962-70. Served from cadet to capt. USAF, 1943-46. Home: Philadelphia PA Died Dec. 6, 1970.

MANNING, WILLIAM ALBERT, mathematician; b. Salem, Ore., Dec. 5, 1876; s. William and Catherine (Kitzmiller) M.; A.B., Willamette U., 1900; Ph.D., Stanford, 1904; studied Sorbonne, Paris, 1904-05; m. Esther Crandall, of San Francisco and Palo Alto, Calif., Sept. 18, 1908; children—Dorothy, Rhoda, Helena, Sylvia, Laurence Albert. Asst. in mathematics Stanford, 1900-02, instr. 1902-04, asst. prof., 1904-13, asso. prof., 1913-21, professor from 1921. Mem. Am. Math Soc., Am. Assn. Univ. Profs., Phi Beta Kappa, Sigma Xi. Author: Primitive Groups (Part 1), 1921. Home: Stanford CA Died Feb. 29, 1972.

MANNY, FRANK ADDISON, teacher; b. Mounds, Brown County, Ill., June 24, 1868; s. William Charles and Mary (Bloom) M.; A.B., U. of Mich., 1893, A.M., 1896; grad. schs. U. of Chicago, Columbia, Harvard, and European schs.; m. Annette Sawyer, June 23, 1904. Prin. high sch., Moline, Ill., 1894-96; asst. in pedagogy, U. of Chicago, 1896-97; supervisor pub. schs., Indianapolis, 1897-98; head edn. dept., State Normal Sch., Oshkosh, Wis., 1898-1900; supt. Ethical Culture Sch., New York, 1900-06; head of edn. and extension depts., Western State Normal Sch., Kalamazoo, Mich., 1908-11; instr. and dir. Allegany County (Md.) Teachers' Continuation Sch., 1909-11; dir. training of teachers, Baltimore, 1911-15; dir. nutrition study Assn. for Improving Condition of the Poor, New York, 1915-18; personnel div. Wm. Filene's Sons Co., 1918-19; nutrition clinics since 1919. Lecturer, Simmons College, Western Reserve, Chicago, Columbia, and Johns Hopkins universities; educational advisor experimental schs., Boston, New York, Chicago. Mem. Phi Beta Kappa. Conglist. Contbr. to Cyclopedia of Edn., ednl. and social jours. Author: City Training Schools for Teachers, 1914; Boxfordians, 1923; Boxford Genealogies, 1926; Time Will Tell—A Tercentenary Pageant (in collaboration), 1930. Home: Boxford, Mass. and 601 1/2 Highland Street, N., St Petersburg FL‡

MANSERGH, ROBERT, British army officer; b. South Africa, May 12, 1900; s. C. L. W. Mansergh; student Royal Mil. Acad., Woolwich, 1919-20. Commd. 2d lt. Royal Artillery, 1920, advanced through grades to gen., 1953; mem. Mil. Mission to Iraq, 1931-35; adj. Royal Mil. Acad., Woolwich, 1935-39; participated liberation of Singapore, World War II; comdr. 15th Indian Corps, 1946; comdr.-in-chief Allied Forces, Netherlands, East Indies, 1946; dir. Territorial Army and Cadets, 1947; mil. sec. Sec. State of War, 1948-49; comdr. Brit. Forces, Hong Kong, 1949-51; dep. comdr.-in-chief, Allied Forces No. Europe, 1951-53, comdr.-in-chief, 1953-55; comdr.-in-chief U.K. Land Forces, 1956-—. Decorated Knight Grand Cross. of the Bath, Knight Comdr. Brit. Empire, Mil. Cross. Clubs: Travellers, United Services (London). Office: London England Died Nov. 1970.

MANSFIELD, GEORGE ROGERS, geologist; b. Gloucester, Mass., Aug. 30, 1875; s. Alfred and Sarah Jane (Hubbard) M.; B.S., Amherst, 1897, M.A., 1901; M.A., Harvard, 1904, Ph.D., 1906; m. Adelaide Claflin, Aug. 18, 1903; children—Harvey Claflin, James Scott, Robert Hubbard, Marion Claflin and Helen Rogers (twins). Teacher, Central High Sch., Cleveland, 1897-1903; instr. in geology, Harvard, 1906-09; asst. prof. geology, Northwestern U., 1909-13; geologist U.S. Geol. Survey since 1913, in charge sect. of non-metalliferous deposits, 1922-27; in charge sect. areal and non-metalliferous geology, 1927-43; editor of geologic maps, 1941-43, retired. Made investigations in phosphate, potash and nitrates in U.S. and dam sites in Puerto Rico, Idaho, and Wyoming, also researches in stratigraphy and structure in Rocky Mountains of Ida. Mem. Nat. Research Council, 1924-27, chmn. com. on tectonics, 1924-34. Fellow Geol. Soc. of America, A.A.A.S. (sec. sect. E. 1926-30; v.p. 1936); mem. Am. Inst. Mining and Metall Engrs., Soc. of Econ. Geologists, Am. Geophysical Union, Washington Acad. Sciences (v.p. 1931), Geol. Soc., Washington (pres. 1930), Phi Sigma Kappa, Phi Delta Theta, Phi Beta Kappa, Sigma Xi. Republican. Conglist. Club: Cosmos. Author of numerous bulls. and professional papers on phosphates in Ida., Fla., greensands in N.J., nitrates in Calif., Tex., Ida. and Ore., potash in Tex. and N.M., and physiography, stratigraphy, and geologic structure in the Rocky Mountains of Ida. Associate editor Am. Jour. Sci., 1938-45. Home: 2067 Park Road, Washington DC‡

MANTER, HAROLD W(INFRED), univ. prof.; b. Anson, Me., June 18, 1898; s. Fred Augustus and Gusta Houghton (Tinkham) M.; A.B., Bates Coll., Lewiston, Me., 1922; A.M., Univ. Ill., 1923, Ph.D., 1925; m. Esther Ruby Welch, Aug. 16, 1927. Instr. in zoology, La. State Univ., 1925-26; asst. prof. zoology, Univ. of Neb., 1926-27, asso. prof., 1927-35, prof. of zoology from 1935; guest investigator, Biol. Lab., Carnegie Instn., Tortugas, Fla., summers, 1930, 31, 32; mem., Third Allan Hancock Expdn. to Galapagos Islands, 1934; Fulbright research scholar in New Zealand, 1951. Mem. A.A.A.S., Am. Soc. Parasit. (mem. council, 1944-46, mem. ed. bd., Jour. Parasit., 1940-43), Am. Micros. Soc., Am. Soc. Zoologists, Soc. System. Zoology, Am. Soc. Limnology and Oceanography; Phi Beta Kappa, Sigma Xi, Author: (monographs) Some North American fish trematodes, 1926; Digenetic trematodes of fishes from the Galapagos Islands and the neighboring Pacific, 1940; The digenetic trematodes of marine fishes of tortugas, Florida, 1947. Contbr. articles on parasitic worms. Home: Lincoln NB Died Apr. 15, 1971; buried Madison ME

MANTLE, GLADYS ANN DOYLE (MRS. ARTHUR CLAUD-MANTLE), civic worker; b. Bridgeport, Conn., Sept. 15, 1896; d. John Thomas and Mary Louise (Ferry) Doyle; grad. high sch.; m. Arthur Claud-Mantle, Apr. 28, 1916 (dec. July 1959); children—Arthur, Jane (Mrs. Charles M. Hall). Exec. sec. Walter C. Mantle Assos., Trumbull, Conn., 1962-69. Treas., March of Dimes, Trumbull, 1930-45, chmn. A.R.C. br., 1943-45; Gray lady St. Vincent's Hosp., Bridgeport, 1949-59; vol. worker St. Joseph's Home for Aged, Trumbull, 1960-69; chmn. fund drive Cerebral Palsy Assn., Trumbull, 1964-66, vice chmn. aux., 1965-69; mem. Trumbull Town Meeting Bd., 1957-59; mem. Sr. Citizen Commn., Trumbull, 1967-69; mem. bldg. coms. Booth Hill and Jane Ryan schs., 1955. Vice chmn. Democratic Town Com., Trumbull, 1965-69; mem. Bd. Tax Rev., Trumbull, 1963-69. Mem. Trumbull Center Library Assn., Hist. Soc. (charter), St. Teresa's Confraternity of Rosary. Clubs: Womens Community, Trulonic (sec. 1929-69). Home: Trumbull CT Died Aug. 22, 1969; interred Middlebrook Burial Ground Trumbull CT

MANTYNBAND, LOUIS M(ARTIN), lawyer; b. San Francisco, Feb. 12, 1897; s. Solomon A. and Mary Esther (Goodkind) M.; Ph.B., U. Chgo., 1918, J.D., 1920; M. Adele B. Weiner, July 14, 1922; children—Babette Marie (Mrs. Irvin F. Richman), Ralph A., Portia Louise (Mrs. Norman B. Kern). Admitted to Ill. bar, 1921, practiced in Chgo., trial lawyer, specializing corporate finance; member of firm Arvey, Hodes & Mantynband, Chgo.; master in chancery Circuit Ct. Cook Co., 1946-48. Vis. trustee U. Chgo. Law Sch. Mem. Am., Ill. Chgo. bar assns., Chgo. Law Inst., Am. Judicature Soc. Home: Chicago IL Died Jan. 1971.

MANTZ, H. J., judge; b. Kozta, Ia., Sept. 23, 1877; s. Samuel Lewis and Harriet (Eddy) M.; LL.B., Drake Univ. Law Coll., 1904; m. Dorothy A. Sandberg, Aug. 27, 1910; children—Paul Samuel, Kathleen Jean (Mrs. Gordon Luce). Private practice, 1904-25; county atty., Audubon County, Ia., 1907-12; mayor, Audubon, 1913-17; mem. Ia. House of Rep., 1917-21, State Senate, 1921-25; judge Dist. Ct., 13th Ia. Judicial Dist., 1925-43; justice Supreme Ct. of Ia. since Jan. 1943. Mem. Iowa State Bar Assn. Republican. Mason. Club: Lions. Home: Audubon IA Office: State Capitol, Des Moines IA*‡

MANUEL, W(ILLIAM) A(SBURY), univ. prof.; b. Freetown, Ind., Jan. 18, 1891; s. Asbury Hill and Sarah Jane (Brown) M.; A.B., DePauw U., 1912; M.S., U. of Ill., 1915; D.Sc., Colo. Sch. of Mines, 1928; m. Lola Warfel, Dec. 25, 1919; children—Elizabeth Lee, Suzanne. Research fellow, Engring. Expt. Sta., U. of Ill., 1915; instr. chemistry, Northwestern U., 1915; ranch sec. Trinchera Ranch Co., Ft. Garland, Colo., 1918-21; prof. chemistry, Western State Coll. of Colo., 1921-29; prof. chemistry, Ohio Wesleyan U., from 1929, head of dept. chemistry, from 1930; consulting chemist. Town trustee, Gunnison, Colo., 1929. Fellow A.A.A.S., Ohio Acad. Sci.; mem. Am. Assn. Univ. Profs., Am. Chem. Soc., Phi Beta Kappa, Sigma Xi, Phi Lambda Upsilon, Omicron Delta Kappa, Phi Gamma Delta. Republican. Methodist. Contbr. articles to chem. jours. Home: Delaware OH Died Aug. 12, 1970.

MANWARING, WILFRED HAMILTON, pathologist; b. Ashland, Va., Sept. 14, 1871; s. Theodore Perry and Mary Frances (Griswold) M.; M.D. Johns Hopkins U., 1904; also studied at Berlin, Leipzig, Frankfort-on-the-Main, Vienna and London, 1907-10; m. Ava Mautner, June 14, 1917; children—John Hamilton, Frederick Wolcott. Fellow and asst. in pathology, U. of Chicago, 1904-05; asso. prof. pathology and bacteriology, Ind. U.; 1905-07; traveling fellow in pathology and bacteriology, Rockefeller Inst. for Med. Research, 1907-08, asst., 1910-13; prof. bacteriology and experimental pathology, Stanford U., 1913-37, emeritus since 1937. Lecturer in functional pathology, Washington U. Med. Sch., St. Louis, Mo., 1920-21, Mem. Soc. for Exptl. Pathology, Am. Assn. Pathologists and Bacteriologists, Am. Assn. Immunologists (pres. 1926), Soc. for Exptl. Biology and Medicine, Soc. Am. Bacteriologists, Sigma Xi; fellow A.M.A., A.A.A.S. Researches in theoretical immunology and experimental pathology. Address: 364 Kingsley Av., Palo Alto CA‡

MAPES, CLAREL BOWMAN, petroleum exec.; b. Laddonia, Mo., Dec. 2, 1902; s. Seth Leslie and Mabel Elizabeth (Bowman) M.; B.S. in Civil Engring., U. Okla., 1922, A.B. in Math., 1923, C.E. (profl.), 1926; m. Elizabeth Celeste Barnes, Sept. 5, 1934; children—Clarel Bowman II. Engr., hwy. and land survey work in Cleve., also McClain, Garvin, Murray counties, Okla., 1918-22; asst. engr. J. C. Milliken, Okla. Gas & Electric Co., 1922, Truxillo R.R. Co., Republic of Honduras, 1923-24; pvt. practice, Norman and Pawhuska, Okla., 1922-23, 24; civil and petroleum engr., dept. econs. Marland Oil Co., Ponca City, Okla., 1924-25; asst. to pres. Carr & McFadden, Inc., 1925-27; asst. gen. sec., technologist Mid-Continent Oil & Gas Assn., Tulsa, 1927-33, acting gen. sec.-treas., 1933-34, gen. sec.-treas., Tulsa, 1934-67, sec.-treas. Kan.-Okla. div., 1931-61, sec.-treas. Osage Oil & Gas Lesses Assn., 1934-67. Profl. engr., Fla., Okla. Mem. Am. Mining Congress, Am. Petroleum Inst., Okla. Safety Council, Am. Econ. Assn., Nat. Oil Scouts and Landmen's Assn. (asso.), Assn. Petroleum Writers (asso.), Am. Inst. Mining, Metall. and Petroleum Engrs., Soc. Am. Mil. Engrs., Nat., Okla. socs. profl. engrs., Am. Statis. Assn., Am. Acad. Polit. and Social Sci., Pub. Relations Soc.

Am., Nat. Tax Assn., Am. Forestry Assn., Transp. Assn. Am., Council for Basic Edn., Phi Beta Kappa, Sigma Tau (nat. sec.-treas.), Scabbard and Blade. Mason (32 deg.). Clubs: Tulsa Press, The Tulsa; Imperial (Dallas). Home: Tulsa OK Died Nov. 23, 1967.

MAPES, VICTOR, playwright; b. New York, Mar. 10. 1870; s. Charles Victor and Martha Meeker (Halsted) M.; A.B., Columbia (first in class), 1891; studied lit. and drama at The Sorbonne, Paris, 1892-93; m. Anna Louise Hoeke, of Washington, June 5, 1900. Resided in Paris, 1892-96, Paris corr. New York Sun; stage mgr. Daniel Frohman's Lyceum Theatre, New York, 1897; dramatic critic, New York World, signing articles Sidney Sharp," 1898-99; gen. stage dir. Daly's Theatre, New York, 1900-01; mgr. Globe Theatre, Boston, 1904-05; dir. New Theatre, Chicago, 1906-07. Mem. Phi Beta Kappa. Clubs: University, Lambs, Columbia, Players, Psi Upsilon. Author: Duse and the French, 1897; Partners Three, 1909; Gilded Way, 1911. Contbr. to mags. Plays: (produced) La Comtesse de Lisne (in French), Theatre Mondain, Paris, May 1895; A Flower of Yeddo, Empire Theatre, New York, Nov. 1898; The Tory's Guest, Empire, Nov. 1900; Don Caesar's Return, Wallack's, New York (by J. K. Hackett), Sept. 1901; Capt. Barrington, Manhattan Theatre, New York, Nov. 1903 (by Charles Richman); The Undercurrent, Studebaker Theatre, Chicago, Jan. 1907 (by Lena Ashwell); The Detective, 1908; The New Henrietta, 1913; The Boomerang (with Winchell Smith), 1915; The Lassoo, 1917; The Long Dash, 1918; The Hottentot, 1919; The Kangaroos, 1921; The Amethyst, 1925. Home: Villa Esperance, Cannes France‡

MARBURY, WILLIAM G., business exec.; b. Farmington, Mo., Mar. 31, 1912; s. Benjamin H. and Anne (Eversole) M.; student Central Coll., Washington U., 1932-35; LL.B., St. Louis U., 1937; m. Frances Steudle, 1938; Frances Anne, Linda. Admitted to Mo. bar, 1937; practice of law, St. Louis, 1937-45; with Miss. River Corp., 1945-71, dir., 1948-71, pres., 1949-56, 65-69, 70-71, chmn. bd., 1956-71; chmn. exec. com. bd. dirs. M.P.R.R., 1960-71, chmn. bd., 1967-71; chmn. bd. C. & E.I. R.R., Miss. River Transmission Corp. Clubs: Mo. Athletic. Noon Day, Racquet (St. Louis); University (N.Y.C.). Home: St Louis MO Died July 11, 1971.

MARCEAU, HENRI, curator; b. Richmond, Va., June 21, 1896; s. Louis and Jeanne (Cotte) M.; B.Arch., Columbia, 1920; fellow in architecture, Am. Acad. Rome, 1922-25 (Rome prize in architecture); A.F.D. (hon.), Temple U., Beaver Coll., Franklin and Marshall; m. Rebecca Alvord, Aug. 17, 1927; 1 dau., Elizabeth. Instr. archtl. design, U. of Pa., 1926, asst. prof., 1927; curator John G. Johnson Collection from 1927; curator fine arts, Pa. Museum of Art, 1929-33, asst. dir., 1933-45, asso. dir., from 1945, acting dir. mus., 1955-56, director 1956-64; adv. com. Walters Art Gallery, Baltimore, chmn., 1946; dir. Phila. Mus. Art, 1956-64, 2d lt. F.A., U.S. Army, World War. Decorated Chevalier, Order of Belgian Crown, 1940; Chavalier, French Order of Legion of Honor, 1947. Fellow Internat. Inst. for Conservation of Mus. Objects; mem. Philadelphia Art Commn. from 1940, v.p., 1945. Mem. Fairmount Park Art Assn. (sec. 1930, v.p. since 1946), Phila. Art Alliance (sec. 1932-33, v.p. 1933), American Philosophical Soc., A.I.A. (hon.), Nat. Soc. Art Dirs., Assn. Art Mus. Dirs., Am. Inst. Designers (hon.), Delta Upsilon. Republican. Home: Philadelphia PA Died Sept. 15, 1969; interred St. Thomas Episcopal Ch., Whitemarsh PA

MARCH, ABRAHAM W., physician; b. East Chicago, Ind., Dec. 11, 1909; s. Wolfe and Bune H. Marcovich; M.D., U. Chgo., 1937; m. Jacqueline S. Front, Oct. 7, 1945; children—Wayne F., Gail A. Intern, U. Chgo. Clinics, 1936-37, asst. resident in radiology, 1937-39, asst. radiologist, 1943-44; cons. in radiology Kellogg Found., 1941-43; asst. prof. radiology U. Chgo., 1943-44; practice medicine specializing in radiology, Dayton, O., 1944-67, ret., 1967; attending staff Miami Valley Hosp., Dayton, Kettering Hosp., Dayton. Diplomate Am. Bd. Radiology. Fellow Am. Coll. Radiology; mem. A.M.A., Radiol. Soc. N.Am., Am. Roentgen Ray Soc., Ohio, Miami Valley (charter, past pres.) radiol. socs. Contbr. articles on Diabetes Mellitus to med. jours. Home: Dayton OH Died June 13, 1969; buried Beth-El Cemetery, East Gary IN

MARCH, HAL, actor, writer; San Francisco, Apr. 22, 1920; s. Leon and Ethel (Schoenfeld) Medelson; student pub. schs.; married Candy Toxton, Feb. 13, 1956; children—Steven, Melissa, Peter, Jeffrey, and Victoria. Started as night club entertainer, Los Angeles, California, 1938-40; singer, comedian in burlesque, San Francisco, 1940-42; announcer radio sta. KYA, San Francisco, 1943; radio actor, Los Angeles, 1944; mem. team Sweeney & March, 1945-47, with guest appearances with Burns and Allen, Jack Benny, Bob Hope, others; vaudeville tour with Jack Carson, 1950; television performer, 1951-54; partner Imogene Coca show, N.Y.C., 1955; master of ceremonies $64,000 Question, N.Y.C., 1954-59; actor plays Two for the Seesaw, 1959-60, Come Blow Your Horn (Broadway), 1961-63. President of Marcan Enterprises, Incorporated. Served with C.A.C., AUS, 1942-43. Recipient Emmy Award, 1956. Look Award, 1956, Sylvania Award, 1956. Mem. Am. Guild Variety Artists, Am. Fedn. Television and Radio Actors. Club: Nat. Press of Washington (hon.). Home: Scarsdale NY Died Jan. 1970.

MARCH, JOHN LEWIS, coll. prof.; b. Easton, Pa., March 11, 1873; s. Francis Andrew and Mildred Stone (Conway) M.; A.B., Lafayette Coll., 1893, A.M., 1896, Ph.D., 1903; unmarried. Taught Latin, Harry Hillman Acad., Wilkes-Barre, Pa., 1893-95; student in Germany, France, Italy, 1895-98; instr., 1899-1903, asst. prof., 1903-04, adj. prof., 1904-22, prof. psychology since 1922, Union Coll. Mem. Delta Kappa Epsilon, Phi Beta Kappa, Sigma Xi. Author: A Book of Verse, 1904; A Theory of Mind, 1908. Home: Schenectady NY*‡

MARCHETTI, ANDREW A., obstetrician, gynecologist; b. Richmond, Va., July 2, 1901; s. Louis and Blanca (Iaccheri) M.; student Johns Hopkins University, 1920-22, M.D., 1928; A.B., University of Richmond, 1924; m. Catherine E. Fopeano, Jan. 2, 1935; children—Marco Anthony, Peter Luigi, Michael Joseph, John Philip. Intern in obstetrics John Hopkins Hosp., 1928-29; assist. resident, later resident, obstetrics and gynecology, Strong Memorial Hospital, Rochester, New York, 1929-31; assistant resident surgery, Cincinnati (Ohio) General Hospital, 1931-32; resident obstetrics and gynecology woman's clinic N.Y. Hospital, 1932-33, attending obstetrician and gynecologist, 1943-47; instr., later asso. prof. obstetrics and gynecology med. coll. Cornell U., 1933-47; prof. obstetrics and gynecology, head dept. Georgetown University School Medicine, 1947-66, professor obstetrics and gynecology, 1947-70; director Georgetown division department of obstetrics and gynecology, D.C. General Hosp.; civilian consultant Army Med. Center, Walter Reed Hosp. Recipient Vicennial medal Georgetown Univ. Diplomate Am. Bd. Obstetrics and Gynecology (dir. 1966-70, pres. 1966-70). Fellow Am. Coll. Obstetricians and Gynecologists (1st v.p. 1958-59), Am. Assn. Obstetricians and Gynecologists, Am. (sec. 1957-61, pres. 1966-67), Washington (pres. 1952-53) gynecol. socs., A.C.S.; mem. Soc. Pelvic Surgeons, A.M.A., Med. Soc. D.C., Kappa Sigma, Alpha Omega Alpha, Alpha Kappa Kappa, Sigma Xi (honorary mem.). Republican. Roman Catholic. Co-author: The Epithelia of Woman's Reproductive Organs, 1948. Home: Silver Spring MD Died June 25, 1970; buried Gate of Heaven Cemetery, Silver Spring MD

MARCO, HERBERT FRANCIS, state ofcl.; b. Auburn, N.Y., Mar. 27, 1907; s. Dominick A. and Rose Mary (Giannino) M.; B.S., Cornell U., 1929; M.S., Syracuse U., 1932; Ph.D. (Charles Boughton research fellow) Yale, 1935; m. Jane Christine Dry, Oct. 26, 1946; children—Teig, Lynn, Gaird. Engineer in charge r.r. constrn. Cady Corp., 1929; mem. Northeastern Forest Expt. Sta., 1935; mem. Conn. Geodetic Survey, 1938-42; dir. project for computation mil. grid coordinates for U.S., Greenland, Iceland, 1941-42; pres. faculty, mem. team for orgn. Air Force Inst. Tech., 1946-56; participant Gatlinburg Conf. Atomic Energy, 1956; dean engring., dir. research and engring. Expt. Sta., S.D. State Coll., 1956-58; tech. specialist Aerojet-Gen. Corp., 1958-65; pres. Guilford Technical Institute, Jamestown, N.C., 1965-68; with Division of State Planning and Community Affairs, Richmond, Va., 1968-69; division mgr., cons. to chmn. bd. Dayco Corporation also cons. to industry at large. Director Rosemont Home Assn. Served maj. AUS, World War II. Decorated Purple Heart, Air medal with cluster. Mem. of the American Society of Engineering Education (nat. chmn. mechanics div., mem. exec. com.), Am. Inst. Aeros. and Astronautics, Sigma Xi, Tau Beta Pi, Gamma Delta, Pi Epsilon Gamma. Mason, Rotarian. Home: Richmond VA Died Oct. 28, 1969; buried Glendale Nat. Cemetery, Richmond VA

MARDEN, JESSE KREKORE, surgeon; b. at Aintab, Turkey, Mar. 10, 1872; s. Henry and Mary (Christy) M.; A.B., Dartmouth, 1895; M.D., U. of Mich., 1898; post-grad. work in Vienna; m. Lucy Morley, of Mentor, O., July, 1908. Med. missionary of A.B.C.F.M. in Turkey, 1898—; in charge Anatolia Hosp., Marsovan, 1903—. Mem. Phi Beta Kappa, Delta Kappa Epsilon, Phi Rho Sigma. Address: Marsovan Turkey‡

MAREK, KURT W. (C.W. CERAM), author; b. Berlin, Germany, Jan. 20, 1915; s. Max and Anna (Mistol) Marek; student Hohenzollern Oberreal Schule, Lessing-Hochschule, Berlin U., 1932; m. Hannelore Schipmann, December 1952; one son, Max Alexander. Began journalistic career, 1932; literature, theatre, film critic Berlin newspapers, 1935; staff Die Welt, 1946-50; editor-in-chief Rowohlt Publs., 1946-52; lived in U.S., 1954-71. Served from pvt. to 1st lt., anti-aircraft unit, German Army, 1938-45. Mem. P.E.N., Archeol. Inst., of Am., Am. Anthropological Assn. Author: Gods, Graves and Scholars, 1951; The Secret of the Hittites, 1956; The March of Archeology, 1958; Yestermorrow, 1961; Archaeology, 1964; Archaeology of the Cinema, 1965; The First American, 1971. Editor: A Woman in Berlin (anonymous), 1954; Lows Kleine Weltgeschichte, 1949; Hands on the Past, 1966. Contbr. articles to profl. publs. Scriptwriter, dir. films for TV. Home: Reinbek bei Hamburg Fed Republic Germany Died Apr. 12, 1972, buried Reinbek near Hamburg Germany

MARES, LUMIR MARTIN, physician; b. Wilber Neb., Nov. 11, 1901; s. M.D., Northwestern U., 1927 married, May 30, 1931 (wife dec. 1965) children—Sam, Robert. Intern St. Lukes Hosp., Chgo. 1927-29; attending physician Deaconess Hosp. Wenatchee, Wash., St. Anthonys-Chelan County Hosp., Wenatchee. Served to lt. col. M.C., AUS 1942-45. Named Wenatchee Pioneer of Year, 1964 Diplomate Am. Bd. Internal Medicine. Mem. A.M.A Home: Wenatchee WA Died May 30, 1967; buried Wenatchee WA

MARGRAF, GUSTAV BERNHARD, lawyer; b. Cape Girardeau, Mo., May 14, 1915; s. William Anton and Mary (Rubel) M.; A.B., S.E. Mo. State Tchrs. Coll. 1936; LL.B., Duke, 1939; m. Grace Margaret Houck Aug. 22, 1939; children—James Houck, Patricia Lee John. Admitted to Mo. bar, 1939, N.Y., 1941, D.C. 1947, Va., 1957; asso. Cahill, Gordon, Reindel & Ohl 1939-48, charge Washington office, 1942-48; v.p., gen atty. NBC, N.Y.C., 1948-53, v.p. for talent, 1953-55 gen. solicitor Reynolds Metals Co., 1955-63, vice pres. 1960-68, general counsel, 1963-68, also dir.; mng. dir. chief operating officer Brit. Aluminum Co. Ltd. London, Eng., 1964-68; pres., chmn. bd. Canadian Brit Aluminum Co., Ltd., Baie Comeau, Can.; vice chmn Manicouagan Power Co., Baie Comeau, 1964-69; chmn Aluminum Wire & Cable Co., Ltd., Swansea, Wales Aluminium Foils Ltd., London, 1964-68, adminstrv v.p., 1968-69; pres. mining and shipping subsidiaries dir. various other subsidiaries Reynolds Metals Co Mem. Am. Judicature Soc., N.Y. County Federal Communications, Va., Richmond bar assns., Assn. Bar City N.Y. Aluminum Fedn. Eng. (pres. 1966-67). Clubs Commonwealth; Country of Va. (Richmond) University (N.Y.C.); Deep Run Hunt (Manakin, Va.) Nat. Lawyer's (Washington); Buck's, Royal Automobile (London). Home: Richmond VA Died July 10, 1969.

MARIENTHAL, GEORGE EDWARD, restauranteur b. Chgo., Sept. 11, 1909; s. Oscar Bernard and Mayme (Ronsiey) M.; student Northwestern U., 1928-30; m Jeanne Prins, Apr. 28, 1950; children—David, James Philip. Account exec. Rothschild & Co., 1929-30; sales mgr. Continental Coffee Co., 1931-43; founder London House, restaurant-night club, Chgo., 1945, now sec. pres. Mister Kelly, Inc., restaurant-night club, Chgo. treas. Happy Medium Inc., theatre club, Chgo.; sec Wacker Parking Co., Chgo. Past chmn. Crusade of Mercy, Chgo. Served with USAAF, 1942-46. Mem Greater N. Michigan Av. Assn. (bd. dirs.). Clubs Standard (past dir.) (Chgo.); Bryn Mawr Country Variety. Home: Chicago IL Died Oct. 26, 1972.

MARITAIN, JACQUES, prof. emeritus; b. Paris France, Nov. 18, 1882; s. Paul and Genevieve (Favre) M.; received degrees Agrege de Philosophie and Licencie en Sciences Naturelles, U. Paris; Ph.D. Roman Universities; student biology scis., Heidelberg U.; m. Raissa Oumancoff. Converted to Catholicism 1906, and began study of scholastic philosophy, 1908 became prof. philosophy, Institut Catholique de Paris 1914, and launched first serious criticism of Bergsonism; founded Bibliotheque Francaise de Philosophie, 1923; directed for Plon, Paris pubs., series of books, Roseau d'or," for 7 yrs.; directed series, Les Iles," for Desclee de Brouwer, from 1934; specialized in scholastic system of St. Thomas and lectured on Thomist philosophy at univs. of Louvain, Geneva Fribourg, Milan, Bonn, Oxford, Santander, Chgo. Angelicim in Rome, and Inst. of Medieval Studies Toronto, Can. Fr. ambassador to the Holy See, 1945-48 Prof., Princeton Univ., 1948-54, prof. emeritus Princeton, 1953-73. Mem. (hon.) Am. Acad., Nat. Inst Arts and Letter. Author numerous books; late publs The Person and the Common Good, 1947; Existence and the Existent, 1948; Man and the State, 1950; The Range of Reason, 1952; Creative Intuition in Art and Poetry, 1953; Approaches to God, 1954; On the Philosophy of History, 1957; Reflections on America 1958; The Degrees of Knowledge, 1959; The Responsibility of the Artist, 1960; On the Use of Philosophy, 1961; Moral Philosophy, 1964; The Peasant of the Garonne, 1968; and also works in French, La Philosophie Bergsonienne, La Philosophie Morale, Le Paysan de la Garonne, 1966, De l'Eglise du Christ, 1970, and articles and pamphlets. Address Princeton NJ Died Apr. 28, 1973.

MARKEE, JOSEPH ELDRIDGE, med. educator; b Neponset, Ill., May 22, 1903; s. Joshua W. and Josephine (Eldridge) M.; student Knox Coll., 1921-24 B.S., U. Chicago., 1924, Ph.D., 1929; m. Myrtle Clapp July 2, 1927; children—Shirley J., Joseph Eldridge Mem. faculty Stanford, 1929-43; prof. anatomy, 1943 prof., dept. anatomy Duke U. Med. Sch., 1943-53 James B. Duke prof., 1953-70, chmn. dept. anatomy 1943-66, asst. dean medical admissions, 1943-66; vis prof. anatomy U. Tennessee Med. Sch., summer 1942 Recipient Golden Apple award Student Am. Med Assn., 1963; Council on Med. Television Roster award posthumously. Commonwealth Fellow, 1966-67. Hon fellow Am. Soc. Orthopedic Surgeons, Am. Orthopedic

Assn.; mem. Assn. Medical Colleges (audio-visual com.), Am. Assn. Anatomist (adv. com. med. Film Inst.; executive committee, 1946-64), American Physiol. Society, American Zool. Soc., N.Y. Acad. Science, Phi Beta Kappa, Sigma Xi, Alpha Omega Alpha. Asso. editor Jour. Morphology. Producer movies on functional anatomy. Home: Durham NY Died Nov. 27, 1970; interred Duke U. Medical Center, Durham NC

MARKEY, JOHN CLIFTON, mfr.; b. Defiance, Ohio, May 31, 1889; s. John Jacob and Catherine (Strusaker) M.; student Ohio Wesleyan Coll., 1910-12; m. Ruth E. Edwards, Oct. 16, 1915 (dec. 1960); children—John R., Catherine (Mrs. M. J. Anderson); m. 2d, Louis Dean Hays, May 20, 1961. Apprentice machinist C. F. Kettering, Defiance, O., 1907-09; founder, propr. metal working firms, 1913-26; founder, propr. Service Sta. Equipment Co., 1926-30; founder, chmn. bd. dirs. The Aro Corp., Bryan, O., from 1930; dir. Dodge Mfg. Corp., Mishawaka, Ind. Trustee Defiance Coll. Mem. Joint Civilian Orientation Conf. Assn., USAF Assn. Methodist. Mason (32 deg., K.T.). Clubs: Old Timers, Toledo, Toledo Country; International-Chicago, Chicago (Chgo.). Home: Bryan Oh Died Dec. 28, 1968.

MARKHAM, GEORGE C., insurance pres.; b. Wilmington, Essex Co., N.Y.; s. Nathan B. and Susan (McLeod) M.; Colonial ancestry; ed. common and select schs., and taught several terms; admitted to bar, Canton, N.Y.; m. Rose S. Smith, of Elizabethtown, N.Y., Aug. 1870 (died 1893). Became resident of Milwaukee, 1869; practiced law until 1895; with Northwestern Mut. Life Ins. Co., 1895, becoming trustee and mem. finance com., July 15, 1895, mem. exec. com., Jan. 29, 1896, 3d v.p., Jan. 30, 1901, 2d v.p., Apr. 20, 1904, v.p., July 19, 1905, and pres., July 15, 1908. Home: 216 Palmetto Drive, Pasadena CA‡

MARKHAM, JAMES WALTER, educator; b. Holland, Tex., Aug. 12, 1910; s. Walter William and Mabel (Goodnight) M.; B.J., U. Tex., 1932, M.A., 1940; Ph.D., U. Mo., 1952; m. Myrtle Sturges, Mar. 14, 1941; children—James David, Sara Hope. Tchr., Austin (Tex.) High Sch., 1933-40; reporter Ft. Worth Press, 1936-37; writer Dallas Jour., 1940-41; adviser student publs. U. Tex., 1941-42; exec. sec. Tex. Bd. Control, 1943-46; asst. prof. Baylor U., 1946-48; asst., then asso. prof. U. Mo., 1948-53; asso. prof., then prof. head dept. journalism Pa. State U., 1953-62; prof., head internat. communication U. Ia., Iowa City, 1962-72, prof. journalism, 1956-72. Cons. Chilton Pub. Co., Phila., 1956-60, U.S. Dept. Agr., 1968-72; lectr. Inter Am. Fedn. Working Newspapermen, Panama City, 1962; mem. workshop Swedish Inst. Peace and Conflict Research, 1967. Mem. Fulbright Journalism Adv. Com., Washington, 1968-70. Recipient award for research in journalism and communication Kappa Tau Alpha, 1954, 67, John Cotton Dana award library promotion, 1961, Iowa Author's award, 1966. Mem. Am. Assn. for Edn. in Journalism (founder internat. div. 1965), UN Assn. U.S.A., Internat. Press Inst., Internat. Assn. Mass Communication Research, Kappa Tau Alpha (nat. sec. 1957-67). Dem. Presbyn. Author: Bovard of the Post-Dispatch, 1954; Voices of the Red Giants: Communications Systems in the USSR and China, 1967; International Images and Mass Communication Behavior, 1967; International Communications as a Field of Study, 1970; also monographs and articles, chpts. in books. Founder, editor Internat. Communications Bull., 1966-72; editor internat. journalism sect. Journalism Quar., 1969-72. Home: Iowa City IA Died Feb. 7, 1972; buried Oakland Cemetery, Iowa City IA

MARKHAM, JOHN RAYMOND, prof. engring.; b. Cambridge, Mass., July 23, 1895; s. John Henry and Mary (Williams) M.; M.E., Mass. Inst. Tech., 1918; m. Genevieve Triquera, June 5, 1921; 1 son, James Paul (killed in action, Mar. 8, 1945). Began as research asso. aeronaut. engring. dept., Mass. Inst. Tech., 1922, prof. aeronaut. engring. from 1946, dir. supersonic lab. from 1947; dir. Wright Bros. Wind Tunnel, Mass. Inst. Tech., cons. engr. Argentine and Brazillian govts. in design of wind tunnels and equipment, also U.S. A.A.F., Boeing Aircraft, United Aircraft Corp. and Gen. Motors Corp.; mem. sci. adv. bd. to U.S.A.A.F., from 1945; chmn. industry and ednl. adv. bd. U.S.A.F. science com. and sub-com. Nat. Adv. Council for Aeros. Chairman bd. Mithras, Inc. (Cambridge, Mass.). Served as capt. AEF, U.S. Army, 1917-19. Recipient USAF medal, 1955. Fellow Inst. Aero. Sci.; mem. Sigma Xi. Contbr. articles to engring. and sci. publs. Home: Belmont MA Died Dec. 12, 1971; buried Belmont Cemetery, Belmont MA

MARKIN, MORRIS, b. Russia, July 15, 1893. Organizer, pres., gen. mgr. Checker Cab. Mfg. Corp. (name changed to Checker Motors Corp, 1958), from 1928; chairman board Parmelee Transportation Co. Address: Kalamazoo MI Died July 1970.

MARKINO, YOSHIO, artist, author; b. Koromo, Japan, Dec. 25, 1874; s. Toshimoto and Katsu (Toyama) M.; ed. Hopkin's Art Sch., San Francisco, 1894-97; South Kensington Art Coll., and Central Sch. of Art and Goldsmith Inst., London, 1898-1902. First came to U.S., 1893, again in 1924. Hon. mem. des peintures modernes de Paris, 1907. Picture: Cornelius' House in Pompeii, in Luxembourg Mus., Paris. Illustrator: The Color of London; of Paris; of Rome; The Charms of London; Oxford Seen From Within; A Little Pilgrimage in Italy; The Story of Yone Noguchi. Author: Little Pilgrimage in Italy; The Story of Yone Noguchi. Author: A Japanese Artist in London, 1910; When I Was a Child, 1911; My Ideal John Bullesses, 1912; My Recollections and Reflections, 1912. Contbr. to British and Am. mags. and newspapers. Address: care The League of Neighbours, 398 Boylston St., Boston MA‡

MARKS, EDWIN I., merchant; b. New York, N.Y., Apr. 19, 1888; s. Isaac D. and Laura (Eppstein) M.; A.B., Harvard Univ.; m. Lucie Loeb, 1930. Vice-pres. and gen. mgr. B. Lowenstein Brothers, Memphis, Tenn.; then gen. mdse. mgr. Stern Bros., New York; divisional mdse. councillor, exec. vice-pres., vice pres. from Apr. 1933, chairman of executive committee from Oct. 1945, R. H. Macy & Co., Inc.; pres. Macy Bank. Dir. Lasalle & Koch Co., Toledo, O., R.H. Macy & Co., Inc., L. Bamberger & Co., Newark, N.J. Trustee Mt. Sinai Hosp., N.Y.C. During World War I, served as lieut. in Air Service, U.S. Army. Clubs: Century Country, Harvard of New York. Home: New York City NY Died Nov. 23, 1970; buried Salem Fields Cemetery, Brooklyn NY

MARKS, J(AMES) CHRISTOPHER, organist; b. Cork, Ireland, July 29, 1863; s. J. Christopher and Marian (Johnston) M.; ed. Royal Sch., Armagh, 1876-81, Trinity Coll., Dublin, 1881-85; Royal Univ. of Ireland, 1883-84; hon. Mus.D., Univ. State of N.Y., 1908; m. Maud Sidley Dowman, Nov. 11, 1886 (died May 2, 1899); children—Malcolm Chamney (dec.), J. Christopher, Jocelyn Gibbons, Dorothy Dowman; m. 2d, Minnie Mae Belcher, Oct. 27, 1903 (died Aug. 31, 1931). Came to U.S., 1902, naturalized, 1919. Began as choir boy Cork Cathedral, 1870; then asst. organist to father at St. Finn Barre's Cathedral, Cork; organist and choirmaster St. Luke's Episcopal Ch., Cork, 1881-1902; organist St. Andrew's Ch., Pittsburgh, Pa., 1902-04; organist and choirmaster Church of the Heavenly Rest, N.Y. City, 1904-29; organist emeritus since 1929. Many prizes for musical compositions, including prize for best song in Great Britain, 1893. Mem. Am. Guild Organists, Nat. Assn. Organists (pres. 1912, 13). Republican. Episcopalian. Mason (33 deg.). Clubs: Bohemians, St. Wilfrid, St. George's Soc., Canadian, British Brooklyn NY‡

MARKS, LEON JOHN, printing and pub. co. exec.; b. N.Y.C., Aug. 9, 1898; s. William M. and Margaret (Whelan) M. student Internat. Corr. Sch., Alexander Hamilton Inst.; m. Marie Olive Brown, 1923; 1 dau., Geraldine (Mrs. John Neal). With J. Horace, MacFarland Co., Harrisburg, Pa., Internat. Textbook Co., Scranton, Pa., also Mt. Pleasant Press, until 1919; with Curtis Pub. Co., Phila., 1919—, asst. to supt. asst. to pres. and supt. 1957-60, v.p., dir. mfg., 1960-63, sr. v.p., dir. mfg., 1963-72; dir. N.Y. & Pa., Co., Inc. Clubs: Seaview Country (Absecon, N.J.); Down Town (Phila.); Drexelbrook Swimming and Tennis (Drexell Hill, Pa.); Brigantine (N.J.) Yacht. Home: Brigantine NJ Died July 24, 1972; buried West Laurel Hill Cemetery, Bala Cynwyd PA

MARKS, SIDNEY JEROME, bldg. materials exec.; b. Chgo., Aug. 15, 1904; s. J. H. and Ann (Lippman) M.; student Crane Coll., Chgo., 1920-22, Kent Coll. Law, Chgo., 1922-23; m. Lenora Jacobs, Dec. 16, 1928; children—Lois I. (Mrs. Howard Tucker), Alan C. With Material Service Corp., Chgo., from 1923, begeinning as clk., successively asst. sales mgr., sales mgr., 1923-32, v.p. sales, from 1932. Clubs: Standard. Home: Chicago IL

MARLATT, ABBY LILLIAN, home economist; b. Manhattan, Kan., Mar. 7, 1869; d. Washington and Julia Ann (Bailey) M.; B.S., Kan. State Agrl. Coll., Manhattan, Kan., 1888, M.S., 1890, D.Sc., 1925; grad. student Clark U., and Brown U. Began as prof. home economics, Utah Agrl. Coll., 1890; instr. home economics, Tech. High Sch., Providence, R.I., 1894-1909; prof. home economics and dir. of courses, U. of Wis., since 1909. Mem. Am. Chem. Soc., A.A.A.S., Am. Home Economics Assn. (ex-pres.), Am. Child Hygiene Assn., Am. Dietetics Assn., Am. Assn. Univ. Women, N.E.A., Omicron Nu, Phi Kappa Phi. Republican. Unitarian. Club: Woman's (Madison, Wis.). Home: 612 Howard Pl., Madison WI‡

MARMER, MILTON JACOB, physician; b. N.Y.C., Mar. 6, 1913; s. Harry and Lina (Kaplan) M.; A.B., U. Mich., 1934, M.D., 1937; M. Med. Sci. in Anesthesiology, N.Y. Med. Coll., 1951; m. Rose Braver, Sept. 15, 1940; children—Stephen Seth, Betty Elisabeth, Richard Franklin. Intern, Bronx (N.Y.) N.Y., 1938-40; instr. anesthesiology N.Y. Med. Coll., 1948-52, Stanford U. Med. Sch., 1952-53; asso. prof. surgery Med. Sch., U. Cal. Los Angeles, 1954-70; chief anesthesiology Cedars of Lebanon Hosp., Los Angeles, 1954-70. Served to 1st lt. M.C. AUS, 1942-44. Diplomate Am. Bd. Anesthesiology. Fellow Am. Soc. Anesthesiologists, Am. Coll. Chest Physicians, Internat. Soc. Anesthesia Research, A.A.A.S., Soc. Clin. and Exptl. Hypnosis. Author: Hypnosis in Anesthesiology, 1959; also articles in profl. jours. Home: Beverly Hills CA Died May 5, 1970.

MARMION, KEITH ROBERT, educator, civil engr.; b. Farmington, Ia., Aug. 15, 1927; s. Robert Samuel and Clara Verne (Mills) M.; B.S. in Civil Engring., U. Denver, 1951; M.S., U. Colo., 1958; Ph.D., U. Cal. at Berkeley, 1961; m. Lois Jane Schallenberger, July 12, 1947; children—Daniel Keith, Shelly Lynn, Cynthia Jane. Constrn. engr. U.S. Corps Engrs., 1951-52; jr. civil engr. Lockwood, Andrews & Newnam, cons. engrs., Victoria, Tex., 1952-55; mem. faculty Tex. Tech. U., Lubbock, 1955-68, prof. civil engring., head dept., 1962-68. Bd. dirs. Day Care Assn. Lubbock, 1962-66, pres., 1964. Served with USNR, 1945-47. Registered profl. engr., Tex. Mem. Nat., Tex. (dir. S. Plains chpt. 1964) socs. profl. engrs., Am. Soc. C.E., Am. Soc. Engring. Edn., Am. Geophys. Union, A.A.A.S., W. Tex. Mus. Assn., Am. Water Resources Assn., Sigma Xi (pres. elect 1968), Phi Kappa Phi, Lubbock TX Died Mar. 17, 1968; buried Resthaven Cemetery, Lubbock TX

MARMUR, JACLAND, author; b. Sosnowiec, Poland, Feb. 14, 1901; s. Max and Gitlia (Rekhnitz) M.; brought to U.S., 1903, citizen through father's naturalization, 1908; grad. Brooklyn Boys High Sch., 1917; m. Vernita Alyce Pellow, Mar. 28, 1921 (deceased 1956); married second to Caroline Welter, 1960. Left home, 1918, going to San Francisco and then to sea for 2 yrs.; crossed Canada afoot to N.Y. returned to West Coast and followed the sea until 1930, settled in Larkspur, Cal.; author short stories and books, from 1927. Fellow International Inst. of Arts and Letters; member U.S. Naval Institute (associate mem.), Authors League America, P.E.N. Mason. Club: San Francisco Press. Author: Ecola1933; The Golden Medallion, 1934; The Sea and the Shore, 1941; Sea Duty, 1944; Andromeda, 1947; The Edge of Chaos, 1969; original story for motion pictures, The Ship of State, and Return from the Sea. Contbr. fiction nat. and British mags. (included in anthologies) Post Stories of 1937, 1940, 1942-45, 1948-49, 1952-56. Home: Larkspur CA Died May 8, 1970; interred Tamalpais Cemetery, San Rafael CA

MAROT, MARY LOUISE, educator; b. Dayton, O., Oct. 16, 1870; d. Benjamin and Harriet (Sowers) M.; student Wellesley, 1889-91; B.S., U. of Chicago, 1894; post-grad. work, same, 1894-95. Founder, with Malvina Howe, of Miss Howe and Miss Marot's Sch., Dayton, O., 1905; moved school, of which is now owner, to Thompson, Conn., 1913; founder and pres. Marot Junior College. Mem. Nat. Assn. Principals of Schs. for Girls, Phi Beta Kappa (Beta Chapter of Ill.). Club: Quinnatisset Golf (Thompson). Home: Thompson CT‡

MARQUARDT, CARL EUGENE, coll. prof.; b. Higginsville, Mo., Sept. 16, 1884; s. Rev. Carl L. and Louise (Guenther) M.; grad. high sch., St. Joseph, Mich., 1905; B.A., U. of Mich., 1909; M.A., Pennsylvania State Univ., 1912; Ph.D., Univ. of Pa., 1915; Ed.M., Harvard University, 1924; m. Delia Florence Schoenbeck, August 17, 1910; children—Helen Louise (Mrs. L. F. Diehl), Gretchen Irmgard, Carl Eugene (dec.), Delia Florence (Mrs. J. W. MacIndoe), Carroll Quentin. Began as instructor in German, Pennyslvania State Univ., 1909-13, asst. prof. and asso. prof., 1913-19, asso. prof. French, 1919-23, prof. Romance philology from 1923, also coll. examiner, 1920-49, later emeritus; asst. dean of admissions, 1948-49; asst. in German, U. of Pa. (on leave of absence), 1913-15; Austin scholar, Grad. Sch. of Edn., Harvard (leave of absence), 1923-24. Mem. bd. mgrs. Pa. Baptist Convention, 1955-61. Fellow A.A.A.S.; mem. Phi Kappa Phi, Tau Kappa Epsilon, Phi Beta Kappa (1st pres. Lambda chapter of Pa.), Phi Delta Kappa, Phi Sigma Iota (1st pres. Beta chapter), Phi Eta Sigma, Kappa Delta Pi, Kappa Gamma Psi. Republican. Baptist. Club: University (hon. life State College). Author of An Entente Cordiale in Civil War Days" (published in Essays in Honor of A. Howry Espenshade, 1937). Home: State College PA Died May 10, 1968; buried Centre County Meml. Park.

MARQUIS, DONALD GEORGE, psychologist, educator; b. Two Harbors, Minn., June 22, 1908; s. William James and Lillian (Holliday) M.; A.B., Stanford 1928; Ph.D., Yale, 1932; m. Peggy L. Cook, Feb. 7, 1959; children by former marriage—Kent Hammond, William James. NRC fellow Yale Sch. Medicine, 1932-33; instr. psychology Yale, 1933-35, asso. prof. psychology, 1938-45, chmn. dept. psychology, dir. psychol. lab., 1941-45; Rockefeller fellow neurology Oxford U. and London U., 1935-36; prof. psychology, chmn. dept. U. Mich., 1945-57; with Social Sci. Research Council, 1957-59; prof. Sloan Sch. Mgmt., Mass. Inst. Tech., 1959-73. Dir. NRC Office of Psychol. Personnel, 1943-45, exec. sec., Armed Forces-NRC vision com., 1944-51; chmn. com. on human resources Research and Devel. Bd., U.S. Dept. Def., 1947-50; pres. Am. Bd. Examiners Profl. Psychology, 1953-57; mem. U.S. Nat. Commn. for UNESCO, 1955-60, 67-70; mem. Nat. Adv. Mental Health Council, 1956-60. Trustee Antioch Coll., 1952-56. Mem. Am. Acad. Arts and Sci. (council 1966-71), Am. Psychol. Assn. (pres. 1947), Soc. Exptl. Psychologists, New Eng. Psychol. Assn. (pres. 1970), Phi Beta Kappa, Sigma Xi. Author: (with E.R. Hilgard) Conditioning and Learning, 1940; (with R.S. Woodworth) Psychology, 1947; (with W.H. Gruber) Factors In the Transfer of Technology, 1969;

(with S. Myers) Successful Industrial Innovations, 1969. Research on mgmt. of sci. and tech., group decision making, social psychology of orgns. Address: Cambridge MA Died Feb. 17, 1973.

MARSH, BENJAMIN CLARKE, b. Eski Zaghra, Bulgaria, Mar. 22, 1877; s. George D. and Ursula (Clarke) M.; B.A., Ia. (now Grinnell Coll.), 1898; post-grad. U. of Chicago, 1899-1900; U. of Pa., 1902-05; m. Eleanor B. Taylor, 1916; children—Michael, Ursula. Special agt. Phila. Soc. for Organizing Charity, 1902-03; sec. Pa. Soc. to Protect Children from Cruelty, 1903-07; exec. sec. Com. on Congestion of Population in New York, 1907-18; sec. N.Y. City Commn. on Congestion of Population and N.Y. State Commn. on Distribution of Population, 1910-11; correspondent First Balkan War, 1912-13; managing director Farmers' Nat. Council, and exec. sec. People's Reconstruction League, 1918-25; sec. The People's Lobby; editor People's Lobby Bulletin. Mem. Phi Beta Kappa. Author: An Introduction to City Planning (with G.B. Ford), 1909; Taxation of Land Values in American Cities. Office: 810 F St. N.W., Washington 4 DC‡

MARSH, RAYMOND E(UGENE), forester, govt. official; b. Westport, N.H., Jan. 27, 1885; s. Walter E. and Jessie H. (Tottingham) M.; B.S., Dartmouth Coll., 1908; M.F., Yale, 1910; m. Lillian M. Sutherland, Sept. Sept. 6, 1913; children—James S., Nancy B. Forest asst., U.S. Forest Service, Ariz. and N.M., 1910-12; dep. forest supervisor, Carson Nat. Forest, N.M., 1912-13, acting supervisor, 1913-14, supervisor, 1914-17; forest supervisor, Coconino Nat. Forest, Ariz., 1917-19; asst. regional forester in charge forest management, S.W. region, Albuquerque, N.M., 1919-26; chief, div. forest economics, also asst. chief, research br., U.S. Forest Service, Washington, 1926-36; asst. chief, U.S. Forest Service, 1936-50. Fellow, Soc. Am. Foresters (former sec.); mem. Orgn. of Professional Employees of Dept. of Agr. (former pres.). Presbyterian. Club: Cosmos (Washington), Contbr. numerous articles to professional jours. and govt. publs. Addressed internat., nat. and local forestry and agr. groups. Home: Washington DC Died June 1971.

MARSH, SUSAN LOUISE COTTON (MRS. EUGENE MARSH), author; b. in Indiana; came to St. Louis, 1890; d. Cullen Columbus and Ann Stonements (Connor) Cotton; grad. high sch.; student Teachers' Training schs., Southern Ind. and Owensboro, Ky., 1889-94; m. Eugene Marsh, of St. Louis, Mo., July 19, 1896; children—Eugenia Louise (Mrs. Howard R. Becker), Wilbur Cotton. Began as a sch. teacher, 1889. Organized Children of Am. Revolution in St. Louis County, 1918; organized St. Louis br., Nat. League Am. Pen Women, 1926, pres., 1926-29; helped organize Snyder Assn. of Universal Culture; an organizer and vice pres. Poet Laureate League of Mo.; graduate of Americanization Class, St. Louis, 1920. Mem. D.A.R. (regent St. Louis County chapter 1915), St. Louis Chapter Daughters of 1812, Colonial Dames of 17th Century, Nat. Magna Charta Dames, St. Louis Tercentenary Shakespeare Soc., The 100 Civic Committee, Woman's Section of Navy League, Paris Art and Lit. Soc. for Goodwill Poems; former vice pres. London Poetical Soc.; etc. First poet laureate of Mo., 1933. Republican. Presbyterian. Club: Shakespeare Drama (president 1920-21). Author: Missouri Centennial, 1928; Young Abe Lincoln, 1929; Missouri Anthology, 1932; American Gallery, 1938; also extensive contbr. of verse. Was author of the Missouri Joint Guardianship Law, 1914. Lecturer. Home: St Louis MO‡

MARSHALL, ALBERT WARE, naval officer; b. Greenville, Tex., Apr. 6, 1874; s. Andrew Soule and Mary Jane (Martin) M.; grad. U.S. Naval Acad., Annapolis, 1896, Naval War Coll., Newport, R.I., 1920; designated naval aviator, Naval Air Sta., Pensacola, Fla., 1926; m. Mabel Flinn, Nov. 14, 1899; 1 son, Ware. Commd. asst. engr., U.S. Navy, 1898; advanced through grades to comdr., 1915, capt., 1920, rear admiral, June 1928. Comd. U.S.S. Baltimore, World War, engaged in mine planting operations off north coast of Ireland, later in North Sea Mine Barrage; comdr. of destroyer squadron, chief of staff to comdr. destroyer squadrons, 1921-22; comdr. aircraft squadrons, Battle Fleet, 1922; in Office of Naval Operations, 1924-27; comdg. U.S.S. Lexington (aircraft carrier), 1927-28; comdr. aircraft squadrons, Scouting Fleet, Sept. 1928-May 1929; comdr. Naval Air Sta., Pensacola, May 1929-July 1931; comdr. Train Squadron 1, Fleet Base Force, 1931-33; sr. mem. Pacific Coast Sect., Bd. of Inspection and Survey, 1933-35; comdr. 15th Naval Dist., Canal Zone, 1935-37; Navy Dept., 1937-38; retired 1938. Mem. Royal Arcanum. Clubs: Army and Navy, Army and Navy Country (Washington); Chevy Chase (Md.); New York Yacht; Army and Navy (Manila, P.I.). Address: Box 342, Pasadena CA*‡

MARSHALL, CLARA, physician; b. West Chester, Pa.; d. Pennock and Mary (Phillips) M.; M.D., Woman's Med. Coll., Pa., 1875. Demonstrator pharmacy, 1875-6, instr. materia medica, 1876, prof. materia medica and gen. therapeutics, 1877-1906, dean since 1888, Woman's Med. Coll.; obstetrician, Phila. Hosp., 1882; attending phys., girls; dept. Phila. House of Refuge, 1886; lecturer, nurses' training sch., Jefferson Med. Coll., 1893. Author: History of The Woman's Medical College of Pennsylvania; also various med. papers. Address: 258 S. 16th St., Philadelphia PA‡

MARSHALL, ELDER WATSON, lawyer; b. Dayton, Pa., Sept. 28, 1883; s. Curtis S. and Tirzah (Elder) M.; B.S., Washington and Jefferson Coll., 1904, LL.D., 1934; LL.B., U. Pitts., 1907, LL.M., 1918; m. Bessie Irvine, Apr. 29, 1909; children—Janice (Mrs. August H. Frye), Betty (Mrs. Gardner A. Mundy), Joseph I., Houston B. Admitted to Pa. bar, 1907, since practiced in Pitts.; judge Ct. Common Pleas, Allegheny County, Pa., 1928-38; from instr. to prof. law U. Pitts., 1904-42; mem. firm Reed, Smith, Shaw & McClay, 1938-68. Pres. Peoples Bank of Unity, Plum, Pa., 1948-68, also dir. Coordinator SSS appeals bd., Allegheny County, 1942-50. Candidate for Pa. Supreme Ct., 1935; del. Republican Nat. Conv., 1948. Pres., life trustee Washington and Jefferson Coll.; corporator Homewood Cemetery, Pitts. Served to capt. U.S. Army, 1918-19. Mem. Am., Pa., Allegheny County (pres. 1951) bar assns., Scotch-Irish Society of the United States of Am. (past pres.), Am. Legion (past post comdr.), Phi Beta Kappa, Alpha Tau Omega, Delta Theta Phi. Presbyn. Clubs: Amen Corner (past pres.), Duquesne, University (Pitts.). Author: Notes on Real Estate in Western Pennsylvania, 1935. Home: Pittsburgh PA Died Jan. 19, 1968; buried Homewood Cemetery, Pittsburgh PA

MARSHALL, ELTON LEWIS, laywer; b. Avalon, Livingston County, Mo., July 29, 1887; s. Andrew and Maggie (Vaughan) M.; Pd.B., Kirksville (Mo.) State Teachers Coll., 1908; A.B., LL.B., U. of Mo., 1912; m. Mabel C. Spain, Oct. 28, 1915; children—Mary Jo, Robert Andrew. Began practice at Chillicothe, Mo., 1912; pros. atty., Livingston County, Mo., 1913-17; spl. asst. atty. gen. of Mo., 1928-29; solicitor (head of legal dept.) U.S. Dept. Agr., 1929-1933; partner Watson, Ess, Marshall & Enggas, Kansas City, Mo.; member board of trustees City Trusts. Del. to Rep. Nat. Conv., 1916. Member American, Mo. State and Kansas City bar assns., Delta Sigma Rho, Phi Alpha Delta, Beta Theta Pi. Presbyterian. Mason, Odd Fellow. Clubs: University, Kansas City, River. Home: Kansas City MO Died Jan. 20, 1970; buried Forest Hills Cemetery.

MARSHALL, HERBERT CAMP, economist, lawyer; b. Zanesville, O., Mar. 8, 1871; s. John Wesley and Rachel Ann (Tanner) M.; A.B., Ohio Wesleyan U., 1891; A.B., Harvard, 1894, A.M., 1895, Ph.D., 1901, LL.B., 1902; m. Mary Emma Griffith, Dec. 20, 1922 (sec. and editor quarterly of Alpha Chi Omega; she died July 25, 1925); 1 dau., Eleanor Griffith. Asst. in economics, Harvard, 1895-96; Henry Lee fellow in economics, same, 1897-98; practiced law, N.Y. City, 1902-16; abroad in Japan, China and Europe, 1906-07; connected with U.S. Dept. Agr. since Nov. 1916. Mem. Assn. Bar City of New York; Am. Econ. Assn., Am. Farm Econ. Assn., Phi Beta Kappa, Delta Tau Delta. Club: Harvard (New York), Cosmos (Washington, D.C.). Author of publications and occasional addresses on prices and marketing and consumption of farm products. Address: 5023 Reno Rd. N.W., Washington DC‡

MARSHALL, HOWARD DRAKE, educator; b. Poughkeepsie, N.Y., Apr. 9, 1924; s. Smith J. and Florence (Drake) M.; A.B., Columbia, 1947, A.M., 1949, Ph.D., 1954; m. Natalie B. Junemann, Aug. 7, 1954; children—Frederick S., Alison B. Mem. faculty Vassar Coll., 1949-72, prof. econs., 1966-72, chmn. dept., 1968-72. Vis. asst. prof. Wesleyan U., Middleton, Conn., 1955-56; tchr. Am. Inst. Banking, IBM Corp., Cornell U. extension; chmn. Hudson Valley Council Econ. Edn., 1965—. Bd. dirs. N.Y. Council on Econ. Edn. Served with AUS, 1943-46. Mem. Am. Econ. Assn., Indsl. Relations Research Assn., Nat. Tax Assn., Am. Assn. U. Profs. Author: The Mobility of College Faculties, 1964; The Great Economists, 1967; Business and Government: The Problem of Power, 1970; Collective Bargaining, 1971. Editor: The History of Economic Thought—A Book of Readings, 1968. Home: NY Died Aug. 15, 1972; buried Pleasant Valley NY

MARSHALL, LENORE G. (MRS. JAMES MARSHALL), author: b. N.Y.C., Sept. 7, 1899; d. Henry A. and Leonie (Kleinert) Guinzburg; A.B., Barnard Coll., 1919; m. James Marshall, Aug. 20, 1919; children—Ellen (Mrs. Roger Scholle), Jonathan. Lit. editor Cape and Smith, 1929-32. Mem. exec. bd. Post War World Council, 1943; co-founder, bd. dirs. Nat. Com. for Sane Nuclear Policy, 1957; co-chmn. program policy com.; exec. bd. P.E.N. Am. Center; founder, co-chmn. Com. for Nuclear Responsibility, 1971; corporate mem. MacDowell Colony. Mem. Women's Internat. League for Peace and Freedom, Authors League, Poetry Soc. Am., Pen and Brush Club, P.E.N. (dir.). Mem. Soc. of Friends. Author: Only the Fear, 1935; Hall of Mirrors, 1937; No Boundary, 1943; Other Knowledge, 1957; The Hill is Level, 1959; Latest Will, 1969; also short stories, poems in various mags., anthologies. Co-author: War, Peace and Disarmament, 1966. Author and reader Spoken Arts record: The Poems of Lenore G. Marshall. Home: New York City NY ALSO New Hope PA Died Sept. 23, 1971; buried Salem Fields Cemetery, Queens NY

MARSHALL, ROY E(DGAR), assn. exec.; b. Arlington, Neb., Feb. 28, 1890; s. Robert C. and Mary (Sharp) M.; B.S., U. Neb., 1913; M.S., Ore. State Coll., 1915; Ph.D., U. Minn., 1931; m. Irene Telford, June 15, 1917; children—Robert T. (dec.), Kenneth. Instr. U. Neb., 1913, Ore. State Coll., 1915-16; extension horticulturist Va. Poly. Inst., 1916-20; asso. prof. horticulture Mich. State U., 1920-34, prof., 1934-50, emeritus prof., 1958-66, asst. dir. Mich. Agr. Expt. Sta., 1950-58; asst. editor Am. Fruit Grower mag., Chgo., 1920; editor Fruits and Gardens mag., Grand Rapids, Mich., 1924-30; exchange asso. prof. horticulture U. Minn., 1928-29; acting head dept. horticulture Wash. State Coll., 1935-36; sec.-treas., mgr. Am. Soc. Hort. Sci., from 1957. Distinguished Achievement award U. Minn., 1962. Mem. A.A.A.S., American Society Hort. Sci. (1st recipient of Appreciation award 1964), Am. Inst. Biol. Scis., Inst. Food Tech., Mich. Assn. Nurserymen (hon.), Sigma Xi, Phi Kappa Phi, Alpha Zeta, Phi Tau Sigma, Farmhouse Frat. Episcopalian. Mason. Author: Cherries and Cherry Products. Home: East Lansing MI Died Aug. 16, 1966.

MARSHALL, THOMAS ALFRED, JR., mech. engr., assn. exec.; b. Savannah, Ga., Jan. 14, 1911; s. Thomas Alfred and Winefred Turner (Miller) M.; B.S. in Aero. Engring., Ga. Inst. Tech., 1932; m. Mary Lucile Bush, May 27, 1933; children—Thomas Alfred III, Susan Marie, Kathryn Penelope (Mrs. T.M. Staph), John Francis. Stationary engr., air conditioning engr.; office mgmt.; sr. analyst mgmt. engring. Met. Life Ins. Co., N.Y.C., 1932-51; exec. sec. Engring. Manpower Commn., Engrs. Joint Council, 1951-54; sec. Engrs. Joint Council, 1953-54; asst. sec. Am. Soc. M.E., 1954-57, sr. asst. sec., 1958-60, exec. sec. Am. Soc. Testing Materials, Phila., 1960-70. Mgr. Nuclear Congress, 1957-59; U.S. rep. com. on English Mgmt. terminology Comite International de l'Orgn. Sci. Served to comdr. USNR, 1940-45. Fellow A.A.A.S., Am. Soc. M.E.; mem. American Soc. Metals, Engring. Inst. Can, Am. Soc. Engring. Edn., U.S. Naval Inst., Soc. Automotive Engrs., Am. Soc. Testing Materials, Am. Water Works Assn., Standard Engrs. Soc., Instn. Mech. Engrs. (Gt. Britain), Tau Beta Pi, Phi Eta Sigma. Clubs: Army and Navy (Washington); Engineers (Phila.). Author articles on mgmt. indsl. engring. and manpower, standards, also profl. devel. engrs. Home: Radnor PA Died Apr. 9, 1970.

MARSHALL, THOMAS CHALMERS, clergyman; b. Wilkingsburg, Pa., Oct. 20, 1868; s. of James Abrahm and Ellen Boyd (Trimble) M.; A.B., Lafayette Coll., 1888, A.M., 1891; U. of Edinburgh, 1888-89; Western Theol. Sem., Allegheny, Pa., 1889-90; grad. Princeton Theol. Sem., 1892; post-grad. work Columbia (S.C.) Theol. Sem., 1896-97; Ch. Div. Sch. of the Pacific, Calif., 1902-03; m. Margaret Steiger, Sept. 28, 1897; children—Margaret Van Patten, Ellen Trimble, Thomas Riley. Ordained Presbyn. ministry, 1892; pastor Lake Crystal and Amboy (Minn.), Auburndale and Winterhaven (Fla.), Ojai Valley (Calif.); deacon, 1902, priest, 1903, P.E. Ch.; in charge St. Peter's Ch., Redwood City, Calif., 1902-04; founded Neighborhood Settlement, Los Angeles, 1904, Episcopal City Mission Soc., 1908, Commn. on Philanthropy and Social Service, 1910; archdeacon Diocese of Los Angeles, 1911-20; rector St. Paul's Ch., Pomona, Calif., 1915-18, St. Athanasius Ch., Los Angeles, 1918-27; dir. Community Welfare Fedn. (Community Chest), 1925-27. Pres. Los Angeles Alliance of Social Agencies, 1921-24; sec. and chaplain, Hosp. Good Samaritan, since 1912. Los Angeles CA‡

MARSHALL, THOMAS FRANKLIN, college pres.; b. Albion, Ia., Jan. 7, 1871; s. Rev. Hugh W. and Hannah Martha (Bamford) M.; Coll. of Emporia, Kan., 1890-2; A.B., Lake Forest (Ill.) Coll., 1894; McCormick Theol. Sem., 1894-6, Danville Theol. Sem., 1897-8; B.D., Union Theol. Sem., 1908; M.A., Columbia, 1908; U. of Cincinnati, 1908-9. Teachers Coll. (Columbia), 1916-18; Johns Hopkins, 1919-20; Ph.D., in honore, Campbell U., Horton, Kan., 1914; m. Edna E. Heller, of Jerseyville, Ill., Sept. 1, 1906. Ordained Presbyn. ministry, 1898; pastor Ironton, Mo., 1898-1902, Linton, Ind., 1902-4, Jerseyville, Ill., 1904-6; dean of Lindenwood Coll., St. Charles, Mo., 1906-7; president Oswego (Kan.) College, 1909-14; dean of Henry Kendall College, Tulsa, Okla., 1914-15; registrar and head department edn., Beechwood Sch., Jenkintown, Pa., 1915-16; asst. minister, Old First Presbyn. Ch., N.Y. City, 1916-18; head dept. edn., Hood Coll., Frederick, Md., 1918-20; pres. Glendale (O.) Coll., 1920—. Mem. Phi Delta Kappa, N.E.A. Home: Glendale OH‡

MARSHALL, WADE HAMPTON, neurophysiologist; b. Pitts., Dec. 17, 1907; s. Francis James and Ann Amos (Miller) M.; student Wooster Coll., 1924-25, U. Pitts., 1925-27; B.S., Beloit Coll., 1927-30; M.S., U. Chgo., 1931, Ph.D., 1934; m. Louise Hanson, Dec. 31, 1934; children—Thomas Hanson, Alice. Instr. physiology George Washington U. Med. Sch., 1934-36; NRC fellow physiology John Hopkins Med. Sch., 1936-38, instr., then asso. lab. physiol. optics Wilmer Opthal. Inst., 1938-43, sr. physicist Applied Physics Lab., 1946-47; engr. Bowen & Co., Bethesda, Md., 1944-46; spl. research fellow Nat. Inst. Mental

Health, 1947-49, neurophysiologist, 1949-53; chief lab. neurophysiology Nat. Insts. Mental Health and Neurol. Diseases and Blindness, 1954-69; chief lab. neurophysiology Nat. Inst. Mental Health, 1969-70; research on nervous system, sensory orgn. of brain, perception, rhythmic activities of nervous system, Leao phenomenon. Mem. Joint Bd. Sci. Edn. for Greater Washington Area, 1957-59. Mem. Washington Acad. Sci., Washington Philos. Soc., Eastern Soc. Electroencephalographers, Am. Assn. Invol. Mental Hospitalization, Am. Neurol. Assn., Am. Electroencephalographic Soc., Am. Physiol. Soc., Soc. Gen. Physiologists, N.Y. Acad. Sci., Brazilian Acad. Sci. (fgn. mem.), Internat. Fedn. Med. Electronics, Biophys. Soc. Clubs: Cosmos, Potomac Appalachian Trail (Washington). Author, co-author numerous sci. and tech. papers. Home: Kensington MD Died Nov. 14, 1972.

MARSHALL, WALTER P(ETER), business exec.; b. Brooklyn, Nov. 20, 1901; s. Peter Walter and Bertha H. (Fredericks) M.; student Pratt Inst., 1918-19, Columbia, 1919-20, Coll. City of N.Y., 1920-21; m. Alice Barnes, 1930; children—Peter Walter, Nancy Alice. Accountant All America Cables and Radio. Inc., Mexican Telegraph Co., 1921-27; accountant Internat. Telephone and Telegraph Corp., 1928-30; chief accountant, Comml. Cable Co., 1930-38; comptroller Mackay Radio and Telegraph Co., 1933-38; Postal Telegraph System, 1930-43, exec. vice-pres., 1943; asst. to pres. Western Union Telegraph Co., 1943-48, treas. 1945-48, v.p. dir., 1946-48, pres. 1948-64, chmn. 1964-67, now dir., dir. Gold and Stock Telegraph Co., other subsidiaries; exec. com., dir. American Express Company, American Broadcasting-Paramount Theatres, Inc. Asso. trustee North Shore Hosp. Mem. Nat. Indsl. Conf. Bd., Edison Birthplace Assn., Inc. (hon. trustee), Newcomen Soc. in N. Am., Financial Execs. Inst. Nat. Assn. Accountants. Republican Lutheran. Clubs: Economic (N.Y.C.); North Hills Country. Home: Manhasset NY Died May 5, 1969; buried Nassau Knolls, Port Washington NY

MARSHALL, WILLIAM LEGRAMD, retail co. exec.; b. Danby, N.Y., July 1 1907; s. William and Bernice Elizabeth (Hubert) M.; Marion Rudolph, June 1, 1936; children—John Thomas, Robert Alan, William Wright. With J.C. Penny Co., from 1927. store mgr., Patchogue, N.Y., 1933-34, Meriden, Conn., 1935-36, Ithaca, N.Y., 1937-39, dist. mgr. St. Louis, 1940-49, West Coast regional mgr., 1949-60, v.p., mem. bd. dirs., 1960-67, also director of stores; dir. J.C. Penny Ins. Co. Chmn Tompkins County United Fund, 1968. Mem. Cal. Retail Assn. (dir. 1954-60), Cal. Chain Store Assn. (v.p. 1950-53), Newcomen Soc. Protestant Episcopalian. Mason (32 deg.), Elk, Kiwanian (past pres. Meriden, Comm.). Clubs: N.Y. Athletic; N.Y. Sales Executive; Travers Island Yaught. Home: Ithaca NY Deceased; buried Maplewood Point, Cayuga Lake NY

MARTENS, WALTER FREDERIC, architect; b. Danville, Ill., Mar. 15, 1890; s. Rev. Ernest and Margarete (Wunder) M., student pvt. and pub. schs., Danville; pvt. study architecture, lang. and music; m. Grayce D. Van Allen, Oct. 24, 1916; 1 son, Robert Erle. Partner Stuche &Co., architects, Danville, 1917-21; pvt. practice architecture, Charleston, W.Va., 1921-40; partner Martens & Son, Charleston, architects, 1940-58, Martens Associated, architects and engrs., 1958-69; designed W.Va. gov.'s mansion, 1927, Davis Elkins (W.Va.) Coll., United Carbon Office Bldg., 1940, sci. hall, mens dorm. W.Va. Inst. Tech., 1952-53, Library-auditorium, girls dorm. Alderson-Broaddus Coll., 1957-58; asso. architect Orchard Manor Housing project, 500 units, Charleston 1952, Charleston Civic Center, 1954, group hdqrs. Columbia Gas System, 1954. Past mem. exec. com. Charleston Symphony Orchestra and Charleston Choral Soc.; pres. Creative Arts Festival of W.Va., 1955-56. Trustee Alderson-Broaddus Coll. President W.Va. Bd. Architects, from 1940. Fellow A.I.A. (pres. W.Va. chpt. 1944-45), Nat. Council Archtl. Registration Bds. (pres. 1958-59); mem. Am. Guild Organists (Kanawha chpt.). Baptist, Mason (Shriner). Club: Executives. Home: Charleston WV Died 1969.

MARTI-IBANEZ, FELIX, physician, editor; b. Cartagena, Spain; M.D., U. Madrid. Apptd. gen. dir. pub. health and social service, Catalonia, 1937, later undersec. pub. health and social service Spain; dir. wartime health edn., Catalonia, 1937-38; with med. dept. Hoffmann-LaRoche Internat. Co., 1941; med. dir. Winthrop Products, Inc., N.Y.C., 1942-46; med. dir. E. R. Squibb & Sons, Internat. and Inter-Am. Cos., N.Y.C. 1946-50; founder MD Publs., Inc., 1950; formerly prof., dir. dept. history of medicine N.Y. Med. Coll.-Flower Fifth Av. Hosps., N.Y.C. Served as maj. M.C., Spanish Air Force. Recipient Order of Carlos J. Finley, Nat. Acad. Scis. Cuba, 1955. Mem. Turkish Soc. for History of Medicine (hon.), Fgn. Press Assn., Overseas Press Club. Author: Centaur: Essays on the History of Medical Ideas, 1958; Men, Molds, and History, 1958; A Prelude to Medical History, 1961; Ariel: Essays on the Arts and The History and Philosophy of Medicine, 1962; All the Wonders We Seek: Thirteen Tales of Surprise and Prodigy, 1963; The Crystal Arrow: Essays on Literature, Travel, Art, Love and The History of

Medicine, 1964; Journey Around Myself, 1964; Waltz and Other Stories, 1965; The Ship in the Bottle, 1968. Editor: Medical Writing, 1955; Health and Travel, 1956; Medicine and Writing, 1956; History of American Medicine, 1958; The Pageant of Medicine, 1960; Henry E. Sigerist on the History of Medicine, 1960; The Epic of Medicine, 1962; Tales of Philosophy, 1967; The Patient's Progress, 1967. Contbr. articles and short stories to popular mags. Home: New York City NY Died June 24, 1972.

MARTIN, CARL NEIDHARD, banker; b. Phila., Pa., Dec. 4, 1874; s. Robert Thomas and Bertha (Neidhard) M.; A.B., Central High Sch., Phila., 1894; Ph.B., U. of Pa., 1896; m. Aline Skillman Taylor, Dec. 5, 1900; children—Carl Neidhard, Evelyn (wife of Edward Jack Wilbraham, M.C., British Army), Hollinshead Taylor, Roberta, Oliver. Clerk with Peter Wright & Sons, shipping, Phila., 1896, Pa. R.R. Co., 1897, Ervin & Co. brokers, 1899; in partnership with father, R.T. Martin & Co., brokers, 1900-12; organizer Martin & Co., investment bankers, 1913, pres. since 1927 of Martin & Co., Inc.; sec. and treas. Trenton, Bristol & Phila. Street Ry. Co., 1909-15, pres. 1915-35; sec. and treas. Salem & Pennsgrove Traction Co., 1916-21, pres., 1921-33; pres. Pa.-N.J. Ry. Co., 1924-35; v.p. Pa. Joint Stock Land Bank, 1928-35; dir. Better Bus. Bur., 1926-33; mem. governing com. Phila. Stock Exchange, 1920-32; mem. exec. com. Eastern Group, Investment Bankers Assn., 1931. Served as pvt. Light Battery, Pa. Vols., Spanish-Am. War; chmn. citizens com., 3d Federal Res. Dist., Liberty Loan campaign, and mem. Selective Draft Bd., World War I. Dir. Phila. Charity Ball Assn. (pres. 1927-32). Mem. Hist. Soc. of Pa., Phila. Soc. for Promoting of Agriculture (founded 1785), Zeta Psi. Republican. Episcopalian, vestryman, Ch. of the Holy Trinity, Philadelphia, since 1912. Clubs: Bond (president 1929), Mask and Wig (pres. 1921-22); Rittenhouse. Home: P.O. Box 577, Paoli, Pa. Office: Packard Bldg., Philadelphia 2 PA‡

MARTIN, CRAWFORD COLLINS, state ofcl.; b. Hillsboro, Tex., Mar. 13, 1916; s. William Marvin and Daisy (Beavers) M.; student U. Tex. Law Sch., 1936-38; LL.B., Cumberland U., 1939; m. Margaret Ann Mash, May 14, 1941; children—Sherry, James, Nancy. Admitted to Tex. bar, 1939; practiced in Hillsboro 1939-63; mem. firm Martin & Martin, 1946-63; sec. state of Tex., Austin, 1962-66, atty. gen. Tex., 1967-72. Chmn. bd. Hillsboro State Bank, 1958-72. Mayor, Hillsboro, 1946-47; mem. Tex. Senate, 1948-63. Served with USCGR, 1942-45. Mem. State Bar Tex. Democrat. Mason. K.P., Lion. Home: Austin TX Died Dec. 29, 1972.

MARTIN, DANIEL J., tool company exec.; b. Lowell, Mass., Sept. 30, 1902; s. David Patrick and Julia Gertrude (Halloran) M.; B.S., U.S. Naval Acad., 1924; Met.E., Stanford, 1931; Sc.D., Harvard, 1934; m. Gertrude Donald, Nov. 27, 1924; children—Joanne (Mrs. James Early), Julia (Mrs. Sam A. Luce). Vice president in charge of engineering Hughes Tool Company, Houston, 1948-62, v.p. research, from 1962, also dir.; dir. Hughes Gun Co., Hughes Tool Co., Ltd. Mem. bd. dirs. Cath. Family and Children Services, Galveston-Houston Diocese; trustee St. Anthony Geriatrics Center. Mem. Senate St. Thomas U. Served with Ord. Dept., USA, 1924-46; ret. as col. Decorated Legion of Merit, Army Commendation ribbon with oak leaf cluster, Def. Service medal; Star of Abdon Calderon (Republic of Ecuador); Cross of Eloy Alfaro Internat. Found. (Republic of Panama); Knight Comdr. with Star, Equestrian Order of Holy Sepulchre of Jerusalem. Mem. Am. Assn. for Advancement of Sci., Am. Ordnance Assn. (bd. dirs.), Am. Inst. Mining and Metall. Engrs., Sigma Xi. Clubs: Houston, Houston Country (Houston). Home: Houston TX Died July 27, 1970.

MARTIN, EARLE D., pub. accountant; b. Stoneham, Mass., Apr. 2, 1890; s. Edwin G. and Mabel H. (Davis) M.; student Northeastern U.; grad. Bentley Coll., 1922; m. Myrtle I. Irwin, Oct. 12, 1922. With Hartshorn and Walter, pub. accountants, Boston, from 1920, partner, 1936-61; pres., dir. Babson's Reports, Inc., 1947-63, treas., dir., 1963-64, controller, dir., from 1964. Mem. Nat. Assn. Accountants, Mass. Soc. C.P.A.'s. Mason, Odd Fellow. Home: Gloucester MA also Lake Wales FL Died Oct. 19, 1969; buried Puritan Lawn Meml. Park, Peabody MA

MARTIN, FLORENCE ARMINTA DELONG (MINTA MARTIN), b. Clark County, Ia., Jan. 11, 1864; d. Andrew Jackson and Alta Myra (Bozarth) DeLong; grad. Afton (Ia.) High Sch., 1881; m. Clarence Y. Martin, Nov. 9, 1882 (died June 1, 1935); 1 son, Glenn Luther. School teacher, Afton, Ia., 1881-82. Actively interested in aviation; adviser and helper to her son, Glenn L. Martin, pres. The Glenn L. Martin Co., airplane mfrs.; one of first women to fly on May 20, 1912; flew with son on flight high over Newport Bay in California, and on Nov. 28, 1913 made flight from Santa Ana to Long Beach, Calif.; flew with son on China Clipper on his 25th anniversary flight from Newport Beach, Calif., to Avalon, Catalina Island, May 10, 1937; travels extensively. Republican. Presbyterian. Home: 3703 Greenway, Baltimore MD‡

MARTIN, GEORGE CURTIS, geologist; b. Cheshire, Mass., July 18, 1875; s. William P. and Fannie M. (Hare) M.; B.S., Cornell U., 1898; Ph.D., Johns Hopkins, 1901; m. Estella A. Wood, of Adams, Mass., Nov. 12, 1903; children—William E., Robert T. (dec.), Louise. Field asst. U.S. Geol. Survey, 1892; asst. Phila. Acad. Natural Sciences, 1897; asst. geologist, Md. Geol. Survey, 1898-1901; instr. geology, Johns Hopkins, 1901-04; geologist Md. Geol. Survey, 1901-04; spl. asst., 1903-04, asst. geologist, 1904-06, paleontologist, 1906-09, geologist, 1909-24, and acting geologist in charge div. of Alaskan mineral resources, 1917-19, and at other times, U.S. Geological Survey. Engaged in investigation of tertiary paleontology of Atlantic Coast, 1897-1901; studied geology of coal fields of Md., Pa., W.Va. and Colo., 1900-08; govt. investigations of Alaskan coal and oil fields and of mesozoic and tertiary stratigraphy of Alaska, 1903-24; in pvt. practice as cons. oil geologist in U.S. and Mexico since 1924. In charge of Nat. Geog. Society's expdn. to Mt. Katmai (Alaska) volcanic Dist., 1912.*‡

MARTIN, GERTRUDE SHORB, educator; b. Decatur, Ill., Oct. 21, 1869; d. William H. and Mary Magdalene (Zorger) Shorb; Ph.B., U. of Mich., 1894; Ph.D., Cornell, 1900; m. Prof. Clarence Augustine Martin, of Cornell U., June 30, 1896; children—Gerturde (Mrs. George G. Neidich), Clarence Augustine. Teacher pub. sch., 1894-96; adviser of women, Cornell U., 1909-16; exec. sec. Assn. Collegiate Alumnae (now Am. Assn. Univ. Women), 1916-22, editor jour. of same; exec. sec. Women's Foundation for Health. Lecturer on ednl. topics. Trustee Keuka Coll. Mem. Bd. of Edn., Ithaca, 1913-21. Mem. League of Women Voters, etc. Baptist. Clubs: University, Ithaca Woman's. Home: 522 Thurston Av., Ithaca NY‡

MARTIN, HAROLD MONTGOMERY, naval officer; b. Bay Mills, Mich., Jan. 18, 1896; s. David A. and Jeanne (Montgomery) M.; student U. of Ill., 1913-14; B.S., U.S. Naval Acad., 1918; m. Elizabeth Risque Bronson, Sept. 26, 1922; 1 son, David Bronson. Commd. ensign, U.S. Navy, 1918, and advanced through the grades to vice adm., 1951; served in U.S.S. Winslow, 1918-19, U.S.S. Nevada, 1919-21; naval aviator, U.S.S. Langley and U.S.S. Saratoga, 1921-38; force aviator, Scouting Force, 1938-40; serving at Naval Air Base, Kaneohe, Oahu, T.H., 1941; comdt. Naval Air Base, Midway, 1942-43; comdg. officer U.S.S. San Jacinto, 1943-44; chief of staff, comdr. air force, Atlantic Fleet, 1944-45; chief naval Air Tech. Training, Memphis, Tenn; comdr. 1st and 7th Fleets; comdr. Air Force Pacific Fleet; ret., 1956. Decorated D.S.M., Gold Star, Bronze Star, Silver Star, Legion of Merit and star, Presidential citation, Unit Citation. Club: Racquet (Phila.). Address: Memphis TN Died Dec. 3, 1972.

MARTIN, HUGH, architect; b. Paducah, Ky., May 11, 1874; s. John and Frances (Dallam) M.; student U. of Tex., 1890-91; B.S. in Arch., Cornell U., 1894; m. Ellie Gordon Robinson, Nov. 11, 1913; children—Hugh, Gordon Dallam, Ellen Lenoir. Mem. firm Miller & Martin, architects, Birmingham, Ala., 1900-35, Miller, Martin & Lewis, architects and engrs., 1935-52; with Hugh Martin, architect, since 1952. Works include: Birmingham Central Library, Birmingham Trust National Bank, 8 buildings for Birmingham Southern College, 40 bldgs. for U. of Alabama, Central City Housing project for 916 families at Birmingham. Served as capt. Air Service, U.S. Army, 1917-18, in France and England, 1918. Fellow A.I.A.; member Alabama Society of Architects; Alpha Tau Omega (past pres.). Democrat. Presbyterian. Clubs: Birmingham Rotary (dir.); Birmingham Country. Address: 1919 S. 15th Av., Birmingham AL‡

MARTIN, LAWRENCE CRAWFORD, newspaperman; b. Pittsburgh, Pa., Nov. 21, 1887; s. Thomas and Kate Moore (Torrance) M.; ed. pub. schs. of Pittsburgh; m. Bertha Schriber, Feb. 13, 1900; children—Richard L., Donald F. Mem. staff Chronicle Telegraph, Pittsburgh, 1905, Cleveland News, Cleveland Plain Dealer, Cleveland Press, 1909-14; editor Akron (O.) Press, 1914-17; with United Press, Washington, D.C., and Washington staff of New York Times, 1917-24; news editor Denver Post, 1924-38, mng. editor 1938-47; asso. editor, 1947-63. Republican. Episcopalian. Home: Denver CO Died Aug. 26, 1970.

MARTIN, LEROY ALBERT, chancellor; b. Morristown, Tenn. Jan. 15, 1901; s. Burton McMahan and Julia (Haggard) M.; student Tenn. Wesleyan Coll., 1921, LL.D., 1959; A.B., U. Chattanooga, 1924, D.D., 1946; S.T.B., Boston U., 1928; A.M., Drew U., 1931; m. Ruth Duckwall, Aug. 10, 1927; children—Julia Carolyn (Mrs. Clifford A. Betts, Junior), Elizabeth Blackburn (Mrs. Archibald Calder Willingham, III). Instructor of the Baylor School, Chattanooga, 1924-25; ordained to ministry the Methodist Church, 1927; minister, Bristol, Tenn., 1928-30. Paterson, N.J., 1932-36. Hackettstown, N.J., 1936-37, Madison, N.J., 1937-45; supt. Western Dist., Meth. Conf., Newark, 1945-50; lectr., practical theol., Drew Theol. Sem., 1948-49; pres. Tenn. Wesleyan Coll., Athens, 1950-59; president University of Chattanooga, 1959-66, chancellor, 1966-72, prof. classics, 1968-72. Exec. com. Chattanooga-Hamilton

County chpt. A.R.C. Dir. Community Found. of Greater Chattanooga. Elected Athens Man of Year, 1955; recipient outstanding civilian service medal Department of Army. Mem. Chattanooga Chamber of Commerce, Newcomen Society, also member of Pi Gamma Mu, Alpha Soc. (U. Chattanooga), Sigma Chi, Blue Key. Clubs: Monday (past pres., N.Y.C.); Rotary (pres. 1968-69), Fairyland, Mountain City. Author: A History of Tennessee Wesleyan College, 1857-1957. Home: Lookout Mountain TN Died Aug. 12, 1972.

MARTIN, PATRICK MINOR, congressman; b. Norfolk, Neb., Nov. 25, 1924; s. Spencer and Augusta (Kesting) M.; B.A., U. Cal. at Berkeley, 1949; LL.B., Hastings Coll. Law, San Francisco, 1953; m. Patricia I. Hamblin, July 17, 1948; children—Lisa, Amy, Tom, Helen, Kurt. Admitted to Cal. bar, 1954; practice in Riverside, 1954-62; mem. 88th Congress 38th Dist. Cal. Served with USCGR, 1943-45. Republican. Home: Riverside CA Died July 18, 1968; buried Arlington Nat. Cemetery, Arlington VA

MARTIN, RALPH ANDREW, oil exec.; b. Cleveland, Apr. 8, 1907; s. Charles Arthur and Anna (Lehman) M.; student Western Res. U., La Salle Extension U.; C.P.A., State of Ohio, 1941; m. Lila Belle Curtis, Nov. 20, 1930; children—Kathryn Anne, Marilyn Edythe. Controller, Standard Oil Company of Ohio, 1949-61, v.p., controller, also subsidiaries, 1961-67, vice president for accounting, since 1967—; v.p., dir. Prospect Internat., C.A. Mem. Am. Petroleum Inst. (past chmn. financial and accounting com), Financial Execs. Inst. (fed. taxation com.), Ohio Soc. C.P.A.s., Am. Inst. C.P.A.'s. Home: Lakewood OH Died Aug. 28, 1967.

MARTIN, RENWICK HARPER, educator, lecturer; b. Sugartree, O., Sept. 14, 1872; s. John and Mary Hannah (McWilliams) M.; A.B., Geneva Coll., Beaver Falls, Pa., 1895; grad. Ref. Presbyn. Theol. Sem., Pittsburgh, 1899; studied Columbia; D.D., Westminster, 1917; m. Alice Anna Garrett, May 14, 1912; children—Renwick Garrett, Robert Donald (dec.), Mary Alice. Ordained ministry Ref. Presbyn. Ch., 1899; pastor College Hill Ch., Beaver Falls, 1899-1916; sec. trustees Geneva Coll., 1907-16; pres. Geneva Coll., 1916-20 (resigned); lecturer for Nat. Reform Assn., 1920-24 (resigned); dir. Sabbath Observance of Presbyn. Ch., 1924-28 (resigned); pres. Nat. Reform Assn. since 1928; moderator of Synod, Ref. Presbyn. Ch. of N.A., 1932-33; pres. Nat. Temperance and Prohibition Council, 1938. Author: The Day (a manual on the Christian Sabbath), 1933; Six Studies on the Day, 1935. Editor of The Christian Statesman. Home: 2 Craig Court, Pittsburgh 34. Office: 209 9th St., Pittsburgh 22‡

MARTIN, ROSCOE COLEMAN, univ. prof.; b. Silsbee, Tex., Nov. 18, 1903; s. Benjamin Wiley and Clara Lee (Mayo) M.; A.B., U. of Tex., 1924, A.M., 1925; Ph.D., U. of Chicago, 1932; m. Mildred Ellis, Sept. 2, 1926; 1 son, Roscoe Coleman. Successively instr., adjunct prof., asso. prof. and prof. of govt., U. of Tex., 1926-37; dir. Bureau Municipal Research, U. of Tex., 1933-37; chief research technician, Nat. Resources Com., 1936; prof. polit. science, U. of Ala., 1937-49; dir. Bur. Pub. Adminstrn., U. of Ala., 1938-49; prof. polit. sci. Syracuse U., from 1949, chmn. dept., 1949-56, Maxwell prof., 1966-72; Haynes Found. lectr. Claremont Grad. Sch., 1958; vis. prof. polit. sci. U. Cal., Berkeley, Cal., 1966-67. Mem. U.S. Nat. Commn. UNESCO, 1948-54, del. 6th gen. conf., Paris, 1951; mem. UN Pub. Adminstrn. Mission to Brazil, 1951-52; Am. specialist abroad U.S. State Dept., 1963-64; cons. numerous govt. orgns. Mem. Am. Polit. Sci. Assn. (mem. exec. council 1937-39, v.p. 1948), Am. Soc. Pub. Adminstrn. (mem. council, 1941-44, v.p., 1944-45, pres. 1949-50), Nat. Civil Service League (member council 1945-60), Nat. Municipal League (member council 1950-53, 54-57), So. (pres. 1941-43), N.Y. (pres. 1950-51) polit. sci. assns., Phi Beta Kappa. Author: People's Party in Texas, 1933; A Budget Manual for Texas Cities, 1934; The Defendant and Criminal Justice, 1934; Urban Local Government in Texas, 1936; The Growth of State Administration in Alabama, 1942; From Forest to Front Page, 1956; TVA; The First Twenty Years, 1956; Grass Roots, 1957; Water for New York, 1960; River Basin Administration and the Delaware (with others), 1960; (with others) Decisions in Syracuse, 1961; Government and the Suburban School, 1962; Metropolis in Transition, 1963; The Cities and the Federal System, 1965; Editor: Public Administration and Democracy, 1965. Mem. board editors American Political Sci. Review, 1941; book review editor, Jour. Politics, 1939-41, mem. adv. Editorial Bd., 1945-53. Address: Syracuse NY Died May 12, 1972.

MARTIN, THOMAS ELLSWORTH, ex-U.S. senator; b. Melrose, Ia., Jan. 18, 1893; s. David J. and Sara A. (Brandon) M.; A.B., State U. of Ia., 1916, J.D., 1927; LL.M., Columbia, 1928; LL.D., Parsons College, Fairfield, Iowa, 1957; m. Dorris Jeanette Brownlee, June 5, 1920;children—Richard Coupland, Dorris Brownlee Reiser. Sales analyst, accountant, Goodyear Tire & Rubber Co., Akron, O. and Dallas Tex., 1916-17, Oklahoma City, Okla. and St. Louis, 1919, 1921. Served as 1st lt. with 35th Inf., U.S. Army, 1917-19, capt., with U.S. Army retired, R.O.T.C. duty State U. of Iowa, 1921-23; accountant Iowa City, Ia., 1923-27; admitted to Ia. bar 1927, U.S. Supreme Court bar, 1939; began practice in Iowa City; city atty., 1933-35; mayor, Iowa City, 1935-37; mem. 76th to 83d Congresses, from 1st Ia. Dist., mem. com. mil. affairs 1939-47, com. on ways and means, 1947-54; United States senator, 1955-61, ret., mem. coms. govt. operations, post office and civil service, 1955-59, interior, pub. works, aero. and space scis., 1959-61. Chmn. Ia. City Community Chest, 1933, 37. Awarded Columbia U. fellowship, 1927-28. Mem. Am. Bar Assn., Ia. Bar Assn., Am. Legion,. Forty and Eight, Phi Delta Phi, Alpha Tau Omega, Order of Coif, Triangle Club, Disabled Am. Vets., Vets. of Fgn. Wars, Omicron Delta Kappa. Republican. Congregationalist. Mason, Elk, Moose, K.P., Rotatarian. Home: Seattle WA Died June 27, 1971; buried National Cemetery, Williamette OR

MARTIN, THOMAS JOSEPH, motion picture exec.; b. N.Y.C., Nov. 10, 1898; s. Owen Thomas and Bridget (Connolly) M.; student Fordham Prep. Sch., 1913-16; B.A., Fordham U., 1920; postgrad. N.Y., 1920-21; m. Lillian Schaeffler, Nov. 7, 1928; children—Joan Marie Shea, Thomas Joseph (Fr. Marius O.C.D.), Lawrence, Virginia (Mrs. George E. Cone), and Therese. Auditor Warner Brothers Pictures, 1925-56, controller, asst. treasurer, 1956, treas., dir., from 1956. Served with S.A.T.C., U.S. Army, 1918. Home: Valhalla NY Died Nov. 19, 1968.

MARTIN, WALLACE HAROLD, lawyer; b. Alto, Ind., Dec. 9, 1894; s. George Clay and Hester (Thorne) M.; A.B., Ind. U., 1917; J.D., N.Y.U., 1922; m. Eleanor Moore, Jan. 31, 1924; 1 son, John Wallace Clay. Admitted to N.Y. bar, 1923, practiced in N.Y.C.; with law firm Nims & Verdi, and successors, 1924-62, partner, 1931-62, Nims, Martin Halliday, Whitman, Howes & Collison, firm specializing in unfair competition and trademark litigation; counsel with Fell, Davis & Murrell, Kokomo, Ind., until 1962. Served as sgt. 42d Rainbow Div., United States Army, Europe, 1917-19. Recipient Distinguished Alumni Service award Ind. U. Fellow Am. Bar Found.; mem. Am. Bar Assn. (chmn. patent, trademark and copyright law sect. 1955-56), N.Y. Patent Law Assn. (pres. 1960-61), U.S. Trade Mark Assn., N.Y. State Bar Assn., Ind. U. Alumni Orgn. (life), Gamma Eta Gamma, Alpha Tau Omega (50 year mem.). Republican. Methodist. Clubs: Kokomo Country, Rotary. Author articles profl. publs. Address: Kokomo IN Died July 11, 1972; buried Sunset Memory Garden Cemetery, Kokomo IN

MARTIN, WILLIAM ELEJIUS, college pres.; b. Tuscaloosa County, Ala., Feb. 21, 1874; s. William Thomas and Mary Lou (Martin) M.; M.A., Birmingham Southern Coll., Ala., 1896; Ph.D., Johns Hopkins, 1901; m. Amelia McTyeire Baskerville, Sept. 19, 1907; children—Janie B., William Thomas, Amelia McTyeire. Prof. history, Emory and Henry Coll., Va., 1901-04; pres. Sullins Coll., Bristol, Va., 1904-10, Woman's Coll. of Ala., Montgomery, 1910-15; v.p. The Ward-Belmont Sch., Nashville, Tenn., 1915; again pres. Sullins Coll. since 1916. Democrat. Methodist. Mem. Phi Beta Kappa, Sigma Alpha Epsilon. Author: History of Internal Improvements in Alabama, 1901. Address: Bristol VA‡

MARTIN, WILLIAM JOSEPH, physician; b. Freehold, N.J., Mar. 19, 1918; s. William Redmond and Julia (Conway) M.; M.D., Georgetown U., 1943; M.Sc. in Medicine, U. Minn., 1952; m. Mary Gertrude Adams, Apr. 22, 1944; children—Mary Jo, Julia (Mrs. Thomas Vitullo), William Joseph II. Intern, Georgetown U. Hosp., Washington, 1944; fellow in medicine Georgetown U., 1944-46; postgrad. in medicine U. Minn.-Mayo Found., Rochester, 1949-53; chmn. div. internal medicine (infectious disease) Mayo Clinic, Rochester; cons. in medicine St. Mary's Hosp., Rochester, Methodist Hosp., Rochester; prof. medicine U. Minn., Mpls. Served to maj., M.C., AUS, 1943-48. Diplomate Am. Bd. Internal Medicine. Fellow A.C.P.; mem. A.M.A., Alpha Omega Alpha. Home: Rochester MN Died May 19, 1970; buried Rochester MN

MARTINEK, FRANK V(ICTOR), b. Chicago, Ill., June 15, 1895; s. Frank and Mary (Koder) M.; ed. pub. schs., business coll. and Acad. of Fine Arts, Chicago; m. Clara Gault Powell, Aug. 14, 1934. Copy boy and cub reporter Chicago Record Herald, 1910-13; identification insp. Chicago Civil Service Commn., 1913-17; spl. agt. U.S. Dept. of Justice, 1921-25; with Standard Oil Co. of Ind. since 1925, asst. v.p., from 1928; created Don Winslow of the Navy," and Bos'n Hal—Sea Scout," newspaper adventure strips, 1934 (Don Winslow of the Navy" also a radio and motion picture feature). Enlisted in United States Navy as seaman, 1917, served as intelligence officer; honorably discharged with rank of lieutenant, 1921; lt. comdr. U.S. Naval Reserve, 1930-41. Decorated with Order of M. R. Stefanik with star (Czechoslovakian); Order of St. Stanislaus (Russia); 5th Class Civil Tiger Decoration (China); Victory medal with Asiatic clasp (United States). Chairman Central and Illinois Gasoline Tax Evasion committees. Member Chicago Association of Commerce, Am. Legion, Am. Petroleum Inst. Mason (32 deg. Shriner). Author: Don Winslow in Ceylon, 1934; Know Your Man, 1936; Don Winslow Series, 1940. Contbr. articles on crime, sabotage, espionage and personnel to mags. Home: Chicago IL Died Feb. 1971.

MARTINELLI, GIOVANNI, tenor; b. Montagnana, Italy, Oct. 22, 1885; s. Antonio and Lucia (Bellini) M.; ed at Montagnana; m. Adele Previtali, Aug. 7 1913; children—Bettina (Mrs. Mario Libotte), Antonio, Giovanna. Sang in Italy, beginning, 1910; came to U.S., 1913, and became a leading tenor of Metropolitan Opera Co. (N.Y.), San Francisco Opera Assn., Chicago City Opera Co., St. Louis Opera Co. Appeared at Ravinia (summer opera) near Chicago, in Buenos Aires, and in principal cities of Europe, U.S. and Canada, Cuba, etc; repertoire of over 50 roles. Catholic. Home: Rome Italy Died Mar. 1969.

MARTINS, MARIA ALVES, sculptor; b. Campanha, Linas, Brazil, Aug. 7, 1900; d. Joao Luis and Fernandina (de Faria) Alves; ed. Rio de Janeiro and Paris, France; m. Carlos Martins P. Sousa, March 27, 1927 (dec.); children—Lucia Maria, Nora Yolanda, Anna Maria. Work represented by statues at Bello Horizonte (Brazil), Met. Mus. Art, Mus. Modern Art (N.Y.C.), Bklyn. Mus., Phila. Mus. Art, Corcoran Art Gallery (Washington), Art Inst. Cleve., Mus. of Art (San Francisco), Mus. of Art (Balt.), Albright Gallery of Art (Buffalo), San Diego Mus., Worcester Mus., Art Inst. Detroit, Art Inst. Chicago, Yale Mus. Modern Art, Cin. Art Inst.; also represented in pvt. collections in France, Belgium, Brazil. Life mem. Mus. of Modern Art and Met. Mus. Art. Roman Catholic. Author: Amazonia (legends of the River Amazon); Poems Gravures (pub. in French), 1946. Home: Rio de Janeiro Brazil Died Mar. 26, 1973.

MARTS, ARNAUD CARTWRIGHT, financial counsellor, univ. pres.; b. Reeds Corners, N.Y., Oct. 9, 1888; s. Rev. William G. and Irene A. (Cartwright) M.; A.B., Oberlin Coll., 1910, LL.D., 1940 LL.D., Hillsdale Coll., 1936; L.H.D., Bucknell, 1946, College of Hobart and William Smith, 1958; m. Ethel A. Dagett, Oct. 16, 1920 (dec. 1953); m. 2d. Anne McCartney, November, 1958. Formerly identified with boys' work, Pittsburgh; became connected Standard Life Ins. Co., Pittsburgh, 1914, elected v.p. and dir., 1917; served as asso. nat. dir. 18,000,000 campaign for War Camp Community Serv., World War, also as mem. Nat. Com. of 35 in charge United War Work Campaign for 175,000,000; after close of the war continued work of raising funds for philanthropic purposes; an organizer, hon. chmn. bd. Marts & Lundy, Inc., financial counsellors for philanthropic insts., , 500,000,000 for colleges, chs., hosps. and other instns.; pres. Bucknell U., 1935-45; apptd. by Governor James exec. dir. of Pa. State Council of Defense, 1941; re-appointed by Gov. Martin, 1943; resigned Feb. 1, 1943, to go to Washington to organize Vol. Port Security Force, U.S. Coast Guard, with rank as capt., U.S. Coast Guard Reserve; named chief of temporary Reserve Div., 1943. Trustee Oberlin Coll.; a founder and trustee Wilkes Coll. Recipient Pa. and Navy Commendation Ribbon. Mem. The Authors Guild, Authors League, S.A.R., American Legion, Phi Beta Kappa, Kappa Delta Omicron. Club: University (N.Y.). Author: Philanthropy's Role in Civilization, 1953; Man's Concern for His Fellow Man, 1961; The Generosity of Americans, 1966; George Lundy of Iowa, 1967. His biography, Arnaud Cartwright Marts-A Winner in the American Tradition, pub. 1970; The Light of Inward Vision: Selected Addresses and Essays of Arnaud C. Marts, 1973. Contbr. mags. Home: New York City NY Died July 11, 1970; buried Oakwood Cemetery, East Aurora NY

MARTWICK, WILLIAM LORIMER, mfg. exec.; b. Chgo., Nov. 7, 1894; s. William Julius and Esther (Abbott) M.; B.S., Haverford Coll.; m. Edith Lackey, Mar. 31, 1918; children—Claire (Mrs. Robert Knowlton), Jean Evans (Mrs. Frank W. Diver, Jr.), Donna Ruth (Mrs. James S. Crothers). Formerly sales engr. Pennsylvania Crusher Co.; then pres. Aero Pulverizer Co.; now chmn. Foster Wheeler Corp., N.Y.C. Home: Plainfield NJ Died Aug. 1968.

MARTZ, HYMAN SCHER, dentist; b. N.Y.C., Oct. 28, 1909; s. Abraham and Sarah (Scher) M.; B.S., N.Y.U., 1929, D.D.S., 1934; M.A., Columbia, 1930; m. Evelyn Pildos, Nov. 16, 1941; 1 dau., Joan. Gen. practice dentistry, N.Y.C., 1934-69, children's dentistry, 1953-69. Participating dentist Dental Health Ins. Plan N.Y.; mem. oral hygiene com. Greater N.Y.; attending dentist N.Y.C. Health Dept., Murray & Leonie Guggenheim Clinic for Children. Served to capt. Dental Corps, AUS, 1942-46. Mem. New York Academy of Science, First District Dental Society, New York Society for Study Orthodontics, Am. Soc. Dentistry Children, International Assn. Orthodontists, N.Y. State Academy General Dentistry. Democrat. Jewish religion. K.P.; mem. B'nai B'rith. Pioneer in use of Andresen activator therapy. Norwegian system functional orthodontics. Address: Bronx NY Died June 5, 1969.

MARVIN, CLOYD HECK, educator; born at Findlay, O., Aug. 22, 1889; s. Cloyd and Gertrude (Heck) M.; student Stanford, 1909-11; B.A., U. of Southern Calif., 1915, M.A., 1916; M.A., Harvard, 1917, Ph.D., 1919; LL.D., U. N.M., 1923; Ph.D., Nihon U., Japan, 1953;

Dr. honoris causa, George Washington U.; m. Dorothy Betts, July 20, 1917; 1 son, Cloyd. Instr. econs. U. So. Calif., 1914-15, asst. professor summer, 1916; Thayer fellow, Harvard, 1916-17; asst. prof. commerce, U. of Calif. at Los Angeles, 1919-20, associate professor, assistant director and dean, 1920-22; professor business administration. Columbia, summers, 1920, 21; prof. economics, U. of Ariz., 1922-27, also pres., 1922-27; pres., George Washington University, 1927-58, president emeritus, 1958-69. Lecturer at the International Inst. Geneva, 1930; pres. Nat. Parks Assn., 1933-35; chmn. of U.S. delegation to 7th Pan-American Scientific Congress, 1935. Chmn. Adv. Com. to the Com. on Edn. of the Ho. of Rep., 1944-45; dep. dir. for research and development, War Dept., 1946-47; spl. adv. to Sec. of War, 1947-49; sec. National Commission on Accrediting, 1949-56; civilian aide to sec. of army for D.C., from 1956. Served as captain Aviation Service, U.S. Army, Aug. 1917-Feb. 1919. Mem. Delta Chi, Phi Beta Kappa, Phi Delta Kappa, Phi Kappa Phi, Sigma Xi. Presbyn. Mason (33 deg.). Clubs: University, Cosmos (Washington). Home: Washington DC Died Apr. 28, 1969; buried Oak Hill Cemetery, Washington DC

MARVIN, DWIGHT, editor; b. Auburn, N.Y., Feb. 7, 1880; s. Dwight Edwards and Ida Norton (Whitman) M.; student Princeton, 1896-98; A.B., Williams, 1901, A.M., 1904; LL.B., Albany Law Sch. (Union U.), 1903; Litt.D., Bates College, Lewiston, Me., 1937; m. Marian Hobbie, Mar. 4, 1909; children—Margaret Ingalls (Mrs. Eric W. Barnes), William Hobbie (dec.), Marian Elizabeth (Mrs. Laurence McKinney), Keith. Practiced law in Troy, New York, 1903-06; reporter, assistant city editor, Troy Times, 1906-07; exchange editor, 1907-08, assistant editor, 1908-11, asso. editor, 1911-15, Troy Record; editor Troy Morning and Evening Record, 1915-35; editor Troy Record and Times Record, 1935-58; mem. bd. directors Troy Record Co. Dir. Troy Chromatic Club; trustee of Emma Williard Sch. (past president). Presidential elector-at-large for N.Y., 1952. Chmn. bd. trustees Hudson Valley Tech. Inst. Mem. Rensselaer County Tb. Assn., Am. Soc. Newspaper Editors (past pres.), N.Y. Soc. Newspapers Editors, Rensselaer County Hist. Assn. (treas.), C. of C., S.R., Phi Delta Theta, Phi Delta Phi, Sigma Delta Chi. Republican. Conglist. Clubs: Tyron Country, Riding and Hunt (Tryon, N.C.); Troy Country, Rotary; Williams, Princeton (N.Y.C.); Troy (N.C.) Country. Author: The Faith I Found, 1954; contbr. mags. Home: Tryon NC Died Jan. 1, 1972; buried Oakwood Cemetery, Troy NY

MARVIN, WALTER S(ANDS), banker, broker; b. Brooklyn, N.Y., June 24, 1889; s. Charles A. and Mabel S. (Metcalf) M.; student Williams Coll., 1913; m. Jean Murray, May 26, 1917; children—Murray Sands, John Howland, Matthew. Reporter New York Sun, 1911-15; stock salesman Am. Philippine Co., 1915-16; bond salesman Hemphill, Noyes & Co., 1916-22, partner, 1922-29; pres. Curtiss-Wright Airports Corp., 1928-29; partner Foster, McConnell & Co., 1931, Foster, Marvin & Company, 1932-42, financial advisor from 1942; director Edward MacDowell Association Incorporated. Served as 1st lt. Gen. Staff, U.S. Army, Washington, D.C., 1917-19. Trustee Montclair Art Museum; mem. budget com. Montclair Community Chest. Mem. Pilgrims Soc., S.A.R., Chi Psi. Republican. Conglist. Clubs: Williams, Borad Street (New York); Montclair Golf; Aviation Country. Home: Montclair NJ Died Apr. 24, 1971; buried Quoque NY

MASHBURN, (ARTHUR) GRAY, lawyer; b. nr. Newport, Ark., Dec. 13, 1873; s. John Alexander and Elizabeth (Fields) M.; grad. in law, U. of Ark., 1909; m. Lillian Richards, Dec. 1912; 1 dau., Lilyan Elizabeth; m. 2d, Ruby McKenzie Frick, June 19, 1919; 1 son, Gray Alexander. Teacher pub. schs. in Ark., 1890-96; teacher in pub. schs. and supt. schs. Little Rock, Ark., 1896-1909; practiced law at Virginia City and Reno, Nev., 1909-31; dist. atty., Virginia City, Nev., 1913-17; atty. gen. of Nev., term 1931-35, re-elected for terms 1935-39, 1939-43. Mem. Am., Nev. State and Calif. State bar assns., Washoe County Bar Assn. (past pres.), Delta Theta Phi, Reno Chamber Commerce. Democrat. Mason, Odd Fellow, K.P., Eagle. Club: Lions. Home: Carson City NV*‡

MASLAND, JOHN W(ESLEY), JR., educator; b. Phila., May 15, 1912; s. John Wesley and Elizabeth (Stager) M.; B.S., Haverford Coll., 1933; M.A., Princeton, 1937, Ph.D., 1938; M.A. (hon.), Dartmouth Coll., 1946; m. Harriet Mary Gilbert, July 22, 1939 (dec.); m. 2d, Mary Sawyer Norton, June 19, 1950; children—Joann Ellis, James Wesley, Thomas Norton, Andrew Tyson; instr., asst. prof., asso. prof. polit. sci. Stanford, 1938-46; prof. govt. Dartmouth Coll., 1946-68, chmn. dept. govt., 1955-59, provost, 1959-67; adviser for edn. for India, Ford Found., 1967-68; divisional assistant Dept. of State, 1942-43; staff Internat. Secretariat, UN Conf., San Francisco, 1945; staff mem., govt. sect. Supreme Comdr. Allied Powers, Tokyo, 1946; dir. studies Nat. War Coll., 1950, 51, mem. board consultants, 1960-63; staff dir. African Study Com., Edn. and World Affairs, 1964-65. Mem. Hanover Sch. Bd., 1957-60; bd. directors U.S. Educational in India; trustee Williston Acad., 1953-58, 63-67, Am. Univs. Field Staff, 1959-66, Inst. Coll. and U. Adminstrs., 1960-66, African Scholarship Program of Am. Univs., 1965-67. Mem. Am. Polit. Sci. Assn., Council Fgn. Relations. Phi Beta Kappa. Club: Cosmos (Washington). Co-author: The Governments of Foreign Powers (Philip W. Buck), 1947, 50; Soldiers and Scholars, Military Education and National Policy (with Laurence I. Radway), 1957; (with Gene M. Lyons) ROTC: Education and Military Leadership, 1959. Home: Hanover NH Died Aug. 3, 1968; buried Hanover NH

MASLOW ABRAHAM HAROLD, educator; b. Bklyn., Apr. 1, 1908; s. Samuel and Rose (Schlosky) M.; B.A., U. Wis., 1930, M.A., 1931, Ph.D., 1934; D. Leg. (hon.), Xavier U., Cin.; m. Bertha Goodman, Dec. 31, 1928; children—Ann (Mrs. Jerome Kaplan), Ellen. Asst. instr. U. Wis., 1930-35; Carnegie fellow Columbia Tchrs. Coll., 1935-37; from instr. to asso. prof. psychology Bklyn. Coll., 1937-51; plant mgr. Maslow Cooperage Corp., 1947-49; asso. prof., prof. Brandeis U., Waltham, Mass., 1951-69, chmn. dept., 1951-61; resident fellow Laughlin Foundation, 1969-70. Named Humanist of Yr., Am. Humanist Assn., 1967. Mem. Am. (council 1946-48, 49-50, 53-56, 58-60), pres. 8th division 1955, president 10th division 1959; nat. pres. 1967), Massachusetts (director 1953-56, pres. 1960-62), New England (pres. 1962-63) psychol. associations, mem. society Soc. Psychol. Study Social Issues (council 1947-49, 51-55, 59-62). Author: Principles of Abnormal Psychology (with B. Mittelmann), 1941; Motivation and Personality, 1954, rev. edit., 1970; Toward A Psychology of Being, 1962, revised, 1968; Religion, Values and Peak-Experiences, 1964, rev. edit., 1970; Eupsychian Management: A Journal, 1965; The Psychology of Science: A Reconaissance, 1966; (with H.M. Chiang) The Healthy Personality: Readings, 1969; Farther Reaches of Human Nature, pub. postumously, 1971; other posthumous publs. include: The Journals of A.H. Maslow; Dominance, Self-Esteem, self. Actualization: Germinal Papers of A.H. Maslow. Editor: New Knowledge in Human Values, 1959; bd. editors profl. jours. Office: Menlo Park CA Died June 8, 1970; cremated.

MASON, C. AVERY, bishop; b. St. Louis, Mo., Aug. 2, 1904; s. Charles Henry and Mary C. (Avery) M.; B.A., Washington Univ., St. Louis, Mo., 1926; B.D., Va. Theol. Sem., Alexandria, Va., 1929; student Gen. Theol. Sem., N.Y. City, 1930-33; S.T.D., Temple U., Phila., 1939; m. Virginia Fear, July 24, 1929; children—Diana Lee, Virginia. Ordained to ministry, P.E. Church, 1928; curate, St. Stephens Parish, Washington, D.C., 1928-29; curate, Trinity Parish (stationed at St. Agnes Chapel), N.Y. City, 1929-30; rector, Ch. of The Ascension, Staten Island, N.Y., 1930-41; rector, Ascension Day Sch., 1933-41; pres. N.Y. Bd. of Religious Edn., 1938-40; dean, Richmond Convocation, Staten Island, N.Y., 1939-41; editor; Action, ednl. mag. Diocese of N.Y., 1939-42; exec. sec. to the presiding Bishop for Forward in Service," 1942; bishop co-adjutor of Dallas, 1945-46, bishop from 1946. Trustee U. of the South, Seabury Western Theol. Sem., Episcopal Theol. Sem. of Southwest. Mem. Chi Delta Phi, Alpha Tau Omega. Author: Where Art Thou?. 1945. Address: Dallas TX Died Mar. 1970.

MASON, CHARLES NOBLE, corp. officer; b. Plymouth, Mass., Dec. 29, 1869; s. Albert and Lydia Finney (Whiting) M.; ed. pub. schs.; m. Emily Elizabeth Reed, June 14, 1909; 1 son, Charles Noble. Began with Thomson-Houston Electric Co., 1887 and upon its absorption by the Gen. Electric Co. continued with the latter until 1902; v.p. United Electric Securities Co. (subsidiary of Gen. Electric Co.), 1902-07; v.p. Electrical Securities Corp. (also subsidiary Gen. Electric Co.), 1907-23; pres. 1923-37, then chmn. bd., now retired. Mem. Acad. Polit. Sci. Clubs: Union, Appalachian Mountain (Boston); Ausable (St. Huberts, New York); Yeamans Hall (Charleston, S.C.). Home: 1020 Fifth Av., New York 28 NY‡

MASON, G(EORGE) GRANT, JR., financier; b. Mason City, Ia., Jan. 2, 1904; s. George and Marion (Peak) M.; student at Browning Sch., New York City, 1912-16, Saint Paul's School, Concord, New Hampshire, 1916-22; A.B., Yale U., 1926; student Guggenheim Sch. of Aviation, N.Y.U., 1926-27; m. Jane Kendall, June 1927 (divorced 1940); children—Anthony, Philip; married 2d, Martha Ashley McMakin, May 1946 (div. Nov. 1968); children—George Grant III, Martha Peak; stepchildren—Richard A., Leigh A. Became district manager new business dept. Corn Exchange Bank, N.Y. City, 1925; one of founders, then rep. of Pan. Am. Airways, Inc., before 21 govts. in Carribbean area, with hdqrs. in Havana, Cuba, 1927-38; pres. and gen. mgr. Compania Nacional Cubana de Aviacion, Havana, 1933-38; mem. Civil Aeronautics Authority, 1938-40, Civil Aeronautics Bd. after reorganization, 1940-42. One of founders, dir. Alloy Products, Inc., Baton Rouge; chmn. bd. Versfelt, Mason & Donegan, Inc., financial services. Pres. Inter-Am. Comml. Arbitration Commn. Apptd. by Pres. Roosevelt, chmn. Am. Del. to 4th Internat. Conf. Pvt. Air Law, Brussels, Belgium, 1938. Administrative asst. in charge South Am. activities, Am. Republics Div., Defense Supplies Corp., Reconstrn. Finance Corp., Jan.-July 1942. Trustee, Skowhegan Sch. Painting and Sculpture. Maj., Air Transport Commands, U.S. Army Air Forces, July 3, 1942; lt. col., A.C., Nov. 6, 1942; asst. chief of staff plans, Air Transport Command, Mar. 6, 1943; lt. col., Gen. Staff Corps, May 11, 1943, col., July 27, 1943; chief Civil Aviation Br., Air Staff Plans, Hdqrs. A.A.F., Sept. 26, 1944. Relieved from active duty, apptd. col., Res. Corps, July 27, 1946. War Dept. rep., world-circling mission with Wendell Wilkie, 1942. Mem. U.S. com. Inter-Am. Arbitration Commn., 1958. Mem. U.S. del. Quadrant" Conf., Quebec, Aug. 1943; Sextant" conf., Cairo, Nov. 1943. Mil. adviser to US-UK Conf. on Civil Aviation, Bermuda, Jan.-Feb. 1946. Various other temporary assignments in all theaters of war in connection with official duties of ATC and subsequently with problems relating to postwar transition from mil. to civil aviation; spl. asst. to Asst. Sec. Air Force, 1948-49, cons. Sec. Air Force, 1949-50; vice chmn. bd. dirs., chmn. exec. com., Vision, Inc., pub. Latin Am. news mags. and U.S. industrial and ednl. services. Decorations and Citations: Legion of Merit; Army Commendation Ribbon; American Asiatic Pacific, European-African-Middle Eastern Campaign Medals, World War II Victory Medal. Mem. Am. Arbitration Assn. (dir. 1956, exec. com. 1957, chmn. membership com. 1958-60, pres. 1960-62, chmn. 1962-65, vice chmn. 1965). Christian Scientist. Clubs: Metropolitan, Yale, F Street, National Aviation (Washington, District of Columbia); Yale, University (New York City); Yeamans Hall (Charleston, S.C.); Mid Ocean (Bermuda); Edgartown Yacht (Martha's Vineyard, Mass). Home: New York City NY Died Oct. 16, 1970.

MASON, GEORGE DEWITT, architect; b. Syracuse, N.Y., July 4, 1856; s. James H. and Zada E. (Griffin) M.; ed. pub. schs. of Detroit and Syracuse; studied in Europe in 1884, 1911, 1924, 1928-30; hon. M.A., Univ. of Mich., 1928; m. Ida Whitaker, May 31, 1882; 1 dau., Lilian (Mrs. James D. Fulton). Began study of architecture in office of Henry T. Brush, Detroit, 1873; mem. firm Mason & Rice, 1878-98; in private practice 1898-1920; as George D. Mason & Co., Inc., since Jan. 1, 1920. Works include the Masonic Temple, Pontchartrain Hotel, Lincoln Motor Car Co. plant, Detroit Yacht Club, Standard Savings and Loan Assn. Bldg., and several churches and theatres, in Detroit, Mich., Cleveland, O., and Quebec and Toronto, Can.; Govt. Appointment for 3 housing projects in Detroit: The Brewster, The Parkside, The Herman Gardens now nearly finished on 160 acres for 2150 families in 239 buildings. First pres. Mich. State Bd. for the Registration of Architects, 1915-20; pres. Nat. Council of Archtl. Registration Bds., 1928. Fellow A.I.A.; mem. Mich. Soc. of Architects, Detroit Engring. Soc., Am. Fedn. of Arts. Democrat. Mason (32 deg.). Clubs: Detroit; Detroit Athletic; Detroit Yacht; Whitenagemote. Home: 746 Collingwood Av. 2. Office: 409 Griswold St., Detroit 26 MI‡

MASON, JAMES MONROE, surgeon; b. Marion, Ala., Nov. 21, 1871; s. James Monroe and Ellen Olivia (Drake) M.; student, Ala. Poly. Inst.; Southern Univ.; M.D., Tulane U., 1899, D.Sc., 1935; m. Grace Hardie Lovelace, Nov. 12, 1901; children—Mrs. J. Rowan Oden, James M. III, Mrs. E. Byron Glenn. Attending surgeon, St. Vincent's, Childrens, and Jefferson-Hillman Hosps., Birmingham, Ala.; prof. surgery Med. Coll. of Ala., 1945-49; chief surgeon Birmingham Electric Co.; chief surg. and med. dir. Ala. Power Co. Fellow A.C.S. (mem. bd. regents); mem. Southern Surgical Assn. (pres.), Am. Surgical Assn. (v.p.). Contbr. of articles to jours. Home: 2721 Niazuma Av. Office: 1023 South 20th St., Birmingham 5 AL‡

MASON, LESLIE FENTON, hosp. adminstr.; b. Tyler, Wash., Jan. 1, 1903; s. Clarence Blanchard and Mabel (Harris) M.; A.B., Wash. State U., 1928, postgrad., 1931; Hum.D., Whitworth Coll., 1964; m. Mary Margaret Lux, Dec. 1, 1928; 1 dau., Marilyn Ann (Mrs. James Cline). Prin. pub. schs., Marcus, Wash., 1924-26; supt. schs., Kettle Falls, Wash., 1928-30, Edwall, Wash., 1930-33; bus. mgr. Lakeland Village Hosp., Medical Lake Wash., 1933-40, supt., 1940-64. Mem. Nat. Assn. Mental Deficiency, Nat. Assn. Mental Health, Spokane Athletic Roundtable, Phi Delta Kappa, Tau Kappa Epsilon. Mason, Elk, Kiwanian (past pres., lt. gov.). Office: Medical Lake WA Died Dec. 9, 1964; buried Holy Cross Cemetery, Spokane WA

MASON, MARY AUGUSTA, prose and verse writer; b. Windsor, N.Y.; d. S. A. and Nancy (Sage) M.; ed. Windsor Acad. and Binghamton Coll.; mem. Daughters of the Am. Revolution; now living at Consulate-General, Constantinople with Charles M. Dickinson and his wife, of whom she is an adopted daughter; frequent contributor to leading mags. and newspapers for several yrs. Author: With the Seasons (collected poems), 1897 R2. Residence: South Mountain Park, Binghamton NY‡

MASON, (MORTIMER) PHILLIPS, prof. philosophy; b. Boston, Mass., Mar. 19, 1876; s. Mortimer Blake and Helena Augusta (Phillips) M.; A.B., Harvard, 1899, A.M., 1900, Ph.D., 1904; grad. student Corpus Christi Coll., Oxford, Eng., 1899-1900,

Heidelberg, Berlin and Marburg, 1900-02, Sorbonne and Coll. de France, Paris, 1902; m. Gertrud (Helene) Natorp, July 2, 1913; children—Helena Elisabeth, Richard Phillips, Adelbert Natorp, (Gertrude) Hildegard (dec.). Instr. in philosophy and psychology, Princeton, 1905-07; asso. in philosophy, Bryn Mawr, 1909-11; lecturer in philosophy, Harvard, 1913-19; prof. philosophy, Bowdoin Coll., since 1920. Mem. Am. Philos. Assn. Democrat. Author: The X of Psychology, 1940. Home: Brunswick ME‡

MASON, ROY MARTELL, landscape painter; b. Gilbert Mills, N.Y., Mar. 15, 1886; s. Frank E. and Elizabeth (Wilson) M.; ed. pub. schs.; studied art under father; m. Lena Adrien Seitz, June 15, 1913. Recipient numerous awards since 1929; represented in many museums and galleries including Met. Mus. Art, N.Y.C., Toledo (O.) Mus., Art Inst. Chgo. Partner, art dir. F.E. Mason & Sons, engravers Asso. Nat. Acad., 1930. Nat. Academician 1940. Recipient many awards and prizes including Gold Medal of Honor for watercolor Allied Artists of Am. Show, 1952-53; Roy Wilhelm Meml. prize North Shore Art Assn. Boston, 1956; 1st watercolor award 1,000, N.Y., N.H. & H. R.R. contest, 1956; Ranger Fund purchase prize Am. Watercolor Soc., 1956; Chautauqua Art Assn. award, 1958; 1st prize American Water Color Society, 1961. Fellow Rochester Mus. of Arts and Scis.; mem. Am. Water Color Soc. (life mem., v.p. 1953, Gold Medal of Honor 1961), Phila. Water Color Soc., Buffalo Soc. Artists, Rochester Art Club, Salmagundi Club, Allied Artists, Audubon Artists. Contbr. artist covers for Readers Digest, others. Home: La Jolla CA Died Aug. 1972.‡

MASON, WILBUR NESBITT, clergyman; b. Mechanicsburg, O., Apr. 15, 1867; s. John Watson and Anna (Nesbitt) M.; A.B., valedictorian, Ohio Wesleyan U., 1890; S.T.B., Boston U. Sch. of Theology, 1896; A.M., Harvard, 1898; D.D., U. of Chattanooga, 1909, Ohio Wesleyan, 1911; LL.D., Baker U., 1925; m. Adelaide A. Green, Sept. 4, 1901; children—Estherline Johnston, Kathleen, Miriam Nesbitt, Sarah Adelaide. Ordained M.E. Ministry, 1895; pastor, Georgetown, O., 1892-93, Epworth Ch., Cambridge, Mass., 1898-1904, Wesley Ch., Salem, Mass., 1904-08, First Ch., Chattanooga, Tenn., 1908-11; pres. Baker U., Baldwin, Kan., Sept. 26, 1911-July 1917; mem. Kan. State Bd. of Adminstrn. (ednl., penal and charitable institutions), 1917-21. Pres. Kan. Conf. of Social Work, 1918-21; pastor First M.E. Ch., Pittsburg, Kan., 1921-27, Country Club M.E. Ch., Kansas City, Mo., 1927-31; supt. Bethany Meth. Hosp., 1931-33; with Kansas City Life Ins. Co., 1933—; supt. Kansas City Dist. of Kansas Ann. Conf. M.E. Ch. since Oct. 1928; supt. Bethany Meth. Hosp., Kansas City, Kan., since 1931. Mem. Phi Beta Kappa. Home: 427 Kansas City MO*‡

MASON, WILLIAM MADISON, journalist; b. Washington, Sept. 21, 1877; s. James Madison and Laura Elizabeth (Pepin) M.; ed. pub. schs., Washington, and 3yrs. at Tufts Coll., Mass.; widower. Engaged in newspaper work since 1897; newspaper corr., P.I., 1899; apptd. lt., U. S. A., at recommendation of Gen. E. S. Otis—declined; with troops at front during campaigns around Manila; went to Martinique on U. S. S. Dixie, on 1st relief expd'n, as sp'l corr. Publishers' Press Assn.; Washington corr. Army and Navy Journal of New York since 1900. Also writes sp'l internat. and mil. articles for Baltimore Sun; has written numerous articles for mags. on eruption of Mont Pelee in Martinique, and on Philippine affairs. Mem. Theta Delta Chi, S. A. R. Episcopalian. Republican. Residence: The Rochambeau. Office: Colo. Bldg., Washington‡

MASSAGLIA, JOSEPH, JR., hotel exec.; b. Trinidad, Colo., Aug. 8, 1908; s. Joseph and Laura (Comoglio) M.; student U. N.M. Asst., later mgr. Joe Massaglia & Co., wholesale grocers, Albuquerque, N.M.; v.p. N.M. Hilton Hotel Corp. (now merged into Hilton Hotel Corp.), 1940-42; pres. owner Massaglia Hotels, from 1945, including Hotel Miramar, Santa Monica, Cal., Hotel Wilton, Long Beach, Cal., Hotel El Rancho, Gallup, N.M., Hotel Franciscan, Albuquerque, N.M., Hotel Park Lane, Denver, Hotel Raleigh, Washington, D.C., Hotel Bond, Hartford, Conn., Hotel Sinton, Cin., Hotel Sherwyn, Pitts., Hotel Waikiki Biltmore, Honolulu, Hotel New Yorker, N.Y.C., Hotel St. Claire, San Jose, Cal. Recipient Columbian award for distinguished merit, 1958; named Ky. col., N.M. col. Mem. Am., Cal., So. Cal., Rocky Mountain hotel assns., Santa Monica C. of C. (dir.). Roman Catholic. Clubs: Optimist; Towne; Searchlight; Indianapolis 500 Car Owner; USAC. Address: Santa Monica CA Died June 23, 1969; buried Holy Cross Cemetery, Los Angeles CA

MASSEE, JASPER CORTENUS, clergyman; b. Marshallville, Macon County, Ga., Nov. 22, 1871; s. Dr. Drew W. and Susan Elizabeth (Bryan) M.; A.B., Mercer U., Ga., 1892, D.D., 1908, Southern Bapt. Theol. Sem., Louisville, 1896, 97; LL.D., Carson and Newman College, Tenn., 1926; m. Mrs. Sallie Stewart, 1893 (died 1895); 1 son, Richard D.; m. 2d, Mary Ola Oliver, June 30, 1896 (died 1932);children—Joseph Carey, Logan Jasper, Marjorie, William Chester; m. 3d, Edna Blair, Aug. 25, 1935. Ordained Baptist ministry, 1893; pastor Kissimmee, Fla., 1893-96, Orlando, Fla., 1897-99, Lancaster, Ky., 1899-1901, Mansfield, Ohio, 1901-03, Raleigh (N.C.) Tabernacle, 1903-08, 1st Ch., Chattanooga, Tenn., 1908-13, 1st Ch., Dayton, O., 1913-19, Baptist Temple, Brooklyn, N.Y., 1920-22, Tremont Temple, Boston, Mass., 1922-29; guest lecturer. Eastern Bapt. Theol. Sem., Phila., 1938-41; now engaged in a nationwide Bible Conf. and Evangelistic ministry; lecturer on Evangelism, Winona Lake Sch. of Theol., 1947, taught homiletics and evangelism, 1947-48. President Home Mission Soc., Northern Baptist Conv., 1918-19. Former trustee Gordon Coll. of Theology and Missions, Northern Bapt. Theol. Sem. Hon. mem. Eugene Field Soc. Author of books and many pamphlets on religious subjects; latest publs., The Holy Spirit; Christ and Human Personality. Home: 1055 Clifton Rd., Atlanta 6 GA‡

MASSMANN, FREDERICK H., pres. Peter Fox Brewing Co.; b. Hanover, Germany, Dec. 1, 1876; s. Carl and Minna (Fricka) M.; brought to U.S., 1884; ed. grammar sch., Chicago, and 6 years in night sch.; m. Elizabeth Dienes, of Springfield, Ill., June 6, 1900; children—Alfred J., Elizabeth R. (Mrs. P. R. Pape). Began as boy in retail grocery store; then with Brookman Mfg. Co., grocery sundries, 1890-95; in employ Durand & Kasper Co., wholesale grocers, 1895-1913; with Nat. Tea Co., wholesale grocers, 1913-39, Peter Fox Brewing Co. since Oct. 1, 1939. Pres. Nat. Chain Store Assn., 1931-33; pres. Nat. Assn. Food Chains, 1933-35. Republican. Mem. Knights of Columbus. Clubs: Lake Shore, Athletic, Ridgemoor Country. Home: 6620 N. Maplewood Av. Office: 2626 W. Monroe St., Chicago IL‡

MASSON, ROBERT LOUIS, educator; b. Washington, Ia., Aug. 31, 1891; s. Daniel John and Matilda Mason (Scofield) M.; A.B., State U. Ia., 1912, A.M., 1915; A.M., Harvard, 1922; m. Henrietta H. Worrell June 18, 1923; children—Helen Elaine (Mrs. Carl H. Engel), Jane Cora (Mrs. Roger S. Jackson), Robert Henry. Supt. schs., Winfield, Ia., 1912-13; prin. Washington (Ia.) High Sch., 1913-14; asst. econs., State U. Ia., 1914-16; asst. econs. Harvard, 1916-17, 1919-20, instr., 1920-22, instr. and tutor, 1922-23; asst. prof. econs., U. Mich., 1923-24, asst. prof. finance, 1924-25, asso. prof. finance, 1925-29; vis. prof. U. Wash., summer, 1928; asso. prof. finance Harvard Grad. Sch. Bus. Adminstrn., 1929-39 prof. finance, 1939-58, emeritus, 1958-70, prof. finance Advanced Mgmt. Program, Honolulu, summers 1958-59, Harvard-Radcliffe Program in Mgmt. Tng., 1958-60, 61-63, Advanced Mgmt. Program in Far East, Baguio, Philippines, summer 1967; prof. finance Institut European d'Adminstrn. des Affairs, Fontainebleau, France, 1960-61; vis. prof. finance Northwestern U., 1964, Morris Harvey Coll., Charleston, W.Va., 1968-69. Mem. bd. dirs. Reliance Coop. Bank. Cons. Indian Inst. Mgmt., Ahmedabad, India, 1964-65, prof. program mgmt. devel., Agra, India, 1966. Member of second O.T.C., Ft. Snelling, Minn., 1st lt. inf., U.S. Res., 1917-18; capt. 1918-19. Recipient Fulbright Act award, lectr. in France, 1960-61. Mem. Am. Econ. Assn., Delta Sigma Rho. Author: Problems in Corporation Finance (with S. S. Stratton), 1935; Financial Instruments and Institutions—A Case Book (with same), 1938; A Case Study of Balloting Regulation: The Boston and Maine Recapitalizes, 1948-53, 1956; New Shares for Old: The Boston and Maine Stock Modification, 1958; (with P. Hunt and R. N. Anthony) Cases in Financial Management, 1960. Home: Centerville MA Died Mar. 14, 1970; buried Beechwood Cemetery, Centerville, Cape Cod MA

MASTERS, HARRIS KENNEDY, cons. engr.; b. N.Y. City, Aug. 6, 1873; s. Hibbert B. and Clara Lovell (Everett) M.; E.M., Columbia Sch. of Mines, 1894; m. Fannie Elliott, June 20, 1908 (dec. 1948). Asst. chemist, asst. supt. Nichols Copper Co., Laurel Hill, L.I., 1895-1902; smelter supt. U.S. Smelting Co., Midvale, Utah, 1902-04; private practice, Salt Lake City, Utah, 1904-05 and 1910-11; gen. mgr. Central Chile Copper Co. (London, Eng.) at Panulcillo, Chile, 1905-10; part owner (v.p.) and operator Ohio Valley Fluorspar Co., Marion, Ky., 1912-13; metall. Griffin Wheel Co., Chicago, 1913-14; gen. foreman bayonet shop Remington Arms Co., Bridgeport, Conn., 1915-16; mgr. metal and ore dept. W.R. Grace & Co., New York, 1916-20; mgr. metal dept. Wah Chang Trading Corp., New York, 1920-24; sec. New York Metal Exchange, 1925-26; mgr. metal and ore dept. Asso. Metals & Minerals Corp., N.Y. City, 1927; v.p. Chas. Hardy, Inc., 1927-40; cons. engr. Molybdenum Corp. of America since 1942. Consultant on antimony and tungsten Advisory Commn. to Council of Nat. Defense, 1940; chief tungsten branch, Office of Prodn. Management, later War Prodn. Bd., 1941-42. Awarded medal for Alumni service, Columbia U., 1936; received Columbia U. medal, 1940. Mem. Mining and Metall. Soc. of Am., Am. Inst. Mining & Metall. Engrs., Iron and Steel Inst., Tau Beta Pi; pres. Columbia Engring. Schs. Alumni Assn., 1921-25; trustee Columbia University in N. Y. City since 1944. Republican. Protestant. Clubs: Columbia University (pres. 1937-40). Mining (N.Y. City). Contbr. to Engineering and Mining Jour. and Am. Soc. for Testing Materials Bulletin. Home: 123 E. 53d St., N.Y.C. 22 NY Office: 500 Fifth Av., NYC 36 NY‡

MASTERS, KEITH, lawyer; b. Morgan County, Ind., Jan. 20, 1903: s. John Volney and Sarah Estella (Keith) M; A.B., Ind. U., 1925; J.D., Harvard, 1929; m. Esther Freeman, July 27, 1929. Admitted to Ill. bar, 1930; asso. firm Kirkland, Fleming, Green, Martin & Ellis (became Kirkland, Ellis, Hodson, Chaffetz & Masters, 1958), Chgo., 1930-73, partner, 1942-73, counsel, Chgo. Better Bus. Bur., Robert R. McCormick Charitable Trust. Dir. Lake Shore Nat. Bank, Chgo. Bd. dirs. Ind. U. Found. Served maj. Judge Adv. Gen. Dept., AUS, 1943-45. Mem. Am., Ill., Chgo. bar assns., Chgo. Law Inst. Phi Beta Kappa. Clubs: Chicago, Legal University, Executives, Mid-America (Chgo.); Westmoreland Country (Wilmette, Ill.). Home: Evanston IL Died Jan. 11, 1973.

MASTERSON, KATE, author; b. Newburgh, N.Y.; educated in convent schs. Began work as matinee girl" on Dramatic Mirror, 1891; editorial staff New York Herald, 1893; corr. New York American during Cuban Insurrection, 1896; London and Paris corr. 1904, 1905, 1907. Won 3d prize Sun contest for best poems answering The Man with the Hoe," 1900; 1st prize, Munsey's Magazine, best topical poem, 1904. Author: The Dobleys, 1900; The Thirteenth Apostle, 1904; A Yellow Primrose" (3-act comedy), 1906. Contbr. to leading mags. and syndicates.*‡

MASTERSON, WILLIAM EDWARD, lawyer, educator; b. Madisonville, Tex.; s. John E. and Frances Elisabeth (Riley) M.; A.B., U. of Tex., 1915; A.M., Harvard U., 1917, LL.B., 1919, S.J.D., 1926; LL.D., U. of London (England), 1928; married Eloise Bordages. Teacher public schools, Texas, 1906-10; admitted to Tex. bar, 1912, and practiced at Dallas and Sinton until 1915; admitted also to bars of Idaho and Missouri; instr. public speaking, U. of Tex., 1913-15; instructural asst. Dept. of English, Harvard, 1915-18; practiced law, Beaumont, 1919-21, N.Y. City, 1921-23; in research abroad, Bur. Internat. Research, Harvard and Radcliffe Coll., 1926-28; asso. prof. law, U. of Ida., 1928-29, prof. law and dean Coll. of Law, 1929-34; prof. law and dean of School of Law, U. of Missouri, 1934-38, prof. of Law, Temple University, 1939-47; acting attorney for Univ. of Missouri, 1935. Asso. law firm Wright, Gordon, Zachri & Cahill, N.Y. City, May-Dec. 1943; cons. Dept. of State Washington, D.C., 1944-47; atty. for State of Tex. in tideland oil litigation. Trustee Daycroft Sch., Stamford, Conn. Adviser on research in international law, Harvard Law Sch.; leader of round tables on international law, Institute of Internat. Relations, Berkeley, California, 1930; founder, former mem. editorial board Idaho Law Journal and editor-in-chief Missouri Law Review. Member United States N.R.F., 1917-18. Formerly chmn. coms. on memorials and on internat. law sources, Assn. Am. Law Schs.; mem. or chmn. of several coms. of Mo. and Am. bar assns., and Inter-American Bar Association; member of Texas Bar Association (honorary), American Legion, Phi Beta Kappa, Phi Kappa Psi, Phi Alpha Delta, Order of Coif. Mason (32 degree), Clubs: Texas of Harvard (pres. 1916-17); Harvard (Phila.). Author: Jurisdiction in Marginal Seas, 1929; co-author of The Internat. Law of the Future." Contbr. to Annual Digest of Pub. Internat. Law Cases, 1925-26, Trans. Grotius Soc. (London), 1928, 29 (addresses), and articles on the law of sales, corps., hovering laws, internat. law constitutional law and jurisprudence, and numerous book reviews, addresses and articles pub. in various legal and religious periodicals and popular mags. and encys., including addresses before the Am. Bar Assn., the Inter-Am. Bar Assn., Internat. Law Association and Inst. of World Affairs. Christian Science practitioner. Home: Philadelphia PA Died Sept. 5, 1967.

MASTICK, SEABURY CONE, lawyer; b. San Francisco, Calif., July 19, 1871; s. William Henry and Laura Jeanette (Mastick) Cone; adopted son of Seabury Lucius and Mary Wood Mastick; grad. Hopkins Acad., Oakland, Calif., 1887; A.B., Oberlin (O.), College, 1891, A.M., 1894, hon. A.M., 1916, Doctor of Humane Letters (honorary), 1962; LL.B., Hastings Coll. Law, U. of Calif., 1894; grad. study Columbia, 1912-17; Sc.D., Pacific U., 1952; LL.D., Wagner Coll., 1953; m. Agnes Warner, Oct. 1, 1896 (dec. 1963); m. 2d, Kathrin Cawein, Apr. 3, 1964. Admitted to Cal. bar, 1893, and began practice in San Francisco; moved to N.Y. City, 1896; v.p. Warner Chem. Co., 1920-28; pres. Westvaco Chlorine Products Co., 1922-27; dir. Warner Brothers Co., Bridgeport, Conn. Successively lt., j.g., lt. and lt. comdr., U.S. N.R. (developer of star shell"), 1917-June 1920. Mem. N.Y. Assembly, 1921-22, N.Y. State Senate, 1923-34 (chmn. com. on taxation and retrenchment and of spl. joint com. on taxation, 1924-32); mem. Suburban Transit Investigating Commn., 1925, Industrial Survey Commn., 1926, Tenement Law Revision Commn., 1927-29; chmn. State Commn. on Old Age Security, 1929-30; mem. Gov.'s Council on Agr., 1929-35; chmn. State Commn. for Revision of Tax Laws, N.Y., 1930-38; chmn. Interstate Commn. on Conflicting Taxation, 1933; vice chmn. Tax Revision Council, 1935; chmn. N.Y. State Tax Assn., 1929-32; adv. director County Trust Co., Pleasantville, N.Y. Chmn. Army and Navy Dept. Com., Y.M.C.A.; mem. Nat. Bd. Y.M.C.A., 1939-46; mem. board dirs. and exec. com. United Service Organizations, 1941-46; member board directors New

York School for the Deaf, White Plains, New York Fellow A.A.A.S.; member Westchester County Historical Soc., S.A.R., Asso. Bar City of New York, American Legion, Phi Lambda Upsilon. Decorated Conspicuous Service Cross, State of N.Y.; spl. letter of commendation (silver star) by secretary of navy. Republican. Episcopalian. Mason. Clubs: University, Columbia University (N.Y.C.); Rotary; Cosmos (Washington). Author: Chemical Patents, 1915. Home: Pleasantville NY Died Aug. 21, 1969.

MASUR, JACK, medical adminstr.; b. Augusta, Ga., June 16, 1908; s. Harry and Jennie (Pearl) M.; B.S., New York University, 1928; M.D., Cornell, 1932; m. Barbara Forsch, June 28, 1943; children—Nancy, Henry, Jenny, Corinne. Intern Bellevue Hosp., N.Y.C., 1932-34; resident medicine Montefiore Hosp., N.Y. City, 1934-36, asst. dir., 1936-40; exec. dir. Lebanon Hosp., N.Y. City, 1941-43; hosp. cons. Fedn. Jewish Philanthropies, N.Y. City, 1946-47; with U.S. Office of Civilian Def., U.S.P.H.S., 1943-44, chief med. officer U.S. Office of Vocational Rehabilitation, Fed. Security Agency, 1944-45, dir. clin. center Nat. Insts. Health, 1948-51, 56-69, asso. dir. for clin. care adminstrn., 1960-69, asst. surgeon gen., chief Bur. Med. Services, Pub. Health Service, 1951-56; lectr. sch. pub. health and adminstrv. medicine Columbia. Commr. Joint Commn. on Accreditation of Hosps., 1954-62; mem. hosp. adv. committee. Kellogg Found., 1955-61. Diplomate Am. Bd. Preventive Medicine and Pub. Health. Fellow A.C.P., Am. Coll. Hosp. Adminstrs., Am. Pub. Health Assn., N.Y. Acad. Medicine; mem. A.M.A., Society of Medical Adminstrs. (pres. 1960-62), Am. Hosp. Assn. (chmn. council hosp. planning and plant operation 1951-53, member board of trustees 1954-57, pres. 1961), Assn. Mil. Surgeons, Phi Beta Kappa. Home: Washington DC Died Mar. 8, 1969.

MATHENY, EZRA STACY, clergyman, architect; b. Columbus, O., Oct. 16, 1870; s. Jacob Sylvestor and Christian Elizabeth (Jackson) M.; ed. common and high schs.; theol. training in Ohio Conf. Course of M.E. Ch., 1897-1906; extension work, U. of Chicago; m. Nellie Maud Beery, Mar. 21, 1895; children—Merrill Everitt, Thelma Elizabeth (wife of Eugene H. Roseboom, Ph.D.), Luella Frances (wife of Elmer R. Rebbeck, M.D.), Margaret Lucile. Apprentice carpenter, 1892-95; ordained M.E. ministry, 1901; successively pastor at Byer, Omego, Piketon, Portsmouth and Crooksville; pastor Columbia Heights Ch., Columbus, 1930-34, Cleveland Avenue Ch., 1934-38; pastor Central Community Church, Columbus, since 1940; chaplain Ohio State Senate since 1921. In business as architect in Columbus, 1913-15; mem. Mathany, Allen & Mounts, 1915-17; mem. Riebel, Sons & Matheny, 1923-29. Has designed 57 public bldgs. including a number of high schs. and churches in Ohio. Was dir. Bur. of Architecture Ohio Council of Chs. With Y.M.C.A. in France, 1918-19. Trustee Industrial Mission. Republican. Methodist. Mason (K.T.). Club: Buckeye Republican. Compiler. American Patriotic Devotions, 1932, 3d edit., 1938 (officially approved by Nat. Council Jews and Christians, by finance com. Ohio State Senate and by Parent-Teacher Assn., regardless of creed, for placement in schs. and libraries throughout the country), 4th edit., under title American Devotion (copies ordered by Ohio legislature for State use, May 24, 1943). Home: Southern Hotel, Columbus OH‡

MATHERS, FRANK C(URRY), prof.; b. Monroe Co., Ind., Feb. 11, 1881; s. (John) Thomas and Elizabeth (Bonsall) M.; A.B., Ind. U., 1903, A.M., 1905; Ph.D., Cornell U., 1907; m. Maud Bowser, July 10, 1911;children—Thomas Nesbit, William Hammond (dec.). Instr. Ind. U., Bloomington, 1903-07, asst. prof., 1907-13, asso. prof., 1913-22, prof. from 1922, then prof. emeritus, until 1973. chmn. chemistry dept., 1945-46; civilian mem. Chem. Warfare Service, Washington, D.C., 1918; project dir. under Office Sci. and Research Development, on lens coating, 1945. Mem. Am. Electrochem. Soc. (pres. 1940-41, dir. numerous research projects), Alpha Chi Sigma, Sigma Xi, Phi Lambda Upsilon. Republican. Author of articles in Guidebook and Directory for Metal Finishing Industries, Nelson's Encyclopedia; also articles on research in electrodeposition of metals, preparation of perchloric acid and use of perchlorates in electroplating, increasing plasticity of lime, preparation of selentates, telluric acid and compounds of indium, also stripping of copper from base metals. Holder of patents on electrodeposition of metals from perchlorate solutions, 1909; coloring liquid and method of staining metals, 1919; electroplating and refining of tin, 1922; electrolytic preparation of fluorine, 1924; electroplating of aluminum, 1940; purification of magnesium fluoride for use in coating lenses, 1948. Home: IN IND Died Mar. 23, 1973.

MATHESON, MARTIN, publisher; b. Jersey City, Feb. 1, 1895; s. Anthony M. and Amelia (Nelson) M.; B.S., Colgate U., 1917; m. Viola M. Wilbur, May 5, 1926; 1 dau., Mary Lee. Tchr. U. Sch., Patterson, N.J., 1920; with U.S. Rubber Co., 1920-24; advt. and sales mgr. John Wiley & Sons, Inc., N.Y.C., 1924-40, dir., 1930-60, asst. v.p., 1941-42, v.p. 1943-56, sr. v.p., sec., 1956-60. Served in U.S. Army, 1917-19; with AEF, France, 1918-19. Mem. Phi Beta Kappa, Lambda Chi Alpha, Alpha Delta Sigma. Republican. Conglist. Clubs: Players, University (N.Y.C.). Author: A History of Forty Eight, 1917-19, 1939. Home: Brookfield Center CT Died 1972.

MATHEWS, JOSEPH HOWARD, chemist; b. Auroraville, Wis., Oct. 15, 1881; s. Joseph and Lydia Tibbets (Cate) M.; B.S., U. of Wis., 1903, A.M., 1905; A.M., Harvard, 1906, Ph.D., 1908; m. Ella Barbara Gilfillan, June 26, 1909; children—Marion Zoe, Jean Barbara. Assistant in chemistry, U. of Wis., 1905; instr. chemistry, Case Sch. of Applied Science, Cleveland, O., 1906-07; asst. prof. chemistry, U. of Wis., 1911, asso. prof., 1917, prof., 1919-52, also chmn. of dept. and dir. course in chemistry. Commd. capt. Ordnance Dept., U.S. Army, July 10, 1917; maj., Jan. 15, 1918; hon. disch., Dec. 16, 1918; went to France as spl. investigator of problems connected with gas warfare, Sept. 1917; returned to U.S., Jan. 1918, and placed in charge offensive gas and research br. of trench warfare sect. Engring. Div. of Ordnance Dept. Criminal identification expert. Fellow A.A.A.S.; mem. Am. Chem. Soc., Sigma Xi, Alpha Chi Sigma, Phi Lambda Upsilon, Phi Kappa Phi. Presbyterian. Clubs: University, Rotary, Professional, Scabbard and Blade (Madison); Black Hawk Country. Co-author: Experimental Physical Chemistry, 1929; author: Firearms Identification, 2 vols., 1962, reprint, with 3 vols., 1973. over 60 papers on scientific subjects. Home: Madison WI Died Apr. 15, 1970; buried Madison WI

MATHEWS, WILLIAM RANKIN, editor, publisher; b. Lexington, Ky., Oct. 15, 1893; s. Robert Trot and Clara (Murry) M.; A.B., U. of Ill., 1917; LL.D., Butler University, 1957, U. Ariz., 1963; m. Betty Boyers, Apr. 12, 1919; children—Elizabeth Bovers (dec.), William Rankin, Charles Dawes and Ann Caro. Advertising salesman for San Francisco Chronicle, 1919-20; business mgr., Santa Barbara Morning Press, 1920-24; general mgr. Arizona Daily Star, Tucson, 1924-30, editor and publisher, 1930-69; dir. El Paso br. Fed. Res. Bank Dallas, 1958-64. Served as 2d lt. USMC, May 1917-July 1918, capt., July 1918-July 1919; wounded at Blanc Mont, France, Oct. 4, 1918; awarded Croix de Guerre with Palm and cited for capture of enemy machine guns and trench mortars and 75 prisoners nr. Vierzy, France, July 18, 1918. Received honorable mention for distinguished editorial writing by Pulitzer prize com., 1934. Mem. adv. com. Columbia Sch. of Journalism (Pulitzer Prize com.), 1944-56. Democratic presidential elector, 1932. Spl. adviser to Sec. of Defense, 1948; mem. bd. of regents U. of Ariz. and State Colls., 1950-61. Dir. Am. Soc. Newspaper Editors, 1950-52. Mason. Clubs: Old Pueblo, Tucson Country (Tucson). Editor: Europe Will Recover, 1947; The White Man's Future in the Orient, 1949; The Marshall Plan Pays Off, 1951; Are We Being Shouted into an Unwanted War?, 1951; Ten Days Behind the Iron Curtain, 1954. Home: Tucson AZ Died Oct. 27, 1969; buried Frankfort Cemetery, Frankfort KY

MATHEWSON, EDWARD PAYSON, metallurgist; b. Montreal, Can., Oct. 16, 1864; s. James Adams and Amelia Seabury (Black) M.; B.S. in mining, McGill, 1885; LL.D., 1922; D.Sc., Colo. Sch. of Mines, 1920; m. Alice Barry, June 25, 1890; children—Alice Seabury (Mrs. E.V. Graybeal), Grace (Mrs. N.C. Streit), Gertrude (Mrs. A.R. Nolin), Mary Elizabeth (Mrs. E.F. Bissantz), Edward Payson. Was assayer, 1886-89, supt., 1889-97, Pueblo (Colo.) Smelting & Refining Co.; joined Guggenheim's Sons tech. staff, 1897, and supt. and mgr. at Perth Amboy, N.J., Monterey, Mex., and Antofagasta, Chile, until 1902; in employ Anaconda Copper Mining Co., 1902-16, mgr. Washoe Reduction Works of company at Anaconda, 1903-16. Mgr. until Jan. 1, 1913, of Internat. Smelting & Refining Co.'s western plants, erecting same at Internat. Utah, and E. Chicago, Ind.; gen. mgr. British Am. Nickel Corp., Ltd., Toronto, 1916-18; dir. and cons. metallurgist, Am. Smelting & Refining Co., New York, 1918-19; cons. metallurgist since 1919; became prof. adminstrn. of mineral industries, U. of Ariz., 1926, now retired. Rep. fellow McGill U., 1923-26. Awarded gold medals, Instn. of Mining and Metallurgy (London), 1911, Mining & Metall. Soc. of Am., 1917. Fellow A.A.A.S.; mem. Am. Inst. Mining and Metall. Engrs. (pres. 1923; made mem. Legion of Honor for 50 years, membership, 1939, Soc. Chem. Industry (London), Tau Beta Phi, Sigma Delta Pi, Theta Tau. Episcopalian. Clubs: Old Pueblo (Tucson); Anaconda (Mont.) Engrs. Contbr. on metallurgy to tech. press and Trans. Inst. Mining Engrs. Inventor of various improvements in blast and reverberatory furnaces for smelting copper and lead ores. Home: 1143 E. Lowell Av., Tucson AZ‡

MATHEY, DEAN, banker; b. Brooklyn, New York, November 23, 1890; s. Louis A. and Josephine (Dean) M.; grad. Pringry Sch., 1908; B.Litt., Princeton, 1912; m. Gertrude Winans, Mar. 26, 1927; children—Dean Winans, Macdonald, David; married second, Helen N. Behr, September 22, 1950 (dec. 1965). With Wm. A. Read & Company, 1912-14; instructor Princeton Prep. School, 1914-15; partner Dillon, Read & Co., investment bankers, 1924-45; chmn. bd. Empire Trust Co., 1945-63, chmn. exec. com., 1963-66; hon. chmn. trustees Bank of N.Y., from 1966, also dir.; dir. Amerada Petrol. Corp., La. Land & Exploration Co., also United N.J. R.R. & Canal Co. Emeritus trustee Princeton. Served as lt. F.A., U.S. Army, 1917-19. Mem. Phi Beta Kappa Assos. Presbyn. Club: Princeton, Brook, Century (N.Y.C.). Author: Fifty Years of Wall Street, 1966. Home: Princeton NJ Died Apr. 1972.

MATHIES, WHARTON, banker, state edn. ofcl.; b. Monroe, Okla., May 14, 1902; s. Christopher C. and Annie Lee (Carnall) M.; student Hendrix Coll., Conway, Ark.; m. Jimmie Ingram, Jan. 14, 1922; children—Lucretia (Mrs. Carl McCoy), Ann (Mrs. Kyle Maxwell). Engaged in ins. bus., from 1922. Mem. Okla. Regents for Higher Edn., from 1941, sec., 1950-58, chmn., 1959-61. Chmn. Pushmataha County Democratic Com., 1938-50. Bd. dirs. Eastern Okla. Frontiers of Sci., Choctaw area Boy Scouts Am. Served with U.S. Navy, 1917-18. Methodist. Mason (Shriner), Lion. Address: Clayton OK Died Nov. 9, 1969.

MATSON, DONALD DARROW, neurosurgeon; b. Ft. Hamilton, N.Y., Nov. 28, 1913; s. Joseph and Kathleen (Connor) M.; A.B., Cornell U., 1935; M.D., Harvard, 1939; m. Dorothy Jean Everett, Sept. 11, 1943;children—Martha Jo, Donald Everett, James Edward, Barbara Baker. Intern Children's Med. Center, Peter Bent Brigham Hosp., Boston, 1939-43, neurosurgeon, 1948-69; resident Duke U. Hosp., 1947-48; pvt. practice, Boston, 1948-69; clin. prof. surgery Harvard Med. Sch., 1961-69; cons. neurosurgery VA Hosp., West Roxbury, Mass., Mass. Hosp. Sch.; mem. spl. med. adv. bd. VA, 1963-69. Served from lt. to maj. M.C., AUS, 1943-46. Decorated Bronze Star medal. Diplomate Am. Bd. Neurol. Surgery (chmn. 1965). Fellow A.C.S.; mem. Nat. Inst. Neurol. Diseases and Blindness (neurology postgrad. tng. com.), A.M.A., Soc. Neurol. Surgeons, Harvey Cushing Soc., Acad. Neurosurgery, Soc. U. Surgeons, Halstead Soc., A.A.A.S., Am. Neurol. Soc., New Eng., Boston surg. socs., Scandinavian Neurosurg. Soc., Am. Surg. Assn. Author: Treatment of Acute Cranio Cerebral Injuries Due to Missiles, 1948; Treatment of Acute Spinal Injuries Due to Missiles, 1948; (with Franc D. Ingraham) Neurosurgery in Infancy and Childhood, 1953; also numerous articles in med. publs. Adv. bd. Medical Specialties. Home: Chestnut Hill MA Died May 1969.

MATSON, MAX M., investment co. exec.; b. Dayton, O., Nov. 30, 1900; s. Isaac and Gertrude Matson; A.B., Ohio State U., 1923, LL.B., 1925; m. Lenore W. Weiss, Mar. 15, 1927; children—Robert I., J. Richard. Admitted to Ohio bar, 1925; practice law, Columbus, Ohio, 1925-30; agt. Mut. Benefit Life Ins. Co., 1932-70; engaged in investments and mergers, 1959-70; pres. Paul Hardeman, Inc., 1968-70. Mem. Zeta Beta Tau. Clubs: Oakwood Country (Cleve.); Palm Beach (Fla.) Country; Harmonie (N.Y.C.); Hollywood (N.J.) Golf. Home: Palm Beach FL Died Aug. 26, 1970.

MATTEI, ALBERT CHESTER, ret. oil exec.; b. Los Olivos, Cal., Mar. 26, 1895; s. Felix and Lucy (Fisher) M.; B.A., Stanford, 1917; m. Beatrice Ferne Orchard, Sept. 5, 1929; 1 son, Peter Orchard. Formerly petroleum geologist Pomeroy & Hamilton, Asso. Oil Co., Gen. Petroleum Corp.; was asst. to pres. Honolulu Oil Corp., San Francisco, pres. 1937-58, chmn. bd., 1958-60, ret., 1960. Mem. Com. Twenty-Five, Palm Springs. Republican. Clubs: Bohemian, Golf, Press and Union League, Pacific Union (San Francisco). Home: San Francisco CA Died Aug. 1, 1969; buried nr. Los Olivos, Santa Ynez Valley CA

MATTESON, VICTOR ANDRE, architect, engr.; b. Chicago, Ill., Aug. 22, 1872; s. Andre and Ellen C. (MacNaughton) M.; grad. Chicago Manual Training Sch., 1891; U. of Ill., 1895. Studied and traveled in Europe. Early associated with various architects' offices in Chicago; now in general pvt. practice alone; architect for a large number of pub. and pvt. bldgs. scattered through U.S. and specializing in waterworks and other pub. utility bldgs. Served as asst. prin. engr., of Construction Div. of the Army, War Dept., Washington, D.C., World War I. Fellow Am. Ins. Architects; mem. Ill. Soc. Architects, S.A.R., U. of Ill. Alumni Assn., Burnham Astron. Soc., Illini Club of Chicago, Sigma Chi. Mason. Office: 20 N. Wacker Drive., Chicago 6 IL‡

MATTFELD, MARIE, mezzo-soprano; b. Munich, Germany; d. Herman Schmid (concert-meister Munich Royal Opera Orchestra); grad. Royal Conservatory of Music, Munich; m. William Mattfeld, of N.Y. City, July 1890. Came to U.S., 1890; with Damrosch Opera Co., 1894-98, Sembrich Opera Co., 1900-01; sang at Stadt Theatre, Bremen, Germany, 1902-03; mem. Met. Opera Co. since 1905; sings in English, Italian, French and German. Home: New York NY*‡

MATTHAEI, FREDERICK CARL, mfg. exec.; b. Detroit, Sept. 17, 1892; s. Konrad Henry and Ottillie (Thiede) M.; B.A., U. Mich., 1914, Dr. Bus. Adminstrn., 1953; LL.D., Wayne U., 1952; D.B.S., Cleary Coll., Ypsilanti, Mich., 1952; m. Mildred Hague, Aug. 7, 1923; children—Frederick Carl, Konrad Henry. Founder, pres. Am. Metal Products Co., Detroit, 1917-54, chmn. bd., 1954-58; now dir.; dir. Detroit Bank & Trust Co., McLouth Steel Corp., Clinton

Engines Corp. Chmn. capital gifts com. Detroit Olympic Com. Established Animal Shelter for Humane Soc. Washtenaw County. Trustee, Evangelical Home for Children and Aged, Detroit; bd. regents U. Mich. Mem. Detroit Bd. Commerce (dir.), Sachem Tribe of Michiguama (hon.). Clubs: Question, Univ., Detroit Golf, Recess (past dir.), U. Mich. (past pres.), M (hon.), Athletic (hon.) (Detroit). Home: Ann Arbor MI Died Mar. 25, 1973.

MATTHEWS CHARLES SAMUEL, physician; b. Buffalo, Mar. 8, 1914; s. Samuel Lowery and Minna (Farbach) M.; Ph.G., U. Buffalo, 1937, B.S. in Pharmacy, 1939, M.A., 1941, M.D., 1944; m. Thelles B. Morgan, Dec. 24, 1944 (dec. July 1967); 1 dau., Penelope Faith; m. 2d, Janet M. Tenglund, Oct. 13, 1967; 1 son, Charles Samuel II. Rotating intern Millard Fillmore Hosp., Buffalo, 1944-45, asst. resident in obstetrics, 1945-46, attending obstetrician and gynecologist, 1950-68; asst. resident in obstetrics Sloane Hosp. for Women, N.Y.C., 1948-49, jr. resident in obstetrics, 1949-50. Vice pres. Houghton Acad. P.T.A., 1969-70. Bd. dirs. Houghton Acad., 1969-70, Wyoming County Cancer Soc., 1969. Served to capt. AUS. Diplomate Am. Bd. Obstetrics and gynecology, Nat. Bd. Med. Examiners. Fellow Am. Coll. Obstetricians and Gynecologists, A.C.S.; mem. A.M.A., Sigma Xi. Silver Springs NY Died Oct. 9, 1970; buried Grace Cemetery Castile NY

MATTHEWS, EUGENE ALEXANDER, lawyer; b. Manila, Ark., Nov. 25, 1908; s. George McDowell and Maggie (Bunch) M.; A.B., Henderson State Coll., 1931; LL.B., Ark. Law Sch., 1933; m. Mary Mildred Balch, Nov. 26, 1936; children—Eugene A., George B. Admitted to Ark. bar, 1932; asst. state counsel Ark. Agy. HOLC, 1934-39, state counsel, 1939-41; pvt. practice of law, Little Rock, 1941-45; mem. firm Wootton, Land & Matthews, Hot Springs, Ark., 1945; spl. chief justice Supreme Ct. Ark., 1970. Pres. Hot Springs YMCA, 1954-55, pres. S.W. area council. Served as pvt. USMC Res., World War II. Mem. Ark. Bar Assn. (pres. 1956-57). Methodist (steward). Clubs: Rotary (past pres.), Hot Springs Golf and Country (Hot Springs). Home: Hot Springs AR Died Sept. 28, 1972.

MATTHEWS, STEPHEN JOHNSON, assn. exec.; b. Emory, Tex., Oct. 30, 1912; s. I. Newton and Carlsie (Johnson) M.; B.S., East Tex. State Coll., 1935, M.S. in Adminstrv. Edn., 1938; courses Internat. City Mgrs. Assn.; m. Dorothy Jo Taylor, Oct. 25, 1944; 1 son, Stephen Taylor. City mgr., Borger, Tex., 1939-40, Pampa, Tex., 1940-42, 1947-48, Lubbock, Tex., 1949-55, San Antonio, 1955-58; exec. dir. Tex. Municipal League, from 1958. Served as lt. USNR, 1943-46. Mem. American Municipal Assn. (mem. exec. bd., 1958-60), Tex. (past pres.), Internat. (v.p.) city mgrs. assns. Mason, Rotarian. Home: Austin TX

MATTHEWS, WILLIAM ALBERT, clergyman, educator; b. Rowley Regis, Staffordshire, Eng., Apr. 6, 1868; s. John and Ann (Smart) M.; came to U.S., 1882; student Shurtleff Coll. (Alton, Ill.), 1890-93, Morgan Park Theol. Sem. (Chicago), 1888-90; A.B., Ewing (Ill.) Coll., 1895, A.M., 1898, Ph.D., 1900; studied U. of Chicago Divinity Sch., 1895-98; m. Della May Burton, June 22, 1892; children—Stewart B., Esther (wife of Dr. W.W. Newcomb), Ruth (Mrs. Peter Drakos), Delight (Mrs. Frank Warren), Wm. A., Dorothy Ann. Ordained Bapt. ministry, 1891; pastor successively St. Louis, Mo., Carbondale, Cambridge, Paw Paw, Aurora and Tabernacle Ch., Chicago (all of Ill.) until 1911; pres. Ewing Coll., 1911-13; pastor Dinuba and Los Angeles, Calif., until 1927; founder, 1927, and since pres. Los Angeles Bapt. Theol. Sem. Editor Rock of Ages," monthly. Address: 2713 Hyannis St., Los Angeles CA*‡

MATTHEWS, WILLIAM HENRY, clergyman; b. McHenry, Ill., July 23, 1868; s. Joseph Jay and Cornelia Maria (Talbot) M.; B.A., Lake Forest (Ill.) Coll., 1892, M.A., 1894, LL.B., Lake Forest U., 1894; student Columbia U. Law Sch.; grad. McCormick Theol. Sem., 1898; grad. work, U. of Chicago and Chicago Theol. Sem.; D.D., Jamestown (N.D.) Coll., 1912, Fargo Coll., 1912; m. Eva Chandler, July 9, 1895; children—Paul Chandler, Ruth Elizabeth (Mrs. Carl J.A. Olsen), William Henry, Edward Talbot, Eva Standish (Mrs. Allen H. Seed, Jr.), Mark Stanley. Ordained Presbyn. ministry, 1898; pastor Marengo, Ill., 1898-1901, Central Ch., Chicago, 1901-06, First Ch., Grand Forks, N.D., 1907-17, Greenwich Ch., N.Y. City, 1918-22; gen. sec. Am. Tract Soc. since 1922-44. Now General Secretary Emeritus. Admitted to Ill. bar, 1894. Built churches at Marengo, Chicago and Grand Forks. Exchange preacher, London, England, three summers, on Carnegie Church Peace Union Foundation. Chmn. Com. on Publication and Sabbath Sch. Work, Gen. Assembly, 1912; apptd. by Gen. Assembly to attend Pan-Presbyn. Council, Aberdeen, Scotland, 1913. Made spl. visit to Bedford and Elstow, Eng., summer, 1927, to secure material for celebration of John Bunyan Tercentenary by Evang. chs. in U.S. in 1928. Contbr. to many ch. periodicals on life and works of John Bunyan, the place of Christian literature in modern life, and home mission work in the northwest. Recorded Pilgrims' Progress as a talking book for the blind, 1935. Republican. Home: Hotel Sheraton, 303 Lexington Av., New York NY‡

MATTHEWS, ZACHARIAH KEODIRELANG, diplomat of Botswana; b. S. Africa, Oct. 20, 1901; s. Peter M. and Martha (Moeketsi) M.; B.A., LL.B., U.S. Africa; M.A., Yale, 1934; LL.D. (hon.), Rhodes U., 1961, Baker U., 1967, Franklin and Marshall Coll., 1967; m. Frieda Bokwe, Dec. 19, 1928; children—Vincent Joseph, Shena Seipelo (Mrs. Maqubela), John Knox, Frieda Lesego (Mrs. Letsunyane), Ethel Pulane (Mrs. Ngcakani). Headmaster, Adams High Sch., Natal, 1925-35; prof. Univ. Coll., Ft. Hare, Alice, S. Africa, 1936-59; engaged in legal practice, 1960-61; Africa sec. World Council Chs., Geneva Switzerland, 1962-66; ambassador of Republic of Botswana to U.S., 1966-68. Mem. Royal Commn. Higher Edn. in E. Africa, 1936-37; pres. Fedn. African Tchrs. Assns., 1942; mem. exec. com. S. African Inst. Race Relations. Mem. S. African Native Rep. Council, 1942-49. Editor: Responsible Government in a Revolutionary Age, 1966. Anthrop. research Barolong of S. Africa, 1936-39. Home: Botswana Died May 11, 1968; buried Gaberones Botswana.

MATTHIAS, JOHN MARSHALL, ret. judge; b. Van Wert, O., Jan. 20, 1903; s. Edward Shiloh and Mary F. (Crouch) M.; A.B., Ohio State U., 1928, law student, 1928-29, Franklin U., 1930; m. Lois Kirkpatrick, Mar. 20, 1939; 1 son, John Edward. Admitted to Ohio bar, 1931; gen. practice law, 1931-40; judge Columbus (O.) Muncipal Ct., 1940-54. Supreme Ct. Ohio, Columbus, 1954-71. Mem. Ohio Jud. Council, 1948-53. Rep. Ohio Legislature, 1935, 39. Mem. Ohio Municipal Judges Assn. (pres. 1948-53), Am., Ohio bar assns., Delta Upsilon, Delta Theta Phi. Presbyn. Mason (33 deg.). Club: University (Columbus). Home: Columbus OH Died Jan. 25, 1973.

MATTIA, VIRGINIUS DANTE, pharm. co. exec.; b. Newark, May 20, 1923; s. Virginius Dante and Laura (Santoro) M.; B.S., Rutgers U., 1944; M.D., N.Y. Med. Coll., 1950; m. Alice Ann Del Tufo, June 16, 1946; children—Peter, Gail, Mark, Barney. Intern St. Barnabas Med. Center, Newark, 1950-51; asso. editor Merck Manual, Merck & Co., Rahway, N.J., 1953-56; dir. med. lit. dept. Hoffmann-La Roche, Inc., Nutley, N.J., 1957-68, president and chief executive officer, 1968-71, also chmn. bd. dirs. and exec. com.; dir. Fidelity Union Trust Co., Newark. Chmn. Rutgers Med. Sch. Adv. Com., 1963. Served to lt. USNR, World War II, Korean War. Decorated knight officer Order Merit Republic Italy; recipient Internat. Humanitarian award B'nai B'rith, 1969. Fellow Internat., Am. colls. angiology, Am. Coll. Cardiology, Am. Coll. Nutrition, N.Y. Acad. Scis.; mem. A.M.A., Assn. Med. Dirs., Pharmaceutical Mfrs. Assn. (mem. board directors), N.J. Acad. Medicine, Essex County Heart Assn. (past pres.). Roman Catholic. Asso. editor: The Merck Manual of Diagnosis and Therapy, 1953-56. Contbr. sect. on Steriods to Practical Therapeutics, 1954. Home: Upper Montclair NJ Died July 4, 1971.

MATTINGLY, FREDERICK BROWNING, farm equipment mfr.; b. Eureka, Kan., Feb. 14, 1901; s. Charles Richard and Addie (Browning) M.; A.B., Kan. U., 1923; m. Frances Lowen, June 7, 1930; 1 dau., Ann. With Internat. Harvester Co., 1923-—, collector, asst. credit mgr., Wichita, Kan., 1926-29, credit mgr., Sweetwater, Tex., 1929-31, Wichita, 1931-35, Kansas City, 1935-42, asst. credit and collection dept., Chgo., 1942-44, mgr. credit and collection dept., 1944-56, dir. credits and collections, prices and contracts, 1956-59, treas., 1959-66, v.p., 1963-66; director LaSalle National Bank Chicago, Internat. Harvester Credit Corp., Chgo., dir. Frank G. Hough Co., Libertyville, Ill. Mem. Alpha Kappa Psi. Republican. Presbyn. Mason (32 deg). Clubs: University, Chicago, Economic, Executives (Chgo.). Home: Evanston IL Died Nov. 17, 1969; buried Memorial Park Cemetery.

MATTOX, WILLIAM EARL, vet. drug co. exec.; b. Portland, Tenn., Mar. 28, 1906; s. Charles and Bertha (Duffer) M.; student Butler U., 1932-33; m. Ruby Small, Dec. 9, 1939; 1 son, Stephen Andrew. With biochem. research div. Eli Lilly & Co., Indpls., 1929-53, successively lab. asst. supr., dept. head antibiotics and crystellization; founder, sec. Mattox & Moore, Inc., 1951-54, pres., 1954-61, chmn. bd., 1961-67. Mem. Am. Chem. Soc., Laurentian Hormone Conf. Republican. Presbyn. Mason. Patentee in field. Contbr. articles to profl. jours. Home: Indianapolis IN Died Dec. 19, 1967.

MATZKE, EDWIN BERNARD, botanist; b. New York City, Aug. 2, 1902; s. Conrad Joseph and Emilie (Frieling) M.; A.B., Columbia, 1924, Ph.D., 1930; student Kaiser Wilhelm Institut for Biology, Berlin-Dahlem and Univ. of Berlin (Cutting travelling fellow), 1928-29; unmarried. Asst. in botany, Columbia, 1924-28, instr. in botany, 1929-33, asst. prof., 1933-43, asso. prof., 1943-47, prof. of botany, 1947-69, chairman of department of botany, 1958-66, chairman of dept. of biological scis., 1966-67, asst. to dean Columbia Coll., 1944-60; lectr. Fordham U., 1942-44; research investigator Marine Biology Lab., summers 1949-56; bd. mgrs.; exec. com. of bd. N.Y. Bot. Garden, 1958-69. Fellow A.A.A.S., N.Y. Acad. Sciences. Member Botanical Soc. of Am., Am. Bryological Soc., Soc. for Study of Evolution, Torrey Botanical Club (treas., 1936, v.p., 1941, sec. 1942-44, pres. 1949, asso. editor 1950-59), Phi Beta Kappa, Sigma Xi. Catholic. Contributor numerous articles on cellular structure of plants, plant growth, floral morphology, coloration in plants, in numerous scientific publications. Researcher on three dimensional shapes of cells, cell division, floral anatomy and pigmentation, developmental morphology of liverworts. Home: Bronx NY Died Sept. 28, 1969.

MAUBORGNE, JOSEPH OSWALD, army officer; b. New York, N.Y., Feb. 26, 1881; s. Eugene Charles and Catherine Elizabeth (McLaughlin) M.; A.B., Coll. of St. Francis Xavier, N.Y. City, 1901; art student Art Students League, N.Y. City, 1901-03, Chicago Art Inst., 1922-23, Corcoran Art Gallery, Washington, D.C., 1923-26; student Army Signal Sch., 1909-10, Army War Coll., 1931-32; m. Katharine Hale Poore, Dec. 3, 1907; children—Joseph Oswald, Benjamin Poore. Commd. 2d lt. inf., U.S. Army, 1903, and advanced through the grades to maj. gen., 1937; with Signal Corps from 1916, chief signal officer, 1937-41, retired; in P.I., France and Panama. Radio pioneer; inventor of numerous radio devices; tech. adviser to U.S. delegations at Inter-Allied Radio Conf., 1919, Internat. Conf. on Elec. Communications, Paris, 1921, Pan-American Com. Conf., Mexico City, 1924, International Telegraphic Conference, Paris, 1925, Washington Radio Conference, 1927; member of the Defense Communications Board, Sept. 1940-Sept. 1941. Portrait painter and etcher, exhibited at Washington, D.C., San Francisco, Dayton, O.; portraits in collections at U.S. Mil. Acad. and in pvt. collections of Mrs. Calvin Coolidge and others. Sci. violin builder; two prizes violin making Internat. Competition, Hague, Holland, 1949. Member Institute Radio Engineers, 1914-25. Awarded D.S.M. (U.S.); Marconi Memorial medal of service by Vet. Wireless Oprs. Assn., 1941. Catholic. Club: Army and Navy (D.C.). Author: Practical Uses of the Wavemeter in Wireless Telegraphy, 1914. Contbr. articles on radio to tech. mags.; author of brochures (U.S. Army) on Cryptanalysis. Home: Little Silver NJ Died June 5, 1971.

MAUGH, LAWRENCE C(ARNAHAN), engr.; b. Wyoming, Ont., Can., Apr. 3, 1901; s. John and Ethel (Lawson) M.; B.S., U. of Mich., 1921, Ph.D., 1934; M.S., S.D. State Coll., 1923; m. Lois Amelia Rowe, June 26, 1931; children—Roger Edward, Lois Ann. Instr. in civil engring., S.D. State Coll., 1921-24; bridge designer, Ind. State High Commn., 1924-25; instr. in civil engring., U. of Mich., 1925-31, asst. prof., 1931-41, asso. prof., 1943-47, prof. civil engring. from 1948; structural cons., Goodyear Aircraft Corp., Akron, O., 1942-43. Member Am. Soc. C.E., Am. Soc. Engring. Edn., Internat. Assn. of Bridge and Structural Engring., Mich. Engring. Soc., Sigma Xi, Tau Beta Pi. Author: Statically Indeterminate Structures, 1946. Contbr. tech. articles on structural analysis in engring. publs. Home: Ann Arbor MI Died Oct. 31, 1971; buried Arborerest Cemetery.

MAULE, HARRY EDWARD, editor; b. Fairmount, Neb., July 13, 1886; s. John Penrose and Mary Katherine (Finigan) M.; ed. common schs. and E. Denver High Sch.; m. Edna J. O'Dell, July 12, 1910; 1 dau., Katherine (Mrs. Clifford Holske). Reporter Denver and N.Y. City, 1903-05; corr. and feature writer in Mexico, 1906-07, mgr. of N.Y., Boston, Detroit, New Haven burs., United Press Assn., 1907-11; editor book dept. Doubleday, Page & Co., v.p., Doubleday, Doran &Co. to June 1939; later with Random House, Inc., book pubs., until 1966; trustee Village of Garden City, 1942-47. Member Authors League America. Episcopalian. Clubs: Century Association (New York); Dutch Treat, Cherry Valley. Editor: A Book of War Letters, 1943, Great Tales of the American West, Modern Library, 1945, The Pocket Book of Western Stories, Pocket Books, 1945. Author: Boys' Book of New Inventions, 1912. Co-editor: The Man From Main Street: A Sinclair Lewis Reader, 1953. Contbr. to mags. Home: Garden City NY Died Apr. 8, 1971.

MAURER, JAMES HUDSON, labor official; b. Reading, Pa., Apr. 15, 1864; s. James D. and Sarah (Lorah) M.; ed. pub. schs., 14 mos.; m. Marj. J. Missmer, Apr. 15, 1886; children—Charles H., Martha M. (Mrs. Ralph Dundore). Newsboy, farm hand, factory worker, and at 15 machinist's apprentice; joined Knights of Labor, 1880, Socialist Labor party, 1898, Socialist party, 1902; candidate of Socialist party for gov. of Pa., 1906; mem. Nat. Exec. Com., same party, 10 yrs.; mem. Pa. Ho. of Rep., 3 terms, 1910, 14, 16, introducing Workmen's Compensation Act, and other labor measures; pres. Pa. Fedn. of Labor, 1912-28; pres. Labor Age Monthly, Workers Ednl. Bur. of America; dir. Brookwood Coll., Katonah, N.Y. Became chmn. Old Age Assistance Commn. of Pa., 1917. Mem. Am. Commn. on Conditions in Ireland, 1920; made tour of Europe with Am. Seminar, 1923; mem. of Am. Fact-finding Commn. to Russia, 1927; mem. City Council, Reading, 1928-32. Socialist candidate for v.p. of U.S., 1928 and 1932, also for U.S. Senate, 1934; now retired. Author: The Far East, 1910; It Can Be Done, 1938. Home: 1355 N. 11th St., Reading PA‡

MAURIAC, FRANCOIS, author; b. 1885. Recipient Nobel prize for lit., 1952. Author: Les Chemins de la mer; Eucharist: the Mystery of Holy Thursday; Letters on Arts and Literature; Mask of Innocence; Unknown Sea (new edit.); Woman of the Pharisees; La chair et le sang, 1912; Le baiser au lepreux, 1922; Feuve de Feu, 1923; Genitrix, 1924; Le Desert de l'amour, 1925; Therese Desqueyroux, 1926; Therese (new edit.); Destins, 1927; Vie de Racine, 1930; Souffrance et Bonheur du Chretien, 1931; Le Noeud des Viperes, 1932; Le Mystere Frontenac, 1932; Proust's Way, 1950; Loved and the Unloved, 1953; River of Fire, 1954; Double Image, 1955; recent publ. of translations into English, include: Kiss for the Leper, 1950; Genetrix, 1950; The Dark Angels, That Which Was Lost, Knot of Vipers, Desert of Love, Men I Hold Great, 1951; Great Men, Little Misery, Stumbling Block, The Enemy, Weakling, 1952; Les chemins de la mer, Eucharist, 1953; Flesh and Blood, 1954, 1955; Stumbling Block, 1956; Lines of Life, 1957; Le Drole, 1957; Questions of Precedence, 1959; The Son of Man, 1959; Second Thoughts, 1961; Cain, Where Is Your Brother, 1963; De Gaulle, 1966. Mem. French Acad., Am. Acad. Arts and Letters, Nat. Inst. Arts and Letters. Address: Paris France Died Sept. 1, 1970.

MAURY, JOHN WILLIAM DRAPER, surgeon; b. New York, Aug. 21, 1871; s. Mytton (q.v.) and Virginia (Draper) M.; student Mass. Inst. Tech., 1891-2; B.S., Harvard, 1895, M.D., Univ. Med. Coll. (New York U.), 1898; m. Alice Hortense Pray, of Shirley, Mass., June 12, 1901. Instr. histology, Univ. Med. Coll., 1900-1; instr. operative surgery, Polyclinic Sch. and Hosp., 1900-2; asst. surgeon to out-patients, orthopedic dept., Bellevue Hosp.; asst. surgeon out-patient dept. Roosevelt Hosp.; instr. experimental surgery, 1905, now adj. in surgery, Columbia; fellow Rockefeller Inst. for Med. Research. Fellow N.Y. Acad. Medicine; mem. A.M.A., N.Y. State Med. Assn., Harvey Soc., Soc. for Med. Research. Club: Harvard. Author: Surgical Differentials, 1905. Contbr. many surg. reviews and editorial matter on surg. topics to Medical News. Address: 264 W. 57th St., New York‡

MAXCY, GARDINER JOSIAH, business exec.; b. Portland, Me., Apr. 15, 1913; s. Robert Farrington and Blanche Rose (Cosley) M.; student Gov. Dummer Acad., 1932; B.S., Bowdoin Coll., 1936; m. Marjorie Jackson, Oct. 4, 1935; children—Anne (Mrs. Jeremiah Dexter Newbury), Robert Farrington, II, Carolyn. With Colonial Press, Inc., from 1936, gen. mgr., from 1951, v.p., dir., from 1953; with C.H. Simonds Co., from 1943, gen. mgr., from 1951, v.p., dir., from 1953; pres. Lexington Press, Inc. (Mass.); v.p., dir. Calais Water and Power Co. Dir. Clinton Home Aged; bd. overseers Squirrel Island, Me. Mem. C. of C. (pres., dir.), Delta Kappa Epsilon. Episcopalian (vestryman). Rotarian (past pres.; dir.). Home: Lexington MA Died Jan. 19, 1971; interred Churchyard of St. Mary's Episcopal Ch., Falmouth Foreside ME

MAXEY, EDWIN, university prof.; b. Royal, Pa., Oct. 26, 1869; s. Thomas and Ann (Price) M.; Ph.B., Bucknell U., 1893; LL.B., Chicago Law Sch., 1896, LL.M., 1897; D.C.L., Ill. Coll. of Law, 1898; Ph.M., University of Chicago, 1899; M.Dip., Columbian University, 1903; (LL.D., Ill. Coll. of Law, 1901). Pres. Palatinate Coll., 1893-5; lecturer Ill. Coll. of Law, 1897-9; dean Aurora Law Sch., 1898-1900; dean law dept. Southern U., 1900-1; fellow polit. science, U. of Wis., 1901-2; lecturer on colonial law and govt., Columbian U., 1902-3; prof. constl. and internat. law, W.Va. U., 1903-6; prof. pub. law and diplomacy, U. of Neb., since 1906. Counsel for Japanese in the case against San Francisco sch. bd.; mem. Com. of One Hundred. Fellow Internat. Soc. of Intellectuals; mem. Phi Alpha Tau, Nat. Geog. Soc. Mason (32 deg., K.T.), K.P. Republican. Author: Some Questions of Larger Politics, 1901; Triumphs of American Diplomacy; International Law, 1906; Suffrage Extension in Rhode Island. Asso. Editor The Arena since 1904; legal editor Delta Chi Quarterly since 1906. Writer of article on Porto Rico in The Making of America; article on Conflict of Laws in Am. Ency. of Law; also monographs on polit. subjects and contbns. to Am., English, Japanese, and French polit. revs. and legal jours. Address: Lincoln NB‡

MAXON, LOU RUSSELL, advertising executive; born Marietta, O., July 28, 1900; s. Frank Louis and Laura Ann (Gilpin) M.; ed. Highland Park High Sch., Muhlenberg Coll.; LL.D., Syracuse (New York) University, 1962; married Ruth Elizabeth Wold, Sept., 1946; children—Alin, Ruth, Frank; children (by a previous marriage)—Lou A., Marjorie B. Began as newspaper reporter and editor, 1915; founder, pres. Maxon, Inc., advertising agency, Detroit, Michigan, 1929; dep. administrator Office Price Adminstrn., 1943. Clubs: Detroit Athletic, Detroit; Duquesne (Pitts.); Grosse Pointe (Mich.) Yacht; Bloomfield Hills (Mich.). Home: Grosse Pointe MI Died May 15, 1971; buried Onaway MI

MAXWELL, ARTHUR FREEMAN, banker; b. Biddeford, Me., June 19, 1899; s. Archie B. and Ina. F. (Welch) M.; ed. Biddeford pub. schs.; m. Rena B. Chappell, Oct. 7, 1922 (dec.); children—Archie B., Richard A., Muriel V.; m. 2d, Clara E. Gray, June 3, 1936; children—Barbara L., Bruce. Teller, First Nat. Bank, Biddeford, 1919-21, asst. cashier, 1921-29, v.p., Biddeford, 1929-43, exec. v.p., 1943-48, pres., 1948-69, chmn. bd., 1969-72, also dir.; pres. trustee Biddeford Savs. Bank; pres. Biddeford & Saco Water Co.; dir. Fed. Res. Bank Boston, 1958-63; dir., exec. com. Central Me. Power Co., Augusta; dir., finance commn. Union Mut. Life Ins. Co., Portland. Past pres., dir. Me. Publicity Bur. Treas., dir. McArthur Library Assn., Greenwood Cemetery Assn., McArthur Home for Aged People, Biddeford. Mem. Me. C. of C. (past pres.), Savs. Bank Assn. Me., Newcomen Soc. Eng., Me. (past pres.), Am. (retirement com.) bankers assns. Republican. Conglist. Mason (Shriner). Club: Portland. Home: Biddeford ME Died Feb. 25, 1972; buried Biddeford ME

MAXWELL, ARTHUR STANLEY, author, editor; b. London, Eng., Jan. 14, 1896; s. George Thomas and Alice Maud (Crowder) M.; student Stanborough Coll. (Eng.), 1912-15; Litt.D., Andrews U., 1970; m. Rachel Elizabeth Joyce, May 3, 1917; children—Maureen, Graham, Mervyn, Lawrence, Malcolm, Deirdre. Came to U.S., 1936. Editor, Present Truth, Stanborough Press, Ltd., Eng., 1920-36, gen. mgr., 1925-32; dir. Pacific Press Pub. Assn., Mountain View, Cal., also editor Signs of the Times, 1937-70. Author: Christ's Glorious Return, 1924; Protestantism Imperilled, 1926; Great Issues of the Age, 1927; This Mighty Hour, 1933; Our Wonderful Bible, 1935; History's Crowded Climax, 1940; War of the Worlds, 1941; Great Prophecies for Our Time, 1943; So Little Time, 1946; God and the Future, 1952; The Coming King, 1953; Your Bible and You, 1959; You and Your Future, 1959; Courage for the Crisis, 1961; Time Running Out, 1963; Under The Southern Cross, 1966; Good News for You, 1967; This is the End, 1967; Man the World Needs Most, 1970; (juvenile) The Bible Story, 10 vols., 1953-57; Uncle Arthur's Bedtime Stories, 48 vols., 1924-71, The Children's Hour, 5 vols., 1945-49; others. Home: Los Altos Hills CA Died Nov. 13, 1970; buried Palo Alto CA

MAXWELL, GAVIN, author; b. Mochrum, Scotland, July 15, 1914; s. Aymer Edward and Mary (Percy) M.; ed. Stowe Sch., Buckinghamshire, Eng.; M.A., Hertford Coll., Oxford U.; m. Lavinia Joan Lascelles, Feb. 1, 1962. Owner, Soay Shark Fisheries, 1944-49; portrait painter, 1949-52; writer, 1952-—. Mem. adv. com. wildlife youth service World Wildlife Fund. Served to maj. Scots Guards, 1939-41, Spl. Operations, 1941-44. Fellow Royal Soc. for Lit., Royal, Am. geog. socs., Zool. Soc. (sci. fellow); mem. P.E.N., Fauna Preservation Soc., Wildfowl Trust (hon. life). Author: Harpoon at a Venture, 1952; God Protect Me from My Friends, 1956; A Reed Shaken by the Wind (Heinemann award Royal Soc. Lit.), 1957; The Ten Pains of Death, 1959; Ring of Bright Water (Book Soc. and Book-of-Month Club selection, 1969; The Otters' Tale, 1962; The Rocks Remain, 1962. Contbr. to New Statesman, Saturday Rev., 20th Century, Nat. Geog., Am. Mag. Natural History, Observer, also other periodicals. Home: London England Died Sept. 1969.

MAXWELL, JOSEPH RAYMOND NONNATUS, college pres.; b. Taunton, Mass., Nov. 7, 1899; s. Richard E. and Caroline (Carpenter) M.; student Holy Cross Coll., 1918-19; Jesuit Novitiate and Juniorate, 1919-23; A.B., Boston Coll., 1925, A.M., 1926; Ph.D., Fordham U., 1930; S.T.L., Weston Coll., 1933; Litt.D., Colegio Real, Bogata, Colombia, 1938; LL.D., Saint Joseph's College, 1943, Tufts U., 1955. Entered Jesuit order, 1919; ordained priest Roman Cath. Ch., 1932; teacher Holy Cross Coll., 1926-29; prof. Weston Coll., 1933-34; private study in Belgium, 1934-35; dean Boston College, Chestnut Hill, Mass., 1935-39, president from 1951; president and trustee Holy Cross Coll., 1939-45; rector Cranwell Prep. School Lenox, Mass., 1945. Ex-mem. bd. Collegiate Authority of Mass.; former mem. exec. com. N.E. Assn. Colls. and Secondary Schs. Decorated Cavalier Royal Crown of Italy. Member Association Am. Colleges (pres. 1955), N.E. Classical Assn. (pres. 1943), Alpha Sigma Nu. Clubs: University, Algonquin, Bostonia. Author: The Happy Ascetic, 1935; Completed Fragments (verse), 1936. Contbr. to America (mag.). Address: Chestnut Hill MA Died Sept. 19, 1971; buried Weston College, Weston MA

MAXWELL, RUSSELL LAMONTE, army officer (retired), executive American Machine & Foundry Co.; b. Oakdale, Ill., Dec. 28, 1890; s. Thomas Samuel and Margaret Alzette (Hildebrand) M.; B.S., U.S. Mil. Acad., 1912; grad. Command and Gen. Staff Sch., 1924; Army Indsl. Coll., 1925, Army War Coll., 1934; Coast Arty. Sch.; m. Katherine Winans, Nov. 3, 1914; children—William Ragland, Robert Edwin, James Winans. Commd. 2d lt. F.A., 1912; served overseas in Army of Occupation, Germany, World War I; comd. ordnance depot near Coblenz, 1918; transferred to Ordnance Dept., Washington, D.C., July 1, 1920; detailed to G.H.Q. Air Force as ordnance officer, 1935; returned to Washington, 1939, to serve on staff of asst. sec. of war; apptd. by President Roosevelt lt. col., adminstr. of export control, July 2, 1940; promoted brig. gen. (temp.), Feb. 1941, major gen., Feb. 1942; in charge of U.S. Mil. Mission in Cairo, 1941; comdr. U.S. forces in Middle East, 1942; assistant chief of staff, G-4, September 1943-46; retired from Army. Elected v.p. Am. Machine & Foundry Co., Aug. 1946, v.p. in charge of personnel and public relations, dir., 1946-56. Episcopalian. Mason. Clubs: University (New York); Army and Navy, Army and Navy Country (Washington); Chevy Chase (Md.). Editor Army Ordnance (mag.), 1925-26. Home: Washington DC Died Nov. 24, 1968; buried U.S. Mil. Acad., West Point NY

MAY, A. WILFRED, executive editor; b. Philadelphia, Pa., April, 5, 1900; s. Morris and Amelia K. May; A.B., Columbia Coll., 1919, A.M., Columbia Univ. Faculty Polit. Sci. 1932; m. Margaret Spiegelberg, May 24, 1926 (div.); 1 son, John Martin; married second, Vivian Reade, Aug. 7, 1949 (div.). Began as woolen mill worker, 1920; purchasing agent and sec.-treas. A.B. Kirschbaum Co., Phila., Pa., 1920-28, sec.-treas. Kempner Realty Corp., 1929; researcher and lecturer, Columbia U., 1930-34; researcher at the London School of Econs., 1936-37; econ. expert Securities and Exchange Commn., Washington, D.C., 1935-36; dir. div. research and statistics, U.S. Treasury War Finance Div. in N.Y. State, 1942-44; fgn. corr. N.Y. Herald Tribune, North Am. Newspaper Alliance, London Financial Times, etc., later exec. editor Commercial and Financial Chronicle, N.Y.C.; sole U.S. correspondent Internat. Economic Conference, Moscow, 1952; accredited press member U.N., mem. faculty New Sch. for Social Research, N.Y. City. Trustee Ednl. Alliance. Stadium Concerts, Silurians Soc., Wine and Food Soc. (emeritus), Overseas Press Corrs. Fund. Mem. Financial Writers Assn., Am. Statis. Assn. (mem. com.), Business Council, N.Y. Security Analysts, Econs. Nat. Committee, National Cultural Foundation, Council on Foreign Relations. Zeta Delta Chi. Clubs: Harmonie, Overseas Press, Dutch Treat, Bohemians (N.Y.C.). Author numerous books and articles in the U.S.A. and Europe and the Far East. Home: New York City NY Died Nov. 12, 1969.

MAY, ALONZO BERYL, educator; b. Joplin, Mo., Mar. 10, 1906; s. Charles A. and Nellie May (Warner) M.; B.S., Kan. State Tchrs. Coll., 1927; A.M., U. Kan., 1935; Ph.D., U. Ia., 1937; advanced study Harvard, Princeton, Columbia; m. Beulah B. Reed, Aug. 12, 1934. Prof. econs. U. Denver, 1936-37, 38-42, 46-—, now prof. econs., chmn. econs. dept.; v.p. Investment Research Corp., mgmt. cons., 1959-68, also dir. organizer 8 comml. banks. Served to lt. USNR, 1943-46; comdr. Res. ret. Fellow Royal Econ. Soc. (Eng.); mem. Am. Econs. Assn., Econs. Club Denver (organizer), Am. Legion, Res. Officers Assn., Alpha Kappa Psi, Beta Gamma Sigma. Republican. Mason. Contbr. articles to mags., econs. jours.; newspaper columnist. Home: Denver CO Died May 20, 1968; buried Hillcrest Meml. Park, Centralia IL

MAY, ARTHUR JAMES, historian; b. Rockdale, Pa., Jan. 21, 1899; s. William and Mary (Mitchell) M.; A.B., Wesleyan U. (Conn.), 1921; M.A., U. Pa., 1923, Ph.D., 1926; student Columbia, 1925; m. Hilda Dewey Jones, June 17, 1926; children—Christopher, Stephen. Asst. instr. history U. Pa., 1921-24, Brown U., 1924-25; instr. U. Rochester, 1925-26, asst. professor, 1926-29, professor, 1929-64, prof. emeritus, univ. historian, 1964-68; staff Duke, summer of 1927; lectr. Austrian, German univs., 1948, 62, 66; lecturer in Poland, 1962. President of the Friends of Rochester Pub. Library, 1953-55. Recipient Adams prize Am. Hist. Assn., 1952; Fulbright scholar, 1955, 61; Guggenheim fellow, 1955. Served U.S. Army, 1918. Mem. Am. Historical Assn., Phi Beta Kappa. Clubs: Philosophers, Rochester City (pres. 1935-36). Author: Contemporary American Opinion of Mid-Century Revolutions, 1927; The Age of Metternich, 1933; Europe and Two World Wars, 1947; The Hapsburg Monarchy, 1867-1914, 1951; A History of Civilization—The Mid-Seventeenth Century to Modern Times, 1956; The Passing of the Hapsburg Monarchy, 1914-1918, 1966; Vienna in the Age of Franz Josef, 1966; Europe Since 1939, 1966. Contbr. to numerous Am., European publs. Home: Rochester NY

MAY, MORTON J., chmn. May Dept. Stores Co., St. Louis; v.p. and dir. Commercial Investment Trust, Shoenberg Real Estate & Investment Co.; dir. Eagle Trading Stamp Co., Associated Retailers, Lesser Goldman Co. Home: St Louis MO Died May 1968.*

MAY, THOMAS, merchandising exec. Vice chmn., dir. May Dept. Stores, Los Angeles; dir. C.I.T. Financial Corp. Home: Beverly Hills CA Died Aug. 1968.*

MAY, WILLIAM HENRY, chmn. bd. and dir. May McEwen Co.; b. Burlington, N.C., Mar. 11, 1875; s. Henry P. and Barbara (Clapp) M.; student Coll.; m. Emma W. Sharpe, Aug. 6, 1906; children—W.H., Jr., S. John Sharpe. With May Hosiery Mills since 1907, became pres., 1912; pres. Vance Knitting Co.; v.p. and dir. Graybur Silk Mills, Dotham Silk Hosiery Co. Office: Burlington NC*‡

MAYBECK, BERNARD RALPH, architect; b. N.Y. City, Feb. 7, 1862; ed. pub. and pvt. schs.; student Ecole Nationale et Speciale des Beaux Arts, Paris, France, 1881-86, and Ecole des Beaux Arts, Arts et Metier,

Louvre and Sorbonne, 1896-98; spl. courses, U. of Calif., 1894-96 and 1898-1900; hon. M.A., Mills College, 1923; LL.D., U. of Calif., 1930; m. Annie White, 1890; children—Wallen White, Kerna McKeehan. Instr. of drawing and descriptive geometry and architecture, U. of Calif., 1894-1900; originator and mgr. Phoebe A. Hearst competition for archtl. design for U. of Calif., 1896-1900; founder dept. of architecture, U. of Calif., 1899; asso. architect Golden Gate Exposition, 1939. Awarded 2 silver medals Ecole des Beaux Arts, 1885, memorial for U. of Calif. competition, A.I.A., 1900; gold medal, St. Louis and San Francisco expns. Supervising architect with U.S. Shipping Bd., for town of Clyde, 1918. Designer: Palace of Fine Arts, Panama-Pacific Expn.; Principia Coll., Elsah, Ill.; gen. plans Mills Coll.; (with Julia Morgan) Phoebe A. Hearst Memorial, Univ. of Calif.; Packard bldgs., San Francisco, Oakland and Los Angeles. Mem. Berkeley City Planning Commn. Hon. mem. San Francisco chapter A.I.A.; pres. Art Assn., San Francisco; founder Council of Allied Arts; mem. San Francisco Soc. Architects, Societe des Eleves de M. Andre. Paris. Republican. Unitarian. Clubs: Bohemian, Commonwealth, Commercial. Off Night (San Francisco); Hillside, Faculty, Cordornices, Cragmont (Berkeley). Home: 2745 Buena Vista Way, Berkeley, Calif. Office: 57 Post St., San Francisco CA‡

MAYBELL, CLAUDE, cartoonist; b. Portland, Ore., May 8, 1872; s. Stephen and Jane M.; ed. pub. schs. and Sch. of Design, San Francisco, 3 yrs.; m. 1896, Ella Crallee. Cartoonist on Chronicle and Examiner, San Francisco, 1891-3, New York Recorder, Brooklyn Citizen, 1893-6, Pa. Grit, Williamsport, Pa., 1896-1900, Phila. Inquirer, 1900-1, Brooklyn Daily Eagle, since Nov., 1901. Residence: 7 E. 135th St., New York‡

MAYER, CHARLES HOLT, lawyer; b. Sturgeon, Mo., Feb. 8, 1876; s. Daniel and Ann Eliza (Welch) M.; ed. Wentworth Mil. Acad., Lexington, Mo.; LL.B., Cornell U., 1898; m. Josephine Thrailkill, Dec. 11, 1906. Admitted to Mo. bar, 1898, and began practice at St. Joseph; mem. firm Mayer, Conkling & Sprague; dir. and gen. counsel Kansas City Gas Co., Wyandotte County Gas Co., St. Joseph Gas Co., St. Joseph Ry. Light, Heat & Power Co. City atty. St. Joseph, 1902-04; mem. Mo. State Senate, 1907-11; judge Circuit Court of Mo., 1912-17. Democrat. Clubs: St. Joseph Country; Kansas City. Home: 2605 Indian Trail Drive. Office: Corby Bldg., St Joseph MO‡

MAYER, EDWARD EVERETT, psychiatrist; b. Allegheny, Pa., June 18, 1876; s. Lippman and Elise (Hecht) M.; B.A., U. of Pittsburgh, 1895, M.A., 1899, M.D., 1897; studied U. of Wuerzberg, Germany, 1897-98, U. of Paris, 1898-99; m. Rose Mae Lamm, June 16, 1902; 1 dau., Catherine (Mrs. Norman J. De Roy). Practiced at Pittsburgh, Pa., since 1900; apptd. Bd. of Health physician, 1900; asso. prof. neurology, U. of Pitt., 1902-10, prof. psychiatry 1910-46, now emeritus; dir. Mental Health Clinic Dept. Pub. Welfare, Pittsburgh, 1922-39; also served as psychiatrist to Montefiore, South Side and Presbyn. hosps.; med. dir. Fairview Sanatorium; supervising dir. Behavior Clinic, Allegheny County. Mem. Am. Med. Assn., Am. Psychiatric Assn., Assn. for Research on Nervous and Mental Diseases, Am. Psychopathol. Assn., Central Neuropsychiatric Assn., Am. Orthopsychiatric Assn. and other med. soc. Ind. Republican. Reformed Jewish religion. Clubs: Concordia, South Hills Golf. Editor: Oppenheim's Diseases of the Nervous System, 1900; (with others) Tice's Practice of Medicine, 1914; (with others) Graham's Surgical Diagnosis, 1931. Home: 5562 Hobart St. Office: 2601 Forbes St., Pittsburgh 17 PA‡

MAYER, ERNEST DE W(AEL), fgn. service officer; b. N.Y. City, Mar. 1, 1903; s. Albert E. and Valentine (De Wael) M.; student Lycee d'Anvers, Stanton Mil. Acad.; pvt. tutors Holland and Eng.; m. Jean Heffernan, Apr. 9, 1928; children—Gerald S., Janet. Newspaper work, N.Y. City, 1921-24, comml. work, 1924-30; apptd. fgn. service officer, v. consul career, sec. Diplomatic Service, 1931; various consular and diplomatic capacities, Havre, France, 1932-35, Southampton, Eng., 1935, Paris, 1935-40, Casablanca and Rabat, Morocco, 1940-44, London, Eng., 1944, Brussels, Belgium, 1944-46, Baden Baden, Germany, 1946-49, Montreal, Que., Can., 1949-51; Am. consul, Quebec City, Can., 1951-53; counselor of embassy, Can., 1953; officer in charge No. European Affairs, Dept. State, 1956-59; dep. chief mission, Accra, Ghana, 1959; consul gen., Tangier, Morocco, from 1960. Decorated Medal of Freedom, 1947. Home: Washington DC Died Dec. 1968.

MAYER, GOTTFRIED OSCAR, meat packer; b. Chgo., Jan. 31, 1908; s. Gottfried and Helen (Jansen) M.; student Amherst Coll., 1925-27; A.B., Harvard, 1929; grad. student Northwestern U.; m. Ruth McKenna, Mar. 4, 1935; children—Roger G., Elsa J. (Mrs. Edward J. Schneiders), G. Philip, Margaret, Louise; m. 2d, Alice A. Husisian, July 11, 1959. With Oscar Mayer & Co., Chgo., 1930-68, sausage foreman, 1933, gen. plant supt., 1934-38, gen. mgr., 1938-43, co. dir., 1938-68, v.p. merchandising, 1942-58, exec. v.p., 1958-60, v.p., 1960-62, v.p. bus. devel., 1962-66, vice chmn. bd., 1966-68; v.p., dir. Kartridg-Pak Machine Co., from 1945. Bd. dirs. Am. Meat Inst. Found.; adv. bd. Wis. Found. Ind. Colls. Mem. C. of C. (dir., pres. 1952), Madison Assns. (pres. 1951). Clubs: Madison Country, Maple Bluff Country (Madison); Chicago Athletic Assn., Synachwine (Chgo.). Home: Chicago IL Died May 1969.

MAYER, HARRY HUBERT, rabbi; b. Pittsburgh, Pa., Jan. 24, 1874; s. Lippman and Alice (Hecht) M.; B.A., U. of Cincinnati, 1896; Rabbi, Hebrew Union Coll., Cincinnati, 1896; grad. study in Germany, 1896-97; m. Cornelia Augusta Ney, Jan. 2, 1905; 1 son, William Lippman. Rabbi of the Temple, Little Rock, Ark., 1897-99, Kansas City, Mo., 1899-1928, rabbi emeritus since 1928. Pres. Kansas City Pure Milk Commn., 1908-18; trustee of Drum Memorial Agrl. Sch.; dir. United Jewish Charities; chaplain Dem. Nat. Conv., 1900. Mem. Central Conf. Am. Rabbis, Franklin Inst. (v.p.), Philos. Soc. of Kansas City, Veiled Prophets, Zeta Beta Tau (dir. nat. ednl. com.); hon. sec. Palestine Exploration Fund of England. Awarded medal by German Red Cross, 1919. Speaker for overseas and war relief campaigns, Executive dir. of Near East Relief com. of Western Mo. Republican. Mason (Shriner), B'nai B'rith. Clubs: Fortnightly, Professional Men's (v.p.), Oakwood Country. Author: Adolf Jellinek (monograph). Editor: Union Hymnal (2d edit.), 1914. Author and editor: The Lyric Psalter, 1940; The Modern Reader's Book of Psalms, 1944. Contbr. essays, reviews, Kansas City MO‡

MAYER, HENRIK MARTIN, painter; b. Nashua, N.H., Dec. 24, 1908; student Manchester Inst. Arts and Sci.; B.F.A., Yale. Asst. dir., instr. painting Herron Art Inst., Indpls., 1933-36; dir., instr. painting Hartford Art Sch., Wadsworth Atheneum, 1946; prof. painting, chmn. faculty Hartford Art Sch., U. Hartford, 1956-73; lectr. pictorial analysis and painting techniques; work exhibited Art Inst. Chgo., Toledo Mus. Art, Nat. Acad. Design, Corcoran Gallery art, Pa. Acad. Fine Arts, Carnegie Inst., Toronto and Montreal museums, Butler Art Inst., Whitney Mus., Herron Art Inst.; represented in collections Ind. U., Indpls. Art Mus.; executed murals Women's Cosmopolitan Club, N.Y.C., Marine Hosp., Louisville, U.S. Post Office, Lafayette, Ind., Aurora, Ind., U. Conn., Wethersfield Library, Marshall Meml., Lexington, Va. Winchester fellow for European study, 1931; recipient award Nat. Acad. Design, 1938, 41, Springfield Art League, 1940, Conn. Acad. Fine Arts, Herron Art Inst. Mem. N.A.D. Home: Essex CT Died Dec. 19, 1973.

MAYER, MARIA GOEPPERT, physicist; b. Kattowitz, Germany, June 28, 1906; d. Friedrich and Maria (Wolff) Goeppert; Ph.D., U. Gottingen, Germany, 1930; Dr. Science (honorary), Russel Sage College, 1960, Mount Holyoke College, 1961, Smith College, 1961; Dr. Science (honorary), Univ. of Portland, 1968; m. Joseph E. Mayer, Jan. 18, 1930; children—Maria Wentzel, Peter C. Came to U.S., 1930, naturalized, 1933. Vol. asso. Johns Hopkins, 1931-39; lectr. Columbia, 1939-46, Sarah Lawrence Coll., 1942-45; physicist SAM Labs., 1942-45; sr. physicist Argonne Nat. Lab., 1946-60; vol. prof. Enrico Fermi Inst. Nuclear Studies, U. Chgo., 1946-59, professor, 1959-60; professor at Revelle Coll. of University Cal. at La Jolla, California, from 1960. Recipient Nobel prize for physics, 1963. Fellow of American Academy of Arts and Sciences; mem. Akademie der Wissenschaften Heidelberg, Philos. Soc., Am. Phys. Soc., Nat. Acad. Scis., Sigma Xi. Author: (with Joseph E. Mayer) Statistical Mechanics, 1940; (with J.H.D. Jensen) Elementary Theory of Nuclear Shell Structure, 1951. Home: La Jolla CA Died Feb. 20, 1972; buried El Camino Meml. Park, San Diego CA

MAYER, RENE, economist, former French govt. ofcl.; b. Paris, France, May 4, 1895; s. Jacob Justin and Marthe Dupont Mayer; degree in philosophy U. Paris, 1913, law degree, 1914; m. Denise Bloch; 1 dau., 1 son (dec.). Sec. communications Gen. Giraud Adminstrn., Algiers, a founder Air France; dir. R.R. Co. of No. France, from 1928, v.p. bd., from 1932; commr. communications and Merchant Navy, French Com. for Nat. Liberation, 1943-44; minister pub. works and transp.; 1944; high commr. for German affairs, 1945-46; minister finance and econ. affairs, 1947-48; minister justice Bidault cabinet, 1949-50, Pleven cabinet, 1950-51, Queuille cabinet, 1951; v.p. council, minister finance and econ. affairs Pleven cabinet, 1951-52; prime minister of France, 1953; chmn. of the high authority European Coal and Steel Community, 1955-57. Mem. 2d Constituent Assembly, 1946, Nat. Assembly, 1946, 51. Served to lt. French Army, 1914-18. Decorated Croix de Guerre, comdr. Legion of Honor. Address: Paris France Died Dec. 13, 1972.

MAYNARD, LEONARD AMBY, univ. prof.; b. Hartford, N.Y., Nov. 8, 1887; s. Edward and Fanny (Cotton) M.; A.B., Wesleyan U., 1911; Ia. State Coll., 1911-12; fellow in chemistry, Cornell U., 1913-15, Ph.D., 1915; Sc.D. (honorary), Wesleyan University, 1945; Rhode Island State University, 1958; married to Helen Jackson, June 3, 1919; children—Patricia, Nancy Faith. Asst. chemist R.I. Expt. Sta., 1912-13; asst. prof. animal nutrition, Cornell U., 1915-17, 1919-20, prof. since 1920, dir. Sch. of Nutrition, 1941-56, professor biochemistry and nutrition, 1944-55, prof. emeritus, 1955-72; vis. prof. University of Nanking, China, 1934. Dir. U.S. Plant Soil and Nutrition Laboratory, 1939-45; mem. Food and Nutrition Bd., NRC; cons. Interdepartmental Com. Nutrition for Defense, from 1956. Served 1st lt. to maj. Chem. Warfare Service, U.S. Army, 1917-19. Recipient Borden Award in Nutrition, 1946; Osborne and Mendel Award in Science of Nutrition, 1954, Order of Rodolfo Robles (Guatemala), 1959. Fellow A.A.A.S., Am. Inst. Nutrition (sec. 1938-41; pres. 1942-43), mem. Nat. Acad. Sci., Am. Chem. Soc., Am. Soc. Biol. Chemists, Am. Soc. Animal Prodn. (pres. 1942-43), Soc. Biology and Medicine, Phi Beta Kappa, Sigma Xi, Phi Kappa Phi, Delta Tau Delta, Gamma Alpha. Presbyterian. Author: Better Dairy Farming, 1923; Animal Nutrition, 1937, rev., 1947, 51, (with J.K. Loosli), 1956, 62. Contbr. to scientific publs. Home: Ithaca NY Died June 22, 1972.

MAYNARD, LESTER, consul gen.; b. San Francisco, Apr. 5, 1877; ed. Polytechnic High Sch.; studied accounting; m. in Paris, France, April 15, 1930. Served as bank clerk 3 yrs., newspaper reporter, war correspondent, publisher and editor; apptd., after examination, consul at Sandakan, June 26, 1906, at Vladivostok, 1908, Harbin, 1911, Amoy, 1912; consul of class 4 by act approved Feb. 5, 1915; detailed to the Dept. of State, Mar. 1, 1916; assigned to Chefoo, 1916, to Alexandria, 1919; promoted class 3, 1920; assigned to Havre, 1923; foreign service officer of class 4, 1924; assigned to Stuttgart, 1929; promoted to class 3 (foreign service), 1929; consul gen. and assigned to Singapore, 1930, to Athens, 1932, to Copenhagen Aug. 23, 1933. Address: Am. Counsulate General, Copenhagen Denmark‡

MAYNARD, ROBERT WASHBURN, merchant; b. Newport, R.I., Oct. 17, 1879; s. Washburn and Bessie (Brooks) M.; B.S., Amherst, 1902, L.H.D., 1942; LL.B., Harvard, 1905; unmarried. With R. H. Stearns Co., dry goods, Boston, from 1905; pres. 1919-46; chmn. bd., 1946-67; dir. New Eng. Tel. & Tel. Co., Mchts. Nat. Bank (now New Eng. Mchts. Nat. Bank), Boston, Brookside Mills. Trustee, chmn. finance com. Amherst Coll.; trustee, chmn. bldg. com. Deerfield Acad. Mem. Alpha Delta Phi. Republican. Conglist. Office: Boston MA Died Oct. 27, 1969; buried Island Cemetery, Newport RI

MAYNARD, ROGER, banker; b. Evanston, Ill., Nov. 27, 1914; s. George S. and Josephine C. (Fleming) M.; B.A., Wesleyan U., Middletown, Conn., 1937; m. Edna M. Mitchell, July 23, 1938; children—Mary (Mrs. Robert W. Anderson), Constance (Mrs. Charles David Mastin), Roger, Douglas, Abigail Abbot. With J. P. Morgan & Co., Inc., 1937-59, v.p., 1953-59; with Morgan Guaranty Trust Company, N.Y.C., 1959-68, senior vice president, 1963-65, executive vice president, 1965-68. Trustee Wesleyan U., 1964-68. Mem. Phi Beta Kappa. Home: Wilton CT Died Mar. 30, 1968.

MAYNARD, WALTER, investment banker; b. N.Y. City, Apr. 19, 1906; s. Walter Effingham and Eunice (Ives) M.; student Groton (Mass.) Sch., 1919-24; A.B., Harvard, 1928; student Trinity Coll., 1928-29; m. Eileen Burden, Feb. 9, 1932; children—Walter, Sheila, John; m. 2d, Augusta P. Billings, December 26, 1957. Entered securities bus., 1929, partner Shearson, Hammill & Co., 1941, 46-64; sr. v.p. Shearson, Hammill & Co., Inc., 1964-69, vice chairman and executive vice pres., from 1969; dir. Spartan Industries, Inc., from 1959; trustee Austen Riggs Center, from 1952; governor of Greenwich House, from 1947. Governor New York Stock Exchange, 1956-62. Served from 1st lt. to lt. colonel U.S.A.A.F., 1942-46. Decorated Legion of Merit, Order Brit. Empire (hon. officer); mentioned in dispatches. Mem. Assn. Stock Exchange Firms (gov. 1948-51, pres. 1951), N.Y. Soc. Security Analysts, Investment Bankers Assn. (gov. 1953-56). Home: New York City NY Died Nov. 27, 1971.

MAYNE, ARTHUR FERDINAND, financial cons.; m. Helen Mary Dunningan, Sept. 4, 1934; 1 son, Patrick James. With Royal Bank of Can., Montreal, Que., 1925, gen. mgr. non-domestic bus., 1960-61, exec. v.p., 1961-69, dir., 1961-72; president, dir. A.F. Mayne & Assos. Ltd., Kennecott Canada Ltd.; dir., dep. chmn. Roy West Banking Corp. Ltd.; dir. Royal Bank Can. (Montreal), B.C. Molybdenum Ltd., Braden Copper Co., Woodward Stores Ltd., Tex.-Park Ltd., United Corps. Ltd., Dominion Bridge Co. Ltd., Campeau Corp. Ltd., Canadian Liquid Air Ltd., Canadian Interurban Properties Ltd., Export Devel. Corp., Kennecott Copper Corp., Pacific Petroleums Ltd., Phillips Petroleum Co., Trust Corp. of Bahamas Ltd., Air Liquids Can. Ltee, Loram Ltd., Roman Corp., Warnock Hersey Internat. Ltd., Chantecler Hotel Co. (1963) Ltd., Chantecler Enterprises Inc., Chantecler Apts. Devel. Co. Ltd., Chantecler Golf Club Inc., Westcoast Transmission Co., Ltd., Consol.-Bathurst Ltd. Clubs: St. James, Royal Montreal Golf, Royal Montreal Curling, Mount Royal, Mattawin Fishing, Montreal Skeet, Chantecler Golf and Country, Forest and Stream, Capilano Country (Vancouver); Lyford Cay (Nassau); The Windsor. Home: Westmount Quebec Canada Died Sept. 17, 1972.

MAYO, EDMUND COOPER, mfr. silverware; b. Old Point Comfort, Va., Jan. 8, 1885; s. Rev. Charles James Stovin and Mary Reynolds (Webber) M.; M.E., U. Md., 1904, D.Eng., 1956; Sc.D. in Bus. administrn., Bryant Coll., 1961; m. Nellie Gordon, Feb. 16, 1909; children—Edmund Cooper, Huntly Gordon. Machinist's helper Newport News Shipbuilding & Dry Dock Co., 1904; mechanic, later asst. to supt. Am. Locomotive Co., Richmond, 1905-06; gen. mgr. Cameron-Tennant Machine Works, 1907; with associates purchased same and renamed it Mayo Iron Works Inc., of which was pres. and gen. mgr., 1907-11; v.p. and gen. mgr. Viaduct Electric Co., Relay, Md., 1911-14; gen. mgr. Worcester Pressed Steel Co., engaged in mfg. munitions, World War, 1914-19; gen. mgr. Am. Tube and Stamping Co., Bridgeport, Conn., 1919, pres., 1920-24; v.p. in charge prodn., also v.p., gen. mgr. Gorham Mfg. Co., Providence, R.I., 1924, president, gen. mgr., 1925-50, pres. 1950-59; pres. Gorham Co., Alvin Corp., 1925-59, chmn., 1959-72; chmn. Gorham Mfg. Co.; dir. Mfrs. Mutual Fire Insurance Company, Industrial Trust Company, also Providence Journal Co., Liberty Mutual Ins. Co., Davol Rubber Co.; mem. Corp. Mass. Inst. of Tech., 1937-42; v.p., trustee R.I. Hosp.; trustee R.I. Sch. Design, 1940-58. Mem. Am. Soc. M.E., Am. Iron and Steel Inst., Newcomen Soc., Soc. Colonial Wars, Sigma Alpha Epsilon, Tau Beta Pi. Episcopalian. Clubs: Hope, Turks Head, Squantum, Agawam Hunt (Providence); University (New York). Home: North Kingstown RI Died Oct. 26, 1972; buried Hollywood Cemetery, Richmond VA

MAYO, FREDERICK JOSEPH, engring. exec.; b. New Haven, July 11, 1906; s. Frederick Alfred and Helen (Rochford) M.; student Georgetown U., 1924-26; C.E., Rensselaer Poly. Inst., 1930; m. Margery Jane Hart, Dec. 2, 1939; children—Susan Jane, Sandra Hart, Margery Ann. Jr. engr. N.Y. State Dept. Pub. Works, 1930-32; engring., adminstrn. teaching, 1932-34, U.S. Govt., 1934-38; cons. engr. Haller Engring. Associates, Cambridge, Mass., 1938-41; engr. F. H. McGraw & Co., Bermuda, 1941-42, project mgr., 1942-43; gen. mgr. Continental Indsl. Development Co. (subsidiary F. H. McGraw & Co.), Rio de Janeiro, Brazil, 1943-45, v.p. charge fgn. operations and N.Y. office, 1946-51, v.p., 1946-54, dir., 1949-72, exec. v.p., 1954-72; corporate officer, project mgr. Atomic Energy Plant, Paducah, Ky., 1951-54; dir., v.p. F. H. McGraw & Co. of Can., Ltd., 1947-58; pres. The Ingalls Shipbuilding Corp., Pascagoula, Miss., 1959-61, pres., 1959-66, chief exec. officer, treas., 1961-72, chairman bd., 1966-72, dir.; vice pres. Litton Industries, Inc., Beverly Hills, Cal.; exec. vice pres. Am. Export Isbrandtsen Co., 1967-72, also dir. Mem. Conn. Soc. Profl. Engrs., Assn. Iron and Steel Engrs., Navy League. Clubs: Metairie Country (New Orleans); Wykagyl Country (New Rochelle, N.Y.); Bel Air Country (Beverly Hills, Cal.); Canadian (N.Y.C.); Propeller of U.S.; Pascagoula Country. Home: Puako HI Died June 1972.

MAYS, CALHOUN ALLEN, lawyer; b. nr. Edgefield, S.C., Nov. 14, 1884; s. Sampson Butler and Ella (Calhoun) M.; A.B., Coll. Charleston, 1906; student law U. Mich., summer 1909; student Columbia, summer 1920; m. Mae Trammell, Nov. 9, 1920 (dec.); children—Nancy (Mrs. Robert A. Trawney, Jr.), Marshall Trammell, Calhoun Allen. Tchr. pub. schs., Elberton, Ga., 1906-08, Waycross, Ga., 1908-10; admitted to S.C. bar, 1910, practiced in Greenwood; partner firm Mays & Mays; service as assistant U.S. atty. Western Dist., 1914-18; spl. judge Circuit Cts. of S.C. Chmn., S.C. Archives Commn. Mem. S.C. Senate, 1942-48. Member Am., S.C. (pres.), Greenwood bar assns., Am. Legion (comdr. 1933, judge adv. dept. S.C. 1936-39), S.C. Hist. Soc., S.C. Hist. Assn. Home: Greenwood SC Died May 18, 1967.

MAYS, DAVID JOHN, lawyer; b. Richmond, Va., Nov. 22, 1896; s. Harvey James and Helga (Nelsen) M.; student Barton Acad., Mobile Mil. Inst.; student Randolph-Macon Coll., 1914-16, 19-20, Litt.D., 1955; LL.B., University of Richmond, 1924; LL.D., University of Richmond, 1954; married Ruth Reams, July 3, 1926. Admitted to Va. bar, 1923, practiced in Richmond, from 1924; mem. Mays, Valentine, Davenport & Moore; law lecturer Univ. of Richmond, 1926-42. Served as 1st lt. infantry, U.S. Army, Mexican Border Service, 1916-17, France, 1918-19. Mem. Virginia State Library Board, 1953-63, chairman, 1954-57. Mem. Va. Constl. Conv., 1956; chmn. Va. Commn. on Constl. Govt., from 1958; Mem. adv. com. McGregor Library, U. Va., 1955-70; mem. exec. com. trustees U. Richmond, from 1959. Mem. Am., Va. (president 1958-59), Richmond (pres. 1955) bar assns., Bar Assn. City N.Y., Fellows Am. Bar Found., Assn. Am. Trial Lawyers, Am. Hist. Assn. (Littleton-Griswold committee), Historic Richmond Found. (dir.), Am. Judicature Soc., Va. Hist. Soc. (pres. 1963-66), C. of C. (dir.), Inst. Early Am. Hist. and Culture (mem. council 1953-56), Phi Beta Kappa, Sigma Nu Phi. Clubs: Golden Horseshoe (Williamsburg, Virginia); Commonwealth, Downtown, Broad Rock, Forum (Richmond). Author: Business Law, 1933; Edmund Pendleton, 1721-1803 (2 volumes), 1952 (winner Award of Merit, American Association State and Local History, 1952, annual award, Inst. Early Am. History and Culture, 1953, Pulitzer Prize, 1953); The Letters and Papers of Edmund Pendleton, 2 vols., 1967. Home: Richmond VA Died Feb. 17, 1971; buried Hollywood Cemetery, Richmond VA

MAZER, JACOB, business exec.; b. N.Y.C., 1898; grad. Bklyn. Poly Inst., 1918; m. Ruth Mazer; children—David, Richard. Chmn. bd., dir. Hudson Pulp & Paper Corp., N.Y.C., until 1965. Home: Purchase NY Died Apr. 1968.

MCADAM, EDWARD LIPPINCOTT, JR., educator; b. St. Paul, May 23, 1905; s. Edward Lippincott and Helen Faith (Martin) McA.; B.A., Carleton Coll., 1927; M.A., U. Minn., 1929; Ph.D., Yale, 1935. Instr. English, Am. U., 1929-32, Yale, 1934-37; asst. prof. to prof. N.Y.U., 1937-69, chmn. Univ. Coll., 1950-69; cons. to founds. on fellowship applications and to bus. orgns. on writing problems of young execs. Served from lt. to lt. comdr., USNR, 1942-51. Guggenheim fellow, 1947. Mem. Modern Lang. Assn. Am. Clubs: Grolier, Century Association (N.Y.C.). Author: Dr. Johnson and the English Law, 1951; also articles, book revs. Editor: (with D. Nichol Smith) Poems of Samuel Johnson, 1942; (with others) A Book of English Literature, 1942; Johnson's Diaries, Prayers, and Annals, 1958; (with G. Milne) Johnson's Dictionary: A Modern Selection, 1963, A Johnson Reader, 1964; (with G. Milne) Poems of Samuel Johnson, 1964; Johnson and Boswell: A Survey of their Writings, 1969. Home: New York City NY Died Apr. 2, 1969.

MCADOO, MARY FAITH FLOYD, author; b. (Floyd) St. Mary's, Ga.; m. William Gibbs McAdoo, A. M., prof. English Univ. of Tenn. (died Aug., 1894). Author: The Nereid; Eagle Bend; also other novels and serials, and the chapters Journalism" and Literature" in Goodspeed's History of Tennessee." Address: 729 N. 3d Av., Knoxville TN‡

MCAFEE, WILLIAM A(RCHIBALD), lawyer; b. Clavevack, N.Y., Mar. 13, 1890; s. William and Flora (Ackley) McA.; A.B., Yale, 1911; LL.B., Harvard, 1915; LL.D., Lake Erie College, Painesville, Ohio, 1960; m. Sarah Edwards McLoud, Oct. 9, 1920; 1 son, Alexander. Admitted to bar, practiced in Cleve.; partner Squire, Sanders & Dempsey. Trustee Lake Erie Coll., Cleve. Symphony Orch., Inst. of Music. Served capt. to maj., F.A., U.S. Army, 1917-19. Mem. Am., Ohio, Cleve. bar assns., Am. Petroleum Inst. Republican. Clubs: Union, Tavern, University (Cleve.); Kirtland Country (Willoughby, O.); Yale of N.Y.; Edgertown Yacht. Home: Cleveland OH Died Sept. 2, 1971.

MCALLISTER, ALAN H., treas. Phoenix Ins. Co. Address: Hartford CT Died Aug. 2, 1967; buried Laconia NH

MCALLISTER, ELLIOTT, former banker; b. San Francisco, Nov. 30, 1898; s. Elliott and Alice (Decker) McA.; A.B., U. Cal., 1920; m. Mary Baldwin, Oct. 11, 1927; children—Elizabeth Cutler, Alice Decker, Alexander Baldwin. With The Bank of Cal. N.A., 1920-63, asst. cashier, 1928, became v.p., 1940, dir., 1948, pres. 1950, chmn. bd., chief exec. officer, 1956-63; dir. Pacific Gas & Electric Co., Del Monte Corp., Stauffer Chem. Co., Rhodes Western Stores. Past mem. fed. adv. council Fed. Res. System. Trustee Cypress Lawn Cemetery Assn. Mem. Kappa Sigma. Clubs: Pacific Union, University (N.Y.C.); Menio Country, San Francisco Golf. Home: San Francisco CA Died Jan. 20, 1973.

MCALLISTER, GEORGE FRANKLIN, teacher; b. Mt. Pleasant, N.C., Feb. 18, 1874; s. Harvey Caswell and Frances (Cook) McA.; grad. prep. dept. North Carolina Coll., Mt. Pleasant, 1893; A.B., N.C. Coll., 1897; studied University of N.C., 1904; M.A., Newberry (S.C.) Coll., 1908; Ped.D. from Gettysburg College, 1933; m. Julia Ethelyn Crabtree, of Salem, Va., June 25, 1913; children—Virginia Shirey, Franklin Grady (dec.), Elizabeth Kate, Carolyn Crabtree, Thomas Caswell. Prin. prep. dept. N.C. Coll., 1897-1902, and co-prin. The Collegiate Inst. (successor to N.C. Coll.), 1902-08; prin. Collegiate Inst., 1908, now pres. Mem. Bd. of Commrs., Mt. Pleasant, 1913-23; mem. County Sch. Bd. of Cabarrus Co., 1903-25. Mem. Am. Acad. Polit. and Social Science, Am. Geog. Soc., Pi Gamma Mu. Mason. Democrat. Lutheran. Home: Mt Pleasant NC‡

MCALLISTER, J(AMES) GRAY, educator, author; b. Covington, Va., Nov. 27, 1872; s. Abraham Addams and Julia Ellen (Stratton) M.; B.A., Hampden-Sydney Coll., Va., 1894; B.D., Union Theol. Sem., Richmond, Va., 1901; Hoge Fellowship, same, 1901-02; D.D., Washington and Jefferson Coll., 1906, Centre Coll., Ky., 1906; LL.D., Southwestern Presbyn. U., Tenn., 1925; Litt.D., Hampden-Sydney Coll., 1926; m. Meta Eggleston Russell, May 18, 1904; children—James Gray, Russell Greenway, Louise (dec.). Editor Bath News, Warm Springs, Va., 1894-95; bus. mgr. Central Presbyn., Richmond, Va., 1895-98; ordained Presbyterian ministry, 1903; asst. prof. Hebrew and Oriental lit., 1902-03, adj. prof., 1904-05, Union Theol. Sem., Richmond, Va.; pastor Farmville, Va., Presbyterian Church, 1903-04; president Hampden-Sydney College, 1905-08; stated supply Hot Springs, Virginia, Presbyterian Church, 1908-09; acting prof., 1909-11, prof., 1911-25, of Bibl. introduction, English Bible and Bibl. theology, Louisville Presbyn. Seminary, Kentucky; professor English Bible, Union Theological Sem., Va., 1925-43, prof. emeritus, 1943-70. Mgr. Southern Presbyn. Confs., Montreat, N.C., 1925-37, 1943-46; hist. research librarian, Union Theol. Sem., 1943-63; instr. Bibl. geography Gen. Assembly's Tng. Sch., Richmond, 1927-38. Mem. Phi Beta Kappa, Omicron Delta Kappa, Pi Kappa Alpha (past nat. officer). Independent Democrat. Author: McAllister Family Records, 1912; Studies in the Gospel of Luke, 1922; Studies in Old Testament History, 1925; Borderlands of the Mediterranean, 1925; Life and Letters of Water W. Moore, 1939; Edward O. Guerrant: Apostle to the Southern Highlanders (co-author), 1950; many monographs. Contributor to encys. and periodicals; conf. lecturer. Editor in chief Union Seminary Review 1932-46. Home: Richmond VA Died Jan. 22, 1970; buried Forest Lawn Cemetery, Richmond VA

MCANALLY, ARTHUR MONROE, librarian; b. Delaware, Ark., Jan. 4, 1911; s. Perry A. and Anne (Humphreys) McA.; A.B., U. Okla., 1933, A.B. in Library Sci., 1935, A.M., 1936; Ph.D., U. Chgo., 1951; m. Lucille McGeorge, Feb. 6, 1935; children—Marilyn Anne (Mrs. Marilyn Anne McAnally Stark), Elizabeth Ann (Mrs. Alexander H. Kunzer), Perry Arthur. Supr. libraries Edinburg (Tex.) Jr. Coll., 1935-38; asst. librarian Knox Coll., Galesburg, Ill., 1939-41; librarian, Bradley U., Peoria, Ill., 1941-44; librarian Wis. State Tchrs. Coll., Milw., 1944-45, U. N.M., 1945-49; asst. dir. U. Ill. Library, 1949-51; dir. libraries U. Okla., 1951-72; spl. reorgn. assignment, library Universidad Nacional Mayor de San Marcos de Lima, Peru, 1948; faculty U. Ankara (Turkey), 1963-64; cons. in field. Mem. A.L.A., Southwestern (pres. 1958-60), Okla. library assns., Okla. Westerners Assn., Phi Beta Kappa. Presbyn. Club: Centennial Rod and Gun. Author numerous articles. Home: Norman OK Died Dec. 1, 1972.

MCANANY, EDWIN SEBAST, lawyer; b. Kansas City, Mo., Feb. 17, 1871; s. Patrick and Helen Winifred (Mansfield) M.; student St. Benedicts Coll., Atchison, Kan., 1884-89; LL.D., St. Mary's (Kan.) Coll., 1919; m. Louise Jameson, Oct. 19, 1907; children—Mary Winifred, Edwin Jameson, Lucie Jane Desloge, Patrick Bevan, Zoe Louise. Admitted to bar, state of Kan., 1892, and since in practice, Kansas City, Kan.; now mem. McAnany, Van Cleave & Phillips; city atty., Kansas City, 1905-07; formerly atty. bd. edn.; pres. Union Mortgage & Investment Co.; director Commercial National Bank, Shawnee State Savings Bank, Fidelity Building and Loan Association. Mem. American Bar Association, Kan. State Bar Assn. (past pres.), Wyandotte County Bar Assn. (past pres.), Kansas City (Kan.) Chamber of Commerce (past dir.); non-resident mem. C. of C. of State of N.Y. Republican. Catholic. K.C. Mem. Equestrian Order of Knights of the Holy Sepulchre. Clubs: University (Kansas City, Mo.). Catholic (New York). Home: 400 N. 17th St. Office: Commercial Nat. Bank Bldg., Kansas City KS‡

MCANDREW, WILLIAM ROBERT, radio and TV news exec.; b. Washington, Sept. 7, 1914; s. William S. and Katherine (Flynn) McA.; A.B., Cath. U., 1935; m. Irene Byrne, June 30, 1937; children—Irene Byrne (Mrs. John Prendergast), Mary Carroll and William Robert. Began career with the United Press, 1935-36; with NBC News, 1936-40, 44-68; chief Washington news staff, 1944-49, sta. mgr. WRC, WRC-TV, 1949-51, mgr. NBC News, 1951-55, director, 1955-58, vice president, NBC News, 1958-62, exec. v.p., 1962-65, pres., 1965-68; with Broadcasting mag., 1940-42; chief information program Bd. Econ. Warfare, 1942; with ABC, 1943-44. Information chmn. President's Com. to Aid Physically Handicapped. Bd. trustees Washington Journalism Center. Decorated Knight of the Holy Sepulchre, Knight Sovereign Mil. Order of Malta. Mem. Nat. Assn. Broadcasters (information com.), Radio-TV Corrs. Assn. Clubs: Siwanoy Country (Bronxville, N.Y.); Nat. Press (Washington); The Players, Dutch Treat (N.Y.C.). Home: Bronxville NY Died May 30, 1968.

MCAVOY, THOMAS TIMOTHY, archivist, historian; b. Tipton, Ind., Sept. 12, 1903; s. Charles Edward and Nora Bernardine (Walsh) McA.; A.B., Univ. of Notre Dame, 1925, A.M., 1930; student Holy Cross Coll., Cath. Univ. of Am., 1925-29; Ph.D., Columbia, 1940. Professed in Congregation of Holy Cross, July 28, 1925; ordained priest Roman Cath. Ch., June 24, 1929; archivist Univ. of Notre Dame Archives (formerly Cath. Archives of Am.) from 1929, instr. history, 1933-35, asst. prof., 1938-44, asso. prof., 1944-48, prof., head dept. history, 1939-60. Mem. Am. Assn. State and Local History, Am. Hist. Assn., History of Sci. Soc., Soc. Am. Archivists (founding mem.), Am. Catholic Hist. Assn., Miss. Valley Hist. Assn., Ind. History Conf., N.E.A., Council for Basic Edn., Am. Studies Assn. Author: Catholic Church in Indiana, 1789-1834, 1940, The Great Crisis in American Catholic History, 1895-1900, 1957 (recipient of John Gilmary Shea prize, 1957); The Americanist Heresy in

Roman Catholicism 1895-1900, 1963; Father O'Hara of Notre Dame, The Cardinal-Archbishop of Phila., 1966; A History of the Catholic Church in the United States, 1969. Joint-author: A History of the United States of America, 1951. Comng. editor Review of Politics 1942-54, acting editor, 1954-55, mng. editor, 1956-69; adv. editor Catholic Hist. Rev., 1944-57; The Image of Man, 1959; book-editor, contbr. Roman Catholicism and American Way of Life, 1960, Le Catholicisme Dans La Vie Americaine, 1963, The Midwest, Myth or Reality, 1961. Contbr. to hist. jours. Address: Notre Dame IN Died July 5, 1969.

MCBEE, EARL THURSTON, chemist; b. Braymer, Mo., July 6, 1906; s. William and Lydia (Post) McB.; A.B., William Jewell Coll., 1929; M.S., Purdue U., 1931, Ph.D., 1936; m. 2d, Viola Renolds, Feb. 15, 1962; children—Beverly Ann, Robert Earl. Prof., Purdue U., 1943, alumni research counselor, 1944-73, head dept. of chemistry, 1949, Shreve prof. indsl. chemistry, 1967-73, ofcl. investigator Nat. Def. Research Com., 1942-43; research cons. U.S. Engr. Office, Madison Square Area, 1945; chmn. adv. bd. U.S. Naval Propellant Plant, 1953-73; chmn. bd., pres., chief exec. officer Great Lakes Chem. Corp.; pres. Ark. Chems., Inc., Bromet Co. Received Modern Pioneer award Nat. Assn. Mfrs., 1940; Certificate of Effective Service in Prodn. of Atomic Bomb, 1945; Certificate of Effective Service in Prosecution of 2d World War, 1945; Ann. Sigma Xi Research award, 1946. Fellow Ind. Acad. Sci., N.Y. Acad. Sci.; mem. Am. Chem. Soc. (chmn. Purdue sect. 1942-43, councilor 1944-45), Mfg. Chemists Assn. (dir.), Am. Inst. Chemists (dir.), Ind. Chem. Soc., A.A.A.S., Sigma Xi, Phi Lambda Upsilon, Alpha Kappa Lambda, Alpha Chi Sigma. Mason (32 deg.), Elk. Clubs: Chemists, Rotary Internat. Contbr. articles to profl. jours. and periodicals, also to publs. Manhattan Project Tech. Series. Home: West Lafayette IN Died Jan. 1973; buried West Lafayette IN

MCBRIDE, GEORGE MCCUTCHEN, univ. prof.; b. Benton, Kan., Oct. 11, 1876; s. James Fleming and Emma Fulton (McCutchen) McB.; A.B., Park Coll., Parkville, Mo., 1898; student Auburn Theol. Sem., Auburn, N.Y., 1898-1901; Ph.D., Yale U., 1921; m. Harriet Luella Fields, Sept. 14, 1907; children—Lester Fields, Emma Louise (dec.), Merle Alexander. Teacher, Instituto Ingles, Santiago, Chile, 1901-06, vice dir., 1904-06; teacher, Colegio Nacional, Oruro, Bolivia, 1907-08; teacher geology and geography and dir. Am. Inst., La Paz, Bolivia, 1908-15; instr. physical geography, Wesleyan U., 1915-17; asst. in Spanish, Yale U., 1916-17; librarian, Am. Geog. Soc. and asst. editor Geographical Review, 1917-19; research asso. Am. Geog. Soc., 1920-22; lecturer, asso. prof. and prof., U. of Calif. at Los Angeles since 1922; visiting prof. in S.A., Carnegie Endowment for Internat. Peace, 1929-30, in C.A., 1938; spl. lecturer Clark U., 1922, U. of Wis., 1923, U. of Okla., 1923, 26, Okla. Southwest Teachers Coll., 1926; instr. Columbia U. summer 1923, San Diego State Coll., summer 1924, 25; United States technical advisor to Ecuador-Peru Boundary Demarcation Commission, 1942-48. Corresponding member Sociedad Geografica, Peru; mem. Pacific Geog. Soc. (regent), Am. Geog. Soc. (hon.), Assn. Am. Geog. (v.p. 1939), Assn. Pacific Coast Geographers (pres. 1937-38), A.A.A.S., Council on Fgn. Policy (pres. 1940-41), Sigma Xi, Pi Gamma Mu, Sigma Delta Pi. Author: Agrarian Indian Communities of Highland Bolivia, 1921; Land Systems of Mexico, 1923; Chile: Land and Society, 1936; Chile: su Tierra y su Gente, 1938. Home: Pacific Palisades (Los Angeles) CA‡

MCBRYDE, CHARLES NEIL, bacteriologist; b. Albemarle County, Va., Feb. 2, 1872; s. John McLaren and Cora (Bolton) M.; B.S., U. of S.C., 1891; M.S., Va. Poly. Inst., 1892; M.D., Johns Hopkins, 1897; Ph.D., George Washington U., 1911; m. Virginia Abbey Sweigard, Sept. 2, 1933. Apptd. interne Johns Hopkins Hosp., 1897 (resigned); bacteriologist, 1901, Biochemic Div., U.S. Dept. Agr., in charge bacteriol. investigations, meats and meat-food products, 1909-16. In charge Exptl. Sta., U.S. Dept. Agr., Ames, Ia., 1928-42. Apptd. chief Biochemic Div., U.S. Dept. Agr., Washington, Nov. 1, 1935 (declined); engaged in research work in the field of animal diseases; retired, 1942. Mem. Sigma Xi, Phi Kappa Phi, Sigma Nu. Club: University (Winter Park, Fla.). Author of numerous papers dealing with diseases of animals and with questions connected with the canning and preservation of meats. Address: Blacksburg VA‡

MCBRYDE, WARREN HORTON, engr., industrialist; Mobile, Ala., Jan. 20, 1876; s. Thomas Calvin and Julia Pierce (Horton) McB.; B.S. in Engring., Ala. Poly. Inst., 1897; LL.D., U. of Santa Clara, 1948; m. Abbie Ford White, Feb. 15, 1905; children—Lucile, Janet (Mrs. James A. Orser), Warren H., Jr. (dec.). Began with Electric Lighting Co., Mobile, Ala., 1897-98; asst. resident engr., Northern Calif., Yuba Elec. Power Co., asst. supt. Peyton Chem. Co., San Francisco and Martinez, asst. to chief engr. Calif. Gas & Elec. Co. (now Pacific Gas & Elec. Co.), 1899-1903; resident engr. E. I. duPont de Nemours & Co., Rapauno plant, Gibbstown, N.J., 1903-05, placed in charge all engring. and constrn. in Calif., 1905, asst. supt. Hercules plant (dynamite and TNT) throughout World War I; asst. to gen. mgr., sec. of the co., and handler engring. problems Calif. and Hawaiian Sugar Refining Co., 1919-27; cons. engr., San Francisco, since 1927. Served with U.S. Lighthouse Dept. and Corps of Engrs., Ft. Morgan, Ala., also chief electrician U.S. Army Transport Sheridan, Spanish-Am. War, 1898-99; served with War Dept., Washington, redesigning mech. equipment Army constrn. program, later standardizing designs and approving plans Army Ordnance and Chem. Warfare Service projects, also chief cons. mech. engr. and chief consultant munitions plants, 1941-42; chief of engring, div. U.S. Army Transportation Corps, 1942-44; subsequently cons. Transportation Corps, U.S. Army, and cons. Army-Navy Explosives Safety Bd., also mem. adv. council Indsl. Coll. Armed Forces. Mem. adv. bd. Richmond (Calif.) branch of Am. Trust Co. Mem. permanent com. Sacramento-San Joaquin Rivers Problems Conf. since 1924; mem. bldg. com. Grade Cathedral, Episcopal, San Francisco; pres. Contra Costa County C. of C.; mem. San Francisco Area Council Boy Scouts America; mem. adv. bd. Salvation Army. Trustee Mech. Inst. Library (San Francisco); mem. adv. bd. Coll. of Engring., U. of Santa Clara. Fellow Am. Soc. M.E. (pres. 1939-40); mem. Newcomen Soc. (vice chmn. Pacific Coast com.). Kappa Alpha, Tau Beta Pi. Republican. Mason. Clubs: Bohemian, Rotary, Commonwealth, Corinthian Yacht (San Francisco). Made 3 circumnavigations of globe, vis. all continents, some 80 countries, 1929-39. Office: 405 Montgomery St., San Francisco CA‡

MCCABE, CHARLES B., newspaper pub. and cons.; b. Cleve., Aug. 26, 1899; s. Charles B. and Caroline (Friedrich) McC.; m. Ruth Starr; children—Charles Bernard III, Robert Andrew, David Allen, Peter Fredrick. Editor Ridgway (Pa.) Record until 1925; with United Press as Washington corr., bur. mgr., Harrisburg, Pa., N.Y.C. wire editor, traveling rep. and Central Div. mgr., Chgo., 1925-35; pub. Denver Rocky Mountain News, 1935; pub. N.Y. Daily Mirror, 1935-63; v.p., dir. Hearst Corp., 1943-64, v.p. and exec. dir. radio and TV div., v.p. N.Y. Mirror div., pres., treas., dir. Mirror Holding Corp., 1940-64; pres. Tannemac Corp.; dir. Bank of Commerce of N.Y. Mem. N.Y. State adv. commn. U.S. Savs. Bond Div. Adviser to pres. Nat. Found.; dir. Boys Life; mem. exec. bd., hon. chmn. Greater N.Y. council, mem. exec. bd. nat. council, chmn. editorial com. Boy Scouts Am.; dir. N.Y. World's Fair 1964-65 Corp., N.Y. Conv. and Visitors Bur. Clubs: Brook, Cloud, Beaverkill Trout, Verbank Hunting and Fishing. Home: Greenwich CT Died May 29, 1970; buried Putnam Cemetery, Greenwich CT

MCCABE, CHARLES MARTIN, merchant, mfr.; b. Nashville, Tenn., Nov. 12, 1870; s. Bernard and Winifred (Feerick) McC.; grad. high sch. and Jennings Business Coll., Nashville; m. Aileen Timothy, of Nashville, Jan. 9, 1907. Pres. Rigo Mfg. Co. since 1903; auditor Tenn. Fertilizer Co., 1916-20; pres. Cotton States Life Ins. Co., 1924-28; v.p. North Am. Nat. Life Ins. Co., 1926-28. City treas., Nashville, 1897-1903; asst. comptroller, Tenn., 1903-12; sec. Com. on Canadian Relations, U.S. Senate, 1912-13; asst. postmaster, Memphis, 1913-14; postmaster, Nashville, 1920-24; pres. park commn., Nashville, since 1927; apptd. commr. of finance and taxation, State of Tenn., Sept. 11, 1929; apptd. U.S. collector of internal revenue, Dist. of Tenn., June 21, 1933. Dir. Nashville Community Chest, Nashville Chamber Commerce (pres. 1925-26), Boys' Club. Democrat. Catholic. Elk. Clubs; Lions (pres. 1925), Hermitage. Home: 3405 West End Av., Nashville TN*‡

MCCABE, EDWARD RAYNSFORD WARNER, army officer; b. Petersburg, Va., July 12, 1876; s. William Gordon and Jane Pleasants Harrison (Osborne) McC.; student Univ. Sch., Petersburg, Va., 1889-96, U. of Va., 1900; grad. Inf., Cav. Sch., Ft. Leavenworth, 1906, Mounted Service Sch., Ft. Riley, Kan., 1907, F.A. Sch., advanced course Ft. Sill, Okla., 1924, Army War Coll., Washington, D.C., 1931; m. Mary Forsyth, Nov. 12, 1908; children—Virginia Harrison Osborne (dec.), Edward Raynsford Warner, Jr. Commd. 2d lt., 1900, advanced through grades to brig. gen., 1944; served in Philippine Islands, 1900-03, 1907-10; in Mexico with Pershing Expedition, 1916; staff and line duty, France and Germany, 1917-19; mil. attache, Am. Legation, Prague, Czechoslovakia, 1920-22, and Am. Embassy, Rome, Italy, 1924-26; prof. mil. science and tactics, Standford U., Calif., 1927-30; mil. attache, Am. Embassy, Rome, Italy, 1931-33; chief of staff, 6th Corps Area, Chicago, 1936-37; chief Mil. Intelligence Div., Gen. Staff, U.S. Army, 1937-40; retired, July 1940; recalled to active service with Army, May 1943; comdt. The Sch. of Mil. Govt., Charlottesville, Va. Jan. 1944-Mar. 1945. Reverted to retired status June 30, 1946. Officer Legion of Honor and Croix de Guerre with Palm (French); Commander Order of Crown (Italian); Military Cross and Commander Order of the White Lion (Czechoslovakia); Commander Polonia Restituta (Poland); Legion of Merit. Mem. Beta Theta Pi, Scabbard and Blade, Soc. of The Cincinnati. Clubs: Colonnade, Farmington Country (Charlottesville, Va.); Chevy Chase, Army and Navy (Washington, D.C.), Saints and Sinners. Home: 1515 Gordon Av., Charlottesville VA‡

MCCABE, FRANCIS XAVIER, clergyman, educator; b. New Orleans, Feb. 6, 1872; s. Hugh and Elizabeth (Gafney) M.; A.B., St. Mary's Sem., Perryville, Mo., 1889, A.M., 1890; also 4 yrs.' course in theology and other ecclesiastical branches, same sch.; LL.D., Ill. Coll. Law, 1912, Notre Dame, 1917. Ordained priest, R.C. Ch., 1896; prof. chemistry, St. Vincent's Coll., Los Angeles, Calif., 1896-1906, v.p., 1902-06; pres. DePaul U., Chicago, 1910-20; rector St. Vincent's Ch., Kansas City, Mo., Apr. 1920-23; dir. Missions for Western Province, Congregation of Missions, 1923-25; pastor St. Stephen's Ch., New Orleans, 1925-26; rector St. Thomas Sem., Denver, Colo., 1926-27; dir. Vincentian Auxiliary, St. Louis, Jan. 1928-36, of Vincentian Missions Western Province U.S., 1936-38. Retreats for laymen of Kansas City since Nov. 1939. Mission work, Chicago, St. Louis, New Orleans, etc., 1906-10. Home: 2015 E. 72d St., Kansas City MO*‡

MCCALEB, WALTER FLAVIUS, author, banker; b. Benton, Tex., Oct. 17, 1873; s. John Lafayette and Elizabeth (Sweeten) McC.; B.Litt., U. of Tex., 1896, M.A., 1897; sr. fellow in history, U. of Chicago, 1897-1900, Ph.D., 1900; m. Idealie Marie McCaleb, June 28, 1901; children—Ethel M., Aurora M., Walter F., Laura; married 2d, Edna Lang, June 11, 1960. Editor on staff New International Encyclopedia, 1901-03; asso. editor Public Ledger, Phila., 1904; also was reviewer on New York Times, The Nation, Am. Hist. Review. Pres. The Continental Bank, Cleveland, O., Dimmitt Co. (Tex.) State Bank, W. Tex. Bank & Trust Co., San Bernardino (Calif.) Valley Bank, Peoples Mortgage Co. of Los Angeles, Am. Home Builders; v.p., dir. San Antonio Life Ins. Co.; v.p. and mgr. Brotherhood of Locomotive Engrs. Nat. Bank; chmn. finance com. Peoples Mutual Life Ins. Co. of Calif.; treas. Crystal City & Uvalde Ry., Globe Fire Ins. Co.; dir., vice-chmn. Federal Reserve Bank, Dallas; mgr. Home Owners Loan Corp., Cleveland Dist.; prin. field rep. Federal Home Loan Bank Bd.; special adviser to Sec. of the Interior, 1937. Lecturer on money and banking, Columbia. Managing dir. Mass. Credit Union Assn.; sec. Nat. Com. on People's Banks; mem. exec. council Am. Bankers' Assn. Fellow Tex. Hist. Assn.; mem. Am. Hist. Assn., Am. Acad. Polit. and Social Science, Nat. Econ. League, Phi Beta Kappa, Nu Alpha. Democrat. Clubs: City (Cleveland); Authors (New York City) Cosmos (Washington). Author of several books since 1903; latest publ.; Conquest of the West, 1947; The Spanish Missions of Texas, 1954; Bigfoot Wallace, 1956; The Alamo, 1956; W.B. Travis, 1957; S.F. Austin, 1957; Sam Houston, 1957; The Mier Expedition, 1959; How Much is a Dollar, 1959; Khorasan, 1962; New Light on Aaron Burr, 1963; Santa Fe Expedition, 1964; No Port of Call, 1964; The Aaron Burr Conspiracy. Home: Austin TX Died 1967.

MCCALL, FRED(ERICK) B(AYS), educator; b. Charlotte, N.C., Oct. 7, 1893; s. Johnston Davis and Sallie Lee (Nooe) McC; A.B., U. of N.C., 1915; LL.B., Yale, 1928; m. Adeline Denham, Sept. 1, 1928. Teacher of Latin and mathematics, Charlotte High Sch., 1915-18, prin., 1918-20; asst. sec. Charlotte C. of C., 1919; admitted to N.C. bar, 1922, and practiced as mem. firm of McCall, Smith & McCall, 1924-26; instr. Latin, U. of N.C., 1922-23; asst. prof. law, 1923-24, 1926-27, asso. prof., 1928-33, prof. of law, from 1933, prof. emeritus, until 1973. Mem. Commn. on revision of laws of N.C. relating to estates, 1935-39. Tympanist, N.C. Symphony Orchestra from 1932, Univ. N.C. Symphony Orchestra since 1926. Mem. N.C. Bar Assn., Order of Coif, Sigma Chi, Phi Delta Phi, Phi Mu Alpha (Sinfonia). Democrat. Methodist. Club: Torch. Contbr. articles in various legal periodicals. Address: Chapel Hill NC Died Apr. 8, 1973.

MCCALLAM, JAMES ALEXANDER, army officer; born Phila., May 13, 1894; s. Thomas and Ellen Jane (Halligan) McC.; V.M.D., U. of Pa., 1917; post grad. Army Veterinary Sch., 1925; grad. Med. Field Service Sch., 1925; m. Lillian Galley, July 24, 1917; children—James A. (killed in action, Italy, June 1944); Doris M. (Mrs. Jack T. Walden). Entered the Veterinary Corps of the United States Army, as 2d lt., July 1917, and advanced through grades to brig. gen., Jan. 24, 1948; army vet., hdqrs. 6th Army, Feb. 1943-Dec. 1945; exec. officer, med. sect. advanced echelon, Hdqrs. 6th Army, Aug. 1943-Feb. 1944; med. insp. med. sect., Apr.-Oct. 1944; exec. officer med. sect. Oct. 1944-Dec. 1945; member mil. commn., Hdqrs. Southwest Pacific Area, Mar.-Sept. 1945; New Guinea (Brit. and Dutch), Leyte and Luzon, P.I., Japan (all in S.W. Pacific Theater Operations). Army vet., hdqrs. 6th Army, Southwest Pacific area, 1943-45; chief, vet. div., Office of Surg. Gen., 1946-53; chief Army Vet. Service, 1946-53. Awarded Legion of Merit medal, Bronze star medal, American Vet. Medical Assn. award, 1958, award of merit, Univ. of Pa. Gen. Alumni Society, 1959. Member U.S. com., XIVth Internat. Vets. Congress, 1948-49; mem. Am. Vet. Medical Assn. (1st. v.p., 1949, pres., 1953, Washington representative), American Public Health Association, Dist. Columbia Vet. Medical Assn. (pres. 1949-50), Pa. State Vet. Medical Association, Association of Military Surgeons, United States Livestock Sanitary Assn., Alpha Psi, Phi Zeta. Mason. Club: Army and Navy. Home: Washington DC Died July 15, 1969; buried Arlington Nat. Cemetery, Washington

MCCALLUM, ANGUS, architect; b. Kansas City, Mo., Nov. 13, 1911; s. James Wood and Nora (Costello) McC.; student Rockhurst Coll., 1927-29, Mass. Inst. Tech., 1929-31; m. Kathleen deSales Foster, Feb. 5, 1945; children—Mary Elizabeth, Lucie Foster. Prin. Angus McCallum & Assos., Kansas City, 1946; works include Avila Coll., Western Miss. Mental Health Center, library Rockhurst Coll., Rehab. Inst., Regional Diagnostic Clinic-Mental Retardation; chmn. adv. council Kansas City U. Coll. Architecture; guest lectr. U. Kan., Kan. State U., Okla. State U. Mem. accreditation coms. Collegiate Schs. Architecture, 1960-65. Dir. Kansas City Philharmonic Assn.; active United Fund, Midwest Children's Center; pres. Kansas City Health and Welfare Council; dir. Kansas City Mental Health Found., Human Resources Corp.; brotherhood chmn. Kansas City region Nat. Conf. Christians and Jews, 1963. Mem. Mayor's Adv. Commn. Served to lt. USNR, 1942-42; PTO. Fellow A.I.A. (pres. Kansas City 1959-60, bd. dirs. 1963-66). Roman Catholic. Mem. Equestrian Order Holy Sepulcre of Jerusalem. Home: Kansas City MO

MCCANDLESS, BRUCE, naval officer; b. Washington, Aug. 12, 1911; s. Byron and Velma May (Kitson) McC.; B.S., U.S. Naval Acad., 1932; student U.S. Naval Postgrad. Sch., 1938-39; M.A. Long Beach State College, 1953; married Sue Worthington Bradley, February 15, 1936; children—Bruce, Sue Worthington, Rosemary, Douglas Montrose. Commd. ensign, U.S.N., 1932, advanced through grades to capt., ret. and advanced to rear adm., 1952; engring., communications, navigation, gunnery, staff and command positions, 1932-52; participated operations Pacific Area, World War II, including battles of Cape Esperance, Guadalcanal, Gilbert Islands, Marshall Islands, Aleutians, Solomon Islands, Iwo Jima, Okinawa; staff Navy Dept., 1946-49; faculty Naval Acad., 1950-52; bd. control, sec.-treas. U.S. Naval Institute 1951-52, editor Proc. 1951-52. Decorated Congl. Medal Honor, Silver Star medal, Purple Heart, Presdl. Unit Citation. Mem. Naval Historical Found., Congl. Medal of Honor Soc., Order of Lafayette, Vets. of Foreign Wars, Naval Inst. Co-author: Naval Leadership, 1959; Service Etiquette. Home: Claremont CA Died Jan. 24, 1968.

MCCANN, HAROLD GILMAN, chemist; b. Kittery, Me., Feb. 9, 1916; s. Harold G. and Cora (Hayden) McC.; B.S., Bates Coll., 1937; M.S., Poly. Inst. Bklyn., 1947; m. Virgilyn Richards Mayo, July 16, 1938;children—Harold Gilman III, Dwight Mayo, Kevin Hayden. Analytical and research chemist Gen. Chem. div. Allied Chem. Co., N.Y.C., 1937-50; prin. investigator Nat. Inst. Dental Research, NIH, Bethesda, Md., 1950-59, chief microanalytical lab. Nat. Inst. Arthritis and Metabolic Diseases, 1959-63; mem. staff Forsyth Dental Center, Boston, 1963-69. Mem. Internat. Assn. Dental Research, Am. Chem. Soc., A.A.A.S. Contbr. articles to profl. jours. Patentee in field. Home: Marblehead MA Died Jan. 18, 1969.

MCCANN, R. L., zinc co. exec.; b. Harrisburg, Pa., Feb. 22, 1896; s. James P. and Nelle (Hammaker) McC.; E.M., Lehigh U., 1917; m. Fleta Munson, July 7, 1923; children—Robert M., Elizabeth L. Alsentzer. With The N.J. Zinc Co., N.Y.C., 1917-71, pres., 1951-66, chmn. bd. 1966-67, ret. 1967, cons., 1967-71, dir., 1951-67; director Gulf and Western Industries, Incorporated, New Jersey Zinc Exploration Company, also Palmer Water Co., Saucon Valley Iron & R.R. Co., Que. Iron & Titanium Corp., Restigouche Mining Corp., Ltd. Mem. Am. Mining Congress; Am. Inst. Mining Metall. and Petroleum Engrs., Newcomen Soc. Am., Tau Beta Pi, Sigma Chi. Clubs: University (N.Y.C.); Saucon Valley Country (Bethlehem, Pa.); Walkill Country (Franklin, N.J.); Lehigh (N.Y.), Down Town Assn., Twenty-Nine. Home: Franklin NJ Died Oct. 14, 1971.

MCCANN, WILLIAM SHARP, physician; b. Cadiz, O., July 6, 1889; s. Dr. Charles Fremont and Carolyn (Sharp) McC.; A.B., Ohio State U., 1911, D.Sc., 1934; M.D., Cornell U., 1915; grad. Army Med. Sch., Washington, 1971; LL.D., Hobart and William Smith Colleges, 1954; m. Gertrude Guild Fisher, M.D., Dec. 29, 1916 (deceased); children—Dorothy Elizabeth, William Peter; married 2d, Ella M. Russ, 1957. Surgical house officer, Peter Bent Brigham Hosp., Boston, 1915-16; Arthur Tracy Cabot fellow in surgery, Harvard, 1916-17; instr. in medicine, Cornell U., 1919-21; research fellow, Russell Sage Inst. of Pathology, 1919-21; adj. asst. visiting physician Bellevue Hosp., 1919-21; asso. prof. of medicine, Johns Hopkins, 1921-24; asso. physician Johns Hopkins Hosp., 1921-24; Charles A. Dewey prof. of medicine, University of Rochester, 1924-57, professor emeritus, 1957-71; vis. prof. adminstrv. medicine Sloan Institute of Hospital Administration, Cornell U., Ithaca, N.Y., 1957-59; physician in chief Strong Memorial and Rochester Municipal hosps., 1924-57. Mem. tuberculosis adv. com., N.Y. State Dept. Health; mem. med. adv. com., Masonic Found. for Health and Human Welfare. Served as lt. M.C., U.S. Army, A.E.F., 1917-19; served from comdr. to capt. MC-USNR, 1942-44. Mem. Naval Research Adv. Com., from 1946; dep. chmn. com. on med. scis. Research and Development Board, Dept. of Defense; consultant in Medicine, Veterans Administration, Branch 2, from 1946. Chmn. American Board Internal Medicine, 1947-48; trustee Asso. Universities, Inc., Brookhaven Nat. Lab., 1950. Fellow A.C.P. (regent; master), N.Y. Acad. Medicine; member Assn. Am. Physicians (pres.), A.A.A.S. (v.p., chmn. section N 1952); Soc. for Clin. Investigation, Harvey Society, Society Exptl. Biology and Medicine, A.M.A., Rochester Acad. Medicine, Am. Inst. of Nutrition, American Society Biological Chemists, American Rheumatism Association, Sigma Xi, Alpha Omega Alpha, Phi Beta Kappa; associate member United States Naval Institute United Presbyterian. Mason. Clubs: Oak Hill Country, Cornell, Fortnightly, University (Rochester). Author: Calorimetry in Medicine, 1924. Contbr. many articles to med. jours. Home: Rochester NY Died June 10, 1971; buried Cadiz OH

MCCARDELL, ROY LARCOM, author; b. Hagerstown, Md., June 30, 1870; s. Thomas F. and Alice Eve M. Began newspaper work on Age-Herald, Birmingham, Ala.; about 1890 went to New York Evening Sun, later on New York World; on editorial staff of Puck, 1893-97; editor Sunday Telegraph, 1898-1900, Metropolitan Magazine, 1901; photoplay author since 1900; was contbr. to New York World. Contbr. prose and verse to magazines and newspapers. Author: My Aunt Angie; My Uncle Oswald; The Singing Stranger (verse); Mr. and Mrs. Nagg, 1906; The Jarr Family, 1907; The Gay Life; and other dramatic compositions. Originator of newspaper colored comic sections, on New York World, 1896. Oct. 15, 1911, won the Leaders of The World" advertising ideas competition from over 10,000 contestants, cash prize of $2,000 and silver trophy valued at $1,000; won $1,000 1st prize in N.Y. Telegraph-Flamingo Film Co. scenario contest, Oct. 1914; Chicago Tribune-N.Y. Globe and American Film Mfg. Co. prize of $10,000 for best moving picture serial-— The Diamond From the Sky"-—from nearly 20,000 contestants, May 1915; United Cigar Stores Better Business Suggestions" contest, first prize of $2,000, from 151,000 contestants, 1922; 3d prize of 200 in Keith Theatres Solution of New York's Traffic Problems," 1923; Pearson's Magazine American Journalism" prize of $200, 1924. Address: 101 W. 52d St., New York NY*‡

MCCARDLE, CARL WESLEY, newspaperman, diplomat; b. Cameron, W.Va., May 31, 1904; s. Daniel Dinsmore and Elma Idella (Hendrickson) McC.; B.S., Washington and Jefferson Coll., 1926, L.D., 1953; LL.B., Temple U., 1931; m. Dorothy Deaderick Bartlett, Sept. 15, 1934; 1 dau., Marcia. Reporter, Moundsville (W.Va.) Echo, 1923. Washington (Pa.) Observer, 1925-26; reporter and rewrite-man, Philadelphia Evening Bulletin, 1926-35, feature writer, 1935-43, diplomatic corr., 1943-45, European corr., 1945-46, national affairs corr., 1948, chief of Washington bur., 1949-53; asst. sec. of state, 1953-57; asst. to chairman bd. Penn-Tex. Corp., 1957-58; exec. of Pan Am. World Airways, Inc., 1959-60; columnist Wheeling Intelligencer, 1963-66; free lance writer, until 1972. Fgn. assignments: Europe, Japan and Korea, U. Pa. award for meritorious achievement in journalism, 1950. Mem. Kappa Sigma. Clubs: Franklin Inn (Phila.); Metropolitan, National Press, (Wash.). Author: These are the Generals (with others), 1943; Ethics in Government (with others), 1952. Contbr. to The Sat. Eve. Post and other mags. Home: McLean VA Died July 10, 1972; buried Potomac Methodist Ch. Cemetery, Potomac MD

MCCAREY, (THOMAS) LEO, producer, dir.; b. Los Angeles, Calif., Oct. 3, 1898; s. Thomas J. and Leona (Mistrot) McC.; LL.D., U. of Southern Calif.; married Stella V. Martin, July 29, 1920; 1 dau., Mary Virginia. Asst. dir. Universal Studios, 1920-23; directed comedies, Hal Roach Studios, 1923-28; dir. various studios, Pathe, Fox, United Artists, Paramount, Columbia and R.K.O., since 1928; directed or produced Kid From Spain," Ruggles of Red Gap," The Milky Way," Make Way for Tomorrow," The Awful Truth," Love Affair," My Favorite Wife," Going My Way," The Bells of St. Mary's." Good Sam, The Cowboy and the Lady, My Son John, Once Upon a Honeymoon, An Affair to Remember, Rally Round the Flag, Boys Santa Monica CA Died July 5, 1969.

MCCARROLL, HENRY RELTON, surgeon; b. Walnut Ridge, Ark., Aug. 6, 1905; s. Horace Rudolph and Pearl Jane (Henry) McC.; grad. Walnut Ridge High Sch., 1923; A.B. magna cum laude, Quachita Coll., Arkadelphia, Ark., 1927; M.D. cum laude, Washington U., 1931; m. Nina Elizabeth Snyder, 1934; children—Henry Relton, Sandra Beth, David Lawrence. Intern in surgery Barnes Hosp., St. Louis, 1931-32, asst. resident surgeon, 1932-33; asst. resident in surgery, Billings Hosp., Chgo., 1933-34; resident in surgery Shriners Hosp. for Crippled Children, St. Louis, 1934-37; asst. surgeon Shriners Hosp., St. Louis, 1937-50; with dept. clin. orthodpedic surgery Washington U., 1937-72, asst. prof., 1944-57, asso. prof., 1957-66, prof., 1966-70, prof. orthopedics, dept. surgery, 1970-72, orthopedic staff Barnes, St. Luke's, St. Louis Children's hosps. Served with Officers Res. Corps, Inf. and Medicine, U.S. Army, 1927-39. Received gold medal, with Dr. C. H. Crego, for exhibit on treatment congenital dislocation of hip Am. Acad. Orthopedic Surgeons, 1939; Distinguished Alumnus award Quachita Coll., 1958. Diplomate Am. Bd. Orthopaedic Surgery. Mem. A.M.A. (vice chmn. orthopedic sect. 1952, chmn. 1953, mem. ho. of dels. 1955-60), Am. Acad. Orthopaedic Surgery (pres. 1959-72), Phi Rho Sigma, Sigma Xi, Alpha Omega Alpha. Contbr. articles to Jour. Exptl. Medicine, Proc. of Soc. for Exptl. Biology and Med., Am. Jour. Physiology, Archives of Surgery, Surgery, Gynecology and Obstetrics, Annals of Surgery, Jour. Bone and Joint Surgery (asso. editor 1947-54), Jour. of A.M.A., Jour. Bone and Joint Surgery (trustee 1958-64); mem. editorial bd. Quar. Rev. of Surgery, 1950-72. Baptist. Home: St. Louis MO Died Feb. 27, 1972; buried Oak Grove Cemetery, St Louis MO

MCCARTHY, EDWARD, lawyer; b. Richmond, Va., Aug. 8, 1893; s. Edward and Deborah Couch (Anthony) McC.; student Richmond Coll., 1916-17; LL.B., George Washington U., 1922; m. Margaret R. Durkee, Nov. 29, 1929; children—Edward, Sarah Allison, Deborah Anthony. Admitted to bar D.C., Va., 1923, Fla., 1927; practicing atty., Washington, 1923-26, Jacksonville, Fla., 1927-67; mem. McCarthy, Adams & Foote. Dir., Atlantic Nat. Bank of Jacksonville; secretary, dir. Jacksonville Shipyards, Jacksonville Dredging Co. Fla. commr. on uniform State Laws, 1939-53. Past pres. Riverside Hosp. Member American, Florida, Jacksonville bar associations, S.A.R., Kappa Sigma. Episcopalian (former vestryman). Mason. Clubs: Timuquana Country, Florida Yacht (Jacksonville). Author: Florida Chancery Act Annotated, 1932. Home: Jacksonville FL Died July 9, 1967.

MCCARTHY, EUGENE ROSS, business exec.; b. Allegan, Mich., Aug. 15, 1882; s. George E. and Annis (Ross) McC.; A.B., Harvard, 1904; Doctor of Laws, Springfield Coll., 1954; married Louise Roblee, Dec. 13, 1913; children—Marjorie (Mrs. G. K. Robins), Carol Louise (Mrs. H. R. Duhme, Jr.), Roblee. Ret. vice chmn. Brown Shoe Co., St. Louis, now dir.; ret. v.p., dir. Moench Tanning Co.; dir. St. Louis County National Bank. President Nat. Council Y.M.C.A., 1949-50, mem. nat. bd., from 1949, chmn., 1951-56, member World Council Y.M.C.A., from 1955. Trustee David Ranken Sch. of Mech. Trades, from 1937. Clubs: University, Mo. Athletic, Bellerive Country (St. Louis). Home: St Louis MO Died Aug. 31, 1971.

MCCARTHY, JUSTIN HOWARD, engr., paper co. exec.; b. Portsmouth, N.H., Sept. 13, 1894; s. Thomas and Ellen (Moorhead) McC.; B.S., Dartmouth, 1915; C.E., Thayer Sch. Engring., 1916; m. Elsie Johnson, Feb. 5, 1929; children—Justin Howard, James H., Ann E. Pulp and paper industry engr., 1916-68, specializing design and constrn. prodn. units; with St. Regis Paper Co., 1946-68, v.p., chief engr., 1955-57, v.p. engring., 1957-68. Mem. Am. Soc. C.E., Am. Soc. M.E. Home: Jacksonville FL Died June 10, 1968.

MCCARTHY, LOUISE ROBLEE (MRS. EUGENE ROSS MCCARTHY), philanthropist; b. St. Louis, Oct. 7, 1888; d. Joseph H. and Florence (Allen) Roblee; grad. Mary Inst., St. Louis, Bradford Acad., Mass.; A.B., Vassar Coll., 1912; H.H.D., Springfield Coll., 1943; m. Eugene Ross McCarthy, Dec. 13, 1913; children—Marjorie (Mrs. G. Kenneth Robins), Carol Louise (Mrs. H. Richard Duhme, Jr.), Roblee. Nat. dir. YWCA of U.S., 1934-64, hon. dir., 1965-70, v.p., 1949-55, chmn. central region, 1946-52, v.p.-at-large, 1952-55; v.p. World YMCA, Geneva, Switzerland, 1955-59; Am. mem. World YWCA Council, 1949-63, mem. exec. com., 1948-59; del. World YWCA Council, Beirut, Lebanon, 1951, Great Britain, 1955, Mexico, 1959, Denmark, 1963; del. membership conf., Whitby, Can., 1950; dir. St. Louis YWCA, 1953-70, pres., 1938-40. Mem. Nat. USO Corp., 1941-47, 51-66, mem. nat. bd., 1948-50, v.p. councils of St. Louis and Mo., 1941-47; nat. v.p. United Def. Fund, 1950-55; former mem. central budget and policy com. St. Louis Community Chest; mem. bd. govs. United Fund of Greater St. Louis, 1955-70; chmn. com. Mo. White House Conf. Com. on Children and Youth to study programs under religious auspices in Mo., 1949-50; mem. Mo. com. White House Conf. on Children and Youth, 1960; mem. Mayor's Race Relations Commn. St. Louis 1943-49; dir. Nat. Conf. Christians and Jews, St. Louis, 1945-55; v.p.-at-large Nat. Council Chs. of Christ in U.S.A., 1945-57, mem. gen. bd., 1954-57, 60-63, mem. div. internat. affairs, 1960-66; exec. bd. Met. Ch. Fedn. St. Louis, 1938-70, v.p., 1956-70. Trustee Vassar Coll., 1933-37, Springfield Coll., 1955-59. Recipient Woman of Achievement citation for nat. service St. Louis Globe-Democrat, 1955; Ecumenical Woman of Yr. citation Met. Ch. Fedn. Greater St. Louis, 1959; citation for notable achievement and service Bradford Jr. Coll., 1961; citation Women of Press, St. Louis, 1964. Mem. Nat. Soc. Colonial Dames Am., Mo. Hist. Soc., Am. Assn. U. Women (pres. St. Louis 1924-26), League Women Voters. Clubs: Vassar (past pres.), Wednesday (hon.), Woman's (St. Louis); Vassar (N.Y.C.) St Louis MO Died Feb. 6, 1970.

MCCARTHY WILLIAM HENRY, postmaster; b. San Francisco, Calif., Dec. 17, 1877; s. Dennis Joseph and

Catherine Cecila (Daly) McC.; grad. Lowell High Sch., San Francisco, 1895; hon. LL.D., U. of San Francisco; m. Retta Helen Haynes, Dec. 30, 1926. Began as office boy in Assay office, San Francisco, 1895; pres. United Workingmen's Boot & Shoe Mfg. Co., 1900-24; receiver Federal Construction Co., 1924-26; pres. Mission Baseball Club, 1927-29; comptroller 450 Sutter Corp., 1929-30; postmaster San Francisco, 1933-48; dir. Macy's, San Francisco; pres. Senator Corporation; former dir. Market Street Railway Co.; chairman board Mark Hopkins, Inc.; president Pacific Coast Baseball League, 1920-24. Mem. Fire Commn. of San Francisco, 1908-10; mem. Bd. of Supervisors, San Francisco, 1912-16; trustee U. of San Francisco (chmn. bd.). Awarded Congressional Medal of Merit. Mem. Nat. Assn. Postmasters (pres. 1935-36). Phi Sigma Kappa. Democrat. Catholic. K.C., Elk. Clubs: Olympic, Bohemian. Home: 1462 Jefferson St. Office: Hobart Bldg., 582 Market St., San Francisco CA‡

MCCARTNEY, JAMES LINCOLN, physician; b. Chungking, China, July 24, 1898 (parents Am. citizens); s. James Henry and Saddie (Kissack) McC.; student Ohio Wesleyan U., 1918-19, Peking Union Med. Coll., 1919; B.S., U. Chgo., 1920; M.D., Rush Med. Coll., 1923; grad. study Columbia, N.Y. Postgrad. Med. Sch., N.Y.U.; m. Edith M. Tufts, Dec. 1924; children—Helen J. (deceased) Helen C. (Mrs. Gettemy), Joan E. (Mrs. Cusick), James Robert. Asst. instr. neurophysiology Peking Union Med. Coll., 1919, U. Chgo., 1920-22; asst. physician St. Elizabeth's Hosp., Washington, 1923-24, 27-29; pvt. practice, China, 1924-27; psychiatry fellow Inst. Child Guidance, N.Y.C., 1928-29; dir. bur. mental hygiene Conn. Dept. Health, 1929-30; psychiatrist, dir. classification clinic Elmira Reformatory, N.Y. State Dept. Correction, 1930-34; dir. Northwest Retreat, Portland, Ore., 1934-35, dept. psychiatry Battle Creek Sanitarium, 1935; psychiatrist N.Y. State Vocational Instn., 1935-38; asso. dir. med. div. Sharp & Dohme, 1939-41; med. dir. W. R. Warner & Co., Inc., 1941-42, Trans-International Psychosomatic Seminars, 1961-69; pvt. practice psychiatry, Garden City, New York, 1946-64, Westhampton Beach, New York, 1964-69; asso. professor Southampton College, L.I.U., 1966-68; cons. Central Suffolk Hosp., Southampton Hosp. Dir. Suffolk County Mental Health Assn. Served active duty USN, 1942-45. Diplomate Am. Bd. Med. Hypnosis. Fellow A.C.P., N.Y., Acad. Medicine (Salmon Meml. award 1933), Med. Writers Assn., Acad. Psychosomatic Medicine, Am. Psychiat. Assn., A.M.A.; mem. Am. Geriatrics Soc., Assn. Exptl. and Clin. Hypnosis, Am. Assn. Clin. Hypnosis, World Med. Assn., Internat. Coll. Internal Medicine, and other profl. orgns., A.A.A.S., Assn. Mil. Surgeons, Ret. Officers Assn. (past pres.), Am. Legion, Phi Chi. Unitarian. Mason. Clubs: China, Shanghai, Tiffin. Author of books, latest being, Understanding Human Behavior, 1956. Home: Westhampton Beach NY Died Nov. 28, 1969; buried Nat. Cemetery at Pinelawn.

MCCARTY, E(DWARD) PROSPER, mining engr.; b. Clifton, Ill., Oct. 1, 1873; s. Andrew F. and Mary (Fogarty) M.; E.M., U. of Minn. Sch. of Mines, 1900; m. Ethel Keefe, of Minneapolis, Sept. 24, 1913; children—Mary Roberta, Jessie Edwarda. Prof. mining, U. of Minn. Sch. of Mines, 1900-17; chief consulting mining engr. to Minn. Tax Commn., 1909-17; consulting mining engr., Minneapolis, 1917-19; mgr. Ajax Mining Co., Biwabik, Minn., 1919-20; prof. mining engring., U. of Wyo., 1920-25; resumed practice as cons. mining engr. Capt. engrs. U.S.A., 1918. Prepared spl. reports on iron mining in Minn., and estimates of iron ore tonnages, 1910, 12, 14, 16. Various papers in trade journals and in Trans. Lake Superior Mining Inst. Mem. Am. Inst. Mining Engrs., Sigma Xi, Tau Beta Pi. Home: 2519 Humboldt Av. S. Office: Roanoke Bldg., Minneapolis MN‡

MCCARTY, SIDNEY LOUIS, clergyman; b. Monroe County, Mo., Jan. 20, 1874; s. Chas. Preston and Elizabeth (Bates) McC.; student Westminster Coll., Fulton, Mo.; A.B., Southwestern Presbyn. U., Clarksville, Tenn., 1897; D.D., Davidson Coll., 1920; student Bibl. Sem. of New York, 1923; m. Louise Miller, Aug. 7, 1902; children—Elizabeth, Charles Raymond (dec.), Sidney Louis. Ordained ministry Presbyn. Ch., 1900; pastor Tallahassee, Fla., 1900-03, Thomasville, Ga., 1903-14. Reid Memorial Presbyn. Ch., Augusta, Ga., 1914-38, pastor emeritus since 1938. Moderator Synod of Ga., 1920; chmn. Synod's com., 1927; commr. to Gen. Assembly, 1933; chmn. Synod's Com. on Business, 1930-36; sec. Synod's Com. on Stated Supply, 1934-38; chmn. Presbytery's Com. on Home Missions, 1917-37. Trustee Davidson Coll., 1922, 28, Thornwell Orphanage since 1936. Mem. Phi Delta Theta, Pi Gamma Mu. Home: Apopka FL‡

MCCARTY, WILLIAM T., clergyman; b. Crossingville, Pa., Aug. 11, 1889; s. Timothy and Margaret (Burns) McC.; ed. St. Mary's Coll., North East, Pa., 1903-09, Mt. St. Alphonsus Sem., Esopus, N.Y., 1910-16. Ordained priest (Redemptorist) Roman Catholic Ch., 1915; prof., St. Mary's Coll., 1916-17, Mt. St. Alphonsus Sem., 1918-30; asst., Mission Ch., Boston, 1930-33; rector, Mt. St. Alphonsus Sem., 1933-39; provincial of Redemptorist Fathers, Brooklyn, N.Y., 1939-43; consecrated bishop, St. Patrick's Cathedral, N.Y. City, Jan., 1943; mil. del. to armed forces, U.S. Army, asst. to Cardinal Spellman, 1943-47; coadjutor bishop, Rapid City, S.D. May 1947, became bishop 1948. Address: Rapid City SD Died Sept. 14, 1972; buried Mt. St. Alphonsus Cemetery, Esopus NY

MCCASH, ISAAC NEWTON, univ. pres.; b. Cumberland County, Ill., June 5, 1861; s. Isaac Sparks and Martha Ann (Van Zandt) McC.; B.S., Nat. Normal U., Lebanon, O., 1882; spl. Summer Sch. of Theology, Harvard, 1899; A.M., Drake U., 1902, LL.D., same; D.D., Phillips U., 1925; m. Marietta Tandy, Oct. 5, 1886; children—Buell, Stella Van Zandt, Lois (dec.), Allegra Ruth. Ordained Disciples of Christ ministry, 1890; pastor University Ch., Des Moines, Ia., 1893-1904; supt. Ia. Anti-Saloon League, 1904-07; mem. nat. hdqrs. com. and secured enactment of Inebriate" bill and Time Limit" bill by Ia. Legislature; life dir., and corr. sec. Am. Christian Missionary Soc., Oct. 1909-14; life dir. Foreign Christian Missionary Soc.; pres. Spokane (Wash.) U., 1913-16; pres. Phillips U., Enid, Okla., 1916-38, pres. emeritus since 1938. President Oklahoma Memorial Assn. since 1944. Trustee, treas. Cottey Coll., since 1932; pres. Nat. Bd. of Edn.; Disciples of Christ, 1919-21; pres. Ia. Children's Home Soc. 10 yrs.; mem. exec. com. Interdenominational Home Mission Council; mem. Federal Council of Chs. of Christ in America; mem. exec. com. North Central Assn. of Colleges, 1933-36; mem. exec. com. Co-ordinating Bd. for Greater U. of Okla., 1933. Mem. Com. on Cultural Relations with Latin America, 1940. Pres. Okla. Ednl. Assn.; mem. Acad. of Science, Okla. Hist. Soc. (dir. since 1944), Pi Gamma Mu, Phi Beta Kappa. Mason (33 deg., K.T., K.C.C.H.); Grand Chaplain Oklahoma Scottish Rites, 1934-35, 1937-38; Grand orator, 1938-39. Clubs: University, Rotary, Philosophical Hi-Twelve. Author: Ten Plagues of Modern Egypt, 1903; Horizon of American Missions, 1912. Editor American Home Missionary, 1909-14. Name placed in Okla. Hall of Fame and bust in Hist. Soc., 1939. Home: 1211 E. Broadway, Enid OK‡

MCCAUSTLAND, ELMER JAMES, prof. civ. engring.; b. Quincy, Wis., Jan. 9, 1864; s. James and Luannia (Winn) M.; B.C.E., Cornell Coll., Ia., 1892; C.E., Cornell U., 1895, M.C.E., 1897; m. Annie Gwynne, Apr. 11, 1893 (died Feb. 18, 1921); children—Gwynne Gravelle, Margaret L.; m. 2d, Mrs. Elinor G. Anderson, Apr. 27, 1922. City engr., Salem, Ore., 1891-93; sec. Salem Improvement Co., 1893-96; instr. Cornell U., 1897-1900; ry. work, Chicago, Ill., 1900-02; asst. prof. civ. engring., Cornell U., 1902-07; prof. civ. engring., U. of Ala., 1907-08; prof. municipal and highway engring., U. of Wash., 1908-14; dean faculty of engring. and dir. Engring. Expt. Sta., U. of Mo., 1914-36, now emeritus, dean, prof. and dir. Pres. State Bd. of Health, Wash., 1912. Progressive. Presbyterian. Fellow A.A.A.S.; mem. Am. Soc. C.E., Pacific N.W. Soc. Engrs., Soc. for Promotion Engring. Edn., Sigma Xi, Phi Beta Kappa. Mason. Contbr. many articles to tech. jours. Club: Engineers (St. Louis). Home: 1501 E. Silver Av., Albuquerque NM*‡

MCCHESNEY, MAY LOUISE (LOGAN), prof. piano; b. Chicago, Ill., Mar. 10, 1875; d. Simon and Sarina (Jones) McChesney; Music B., Coll. Fine Arts, Syracuse U., 1902. Teacher, piano and theory, Mansfield, Pa., 1902-04; teacher studied piano, Fine Arts Coll., Syracuse Univ., 1904-45 (also studied 3 yrs. abroad with Paul Braud, Conservatoire in Paris; Tobias Mathay, London); prof. emeritus since 1945. Mem. Am. Assn. Univ. Profs., Am. Aid for France, Morning Musicals, Gamma Phi Beta. Methodist. Home: (summer) Old Forge Hotel, Old Forge, N.Y.; (winter) Gayfair Hotel, St. Petersburg FL‡

MCCLAIN, DAYTON ERNEST, clergyman, educator; b. Gumboro, Del., May 15, 1879; s. Levin White and Mary Ellen (Culver) McC.; A.B., Dickinson Coll., 1906; M.A., Harvard U., 1907; Ph.D., Boston U., 1909, S.T.B., 1917 (as of 1909); LL.D., American Univ., 1939; L.H.D., John Brown U., 1950, D.S.T., 1954; D.D. (honorary), Wofford College, 1959; married Edna May Insley, Mar. 27, 1901 (dec. 1957); children—Mae Elizabeth (wife of Dr. Alpine W. McGregor), Preston LeRoy; m. 2d, Myrtle D. Derrickson, June 13, 1959. Principal Tyaskin (Md.) Grammar Sch., 1900-01. Ordained to ministry, Methodist Episcopal Ch., 1909; paster Milo Junction and Milo (Me.) Chs., 1909-14, Knight Memorial, Calais, Me., 1914-16, Bar Harbor, Me., 1916-18; dir. of finance in Centenary Movement, 1918-20; mem. finance dept., Board Edn., 1920-26; dir. finance Am. Univ., 1926-32, v.p. from 1939; pastor Deals Island (Md.) Ch., 1934-37, Zion M.E. Ch., Cambridge, Md., 1937-39. Supt. Anti-Saloon League of Del., 1933-34. Del. to Methodist Northeastern Jurisdictional Conf., 1952. Mem. Washington Bd. Trade since 1939; Phi Beta Kappa. Methodist. Mason (32 deg., K.T., Shriner), Odd Fellow, Granger. Club: Universities. World's strawberry picking record, 787 qts. 1 day. Author: The Sin of Omission, 1959; The Miracle of Two Cents, 1968. Contbr. articles to papers and mags. Home: Gainesville FL Died Sept. 1971.

MCCLAIN, JOSEPH A., JR., state senator; b. Ringgold, Ga., May 1, 1903; s. Joseph A. and Robert Emily (Jones) McC.; B.A., Mercer University, 1925, LL.B., 1924, LL.D., 1941; J.S.D., Yale, 1929; LL.D., Tulane University, 1944; m. Laura Elizabeth Burkett, Sept. 15, 1926; children—Joseph A., Laura Elizabeth, David Hollingsworth. Admitted to the Georgia bar, 1924, Missouri bar, 1942; associated firm Slade & Swift, Columbus, Ga., 1925-26; prof. of law, Mercer U., 1926-27; prof. and dean, Mercer U. Law Sch., 1927-33; prof. of law, U. of Ga., 1933-34; dean and prof. of law, U. of Louisville, 1934-36; dean of Washington U. Law Sch., 1936-42; dean of Duke University Law School, 1950-56; instr. Stetson U. Law Sch., 1956-61; partner McClain & Smiley, Sarasota, Fla., 1956-57, Mabry, Reavies, Carlton, Fields & Ward, Tampa, 1957-62, McClain, Cason & Turbiville, Tampa, Florida, 1962-64; partner of McClain & Turbiville, Tampa, 1964-70; v.p., general counsel Terminal R.R. Assn. St. Louis, Mo., 1942-45; general counsel Wabash Railroad, 1945-50; mem. Fla. Senate, 1967-70, recipient Allen Morris award for most valuable 2d term senator. Chairman Enemy Alien Hearing Bd., Fed. Eastern Dist. of Missouri, 1941-46. Chmn. citizens com. which successfully campaigned for charter amendment establishing Merit System for St. Louis, 1941. Pres. Social Planning Council of St. Louis and St. Louis County, 1942-44 (mem. council, 1940-44), Fedn. of Merit System. Mem. City Plan Commn. since 1946 (chmn. 1947-50); v.p. of adult edn. of Council of Greater St. Louis; dir. St. Louis C. of C. 1945-50 (chairman members' assembly com., 1945-47); chmn. Citizens' Area Planning Group of St. Louis of the Metropolitan Plan Assn., 1946-50; chmn. Citizens' Sch., Tax Increase and Bond Issue Campaign Com., 1947; chmn. spl. com. appointed by State Bar of Calif. to make survey legal edn. and admissions to bar Cal. Law Schools, 1948-49, Florida, 1954. Member Georgia, Missouri, Florida (chmn. com. no legal edn. and admissions to bar), North Carolina bars, American Bar Association (member council on legal edn. 1942-50, chmn. 1945-47; mem. ho. dels. 1945-50, chmn. com. civil service; assembly delegate, house of delegates, 1961-64), Bar of U.S. Supreme Ct., St. Louis Bar Association (vice pres. 1944-45), Am. Law Inst., Pi Kappa Phi, Phi Alpha Delta, Order of Coif. Republican. Baptist. Mason (Shriner). Contbr. articles in various law jours. Home: Tampa FL Died Mar. 18, 1970.

MCCLASKEY, HENRY MORRISON, JR., advt. exec.; b. Louisville, Feb. 13, 1919; s. Henry Morrison and Lottye McClaskey; student Princeton, 1941; m. Ann Foree McMullen, July 11, 1942; children—Henry Morrison III, Malcolm, Heather. Reporter, Louisville Courier-Journal, 1942; with Zimmer-McClaskey-Lewis, Louisville, 1947-70, pres., 1964-70. Served as officer USAAF, 1942-45. Home: Anchorage KY Died Apr. 18, 1970.

MCCLEARY, ROBERT ALTWIG, educator; b. Dayton, O., Jan. 9, 1923; s. Harold and Mae (Altwig) McC.; B.A., Harvard, 1944; M.D., Johns Hopkins, 1947, Ph.D. in Psychology, 1951; m. Nan Sarah Brown, Feb. 3, 1945; children—Robert Edward, Beverly Nan, Susan Elaine. Intern internal medicine Barnes Hosp., St. Louis, 1947-48; from asst. prof. to asso. prof. psychology U. Mich., 1953-61; prof. psychology and physiology U. Chgo., 1961-73; cons. Aerospace Med. Center, Brooks AFB, 1961-73, Nat. Insts. Mental Health, 1961-73. Served to capt. USAF, 1951-53. USPHS fellow, 1953-55; Carnegie Sr. Research fellow U. Oslo (Norway), 1957-58. Fellow Am. Psychol. Assn.; mem. Psychonomics Soc., Soc. Exptl. Psychologists. Spl. research exptl. analysis brain-mechanisms of behavior. Home: Chicago IL Died Mar. 20, 1973.

MCCLEAVE, ROBERT, army officer; b. Ft. Union, N.M., Sept. 9, 1874; s. William and Mary (Crooke) McC.; grad. high sch., Berkeley, Calif.; student Merrill Bus. Coll., San Francisco, Calif.; student U. of Calif.; m. Etta Bartlett, 1898; children—Phyllis (dec.), Robert B., Mildred (wife of Newell E. Watts, U.S. Army). Enlisted as pvt., inf., 1894, advanced through grades to col., July 1, 1920; brig. gen., Dec. 13, 1929; now retired. Served in Spanish-Am. War (silver star citation for distinguished service at Battle of Santiago), Philippine Campaign, 1902-03; asst. chief of staff, 1st Am. Army, World War; observation duty, Brit. and French armies, 1917; as chief of operations sect. directed planning and operations of battles of St. Mihiel and Meuse-Argonne. Awarded D.S.M. for World War services. Presbyn. Mason. Club: San Diego (Calif.) Athletic. Address: 5555 Hollywood Blvd., Hollywood CA*‡

MCCLELLAND, ROSS ST. JOHN, engr., banker; b. Hillsdale, Ia., Oct. 7, 1878; s. William Dunlap and Ada (Moore) McC.; ed. Highland Park Coll., Des Moines; Iowa State Coll. Agriculture and Mechanic Arts, 1903; Stanford, 1904; B.Sc., Union Coll. Schenectady, N.Y., 1905; married; 1 son, Roswell D. Constructing engr. on Pacific Coast and in Mexico, chief engr. Electric Bond & Share Co., New York, 1906-19; pres. R.J. McClelland Co., investments, 1923-31, investment banking, London, Paris, Edinburgh and Zurich. A pioneer in long-distance electric power transmission, and writer on tech. and economic topics pertaining thereto. Life mem. Union Interalliee (Paris), Lake Placid Club (N.Y.). Home: 16780 Oak View Drive, Encino, Los Angeles CA‡

MCCLENAHAN, PERRY EUGENE, educator; b. in Keokuk County, Iowa, 1873; s. Winfield Scott and Frances (Meade) M.; B.Di., Ia. State Teachers Coll., 1898, M.Di., 1899; Ph.B., State U. of Ia., 1905, M.A., 1906; m. Alta Birdsall, of Cedar Falls, 1899; children—Dorothy, Ruth, Genevieve. Teacher rural schools, principal schools, Baldwin, Iowa, supt. schs., Winterset, until 1904; prin. secondary edn., N.M. Coll. Agr. and Mechanic Arts, 1907-09; dean liberal arts, Highland Park Coll., Des Moines, Ia., 1909-11; high sch. insp. for State Bd. of Edn., Ia., 1911-16; state supt. pub. instrn., Ia., term 1920-24. Republican. Methodist. Mason, K.P., Elk. Home: Iowa City IA‡

MCCLENAHAN, ROBERT STEWART, missionary educator; b. Wyoming, Ia., June 5, 1871; s. James Urie and Margaret Ann (Lorimer) McC.; A.B., Tarkio (Mo.) Coll., 1893, A.M., 1906; A.B., Yale, 1896, A.M., 1919; LL.D., Westminster, 1913; m. Margaret Jeannette Wallace, Sept. 1, 1897; children—William Urie, Robert Wallace, Helen Jeannette, John Lorimer. Teacher in Mission Coll., Norfolk, Va., 1893-95, Phillips Acad., Andover, Mass., 1896-97; teacher of religion and ethics, Assiut Coll., Egypt, 1897-1910, pres., 1910-18; dean Coll. of Arts and Science, Am. Univ., Cairo, 1918-28, dean of univ., 1928-32, dean of School of Oriental Studies, 1932-39; emeritus. Chairman Committee on Missions and Govts. of Egypt Intermission Council, 1931-39; mem. of The Com. on Africa, The War and Peace Aims, 1942. Mem. Am. Acad. Polit. and Social Sciences. Presbyn. Men's Social Union, Phi Beta Kappa (Yale Chapter). Club: Contemporary. Address: 902 Land Title Bldg., Philadelphia PA‡

MCCLINTIC, ROBERT HOFFERD, business exec.; born Pitts., 1901; m. Jean T. McClintic; children—Robert Hofferd II, William H., Ronnald T., David W. Chmn. bd., treas. Gordon Terminal Service Co., MeKees Rocks, Pa.; chmn. bd. Tioga Pipeline Co., Pitts.; mem. exec. com., dir. Koppers Co., Inc. Honorary director School for Blind Children, Western Pa. Hosp. (Pitts.). Home: Ligonier PA Died Jan. 25, 1970; buried St. Michael's of the Valley Cemetery, Rector PA

MCCLINTOCK, EUPHEMIA E., educator; b. Newberry, S.C.; d. Ebenezer Pressley and Elizabeth Jane (Young) M.; A.B., Woman's Coll. of Baltimore, 1893; A.M., U. of Chicago, 1916. Pres. Coll. for Women, Columbia, S.C., 1902-15; prin. the Erskine School, Boston, since 1920. Mem. Phi Beta Kappa. Address: 129 Beacon St., Boston MA‡

MCCLINTOCK, HARRY WINFRED, supt. schs.; b. Johnston City, Ill., May 22, 1907; s. Moses E. and Flora B. (Mosley) McC.; Ph.B., Shurtleff Coll., 1929; M.A. in Edn., U. Ky., 1941; postgrad. Dartmouth, 1943, Ill. State U., 1963; m. Harriet K. Christoe, June 10, 1931; 1 dau., Katheryn Anne. Tchr., Frankfort Community High Sch., West Frankfort, Ill. 1929-43; pub. relations Tomlinson Motors, West Frankfort, 1947-54; co-owner Mack's Super Market, West Frankfort, 1954-55; asst. dir. Ill. Dept. Pub. Welfare, Springfield, 1955-61; tchr. high sch., Springfield, 1961; supt. schs., Gridley, Ill., 1961-69. Mem. Bd. Spl. Edn., McLean County, Ill., 1965-69. Mem. Ill. Ho. of Reps., 1947-55, chmn. mil. affairs com., sec. sch. problems com., 1951-55. Served to lt. comdr. USNR, 1943-46. Mem. Am. Assn. Sch. Adminstrs., N.E.A., Ill. Edn. Assn., Am. Legion. Republican. Mem. United Ch. of Christ. Kiwanian. Club: Community (West Frankfort). Home: Gridley IL Died May 8, 1969.

MCCLINTOCK, JOHN CALVIN, thyroid surgeon; b. Iowa City, Mar. 2, 1906; s. John T. and Beulah (George) McC.; B.S., State U. Ia., 1927, M.D., 1929; m. Martha Mumma, July 11, 1930; children—Gail (Mrs. David Pike), Beulah Janes (Mrs. Russell Weidman), John T. II. Intern Montreal Gen. Hosp., 1929-30; fellow surgery Cleve. Clinic Found., 1930-32; clin. asst. surgery Northwestern U., 1933-34; mem. faculty Albany (N.Y.) Med. Coll., 1942-69, asso. clin. prof. surgery, 1956-69; mem. staff Albany Med. Center Hosp., 1937-69, attending surgeon, 1957-69. Served to maj., M.C., AUS, World War II. Fellow A.C.S. (past bd. govs.); mem. Albany County Med. Soc. (pres. 1955-56), Med. Soc. State N.Y. (exec. council 1955-65), A.M.A. (ho. of dels. 1957-69), Excelsior Surg. Soc., Am. Thyroid Assn. (pres. 1962-63; Distinguished Service award 1965), Pan-Pacific Surg. Assn., Sigma Xi, Alpha Slingerlands NY Died Feb. 3, 1969; buried Graceland Cemetery, Delmar NY

MCCLOSKEY, MANUS, army officer, hosp. supt.; b. Pittsburgh, Pa., Apr. 24, 1874; s. James E. and Catherine McC.; B.S., U.S. Mil. Acad., 1898; honor grad. Army Sch. of the Line, 1909; grad. Army Staff Coll., 1910; grad. General Staff Coll., Washington, D.C., 1920; m. Sara Monro, Aug. 14, 1901; children—Monro, Sally. Commd. 2d lt. 5th Arty., Apr. 26, 1898; promoted through various grades to col., May 15, 1917; brig. gen. (temp.), Aug. 8, 1918; brig. gen. (permanent), Sept. 1, 1930. At Santiago, Cuba, Aug. 10-19, 1898; comdr. platoon of light battery at Mil. Athletic Tournament, Madison Sq. Garden, N.Y. City, Mar. 20-25, 1899; in Philippines and China, 1899-1901; wounded in action, Oct. 3, 1899; participated in march to Peking and rescue of Legation, Aug. 1900; again in Philippines, 1907; comdg. West Point Battery at U.S. Mil. Acad., 1911-12, 1st Batn., 3d Field Arty., Tex., 1913-14; instr. Nat. Guard F.A., at Tobyhanna, Pa., 1915; comdg. regt. of Va. and N.H. F.A., in Tex., Sept. 1916-May 1917; organized 12th Regt. F.A., U.S. Army, June 1917; took regt. to France, Jan. 1918, and comd. it in action at Verdun, Chateau Thierry, Belleau Wood and Soissons, Mar.-Aug. 1918; wounded in action at Soissons, July 19, 1918; comd. 152d Brigade F.A., 77th Div., in action on the Vesle and through the Argonne-Meuse operations until armistice, and until Feb. 1919; comdg. 2d Brigade F.A., 2d Div., in Germany, until July 1919; comdg. Camp Knox, Ky., Aug. 1920; on Gen. Staff hdqrs., 6th Corps Area, Chicago, Ill., Jan. 1921-June 30, 1924; on organized reserve duty as chief of Staff, 6th Corps, July 1, 1924-Dec. 29, 1925; comdg. 11th Field Arty., Hawaii, 1926-28; organized reserve duty, N.Y. City, Jan.-Apr. 1929; chief of staff Arty. Group, Chicago, Apr. 1929-Aug. 31, 1930; comd. Ft. Sheridan, Ill., to May 23, 1931, Ft. Bragg, N.C., June 3, 1931-Apr. 30, 1938; now retired. Organized, 1933, and administered Civilian Conservation Corps in N.C., 1933-36; supt. Cook County Hosp., Chicago, 1938-47. D.S.M., Silver Star with oak-leaf cluster, Purple Heart with oak-leaf cluster (U.S.); Legion of Honor, Croix de Guerre (French); Crown of Italy (Italian). Mem. Am. Coll. Hosp. Adminstrs. Club: Army and Navy (Washington). Home: 181 Sheridan Rd., Winnetka IL‡

MCCLOSKEY, MATTHEW H., builder; b. Wheeling, W.Va., 1893. Founder McCloskey & Co., Phila., 1911; ambassador to Ireland, 1962-64. Treas., Nat. Democratic Com., 1954-62. Inventor 100-a-plate campaign fund-raising dinner, 1935. Home: Philadelphia PA Died Apr. 1973.

MCCLOSKEY, ROBERT GREEN, educator; b. Wisconsin, Rapids, Wis., Jan. 8, 1916; s. John Stewart and Margaret (Green) McC.; B.A., U. Wis., 1942; M.A., U. Mich., 1944; M.P.A., Harvard, 1946, Ph.D., 1948; m. Helen Stueland, Aug. 23, 1941; children—Donald, Laura, John. Faculty Harvard, 1948-69, prof. of government, 1958-69, formerly chairman of the department. Administrative asst. to governor of Mich., 1944-45. Author: American Conservatism in the Age of Enterprise, 1951; The American Supreme Court, 1960. Editor: Essays in Constitutional Law, 1957. Contbr. profl. jours. Home: Arlington MA Died Aug. 4, 1969; buried Mt. Auburn Cemetery, Cambridge MA

MCCLOSKEY, THOMAS DAVID, lawyer, corp. official; b. Somerville, Mass., Jan. 7, 1873; s. Thomas and Abigail (Warnock) McC.; A.B., Geneva Coll., Beaver Falls, Pa., 1893; LL.B., Harvard, 1899; m. Grace P. Moorhead, Nov. 4, 1904 (died Dec. 27, 1925); m. 2d, Elizabeth Wood Lilley, Apr. 20, 1933. Admitted to Mass. bar, 1899, Pa. bar, 1900; in practice, Pittsburgh, since 1901; member firm McCloskey, Best & Leslie; director Thompson & Company, Western Savings & Deposit Bank. Presbyterian. Club: Duquesne. Home: 1311 Squirrel Hill Av. Office: Oliver Bldg., Pittsburgh 22 PA*‡

MCCLURE, HOWARD (ORTON), b. Wabash, Ind., Dec. 23, 1865; s. Thomas W. and Anna (Silver) McC.; ed. pub. schs.; m. Matie Parcells, June 29, 1892; 1 dau., Sarah Loraine. Locomotive engr., C.&W.I. R.R., 1887-91; in hardware business, Chicago, Ill., 1891-1905; same, Tulsa, Okla., 1905-18; pres. Atlas Life Ins. Co., 1918-29; dir. 1st Nat. Bank, Tulsa; pres. 4th Nat. Bank since April 20, 1933. Pres. Bd. of Edn., Tulsa, 1908-15; pres. Tulsa Chamber Commerce, 1908, 23. Republican. Club: Tulsa. Home: 1437 Terrace Drive, Tulsa OK‡

MCCOBB, PAUL (WINTHROP), designer; b. Boston; s. Raymond and Winifred (Caulfield) McC.; ed. pvt. tutors; studied painting Vester Sch. Fine Arts, and with various individual artists; m. Mary Frances Rogers. Founder Paul McCobb Design Assos., N.Y.C., 1945, furniture design added to program, 1950; designs now manufactured in U.S.A., Can., Holland, Germany, Denmark, Japan; cons. indsl. design various indsl. orgns.; designs included exhbns., including Am. exhibit Milan Triennale, world trade fair, Italy, 1957; design selected for many fairs including Brussels Fair, 1958. Bd. govs. Phila. Mus. Art. Served with Camouflage Corps, AUS, World War II. Recipient many design awards including Mus. Modern Art, 1950, 51, 53, 54, 55, ann. award Hardwood Inst., 1953, Trail Blazers award Home Fashions League, 1953. Mem. Am. Inst. Decorators, Am. Soc. Indsl. Designers. Home: New York NY Died Mar. 12, 1969.

MCCOLL, ROBERT BOYD, locomotive mfg.; b. Kilmarnock, Scotland, Jan. 1, 1882; s. Hugh and Jane (Boyd) McC.; student Kilmarnock Acad., Science and Art Coll., 1897-1902; m. Mary Ann MacLennan, June 24, 1908. Came to U.S., 1905; naturalized citizen, 1929. Apprentice Glasgow Southwestern R.R., Kilmarnock, Scotland, 1897-1902; draftsman Robert Stephenson & Co., Darlington, Eng., 1904-05; successively small tool supervisor, gen. machine shop foreman, asst. supt., supt. and works mgr. Montreal Locomotive Works, Ltd., Montreal, Can., 1905-18; gen. mgr. Sir K.G. Armstrong Whitworth Co., Newcastle-on-Tyne, Eng., 1919-22; mgr. Schenectady plant Am. Locomotive Co., 1922-31, pres. McIntosh & Seymour Diesel Engine Corp., Auburn, N.Y., and Alco Products, Inc., subsidiaries, 1931-40; v.p. in charge mfg. Am. Locomotive Co., also Montreal Locomotive Works, Ltd., Mar. 1940-Sept. 1945, exec. v.p. (both cos.), Sept.-Dec. 1945, pres. both cos. 1945-50, also dir.; dir. Schenectady Trust Company, Beaumont (Tex.) Iron works, Gen. Steel Castings Corp. Mem. Inst. Mech. Engrs. (London), Newcomen Soc., St. Andrews Soc., A.S.M.E. Presbyn. Clubs: Metropolitan, Railroad-Machinery, Blind Brook, Westchester Country, Mohawk, Mohawk Golf. Home: New York City NY Died May 23, 1972.

MCCOLLOCH, FRANK CLEVELAND, lawyer; b. Portland, Ore., Aug. 25, 1892; s. Charles Henry and Mary (Wooddy) McC.; LL.B., Stanford, 1917; m. Elizabeth Susanne Meyer, Aug. 15, 1917; 1 son, Charles Koerner. Admitted to Ore. bar, 1919; practiced in Baker, 1919-35; pub. utilities commnr. Ore., 1935-37; partner firm McColloch, Dezendorf & Spears, and predecessors, Portland, 1937-68. Chmn. Ore. Bd. Geology and Mineral Industries, 1961-68; adv. bd. Am. Petroleum Inst., 1961-68; mem. Ore. Interim Com. Water Resources, 1953-55. Served as maj., inf., U.S. Army, 1917-19; AEF in France and Belgium. Decorated Purple Heart; Croix de Guerre with palm (France). Mem. Am., Ore. bar assns., Am. Judicature Soc., Portland C. of C., Phi Delta Phi. Democrat. Mason (32 deg.). Author Ore. ground water act, 1955; co-author Ore. water resources act, 1955. Home: Portland OR

MCCOMAS, HENRY CLAY, psychologist; b. Baltimore, Md., Dec. 21, 1875; s. Henry Clay and Mary (Parker) M.; A.B., Johns Hopkins, 1897; A.M., Columbia, 1898; grad. Union Theol. Sem., New York, 1900; Ph.D., Harvard, 1910; m. Edith R. Gates, Oct. 20, 1897. Ordained Congl. ministry, 1900; pastor North Attleboro, Mass., 1900-03, Cadillac, Mich., 1903-07; instr. psychology, Princeton, 1909-12, asst. prof., 1912-21, asso. prof., 1921; pres. H.C. McComas Coal Co. since 1927; pres. Baltimore Coal Exchange, 1930-33; lecturer in psychology, Johns Hopkins U., since 1928. Collaborator on Psychol. Index, 1909-11; sec. Psychological Review Pub. Co. Capt. Sanitary Corps, U.S. Army, 1918-19. Fellow A.A.A.S.; mem. Am. Psychol. Assn., New York Acad. Sciences, Phi Gamma Delta, Sigma Chi. Author: Some Types of Attention, 1911; The Psychology of Religious Sects, 1912; The Aviator, 1921; Ghosts I Have Talked With, 1935. Home: 320 Hawthorne Rd., Roland Park MD‡

MCCONACHIE, LAUROS GRANT, publicist; b. Sparta, Ill., Jan. 18, 1866; s. David and Eliza (Foster) M.; A.B., Knox Coll., Galesburg, Ill., 1890, A.M., 1893; Johns Hopkins, 1892-93; U. of Pa., 1893-94; Ph.D., Cornell, 1896; m. Martha Marion Fay, Oct. 30, 1909 (died Oct. 21, 1918); 1 dau., Janet Alden. In ednl. service P.I., 1901-05; instr. polit. science, U. of Wis., 1905-09; with Legislative Reference and Research depts., Wis. and N.Y., 1908-14; expert, N.Y. State Dept. of Labor, 1914-37. Unitarian. Author: Congressional Committees (vol. of Crowell's Library of Economics and Politics), 1898. Editor bulls. on workmen's compensation; contbr. to Nelson's Loose Leaf Ency., and on politics to periodicals. Home: 4 Pine St., Albany NY‡

MCCONIHE, MALCOLM STUART, Dem. nat. committeeman; b. Troy, N.Y., Aug. 21, 1872; s. Isaac and Phoebe McKean (Warren) McC.; A.B., Trinity Coll., Hartford, Conn., 1892; m. Eleanor Berger Moran, Nov. 18, 1903; children—F. Moran, Malcolm Stuart. Engaged in real estate business, Washington, D.C., since 1927; receiver of nat. banks in N.M., Tex., S.C., N.C., pres. Wm. Corcoran Hill Co., Inc., since 1930; treas. Rosslyn Steel and Cement Co. since 1934. Mem. Dem. Nat. Com. from D.C., since 1936. Served in O.T.C. during World War. Mem. Am. Legion. Elk. Clubs: University (N.Y. City), Travellers (Paris, France); Metropolitan (Washington, D.C.); Alfalfa, Chevy Chase (Washington, D.C.); Dunes (Narragansett, R.I.). Home: 2817 Woodland Drive. Office: 712 Jackson Pl., Washington DC*‡

MCCONNEL, ROGER HARMON, mining geologist; b. Caldwell, Ida., Dec. 8, 1908; s. Fred Homer and Ellen (Harmon) McC.; student Coll. of Ida., 1927-30; B.S. in Geology, U. Ida., 1932, M.S., 1936; m. Harriet Idell Smith, Nov. 3, 1934; children—Stephen S., Mary Alice. Jr. topographic engr. U.S. Geol. Survey, summers, 1934-35, field asst., 1936-37; geologist Bunker Hill Co., Kellog, Ida., 1938-40, chief geologist, 1940-42, 46-66, chief exploration geologist, 1967, geology cons., 1967-71. Served as capt. AUS, 1942-46; ETO. Fellow Geol. Soc. Am.; mem. Am. Inst. Mining, Metall. and Petroleum Engrs. (Engr. of Year Columbia sect. 1968); N.W. Mining Assn. (life); Mining and Metall. Soc. Am., Soc. Econ. Geologists (pres 1971); Societe de Geologique Appliquee Aux. Gites Minereaux. Contbr. articles to tech. jours. Home: Kellogg ID Died June 19, 1971; buried Greenwood Cemetery, Kellogg ID

MCCONNELL, ANDREW M., scientist and author; b. Blount Co., Ala., 1873; s. W. T. and A. M. McC.; grad. Blount Coll., Blountsville, Southern Univ., Greensboro, Ala.; m. Atlanta, Ga., Jan., 1898, Marion Delana

Daniel. In 1898 purchased The Alkahest, a Southern mag.; inaugurated also the Alkahest Lyceum system, a cooperative plan for furnishing Southern towns with popular and edn'l entertainments, lectures, music, etc., of which he was pres.; also lecturer; founder McConnell Library Assn., giving pub. libraries free through lecture courses; 190 libraries established in 1st year's work; founder Consumers' Co-operative Union, a buying union for reducing the expenses of workingmen. Author: Echoes from the Heart, poems, 1896; Just Understand, 1906; Organic Electricity, 1907; Scientific Mind Healing. Address: Birmingham AL‡

MCCONNELL, FRANZ MARSHALL, clergyman; b. Buffalo, Mo., Oct. 6, 1862; s. Joseph Marshall and Samantha (Williams) McC.; ed. Clarke's Acad., Berryville, Ark.; admitted to bar, 1885; D.D., Okla. Bapt. Coll., 1911, Okla. Baptist U., 1921, Baylor U., 1931; LL.D., Howard Payne Coll., 1939; m. Della Friedly, 1886 (died 1896); 1 son, Franz Bruce; m. 2d, Lenore Young, Dec. 23, 1897; children—Miriam, Manon. Admitted to bar, 1885; ordained Bapt. ministry, 1886; pastor various chs. until 1899; evangelist, 1899-1903; pastor Brownwood, Tex., 1903-06; again evangelist, 1906-10; corr. sec. Bapt. Gen. Conv. of Tex., 1910-14; supt. dept. of evangelism, Southwestern Bapt. Theol. Sem., 1915; corr. sec. Bapt. Gen. Conv. of Okla., 1916-22; pres. Burleson (Tex.) Coll., 1922-24; pastor First Bapt. Ch., Bonham, Tex., 1924, 25, Calvary Ch., San Antonio, 1927; exec. sec. Baylor Hosp., Dallas, 1925-27; editor The Baptist Standard, Dallas, Tex., since 1928. Collected over $2,000,000 for Bapt. work. Democrat. Author: Winning Souls and Strengthening Churches, 1913; The Deacon's Daughter, 1918; After the Feast, 1934; The Rights and Obligations of Labor, 1936. Editor Questions Answered" dept. of Bapt. Standard, Dallas, Tex. Home: 6048 Bryan Parkway. Office: Burt Bldg., Dallas TX*‡

MCCONNELL, HERBERT S(TEVENSON), lawyer; b. Temple, Tex., May 25, 1905; s. Francis W. and Maymee (Nichols) McC.; A.B., Rice Inst. (now Rice U.), 1928; LL.B., Harvard, 1931; m. Virginia Glines, June 20, 1933; children—Walter Glines, Frank Winston. Admitted to Tex. bar, 1931, P.R. bar, 1935; asst. atty. gen. P.R., 1932; mem. firm Fiddler, Cordova & McConnel, and successor firm Fiddler, McConnell & Gonzalez, 1934-42; partner firm McConnell & Valdes (name now changed to McConnell, Valdes, Kelley & Sifre), San Juan, P.R., from 1946. Mem. Am. Bar Assn., Fed. Bar Assn. P.R. (bd. dirs.), Colegio de Abogados de P.R. Home: St Thomas VI Died June 5, 1971; buried Cuernavaca Mexico

MCCONNELL, ROBERT DARLL, b. Montrose, Colo., Mar. 30, 1889; s. Charles E. and Coie (Earll) McC.; student U. of Colorado, 1905-07; Columbia Univ., 1910 (Engineer of Mines); m. Caryll N. Esterbrook, Dec. 28, 1918; children—Mildred, Robert, Elizabeth, Richard, Caryll. Assistant engineer Chino Copper Co., 1910-11; superintendent various mines, 1911-15; examining engr. S. W. Mudd & Associates, 1915-17; mining engr., 1920-31; partner Foster McConnell & Co. (mems. New York Stock Exchange), 1922-31; pres. and dir. Centrifugal Pipe Corp., Mayflower Associates, Inc., Mayflower Consol, Inc., 1924-39; pres. and dir. Pilgrim Exploration Co., 1937-47; dir. Rhokana Corp., Cyprus Mines Corp., Hazeltine Corp., Esterbrook Steel Pen Mfg. Co., Simmons Co., Fohs Oil Co.; bus. adviser to Dept. of Commerce, Sept. 1939-Aug. 1940; consultant Office of Production Management, Mar. 1941-Mar. 1942; apptd. by Sec. of Treasury of U.S. and Alien Property Custodian as chmn. bd. and pres. Gen. Aniline & Film Corp., Mar. 1942-July 1943; consultant, Treas. Dept., Washington, D.C., 1943-44; dep., Civil Affairs Div., War Dept., Apr.-Dec. 1945. Mayor Town of Jupiter Island, Hobe Sound, Fla., 1955-61. Member board of trustees Robert Earll McConnell Foundation. Served as lt., U.S.N.R., 1917-19. Mem. Am. Inst. Mining and Metall. Engrs., Mining and Metall. Soc. Am., Delta Tau Delta, Sigma Xi. Clubs: Links, Recess, Blind Brook, Seminole. Home: Hobe Sound FL Died Apr. 16, 1971; buried Middleburg VA

MCCONNELL, ROBERT PERCHE, ret. naval officer b. Oakland, Cal., July 8, 1895; s. James Joseph and Augusta (Lehnig) McC.; student U. Cal., 1915-16; m. Mildred Schafer, Apr. 17, 1920 (dec. 1946); children—Doreen (Mrs. Edward Beverly Johnson), Mildred (Mrs. Albert Kyle Earnest), Josephine (Mrs. Edward Crozer Rutherfurd); m. 2d, Melinda Alexander, 1946. Entered Navy as seaman 2d class, U.S.N.R.F., 1917; commd. ensign Naval Res., 1918, advancing through grades to rear adm., U.S.N., 1946 continuous duty in naval aviation; at sea in observation and scouting squadrons, U.S.S. Arizona, Omaha, Lexington and Saratoga, 1925-36; gen. insp. naval aircraft, central dist., Dayton, O., 1932-34; comd. U.S.N.R. Aviation Base, Miami, Fla., 1937-40, U.S.S. Langley (vessel sunk as result of engagement with Japanese bombers in Indian Ocean south of Java, Feb. 27, 1942), U.S.S. Cowpens, 1943-44; on duty with joint chief of staff, Washington, 1944-46; comdr. Carrier Div. 15, 1947; comdr. Fleet Air Wing One 1947-49; mem. Gen. Bd. of Navy, 1949-50; pres. Bd. of Review, Discharges and Dismissals, 1950-53; pres. Naval Retiring Review Bd., 1951-53, sr. mem. Naval Clemency Bd., 1951-53; retired as vice adm., June 1953. Decorated Silver Star Medal, Navy Unit Commendation Ribbon (Navy). Home: AshevilleNC Died Feb. 10, 1973.

MCCONNICO, ANDREW JACKSON, foreign service; b. Vaiden, Miss., Feb. 20, 1875; s. Samuel Edward and Margaret (Wyse) McC.; prep. edn., high sch., Vaiden, and Mt. Hermon (Mass.) Boys' Sch.; Ph.B., Brown U., 1899; m. Mayvelle L. Crook, of Providence, R.I., Feb. 20, 1901;children—Andrew Jackson, Berenice Linnette. In practice of law at Vaiden, 1902-09; consul at St. John's, Quebec, Can., 1909-13, Trinidad, B.W.I., 1913-17, Corinto, Nicaragua, 1917-19, Guadalajara, Mexico, 1919-24, Bluefields, Nicaragua, 1924-28, Yarmouth, N.S., June-Aug. 1928, Charlottetown, Prince Edward Island, Sept.-Oct. 1928, Hull, Eng., 1929-36. Mem. Beta Theta Pi. Episcopalian. Mason. Home: 2355 Maine Av., Long Beach, Calif. Address: Am. Consulate, Hull England‡

MCCORD, JAMES NANCE, ex-gov.; born at Unionville, Tenn., March 17, 1879; s. Thomas Newton and Iva (Steele) McC.; ed. pub. schs. of Tenn.; m. Vera Kercheval, May 22, 1901 (dec. 1966). Clerk in hardware store, 1894; mem. firm McCord Bros., books and stationery, 1897-1900; traveling salesman, 1900-10; pub. Marshall Gazette, Lewisburg, Tenn., 1910-68; auctioneer since 1920; mem. 78th Congress (1943-45), 5th Tenn. Dist.; gov. of Tenn., 1947-49. Mayor of Lewisburg, 1916-42. Dir. First Nat. Bank, Lewisburg. Mason. Clubs: Rotary, Chamber of Commerce. Home: Lewisburg TN Died Sept. 2, 1968.

MCCORMACK, BUREN H., newspaper executive; b. Jamestown, Indiana, March 4, 1909; s. Kise R. and Louella (Cook) McC.; A.B., DePauw University, 1930, D.Litt. (honorary), 1963; m. Kathryn Tofaute, Oct. 20, 1933 (deceased); children—Susan (Mrs. Hollinshed T. Knight), James, Judith; m. 2d, Edna Hanson Marshall, 1966. Engaged as reporter, copy desk man, copy desk head, feature writer, news editor The Wall St. Jour., N.Y.C., 1931-43, asst. mng. editor, 1943-46, mng. editor, 1946-50, sr. asso. editor, 1950-51, exec. editor, 1951-55, bus. mgr., treas., 1955-56, bus. mgr., treas., v.p., 1957, treas., v.p., editorial dir., 1958-60; v.p., gen. mgr., editorial dir., Dow Jones & Co., 1961-66, dir., 1965-72, exec. v.p., 1966-72; dir. West Tacoma Newsprint Co. Former chmn. bd. trustees Masters Sch.; former chmn. Irvington (N.Y.) Pub. Library. Mem. Sigma Delta Chi (past pres.), Phi Gamma Delta. Episcopalian (council of Diocese). Clubs: Harbor View (N.Y.); Union (Cleve.); Sleepy Hollow Country; Recess (N.Y.C.). Home: Mathiessen Park NY Died Feb. 28, 1972; buried Sleepy Hollow Cemetery, Tarrytown NY

MCCORMACK, M. HARRIET JOYCE (MRS. JOHN W. MCCORMACK), b. Boston; m. John W. McCormack, 1920. Operatic contralto, artist. Recipient Order of Queen Isabella, Spanish Govt.; Papal Order of ProEcclesia Pontifica, Pope Pius XII. Home: Boston MA Died Dec. 1971.*

MCCORMICK, CHARLES PERRY, manufacturing executive; born in Morelia, Mexico (of American parents) June 9, 1896; s. Rev. Hugh Pendleton and Anne Pauline (Perry) McC.; ed. schools in Puerto Rico, Birmingham, Ala., Paris, France, grad. Baltimore City Coll., 1915; Johns Hopkins, 1919; LL.D. (honorary), Presbyterian College;children—Rosalie McC., Charles Perry, John G., and Robert N. Joined United States Navy, April 17, 1917; athletic director 5th Naval District for 9 months; served overseas on S.S. Edgar F. Luckenbach; hon. disch., 1919. With McCormick & Co., Inc., importers, exporters, grinders, Balt.; v.p., 1928-32, pres., 1932-55, then chmn., now dir.; chmn. McCormick Foods (U.K.), Ltd., London, Eng.; past chmn. bd. Balt. br. Fed. Reserve Bank, 1939; formerly dir., chmn. and fed. agt. Richmond (Va.) Fed. Reserve Bank; dir. Mass. Mut. Life Ins. Co., Equitable Trust Co. Balt. Chmn. Md. Bd. Agr. Past v.p. Am. Heart Fund, 1960-61; chmn. Civic Center Commn. Balt., 1956-65; past pres. Balt. Conv. Bur. Past dir. C. of C. U.S.; grad. mem. Bus. Council, 1947-66, hon. mem., 1967-70, former mem. import adv. com. U.S. Dept. Commerce; past dir. Coun. of U.S. Assos. of Internat. C. of C., Inc., past trustee Nutrition Found.; chmn. bd. regents U. Md.; dir. Boys Clubs Am., Inc., C. of C. Met. Balt. (v.p.); past pres. Better Bus. Bur. Balt.; Md. chmn. Savs. Bonds Adv. Com., 1963-64; past chmn. Army & Navy, Inc. (3d Corps Area); U.S. Employer delegate to Internat. Labor Orgn., 1949-52, v.p. Conf., 1952; past pres. Internat. Orgn. Employers; adv. Senate sub-com. on relations with Internat. Orgns.; formerly v.p., pres., chmn. bd. Q.M. Assn. Past dir. Balt. Sch. Commrs. (1939), Am. Mgmt. Assn.; past pres. Balt. Export Mgrs. Club, Mayonnaise Products Mfrs. Assn. of Am., Inc., Nat. Assn. Insecticide & Disinfectant Mfrs. Past mem. Baltimore Criminal Justice Commn.; adv. council, past chmn. Md. Employment Service. Mem. Royal Soc. Arts London, Md. Hist. Soc., Acad. Polit. Sci., U.S. Jr. C. of C. (hon. life), Jr. Chamber Internat. (senator; hon. life mem.), Am. Legion (hon. life), Phi Gamma Delta, Delta Sigma Pi (honorary member), Beta Gamma Sigma (honorary member), also member of Omicron Delta Kappa. Mason (32 deg., K.T., Shriner, Jester). Clubs: Baltimore Country, Maryland, Alfalfa, Asparagus (hon.), Annapolis Yacht; Center. Author: Multiple Management, 1938 (8th edition; also Spanish, Japanese, French and Mexican editions); Sparks, 1941 (9th edition); The McCormick System of Management (Eng. edit.); The Power of People, 1949 (3d edition, Japanese 1952); Sparks II, 1953. Contbr. articles on mgmt., the McCormick System, etc., to jours. Citation and medal for Human Relations by Soc. Advancement of Mgmt., 1946; citation of honor S. Atlantic Assn. Amateur Athletic Union U.S., 1950; citation Md. region Nat. Conf. Christians and Jews, 1958, Sports Boosters and Writers Md., 1958; named Big. Bro. of Year for Md., 1959; Gantt Gold Medal Am. Mgmt. Assn., Am. Soc. M.E., 1960; Gold Heart award Nat. Heart Fund; Silver Recognition award Md. Heart Assn., 1961; named Man of Year, Advt. Club Balt., 1962; Distinguished Service award U.S. Treasury, 1964; Distinguished Merit citation Nat. Conf. Christians and Jews, 1965; Herbert Hoover award Nat. Am. Wholesale Grocers Assn., 1968. Home: Baltimore MD Died June 16, 1970.

MCCORMICK, CYRUS, b. Chicago, Sept. 22, 1890; s. Cyrus Hall and Harriett (Hammond) M.; grad. Hotchkiss Sch., 1908; A.B., Princeton, 1912; grad. student Oxford U. (Eng.), 1912-14; m. Dorothy C. Linn, Feb. 13, 1915; m. 2d, Florence Sittenham Davey, Mar. 14, 1931; 1 stepson, William Davey. Salesman for Internat. Harvester Co., 1914-16, br. mgr., 1916-17, works mgr., 1919-22, v.p. mfg., 1922-31, retired, 1931; owner El Nuevo Mexicano; dir. Internat. Harvester Co.; chief automobile and truck price sect. OPA, 1941-42. Rep. Nat. committeeman for State of N.M., 1936-42. Served as lt. Air Service, U.S. Army, 1918-19; major, Ordnance, U.S. Army, serving in Eng., 1942-43. Trustee Industrial Relations Counselors, Inc. Presbyn. Elk. Clubs: University (N.Y.C.); Chicago, Tavern (Chgo.). Author: The Century of the Reaper, 1931. Home: Santa Fe NM Died Apr. 1970.

MCCORMICK, FOWLER, former chmn. Internat. Harvester Co.; b. Chgo., Nov. 15, 1898; s. Harold F. and Edith (Rockefeller) McC.; A.B., Princeton; m. Anne U. Stillman, June 4, 1931. Took student's course in mfg., engring. and sales, 1925-298 dist. mgr. Internat. Harvester Co., 1930, regional sales mgr., 1931-32, asst. domestic sales mgr., 1933, v.p., 1934, second v.p., 1935-41, dir., 1936-59, pres., 1941-46, chmn., 1946-51. Bd. dirs. Chgo. Crime Commn.; trustee Art Inst. Chgo. Clubs: Chicago, Tavern, Casino, Mid-America, Commercial, Wayfarers (Chicago); Racquet and Tennis, Princeton (N.Y.). Home: Chicago IL Died Jan. 6, 1973.

MCCORMICK, GEORGE CHALMERS, newspaper pub.; b. Sandyville, Ia., Oct. 20, 1872; s. Montgomery and Harriet (Kitchell) McC.; B.Ph., Amity Coll., College Springs, Ia., 1897; m. Carrie Sherman, June 22, 1897 (dec. 1948); children—Paul S., Ruth; m. 2d, Gertrude York (dec. 1953); m. 3d, Letha Wolfe, 1954. Began as pub. Current Press, College Springs, 1897; pub. Albia Republican, 1899-1907; pub. Ft. Collins (Colo.) Morning Express and Evening Express-Courier, 1907-28; pub. Independent Record, Thermopolis, Wyo., 1928-1941; pres. Midwest Outdoor Adv. Co., Caper, Wyo.; identified with real estate. Democrat. Presbyterian. Mason. Mem. Selective Service Draft Bd. Author: (genealogy) John Kitchell and Esther Peck, 1913, 2d edit., 1963. Home: Thermopolis WY Died Feb. 16, 1968; buried Thermopolis WY

MCCORMICK, GERTRUDE HOWARD (MRS. VANCE C. MCCORMICK), newspaper exec., publisher; b. Richmond Va., May 7, 1874; d. Conway Robinson and Jeannie (Colston) Howard; m. Marlin Edgar Olmsted, Oct. 26, 1899 (died July 12, 1913); children—Marlin Edgar (died, 1930), Gertrude Howard (Mrs. Spencer G. Nauman), Henry Cushing, Conway Howard, Jane (Mrs. Hugh McMillan); m. 2d. Vance Criswell McCormick, Jan. 5, 1925 (died, June 16, 1946). V.p. Patriot Co.; pub. Harrisburg (Pa.), Patriot and Evening News until 1948. Mem. Valley Forge Park Commn. of Pa., 1935-39. Hon. v.p. Girl Scouts of Am.; former mem. bd. nat. Y.W.C.A.; hon. vice president Civic Club, Harrisburg, Art Association of Harrisburg; 1st v.p. Symphony Soc.; chmn. Dauphin County Com. of Pa. Soc. of Colonial Dames of Am. Episcopalian. Clubs: Colony (New York); Sulgrave (Washington, D.C.); Mt. Vernon (Baltimore); Yeaman's Hall (Charleston, S.C.). Home: 105 N. Front St. and Cedarcliff Farms. Office: 242 N. Third St., Harrisburg PA‡

MCCORMICK, JOHN HENRY, educator; b. Washington, Mar. 25, 1870; s. John H. and Julia A. McC.; ed. pub. and high schs. and Georgetown Coll., Washington; grad. M. D., Nat. Univ., 1890; m. Washington, Sept. 16, 1890, Aimee Sioussat, Asst. Surgeon, Johns Hopkins Hosp., 1891-2; prof. natural sciences, Mt. Vernon Sem., 1890-1; same, Washington Sem., 1892-6; sec. Anthropol. Soc., 1893-1900; asst. sec. Am. Folk-Lore Soc.; asso. editor Am. Antiquarian, 1894-6; practiced medicine, Washington, 1890-1904; sec. 8th Internat. Geog. Congress, 1904. Wrote articles on medicine and anthropology for various scientific publs., etc. Address: Masonic Temple Mobile AL‡

MCCORMICK, JOHN VINCENT, ret. judge; b. Mineral Point, Wis., 1891; s. John and Annie Loretta

(Laverty) McC.; grad. of high sch. Mineral Point, 1910; A.B., U. Wis., 1914; J.D., U. Chgo., 1916; m. Adeline M. Ulias, Mar. 17, 1928; 1 dau., Patricia (Mrs. Francis W. Huston) (dec.). Admitted to Ill. bar, 1916; atty. Legal Aid Soc., Chgo., 1916-17; mem. firm Fulton, McCormick & Fulton, Chgo., 1917-24; sec. and acting dean Loyola U. Sch. Law, 1924-27, dean, 1927-38; judge of Municipal Ct. of Chgo., 1936-53; judge Superior Ct. Cook County, 1953, apptd. judge Appellate Ct. of Ill., 1954-64, justice, 1964-71. Mem. Am., Ill., Chgo. bar assns., Am. Legion, Artus, Pi Gamma Mu, Chi Phi, Delta Theta Phi. Democrat. Roman Catholic. K.C. Home: Chicago IL Died Nov. 30, 1971.

MCCORMICK, ROBERT ELLIOTT, lawyer; b. Peoria, Ill., May 12, 1903; s. Robert Nish and Adele (Elliott) McC.; student Phillips Acad., Andover, Mass., 1919-20; A.B., Amherst Coll., 1924; LL.B., Harvard, 1927; m. Helen Roberts, June 25, 1927 (dec. May 15, 1942); children—Shirley, Sanford Elliott; m. 2d, Clotilde Knapp Sierstorpff, Jan. 5, 1950; 1 son, Michael. Admitted to N.Y. bar, 1928; asso. Alexander & Green, N.Y.C., 1927-38, mem. firm, 1938-54; counsel U.S. Commercial Co., 1942; spl. counsel Def. Supplies Corp., 1943; chief rep. Fgn. Bondholders Protective Council, Rio de Janeiro, 1943; gen. counsel Internat. Hotels Corp., 1946-52; gen. counsel Olin Mathieson Chem. Corp., N.Y.C., 1955-59, v.p., sec., 1955-62; member of the board directors U.S. Minerals Corp., Wallace, Clark & Company. Member board of trustees Boys' Athletic League, Inc., N.Y., Eye Bank, Retina Found., Research to Prevent Blindness, Am. Found. for Blind. American Foundation for Overseas Blind. Recipient Citizens award Med. Soc. County N.Y., 1969. Mem. of Am. Bar Assn., Delta Kappa Epsilon. Democrat. Clubs: Links Golf (Roslyn); The Links, Racquet and Tennis, River (N.Y.C.). Home: New York City NY Died Nov. 25, 1969; cremated.

MCCORMICK, WILLIAM BERNARD, editor; b. Brooklyn, June 1, 1868; s. Bernard Augustus and Sarah Elizabeth (Teevan) M.; pub. sch. edn.; m. Katharine Fine, Nov. 5, 1903 (died 1923). Correspondent and editor Associated Press, 1894; lit. and art editor and editorial writer New York Press, 1895-1915; art critic, New York Evening Mail, 1915-16; asso. editor Army and Navy Journal, 1916-21. Contbr. art articles to Am. Year Book, 1916-21; lit. staff, New York Sun and New York Herald, 1918-24; asst. editor Internat. Studio, 1922-25, editor, 1925-28; art critic New York American, 1925-30. Special art column, Hearst newspapers, 1931-33. Democrat. Catholic. Contbr. short stories and articles to mags. Home: 680 Madison Av., New York NY‡

MCCOWN, CHESTER CHARLTON, educator; b. Orion, Henry County, Ill., Nov. 26, 1877; s. David Sylvester and Henrietta (Stevenson) McC.; B.A., De Pauw U., 1898; B.D., Garrett Bibl. Inst., 1902; studied Heidelberg and Berlin, 1906-08; Ph.D., U. of Chicago, 1914; D.D., Garrett Bibl. Inst., 1919; D.D., Pacific Sch. Religion, 1947; LL.D., De Pauw U., 1948; m. Harriet M. Doney, Dec. 19, 1905 (dec. Sept. 1956); children—Theodore D., Donald Eugene, Dorothy Beatrice (Mrs. Gordon H. Mattison). Ordained Methodist ministry, 1898; prin. Am. Meth. Instn., Calcutta, India, 1902-06; prof. Bibl. lit., Wesley Coll., Grand Forks, N.D., 1909-12, Y.M.C.A. Coll., Chicago, 1912-14; prof. N.T. lit. and interpretation, Pacific Sch. of Religion since 1914, dean, 1928-36, 1945-46; emeritus, 1947; director Palestinian Archeological Institute, 1936-47; on leave as Thayer fellow, Am. School Oriental Research, Jerusalem, 1920-21, as dir., 1929-31, as annual prof. and acting dir., 1935-36; joint dir. Yale Univ.-Am. Sch. Expdn., at Jerash (Gerasa), 1930-31. Dir. religious work, Army Y.M.C.A., 1918-19. Lectr. Haskell Found., Oberlin Coll., 1947, and various others; vis. prof. several colls. and univs., 1924-—. U. of Ore., 1949. Ecumenical study group World Council of Chs., 1951-52. Mem. Archeol. Adv. Bd. of Palestine Govt., 1929-31, 1935-36, Internat. Congress of Orientalists, Rome, 1935. Mem. Soc. Bibl. Lit. (pres. 1940), Philol. Assn. Pacific Coast (pres. 1940), Archeol. Inst. Am. (hon. v.p. 1948), several profl. assns. in fields of religion, archeology and philology. Mason. Clubs: Faculty, City Commons (v.p. 1942, pres. 1943-44). Author Search for the Real Jesus, 1940; Ladder of Progress in Palestine, 1943; Tellen-Nasbeh Excavations, 1947; also articles, monographs and books on bibl., geog. and archael. themes. Home: 1611 Scenic Av., Berkeley 9 CA‡

MCCOWN, THEODORE DONEY, educator; b. Macomb, Ill., June 18, 1908; s. Chester Charlton and Harriet M. (Doney) McC.; A.B., U. Cal., 1929, Ph.D., 1939; research fellow Am. Sch. Prehistoric Research, 1932, 35-37; m. Elizabeth A. Richards, Aug. 31, 1946; children—Ann Elizabeth, Jean Keith, Faith Carol. Taussig traveling fellow, 1933-34, Amy Bowles Johnson traveling fellow, 1934-35; archeol. asst. joint expdn. Am. Sch. Prehistoric Research-Brit. Sch. Archeology, Jerusalem, Mt. Carmel, Palestine, 1930-31, field dir., 1932, supervisor project Inst. Andean Research, North Peru, 1941-42; instr. anthropology U. Cal. at Berkeley, 1938-41, asst. prof. anthropology, asst. curator phys. anthropology, 1941-46, asso. prof., 1946-51, prof. since 1951, asso. curator, 1946-48, curator phys. anthropology R. H. Lowie Mus. of Anthropology, 1957-69, chairman of dept. of anthropology, 1950-55, associate dean College of Letters and Science, 1956-61, also chmn. S.Asian studies, dir. U. Cal. at Berkeley and Deccan Coll. Joint Expdn. to India, 1957, 64. Served with U.S. Army, 1942-45. Fellow Am. Anthrop. Assn., Royal Anthrop. Inst. Gt. Britain and Ireland, member American Association Physical Anthropologists, Soc. Am. Archeology, A.A.A.S., Prehistoric Society, Sigma Xi, Phi Beta Kappa. Author: The Stone Age of Mt. Carmel, Vol. II (with Sir Arthur Keith), 1939; Pre-Incaic Huamachuco, 1945; The Genus Palaeoanthropus and The Problem of Superspecific Differentiation among the Hominidae, 1950; Antiquity of Man in South America, 1963, (with K.A.R. Kennedy) Climbing Man's Family Tree, 1972. Home: Berkeley CA Died Aug. 17, 1969.

MCCOY, BERNICE, state sch. supt.; b. Portland, Ore.; d. J. B. and Harriet G. (Hald) M.; grad. State Normal Sch., Lewiston, Ida., 1898; post-grad. work, Teachers Coll. (Columbia U.), 1909. Teacher in rural and city schs., 1894-1903; supt. schs., Nez Perce Co., Ida., 1903-9; grammar grade critic Lewiston (Ida.) State Normal Sch., 1910-11; asst. state supt. pub. instrn., 1911-14, state supt., 1915-17; dean of women, Lewiston State Normal Sch., 1917-18. Republican. Presbyn. Address: Lewiston ID‡

MCCOY, GEORGE WALTER, sanitarian; b. Cumberland Valley, Pa., June 4, 1876; s. Osborne George and Levanda (Walter) M.; M.D., U. of Pa., 1898; hon. D.Sc., U. of La.; m. Edith Miller, Mar. 17, 1901;children—George, Edith (Chappelear). Apptd. asst. surgeon, Pub. Health and Marine Hosp. Service, 1900; surgeon Public Health Service, 1913, and appointed medical dir. of same, July 1, 1930. In charge U.S. Plague Lab., San Francisco, 1908-11; dir. U.S. Leprosy Investigation Sta., 1911-15; sanitary adviser, Hawaiian Govt., 1911-15; dir. Nat. Inst. of Health, 1915-37; prof. preventive medicine and pub. health, Sch. of Medicine, Louisiana State University, 1938-47, professor emeritus since 1947; acting dean, 1945-46. Member A.M.A., Am. Society Tropical Medicine, Am. Assn. Pathol. and Bacteriol., Council on Pharm. and Chem. (chmn. com. on biol. products), Assn. Mil. Surgeons, Am. Pub. Health Assn., Nat. Bd. Med. Examiners, 1921-40, Pathol. Soc. of Phila., Calif. Acad. Med. U.S. Pharmacopoeia Revision (com. on biol. products), Washington Acad. of Science (pres. 1935), Assn. Am. Physicians, Am. Coll. Physicians, mem. USPHS Spl. Adv. Com. on Leprosy, Sigma Xi. Democrat. Mem. Ref. Ch. Club: Cosmos. Author numerous papers on bacteriology and pub. health subjects, particularly in regard to plague and leprosy. Home: 1532 Foucher St., New Orleans 15 LA‡

MCCOY, WHITLEY PETERSON, arbitrator; b. Washington, D.C., Oct. 26, 1894; s. Joseph Melville and Ellen (Peterson) M.; A.B., Dartmouth Coll., 1916; LL.B., George Washington U., 1921; m. Dorothy Dawson McConnel, Apr. 16, 1936; 1 dau., Juliet Granville. Admitted to D.C. bar, 1921; asso. prof. law, U. of Ala., 1921-22; asst. prof. law, U. of S.D., 1922-23, George Washington U., 1923-24; practiced law as partner Chilton & McCoy, Montgomery, Ala., 1924-26; with Shackelford & Brown, Tampa, Fla., 1926-27; professor of law, University of Alabama, 1927-53; visiting professor of law, George Washington U., 1945; trial examiner for Nat. Labor Relations Bd., summers 1938-39; arbitrator of U.S. Conciliation Service, Nat. War Labor Board, and Am. Arbitration Assn., 1941-71; dir. Fed. Mediation & Conciliation Service, Washington, 1953-54, ret. lt. (j.g.), U.S.N., 1917-19. Mem. executive committee Assn. Am. Law Schs., 1945; vice president of the National Academy of Arbitrators, 1947, 48. Member Labor Relations Research Assn., Am. and Ala. State bar associations. Order of the Coif, Delta Tau Delta, Phi Alpha Delta. Democrat. Episcopalian. Author: Judicial Procedure in Alabama (brochure), 1935; (with Clarence M. Updegraff), Arbitration of Labor Disputes, 1946. Editor: Cases and Statutes on Trial and Appellate Practice in Alabama, 1932, ed. 1948. Contbr. to law jours. Home: Tuscaloosa AL Died Jan. 21, 1971.

MCCOY, WILLIAM DANIEL, business exec.; b. Chicago, Mar. 28, 1896; s. William Forest and Mary Ellen (Fahey) McC.; ed. parochial and pub. schs., St. Louis; student extension accounting courses, 1915-20; m. Ruby E. Jordan, Dec. 28, 1922; children—Joyce (Mrs. John R. Hupper), Jean, Joan, William. Printing house messenger Con. P. Curran Printing Co., St. Louis, 1910-12; customers accounts bookkeeper Brown Shoe Co., St. Louis, 1912-18; bookkeeper-credit mgr. Meyer Bros. Drug Co., St. Louis, 1918-19; accountant-cost accountant Forked Leaf Lumber Co., West Eminence, Mo., 1919; pub. accountant, income tax specialist, St. Louis, 1920-22; auditor Von Hoffmann Corp., St. Louis, 1922-28, gen. mgr., 1928-29, vice pres. and gen. mgr. sales agts., 1929-47, pres., 1947-65, vice chmn. bd., 1966-67; pres. Von Hoffmann Realty & Mortgage Co., St. Louis, 1955-67; dir. N. Am. Rare Metals, Ltd., Toronto; v.p., dir. Publishers, Lithographers, Inc.; v.p. Von Hoffman Press, St. Louis, Jefferson City; dir. Mistang River Mines, Ltd., Toronto; dir. Eagle Rock Iron Mines, Ltd. (Toronto, Can.). Mem. Telephone Pioneers of Am. (hon.). Congregationalist. Elk. Clubs: Glen Ridge (New Jersey) Country; Mo. Athletic (St. Louis); Brae Burn Country (West Newton, Mass.); Everglades Yacht and Tennis (Ft. Lauderdale, Fla.). Oyster Harbors (Osterville, Mass.); Marco Polo (Waldorf, N.Y.); Yachting of Am. (gov. 1966). Home: Waban MA Died Aug. 11, 1967.

MCCRACKEN, ROBERT JAMES, clergyman; b. Motherwell, Scotland, Mar. 28, 1904; s. Joseph and Sarah (Carson) McC.; M.A., U. Glasgow, 1925, B.D., 1928; student Cambridge, 1937-38; D.D., McMaster U., Ont., 1946, Bucknell University, 1947, U. Glasgow, 1949, Colgate U., 1950; S.T.D., Columbia, 1950; L.H.D., Bates College, 1951, Shurtleff Coll., 1952, Pratt Inst., 1958; D.D., Denison U., 1953, U. Vt., 1956, Princeton, 1956, Wake Forest Coll., 1958, Colby Coll. 1960, Lafayette Coll., 1968; m. Maud Orr Ibbotson, Mar. 1929 (dec. 1969); children—James Desmond, Richard Norman; m. 2d, Sally Koch, July 1972. Moved to Canada, 1938, to U.S., 1946. Ordained to ministry Bapt. Ch., 1928; pastor Marshall St. Baptist Church, Edinburgh, Scotland, 1928-32; Dennistoun Bapt. Ch., Glasgow, 1932-37; lecturer in systematic theology, Bapt. Theol. Coll. of Scotland, 1932-37; asso. prof. Christian theology and philosophy of religion McMaster U., Hamilton, Ont., 1938-44, head dept. Christian theology and philosophy of religion 1944-46; pastor Riverside Ch., N.Y. City 1946-67, minister emeritus, since 1967-73; lecturer in practical theology, Union Theol Sem., N.Y.C., 1949-54, asso. prof., 1954-66, adj. prof., 1966-67. Sprunt lecturer, Union Theol. Sem., Richmond, Va., 1952; Shaffer Found. lectr. Yale, 1950; Stone lectr. Princeton Theol. Sem., 1954; and other named lectureships schs., colls. and sems. Pres. Bapt. Conv. of Ont. and Que., 1945-46; del. to World Conf. on Faith and Order, Lund, Sweden, 1952; del. World Conf., Faith and Order, Edinburgh, 1937. Vice chmn. bd. Correction, N.Y.C., 1958. Trustee Colgate Rochester Divinity School, 1960-64; pres. bd. trustees Inst. Religious and Social Studies, N.Y.C.; past dir. Morningside Heights, Inc. Mem. St. Andrew's Soc. of State N.Y., Century Assn. Club: Canadian of N.Y. (honorary). Author: Questions People Ask, 1951; The Making of the Sermon, 1956; Putting Faith to Work, 1960; What Is Sin? What is Virtue?, 1966. Office: New York City.NY

MCCRACKEN, ROBERT MCDOWELL, ex-congressman; b. Vincennes, Ind., Mar. 15, 1874; s. Robert D. and Ella (Myrick) M.; ed. pub. schs., Carmi, Ill.; m. Mida Ezell, of Malad, Ida., formerly of Princeton, Ky., Dec. 15, 1898 (now dec.); children—Fred (dec.), Frances (Mrs. Hugh Ramsay), Mida (Mrs. Frederick A. Bartlett), Jean (Mrs. Gilbert Conley). Admitted to Ida. bar 1902, and began practice at Blackfoot, at Boise since 1907; prosecuting attorney of Bingham County one term; mem. Idaho House of Representatives, two terms; author of prohibition and child-labor laws; mem. 64th Congress (1915-17), Ida. at large. Capt. Chem. Warfare Service, World War. Referee in bankruptcy. Republican. Baptist. Home: Boise ID‡

MCCRADY, JOHN, artist, teacher; b. Canton, Miss., Sept, 4, 1911; s. Edward and Mary Ormond (Tucker) McC.; student U. of Miss., U. of Pa., 1930-32, New Orleans Art Sch., 1933, Art Students' League of New York, 1934; m. Mary B. Basso, Sept. 11, 1937; 1 dau., Mary Tucker. Director of the John McCrady Art Sch., New Orleans. Permanent exhibits: High Museum of Art, Atlanta, Ga., Art Museum, St. Louis, Mo., Newark (N.J.) Art Mus., San Francisco Art Mus., Swope Mus. Art, Terre Haute, Ind., Nat. Business Machine Corp., Mary Buie Mus., Oxford, Miss.; one-man shows at Downtown Gallery, New Orleans, Mary Buie Museum. Completed series of paintings for U.S. Navy, The Story of the Building of the PBY, 1945. Executed mural, Holy Communion, New Orleans, 1954, Bank of Oxford (Miss.), 1969. Awarded Art Students' League nat. scholarship, 1934, Guggenheim fellowship, 1939, Blanche Benjainine prize, 1942, first prize, Arst and Crafts Club, 1938, first prize La. Art Commn., 1939, 40, first prize in lithography, Southern States Art League, 1946, first prize in painting, New Orleans Art Association, 1946. Selected by Time Magazine as outstanding regional painter, 1938; 1st prize oil painting Art League. 1949; awarded Grant Nat. Inst. Arts and Letters, 1949. Home: New Orleans LA Died Dec. 24, 1968; buried New Orleans LA

MCCRARY, JOHN ALVA, banker; b. Warnerville, Ga., Nov. 9, 1871; s. John Matthew and Mary E. (Boyd) McC; ed. Georgia Sch. of Tech., Atlanta, Ga.; m. Dollie Rogers, 1898; children—Mary Louisa (Mrs. Robert Davis), Dorothy (dec.); m. 2d, Florrie J. Bennett, 1912; 1 dau., Margaret Boyd (dec.). Began with Farmers & Merchants Bank, Senoia, Ga., 1892; cashier Farmers & Merchants Bank, Tennille, 1894-1901; cashier and v.p. First Nat. Bank, Barnesville, 1901-11; v.p. and treas. J.B. McCrary Co., dealers in bonds, also engring. and constn. municipal improvements, Atlanta, since 1911. Organized and supervised banks in Tennille, Harrison, Talbotton, Barnesville and Senoia; mem. bd. dirs. Federal Reserve Bank, Atlanta, Ga., since 1914. Democrat. Mem. Methodist Ch. Mason (32 deg., Shriner), Old Fellow, K.P. Originator of a number of bank form books. Home: 415 Sycamore St., Decatur GA Office: Marietta St. Bldg., Atlanta GA‡

MCCREARY, GEORGE BOONE, clergyman, educator; b. New Concord, O., Dec. 9, 1875; s. Henry (M.D.) and Samantha Ann (Stevenson) McC.; B.A., Muskingum Coll., New Concord, O., 1895; M.A., 1902, D.D., 1924; Ph.D., Grove City (Pa.) Coll., 1914; grad. Pittsburgh Theol. Sem., 1898; student U. of Chicago, 1901; m. Lova Ruth Fowler, Sept. 24, 1901; children—Dorothy, Jane Elizabeth, Robert Henry. Ordained ministry U.P. Ch., 1900; pastor Pretty Prairie, Kan., 1900-01; teacher Ingleside Academy, Burgettstown, Pa., 1902-03; pastor Hobart, Okla., 1903-05; prof. Greek, Bible and philosophy, Epworth U., Oklahoma City, Okla., 1905-08; prof. Bible and philosophy, also registrar Sterling Coll., 1908-14; prof. Bible and philosophy, Hope Coll., Holland, Mich., 1914-17; prof. Greek, Muskingum Coll., 1917-20, also acting prof. Bible, 1917-19; prof. philosophy, same coll., 1920-24; prof. philosophy of religion and applied Christianity, Xenia Theol. Sem. (now Pittsburgh-Xenia Theol. Sem.), 1924-46; retired. Lecturer on war aims, S.A.T.C., World War. Mem. S.A.R. Address: 777 Berkeley Av., Claremont CA‡

MCCRORY, WILTON WADE, judge; b. Air Mount, Miss., Jan. 27, 1873; s. Stephens S. and Elizabeth Sofia (Hall) McC.; student U. of Miss., 1889-91; LL.B., U. of Tex., 1897; m. Ethel Gaither, Mar. 10, 1902;children—Hall (dec.), Marion Elizabeth (Mrs. Travis B. Moursund). Admitted to Tex. bar, 1897, and began practice at Edna; moved to San Antonio, 1920; pres. Allen Nat. Bank, Edna; dir. Smith Bros. Properties, Inc., San Antonio; owner cotton, corn and rice farms. County atty. Jackson County, Tex., 1900-12; mem. Tex. Ho. of Rep., 1913-15; county judge, Jackson County, 1916-20; mem. Tex. State Highway Commn., 1921-23; judge of Criminal Court, San Antonio, since 1923. Mem. Nat. Crime Commn. Mem. Sigma Alpha Epsilon. Democrat. Unitarian. Mason, Odd Fellow, Elk, Woodman. Clubs: San Antonio, San Antonio Athletic, Alamo Country. Home: 127 E. Mistletoe St. Office: Court House, San Antonio TX*‡

MCCROSKY, THEODORE TREMAIN, cons. engr.; b. Tecumseh, Neb., June 12, 1902; s. James Warren and Josephine (Tremain) McC.; grad. Barnard Sch., N.Y.C., 1919; B.S. summa cum laude, Yale, 1923; Ingenieur Constructeur, U. Catholique de Louvain, 1925; m. Agnes Herriott James, Sept. 2, 1925; children—Marion Currie (dec.), John Warren James. Instr. engring. mechanics and strength of materials Yale, 1923-24, 25-27, also engring. asso. Eno Found. for Hwy. Traffic Research, 1925-27; editorial asst. to gen. dir. Regional Plan of N.Y. and Its Environs, 1928; resident engr. for Ernest P. Goodrich, also planning engr. City of Nanking, China, 1929-30; planning dir., Yonkers, N.Y., 1931-37, also cons. Mayor's Com. on City Planning, City of N.Y., 1934-37, mem. and exec. officer Yonkers Municipal Housing Authority, 1935-37; regional project adviser U.S. Housing Authority, 1938; dir. planning N.Y.C. Dept. City Planning, 1938-40; exec. dir. Chgo. Plan Commn., 1941-42, Greater Boston Development Com., 1946-48; cons. engr., N.Y.C., 1948-68; partner McCrosky-Reuter, 1962-66, cons., 1966-68, specializing in regional and community planning, traffic engring., zoning, capital programming, and related work. Vis. lectr. various univs. Bd. dirs., mem. Belgian-Am. Ednl. Found. Served lt. comdr. to comdr., USNR, 1943-45, ret. Licensed profl. engr., N.Y., N.J., Conn. Fellow Am. Soc. C.E.; mem. American Inst. Cons. Engrs. (secretary), Inst. Traffic Engrs., Am. Inst. Planners (v.p. 1943), Yale Engring. Assn., Am. Soc. Planning Ofcls., Sigma Xi, Tau Beta Pi, Lambda Alpha, Theta Xi. Clubs: RNVR (London England); University (New York City); Yale (New York City). Author of: Surging Cities (with Chas. A. Blessing and J. Ross McKeever), 1948. Contbr. American Civil Engineering Practice, 1956, and articles profl. jours. Home: New York City NY Died Juyly 1968.

MCCRUM, BLANCHE PRICHARD, librarian; b. Lexington, Va., Nov. 2, 1887; d. R. Barton and Martha Ann (White) McCrum; certificate Drexel Inst. Library Sch., 1913; student U. of Wis., Harvard U. and U. of Va., summers 1920-29, Radcliffe Coll., 1925-26; B.S., Boston U., 1930; M.A., U. of Calif., 1931; unmarried. First asst. of branch library, Carnegie Library of Pittsburgh, 1913-16, branch librarian, 1916-17, head central circulation room, 1917-18; asst. librarian Washington and Lee U., 1918-22, librarian, 1922-37; librarian Wellesley Coll., 1937-47; member of the general reference and bibliography division, Library of Congress, since 1947, specialist in documentation, 1952-55; lecturer in reference and bibliography University of Calif. at Los Angeles, summer 1939; lectr. in coll. library adminstrn., U. of Ill., summer 1941. Awarded Carnegie Corp. fellowship at Columbia U., 1936-37. Mem. Am. Library Association (member council 1941-43), Bibliographical Society of America; president Virginia State Library Association, 1934-36; president Assn. Coll. and Reference Libraries, 1945-46. Presbyn. Author: An Estimate of Standards for a College Library, 1933, 2d edit. (revised), 1937; Bibliographical Procedures & Style (with Helen D. Jones), 1954. Contbr. articles and book reviews to Am. Library Assn. Bull., College and Research Libraries. Address: Arlington VA Died Aug. 1969.

MCCULLEY, BRUCE, coll. prof.; b. Chatham, Ont., June 5, 1873; s. Cyrus and Elizabeth (Richardson) M.; A.B., Hiram (O.) Coll., 1899; A.M., U. of Chicago, 1901; Ph.D., Harvard, 1910; m. Katharine Weeks, of St. Lawrence, S.D., Aug. 20, 1901; children—Alice Virginia, Edward Bence, Katharine, Margaret, Robert Douglas. Prof. English and head of dept., State Coll. of Wash., 1910-20; prof. English lit. and head dept. Pomona Coll., 1921—. Mem. Modern Lang. Assn. America, Am. Assn. Univ. Profs. Conglist. Contbr. papers before Am. and Wash. State philol. assns. Home: Claremont CA‡

MCCULLOCH, WALTER FRASER, educator; b. Vernon, B.C., Can., Mar. 21, 1905; s. Arthur Caldwell and Elsie Adelaide (Fraser) McC.; B.A., U. of Brit. Columbia, 1925; grad. student U. of Wash., 1927-28; M.S., N.Y. State Coll. of Forestry (at Syracuse U.), 1936; Ed.D., U. of Ore., 1947; m. Margaret Mildred Neher, Aug. 5, 1931. Came to U.S. 1926, naturalized. With Brit. Columbia Forest Service, Victoria, 1923-26; with Erie R.R., 1930-34; dir. Mich. State Forest Expt. Sta., Sault Ste. Marie, 1936-37; asst. prof., Sch. Forestry, Ore. State Univ., 1937-42, prof., dept. head, 1945-73, dean, 1955-66; asst. state forester of Ore., 1942-45. Fellow of the Forest History Society, Society of the American Foresters. Author: Conservation Education in the Pacific Northwest, 1940; The Cascades, Mountains of the Northwest (with others), 1949; Forest Management Education in Oregon, 1949; The Forester on the Job, 1950; Woods Words, 1958; also numerous bulls. and profl. articles. Home: Corvallis OR Died Jan. 27, 1973.

MCCULLOH, JAMES SEARS, retired telephone official; b. Englewood, N.J., Sept. 5, 1868; s. James William and Isabella Steel (Walker) McC; ed. Englewood Sch. for Boys, and Stevens High Sch., Hoboken, N.J.; m. Sara May White, April 27, 1898 (died July 19, 1933); 1 son, Gordon; m. 2d, Eleanor Silkman Gilman, Jan. 11, 1936. Began as clerk with the West Shore R.R., 1885, later sec. to gen. supt., asst. to supt. telegraph and signals, and div. operator; joint rep. Western Union Telegraph Co. and West Shore R.R. Co., 1890-93; with Am. Telephone & Telegraph Co., 1893-1903; appointed superintendent buildings New York Telephone Company, 1903, and promoted through various positions to president, Sept. 24, 1924, director 1933-38; retired October 1, 1933; trustee Bowery Savings Bank; president Rye National Bank, 1934-41, chairman board since 1941. Mem. Am. Mus. Natural History, Burns Soc., Met. Mus. Art, New York Zool. Soc., St. Andrews Soc., Legislative Corrs. Assn. of Albany, N.Y. (hon.). Democrat. Presbyterian. Clubs: Railroad, Apawamis, Manursing Island, Am. Yacht, Sebatis Fish and Game (N.B., Can.). Home: NY‡

MCCULLOUGH, CAMPBELL ROGERS, nuclear and chem. engr.; b. Washington, Apr. 12, 1900; s. Charles Edmund and Emma (Rogers) McC.; A.B., Swarthmore Coll., 1921; M.S., Mass. Inst. Tech., 1922, Ph.D. (DuPont fellow 1927-28), 1928; m. Exia Drummond, Oct. 16, 1936; children—David Rogers, Diane Exia. Chemist, Hygrade Lamp Co., 1922-26; chemist, chem. engr. prodn. and devel. organic and inorganic chemicals Monsanto Chem. Co., 1928-60; project mgr. NDRC Rocket Propellant Pilot Plant, 1944-46; dir. Power Pile div. Clinton Labs, 1946-47; v.p., dir. Nuclear Utility Services, Inc., 1960-65; consulting nuclear and chemical engr., technical director Southern Nuclear Engineering, Inc., 1965-70; Atomic Indsl. Forum; consultant CNEN of Italy. Chmn., mem. adv. com. on reactor safeguards AEC, 1951-59, vice chmn., 1960-61; sci. adviser U.S. delegation Internat. Conf. for Peaceful Uses of Atomic Energy, Geneva, 1955, 58. Recipient Presidential Certificate of Merit, 1949. Member of American Nuclear Society (president 1956-57), Am. Chemical Soc., Am. Inst. Chem. Engrs., Phi Beta Kappa, Sigma Xi. Editor: Safety Aspects of Nuclear Reactors, 1957. Contbr. to Handbook on Nuclear Engineering, Modern Nuclear Technology Mills, others. Home: Rockville MD Died Jan. 13, 1970; buried Anniston AL

MCCULLOUGH, MYRTLE REED, author; b. Chicago (Norwood Park), Sept. 27, 1874; d. H. V. and Elizabeth A. Reed; grad. West Div. High Sch., Chicago, 1893; m. James Sydney McCullough, Oct. 22, 1906. Mem. Ill. Woman's Press Assn. Club: Little Room. Author: Love Letters of a Musician, 1899; Later Love Letters of a Musician, 1900; The Spinster Book, 1901; Lavender and Old Lace, 1902; Pickaback Songs, 1903; The Shadow of Victory, 1903; The Master's Violin, 1904; The Book of Clever Beasts, 1904; At the Sign of the Jack o'Lantern, 1905; A Spinner in the Sun, 1906; Love Affairs of Literary Men, 1907; Flower of the Dusk, 1908; Old Rose and Silver, 1909. Address: Chicago IL*

MCCUNNIFF, WILLIAM BARLOW, physician; b. Antonito, Colo., Nov. 25, 1920; s. Francis A. and Grace (Barlow) McC.; B.S., Creighton U., 1941, M.D., 1943; postgrad. Washington U., St. Louis, 1949-50; m. Sara Christine Jeffers, Apr. 11, 1953; children—Michael David, Thomas Vincent, Mary Christine. Intern, St. Josephs Hosp., Kansas City, Mo., 1944, surg. resident, 1947-49, member staff, 1950-67, pres. staff, 1965; practice medicine, specializing in gen. surgery Kansas City, Mo., 1950-67; physician Sheffield div. Armco Steel Co., Kansas City, 1951-67, Butler Mfg. Co., Kansas City, 1956-67. Served to capt. M.C., AUS, 1944-46. Mem. nat. bd. govs. Creighton U., 1958-67; bd. dirs. Kansas City Goodwill Industries, 1952-60. Diplomate Am. Bd. Surgery. Fellow Internat., Am. colls. surgeons; mem. Am., Mo., Jackson County med. assns., Am. Med. Writers Assn., S.W. Clin. Soc., Indsl. Med. Assn., Mo. Surg. Soc., Great Plains Indsl. Medical Association. Democrat. Roman Catholic. Asso. editor: Mo. Medicine, 1953-54, contbg. editor, 1954-67; asso. editor: Jackson County Med. Bull., 1960-62. Home: Kansas City MO Died Dec. 30, 1967.

MCCURDY, MERLE M., U.S. atty.; b. 1912; LL.B., Western Res. U. Admitted to bar, 1947; U.S. atty. No. Dist. Ohio, until 1968. Mem. Am. Bar Assn. Address: Cleveland OH Died May 6, 1968.

MCCUTCHAN, ROBERT GUY, hymnologist; b. Mt. Ayr, Ia., Sept. 13, 1877; s. Erastus G. and Margaret (Edie) McC.; student Park Coll., Parkville, Mo., 1893-94; Mus.Bac., Simpson Coll., 1904, Mus. Doc., 1927; D. Sacred Music, Southern Meth. U., 1935; D.Litt., Southwestern U., 1943; studied in Berlin and Paris; m. Carrie Burns Sharp, Nov. 23, 1904 (died July 20, 1941); 1 son, Robert John; m. 2d, Helen L. Cowles, Dec. 11, 1944. With Baker University, 1904-10, first as teacher of singing then organized Conservatory of Music, of which was director, 1906-10; organizer and dir. Summer Sch. of Music, Mt. Lake Park, Md., 1912-13; organizer community music activities for Indiana State Council of Defense, 1917-18; organizer and dir. Summer Sch. of Music, Bay View, Mich., 1919-27; dir. Summer Sch. of Music, Winona Lake, Ind., 1928-29; dean School of Music, De Pauw Univ., 1911-37, dean emeritus since 1937; lecturer Summer Conf. on Church Music, Northwestern, 1938-39, 41-42, 44-45, University of Montana, 1939; special lecturer on religious music, Claremont Graduate School, since 1939; an Earl lecturer Pacific School of Religion, 1942; Southwestern University Foundation lectures, 1943; director choirs and festival organizations; member Commission on Church Music, M.E. Church, 1924-28; Mem. Joint Commn. on Revision of Methodist Hymnal and Psalter, 1928-35; mem. Gen. Conf. on Music, M.E. Ch. since 1937; del. at large, Uniting Conf. Meth. Churches, Kansas City, 1939; mem. Gen. Conf. Commn. (Meth.) on Ritual and Orders of Service, 1940 (ed. com. 1942); mem. Gen. Conf. (Meth.) Ecumenical Commn., 1944, So. Calif.-Ariz. Conf. (Meth.) Com. on Grad. Sch. of Religion, Univ. of Southern Calif., 1940. Mem. Music Teachers Nat. Assn. (ex-sec.), Indiana Music Teachers' Assn. (ex-pres.), Hymn Soc., American Musicalogical Society, Nat. Assn. Ch. Choir Directors (nat. ex-pres.) Com. on Worship of Federal Council of Chs. in America, Phi Mu Alpha, Pi Kappa Lambda (ex-president general). Mason. Clubs: University (Claremont); Rotary (hon.). Author numerous books since 1937; latest publ.; Hymns of the American Frontier, 1950. Home: 790 Mayflower Rd., Claremont CA‡

MCCUTCHEON, KEITH BARR, marine corps officer; b. E. Liverpool, O., Aug. 10, 1915; s. Merle D. and Louise Alberta (Sturtevant) McC.; B.S. in Mgmt. Engring., Carnegie Inst. Tech., 1937; M.S. in Aero Engring., Mass. Inst. Tech., 1944; grad. Nat. War Coll., 1960; m. Marion Postles Thompson, Nov. 1, 1947; children—Marion Louise, Keith Barr. Commd. 2d lt. USMC, 1937, advanced through grades to lt. gen., 1970; assigned U.S.S. Yorktown, 1938-39. flight tng., 1940; served PTO, World War II; assigned Bur. Aero., 1946-49; designated helicopter pilot, 1950; assigned Korea, 1951-52, staff CINCEUR, 1952-54, Marine Corps Equipment Bd., 1954-57; comdr. helicopter group, 1957-59; dir. Marine Corps Aviation, 1961; comdg. gen. 1st Marine Brigade, Hawaii, 1962; asst. chief staff operations, staff CINCPAC, 1963-65; comdg. gen. 1st Marine Aircraft Wing, also dep. comdr. III MAF, Vietnam, 1965-66; dep. chief staff (air) Hdqrs. USMC, 1966-70; comdg. gen. III Marine Air Force, Vietnam, 1970; ret., 1971. Bd. dirs. Naval Mut. Aid, 1968-71. Decorated D.S.M., Silver Star, Legion of Merit, D.F.C., Air medal. Mem. Am. Helicopter Soc. (bd. dirs.), Marine Corps Assn. (bd. govs.), Beta Theta Pi, Tau Beta Pi, Pi Delta Epsilon. Presbyn. Author articles. Home: Alexandria VA Died July 13, 1971; buried Arlington Nat. Cemetery, Arlington VA

MCCUTCHEON, MALCOLM WALLACE, Canadian govt. ofcl.; b. London, Ont., May 18, 1906; s. Frederic W. C. and Mary (Vining) McC.; B.A., Victoria Coll., U. Toronto, 1926; LL.D., St. Francis Xavier U., U. Western Ont.; m. Eva Trow Borland, Dec. 14, 1934; 3 sons, 2 daus. Called to Ont. bar, 1930; King's counsel, 1947, Queen's counsel, 1953; practice with firm Osler, Hoskin & Harcourt, Toronto, 1930-34; asst. to pres. Nat. Life Assurance Co. of Can., 1934-37, sec., 1937-38, asst. gen. mgr., 1938; v.p., mng. director Argus Corp., Ltd., 1945-62; senator Govt. of Can., 1962-69, minister-without-portfolio, 1962; minister trade and commerce, 1963; chmn. bd. Nat. Life Assurance Co. Can.; counsel Shibley, Righton, & McCutcheon, Toronto; dir. Montreal Trust Co., Glens Falls Ins. Co. (N.Y.), Canadian Enterprise Development Corporation, Limited, Longmans Can., Limited. Mem.

Wartime Prices and Trade Board, 1941-46, deputy chairman board, 1945-62. Chairman, Ontario Cancer Inst., Princess Margaret Hosp. Bd. dirs. Royal Agrl. Winter Fair; bd. govs. St. Francis Xavier U., U. Toronto; adv. bd. St. Michael's Hosp.; bd. mgmt., v.p. Victorian Order Nurses for Can.; mem. senate Stratford Shakespearean Found. Can.; trustee United Community Fund Met. Toronto. Decorated comdr. Order Brit. Empire. Mem. Pvt. Planning Assn. Can. (Can.-Am. com., Can. trade com.), Can. Inst. Internat. Affairs (hon. vice chmn.). Mem. United Ch. of Can. Mason. Clubs: Toronto, Rosedale Golf, Albany, Tadenac, University, Granite, National, York (Toronto); Montreal, Mt. Royal (Montreal); London; Rideau, Country (Ottawa); Vancouver (B.C.). Home: Gormley ON Canada Died Jan. 23, 1969; buried Toronto, Ont., Can.

MCDANIEL, HENRY BONNER, educator; b. Hico, Tex., March 20, 1903; s. Henry Blake and Maude (Roberts) McD.; A.B., U. of Ariz., 1925; A.M., 1935; Ph.D., Columbia, 1940; m. Estella Brown, Aug. 25, 1930; children—Judith, Rodney. High sch. teacher, Ariz. and Calif., 1925-38; research asst., Teachers Coll., Columbia, 1938-40; coordinator of guidance, San Diego (Calif.) Pub. Schs., 1940-42; chief, bur. of guidance, Calif. State Dept. Edn., 1942-46; mem. faculty, sch. edn., Stanford, from 1946, prof. of edn. and psychology from 1949; vis. prof., Columbia, 1941, U. of Calif., 1942, 43, U. of Calif., Los Angeles, 1944; consultant to sch. systems, Calif., Wash., Mont., Utah, and Alberta, Can. Diplomate Am. Bd. Psychol. Examiners; fellow Am. Psychol. Assn. (div. of counseling), Nat. Vocational Guidance Assn. (trustee 1942-49), Calif. Soc. for Secondary Edn. (bd. dirs.). Unitarian. Contbr. to various ednl. jours. Speaker ednl. and civic orgns. Home: Stanford CA Died Feb. 20, 1972.

MCDANIEL, WALTON BROOKS, coll. prof.; b. Cambridge, Mass., Mar. 4, 1871; s. Samuel W. and Georgianna F. (Brooks) M.; A.B., magna cum laude, Harvard, 1893, A.M., 1894, Ph.D., 1899; m. Alice C. Garlichs, Aug. 2, 1899. Asst. in Greek and Latin, 1896-97, instr., 1899-1901, Harvard; also instr., Radcliffe, 1900-01; became prof. Latin, U. of Pa., 1909. Prof. Am. Acad. in Rome, 1920-21. Democrat. Unitarian. Mem. Delta Upsilon, Phi Beta Kappa, Am. Philos. Soc., Am. Philol. Assn. (ex-pres.), Archaeol. Inst. America, Classical Assn. of Atlantic States, Am. Classical League, The Mediaeval Acad. of America, Classical Assn. of England and Wales, Societe des Etudes Latines of France; charter mem. Am. Assn. Univ. Profs.; fellow A.A.A.S. Author: Roman Private Life and Its Survivals, 1924; Guide for the Study of English Books on Roman Private Life, 1926; Conception, Brith and Infancy in Ancient Rome and Modern Italy; Riding a Hobby In the Classis Lands. Contbr. numerous articles to Am. and foreign philol. jours. Address: 4082 Malaga Av., Coconut Grove FL‡

MCDERMOTT, JAMES THOMAS, congressman; b. Grand Rapids, Mich., Feb. 13, 1872; ed. St. Andrew's Cathedral there; telegrapher with Western Union Telegraph Co. at Detroit, 1884-9; went to Chicago, 1889; m. Nellie Fleming. Mem. 60th. to 63d Congresses (1907-15), 4th Ill. Dist.; resigned July 21, 1914, and reelected to 64th Congress (1915-17), same dist. Address: 4524 Union Av., Chicago IL‡

MCDERMOTT, R. THOMAS, chmn. bd. J. Ray McDermott & Co., Inc. Address: Houston TX Died July 27, 1970.

MCDEVITT, GEORGE EDWIN, lawyer; b. Keokuk, Ia., Jan. 19, 1910; s. Daniel W. and Susan (Baldwin) McD.; A.B., U. Ill. at Urbana, 1932; LL.B., Harvard U., 1936; m. Alice Schaefer, Aug. 19, 1933; children—Peter M., Susan A. Admitted to N.M. bar, 1937; practicing atty., Gallup, N.M., 1937-71; Gallup city atty., 1937-58; spl. asst. N.M. Atty. Gen., 1960-71. Served to lt. (s.g.) USNR, 1943-46. Mem. N.M., McKinley County bar assns., Harvard Law Sch. Assn. N.M. (pres. 1963-64), V.F.W. Elk, Kiwanian. Home: Gallup NM Died Jan. 6, 1971.

MCDONALD, BILL, assn. exec.; b. Guntersville, Ala., Oct. 17, 1909; s. James D. and Vida N. (Perkins) McD.; grad. accounting, Massey Coll., 1928; LL.B., Columbus U., 1941; m. Mary V. Simms, June 15, 1934. Probate ct. clk., Marshall County, Ala., 1929-33; adminstrv. asst. N.R.A., 1933-36; field rep., adminstrv. officer soil cons. service Dept. Agr., 1936-41; from adminstrv. officer to asst. nat. dir. U.S. Savs. Bond div. Treasury Dept., 1941-66; mgr. C. of C., Guntersville, Ala., from 1966. Served with AUS, 1943-45. Mem. Am. Farm Bur. Fedn., Ala. Soc., Am. Legion. Democrat. Methodist. Club: Val Monte Country (Guntersville, Ala.). Home: Guntersville AL Died Mar. 5, 1969.

MCDONALD, CHARLES HENRY, lawyer, retired army officer; b. Manchester, Wisconsin, October 16, 1872; s. Daniel and Anne (McLaughlin) M.; preparatory education at the State Normal School, Oshkosh. Wis.; LL.B., Chicago (Ill.) Law Sch., 1897; m. Ella Meisner, Aug. 12, 1902; children—Isabel Anne, Mildred Meisner, John Charles. Practiced at Wittenberg and Oshkosh, Wis., 1897-1913; atty. for Bur. of Corps., Dept. of Commerce, 1913-15; chmn. of Law and Joint Boards of Review of Federal Trade Commn., Washington, D.C., 1915-18. Counsel in charge of administration of Trading with the Enemy Act by the Federal Trade Commn., 1917-18; legal advisor to Am. Forces in Germany on civil affairs, 1919-20. Commd. maj., Judge Advocate's Dept., U.S. Army, 1918, lt. col., 1932; judge advocate 6th Corps Area, 1932-35; ordered to active duty, 6th Service Command, March 1, 1943; law mem. Permanent General Court Martial, World War II. Mem. K.C., Mil. Order of World War, Am. Legion, Am. Bar Assn. Clubs: Union League, Chicago Athletic, South Shore Country (Chicago). Home: 1857 N. Prospect Av., Milwaukee WI‡

MCDONALD, EDWIN C., banking exec.; born Columbus, O., July 9, 1897; s. Morton and Stella (Breyfogle) McD.; student Culver (Ind.) Mil. Acad., 1911-15, Ohio State Univ., 1915-17; m. Elizabeth Hann, Sept. 2, 1918; children—Edwin C., Betty Lynn (Mrs. O. W. Hickel, Jr.). Vice pres. Met. Life Ins. Co. charge group ins. activities, 1953-59, dir., 1957-72, sr. v.p., 1960-62, exec. v.p., 1963-64; chmn. bd. Royal Bank of Can. Trust Co., N.Y.C., 1964-72; chmn., dir. Thomson Newspapers, Inc.; chmn. bd., dir. Exec. Fund of Can.; dir. Downe Communications, Inc., Internat. Minerals and Chemical Corporation (Canada) Ltd., Versafoods, Ltd., Crush Internat., Standard Packaging Corp., Automatic Retailers of Am., Inc., Pacific Petroleums, Ltd., Diners Club, Inc., Diners Club Gt. Britain, Franklin. Custodian Funds, Inc., General Bakeries Ltd., Met. Life Ins. Co., Royal Bank of Can. Internat., Ltd., Western World Ins. Co., Vancouver Wharves, Ltd., Lord Hardwicke, Ltd., Maxwell Labs. Inc., Sci., Systems & Software Incorporated, Union Bank of Los Angeles, Royal Bank of Canada, Frontier Airlines, Gen. Host Co., May Dept. Stores Co. Served as lt. and capt. U.S. Marines, 1917-19. Bd. dirs. Culver Ednl. Found., Am. Red Cross, University Western Ontario. Mem. Can. Life Ins. Officers Assn. (pres. 1946-47), Beta Theta Pi. Clubs: Mount Royal (Montreal); Toronto; Blind Brook, Union League (N.Y.C.); Siwanoy Country; Lyford Cay (Nassau, Bahamas); American, Buck's (London, Eng.); Los Angeles. Home: New York City NY Died 1972.

MCDONALD, ETTA AUSTIN BLAISDELL, author; b. Manchester, N.H., Mar. 20, 1872; d. Clark and Clara M. Blaisdell; grad. State Normal Sch., Framingham, Mass., 1891; m. James Richard McDonald, Aug. 3, 1899. Taught sch. in Mass., 1892-96; supervisor primary schs., Brockton, Mass., 1896-99; dir. Chandler Secretarial Sch., Boston, 1918-27. Author: (with sister, Mary Frances Blaisdell) Child Life, 1899; Child Life in Tale and Fable, 1899; Child Life in Many Lands, 1900; Child Life in Literature, 1900; The Child Life Primer, 1901; The Blaisdell Spellers, 1901; The Child Life Fifth Reader, 1902; Boy Blue and His Friends, 1907; Manuel in Mexico, 1909; Ume San in Japan, 1909; Rafael in Italy, 1909; Kathleen in Ireland, 1909; Fritz in Germany, 1910; Gerda in Sweden, 1910; Boris in Russia, 1910; Betty in Canada, 1910; Marta in Holland, 1911; Hassan in Egypt, 1911; Donald in Scotland, 1912; Josefa in Spain, 1912; Colette in France, 1913; Chandra in India, 1916; Mother Goose Children, 1916; Rhymes and Tales for Children, 1918; The Kelpies, 1924; Toy Town, 1927; My Garden of Stories, 1929; The Kelpies Run Away, 1930. Home: Mount Dora‡

MCDONALD, FREDERICK HONOUR, cons. engr.; b. Charleston, S.C., Aug. 16, 1892; s. William Ogier and Katie (St. Clair) McD.; B.S., in Elec. and Mech. Engring., Clemson (S.C.) Coll., 1914; post grad. extension work, U. of Pittsburgh, 1915-16; m. Katharine Steed Everett, Dec. 1919; children—Mary Fay (Mrs. Lester MacLean), Katharine Everett (Mrs. John T. Jeter), Jane Honour (Mrs. William E. Craver), Anne Ewing (Mrs. James E. Bell). With Westinghouse Electric & Mfg. Co., 1914-16; field engr. Hope Engring. & Supply Co., Tulsa, 1916-17; industrial engr. Lockwood Greene & Co., Atlanta, 1921-23; dir. and chief engr. Ga. Industrial Bur., Atlanta, 1923-24, pres. McDonald & Co., engrs. and architects, 1924-32, private practice as cons. engr., Atlanta, 1932-39; founder community research Inst. and director, from 1939; president Management Research Institute; development and industrial engineer S.C. Pub. Service Authority, 1939-41; cons., industrial engr., Charleston, S.C., specializing in plant location, power developments, and mgmt., from 1941; publisher and editor of Dixie Magazine, 1947-49; dir. Ga. Geodetic Control Surveys, 1934-39. Served as 1st lt. Engr. Corps, U.S. Army, 1917-21, Chairman of the Board of Archtl. Review for Old and Historic Charleston, S.C., from 1951. Decorated Military Order of Purple Heart (U.S.). Mem. Am. Inst. Consltg. Engrs., Am. Soc. Civil Engrs. (dir. 1934-36; organized Engring. Economics Div., 1931, sec. 1931-37, chmn. 1938-39), S.C. Soc. Engrs., Huguenot Soc. of S.C., Charleston Rotary Club (pres. 1943-44), Civil Engrs. Club Charleston (co-founder, hon. life mem., recipient citation from young engrs.). Independent Democrat. Presbyterian Church. Club: Cosmos (Wash.). Author: How to Promote Community and Indsl. Development, 1938; Geodetic Survey of Georgia, 1939; Manual for the Business Aid Clinic, 1940; Manual on Manpower and Incentive Principals, 1951; The Citadel of Business, 1952; Education and Race Relations, 1954; Creative Management, 1956; The New Art of Fabrication Engineering, 1958; also tech., econ. articles in profl. and Charleston SC Died Aug. 2, 1972.

MCDONALD, JOSEPH JOHN, surgeon, educator; b. Seattle, Feb. 25, 1913; s. Joseph and Nellie Eva (Nicholson) McD.; B.S., U. Wash., 1935; M.S., Northwestern 1939, M.D., 1940; D.M.S., Columbia, 1946; m. Jo-Janette Gilbert, Sept. 9, 1943; children—Ann Laura, Joseph Gilbert. Served as intern Passavent Meml. Hosp., Chgo., 1940; asst. resident, resident surgery Presbyn. Hosp., N.Y.C., 1941-43, asst. resident plastic surgery, 1943-45, instr. surgery, asst. attending surgeon, 1945-46, attending surgeon, 1951-53; asso. prof., chmn. dept. surgery Am. U., Beirut, Lebanon, 1946-48, prof. surgery, 1948-53, Columbia Coll. Phys. and Surgs., 1951-53; pvt. practice specializing in plastic, reconstructive and cancer surgery, N.Y.C., 1951-53; vis. surgeon, dir. surg. service Francis Delafield Hosp., N.Y.C., 1951-53; surg. prof. & med. dean, Am. U., Beirut, Lebanon, 1953-67. Recipient of Lebanese gold medal of merit, 1955. Diplomat Am. Bd. Surgery, Nat. Bd. Med. Examiners. Fellow A.C.S.; mem. Am. Soc. for Surgery Hand, Soc. U. Surgeons, Alpha Omega Alpha, Sigma Alpha Epsilon, Nu Sigma Nu. Author: Correlative Neuroanatomy and Functional Neurology (with Joseph G. Chusid), 1962. Co-editor: Handbook of Surgery, 1960. Contbr. to sci. jours. Producer ednl. films on surgery and embryology of face, gastro-intestinal tract and nervous system. Address: Beirut Lebanon Died Apr. 11, 1967.

MCDONALD, KAROLA JENNY, coal co. exec.; b. nr. Stuttgart, Germany, Apr. 13, 1920; d. George and Maria (Laechele) Lind; degree in bus. adminstrn. Hohere Handelsschule, Ludwigsburg, Germany, 1938; grad. Classical Music Acad., Germany 1948; m. James P. McDonald, Apr. 7, 1956 (annulled Nov. 1959); m. William Wildermann, Nov. 6, 1960 (div. May 1963). Came to U.S., 1953, naturalized, 1958. Profl. opera singer, Germany, 1948-49; founder Kadostahl, Inc., 1956, pres., 1956-70; U.S. rep. Wartsila-Koncer-ner A/B Ship Bldg. Division, Helsinki, Finland. Member German-American Finnish-Am., Italian-Am., Am.-Israel chambers commerce Met. Opera Guild, Opera Soc. Stuttgart. Address: Forest Hills NY Died Mar. 31, 1970.

MCDONALD, MARGARET PUTH (MRS. THOMAS H. MCDONALD, JR.), journalist; b. Appleton, Wis.; d. George J. and Marie Elizabeth (Roemer) Puth; B.A. cum laude, Lawrence Coll., 1944; postgrad. Syracuse U.; m. Thomas H. McDonald, Jr., Apr. 28, 1947; children—Brian Causey, Tracy Anne. Reporter, Batavia Daily News, Batavia, N.Y., 1945-49; corr. for Rochester (N.Y.) Times-Union and free lance writer, 1949-50; feature writer, reporter, critic Shreveport (La.) Times, 1950-55; dir. News Bur. at Centenary Coll., Shreveport, 1955-62; amusements editor, feature writer Shreveport Jour., 1962-68, twice-weekly column Off Stage and On, 1962-68; also free lance work. Bd. dirs. Shreveport Blood Bank, 1955. Mem. La. Press Women (v.p. 1965-67), Am. Fedn. Musicians, Pi Beta Phi, Mortar Bd. Roman Catholic. Democrat. Editor cookbook: Favorite Recipes of the Red River Valley, 1953; contbr. articles and poetry to nat. Shreveport LA Died Oct. 1, 1968.

MCDONALD, ROY WILLIAM, lawyer; b. Austin, Tex., June 20, 1905; s. John Philo and Tennie (Ford) McD.; LL.B., U. Tex., 1927; B.S., So. Meth. U., 1940; LL.M., Columbia, 1941, J.S.D., 1952; m. Gladys Eugenia Castle, Nov. 27, 1930. Admitted to Tex. bar, 1927, U.S. Supreme Ct. bar, 1944, N.Y. bar, 1945, D.C. bar, 1958; practiced law, Dallas, 1927-38; spl. lectr. law Dallas Sch. Law, 1929-37; prof. law So. Meth. U., 1938-45 (on leave 1943-45); vis. prof. law U. Tex., summer 1939, U. Mich., summer 1942, Columbia, summer 1946; faculty George Washington U., 1942-43; staff of gen. counsel Bd. Econ. Warfare, Washington, 1943, acting asst. gen. counsel, Apr.-Aug. 1943; asst. chief enemy br. Fgn. Econ. Adminstrn., Aug.-Sept. 1943, chief econ. intelligence div., Sept. 1943-Apr. 1944; asso. Donovan, Leisure, Newton & Irvine, 1944-48, partner, from 1948. Mem. adv. com. on rules of civil procedure Supreme Ct. Tex., 1940-48, com. reporter, 1940. Nat. council chief Lone Scouts of Am., 1925; nat. chmn. Lone Scout div. Boy Scouts Am., 1927. Mem. chancellor's council Univ. Tex., from 1966. Fellow Am. Coll. Trial Lawyers, Am. Bar Found.; mem. Am. Law Inst., Am., N.Y., Tex., Fed., Internat. bar assns., Association Bar City N.Y., Nat. Legal Aid Soc., Order of Coif, Delta Theta Phi, Alpha Phi Epsilon, Phi Delta Gamma, Chancellors. Member of the Baptist Church. Mason. Clubs: Downtown Assn. (N.Y.C.); Town, Scarsdale Golf. Author: Texas Civil Procedure, 1950, and biennial supplements; Alternative Pleading, 1952; Jurisdiction-Venue, 2d edit., 1965; Pleading-Discovery, 2d edition, 1969. Contbr. articles to legal publs. Home: Scarsdale NY Died Apr. 3, 1972; buried Laurel Land Meml. Park, Dallas TX

MCDONALD, SAMUEL F., baking co. exec.; b. Biggsville, Ill., July 9, 1871; s. William and Rebecca (Nelson) M.; m. Kate E. Prest, Jan. 16, 1896; 1 son, S. Floyd. Asso. with Kelley, Lysle Milling Co.,

Leavenworth, Kan., 1887-99; in baking bus., Memphis, 1900-22; sold bus. to Continental Baking Co., 1922, v.p., 1922-51, ret. 1951, mem. bd govs. Chmn. ways and means com. New Rochelle Hosp. Republican. Episcopalian. Club: Wykagyl Country. Home: 395 Williamsburg Lane, Memphis TN‡

MCDONNELL, DONALD N., investment co. exec.; b. Des Moines, Ia., 1899; student U. Wash., 1922, Harvard, 1925. Vice chmn. bd. Blyth & Co., N.Y.C., 1965-66; dir. Halliburton Co., Magnovox Co., Chgo. Pneumatic Tool Co., U.S. Bank Note Corp., Weybright & Talley, Ltd., Mich. Gas Utilities Co.; exec. com., dir. Gen. Dynamics Corp. Office: New York City NY Died Sept. 28, 1969.

MCDONOUGH, GORDON LEO, congressman; b. Buffalo, N.Y., Jan. 2, 1895; s. Sylvester Henry and Ellen (Parker) McD.; ed. Emporium (Pa.) High Sch.; studied chemistry with spl. instrs.; m. Catherine Ann McNeil, Feb. 11, 1896; children—Gordon Leo, Marie Louise (Mrs. Richard H. Miller), Paul McNeil, Vincent Sylvester, Thomas Cornelius, James Quentin, Lucile Elaine (Mrs. John F. Mannelly). Began as assistant chemist, Emporium (Pa.) Iron Co., 1911-13, Aluminum Co. of America, Niagara Falls, N.Y., 1913-15, Aetna Explosions Co., Emporium, 1915-17; chem. salesman Scientific Materials Co., Pittsburgh, 1917-18; chemist Warman Steel Castings Co., Los Angeles, Calif., 1918-20, Raymond Osborne Testing Lab., Los Angeles, 1920-22; salesman Great Western Milling Co., Los Angeles, 1922-27; Indsl. engr. Los Angeles Chamber of Commerce, 1927-33; Los Angeles County supervisor, 1933-45; mem. 79th to 87th Congresses, from the 15th Calif. Dist.; mem. House Science and Astronautics Com. 1st chairman Los Angeles County War Council; mem. exec. bd. Los Angeles met. area council Boy Scouts Am. Awarded citation, USN, U.S. Treasury; Award of Merit, D.A.R., Nat. Assn. Co. Officials, Vets. Fgn. Wars (hon.). Republican. Roman Catholic. K.C. (4 deg.), Kiwanian. Home: Los Angeles CA Died June 25, 1968; buried Holy Cross Cemetery, Los Angeles CA

MCDONOUGH, JAMES BUCHANAN, lawyer; b. Bloomer, Ark., Nov. 24, 1865; s. Wesley Farmer and Sarena (Smith) McD.; student Buckner Coll., Witcherville, Ark.; A.B., U. of Ark., 1886; m. Sara Mason Martin, Apr. 27, 1897 (died 1915); children—Lucy Mason (Mrs. Joseph R. Brown), James Buchanan, John Martin; m. 2d, May Robins, 1922; step-sons—John S. Robins and Delma H. Robins. Admitted to Ark. bar, 1889, and began practice at Fort Smith; atty. K.C.S. Ry. since 1903; pres. Ark. Western Ry. Co., Fort Smith & Van Buren Ry. Co.; gen. counsel Fort Smith, Subiaco & Rock Island R.R. Co.; dir. and atty. City Nat. Bank. Asst. U.S. atty. Western Dist. of Ark., 1893-97; pros. atty. 12th Dist. of Ark., 1892; mem. Ark. Ho. of Rep., 1887-89. Successfully prosecuted in U.S. Court, 1914, the case of the Coronado Coal Co. et al. vs. the United Mine Workers of America, successfully establishing the principle, previously unkown in jurisprudence, that under the Sherman and Clayton acts of Congress unicorporated assns. might be sued for violations of said acts of Congress. Mem. Am. and Ark. State bar assns., Acad. Polit. Science, Phi Beta Kappa. Democrat. Episcopalian. Elk. Clubs: Rotary, Hardscrabble Country. Contbr. to Am. Law Rev., Va. Law Rev., Central Law Jour. Home: Free Ferry Rd. Office: Merchants Nat. Bank Bldg., Fort Smith AR*‡

MCDOUGAL, MYRTLE ARCHER (MRS. DANIEL ARCHIBALD MCDOUGAL), b. Baldwyn, Miss.; d. George Washington and Sarah Jane (Welch) Archer; ed. pub. sch. and pvt. tutors; m. Daniel Archibald McDougal, of Savannah, Tenn., Feb. 12, 1888;children—Jennie Myrtle (Mrs. Hugh Mackay), Mary Carmack (Mrs. Iver Axelson), Violet. Mem. Dem. Nat. Com. since 1924 (mem. conv. arrangements com., 1924); ex-pres. Okla. Fed. Women's Clubs; a founder, 1st pres. Fla. League Am. Pen Women. Lecturer, short story and feature writer. Engaged in Red Cross work and hospitality work, World War. Mem. Christian (Disciples) Ch. Home: Washington DC‡

MCDOUGALL, EDWARD GEORGE, packer; b. Fargo, Mich., Apr. 6, 1875; s. John D. and Christy Ann (Monroe) McD.; ed. high sch.; m. Alice L. Filmore, June 28, 1904; children—Clarice Louise, Chesley Edward, Lorna Lee. Began as clk. with Libby, McNeill & Libby, Chicago, 1901, elected v.p., 1915; pres. and gen. mgr. since Apr. 29, 1922. Served as lt. Spanish-Am. War. Republican. Protestant. Clubs: Union League, South Shore Country, Beverly Country. Home: 6905 Bennett Av. Address: Union Stock Yards, Chicago IL‡

MCDOUGLE, ERNEST CLIFTON, clergyman, lawyer; b. Keno, Meigs County, O., Mar. 16, 1867; s. Samuel Benjamin and Charlotte Adelia (Cowdery) McD.; B.S., Nat. Normal U., Lebanon, O., 1891; A.B., Southern Normal U., Huntingdon, Tenn., 1893, A.M., 1895; Ph.D., Clark U., 1914; m. Linna Alice Caldwell, Aug. 25, 1891 (died Apr. 9, 1939);children—Ivan Eugene, Miree, dec. (wife of Dr. B. M. Brown), Earl Caldwell (dec.), Marion Everett; m. 2d, Mrs. Minnie Gibson Long, March 6, 1943. V.p. Southern Normal Univ., 1893-96; prof. belles lettres, Nat. Normal U., 1896-1901; pres. Southern Normal U., 1901-02; pres. Georgie Robertson Christian Coll., Henderson, Tenn., 1902-07; asst. in edn. and business dir., 1907-10, prof. edn., 1910-21, dean, 1915-21, Eastern Ky. State Normal Sch., Richmond; clergyman (Christian Disciples) in regular pastorates; elected county judge, Madison County. Ky., Nov. 3, 1925, without opposition, for term 1926-30 (only Dem. official to win). Admitted to Ky. bar, 1929, all state and federal courts, 1930. Lectured in over 100 teachers' insts. in Ky., Ohio and W.Va. Author: The Pedagogy of Arithmetic, 1914. Richmond KY‡

MCDOWALL, ROBERT EDWARD, electronics co. exec.; b. Carson, N.D., Apr. 29, 1927; s. Harvey W. and Dorothy (Gross) McD.; B.S. in Bus. Adminstrn., U. Cal. at Los Angeles, 1954; m. Lois Ann Solberg, Dec. 26, 1949; children—Sandra Diane, Douglas Jeffrey. With Arthur Young & Co., C.P.A.'s, Los Angeles, 1954-58; with Cohu Electronics Inc., San Diego, 1958-68, exec. v.p., 1965-68, also dir. Served with USMCR, 1945-48, 51-52. C.P.A., Cal. Mem. C.P.A. Soc. Cal., Nat. Assn. Accountants. Presbyn. Home: La Mesa CA Died Nov. 8, 1968.

MCDOWELL, PHILETUS H(AROLD), clergyman; b. Montgomery County, Kan., Dec. 28, 1873; s. James Perry and Sarah (Biddle) McD.; A.B., Central Coll., Pelia, Ia., 1897, D.D., 1909; grad. Rochester (N.Y.) Theol. Sem., 1900; m. Jessie Elizabeth Alexander, June 20, 1900; 1 dau., Mary Elizabeth. Ordained ministry Bapt. Ch., 1896; pastor successively at Malvern and Winterset, Ia., Omaha, Neb., Davenport, Ia., Melrose, Mass., until 1923, First Ch., Glens Falls, N.Y., 1923-39. Mem. bd. mgrs. Am. Bapt. Home Mission Soc., 1922-41; past v.p. N.Y. Bapt. Missionary Conv. With 90th Div., A.E.F., in France and Germany, 1918-19; religious dir. and div. sec. Y.M.C.A., overseas. Republican. Kiwanian. Home: Kenworthy Av., Glens Falls NY‡

MCEACHERN, DANIEL VICTOR, constrn. engr.; b. Port Huron, Mich., Mar. 9, 1879; s. Alexander and Jane (McClellan) McE.; LL.D., Pepperdine Coll., 1958; m. Ida J. Peters, 1904 (dec. Sept. 1965); children—Franklin Wallace, Robert Burns; m. 2d, Juanita Rainey Fogarty, Oct. 25, 1967. Founder Highline Savs. & Loan Assn., Seattle, 1948, dir., from 1948; with General Construction Co., Seattle, from 1926, trustee, from 1929, pres., 1952-55, chmn. bd., from 1955; dir. Kaiser Industries, Permanente Cement (both Oakland, Cal.), Northwestern Glass Co. (Seattle). Recipient achievement medal citation U. Tampa; named Christian layman Bethany Coll., W.Va., 1959. Home: Seattle WA Died Jan. 28, 1971.

MCELROY, JAMES W., banker; b. Baltimore Co., Md., Apr. 26, 1892; s. Anthony Bonn and Elizabeth Williams (Morrison) McE.; student Baltimore City College, evening courses, Johns Hopkins U.; married Katharine Myers, June 10, 1915; children—James W., Thomas Anthony. Began banking career with Fed. Res. Bank, Richmond, Va.; joined First Nat. Bank of Balt., 1923, past pres., dir.; dir. Eutaw Savs. Bank Balt., Samuel Kirk & Son, Inc., Balt. Chmn. investment adv. com. Retirement Systems Md. Pres. bd. trustees Boys' Latin School of Balt.; board of directors Mercy Hosp., Balt. Served as 1st lt., inf., U.S. Army, World War I. Clubs: Maryland, Elkridge. Home: Baltimore MD Died June 16, 1971; buried Druid Ridge Cemetery, Baltimore County MD

MCELROY, NEIL H., bus. exec.; b. Berea, O., Oct. 30, 1904; s. Malcolm Ross and Susan Harriet (Hosler) McE.; A.B., Harvard, 1925; m. Mary Camilia Fry, June 29, 1929; children—Nancy Sue (Mrs. Lee M. Folger), Barbara Ellen (Mrs. David Dimling), Malcolm Neil. With Prctor & Gamble Co., Cin., 1925-72, entered advt. dept., 1925, mgr. promotion dept., 1929-40, mgr. advt. and promotion, 1940-43, v.p. in charge advt., 1943-46, v.p., gen. mgr., 1946-48, pres., 1948-57, chmn. bd. 1959-72. Sec. def., Washington, 1957-59; dir. Gen. Electric Co., Chrysler Corp., Equitable Life Assurance Soc. U.S. Trustee Nat. Safety Council; dir. Atlantic Council of U.S., Inc.; mem. nat. council United Negro Coll. Fund; vis. com. Harvard Center Internat. Affairs; vice chmn. Bus. Council; past mem. or exec. officer several nat. citizens orgns. for edn. and community welfare; chmn. com. univ. resources Harvard; mem. Washington Office Consumer Affairs, Better Bus. Bur.; mem. Com. Corporate Support Am. Univs.; nat. adv. council Girl Scouts U.S.A.; exec. com. Cin. Inst. Fine Arts. Clubs: Bohemian (San Francisco); Harvard (Boston and N.Y.C.); Cincinnati Country, Commonwealth Commercial (pres. 1960-61), Camargo, Queen City (Cin.); Links, 29 (N.Y.C.); Chevy Chase, 1925 F St (Washington). Home: Cincinnati OH Died Nov. 30, 1972.

MCELWAIN, CHARLES CHURCH, ins. exec.; b. Springfield, Mass., May 14, 1872; s. Edwin and Caroline (Church) McE.; student pub. schs. Springfield; m. Greta Parks, Nov. 8, 1899; 1 son, Edwin. Employee Kibbe Bros. & Co., candy mfrs., Springfield, 1890, prin. owner, pres., treas., 1911-33; dir. Mutual Fire Assurance Co. of Springfield since 1914, pres., since 1923; dir. Mass. Mutual Life Ins. Co. of Springfield, since 1922, mem. exec. com. since 1924; dir. United Electric Light Co. of Springfield, 1924-42, Western Mass. Electric Co., since 1943, Springfield Safe Deposit & Trust Co., 1911-31, Chapman Valve Mfg. Co. of Springfield, 1911-36; trustee Western Mass. Cos. since 1927. Trustee Springfield Hosp., 1916, Springfield Cemetery Assn. Mem. S.A.R., Newcomen Soc. of Eng. Conglist. Mason. Club: Colony (Springfield). Home: 230 Forest Park Av. Office: 145 State St., Springfield 3 MA‡

MCELWAIN, WILLIAM HENRY, banker; b. Amsterdam, N.Y., Jan. 2, 1904; s. Judson Parr and Sarah (Dean) McE.; student Rensselaer Poly. Inst., 1926; m. Carolyn Thomas Daley, Sept. 21, 1951; 1 son, William Parr, Div. mgr. N.Y. State Electric & Gas Corp., 1926-49; v.p. Met. Edison Co., Reading Pa., 1949-56; with Jersey Central and N.J. Power & Light Cos., 1956-69, pres., 1961-69; chmn. bd., chmn. exec. com. First Nat. Iron Bank, Morristown, N.J., 1970-72; First Nat. Bank, Asbury Park, N.J. Trustee Sommerset Hills (N.J.) chpt. A.R.C.; bd. overseers Newark Grad. Coll. Engrng.; trustee Stevens Inst. Tech., Morris Mus. Arts and Scis. Home: Basking Ridge NJ Died Nov. 21, 1972.

MCENTEGART, BRYAN J., bishop; born at New York City, New York, January 5, 1893; s. Patrick and Kate (Roe) McE.; B.A., Manhattan Coll., 1913, LL.D., 1939; M.A., in sociology, Catholic Univ., 1918; grad. N.Y. Sch. of Social Work, 1920; LL.D., Fordham, 1946, St. Bonaventure, 1951, St. Michaels, 1953, University Coll., Dublin, 1954, St. Francis College, 1958, The Catholic University of America, 1966; L.H.D. (hon.), St. John's U., 1957. Ordained priest Cath. Ch., 1917, made domestic prelate, 1941, consecrated bishop of Ogdensburg, 1943-53; became rector Cath. U. Am., Washington, 1953; bishop of Brooklyn Diocese, 1957-68. Became archbishop-bishop of Brooklyn, 1966. Asso. dir. archdiocesan survey of Catholic charitable agencies, 1919; dir. div. of children N.Y. Cath. Charities, 1920-41; nat. sec. Cath. Nr. East Welfare Assn., 1941-43, exec. dir. war relief services Nat. Cath. Welfare Conference, 1943. Member advisory committee on child welfare, President's Council on Econ. and Social Security, 1934; mem. bd. dirs. Child Welfare League of America, 1931-37; vice chmn. report com., White House Conf. on Children, 1940; member exec. com. Welfare Council of N.Y. City, 1930-41; mem. central admission and distbn. com. Greater N.Y. Fund, 1938-41; chmn. Diocesan Dirs. of Charities, 1940; pres. N.Y. State Conf. on Social Work, 1940; 1st v.p. Nat. Conf. on Social Work, 1942; pres. Nat. Conf. of Catholic Charities, 1941; mem. bd. dirs. U.S.O.; exec. com. Nat. Catholic Community Service. Address: Brooklyn NY Died Sept. 30, 1968; buried Cathedral Coll. Sem. of Immaculate Conception, Douglaston NY

MCFADDEN, EFFIE BELLE, author; b. Delhi, N.Y., Sept. 1, 1872; d. Archibald and Bettie (Christie) McF.; A.B., Stanford, 1900; student U. of Calif., 1897-98; unmarried. Teacher pub. schs. Orange Co., Calif., 1891-93; supervisor pub. schs., Oakland, Calif., 1897-1900; supervisor State Teachers College, San Francisco, 1900-27, professor of biology since 1927. Lecturer teachers' associations and summer schools. Mem. Nat. Edn. Assn., Am. Association of University Women, Kappa Delta Pi Sorority. Author: Methods of Teaching Language, 1904; A Course of Study in Language for Elementary Schools, 1909; Teaching of Composition, Language and Spelling, 1912; McFadden Language Series, 1915; McFadden-Ferguson Language Series, 1918; McFadden English Series, 1923. Joint Author: Juniors Own Composition Book, 1928; Self-Instruction Exercises in Formal Language. Home: 496 Crestlake Drive, San Francisco CA‡

MCFARLAND, EARL, army officer; b. Topeka, Kan., July 7, 1883; s. James Davis and Mathilda (Steele) McF.; B.S., U.S. Mil. Acad., 1906; grad. Ordnance Sch. Tech., 1911, Ordnance Sch. of Application, 1912; M.E., Worcester Poly. Inst., 1923, Command and Gen. Staff Sch., 1931, Army Industrial Coll., 1933, Army War Coll., 1934; m. Mary Edith Cole, June 30, 1911; children—Mary Ann (Mrs. Hamilton Austin Twitchell), Cole, Earl. Commd. 2d lt., arty., 1906, and advanced through grades to brig. gen., 1938; prof. ordnances and gunnery and head dept. U.S. Mil. Acad., 1924-29; asst. Chief of Ordnance, U.S. Army, 1938-42; became comdg. officer Springfield (Mass.) Armory, June 1942; retired from active service, 1943. Elected supt. Staunton (Va.) Mil. Acad. Awarded D.S.M., Legion of Merit, Army Citation. Clubs: Army and Navy, War College (Washington); Colony (Springfield) Author of a U.S. Mil. Acad. textbook. Address: Staunton VA Died Jan. 1, 1972.

MCFARLAND, GARY, composer; b. Los Angeles, Oct. 23, 1933; s. Bovy Eugene and Mary Mildred (Fillion) McF.; student U. Ore., 1952-53, Berklee Sch. Music, U. Ore., fall 1955, 59, Los Angeles City Coll., fall 1956, E. Los Angeles Jr. Coll., spring 1957, San Jose City Coll., fall 1957, spring 1958; m. Gail Evelyn Frankel, Oct. 13, 1963; 1 son, Milo. Musical dir./conductor Downbeat Jazz Festival, Chgo., 1965; conductor U. Cal. at Los Angeles Jazz Festival, 1967; co-dir. TV music prodn. co., Composers' Collaborative; composed, orchestrated jazz ballet Reflections in the Park, 1964; composed, orchestrated, conducted Profile, concert contemporary music, 1966; recording artist for Impulse Skye records; composer film score 13, 1966, Sole Art, 1967; composer spl. arrangements numerous jazz musicians. Co-founder Willie Dennis Meml. Scholarship, 1966; founder Gary McFarland Student Scholarship, 1967. Served with AUS, 1954-55. Recipient Best New Composer award Down Beat mag., 1963. Mem. A.F.T.R.A., A.S.C.A.P., Am. Fedn. Musicians, Home: East Hampton LI NY Died Nov. 1971.

MCFARLAND, GREYBLE LEWIS, JR., orgn. exec.; b. nr. Southport Ind., Nov. 18, 1919; s. Greyble Lewis and Pearl Agnes (Johnson) McF.; A.B., Wabash Coll., Crawfordsville, Ind., 1941. With Golden Guernsey Farms, Inc., Indpls., from 1946, pres., from 1963; president Golden Guernsey, Incorporated, Peterborough, New Hampshire, from 1965; mng. director McFarland Found., Indpls., from 1964; pres., chmn. bd. Am. Guernsey Cattle Club, from 1965. Pres. Met. Plan Commn., Marion County, Ind., 1959-63; vice chmn. Ind. Office Bldg. Commn., from 1966; chmn. dairy adv. com. Ind. Bd. Health, 1954-66; chmn. Milk Industry Found., 1954-58. Chmn. Ind. March of Dimes, 1955-60; life mem. Nat. Trust for Great Britain. Mem. Ind. Senate from Marion-Johnson Counties, 1949-53; chmn. platform adv. com. Ind. Democratic Com., 1954-65. Served to lt. USNR, 1942-46. Named Ky. col., 1965. Mem. Farm Bur., Farmers Union, Indpls. C. of C., Delta Tau Delta. Presbyn. Club: Indpls. Athletic. Home: Indianapolis IN Died Sept. 12, 1971; buried Greenwood IN

MCFARLAND, JOHN CLEMSON, retired govt. official; b. Cedar County, Mo., Oct. 22, 1877; s. Thomas Jefferson and Mary Jane (Pruet) McF.; LL.B., National Univ., 1910; LL.M., 1911; m. Ruth E. Allee, June 1899 (died 1903); children—Louise (Mrs. Donald A. Hipkins), Thomas Princeton; m. 2d, Alice Prescott, July 1906 (died 1928); m. 3d, Marie Prescott, Sept. 1929. Teacher in business coll., 1896-98; clerk in office of auditor for War Dept., Washington, 1904-08; transferred to office of Comptroller of the Treasury, 1908, law clerk, 1911-17, chief clerk of branch office, Paris, France, 1917-19, atty., 1919; in Gen. Accounting Office since 1921, atty., 1921-26, asst. gen. counsel, 1926-39, gen. counsel since 1939. Mem. Federal Bar Assn. Mason (32 deg., Shriner). Home: 6706 Meadow Lane Chevy Chase MD‡

MCFARLAND, KERMIT, writer; b. Grand Junction, Ia., Aug. 3, 1905; s. Edgar Bertrand and Mary Rosella (Thomas) McF.; B.A. in Journalism, U. Ia., 1928; m. Marjorie Beglinger, Jan. 23, 1956. Corr., Des Moines Register, other newspapers, 1921-28; polit. writer Harrisburg (Pa.) Patriot, 1928-29; polit. writer Pitts. Press, 1929-40, asso. editor, polit. columnist, 1940-51; editorial writer Scripps-Howard Newspaper Alliance, Washington, 1951-72, chief editorial writer, 1967-72. Chmn. exec. com., v.p., dir. Nat. Press Bldg. Corp.; pres. Pitts. Newspaper Guild, 1933, Pa. Legislative Corr. Assn., 1937-39; bd. govs. Nat. Press Club, Washington, 1955-65, chmn., 1959-65. Pres., Raymond Clapper Meml. Assn., 1969-72. Recipient Roy W. Howard Meml. award for extraordinary service Scripps-Howard Newspapers, 1972. Mem. Sigma Delta Chi, Sigma Phi Epsilon. Home: Washington DC Died Nov. 26, 1972; buried Nat. Meml. Park, Falls Church VA

MCFARLAND, RAYMOND, author; b. Lamoine, Me., Apr. 15, 1872; s. Daniel Y. and Hannah (Brooks) M.; B.A., Amherst Coll., 1897; M.A., Yale, 1902; m. M. Elizabeth Bacon, June 29, 1904; children—Hannah Elizabeth (Mrs. R. D. Silliman), Raymond Bacon, Eleanor Grace (Mrs. J. A. Barone), Florence Adella (Mrs. Joseph F. Bragg), Helen Caroline, Donald Joyce. Began teaching in Me. public schs., 1897; teacher, Normal Sch., Castleton, Vt., 1902-03; prin. Leicester (Mass.) Acad., 1903-08, Ithaca (N.Y.) High Sch., 1908-09; prof. secondary edn., Middlebury Coll., 1909-20; prin. Vermont Acad., 1920-23; purchasing agt. Art Work Shop, Buffalo, 1923-30; asst. in English and pub. speaking Buffalo State Teachers Coll., Mar.-Aug., 1933; teacher East Aurora High Sch., 1933-—; Vt. exec. sec. Interch. World Movement, 1919. Collaborator Carnegie Instn., Washington, 1904-07; leader of scientific expdn. into Labrador, 1910; lecturer, U. of Va., summer, 1915; 2d lt. inf., U.S. Army, 1918. Mem. Am. Legion, Phi Kappa Psi. Prog. Rep. Baptist. Mason. Author: A History of New England Fisheries, 1911; Skipper John of the Nimbus, 1918; Sons of the Sea, 1920; The Sea Panther, 1928; On the Roof of Labrador, 1935; Notable Short Stories, 1937; The Masts of Gloucester, 1937; Sea Adventure, 1938; also (brochures) Secondary Education in Vermont; Beyond the Height-ofLand; On the Roof of Labrador; etc. Home: East Aurora NY‡

MCFARLAND, RUSSELL S(COTT), petroleum exec.; b. Denver, Aug. 29, 1893; s. James and Helen (Russell) McF.; A.B., Park College, 1915; A.B., University of Missouri, Columbia, also graduate work, 1916; m. Jeannie L. McRuer, Oct. 25, 1917; children—Howard Russell, John Douglas, Jean Elizabeth. Petroleum geologist Empire Gas & Fuel Co., Wyo., Colo., Mont., and Tex., 1916-18; cons. geologist, Dallas, 1918-20; sec. and supt. land geol. dept. Twin States Oil Co. (subsidiary Sun Oil Co.), Tulsa, 1920-29; dir., v.p., gen. mgr. Sunray Oil Co., 1929-31; vice pres. Seaboard Oil Co., Dallas, gen. mgr. Mid-Continent operations, 1931-52, exec. v.p. in charge Seaboard operations, 1952-53, pres. from 1953, bd. dirs. from 1945. Mem. Am. Petroleum Inst. (dir.), Nat. Petroleum Council, Am. Inst. Mining and Metall. Engrs., Am. Assn. Petroleum Geologists (pres., 1928), Mid-Continent Oil and Gas Assn. (exec. com. and dir.; award 1949), Ind. Petroleum Assn. Am. (dir.), Dallas C. of C. (dir.). Clubs: Dallas Country, Athletic, Engineers, Petroleum (Dallas); University (N.Y.C.). Home: Dallas TX Died July 1968.

MCFARLANE, CHARLES T., prof. geography; b. New Berlin, Chenango Co., N.Y., May 5, 1872; s. James and Martha (Tinker) M.; student Coll. City of New York; B.Pd., N.Y. State Normal Coll., 1893, D.Pd., 1903; M.Pd., Mich. State Normal Coll., 1901; U. of Vienna, Harvard Grad. Sch.; m. Lena Faxon Worden, of Ypsilanti, Mich., Dec. 24, 1895; children—David Eugene, James Worden. Prof. geography, Mich. State Normal Coll., Ypsilanti, 1893-1901; prin. N.Y. State Normal Sch., Brockport, N.Y., 1901-10; controller, 1910-27, prof. geography, 1913-27, Teachers Coll. (Columbia); treas. and comptroller Fred F. French Co., N.Y. City. Home: Ashford Av., Dobbs Ferry NY‡

MCFAYDEN, DONALD, educator, clergyman; b. Owen Sound, Ont., Can., March 26, 1876; s. Charles and Mary Ann (Kennedy) M.; B.A., U. of Toronto, 1896; M.A., Harvard, 1901; Harvard Div. Sch., 1901-02; S.T.B., Andover Theol. Sem., 1904; U. of Marburg, Germany, 1904-05, U. of Cambridge, Eng., 1905-06; Ph.D., Chicago, 1917; m. Edith Tyer, 1908; 1 dau., Mary Catherine. Came to U.S., 1900, naturalized citizen, 1917. Deacon, 1904, priest, 1905, Church of Eng.; curate, Bishop Monkton, Leeds, Eng., 1904, Godmanchester, Huntingdon, Eng., 1905-08; rector Grace P.E. Ch., Amherst, Mass., 1908-11; instr. ancient and Bible history, U. of Colo., 1911-19; asst. prof. history, U. of Neb., 1919-22; prof. history, Washington, U., St. Louis, 1922-44. Professor Emeritus, 1944. Author: History of the Title Imperator under the Roman Empire, 1920; Understanding the Apostles' Creed, 1927. Editor of chapter on Greek History in Am. Hist. Assn. Guide to Historical Literature. Republican. Home: 125 N. Hanley Rd., Clayton 5 MO‡

MCFETRIDGE, WILLIAM LANE, labor union exec.; b. Chgo., Nov. 28, 1893; s. William F. and Wilhelmina (Quesse) McF.; ed. pub. schs.; LL.D. (hon.), St. Joseph's College, 1963; m. Barbara A. Werner, Oct. 22, 1923; 1 dau., Dorothy (Mrs. Theodore A. Krueger). Mem. Bldg. Service Employees Internat. Union, 1923-69, v.p., 1926-40, pres., 1940-60, pres. local 46, 1927-48; pres. Chgo. Flat Janitors Union, 1937-69; organized Chgo. Met. Area Joint Council No. 1, Bldg. Service Employees Internat. Union, 1941; v.p. Ill. Fedn. Labor, 1939-50; v.p. AFL, 1950-69; v.p., mem. exec. council and coms. AFL-CIO, 1950-69; AFL cons. Internat. Labor Orgn. Conf., Geneva, 1949; del. Internat. Confedn. Free Trade Unions, Mexico City, 1951. Mem. Chgo. Police Bd., 1960-—; pres. Marina City Bldg. Corp.; Mem. Ill. Mediation and Conciliation Dept., 1929-41; dir. salvage Chgo. Met. Area, World War II; commr. Chgo. Park Dist., 1945-69, v.p., 1946-69; mem. Ill. Pub. Bldg. Commn., 1956-69; mem. Rail Terminal Authority, Chgo., 1957-69; chmn. Citizens Com. for a Cleaner Chgo., 1955; mem. fiscal adv. commn. Chgo. Bd. Edn., 1957. Active Am. Heart Assn., Nat. Conf. Christians and Jews, Parents Assn. for Cerebral Palsy Children, Urban League, Israel Bond Com. Recipient certificate for good citizenship and civic mindedness, Am. Legion, 1950; named asso. Northwestern U., 1951; selected one of Chgo.'s one hundred outstanding citizens, 1957; recipient Green-Murray award Frat. Order Eagles, 1958; award of merit, Dept. of Labor, 1960; Daniel H. Burnham award, Roosevelt U., 1962; honorary fellow Bar-Ilan University, Israel, 1962. Home: Chicago IL Died Mar. 15, 1969.

MCGAHAN, PAUL JAMES, newspaperman; b. Phila., Pa., Dec. 2, 1888; s. John Paul and Katherine Cecelia (Burke) McG.; ed. pub. schs.; unmarried. Began as office boy Phila. Press, 1904, reporter, 1905-09; news editor Coatesville (Pa.) Record, 1909-10; asst. city editor Phila. Press, 1910-12; with Phila. Inquirer, 1912-62, author weekly agrl. column, Sunday edition, 1954-62; with Washington Bureau since 1920, chief of bureau, 1930-37. Served as pvt. and 1st lt., inf., U.S. Army, 1917-18; commd. in O.R.S., 1919; mem. War Dept. Gen. Staff, May-Sept. 1925; in active service, major, inf., March 1942; assigned as dep. pub. relations officer Hdqrs. 3d Service Command, Baltimore, Md.; promoted lt. col., Sept. 1942, col., Oct. 1946; public relations officer 3d Serv. Command and Hdqrs. 2 Army; disch. Dec. 1946; ret. as Col. A.U.S., 1949 after 31 years service. Dept. commander District of Columbia American Legion, 1923-24; member national executive committee American Legion, 1924-30 and 1936-42; national historian Forty and Eight, 1920-37; state comdr. D.C. Mil. Order of World War, 1929; comdr. D.C. Comdry. Mil. Order Foreign Wars, 1932. Mem. President Hoover's Inaugural Com. 1929; accompanied President Hoover on trip to Virgin Islands and Puerto Rico, 1931; mem. (sec. 1935-36) Standing Com. of Corrs. controlling Press Galleries of 74th to 76th Congresses, 1935-41; mem. President Roosevelt's Inaugural Committees, 1937, 1941. In charge of assignment of press seats and arrangements at Rep. and Dem. nat. convs., 1936, 40. Mem. bd. management, Temp. Home ex-Union Soldiers, Sailors and Marines (G.A.R.), since 1924. Awarded Army Commendation Ribbon with three oakleaf clusters. Hon. mem. United Spanish War Vets., Vets. of Foreign War; member Phi Upsilon Rho Fraternity, Sigma Delta Chi Fraternity. Republican. Roman Catholic. Clubs: Army and Navy, Overseas Writers, Nat. Press (Washington); Pen and Pencil (Philadelphia). Home: Philadelphia PA Died Sept. 7, 1972.

MCGANN, MARION EUDORA HOTCHKISS (MRS. JAMES MCGANN), artist; b. Providence; d. Arthur B. and Marion (Otis) Hotchkiss; student R.I. Sch. Design, 1924-26, Queens Coll., 1950-53, Art Students League Manhattan, 1959-61; studied with Leslie Fleigel, 1957-66; m. James A. McGann, Apr. 27, 1932; children—John A., James R., Dorothy (Mrs. Rayman O. Bowen). Exhibited one man shows Attleboro (Massachusetts) Savings Bank, 1958, Leslie Fleigel Gallery, Kew Gardens, L.I., 1963; exhibited group shows R.I. Sch. Design, Providence, 1924, Art Students League, N.Y.C., 1959, Art League L.I., 1958-67, Macy's Dept. Store, B. Altman's, 1958-66, Suffolk (L.I.) Mus., 1961, Gertz Dept. Stores, Jamaica, N.Y., 1950-60, Roosevelt Raceway, L.I., 1964, aboard S.S. France, Manhattan, 1964, fine arts collection Smithsonian Instn., Washington, 1966. Recipient Colt Meml. award R.I. Sch. Design, 1924; 1st prize Nat. Glamorine contest Nassau County Region, 1964; Grumbacher award, 1964; 1st prize, gold plaque Nat. League Am. Pen Women, Nassau County Ann. Juried Exhibit, 1967. Mem. Art Students League, Nat. League Am. Pen Women, Art League L.I., Suburban Art League L.I. Home: Williston-Park NY Died Feb. 17, 1969; buried of Holy Rood Westbury NY

MCGARRY, WILLIAM RUTLEDGE, foreign trade counsel; b. N.Y. City, Apr. 29, 1872; s. James Adams and Catherine (Rutledge) M.; U. of Minn., 1889-93, later studied at U. of Paris, and in France, Germany, Russia, Asia Minor and Far East; m. Margaret Hoche Doscher, of London, Eng., 1894 (died 1906); children—James Giles (dec.), Ruth Elaine (Mrs. William C. Tesche), Mark Rutledge; m. 2d, Emily Graves, of Los Angeles, Calif., 1919. Ry. service until 1904; pres. Chetlo Harbor (Wash.) Packing Co., 1906-10; chmn. bd. Federal Gas Co., Mackie Steel Tube Works, 1905-07; traveled widely abroad in interest of Am. foreign trade, touring world, 1922-24, making survey of polit. and economic possibilities of principal commercial nations; active in promotion of interest in Nicaraguan and Panama Canal projects, deepening of rivers and harbors, Am. merchant marine, Cape Cod Ship Canal, development of Gogebic and Messaba iron fields. Drafted plan for stabilizing finances in Nicaragua, first plan for selection of U.S. senator by popular vote, in Ore.; counsel in case of Hibbard vs. Belding, controversy over boundary line between N.C. and Tenn., etc. Mem. Am. Bar Assn., Pan Pacific Union, Am. Asiatic Assn., Japan Soc., Latin Am. Assn., Foreign Legion, etc. Mason, K.P., Red Man, Woodman. Clubs: Commercial, Foreign Trade. Author: From Berlin to Bagdad, 1914; Rescuing the Czar, 1919. Contbr. numerous articles on foreign trade to mags.*‡

MCGAURAN, JOHN BAPTIST, surveyor gen.; b. Dubuque Co., Ia., Jan. 19, 1872; s. Thomas and Emily (Fitz Gerald) M.; ed. pub. schs., and Coll. of Sacred Heart, Denver; unmarried. Editor The Denver Catholic Register, 1908-10; deputy city auditor, 1900-1; elected supervisor, City and County of Denver, on Citizens' ticket, defeating Dem. and Rep. opponents, May 17, 1909, pres. of bd., 1912-13; U.S. surveyor gen. for Colo., since June, 1914. Mem. exec. bd. Colo. Direct Legislation League; v.-p. Colo. Single Tax Assn. Mem. Reconstruction Com. for Colo. of Nat. Catholic War Council. Home: 2064 Emerson St. Office: Post Office Bldg., Denver CO‡

MCGAVIN, CHARLES, ex-congressman; b. Riverton, Sangamon Co., Ill., Jan. 10. 1874; s. James and Mary Ann (Farley) M.; ed. pub. schs. of Springfield and Mt. Olive (Ill.) High Sch.; m. at Newark, N.J., Mabel E. Talty, of Washington, June, 1909. Admitted to bar, 1897; in practice at Chicago since 1899. Candidate for alderman, 18th Ward, 1903; asst. city atty., July, 1903; mem. 59th and 60th Congresses (1905-9), 8th Ill. Dist.; Republican. Presbyn. Home: 3329 Washington Boul. Office: 1031 Unity Bldg., Chicago‡

MCGAVRAN, EDWARD G(RAFTON), pub. health adminstr.; b. Pachmari, C.P., India (parents U.S. citizens), May 14, 1902; s. John Grafton and Helen (Anderson) McG.; A.B., Butler U., 1924, D.Sc., 1955; M.D., Harvard U., 1928, M.P.H., 1935; m. Mary Graydon Payne, Oct. 26, 1927; children—Edward G., Jr., Merrill P., Mary Katharine. Interne Rochester Gen. Hosp., 1928-29; teaching fellow, Harvard Medical Sch., 1926-28; med. research, Rockefeller Foundn., Egypt, 1927; gen. practice med., Sidel, Ill., 1929-33; county health officer, Hillsdale, Mich., 1934-39; dir. health, W. K. Kellogg Found., 1934-39; survey and study health conditions sugar industry in Hawaii, 1939-40; dir. W.Va. Pub. Health Training Center, Monongalia County Health Dept., Morgantown, W.Va., 1940-41; health commr., St. Louis County, Mo., 1941-46. Asso. prof. pub. health, Washington U. Med. Sch., 1941-43; Assn. Am. Medical Colls., tropical disease studies, Central Am., 1943; prof. pub. health, Washington U. Med. Sch., 1943-46; acting head dept. pub. health and preventive med., 1943-45; prof. pub. health and preventive med., head dept., U. of Kan. Sch. Med., 1946-47; prof. epidemiology, dean sch. pub. health, U. of N.C., 1947-63, professor emeritus, 1963, prof. continued edn. dept., 1969-72; consultant to the Ford Foundation and Indian government, 1963-69; national cons. to surgeon gen. USAF, 1963. Consultant, WHO Expert Com. on Edn. Med. and Auxiliary Personnel, Geneva, Switzerland, summer 1952; -Catedratico Honororio, hon. chair san. engring. National Univ. Engring., Lima, Peru, 1957. Formerly member board Civilian Defense Council for St. Louis County; chmn. med. service com. and health com., incident officer, Civilian Service Corps.; local and area War Priority Bd. Pres. N.C. Health Council, 1954-55, exec. com., 1955-—; mem. cancer control com. Nat. Insts. Health. Diplomate Am. Bd. Preventive Med. and Pub. Health. Fellow Am. Pub. Health Assn.; mem. A.M.A., N.C. Public Health Assn. (pres. 1956-57), N.C. Acad. Pub. Health (pres. 1953), Elisha Mitchell Sci. Soc., Tau Kappa Alpha, Delta Omega (nat. pres. 1955). Chmn. editorial bd. Public Health Reports, 1952-59. Home: Chapel Hill NC Died Aug. 29, 1972; buried Chapel Hill NC

MCGAW, ALEX JAMES, civil engr.; b. Belfast, Ireland, Mar. 2, 1909; s. Robert and Mina (McClue) McG.; came to U.S., 1912, naturalized, 1938; A.B., U. Wyo., 1933, B.S. with honor, 1934, C.E., 1937; m. Margaret Hopkins, Dec. 20, 1931; children—Jo Ann, Michael Robert, Nancy Kathleen. Asst. combustion engr. Standard Oil Co., Ind., Aruba, N.W.I., 1929-31; structural engr. Standard Oil Co., N.J., Aruba, N.W.I., 1934; spl. engr. Wyo. State Engrs. Office, 1935; mem. faculty U. Wyo. since 1935, prof. civil engring. since 1943, head dept. civil and archtl. engring. since 1948, acting dean, grad. sch., 1949, coll. engring., 1952, dean of engineering, since 1964-—; city engineer, City of Laramie, Wyo., 1940, 41; head structural design Toltz, King & Day, engrs., architects, air base, Casper, Wyo., 1942; cons. engr., 1940-—. Trustee Ivinson Memorial Hospital. Fellow A.A.A.S., Am. Soc. C.E. (president Wyoming sect. 1940); Wyo. Engring. Society (pres. 1955), Wyo. Reclamation Soc., Laramie Zoning Commn. (chmn. 1941-46), Bldg. Code Com. (chmn.), Am. Soc. Testing Materials (mem. Rocky Mountain council 1958-60), Am. Soc. Engring. Edn. (chmn. archtl. engring. div. 1957, member general council 1958-60), Nat. Soc. Profl. Engrs. (dir.), Laramie Planning Bd. (sec. 1943-45), Laramie C. of C. (dir. 1941-43), Sigma Xi, Sigma Tau, Sigma Alpha Epsilon. Republican. Episcopalian. Clubs: Laramie Country (pres. 1948), Rotary. Home: Laramie WY

MCGEEVER, JOHN F., educator; born at Homestead, Pa., December 29, 1912; s. Thomas Joseph and Anna (Dunlap) McG.; B.S., Duquesne U., 1933, M.A., 1940; Ed.D., Columbia 1959; m. Margaret Elizabeth Cook, Oct. 8, 1943; one daughter, Kelly Ann. Began career with chem. social studies dept., coach Linesville (Pa.) High Sch., 1934-39; supervising prin. Linesville Sch. Dist., 1939-40; basketball coach Allegheny Coll., Meadville, Pa., 1941-42; athletic dir. Linesville-Conneaut-Summit Sch. Dist., 1946-51; dir. Linesville Community Recreation Program, 1948-54; jr. occupational co-ordinator Miami Springs Jr. High Sch., Miami, Fla., 1955-57; dir. guidance Riviera Jr. High Sch., Miami, 1957-60; prof. edn. Western Carolina Coll., Cullowhee, N.C., 1961-63; dean student personnel Palomar Coll., San Marcos, Cal., 1963-65; prof. edn., chmn. edn. dept. University of San Diego, Call. for Men, 1965-69. Served with AUS, 1942-46. Mem. Am. Assn. Sch. Adminstrs., N.E.A., Am. Personnel and Guidance Assn., Council Exceptional Children, Nat. Vocational and Rehab. Council, Nat. Council Family Relations, Am. Assn. U. Profs., Phi Delta Kappa, Kappa Delta Pi. Author: Curriculum Guide for the Educable Mentally Retarded, 1965. Contbr. articles to profl. publs. Home: San Diego CA Died Jan. 10, 1969.

MCGEHEE, HARVEY, judge; b. Little Springs, Miss., June 11, 1887; s. John Hiram and Alice (Ford) M.; Ph.B., Mississippi Coll., Clinton, Miss., 1908; student U. of Miss. Law Sch., 1908-09; m. Willie-Belle Brinson, Apr. 18, 1916; children—Billy, Helen. Admitted to Miss. bar, 1909; county prosecuting atty., 1909-10; mem. State Senate, 1916-20; chancery judge, 1926-28; circuit judge, 1933-37; justice and chief justice Miss. Supreme Court, from 1937. Baptist. Mason, K.P. Club: Kiwanis (Jackson, Miss.). Address: Jackson MS Died Nov. 1965.

MCGILL, RALPH EMERSON, pub.; b. Soddy, Tenn., Feb. 5, 1898; s. Benjamin Franklin and Lou (Skillern) McG.; ed. McCallie Prep. Sch., Chattanooga, Tenn., 1913-17; student Vanderbilt U., 1917, 1919-22; LL.D., U. Miami, 1959, Colby Coll., 1960, Mercer U., 1961, Harvard U., 1961, Morehouse College, 1962. St. Bernard Coll., 1963, Wayne State U., 1963, Atlanta U., 1965; L.H.D., Brandeis U., 1963, Kenyon Coll., 1964, Tufts U., 1965, Ohio No. U., 1967; Litt.D., Notre Dame U., 1963, Oberlin Coll., 1963, Columbia, 1963 Emory U., 1963, Brown U., 1964, DePaul U., 1965, Temple U., 1967; m. Mary Leonard, Sept. 4, 1929 (dec. March 1962); children—Elizabeth (dec.), Virginia (dec.), Ralph E.; m. Mary Lynn Morgan, Apr. 20, 1967. Reporter, sports editor, The Banner, Nashville, Tenn., 1922-28; sports editor The Constitution, Atlanta, Ga., 1929-38, exec. editor, 1938-42, editor, 1942-60, pub., 1960-69. Dir. Fund for the Advancement of Edn.; trustee Carnegie Endowment for Internat. Peace, hon. mem., 1968-69. Served with USMC, 1918-19. Awarded Rosewald fellowship, 1937-38, for travel in Europe; Pulitzer prize for editorial writing, 1958, Presidential Medal of Freedom, 1964. Member of the Sigma Chi. Episcopalian. Author: The South and the Southerner (Atlantic nonfiction prize $5000), 1963. Home: Atlanta GA Died Feb. 3, 1969; buried Westview Cemetery, Atlanta GA

MCGILL, STEPHENSON WATERS, Christian education; b. Louisville, Ky., Nov. 24, 1870; s. David Thomas and Harriet (Waters) McG.; ed. Sheldon Sch. of Business, Y.M.C.A. Coll., Chicago, and Lake Geneva, Scofield Bible Sch., Chicago; student Presbyn. Theol. Sch., Louisville, Ky., 1895-97; Th.D., Vanderbilt, 1910; D.D., Southwestern U., 1922, Centre Coll., Ky., 1923; m. Frances Phillips Wilson, of Louisville, Feb. 16, 1899; children—Anne Kendrick, Stephenson Waters. Traveling salesman for machinery, 7 yrs.; ordained Ministry Presbyn. Ch. in U.S., 1898; Y.M.C.A. local sec., 8 yrs., state sec., Tenn., 12 yrs.; taught business management, social service and sociology, public speaking, evangelism and English Bible, summers; gen. field supt., religious work, A.E.F., and press corr. in France and Germany, 1918, 19; field sec. Southern Presbyterian Church, 1919-22. Trustee Y.M.C.A. Coll., 1910-15; mem. Tenn. State Bd. Charities and Corrections, 1908-14. Democrat. Mason (32 deg.). Clubs: Quest, Commercial. Author: Financing Religious Programs, 1926; Prolonging Personality, 1931. Editor: Better Nashville, 1906-18; Presbyterian Viewpoint, 1919-22. Assisted in raising $50,000,000 for edn. and philanthropy. Home: 3212 Indiana Av. Office: Lincoln Tower, Ft Wayne IN‡

MCGINNIS, PATRICK BENEDICT, r.r. executive; b. Palmyra, N.Y., May 23, 1904; s. Patrick and Ann (Mulgannon) McG.; B.S., St. Lawrence U., 1926; student N.Y.U., 1926-29, Bklyn. Law Sch., 1935, Columbia University, 1929-31; married Lucile Whitney, Aug. 4, 1930; children—Patrick Benedict, Carol Iveagh (Mrs. Edward McGrath). Manager of railroad bond dept. Lehman Bros., 1930-31; with Pflugfelder, Bampton & Rust, mems. N.Y. Stock Exchange, 1937-46, partner, 1943-46; sr. partner McGinnis, Bampton & Sellger, mems. N.Y. Stock Exchange, 1946-48, McGinnis & Co., 1949-56; president, chmn. bd. John L. Roper Lumber Co., McGinnis Indsl. Center; dir., chmn. bd. Norfolk So. Ry. Co., 1947-52; pres., dir. N.Y. N.H.&H. R.R. Co., 1954-56; president Boston and Maine R.R., 1956-62, chmn. board, 1962-73; cons. Highway Trailer Industries, Incorporated, New York; director subsidiaries Norfolk So. Bus. Company; expert I.C.C. and U.S. Dist. courts in formulating most of current plans of re-orgn. for Class I, R.R.; lectr. N.Y. Inst. Finance, 1940-73. Mem. bd. dirs. N.Y. Conv. and Visitors Bureau, Inc. Decorated Knight of Malta. Mem. Assn. Am. Railroads (dir.), N.Y. Soc. Security Analysts, Alpha Tau Omega. Roman Catholic. Clubs: Princess Anne Country (Virginia Beach, Va.); Seaview Country (Absecon, N.J.); New Haven Country, New Haven Lawn. Editor of bi-annual book Guide to Railroad Reorganization Securities. Home: Staten Island NY Died Feb. 20, 1973.

MCGOHEY, JOHN F. X., ret. U.S. judge for So. dist. of N.Y. Home: New York City NY Died July 7, 1972.

MCGOWN, CHESTER STOWE, educator; b. Lawrence, Mass., June 29, 1870; s. George H. and Mary Anne (Timmons) McG; grammar sch., high sch. and business training; grad. Y.M.C.A. Internat. Coll., 1895; m. Jennie Gertrude Miller, Dec. 29, 1897. Connected with Am. Internat. Coll. since 1910, president since Dec. 12, 1911. Mem. at large of Sch. Bd., Springfield. Mem. Springfield Chamber Commerce. Conglist. Mason. Rotarian.‡

MCGRANAHAN, RAYMOND DEPUE, business exec.; b. Harmonsburg, Pa., Mar. 8, 1914; s. Harry Raymond and Mabel P. (DePue) McG.; A.B., Allegheny Coll., 1938; M.B.A., Harvard, 1940; m. Elizabeth Warner, June 8, 1944; children—Christopher, Candace, Cynthia. With Nat. Refining Co., Cleve., 1940-41, Westinghouse Electric Corp., Pitts., 1941-47; dir. purchases Nuttall, constrn., radio and radar divs. Gulf Oil Corp., Pitts., 1948-60, dir. coordination, v.p., 1954-60, adminstrv. v.p., coordinator transportation, pres., dir. subsidiary cos. until 1960; pres. Wilshire Oil Co. of Cal., Los Angeles, 1960-63; exec. v.p., dir. Times-Mirror Co., 1963-65; pres. paper division Champion Papers, Inc., 1965-70, corporate vice pres., 1965-70; vice president, director Kuwait Tankers, Inc.; v.p. Project Five Pipe Line Corp.; dir., mem. exec. com. Curtis Publishing Company. Fgn. supply and transportation com. Petroleum Adminstrn. for Def.; mem. Mil. Petroleum Adv. Bd.; mem. com. on tanker requirements Nat. Petroleum Council. Mem. Pa., Pitts. C.'s of C., Am. Petroleum Inst. Clubs: Harvard - Yale - Princeton, Duquesne (Pitts.); Harvard (N.Y.C.). Home: CA Died Dec. 1970.

MCGRATH, SISTER MARY, psychologist, educator; b. Fitchburg, Mass., Aug. 24, 1896; d. Francis and Nora (Ryan) McGrath; A.B., U. Mich., 1918; M.A., U. Pitts., 1920; Ph.D., Catholic U. Am., 1922. Mem. Congregation of Sisters, Servants of Immaculate Heart of Mary, 1914-70; tchr. Pitts. pub. schs., 1918-19, Swissvale (Pa.) High Sch., 1919-20; faculty St. Mary Coll. and Acad., Monroe, Mich., 1922-27, Marygrove Coll., Detroit, 1927-70; conducted psychol. clinic, 1930-70, dir. preschool lab., 1942-70; cons. psychologist. Dir. social work relief effort Bishop's Polish Relief Program, 1941-45. Mem. Am., Am. Catholic, Mich., Detroit psychol. assns., Nat. Council Cath. Women, Mich. Assn. for Emotionally Disturbed Children. Home: Monroe MI Died Apr. 25, 1970; buried Monroe MI

MCGRATH, RAYMOND DYER, corp. exec.; b. Keokuk, Ia., Nov. 21, 1890; s. Thomas J. and Edith (Limback) McG.; B.S., U. of Wis., 1913; m. Anne Serre, June 4, 1931; children—Mary C., Anne D. Assistant treas. Continental Ins. Co., New York, 1922-24; mem. banking firm of Lazard Freres, New York, 1924-39. Dir. International Silver Co. Served as 1st lt. to maj., Ordnance Dept., 1917-19, World War I. Clubs: Racquet and Tennis, University (New York); Metropolitan (Washington). Home: Warrenton VA Died Apr. 8, 1971.

MCGRAW, JAMES H., JR., pub. and mfr.; b. Madison, N.J., May 9, 1893; s. James H. and Mildred (Whittlesey) McGraw; A.B., Princeton U., 1915; D.Eng., Rensselaer, 1945; D.C.S., N.Y.U., 1950; m. Lois Durand Scheerer; children—Mrs. Stanley A. Sweet, Jr., James H. III. Successively sec. treas., v.p. and treas., exec. v.p., McGraw-Hill Pub. Co., chmn. bd., 1935-50, pres., 1937-50; chmn. bd. and dir., McGraw Hill Book Co., pres. Internat. Corp., 1925-50; dir. McGraw-Hill Pub. Co., 1915-50; pres., chmn. bd. Old Town Corp., N.Y. Trustee Com. Econ. Development. Adv. bd. Chem. Warfare Service; mem. Nat. Adv. Council Jr. Achievement Inc.; mem. class endowment fund Princeton U. Alumni Assn. Mem. Army Ordnance Assn. (com. on endowment), Am. Soc. M.E., Am. Standards Assn. (adv. com.) Council on Foreign Relations, Am. Mus. of Natural History (men's com.), Am. Arbitration Assn. (dir.), Air Power League, Washington Assn. of N.J., Mem. Council on Fgn. Relations; mem. Bus. Council. Republican. Presbyn. Clubs: University, Links, Century Assn. (N.Y.); Metropolitan (Washington); Chicago; Everglades (Palm Beach). Home: New York City NY Died Feb. 20, 1970.

MCGREGOR, GORDON ROY, business exec.; b. Montreal, Que., Can., Sept. 26, 1901; s. Thomas Daniel and Florence May (Morris) McG.; student St. Andrew's Coll., Toronto, Can.; student McGill U., Montreal, LL.D.; m. Alexandra May Ramsay, June 29, 1928. With Bell Telephone Co., Montreal, 1923-39, with Trans-Can. Air Lines (name later changed to Air Canada), Montreal, 1945-68, general traffic mgr., 1946-48, pres. and dir., 1948-68; dir. Hawker Siddeley Can. Ltd., 1969-71; chmn., dir. Orenda Ltd., 1969-71. Board of management Montreal General Hospital. Served with R.C.A.F., overseas, demobilized as group capt., 1945. Decorated Order Brit. Empire, D.F.C., Croix de Guerre (France); Comdr. Order of Orange Nassau (Netherlands); War Cross (Czechoslovakia); companion Order of Can., comdr. brother Order St. John. Fellow of Royal Aeronautical Society (hon.), Canadian Aeronautics and Space Inst. (hon.); member Royal Canadian Air Force Assn. (grand pres. 1970), Air Force Vets. Assn. Mason (Scottish Rite). Presbyterian. Clubs: Mount Bruno, Forest and Stream Club (Montreal); Royal Ottawa Golf. Home: Montreal PQ Canada Died Mar. 8, 1971; buried Mt Royal Cemetery, Montreal Que Can

MCGREGOR, WILLIAM MORRELL, banker; b. Talladega, Ala., July 31, 1869; s. William Morrell and Emma (Cousins) M.; ed. pub. sch.; m. Kate Carter, of Palo Pinto, Tex., July 24, 1890; children—Lillian (Mrs. Lester T. Burns), Carter. Entered banking business with First Nat. Bank, Wichita Falls, Tex., 1888, now pres. Democrat. Episcopalian. Mason (Shriner), K.P. Clubs: Wichita, Knife and Fork, Wichita Falls Golf and Country, Lions. Home: 1310 10th St., Wichita Falls TX*‡

MCGREW, CLARENCE ALAN, newspaper editor; b. Camden, N.J., Mar. 20, 1875; s. Gifford H.G. and LaDelia (Chapman) McG.; A.B., Harvard, 1897; m. Helen Ried, Sept. 30, 1897. Reporter N.Y. Sun, 1897-1904; editorial staff N.Y. Times, 1904-06; editorial work Berkeley (Cal.) Independent and S.F. Bull., 1906-07; editor San Diego (Cal.) Sun, 1908-15; city editor San Diego Union, 1915-34, editor, 1933-51, editor emeritus since Jan. 1951. Home: 8397 Dexter Dr., La Mesa CA Office: care San Diego Union, San Diego 12 CA‡

MCGREW, HENRY EDWIN, coll. pres.; b. LeGrand, Marshall County, Ia., Mar. 4, 1868; s. David Davis and Alpha (Pearson) McG.; grad. LeGrand Friends Acad., 1887, Capital City Commercial Coll., Des Moines, 1890; B.S. Penn Coll., Oskaloosa, Ia., 1895, M.S., 1898; A.M., Haverford Coll., 1904; D.D., Whittier Coll., 1918; Litt.D., William Penn Coll., 1942; m. Edith B. Ware, Nov. 24, 1892 (died 1919); 1 dau., Marion Edwina; m. 2d, Frances W. Mitchell, July 28, 1921. Gen. sec. Y.M.C.A., Clinton, Ia., 1895-96; prin. Penn Acad., Oskaloosa, Ia., 1896-97; pastor and teacher, Earlham, Ia., 1897-1900; pres. Pacific Coll., Newberg, Ore., 1900-07; pastor First Friends Ch., Los Angeles, 1908-10, Whittier, Calif., 1910-18; pres. Penn Coll., Oskaloosa, Ia., 1918-28; pastor First Friends Ch., Pasadena, Calif., 1928-37; pres. William Penn Coll., 1937-42, emeritus. Mem. Pi Gamma Mu. Republican. Club: Rotary (Oskaloosa). Address: William Penn Coll., Oskaloosa IA and 2135 Navarro Av., Altadena CA‡

MCGREW, JOHN GILBERT, economist, educator; b. Charleston, W. Va., Sept. 14, 1910; s. Frank A. and Sadie (Safreed) McG.; A.B., W.Va. Inst. Tech., 1932; M.A., W.Va. U., 1937; Ph.D., U. Ill., 1941; m. Jessie Given, Dec. 25, 1934 (dec. Apr. 1963); 1 son, John Gilbert; m. 2d, Florence Lane, Sept. 1, 1966. Prof. econs. Concord Coll., 1941-45; prof., chmn. dept. econs. Cleveland State University, 1945-68, chairman dept. econs., 1965-68, also chmn. Bur. Bus. Research Sch. Bus. Adminstrn.; vis. lectr. Cleve. Coll., Western Res. U. Capt. local Community Fund, 1952-59; cubmaster Cleve. Council Boy Scouts Am., 1955-58, chmn. troop exec. com., 1962-68. Republican precinct committeeman, 1942-68. Mem. Am. Econ. Assn., Am. Assn. U. Profs., Tau Kappa Epsilon. Mason (Shriner). Author: History of Ripley, West Virginia, During the Civil War, 1939; Monetary and Banking Investigations in the United States and Great Britain Since 1900, 1941; Principles of Economics, 1954. Home: Bay Village OH Died June 7, 1968.

MCGUIGAN, HUGH (ALISTER), pharmacologist; b. Lisnoe, Lisburn, County Down, Ireland, Mar. 29, 1874; s. Bernard and Susanna (Alister) McG.; B.S., N.D. Agrl. Coll., 1898; student U. of Mich., 1901-02; Ph.D., U. of Chicago, 1906; M.D., Rush Med. Coll., Chicago, 1908; student U. of Heidelberg, 1908-09; m. Mabel Leininger, June 20, 1906. Asst. prof. chemistry, N.D. Agrl. Coll., 1902-03; asst. in biologic chemistry, U. of Chicago, 1903-06; asst. prof. pharmacology, Washington U., St. Louis, 1906-10; prof. pharmacology, Northwestern U. Med. Sch., Chicago, 1910-17; prof. pharmacology and therapeutics, U. of Ill. Coll. of Medicine, Chicago, 1917-42, professor emeritus since 1942. Fellow American College of Physicians, Internat. Coll. Anesthetists; mem. American Biochem. Soc., Am. Physiol. Soc., Society Pharmacology and Experimental Therapeutics, Inst. Medicine Chicago, Nu Sigma Nu Sigma Xi, Mason. Episcoplaian. Club: University (Chicago). Home: 2418 Park Place, Evanston IL‡

MCGUIGAN, JOSEPH J., lawyer; b. Wilkes-Barre, Pa., Mar. 17, 1876; s. Patrick Henry and Ellen (Gallaher) McG.; ed. pub. sch., Wilkes-Barre, Pa.; studied law with Martin, Thornton and Ward, Wilkes Barre, 1895-1898; m. Irene Pittman Gayle, Feb. 15, 1911; children—Edmund Gayle, Rose Agatha, Kathleen Mary. Served with 40th Regt. Vols., U.S. Army, in Philippines, 1899-1901; with Philippines Civil Service, Philippines, 1902-05; with Panama Canal Service since Jan. 1906 (except service as sanitary expert during occupation of Vera Cruz, Mexico, 1914); admitted to Luzerne Co., Pa. bar, 1898; asst. dist. atty., later dist. atty., Canal Zone, since 1921. Democrat. Catholic. Home: Balboa Heights. Office: Ancon CZ‡

MCGUIRE, MARTIN RAWSON PATRICK, univ. prof.; b. Whitinsville, Mass., Dec. 30, 1897; s. Martin and Mary Ann (Sheehan) McG.; A.B., Coll. of the Holy Cross, Worcester, Mass., 1921; A.M., Cath. Univ. of America, 1925, Ph.D., 1927, L.H.D., 1969; L.H.D., Coll of the Holy Cross, 1946; m. Florence Teresa Mattimore, Aug. 20, 1929; children—John Martin, Agnes Elizabeth, Helen Teresa, Patrick Andrew, James Harold, Florence Maureen and Joseph Francis. Teacher of Spanish, Latin, and history, Georgetown Prep. Sch., 1921-24; asst. in Greek and Latin, Cath. U. of Am., 1924-27, instr., 1927-34, asso. prof., 1934-36, professor since 1946, dean of the Graduate School of Arts and Sciences, 1937-48, prof. since 1948. Mem. President's Commn. on Higher Edn., July 1946-Dec. 1948. Served as 2d lt. Inf., U.S. Army, Sept. 1918 to April 1919; 2d lt. Inf. Res., 1919-24. Recipient Spellman award Cath. Theologian, 1968. Mem. U.S. Adv. Commn. on Ednl. Exchange, 1948-54; mem. Fulbright Bd. Fgn. Scholarships, 1947-54. Mem. Am. Cath. (pres. 1942), American historical associations, Renaissance Society of America, American Philol. Assn., Medieval Acad. of Am., Riccobono Seminar of Roman Law in Am. Asso. editor of The Catholic Historical Review. Co-editor: Patristic Studies, and Studies in Medieval and Renaissance Latin Language and Literature (Cath. U. of Am.); mem. editorial bd. Fathers of Church, A New Translation, 1946. Author: (with James M. Campbell) The Confessions of St. Augustine, Books I-IX (Selections), 1931; Introduction to Classical Scholarship: A Syllabus and Bibliographical Guide, published in 1958; Introduction to Mediaeval Latin Studies: A Syllabus and Bibliographic Guide, 1964. Sr. editor New Catholic Encyclopedia; president Corpus Instrumentorum. Translator: (with E. P. Arbez) Robert Tricot Guide to the Bible, Volume I, published 1951, Volume II, 1955, second revised edit., 1960. Editor: Teaching Latin in the Modern World, 1960. Mem. exec. com. Medieval and Renaissance Latin Translations and Commentaries. Home: Washington DC Died Mar. 15, 1969; buried Mt. Olivet Cemetery, Washington DC

MCHARG, ORMSBY, lawyer; b. Wauzeka, Wis., Apr. 11, 1871; s. John and Fanny (Ormsby) McH.; studied U. of Mich.; LL.B., U. of Mich., 1896; LL.M., Columbian (now George Washington) U., 1900, M.Dip., 1901, D.C.L., 1902; M. Grace Stevens, Nov. 15, 1900; 1 dau., Elizabeth. Practiced at Jamestown, N.D., 1896-99; mem. N.D. Ho. of Rep., 1899-1900; instr. public internat. law, in association with Justice Brewer of Supreme Court of U.S., and in administrative, pub. utility law, George Washington U., 1900-06; practiced at Seattle, Wash., 1906-07, N.Y. City, 1909-21; asst. to atty. gen. of U.S., 1907-08; resigned at request of President Roosevelt to assist in nomination of William H. Taft to the presidency, represented Taft interest in delegate contests at 1908 convention; general counsel Rep. Nat. Com., 1908 campaign; asst. sec. Dept. of Commerce and Labor, 1909. At request of friends of Col. Roosevelt, with his knowledge, organized campaign for his nomination for president, 1912; had charge of delegate contests at convention, June 1912, outcome of which caused Roosevelt to organize his separate party; remained regular Republican; now engaged in financing chemical research. Member Phi Delta Phi, Kappa Alpha (Southern). Presbyn. Address: 116 Norman Av., Brooklyn 22 NY‡

MCHATTIE, WILLIAM ALEXANDER, steel tubing co. exec.; b. Chgo., Sept. 30, 1902; s. William Alexander and Louise (Jewel) McH.; grad. Northwestern Mil. and Naval Acad., Lake Geneva, Wis., 1920; m. Nancy McMunn, Apr. 10, 1930; children—Janet (Mrs. Carl E. Pfeiffer), William Northrop. With Michigan Seamless Tube Co. South Lyon, Mich., 1933-72, chief exec. officer, chmn. bd., dir. pres. Gulf States Tube Corp., Rosenberg, Tex., 1956-72, also dir. chmn. bd. Standard Tube Co., Detroit. Clubs: Oakland Hills Country (Birmingham, Mich.); Bloomfield Open Hunt (Bloomfield Hills, Mich.); Detroit Athletic; Lakeside Country, Houston (Houston). Home: Houston TX Died Aug. 27, 1972.

MCHENDRIE, ANDREW WATSON, lawyer; b. Bellevue, Ia., Jan. 6, 1874; s. Andrew Gregg and Eliza Jane (Kiskaddon) McH.; grad. Tillotson Acad., Trinidad, Colo., 1896; A.B., Colo. Coll., Colo. Springs, 1899; m. Frances E. Hamilton, Dec. 17, 1902; children—Janet Hamilton, Andrew Douglas. Admitted to Colo. bar, 1903; now mem. McHendrie, Burris & Pointer; began as legal stenographer, 1893; court reporter 3d Judicial District, Colo., 1899-1903; dist. atty. same, 1905-13; judge Dist. Court, 3d. Dist., 1913-19; gen. law practice since 1919. Trustee Colo. Coll. Mem. Am. Bar Assn., Colo. Bar Assn. (pres. 1930), Pueblo County Bar Assn., Phi Gamma Delta. Republican. Presbyterian. Mason (K.T.) Club: Pueblo Rotary. Address: 140 Marion Dr., Pueblo CO‡

MCHENRY, DONALD EDWARD, naturalist; b. Great Bend, Pa., Aug. 28, 1895; s. Edward James and Elizabeth Louise (Rooker) McH.; A.B., U. Wyo., 1928; M.A. (research fellow), U. Colo., 1929; m. Bona May Ford, July 14, 1928; children—Douglas Bruce, Donald Keith (dec.). Asst. prof. botany Okla. State U., 1929-32; jr. park naturalist Grand Canyon Nat. Park, 1932-36; park naturalist Nat. Capital Parks, Washington, 1936-47; chief park naturalist, Yosemite Nat. Park, 1947-56; ret. 1956; cons. natural history Saratoga (Cal.) Sch. Dist. and Santa Clara County Cal., Boy and Girl Scouts, also Campfire Girls. Sub-dean and dir. Santa Clara County Am. Guild Organists, 1957-70; v.p., dir. Saratoga Hist. Found., 1959-70; dir. Los Gatos Community Concert Assn., 1958-70; bd. San Jose Symphony, Los Gatos-Saratoga Symphony. Served to sgt. U.S. Army, 1914-17. Mem. A.A.A.S., Audubon Naturalist Soc. (hon. v.p.). Episcopalian. Lion (past pres., dir.). Author articles profl. jours. Address: Los Gatos CA Died Dec. Dec. 28, interment Grand Canyon.

MCHUGH, JAMES F. (JIMMY), composer; b. Boston, Mass., July 10, 1894; s. James Andrew and Julia Anne (Collins) McH.; student St. John's Prep. Sch.; also student Holy Cross College (Massachusetts); hon. Dr. Oratory, Staley Coll., Brookline, Mass., 1939; hon. Dr. of Music, Los Angeles College, Calif., 1941; 1 son, James Francis, Junior. Competed in Aviation Meet, Squanton, Mass., 1914; office boy Boston Opera House, 1914; pianist Irving Berlin Pub. Co., music pubs., N.Y. City, 1916; composer popular songs, scores for musical shows, motion pictures, etc., 1920-69. Served with Mass. Cavalry, 1917. Composer (popular songs) I Can't Give You Anything But Love, Baby"; I'm in the Mood for Love"; South American Way," for Carmen Miranda; Hiting a New High," for Lily Pons; Cuban Love Song," for Lawrence Tibbett; Youre a Sweetheart," for Alice Fay; for the Deanna Durbin pictures: My Own," I Love to Whistle," You're Pretty as a Picture," Black Birds of 1928;" Internat. Review for Gertrude Lawrence and Harry Richman; (songs) Exactly Like You," On the Sunny Side of the Street," Streets of Paris," 1938; (scores for motion pictures) My Dancing Lady, Dinner at Eight, That Certain Age, Mad About Music, Seven Days Leave, Happy Go Lucky, Hers to Hold, (Broadway musical songs) Strip for Action, 1956; also song hit of aviators of World War II, Comin' in on a Wing and a Prayer;" Say a Prayer for the Boys Over There," for Deanna Durbin; songs for Frank Sinatra's first picture, Higher and Higher," I Couldn't Sleep a Wink Last Night" and The Music Stopped," also 8th and 9th U.S. war bond official songs: Buy, Buy a Bond; We've Got Another Bond to Buy; (popular song) Hubba, Hubba, Hubba; song, It's A Most Unusual Day, for picture, A Date With Judy; songs for Broadway musical show I Must Have That Man, Winter Garden Theatre, 1948, Home Before Dark for Jean Simmons film of same name, 1958, U.S. Navy recruiting song The Navy Swings (spl. citation), Reach for Tomorrow for Ella Fitzgerald film Let No Man Write My Epitaph, Where the Hot Wind Blows for Gina Lollobrigida, First Lady Waltz for Mrs. John F. Kennedy; other songs include, Don't Blame Me, I Feel a Song Comin' On, When My Sugar Walks Down the Street, Lost in a Fog, Let's Get Lost, Can't Get Out of this Mood, I'm Shooting High, Lovely Lady, Diga, Diga, Doo, Where Are You?, With All My Heart, There's Something in the Air, Where the Lazy River Goes, With a Banjo on My Knee, You've Got Me this Way, I'd Know You Anywhere, The Bad Humor Man, Something for the Boys, Nob Hill, Doll Face, I Wish We Didn't Have to Say Goodnight, I'm in the Middle of Nowhere, I Walked in with My Eyes Wide Open, Hubba, Hubba, Hubba, Here Comes Heaven Again; scores for Smash-Up, Hit Parade of 1947, Calendar Girl, If You Knew Susie, His Kind of Woman; appeared on numerous TV shows including Patti Page, Perry Como, Ed Sullivan, Arthur Murray, Kate Smith; Hollywood Bowl Concert, 1959, 62, Pasadena Symphony Concert, 1960, Seattle World's Fair, 1962, A.S.C.A.P. Concert, Lincoln Center, N.Y.C.; TV spectaculars. Chmn. Beverly Hills A.R.C., 1959-60, Founder, president Jimmy McHugh Polio Found., Jimmy McHugh Charities, Incorporated. Member A.S.C.A.P. (vice president, dir.), Beverly Hills C. of C. (past president, director), The Amateur Athletic Union of the United States (life mem.). Recipient Presdl. Citation Certificate of Merit, 1947; Man of Year award 1955; Ct. of Honor award Am. Legion, 1960. Command performance before Queen of England and Duke of Edinburgh, 1951, also citations and plaques from Los Angeles City Council. Address: Beverly Hills CA Died May 23, 1969; buried Calvary Cemetery and Mausoleum, Los Angeles CA

MCINERNEY, JAMES LAWRENCE, mfg. exec.; b. Elmira, N.Y., Jan. 17, 1888; s. Charles A. and Nellie (Coppenger) McI.; student pub. schs., Elmira and Leonardsville, New York, Doctor of Laws, Aquinas College, 1962; m. Kathryn M. Kellar, July 2, 1913; children—Catherine R. (Mrs. Robert N. Alt), James M., William K. Clk. Gen. Store, Leonardsville, 1903-09; clerk, department manager Sears, Roebuck & Co., Chgo., 1909-25; pres. Nat. Spring & Wire Co., Grand Rapids, Mich., 1925-31; pres. McInerney Spring & Wire Co., Grand Rapids, Michigan, 1931-53, chmn., 1953-68. Dir. Grand Rapids Hosp. Council, St. Mary's Hosp., St. John's Orphan's Home. Republican. Roman Catholic. K.C., Knight Comdr. St. Gregory. Clubs: Peninsular, Blythefield Country (Grand Rapids). Home: Grand Rapids MI Died Jan. 29, 1968.

MCINNIS, CHARLES BALLARD, lawyer; b. Repton, Ala., Dec. 27, 1899; s. John Edward and Louie (Ballard) McI.; grad. Pace Inst. Accounting (now Benjamin Franklin U.), 1921; LL.B., George Washington U., 1924, A.B., 1927; m. Ruby Lucille Kidd, June 26, 1928; children—Elizabeth Ann (Mrs. Randolph Maury Browne III), Jean Ballard (Mrs. Paul Nicolai). Admitted to Ala. and District of Columbia bars, 1924, N.Y. bar, 1927, Maryland bar, 1960; practiced in Washington and N.Y. City since 1926; auditor and atty. U.S. Bur. Internal Revenue, 1920-25; asso. Holmes, Paul & Havens, N.Y. City, 1926-30; partner and Washington mgr. Olcott, Holmes, Glass, Paul & Havens and Olcott, Paul, & Havens, 1930-36, sr. partner Roberts & McInnis, Washington, 1936-65, McInnis, Wilson, Munson and Woods, 1965-69, McInnis, Munson, Muzzall & Tansill, 1969-70; v.p., sec., dir. Big Horn-Powder River Corp., Denver; dir. Pulitzer Pub. Co., St. Louis, KVOA Television, Inc., Tucson, KOAT Television, Inc., Albuquerque, Magness Petroleum Corp., Oklahoma City. Trustee Eastern Baptist Theological Seminary, Eastern Baptist College, Phila. Trustee, treas. D.C. Baptist Convention Foundation. Treasurer of the board of trustees of Bapt. Home, Washington. Fellow Internat. Acad. Trial Lawyers; mem. Am., D.C. bar assns., National Tax Assn., Knights of the Round Table, Civil War Round Table, Washington Board of Trade, Sigma Phi Epsilon, Phi Alpha Delta. Baptist (trustee). Mason. Club: Congressional Country (Washington). Collaborator: Law of Fed. Income Taxation (with Randolph E. Paul and Jacob Mertens, Jr.), 1934, rev. edit. (with Jacob Mertens, Jr.), 1942; also articles on fed. taxation in legal publs. Home: Bethesda MD Died Aug. 11, 1970; buried Repton AL

MCINTIRE, WALTER OSCAR, prof. philosophy; b. Manchester, O., July 4, 1875; s. Andrew James and Sarah Jane (Davis) McI; A.B., Coll. of Wooster, 1898; grad. McCormick Theol. Sem., 1901; A.M., Johns Hopkins, 1909; Ph.D., Harvard, 1914; L.H.D. Wheaton Coll., 1941; m. Rebecca Elizabeth Berry, Feb. 29, 1904; children—Raymond Andrew, David Prigmore. Ordained Presbyn. ministry, 1901; missionary and teacher, Silliman Inst., Dumaguete, P.I., 1901-11; asst. in philosophy, Harvard, 1912-14; prof. philosophy, Wheaton Coll., Norton, Mass., 1914-41, prof. emeritus since 1941. Mem. Am. Philos. Assn., Phi Beta Kappa, Alpha Tau Omega. Republican. Presbyterian. Home: R.D. 1, Middleboro MA‡

MCINTOSH, CHARLES HERBERT, lawyer; b. Elko, Nev., Aug. 9, 1875; s. John Albert and Mary Hathaway (Munson) McI.; prep. edn., high sch., Berkeley, Calif., student Hastings Coll. of Law (U. of Calif.); m. Pearl Marie Hunt, of Berkeley, 1900; children—Phyllis Merrill, John Hunt, Harriet Heywood, Mary Hathaway; m. 2d, Sadie Evelyn Archibald, of Reno, Nev., June 8, 1921. Admitted to Nev. bar, 1901, and began practice in Humboldt Co.; mem. firm McIntosh & Cooke, Tonopah, 1907-13; practiced alone at Reno, 1913-23; has successfully handled many grub stake" and apex" mining suits; dir. and counsel Venezuela Gold, Inc., Little Rock Power &Water Co., Belmont Engels Copper Co., Granite Power & Light Co., etc. Formerly sergt. Co. E, Nev. N.G. Sec. Nev. State Senate, 1903-05; dem. primary candidate for U.S. Senate, 1910, 26; chmn. Dem. State Central Com., 1912. Mem. Am., Nev. State and Calif. State bar assns. Episcopalian. K.P., Elk. Home: Santa Monica, Calif. Office: Rowan Bldg., Los Angeles CA‡

MCINTYRE, ROBSON DUNCAN, univ. prof.; b. Wilmington, Ill., Mar. 11, 1899; s. Daniel J. and Mary R. (Robson) McI.; B.S., U. of Ill., 1921, M.S., 1923; grad. work U. of Ill., 1921-23, Northwestern, 1927, N.Y. Univ., 1937-38. Instr. in commerce, U. of Ill., 1921-23; salesman Marshall Field & Co., Chicago, 1923-25; prof. marketing, Coll. of Commerce, U. of Ky., since 1925. Served as pvt., Inf., U.S. Army, 1918-19; major, A.A.F., 1942-46; chief of information and edn. sect., Santa Ana Army Air Base. Recipient Army Commendation ribbon, 1946. Mem. Am. Marketing Assn., Am. Assn. Univ. Profs., Community Concert Assn. of Central Ky. (pres. 1934-71), Omicron Delta Kappa (nat. treas.), Beta Gamma Sigma, Delta Sigma Pi, Alpha Delta Sigma. Republican. Presbyterian. Club: Optimist. Home: Lexington KY Died Feb. 26, 1971; buried Lexington Cemetery, Lexington KY

MCKAY, CLAUDE, author Selected Poems; The Dialect Poetry of Claude McKay; Home to Harlem; Gingertown; Banjo; A Long Way from Home; Harlem: Negro Metropolis; Banana Bottom; The Passion of Claude McKay. Address: New York City NY Died May 22, 1948; buried Calvary Cemetery, Woodside NY

MCKAY, DAVID O., church official; b. Huntsville, Utah, Sept. 8, 1873; s. David and Jennette (Evans) McK.; student U. of Utah, 1894-97, Litt.D. (honorary), 1951; hon. M.A., Brigham Young U., 1922, H.H.D. (honorary), 1951; LL.D. (honorary), Utah State Agrl. Coll., 1950; Litt.D. (hon.), Temple University, 1951; Doctor of Humanities, Weber State Coll., 1965; m. to Emma Ray Riggs, January 2, 1901; children—David Lawrence, Llewelyn Riggs, Royle Riggs (dec.), Lou Jean (wife of Dr. Russell H. Blood), Emma Rae (Mrs. Conway Ashton), Edward Riggs, Robert Riggs. Pres. Scottish Conf. of Church of Jesus Christ of Latter-Day Saints, Mar. 1898-Aug. 1899; 2d asst. supt. Weber Stake Sunday Schs., 1899-1906; prin. Weber Coll., Ogden, Utah, 1902-08; mem. Deseret Sunday Sch. Gen. Bd. Ch. Jesus Christ of Latter-Day Saints, 1906-18; 2d asst. gen. supt. Church-wide Sunday Schools, 1906-09; 1st asst. gen. supt. Church-wide Sunday Schs., 1909-18, gen. supt., 1918-34; mem. Council of the Twelve Apostles, 1906-34; 2d counselor in 1st Presidency of Church of Jesus Christ of Latter-Day Saints, 1934-51, pres., 1951-70; pres. Council Twelve Apostles, 1950-51. President European Missions of Church, 1922-24; commr. of Church Schs., 1917-22; mem. Church Bd. of Edn. since 1906; regent U. of Utah, 1919-22; mem. bd. trustees Utah State Agrl. Coll., 1940-41; president bd. trustees, Brigham Young U. Pres., dir. Zion's Securities Corp.; chairman bd. Hotel Utah, Beneficial Life Ins. Co., Zion's Coop. Mercantile Instn., Utah-Ida. Sugar Co., also chmn. Radio Service Corporation of Utah. Pres. Ogden Betterment League, Ogden, Utah, 1914-17; mem. Red. Cross exec. bd. of Weber County, Utah, 1915; appointed chairman of the Utah Council for Child Health and Protection, 1932; chairman of the Utah Centennial Commission, 1938-47; chmn. Utah State Advisory Com. of Am. Red Cross, Jan. 1942-May 1943; hon. mem. nat. council Boy Scouts of America. Awarded Silver Buffalo; Nat. Council Boy Scouts Am., 1953, Silver Beaver award Great Salt Lake Council, 1956; Cross of Comdr. Royal Order Phoenix (Hellenes), 1954; Golden Medall of Greek Archdiocese of N. and S.A., 1955, Distinguished Leadership award Nat. Dairy Council, 1963, Ten Commandments award Fraternal Order Eagles, 1963, citation for dedicated leadership Nat. Ret. Tchrs. Assn. and Am. Assn. Ret. Persons, 1963. Mem. Newcomen Soc., N.Y. Acad. Sci., Nat. Congress Parents and Tchrs. (hon. life), Blue Key. Clubs: Ogden Rotary (hon.), Bonneville, Nat. Travel. Author: Ancient Apostles, 1918; also numerous Priesthood Manuals for the Church. Home: Salt Lake City UT Died Jan. 18, 1970.

MCKAY, PAUL LEONARD, univ. pres.; b. Laclede, Ill., June 29, 1917; s. Rev. Elmer and Eva (Hulen) McK.; A.B., Greenville Coll., 1939; M.A., N.Y. U., 1941, Ph.D., 1945; B.D., Union Theol. Sem., 1945; LL.D., Lincoln Coll., 1964; m. Geraldine Lindley, Nov. 18, 1941; 1 dau., Mary Ruth (Mrs. Terry Gaines). Ordained to ministry Presbyn. Ch., 1943; asso. minister Marble Collegiate Ch., N.Y.C., 1944-46; minister First Presbyn. Ch., Akron, O., 1946-57; lectr. philosophy and religion U. Akron, 1947-49; pres. Millikin U., Decatur, Ill., 1957-71. Chmn. Com. Coop. Higher Edn., State Ill., 1961. Moderator Presbytery Cleve., 1954. Pres. Mental Health Assn. Summit County, Ohio; trustee Assn. Commerce, YMCA, Decatur, Decatur and Macon County Hosp. Recipient Distinguished Service award, Akron, 1951. Mem. Asso. Colls. Ill. (chmn. bd. 1966-68), Presbyterial coll. Union (pres. 1967), Central States Coll. Assn. (chmn. bd.), Alpha Kappa Psi, Phi Kappa Phi, Kappa Delta Pi, Phi Delta Kappa. Clubs: University, Country of Decatur, Decatur; Union League (Chgo.). Home: Decatur IL Died Feb. 2, 1971.

MCKAY, SETH SHEPARD, coll. prof.; b. Holland, Tex., Jan. 12, 1888; s. Albert Johnson and Jane Elijah (Sparks) McK.; B.A., U. of Tex., 1912, M.A., 1919; Ph.D., U. of Pa., 1924; m. Bama Lawson Camp, Oct. 21, 1914; children—Seth Shepard (dec.), Lafayette Camp, Mary Lamartine. With North Tex. Teachers Coll. as instr. Am. history, 1916-17, asst. prof., 1917-19, asso. prof., 1919-21; teaching asst. in Am. history, U. of Pa., 1921-22; adj. prof. history U. of Tex., 1922-23, summers 1923-25, 47, 49; lecturer on Am. hist., Ohio State U., 1923-24; prof. history, Furman U., 1924-28; prof. hist., Tex. Tech. Coll., from 1928, chmn. dept. 1939-44; visiting professor, University of Texas, 1948-49. Mem. Govs. com. for study Constl. Revision in Texas. Member Am. Hist. Assn., Miss. Valley Hist. Assn., Tex. State Hist. Assn., West Tex. Hist. Assn., Am. Polit. Science Assn., Southwestern Polit. Science Assn., Pi Gamma Mu. Democrat. Mem. Disciples of Christ, Club: Lions (ex-pres.). Author: Making the Texas Constitution of 1876, 1924; Debates in the Texas Convention of 1875, 1930; Seven Decades of the Texas Constitution of 1876, 1945; W. Lee O'Daniel and Texas Politics, 1938-1942, 1945; Texas Politics, 1906-1944, 1952; Texas and the Fair Deal, 1945-52, 1954; (with Odie B. Faulk) Texas After Spindletop, 1965. Contbr. Dictionary Am. Biography, Dictionary Am. History, West Texas Hist. Assn. Year Bk., Southwestern Hist. Quarterly, Handbook of Texas, Southwestern Social Science Quarterly. Home: Lubbock TX Died June 4, 1969; buried Resthaven Meml. Park, Lubbock TX

MCKAY, THOMAS CLAYTON, lawyer; b. Chgo., Feb. 2, 1922; s. Charles Edward and Rebecca (Decker) McK.; A.B., Graceland U., 1940; LL.B., U. Conn., 1948; m. Rita Duffy, Oct. 14, 1944; children—Sharyn, Robin, Denise. Admitted to Conn. bar, 1948, Ill. bar, 1949, U.S. Supreme Ct. bar, 1957; practiced in Hartford, Conn., 1948-49, Chgo., 1949-69; mem. firm Pam, Hurd and Rickman, Dallstream, Schiff et al, Chicago Heights, Ill., 1969-71; sr. partner McKay, Moses, McGarr and Gibbons, Chgo., 1955-67; chmn. bd. Hamler Industries, Inc., Chicago Heights, 1957-71; owner, operator Triple R Ranch, Frankfort, Ill., 1960-71. Pres., Community Council, Park Forest, Ill., 1949-50, Community Chest Park Forest 1950-52. Mem. Am., Chgo. (ethics com.) bar assns., Legal Club Chgo., Phi Kappa Psi. Republican. Mem. Christian Ch. Clubs: Executive, Union League (Chgo.); Lincolnshire Country (Crete, Ill.); Woodmar Country (Hammond, Ind.); Prestwick Country (Frankfort, Ill.); Olympia Fields (Ill.) Country. Home: Frankfort IL Died Sept. 23, 1971.

MCKECHNIE, NEIL KENNETH, author, artist; b. London, Eng., Sept. 4, 1873; s. Donald and Marian (Evans) McK.; ed. St. Mark's Coll., London, and in Germany until 1890; studied Academie Julian, Paris, 1890-91; Lambeth Art Sch., London, 1891-92; Royal Acad. Schs., 1892-96; again Academie Julian, 1896-97; unmarried. Winner 2d Armitage prize for best picture at Royal Acad. Schs., 1894; took up book illustration but eyesight failed and emigrated to Canada to farm; eyesight recovered; became artist on staff of Ralph & Clark, lithographers, Toronto; served as capt. inf. in World War 3 1/2 yrs., 14 mos. in France; free lance artist in N.Y. City since 1925. Mem. Canadian Graphic Arts Soc. Protestant. Author: Heir of All the Ages, 1926. Home: 3 Springbank Av., Toronto, Can. Studio: 246 W. 21st St., New York NY‡

MCKEE, ARTHUR G., cons. engr.; b. State College, Pa., Jan. 12, 1871; s. Prof. James Y. and Margaret Anne (Glenn) McK.; B.S., Pennsylvania State College, 1891, M.E. from same, 1899; D.Engring., Case School of Applied Science, Cleveland, Ohio, 1941; m. Marion Fairbanks Deane, Apr. 20, 1899; children—Mary Katherine (Mrs. Paul O. Semon, Jr.), Marion Deane (Mrs. John Latta). Engr. Edison Gen. Electric Co., Chicago, 1891-92; gen. contracting, State College, Pa., 1893-95; mining and mech. engr., H.C. Frick Coke Co., Scottdale, Pa., 1895-96; with Duquesne & Edgar Thomson Works, Carnegie Steel Co., 1896-98; asst. chief engr., Ohio Steel Co., Youngstown, O., 1898-1900; blast furnace engr., Julian Kennedy Co., Pittsburgh, 1900-01; dist. engr. Am. Steel & Wire Co., Cleveland, O., 1901-05; in practice as cons. and Wire Co., Cleveland, O., 1901-05; in practice as cons. and contracting engr., Cleveland, since 1905, operating under name of Arthur G. McKee & Co. since 1915, pres. 1915-46, chmn. of advisory com. since 1946. Mem. Cleveland Chamber of Commerce, Am. Iron and Steel Inst., Am. Inst. Mining and Metall. Engrs., Am. Inst. Mech. Engrs., Iron and Steel Engrs., Eastern States Blast Furnace and Coke Oven Assn., Blast Furnace and Coke Oven Assn. of Chicago Dist., Cleveland Engring. Soc., Iron and Steel Inst. (Eng.), Am. Hort. Council, Inc., Cleveland Orchid Soc. Presbyterian. Republican. Clubs: Union, Mayfield Country (Cleveland); Duquesne (Pittsburgh); Riomar (Vero Beach, Fla.) Country. Home: 2219 Chestnut Hills Drive. Office: 2300 Chester Av., Cleveland OH‡

MCKEE, RALPH HARPER, chemical engr.; b. Clinton, Mo., June 20, 1874; s. James Thomas and Mary Frances (Ricketts) McK.; A.B., U. of Wooster, 1895, A.M., 1897; Ph.D., U. of Chicago, 1901; LL.D., Carthage (Ill.) Coll., 1924, U. of Me., 1929; Sc.D., Coll. of Wooster, 1929; D.Nat.Ph., U. of Tartu, Estonia, 1932; m. Mary Coyle Noyes, June 26, 1902 (divorced); children—Margaret Harper, William Noyes; m. 2d, Marian E. Winter, Sept. 10, 1931. Prof. chemistry, Lake Forest (Ill.) U., 1901-09, U. of Me., 1909-16; prof. chem. engring., Columbia, 1917-39; retired. Chem. engr. Tenn. Copper Co.; president Swiss Borvisk Company; director Kerogen Oil Co.; pres. McKee Poplar Forestation, Inc. Dir. (United States) Ordnance School of Explosives Mfg., 1918-19. Member Perkin Medal Com., 1906, 07, 19, 20, 22, 23. Fellow A.A.A.S.; mem. Am. Chem. Soc. (councilor at large; chmn. N.Y. sect. 1920), Am. Inst. Chem. Engrs., Tech. Assn. Pulp and Paper Industry, Soc. for Promotion Engring. Edn., N.Y. Soc. Profs. Engring. Comdr. Order of Polonia Restituta. Republican. Presbyterian. Club: Chemists (New York). Contbr. about 100 scientific and technical papers in Am. and European periodicals; devised and developed to commercial success several new chem. processes. Home: 635 Riverside Drive, New York 31 NY‡

MCKEE, ROSE, former govt. ofcl.; b. Wabasso, Minn.; d. Robert Earl and Rosa (Lucas) McKee; B.S., U. N.D. With St. Paul Daily News, 1929-34, Japan Times, Tokyo, 1934-36, Phila. Inquirer, 1937-44, Senate corr. INS, 1944-58; feature editor Nat. Assn. Home Builders 1958-64; dir. Office Information, Small Bus. Adminstrn., 1964-66; dir. Office Pub. Information, Econ. Devel., U.S. Dept. Commerce, 1965-69. Recipient George R. Holmes Meml. award, 1952. Mem. Women's Nat. Press Club, Am. Newspaper Women's Club. Home: Washington DC Died 1971.

MCKEEN, WILLIAM RILEY, mechanical engr., inventor; b. Terre Haute, Ind., Oct. 2, 1869; s. William Riley M., Sr.; B.S., Rose Poly. Inst., Terre Haute, 1889, M.S., 1896, M.E., 1897; post-grad. work, Johns Hopkins, 2 yrs., Polytechnikum, Berlin, Germany, 1 yr. Spl. apprentice Pittsburgh, Columbus, Cincinnati & St. Louis Ry. shops, Columbus, O., 1892-3; master car builder and gen. foreman car and locomotive shops, Vandalia Line, Terre Haute, Ind., 1893-7; dist. foreman, North Platte, Neb., 1898-01, master mechanic, Wyo. div., Cheyenne, 1901-2, supt. motive power and machinery, Omaha, 1902-8, consulting engr. motor cars, 1908-—. U.P. R.R.; pres. and gen. mgr. McKeen Motor Car Co., Aug. 1, 1908-21. Inventor McKeen 200 h.p. gasoline motor car for rys., and various devices for use of rys. Mem. Am. Soc. Mech. Engrs., Ry. Master Mechanics' Assn., Master Car Builders' Assn. Home: 205 Coast Highway, Santa Barbara, CA‡

MCKEEVER, FRANCIS MICHAEL, orthopedic surgeon; b. Santa Ana, Cal., May 8, 1901; s. Thomas and Margaret (Devin) McK.; B.A., U. Cal., 1922, M.D., 1927; m. Catherine Patricia O'Malley, Jan. 19, 1946; children—Shelia, Michael and Patricia. Post graduate tng. in orthopedic surgery Mass. Gen. and Boston Children's Hosps., 1929-31; began practice of orthopedic surgery, Los Angeles, 1931; vis. orthopedic surgeon Los Angeles Gen. Hosp., Los Angeles Children's Hosp.; prof. orthodpedic surgery emeritus U. So. Cal. Sch. Medicine. Served with M.C., AUS, chief orthopedic service and chief surg. service Percy Jones Gen. and Convalescent Hosp., Battle Creek, Mich. Apptd. to Nat. Adv. Council for care of Vets., 1946. Trustee Orthopedic Research and Edn. Found.; bd. regents Loyola U., Los Angeles, 1957-73. Decorated Legion of Merit, 1946. Mem. Am. Bd. of Orthopedic Surgery. Fellow A.C.S. (regent 1958-73; first v.p. 1968-69); mem. A.M.A. (exec. com. orthopedic sect.), Am. Orthopedic Assn., Am. Surg. Assn., Pacific Coast Surg. Soc., Am. Acad. Orthopedic Surgeons (pres. 1952-53), Chgo. Surg. Soc., Western Orthopedic Assn., Calif. Med. Soc., Los Angeles County Med. Assn. Roman Catholic. Home: Los Angeles CA Died Apr. 2, 1973.

MCKELVEY, GRAHAM NORTON, fgn. service officer; b. Philipston, Pa., July 31, 1907; s. Frank Bell and Fonda (Barras) McK.; m. Ruth Nadyne South, June 6, 1942; children—Stephen Fred, Michael John. Stock and bond brokerage, Chgo., 1927-39; occupation analyst USES, Chgo., 1939-42; adminstrv. officer Office Mil. Govt., Germany, 1946-48; chief labor supply and employment sect. ECA, Office Spl. Representative, Paris, 1948-50; labor attache Fgn. Service, Manila, P.I., 1950-52, Bonn, Germany, 1952-56, Dept. of State, 1956-58, Singapore, Fedn. of Malaya, 1958-61, Australia, 1961-62, Belgium-Luxembourg, 1962-70; dir. dept. nat. and internat. affairs United Mine Workers, 1970-72. Served from pvt. to lt. AUS, 1942-46. Home: Washington DC Died May 2, 1972.

MCKELVEY, S. WILLIS, clergyman; b. Sparta, Ill., Apr. 30, 1869; s. Samuel Wylie and Nancy Therissa (McGuire) McK.; B.A., Monmouth (Ill.) Coll., 1894, D.D., 1918; B.Th., Xenia (O.) Sem., 1897; LL.D., Mo. Valley Coll., Marshall, Mo., 1929; m. Bessie R. Liggett, Nov. 3, 1897; children—Frances L., S. Warren, Randolph T., Donald L., Justin E. Ordained ministry United Presbyn. Ch., 1897; pastor Harrisville, Pa., 1897-99, 2d U.P. Ch., Mercer, 1899-1903, 2d U.P. Ch., Pittsburgh, 1903-12, 2d Presbyn. Ch., Wilkinsburg (Pittsburgh), 1912-21, St. Paul Ch., Phila., 1921-26, 2d Ch., Kansas City, Mo., since Feb. 1926. Mem. Bd. of Nat. Missions Presbyterian Ch. U.S.A.; mem. bd. dirs. Mo. Valley Coll., U. of Mo. Bible Coll. Chaplain St. Andrew's Soc., Kansas City. Club: University. Author: The Church—Its Privileges; The Flag-The Meaning of The Red, The White, The Blue; The Essential Spirit of Jesus. Home: 25 E. 56th St., Kansas City MO*‡

MCKENDRICK, EDWARD JOHN, investment broker; b. St. Paul, Apr. 12, 1899; s. Mark D. and Anne (Anderson) McK.; student accountancy, La. Salle Extension U., 1919-21, bus. adminstrn. evening sch., U. Minn., 1920-29; m. Evelyn Nelson, Nov. 25, 1937; children—John, Sally, Mary. Credit mgr. No. States Power Co., 1921-23, accountant, 1923-26, securities salesman, 1926-28, 30-35; securities salesman Halsey-Stuart & Co., 1928-30; sec.-treas. Delanet-Johnson-McKendrick, Mpls., 1935-42; sec.-treas. WPB, 1942-45; v.p. Johnson-McKendrick, Mpls., 1945-53, pres., 1953-55; pres. McKendrick-Haseltine & Wilson, Mpls., 1957-59; mgr. Dempsey-Tegeler & Co., mems. N.Y. stock exchange, 1959-62; partner M. H. Bishop & Co., 1961-68. Chairman of governors district 4 Nat. Assn. Securities Dealers; gov. Midwest Stock Exchange. Clubs: Twin City Bond, Interlachen Golf, Twin City Bond Traders (Mpls.); Newman (U. Minn.). Home: Minneapolis MN Died Jan. 25, 1968; buried Lakewood Cemetery, Minneapolis MN

MCKENNA, PHILIP M., manufacturer; b. Pitts., June 16, 1897; s. Alexander G. and Eliza DeHaven (Mowry) McK.; A.B., George Washington U., 1921; children—Philip C., Carol E. Chemist helper, analytical lab. U.S. Bur. Standards, 1913-14; chemist Chem. Products Co. of Washington, 1914-16, gen. mgr., v.p., 1916-20; chem. process cons. Vanadium Alloys Steel Co., 1916-17, research dir., v.p., 1928-38; privately engaged, 1922-25; sole propr. McKenna Metals Co., 1938-40, partner, 1940-43; pres., dir. Kennametal, Inc., chmn.; chmn. Kennametal Co. O.; director Kennametal Overseas Corp. Fellow American Association for Advancement of Science; member Gold Standard League (nat. chairman 1949-55), American Chem. Soc., Am. Institute Mining and Metall. Engring., Am. Soc. Tool Engrs., A.S.M.E. (named Towne lectr. 1953; Holley medal, 1953), Am. Acad. Polit. Scis. Clubs: University, Duquesne (Pitts.); Engineer's (N.Y.C.). Author articles tech. press. Evolved processes of extracting and refining metals, particularly tungsten; experiments instrumental in discovery intermetallic compound tungsten-titanium-carbide. Home: Greensburg PA Died Aug. 16, 1969.

MCKENNEY, RUTH, author; b. Mishawaka, Ind., Nov. 18, 1911; d. J. S. and Marguerite (Flynn) McK.; student Ohio State U., 1932; m. Richard Bransten, Aug. 12, 1937 (dec. 1955); 1 dau., Eileen Edith Celia. Reporter, N.Y. Post, 1934-37. Author: My Sister Eileen, 1938 (became Broadway play, motion picture, musical Wonderful Town) Industrial Valley, 1939; The McKenneys Carry On, 1940; Jake Home: 1943; Loud Red Patrick, 1947 (became Broadway play); Love Story, 1950; Here's England, 1950; All About Eileen, 1952; Far Far From Home, 1954; Mirage, 1956; (with Eileen Bransten) Statements On The Tourist Racket, 1960. Home: Columbus OH Died July 25, 1972.

MCKENZIE, WILLIAM DEXTER, retired vice president, Quaker Oats Co.; b. Hampton, Iowa, Feb. 13, 1873; s. James Wheeler and Ruth Delia (Hemingway) McK.; A.B., Univ. of Mich., 1896, hon. M.A., 1936; m. Charlotte G. Lane, June 21, 1906; children—Roderick, Roxane McKenzie Price. Teacher Austin High Sch., Chicago, 1897-1902; admitted Ill. bar, 1901, practice in Chicago since 1902; asso. Knapp & Campbell, 1908-20, mem. from 1916; gen. counsel The Quaker Oats Co., 1920-46, vice pres., 1934-49. Trustee New Trier Township High Sch., Winnetka, Ill., 1910-16, pres., 1913-14; pres. village Winnetka, 1917, 18; trustee Winnetka Congl. Ch., Hadley Sch. for the Blind, Winnetka. Mem. Psi Upsilon. Republican. Clubs: University, Law (Chicago); Indian Hill (Winnetka, Ill.); Lawyer's (Ann Arbor, Mich.); Biltmore Forest Country (Asheville, N.C.). Home: 1190 Oakley Av., Hubbard Woods IL‡

MCKENZIE, WILLIAM WHITE, physician; b. Salisbury, N.C., Oct. 12, 1869; s. Charles Harris and Ellen (Sumner) M.; U. of N.C., 1888-91; M.D., Jefferson Med. Coll., Phila., 1893; post-grad. work, New York Post-Grad. Sch. and Hosp.; m. Alice Caldwell, of Salisbury, N.C., Oct. 10, 1894 (died Jan., 1909). Practiced, Salisbury, 1893—; phys. to Whitehead-Stokes Sanitarium, Salisbury; local surgeon Southern Ry.; city health phys., Salisbury, 1904-12; pres. Bd. Med. Examiners of N.C., 1908—. Mem. A.M.A., N.C. Med. Assn. (v.-p. 1903—), Tri-State Med. Assn. (v.-p. 1908—), Rowan Co. Med. Soc. (pres. 1900-1), etc. Democrat. Episcopalian. Mason. Clubs: Old Hickory, Elks, Salisbury Country. Address: Salisbury NC‡

MCKERNAN, MAUREEN (MRS. JOHN COOPER ROSS), publisher; b. White Cloud, Kansas, June 18, 1893; d. John Franklin and Eva (Fleming) McKernan; B.A., U. Kan., 1916; m. John Cooper Ross, Nov. 4, 1928. Reporter, woman's editor Topeka (Kan.) Daily Capital, 1918-22; reporter Kansas City (Mo.) Jour., 1922-24, Chgo. Tribune, 1924-27, Westchester County Publishers, White Plains, N.Y., 1931-36, N.Y. Post, N.Y.C., 1936, 42, The Record, Phila., 1942-43; publicist, 1927-31; reporter, editor Westchester County Publishers, White Plains, N.Y., 1943-61, cons., 1961-65; pub. pres., The Ripley Review, Inc., 1965-68. Mem. Theta Sigma Phi, Alpha Chi Omega. Club: Women's Press. (N.Y.) Author: The Amazing Crime and Trial of Leopold and Loeb, 1924. Home: Westfield NY Died Apr. 29, 1968.

MCKIMMON, JANE SIMPSON (MRS. CHARLES MCKIMMON), home economist; b. Raleigh, N.C., Nov. 13, 1869; d. William and Ann Cannon (Shanks) Simpson; grad. Peace Inst., Raleigh, 1885; B.S., N.C. State Coll. Agr. and Engring., 1926, M.S., 1928; LL.D., University of North Carolina, 1934; m. Charles McKimmon, of Raleigh, Nov. 10, 1886; children—Charles, Anne (Mrs. Robert W. Winston), Wm. Simpson, Hugh. Dir. Women's Institutes of the N.C. Farmers' Institutes, 1908-10; organizer State Fed. Home Demonstration Clubs for farm women and 4-H clubs for farm girls; state home demonstration agt. of N.C. since 1911; asst. dir. N.C. Extension Service since 1924; member N.C. Rural Electrification Authority, 1935-40; member board dirs., Farmers Cooperative Exchange. Organized over 60,000 farm women and girls into 2,500 clubs for better rural life. North Carolina state home economics supervisor during World War. Trustee Olivia Raney Library, Raleigh. Awarded distinguished service ruby by Epsilon Sigma Phi. Mem. Am. Econ. Assn., N.C. Home Econ. Assn., N.C. Hist. Assn., House of Pioneers of Epsilon Sigma Phi. Democrat. Episcopalian. Clubs: Raleigh Woman's, Fortnightly Review Book, Carolina Country. Home: 123 New Bern Av. Office: State College of Agriculture and Engineering, Raleigh NC‡

MCKINLAY, CHAUNCEY ANGUS, physician; b. Wichita, Kan., Aug. 9, 1890; s. Lincoln and Jennie (Knickerbocker) McK.; B.A., U. Kan., 1914, M.D., 1916; m. Kathryn Christine Thorbus, Sept. 5, 1921; children—Donald Thorbus (dec.), Gordon Lynn, Robert Chauncey, Eleanor Jean (dec.). Intern, Montreal (Que., Can.) Gen. Hosp., 1916-17; resident in pathology New Haven Hosp., 1917-18; resident in medicine U. Minn. Hosp., Mpls., 1919-21; practice medicine specializing in internal medicine, heart and cardiovascular disease, Mpls., 1921-58; cons. health service staff U. Minn., from 1920, clin. asso. prof. medicine, until 1958; former mem. staffs Mpls. Gen., Asbury, Methodist, Northwestern hosps. Dir., Minn. Med. Service, Inc., 1947-59, pres., 1959-60; mem. local med. adv. bd. SSS, 1942. Served to 2d lt. U.S. Army, 1918-19. Diplomate Am. Bd. Internal Medicine. Mem. A.M.A., A.C.P., Central Soc. Clin. Research, A.A.A.S., Am. Coll. Chest Physicians, Am. Heart Assn., Minn. Med. Assn., Hennepin County Med. Soc. (past 1st v.p.), Minn., Mpls. socs. internal medicine, Minn., Mpls. acads. medicine, Minn. Path. Soc. (pres. 1949-50), Minn. Tb and Health Assn. (pres 1959), Soc. Mayflower Descs., Sigma Xi, Gamma Alpha, Alpha Kappa Kappa. Republican. Presbyn. (elder). Mason, Optimist. Co-editor, contbr. to Diseases of Chest and Heart, 2 vols., 1949. Contbr. numerous articles to med. jours. Reserach on infectious mononucleosis. Home: Minneapolis MN Died Nov. 12, 1969 buried Sunset Meml. Park, Minneapolis MN

MCKINLEY, CHARLES ETHELBERT, clergyman; b. Anita, Ia., May 18, 1870; s. Isaac Addison and Mary (Allspaugh) M.; ed. country dist. schs., Anita High Sch., Grinnell (Ia.) Acad., Iowa Coll., A. B., 1891, Chicago Theol. Sem., Sept.-Dec., 1891, Andover Theol. Sem., 1894; m. Clinton, Ia., Aug. 30, 1894, Fannie B. Keister. Asst. sec. and later gen. sec. Grinnell (Ia.) Y.M.C.A., 1889; in charge of a mission ch., Cedar Rapids, Ia., Jan.-Oct.. 1892; ordained to ministry, 1894; pastor 1st Parish Cong'l Ch., Yarmouth, Me., 1894-6, Union Cong'l Ch., Rockville, Conn., since Sept. 1, 1896. Author: Educational Evangelism, 1905 P8. Address: Rockville CT‡

MCKINNEY, ANNIE (VALENTINE) BOOTH, author; b. Warren Co., Miss.; d. Col. S. S. and Anne (Valentine) Booth; grad. Hillman Coll., Clinton, Miss.; m. at Vicksburg, Miss., Samuel McKinney, Feb. 14, 1878. Pres. Tenn. Woman's Press and Authors Club; pres. Knoxville chapter, Daughters of the Confederacy; mem. Bonny Kate Chapter, D.A.R.; ex-pres. Ossoli Circle, first federated club in South; founder and v.-p. Woman's Building Bd.; ex-dir. Gen. Federation of Women's Clubs; hon. mem. New York Woman's Club. Author: Mistress Joy (with Grace MacGowan Cooke (q.v.), 1898. Has contbd. to Harper's Bazar, Munsey's, Vogue and Town Topics, etc. Address: 604 W. Main St., Knoxville TN‡

MCKINNEY, IDA SCOTT TAYLOR, song writer; b. Springfield, Ill.; d. Thomas G. and Eliza Helen (Chappell) Taylor; grad. Jacksonville (Ill.) Acad. for Young Women, 1874; studied music and painting; m. at Jacksonville, Ill., William E. McKinney, June 5, 1895. Author: Story of Columbus Told in Rhyme; Baby's Journal; Year Book of American Authors; Year Book of English Authors; also booklets, A Little Quaker Meeting; In His Name; Forsake Me Not; The Little Quaker Meeting; In His Name; Forsake Me Not; The Beatitudes; etc. Has written for local papers, mostly verse, since 14 or 15.*‡

MCKINNEY, LAURENCE, author, manufacturer; b. Albany, N.Y., June 2, 1891; s. Edward N. and Marion Louise (Roessle) McK.; grad. Albany Acad., 1908; A.B., Harvard, 1912; m. Alice Williams, 1917 (divorced 1942); m. 2d, Betsy Marvin, May 11, 1943; children—Laurence Osborne, Reinold Marvin, Andrew Reid. Chmn. James McKinney & Son, Inc., steel fabricators. Served as lt., Field Arty., A.E.F., 1917-18. Past pres. Albany Symphony Orch. Inc.; pres. Albany Inst. of History and Art; dir. Albany Chamber Music Soc., Albany Council N.Y. Com. for human rights. Director Albany Boys Club, Mohawk-Hudson Council Ednl. TV; mem. adv. com. Salvation Army; nat. asso. Boys' Clubs Am.; dir. Albany League of Arts. Presbyn. Clubs: University, Rotary, Fort Orange, Schuyler Meadows (Albany); Harvard, P.E.N., Coffee House (N.Y.); Stone Horse Yacht, also Wychmere Harbor (Harwich Port). Author of: People of Note: A Score of Symphony Faces, 1940; Garden Clubs & Spades, 1941; Lines of Least Resistance, 1941. Contbr. light verse and humorous articles to numerous mags. Home: Loudonville NY Died Apr. 21, 1968; buried Albany Rural Cemetery Albany NY

MCKITTRICK, THOMAS HARRINGTON, banker; b. St. Louis, Mo., Mar. 14, 1889; s. Thomas Harrington and Hildegarde (Sterling) McK.; student St. Louis (Mo.) Manual Training Sch., 1903-05, Hackley Sch., Tarrytown, N.Y., 1905-07, St. Louis U. Law School, 1914-15; A.B., Harvard, 1911; married Marjorie Benson, November 9, 1921; children—Marjorie Sterling (Mrs. Neil E. Handel, Elisabeth Benson (Mrs. Paul E. Booz), Mary, Frances Anne. With Hargadine, McKittrick Dry Wholesale Goods Co., 1911-14, St. Louis Union Trust Co., 1914-15; National City Bank of N.Y. in N.Y. City, 1916, in Genoa, Italy, 1916-18; with Lee Higginson & Co. in N.Y. City, 1919-21; with Higginson & Co., London, 1922-39, partner, 1924-39; pres. Bank for Internat. Settlements, Basle, 1940-46; chmn. No. Paper & Pulp Works, Tallinn, Estonia, since 1935; v.p. Chase Nat. Bank, N.Y., 1946-49, sr. v.p. since 1949; dir. Chase Bank since 1946. Chief, Trade and Payments Div. Office of Spl. Rep., Econ. Co-op. Adminstrn., Am. Embassy, Paris, France, June-Dec. 1948; acting chief Mission to United Kingdom, Econ. Cooperation Adminstrn., London, Aug.-Sept., 1949. Director American Chamber of Commerce, London, Eng., 1930-39; v. chmn. U.S. council International C. of C.; first vice chairman committee on Monetary Relations. International C. of C., 1947; mem. advisory group to N.A.M. Committee on Internat. Economic Relations, 1947; chmn. foreign securities com. Investment Bankers Assn. of Am., 1948; pres. Am.-Brit. Found. for European Edn., Inc. since 1949; mem. German Credits Arbitration Com., 1931-39 (vice chmn. 1933); mem. exec. com. and hon. treas. Am. Relief Soc., London, England, 1930-39. Served as 2d lt., A.E.F., 1918, 1st lt., 1919; cited for meritorious service. Decorations: Knight Grand Cross Order Crown of Roumania, 1948; Commanderie de l'Ordre de la Couronne, Belgium, 1948. Mem. Brit. Ornithol. Union; asso. mem. Am. Ornithol. Union; mem. Am. Geog. Society, Academy Polit. Science; corr. mem. Statistisch-Volkwirtschhaftliche Gesellschaft, Basel. Clubs: University, Harvard (N.Y. City); American (London). Contbr. to Blairstown NJ Died Jan. 21, 1970.

MCKNIGHT, GEORGE HARLEY, prof. English; b. Sterling Valley, N.Y., Apr. 24, 1871; s. James and Letitia Jane (Cooper) McK.; A.B., Cornell U., 1892, Ph.D., 1896; studied Freiburg U. and the Sorbonne, 1897-99; m. Sarah Watson Forrest, June 16, 1909. instr. in English, Cornell U., 1892-97; asst. prof. rhetoric, Ohio State U., 1899-1907, prof. English, 1907-41, professor English emeritus since 1941. Member Modern Language Association of America (exec. council; mem. editorial com. 1925-29), Phi Beta Kappa. Republican. Presbyterian. Club: Faculty. Author: St. Nicholas, 1917; English Words and Their Background, 1923; Modern English in the Making, 1928; A Grammar of Living English (with W. W. Hatfield and T.B. Haber), 1939. Editor: King Horn, Floriz and Blauncheflur, The Assumption of Our Lady, 1901; Middle English Humorous Tales in Verse, 1913. Contributor to periodicals. Member advisory board of editors American Speech, 1930-32; mem. editorial advisory com. Thorndike Century English Dictionary; cons. in pronunciation for Webster Internat. Dictionary. Home: 725 Franklin Av., Columbus 5 OH‡

MCKNIGHT, HENRY TURNEY, b. Mpls., April 2, 1913; s. Sumner Thomas and Henriette Denny (Turney) McK.; grad. St. Paul's Sch., Concord, N.H., 1928-32; A.B., Yale, 1936; m. June Hanes, Apr. 11, 1942;children—Henry T., Sumner T. II, Christina Agnes; m. 2d, Grace Carter Lindley, Feb. 1, 1958; children—Clarkson and Kristine Lindley. Began as advertising salesman N.Y. Herald Tribune, 1936-39; account exec. Batten, Barton, Durstine & Osborn, 1939-41; publisher's asst. LOOK mag., 1946-47; owner and operator McKnight Angus Farm, Victoria, Minn.; chmn. bd. Impro Sales, Inc.; pres. Bright Futures, Inc., Carver Co., Ace Development Corp.; vice president S. T. McKnight Co., Mpls. Mem. Minn. Senate, from 1962. Apptd. sec. Nat. Agrl. Adv. Com., 1952; v.p. Keep Minn. Green, Inc.; chmn. Minn. Natural Resources. Served from ensign to lt. comdr., USNR, 1941-45. Decorated Bronze Star. Mem. Mpls. Soc. Fine Arts (trustee), Am. Forestry Assn. (mem. executive com.), C. of C. Clubs: Chicago; Metropolitan (Washington); Links (N.Y.C.); Minneapolis (Mpls.); Wayzata Country, Woodhill Country (Wayzata, Minn.). Home: Wayzata MN Died Dec. 30, 1972.

MCLANE, A.V., lawyer; b. Lewisburg, Tenn., Aug. 30, 1874; s. Gustavus Adolphus and Margaret Eliza (Whitsett) McL.; ed. public schools and Haynes-McLean Coll., Lewisburg; b. Ruby Donna Roach, June 8, 1904; 1 dau., Elizabeth. Admitted to bar, 1895, and began practice at Lewisburg; U.S. atty., Middle Tenn. Dist., 1922-34; now in practice at Nashville. Republican. Presbyterian. Home: 3708 Richland Av., Nashville TN Office: Third Nat. Bank Bldg., Nashville TN; also First Nat. Bank Bldg., Lewisburg TN*‡

MCLANE, CHARLES LOURIE, educator; b. Scotland County, Mo., Apr. 4, 1862; s. Daniel and Drusilla (Bennett) McL.; B.S., Valparaiso (Ind.) U., 1887; post-grad. study, U. of Calif., U. of Chicago, and Harvard U.; m. Demma F. Best, Dec. 26, 1891 (died 1931); 1 dau., Marguerite Harris; m. 2d, Elizabeth J. Price, Dec. 21, 1933. Teacher public schs., Ia. and Mo., 1882-90; admitted to bar of Mo., 1889, Calif., 1891; teacher pub. schs., Fresno, Calif., 1891-93; prin. high sch., Virginia City, Nev., 1893-96, Fresno, Calif., 1896-99; supt. schs., Fresno, 1899-1913; pres. Fresno State Teachers Coll., 1911-27; pres. Calif. State Bd. of Edn., 1927-33. Organized first jr. coll. in Calif., at Fresno, 1910. Republican. Mason (K.T., 32 deg.). Home: Fresno CA‡

MCLANE, JOHN ROY, lawyer; b. Milford, N.H., Jan. 7, 1886; s. John and Ellen Luetta (Tuck) McL.; student St. Paul's Sch., Concord, 1900-03; A.B., Dartmouth, 1907, hon. M.A., 1926; Rhodes scholar from N.H. at Oxford U., Eng., 1907-09, B.A., 1909; LL.B., cum laude, Harvard, 1912; m. Elisabeth Bancroft, June 12, 1915; children—John Roy, Charles Bancroft, Elisabeth Bancroft (Mrs. David J. Bradley), Malcolm, Mary Craig. Admitted to New Hampshire bar, 1912, practicing at Manchester, N.H.; member law firm Taggart, Burroughs, Wyman & McLane, 1916-18; now McLane, Carleton, Graf, Greene & Brown; dir. Nat. Life Ins. Co.; pres. Manchester Savs. Bank; Chief of Industrial Relations br. Q.M. Corps. U.S. Army, 1918-19; chmn. N.H. State Bd. of Arbitration and Conciliation, 1925-40. Trustee Dartmouth College. Member of American N.H. and N.Y. State bar assns., Delta Kappa Epsilon. Republican. Manchester NH Died Apr. 21, 1969.

MCLANE, PATRICK, congressman; b. County Mayo, Ireland, Mar. 14, 1875; came with parents to Scranton, Pa., 1882; ed. pub. schs. 3 yrs. Worked in coal mines 10 yrs.; entered ry. service and advanced to locomotive engr.; mem. 66th Congress (1919-21), 10th Pa. Dist. Served as pvt. Co. E, 11th U.S. Inf., Spanish-Am. War, 1898-9. Mem. Sch. Bd., Scranton, 8 yrs. Democrat. Roman Catholic. Home: 535 Broadway, Scranton PA‡

MCLAREN, WALTER WALLACE, economist; b. Renfrew, Ont., Can., Mar. 4, 1877; s. John and Emma (Beal) McL.; M.A., Queens U., Can., 1899, B.D., 1902; Ph.D., Harvard, 1908; LL.D., Lawrence Coll., 1927, Queen's University, Canada, 1948; married Zaidee Rogers, 1910;children—Walter Rogers, Zaidee, Mary Catherine. Pastor St. Andrew's Church, Picton, Ontario, Can., 1902-05; professor economics and politics, Keiogijuku, Tokyo, 1908-14; editor Transactions Asiatic Soc. of Japan, 1912-14; prof. economics, 1914-45, Williams College, Williamstown, Mass.; prof. econ., Hamilton Coll., 1945-46. Began teaching in Tokyo. Economist for Far Eastern countries in Department of State, Washington, 1920-21; sec. to Am. delegation and chief Internat. Secretariat at Washington Conf. on Electrical Communications, 1920; exec. sec. Inst. of Politics, Williamstown, Mass.; chmn. exec. com. Conf. on Canadian-Am. Affairs, 1935. Fellow Am. Acad. of Arts and Sciences; mem. Am. Econ. Assn. Asiatic Soc. Japan, Kappa Alpha. Prebyterian. Author: Political History of Japan, 1916; Present Day Japanese Government, 1919. Editor: Japanese Government Documents (Asiatic Soc.), 1914; Proceedings of Conf. on Canadian-Am. Affairs, 1936, 38, 40. Home: 8 Prospect Rd., Williamstown MA‡

MCLAREN, WILLIAM GARDNER, lawyer; b. Jasper County, Ia., Oct. 28, 1875; s. Robert and Agnes (Gardner) M.; A.B., Grinnell Coll., 1898, LL.D., (hon.) 1948; Ia. State U. Law Sch., 1900-02; m. Nelle Stubbs, Sept. 21, 1909. Admitted to Wash. bar, 1902; member law firm McLaren & Shorett, Everett, Wash., 1902-08, Bell, Anderson & McLaren, Shorett, Everett, Wash., 1902-08, Bell, Anderson & McLaren, Everett, 1908-10, Shorett, McLaren & Shorett, Seattle, 1910-29; since 1929, Peters, Powell, Evans & McLaren, now Evans, McLaren, Lane, Powell & Beeks. City atty., Everett, Wash., 3 terms, 1906-10; asst. U.S. Dist. Atty., Western District of Washington, 1908-12; appointed member Washington State Board of Law Examiners by Supreme Court of Washington, 1926, resigned, 1929. Member Board of Uniform Law Commrs. for State of Wash. since 1940. Mem. Am. Bar Assn. (mem. board govs., 1937-40), (State del. 1940-48). Am. Law Institute, Seattle Bar Assn. (pres. 1920), Wash. State Bar Assn. (pres. 1936), Am. Judicature Society (director), Phi Delta Phi, Phi Beta Kappa. Republican. Presbyterian (sec. bd. trustees 1st Ch. of Seattle). Clubs: Rainier, Seattle Golf and Country, Broadmoor Golf (Seattle). Contributor to legal periodicals. Home: 1214 Parkside Dr., Seattle 2. Office: Dexter Horton Bldg., Seattle 4 WA‡

MCLAUGHLIN, ALLAN JOSEPH, sanitarian; b. London, Ont., Can., June 26, 1872; s. Patrick Hugh and Katherine (MacLean) M.; grad. London Collegiate Inst., 1888; M.D., Detroit Coll. Medicine, 1896; m. Susan Mars, July 16, 1901. Appointed acting asst. surgeon, U.S. Pub. Health Service, Mar. 1900; commd. asst. surgeon, Apr. 1900; passed asst. surgeon, Apr. 1905; surgeon, Dec. 1, 1912. Served in New York, Washington, Naples, Italy, Hamburg and Berlin, Germany, Trieste, Austria, and San Francisco acting dir. of health for P.I., 1908-09; in charge federal investigation sewage pollution of Great Lakes and Missouri River, 1911-12; chief sanitary expert and director field work, Internat. Joint Commn., 1913-14; Mass. state commr. of health, 1915-17; appt. asst. surgeon gen. U.S. Pub. Health Service, 1918; served in N.Y. City, St. Louis and as dir. Dist. No. 3, hdqrs. Chicago; med. dir. U.S.P.H.S. since 1930; chief med. officer U.S. Coast Guard, 1932-36; professorial lecturer in communicable diseases and epidemiology, Div. of Hygiene and Pub. Health, U. of Michigan, 1936-40; medical administrative consultant, Ill. State Dept. of Public Health, 1942-44. Member com. making public health survey of Greece for League of Nations, 1929. Mem. Am. Med. Assn., Mass. Medical Society, American Pub. Health Assn. (pres. 1922). Author: Communicable Diseases, 1923; (with J. A. Tobey) Personal Hygiene (brochure), 1923. Contbr. many articles to med. jours. and to publs. U.S.P.H.S. Home: 107 Glenbrook Rd., Bethesda 14, Md. Address: U.S. Public Health Service, Washington DC‡

MCLAUGHLIN, CHARLES V(INCENT), Asst. Sec. of Labor; b. North Platte, Neb., Apr. 5, 1875; s. Michael M. and Rose (Daugherty) McL.; m. Alice M. Talbot, Jan. 18, 1899. Fireman U.P.R.R., 1898-1902, locomotive engr., 1902-10; mem. Assn. of Locomotive Firemen and Enginemen since 1900, v.p. since 1910; Asst. Sec. of Labor, Jan. 6, 1938-Aug. 1, 1941; now retired. Home: 3500 75th Pl., Inglewood CA*‡

MCLAUGHLIN, EMMA MOFFAT (MRS. ALFRED MCLAUGHLIN), civic worker; b. San Francisco, Calif., Sept. 21, 1880; d. Henry and Adrianna Green (Swett) Moffat; A.B., U. Cal., 1902, L.H.D., 1960; M.A. Mills Coll., 1942, LL.D., 1962; m. Dr. Alfred McLaughlin, Oct. 29, 1904; 1 dau., Jean (Mrs. Jefferson J. Doolittle). Chmn. Baby Hygiene Com., Am. Assn. Univ. Women, 1916-18; dir. Pub. Edn. Soc., 1917-32; mem. Calif. State Com. of Children's Year, 1917-22, San Francisco chmn., 1918; v.p. Progress Co., 1919; pres. San Francisco Center, Calif. League Women Voters, 1920-21, mem. bd. of dirs., 1921-29; dir. Community Chest, 1921-26; chmn. Dept. of Internat. Cooperation to Prevent War, Calif. League Women Voters, 1928-29; mem. bd. Dept. of Social Welfare of State of Calif., Dec. 1930-Feb. 1932; member Library Commission of San Francisco; mem. Art Commn. of City of San Francisco, 1932-33; as mem. attended Inst. of Pacific Relations meetings, Honolulu, 1927, Kyoto, 1929, Banff, 1933; sec. San Francisco Bay Region Com. of the Inst. since 1928; vice chmn. San Francisco Bay Region Group of Inst. of Pacific Relations, 1935; vice chmn. Motion Picture Research Council, California Chapter, 1935; mem. presidential and gubernatorial campaign coms.; No. Calif. chmn. govt. and foreign policy, League of Women Voters; dir. League for Planned Parenthood. Mem. bd. dirs. Internat. House U. of California, 1952-58; second vice pres. Alumni Assn. U. of California, 1944-45. Trustee of the World Affairs Council of Northern Calif., since 1947; mem. Distbn. Com., San Francisco Found., 1948-68. Dir. Children's Hosp., San Francisco, 1917-34, Community Chest; mem. women's com. Golden Gate Internat. Expn. Mem. Kappa Gamma. Unitarian. Clubs: Century, Women's Athletic, Women's City, Women's Faculty (Berkeley). Home: San Francisco CA Died Aug. 7, 1968.

MCLAUGHLIN, HAROLD NEWELL, lawyer; b. Cleve., Mar. 19, 1896; s. James R. and Lillian (Newell) McL.; grad. Wooster Acad., 1913; Ph.B. with spl. honors in polit. sci., Coll. of Wooster, 1917; LL.B., Western Res. U., 1922; m. Jeanne Haskins Hoffman, Sept. 8, 1928; children—Robert James, Jane Cynthia (Mrs. Henry Fleming Decker). Admitted to Ohio bar, 1922, U.S. Supreme Ct. bar, 1934, ICC bar, 1931, FCC bar, 1946, CAB bar, 1945; practice in Cleve., 1922-67; partner firm Marshman, Hornbeck, Hollington, Steadman & McLaughlin, 1961-66; asso. Marshman, Hornbeck & Hollington, 1966-67. Asst. sec., dir. Cleve. Broadcasting, Inc., 1946-67; sec., dir. Alraydan Mining Co., Inc., 1952-67. Treas., mem. exec. com. Cleve. Ch. Fedn., 1950-53. Trustee Belvoir Gardens Assn. Served as ensign USN, World War I. Mem. Am. (past mem. com. on ry. labor law), Cleve. bar assns., Delta Sigma Rho, Delta Theta Phi. Republican. Presbyn. Mason (32 deg., Shriner). Home: Shaker Heights OH Died Dec. 31, 1967; buried Riverside Cemetery, Cleveland OH

MCLAUGHLIN, PAUL, city ofcl.; b. Boston, Oct. 17, 1900; s. Francis Joseph and Frances (Gorman) McL.; grad. Boston Latin Sch., 1916; m. Elizabeth M. Gorry, Oct. 19, 1946. Asst. mgr. F. H. Birch Co., Boston, 1921-25; spl. rep. marketing Emerson Radio of Conn., Hartford, Conn., 1945-51; S.E. rep. and regional mgr. Bendix Aviation Corp. (name changed Bendix Corp.), Balt., 1951-56; v.p. charge of sales Calcintor Corp., Bay City, Mich., 1956-60; indsl. coordinator Town of Southington (Conn.), 1960-71. Spl. cons. Southington Bank & Trust Co., 1963-71. Exec. dir. Southington Community Chest, 1963-71; chmn. Southington chpt. ARC, 1947-49. Served with USNR, 1917-19, 42-45. Mem. Conn. Assn. Municipal Devel. Commn. (mem. ethics com. 1965-71), N.E. Indsl. Developers Assn., Am. Legion, Police Commrs. Assn. Conn. Democrat. Home: Southington CT Died Mar. 5, 1971.

MCLAUGHLIN, ROBERT SAMUEL, business exec.; b. Enniskillen, Ont., Can., 1871. Chmn. bd., dir. Gen. Motors Can., Ltd.; v.p. Gen. Motors Corp.; dir. C.P. Ry. Co., Canadian Consol. Mining and Smelting Co. of Can., Ltd., Internat. Nickel Co. of Can., Ltd., Moore Corp., Ltd. Home: Parkwood, Oshawa. Office: Oshawa ON Canada

MCLAUGHLIN, ROLAND RUSK, educator; born Toronto, Ont. Can., Mar. 16, 1901; s. John James and Maude (Christie) McL.; B.A.Sc. in Chem. Engring., U. Toronto, 1922, M.A.Sc., 1923, Ph.D., 1926; D.Sc. (hon.), Assumption U., Windsor, Ont., 1961; m. Marjorie Jean McLay, Sept. 16, 1925; 1 dau., Julia. With Canada Dry Ginger Ale, Inc., 1923-26; Grocer's Co. scholar biochemistry Lister Inst. Preventive Medicine, London, Eng., 1930; prof. chem. engring. U. Toronto, 1931-—, chmn. dept., 1946-60, dean faculty applied sci. and engring., 1954-66, chairman of planning division, 1966-—. Chairman committee reorgn. Canadian Chem. Socs., 1943-44. Fellow Chem. Inst. Can. (pres. 1945-46), Engring. Inst. Can., Chem. Soc. (London); mem. Canadian Inst. Chemistry (v.p. 1942-43), Canadian Chem. Assn. (pres. 1943-44), Am. Soc. Engring. Edn., Sigma Chi. Clubs: University, York (Toronto). Toronto ON Canada Died Sept. 10, 1970.

MCLAUGHLIN, STUART WATTS, accountant; born Newark, Nov. 29, 1905; s. John W. and Evelyn Nichols (Watts) McL.; A.B., Colgate U., 1926; grad. study N.Y.U., 1927-29, Harvard Grad. Sch. Bus. Adminstrn., fall 1948; C.P.A., N.J., 1935, and New York State, 1936; married Bette Warren Hickok, December 1940; children—Janet, Bruce Campbell, John Ware. Mng. accountant Price Waterhouse & Co., N.Y. City, 1928-45; asst. comptroller W.Va. Pulp and Paper Co., N.Y. City, 1945-49, comptroller, 1949-61; controller F. W. Dodge Corp., 1962-64; pvt. practice as C.P.A., N.Y.C., 1964-67. Mem. Am. Inst. C.P.A.'s, Financial Execs. Inst., Am. Mgmt. Assn., N.Y. State Soc. C.P.A.'s, Kappa Delta Rho. Club: Colgate University (pres. 1966-67) (N.Y.C.). Home: New York City NY Died Apr. 20, 1967.

MCLEAN, EDWARD COCHRANE, judge; b. Hoosick Falls, N.Y., Oct. 16, 1903; s. Edward K. and Irene M. (Cochrane) McL.; A.B., Williams Coll., 1924; LL.B., Harvard, 1929; m. Louise D. Hunter, Sept. 5, 1931; children—Edward C., Alan. Admitted to N.Y. bar, 1929; mem. Debevoise, Plimpton & McLean and predecessor firms, 1943-62; probate judge of Darien, Conn., 1957-62; U.S. dist. judge So. Dist. N.Y., 1962-72; dep. asst. dist. atty. N.Y. County, 1935-36.

Fellow Am. Coll. Trial Lawyers; mem. Am. Law Inst., Am., N.Y. State, N.Y. City bar assns., Phi Beta Kappa, Phi Sigma Kappa, Delta Sigma Rho. Republican. Episcopalian. Clubs: Down Town Assn., Century Assn. Harvard (N.Y.C.). Home: Darien CT and New York City NY Died Oct. 12, 1972; buried Roxbury CT

MCLEAN, FRANKLIN CHAMBERS, univ. prof.; b. Maroa, Ill., Feb. 29, 1888; s. William Thomas and Margaret Philbrook (Crocker) McL.; B.S., U. of Chicago, 1907, Ph.D., 1915; M.D., Rush Med. Coll., 1910; M.D. (hon.), University of Lund, Sweden, 1957; m. Helen Vincent, June 11, 1923; 1 son, Franklin Vincent (died May 31, 1948). Interne Cook County Hospital, 1910-11; professor pharmacology, University of Oregon, 1911-14; member staff Hosp. of Rockefeller Inst. for Med. Research, New York, 1914-16; dir. Peiping (China) Union Med. Coll., 1916-20, prof. medicine, 1916-23; prof. medicine U. Chgo., 1923-32, prof. pathol. physiology, 1933-53, emeritus, 1953-65, dir. univ. clinics, 1928-32, dir. toxicity lab., 1941-43, dir. spl. AEC project, 1948-51, dir. special project for USAF, 1951-54; visiting professor, department of histology, University of Illinois College Dentistry, 1966-68. Cons. to Santa Fe Operations office, AEC, Los Alamos, N.M., 1947-49; mem. spl. panel AEC, Washington, 1948-50; dep. chmn. Joint Panel on Med. Aspects of Atomic Warfare, 1949-53; mem. tech. adv. panel on biol. and chem. Warfare Office Asst. Sec. of Def., 1955-60; member subcommittee on Skeletal system NRC, 1952-58. Served as 1st lt. to maj. M.C., U.S. Army, World War; sr. consultant in gen. medicine, A.E.F., 1918. Served as civilian in connection with chem. warfare preparedness, Office Sci. Research and Development, 1941-43; lt. col. and col., Med. Corps A.U.S., assigned to Chem. Warfare Service, 1943-45. Mem. Research Council of Chem. Corps Adv. Bd., 1947-49. Awarded Legion of Merit, 1945, Army Commendation Ribbon, 1947; War and Navy Depts. certificate Appreciation, 1947. Trustee Easter Seal Research Found., 1960-68, past chmn.; dir., sec.-treas. Nat. Med. Fellowship, Inc., Chicago; trustee Fisk U. (chmn. bd. 1951-55). Mem. Assn. Am. Physicians, Harvey Soc., Institute of Medicine (pres. 1959) (Chgo.), Chicago Soc. Internal Medicine, American Physiol. Soc.; Am. Acad. Orthopaedic Surgeons (hon.), Assn. Bone and Joint Surgs. (hon.). Clubs: Tavern, Quadrangle (Chgo.); Cosmos (Washington). Author: (with Marshall R. Urist) Bone: An Introduction to the Physiology of Skeletal Tissue, 1955; (with Ann M. Budy) Radiation, Isotopes, and Bone, 1964). Co-editor: Radioisotopes and Bone, 1962. Home: Chicago IL Died Sept. 10, 1968.

MCLEAN, HEBER HAMPTON, ret. naval officer; b. Llano, Tex., Dec. 9, 1899; s. John Hiram and Minnie (Button) McL.; B.S., U.S. Naval Acad.; m. Evelyn Winston Lane, Dec. 11, 1923; 1 dau., Evelyn Lane Ghormley; m. 2d, Ellen Burkhardt Knox, Feb. 25, 1953; 1 dau., Mary Ann. Commd. ensign USN, 1920, and advanced through various grades to rear admiral; ret. 1954 with rank of v. admiral. Awarded Legion of Merit, awarded Gold star in lieu of 2d and 3d awards, Grand Cruz di Aviz (Portugal), Order of St. Charles (Monaco), Order of Military Merit (Korea). Methodist. Mason. Club: Army and Navy Country. Home: San Antonio TX Died Sept. 9, 1971.

MCLEAN, JOHN M(ILTON), physician; b. N.Y.C., Oct. 24, 1909; s. William and Ella Louise (Powel) M.; M.E., Stevens Institute Technology, 1930, Doctor of Education (honorary), 1965; M.D., Cornell U., 1934; m. Mary Lou Carlon, June 14, 1941; children—Ann Powel, Mary Margaret, John Brandon, Ellen Steele. Intern ophthalmology Johns Hopkins Hosp., 1934-35, asst. resident, 1935-38, resident, 1938-39; asst. ophthalmology Johns Hopkins Med. Sch., 1935-38, Mellon fellow, 1936-37, asso., 1939-41; asso. prof. ophthalmology Cornell U. Med. Coll., 1941-42, prof., 1942-68, prof. clin. surgery, 1942-68; dir. dept. ophthalmology N.Y. Hosp., attending surgeon ophthalmology, 1941-68; cons. ophthalmologist N.Y. Eye and Ear Infirmary, U.S. Naval Hosp., St. Albans, Hosp. Spl. Surgery, Phelps Meml. Hosp., Meml. Hosp. Center, Manhattan Eye, Ear and Throat Hospital. Member advisory bd. N.Y. State Athletic Commn. Mem. Am. Ophthal. Soc., Assn. Research Ophthalmology, A.A.A.S., N.Y. State, N.Y. County med. socs., A.M.A., N.Y. Acad. Med., Am. Acad. Ophthalmology and Otolaryngology, Internat. Congress Ophthalmology, ophthal. socs. Peru, Brazil, Mexico, Chile, Pan Am., N.Y., Miss.-La. ophthal. socs., Harvey Soc., Alpha Omega Alpha, Chi Phi, Tau Beta Pi, Nu Sigma Nu. Presbyn. Club: Univ. (N.Y.C.); Pelham Co. Author eye surgery textbooks. Contbr. sci. articles med. jours. Home: Pelham Manor NY Died May 2, 1968.

MCLELLAN, HUGH DEAN, lawyer; b. Belfast, Me., Sept. 10, 1876; s. William Henry and Angeline (Nickels) McL.; A.B., Colby Coll., 1895; LL.B., Columbia, 1902; LL.D., Colby, 1934, Bowdoin College, 1935; m. Nina Poor, Jan. 1, 1908; children—Janet M. (Mrs. Janet M. Russell), Nancy F., Nina P. Admitted to Me. bar, 1897; prin. high sch., Belfast, Me., 1897-99; in practice of law at Boston, Mass., 1902-32; mem. McLellan, Brickley & Sears, 1913-32; lecturer in agency, Boston U. Law Sch., 1929-38; lecturer in brief making and preparation of cases, Harvard U. Sch. of Law, 1935-42; judge U.S. Dist. Court, Mass. Dist., 1932-41, resigned; in general practice since Oct. 1941; chmn. Enemy Alien Bd. for Mass., since 1941. Apptd. by Supreme Ct. mem. Adv. Com. on Rules of Criminal Procedure. Mem. Am., Middlesex and Boston bar assns. Club: Curtis (Boston). Author of Some Aspects of Court and Office Practice," 1939, also A Case Book on Contracts (with John T. Noonan). Home: 45 Percy Rd., Lexington, Mass. Office: 1 Federal St., Boston MA‡

MCLELLAN, THOMAS GEORGE, physician; b. Weston, Ont., Can., Oct. 28, 1898; s. Thomas and Isabell (Cruickshank) McL.; M.D., U. Toronto, 1924; m. Mary George, Oct. 17, 1927; 1 son, Thomas George. Came to U.S., 1924, naturalized, 1932. Rotating intern Westmoreland Hosp., Greensburg, Pa., 1924-25, Western Pa. Hosp., Pitts., 1925-26; resident Wills Eye Hosp., Phila., 1929-30; opthalmologist Connellsville (Pa.) State Hosp., also past pres. bd. Bd. dirs. Carnegie Library. Served with 1st Canadian Tank Bn., World War I. Diplomate Am. Bd. Opthalmology. Mem. A.M.A., Am. Acad. Opthalmology and Otolaryngology, Fayette County Med. Soc. (pres. 1943), Pa. (v.p.), Pitts. (pres.) opthalmology socs. Mason (32 deg., Shriner). Home: Connellsvilee PA Died July 2, 1969; buried Greenwood Cemetery, Connellsville PA

MCLEMORE, ALBERT SYDNEY, officer U.S.M.C.; b. Franklin, Tenn., May 23, 1869; grad. U.S. Naval Acad., 1891. Apptd. 2d lt. U.S.M.C., July 1, 1893; promoted 1st lt., June 14, 1896; capt., Mar. 3, 1899; asst. adj. and insp. with rank of maj., Dec. 15, 1904; same, with rank of lt. col., Aug. 29, 1916; same, with rank of col., Aug. 29, 1916. Bvtd. capt. for distinguished conduct and pub. service at Guantanamo, Cuba; brigade adj. and insp., 1st Brigade of Marines, Manila, P.I., 1908-09; in charge S. Atlantic Insp. Dist., Norfolk, Va., 1910-11; assigned duty office of adj. and insp. Marine Corps Hdqrs., Navy Dept., May 23, 1911; asst. adj. and insp., San Francisco, Aug, 1919-—. Home: Murfreesboro TN‡

MCLENDON, LENNOX POLK, lawyer; b. Wadesboro, N.C., Feb. 12, 1890; s. Walter Jones and Sarah J. (Polk) McL.; B.S., N.C. State Coll., 1910, H.H.D., 1962; LL.B., U. of N.C., 1912, LL.D., 1955; Dr. of Laws (hon.), University N.C. at Greensboro, 1964; m. Mary Lilly Aycock, June 27, 1917; children—Mary Louise (Mrs. E. K. Atkinson), Lennox Polk, Charles Aycock, William Woodard, John Aycock. Admitted to N.C. bar, 1913; mayor of Chapel Hill, N.C., May-Dec. 1913; practiced law, alone, Durham, N.C., 1914-16; sr. mem. McLendon & Hedrick, Durham, 1919-33; partner McLendon, Brim, Brooks, Hedrick, Durham, 1919-33; partner McLendon, Brim, Brooks, Pierce & Daniels, Greensboro, 1933-68; solicitor 10th Judicial Dist., 1921-24. Mem. N.C. Gen. Assembly, 1917; chmn. State Bd. of Elections, 1932-36; chmn. Commn. on State Dept. of Justice for N.C., 1937-38; mem. N.C. Probation Commn., 1939-54; declined appointment to the N.C. Supreme Court, 1936. Gen. counsel U.S. Senate Com. Rules and Adminstrn., Baker Investigation, 1963-65. Served as 1st lieutenant N.C. Nat. Guard, Mexican border, 1916; capt. field arty., U.S. Army, 1917, and recruited Battery C, 113th F.A.; sent to France with Advanced Sch. Detachment, 30th Div., May 1918, rejoining 113th F.A., Aug. 1918; participated Battle of St. Mihiel and Argonne Forest Offensive; with Army of Occupation; disch. maj., Mar. 1919. Trustee Cone Meml. Hosp., Greensboro, N.C. Fellow Am. Bar Assn. Found. Mem. N.C. State Bar (pres. 1940-41), Am., N.C. bar assns., N.C. State Bd. Higher Edn. (vice chmn. 1955-60, chmn. 1960-63), Kappa Sigma. Democrat. Baptist. Club: Greensboro Country. Home: Greensboro NC Died Aug. 7, 1968.

MCLEOD, MARY LOUISE DEMARCO, lawyer; b. Detroit, Aug. 21, 1914; d. Charles and Antonia (DeMarco) DeMarco; student Coll. Liberal Arts, Wayne U., 1931-34, LL.B., 1938; m. Clarence J. McLeod, Feb. 9, 1959 (dec. May 1959). Admitted to Mich. bar, 1938, pvt. practice, 1938; tchr. lecture discussion course law for the Layman at YWCA, 1942-43; 1st woman atty., rent control div. OPA, 1942-43; pvt. practice, mem. law firm McLeod, Fixel and Fixel, 1940-47; asso. Clarence J. McLeod, 1947-59, Henry P. Rosin, 1959-68; civilian legal assistance officer U.S. Army, Army Ground and Service Forces Redistbn. Center, Miami Beach, Fla., 1944-45; civilian claims officer Kennedy Gen. Hosp., Memphis, 1946; adjudicator VA, Detroit, 1947. Named one of Top Ten Working Women in Mich., 1967. Mem. Fed., Am. (chmn. subcom. inter-country adoptions 1961-63, Mich. membership chmn., sect. gen. practice), Detroit bar assns., State Bar Mich., Women Lawyers Assn. Mich., Nat. Assn. Women Lawyers (editor jour. 1963-64, pres. 1966-67), Internat. Fedn. Women Lawyers (chmn. scholarship com., N.Am. editor 1964-68), Phi Delta Delta. Clubs: Detroit Athletic. Women City. Established scholarship at U. Detroit in memory of husband. Home: Detroit MI Died July 31, 1968.

MCLEOD, N.H.F., sec.-treas. Parke, Davis & Co.; b. London, Ont., Can., Feb. 12, 1875; s. Robert and Ann (McIvor) McL.; m. Maude Annie Evans, May 13, 1896; children—Rodina (Mrs. Gilbert H. Whelden), Margaret (Mrs. Fred A. Hughes). Associated successively with Canadian Bank of Commerce, Detroit-Michigan Stove Co., Parke, Davis & Co.; resigned from Parke, Davis & Co., Nov. 1946. Republican. Presbyn. Clubs: Detroit, The Country, Detroit Boat. Home: 8120 E. Jefferson Av. Office: Buhl Bldg., Detroit MI‡

MCLIN, ANNA EVA, pre-school educator; b. Houston, d. Robert W. and Christine E. (Tuffly) McLin; grad. Wheelock Kindergarten Training Sch., Boston, 1907; grad. Second Internat. Montessori Training Course, Rome, Italy, 1914; courses at Teachers Coll., Columbia, and New Sch. of Social Research, New York; also specialized courses in European Centers. Began as teacher, 1907; a pioneer in the nursery school field; served as dir. kindergarten, at Hope Farm, Verbank, N.Y., as dir. Model Kindergarten and instr. Kindergarten Training Sch., Dallas, Tex., and dir. Pub. Sch. Kindergarten, Trenton, N.J.; dir. Kindergarten of Alfred Corning Clark Neighborhood House, N.Y. City, 1914, establishing the first nursery sch. in U.S.; then dir. kindergarten dept. City Training Sch., Trenton and twice returned to the Neighborhood House; dir. kindergarten, Primary Training and Normal Training Sch., Stevens Point, Wis., summer 1915; apptd. prin. Child Edn. Foundation Tng. Sch., 1918; dir. Child Edn. Found., 1918-53, emeritus; consultant in education and human relations. Mem. of original Nat. Com. on Nursery Schs., 1926; mem. kindergarten com. Assn. for Childhood Edn.; mem. advisory com. on Emergency Nursery Schs., N.Y. City; del. to New Edn. Fellowship Conf., Elsinore, Denmark, 1929; del. to White House Conf. on Child Health and Protection, Nov. 1930; del. Midcentury White House Conf. on Children and Youth, 1950; mem. adv. com. Nat. Fedn. Day Nurseries; with Non-Govtl. Orgn. of UN. Mem. Mus. Modern Art; dir. emeritus School of Education, Syracuse U., from 1958. Mem. English-Speaking Union (edn. com.), Nat. Assn. for Nursery Edn., N.Y. State Assn. for Nursery Edn. Presbyn. Club: Cosmopolitan. Author of ednl. charts, pamphlets and articles, and lecturer before ednl. assns., clubs, parents' forum, radio broadcasts, etc. Home: New York City NY Died July 19, 1970; buried Hempstead TX

MCMAHAN, GEORGE THOMAS, hosp. adminstr.; b. Van Alstyne, Tex., Feb. 13, 1901; s. Eli F. and Minnie (Fowler) McM.; student Austin Coll., 1924-25; M.D., Baylor U., 1928; postgrad. neurology and psychiatry, Columbia, 1941; m. Martha Ruth Dalton, Feb. 14, 1947; one daughter, Mrs. R. D. Howell. Engaged as assistant physician San Antonio State Hosp., 1928-30, physician, 1930-35; intern Parkland Hosp., Dallas, 1930; pvt. practice, Burnet, Tex., 1935-37; supt. Big Spring (Tex.) State Hosp., 1937-41; chief neuropsychiat. service William Beaumont Gen. Hosp., El Paso, Tex., 1942-46; chief med. officer Waco (Tex.) VA Center, 1946-47; dir. VA Hosp., Gulfport, Miss., 1947-49; mgr. Waco VA Center, 1949-59; dir., Waco VA Hosp., 1959-67. Bd. dirs. Waco United Fund, 1952-67, bd. trustees 1952-54; bd. dirs. Waco Goodwill Industries, 1955-56. Served to col., M.C., AUS, 1942-46. Diplomate Am. Bd. Psychiatry and Neurology. Fellow Am. Psychiat. Assn.; mem. Am., Tex. med. assns., McLennan County Med. Soc., Assn. Med. Supts. Mental Hosps., Assn. Hosp. Adminstrs., Fed. Hosp. Inst. Alumni Assn., Am. Legion, Waco C. of C. (hon. mem. bd. 1960-67). Rotarian. Home: Waco TX Died Dec. 31, 1967; buried Howe Cemetery, Howe TX

MCMAHON, ALPHONSE, physician; b. St. Louis, Mo., Aug. 4, 1895; s. John Francis and Margaret Elizabeth (Murphy) McM.; A.B., St. Louis University, 1915, M.D., 1919, M.A., 1935; married Mary Celeste Dolan, December 31, 1954. Intern St. Luke's Hosp., St. Louis, Mo., 1919; St. Vincent's Hosp., Los Angeles, Calif., 1920; asst. resident, Pottenger Sanitorium, Monrovia, Calif., 1920-21; practice of internal medicine, St. Louis, Mo., 1921-42; mem. faculty of sch. of medicine St. Louis Univ.; 1922-46, associate professor medicine, from 1946; chief of staff of St. John's Hospital, 1951. Cons. internal medicine to Surgeon Gen. U.S. Navy. Served as member M.C., U.S.N.R., from 1935; called to active duty, 1942; promoted to rank of commodore, 1945; comdg. officer Naval Res. Med. Co. 9-1; rear adm., 1953. Mem. St. Louis Smoke committee, 1939; mem. bd. St. Louis Opera Guild, 1939. Received Letter of Commendation for Naval Med. Service at base hosp. in South Pacific; awarded Distinguished Service Medal of Miss. Valley Med. Assn., 1944. Diplomate Am. Bd. Internal Medicine. Fellow A.C.P., Assn. Mil. Surgeons, Soc. Med. Cons. to Armed Forces; mem. St. Louis Med. Soc. (pres. 1939), A.M.A. (v.p. 1940, chmn. council on sci. assembly), Soc. Internal Medicine, Am. Therapeutic Soc. (pres. 1938), Nat. Tb Assn., Am. Heart Assn., So. Med. Assn. (councilor 1936-41, pres. 1953-54), Alpha Omega Alpha, Sigma Psi, Alpha Kappa Kappa. Roman Catholic. Knight of Malta, K.C. Club: University (St. Louis). Author med. articles. Home: St Louis MO

MCMAHON, ARTHUR LAURENCE, priest; b. Waterbury, Conn., Sept. 14, 1863; s. Patrick and Ellen (Carroll) McM.; Dominican Coll., Springfield, Ky., and

Somerset, O., 1887-90; Dominican House of Studies and U. of Louvain, Belgium 1890-94, ordained, 1892: Dominican House of Studies, Vienna, 1894-95, Lectoı of Theology, 1896; Dominican Bibl. Coll. of St. Stephen, Jerusalem, 1895-97, and traveled extensively through Bibl. lands; B.Th., Rome, 1907, M.Th., 1913. Novice master, St. Joseph's Convent, Somerset, O., 1897-1904; prof. theology and sacred scripture, Dominican House of Studies, Somerset, 1897-1905; Dominican House of Studies, Washington, D.C., 1905-07; definitor and sec., Gen. Chapter Dominican Order, Viterbo, Italy, 1907; vicar-gen. Dominican Order West of Rocky Mountains (Congregation of Calif.), 1907-12, and provincial same, after its erection into a province, 1912-26. Se. Gen. Chapter Dominican Order, Fribourg, Switzerland, 1916; mem. commn. revising Constitutions of Dominican Order, Rome, 1928-29; treas. Dominican House of Studies, Washington, D.C., 1929-39. Contbr. to Catholic New Haven CT‡

MCMAHON, HENRY GEORGE, educator, lawyer; b. New Iberia, La., Dec. 27, 1900; s. Richard Supple and Mathilde (Dansereau) McM.; A.B., La. State U., 1923, LL.B., 1925, A.M., 1937; LL.D., Loyola U. of South, 1962; research asso. Raymond Found., Northwestern U., 1940-41; m. Neenah Webster, Dec. 27, 1927; children—Henry George, Philip, Dan, Nancy (Mrs. Charles M. Pecot, Jr.), John. Admitted to La. bar, 1925; practiced in New Orleans, 1926-36; with Normann, McMahon & Breckwoldt, later Normann & McMahon, 1929-36; mem. law faculty Loyola U. of South, 1929-37; prof. law Louisiana State University, 1937-62, Boyd professor, 1962-66, acting dean, 1942, 47-48, dean, 1949-52. Res. counsel The California Co., New Orleans, 1945-46; city-parish atty., Baton Rouge, Parish of East Baton Rouge, 1949; coordinator, reporter La. Code Civil Procedure. Served to lt. comdr. USNR, 1942-45. Recipient Hatton W. Summers award for outstanding services in improvement adminstrn. justice Southwestern Legal Found. Mem. Am., La. (gov. 1941-42, 48-49, 54-55, 58-59, 64-65) bar assns., La. Law Inst. (council 1938-66), Am. Judicature Soc., Phi Kappa Phi, Kappa Sigma, Phi Delta Phi. Democrat. Roman Catholic. Club: Boston (New Orleans). Author: McMahon on Louisiana Practice, rev. edit., 1949; (with Rubin) Anno. La. Pleadings, 1963. Contbr. articles law jours. and reviews. Home: Baton Rouge LA Died Oct. 30, 1966; buried Roselawn Cemetery, Baton Rouge LA

MCMANES, KENMORE MATHEW, naval officer; born Galion, O., May 22, 1900; s. Albert Flynn and Emma (Olson) McM.; B.S., U.S. Naval Acad., 1922; J.D., George Washington U., 1937; m. Virginia Reed, Oct. 15, 1930; children—Kenmore Reed, Albert Spencer. Commd. ensign, U.S. Navy, 1922, advanced through grades to rear adm., 1950; duty in battleships, submarines, light cruisers, 1922-34; command USS Monoghan, 1939-40; asst. naval attache Am. Embassy, London, 1941-43; comdr. Destroyer Squadron 24, Pacific Fleet, 1943-45, U.S. Naval Group, France, 1945; duty Office Judge Advocate Gen., Navy Dept., 1946; comdr. USS Houston, 1947; with Gen. Planning Group, Office Chief Naval Operations, Navy Dept., 1948-50; comdr. Destroyer Flotilla One, Pacific Fleet, 1950-51; comdr. fleet activities Japan-Korea, 1951-52; asst. chief of naval operations, Naval Reserve, 1953-58; deputy chief of naval operations, 1958-59; comdt. 6th Naval Dist., Charleston (S.C.) Naval Base, 1959-62; ret., 1962; exec. dir. Easter Seal Med. Center, Rockville, Md., 1962-71. Decorated Navy Cross, Legion of Merit (combat), Order Brit. Empire (hon. comdr.), 1943. Episcopalian. Mason. Clubs: Army and Navy (Wash.); Kenwood (Bethesda, Md.). Home: Bethesda MD Died Jan. 20, 1973; buried Annapolis MD

MCMANIS, JOHN THOMAS, author; b. Wabash, Ind., 1870; s. John Newton and Julia Ann (Jones) M.; student Ind. State Normal Sch., Terre Haute, Ind., 1890-3, Ind. U., 1895-6; A.B., Leland Stanford Jr. U., 1897, A.M., 1902; Ph.D., U. of Chicago, 1904; m. Olive J. Breese, of Galesburg, Mich., June 19, 1914. Teacher pub. schs., Ossian, Ind., 1893-5; prin. high sch., Los Banos, Cal., 1897-1900; head dept. of psychology and edn., Western Mich. State Normal Sch., Kalamazoo, 1904-8; head dept. of edn., Chicago Normal Coll., since 1908. Unitarian. Author: Ella Flagg Young, 1916; Study of Behavior of an Individual Child, 1916. Home: 6946 S. Michigan Av., Chicago IL‡

MCMANUS, GEORGE HENRY, army officer (ret.); b. Hudson, Ia., Dec. 23, 1867; s. Thomas Pierson and Sarah (Rupp) McM.; B. Didactics, Ia. State Teachers Coll., 1887; B.S., U.S. Mil. Acad., 1893; m. Emilie Gertrude Kessler, Jan. 7, 1897; children—Sarah Catharine (Mrs. H.W. McCurdy), George Henry Jr., Thomas Kessler, Mary Alice. Commd. 2d lt., U.S. Army, June 12, 1893, and advanced through grades to brig. gen., Oct. 1, 1918; assigned to Coast Arty., 1893, and served on Atlantic and Pacific coasts, in Alaska, China, Philippines and Canal Zone; served as troop movement officer. Port of Embarkation, Hoboken, N.J., Nov. 1917; ret. Dec. 31, 1931. Awarded D.S.M., Navy Cross. Club: Army, Navy and Marine Corps Country (Washington). Home: 7 Newport Rd., Cambridge 40 MA‡

MCMARTIN, WILLIAM JOSEPH, physician; b. Omaha, Sept. 26, 1904; s. Charles and Mary (O'Kelly) McM.; student U. Chgo., 1923-25, U. Neb., 1925-27; m. Barbara Caroline Baird, Nov. 2, 1935; children—Ray Baird, Walter Richard. Bishop Matthew fellow urology, resident U. Pa. Hosp., 1931-33; mem. faculty Creighton U. Sch. Medicine, 1933—, prof. urology, chmn. dept., 1954—. Mem. Omaha Bd. Health, 1949-55, pres., 1953. Fellow A.C.S.; mem. Am. Urol. Assn. (pres. 1955-56), Western Assn. Ry. Surgeons (past pres.),Internat. Soc. Urology, Belgian Soc. Urology (asso.), Chi Psi. Republican. Presbyn. Author: (with Thomas McCurdy) The Kidney in Hypertension, 1942; also numerous articles. Home: Omaha NB Died Mar. 26, 1971; buried Omaha NB

MCMASTER, FITZ HUGH, newspaper editor; b. Winnsboro, S.C., July 22, 1867; s. George Hunter and Mary Elizabeth (Flenniken) McM.; prep. edn., Mt. Zion Acad., Winnsboro; A.B., U. of S.C., 1888, LL.B., 1889; m. Elizabeth S. Waring, Nov. 2, 1892. Reporter Columbia (S.C.) Record, 1890-91, The State, Columbia, 1893-95; mgr. Evening Post, Charleston, S.C., 1895-1903; circulation mgr. The State, 1903-08; ins. commr. of S.C., 1908-18; city editor The State, 1917-20; asst. mgr. Carolina Life Ins. Co., 1929; editor Columbia Record, 1929-31; then served as reporter on The State; mgr. Standard Cotton Warehouse, Columbia, 1934-41, retired. Sec. and treas. Nat. Conv. of Ins. Commrs., 1912-17. Mem. S.C. Ho. of Rep., 1900-02; mem. S.C. Hist. Commn., 1905-08. Chmn. Columbia Chapter Am. Red Cross, World War, also of Salvation Army Campaign. Chmn. Commn. of Confederate Home, 1924-34; chmn. com. which purchased boyhood home of Woodrow Wilson in Columbia for the State of S.C. Mem. S.R., Sons of Confederacy, Phi Beta Kappa, Sigma Alpha Epsilon, Sigma Delta Chi; State chief of McMaster Clan in America. Democrat. Ruling elder First Presbyn. Ch., Columbia, since 1915. Mason. Club: Kosmos, Rotarian. Apptd. chmn. S.C. ration board, Jan. 1942, retired, July 1943. Home: 1428 Laurel St., Columbia SC‡

MCMASTER, PHILIP DURYEE, research physician; b. Phila., Sept. 14, 1891; s. John Bach and Gertrude (Stevenson) McM.; student pvt. schs., Phila.; B.S., Princeton, 1914; M.D., U. Pa., 1918; spl. student U. Freiburg, Germany, 1914, Columbia, 1921; m. Elizabeth Parsons Dwight, Oct. 13, 1923; children—Gail Parsons (Mrs. Charles Booth Alling, Jr.), Philip Robert Bache. Resident physician U. Pa. Hosp., 1917-19; fellow Rockefeller Inst. Med. Research, 1919-20, asst., 1920-22, asso., 1922-26, asso. mem., 1926-51, mem., prof., 1951-62, prof. emeritus, 1962-73; fellow research psychology Harvard, 1929-30. Served 1st lt. U.S. Army, 1918. Fellow A.A.A.S.; member of Nat. Acad. Scis., N.Y. Acad. Sci., N.Y. Acad. Medicine, Harvey Soc. (sec. 1927-28), Am. Assn. Immunologists, Am. Soc. Exptl. Pathology, Am. Assn. Pathologists and Bacteriologists, Am. Soc. Exptl. Biology and Medicine, Sigma Xi, Alpha Omega Alpha. Clubs: Princeton (New York); Riverside (Conn.) Yacht; Century. Home: Cos Cob CT Died Mar 1973.

MCMASTER, WILLIAM HENRY, senator; b. Ticonic, Ia., May 10, 1877; s. Samuel Alden and Sarah Jane (Woodsum) M.; Beloit (Wis.) Coll., 1895-99; m. Harriet R. Reustle, of Beloit, Apr. 16, 1902; children—William Henry, Dorothy. Banking business (country banks), 1901-66. Mem. S.D. Ho. of Rep., 1911, Senate 1913-15; lt. gov. of S.D., 1917-19, gov., terms, 1921-23, 1923-25; started gasoline war, 1923, that resulted in lower price of gasoline throughout U.S.; mem. U.S. Senate, term 1925-31; pres., chmn. bd. Dixon Nat. Bank (Ill.), 1933-66. Republican. Episcopalian. Trustee Yankton (S.D.) Coll. Mason, Odd Fellow, Elk. Mem. Beta Theta Pi. Home: Dixon IL Died Sept. 16, 1968.

MCMASTER, WILLIAM HENRY, coll. pres.; b. Centerville, O., Sept. 17, 1875; s. James Nelson (M.D.) and Susan Elizabeth (Neff) M.; Ph.B., Mt. Union Coll., Ohio, 1899; B.D., Drew Theol. Sem., 1902, United Free Ch. Coll., Glasgow, Scotland, 1903-04; M.A., New York University, 1905, D.D., Ohio Wesleyan U., 1911, LL.D., U. of Pittsburgh, 1926; m. Isabella Thoburn Mills, of Cleveland, O., May 8, 1907; children—Isabella Thoburn, William Henry, Janet Lyle. Ordained M.E. ministry, 1899; pastor Bronxdale, New York City, 1899-1901, Elmhurst, New York City, 1901-06, Embury Memorial Ch., Brooklyn, 1906-09, pres. Mt. Union Coll. since 1909. Pres. Ohio Council Chs.; mem. Gen. Conf. M.E. Ch., 4 times to 1932. Mem. Sigma Alpha Epsilon. Mason (32 deg.); past chaplain Ohio Grand Lodge, F. and A.M. Home: Alliance OH‡

MCMATH, ROBERT EDWIN, steel mfr.; b. Oct. 21, 1886; s. Edwin Augustus and Harriet C. (Lapham) McM.; A.B., Harvard University, 1908, LL.B., 1910; LL.D. (honorary), Lehigh University, 1958; married Grace E. Richman, Sept. 9, 1914. Admitted to N.Y. bar, 1911; practiced law, 1911-18; asst. sec. Bethlehem Steel Corp., 1918-19, sec., 1919-57, financial v.p., 1930-68, financial vice president, chmn. finance com., 1957-68. Trustee Nat. Foundation for Infantile Paralysis since 1937; trustee and chmn. of finance com. Lehigh Univ., 1942-57. Republican. Clubs: Harvard, University, The Links, Metropolitan (New York). Home: Lake Wales FL Died Mar. 23, 1968.

MCMILLAN, ALFRED E., public relations co. exec.; b. Centralia, Ill., Feb. 2, 1900; ed. U. Ill. Reporter Centralia Eve. Sentinal; sports writer Miami (Fla.) Daily News; sports editor Daytona (Fla.) New Jour., then Palm Beach (Fla.) Post-Times; with Carl Byoir & Assos., Inc., 1937-68, exec. v.p. Mem. Pub. Relations Soc. Am., Artists and Writers in Business. Home: West Palm Beach FL Died 1972.

MCMILLAN, GEORGE SCHOLEFIELD, businessman; b. Canon City, Colo., July 26, 1895; s. A.C. and Virginia (Scholefield) McM.; ed. schs. of Yonkers, N.Y.; A.B., Hamilton Coll., 1916; m. Elizabeth Forsyth, 1922; 1 dau., Virginia S. (dec.). Editorial work on business publs., advertising work as sec., Assn. Nat. Advertisers, Inc.; dir. pub. relations, Bristol-Myers Co., 1944-45, sec., 1945-48, v.p. from 1948. Served as pvt., U.S. Army Hosp. Unit B, France, 18 mos., U.S., 8 mos., World War I. Mem. bd. Advt. Fedn. of Am. (past chmn.); former vice chairman of the board U.S. Trademark Assn.; former mem. exec. com. Proprietary Assn. Am. (chmn. Nat. Relations com.); member steering committee Bureau of Education on Fair Trade; member committee on distbn. Nat. Assn. Mfrs.; mem. com. advt. C. of C. of U.S.; chmn. govt. relations com. Assn. Nat. Advertisers; past mem. bd. Brand Names Found. Mem. N.Y. State C. of C., St. Andrews Soc. State of N.Y., American Legion, Alpha Delta Phi. Clubs: Univ., Sales Exec., Advt. (v.p.), Caledonian Curling (N.Y. City); N. Broadway Marching and Chowder, Hudson River Country (Yonkers, N.Y.); Spencertown Rod and Gun, National Press, Capitol Hill (Washington). Republican. Presbyn. Contbr. arts to advt. jours. Home: Yonkers NY

MCMILLAN, WILLIAM JOSHUA, clergyman; b. nr. Acworth, Ga., Apr. 11, 1870; s. Robert Huie and Margaret (Prichard) McM.; prep. edn., high sch., Acworth; student Davidson (N.C.) Coll., 1889-90; A.B., Southwestern Presbyn. U. Clarksville, Tenn. (now at Memphis), 1893, and student theol. dept., 1894-96; D.D., Southwestern, 1911; m. Florence Willie Hodge, of Ruston, La., July 26, 1897 (died 1900); 1 son, William Erwin; m. 2d, Emma Belle Smith, of Baltimore, Md., Apr. 30, 1928. Ordained ministry Presbyterian Church in United States, 1896; evangelist New Orleans Presbytery, 1896-1897; pastor successively First Church, Brownwood, Texas, and Franklin, Tenn., until 1912, Maryland Av. Ch., Baltimore, Maryland, 1912-31; superintendent of Home Missions, Potomac Presbytery, 1931-33; supply preacher since 1933. Commissioner Gen. Assembly Presbyn. Ch. 5 times to 1927; del. Alliance Ref. Chs. holding Presbyn. System, Pittsburgh, 1921, Cardiff, Wales, 1925; moderator Synod of Tenn., 1911. Mem. bd. dirs. Mary Baldwin Coll., Staunton, Va., 1925-32. Democrat. Home: Old Hickory TN‡

MCMILLEN, DALE WILMORE, bus. exec.; b. Van Wert, O., Jan. 27, 1880; s. Joseph Warren and Mary Jane (Wilmore) McM.; student Oberlin (O.) Coll., 1899-1901; m. Agnes Dell Stewart, Feb. 22, 1904; children—Stewart W., Harold W., Mary Jane (Mrs. Charles W. Crowe), Dale Wilmore. Founder The McMillen Co., Ft. Wayne, Ind., 1916, company merged with Am. Milling Co. to form Allied Mills, Ft. Wayne, 1929, pres., 1929-33; founder Central Sugar Co., Decatur, Ind., 1933, chmn. bd., 1933-44; founder and chmn. bd. Central Soya Co., Inc., Ft. Wayne, Ind., 1934-54. Created McMillen Foundation for support of public projects, Ft. Wayne. Presbyterian. Mason (33deg, K.T.). Home: Fort Wayne IN Died Apr. 20, 1971; buried Fort Wayne IN

MCMULLEN, ADAM, ex-gov.; b. Wellsville, N.Y., June 12, 1874; s. John H. and Mary (Harbison) McM.; grad. high sch., Wymore, Neb., 1889; A.B., U. of Neb., 1896; LL.B., Columbian (now George Washington) U., 1899; m. Cora Greenwood, of Wymore, June 5, 1901. Settled with parents in Neb., 1884; admitted to Neb. bar, 1902; began practice at Wymore; served as mayor also as pres. Sch. Bd., Wymore; mem. Neb. Ho. of Rep., 1905-07, Senate, 1917; gov. of Neb. 2 terms, 1925-29; postmaster, Beatrice, Neb., 1932-36; extensively engaged in farming. Mem. Delta Tau Delta. Republican. Episcopalian. Mason (32 deg., K.C.C.H., K.T.), Odd Fellow. Home: Beatrice NE‡

MCMULLEN, CHARLES BELL, prof. philosophy; b. Greenville, Indiana Co., Pa., Apr. 14, 1871; s. Thomas and Rebecca Jane (Swan) McM.; A.B., Tarkio (Mo.) Coll., 1894; A.B., magna cum laude, Coll. of N.J. (now Princeton), 1896, Ph.D., Princeton, 1909; B.D., Princeton Theol. Sem., 1901; post-grad. study, Yale and Princeton; m. Lille Callabaius Haynes, of Leesville, S.C., Aug. 17, 1909; children—Charles Haynes, Sarah Catherine, Bryce Herbert. Prof. Latin and Greek, Hayward Coll., Fairfield, Ill., 1896-97; prof. philosophy and psychology, Tarkio Coll., 1901-24; prof. philosophy and ethics, Centre College, Danville, Kentucky, since 1924. Member A.A.A.S., Midwestern Psychological Association, Phi Beta Kappa; asso. mem. Am. Psychol. Assn. Republican. Presbyterian. Author: The Logic of Evolution, 1925. Home: Ky. Coll. for Women Campus, Danville KY‡

MCMULLEN, JOHN JOSEPH, editor, publisher; b. Cumberland, Md., Oct. 17, 1901; s. Hugh A. and Anna Mary (Mulledy) McM.; A.B., Mt. St. Mary's Coll., Emmitsburg, Md., 1922; m. Louise Gable Sept. 28, 1927; children—Hugh Aloysius, Louise, Mary John Joseph, Daniel Francis. Partner, McMullen Bros. Dept. Store, Cumberland, 1922-36; sec. treas. The Times and Alleganian Co., publs. of The Cumberland News, The Evening Times and The Sunday Times newspapers, 1936-43, pres., 1943-70; also chmn. bd. and pub. Sunday Times Newspapers; dir. Liberty Trust Co.; Potomac Edison Co., Cumberland; Fidelity Savings Bank, Frostburg, Md. Chmn. Upper Potomac River Commn.; mem. Md. State Planning Commn., 1942-46; mem. Md. States Roads Commn., 1955-70, chmn., 1959. Treas. Democratic State Central Com.; del. to Dem. Nat. Conv., 1948. Democrat. Roman Catholic Elk. Clubs: Country Cumberland MD Died Apr. 1970.

MCMURRAY, JAMES DONALD, newspaper pub.; b. Oneida, Ky., Apr. 7, 1911; s. Harry Logan and Junia (Johnstone) McM.; Ph.B., U. Wis., 1935; m. Carol Starbuck, July 28, 1939; children—Martha Johnstone, Ann Starbuck. Grad. instr. sociology U. Wis., 1935-36; with Indsl. Commn. Wis., 1936-39; sociologist bur. agrl. econs. U.S. Dept. Agr., 1939-41; reporter, editorial writer Racine (Wis.) Jour. Times, 1941-51, pres., pub., editor, 1951-69; pres. Racine Broadcasting Corp.; dir. First Nat. Bank & Trust Co. (Racine). Pres., mem. operating bd. St. Luke's Hosp., Racine. Mem. Wis. Daily Newspaper League (pres.), Sigma Delta Chi. Elk. Home: Racine WI Died May 30, 1969.

MCMURRAY, JOHN, banking, stock raising; b. Grantsville, Utah, June 12, 1873; s. Charles K. and Mary Ann (Hudson) McM.; student Agrl. Coll. of Utah, 1898-99; m. Lula Clara Dahlquist, Aug. 22, 1900; children—Thelma Clara (Mrs. James E. Dayley), John Odell, Raymond William, Mez, Kay, Norma Lu. Stock raiser and farmer nr. Oakley, Ida., since 1900; pres. Farmers Commercial & Savings Bank, Oakley, since 1912; county commr., Cassia Co., Ida., 1912-14; mem. Ida. Ho. of Rep., 1914-16, Ida. State Senate, 1918-29 (pres. pro tem. and majority floorleader 3 terms); chmn. Rep. State Com., 1924-30; Rep. candidate for gov. of Ida., 1930. Mormon. Home: Oakley ID‡

MCNAGNY, PHIL MCCLELLAN, lawyer; b. Columbia City, Ind., Feb. 27, 1886; s. William Forgy and Effie Jane (Wunderlich) McN.; student Culver Mil. Acad., 1901-04; A.B., U. Va. (scholarship), 1907; m. Lucy Cole, Apr. 7, 1920; children—William Forgy, Phil McClellan, Bayard Cole, Lucy McIntosh. Admitted to Ind. bar, 1910; instr. English, French and Latin, Culver Mil. Acad., 2 yrs.; practicing lawyer, Whitley Co., 1910-24, Ft. Wayne, from 1924; mem. Barrett, Barrett & McNagny, specializing in trial law. Mem. Ind. State Legislature, 1917. Served as maj., 46th Inf., U.S. Army, 1917-19. Fellow Am. Coll. Trial Lawyers; mem. American Judicature Soc., Bar Assn. of the Seventh Federal Circuit, Am., Ind. State and Allen Co. bar assns., Am. Legion, Nat. Assn. R.R. Trial Counsel. Episcopalian. Mason. Home: Ft Wayne IN Died Aug. 3, 1969; buried Green Lawn Meml. Cemetery, Fort Wayne IN

MCNAIR, JAMES BIRTLEY, chemist, botanist; b. Hazleton, Pa., Mar. 18, 1889; s. Thomas Speer and Mary (Stevens) McN.; Pomona College, Claremont, Calif., 1912-13; A.B., U. of Calif., 1916, A.M., 1917; studied U. of Pa., 1918, U. of Chicago, 1922-25, U. of Southern Calif., 1934, Chemical Warfare Sch., Edgewood, Md., 1929, 1943. Asst. in U. of Calif., 1914-16; research chemist Nev. Agrl. Expt. Sta., 1917; asst. chemist Citrus By-Product Lab., Bur. Chemistry, U.S. Dept. Agr., Los Angeles, Calif., 1919; chemist in charge Chem. Econ. Co., Los Angeles, 1920; jr. chemist Dairy Div. Bur. Animal Industry, U.S. Dept. Agr., Washington, D.C., 1920-21; asst. Fishery Food Lab., Bur. Fisheries, Washington, D.C., 1921-22; asst. chemist Bur. Internal Revenue, Treas. Dept., Chicago, Ill., May-Oct. 1922; asso. in econ. botany, 1925-26, asst. curator of econ. botany, Field Museum Natural History, Chicago, 1926-32; cons. in ethnobotany, Southwest Museum, Los Angeles, since 1929; asst. wine maker and chemist, Pacific Wines, Inc., Los Angeles, from 1945. Pvt. Med. Enlisted Reserve Corps, U.S. Army, June 1918-Apr. 1919; served in C.W.S., World War II. Awarded Certificate of Merit by Institute of Am. Genealogy, 1939. Fellow A.A.A.S., Soc. Antiquaries of Scotland; mem. profl. assns. Republican. Presbyn. Mason (32 degree, Shriner). Club: Sierra. Author: McNair, McNear, and McNeir Genealogies, 1923, supplement, 1928; Rhus Dermatitis, Its Pathology and Chemotherapy, 1923; Citrus Products, Part I, 1926, Part II, 1927; The Analysis of Fermentation Acids, 1947 (reprint 1952); Simon Cameron's Adventure in Iron, 1949; With Rod and Transit; the engineering career of Thomas S. McNair, 1951; Chemical Plant Phylogeny, 1965. Contbr. Dictionary of Am. Biography, Collier's Med. Ency.; McNair, McNear and McNeir Geneologies Supplement, 1955. Investigations in economic botany, analysis of acids, interrelation between chemical substances in plants, taxonomic and climatic distribution chemical products in plants, chem. products in relation to plant and animal evolution; also plant forms, habits and habitats, law of mass action and production of alkaloids, etc. Home: Los Angeles CA Died Dec. 31, 1967.

MCNAIR, JOHN BABBITT, lt. gov. N.B.; b. Andover, N.B., Can., Nov. 20, 1889; s. James and Frances Ann (Lewis) McN.; B.A., U. N.B., 1911, LL.D., 1938; B.A., Oxford (Eng.) U., 1913, B.C.L., 1914; D.C.L., Mt. Allison U., 1951; m. Marion M. Crocket, May 17, 1921 (dec. Aug. 1961); children—John C., Nancy M. (Mrs. Robert L. Moodie), Marion M. (Mrs. H. Harrison McCain), Janet E. (Mrs. Jeremy C. Scarfe); m. 2d, Margaret Jones, Apr. 27, 1963. Admitted to N.B. bar as barrister, solicitor, 1919; practiced in Fredericton, 1919-55; mem. firms Winslow & McNair, 1920-45, McNair & McNair, 1953-55; mem. Legislative Assembly N.B., 1935-52, atty. gen., 1935-52, premier, 1940-52; chief justice Supreme Ct. N.B., 1955-64; re-admitted to N.B. bar, 1964; lt. gov. N.B., Fredericton, 1965-67. Served as lt., arty., Canadian Expeditionary Force, Canadian Army, 1915-19. Mem. Liberal Fredericton NB Canada Died June 14, 1968; buried Fredericton, NB Can

MCNALLY, JOSEPH THOMAS, editor; b. Albany, N.Y., Oct. 25, 1869; s. Thomas and Maria (Nolan) M.; ed. Villanova (Pa.) Coll.; m. Agnes E. Bulger, of Albany, June 22, 1910. Reporter Albany Evening Union, 1890; telegraph editor Albany Times-Union, 1891-94; telegraph editor, 1895-1905, mng. editor, 1905-11, editor, 1911-—, The Argus. Member advisory board on vocational schs., Albany. Democrat. Member N.Y. State Dem. Editorial Assn. Home: 8 Magnolia Terrace, Albany NY*‡

MCNAMARA, JOSEPH AUGUSTINE, lawyer; b. Fair Haven, Vt., Aug. 4, 1892; s. James and Catherine (Foy) McN.; student St. Michaels Coll., 1910-11; A.B., Coll. of Holy Cross, Worcester, Mass., 1915, A.M., 1925, LL.D., 1953; grad. Harvard Law Sch., 1918; m. Mary P. Magner, June 29, 1922; children—Maureen, Nancy, James, Martha. Admitted to Vt. bar, 1919, practicing in Burlington; judge city ct., 1921-23; U.S. dist. atty. for Vt., 1933-53. Served in 87th Div., U.S. Army, World War. Candidate for Congress, 1930, 32. Mem. Am., Vt. bar assns. Democrat. Catholic. K.C., Elk. Club: Burlington Country. Home: Burlington VT Died Mar. 1972.

MCNAMARA, ROBERT CHARLES, book publisher; b. Redfield, N.Y., May 28, 1881; s. Thomas and Mary (Comiskey) McN.; B.A., Princeton, 1903; m. Elva McCormick, Nov. 24, 1904; children—Ruth M. Felton, Robert Charles, Donald McCormick; m. 2d, Helen Dewey Kingsley, Oct. 1, 1924. Began active career as salesman firm of Hinds, Noble & Eldrege, at N.Y. City, 1903; with Princeton Univ. Store, 1905-08; with Scott, Foresman & Co., ednl. pubs., from 1908, pres., 1943-55, chmn., 1955-61, also dir. Clubs: Chicago, University, Lake Shore (Chgo.); Indian Hill (Winnetka, Ill.); Nassau (Princeton). Home: Winnetka IL Died Sept. 23, 1967; cremated.

MCNAMEE, LUKE, radio exec. (ret.); b. Mt. Hope, Wis., Apr. 4, 1871; grad. U.S. Naval Acad., 1892; Naval War Coll., 1916-17. Commd. ensign, U.S.N., July 1, 1894; advanced through grades to rear admiral. Served on Princeton, Spanish-Am. War, 1898; Naval Sta., Guam, 1905-08; insp. ordnance, Gen. Electric Co., Schenectady, N.Y., 1908-10; navigator, Connecticut, 1910-11; insp. engring. material, Mass. Dist., 1912-14; comd. Sacramento, 1914-15; apptd. chief of staff Pacific Fleet, Apr. 30, 1917; on staff of Adm. Benson, Jan.-Sept. 1918, of Adm. Sims, London, Sept.-Dec. 1918; mem. naval adv. staff to Am. Commn. to Negotiate Peace, Paris, Dec. 1918-Aug. 1919; on staff Adm. Sims, U.S. Naval War Coll., Aug. 1919; comd. U.S.S. Nevada, 1920-21; dir. Naval Intelligence, 1922-23; comd. U.S.S. Tennessee, 1923-24; U.S. naval attache Am. Embassy, London, 1924-25; comdr. Destroyer Squadrons, Battle Fleet, 1926-27; dir. fleet training, Navy Dept.; vice adm. comdg. battleships, Battle Force, 1931-32; adm. comdg. Battle Force, 1932-33; pres. Naval War Coll., 1933-34; retired, 1934; permanent rank, adm.‡

MCNARNEY, JOSEHH T., corp. exec.; b. Emporium, Pa., Aug. 28, 1893; s. James Pollard and Helen (Taggert) McN.; B.S., U.S. Mil. Acad., 1915; grad. Air Corps Tactical School, 1921, Command and Gen. Staff School (honor grad.), 1926, Army War Coll., 1930; m. Helen Wahrenberger, June 30, 1917; 1 dau., Betty Joe. Commd. 2d lt., U.S. Army, 1915, and advanced through the grades to major general (permanent), 1943, to general permanent), 1952; with aviation section, Signal Corps, 1916; comdg. corps observation groups, overseas, 1917-19; instr. Air Corps Tactical School, 1921-25; mem. gen. staff, War Dept., 1926-29; comdg. March Field, Calif., 1930-31, 7th Bombardment Group, 1932-33; instr. Army War Coll., 1933-35; staff G.H.Q. Air Force, 1935-38; comdg. 7th Bomber Group, 1939; gen. staff, War Dept., 1939-41; apptd. chmn. War Dept. Reorganization Committee, Jan. 1942; apptd. deputy chief of staff, U.S. Army, Mar. 1942; mil. observer, London, 1941; appointed member bd. of experts to investigate Hawaiian surprise attack, December 7, 1941. Appointed Deputy Supreme Commander-in-Chief Mediterranean and commanding gen. U.S. Mediterranean Theater of Operations, Oct. 23, 1944; acting Allied supreme comdr. in Mediterranean area, October 1, 1945; comdr. U.S. Forces in Europe, Nov. 1945. Apptd. Army Air Force rep., Mil. Staff Com., United Nations, 1947, comdg. gen. materiel command, Wright Field, Dayton, Ohio, 1947, retired, 1952; president Conviar division General Dynamics Corp., senior v.p. General Dynamics Corp., 1952-58, past dir. Appointed mem. U.S.-Canadian Permanent Joint Bd. of Defense, August 1940. Named chairman Nat. Def. Management Com., 1949. Member Order of Daedalliens. Clubs: Army and Navy, Army, Navy and Marine Corps Country (Washington). Home: Alhambra CA Died Feb. 1, 1972.

MCNAUGHTON, WILLIAM FRANCIS, judge; b. Earling, Ia., Nov. 30, 1876; s. Findley Jackson and Melissa (Washburn) McN.; grad. Woodbine (Ia.) Normal Sch., 1897; completed prep. course, U. of Neb.; LL.B., same univ., 1901; m. Mame Johnson, Apr. 6, 1904; children—Marjorie, Josephine, Frances. Began practice at Sioux Falls, S. Dak., 1901; opened office in Coeur d'Alene, Ida., 1909; apptd. judge Dist. Court, 1920; justice Supreme Court of Ida. since Jan. 1930. Presbyn. Mason (32 deg.). Rotarian. Home: Coeur d'Alene, Ida. Address: State Capital Boise ID‡

MCNEELY, HARRY G(REGORY), bus. exec.; b. West Union, Minn., May 9, 1887; s. Austin W. and Mary (Cannon) McN.; student Coll. of St. Thomas, St. Paul, 1904-08; m. Adelaide Frenzel, Sept. 24, 1913; children—Donald Gregory, Rosemary Jean, Audrey Adelaide, Harry Gregory, Jr. Pres. St. Paul Terminal Warehouse Co. since 1916, Minneapolis Terminal Warehouse Co. since 1929, Witte Transportation Co. since 1930, N.Y. Terminal Warehouse Co. since 1939, Capital Warehouse Co., Inc. since 1942, Terminal Transport Co. since 1942, Transport Leasing Corp. since 1941, Terminal Dist. Co., 1947-68, Northern Waterways Terminals Corp., 1949-68; dir. C. & N.W. Ry. System, Minn. Fed. Savings & Loan Assn., N.W. Publs., Inc. Mem. Nat. Freight Traffic Assn. Clubs: Minnesota, Somerset Country, Athletic, Town and Country (St. Paul); Minneapolis (Minn.); Los Angeles Country (Los Angeles); Indian Creek MN Died Jan. 2, 1968.

MCNEELY, ROBERT WHITEHEAD, naval officer; b. Salisbury, N.C., Aug. 11, 1873; s. William Gaither and Mildred Ann (Hunt) M.; grad. U.S. Naval Acad., 1894; m. Marie Calhoun Butler, of Edgefield, S.C., Feb. 15, 1900. Promoted through various grades to capt.; served at sea 14 yrs., on shore 12 yrs. Has specialized in naval ordnance; introduced improved method of obtaining velocity at high angles of gun fire; improved methods of placing rotating bands on large caliber projectiles; improvements in naval primers. Episcopalian. Clubs: Army and Navy (Washington), Chevy Chase (Md.). Address: Navy Dept., Washington DC‡

MCNEIL, KENNETH GORDON, ins. underwriter; b. London, Eng., Sept. 30, 1902; s. David and Evelyn Louise (Schwarz) McN.; student Merton Coll., Oxford U., 1922-24; m. Eleanor Mary MacGregor, July 4, 1931; children—Fiona Ann, Ian David, Andrew Ross, Alison Mary. With Lloyd's of London, from 1924, underwriting mem., from 1926, underwriter for Lion Motor Policies, 1931-56, mng. dir. K.G.M. Motor Policies, from 1957, com. of Lloyd's, 1947-50, 52-55, 57-60, and from 1962, dep. chmn., 1954-55, 65; chmn. Lloyd's Motor Underwriters' Assn., 1940-46; dir. Fenchurch Ins. Holdings Ltd.; v.p. of Chartered Insurance Inst., from 1963; dir. Additional Securities, Ltd. Justice of the Peace for County of Surrey, from 1961. Member War Office Claims Commn., from 1949. Gov. King's Coll. Sch., from 1948; gov. Benenden Sch., from 1956. Decorated commander Order of British Empire. Mem. Governing Bodies Assn. Home: Lingfield Surrey England Died July 2, 1970.

MCNEIL, SISTER MARY DONALD, educator; b. Antigo, Wis., Mar. 31, 1899; d. Michael Alexander and Margaret (Harrington) McNeil; A.B., Clarke Coll., Dubuque, Ia., 1920; M.A., U. Ill., 1928, Ph.D., 1934. Joined Order of Sisters of Charity, B.V.M., 1921; instr. Immaculata High Sch., Chgo., 1923-28; mem. faculty Mundelein Coll., Chgo., 1930-—, prof. classics, 1938-—, chmn. dept., 1930-—, dean studies, 1955-61; vis. prof. Loyola U., Los Angeles, summer 1956; vis. lecturer Loyola U., Chgo., 1966-67. Mem. Ill. Curriculum Council, 1957-—. Mem. Am. Philol. Assn., Classical Assn. Middle West and South, Ill. Classical Conf. (pres. 1965), Chgo. Classical Club, Vergilian Soc. Address: Chicago IL Died Aug. 21, 1969.

MCNEIL, ROBERT LINCOLN, pharm. mfr.; b. Phila., Pa., May 4, 1883; s. Robert and Mary Hubbard (Urwiler) McN.; B.S. in economics, U. of Pa., 1904; D.Sc. (hon.), Phila. Coll. Pharmacy and Sci., 1964; m. Grace Fannie Slack, Oct. 2, 1914; children—Robert Lincoln, Jr., Henry Slack. Executive partner in firm of Robt. McNeil, 1914-33; founded McNeil Labs., 1933, president, 1933-55, hon. chariman board, 1966-68; an organizer of the Pharm. Contact Com. (to cooperate with U.S. Dept. of Agr. for establishing standards of nonofficial pharm. preparations), co-chmn., 1924-27. Hon. dir. U.S. committee of World Medical Assn.; member of Am. Drug Mfrs. Assn. (dir. 1929-58; treas. 1936-44; v.p. 1944-48; pres. 1948-50). Mem. American

Pharm. Mfrs. Assn. (dir. 1919-58 pres. 1927-29; chmn. bd. dirs. 1929-33), Drugs Resources Committee (advisory to U.S. Army and Navy Munitions Bd.), 1939-44, Pharm. Industry Advisory Com. U.S. W.P.B., 1944-45; mem. Pharm. Drug Mfrs. industry adv. com. U.S. O.P.S., 1951-53; mem. bd. grants Am. Found. Pharm. Edn., 1952-68. Recipient Procter medal Phila. Drug Exchange, 1961. Mem. Clan Macneil Assn. Am. (hon. v.p. 1960-68), Kappa Sigma, St. Andrew's Soc.; hon. mem. Phila. Drug Exchange, Vet. Guard of Nat. Guard of Pa. Presbyn. Mason. Clubs: Union League. Home: Philadelphia PA Died 1968.

MCNEILL, EDWIN RUTHVEN, judge, lawyer; born Onawa, Iowa, January 5, 1880; son Edwin Ruthven and Louisa Irene (Younkin) McNeill; graduate Onawa High School, 1899; A.B., University of Minnesota, 1905; LL.B., Chicago-Kent College of Law, 1910; married Louise Campbell Clark, September 3, 1913. Admitted to Illinois bar, 1910, to Oklahoma bar, 1914; practiced in Pawnee as partner McNeill & McNeill, 1914-17; county registrar Pawnee County, 1918-23; dist. judge 21st Jud. Dist., 1923-31; justice Supreme Court of Okla., 1931-37; chief justice, 1935-37; a brother, Neal E., also was formerly chief justice; later in practice of law at Pawnee, Okla. Chmn. Pawnee County local exemption bd., mem. bd. dirs. Pawnee County Red Cross, World War; chmn. of Selective Service Bd. of Pawnee County, Okla., World War II. Chairman local board of Pawnee County under present Selective Service system. Member board directors Oklahoma Library, secretary, 1931-33, chairman 1933-35. Mem. Am., Okla., Pawnee Co. (pres. 1939-40), bar assns., Phi Alpha Delta. Democrat. Mem. Christian Disciples Ch. Address: Pawnee OK Died Sept. 22, 1962.

MCNICHOL, PAUL JOHN, govt. ofcl.; b. Phila., July 25, 1908; s. Anthony Drew and Anna (Watson) McN.; B.S. in Journalism, St. Joseph's Coll., Phila., 1932; m. Ruth Alexander, Mar. 1, 1941; children—David, Deborah (Mrs. J. Fernando Barrueta), Daniel, Nancy, Kathleen. Spl. agt. with the FBI, 1941-52; manager finishing dept. Glasco, Ltd., Phila., 1952-53; chief investigations div. Office Security, U.S. Information Agy., 1953-56, dep. dir., 1956-58, asst. dir. (security), 1958-71. Recipient Superior Honor award, presented posthumously. Home: Rockville MD Died Dec. 6, 1971; buried Gate of Heaven, Silver Spring MD

MCNIECE, HAROLD FRANCIS, educator; b. N.Y.C., Mar. 20, 1923; s. John and Alice (Foley) McN.; B.S. cum laude, St. John's U., 1944, LL.B. summa cum laude, 1945; J.S.D., N.Y. U., 1949. Admitted to N.Y. bar, 1945; with firm Davis, Polk, Wardwell, Sunderland & Kiendl, N.Y.C., 1945-46; faculty St. John's U. Law Sch., 1946-72, prof. law, asso. dean, 1957-60, dean, 1960-70. Vice chmn. N.Y. State Joint Legislative Com. Implement Ct. Reorgn., 1961-72; chmn. adv. council N.Y. State Joint Legislative Com. Matrimonial and Family Laws, 1961-72; mem. exec. com. N.Y. State Conf. Legal Edn., 1961-72; exec. dir. jud. com. N.Y. Constl. Conv. Dir. City Title Ins. Co. Adv. council N.Y.C. Bd. Pub. Welfare, 1960-72, Cath. Charities Diocese Bklyn., 1960-72. Bd. dirs., sec. Community Council Greater N.Y., 1957-72; bd. dirs., pres. Bklyn. Soc. Prevention Cruelty to Children, 1962-72. Mem. Am. (vice chmn. workmens compensation and employers liability ins. law com. 1960-72), N.Y. State, Bklyn. (chmn. com. law student activities 1958-72) bar assns., Fed. Bar Assn. N.Y., N.J., and Conn., Assn. Bar City N.Y., Cath. Lawyers Guild (pres. Bklyn. 1956-57), Phi Delta Phi. Roman Catholic (trustee). Clubs: Brooklyn, Lawyers (N.Y.C.). Author: Cases and Materials on Torts, 1947; Heart Disease and the Law, 1961. Co-author: Cases and Materials on Security Transactions, 1947. Home: Brooklyn NY Died Dec. 27, 1972.

MCNULTY, FRANK J., congressman; b. Ireland, Aug. 10, 1872; s. Owen McN.; father a vet. of Union Army in Civil War, moved to Ireland and returned in 1876; ed. pub. schs.; m. Edith H. Parker, of Jersey City, N.J., 1893 (died 1920). Elected v.p. Internat. Brotherhood Elec. Engrs., 1901, pres., 1903-18. chmn. internat. bd. same; mem. commn. to study municipal and pub. ownership in British Isles, 1906; v.chmn. Ry. Bd. of Adjustment No. 2, World War; visited Italy and France during the war at request of Govt.; dep. dir. pub. safety, Newark, N.J., 4 yrs.; mem. 68th Congress (1923-25), 8th N.J. Dist. Democrat. Catholic. Home: Newark NJ‡

MCNULTY, JAMES, bishop; b. N.Y.C., Jan. 16, 1900; student Seton Prep. Sch. and Coll., Immaculate Conception Sem., N.J., Louvain U., Belgium. Ordained priest, Roman Cath. Ch., 1925; pastor, Jersey City and Newark; diocese dir. Confraternity of Christian Doctrine, moderator Mt. Carmel Guild, dir. C.Y.O.; faculty Tchrs. Inst. for Religious; titular bishop of Methone, auxiliary bishop of Newark, 1947-53; former bishop of Paterson; now bishop Buffalo. Home: Buffalo NY Died Sept. 4, 1972; buried Gate of Heaven Cemetery, East Hanover NJ

MCNUTT, ANNA MARY, orgn. exec.; b. Festus, Mo.; d. Francis A. and Alice F. (Doak) McNutt; A.A., George Washington U., 1947. Accountant, U.S. Dept. Agrl. Office Budget and Finance, Washington, 1913-53; asst. to chief Bus. Press News Bur., Washington, 1953-61. Recipient Medal of Appreciation S.A.R., 1965. Mem. D.A.R. (v.p. gen. 1967-69, D.C. regent 1964-66). Presbyn. (trustee 1955-69). Home: Washington DC Died July 5, 1969.

MCPHERREN, CHARLES ELMO, lawyer; b. Pleasant Grove, Miss., June 16, 1875; s. Andrew M. and Fanny E. (Boxley) McP.; student Franklin Coll., Pilot Point, Tex., 1889-93; LL.B., U. of Miss., 1896; m. 2d, Maude A. Moore; children—(by first marriage)—Charles J. (lt. 7th Cavalry, U.S. Army), Margaret Jane, John Martin (sgt. U.S. Army), David A. Admitted to Tex. bar, 1896, practicing at Pilot Point; practiced at Caddo and Durant, Okla., 1897-1924, at Oklahoma City since 1924; mem. firm McPherren & Mauer. Sergt. U.S. Vol. Cav. (Roosevelt-Rough Riders), 1898; now major general, retired, U.S. Army; grad. Army War Coll., Command and Gen. Staff Sch. at Ft. Leavenworth (Kan.); former comdg. gen. 45th Div., U.S. Army. Mem. Okla. State Senate, 1921-25. Mem. Am. Bar Assn., Okla. State Bar Assn., Alpha Sigma Phi. Democrat. Methodist. Clubs: Oklahoma, Army and Navy Club. Home: 1220 W. 20th St. Office: Suite 708-709, Perrine Building, Oklahoma City OK*‡

MCQUADE, VINCENT AUGUSTINE, coll. pres., clergyman; b. Lawrence, Mass., June 16, 1909; s. Owen Francis and Kathryn M. (McCarthy) McQ.; grad. Augustinian Acad., S.I., N.Y., 1926; A.B., Villanova Coll., 1931; A.M., Cath. U. Am., 1934, Ph.D., 1938; LL.D., Villanova U., 1956; Ed.D., Suffolk U., 1957; Sc.D., Lowell Technological Inst., 1959. Entered Order of Hermits of Saint Augustine, 1926; ordained priest, Roman Cath. Ch., 1934; asst. prof. sociology Villanova Coll., 1937-46; asst. to the pres., 1940-42, dean, dir. Navy V-12 program, 1942-44, chmn. vets. guidance com., 1944-46; first pres. Merrimack Coll., Andover, Mass., 1947-68, also trustee and treas. bd.; dir. Augustinian Ednl. Assn., also treas. Province of St. Thomas of Villanova, 1968-71. Member Mass. Board of Educational Assistance, 1958-71. Mem. Greater Lawrence Indsl. Development Com. Trustee Villanova U. Mem. Augustinian Ednl. Assn. (pres.), Am. Anthropol. Assn., Nat. Cath. Ednl. Assn. (pres. N.E. div. 1956). Association of American Colleges (member board directors 1956-60), Catholic Anthropol. Assn., Am. Cath. Sociol. Assn. Author: American Catholic Attitudes on Child Labor, 1937. Lectr. and writer on ednl. and social-religious subjects. Address: Villanova PA Died Feb. 11, 1971; buried St. Mary's Cemetery, Lawrence MA

MCQUEEN, L(OREN) A(NGUS), business exec.; b. Superior, Wis., Jan. 5, 1893; s. Angus and Katherine (McLean) McQ.; A.B., U. Wis., 1916; m. Mary L. Jillson, July 25, 1917. Corr. clerk The B. F. Goodrich Co., Akron, O., 1917-25; gen. sales mgr., 1925-29, v.p. Gen. Tire & Rubber Co., 1929-60, exec. v.p., 1960-71, also honorary chmn. bd., chmn. executive committee; dir. Aerojet-Gen., Los Angeles, CPA Ins. Corp., Detroit, Midland Steamship Line, Inc., Cleve., A. M. Byers Co., Pitts. Republican. Conglist. Mason (32 deg.). Clubs: Shriner, Portage Country, Pepper Pike Country, Gulf Stream Golf. Home: Akron OH Died Apr. 20, 1971; buried Akron OH

MCREYNOLDS, FREDERICK WILSON, lawyer; b. Delphi, Ind., Sept. 11, 1872; s. Lafayette Emerson and Mary Belle (Wilson) McR.; A.B., Dartmouth; LL.B., Columbian (now George Washington) U.; m. Jessie Brooke Stabler, Oct. 9, 1894; children—George Brooke (colonel U.S.A.), Catherine (Mrs. Robert Leighton Barnes), Alice Brooke. Admitted to D.C. bar, 1896, and engaged in practice at Washington, 1896-1915; asst. prof. law and finance, Tuck School of Administration and Finance, of Dartmouth Coll., 1915-19; counsel for War Trade Bd. and Com. on Pub. Information, 1917-18; spl. atty. in charge of Internal Revenue litigation, 1919-22; private practice since 1922. Chmn. Bd. of Pub. Welfare of D.C., 1933-43. Democrat. Episcopalian. Mem. Sigma Chi, Soc. of the Cincinnati. Clubs: Chevy Chase, Nat. Press, Lawyers', Cosmos. Home: 2039 New Hampshire Av. N.W. Office: Union Trust Bldg., Washington DC‡

MCSKIMMON, WILLIAM BINGHAM, corp. official; b. Bangor, Me., Mar. 2, 1872; s. David and Mary (Clarke) M.; student Bangor High Sch., 1886-90; m. Mary K. Monahan, Jan. 2, 1896; children—Donald, Madeline (Mrs. John Marshall Duane). Began with Brown & Sharpe Mfg. Co., Providence, R.I., 1892; now treas. Union Twist Drill Co., pres. O.S. Walker Co., J. T. Slocomb Co., Vitrified Wheel Co., New England Drawn Steel Co. Mason. Clubs: Engineers (Boston); Woodland Golf (Auburndale, Mass.); Petersham (Mass.) Golf. Home: East Jeffrey, N.H. Office: Union Twist Drill Co., Anthol MA*‡

MCSPARRAN, JOHN ALDUS, farmer; b. Lancaster County, Pa., Oct. 22, 1873; s. James G. and Sarah Margaret (Collins) McS.; Ph.B., Lafayette Coll., 1893; m. Betty Harrison Goodwin, Dec. 2, 1902; children—Sarah Margaret (Mrs. Sam B. Long), Lucy Isabella (Mrs. George W. Buller), Charles Goodwin, John Collins; m. 3d, Laura McCullough, Jan. 30, 1926; children—Donald Harry, Gray Fleming. Engaged in farming since 1894; master Pa. State Grange, 1914-24; sec. Agriculture of Pa., 1931-34. Candidate for gov. of Pa., Dem. Party, 1922. Mem. Patrons Husbandry. Republican. Methodist. Home: Greene PA‡

MCSWEENEY, JOHN, congressman, university trustee; b. Wooster, O., Dec. 19, 1890; s. John and Ada Jane (Mullins) McS.; Ph.B., Wooster Coll., 1912, LL.D., 1931; student law Inns of Court, London, Eng., 1918-19, also Trinity Coll., Dublin; m. Abby Schaefer, July 9, 1924. Mem. engring. corps Pa. R.R., 1912-13; tchr. Wooster High Sch., 1913-17, 19-22; admitted to Ohio bar, 1925; practice in Wooster, 1925-31; dir. pub. welfare Ohio, 1931-35; fgn. rep. Am. Relief for Italy, 1946-47. Commr. Am. Legion council Boy Scouts Am. Mem. Wooster Sch. Bd. Mem. 68-70th Congresses, also 81st Congress, 16th Ohio Dist., mem. 75th Congress, Ohio-at-large; candidate U.S. Senate from Ohio, 1940, candidate for gov., 1942; mem. Wooster City Council. Member board trustees Kent (Ohio) State University. Served to capt., inf., U.S. Army, 1917-19, to lt. col. AUS, 1943-47. Decorated Purple Heart with cluster, Legion of Merit, Croix de Guerre (France); commandatore Crown Italy, Italian Red Cross medal; commandatore Order Malta, Order St. George, Order St. Hubert, medal Pope Pius XII. Mem. Am. Legion Disabled Am. Vets. Am. Forestry Assn. (past (v.p.), Ohio Soc. Washington (pres. 1950), Phi Gamma Delta. Democrat. Episcopalian. Clubs: Lamplighters (hon.) (Wooster); University (Cleve.). Home: Wooster OH Died Dec. 14, 1969.

MCVINNEY, RUSSELL J., clergyman; b. Warren, R.I., Nov. 25, 1898; s. Thomas and Catherine (Blessington) McV.; Grad. LaSalle Acad., Providence, 1916; student St. Charles Coll., Catonsville, Md., 1916-18, Seminaire de Philosophie, Montreal, Can., 1918-20, St. Bernard's Sem., Rochester, N.Y., 1920-21, Am. Coll., Louvain U., Belgium, 1921-24; student Notre Dame, 1935; LL.D. (hon.), Providence Coll., 1946, St. Michael's Coll., 1955, Stonehill Coll., 1954, Manhattan Coll., 1957, U. Louvain, 1957, Boston Coll., 1960, L.H.D. (hon.), R.I. State Coll., 1949, Salve Regina Coll., 1960, Suffolk U., 1960, Bryant Coll., 1970. Ordained priest Roman Cath. Ch., Louvain, Belgium, 1924; asst. St. Patrick's Ch., Harrisville, R.I., 1924-29, St. Edward's Ch., Pawtucket, R.I., 1929-35 (also teacher St. Raphael's Acad.), S.S. Peter and Paul's Cathedral, Providence, 1936-41; rector Our Lady of Providence Sem., Warwick Neck, R.I., 1941-48, consecrated Bishop of Providence July 14, 1948; pres. and treas. all Diocesan Corps. in State of R.I. Dir. diocesan pilgrimage to Eucharistic Congress, New Orleans, 1938. Mem. Internat. Fedn. Catholic Alumnae (moderator, 1940-48). K.C. (4 deg.). Club: Notre Dame of R.I. (chaplain 1937-48). Asso. editor The Providence Visitor. Home: Providence RI Died Aug. 10, 1971; buried Warwick Neck RI

MCWILLIAMS, JOHN PROBASCO, industrialist; b. Chillicothe, O., Jan. 8, 1891; s. Rev. Thomas S. and Susan Probasco (Nipgen) McW.; C.E., Princeton, 1913; m. Ella Brooks Barlow, Sept. 29, 1928; children—W.J. Barlow, Suzanne Brooks (Mrs. Frank T. Murray), Marianne (Mrs. Donald M. Allen), John Probasco. Timekeeper, railroad construction, 1913; with Oxweld Acetylene Co., 1914-17; Oxweld Railroad Service Co., 1917-24; founded Youngstown Steel Door Co., 1924, v.p., gen. mgr., 1924-33, pres. 1933-47, Chairman of the board, 1948-58, director, 1924-68, chairman executive committee, 1958-68; dir. Eaton Manufacturing Co. Mem. bus. adv. council to Dept. of Commerce, from 1949. Trustee Western Res. U., U. Hosps. Cleve., Ch. of Covenant. Clubs: Union, Tavern (Cleveland); Kirtland Country (Willoughby, O.); Winous Point Shooting (Port Clinton); Links (N.Y.). Home: Cleveland OH Died July 14, 1972; interred Lake View Cemetery, Cleveland OH

MEACHAM, W(ILLIAM) BANKS, osteopathist; b. Senatobia, Tate Co., Miss., Aug. 1, 1873; s. Henry Banks and Mary Ann (Robinson) M.; A.B., Miss. Coll., Clinton, Miss., 1895; A.B., Harvard, 1898; D.O., Boston Inst. Osteopathy, 1901; m. Genevieve Cochran, of Meridian, Miss., Dec. 27, 1901. Sec.-treas. N.C. State Bd. of Osteopathic Examination and Registration; owner and phys. in charge Ottari," an instn. for treatment of non-communicable diseases. Trustee A. T. Still Research Inst., Chicago. Mem. Am. Osteopathic Assn. (pres. 1916-17), N.C. State Osteopathic Soc. (1st sec.). Democrat. Unitarian. Mason (32 deg.). Clubs: Rotary, Asheville Country. Home: Asheville NC‡

MEAD, EDWARD SHERWOOD, educator; b. Medina, O., Jan. 25, 1874; s. Giles F. and Martha A.M.; A.B., DePauw U., 1896; fellow U. of Chicago, 1896-98, U. of Pa., 1898-1900 (Ph.D., 1899); m. Emily Fogg, June 1, 1900; children—Margaret, Richard Ramsay, Katherine (dec.), Elizabeth, Priscilla. Instr. in commerce and industry, 1900-04, asst. prof. finance, 1904-07, prof. since 1907, now prof. of finance emeritus, chmn. Extension Sch. Com., 1913-14, Wharton Sch. of Finance and Commerce, U. of Pa. Dir. Evening Sch. of Accounts and Finance, 1904-13; financial editor Phila. Public Ledger, 1910; spl. corr. for Asso. Press, 1931. Expert witness in rate and merger cases, 1943, 44; instr. on contract termination loans, U. of Pa., 1944-45; spl. courses in finance, East Pa. div., Investment Bankers

Assn., 1945-47. Served as govt. rep. under NRA. Mem. Am. Econ. Assn., Phi Beta Kappa, Delta Upsilon, Beta Gamma Sigma. Clubs: University (Phila.); Lenape. Author: Business Georgraphy, 1902; Economics of Business, 1909; Trust Finance, 1903; Story of Gold, 1908; Corporation Finance, 1910. 7th edit., 1933; The Careful Investor, 1914; Harvey Bauma Study of the Agricultural Revolution (with Bernhard Ostrolenk), 1928; Voluntary Allotment (with same), 1933; The Ebb and Flow of Investment Values (with Julius Grodinsky), 1939; The Business Corporation-Its Financial Organization and Operation (with D. B. Jeremiah and W. E. Warrington), 1941. Contributor to economic journals and to reviews on topics in finance, commerce and industry. Home: 214 S. McAlpin St., Philadelphia 4 PA‡

MEAD, SOLOMON CRISTY, past secretary Merchants' Assn. of N.Y (now Commerce and Industry Assn. of New York, Inc.); b. Greenwich, Conn., Nov. 26, 1867; s. Solomon and Mary Elizabeth (Dayton) M.; prep. edn., Greenwich Acad., and Phillips Acad., Andover, Mass.; A.B., Yale, 1890, LL.B., 1892; m. Frances Ripley Boss, June 26, 1890; 1 son, Kenneth Ripley. Admitted to N.Y. bar, 1892, and practiced with Dill, Chandler & Seymour, N.Y. City, until 1897; asst. sec. Merchants' Assn. of New York, 1897-1904, sec., 1904-41. An organizer, 1912, and nat. councillor Chamber Commerce of U.S.; vice chmn. and sec. com. on permanent orgn. and hon. sec. orgn. meeting of Internat. Chamber Commerce, Paris, 1920; was pres. Am. Assn. Commercial Executives and a founder, and 1st pres. of its successor, The Nat. Assn. of Commercial Orgn. Secretaries, 1914; pres. emeritus National Inst. Commercial and Trade Orgn. Execs.; member N.Y. State Waterways Assn. (exec. com.), Nat. Inst. Social Sciences, Phi Gamma Delta. Pres. N.Y. State Commn. of S.C. Interstate and West Indian Expn., Charleston, 1902. Chevalier Order Crown of Italy. Republican. Conglist. Clubs: Yale, Phi Gamma Delta (New York). Home: 41 Washington Av., Greenwich CT Office: 233 Broadway, New York NY‡

MEAD, STERLING V., dentist; b. Hutchinson, Kan., Oct. 16, 1888; grad. Emerson Inst., Washington, D.C., 1911; D.D.S., George Washington U., 1914; B.S. Dentistry, Georgetown U., 1929, M.S., 1930, D.Sc., 1952. Pvt. practice dentistry, Washington, 1914-69; founder Mead Dental Hosp., 1959-66; prof. oral surgery, diseases of mouth, radiography and dir. research, Georgetown Univ. for many years; past pres. Am. Dental Assn. Fellow Am. Coll. of Dentists; mem. D.C. Dental Soc. (pres. 1929), Am. Soc. Oral Surgeons, Psi Omega. Recipient award by Internat. Research Soc., 1935, Conn. Dental Assn., 1944. Author: (books) Diseases of the Mouth; Oral Surgery; Anesthesia; also numerous sci. papers. Address: Washington DC Died Dec. 9, 1972.

MEAD, WILLIAM EDWARD, univ. prof.; b. Gallupville, N.Y., Oct. 25, 1860; s. Rev. Merritt Bates and Lucenia A. (Tucker) M.; B.A., Wesleyan U., 1881, grad. student and asst. librarian, 1881-82; Ph.D., U. of Leipzig, 1889; studied at U. of Berlin, Ecole des Chartes, Paris, Bibliotheque Nationale, Paris, British Mus. and Inner Temple, London; m. Kate Campbell Hurd, June 21, 1893 (died Jan. 1, 1941). Prof. English lang., Wesleyan U., 1890-1925; lit. investigations in European libraries, 1925-29; prof. Middle English, U. of Chicago, summer quarter, 1903; lecturer on English, Columbia summer session, 1911; editor Dialect Notes, 1906-12. Sec. pedagog. sect. Modern Lang. Assn., 1897-1903; v.p. Am. Dialect Soc., 1904-05 (sec.-treas. 1906, sec. 1907-12, pres. 1912-15); mem. Psi Upsilon, and Phi Beta Kappa. Author: The Versification of Pope in Its Relations to the Seventeenth Century, 1889; Elementary Composition and Rhetoric, 1894; Outlines of the History of the Legend of Merlin, 1899 (Early English Text Soc., London); Practical Composition and Rhetoric, 1900; Language Lessons (joint author), 1903; Grammar Lessons (joint author), 1904; The Grand Tour in the Eighteenth Century, 1914; The English Medieval Feast, 1931. Editor: Selections from Malory's Morte d'Arthur, 1897; The Squry of Lowe Degree, 1903; Chinon of England (1597), 1925; John Leland's Assertio Inclytissimi Arturii (1544), with Richard Robinson's English Version (1582), 1925; The Pastime of Pleasure by Stephen Hawes (E.E.T.S.), 1927. Contbr. to lit. revs. and philol. jours. Since 1884 has spent more than 10 yrs. in travel and research in Europe. Home: Haddam CT*‡

MEADE, ELEANORE HUSSEY, educator; b. Huntsville, Alabama, August 17, 1884; the daughter of William Baker and Ella (Moss) Hussey; grad. of George Peabody Coll. of Tchrs., 1904, student summers, 1906-08; student U. Mich., summer 1914; m. George Peterkin Meade, Aug. 7, 1912. Tchr. English, Gastonia (N.C.) High Sch., 1904-06, Abbeville (La.) High Sch., 1906-09; asst. prin. Lutcher (La.) High Sch., 1909-12; tchr. English, Presbyn. Sch., Cardenas, Cuba, 1914-17; tchr. bible class Lutcher Community Ch., 1925-56; mem. La. State Bd. Edn., 1927-63, v.p., 1936-53, pres., 1953-54. Mem. Gov.'s Adv. Commn. Higher Edn. Sec., home service chmn. St. James chpt. A.R.C., 1939-56; life trustee Peabody Coll. Tchrs. Eleanore Hussey Meade Honor Professorship established La. State Coll., 1967. Mem. P.T.A. (state pres. 1928-32, state treas. 1945-54, state historian 1954-56), New Orleans Philharmonic, New Orleans Opera House Assn., Le Petit Theatre du Vieux Carre, New Orleans Edn. TV. Found., U.D.C., D.A.R., Am. Assn. U. Women, Nat., La. edn. assns., Delgado Mus. Art Assn., Delta Kappa Gamma, Phi Lambda Pi. Ind. Democrat. Episcopalian. Club: Orleans (New Orleans). Home: New Orleans LA Died Dec. 5, 1969; buried Nashville TN

MEADE, GEORGE EDWARD, govt. ofcl.; b. Midsomer, Norton, Eng., Mar. 27, 1914; s. Edward and Mary (Smith) M.; brought to Can., 1928; student U. Leeds (Eng.), 1944-45, U. Paris (France), 1945-46; m. Dorothy Leone Sheriff, Sept. 23, 1944. Journalist, outdoor editor The Vancouver Province, 1946-55; mgr. Wildlife Fedn. B.C., Vancouver, 1955-63; mgr. Vancouver office Dept. Travel Industry, Province of B.C., 1963-72. Bd. dirs. Natural Resources Conf. B.C., Vancouver, pres., 1962. Home: Richmond British Columbia Canada Died July 11, 1972.

MEADOWS JAMES ALLEN, physician; b. Miss., May 24, 1884; s. Columbus and Polly Meadows; M.D., U. Ala., 1912; m. Minna Mundt, May 9, 1917; children—James Allen, Edward R., Margaret Morgan. Intern, Providence Infirmary, Mobile, Ala., 1911-12; intern St. Vincent's Hosp., Birmingham, Ala., 1912-13, radiologist, until 1970; radiologist Anti-Tb Clinic, Children's Hosp., South Highlands Infirmary. Diplomate Am. Bd. Radiology. Fellow Am. Coll. Radiology; mem. A.M.A., Soc. Med. Assn., Radiol. Soc. N.Am., Am. Roentgen Ray Soc. Home: Birmingham AL Died June 3, 1970; buried Birmingham AL

MEANEY, THOMAS FRANCIS, judge; b. Jersey City, N.J., Sept. 6, 1888; s. Thomas F. and Mary (Kinkead) M.; A.B., St. Peters Coll., Jersey City, 1908, A.M., 1909; LL.B., Fordham, 1911; unmarried. Hudson common pleas judge, 1934-39; U.S. dist. judge for N.J., 1942-66, sr. judge, until 1966. Served in France and with Army of Occupation, 1917-19. Democrat. Roman Catholic. Home: Jersey City NJ Died May 1968.*

MEANS, EMILY ADAMS, academy prin.; b. at Groton, Mass.; d. Rev. James and Elizabeth Phebe (Johnson) M.; sister of David MacGregor M. (q.v.); ed. pvt. tutors, Abbot Acad., Andover, Mass., in Paris, study and travel 4 yrs. Taught art, Kent Pl. Sch., Summit, N.J., 8 yrs.; instr. art, 12 yrs., prin. since 1898, Abbot Acad. Has lectured on art subjects and contbd. revs. to Nation and Outlook. Address: Andover MA‡

MEANS, THOMAS HERBERT, consulting engr.; b. Waterford, Va., Nov. 15, 1875; s. Samuel C. and Rachael Ann (Bond) M.; B.S., Columbian (now George Washington) U., 1898, M.S., 1901; m. Constance Adams, Nov. 6, 1900; children—Alice Adams (now Mrs. Lloyd Eric Reeve), Thomas Moore. In charge Soil Survey of U.S. since 1900; engr. of soils, U.S. Reclamation Service, since 1904; project engr. U.S. Reclamation Service, 1910; consulting engr., San Francisco, since 1910, specializing in irrigation and agrl. engring. Mem. Am. Soc. C.E. Club: Engineers. Author several Dept. Agr. publs. and engineering articles. Home: 2729 Forest Av., Berkeley, CA Office: 111 Sutter St., San Francisco CA‡

MEARS, LOUISE WILHELMINA, educator, writer; b. Beatrice, Neb., Mar. 12, 1874; B.E., Neb. State Teachers Coll., 1909; A.M., U. of Neb., 1912; also undergrad. and grad. study Harvard, U. of Chicago, Cornell U., Clark U., U. of Wis., U. of Minn. Seaside Lab., Vancouver Island, Can., Marquette U., Milwaukee, Wis. Critic, Neb. State Teachers Coll., Peru, 1897-1900; head of dept. geography, State Teachers Coll., Moorhead, Minn., 1901-07, Neb. State Teachers Coll., 1907-12; prof. of geography, State Teachers Coll., Milwaukee, Wis., 1912-40, was also head of dept. Pres. geography sect., Wisconsin State Teachers Colls., 1930-32. Founder and donor Louise Mears medal award for geographic research, State Teachers Coll., Peru, Neb. Del. Pan-Pacific Sci. Conference, Hawaiian Islands, 1920; delegate to World Education Conf., Toronto, Can., 1927, World Fedn. Ednl. Assns., Oxford, Eng., 1935, Rio de Janeiro, 1939. Mem. N.E.A., Nat. Council Administrative Women in Edn. Y.W.C.A. (life), Neb. Writers Guild, Am. Assn. Univ. Women, Neb. State Hist. Society, Delta Kappa Gamma (life); fellow Royal Soc. Arts and Sciences. Protestant. Author: The Hills of Peru, 1912, 48; American's Fairyland—the Hawaiian Islands, 1922; Wisconsin—A Geographical Reader (with J. A. Merrill), 1931; Life and Times of a Midwest Educator, Carroll Gardner Pearse, 1944; also numerous monographs and mag. articles. Founder and donor of William Gaede Memorial Collection, Pub. Library, Auburn, Neb. Address: Box 663, Nebraska City NE‡

MEARS, MARY, author; b. Oshkosh, Wis.; d. John H. and Elizabeth (Farnsworth) M. (whose pen-name was Nellie Wildwood"); ed. State Normal Sch., Oshkosh, Wisconsin, and abroad; unmarried. Author: Emma Lou—Her Book, 1896; Breath of the Runners, 1906; The Bird in the Box; Rosamond the Second; The Forbidden Thing. Clubs: MacDowell, Pen and Brush (N.Y.); Provincetown Art. Lectures on The Life and Work of Helen Farnsworth Mears. Address: Pen and Brush Club, 16 E. 10th St., New York NY‡

MEBANE, HARRY BARTLETT, JR., knitting co. exec.; b. Graham, N.C., 1909. Pres., dir. Standard Knitting Mills, Inc. Home: Knoxville TN Died July 30, 1967; buried Knoxville TN

MECH, STEPHEN JOHN, agrl. engr.; b. Poland, Aug. 3, 1909; s. Pawel and Ulianna (Kondzela) M.; came to U.S., 1913, naturalized, 1921; B.S., Pa. State U., 1933; postgrad. Tex. A & M U., 1933-34; m. Eunice Samson, June 24, 1935; children—Cecile (Mrs. Thomas K. Gurney), Stephen John, William P., Mary A. Forester engr. Pa. Dept. Forest and Waters 1933; mem. staff U.S. Dept. Agr., 1934-68, engr. Soil Conservation Service, Lindale, Tex., 1934-35, engr., soil conservationist Erosion Control Research, Lindale, Pullman, Wash., Marcellus, N.Y., LaCrosse, Wis., 1935-43, research engr. irrigation div., Prosser, Wash., 1943-60, research investigation leader, Fort Collins, Colo., 1960-61, project leader, research investigation leader Agrl. Research Service, Pullman, 1961-66, research agrl. engr. Irrigation Agr. Research Center, Prosser, 1966-68. Mem. A.A.A.S., Am. Soc. Agrl. Engring., Am. Soc. Agronomy, Soil Conservation Soc. Am., Am. Geophys. Union. Episcopalian. Mason. Home: Prosser WA Died July 8, 1968.

MECHEM, PHILIP, author, law educator; b. Detroit, Dec. 12, 1892; s. Floyd Russell and Jessie (Collier) M.; grad. Hotchkiss Sch., 1911; student Harvard, 1911-14; B.A., Stanford, 1921; LL.B., U. Colo., 1922; J.S.D., U. Chgo., 1925; m. Catharine B. Evans, Sept. 9, 1922; 1 son, Charles E. Asst. prof. law U. Ida., 1922-24; teaching fellow law U. Chgo., 1924-25; prof. law U. Kan., 1925-28; acting dean law, 1928-29; prof. law Washington U., St. Louis, 1929-30; prof. law U. of Ia., 1930-48, U. Pa., 1948-63. On leave of absence as head atty. claims div. Dept. of Justice, Washington, 1942-44. Mem. Assn. Am. Law Schs. (pres. 1957), Phi Delta Phi, Order of Coif. Democrat. Clubs: Merion Cricket, Franklin Inn (Phila.). Author: Mechem and Atkinson, Cases on Wills (with Prof. T. E. Atkinson), 4th edit., 1954; The Columbine Cabin Murders, 1932; Mechem's Cases on Agency, 4th edit., 1953; And Not for Love, 1942; Mechem, Outlines of Agency, 4th edit., 1952; Mechem, Cases on Future Interests, 1958. Contbr. legal jours. Home: Merion PA Died Mar. 1969.

MECKLIN, JOHN MARTIN, mag. editor; b. Pitts., Jan. 29, 1918; s. John Moffatt and Hope (Davis) M.; grad. Deerfield (Mass.) Acad., 1935; B.A., Dartmouth, 1939; m. Shirley Elaine Karr, Apr. 26, 1943;children—John Davis, William Alexander. Newspaper reporter, 1939-42; war corr. in N. Africa and Western Europe, 1942-45; fgn. corr. in Italy, 1945-47; writer N.Y. Times, 1947; foreign correspondent in Canada, London, S.E. Asia, Middle East and Central Europe for Time, Incorporated, 1948-61, bureau chief, San Francisco, California, 1964-66; public affairs adviser United States mission to Orgn. Econ. Coop. and Devel., Paris, France, 1961-62; pub. affairs officer Am. embassy, Saigon, 1962-64; asso. editor Fortune mag., N.Y.C., 1966-68, mem. bd. editors, 1968-71. Mem. Theta Delta Chi. Conglist. Club: Overseas Press (N.Y.C.). Author: Mission in Torment, 1965. Home: Westport CT Died Oct. 29, 1971.

MEDEARIS, T(HOMAS) W(HITTIER), clergyman; b. Columbus, Ind., Apr. 11, 1889; s. Thomas Whittier and Susan M. (Carns) M.; A.B., William Jewell Coll., LL.D., 1953; B.D., Kansas City Sem. (now Central Baptist), 1923, D.D., Okla. Baptist U., 1936; m. Mara E. Miller, Jan. 13, 1913; children—Allen Miller, Roger Norman, Dorothy Lou, Marian Adell. Pastor, Lamar, Fayette, Leeds, Bolivar (Mo.), 1918-25; head Bible Dept., Southwest Baptist Coll., Bolivar, 1925-28; pastor First Baptist Chs., Bristow (Okla.) 1928-34, Miami (Okla.), 1934-42; Gen. Supt. Mo. Bapt. Conv., 1942-54; interim pastor College St. Ch., Springfield, Mo., 1954-55; pastor Magnolia Av. Ch., Riverside, Cal., 1955-56; acting president California Baptist College, 1957-58; acting exec. sec. Mo. Baptist Foundation, 1946-49, sec.-treas. Mo. Assn. Free Public Schools; pastor Calvary Baptist Church, 1962-63; chairman of religious advisory committee Civil Defense Orgn., Mo. Trustee Central Baptist Seminary; mem. exec. committee board trustees Cal. Baptist Coll., Riverside. Member Pasadena Bd. Realtors. Recipient of Achievement Citation, William Jewell Coll., 1944. Vice-pres. Okla. Bapt. Conv., 1930; pres. bd. trustees Okla. Bapt. U., 5 years; mem. Fgn. Mission Bd., Southern Bapt. Conv., 1934-42 (visited missions in Europe, Palestine, Syria, 1939, Mexico, 1942, Europe 1947). Chaplain's Training School and commissioned O.R.C., World War I. Contributor church publs. Home: Pasadena CA Died July 7, 1970; buried Carthage Cemetery, Carthage MO

MEDFORD, WILLIAM, U.S. atty.; b. Bryson City, N.C., Jan. 29, 1909; s. Allen Thurman and Verna (Welch) M.; A.B., U. N.C., 1931, LL.B., 1933; m. Martha Jeanette Mock, Nov. 23, 1940; 1 son, James Allen. Admitted to N.C. bar, 1933; practice in Waynesville, 1933-61; U.S. atty. Western Dist. N.C., 1961-69. Dir. Welco Ro-Search, Umagusta Mfg. Co., Carolina Woodturning Co., Giles Chem. Corp., Balsam Gap Co. Chmn. N.C. Nat. Park Commn., 1954-63;

mem. N.C. Adv. Com. Edn., 1955-57, N.C. Jud. Council, 1955-57. Mem. N.C. Senate, 1947, 51, 55, 59. Trustee U. N.C., 1961-69. Served to lt. comdr. USNR, 1942-45. Mem. Am., N.C. bar assns., (v.p. 1959). U. N.C. Law Sch. Alumni Assn. (pres. 1963). Rotarian. Home: Waynesville NC Died Apr. 27, 1969; buried Greenhill Cemetery, Waynesville NC

MEDSGER, OLIVER PERRY, naturalist and educator; b. Jacob's Creek, Pa., Nov. 1, 1870; s. Henry Harrison and Elizabeth (Hough) M.; B.S., Ohio Northern U., Ada, 1898; student Columbia, 1904-05; m. Jennie A. Arnold, Aug. 24, 1905; children—Henry Otis, Thomas Arnold, Oliver Perry. Civil engr. Westmoreland County, Pa., 1898-99; prin. E. Huntington Twp. Schs., 1899-1900, and 1902-04; teacher sciences, high sch. Salem, O., 1900-01; head science dept. and vice prin., Kearny (N.J.) High Sch., 1904-09; teacher science, Dickinson High Sch., Jersey City, 1909-12; head science dept., Lincoln High Sch., Jersey City, 1912-32, asst. prin., 1932-33; prof. nature edn., in charge visual instrn., Pennsylvania State Coll., 1934-37, now emeritus; writing and lecturing since 1937. Organized and directed nature study in summer camps, 1917-27; naturalist, instr. dept. nature education, Pa. State Coll., summer sch., 1928-33; nature study courses, Rutgers U., 1929-33. Dir. Am. Nature Study Society since 1936. Member Kearny Shade Tree Commission, 1909-33, pres. or v.p., 1920-1933 and 1938-1943; chmn. biology sect. N.J. State Science Teachers Association, 1927-29, president, 1920-31; director New Jersey Federation Shade Tree Commissions since 1930, president, 1941-43; member advisory board N.J. State League of Municipalities. Fellow A.A.A.S.; mem. Torrey Bot. Club, John Burroughs Assn. (pres. 1942-44), Amateur Astronomers' Assn. of N.Y. (vice-pres.), Phi Delta Kappa Fraternity. Republican. Methodist. Club: Winter Park University (1st v.p., 1948-49). Author: Nature's Secrets (Vol. 12), 1921; Nature Rambles—Spring (1931)—Summer (1932)—Autumn 1932)—Winter (1932), and awarded John Burroughs medal for same, 1933; Edible Wild Plants, 1939. Co-author: Through Field and Woodland, 1925. Made large collections of plants for Carnegie Mus., Pittsburgh, etc.; assisted in botanical survey, San Jacinto Mtn., Calif., 1901; discovered cassia medsgeri, wild flower named in his honor. Has assembled one of best seed herbaria in U.S. Contbr. nature articles to mags.; lecturer. Mem. Winter Park (Fla.) University Club. Address: 509 Greely St., Orlando FL‡

MEEK, EDWARD ROSCOE, ex-judge; b. Davenport, Ia., Dec. 23, 1865; s. Aaron and Rhoda (Gardner) M.; A.B., State U. of Ia., 1887, LL.B., 1889, A.M., 1891; m. Elizabeth, d. R. P. Clarkson, Oct. 2, 1890. Admitted to bar, 1889; practiced at Ft. Worth, Tex., 1889-98; became U.S. dist. judge, Northern Dist. of Tex., July 1898, retired, Feb. 15, 1936. Mem. Phi Kappa Psi. Republican. Address: Dallas TX*‡

MEEK, HOWARD BAGNALL, educator; b. Chelsea, Mass., Oct. 30, 1893; s. Warren Lee and Eliza Fowler (Reed) M.; S.B., Boston U., 1917, D.Sc. in Edn. (hon.), 1949; M.A., U. Maine, 1920; Ph.D., Yale, 1933; m. Lois Ann Farmer, Sept. 4, 1924; children—Lois Jean, Donald Bagnall. Organizer, Sch. Hotel Adminstrn., Cornell U., 1922, dean, 1954-61, exec. dir. Council on Hotel Restaurant and Instnl. Edn., 1961-69. Past pres. N.Y. State Minimum Wage Bd. for Hotel Industry; cons. OPA, Point IV aid programs. Past pres. Tompkins County Hosp., Ithaca Reconstrn. Home. Mem. Am. Statis. Assn., Am. Econ. Assn., Nat. Restaurant Assn. (life), Club Mgrs. Assn. Am., N.Y. State Hotel Assn. Author: A Theory of Hotel Rates, 1938; Public Hospitalities Around the World, 1938; The Hotels of Latin America, 1952; Code of Minimum Standards for the Hotels of Puerto Rico, 1953; The Hotel Industry Ithaca NY Died July 16, 1969; buried Ithaca NY

MEEK, JOSEPH A(ICINUS), tire and rubber co. exec.; b. East Palestine, O., Sept. 27, 1904; s. Joseph A. and Fannie (Chamberlain) M.; B.A., Ohio Wesleyan U., 1925; m. Clara Phillips, July 10, 1931; children—Donald, Phillip, Marilyn. With Firestone Tire & Rubber Co., Akron, 1925-71, beginning as cost clk., successively times study engr., indsl. relations and prodn. mgr., ordnance plant mgr., dept. field dir. ammunition plants (U.S. Army), asst. dir. indsl. relations, gen. factory mgr., 1925-53, dir. indsl. relations, 1953-58, v.p., 1958-71. Regional executive committee, president Akron Area council of Boy Scouts of America. Bd. trustees Wesleyan University. Member of Phi Gamma Delta frat. Presbyterian Ch. Club: Portage Country, University (Akron). Home: Akron OH Died Feb. 27, 1971; buried East Palestine OH

MEEK, STERNER ST PAUL, author; b. Chgo., Apr. 8, 1894; s. John Washington and Ella (Sterner) M.; student U. Chgo.; B.S. U. Ala., 1915, postgrad. U. Wis., Mass. Inst. Tech.; m. Edna Brundage Noble, July 12, 1927; 1 son, Noble Stafford. Commd. 2d lt., inf. U.S. Army, 1917; transferred to ordnance dept. 1920; advanced through grades to col., 1942; dir. small arms ammunition research U.S. Army, 1923-26; ret. 1947. Mem. N.Am. com. 1000, Christian Children Fund. Mem. Phi Beta Kappa, Pi Tau Phi. Mason (K.T., 32). Club: Pacific Sailfish (Balboa, C.Z.); Seagate (Delray Beach, Florida). Author numerous books including: Hans, A Dog of the Border Patrol, 1950; Surfman, The Adventures of the Coast Guard Dog, 1950; Pagan, A Border Patrol Horse, 1951; Red, ATrailing Bloodhound, 1951; Boy, An Ozark Coon Hound, 1952; Rip, A Game Protector, 1952; Omar, A State Police Dog, 1953; Bellfarm Star, 1955; Pierre of the Big Top, 1956; The Drums of Tapajos, 1961; Troyana, 1961; Frog—Story of A Horse that Knew no Master; Rusty—A Cocker Spaniel; So You're Going to Get a Puppy. also serials, novelettes, short stories and articles in nat. mags. Numerous basic patents on modern tracer ammunition. Breeder, trainer, handler and exhibitor of dogs; judge bench shows, hunting dog field trials; lectr. on dogs and kindred subjects. Home: Delray Beach FL Died June 10, 1972.

MEEKER, ARTHUR, author; born Chicago, Illinois, Nov. 3, 1902; s. Arthur and Grace (Murray) M.; student Chicago Latin Sch., 1916-20, Princeton, 1921-23, Harvard, 1923-24. Press rep. in Santa Barbara, Calif., 1925; reporter on Chicago Herald and Examiner, 1925-26; free lance corr. and mag. writer in U.S. and Europe, 1926-50; travel correspondent for the Chicago Tribune, 1950—. Chmn. bd. Bay Chamber Concerts, Camden, Me. Mem. Soc. of Midland Authors (dir. 1930-71, pres. 1941-43; v.p. Ill., internat. rep.), P.E.N. (sec. Chicago sect.), Authors Guild of Authors League of America; mem. bd. dirs. Midwestern Writers' Conf. Clubs: Arts of Chicago (Chgo.). Author: American Beauty, 1929; Strange Capers, 1931; Vestal Virgin, 1934; Sacrifice to the Graces, 1937; The Ivory Mischief, 1942, The Far Away Music, 1945; Prairie Avenue, 1949; The Silver Plume, 1952; Chicago, Santa Barbara CA Died Oct. 20, 1971; buried Graceland Cemetery, Chicago IL

MEFTAH, DAVOOD KHAN, diplomat; b. Teheran, Persia, 1873. Entered service of Foreign Office of Persia, 1893; advanced to head of English dept.; counsellor spl. mission to Edward VII of Eng., 1905; undersec. of Foreign Office, 1909-11; counsellor spl. embassy to coronation George V of Eng., 1911; to King of Italy for 50th Jubilee of Unite Italianne, 1911; rep. of Persia at Durbar of King George V, Delhi, India, 1911; consul gen. to India, 1912-19; minister of Persia, London, 1920-24; undersec. to Foreign Office, acting minister for Foreign Affairs, 1924-26; E.E. and M.P. to U.S. since Nov. 1926. Address: Persian Legation, 2620 16th St., N.W., Washington DC‡

MEGGINSON, WILLIAM, clergyman; b. Greenville, Tenn., July 30, 1869; s. John Thomas and Sarah E. (Smith) M.; grad. Presbyn. Sem. of Ky., 1897, post-grad. same, 1901; m. Amy Leonard Allen, Apr. 27, 1908. Ordained ministry, Presbyn. Ch. U.S., 1897; pastor Utica Ch., San Antonio, Tex., 1897-1901, Elizabethtown, Ky., 1902-05; dist. supt. S.S. work of Southern Presbyn. Ch., 1905-09; pastor 1st Ch., Biloxi, Miss., 1909-14; dean of Assembly's Training Sch. for Lay Workers, Richmond, Va., 1914-18, also prof. Christian doctrine and O.T. history, same; supt. Presbyn. Orphans' Home, Lynchburg, Va., June 1, 1918-June 1, 1943, now retired. Home: Staunton VA‡

MEHLBERG, JOSEPHINE JANINA BEDNARSKI SPINNER (MRS. HENRY MELHBERG), mathematician, educator; b. Zurawno, Poland, May 1, 1915; s. Paul and Antonia (Morganowska-Suchodolska) Bednarski; M.S., Johannes Casimirus U., Lwow, Poland, 1936, M.A., 1937, Ph.D., 1938; postgrad. Sorbonne, 1938; m. Henry Mehlberg, Aug. 6, 1933. Came to U.S., 1956; naturalized, 1962. Lectr., Coll. of Lwow, 1939-41, mem. Inst. for Postgrad. Tng. High Sch. Tchrs., 1939-41; asso. dir. Polish Council Social Welfare, 1941-42; dir. gen., 1943-50; lectr. math. U. Toronto, Ont., Can., 1951-56; sr. mathematician, study coordinator Inst. for System Research, U. Chgo., 1957-61; asso. prof. math. Ill. Inst. Tech., 1961-66, prof., 1966-69. Mem., v.p. Coordinating Com. for Child Welfare in Poland, 1945-50; mem. exec. com. Internat. Union for Child Welfare, Geneva, Switzerland, 1948-52; v.p. gen. assembly Internat. Conf. Instns. for Child Welfare, Stockholm, Sweden, 1951; del. 9th nat. conf. UNESCO, Chgo., 1963. UN fellow, 1948-49. Mem. Am. Soc. Engring Sci. (founder), Am. Math. Soc., Am. Math. Assn., A.A.A.S., Am. Inst. Aeros. and Astronautics (treas. Chgo. sect.), Am. Soc. Engring. Edn., Canadian Math. Congress, Sigma Xi. Author: Analysis of Axiomatic Foundations of Probability, 1961. Contbr. articles profl. publs. Home: Chicago IL Died May 26, 1969; buried Chicago IL

MEHLIN, THEODORE GREFE, educator; b. Des Moines, June 13, 1906; A.B., Drake U., 1927, A.M., 1930; postgrad. U. Chgo., 1930-31; Ph.D., Yale, 1935; m. Helen M. Roche, Aug., 1936; children—Peter, David. Asst. prof. Drake U., 1936-38, asso. prof., 1938-40, prof., 1940-42; with Williams Coll., Williamstown, Mass., 1942-71, Field Meml. prof. astronomy, dir. Willis I. Milham Planetarium. Author: Astronomy, 1959; Astronomy and the Origin of the Earth, 1968. Address: Williamstown MA Died Dec. 5, 1971.

MEIDELL, HAROLD M., banker; b. Chicago Heights, Ill., Feb. 12, 1910; s. Stephen J. and Ragnhild (Halvorsen) M.; student Northwestern U.; m. Dorothy Eckfeldt, Sept. 19, 1935 (dec. Sept. 1966); children—Karen (Mrs. A. Grant Bohl), John E., Marian; m. 2d, Dorothy H. Healy, Oct. 21, 1967. With First Nat. Bank, Chicago Heights, 1929-46, v.p., cashier, 1939-46; with LaSalle Nat. Bank, Chgo., 1946-68, chmn. bd., pres., 1962-64, chmn., 1964-68, also dir.; dir. No. Ill. Gas Co., NI-Gas Energy, Inc. Treas. for Ill., Fed. Service Joint Crusade, 1960-68. Dir., mem. exec. com. Chgo. chpt. A.R.C.; mem. board govenors Crusade of Mercy; member board dirs. United Charities Chgo.; mem. Northwestern U. Assos., mem. bd. govs. Glenwood Sch. for Boys; citizens board University Chicago. Mem. Chgo. Assn. Commerce and Industry, Chgo. Better Bus. Bur., Execs. Club Chgo., Assn. Res. City Bankers. Clubs: Chicago, Bankers, Commercial, Attic (bd. govs.), Mid-Day, Mid-Am. (Chgo.); Flossmoor Country. Home: Flossmoor IL Died Oct. 3, 1968.

MEIGS, ROBERT VAN, clergyman; b. Pineville, Mo., Jan. 21, 1873; s. Maj. James Madison Monroe and Nanie Edonia (Chilton) M.; B.A., Bacone Coll., 1894; B.D., Div. Sch., U. of Chicago, 1898, post-grad. work, 1903; m. Ida May Holch, Dec. 20, 1899; children—James Samuel (dec.), Esther Geraldine, Frederick Madison, Elizabeth Edonia (Mrs. James R. Morford). Began ministry Bapt. Ch. as student pastor, 1895, evangelist, 1899-1900; pastor successively First Ch., Quincy, First Ch., Urbana, Ill., Muscatine, Ia., and Muskogee, Okla., until 1918; again at Quincy as pastor Central Ch. (consol. of First and Second chs.), 1918-26, Immanuel Ch., Chicago, 1926-28, Logan Sq. Ch., Chicago, 1929-Apr. 1941; pastor First Baptist Ch., Arthur, Ill. to 1943. Retired June 1943; acting pastor Congregational Ch., Shelby, Michigan for duration World War II, pastor First Congl. Church, Interlachen, Fla. since 1947. Offered harmony resolution adopted by Northern Bapt. Conv., at Seattle, Wash., 1925, when a division between fundamentalists and modernists seemed inevitable; has served on Bapt. Conv. Bds.; pres. Chicago Bapt. Ministerial Union, Oct. 1929-Apr. 1930. Republican. Wrote: Deity in the School of Fallen Humanity, The Insignificance and Dignity of Man; Christ and Creation; The Door of Power and Privilege; The Hand of God in the Life of Lincoln; Lincoln's Christianity; Washington's Christianity; Evangelism, the Supreme Function of the Church. Home: Interlachen FL‡

MEIKS, LYMAN THOMPSON, physician, educator; b. Shelbyville, Ind., Oct. 22, 1902; s. George H. and Stella (Thompson) M.; A.B., DePauw U., 1923; M.D., Johns Hopkins, 1927; m. Marie Olsen, Feb. 14, 1931; 1 dau., Karen. Intern Johns Hopkins Hosp., 1927-28; asst. resident, resident New Haven Hosp., 1928-30; chief pediatrician Riley Hosp., 1931-70; prof. pediatrics Ind. U. Sch. Medicine, 1950-70, chmn. dept. 1951-67. Mem. A.M.A., Am. Acad. Pediatrics, Am. Pediatric Soc. Home: Indianapolis IN Died Jan. 25, 1972.

MEIN, JOHN GORDON, fgn. service officer; b. Cadiz, Ky., Sept. 10, 1913; s. John and Elizabeth M. (Fehsenfeld) M.; A.B., Georgetown Coll., 1936; LL.B., George Washington U., 1939; m. Elizabeth Ann Clay, June 15, 1946; children—David Gordon, Marilyn Elizabeth, Eric Alan. With Dept. Agr., 1936-41, Dept. of State, 1941-42, and 1944-47; assigned Am. Embassy, Rio de Janeiro, 1942-44; fgn. service officer, consul career, sec. Diplomatic Service since 1947, 1st as 2d sec. Am. Embassy, Rome, Italy, later 1st sec. Am. Embassy, Oslo, Norway; student Nat. War Coll., 1953-54; 1st sec. Am. embassy, Djakarta, Indonesia, 1954, counselor, 1955-56; dep. dir., office of Southwest Pacific Affairs, Dept. of State, Washington, 1956-57, dir., 1957-60; minister counselor Am. embassy, Manila, 1960-63, Am. embassy, Rio, 1963-65; ambassador to Guatemala, 1965-68. Mem. Bar Assn. D.C. Guatemala City Guatemala First Am. ambassador to be assassinated. Died Aug. 28, 1968; buried Washington DC

MEINE, FRANKLIN JULIUS, editor, author; b. Chgo., May 18, 1896; s. Frank Henry C. and Theresa (Salomon) M.; Ph.B., U. Chgo., 1917, grad. work, 1923-24; A.M., Carnegie Inst. Tech., 1919; grad. work econs. Harvard, 1921-23; m. Helen Lomax, May 18, 1926; children—Frank Carden, Frederick. Research fellow Carnegie Inst. Tech., 1917-18; asst. personnel mgr. Dennison Mfg. Co., Framingham, Mass., 1919-21; research fellow U. Chgo., 1921-23; pres., mgr. Chgo. Book and Art Auctions, 1930-36; author editor Consol. Book Publs., editor The Am. Peoples Ency., Chgo., from 1937; Cresap research fellow Am. lit. Northwestern, 1938-40. Asso. mem. Com. Classification Personnel in Army, World War I. Mem. Soc. Applied Anthropology, Am. Geog. Soc., Am. Acad. Polit. and Social Sci., Soc. Midland Authors (past president), American Folklore Society (council), Miss. Valley Hist. Assn. Clubs: Caxton (pres.); Cliff Dwellers (past pres.) (Chgo.). Author: Job Specifications, 1919; Tall Tales of the Southwest, 1930; Mike Fink, King of the Keelboatmen (with Walter Blair), 1933. Editor: Great Leaders of the World, 1937; Stories of the Streets and of the Town, 1940; Story of America in Pictures, 1944; John McCutcheon's Book, 1948; Mark Twain's First Story,

1952; The Davy Crockett Almanacs, 1955. Collector Am. humor, Am. folk lit.; exhibited collection Am. humor Newberry Library, Chgo., 1939. Home: Chicago IL Died Dec. 1968.

MEINHOLD, H. E., chmn. bd. dirs. Duffy-Mott Co. Address: New York City NY Died Mar. 28, 1971.

MEISLE, KATHRYN (MRS. CALVIN M. FRANKLIN), contralto; b. Phila., Pa., Oct. 14, 1899; d. Adam and Isabelle (Meisle) Meisle; musical training in U.S.; m. Calvin M. Franklin, Nov. 9, 1917. Debut as Erda, in Siegfried," with Chicago Civic Opera Co., 1923; debut as Amneris in Aida" with Met. Opera Assn., 1935; has appeared as soloist with Boston Symphony Orchestra, Phila. Orchestra, Chicago Symphony Orchestra, Detroit Symphony Orchestra, Minneapolis Symphony Orchestra, etc.; principal roles: Amneris in Aida"; Delilah in Samson and Delilah"; Azucena in Il Trovatore"; Erda in Siegfried"; Fricka in Die Walkure"; etc. Address: New York City NY Died Feb. 1970.

MEISTEN, JOHN NICHOLAS, transp. co. exec.; b. N.Y.C., May 11, 1909; s. John Nicholas and Johanna (Krause) M.; B.A., Col. City N.Y., 1930; LL.B., St. John's U., 1935; grad. Advanced Mgmt. Program, Harvard, 1954; m. Melva Delsemme, Oct. 8, 1939; 1 son, John Nicholas III. With Railway Express Agy., Inc., N.Y.C., 1930-—, dir. labor relations, 1953-54, v.p. personnel, from 1954; v.p. Railway Express Motor Transport, Inc., Indpls., from 1955, Railway Express Agy. of Cal., from 1955. Admitted to N.Y. bar, 1936. Bd. mgrs. Grand Central YMCA. Mem. N.Y. County Lawyers Assn. Commerce and Industry Assn. N.Y.C., Harvard Bus. Sch. Assn., N.Y.C. Traffic Club, Newcomen Soc., Theta Delta Chi. Democrat. Episcopalian. Clubs: University (Nassau) (N.Y.); Rockville (N.Y.) Links; Union League (Chgo.). Home: Lynbrook NY Died Aug. 9, 1971; buried Greenfield Cemetery.

MEITNER, LISE, Austrian physicist; b. Vienna, Austria, Nov. 7, 1878; d. Philipp M. and Hedwig (Skovran) Meitner; Ph.D., U. Vienna, 1906; studied with Dr. Max Planck, Berlin, Germany, also Dr. Otto Hahn; hon. degrees univs. Rochester, Rutgers, Stockholm, Berlin, also Adelphi Coll., Smith Coll. Asst., Inst. Theoretical Physics, U. Berlin, 1912-15, lectr. U. Berlin, 1922, extr. prof., 1926; head phys. dept. Kaiser Wilhelm Inst. for Chemistry, 1917-38; staff Novel Inst., Stockholm, Sweden, 1938-48. Recipient Leibnitz medal Berlin Acad. Scis., 1924, Lieben prize Austrian Acad. Scis., 1925; prize in sciences City of Vienna, 1947; Planck medal, 1949; Enrico Fermi award Atomic Energy Commn., 1966. Fgn. mem. Swedish, Copenhagen, Goteborg, Vienna, Berlin, Gottingen, Stockholm acads. scis., Royal Soc. London. Address: Cambridge England Died Oct. 28, 1968.

MELCHIOR, LAURITZ LEBRECTH HOMMEL, tenor; b. Copenhagen, Denmark, Mar. 20, 1890; s. Jorgen Conradt and Julie (Moeller) M.; ed. Melchior's Sch., Copenhagen, 1896-1905; L.H.D., Wagner College, Staten Island, 1951; H.H.D., Philothea Coll., London, Can.; Dr. of Literature, Trinity Southern Bible Coll. of S.C. Am. Inger Nathansen, Nov. 1915 (dec.); children—Ib Jorgen, Birte Inger; m. 2d, Maria Hacker, May 26, 1925 (dec.); m. 3d, Mary Markham, May 23, 1964 (div. 1965). Debut baritone, Copenhagen Opera, Apr. 2, 1913; tenor, Oct. 8, 1918; has sung Covent Garden, London, 1925-72, at Wagner festivals, Bayreuth, 1925-72; with Metropolitan Opera Co., 1926-50; has appeared with marked success in Paris, Berlin, Vienna, Hamburg, Buenos Aires, etc.; singer to Royal Court of Denmark Kammersanger; also a career in TV, radio and motion pictures, latest picture; (Paramount) The Stars Are Singing; founder adminstr. Heldentenor Found., 1968-73. Spl. lectr. for handicapped, Tchrs. Coll. Columbia U. Pres. Royal Guard Outside Denmark. Decorated grand cross comdr. Knightly Order of St. Brigitte; Comdr. of Dannebrog (Denmark), and Dannebrogsmand; Comdr. Order of the White Rose of Finland; El Merito of Chile; Grand Verdienstkreutz (Germany); Legion of Honor (France); various other European decorations. Mason. Address: Beverly Hills CA Died Mar. 18, 1973; buried Copenhagen Denmark

MELDRUM, A(NDREW) MACKENZIE, clergyman, educator; b. Kilwinning, Ayrshire, Scotland, Sept. 6, 1876; s. Andrew and Isabella Scott (Smith) M.; came to U.S.A., 1894, naturalized citizen, 1913; M.A., Ky. U.; grad. Coll. of Bible, Lexington, Ky., 1902; studied in Australia and Scotland, 1903-08; D.D., Spokane U., 1921; m. Helen Scott, d. late Capt. Peter Campbell Crockatt, of Glasgow, Scotland, Sept. 2, 1908 (died 1922); m. 2d, Louise Mitchell, of Melbourne, 1925. Ordained ministry Ch. of Christ, 1902; minister Swanston St. Ch., Melbourne, Australia, 1903-06; traveled widely in the Orient and Europe, 1906-08; minister Pendleton and Athena, Ore., 1908-14; field sec. and lecturer, 1914-16; pres. Spokane U., 1916-24; pres. Pacific Bible Sem., Los Angeles, since 1929. Mason. Lecturer. Exploration and research South Sea Islands, 1923-27. Address: 321 Prospect Av., Los Angeles CA‡

MELDRUM HERBERT ALEXANDER, merchant; b. Buffalo, N.Y., Feb. 15, 1870; s. Alexander and Ann Elizabeth (Webster) M.; ed. grammar and high schs., Buffalo; m. Louise Hingston, Sept. 23, 1895. Began in dry goods under father, 1890; was pres.-treas. H. A. Meldrum Co. dept. store; chmn. trustees Am. Savings Bank (ex-pres.); dir. Bankers Trust Co., Federal Telephone & Telegraph Co.; dir. and sec. Penn-York Oil Corp. Apptd. by Gov. Hughes mem. bd. mgrs. Buffalo State Hosp., 1907; pres. Chamber of Commerce, Buffalo, 3 terms, 1913-15; life mem. Albright Art Gallery, Grosvenor terms, 1913-15; life mem. Albright Art Gallery, Grosvenor Library, Buffalo Pub. Library, Automobile Club of Buffalo (bd. dirs. 1903-06, pres. 1906); mem. Am. Automobile Assn. (v.p. 3 terms, 1927-29 inclusive; dir.), N.Y. State Automobile Assn. (pres. 3 terms to 1928), Automobile Old Timers. Republican. Presbyterian. Home: 945 Lafayette Av., Buffalo 9 NY‡

MELHORN, NATHAN R., clergyman, educator; b. Ada, O., Dec. 23, 1871; s. Michael S. and Martha (Ahlefeld) M.; A.B., Ohio Northern U., 1890; grad. Luth. Theol. Sem., Phila., 1897; D.D., Muhlenberg, 1917; Litt.D. from Carthage (Ill.) College, 1926; LL.D., Midland College, Fremont, Neb., 1938; m. Florence L. Richmond, 1901; children—Nathan R., Henry B. Ordained Luth. ministry, 1897; editor of The Lutheran, 1920-45, retired since 1945. Trustee Lankenau Hosp. and Drexel Motherhouse of Deaconesses, Philadelphia, Pa. Republican. Home: 4720 Warrington Av. Office: Muhlenberg Bldg., Philadelphia PA‡

MELIODON, JULES ANDRE, sculptor, b. Paris, France, June 1, 1867; s. Jules Antoine and Jeanne Francoise Catherine (Van Cutsem) M.; ed. Nat. Decorative Art Sch., Nat. Beaux Arts, Jardin des Plantes Sch., France; m. Louise Gabrielle Hugot, Feb. 3, 1904; children—Louis Edward, Andree. Came to U.S., 1904, naturalized, 1911. Works: bust of Francollin, bust of Lesueur, France; soldiers memorial, Bloomingdale, N.J.; busts of Senator Chase, Fred Stevens, Ferdinand Roebling, Simon Gratz; bronze memorial, Ch. of St. Thomas the Apostle, New York; Alpha and Omega frieze, St. Elizabeth Ch., Phila. Decorated Officer of Academy by French Govt., 1898; Officer of Public Instrn., 1904; hon. mention Salon of Artistes Francais, 1902. Served as pvt. in French Army, 1891-93. Mem. Art Alliance (Phila.), Am. Artists Professional League. Home: 2612 S. 12th St. Studio: 1840 S. Bancroft St., Philadelphia PA*‡

MELISH, JOHN HOWARD, clergyman; b. Milford, O., Oct. 12, 1874; s. Thomas Jefferson and Maria (Bromwell) M.; student U. of Cincinnati, 1892-95, LL.D., 1931; student Harvard, 1895-96, Episcopal Theol. Sch., Cambridge, Mass., 1895-98; D.D., U. of Ga., 1926; m. Marguerite McComas, 1899. Deacon, 1898, priest, 1899, P.E. Ch.; pastor Associate Missions, 1898-1900; univ. chaplain, U. of Cincinnati, 1899-1904; asso. pastor Christ Ch., Cincinnati, 1900-04; rector Holy Trinity Ch., Brooklyn, 1904-51. Fraternal del. Central Trades Council of Greater N.Y.; chmn. Brooklyn Housing Com. Mem. City Affairs Com. of N.Y. Clubs: City, Rembrandt. Author: Franklin Spencer Spalding, Man and Bishop, 1917; Paul Jones, Minister of Reconciliation, 1942. Co-author: Getting Together, 1913; A Free Pulpit in Action, 1931; In That Case, 1938. Address: 126 Pierrepont St., Brooklyn NY‡

MELLON, RICHARD KING, banker; b. Pittsburgh, Pa., June 19, 1899; s. Richard Beatty and Jennie Taylor (King) M.; student Princeton Univ.; hon. LL.D., Waynesburg Coll., 1946, Washington and Jefferson Coll., 1947; hon. S.P.D., St. Vincent Coll., Latrobe, Pa., 1946; LL.D. (honorary), University of Pitts., 1948; Pa. Mil. Coll., 1954; D.C.S. (honorary) N.Y. U. Sch. Commerce, 1950; E.D. (hon.), Duquesne U., 1953; Sc.D., Carnegie Institute Technology, 1956; m. Constance Prosser, April 1936; children—Richard, Cassandra, Constance, Seward. Began as messenger Mellon Nat. Bank, 1920, assistant cashier, 1924-28, vice pres. 1928-34, pres. 1934-46; chmn. bd. Mellon Nat. Bank & Trust Co., 1946-66, honorary chairman of the bd., 1967-70; governor and pres., T. Mellon & Sons; director Aluminum Co. of Am., Gen. Motors Corporation, also director Gulf Oil Corporation. Served as student pilot, A.C., 1918; commd. maj. AUS, 1942, promoted lt. col., Oct. 2, 1942; col., April 3, 1943; served as dir. Selective Service, State of Pa.; asst. chief of staff, Internat. Div. War Dept., Washington, D.C.; disch. as col., 1945; brig. gen., 1948, lt. gen. res., 1961. Decorated D.S.M.; recipient Andrew Heiskell Award for civic statesmanship, Action, Inc., 1963; annual citation Midwest Research Inst., 1964. Member bd. trustees Carnigie Inst. Republican. Presbyn. Home: Ligonier PA Died June 3, 1970.

MELLUISH, JAMES GEORGE, sanitary engr.; b. Bloomington, Ill., Feb. 25, 1870; s. Joseph Henry and Hannah (Bell) M.; grad. Lawrenceville (N.J.) Sch., 1891; spl. student U. of Ill., 1895; B.S., Mass. Inst. Tech., 1896; m. Ruth Kershaw, of Bloomington, Ill., Oct. 15, 1903; 1 son, James Kershaw; m. 2d, M. Teresa Galvis, Bucaramanga, S.A., May 11, 1929; 1 daughter, Gladys. Researches in sanitary biology, Massachusetts Institute of Technology, with Prof. W. T. Sedgwick, 1897; designed sanitary engring. works of Ill. State Normal U. and Ill. Soldiers Orphans Home, 1898-1900; supt. Union Gas & Electric Co., Bloomington, Ill., 1900-01; sanitary and engring. investigations in Ia., Ill., N.Y., Fla. and La., also sewerage and sewage disposal, etc., 1901-19; project engr. U.S. Housing Corpn., Alton (Ill.) Dist., 1918; dist. dir. Div. of Industrial Hygiene and Medicine, St. Louis, 1919; capt. U.S.P.H.S., rank of asso. sanitary engr.; sanitary engr. Pearse, Greeley & Hansen, 1923-28; engr. sewerage system, Barranquilla, Colombia, 1928-—. Mem. Am. Soc. C.E., Ill. Soc. Engrs., Phi Delta Theta. Republican. Unitarian. Chicago IL*‡

MELONEY, WILLIAM BROWN, author; b. N.Y.C., May 3, 1905; s. William Brown and Marie (Mattlingly) M.; student Williams Coll., 1924-25; A.B., Columbia, 1926, grad. student, 1928-31, law sch., 1930-31; fellow U. Paris, 1927-28; m. Elizabeth Symons, Mar. 5, 1927; children—William Brown Peter; m. 2d, Rose Franken, Apr. 29, 1937. Lectr. English and comparative lit. Columbia, 1927; with law firm William J. Donovan, 1930-32, mgr. gubernatorial campaign William J. Donovan, N.Y., 1932; pub., editor weekly newspaper chain, Dutchess Co., N.Y., 1932-36; producer N.Y. stage plays: Outrageous Fortune, Doctors Disagree, Soldier's Wife, The Hallams; producer, dir. Claudia radio series; partner Pynekeudall & Hollister, 1954-71. Clubs: Players, Dutch Treat, Columbia, N.Y. Athletic. Author: Rush to the Sun, 1937; In High Places, 1939; Beloved Enemy, 1936; Call Back Love, 1938; Strange Victory, 1939; When Doctors Disagree, 1940; American Bred, 1941; Money, 1952; Many Are the Travelers, 1954. Contbr. articles, short stories to mags. Home: Kent CT Died May 1971.

MELVIN, MARION EDMUND, clergyman, educator; b. Camden, Miss., Sept. 23, 1876; s. Edmund Waller and Elizabeth Ann (McMurtray) M.; grad. with first honors, French Camp (Miss.) Acad., 1895; A.B., Southwestern Presbyn. U., Clarksville, Tenn., 1898, A.M. and B.D., 1900, D.D., 1912; m. Susie Priestly Reid, of Canton, Miss., Nov. 1900; 1 dau., Margaret (adopted). Ordained ministry Presbyn. Ch. in U.S., 1900; pastor Brandon and Forest, Miss., 1900-04, Port Gibson, 1904-08; pres. Chamberlain Hunt Acad., Port Gibson, 1908-14; supt. schs. and colleges for Synod of Miss. (Presbyn. Ch. in U.S.), 1914-17; field sec. Dept. of Edn., same denom., 1917-21, raising abt. $5,000,000 for colleges; gen. sec. Dept. of Stewardship and Ch. Finance, same denom., 1921-27; pres. Westminster Coll., Fulton, Mo., since June 1, 1927. Pres. United Stewardship Council, Chs. of Christ in America, 1924, 25; moderator Synod of Miss., 1917. Mason. Rotarian. Author: Royal Partnership, 1926; also writer of pamphlets on stewardship and Christian edn. Home: Fulton MO‡

MENDEL, WARNER H(UMPHREY), life ins. exec., lawyer; b. Knoxville, Tenn., Oct. 2, 1906; s. Maurice H. and Nell (Warner) M.; B.A., Columbia, 1927, LL.B., 1930; m. Betty Rose Herschman, Oct. 5, 1934. Admitted to N.Y. bar, 1930 since practiced in N.Y.C.; research asst. Columbia Law Faculty, 1930-33; mem. staff of pres. Equitable Life Assurance Soc. U.S., 1933-41, asst. counsel, 1941-44, asso. counsel, 1944-51, counsel, 1951-55, v.p., counsel, 1955-59; v.p., gen. solicitor, 1959-67. Trustee Montefiore Hosp., N.Y.C. Mem. Am., N.Y. State N.Y.C. bar assns., Assn. Life Ins. Council, Am. Life Conv., Life Ins. Assn. Am., N.Y. C. of C., Phi Beta Kappa, Zeta Beta Tau. Home: Hampton Bays NY Died Oct. 22, 1967.

MENDELL, CLARENCE WHITTLESEY, educator; b. Norwood, Mass., June 3, 1883; s. Ellis and Clara Eliza (Whittlesey) M.; B.A., Yale, 1904, M.A., 1905, Ph.D., 1910; m. Katharine DeFord Webb, April 14, 1914 (died Jan. 21, 1919); m. 2d, Elizabeth Bailey Lawrence, July 10, 1930. Instr. Latin, 1907-11, asst. prof. Greek and Latin, 1911-19, Yale; apptd. Dunham prof. Latin lang. and lit., same, 1919; dean Yale Coll., 1926-37; chmn. Bd. of Athletic Control, Yale, 1919-25; master Branford Coll., 1932-43, Sterling prof., Yale, from 1947, public orator from 1947. Annual prof. Am. Acad., Rome, 1932-33. With Am. Mil. Intelligence, Paris, 1918; asst. to territorial experts of Am. Commn. to Negotiate Peace, Paris, 1918-19. Served as lt. comdr., U.S.N.R., June 1942; comdr. U.S.N.R., Nov. 1944. Awarded Legion of Merit, Dec. 1945. Chmn. bd. trustees, Salisbury School; trustee Am. Acad. in Rome. Mem. Am. Philological Association, Classical Association Great Britain, Beta Theta Pi, Phi Beta Kappa. Republican. Episcopalian. Clubs: Graduate, Elizabethan, Lawn (New Haven); Yale, Century (N.Y.). Author: Sentence Connection in Tacitus, 1911; Latin Sentence Connection, 1917; Prometheus, 1926; Jeanne d'Arc, 1931; Our Seneca, 1941; Tacitus, The Man and His Work, 1960; Latin Poetry, The New Poets and the Augustans, 1965; Latin Poetry, The Age of Rhetoric and Satire, 1967; Lanx Satura, 1969. Contbr. on classical subjects. Home: Bethany CT Died Dec. 14, 1970.

MENEFEE, F(ERDINAND) N(ORTHRUP), educator, cons. engr.; b. Columbus Kan., Jan. 7, 1886; s. Harry Bostwick and Alice DiaDame (Hodgen) M.; B.S. in Civil Engring., U. Neb., 1908, C.E., 1932; C.E.,

Cornell, 1910; D.Eng., Lawrence Inst. Tech., Detroit, 1937; m. Lucile Cull, Sept. 17, 1909; children—Charles Cull, Ruth. Instr. civil engring., Cornell U., 1910; instr. U. Mich., 1910-13, asst. prof. drawing, 1914, asst. prof. engring. mechanics, 1915-16, prof., from, 1919, prof. emeritus, until 1973; sec. United Engring. Corp., Detroit and Ann Arbor, 1919-20, v.p., 1920-29; firm Menefee and Dodge, 1925-35; pres. Oak Park Land Co., 1925-73; ex-chmn. bd. Lus-Trus Plastics, Inc.; treas. Dana Fiduciary; dir. Am. Cement Corp. Mem. nat. council YMCA, 1927-32, state com. 1927-35, pres. Ann Arbor, 1923, dir., 1921, 22; bd. dirs. Student Christian Assn., 1929-36; mem. U. Mich. Fresh Air Camp Com., chmn. 1923-46; pres. Community Fund Assn., Ann Arbor, 1927. Mem. Ann Arbor Bd. Pub. Works, 1925-49, pres., 1935-40. Served to maj., Ordnance Dept., World War I. Mem. Am. Soc. C.E. (pres. Mich. sect. 1948, vice chmn. com. on water diversions), Am. Soc. Testing Materials, Am. Concrete Inst. (past chmn. precast floor constrn. com., dir. 1952-55), Mich. Engring. Soc. (pres. 1930), Mich. Patent Law Assn., Engring. Soc. Detroit, Am. Legion, Kappa Sigma, Sigma Xi, Sigma Tau, Sigma Rho Tau (former nat. pres.). Republican. Mem. Conglist. Ch. Clubs: Rotary (dir. 1932), Michigan Union. Author: Materials Testing Manual, 1932; St. Lawrence Seaway, 1940; Structural Members and Connections (co-reviser with R.R. Zipprodt), 1943. Editor: Michigan Engineer, 1927-37. Contbr. reports and engring. articles. Home: Ann Arbor MI Died Feb. 12, 1973.

MENTON, A(NDREW) PAUL, sports commr.; b. Sparrows Point, Md., Oct. 23, 1901; s. John Aloysius and Anna (Hurn) M.; A.B., Loyola Coll., 1922; m. Jean Taylor Dawson, Apr. 18, 1927; children—John, James Paul (dec.). Sports writer Balt. (Md.) Am., 1922, Balt. Post, 1923, Balt. Evening Sun, 1923-25; sports editor Baltimore Evening Sun, 1925-67, ret.; commr. Maryland Scholastic Assn., 1922-69; v.p., Hoban, Inc., Baltimore, 1939-44; commr. Mason-Dixon Intercollegiate Conf. 1940-69, football ofcl., 1923-54, basketball ofcl., 1920-53; treas. Monumental Adhesive Co., 1952-57. Member Joint Basketball Rules Committee, 1927-36. Consultant to U.S. Army Service Forces Athletic Com., 1944. Dir. Camp Ha-Wa-Ya, Harrison, Me., 1945-61. Dir. Eastern Assn. Intercollegiate Football Ofcls., 1945-53 (pres. 1947); dir. So. Football Ofcls. Assn., 1929-49. Trustee U. Balt., 1958-69, chmn., 1967-69; mem. selections com. Md. Hall Fame, 1956-65; pres. Balt. Colts Found. Democrat. Roman Catholic. Home: Baltimore MD Died Nov. 21, 1969; buried New Cathedral Cemetery, Baltimore MD

MENTZER, WILLIAM CYRUS, ret. air transp. exec.; b. Knoxville, Ia., May 27, 1907; s. William C. and Maude (Gilson) M. A.B. in Journalism, U. Neb. 1929; B.S. in Aero. Engring., Mass. Inst. Tech., 1931; postgrad. Harvard Grad. Sch. Bus., 1943-44; m. Mary Esther Cruickshank, Sept. 19, 1933; children—William Cyrus, Molly E., Sally G. Engr., Boeing Airplane Co., 1931-34; with United Air Lines, Inc., 1934-71, v.p. engring., 1958-62, sr. v.p. engring. and maintenance, San Francisco, 1962-70, sr. v.p., asst. to gen. mgr., 1970-71. Vis. com. Stanford U. Sch. Medicine; adv. com. Inst. Transp. and Traffic Engring., U. Cal.; corp. devel. com. Mass. Inst. Tech. Recipient Distinguished Service award FAA, 1969, Daniel Guggenheim medal, 1972. Fellow Am. Inst. Aeros. and Astronautics; mem. Soc. Automotive Engrs., Nat. Acad. Engring., Phi Delta Theta. Home: Palo Alto CA Died Dec. 23, 1971.

MENZIES, ALAN WILFRID CRANBROOK, prof. chemistry; b. Edinburgh, Scotland, July 31, 1877; s. Thomas Hunter and Helen Charlotte (Cranbrook) M.; M.A., Edinburgh U., 1897, B.Sc., 1898; studied univs. of Leipzig and Aberdeen; Ph.D., U. of Chicago, 1910; m. Mary Isabella Dickson, of Edinburgh, Mar. 20, 1908; 1 dau., Elizabeth Grant Cranbrook. Asst. prof. and prof. chemistry, Edinburgh and Glasgow until 1908; organizer and dir. summer courses for science teachers, Ireland, 1904-08; came to U.S., 1908; asst. prof. chemistry, U. of Chicago, 1911-12; prof. chemistry, Oberlin Coll., 1912-14; prof. chemistry, Princeton, 1914—. Mem. A.A.A.S., Sigma Xi; fellow Royal Soc. Edinburgh, Chem. Soc. London. Home: Princeton NJ‡

MERCER, HUGH VICTOR, lawyer; b. Salem, Ill., Jan. 26, 1869; s. Silas and Caroline (Gaston) M.; ed. pub. and normal schs. and pvt. study; LL.B., U. of Minn., 1894, LL.M., 1897 (D.C.L., 1911); m. Edith Huling Crawford, of Marietta, O., later St. Paul, Minn., Aug. 18, 1904; children—Caroline Gaston, Victoria Louise. Admitted to Minn. bar, 1894 and since in practice at Minneapolis, now sr. mem. H. V. Mercer & Co. Lecturer on equity practice and procedure in U.S. Court, U. of Minn. Pres. Minn. Workmen's Compensation Com., 1909-11; official of 1st 4 interstate confs. to formulate the workmen's compensation movement, and chmn. com. of 4th conf. to draft bills as a guide for the states for the two theories of compensation to workmen. Mem. Am. Bar Assn. (v.p. for Minn. 1 yr.), Minn. State Bar Assn. (ex-pres.), Minneapolis Bar Assn. (pres.). Mem. Minn. Com. on Uniform State Laws. Republican. Clubs: Minneapolis, Minikahda, Minneapolis Automobile, Encampment Forest, Six-o'clock, Professional Men's, Dinner (Minneapolis); Cosmos (Washington). Home: 3800 Zenith Av. So. Office: Foshay Tower, Minneapolis MN‡

MERICKA, WILLIAM JOHN, corp. exec.; b. Cleve., Dec. 2, 1898; s. Michael and Julia (Banking) M.; m. Lauretta E. Popp, Dec. 21, 1925; children—James Robert, William A. With Herrick Co., Cleve., 1916-30, v.p., 1928-30; pres. William J. Mericka Co., Cleve., 1930-65, also dir.; chmn. bd. Van Norman Industries, New Bedford, Mass., 1960-65, Delphos Soya Co., 1950-65, Reedy Fork Ranch, Inc., 1951-65; dir. Vernors Ginger Ale Company. Clubs: Union, Canterbury Country, Midday (Cleve.); Sedgefield Country (Greensboro, N.C.). Home: Cleveland OH Died Oct. 1965.

MERIGOLD, BENJAMIN SHORES, prof. chemistry; b. Taunton, Mass., July 24, 1873; s. Samuel and Sarah Amelia (Shores) M.; A.B., Harvard, 1896, A.M., 1897, Ph.D., 1901; hon. Sc.D., Clark U., 1941; m. Mary Edith Sayward, July 10, 1930. Asst. in chemistry, Harvard, 1896-1900; instr. in chemistry, 1900-03, Worcester Poly. Inst.; asst. prof., 1903-08, prof. 1908-46, Clark U. Mem. Am. Chem. Soc., A.A.A.S. Home: 17 Charlotte St., Worcester MA‡

MERITT, EDGAR BRIANT, b. Columbia Co., Ark., Nov. 16, 1874; s. William Cass and Lucinda Jane (Briant) Meritt; attended pub. schs. in Arkansas; grad. Wood's Commercial College, Washington, D.C.; LL.B., Georgetown U., 1898; LL.M., George Washington U., 1899; spl. studies in diplomacy, internat. and civil law, and polit. economy, same univ.; m. Katharine Kidd Spencer, of Ionia, Mich., Oct. 11, 1909. Compositor and proofreader Govt. Printing Office, Washington, D.C., 10 yrs.; with Indian Service since 1906; chief law officer Indian Service, 4 yrs.; asst. Indian commr. since Oct. 23, 1913. In charge legislation for Indian Bur. since 1911. Mem. Southern Soc. (v.p.), Arkansas Club of Washington (ex-pres.), Federal Club Washington Bd. of Trade. Methodist. Mason. Has written extensively on the Am. Indian. Home: 1345 Jefferson Av. N.W., Washington DC‡

MERKER, HARVEY MILTON, chem. engr.; b. Detroit, Feb. 24, 1888; s. Herman and Rosa (Walz) M.; B.S., U. Mich., 1909, M.S., 1940, D.Eng. (hon.), 1953; D.S., Wayne U., 1943; m. Buda Overesch Martin, June 27, 1911; children—Henry M., Marjorie (Mrs. Rudolph Sell). Chem. engr. Parke, Davis & Co., 1909-29, supt. mfg., 1929-53, dir. sci. relations, 1953-57, ret.; dir. Mich. Life Ins. Co. Pres. Detroit Pub. Library Commn., from 1953; chmn. nat. adv. com. Mich. Meml.-Phoenix Project; adv. com. Franklin Settlement. Dir. Detroit Council Churches; trustee Detroit Historical Society, Metropolitan Society for the Blind; commissioner, president Detroit Public Library; trustee, past president Detroit Institution, Cancer Research; vice pres., trustee Kresge Eye Institute, Edwin S. George Found.; trustee, sec. Cranbrook Inst. Sci.; trustee Alma Coll.; gov. Rackham Research Found. Mich. State Coll.; pres. Kresge-Hooker Scientific Library Associates; director Junior Achievement of S.E. Mich., Meth. Children's Village, Detroit chapter UN, Detroit Sci. Museum Soc., World Medical Relief, Incorporated. Member adv. bd. Detroit Dist. Nurses Assn., Nat. Fedn. of Settlements and Neighborhood Centers. Named First Citizen of Detroit, 1957; Midwest citation of honor Ind. Tech. Coll., 1958. Fellow A.A.A.S.; member Am. Chem. Soc., Am. Institute Chem. Engrs., Engring. Soc. Detroit (past pres.), Better Bus. Bur. Detroit (dir.), Sigma Rho Tau, Tau Beta Pi. Presbyn. Clubs: Torch, Orpheus, Detroit Boat, Detroit Athletic, Forest Lake Country (Detroit). Author: Book of Stainless Steels, 1933; Encyclopedia of Chemical Technology (with A.R. Whale), 1953; Centennial History of the Engineering College of the U. of Michigan, 1953. Contbr. profl. pubs. Home: Detroit MI Died May 4, 1970; interred Evergreen Cemetery, Detroit MI

MERNER, GARFIELD DAVID, business exec.; b. Cedar Falls, Ia.; s. David C. and Emma Louise (Pfeiffer) M.; LL.D. (hon.), Ill. Wesleyan U., 1947. Chungang Univ. (Seoul, Korea), 1956; L.H.D. (hon.), Pfeiffer College, 1962; married to Benetta Delight Ward (deceased); children—Benetta Delight (Mrs. Charles W. Sciutto), Ward Pfeiffer, Mary Louise (Mrs. Merner McAfee), David Robinson (deceased); second marriage to Ruth Conklin Geggie, 1959. Vice pres. and gen. mgr. William R. Warner & Co., Inc., St. Louis Labs., 1908-20; vice pres. and a founder Merner Lumber Co., Palo Alto, Cal., 1923-29; mem. bd. of dirs. Garfield, Inc., Palo Alto, Cal. Served as dir. of supply service Pacific area nat. A.R.C., 1943-44. Co-founder Allied Arts Guild Cal. Ltd., 1929; v.p., dir. Gustavus and Louise Pfeiffer Research Found., N.Y.; trustee Atlanta U., Am. Found. for Blind, Inc., Am. Found. for Overseas Blind, Inc., Bennett Coll., Clark Coll., Ill. Wesleyan U., Ohio Wesleyan U. (Del.), Pfeiffer Coll.; trustee, Cal. Coll. Arts and Crafts, Oakland; pres. Albert Baker Meml. Scholarship Fund for Higher Edn.; bd. dirs., vice chmn. Am. Korean Found. N.Y. Mem. Cal. Acad. Scis., Cal. Hist. Soc., English Speaking Union, Friends Bancroft Library, World Affairs Council No. Cal. Mason (32 deg.). Clubs: Bohemian, Book of California, Commonwealth of Cal., Roxburghe, Sierra (San Francisco). On Flight to North Pole, 1949. Home: San Francisco CA Died Feb. 27, 1972.

MERORY, JOSEPH, author; b. Patrauti, Bucovina-Austria; Jan. 6, 1895; s. Jacob and Esther (Weidenfeld) M.; student Technische Hochschule, Vienna, Austria, 1919-21; Chem. Engr., Inst. Sup. Techn. et Coll., Liege, Belgium, 1927; m. Sarah Leibovich, Aug. 22, 1944; 1 dau., Edith (Mrs. Even T. Collinsworth, Jr.); came to U.S., 1937; naturalized, 1944. Developer fruit flavorings, Fries & Bro., Bloomfield, N.J., 1938-41, Van Ameringen-Haebler, Elizabeth, N.J., 1941-43; mgr. flavor dept. Joe Lowe Corp., N.Y.C., 1944-48; mgr. prodn., sale fruit flavoring, Givaudan-Delawana, N.J., 1948-52; pres. Merory Flavors, Inc., 1952. Mem. Inst. Food Tech., International Assn. Mason. Author: Food Flavorings, 1960, rev. 1968. Patentee food flavoring prodn., methods. Home: Lake Hiawatha NJ Died July 6, 1970.

MERRICK, EDWARD STEELE, lawyer; b. Cleve., Jan. 30, 1904; s. Walter C., and Elizabeth (Steele) M.; student Williams Coll., 1923-25; B.A., Ohio Wesleyan U., 1927; LL.B., Western Res. U., 1935; m. Beatrice E. Bolton, Oct. 14, 1939; children—Bonnie (Mrs. Anthony S. Baker), Beatrice Elizabeth (Mrs. Richard D. Wills). With Nat. Screw & Mfg. Co., Cleve., 1927-31; admitted to Ohio bar, 1935; practiced in Cleve., 1935-68; partner McKeehan, Merrick, Arter & Stewart, 1945-55; partner Arter, Hadden, Wykoff & Van Duzer, 1955-68. Pres., Civil Service Commn., Cleveland Heights, 1951-68. Past pres., trustee Childrens Services; trustee Golden Age Center. Mem. Am., Ohio, Cleve. bar assns., Am. Judicature Soc., Cleve. C. of C., Ct. Nisi Prius, Alpha Delta Phi, Phi Delta Phi. Republican. Presbyn. Clubs: Mid Day, Mayfield Country (past pres., trustee). Home: Cleveland OH Died Sept. 28, 1968; buried Lake View Cemetery Cleveland OH

MERRICK, HARRY HOPKINS, b. Minneapolis, Minn., Oct. 15, 1873; s. Ambrose Newell and Sarah Bates (Warriner) M.; LL.B., U. of Minn., 1892; m. Edna Marshall Fuller, of Tampa, Fla., Mar. 21, 1894; children—Marlowe M., Dixie A. (dec.). Admitted to bar, 1892, and began practice in Minn.; moved to Sioux City, Ia., 1893, and became house atty. for Tolerton & Stetson Co.; credit mgr. Hammond Packing Co., Omaha, also of T. M. Sinclair Packing Co., Cedar Rapids, Ia.; gen. mgr. credits for Armour & Co., Chicago, 1901-18; v.p. Central Trust Co. of Ill., July 1918-May 1919; pres. Great Lakes Trust Co., Chicago, 1919-21; a v.p. Central Trust Co. of Ill. (which absorbed Great Lakes Trust Co.), 1921-22; moved to Los Angeles, 1922, and formed Merrick & Ruddick, Inc., gen. ins. and real estate, title of firm now Harry H. Merrick & Co., Inc. Pres. Hollywood Foothills Improvement Assn. Pres. Chicago Br. Nat. Security League, 1916-19; chmn. draft bds., also of Coal Crisis Com. of Ill. and pres. Selective Service Assn., 1917-18, World War. Mem. Chicago Assn. Commerce (gen. treas. 1917, v.p. interstate and foreign trade div. 1918, pres. 1919); mem. Chicago Assn. Credit Men (pres. 1918-19), Miss. Valley Assn. (pres. 1919-20), Great Lakes-St. Lawrence Tide Water Assn. (pres. 1920-21), Greater Los Angeles Assn. (pres.), Central Motion Picture Dist., Inc. (v.p.). Mem. Delta Chi. Republican. Clubs: Jonathan, El Caballero, Surf and Sand. Home: 3404 Troy Drive. Office: 139 N. Broadway, Los Angeles CA‡

MERRILL, AMOS NEWLOVE, educator; b. Richmond, Utah, Mar. 15, 1875; s. Marriner Wood and Sarah Ann (Atkinson) M.; B.S., Utah State Agrl. Coll., 1897; M.S., U. of Ill., 1908; Ph.D., Stanford U., 1926; grad. student, Harvard, 1938; travel in Europe, 1938; m. Eliza Drysdale, Apr. 25, 1900; children—Amos Lyman, Vernon Newlove, Erma Janet (Mrs. DeCosta Clark, now dec.), Sarah Lucile (Mrs. Melvon McDonald), David Marriner, Alton Drysdale. Began as teacher, 1902; prof. of agr., Brigham Young Coll., 1905-09, Brigham Young U., 1909-22; dean Church Teachers Coll., Brigham Young U., 1917-23, prof. of secondary education since 1924, acting dean, 1930-39, dean of education, 1939-46, prof. emeritus since 1946; exchange professor of education, University of Maine, 1940. Member Board of Education of Provo, Utah (president, 1941-47). Member Utah Educational Association (past pres.), Utah Acad. Science, Phi Delta Kappa. Author: A Reader for Junior Students, 1928; Balance Wheels, 1932; Recent Trends in Organization of State Depts. of Education, 1934; Improved Teaching (German translation), 1936. Home: 279 N. 4th Provo UT‡

MERRILL, CHARLES WHITE, mining engr.; b. La Crescenta, Cal., July 22, 1900; s. Samuel and Emilie (Scherb) M.; A.B. in Geology, Stanford, 1922, E.M., 1924; m. Lillian M. Dobbel, Aug. 15, 1925; children—Lillian D. (Mrs. Archibald C. Coolidge, Jr.), Charles White, Celine W. (Mrs. Francis B. Birkner), Henry D. With various mining cos. in U.S. and Mexico, 1924-28; with U.S. Bur. Mines, San Francisco and Washington, 1928-70, chief div. of minerals Washington, 1955-70; asso. Behre Dolbear & Co., N.Y. 1970-72. Mem. U.S. delegations Tin Study Group Meetings, 1947-53, U.S. Tin Mission to Malaya, 1951, head U.S. delegation subcom. mineral resources Econ. Commn. Asia and Far East, Tokyo (UN), 1960. Served as pfc., Tank Corps, U.S. Army, 1918-19; capt. specialist res., 1931-42. Mem. Am. Inst. Mining Engrs. (dir.

1955-56, chmn. mineral econs. div. 1955-56; Mineral Economics award 1967), Mining and Metall. Soc. Am. Club: Cosmos (Washington). Author articles mining engring., mineral econs., strategic minerals in govt., profl. and tech. publs., jours. Home: Washington DC Died May 1, 1972.

MERRILL, FRANCIS ELLSWORTH, educator; b. Ft. Dodge, Ia., May 21, 1904; s. Roy Willard and Anna (Farrell) M.; A.B., Dartmouth, 1926; A.M., U. Chgo., 1934, Ph.D., 1937; m. Emily W. Archibald, Mar. 30, 1934. Instr. sociology U. Kan., 1931-32; asst. prof. sociology Roosevelt Coll., Chgo., 1932-35; with Dartmouth, 1935-68, professor of sociology, 1946-69; Fulbright lectr. U. Rennes, University of Aix-en-Provence, France, 1959-60; also at University of Nice (France), 1966-67, 68-69. Priority specialist WPB, Wash., 1941-42; intelligence officer Bd. Econ. Warfare, Washington, 1942-43. Mem. Eastern Sociological Soc. (v.p. 1961-62), Am. Sociol. Soc., Phi Beta Kappa, Alpha Delta Phi. Author: Social Disorganization (with M. A. Elliott), 1961; Marriage and the Family in American Culture (with A. G. Truxal), 1947; Social Problems on the Home Front, 1948; Courtship and Marriage, 1959; Social Problems (with others), 1950; Culture and Society (with H. W. Eldredge), 1952; Society and Culture, 1969; also articles sci. jours. Home: Hanover NH Died Nov. 22, 1969: buried Cimetiere de l'Est, Nice France

MERRILL, FREDERICK AUGUSTUS, author; b. at Boston, June 15, 1875; s. Samuel and Lucy (Urann) M.; B.S., Mass. Agrl. Coll., 1899; B.Sc., Boston U., 1899; m. Effie Smith Myddleton, of Valdosta, Ga., Dec. 22, 1909 (died 1927). Was teacher in schs. of Ga.; prof. science, Union Bapt. Inst., Mt. Vernon, Ga., 1906-08; prof. geography and nature study, State Normal School, Athens, Ga., 1908-14, prof. rural economics and sociology, dir. Ga. Club, 1914-18; head dept. of geography, U. of Ga. Summer Sch., 1906-15; prof. geography, Summer Sch. of the South, U. of Tenn., 1915-—; lecturer summer session Johns Hopkins U., 1917; institute lecturer. Democrat. Charter mem. Burroughs Nature Club; mem. Southern Geol. Soc. Clubs: University, Peabody. Author: What to Teach in Nature Study, 1909; Field and Laboratory Note Book in Physical Geography, 1911; Geography of the Soils of Georgia, 1911; Primary Geography of Georgia, 1913; Advanced Geography of Georgia, 1913; Practical Lessons in Agriculture (with Lester S. Ivins), 1913; Geographic Readers (4 vols.). Editor and pub. The Educational Monthly. Regional dir. U.S.S.G., Bur. of Edn., Washington, D.C., 1918-20; asst. in agrl. edn., U.S. Dept. of Agr., 1920-29; editor Cooperative Extension Work, 1929-—. Address: Dept. of Agriculture, Washington DC‡

MERRILL, JOHN LISGAR, engring., investment exec.; b. Oakland, Cal., Mar. 29, 1903; s. Charles Washington and Clara (Robinson) M.; B.S., U. Cal. at Berkeley, 1924; B.A. (Rhodes scholar), Oxford U., 1927, B.S., 1953, M.A., 1953; M. Natalie O'Maley, December 17, 1935; children—Jacqueline (Mrs. Philip E. Rollhaus), Steven, Deborah. Employed as engineer Blair & Co., 1928-31. mgr. Flintock Co., 1932-33; engr. to pres. and dir. Merco Centrifugal Co., 1933-56; pres., dir. Merrril Co., Merrill Estate Co., 1953-69; pres., dir. Merrill-Brose Co., 1949-69, J.L.M. Co., 1958-69; v.p., dir. Central Natural Gas Co., Vermillion, S.D., 1939-69; pres., dir. Metals, Inc. (war prodn. work; Army and Navy E award), 1942-45, Merrill Products Co. (war prodn. work; Navy Certificate award), 1943-45; dir. Bank of Cal. NA, Gulf Resources & Chem. Corp., Arthur D. Little, Inc., Pacific Tel. & Tel. Co., Rockwell Mfg. Co., Victor Equipment Co.; dir., mem. exec. com. U.S. Leasing Corp. Pres. San Francisco Planning and Urban Renewal Assn., 1960-61, vice chmn. exec. com. 1962-67, chmn., 1967-69; mem. Redevel. Agy. City and County San Francisco, 1957-59. Hon. chairman executive committee Golden Gate chapter American Red Cross; director Bay Area Ednl. TV Assn., San Francisco Civic Light Opera Assn., San Francisco Museum of Art; mem. bd. directors Assn. Am. Rhodes Scholars. Member Am. Inst. Mining, Metall. and Petroleum. Engrs., Am. Chem. Soc., Cal. Acad. Scis., Cal. Hist. Soc., English Speaking Union (San Francisco past pres.), Assn. Am. Rhodes Scholars (mem. bd. dirs.), Phi Delta Theta, Tau Beta Pi. Clubs: Pacific Union, Bohemian, Commonwealth, University (San Francisco); Burlingame (Cal.) Country. Home: San Francisco CA died Jan. 9, 1969.

MERRILL, JOSEPH L., investment banker; b. Boston, Sept. 27, 1899; s. John L. Merrill; A.B., Harvard, 1910; m. Kathleen Cushman, June 10, 1920; children—Arthur Cushman, Robert Gordon. With W. H. McElwain & Co., Boston, 1910-20; partner Merrill Lynch & Co., 1920-40; pres. and dir. Sterling Holding Corp., Wilmington, Del., 1940-70; vice pres. in charge finance and dir. Melville Shoe Corp., N.Y.C., 1940-70; dir. J. F. McElwain Co. Past dir. A. S. Beck Shoe Co., Diamond Shoe Corp., G. R. Kinney Co., Feltman & Curme Shoe Stores, Central Shoe Co., Waldorf System, Inc., Lane Bryant, Inc., Adams-Hills Corp., Struthers Wells, Inc., Beechvale Investments, Ltd., Bird Grocery Stores, Daniel Reeves, Inc., Nat. Tea. Co., Safeway Stores, Inc. Served as capt., U.S. Army, World War I. Owner of Feather," winner championship Yacht Racing Assn. of L.I. Sound, 1940, 41, 46, 47; and Royal Bermuda Yacht trophy. Clubs: New York Yacht, American Yacht, Southhampton Yacht; Meadow (Southhampton); Harvard (New York); Piping Rock, National Golf Links of America. Home: Locust Valley NY Died May 7, 1970.

MERRIMAN, MYRA HUNT KINGMAN (MRS. JOSIAH C.), b. Tremont, Ill., Nov. 2, 1873; d. Lysander Philip and Susan Wilde Pettes (Hunt) Kingman; ed. Miss Fenner's Sch. (Tremont, Ill.), Ill. State Normal School; also studied journalism, civics and philanthropy; m. George Alonzo Miller, of Tremont, Ill., June 26, 1895 (died Nov. 15, 1916); m. 2d, Dr. Josiah C. Merriman, Aug. 6, 1921. Was member staff Peoria (Ill.) Transcript, Chicago Chronicle; traveling correspondent in South and Central America, for Chicago Record; settled in Cal., 1894; mem. staff Long Beach (Cal.) Tribune, later staff of Telegram; editor Sierra Magazine, 1908. Pres. College Women's Club, of Long Beach, Cal., 1912-15; del. to biennial Nat. Federation of Coll. Women, San Francisco, 1915 (v.-p. 1916, and pres., 1917-18-19); apptd. by Sec. Labor Wilson mem. bd. dirs. Bur. of Registration for Woman's Service, 1917; mem. advisory com. Woman's Liberty Loan Com., advisory com. Woman's Com. National Council of Defense; etc. Mem. nat. com. D.A.R. On editorial and lecture staffs Community Motion Picture Bur., N.Y.; chmn. Foreign Film Reconstruction Unit, 1919; exec. sec. Nat. Federation Better Film Workers; sec. Nat. Council of Women of U.S.A., 1920-21; del. Internat. Council of Women, 1921; chmn. official delegation of 40 women investigating conditions in Europe, 1921; mem. advisory bd. to 9 nat. organizations. Home: The Commodore, New York NY‡

MERRITT, DIXON LANIER, editor; b. Wilson County, Tenn., July 9, 1879; s. Hatton and Fannie (Merritt) Abernathy; adopted son of his uncle, L. Willis Merritt, and assumed uncle's surname at 21; ed. country schools and U. of Nashville; m. Harriote Johnson, Mar. 1903; children—Alice Philippa (Mrs. Norwood Gant), Dixon Lanier; m. 2d, Ruth Eloise Yates, Aug. 1922; children—Stanley Yates, Robert Lewis. Began newspaper work on the Nashville Banner, 1901; then became city editor Owensboro Messenger, 1902-09; staff corr. Nashville Banner, 1909-10; sec. Nashville Industrial Bur., 1911; asso. editor, Nashville Banner, 1911-14; editor Nashville Tennessean-American, 1915-17; war emergency work, office of asst. sec. of agr., Washington, Aug. 1917-Dec. 1918; editor in Office of Information, Department of Agr., 1919-20; chief press service, same, 1920-22; editorial corr. of The Outlook, 1923-26, asso. editor, 1927-29; editor Lebanon Democrat, 1929-38; dir. of public safety for the State of Tenn., 1933-37; prof. of journalism, Cumberland U., since 1937; editor Murfreesboro Daily News Journal, 1939-40; in defense emergency work, Rural Electrification Administration, U.S. Dept. of Agriculture, 1941-46. Member American Press Humorists (pres. 1916-17), Tenn. Ornithol. Soc. (founder), A.A.A.S. Club: Nat. Press. Author: Audubon in Kentucky, 1908; History of Tenneseee, 1913; Department of Agriculture in the War, 1919; The Seventeen-Year Locust, 1919; Sons of Martha, 1928. Also monographs on Masonic law, poems and sketches. Home: Lebanon TN Died Jan. 9, 1972.

MERRITT, EMMA LAURA SUTRO (MRS. GEORGE WASHINGTON MERRITT), physician; b. San Francisco, Cal.; d. Adolph and Leah (Harris) Sutro; A.B., Vassar Coll., 1877, A.M., 1882; student Woman's Med. Coll. of New York Infirmary; M.D., U. of Cal., 1881; post-grad. work Ecole de Medicine, Paris; m. George Washington Merritt (M.D.), of San Francisco, Mar. 27, 1883. Clinician to Dispensary of Children's Hosp., 1887-1906; surgeon Hosp. for Children, 1887-1909; now mgr. Sutro Estate in Cal. Mem. A.M.A., Med. Soc. State of Cal. Club: Century of Cal. Home: Sutro Heights, San Francisco CA‡

MERRITT, WALTER GORDON, lawyer; b. Danbury, Conn., Jan. 4, 1880; s. Charles Hart and Luana (Kniffin) M.; grad. Gunnery Sch., Washington, Conn., 1898; A.B., Harvard, 1901; LL.B., N.Y. Law Sch., 1903; m. Isabel K. Hooker, July 26, 1919 (dec. Feb. 1963); m. 2d, Mary Shawah, Dec. 30, 1966. Admitted to the New York bar, 1903, practiced in N.Y. City; member Windels, Merritt & Ingraham. Dir. Legal Aid Soc. N.Y.; bd. mgrs. Danbury (Conn.) Hosp. Recipient outstanding achievement certificate Gunnery Sch., Washington, Conn., 1955. Republican. Conglist. Clubs: Century, Harvard (N.Y. City); Cosmos (Washington). Author: Destination Unknown: Fifty Years of Labor Relations, 1956. Contbr. mags. Home: New Fairfield CT Died Sept. 13, 1968.

MERRY, JOSEPH JAMES, electric co. exec.; b. Boston, Aug. 5, 1901; s. John Christopher and Hannah Elizabeth (Moore) M.; LL.B., Fordham U., 1931; LL.M., N.Y.U., 1934. Admitted to N.Y. State bar, 1934; with Western Electric Co., Inc., 1917-66, sec., 1959-66; sec. Teletype Corp., Chgo., Mfrs. Junction Ry. Co., Cicero, Ill. Home: New York City NY Died May 1968.

MERSETH, SIDNEY INGMAR, lumber co. exec.; b. Clearwater County, Minn., Jan. 10, 1913; s. Barninus M. and Signora (Kvaale) M.; grad. Augsburg Acad., 1930; m. Kate C. Lidstone, Jan. 7, 1936; children—Gordon L., Gale D. Laborer, Shevlin-Hixon Lumber Co., Blind River, Ont., Can., 1930-32; mgr. Queen's Tea Room, 1932-35; with Edward Hines Lumber Co., 1932-67, plant supt., 1962-63, personnel and safety dir. Ponderosa Pine div., Hines, Ore., 1963-67; dist. rep. Fraternal Life Ins. Co., Eugene, Ore., 1967-68. Hines City recorder, 1952-56, councilman, 1960-67. Chmn. bd. dirs. Sch. Dist. 30, 1949-61; dir. Rural Sch. Bd., 1961-67. First aid instr. A.R.C.; mem. indsl. safety com. Asso. Ore. Industries; dir. County United Fund; bd. govs. Ore. United Fund; mem. County Welfare Bd., 1964-68, Mental Health Com., 1962-68, Ore. Sch. Bds. Assn., 1964-68; sec. Harney County Swim Pool Assn., 1961-68. Mem. Western Wood Products Assn., Western Pine Assn., Harney County C. of C. (pres. 1965), Hoo-Hoo Order. Democrat. Lutheran. Rotarian (past pres.). Home: Eugene OR Died Mar. 3, 1968; interred Sunset Hills Meml. Gardens Eugene OR

MERSHON, MARTIN LUTHER, lawyer; b. Brunswick, Ga., Aug. 10, 1891; s. Martin Luther and Belle (Bearden) M.; LL.B., U. of Fla., 1912; m. Marie Turner, Dec. 4, 1927; children—Nancy Belle, Betty Marie. Admitted to Florida bar, 1912, in practice at Leesburg, Fla., 1912-13, at Ocala, Fla., 1913-18; founded, with W. I. Evans, firm of Evans & Mershon, Miami, 1920, sr. mem. Mershon, Sawyer, Johnston, Dunwody & Cole; dir. Miami Beach First National Bank, United Bancshares Florida, Incorporated. Trustee Dade County Law Library; vice president, director Miami Heart Inst. Served in U.S. Army, 1918-19. Mem. Fla. Bd. Law Examiners, 1930-33; dir., past pres. S.E. Div. of Childrens Home Soc. of Fla. Mem. Fla. State Bd. Control, 1944-47. Mem. Am., Dade County (past pres.), Fla. State bar assns., Alpha Tau Omega. Democrat. Methodist. Home: Coral Gables FL Died Sept. 21, 1968; buried Woodlawn Park Cemetery, Miami FL

MERSON, ALEXANDER J(AMES), packing exec.; b. Newcastle-under-Lyme, Eng., July 30, 1905; s. Alexander Stuart and Lettice Maude (Mee) M.; privately educated; m. Joyce Stewart, Apr. 9, 1941; 1 son, Christopher Stewart. Naturalized U.S. citizen, 1957. With Price Waterhouse Peat & Co., Argentina and Chile, 1930-39, Swift Internat. Co., Buenos Aires, 1939-58, dir., 1945-58; treas., dir. Internat. Packers, Ltd. (name changed to IPL, Inc., 1968), Chgo. 1952-71, v.p., 1962-71, chmn. finance com. 1968-71; pres. Deltec Banking, Nassau, Bahamas, 1969-71. Home: Sotogrande Cadiz Spain Died July 27, 1971; buried Spain

MERTINS, GUSTAVE FREDERICK, author; b. Evergreen, Ala., Aug. 19, 1872; s. of Gustave Ferdinand and Jennie A. L. W. (Stahl) M.; ed. Coll. of St. Anthony, Geneva, Switzerland; pvt. tutelage, Kolmar, Posen, Germany; acad. and the law depts., Washington and Lee U., 1887, 1888, 1890-3; m. Bessie P. Screws, of Montgomery, Ala., Feb. 26, 1908. Practiced, Montgomery, Ala., 1893-—; spl. asst. to atty.-gen. of U.S. in bankruptcy fraud prosecutions, 1910. Democrat. Episcopalian. Mem. Ala. State Bar Assn. Mason (K.T., Shriner). Author: The Storm Signal, 1905; A Watcher of the Skies, 1911. Home: 10 N. McDonough St. Office: Vandiver Bldg., Montgomery AL‡

MERTINS, MARSHALL LOUIS, author; b. Jackson County, Mo., Dec. 7, 1885; s. Carl Henry and Mary E. (Koger) M.; student Kansas City Sem., 1906-07; student William Jewell Coll., 1905-10, LL.D., 1939; m. Lena Lee Holman, Sept. 28, 1907; children—Blanche (Mrs. Louis Garcia), Virginia Lee (Mrs. Lee McIntosh), Sara (Mrs. Malcolm Dewees), Louis II; m. 2d, Esther Pedersen Erickson, May 12, 1939. Ordained to ministry Baptist Ch., 1906; organizer, pastor Swope Park Ch., Kansas City, Mo., 1911-15; pastor 1st Ch., Nevada, Mo., 1915-16; Chautauqua and lyceum lectr., 1910-26; columnist, radio commentator, 1926-56; lectr. world lit. Valley Coll., San Bernardino, Cal., 1956-63. Dir. Progressive-Commonwealth Fedn. Mem. Cal. Writers Guild (founder 1932; mem. exec. bd.; v.p. 1959), Internat. Mark Twain Soc. (hon.), Sigma Tau Delta, Pi Gamma Mu, Lambda Chi Alpha. Mem. Mystic Order Pyramids (supreme council). Clubs: E. Clampus Vitus, P.E.N. (pres. Los Angeles chpt. 1965-66), Beloved Vagabonds; Fortnightly (past pres.). Author books, 1917, latest publs. including: (with Esther Mertins) The Intervals of Robert Frost, 1947; Robert Frost; Life and Talks-Walking, 1965; The Blue God An Epic of Mesa Verde, 1968. Home: Redlands CA Died Jan. 17, 1973; interred Hillside Cemetery, Redlands CA

MERTON, THOMAS, clergyman, author; b. Prades, France, Jan. 31, 1915; s. Owen and Ruth (Jenkins) M.; student Lycee de Montauban, France, 1927-28, Oakham Sch., Eng., 1929-32, Clare Coll., Cambridge, 1933-34; B.A., Columbia University, 1938, M.A., 1939; LL.D., University of Kentucky, 1963. Instr. English, univ. extension Columbia, 1939; prof. English St. Bonaventure U., 1940-41; entered Trappist monastery of Gethsemani, 1941, ordained priest, 1949; master of students Abbey of Gethsemani, 1951-55, master of novices, 1955-65. Mem. Cistercians of the Strict Observance. Recipient medal of Excellence, Columbia U., 1963. Author: Thirty Poems, 1944; A Man in the Divided Sea, 1946; Figures for an Apocalypse, 1947; Seven Storey Mountain, 1948; Exile Ends in Glory, 1949; Seeds of Contemplation, 1949; Waters of Siloe, 1949; Tears of the Blind Lions, 1949; What Are These Wounds?, 1950; The Ascent to Truth, 1951; Sign of Jonas, 1953; Bread in the Wilderness, 1953; Last of the Fathers, 1954; No Man is An Island, 1955; The Living Bread, 1956; The Silent Life, 1957; The Strange Islands, 1957; Thoughts in Solitude, 1958; The Secular Journal of Thomas Merton, 1959; Selected Poems of Thomas Merton, 1959; Disputed Questions, 1960; Spiritual Direction and Meditation, 1960; Disputed Questions, 1960; Behavior of Titans, 1961; Wisdom of the Desert, 1961; The New Man, 1962; A Thomas Merton Reader, 1962; New Seeds of Contemplation, 1962; Original Child Bomb, 1962; Life and Holiness, 1963; Emblems of a Season of Fury, 1963; Seeds of Destruction, 1964; Seasons of Celebration, 1965; The Way of Chuang Tzu, 1965; Raids on the Unspeakable, 1966; Conjectures of a Guilty Bystander, 1966; Mystics and Zen Masters, 1967; Cables to the Ace, 1968; Faith and Violence, 1968; Zen and the Birds of Appetite, 1968; My Argument with the Gestapo, 1969; The Geography of Lograire, 1969; The Climate of Monastic Prayer, 1969; Contemplative Prayer, 1969; The True Solitude, Selections from the Writings of Thomas Merton, 1970; Contemplation in a World of Action, 1971; Thomas Merton on Peace, 1971; Opening the Bible, 1971; The Asian Journals of Thomas Merton, 1973. Editor: Break Through to Peace, 1962; Gandhi on Non-Violence, 1965. Monks Pond (mag.), 1968. Contrbr. to jours., lit. revs., anthologies. Home: Trappist KY Died Dec. 10, 1968; buried Abbey of Gethsemani, Trappist KY

MERWIN, LORING CHASE, publisher; b. Bloomington, Ill., Mar. 26, 1906; s. Louis Buckley and Jessie Fell (Davis) M.; ed. Choate Sch., 1921-24; B.S., Harvard, 1928; Dr. Pub. Service, Ill. Wesleyan U., 1968; m. Marjorie Sward, Jan. 5, 1935; children—Amanda Fell, Susan, Miles. Chmn. bd. Daily Pantagraph, Bloomington; pres. Bloomington Broadcasting Corp. (operating radio sta. WJBC, Bloomington, and sta. WROK, Rockford, Ill.). Trustee Ill. Wesleyan U.; mem. adv. council Ill. State Normal U.; mem. adv. bd. Ill. Dept. Conservation; pres. Bloomington Unlimited, 1969; v.p. Park Lands Found. Served to lt. USNR, 1942-45. Mem. Bloomington Assn. Commerce (dir. 1950-58, chmn. 1956-63), Living Desert Assn. (bd. govs.), Harvard Alumni Assn. (dir.), Inland Daily Press Assn. (pres. 1960-61), Sigma Delta Chi. Unitarian. Clubs: Press, Harvard, Racquet (Chgo.); Iroquois (Harvard Coll.); Bloomington Country; Overseas Press (N.Y.C.); Old Elm (Lake Forest Ill.), Thunderbird (Palm Springs, Cal.); Country of Fla. (Delray Beach). Home: Bloomington IL Died Sept. 6, 1972.

MESSINA, ANGELINA ROSE, micropalentologist; b. N.Y.C., Apr., 23, 1910; d. Michaelangelo and Josephine (Sperrazza) Messina; B.A., N.Y.U., 1932; M.A., Columbia, 1935; Ph.D., h.c., U. Basel (Switzerland), 1967. Asst. geology N.Y.U., 1932-33; instr. geology Bklyn. Coll., 1933-34; asso. dir. research project on Foraminifera, Am. Mus. Natural History, 1934-41, asso. curator dept. micropaleontology, 1941-67, chmn., curator dept. micropaleontology, 1967-68; adj. prof. geology Rutgers U.; collector, research Mediterranean and Caribbean microfaunas. Recipient Amita award, 1965. Fellow Am. Assn. Advancement Sci., Geol. Soc. Am. N.Y. Acad. Sci. (chmn. sect. geology 1953-54); mem. Am. Assn. Petroleum Geologists (sec. Eastern sect. 1952-53), Paleontological Society, Society of Economic Paleontologists and Mineralogists, Societa Paleontologica Italiana, Soc. Paleontol. Japan, Deutsche Geologische Gesellschaft, Sigma Xi. Author: (with Brooks F. Ellis) Catalogue of Ostracoda, Catalogue of Foraminifera. Editor Micropaleontology (quar.). Home: New York City NY Died Nov. 20, 1968.

MESSING, ABRAHAM JOSEPH, college prof.; b. Chicago, Aug. 4, 1873; s. Aaron Joseph and Fannie (Livingston) M.; B.H., Hebrew Union Coll. Cincinnati, 1892, rabbi, 1896; B.A., U. of Cincinnati, 1896; LL.B., Ill. Wesleyan U., 1907; m. Florence Schwabacher, of Peoria, Ill., Aug. 17, 1898. Prof. internat. and constl. law, Ill. Wesleyan U., 1909—. V.-p. Withers Pub. Library, Bloomington, Ill. Democrat. Jewish religion. Mem. Phi Delta Phi. Mason. Author: (with R. M. Benjamin) Cases on The American Law of Contract, 1911. Address: Bloomington IL‡

MESSLER, EUGENE LAWRENCE, engr.; b. Pittsburgh, Pa., Apr. 6, 1873; s. Thomas D. and Maria R. (Varick) M.; B.Ph., Sheffield Scientific School (Yale), 1894; m. Elizabeth V. Long, Dec. 31, 1898; children—Thomas D., E. Lawrence. Began as pattern maker and moulder, Edgar Thompson Works of Carnegie Steel Co.; successively civ. engr., gen. supt. labor and transportation and asst. blast furnace supt., Duquesne Works, Carnegie Steel Co., Pa., 1895-99; supt. and gen. supt. Eliza Furnaces, Coke Works, Jones &Laughlin Steel Co., 1899-1911; asst. to pres. Riter-Conley Mfg. Co., 1912-15; v.p. and gen. mgr. Witherow Steel Co., 1916-18; also pres. Eureka Fire Brick Works; dir. Pittsburgh, Fisher Scientific Co. Commd. capt. engrs., May 20, 1918; comdg. Co. G., 21st Engrs., 1st Army A.E.F., Sept. 1918-May 1919; participated in St. Mihiel, defensive sector and Meuse-Argonne offensives; lt. col. Engr. Reserves, to 1938, now inactive due to age limit. Member American Iron and Steel Inst., Am. Inst. M.E., Am. Refractories Inst., Am. Soc. Mil. Engrs., Vets. of Foreign Wars, Engring. Soc. Western Pa., British Iron and Steel Inst., S.A.R., Am. Legion, Reserve Officers Assn. Clubs: Yale (New York); Harvard-Yale-Princeton, Cloister, Pittsburgh Golf, Rolling Rock. Home: 5423 Forbes St. Office: B. F. Jones Bldg., Pittsburgh PA‡

MESTERN, H. EDWARD, patent agt.; b. Berlin, Germany, Dec. 31, 1909; s. Armand E. and Gertrud (Wurceldorf) M.; M.A., U. Berlin, 1933; Ph.D. cum laude, U. Munster (Germany), 1936; m. Elsa Catherine Sapp, Jan. 24, 1956; 1 son by previous marriage, Douglas Kemp. Came to U.S., 1936, naturalized, 1943. Consultant to U.S. Air Force, 1953, 1956-68. Served to lt. colonel in USAF Res., 1951-53. Mem. Chemists Club, Am. Chem. Soc., Res. Officers Assn. U.S. (pres. Westchester 1959, dist. v.p. 1960-62). Home: Yonkers NY Died Feb. 29, 1968.

METTEN, JOHN FARRELL, shipbuilding engr.; b. Kent County, Del., Dec. 15, 1873; s. Alexander and Elizabeth (Hoffecker) M.; student Middletown (Del.) Academy honorary; Dr. Engring., Lehigh University, 1928 and University of Delaware, 1942; unmarried. Began as draftsman, 1894; chief engineering, draftsman, William Cramp & Sons Ship & Engine Bldg. Co., Philadelphia, 1904-09, chief engr., 1909-25, v.p. in charge of engring., 1925-27; pres. Marine Engring. Corp., Phila., 1927-31; consulting engr., Phila., 1931-35; became pres. and dir. N.Y. Shipbuilding Corp., Camden, N.J., 1935, later chmn. bd. dirs. Mem. A.A.A.S., Am. Soc. Naval Engrs., Am. Soc. Naval Architects and Marine Engrs., British Inst. Naval Architects (London), Franklin Inst., Newcomen Soc., N.Y. Geog. Soc. Club: Union League (Phila.). Office: Camden NJ Died Sept 16, 1968.

METTEN, WILLIAM F., newspaper exec.; b. nr. Milford, Del., Feb. 6, 1871; s. Alexander and Elizabeth M.; ed. country sch.; m. Elizabeth Janvier Murray, Nov. 1900 (died Apr. 1910); children—W. Murray, Elizabeth; m. 2d, Meta McSorley, Nov. 14, 1913; children—John F., Miriam, William. Began as reporter Every Evening, Wilmington, Del., 1895, pub. of same, 12 yrs. until 1933; bus. mgr. News-Journal Co. until retirement. Director of Security Trust Company, Artisans Savings Bank. Mem. Bd. Park Commrs. (Wilmington), State Welfare Commn. Ex-pres. Wilmington Chamber Commerce. Democrat. Methodist. Clubs: Wilmington, Wilmington Country (dir.). Home: 2209 Boulevard. Office: 831 Orange St., Wilmington DE‡

METTS, JOHN VAN BOKKELEN, adjutant general of N.C.; b. Wilmington, N.C., Dec. 17, 1876; s. James Isaac and Cornelia (Frothingham) M.; student Tilston Normal Sch., Cape Fear Acad., and Morrell Sch., Wilmington, N.C.; m. Josephine Budd, Nov. 20, 1906 (dec.); children—Josephine (Mrs. Spotswood Hatherway Huntt), John Van Bokkelen. Owner and operator of fire insurance agency, Wilmington, N.C., 1902-17. Enlisted N.C. Nat. Guard, 1894; commd. 2d lt., 1899, and advanced through grades to maj. gen., 1949; selective service on Mexican Border, 1916-17; comdr. 119th Inf., 30th Div., U.S.A., A.E.F.; adjutant gen. of N.C., since 1920; dir. N.C. Selective Service, 1940-50. Awarded Distinguished Service Medal. Mason. Home: 730 N. Blount. Office: Justice Bldg., Raleigh NC‡

METZGER, RALPH ALFRED, ins. exec.; b. Akron, O., Dec. 3, 1897; s. William John and Clementine (Braucher) M.; student pvt. schs., U. Pa.; B.S., Ohio State U., 1922; m. Catherine Tieleman-Hoogeveen, Jan. 17, 1951. With Union Central Life Ins. Company, Cincinnati, from 1939, v.p., 1940-59, exec. v.p., 1959-72, also dir.; dir. Central Bancorp. Mem. Am. Legion, Sigma Nu, Alpha Kappa Psi, Beta Gamma Sigma. Mason. Clubs: 100 (charter), Bankers (Cin.). Home: Milford OH Died Jan. 8, 1972.

MEYER, BALTHASAR HENRY, economist; b. Mequon, Ozaukee County, Wis., May 28, 1866; s. Henry and Louise (Wiepking) M.; grad. Oshkosh Normal Sch., 1893; B.L., U. of Wis., 1894, Ph.D., 1897, LL.D., 1914; grad. study U. of Berlin, 1894-95; m. Alice Elizabeth Carlton, Aug. 29, 1901; children—Carleton Wiepking, Thomas Balthasar, Sylvia Elizabeth (Mrs. Oliver Gasch). Taught district school, 1884-86; principal schools, Fredonia, Wisconsin, 1887-89; principal high sch., Port Washington, Wisconsin, 1889-92; hon. fellow, 1895-96, univ. fellow, 1896-97, extension lecturer, 1895-97, instr. sociology, 1897-99, asst. prof. sociology, 1899-1900, prof. polit. economy, 1900-10, U. of Wis.; granted leave of absence from univ. to accept apptmt. as mem. of R.R. Commn. of Wis., July 1905; chmn. R.R. Commn. of Wis., 1907-11; apptd. by Presdient Taft mem. R.R. Securities Commn., Aug. 1910, and mem. Interstate Commerce Commn., Jan. 1, 1911-May 1, 1939; now engaged in constl. and mediation in transportation. Mem. various scientific and other orgns. Author: Railway Legislation in the United States, 1903; History of Transportation in the U.S. before 1860. 1917; also monographs and articles on ry. legislation and administration and other econ. subjects. Active in a number of local social agencies. Home: 3327 P St. N.W. Office: Shoreham Bldg., Washington 5 DC‡

MEYER, CHARLES ZACHARY, banker; b. Chicago, July 21, 1895; s. William John and Dora (Walther) M.; student Northwestern U., 1914; m. Ruth E. Carlson, Oct. 30, 1920; children—Charles Orville, Charlotte Ruth (Mrs. Harry P. Maxwell). Clerk, First Nat. Bank, Chicago, 1912-30, asst. cashier, 1930-32, auditor, 1932-38, comptroller 1938-51, vice president and comptroller, 1951-58, sr. v.p., comptroller, 1959-60; chmn. bd. Upper Avenue Nat. Bank, Chgo., from 1961; dir. A.Y. McDonald Mfg. Co. (Dubuque, Ia.). Dir. Chgo. Ordnance Dist. Trustee, pres. Glenwood Sch. Boys. Served as sgt., inf. A.E.F., 1917-19; lt. col., Office Chief Ordnance, U.S. Army, 1942-45. Awarded Legion of Merit. Mem. Financial Execs. Inst. (pres. 1951), Nat. Assn. Bank Auditors and Comptrollers (pres. 1940), Mil. Order World War, Am. Ordnance Assn. Presbyn. Clubs: Chicago, MidDay, Economic, Sojourners, Chicago IL Died Feb. 11, 1971.

MEYER, ELY, mfg. co. exec.; b. Rochester, N.Y., Oct. 15, 1890; s. Ely and Esther (Simon) M.; student U. Rochester, 1907-10, Harvard, 1911; m. Corinne Wellhouse, May 6, 1914 (dec. Sept. 1950); children—Jane W., Gloria (Mrs. Walter Gold). Paper converter and mfr., 1914-71; chmn. Sterling Pulp & Paper Co.; pres., treas. United Paper Co. Asso. dir. Boys' Club Am. Mem. Pulp and Paper Industry, T.A.P.P.I. Mason (Shriner). Clubs: Palma Cia Golf, Yacht (Tampa). Home: Tampa FL Died Nov. 5, 1971.

MEYER, ESTELLE REEL (MRS. CORT F. MEYER), educator; b. Pittsfield, Ill., Nov. 26, 1862; d. M.A.L. Reel; ed. Chicago, St. Louis and Boston; m. Cort F. Meyer. Became teacher; county supt. schs., Laramie, Laramie County, Wyo., 1887, and state supt. pub. instrn., 1894-98; became gen. supt. Indian schs., June 1898, now retired. Home: Toppenish WA‡

MEYER, FRANK STRAUS, author, editor; b. Newark, May 9, 1909; s. Jack F. and Helene (Straus) M.; student Princeton, 1926-28; B.A., Balliol Coll., Oxford (Eng.) U., 1932, M.A., 1954; student London (Eng.) Sch. Econs., 1932-34, U. Chgo., 1934-38; m. Elsie Bown, Oct. 11, 1940; children—John Cornford, Eugene Bown. Mem. staff National Rev., 1955-72, sr. editor, 1957-72; editorial adviser Modern Age, 1960-72; cons. Lilly Endowment, Inc., 1962-66. Mem. nat. adv. com. Young Americans for Freedom, 1961-72; mem. exec. com., chmn. com. internat. affairs Conservative Party N.Y. State, 1962-72, vice chairman 1968-72; member board directors Am. Conservative Union, 1965-72, also treas., 1965-66; dir. U.S. Chess Fedn. Bd. dirs. Am. Afro-Asian Ednl. Exchange Grantee Fund for Republic, 1957, William Volker Fund, 1954; grantee Relm Found., 1965. Served with AUS, 1942-43. Mem. Philadelphia Soc. (1st v.p. 1964-67), Am. Polit. Sci. Assn., Am. Legion. Clubs: Princeton (N.Y.C.); Nat. Press (Washington); Athenaeum (Boston). Author: The Moulding of Communists, 1961; In Defense of Freedom, 1962; The Conservative Mainstream, 1969; (with others) What is Conservatism?, 1964, Left, Right and Center, 1965. Editor: The African Nettle, 1965; Home: Woodstock NY Died Apr. 1, 1972; buried Woodstock NY

MEYER, FREDERICK H., b. Hamelin, Germany, Nov. 6, 1872; s. Moritz and Amanda (Loges) M.; grad. Royal Art Sch., Berlin, 1896; grad. Pa. Mus. and Sch. of Industrial Art, Phila., 1897; m. Laetitia Summerville, of Boston, Mass., June 1902. Came to U.S., 1888; supervisor drawing, Stockton (Calif.) pub. schs., 1898-1902; instr. drawing, U. of Calif.; prof. applied art Mark Hopkins Inst. of Art, San Francisco, 1902-06; founder, pres. and trustee Calif. Coll. of Arts and Crafts since 1907; dir. of art Oakland pub. schs., 1913-19. Medal of Honor, San Francisco Expn., 1915. Progressive Republican. Protestant. Clubs: Faculty Rotary, Business Men's Garden Club. Specializes in architectural designing, interior decorating and landscape gardening. Home: Broadway at College Oakland CA‡

MEYER, FREDRIK, steel co. exec.; b. Jan. 28, 1898 ed. U. Cape of Good Hope, U. Steelenbosch (Germany) Tech. U. Charlottenburg (Germany). Chem. E. 1924-25; govt. adviser indsl. devel., South Africa 1926-28; with South African Iron & Steel Industries Corp. Ltd., Pretoria, 1928—, chmn., 1949—. Dir Babcock & Wolcox Africa; chmn. African Metals Corp. Vanderbijl Engring. Corp. Ltd., Vanderbijl Parb Estate Co., Ruberowen Ltd., Steel Wheel and Axle S.A. Ltd Trustee South African Founds. Mem. South Africa Inst Mining and Metallurgy, The Africa Inst., Die Ekonomies Instituut, South African Chem. Inst., Nat Devel. and Mgmt. Found. South Africa (pres.), Assn Sci. and Tech. Socs. South Africa (pres.). Address Pretoria South Africa Died June 7, 1972; buried Pretoria Western Cemetery, Pretoria South Africa

MEYER, HERBERT ALTON, JR., newspaper editor and publisher; b. Staunton, Va., Sept. 15, 1912; s. Herbert Alton and Mary Davis (Watts) M.; B.A., U. Kan., 1936; m. Mary Janet McDonald, Jan. 23, 1941; children—Herbert Alton III, Mary Lourene. Advt. sales and advt. mgr. Capper Publns., Inc., Topeka, 1936-40; with Independence Daily/Sunday Reporter, 1940-71, pub., 1950-71, editor, 1957-71; pres., dir. Reporter Pub. Co., Inc. Mem. Kan. Banking Bd., 1965-69, chmn., 1968-69. Trustee William Allen White Found., 1957-71, pres., 1966-68. Served to lt. USNR, 1942-45. Recipient William Allen White Found. State award journalistic merit, 1969. Mem. Kan. Press Assn. (pres. 1951), Midwest Newspaper Advt. Execs. Assn. (pres. 1951), Kan. A.P. Assn. (chmn. 1962-63), Independence C. of C. (pres. 1964), U. Kan. Alumni Assn. (nat. pres. 1955), V.F.W., Am. Legion, Sigma Chi, Sigma Delta Chi. Republican. Episcopalian. Rotarian. Elk. Club: Kansas City (Mo.) Press. Home: Independence KS Died May 22, 1971; buried Mt. Hope Cemetery, Independence KS

MEYER, HERBERT WILLY, surgeon; b. N.Y.C., Apr. 26, 1896; s. Willy and Lilly O. (Maass) M.; A.B., Columbia Coll., 1916, M.D., 1919; m. Emmy-Dorothy Kaesche, Apr. 29, 1926; children—Dorothy E. Craig, Audrey E. Sargent. Cons. surgeon University Hosp., Bellevue Hosp., Lenox Hill Hosp. (N.Y.C.), USN Hosp. (San Diego), Scripps Meml. Hosp. (La Jolla), Palomar Meml. Hosp. (Escondido), U.S. Naval Hosp. (Camp Pendelton, Cal.); hon. staff Children's Hosp. San Diego, Long Beach Surg. Soc., Tri-County Surg. Soc. So. Cal., Soc. Gen. Surgeons San Diego (all Cal.). Served with AUS, M.C., World War II. Diplomate Am. Bd. Surgery, Am. Bd. Plastic Surgery, Am. Bd. Thoracic Surgery. Mem. Am. Assn. Thoracic Surgery, A.M.A., Am. Cancer Research, Am. Surg. Assn., Am. Assn. Mil. Surgeons, Internat. Soc. Surgery, A.C.S. (life), Pacific Coast Surg. Assn., Ewing Soc. Phi Delta Theta, Nu Sigma Nu, Alpha Omega Alpha. Club: Columbia University. Contbr. articles to med. jours. Home: Santa Fe CA Died Jan. 26, 1973.

MEYER, JOHN JACOB, university prof.; b. at Frankenmuth, Saginaw Co., Mich., Apr. 25, 1870; s. John Michael and Anna Katherine (Engel) M.; A.B., Concordia Coll., Ft. Wayne, Ind., 1891; grad. Concordia Theol. Sem., St. Louis, 1894; grad. student, U. of Chicago, 1898-1900, fellow, 1899-1900, Ph.D., 1900; has made extensive researches in Sanskrit and Finnish langs. and lits. m. Felicie Calonder, of Pontresina, Switzerland, Sept. 4, 1904. Instr. Sanskrit, 1901-6, asst. prof. German, 1910-—, U. of Chicago. Corr. mem. Suomalaisen Kirjallisuuden Seura (Soc. of Finnish Literature). Author: Dandins Dacakumaracaritam, 1902; Kshemendras Samayamatrika, 1903; Damodaraguptas Kuttanimatam, 1903; Kavyasamgraha, 1903; Asanka, Sudschata, Tangara und andre Dichtungen, 1903; Felicie, Liebes u. Wanderlieder, 1905; Am. Strand gefunden, Gedichte, 1908, Vom Land der tausend Seeen, 1910; Das Engadin, 1912; Isolde's Gottesurteil, 1914; Das Weib im altmdischen Epos, 1915. Translator: Gedichte von W. A. Koskenniemi (from the Finnish), 1907; Hindu Tales (from Maharashtri), 1909; also numerous other writings. Address: Chicago IL

MEYER, KARL ALBERT, surgeon; b. Gilman, Ill., Sept. 28, 1886; M.D., U. of Ill. Coll. of Med., 1908; m. Faye Hart, Nov. 10, 1918; children—Mary Ann Daro, Nancy Ruth Eldert, Robert. Intern Univ. and Cook County hosps., 1908-10; in gen. practice, Chicago, 1910-14; med. supt. Cook County (Ill.) Hosp., 1914-68 (attending surgeon); asst. clin. surgery, U. of Ill. Coll. of Medicine, 1914-20, prof. clin. surgery, 1920-25; asso. prof. surg., Northwestern University Med. Sch., 1925-45, prof. surgery, 1925-54, emeritus, 1954-72; surgeon-in-chief Columbus Meml. Hosp.; pres. Cook County Grad. Sch. Medicine. Vice president Medical Center Commn. Pres. Chgo. Foundling Home. Trustee Lincoln (Illinois) Coll. Fellow A.C.S.; member A.M.A., Illinois and Chgo. (pres.) 1956 med. socs., Chgo. Surg. Soc., Western Surg. Soc., Internat. Surg. Soc., Internat. Coll. Surgeons, Alpha Omega Alpha. Clubs: Bob O'Link, Chicago Athletic, University (Chgo); Exmoor Country (Highland Park, Ill.). Died Jan. 6, 1972.

MEYER, LOTHAR, chemist; b. Breslau, Germany (now Wroclaw), Poland, July 13, 1906; s. Gotthold and Selma (Heimann) M.; Dr.Engring., Inst. Tech., Breslau, 1930; m. Marion Meyer, Mar. 25, 1935. Came to U.S., 1946, naturalized, 1952. Asst. U. Gottingen, 1930-32; mgr. patent dept. Gesellschaft fuer Linde's Eismaschinen, Munich, Germany, 1932-39; research asso. U. Leiden (Holland), 1939-46; with U. Chgo., 1947-71, prof. chemistry, 1953-71; Gauss prof. U. Gottingen, 1961-62. Fellow Am. Phys. Soc.; mem. Faraday Soc. London, Sigma Xi. Research, numerous publs. on superfluid behavior of liquid helium, adsorption, quantum hydrodynamics, chem. reactions at hot surfaces, crystal structures at low temperatures. Home: Chicago IL Died Feb. 1, 1971; buried Chicago IL

MEYER, MAX F(RIEDRICH), psychologist, university professor; b. at Danzig, June 15, 1873; s. of Hermann and Sophie (Luschnath) M.; grad. Municipal Gymnasium, Danzig, 1892; Ph.D., Univ. of Berlin, 1896, research work, 1896-98; came to U.S., 1899; m. Stella Sexton, Feb. 13, 1904; children—Dorothy, Harold, Otto, Katherine, Sophie. Prof. psychology, U. of Mo., since 1900; exchange prof. U. of Chile, Sept.-Dec. 1929; visiting prof. U. of Miami, Fla., since 1932 (leave of absence). Fellow A.A.A.S.; mem. Am. Psychol. Assn., Acoustical Soc. Am., Phi Beta Kappa, Sigma Xi, Phi Mu Alpha, Translator: Adolf Hildebrand's Problem of Form in Painting and Sculpture (with R. M. Ogden), 1907. Translator and editor: Ebbinghaus's Psychology, 1908. Presbyn. Author several books since 1907; latest publ.: How We Hear (How Tones Make Music), 1950. Address: 3939 Loquat Av., Miami 33 FL*‡

MEYER, SCHUYLER MERRITT, lawyer; b. N.Y.C., Oct. 27, 1885; s. Charles B. and Virginia H. (Hoyt() M.; A.B., Yale, 1907; LL.B., N.Y.U., 1910; m. Helen Martin, Sept. 19, 1914. Admitted to N.Y. State bar, 1910, since practiced in N.Y.C.; mem. firm Seward & Kissel, (and predecessors), 1917-70. Chairman New York State Joint Legislative Com. to Investigate Affairs City N.Y., 1920-21. Mem. N.Y. State Assembly, 1914-17, 21, N.Y. State Senate, 1920-21. Trustee Edwin Gould Found. for Children, Edwin Gould Services for Children; board dirs. Sheltering Arms Childrens Service, N.Y.C. Mem. Am. Bar Assn., Assn. Bar City N.Y. Clubs: Yale, Down Town Assn. (N.Y.C.). Home: Hanover NH Died June 21, 1970.

MEYER, WALLACE, advt. agy. exec.; b. Oshkosh, Wis., Jan. 14, 1888; s. Fred A. and Sophia (Zellmer) M.; A.B., U. Wis., 1916; m. Ruth Genevieve Richtmeyre, Jan. 17, 1920 (div. Aug. 1962); children—Michael W. R., Richard F.; m. 2d, Elinor M. Carlstrand, Sept. 5, 1963. Reporter, Oshkosh Daily Northwestern, 1908-12; copywriter J. Walter Thompson, Advt., Chgo., 1916-17; contact Charles F. W. Nichols, Advt., Chgo., 1917, 19-25; mem. staff Reincke, Meyer & Finn, Advt., Chgo., 1925-71, exec. v.p., 1932-46, pres., 1946-71, chmn., 1960-71. Bd. dirs. U. Wis. Found. (chmn. information com., Journalism citation 1961). Served with Signal Corps, U.S. Army, 1918-19. Mem. Chgo. Athletic Assn., Acacia, Sigma Delta Chi. Contbr. articles to profl. jours. Home: Chicago IL Died Jan. 8, 1971.

MEYERDING, HENRY WILLIAM, surgeon; b. St. Paul, Minn., Sept. 5, 1884; s. Henry John and Adelgunda (Rosenkranz) M.; B.Sc., U. of Minn., 1907, M.D., 1909, M.Sc. in orthopedic surgery, 1918; m. Lura Abbie Stinchfield, Feb. 12, 1912 (dec. Apr. 1960); children—Augustus (dec.), Edward Henry, Anne (dec.). House surgeon Mayo Clinic, 1911-12, attending physician, 1912-14, asst. orthopedist, 1914-15, asso. orthopedic surgeon, 1915, surgeon from 1915; orthopedic surgeon St. Mary's and Colonial hosps., 1915; instr. orthopedic surgery Mayo Foundation, U. Minn. Grad. Sch., 1918-20, asst. prof., 1920-22, associate professor, 1922-37, prof. 1937-49, emeritus, 1949-69. Served in Minn. Nat. Guard, 1st lt. M.C., 1909, col. 1938. Recipient Gold medals, Am. Med. Assn., 1939; gold medal, Am. Cong. Phys. Therapy, 1939. First award, Chgo. Med. Soc., 1947; medal of honor, from the University of Bordeaux, 1952; Certificate of Merit, U. Minn., 1952. Diplomate Am. Bd. Orthopedic Surgery. Fellow A.C.S. (gov. 1946-53), Internat. Coll. Surgeons (pres. U.S. sect. 1950-51, internat. president 1958), Acad. Surgery, Spain (hon.); mem. Am. Fracture Assn. (pres. 1952-56), Internat. Soc. Orthopaedic Surgery and Traumatology (nat. chmn. U.S. sect., pres. 6th congress 1948; chmn. U.S. delegations 1946-55), hon. mem., corr. mem. fgn., internat. and nat. profl. and scientific orgns. and assns. Italian, Brazilian, Argentine and including hon. memberships in: French Socs. Orthopedic Surgery and Traumatology, Internat. Surg. Soc., World Med. Assn., Netherlands Orthopaedic Soc., Belgian, Czechoslovak, Bordeaux, Madrid, Internat. surg. socs., Brazilian Acad. Medicine, Philippine Coll. Surgeons, Turkish Assn. Surgeons. Conglist. Mason (32 deg., Shriner). Club: University. Home: Rochester MN Died Aug. 1969.

MEYERHOLZ, CHARLES HENRY, educator; b. nr. Wapello, Ia.; s. Henry and Leise (Burchold) M.; M.Di., Ia. State Teachers Coll., 1898; Ph.B., Ia. State Univ., 1902, M.A., 1903; A.M., Harvard University, 1905; studied and traveled in Europe, 1905-08; Ph.D., Leipzig, 1907; studied law and ednl. administration, Harvard, 1912-13; unmarried. Teacher rural schs., 1894-96; supt. schs., Ia., 1898-1901; prof. history U. of Me., summer, 1905; prof. history State Normal Coll., Emporia, Kan., 1907-08; head depts. of govt. and economics, Ia. State Teachers Coll., 1908-22; dir. S.A.T.C., 1917-18; prof. ednl. administration and asso. dir. extension, U. of Pittsburgh, 1922-31; educational dir. Oxford Institute since 1935. Lecturer on education and social sciences at teachers' institutes. Member N.E.A., Am. Polit. Science Assn., Am. Hist. Assn. (life), Am. Economic Assn., Ia. State Teachers' Assn., Ia. Social Science Teachers (pres.), Phi Delta Kappa. Republican. Methodist. Mason. Clubs: Faculty, University. Author: Federal Supervision Over Territories of the United States, 1907; The Federal Convention of 1787, 1906; History and Government of Iowa, 1912; Government of Iowa and the United States, 1916; State Course of Study in Citizenship, 1921. Joint Author: The Short Constitution, 1921; American History in Outline, 1927. Address: 5350 Drexel Boul., Chicago IL‡

MEYERS, CARLISLE PAUL, lawyer; b. Lincoln, Neb., Sept. 25, 1915; S. William H. and Geraldine (Ankeny) M.; A.B., U. Neb., 1936, J.D., 1939; m. Emma White, June 1966 (dec. June 1972); children (by previous marriage)—Neil Peets, Lynn Ann. Admitted to Neb. bar, 1939, Pa. bar, 1955; practiced in Lincoln, 1939-41; lawyer anti-trust div. Dept. Justice 1941-48; with Westinghouse Electric Corp., 1948-72, head law dept., N.Y.C., 1951-52, Pitts., 1952-55, gen. counsel, 1955-72, sec., 1958-72, v.p., 1961-72; dir. Westinghouse Broadcasting Co., Inc. Bd. dirs., pres. Met. Pitts. YMCA; trustee Westinhouse Electric Fund. Served as 1st lt., F.A., AUS, 1943-46. Mem. Am. Soc. Corporate Sec. (pres. Pittsburgh), Phi Delta Theta. Republican. Presbyn. Clubs: University, Chartiers Country, Duquesne (Pitts.). Home: PA Died June 14, 1972.

MEYERS, JOSEPH HUGH, consultant; b. Balt., July 1, 1904; s. J. Herman and Catherine M. (King) M.; student U. Mich., 1923-26; LL.B., Cath. U. Am., 1933, LL.M., 1940; M. Hollis V. Carder, Aug. 21, 1934(dec. June 1966); children—Judith, Thomas, John, Mary; m. 2d, Mary M. Morrison, July 11, 1970. Admitted to D.C. bar, 1934; atty. Dept. Health, Edn. and Welfare, and predecessors, 1936-60, dept. commr. Social Security, 1960-63; dept. commr. welfare Dept. Health, Edn. and Welfare, 1963-67, acting commr. welfare, 1967, dep. adminster, social and rehab. service, 1967-70; cons. pub. welfare, 1970-72; lectr. Barry Coll. Sch. Social Welfare, Miami Shores, Fla., 1970-72. Trustee William J. Kerby Found. Served to maj. AUS, World War II. Mem. Am. Pub. Welfare Assn. (2d v. p. 1969-71), Fed. Bar Assn., Fla. Health and Welfare Council (mem. bd.). Home: Miami Beach FL Died Dec. 29, 1972; buried Arlington Nat. Cemetery.

MEYERS, SIDNEY STUYVESANT, lawyer; b. New Orleans, La., Jan. 16, 1876; s. Henry and Rosalie (Lang) M.; A.B., Columbia, 1895; LL.B., New York U., 1897; unmarried. Practiced in N.Y. City since 1897; gen. counsel for Motor and Accessory Mfrs., comprising 90 per cent of mfrs. of automobile parts and supplies in U.S.; represented automobile tire mfrs., 1911, before legislature of N.Y. State in opposition to bill compelling branding and marking of tires with date of manufacture; counsel and mem. creditors' com. U.S. Motor Co., 1912, gen. counsel Fisk Rubber Co.; selected as counsel for Rubber Assn. of America, 1914, and assisted in arranging details for modification of embargo of Great Britain on rubber; etc. Wrote brief on proposed imposition of tax on crude rubber and submitted same to chmn. ways and means com., Nat. Ho. of Rep., 1915. Represented Western Electric Co. in purchase of license of De Forest radio patents, 1914; represented merchandise creditors of Locomobile, Sheldon and Bethlehem Motor cos., 1923; became asso. counsel firm Wellman, Smyth & Scofield, 1925. Democrat. Mem. Am. Bar Assn. Home: 2975 New York NY‡

MEYNE, GERHARDT, constrn. contractor; b. Chgo., Dec. 30, 1880; s. William and Wilhelmine (Hinrichs) M.; student parochial schs., Chgo.; m. Elizabeth Starrett Ernst, Feb. 7, 1911 (dec. 1919); m. 2d, Hilda Beatrice Brown, Jan. 31, 1928. Apprentice carpenter, 1899; president Gerhardt F. Meyne Co., specializing indsl., comml. bldgs. involving extraordinary structural engineering and arichtectural problems, 1912-65, later director, adminstrative consultant; pres. 1448 Lake Shore Dr. Bldg. Corp.; dir. Lake Shore Nat. Bank, Republic Realty Mortgage Co. Vice pres. Chgo. Crime Commn., Adult Edn. Council; mem. exec. com. Chgo. Plan Commn.; mem. Met. Housing Council; vis. com. to div. humanities U. Chgo. Trustee Union League Found. for Boys Clubs, Field Mus. Natural History. Mem. Chgo. Assn. Commerce and Industry (v.p., dir.), Chgo. Hist. Soc., Symphony Orchestra Assn., Am. Acad. Polit. and Social Sci., Asso. Gen. Contractors Am., Western Soc. Engrs., Builders Assn. Chgo., Builders League (dir.), Bldg. Constrn. Employers Assn. Chgo., Assn. Employers Ill. (dir.), Nat. Com. Uniform Lien Laws. Republican. Lutheran. Clubs: Union League, Architects, Lake Shore Athletic, Yacht, Rotary (Chicago); Evanston Golf. Home: Chicago IL Died Nov. 22, 1966; buried Concordia Cemetery, Forest Park IL

MEZZROW, MEZZ, (MILTON MESIROW), jazz musician; b. Chgo., Nov. 9, 1899. Played sax and clarinet with Teschemacher, McPartland, others and Austin High gang, also with Jungle Kings, Chgo. Rhythm Rings, Eddie Condon, 1920's; championed early New Orleans Jazz style, influential in devel. Chgo. Style; recorded with Art Hodes, played club dates, 1940's; recorded on own label, King Jazz, 1945-48; influenced Hugues Panassie, French jazzologist; with small jazz groups in France, 1948-72. Author: (autobiography, with Bernard Wolfe) Really the Blues, 1946. Died Aug. 1972.

MICHAELIS, GEORGE V. S., publicity expert and industrial statistician; b. U.S. Arsenal, Watertown, Mass., June 21, 1873; s. Maj. Otho E. (U.S.A.) and Kate (Woodbridge) M.; ed. by mother and grad. high sch.,

Augusta, Me., 1891; unmarried. In chief eng'rs office, N.Y. & N. E. R. R., 1888-9; asst. supt. of a pulp mill, 1890; in newspaper, editorial and business work on Kennebec Journal, Augusta, Me., Boston Globe, Boston Journal, 1890-9; founded and became pres. and gen. mgr., 1900, Publicity Bureau; mng. partner, Michaelis & Ellsworth, industrial statisticians and corp'n advisers, 1904. Dir. Caucus Reform League of Mass.; mem. Am. Acad. Polit. and Social Science; mem. industrial dept., Civic Federation; mem. exec. coms., Mass. and Cambridge Civil Service Reform assns. Clubs: Reform, Nat. Arts, New York, Nassau Country (New York), Papyrus, Copley Soc. (Boston). Residence: 123 Oxford St., Cambridge, Mass. Office: 126 State St., Boston MA‡

MICHAELS, ERNEST EDWIN, engr., b. Watertown, S.D., Sept. 30, 1897; s. Herman Frederick and Bertha (Rau) M.; B.S., South Dakota State College, 1920, Dr. Engring., 1959; M.S., University of Ill., 1922; m. Emily Elizabeth Shedd, June 12, 1926; children—Elizabeth Ann, Edwin Shedd. Engr. S.D. Hwy. Commn., 1920; research grad. asst. U. Ill., 1920-22; engr., asst. chief engr. Chgo. Bridge & Iron Co., 1922-24, chief draftsman, 1924-27, asst. mgr. operations, 1927-30, mgr. Birmingham plant, 1930-47, v.p., dir., 1946, mgr. operations, 1947, exec. v.p., 1952-56, pres., 1956-70. Served as sgt. U.S. Army, 1917-19. Fellow Am. Soc. C.E.; mem. Western Soc. Engrs., Welding Research Council (chmn.), Am. Welding Soc., Sigma Xi. Republican. Home: Chicago IL Died July 1970.

MICHEL, CHARLES E(UGENE), business exec.; b. St. Louis, Mo., July 19, 1875; s. Dr. Charles E. and Celeste Pratte (Nidelet) M.; student Va. Mil. Inst., Lexington, Va., 1892-96; m. Marie von Phul, Apr. 10, 1901; children—Celeste (Mrs. Carlos Reese), Marie (Mrs. Eugene Kilgen), Charles E. Passenger rep., Burlington R.R. Co., St. Louis, Mo., 1896 to 1907; dept. head Union Electric Co. of Mo., 1907-35, sales mgr. vice pres. in charge of sales 1935-46, dir. since 1941; vice pres. Union Elec. Power Co., 1945-49, director since 1941; dir. Union Colliery Co. Mem. Edison Elec. Inst., Assn. Edison Illuminating Cos. Roman Catholic. Clubs: Rotary, University, Racquet. Home: 470 Lake Ave., St. Louis 8 MO Office: 315 N. 12th Blvd., St. Louis 1 MO‡

MICHEL, LINCOLN MATTHEUS, ins. co. exec.; b. Jersey City, Feb. 12, 1911; s. Alexander and Meta (Mattheus) M.; B.A., Williams Coll., 1932; m. Dorothy Margaret Kelley, Apr. 23, 1935; children—Mark, Paul, Peter, Timothy. Field agt. Fire Assn., 1933-37, staff N.Y. office, 1937, spl. agt. Phila. office, 1938-44, sec., 1944-49, v.p., dir., 1949-66; v.p., mgr. Pacific Coast region Reliance Ins. Co., San Francisco, 1966-67, also dir.; v.p. Excess & Treaty Mgmt. Corp., 1967-68, exec. v.p., 1968-72; dir. Planet Ins. Co., Reliance Life Ins. Co., Gen. Casualty Co. Wis. Mem. governing com. Pacific Fire Rating Bureau. Mem. Factory Ins. Assn. (exec. com.), Nat. Bd. Fire Underwriters., Assn. Fire Underwriters (chmn. bd. govs. middle dept.), Excess and Casualty Reins. Assn. (exec. com.), Ins. Soc. Phila. (pres.), Delta Upsilon. Clubs: Williams, Drug and Chemical, Down Town Assn. (N.Y.C.); St. David's Golf, Down Town, Racquet (Phila.); Montclair (N.J.) Golf. Home: Montclair NJ Died Mar. 20, 1972; cremated.

MICHEL, WILLIAM C., motion picture exec.; b. N.Y.C., 1894. Began career as comptroller Precision Machine Co., 1914; v.p., treas. Internat. Projector Corp. to 1930, Fox Film Corp., 1930-32; exec. v.p. 20th Century-Fox Film Corp., N.Y.C., 1932-70, also mem. bd., exec. com.; vice chmn. 20th-Fox Internat. Corp.; pres. Movietonews, Inc. Mem. Motion Picture Pioneers. Club: New York Athletic. Address: New York City NY Died Oct. 1970.

MICHELS, NICHOLAS ALOYSIUS, educator; b. St. Paul, Oct. 1, 1891; s. Jean Pierre and Katherina (Kraemer) M.; B.A., St. Thomas Coll., 1914; S.T.B., Cath. U., 1918; M.A., U. Minn., 1920; D.Sc., U. Louvain, Belgium, 1922; postgrad. Sorbonne U., Paris, 1923, Siena U., Italy, 1923, U. Chgo., 1925; m. Martha A. Tweeddale, June 1929 (dec. Nov. 1939); children—Adelle (Mrs. Sidney Parsons Jr.), Harvey; m. 2d, Hilda B. Datty, June 1942. Research with Dr. Ferrata. Siena U., Dr. Alexander Maximow, U. Chgo., also N.Y.U., Bellevue and Mt. Sinai hosps., 1926-28; asst. prof. biology, histology St. Louis U., 1926-27; asso. prof. anatomy Creighton U., 1927-29; asso. prof. (Jefferson Med. Coll., 1929-48, prof. anatomy, from 1948. Fellow A.A.A.S.; mem. Am. Assn. Anatomists, Soc. Exptl. Biology and Medicine, Internat. Soc. Hematology, Internat. Coll. Surgeons (chmn. anatomy, allied sci. sect.), N.Y. Acad. Sci., Am. Assn. Phys. Anthropologists, Societe d'Antropologie de Bruxelles, Am. Soc. Hematology, Sigma Xi, Phi Beta Pi, Alpha Omega Alpha. Author: Blood Supply and Anatomy of the Upper Abdominal Orgns., 1955. Research in and reports on cell biology, including mast cells, plasma cells, erythrocyte, lymph nodes, Russell body cells, also anatomical structure upper and lower abdomen. Home: Hatfield PA Died Oct. 27, 1969.

MICHELSON, ARNOLD, regulator exec.; b. Bismark N.D., July 7, 1893; s. Herman L. and Justyni (Maska) M.; A.B., U. Minn., 1916; m. Esther E. Erickson, Oct. 30, 1920; children—James, Virginia. Sales dept. Northwestern Fuel Co., Duluth, St. Paul Minn., 1918-19, joined Minneapolis Honeywell Regulator Co., 1920, v.p., 1928-64, regional mgr. eastern operations 1934-54, regional v.p., 1954-64. Capt. U.S. Army, 1917-18. Mem. Oil Heat Inst. N.Y. Oil Trades Assn., N.Y., N.J. fuel assns. Beta Theta Pi. Mason. Clubs: Sales Executives (N.Y. City); Lake Placid. Home: New York City NY Died Aug. 1969.

MICHELSON, HENRY E(RNEST), dermatologist; b. Bismarck, N.D., Sept. 22, 1888; s. Herman L. and Justyna (Aurbach) M.; B.S., U. of Minn., 1910, M.D., 1912; study, London, Paris, Vienna, 1921, 29; married Dalie Lindsay, August 14, 1916; children—Robert, Margery (Mrs. Scotson Webbe). Interne, City and County Hospital, St. Paul, Minn., 1912-13; practiced at Virginia, Minn., 1913-15; assistant in dermatology, U. of Minnesota, 1915-20, associate professor dermatology, 1923-26, prof., dir. div. dermatology and syphilology, 1927-66, prof. emeritus, 1966-72. Chmn. Bd. Dermatology, Am. Med. Assn. of U.S., from 1947; hon. pres. Internat. Congress Dermatology, 1962. Recipient Gold medal award Am. Acad. Dermatology, 1962. Mem. Am. Dermatology Assn. (pres. 1951), Minn. Dermatology Soc., Chgo. Dermatology Soc., Am. Bd. of Dermatology and Syphilology from 1939, Vienna Dermatol. Soc., Beta Theta Pi, Nu Sigma Nu, Alpha Omega Alpha, Sigma Xi; corresponding member French, Danish, Italian, Swedish dermatol. socs.; hon. mem. Brit., German, Venezuelan, Austrian dermatological socs., Royal Society of Medicine London. Clubs: Minneapolis; Tavern (Chicago, Ill.). Home: Minneapolis MN Died May 10, 1972.

MICHIE, H(ENRY) STUART, b. Fergus, Ont., Can., May 16, 1871; s. Henry and Anne (Argo) M.; student Upper Can. Coll., Toronto, Ont., 1888-90, Toronto U., 1890-92, Pratt Inst., Brooklyn, N.Y., 1898-1901, Central and Camberwell Schs. Arts and Crafts, London, Eng., 1905-06; m. Jeanne Hatch, of Camden, N.J., June 2, 1910;children—Henry (dec.), Jean, Forbes, Estes (dec.), Anne. Instr., McKinley Manual Training Sch., Washington, D.C., later with Minneapolis (Minn.) Guild of Handicraft until 1906; head of arts and crafts dept., George Washington U., 1907-09; prin. Worcester (Mass.) Art Mus. Sch., 1909-38; retired. Mem. Soc. Arts and Crafts, Audubon Soc., Japan Soc., New York, Japan Soc., Boston. Conglist. Clubs: Worcester, Bohemian, Tatnuck Country; University. Contributor on textiles, crafts and Japanese prints. Collector of Japanese print, Oriental textiles, etc. Home: 10 Military Rd., Worcester MA‡

MICHIE, THOMAS JOHNSON, U.S. district judge; b. Northport, N.Y., June 7, 1896; s. Thomas Johnson and Emily (Hewson) M.; A.B., U. Va., 1917, A.M., 1920, LL.B., 1921; m. Marcella Guidotti, Jan. 7, 1947; children—Cordelia Ruffin (Mrs. Walter C. Plunkett, Jr.), Thomas Johnson, Emily (Mrs. John Gennari), Virginia. Admitted Va. bar, 1921, partner Allen, Walsh & Michie, Charlottesville, 1921-26; legal dept. Koppers Co., Pitts., 1926-42, chief counsel, 1937-42; partner Michie, Taylor, Camblos & Deets and predecessor firms, 1946-61; U.S. dist. judge Western Dist. of Va., 1961-67. Lectr. U. Va. Law Sch., 1946-61. Mayor of Charlottesville, 1958-60. Dir. Thomas Jefferson Meml. Found. Served as 2d lt. A.C., U.S. Army, 1917-19, lt. col. U.S.A.A.F., 1942-46. Decorated Legion of Merit, Bronze Star, Order Brit. Empire, Order Crown of Italy, Croix de Guerre (France). Home: VA Died Apr. 9, 1973.

MICHLER, FRANCIS, capt. U.S.A.-lt.-col. and asst. adj-gen. U.S. vols.; b. in N.Y.; apptd., 1866; grad. West Point, 1870; 2d lt., June 15, 1870; 1st lt., Nov. 12, 1876; capt., May 22, 1888; apptd. lt-col., U.S. vols., 1898; aide-de-camp, on staff Gen. Miles; took part in campaigns against Apaches in Arizona, 1872-3. Residence: Metropolitan Club, Washington DC‡

MICKEY, HAROLD CHANDLER, hosp. adminstr.; b. Denver, Nov. 13, 1908; s. Chandler Stephenson and Hazel (Brock) M.; B.B.A., U. Colo., 1931; m. Frances Combs, Mar. 5, 1932; children—Nancy Louise (Mrs. Stanley R. King), Susan Ann (Mrs. John W. Bales), Stephen Linwood. Investigator, Retail Credit Co., Denver, 1931-36; asst. supt., then supt. Duke U. Hosp., 1936-49; asso. hosp. adminstrn. Duke Sch. Medicine; hosp. cons. James A. Hamilton & Assos., Mpls., 1949-54; asso., grad. faculty U. Minn.; adminstr. Rochester Meth. Hosp., 1954-66, exec. dir., 1966-68. Trustee Hosp. Care Assn., Durham, N.C., 1944-49; bd. dirs. Hosp. Bur., Inc., 1964-68, v.p., 1966, pres., 1968. Fellow Am. Coll. Hosp. Adminstrs.; mem. Am. Hosp. Assn. (ho. dels. 1963-65, trustee 1965-67), Minn. Hosp. Assn. (dir. 1957-59, pres. 1960), Upper Midwest Hosp. Assn. (pres. 1958-59), Am. Pub. Health Assn., Internat. Hosp. Fedn., Delta Sigma Pi, Sigma Phi Epsilon. Baptist. Clubs: Kiwanis, Rochester Rotary (pres. 1956-57). Contbr. articles hosp. jours. Home: Rochester MN Died Dec. 22, 1968; buried Oakwood Cemetery, Rochester MN

MIDDLEBUSH, FREDERICK ARNOLD, univ. pres.; b. Grand Rapids, Mich., Oct. 13, 1890; s. Wietsche and Nellie (Masternbroek) M.; A.B., U. Mich., 1913; A.M., 1914, Ph.D., 1916, LL.D., 1953; LL.D., Knox Coll., 1937, Hope Coll. 1937; LL.D., Washington U. (St. Louis), 1944; research work, London, Paris and The Hague, 1920-21, Geneva, 1931-32; m. Catherine Sofie Paine, Sept. 1, 1917. Teacher country and pub. schs., until 1912; instr. history and polit. science, Knox Coll., 1915-16, asst. prof., 1916-17, prof. 1918-22; asso. prof. polit. science and pub. law, U. of Mo., 1922-23, prof. from 1923; acting dean, Sch. of Business and Pub. Adminstrn., U. of Mo., 1925-26, dean, 1926-35; acting president, June-Oct. 1931, and from September, 1934-July, 1935, president 1935-54, pres. emeritus, 1954-71; dir. U. Mo. Development Fund, from 1954; vis. prof. polit. science, Stanford Summer 1927. Dir. war aims courses, Knox Coll., S.A.T.C. Mem. European Conf., Profs. of Internat. Law and Relations, 1926. Mem. bd. trustees, The Carnegie Foundation from 1937, vice chairman 1951-52, chmn. from 1952. Vice chairman Navy Civilian Adv. Com., 1946; member American Political Science Association (exec. council 1925-27; 2d v.p. 1942), Am. Soc. Internat. Law (exec. council, 1928-30), Am. Assn. of University Professors; trustee, gov. Midwest Research Institute from 1944. Mem. Nat. Commn. on Liberal Arts College, 1942; vice pres. Nat. Assn. State Universities, 1943 (mem. exec. com. 1944-50, pres. 1948-49) pres. Assn. Am. Us. 1950-52; member National Science Bd.; member exec. com. Assn. of Land-Grant Colls. and Univs., 1948-49; mem. Citizens Com. on Reorgn. Fed. Govt.; mem. academic adv. bd. U.S. Merchant Marine Acad., 1948-49; mem. Commn. on Organization of Executive Branch of Govt., 1948-49, Commn. on Financing of Higher Edn., and Research Service Academy Board, 1949-50; mem. adv. com. Educational Opportunities in Armed Forces from 1952; mem. com. Univ. Pres. William Rockhill Nelson Trust. Mem. 1946-48 Bd. of Visitors, Naval Acad., Annapolis, Panel of Polit. Scientists of Am. Polit. Sci. Assn., 1946, Alpha Pi Zeta (nat. pres. 1929-31). Presbyn. Clubs: Quadrangle (U. of Mich.); University (Columbia, Mo.). Editor: The Dispatches of Thomas Chudleigh and Thomas Plott, 1681-1685, 1926. Co-author: (with Dr. Chesney Hill) Elements of International Relations, 1940. Contbr. spl. articles, reviews, to profl. jours. Mem. bd. editors Am. Polit. Science Rev., 1932, 34. Home: Columbia MO Died 8, 1971; buried Columbia Cemetery, Columbia MO

MIEDEL, ROBERT EUGENE, cons. co. exec.; b. Zanesville, O., June 3, 1920; s. Charles A. and Olive (Scott) M.; student extension Am. U. Law Sch.; m. Eugenia M. Weldon, July 30, 1942. Civilian with U.S. Army, then USAAF and USAF, 1939-69; joint services project officer Distant Early Warning Line, 1953-55; dep. dir. procurement ARDC, 1955-61, asso. dir. procurement AFSC, 1961-63, asso DCS procurement and prodn., 1963-66; ret. 1966; founder W-M Consultants, Inc., Costa Mesa Cal., 1966, owner, pres., 1966-69. Pres. Camp Springs Citizens Assn., 1958-69. Served with USAAF, 1942-45. Recipient USAF exceptional civilian service award, 1958, Dept. Def. exceptional civilian service award, 1958, USAF award for meritorious civilian service, 1966. Address: Costa Mesa CA Died Mar. 24, 1969.

MIERS, EARL SCHENCK, author; b. Bklyn., May 27, 1910; s. William Schenck and Emma (Swanell) M., Litt.B., Rutgers U., 1933, M.A., 1943, Litt.D., 1963; L.H.D., Lincoln Coll., 1962; m. Agnes Starling Wyckoff, Aug. 25, 1934; children—David, Meredith, William. Asso. editor Univ. Publs., Rutgers U., 1935-42; editor Westminister Press, Phila., 1942-44; dir. Rutgers U. Press, 1944-49; editor Alfred A. Knopf, Inc., 1949-51, World Pub. Co. 1951-54. Mem. Nat. Soc. Crippled Children and Adults, Mem. N.J. Hist. Commn., Phi Beta Kappa. Clubs: Cosmos (Washington); University (N.Y.C.). Author: (with Ernest E. McMahon) The Chronicles of Colonel Henry, 1936; Backfield Feud, 1936; Composing Sticks and Mortar Boards, 1941; Career Coach, 1941; Bookmaking and Kindred Amenities, 1942; Big Ben, 1942; Valley in Arms, 1943; Grass Roots, 1944; The Ivy Years, 1945; (with Richard A. Brown) Gettysburg, 1948; The General Who Marched to Hell, 1950; The Christmas Card Murders (pseud. David Wm. Meredith), 1950; Monkey Shines, 1952; Touchdown Trouble, 1953; The Kid Who Beat the Dodgers, 1954; The Rainbow Book of American History, 1955; Web of Victory, 1955; The Story of Thomas Jefferson, 1955; (with Paul M. Angle) The Living Lincoln, 1955; Robert E. Lee, 1956; Ball of Fire, 1956; The American Story, 1956 Rebel's Roost, 1956; The Guns of Vicksburg, 1957; Mark Twain on The Mississippi, 1957; Blood of Freedom, 1958; Why Did This Have to Happen?, 1958; When Washington Won at Yorktown, 1958; The Great Rebellion, 1958; American and Its Presidents, 1959; Billy Yank and Johnny Reb, 1959; The Storybook of Science, 1959; When Grant Met Lee at Appomattox, 1960; (with Paul M. Angle) Tragic Years 1860-1865, 1960; The American Civil War, 1961; Our Fifty States, 1961; With Lincoln in the White House, 1963; Yankee Doodle Dandy, 1963; Golden Book of American History, 1963; Wild and Woolly West, 1964; The Story of John F. Kennedy, 1964; Where the Raritan Flows, 1964; New

Jersey and the Civil War, 1964; Abraham Lincoln in Peace and War, 1964; Freedom, 1965; Men of Valor, 1965; Where Liberty Stands Guard, 1966; The Trouble Bush, 1966; Baseball, 1967; Football, 1967; That Lincoln Boy, 1968; The Bill of Rights, 1968; The Magnificent Mutineers, 1968; Basketball, 1969; The Night We Stopped the Trolley, 1969; Emancipation, 1969; Black Americans, 1969; A Blazing Star, 1970; The Golden History of the United States, 1970; That Jefferson, Boy, 1970; Crossroads of Freedom, 1971. Editor: When the World Ended, 1957; Rebel War Clerk's Diary, 1958; Lincoln Day by Day, 1960; Ride to war, 1961; The Last Campaign, 1972; Down in Jersey, 1973. Home: Edison NJ Died Nov. 17, 1972.

MIERS, HENRY VIRGIL, newspaper editor, critic; b. Texarkana, Tex., Jan. 19, 1925; s. Henry Virgil and Willa Neta (Castleman) M.; B.A., Tex. Tech. Coll., 1947; m. Patricia Nancy Locke, Aug. 7, 1954;children—Peggy Castleman, Roslyn Southwick, Douglas Locke. With Dallas Times Herald, 1947-67, amusements editor, 1953-67; critical writer Christian Sci. Monitor, others, 1956-67. Mem. Margo Jones Nat. Award Com., mem. regional com. ANTA; program com. YMCA; mem. Dallas profl. Arts Alliance. Served with USNR, 1944-46. Mem. Nat. Screen Council, Broadway Theater League (dir.), Alpha Tau Omega. Club: Variety. Home: Dallas TX Died Nov. 27, 1967; buried Dallas TX

MIES VAN DER ROHE, LUDWIG, architect; b. Aachen, Germany, Mar. 27, 1886; D. Engring., Inst. Tech., Karlsruhe, Germany, 1950, Tech. Inst., Braunschweig, 1950, Ill. Inst. Tech., 1966; LL.D., North Carolina State College, 1956; A.F.D., Carnegie Inst. Tech., Pitts., 1960, Northwestern U., 1963, U. Ill., 1964; H.H.D., Wayne State U., 1961. Came to United States, 1938, naturalized Am. citizen. Began as apprentice to famous deisgners and architects of Europe; with Bruno Paul, furniture designer, Berlin, 1905-07; apprentice, Peter Behrens, 1908-11; projected designs for steel and glass skyscrapers, 1919-21, for concrete office bldg., 1922-69; fgn. archtl. designs include, German bldg. Internat. Expn., Barcelona, Spain, 1929, Tugendhat house, Brno, Czechoslovakia, 1930, skyscraper on Friedrichstrasse, Berlin, Bacardi Office Bldg., Mexico City, Seagram bldg., N.Y.C., 26-story apt. bldgs., 860 Lake Shore Dr., Chgo.; dir. Bauhaus School in Germany, 1930-33; dir. Sch. Architecture, Ill. Inst. Tech., 1938-58; designer of institute's campus, Chgo.; also designer of steel furniture. Served as 1st v.p. Deutscher Werkbund (orgn. to improve quality of indsl. design), 1927. Dir. Weissenhofsiedlung Exhbn. at Stuttgart, 1927; had one-man show of work Mus. Modern Art, N.Y.C., Art Inst. Chgo. Recipient medal of honor VII Congress of Pan-Am. Architects, award of merit Ruskin Soc. of Am., Feltrinelli Internat. prize for architecture, Rome, Italy; Presidential Medal of Freedom, U.S.; numerous other medals and honors. Life mem. Order Pour le Merite (Germany). Fellow A.I.A., Am. Acad. Arts and Scis.; mem. Prussian Acad. Art, soc. Mex. Architects (hon.), Royal Inst. Brit. Architects, Internat. Congress Modern Architecture, Ill. Soc. Architects, Am. Assn. U. Profs., Am. Soc. Engring. Edn., Coll. Art Assn. of Am., Am. Inst. Arts and Letters, Nat. Inst. Arts and Letters (hon.). Home: Chicago IL Died Aug. 17, 1969; buried Graceland Cemetery, Chicago IL

MIGNONE, ALBERT EDMUND, mfg. co. exec.; b. Providence, Apr. 25, 1914; s. Ettore A. and Ruby A. (Granata) M.; Sc.B. in Elec. Engring., Brown U., 1935; m. Gilda Cirelli, Oct. 25, 1940; children—Robert, Paula, Richard, Thomas, Karen, James, Patricia. Design engr. Builders Iron Foundry, 1936-37; insp. U.S. Army Engrs., 1937-38; asst. supr. tabulating R.I. Unemployment Comepnsation Bd., 1938-40; research adminstr. U.S. Naval Torpedo Sta., 1940-47; v.p. Arthur D. Little, Inc., Cambridge, Mass., 1947-63; v.p. research and engring. Addressograph-Multigraph Corp., 1963-68, adminstrv. v.p. research and engring., from 1968; dir. Wellesley Booster, Inc., Elgin Electronics. Chmn. subcom. on NASA, U.S. C. of C., from 1962, also mem. com. sci. and tech. Mem. Am. Ordnance Assn., A.A.A.S., N.Y. Acad. Scis., Indsl. Research Inst., Am. Inst. Physics, Cleve. Engring. Soc. (bd. govs.), Brown Engring. Assn. Club: Brown (Boston). Home: Shaker Heights OH

MIKESELL, JEROME BYRON, lawyer, corp. exec.; b. Atwood, Kan., June 30, 1901; s. Elihu A. and Sarah Catherine (Fleming) M.; student U. Kan., 1920-21, De Pauw U., 1921-23; LL.B., U. Mich., 1927; m. Ruth Annette Weaver, June 14, 1930 (dec. 1949); m. 2d, Rosalind Mary Snow, Dec. 4, 1951; children—Jerome Jay, Rodney Byron. Admitted to Mich. bar, 1927, Ill. bar, 1928, pvt. practice, Chgo., 1928-38; asso. with Power's Service, Inc., 1938-68, pres., dir., 1950-68. Mem. Am., Ill., Chgo. bar assns., Am. Judicature Soc., Chgo. Hist. Soc. (life mem.), Soc. Mayflower Descendants, Chgo. Assn. of Commerce and Industry, Lambda Chi Alpha, Delta Sigma Rho. Clubs: South Shore Country, Illinois Athletic, Chicago Executives. Author articles on lawn bowling and credit. Editor: South Shore Country Club Mag., 1957-60. Home: Chicago IL Died June 22, 1968; buried Oak Woods Cemetery Chicago IL

MIKESELL, WILLIAM HENRY, psychologist; b. Md.; s. William Augustus and Lucinda Magdalena (Harner) M.; A.B. cum laude, Western Md. Coll., 1912; A.M., Harvard, 1914; Ph.D., U. of Ill., 1926; m. Patricia Rand Patterson, June 16, 1923; children—Ritchie Patterson, William Henry. Ednl. dir. Y.M.C.A., France, World War I; instr. public speaking, U. of Tex., 1916-18; instr. public speaking and dramatics, U. of Ky., 1920-22, U. of Mo., 1922-23; instr. public speaking, U. of Ill., 1923-26; dean, Coll. Liberal Arts, Municipal U., Wichita, Kan., 1926-29; head dept. psychology, Wichita U., 1926-42; head psychology, Municipal U. Washburn, Topeka, Kan., 1947; formerly co-ordinator of guidance, Miss. State Coll. for Women; with Anderson (Ind.) Coll., until 1964; dir. guidance Roswell Community Coll., from 1964. Chief psychologist Mental Hygiene Clinic Vets. Adminstrn. Denver, 1946. Served as capt. (psychologist), U.S. Army, 1942-46. Fellow Am. Psychol. Assn. Conglist. Mason (32 deg.). Author: Mental Hygiene, 1939; How to Study, 1940. Co-author: Psychology of Adjustment (with Hanson), 1952; Techniques of Living, 1953; The Power of High Purpose, 1960; Counseling for Ministers, 1961. Editor: Psychology and Life, 1932; Modern Trends in Abnormal Psychology, 1949; also other text books. Lecturer on applied psychology, Chicago Speaking Bureau. Address: Roswell NM Died Mar. 1969.

MIKHALAPOV, GEORGE SERGEI, metals co. exec.; b. Kiev, Russia, Jan. 26, 1906; s. Sergei and Anastasia (Laboutine) M.; came to U.S., 1923, naturalized, 1929; B.S. in Elec. Engring., Mass. Inst. Tech., 1926; m. Priscilla Sinnickson, Oct. 9, 1937; 1 dau., Ruth; m. 2d, Anne Biddle, June 2, 1956. Jr. engr. Stone & Webster Engring. Corp., 1926-33; engr. Heintz Mfg. Co., Phila., 1933-40; dir. research Taylor-Winfield Corp., Warren, O., 1940-41; research supt. war metallurgy com. OSRD, 1941-44; mgr. apparatus research dept. Air Reduction, Inc., 1944-49; mgr. engring. Knolls. Atomic Power Lab., Gen. Electric Co., Schenectady, 1951-54; pres. Coast Metals, Inc., Little Ferry, N.J., 1954-57; exec. v.p. Brush Beryllium Co., Cleve., 1957-59, president, 1959-65, chief executive officer, 1962-67, chairman of the board, 1965-67, cons., 1967-71. Mem. of Am. Soc. Mech. Engrs., Am. Soc. Testing Materials, Am. Welding Soc., Am. Mgmt. Assn., Am. Nuclear Soc. Home: Devon PA Died Nov. 1971.

MILAS, NICHOLAS ALTHANASIUS, educator; b. Candia, Crete, Greece, Jan. 1, 1897; s. Althanasius E. and Mary Milas; B.S., Coe Coll., Cedar Rapids, Ia., 1922, Sc.D., 1957; M.S. U. of Chicago, 1923, Ph.D., 1926; m. Georgia C. Despotes, Feb. 23, 1929; children—Beatrice Mary (Mrs. B. M. Wyse), Helen Frances. Entered U.S., 1912; naturalized, 1918. Asst., U. of Chicago, 1922-26; Nat. Research fellow, Princeton, 1926-28; research asso., Mass. Inst. Tech., 1928-35, asst. prof. chemistry, 1935-41, asso. prof., 1941-62, prof. emeritus, lectr., 1962-71; lectr. fgn. univs. Visiting and adv. com. Coe Coll. Pvt. Signal Corps, 1918-19; 1t. Chem. Warfare Service Reserve, 1925-40. Fellow Am. Acad. Arts and Sciences, N.Y. Acad. Scis.; mem. A.A.A.S. Mem. Assn. Am. Univ. Profs. (pres. M.I.T. chapter since 1945), Am. Chem. Soc.; Science History Soc., Acad. Applied Sci., Croatian Chem. Soc. (hon.), Sigma Xi, Gamma Alpha, Alpha Chi Sigma. Protestant. Republican. Contbr. to scientific jours. Synthetized Vitamin A. Holder numerous patents. Consultant. Home: Belmont MA Died Jan. 25, 1971.

MILBANK, JEREMIAH, corp. exec.; b. New York, Jan. 24, 1887; s. Joseph and Ella (Dunlevy) M.; prep. edn., Cutler Sch., N.Y. City; A.B., Yale, 1909; Doctor of Agricultural Industries, Clemson Agrl. Coll., 1951; L.H.D., New York University, 1959; LL.D., George Washington U., 1960, The Citadel, 1962; m. Margaret Schulze (dec. 1917); m. 2d, Katharine Schulze, June 21, 1919; children—Margaret (Mrs. H. Lawrence Bogert), Jeremiah, Jr., Nancy (Mrs. Charles Cooke Spalding). Dir. Metropolitan Life Ins. Co., So. Ry.; trustee Provident Loan Soc. Eastern treas. Rep. Nat. Com., 1928-32. Trustee Inst. for Crippled and Disabled, Community Service Society of N.Y.; director Boys' Clubs of America. Member Zeta Psi. Republican. Presbyn. Clubs: University, Yale, Union League, Down Town, Racquet and Tennis, Links, Apawamis, Blind Brook, New York Yacht, Indian Harbor Yacht, Bohemian. Home: Byram NC Died Mar. 22, 1972.

MILBURN, EDWARD GARLAND, chain store exec.; b. Balt., Apr. 26, 1919; s. Garland and Elsie (Cupero) M.; B.A., St. Lawrence U., 1942; m. Nancy Hatch, July 12, 1945; children—Jeffrey, Susan. With W.T. Grant Co., 1946-71, personnel dir., 1962-64, v.p., comptroller, 1964-66, v.p. Western region, 1966-69, v.p. eastern region, 1969-71. Home: West New York NJ Died Feb. 12, 1971; buried George Washington Meml. Park Cemetery, Paramus NJ

MILES, PERRY LESTER, army officer; b. Westerville, O., Oct. 15, 1873; s. James A. and Mary (Longwell) M.; grad. U.S. Mil. Acad., 1895, Army Sch. of the Line, 1916, Gen. Staff Sch., 1920, Army War Coll., 1921; m. Mary Latta Stott, Dec. 28, 1921. Commd. 2d lt. inf., U.S. Army, June 12, 1895, and advanced through grades to col., July 1, 1920; brig. gen., Feb. 1, 1932. Comd. 1st, 2d, 16th Brigs. and 1st Div.; served in Spanish-Am. War, Philippine Insurrection, Mexican border, World War; retired Oct. 31, 1937. Awarded D.S.C., D.S.M., Spanish-Am. War, Philippine Insurrection, Mexican Border and Victory medals (U.S.); officer Legion of Honor, Croix de Guerre with Palm (France). Protestant. Chmn. Shenandoah Valley Regional Defense Council, 1941; chmn. Staunton and Augusta County War Finance Com., 1943-45; chmn. Staunton Salvage Com., 1942-45. Clubs: Army and Navy (Washington); University (Winter Park, Fla.). Author: The Infantry Soldier: Notes for the Private and Corporal. Co-Author: Vol. 4 of Tactical Principles and Decisions, 1923; contbr. articles on military subjects. Home: 501 E. Beverly Staunton VA‡

MILLAR, ROBERT CAMERON, publisher; born Glasgow, Scotland, Feb. 15, 1900; s. John and Janet (McArthur) M.; m. Anne Gilbert, Nov. 25, 1926; children—Robert Cameron, Janet Claire (Mrs. Janet M. Rowland). Pres. Fla. Pub. Co., 1948-66; gen. mgr. Fla. Times-Union and Jacksonville Jour. Mem. So. Newspaper Publs. Assn. (pres. 1960-61). Democrat. Presbyn. Clubs: Rotary, San Jose Country, Florida Yacht. Home: Neptune Beach FL Died May 25, 1971; buried Oaklawn Cemetery, Jacksonville FL

MILLARD, EARL, corp. exec.; b. Rushville, Ind., Mar. 6, 1905; s. John Akard and Pearl (Faught) M.; D.D.S., Washington U., 1929; m. Dorothy Nester, Oct. 28, 1933 children—Joseph Nester, Earl, Jr. Practiced dentistry, East St. Louis, Ill., 1929-48; exec. v.p. Obear Nester Glass Co., East St. Louis, State Savs. & Loan Assn., East St. Louis; director U.S. Partition & Packaging Corp., Milw., 1st Nat. Bank, E. St. Louis, Ill. Served as lt. comdr., USN, 1942-45; Mem. United States Brewers Association (bd. dirs.), Jr. C. of C. (past pres.), Beta Theta Pi. Clubs: Noonday, Old Warson, University (St. Louis); St. Clair Country (Belleville, Ill.), Racquet (St. Louis). Home: Belleville IL Died Jan. 1970.

MILLARD, WILLARD B(ARROWS), JR., banker; b. Omaha, Sept. 24, 1900; s. Willard B. and Frances (Barton) M.; Ph.B., Yale, 1924; m. Nancy Dolman, May 7, 1942; 1 dau., Nancy. Clk. Omaha Nat. Bank, 1924-27. asst. cashier, 1927-29, v.p., 1929-46, sr. v.p., 1946-49, pres., 1949-62, chmn., 1962-69, dir., 1933-69; dir. Bankers Life Ins. Co. Neb., U.P.R.R. Nat. dir. Boys Clubs Am.; regent Creighton U. Mem. C. of C., Assn. Res. City Bankers, Ak-Sar-Ben Knights. Clubs: Omaha, Athletic, Country (Omaha). Home: Omaha NB Died Jan. 3, 1969.

MILLBERRY, GUY STILLMAN, dental educator; b. Menominee, Mich., Nov. 3, 1872; s. Frank Samuel and Mary Amy (Ingalls) M.; D.D.S., U. of Calif., 1901; m. 2d, Gertrude Mann, May 27, 1936. Began practice at San Francisco, 1901; prof. chemistry and metallurgy, U. of Calif. Coll. of Dentistry, since 1910, dean 1914-39, retired June 30, 1940, as prof. Dental Health Education emeritus; dir. and sec. Medico-Dental Bldg. Corp. Mem. and chmn. bd. dirs. Good Teeth Council for Children, Inc., Chicago. Fellow A.A.A.S., Am. Pub. Health Assn.; mem. Am. Acad. Political and Social Science, California Academy of Science, American Dental Assn. and affiliated California societies, Xi Psi Phi, Epsilon Alpha, Sigma Xi, Delta Omega. Fellow California Academy of Sciences. Member Dental Advisory Committee, Procurement & Assignment Service, WMC, Republican. Clubs: Faculty (Berkeley, Calif.). Revising editor of Hodgen's Dental Metallurgy, 4th, 5th and 6th edits.; contbr. chapter to Brenneman's practice of Pediatrics. Home: Route 2, Box 181, Los Gatos CA‡

MILLER, ANDREW, b. Denmark, Nov. 16, 1870; s. Andrew and Marie (Mungenson) M.; brought to America at age of 2 yrs.; ed. pub. schs.; m. Ava Mabel Wing, May 28, 1896; children—Max Wing, Milo Vernon, Kenneth Leroy (dec.), Eleanor Frances. Admitted to Iowa bar, 1894; began practice at Buffalo Center; elected county atty., Winnebago County, Ia., 1896; removed to Forest City; mayor Forest City 2 terms, 1897-1901; located in Bismarck, N.D., 1905; asst. atty. gen. of N.D., 1907-08, atty. gen. 3 terms, Jan. 1909-Jan. 1915; mem. Miller & Zuger until 1922; judge U.S. Dist. Court, Dist. of N.D., by apptmt. of President Harding, Feb. 2, 1922-Mar. 29, 1941; retired. Republican. Lutheran. Home: Fort Lauderdale FL‡

MILLER, ANNA JENNESS, author, lecturer; b. in N. H.; d. S. Jenness; resided in Boston prior to her marriage in 1884; for several yrs. was editor and propr. Jenness Miller Monthly, a mag. devoted to physical development, improved dress and correct living; has given over 1,100 lectures upon Physical Culture and Dress in U.S. and Canada; now principally engaged in literary work and in collecting paintings and curios in Europe. Author: Barbara Thayer, 1884 L3; Twixt Love and Law; Mother and Babe, 1892 A7; How to Finish and Furnish a Home, 1892 A7; Creating a Home, 1896 A7; Physical Beauty; Philosopher of Driftwood, S28; Mother's Health and Baby's Welfare, 1905. Wrote chapter on Dress, Johnson's Revised Ency.; also various essays on art subjects. Address: Washington DC‡

MILLER, ARTHUR W., veterinarian; b. Manchester, N.H., Sept. 27, 1876; D.V.S., Kansas City Veterinary Coll., Kansas City, Mo., 1901; m. Mary Gertrude Beagle, Aug. 26, 1902; children—Merle B., Nina, Robert Mayo, Donald. Veterinary inspector, bureau animal industry, U.S. Dept. Agr., 1901-07, inspector in charge and travelling inspector, 1907-17, chief, field inspection div., Washington, D.C., 1917-28; asst. chief, bur. animal industry, 1928-43, chief since 1943. Fellow A.A.A.S.; mem. Am. Vet. Med. Assn., Nat. Assn. Bureau Animal Industry Vets., Am. Genetic Assn. Home: 6833 Piney Branch Road, Washington 12. Office: U.S. Department of Agriculture, Washington DC‡

MILLER, BARSE, artist; b. N.Y.C., Jan. 24, 1904; s. Warren Hastings and Susan (Barse) M.; ed. pvt. tutors; student Sch. of Pa. Acad. of Fine Arts, 1920-24; m. Mary Elizabeth Smith, Feb. 25, 1925 (div.); children—Barse Purviance (dec.), Mills Wagner, Helen Woolston; m. 2d, Betty Thompson, Oct. 22, 1947; 1 dau., Susan Barse. Held first exhbns. at Pa. Acad. Fine Arts and Salon d'Autome, Paris, 1923; tchr. of art, Cal., 1925-39; guest instr. U. Vt., Pa. Acad. of Fine Arts, 1939-41; prof. art, Queens Coll., City U. of N.Y.; exhibitor, leading U.S. exhbns.; rep. museums, Bklyn., N.Y.C., Los Angeles, San Diego, Chgo. Art Inst. Glasgow, etc. Commd. capt., U.S. Army engrs., 1942, Gen. MacArthur's hdqrs., Australia to paint New Guinea, Bismark Sea, Philippine campaigns; served in Japan, N. China with occupation forces; ret. as maj. C.E., R.C., 1946. Decorated Legion of Merit, recipient Dalzel Hatfield gold medal, Calif., 1929, Guggenheim post service fellowship for creative work in painting, 1946-47, Dana medal, Pa. Acad. Fine Arts, 1936; Lena Newcastle Meml. award, Am. Watercolor Soc., 1954; Adolph & Clara Obrig prize, Nat. Acad. Design, 1955. Fellow Pa. Acad. Fine Arts; mem. Los Angeles Jury for Painting, N.Y. World's Fair, 1940; mem. Nat. Acad. Design (elected to council 1960-66; asst. corr. sec. 1968-73), Cal. Nat. Watercolor Soc. (pres. 1937-39), Am. Watercolor Soc. (bd. control 1959). Democrat. Episcopalian. Club: Port Washington Yacht. Home: Plandome Manor NY Died Jan. 23, 1973.

MILLER, BERTHA EVERETT MAHONY, editor, publisher; b. Rockport, Mass., Mar. 13, 1882; d. Daniel and Mary Lane (Everett) Mahony; grad. secretarial course, Simmons Coll., 1903; m. William D. Miller, Sept. 7, 1932. Organized bookshop for boys and girls for Women's Ednl. and Indsl. Union Boston, 1916, editor Horn Book mag., pub. by union, 1924-36; purchased mag. from union, 1936; editor Horn Book mag., 1924-50; chmn. Horn Book, Inc., 1963-69. Recipient Constance Lindsay Skinner award Simmons Coll., 1955, citation children's services div. A.L.A., 1959; Regina award Catholic Library Association, 1967. Mem. Am., Mass. library assns., New Eng. Round Table Children's Librarians, Am. Assn. UN, Mass., Fla. Audubon socs., Am. Civil Liberties Union, Mass. Hor. Soc. Conglist. (auxiliary). Clubs: College (Boston); Ashburnham Olio Woman's. Compiler: (with Elinor Whitney) Realms of Good in Children's Books, 1929, Five Years of Children's Books, 1936; with (Louise P. Latimer and Beulah Folmshee (Illustrators of Children's Books, 1947); others. Home: Ashburnham MA Died May 14, 1969; buried Mt. Adnah Cemetery, Annisquam MA

MILLER, CHARLES FRANKLIN, supt. schs.; b. Fountain County, Ind., 1875; s. James P. and Elmira (Shroyer) M.; A.B., De Pauw U., 1896; post-grad. work, U. of Chicago, 1913-14; m. Rose Wood; 1 son, Douglass. Prin. sch., Kingman, Ind., 1896-1900; supt. schs., successively, Boswell, North Manchester and Napanee, Ind., until 1921; county supt. schs., Elkhart County, Ind., 1921-27; Ind. state supt. pub. instrn., 1927; supt. city schs., Indianapolis, Ind., since 1927. Mem. bd. dirs. Ind. State Tuberculosis Assn., Ind. Parent Teachers' Assn.; del. to World's Fed. of Ednl. Assns., Geneva, Hist. Assn., N.E.A., Ind. Teacher's Assn., Phi Beta Kappa. Switzerland, 1929. Mem. Am. Republican. Methodist. Mason. Odd Fellow. Home: 5766 Central Av., Indianapolis IN‡

MILLER, DAVID LEWIS, airlines exec.; b. Johnstown, Pa., Mar. 24, 1904; s. Lewis Clarke and Olive (de Lozier) M.; student Bucknell U., Temple U.; M.A., St. Vincent Coll.; m. Jeanne Stratton Porter, Mar. 7, 1943; children—Jan David, Hugh Clark, Brent Lewis. With Allegheny Airlines, Washington, 1942-70, dir. sales, 1949-51, v.p. sales, 1951-59, sr. v.p., dir., 1959-70. Episcopalian. Home: Arlington VA Died July 15, 1970; buried Westmoreland County Meml. Park, Greensburg PA

MILLER, DICK, banker; b. Parke County, Ind., Jan. 12, 1871; s. James N. and Sarah A. (Snow) M.; prep. edn., Friends Bloomingdale Acad.; A.B., Ind. U., 1894; LL.B., Ind. Law Sch., 1896; m. Cathrine Trimble, of Indianapolis, Ind., June 28, 1906; children—Genevieve (Mrs. John M. Moore), and Juanita (both adopted). Practiced at Terre Haute, Ind., 1897-1901; entered bond business as salesman, 1901; organized firm Miller & Co., 1907; sold business 1918, to City Trust Co., of which was pres. until 1931; pres. Postal Station State Bank until 1931. Mem. Ind. House of Rep., 1897; Dem. candidate for mayor of Indianapolis, 1918. Pres. Indianapolis Chamber Commerce, 1926-27. Mem. Phi Gamma Delta. Methodist. Mason, Elk. Clubs: Ind. Democratic, Highland Golf and Country. Home: 3130 N. Delaware St., Indianapolis IN*‡

MILLER, DON CLARK, corp. exec.; b. Marion, Ind., Aug. 9, 1914; s. John Hyson and Marguerite (Cornell) M.; A.B., U. Mich., 1938; m. Carolyn Edison Morse, 1937; children—Don Curry, Claire Morse. With Campbell-Ewald Co., 1936-42, v.p., gen. mgr. subsidiary Motor City Pub. Co., 1940-42; manager orgn. and analysis dept. Packard Motor Co., 1946-48; sr. v.p., dir. Kenyon & Eckhardt, Inc., 1948-59; vice pres. marketing B. F. Goodrich Co., 1959-64; v.p. Gen. Aniline & Film Corp., N.Y.C., 1965-67; v.p. Textron Inc., 1967-70. Chief promotion specialist War Finance Div., asst. to dir.-gen. WPB, 1942-44. Served as lt. USNR, 1944-46. Mem. Phi Kappa Psi. Club: University (N.Y.C.); Rhode Island Country (Barrington). Home: Newton CT Died Jan. 2, 1970; buried Village Cemetery, Newtown CT

MILLER, DON HUGO, oil co. exec.; b. Kansas City, Mo., June 9, 1909; s. Arden T. and Blanche Beatrice (Beard) M.; B.A., U. Mo., 1932; m. Mary Finch, Oct. 17, 1937; children—Randall, Lawrence. With Skelly Oil Co., Tulsa, 1932-68, wholesale sales mgr. marketing dept., 1953-57, asst. to v.p. marketing, 1956-57, gen. mgr. marketing, 1957-59, pres., 1959-68, also dir.; dir. Mission Corp., Great Lakes Pipe Line Co., 1st Nat. Bank & Trust Co., Tulsa. Trustee U. Tulsa, Midwest Research Inst. Mem. Am. Petroleum Inst. (dir.), Nat. Petroleum Council, Tulsa C. of C. (dir.), Kappa Sigma. Clubs: Tulsa; Kansas City; Southern Hills Country. Home: Tulsa OK Died Apr. 7, 1968.

MILLER, DUDLEY LIVINGSTON, lawyer; b. N.Y.C., Apr. 28, 1921; s. Andrew Otterson and Gretchen (MacDowell) M.; grad. cum laude Hotchkiss Sch., 1939; B.A., Yale, 1942; postgrad. sch. medicine, 1943, LL.B., 1945; J.S.D., N.Y. U., 1946-49; m. Marilyn M. Mattews Dec. 22, 1962; children—Dudley L., Jr., Alexandra C., Courtlandt G. Admitted to N.Y. bar, 1945, since practiced N.Y.C.; law clk. to U.S. Circuit Ct. judge Augustus N. Hand, 1945-46; asso. Miller, Montgomery & Spalding and predecessor firms, 1945-69, sr. partner, 1959-69; dir. Fuqua Industries, Atlanta, 1966-69, Knapp Bros. Shoe Mfg. Co., Brocton, 1947-69, Homes Leather Co., Boston, 1946-69, Realty & Indsl. Corp., N.Y.C., 1951-69. Teaching fellow law N.Y. U., 1946-52. Trustee, sec. Boys Harbor, N.Y.C. and E. Hampton, N.Y., 1964-69. Mem. Skull and Bones, Am., N.Y., bar assns. Assn. Bar City N.Y., Order of Coif, Yale Alumni Fund (bd. dirs. 1950-55), Phi Beta Kappa, Zeta Psi. Contbr. articles in field to profl. jours. Home: NYC NY Died Jan. 11, 1969.

MILLER, E(UGENE) K(EARFOTT), steel exec.; b. Scottdale, Pa., Sept. 7, 1890; s. J.P.K. and Sara M. (Pegg) M.; student Lafayette Coll., 1909-12, Sheffield Sci. Sch., Yale, 1912-13; m. Roberta Kyser, Oct. 4, 1916; children—Eugene Kearfott, John K. Asst. supt. blast furnaces Tenn. Coal, Iron & R.R. Co., div. U.S. Steel Corp., 1913-24, supt. blast furnaces, 1924-29; with Jones & Laughlin Steel Corp., from 1929, successively asst. gen. supt. Aliquippa works, gen. supt., asst. v.p. prodn., v.p. prodn., from 1953, cons., from 1954; pres., dir. Union Dock Co.; v.p., dir. Magdalena Mining Co., Jalore Mining Co., Ltd.; director Eichleay Corporation, (Pittsburgh), S.P. Kinney Engineers, Incorporated. Member American Iron and Steel Inst., Am. Inst. Mining and Metall. Engrs. (chmn. blast furnaces, coke oven and raw material sect. 1952), Eastern States Blast Furnace and Coke Assn., Am. Ordnance Assn., C. of C., Assn. Masonic Vets, Western Pa., Theta Delta Chi. Mason (32 deg., Shriner). Clubs: St. Clair Country, Pittsburgh Athletic Association, Duquesne (Pitts.). Home: Pittsburgh PA Died Jan. 27, 1968; buried Elmwood Cemetery, Birmingham AL

MILLER, EDGAR CALVIN LEROY, bacteriologist; b. Pelham, Mass., Aug. 24, 1867; s. Lorenzo Wallace and Helen Elizabeth (Rice) M.; grad. Neb. State Normal Sch., 1887; studied Oberlin Coll., 1888-90; M.D., U. of Mich., 1894; m. Lillian Belle Carpenter, Sept. 17, 1890; children—Leland Hubert, Pyari Frances Geraldine, Louis Charles, Gwendolyn Lucile. Instr., U. of Mich., 1894-95; med. missionary, India, 1895-1900; mem. research staff, Parke, Davis &Co., Detroit, Mich., 1900-10; prof. bacteriology, Medical College Va., 1911-29, directing librarian since 1930, ret. Mem. A.M.A., A.A.A.S., Soc. Chemical Industry (London), Am. Assn. Immunologists, Med. Soc. of Va., Richmond Acad. Medicine, Va. Acad. Science (sec.-treas. since 1923), fellow Chem. Soc. (London). Collaborator Am. Illustrated Med. Dictionary since 1922. Home: 2915 Seminary Av., Richmond VA‡

MILLER, EDWARD GODFREY, JR., lawyer; born San Juan, P.R., Sept. 27, 1911; s. Edward Godfrey and Nora (Elizardi) M.; grad. St. Paul's Sch., Concord, N.H., 1929; A.B., Yale, 1933; LL.B., Harvard, 1936; m. Carol H. Prichitt, Feb. 3, 1939 (div. 1967); children—Rebecca P., Jane G. Admitted to N.Y. bar, 1938; asso. lawyer Sullivan & Cromwell, N.Y.C., 1936-41, partner, 1947-49, 53-58; partner Lazard Freres & Co., N.Y.C., 1958-60; Paul, Weiss, Rifkind, Wharton & Garrison, 1960-64; counsel Curtis, Mallet-Prevost, Colt & Mosle, 1967-68; asst. chief fgn. funds control div. Dept. State, Washington, 1941-42; spl. asst. U.S. ambassador, Rio de Janeiro, 1942-43, spl. asst. under-sec. state, 1944-46, asst. sec. state, 1949-52. Member board of directors Pan-Am. Capital Corp. Mem. U.S. del. UN Conf., Bretton Woods, 1944, San Francisco, 1945; spl. ambassador, inauguration presidents of Costa Rica, 1949, Uruguay, 1951, Panama, 1952; prin. adviser U.S. delegation 4th meeting Ministers Fgn. Affairs, Washington, 1951; chief U.S. del. Inter-Am. Econ. Confs., 1951-52; chmn. Mayor's Com. on Puerto Rican Affairs, N.Y.C., 1954-56. Decorated Order of Southern Cross (Brazil); Great Cross of Boyaca, Great Cross of San Carlos (Colombia); Order of Ruben Dario (Nicaragua); Order of Honor and Merit (Haiti). Mem. Council Fgn. Relations N.Y. Democrat. Episcopalian. Clubs: Knickerbocker, River, India House (N.Y.C.); Metropolitan (Washington). Home: New York City NY Died Apr. 1968.

MILLER, EMMA GUFFEY, Dem. nat. committeewoman; b. Guffey Station, Westmoreland Co., Pa.; d. John and Barbaretta (Hough) G.; A.B., Bryn Mawr, 1899; m. Carroll Miller, Oct. 28, 1902; children—William Gardner III, John Guffey, Carroll Jr., Joseph F. Guffey. Woman suffrage worker 1910-20; mem. Consumers League 1910-14; Parent Teachers 1915-18. League of Women Voters 1921-25. Delegate National Democratic Conventions, 1924, 28, 32, 36, 40, 44, 48, 52, 56, 60, 64, mem. conv. platform com., 1944, 48, 52, 56, 60, 64. Democratic nat. committeewoman, 1932-70; first woman to receive vote for nomination for Pres. in nat. conv. 1924; seconded nomination of Gov. Smith 1924, 1928; seconded Pres. Roosevelt 1932, 1936; mem. mayor's com. Pittsburgh, George Washington Bicentennial 1932; mem. nat. advisory bd. Womens Orgn. Nat. Prohibition Reform 1929-33; chairman bd. trustees State College, Slippery Rock, Pa., 1956-70, also Assn. of Pa. Teachers colls. 1937-39; member planning committee Japan International Christian University Foundation, 1958; member Pennsylvania State Council of Edn. and Pa. State Welfare Com., 1935-39; chmn. Women's Activities, Pa. Fed. Constitution Commemoration, 1937-38; vice chmn. Pa. 300th Anniversary Com. 1938-39; chmn. advisory bd. Pa. Nat. Youth Administrn. 1935-43; presidential elector, 1940, 44, 60, 64, 68. Mem. Gov's Def. Com. Pa., 1949; mem. Nat. Woman's Party Equal Rights Amendment, chmn., 1961-65, life pres., 1965-70. Named Distinguished Dau. of Pa., 1955; recip. citation Am. Jewish Congress, 1960. Mem. Am. Jewish Congress (hon. Eleanor Roosevelt chpt.), Pi Delta Phi (asso.). Home: Washington DC Died Feb. 23, 1970; buried Hollywood Cemetery, Richmond VA

MILLER, ERNEST IVAN, librarian; b. Harvard, Neb., Feb. 27, 1907; s. John P. and Alice (Keller) M.; A.B., Elmhurst Coll., 1931, L.L.D., 1962; B.S., U. Ill., 1932; M.A., U. Tenn., 1939; m. Elinor Ross, Sept. 27, 1936; children—David L., Margaret R. Serials asst. U. Neb. Library, 1933-34; asst. librarian TVA Tech. Library, 1934-41; tech. librarian Detroit Pub. Library, 1941-47; asst. librarian Cin. Pub. Library, 1947-53, dir., 1955-72. Mem. A.L.A., Mich (past pres.), Ohio (past pres.) library assns., Engring. Soc. Cin., Cincinnatus Assn. Clubs: Rotary, Literary (Cin.). Home: Cincinnati OH Died July 1972.

MILLER, GALEN, mfg. exec.; b. Shanesville, O., Apr. 25, 1895; s. Aaron T. and Mary Catherine (Schott) M.; student Oberlin Coll., 1913-16; B.A., Ohio State U., 1917; m. Ida Marjorie Collom, Jan. 15, 1930 (dec. Jan. 1953); 1 dau., Joan (Mrs. James T. Lynn); m. 2d, Mary Elizabeth May, Dec. 7, 1962. Salesman, sales mgr. Hayden, Miller and Co., 1917-35, partner, 1936-63, sec., dir. Towmotor Corp., 1943-46, treas., 1946-59, v.p., 1951-59, exec. v.p., 1959-61, pres., 1961-65, vice chmn., from 1965, also chief executive officer; dir. S.K. Wellman Company, Anchor Hocking Glass Corporation. Pres. Cleve. Welfare Fedn., 1953-56, United Appeal, from 1962; trustee Cleve. Community Fund, Blind Soc. of Cleve., Health Fund Cleve. Trustee Fenn Coll. Served with U.S. Army, World War I. Clubs: Union, Mayfield Country, Tavern (Cleve.). Home: Shaker Heights OH

MILLER, GEORGE ABRAM, mathematician; b. Lynnville, Pa., July 31, 1863; s. Nathan and Mary Miller (Sittler) M.; A.B., Muhlenberg (Pa.) Coll., 1887, A.M., 1890; Ph.D., Cumberland U., 1893; student Univs. of Leipzig and Paris, 1895-97; m. Cassandra Boggs, Dec. 23, 1909. Prin. schs., Greeley, Kan. 1887-88; prof. mathematics, Eureka (Ill.) College 1888-93; instr. mathematics, U. Mich., 1893-95 Cornell, 1897-1901; asst. prof. mathematics Stanford 1901-02, asso. prof., 1902-06; asso. prof. mathematics U. Ill., 1906-07, prof., 1907-31 when retired; prof. mathematics U. Chicago summer 1912, U. Calif., summer 1913. Co-editor Am. Year Book School Science and Mathematics, and Ency. des Sciences Mathematiques. Winner internat., math. prize, 1900 Fellow Am. Acad. Arts and Sciences, A.A.A.S. (sec Sect. A., 1907-12, chmn., 1921-22; chmn. math sub-com. on com. of 100 on sci. research); mem. Nat Acad. Sciences, Math. Assn. Am. (v.p., 1916, pres.

1921), Am. Math. Soc. (v.p. 1907-08), London Math. Soc., Deutsche Mathematiker Verein; corr. mem. Spanish Mathematic Soc.; hon. mem. Indian Mathematic Soc. Author: Determinants, 1892; Mathematical Monographs (co-author), 1911; Theory and Applications of Groups of Finite Order, 1916, rev. ed., 1938; Historical Introduction to the Mathematical Literature, 1916; College Teaching, 1919; Collected Works (Vol. I), 1935, (Vol. II), 1938; also articles on the theory of groups and the history of mathematics in Am. and fgn. jours. Home: 1203 W. Illinois St., Urbana IL*‡

MILLER, GEORGE HENRY, clergyman; b. Dundee, Mich., May 12, 1871; s. Clark Nelson and Elizabeth Caroline (Ashley) M.; A.B., Adrian (Mich.) Coll., 1900; student U. of Chicago 1 term, D.D., Western Md. Coll., Westminster, Md., 1915; m. Stella May Wolcott, of St. Johns, Mich., Nov. 29, 1900. Ordained M.P. ministry, 1900; pastor 1st Ch., Steubenville, O., 1900-16; 1st sec. Bd. Edn. M.P. Ch., May 1916-Aug. 1924; pastor 1st M.P. Ch., Cambridge, O., since Aug. 1924. Trustee Adrian Coll. Mem. Sigma Alpha Epsilon. Home: Cambridge OH‡

MILLER, GEORGE STEWART, educator and banker; born Lawrence, Mass., May 12, 1884; s. James Bruce and Katherine (Stewart) M.; student Phillips Andover Acad., 1901-02; A.B., Tufts Univ., 1906, A.M., 1907, Litt.D., from same, 1941; m. Marion Folsom Stratton, Aug. 14, 1913; children—Ruth Stratton (Mrs. Chester A. Foss), Doris Folsom (Mrs. Ralph A. Slater). Teacher high sch., Concord, Mass., 1907-09; asst. prin. Monson Acad., 1909-12; head of history dept. high sch., Medford, Mass., 1912-16; asst. to pres. Tufts Univ., 1916-37, acting pres., 1937-38, asst. to pres., 1938-39, v.p. and dean faculty of arts and scis., 1939-51, dean adminstrn., 1951-56, emeritus dean, 1956-71; pres., dir. Hillside Cambridge Coop. Bank; member corporation Medford Savings Bank. Cons. Lincoln Filene Center for Citizenship and Pub. Affairs, Tufts U. Member School Com., Medford, Mass., 1920-27, chmn. of com., 1924-27; chmn. nursing sch. adv. bd. Meml. Hosp., Medford. Del. to Rep. Nat. Conv., Chicago, 1932. Trustee Monson Academy; member board of govs. Huntington School, Mass.; trustee, chmn. exec. com. Civic Edn. Found. Mem. nat. advisory com. Armed Forces Inst., 1942-46. Mem. Tufts Univ. Alumni Assn. (president 1954-60), N.E. Assn. Colls. and Secondary Schs., (sec.-treas. 1930-47, pres., 1947-48), Alpha Tau Omega, Phi Beta Kappa. Republican. Conglist. Mason Clubs: Republican of Massachusetts, Mass. Schoolmasters (pres. 1947-48). Home: West Medford MA Died June 22, 1971; buried Hudson MA

MILLER, GILBERT HERON, theatrical producer; b. N.Y.C., July 3, 1884; s. Henry and Helene (Stoepel) M.; student De La Salle Inst., New York, 1894-96, Freres des Ecoles Chretiennes-Passy, Paris, 1896-98, Muller-Gelenick Realschule, Dresden, 1898-99, Bedford County Sch., Bedford, England, 1899-1900; m. Kathryn King Bache, July 16, 1927. Theatre mgr. since 1907, producer since 1916; v.p. Charles Frohman, Inc., 1921-32; lessee Henry Miller's Theatre, N.Y. City, since 1926. St. James Theatre, London, since 1921, Lyric Theatre, London, England, since 1919; producer numerous successful plays, most recent among them: Edward, My Son, 1948; The Cocktail Party, 1950; Gigi, 1951; Caesar and Cleopatra and Antony and Cleopatra, 1951; and also Witness for the Prosecution, 1954; The Reluctant Debutante, The Sleeping Prince, 1956; Under Milkwood, 1957; Rope Dancers, 1957; Patate, 1958; The Golden Fleecing, 1959; The Caretaker, 1961; The White House, 1964; Diamond Orchid, 1965. First lieutenant in A.E.F., Intelligence Dept., 1918-19. Served as aviation technician U.S.S. Shangri-La, Sept. 1944-Feb. 1945. Decorated Ofcr. Legion of Honor (French). Catholic. Clubs: Players (N.Y.C.); Bucks (London); Travellers (Paris). Home: New York City NY Died Jan. 1969.

MILLER, HARLAN, writer, columnist; s. Morris and Leah (Patton) M.; student engring. Ia. State Coll., Drake U. Coll. Law; m. Doris Green, Mar. 27, 1929; children—Doris, Harlan, Quentin. Writer Des Moines Register, United Press (bur. chief), N.Y. Eve. Post, Miami (Fla.) Daily News, N.Y. Herald Tribune; columnist Des Moines Register, Des Moines, 1927-37, and from 1940; columnist Washington Post and Pubs. Syndicate, 1937-40; originator The Man Next Door in Better Homes and Gardens, 1935-49, author monthly page There's a Man in the House, Ladies Home Jour., from 1949. Vol. overseas duty with War Dept., 1917, with A.S., AEF, 1917-19; mem. Hoover Mission, Warsaw and Danzig, 1919; active duty as capt., liaison officer, 1942; maj., 1943; overseas, 1943-45; lt. col., 1943; campaigns: Normandy, France, Germany, liberation of Paris. Recipient citation for meritorious and conspicuous services AEF by Gen. Pershing; decorated Order White Eagle, Polish Govt. Mem. Fgn. Press Assn., Tennis Umpires Assn. Forest Hills, Sigma Delta Chi. Clubs: Des Moines, Embassy (Des Moines, Ia.); Okoboji (Ia.) Yacht; Authors, Overseas Writers, Nat. Press (Washington); Churchill (London). Contbr. to nat. mags.; authors articles on S.Am. and Europe airplane trips around S.Am. 1930, 50), series on Russia, 1936, 56, also series on Europe, Africa, Asia, 1948, 50, 51, 54, 58, 61. Author: (book) There's a Man in the House, 1955. Office: Des Moines IA Died Aug. 7, 1968; buried Des Moines IA

MILLER, HARRY (MCKINLEY), utility exec.; b. Gallia, O., May 8, 1903; s. Arthur and Amelia (Miller) M.; student Ohio Wesleyan 1921-24; LL.B., Ohio State U., 1927; m. Ernestine Biddle, June 14, 1928; children—Donn B., Arthur, Marjorie. Admitted to O. bar, 1927, practiced law, in Gallipolis, 1927-38; exec. sec. Gov. of Ohio, 1939-40; mem. Pub. Utilities Commn. Ohio, 1940-51, chmn., 1947-49; v.p. Columbus & So. Ohio Electric Co., Columbus, 1951-52, executive vice pres., 1952-56, pres., board chmn., 1956-66, chmn., 1966-69; dir. Ohio Valley Bank Co., Galipolis, Huntington Nat. Bank Co., Buckeye Fed. Savs. & Loan Co. Chmn. bd. Battelle Meml. Institute. Mem. Nat. Assn. R.R. and Utilities Commrs. (pres. 1950), Phi Delta Phi, Phi Kappa Psi, Sigma Chi. Home: Columbus OH Died Feb. 9, 1969.

MILLER, HERBERT ADOLPHUS, sociologist; b. Tuftonboro, N.H., June 5, 1875; s. William Magnus and Ellen (Thompson) M.; A.B., Dartmouth, 1899, A.M., 1902; Ph.D., Harvard, 1905; studied U. of Chicago, 1911; m. Elizabeth Northway Cravath, of Nashville, Aug. 22, 1903; children—Gustova C., Maurice C. Instr. Latin and Greek, Fisk U., 1899-1902; asst. prof. philosophy and sociology, Olivet (Mich.) Coll., 1905-07, prof., 1907-14; prof. sociology, Oberlin Coll., 1914-25, U. of Calif., summer 1922; prof. sociology, Ohio State U., 1924-31, Summer Sch., Northwestern Univ., 1932; lecturer on social economy, Bryn Mawr College since 1933; gave courses at Yenching U., Peiping, China, and lectured at univs. of China, India, Syria, 1929-30. Mem. bd. dirs. Internat. Inst. of Phila. (pres.), National Institute for Immigrant Welfare. Made survey of immigrant conditions and school facilities for immigrants, Cleveland, Ohio, for Russell Sage Foundation, 1915; chief of div. on immigrant heritages Carnegie Corpn. Organizer and dir. Mid. European Union. Chmn. Ohio Com. on Penal Conditions. Mem. Am. Sociol. Soc. (com. on internat. relations), A.A.A.S., Phi Beta Kappa (hon.). Conglist. Club: Contemporary (Phila.). Author: The School and the Immigrant, 1916; Old World Traits Transplanted (joint author), 1921; Races, Nations and Classes, 1924; The Beginnings of Tomorrow, 1933; also articles on social and national questions. Home: 229 Roberts Rd., Bryn Mawr PA‡

MILLER, IRVING ELGAR, psychologist; b. W. Springfield, Pa., Sept. 15, 1869; s. Henry and Sarah (Elgar) M.; A.B., U. of Rochester, 1894 (valedictorian), A.M., 1888; fellow U. of Chicago, 1900-1, 1903-4, A.M., 1903, Ph.D., 1904; m. Lily Rose Fuenfstueck, Wausau, Wis., Nov. 28, 1907. Prin. Union Sch., Ontario, N.Y., 1894-5; prof. mathematics, Colby Acad., N.H., 1895-9; asst. prof. philosophy and edn., Ill. Coll., Jacksonville, 1901-2; prof. psychology and pedagogy, 1904-9, asst. in supervision of practice teaching, 1906-9, State Normal Sch., Milwaukee; prof. science of edn. and dean of graduate and professional work, The State Teachers' College of Colorado, Greeley, 1909-14; assistant professor of philosophy and education, University of Rochester, since 1914. Member N.E.A., National Society Scientific Study of Edn., Phi Beta Kappa. Baptist. Author: The Significance of the Mathematical Element in Plato's Philosophy, 1904; The Psychology of Thinking, 1909; also chapter Psychology in the High School Curriculum," in Johnston's High School Education," 1912. Address: University of Rochester NY‡

MILLER, JAMES DECATUR, JR., educator; b. Liberty Hill, Tex., Jan. 9, 1897; s. James Decatur and Lula Della (McFarlin) M.; A.B., Austin Coll. (History scholarship 1920, All-round award 1921), 1921, M.A., 1922, Litt.D., 1946; grad. student U. Tex.; m. Allene Sanders, June 1, 1925; children—Allene, Barbara Annelle. Faculty Tex. Mil. Inst., 1926, bd. dirs., 1927-52, supt., 1947; asst. to president Westminister Schools, Atlanta; retired president Howey Acad., Howey-in-the Hills, Fla.; now counselor Bexar County Schs., San Antonio. Ret. baseball commr. Little League. Alamo Heights Recreational Council. Recipient Austin Coll. Meritorious Service award and Hall of Fame. Mem. Tex., San Antonio (pres. 1951) hist. socs., So. Assn. Ind. Schs (pres. 1949), Tex. Assn. Independent Schs. (pres. 1951-53), Nat. Assn. Secondary Sch. Prins., American Personnel and Guidance Association, Georgia, South Tex. guidance associations, Amateur Athletic Union (sec.-treas. Tex. 1947—), Phi Delta Kappa. Methodist (pres. San Antonio Bd. Missions 1951). Mason (Shriner). Home: San Antonio TX Died Mar. 10, 1969.

MILLER, JAMES KENNETH, clergyman; b. Venetia, Pa., Nov. 23, 1904; s. James Hunter (D.D.) and Armitta Dales (Buck) M.; A.B., Muskingum Coll., New Concord, O., 1926; Th.B., Pittsburgh Theol. Sem., 1929; A.M., Columbia Univ., 1942; D.D., Muskingum Coll., 1946; m. Margaret Campbell, Apr. 18, 1933; children—Marjorie Lois, Marion Campbell, Doris Eleanor. Ordained to ministry of United Presbyterian Ch., 1929; pastor, Boston, Pa., 1929-37, Garden City, N.Y., 1937-67; asso. pastor Webster Groves (Mo.) Presbyn. Ch., from 1967; stated clk. United Presbyn. Synod of N.Y., 1942-58. Director Pittsburgh Xenia Theol. Sem., Pittsburgh, Pa., pres. bd., 1946; United Presbyn. Ch. prin. del. to Constituting Assembly, World Council of Chs., Amsterdam, 1948, to 2d Assembly, Evanston, Ill., 1954, mem. exec. com. U.S.A. mem. chs., 1948-61; mem. United Presbyn. World Service Com., 1944-58; mem. Com. World Relief and Emergency Service, United Presbyn. Ch. U.S.A.; mem. Commn. on Ecumenical Mission and Relations, United Presbyn. Ch. 1958-63; b. mgrs. Dept. of Church World Service, vice chmn., 1955-62; chmn. personnel, div. Overseas ministries, 1965-67; mem. World Presbyn. Alliance, N. Am. area, from 1959. Moderator Synod of N.Y., United Presbyn. Ch. 1959. Home: Glendale MO Died Sept. 26, 1971.

MILLER, JOHN ANTHONY, coll. prof.; b. Greensburg, Ind., Dec. 16, 1859; s. Bruno Brunen and Katherine (Arnold) M.; A.B., Indiana U., 1890, LL.D., 1928; A.M., Stanford U., 1893; Ph.D., U. of Chicago, 1899; m. Mary Catharine Goodwine, Dec. 24, 1880; children—Max B., Harry L.; m. 2d, Frances Morgan Swain, June 23, 1932. Supt. schs., Rockville, Ind., 1890-91; instr. mathematics, 1891-93, asst. prof., 1893-94, Stanford; prof. mathematics, 1894-95, mechanics and astronomy, 1895-1906, Ind. U.; prof. astronomy, and dir. Sproul Obs., Swarthmore Coll., 1906-32, v.p. Swarthmore College, 1914-29, prof. of astronomy emeritus since 1932. Chief of expedition sent by Indiana Univ. to Spain, 1905, to observe total eclipse of the sun, and of expdn. sent by Sproul Obs. to observe total eclipse of sun, 1918, and to Mexico, 1923, by Swarthmore Coll. to observe total eclipse of sun, to New Haven, Conn., 1925, to Sumatra, 1926, 29, to Vermont, 1932; technicolor dir. expdn. by Hayden Planetarium to Peru, 1937. Fellow Am. Acad. Arts and Sciences, A.A.A.S., Indiana Academy Science, Royal Astron. Soc.; mem. Am. Math. Soc., Am. Astron. Soc., Am. Philos. Soc. (ex-sec.), Sigma Xi, Phi Beta Kappa. Republican. Friend. Author: Trigonometry for Beginners, 1896; Analytic Mechanics, 1915 (revised 1935). Contbr. to math. and astron. publs. Home: Wallingford PA*‡

MILLER, JULIAN CREIGHTON, horticulturist; b. Lexington, S.C., Nov. 29, 1895; s. Simeon Jeremiah and Plumie Elizabeth (Shull) M.; B.S., Clemson Coll. 1921, honorary doctor's degree, 1961; M.S., Cornell University, 1926, Ph.D., 1928; m. Caroline Stone Leichliter, Dec. 26, 1923; children—Rodman B., Julian Creighton. Instr. horticulture, N.C. State Coll., 1921-23; county agrl. agt., S.C., 1923-25; asst., Cornell U., 1925-28; asso. prof. horticulture and research, Okla. Agr. and Mech. Coll., 1928-29; prof. horticulture and head dept., La. State U. 1929-71, emeritus, 1971—; developing technics for breeding vegetable crops. Agr. advisor to P.R. and Central Am.; plant exploration for Ipomea species, economic medicinal plants in West Indies in cooperation with U.S. Dept. Agr., 1953; U.S. del. to Internat. Hort. Congress, 1955. Served with U.S. Navy, 1917-19, seaman, line officer as ensign and lt. (j.g.); developed process for dehydrating sweet potatoes for Army, World War II. Named Progressive Farmer's Man of Year 1940 for La., Man of South, 1947; awarded Wilder Medal for breeding and introdn. of Klonmore strawberry, also plaques for services rendered hort. field; named Vegetable Man of the Year, Vegetable Growers Association America; recipient Presdl. commendation, 1971. La. State U. Alumni Distinguished Faculty fellow, 1967. Fellow A.A.A.S., Am. Hort. Soc. (pres. 1942, chmn. So.; mem. Am. Genetic Assn., Potato Assn. Am. (pres. 1938), Assn. So. Agr. Workers, So. Assn. Sci. and Industry, Am. Inst. Biol. Scis., La. Farm Bur. Fedn. (hon. life mem.), So. Seedsmen's Assn. (hon. life mem.). Phi Kappa Phi (provincal sec. so. sect. 1935-52; nat. regent), Sigma Xi, Omicron Delta Kappa, Alpha Gamma Rho, Alpha Gamma Delta, Alpha Zeta (Centennial hon. mem.). Democrat. Presbyn. (ruling elder). Mason. Kiwanian. Author numerous expt. sta. bulls., spl. feature articles on research; contbr. to sci. jours. Home: Baton Rouge LA Died Apr. 13, 1971; buried Roselawn Meml. Park, Baton Rouge LA

MILLER, JUSTIN, association executive, government official; born in Crescent City, California, Nov. 17, 1888; son Robert Willis and Matilda (Morrison) M.; A.B., Stanford, 1911, J.D., 1914; LL.B., Univ. of Montana, 1913, LL.D., 1941; D.C.L., Yale, 1934; LL.D., Franklin and Marshall College, 1945, Boston U., U. Ariz., 1948, Ithaca Coll., 1951; married May Merrill, June 20, 1915;children—Jean Marian (Mrs. Edwin Ball Abbott), Merrill Justin. Admitted to bar Mont., 1911, Calif. 1913, Minn., 1924, N.C., 1931, Supreme Court of U.S., 1934, United States Court of Appeals for D.C., 1946. Assistant in economics, 1910, in history, 1911, Stanford; asst. instr. in law, U. of Montana, 1912-13; instr. in English, Stanford, 1913-14; clk. law office of McCutcheon, Olney & Willard, San Francisco, 1914; engaged in general practice of law in Hanford, Fresno and San Francisco, Calif., 1914-21; district atty. Kings County, Calif., 1915-18; mem. Harris & Harris, Fresno, 1919; atty. and exec. officer Calif. State Commn. of Immigration and Housing, 1919-21; lecturer U. of Calif., summer 1921; prof. law, U. of Ore., 1921-23, Univ. of Minn., 1923-26; sec. Minn. Crime Commn., 1926; mem. Calif. Crime Commn., 1927-30; editor in chief Ore. Law Rev., 1921-23; asso. editor Minn. Law Rev., 1923-26; prof. law Stanford U., summer, 1926; prof. law, U. of Calif., 1926-27; dean of the Sch. of Law, U. of Southern Calif., 1927-30; visiting prof. of law, Columbia Univ., summer 1929; dean Sch. of Law, Duke University, 1930-35; spl. asst. to atty. gen. of U.S., 1934-36; chmn. atty. gen.'s Advisory Com. on Crime, 1935-37; mem. U.S. Board of Tax Appeals, 1937; asso. justice U.S. Court of Appeals, Washington, 1937-45; chmn. Salary Stabilization Bd., 1951-52. Pres. Assn. Broadcasters, 1945-51; chmn. bd. and gen. counsel Nat. Assn. Radio and Television Broadcasters since 1951. President Southern Calif. Acad. Criminology, 1929; pres. Calif. Conf. Social Work, 1929-30; pres. N.C. Conf. of Social Service, 1933-34; vice chmn. Govt. Div. of Community Chest, Washington, D.C., 1936-37; mem. bd. dirs. Nat. Probation Assn., 1929-30, v.p., 1930-36; chmn. com. on cooperation with law schs. of Nat. Assn. Legal Aid Orgns., 1930; mem. Human Betterment Foundation (v.p. 1930-32); hon. mem. Internat. Assn. of Chiefs of Police; chmn. com. on survey of criminal law and procedure, Assn. of Am. Law Schs., 1925-33 (chmn. Round Table on Remedies, 1925, 26, Round Table on Wrongs, 1932). Mem. Pres. Truman's Famine Emergency Com.; mem. U.S. Nat. Commn. for UNESCO (vice chairman and mem. executive com., 1947-50); mem. Nat. Commn. on Youth and Children; chmn. Radio Div. of March of Dimes; mem. exec. com. Fed. Radio Edn. Com.; adv. com. Cal. Legislative Constl. Revision Com.; chmn. bd. Broadcast Music, Inc.; member United States Advisory Commission on Information (chairman radio advisory committee); chairman Attorney General's Adv. Com. on Citizenship; chmn. American Bar Assn. Com. on Cooperation with Laymen. Served as private, Calif. Nat. Guard on Mexican border, 1916. Mem. Am. Bar Assn. (chmn. sect. on criminal law, 1927-37; chmn. com. Pacific coastal fisheries, 1939, Sect. of Internat. Law, mem. pub. relations com., com. on motion pictures, radio broadcasting and comic strips), American Judicature Soc. (vice president 1932), Federal Bar Assn. (pres. 1935-37; chmn. war wk. com. 1942-44), California State Society of Washington, D.C. (pres. 1939, 1940), California State Bar, Los Angeles County Bar Assn. (chmn. com. on Juvenile Courts, 1929-30), North Carolina State Bar Association (chairman com. on uniform state laws, 1932-35), American Soc. Internat. Law, Am. Law Inst. (life). Member Fed. Communications Bar, National Legal Aid Association (member board dirs.), Delta Sigma Rho, Delta Chi, Alpha Pi Zeta, Phi Delta Phi, Order of the Coif, Phi Kappa Phi, Pi Sigma Alpha, Omicron Delta Kappa, Phi Beta Kappa (past chmn. western div.), Pi Gamma Mu, Sigma Nu Phi. Democrat. Episcopalian. Author: Miller on Criminal Law, 1934. Contbr. to legal and other periodicals. Home: Los Angeles CA Died Jan. 17, 1973.

MILLER, KNOX EMERSON, U.S. Pub. Health Service; b. Norton, Kan., Nov. 26, 1886; s. Joseph Medford and Martha Washington (Whiteman) M.; A.B., William Jewell Coll., Liberty, Mo., 1908; M.D., Johns Hopkins, 1912; m. Noxie Bliss Miller, Oct. 29, 1915; children—Martha Vincent (Mrs. Pope A. Laurence), Betty Bow (Mrs. Richard O. Madson). Knox Emerson. Staff mem. Va. State Health Dept., 1912-14; commd. asst. surgeon U.S.P.H.S., 1914, passed asst. surgeon, 1918, surgeon, 1922, senior surgeon, 1934, medical director, 1940; research in rural health adminstrn., 1917-19; spl. consultant and dir. rural health adminstrn. N.C. State Dept. of Health, 1919-23; same La. State Dept. of Health, 1923-27; exec. officer Marine Hosp., N.Y., 1927-28; med. officer in charge Marine Hosp., Evansville, Ind., 1928-31; dir. rural health, Tex. State Dept. of Health, 1931-34; health consultant to states of Gulf region and Pacific Southwest, 1934-35, to states of Great Lakes region, 1935-36; asst. to asst. surgeon gen. in charge Domestic Quarantine Div., 1936-38; dir. Med. Research and Advisory Div., Federal Trade Commn., 1938-40; liason officer, 8th Service Command Headquarters, U.S. Army, Dallas, 1940-46; dist. dir. 9th Dist., U.S.P.H.S., Dallas, 1941-49, ret.; asst. state health officer of Fla. from 1949; dir. Chicago-Cook County Health Survey. Member mission to study strategic bombing in Japan. Diplomate, Am. Bd. Preventive Medicine and Pub. Health. Fellow A.M.A., Am. Pub. Health Assn.; mem. Assn. Mil. Surgeons (life), A.A.A.S., Asociacion Nacional de Venereolgia (Mexico), Tex. Acad. Sci., Sci. Soc., San Antonio, U.S.-Mexico Border Pub. Health Assn., Alpha Omega Alpha, Phi Chi, Lambda Chi Alpha, Pi Gamma Mu, Celsus Soc., Ho Din of Southwestern Medical Foundation. Clubs: Cosmos (Washington, D.C.). Contbr. professional articles to med. and pub. health mags. Home: Jacksonville FL Died May 1969.

MILLER, LEO L., govt. official; b. Adams County, Ind., Oct. 6, 1901; s. John B. and Inez (Andrews) M.; educated high school; m. Mildred L. Davison, May 28, 1921; children—Mrs. Vivian Maxine Graff, Richard. Clerk, Ft. Wayne Rolling Mills, 1922-25; traffic mgr. McDougall Co., Frankfort, Ind., 1925-32; agent, People's Life Ins. Co., Indianapolis, Ind., 1932-33; clerk, Governor's Commn. for Unemployment Relief, Indianapolis, Ind., 1933-35; accountant in charge, U.S. Treasury Dept., Indianapolis, 1935-39; budget officer, Federal Security Agency, Washington, 1939-43, exec. asst. to adminstr., 1943-54; chief fiscal analysis office, budget div. Comptroller of Army 1954-58; exec. officer Food and Drug Adminstrn., Dept. Health, Edn., and Welfare, 1958-61, asst. commissioner, from 1961. Mem. Am. Acad. Polit. Sci. Presbyterian. Mason. Home: Washington DC Died June 23, 1969

MILLER, LESLIE ANDREW, found. exec.; b. Junction City, Kan., Jan. 29, 1886; s. Andrew Early and Anna Belle (Orr) M.; LL.D., Wyo. U., 1951; m. Margaret May Morgan, Mar. 31, 1909; children—Katherine Mabee, John Selden. Mem. Wyo. Legislature, 1911-12, 23-24, 29-31, 45-49; collector internal revenue, Wyo., 1919-21; gov. Wyo., 1933-38. Chmn. natural resources task force Hoover Commn., 1947-48, vice chmn. task force on water resources and power, 1953-54. Dir. Resources for Future, Inc. (Ford Found. affiliate), Jackson Hole Preserve, Inc. (Rockefeller conservation orgn.), Grand Teton Lodge Co. (Rockefeller resort operations). Served with USMC, 1918-19. Author articles on natural resources. Home: Cheyenne WY Died Oct. 1970.

MILLER, LOYE HOLMES, biology; b. Minden, La., Oct. 13, 1874; s. George and Cora (Holmes) M.; B.S., U. of Calif., 1898, M.S., 1903, Ph.D., 1912; m. Anne Lucia Holmes, Aug. 1, 1901; children—Alden Holmes, Holmes Odell. Instr. in natural science, Oahu Coll., Hononlulu, T.H., 1900-03; instr. biology, State Normal Sch., Los Angeles, Calif., 1904-18; asst. prof. biology, U. of Calif., 1919-20, asso. prof., 1920-23, prof., 1923-43 (emeritus). Served as expert with U.S. Bur. of Fisheries, U.S. Dept. Agr. Fellow Am. Assn. for Advancement of Science Am. Ornithol. Union; mem. Am. Soc. Naturalists, Cooper Ornithol. Club (pres. bd. govs.), Sigma Xi, Phi Beta Kappa, Thanic Shield (U. of Calif.). Conglist. Contbr. 100 papers on fossil and recent vertebrates of Pacific Coast to geol. publs. U. of Calif., publs. Carnegie Inst., Science, Jour. Mammalogy, etc. Home: Los Angeles CA Died Apr. 6, 1970.

MILLER, LUTHER DECK, army officer; b. Pennsylvania, June 14, 1890; B.D., Chicago Theol. Sem., 1917; grad. Chaplains Sch., 1922. Commd. 1st lt., chaplain, U.S. Army, 1918, and advanced through the grades to maj. gen., 1945; chief of chaplains, U.S. Army. Elected canon and mem. Presbytery of Washington Cathedral. Home: Washington DC Died Apr. 27, 1972.

MILLER, MAX, author; b. Traverse City, Mich., Feb. 9, 1899; s. William Wesley and Bessie (Adams) M.; B.A., U. Wash., 1923; m. Margaret Ripley, Aug. 23, 1927. Began as reporter on Everett (Wash.) News. Served in U.S. Navy, 1917-18. Mem. Sigma Alpha Epsilon. Author: I Cover the Waterfront, 1932; He Went Away for a While, 1933; The Beginning of a Mortal, 1933; The Second House from the Corner, 1934; The Man on the Barge, 1935; The Great Trek, 1935; Fog and Men on Bering Sea, 1936; For the Sake of Shadows, 1936; Mexico Around Me, 1937; A Stranger Came to Port, 1938; Harbor of the Sun, 1940; Reno, 1941; It Must be the Climate, 1941; Land Where Time Stands Still, 1943; Daybreak for Our Carrier, 1944; The Far Shore, 1945; It's Tomorrow Out Here, 1945; The Lull, 1946; The Town With the Funny Name, 1948; No Matter What Happens, 1949; I'm Sure We've Met Before, 1951; The Cruise of the Cow, 1952; Always the Mediterranean, 1952; Speak to the Earth, 1955; Shinny on Your Own Side, 1958; And Bring All Your Folks, 1959; Holladay Street, 1962; also mag. articles. Served in USNR, 1942-45; comdr. Res.; recalled to active duty, 1950-53. Home: La Jolla CA

MILLER, MERRITT FINLEY, univ. prof.; b. Grove City, O., July 7, 1875; s. Edward and Eliza (Demorest) M.; student Ohio Wesleyan U., 1895-96; B.S.A., Ohio State U., 1900; M.S.A., Cornell U., 1901; student Univ. of Gottingen, 1910-11, U. of Munich, 1933-34; hon. D.Sc., Kan. State Coll., 1938, Ohio State U., 1939; m. Flora Grace Ernst, Dec. 19, 1914; children—Edward Ernst, Elizabeth Marie, Robert Demorest, Daniel Weber. Soil surveyor U.S. Dept. Agr., 1901-02; instr. in agronomy, Ohio State U., 1902-03, asst. prof., 1903-04; prof. of agronomy, U. of Mo., 1904-14, prof. of soils, 1914-38, asst. dean Coll. of Agr., 1928-38, dean Coll. of Agr., dir. Agrl. Exptl. Sta. 1938-45; dean emeritus since Sept. 1945. Fellow A.A.A.S., Am. Soc. Agronomy; mem. Am. Soc. Soil Science, Internat. Soc. Soil Science, Sigma Xi, Alpha Zeta, Gamma Sigma Delta, Acacia, Farm House. Episcopalian. Mason. Clubs: Kiwanis (Columbia, Mo.); University (U. of Mo.). Author: The Soil and Its Management, 1924; also bulletins of Mo. Agrl. Expt. Sta. Contbr. to tech. jours. Home: 514 High St., Columbia MO‡

MILLER, MILTON, editor; b. N.Y.C., Dec. 10, 1911; s. Henry Nathan and Minnie (Kreiner) M.; student N.Y. U., 1931-36; m. Irma Jean Ganz, Sept. 3, 1939; children—Jeffrey Harold, Lee James. Sports reporter N.Y. American, 1932-36; sports editor Wilkes Barre (Pa.) Record, 1936-43; reporter, deskman, makeup man, asst. sports editor PM, N.Y., 1943-46; night sports editor N.Y. Post, 1946-47; editor Frontpage, 1947-55; editor 338 News, 1955-69; editor Soccer News, 1950-69; soccer editor L.I. Press, also L.I. Star-Jour., 1946-69; mng. editor 888 Leader, 1963-69; editor Leisure Time; pres. SportShelf. Labor press cons. Muscular Dystrophy AA, 1968-69. Mem. Am. Newspaper Guild, The Lambs, Soccer Writers Assn. (pres.), Eastern League Baseball Writers Assn., Nat. Sportscasters and Sportswriters Assn. Clubs: Overseas Press, Silurians. Mem. Sports Lodge (past New Rochelle NY Died Dec. 15, 1969.

MILLER, PLEASANT THOMAS, coll. dean; b. Bell County, Tex., July 24, 1875; s. Thomas Lively and Cynthia Rosa (Ranne) M.; A.B., U. of Tex., 1918, A.M., 1918; student U. of Chicago, 1925-26, 1928-29; m. Lynn Etta Witt, Aug. 15, 1900; children—Robert Bruce, Thomas Harold. Teacher of rural sch., Bell County, Tex., 1896-97, village sch., Killeen, Tex., 1898-99; teacher Temple (Tex.) High Sch., 1900-02, Austin (Tex.) High Sch., 1902-06; teacher of chemistry and physics, Southwest Tex. Teachers Coll., San Marcos, 1906-17; prof. of chemistry, U. of Wyo., 1918-46, dean of liberal arts, 1929-46; dean emeritus, prof. emeritus of chem., since July 1946. Mem. Am. Chem. Soc., A.A.A.S., Colo.-Wyo. Acad. of Sciences, Phi Beta Kappa, Sigma Xi, Phi Kappa Phi. Democrat. Baptist. Mason. Home: 906 Ivinson Av., Laramie WY‡

MILLER, ROBERT FREDERICK, educator; b. nr. Continental, O., Aug. 16, 1929; s. Adolf Frederick and Edna (Kirkendall) M.; B.S., Ohio State U., 1952, M.S., 1957, Ph.D., 1961 Miriam Sherman, Mar. 24, 1951; children—Stephen, Susan,; m. Bruce, Cynthia. Instr. indsl. engring. Ohio State U., Columbus, 1956-61, asst. prof., 1961-65, asso. prof., 1965-72, asst. dean Grad. Sch., 1966-69, research asso. Engring. Exptl. Sta., 1957-61. Served from ensign to lt. USNR, 1952-55. Registered profl. engr., Ohio. Fellow A.A.A.S.; member Inst. Mgmt. Sci., Am. Soc. Engring. Edn., Inst. Indsl. Engring., Texnikoi, Sigma Xi, Sigma Phi Epsilon. Home: Columbus OH Died May 16, 1972.

MILLER, ROBERT ROWLAND, aircraft mfr.; b. Santa Monica, Cal., July 29, 1903; s. Robert M. and Nettie R. (Rowland) M.; A.B., U. Cal. at Berkeley, 1926; m. Mary Mattison, Mar. 21, 1934. Salesman Wm. Cavalier & Co., Los Angeles, 1926-28; customers man Sutro & Co., mem. N.Y. Stock Exchange, Los Angeles, 1928-35, resident partner, 1935-40; exec. v.p. Menasco Mfg. Co., Burbank, 1940-47; asst. to pres. Republic Aviation Corp., N.Y.C., 1948-50; with Northrop Corp., from 1950, assistant to president 1954, adminstrv. v.p., 1955, v.p., gen. mgr., dir. 1955-58, sr. v.p., dir. from 1958; pres. Alexander Hotel Co., Long Beach, from 1945. Mem. Conquistadores Del Cielo. Clubs: Burning Tree; Los Angeles Country, California. Home: Los Angeles CA Died Dec. 19, 1971; buried Woodlawn Cemetery, West Los Angeles CA

MILLER, ROBERT WATT, corporation executive; b. Oakland, Calif., Oct. 10, 1899; s. C. O. G. and Janet (Watt) M.; Yale, 1920; m. Elizabeth Folger, Nov. 15, 1921; children—Robert Folger, Paul Albert, Richard Kendall, Marian Madelaine. With Pacific Lighting Corp. since 1924, exec. v.p., 1929-41, pres., 1940-56, chmn. bd., 1956-70; director American Air Lines, Wells Fargo Bank, Fibreboard Paper Products, Incorporated, and The Caterpillar Tractor Co. Chmn. San Francisco Opera Association. Served from captain to colonel U.S. Army, 1942-45. Decorated Legion of Merit, Star of Solidarity (Italy); Das Grosse Ehrenzeichen (Austria). Clubs: Pacific Union, Bohemian, California (Los Angeles); Recess, Links (N.Y.C.); Burlingame (Cal.) Country. Home: San Francisco CA Died Feb. 19, 1970.

MILLER, SAMUEL HOWARD, univ. dean, clergyman; b. Phila., Feb. 3, 1900; s. Howard and Martha (Edmondson) M.; student Mass. Inst. Tech., 1917-18; B.Th., Colgate U., 1923, D.D., 1953; Litt.D., Clark U., 1959; D.D., Chgo. Theological Sch., 1960, Kalamazoo Coll., 1962; M.A. (honorary), Harvard, 1959; D.Ed., U. Chattanooga, 1961; D.D., Denison U., 1962; LL.D., Franklin, 1964; m. Myra Studley, 1918; children—Myra Theresa (Mrs. Richard Bryan), S. Howard, Albert S., F. William. Ordained to ministry Bapt. Ch., 1923; minister Calvary Bapt. Ch., Belmar, N.J., 1923-28, Arlington, N.J., 1928-30, First Bapt. Ch., Clifton, N.J., 1930-35, Old Cambridge Bapt. Ch., (Mass.), 1935-59; adj. prof. philosophy of religion Andover Newton Thel. Sch., 1951-58; lectr. Harvard Div. Sch., 1954-58, prof. pastoral theology, 1958-59, dean, 1959-68. Sec. commn. on worship and arts Nat. Council Chs. Fellow Acad. Arts and Scis. Author: The Life of the Soul, 1951; The Life of the Church, 1953; Great Realities, 1955; Prayers for Daily Use, 1957; The Dilemma of Modern Belief; Man the Believer, 1968; Religion in a Technical Age, 1968. Home: Cambridge MA Died Mar. 20, 1968; interred Mt. Auburn Cemetery Columbarium.

MILLER, STEPHEN IVAN, educator; b. at Howell, Mich., July 4, 1876; s. Stephen I. and Betsey R. (Hosley) M.; U. of Mich., 1894-97, LL.B., 1896; A.B., Stanford, 1898; LL.D., University of Southern California, 1927; post-grad. work Heidelberg, U. of Mich. and Harvard; m. Florence I. Dunston, of Fowlerville, Mich., Sept. 16, 1896; 1 dau., Charlotte Lahring. With U.S. Forest Service, 1908-10; instr. Stanford, 1912-14; Austin scholar at Harvard, 1914-15; asst. prof. economics, Stanford, 1915-17; spl. investigator Federal Trade Commn., 1917-18; prof. mil. transportation and European economics, S.A.T.C., Washington, 1917-18, also dir. war course in employment management for Pacific Northwest; dean Coll. of Business Administration, U. of Wash., 1918-23; federal counselor for vocational edn. in Pacific Northwest Dist., 1918-22; exec. mgr. Northwest Electrical Service League, 1921-22; nat. ednl. dir. Am. Inst. of Banking, 1923-27; exec. mgr. Nat. Assn. of Credit Men since Nov. 1, 1927; exec. with R. G. Dun & Co. Mem. Alpha Tau Omega, Alpha Kappa Psi, Beta Gamma Sigma, Phi Alpha, Beta Alpha Psi, Panxenia. Republican. Unitarian. Author monographs and articles on industrial topics; also of Standard Economics, Investments of the Am. Inst. of Banking Series. Editor of Resources of the Pacific Northwest." Lecturer. Home: 44 Gramercy Park N. Office: 290 Broadway, New York NY‡

MILLER, WILHELM, teacher; b. Duane, King William Co., Va., Nov. 14, 1869; s. Albert and Olive Coit (Tyler) M.; A.B., U. of Mich., 1892; A.M., Cornell U., 1897, Ph.D., 1899; m. Mary Farrand Rogers (q.v.), June 8, 1899. Asso. Editor Cyclopedia of American Horticulture, 1897-1901; editorial staff of Country Life in America, 1901-12; editor The Garden Mag., 1905-12; asst. prof. landscape horticulture, U. of Ill., 1912-—. Mem. Phi Beta Kappa, Sigma Xi, Psi Upsilon, Cliff Dwellers, Friends of Our Native Landscape, Prairie Club, Michigan Union. Mem. Soc. of Friends. Author: What England Can Teach Us About Gardening; The Illinois Way of Beautifying the Farm; The Prairie Style of Landscape Gardening; compiler of How to Make a Flower Garden, 1904. Home: Urbana IL‡

MILLETT, GEORGE VAN, artist; b. Kansas City, Mo., Apr. 5, 1864; s. Henry Shirley and Elizabeth M. (Ferguson) M.; student Cincinnati Art Sch., 1884-85, Royal Acad. Fine Arts, Munich, Germany, 1886-90; m. Mary Mimms McKee, July 19, 1899; children—Mrs. Elizabeth M. Robinson, George Van, Jr., Mary Catherine, John McKecknie. Specialized in portraits and Missouri interiors with figures; restorer of valuable oil paintings; artist for Kansas City Bd. of Edn. Mem. Kansas City Art Commn. Awarded silver medal, Royal Acad. of Fine Arts, Munich, 1889. Democrat. Methodist. Mason (32 deg., Shriner). Home: 421 W. 61st Terrace. Studio: 520 Studio Bldg., Kansas City MO‡

MILLIKAN, MAX FRANKLIN, economist; b. Chgo., Dec. 12, 1913; s. Robert Andrews and Greta (Blanchard) M.; student Cal. Inst. Tech., 1931-33; B.S. in Physics, Yale, 1935, Ph.D. in Econs., 1941; student Cambridge U., 1935-36; m. Jeanne MacBeath Thomson, July 14, 1937; children—Jane Andrews, Nicholas Thomson, Abigail. Instr. econs. Yale, 1938-41, asst. prof., 1941-42, research asso., 1942-49; on leave, 1942-46, as sr. bus. specialist OPA, 1942, prin. economist War Shipping Adminstrn., 1942-44, asst. dir. div. ship requirements, 1944-46, chief econ. intelligence br. div. research for Europe, Dept. of State, 1946, asst. exec. sec. President's Com. on Fgn. Aid, 1947, cons. Ho. of Reps. Select Com. on Fgn. Aid, 1947; asso. prof. Mass. Inst. Tech., 1949-51, prof. econs., 1952-69, dir. Center Internat. Studies. 1952-69; on leave, 1951-52, as asst. dir. CIA, Washington; member President's Task Force Fgn. Aid, 1961. President World Peace Foundation, 1956-69; trustee Carnegie Endowment for Internat. Peace, 1964-69. Mem. Am. Econ. Assn., Econometric Soc., Royal Econ. Soc., Inst. Math. Statistics, Am. Statis. Assn., Council Fgn. Relations, Inc., American Academy of Arts and Sciences. Clubs: Cosmos (Washington); Yale (N.Y.C.). Editor and co-author: Income Stabilization for a Developing Democracy, 1953. Author: (with W. W. Rostow) A Proposal—Key to a More Effective Foreign Policy, 1957. Editor and co-author: (with D. L. M. Blackmer) The Emerging Nations—Their Growth and United States Policy, 1961. Home: Cambridge MA Died Dec. 14, 1969.

MILLIN, SARAH GERTRUDE, author; b. S. Africa; d. Isiah and Olga Liebson; ed. schools of S. Africa; m. Philip Millin, judge of the Supreme Court of South Africa (dec. 1952). Began writing at age 19. Author: Dark River, 1920; Middleclass, 1921; The Jordans, 1923; God's Stepchildren, 1924; Mary Glenn, 1925; The South Africans, 1927, rev. edit., 1954; Artist in the Family, 1928; Coming of the Lord, 1928; The Fiddler, 1929; Men on a Voyage, 1930; Adam's Rest, 1930; The Sons of Mrs. Aab, 1931; Cecil Rhodes, 1933; General Smuts, 1936; Three Men Die, 1934; What Hath a Man?, 1938; Herr Witch Doctor, 1941; The Dark Gods, 1941; The Night Is Long, 1941; No Longer Mourn, a play based on Mary Glinn produced in London, 1937; General Smutz (radio play), 1943; War Diaries (6 vols.); World Blackout, 1944; The Reeling Earth, 1945; The Pit of the Abyss, 1946; The Sound of the Trumpet, 1947; Fire Out of Heaven, 1947; The Seven Thunders, 1947; King of Bastards, 1949. Home: Johannesburg South Africa Died July 1968.

MILLIS, WALTER, journalist; b. Atlanta, Ga., Mar. 16, 1899; s. John and Mary (Raoul) M.; A.B., Yale University, 1920; m. Norah Kathleen Thompson, Apr. 11, 1929; children—Walter, Sarah; m. 2d, Eugenia Benbow Sheppard, May 6, 1944. Editorial writer Baltimore News, 1920-23, New York Sun and Globe, 1923-24; editorial and staff writer New York Herald Tribune 1924-54; staff dir. Fund for Republic, Inc., from 1954. Served as 2d lt. F.A., (in U.S.), 1918. Clubs: Elizabethan (New Haven); Century (N.Y.C.); Orient Yacht. Author: The Martial Spirit, 1931; Road to War, 1935; Why Europe Fights, 1940; The Last Phase, 1946; This is Pearl1947; Arms and Men, 1956; An End to Arms, 1965. Co-author: Arms and the State, 1958; The Abolition of War, 1963. Editor: The Forrestal Diaries, 1951; American Military Thought, 1966. Contbr. to mags. Home: Glen Head NY Died Mar. 17, 1968.

MILLOY, JAMES S., publishing exec.; b. Peterboro, Can., Sept. 27, 1895; s. Peter and Katherine (Farrell) M.; ed. parochial sch., high sch. and bus. coll., Peterboro; m. Winnifred Blakey, July 16, 1919 (dec. 1953); children—James, Peter, Kathleen (Mrs. J. R. Pope), Richard P., Donald (dec.). Reporter, 1913-21; exec. sec. Minot (N.D.) Chamber of Commcerce, 1921-25; exec. sec. Greater N.D. Assn., 1925-31; joined Minneapolis Tribune, Oct. 1, 1931, as northwest development editor and asst. to pub.; in Washington for Minneapolis Tribune, 1932-41; executive Cowles Mags. & Broadcasting Co., Inc., publisher of Look; Des Moines Register and Tribune, Minneapolis Star and Tribune, 1941-71. Republican. Roman Catholic. K.C. Club: Nat. Press (Washington). Home: Arlington VA Died Mar. 19, 1971.

MILLS, DWIGHT M., advertising agency executive; born at Arcola, Ill., Dec. 9, 1901; son Arthur W. and Laura E. Mills; B.S., Northwestern U., 1923; married Adella Mitchell, 1925; 1 son, Mitchell; married second, Katherine P. Cole, 1943. Began as stock boy S. H. Kress &Co., 1923; later with A. W. Shaw Co., then with McGraw Hill Pub. Co.; pres. Kenyon & Eckhardt, Inc., advertising agency, 1949-51, chmn. exec. com. from 1951. Mem. Sigma Nu. Republican. Methodist. Clubs: University (N.Y.C.); Detroit Athletic, Turf and Field. Home: Lake Placid NY Died Apr. 25, 1969.

MILLS, EARLE WATKINS, corp. exec.; born Little Rock, Ark., June 24, 1896; s. Elisha Wright and Angie Irwin (Stansberry) M.; ed. U. of Ark., 1913-14; B.S., U.S. Naval Acad., 1917; post grad. 1922-23; M.S., Columbia U., 1924; D.Eng. (honorary), Univ. of Louisville, 1944; m. Carolyn Hayes Park, July 6, 1918; 1 dau., Shirley Marian. Ensign, 1917; advanced through grades to vice adm., 1945; splty. naval engring.; dep. chief Bur. Ships, 1942-46, chief, 1946-49; ret. as vice adm., 1949. Mem. Research and Development Board, Nat. Mil. Establishment, 1948; later chmn., dir. Foster Wheeler Corp., N.Y.C.; chmn. Nuclear Engring. Co., Walnut Creek, Cal., 1966-68; dir. Liberty Mut. Ins. Co., Boston. Decorated D.S.M., Victory, Am. Def., Pacific, European and Am. Theatre medals; Comdr. Order British Empire. Member Newcomen Soc. Am. Soc. Naval Engrs., Soc., Naval Architects and Marine Engrs. (David W. Taylor medal for achievement in marine engring., 1948), Am. Soc. M.E. Clubs: Army and Navy Country (Washington); Bankers, India House, University (N.Y.C.); Baltusrol Golf (Springfield, N.J.). Home: Walnut Creek CA Died Aug. 1968.

MILLS, HERBERT HAGERMAN, conservationist; b. Langhorne, Pa., Sept. 11, 1910; s. Everett Walker and Frances Shoemaker (Hagerman) M.; student Rollins Coll., 1933; m. Helen E. Strouse, June 15, 1935 (div. 1946); 1 dau., Sallie Ann. Engaged as farmer, mfg. and bus. cons., 1935-62; bd. dirs. Nat. Audubon Soc., 1957-64, chmn. exec. com., 1959-61, chmn. bd. 1962-64, v.p. 1965; exec. v.p. World Wildlife Fund, Inc., Washington, 1966-71. Mem. exec. com. World Wildlife Fund Internat.; mem. survival service commn. Internat. Union Conservation Nature and Natural Resources; bd. dirs. Phila. Conservationists, Inc., Natural Lands Trust, Citizens Com. Natural Resources; founder, pres. S. Jersey Wetlands Inst., 1969-72. Fellow Delaware Valley Ornithol. Club: mem. Am., Wilson, Delaware Valley ornithol. socs., Cornell Lab. Ornithology (dir.), Cumberland County Hist. Soc. (dir.). Mem. Soc. of Friends. Address: Bridgeton NJ Died Oct. 21, 1972.

MILLS, LENNOX A(LGERNON), university prof., radio commentator; b. Vancouver, Can., July 30, 1896; s. John Algernon and Margaret (Murchie) M.; A.B., Univ. of B.C., 1916; A.M., Univ. of Toronto, 1918; student Univ. of Calif., 1918-19, Harvard, 1919-20; A.B., Oxford (Rhodes scholar, 1920-23), 1923, Ph.D., 1924; Guggenheim Travelling Fellowship for travel and research in Ceylon, Malaya, Dutch East Indies, P.I., Hongkong, and Eng. 1936-37; m. Joan Shoolbred, June 16, 1928. Came to U.S., 1927. History tutor, Oxford, 1924-25, prof. of polit. sci. specializing in internat. relations and modern imperialism. Univ. of Minn., 1928-63, professor history Acadia University, Canada, 1963-65; radio commentator, Minneapolis, 1943-48; columnist, Minneapolis Shopping News, 1943-48. Recipient Guggenheim Fellowship, 1936, 56, 60. Member Royal Inst. Internat. Affairs, Royal Commonwealth Soc., London, Eng. Episcopalian. Author: British Malaya 1824-1867, 1925; British Rule in Ceylon 1795-1932, 1933; British Rule in Eastern Asia, 1942; Govt. and Nationalism in S.E. Asia (with R. Emerson and V. Thompson), 1942; Malaya. A. Political and Economic Appraisal, 1958; Southeast Asia, Illusion and Reality in Politics and Economics, 1964. Editor: The Annals of S.E. Asia and P.I., Vol. 226, 1943; The New World of S.E. Asia (part author), 1949; (with C.H. McLaughlin) World Politics in Transition, 1955. Contbr. articles on British, Dutch or American Asiatic dependencies. Home: Wolfville NS Canada. Died Dec. 23, 1968; buried Anglican Ch. Cemetery, Wolfville.

MILLS, MATTHEW, lawyer; b. Chicago, Aug. 30, 1877; s. Luther Laflin and Ella Jessup (Bates) M.; prep. edn. Lake Forest (Ill.) Acad., U. Chicago; A.B., Yale, 1900; LL.B., Northwestern, 1903. Admitted to Ill. bar, 1903, practiced in Chicago since 1903; mem. firm Deprees, Fiske, O'Brien & Momson since 1920; asst. atty. gen. Ill., 1916-20; counsel Ill. Pub. Utilities Commn., 1916-20. Mem. Ill. Legislature, 1907-11. Mem. Am. and Chicago bar assns., Phi Delta Phi, Psi Upsilon, Scroll and Key. Clubs: Chicago Law, Union League. Home: 65 West Jackson Blvd., Chicago 4. Office: 105 LaSalle St., Chicago IL‡

MILLWARD, RUSSELL HASTINGS, explorer; b. Cincinnati, O., Apr. 5, 1877; s. Capt. Frank and Margaret Ann (Jones) M.; student Rockville (Md.) Acad., 1889-93, Emerson Inst., Washington, D.C., 1893-94, Columbia, 1901-02; m. Edna P. Boyden, Aug. 27, 1914; 1 dau., Edna Boyden. Assisted in survey of Yavapai County, Ariz., 1902-03; in charge exploring expdns. in Africa and S. America, 1903-06; Am. v-consul gen., Boma, Congo Free State, 1906-07; v-consul Durban, Natal, Jan.-Aug. 1907, Tampico, Mexico, 1907-08; in charge various exploring expdns. since 1908; holder of world's record in distance covered on foot, traveling over 20,000 miles in uncharted portions of Africa, S. and Central America and Mexico; completed charting, Dept. of Peten and Ty. of Quintana Roo, Yucatan, July 1913. Charted 1st Am. Airway, coast to coast, known as the Woodrow Wilson Airway, 1918. Dir., instr. Free Sch. Printing, Occupational Therapy; founder, Nat. Pet Therapy. Made many important contbns. in zoology, archaeology and ethnology, to museums and scientific instns. Possessor 57 decorations, hereditary and earned. Fellow Royal Geog. Soc., Royal Soc. Arts, London; mem. Am. Mus. Nat. Hist. (life), Am. Geog. Soc., N.Y. Acad. Sciences, Am. Genetic Assn., New York Zool. Soc. (life corr.), Mil. Order Loyal Legion, Army and Navy League of U.S., Sigma Chi, Lambda Epsilon, etc. Clubs: Nat. Press, Army and Navy (Washington, D.C.); Explorers, Aero of America, etc. Contbr. numerous articles to Am. and foreign mags. and newspapers. Address: 3100 Connecticut Av., Washington 8 DC‡

MILNE, FRANCES MARGARET (TENER), librarian, author; b. Tattykeel, nr. Cookstown, Co. Tyrone, Ireland; d. Isaac William and Frances Margaret (Evans) Tener; brought by parents to U.S. when 3 yrs. old; ed. pub. schs., Allegheny, Pa., and afterward at home; m. at Santa Cruz, Cal., James Proven Milne, Dec. 26, 1878 (now deceased). Librarian Free Pub. Library, San Luis Obispo, Cal., since 1899. Mem. Library Assn. of Cal., Single Tax Soc. of San Francisco, Woman's Single Tax League, Washington; v.-p. Am. Single Tax League. Mem. Disciples of Christ (Christian Ch.). Author: Rose Carleton (for children), 1872; For To-day (poems), 2 edits., 1894, 1905; Heilotrope (sketches for young people), 1897; A Cottage Gray, and Other Poems, 1895; Our Little Roman (verses of childhood), 1902; The Passing of the Village, 1902. Address: San Luis Obispo CA‡

MILNER, ROBERT TEAGUE, ex-educator; b. in Alabama; s. Arnold and Mary M.; family removed to Tex., 1851; ed. Henderson Coll.; m. Mary L. Hawkins, of Henderson, Tex., Oct. 3, 1882. Speaker Tex. Ho. of Rep., 1891; pres. Agrl. and Mech. Coll. of Tex., Sept., 1908-1914. Home: Henderson TX‡

MILOFSKY, ALLAN HENRY, physician; b. Washington, Apr. 25, 1933; s. Morris and Sophia Milofsky; M.D. cum laude, Yale, 1958; m. Eva Schur, Jan. 25, 1959; children—Michael, Robert. Mixed med., chest and pathology intern Columbia Med. Div., Bellevue Hosp., N.Y.C., 1958-59; resident in psychiatry Boston Psychopathic Hosp. and Southard Clinic, Mass. Mental Health Center, Boston, 1959-61, resident in psychiatry children's unit, 1961-62; resident James Jackson Putnam Children's Center, 1964-65, staff psychiatrist, until 1971. Served to sr. surgeon USPHS 62-64. Diplomate Am. Bd. Psychiatry and Neurology. Mem. Am. Psychiat. Assn., Phi Beta Kappa, Alpha Omega Alpha. Home: Belmont MA Died Sept. 6, 1971; buried Sharon Meml. Park, Sharon MA

MILTOUN, FRANCIS (FRANCIS MILTOUN MANSFIELD), author; b. Lynn, Mass., Feb. 14, 1871; m. Blanche McManus, Oct. 12, 1898. Officier du Nicham Iftikhar of Tunisia. Was consular agt., Toulon, France, 1909-13; vice and deputy consul-gen., Barcelona, Spain, 1913-14. Collaborator U.S. Office of Pub. Roads. Mem. Assn. Internat. des Congres de la Route, Ligue Internat. des Assn. Touristes, Touring Club d'Italia. Clubs: Salmagundi (New York); Touring Club de France, Anglo-American Press Assn., American Club (Paris). Foreign touring expert, Am. Automobile Assn. and asso. editor, Am. Motorist (official organ). Paris corr. Phila. Press, 1917-20; accredited corr. to Am., British, French and Belgian fronts, 1916-18. Paris corr. Motor Life (N.Y.) and Iron

Trade Review (Cleveland). Continental rep. Automobile Assn. and Motor Union (London); Paris rep. Detroit Automobile Club. Member Anglo-Am. Press Assn. Paris, Authors' League America. Mem. Am. Com. on Pub. Information, Paris, 1918-19. Paris corr. Cleveland Plain Dealer since 1924. American Machinist since 1924; tech. press corr. at League of Nations, Geneva, since 1927. Author: Stevensoniana: A Kipling Note Book All About Ships and Shipping; Dickens' London, 1903; Cathedrals of Northern France, 1903; Cathedrals of Southern France, 1904; Dumas Paris, 1904; Cathedrals of the Rhine, 1905; Rambles in Normandy and Brittany, 1906; Among the Chateaux ef Touraine, 1906; Among the Chateaux of Old Navarre, 1907; The Automobilist Abroad, 1907 (all illustrated by Blanche McManus); also (with Blanche McManus) Romantic Ireland, 1905; Italian Highways and Byways From a Motor Car, 1909; Royal Parks and Palaces, 1910; A Road Book to the Chateau Country, 1913; The Ideal Tour of France, 1913; Old and New France, 1915. Staff corr. New York Sun at League of Nations, also del. Mid-west Am. League of Nations Assn., at Geneva, 1913-—. Address: 9 Rue Falguiere, Paris France‡

MINAHAN, DANIEL FRANCIS, ex-congressman; b. Springfield, O., Aug. 8, 1877; s. Daniel F. and Mary E. (Murphy) M.; ed. Seton Hall Coll., South Orange, N.J.; m. Genevieve R., d. Lawrence T. Fell, of Orange, N.J., Feb. 17, 1919. Mayor of Orange, N.J., 1914-19; mem. 66th Congress (1919-21) and 68th Congress (1923-25), 9th N.J. Dist. Democrat. Catholic. Home: 415 Fairview Av., Orange, N.J. Office: Lefcourt Bldg., Newark NJ‡

MINCHIN, NINA MESIROW, pianist; B. Chgo.; d. Elias B. and Rebecca (Halfand) Mesirow; student with Godowsky, Moritz Rosenthal, J. Lhevinne, F. Bloomfield-Zeisler, Heniot Levy; children—Jarvis, Gloria. Debut, 1924; founder, 1931, since pianist-mus. dir. Pro Musica Trio, devoted entirely to chamber music concerts; founder Chgo. Chamber Music Soc., 1935, monthly series until 1957; trio made N.Y.C. debut, 1937, toured nationally, pioneered in chamber music in U.S., 1957-72, gave monthly concerts in Chgo.; founder, mus. dir. Pro Musica Soc. of Chgo., 1957-72; performed with leading symphony orchs.; recs. for Pro Musica Records; Juilliard quartet in series at Orch. Hall. Club: Arts (Chicago). Address: Chicago IL Died Aug. 27, 1972; buried Ridgelawn Cemetery, Chicago IL

MINER, ROBERT BRADFORD, educator; b. Conneaut, O., June 1, 1916; s. Charles Warren and Cora Ruth (Carr) M.; student Allegheny Colo. 1934-36; B.S.C., Ohio U., 1938, M.S., 1940; Ph.D., Ohio State U., 1948; m. Margaret Louisa Earnhart, June 5, 1942; children—Richard Lee, Allan Bradford. Asst. price specialist OPA, 1942-43; mem. faculty Ohio State U., 1946-—, prof. bus., 1958-—, chmn. dept. bus. orgn., 1957-68; vis. lectr. U. Wis., summer 1950. Served to 1st lt. AUS, 1943-46. Mem. Am. Marketing Assn. Co-author: Introduction to Business Management, 1951; Distribution Costs, 1953. Contbg. editor Accountants Handbook, 1956, 70; Marketing Handbook, 1965. Home: Columbus OH Died Feb. 6, 1971.

MINGENBACK, EUGENE CARL, ins. co. exec.; b. Greensburg, Kan., Apr. 8, 1888; s. C. F. and Julia J. (Miller) M.; student St. Edwards Coll., Austin, Tex.; m. Mary J. Aske, 1916; 1 dau., Julia Luisa (Mrs. William W. Shanks). Chmn. bd., gen. mgr. Farmers Alliance Mut. Ins. Co.; dir. Alliance Mut. Casualty Co. and Alliance Life Ins. Co., McPherson, Kan., sec., gen. mgr., pres.; pres. State Investment Co., McPherson. Mem. Kan. C. of C. (past pres.). Elk, Rotarian. Home: McPherson KS

MINIFIE, WILLIAM CHARLES, clergyman, lecturer; b. London, Eng., Mar. 8, 1869; s. John Holloway and Isabella (Curtis) M.; ed. Sherborne Grammar Sch., and Met. College, London, 1886-9; (D.D., Washington and Tusculum Coll., Tenn., 1901; D.C.L., Potomac U., 1905, Ph.D., 1908; Litt.D., Alfred University, N.Y., 1914); m. Ivy H. L. Rossiter, of Weston-Super-Mare, Eng., Mar. 1890; 2d, Ellen G. Brown, of Newburyport, Mass., 1917. Ordained Baptist ministry, 1889; pastor Clarendon St. Bapt. Ch., Boston, 1907-9. Has lectured extensively in Great Britain and America; was for some time asst. private sec. to C. H. Spurgeon. Dir. Internat. Bible Inst. Fellow Royal Geog. Soc., Royal Soc. of Literature; mem. Royal Soc. Arts, London, Philos. Soc. Great Britain. Mason. Author: The Mask Torn Off, 1901; The Well in the Wilderness, 1902; The Search-Light Pulpit, 1902. Home: Newburyport, Mass. Office: Tremont Temple, Boston MA‡

MINITER, EDITH (DOWE), editor; b. Wilbraham, Mass., May 19, 1869; d. William Hilton and Jennie E. (Tupper) Dowe; grad. Mrs. Woodford's Sch., Worcester, 1886; m. at Worcester, John T. F. Miniter, Sept. 19, 1887 (now deceased). In editorial work since 1887; in 1890 was city editor Manchester Press (daily) and only woman city editor of a daily in N.E.; editor Boston Home Journal, 1895-1906; later Home and Abroad. Ex-pres. Nat. Amateur Press Assn. (1st woman pres.), and Interstate Amateur Press Assn. Her article How to Dress on $40 a Year." in Boston Globe, 1888, attracted wide discussion and notice. Author: Our Natupski Neighbors, 1916. Home: 20 Webster St., Allston MA‡

MINNAERT, MARCEL GILLES JOZEF, astrophysicist; b. Bruges, Belgium, Feb. 12, 1893; s. Jozef and Jozefina (van Overberge) M.; D.Biology, U. Ghent, 1914; D.Math. and Physics, U. Utrecht, 1925; Hon. Dr., univs. Heidelberg and Moscow; m. Marla Bourgonje Coelingh, Dec. 20, 1929; children—Koenraad, Boudewijn. Lectr., U. Ghent, 1916-18; observer U. Utrecht, 1920-37, prof. astronomy, dir. obs., 1937-63; ret. Active Flemish nat. movement, action against nuclear weapons, action against Viet Nam war. Recipient Gold medal Royal Astron. Soc. London, 1947, Bruce medal Astron. Soc. Pacific, 1951, Janssen medal Soc. Astronomique de France, 1966. Order du Merite, Societe pour a Recherche et l'Invention, 1964. Mem. Acad. Amsterdam; fgn. mem. acads. Brussels Boston, Wash., Coimbra, Uppsala, Academia Leopoldina in Halle, Academia d Lincel in Rome. Contbr. articles to Kuiper, The Solar System, Photometric Atlas of the Solar Spectrum. Author: De Natuurkunde van 't Vrije Veld, 3 vols (English trans. of 1st part; Light and Color), 1937, 39, 40; Practical Exercises in Elementary Astronomy, 1968. Research and publs. on solar physics, other astrophys. subjects, particularly Fraunhofer lines. Home: Utrecht Netherlands Died Oct. 26, 1970.

MINNICK, JOHN HARRISON, teacher; b. Somerset, Ind., Oct. 26, 1877; s. David Monroe and Mary (Okley) M.; grad. Marion (Ind.) Normal Sch., 1903; A.B., Ind. U., 1906, A.M., 1908; grad. student U. of Illinois, U. of Chicago, Columbia U.; Harrison fellow in mathematics, 1909-10 and in education, 1915-16, Univ. of Pa.; Ph.D., Univ. of Pa., 1918; m. Eva Smith, August 8, 1908; 1 dau., Mrs. Marjorie Inez Donaldson. Teacher high schs., Ind. and Ill., various periods; critic teacher mathematics, Ind. U., 1911-13; instr. mathematics, Horace Mann Sch., (Columbia), 1913-15; instr. mathematics, 1916-17, asst. prof. edn., 1917-20; prof. edn. since 1920, dean Sch. of Edn., U. of Pa., 1921-48; prof., 1920-48; professor education emeritus since 1948. Mem. N.E.A., Nat. Council Teachers of Mathematics, Nat. Assn. Coll. Teachers of Edn., Phi Delta Kappa, Pi Mu Epsilon, Phi Beta Kappa, Sigma Xi, Kappa Phi Kappa, Theta Chi. Mem. United Presbyn. Ch. Editor: The Educational Outlook. Author: An Investigation of Abilities Fundamental to Geometry, 1918; Teaching Mathematics in the Secondary Schools, 1939. Developed standardized tests in Philadelphia 43 PA‡

MIRISCH, HAROLD JOSEPH, motion picture exec.; b. N.Y.C., May 4, 1907; s. Max and Flora (Glasshut) M.; ed. pub. schs.; m. Lottie Mandell, Aug. 25, 1930; children—Maxine F. (Mrs. Jerome M. Siegel), Robert Alan. With Warner Bros., 1922-39; partner Walter Anneberg in operation Oriental and Tower theatres, Milw., 1939-40; organized Theatre Candy Co., Milw., 1940; film buyer RKO, N.Y.C., 1942-47; v.p. Allied Artists Picture Corp., 1947-57; organized, pres. Mirisch Co., Los Angeles, from 1957. Chmn. Western div. Am. Israel Cultural Found. Clubs: Hillcrest Country (Beverly Hills, Cal.); Tamarisk Country, Racquet (Palm Springs). Home: Beverly Hills CA also Palm Springs CA Died Dec. 5, 1968; buried Hillside Meml. Park and Mausoleum.

MIRZA, ISKANDER, former pres. Islamic Republic of Pakistan; b. Nov. 13, 1899; ed. Ephinstone Coll., Bombay; selected cadet Royal Mil. Coll. at Sandhurst, 1918, on completion of course became first cadet from India to be gazetted into the Army; joined the Cameronians (2d Scottish Rifles) at Kohat in 1921, participated in Khoodad Khel operations; posted 17th Poona Horse at Jhansi, participated Waziristan operations, 1924; selected from Indian Polit. Service, 1926, served as asst. commr., Abbottabad, Bannu, Nowshera and Tank; dep. commr. Hazara and Mardan, 1931-36; polit. agt., Khyber, 1938; dep. commr. Peshawar, 1940; polit. agt. Orissa States, 1945; joint sec. Govt. of India, Ministry of Def., 1946; on partition apptd. def. sec. Pakistan Govt., 1947; gov. East Pakistan, 1954; minister for interior, states and frontier regions Govt. of Pakistan, 1954; acting gov.-gen. of Pakistan, 1955; gov.-gen., 1955-56; pres. Islamic Republic of Pakistan, 1956-58. Decorated Officer Order Brit. Empire, Companian Order Indian Empire. Address: Karachi Pakistan Died Nov. 1969.

MISER, HUGH DINSMORE, geologist; b. Pea Ridge, Ark., Dec. 18, 1884; s. Jordan Stanford and Eliza Caroline (Webb) M.; A.B., University of Arkansas, 1908, A.M., 1912, Doctor of Laws, 1949; m. Mary Kate Goddard, Sept. 21, 1910 (dec. 1963); d., Mrs. Catherine M. Kayser. Joined U.S. Geol. Survey as field asst., 1907, jr. geologist, 1911, asst. geologist, 1912, asso. geologist, 1913-18, geologist, 1919-54, in charge sect. areal geology, 1927, regional geologist for eastern United States, 1942; chief, fuels sect., 1928-47, staff geol., 1947-54, scientific staff assistant Office of Dir., 1955-69; cons. geologist Ark. Geol. and Conservation Commission, 1959-69; geologist Ark. Geological Survey, 1907-10; geologist Tenn. Geol. Survey, 1912 and 1917; state geologist of Tennessee, 1926; acting prof. geology, U. of Ark., and state geologist of Arkansas, 1920. Made investigation of manganese deposits in U.S. during World Wars I and II; author first multicolored geologic map of Okla., 1926, 2d, 1954; geologist to engring. party that explored and mapped San Juan Canyon, Utah, 1921. Dir. Sibley Memorial Hosp., (1925-44; chmn. bd. 1936-37). Recipient Distinguished Service Medal, U.S. Dept. Interior 1955. Mem. Am. Assn. Petroleum Geologists (hon. mem. 1948), Soc. Econ., Geologists, Geol. Soc. Am., Geol. Soc. Washington (pres. 1938), Washington (v.p. 1939), Tenn. acads. scis., Mineral Soc. Am., N.M. (hon.), Tulsa (hon.), Oklahoma City (hon.) geol. socs., Okla. Mineral and Gem Soc. (hon.), Okla. Acad. Sci., Sigma Gamma Epsilon (hon.). Donated collection of 5700 rare and select Ark. quartz crystals to U. Ark. Mus., 1954. Home: Washington DC Died Aug. 1, 1969

MISHIMA, YUKIO, (KIMITAKE HIRAOKA), novelist; b. Tokyo, Japan, Jan. 14, 1925; grad. Peers' Coll., 1944; LL.B., Tokyo Imperial U., 1947; m. Yoko Mishima; 1 son, 1 dau. Worked briefly in Ministry of Finance, resigned to devote full time to writing; toured S. Am. and Europe, 1952. Mem. Japan Pen Club, Japan Lt. Assn., Internat. Riding Club: Author: Sound of Waves, Five Modern No Plays, Confessions of a Mask, Temple of the Golden Pavilion, After the Banquet, The Sailor Who Fell from Grace with the Sea, Forbidden Color, Death in Midsummer, the Sea of Fertility, a tetralogy, and other stories. Address: Tokyo Japan Died Nov. 25, 1970; buried Tokyo Japan

MITCHEL, EDWIN KENT, publisher; b. East Orange, N.J., Apr. 23, 1901; s. Frederick Augustus and Maria Letita (Goold) M.; B.S. in Chemistry, Lafayette Coll., 1923; m. Arlene Pierson Lee, June 25, 1925; 1 son, Frederick Kent. With Federal Advt. Agy., 1923-25, J. Walter Thompson Co., 1925-26; field promotion mgr. Pacific Mills, 1927-30; mdse. mgr. Cheney Bros., 1930-35; gen. mgr. Essley Shirt Co., 1935-36; with Curtis Publishing Co., 1936-63, sales staff Sat. Eve. Post, 1936-45, sales mgr. Holiday, N.Y., 1945-48, sales mgr., 1948-57, v.p., advt. dir. Holiday, 1957-58, pub. Am. Home mag., 1958-61, sr. pub. Am. Home mag. and Ladies Home Jour., 1961-62, sr. v.p. mag. div. of co., 1962-63, ret. Club: University (N.Y.C.). Home: North Sandwich NH also Harbour Island Bahamas Died Jan. 1, 1972.

MITCHELL, ALFRED NEWTON, ins. exec.; b. Newtonville, Ont., Can., Apr. 25, 1876; s. Dr. John C. and Effie M. (Jardine) M.; B.A., U. of Toronto, 1900; m. Florence Tilley, June 23, 1903. Advt. mgr. Mfrs. Life Ins. Co., Toronto, 1901-06, asst. sec., 1906-11; asst. gen. mgr. Fed. Life Ins. Co., Hamilton, Ont., 1911-12, gen. mgr., 1912-15; with The Canada Life Assurance Co. since 1915, asst. gen. mgr., 1926-30, gen. mgr., 1930-35, v.p., 1935-38, pres., 1938-46, chmn. bd., 1946-51, dir. since 1930; v.p. Nat. Trust Co., Ltd., since 1939; dir. Canadian Bank of Commerce. Mem. Delta Kappa Epsilon. Mason. Clubs: National, Toronto Golf, Toronto Hunt, Ontario Jockey. Home: 225 Russell Hill Rd., Toronto 5. Office: 330 University Av., Toronto ON Canada‡

MITCHELL, ARTHUR W., congressman; b. Chambers County, Ala., Dec. 22, 1883; son of ex-slaves; student Tuskegee Inst., Columbia and Harvard; LL.D., Wilberforce U.; m. Annie Harris; 1 son, Arthur W. Taught school in rural sections of Ala. for many years; founded and was pres. Armstrong Agr. Sch., West Butler, Ala. Admitted to D.C. bar and practiced law in Washington, D.C., 10 years, also real estate; practiced in Chicago, 1929-39; mem. 74th to 77th Congresses (1935-43), 1st Ill. Dist., succeeding Oscar De Priest (first Negro Democrat to be elected to Congress). Mem. Phi Beta Sigma (nat. pres. 10 yrs.). Democrat. Address: Chicago IL Died May 1968.*

MITCHELL, CHARLES FRANKLIN, surgeon; b. 1875; M.D., U. of Pa., 1898. Practiced at Phila. since 1898; asso. prof. surgery Grad. Sch. of Medicine, U. of Pa. Mem. Am. Surg. Assn., A.M.A., Med. Soc. State of Pa. Address: 2003 Pine St., Philadelphia PA‡

MITCHELL, CHARLES SCOTT, corp. ofcl.; b. Spring Hope, N.C., Sept. 22, 1909; s. Charles Scott and Harriet Elizabeth (Edwards) M.; B.S. in Engring., N.C. State Coll., 1930; D.Sc. (hon.), N.C. State University at Raleigh; m. Margaret Louise Stein, Mar. 28, 1937; children—Georgeanne Elizabeth, Charles Scott, Robert Bruce. Jr. engr. Cities Service Oil Co., 1930-31; with meter dept. Cities Service Gas Co., 1931-37, asst. supt. panhandle operations and sales engr., 1937-39; buyer purchasing dept. Cities Service Oil Co. (Del.), 1939-43, asst. purchasing agt., 1943-47, successively engr. marketing div., mgr. crude oil purchase and sales div., mgr. crude oil supply and transportation div., 1947-55; pres. Cities Service Pipe Line Co., 1951-55; dir., mgr. transp. and supply Cities Service Co., 1950-54, v.p., 1956-59, sr. v.p., 1959-64, exec. v.p., 1964-66, dir., 1955-72, pres., mem. exec. com., 1966-68, chmn. bd., chief exec. officer, chmn. exec. com., 1968-72; director Cities Service Research & Development Company; president of Cities Service Athabasca, Inc.; dir. Cities Service Gas Co.; Columbia Carbon Co.; pres., dir. Cities Service Internat. Inc.; dir., mem. exec. com. Tennessee,

Corp. Vice pres., mem. exec. com., dir. N.C. Engring. Found.; bd. assos. Meredith Coll. Mem. Nat. Soc. Profl. Engrs., Am. Petroleum Inst., Nat. Petroleum Council (dir.), Newcomen Soc. N.Am., 25 yr. Club Petroleum Industry, Newcomen Soc., Phi Kappa Phi, Tau Beta Pi, Sigma Chi. Clubs: Economic, Metropolitan. Home: New York City NY Died Jan. 1972.

MITCHELL, CLARENCE BLAIR, lawyer; b. New York, N.Y., Nov. 4, 1865; s. Clarence Green and Aurelia Ann (Blair) M.; ed. Harrington Sch., 1878-80, St. John's Sch., 1880-83; Princeton U., 1885-89 (B.A.); Columbia Law School, 1889-91; m. Lucy Mildred Matthews, Dec. 4, 1889; children—Clarence Van Schaick, Dorothy (Mrs. De Coursey Fales), Lucy Virginia (Mrs. Frederick H. Prince, Jr.), Mildred Aurelia (Mrs. John W. Brock), Caroline Winifred (Mrs. Edward T. Look). Admitted to N.Y. bar, 1891; with Dillon & Swayne, 1891-93, Hon. John F. Dillon, 1893-1912, Choate, & Laroque, 1912-13; mem. firm Choate, Laroque & Mitchell, 1913-37, Choate, Laroque, Mitchell & Ely, 1937-41, Choate, Mitchell Ely since 1941; trustee Princeton University Press; dir. v.-pres. Am. Platinum Co., Baker & Co., Inc., Hanovia Chem. & Mfg. Co., Irvington Smelting & Refining Co. Mem. Ivy Club of Princeton. Clubs: Union, Century Assn., Downtown, Ch. (New York); Essex Fox Hounds, Sons of the Revolution (N.J.). Editor: Mitchell-Boulton correspondence; with a Military Ambulance in France; Letters from a Liaison Officer; An American Girl in the War Zone. Author: Mitchell Record, 1925; The A B C of Riding to Hounds, 1916; History of the Ivy Club, 1929. Address: Pennbrook House, Far Hills, N.J. Address: 41 Broad St., New York NY‡

MITCHELL, DAVID RAY, consulting engineer; b. Bells Landing, Pa., June 12, 1898; s. John Francis and Gertrude (Johnson) M.; B.S. in Mining Engring., Pa. State Coll., 1924, M.S., 1927; E.M., U. of Ill., 1931; m. Lois Rishell, Mar. 12, 1925; children—David Ray, Mary Patricia. Worked in coal and clay mines of Pa., 1917-27; prof. mining and metall. engring. U. of Ill., 1927-38; chmn. div. of mineral engring., Pa. State Univ., 1938-60, past associate dean college of mineral industries, dean College Mineral Industries, 1960-63; consultant mining engineer, 1963-72. Served as private, Signal Corps, U.S. Army, 1918-19. Certified fire boss and mine foreman, Pa.; professional engr., Pa. Hon. mem. Mark Twain and Eugene Field socs. Mem. Am. Inst. Mining Engrs. (sec., coal div.), Am. Mining Congress, Coal Mining Inst. Am. Ill. Mining Inst., Sigma Xi, Sigma Gamma Epsilon. Methodist. Editor and co-author: Coal Preparation, 1943, 50. Contbr. numerous tech. papers on mining and mineral preparation to professional publs. Home: State College PA Died Sept. 22, 1972.

MITCHELL, EMORY FORREST, ry. official; b. McVeytown, Pa., July 19, 1864; s. George and Rebecca G. M.; ed. pvt. schs.; m. Catherine West, May 1887. Began as axman in engring. dept., Pa. R.R., 1882, and later miscellaneous engring. work maintenance of way dept., same rd.; asst. engr. N.&W. Ry., 1887-88; div. engr. maintenance of way dept. same rd., 1888-90; asst. engr. D.&R.G. R.R., 1890-92; pvt. practice, Colo. and U.S. dept. mineral surveyor until 1900; asst. engr. D.&R. G. R.R., 1900-01; chief engr. and supt. San Luis Valley Mining Co., Colo., 1901-04; engr. constrn. and chief engr. M.P. Ry. System, 1905-12; engr. Western Group, engring. com. of President's Conf. Com. on Federal Valuation of Railroads, 1916-17; chief engr. T. & P. Ry., 1917-Aug. 1, 1941, now cons. engineer for T.. Ry. Democrat. Presbyterian. Club: University. Home: 312 N. Henderson St. Office: T.&P. Bldg., Dallas TX‡

MITCHELL, F. EDWARD, lawyer; b. Washington, D.C., Oct. 5, 1871; s. Joseph T. and Margaret A. T. (Martin) M.; ed. parochial and pub. schs.; studied law, Georgetown U.; LL.B., Nat. Univ. Law Sch., Washington, 1894; m. Anna M. Wheatley, of Washington, Apr. 24, 1895; children—Joseph Albert (dec.), William Edward, Walter Scott, Anna T. Admitted to D.C. bar, 1894; practiced as title examiner with Dist. Title Ins. Co., 1894-96; gen. practice till 1923; mem. firm Turner & Mitchell, 1898-1903; spl. asst. to atty. gen. in war transaction sect., Dept. of Justice, 1923-25; U.S. dist atty. for Canal Zone, by apptmt. of President Coolidge, since Feb. 16, 1925. Originally a Democrat but organized Harding Dem. Club, Washington, in opposition to League of Nations. Catholic. Club: Union (Panama). Address: Ancon CZ‡

MITCHELL, HAZEL HAYNES, educator; b. West Monroe, La.; d. Fred R. and Margarette (Haynes) Mitchell; A.B., Brenau, 1936; M.A., La. State U., 1938, Ph.D., 1964. Faculty, N.E. La. Coll., Monroe, 1940-70, prof. Spanish. Pres., Jr. Charity League, 1950-51. Mem. Am. Assn. U. Women (past pres.), v.p. La. div. 1968-70), S. Central Modern Lang. Assn., La. Tchrs. Assn., La. Fgn. Lang. Tchrs. Assn., Assn. Higher Edn., Modern Lang. Tchrs. Assn., Delta Kappa Gamma, Alpha Lambda Delta, Sigma Tau Delta, Alpha Gamma Delta. Episcopalian. Home: Monroe LA Died Jan. 29, 1970.

MITCHELL, HUGH GORDON, former U.N. ofcl.; b. Statesville, N.C., Oct. 5, 1902; s. Richard Page and Amelia (Leinster) M.; B.S., U. of N.C., 1924; student of law, 1924-26; unmarried. In practice of law from 1926, atty., 3d v.p. Alexander R.R. Co.; state senator, N.C., 1943, 1945; delegate from N.C. Nat. Dem. Conv., 1936, 1940, 1944, 56, 60; spl. legal advisor on adminstrv. matters for U.N., 1946-48. Alt. del., Nat. Democratic Conv., 1948; Iredell County (N.C.) attorney, 1956-62. Former dir. N.C. Assn. for the Blind; chmn. Zebulon Baird Vance Memorial Commn. of N.C.; chmn. War Savings Staff, Iredell Co., N.C., 1942; govt. appeal agent, Selective Service, Iredell Co., Bd. No. 1, 1940-42, Bd. directors Patterson Sch., 1959-70. Mem. nat. awards jury for Freedoms Found., 1951. Mem. Am. Coalition Patriotic, Socs., Inc. (pres. 1965-71, gen. counsel), Lions Internat. (Internat. counsellor, president's award, 1956-57, dist. chmn. internat. relations com. 1963-71), Patriotic Order Sons Am. (pres. N.C. State Camp, 1928-31, nat. pres., 1935-43, 1949-51, nat. dir.-gen. 1951, nat. sec. 1951-71, merit award 1954), Am., N.C. State, Iredell County (pres. 1964-65), N.C. 22d Jud. Dist. (v.p. 1970-71) bar assns., Am. Judicature Soc., Delta Sigma Phi. Democrat. Presbyterian. Clubs: Statesville City, Statesville Country. Home: Statesville NC Died Apr. 10, 1972; interred Oakwood Cemetery, Statesville NC

MITCHELL, JOHN BLANTON, banker; b. St. Louis, Aug. 31, 1917; s. Moreh L. and Louise A. (Shipp) M.; student Washington U., 1936-37, St. Louis U., 1937-40, Rutgers U., 1950; m. Genevieve Mullins, Oct. 12, 1940; children—Nicola Susan, John Blanton. With Mercantile Commerce Bank & Trust Co., 1937-49; v.p. Mercantile Commerce Nat. Bank, 1940-50; v.p. Mfrs. Bank & Trust Co., 1950-55; v.p. First Nat. Bank, St. Louis, 1955-60, exec. v.p., 1960-62, pres. 1962-68, also dir.; dir. Pet Inc., Alton Box Board Co., Alton, Ill., Curlee Clothing Co., St. Louis, St. Louis Union Trust Co., Gen. Am. Life Ins., U.S. Paint Co., St. Louis, Volkswagen Ins., St. Louis. Chmn. adv. com. on banking policies and practices 10th Nat. Bank Region, Office Controller Currency. Trustee Found. for Comml. Banks; bd. dirs. St. Louis YMCA, St. Louis Children's Hosp., St. Louis Symphony Soc., Jr. Achievement Miss. Valley Area, council Boy Scouts of America; bd. dirs. Mo. Pub. Expenditure Survey, pres., 1967-71; member of the president's council St. Louis Univ. Served with USCGR, World War II. Mem. Am. Bankers Assn. (banking and financial com.), Assn. Res. City Bankers (corr. bank com.), Mo. C. of C. (dir.). Presbyn. (deacon.) Clubs: Bellerieve Country, Bogey, Racquet, University (St. Louis). Home: St Louis MO Died Nov. 29, 1968; interred Oak Grove Mausoleum, St. Louis MO

MITCHELL, JOHN DOYLE, accountant; b. Pasadena, Cal., Nov. 16, 1936; s. Edwin E. and Mary (Miner) M.; B.S., Fresno State Coll., 1960; M.B.A., U. Cal., Los Angeles, 1961, postgrad.; m. Patricia E. Wittle, Sept. 14, 1962; children—John Doyle, Lisa Renee. With Bradford, Stark & McGhee, C.P.A.s, Fresno, Cal., 1958-60, Garfield Goldfarb & Co., C.P.A.s, Studio City, Cal., 1960-62; practice pub. accounting, Sherman Oaks, Cal., 1962-65; teaching asst. U. Cal., Los Angeles, 1960-65; asst. prof. accounting and quantitative studies Fresno State Coll. Alpha Kappa Psi scholar, 1959-60, Price Waterhouse scholar, 1962-63, Haskins & Sells Found. scholar. Mem. Am. Accounting Assn. (membership chmn.), Am. Assn. U. Profs., Am. Inst. C.P.A.'s, Cal. Soc. C.P.A.'s, Alpha Kappa Psi, Beta Gamma Sigma. Home: Fresno CA Deceased.

MITCHELL, JOHN MARVIN, industrialist; b. Maryville, Tenn., Jan. 23, 1908; s. John Harmon and Myrtle (George) M.; student U. Fla., 1925-26, U. Tenn., 1926-29; m. Eleanor Martin Smith, Feb. 14, 1931. With Aluminum Co. Am., 1929-37, 43-47, 50-55, 58-—, successively clk., sales and operating trainee, market research analyst, sales engr., 1929-37, personnel and indsl. relations mgr., New Castle, Pa., mgr. wage stblzn. non-employees, Pitts., spl. assignment fgn. sales, 1943-47, mgr. export and comml. research divs., Pitts., 1950-55, gen. mgr. internat. div., 1958-61; v.p. Aluminum Co. of Am., 1961-63, exec. v.p., dir., 1963-72; br. sales mgr. H.D. Catty Corp., Phila. 34-40, br. mgr., Buffalo, 1941; with aluminum-magnesium div. WPB, Washington, 1942; gen. mgr. Alcomex S.A., Monterey, Mexico, 1948-49; pres., dir. Ekco-Alcoa Containers, Inc., Wheeling, Ill., 1955-58; pres. Alcoa Internat., Inc., 1958-61; dir. Aluminio, S.A. de C.V., Mexico City, Alcoa Australia, Ltd., Melbourne. Mem. Hosp. Council Western Pa., Community chest Allegheny County, Center for Internat. Relations; chmn. health task force Health and Welfare Assn.; Pres., Pitts. Council for Internat. Visitors Bd. dirs. World Affairs Council Pitts., stateside bd. mem. U. Americas; trustee U. Ams. Found., Health Research and Services Found.; bd. dirs. Shadyside Hosp. Decorated Fundacion Internacional Elroy Alfaro (Panama City). Mem. Am. Marketing Assn., Newcomen Soc. N.Am., Pa. Soc., Pi Kappa Alpha. Clubs: Duquesne, Fox Chapel Golf (dir.), University (Pitts.); Rolling Rock, Laurel Valley Golf, Pike Run (Ligonier, Pa.); Internat. (Washington). Home: Pittsburgh PA Died Oct. 18, 1972; buried Maryville TN

MITCHELL, JOHN MCKENNEY, physician; ednl. dir.; b. Centreville, Md., Sept. 23, 1895; s. James Archibald and Eleanor Lux (McKenney) M.; A.B., Trinity Coll., 1920, Sc.D. (hon.), 1949; M.D. cum laude, Yale, 1924; LL.D. (hon.), Temple U., 1951; Sc.D., Dickinson Coll., 1953, Union U., 1958; m. Eleanor A. Janeway, Sept. 12, 1925; children—James Andrew. Eleanor Janeway (Mrs. Robert A. Huggins); m. 2d, Harriet Taylor Mauck, September 16, 1961. Intern-Resident New Haven Hosp., 1924-27; practice, specializing in pediatrics, Phila., 1927-42; faculty, sch. medicine U. Pa., 1927-62, prof. pediatrics, 1952-69, dean sch. medicine, 1948-62; dir. med. edn. Bryn Mawr Hosp., Pa., 1962-66; dir. study pediatric edn. Am. Acad. Pediatric Education, Commonwealth Fund, 1949. Served as 1st lt. Inf., U.S. Army, World War I; col. M.C., A.U.S., China-Burma-India Theatre, 1942-45; col. Medical Corps. Ret. Decorated Silver Star; recipient Abraham Jacobi award Am. Med. Assn., 1964. Exec. sec. Am. Bd. of Pediatrics since 1948. Fellow A.M.A., Am. Acad. Pediatrics (recipient Clifford Grulee award 1966); mem. Am. Pediatric Soc., Soc. for Pediatric Research, Assn. Am. Med. Colls. (pres. 1958-59), adv. bd. Med. Spltys. (pres. 1956-58), Assn. Hospital Directors of Medical Education, Sigma Xi, Alpha Omega Alpha, Delta Psi, Nu Sigma Nu. Author articles med. jours. Home: Rosemont PA Died Sept. 18, 1969.

MITCHELL, JULIAN, lawyer; b. Flat Rock, N.C., Nov. 21, 1867; s. Julian and Caroline Phoebe (Pinckney) M.; student Harvard and Univ. of Va.; m. Belle Thekla Witte, May 14, 1895; children—Julian, 3d, Cotesworth Pinckney. In active practice of law at Charleston, 1890-1931; mem. firm Mitchell & Horlbeck, 1931-49; pres. and chmn. bd. S.C. National Bank. Office: 31 Broad St., Charleston SC‡

MITCHELL, MARGARET JOHNES, teacher domestic science; b. Chicago, Dec. 26, 1869; d. Arthur and Harriet Edith (Post) M.; grad. Drexel Inst., Phila., 1900. In charge of dept. of vocal music, Oxford (O.) Coll., 1896-8; dietitian, Manhattan State Hosp., 1900-1; dir. domestic science, pub. schs., Bradford, Pa., 1902-6; instr. domestic science, Drexel Inst., 1906-7. Mem. Lake Placid Conf. Home Economics. Author: Course in Cereal Foods and Their Preparation, for Movable Schools of Agriculture, 1908; The Fireless Cook Book, 1909. Address: 414 W. 118th St., New York‡

MITCHELL, RALPH CLINTON, JR., transformer mfg. exec.; b. Brinkley, Ark., Nov. 3, 1913; s. Ralph Clifton and Lillie (Wade) M.; grad. Pine Bluff (Ark.) High Sch., 1932; m. Marian Estelle Taylor, Sept. 10, 1932; children—Ralph Clifton III, William Taylor. Distbr., Cities Service Products, 1935-53; with Central Transformer Corp., Pine Bluff, 1953-72, pres., 1962-72, chmn. bd., 1964-72, also dir.; chmn. bd. Moloney Electric Co., St. Louis, 1965; sr. v.p., dir. Colt Industries, Inc.; dir. Simmons First Nat. Bank, Pine Bluff. Bd. dirs. Jefferson Hosp., Pine Bluff. Served with AUS, 1944-46. Mem. Pine Bluff C. of C. (past pres.), Nat. Elec. Mfrs. Assn., (bd. dirs. power systems div.), U.S. C. of C. Methodist (ofcl. bd.). Lion (past pres. Pine Bluff). Home: Pine Bluff AR Died Nov. 14, 1972.

MITCHELL, RICHARD F(URLONG), judge; b. Fort Dodge, Ia., Oct. 11, 1889; s. Peter M. and Sarah (Furlong) M.; A.B., State University of Iowa, 1912, LL.B., 1913; M. Miriam Reynolds, Oct. 1936; children—Marcia Miriam, Katherine Victoria. Began practice of law at Fort Dodge, 1914; pres. Mitchell Investment Co. Was 1st lt. Air Service, U.S. Army, 1917-July 1919, 11 months overseas. Mem. Dem. State Central Com., Ia., 1924-31, and served as chmn.; elected mem. Dem. Nat. Com., 1919; mem. Supreme Court of Iowa, Nov. 1932-47, chief justice, 1934-39; commnr. ICC, 1947-60, chmn. 1954-57. Mem. Ia. State Bar Assn., Am. Law Inst., Order of Coif, Phi Delta Phi, Sigma Chi. Catholic. Clubs: National Press, Kenwood Country. Home: Chevy Chase MD Died Aug. 2, 1969; buried Gates of Heaven Cemetery, Montgomery County MD

MITCHELL, ROSCOE LEE, health officer, b. Hudson, Me., Apr. 7, 1877; s. Alphonso Hartley and Jenny Maria (Hubbard) M.; student Higgins Classical Inst., Charleston, Me.; M.D. cum laude, Univ. of Vt., 1908; postgrad. study Phila. Lying-in Hosp., 1908; married Georgia Lavinia Moores, August 1, 1917; children—Barbara Nadine, Eleanor Lee (Mrs. Philip Mazzulo). Principal Robie High School, Gorham, Me., 1899-1901; assistant interne Bridgewater State Hospital, 1902-05; medical and surgery residency Phila. Polyclinic Postgrad. Hosp., 1909; in gen. practice medicine and surgery, Portland, Me., 1909-10; co. surgeon Androscoggin Reservoir Co., Aziscohos Falls, 1910; in gen. practice, Carmel, Me., 1911-30; dist. Health officer Dist. 2, State Dept. of Health, Lewiston, Me., 1930-34, asst. dir. of health organizing maternal and child health program, 1935-37, venereal disease program, 1937-39, dir. Bur. of Health and State Health Officer. State Dept. Health and Welfare, Augusta, Me., 1939-47; organized Tuberculosis Control program, 1940. Member Penobscot County Rep. Com., 1918-20. Volunteered for M.C., U.S. Army, 1918 (not called); med. adviser to chief, Selective Service, 1944-46. Recipient Presidential certificate of commendation for work in connection with med. activities in Selective Service, Mem. A.M.A., Kennebec County Med. Assn., Am. Pub. Health Assn., Assn. State and Provincial Health Officers (past v.p.), Me. Public Health Assn. (dir.). Mason (32 deg.). Author various professional radio scripts. Contbr. to med. pubs. Home: 111 Western Av., Augusta, Me. Office: 97 Water St., Hallowell ME‡

MITCHELL, SYDNEY KNOX, prof. history; b. Lakeville, N.Y., Jan. 28, 1875; s. John and Caroline Stewart (Knox) M.; State Normal Sch., Geneseo, N.Y.; B.A., Yale, 1898, Ph.D., 1907; m. Mary Cornwall Hewitt, of New Haven, Conn., Sept. 1, 1909; 1 son, John Hewitt. Began teaching at Manila, P.I., 1901; mem. faculty, Yale, since 1907, asst. prof. history, 1910-20, prof. since 1920. Trustee Yale in China. Mem. Am. Hist. Assn., Beta Theta Pi, Phi Beta Kappa. Conglist. Club: Graduate. Author: Studies in Taxation under John and Henry III, 1914. Home: 273 Norton St., New Haven CT‡

MITCHELL, THOMAS A., business exec.; b. Manlyville, Tenn., Sept. 30, 1892; s. Thomas A. and Fredona V. (Turnbow) M.; student West Tenn. Coll.; m. Lavinia M. McCue, Jan. 2, 1920; children—Thomas A., Sue L. Chief clk. Tenn. Copper Co., 1922-28, asst. mgr., 1928-46, mgr., 1946-49, gen. mgr., from 1949, pres., from 1957; dir. Tenn. Corp.; pres., chmn. bd. First Nat. Bank of Polk Co., Copperhill, Tenn., 1935-52. Mem. Am. Legion, Am. Inst. Mining and Metall. Engrs. Mason (Shriner, 32 deg.), Kiwanian. Home: Copperhill TN Deceased.

MITCHELL, WALTER LEE, labor union exec.; b. Florence Ala., Jan. 30, 1915; s. Goodlow S. and Exel T. (Hendon) M.; LL.B., Atlanta Law Sch., 1950, LL.M., 1951; student U. Ga., 1951-52; m. Ruby A. Jenkins, Apr. 8, 1936 (div. Apr. 1954); children—Joyce, William S.; m. 2d, Lucille Snowden, Dec. 24, 1955. Chem. plant employee TVA, 1933-42; organizer AFL, 1942-44, 46; v.p. Internat. Chem. Workers Union, AFL, 1946-56, pres., from 1956. Vice pres. Indsl. Union Dept., AFL-CIO, 1962, exec. bd. Maritime Trades Dept., 1962; del. Internat. Labor Orgn.'s Chem. Industries Com., Geneva, Switzerland, 1962, chmn. com. representing workers. Mem. nat. bd. Americans for Dem. Action; mem. nat. bd., exec. com. Citizens Crusade Against Poverty. Mem. Am. (labor relations sect.), Atlanta, Ga. bar assns., Sigma Delta Kappa. Home: Akron OH Died Sept. 19, 1968; buried Florence AL

MITCHELL, WILLIAM JOHN, educator; b. N.Y.C., Nov. 21, 1906; s. Philip Alfred and Louise (Goering) M.; A.B., Columbia, 1930, A.M., 1938; m. Adelheid Ida Wagner, 1933 (div.); children—Judith Ann, Thomas William; m. 2d, Alice Levine; children—Philip Andrew and Aaron Peter (twins), Susan. Instr. music Columbia, 1932-41, asst. prof., 1941-47, asso. prof., 1947-52, prof., 1952-72, asst. to dean, 1948-58, member of the committee on instruction, 1957-72; vis. professor U. Cal. at Los Angeles, spring 1957; lectr. Mannes Coll. of Music, 1957-72. Director Walter W. Naumburg Found., 1950-72. Mem. Am. Musicol. Soc. (sec. 1949-52), College Music Society, Society for Music Liberal Arts Coll. (chmn. 1953). Author: Elementary Harmony, 1939, rev. edit., 1949; Essay on the True Art of Playing Keyboard Instruments, 1949. Contributing editor: Piano Quarterly Newsletter, 1954-71; editor: Pianist's Page, Etude, 1956-57. Contbr. edn. jours. Home: New York City NY Died Aug. 17, 1972.

MITCHELL, WILMOT BROOKINGS, coll. prof.; b. Freeport, Me., Aug. 24, 1867; s. Parmenas and Priscilla Williams (Belcher) M.; A.B., Bowdoin, 1890, A.M., 1907; studied at Harvard University, 1895-96; Litt. D., Grinnell College, 1920; L.H.D., Bowdoin College, 1938; Litt.D., University of Maine, 1944; m. Alice Merrill, Dec. 26, 1892; children—Helen Belcher (Mrs. Loren F. Richards), Hugh Addison, Esther Merrill (Mrs. Charles N. Cutter). Prin. Freeport High Sch., 1890-93; instr. rhetoric, 1893-97; prof. rhetoric and oratory, Bowdoin Coll., since 1897, acting dean, 1928 and 1934-35. Author: School and College Speaker, 1901; Elijah Kellogg—The Man and His Work, 1903; Abraham Lincoln—The Man and the Crisis, 1910; Education in Maine, 1919. Address: Brunswick ME‡

MITKE, CHARLES A., mining engr.; b. Dorrance, Pa., Aug. 14, 1881; s. Theodore and Amelia (Zoepke) M.; ed. Stroudsburg State Normal Sch., Pa.; B.A., Yale, 1908, Ph.B., 1910; m. Jessy Grant, June 11, 1917. Mining engr. Phelps Doge Corp., 1910-16, cons. engr. 1917-70; v.p. Manila Mining Corp.; pres. Cebu Mining Corp.; cons. engr. Inspiration Consol. Copper Co., Calumet & Ariz. Copper Co., United Verde Extension Mining Co., Cia de Sta. Gertrudis. Pachuca, Mexico; Cerro de Pasco Copper Corp., Peru; Roan Antelope Copper Mines, Ltd., No. Rhodesia, S.A.; Mt. Isa Mines Ltd., Northwestern Queensland, Australia; Broken Hill Mines, South Australia; New Guinea Goldfields; Cyprus Mines Ltd.; Phila. & Reading Coal and Iron Co., Bethlehem Steel Co., Cornwall, Pa.; dir. cons. engr. Masbate Consol. Gold Mining Co., Philippines, 1938; adviser to Metals Reserve Corp., Washington (in Philippine Islands) for strategic materials, 1941; prisoner in Japanese internment camp, Santo Tomas, 1944-45; rep. of U.S. High Commr. to Philippines, in Japan, on reparations, Jan.-July 1946; developing mines in Philippines, 1946-58; examining manganese mines in India, chrome mines in Turkey, 1950; investigated copper range mine, No. Mich., for Def. Minerals Adminstrn., Washington, 1951; developing tin mines in Southwest Africa for Ventures Ltd. of Toronto, Ont., Can., 1952-54. Member Am. Inst. Mining and Metall. Engrs., N.Y. Mining and Metall. (London), Kappa Epsilon. Republican. Presbyn. Club: Bankers (N.Y.). Author: Standardization in Mining Methods, 1919, Mining Methods, 1930. Address: Tucson AZ Died Feb. 22, 1970; cremated.

MIXTER, GEORGE, business exec.; b. Boston, Jan. 16, 1889; s. Samuel Jason and Wilhelmina (Galloupe) M.; A.B., Harvard, 1908, A.M., 1909, M.E.E., Harvard Grad. Sch. Applied Sciences, 1911; m. Muriel Eaton, Aug. 12, 1914; children—George, James Murchie, Robert Cutler. Began with Stone & Webster, 1911, in the Key West Electric Co.; joined Am. Internat. Corp., N.Y., 1916; v.p. Am. Balsa Corp., 1920; rejoined Stone & Webster, Inc., 1923, v.p., 1929; became sec. and treas. U.S. Smelting, Refining and Mining Co., 1934, exec. v.p. 1945, ret. 1954, also dir.; dir. Pan Am. Airways, Ware Trust Company, The West End House, Inc. and West End House Camp. Director Massachusetts Heart Association; trustee American Child Guidance. Found. Eaton & Howard Funds. Fellow Royal Geog. Soc., London, Nat. Geog. Soc.; mem. Hardwick Hist. Soc. (life), Mining and Metallurgical Soc. of Am. Clubs: St. Bernard Fish and Game; Sombrero Yacht and Golf; Harvard Travellers (fellow), Country, Somerset (Boston). Home: Hardwick MA Died Nov. 14, 1968; buried Hardwick MA

MOBLEY, RADFORD E., newspaperman; b. Eutaw, Ala., Apr. 7, 1905; s. Radford E(llis) and Hortense (Lucius) M.; A.B., U. of Alabama, 1927; m. Barbara Martin, Feb. 21, 1934; children—Kuulei, Patricia Ann, Kate. Newspaperman, 1927-69; Washington (D.C.) correspondent 1928-69, representing Knight newspapers: Akron Beacon Journal, Miami Herald, Detroit Free Press, Chicago Daily News; also Honolulu Star-Bulletin; asst. to pres., Knight Newspapers, 1956-69. Member of Phi Beta Kappa, Dleta Tau Delta, Sigma Delta Chi. Clubs: Gridiron, National Press (former pres.) (Washington). Home: Washington DC Died Nov. 12, 1969; buried Christmas Cove ME

MOCK, CHARLES ADOLPHUS, prof. of theology; b. Bedford County, Pa., Aug. 7, 1873; s. David B. and Elizabeth (Colebaugh) M.; B.A., Central Pa. Coll. (now merged with Albright Coll., Reading, Pa.) 1898, M.A., 1905; Ph.D., Grove City Coll., 1905; M.A., and B.D., Yale, 1911; m. Sue Elizabeth Allison, Dec. 15, 1897; children—Byron Fay, Charles Edgar, Grace Lillian. Ordained ministry Evang. Ch., 1898; pastor Oil City, Pa., 1898-1901, Johnstown, 1901-05, prof. Greek and Latin, Dallas (Ore.) Coll., 1905-09; pres. Western Union Coll., Le Mars, Ia., 1911-30; asso. editor Evangelical Messenger, 1930-34; prof., and head of dept. of systematic theology, Evang. Sch. of Theology, Reading, 1934-45; prof. emeritus of systematic theology, since 1945. Republican. Address: 1403 Midway Windber PA‡

MOCKRIDGE, JOHN CHARLES HILLIER, clergyman; b. in Can., Sept. 8, 1872; s. Rev. Charles Henry and Sophia Ridley (Grier) M.; King's Coll. Sch., Windsor, N.S.; B.A., U. of Trinity Coll., Toronto, 1893, M.A., 1894, B.D., 1914; D.D., St. Stephen's Coll., 1913; m. Beatrice B., d. of Hon. F. Osler, 1899; children—Elisabeth, Harold C. F., Beatrice, John B. O. Deacon, 1894, priest, 1896, P.E. Ch.; asst. St. Luke's Ch., Toronto, 1894-97; rector Ch. of Messiah, Detroit, 1897-1903, St. Andrew's Memorial Ch., Detroit, 1903-07, St. Paul's Ch., Louisville, Ky., 1907-10; vicar Trinity Chapel, Trinity Parish, New York, 1910-14, Trinity Ch., New York, 1914, 15; rector St. James' Ch., Phila., since 1915, also of St. Mary's Ch., 1933. Mem. bd. overseers Phila. Divinity Sch., 1936-39; mem. Gen. Conv. P.E. Ch. 4 times to 1934; pres. Episcopal Acad., 1938-40; founder, 1937, St. James' Choir Sch. Chaplain Pa. Soc. Colonial Wars, 1922. Club: Union League. Address: 132 S. 22d St., Philadelphia PA*‡

MODELL, CLARION, coll. ofcl.; b. N.Y.C.; d. Harry and Gussie (Egdol) Modell; B.S. in Edn., U. So. Cal., 1936, M.S. in Edn., 1938. Tchr., Ventura, Cal., 1938-42; personnel technician U.S. Govt., Sacramento and Washington, 1942-47; asst. dir., counselor exec. placement Vocational Placement Bur., U. So. Cal. at Los Angeles, asst. dir., dir. careet Planning and Placement Center, 1968. Mem. Los Angeles County Youth Employment Com., 1956-61, Fedn. Community Coordinating Councils, 1956-61; mem. Los Angeles Mayor's Com. for Handicapped. Mem. Am. Personnel and Guidance Assn. (Cal. State Membership Coordinator), Nat. Vocational Guidance Assn. (past pres. Los Angeles), Am. Coll. Personnel Assn., Cal. Counseling and Guidance Assn. (chmn. placement com.), Western Coll. Placement Assn., Bus. and Profl. Women's Clubs, Personnel and Indsl. Relations Assn., Cal. Personnel and Guidance Assn., Los Angeles C. of C. (personnel mgr.'s com.), Omega Alpha Delta. Died May 26, 1970.

MOE, ALFRED KEAN, lawyer; b. Buffalo, N.Y., Oct. 5, 1874; s. Alfred Myron and Sarah (Mahony) M.; B.A., Harvard, 1897; Harvard Law Sch., 1 yr.; master patent law, Columbian (now George Washington) U., 1901; m. Charlotte Campbell, June 6, 1906. Admitted to N.J. bar, 1898; counsellor, N.J., 1901, N.Y., 1904; Am. consul at Tegucigalpa, Honduras, 1902-04, at Dublin, Ireland, 1904-09, at Bordeaux, France, Apr. 9, 1909-Jan. 1914; resigned to engage in pvt. practice of internat. and gen. law. Mem. commn. to acquire new water works and water supply for Elizabeth N.J.; commr. public works, City of Elizabeth, 1926-32. Clubs: Harvard (New York); Masonic, Carteret (Jersey City); Bordeaux (France) Golf; Harvard (N.J.). Author: History of Harvard (humorous), 1896; Handbook of Honduras (U.S. Govt. official). Home: 1272 Clinton Pl. Office: Hersh Tower Bldg., Elizabeth NJ‡

MOELLER, HAROLD FREDERICK, banker; b. N.Y.C., Oct. 3, 1904; s. Carl L. and Katherine (Dauer) M.; spl. courses N.Y.U., 1926-28; grad. Am. Inst. Banking, Advanced Mgmt. Program, Harvard; m. Gertrude Simonson, June 2, 1934; 1 dau., Gail Meredith. With Am. Banknote Co., 1918-19; machine operator Chase Manhattan Bank, N.Y.C., 1919, asst. mgr., 1928-30, asst. cashier, 1930-41, 2d v.p., 1941-45, v.p., 1945-57, exec. v.p., 1957-67; treas., dir. Fed. Hall Meml. Assos., N.Y.C., 1958-67. Mem. English-Speaking Union, N.Y. C. of C. Mason. Clubs: North Hempstead Country (Port Washington, L.I., N.Y.); Rockefeller Center, Union League (N.Y.C.); Ekwanok Country (Manchester, Vt.). Home: Sands Point NY Died May 8, 1967.

MOELLMANN, ALBERT, govt. ofcl.; b. Kronau, Ukraine, U.S.S.R., Sept. 3, 1904; s. Frederick and Marie (Guenther) M.; B.A., U. Sask., 1930, M.A., 1933; M.A., McGill, 1935; Ph.D., Philips U., Marburg, Germany, 1937; m. Ruby Elizabeth Kaufman, Aug. 5, 1939; children—Richard Alexander, Robert Frederick. Tchr. pub. and high schs., Sask., Can., 1924-31; salesman Can. Life Assurance Co., Montreal, 1935; asst. librarian Inst. fuer Grenzund Auslandsdeutschtum, Marburg, Germany, 1935-37; instr. Bach's Fremdsprachler Faschschule, Leipzig, Germany, 1937; prof. econs. and bus. adminstrn. Waterloo (Ont.) Coll., 1937-40; statistician Dominion Bus. Statistics. Ottawa, Ont., 1940-42; indsl. engr. John Inglis Co., Toronto, 1943-44; market researcher Maclean-Hunter Publ. Co., Toronto, 1944-45; market analyst The Detroit News, 1945-56, research mgr., 1956-63; pres. Realty Research Counselors, 1955-65; chief consumer surveys br., div. consumer edn. Bur. Edn. and Voluntary Compliance, FDA. U.S. Dept. Health, Edn. and Welfare, Washington, 1965-67; social ins. research analyst Social Security Adminstrn., 1967-68; agrl. statistician Bur. Census, Dept. Commerce, Washington, 1968-69. Lectr. marketing research Wayne State U., Detroit, 1948-49, 57, Oakland U., 1964, U. Detroit, 1965. Mem. Southfield (Mich.) Planning Commn., 1957-61; chmn. Detroit Census adv. com. Bur. Census, 1956-65; past pres. Brotherhood of Mich. Synod, United Luth. Ch. Am. Mem. Ch. Am. Marketing Assn., Am. Statis. Assn. Lutheran. Author: Das Deutchtum in Montreal, 1937. Home: Washington DC Died May 26, 1969.

MOENKHAUS, WILLIAM J., univ. prof.; b. Huntingburg, Ind., Jan. 6, 1871; s. William and Fredricka (Ramsbrook) M.; grad. Ind. State Normal Sch., Terre Haute, 1892; A.B., Ind. U., Bloomington, 1894, A.M., 1895; studied Harvard, 1896-99; U. of Chicago, 1899-1901, Ph.D., 1903; m. Sara Katherine Rettger, of Bloomington, Sept. 10, 1901; children—William Ernest, Charles Augustus. Asst. dir. State Museum, Sao Paulo, Brazil, 1897-98; asst. prof. zoology, 1901-04, asso. prof. physiology, 1904-05; jr. prof., 1905-08, prof., since 1908, Ind. U. Fellow A.A.A.S., Ind. Acad. Science; mem. Am. Soc. Naturalists, Am. Soc. Zoologists, Phi Gamma Delta, Phi Beta Kappa, Sigma Xi. Contbr. to scientific jours. on exptl. biology. Home: Bloomington IN‡

MOFFATT, LUCIUS GASTON, educator; b. Chester, S.C., Mar. 14, 1899; s. James Strong Moffatt and Jennie Moffatt Grier; A.B., Erskine Coll., 1921, Litt.D. (hon.), 1937; student Army School, Beaune, France, 1919; U. of Paris and Ecole Normale Superieure, Paris, 1924-26; U. of Madrid (Spain), 1926; A.M., Harvard, 1928, Ph.D., 1929; Fellow, McKenzie Coll., Sao Paulo, Brazil, 1921-22; m. Susie Gatewood Cathcart, Oct. 18, 1923; children—Suzanne, Lucie Gaston. High sch. prin., Pageland, S.C., 1922-23; instr., English-French, Clemson (S.C.) Coll., 1923-24; instr., tutor, Harvard, 1928-29; asso. prof. Romance langs., Syracuse U., 1929-37; prof. and chmn. dept. Romance langs., 1937-41; prof. and chairman School of Romance Languages, U. of Va., 1941-64, professor of romance philology, 1964-71. Served with U.S. Army, 1917-19; sgt., A.E.F., Jan. 1918-Aug. 1919; awarded Bronze star for service in Aisne-Marne offensive, Aisne-Marne defensive; Saint-Mihiel, Meuse-Argonne. Mem. Com. on Intellectual Co-operation with Latin-Am. Univs., since 1942; mem. Am. Assn. Univ. Profs. (mem. nat. council 1943-46), Am. Assn. Tchrs. French, Raven Soc. Am. Assn. Tchrs. Spanish and Portuguese, Modern Lang. Assn. of Am., Modern Lang. of Va. (pres., 1942-43, 1950-51), Phi Beta Kappa, Tau Kappa Epsilon.

Democrat. Presbyn. Clubs: Rotary, Farmington Country (Charlottesville). Author: Letters of Court of John III, King of Portugal (with J. D. M. Ford), 1933; reviser and co-author Portuguese Grammar (with Hills, Ford, Coutinho), 1944; contbr. Dictionary of Modern European Literature, 1947. Author: Merlusse, 1937. Contbr. articles on French, Spanish, Portuguese linguistics and lit. in various publs. Travel and study in France, Spain, Portugal, and Brazil. Home: Charlottesville VA Died June 2, 1971; buried Alicante, Spain

MOFFETT, ELWOOD STEWART, labor union exec.; b. Williamstown, Pa., Apr. 30, 1908; s. Alfred and Jennie A. (Showers) M.; grad. high sch.; m. Hannah Pauline Ely, Jan. 31, 1931; children—Kenneth Elwood, Alfred Robert, Brent Arthur, John Paul. Mine worker, Williamstown, 1924-42; pres. local union United Mine Workers Am., 1935-42; mem. Dauphin County (Pa.) Bd. Pub. Assistance, 1937-38, Anthracite Coal Scale Com. United Mine Workers Am., 1939-40, rep., 1942-46, regional dir., 1946-48, asst. to pres., 1948-58, v.p. Dist. 50, 1958-62, pres. Internat. Dist. 50, 1962-72. Mem. Nat. Labor Adv. Com. to Sec. Treasury for Savs. Bonds, 1956-72. Trustee John L. Lewis Scholarship Fund. Democrat. Methodist (trustee). Home: Takoma Park MD

MOFFETT, LOUIS BURDELLE, b. Swedesboro, N.J., Mar. 22, 1874; s. Biddle Reeves and Mary Emma (Eastlack) M.; grad. Peirce Sch. Business Administration, Phila., Pa., 1892; m. Mary Lewis Quinn, July 3, 1894; 1 son, Louis Burdelle. With Peirce Sch. of Business Administration since 1892, sec., 1896-1900, later dir., retired, 1934; now pres. of Woodbury Trust Co. (Woodbury, N.J.). Member N.J. State Fuel Administration, World War. Sec., treas. Sinking Fund Commn., Woodbury, N.J. Mem. N.J. Soc. of Pa. (sec.), Geneal. Soc. of Pa. (dir.). Republican. Methodist. Mason (32 deg.). Clubs: Phila Rotary (pres. 1931), Union League (Phila.). Author: Money and Banking, 1915. Home: Woodbury NJ‡

MOFFIT, ALEXANDER, librarian; b. Primghar, Ia., Mar. 24, 1902; s. Cassius Clay and Harriet (Adams) M.; student Ia. State Coll., 1920-23; A.B., U. Ia., 1926; B.L.S., U. Ill., 1931, M.S., 1935; m. Catherine Leytze, Aug. 17, 1929 (dec. Aug. 1968); children—Ann, Constance. Successively exchange asst., documents asst., reference asst., chemistry librarian U. Ill. Library, 1931-36; asso. univ. librarian U. Tex. Library, 1936-45, librarian from 1945. Mem. Am. Tex., S.W. library assns. Contbr. articles periodicals. Home: Austin TX Died May 21, 1969.

MOFFITT, HERBERT CHARLES, physician; b. San Francisco, Dec. 9, 1867; s. James and Delia (Kennedy) M.; B.S., U. of Calif., 1889, LL.D., 1919; M.D., Harvard Med. Sch., 1894; D.Sc., Harvard, 1921; m. Margaret Joliffe, June 15, 1899; children—James (killed in action, July 2, 1943), Alice, Herbert Charles. Practiced at San Francisco since 1898; emeritus prof. medicine, U. of Calif. Home: 1818 Broadway, San Francisco CA‡

MOFFITT, WALTER VOLENTINE, investment banker; b. Lancaster, Tex., Sept. 17, 1905; s. William Alfred and Marian Ada (Price) M.; B.B.A., U. Chattanooga, 1927; M.A., Duke, 1928; post grad; student Columbia, 1929-30; m. Martha Meredith Moore, Oct. 2, 1936; children—Martha Meredith (Mrs. Robert J. Osterhus), Ann Price (Mrs. Theodore Wickersham). Various positions Guaranty Trust Co. of N.Y. and affiliate Guaranty Co. of N.Y., 1928-33, trust investment and security analysis div., 1933-35; research and security underwriting Kidder, Peabody & Co., N.Y.C., 1935-39, mgr. research and statis. div., 1939-44, gen. partner, specializing in corporate finance, merger negotiations, investment and corp. analysis, 1944-65, later dir., mem. exec. com. Kidder, Peabody & Co., Inc.; dir., mem. exec. and finance coms. Benjamin Moore & Co., N.Y.C.; dir., mem. finance com. Thalhimer Bros. Inc., Richmond, Va.; dir. Penn Worsted Co., Duffy-Mott Co., Inc. (N.Y.C.). Director and member finance committee Huntington (Long Island) Hosp.; director, member finance coms. Manhattan Eye, Ear and Throat Hosp. Mem. Am., N.Y. Soc. Security Analysts, Phi Delta Theta. Republican. Episcopalian (vestryman). Clubs: University, Recess, Bond, Economic (N.Y.C.); Huntington Country; Cold Spring Harbor (L.I.) Beach; Lloyds Neck (L.I.) Bath. Home: Cold Spring Harbor LI NY Died Apr. 15, 1968; buried St. John's Ch. Meml. Cemetery, Cold Spring Harbor NY

MOHLER, JOHN ROBBINS, pathologist; b. Phila., Pa., May 9, 1875; s. William Casper and Harriet Robbins (Hart) M.; Central High Sch.; Phila., 1888-92; Temple U., 1892-93; V.M.D., U. of Pa., 1896, hon. D.Sc., 1925; Med. Dept., Marquette U., 1897-99; hon. D.Sc., Iowa State Coll., 1920; hon. D.Sc., U. of Md., 1928; m. Clara Moffett Clarke, Dec. 23, 1897; children—William Melvin, Miriam Clarke. Practiced as veterinarian, 1896-97; asst. insp., Bur. Animal Industry, Dept. of Agr., 1897-99; asst. pathologist, 1899-1901, zoologist, 1901-02, chief pathol. div. of the bureau, 1902-14; asst. chief of the Bur. of Animal Industry, 1914-17; chief of that bureau 1917-1943, when he retired. Baptist. Member American Veterinary Med. Assn. (pres. 1913), Soc. Am. Bacteriologists, Soc. Exptl. Biology and Medicine, Pa. State Vet. Assn., Internat. Vet. Congress (president 1934), Am. Pub. Health Assn., Washington Acad. of Sciences, U.S. Livestock Sanitary Assn. (pres. 1925), Soc. of Animal Production, D.C. Bd. of Veterinary Examiners, Washington Acad. Medicine, Royal Soc. of Medicine (Great Britain), Sigma Xi; hon. mem. Alpha Psi, Phi Kappa Phi. Hon. prof. U. of Havana, 1944. Awarded 12th Internat. Veterinary Congress prize, 1940; Dr. George Martin Kober Foundation lectureship for 1941 by the Medical Society of the D.C.; A.V.M.A. Award as Investigator and Administrator, Boston, 1946. Translator: Edelmann's Meat Hygiene, 1908 (also editor) Hutyra and Marek's Special Pathology and Therapeutics, 1912, 4th Edition, 1938; Ernst's Milk Hygiene, 1914. Author numerous articles on pathology, bacteriology and meat inspection, in govt. publs., med. jours. and encys. Home: 1620 Hobart St. N.W., Washington DC‡

MOHLER, SAMUEL LOOMIS, educator; b. Baltimore, Mar. 29, 1895; s. John Fred and Sarah (Loomis) M.; A.B., Dickinson Coll., 1914; A.M., Harvard, 1918; Ph.D., U. of Pa., 1926; m. Harriet Holmes Stuart, June 22, 1918; children—Mary Baird, Sarah Loomis (Mrs. Henry J. Stojowski). Latin and Greek teacher Wilmington Conf. Acad., 1914-16, Loomis Inst., 1918, Camden (N.J.) High Sch., 1919-20, Chester (Pa.) High Sch., 1920-21; instr. Latin, U. of Pa., 1921-26; mem. faculty Franklin and Marshall Coll., Lancaster, Pa., from 1926, prof. classics from 1932. Mem. Am. Philol. Assn., Classical Assn. Atlantic States, Pa. State Assn. Classical, Teachers, Phi Beta Kappa. Contbr. to classical jours. Home: Lancaster PA Deceased.

MOHR, CHARLES ADAM, college prof.; b. Macungie, Pa., May 29, 1869; s. Herman and Sarah Anna (Smith) M.; B.E., Keystone (Pa.) State Normal Sch., 1890; A.B., Franklin and Marshall Coll., Lancaster, Pa., 1896; B.D., Union Theol. Sem., 1899; grad. student, Columbia, and univs. of Berlin and Heidelberg, 1909-13; Ph.D., U. of Chicago, 1913; unmarried. Ordained Congl. ministry, 1901; pastor Ft. Recovery and Marblehead, O., later Silverton, Colo., 1901-7; spl. editor Schaff-Herzog Ency., 1908-9; asso. prof. philosophy and logic, Ind. U., 1913-14; prof. philosophy and psychology, Fargo Coll., N.Dak., 1915-18, Lawrence Coll., Appleton, Wis., 1918-19; prof. edn., Dak. Wesleyan U., since Sept. 1919. Spl. investigator N.Y. State Tenement House Commn., 1900. Home: Mitchell SD‡

MOLDVEEN-GERONIMUS, MIRIAM ESTHER, physician; b. N.Y.C., Feb. 8, 1925; d. Isadore and Anna Moldveen; M.D., Woman's Med. Coll., Phila., 1951; m. Lippman Hart Geronimus, Mar. 15, 1952; children—Edith Olivia (Mrs. Timothy Nason), Arline Tabitha, Susan Rebecca. Intern, Queens Gen. Hosp., 1951-52; resident in pathology Mt. Sinai Hosp., N.Y.C., 1952-53, Bronx (N.Y.) VA Hosp., 1953-55, Peter Bent Brigham Hosp., Boston, 1955-56; asst. pathologist Faulkner Hosp., 1956-57, Boston VA Hosp., 1958-70; instr. pathology Harvard, Tufts U.; asst. prof. pathology Boston U. Med. Sch. Diplomate Am. Bd. Pathology. Mem. New Eng. Pathol. Soc. Home: Brookline MA Died Sept. 23, 1970; buried Lindwood Park, Randolph MA

MOLEEN, GEORGE ARNOLD, M.D.; b. E. St. Louis, Ill., Nov. 16, 1876; s. Alfred and Mary E. (Pelissier) M.; Ph.G., Phila. Coll. Pharmacy, 1896; M.D., Gross Med. Coll. (U. of Denver), 1900; m. May Luff Conway, of Denver, July 20, 1916. Practiced in Denver, 1900; work practically confined to consultation in nervous and insane diseases and expert court work. Asst. prof. neurology, Med. Dept. U. of Colo. Acting steward and steward, Hosp. Corps, Colo. N.G., 1897-1900. Mem. A.M.A., Colo. State Med. Soc., Med. Soc. City and Co. of Denver (pres. 1918-19), Denver Clin. and Pathol. Soc., Assn. for Research in Nervous and Mental Disease, Colo. Neurol. Assn. (a founder). Clubs: Denver Athletic, Mt. Vernon Country. Catholic. Address: 719 Gaylord St. Office: Mack Bldg., Denver CO‡

MOLINEUX, MARIE ADA, lecturer; b. Centreville, Cal.; has lived at Boston, from childhood; A.B., Boston U., 1879, A.M., 1880, Ph.D., 1882; studied Mass. Inst. Tech., 1890. Bacteriologist, teacher of psychology, essayist; lecturer on literary, artistic and scientific topics. Corr. sec. Boston Browning Soc.; life mem. N.E. Women's Club. Author: A Phrase Book from the Poetic and Dramatic Works of Robert Browning, 1896. Address: 2 Regent Circle, Brookline MA‡

MOLITOR, HANS, pharmacologist; b. Maffersdorf, Czechoslovakia, Aug. 10, 1895; s. Emil and Lydia (Schmid) M.; grad. Volkesschule, Maffersdorf, 1905, Staatsgymnasium Reichenberg, Czechoslovakia, 1913; Abiturium, M.D., U. of Vienna, Austria, 1921; unmarried. Came to U.S., 1932, naturalized, 1937. Asst. prof. pharmacology U. of Vienna Med. Sch., 1922-26; Rockefeller traveling fellow Edinburgh and London, 1924; privat-dozent (lectr.) pharmacol. and toxicol., U. of Vienna Med. Sch., 1927-28, asso. prof., 1928-32; dir. Merck Inst. for Therapeutic Research, Rahway, N.J., 1932-55, chmn. bd. 1955-70; dir. sci. relations, Merck Sharp & Dohme Research Labs., div. Merck & Co., Inc., 1956-70. Fellow A.A.A.S., Internat. Coll. Anes, N.Y. Acad. Sci. (councillor 1946-48, v.p. 1948); Royal Soc. Medicine (1956); mem. Am. Physiol. Soc. Am. Soc. Pharmacol. and Exptl. Therapy, Soc. Exptl. Biol. and Med., Am. Soc. Trop. Med., Nat. Malaria Soc., Southern Med. Assn., Phila. Physiol. Soc. Club: Colonial Country (Rahway). Contbr. over 100 research articles to sci. jours. Home: Metedeconk NJ Died Sept. 1970.

MOLLISON, JAMES ALEXANDER, army officer; b. Smith Center, Kan., July 9, 1897; commd. 2d lt. Air Service, July 1920, and advanced through the grades to brigadier general, Nov. 1942; married Betty Bulkeley, March, 4, 1924; children—Lt. Col. Douglas Alexander, Armored Force, United States Army, Molly Bulkeley Kalish, Betsey Barrington Volkert; assigned 2d Air Service Area Command. Ft. Worth, Tex. July 1942. comdg. gen., 1942; became chief, Personnel Training Div., Air Service Command, Patterson Field, O., Dec. 1942. Became comdg. gen., Mobile Air Service Command, Feb. 1943-Sept. 1944; comdg. gen. XV Air Force Service Command, September 1944-May 1945; comdg. gen. XV Air Force, May 1945-July 1945; comdg. gen. Mediterranean Air Force, July 1945-Aug. 1945; joint chief of Staff, Wash., D.C., Sept. 1945-Dec. 1945; chief of Air Installations in Office of comdg. gen. Army Air Forces, Dec. 1945-Jan. 1946. Loaned by War Dept. to War Assets Adminstrn. as dep. adminstr. for aircraft disposal, Jan. 1946-Nov. 1946; vice administr. for Staff Operations, War Assets Adminstrn., 1946-48; retired from U.S. Air Force, June 1948. Dir. McClanahan Oil Co.; exec. v.p. and dir., Great Lakes Chem. Corp.; v.p. Ewin Engring. Corp., D.G. Volkert & Assos. Mem. Washington Bd. Trade. Rated command pilot and combat observer. Home: Washington DC Died Feb. 4, 1970; buried Arlington Nat. Cemetery, Arlington VA

MOLNAR, JULIUS PAUL, physicist; b. Detroit, Feb. 23, s. Joseph and Elizabeth (Goeney) M.; A.B., Oberlin Coll., 1937; Ph.D., Mass. Inst. Tech., 1940; Margaret Hale Andrews, July 12, 1941; 1 son, Peter Hale. Tech. aide Nat. Def. Research Com., 1940-42; physicist Gulf Research and Development Co., 1942-45; mem. tech. staff Bell Telephone Labs., 1945-49, electron tube development systems development, 1955-57, dir. mil. development engr., 1950-54, dir. electron tube development, 1955, dir. mil. development, 1957, v.p., 1957-58; v.p. Western Electric Co., 1958-60; exec. v.p. Bell Telephone Labs., Inc., 1960-73; pres. Sandia Corp., 1958-60. Mem. Am. Phys. Soc., Optical Soc. Am., Inst. Radio Engrs. Home: Summit NJ Died Jan. 11, 1973.

MOLOHON ALBIN D(UNLAP), govt. ofcl.; b. Jacksonville, Ill., Mar. 7, 1900; s. Henry Albin and Stella Roberta (Dunlap) M.; student U. Ariz., 1925; M.Agr. (hon.), Ore. State Coll., 1939; hon. degree, Eastern Mont. Coll. Education, 1953; m. Josephine Louise Doenges, Nov. 24, 1920; children—Kathleen Patricia (Mrs. Vernon D. Adams), Michael Dunlap, Packer and powderman for the U.S. Forest Service, 1924-25, asst. forest ranger, 1926, sr. forest ranger, 1929, grazing asst., 1931, asst. forest supervisor, 1934; regional grazer U.S. Grazing Service, 1935, chief range surveys, planned, developed Magdalena Stock Driveway, N.M., 1936, planned, organized, directed range surveys grazing dists. 10 western states, 1936-38, reorganized range improvement program, 1939, established program soil and moisture conservation grazing dists., 1940, chief range management, 1941; spl. asst. to dir., planning orgn. Bur. Land Management, 1946, regional adminstr. Mo. Basin Region, 1947-52; chief agriculturist, U.S. Operations Mission Israel, 1953-56. U.S. Operations Mission Ethiopia, 1956-60. ret.; cons. Agency Internat. Development, 1960-68; guest lectr. Ore. State Coll., 1935-39; collaborator in planning and constructing Squaw Butte Range Expt. Sta., Burns, Ore., 1935-40; lectr. Mediterranean Tng. Centre, Ankara, Turkey, 1951; range management cons. Hashemite Kingdom of the Jordan, Point 4 Program, 1953; collaborator in establishment of course of conservation edn. Eastern Mont. Coll. Edn., 1949-52. Mem. Pres. Com. on Shelf of Post War Projects, 1939-40; mem. Nat. Com. Policies in Conservation Edn. since 1948; mem. Mo. Basin field com. Dept. Interior, 1947-52. Served as sgt. Inf. U.S. Army, 1917-19, maj. Inf., 1942-46, hdqrs. comdt., Ft. Lewis, Wash., 1943-46. Decorated Army Commendation ribbon, Purple Heart, Distinguished Service Unit Plaque, campaign ribbons World War I and II. Mem. Am. Legion (past post comdr.). Episcopalian (vestryman, ordained perpetual deacon 1969). Mason (Shriner). Dunnellon FL Died Nov. 10, 1970; buried Arlington Nat. Cemetery.

MOLONEY, WILLIAM CURRY, physician, educator; b. Boston, Dec. 19, 1907; s. Francis and Elizabeth (Curry) M.; M.D., Tufts U., 1932; m. Josephine O'Brien, Nov. 1933; children—Patricia, William Curry, Elizabeth, Thomas. Prof. medicine Harvard Med. Sch.; also physician Peter Bent Brigham Hosp. Dep. dir. Atomic Bomb Casualty Commn., Hiroshima, Japan, 1952-54. Served as maj., M.C., AUS,

World War II. Diplomate Am. Bd. Internal Medicine. Fellow A.C.P., Internat. Soc. Hematology, Am. Assn. Cancer Research, Mass. Med. Soc.; mem. A.M.A., Asso. Am. Physicians, Alpha Omega Alpha. Office: Boston MA Died Feb. 21, 1972.

MONACHESI, ELIO DAVID, sociologist; b. Macerata, Italy, July 19, 1905; son of Armando and Nera (Vitaloni) Monachesi; came to U.S, 1912, naturalized, 1931; A.B., U. of Mo., 1927, A.M., 1928; Ph.D., U. of Minn., 1931; m. Marjorie F. Diddy, Jan. 31, 1936 (dec. Jan. 1972); children—Livia, Aleeta. Undergrad. asst. in polit. sci., U. of Mo., 1926-27, grad. asst. in sociology, 1927-28, instr. sociol., U. of Minn., 1928-32, asst. prof., 1934-39, asso. prof., 1939-45, prof. sociol. 1945-71, chmn. dept. sociology, 1951-71; vis. prof. University of Oregon, summer 1958. Post-doctoral fellow, Social Science Research Council, Boston, and Italy, 1932-34. Fellow A.A.A.S. Am. Sociol. Soc., Sociol. Research Assn., Am. Assn. Social Workers, Am. Assn. Univ. Profs., Big Brothers, Inc., Midwest Sociological Society (pres. 1958-59), Phi Beta Kappa, Alpha Pi Zeta, Alpha Kappa Delta. Author: Prediction Factors in Probation, 1932; The Rehabilitation of Children (with Edith M. H. Baylor), 1939; Elements of Sociology (with Don Martindale), 1951; Analyzing and Predicting Juvenile Delinquency with the MMPI (with Starke R. Hathaway), 1953; (with Starke R. Hathaway) An Atlas of Juvenile MMPI Profiles, 1961, Adolescent Personality and Behavior, pub. 1963. Contbr. to profl. jours. Home: Minneapolis MN Died June 28, 1971; buried Sunset Meml. Cemetery, Minneapolis MN

MONAHAN, ARTHUR COLEMAN, educational expert; b. Framingham, Mass., Mar. 24, 1877; s. Michael and Johannah (Coleman) M.; B.S., Mass. Agrl. Coll., 1900; m. Mary Ellen Cody, June 30, 1904. Instr. Mass. Agrl. Coll. and asst. at Expt. Sta., 1900-01; teacher and prin. pub. high schs., 1901-10; specialist in rural and agrl. edn., U.S. Bureau of Edn., Washington, July 1, 1910-Jan. 8, 1918; maj., U.S. Army, Jan. 8, 1918-Jan. 1, 1921; attached to surgeon general's office in ednl. service, div. of reconstruction, 1918-19; lt. col. U.S. Army Reserves (med. dept.), S.C.; chief of ednl. service, Walter Reed Gen. Hosp., 1919-20; dir. bureau edn., Nat. Catholic Welfare Council, 1921-22, editor and ednl. adviser, 1923-32; asst. to commr. in charge of property, U.S. Office of Indian Affairs, since 1932. Mem. N.E.A. Lecturer on sch. administration and edn.; author various bulletins and contbr. on ednl. topics. Address: 3700 13th St. N.W., Washington DC‡

MONHELM, LEONARD MYERS, educator; b. Clairton, Pa., June 7, 1911; s. Charles and Julia (Feldstein) M.; B.S., U. Pitts., 1933, D.D.S., 1933, M.S., 1953; m. Marion Altman, Dec. 3, 1950; children—Charles William, Lisa Rae. Prof. anesthesiology U. Pitts. Schs. Medicine and Dentistry, 1948-71, prof. pharmacology Sch. Dental Medicine, 1965-71, prof. Grad. Faculty, 1955-71; anesthesiologist Presbyn. U. Hosp., Pitts., 1938-71, twice pres. med. staff. Mem. Allegheny County (Pa.) Bd. Helath, 1960-71; adv. com. Western Pa. Regional Med. Program, 1965-70. Served with AUS, 1942-46; PTO. Recipient Heidbrink award Am. Dental Soc. Anesthesiology, 1957, Horace Wells award, 1961. Mem. Am. Soc. Anesthesiologists, Dental Soc. Anesthesiologists, Internat. Anesthesia Research Soc., N.Y. Acad. Scis., Sigma Xi. Author: Local Anesthesia and Pain Control in Dental Practice, 4th edit., 1969; General Anesthesia in Dental Practice, 3d edit., 1969. Anesthesia editor Jour. Oral Surgery, 1963, Triple O. Jour., 1963-70. Home: Pittsburgh PA Died Oct. 18, 1971.

MONNETT, VICTOR, geologist; b. Hale, Mo., Dec. 1, 1889; s. Ira and Ann (Todd) M.; A.B., U. of Oklahoma, 1912; student U. of Mich., 1912-13; Ph.D., Cornell, 1922; m. Kathryn Brown, Aug. 16, 1915; 1son, Victor Brown. Began as teacher of geology; asst. prof. geology, U. of Okla., 1917-22, prof., 1922-60, David Ross Boyd emeritus prof. geology, 1960-72, dir. Sch. of Geological Engring., 1922-42, Sch. of Geology 1930-55, dean of grad. sch., and dir. research inst., 1944-46. Mem. Sigma Xi, Phi Beta Kappa, Sigma Gamma Epsilon, Sigma Tan. Methodist. Club: Lions. Home: Norman OK Died Sept. 18, 1972.

MONRO, CHARLES BEDELL, aviation co. exec.; b. Pitts., Feb. 26, 1901; s. William L. and Violet K. (Bedell) M.; student Philips Exeter (N.H.) Acad., 1916-19; A.B., Harvard, 1923; M.A., U. Pa., 1926; LL.D., Marietta Coll., 1944; m. Marjory Boyd Hill, June 3, 1926; 1 son, Charles B. Instr. U. Pitts., 1924-29; sec. Pitts. Aviation Industries Corp., 1928-30, dir., 1930, v.p., sec., 1931-32, exec. v.p. and sec., 1933-34; sec.-treas. Pa. Airlines, Inc., 1930-31, dir., 1930, v.p. and sec., 1931-32, exec. v.p. and sec., 1933-34; exec. v.p. and dir. Pa. Airlines & Transport Co., 1934, pres., 1934-36; pres. Pa.-Central Airlines Corp., (name changed to Capital Airlines, Inc.), 1936-47; dir. Capital Airlines, Inc., 1936-61, exec. com., 1956-61; pres. and dir. United Service Assos., 1947-72. Episcopalian. Clubs: Congressional, Burning Tree (Washington). Co-author: Quest of Chevy Chase MD Died June 30, 1972.

MONROE, DANIEL L., investment co. exec.; grad. Princeton, 1926; m. Marjorie Coe; children—Daniel C., Mrs. John M. Emery. Partner Ingalls & Snyder, N.Y.C. Bd. dirs. Five Towns Community House; past bd. dirs., pres. Lawrence Country Day Sch.; trustee Hofstra U., 1949-73, pres. bd. trustees, 1963-67; trustee, treas. Woodrow Wilson Found.; trustee Hackley Sch. Recipient Class Achievement award Princeton, 1972. Home: Lawrence NY Died Apr. 10, 1973.

MONROE, LAWRENCE ALEXANDER, chem. engr.; b. Peoria, Ill., Aug. 10, 1912; s. Edward Daniel and Sara (Weatherwax) M.; student Bradley U., 1928-30; B.S., U. Ill., 1932; S.M., Mass. Inst. Tech., 1934, Sc.D., 1936. Asst. prof. chem. engring. Mass. Inst. Tech., 1938-40; chem. engr. Allied Chem. Corp., Phila., 1940-42; chief, chem. industries br. Office Prodn. Research and Devel., WPB, Washington, 1944-45; engr. Ethyl Corp., N.Y.C., 1945-49; engr. R. R. Donnelley & Sons Co., Chgo., 1960-69. Mem. Am. Chem. Soc., T.A.P.P.I., A.A.A.S., Am. Inst. Chem. Engrs., Alpha Chi Sigma, Phi Lambda Upsilon, Delta Sigma Phi. Club: Mass. Inst. Tech., Chgo. Home: Evanston IL Died July 1969.

MONSMAN, GERALD, lawyer; b. Berlikum, The Netherlands, Apr. 19, 1899 (derivative citizenship); s. John and Helen (Kikstra) M.; came to U.S. 1902; A.B., Calvin Coll., 1926; LL.B., U. Md., 1934; J.D., Georgetown U., 1935; student U. Mich., Johns Hopkins; m. Diana de Kryger, Dec. 31, 1927; 1 son, Gerald Cornelius. High sch. tchr., 1926-34; admitted to Md. bar, 1934; atty. Mexican Claims Agy., Dept. of State, 1935-36; atty., exec. dir. Legal Aid Bur., Balt., 1937-54, also supvr. legal aid clinic Law Sch. U. Md.; counsel, exec. sec. United Christian Citizens, Inc., Balt., 1954-59; exec. director State Coordinating Commission on the Problems of the Aging, 1959-68. Director, exec. com. Nat. Legal Aid Assn., 1940-54; pres. pub. relations council Balt. Community Chest Agencies, 1943-45; sec. Gov.'s Commns. to Study Child Placement and Adoption Laws, 1946-47, 53-54; pres. Md. Conf. Social Welfare, 1950-52; counsel, mem. bd. Fight Blight, Inc., Balt., 1950-55; mem. adv. bd. Fight Blight Fund, 1953-55. Member Maryland Bar Association, Bar Association of Baltimore City, Order of Coif. Democrat. Presbyn. (clk.). Contbr. legal jours. Home: Towson MD Died May 4, 1970; buried Fremont MI

MONTAGUE, FAIRFAX EUBANK, physician; b. Raleigh, N.C., Mar. 7, 1925; s. Edgar Burwell and Mary (Read) M.; M.D., Emory U., 1952; m. Barbara Lucile Wilson, June 4, 1949; children—Sally Paige, David Fairfax, Tyler Clark, Lisa Ashlyn. Intern, Duke Hosp., Durham, N.C., 1952-53; asst. resident in surgery Emory U. Hosp., Atlanta, 1953-54, sr. resident in surgery and neoplastic disease Winship Clinic, 1956-57; asst. resident in surgery Atlanta VA Hosp., 1954-56, sr. resident in surgery and neoplastic disease, 1956-57; mem. staff Putnam Hosp., Palatka, Fla., until 1971, chief staff, 1970. Med. dir. Putnam County Blood Bank, 1957-71. Chmn. Citizens Adv. Com. for Schs., 1967; pres. Putnam County Taxpayers League, 1968. Served with AUS, World War II; ETO. Decorated Bronze Star. Diplomate Am. Bd. Surgery. Fellow A.C.S.; mem. A.M.A., So., Fla. (chmn. com. on blood banks 1965-68), Putnam County (pres. 1967) med. assns., Southeastern Surg. Congress, Putnam C. of C. (dir. 1968-70), Phi Beta Kappa, Alpha Omega Alpha, Sigma Chi. Presbyn. (deacon 1955-57, elder 1958-71). Home: Palatka FL Died July 15, 1971; buried Palatka Meml. Gardens, Palatka FL

MONTAGUE, HELEN WEYMOUTH, M.D.; b. Cambridge, Mass., Sept. 22, 1876; d. Aaron and Georgianna (Ellis) Robinson; student U. of Calif., 1900-03, Barnard Coll. (Columbia), 1904-06; M.D., Woman's Med. Coll. of Pa., 1910; m. William Pepperell Montague, Aug. 5, 1896; children—William Pepperell, Robinson Prescott Cary. Began practice N.Y. City, Oct. 1912; psychiatrist to Children's Court, N.Y. City, since 1917, dir. psychiatric clinic of same since 1928; psychiatrist Inwood House (custodial instn. for girls), N.Y. City, since 1915; mem. bd. mgrs. N.Y. State Training Sch. for Girls, Hudson, N.Y., since 1922; attending phychiatrist State Psychiatric Inst. of N.Y. Mem. Am. Med. Assn., N.Y. County Med. Soc., Am. Women's Assn., Med. Jurisprudence Soc. Democrat. Club: Women's City. Home and Office: 27 W. 9th St., New York NY*‡

MONTAGUE, JAMES EDWARD, JR., lawyer; b. Washington, Aug. 3, 1903; s. James Edward and Marion (Chapin) M.; student Carleton Coll., 1921-23; B.A., U. Minn., 1926, LL.B., 1927; M. Dorothy Reece, Aug. 14, 1929; children—James Edward III, Jane Elizabeth (Mrs. Arlan Brugman). Admitted to Minn. bar, 1927; practice in Virginia, Minn., 1927-39; city atty., Virginia, 1935-37; practice in Duluth, 1939-66; partner firm Montague, Applequist, Lyons, Nolan, Donovan & Knetsch, 1941-66. Pres. Gretmar, Inc., mineral properties. Duluth, 1955-66; dir. Zalk-Josephs Company, Duluth. Sec., treasurer of The John C. Dwan Ednl. Found.; treasurer of the Marshall H. and Nellie Alworth Meml. Fund. Fellow American Bar Foundation, American College of Trial Lawyers; mem. of Am., Minnesota (mem. bd. of govenors 1951-52, president 1965-66), District (president 1950) bar associations, also mem. Duluth C. of C., Delta Sigma Rho, Zeta Psi. Conglist. (trustee). Clubs: Kitchi Gammi (dir.), Northland Country (Duluth). Home: Duluth MN Died Sept. 23, 1966; buried Forest Hill Cemetery, Duluth MN

MONTAGUE, ROBERT LATANE, marine corps officer (ret.); b. Danville, Va., Apr. 2, 1897; s. Andrew Jackson and Elizabeth Lyne (Hoskins) M.; B.S., Univ. of Va., 1920; student, Univ. of Grenoble, France, 1919; grad. Army Inf. Sch., 1926, Ecole Superieure de Guerre, Paris, 1935, U.S. Naval War Coll., 1941; m. Frances Breckinridge Wilson, June 30, 1932; children—Robert Latane III, Francis Breckinridge. Commd. 2d lt. U.S.M.C., 1917, and advanced through grades to brig. gen., 1946; served in command and staff assignments, World Wars I and II; ret. from active duty, 1946. Awarded Army D.S.C., Navy Cross, Legion of Merit, 2 Presidential unit citations, Cloud and Banner (China). Democrat. Episcopalian. Clubs: St. Anthony, Army Navy (Washington), Country (Texarkana). Home: Urbanna VA Died May 1972.

MONTAVON, WILLIAM FREDERICK, commercial attache; b. in Scioto Co., O., July 17, 1874; A.B., Notre Dame U., Ind., 1898; studied Inst. de Sainte Croix, Paris, and Catholic U. of America, 1908-11. Was teacher and supt. schs., Philippines; commercial attache of U.S. to Peru, Ecuador and Bolivia, 1916-18; exec. rep. of Internat. Petroleum Co., Ltd., on the West Coast of S.A., 1918-—. Address: Apartado 960, Lima Peru‡

MONTEITH, WALTER E(MBREE), judge; b. Belton, Tex., Sept. 9, 1877; s. Arthur M. and Wilhoit (Embree) M.; grad. Belton Male Acad., 1896; LLB., U. of Tex., 1901; m. Vera Morey, Feb. 27, 1908; 1 son, Arthur Morey (dec.). In practice, Belton, 1904-06; land commr. for receivers Kirby Lumber Co., 1906-09; resumed practice of law, Houston, Tex., 1909; judge of County Court at Law, Harris County, Tex., 1916-19; judge Dist. Court, 61st Jud. Dist., 1919-28; mayor of Houston, 1929-33; elected chief justice Court of Civil Appeals, 1st Supreme Judicial Dist. of Tex., 1938. Mem. Tex. Bar Assn., Houston Bar Assn. (pres. 1938), Am. Bar Assn., Am. Judicature Soc., Am. Legion, Kappa Alpha. Democrat. Presbyterian. Mason (32 deg., K.T., Shriner). Clubs: Houston, Houston Country. Home: 5 Shadow Lawn, Houston, Tex. Office: Court Civil Appeals, Galveston TX‡

MONTGOMERY, A.E., treas. Boise Cascade Corp. Address: Boise ID Died Aug. 12, 1971.

MONTGOMERY, BENJAMIN F., army officer; b. Petersburg, Va., s. Joseph R. and Anne E. (Griffin) M.; ed. pub. and high schs., Petersburg, Va., and Va. Acad.; m. Petersburg, Va., Dec. 27, 1877, Ella Franklin. Electrician; practical telegrapher; early life associated with Western Union and other co's; entered U.S. signal service, 1875; served at hdqrs. chief signal officer of the Army, 1875-7; on detached duty with Presidents Hayes, Garfield and Arthur, 1877-82, at exec. mansion; on exec. staffs Presidents Arthur and Cleveland, 1882-9; exec. clerk and actg. asst. sec. to Presidents Harrison and Cleveland, 1889-97; apptd. by President McKinley, May, 1893, capt. signal corps, U.S.A. Upon declaration of war assigned to duty as chief Telegraph and Cipher Bureau in office of the President, commissioned, Aug. 1, 1898, lieut. col. and chief signal officer 6th army corps. Upon reorganization of the army, Feb. 2, 1901, reassigned to duty, charge of Telegraph and Cipher Bureau, Exec. Office. In Mar., 1903, apptd. by President Roosevelt Chief of Telegraph and Cipher Bureau of the Executive Office and commissioned maj. Washington DC‡

MONTGOMERY, EDNA MORLEY, research chemist; b. National City, Cal., Apr. 15, 1896; d. James M. and Jessie M. (Parker) Montgomery; B.A. in Chemistry, U. Mont., 1919; M.A. in Chemistry, U. Ill., 1924. Instr. Whitworth Coll., Spokane, Wash., 1924-25; jr. chemist Nat. Bur. Standards, Washington, 1926-28; asst., asso. chemist NIH, Bethesda, Md., 1929-44; with U.S. Dept. Agr., 1945-70, Ccrn Ind. Research Found., Peoria, Ill., 1945-50, asso. chemist, then chemist No. Regional Research Lab., Peoria; chemist S. African Council Scientific and Indsl. Research, Pretoria, 1966; ret. Recipient Dunniway award in chemistry, 1919. Mem. Am. Chem. Soc., Am. Assn. Cereal Chemists, Alpha Phi. Author articles profl. jours. Patentee. Home: San Diego CA Died May 10, 1970; buried Chinook Cemetery, Chinook MT

MONTGOMERY, EMILY P. (MRS. E. GEOFFREY MONTGOMERY), civic worker; b. Dec. 3, 1897; d. George A. and Edith (Taylor) Pope; student pvt., pub. schs.; m. E. Geoffrey Montgomery, July 4, 1947; 1 dau., Emily Taylor (Mrs. A. Andrews, Jr.). Mem. women's bd. St. Luke's Hosp., 1952-71; bd. mgrs. Mills Meml. Hosp., 1953-71, San Francisco Opera Guild, 1956; dir. Hillsborough Garden Club, 1954-58; mem. Redwood Grove com. Garden Clubs of Am., 1954. Home: Burlingame CA Died May 25, 1971.

MONTGOMERY, JACK PERCIVAL, prof. chemistry; b. Columbus, Miss., July 18, 1877; s. David

Hugh and Annie (Stinson) M.; prep. edn., Franklin Acad., Columbus, Miss., and Howard Coll., Birmingham, Ala.; A.B., Southwestern Presbyn. U., Clarksville, Tenn., 1899, A.M., 1900; Ph.D., U. of Va., 1903; studied Armour Inst. Tech., Chicago; summer courses at Columbia U., Johns Hopkins and U. of Chicago; m. Adeline Hudson Harrison, July 18, 1917; 1 dau., Belle R. Asso. prof. chemistry, Miss. Agrl. and Mechanical College, 1903-11; professor organic chemistry, University of Ala., 1911-47, prof. emeritus since 1947; professor chemistry, University of Virginia, summer 1926, 27; also consulting practice. Member Am. Inst. Chemists, Am. Chem. Soc., Ala. Acad. Science, Chem. Soc. (London), Pi Kappa Alpha, Phi Beta Kappa, Alpha Epsilon Delta, Gamma Sigma Epsilon, Omicron Delta Kappa, Phi Beta Pi, Phi Eta Sigma, Chi Beta Phi. Democrat. Baptist. Kiwanian. Author: Laboratory Manual in General Chemistry, 1918, 25; Laboratory Manual in Organic Chemistry, 1927; also articles giving results of original researches in organic chemistry, colloid chemistry, etc. Cons. editor Handbook of Chemistry and Physics; asst. editor Outline of Organic Chemistry; asso. editor Fundamental Organic Chemistry. Home: 1918 9th St., Tuscaloosa AL‡

MONTGOMERY, JAMES ALAN, clergyman; b. Germantown, Phila., June 13, 1866; s. Thomas Harrison and Anna (Morton) M.; A.B., U. of Pa., 1887, Ph. D., 1904, S.T.D., 1908; grad. Phila. Div. Sch., 1890; univs. of Greifswald and Berlin; Grad. Sch. U. of Pa., 1904; m. Mary Frank Owen, Aug. 1, 1893 (died 1900); m. 2d, Edith Thompson, June 17, 1902; children—James Alan, Newcomb T., George M. Deacon, 1890, priest, 1893, P.E. Ch.; curate Ch. of Holy Communion, New York, 1892-93, St. Paul's, W. Phila., 1893-95, St. Peter's, Phila., 1895-99; rector Epiphany, Germantown, 1899-1903; assistant editor Church Standard, 1897-99; instr. and prof. O.T., Phila. Div. Sch., 1899-1935; became lecturer and prof. Hebrew, Grad. Sch., U. of Pa., 1909; now emeritus. Dir. Am. Sch. of Oriental Research in Jerusalem, 1914-15; pres. Am. Schs. of Oriental Research, 1921-33. Editor Jour. Bibl. Lit., 1910-14; editor Jour. Am. Oriental Soc., 1916-22. Mem. Soc. Bibl. Lit. and Exegesis, Am. Oriental Soc., Archeol. Inst. America, Am. Philos. Soc., Phila. Oriental Club, Zeta Psi, Phi Beta Kappa. Author: The Samaritans, the Earliest Jewish Sect, 1907; Aramaic Incantation Texts from Nippur, 1913; Religions of the Past and Present; Commentary on Daniel, 1927; History of Yaballaha III, 1927; Arabia and the Bible, 1934; Hebraic Mythological Texts from Ras Shamra, 1935. Contbr. to theol. and Oriental jours. Home: 6806 Greene St., Germantown, Philadelphia PA‡

MONTGOMERY, JAMES LLEWELLYN, architect; b. Montgomery, W.Va., Aug. 24, 1869; s. Henry S. and Mary Elizabeth (Jones) M.; student U. of W.Va., 1885-87; m. Eva M. Brinson, Apr. 19, 1892; children—Henry B., Henry (dec.). Practice of architecture in Ga., 1896-1905, Ala., 1905-08, La., 1908-09, Charleston, W.Va., since 1909; co-partner Montgomery and Patteson, Charleston, since 1928. Fellow Am. Inst. Architects. Baptist. Mason. Home: 3 Veazey St. Office: 604 National Bank of Commerce Bldg., Charleston 1 WV‡

MONTGOMERY, MARY WILLIAMS, Orientalist; b. Marash, Turkey, Nov. 21, 1874; d. Giles F. and Emily (Redington) M.; grad. Wellesley Coll., 1896; Ph.D., Berlin, 1901 (dissertation Briefe aus der Zeit Hammurabis-e. B. C. 2500); unmarried. Now engaged in lit. work in Oriental subjects. Author (with Mrs. Izora Chandler); Told in a Garden of Araby; articles for Jewish Ency. Member Deutsche Orient Gesellschaft, Vorderasiatische Gesellschaft. Club: Women's University. Now mgr. Singer Co., pubs. Residence: 126 W. 104th St. Office: 55 E. 20th St., New York‡

MONTGOMERY, MORRIS CARPENTER, judge; b. Hustonville, Ky., Apr. 1, 1907; s. Charles Francis and Mary Allene (Carpenter) M.; A.B., Transylvania Coll., 1928; student U. Ky., 1927; LL.B., Washington and Lee U., 1930; m. Phoebe Frances Wash., Aug. 22, 1936 (dec. Sept. 1969); 1 dau., Lydia Morris. Admitted to Ky. bar, 1930; practice of law, 1930-54; police judge, 1935-36; city atty., Liberty, Ky., 1938-51, 52-53; commonwealth atty. Commonwealth Ky., 1951-52; judge Ct. Appeals Ky., 1954-69, chief justice, 1959-60. Mem. Ky. Senate, 1954; mem. exec. council Nat. Conf. Chief Justices, 1959-60. Served USAAF, 1942-46; lt. col. Res. Mem. Inst. Judicial Adminstrn; Am. Judicature Soc., Am. Law Inst., Ky. Jud. Council (chmn.), Phi Delta Phi, Kappa Alpha. Mem. Christian Ch. Home: Lawrenceburg KY Died Sept. 3, 1969; buried Lawrenceburg KY

MONTHERLANT, HENRY DE, writer; b. 1896; ed. Lycee Janson-de-Sailly, also Ecole Sainte-Croix Neuilly. Plays produced by Comedie Francaise; war corr. World War II. Served with French Army World War I. Recipient Grand Prix de Litterature, French Acad., 1934. Mem. Acad. Francaise. Author: La Releve du Matin, 1920; Le Songe, 1922; Les Olympiques, 1924; Chant Funebre pour les Morts de Verdun, 1924; Les Bestiares, 1926; Aux Fontaines du Desir, 1927; Le Petite Infante de Castille, 1929; Mors et Vita, 1923; Encore un Instante de Bonheur, 1934; Les Celibataries, 1934; Service Inutile, 1935; Les Jeunes Filles, Pitie pour les Femmes, 1936; L'Equinoxe de Septembre, 1938; Les Lepreuses, 1939; Le Solslice de Juin, 1941; La Reine Morte, 1942; Fils de Personne, 1943; Malatesia, 1946; Le Maitre de Santiago, 1947; Demain il fera jour, 1949; Celles qu'on prend dans ses bras, 1950; La Ville dout le Prince est un Enfant, 1951; Port-Royal, 1954; Don Juan, 1958; Le Cardinal d'Espagne, 1960; Le Chaos et la Nuit, 1963; La Guerre Civile, 1964. Address: Paris France Died Sept. 1972.

MONTZHEIMER, ARTHUR, civil engr.; b. Sharpsburg, Pa., Jan. 23, 1869; s. Julius H. G. and Isabel G. (Hillock) M.; prep. edn., high sch., Webster City, Ia.; grad. Dixon (Ill.) Coll. Civ. Engring., 1888; m. Julia McClellan Mosher, of Racine, Wis., June 28, 1893; children—Gertrude E. (dec.), Marie (Mrs. Leonard W. Gesler), Arthur M. Began with Chicago & Northwestern Railway, 1886; rodman, transitman, draftsman and asst. engr., same rd., 1889-95, and supt. bridges, hdqrs. Milwaukee, Wis., 1895-1903; chief engr. Elgin, Joliet & Eastern Ry. Co. since 1903; chief engr. Chicago, Lake Shore & Eastern Ry., 1903-09, and of Chicago, Milwaukee & Gary Ry., under U.S. R.R. Administration, Jan. 1918-Mar. 1920. Mem. engring. com. of Real Estate Advisory Commn. of Sanitary Dist. of Chicago. Mem. Am. Soc. C.E., Western Soc. Engrs., Am. Ry. Engring. Assn., Am. Ry. Bridge and Building Assn. (ex-pres.), Am. Ry. Signal Assn., Am. Wood Preservers' Assn., Chicago Regional Planning Assn. Republican. Presbyn. Mason (K.T., Shriner). Clubs: Engineers', Rotary, Shabbona, Shriners. Home: 602 Wilcox St. Office: Joliet Nat. Joliet IL‡

MOODIE, CAMPBELL, Canadian diplomat; b. Capetown, S. Africa, Aug. 30, 1908 (parents Canadian citizens); s. Walter H. and Marcella (Twiss) M.; ed. McGill U., also N.Y.U.; m. Mary Galtrey Pearson; children—Virginia (Mrs. Jose de Brito), Dominic C. Formerly with Agy. Bank of Montreal, N.Y.C., joined Canadian Dept. External Affairs, and assigned London, Eng., until 1960; counsellor Canadian mission to UN, 1960-64; consul gen. in Seattle, 1964-70. Mem. Zeta Psi. Served with Canadian Army, World War II. Clubs: Knickerbocker (N.Y.C.); Turf (London); Washington Jockey; Rainier (Seattle); United Hunts (N.Y.C.); Seattle Yacht, Seattle Tennis. Home: Seattle WA Died June 1970.

MOONEY, EUGENE FRANCIS, tobacco co. exec.; b. Pawtucket, R.I., Mar. 18, 1907; s. Lawrence Sylvester and Katherine (Radigan) M.; student Providence Coll., 1930; m. Virginia Randall, Dec. 29, 1941. With Am. Tobacco Co., 1933-71, dir. sales, 1963-66, vice president sales, 1966-71, also dir. Served to comdr. USNR, 1942-45. comdr. Res. Catholic. Club: Greenwich Country. Home: Greenwich CT Died Oct. 1971.

MOONEY, JAMES ELLIOTT, Polar authority, editor, author, ex-univ. pres.; b. Dansville, N.Y., July 30, 1901; s. Edward S. and Ellen Jane (Massey) M.; grad. N.Y. State Tchrs. Coll., Geneseo, 1922; Ed.D., Duquesne U., 1933; L.H.D., Beaver Coll., 1938; D.Sc., Rider Coll., 1939; m. Mildred Charlotte Montgomery, Aug. 8, 1922; children—Ellen Mooney McGuire, James Elliott, Richard Edward, Stewart Walter. Prin. jr. high sch., Penn Yan. N.Y., 1922-26; dir. English research Ridgefield Park (N.J.) pub. schs., 1927, Charles Scribner's Sons, 1927-38; acting pres. Beaver Coll., 1938-40; pres., editor Youth's Digest, 1938-40; pres. U. Tampa (Fla.), 1940-45; dir. Pinellas Co., aviation, 1945-50; asso. Adm. Richard E. Byrd devel. U.S. Antarctic policy programs, 1953-57; dep. and acting U.S. Antarctic Projects officer, 1957-66. Devel. projection future trans-Antarctic air routes; adviser to mems. Congress on Antartic affairs; coordinated internat. dedication, also named Amundsen-Scott S. Pole sta., 1956; mem. inter-deptl. com. Antarctic programs; prin. exponent U.S. nuclear reactor devel. in Antarctics, also planned modernized living quarters; past adviser Am. Acad. Air Law, N.Y.U., also Air Youth Am.; consul for El Salvador, Guatemala; adviser SECNAV dirigible devel. Founder, past pres. Beaver Found. Advancement Edn.; mem. adv. coms. Flas. State Parks, World Trade Council, Fla. Def. Council, Air League British Empire; mem. coll. council NYA; chmn. nat. educators tribute to Adm. Byrd, 1938. H.C. Frick edn. fellow, Eng. and France, 1934; recipient Am. Polar Explorers award, 1938, award of merit U.S. Navy, 1943; mountain in Antarctica named in his honor by Adm. Byrd, 1938; recipient commendation Chmn. Joint Chiefs Staff, 1955, Chief Naval Operations, 1958; Distinguished Pub. Service medal U.S. Navy, 1959, Congl. medal for Antarctic service, 1961; Sec. Def. medal distinguished service, 1963; Order of Crown (Belgium), 1965; Place of Honor by Explorers Club, 1966; Congl. resolution of commendation for distinguished pub. service and contbns. to U.S. policy and internat. coop. in Antarctica, 1966. Life mem. Nat. Geog. Soc. (spl. commendation 1966), Explorers Club, St. Petersburg (Fla.) Aero Club; mem. Pi Gamma Mu, Pi Delta Epsilon, Junto. Author numerous books, most recent being Knight Withour Armor, French in Florida, French in Louisiana, Wheels Up, Roaring Wheels and Shining Rails, I Am Aviation, Airport Area Planning, Flight to Nature's Wonderlands, Aviation Economic Study of Pinellas County, 2 vols.; study and report with Adm. Byrd of establishment Antarctic Commn.; also series articles on airport operations and mgmt.; co-author: Songs of the South Pole. Editor Courage and Beaver Found. Jour., also Each Tomorrow, editor series monographs on Antarctica; author bills for Congress recommendations for future U.S. activities in Antarctica for SECDEF and SECNAV, 1966; contbg. editor history text books; assisted writing, negotiating Antarctic Treaty; author, cons. aero. edn. larger sch. systems, 1928-30. Lectr. radio programs This Week in Defense, Our Latin Am. Neighbors, also on Antarctics; newspaper column Aviation and Us. Co-namer Navy satellite Explorer; with 8 other made 1st flight over N. and S. poles on continuous flight plan, 1957. Potomac MD Died Oct. 1968; buried Washington DC

MOONEY, JAMES GARTH, orthopedic surgeon; b. Cle Elum, Wash., Feb. 23, 1921; s. James Potter and Martha (Jones) M.; B.S., U. Wash., 1942; M.D., U. Ore., 1945; m. Verna Lucille Jacobson, Aug. 30, 1941; 1 dau., Marilee. Intern, King County Hosp., 1945-46; resident Children's Orthopedic Seattle, 1949-50, Providence Hosp., Seattle, 1950, Swedish Hosp., Seattle, 1950-51, Mt. Elizabeth Hosp., Sitka, Alaska, 1951, King County Hosp., Seattle, 1952; orthopedic surgeon Terr. Alaska Dept. Health, Mt. Edgecumbe, Alaska, 1952; orthopedic surgeon Seattle Orthopedic, Fracture and Rehab. Clinic, Seattle, 1954-71; clin. asst. prof. div. orthopedic surgery U. Wash. Sch. Medicine, part time since 1954-71; staff Swedish, Children's Orthopedic, King County, Doctors, Providence hosps. (all Seattle). Served with M.C., AUS, 1946-58. Mem. N. Pacific, Western orthopedic socs., Am. Acad. Orthopedic Surgery, Seattle Surg. Soc., Wash., King County med. assns., A.M.A., Am. Acad. Cerebral Palsy, Theta Chi. Republican. Lutheran. Mason (Shriner). Home: Bellevue WA Died Apr. 3, 1971.

MOORA, ROBERT L(ORENZO), newspaperman; b. Newark, N.J., June 25, 1912; s. Godfrey and Lillian (Brown) M.; educated in Montclair, New Jersey public schools; m. Alison Merrill, Mar. 1, 1947; children—Michael W., Christopher M., Kathleen A. Employed Newark Sunday Callas reporter, feature writer, gravure editor and asst. city editor, 1930-40; asst. night city editor, N.Y. Herald Tribune, Oct. 1940-Mar. 1946. Sunday editor, Mar. 1946-49; news editor Washington bureau, 1949-53, member of editorial staff in New York City, 1953-71. Served as 1st lt., U.S. Army, Feb. 1942-Dec. 1945; mng. editor Stars and Stripes, E.T.O., London, Paris, Frankfurt, 1942-45; opened London bur. of Yank. July 1942 and served as bur. chief to Oct. 1942; helped establish daily Stars and Stripes, London, Nov. 1942, directed establishment Stars and Stripes editions in Rennes, Brittany, Aug. 1944, Paris, Sept. 1944 and Frankfurt (Pfungstadt). Apr. 1945; Stars and Stripes news service for Euorpean editions, Paris, Dec. 1944. Mem. Am. War Corrs. Assn. Clubs: Overseas Press of America, National Press. Home: Union NJ Died Apr. 1971.

MOORE, ALLEN FRANCIS, retired capitalist; b. St. Charles, Ill., Sept. 30, 1869; s. Henry Van Rensallaer and Alzina W. (Freeman) M., A.B. Lombard Coll. Ill., 1889; m. Madora Bradford of Quincy, Ill. Mar. 20, 1895; children—Bradford V. R., Mary A. (dec.), Allen F. Began as manufacturer, at Monticello, 1899; now president The Moore Investment Company. Mayor of Monticello, 1901-03; mem. 67th and 68th Congresses (1921-25), 19th Ill. Dist. Mem. Rep. Nat. Com. 1925-28. Trustee U. of Ill., 1908-14. Republican. Universalist. Mason, K.P., Elk. Clubs: Union League, Chicago. Home: Monticello IL‡

MOORE, ANSLEY CUNNINGHAM, clergyman; b. Atlanta, Aug. 28, 1903; s. James Linton and Susan (Ansley) M.; Ph.B., Emory U., 1925; B.D., Columbia Theol. Sem., 1930; D.D. (hon.), Southwestern Coll., 1944; LL.D. (hon.), Davidson Coll., 1967; grad. student U. Chgo. Div. Sch., Union Theol. Sem., N.Y.C., also Richmond Va.; m. Margaret Haynie, June 18, 1929; children—Margaret Ansley (Mrs. James M. Hutchinson) Sally (Mrs. Frederic Sharaf). Ordained to ministry Presbyn. Ch., 1930; pastor in Ga., 1930-37, Fla., 1937-42, Ala., 1942-47, Pa., 1947-60; pres. St. Andrews Presbyn. Coll., 1960-69; minister Sixth United Presbyn. Ch.; midnight minister Pitts. radio sta.; columnist Pitts. Sun-Telegraph; exchange preacher, Europe, 1939. Mem. Pitts. (pres.), Nat. (past mem. gen. bd.) councils chs., N.Y. So. Soc., Alpha Tau Omega, Omicron Delta Kappa. Rotarian. Asso. editor Presbyn. Outlook. Laurinburg NC Died Mar. 25, 1973.

MOORE, CARL VERNON, physician, educator; b. St. Louis, Aug. 21, 1908; s. Carl V. and Mary (Kamp) M.; student Elmhurst Coll., 1924-27, LL.D., 1955; A.B., Washington U., 1928, M.D., 1932; m. Dorothy Adams, May 25, 1935; 1 dau., Judith. NRC fellow in medicine Ohio State U., 1934-35, asst. prof. medicine, 1935-38, asst. prof. medicine Washington U., 1938-41, asso. prof., 1941-46, prof., 1946-72, dean Sch. Medicine, 1954-55, head dept. medicine, 1955-72, vice chancellor for medical affairs, 1964-65. Chmn. hematology study sect. USPHS, 1952-56; chmn. com. blood and blood derivatives NRC, 1953-60; mem. adv. com. on biology and medicine AEC, 1960-66; mem. sci. adv. bd. Nat.

Cancer Inst., 1957-59; mem. council Nat. Arthritis and Metabolic Diseases Inst., Nat. Insts. Health, 1958-62, 68-72; drug research bd. NRC, 1962-66. Jacobeus lectr. Sweden, Malthe Lectr., Norway, 1955; George Minot lectr. A.M.A. 1958; McIlrath vis. prof. U. Sydney, Australia, 1962; Stratton lectr., medal Internat. Soc. Hematology, 1964. Recipient Joseph Goldberger award, A.M.A., 1959. Fellow A.C.P. (gov. 1958-60, v.p. 1962-62, regent 1962-72; John Phillips Meml. award 1970); mem. Nat. Acad. Scis., Am. Acad. Arts and Scis., Assn. Am. Physicians (pres. 1963-64), Am. Soc. Clin. Investigation (pres. 1954), Central Soc. Clin. Research (pres. 1947), Am. Soc. Exptl. Pathology, Soc. Exptl. Biology and Medicine, Inst. Nutrition, Internat. (councillor 1953-58, pres. 1966-68), Am. (pres. 1959) socs. hematology, Am. Assn. Med. Colls. (Abraham Flexner award 1971), Alpha Omega Alpha, Sigma Xi. Editor Jour. Lab. and Clin. Medicine, 1944-49; asso. editor Blood, The Jour. of Hematology, 1946-72, Am. Jour. Medicine, 1955-72; co-editor Progress in Hematology. Home: University City MO Died Aug. 13, 1972.

MOORE, CHARLES LOTHROP, banker; b. Belmont, Mass., Oct. 21, 1915; s. Herbert Lincoln and Elizabeth (Lothrop) M.; grad. Harvard, 1938, grad. student, 1940; m. Alice Lyman, May, 27, 1944; children—Harrison Lyman, Elizabeth Lothrop, Charles Lothrop. With First Nat. Bank Boston, 1940, asst. v.p., 1953-54, v.p., 1954-67, sr. v.p., 1967-72; dir. Gen. Cinema Corp., Geartronics, Inc.; trustee Winchester Savs. Bank (Mass.). Past trustee Belmont Hill Sch.; bd. dirs. Winchester Hosp. Served from ensign to lt. comdr., SeaBees, USNR, 1942-43; charge surplus disposal for Bethlehem Steel, Navy, 1944. Decorated Letters of Commendation. Republican. Conglist. Clubs: Algonquin, Harvard (Boston); Annisquam Yacht; Winchester Country; Boothbay Harbor Yacht. Home: Winchester MA Died July 2, 1972; buried Winchester MA

MOORE, CLARENCE KING, univ. prof.; b. New York, Oct. 1, 1873; s. James Morrison and Angela Starr (King) M.; A.B., Harvard, 1897, A.M., 1898, Ph.D., 1906; post-grad. study Stanford, Ecole des Hautes Etudes, Paris, U. of Madrid, U. of Rome, U. of Florence; m. Rida Saunders, 1900. Prof. Romance langs., U. of Rochester, since 1904. Mem. Phi Beta Kappa. Home: 53 Girton Pl., Rochester NY‡

MOORE, DEWITT VAN DEUSEN, civil engr.; b. Perry, Lake Co., O., Apr. 6, 1874; s. Webster Oliver and Anna Electa (Van Deusen) M.; ed. Hiram (O.) Coll.; m. Flora Mable Berg, June 14, 1898, 2d, Dorothy Daisy Comer, of Indianapolis, Nov. 19, 1902. Asst. engr. Indianapolis Union Ry., 1895-02; same Pa. Lines West, at Indianapolis, 1897-02; v.-p., sec. Moore-MansfieldConstn. Co., Indianapolis, 1902-11; consulting engr., Indianapolis, 1911-13; dist. engr., central dist., div. of valuation, Interstate Commerce Commn., since Sept. 1, 1913. Dir., charter mem. Am. Soc. Engring. Contractors; mem. Ind. Engring. Soc. (ex-pres.). Republican. Mem. Disciples of Christ. Wrote: Forty-one Concrete Reasons; Contracting Practice; Cost Analysis Engineering; also many papers on cost keeping, analysis and related topics. Home: 5310 Cornell Av. Office: Karpen Bldg., Chicago‡

MOORE, DOUGLAS STUART, coll. prof.; composer; b. Cutchogue, L.I., Aug. 10, 1893; s. Stuart Hull and Myra (Drake) M.; B.A., Yale Coll., 1915, Mus.B., Yale Sch. of Music, 1917; student Schola Cantorum, Paris, 1921; Cleveland Inst. Music, 1924; Hon. Mus. Dr., Cin. Conservatory Mus., 1946, U. Rochester, 1947, Yale U., 1955; L.H.D., Columbia University, 1963; m. Emily Bailey, Sept. 16, 1920; children—Mary, Sarah. Dir. music, Mus. of Art, Cleveland, 1921; asso. Dept. of Music, Columbia U., 1926, asst. prof., 1927, asso. prof., 1928, prof. and chmn., 1940, MacDowell prof. of music, 1943-62, emeritus. Yale Alumni Council, 1947. Pulitzer scholarship, 1925; Guggenheim fellowship, 1934, N.Y. Critics Circle award for opera, 1958. Mem. bd. directors American Academy in Rome, 1945. Recipient Pulitzer prize in music, 1951, Huntington Hartford Found. Award for lit. and composition, 1960. Mem. Am. Acad. Arts and Letters (pres. 1959-62), A.S.C.A.P.; mem. Nat. Inst. Arts and Letters (pres. 1946-53). Served lt. (j.g.) USN, 1917-19. Conglist. Clubs: Faculty of Columbia, Century (N.Y.C.). Compositions include works for orchestra, chorus and orchestra, chamber music, opera; latest operas include: Giants in the Earth, 1950; The Ballad of Baby Doe, 1955; Gallantry: A Soap Opera, 1957; The Wings of the Dove, 1961; Carry Nation, 1966. Author: Listening to Music, 1932; From Madrigal to Modern Music, 1942. Contbr. revs. and articles to mags. Home: New York City NY Died July 25, 1969; buried Cutchoque NY

MOORE, ERNEST CARROLL, JR., lawyer; b. Youngstown, O., Sept. 6, 1913; s. Roy John and Margaret (Brownlee) M.; B.A., U. Cal. at Los Angeles, 1935; LL.B., Harvard, 1939; m. Frances Marian Miller, Oct. 4, 1943; children—Ernest Carroll III, Meredith Brownleigh. Admitted to Hawaii bar, 1941; with Dillingham Corp., Honolulu, 1940-42; practiced in Honolulu, 1946; partner firm Moore, Torkildson & Schulze, 1967-72. Pres. Duraast, Inc., 1969-72. Bd. govs. Am. Nat. Red Cross 1967-72. bd. dirs., exec. com. Aloha United Fund, 1966; trustee Hawaii Sch. Girls, 1967-72. Served to lt. col. AUS, 1942-46. Decorated Bronze Star. Mem. Am. Bar Assn. (co-chmn. subcom. state labor legislation 1966-67, antitrust devel. 1968-69), Honolulu Wine and Food Soc., U.S. C. of C., C. of C. Hawaii (dir. 1969-72), Phi Beta Kappa. Club: Pacific (bd. govs. 1952-61, pres. 1958-59) (Honolulu). Home: Honolulu HI Died Nov. 4, 1972.

MOORE, FRANK HORACE, railway lawyer; b. Mantua, O., Sept. 1, 1872; s. Horace Ladd and Esther Amelia (Harmon) M.; A.B., Univ. of Kan., 1894; LL.B., Columbian Univ. (now George Washington Univ.) Law Sch., 1896; m. Nerva M. Duff, Sept. 26, 1900; children—Horace D., Esther L. (Mrs. Wallace E. Bohannon), Lewis H. Admitted to the Mo. bar, 1896; gen. practice of Law, Kansas City, Mo., 1896-1900, Albuquerque, N.M., 1900-10; asst. atty. K.C.S. Ry., Kansas City, Mo., 1910-11, asst. gen. solicitor, 1911-20, general solicitor, 1920-36, general counsel, 1936-44, vice president law, 1944 of K.C.S. Railway and Louisiana & Arkansas Railway Co.; officer and dir. various subsidiary and affiliated cos. of K.C.S. Ry. Co., 1920-46; retired Apr. 1, 1946; consultant since 1946. Dir. Parking Systems, Inc., Kansas City. Mem. Am., Mo., Kansas City bar assns., Mo. Lawyers Assn., Kansas Hist. Assn., Assn. Am. R.R. (law com.), Kansas City C. of C., Sons of Am. Revolution, Phi Beta Kappa, Phi Delta Pi. Rep. Presbyn. Mason. Clubs: Kansas City, Professional Men's. Home: 5318 Sunset Dr., Kansas City 12. Office: 314 Kansas City Kansas City 6 MO‡

MOORE, FREDERICK, author; b. New Orleans, November 17, 1877; s. Frederick and Annie Louise (Cook) M.; student Harvard, 1906; m. Edith Mary Thomson, of Plymouth, Eng., May 1, 1908; children—David Lewis, Margaret Mary, John Stewart, Jane Lucilla. As corr. for leading Am. or English newspapers, including N.Y. Times, London Times, Asso. Press, Reuter's Agency, was located in Washington, 1900, 01, London, 1902, Balkan States, 1903-04, London, 1905, Morocco, 1907, Turkey, 1908-09, China, 1910-16; mng. editor Asia Magazine, New York, 1917; at Peace Conf., Paris, 1919; at League of Nations Assembly, Geneva, 1920; foreign councillor to Japanese ministry for Foreign Affairs, 1921-26; corr. in China, 1927. Mem. Japanese delegation to Geneva, regarding Manchurian Question, 1932-33. Clubs: Century (New York); Cosmos (Washington); Tokyo (Tokyo); Savage (London). Author: The Balkan Trail, 1906; The Passing of Morocco, 1908; The Chaos in Europe, 1919; America's Naval Challenge, 1929. Address: Cosmos Club, Washington DC‡

MOORE, FREDERICK FERDINAND, editor, author; b. Concord, N.H., Dec. 24, 1877; s. James Bell and Nell (Collins) M.; ed. Boston Coll.; m. Florence Frisbee, San Francisco, Aug. 25, 1906; 1 dau., Marjorie. m. 2d, Eleanor Gates, dramatist and author, Oct. 18, 1914. Ran away to sea when a boy and served as a sailor, soldier, civilian scout, and war corr. in various parts of world; served in 2d U.S. Cav. in Philippines, but discharged own application, to resume newspaper work during Russo-Japanese War. Arrived San Francisco from Far East, 1905; editorial staff San Francisco Examiner, 1905-13; editor The Argosy, New York, Jan. 1913-15; established Book Dealers Weekly, 1925. Capt. Intelligence Div., Gen. Staff U.S.A., 1918-19, in Siberia (Amur region, and Chita, Trans-Baikalia with Cossack Ataman Semenoff and Lt. Gen. Oba, Japanese forces). Decoration, Order Rising Sun, Japan; Victory medal, Siberian clasp. Contbr. short stories and critical articles on mil. and naval topics. Author: The Devil's Admiral, 1913; Siberia To-Day, 1919; Sailor Girl, 1920; Isle o' Dreams, 1920; The Samovar Girl, 1921. Home: 66 Fifth Av. Office: 730 New York NY‡

MOORE, GEORGE CURTIS, fgn. service officer; b. Toledo, Sept. 7, 1925 s. Paul H. and Lucille (Munn) M.; B.A., U. So. Cal., 1949, M.A., 1951; m. Sarah Anne Stewart, June 21, 1950; children—Lucy Anne, Catherine Jane. Joined U.S. Fgn. Service, 1950; assigned Kaufbeuren and Wuerzburg, Germany, 1950-53; vice consul, Cairo, Egypt, 1953-55; detailed Arabic lang. and area specialization, Beirut, Lebanon, 1956-57; consul, Asmara, Eritrea, 1958-59; polit. officer, Benghazi and Tripoli, Libya, 1959-63; officer in charge Arabian peninsula affairs State Dept., Washington, 1964-67, personnel chief Bur. Near East and South Asia, 1967-68, assigned to Nat. War Coll., 1968-69; charge d'affairs Am. embassy, Khartoum, Sudan, 1969-73. Served with AUS, 1944-46; ETO. Mem. Phi Beta Kappa, Chi Phi, Delta Phi Epsilon. Rotarian. Club: Blue Nile Sailing. Home: Washington DC Died Mar. 2, 1973; buried Arlington Nat. Cemetery, Washington DC

MOORE, GEORGE GAIL, physician; b. Wayne County, Ill., Mar. 14, 1889; s. Wlater Jackson and Mary Florence (Shelton) M.; student Ewing Coll., 1905; B.S., So. Ill. Normal U., 1908; M.D., St. Louis U., 1913; m. Maidia Grace Carruthers, Dec. 29, 1951 (dec. Dec. 1970); children—Homer Gail, Dorothea Jean (Mrs. Richard Clay Wilson). Intern, Mo. Baptist Hosp., Kansas City, 1913-14; practice medicine specializing in gen. practice, Wardell, Mo., 1914-18, Dahlgren, Ill., 1918-1920, Benton, Ill., 1920-70. Recipient Civilian medal for meritorious service, 1946. Mem. A.M.A., Am. Polled Hereford Assn. (charter mem.), Phi Chi. Democrat. Baptist. Elk. Home: Benton IL Deceased.

MOORE, HARRISON BRAY, pres. New York Lighterage and Transportation Co. since 1874; b. Windham, Me.; ed. public schools; started, 1863, in the lighterage business, which was incorporated, 1874; connected for yrs. with N. Y. militia with rank of maj.; m. 1866, Marietta H. Christie. Residence: 126 Pierrepont St., Brooklyn. Office: 6 Broadway, New York‡

MOORE, HARRY TUNIS, bishop; b. Delavan, Wis., Oct. 4, 1874; s. Tunis and Hannah (Rector) M.; B.A., Hobart Coll., Geneva, N.Y., 1899; grad. Western Theol. Sem., Chicago, 1902; m. Annette Irene Reeme, Aug. 8, 1907; children—Harry Reeme, Reeme. Deacon and priest, 1902, P.E. Ch.; asst., Delevan, Wis., 1902; rector St. James Ch., Fremont, Neb., 1902-04, St. Mark's Ch., San Antonio, Tex., 1904-05, Grace Ch., Chicago, 1905-06, Emmanuel Ch., Champaign, Ill., 1906-07, St. Matthew's Cathedral, Dallas, Tex., 1907-17; coadjutor bishop Diocese of Dallas, 1917-24; bishop of Dallas, 1924-46. Member of Theta Delta Chi, Phi Beta Kappa. Republican. Mason (hon. 33 deg., Shriner). Clubs: City, Dallas Country. Address: 5100 Ross Av., Dallas TX*‡

MOORE, HUGH, mfr.; b. Ft. Scott, Kan., Apr. 27, 1887; s. John James and Alice Elizabeth (Harbison) M.; student Harvard Coll., 1910; LL.B., Lafayette Coll., 1961; m. Berenice Brown, Sept. 15, 1917 (div. 1947); children—Craig, Hugh; m. 2d, Louise Wilde, 1947. Co-founder first paper drinking cup co. in U.S. upon leaving college founder Paper Cup and Container Inst.; founder, chmn. bd. Dixie Cup Co.; cons. Am. Can Company. Served as capt. U.S. Army, Intelligence officer Eastern Dept., 1918. Chmn. exec. com. Com. to Defend Am. by Aiding the Allies, 1940; treas. Com. for Marshall Plan, 1948; chmn. Finance Com., Woodrow Wilson Found., 1951-52. Chmn. bd. St. Lawrence Seaway Devel. Corp. 1960. Chmn. bd. dirs. Population Reference Bur., Atlantic Union Com., 1949-60; Am. Assn. U.N., 1940-54; code dir. NRA; v.p. Internat. Planned Parenthood Fedn., 1964; co-founder Population Crisis Com., 1965, World Organization; consultant UN Conference, San Francisco, 1945; mem. U.S. Commn. NATO, 1961-72. Mem. Hugh Moore Pkwy. Commn., Easton, 1968. Pres. Hugh Moore Fund. Member vis com. Harvard Sch. of Pub. Health. Recipient medal U. Bologna, 1950; Nat. Conservation medal Am. Motors Co., 1971. Mem. Council Fgn. Relations (N.Y.) Democrat. Unitarian Mason. Clubs: Harvard, Century (N.Y.), Northampton County (Easton). Address: Easton PA Died Nov. 25, 1972; cremated.

MOORE, HUGH BENTON, ry. official; b. Huntland, Tenn., Jan. 11, 1874; s. Horatio R. and Annie (Hunt) M.; ed. common schs.; m. Helen Edmunds, of Kansas City, Mo., Sept. 5, 1905. Began as messenger T. & P. Ry. Co., Dallas, Tex., 1890; pres. and gen. mgr. Tex. City Terminal Ry. Co. since 1917. Commd. capt. O.R.C., 1917; apptd. transportation officer on staff of Gen. Pershing, May 1917; arrived in France, June 10, 1917; supt. Army Transport Service at St. Nazaire, later gen. supt. at principal ports of France; promoted to newly created position of dir. Army Transport Service of all ports and steamship operations of A.E.F. in Europe, Jan. 1918; promoted col.; hon. discharged Feb. 1919. Awarded D.S.M. (U.S.); Legion of Honor (French). Mem. Christian (Disciples) Ch. Mason (K.T., 32 deg., Shriner). Home: Texas City TX‡

MOORE, IRWIN L., electric utility exec.; b. Hoboken, N.J., May 7, 1896; s. Samuel C. and Emma V. (Likely) M.; A.B., Cornell U., 1917; B.S., Mass. Inst. Tech., 1920; m. Pamela L. Thompson, June 18, 1921; children—Donald Campbell, John Irwin; m. 2d, Cecilia H. McCarthy, Dec. 30, 1964. Asst. chemist Bur. Standards, 1917-19; student instr. elec. engr. Mass. Inst. Tech., 1919-20; engring. asst. Aluminum Co. Am. 1920; with operating dept. New Eng. Power Co., Providence, 1920-25, asst. to gen. mgr., Worcester, Mass., 1926; engring. asst. to pres. Internat. Paper Co., N.Y.C., 1926-36; pres. New Eng. Electric System, 1941-59, chmn., chief exec. officer, 1959-61, vice chmn., 1961-72. Home: Waban MA Died July 21, 1972; buried Newton Cemetery, Newton MA

MOORE, ISAAC SADLER, banker; b. Abingdon, Md., May 25, 1870; s. James Gibbons and Caroline Anne (Sadler) M.; ed. pub. schs.; m. Katherine May Long, of Duluth, Minn., May 16, 1893; children—Carolyn Bernice, Virginia May (Mrs. Warren F. Starkey). In ins. business, Baltimore, Md., 1884-87; with Am. Exchange Nat. Bank, Duluth, 1887-1929, pres. until 1929; pres. 1st & Am. Nat. Bank since 1929; dir. Northwest Bancorporation. Republican. Methodist. Clubs: Kitchi Gammi, Northland. Home: 124 N. 23d Av. E. Office: 1st and American Nat. Bank, Duluth MN‡

MOORE, J(OSEPH) HAMPTON, ex-mayor, ex-congressman; b. Woodbury, N.J., Mar. 8, 1864; s. Joseph B. and Mary J. (Dorff) M.; ed. pub. schs.; LL.D.,

Ursinus Coll., 1920; LL.D., Hahnemann Med. Coll., 1933; m. Adelaide Stone, Jan. 16, 1889; children—Clayton F. (dec.), Dorff, Edward M., Harvey, Mark M. (dec.), Sevena C. (Mrs. H. Paul Barnes), Julia D. (Mrs. Fredk. G. Eisley), Richard O. (dec.). Court reporter; reporter and editorial writer, Phila. Public Ledger, 12 yrs.; chief clerk to city treas., Phila., 1895-97, sec. Peace Jubilee, 1898; sec. to mayor of Phila., 1898-99; sec. Citizens' Com. Nat. Rep. Conv., Phila., 1899; city treas., Phila., 1901-03; chief, Bur. of Mfrs., Dept. Commerce and Labor, Washington, Jan.-June, 1905; elected to 59th Congress for an unexpired term; reelected 60th and 66th Congresses (1907-21), 3d Pa. Dist.; resigned from Congress, 1920, on being elected mayor of Phila., served as mayor, 1920-23 and 1932-35. Pres. Allied Rep. Clubs of Phila., 1900-06, Pa. State League Rep. Clubs, 1900-01, Nat. League Rep. Clubs, 1903-06; del. at large Nat. Republican Conv., 1920; Presidential elector, 1932; pres. Atlantic Deeper Waterways Assn. since 1907. Mem. N.J. Soc. of Pa., Pa. Hist. Soc.; decorated Chevalier Order of the Crown (Italy), 1921. Clubs: Five O'Clock, Union League (Phila.); National Press, Congressional Country, Alfalfa (Washington). Wrote: History of Five O'Clock Club, 1891; Fiveoclockiana (poems), 1898; Through the Tropics, 1907; Roosevelt and the Old Guard, 1925; also various polit. pamphlets. Home: 319 W. Carpenter Lane. Office: Widener Bldg., Philadelphia PA*‡

MOORE, J.W.E., lawyer; b. in Haywood Co., Tenn.; s. John and Judith Belle (Estes) M.; ed. in local schs. and Univ. of Va.; m. Mary M., d. Col. James P. Wood. Admitted to bar at 21; ever since practicing law in Hayward and adjoining cos. of Tenn., and in Federal Court at Memphis. Mem. Tenn. Bar Assn. Del. Universal Congress Lawyers and Jurists, St. Louis, 1904. Address: Memphis TN‡

MOORE, JAMES GREGORY, educator; b. Augusta, Ill., May 8, 1870; s. Samuel R. and Jemima (Alter) M.; grad. Oberlin (O.) Acad., 1891; student Oberlin Coll., 1891-93; B.S., U. of Ill., 1924; m. Flora Powell, of Monmouth, Ill., June 18, 1903; children—Gregory Powell, Albert Fleming, Sarah Letitia (Mrs. William H. Lyons), Rollin Samuel, Ruth Jemima, James Alter. Village sch. teacher, Ill., 1893-98; admitted to Ill. bar, 1902; with Met. Life Ins. Co., 1902-03, Western Stoneware Co., 1903-04; supt. schs. Blandinsville, Ill., 1904-06, Lexington, Ill., 1906-11, Streator, 1911-14, Paris, 1914-16, Superior, Wis., 1916-21, Fargo, N.D., 1921-35. Pres. Ill. City Supts'. Assn., 1914-15, N.D. City Supts. Assn., 1931-32, N.D. Edn. Assn., 1933-34. Mem. N.E.A. (life dept. of superintendence), Pi Gamma Mu. Contbr. of articles, stories and verse to various publs. Home: 408 8th Av. S., Fargo ND‡

MOORE, JOHN CECIL, author; b. Tewkesbury, Eng., Nov. 10, 1907; s. Cecil Charles and Eliza Georgina (Moore) M.; student Malvern Coll.; m. Lucile Douglas Stephens, Apr. 1, 1944. Dir. Tewkesbury Play Festival, 1934-39; dir. Cheltenham Festival Contemporary Lit., 1949-56. Fellow Royal Soc. Lit., British Soc. Authors (past chmn.). Author: The Fair Field (Portrait of Elmbury), 1945; Brensham Village, 1946; The Blue Field, 1948; Dance and Skylark, 1951; September Moon, 1957; You English Words, 1962; The Waters Under the Earth, 1965; Among the Quiet Folks, 1967. Home: Tewkesbury Gloucester England Died July 27, 1967; interred Cloister Garth, Tewkesbury Abbey, Gloucester England

MOORE, JOHN FERGUSON, author; b. Albany, N.Y., Aug. 22, 1868; s. Levi and Ida Louisa (Ferguson) M. ed. public schs.; m. Anne E. Fuller, Apr. 6, 1882 children—John Ferguson, Gertrude Fuller. Began as cash boy, 1879; later salesman; with Y.M.C.A. as local and state sec., 1881-89, internat. sec., 1889-1928; made tour of world for Y.M.C.A., 1913; research work in Europe 6 mos., 1925; editor Railroad Assn. Magazine, 1914-24. Decorated with Order of the Rising Son (Japan). Republican. Presbyn. Mason. Author: Story of the Railroad Y, 1930; Will America Become Catholic? 1931; The Y in Rhyme, 1940. Home: 80 Pintard Av., New Rochelle NY‡

MOORE, JOHN SMALL, b. New Castle, Pa., Mar. 12, 1876; s. John Small and Sarah Zemyrah (Shields) M.; student Parsons Coll., 1894-96; grad. student U. of Neb., 1898-1901, U. of Mo., 1909-11; M.A., Grove City Coll., 1906; Dr. Humane Letters (hon.) Parsons College, 1945; m. Jennie Tidrick, August 30, 1900; children—Ruth Agnes Dawson, Virginia Emily Schott, John Shields, Burt Dix, June Alice Benner. Traveling rep. for Y.M.C.A., 1901-09; social, ednl. and religious activities, U. of Missouri, 1909-17; Y.M.C.A. war work, Camp Knox, Camp Taylor, Ky., 1917-20; religious work dir. Y.M.C.A., Dayton, O., 1920-28; spl. corr. League of Nations, Geneva, summers, 1926-28 and 1929-30; spl. corr. to Mexico, summer, 1927, World Economic Conf., London, summer, 1933; fellowship Carl Schurz Memorial Foundation, Germany, summers, 1933, 34, 36; spl. mission Japan, Manchuria, China, summer, 1935; contbg. editorial writer Dayton Daily News, Springfield Sun, 1937; lecturer internat. affairs on pub. forums under auspices of Federal Commn. of Edn.; dir. League of Nations Assn. of Ohio since 1929. Contbr. to Rotarian. Mem. Am. Seminar in England and Germany, summer, 1939; also represented Dayton Daily News as spl. corr. in Warsaw, Krakow, Geneva, Paris; mem. Mexican Seminar early in 1941. Dir. U.N. Assn.; press. rep. orgn. U.N.R.R.A., Atlantic City, 1943; San Francisco Peace Conf., 1945; Assembly U.N., Flushing Meadows, 1946. Presbyterian. Club: Town and Gown (Antioch College). Home: 29 South Dixie Av. Dayton 9 OH‡

MOORE, KENNETH W., banker; b. Endeavor, Wis., May 16, 1902; s. John and Edna (Dorr) M.; ed. Christian Endeavor Acad.; m. Bettice Marriott McClevey, Sept. 6, 1930; 1 dau., Joan Marriott. Purchasing agt. Chgo. Title & Trust Co., 1926-38, office mgr., 1938-45, asst. v.p. 1945-47, v.p. since 1947. Mem. Office Management Assn. Chgo., Nat. Office Management Assn. (pres.), Purchasing Agts. Assn. Chgo., Nat. Assn. Purchasing Agts., Chgo. Real Estate Bd., Chgo. Assn. Commerce. Republican. Conglist. Clubs: Hinsdale (Ill.) Golf; Chicago Athletic. Home: Western Springs IL Died Oct. 1971.

MOORE, MARIANNE CRAIG, writer; b. St. Louis, Mo., Nov. 15, 1887; d. John Milton and Mary (Warner) Moore; prep. edn., Metzger Inst., Carlisle, Pa., 1896-1905; A.B., Bryn Mawr, 1909; grad. Carlisle Commercial Coll., 1910; Litt.D., Wilson College, Chambersburg, Pa., 1949, Mount Holyoke College, 1950, U. Rochester, 1951, Dickinson Coll., 1952; L.I. Univ., 1953; L.H.D., Smith Coll., 1950, Pratt Inst., 1958; Litt.D., Douglass Coll., Rutgers University, 1967, St. John's University 1968, Princeton, 1968. Teacher, Carlisle (Pennsylvania) U.S. Indian Sch., 1911-15; vis. lectr. Bryn Mawr Coll., 1953; asst. N.Y. Pub. Library, 1921-25; acting editor The Dial, 1925-29. Received Dial Award, 1924; Helen Haire Levinson prize, 1933; Ernest Hartsock Memorial prize, 1935; Shelley Memorial Award, 1940; Contemporary Poetry's Patrons' Prize, 1944; Harriet Monroe Poetry Award of 1944; Guggenheim Memorial Fellowship, 1945; Nat. Inst. Arts and Letters award, 1946; Bollingen prize, poetry, Yale U. Library, 1951; Nat. Book Award, 1951; Pulitzer Prize, poetry, 1951; M. Carey Thomas Award, 1953; Nat. Inst. Arts and Letters gold medal, poetry, 1953; gold medal Poetry Soc. Am., 1960, 67; award for poetry Brandeis U., 1963; MacDowell Medal, Peterborough, N.H., 1967; decorated Cross Legion Honor Order Arts and Letters (France); fellowship Acad. Am. Poets, 1965; named Woman of Achievement, N.Y., Am. Assn. U. Women, 1968. Mem. Nat. Inst. Arts Letters, Am. Acad. Arts and Letters. Presbyn. Author: Poems, 1921; Observations, 1924; Selected Poems, 1935; The Pangolin and Other Verse, 1936; What Are Years, 1941: Nevertheless, 1944; Collected Poems, 1951; The Fables of La Fontaine (transl.), 1954; Predilections, 1955; Like a Bulwark, 1956: O To Be a Dragon, 1959; A Marianne Moore Reader, 1961; Three Classic Tales (translation), 1963; The Arctic Ox, 1964; Tell Me, Tell Me, 1966; Complete Poems, 1968. Contrb. criticism and verse to mags. Home: New York City NY Died Feb. 5, 1972.

MOORE, MARK EGBERT, educator; b. Lamont, Tenn., June 22, 1871; s. Jerome Egbert and Rebecca (Litzy) M.; student Orlinda Prep. Sch., 1883-87; A.B., Southern Normal U., 1900; A.M., U. of Kan., 1916; m. Bettie Pearson, of Lamont, Tenn., Oct. 2, 1892; children—Mary Constance (Mrs. Willis L. Short), Ruby Pearson (Mrs. Clyde Cobbs), Lillian Dent (Mrs. Haskell Porter), Mark Edwin. Began as teacher in rural schs., 1888; county high sch. prin., Coopertown, Tenn., 1891-95; prin. city elementary sch., Springfield, Tenn., 1895-97; co. high sch. prin., Pleasant View, Tenn., 1897-1900; in real estate business, 1900-02; supt. schs., Marietta, Okla., 1902-09; pres. Teachers' Coll., Durant, Okla., 1909-12; supt. schs., Leavenworth, Kan., 1912-19, Beaumont, Tex., 1919-38. Mem. Safety Council, Ft. Leavenworth, during World War, in charge social and hygienic dept. Baptist. Mason, K.P. Clubs: University, Rotary (past pres.). Author: Parent, Teacher and School, 1923. Home: 2337 Broadway, Beaumont TX‡

MOORE, MARY NORMAN, college pres.; b. at Huntsville, Madison Co., Ala., Aug. 6, 1874; d. William Henry and Mary Prince (Poe) Moore; grad. (Master of English and Latin) Huntsville Female Coll., 1890; pvt. courses of study in lit. and philosophy, Harvard U. Summer Sch.; unmarried. Teacher pvt. and pub. schs. of Ala. and Ark., 1892-9; commercial business, 1899-02; sec. Alabama Christian Advocate, Birmingham, Ala., 1902-4; pres. Athens (Ala.) Coll., 1904-—. Pres. Woman's Missionary Soc. of Ala. Conf. M.E. Ch., S. Speaker and writer on religious, ednl. and philanthropical subjects. Home: Athens Limestone Co AL‡

MOORE, MILTON HARVEY, supt. schs.; b. Bedford, Tarrant Co., Tex., July 27, 1871; s. Milton and Margaret M.; grad. Sam Houston State Normal Inst., Huntsville, Tex., 1894; grad. Texas Christian U., Fort Worth, Tex.; m. Anna Pearl Preston, of Irving, Tex., June 23, 1892; children—Harry M. (dec.), Homer T., Joe T., J. Calvin, Marcus H., Margaret. Teacher rural schs., Tarrant and Hood cos., Tex., 1890-1900; supt. Tarrant Co. schs., 1900-04, N. Ft. Worth schools, 1904-09; prin. North Side High Sch., Ft. Worth, 1909-14; asst. supt. schs., Ft. Worth, 1914-15, supt. 1915-—. Pres. Tex. State Teachers' Assn., 1921-22. Democrat. Mem. Ch. of Christ. Mason, Woodman. Clubs: Rotary, Lions. Office: 409 E. Weatherford St., Ft Worth TX‡

MOORE, RANDLE T., banker; b. on farm, Caddo Parish, La., Mar. 15, 1875; s. John M. and Jennie Elizabeth (Jones) M.; ed. pub. schs.; m. Susie Frost, of Texarkana, Ark., Dec. 19, 1900; children—Wesley Frost, Virginia Elizabeth, Edwin Ambrose, Randle Thomas. Began as clk. in store; entered gen. mercantile business, on own account, 1895, lumber mfg., 1901; became connected with Frost-Johnson Lumber Co., Mansfield, La., 1905; an organizer Peavy-Moore Lumber Co., 1919. Chmn. board, Commercial National Bank, Shreveport, La., since 1924; chmn. bd. Continental-American Bank & Trust Co.; v.p. Peavy-Wilson Lumber Co., Peavy-Moore Lumber Co., Bank of Commerce & Trust Co. (Mansfield); dir. Louisiana & Arkansas Ry., Sabine & Neches Valley R.R. Mem. bd. U.S. Chamber of Commerce, 1924-26. Trustee Centenary Coll., Shreveport. Chmn. ednl. drive of M.E. Ch., La. Conf. Democrat. Mason (32 deg., K.T., Shriner). Clubs: City, Rotary, Shreveport Country. Home: Shreveport LA‡

MOORE, ROBERT ALLAN, physician, educator; b. Chgo., Ill., July 12, 1901; s. Ellis Philip and Nelly (Clymer) M.; A.B., Ohio State U., 1921, M.D., 1928, M.Sc., 1927, D.Sc., 1956; Ph.D., Western Res. U., 1930; D.Sc. (hon.), Ohio State U., 1954, Union Coll., 1954, Waynesburg, 1957; L.H.D., U. Miami, 1956; LL.D. (honorary), Long Island University, 1959; m. Ruth Miller, June 15, 1922; children—Richard Allan, Calvin Cooper. Instr. pathology, O. State U., 1924-28; research fellow, pathology, Western Res. U., 1928-30, instr., 1930-33; asst. prof. pathology, Cornell U., 1933-37, asso. prof., 1937-39; prof. of pathology, Washington U., St. Louis, Mo., 1939-54; dean, Washington U. Sch. Medicine, 1946-54; vice chancellor schs. of health professions, Univ. Pitts., 1954-57, prof. pathology 1954-57; pres. Downstate Med. Center, dean Coll. Medicine State U. N.Y., 1957-66; Guiteras lectr., Am. Urol. Assn., 1950; Poynter lecturer University Nebraska, 1951; Melon lecturer, University Pittsburgh, 1951; Luis Guerrero lecturer, U. Santo Tomas, 1952; Macgregor lectr. U. Western Ontario, 1952; Ballenger lectr., Southeastern Sec., Am. Urol. Assn., 1956; sr. cons. path. surgeon gen., AUS; mem. com. pathol., 1942-58, Nat. Research Council; civilian adviser on epidemic diseases to secretary of war, 1942-46; spl. consultant to surgeon gen., U.S. Army; scientific adv. bd. Army Inst. Pathol. (chmn. 1953); mem. adv. com. VA; adv. com. med. pub. health Rockefeller Found.; mem. Am. Bd. Pathology (pres. 1951-53); advisory committee Cancer Control USPHS (chmn. 1952-55); hon. cons. surgeon gen. USN, 1956-59; Nat. adv. council Health Research Facilities, USPHS, 1956-60. Coordinating dir. U. Pitts. Health Center, 1954-57; mem. bd. trustees Nat. bd. Medical Examiners, 1948-60, pres. 1954-57, China Med. bd. N.Y., 1955-71; adv. council Med. Edn., 1950-56; adv. com. Nat. Com. Resettlement Fgn. Physicians, 1956-63; adv. bd. Med. Specialties, pres. 1953-57; Mem. Am. Assn. Pathol. and Bacteriol. (president 1952), Federation Biol. Societies, Club for Rsrch. on Aging, Soc. Exptl. Pathol., Am. Soc. Clin. Pathol., Am. Soc. Cancer Research. Gerontological Soc. (pres. 1951), Internat. Soc. Geographic Pathology (pres. 1952-54), Coll. Am. Pathol., Am. Soc. Clin. Pathologists, Mexican Association of Pathologists (hon.), Alpha Omega Alpha, Sigma Xi. Republican. Episcopalian. Author: Textbook of Pathology, 1944, 1951. Contbr. sci. jours. Christian Fenger lectr. Chgo. Inst. Medicine, 1947. Home: Pittsburgh PA Died Sept. 24, 1971; buried Woodland Cemetery, Van Wert OH

MOORE, ROBERT H(ARRIS), labor mediator; b. Excelsior Springs, Mo., Dec. 28, 1907; s. Harris L. and Nancy (Jones) M.; student U. Mo., 1925, Kansas City Law Sch., 1927-30; m. LaVerne Brown, Nov. 9, 1933; 1 son, Jon Richard. Publicity dir. Ball Clinic, Excelsior Springs, 1927-31; admitted to Mo. bar, 1931; practice of law, Excelsior Springs, 1931-42; commr. U.S. Conciliation Service, 1942-43, 46-47; commr. Fed. Mediation and Conciliation Service, 1947-53, regional dir., 1954-55, spl. asst. to dir., 1955-56, dep. dir., 1956-70. Mem. Fed., Mo., Kansas City bar assns., Vets. Fgn. Wars, Am. Legion. Elk. Home: Arlington VA Died Jan. 1972.

MOORE, ROBERT LEE, college pres.; b. Globe, N.C., Sept. 8, 1870; s. Jesse Daniel and Mary Ann (Berry) M.; A.B., Wake Forest (N.C.) Coll., 1892; student summer, U. of N.C., 1897, Chautauqua, N.Y., 1905; Ed. D., Wake Forest (N.C.) College, 1927; m. Edna S. Corpening, of Morganton, N.C., June 11, 1895 children—Nona (Mrs. Roberts), Everett (dec.), Ernest Corpening. Prin. Amherst Acad., Morganton, 1892-97; pres. Mars Hill (N.C.) Coll. since 1897. Supt. pub. instrn., Madison Co., N.C., 1901-03. Trustee Wake Forest Coll., Mills Home (Thomasville); former chmn. Bd. of Edn., Madison Co. Home: Mars Hill NC‡

MOORE, ROBERTS COSBY, banker; b. Newport News, Va., Aug. 29, 1905; s. Roberts Bledsoe and

Margaret (Eggleston) M.; student Coll. William and Mary, 1924-26; grad. Stonier Sch. Banking, 1953; m. Dorothy Harrison Garrett, June 7, 1941; children—Grace Elizabeth (Mrs. Timothy O. Tobin), Margaret Garrett (Mrs. Conrad M. Hall). With Trust Co. Norfolk (Va.), 1925-27; bank aquired by Nat. Bank Commerce, Norfolk, 1927, pres., 1961-63, also dir.; bank merged with Peoples Nat. Bank Central Va., Charlottesville, 1963, to form Va. Nat. Bank, Norfolk, vice chmn. bd., 1963-64, chmn. bd., chief exec. officer, 1964-69; dir. Am. Heritage Life Ins. Co. Chmn., Norfolk Bd. Sinking Fund Commnrs., 1964-69; chmn. Norfolk Municipal Bond Commn. Mem. Norfolk Citizens Adv. Com. Civil Def., Va. Commn. Higher Edn., central command/community relations com. 5th Naval Dist.; bd. dirs. Norfolk Devel. Found.; trustee Tidewater Va. Devel. Council; chmn. Va. campaign com. United Negro Coll. Fund. Bd. dirs. United Communities Fund (pres. 1966), Norfolk Gen. Hosp.; trustee Va. Wesleyan Coll., Norfolk Acad.; chmn. adv. com. Norfolk Area Med. Center Authority; chmn. trustee com. Norfolk Found.; trustee Endowment Assn. Coll. William and Mary; mem. Taylor Murphy Inst., U. Va. Mem. Am., Va. bankers assns., Va., Norfolk (pres. 1964) chambers commerce, Hampton Roads Maritime Assn. (bd. dirs.), Navy League (bd. dirs. Hampton Road council), Newcomen Soc. N. Am. Pi Kappa Alpha. Presbyn. Mason. Clubs: Cedar Point (Nansemond Country); Farmington Country (Charlottesville); Princess Anne Country, Cavalier (Virginia Beach); German, Yacht and Country (Norfolk). Home: Norfolk VA Died Aug. 2, 1969; buried Forest Lawn Cemetery, Norfolk VA

MOORE, ROY W., hon. chmn. Canada Dry Corp.; b. Macon, Ga., Feb. 27, 1891; s. John T. and Carrie (Worsham) M.; B.S., Ala. Polytechnic Inst., 1910; Cornell University, 1911; LL.B., Harvard Law Sch., 1915; m. Nona Stewart Shaw, June 20, 1916; children—Nona Stewart, Roy Worsham, Josephine Shaw. Practicing atty., Macon, Ga., and served 10 yrs. as state's attorney of Georgia (prosecuting attorney); local counsel, Central of Ga. Ry., 1917-18; in trust dept. Guaranty Trust Co. of New York, 1929-32; exec. v.p., Long-Beach-on-the-Ocean, Inc., 1932-34; v.p., gen. mgr. Can. Dry Corporation, 1934, pres., gen. mgr. 1935-57; chmn. bd., chief exec. officer, 1957-60, chmn. bd., 1960-66, hon. chmn., 1966-71; dir. Emery Air Freight Corp., Irving Trust Co., U.S. Pipe & Foundry Co. Asso. mem. W.L.B., 1942-43. Dir. N.Y. Bd. of Trade, 1940-41; dir. YMCA, 1943. Former treas. Jr. Achievement, Inc.; chmn. Greater N.Y.C. Campaign March Dimes; dir. Nat. Multiple Sclerosis Soc., trustee Nat. Foundation; chmn. founders bd. Salk Inst. Biol. Studies. Served in U.S.A., 1918. Mem. N.A.M., Asso. Grocery Mfg. Assn., Am. Legion (post comdr. 1921), Kappa Sigma. Clubs: Economic of N.Y. (dir. 1942-45); Union League; Fairfield (Connecticut) Country; Racquet and Tennis, Harvard. Vestryman, senior warden, Trinity Epis. Ch., Southport, Conn., 1939-44. Home: Southport CT Died Sept. 29, 1971; buried Oaklawn Cemetery, Fairfield CT

MOORE, RUPERT EASTMER, banker; b. on farm in Eastern Kan., Sept. 5, 1872; s. Reuben Francis and Georgia Ann (Pieratt) M.; ed. acad. and business coll.; m. Louise A. Wilcox, of El Paso, Tex., June 30, 1904. Began with Western Security Co., Kansas City, Mo., 1892; with First Nat. Bank, El Paso, Tex., 1894-96, Am. Smelting Co., in Mexico, 1897-1904, Gila Valley Bank & Trust Co., Globe, Ariz., 1905-14; with the Valley Bank, Phoenix, since 1914, pres. since 1921; pres. Maricopa Credit Corpn., Phoenix, v.p. Salt River Valley Bank, Salt River Trust and Savings Bank, both of Mesa, Ariz.; dir. First Nat. Bank, Glendale, Ariz. Republican. Mason, Elk. Home: Phoenix AZ‡

MOORE, THOMAS VERNER, clergyman, educator; b. Louisville, Ky., Oct. 22, 1877; s. John Neuton and Charlotte (McIlvain) M.; Ph.D., Catholic U. of America, 1903, student of philosophy, U. of Leipzig, 1904-05; studied medicine Georgetown U., 1911-13, Munich, Germany, 1913-14; M.D., Johns Hopkins, 1915. Ordained priest R.C. Ch., 1901; fellow in psychology, Catholic U. of America, 1903; lecturer Inst. of Pedagogy, same univ., New York, 1903-04; fellow in pyschology, U. of Calif., 1909; prof. philosophy, St. Thomas Coll., Washington, D.C., 1909-11; instr. psychology, Catholic U. of America, 1910-16, asso. prof., 1916-22, prof., 1922-47, head dept. psychology and psychiatry, 1939-47. Benedictine Monk from 1923; joined Carthusian Order, Burgos, Spain, 1947, spent last 20 years in contemplative life there. Served as capt. and maj. M.C., U.S. Army, France, World War, 1918-19. A founder, first pres., Benedictine Foundation, Washington, D.C.; dir. clinic for mental and nervous diseases, Providence Hosp., Washington, D.C., 1916-39. Founded St. Gertrude's Sch. of Arts and Crafts, 1926, a training sch. for girls of borderline intelligence, and acted as dir. Spl. lecturer on psychology, U. of Madrid, Spain, 1947. Author: A Historical Introduction to Ethics, 1915; Dynamic Psychology, 1924; Prayer, 1931; The Essential Psychoses, 1933; Principles of Ethics, 1935; Consciousness and the Nervous System, 1938; Cognitive Psychology, 1939; The Nature and Treatment of Mental Disorders, 1943; Personal Mental Hygiene, 1944; The Driving Forces of Human Nature and Their Adjustments, 1948; Home and its Inner Spiritual Life, 1952; The Life of Man with God, 1956; Heroic Sanctity and Insanity, 1959. Home: Burgos Spain Died June 5, 1969; buried Miraflores, Burgos, Spain

MOORE, THOMAS WATERMAN, physician; b. Catlettsburg, Ky., Oct. 4, 1866; s. Vincent Morgan and Addie Marian M.; M.D., Medico-Chirurgical Coll., Phila., Pa.; m. Harriet Prentice Hallock, June 28, 1899; children—Joseph Hallock (dec.), Thomas Waterman. Began practice, Everett, Pa., 1893; removed to Huntington, W.Va., 1897; specialist in ophthalmology. Dir. First Huntington Nat. Bank. Pres. C.&O. Ry. Surgeons Assn., 1941-48. Hon. fellow Am. Bronchoscopic Soc., Southeastern Surg. Congress. Fellow Am. College Surgeons; mem. A.M.A., Southern Med. Assn. (pres. 1929), W.Va. State Med. Soc. (pres. 1910), Acad. Ophthalmology and Otolaryngology, Am. Laryngol., Rhinol. and Otol. Soc. Republican. Mason (32 deg., K.T.). Home: 1209 Rugby Rd. Office: 1st Huntington National Bank Bldg., Huntington WV‡

MOORE, VICTOR F., actor; b. Hammonton, N.J., Feb. 24, 1876; s. Orville E. and Sarah Annett (Davis) M.; ed. pub. schs. of Hammonton; m. Emma Littlefield, of New York, June 26, 1903. Debut, Boston, Sept., 1896; has since appeared with John Drew Co., in Girl From Paris," A Summer Shower," Coon Hollow," 45 Minutes From Broadway"; starred in The Talk of New York"; in The Happiest Night of His Life," 1911; Shorty McCabe," vaudeville, 1912-14 and 1919-22. Starring in motion pictures, 1915—. Republican. Universalist. Elk. Clubs: Green Room, Friars, South Shore Yacht (life). Home: Baldwin LI NY‡

MOORE, WILLIAM GEORGE, physician; b. Denver, Dec. 8, 1934; s. Clarence Carl and Dorothy Evelyn (Holtz) M.; M.D., Northwestern U., 1961; m. Anneke Y. Schmidt, Sept. 9, 1961; children—Linda Evelyn, Ellen Louise. Intern Cook County Hosp., Chgo., 1961-62, resident orthopedics, 1965-66; resident gen. surgery Chgo. Wesley Meml. Hosp., 1962-63, resident orthopedics, 1963-64; resident orthopedics ALL Childrens Hosp., St. Petersburg, Fla., 1966-67; chmn. dept. surgery Kootenai Meml. Hosp., Coeur d'Alene, Ida., 1969-70; dir. N. Ida Crippled Children's Service. Bd. dirs. YMCA, 1969-70. Mem. Ida. Orthopedic Soc., Kootenai Med. Soc. Home: Coeur d'Alene ID Died Oct. 3, 1970; buried Coeur d'Alene ID

MOORHEAD, DUDLEY THOMAS, coll. dean; b. San Jose, Cal., Mar. 12, 1913; s. Thomas James, Jr., and Hazel Caroline (Green) M.; B.A., San Jose State Coll., 1934; M.A., Stanford, 1938, Ph.D., 1942; m. Lucille Evelyn Meyer, Dec. 19, 1936; 1 son, Dudley Thomas II. High sch. tchr., Salinas, Cal., 1936-38; head social sci., city secondary schs., San Luis Obispo, Cal., 1938-42; from instr. to prof. dept. history San Jose State Coll., 1946-57, head dept. history, econs. and geography, 1954-57, dean instrn. div. humanities and art, 1957-66, acting acad. v.p., 1966-67, dean Sch. Humanities and Arts, 1967-72, 1st chmn. faculty council, 1953-54. Served from pvt. to capt., USAAF, 1942-45; hist. officer XIII Bomber Command, 13th Air Force, 1944-45. Mem. Cal. Employees Assn. (chpt. pres. 1952), Am. Assn. U. Profs. (chmn. San Jose chpt. 1952-53), Am. Hist. Assn., Phi Alpha Theta, Alpha Kappa Delta, Iota Delta Phi, Tau Delta Phi. Club: Commonwealth of Cal. Contbr. to Ency. Britannica, other publs. Home: San Jose CA Died June 30, 1972.

MOORHEAD, MAXWELL K., consular service; b. Pittsburgh, Pa., July 14, 1877; s. William Jefferson and Emily Butler (Black) M.; Ph.B., U. of Chicago, 1904; m. Muriel Ermatinger, of St. Thomas, Ont., May 16, 1906. Employed in mercantile and ry. business, Pa., until 1900; apptd. by Pres. Roosevelt consul at St. Thomas, Ont., June 26, 1905; consul at Belgrade, Servia, 1906-08; Acapulco, Mex., 1908-09, St. John, N.B., 1909-10, Rangoon, India, 1910-15, Swansea, Wales, 1915-19, Nantes, France, 1919-22, Stuttgart, Germany, 1922-24, Dundee, Scotland, 1924-28, Johannesburg, 1929-34; consul gen. since 1931; at Istanbul since Feb. 1935. Companion, 1st Class, Mil. Order Loyal Legion. Presbyn. Home: 5308 Ellsworth Av., Pittsburgh, Pa. Address: Am. Consulate General, Istanbul Turkey‡

MOORHEAD, ROBERT LOWRY, publisher; b. Indianapolis, Ind., Sept. 15, 1875; s. Thomas W. and Alice (Griffith) M.; ed. high sch., Indianapolis, and Butler Univ.; m. Roxanna Sanders, Dec. 1, 1916. With The Bobbs-Merrill Co., book pubs., Indianapolis, since 1894, v.p., 1922-29, sec.-treas., 1929, treas., since 1948. Mem. Indpls. Light Inf., 1892; mem. Ind. N.G., 1892-1917, sergt. maj., Ind. Vol. Inf., Spanish-Am. War; served as col., F.A., U.S.A., with A.E.F. in France, 1917-19; col., F.A. Res. Mem. Ind. State Sen., 1921-32, (chmn. budget com. 1924-26). Mem. Warren Township Adv. Bd. since 1938. Mem. Ind. State Armory Bd., 1919-33, and 1945-49. Mem. S.A.R. (p. pres. Ind. Soc.), Ind. Society of War of 1812 (pres. 1947-53), Soc. Ind. Pioneers, Military Order Foreign Wars (past commander Ind. Commandery), Reserve Officers Association of U.S. (president Ind. Dept. 1933-35, 1946; pres. 5th Corps Area 1938-39), Am. Legion (mem. nat. exec. com.), 40 and 8 (Grand Chef de Gare, Indiana Passe), Soc. Am. Legion Founders, Army, Navy and Air Force Vets. of Can., Indpls. C. of C., Phi Delta Theta, Scabbard and Blade (hon.). Republican. Methodist. Mason. Clubs: Century (ex-pres.), Columbia, Rotary. Author: The Story of the 139th F.A., 1921. Home: Wildwood," Brookville Rd. Office: 724 N. Meridian St., Indianapolis IN‡

MORA MIRANDA, MARCIAL, ambassador; b. Chilian, Chile, Jan. 12, 1895; s. Victor Marcial Mora Arenas and Semiramis Miranda Rojas; B.A., Lyceum Chilian Instituto Pedagogico, Santiago, Chile; State prof., U. of Chile; lawyer; m. Elena Wackenhut, May 19, 1920; children—Marcial, Elena, Gabriela. Prof. history and geography, Lyceum of Chilan; dir., El Dia, daily newspaper, Chilian; in practice of law with Luis Alamos Barros, Santiago de Chile; now ambassador of Chile to U.S. Served with Chilean Govt. as mem. Chamber of Deputies for Nuble; dir. gen. of nails and telegraph; dir. Amortization Bank; minister of interior, foreign affairs and finance; pres. Nat. Savings Bank, 1933-39; pres. Central Bank of Chile. Pres. Union for Victory (pro-United Nations democratic orgn.). Mem. governing bd. Pan Am. Union. Clubs: Union; Automobile Club of Chile. Home: DC also Santiago de Chile Died May 13, 1972.

MORAN, JOHN JOSEPH, electronics mfg. co. exec.; b. Boston, Jan. 21, 1915; s. Thomas H. and Ida (Bowman) M.; B.B.A., Northeastern U., 1954; m. June H. Peterson, May 9, 1936; children—John F., Janice R., Jane L. Store mgr. H. P. Hood Co., Boston, 1933-41; with Sigma Instruments, Inc. and Fisher Pierce Co., Braintree, Mass., 1941-69, gen. mgr., 1957-69; pres. Sigma Instruments, Inc. 1965-69, Sigma Instruments (Canada) Limited, 1966-69; director Town Moderator. Mem. finance com. Town Marshfield, Mass., 1958-69. Republican. Home: Marshfield MA Died Apr. 10, 1969.

MORAN, RICHARD BARTHOLOMEW, army officer; b. Florence, Colo., Nov. 26, 1895; s. William George and Mary Jane (Coyle) M.; student Colo. State Coll., 1914-17; m. Thelma Thickins, July 15, 1917 (divorced); m. 2d, Blanche Ruth Bird, Feb. 21, 1949. Commd. 1st lt., U.S. Army, May 6, 1917, and advanced through grades to brig. gen., 1942; served World War I; overseas assignment with 5th Army and 15th Army Group in Italy; in Africa and Austria with (General Mark W. Clark; signal officer, 4th Army, Fort Sam Houston, 1947-50; gen. mgr. Imperial Bd. Telecommunications of Ethiopia, 1951-52; now adminstr. civil def. Kerr County, Tex. Decorated D.S.M., Legion of Merit (United States), Comdr. Brit. Empire (Gt. Britain), Croix de Guerre (France), Grand Officer, Crown of Italy, Military Medal (Italy), War Medal (Brazil). Mem. Am. Legion, Sigma Chi. K.C. Retired. Home: Kerrville TX Died Feb. 13, 1972; buried Ft. Sam Houston Nat. Cemetery.

MORAN, WILLIAM EDWARD, JR., assn. executive; b. Herkimer, N.Y., Jan. 8, 1916; s. William Edward and Esther Florence (Henry) M.; A.B., Syracuse U., 1937, LL.B., 1940; M. Phyllis Marie Duffy, May 17, 1941; children—William Edward III, Patricia Marie. Asst. dir. ECA Mission to Belgium, 1949-52; chief dependent overseas territories br. ECA, Mut. Security Agy., 1952-53; dir. Africa div. FOA, 1953-57; dep. dir. ICA Mission to Morocco, 1957-59; head Africa program Stanford Research Inst., 1959-62; dean sch. fng. service, Georgetown U., 1962-66; v.p., exec. dir. Internat. Econ. Policy Assn., Washington, 1966-68; pres. Population Reference Bur., Washington, 1968-70. Fellow African Studies Assn.; mem. Population Reference Bureau (v.p.), Cath. Association for International Peace (pres.), Council Fgn. Relations, Washington Inst. Fgn. Affairs, Phi Delta Phi. Co-author: Handbook on African Economic Development, 1962. Editor: Population Growth: Threat to Peace? Home: Washington DC Died Mar. 8, 1970; buried Gate of Heaven Cemetery.

MORE, HERMAN, ret. mus. dir., artist; b. Medford, Mass., July 15, 1887; s. Charles Herbert and Mary Emma (Rhinehart) M.; art edn., Art Inst. of Chicago, Art Students' League of New York, ind. study in Paris; m. Edna Amelia Robeson, 1923. Dir. and instructor drawing and painting, Davenport Art League, Ia., 1919-24; instr. of drawing and painting Davenport Municipal Art Gallery, 1926-29, dir. of museum, 1928-29; curator Whitney Museum of Am. Art, N.Y.C., 1931-48, dir., 1948-58, ret.; paintings exhibited in Carnegie Inst., Pitts., A Century of Progress, Art Inst. of Chicago, 1933, Golden Gate Internat., San Francisco, 1939; also the Multi-National, London and Paris, and Nat. Museums of Canada; mem. Jury of Selection, New York World's Fair, 1939; organized sect. of Am. Painting, Golden Gate Expn., San Francisco, 1940; organized Centenary Exhbn. Art, State of Utah Centennial, 1947. Asso. dir. Am. Art Research Council; mem. exhbn. com. Am. Fedn. Arts. Trustee Whitney Museum of American Art. Recipient Art in America award Contribution to Am. art. Mem. Coll. Art. Assn., Am. Assn. Mus., Assn. Art Mus. Dirs., Woodstock NY Died Dec. 1968.

MORE, JOHN HERRON, lawyer; b. Cin., Dec. 2, 1903; s. Louis Trenchard and Eleanor (Herron) M.;

grad. Taft Sch., Watertown, Conn., 1920; A.B., Yale, 1924; LL.B., Harvard, 1928; m. Margaret Rapp, Nov. 23, 1935; children—John Herron, Timothy Trenchard. Admitted to Ohio bar, 1928, since practiced in Cin.; partner firm Taft, Stettinius & Hollister, 1935-70. Dir. various corps. Trustee Cin. Symphony Orch., Louise Taft Semple Found. Mem. Am., Ohio, Cin. bar assns. Republican. Episcopalian. Clubs: Cin. Country, Racquet, Camargo Country, Literary (Cin.). Home: Cincinnati OH Died Nov. 9, 1970.

MOREHOUSE, LYMAN FOOTE, telephone engr.; b. Big Rapids, Mich., Oct. 21, 1874; s. Amos Robert and Lucy P. (Foote) M.; B.S. in E.E., U. of Mich., 1897, A.M., 1904; Dr. Engring. (hon.), 1934; grad. student in analyt. chemistry, U. of Chicago, and in mathematics, physics, and elec. engring., U. of Mich.; m. May Cornelia Wyman, June 25, 1904 (died Feb. 12, 1921); children—Dorothy May, Marjorie Lucellen; m. 2d, Mary Spencer Schuessler, Sept. 30, 1922. Instr. in physics, Washington U., 1901; instr. in physics, U. of Mich., 1902-04, instr. and later asst. prof., elec. engring., 1904-06; transmission engr. Western Electric Co., London, Eng., 1906-09; equipment engr. Am. Telephone & Telegraph Co., New York, 1909-19; equipment development engr. same co., 1919-33; asst. dir. of systems development, Bell Telephone Labs., 1933-35; tech. rep. Am. Telephone & Telegraph Co. and Bell Telephone Labs. in Europe since 1935. Mem. N.J. State Board of Education, 1928-35. Fellow Am. Inst. E.E. (mgr. 1919-23; v.p. 1925, 26); fellow A.A.A.S.; mem. British Instn. of Elec. Engrs., Sigma Xi, Tau Beta Pi. Republican. Methodist. Home: 30 Draper Terrace, Montclair, N.J.; 40 Landsdowne House, Mayfair, London, England. Office: Bush House, London Eng*‡

MOREHOUSE, P. GAD BRYAN, lawyer; b. Ogden, Utah, Jan. 10, 1893; s. Jack A. and Lotta Hannah (Bryan) Russell (took name of Morehouse from stepfather, Alanson David Morehouse); student Cornell Coll., Mt. Vernon, Ia., 1908-09; LL.B., George Washington U., 1916, LL.M., 1917, A.B., 1918; m. Anne Elizabeth Shelton, Nov. 10, 1934; children—Peter Gad, William Jonathan. Stenographer Indian Service, Keams Canyon, Ariz., 1910-13; admitted to Dist. of Columbia bar, 1916, and in general practice, 1916-30; trial atty. Fed. Trade Commn., 1930-38; dir. Division of Stipulations, Fed. Trade Commn., 1938-51, asst. dir. Bur. Industry Co-op., chief div. Trade Practice Confs. 1951-52, asst. gen. counsel from 1952. Member Kappa Alpha, Delta Sigma Rho. Democrat. Episcopalian. Mason (Shriner), Kt. York Cross of Honor. Home: Silver Spring MD Died Dec. 8, 1962.

MORELL, WILLIAM NELSON, lawyer; b. Grandy, Minn., Feb. 17, 1898; s. Swen S. and Anna (Nelson) M.; ed. Macalester Coll.; Univ. of Minn., Southeastern Univ. Law Sch.; J.D., Nat. Univ. Law Sch., 1922, LL.M., 1923; m. Blanche Louise Cox, June 9, 1919; children—William Nelson, Charles Acker, Caroline (Mrs. John Morgan Parker), Marcia (Mrs. Edward Painter Crockett), Constance (Mrs. Robert Carson Fraser). Began career as editor Foreign Service Mag., 1920-21; atty. Compensation and Ins. Div., Vets. Bur., 1922-24; asso. counsel, Solicitor's Office, 1924-29; chief legal adviser. Ins. Claims Council, Vets Adminstrn., 1929-33; mem. U.S. Bd. Vets. Appeals, 1934-60, chief mem. 1960-61; legal adminstrv., ins. law cons., 1961-71; chmn. Annual Nat. Conf. on Adminstrv. Law, Fed. Bar Assn., 1938; chmn. Annual Nat. Conf. on Civil Service of Fed. Bar Assn., 1939; bd. trustees Suburban Hosp., Bethesda, Md., 1942-71, member executive committee of board, chmn. planning com.; pres. Fed. Bar Assn., 1939-40, mem. exec. com. 1933-42, mem. veterans affairs committee; chairman National Pilgrimage Committee American Legion, 1933-36; mem. com. on Pacific settlement of internat. disputes, Am. Bar Assn., 1939-40; chmn. Delaware Valley Tercentenary Com. of D.C., 1938; chmn. D.C. Com. Wings for Norway, 1942; pres. Minn. State Soc., 1942; mem. United Nations League of Lawyers, exec. council, 1948-49, pres. U.S. div., 1950-51; member of the board of trustees Community Chest, Montgomery Co., Md., 1944-45; delivered memorial address on Justice Holmes, Sesquicentennial of the Supreme Court of the U.S. under auspices of Joint Committee of Congress. Member Hospital Council of Maryland. Enlisted as volunteer, U.S. Navy, Apr. 28, 1917; served to Aug. 1919. Recipient certificate distinguished service Fed. Bar Assn., 1955; superior performance award, U.S. Bd. Vets. Appeals. Mem. Fed. (nat. council), Am. bar assns., Md. Hist. Soc., John Hanson Soc. Md., Minn. State Soc., Am. Judicature Soc., Suburban Hosp. Assn., Am. Legion. Post Mortem, Sigma Chi, Sigma Delta Kappa. Rep. Lutheran. Author: Govt. Insurance Bethesda MD Died Oct. 16, 1971; buried Parklawn Cemetery, Rockville MD

MORELOCK, HORACE WILSON, education; b. Cleo, Tenn., May 16, 1873; s. William M. and Sarah Lucretia (Weatherly) M.; A.B., U. of Tenn., 1902; A.M., Harvard, 1918; LL.D., Trinity U., Waxahachie, Tex., 1925; m. Willa Royston Battaile, June 24, 1907; children—Horace Weatherly (comdr., officer, Armed Guard, U.S.N.R.; killed in Mid-Pacific action, May 1945), Willa Battaile (Mrs. John W. Washington), Frances Stones (wife of Dr. Malone V. Hill). Supt. of schools, Kerrville, Tex., 1905-10; head dept. of English, West Texas State Teachers Coll., Canyon, Tex., 1910-23; pres. Sul Ross State Teachers Coll., Alpine, Tex., 1923-45; resigned Aug. 31, 1945. Vice pres. Big Bend Park Assn.; pres. Highway 67 Assn. Mem. Phi Kappa Phi. Mason, Rotarian. Author of (articles), Midnight Meditations, Living Memorials, Town and Gown on the Last Frontier, Turning in the Keys. Active in study and surveys relating to allocation of surplus war goods. Advocate of an international holiday, International Peace Day, to be observed by nations throughout the world. Home: Alpine TX*‡

MORESCHI, JOSEPH V., pres. Hod Carriers, Bldg. and Common Laborers Union of America, A.F. of L. Home: Washington DC Died Apr. 1970.

MORGAN, ALFRED POWELL, electrical engr.; b. Brooklyn, N.Y., Apr. 15, 1889; s. Frederick Powell and Margaret (Pattison) M.; grad. Montclair (N.J.) High Sch., 1908; student Mass. Inst. Tech.; m. 2d, Ruth Whigham Shackleford, Nov. 19, 1927; children—by 1st marriage, William; by 2d marriage, Alfred Powell, Charles Shackleford, Thomas Burris. Formerly president Adams-Morgan Co., Inc., Cole & Morgan, Inc., Morgan-Kline, Inc., A.P. Morgan, Inc., R.H. McMann, Inc.; formerly editor mechanical and electrical department Boys' Magazine. Author books on elementary sci. handcraft and engring.; latest: Home Electrical Repairs, 1950; 1st Chemistry Book for Boys and Girls, 1950; A Boy's First Book of Radio and Electronics, 1954; A Boy's Second Book of Radio and Electronics, 1956; A Boy's Third Book of Radio and Electronics, 1962; A Boy's Fourth Book of Radio and Electronics, 1969. Contributed to devel. of radio telegraphy; developed and produced the first short wave regenerative receivers, with Paul Godley; holder of U.S. patents covering radio and mech. devices. Home: Upper Montclair NJ Died Mar. 16, 1972; buried Mt. Hebron Cemetery, Upper Montclair NJ

MORGAN, BROOKS SANDERSON, mfr.; b. nr. Lexington, Ky., Sept. 22, 1877; s. William Garrard and Frances (Brooks) M.; ed. Kentucky U., 1898-1902; m. Mignon McCarty, of Atlanta, Ga., Oct. 4, 1916. Began as clk. in office of Southern Ry., Lexington, Ky., 1903; asst. gen. pass. agt. same, Washington, D.C., 1907-08 (resigned); pres. and gen. mgr. Block Candy Co., mfg. confectioners and biscuit mfrs., Atlanta, since 1908; ex-pres. Biscuit & Crackers Mfrs.' Co., New York; ex-v.p. Atlanta, Birmingham & Atlantic Ry.; dir. Morris Plan Banks of Georgia. Ex-pres. Biscuit & Cracker Manufacturers' Association of America; ex-v.p. Atlanta Chamber Commerce; mem. exec. com. Nat. Confectioners' Assn. (regional dir. industrial recovery div.). Pres. Atlanta Mfrs.' Expn. Co.; dir. Ga. Mfrs.' Assn. Chmn. Bankers' Committee, U.S. Food Administration, World War. Clubs: Piedmont (v.p.), Capital City, Druid Hills. Home: 1285 Peachtree St. Office: 160 Garnett St. S.W., Atlanta GA‡

MORGAN, CAROLINE STARR, author; d. Frederick Starr; m. Thomas J. Morgan, 1870 (died July 13, 1902). Was associated with her husband in lit. work. Author: Ways That Win; Esther Lawrence; Charlotte's Revenge; Marmaduke Multiply Stories; A Sheaf of Happy Holidays, 1907; also numerous short stories for children. Address: Rochester NY‡

MORGAN, ELFORD C(HAPMAN), educator; b. Spartanburg, S.C., June 28, 1905; s. Jo Elford and Nancy Gertrude (Chapman) M.; A.B., Wofford Coll., Spartanburg, 1927; A.M., U. of N.C., 1932, Ph.D., 1941; Litt.D., Wofford College, 1958; was married to Martha Hamilton, June 9, 1932; children—Elford Hamilton, Charles Hamilton. Teacher of English, Spartanburg High Sch., 1927-29; instr. English, Wofford Coll., 1929-30, Converse Coll., Spartanburg, 1932-34, asst. prof., 1934-36, asso. prof., 1936-41, prof. English and dean of faculty, 1941-55, acting pres., 1955-56, dean of adminstrn., 1956-62; prof. English, head of dept., Coll. of Charleston, S.C., 1962; project director program institutional evaluation and visitation So. Assn. Colls. and Universities, 1958-59, 60-62. Member S.C. Council on tchr. edn., 1944-60. Mem. So. Assn. Commn. Colls. and Univs. (sec. 1953-57, chmn. 1957-58), Modern Lang. Assn., S. Atlantic Modern Lang. Assn., Pi Kappa Phi, Sigma Upsilon, Phi Beta Kappa, Blue Key. Democrat. Presbyn. Clubs: Rotary, Piedmont. Home: Landrum SC Died Oct. 18, 1962; buried Spartanburg SC

MORGAN, FREDERIC LINDLEY, architect; b. Loda, Ill., Jan. 6, 1889; s. Joseph Sidney and Maud (Lindley) M.; B.S. in Architecture, U. Ill., 1912; studied abroad. With Louisville Bd. Edn., 1913-15; with archtl. firm Malchonron & Higganbothan, Detroit, 1916, Smith, Hinchman & Grilles, Detroit, 1917-19; asso. Nevin & Henry, architects, Grilles, Detroit, 1917-19; asso. Nevin & Henry, architects, Louisville, 1919, Nevin, Wischmeyer & Morgan, 1921-29, Nevin, Morgan & Holbrook, 1929-42, Nevin & Morgan, 1942-70. Fellow A.I.A. Clubs: The Arts, Filson (Louisville). Home: Louisville KY Died May 29, 1970.

MORGAN, GEORGE ALLEN, clergyman, educator; b. nr. Shelbyville, Tenn.; s. German Baker and Isadora Alice (Holt) M.; grad. Webb Sch., Bell Buckle, Tenn.; B.A., Vanderbilt, 1897; D.D., Emory U., 1920; m. Effie Verner Kennedy, of Cornersville, Tenn., June 12, 1901; 1 son, George Allen. Ordained M.E. Ch., S., ministry, 1890; pastor in Tenn. at Lewisburg, 1897-1900, Fayetteville, 1900-04, Murfreesboro, 1904-08, Pulaski, 1908-12, West End, Nashville, 1913-18; pres. Martin Coll., Pulaski, Tenn. (for girls and young women), 1918-29; pastor, Lebanon, Tenn., 1930-31; presiding elder, Murfreesboro Dist., Tenn. Conf., 1931-35; pastor Pulaski, Tenn., 1935-39; prof. Bible, and Chaplain Martin Coll. Mem. Delta Kappa Epsilon. Democrat. K.P. Home: Pulaski TN‡

MORGAN, GEORGE WILSON, lawyer, pub.; b. N.Y.C., Sept. 8, 1907; s. George Wilson and Helen E. (Demuth) M.; student Hotchkiss Sch., 1921-25; A.B., Trinity Coll., Conn., 1929; J.D., N.Y.U., 1934; m. Angela de R. Stevenson, Jan. 17, 1938 (dec. 1959). Admitted to N.Y. State bar, 1934, since practiced law in N.Y.C.; formerly partner in firm of Maclay, Morgan & Williamson; spl. counsel Assn. Am. Ship Owners, 1944, pres., 1945-69; com. finance, ins., mgmt. Nat. Cargo Bur., Inc.; publisher The Inquirer & Mirror, Nantucket, Massachusetts; president The Inquirer & Mirror, Inc. Mem. Am., N.Y. bar assns., Assn. Bar City of New York, N.Y. County Lawyers Assn., Maritime Law Association United States. Clubs: Tuxedo (Tuxedo Park); University, City Mid-day, Union, River (N.Y.C.); Metropolitan (Washington); Mid-Ocean (Bermuda). Editor of Shipping Survey, 1948-69. Author New York City NY Died June 28, 1969; buried Sleepy Hollow Cemetery, Tarrytown NY

MORGAN, IKE, illustrator; b. Grand Tower, Ill., June 28, 1871; father German, mother Scotch-Irish; ed. pub. schs. St. Louis; studied drawing and painting St. Louis Sch. of Fine Arts; m. June 28, Pauline Swain. Did 1st illustrating for St. Louis Republic; since 1896 in Chicago, doing sp'l work for Record-Herald. Illustrated: Kids of Many Colors, 1901; Pickaback Songs, P2. Residence: 386 Dearborn Av. Studio: Record-Herald Bldg., Chicago‡

MORGAN, JACOB L., clergyman; b. Rowan County, N.C., Feb. 7, 1872; s. Jacob and Sallie (Hodge) M.; A.B., North Carolina College, 1899; grad. Southern Luth. Theol. Sem., 1902; D.D., Lenior Rhyne Coll., 1922, LL.D., 1945; m. Virginia C. Shoup, May 25, 1903; children—Gladys, Ruth (dec.), Karl Z., Katharine, Lois. Ordained Luth. ministry, 1902; pastor Haven Luth. Ch., Salisbury, and Enochville, Pastorate, Rowan County, N.C., until 1907; sec. Synodical Home Missions of N.C. Luth. Synod, 1907-17, organizing and building chs. at High Point, Greensboro, Mooresville, Landis, Liberty and Raleigh, N.C.; pastor Holy Trinity Ch., Raleigh, 1911-19; pres. United Luth. Synod of N.C., 1919-47; ret. 1947; mem. Bd. Fgn. Missions United Luth. Ch. in America; ex-officio mem. Bd. Ednl. Instns. of Luth. Synod of N.C.; del. N.C. Luth. Synod to Merger Conv., New York, 1918, when United Luth. Ch. in America was organized, and since chmn. N.C. delegation to biennial conventions of same, also mem. exec. bd. United Luth. Ch. in America, and mem. Bd. of Am. Missions. Camp pastor for Lutherans at Camp Polk, Salisbury NC‡

MORGAN, JOHN HEATH, foreign service officer; b. Lynn, Mass., Dec. 6, 1901; s. Edward and Martha Ambler (Heath) M.; S.B., Harvard, 1924; m. Katherine Louise Whelchel, June 18, 1926; children—Louise Longstreet, John Heath. Foreign service officer since 1925; vice consul, Budapest, 1926-30, consul, 1930; consul, Berlin, 1931-33; with western European div. Dept. of State, 1933-37; 2d sec., Vienna, 1937-39, Madrid, 1939-42, Bogota, Colombia, 1942-44; asst. chief, Div. of Northern European affairs, Dept. of State, 1944-47, chief, 1947-71; adviser Am. delegation West Indian Conference, St. Thomas, Virgin Islands, Feb. 1946; 1st sec., Rekjavik, Iceland, June-July 1946; became asso. chief Northern European Div., Nov. 1946; Counselor of Embassy, Ottawa, 1951-71; counselor of Embassy, Helsinki, 1953-56; Dept. of State adviser Army War Coll., 1956-58; examiner Bd. Examiners Fgn. Service, Dept. State, 1958-60, spl. asst. to dir., Hist. Office, 1960-71. Home: Chevy Chase MD Died May 1971.

MORGAN, JOHN THOBURN, ret. elec. supply co. exec.; b. Charleston, W.Va., Nov. 25, 1889; s. Benjamin Stephen and Annie (Thoburn) M. student W.Va. U., 1906-09; m. Rebecca Putney, Sept. 17, 1919; children—John Thoburn (dec.) and Rebecca Putney (Mrs. P.J. Beattie, Jr.) (twins), Joanne Thoburn (Mrs. J.R. Hartman). Salesman Charleston Elec. Supply Co., 1909-13, sales mgr., 1919-21, sec., dir., sales mgr., 1921-40, pres., dir., chmn., 1940-55, chmn., dir., 1955-60, retired; active in land development projects; dist. sales rep. Ohio Brass Co., 1913-17; dir. Chesapeake & Potomac Telephone Co. W.Va., Kanawha Banking & Trust Co., Charleston. Past chmn. adv. bd. W.Va. Dept. Pub. Assistance. Mem. bd., past chmn. Kanawha-Clay chpt. A.R.C.; mem. bd. Charleston Civic Center, from 1957, also past chmn. bd. Served from 2d lt. to capt., Engrs., U.S. Army, World War I; 80th Div. in France,

3d Army in Germany. Profl. engr., W.Va. Mem. Charleston C. of C. (past pres.), 80th Div. Vets. Assn. (past nat. comdr.), Am. Legion, Soc. Am. Mil. Engrs. (charter mem.), Am. Soc. M.E., Nat., W.Va. socs. profl. engrs., Telephone Pioneers Am., Nat. Assn. Elec. Distbrs. (hon. life), Newcomen Soc., Phi Sigma Kappa. Presbyn. (deacon 30 years, trustee 10 years). Mason (Shriner). Clubs: Rotary, Edgewood Country, Press (Charleston); Metropolitan (Washington). Home: Charleston WV Died Jan. 31, 1970; buried Spring Hill Cemetery, Charleston WV

MORGAN, LEWIS LOVERING, congressman; b. Mandeville, La., Mar. 2, 1876; ed. St. Eugene's Coll. of St. Tammany Paris, La.; LL.B., Tulane U. Law Dept., 1899; m. Lenora Cefalu, 1903. Admitted to La. bar, 1899; mem. La. Ho. of Rep., 1908; served as dist. atty.; mem. 62d, 63d and 64th Congresses (1911-17), 6th La. Dist. Democrat. Home: Covington LA‡

MORGAN, MINOT CANFIELD, clergyman; b. Princeton, N.J., Sept. 17, 1876; s. Rev. Minot Spaulding and Anna Corilla (Green) M.; A.B., Princeton, 1896, A.M., 1900; grad. Princeton Theol. Sem., 1900; D.D., Lafayette Coll., 1917, Southwestern, 1917; m. Margaretta Webb Holden (A.B., Vassar), May 11, 1911; children—Minot Canfield, Edward Holden, Henry Green. Ordained Presbyn. ministry, 1900; asst. to pastor Tenth Ch., Phila., 1900-01; pastor successively First Ch., Far Rockaway, N.Y., Central Ch., Summit, N.J., Fort Street, Ch., Detroit, Mich., until 1926; co-pastor Fifth Av. Ch., New York, 1926-33; pastor First Ch., Greenwich, Connecticut, 1933-50; moderator of New York Presbytery, 1931-33. Camp religious work dir. Y.M.C.A., 1918; capt. reserve chaplain, U.S. Army, 1925-35. Rec. sec. Presbyn. Bd. of Christian Edn., 1923-45. Trustee Princeton Theol. Sem., since 1911. Mem. S.A.R. Republican. Traveled around the world visiting mission fields, 1908, 09. Home: 47 Hawthorne Av., Princeton NJ‡

MORGAN, THEOPHILOUS JOHN, artist; b. Cincinnati, O., Nov. 1, 1872; s. Theopilous John and Laura (Finch) M.; student St. Francis Xavier Coll., 1884-90; studied Cincinnati Art Sch., pupil of Rebisso Duveneck, Meakin, Lutz, Noble; m. Helice Marie Tracy, 1925. Works: Long Point Lighthouse," Witchery of the Moon," The Road to Truro," The Path of the Moon," In Arcadia," Old Willows," Town Hall," Fishing Boats." Represented in Lessing Rosenwald Collection, Phila.; Delgado Mus. of Art, New Orleans; Univ. of Ind.; Women's Hosp., Cleveland; Springville (Utah) Art Mus.; Aurora (Ill.) Museum; Museum of Fine Arts, Houston; Witte Memorial Museum, San Antonio; Women's Club Galleries, Harlingen, Tex.; Montgomery (Ala.) Women's Coll. Museum; Girl Scouts Galleries, San Antonio; Los Angeles Museum of Fine Arts; Highland Park, Society of Artists, Dallas, Art Museum, Binghamton, New York. Director Sears Roebuck Art Galleries, Washington, D.C., 1932, East High School Galleries, Salt Lake City, 1934. Awards: First prize ($2500) Tex. Wild Flower Competition, 1928; gold medal, Davis Wild Flower Competition, also hon. mention, 1929; 1st prize Springfield Art Assn., Utah, 1930; Edgar B. Davis prize 1928-30; Pabst gold medal, 1929. Mem. San Antonio Palette Assn., Washington Soc. of Artists, San Diego Art Assn., San Antonio Art League, Southern States Art League. Clubs: Washington Art; New York Water Color; Beachcombers (Provincetown, Mass.). Home: Forest Glen MD Studio: 456 N St., S.W., Washington DC*‡

MORGAN, THOMAS FRANCIS, JR., philanthropic financial counsellor; b. Paterson, N.J., July 18, 1895; s. Thomas Francis and Jennie Bell (Walker) M.; student U.S. Mil. Acad., 1918-19; B.S., Bucknell U., 1921; m. Edith Florence Somers, Sept. 11, 1944; children—Linda Winifred, Thomas Francis III. With firm Ward, Wells & Dreshman, fund raisers, N.Y.C., 1921-25; asso. dir. 15 Million Presbyn. Pension Fund Appeal, N.Y.C., 1925-26; with Marts & Lundy, Inc., financial counsellors for philanthropic instns., N.Y.C., from 1926, v.p., 1952-56, pres., from 1956, also dir.; dir. $20 Million Mid-Century Fund, Mass. Inst. Tech., 1949-50. Bd. dirs. John E. Mason Meml. Found. aiding young men planning govt. careers, from 1955, v.p., 1955; trustee Wilkes Coll. Served as 1st lt. U.S. Army, 1919. Mem. Am. Assn. Fund Raising Counsel (dir., exec. com.), Lambda Chi Alpha (nat. treas.). Presbyn. Home: Lewisburg PA Died Jan. 9, 1970.

MORGAN, WILLIAM CONGER, chemist; b. at Albany, N.Y., June 21, 1874; s. William and Josephine Amelia (Conger) M.; B.A., Yale, 1896, Silliman fellow in chemistry, Ph.D., 1899; m. Charlotte Elizabeth Lansing, of Albany, June 21, 1900. Instr. chemistry, 1899, prof., 1900-1, Washburn College, Topeka, Kan.; instr. chemistry, 1901-6, asst. prof. since 1906, U. of Cal. Fellow A.A.A.S.; mem. Am. Chem. Soc., Deutsche Chemische Gesellschaft. Sigma Xi, Phi Beta Kappa. Congregationalist. Clubs: Outlook (Oakland), Faculty (Berkeley). Author: Qualitative Analysis as a Laboratory Method for the Study of General Inorganic Chemistry, 1906; also numerous papers on chemistry and edn. Address: 2440 Hillside Av., Berkeley CA‡

MORGAN, WILLIAM SACHEUS, theologian; b. Rhymney, Monmouthshire, Wales, Feb. 3, 1864; s. Paul and Sarah (Webley) M.; A.B., Pontypool Coll., Wales, 1889; B.D., Yale, 1892, Ph.D., 1895; S.T.D., Pacific Unitarian Sch. for Ministry, 1929; m. Leolyn Smith Beard; children—Leolyn S., Gwendolen S., Elaine W., William R., Pauline W. Ordained Bapt. ministry, 1890; pastor Greenport Ch., L.I., N.Y., 1895-99; asst. pastor Madison Av. Ch., New York, 1899-1900; prof. logic and psychology, Amity Theol. Sch., New York, 1890-1900; joined Unitarian Ch., 1900; pastor Unitarian Ch., Derby, Conn., 1900-06, First Ch., Albany, N.Y., 1907-10; prof. philosophy and psychology of religion and sec. of faculty, Pacific Unit. Sch. for the Ministry, Berkeley, Calif., 1910-41, Cutting professor of philosophy, emeritus, since 1941, also acting dean, 1924-25, acting pres. later pres. bd. trustees, 1931-32; pres. Pacific Unitarian Sch. for the Ministry, 1932-41; travel and study in Europe, 1925-26; lecturer history of philosophy, Yale, 1894-95; Carnegie Foundation lecturer, U. of Ore. Summer Sch., 1915. Pres. Pacific Coast Conf. Unitarian Ch. Investigated European municipalities, 1910. Mem. Berkeley Traffic Safety Commn. (life mem.; pres. 1928); chmn. com. for zoning of Berkeley; mem. Berkeley Bd. of Edn., 1931-35; moderator Pacific Coast Conf. Unitarian Ch., 1932-40. Made hon. mem. of Bible Foundation, 1937. Mem. Am. Philos. Soc., A.A.A.S., American Assn. for the United Nations, Yale Alumni Assn., Soc. for Religious Culture, Mark Twain Society, English-Speaking Union, Pi Gamma Mu. Mem. American Unitarian Assn. (life), Hosmer Chapter, Unitarian Laymen's League (pres.). Clubs: Faculty of U. of Calif. (hon.), City Commons (pres. 1940-41), Hillsdale, Calif. Writers (hon.). Trustee First Unitarian Ch., 1940-43. Author: Modern Philosophy and the Religious Life, 1902; Nuggets of Gold, 1909; Modern Cities (with Horatio M. Pollock), 1913. Mem. Calif. War Price and Rationing Bd. (83: 1-8), 1942-46. Home: 1683 La Loma Av., Berkeley 9 CA‡

MORGULIS, SERGIUS, biochemist; b. Russia, Aug. 6, 1885; s. Samuel and Hannah (Spigel) M.; Ananieff Gymnasium; A.M., Columbia, 1907; Ph.D., Harvard, 1910; studied in Vienna, Berlin, Naples, Woods Hole, etc.; m. Fannie Bashkirtzeva, 1911. Came to U.S., 1904, naturalized citizen, 1910. Austin teaching fellow, Harvard, 1909; traveling fellow from Harvard, 1910-12; asso. in animal metabolish, Carnegie Instn., 1912-13; asso. in biochemistry, Coll. Physicians and Surgeons (Columbia), 1913-16; spl. research asso., U.S. Bur. Fisheries, 1914-16; prof. physiology and biochemistry, Creighton U., Omaha, Neb., 1916-21; prof. biochemistry, U. of Neb. Coll. of Medicine, from 1921. Fellow A.A.A.S.; mem. Soc. Biol. Chemistry, Am. Physiol. Soc., Am. Soc. Zoologists, Biochem. Assn., Societe Chimie Biologique, Paris, 1934, Biochem. Soc. (Great Britain), Sigma Xi. Author: Fasting and Undernutrition, 1923; Experiments in Physical and Physiological Chemistry, 1929; Nutritional Muscular Dystrophy, 1938; (with Oparin) The Origin of Life, 1938; Biochemical Evolution (with Florkin), 1949; also numerous exptl. and general articles in mags. Address: Omaha NB Died Dec. 20, 1971; cremated.

MORIARTY, EUGENE, exec. editor Boston Herald, Traveler. Address: Boston MA Died Apr. 1970.

MORISSE, RICHARD DIEHM, univ. adminstr.; b. St. Louis, Jan. 3, 1914; s. William J. and Alice (Seidler) M.; grad. St. Louis U., 1939; m. Harriet M. Mac Gregor, Nov. 10, 1938; children—Marian (Mrs. Lyle Irving Van Vleet), Ralph D. Auditor Price, Waterhouse & Co., St. Louis, 1935-37; auditor Kerber, Eck & Braeckel, St. Louis, 1937-42; auditor of Lybrand, Ross Bros. & Montgomery, St. Louis, 1942-46; internal auditor U. So. Cal., Los Angeles, 1946-68. Mem. Am. Inst. C.P.A.'s, Cal. Soc. C.P.A.'s Clubs: Town Hall. Home: Arcadia CA Died Sept. 27, 1968.

MORITZ, RICHARD DANIEL, educator; b. Emden, Germany, May 10, 1872; s. Karl Fredrich and Maria (Stalhut) M.; came to U.S., 1880; naturalized, 1896; B.S., Hastings (Neb.) Coll., 1899; B.E., State Coll., Peru, Neb., 1912; grad. work Columbia, 1922; m. M. Genevieve Richards, Dec. 22, 1897; children—Alan R., John R., Genevieve R. (Mrs. Lowell Beer). Supt. schs. Adams County, Neb. (Hastings), 1897-1901; Blue Hill, Neb., 1901-07, Red Cloud, 1907-14; state normal training insp., Lincoln, Neb., 1914-16; supt. schs. Seward, Neb., 1916-24; dean summer sessions and dir. dept. ednl. service, U. of Neb., since 1924. Mem. N.E.A., Am. Personnel Assn., American Assn. Summer Sch. Deans and Dirs., Neb. State Edn. Assn. Democrat. Conglist. Mason. Elk. Home: 3816 Orchard St., Lincoln NB‡

MORLEY, CLARENCE JOSEPH, governor; b. Dyersville, Ia., Feb. 9, 1869; s. John and Mary Dyer (Plaister) M.; grad. high sch., Cedar Falls, Ia., 1886; LL.B., U. of Denver, 1899; m. Maud M. Thompson, of Cedar Falls, July 2, 1893; children—Mrs. Katharine Morley Shelton, Harold T., Clarence J., Mary C. Admitted to Colo. bar, 1897; connected with law firm of Teller, Orahood & Morgan, 1900-06, Teller & Dorsey, 1906-10; in partnership with Frank McDonough, Sr., 1910-16; associated with Thomas E. Walters, 1916-23. Served as pub. administrator, Denver, 4 yrs.; mem. State Bd. of Pardons 4 yrs.; judge Dist. Court, 1919-25; gov. of Colo., term 1925-27. Mem. Colo. and Denver bar assns. Republican. Methodist. Mason (32 deg., K.C.C.H.). Clubs: Cosmopolitan, Lions (hon.), High Twelve (hon.).*‡

MORON, ALONZO GRASEANO, housing ofcl.; b. St. Thomas, Virgin Islands, Apr. 12, 1909; Ph.B., Brown U., 1932; M.A., U. Pittsburgh, 1933; LL.B., Harvard, 1947; LL.D., Wilberforce U., 1950, Brown U., 1955; married Leola Churchill, Sept. 12, 1932. Commr. pub. welfare Govt. of Virgin Islands, 1933-36; housing mgr. Atlanta Housing Authority, 1936-44; gen. business mgr. Hampton (Va.) Inst., Feb. 1947-Apr. 1949; acting pres. and gen. bus. mgr., Oct. 1948-Apr. 1949, pres., 1949-59; asst. gov. Virgin Islands, 1959, commr. edn., 1960; asst. to regional adminstr. HHFA; deputy regional adminstr. Dept. Housing and Urban Devel., San Juan, Puerto Rico. Member National Manpower Council. Member Nat. Assn. Housing and Redevelopment Ofcls., NAACP, Internat. Conf. Social Work, Sigma Pi Phi, Phi Beta Kappa, Alpha Phi Alpha. Rotarian. Contbr. articles on housing to Social Forces, Am. City and Phylon. Home: Santurce PR Died Oct. 31, 1971.

MORONEY, JAMES MCQUEEN, corp. exec.; b. Dallas, Tex., July 10, 1894; s. James and Lenora Bush (McQueen) M.; student Holy Trinity Coll., Dallas, 1907-11, Georgetown U., 1911-14; m. Maidie Dealey, Apr. 10, 1917; children—Mrs. George H. Norsworthy, Mrs. James J. Laney, James McQueen, Jr. Pres. Moroney Hardware Co., Dallas Tex., 1915-26; personal investment business, Dallas, 1926-34; dir., mem. exec. dept. A.H. Belo Corp., publs. The Dallas Morning News and Tex. Almanac and owners sta. WFAA (AM-FM-TV), Dallas, 1934-35. dir., acting sec.-treas., 1935-38, dir., sec.-treasurer, 1938-39, v.p., sec., dir., 1940-55, sr. v.p., dir., 1955-60, vice chairman of board of directors, 1960-64, chairman board dirs., dir., from 1964. Councilman for Highland Park, Tex., 1930-34. Member exec. com. Dallas Co. chapter. A.R.C., 1931-50, vice chmn. Dallas County Chapter, 1933-34, chmn., 1935; dir. Freeman Memorial Clinic, Children's Hosp. of Texas, State Fair of Tex.. Mem. Dallas Hist. Soc. (trustee), Dallas Branch of English Speaking Union, Delta Sigma Chi. Ind. Democrat. Roman Catholic, K.C. Clubs: Dallas Country, Serra, City (Dallas). Home: Dallas TX Died Sept. 23, 1968.

MOROSCO, OLIVER, theatrical producer; b. Logan, Utah, 1876; ed. pub. schs. Began as acrobat in father's troup, later asst. theatrical mgr. and press agt. in Calif.; became mgr. Majestic Theatre, Los Angeles, 1908; propr. Morosco Theatre, New York and Los Angeles. Produced The Fox," 1909; later Bird of Paradise"; Peg o' My Heart"; The Unchastened Woman"; etc. Author: (with others) The Judge and the Jury"; The Society Plot"; So Long, Letty"; Merely Mary Brown."*‡

MORRILL, WILLIAM KELSO, univ. dean; b. Balt., Dec. 15, 1903; s. Bert S. and Edna (Fort) M.; A.B., Johns Hopkins, 1925, M.A., 1927, Ph.D., 1929; m. Mary C. Kirk, Aug. 15, 1934; children—William Kelso, Jean Elizabeth. Mem. faculty Johns Hopkins, 1930-68, asso. prof. math., 1945-68, dean students, 1958-67. Univ. rep. to bd. dirs. Balt. YMCA. Mem. Balt. bd. dirs. Camp Fire Girls Am. Elected to Lacrosse Hall of Fame, 1963, Baltimore City College Hall of Fame, 1965. Mem. Am. Math. Soc., Am. Math. Assn., Sigma Xi, Omicron Delta Kappa (faculty adviser), Kappa Alpha. Presbyn. (deacon). Author: Trigonometry, 1946; Lacrosse, 1952; Analytic Geometry, 1951; Calculus, 1956. Home: Baltimore MD Died Apr. 11, 1968; buried New London PA

MORRIS, ALICE A. PARMELEE, author; b. New Haven, Conn.; d. Andrew Y. and Sarah E. (Farren) Parmelee; ed. in Europe; m. Robert Clark Morris, June 24, 1890. Author: Dragon and Cherry Blossoms, 1896. Commd. by Dept. Interior, 1917, to prepare complete system of trails for horses in and about Yellowstone Nat. Park; rode in saddle over 1,500 miles, making map of existing trails and laying out proposed trails; filed detailed map and 2 reports for which received thanks of dept. Address: Care Robert C. Morris, 27 Pine St., New York NY‡

MORRIS, CHARLES HARWOOD, lawyer; b. Shelbyville, Ky., Mar. 20, 1871; s. James Smith and Margaret Laetitia (Scearce) M.; ed. common schs.; m. Agnes White Crutcher, May 10, 1910. Admitted to Ky. bar, 1895, and practiced at La Grange; chmn. Oldham County Dem. Com., 15 yrs.; entered office of atty. gen. as clk., 1904, later asst. to atty. gen.; elected atty. gen. of Ky., Nov. 1917, to fill vacancy expiring Jan. 1, 1920; commr. Ky. Court of Appeals since Oct. 1934. Democrat. Baptist. Mason (K.T., Shriner), Elk. Author: Kentucky Laws Made Plain, 1907; Banking Laws of Kentucky, 1922. Home: 417 Shelby St., Frankfort KY*‡

MORRIS, CHESTER, actor; b. N.Y.C., Feb. 16, 1901; s. William and Etta (Hawkins) M.; grad. high sch.; m. Suzanne Kilborn, Nov. 8, 1926; children—Brooks, Cynthia; m. 2d, Lili Kenton, Nov. 30, 1940; 1 son, Kenton. Began career with Lionel Barrymore in The Copperhead, Shubert Theatre, N.Y.C., 1918; other plays include Turn to the Right, Thunder, Crime, (with Geoge M. Cohan) Yellow, Home Towners, Whispering Friends; motion pictures include Alibi, 1928, The Big House, 1933, Divorcee, 1934, Unchained, 1953, also Boston Blackie series; appeared Broadway play, Blue Denim, 1957-59, Advise and Consent, 1963; film The Great White Hope, 1970; appeared on TV shows, 1964; Broadway and on tour Subject Was Roses, 1966-67. Home: New York City NY Died Sept. 11, 1970.

MORRIS, CLAUDE FRANK, judge; b. Ralls County, Mo., Jan. 10, 1869; s. Harrison Franklin and Nancy Catherine (Domigan) M.; LL.B., George Washington U., 1902; m. Alice Carey Manwaring, Oct. 25, 1905; children—Catherine (Mrs. Wilbur Fisk Sanders, 2d), Phillip Manwaring, Richard McKennan (dec.). Admitted to D.C. bar, 1902, Mont. bar, 1903; clk. in U.S. Dept. of Agr., 1899-1903; sec. and trust officer Union Bank & Trust Co., Helena, Mont., 1903-06; bank dir. and practicing atty., 1907-21; activities extended to ranching 1922-32; mem. Mont. State House of Reps., 1914-16, State Senate, 1916-20; asst. atty. gen., 1932-34; mem. Havre City Council, 1912-18; asso. justice Mont. Supreme Court for term 1934-40, re-elected Nov. 1940, for 6-yr. term; now practicing law, Great Falls, Mont. Mem. Kappa Sigma. Democrat. Presbyterian. Mason (32 deg., Shriner), Elk. Club: Montana (Helena). Home: Lorraine Apts., 2d Av. N. and Park Dr. Office: Electric Bldg., Great Falls MT‡

MORRIS, CLYDE TUCKER, prof. civil engring.; b. Morrow County, O., Apr. 19, 1877; s. Byrant Washington and Adelade (Ashley) M.; C.E., Ohio State U., 1898; m. Mabel Taylor, Oct. 18, 1899; children—Ruth Elizabeth (Mrs. F. D. Young), Wilametta Esther (Mrs. Warren R. Sisson), Eugene Bryant. Began as draftsman with Columbus Bridge Co., Columbus, O., 1898-99, Youngstown (O.) Bridge Co., 1899-1901, King Bridge Co., Cleveland, O., 1901-02; asst. engr. Puget Sound Bridge & Dredging Co., Seattle, Wash., 1902-04, King Bridge Co., 1904-06; asso. prof. structural engring., Ohio State U., 1906-08, prof. civil engring. since 1908, chmn. dept. civil engring., 1938-47; emeritus prof. of civil engring., since 1947. Mem. American Soc. C.E., American Concrete Inst., Am. Society for Engring. Edn., Sigma Xi, Tau Beta Pi. Acacia, Triangle. Republican. Mason (32 deg.). Clubs: Faculty, Engineers. Author: Steel Structures, 1909; Stresses in Structures (with A. H. Heller), 1916; Structural Frameworks (with S. T. Carpenter), 1943. Contbr. on engring. Home: 2442 Northwest Blvd., Columbus 12 OH‡

MORRIS, EDWIN BATEMAN, architect; b. Phila., Nov. 18, 1881; s. Robert C. and Grace P. (Powell) M.; B.S. in Architecture, U. Pa., 1904; m. Faith Farquhar, Sept. 28, 1910; children—Edwin Bateman, Kay (Mrs. L. H. Mills), Martha (Mrs. H. W. Stabler). With Office Supervising Architect, Treasury Dept., Washington, 1906-42, chief architecture, 1934-42; v.p. Tile Mfrs. Assn., 1942-60. Mem. Washington Bldg. Congress, 1945-71; organizer Constrn. Specification Inst., 1948; pres. Thornton Soc. Preservation Historic Structures, 1942-71. Fellow A.I.A. (Gold medal outstanding achievement fed. architecture 1952). Author: (novels) The Narrow Street, 1924, Blue Anchor Inn, The Millionaire, Our Miss York, Or Else a Park Bench, The Road to Santa Fe, The Cresting Wave, Riches for Caroline, The Open Door, The Silk Coquette, Copper Moon, Mere Man; (plays) College Comedies. also articles. Editor The Fed. Architect, 1930-45. Home: Bethesda MD Died May 24, 1971; buried Sandy Spring Friends Cemetery, Sandy Spring MD

MORRIS, ELISABETH WOODBRIDGE (MRS. CHARLES GOULD MORRIS), author; b. Brooklyn, N.Y., June 16, 1870; d. Charles Lester and Irene Augusta (Cartwright) Woodbridge; prep. edn., Packer Collegiate Institution, Brooklyn; A.B., Vassar College, 1892 (Phi Beta Kappa); Ph.D., in English, Yale University, 1898; m. Charles Gould Morris, of New Haven, Conn., Sept. 27, 1899; children—Laura Wylie (Mrs. John S. Burnett), Woodbridge Edwards, Martha Cartwright (Mrs. George B. Vaughan), Daniel Luzon, Charles Lester, Elisabeth Woodbridge (Mrs. Earl Jackson). Teacher English and History, Packer Collegiate Institute, 1894-95; teacher English, Vassar, 1898-99. Club: Saturday Morning (New Haven). Author: Studies in Jonson's Comedy, 1898; The Drama—Its Law and Its Technique, 1898; Course in Expository Writing (with Prof. Gertrude Buck), 1899; Course in Narrative Writing (with same), 1906; The Jonathan Papers, 1912; More Jonathan Papers, 1915; Days Out, 1917; Isaiah—Incorporated, 1920; The Crusade of the Children, 1923; The Summoning of the Nations (peace pageant), 1934; Episodes from Colonial Connecticut (tercentenary series, with Alice J. Walker), 1935. Home: 230 Prospect St., New Haven, Conn.; (summer) Sandy Hook CT‡

MORRIS, FREDERICK WISTAR, III, investment banker; b. Wyncote, Pa., Aug. 11, 1905; s. Frederick Wistar, Jr. and Sophia (Starr) M.; grad. St. Paul's Sch., Concord, N.H., 1925; Ph.B., Yale, 1929; m. Mildred Dickinson, June 29, 1933; children—Frederick Wistar IV, Meredith D. (Mrs. E. Anthony Newton), Philemon D. With Charles D. Barney & Co., 1933-36; with Smith, Barney & Co., Phila., 1936-71, partner, 1963-64, v.p., dir., 1964-68, sr. v.p., dir., 1968-71, mem. adv. bd., 1971. Bd. govs. Phila.-Balt.-Washington Stock Exchange, 1964-68, PNB Marketing and Realty Investors Trust, 1970-71. Bd. dirs. United Cerebral Palsy Phila.; trustee Am. Oncologic Hosp. Phila. Served to lt. comdr. USNR, 1942-46. Home: Plymouth Meeting PA Died Nov. 10, 1971.

MORRIS, JOSEPH CHANDLER, educator; b. New Orleans, May 29, 1902; s. Joseph Chandler and Margaret Moore (West) M.; B.S., Tulane U., 1921, M.S., 1923; M.A., Princeton, 1926, Ph.D., 1928; m. Grace Elwood Oldfather, June 9, 1934; children—Grace Elwood (Mrs. Grace Morris Williamson), Joseph Chandler. Instr. physics Princeton, 1923-25, 1926-28, fellow, 1925-26, asst. prof. 1928-38; instr. physics Tulane U., New Orleans, 1921-23, prof., 1939-70, head dept. physics, 1945-60, v.p., 1949-70. Dir. Internat. City Bank 7Trust Co.; director, v.p., Central Gulf Steamship Corp. Dir. office sci. personnel, Nat. Research Council, 1941-43; asst., later asso. dir. tng. program San Diego Labs. Div. war research U. Calif., 1943-45; personnel procurement officer Applied Physics Lab., Johns Hopkins, 1945; cons. Nat. Roster Sci. and Specialized Personnel, 1941-45, Office of Edn., 1949-70; mem. bd. Nat. Sci. Found., 1950-66; dir. Council Library Resources, Inc., Washington; mem. commn. grad. edn. Bd. Control So. Regional Edn. Mem. A.A.A.S., Am. Assn. Physics Tchrs., Am. Phys. Soc., Inst. Radio Engrs., Sigma Xi, Sigma Pi Sigma. Democrat. Presbyn. Clubs: Round Table, Louisiana, Boston, Pickwick, Plimsoll (New Orleans); Cosmos (Washington); Princeton (N.Y.C.). Home: New Orleans LA Died Apr. 5, 1970; buried Metairie Cemetery, New Lrleans LA

MORRIS, PERCY AMOS, author; b. Seymour, Conn., Jan. 2, 1899; s. John H. and Virginia (Wyant) M.; spl. student Yale; m. Violet Catherine French, Sept. 3, 1922; 1 dau., Marion Louise (Mrs. Ralph R. Rasey). With Peabody Mus. Natural History, Yale U. Served with USNRF, 1917-18. Mem. Am. Malacol. Union, New Haven (Conn.) Bird Club (pres.). Author: Nature Photography Around the Year, What Shell is That, 1939; They Hop and Crawl, 1944; A Field Guide to the Shells of our Atlantic and Gulf Coasts, 1947, 3d edit., 1973; Boys Book of Snakes, 1948; A Field Guide to the Shells of the Pacific Coast and Hawaii, 1952, 2d edit., 1966; Boys Book of Turtles and Lizards, 1959; Boys Book of Frogs, Toads and Salamanders, 1957; Nature Study at the Seashore, 1962. Home: New Haven CT Died Dec. 13, 1969; interred Beaverdale Meml. Park Hamden CT

MORRIS, ROBERT EUGENE, newspaper pub.; b. Beatrice, Neb., Sept. 1, 1930; s. Harry Frances and Jenny (Wisdom) M.; B.A. in History, U. Omaha, 1957; m. Helen Kay Christoffel, Aug. 14, 1954; children—Kerry, Bradley, Lisa. Shop work Beatrice (Neb.) Times Company, 1942-48, gen. news reporter, 1948-50, sports editor 1950-52; editor Dundee-West Omaha News, Omaha, Neb., 1955-57; pub. editor The Wymore (Neb.) Arbor State, 1957-67; pub. The Cortland (Neb.) News, 1963-67. Served from pvt. to sgt., AUS, 1952-53. Mem. Mid-East Neb. Sports Writers Assn. (pres. 1949-52), Southeast Neb. Press Assn. (pres. 1960, dir.), Neb. Press Assn. (dir. 1960-67, treas. 1966-67). Home: Wymore NE Died Mar. 24, 1967.

MORRIS, ROBERT SEYMOUR, investment banker; b. Hartford, Conn., July 2, 1893; s. William S. and Alice (Oakes) M.; B.S., Trinity Coll., 1916, M.S., 1917; Doctor of Laws, Trinity Collge, 1965; m. Helen Loveland, June 1, 1920; one daughter, Barbara (Mrs. Arthur E. Davis). Underwriter, Aetna Casualty & Surety Co., 1916-18; salesman Tripp & Andrews, 1919-29; partner E. T. Andrews & Co., 1929-32; propr. Robert S. Morris & Co., Hartford, Conn., since 1932. Dir. U.S.O. Council, 1941-46, Hartford C. of C., 1945-48; mem. finance com. Conn. Prison Assn., 1938-59, Hartford YMCA, 1938-41; member Conn. Council Mental Retardation, 1962-68, Conn. Adv. Planning Com. Mental Retardation, 1964-66, Conn. Advisory Council Mental Retardation Facilities Construction Program, 1964-71; scout commr. Charter Oak council Boy Scouts Am., 1929-30; pres. Conn. Council of Chs., 1942-45; mem. Hartford (Conn.) adv. bd. Salvation Army, 1939-60, sec., 1941-59, chairman, 1959-60. Director of Hartford County Air Training Corporation of America, 1942, Conn. Society for Crippled Children and Adults, 1943-60 (chmn. finance com. 1954-60); trustee of Conn. Ednl. Television Corp., 1961-71; mem. Govs. Com. on Mentally Retarded Children in Conn., 1956. Trustee Trinity College, 1941-63 (bd. fellows, 1928-41, chairman 1938-40, alumni and spl. gifts chmn. 125th development program 1946-48, nat. chmn. program of progress 1955-58), Southbury Tng. School, 1948-71, Wadsworth Atheneum, 1949-67; dir. Ind. Social Center, 1949-51; dir. Hartford Sch. Music, 1944-50. Served as ensign U.S. Navy, World War I. Winner Alumnus-of-the-Year Award, Trinity Coll., 1949, Alumni Fund Cup, 1949-55. Mem. Nat. Assn. Securities Dealers (gov. 1944-47; exec. com. 1946-47), Investment Bankers Assn., Conn. Investment Bankers Assn. (pres. 1939-41), Nat. Securities Traders Assn., Open Hearth Assn. (trustee 1929-67, v.p., chmn. finance com. 1935-71), Hartford Better Business Bur., N.E. Council, Conn. Hist. Soc., S.A.R., Soc. Colonial Wars, Soc. Descs. Founders Hartford, Mil. Order Fgn. Wars, Am. Legion, Trinity Coll. Assos. (adv. council), Trinity Coll. Alumni Assn. (pres. 1940-42), Am. Assn. Mental Deficiency, Weekapaug (R.I.) Dunes Assn. (chmn. 1957-59), Alpha Chi Rho. Republican. Conglist. Mason. Clubs: University (past dir.), Rotary, (pres. 1946-47), Choral (sec. 1925-32, pres. 1933-38, historian 1932-51, bus. mgr. 1945-51), 20th Century (Hartford); Weekapaug (R.I.) Yacht; Armed Forces (director 1942-45). Author: Pigskin Parade Track at Trinity; A History of the Choral Club of Hartford; also articles for coll. archives and bus. publs. Compiler, editor: Trinity College Song Book, 1938, Chronology of Trinity College. Home: West Hartford CT Died Mar. 28, 1971; buried Fairview Cemetery, West Hartford CT

MORRIS, WILLIAM HENRY HARRISON, army officer; born Ocean Grove, N.J., March 22, 1890; son Howard F. and Mary (Van Dyke) M.; B.S., U.S. Mil. Acad., 1911; grad. Command and Gen. Staff Sch., 1925, Army War Coll., 1930; m. Marguerite Downing, Dec. 14, 1915. Commd. 2d lt., U.S. Army, June 11, 1911, and advanced through the grades to maj. gen., May, 1942; served as lt. col., 90th Div., World War I; mem. War Dept. Gen. Staff, 1938-40; comdg. gen. 6th Armored Div., Jan. 20, 1942-May 14, 1943; comdg. gen. II Armored Corps, May-Sept. 1943, XVIII Corps, Oct. 1943-July 1944, 10th Armored Div., July 1944-May 1945, VI Corps, May-Sept. 1945; Office of Secretary of War, 1945-47; became senior mem. Joint Brazil-United States Mil. Commn., June 1947; comdr. in chief, with rank of lt. gen., Caribbean command, 1949-52. Commanded 10th Armored Division in capture of Metz, Battle of Bulge (including defense of Bastogne), capture of Trier, breakthrough to the Rhine, capture of Heidelberg and Ulm, crossing Danube River, drive through Alps to Garmisch-Partenkirchen. Decorated D.S.C., D.S.M., Purple Heart, Silver Star, Legion of Merit, Bronze Star Medal (U.S.), Legion of Honor, Croix de Guerre with palm (France), Croix de Guerre (Belgium), Order Mil. Merit grade comdr. (Brazil); Order Vasco Nunez de Balboa (Panama); Order Abdon Calderon (Ecuador). Clubs: Army and Navy, Army-Navy Country (Washington). Home: Washington DC Died Mar. 31, 1971.

MORRIS, WILLIAM HICKS, oil co. exec.; b. Tulsa, Jan. 19, 1916; s. George W. and Elizabeth (Best) M.; student John Brown U., U. Tulsa, 1932-35, Harvard Grad. School of Business, 1956; m. to Vera Davis, Jan. 1, 1937 (dec.); 1 son, William Hicks; m. 2d, Renee Sorensen, December 1, 1952; children—Robert Lee and Michael James Morris. Vice pres., dir. Sinclair Oil Corp., Pres. 2 subsidiaries, 1936-64; pres., chief exec. officer, dir. Gt. Yellowstone Corp., 1964-69; dir. Frontier Pipeline Corp., Union Bank, Republic Gas Pipeline Corp., Midwest Natural Gas Co., Struthers Thermo-Flood Corp. Bd. dirs. Tulsa Council Alcoholism, Inc., Tulsa Philharmonic Soc. Trustee Tulsa U., John Brown U., Mem. Ind. Petroleum Assn. Am., Am. Petroleum Inst., Newcomen Soc. Methodist (dir.). Mason (32 deg., K.T., Shriner, Jester), Elk. Clubs: Alta (Salt Lake City); Country, University, Antelope Hunt (Lander, Wyoming); Tulsa, Southern Hills One Shot Petroleum (Tulsa); Seaview Country (Absecon, N.J.); 25 Year of Petroleum Industry. Home: Tulsa OK Died Dec. 27, 1969.

MORRISON, CHARLES SAMUEL, agrl. engr.; b. Black Lick, O., Sept. 10, 1919; s. Samuel Melville and Mary (Palmer) M.; B.S. in Agr., Ohio State U., 1941, B.Agrl. Engring., 1942; M.S. in Agrl. Engring., Ia. State U., 1946; m. Nina B. Smith, Sept. 21, 1944; children—James Robert, Charles Richard, Janet Ann, Sandra June. With Huber Mfg. Co., Marion, O., 1941; farmer, Black Lick, 1942; with Deere & Co., Moline, Ill., from 1947, mgr. product research and devel., 1960-63, mgr. agrl. engring. research, from 1963. Patron Tri City Symphony Orch. Served to lt. USNR, 1942-46. Registered profl. engr., Ill. Mem. Am. Soc. Agrl. Engrs. (chmn. power and machinery div. 1957-58, chmn. quad city sect. 1956-57, v.p. 1962-64, pres. elect 1964-65, pres. 1965-66), Chemurgie Council (bd.), Farm and Indsl. Equipment Inst. (adv. engring. com.), Soc. Automotive Engrs., Am. Soc. Metals, Ill. Soc. Profl. Engrs., Agrl. Research Inst., Tau Beta Pi, Gamma Sigma Delta, Phi Eta Sigma, Alpha Gamma Sigma. Meth. Club: Short Hills Country (E. Moline, Ill.). Home: Moline IL Died July 8, 1967.

MORRISON, HARRY WINFORD, contractor; b. Tunbridge Twp., DeWitt County, Ill., Feb. 23, 1885; s. George William and Amy Maria (Hawkins) M.; Dr. of Sci. (honorary), University of Idaho; LL.D., U. Portland (Ore.); LL.D., Coll. Ida., 1959; m. Anna Daly, Dec. 12, 1914 (dec. Oct. 1957); m. 2d, Velva V. Shannon, July, 1959. Water boy, later timekeeper, Bates & Rogers Constrn. Co., Chicago, 1902-05; successively axman, chainman, rodman, levelman, inspector, foreman, draftsman and supt. U.S. Bur. of Reclamation, Boise, Ida., 1906-12; partner, acting as v.p. and gen. mgr., Morrison & Knudsen, general contractors, 1912-23; v.p., gen. mgr. Morrison-Knudsen Co., Ida. corp.,

1923-34, Del. corp., 1935-39, pres., gen. mgr., 1940-46, pres., 1947-60, now chmn.; organizer, pres. Six Cos., Inc., builders of Hoover and Parker Dams; past chmn., dir. Morrison-Knudsen Co., Inc.; chmn., dir. Pakistan Constructors Corp., Ltd.; dir. Ida. 1st Nat. Bank and 44 branches in Ida. Recipient Econ. Statesmanship award Seattle U., 1958; Ida. Bus. Man. of Year award Ida. State U., 1963. Hon. life mem. Ida. Soc. Engrs.; hon. mem. The Moles (N.Y.C.). Home: Boise ID Died July 19, 1971; buried Morris Hill Cemetery, Boise ID

MORRISON, JACK HAROLD, govt. ofcl.; b. Abilene, Kan., May 17, 1911; s. Hope Harold and Lora Stone (Shearer) M.; student Kan. U., 1929-31, George Washington U., 1931-34; m. Helen Patricia Brewer, Sept. 1, 1934 (dec. 1961); children—Susan Hope, Patricia (dec.), Michael (dec.); m. 2d, Marlene Lucille Nettleingham, December 28, 1962; children—Tracy, Alison, Kelly; one step-son, Hilton Glynn. With U.S. Dept. Agr., 1934-69, beginning as file clk., successively adminstrv. asst., 1934-50, Southwest area dir. Fed. Crop Ins. Corp., 1950-60; dep. mgr. Fed. Crop Ins. Corp., 1961-69. Served as staff sgt. 88th Inf. Div., AUS, World War II. Mem. Vets. Fgn. Wars, Am. Legion, Delta Tau Delta. Home: Great Bend KS Died Oct. 17, 1969; buried Great Bend Cemetery, Great Bend KS

MORRISON, JIM, singer; b. Melbourne, Fla., 1944; student St. Petersburg Jr. Coll., Fla. State U., U. Cal.; m. Pamela Morrison. Vocalist, lyricist The Doors. Died July 1, 1971; buried Pere-Lachaise Cemetery, Paris France

MORRISON, JOSEPH L(EDERMAN), author; b. N.Y.C., May 28, 1918; s. Morris and Rose (Spitz) L.; A.B., U. N.C., 1940; M.A., Columbia, 1958; Ph.D., Duke, 1961; m. Pearl Penner, Sept. 7, 1946; children—Lucy, Peter. Reporter, Norfolk (Va.) Virginian-Pilot, 1941; mem. faculty U. N.C., 1946-70, professor of journalism; violinist Univ. Symphony Orch. Served to 1st lt. USAAF, 1942-45. Recipient internship Nat. Assn. Broadcasters, 1947; fellow CBS Found., 1957. Mem. Assn. Edn. in Journalism, Phi Beta Kappa, Sigma Delta Chi. Author: Josephus Daniels Says... An Editor's Political Odyssey from Bryan to Wilson and F.D.R., 1894-1913, 1962; Josephus Daniels: The Small-d Democrat, 1966; W. J. Cash: Southern Prophet, 1967; governor O. Max Gardner: A Power in North Carolina and New Deal Washington, 1971; also articles. Home: Chapel Hill NC Died Nov. 11, 1970.

MORRISON, OCIE BUTLER, JR., naval officer; b. Petersburg, Va., Nov. 20, 1896; s. Ocie Butler and Mary Young (Barner) M.; M.D., U. Va., 1925; postgrad. U.S. Naval Med. Sch., 1935-36. U.S.M.C. Staff and Command Sch., 1944; m. Stella Holcombe Moodey, August 6, 1919 (dec. Mar. 1966); children—Robert Holcombe, Mary Barner (wife William W. South, U.S.N.); m. 2d, Mary June Clark, Oct. 8, 1966. Commd. lt. (j.g.), M.C. U.S.N., 1925, advanced through grades to vice adm., 1958; intern, staff Naval Hosp., Norfolk, Va., 1925-27; various assignments, 1927-34; staff U.S. Naval Academy, 1936-40; senior medical officer of U.S.S. Chicago, Pearl Harbor, T.H., 1940-42; profl. asst. comdg. med. officer Naval Hosp., Seattle, 1942; comdg. med. officer Armed Guard Tng. Center, Gulfport, Miss., 1942, sr. med. officer Armed Guard Sch., Advance Base Depot, Receiving Barracks, 1943; corps surgeon 1st Marine Amphibious Corps (later designated Third Amphibious Corps), 1944-45; chief surgery, later exec. officer Naval Hosp., Santa Margarita Ranch, Oceanside, Cal., 1945-48; exec. officer Naval Hosp., Portsmouth, Va., 1948-49; dir. personnel div., bur. medicine and surgery Navy Dept., Washington, 1949-50; comdg. officer Naval Hosp., San Diego, 1950-52; med. officer staff Comdr. Naval Forces Far East, 1952-53; dist. med. officer 1st Naval Dist. Hdqrs., Boston, 1953; dir. for planning and liaison, office or Asst. Sec. Defense, 1953-54; comdg. officer U.S. Naval Hosp., Portsmouth, Va., 1955-57; dist. med. officer Fifth Naval Dist., Hdqrs., Naval Base, Norfolk, 1957-58; dist. med. officer 11th Naval Dist., San Diego, Cal., from 1958. Decorated Legion Merit with gold star and oak leaf cluster, Bronze Star Medal with gold star. Presdl. Unit Citation, Navy Unit Commendation, Breast Order on Yun Hui (China); Danish Red Cross medal; Nat. Def., Korean, UN service medals. Fellow A.C.S.; mem. Assn. Mil. Surgeons, A.M.A. Mason (32 degree). Rotarian. Home: San Diego CA Died Sept. 21, 1969.

MORRISON, PHOEBE, lawyer; b. Takoma Park, Md., June 21, 1902; d. Lisle and Isabel (Fechtig) Morrison; A.B., Vassar Coll., 1924; LL.B., George Washington U., 1927; J.S.D., Yale, 1928. Carnegie fellow internat. law, 1927-28; research asst. to Hon. John B. Moore, 1928-30, to Edwin Borchard, 1930-42 (rank of asst. prof., 1937-39, asso. prof., 1939-42; admitted to Conn. bar, 1931; trial justice, probate judge, Killingworth, Conn., 1939-44; dist. rationing officer O.P.A., Hartford, Conn., 1942-43; spl. asst. to dir. research and analysis OSS, 1943-45; exec. sec., dir. Research Found. for Fgn. Affairs, Washington, 1945-48; internat. relations asso. Am. Assn. U. Women, 1948-51; asso. prof., 1952-60, professor govt., 1960-67, executive officer, dept. govt. Barnard Coll., 1952-56, 59-65, sr. fellow Yale Law Sch., 1958-59; staff Middlesex Community Coll., Conn., 1967-68. Recipient Founders' award Am. Assn. U. Women. 1958-59. Mem. Am. Soc. Internat. Law, Am. Polit. Sci. Assn., Am. Acad. Polit. Sci., Order of Coif, Phi Beta Kappa, Delta Sigma Rho, Phi Delta Delta. Home: Chester CT Died Sept. 30, 1968.

MORRISON, ROBERT HUGH, univ. dean; b. Pioneer, O., Jan. 19, 1893; s. Lyman H. and Caroline (Seeley) M.; A.B., Mich. State Tchrs. Coll., 1923; A.M., Colo. State Coll. Edn., 1926; Ph.D., Columbia, 1933; m. Mabel Hebeler, Apr. 17, 1918; children—Robert J., John H. Elementary sch. prin., Flint, Mich., 1917-23; prof. edn. State Tchrs. Coll., Greely, Colo., 1925-35; pres. State Tchrs. Coll., Paterson, N.J., 1935-37; state dir. tchr. edn., Trenton, N.J., 1937-45, asst. commr. higher edn., State of N.J., 1945-55; provost sch. edn. Seton Hall U., 1955-59, dean of graduate studies, South Orange, N.J., from 1959. Served as 2d lt. AUS, World War I. Mem. N.E.A., N.J. Council Adult Edn., Kappa Delta Pi. Author: Internal Organization and Administration of Teachers Colleges, 1933; The Morrison Rating Scale Profile for Teachers, 1944; Diagnostic Test of Speech Habits. Home: Chula Vista CA Died Mar. 25, 1973.

MORRISON, SARAH ELIZABETH, author; b. nr. Madison, Jefferson Co., Ind.; d. Hiel (M.D.) and Anna Sophia (Martin) M.; pvt. edn.; unmarried. Author: Chilhowee Boys, 1893; Chilhowee Boys in War Time, 1895; Chilhowee Boys at College, 1896; Chilhowee Boys in Harness, 1898. Address: 4541 Chestnut St., Philadelphia PA‡

MORRISON, ZAIDEE LINCOLN, artist; b. Skowhegan, Me., Nov. 12, 1872; d. Lucius Lincoln and Ellen Estella (Sawyer) M.; student Art Students League, 1891-92 and 1899-1905, Nat. Acad. of Design, 1890-91, Cooper Union Art Sch., 1899-1900; pvt. instruction in painting, N.Y. City; studied piano and organ under various instrs.; studied and taught piano under Kate S. Chittendon; Bach interpretation under Jean Sinclair Buchanan; student of piano at Carleton Coll., 1898-99. Supervisor of art, Skowhegan (Me.) Pub. Schs., 1896, Palmer (Mass.) Pub. Schs., 1897-98; dir. of art, Carleton Coll., 1898-99; asst. instr. of piano Vassar Coll., 1907-08; instr. of art, Buchanan Sch. (Mt. Kisco, N.Y.), 1921-1922. Portraits of Thuel Burnham, Mrs. John Bovcock, Blair Thaw, Gavin Dhu High, Mrs. Horace M. Biddle, Mr. and Mrs. Morgan Wing and others; miniatures of Mrs. E. S. Buchanan, Mrs. George Otis Smith, Mrs. Alexander Whiteford, Gen. Thomas Palmer. Represented in exhbns. of Am. Miniature Soc., Grand Central Galleries, Nat. Gallery of Art, Mt. Holyoke Coll., Brooklyn Soc. of Miniature Painters, Baltimore Water Color Soc., New York Water Color Club, Portland (Me.) Mus., North Shore Art Assn., N.Y. Water Color Soc., Orgunquit Art Centre, Palm Beach Art Centre. Mem. D.A.R., Gamma Delta. Republican. Conglist. Home: 57 W. 58th St., New York NY‡

MORRISON, ZELMA REEVES, mem. Democratic Nat. Com.; b. Wenatchee, Wash.; d. Frank and Belle (Culp) Reeves; B.A., U. Wash.; grad. student N.Y.U., summers 1949-50; m. Raymond R. Morrison; children—Frank R. (USAF). Betty Belle (Mrs. R.A. Vitousek, Jr.), Raeburn Rose (Mrs. Wayne Hagen). Complaint adviser Spokane County Welfare Dept., 1936-41; information exec. OPA, 1943-46; faculty pub. relations Eastern Wash. Coll. Edn., 1946-51; information dir. OPS, Spokane, 1951-53; chief staff services Wash. State Dept. Licenses, from 1960. Active Dem. Party, from 1932; pres. Wash. State Fedn. Dem. Women's Clubs, 1955-59; vice chmn. Wash. State Dem. Central Com., 1955-59; mem. Dem. Nat. Com. from Wash. State, from 1960. President of the Spokane City Pan Hellenic, 1957-58. Chmn. bd. trustees Eastern Wash. Coll. Edn., 1957-61; personnel bd. Eastern Wash. State Coll., from 1961, chmn., 1961-65; sec. adv. bd. Booth Meml. Hosp., pub. relations chmn., from 1965. Named Dem. Woman of Year Wash. State Fedn. Dem. Women's Clubs, 1959. Mem. Am. Assn. U. Women (chmn. higher edn. Washington State 1959-63), D.A.R., Nat. Assn. Parliamentarians, League Women Voters, Rebekah Assembly, Lady Lions, Chi Omega. Episcopalian. Address: Spokane WA

MORRISS, ELIZABETH CLEVELAND (MRS. JOHN), educator; b. Selma, Ala.; d. William Calloway and Frances Cornelia (Lide) Cleveland; A.B., Judson Coll., Marion, Ala., 1895; L.I., Peabody Coll. for Teachers, Nashville, 1898; spl. work, U. of Va. and U. of Wis.; B.Sc., Teachers Coll. (Columbia), 1932, M.A., 1933; m. John Morriss, Sept. 1908 (now dec.). Teacher pub. schs., Birmingham, 1900-01, Selma, 1901-04; teacher Margaret Allen Sch., Birmingham, 1904-08. Began organizing community schs. for adult illiterates in Buncombe County, 1919; has developed plans for standardizing schs. for native illiterates; mem. Nat. Com. of 9 that outlined courses of study, etc., for same; made film for depicting problmes of adult illiteracy; later dir. adult elementary edn. of Buncombe County; then asso. in adult edn., Teachers Coll. (Columbia); dir. Adult Edn. Div., State Department of Public Instruction and Works Progress Administration in North Carolina, 1936-40; dir. Adult Education Div. State Department Public Instruction, 1940-41; retired July 1941. Active in war work World War; chairman illiteracy committee N.C. State Federation Women's Clubs, 1924-30; chmn. State Literacy Commission since 1928. Mem. N.E.A. (life; exec. dir. dept. adult edn. 1929-31, v.p., 1938, 40), N.C. Ednl. Assn., D.A.R., Pi Lambda Theta, Kappa Delta Pi. Democrat. Episcopalian. Clubs: Teachers Coll. Country; Nineteenth Century (Birmingham). Author: Writing and Composition Book for Adult Beginners, 1921; Citizen's Reference Book, 1922; Adult Adventures in Reading, 1939; (bull.) Elementary Instruction of Adults (Nat. Bur. Edn.); also a textbook for adult beginners, containing, among other things, 12 reading lessons by prominent men and women of U.S., 1926. Home: 514 19th St., N.W., Washington DC‡

MORRISSEY, JAMES PETER, university pres.; b. Santa Cruz, Cal., 1872; B.Sc., U. of Santa Clara; post-grad. work in Germany and Italy; Ph.D.; (D.D.). Began teaching, St. Ignatius Coll., San Francisco, 1895; now pres. U. of Santa Clara. Commr. Cal. Redwood Park. Democrat. Mem. Soc. of Jesus. Address: University of Santa Clara, Santa Clara CA‡

MORROW GLENN R., edcuator; b. Calhoun, Mo., Apr. 29, 1895; s. Charles Sumner and Bessie (Bronaugh) M.; A.B., Westminster Coll., Fulton, Mo., 1914, LL.D., 1951; student Louisville Presbyn. Theol. Sem., 1916-17; A.M., U. Mo., 1918; Ph.D., Cornell U., 1921; student U. Paris, 1921-22, univs. Munich and Vienna, 1933-34; L.H.D., U. Pa., 1966; m. Dorrice Richards, July 11, 1923. Instr. Greek, Westminster Coll., 1914-16; lectr. philosophy Cornell U., 1922-23; asst. prof., later asso. prof. philosophy U. Mo., 1923-29; prof. philosophy U. Ill., 1929-39; prof. philosophy U. Pa., 1939-73, dean Coll., 1944-52, Adam Seybert prof. moral and intellectual philosophy, 1947-65, now emeritus. Del. Am. Council Learned Socs., 1937-50, exec. com., bd. dirs., 1945-47. Served as 2d lt., F.A., U.S. Army, 1918-19. Guggenheim fellow Am. Sch. Classical Studies, Athens, 1952-53; Am. Field Service fellow in France, 1921-22; Fulbright scholar, Oxford, 1956-57. Mem. Am. Philos. Assn. (pres. Western div. 1940, Eastern div. 1953), Am. Assn. U. Profs. (council 1955-57, v.p. 1958-60, chmn. self-survey com. 1963-65), Am. Philol. Assn., Archaeol. Inst. Am., Phi Beta Kappa, Phi Kappa Phi. Club: Lenape (Phila.). Author: The Ethical and Economic Theories of Adam Smith, 1923; Studies in the Platonic Epistles, 1935; Plato's Law of Slavery in its Relation to Greek Law, 1939; Plato's Cretan City, 1960; Plato's Epistles, 1962; (transl.) Proclus' Commentary on the First Book of Euclid's Elements, 1970. Am. editor Archiv fur Geschichte der Philosophie, 1960-65. Contbr. articles to philos. and philol. jours. Home: Swarthmore PA Died Jan. 31, 1973; interred Gettysburg Nat. Mil. Park.

MORROW, JOHN D. A., manufacturer; b. Campbellstown, O., June 10, 1881; s. Richard Edwin and Martha Joanna (Adams) M.; B.L., Ohio Wesleyan U., 1906; m. Jessie Lehmer Bowers, Dec. 1911; children—Richard Stevens (dec.), Alan Bowers, Nancy, John Stuart. Asst. sec. Federal Trade Commn., Washington, 1916; resigned, 1916, to organize Pittsburgh Coal Producers Assn.; elected gen. sec. Nat. Coal Assn., Sept. 1917; apptd. gen. dir. coal and coke distribution, U.S. Fuel Adminstrn., Feb. 1, 1918, and organized and directed the work until June 30, 1919; v.p. and active exec. Nat. Coal Assn. until Dec. 1, 1922; pres. Pittsburgh (Pa.) Coal Co. to Sept. 1, 1940; pres. and dir. Joy Mfg. Co. (Pennsylvania), 1940-56, chmn. bd., 1956-57, ret., dir., mem. exec. com.; bd. mgrs. Adams Express Co. Mem. council, chmn. police and pub. safety com. Edgeworth (Pa.) Borough, 1931-70. Decorated Chevalier Legion of Honor, 1955 (France); recipient outstanding leadership award, Industry-Sponsored Coal Research, 1959. Mem. Engrs. Soc. Western Pa., Am. Inst. Mining and Metall. and Petroleum Engrs., Phi Beta Kappa. Republican. Clubs: Duquesne, Allegheny Country, Edgeworth. Home: Edgeworth PA Died Feb. 3, 1971; buried Sewickley (Pa.) Cemetery.

MORROW, MARCO, journalist; b. Foster's, Ohio, July 18, 1869; s. William Finley and Priscilla Catherine (Rhine) M.; grad. high sch., Springfield, O., 1888; m. Mary Lynn, 1892; m. 2d, Ida McCoskrie, 1910; 1 son, Richard Mac. Reporter Springfield Republic-Times, 1890-94; editor of Womankind, Springfield, Ohio, 1895-1899; editor of Agricultural Advertising, Chicago, 1899-1906; sec. Long-Critchfield Corp., Chicago, 1906-08; dir. adv., 1908-19, asst. pub., 1919, v.p., 1938-41, Capper Publications, Inc., Topeka, Kansas; president Topeka Broadcasting Association, 1934-42. Mem. Agricultural Publishers Assn. (president 1920-21, 1924-25), Audit Bureau of Circulations (dir.), Sigma Delta Chi (hon. nat. pres. 1941-46), Tau Delta Pi (hon.). Republican. Mason (32 deg.). Home: 1028 Western Av., Topeka KS‡

MORROW, WINSTON VAUGHAN, b. Cincinnati, O., Sept. 16, 1886; s. Worcester Beach and Caroline (Caine) M.; A.B., Kenyon Coll., Gambier, O., 1908; student Cincinnati Coll. Finance, Commerce and Accounts; m. Selma Caroline von Egloffstein, July 22, 1916; children—Thomas Camill, Winston Vaughan.

With Cincinnati Commercial Tribune, 1908-12, Cincinnat Times-Star, 1912-13; editor Livingston (Mont.) Enterprise and Livingston Post, 1914-15, Douglas (Ariz.) Dispatch, 1915-16; editor Furniture Mfr. and Artisan, 1922-28; former asso. editor Grand Rapids Furniture Record; editor Metalcraft, 1928-31; asso. editor Furniture Index, Woodworking Industries, 1928-31; publisher rep. from 1931; instructor of journalism Stetson U., 1949-52; dep. dir. Fla. Civil Defense Agency, 1952-53. Served as second lieutenant World War; capt. 392d Inf., O.R.C., from 1922; active duty comdg. officer, U.S. Army recruiting service, later with Armed Forces Induction Station, Buffalo, N.Y. July 1940; pres. aviation cadet exam. bd., A.A.F. exam. bd.; P.R.O. Japan, Aug., 1946-47; ret. as lt. col., 1948. Vocational adviser Federal Bd. Vocational Edn., 1919-21; officer U.S. Vets. Bur., 1921. Mem. exec. com. Nat. Conf. of Business Paper Editors, 1925-28. Mem. Am. Legion, Ret. Officers Assn. Episcopalian. Mason (32 degree, Shriner), Sojourner. Club: University Terrace. Writer for numerous publs., from 1931. Home: Deland FL Died Feb. 26, 1972; buried Wesleyan Cemetery, Cincinnati OH

MORROW, WRIGHT CHALFANT, judge; b. in Ky., Oct. 12, 1858; s. William W. and Gabriella (Chalfant) M.; ed. pvt. schs. and summer lectures, Univ. of Va.; m. Fanny Tarlton, Jan. 8, 1884 (died 1920);children—John Tarlton, William C., Lyde (Mrs. Roger W. Guthrie), Wright. Began as druggist, 1880; admitted to Tex. bar, 1887, and practiced at Hillsboro, Tex., until 1917; mem. Tex. Senate, 1913-17; became judge Court of Criminal Appeals, Tex., 1917, presiding judge, 1921, resigned Oct. 15, 1939. Mem. Tex. State Bar Assn. Democrat. Episcopalian. Mason. Home: 1304 San Antonio St., Austin TX*‡

MORSCH, LUCILE M., librarian; b. Sioux City, Ia., Jan. 21, 1906; d. Jacob and Lydia (Meyer) Morsch; A.B., State U. Ia., 1927; B.S., Columbia (Lydia Roberts fellowship), 1929, M.S. (Lydia Roberts fellowship), 1930; m. Werner B. Ellinger, May 20, 1944. Asst. preparations div. N.Y. Pub. Library, June-Aug. 1929; cataloger, later 1st asst. catalog dept. State U. Ia., 1927-28, 30-35; asso. head, later head catalog dept. Enoch Pratt Free Library, Balt., 1935-40; chief descriptive cataloging div. Library of Congress, Washington, 1940-51, 52-53, 62-65, chief gen. reference and biblio., 1951-52, dep. chief asst. librarian, 1953-62; instr. cataloging and classification La. State u., summer 1930; instr. sch. library service, Columbia, summers 1937-39. Member of U.S. National Commission for UNESCO. First recipient Margaret Mann Citation in Cataloging and Classification, 1951. Mem. A.L.A. (council member 1940-44, 52-55, and 56-72, president 1957-58, pres. cataloging and classification div. 1943-45), Assn. Coll. and Research Libraries (dir. 1960-72), D.C. Library Assn. (pres. 1954-55), Am. Assn. U. Women, Mortar Bd., Beta Phi Mu, Alpha Xi Delta. Author: New Jersey Imprints, 1784-1800, 1939; Catalog Department Manual, 1940; also articles periodicals and yearbooks. Editor: Library Lit. 1921-32, 1934. Home: Alexandria VA Died July 3, 1972.

MORSE, ALBERT LAVERNE, banker; b. Orchard, Ia., July 3, 1919; s. Clarence M. and Minnie (Mielahn) M.; grad. high sch.; m. Ruth M. Smith, May 12, 1950; children—Stanley A., Rebecca R., Sarah M. With Home Trust &Savs. Bank, Osage, Ia., 1947-72, exec. v.p., 1964-72. Served Savs. Bank, Osage, Ia., 1947-72, exec. v.p., 1964-72. Served with USAAF, 1942-46. Mason. Home: Osage IA Died Mar. 4, 1972.

MORSE, ARTHUR DAVID, author, TV producer; b. Bklyn., Dec. 27, 1920; s. Frank and Henrietta (Mensher) Moskowitz; B.A., U. Va., 1941; m. Joan Berend, June 17, 1945; children—Ann Bramson, Jonathan. Pub. relations dir. Parents' Inst., 1945-46; writer for nat. magazines, 1946-54; reporter-dir. for See it Now TV programs, CBS, 1954-59; prodn. include Clinton and the Law (Robert E. Sherwood award Fund for Republic), 1957; Ballots at Bear Creek (Nat. Sch. Bell award), 1956; Atomic Timetable (Sylvania TV award), 1957; The Lost Class of '59 (George Foster Peabody award, Nat. Sch. Bell award, Ohio State U. First award, Inst. for Edn. by Radio-TV), 1959; producer-writer CBS Reports, documentaries, 1960-64, exec. producer, 1964-71; prodns. include Who Speaks for the South? (Nat. Sch. Bell award, Nat. Council Christians and Jews Brotherhood award), 1960; The Other Face of Dixie, 1962; The Influential Americans (Ohio State U. First award), 1960; The Catholics and the Schools (Nat. Sch. Bell award), 1964; Can We Disarm?, 1961; Censorship and the Movies, 1961; exec. dir. Internat. Broadcast Institute, 1969-71. President Citizens Sch. League, Stamford, Conn., 1960. Served as officer USNR, 1941-45; PTO. Recipient Distinguished Pub. Service Journalism award Sigma Delta Chi, 1951; Sidney Hillman Found. award, 1951; Annual award Ednl. Writers Assn., 1951; Freedoms Found. award, 1950; magazine award Christophers, 1956. Mem. Inst. Current World Affairs (bd. govs.), Internat. Broadcast Inst., Soc. Mag. Writers. Democrat. Jewish religion. Author: Schools of Tomorrow—Today, 1960. Contbr.: Freedom and Public Education, 1953; Prose for Professionals, 1961; While Six Million Died, 1968. Home: Scarsdale NY Died June 1, 1971.

MORSE, DAVID SHERMAN, educator; b. Roxbury, N.Y., Sept. 16, 1892; s. Herbert G. and Carrie Estelle (Dean) M.; A.B. cum laude, N.Y.U., 1917, Pd.M., 1917; A.M., Harvard, 1918; Ph.D., Cornell, 1923; m. Nellie Louise Ayling, June 17, 1918. Instr. mathematics Cornell, 1920-24; Union Coll., Schenectady, N.Y., 1918-20, asst. prof., 1924-27, asso. prof., 1927-31, prof., 1931-69, chmn. dept. mathematics, 1944-69, chmn. div. sci., 1943-55, Marie Louise Bailey prof. mathematics, 1952-69; teacher summer sessions N.Y.U., 1916-17, Cornell, 1920-24, Syracuse (N.Y.) U., 1927. Fellow A.A.A.S.; mem. Am. Math. Soc., Math. Assn. Am., Am. Assn. U. Profs., Phi Beta Kappa (chpt. pres. 1932-39, pres. Upper Hudson Assn. 1949-50, chmn. Middle Atlantic dist. 1940-49, senator united chpts. 1944-46), Sigma Xi, Phi Kappa Phi. Republican. Home: Schenectady NY Died Jan. 9, 1969; buried Schenectady NY

MORSE, ELMER ADDISON, ex-congressman; b. Franksville, Wis., May 11, 1870; s. Addison J. and Suzette (French) M.; A.B., Ripon (Wis.) Coll., 1893; co. supt. schs., Racine Co., 1894-8; studied U. of Wis. Law Sch., 1898-1900; m. Myra Tradewell, of Racine, Wis., 1896. Admitted to bar, 1900; city atty., Antigo, Wis., 1900-6; mem. 60th, 61st, 62d Congresses (1907-13), 10th Wis. Dist. Republican. Address: Antigo WI‡

MORSE, IRA HERBERT, b. Chester, New Hampshire, Jan. 4, 1875; s. Samuel Sanborn and Luella Helen (Merrill) M.; student Warren (N.H.) Grade School, 1880-90; awarded hon. D.Sc., Norwich Univ.; m. Lillian Little, Sept. 7, 1898 (died 1942); children—Herbert (dec.), Philip; m. 2d, Julie Burke Mahoney, d. Judge John C. Burke, Mar. 12, 1931; 1 son, John Burke. Pres. I.H. Morse Shoe Stores, Inc. Big game hunter, fisherman, curio collector; founder and owner Morse Museum, Warren, N.H.; world traveler, lecturer. Mem. N.E. Shoe Dealers' Assn. (pres. 1925), New Eng. Historic Geneal. Soc., Am. Museum of Natural Hist. Republican. Methodist. Mason, Odd Fellow. Clubs: Yorick, Vesper (Lowell, Mass.); Golf (Tyngsboro, Mass.); Tuna Club of America (Catalina Island); Izaak Walton (Useppe Island, Fla.); Bimini Rod and Gun (Bimini, Bahama Islands). Author: 1 Yankee in Africa, 1936. Dir. 6 Morse Museum expdns. to Africa, India and Far East. Home: Warren, N.H., and 292 Andover St., Lowell, MA Office: I. H. Morse Shoe Stores, Lowell MA*‡

MORSE, IRVING HASKELL, sugar chemist; b. Emporia, Kan., Mar. 24, 1868; s. Grosvenor C. and Abby Prentis (Barber) M.; student Emporia Coll., 1885-87; B.S., U. of Kan., 1891; 3 months' spl. work in U. of Chicago, 1894; m. Caroline Johnston, July 31, 1902; 1 són, James Johnston. Factory chemist for Miles Planting & Mfg. Co., New Orleans, 1891-1901; for Cuban-Am. Sugar Co., Tinguaro, Cuba, 1901-03; chief chemist for Longmont (Colo.) Sugar Co. and supt. of cane sugar factory Mercedita," in Cuba, 1903-10; supervising chemist for La. Sugar Co., New Orleans, 1910-13; pres. Morse Lab. Co., Inc., since 1917. Inventor apparatus for separating impurities from cane juice or other liquors. Author: Calculations Used in Cane-Sugar Factories, 1904; Laboratory Record, 1911. Developed open kettle" system of mfg. pure sugar direct from cane. Home: 2806 State St., New Orleans LA‡

MORSE, LESTER SAMUEL, shoe co. exec.; b. Sommerville, Mass., Jan. 10, 1897; s. Morris and Harriet (Phillips) M.; student Dartmouth, 1916, Boston U., 1917, 18; m. Ruth Schwartz, Feb. 14, 1927; children—Lester Samuel, Richard P. With Morse Shoe, Inc., Canton, Mass., 1922-70, chmn. bd., 1958-70. Trustee Children's Hosp., Boston, 1966-70, Frances Ouimet Scholarship Fund, 1953-70; trustee, mem. exec. com. Combined Jewish Philanthropies; fellow Brandeis U. Served with U.S. Army, 1916-17. Home: Chestnut Hill MA Died Feb. 1970.

MORSE, MARGARET FESSENDEN, author; b. Jamaica Plain, Mass., Nov. 28, 1877; d. Robert McNeil (q.v.) and Anna E. (Gorham) M.; ed. pvt. schs. and Mass. Inst. Tech.; unmarried. Author: The Spirit of The Pines, 1906; On the Road to Arden, 1909; Scottie and His Lady, 1910. Address: Jamaica Plain MA‡

MORSE, SAMUEL FINLEY BROWN, realtor; b. Newton, Mass., July 18, 1885; s. George W. and Clara (Bolt) M.; grad. Phillips Andover Acad., 1903; B.A., Yale Univ., 1907; LL.D., University California, 1966; m. Maurine C. Dalton, November 11, 1952; children—Samuel Finley Brown (dec.), John B., Nancy (Mrs. William F. Boland), Mary (Mrs. W. V. Shaw). Manager land development project for John Hays Hammond, Cal., 1907-10, Crocker-Huffman Land & Water Co., Merced, Cal., 1910-15, Pacific Improvement Co., 1915-19; pres., organizer Del Monte Properties Co., San Francisco, 1919-69, chmn. board; sr. dir. Crocker 1st Nat. Bank, 1916-56; adv. council Crocker-Anglo National Bank, San Francisco, U.S. Leasing Corp. Associate fellow of Morse College. Yale University. Clubs: Links, Racquet and Tennis (New York City); Pacific-Union (San Francisco); Burlingame (Cal.) Country; Cypress Point (Pebble Beach, Cal.). Pebble Beach CA Died May 10, 1969.

MORSTEIN MARX, FRITZ, polit. scientist; b. Hamburg, Germany, Feb. 23, 1900; s. Ludwig and Amada (Plumhof) Morstein Marx; student U. Hamburg, U. Freiburg, U. Munich, 1919-22; Ph.D., U. Hamburg, 1922, research asso., 1920-33. Adminstrv. career officer State of Hamburg, 1922-33; Rockefeller research fellow, 1930-31; mem. faculty Princeton, 1934-35, Harvard, 1935-39, Queens Coll., 1939-42; cons. adminstrv. mgmt. div. Bur. Budget, Exec. Office of the President, 1942-45, staff asst. Office of Dir., 1945-60; lectr. Am. U., 1944-50, adj. prof., 1950-60; prof. polit. sci., dean adminstrn. Hunter Coll., 1960-62; prof. comparative adminstrv. sci. and pub. law Hochschule fur Verwaltungswissenschaften, Speyer, Germany, from 1962; vis. professor govt. Howard U., 1948-50, U. Wash., 1957, U. So. Cal., 1959, U. Tibingen, from 1963, University of Heidelberg, from 1963; Ford Found. research prof. govt. affairs Princeton, 1959-60. Chmn. Citizens Commn. Ethics in Govt., Arlington County, Va., 1951-52. Author: Government in the Third Reich, rev. edit., 1937; The Pres. and His Staff Services, 1947; The Adminstrv. State, 1957; Einfuhrung in die Burokratie, 1959; Amerikanische Verwaltung, 1963; Das Dilemma des Verwaltungsmannes, 1965. Editor: Elements of Public Adminstration, rev. edit., 1959; Foreign Governments, rev. edit., 1952; Verwaltung, 1965. Co-editor: Verwaltungsarchiv, 1963—. Editor-in-chief Public Adminstrn. Rev., 1949-51. Editorial bd. Am. Polit. Sci. Rev., 1945-50. Address: Speyer Germany Died Oct. 1969.

MORTENSEN, MARTIN, prof. of dairy industry; b. Sindal, Denmark, May 29, 1872; s. Peder Christian and Juliana Marie (Larsen) M.; student Royal Teachers Sem., Ranum, Denmark, 1889-92; B.S.A., Ia. State Coll., 1909; LL.D., Kan. State Coll., 1934; m. Ane Emelia Christensen, Nov. 14, 1900; children—Marie Christine (Mrs. Will Moore Beale), Edna Julia (Mrs. Vernon Roger Kiely). Came to U.S., 1893, naturalized, 1900. Teacher in rural sch., Denmark, 1892-93; buttermaker Iowa Center (Ia.) Creamery, 1894-97; mgr. Willow Creek (Ia.) Creamery, 1899; supt. Hanford Hazelwood Creamery Co., Sioux City, Ia., 1900-04; mgr. Hazelwood Creamery Co., Portland, Ore., 1904-08; prof. and head dept. dairy industry, Iowa State College, 1909-38, prof., 1938-43, professor emeritus since 1943. Representative U.S. Dept. of Agriculture to Great Britain and Denmark, 1900; U.S. rep. Internat. Dairy Congress, Copenhagen, 1931. Awarded Ridder (Knight) of Dannebrogsordenen (Denmark), 1927; Scroll of Am. Dairy Science Assn., 1935; Alumni merit award, Chicago Alumni Assn. of Iowa State Coll., 1942. Mem. Am. Dairy Science Assn., Royal Agrl. Soc. of Denmark, Sigma Xi, Phi Kappa Phi, Phi Lambda Upsilon, Alpha Zeta, Gamma Sigma Delta. Republican. Congregationalist. Club: Rotary (Ames, Ia.). Author: Management of Dairy Plants, 1920, rev. edit., 1938. Contbr. to dairy jours.; author of bulletins on dairy industry. Home: 126 N. Riverside Drive, Ames IA‡

MORTENSON, ERNEST DAWSON, civil engr.; b. Boston, Oct. 31, 1895; s. Nils and Mary (Wyke) M.; B.S., Tufts U., 1917; m. Gladys Fullerton Hill, July 27, 1922; children—Olive (Mrs. Kenneth Ernest Blackwell), Leonard Earl, Judith (Mrs. Robert Twarog). Spl. agt. engr. New Eng. dist. PWA, 1935-37; contract, specification engr. Met. Water Supply Commn., Boston, 1938-40; supervising engr. U.S. Navy Quonset Air Sta., R.I., 1940-46; asst. city plan engr. New Haven, 1946-47; chief and asso. engr. Lyons & Mather Architects, Bridgeport, Conn., 1947-66, exec. engr., 1966-68. Cons. engr. various firms New Eng., 1935; lectr. Franklin Tech. Inst., Boston, 1933-40, Bridgeport Engring. Inst., 1950-52. Mem. Melrose (Mass.) City Plan Commn., 1934-40; advancement chmn. Boy Scouts Am., Melrose, 1938-40. Registered profl. engr. Mass., Conn., R.I. Fellow Am. Soc. C.E.s; mem. Greater Bridgeport Engring. Socs. Council, Nat. Soc. Profl. Engrs. (pres. Conn. 1938-39), Am. Concrete Inst., Boston Tufts Club. Mason (32 deg.). Home: Stratford CT Died May 1968.

MORTON, CONRAD VERNON, botanist; b. Fresno, Cal., Oct. 24, 1905; s. Walter Crow and Noma (Bartholomew) M.; B.A., U. Cal. at Berkeley, 1928. Aide div. plants' U.S. Nat. Museum, Smithsonian Instn., 1928-38, asst. curator, then asso. curator, 1938-48, curator div. ferns, 1948-70, sr. botanist, 1970-72; asso. editor Am. Fern Jour., 1940-47, editor-in-chief, 1948-61, asso. editor, 1962-72; editor for pteridophyta Biol. Abstracts, 1946-72. Guggenheim fellow, 1954. Mem. Phi Beta Kappa, Sigma Xi, Phi Sigma. Author numerous articles in field. Home: Washington DC Died July 29, 1972.

MORTON, JACK A., engineer; b. St. Louis, Sept. 4, 1913; s. Mack Ray and Minette (Hirsfeld) M.; B.Sc., Wayne University, 1935, D.Sc. (honorary), 1956; M.Sc., University Michigan, 1936; graduate study Columbia, 1937-41; Ph.D. (hon.), Ohio State U., 1954; m. Helen Read, May 27, 1938; children—Kim, Mack. Asst. dir. electronic apparatus development Bell Telephone Labs., Inc., Murray Hill, N.J., 1952-53, dir. transistor development, 1953-54, dir. development solid state devices, 1954-55, dir. device development, 1955-58, v.p., 1958-71. Mem. planning bd. Hillsborough (N.J.) Twp. Recipient Univ. Alumni award Wayne U., 1951, Certificate of Merit, 1958.

Distinguished Alumnus citation U. Mich., 1953; David Sarnoff award, 1965. Fellow Inst. Elec. and Electronics Engrs. (chmn. electron tube conf. 1949); mem. MacKenzie Honor Soc., National Academy Engineering, Phi Beta Kappa, Sigma Xi, Eta Kappa Nu, Alpha Delta Psi, Phi Kappa Phi, Tau Beta Pi. Home: South Branch NJ Died Dec. 11, 1971.

MORTON, JAMES GEARY, trade assn. ofcl.; b. Pitts., Aug. 4, 1916; s. James C. and Eleanor (Geary) M.; A.B., The Citadel, 1938; m. Love Brice, Nov. 13, 1945; 1 son, Geary. Advt. staff N.Y. Sun, 1938-39; advt. staff N.Y. Jour-Am., 1939-42, editorial dept., 1942-48, editorial exec., 1948-56, promotion mgr., 1956-57; exec. staff Am. Weekly, 1958-61; v.p. Hearst Pub. Co., 1959-61; spl. asst. to Fed. Hwy. Adminstr., U.S. Bur. Pub. Roads, 1962; spl. asst. to U.S. Sec. Commerce, 1962-63, asst. to U.S. Sec. Commerce, 1963-67; dir. govt. relations Mfg. Chemists Assn., 1967-73. Organizing com. 9th Pan Am. Hwy. Congress, del., 1964, 67. Served from 2d lt. to capt., 506th Parachute Regt., 101st Airborne Div., AUS, 1942-46. Decorated Bronze Star medal (3), Purple Heart (2), Presdl. citation with oak leaf cluster (U.S.); Belgian Fourragere; Dutch Orange Lanyard; N.Y. Conspicuous Service Cross; gold citizenship medal S.A.R., 1954; Freedoms Found. award, 1955-57; Amigo award Mexican Hwy. Assn., 1966. Mem. Hon. Tar Heels N.C., Mil. Order World Wars, 101st Airborne Assn., Silurians. Democrat. Episcopalian. Clubs: Nat. Capital Democratic (gov.), Army Navy (N.Y.C.); Overseas Press; Nat. Press; George Town (Washington). Home: Nags Head NC Died Jan. 12, 1973; buried Arlington Nat. Cemetery, Arlington VA

MORTON, JAMES PROCTOR, naval officer; b. Rockford, Tenn., Feb. 8, 1874; s. Henry Thomas and Mary Arvilla (Proctor) M.; student U. of Mo., 1890-1; grad. U.S. Naval Acad., 1895; m. Grace L. Howard, of Washington, D.C., Mar. 21, 1911. Promoted ensign, June 1897; advanced through various grades to capt., Oct. 15, 1917. Served on Marblehead and Vixen, Spanish-Am. War, 1898; promoted for spl. service on blockade of Santiago de Cuba; on Monadnock and Bennington, in Philippine Island, 1898-1901, assisting to land the army; head of Post-Grad. Sch. for Officers of Navy, at Annapolis, Md., 1912-15; organized sch. for advanced work in engring., electricity and ordnance, 1912. Naval attache to Turkey, 1915-17, comd. transport President Grant, landing troops in France, Aug. 1917-Feb. 1918; apptd. comdr. battleship Kentucky, Feb. 18, 1918. Mem. Am. Soc. Naval Engrs., Sigma Alpha Epsilon. Medals Spanish-Am. War, West Indies Campaign, Philippine Insurrection. Presbyn. Clubs: Army and Navy, Chevy Chase (Washington, D.C.); Racquet (Philadelphia); New York Yacht. Home: 3009 DeGraff Way, Kansas City MO‡

MORTON, ROSALIE SLAUGHTER, surgeon; b. Lynchburg, Va., Oct. 28, 1876; d. John Flavel and Mary Haines (Harker) Slaughter; student pvt. schs., Va. and Md.; M.D., with honors, Woman's Med. Coll. of Pa., 1897; interne City Hosp., Phila., 1897; resident physician Alumni Hosp. and Dispensary Woman's Med. Coll. of Pa., 1897-98; post-grad. study in nervous diseases, gynecology and surgery, Berlin, Vienna, Paris and London, 1899-1901; tropical diseases, Ceylon and India, 1901; hon. Dr. Humanities, Rollins Coll., 1929; D.Sc., Rutgers, 1939; m. George B. Morton, Jr., Sept. 1905 (died 1912). Practiced at Washington, 1902-05, New York, 1906-29; at Winter Park, Florida, since 1930, specializing in endocrinology and arthritis; clin. asst. and instr. gynecology, 1912-14, lecturer on surgery, 1914-16, adj. prof. gynecology, 1916-18, N.Y. Poly. Med. Sch. and Hosp.; attdg. surgeon, Vanderbilt Clinic of Coll. Physicians and Surgeons (Columbia), 1916-18; founded social service dept. N.Y. Polyclinic Hosp., 1917; visiting surgeon and consultant Volunteer Hosp., 1919-23; mem. visiting staff Orange Gen. Hosp. since 1930. Specialist in treatment of arthritis since 1929. Active service in France and on Salonica front, 1916; was first chmn. war service com. of Am. Women's Nat. Assn.; founder and first chmn. of Am. Women's Hosps.; under apptmt. of U.S. Govt. represented 6,000 women physicians on U.S. Council Nat. Defense, Washington, 1917-18, World War; provided hosp. equipment for 2 Yugoslav hosps., and tuberculosis camp for children under Serbian Red Cross, 1919; founder and chmn. Internat. Serbian Ednl. Com., under which 60 Yugoslav students were educated in Am. univs., 1919-28. Lectured widely in U.S., also in Serbia, Australia and S. Africa. Commr. on Internat. Education to Eng., France, Germany and Italy, 1921-26; from League of Am. Pen Women and Women's Med. Soc. of N.Y. State to S. Africa, 1926, to Iraq and Iran, 1935; del. Pan Pacific Scientific Congress, Australia, 1923; to Congress of Socs. to Promote League of Nations, France, 1924; ambassador of good will from various organizations to Mexico, Hayti and Porto Rico, 1928, 29; hon. pres. and ambassador of good will to med. women in Near and Middle East, summer 1935; business and professional commr. of nat. and internat. assns. to Greece, Turkey and Syria, summer 1935. For distinguished services on Salonica front, on Mediterranean, in Serbia, Yugoslavia and France, was decorated 9 times by France, Serbia and State of N.Y., 1916-23; tree in Honor Grove, Central Park, New York, planted in her honor for distinguished patriotic service," 1926; awarded Palm of Officer French Acad., 1927; presented with loving cup by a group of members of Am. Med. Assn., 1934. Fellow A.M.A.; mem. Fla. Med. Assn., Orange County Med. Soc. (Fla.) Women's Med. Assn. N.Y. City (pres. 1917-18), Woman's Med. Soc. State of N.Y. (pres. 1927-28), Nat. Inst. Social Sciences, Colonial Dames, D.A.R., U.D.C., Nat. Soc. Patriotic Women of America, Soc. of Va. Women in New York, Vets. of Foreign Wars, Am. Assn. Univ. Women, League of Am. Pen Women, Inst. of Internat. Edn., N.Y. Acad. Sciences, Am. Red Cross (life mem.), Assn. of Mil. Surgeons of the U.S., Am. Inst. for Iranian Art and Archaeology, Sociedad Medica Yucateca (hon. since 1928), Zeta Phi (pres. 1926-28), etc. Episcopalian. Club: Zonta (twice pres.). Has studied sociological and economic problems in Sweden, Finland, Estonia, Latvia and Lithuania. Author: A Woman Surgeon (autobiography; pub. U.S., Eng. and Sweden), 1937; A Doctor's Holiday in Iran, 1940. Invented 9 surg. instruments and appliances; author of numerous articles on gynecol., arthritis and other scientific subjects. Home: 667 Osceola Av., Winter Park FL‡

MOSELEY, FREDERICK S., JR., assn. ofcl. Ltd. partner Wood, Struthers & Winthrop, mems. N.Y. stock Exchange. Bd. dirs. N.Y. Lighthouse Assn. for Blind, 1947-72, pres., 1967-72; past v.p. N.J. State Med. Hosp., Greystone Park; now v.p. N.Y. Bot. Garden. Address: New York City NY Died Feb. 1, 1972.

MOSELY, PHILIP EDWARD, prof. internat. relations; b. Westfield, Mass., Sept. 21 1905; s. Arthur Chauncey and Eliza Harvey (Rust) M.; A.B., Harvard, 1926, Ph.D., 1933; LL.D., U. Notre Dame, 1956, Union Coll., 1959; LL.D., Middlebury Coll., 1964; D.I.L., Susquehanna U., 1969; m. Ruth Bissell, Apr. 2, 1939; children—Patricia, Ann. Instr. Princeton, 1929-30; historical research, Moscow, 1930-32; instr. Union Coll., 1933-35; research in Balkans, 1935-36, 38; asst. prof. Cornell, 1936-40; asso. prof., 1940-43; prof. internat. relations Russian Inst., Columbia, 1946-55, adj. prof., 1955-63, Adlai E. Stevenson prof. internat. relations, dir. Inst. on Western Europe, asso. dean faculty internat. affairs, 1963-72. Trustee The Rand Corp. Pres. E. European Fund, 1952-61; dir. research program on USSR, 1951-61; dir. Russian Institute, 1951-55; dir. studies Council Fgn. Relations, 1955-63; officer Dept. State, 1942-46, asst. chief, div. polit. studies, chief div. territorial studies, adviser U.S. delegation Moscow Conf., 1943, polit. adviser U.S. delegation European Adv. Commn., London, 1944-45, Potsdam Conf., 1945, Council Fgn. Ministers, London and Paris, 1945-46; U.S. rep. Commn. Investigation Yugoslav-Italian Boundary, 1946. Mem. Am. Hist. Assn., Council Fgn. Relations, Am. Polit. Sci. Assn., Fgn. Policy Assn. (trustee 1961-70). Episcopalian. Clubs: Cosmos (Washington); Century (N.Y.C.). Author: Russian Diplomacy and the Opening of the Eastern Question in 1838 and 1839, 1934; The Kremlin and World Politics, 1960. Contbr. scis. revs. Home: New York City NY Died Jan. 13, 1972; buried Pine Hill Cemetery, Westfield MA

MOSER, ALFRED A., past pres. Merchants Fire Assurance Corp.; b. New York, Apr. 13, 1873; ed. public schools, N.Y. City. With North British & Mercantile Co., 13 yrs.; with Crum and Foster, 13 years; with Merchants Fire Assurance Corp., N.Y. City, 1916-49, ret. as pres.; v.p. Washington Assurance Corp. of N.Y. and of Merchants Indemnity Corp. of N.Y. Mem. Drug and Chemical Club. Club: Echo Lake Country (Westfield, N.J.). Home: 535 Tremont Av., Westfield, NJ Office: 45 John St., New York NY‡

MOSER, CHARLES KROTH, consul; b. Marion, Smythe Co., Va., Aug. 27, 1877; s. Jacob Shaffer and Sarah Elizabeth Virginia (Scherer) M.; ed. U. of Cal., 1901; m. Helen Marian Place, of Cortland, N.Y., July 7, 1906. In editorial dept., San Francisco Chronicle, 1900-4; practiced law, San Francisco, 1902-4; mag. writer, 1904-7; an asso. editor Washington Post, 1907-9; apptd. consul at Aden, Arabia, May 31, 1909; consul at Colombo, Ceylon, Aug. 19, 1911-July, 1914, at Harbin, China, July 12, 1914-—. Lutheran. Member Royal Asiatic Society of Great Britain (Ceylon br.), Kappa Alpha. Clubs: Washington Country (Washington), Colombo Golf. Contbr. travel articles to mags. Home: Roslyn, Va. Address: American Consulate, Harbin China‡

MOSER, CLARENCE PATTEN, lawyer; b. Rochester, N.Y., Feb. 5, 1876; s. Alexander M. and Elizabeth C. (Patten) M.; A.B., U. Rochester, 1897; LL.B., N.Y.U., 1899; m. Helen Louise Hardison, Sept. 8, 1906;children—John H., Richard G., Robert F. Admitted to N.Y. bar, 1899, practiced in N.Y. City, 1899-1910, Rochester, since 1910; mem. Moser, Johnson & Reif since 1944; dir. Todd Co., Inc. Mem. Am. and N.Y. State bar assns., Am. Law Inst., Am. Judicature Soc., Psi Upsilon. Clubs: Genesee Valley, Country of Rochester (Rochester); University (N.Y. City). Home: 209 Culver Rd., Rochester 7 NY Office: 47 S Fitzhugh St., Rochester 14 NY‡

MOSER, HENRY S., lawyer; b. Steger, Ill., Oct. 27, 1900; s. Sol and Emma (Bishop) M.; B.S., Crane Coll., 1918; LL.B., John Marshall Law Sch., 1921; m. Freda Grossman, Aug. 27, 1921 (dec. 1952); children—Allan Henry, William Paul; m. 2d, Ruth Coy, Nov. 24, 1953 (dec. 1962); m. 3d, Freda Sanders Greene. Admitted to Ill. bar, 1921; pvt. practice law, 1921-53; gen. counsel Allstate Ins. Co., Skokie, Ill., 1932-71, dir., 1942-71, v.p., 1953-57, sr. v.p., 1957-60; counsel to firm Sonnenschein, Levinson, Carlin, Nath & Rosenthal, Chgo., 1960-64; dir. Allstate Ins. Co., Nat. Emblem Ins. Co., Allstate Enterprises, Inc.; v.p., dir. La California Compania Gen. de Seguros, S.A.; vice chmn. bd. Allstate Internat., S.A., Zurich, Alstadt Versicherungs-Aktiengesell-schaft. Trustee John Marshall Law Sch., 1954-71. Clubs: Standard, Northmoore Country (Chicago); Cuernavaca Mexico Died Mar. 11, 1971.

MOSHER, SAMUEL BARLOW, oil co. exec.; b. Carthage, N.Y., 1892; ed. U. of Cal., 1916; m. Margaret Clinch McGann. Hon. chmn. bd. Signal Cos., Inc. Mem. Nat. Petroleum War Council, 1940-47. Mem. Delta Sigma Phi. Mason. Clubs: Jonathan, California. Home: Santa Barbara CA Died Aug. 4, 1970; buried Santa Barbara CA

MOSHER, WILLIAM ALLISON, chemist; b. Salem, Ore., Dec. 26, 1912; s. Daniel Harrison and Maud (Stone) M.; B.A., Willamette U., 1935, D.Sc., 1961; M.S., Ore. State U., 1936; student U. Mich., 1937; Ph.D., Pa. State U., 1940; m. DeLaurice E. Yarnes, Oct. 3, 1936; children—Allison Jean, Carol Anne. Food chemist, Reid, Murdock & Co., Salem, Ore., 1932-36; research fellow, asst., Ore. State Coll., 1935-37; asst. prof. chemistry, Willamette U., 1937-38; asst. fellow, Pa. State U., 1938-40; research chemist Hercules Powder Co., Wilmington, Del., 1940-41; asst. to dir. research Hercules Powder Co., 1941-45; prof. chemistry, head dept. chemistry, U. Del., 1945-72, Willis F. Harrington Prof. and chmn., 1962-—; Lank lectr. U. Montreal, 1960; Zinn lectr., Gettysburg, 1962; Baugher lectr., Elizabethtown, 1962; mem. adv. council Biochemical Research Found., Franklin Inst. since 1946; chem. advisor Biochem. Research Found. since 1948; gas cons. Del., 1942-45; Fulbright lectureship in Austria, 1952-53; cultural del. to Rumania, 1958; cons. to Army Chem. Corps. Served with Chem. Corps. Res. as 1st lt. Member Am. Chem. Soc., Chem. Soc. (London), Nat. Com. Professional Relations, A.A.A.S., N.Y. Acad. Sci., Franklin Inst., Sigma Xi, Phi Kappa Phi, Alpha Chi Sigma, Phi Lambda Upsilon, Alpha Tau Omega. Theta Alpha Phi, Tau Kappa Alpha, Blue Key. Republican. Methodist. Contbr. scientific articles profl. jours. Home: Newark DE Died July 23, 1972; interred Gracelawn Meml. Park, New Castle DE

MOSIER, HAROLD GERARD, ex-congressman; b. Cincinnati, Ohio, July 24, 1889; s. M. G. and Anna (Hogsett) M.; A.B., Dartmouth College, 1912; LL.B., Harvard, 1915; m. Grace Hoyt Jones, 1918. Admitted to Ohio bar, 1916; practiced in Cleveland, O., 1916-42; member firm Minshall and Mosier, 1930-42. Member Ohio State Senate, 1933-34; lt. gov. Ohio, 1935-36; member 75th Congress (1937-39), Ohio at large. Admitted to Md. Bar, 1943; counsel The Glenn L. Martin Co., Baltimore, 1942-52; legislative adviser Aircraft Industries Association, Washington, 1952-60, ret. Mem. Am. Bar Assn., Newcomen Soc. N.A., Delta Kappa Epsilon. Democrat. Episcopalian. Clubs: Wings (N.Y.C.); Aero, Nat. Aviation (Washington). Died Aug. 7, 1971; buried Ft. Lincoln Cemetery MD

MOSS, CHARLES MCCORD, newspaper exec.; b. Nashville, July 30, 1902; s. Charles Thomas and Annie Lee (McCord) M.; student Vanderbilt U., 1920-24; honorary alumnus of the University of the South; m. Elizabeth Buford Yerger, July 19, 1924; 1 son, Michael Yerger. Reporter Nashville Banner, 1926-29, city editor, 1929-36, mng. editor, 1936-50, exec. editor, 1950-71. Mem. bd. dirs. So. Education Reporting Service. Mem. Am. Soc. Newspaper Editors, Asso. Press Mng. Editors, Sigma Chi. Episcopalian. Home: Nashville TN Died Feb. 16, 1971; buried Mt. Olivet Cemetery, Nashville TN

MOSS, EMMA SADLER, physician, educator; b. Pearlington, Miss., Sept. 19, 1898; d. Paul H. and Lou (Cowart) Sadler; B.S., Miss. State Coll. Women, 1919; M.B., La. State U., 1934, M.D., 1935; m. John Wellford Moss, Nov. 26, 1921 (dec.). Med. technologist VA hosps., 1919-30; intern, resident pathology Charity Hosp., New Orleans, 1934-39, dir. pathology, 1939-70; successively asst., instr., asst. prof., clin. asso. prof. pathology La. State U., 1934-51, clinical professor, 1951-69, clinical professor emeritus, 1969-70. Bd. dirs. Miss. State College Women Found. Recipient gold medal Am. Soc. Clin. Pathologists, 1944, 51, silver medal, 1947, Billings gold medal A.M.A., 1954. Diplomate Am. Bd. Pathology. Fellow A.C.P., Coll. Am. Pathologists, Am. Soc. Clin. Pathologists (pres. 1955-56, exec. com.); mem. Soc. Am. Bacteriologists, Assn. Pathologists and Bacteriologists, Am. Soc. Tropical Medicine and Hygiene, Am., So., La., Orleans Parish med. assn., La. Pathology Soc. (past v.p.), Alpha Omega Alpha, Beta Beta Beta, Alpha Epsilon Delta, Beta Epsilon Upsilon. Co-author: Atlas Medical Mycology, 3d edit., 1969. Home: New Orleans LA Died Apr. 30, 1970; buried Highland Park Cemetery, Hattiesburg MS

MOSS, FRANK J., mfr.; b. Moundville, Wis., Mar. 20, 1863; s. Thomas and Fannie (Bonell) M.; ed. country sch., Moundville, and night sch., Iowa City, Ia.; m. Grace Flint, 1896; 1 dau., Mary Frances (Mrs. Alexander Hamilton). Began as photographer's apprentice, Hudson, Wis., 1882; in photograph and picture frame business, Chicago, Ill., 1883; salesman of photog. dryplates, 1884; photographer, Iowa City, 1885-86; with Huttig Mfg. Co., Muscatine, Ia., 1887-92; sec. and mgr. Huttig Moss Mfg. Co., St. Joseph, Mo., 1892-1906; organizer, 1906, pres. since 1906, Am. Sash & Door Co. (absorbed Huttig Moss Mfg. Co. and Roach & Kingle Sash & Door Co.); pres. and gen. mgr. Am. Industrial & Warehouse Co., Am. Lumber Co. (Denver, Colo.); dir. Mo. River Navigation Co. Independent Republican. Episcopalian. Clubs: Kansas City, Kansas City Country. Contbr. on scientific taxation. Home: 5212 Bellview Av. Office: 16th St. and Bellfontane Av., Kansas City MO‡

MOSSER, CHARLES MARCEL, constrn. co. exec.; b. Fremont, O., Dec. 3, 1908; s. Louis and Theresia (Lehman) M.; student parochial schs., Fremont; m. Virginia Alice Miller, Oct. 18, 1947; children—Janet (Mrs. Robert P. Sweeney), Charles Norman. Pres., chmn., dir. Mosser Constrn., Inc., Fremont, 1946-72; pres., dir. Fremont Drive-in Theatres, Inc., 1947-72, Fremont Rental & Sales, Inc., Fremont, Sandusky, O., 1953-72, Innkeepers of Fremont, Inc., 1971-72, U.S. Financial Co., San Diego, Indepedence Nat. Co., Columbus, O. Mem. Fremont C. of C. Roman Catholic. Elk. Home: Fremont OH Died Oct. 30, 1972.

MOSSMAN, B. PAUL, ret. mfg. exec.; b. Coesse, Ind., Oct. 23, 1870; s. William E. and Lois (Douglas) M.; A.B., U. Mich., 1891; s. Emma Seymour, Dec. 22, 1897; children—William S., Dorothy E. Pres. Mossman Yarnelle Co., Ft. Wayne, Ind., 1918-30, ret. 1930; dir. Lincoln Nat. Life Ins. Co., Home Telegraph & Telephone Co., Ft. Wayne Nat. Bank. Republican. Conglist. Mason (33 deg.). Home: 230 Pearl St., Ft Wayne 2 IN‡

MOSTELLER, L. KARLTON, lawyer; b. Bartow County, Ga., Nov. 28, 1895; s. Jefferson and Ida (Woodall) M.; grad. Sch. Fgn. Service, Georgetown U. and George Washington U.; m. Helen Briggs, June 22, 1940. Admitted to D.C. and Okla. bars; mem. firm Mosteller, Andrews & Mosberg, Oklahoma City. Mason. Contbr. articles legal jours. Office: Oklahoma City OK Died Dec. 23, 1966.

MOTE, DONALD ROOSEVELT, judge; b. nr. Union City, Ind., Apr. 27, 1900; s. Oliver Perry and Emma Alice (Thomas) M.; student DePauw U., 1919-22; A.B., Wabash Coll., 1923; LL.B., George Washington U., 1927; m. Flora Elizabeth Hunter, Apr. 20, 1932; children—Virginia (Mrs. Richard L. Walsman), Thomas N. Admitted to Ind. bar, 1927; practice law, Indpls., 1927-36, North Manchester-Wabash, 1937-62; dep. atty. gen., Ind., 1928; city atty., North Manchester, 1948-52; county atty., Wabash County, Ind., 1957-62; judge Ind. Appellate Ct., 1963-66, Ind. Supreme Ct., Indpls., 1966-68. Mem. Ind. Soc. Chgo., Wabash C. of C., Wabash County Hist. Soc., Delta Tau Delta, Phi Delta Phi, Phi Delta Kappa. Mason (Shriner, Jester), Elk. Presbyn. Home: Wabash IN Died Sept. 17, 1968.

MOTLEY, WARREN, lawyer; b. Boston, May 14, 1883; s. Thomas and Eleanor (Warren) M.; grad. Groton Sch., 1900; A.B., Harvard, 1904, LL.B., 1906. Admitted to Mass. bar, 1906, practiced in Boston; partner firm Gaston, Snow, Motley & Holt, and predecessors. Office: Boston MA Died Nov. 18, 1971.

MOTT, CHARLES STEWART, dir. Gen. Motors Corp.; b. Newark, N.J., June 2, 1875; s. John Coon and Isabella Turnbull (Stewart) M.; M.E., Stevens Inst. Tech., 1897, E.D., 1937; studied zymotechnology in Denmark, 1894, chemistry in Germany, 1895; m. Ethel Harding, 1900 (died 1924); children—Aimee (Mrs. Patrick Butler), Elsa Beatrice (Mrs. Hamish Mitchell), Charles Stewart Harding; m. 2d, Mrs. Mitties Rathbun (died 1928); m. 3d, Miss Ruth Rawlings, Oct. 13, 1934; children—Susan Elizabeth, Stewart Rawlings, Maryanne Turnbull. Secretary and superintendent Weston-Mott Company, 1900-03, president, 1903-13; director General Motors Corporation since 1913, mem. exec. com., 1922-29, vice-pres., 1916-37; mem. finance com., 1929-37, audit committee since 1942; chmn. bd. U.S. Sugar Corp.; pres. Northern Ill. Water Co. Served in U.S. Navy, Spanish-Am. War; colonel Ordnance R.C. President Charles Stewart Mott Foundation. Trustee Stevens Inst. Tech., 1938. Vice-chairman Flint Office Civilian Defense, since 1942; chairman exec. com. Flint War Board, 1942. Fellow American Soc. of M.E., Soc. Automotive Engrs., Detroit Aviation Soc., Spanish War Vets., Vets. Foreign Wars, Am. Legion Army Ordinance Association, Reserve Officers Association. Republican. Episcopalian. Mason (33 deg., K.T.), Elk, Moose. Clubs: Detroit, Detroit Athletic, Army and Navy, Kiwanis (Detroit); Rotary, Kiwanis, Civitan, Lions, Army and Navy, Flint City, Flint Golf (Flint); Metamora (Mich.) Hunt; Royal Bermuda Yacht. Home: 1400 E. Kearsley St., Flint 3, MI; also Parapet, Somerset, Bridge, Bermuda. Office: 500 Mott Foundation Bldg., Flint 3 MI‡

MOTT, RODNEY LOOMER, polit. scientist; b. Pullman, Wash., Nov. 2, 1896; s. Albert Washington and Mary Elizabeth (Loomer) M.; A.B., Stanford U., 1917; A.M., U. of Wis., 1918, Ph.D., 1922; m. Harriet Lavinia Minton, July 12, 1923; 1 dau., Patricia. Instr. in English and history Eureka Jr. Coll., 1919-20; instr. in polit. science U. of Minn., 1922-23, U. of Chicago, 1923-26, asst. prof., 1926-33; prof. polit. science and dir. Div. of Social Sciences, Colgate U., 1934-59, Charles Evans Hughes professor govt. and jurisprudence, from 1959, director div. social sciences, 1959-62. Specialist in government finance HICOG, Germany, 1950-51; Fulbright research scholar, Australia, 1953-54; dir. Am. Studies Seminar, Kyoto, Japan, 1954-55; mem. 9th Selection Boards, U.S. Dept. of State, 1955. Served as pvt. infantry, 1918, maj. and comdt. cadets, Nat. Guard of Calif., 1919-20; major Army Specialists Reserve Corps, 1943-45; mil. govt.; lt. col. Gen. Staff Corps, 1945-46, military govt. (Germany). Awarded Legion of Merit, Oct., 1945; Army Commendation Ribbon, July, 1946. Research consultant and managing editor of State Government, American Legislators Association, 1930-34; member Governors Committee on N.Y. Non-competitive Civil Service, 1939-41. Fellow Social Science Research Council, 1929; mem. Am. Polit. Science Assn. (exec. council, 1939-42), Am. Judicature Soc., Nat. Municipal League, Phi Beta Kappa. Baptist. Mason. Club: Torch. Author: Materials Illustrative of American Government, 1925; Due Process of Law, 1926; Constitutions of the States and the United States (with W.L. Hindman), 1938; Men, Groups and the Community (with T.H. Robinson and others), 1940; Home Rule for American Cities, 1949; Governing Post War Germany (with Litchfield and others), 1953; The First Freedom, 1960. Home: Hamilton NY Died Dec. 9, 1971; buried Colgate U. Cemetery, Hamilton NY

MOTTET, JEANIE GALLUP (MRS. HENRY MOTTET), artist; b. Providence, R.I.; d. Albert S. and Jane Adams (Balch) Gallup; studied at Art Students' League, New York, and in Europe, with William M. Chase, Richard Miller, E. Ambrose Webster and others; m. Rev. Henry Mottet, D.D., rector Ch. of Holy Communion, New York, May 14, 1895. Painter of portraits, figures, still life and flowers; exhibited Nat. Acad. of Design, Corcoran Gallery (Washington, D.C.), Toledo Art Museum, Newport Art Assn., Boston Art Club, etc. Curator of painting, Mus. of French Art, New York; member of Art Com. Roosevelt House. Mem. Nat. Assn. Women Painters and Sculptors (pres. 1918, 19), Boston Art Club, Providence Art Club, Nat. Soc. Colonial Dames, State of N.Y.; chmn. bd. mgrs. Home for the Destitute Blind, New York. Decorated Officier d'Academie, by Minister of Beaux Arts, Paris, 1918, and Officier de'l Instruction Publique, 1929. Represented in Musee du Luxembourg, Paris, Brooklyn Museum, etc. Democrat. Club: Colony. Home: 157 E. 72d St., New York NY‡

MOTZKIN, THEODORE S., educator, mathematician; b. Berlin, Germany, 1908; s. Leo and Pauline M.; student University of Berlin, 1924-27, U. Goettingen (Germany), 1928, U. Paris (France), 1930; Ph.D., U. Basel (Switzerland), 1934; m. Naomi Orenstein; children—Aryeh Leo, Joseph J. Elbanan, Gabriel G. H. Naturalized U.S. citizen, 1958; mem. faculty U. Jerusalem, 1936-48, Boston Coll., 1950; mem. faculty U. Cal. at Los Angeles, 1950-70, prof. math.; vis. prof. U. Jerusalem, 1968, Rockefeller U., 1966; cons. U. Chgo., 1953. Harvard Research fellow, 1948; NSF sr. postdoctoral fellow, U. Copenhagen (Denmark), 1963. Mem. Am., Danish, France, Israel (pres. 1936-48), London, Switzerland math. socs. Editorial bd. Jour. Approximation Theory, Jour. Combinatories, Jour. Lin. Algebra and Applications. Author articles abstract structures, polynomial alegebra and geometry, convexity and approximations theory. Died Dec. 15, 1970.

MOUDY, WALTER FRANK, lawyer; b. Cassville, Mo., Dec. 19, 1929; s. Ernest and Maxine (Brown) M.; A.B., U. Mo., 1954, LL.D., 1957; m. Marguerite Boldin, Apr. 21, 1952; children—Anthony Roger, Christopher Brian, Jennifer Lynn. Admitted to Mo. bar, 1957; asso., partner firm Caldwell, Blackwell, Oliver & Sanders, 1957-63; partner firm Morris, Foust, Moudy & Beckett, Kansas City, 1963-73. Served with AUS, 1950-53. Decorated Air medal. Mem. Order of Coif, Phi Beta Kappa. Author: No Man on Earth, 1964, The Ninth Commandment. Contbr. articles to profl. jours. Home: Kansas City MO Died Apr. 13, 1973.

MOUHTAR BEY, AHMED, ambassador; b. Constantinople, Turkey, May 13, 1871; s. Hassan Tahsin and Fatma Zehra; grad. Ecole Superieure de Science Politique, Stamboul; law degree, University of Constantinople; m. Kerimeh Hanim, of Magnesia, 1897; children—Enver Bey, Nebil Bey. Sec., office of foreign corr., Ministry of Foreign Affairs, Turkey, later 2d sec. legation, Stockholm, Sweden, 1898-99, 1st sec., 1900; successively to asst. to legal counsellor, Sublime Porte, and chief of office of foreign corr., Grand Vizierate, 1900-05; consul gen., Budapest, Hungary, 1905-17, E.E. and M.P., Athens, Greece, 1917; deputy to Turkish parliament, later to Great Nat. Assembly, 1920; acting minister for foreign affairs, 1920, minister, 1921; on spl. missions, 1922; ambassador to Moscow, 1923-24; mem. Great Nat. Assembly, 1924-26; ambassador to U.S., Washington, D.C., since 1927. Address: 1708 Massachusetts Av. N.W., Washington DC‡

MOUNTCASTLE, GEORGE WILLIAMS, banker, mfr.; b. Jefferson City, Tenn., Feb. 2, 1871; s. Andrew Jackson and Cornelia Frances (Williams) M.; A.B., Carson and Newman Coll., Jefferson City, 1888; student Eastman Bus. Coll., Poughkeepsie, N.Y., 1888; m. Frances Louise Hunt, Jan. 12, 1892; children—Chas. Andrew, Kenneth F., Frances Holt (Mrs. Woodrow McKay). Cashier, Bank of Lexington, 1889-94, pres., 1894-1928, chmn. bd. since 1928; pres. Mountcastle Knitting Co., Lexington Perpetual Bldg. & Loan Assn.; v.p. Erlanger Cotton Mills Co.; sec. and treas. Lexington Telephone Co.; v.p., dir. Hoke Realty Co.; dir. Mooresville Cotton Mills, Southeastern Cotton Co., B.V.D. Corp. (New York), Dacotah Cotton Mills, N.C. R.R. Co., Midland R.R. Co., Commercial Bank of Lexington. Chmn. 5 Liberty Loan campaigns, World War. Chmn. War Finance Victory Loan. Ex-pres. N.C. Bankers Assn. Democrat. Presbyterian. Mason, K.P. Clubs: Lexington Country, Forsyth Country. Home: Lexington NC*‡

MOURSUND, ANDREW FLEMING, JR., educator; b. Fredericksburg, Tex., Dec. 4, 1901; s. Andrew Fleming and Therese (Wahrmund) M.; A.B., U. Tex., 1923, A.M., 1927; Ph.D., Brown U., 1932; m. Lulu Amelia Vorleck, June 29, 1931; children—Robert Andrew, David Garvin, Anne Loreen, Peter Douglas Tchr. math. high schs. in Mason and Austin, Tex., 1924-27; instr. math. Tex. Tech. Coll., Lubbock, 1927-28; instr. math. U. Ore., 1931-34, asst. prof., 1934-36, asso. prof., 1936-43, head dept., 1939-43, prof., head dept., 1943-70, prof., 1970-72. Mem. Am. Math. Soc., Math. Assn. Am. Assn. Profs., Inst. Math. Statistics, Sigma Xi. Club: Faculty U. Ore. (Eugene). Contbr. articles math. jours. Home: Eugene OR Died Oct. 14, 1972.

MOUSEL, LLOYD HARVEY, physician; b. Cambridge, Neb., 1903; M.D., U. Neb., 1930; M.Sc. in Anesthesiology, U. Minn., 1939. Intern Takoma Gen. Hosp., 1930-31; surg. asst., 1931-35; fellow anesthesiology Mayo Found., U. Minn., 1936-39; cons. anesthesiologist Mayo Clinic, 1939-46; dir. anesthesiology Gallinger Municipal Hosp., Wash., 1946-50; chief anesthesiology br. sect. VA Hosp., 1946-52; dir. anesthesiology George Washington U. Hosp., 1946-50; dir. depts. anesthesiology and oxygen therapy Swedish Hosp., Seattle, 1950-70; instr. anesthesiology Mayo Found., U. Minn., 1939-43; asst. prof. anesthesiology U. Minn., 1943-46; clin. prof. anesthesiology George Washington U., 1946-48, prof., 1948-70; clin. asso. prof. anesthesiology U. Wash., 1950-70. Served to lt. col. M.C., AUS, 1942-46. Address: Seattle WA Died June 1970.

MOWAT, MAGNUS, cons. engr.; b. Bombay, India, Nov. 10, 1875; s. Hon. Magnus and Jane (Stodart) M.; ed. Aberdeen Grammar Sch. and Kings Coll., London; unmarried. Apprentice in locomotive work, North British Ry., Glasgow, Scotland; asst. engr. on construction Great Central Ry. (Leicester sect.), Indian Midland Ry., Jhansi, India; resident engr. G.I.P. Ry., Agra, India; chief engr. Millwall Dock Co., London; dir. engrng. firm Southern Counties. Comd. Royal Engrs. of A Div., 2 yrs. during World War I, later dir. of roads at War Office, 1919-20. Mem. council and fellow King's Coll., London. Vice pres. The Roads Improvement Assn. Fellow Royal Soc. Engrs. (hon. life mem.), Am. Soc. Mech. Engrs.; mem. Inst. Civil Engrs., Inst. Mech. Engrs. (sec. emeritus), Inst. Engrs. and Shipbuilders (Scotland). Decorated Comdr. Order of British Empire, Territorial Decoration. Address: Ebor House, Sheen Gate Gardens, East Sheen, London SW 14 Eng*‡

MOWRER, FRANK ROGER, ex-consul gen.; b. Xenia, O., July 7, 1870; s. Isaac S. and Hannah (Maley) M.; student Ohio Wesleyan U., 1888-90; LL.B., Cornell, 1894; m. Genevieve Winterbotham, of Chicago, Oct. 18, 1908; 1 daughter, Frances; m. 2d, Blanche Van Horn Armstrong, of Evansville, Ind., Apr. 17, 1918. Admitted to Ohio bar, 1895; practiced law in Xenia, 1895-97; apptd. marshal of the Consular Ct., Yokohama, Dec. 18, 1897; retired by operation of treaty, July 16, 1899; apptd. marshal of the Consular Court, Canton, China, July 22, 1899; consul at Antigua, British West Indies, Jan. 1901, Ghent, Belgium, Nov. 1901; consul gen. at Addis Ababa, Abyssimia, 1906-07; consul Leghorn, Italy, 1907; consul gen., Copenhagen, 1907-09 (resigned); admitted to California bar December 13, 1909. Developed Hot Springs Ranch," in Owens Valley, Calif., 1910-12; first industrial agent of Modern Industrial Town," of Torrance, Calif., 1915; with West India Oil Co. and Standard Oil Co. of Calif., 1916-22, Union Oil Co. of Calif., 1923-24, Security-First Nat. Bank of Los Angeles, 1925-29 (retired). Decorated by Menelik II, King of Ethiopia, with the Grand Cordon, Order of Star of Ethiopia, as the first resident American diplomatic representative in Ethiopia. Mem. Phi Gamma Delta. Mason. Methodist. Clubs: University, Cornell. Home: 346 South Benton Way Los Angeles CA‡

MOWRER, PAUL SCOTT, writer; born Bloomington, Ill., July 14, 1887; s. Rufus and Nellie (Scott) M.; grad. Hyde Park High Sch., Chicago, 1905; spl. student, University of Michigan, 1906-08, hon. LL.D., same, 1941; married Winifred Adams, May 8, 1909; children—Richard, Scott, David Adams; m. 2d, Hadley Richardson Hemingway, 1933. Began as reporter, Chicago Daily News, 1905; apptd. Paris corr., same newspaper, Apr. 1910; corr. with allied armies, first Balkan War., 1912-13; organized and directed Chicago Daily News war service in France, 1914-Nov., 1918; permanently accredited to French armies as official war corr., July 1, 1917, to end of war; dir. Chicago Daily News Peace Conf. Bur., Nov. 11, 1918-Aug. 31, 1919; war correspondent Moroccan campaigns in Riff, 1924, 25; asso. editor and chief editorial writer Chicago Daily News, 1934-35, editor, 1935-44; European editor, New York Post, 1945. Pulitzer prize for best foreign correspondent, 1928; Sigma Delta Chi national scholarship award for foreign correspondence, 1932. Awarded Legion of Honor, French General Headquarters, April 1918, promoted Officer, 1933. Author: Hours of France (poems) 1918; Balkanized Europe—A Study in Political Analysis and Reconstruction, 1921; The Good Comrade (poems), 1923; Our Foreign Affairs, 1924; Poems Between Wars, 1941; The House of Europe, 1945; On Going to Live in New Hampshire (poems), 1953; And Let the Glory Go (poems), 1955; Fifi (verse play), 1956; Twenty-one and Sixty-five (poems), 1958; The Mothering Land (poems), 1960. High Mountain Pond (poems), 1962; School for Diplomats (poems), 1964; (poems) This Teeming Earth, 1965; (poems) The Island Ireland, 1966; Poems (complete, 1968; Six Plays (theatre), 1968. Mem. Poetry Soc. N.H. (laureate). Club: New England Poetry. Home: Chocorua NH Died Apr. 5, 1971; buried Chocorua Cemetery.

MOYER, BURTON JONES, coll. dean, physicist; b. Greenville, Ill., Feb. 24, s. Jacob and Mabel(Jones) M.; A.B., Seattle Pacific Coll., 1933, Sc.D. (hon.), 1955; Ph.D., U. Wash., 1939; m. Lela Brushwood, June 22, 1937; children—Burton Jones, John Howard, Robert Philip, Lela Virginia. Tchr. physics and math. Greenville Coll., 1939-42; physicist Lawrence Radiation Lab., 1942-70; with Manhattan Dist., Berkeley and Oak Ridge, 1942-45 mem. faculty U. Cal. at Berkeley, 1947-70, prof. physics, 1954-70, chmn. dept., 1962-68, prof. emeritus, 1971-73; dean Coll. Liberal Arts, U. Ore., 1971-73; cons. nucleonics and radiation Shielding. Staff mem. Kanpur Indo-Am. programs, 1965-66. Fellow Am. Phys. Soc. Presbyn. (elder). Author articles on meson physics, high energy nuclear physics. Home: Eugene OR Died Apr. 21, 1973.

MOYER, DAVID GURSTELLE, corp. exec., lawyer; b. nr. Frederick, Ill., May 2, 1900; s. Archie G. and Laura (Gragg) M.; LL.B., U. Ill., 1929; m. Margaret Curtis, Sept. 22, 1928; children—Mary Ann, Sarah Jane. Admitted to Ill. bar, 1930; with Little & Finfrock, Urbana, 1929-31; mem. firm Moyer & Mix, Jacksonville, 1931-33; staff collection dept. Internat. Harvester Co., Peoria, Ill., 1933, law dept., 1934-65, gen. atty., 1944-57, gen. counsel, v.p., 1957-65, also dir. Mem. Am., Ill., Chgo. bar assns., Phi Delta Phi, Acacia. Republican. Conglist. Club: University (Chgo.). Home: Sturgeon Bay WI Died May 8, 1971; buried Bay Side Cemetery, Sturgeon Bay WI

MOYER, JOSEPH KEARNEY, lawyer; b. Pottsville, Pa., Dec. 22, 1890; s. Morgan G. and Fannie C. (Smith); B.C.S., cum laude, New York U., 1917; LL.B., Southeastern U., Washington, D.C., 1926; spl. course, Cornell, 1912; LL.D. (honorary), Southeastern University, 1947; married Alta C. Turner, Oct. 14, 1922. Bank clerk, 1908; asst. nat. bank examiner, 1912; teacher, 1911-17; U.S. treas., Bur. Internal Revenue, 1919-34; private law practice from 1934; dean, Southeastern U. Served to 2d lt., Chem. Warfare Service, 1918-19; 1st lt., capt. Army Reserves, 1919-34. Mem. Am. Bar Assn., Am. Inst. Accountants, Beta Gamma Sigma. Republican. Lutheran. Mason (Shriner), Rotarian. Author articles on fed. taxation. Home: Washington DC Died Aug. 1969; buried Genoa, OH

MOYLE, WALTER GLADSTONE, lawyer; b. Salt Lake City, Mar. 13, 1895; s. James Henry and Alice (Dinwoody) M.; A.B., U. Utah, 1915; Ph.B., U. Chicago, 1915, J.D., 1919; student Harvard Law Sch., 1916-17; m. Joyce Martineau Nebeker, Aug. 28, 1922; children—Walter Gladstone, Joyce N. (Mrs. Ralph E. Ladue, Jr.); m. 2d Irene VanOvermeer, Sept. 25, 1940. Admitted to Utah bar, 1919, D.C. bar, 1924; spl. asst. atty. gen., U.S., 1919-21; spl. asst. legal unit Office Commr. Internal Revenue, 1921-22; pvt. practice law, specialist corporate law, fed. taxation, Washington, 1922-70. Mayor Bethany Beach, Del., 1938-39. Served with AUS, 1917-18, AEF, 1918, 2nd lt., 139th F.A. Mem. Am. Legion, Am., D.C. bar assns., S.A.R. The Inquirendo (a founder 1930), Phi Alpha Delta. Mem. Ch. of Jesus Christ Latter-day Saints. Clubs: Ye Olde Bailey (Harvard Law Sch.); Harvard (Washington); U. Utah (past pres.), U. Chicago, Chatterbox, Congressional Country (Washington); La Gorce Country (Miami Beach, Fla.). Home: Key Biscayne FL Died Nov. 1970.

MUELLER, FRED WILLIAM, ch. official; b. Sandusky, O., Aug. 21, 1871; s. August Fred and Anna (Wekerlin) M.; prep. edn., Acad. Marietta Coll.; A.B., Baldwin Wallace Coll., Berea, O., 1893, D.D., 1915, Gammon Theol. Sem., D.D., 1938; student Sem. U.P. Ch., Pittsburgh, Pa., 1900, Nast Theol. Sem. and Baldwin Wallace Coll., Berea, 1915; m. Ellen Mack, Sept. 11, 1899; 1 dau., Ruth Hilda; m. 2d, Mrs. Beulah Vandervort, Sept. 29, 1944; 1 dau., Gretchen. Ordained ministry M.E. Ch., 1893; pastor chs. in Ohio and Pa. until 1910; dist. supt., Ohio and Mich., 1911-20; spl. editor Christliche Apologete, Dec. 1918-Apr. 1919; asso., ch. extension dept., Bd. Home Missions and Ch. Extension, M.E. Ch., 1920-28, supt. of dept. since 1928 and assistant treas., 1931-34, comptroller since 1934; dir. Nast Theol. Sem., 1918-29; trustee Baldwin-Wallace Coll., 1927-30; chmn. exec. com., treas. and trustee Children's Home, Berea, since 1903; vice pres. Bethesda Hosp. Cincinnati, 1911-28; delegate general Conference M.E. Ch., 4 times to 1928; delegate Ecumenical Conference, Atlanta, Ga., 1931; Springfield, Mass., 1947; member Joint Methodist Unification Commission since 1928; delegate Uniting Meth. Conf., 1939; del. to First Gen. Conference of United Methodism, 1940; member committee on religious work in the Canal Zone, 1941; exec. sec. Board of Home Missions and Church Extension since 1940; mem. exec. com. Home Missions Council, 1940, exec. sec. Gulfside Assembly, Waveland, Miss., since 1946. Mem. Kappa Nu. Office: 1908 Grand Av., Nashville 5 TN‡

MUELLER, KARL ANTON, bishop; b. Zeidler, Bohemia, Sept. 6, 1867; s. Joseph and Maria (Hesse) M.; grad. Moravian Theol. Sem., Pa., 1890, D.D., 1917; m. Pauline Purat; children—Theophil Herbert, John A. C., P. Gerhardt, J. Margaret, Gertrude E., Joseph (dec.). Came to America, 1887; ordained ministry Moravian Ch. in America (Unitas Fratrum), 1890; pastorates, Mamre and Gerah, Wis., 1890-93, Ebenezer (Watertown P.O.), Wis., 1893-1900; mem. Dist. Exec. bd. Moravian Ch., 1897-1941; editor Der Brueder-Botschafter, 1899-1941; consecrated bishop, 1908; mem. Provincial Elders' Conf. (exec. bd. Moravian Church in America), 1913-41; elected v.p. Unity's Elders Conf., 1931; exec. chmn. Unity's Elders Conf. (exec. bd.) United Fratrum or Moravian Ch. in gen., including Europe, 1937-41. Home: 530 S. Clifton Av., Park Ridge IL‡

MUENCH, HUGO, JR., physician; b. St. Louis, Oct. 17, 1894; s. Hugo and Eugenia (Thamer) M.; A.B., Cornell, 1915; M.D., Washington U., 1918; Dr.P.H., Johns Hopkins, 1932; A.M. (hon.), Harvard, 1946; m. Helen Ruth Harrison, Dec. 28, 1920; 1 son, James Frederick. Intern mil. hosps., 1917-20; county health officer Bertie County, Windsor, N.C., 1920-21; mem. field staff, internat. health div., Rockefeller Found., 1921-46, charge statis. work, 1932-37, fellowship adviser, 1937-46; prof. biostatistics Harvard Sch. Pub. Health, 1946-72, asst. dean, 1946-54. Mem. commn. on evaluation Poliomyelitis vaccine. Diplomate (founders group) Am. Bd. Preventive Medicine and Pub. Health. Fellow A.A.A.S., Am. Statis. Assn., Am. Pub. Health Assn.; mem. Institute of Math. Statistics, American Epidemiological Society, Delta Omega (past national pres.). Author: Catalytic Models in Epidemiology, 1959. Contbr. papers, book chapters, articles in gen. field of statistics applied to pub. health, med. and lab. problems. Home: Cambridge MA Died Nov. 16, 1972.

MUHLEMAN, GEORGE WASHINGTON, chemistry; b. Hannibal, O., Apr. 26, 1871; s. John Godfrey and Margaret Magdalena (Anshutz) M.; B.S., Northwestern U., 1899; M.S., State U. of Ia., 1912; D.Sc., U. of Geneva, Switzerland, 1927; m. Pamelia Florence Woods, Sept. 7, 1898. Teacher of Science, prin. and supt. pub. schs., Wis. and Ill., 1899-1910; instr. chemistry, Ia. State Teachers Coll., 1910-11; prof. chemistry, Meth. U. of Okla., 1913-15; business adminstr., Davenport, Ia., 1915-16; prof. chemistry, Mount Union Coll., Alliance, O., 1916-18, Hamline Univ. St. Paul, 1918-41, retired by bd. of trustees, June 1941; visiting prof. Alma (Mich.) Coll., 1941-42; head of dept. of inorganic chemistry, N.D. Agrl. College, 1942-43; instr. chemistry University of Florida, 1943-47; acting assistant Prof. of Chem., 1944-47; president Prairie-Garfield Co.; research Minn. Mining & Mfg. Co., summer 1944; delegate to 6th Congress of Industrial Chemists, Brussels, 1926; rep. of St. Paul Pioneer Press-Dispatch at Council of League of Nations, Mar.-June 1927; mem. Com. One Hundred for Law Enforcement, pres. Hamline Branch Library Council, St. Paul, since 1937, made life mem., 1940. Author of the nine papers read before sections of the Am. Chem. Society at different meetings. Received Merit Award of Northwestern Univ. Alumni Assn., 1941. Fellow A.A.A.S.; mem. Am. Chem. Soc., Swiss Chem. Soc., Am. Assn. Univ. Profs. (pres. 1932), Am. Men of Science, Leaders in Education, Twin City Northwestern University Alumni Assn. (pres.), Phi Beta Kappa, Sigma Xi. Republican. Presbyn. Mason; mem. Eastern Star. Author: Qualitative Analysis, 1926; Teaching of Chemistry in Colleges and Universities, 1921; Lecture Demonstrations in General Chemistry, 1934; Chemical Elements and their Discoverers (chart), revised, 1946; Must Life End at Sixty-Five (bulletin). Joint author: General Chemistry, 1926. Editor and joint author of General Chemistry, 1937, 38, 39. Contbr. to scientific publs. Lecturer on chemistry. Studied and traveled in Europe and British Isles, 1926-27. Inventor of fume hood for chem. labs. Home: 1450 Englewood Av., St Paul E 4 MN‡

MUIR, ANDREW FOREST, educator; b. Houston Heights, Tex., Jan. 8, 1916; s. Joseph Bailey and Annie Jane (James) M.; B.A., Rice Inst., 1938, M.A., 1942; Ph.D., U. Tex., 1949. Tchr., Tex., Hawaii and P.R., 1941-69; mem. faculty Rice U., 1958-69, prof. history, 1965-69, Guggenheim fellow, 1957. Fellow Tex. Hist. Assn., 1967. Democrat. Episcopalian. Editor: Texas in 1837, 1958. Asso. editor Jour. So. History, 1960-65; mem. editorial bd. Hist. Mag. of the Protestant Episcopal Church, 1962-69; mem. editorial adv. bd. Southwestern Hist. Quar., 1960-69. Home: Houston TX Died Feb. 3, 1969; buried Forest Park Lawndale Cemetery.

MUIR, JERE T., ex-college pres.; b. Trimble Co., Ky.; s. Robert and Ann M. (Bartlett) M.; A.B., LaGrange Coll., Mo., 1877, A.M., 1880 (LL.D., 1896); m. Elma Hay, of LaGrange, Mo., Oct. 2, 1879. Admitted to Mo. bar, 1882; teacher State Normal Sch., Kirksville, Mo., 1887-94; pres. LaGrange Coll., 1896-1905; field rep., State Normal Sch., Kirksville, 1907; now pres. La Grange (Mo.) Coll. Mem. 43d to 45th Gen. Assemblies of Mo. Author: Orthoepy, 1892; History and Government of Missouri, 1908; also ednl. articles. Address: La Grange MO‡

MULFORD, RAYMON HOWARD, glass exec.; b. San Francisco, Sept. 15, 1909; s. George Bacon and Sara Ann (Inskip) M.; B.A., Leland Stanford Jr. U., 1931; M.B.A., Harvard, 1933; 1933; LL.D., Bowling Green State U., 1965, U. Toledo, 1968; m. Jane L. Gould, July 1, 1938; children—Marilyn Helen, Louis (dec.), Sara Ann. Indsl. engr. Owens-Ill. Glass Co., Toledo, 1933-40, plant mgr., 1940-46, gen. factories mgr. Pacific Coast div., 1946-49, v.p., dir. personnel relations, 1949-53, v.p., gen. mgr. Kimble Glass Co., subsidiary, 1953-55, pres., 1956-60; v.p. Owens-Ill. Glass Co., 1956-60, exec. v.p., 1960-61, pres., dir., 1961-68, chief exec. officer, 1965-68, chmn. bd., chief exec. officer, 1968-73, pres. Glass Container div., 1960-73; dir. Ohio Citizens Trust Co., Nat. Petro Chems. Corp., Marathon Oil Co. Dir., N.Y. Stock Exchange. Mem. Nat. Bus. Council for Consumer Affairs, Nat. Center for Vol. Action; chmn. bus. structure and performance subcom. Com. for Econ. Devel. Trustee Toledo Museum Art, Nat. Cystic Fibrosis Research Found.; mem. adv. council Grad. Sch. Bus., Stanford U. Mem. Am. Soc. Corporate Execs. Congregationalist. Clubs: Toledo, Inverness, Toledo Country, Harvard Business School (Toledo); Seaview Country (Absecon, N.J.); Belmont Country (Perrysburg, O.); Cloud, Links (N.Y.C.); Cotton Bay (Eleuthera). Home: Toledo OH Died Feb. 1973.

MULFORD, ROLAND JESSUP, b. Friendsville, Pa., May 27, 1871; s. Elisha (LL.D.) and Rachel Price (Carmalt) M.; A.B., Harvard University, 1893, LL.B., 1896; fellow in politics, Johns Hopkins, 1901, Ph.D., 1903; m. Margaret Biddle Guest Blackwell, of Baltimore, Dec. 21, 1901. Master, St. Mark's Sch., Southboro, Mass., 1893-4, Pomfret (Conn.) Sch., 1896-9; head master Country Sch. of Baltimore, 1901-3, Cheshire (Conn.) Sch., 1903-7, Ridgefield (Conn.) Sch., 1907-22; instr. in Latin, Princeton, 1923—. Ordained deacon P.E. Ch., 1910, priest, 1922. Mem. Alpha Delta Phi, Headmasters' Assn. Clubs: University (New York), Nassau (Princeton). Dir. Camp Choconut, Friendsville, Pa., 1896-16. Home: 25 Wiggins St., Princeton NJ‡

MULFORD, WALTER, ret. educator; b. Millville, N.J., Sept. 16, 1877; s. Furman L. and Anna (Lloyd) M.; B.S.A., Cornell Univ., 1899; F.E., 1901; hon. Sc.D., U. of Mich., 1938; m. Vera Wandling, July 1, 1903. Forester to Conn. Agrl. Expt. Sta. and state forester of Conn., 1901-04; with U.S. Forest Service, 1904-05. Asst. prof. forestry, U. of Mich., 1905-07; jr. prof. forestry, same, 1907-11; prof. forestry, in charge dept. of forestry, Cornell U., 1911-14; prof. forestry, and chief of div. of forestry, U. of Calif., 1914-39, chmn. dept. forestry, 1939-46, dean School of Forestry, 1946-47; chmn., Executives Heads of Forestry Schools, 1946-48. Vice-pres. 1st World Forestry Congress, Rome, Italy, 1926, Calif. State Bd. of Forestry, 1928-30, since 1945; pres. bd. trustees Institute of Forest Genetics, 1932-33. Fellow Society American Foresters (pres. 1924); mem. Sigma Xi, Alpha Zeta, Xi Sigma Pi, Phi Sigma. Cons. ed. American Forestry Series since 1933. Home: 1775 Spruce St., Berkeley 9 CA‡

MULHOLLAND, JOHN, magician; b. Chicago, Ill., June 9, 1898; s. John and Irene May (Wickizer) M., ed. high sch. and spl. courses Columbia and Coll. City of N.Y.; m. Pauline Pierce, 1932. Began practicing magic at 5 years of age as a hobby, and entered field professionally while in sch.; teacher of industrial arts, Horace Mann School for Boys, New York, 6 yrs.; formerly identified with the World Book Co.; editor The Sphinx (magicians mag.), 23 yrs.; gave exhibitions of magic and lectured upon magic in principal countries of the world. Lifetime collection of books and memorabilia on magic given to the Walter Hampden Meml. Library at the Players, New York City. Member of Society American Magicians, Inner Magic Circle, British Magical Society, Indian Magicians' Club (Calcutta), and many others. Republican. Protestant. Clubs: Players, Circumnavigators, Dutch Treat (New York City). Author: Magic in the Making (with Milton Smith), 1925; Quicker Than the Eye, 1932; Story of Magic, 1935; Beware Familiar Spirits, 1938; The Girl in the Cage (with Cortland Fitzsimmons), 1939, The Art of Illusion, 1944; Book of Magic, 1963; Magic of the World, 1965; (with Dr. George N. Gordon) The Magical Mind, 1967; spl. ed. Webster's Unabridged Dictionary, 2d edit. Contbr. to Ency. Brit., Britannica Jr., Compton's World Book, also mags. and newspapers. Home: New York City NY Died Feb. 25, 1970; buried Woodlawn Cemetery.

MULL, JOHN WESLEY, ret. mfg. co. exec.; b. St. Louis, Mo., Aug. 10, 1887; s. John Wesley and Nellie (Nowath) M.; student public schools; m. Ida Merkel, Sept. 9, 1908 (deceased); one daughter, Bernice (Mrs. R. H. Thompson). Salesman St. Louis Machinist's Supply Co., 1905-15, Union Twist Drill Co., Athol., Mass., 1915-20, Vonnegut Machinery Co., Indpls., 1920-23; mfrs. rep. J. W. Mull, Jr., 1923-58, retired, 1958. Member of the Soc. Automotive Engrs., Am. Soc. Tool Engrs., Soc. Am. Mil. Engrs., American Ordnance Association Committee of One Hundred, Navy League of U.S. Clubs: Indianapolis Athletic, Columbia, Automobile Old Timers (Indpls.); Rotary. Address: Indianapolis IN

MULLANEY, JOHN BARRY, newspaperman; b. Elmira, N.Y., Oct. 24, 1900; s. David and Anna M. (Barry) M.; student Cornell, 1918-21; m. Irene S. Riffle, Nov. 16, 1921; children—Elinor Jane (Mrs. Willard N. Adams), Irene Ann (Mrs. R. L. Traxler), Emily (Mrs. J. L. Rice). With Corning (N.Y.) Evening Leader, 1916-18, Ithaca (N.Y.) News, 1918-20; Buffalo Courier, 1921-22; news editor Rochester (N.Y.) Jour.-Am., 1922-29; news editor Cleveland News, 1929-43, associate editor, also chief editorial writer, 1943-53, managing editor, 1953-71; assistant editor Cleveland Plain Dealer, 1960-71, assistant to the publisher, 1963-71. Mayor of Beachwood Village, Ohio, 1945-52. Trustee Family Service Association, Cleveland, also Welfare Fedn. Mem. Am. Soc. Newspaper Editors, Nat. Conf. Editorial Writers (chmn. 1952), C. of C., Asso. Press Managing Editors Association (director) American Council on Education for Journalism, Sigma Delta Chi. Clubs: Cleveland City (pres. 1952), Canterbury Golf, National Press (Washington). Home: Beachwood OH Died Sept. 18, 1971.

MULLEN, RUTH ACKERMAN (MRS. FRANK A. MULLEN), assn. exec. Adminstr. Queensboro Soc. Prevention Cruelty to Children, N.Y.C.; asst. adminstr. YWCA. Address: Jamaica Estates NY Died Oct. 15, 1969; buried Hamden CT

MULLEN, WILLIAM E., lawyer; b. in Ill., July 25, 1866; LL.B., U. of Mich., 1893. Practiced in Wyoming since 1895; atty gen. of Wyo., 1905-11; commr. to compile laws of Wyo., 1910-20; Supreme Court reporter, Wyo., since 1915; dir. and gen. counsel Am. Nat. Bank. Trustee Pershing Memorial Hosp. Republican. Clubs: Chamber of Commerce, Cheyenne Country. Home: 420 E. 22d St. Office: Hynds Bldg., Cheyenne WY*‡

MULLER, ADOLF LANCKEN, architect; b. Bklyn., Feb. 24, 1898; s. Adolf and Alice Marie (von der Lancken) M.; grad. Poly. Prep. Sch., Bklyn., 1915; B.S., Mass. Inst. Tech., 1918; M.S., Columbia, 1922; m. Eleanor Elizabeth Benger, Apr. 26, 1924; 1 dau., Elizabeth (Mrs. James A. Daugherty, Jr.). Archtl. Designer George B. Post, Alfred Bossom, also Starrett & Van Vleck, 1919-25; designer Halsey McCormack & Helmer, Inc., N.Y.C., 1925-32, architect, 1935-72, exec. v.p., 1935-54, pres., treas., 1954-68, then cons.; pvt. archtl. practice, 1932-35; designer banks, N.Y.C. area. Served as sgt. 1st class, C.W.S., U.S. Army, World War I. Mem. A.I.A., L.I. Hist Soc., Beta Theta Pi. Club: Mass. Institute Technology (N.Y.C.). Home: Brooklyn NY Died Nov. 21, 1972.

MULLER, JONAS NORMAN, physician, pub. health adminstr., educator; b. N.Y.C., Feb. 7, 1920; s. Henry and Dorothy (Peristein) M.; B.S. magna cum laude, Harvard, 1940; M.D., Columbia, 1943; M.P.H., U. Mich., 1948; D.Sc., N.Y. Med. Coll., 1967; m. Charlotte Feldman, Mar. 14, 1942; children—Jeremy Lewis, Sara Linda. Pub. health med. officer Cal. Health Dept., 1947-48; asst. health officer, Oakland, Cal., 1948-50; staff dir. med. care Am. Pub. Health Assn., 1952-56; asso. prof. pub. health Yale, 1952-56; prof., chmn. dept. preventive medicine N.Y. Med. Coll., 1956-69. Vice chmn. East Harlem Council Community Planning; mem. Nat. Bd. Med. Examiners. Recipient Haven Emerson award N.Y. City Pub. Health Assn., 1968. Diplomate Am. Bd. Preventive Medicine. Fellow Am. Pub. Health Assn. (vice chmn. tech. devel. bd.); Am. Coll. Preventive Medicine; mem. N.Y. State Acad. Preventive Medicine (past dir.), N.Y. State, N.Y. County med. socs., Assn. Tchrs. Preventive Medicine (exec. com.), A.M.A. Alpha Omega Alpha, Phi Beta Kappa, Phi Kappa Phi, Delta Omega. Editor: (with others) Readings in Medical Care. Home: Leonia NJ Died Mar. 26, 1969.

MULLER, SIEMON WILLIAM, educator; born Blagoveshchensk, Russia, May 9, 1900; s. Wilhelm Peter and Evdokiia (D'iachkova) M.; candidate of commerce, Comml. Coll., 1917; B.A., U. Ore., 1927; M.A., Stanford, 1929, Ph.D., 1930; m. Vera Alexander Vilamovsky, June 23, 1928; 1 son, Eric Siemon. Instr. Stanford, 1927-30, asst. prof., 1930-36, asso. prof., 1936-41, prof. geology, 1941-70; geologist U.S. Geol. Survey, 1931-70; mem. Mil. Geology Unit, 1942-43; cons. USAAF constrn. permafrost areas, Alaska, 1943-45. Awarded Silver medal by Comml. Coll.; citation for meritorious service with Armed Forces in Arctic; Freedom medal. Fellow Geol. Society of America (council 1948-51); member of Paleontological Society (president 1963-64), Geol. Society London, Calif. Acad. Scis., American Assn. Petroleum Geologists, Sigma Xi. Home: Palo Alto CA Died Sept. 9, 1970; ashes interred Skylawn Memorial Parks, San Mateo CA

MULLIGAN, CATHARINE A(RCHER), home economist; b. Spartanburg, S.C., Sept. 29, 1875; d. Alfred B. and Florence Carroll (Archer) M.; B.E. and B.A., Converse (S.C.) Coll., 1895; grad. Oread Inst., Worcester, Mass., 1902; unmarried. Teacher Spartanburg city schs., 1896-01; head of dept. home economics, Ga. Normal and Industrial Coll., Milledgeville, Ga., 1902-4; head of dept. domestic science, Winthrop (S.C.) Normal and Industrial Coll., 1904-8; head of dept. home economics, Fla. State Coll., for Women, 1908-9; dean of women and asso. prof. home economics, U. of Tenn., 1909-14; prof. home economics, Converse Coll., 1914—. Mem. council Am. Home Economics Assn., 1908-19. Methodist. Address: Spartanburg SC‡

MULLIGAN, CHARLES WISE, clergyman; b. St. Louis, Oct. 12, 1905; s. Charles G. and Mary E. (Wise) M.; A.B., St. Louis U., 1928, M.A., 1933. Ordained priest Roman Catholic Ch., 1939; redactor Modern Schoolman, 1943-69; librarian Fusz Meml. Coll. Philosophy and Letters St. Louis U., 1952-69, instr., 1960-69. Recipient Austin G. Schmidt, S.J. certificate of merit Loyola U. Press, 1962. Mem. Am. Acad. Polit. and Social Sci., Alpha Sigma Nu. Author: (with Kammer and Diebold) Correct Writing, 1952, Adult Writing, 1953; (with Kammer) Writing Handbook, 1953; For Writing English, 1960. Address: St Louis MO Died June 3, 1969.

MULLIKEN, OTIS E., govt. official; b. Medford, Mass., March 20, 1907; s. William Emery and Edith Jennie (Otis) M.; student Lexington High Sch. Lexington, Mass., 1920-24; A.B., Harvard U., 1928, M.A., Ph.D., 1934, grad. student, 1932-34; m. Jean Buford Hayden, May 4, 1935; children—Carolyn Weymouth (Mrs. Hubert R. Halkin), Sherrill Jean (Mrs. Arthur Amory Houghton III). Tchr. econs., 1930; instr. economics, University of California, Los Angeles, 1930-32; chief of labor division agricultural adjustment administration department agr., chief labor div., office of agrl. war relations, 1935-43; dept. of state, 1943; chief, div. of internat. labor, social and health affairs, 1943; advisor Internat. Labor Conf., Phila., 1945, Paris, 1946; United Nations Conf. on Internat. Orgn., San Francisco, 1945, Gen. Assembly and Econ. and Social Council of United Nations, London, 1946, Economic and Social Council of U.N., New York, May 1946, Sept. 1946; later spl. asst. to dir. Office of International Economic and Social Affairs, Dept. of State, chief Bur. Human Resources, until 1970; adviser International Labor Conference, 1952-58; professorial lecturer at the American University. Officer in charge of the United Nations Social Affairs; adviser 9th Internat. Conf. Am. States, Bogota, Colombia, 1948; adviser 3d Gen. Conf. UNESCO, Beirut, Lebanon, 1948, 4th Gen. Conf., Paris, 1950, 5th, Florence, Italy, 1951, others; alternate mem. bd. UNICEF. Mem. Am. Econ. Assn., Delta Upsilon. Contbr. to Inter-American Affairs and to International Problems of Peace. Home: Washington DC Died Oct. 31, 1972; buried Lexington MA

MULLIN, SAM S., mfg. executive; born Syracuse, N.Y., Nov. 28, 1914; s. Sam S. and Ann Frances (McGourty) M.; A.B., Holy Cross Coll., 1937; LL.B., Yale, 1940; m. Margaret Fulham, July 12, 1947; children—Ann Frances, Mary Ellen, Sam S., III, John F., Margaret J., Barbara. Admitted to N.Y. bar, 1940; atty. U.S. Treas. Dept., 1940; asst. to gen. counsel Lend Lease Adminstrn. and Office Emergency Mgmt., 1940-41; gen. mgr. adminstrn. Textron, Inc., 1946-48; v.p. Cleve. Pneumatic Tool Co., 1948-49, pres., 1949-60; pres. Pneumo Dynamics Corp., 1960-69, Cleve. Pneumatic Tool subsidiary. Mem. devel. and adv. coms. Case Inst.; trustee Cleve. Community Chest, Cath. Charities, Cleve., St. Vincent Charity Hosp., Cleve.; asso. bd. trustees Holy Cross Coll.; member adv. bd. Ursulline College for Women, Cleve. Served as lt. col. USAAF, 1941-45. Decorated Legion of Merit. Mem. Aerospace Industries Assn., National Machine Tool Builders' Association, Navy League U.S. Clubs: Cleveland Skating, Union, Shaker Heights Country (Cleve.); Wing's (N.Y.C.); Metropolitan (Washington). Home: Cleveland Heights OH Died Apr. 6, 1969.

MULLINS, THOMAS C., coal co. exec.; b. 1922; B.S. in Mech. Engring., Purdue U. Formerly with No. Ill. Coal Corp.; pres. Midland Electric Coal Corp.; exec. v.p. Peabody Coal Co. (subsidiary of Kennecott Copper Corp.), St. Louis, 1963-64, sr. exec. v.p., 1964-65, pres., 1965-68, pres., chief exec. officer, 1968-71. Died Apr. 26, 1971; buried Flossmoor IL

MULROONEY, EDWARD PIERCE, b. N.Y. City; ed. pub. schs.; married; children—Helen, Elizabeth. Began as patrolman N.Y. City police force, 1896, police commr., 1930-33; chmn. Alcoholic Beverage Control Bd., State of N.Y., 1933-36; commr. N.Y. State Dept. Correction, 1936-39; impartial chmn. of hotel industry, City of New York, since Mar. 1, 1939. Catholic. Home: 180 E. 79th St., New York. Office: 41 E. 57th St., New York NY‡

MUMMA, HARLAN L., army officer; b. Findlay, O., Dec. 6, 1894; s. Eber Leslie Edward and Sarah Amanda (Waltz) M.; student Ohio Northern University, Ada, O., 1910-11; B.S., U.S. Military Academy, 1916; m. Juliette Rathbone; children—Juliette Cherie (wife of Lt. Comdr. J. H. Redington, U.S.N.R.), John Rathbone, Harlan L. Commd. 2d lt., U.S. Army, 1916, and advanced through the grades to brig. gen., 1944. Decorations: Legion of Merit, oak leaf cluster; commendation ribbon, oak leaf cluster. Mem. Scabbard and Blade, Torch and Serpent, The Mountain (W.Va. Univ.). Home: Clearwater Beach FL Died Apr. 1972.

MUMMA, JAMES HEBRON, mgmt. cons.; born Lancaster, Pa., Apr. 29, 1915; s. J. Hebron and Grace Wilhelmina (Frey) M.; B.S., Franklin and Marshall Coll., 1940; postgrad. N.Y.U., Cornell U., 1951-53; m. Marjorie Carson, May 19, 1944; children—Marjorie Anne, James, Thomas, William, Phyllis Ann. Personnel asst. Richardson-Merrell, Inc., N.Y.C., 1940-47; personnel mgr. Bigelow Sanford Co., N.Y.C., 1947-55; dir. personnel Continental Baking Co., Rye, N.Y., 1955-60; dir. personnel adminstrn. Raytheon Co., Lexington, Mass., 1960-64; staff v.p. personnel relations Eastern Air Lines, New York City, 1964-66; management consultant, from 1966. Member of Boston Council Against Discrimination, 1961-63; vice president Little League, Rye, 1958-59; mem. personnel adv. com. Winchester Schs., 1962-63. Bd. dirs. United Fund. Served to capt. AUS, 1941-46. Mem. Am. Mgmt. Assn., N.Y. Personnel Mgmt. Assn., N.Y.C. C. of C., Alpha Delta Sigma, Pi Gamma Mu, Sigma Pi. Presbyn. Lion. Address: Rye NY Died Sept. 28, 1971; buried The Columbarium, Presbyn. Ch., Rye NY

MUMMA, MORTON CLAIRE, JR., naval office (ret.); b. Manila, P.I., Aug. 24, 1904; s. Morton Claire and Gail Cass (Zugschwert) M.; B.S., U.S. Naval Acad., 1925; grad. U.S. Submarine Sch., 1928; m. Virginia Page Elder, Oct. 7, 1925; children—Morton Claire, Ann (Mrs. Ralph Meade Dorsey). Commd. ensign U.S. Navy, 1925, and advanced through grades to rear adm., 1946; served at sea in battleships, destroyers, submarines, 1925-42; coach U.S. Navy rifle team, 1927, 28; comdr. U.S.S. S-43, 1935-38, U.S.S. Sailfish, 1940-41; staff mem., submarines of Asiatic fleet, naval liaison with 5th air force, comdr. motor torpedo boat squadrons, 7th Fleet, 1943-44; naval aide to Under-Sec. of Navy, Forrestal, 1944; planning div., Bur. of Naval Personnel, 1944-46; ret. Aug. 1, 1946, advancing to grade of rear adm.; sec.-treas., Jefferson Pub. Co., Inc. and mng. editor, Spirit of Jefferson-Advocate (newspaper), Charles Town, W.Va., from 1946. Dir. and mem. exec. com., Winchester Memorial Hospital. Awarded Navy Cross, Legion of Merit and Gold Star, Army Distinguished unit badge, Sec. of Navy. unit citation, distinguished marksman and pistol expert medals, campaign, service and area medals; decorated with Order of Brit. Empire. Mem. exec. com. and life mem., Nat. Rifle Assn. of Am.; nat. dir. and v.p., Va. div. Izaak Walton League of Am. Episcopalian. Mason. Club: Army Navy (Washington). Ofcl. referee, Nat. Rifle Assn. registered tournaments. Home: Tucson AZ Died Aug. 1968.

MUNDT, WALTER J., controller, sec. Peoples Trust. Co. Address: Hackensack NJ Died Mar. 22, 1971.

MUNGER, HAROLD HENRY, architect; b. Perrysburg, O., July 29, 1890; s. George and Elizabeth (Amon) M.; B.S. in architecture, U. Notre Dame, 1915; m. Lela Marie Hoffman, Oct. 6, 1921; 1 son, Harold C. With Thomas F. Huber, architect, Toledo, 1915-18; designer Stophlet & Stophlet, 1919, C. Howard Crane, Detroit, 1920; archtl. Stophlet, 1919, C. Howard Crane, Detroit, 1920; archtl. designer, supt. constrn. Bd. Edn., Toledo, 1920-23, supervisor constrn. Toledo City Hall, 1923-27; partner C. C. Britsch 1927-55; partner Munger & Munger Assos., 1955-70. Principal works include schools, churches, hospitals, coll. dormitories, and housing projects in Toledo. Member Village Planning Commission, Perrysburg, O., 1939-53, mem. Way Library Bd.; mem. Toledo Port Survey Com., 1942-43; mem. residential areas com. Toledo Planning Commn. for Toledo and Lucas Co.; mem. Ohio State Bd. Examiners of Architects, 1945-70; pres., 1950, 54, 57, 63. Mem. Community Improvement Corp. Perrysburg. Served sgt., U.S. Army, 1918-19. Fellow A.I.A. (pres. Toledo chpt. 1942, 43); mem. Architects Soc. Ohio,

Am. Legion (comdr. 1919-20), Toledo C. of C. (chmn. met. planning com.), Regional Planning Assn. Toledo, Perrysburg Civic Assn., Notre Dame Alumni Association. Roman Catholic. Kiwanian. Clubs: Kiwanis, Notre Dame (Toledo). Author articles in profl. jours. Home: Perrysburg OH Died Nov. 16, 1970; buried St. Rose Cemetery, Perrysburg OH

MUNOZ GRANDES, AGUSTIN, Spanish govt. ofcl.; b. Madrid, Spain, Jan. 27, 1896; s. Fernando Munoz and Maria Grandes; ed. Mil. Acad.; m. Maria Galilea de Munoz, May 12, 1927; 1 son, Agustin. Commd. 2d lt. Spanish Army, 1913, advanced through grades to capt. general, 1957; now v.p. Spanish govt., chief high staff. Recipient numerous decorations, from China, Cuba, Dominican Republic, France, Germany, Italy, Jordan, Portugal, Spain, U.S., Thailand, Venezuela. Roman Catholic. Home: Madrid Spain Died July 11, 1970.

MUNRO, DONALD, neurological surgeon; b. Boston, Mass., Aug. 10, 1889; s. John Cummings and Mary (Squibb) M.; A.B., Harvard, 1911, M.D., 1914; m. Margaret Harbison, May 1, 1928, 1 dau., Mary Frances. Formerly asst. prof. neurol. surgery Harvard Med. Sch., asso. prof. neurosurgery, Boston U. Sch. Med. surgeon in chief and dir. dept. neurosurgery Boston City Hosp. then consultant. Diplomate Am. bds. surgery and neurosurgery; mem. N.E. Surg. Soc., Am. Neurol. Soc., Soc. Neurol. Surgeons, Boston Surg. Soc., Boston Soc. Neurology and Psychiatry, Harvey Cushing Society, A.C.S., A.M.A., Societe de Neuro-Chirurgei de langue Francaise (honorary). Author: Craniocerebral Injuries, 1938; Injuries to the Nervous System, 1952. Contbr. articles on neurosurgery to med. jours. Home: Milton MA Died Mar. 10, 1973.

MUNRO, JAMES ALAN, clergyman; b. Winnipeg, Man., Can., July 7, 1898; s. Archibald and Isabel (Stewart) M.; B.A., tchrs. certificate with 1st class honors, U. Sask.; D.D. (hon.), Knox Coll., Toronto, Can.; m. Donelda Morrison, July 10, 1933 (dec. Oct. 1967). Ordained to ministry of Presbyterian Church; was minister in Rosetown. Sask., then Chilliwack, B.C.; tchr., Zeacandia, Sask., then Coleville, Sask.; sec. nat. missions Presbyn. Ch. Can., 1946-67, exec. dir. Nat. Devel. Fund, 1967-72. Moderator Presbyn. Ch. Can., 1965-66; chmn. nat. religious adv. com. Canadian Broadcasting Co. Trustee United Appeal Met. Toronto. Served to lt. col., Chaplains Corps, Canadian Army. 1940-46. Decorated Mil. Cross. Home: Toronto Ontario Canada Died June 19, 1972.

MUNRO, ROBERT FRATER, corporation dir.; s. William and Margaret (Frater) M.; ed. at Inverness, Scotland; m. A. Nada Swasey, of Boston, June 1, 1891. Ex-pres., now dir. Am. Cotton Oil Co. Mem. St. Andrew's Soc. of N.Y. Clubs: Lawyers, British Schools and Universities. Office: 120 Broadway, New York NY‡

MUNROE, JOHN ALEXANDER, railway official; b. Bradford, Mass., Aug. 18, 1853; s. Rev. Nathan and Lucelia T. M.; Dartmouth, 1871-73, A.M., 1916; m. Hattie Baker, Jan. 18, 1888 (died Apr. 30, 1921). Began as clerk Green Bay & Minn. R.R., 1873; gen. agt., C.,St.P.,M.&O. Ry., at Omaha, Neb., 1881; asst. traffic mgr., same, at Minneapolis, 1882; asst. gen. freight agt. U.P. R.R., 1882-1901; freight traffic mgr. same, 1901-11, in charge of traffic and v.p., 1911-18; traffic mgr., U.P. R.R., Ore. Short Line R.R., L.A.&S.L. R.R., and St. Joseph & Grand Island R.R., Aug. 22, 1918-20, retired; was v.p. Omaha & Council Bluffs St. Ry. Co., retired 1926, now dir. Republican. Home: 3870 Harney St., Omaha NE‡

MUNSON, EDWIN STERLING, ophthalmologist; b. Earlville, Ill., May 8, 1870, M.D., New York Medical College and Flower Hospital, New York, N.Y., 1894. Practiced in New York City, since 1894; formerly prof. ophthalmology and dean College of N.Y. Ophthalmic Hospital; prof. ophthal., N.Y. Med. Coll. and Flower Hosp.; surgeon N.Y. Ophthalmic Hospital; consultant ophthalmologist Flower-Fifth Avenue Hospital, Yonkers General Hospital, State Hospital, Middletown, N.Y., Brunswick General Hospital, Amityville, N.Y. Fellow American College Surgeons; member American Institute Homeopathy, Am. Homoe. Ophthal. Otol. and Laryngol. Soc., Alpha Kappa Kappa. Address: 133 E. 58th St., New York 22 NY‡

MUNSON, GORHAM B., educator, writer, editor; b. Amityville, N.Y., May 26, 1896; s. Rev. Hubert Barney and Carrie Louise (Morrow) M.; A.B., Wesleyan U., Conn., 1917; studied and traveled in Europe, 1921-22; m. Elizabeth Delza (profl. dancer), Apr. 2, 1921. Tchr. English, Ridgefield (Conn.) Sch., 1917-18, 1920-21, Riverdale Country Sch., N.Y. City, 1918-19; free lance journalist until 1924; editor Secession Mag., 1922-24; mng. editor Psychology Mag., 1924-26; mng. editor Grant Publs., 1926-28; editorial adviser Doubleday, Doran & Co., 1928-30, Thos. Y. Crowell Co., 1934-37; lectr. New Sch. for Social Research from 1927; mem. adminstrv. staff Work Projects Adminstrn. Washington, 1939-41; asso. editor Greystone Press, N.Y.C., 1941-42; editor Robert M. McBride Co., 1943, Prentice-Hall, 1944-48, Hermitage House, 1951-55, Thomas Nelson and Sons, New York City, 1955-60; asst. prof. English, Fairleigh-Dickinson U., 1961-66; prof. University of Cal. at Davis, 1966-67; fellow Center for Advanced Studies, Wesleyan U., Conn., 1967-68; distinguished prof. Am. lit. U. Hartford, 1968-69. Recipient Spl. citation New Sch. for Social Research, 1962. Mem. Am. Social Credit Movement (gen. sec. from 1938), Poetry Soc. Am., Delta Kappa Epsilon. Author: Waldo Frank—A Study, 1923; Robert Frost—A Study in Sensibility and Good Sense, 1927; Destinations—A Canvass of American Literature since 1900, 1928; Style and Form in American Prose, 1929; The Dilemma of the Liberated, 1930; Twelve Decisive Battles of the Mind, 1942; Aladdin's Lamp, 1945; The Written Word, 1949; The Writer's Workshop Companion, 1951; Penobscot: Down East Paradise, 1959; Robert Frost: Making Poems for America, 1962; Biography of Walt Whitman, pub. posthumously, 1970. Editor: Best Advice on How to Write, 1952. Collaborator: Humanism and America, 1930; Behold AmericaEditor of New Democracy, 1933-39. Editorial cons. Parapsychology Found., Inc., 1961-65. Contbr. to publs. including Saturday Rev., Yale Rev., The Atlantic, Kenyon Rev., Lit. Rev., Am. Literary Scholarship. Club: The Players. Home: New York City NY Died Aug. 15, 1969; buried Mountain View Cemetery, Camden ME

MUNSON, LEWIS S., JR., chmn. bd. Wilmington Trust Co. Died Jan. 18, 1971.

MUNSON, SAMUEL EDGAR, physician; b. Sangamon County, Ill., Aug. 25, 1866; s. Joel Martin and Elizabeth Frances (Van Hook) M.; student Valparaiso (Ind.) U., 1887-89; M.D., Northwestern U., 1893; post grad. work U. of Gottingen, Germany, 1898, U. of Vienna, 1899; m. Daisy North, June 9, 1897; 1 dau., Mary Elizabeth. Practice in Mt. Pulaski, Ill., 1893-98, in Springfield, Ill., since 1899; mem. Springfield Hosp. staff since 1900, pres., 1910; mem. med. advisory bd. Dept. Pub. Health, State of Ill., 1936-41. Served as mem. Med. Advisory Bd. during World War. Fellow Am. Coll. Physicians (gov. for Ill., 1923-41; v.p., 1941); diplomate Am. Bd. Internal Medicine; mem. A.M.A., Ill. State Med. Soc. (pres. 1938), Miss. Valley Med. Soc., Central Il. Dist. Med. Soc. (past pres.), Sangamon County Med. Soc. (past pres.), Phi Rho Sigma. Democrat. Member Christian Church. Mason (K.T., 32 deg.). Clubs: Kiwanis and Illini Country (Springfield). Contbr. med. articles to jours. Home: 712 S. 2d St. Office: Ridgely Bank Bldg., Springfield IL‡

MURALT, CARL LEONARD DE, cons. engr.; b. Brooklyn, N.Y., Jan. 29, 1873; s. Carl and Lily (Wegmann) de M.; M.E. and E.E., Polytechnic of Zurich, Switzerland, 1895; post-grad. work, U. of Munich; m. Jeanette Lathrop, Dec. 10, 1898. Entered employ of Gen. Electric Co., 1895, first in shops, then in engring. dept., Schenectady; detailed to German branch of the co., 1897, as engr. of lighting and power dept. and built some of the most important electric plants in Europe; entered employ of Brown, Boveri & Co., Swiss engrs., 1900; original work in high tension power transmissions and electrification of mountain rys.; returned to U.S., 1902, and established firm of Muralt & Co., engrs., in N.Y. City; prof. elec. engring. U. of Mich., 1907-13; cons. engr. since 1913. Mem. Am. Inst. E.E., Am. Soc. C.E., Verein Deutscher Ingenieure, Elektrotechnischer Verein, Gesellschaft Ehemaliger Polytechniker. Clubs: University (Ann Arbor, Mich.); Players (New York); Herrenclub (Munich). Contbr. to Trans. of Am. Inst. Elec. Engrs. Portrait painter. Address: 23 Fuersten St., Munich Germany‡

MURCHISON, CLAUDIUS TEMPLE, econ. advisor Am. Cotton Mfrs. Inst.; b. Hickory, North Carolina, April 17, 1889; son Claudius Murat and Alice Penelope (Temple) M.; A.B., Wake Forest (N.C.) College, 1911; Ph.D., Columbia University, 1919; married Constance Waterman, June 24, 1916; children—Nancy Croom, Cameron, David Claudius; married 2d, Esther L. Devine, August 21, 1951. Lecturer in economics, Columbia, 1915-16; assistant professor economics, Miami Univ. 1916-18, Hunter Coll., 1918-20, New York U., 1920-21; asso. prof. U. of N.C., 1921-22, prof. 1922-34, dir. U.S. Bur. Foreign and Domestic Commerce, mem. exec. com. Commercial Policy Com. of U.S., mem. bd. Export-Import Bank of Washington, 1934-35; pres. Cotton Textile Inst., 1935-49, econ. advisor; mem. Cotton Mill Adv. Comm. to W.P.B., 1942-45, and to O.P.A., 1943-46; advisor U.S. delegation Internat. Cotton Conf., 1954. Mem. Am. Econ. Assn., Am. Statis. Assn., Alpha Chi Rho, Episcopalian. Club: Merchants (N.Y.C.), Author: Resale Prize Maintenance, 1919; King Cotton is Sick, 1930; Japan and the World Cotton Goods Trade, 1952; World Trade and the United States, 1953. Co-author: Management Problems, 1931; Culture Below the Potomac, 1933. Contbr. on econ. subjects. Home: Arlington VA Died Aug. 1968.

MURCHISON, CLINTON WILLIAMS, industrialist; b. Athens, Tex., 1895; student Trinity U., San Antonio; married; children—John Dabney, Clinton Williams, Burk (dec.). Pres. Delhi Oil, 1948—; owner First Nat. Bank of Athens, City Transportation, Dallas, Royal Gorge Bridge and Amusement Co., Colo.; partner with Howard Reed in raising Brahman cattle, Acuna Ranch, Mexico; other large company interests and holdings include many connected with railroads, steamships, real estate, gas, oil, publishing, office equipment, insurance, motion picture theatres, restaurants, fishing tackle. Office: Dallas TX Died June 20, 1969; buried Athens TX

MURDOCK, HENRY TAYLOR, drama, movie critic; b. Phila., Mar. 7, 1902; s. Samuel George and Katherine (Taylor) M.; m. Martha M. McConnell; children—Margery Ann, David Henry. Formerly drama, movie critic Pub. and Evening Ledgers, Phila., Chgo. Sun, Phila. Inquirer; publicity for Columbia Pictures, N.Y.C., RKO-Radio, Hollywood, Cal., Robin Hood Dell. Recipient Front Page award for drama criticism Chgo. Sun, 1946. Democrat. Home: Philadelphia PA Died Apr. 20, 1971; buried West Laurel Hill Cemetery, Philadelphia PA

MURDOCK, JOHN ROBERT, congressman; b. Lewis County, Mo., Apr. 20, 1885; s. John and Elizabeth (Wallace) M.; A.B., Kirksville (Mo.) State Teachers Coll., 1912; A.M., State U. of Ia., 1925; grad. work U. of Ariz., 1923, U. of Calif., 1929; m. Myrtle M. Cheney, Aug. 27, 1906; children—Rachael Weber, David Nathaniel, John Benjamin. Country school teacher, 1904-07; high sch. prin., 1908-10; instr. Tempe Teachers Coll., Tempe, Ariz., 1914-32, U. of Calif., 1929, on leave; dean Ariz. State Teachers Coll., 1933-37; mem. 75th to 82nd Congresses (1937-53), Ariz. 1st dist. Mem. Phi Delta Kappa. Democrat. Conglist. Mason (32 deg.), K.P. Author: Constitution of Arizona, 1929; Constitutional Development of Arizona, 1933. Home: Tempe AZ Died Feb. 1972.

MURDOCK, MARCELLUS MARION, publisher; b. Wichita, Kan., Feb. 14, 1883; s. Marshall Mortimer and Victoria (Mayberry) M.; ed. Wichita grade and high schs.; m. Mabelle Claire Armour, July 23, 1902 (dec.); children—Marshall Mayberry, Victoria (Mrs. Robert Bloom), Janet Mary (Mrs. Foster Jennings), Jane (Mrs. Ward Colwell). With Wichita Eagle and Beacon, 1902-70, beginning as reporter, held various positions, became pub., now chmn. bd., pres.; exec. vice pres. Radio Station KFH; Pres. The Wichita Eagle and Beacon Pub. Company, Inc. Mem. Community Chest, Library Bd. and Y.M.C.A. Served with M.I. in World War I. Breveted aviation pilot by Orville Wright, July 2, 1929. Capt. Kansas Wing, Civilian Air Patrol. Mem. Wichita Chamber of Commerce (chmn. aviation com. 10 yrs.), Aero Chamber of Commerce, National Aeronautical Assn. (treas. Wichita chapter), AOPA, The Air Force League, Sigma Delta Chi, Conquistadores Del Cielo. Republican. Methodist. Mason (past potentate Midian Shrine), (dir. Royal Order of Jesters), Clubs: Wichita, Wichita Flying, Quiet Birdmen; Prairie. Home: Wichita KS Died Mar. 10, 1970.

MURLIN, JOHN RAYMOND, b. Auglaize County, O., Apr. 30, 1874; s. John A. and Isabel (Hamilton) M.; B.S., Ohio Wesleyan U., 1897, A.M., 1899; Ph.D., U. of Pa., 1901; D.Sc., Ohio Wesleyan, 1918, Ursinus Coll., Collegeville, Pa., 1928; m. Josephine Seaman (A.B., Ohio Wesleyan, 1897), Sept. 7, 1899. Prof. biology, Ursinus College, Collegeville, 1901-03; instr. and asst. prof. physiology, New York U., 1903-09; asst. prof., Cornell U. Med. Coll., 1909-17; Harvey lecturer, New York Acad. of Medicine, 1917; prof. physiology and dir. Dept. of Vital Economics, U. of Rochester, 1917; emeritus, 1945; Mellon lecturer at the Univ. of Pittsburgh, 1945; apptd. dir. div. food and nutrition Med. Dept., U.S. Army, Sept. 1917. Chmn. com. on food and nutrition Nat. Research Council, 1919-22. Commd. maj., San. Corps., A.U.S., 1917, lt. col., 1918; col. San. Res. Corps, 1919. Mem. Am. Physiol. Soc., Am. Soc. Biol. Chemists, Soc. Exptl. Biology and Medicine, Harvey Soc., A.A.A.S., Am. Chem. Soc. Am. Phil. Soc., Am. Inst. Nutrition (pres. 1934-36), Rochester Academy of Medicine (honorary life mem.), Sigma Xi, Phi Beta Kappa, Sigma Alpha Epsilon. Translator and editor: Tigerstedt's Text-Book of Physiology, 1906. Contbr. numerous papers on physiol. research, especially nutrition, also chapters on energy metabolism in Abt's System of Pediatrics, 1923, and Barkers' Endocrinology and Metabolism, 1922. Editor Jour. of Nutrition, 1928-39. Mem. White House Conf. on Child Health and Protection, 1930, 31; del. to Internat. Conf., Health Sect., League of Nations, Berlin, 1932; mem. Food and Nutrition Bd., Nat. Research Council 1941-45. Received scientific distinction award, A.G.M.A., 1940. Home: 55 Oak Lane (10). Office: U. of Rochester Sch. of Medicine, Rochester 7 NY‡

MURNANE, GEORGE, b. Brooklyn, N.Y., Sept. 13, 1887; s. William and Katherine (McNamara) M.; C.E., Lehigh U., 1910; m. Edith Pinkney, Oct. 7, 1914. With New York Telephone Co., 1910-12, H. K. McCann Co., 1912-18; deputy commr. for France, Am. Red Cross, May 1918-May 1919; v.p. New York Trust Co., 1919-28; mem. Lee, Higginson & Co., 1928-35. Monnet, Murnane & Co., 1935-45; partner Lazard Freres & Co., 1945; dir. Corning Glass Works, Magma Copper Co., Internat. Minerals & Metals Corp., Wyandotte Chem. Corp. Trustee emeritus of the Rockefeller Univ. Republican. Roman Catholic. Clubs: Racquet and Tennis, Piping Rock. Home: Brookville LI NY Died Feb. 20, 1969.

IURPHEY, ROBERT JOSEPH, bus. cons.; b.)ecatur, Ill., Aug. 7, 1898; s. Joseph M. and Ella (Rike) 1.; B.S., University of Pennsylvania, 1922; C.P.A., U. 'l., 1923; m. Phillis Hamman, Apr. 21, 1923 (dec. July 966); children—Myram (Mrs. R. L. Condon), Martha Mrs. D. L. Trimmer); m. 2d, Gladys Goltermann, Oct. 969. Mem. firm Murphey, Jenne & Jones, C.P.A.'s,)ecatur, Ill., 1922-67; bus. cons. 1967-70; director of Vagner Castings Co., A. E. Staley Mfg. Co. (Decatur), 'itizens Bldg. Corp., Miss. Valley Structural Steel Co. 1em. Council Theol. Edn. United Presbyn. Ch. U.S.A., 961-64. Mem. Am. Inst. C.P.A.'s (v.p. 1958-59, mem. ccounting prins. bd.), Ill. C. of C. (past dir.), Ill. Soc. :.P.A.'s (pres. 1957-58), Beta Alpha Psi, Beta Theta Pi. 'resbyn. Mason (32 deg.). Clubs: Country of Decatur,)ecatur: Union League (Chgo.). Home: Decatur IL)ied June 28, 1970.

IURPHY, D. HAYES, elec. supply mfr.; b. 'rovidence, Nov. 24, 1877; s. Daniel E. and Rosalie Maher) M.; B.S., University Wisconsin, 1900; LL.D., Jniversity of Hartford, 1959; married Jessica Esther)avis, January 20, 1904 (deceased, January 22, 1958); hildren—Rosalie (Mrs. Ambrose Judd Massey), essica (Mrs. Edward Phillip Jones), Marjorie (Mrs. Jerard Hassett Morrissey), John Davis, Robert Henry. ec., treas. Am. Interior Conduit Co., Milw., 1900-02; en. mgr. Safety Armorite Conduit Co., Pitts., 1902-09; ec., treas. Am. Conduit Mfg. Co., Pitts., 1909-10, pres., 910-13, pres. treas., 1913-19 (name of company hanged to The Wiremold Co., and located at Hartford, 'onn., 1919); pres. The Wiremold Co., 1919-55, chmn. f the board, from 1955; dir. Conn. Bank & Trust Co.)ir. St. Francis Hosp.; Am. Sch. for the Deaf, W. Iartford; mem. Jr. Achievement of Hartford, Inc. Jr. Achievements, Inc., Nat. Conf. Christians and Jews, nc., N.Y.C.; bd. adv. St. Joseph Coll. Mem. bus. adv. ouncil Dept. Commerce; chief, certification sect.)PM, Washington, 1941-42. Mem. West Hartford 'own Council, 1935-37, 37-39, chmn. bldg. com., 935-36, v.p., 1937-39. Mem. Mfrs. Assn. of Hartford 'ounty (dir.), Mfrs. Assn. of Conn., Inc. (treas. 1944), Jat. Elec. Mfrs. Assn. (pres. 1938), National Association of Manufacturers (member clergy industry elations advisory committee), Boy Scouts Am., Iartford C. of C. (dir. 1941-44), West Hartford C. of C. chmn. mfrs. div. 1948-49), YMCA (dir. 1940-46, hmn. indsl. com. 1940-50, trustee from 1950), Nat. 'onf. Christians and Jews, Inc. (regional co-chairman), igma Chi. Clubs: Civitan, Electrical Manufacturers president 1942, 43), Hartford, Wampanoag Country past president). Recipient McAuliffe medal Diocesan abor Inst. of Conn., 1949. Home: West Hartford CT lso Groton Long Point CT

IURPHY, DANIEL JOSEPH, lawyer, govt. ofcl.; b.)orchester, Mass., Aug. 17, 1896; s. Andrew P. and Annie (McGivern) M.; A.B., Boston Coll., 1918; tudent Harvard Cadet Sch., 1919, Harvard University, 920, Catholic University of America, 1921; LL.B., Boston U., 1922; m. Esther M. Lydon, Oct. 19, 1929; 1 lau., Elizabeth Ann. Admitted to Mass. bar, 1922, Fed. ar, 1923; pvt. law practice, Boston, 1922-35; litigation tty. N.R.A., Washington, 1935; principal atty. Fed. Trade Commn., Washington, 1935, chief div. litigation rom 1946, asst. dir. Bur. Antideceptive Practices, 950-53, dir. 1953-54, legal advisor on deceptive ractices Bur. of Litigation, FTC, 1955-57, assistant lirector of the Bur. Litigation, 1957-62, director Bur.)eceptive Practices, 1962-65. Past pres. trade com. 'ed. Credit Union. Mem. Mass., Fed., U.S. Supreme Ct. ar assns., Am. Legion. Roman Catholic. Westmoreland Hills MD Died Aug. 18, 1970.

MURPHY, EDMOND GEORGE, banker; b. Bklyn., May 18, 1910; s. John A. and Irene (Swift) M.; B.S., N.Y.U., 1941; m. Joanna J. Wirska, Apr. 14, 1942; hildren—Joan, Barbara, Edmond, Thomas. With 'hase Nat. Bank, N.Y.C., 1925-27; asst. mgr. Mfrs. Trust Co., N.Y.C., 1927-39; examiner N.Y. State Banking Dept., 1939-49; with Lincoln Savs. Bank, 3klyn., 1949-73, pres., chief exec. officer, 1970-73, also rustee; dir. Savs. Bank Trust Co. Trustee St. Francis 'oll., Bklyn. Served to comdr. USNR, 1942-46. Mem. Am. Inst. C.P.A.'s, N.Y. Soc. C.P.A.'s. Clubs: Brooklyn; Jnion League (N.Y.C.); Cherry Valley (Garden City). Home: Garden City NY Died 1973.

MURPHY, (MERLE) FARMER, newspaper corr.; b. Vapello, Ia., June 29, 1871; s. Rev. Samuel Soule and 'rudence Matilda (Kibben) M.; student Baker Univ., 3aldwin, Kan., 1887-89; B.A., Williams College, 1893; n. Beatrice Landon Goodrich, June 19, 1899; hildren—Goodrich Kibben, Harriet Prudence (Mrs. 'aul A. Borglum). Began with Topeka State Jour., 1893, Washington corr., 1895-96; with Chicago Tribune, 1897-1919, New York corr., 1897-1917, mgr. Tribune European Bureau and pub. Army Edition of Tribune, 'aris, 1918, corr. Central Europe, hdqrs. Vienna, 1919; with Am. Relief Adminstrn. in Central Europe and Russia, 1919-23; with Baltimore Sun as corr., N.Y. City, 1925, Washington, 1926, 1929-31, 1933-34, London, 1927-29, 1932, Berlin, 1931; in Trade Agreements Div., Dept. of State, 1934-35; Publicity Div. Dem. Nat. Com., Washington, 1936, 42. Mem. Am. Geog. Soc. Clubs: Nat. Press (Washington); Williams (New York). Home: New Canaan CT‡

MURPHY, FRANCIS DANIEL, physician; b. New Diggings, Wis., Nov. 7, 1895; s. Michael J. and Mary (Driscoll) M.; B.S., Marquette U., 1918, M.D., 1920, LL.D., 1961; M.S., U. Pa., 1924; m. Madaline McNamara, June 27, 1925; children—Joan Ellen, Francis Daniel. Began practice in Milwaukee, 1920; specializes in internal medicine; clin. dir. Milwaukee Co. Hosp., 1924-58, emeritus; prof. medicine, Marquette U., 1928-58, emeritus; chief staff emeritus St. Joseph's Hosp. Certificate of Honor, A.M.A., 1933, for special work on Bright's Disease; special research on nephritis at Milwaukee County Hosp. Named Marquette U. Alumnus of year, 1956, Francis D. Murphy Chair Medicine established Marquette U., 1957. Fellow Am. Coll. Physicians, A.M.A., Am. Coll. Dentists (hon.); mem. Central Soc. for Clin. Research, Wis. State and Milwaukee County med. socs., Milwaukee Acad. Medicine, Chicago Soc. of Internal Medicine, Milwaukee Surg. Soc., Am. Therapeutic Soc., Am. Heart Assn., Soc. Internal Medicine (Am. bd.), Wis. Hist. Soc., A.A.A.S., American Soc. for Study of Arteriosclerosis, Am. Found for High Blood Pressure, American Geriatric Society, Alpha Sigma Nu, Alpha Omega Alpha, Phi Beta Pi. Catholic. Clubs: University, Wisconsin. Author: Dr. Murphy's Bedside Clinics (8 vols.), 1934-39; Medical Emergencies, 1955. Wrote section on Bright's Disease, Tice's Practice of Medicine, 1937; Lipoid Nephrosis; Acute Diffuse Glomerular Nephritis; Phases of Renal Edema. Contbr. numerous articles to med. pubs. and yearly review on Bright's Disease for Cyclopedia of Medicine. Home: Milwaukee WI Died June 15, 1968.

MURPHY, FRANCIS S., publisher; b. New Haven, Conn., October 12, 1882; s. Henry J. and Mary A. (Dunn) M.; ed. Hartford grammar and high schs.; A.M. (honorary), Trinity College; married Iva (Marsh) Murphy, October 16, 1907; 1 son, Warner. Began as errand boy Hartford Times, 1898, and since in their employ, pub. in 1936 and sec. of corp., 1928-71; trustee Mechanics Savs. Bank. Life director of New England Council; chairman of Conn. aeronautics commission. Trustee Gannett Newspaper Foundation, Julius Hartt Foundation Corporation, American Sch. for the Deaf. Director Family Service Soc., Hartford County Y.M.C.A., Conn. State Chamber of Commerce, Hartford Chamber of Commerce (vice pres.); mem. U.S. Civil Service Loyalty Bd. for New England; dir. Newington Home for Crippled Children. Recipient Presidential Citation Medal for Merit. Mem. National Planning Assn. of New England. Clubs: Hartford, University (Hartford); Wings (New York); Farmington Country. Home: West Hartford CT Died Aug. 17, 1971; buried Fairview Cemetery, West Hartford CT

MURPHY, HENRY KILLAM, architect; b. New Haven, Conn., Aug. 10, 1877; s. John and Alice Button (Killam) M.; A.B., Yale, 1899, grad. study, 1899-1900, hon. B.F.A., 1913; student Atelier Masqueray, N.Y. City; m. Rosalie Smith Exum (widow of Dr. Wyatt P. Exum), Feb. 28, 1949. Began practice N.Y. City, 1906; mem. firm Murphy & Dana, 1908-20, Murphy, McGill & Hamlin, 1921-23, alone since 1924. Prin. works: Loomis Inst., Windsor, Conn., 1912; Yale-in-China, Changsha, China, 1913-23; Yenching U., Peking, China, 1918-32; Pacific Bldg., Manila, P. I., 1920; Security Ins. Bldg., New Haven, Conn., 1924. Apptd. archtl. adv. to Nat. Govt., China, 1928, architect for city planning of Nanking as capital of China, 1929, for Revolutionists Memorial Group, Nanking, 1930-34. Mem. Chinese-Am. bd. of trustees Nat. Cultural and Econ. Inst., Peiping. Republican. Clubs: Yale (New York); Graduate (New Haven); American (Shanghai, China). Author of chapter on Chinese architecture in China volume of United Nation's Series. Lecturer on New China," Consultant U.N.R.R.A., 1945-46. Address: Yale Club., N.Y.C.; also 140 E. NYC NY‡

MURPHY, JAMES SHIELDS, mining man; b. Boston, Mass., Dec. 1, 1870; s. John White and Margaret (Colford) M.; spl. studies Boston Coll., Holy Cross Coll., Columbia U.; unmarried. Began as reporter Boston Herald, later N.E., rep. Week's Sport, Sporting Times, Dramatic News; publisher The Referee, first sporting paper, Boston, The Golfer, first golf publn. in America, Motors, first motor publn. in America, Land and Water, first of its kind in America; moved to San Francisco, 1910; now pres. and mgr. Murphy Mining Co., and is largely interested in other mines in Calif., Nev. and Ariz. Mem. Arts and Crafts Soc., Theosophical Soc., Hindu Club. Catholic. Home: 1678 Sacramento St., San Francisco, Calif. Address: Tonopah NV*‡

MURPHY, JOHN PATRICK, business exec.; b. Westboro, Mass., Apr. 25, 1887; s. Patrick and Margaret (Mahoney) M.; student Holy Cross College, Worcester, Mass., 1906-08; LL.B., Univ. of Notre Dame, 1912; LL.D. (hon.), John Carroll U., U. Notre Dame; married to Gladys Tate, June 30, 1924. Admitted to bar of Minn., 1913, in gen. law practice, Minneapolis, 1913-15, Wolf Point, Mont., 1915, Glasgow, Mont., 1916-17; sen. counsel U.S. Spruce Prodn. Corp., Portland, Ore., 1918; atty. for Van Sweringen interests, Cleveland, O., 1920-37; dir. several Van Sweringen Cos. including N.Y., C. & St.L. R.R. Co. (Nickel Plate Rd.); pvt. practice of law as partner firm of Morley, Stickle and Murphy, Cleveland, Ohio, 1938-44, firm of Morley, Stickle, Keeley and Murphy, Cleveland, from 1944; pres., dir. The Higbee Co., 1944-62, chairman of board of directors, 1962-68, hon. chmn., 1968-69; director Medical Mutual of Cleveland, Incorporated, Associated Merchandising Corporation, Cleveland Trust Co., Pioneer Alloy Products Co. Mem. lay bd., trustees John Carroll U., Notre Dame U.; trustee St. Vincent Charity Hospital, Cleve. Development Foundation, Air Found.; dir. Greater Cleveland Hosp. Fund. Enlisted U.S. A.C., 1917, commd. 2d lt., 1918, assigned Kelley Field. Director Cleveland Chamber of Commerce, member Northern Ohio Opera Association (exec. com.), Newcomen Soc. Roman Catholic. Clubs: Union, Country, Mid-day, The Court of Nisi Prius, Skating, Kirtland Country (Cleve.); University (N.Y.C.). Home: Cleveland OH Died July 15, 1969; buried St. Luke's Cemetery, Westboro MA

MURPHY, JOSEPH DUDLEY, business exec.; b. Chgo.; s. Michael N. and Jane (Irwin) M.; m. Jane O'Connell, Dec. 5, 1931; 1 dau., Jane. With Stifel, Nicolaus & Co., Chgo., since 1931, pres., 1940-69; v.p., dir. No. Ill. Water, St. Louis County Water, Gary-Hobart Water Corp.; dir. U.S. Sugar Corp., Long Island Water. Mem. Chgo. Art Inst., Mus. Natural History, Chicago Historical Society. Clubs: The Chicago Club, Chicago Yacht, Attic (Chgo.); Edgewood Valley Country; Butterfield Country; Racquet (St. Louis). Home: La Grange IL Died Dec. 11, 1969.

MURPHY, LAWRENCE WILLIAM, journalism; b. Madison, Wis., Oct. 18, 1895; s. Lawrence Bartholomew and Lillian (Nicodemus) M.; B.A., U. of Wis., 1921, grad. study, 1921-23; M.A., U. of N.D., 1923; grad. study, U. of Ill., 1925-29; Litt.D., Marquette U., 1933; m. Alice Harrington, Dec. 26, 1921; 1 son, Lawrence William. Reporter Madison Democrat, 1916; with various newspapers, Wis., Minn., N.D. and Ill., 1916-24; organizer, 1921, head dept. of journalism, Univ. of N.D., 1921-24, asst. prof., 1924-25, acting dir., later dir. courses in journalism, 1925-27, asso. prof. and acting dir. Sch. of Journalism, 1927-29; prof. journalism and dir. Sch. of Journalism, 1929-40; prof. journalism, U. of Ill., 1929-50, professor journalism and communications since 1950; lecturer, Medill Sch. of Journalism, Northwestern U., 1927, Miami U., 1960. Mem. Pub. Relations Council on Edn. Lt. AEF, 1918-19. Mem. ednl. adv. council Pub. Relations Soc. Am., 1964; chmn. Nat. Council on Education for Journalism, 1935-40. Fellow Found. Pub. Relations Research and Edn., N.Y.; mem. Ill. Press Assn. (hon.), Am. Assn. Teachers of Journalism (pres. 1930-31), Am. Assn. Sch. and Depts. Journalism (pres. 1936-37), Am. Legion, Chi Phi, also mem. Kappa Tau Alpha (first national pres. 1966-69). Rotarian. Author: Introduction to Journalism, 1929. Mem. adv. bd. editors Journalism Quar., 1964 (founder, 1st editor). Contbr. to Editor and Publisher. Home: Champaign IL Died Nov. 1969.

MURPHY, MABEL ANSLEY, author; b. Plumville, Pa., Feb. 21, 1870; d. W. B. (M.D.) and Mary Alice (Wood) Ansley; grad. State Teachers' Coll., Indiana, Pa., 1890; post-grad. work, Knox Coll., Galesburg, Ill., 1916-17, Columbia, 1920-23; m. John Davidson Murphy, 1894 (died 1941); children—Howard Ansley, William Donald. Republican. Conglist. Mem. D.A.R. Clubs; League of Am. Penwomen, Writers' (New York). Author: Great Hearted Women, 1920; American Leaders, 1920; Timoleon, 1921; The Torchbearers, 1924; When Rome Reigned, 1926; When Washington Was Young (serial), 1928, (book), 1931; Theodosia (serial) 1930; Thomas Jefferson Goes to College (serial), 1932; Out and Beyond (serial), 1933; Trails (The Evolution of Roads), 1934; They Were Little Once (book), 1939. Specializes in hist. fiction. Pseudonym, Anne S. Lee. Home: Greenridge Ct. Apts., White Plains NY*‡

MURPHY, MORGAN, publisher; b. Superior, Wis., May 28, 1903; s. John T. and Elizabeth (Flynn) M.; student Superior State Teachers Coll., 1920-22; B.S. U. Wis., 1924; student Harvard Grad. Sch., 1924-25; Litt.D., St. John's U.; m. Elizabeth M. Beck, June 24, 1931; children—Elizabeth (Mrs. Duane Schirmer), and John. President, director Evening Telegram Co. (Superior), Fremont Cable TV (Cal.), Mesabi Pub. Co., Virginia, Minn., Ashland Pub. Corp. (Wis.), Pacifica Cable Co. (Cal.), Crystal-Brite Television, Inc., Half Moon Bay, California, Dunedin (Florida) Times. West Coast Printing Company, Pinellas Park, Florida, Largo (Florida) Sentinel, Hibbing (Minn.) Tribune, KTHI-TV, Fargo, N.D., Television Wis., Inc., Madison, Spokane Television, Inc. (Wash.), Apple Valley Broadcasting Co., Yakima, Wash. Trustee Northland College. Mem. Delta Upsilon. Roman Catholic. Elk. Clubs: Kitchi Gammi, Northland Country (Duluth); Madison (Wis.). Home: Superior WI Died Feb. 6, 1971.

MURPHY, ROBERT CUSHMAN, naturalist; b. Brooklyn, N.Y. Apr. 29, 1887; s. Thomas D. and Augusta (Cushman) M.; Ph.B., Brown U., 1911; A.M., Columbia, 1918; D.Sc., honoris causa, Univ. of San Marcos, Lima, Peru, 1925, Brown, 1941; D. Sc. (hon.), Long Island U., 1964; m. Grace E. Barstow, Feb. 17, 1912; children—Alison M. Conner, Robert Cushman, Amos Chafee Barstow. Curator of mammals and birds,

Brooklyn Mus., 1911-17, curator of the dept. natural sci., 1917-20; asso. curator of birds, Am. Mus. Natural History, 1921-26, asst. dir., 1924-36, curator of oceanic birds, 1927-42, chmn. dept. of birds 1942-54, Lamont curator of birds, 1948-55, emeritus 1955-73, research asso., 1955-73. Leader expedition for Am. Mus. Natural History and Brooklyn Mus. into tropical and sub-antarctic Atlantic Ocean, 1912-13; into Lower Calif., Mexico, for Brooklyn Mus., 1915; to coast and islands of Peru for Brooklyn Mus., Am. Mus. Natural History and Am. Geog. Soc., 1919-20; to Peru and Ecuador for Am. Mus. Natural History, 1924-25; to western Mediterranean, 1926; to Pacific Coast of Colombia, 1937, and 1941; to Pearl Islands, 1945; to New Zealand and Islands to the South, 1947-49. Bermuda, 1951, 71, Venezuela and Caribbean Islands, 1952; Peru, 1953-54; Bahama Islands, 1953-54; Antarctica, 1960; del. 3d PanAm. Sci. Cong., Lima, 1924; to 6th Internat. Ornithol. Cong., Copenhagen, 1926; to Brit. Assn. Advancement of Sci., Oxford, 1926; to 7th Pacific Sci. Congress, New Zealand, 1949, Internat. Ornithol. Congress, Upsala, 1950; U.S. delegate 8th Pacific Sci. Congress, P.I. 1953, 9th Pacific Sci. Congress Bangkok, 1957, 12th Pacific Sci. Congress, Canberra, Australia, 1971; pres. Cold Spring Harbor Lab., 1940-52. Mem. Antarctic programs com. NSF, 1963-67; adv. commn. Fire Island Nat. Seashore, 1965-73; exec. council L.I. Univ. at Brookhaven, 1964-73. Recipient Congl. medal for Antarctic Service, also numerous other awards and medals. Fellow Am. Geog. Soc. (councilor), N.Y. Acad. Sci. (v.p. 1924), Am. Ornithologists' Union, A.A.A.S., N.Y. Zool. Soc., Zool. Soc. London; mem. L.I. Biol. Assn., Assn. Am. Geographers, Am. Geophys. Union, Am. Philos. Soc., Nat. Audubon Soc. (past and hon. pres.), Cal. Acad. of Scis., Linnaean Soc. of N.Y., Royal Soc. of N.Z. corr. mem. Deutsche Ornithologische Gesellschaft, Sociedad Ornitologica del Plata (Argentina); Royal Australasian Ornithologists Union; hon. mem. Royal Hungarian Inst., Sigma Xi, Phi Beta Kappa. Unitarian. Clubs: Explorers, Century Assn. Author 12 books. Contbg. editor Geog. Rev. Home: Stony Brook NY Died Mar. 1973.

MURPHY, STANWOOD, lumber co. exec.; b. Pasadena, Cal., 1919. Pres., dir. Pacific Lumber Co.; dir. Bank of Cal. Address: Scotia CA Died Aug. 1972.

MURPHY, TIMOTHY FRANCIS, physician, statistician; b. Lewiston, Me., Dec. 5, 1875; s. Thomas and Mary (Downey) M.; student Bowdoin Coll., 1894-98, Me. Med. Sch., 1899-1902; M.D., George Washington U., 1906; m. Juliana Randall Elliott, Apr. 26, 1910; 1 son, Elliott Munroe. Chief statistician Div. Information, Publication and Records, Bur. of Census. Mem. Nat. Conf. on Nomenclature of Disease. Fellow Am. Pub. Health Assn., A.M.A., Southern Medical Assn. Mem. Society for Prevention of Asphyxial Deaths, American Statistical Assn., Zeta Psi, Phi Chi. Club: University. Author and compiler of statistical articles and reports. Home: 1673 Columbia Rd. N.W. Address: Bureau of the Census, Washington DC*‡

MURPHY, W. LEO, transp. co. exec.; b. La Crosse, Wis., June 21, 1903; s. Michael Pierce and Anna (O'Connor) M.; student La Crosse State U., U. Minn., Marquette U.; m. Mary Agnes Daly, Aug. 27, 1932; children—John Daly, Terrance Michael, Jane Ann, (Mrs. James P. McCormick), Pierce Michael, with Sears Roebuck & Co., 1925-26, Nat. Cash Register Co., 1926-27; with Gateway Transp. Co., Inc., 1928, chmn. bd., from 1960, also dir.; dir. Choats Realty Co., Viterbo Coll., La Crosse, La Crosse Planning Corp. Mem. Viterbo Adv. Bd., 1954-66; mem. La Crosse Police and Fire Commn., 1945-50. Bd. Dirs. Wis. Found. Ind. Colls., from 1954, Viterbo Coll., from 1966; mem. regional council Boy Scouts Am. Decorated Knight comdr. St. Gregory; recipient Silver Beaver award Boy Scouts Am., Catholic Boy Scouts award, 1967. Mem. La Crosse (pres. 1942), Wis. (bd. dirs. 1941-42) C.'s of C. Chgo. Traffic' Club. Roman Catholic. Clubs: La Crosse, La Crosse Country. Elk, K.C. Home: La Crosse WI Deceased.

MURRAY, CHARLES, dean emeritus, veterinarian; b. Greenfield, O., Feb. 8, 1876; s. Philip Oliver and Edith Gertrude (Boyd) M.; B.Pd., Drake U., 1906; student U. of Chicago, 1901; B.S., Ia. State Coll., 1910; D.V.M., Ia. State Coll., 1912; m. Minnie Best, June 2, 1897; children—Herbert St. Clair (dec.), Eleanor Miriam (Mrs. J. H. Watkins), Gertrude Elizabeth (Mrs. Clarence D. Platt), Lois Madelyn (Mrs. Jerome C. Miller). Public sch. teacher, Woodburn, Ia., 1894; supt. high sch., Lucas, Ia., 1898, Tingley, 1900-08, instr. Ia. State Coll., 1908-12, asst. prof. bacteriologist, 1912-16, prof. and head veterinary research inst., 1916-36, dean, Coll. Veterinary Medicine, and dir. Veterinary Research Inst., 1936-43, dean emeritus since 1943. Mem. Ames City council, 1914-16. Mem. Am. Veterinary Med. Assn., Ia. State Veterinary Assn., U.S. Livestock Sanitary Assn., Nat. Research Council, Am. Conf. Research Workers in Animal Diseases, Sigma Xi, Phi Beta Kappa, Phi Kappa Phi, Phi Zeta, Gamma Sigma Delta. Republican. Presbyterian. Club: Osborn Research (Ia. State Coll.). Author: Buchanan's Veterinary Bacteriology (with R.E. Buchanan), 1916; History of Iowa State College, 1947; Diseases of Poultry, 1948. Home: 3503 Woodland Av., Ames IA‡

MURRAY, JAMES P., vice pres. Boeing Airplane Co.; b. Mystic, Conn., Nov. 23, 1892; s. Patrick F. and Margaret (Donovan) M.; student Norwich (Conn.) Free Acad., 1908-11; B.S., Trinity Coll., Hartford, Conn., 1914; m. Evelyn Jensen, Sept. 15, 1926;children—James P., Jr., Ruth Elizabeth. Began as teacher at boys prep. school, 1914; joined Royal Flying Corps, June 1917, and served in Great Britain, 1917-19; flew mail for Post Office Dept., 1920-26; with Boeing Air Transport Co. from 1926, flying mail, 1926-28, Washington rep. from 1928, vice pres. from 1933. Sec. and mem. bd. of govs. Mfrs. Aircraft Assn. Mem. Phi Gamma Delta. Home: Washington DC Died Jan. 20, 1972.

MURRAY, JAMES T., business exec.; b. N.Y. City, Nov. 14, 1897; s. James and Ellen (Lucey) M.; student Harvard; B.A., Fordham U., 1921; LL.B., cum laude, 1923, LL.D., 1951; m. Mary Fraser Macdonald, June 15, 1929. Admitted to bar; in practice law with Hayward & Murray, and predecessors, N.Y. City, from 1921; chairman of board Coca-Cola Bottling Co. of N.Y. and Chas. E. Culpeper Found., Inc. Pres. Murray-Macdonald Found. Clubs: Harvard, Union League (N.Y.C.). Home: New York City NY Died Nov. 13, 1968; buried Alexandria, ONT Canada

MURRAY, JENNIE SCUDDER (MRS. C. EDWARD MURRAY), orgn. exec.; b. nr. Elkton, Md., Aug. 1, 1874; d. Jonathan Montgomery and Isabella D. (Gilbert) Scudder; student Model Sch., Trenton, N.J., 1891-94, Rider Coll., Trenton, 1894-95; m. Stephen F. Reed, Aug. 1, 1900 (died Nov. 5, 1900); m. 2d, Gen. Thomas Stryker Chambers, July 25, 1916 (died Oct. 21, 1919) m. 3d, Gen. C. Edward Murray, Oct. 6, 1921 (died Jan. 12, 1943). Vice regent Gen. David Forman chapter D.A.R., Trenton, N.J., 1920-24, regent, 1924-29; N.J. state regent D.A.R., 1929-32, hon. state regent since 1932; vice pres. gen. Nat. Soc. D.A.R., 1932-35, curator gen., 1941-44, 2d v.p. gen., 1944-47, nat. chmn. printing com., 1944-47, Constitution Hall com. since 1944, also hon. 2d vice president general of nat. soc., D.A.R. Pres. N.J. Soc. Colonial Dames, 1934-38; pres. Daus. Colonial Wars, 1935-38; 1st state vice regent Daus. Am. Colonists, 1924-27; nat. chaplain Daus. Founders and Patriots, 1944-46. Exec. chmn. Trenton Red Cross, 1917-19, chmn. womans div. A.R.C. campaign, Trenton, 1941, mem. A.R.C. board, Trenton, since 1922; honorary member of the A.R.C. Board since 1948. Mgr. N.J. State Hosp. Bd. since May 1934; pres. woman's board Mercer Hosp., Trenton, 1915-17, hon. vice pres. since 1917, chmn. library com.; mem. bd. mgrs. William Trent-House Assn.; exec. chmn. woman's div., 2d, 3d, 4th Liberty Loan; vice chmn. woman's div., Southern Dist. N.J., 5th Liberty Loan; past v.p. Scudder Assn. Mem. Order of Crown, Daus. of Holland Dames, Daus. of Barons of Runnymede, Jinnie Jackson Soc., Children Am. Revolution (organizing pres.), N.J. and Monmouth County hist. socs. Clubs: Ex-Regents D.A.R., Nat. Officers D.A.R., State Officers D.A.R., Contemporary (v.p. 1926-28). Republican. Presbyterian. Received 25th service bar, Trenton chapter, A.R.C., 1945. Home: 301 W. State St., Trenton NJ‡

MURRAY, JOHN TUCKER, educator; b. Rio de Janeiro, Brazil, July 31, 1877; s. David and Mary Alice (Smith) M.; A.B., Dalhousie U., Halifax, N.S., 1897; A.B., Harvard, 1899, A.M., 1900; m. Mabel Wesson, June 25, 1907; children—Jean Wesson, Alisoun Tucker, Beatrice Lovell, David Hill. Mem. faculty, Harvard, since 1919, prof. English, 1929-39, emeritus; dir. Harvard Summer Sch., 1920-24. Enlisted as pvt., inf., British Army, Sept. 1914; detailed to Pub. Sch. Corps, London, later to 3d Batt., Duke of Wellington's Regt., 1915; commd. lt., 1915; later capt.; demobilized 1919. Mem. Phi Beta Kappa, Cambridge Folk-Lore Society. Episcopalian. Clubs: Harvard; Jr. Army and Navy Club (London). Author: English Dramatic Companies (1558-1642), 2 vols., 1910. Address: San Clemente CA‡

MURRAY, LAWRENCE N(EWBOLD), banker; b. N.Y.C., Dec. 20, 1894; s. Francis W. and Mary Gertrud (Lawrenc) M.; grad. St. Paul's Sch., Concord N.H., 1913; B.A., Yale, 1917; m. Mary Brewster Trowbridge, 1918; children—Caroline L., Frank T., Margaret T. Asst. cashier Nat. Comml. Bank, Albany, N.Y., 1922-25; with Koppers Co., Inc., Pitts., 1925, now dir.; asst. cashier Mellon Nat. Bank, Pitts., 1925-29, v.p., dir., 1929-46, pres., dir. Mellon Nat. Bank & Trust Co., Pitts., 1946-58, now dir.; dir. Am. Brake Shoe Co. Alco Products, Incorporated. Republican. Mem. Epsicopalian Ch. Clubs: Duquesne, Pitts. Golf, Rolling Rock (Pitts.); Links, Yale (N.Y.C.). Home: Pittsburgh PA Died May 5, 1971; buried St. Michaels of the Valley Cemetery, Rector PA

MURRAY, O. WILLARD, motion picture co. exec.; b. Norfolk, Va. Oct. 28, 1914; s. Otis Lepage and Lessie (Holstein) M.; B.S., Coll. William and Mary, 1936, M.A., 1937; m. Nancy Christiana Sparks, July 26, 1935 (dec. 1967); children—Julia Christiana (Mrs. Paul Schottler), Willard Burkitt; m. 2d, Kathaleen Ellis, July 1967. Research engr. E.I. duPont de Nemours & Co., Inc., Parlin, N.J., 1937-46; successively research dir., v.p., pres., dir. Color Corp. Am., Burbank, Cal., 1947-54; successively v.p., exec. v.p., pres., dir. Pathe Labs. Inc., Hollywood, Cal., 1954-66, pres., di 1970-73; dir. Chesapeake Industries Inc., 1963-65; v.p dir. Republic Corp., 1963; v.p. Universal TV Inc 1966-70. Registered profl. engr., Cal. Mem. Am. So Cinematographers, Acad. Motion Pictures Arts an Scis. Episcopalian (sr. warden). Home: Van Nuys C. Died 1973.

MURRAY, ROBERT B(LAINE), JR., airline exec.; Hampstead, Md., Jan. 31, 1911; s. R. Blaine and Mab Fairfax (Abbott) M.; student Mercersburg Acad 1927-30; A.B., Harvard, 1934; m. Elinor Leverin Lindley, Dec. 9, 1939. Investment banker C. Williams & Co., Balt., 1934-35, Tucker Anthony & Co N.Y.C. (mem. N.Y. Stock Exchange), 1935-40, N.Y Trust Co., 1940-41; pres. Pa. Economy League, Inc Harrisburg, 1946-53; undersec. commerce fo transportation, 1953-55; v.p., dir. and asst. to pre Baldwin-Lima-Hamilton Corp., Phila., 1955-56; becam v.p. Pam American World Airways, Inc., 1956; di Andrade & Co., Ltd., Honolulu. Mem. board director San Francisco chpt. Am. Nat. Red Cross, Interna Hospitality Center; trustee World Affairs Council N Cal., from 1959; gov. San Francisco Bay Area Counc chmn. San Francisco Pacific Festival, 1958, 59, hor chmn., 1960; chmn. exec. com. Invest-in-Am. Week 1959, general chairman, 1960; v.p. Governmenta Research Council; pres. San Francisco Airport Soun Abatement Committee. Secretary United Republica Finance Committee, Met. N.Y., 1938-40, chmn. 194 exec. com. Eisenhower Nat. Finance Com., 1952; mem Rep. Nat. Finance Com., 1952. Chmn. air coordinatin com., chmn. transportation and storage com. O.D.M mem. bd. N.A.C.A.; chmn. Am. Delegation to Interna Civil Aviation Orgn. Conf., Brighton, Eng., 1953; mem Air Naviagation Development Bd., 1953-56; vice chmr White House Conf. on Hwy. Safety, 1955; mem. Pres Adv. Com. on Weather Control, 1954-56. Truste United Seaman's Service. Bd. assos. Sch. World Bu and Internat. Development at the San Francisco Stat Coll., California. Served as a colonel USAAF, 1942-4 Decorated Legion of Merit, Army Commendatio Medal with 3 oak leaf clusters. Mem. Soc. Nava Architects and Marine Engrs., Govtl. Research Assn Am.-Australian Assn. Cal. (v.p. 1958, pres. 1959), Sa Francisco C. of C. (dir.), Mercersburg Acad. Alumr Council, American Acad. Polit. Sci., Nat. Tax Assn Nat. Def. Transportation Assn. Republican. Clubs Racquet (Phila.), Midday (Phila.); Pilgrims, Pinnacl (New York City); Burlingame (Cal.) Country; 1925 St., Chevy Chase (Washington); San Francisco Gol Home: Hillsborough CA Died June 1969.

MURRAY, TOM, congressman; b. Jackson, Tenn Aug. 1, 1894; B.A., Union U.; LL.B., Cumberland U Began law practice, Jackson, Tenn.; elected dist. att gen. 12th Judicial Circuit, Tenn., 1922-33; with Offic of the Solicitor, Post Office Dept., Washingtor 1933-42; mem. 78th to 82d Congresses 8th Tennesse Dist., 83d-89th Congresses 7th District. Dem. Chmr Dem. Exec. Com., Madison County, Tenn., 1924-3 former mem. State Dem. Exec. Com. Tenn.; del. Dem Nat. Convs., 1928, 32, 36. Served in A.E.F., Franc World War I. Served as comdr. John A. Deaver Pos Am. Legion, Jackson, v.p. State of Tenn.; mem Veterans of Fgn. Wars, Sigma Alpha Epsilon. Hom Jackson TN Died Nov. 1971.

MUSCHAMP, GEORGE MORRIS, mfg. co. exec.; b Phila., Aug. 29, 1908; s. Herbert William and Letiti (Morris) M.; M.E., Drexel Inst. Tech., 1935; m. Sylvi T. Hickman, Jan. 28, 1944; children—George Morris Herbert Mitchell, Robert William, Muriel Anne. Wit Brown Instrument Co., 1930-49, v.p. engring., dir 1943-49; v.p. charge engring. Brown div. Mpls Honeywell Co., 1949-58, v.p. charge engring. inds products groups, 1958-65, v.p. engring. internationa operations, 1965-69. Active local United Communit Fund, Community Assn. Recipient Distinguishe Alumni award Drexel Inst. Tech., 1951; Mary Iric Drexel award, 1962. Registered profl. engr., Pa. Fello Am. Soc. M.E. (dir., mem. exec. and finance coms. A.A.A.S., Instrument Soc. Am.; mem. Franklin Inst Soc. Advancement Mgmt., English Speaking Union U.S. Figure Skating Assn., Germantown Hist. Soc., Soc Antiquaries New Castle-Upon-Tyne, Newcomen Soc N.A. Clubs: Cricket, Engineers, Germantown Cricke Wissahickon Skating (Phila.). Author articles o automation. Home: Clearwater FL Died June 1969.

MUSE, WILLIAM TAYLOR, coll. dean, lawyer; b Gloucester Co., Va., Nov. 27, 1906; s. Peachy Elber and Annie Valentine (Haywood) M.; B.A., U Richmond, 1928, LL.B., 1930; S.J.D., Harvard, 193 m. Alice Harper, Nov. 15, 1941; 1 son, William Wayne Admitted to Va. bar, 1929; partner Patteson & Muse Richmond, 1930-31, asso. Shewmake & Gary, 1931-3 asso. prof. U. Richmond from 1931, prof. law fro 1932, dean law sch. from 1947; vis. prof. law sch. U. Va 1945-46; research fellow law sch. Harvard, 1933-3 40-41. Vice pres. Richmond chapter Am. Red Cros Mem. bd. trustees So Baptist Theol. Sem., Louisvill Dir. Camp Service, A.R.C., ETO, World War II. Pres chmn. bd. U. Richmond Publs., Inc. Mem. Am., V (past pres.), City of Richmond bar assns., Am. La Inst., Phi Beta Kappa, Lambda Chi Alpha, Delta Thet Phi, Omicron Delta Kappa, Pi Delta Epsilon, Ta

Kappa Alpha. Baptist. Mason (Shriner). Author: Virginia Annotations to the Restatement of Torts, 1944. Editor Annual Reports, Va. State Bar Assn., 1941-60. Home: Richmond VA Died Oct. 31, 1971; buried Hollywood Cemetery, Richmond VA

MUSICK, CHARLES ELVON, lawyer; b. Fresno, Cal., Jan. 16, 1890; s. Henry Lewis and Viola Lois (Ayers) M.; student Occidental Coll.; LL.B., University of Southern California, 1915, LL.D., 1958; married to Mabel Ayers, Aug. 6, 1914. Admitted to Cal. bar, 1914; trust counsel Title Ins. & Trust Co., 1920-23; with Musick, Burr & Pinney, 1923-27, Woodruff, Musick, Pinney & Hartke, 1927-31, Faries, Williamson & Musick, 1931-34; sr. mem. Musick & Burrell, 1934-53, Musick, Peeler & Garrett, Los Angeles, 1954-68; chmn. bd., counsel Pineapple Growers Assn. of Hawaii; dir. Western Bancorporation, Rancho Palos Verdes Corp.; v.p., dir. Davis Petroleum Co.; chmn. bd., dir. Missiana Land and Exploration Co.; v.p., counsel Pineapple Research Inst. of Hawaii; dir. Linda Petroleum Co., Walker Lake Land Co. Inc., United Cal. Bank, East Highlands Orange Co. Trustee, U. So. Cal. Mem. State Bar of Cal., Am. Bar Assn., Cal. Inst. Assos. Clubs: California, Los Angeles Country, Bohemian; Pacific (Honolulu). Home: Los Angeles CA Died May 16, 1968.

MUSMANNO, MICHAEL ANGELO, judge; b. nr. Pitts., Apr. 7, 1897; s. Antonio and Maddelena (Castellucci) M.; graduate of George Washington, Georgetown, American and National Univs., U. Rome. Admitted to Pa. bar, 1923; trial lawyer Phila. and Pitts., 1923-31; judge Co. Ct., 1932-34, Ct. Common Pleas, 1935-51; judge Pa. Supreme Ct., 1952-68. Mem. Pa. State Legislature, 1929-31. Mem. Commn. on Internat. Rules of Jud. Procedure; mem. National Citizens Com. on Civil Rights Act. Served as capt. USNR, World War II; aide to Gen. Mark W. Clark; pres. U.S. Bd. Forcible Repatriation, Austria; judge Internat. War Crimes, Tribunal II. Nuremberg. Mem. Am. Legion, Nat. Confedn. Am. Ethnic Groups (president), Vets. Fgn. Wars, Disabled Am. Vets., Mil. Order Purple Heart. Author: Proposed Amendments Constitution, 1929; Black Fury, 1935; After Twelve Years, 1939; The Soldier and the Man, 1946; Listen to the River, 1947; War in Italy, 1948; Ten Days to Die, 1950; Across the Street from the Courthouse, 1954; Justice Musmanno Dissents, 1955; VerdictKommandos, 1961; The Story of the Italians, 1965; An American Replies, 1966; That's My Opinion, 1966; Columbus Was First, 1966; The Glory and the Dream, 1967. Contributor articles mags.; authored bill in Pa. Legislature which outlawed Communist Party, 1951; co-author Federal Communist Control Act, 1954. Home: McKees Rock PA Died Oct. 12, 1968; buried Arlington Nat. Cemetery, Arlington VA

MUSSELMAN, J(OHN) ROGERS, univ. prof.; born Gettysburg, Pa., Dec. 1, 1890; s. John Elmer and Euphemia Duncan (Rogers) M.; student Gettysburg Acad., 1906; A.B., Gettysburg Coll., 1910, A.M., 1913; Ph.D., Johns Hopkins U., 1916; m. Paula Wilson, May 23, 1925; 1 son, Peter Rogers. Instr. math., U. of Ill., 1916-18; statistician, U.S. Food Adminstrn., Feb.-May 1918; instr. math., Washington U., 1919-20; asso. math., Johns Hopkins, 1920-25, asso. prof., 1925-28; prof. math. Western Reserve, 1928-61, chmn. div. math., 1935-59. University scholar, Johns Hopkins Univ., 1913-14, univ. fellow, 1914-16. Served as 1st lt., statistics br., Gen. Staff, U.S. Army, 1918-19. Fellow A.A.A.S.; mem. Am. Math. Soc., Math. Assn. Am., Phi Delta Theta, Gamma Alpha, Phi Beta Kappa, Sigma Xi. Republican. Asso. editor: Am. Mathematical Monthly, 1928-43. Contbr. tech. articles to Am. Cleveland OH Died Aug. 1968.

MUTESA, EDWARD FREDERICK WILLIAM WALUGEMBE MUTEBI LUWANGULA, II, former pres. of Uganda; s. Daudi Chaw II; ed. King's Coll., Buddo, Buganda Makerere U. Coll., Uganda, Magdalene Coll., Cambridge (Eng.) U.; m. Damali Kisosonkole, 1948. Kabaka of Buganda, 1939-69, crowned, 1942, exiled, 1953-55; 1st pres., comdr.-in-chief State of Uganda. Created knight British Empire; decorated comdr. Order Shield and Spears (Buganda); knight grand cross Order Phoenix (Greece); grand cordon Order Queen of Sheba (Ethiopia), 1962; hon. lt. col. in Grenadier Guards. Address: Kampala Uganda Died Nov. 1969.

MUZZY, H(ENRY) EARLE, business exec.; b. Paterson, N.J., June 24, 1890; s. Henry and Hattie Schuyler (Goodspeed) M.; A.B., Princeton, 1912; m. Margaret Henrietta Dows, May 14, 1929 (dec. Mar. 9, 1935); m. 2d, Margaret Von Maur Hopkins, Oct. 2, 1943. Exec. vice-pres. The Quaker Oats Co., Chgo., dir., 1947, pres., 1953, now vice chmn. of board; dir. E. L. Bruce Co. (Memphis), Mickelberry's Food Products, Inc. Trustee Coe Coll. Served as 1st lt., 313th F.A., U.S. Army, World War I. Republican. Presbyterian. Clubs: Casino, Attic (Chicago); Onwentsia (Lake Forest); Shoreacres (Lake Bluff). Home: Evanston IL Died Mar. 1972.

MYER, JOHN WALDEN, museum dir.; b. London, Eng., Sept. 18, 1901 (parents U.S. citizens); s. Albert James and Gertrude (Sharp) M.; B.S., Harvard, 1923, grad. study archtl. sch., 1924-27, grad. sch., 1927-28; m. Martha Rosalie Humphrey, Sept. 8, 1934; children—Theodore Humphrey, Martha Elizabeth. Asst. to dir. Mus. City of N.Y., 1929-34, v. dir., 1934-51, dir., 1951-58. Fellow The Pierpont Morgan Library. Served as maj., USAAF, 1942-45. Mem. Nat. trust for Hist. Preservation. Mem. Mus. Council N.Y.C., Soc. for Preservation of L.I. Antiquities (pres. 1961-64), Am. Assn. Museums, Archives Am. Art, Soc. Archtl. Historians, Municipal Art Soc. N.Y.C. (member of the historic buildings committee), Holland Society N.Y., Colonial Lords of Manors in America. Clubs: Century Assn. (N.Y.C.); Piping Rock (Locust Valley, N.Y.). Contbr. profl. publs. Home: Wiscasset ME Died Mar. 14, 1972.

MYER, SEWALL, lawyer; b. Plantersville, Tex., Oct. 11, 1884; s. I. S. and Susie (Sterling) M.; LL.B., Tex. U., 1906; m. Emily Kohli, Aug. 5, 1939. Admitted to Tex. bar 1906, practiced law Houston, ret.; city atty., 1921-29, 39-40. Commr. Houston Port, 6 yrs. Mem. Am., Houston bar assns., State Bar Tex., C. of C., Mus. Fine Arts, U. Tex. Ex-Students Assn. (Blue Book life), Kappa Sigma. Episcopalian. Mason, Elk. Clubs: Houston, Warwick (Houston). Home: Houston TX Died Nov. 14, 1967.

MYERS, ALBERT COOK, historian; b. York Springs, Adams County, Pa., Dec. 12, 1874; s. John T. and Sarah A. (Cook) M.; grad. Martin Acad., Kennett Sq., Pa., 1894; grad. Swarthmore Coll. (Bach. Letters), 1898, M.L., 1901; Litt.D., Franklin and Marshall College, 1932; unmarried. In shipping business, Phila., also editor hist. dept. Literary Era, 1898-1900; made hist. researches, Brit. Isles, 1900, 03, 11, 12-13, 14-17; registrar, instr. Swarthmore Coll., 1900-02; hon. curator Friends' Hist. Library, 1924-36; grad. student in History, U. of Pa., 1901-03; Joshua Lippincott traveling fellow of Swarthmore Coll., 1903-04, at U. of Wis. (as hon. fellow in Am. history), and at Harvard. Dir. Pa. State hist. exhibit and supt. hist. exhibits, Jamestown Expn., 1907; mem. mayor's hist. com. and dir. and curator of historic industries Loan Exhibit, Founders' Celebration, Phila., 1908; mem. Pa. Com. Sch. History Text Books, 1923-24; Pa. state commr., sec., chmn. hist. com., Valley Forge Park, 1923-35; commr., sec. Pa. State Hist. Commn., 1923-27, 1932-36, erecting 37 stone and bronze markers, also dir. Wm. Penn Commemoration, 1932; editing Complete Works of William Penn since 1910, and internationally known as authority on Penn, his associates and associations. Mem. Delaware, Chester, Adams, York counties hist. socs., Pa. Fedn. Hist. Socs. (ex-pres.), Friends' Hist. Assn., Phila., Friends' Hist. Soc. England (ex-pres.), N.E. Hist. Genealogical Society, Pennsylvania Historial Association. Member Mayor's Committee Sesquicentennial, Phila., 1925; mem. Bushy Run Battlefield Commn., State of Pa., 1932-35. Served as officer War Camp Community Service, Phila., and chmn. exec. com. Hist. Soc. Pa., entertaining soldiers and sailors, 1918-19. Mem. Society of Friends. Author (or editor): Immigration of the Irish Quakers Into Pennsylvania, 1682-1750, 1902; Quaker Arrivals at Philadelphia, 1682-1750, 1902; Sally Wister's Journal, 1902; Hannah Logan's Courtship, 1904; Publications of the Pennsylvania History Club, 1909; Narratives of Early Pennsylvania, New Jersey and Delaware, 1630-1707, 1912; For Soldiers-Sailors-Marines, What to See in Historic Philadelphia, 1918; A Relic of the Susquehanna Indian, 1922; Memorial Exhibition of Portraits of Thomas Sully, 1922; William Penn's First Charter to Pennsylvania (1682), 1925; Marking the Historic Sites of Early Pennsylvania, 1926; Memoir of Gilbert Cope, 1929; Benjamin West's Mother, 1929; William Penn—His Own Accounts of the Delaware Indians, 1683, 1937; The Boy, George Washington—His Own Account of an Iroquois Indian Dance, 1748, 1932; Robert Wade, First American Host of Penn (1682), 1932; Records of the Court of New Castle on Delaware (1681-1699), 1935; William Marshall Swayne, Chester County's Sculptor of Lincoln, 1936; William Penn's Early Life in Brief, 1644-1674, 1937. Editor many works on hist. subjects and hist. cartographer. Presented to King George V, Court of St. James, London, 1911. Home: Moylan Delaware County PA‡

MYERS, ALONZO FRANKLIN, educator; b. Grover Hill, O., Apr. 6, 1895; s. Louis and Emma (Evans) M.; A.B., Tri-State Coll., Ind., 1915; A.M., Columbia, 1924, Ph.D., 1927; Litt.D., Newark State Coll., 1962; LL.D., Tri-State Coll., 1959; D.H.L., Pa. Mil. College, 1960; married to Rose M. Chilcote, Sept. 21, 1917; children—John, Alice, Martha, Rose Anne; m. 2d, Louise M. Kifer, 1938. Supt. of schools, Hudson, Ind., 1915-16; prin. high school, Edgerton, O., 1916-17; supt. schs., Edgerton, 1919-20, Port Clinton, O., 1920-22; prof. edn. and dir. teacher training, Ohio, U., 1922-28; dir. teacher preparation Conn. State Bd. of Edn., and dir. summer Normal Sch., 1928-30; prof. edn., New York U. since 1930; chmn. dept. of higher edn., 1941-60; director retirement counseling center, 1955-60; distinguished vis. prof. higher edn. So. Ill. U., from 1960; lectr. sch. administrn., Yale, 1935-36 and 1936-37. Delivered annual Sir John Adams Lecture at U. of Calif. in Los Angeles, 1941. Capt. inf., U.S. Army, 1917-19. Recipient Great Teacher award for outstanding teaching by the New York Univ. Alumni Fedn., 1959. Mem. Accrediting Com. Am. Assn. of Tchrs. Coll., 1936-41, chmn., 1940-41; chairman National Education Assn. Commn. on Defense of Democracy Through Education, 1941-47; mem. exec. com., 1944-46, vice pres., 1946-47; president Department of Higher Education, Nat. Edn. Assn., 1947-48. Mem. Eastern States Assn. Professional Schools for Teachers (pres. 1933-36), National Assn. Supervisors of Student Teaching (pres. 1935-36), New York Adult Education Council (dir. from 1946), Phi Delta Kappa, Kappa Delta Pi. Author or co-author of publications relating to field. Home: Venice FL Died May 24, 1970; buried Ashland KY

MYERS, DAVID JACKSON DUKE, consular service; b. La Fayette, Ga., Apr. 5, 1877; s. William Winfield Scott and Sarah Ann Elizabeth (Calhoun) M.; A.B., U. of Ga., 1900; m. Susan Elizabeth McCoy, of Jefferson, Ga., Feb. 18, 1909; children—Sarah Adaline McCoy, Mary Elizabeth McCoy. Teacher pub. schs., Ga., 1900-01, and in Philippine Islands, 1901-03 and for 6 mos., 1905; civ. engr. Imperial Chinese R.R. Administration, Canton, China, 1903-04; surveyor, Bureau of Lands, P.I., 1905-12; consul at Puerto Cortes, Honduras, 1912-14, Iquique, 1914-15, Punta Arenas, Chile, 1915-17; detailed to Buenos Aires, Nov. 3, 1917; consul at Montevideo, Uruguay, 1919-23, San Luis Potosi, Mexico, 1923, Durango, Mexico, Oct. 2, 1923-28, Chihuahua, Mexico, 1928-29, Tegucigalpa, Honduras, 1929-31, San Jose, Costa Rica, 1931-33, Tenerife, Canary Islands, 1933-35; assigned to Dept. of State, Washington, D.C., 1935-36; retired, Apr. 30, 1936. Mem. Pi Gamma Mu. Democrat. Presbyn. Mason (32 deg.). Clubs: Union, Aleman, San Jose Golf; Casino Principal, Nautico, Tenerife Golf (Santa Cruz de Tenerife, Canary Islands). Home: La Fayette‡

MYERS, EDWARD DELOS, educational adminstr.; b. Martinsville, Va., May 18, 1907; s. Ernest DeLos and Pattie Lee (Foster) M.; A.B. Roanoke Coll., 1927; M.A., Princeton University, 1928; Ph.D., 1931; LL.D., Roanoke Coll., 1963; student Gen. Theol. Sem. N.Y., 1933-35, summer seminar in Arabic and Islamic studies, Princeton, 1935, summer sch., Denmark, 1939; m. Dorothy Louise Gills, Dec. 19, 1942; children—Jay Foster, Richard Anthony, Ann, Catherine, Deborah. Student instructor, Gen. Theol. Sem., 1933-35; instructor, Birmingham-Southern Coll., 1936-37; asst. prof. of linguistics, Trinity Coll., 1937-45, sec. of admissions, 1942, dean of freshmen, 1943-45, dean and prof. in humanities Roanoke Coll., 1945-49; prof. of philosophy Washington and Lee U., 1949-61; cultural attache for U.S. in Germany, 1958-60, vis. prof. Free Univ., Berlin, summer 1959; Taft lecturer U. Cin., 1946; cultural attache USIS, Am. Embassy, London, 1961-64; academic vice president Haile Sellassie I University, Addis Ababa, Ethiopia, 1964-66; cultural attache Am. embassy, London, Eng., 1966-69. Mem. Southern Soc. Philosophy Religion (past pres.), Am. Philos. Assn., Guild Scholars in Episcopal Ch. (past pres.), So. Humanities Conf. (past chmn.), Am. Assn. U. Profs., Va. Philos. Assn. (past pres.). Club: Athnaeum. Author: The Foundations of English, 1940; Christianity and Reason, 1951; A Study of History, vol. XI (with Arnold J. Toynbee), 1959; Education in the Perspective of History, 1960; also articles. Died Jan. 13, 1969; buried Roanoke VA

MYERS, ELIZABETH (FETTER) LEHMAN (MRS. J. UPTON MYERS), author; b. Bethlehem, Pa., June 29, 1869; d. Bernhard E. and H. Matilda (Fetter) Lehman; descendant of pioneer Moravians of Pa.; grad. Linden Hall Sem., Lititz, Pa., 1886; m. J. Upton Myers, of Bethlehem, May 23, 1900. State Chmn. Needlework Guild America and pres. Bethlehem br.; mem. bd. dirs. Associated Charities, Bethlehem br. Am. Red Cross. Mem. Moravian Hist. Soc., Pa. Hist. Soc., Northampton Co. Hist. Soc. Moravian. Clubs: Bethlehem Woman's, Northampton Country. Author: A Century of Moravian Sisters—A Record of Christian Community Life, 1918; also numerous papers on hist. subjects. Home: 228 Market St., Bethlehem PA‡

MYERS, GARRY CLEVELAND, psychologist; b. Sylvan, Pa., July 15, 1884; s. John A. and Sarah A. (Besore) M.; grad. Cumberland Valley State Normal Sch. 1905; A.B., Ursinus Coll., Collegeville, Pa. 1909; student U. Pa., 1909-10; Ph.D., Columbia, 1913; m. Caroline Elizabeth Clark, June 26, 1912; children—John, Elizabeth Clark, Garry Cleveland (dec.). Prof. psychology and social sciences Juniata Coll., Huntingdon, Pa., 1912-14; prof. psychology and edn. Bklyn. Tng. Sch. for Teachers, 1914-18; head dept. psychology Cleveland School Edn., also chmn. div. of psychology, Sr. Coll. of Western Res. U. and Cleveland Sch. of Edn., 1920-27; head div. parent edn. Cleveland Coll. of Western Res. U., June 1927 to June 1940; lectr. child psychology; certified consulting psychologist. Commd. 1st lt. San. Corps. U.S. Army, Mar. 16, 1918; capt. Nov. 8, 1918; dir. edn. Camp Upton; dir. Americanization program. Leader of pub. forums for U.S. Office Edn., 1937-39. Recipient citation of merit Nat. Assn. Gifted Children, 1966. Fellow A.A.A.S., Ohio Acad. Sciences (v.p. 1936-37), Am. Ednl.

Research Assn., Am. Psychol. Assn., Soc. for Research in Child Development; mem. Nat. Soc. for Study of Edn., Pres. Honesdale (Pa.) Rotary Club, 1948-49. Author or co-author numerous books; latest: For Beginning the School Day; Creative Thinking Activities; Headwork for Pre-school Children; Headwork Elementary School Children; Your Child and You; Wishes; Christmas Wishes. Founder, editor Highlights for Children. 1946, Highlights for Children incorporating Children's Activities, from 1960; writer syndicated newspaper column, The Parent Problem, from 1932. Contbr. to sci. ednl. jours. and popular mags. Home: Boyds Mills PA Died July 19, 1971; buried Calkins PA

MYERS, GEORGE EDMUND, educator, b. Massillon, Ia., Nov. 26, 1871; s. John Robert and Clara (McLeod) M.; A.B., Ottawa (Kan.) U., 1896; A.M., U. of Chicago, 1901; Ph.D., Clark U., 1906; studied Columbia, 1914-15; m. Harriet Blackstone, Aug. 20, 1902. Prin. high sch., Colorado Springs, Colo., 1902-04; prin. McKinley Manual Training Sch., Washington, D.C., 1906-11; pres. Kan. State Manual Training Normal Sch., 1911-13; supervisor vocational edn., N.Y. City sch. system, 1914-17; prof. vocational edn. and guidance University of Mich., Nov. 1917-Feb. 1942; professor emeritus of education since Feb. 1942. Lecturer on education, George Washington University, 1907-10; prof. vocational edn., Ind. U., Summer 1915, New York U., summer, 1917, U. of Calif., summer, 1928; U. of Colo., summer, 1942. Investigated industrial schools in England, France and Germany, 1913-14. Mem. N.E.A., Am. Vocational Assn., Nat. Vocational Guidance Assn. (pres. 1931-32), Phi Delta Kappa. Joint Author: Moral Training in Public Schools, 1907; Planning Your Future, 1930; Industrial Arts in Modern Education, 1934. Wrote: Some Problems of Vocational Education in Germany (Bull. 33, U.S. Bur. Edn.), 1915; The Problem of Vocational Guidance, 1927; Principles and Techniques of Vocational Guidance, 1941. Home: 509 Linden St., Ann Arbor MI‡

MYERS, HARRY WHITE, missionary; b. Lexington, Va., May 20, 1874; s. Henry H. and Mary Ella (Nelson) M.; B.A., Washington and Lee U., 1894, M.A., 1897, D.D.; awarded Robinson medal and Franklin scholarship at univ.; B.D., Ky. Theol. Sem., Louisville, Ky., 1897; m. Grace K. Field, of Lexington, Mo., Nov. 29, 1897; children—Wentworth Field, Henry Nelson, Frances Caroline (Mrs. George Dickely). Ordained ministry Presbyn. Ch. in U.S., 1897; missionary in Japan since 1897; now pastor Kobe Union Ch.; prof. N.T. Greek, etc., Kobe Theol. Sch. Mem. Am. Assn. of Kobe, British and Foreign Bible Soc., Delta Tau Delta, Phi Beta Kappa. Author: Christianity Preeminent (in Japanese), 1912. Address: 112 Yamamoto Dori, 4 Chome, Kobe Japan‡

MYERS, JACK ALLEN, pipe line co. exec.; b. Des Moines, Mar. 1, 1927; s. Robert William and Ione Florell (Hanks) M.; A.A., Long Beach City Coll., 1949; B.S., Rockhurst Coll., 1951; m. Jo Ann Royer, Nov. 19, 1948; children—Marsha Jan, Monica Jane, Jack Allen, Melissa Jo, Frederick William. Sr. accountant Touche Ross & Co., 1951-56; asst. controller Allied Labs., Inc., 1956-62; tax mgr. Panhandle Eastern Pipe Line Co., Kansas City, Mo., 1963-71. Served with USN, 1945-46. Mem. Am. Inst. C.P.A.'s. Democrat. Presbyn. Home: Prairie Village KS Died Dec. 5, 1971.

MYERS, JOHN LLEWELLYN, physician; b. Livingston County, Mo., Mar. 29, 1872; s. Simeon and Susan Leaton (Alexander) M.; A.B., Park Coll., Parkville, Mo., 1901; M.D., Physicians and Surgeons Med. Coll. (now med. dept. U. of Kan.), 1904; studied in London, Eng. and N.Y. City, 1914-15; m. Florence Alverda Young, Apr. 8, 1904. Practiced at Ketchikan, Alaska, 1904-14; specializing in eye, ear, nose and throat work, Seattle, Wash., 1915-16; with Dr. J. E. Sawtell, Kansas City, Mo., 1916-18; together with his brothers, Dr. B. L. Myers and Dr. W. A. Myers, organized and conducted Myers' Clinic since 1919, University of Kansas Medical School, since 1926, now associate professor emeritus. Captain M.R.C., U.S. Army, 1918. President board med. examiners, Alaska, 1912-14; pres. Kansas City Eye, Ear, Nose and Throat Soc., 1921-22, Kansas City-Southwest Clin. Soc., 1931-32; sec. ear, nose and throat sect. Am. Acad. Ophthalmology and Otolaryngology, 1926-42. Fellow Am. Coll. Surgeons, A.M.A., Am. Congress Physical Therapy; mem. A.A.A.S., Am. Laryngol. Assn. Republican. Presbyn. Mason; mem. I.O.O.F., Eastern Star, Redmen. Home: 5401 W. 67th St., Mission P.O., Kan. Office: Shukert Bldg., Kansas City MO‡

MYERS, JOHN SHERMAN, univ. dean; b. Bklyn., Apr. 7, 1897; s. John A. and Sarah Ann (Sherman) M.; B.S., Harvard, 1919, LL.B. cum laude, 1925; m. Alvina Reckman, Dec. 22, 1928. Admitted to Mass. bar, 1925, N.Y. bar, 1926; with firm Hughes, Schurman & Dwight, N.Y.C., 1925-31; v.p., gen. counsel, then pres. and chmn. Distributors Group, N.Y.C., 1931-37; v.p., gen. counsel, co-owner Lord, Abbott & Co., N.Y.C., 1937-41; prof. law U. Colo., 1941-42; prof. law Washington Coll. Law, Am. U., 1947-69, dean, 1956-67, dean emeritus, research prof. law, 1967-69. Served to colonel U.S. Army and AUS, 1918, 42-47. Decorated Legion of Merit. Mem. Am., D.C. bar assns., Assn. Bar City N.Y., Am. Law Inst., Assn. Am. Law Schs. Mason. Clubs: Cosmos, Congressional, Nat. Lawyers (Washington); Augusta (Me.) Country. Contbr. articles profl. publs. Home: Washington DC Died Jan. 24, 1969; buried Gettysburg Nat. Cemetery, Gettysburg PA

MYERS, JOHN TWIGGS, lt. gen.; b. of Am. parents at Wiesbaden, Germany, Jan. 29, 1871; s. Abraham Charles and Marion Ysabelle (Twiggs) M.; grad. U.S. Naval Acad., Annapolis, Md., 1892; Naval War Coll., 1896, 1905; grad. Army War Coll., 1912; m. Alice G. Cutts, Apr. 30, 1898. Commd. 2d lt., U.S. Marine Corps, Mar. 7, 1895, and advanced through grades to lt. gen., May 1942. Served in Spanish American War, Philippine Insurrection, Boxer uprising, China (pvt. maj. while comdr. Legation Guard, Siege of Pekin, 1900), Punitive Expdn., Mexico, World War I. Served as fleet marine officer, European, Asiatic, Pacific and Atlantic fleets; comdr. posts Parris Island, San Diego, Quantico; retired (for age) Feb. 1, 1935. Mem. Aztec Society, Military Order Dragon, Military Order Carabao, Naval and Mil. Order Spanish-Am. War, Spanish War Vets., Am. Legion. Episcopalian. Clubs: Army and Navy, Army Navy Country (Washington). Address: 3919 Braganza Av., Coconut Grove FL‡

MYERS, LOUIS ROBERT, collection bur. exec.; b. Johnstown, Pa., Aug. 28, 1902; s. Samuel and Mary (Beerman) M.; student U. Pa., 1921-23; m. Minna Helen Schapiro, June 26, 1929; 1 son, Blake Millard. Mgr. various dept. stores, Harrisburg, Pa., Troy, N.Y., Akron, O., 1923-39; mgr., owner United Personnel & Adjustment Bur., Canton, O., 1940-68. Active in various community fund drs. Past dir. Jewish Community Fedn. Mem. Ohio Collectors Assn. (past pres.), Am. (past dir.), Ohio (past pres.) collectors assns., Phi Sigma Delta. Jewish religion (past pres. Temple Israel Men's Club). Mason (32 deg., Shriner). Club: Arrowhead Country.

MYERS, WILL MARTIN, scientist, educator; b. Bancroft, Kan., June 11, 1911; s. Samuel Edwin and Amelia Askew (Woodall) M.; B.S., Kan. State Coll., 1932; M.S., U. Minn., 1934, Ph.D., 1936; m. Emma Louise Manchester, June 1, 1935; children—Susan Louise, Mary Jane, James Martin. Instr. U. Minn., 1932-37, prof., head dept. agronomy and plant genetics, 1952-63, dean of Office of Internat. Programs, 1963-65; associate geneticist, later geneticist U.S. Regional Pasture Research Lab., Dept. of Agr., 1937-46, sr. geneticist, 1947-49, head agronomist charge div. forage crops and diseases Bur. Plant Industry. Soils and Agr. Engring., 1949-51, dir. field crops research, 1951-52; head agrl. research br., agr. div. Natural Resources Sect., G-Hdqrs., Supreme Comdr. Allied Powers, Tokyo, Japan, 1946-47; prof. cytogenetics Pa. State U., 1947-49; asso. dir. agrl. sciences Rockefeller Found., 1965-67, vice president, 1967-70. Vice chmn. organizing com., chmn. exec. com., chmn. program com., sec. gen. 6th Internat. Grassland Congress; spl. consultant Rockefeller Found., 1959-60. Recipient Stevenson award Am. Soc. Agronomy, 1949; Outstanding Achievement award U. Minn., 1951; Distinguished Service award Kan. State U., 1970. Fellow Am. Soc. Agronomy (chmn. crops div. 1947, pres. 1958); mem. Bot. Soc. Am., Am. Soc. Naturalists, Am. Genetic Assn., Genetics Soc. Am., Am. Soc. Range Mgmt., Sigma Xi, Alpha Zeta, Phi Kappa Phi. Home: Port Chester NY Died July 26, 1970; buried Sunset Meml. Park, Minneapolis MN

MYNDERS, ALFRED D., editor; b. Hartsville, Tenn., Aug. 13, 1888; s. Seymour Allen and Pobrecita (Richeson) M.; student U. of Tenn., 1906-09; unmarried. On editorial staff, Knoxville Sentinel, 1909; asso. editor, Chattanooga News, 1909-17, 1928-39; news editor, Memphis Commercial Appeal, 1919-28; asso. editor, Chattanooga Evening Times, 1940-41; editor, The Chattanooga Times, 1942-58. Editorial staff Paris edit. Chicago Tribune. Served as 2d lt. 6th Div., Inf., France, Germany, 1918-19. Dir. Chattanooga Symphony Assn.; dir., sec. of bd., Chattanooga Y.M.C.A.; mem. Chattanooga adv. com. to U.S. Army. Mem. Internat. Press Inst., Atlantic Union (nat. council), Am. Soc. Newspaper Editors, Nat. Conf. Christians and Jews, So. Regional Council, Phi Gamma Delta. Episcopalian. Democrat. Clubs: Rotary, Executives, Chattanooga Writers, Cumberlands Hiking. Home: Chattanooga TN Died Mar. 1969.

MYRICK, ARTHUR BECKWITH, coll. prof.; b. N.Y. City, June 27, 1875; s. Franklin Brown and Sarah (Beckwith) M.; A.B., Harvard, 1900; A.M., 1901, Ph.D., 1904; m. May Edwards Selfe, June 11, 1903. Austin teaching fellow, Harvard, 1902-04; prof. incaricato of English lit. and philology, Accademia Scientifico-letteraria, Milan, Italy, 1904-05; professor Romance languages, University of Vermont, since 1905, prof. emeritus since June 1945. Decorated Chevalier honoraire de la Societe du Bon Parler Francais. Mem. Modern Lang. Assn. Am. and New England, Am. Assn. Univ. Profs., Am. Assn. Teachers of French, Mediaeval Acad. America, Phi Beta Kappa, Sigma Alpha Epsilon. Republican. Conglist. Translator: Beaumarchais' Barber of Seville, 1905; de Banville's Gringoire, 1916; Il Filostrato of Boccaccio (with N.E. Griffin), 1929; Short Stories from French and Spanish. Contbr. articles and notes in philol. revs. Club: Theatre. Home: 146 Summit St., Burlington VT‡

MYRICK, JULIAN SOUTHALL, life ins. cons., assn. exec.; b. Murfreesboro, N.C., Mar. 1, 1880; s. Charles English and Blanche (Colton) M.; m. Marion Washburn, Jan. 1, 1910; children—Cynthia S. (Mrs. Charles E. Saltzman), Marion D. (Mrs. John E. MacCracken), Shirley (Mrs. William H. Cyde), William W. Clk., Charles H. Raymond & Co., gen. agts. Mut. Life Ins. Co., 1898; gen. agt. Washington Life Ins. Co. 1907-09; mgr. Mut. Life Ins. Co., 1909, 2d v.p., 1941, ret., 1949; life ins. cons., from 1953. Mem. Am. Coll. Life Underwriters (past chmn.), N.Y. State Assn. Life Underwriters (hon. pres.), Life Underwriters Assn. N.Y.C. (past pres.), Nat. Assn. Life Underwriters (past pres.), N.Y. C. of C., U.S. Lawn Tennis Assn., Pilgrims Soc., Down Town Assn. Clubs: Links, Racquet and Tennis, Church, Seabright Lawn Tennis New York City NY Died Jan. 8, 1969; buried East Hampton NY

NABOURS, ROBERT KIRKLAND, zoologist; b. Many, La., Nov. 5, 1875; s. George Maston and Mary Elizabeth (Gibson) N.; diploma La. State Normal Sch., 1900; B.Ed., U. of Chicago, 1905, Ph.D., 1911; m. Mayme T. Davis (B.S., Ohio State U.), June 3, 1916; children—Elizabeth Frances, Robert Kirkland, Catherine Ann, Richard Davis. Asst. in museum and teacher natural history, Sch. of Edn., U. of Chicago, 1906-09, asst. in zoology, 1909-10; instr. zoology, 1910-12, prof. and head of dept. 1912-44, Kan. Agrl. Coll.; zoologist and experimenter in genetics, Expt. Sta. same since 1944; zoologist Kan. State Bd. Agr.; asso. in genetics Carnegie Instn., 1929-30. Made expdn. to Russia and Bokhara., Central Asia, 1914, to study Karakul sheep; trip around world for further study of sheep, 1916; also trip, 1920, to reopen trade in furs with Bokhara. Fellow A.A.A.S., Am. Soc. Zoologists; mem. Am. Soc. Naturalists, Kan. Acad. Science (ex-pres.), Sigma Xi, Alpha Zeta, Phi Kappa Phi, Phi Sigma Kappa. Conglist. Home: Manhattan KS‡

NAFF, GEORGE TIPTON, lawyer; b. Bastrop, La., Nov. 11, 1900; s. George W. and Irene (Huffman) N.; B.S., Ala. Polytechnic Inst., 1924; LL.B., Univ. of Ala. 1927; m. Myrtle Johnson, Oct. 21, 1924; 1 dau. Caroline. Admitted to La. bar, 1928, gen. practice of law as asso. or partner in firm Wilkinson, Lewis & Wilkinson, Shreveport, La., 1927-41; gen. counsel prin. subsidiaries of United Gas Corp., 1941-45, also vice pres. and gen. counsel from 1945. Former dir. and gen. counsel Union Producing Co., United Gas Pipe Line Co. United Oil Pipe Line Co.; exec. v.p. Tex. Eastern Transmission Corp. 1948-54, pres. 1954-56, vice chmn. 1956-57; pvt. law practice, 1957-68. Mem. Kappa Sigma, Phi Beta Kappa. Episcopalian. Home: Shreveport LA Died June 17, 1968.

NAGEL, CONRAD, actor, dir.; b. Keokuk, Ia., Mar. 16 1897; s. Frank and Frances (Murphy) N.; B.O., Highland Park Coll., Des Moines, 1914; m. Ruth Helms, 1919 (div. 1935); 1 dau., Ruth Margaret; m. 2d, Lynn Merrick (div. Mar. 1947); m. 3d, Michael Coulson Smith, 1955. Began with Princess Stock Co., Des Moines, later appeared in The Natural Law, Experience, The Man Who Came Back, Forever After; appeared numerous motion pictures, 1919—; silent and talking pictures include Midsummer Madness, What Every Woman Knows, Tess of the D'Urbervilles, 1924, Tin Hats, 1926, Quality Street, Dynamite, The Swan, Sacred Flame, Navy Spy, Gold Racket, 1937; dir. Love Takes Flight; narrator One Million B.C., United Artists-Roach; stage appearances, 1933-70, The First Apple, The Shining Hour, Skin of Our Teeth (Pulitzer prize play) State of the Union (Pulitzer prize play), Tomorrow the World, A Goose for the Gander, For Love or Money, Goodbye My Fancy, The Captains and the Kings; appeared on New York stage in Tomorrow the World, 1944; became dir. Silver Theatre radio broadcasts, 1937, host Celebrity Time, ABC-TV, 1948 host on Broadway to Hollywood TV show; dir. Radio Reader's Digest, 1941-45. Past pres. Motion Picture Relief Fund. Served as seaman U.S. Navy, World War I. Mem. Actors Equity Assn., Acad. Motion Picture Arts and Scis. (founder, past pres., hon. life mem.), Beverly Hills C. of C. (adv. bd., dir.), Am. Legion, Am. Fedn. Radio and TV Artists (v.p.). Republican. Christian Scientist. Mason (Shriner), Elk. Clubs: Hollywood Athletic, Riviera Country (Hollywood); Lambs, Athletic (N.Y.C.). Died Feb. 24, 1970.

NAGEL, JOSEPH DARWIN, physician; b. Galgocz Hungary, Nov. 20, 1867; s. Adolphe and Therese N.; A.B., Evang. Luth. Gymnasium, Budapest, Hungary 1885; went to Vienna, Paris and Amsterdam; M.D., Coll. Physicians and Surgeons (Columbia), and received Harzen prize medal, 1889; m. Dolly Adelaide Rogers, June 14, 1893; children—Joseph Darwin, Katharine R. Engaged in practice at New York since June 1889; cons. physician French Hosp. Decorated Medaille d'Hygiene Publique (France). Mem. A.M.A., Med. Soc. State of N.Y., N.Y. County Med. Soc., Am. Acad. Gen. Practice, Societe Royale Medicale de Belgique. Mason. Author: Diseases of the Nervous System, 1892; Diseases of the Mind and Nervous System, 1904. Home: Game Cock

Island, East Port Chester, Conn. and 154 E 71st St., New York, N.Y. Office: 10 Park Av., New York NY‡

NAGEL, STINA (MRS. LEON HILL), artist; b. Ann Arbor, Mich., Jan. 25, 1918; d. Gottlieb and Rose (Haab) Nagel; B. Design, U. Mich., 1940; m. Leon Hill, July 2, 1944; children—Desha Robin; Frank Dushan. One-man shows at Mint Mus., North Carolina; 1957, and Koltnow Gallery, 1961; exhibited in group shows at Oakland (Cal.) Ann., Audubon Ann., Allied Am. Artists, Newport Assn. Ann., Nat. Assn. Women Artists, Butler Inst. Ann., Davidson Coll. and others. Recipient Jane Higbee award U. Mich., 1939. Mem. Audubon Artists Assn., Artists Equity Assn., Alpha Alpha Gamma, Tau Sigma Delta, Phi Kappa Phi. Illustrator books and mags. Address: New York City NY Died Mar. 14, 1969.

NAGER, RUDOLF FELIX, investment banker; b. Zurich, Switzerland, Oct. 17, 1911; s. Felix Robert and Hedwig (Naef) N.; student Univ. Coll., Oxford, Eng., 1931-32, Catholic U., Paris, France, 1932-35; Ph.D. in Philosophy, Fribourg (Switzerland) U., 1938; m. Margaret M. Beitz, Dec. 13, 1952. Came to U.S., 1963. With Swiss Credit Bank, Zurich, N.Y.C., 1939-58, mgr., Zurich, 1951-58; mng. dir. August Thyssen-Bank, A.G., Dusseldorf, Germany, 1958-63; with Swiss Am. Corp., N.Y.C., 1963-70 pres., 1964-70; mem. U.S. adv. bd. Zurich Insurance Co., Chgo.; dir. Am. Guarantee and Liability Ins. Co., Chgo., Zurich Life Ins. Co., N.Y.C. Rotarian. Home: Greenwich CT Died 1970.

NAIR, JOHN HENRY, JR., cons. indsl. chemist; b. Chgo., Feb. 20, 1893; s. John H. and Isabel Bratton (Painter) N.; B.S. cum laude, Beloit Coll., 1915; D.Sc., 1958; student Syracuse U. 1916-17; m. Claire Louise Cook, Mar. 22, 1920; children—John, Janet Cook (Mrs. Clarence L. Adams). Chemistry instr. Wausau (Wis.) High Sch., 1915-16, Syracuse U., 1916-17; research chemist Merrell-Soule Co., Syracuse, N.Y., 1919-28; asst. dir. research Borden Co., Syracuse, 1928-38; tech. sales Borden Co., N.Y.C., 1938-42; asst. dir. research T. J. Lipton, Inc., Hoboken, N.J., 1942-57; v.p., dir. L & N Corp., Raleigh, N.C.; secretary-treas. Elmenair Corporation, Raleigh, N.C. Member advisory board Jour. Agrl. and Food Chemists, 1953-57; dir. Avi Pub. Co.; vis. prof. N.C. State Coll., U.N.C., 1963-64. Trustee Beloit Coll., 1961-64. Served as capt. Signal Corps C.W.S., AEF, 1917-19. Mem. Am. Chem. Soc. (nat. councillor, 1929-35, 1945-63, dir. 1964-71), Inst. Food Technologists (chmn. N.Y. sect. 1946-47, nat. council 1947, 51-53, 57-59, pres. elect 1965-66), Am. Inst. Chemists (nat. councilor 1957-61, pres. 1956-57, hon. mem. 1962-71), N.A.M. (research com.), Assn. Research Dirs. (pres. 1956-57), American Dairy Science Assn., Sci. Research Soc. of Am., Society Chimie Industrielle, also Sigma Xi, Phi Tau Sigma, Delta Sigma Rho, Alpha Chi Sigma, Tau Kappa Epsilon. Mason. Clubs: Chemists (N.Y.C.); Raleigh (N.C.) Country; North Carolina State Faculty. Contributing author: Handbook of Food and Agriculture, 1955; Food Dehydration, volume 2, 1964. Contributing editor Food Engring. Author numerous articles on chem. research. Home: Raleigh NC Died July 25, 1971.

NAMM, BENJAMIN HARRISON, business exec.; b. Brooklyn, N.Y., Nov. 29, 1888; s. Adolph Isaac and Cecilia (Meyer) N.; grad. Peekskill (N.Y.) Mill. Acad., 1905; student Brooklyn Polytech. Inst., Brooklyn, 1906-07; m. Margaret Alice Wolf, May 15, 1922; children—Andrew Irving, Peggotty Hanks. Salesman, The Namm-Loeser Store, Bklyn., 1910-16, pres. 1916-46, former chairman of board; chmn. bd. Arebec Corp.; dir. Avco Mfg. Corp., Equitable Fed. Savs. & Loan Assn. Chmn. retail advisory committee U.S. Treasury, 1941; spl. asst. to dir. U.S. Office of Civilian Defense, 1942; exec. dir. U.S. Purchasing Commn. for Brazil, 1943; consultant to State Dept. at U.N. Conf. on Internat. Orgn., San Francisco, 1945; observer to U.N. Conf., Lake Success, New York. Served overseas as chief gas officer of 5th div. World War I; served overseas as civilian cons. U.S. Army, World War II. Decorated Officer French Legion of Honor, Brazilian Southern Cross, Luxemborg Order of Duchy, Italian Legion of Honor, Swedish Royal Order of Vasa. Former chmn. bd. trustees N.Y. City Community Coll.; hon. chmn. Lafayette Fellowship Found.; past chmn. Conf. of National Orgns.; ex-gov. Am. Stock Exchange. Dir. Bklyn. chpt. ARC. Mem. Nat. Retail Merchants Assn. (pres. bd. dirs., winner gold medal award in 1941, chmn. internat. com.), Downtown Bklyn. Assn. (gold medal award), N.Y. U. Sch. of Retailing (mem. adv. com.), U.S. C. of C. (domestic distbrn. com.), Bklyn. C. of C. (dir.). Author: Advertising the Retail Store (forward by Arthur Brisbane), 1924; Would You Enter A Door Marked Socialism. Home: New York City NY Died Aug. 1969; buried Salem Fields Cemetery, Brooklyn NY

NANCE, WILLIS DEAN, lawyer; b. Chgo., Sept. 28, 1896; s. Willis O. and Zelma (Arter) N.; A.B., U. Mich., 1917; LL.B., Northwestern U., 1920; LL.D. (hon.), John Marshall Law Sch., 1960; m. Louella Paul, Apr. 4, 1923; 1 dau., Elizabeth (Mrs. John D. Mall). Admitted to Illinois bar, 1920, U.S. Supreme Ct., 1924; practice in Chgo., 1920-68; partner firm Kirkland, Ellis, Hodson, Chaffetz & Masters, 1931-68; spl. atty. U.S. Treasury Dept., 1924-25; Masters, 1931-68; spl. atty. U.S. Treasury Dept., 1924-25; village atty., Wilmette, Ill., 1931-35. Bd. dirs. Chgo. Bar Assn. Found., pres., 1962-65. Trustee Weymouth Kirkland Found., Ill. Children's Home and Aid Soc.; gov. life mem. Art Inst. Chgo.; mem. Northwestern U. Assos. Served to 1st lt. U.S. Army, 1917-19. Recipient award of merit Northwestern U., 1961. Fellow Am. Bar Found.; mem. Am. (ho. of dels. 1959-60, 62-68), Internat., Ill. (chmn. sect. taxation 1927), Chgo. (pres. 1959-60) bar assns., Nat. Tax Assn., Chgo. Fed. Tax Forum (past chmn.), Northwestern U. Sch. Law Alumni Assn. (pres. 1965-68), Delta Upsilon, Phi Delta Phi. Presbyn. (v.p. bd. trustee). Clubs: University (pres. 1953-55), Law, Legal, Chicago, Mid-America (Chgo.); Lawyers (U. Mich.); Indian Hill (Winnetka, Ill.); Presidents (U. Mich.); John Evans, John Henry Wigmore (life) (Northwestern U.). Home: Kenilworth IL Died July 17, 1968.

NANKIVELL, FRANK ARTHUR, artist; b. Maldon, Victoria, Australia, Nov. 16, 1869; s. John and Annie (Green) N.; ed. Wesley Coll., Melbourne; children—Francis John, Edith Anne, (by second marriage) John Elbert, Ronald Thomas. Studied architecture and engineering in Melbourne, Australia, and practiced engineering on Victorian railways until 1891; contbg. occasionally to Australian publs.; worked and studied art in Japan, 1891-94, in San Francisco, 1894-96. Published and illustrated fortnightly mag. Chic," and made drawings for San Francisco Call, Examiner, and Chronicle; to New York, 1896, illustrated daily papers; joined staff of Puck, May 1896, as cartoonist and caricaturist. Studied portrait painting in New York and London; now occupied as painter and etcher. Represented in Brooklyn Museum, Harvard U. Law Sch., U. of N.C., State Hist. Soc. of Mo., Duke U., Metropolitan Museum, N.Y. Pub. Library, Congressional Library (Washington, D.C.). Mezzotint portrait of Mark Twain in 40 museums and libraries in the U.S. Produced first complete reel motion picture animation in full color. Member of the Society of American Etchers. Club: Circumnavigators'. Home: Walton, N.Y. Studio: 35 W. 14th St., New York NY*‡

NAON, ROMULO S., diplomat; b. Buenos Aires, Argentine Republic, Feb. 17, 1875; Dr. Jurisprudence, Buenos Aires U. (gold medal and diploma of honor), 1896; (LL.D., U. of Pittsburgh, Yale, Harvard, and Brown); m. Isabel de Naon, of Buenos Aires, July 1, 1899. Sec. govt. of Buenos Aires State; rep. to Nat. Congress, 1902; reelected 1906; minister of justice and pub. instrn., 1908; E.E. and M.P. to U.S., 1911-14; first ambassador Argentine to U.S., 1914-—. Reelected to Nat. Congress, 1912, but resigned to remain in U.S. Was formerly professor philosophy, Colegio Nacional de Buenos Aires; prof. constl. law and mem. directive council faculty of law and social sciences, Buenos Aires U.; mem. directive council, Mortgage Bank of the State of Buenos Aires. Gen. sec. Argentine delegation 2d Peace Conference, The Hague; mem. directive council, Superior Normal Sch.; spl. ambassador Centennial of Independence U.S. of Venezuela, and at the inauguration of the President of Chile, Dec. 1915. Negotiated and concluded treaties of gen. arbitration with Venezuela, Ecuador and Colombia, as well as others, and treaties and conventions with the U.S.A. Del. to several internat. congresses and confs.; pres. several dist. councils of primary edn.; hon. pres. several ednl. instns. and scientific congresses; etc. Rep. of Argentine in mediation conf., Niagara Falls, 1914, bet. reps. of Argentine, Brazil and Chile and U.S. and Mex., to avoid a war bet. the latter, and for which was voted a gold medal and resolution of thanks of Congress; del. Pan-Am. conf., 1915, that brought about the recognition of the de facto govt. in Mex.; addressed joint session of Pa. Legislature by invitation; etc. Decorations: Great Cross of Isabel the Catholic of Spain; Grand Officer of the Crown of Italy; Comdr. Legion of Honor of France; 2d class Cross of Liberator Bolivar of Venezuela; medal of Queen of Holland; medal of Pennsylvania Soc., Medal for the Merit of Chile. Author of various works on political science and constl. law and on ednl. subjects. Home: Buenos Aires, Argentina. Address: 1600 New Hampshire Av., Washington DC‡

NAPOLI, ALEXANDER J., U.S. judge; b. Chgo., Oct. 7, 1905; s. Vincenzo and Catherine (Basile) N.; Ph.B., U. Chgo., 1927, J.D., 1929; m. Helen Martha Bibb, Feb. 25, 1936; children—Thomas J., Robert A., Richard G. Admitted to Ill. bar, 1929; practiced in Chgo., 1929-33; asst. state's atty. Cook County, 1933-50; judge Municipal Ct. Chgo., 1950-60, Superior Ct., Cook County, 1960-63; judge No. dist. Ill., U.S. Dist. Ct., 1966-—. Mem. Am., Ill., Chgo. bar assns. Democrat. K.C. Home: Chicago IL Died July, 1972.

NASH, C(ARLTON) STEWART, otolaryngologist; b. Ontario Center, N.Y., Nov. 14, 1893; s. Charles J. and Sarah L. (Fish) N.; A.B., U. of Rochester, 1915; M.D., U. of Mich., 1919; m. Grace V. Connor, Sept. 29, 1920; 1 son, Donald S. Chief of staff, dept. of otolaryngology, Rochester Gen. Hosp. from 1921; asso. otolaryngologist, Strong Memorial and Municipal hosps since 1925; cons. otolaryngologist, Genesee, Highland, St. Mary's and Rochester state hosps., also Convalescent Hosp. for Children; cons. otolaryngol., Lakeside Meml. Hosp., Brockport, N.Y.; instr. otolaryngology, Med. Sch., U. of Rochester from 1930; faculty consultant sch. medicine and dentistry; lecturer, anatomy and physiology, Eastman Dental Dispensary. Served with Med. Res. Corps, U.S. Army, during World War I. Dir. Am. Bd. Otolaryngology, Am. Soc. Advancement of Speech, Rochester Sch. for Deaf. Fellow Am. Coll. Surgeons; mem. Am. Med. Assn., Am. Acad. Ophthalmology and Otolaryngology (vice pres.), Am. Laryngol., Rhinol. and Otol. Soc. (sec. 1936), Am. Otol. Soc., Am. Laryngol. Assn., Am. Hearing Society (pres.), Medical Society County of Monroe (pres.). Club: University (Rochester). Contbr. numerous articles to sci. publs. Home: Rochester NY Died May 1, 1971; buried Ridge Chapel Cemetery, Williamson NY

NASH, ELLIOTT E., ry. official; b. Hudson, Wis., Mar. 28, 1870; s. Lester A. and Mary E. Prey; ed. high sch., Hudson; m. Jessie W. Von Valkenburgh, of Hillsdale, Mich., Dec. 23, 1896 (died Feb. 10, 1922); children—Margaret Elizabeth, Mary Agnes. Began with C.,St.P.,M.&O. Ry., June 1886, and successively clk. at Hudson, Wis., 1888, clk. auditor's office, St. Paul, 1888-91, traveling auditor, 1891-92, agt. at Ashland, Wis., 1892-98, at St. Paul, 1898-99, Minneapolis, 1899-1905, asst. supt. at Itasca, Wis., 1905, Eau Claire, 1905-10; with C.&&N.W. Ry., spl. work in president's office, Chicago, 1910-11, supt. Minn. Div. at Winona, 1911-12, Madison Div., Baraboo, Wis., 1912-13, asst. gen. supt. lines E. of Mo. River (except Ia., Minn. and Dak. divs.), at Chicago, 1913-17, asst. gen. supt. Ia. territory, 1917-18, asst. to federal mgr., at Chicago, 1918-20; gen. mgr. M&St.L. R.R., at Minneapolis, 1920-21, v.p. and gen. mgr., 1921-22; western rep. Am. Locomotive Co., Chicago, June-Oct. 1922; again v.p. M.&St.L. R.R., 1922-23, v.p. and chief operating officer since July 1923; pres. Minn. Transfer Ry. Co., 1925-27; v.p. Ry. Transfer Co. (Minneapolis), Hocking (Ia.) Coal Co. Republican. Christian Scientist. Clubs: Traffic, Minneapolis, Minikahda Country, Union League, South Shore Country (Chicago). Home: 510 Groveland Av. Office: 317 2nd Av. So., Minneapolis MN‡

NASH, ISAAC H(ENRY), land examiner; b. Franklin, Ida., Jan. 28, 1872; s. Isaac B. and Martha (Howland) N.; ed. Oneida Stake Acad., Preston, Ida., 1895-97; m. Amanda May West, Nov. 19, 1897; children—Lyn W., Josie May (Mrs. Kenneth Anderson), Alton, Alice (Mrs. Eugene Jenkins), Isaac B. Teacher rural schs., Ida., 1900-03; county assessor, Oneida Co., Ida., 1904-05, 1907-08; Ida. state land selector and appraiser, 1909-16; mem. Ida. State Senate, 1919-20; state land commr., Ida., 1919-31; examiner, Salt Lake Div. Gen. Land Office, since 1931; pres. I. H. Nash & Sons Land &Live Stock Co., Twin Lakes Federal Farm Loan Assn.; v.p. Twin Lakes Canal Co. Mem. Com. on Conservation of Pub. Lands, 1930-31. Chmn. Ida. Rep. State Com., 1922-23, mem. many yrs.; also mem. Oneida Co. Rep. Com. many yrs. Ex-pres. Southern Ida. Timber Protective Assn. Mormon. Address: Field Div. Gen. Land Office, Salt Lake City UT*‡

NASH, LOUIS ROGERS, hosp. adminstr., physician; b. Omaha, Feb. 23, 1907; s. Louis C. and Janet E. (Rogers) N.; B.S., Georgetown U., 1929, M.D., 1933; grad. hosp. adminstrn. devel. program, Cornell U., 1962; m. Madalon Wagner, July 6, 1940; children—John B., Robert J., Louis C. Intern N.Y. Postgrad. Hosp., N.Y.C., 1934; research field work Rockefeller Inst., W. Indies, 1934-35; psychiat. resident, staff psychiatrist Hastings (Neb.) State Hosp., 1937-38, asst. supt., 1938-39; postgrad. psychiatry and neurology Neuropsychiat. Inst., Columbia, 1939; staff psychiatrist Camarillo (Cal.) State Hosp., 1941-48, asso. supt., 1948-53, supt.-med. dir., 1963-68; acting supt. Atascadero (Cal.) State Hosp., 1960-61. Bd. dirs. So. Coast Service Area, United Fund Ventura County. Served with M.C., AUS, 1939-41. Fellow Am. Psychiat. Assn.; mem. Am., Cal. med. assns., Ventura County Med. Soc., A.A.A.S., Royal Soc. Health, Los Angeles County Assn. Mental Health. Author articles in field. Home: Camarillo CA Died July 11, 1968; buried Conejo Mountain Meml. Park, Camarillo CA

NASH, LUTHER ROBERTS, engineer; b. Ridgefield, Conn., Jan. 22, 1871; s. John D. and Sarah J. (Holmes) N.; S.B., Mass. Inst. Tech., 1894; S.M., Harvard, as of 1898; m. Bonnibel Remington, of Boston, Mass., Oct. 15, 1896; 1 son, Frank Remington (dec.). With Stone & Webster, Inc., Boston, since 1895; designing and constg. engr., 1895-1904, mgr. pub. utilities, 1904-08; appraisal engr. and rate expert, 1908-19; consultant on regulation, rates, taxation, depreciation and pub. relations, 1919-32; v.p. Stone & Webster Engring. Corpn., in charge appraisals and rate Webster Engring. Corpn., in charge appraisals and rate investigations, 1933-37, cons. engr. since 1937; pres. Acorn Press, Inc., since 1938. Lecturer at Mass. Inst. Tech., Harvard and Mass. Dept. of Edn. Mem. Am. Inst. Elec. Engrs., Edison Electric Inst., Am. Gas Assn., Chi Phi. Republican. Conglist. Clubs: Silver Spring Country, Lions. Author: Economics of Public Utilities, 1931, Public Utility Rate Structures, 1933; also monographs and papers on utility and economic subjects. Home: 155 Main Street, Ridgefield, Conn. Office: Stone and Webster Building, 90 Broad Street, New York NY‡

WHO WAS WHO 526

NASH, OGDEN, writer; b. Rye, N.Y., Aug. 19, 1902; s. Edmund Strudwick and Mattie (Chenault) N.; student St. George's Sch., Newport, R.I., 1917-20, Harvard, 1920-21; m. Frances Rider Leonard, June 6, 1931; children—Linell Chenault, Isabel Jackson. Member of American Academy of Arts and Sciences, National Institute of Arts and Letters. Author: Hard Lines (verse), 1931; Free Wheeling, 1931; Happy Days, 1933; The Primrose Path (verse), 1935; The Bad Parents' Garden of Verse, 1936; I'm a Stranger Here Myself, 1938; Face is Familiar, 1940; Good Intentions, 1942; Many Long Years Ago (verse) 1945; Versus, 1949; Parents Keep Out, 1951; The Private Dining Room, 1953; You Can't Get There From Here, 1957; The Christmas That Almost Wasn't, 1957; (with Kurt Weill and also S.J. Perelman) One Touch of Venus (musical comedy), 1943; Verses from 1929 On, 1959; Everyone But Thee and Me, 1962; Marriage Lines—Notes of a Student Husband, 1964; Cruise of the Aardvark, 1967; There's Always Another Windmill, 1968. Frequent contbr. verse to leading mags. Died May 19, 1971; buried North Hampton NH

NASH, WALTER, former prime minister New Zealand; b. Kidderminster Eng., Feb. 12, 1882; s. Alfred Arthur and Amelia (Randle) N.; ed. St. John's Church Sch., Kidderminster; LL.D., Cambridge, (Eng.), 1937, Temple U., Tufts Coll. (U.S.); m. Lotty May Eaton, June 16, 1906;children—Clement Walter (dec.), Leslie Richard, James Archibald D. Began in mfg. bus., later became wholesale merchant, Birmingham, Eng.; moved to New Zealand, 1909; salesman woolen goods, then mfrs. and pubs. rep.; mem. of Parliament, 1929-68; minister of finance and customs, 1935-49; deputy prime minister, 1940-49; Leader of the Opposition, 1950-57, 60-63; prime minister New Zealand, minister external affairs, minister Maori affairs, 1957-60; minister of social security, 1938; minister of marketing, 1936-41; minister to United States 1942-44. Mem. Nat. Exec. Labour Party, 1919-37, 50-63; sec. New Zealand Labour Party, 1922-32, nat. pres., 1935-36; v.p. New Zealand Inst. Internat. Affairs, 1936; member Wellington Harbour Bd., 1933-38; mem. New Zealand War Cabinet, 1939-45. Pacific War Council, Washington, 1942-44; del. 2d ILO Conf., Geneva, 1920, Inst. Pacific Relations confs., Honolulu, 1927, Banff, 1933, Mont Tremblant, Can., 1942, Brit. Commonwealth Relations Conf., Toronto, Ont., Can., 1933; pres. ILO Conf., Phila., 1944; leader New Zealand del. Internat. Monetary Conf., Bretton Woods, 1944; del. Brit. Commonwealth Prime Ministers Conf., London, 1946, 60; leader del. to confs. on trade and employment, Geneva, 1947, Havana, 1947, 48; leader New Zeland del. 14th session Ecafe Kuala Lumpur, 1958; 4th session SEATO council ministers, Manila, 1958; UN general assembly, N.Y., Columbo Plan Meeting, Seattle, 1958, Wellington, New Zealand, 1959, Washington, 1960; leader New Zealand delegation UN, 1958-60, Antartic Conf., Washington, 1959. Mem. Privy Council. Decorated knight grand cross Order St. Michael and St. George, Companion of Honour. Home: Lower Hutt New Zealand Died June 4, 1968; inurned Karori Cemetery, Wellington New Zealand

NASON, LEONARD HASTINGS (STEAMER), author; b. Somerville, Mass., Sept. 28, 1895; s. Frank Leonard and Jennie Rand (Allen) N.; grad. Newton Tech. High Sch., B.Sc., Norwich U., 1920; m. Lucia Millet, Aug, 12, 1920; children—Jane, Priscilla, Leonard H. In Mexican border service, with 1st Vt. Inf., 1916; sergt. Battery A, 76th F.A., A.E.F.; wounded Mont St. Pere, July 1918, and Montfaucon, Oct. 1918; cited for gallantry in action" by Gens. Pershing and Howze (2 citations); active duty with U.S. Army, 1941-45; lt. col., cav. (Armored Force), Army U.S., 1942; made initial landing with U.S. forces, Morocco, 1942; mil. gov. of Rabat Dist., 1942; in Tunisian campaign, 1943; campaign of France, and the liberation of Paris, 1944. Sgt.-maj. of honor, Moroccan Regt. of Colonial Inf. (R.I.C.M.), 1943; col. Cavalry, U.S. Army Reserve. Decorated Bronze Star (combat), Purple Heart and Silver Star (U.S.); Ouissam Alaouite (Morocco). Mem. Ancient and Hon. Arty. Co. of Boston, Am. Legion, Soc. Third Division, Sigma Phi Epsilon, S.A.R. Conglist. Clubs: Norwich, Algonoquin (Boston); Cercle Internallie (Paris); Chiberta Country (Biarritz). Author: Chevrons, 1926; Three Lights from a Match, 1927; Sergeant Eadie, 1928; The Top Kick, 1928; The Man in the White Slicker, 1929; Incomplete Mariner, 1929; Livingstone Brothers, 1930; A Corporal Once, 1930; Defenders of the Bridge, 1932; Among the Trumpets, 1932; (screen play) Rodney, 1933; (screen play) Red Night, 1935; Eagles Eastward, 1936; I Spy Strangers, 1940; Approach to Battle, 1941; Contact Mercury, 1946; The Barbary Voyage, 1949. Contbr. stories to Adventure, Saturday Evening Post, Am. Legion Mag., also verse in the Line o'Type," Chicago Tribune, under pen name of Steamer." Home: New York City NY Died July 25, 1970; buried Arlington Nat. Cemetery, Arlington VA

NASON, THOMAS WILLOUGHBY, artist, engraver; b. Dracut, Mass., Jan. 7, 1889; s. William Walton and Kate Julia (Hooker) N.; educated in public schools; A.M. (hon.), Tufts College; married Margaret Warren, May 10, 1919. Represented in permanent collections of notable galleries and museums in U.S. and abroad, also private collections. Recipient of numerous prizes and awards. Served with 26th Div., A.E.F., U.S. Army, 1917-19. Fellow Am. Acad. Arts and Sciences; Nat. Acad., Nat. Inst. of Arts and Letters, Lyme Art Assn. Home: Lyme CT Died 1971; buried Cove Cemetery, Lyme CT

NASSER, GAMAL ABDEL, president of United Arab Republic, chmn. Supreme Arab Socialist Union com.; b. Alexandria, Egypt, Jan. 15, 1918; grad. Mil. Acad., 1938, Army Staff Coll., 1948; m. 1944; children—Khaled, Abdel Hamid, Abdel Hakim, Hoda, Mona. Comdr. inf. platoon, Assiout barracks, 1937; advanced lt. col. Egyptian Army; instructor Military Academy; in active service with army, World War II; head of 12-man Revolutionary Command Council which planned and led revolution to gain control of army and force abdication of King Farouk, July 1952; proclaimed Egypt a republic, ending reign of King Admed Fuad II (son of ex-King Farouk), June 1952, and became deputy premier and minister of interior; prime minister, head revolution command council, 1952-56, pres. Republic of Egypt, 1956; pres. UAR, 1958-70; chmn. Supreme Arab Socialist Union Com., 1962-70; nationalized Suez Canal Co., 1956; realized unity between Egypt and Syria, 1958; proclaimed Socialist laws, 1961, 63; diverted course of Nile, 1964. Address: Cairo UAR Died Sept. 28, 1970; buried Gamal Abdel Nasser's Mosque, Manshiet El Bakri, Cairo UAR

NATELSON, MORRIS, business exec.; b. N.Y.C., Nov. 16, 1904; s. Max and Bessie Hannah (Melinkoff) N.; B.B.A., Coll. City N.Y., 1925; m. Ruth Norton, Feb. 1, 1931; children—Maryanna, David; m. 2d, Ruth Gormley, Sept. 28, 1943; 1 dau., Pamela Adelaide. Office mgr. Crescent Leather Goods Co., 1925-27; asso. Lehman Bros., 1928-49, partner, 1950-72; dir. Bond Stores, Inc., Edison Bros. Stores, Inc., Zayre Corp., Maryland Cup Corp., Commerce Oil Refining Corp., United Piece Dye Works, Harvard Industries, Inc., Beneficial Standard Corp., Beneficial Nat. Corp. Home: Port Washington NY Died Aug. 23, 1972.

NATHAN, J(ACOB) PHILIP, banker; b. Chgo., July 27, 1905; s. Samuel and Annie (Shorris) N.; student Internat. Accountants Soc., 1922-26, Am. Inst. Banking, 1921-27; m. Annette E. Quartararo, Sept 5, 1936; 1son, David Paul. With Anglo Cal. Nat. Bank of San Francisco, 1921-56, v.p., controller, 1950-56; v.p., controller Crocker-Anglo Nat. Bank, also Crocker-Citizen Nat. Bank, San Francisco, 1956-70. Mem. Financial Execs. Inst., San Francisco Comml. Club. Home: San Francisco CA Died 1970.

NATIONS, GILBERT OWEN, lawyer, educator; b. Perry County, Mo., Aug. 18, 1866; s. James W. and Caroline L. (Hart) N.; B.S., Lebanon (Ohio) U., 1890; Ph.M., Hiram (Ohio) Coll., 1900; Ph.D., American U., 1919; LL.D., Eugene (Ore.) Bible University, 1927; m. Sallie E. McFarland, Dec. 5, 1886 (died Feb. 13, 1940); children—Reginald Heber, Zora Caroline (Mrs. Leonard S. Ritter), Gus Orville (dec.), Myrtle Frances (Mrs. Roy Ellis), Paul Douglass, Florence Emily (Mrs. Alfred Pyatt), Karl McFarland. Practiced law in Mo. until 1916; judge Probate Ct., Farmington, Mo., 1903-11; prof. Roman law, canon law and legal history, Am. U., 1920-34; pub. The Protestant, 1921-31; editor The Fellowship Forum, 1931-36. Nominee of Am. Party for president of U.S., 1924. Mem. Christian Ch. Mason (32 deg.). Author: Papal Sovereignty, 1917; Canon Law of Papal Throne, 1926; Political Career of Alfred E. Smith, 1928; Roman Catholic War on Public Schools, 1931. Home: 1506 Grace Church Rd., Silver Spring MD‡

NAUMBURG, GEORGE WASHINGTON, retired banker; b. New York, N.Y., July 4, 1876; s. Elkan and Bertha (Wehle) N.; student Phillips Exeter Acad., 1894; A.B., Harvard, 1898; m. Emma Adler, May 28, 1900; children—Bertha (dec.), Virginia; m. 2d, Ruth Morgenthau, Apr. 30, 1917; children—George W., Philip Henry, Ellin; m. 3d, Cecile Louchheim Steppacher, Nov. 24, 1937. Mem. E. Naumburg & Co., New York, 1899-1932; pres. N.Y. Guaranteed Mortgage Protection Corp., 1933. Mem. exec. com. Citizens Budget Commn. Asst. chief cotton sect. War Industries Bd., methods sect. Gen. Staff World War I. V.p. Parents Inst. (pub. Parents Mag.); pres. Baron de Hirsch Fund; pres. Naumburg Orchestral Found. Com. Finance and Currency C. of C., N.Y. Refugee Econ. Corp., Hawthorne Sch. for Delinquent Boys and Girls, Beckman Hosp., Ossining Hosp.; mem. overseers vis. com. dept. social relations dept., Harvard. Chmn. finance com., mem. distribution com., trustee, v.p. citizens budget commn. Fedn. Support of Jewish Philanthropies of N.Y. Clubs: Terrace, Harvard, Bohemians, Harmonie, Bankers, 60 East, Chemists. Home: Croton-on-Hudson NY Died June 23, 1970.

NAUSS, HENRY G., educator; b. Wappingers Falls, N.Y.; d. Louis George and Mary Ann (Rode) Lauber; grad. N.J. State Tchrs. Coll., 1916; B.S. in Edn., Wayne State U., 1943, M.A. in Sociology and Clin. Psychology, 1950; postgrad. Western Carolina U., 1962; m. Henry G. Nauss, June 29, 1920. Tchr., Demarest (N.J.) Pub. Schs., 1916-20; tchr., sch. psychologist spl. edn. dept. Bryson City (N.C.) Schs., 1956-71. Sec., organizer Sarasota (Fla.) Mental Health Soc., 1951-53. Recipient commendation N.C. Dept. Pub. Instrn., 1965. Mem. Am. Sociol. Assn., Am. Assn. Mental Deficiency, Nat., N.C., Bryson City congresses parents and tchrs., N.E.A., N.C. Edn. Assn., Classroom Tchrs. Assn., Detroit Fedn. Women's Clubs (social welfare chmn. 1945-50), Council for Exceptional Children, Am. Assn. U. Women (nomination chmn. Bryson City chpt. 1966, pres. 1967-69), Bus. and Profl. Woman's Club (v.p. Bryson City chpt. 1966), P.E.O., Bryson City NC Died June 22, 1971; buried Swain Meml. Park Cemetery Bryson City NC

NAVIN, ROBERT B(ERNARD), clergyman, coll. pres.; b. Youngstown, O., Apr. 27, 1895; s. John and Bridget (Kenney) N.; student St. Charles Coll., 1913-17; S.T.D., Collegium Urbanum, Rome, Italy, 1923; M.A., Cath. U., 1932, Ph.D., 1935. Ordained priest, Roman Cath. Ch., 1923; dean St. John Coll., Cleveland, 1929-48, pres. since 1948. Mem. Cleveland Welfare Fedn., bd. of dirs. of ACTION: mem. Community Relation Bd. Cleveland. Mem. Am. Cath. Ednl. Assn., Am. Cath. Sociol. Soc. (pres. 1949), Am. Sociol. Soc., Cleve., Council of World Affairs (bd. trustees). Home: Cleveland OH Died Feb. 12, 1970.

NAYLON, EDMUND BARRY, lawyer; b. Schenectady, Nov. 18, 1900; s. Daniel and Delia (Barry) N.; B.S., Union Coll., 1923; LL.B., Bklyn. Law Sch., 1926; m. Marion C. O'Keefe, Aug. 6, 1932. Admitted to N.Y. bar, 1927; with Title, Guarantee & Trust Co., N.Y.C., 1923; legal dept. Asso. Gas & Electric System, 1924-35; pvt. law practice, 1935-40; sr. partner firm Naylon, Huber, Magill, Lawrence & Farrell, and predecessors, 1940-72, specializing in corp. law. Mem. Am., N.Y. State bar assns., New York County Lawyers Assn., Assn. Bar City N.Y., Phi Beta Kappa, Kappa Alpha. Home: New York City NY Died Mar. 28, 1972.

NEAL, ERNEST EUGENE, fgn. service officer; b. Chattanooga, Tenn., June 21, 1911; s. Orange Marion and Mamie Louise (Shepherd) N.; B.S., Knoxville Coll., 1935; M.A., Fisk U., 1938; grad. student sociology, U. Mich., 1942-43, 47-48; LL.D. (hon.), Texas Coll., 1956; m. Pearl J. Johnson, July 23, 1944 (div. 1965); children—Kathleen Juette, Ernest Eugene (dec.); m. 2d, Judith L. Strack, May 25, 1965; 1 dau., Amy Louise. Chmn. dept. social sci. Texas Coll., 1939-42; information specialist regional office, OPA, Dallas, 1944-45; prof. sociology and econs. N.C. Coll., 1945-46; dir. applied edn. Bishop Coll., Marshall, Tex., 1947-48; dir. rural life council Tuskegee Inst., 1948-54; community development adviser U.S. mission to India, New Delhi, 1954-56; spl. asst. for community development U.S. mission to Philippines, Manila, 1956-58; dep. dir. U.S. mission to Liberia, Monrovia, 1958-60; dir. U.S. mission to Sierra Leone, 1960-63; dep. dir. rural and community devel. AID, Wash., 1963-64; dep. dir. U.S. AID Mission to Philippines, 1964-69; regional population officer, Accra, Ghana, 1969-71. Cons. Hogg Found. Mental Hygiene, University of Texas, from 1940; consultant regional studies division TVA, 1948-54; adviser child labor Dept. of Labor, 1950-54. Gen. Edn. fellow, 1942-43, 47-48; recipient Certificate of Merit (Philippines), 1958. Fellow Am. Social Soc.; mem. Rural Sociol. Soc., Soc. Internat. Development, Am. Acad. Polit. and Social Sci. Baptist. Home: Reston VA Died Jan. 14, 1972; buried Greenwood Cemetery, Tuskegee Institute AL

NEAL, MILLS FERRELL, mfr.; b. Richmond, Va., Aug. 29, 1893; s. Thomas David and Fannie (Mills) N.; ed. pub. schs., Richmond; student bus. adminstrn., 1909-12, Army War Coll., 1934. With Neal & Binford (tobacconists supplies), 1912-27; organized firm M. F. Neal & Co., Inc., 1927, pres., 1927-70; pres. Tuckahoe Warehouse Corp.; dir. Bank of Va. Bd. visitors Va. Mil. Inst. Served to lt. col. Va. N.G., 1911-17, 20-40, in Fed. service on Mex. border 1917; served from 2nd lt. to 1st lt. U.S. Army, 1917-19; to col. AUS, 1940-46; dir. Selective Service for Va., with Supreme Hdqrs. Allied Expeditionary Forces; ETO. Decorated D.S.M. Clubs: Commonwealth, Country Club of Virginia (Richmond). Author of Selective Service Plan for State of Virginia. Home: Richmond VA Died Sept. 1972.

NEAL, PHIL HUDSON, mining and mfg. co. exec.; b. Ridgeway, Ga., July 6, 1894; s. George G. and Kate C (Brannon) N.; student U. Ill., 1911-12; m. Amy R Gross, Mar. 10, 1921; 1 son, Phil Hudson. Asso. Ala By-Products Corp. as mgr. coke and coal and chemica sales, v.p., asst. to pres., and pres., Birmingham 1946-68, dir. mem. exec. com., 1968; pres., dir Smokeless Fuel Co., Birmingham, 1946-68; pres., di Ketona Chem. Corp., Ketona, Ala., 1954-68, dir., 1968 Mem. Birmingham's Com. of 100. Bd. govs. Ala Mining Inst. Mem. Am. Coke and Coal Chems Inst Civic Symphony Assn., Asso. Industries Ala. (hon. dir. C. of C., Newcomen Soc. Episcopalian. Rotarian. Clubs Birmingham Country, Vestavia Country, Down Town The Club (Birmingham). Home: Birmingham AL Die Apr. 28, 1972.

NEAL, WILLIAM WATT, advt. agy. exec.; Kernersville, N.C., Apr. 9, 1908; s. William Watt an ucy Bell (Vance) N.; A.B., U. N.C., 1928; m. Fort ott Meador Willingham, Jan. 1, 1964; ildren—Polly Vance (Mrs. Al B. Braselton), Belle illingham (Mrs. George Kirkpatrick), Thomas Irving illingham, Anna Willingham (Mrs. Galen Kilburn, .), William Watt. With James A. Greene & Co., tlanta, 1928-29; sec. Gottschaldt-Humphrey, Inc., tlanta, 1929-36; with Phillips Granite Co., Rion, S.C.,)36-39, Freitag Advt. Agy., Atlanta, 1939-40; chmn. I. Liller, Neal, Battle & Lindsey, Inc., Atlanta. Dir. esbyn. Survey Mag. Vice pres. Met. Atlanta ommunity Services, 1954, 65. Bd. dirs. Atlanta Tb. ssn., Ga. Soc. for Crippled Children and Adults, U. .C. Alumni Bd., 1962-67. Mem. Am. Assn. Advt. gys. (past sec.-treas, dir.), Atlanta Advt. Club (past es.), Phi Beta Kappa, Sigma Phi Epsilon, Alpha Delta gma. Presbyn. (elder), Clubs: Atlanta Athletic, edmont Driving, University Yacht (Atlanta), Ansley olf. Home: Atlanta GA Died Feb. 6, 1970.

EBEKER, FRANK KNOWLTON, lawyer; b. aketown, Utah, May 15, 1870; s. Ira and Delia (Lane) .; LL.B., Cornell, 1895; m. Lillian Martineau, July 10, 390; children—Frank Knowlton, Mrs. Marjorie oung, Lyman Martineau, Mrs. Joyce N. Mueller, Mrs. elia N. Taylor, Mrs. Ruth N. Hannegan. In practice at ogan, Utah, Jan. 1896-1909; in private practice Salt ake City, 1909-17; asst. gen. atty. Ore. Short Line R.R. o., Salt Lake City, 1909-12; county atty., Cache ounty, Utah, 1896-1900; dist. atty., 1st Jud. Dist., 00-04; Utah mem. Dem. Nat. Com., 1908-16; spl. st. to U.S. atty. gen., in charge of prosecution in hicago of W.D Haywood and other leaders of the W.W., Aug. 1917-Sept. 1918; asst. atty. gen. in charge b. lands div., Washington, June 1919-Nov. 1920; asst. atty. gen. in charge anti-trust div. Dept. of Justice, ov. 1920-Mar. 1921; in gen. practice, Washington, nce Mar. 1921; spl. asst. to atty. gen. in charge U.S. vs. eirton Steel Co., Apr. 1934-June 1935. Mem. Am. aw Inst., Am. Bar Assn. Club: Nat. Press. Home: 3409 oodley Rd., N.W. Office: Tower Bldg., Washington C*‡

EDVED, ELIZABETH KIMBALL (MRS. UDOLPH JAMES NEDVED), architect, atercolorist; b. Chgo., Oct. 26, 1897; d. Ernest Morton d Jessie (Wilson) Kimball; student Northwestern U., 15-16, Ch. Sch. Art, Chgo., 1916-18, U. Ill., 1921-22; S., Armour Inst. Tech., 1925; m. Rudolph James edved, Sept. 4, 1923; children—Kimball, Rudolph mes, Antonia Elizabeth. Architect, Nedved & mball, Architects, Chgo., 1926-69; with Bur. Ships SN, Washington, 1943; exhibited in group shows Art st. Chgo., 1920's, Corcoran Gallery, Washington, 36; Cliff Dweller, 1965; tchr. watercolor classes. em. A.I.A. Important works include Sunset Point tate, Eagle River, Wis. Home: Glencoe IL Died Apr. 1969.

EEDHAM, DANIEL, lawyer; b. Groton, Mass., Feb. 1891; s. Daniel and Ellen Mary (Brigham) N.; ed. roton pub. schs., Phillips (Andover) Acad.; A.B., arvard, 1913, LL.B., 1916; m. Frances Sarah Topping, pr. 27, 1921; children—Daniel, Jr., Nathalie. dmitted to Mass. Bar, 1917; since engaged in gen. actice at Boston; mem. firm Sherburne, Powers & eedham, 1919-71; vice president, dir. Nat. Fireworks dnance Corp., Clark-Babbitt Foods, Inc., Babbitt pe Co., Inc., Nat. Coating, Inc., Babbitt Missile Co.; ., clk. Waterfront Service Company, Incorporated; ustee Nat. Assos. Commr. pub. safety Mass., 1933-34; em. Mass. Bd. Probation, 1938-41, Mass. Crime ommission, 1956-58, Electoral Coll., 1956, Assay ommn., 1960; chmn. gov.'s adv. com. civil def. Dir. oston Met. chpt. A.R.C., chmn., 1956-58; dir. United nd Greater Boston, Blood Research Institute. Pres. ard trustees Lawrence Acad. Lt. and capt., 26th Div., S. Army, World War I, maj. gen. comdg. 26th Div. ass. N.G., 1934-39; honored by 2 citations (U.S.). ecorated Silver Star. Mem. Am., Mass., Middlesex, oston bar assns., Pi Eta. Republican. Mason. Clubs: nion, YD, Harvard (Boston); Brae Burn Country, urtis, Middlesex. Home: West Newton MA Died June 71.

EEDLES, ENOCH RAY, cons. engr.; b. Brookfield, o., Oct. 29, 1888; s. Sim Gesmer and Elma (Bray) N.; S., Mo. Sch. Mines, 1914, C.E., 1920, D.Eng. (hon.), 37; m. Ethel Schuman, Sept. 12, 1916; ildren—Elma (Mrs. J.W. Wight), Margaret (Mrs. P. Williams), Mary (Mrs. H.P. McJunkin), Thomas Carolyn (Mrs. C.E. Homer), Sally Jane (Mrs. H.J. ffey). Various engring. positions, 1914-28; partner oward, Needles, Tammen & Bergendoff, cons. engrs., Y.C., also Kansas City, Mo., from 1928; prin. projects clude: Del. Meml. Bridge, Pulaski Skyway, Harlem ver Lift Bridge, Me. Turnpike, N.J. Turnpike, W.Va. rnpike, Ohio Turnpike, 5 other state turnpikes, merous other state and fed. projects, various Miss. ver bridges. Served as col., Corps. Engrs., AUS, 42-45. Decorated Legion of Merit; recipient UMR ver Centennial medal honor, 1971. Mem. Am. Road ilders Assn. (pres. 1949-50), Am. Soc. C.E. (pres. 55-56), Am. Inst. Cons. Engrs. (pres. 1946), Soc. Am. il. Engrs., Nat. Soc. Profl. Engrs., Am. Association for dvancement of Science, Engineers Joint Council esident 1958-59), Newcomen Soc., Tau Beta Pi, Phi Kappa Phi, Chi Epsilon, Pi Kappa Alpha. Clubs: Bankers, Engineers (N.Y.C.); Canoe Brook (N.J.) Country; Morris County (N.J.) Golf. Webhannet (Me.) Golf; Army and Navy (Washington). Home: New Vernon NJ Died Jan. 5, 1972; buried New Vernon NJ

NEEF, FREDERICK EMIL, surgeon; b. Springfield, Ill., July 11, 1872; s. Emil and Caroline (Armbruster) N.; B.S., Notre Dame U., 1892, B.L., 1893, M.L., 1895; M.D., Columbia, 1904; m. Kathryn M.E. Brandt, Oct. 11, 1912; children—Kathryn Marie Caroline, Frederick Emil, Dorothy Eileen, Alice Hopeful. Began practice at New York, 1907; served as jr. surgeon, Lincoln Hosp., attending surgeon, St. Elizabeth's Hosp. and N.Y. City Cancer Inst.; taught at Fordham U., 13 years, dean, dept. of gynecology and obstetrics, 1919-21; post grad. teacher, N.Y. City Cancer Inst., dir. gynecology, Misericordia Hosp. since 1935; cons. in gynecology, Lenox Hill, Rockaway Beach and St. Francis hosps. Fellow Am. Coll. Surgeons; mem. Clin. Soc., German Med. Soc. Republican. Author: Practical Points in Anesthesia, 1908; Guiding Principles in Surgical Practice, 1914; Surgical Nursing, 1933, Contbr. to med. jours. Home: Smithridge Rd., Lewisboro, N.Y. Office: 1070 Park Av., NYC 28‡

NEELANDS, THOMAS D., JR., financial cons.; b. Chicago, July 31, 1902; s. Thomas D. and Catherine E. (Metaxas) N.; ed. Phillips Acad., Andover, Mass., Sheffield Scientific Sch., Yale, 1923; Princeton, 1924; m. Katherine M. O'Connor, July 28, 1934; two children. Asso. with Jackson & Curtis, investment bankers, N.Y. City, 1923-32; pres. and chmn. bd. dirs. N.R. Airways, Inc., N.Y. City, 1927-30; financial cons. Travel Air Airplane Co., Wichita, Kan., 1926-29; Boettcher Newton & Co., investment bankers, N.Y. City, 1932-34; sr. partner Neelands Platte (changed to T.D. Neelands, Jr., & Co.), investment bankers, 1934-42; pres. and chmn. bd. dirs. Kathlands Development Corp., N.Y. City, since 1936; financial consultant Beech Aircraft Corp., Wichita, Kansas, 1941-42, 45-53; chmn. finance com. Robinson Aviation, 1958-72; chmn. bd. dirs. Silex Co., Hartford, Conn.; chmn. bd., mem. exec. com. Capital Airlines, Inc., Wash., 1960-72; chmn. finance com., mem. exec. com., dir. Proctor-Silev Corp., Philadelphia. Served as major, United States Army, Office of Fiscal Dir., Chief of Loan Sect., 1942-45. Mem. N.Y. C. of C. Clubs: Book and Snake (Yale) N. Hempstead (L.I.) Country, Midday, Wall Street, Candian (N.Y.C.); Sands Point Golf. Home: Oyster Bay LI NY Died Jan. 1972.

NEELEY, JOHN LAWTON, lawyer; b. Jefferson Co., Fla., Sept. 17, 1877; s. Samuel Villepigne and Sarah (Arendal) N.; ed. pub. schs. and under pvt. tutors; m. Russell DeWitt Lott, of Gadsden Co., Fla., June 5, 1902. Sec. to Railroad Commn. of Fla., 1897-1901; admitted to Fla., bar, 1898; mem. Fla. Ho. of Rep., from Leon Co., 1909; again elected, 1915, but resigned to become U.S. atty. for Northern Dist. of Fla.; reapptd., 1916, for term 1916-20. Chmn. bd. Fla. State Coll., 1902-5. Democrat. Methodist. Mason, Odd Fellow, K.P. Home: Pensacola FL‡

NEELY, JOHN MARSHALL, III, physician; b. Elmwood, Neb., 1904; s. John Marshall and Edna (Perry) N: M.D., U. Neb., 1930; m. Mary Foulon Barlow, July 9, 1929; children—Mary Jean, Hugh Williams. Intern, U. Neb. Hosp., Omaha, 1930; intern Ancker Hosp., St. Paul, 1930-31, resident in pathology, 1931-32, resident in roentgenology, 1933; postgrad. course U. Minn., 1931-32; resident in radiology Lincoln (Neb.) Gen. Hosp., 1936-37, pathologist and radiologist, until 1969; radiologist Neb. Orthopaedic Hosp.; attending radiologist VA Hosp., St. Elizabeths Hosp, Neb. State Orthopaedic Hosp. (all Lincoln), Lutheran Hosp., Beatrice, Neb.; sr. instr. radiology U. Mich., 1938-39; asst. prof. radiology Creighton U., until 1969. Chmn., Neb. Bd. Med. Examiners, 1949-59. Pres., Lincoln Symphony. Served to capt., M.C., USNR, 1942-45. Diplomate Am. Bd. Radiology. Fellow Am. Soc. Clin. Pathology, A.C.P., Am. Coll. Radiology; mem. A.M.A., Radiol. Soc. N.Am., Am. Radium Soc., Lancaster County Med. Soc. (pres.), Alpha Sigma Phi, Nu Sigma Nu. Elk. Home: Lincoln NE Died May 9, 1969.

NEFF, ELIZABETH HYER, author; b. Greenfield, O.; d. Col. Jacob and Amanda C. (Sayre) Hyer; M.L.A., Ohio Wesleyan Univ., 1874; m. William B. Neff, of Cleveland. Author: Altars to Mammon, 1908. Address: Tynewald," Gates Mill, O., and Cleveland‡

NEFF, GROVER CLEVELAND, chmn. Wis. Power & Light Co.; b. Milford, Ind., Aug. 12, 1886; s. James and Mary (Miller) N.; B.S. in C.E., Purdue U., 1907, C.E., 1911, E.D., 1952; m. May Prehn, Dec. 31, 1910;children—Mary Louise, William James. With Wis. Power & Light Co., from 1908, pres. 1934, chmn. 1954-63. Chmn. rural electric service com. Nat. Electric Light Assn., 1922-27; sec. and treasurer Com. on Relation of Electricity to Agrl., 1923-39; pres. Edison Electric Institute, June 1946-47. Mem. Am. Inst. E.E., Am. Soc. Agrl. Engrs., Wis. Utilities Assn., Tau Beta Pi. Mason. Clubs: University, Maple Bluff Country, Madison Technical, Rotary. Contbr. on rural electrification. Address: Madison WI Died Oct. 30, 1970.

NEFF, HAROLD HOPKINS, lawyer; b. Harrisonburg, Va., Oct. 8, 1891; s. Dr. John H. and Brownie (Morrison) N.; B.S., M.A., LL.B., U. of Va., 1917; student U. of Berlin, U. of Marburg, Germany, U. of Caen, France, 1912-13; m. Henriette Thomas, Dec. 16, 1918 (div. Feb. 1950); children—Philippe, Jacqueline (Mrs. Wright). Yvonne (Mrs. Calomeris); m. 2d, Irene F. Getz, Oct. 28, 1950; 1 stepson, Harry D. Getz. Admitted to N.Y. bar, 1917; practiced law in N.Y. City, 1921-24; prof. internat. law, U. of Va., 1924-26; practiced law in Paris, France, 1927-31; represented Am. interests in Europe during liquidation of Kreuger Cos., 1932; spl. adviser to State Dept., 1933; dir. Export-Import Bank, 1933-35; asst. chief securities div. FTC, 1933-34; asst. gen. counsel SEC, 1934-35, dir. forms and regulations div., 1936-38, European rep. in London, Eng., 1939, foreign expert, 1940; spl. asst. to under sec. of war 1941-47; spl. asst. to sec. of army, 1947-48; Am. del. to Internat. Trade Conf., Geneva, Switzerland, 1947; War Dept. rep. on policy com. Bd. Econ. Warfare, Exec. Com. Econ. Fgn. Policy, Trade Agreements Com., Com. for Reciprocity Information, Nat. Munitions Control Bd.; ret. Served as 2d lt., U.S. Army Tank Corps, A.E.F., 1917-19. Recipient Exceptional Civilian Service award, 1946. Mem. Am. Bar Assn., Am. Soc. of Internat. Law, Raven Soc., Phi Beta Kappa, Sigma Chi. Clubs: Army and Navy Country, University (Washington, D.C.). Contbr. articles to law jours. Home: Washington DC Died Apr. 15, 1971; buried Culpeper (Va.) Nat. Cemetery.

NEFF, J. LOUIS, public health executive; b. Brooklyn, N.Y., Feb. 25, 1894; s. Louis and Viola M. (Fallshaw) N.; Cornell U., 1916; m. Maron Hanson, March 2, 1929; children—Louis Eaton, James Allan. Exec. sec. Nassau Co. Med. Soc., 1923-43; editor Nassau Med. News, 1927-43; sec. Nassau County Cancer Com., 1928-43; exec. dir. Am. Soc. for Control Cancer, Inc., New York City, 1944-46, Texas Division, Houston, Tex., 1946-55; exec. sec. Nassau Co. Med. Soc. and Acad. Medicine, from 1955. Del. mem. Am. Cancer Soc.; mem. exec. com., Nassau div., 1958. Dir. Nassau Co. Tb. and Pub. Health Assn., 1934-44; asst. editor Jour Aviation Medicine, 1944-46; chmn. Nassau County chpt. Nat. Multiple Sclerosis Soc., 1955-56. Fellow Am. Pub. Health Assn., Pub. Heath Cancer Assn. Am. (charter mem.); hon. mem. Asso. Physicians of L.I. (sec.), Society Pub. Health Educators (sec.), mem. Alpha Gamma Rho. Episcopalian. Mason. Club: Cornell, N.Y. City. Contbr. health edn. articles to nat. jours. Office: Garden City NY Died Jan. 1963; buried Mt. Olivet Cemetery, Brooklyn NY

NEFF, JOSEPH A., business exec., b. Phila., 1900. Chmn. bd., mem. exec. com., dir. D.A. Schulte & Co.; pres., dir. Jan Products Co., Neff & Co., Inc.; pres. Cigarette Lighter Mfrs. Home: New York City NY Died June 1969.*

NEILL, LELIA WINSLOW BRAY (MRS. CHARLES R. NEILL), artist, orgn. exec.; b. Kansas City, Mo., Jan. 24, 1892; d. George Thatcher and Hattie (Debord) Bray; student pub. schs.; m. Charles R. Neill, Nov. 3, 1917; children—John R., Charles R., Anne (Mrs. Glenn Stubbs). Tchr. pub. schs., Kansas City Mo., 1909-17; partner Charles R. Neill Agy., real estate and ins., 1930-60; treas., clk. City of Hotchkiss, 1941-46; treas., mgr. Local Credit Union, 1941-46; artist, 1961-69; one-man show Komac Gallery; exhibited in group shows various cities in Colo.; represented in pvt. collection throughout U.S. Recipient numerous awards, first and second prizes, best of show. Local pres. W.C.T.U., 1955-58, dist. pres., 1958-62; Colo. state v.p., 1959-65. Mem. Bus. and Profl. Woman's Club, Nat. Fedn. Women's Clubs (past pres., dist. officer, recipient award for outstanding leadership 1966). Democrat (del. Colo. Conv. 1964). Methodist (chmn. ch. commn. on Christian social concerns 1960-65). Clubs: Federated Woman's. Home: Hotchkiss CO Died Jan. 13, 1969.

NEILSON, JASON ANDREW, banker, mcht.; b. N.Y. City, June 3, 1872; s. Jason Androscoggin and Margaret (Hay) N.; m. Charlotta Isabel, of Phoenixville, Pa., Jan. 1919; 1 son, Jason Andrew. With Stern Bros., dry goods, New York, 1883-1902; Brown Bros. & Co., bankers, 1902-17; v.p. Mercantile Bank of the Americas, 1917-21, Nat. Bank of Nicaragua, 1912-21, Banco Mercantil Americano del Peru, 1917-20. Republican. Episcopalian. Club: Commonwealth of Calif. Home: Fairmont Hotel. Office: 310 Sansome St., San Francisco CA‡

NEILSON, NEVIN PAUL, fgn. service officer; b. Allentown, Pa., June 25, 1915; s. Jay Arden and Florence Marie (Ranck) N.; A.B., La. State U., 1940; grad. Air War Coll., 1958; m. Rhoda Marathea Arneson, Oct. 9, 1948; 1 dau., Perl Alain. Newspaper reporter, 1935-36; editor Press Assn., Inc., 1940-43; radio news commentator ABC, N.Y.C., 1943-45; pub. relations Hill & Knowlton, N.Y.C., 1945-46; radio news commentator CBS, MBS, 1946-48; fgn. service officer Dept. State, 1948-71; assigned U.S. Information Agy., Indonesia, Japan, Thailand, Indo-China, Burma, then asst. dir. Far East to 1962; counselor of embassy for public affairs, Djakarta. R.I. (Indonesia), 1962-65; counselor for pub. affairs United States Mission, Geneva, Switzerland, 1965-67; pacification adviser U.S.

embassy, Saigon, 1967-69; pub. affairs adviser Bur. E. Asia, Pacific; Dept. State, 1969-71; adviser U.S. delegation SEATO Conference, Manila, P.I., 1954, UN Emergency Session on Middle East, 1958. Recipient meritorious service award U.S. Information Agy., 1956. Mem. Am. Acad. Polit. Sci., Fgn. Policy Assn., Sigma Delta Chi, Theta Xi. Clubs Chicago Press, Tokyo Press. Home: Washington DC Died Feb. 19, 1971.

NEL, LOUIS TAYLOR, geologist; b. Wolmaransstad, South Africa, Feb. 24, 1895; s. Paul and Mabel (Taylor) N.; M.Sc. cum laude, U. Stellenbosch, South Africa, 1920, D.Sc., 1927; postgrad. U. Feiburg U. Bonn, 1930; m. Muriel Isabelle Malherbe, Mar. 15, 1932; children—Paul Malherbe, Muriel Mabel (Mrs. J.G.M. Antelme), Louis Hubert Alvin. With Geol. Survey of South Africa, 1920-55, dir., 1948-55, ret., 1955; geol. adviser Atomic Energy Bd. South Africa, 1955-68. Bd. curators Transvaal Mus., 1944-63; mem. mgmt. com. Govt. Metall. Lab., 1948-60; mem. Nat. Com. for Advancement Sci., 1955-62. Recipient Prix Spendiaroff, Internat. Geol. Congress, 1929. Fellow Geol. Soc. London; mem. Geol. Soc. S. Africa (Draper Meml. medal 1943, council 1937-64, pres. 1942), S. African Assn. Advancement Sci. (life), S. African Acad. Sci. and Arts (Havenga prize 1955). Author: The Geology of the Country Around Vredefort, 1927; Geology of the Postmasburg Manganese Deposits, 1929; Geology of the Kierksdorp and Ventersdorp District, 1935; also articles, ofcl. publs. Research on Witwatersrand System, Dredefort Dome, genesis of gold and uranium deposits, resources of nuclear raw materials in S. Africa. Home: Pretoria Republic of South Africa Died June 1968.

NELSON, BURTON EDSAL, educator; b. July 30, 1867; s. John and Susan (Cypher) N.; grad. Whitehall Acad., Camp Hill, Pa., 1882; grad. Pa. State Normal Sch., Millersville, Pa., 1884; B.S., Western Normal Coll., Bushnell, Ill., 1891, M.S., 1895. Teacher rural schools until 1889; principal high schs., Bushnell, 1891-93; supt. schs. Lewistown, Ill., 1893-1900, Lincoln, 1900-04, Racine, Wis., 1904-18; sales mgr. and lecturer on visual edn., Keystone View Co., 1918-23; pres. The Stout Inst., Menomonie, Wis. (state coll., training teachers of home economics and industrial education), 1923-45; retired Nov. 1, 1945. Home: Menomonie WI‡

NELSON, CHARLES DONALD, educator; b. Stratford, Ont., Can., Sept. 16, 1927; s. Albert Ernest and Grace (Mitchell) N.; student Ont. Normal Sch., 1946; B.A. with honours, Queen's U. at Kingston, 1951, M.A., 1952, Ph.D., 1955; m. Frances McEwen, Aug. 22, 1953; children—Nancy, Barbara, Elizabeth, Donald. Tchr. elementary schs., Ottawa, Can., 1946-48; tchr. secondary schs., Ottawa, 1949; research asso. Atomic Energy of Canada, Ltd., Chalk River, Can., 1952; instr. U. Pa., 1953; research officer NRC, Ottawa, 1955-59; asst. prof. Queen's U., Kingston, 1959-60, asso. prof., 1960-65, chmn. dept. biology, 1964-65; prof., head dept. biol. scis. Simon Fraser U., Burnaby, B.C., 1964-68, dean sci., 1965-68. Mem. com. plant sci. NRC, 1966-68. Mem. Acad. Bd. of B.C. Gov., Vancouver Aquarium Assn. Fellow Royal Soc. Can., N.Y. Acad. Sci.; mem. Canadian Soc. Plant Physiologists, Am. Soc. Plant Physiologists. Research in translocation of organic compounds in plants; photosynthesis, primary productivity, and photorespiration; patentee herbicides. Home: Burnaby BC Canada Died June 22, 1968; interred Fife Cemetery Keene Ontario Canada

NELSON, CLARENCE, clergyman; b. St. Paul, Sept. 8, 1900; s. John Nicholas and Amelia (Swenson) N.; student North Park Theol. Sem., Chicago, 1918-20; L.H.D., 1964, A.B., Macalester College, 1930, D.D., 1955; student University of Chicago, 1929, The University of Minnesota, 1932-34; m. Blanche A. Nordell, Oct. 27, 1926; 1 son, Craig W. Ordained to ministry of the Evangelical Covenant Ch., June, 1927; served as asso. pastor, 1st Covenant Ch., St. Paul, 1921-24; pastor, Mission Covenant Ch., Evanston, Ill., 1926-29, Salem Covenant Ch., Minneapolis, 1929-45; pres. Minnehaha Acad., 1943-50, North Park Coll. and Theol. Sem., 1950-59, The Evangelical Covenant Ch. of Am., 1959-67; pres. Covenant Palms of Miami (Fla.), 1967-71. Vice pres. and vice sec. Evangelical Covenant Ch. of Am., 1938-50. Trustee Swedish Hosp., Minneapolis, 1946-50. Decorated Commandeur de l'Ordre de St Paul MN Died July 21, 1971; buried Lakewood Cemetery, Minneapolis MN

NELSON, JOHN MANDT, ex-congressman; b. Town of Burke, Dane Co., Wis., Oct. 10, 1870; s. Christopher and Elsie N.; A.B., U. of Wis., 1892, LL.B., 1896; post-grad. studies, 1901-03; m. Thea Johanna Stondall, July 25, 1891. Co. supt. of schs., Dane Co., Wis., 1892-94; admitted to bar, 1896. Mem. Rep. State Central Com., 1901-05; elected to 59th Congress, Sept. 4, 1906, for unexpired term (1906-07), reelected 60th to 65th Congresses (1907-19) and 67th to 72d Congresses (1921-33), 3d Wis. Dist. Chmn. Progressive group, House of Reps., 68th Congress; mgr. Independent Progressive campaign of La Follette and Wheeler, 1924. Home: 345 Lakewood Boul., Madison WI‡

NELSON, MARTIN, agronomist; b. Crawford County, Wis., Dec. 12, 1871; s. Erik and Christene (Oleson) N.; grad. State Normal Sch., Stevens Point, Wis., 1900; B.S., University of Wisconsin, 1905, M.S., 1906; LL.D., (hon.) U. of Arkansas, 1945; m. Maude Agnes Farnham, Jan. 22, 1910; children—Helen Christine, Isabel May. Teacher pub. schs., Vernon County, Wis., 1896-97; prin. Star Lake (Wis.) High Sch., 1900-02; adj. prof. agronomy, 1906-07, asso. prof., 1907-08, Coll. of Agr. and Expt. Sta., Univ. of Neb.; prof. agronomy, 1908-13, dean and dir., 1913-20, vice dean and dir. Coll. of Agr. and Agrl. Expt. Sta., vice dean and head dept. agronomy, 1920-41; prof. emeritus since 1941, U. of Arkansas. Presbyterian. Mem. Am. Soc. Agronomy, Am. Genetic Assn., A.A.A.S., Alpha Zeta, Pi Gamma Mu. Home: Fayetteville AR‡

NELSON, MARTIN JOHAN, educator; b. Windsor, Wis., Jan. 24, 1894; s. Andres and Petrine (Erickson) N.; A.B., Luther Coll., Decorah, Ia., 1916; M.A., U. of Wis., 1924, Ph.D., 1928; m. Cora Geneva Jenson, Aug. 27, 1919; children—Morton James, Marjorie Joyce. Prin. and supt. in pub. schs. of N.D., 1916-17, 1919-22; prof. edn., Ia. State Teachers Coll., 1924-29, dir. of research, 1929-30, head of dept. of edn., 1930-34, dean of the faculty, 1934-54, dean of instruction of the college 1954-70. Served as private 89th Division, U.S. Army, World War. Fellow, Am. Psychological Association, A.A.A.S. Mem. Am. Ednl. Research Assn., Nat. Soc. Coll. Teachers Edn., Nat. Soc. Study Edn., N.E.A., Ia. State Edn. Assn., Am. Legion, Phi Delta Kappa. Lutheran. Club: Lions. Author or co-author several books relating to field. Mem. editorial bd. Jour. Ednl. Research. Home: Cedar Falls IA Died Nov. 1, 1970; buried Concordia Gardens Cemetery, Fort Wayne IN

NELSON, ORVILLE NORMAN, physician; b. Battle Lake, Minn., Apr. 21, 1896; s. Ole Christian and Mathilda (Mickelson) N.; M.D., U. Minn., 1920, M.Sc., Mayo Found. Grad. Sch., 1920; m. Jane Sherwood, June 30, 1937; children—Robert S., Susan (Mrs. Robert F. Moore). Intern, Univ. Hosps., Northwestern Hosp., Mpls., 1920-21; postgrad. Mayo Found. Grad. Sch., U. Minn., Postgrad. Sch., Vienna (Austria) U.; gen. practice medicine, Battle Lake, 10 years, specializing in eye, ears, nose and throat, Fergus Falls, Minn., 14 years, St. Petersburg, Fla., 26 years; cons. eye, ears, nose and throat service VA Facility, Bay Pines, Fla.; mem. med. staff St. Anthony's, Mound Park, Am. Legion Crippled Children's, All Children's, Palms of Pasadena, St. Petersburg Gen. hosps. (all St. Petersburg). Served with U.S. Army, 1917-18. Diplomate Am. Bd. Ophthalmology Am. Bd. Otolaryngology. Fellow A.C.S., Internat. Coll. Surgeons; mem. A.M.A., So. Med. Assn., Am. Acad. Ophthalmology and Otolaryngology, Assn. Mil. Surgeons U.S., Pan Am. Assn. Ophthalmology, Pan Am. Assn. Otolaryngology, Phi Rho Sigma. Republican. Lutheran. Home: St Petersburg FL Died Dec. 27, 1970; buried St Petersburg FL

NELSON, PERRY ALBERT, communications exec.; b. Rockland, Ida., Dec. 21, 1916; s. Bert Albert and Polly May (Perry) N.; student Ida. State Coll., 1935-36, 40; m. Helen Eleanor Lindsay, Dec. 21, 1941; children—James P., Richard D., Steven B., Connie Jean. Ida. safety dir., 1941; exec. sec. Ida. traffic adv. com. to War Dept., 1942; clk. irrigation and reclamation com. U.S. Ho. of Reps., 1942-43; field rep. Ida. Planning Bd., 1946-47; dist mgr. No. Life Ins. Co., 1947-49; owner Western Real Estate & Ins. Co., Pocatello, Ida., 1949-68; member board of directors Idaho Radio Corporation, Mountain States Tel. & Tel. Co., Denver, also mem. Ida. adv. bd. Power County rep. Ida. Senate, 1941; candidate U.S. Congress, 2d Dist. Ida., 1946. Past pres. Pocatello Real Estate Bd.; member of Idaho Nuclear Commission; vice president Bannock County Centennial Commn. Spl. agt. U.S. Mil. Intelligence, World War II. Decorated Legion of Merit; Man of Year award Jr. C. of C.; Pocatello Chief award for outstanding community service; Ida. Realtor of Year, 1968. Member of Idaho (president 1963-64, dir., member executive committee), Pocatello (past pres.) chambers commerce, Pocatello Property Owners Assn., Ida. Real Estate Assn. (past pres.), Inst. Real Estate Mgmt., Internat. Real Estate Fedn., National Institute of Real Estate Brokers, National Association of Real Estate Bds. (director). Elk (past exalted ruler), Rotarian (past pres. Pocatello). Home: Pocatello ID Died Sept. 28, 1968; buried Rockland ID

NELSON, RALPH THOMAS, army officer; b. Lebanon, Ind., June 19, 1902; s. Lloyd T. and Florence E. (Alexander) N.; student Purdue U., 1920-23; B.S., U.S. Mil. Acad., 1928; grad. Indsl. Coll. of Armed Forces, 1953; m. Christine Clarke, Oct. 10, 1929; children—Thomas C. (U.S. Army), Alexa N. Plantz. Commd. 2d lt. U.S. Army, 1928, advanced through grades to maj. gen., 1958; inf. assignments, U.S. and Hawaii, 1928-42; signal officer, 4th Div., 1942; signal officer 9th div. XV Corps, also dep. signal officer 15th Army and U.S. Forces, Austria, 1943-46; various assignments U.S., 1947-53; signal officer X Corps and 8th Army, Korea, 1953-54; comdg. gen. Signal Tng. Center, Ft. Gordon, also comdg. gen. Electronic Proving Ground, Ft. Huachuca, Ariz., 1955-58; dep. chief signal officer U.S. Army, 1958-59, chief sign officer, 1959-62. Decorated D.S.M., Legion of Mer Bronze Star, Purple Heart; Ulchi medal (Korea). Mer Armed Forces Communications and Electronics Ass (3d v.p.). Home: Arlington VA Died Oct. 1, 196 buried Arlington Nat. Cemetery, Arlington VA

NELSON, ROBERT OLIVER, educator; b. Havan Ark., October 9, 1899; son Melville M. and Sara (Fergeson) N.; A.B., Erskine College, Due West, Sou Carolina, 1916-20; M.A., Peabody College, 193 Ph.D., U. Ga., 1941; m. Frances Hawkins, June 7, 193 1 dau., Nancy (Mrs. Robert E. Diggs). Elementary ar secondary sch. prin., Columbia, S.C., 1930-43; ass supt. schs., Richmond, Va., 1943-45; supts. Martinsvil (Va.) pub. schs., 1945-46; supt. Newport News (Va pub. schs., 1946-65; prof. edn. Coll. William and Mar 1965-66, 68-70, acting dean Sch. Edn., 1966-68. B dirs. local YMCA, Boy Scouts Am., A.R.C. Men N.E.A., Am., Va. (past pres. assns. sch. adminstrs.). V P.T.A. Kiwanian (past pres. Newport News). Clu Peninsula Executives (Hampton and Newport New Va.). Author: The Annual Report of the Superintende of Schools, 1930; South Carolina Newport News V Died Jan. 16, 1970; buried Peninsula Meml. Par Newport News VA

NELSON, ROBERT WILLIAM, b. Patton, Ala., Ap 13, 1894; s. Robert and Elvira Anne (Clark) N.; gra Gilman Sch., Baltimore, 1912; B.S. in Engring., Joh Hopkins, 1915; m. Dorothea Harper Pennington, Ap 15, 1918 (div.); children—Dorothea, Robert, Ronc Elizabeth; m. 2d, Frances Pogue, Dec. 14, 1945. Mec engr. Bartlett Hayward Corp., mfrs. gas apparatus an munitions, Baltimore, 1915-25, Industrial Bur. Baltimore Assn. Commerce, 1925-26; gen. mgr. Oh Valley Industrial Corp., Wheeling, W.Va., 1926-3 exec. v.p. Cincinnati Chamber Commerce, 1931-36; v. charge corporate bus. devel. First Nat. Bank of Cir 1937-70, also dir. Mem. Alpha Delta Phi. Repu Episcopalian. Clubs: Queen City, Cincinnati Countr Home: Cincinnati OH Died Dec. 20, 1970; burie Spring Grove Cemetery, Cincinnati OH

NELSON, RUFUS JERRY, editor; b. Washingtc Co., Ark., Dec. 6, 1870; s. Sam Houston and Alice (Wyatt) N.; normal diploma, U. of Ark., 1903, B.S. Agr., 1904, M.S., 1907; studied Cornell U., summ 1908; m. Flossie Ella Sanderford, Ranger, Tex., June 2 1908; children—Rufus J. (dec.), Alice Ella, Edna Lucil Arthur Lee, Helen Elizabeth, Margaret Jean. Asst. sup horticulture, St. Louis Expn., 1904; field agt. Ark. Agr Expt. Sta., 1904-07; prof. agr. and prof. agrl. edn., U. Ark., 1907-10; editor-in-chief Farm and Ranc 1910-20; organizer of Self-Help Community clubs rural school houses in Southwest; seed breeder, fru grower; pub. Arkansas Countryman; mem. Ge Assembly, Ark., 1933, 34; asst. agrl. aide Sc Conservation Service, U.S. Dept. Agr. Democra Missionary Baptist. Accomplished notable work developing the rice industry in Ark., 1904-07. Auth bulls. on rice growing. Home: 305 Cypress, Park Hi North Little Rock AR‡

NELSON, WILLIAM, mgmt. exec., ret. naval office b. Minn., May 23, 1893; s. C. and M. (Christen) N.; B.S U.S. Naval Acad., 1915; M.S., Mass. Inst. Tech., 192 m. Faye Callison, Mar. 6, 1918; children—Willia Ross, Naida (Mrs. John Salberg) (dec.). Commd. ensig USN, 1915, advanced through grades to capt., 194 engaged in naval constrn., World War I; gen. insp. nav aircraft Eastern U.S., 1930-34; naval observer, 193 chief engr. Naval Aircraft Factory, 1938-40; gen. re Bur. Aero., 1944-45; ret., 1945; asst. to pres. Gar Woc Industries, 1947-49; with ACF Brill Motors Co., Phila 1950-55, pres., 1954-55; div. mgr. Hall-Scott, Inc 1950, pres., 1957-60; pres. J. G. Brill Co., 1956-5 chmn. bd. Teleregister Corp., Stamford, Conr 1960-61; vice chmn. bd. DuBois Chems., Inc., Cir 1960-63, dir., 1960-64; cons. W. R. Grace & Cc 1964-67; dir. Nelson Knitting Works, 1950-62; di Altamil Corp., Indpls., 1958-69, chmn. bd., 1961-6 dir. Alson Industries, Inc., 1970-71. Mem. U.S. Nav Inst., U.S. Navy Acad. Alumni Assn. Author: Sea Plar Design, 1936; Airplane Lofting, 1941. Home: Porto Valley CA Died Dec. 8, 1971.

NEMEYER, S(IDNEY) LLOYD, utilities exec.; Tacoma, Dec. 4, 1916; s. Sidney Herbert and Bert Eulalia (Niman) N.; B.S., U. Ill., 1938; m. Ruth M Rennick, Sept. 18, 1943; children—Linda Anne, Sus Ruth, David Lance. With Arthur Andersen & Cc 1940-55, partner, 1949-55; pres., dir. Milw. Gas Lig Co., 1955-68; dir. Am. Natural Gas Co., Marine N Exchange Bank. Dir. Milw. Better Bus. Bur. Mer Milw. Assn. Commerce (dir.), Am. Gas Assn. (dir.), P Kappa Psi. Clubs: Chicago (Chgo.); Milwaukee. Hom Shorewood WI Died Jan. 24, 1968.

NERLOVE, SAMUEL HENRY, economist, educatc b. Vitebsk, Russia, Dec. 19, 1901; s. Max and Ma (Lissner) N.; brought to U.S., 1905; Ph.B., U. Chg A.M., 1923; m. Evelyn Andelman, Mar. 24, 193 children—Marc Leon, Harriet Jane, Sara Beth. Began statistician and accountant with Labor Bur., Inc., 192 asst. Sch. of Business, U. Chgo., 1922-23; dir. eco research, Independent Oil Men's Assn., 1925; researc prof. Inst. of Law, Johns Hopkins, 1928; sr. financial economist, U.S. Treasury, 1930-31; trustee Security Life Ins. Co. of Am. Trust, 1936-45; prof. bus. econ. and policy U. Chgo., 1943-63; vis. prof. bus. adminstrn. Graduate School of Business Administration, University of California at Los Angeles, 1962-64, prof., 1964-72, senior lectr. bus. econs. and policy, 1965, prof. econs., bus. policy in residence, 1968-72. Mem. Am. Econ. Assn., Am. Assn. of University Professors. Author: (with others) Outline of Economics, 1930; A Decade of Corporate Incomes (1920-29), 1930. Contbr. articles on investments, ins. and bus. econs. Home: Los Angeles CA Died Feb. 13, 1972.

NESBIT, OTIS BURGESS, M.D.; b. Severance, Kan., Jan. 31, 1871; s. Samuel F. and Mary (Templar) N.; pharm. dept. Valparaiso U., 1899; M.D., Bennett Med. Coll., Chicago, 1902; m. Alice A. Vincent, of Valparaiso, Ind., June 22, 1897; children—Allegra M., Beatrice T. (wife of Oppenheim Alexander of Raffles Coll., Singapore, S.S.). Practiced in Valparaiso, 1902-13; prof. therapeutics, Valparaiso U., 1903-13; pres. Valparaiso Bd. of Health, 1910-14; dir. of med. inspection Gary pub. schs. since 1913; chmn. child hygiene sect. N.E.A., 1920-—. Fellow Am. Coll. Physicians, Am. Med. Assn. Editor: Nesbet Family Letters. Home: 444 Jackson St., Gary IN‡

NESLEN, CLARENCE CANNON, lawyer; b. Salt Lake City, Jan. 14, 1907; s. Charles Clarence and Grace (Cannon) N.; A.B., U. Utah, 1933; J.D., George Washington U., 1937; M. Leone Rockwood, Apr. 7, 1937; children—Clarence Cannon, Richard R., Roger H., Elizabeth. Admitted to D.C. bar, 1936, Utah bar, 1937, U.S. Supreme Ct., 1955, U.S. Ct. Mil. Appeals, 1955; review atty. Social Security Bd., 1936-39; area adminstr. Railroad Retirement Bd., Utah, Ida., Nev., 1939-40; counsel Utah Tax Commn., 1946-47; mem. firm Neslen & Mock, Salt Lake City, 1958-70. Dir. Lone Star Mining & Devel. Corp., Monte Cristo Corp. Chairman, Utah Merit Council. Served to lt. col. AUS, 1940-46. col. Judge Adv. Gen. Corps Res.; civilian aide for Utah to Secretary of Army. Decorated Bronze Star medal. Mem. Am. Legion (state comdr. 1949-50), Beta Theta Pi. Mem. Ch. Jesus Christ of Latter-day Salt Lake City UT Died May 2, 1970; buried Salt Lake City Cemetery.

NETHERCUT, EDGAR S., sec. emeritus Western Soc. Engrs.; b. Lake Geneva, Wis., June 12, 1866; s. George S. and Mary Bell (McConnell) N.; B.C.E., U. of Wis., 1889; m. Grace E. Goodenough, Apr. 28, 1896 (died 1934). Chief engr., sales mgr. and dir. Paige Iron Works, and Buda Co., Chicago, 1890-1908; cons. civil engr., Chicago, New York and Washington, D.C., 1908-17; sec. Western Soc. Engrs., 1917-35. Mem. Am. Society Civil Engrs., Western Society Engineers, Franklin Institute, Borrowed Time Club, Evanston; hon. mem. Chi Epsilon, Univ. of Wisconsin Glee Club. Republican. Clubs: University (Chicago); University (Evanston). Home: University Club, 1704 Hinman Av., Evanston IL‡

NEUHOFF, CHARLES SIDNEY, lawyer; b. St. Louis, May 4, 1897; s. Fritz and Mary Ethel (Coulter) N.; student Boston U., 1921-23, Wash. U., 1923-27; m. Ula Howorth, Nov. 16, 1935. Clk. The Tex. Co., St. Louis, 1916-20, supr. expense, Boston office, 1921-23; admitted to Mo. bar, 1927, since practiced in St. Louis; mem. of the law firm Stamm, Millar & Neuhoff and preceeding firms, St. Louis, Mo., 1954-67. Mem. Am., Mo., St. Louis bar assns., Am. Legion, Phi Delta Phi, Kappa Alpha. Unitarian. Home: University City MO Died June 8, 1967.

NEUMAN, ABRAHAM C., educator; b. Brezan, Austria, Sept. 23, 1890; s. Max and Rachel (Rose) N.; brought to U.S., 1898; B.S., Columbia, 1909, M.A., 1912; rabbi Jewish Theol. Sem., 1912, D.H.L., 1914, Litt.D., 1947, LL.D., U. of Pa., 1945; D.H.L. Hebrew Union Coll., 1945; L.H.D., New York Univ., N.Y.C., 1955; married Gladys Reed, April 30, 1919; 1 son, Cyrus Adler; m. 2d, Elsie Guggenheim, Dec. 10, 1944. Inst. history Teachers Inst., Jewish Theol. Sem., 1912; instr. history, Dropsie Coll. for Hebrew and Cognate Learning, 1913-23, associate professor, 1923-34, professor, 1934-41, pres., 1941-66, honorary president, 1966-70; rabbi Congregation B'nai Jeshurun, Philadelphia, 1919-27, Congregation Mikveh Israel, Phila., 1927-43, hon. rabbi, 1943-70. Trustee, chmn. coll. com. Gratz Coll., Phila., mem. bd. overseers; Rabbinical Assembly, Pa. Constitution Commemoration Com., 150th Anniversary; mem. advisory com. Adult Edn. Council of Phila., and of Better Phila. Com.; dir. A Modern Constitution for Pa., Inc. Editor Jewish Quarterly Review; mem. publ. com. Jewish Publ. Soc. of Am.; revising editor Universal Jewish Ency.; chmn. Editorial Bd. Jewish Apocryphal Lit. Member executive council, vice president American Jewish Hist. Soc., 1949-63, Jewish Hist. Soc. of Israel, Am. Hist. Soc., Am. Oriental Soc., Historical Soc. of Pa.; hon. fellow Jewish Acad. Arts and Sciences; hon. mem. Am. Acad. for Jewish Research; corr. mem. of Jewish Historical Society of England. Dem. presdl. elector for State of Pa., 1940. Clubs: Round Table, Oriental, Philmont Country, Contemporary (Phila.). Author several books since 1940. Home: Elkins Park PA Died Nov. 20, 1970; buried Adath Jeshurun Cemetery.

NEUMANN, EDWARD MORSBACH, ins. exec.; b. Newark, June 15, 1905; s. Edward David and Paulene (Morsbach) N.; B.Sc., Rutgers U., 1926; m. Arlene Pierce, Nov. 29, 1928 (dec.); 1 dau., Lois (Mrs. John G. Rathman); m. 2d, Elin H. F. Anderson, Aug. 23, 1961; children—Mrs. Robert G. Dluhy, Geoffrey G. Tegnell. With Prudential Ins. Co. of Am., Newark, 1926-71, beginning as actuarial clk., successively asst. mathematician, mathematician, asst. actuary, asso. actuary, 2d v.p. and asso. actuary, 1926-54, v.p. and asso. actuary, 1954-59, vice president, actuary, 1959-71. Trustee Rutgers University, 1957-71. Fellow Society Actuaries; member Internat. Congress Actuaries, Rutgers Alumni Assn. (pres. 1955-56), Lambda Chi Alpha. Clubs: Ponta Vedra (Fla.); Rock Spring (West Orange, N.J.). Contbr. articles profl. publs. Short Hills NJ Died Oct. 13, 1971.

NEUMANN, WILLIAM LOUIS, educator, historian; b. Buffalo, Mar. 4, 1915; s. William L. and Elizabeth (Boller) N.; B.S., N.Y. State Coll. at Buffalo, 1938; M.A., U. Mich., 1939, Ph.D., 1948; m. Doris E. McGlone, Dec. 26, 1941; children—Christopher R., Gregory A. Lectr., Howard U., 1946-47; asst. prof. U. Hawaii, 1948-49; editor American Perspective, 1949-51; cons. fgn. affairs U.S. Senate, 1952-53; mem. faculty Goucher Coll., 1954-—, now prof. history, chmn. Am. studies program; vis. prof. U. Md., U. Va., U. Wis., R.I. U., Johns Hopkins, Morgan State Coll., Balt. Mem. internat. conf. and seminar program Am. Friends Service Com., 1962-—. Rockefeller fellow, 1961-62; Social Sci. Research Council fellow, 1956. Mem. Am. Hist. Assn., Am. Assn. U. Profs., Am. Civil Liberties Union, Fellowship of Reconciliation, Sane Nuclear Policy Com., Citizens Planning and Housing Assn. Author: Genesis of Pearl Harbor, 1945; Recognition of Governments in the Americas, 1947; Making the Peace, 1941-45, 1950; America Encounters Japan, 1963; After Victory: Churchill, Roosevelt and Stalin, 1967. Home: Timonium MD Died Sept. 30, 1971.

NEUMEYER, ALBERT GUSTAVE, banker; b. N.Y.C., Oct. 20, 1910; s. Gustave Henry and Amy (Hirsch) N.; student U. Pa. Wharton Sch. Finance and Commerce, 1930; m. Sally Wohl, June 26, 1943; children—Richard Albert, Louise Elaine. Sec., treas. Tropauer & Neumeyer Realty Co., 1930-32; Pfeiffer-Neumeyer Constrn. Co., N.Y.C., 1932-37; mfg. rep. A.G. Neumeyer, Los Angeles, 1937-52; sec.-treas. Hirsch Lumber Co., N.Y.C., 1952-54; owner, mgr. A.G. Neumeyer, real estate investments, Las Vegas, Nev., 1954-58; pres. State Realty Co., Las Vegas, 1955-57; pres. First Western Savs. & Loan Assn., Las Vegas, 1958-63, chmn., 1959-64; chmn. exec. com., dir. First Western Financial Corp., Las Vegas, 1960-64; past pres., chmn. bd. S.W. Devel. Co., Inc., Los Vegas; dir. Fed. Home Loan Bank of San Francisco, 1962-64; past pres., chmn. bd. First Western Devel. Co., Beverly Hills, Cal. Vice pres., treas. United Fund of Clark County, 1959-61; chmn. Nev. Gov.'s Survey for Mental Health, 1958; co-chmn. fund dr. A.R.C., Las Vegas, 1958. Bd. dirs. Las Vegas Symphony Soc. Mem. Nat. League Insured Savs. Assns. (bd. govs. 1959-64), Phi Epsilon Pi. Home: Los Angeles CA Died May 15, 1970.

NEUPERT, CARL NICHOLAS, physician, pub. health adminstr.; b. London, Wis., May 31, 1897; s. Otto and Augusta (Punzel) N.; diploma, Stout Inst., Menominie, Wis., 1917; student Univ. of Wis., 1919-21; M.D., Washington Univ., 1925; M.S.P.H., Univ. of Mich., 1941; m. Melba de Shazer, June 14, 1925; children—Carl David, John Cornelius. Teacher Oak Park (Ill.) Pub. Schs., 1917-18; rotating internship Mo. Baptist Sanatorium, St. Louis, 1925-26; pvt. practice medicine, Janesville, 1926-28; pediatric intern. Univ. Rochester Strong Memorial Hosp., 1928-29; pediatric practice Janesville, Wis., 1929-36; supervisor local pub. health service, Wis. State Bd. Health, 1936-39; asst. state health officer, Wis. State Bd. Health, 1939-43, state health officer and exec. sec., Madison, Wisconsin, 1943-65; deputy director Community Health Services, from 1965. Mem. U.S. delegation to 6th World Health Assembly, World Health Organization, 1953. Served as ensign, U.S. Navy, R.F., 1918-19; past president, Assn. State and Territorial Health Officer. Diplomate, Am. Bd. Preventive Medicine and Pub. Health. Fellow Am. Pub. Health Assn., A.M.A.; mem. Dane Co., Wis. State med. assns., Conf. State and Provincial Health Authorities N.A. (past pres.), Delta Sigma Phi, Phi Beta Pi, Delta Omega. Conglist. Home: Madison WI Died May 22, 1968.

NEUTRA, RICHARD JOSEPH, architect; b. Vienna, Austria, Apr. 8, 1892; s. Samuel and Elizabeth (Glaser) N.; grad. Poly Coll., U. of Vienna; diploma with distinction, U. of Zurich, Switzerland, 1918; honorary Doctor's Degree univs. of Graz and Berlin; D.F.A. (hon.), Adelphi University, 1963; hon. doctorate U. of Rome, 1965, U. Cal., Los Angeles, 1969; m. Dione Niedermann, December 22, 1923; children—Frank Lucian, Dion, Raymond Richard. Came to U.S., 1923, naturalized, 1929. Began as architect, city planner, Switzerland, 1919-23; asso. with Holabird & Root, Frank Lloyd Wright, 1923-25; own practice, Los Angeles, 1926-66; mem. Richard and Dion Neutra, Architects and Assos., 1966-70; cons. Richard J. Neutra Insts., Cal., Switzerland. Designed and built large and small dwellings, many office bldgs., open air schs.; universities in U.S.A., East and West Pakistan; architect for resident centers for National Youth Administration, 1940-41; 5 pub. housing projects, 1939-41. Channel Heights, 160 acres postwar housing project with full traffic segregation, 1943; housing project in Spain, Germany, Italy. Lectr. Harvard, Princeton, Columbia, other colls. U.S., Mexico, Japan, Switzerland, Belgium, and many other countries; recent work includes: Mathematics Park, Princeton, Benmore Gardens Housing Project, Johannesburg, S. Africa, U. Pa. Grad. Student Housing, Orange County Courthouse, Santa Ana, Cal., Roberson Meml. Cultural Center, Binghamton, N.Y.; consultant, National Youth Adminstrn., U.S. Housing Authority, Fed. Works Agy., Fed. Pub. Housing Authority, 10 year devel. plan for Guam; redevel. plans for Sacramento and Tulsa; chmn. Cal. Planning Bd. Mem. Calif. Bd. Examiners, Architect and consultant for hosps., schs., Govt. of Puerto Rico. Recipient over 50 1st and 2d prizes in competitions for projects and executed comml. and residential designs. Awards from World Expn., Paris 1938, Hall of Fame, N.Y. World's Fair, 1940; German Great Cross of Merit; God medal Ethiopia; hon. ring City of Vienna; award of excellence Am. Institute Steel Construction, 1962. Member advisory board for schoolhouse planning U.S. Dept. of Edn. American International Congress for Modern Architecture; special consultant to government of Austria, 1969; mem. adv. bd. Los Angeles Internat. Design Center; mem. Joint A.I.A.-A.M.A. Com. on Environmental Health; mem. archtl. rev. and adv. panel U.S. Navy. Benjamin Franklin fellow Royal Soc. Arts, London. Fellow A.I.A. (residential honor award 1954), Sociedad Central de Arquitectos Argentina (hon.); hon. mem. Academia de Belle Arti de Venzia, Academia Lucca, Assn. Mexican Architects. Assn. of Cuban and of Bolivian architects, Royal Inst. British Architects, Society of German Architects (hon. pres. 1969); member of French Acad. of Architecture, N.A.D., Nat. Inst. Arts and Letters, Assn. Argentinian (hon.), Assn. Peruvian Architects (hon. mem.). Author: How America Builds, 1926; America New Building in the World, 1929; Mystery and Realities of the Site, 1951; Buildings &Projects, 1952, vol. 2, 1959, vol. 3, 1961-66; Therapy by Design, published 1965; Naturnahes Bauen, 1970; co-author Preface to a Master Plan, 1941; New Architecture and City Planning; Architecture of Social Concern (Portuguese and English), 1949; Survival through Design, 1954; World and Dwelling, 1962; Life and Shape, 1962; Life and Human Habitat, Spl. Neutra edition of French mag. L'Architecture d'Aujourd'hui. Principal several feature mag. stories. Home: Los Angeles CA Died Apr. 16, 1970.

NEUWIRTH, ISAAC, educator; b. N.Y.C., Dec. 15, 1894; s. Samuel and Pearl (Berger) N.; B.S., Cornell U., 1914, Ph.D., 1927; m. Gladys Bellin, Nov. 11, 1919; children—Berle Eleanor (Mrs. Clement Geronemus). Martha Ellen (Mrs. Ben Fledel), S. Edward. Chemist, British Ministry of Foods, Schwarz Labs., Pease Labs., N.Y.C., 1919-20; instr. biochemistry, lectr. pub. health and hygiene N.Y. Homeopathic Med. Coll., 1920-24; asst. cons. chemist Flower Hosp., N.Y.C., 1920-24; instr. physiology and pharmacology U. Louisville Med. and Dental Schs., 1924-25; instr. pharmacology and therapeutics N.Y.U. Coll. Dentistry, 1925-26, asst. prof., 1926-32, asso. prof. pharmacology, therapeutics and preventive dentistry, 1932-38, asso. prof. pharmacology and therapeutics, 1938-47, head dept., 1945-47, prof. pharmacology, head dept., 1947-54, prof. pharmacology, chmn. dept., 1954-60; vis. prof. biochemistry New York Medical College, 1960-63, visiting lecturer, 1947; adjunct professor chemistry, Pratt Institute, 1963-72. Recipient of Great Teacher award, N.Y.U., 1959. Served with San. Corps, U.S. Army, 1917-19. Fellow N.Y. Acad. Sci., A.A.A.S.; asso. fellow N.Y. Acad. Medicine; mem. Am. Chem. Soc., Am. Soc. Biol. Chemists, Am. Soc. Pharmacology and Exptl. Therapeutics, Soc. Exptl. Biology and Medicine, Harvey Soc., Internat. Assn. Dental Research, Sci. Research Soc. Am., Sigma Xi, Omicron Kappa Upsilon. Home: Forest Hills NY Died Nov. 26, 1972; buried Mt. Zion Cemetery, Maspeth NY

NEVADA, EMMA (MRS. RAYMOND PALMER), prima donna; b. (Emma Wixon) Austin, Nev.; studied under Mme. Marchesi, Paris; m. Dr. Raymond Palmer, Oct. 1, 1885. Debut, Her Majesty's Theatre, London, May 17, 1880, as Amina in La Sonnambula"; sang in Italy in 1883, appearing as Mysole in La Perle de Bresil" and afterward as Mignon; sang at Norwich festival, 1884, and in 1885 made tour of U.S.; later appeared many times in U.S. and Europe. Lives in Paris France*‡

NEVILLE, DONALD WESTON, civil engr.; b. Lawrence, Mass., Mar. 11, 1912; s. George Duncan and Alice (Weston) N.; student Clark Sch., Hanover, N.H., 1932, Colgate U., 1936; m. Dorothy Price, July 13, 1935; children—Patrick Richard, Susan Alice. Constrn. engr. United Engrs. & Constructors, Phila., 1934-35, TVA, 1935-38. Stone & Webster, 1938; engring. in field, advancing to dist. mgr., vice president director F. H. McGraw & Co., Chgo., 1939-59, sr. v.p., dir. 1959; pres., dir. McGraw Terminals, Inc., Burnside, La., 1957-59; pres. D. W. Neville & Assos., Chgo., 1960-62, Edward Gray Corp., Chgo., 1962-—; chmn. bd. Great

Lakes Supply Corp., Chgo. Clubs: Union League, Chicago Athletic Assn. (Chgo.); Evanston (Ill.) Golf; Alta (Salt Lake City); Bull Valley Hunt (Woodstock, Ill.). Home: Skokie IL Died Mar. 26, 1971.

NEVILLE, PAUL EDWIN, newspaper editor; b. Ware, Mass., May 8, 1919; s. John A. and Elizabeth (McLaughlin) N.; A.B., U. Notre Dame, 1942; m. Lillian M. Foster, Oct. 29, 1946; children—Peter, John, Patricia, James, Ruth. Mng. editor S. Bend (Ind.) Tribune, 1952-57; asst. to editor Buffalo Evening News, 1957-59, mng. editor, 1959-66, exec. editor, 1966-69. Bd. dirs. Rosary Hill Coll., Sisters of Mercy Hosp., Studio Arena Theatre, Buffalo. Served with USAAF, World War II. Decorated Bronze Star. Mem. Am. Soc. Newspaper Editors, N.Y. State Soc. Newspaper Editors (pres.), A.P. Mng. Editors Assn. (dir.). Club: Buffalo Athletic. Home: Buffalo NY Died June 1969.

NEVILLE, ROBERT, fgn. corr.; b. Vinita, Okla., May 12, 1905; s. Oliver and Alice (McClure) N.; student U. Cal.; Litt.B., Columbia, 1928, M.S., 1929; m. Mary Sentinelli, 1947. Typesetter Campbell Co. Record, Gillette, Wyo., 1919; reporter N.Y. Post, N.Y. Times, 1929; reporter N.Y. Herald Tribune, 1929-36, fgn. corr., 1936-37; fgn. news writer Time, 1937, fgn. news editor, 1938-40; fgn. news editor PM, 1940-41; head news bur. Time-Life, New Delhi, India, 1946-48, Buenos Aires, 1948-50. Far East corr., Hong Kong, 1950-53, head news bur., Rome, 1953-56, head news bur., Istanbul, Turkey, 1956-59; contbr. Look, Harper's, Encounter on Vatican affairs, 1959-70. Served as lt. col., AUS, 1942-46; editor, publs. officer Stars and Stripes, Mediterranean. Decorated, Legion of Merit. Club: Overseas Press (N.Y.C.). Author: The World of the Vatican, 1962. Died Feb. 1970.

NEVIN, WILLIAM LATTA, capitalist; A.B., U. of Pa., 1879, LL.B., 1880; m. Mary G. Hall; 1 dau., Francis H. Apptd. one of executors of Rodman Wanamaker's Estate; formerly pres. John Wanamaker, Philadelphia, and John Wanamaker, New York (dept. stores); v.p., trustee Wanamaker Inst. of Industries; and officer or dir. various other corpns. Mem. Am. Bar Assn. Clubs: University, Merion Cricket, Philadelphia Country. Home: 329 S. 16th St. Office: 13th and Market Sts., Philadelphia PA*‡

NEVINS, ALLAN, educator, author; b. Camp Point, Ill., May 20, 1890; s. Joseph Allan and Emma (Stahl) N.; A.B., U. of Ill., 1912, A.M., 1913; Litt. D., Union, 1935, Datmouth, 1936; LL.D., Washington and Lee Univ., 1935, Miami U., 1937; Litt.D., Oxford, 1965; Litt.D., Trinity Coll., 1948, University of Illinois 1953, Lincoln Coll., Gettysburg College, Lehigh University, Grinnell College, Columbia, 1960, Loyola U., 1961, U. of So. Cal., U. Cal., 1963, Oxford U., 1965; L.H.D., Ill. Coll., 1953; LL.D., Dartmouth College, 1958, Occidental Coll., 1967, L.I. University, 1968; married Mary Fleming Richardson, December 30, 1916; children—Anne Elizabeth, Meredith. Instructor English, U. of Ill., 1912-13; editorial writer New York Evening Post, 1913-23; editorial writer the Nation, 1913-18; lit. editor New York Sun, 1924-25; editorial staff New York World, 1925-27; prof. American history, Cornell U., 1927-28; asso. in history, Columbia, and mem. editorial staff New York World, 1928-31; prof. Am. history, Columbia, 1931-58, senior research associate at the Huntington Library, San Marino, California, 1958-71; Sir George Watson chair of American history, literature, and instns. in Great Britain, 1934-35; visiting prof. Calif. Inst. Tech., 1937-38; visiting scholar Huntington Library, 1937; Harmsworth prof., Oxford U., 1940-41, 64-65; spl. rep. Office War Information in Australia and New Zealand, 1943-44; chief public affairs officer, Am. embassy, London; 1945-46; visiting prof. Hebrew U. of Jerusalem, 1952. Trustee Woodrow Wilson Internat. Center for Scholars, at the Smithsonian Institution, 1969-71. Member of American Hist. Assn. (past pres.), Am. Acad. Arts and Letters (pres. 1966-68), Council on Foreign Relations; hon. fellow New York State Hist. Assn.; corr. member Mass. Hist. Soc.; past pres. Soc. of Am. Historians; member N.Y. Hist. Soc. Presbyn. Clubs: Lotos, Century, (N.Y.C.); National Press (Washington); Atheneum (London). Author or co-author, 1914-71; latest publs.: The Emergence of Lincoln, 2 vols., 1952; Statesmanship of the Civil War, 1953; Study in Power, 1953; Ford: the times, the man, the company (with Frank E. Hill), 1954, 2d vol., 1957, 3d vol., 1963; The War for the Union, 2 volumes, 1959, 2 vols., 1961; Herbert H. Lehman and His Era, 1963. Editor books, 1927-71; latest: Diary of George Templeton Strong. pub. in 1952; Leatherstocking Saga (James Fenimore Cooper), 1954; James Truslow Adams: Historian of the American Dream, 1968. Gen. editor of Am. Polit. Leaders series; Yale Press Chronicles of America, new series, D.C. Health Colleges and University History series. Recipient Pulitzer prize for biography, 1932, 1937, Scribner Centenary prize and Bancroft prize, 1947, Gold Medal for history and biography Nat. Inst. Arts and Letters, 1957; Gold medal. N.Y. Hist. Soc., 1958, Commonwealth Club of Cal., 1960, Rice U., 1962; Golden Plate award Am. Acad. Achievement, 1966; Alexander Hamilton award, Columbia U., 1968. Home: San Marino CA Died Mar. 5, 1971.

NEW, CATHERINE MCLAEN, author; b. Toronto, Can., Feb. 8, 1870; ed. Ursuline Convent, Chatham, Ont.; m. at New York, Harry S. New (q.v.), Aug. 18, 1891. Author: A Woman Reigns, 1895. Address: 1002 Capitol Av., Indianapolis IN‡

NEWBERRY, FARRAR, insurance exec.; b. Gurdon, Ark., July 30, 1887; s. Lawrence Clinton and Martha Ann (Harris) N.; A.B., Arkadelphia (Ark.) Meth. Coll. (now Henderson State Teachers Coll.), 1906; A.M., Vanderbilt U., 1908; m. Lila Lee Thonasson, June 22, 1911; children—Farrar, Nick T. Teacher, Union City (Tenn.) Training Sch., 1908-09, Arkadelphia Meth. Coll., 1909-11; acting prof. of history, U. of Ark., 1911; served one term in Ark. legislature; head consul Woodmen of World, 1915; field man, Woodmen of World Life Ins. Soc., 1915-18, state mgr., 1918-36, dir., 1932-50, sec., 1937-43, pres. 1943-55; dir. Northern Natural Gas Co., Neb. Savings & Loan Assn. Pres. Nat. Fraternal Congress of Am., 1944-45. Dir., pres. Omaha C. of C., 1944, 45; past dir. Omaha Community Chest and United War and Community Fund; past dir. Covered Wagon Council of Boy Scouts of Am.; dir. Greater Omaha Assn. (v.p.); Douglas Co. chpt. A.R.C.; past mem. bd. regents Univ. of Omaha. Mem. Phi Kappa Sigma. Mason. Clubs: Omaha Country, Omaha Athletic, Ak Sar Ben, Rotary, Ad-Sell. Author: A Life of Mr. Garland of Arkansas, 1908; The Life of J. C. Root and the Glories of Perfected Woodcraft, 1913; James K. Jones, the Plumed Knight of Arkansas, 1914. Home: Omaha NB Died Aug. 1968.

NEWBORG, LEONARD DAVID, investment banker; b. Rumson, N.J., Aug. 19, 1894; s. Joseph L. and Goldie (Stachelberg) N.; B.A., Williams Coll., 1916. With Hallgarten & Co., N.Y.C., 1919, partner, 1935. Served to 1st lt., inf., U.S. Army, 1917-19. Home: New York City NY Died Oct. 4, 1972; buried Beth-el Cemetery.

NEWBURY, FRANK DAVIES, economist; born Bklyn., June 9, 1880; s. Henry Fitch and Anna Eliza (McAllister) N.; M.E., Cornell, 1901; m. Mary Grace Lincoln, Aug. 28, 1907; children—Constance (dec.), Paul Lincoln, Marshall McAllister (dec.). With Westinghouse Electric Corp. from 1901, design engr., 1903-07, sect. engr. power div., 1907-11, div. engr., 1911-20, mgr. power engring. dept., 1920-30, gen. mgr. machinery engring., 1931-35, asst. to v.p., 1935-37, economist from 1937, mgr. new products div., 1938-47, mgr. emergency products div., 1940, v.p., 1941-47, dir., 1946-47, cons. economist from 1947; asst. sec. def. Dept. Def., Washington, 1953-57; dir. Nat. Securties and Research Corp., N.Y.C. Trustee Chatauqua (N.Y.) Inst. Republican. Home: Washington DC Died Mar. 26, 1969; buried Homewood Cemetery, Pittsburgh PA

NEWBURY, MICHAEL, assn. exec., social service leader. Treas. John Howard Assn., Chgo. Died Dec. 25, 1970.

NEWCOMB, WYLLYS STETSON, lawyer; b. Norwalk, Conn., Sept. 4, 1907; s. Josiah Turner and Emily Louise (Stetson) N.; student Fessenden Sch., West Newton, Mass., 1920-21, Phillips Acad., Andover, Mass., 1921-26; A.B., Williams Coll., 1931; LL.B., Harvard, 1934; m. Frances Annette League, Aug. 12, 1944; children—Wyllys Stetson, Thomason League, Josiah Turner, Charles Francis. Admitted to N.Y. bar, 1935; asso. Hunges, Scherman & Dwight, 1934-37, Dwight, Harris, Koegel & Caskey, 1937-42; asst. dist. atty. N.Y. Co., 1944-49; spl. asst. atty. gen., N.Y. State, 1951-53, U.S. 1953-57; mem. firm Newcomb & Cantor, 1952-59. Royall, Koegel & Rogers and predecessor firms, 1960-68; dir. Northeastern Life Ins. Co. Mem. N.Y. Bar Assn., Bar Assn. City N.Y. Clubs: Williams (N.Y.C.); Knollwood Country. Home: White Plains NY Died Aug. 29, 1968.

NEWELL, CLARENCE DEROCHA, advertising executive; b. Orange N.J., Feb. 5, 1876; s. Clarence DeRocha and Harriet (Williams) N.; m. Alberta Sayres Dunn, Jan. 2, 1900; 1 dau., Barbara Newell Bowen. With Frank Seaman, Inc., 1904-19; partner Newell-Emmett Co., N.Y. City, since 1919. Clubs: Union League (New York); Glen Ridge Country; Woodway Country (Stamford, Conn.). Home: 10 Crestmont Rd., Montclair NJ‡

NEWELL, HENRY CLINTON, clergyman, educator; b. Springfield, Mass., Oct. 12, 1875; s. Roscius Clinton and Sarah Allerton (Cushman) N.; B.S., Amherst, 1901; B.D., Hartford Theol. Sem., 1916; D.D., Piedmont Coll., 1928; m. Ruth Anne Johnson, 1904 (died 1905); m. 2d, Mary Aurelia Bates, 1907 (died 1931); m. 3d, Edith Harrison Andrews, 1932. Member of faculty of Piedmont Coll., 1904-13; ordained Congregational ministry, 1908; pastor Middlebury, Vt., 1916-30; pres. Piedmont Coll., 1930-36; pastor of First Congl. Ch. Harwich, Cape Cod, Mass., 1936-45; pres. emeritus, Piedmont Coll., since 1945; trustee Piedmont Coll. Mem. Soc. Bibl. Lit. and Exegesis, Phi Kappa Psi. Mason. Clubs: Kiwanis, Rotary of Middlebury (hon.). Home: Springfield MA‡

NEWELL, JAMES W., ry. official; b. Plattsmouth, Neb., May 29, 1875; s. William Henry and Mildred (Searle) N.; student Neb. Wesleyan U.; m. Hallie Atwood, of Plattsmouth, Oct. 18, 1899. Began with C.,B.&Q. R.R., as messenger, June 18, 1895, and continued as telegraph operator, station agt. and various positions, and auditor freight accounts until 1916; with Lehigh Valley R.R. as auditor revenues, 1917-18; comptroller U.S. R.R. Administration, 1918-20; comptroller and v.p. Wabash Ry., 1920-25, v.p. since May 1, 1925; v.p. Ann Arbor R.R. Co., Manistique & Lake Superior R.R. Co., Lake Erie & Fort Wayne R.R. Co.; comptroller New Jersey, Indiana & Ill. R.R. Co. Republican. Episcopalian. Mason. Clubs: Glen Echo, Racquet, Noonday. Home: 484 Lake Av. Office: Railway Exchange, St Louis MO‡

NEWELL, JESSIE EDNA WHITEHEAD, educator; b. Carbon Hill, Ala., Jan. 25, 1913; d. William Henry and Belle (McLain) Whitehead; B.S., Ala. Coll., 1934; M.A., U. Ala., 1955; m. Clois Frank Newell, June 5, 1937; children—Janice (Mrs. Robert Earle Grogan Jr.), John William, Clois Frank. Tchr. high sch., Weogutka, Ala., 1934-37; tchr. Cliburn County High Sch., Heflin, Ala., 1941-43, Walker County High Sch., Jasper, Ala., 1943-45, Laboratory High Sch., Jacksonville, Ala.; instr. Ky. Home Economics Tchrs. Workshop, 1955; mem. workshop planning com. Ala. Home Economics Tchrs., 1952, co-chmn., 1953, chmn., 1954; chmn. housing sect. Study of Curriculum for Ala. Home Economics Tchrs., 1961. Mem. Ala. Vocational Assn. (county chmn., 1953-54, Northeast dist. chmn., 1961-62, state v.p., 1961-62, state pres., 1962-63), Delta Kappa Gamma (v.p. 1962-63). Baptist (dept. supt. Sunday sch., Anniston AL

NEWELL, WILLIAM REED, Bible teacher; b. Savannah, O., May 22, 1868; s. David Ayers and Elizabeth (Reed) N.; student Grove City (Pa.) Coll., 1886-87; grad. U. of Wooster (now Coll. of Wooster), Ohio, 1891; student Princeton Theol. Sem. (non-grad.); m. Mellicent Woodworth, June 9, 1896; children—David, Philip, John, Harriet (dec.). Pastor Bethesda Congregational Ch., 1895-96; asst. supt. Moody Bible Institute, Chicago, 1896-98; Interdenominational popular Bible Class teacher since 1897, at Chicago, St. Louis, Detroit, Toronto, London, Cairo, Shanghai, etc. Author: Old Testament Studies, 1905; Romans (with outline of Acts), 1925; Peter vs. Paul, 1927; The Book of Revelation, 1935; Extracts from David Brainerd's Journal, 1900; Commentary on Romans Verse by Verse, 1938; (revised edition) 1945; Commentary on Hebrews, also various Bible tracts. Home: 419 E. New York Av., De Land FL‡

NEWENS, ADRIAN M., mgr. Ithaca College Council; b. Medina, O., Sept. 15, 1871; s. James and Augusta A. (Post) N.; student Hiram Coll., Ohio; B.O., A.B., Drake U., Des Moines, Ia., 1898; m. Hattie Eleanor Miller, 1896 (died 1910); children—Frances Eleanor, Adrian Miller, William James, Harriette Augusta; m. 2d, Margaret F. Scott, Oct. 4, 1911; 1 son, Richard Scott. Teacher Drake U., 1894-95; instr. pub. speaking and asso. prof. English, 1896-99, prof. pub. speaking, 1899-1908, Ia. State Coll.; monologue lecturer; program dir. and critic with Redpath Lyceum Bur., 1908-15; head dept. speech arts, Horner Inst., Kansas City, Mo., 1914-17; dir. and pres. Univ. School of Music, Lincoln, Neb., 1918-30; dir. Conservatory of Music, 1931-32, and Sch. of Speech and Drama, 1932-38, Ithaca (N.Y.) Coll., mgr. council since 1938, editor Speech Arts, Service Bulletin. President Friends of Fine Arts, Lincoln, 1920-22; pres. National Speech Arts Assn., 1910-12; mem. International Lyceum Assn., Neb. Music Teachers' Assn., Sinfonia, Neb., Writers Guild; Nat. Theatre Conf., Nat. Assn. Teachers of Speech, Ithaca Chamber of Commerce, Theta Alpha Phi, Phi Mu Alpha, Phi Beta Kappa, Pi Kappa Lambda. Republican. Mem. Christian (Disciples) Ch. Pres. Lincoln Rotary Club, 1923-24; mem. Ithaca Rotary Club; gov. Dist. 172, Rotary International, 1938-39. Home: 110 Eddy, Ithaca NY‡

NEWHALL, CHARLES FRANCIS, banker; b. Chgo., Sept. 17, 1910; s. R. Frank and I. Myrtle (Carlson) N.; student U.Ill., 1930-31; student Rutgers U. Grad. Sch. Banking, 1947-48; m. Suzanne J. Ray, Aug. 10, 1946; children—Cynthia, Margery. With First Nat. Bank of Chgo., 1931-67, v.p. charge banks and bankers div., 1959-67. Mem. Chi Psi. Republican. Methodist. Clubs: Executives, Bankers, University (Chgo.); Barrington Hills (Ill.) Country. Home: Barrington IL Died July 17, 1967.

NEWHALL, HENRY WHITING, publisher and printer; b. Boston, Mass., May 14, 1875; s. Henry Sylvanus and Elizabeth Warren (Upham) N.; ed. pub. schs.; m. Lida Margaret Preston, of Santa Rosa, Calif., Dec. 16, 1901; children—Dorothy Florence, Robert Preston, Roger Warren, Henry Sylvanus. Partner, Curtis, Newhall Co., advertising agts., Los Angeles, Calif., 1897-98; mem. firm Newhall & Fenner, importers and exporters, Manila Truck-Transport Co., Travelers Transfer Co. (all of Manila, P.I.), 1899-1902; with Priscilla Pub. Co., since 1904, pres. since 1920; pres. Southgate Press since 1916; treas. Southgate Machinery Co.; dir. Beacon Trust Co. Mem. U.S. Chamber Commerce (nat. councilor), Boston Chamber Commerce. Trustee N.E. Bapt. Hosp.; dir. Nat. Pubs. Assn. Baptist. Clubs: City, Advertising, Baptist Social

Union (Boston); Advertising (New York). Home: 34 Bonad Rd., West Newton, Mass. Office: 470 Atlantic Av., Boston MA‡

NEWHOUSE, WALTER HARRY, geologist; b. Fisher, Pa., Dec. 13, 1897; s. Edward Winfield and Hattie May (Elder) N.; B.S., Pa. State Coll., 1921; M.S., Mass. Inst. Tech., 1923, Ph.D., 1926; m. Grace Edna Brown, June 30, 1923; 1 child, Jan. Mem. staff Mass. Inst. Technology, 1923-46, prof. of econ. geology, 1944-46; chmn. dept. of geology U. Chicago, 1946-57; consulting work various mining companies. Mem. Geol. Soc. of America, Soc. Econ. Geology, Am. Inst. M.E., Can. Inst. Mining Engrs., Am. Acad. Arts and Scis., Ill. State Bd. Natural Resources and Conservation. Soc. Geology de Belgigue, Sigma Xi. Editor: Ore Deposits as Related to Structural Features, 1942. Mem. editorial bd. Jour. Geology. Contbr. articles to sci. jours. Home: Chicago IL Died Sept. 21, 1969.

NEWMAN, ALFRED, composer, condr., mus. dir.; b. New Haven, Mar. 17, 1901; studied music privately; m. Martha Montgomery; children—Tony, Tim, Lucy, Fred, David, Tommy, Maria. Gave first pub. concert, 1908; piano soloist in childhood; debut as condr. with Scandals; conducted Gershwin shows; guest condr. many symphony orchestras; formerly in charge music for United Artists, Samuel Goldwin, 20th Century Fox; music dir. 20th Century Fox Films Corp. until 1960; pictures include People Will Talk, David and Bathsheba, Viva Zapata, Stars and Stripes Forever, Tonight We Sing, How to Marry a Millionaire, The President's Lady, The Robe, Hell and High Water, Diary of Anne Frank, How the West Was Won, The Greatest Story Ever Told. Recipient Academy Awards for mus. scoring Alexander's Ragtime Band, 1938, Tin Pan Alley, 1940, Song of Bernadette, 1943, Mother Wore Tights, 1947, With a Song in my Heart, 1952, Call Me Madam, 1953, Love is a Song in my Heart, 1952, Call Me Madam, 1953, Love is a Beverly Hills CA Died Feb. 17, 1970.

NEWMAN, BARNETT, painter; b. N.Y.C., Jan. 29, 1905; s. Abraham and Anna (Steinberg) N.; A.B., Coll. City N.Y., 1927; student Cornell U., 1941, Art Students League, N.Y.C., 1922-24, 29-30; m. Annalee Greenhouse, June 30, 1936. One man shows include Betty Parsons Gallery, N.Y.C., 1950, 51, Bennington (Vt.) Coll., 1958, French & Co., N.Y.C., 1959, (with DeKooning) Allan Stone Gallery, New York City, 1962, Guggenheim Mus., 1966, also Knoedler and Company, 1969, Pasadena Art Mus., 1970; represented various national shows; 1947-70, latest being Mus. Modern Art Traveling Show, Ben Heller Coll., 1961, Am. Abstract Expressionists and Imagists, Guggenheim Mus., 1961, Decisive Years, Inst. Contemporary Art, U. Pa., 1965, lithographs Mus. Modern Art, 1964, Recent Am. Synagogue Architecture, Jewish Mus., 1963, New Directions in Am. Painting, Poses Inst. Fine Art, Brandeis U., 1963, Am. drawings Guggenheim Mus., 1964, Between the Fairs, Whitney Mus., 1964, N.Y. Sch., Los Angeles County Mus., 1965, Art of U.S., and Sculpture Ann., Whitney Mus., 1966, 68, Two Generations, Sidney Janis Gallery, 1967, Contemporary Sculpture, Corcoran Gallery Art, 1967; rep. internat. shows, 1958-70; latest being Vanguard Am. Painting for USIA in Yugoslavia, Austria, Poland and Eng., 1962, Seattle World's Fair, 1962, Oshkmuseet, Moderns Museet, Stockholm, Sweden, 1963, Dunn Internat., Can. and London, Eng., 1963, Painting and Sculpture of a Decade, Gulbenkian Found., London, 1964, Amerikaanse Grafiek, Stedelijk Mus., Amsterdam, Holland, 1964, Guggenheim Internat. Show, 1964, Bilanz Internat., Basel, Switzerland, 1964, Contemporary Am. Sculpture, Paris, Germany and Scandinavia, 1965-66, U.S. Sect VIII Sao Paulo Biennial Exhbn., Brazil, 1965, Kompas III, Einhoven, Holland, 1967, Rose, Dublin, Ireland, 1967, Documanta IV Kassel, Germany, 1968; rep. permanent collections Mus. Modern Art, Kunsthalle Mus., Basel, Whitney Mus., Hartford Mus., Moderna Museet, Stockholm, Stedelijk Mus., Amsterdam, Holland, Met. Mus. N.Y. Tate Gallery, London, Allen Meml. Art Mus., Oberlin; also pvt. collections; retrospective exhbns. Mus. Modern Art, 1971-72, Stedelijk Mus., Amsterdam, 1972, Tate Gallery, London, 1972, Grand Palais, Paris, 1972; co-founder Subjects of the Artist, N.Y.C. Art Sch., 1948; leader art workshop U. Sask. (Can.), 1959; condr. grad. seminars U. Pa., 1962, 63, U. Bridgeport, 1968. Author articles in field. Recipient Brandeis U. Creative Arts award in painting, 1969-70. Home: New York City NY Died July 4, 1970.

NEWMAN, BERNARD, author, lectr.; b. Ibstock, May 8, 1897; s. William Betteridge and Annie (Garner); m. Marjorie Donald, Aug. 23, 1923; children—Margaret (Mrs. Jeremy Potter) Hilary (Mrs. Richard Hipkin) (dec. 1967), Lauriston (Mrs. Malcolm Norris); m. second, Helen Johnston, July 20, 1966. Lecturer in the United States, Japan, also Russia, other countries, 1925-—. Served with British Army, 1914-19. Decorated Legion of Honor (France). Fellow Royal Soc. Arts; mem. Royal Inst. Internat. Affairs, P.E.N., Soc. Authors, Crimewriters Assn. Author: They Saved London, Taken at the Flood (both also produced as motion pictures); The Cavalry Goes Through, 1930; Spy, 1935; The Three Germanies; Portrait of Poland; Danger Spots of the World; Visa to Russia; Speaking From Memory (autobiography); Far Eastern Journey; The Blue Ants; Mr. Kennedy's America; Unknown France; The World of Espionage: Round the World in 70 Days, South African Journey; Background to Vietnam; Spain Revisited, 1966; To Russia and Back, 1967; Turkey and the Turks, 1968; The New Poland, 1968; The History of the British Secret Service, pub. posthumously, 1969; numerous others. Home: Harrow Middlesex England Died Feb. 19, 1968.

NEWMAN, CHARLES MOREHEAD, realtor, cattleman; b. St. Louis, Mo., May 11, 1876; s. Ezekiel Simion and Fanny (Morris) N.; ed. pub. schs., El Paso, Tex., and New York Mil. Acad., Cornwall; m. Ann Butterfield, of Farmington, Mo.; 1 son, Charles Morehead. Began in real estate business with Newman Investment Co., founded by father, head of firm since 1903; pres. Travelers Aid. Pres. El Paso Internat. Museum Assn.; chmn. bd. Salvation Army; mem. bd. dirs. El Paso Pub. Library. Baptist. Mason, Odd Fellow, K.P. Home: 2601 Altura Boul. Office: El Paso TX

NEWMAN, DORA LEE, educator; b. Moundsville, W.Va., Sept. 5, 1876; d. Lewis Steenrod and Clementine (Pickett) N.; grad. high sch., Moundsville, 1893; student W.Va. U. Teacher pub. schs., Moundsville, 1902-07; head of English and history depts., high sch., Cameron, W.Va., 1907-12; head of history and civics dept. high sch., Fairmont, W.Va., 1912-20; instr. in history and govt., Fairmont State Normal Sch., 3 summers; prin. Cathedral Sch. for Girls, Orlando, Fla., 1922-23; prin. Brownell Hall, Omaha, Neb., 1923-25; dir. Cummock Sch., Los Angeles, Calif., 1927-30. Served in France with Am. Red Cross, 1918, Y.W.C.A., 1919; on hdqrs. staff Penn.-Del. div. Am. Red Cross, 1920-21; asso. dir. Junior Am. Red Cross, Atlantic div., 1921-22. Mem. W.Va. Hist. Soc. (1st sec.-treas.), Assn. Head Mistresses of Pacific Coast. Episcopalian. Author: Marion County in the Making, 1916. Contbr. verse to mags. Home: 1724 Edgemont St., Los Angeles CA‡

NEWMAN, ERWIN WILLIAM, physician; b. Minn., 1903; M.D., U. Minn. Intern, Letterman Gen. Hosp., San Francisco, 1931-32; resident in opthalmology U. Minn., Mpls., 1933-34, Ia. State U., Iowa City, 1934-37; staff mem. Meml. Hosp. of Laramie County, Cheyenne, Wyo; cons. opthalmologist VA Facility. Served with U.S. Army. Diplomate Am. Bd. Opthalmology. Mem. A.M.A., Am. Acad. Opthalmology and Otolaryngology. Home: Cheyenne WY

NEWMAN, HERMAN, editor; b. Roberts, Ill., Oct. 22, 1874; s. William R. and Sarah Hamilton (Peacock) N.; Penn. Coll., Oskaloosa, Ia., 1897-98; A.B., Friends U., Wichita, Kan., 1901; A.B., Haverford Coll., 1902, A.M., 1906; grad. work in sociology, U. of Pa., 1906-7, 1907-8; m. Emma J. Broomell, of Baltimore, Aug. 15, 1907. Teacher dist. sch., 4 yrs.; instr. history, Friends U., 1901-2; recording clerk Kansas Yearly Meeting Soc. of Friends, 1905, 1906; recorded a minister by monthly meeting, Hargrave, Kansas, 1901; asst. editor The American Friend, 1902-7; editor same, Jan. 1, 1907-—. Mem. Corpn. Haverford Coll. Home: Lansdowne, Pa. Office: 1010 Arch St., Philadelphia‡

NEWMAN, JAMES JOSEPH, corp. exec.; b. Brooklyn, N.Y., March 11, 1889; s. Dr. Charles F. and Margaret F. (McNally) N.; B.C.S., New York U., 1912; m. Marie Louise Kevin, April 14, 1920; children—Patricia (Rummage), James Kevin. Pub. accountant 1908-19; treas., v.p., Loft, Inc., 1919-27; treas. Stanley Co. Am., 1927-29; pres. Pick, Barth Holding Co., 1929-31; v.p. The B.F. Goodrich Co., 1931-53; special cons. U.S. Treasury Dept., from 1953. Served as capt. and maj. Signal Corps, U.S. Army, A.E.F., 1917-19. Dir. and trustee several civic organizations, C.P.A., N.Y. Clubs: Paradise Valley Country (Scottsdale, Ariz.); Metropolitan (N.Y.C.); Portage Country (Akron, O.); Union (Cleve.). Home: Scottsdale AZ Died July 27, 1971; buried St. Francis Cemetery, Phoenix AZ

NEWMAN, LOUIS ISRAEL, rabbi; b. Providence, R.I., Dec. 20, 1893; s. Paul and Antonia (Hecker) N.; A.B., Brown U., 1913; fellow, Columbia, 1916, Ph.D., 1924; A.M., U. of Cal., 1917; D.D., Brown U., 1942; m. Lucile Helene Uhry, June 14, 1923; children—Jeremy Uhry, Jonathan Uhry, Daniel Uhry. Asst. to Rabbi Stephen S. Wise, Free Synagogue, N.Y. City, 1917; rabbi Bronx Free Synagogue, 1917-21; asso. rabbi Temple Israel, N.Y. City, 1921-24; spl. lecturer, Columbia, 1923; mem. faculty, dept. apologetics, Jewish Inst. Religion, N.Y. City, 1922-24, 1931-33; rabbi Temple Emanu-El, San Francisco, 1924-30; rabbi Congregation Rodeph Sholom, N.Y.C., 1930-72. Ofcl. observer Central Conference of Am. Rabbis at UN, 1946-50; founder Acad. for Liberal Judaism, dir. 1955-56; hon. chmn. Tel Hai Fund (Revisionist-Zionist); acting chmn. Palestine Mandate Defense League since 1936; hon. chmn. Am. Friends of a Jewish Palestine since 1939; vice chmn. of Friends of the John Hay Library at Brown U., 1939-42; mem. adminstrv. com. Zionist Orgn. Am., 1930-31; mem. bd. trustees Fedn. for Jewish Philanthropies, N.Y.; Jewish Edn. com., N.Y. Mem. Archaeol. Soc. America (served as mem. exec. com. San Francisco br.), various academic, Zionist and communal orgns. in N.Y.C. and throughout U.S.; ex-pres. Intercollegiate Menorah Assn., Nat. Young Judea. Author numerous books, 1918-62, including: Studies in Bibical Parallelism (with William Popper), 1918; Jewish Influence on Christian Reform Movements, 1924; The Hasidic Anthology (with Samuel Spitz), 1934; The Talmudic Anthology (with Samuel Spitz), 1945; A Chief Rabbi of Rome Becomes a Catholic, 1946; Collections of Sermons, 1946-54; Pangs of the Messiah and Other Plays, Pageants and Cantatas, 1957; The Jewish People, Faith and Life, 1957; The Woman at the Wall, 1958; The Little Zaddik (play), 1961; Maggidim and Hasidim: Their Wisdom, 1962. Contbr. weekly column. Telling It In Gath, to syndicate of Jewish newspapers; formerly feature writer San Francisco Call-Bulletin. Home: New York City NY Died Mar. 9, 1972; buried Union Field Cemetery, Queens NY

NEWMAN, OLIVER PECK, b. Lincoln, Neb., Apr. 20, 1877; s. George Clyde and Sallie Nicholson (Shivers) N.; ed. Des Moines Coll., Highland Park Coll., Des Moines, Ia.; U.S. Mil. Acad., 1897-98; m. Mrs. Jennie E. Bixby, of Beaumont, Tex., Sept. 19, 1904. Began as reporter Des Moines Leader, 1898; civilian officer, U.S. Tuberculosis Sanitarium, Ft. Stanton, N.M., 1902-04; reporter Washington Post and Washington Times, 1901-02, Beaumont (Tex.) Enterprise, 1904, San Antonio Express, 1905; polit. editor Des Moines News, 1906; editor Sioux City News, 1907-09; St. Joseph (Mo.) Star, 1909; mng. editor Lincoln Star, 1910; chief editorial writer Washington (D.C.) Times, 1911-12; commr. D.C. by apptmt. of President Wilson, term 3 yrs., and elected pres. of bd.; reapptd. 1916 (resigned 1917). Student 1st Mil. Training Camp, Ft. Myer, Va., 1917; commd. maj. and assigned 313th F.A., 80th Div., Camp Lee, Va.; grad. Sch. of Fire for F.A., Ft. Sill, Okla., 1918; sailed with 80th Div., May, 1918; served in France with 80th Div. and as counter battery officer Arty. Information Service, 1st Am. Army, on staff of comdr. of arty. in Meuse offensive; journalist since 1919; v.p. Thomas R. Shipp, Inc., advertising and publicity counsellors, Washington, 1926. Democrat. Club: Cosmos. Contbr. mag. articles on Nat. politics and govt. Home: Mayflower Hotel, Washington DC‡

NEWSOM, HERSCHEL D., government ofcl.; born Columbus, Ind., May 1, 1905; s. Jesse and Nellie (Davis) N.; A.B., U. Ind., 1926; m. Blanche Hill, Oct. 26, 1929; children—Jesse R., David H. Farmer, Bartholomew Co., Ind.; master Ind. State Grange 1937-50, mem. exec. com. Nat. Grange, 1946-50, chmn., 1948-50, master, 1950-68; commr. U.S. Tariff Commn., Washington, 1968-70; dir., v.p., Farmers and Traders Life Ins. Co.; dir. Nat. Grange Mut. Ins. Co. Mem. Research Marketing Adminstrn. adv. com., Dept. Agr., 1950-56, public advisory board Mutual Security Adminstrn., 1952-53; mem. Fgn. Operations Adv. Bd., 1954-55; Nat. 4-H com., 1950-69; citizens com. reorgn. exec. br. govt., 1953-58; exec. com. Ind. Flood Control Commn., 1946-51; mem. Internat. Development Adv. Bd. 1950-58; mem. Citizens Com. Internat. Devel., Internat. Cooperation; nat. com. Am. Mus. of Immigration; mem. Citizens Com. Tax Reduction and Revision, 1963; mem. Pres.'s com. People to People Program; nat. policy bd. Am. Assembly; mem. Com. Latin Am. Econ. Relations; trustee Joint Council Econ. Edn.; dir., mem. exec. committee CARE-Agy. Internat. Devel. Com. Coop. Training Program; chairman World Food Crises Committee, 1966-69. Dir. Nat. Highway Users Conf. (v.p.), Nat. Fund Med. Edn.; dir. Blue Cross Hosp. Service, 1941-64. Blue Shield (Ind.) 1946-55, Bartholomew County Hosp. Bt. Trustees, 1945-51. Dir. Found. Am. Agr., U.S. Com. for UN; nat. council Boy Scouts Am.; mem. exec. com. Farm Film Found.; Inter-Am. Economic Policy Committee; trustee Am. Inst. Co-op.; mem. bd. Automotive Safety Found.; bd. govs. Agrl. Hall Fame. Recipient distinguished service alumni award, Ind. U., 1960; hon. Am. Farmer degree Future Farmers Am., 1951. Mem. Ind. University Alumni Council, Nat. Planning Association, Internat. Fedn. Agricultural Producers (pres. 1963-66, dir.). Member Society of Friends. Mason (Shriner). Home: Washington DC Died July 2, 1970; buried Garland-Brooke Cemetery, Columbus IN

NEWTON, CHARLES BERTRAM, head master; b. Sabathu, India, July 17, 1871; s. John and Sarah Estelle (Wigfall) N.; A.B., Princeton, 1893; Harvard Grad. Sch., 1 yr.; m. Carol Hall Cooke, of Brooklyn, June 28, 1899. Teacher, Germantown (Pa.) Acad., 1893-7, Lawrenceville (N.J.) Sch., 1898-1911; head master Blake Sch., Minneapolis, Sept., 1911-—. Asso. editor History Teachers' Mag. 2 yrs. Presbyn. Clubs: Six O'Clock, Skylight. Author of 4 booklets. Outlines for Review in English. American, Greek, and Roman History, 1908. Home: 2008 Aldrich Av. S. Address: The Blake School, Minneapolis MN‡

NEWTON, GLENN D., lawyer; b. Bainbridge, Ind., Dec. 12, 1902; s. O. M. and Lilly A. (Dobbs) N.; A.B., Stanford, 1924, J.D., 1929; m. Virginia Young, Sept. 6, 1930; children—Joan, Patricia. Head history dept. Shasta Union High Sch., Redding, Cal., 1925-28; admitted to Cal. bar, 1930, since practiced at Redding; dist. atty. Shasta County, Cal., 1935-39; city atty.

Redding, 1939-46. Past chmn. Shasta County Republican Central Com., Cal. Central Com. Dir. No. Def. Co. Assn. Fellow Am. Coll. Probate Counsel; mem. Nat. Assn. R.R. Def. Counsel, Redding C. of C. (dir., past pres.), Shasta Cascade Wonderland Assn., Am. Judicature Soc., State Bar Cal. (conf. com. 1964-65). Episcopalian. Elk. Clubs: Rotary (past pres.), Shasta Dinner (v.p.), Riverview Golf and Country; Commonwealth. Home: Redding CA Died Feb. 8, 1969; interred Redding Cemetery Redding CA

NEWTON, JOHN WHARTON, investor; b. Dallas, May 8, 1892; s. Isaac Henry and Nancy Rebecca (Dean) N.; student Allen Acad., 1909; B.S. in Chem. Engring. Tex. A. and M. Coll., 1912; m. Anne Lee Ellis, June 2, 1915; 1 son, John Wharton. Chemistry instr. Tex. A. and M. Coll., 1912-14; with Magnolla Petroleum Co., Beaumont, Tex., 1914-57, v.p., dir., 1938-57; pres., dir. Norvell-Wilder Supply Co., 1957-62; commr., chmn. Beaumont Navigation Dist., 1938-71; dir. Am. Nat. Bank of Beaumont; v.p. Beaumont Savs. Assn.; dir. Lower Neches Valley Authority. Mem. refining panel, chmn. refining com. for Dist. 3 Mil. Petroleum Adv. Bd., 1950-51; chmn. refining com., mem. gen. com. Dist. 3 Petroleum Adminstrn. War, 1941-45; council mem. com. refining Petroleum Industry War Council, 1941-45. Mem. spl. adv. com. on higher edn. Tex. Legislative Council, 1950-52; mem. Gov. Tex. Statewide Water Com., 1954-62; dir. Tex. Econ. Commn., 1950-52; bd. dirs. Tex. A. and M. Coll. System, 1945-51, 59-65, v.p., chmn. exec. com., 1949-51, 59-65; chmn. 75th Anniversary com., Tex. A. & M. Coll., 1951; chmn. Spindletop 50th Anniversary Commn., 1950-51; mem. Tex. Commn. Higher Edn., 1955-59. Councillor Texas A. and M. Research Found. (trustee 1952-55); hon. trustee Bapt. Hosp. South East Texas; trustee Houston Baptist Coll. Named Distinguished mem. honor Tex. A. and M. U., 1962. Mem. N.A.M. (bd. dirs. 1949-52), Am. Petroleum Inst. (chmn. com. smoke and fumes 1955-56, v.p. refining., dir., mem. exec. com., chmn. gen. com. div. refining, 1953-54), Tex. Mfrs. Assn. (bd. dirs., exec. com. 1946-49), East Tex. (dir. 1947), Beaumont (dir. 1943-46) chambers commerce, Beaumont Com. Econ. Develop. (community chmn., 1943-46), Assn. Governing Bds. State Univs. (exec. com., pres. 1962-63), Intracoastal Canal Assn. (dir. 1956-71), Texas Water Conservation Assn. (dir.), Vets. Service Council Beaumont (pres. 1944-46), Newcomen Soc. Eng., Tau Beta Pi. Baptist. Mason. Clubs: 25 Year (American Petroleum Industry); Rotary, Beaumont, Texas A. and M., Beaumont Country, Town (Beaumont); Petroleum (Houston). Home: Beaumont TX Died July 20, 1972; buried Forest Lawn Meml. Cemetery, Beaumont TX

NEWTON, MAURICE, investment banker; b. Elberon, N.J., July 2, 1892; s. Sigmund and Agnes Richard N.; A.B., Princeton, 1913; m. Marguerite Storm, Oct. 4, 1924; children—Joan, Diane; m. 2d, Lucienne Legarcon, Sept. 11, 1937. Began as statistician, 1914; in statistical dept., Hallgarten & Co., 1914-17; mem. N.Y. Stock Exchange, 1919-21; partner Hallgarten & Co., investment banking, from 1921; member of the executive committee, and of the bd. mgrs. Adams Express Co.; dir. Frederick H. Cone and Co.; dir. Hotel Waldorf-Astoria Corp.; dir., mem. exec. com. Am. Internat. Corp.; dir., mem. exec. com., Austin, Nichols & Co.; dir. The Anaconda Company. Served as major, Quartermaster Corps, U.S. Army, World War I. Clubs: Princeton, Leash, Recess, Madison Square Garden, Turf and Field (N.Y.C.); Saint James (London, Eng.); Saint Cloud Country (Paris); Deepdale Gold (Manhasset, N.Y.); The Travellers (Paris); Meadow Brook Old Brookville LI NY Died Apr. 25, 1968.

NICHOL, EDWARD STERLING, physician; b. Granville, O., Oct. 14, 1894; s. Edward Apollis and Lydia (Greene) N.; student Ohio State U., 1913-15, 1919-20, University of Illinois, 1916-17, (A.B.), Northwestern University, 1920-23 (M.D.); married Dorothy M. Evans, June 21, 1924 (div. 1955); children—Nancy Evans (Mrs. James W. McLamore) Dorothy Patricia (Mrs. Richard Barnes); m. 2d Polly Edgeworth Davidson, July 19, 1956; stepchildren—Carolyn (Mrs. Ferdinand Kuehn), Richard Davidson. Interne, Children's Meml. Hosp., Chgo., 1923, Cook Co. Hosp., Chgo., 1924-25; practicing physician, specializing in heart diseases, Miami, Fla., 1925-70; asso. clin. prof. Med. U. of Miami Sch. of Medicine; Founder Miami Heart Institute, director of professional services, 1960-70. Fellow International College of Angiology, A.C.P., American College Chest Physicians; mem. Am., Fla. (pres. 1949, dir.), Miami (pres. 1939, dir.) heart assns., Am., So. (chmn. med. sect. 1949), Fla. Med. assns., Dade County Medical Society, Am. Geriatrics Society, Am. Coll. Cardiology (vice president 1961), American Therapeutic Society (president 1945, chairman council 1956), Phi Kappa Psi, Alpha Kappa Kappa. Served as 1st lt. comdg. Sect. 534, U.S. Army Ambulance Service (France), 1917-19. Awarded Croix de Guerre with silver and gold stars (France). Republican. Presbyn. Clubs: Bath, La Gorce Country, Committee of 100 (Miami Beach); University (Chgo.). Home: Miami Beach FL Died June 24, 1970.

NICHOLAS, WILLIAM OLIVER, univ. adminstr.; b. New Britain, Conn., Aug. 21, 1913; s. Oliver Howard and Edna (Moore) N.; A.B., Syracuse U., 1938, M.B.A., 1950; m. Charlotte Elizabeth Stamper, Dec. 20, 1941; children—Jerry Oliver, Robert William. Accountant Underwood Typewriter Co., Hartford, Conn., 1933-34, 1938-39; asst. to treas. Whitney Blake Co., Hamden, Conn., 1939-40; asst. to office mgr. Handy and Harman, Fairfield, Conn., 1940-42; mgr. Credit Rating Bur., Danbury, Conn., 1946-47; asst. bus. mgr. Syracuse U., Syracuse, N.Y., 1947-53; V.P., treas., bus. mgr. Am. U., Washington. Served to lt. USNR, 1943-46. Mem. Delta Upsilon. Methodist. Home: Washington DC

NICHOLLS, GEORGE HEATON, former commr. for Union of S. Africa; b. Hounslow Eng., 1876. Served in British Army in India; joined Sarotse Native Police, S. Africa, during Boer War; 1st collector Northern Western Rhodesia; dist. commr. of Kafuwe Dist.; gold warden; commandant Native Armed Terr., Papua, British New Guinea; mem. Union Parliament for the Zululand Constituency, S. Africa; leader Natal Parliamentary group; mem. S. African del. of Empire Parliamentary Tour, Can., 1928; rep. sugar industry as advisor Imperial Conf., London, 1931; rep. S. African Agrl. Union and Co-operative Socs., Imperial Conf., Ottawa, Can.; mem. Indian Round Table Conf., Cape Town; Indian Colonization Commn.; permanent Native Affairs Commn.; High Commr. for Union of S. Africa, London, 1944-47. Leader S. African del. to Prep. Commn., Nov.-Dec. 1945; leader S. African del. to 1st part of 1st session Gen. Assembly, Jan. 1946. Author: Bayete; contbr. numerous pamphlets. Office: South Africa House, Trafalgar Sq., London WC 2 Eng*‡

NICHOLLS, THOMAS DAVID, congressman; b. Wilkes-Barre, Pa., Sept. 16, 1870; s. Alfred and Ann (Davis) N.; ed. pub. schs. until 9; studied mining by correspondence course; m. Sarah Ann Hughes, of Nanticoke, Pa., Feb. 26, 1896. Worked in coal mines since 9 yrs. of age as breaker boy and miner; pres. Dist. No. 1, United Mine Workers of America, 1899-1909. Mem. 60th and 61st Congresses (1907-11), 10th Pa. Dist. Democrat. Address: Scranton PA‡

NICHOLS, ARTHUR BURR, ry. official; b. Bernardston, Mass., Aug. 28, 1876; s. Walter Edmund and Emma Frances (Albee) N.; student Powers Inst., Bernardston, Mass., 1889-93; m. Eva O. Mitchell, May 25, 1899; 1 dau., Dorothy. In employ Boston & Maine R.R. continuously since 1894, stenographer, then sec. in president's office, 1894-1912, clerk of corp. since 1912, asst. to pres., 1914-16, asst. to temporary receiver, 1916-18, treas. of corp. under Federal Adminstrn., 1918-20; v.p. Boston & Maine R.R. since 1929, also represents that co. as dir. and officer of numerous affiliated corps. and subsidiaries. Republican. Unitarian. Home: 98 Walton Park, Melrose, Mass. Office: 150 Causeway, Boston MA*‡

NICHOLS, CLARK ASAHEL, author; b. Warner, N.Y., Jan. 28, 1875; s. Erwin F. and Eunice D. (Clark) N.; student U. of Denver, 1894-95, LL.B., U. of Colo., 1896; m. Gladys Ruggles Bell, of Hurley, Wis., Feb. 24, 1934. Admitted to Calif. bar, and practiced in San Diego. Republican. Author: Nichols New York Practice, 1904; Nichols Annotated Forms, 1925; Nichols Applied Evidence, 1928; Nichols Cyclopedia of Legal Forms, 1936. Editor: Cyclopedia of Federal Procedure (Vol. 8), 1930. Address: 1121 Balboa Av., Burlingame CA‡

NICHOLS, FREDERICK DAY, publisher; b. Plainfield, Ia., 1870; s. Horace (M.D.) and Sarah (Robinson) N.; prep. ed'n, Cedar Valley (Ia.) Sem. and Morgan Park (Ill.) Acad.; grad. Univ. of Chicago, 1897; grad. study in English, Univ. of Chicago, and Oxford (Eng.), 1897-1900; m. Kenilworth, Ill., 1897, Harriet Campbell Rew. Asso. in English, Univ. of Chicago, 1897-1900; asst. editor, Ginn & Co., 1900-5; charter mem., treas. Council of Soc. of Printers, 1905-6; pres. F. D. Nichols Co. Club: Quadrangle (Chicago), Alpha Delta Phi. Editor: Milton's Shorter Poems and Sonnets, 1899 A2. Residence: 622 W. 114th St. Office: 31 Union Sq., New York‡

NICHOLS, JOHN FRANCIS, mech. engr.; b. Bay City, Mich., June 19, 1873; s. Frederick A. and Emma (Luxton) N.; B.S., U. of Mich., 1895; m. Florence Maude Evans, Oct. 12, 1897 (died Feb. 17, 1937); children—Marian Maude (Mrs. Michele A. Fiore), Elizabeth (dec.), Norman Montgomery (dec.), John Evan; m. 2d, Elinor L'Amoureux Hayes, Sept. 1, 1938. Began as draftsman, Newport News Ship-building and Dry Dock Co., 1898, chargeman, 1900-08, chief draftsman, 1908-13, asst. chief engr., 1913-18, chief engr., 1918-41, dir. engring., 1941-47, now retired; dir. Newport News Bldg. & Loan Assn. Trustee county schs., Elizabeth City Co., 1918-20. Council mem. Soc. Naval Architects and Marine Engrs.; mem. Am. Soc. Naval Engrs., North-East Coast Inst. of Engineers and Shipbuilders, Am. Bureau Shipping (special sub-committee on marine engineering). Republican. Episcopalian. Club: James River Country. Home: 108 Holly St., Hampton VA‡

NICHOLS, MARK LOVEL, agricultural engr.; b. Bellevue O., Jan. 24, 1888; s. Mark Richie and Allie (McCrillis) N.; B.S., O. State Coll., 1912; M.S., U. of Del., 1916; Sc.D., Clemson Coll., 1937; m. Nina Agnes Griffin, 1913; children—Mark Richard, Dorothy Jean. Began as farmer in O., 1912-14; teacher of engring., agronomy, T.N. Vail Agrl. Sch., 1915; asst. prof. agronomy, state agronomist, U. of Del. and Del. Agrl. Expt. Station, 1915-17; agrl. engr., Va. Poly. Inst., doing food prodn. work, 1917-19; head dept. of agrl. engring., Ala. Poly. Inst., Ala. Agrl. Expt. Station, 1919-36; regional engr., Soil Conservation Service, U.S. Dept. of Agr., 1936-37; asst. chief of research, 1937-38, chief, 1938-53; formerly with Bureau Plant Industry, Soils, and Agrl. Engring.; past head tillage machinery lab. sect. agrl. engring. research branch Agrl. Research Service; lectr., collaborator U.S. Dept. Agr., from 1958. Received McCormick Medal for outstanding engring. contbrns. to agr., 1934. Fellow Am. Soc. of Agrl. Engring. (pres. 1946-47); mem. Nat. Research Council, Washington Acad. Science, Phi Kappa Phi, Gamma Sigma Delta, Sigma Psi, Alpha Zeta. Home: Auburn AL Died July 7, 1971; buried Auburn AL

NICHOLS, ROY FRANKLIN, educator; b. Newark, Mar. 3, 1896; s. Franklin C. and Anna (Cairns) N.; A.B., Rutgers U., 1918, A.M., 1919, L.H.D., 1941; Columbia U. fellow, 1920-21, Ph.D., 1923; Litt.D., Franklin and Marshall Coll., 1937, Muhlenberg Coll., Pa. 1956; Ph.D., Susquehana, 1964, M.A., Cambridge U. (Eng.), 1948, fellow Trinity Coll., 1948-49; LL.D., Moravian Coll., 1953, Lincoln U., 1959, Knox Coll., 1960; D.Sc., Lebannon Valley, 1961; Dr. Civil Law, U. Pa., 1966; m. Jeannette Paddock, 1920, Instr. history Columbia, 1922-25; asst. prof. history U. Pa., 1925-30, prof., 1930-66, prof. history emeritus, 1966-73, dean grad. sch. arts and scis., 1952-66, vice provost, 1953-66; vis. prof. Columbia, 1944-45; vis. prof. Am. history Cambridge U., 1948-49; vis. prof. Stanford, 1952. Trustee Rutgers U., 1950-73, bd. govs., 1958-73; chmn. Social Sci. Research Council, 1949-53; Fulbright lectr., India and Japan, 1962. Recipient Putlizer prize in history, 1949; Haney medal, Athenaeum award, 1962. Mem. Am. Acad. Polit. and Social Sci. (dir.), Soc. Am. Studies, Presbyn. Hist. Soc., (dir.), Library Co. Phila. (dir.), Athenaeum Phila. (v.p.), Am. Philos. Soc. (v.p. 1962-65), Am. Hist. Assn. (mem. council 1943-47; exec. com. 1945-47; pres. 1966), Assn. Grad. Schs. (pres. 1964), Council Grad. Schs. U.S. (chmn. 1965), Middle States Assn. History Tchrs. (pres. 1932-33), Pa. Hist. Assn. (pres. 1936-39), Pa. Fedn. Hist. Socs. (pres. 1940-42), Pa. Hist. Commn. (1940-43), Hist. Soc. Pa. (v.p.), Soc. Am. Historians, Gen. Soc. Am. (pres. 1946-57), Phila. Hist. Commn. (chmn. 1968), Am. Assn. U. Profs., Am. Assn. State and Local History, Phi Beta Kappa (senator 1961-73), Pi Gamma Mu, Phi Alpha Theta. Baptist. Clubs: The Rittenhouse, Franklin Inn, Lenape (Phila.), Cosmos (Washington); Authors (London, Eng.); Century Club (N.Y.C.). Author: The Democratic Machine (1850-54), 1923; Syllabus for History of Civilization (joint author), 1927; America Yesterday and Today (with C.A. Beard and W.C. Bagley), 1938; Growth of American Democracy (with Jeannette P. Nichols), 1939, The Republic of the United States: a History (with Jeannette P. Nichols), 1942; A Short History of American Democracy (with Jeannette P. Nichols), 1943; Franklin Pierce, 1931; Disruption of the American Democracy, 1948; Advance Agents of American Destiny, 1956; Religion and American Democracy, 1959; States of Power, 1845-1877, 1961, Blue Prints for Leviathan, American Style, 1963; The Invention of the American Political Parties, 1967; A Historian's Progress, 1968. Home: Philadelphia PA Died Jan. 11, 1973.

NICHOLS, THOMAS FLINT, educator, eng'r; b. Pownal, Me., Nov. 10, 1870; s. Charles Lewis and Anna (Flint) N.; grad. Bowdoin Coll., A.B., 1892. Clark Univ., Ph. D., 1895; m. Clinton, N. Y., Dec. 20, 1900, Alice Gordon Root. Asst. mathematics, Univ. of Wis., 1895-6; asst. prof. mathematics, 1896-1904, prof. applied mathematics since 1904, Hamilton Coll. Eng'r for Franklin Iron Mfg. Co. since 1899. Member eng'r corps Glenfield & Western R. R., N. Y. Central & Hudson River R. R., and now mem. N. Y. State Eng'rs Corps. Mem. Am. Math. Soc. Congregationalist. Republican. Address: Clinton NY‡

NICHOLS, WALTER EDMOND, physician; b. Hoboken, N.J., Apr. 28, 1875; s. Frank (M.D.) and Mary Ann (Barton) N.; grad. Peddie School, Hightstown, N.J., 1895; A.B., Stanford University, Calif., 1899; M.D., New York Med. Coll., Flower and Fifth Avenue Hospitals, 1903; m. Ettilla Bethell, July 29, 1903; children—Winifred Barton Carr, Eleanor Mary Skoog, Walter Frederick. Practiced, Pasadena, since 1903; mem. staff Huntington Memorial Hosp. Republican. Mem. A.M.A., Calif. State and Los Angeles Co. Med. Socs., Am. Inst. Homeopathy, Calif. and Los Angeles County Homeo. Med. Socs., Alpha Sigma. Mason (32 deg.). Mem. bd. trustees Neighborhood Ch. Club: University (bd. govs.). Home: 120 S. San Rafael Av., Pasadena 2. Office: Professional Bldg., 65 N. Madison Av., Pasadena 1 CA‡

NICHOLSON, EDWARD EVERETT, univ. prof.; b. Yellow Springs, O., Feb. 9, 1873; s. Hudson Henry and

Jennie (Higgins) N.; B.S., U. of Neb., 1894, A.M., 1896; m. Emma Pearle Camp, of Lincoln, Neb., June 1894; 1 son, Edward Camp. Asst. chemist U.S. Dept. Agr., 1892-93; instr., 1895-1900, asst. prof. since 1900, U. of Minn.; chmn. administrative bd., Coll. of Science, Lit. and Arts, same, 1913; chmn. joint bd. for Science, Lit. and Arts and Coll. of Edn., 1915; asst. dean, Coll. of Science, Literature and Arts, rank of prof., 1915, and dean of student affairs, 1917. Sent on special commission by Gov. John A. Johnson, of Minn., to Sweden, 1910. Mem. Am. Chem. Soc., Beta Theta Pi, Alpha Chi Sigma. Republican. Presbyn. Scottish Rite Mason. Clubs: Athletic, Campus, Rotary. Educational dir. for War Dept. of S.A.T.C. for states of Minn., Ia., Neb., N.D. and S.D., 1918. Home: 806 Superior St., S.E., Minneapolis MN‡

NICHOLSON, GEORGE MANSEL, lawyer; b. Riley County, Kan., May 30, 1874; s. George E. and Ida (Carpenter) N.; ed. pub. schs.; m. Julie Sheldon, Sept. 1, 1903 (died Dec. 29, 1919); m. 2d, Edith Cole, July 31, 1927. Admitted to Kan. bar, 1894, and began practice at Ness City; moved to Lincoln, Neb., 1898, Sulphur Ind. Ty., 1903, Oklahoma City, 1921; asso. justice Supreme Court, Okla., 1921-27, chief justice, 1925-27; practice since 1927. Mem. Am. and Okla. State bar assns. Republican. Methodist. Home: 1521 W. 18th St. Office: Perrine Bldg., Oklahoma City OK*‡

NICHOLSON, HAROLD GEORGE, statesman, author; b. Tehran, Iran, 1886; s. 1st Baron Carnock; ed. Wellington, Balliol Coll., Oxford U.; hon. dr. Univs. Athens, Grenoble, Glasgow, Dublin, Durham; m. Victoria Mary Sackville-West, 1913 (dec. 1962); 2 sons. With Brit. Fgn. Office, 1909, assigned to Madrid, 1910, Constantinople, 1911, Fgn. Office, 1914, mem. Brit. delegation to Peace Conf., 1919, 2d sec. Diplomatic Service, 1919, 1st sec., 1920, counsellor, 1925, Tehran, 1925, Berlin, 1927, resigned, 1929; mem. editorial staff Evening Standard, 1930; M.P., 1935-45; Parliamentary Sect. to Ministry Information, 1940-41; joined Labour Party, 1947; gov. BBC, 1941-46; chmn. Com. London Library, 1952-57; vice chmn. of exec. Nat. Trust; hon. fellow of Balliol. Trustee, Nat. Portrait Gallery, 1948-64. Decorated comdr. Legion of Honour, knight comdr. Royal Victorian Order, Companion of St. Michael and St. George. Fellow Royal Soc. Lit.; mem. Classical Assn. (pres. 1950-51), N.Y. Acad. (hon.). Clubs: Travellers, Beefsteak. Author numerous books, 1921—, latest being King George V: His Life and Reign, 1952; Evolution of Diplomatic Method (Chichele Lectures), 1954; Good Behavior, 1955; Sainte-Beuve, 1957; Journey to Java, 1957; The Age of Reason, 1960; Monarchy, 1962; Diaries and Letters, 3 vols., 1966-68. Address: Sissinghurst Castle Kent England Died May 1, 1968.

NICHOLSON, JAMES THOMAS, executive vice president American National Red Cross; born Leominster, Mass., Oct. 31, 1893; s. Joseph and Elizabeth (Ayers) N.; B.S., Massachusetts State College, 1916, LL.D., 1946; married Marguerite Elaine Dobson, Nov. 9, 1918; children—Elizabeth, James T. Dir. Junior Red Cross, Atlantic Div., New York City, 1919-22, asst. nat. dir., Washington, D.C., 1922-24, asst. mgr. eastern area, Am. Nat. Red Cross, Washington, D.C., 1924-30, mgr. Chicago Chapter, Chicago, Ill., 1930-39; nat. dir. Am. Junior Red Cross, Washington, D.C., 1939-42; vice chmn., Am. Nat. Red Cross, Washington, D.C., from 1942, exec. v.p., Am. Red cross, until 1969; delegate, Internat. Conf. of Social Work, Paris, 1928, London, 1936 (chmn.); mem. Am. Red Cross delegation to the XIV Internat. Red Cross Conf., Tokyo, 1934, XV Conf., London, 1938; XVII Conf., Stockholm, 1948; XVIII Conf., Toronto, Canada, 1952; XIX Conference New Delhi, 1957; member of the Standing Commn. Internat. Red Cross Conf.; vice chmn. League Red Cross Socs., Toronto, 1952; del. to Germany for Poland, Am. Red Cross War Mission to Europe, 1939-40; mem. A.R.C. delegation to IV Pan-Am. Red Cross Congress, Chile, 1940, V Cong., Venezuela, 1948, VI Conf., Mexico City, 1951; Am. Red Cross del. to the U.S.S.R., accompanying the Am. and British Special Missions, 1941. Served as 2d lt., 41st Machine Gun Batt., 14th Div., U.S. Army, World War I. Chmn. Chicago Chapter, Am. Assn. of Social Workers, 1937-39, mem. bd. dirs., Council of Social Agencies, Chicago, 1931-39; Traveller's Aid Soc., Chicago, 1937-39, Chicago Community Fund, 1934-39; mem. adv. bd. Cook County Bur. of Public Welfare, 1932-39; mem. bd. dirs. Cook County Training Sch. for Nurses, 1937-39. Mem. Am. Assn. of Social Workers, Belgian, Cuban, Danish, French, Chilean and Bulgarian Red Cross socs., (hon.) Brazilian Red Cross, Sigma Phi Epsilon. Episcopalian. Contbr. articles to Red Cross periodicals and pamphlets. Completed negotiations with German Govt. whereby relief for Poland was effected after occupation in 1939 and 1940, and distributed without diversion on basis of need and without regard to race, religion or politics. Recipient annual award from Parents' Mag. for outstanding service to children, 1943; Officer's Cross of Polona Restituta (Poland); Grand Cross, Order of Honor and Merit (Cuba); Officer French Legion of Honor; Comdr. Royal Order of Dannebrog (Denmark); Associate Commander Order of St. John of Jerusalem; Royal Gold Medal, Swedish Red Cross; Finnish, Greek, German (Fed.), South Korean, Mexican, Netherlands, Norwegian, Polish Red Cross honors and medals; Grand Silver medal (Austria). Home: Washington DC Died Apr. 15, 1969.

NICHOLSON, NORMAN EDWIN, assn. exec.; b. Goshen, N.Y., Jan. 18, 1923; s. Edwin and Pauline Josephine (Nelson) N.; B.A., Tufts U., 1943; m. Barbara J. Casey, Nov. 12, 1948. Engaged in newspaper work in Mass., Pa. and Tenn., 1943-46; automotive writer U.P.I., 1946-50; bur. chief Newsweek mag., Detroit, 1950-55, Time, Inc., 1955-58; with Kaiser Industries Corp., 1958-72, v.p., asst. to pres.-communications, 1964-72; v.p. charge pub. affairs Hwy. Users Fedn. for Safety and Mobility, 1972. Mem. President's Commn. Status Women, 1962; member of the citizens adv. council to the Interdeptl. Commn. Status Women, 1963-66; alternate mem. Pres.'s Missile Sites Labor Commn., 1961—; vice chairman Oakland Economic Development Com.; vice chmn. employment devel. com. Adult Minority Employment Project, Oakland, 1964-66; 1st v.p., dir. San Francisco Bay Area Urban League; mem. steering com. Nat. Adv. Council Plans for Progress. Recipient Urban Service award OEO, 1967; Delta Tau Delta (pres. Beta Mu chpt. 1943). Club: Detroit Press (organizing bd. govs. 1958). Home: Potomac MD Died May 30, 1972.

NICHOLSON, RALPH, newspaper publisher and exec.; b. Greens Fork, Ind., Feb. 12, 1899; s. F.C. and Fannie (Davis) N.; A.B., Earlham Coll., 1920; student Harvard Grad. Sch. Arts and Scis., 1921-22; M.A., 1941; LL.D., Earlham College, 1962; m. to Jane E.B. Harvey, April 5, 1926; children—Martha Jane, Anne Blayney. President of Interstate Oratorical Assn., 1918-20; began as carrier boy, 1912-16; part time reporter, 1916-20, Richmond (Ind.) Item; European correspondent Philadelphia Public Ledger, 1920-21; vice president and treasurer Editorial Research Association (New York), 1923-25; production manager New York Evening Post, 1925-27; gen. mgr. Japan Advertiser and Trans-Pacific Advertising Agency (Tokyo), 1927-28; production mgr. New York Telegram, 1928-29; asst. business mgr. Pittsburgh Press, 1929-30; mgr. dept. pub. relations Gen. Motors Corp., 1930-31; gen. mgr. McFadden Newspapers, 1932; asst. pub. New York Daily Mirror, 1932-33; gen. mgr., treas. Tampa Times Co. (Tampa Daily Times, Radio Station WDAE), 1933-41, v.p., dir., 1933-51; pres., pub. New Orleans Item, 1941-49; spl. cons. Sec. Army, 1949; dir. office Pub. Affairs, U.S. High Commn., Germany, 1949-50; pres. and pub. St. Petersburg (Fla.) Ind., 1950-52, The Charlotte Observer, 1951-53; owner, pres., pub. Dothan (Ala.) Eagle, 1955-66, The Troy (Ala.), Messenger, 1960-66, The Brundidge (Ala.) Banner, 1961-66, Chronicle, Pascogoula-Moss Point, Miss., 1963-66; director Pullman Co., 1947-50, Tallahassee Bank & Trust Company, 1959-64; sr. adviser to Freedom Newspapers for Acquisitions in Southeastern States, from 1968; adviser to pres., pub. Gate City daily newspaper, Keokuk, Ia. Mem. Judicial Council, Fa., 1955-60, vice-chmn., 1957-60; member National Defense Executive Reserve, from 1959. Served as student pilot Flying Corps, U.S.N.R., 1918-19. Trustee Earlham Coll., 1948-51. Mem. Associated Dailies of Fla., 1934-41 (v.pres. 1936-37, president 1937-38); Chmn. Business Affairs Com. of Southern Newspaper Pub. Assn., 1936-37, chmn. Pub. Relations Com., 1941-44, dir., 1937-39, treas., 1947-49; chmn. New Orleans Red Cross Fund, 1944; La. chmn. Ducks Unlimited, 1944-49. War corr. European Theater of Operations, 1944. Mem. Newcomen Soc., Soc. Friends, So. (chmn. postal com.) Am. newspapers pub. assns., Sigma Delta Chi. Episcopalian. Mason. Clubs: Metropolitan, Nat. Press (Washington); Boston; New Orleans; Harvard (N.Y.C.). Home: Tallahassee FL Died July 10, 1972; buried Episcopal Cemetery, Tallahassee FL

NICHOLSON, ROBERT HARVEY, utility exec.; b. Anderson, Cal., Nov. 25, 1889; s. William Drake and Abigail (Cochrane) N.; student pub. schs., Cal.; m. Leona Browne, Aug. 1912; 1 dau., Nadine R. (Mrs. Merideth E. Moseley); m. 2d, Helene Strauss, Sept. 21, 1929; children—Nancy H. (Mrs. Cunningham), Robert Harvey. Engr. Santa Fe Ry., Oakland, Cal., and Cal. R.R. Commn., 1913-22; cons. engr., Los Angeles, 1923-26; pres. So. Cal. Utilities, Inc., 1926-28; pres. San Gabriel Valley Water Co., El Monte, Cal., 1936-59, chmn. bd., 1959-69. Served as capt. Engrs., U.S. Army, AEF, 1917-20, col., C.E., 1941-45; ETO. Clubs: California (Los Angeles); Annandale Golf (Pasadena); Newport Harbor Yacht, Irvine Coast Country (Newport Beach, Cal.). Home: Pasadena CA Died May 8, 1969.

NICHOLSON, SAMUEL THORNE, b. Halifax Co., N.C.; s. Thomas W. and Martha E. (Thorne) N.; grad. Horner Sch.; classical and lit. course U. of Va.; studied law, same; m. Jennie Conwill, of Selma, Ala., Dec. 26, 1899 (died July 10, 1919); m. 2d, Eva S. Moore, nee Spence, Feb. 9, 1922. Formerly in ins. business; became interested in reform work; called and managed Nat. Christian Conf., 1895; called another nat. conf. 1897, which organized Nat. Good Citizenship League, of which was made gen. sec.; was v.p. Initiative and Referendum League of America; sec. Southern Christian Citizenship Congress, Atlanta, 1913; candidate of Union Reform Party for v.p. of U.S., 1900; now mgr. Am. Law & Credit Service. Methodist. Sec. Bible League of America. Club: Commonwealth (New York). Office: 825 Vermont Av. N.W., Washington DC‡

NICKELS, MERVYN MILLARD, physician; b. New Brighton, Pa., Aug. 4, 1898; s. John Hobbs and Viola May (McFarland) N.; M.D., Loyola U., Chgo., 1927; m. Loretta Nickels; children—Nedra (Mrs. Fitch Williams III), Rita (Mrs. John Selden), Michael David and Daniel Arthur (twins). Intern, Grace Hosp., Detroit, 1927-28; asst. physician Traverse City (Mich.) State Hosp., 1936-39, clin. dir., 1942-46, asst. supt., 1946-70, acting supt., 1955-56. Served to comdr., M.C., USNR, 1943-46. Diplomate Am. Bd. Psychiatry and Neurology. Mem. Am. Psychiat. Assn. Home: Traverse City MI Died Apr. 16, 1971; buried Oakwood Cemetery.

NICKS, F. WILLIAM, banker; b. Winnipeg, Man., Can., Oct. 9, 1906; s. Frank W. and Elizabeth (Morrow) N.; ed. St. John's Sch., Winnipeg; D.C. L. (hon.), Mt. Allison U., Sackville, N.B., Can., 1960; m. Katherine Honora Simser, Oct. 23, 1937. With Bank of N.S. (Can.), 1923-72, accounting and managerial positions, various locations, 1923-52, asst. gen. mgr., Toronto, Ont., Can., 1952-54, gen. mgr., 1954-57, v.p., 1957-58, pres., chief exec. officer, 1958-62, chmn. bd., pres., 1962-72, also dir.; chmn. Bank of N.S. Trust Co. (Bahamas) Ltd., Bank of N.S. Trust Co. Jamaica Ltd., Bank of N.S. Trust Co. West Indies Ltd., Bank of N.S. Trust Co. of N.Y., Mortgage Ins. Co. Can.; dir. Nat. Trust Co. Ltd., Can. Life Assurance Co., Siemens Overseas Investments Ltd., Elican Devel. Co. Ltd., Adela Investment Co. S.A. Mem. Internat. C. of C. (Canadian council), Newcomen Soc. N. Am., Canadian Bankers Assn. (past pres.). Clubs: York, Toronto, Royal Canadian Yacht, Toronto Hunt, Empire, Board of Trade, Canadian National Caledon Mountain Trout; Canadian (N.Y.); Halifax (N.S.); Mount Royal (Montreal). Home: Toronto ON Canada. Died Jan. 4, 1972; buried Elmwood Winnipeg Winnipeg, Manitoba Canada

NICOL, JACOB, senator, newspaper pub.; b. Roxton-Pond, P.Q., Can., 1876; s. Philippe and Sophie (Cloutier) N.; student Feller Inst., Quebec; A.B., McMaster Univ., Toronto, 1900, LL.D., 1929; LL.M., Laval Univ., Quebec, 1904; D.C.L., Bishop's Univ., Lennoxville, Quebec, 1927; m. Emelie Couture, 1909. Admitted to Can. bar, 1904; practised under the firm name of Nicol, Lazure & Couture, Sherbrooke, 1905-35; pub. daily newspapers: Le Soleil since 1929, l'Evenement, since 1930, Quebec City; Le Nouvelliste, Three-Rivers, P.Q., since 1932; La Tribune, Sherbrooke, P.Q., since 1910; these papers control radio stas. Pres. Stanstead & Sherbrooke Ins. Co. since 1921, The Missisquoi & Rouville Mutual Fire Ins. Co. since 1923, The Sterling Ins. Co. of Can. since 1940 (dir. of 5 other ins. cos.); vice pres. Canadian National Bank in Montreal since 1942. Dir. General Trust of Canada, Montreal, Southern Canada Power Co., Montreal, Sherbrooke Trust Co. Batonnier of the Dist. of Saint-Francis, 1918-20, 1924-26, dist. atty., 1906-21, treas. of P.Q., 1921-29; mem. legislative council since 1929; speaker of body 1930, resigned to become Leader in 1934. Apptd. to Canadian Senate in 1944. Liberal. Clubs: Garrison (Quebec); Universetaire (Montreal and Quebec), Reform (Montreal); Hermitage, Magog, Que., St. George (Sherbrooke). Office: Sherbrooke Province of PQ Canada‡

NICOLASSEN, GEORGE FREDERICK, prof. ancient langs.; b. Baltimore, Md., Dec. 15, 1857; s. Albert and Mary Eliza (Coulson) N.; grad. Baltimore City Coll., 1874; A.B., U. of Va., 1879; A.M., 1880; Ph.D., Johns Hopkins, 1882; studied Harvard and Columbia, 1915-16; married Eliza Trueheart Graves, July 11, 1888; children—Agnes Tinsley (Mrs. T.J. Wharton), Augusta Graves, Elizabeth. Fellow in Greek, 1879-81, instr. Greek and Latin, 1881-82, Johns Hopkins; prof. ancient lang., 1882-91, prof. Greek and German, 1891-1915. v. chancellor 1897-1906. 1909-14. Southwestern Presbyterian U., Clarksville, Tenn. (now Southwestern Univ., Memphis); prof. ancient langs., dean sch. liberal arts, Oglethorpe U., 1916-45. Mem. Rhodes scholarship committee for Tennessee, 1910-15. Moderator Synod of Tenn., Presbyn. Ch. U.S., 1914. Mem. Classical Assn. Middle West and South, Chi Phi. Democrat. Author: Notes on Latin and Greek, 1890; Greek Notes, revised, 1896; The Book of Revelation, 1917. Editor of Digest, Gen. Assembly Southern Presbyn. Ch., 1911 and 1922. Address: 176 Westminster Dr., N.E., Atlanta GA‡

NIEBUHR, REINHOLD, clergyman; b. Wright City, Mo., June 21, 1892; s. Gustave and Lydia (Hosto) N.; student Elmhurst (Ill.) Coll., 1910; Eden Theol. Seminary, St. Louis, Mo., 1913; D.D., Eden Theological Seminary, 1930; B.D., Yale Divinity School, 1914, A.M., 1915; D.D., Grinnell College, 1936, Wesleyan Coll., 1937, U. of Pa., 1938, Amherst, 1941, Yale, 1942, Oxford, 1943, Harvard, 1944, Hobart Coll., 1948, Dartmouth Coll., 1951; LL.D., Occidental Coll., Los Angeles, Calif., 1945; D.D., Princeton, Univ., 1946,

Glasgow U., 1947, New York Univ., 1947; Litt.D., New Sch. Social Research, 1951; D.D., Manchester University, England, 1954, Hebrew U., Jerusalem, 1967; married Ursula Keppel-Compton, 1931; children—Christopher Robert, Barbara Elizabeth. Ordained ministry Evangelical Synod of North America, 1915; pastor at Detroit, 1915-28; associate professor philosophy of religion, Union Theol. Seminary, 1928-30, prof. Christian ethics, 1930-60, now emeritus; was research asso. Inst. War and Peace Studies, Columbia. Recipient Presdl. Medal of Freedom, 1964. Mem. Am. Acad. Arts and Letters, Inst. Arts and Scis., Alpha Sigma Phi. Author several books since 1927, including Moral Man and Immoral Soc., 1932; Nature and Destiny of Man, 1941; Christian Realism and Political Problems, 1953; The Self and the Dramas of History, 1955; Structure of Nations and Empires, 1963; Man's Nature and His Communities, 1965; Faith and Politics, 1968. Editor of bi-weekly Christianity and Crisis, 1941-66. Home: Stockbridge MA Died June 1, 1971.

NIEHAUS, FREDRICH WILHELM, physician; b. Treynor, Ia., Feb. 11, 1889, s. Friedrick Karl and Rosetta (Huelle) N.; M.D., U. Neb. 1916; postgrad. U. Vienna (Austria), 1929-30; m. E. Effie Ruth Kelley, Aug. 5, 1918; children—Virginia (Mrs. Robert Auracher), Karl Friedrich. Intern Bishop Clarkson Meml. Hosp., 1916-17, later chief staff; staff Bellevue Hosp., N.Y.C., also St. Vincent's Hosp., N.Y.C., 1917-18; later U. Neb. Hosp. Prof. medicine U. Neb., from 1935, prof. emeritus, 1954-69, also sr. cons. Served to capt. M.C., U.S. Army, World War I. Diplomate Am. Bd. Internal Medicine. Fellow Am. Heart Assn., A.C.P., Am. Coll. Chest Physicians; mem. A.M.A., Neb., Omaha-Douglas County med. socs., Midwest Clin. Soc. (founder, pres.), Alpha Omega Alpha, Phi Rho Sigma. Contbr. papers to profl. publs. Home: Omaha NE Died Oct. 6, 1969; buried Fairview Cemetery, Treynor IA

NIELSEN, HARALD HERBORG, retired educator, physicist; b. Menominee, Mich., Jan. 25, 1903; s. Knud and Maren (Nielsen) N.; student St. Olaf Coll., Northfield, Minn., 1923-25; B.S., U. Mich., 1926, A.M., 1927, Ph.D., 1929; student U. Copenhagen (Universitetets Institut for Teoretisk Fysik), 1929-30; Dr. Honoris Cause, U. Dijon (France), 1965; m. Martha Ann Evans, Sept. 18, 1943; 1 son, Peter Herborg. Am. Scandinavian fellow, 1929-30; mem. faculty Ohio State U., 1930-71, prof. physics, 1943-71, emeritus, 1971-73, chmn. dept., 1946-67; tech. rep. NDRC, 1942-44; Fulbright lectr. U. Paris, 1958-59; vis. prof. U. Copenhagen, 1968-69; Dept. State sci. attache, Stockholm, Sweden, 1952-53; pres. commn. on symbols, units and nomenclature Internat. Union Pure and Applied Physics, 1952-60, v.p., 1960-61, sec. triple commn. spectroscopy, 1960-63, pres., 1963-64, v.p. U.S.A. nat. com., 1958-61, sec. U.S.A. com., 1961-69; cultural exchange trip, USSR, 1958; chmn. NRC com. symbols, units and nomenclature, 1956-61, mem., 1962-65, mem. div. chemistry and chem. tech. com. phys. chemistry; cons. to sci. adviser to sec. state, 1958-60. Decorated cross of Leopold (Belgium); medal of U. Liege (Belgium), 1949; cross Order of Knight of Dannebrog (Denmark), 1957; Guggenheim fellow, 1949-50; Fellow Am. Phys. Soc., A.A.A.S.; mem. Am. Assn. Physics Tchrs., Am. Scandinavian Found. (asso.), Optical Soc. Am., Am. Nat. Rebild Com., Societ Royale des Sicences de Liege, Societe Francaise de Physique, Royal Danish Acad. Scis. and Letters, Phi Beta Kappa, Sigma Xi, Sigma Pi Sigma. Clubs: Cosmos; Torch; Ohio State Faculty. Co-author: Rotation-Vibration of Polyatomic Molecules. Editor Jour. Molecular Spectroscopy; asso. editor Phys. Rev., 1945-48, Jour. Chem. Physics, 1952-55. Home: Columbus OH Died Jan. 8, 1973; buried Green Lawn Cemetery Mausoleum, Columbus OH

NIELSEN, JOHANNES MAAGAARD, psychiatrist, neurologist; b. Denmark, Oct. 17, 1890; s. Soren Peter and Elise (Maagaard) N.; brought to U.S., 1896, naturalized, 1913; B.S., U. Ill., 1921, M.D., 1923; m. Celia Evelyn Owens, July 20, 1922 (dec.); children—Robert Johannes, Theodore Milton, Lois Evelyn, Paul Vernon; married second, Dorothy Cadwell, April 1, 1947 (died 1958); one daughter, Dorothy. Intern Los Angeles County Hospital, 1923-24; asst. in neurology and psychiatry, sanitarium, Battle Creek, Mich., 1924-26, asso., 1926-30; asso. prof. neurology Coll. Med. Evangelists, Los Angeles, 1930-31; asso. clin. prof. neurology and psychiatry U. So. Cal., 1931, clin. prof., 1948-52; now clin. prof. neurology U. Cal. at Los Angeles; pvt. practice neurology and psychiatry, Los Angeles, 1930-69. Chief cons. in aphasia VA, Washington; sr. cons. neurology Long Beach VA Hosp. Fellow A.C.P., Am. Acad. Neurology, Am. Psychiatric Assn.; hon. mem. Phila., N.Y. neurol. socs., Northwest Soc. Neurology and Psychology, Am. Paraplegic Soc.; member A.M.A., American Neurological Association (president 1955-56), Assn. for Research Nervous and Mental Diseases, Harvey Cushing Soc., Soc. Biol. Psychology (past pres.), A.A.A.S., Alpha Omega Alpha, Phi Chi. Author: Agnosia, Apraxia, Alphasia, 1936; Clinical Neurology, 1941; Engrammes of Psychiatry (sr. author); Memory and Amnesia. Contbr. sci. jours. Home: Los Angeles CA Died Dec. 12, 1969.

NISBET, WALTER OLIN, JR., investment banker; b. Charlotte, N.C., Sept. 18, 1906; s. Walter Olin and Eugenia A. (Heath) N.; B.S., Davidson Coll., 1928; M.B.A., Harvard, 1930; m. Rebecca Wise Jones, Aug. 1, 1931; children—Mary Jane (Mrs. Seddon Goode, Jr.), Rebecca Jones (Mrs. Edwin R. Rencher, Jr.), Walter Olin III. With R. S. Dickson & Co., 1930-32; with Interstate Securities Corp., Charlotte, 1932-69, pres., 1950-64, chmn. bd., 1964-69; vice president, director Sterling Investment Fund; dir., mem. exec. com. Mineral Research and Devel. Corp.; Manetta Cotton Mills, Mt. Mitchell Broadcasters, Inc., Melodaire, Inc., Western Carolina Telephone Co., Thermo Plastics Corp.; cons. Calvin Bullock, Ltd. Trustee Davidson Coll., 1949-64, bd. govs., 1964-—. Served to lt. USNR, 1943-46. Mem. Investment Bankers Assn. Am. (bd. govs. 1959-63), N.Y., N.C. (charter) socs. financial analysts, Omicron Delta Kappa, Beta Theta Pi. Presbyn. Clubs: Kiwanis, Charlotte Country, City (bd. govs.), Charlotte Textile, Charlotte Executives (Charlotte); Quail Hollow Country; Biltmore Forest Country; Harvard (N.Y.C.). Home: Charlotte NC Died Aug. 22, 1969.

NISONGER, HERSCHEL WARD, assn. exec.; b. Ithica, O., Mar. 18, 1890; s. Perry and Laura (Crawford) N.; B.S. in Agr., Ohio State U., 1914; M.A., Columbia, 1926; student U. Chgo., summers 1916, 17; m. Ethel Peffly, Aug. 21, 1914; children—Emmagene, Joseph. Tchr. sci., Bradford, O., 1914-16; prin. high sch., Versailles, O., 1916-19; instr. agrl. edn. Ohio State U., 1919-22, asst. prof. agrl. edn., 1922-26, prof., 1926-28, jr. dean Coll. Agr., 1928-36, prof. adult edn. Coll. Edn., 1936-45, din. bur. spl. and adult edn., 1945-57, dir. bur. ednl. research and service, 1957-60, prof. emeritus, until 1969; pres. American Assn. Mental Deficiency, 1961-62. Adult edn. cons. Mil. Govt., Germany, 1949. Pres. Ohio Citizens Council Health and Welfare, 1947-49, Ohio Welfare Conf., 1948; dir. AAMD research project Tech. Planning in Mental Retardation, from 1956. Member American Hearing Society (president 1954-57), Adult Education Association United States, Nat. Edn. Assn., Internat. Council Expectional Children, Phi Delta Kappa. Conglist. Home: Columbus OH Died May 18, 1969.

NIXON, EUGENE WHITE, educator; b. Marissa, Ill., Jan. 6, 1885; s. John Thomas and Margaret Jane (White) N.; A.B., Monmouth (Ill.) Coll., 1907; student, U. of Ill., 1916, U. of Calif., 1918; M.A., Columbia U., 1932; m. Edna Maude Blair, June 30, 1909 (div.); children—Eugene Blair (dec.), John Erskine; m. 2d, Mrs. Patricia Davies Baldwin, May 26, 1942. Began as teacher, St. Matthews School, Burlingame, Calif., 1907-09 at Davenport (Ia.) High Sch., 1909-16; prof. phys. education, Pomona Coll., Claremont, Calif., 1916-50; instr., U. of Calif. at Los Angeles, summers 1932, 36; former mem. Claremont Sch. Bd. Served as 2d lt. inf., U.S. Army, 1917-18. Rep. candidate for for Cong., 12th Calif. Dist., 1938. Honor award for distinguished service in phys. edn., 1937, citation of honor from Football Writers Assn. Am. Mem. Cal. Assn. for Health, Phys. Edn. and Recreation, Am. Legion, Phi Kappa Pi. Author: The Athlete in the Making (with Jesse F. Williams), 1932; Introduction to Physical Education (with F.W. Cozens), 3d edit., 1947; 4th edit., 1952 (translated Japanese, auspices U.S., 1950), 5th edit., 1959. Contbr. articles Hygeia, Todays Health, Field and Stream, Popular Mechanics, McClures and others. Home: Claremont CA Died Mar. 5, 1969.

NIXON, THOMAS CARLYLE, lawyer; b. Rochester, N.Y., July 3, 1890; the son of William Henry and Blanche (Gage) Nixon; LL.B., Union Coll., 1911, LL.D., 1963; m. Helen McElwain, July 28, 1917; 1 dau., Patricia (Mrs. Arthur A. Arms, Jr.). Admitted to N.Y. bar, 1911, since practiced in Rochester; mem. Nixon, Hargrave, Devans & Doyle, and predecessors, 1921-—, specialist in corp. law; dir. Bausch & Lamb Optical Co., Rochester Gas & Electric Corp., Rochester Telephone Corp. Trustee Albany (N.Y.) Law School, U. Rochester. Mem. Am., N.Y. State, Rochester bar assns., American Legion. Clubs: Rochester, Genesee Valley, Country. Home: Rochester NY Died Oct. 14, 1967; buried Rochester NY

NKRUMAH, KWAME, ex-pres. Republic Ghana, Africa; b. Brit. W. Africa, Sept. 21, 1909; student Achimota Coll., Tchr. Tng. Coll., Achimota, Gold Coast; B.D., LL.D., Lincoln U., Pa.; S.T.B., M.A., M.Sc., U. Pa.; student London Sch. Econs. Schoolmaster primary schs., Elmina and Axim, 1931-34, Roman Catholic Seminary, Amissano, Gold Coast, 1934-35; student United States 1935-45, England, 1945-47; married Fathia Halim Ritzk, 1958; children—Gamal, Samia, Sekou. Gen. sec. West African National Secretariat, joint sec. Pan African Congress, London, editor New African, London; returned to Gold Coast, 1947; former mem., first gen. sec. polit. party, United Gold Coast Conv.; formed Convention People's Party, 1949; imprisoned for inciting strikes, 1949; municipal mem. from Accra, in first gen. election, 1951, released from prison to become leader Govt. Bus. in Legislative Assembly; prime minister, Gold Coast, Africa, 1952-57; prime minister Ghana, Mar. 1957-60, pres., 1960-67. Life chmn. Convention People's Party. Chancellor U. Ghana, Legon, Kwame Nkrumah U. Sci. and Tech. Author: Towards Colonial Freedom; Ghana the Autobiography; I Speak of Freedom; Africa Must Unite; Consciencism. Address: Accra Ghana Africa Died Apr. 27, 1972.

NOA, ERNESTINE, welfare and civic work; b. Baltimore, Nov. 23, 1871; d. Ismar and Rose B. (Loveman) N.; ed. Chattanooga U., Women's (Goucher) Coll., Baltimore, Cleveland (O.) Kindergarten Coll.; unmarried. Writer advertising for D. B. Loveman Co., Chattanooga, Tenn., 1896-01; sec. and bookkeeper to father in real estate and building business, 1905-7 and continued business alone after his death. Industrial and vocational investigation, Eastern and Northern Cities, 1909; continued investigation in Europe, 1910-12; spl. commr. Southern Commercial Congress, for study of cooperation in Europe, 1912-—; mem. Am. commn. to investigate rural cooperation in Europe, 1913. Chairman industrial edn. Tenn. Federation Women's Clubs, 1908-10; mem. Tenn. Women's Press and Authors' Club (founder, 1899). Home: Lookout Mountain TN‡

NOAKES, FRANK LEROY, labor union exec.; b. Chgo., July 4, 1903; s. Lewis Henry and Mayme (O'Keefe) N.; ed. pub. schs., Chgo.; m. Doris Mitchell, Feb. 19, 1921 (dec. 1966); 1 dau., Lois (Mrs. O.E. Sabatke). Mem. Brotherhood of Maintenance of Way Employees, 1923-—, gen. chmn., Chgo. chpt., 1927-47, nat. dir. research, 1947-56, grand lodge sec.-treas., 1956-—. Chmn. U.S. sect. Joint U.S.-Mexico Trade Union Com., 1951-—; mem. farm labor adv. com. Dept. Labor, 1947-—; nat. reporting officer R.R. Retirement Bd., 1956-—; mem. community adv. council and labor adv. com. Inst. Labor and Indsl. Relations, U. Mich.-Wayne State U., 1951-—. Mem. Gov. Mich. Study Commn. Prepaid Hosp. Care Plans. Clubs: Nat. Capital Democratic (Washington); Lakepointe Country (St. Clair Shores, Mich.); Kenwood Golf and Country (Bethesda, Md.). Home: Grosse Pointe MI Died May 6, 1971.

NOBLE, CHARLES C(ASPER), clergyman; b. Washington, Jan. 1, 1898; s. Charles Thompson and Bessie Summerfield (Cline) N.; A.B., Williams Coll., 1921, D.D. (hon.), 1949; B.D., Union Theol. Sem., 1924; M.H. (honorary), Springfield Coll., 1949; D.S.T. (honorary), Northwestern University, 1957; LL.D., George Williams College, 1962, Syracuse U., 1967; m. Grace Myra Kepner, June 4, 1925; children—Anne Elizabeth, Margaret Helen, Carolyn Jane. Ordained to ministry of Meth. Ch., 1923, pastor, The Bronx, 1924-27, Brooklyn, 1927-30, Hartford, Conn., 1930-34, Glens Falls, 1934-41, Syracuse, N.Y., 1941-45, dean Chapel of Syracuse U., from 1945; Merrick lecturer Ohio Wesleyan U., 1957. Member internat. bd., state dir., chmn. nat. adv. com. on camping YMCA. Trustee Brewster Acad., Wolfeboro, N.H. Member of National Association of Coll. and U. Chaplains (pres. 1948-49). Clubs: Rotary (Glen Falls and Syracuse). Author: Faith for the Future, 1950. Home: Syracuse NY Died July 1, 1968.

NOBLE, GEORGE BERNARD, former govt. cons.; b. Leesburg, Fla., July 11, 1892; s. Charles Samuel and Eva Susanna (Hall) N.; ed. U. Wash., 1910-13; B.A., Oxford U. (Rhodes scholar, 1913-16), Eng., 1915, M.A., 1923; U. of Wis., 1916-17; Columbia 1919-20, 1925-26, Ph.D., 1935; LL.D. Reed Coll, 1962; m. Matilda Thomas, Dec. 24, 1917. Reporting on French opinion U.S. commn. to Negotiate Peace, 1918-19; asst. prof. polit. sci. U. of Neb., 1920-22; asst. prof. polit. sci., Reed Coll., Portland Ore., 1922-28, prof., 1928-43; vis. lecturer polit. sci., Barnard Coll., 1926-27; chmn. 12th Regional W.L.B., 1943-45; asst. chief div. research and publ., Dept. of State, Mar.-Sept. 1946, chief div. hist. policy research, 1946-53, chief hist. div., 1953-59, director historical office, 1959-62; cons. to Dept. State Pub. Affairs Bur., 1962-65. Member Oregon State Senate, 1941-42; chmn. Oregon State Adjustment Bd. (N.R.A.), 1934-35. Served as 1st lt., 168th inf., World War I. Decorated Distinguished Service Cross, 1918. Mem. Am. Polit. Sci., Am. Soc. Internat. Law, Am. Hist. Assn., Alpha Delta Phi, Phi Beta Kappa, Unitarian. Club: Cosmos (Washington). Author: Policies and Opinions at Paris, 1919, 1935; Christian A. Herter, 1970; various articles. Home: Falls Church VA Died Nov. 28, 1972.

NOBLE, JOHN MARTIN, retired telephone official; b. Christian County, Ill., Aug. 23, 1869; s. James Alexander and Marie K. (Orr) N.; student U. of Kan., 1887-91; m. Anna May Martin, Nov. 29, 1892. Came to Okla., 1903; served as pres., gen. mgr., etc., Southwestern Bell Telephone Co. and predecessors, since 1903; now v.p. Southwestern Bell Telephone Co.; dir. First Nat. Bank & Trust Co., Alexander Drug Co. Home: 501 N.W. 15th St., Oklahoma City OK‡

NOBLE, MERRILL EMMETT, lawyer, state supreme court justice; born in Savoy, Ill., December 5, 1896; s. James Houston and Harriett (Baird) N.; LL.B., U. Ill., 1920; LL.D., New Mexico Highlands Univ. 1963; m. Martha Van Petten, June 19, 1920; children—James Van Petten, Merrill Emmett, Margaret (Mrs. R. D. Bentley). Admitted to N.M. bar, 1920; mem. firm

Hunker & Noble, 1920-33; pvt. practice law, Law Vegas, N.M., 1933-37; mem. firm Noble & Spiess, 1937-49, Noble, Spiess & Noble, 1949-55, Noble & Noble, Las Vegas, 1956-60; city atty. Las Vegas, 1924-25, 49-53; dist. atty. 4th Jud. Dist. N.M., 1937-45; mem. N.M. State Bar Commn., 1950-57; justice N.M. Supreme Court, 1960-69. Member N.M. Democratic Central Com., 1942-53, state executive committee, 1946-50. President board regents New Mexico Highlands Univ., 1937-43; trustee Southwestern Legal Center, 1955-56. Mem. Am. (N.M. chmn. com. retirement benefits 1956-57), N.M. (chmn. com. ethics, grievances and discipline 1952-55, president 1955-56), San Miguel Co. (president 1939-42) bar associations, Chamber of Commerce, Theta Delta Chi, Phi Delta Phi. Elk. Home: Santa Fe NM Died Nov. 13, 1969.

NOBLE, RALPH EDWARD, coll. pres.; b. Randolph, Vt., June 29, 1899; s. Henry John and Bertha (Dearing) N.; A.B., Dartmouth Coll., 1923; A.M., University of Vermont, 1932, Ed.M., 1940; Pd.D., Middlebury College, 1942; LL.D., Norwich University, 1948; married to Bertha D. Eddy, June 25, 1924; 1 son, John Will. Principal Underhill (Vt.) High Sch., 1923-25; teacher English, Peoples Acad., Morrisville, Vt., 1925-31; supt. schs., Lamoille S. dist., Vt., 1931-32; prin. Peoples Acad., 1932-34; supt. city schs., Barre, 1934-35; state dir. secondary and vocational edn., 1935-40, state commr. edn., 1940-49; pres. Vermont Junior Coll., Montpelier, 1949-66. Past pres. N.E. Jr. Coll. Council. Home: Montpelier VT Died Mar. 16, 1972

NOBLE, ROBERT PECKHAM, business exec.; born Gouverneur, N.Y., Oct. 1, 1880; s. Harvey H. and Edna (Wood) N.; B.S. in M.E., Purdue U., 1903; m. Meta Buehner, Jan. 15, 1912; children—Robert Philip, Edward John, Margarita Elizabeth. Northwest rep. Westinghouse Air Brake Co., Portland, Ore., 1907-12; v.p. and sec. Carlton Lumber Co., Portland, 1913-16; v.p. and sec. Life Savers Corp., Port Chester, N.Y., 1916-49, pres., 1949-73, chmn. bd., 1955-56; co. merged with Beech-Nut Packing Co., 1956, vice chmn. bd. of merger Beech-Nut Life Savers, Inc., 1956-65; founder, president, dir. Petroleum Exploration Co., 1939-54; director of the merged company, Drilling and Exploration Company; president Allied Industries, Greenwich, Conn., 1930-73; dir. Putnam Trust. Mem. Phi Kappa Psi. Republican. Unitarian. Clubs: University, Racquet & Tennis (N.Y. City); Greenwich CT Died Mar. 1973.

NOEL, CLEO ALLEN, JR., fgn. service officer; b. Oklahoma City, Aug. 6, 1918; s. Cleo Allen and Mary Pearl (Hand) N.; A.B., U. Mo., 1939, M.A., 1940; M.A., Harvard, 1948; m. Lucille McHenry, Sept. 1, 1951; children—John Francis, Janet Elizabeth. Joined U.S. Fgn. Service, 1949; vice consul, Genoa, Italy, 1949-51, Dhahran, Saudi Arabia, 1952-54; consul, Marseille, France, 1954-55; Arabic lang. tng., Washington, also Beirut, Lebanon, 1956-57; 2d sec. embassy, Jedda, Saudia Arabia, 1957-58, Khartoum, Sudan, 1958-61; officer charge Sudanese affairs State Dept., 1961-63; chief Far East br. personnel operations div. State Dept., 1963-65; polit. counselor, the Hague, 1965-67, Khartoum, 1967-72; ambassador to Sudan, 1972-73. Served to lt. comdr. USNR, 1941-45. Home: Bethesda MD Died Mar. 1973.

NOFFSINGER, HUGH GODWIN, coll. pres.; b. Botetourt County, Va., Nov. 27, 1873; s. Samuel and Hettie M. (Owens) N.; Alleghany Inst., Roanoke, Va., 1892-96; A.B., U. of Richmond, 1898, A.M., 1899; Litt.D., U. of Richmond, 1937; LL.D., King College, Bristol, Tenn., 1937; m. Civilla W. Brock, June 18, 1901; children—Hugh Godwin, Margaret E. (dec.). Teacher Windsor (Va.) Acad., 1899-1904; prin. Franklin Acad., 1904-07; pres. Southside Inst., Chase City, Va., 1907-12; v.p. Va. Intermont Coll., 1912-14, also teacher psychol.; pres. 1914-45; retired. Mem. bd. dirs. First Nat. Bank, Chase City, Va. Pres. Am. Assn. Jr. Colls., 1925, Va. Assn. Colleges, 1932. Mem. state membership com. Va. Museum Fine Arts. Mem. Phi Beta Kappa. Democrat. Baptist. Club: Kiwanis (pres. 1922). Home: Bristol VA‡

NOLAN, WILLIAM IGNATIUS, ex-congressman; b. St. Paul, Minn., May 14, 1874; s. James Henry and Anna Elizabeth (Dixon) N.; ed. pub. schs., Minneapolis, Minn.; m. Matea E. Solem, of Rochester, Minn., Mar. 10, 1894 (died Sept. 2, 1927); children—Marjorie Dorris (dec.), Genevieve Ann (Mrs. Frank Beddor), Mercedes Isabel (dec.), Agnes Bruce (Mrs. Charles Gehrke), Edwina Henrietta, Wilhelmina Elizabeth (Mrs. Hubert P. Hartigan), Theodora Antoinette (Mrs. Thomas Dudley), Alice Germaine (Mrs. Donald Berent), Rowena Patricia (Mrs. John W. Palmer, Jr.); m. 2d, Estelle A. Flanders, of Minneapolis, Minn., December 21, 1929; 1 son, William I. Began as entertainer and humorist, 1894, later son, William I. Began as entertainer and humorist, 1894, later Chautauqua lecturer. Mem. Minn. Ho. of Rep., 1903-13, 1917-23 (speaker of House 1919-21, 1923); lt. gov. of Minn., 1925-29; mem. 71st and 72d Congresses (1929-33), 5th Minn. Dist. Mem. Minn. N.G., 1891-96. Chmn. Minn. Reforestation Commn., 1927. Mem. Izaak Walton League, Minn. Soc. Fine Arts. Republican. Congregationalist. Mason (Shriner), Elk; member Royal Arcanum. Clubs: Minneapolis Athletic, Naniboujou, Hennepin City Sportmen's, Calhoun Beach. Home: 4041 Bryant Av. S., Minneapolis MN‡

NOLAND, EDGAR SMITH, investment banker; b. Mt. Sterling, O., May 23, 1902; s. Frank Edgar and Laura W. (Smith) N.; A.B., Ohio Wesleyan U., 1924; m. Mary Katherine Thomson, July 31, 1925; children—Nancy A. (Mrs. Fred B. DeCamp), M. Diane (Mrs. George W. Byers, Jr.). With Citizens Trust and Savs. Bank, Columbus, O., 1924-25; with Ohio Co., Columbus, 1925-—, treas., 1930-64, exec. v.p., 1963-64, pres., 1964-—; v.p., sec., dir. Ohio Capital Fund, Inc.; pres., dir. Knowledge Communications Fund, Incorporated; mem. Midwest Stock Exchange; dir. Atlas Realty Inc., Del. Gazette Co., Nat. Bldg. Co., Ohio Valley Pub. Co., Federated Publs. Inc., Ohio Company, Cambridge Time Manufacturing Company. Mem. Beta Theta Pi. Mason. Clubs: Columbus Country, University (Columbus); London (O.) Country. Home: Columbus OH Died Sept. 2, 1971; buried Oak Hill Cemetery, London OH

NOLAND, LOWELL E(VAN), univ. prof.; b. Lee, Ind., July 15, 1896; s. David Evan and Mary Emma (Matthews) N.; B.A., DePauw U., 1917; student U. of Montpellier, France, 1918, Marine Biol. Lab., Woods Hole, Mass., 1922; M.A., U. of Wis., 1921, Ph.D., 1924; m. Ruth Wayland Chase, Sept. 6, 1923; children—Wayland Evan, Ruth Mary. Editor and pub. Rolling Prairie (Ind.) Record, 1912-13; high sch. teacher, Mitchell, Ind., 1917-18 and 1919-20; asst. in zoology, U. of Wis., 1920-21, instr., 1921-25, asst. prof., 1925-31, asso. prof., 1931-35, prof. from 1935, chmn. dept. zoology, 1945-48, prof. integrated liberal studies from 1948; research, U. of Wash. Biol. Sta., Friday Harbor, Wash., summer 1933; instr. U. of N.H. Biol. Sta., Isles of Shoals, summer 1934; research, U.S. Bur. Fisheries Sta., Beaufort, N.C., and Bass Biol. Lab., Englewood, Fla., 1934; vis. prof. U. of Hawaii, Honolulu, 1944. Bd. dirs., U. of Wis. Y.M.C.A., 1947-53; hon. dir. Dane County Humane Soc. Served as cpl. medical dept., U.S. Army, 1918-19. Fellow A.A.A.S.; mem. Am. Soc. Zooligists, Am. Microscop, Soc. (pres. 1939), Ecol. Soc. Am., Limnol. Soc. Am., Am. Soc. Parasitology, Entomol. Soc. Am., Am. Soc. Naturalists, Soc. Protozoologists (president 1954-55), Wisconsin Academy of Sciences, Arts and Letters (sec.-treas. 1930-33, president 1946-48), Wis. Hist. Soc., Am. Inst. Biol. Scis., Biol. Stain Commn., Nat. Assn. Biology Tchrs., Soc. Syst. Zoology, Am. Assn. U. Profs., Wis. Edn. Assn., Depauw Univ. Alumni Assn., University of Wisconsin Alumni Assn., Madison Audubon Soc. (pres. 1969-71), Madison Art Assn., Madison Civic Music Association, Madison Philharmonic Chorus, Friends of U. of Wis. Library, Societe des Amis de la Maison Francaise, Phi Beta Kappa, Sigma Xi, Gamma Alpha, Phi Sigma, Tau Kappa Epsilon. Clubs: Kumilen (ornithology), University (Madison), Wisconsin Union (U. of Wis.), University Heights Poetry. Author numerous articles relating to field. Home: Madison WI Died Jan. 3, 1972; buried Forest Hill Cemetery Madison WI

NOLDE, O. FREDERICK, seminary prof.; b. Phila., Pa., June 30, 1899; s. Antone Harry and Ida (Fuchs) N.; A.B., Muhlenberg Coll., 1920, D.D., 1932, LL.D., 1946; B.D., Lutheran Theol. Sem., Phila., 1923; Ph.D., U. of Pa., 1928; L.H.D., Wittenberg College, Pennsylvania, 1951; Litt.D., Temple University, 1957; m. Ellen Jarden, June 21, 1927 (dec.); children—Anthony, Susanne Van Loehr, Fredericka (Mrs. Bruce Berger), Walter (dec.); m. 2d, Nancy Lawrence, Jan. 12, 1966. Instr. religious edn., Luthern Theol. Sem., 1925-28, assistant professor, 1928-31, professor from 1931, dean of graduate school, 1943-62; instr. religious edn., U. of Pa., 1925-28, asst. prof., 1929-35, lecturer, 1936-43. Mem. Dept. of Internat. Justice and Goodwill; asso. gen. sec. (for internat. affairs) of World Council Chs., from 1948; dir. Commn. of Chs. on Internat. Affairs, from 1946; mem. Commn. to Study Orgn. of Peace. Associate cons. to U.S. delegation at UN Conf., San Francisco, 1945. Mem. executive committee of bd. trustees Carnegie Endownment for Internat. Peace, from 1951, also vice chmn. bd. Fellow Internat. Inst. Arts and Letters; mem. Acad. Polit. and Social Sci., Phi Kappa Tau, Phi Delta Kappa, Kappa Phi Kappa. Clubs: Century (New York City); Philadelphia Cricket (Philadelphia); Mantoloking Yacht, (Mantoloking, New Jersey). Author: Guidebook in Catechetical Instruction, 1932; Yesterday, Today, Tomorrow, 1933; The Church Worker (with Paul J. Hob), 1934; Truth and Life, 1937; Christian World Action, 1942; Christian Messages to the Peoples of the World, 1943; Power for Peace, 1946; Free and Equal-Human Rights in Ecumenical Perspective, 1968; The Churches and the Nations, 1970. Contbr. to religious and ednl. jours. Home: Philadelphia PA Died June 17, 1972.

NOON, MALIK FIROZ KHAN, govt. ofcl., mem. parliament, Pakistan; b. Hamoka, Punjab, West Pakistan, May 7, 1893; s. Nawab Sir Muhammad Hayat Noon; student Aitcheson Co., Lahore, 1906-12; M.A., Oxford U., Eng., 1916; LL.D., U. Toronto, Can.; m. Elizabeth Rick, 1945. Advocate, Lahore High Ct., 1917-26; mem. Punjab legislature, 1920-36; minister Local Self-Govt., 1927-30, edn. minister, 1931-36 (all Punjab); high commr. for India in U.K., 1936-41; labor mem. Viceroy's Exec. Council, India, 1941-42; defense mem. India, 1942-45, also rep. India on Brit. War Cabinet, 1944-45; rep. India at UN Conf., San Francisco, 1945; mem. Punjab Provincial Legislature and All Pakistan Constituent Assembly and Legislature, 1947-55; gov. East Pakistan, 1950-53; chief minister, Punjab, 1953-55; fgn. minister Pakistan, 1956-57, prime minister, 1957-58. Leader delegations to ILO, SCAFE, UN, Baghdad Pact, Commonwealth Relations, on numerous occasions; leader Muslim League, Punjab; leader Republican Party Central Assembly, 1957. Fellow Wadham Coll. Knight Bachelor, Knight of St. John of Jerusalem, Knight Comdr. Indian Empire, Knight Comdr. Star of India. Author: Scented Dust; Canada and India; Wisdom from Fools; From Memory (autobiography). Home: Lahore Pakistan Died Dec. 9, 1970; buried Nurpur Noon, Punjab, Pakistan

NOON, PAUL A.T., librarian; b. Columbus, O., June 18, 1901; s. John Thomas and Ella Veronica (Welch) N.; A.B., Ohio State U., 1930; B.L.S., Columbia, 1932; M.A., New York U., 1933; m. Grace Ballard Rinard, June 21, 1947; 1 son, Christopher. Asst. Coll. of Edn. Library, Ohio State U., 1927-30; res. librarian Teachers Coll. (Columbia), 1930; chief res. div., New York U. Library, 1930-31, order librarian, 1931-33; librarian State Library of Ohio, 1933-42; Lansing (Mich.) Public Library, Oct. 1943-45; dir. regional library service, 1945-47; asso. librarian, Jacksonville Pub. Library, 1947-54; dir. Canton (O.) Pub. Library, 1954-63; instructor of sociology, associate librarian Walsh College, Canton, O., 1963-64; asst. prof. Kent (O.) State U., from 1964; instructor Ohio State University, summer 1936-37. Private, corp., sergt., U.S. Army, 1943; master sergeant and sergeant major, 119th Armored Engineer Batn., 12th Armored Division; honorary discharge, Sept. 20, 1943; librarian Lansing (Michigan) Public Library Oct. 5, 1943-Oct. 15, 1945; dir. Regional Service, Illinois State Library, 1945-47. Member A.L.A. (mem. council), Fla. Library Assn. (pres. 1951), Nat. Assn. State Librarians (pres. 1937-39), League Library Commns., Southeastern Library Assn. (chmn. pub. library div.). Contbr. to Library Jour., Publishers Weekly, Am. Library Assn. Bull., Wilson Library Bull. Editor and compiler of Ohio Library Laws in force Jan. 1, 1940: Address: Canton OH Died Nov. 1971.

NOONAN, EDWARD J., cons. civil engr.; b. La Salle, Ill., Apr. 24, 1874; s. Edward and Catherine (Golden) N.; ed. St. Patrick's Acad., La Salle; m. Josephine Hayden, June 8, 1897; children—Helen Marie, Eddy Jo. Engaged in municipal work, 1891-1901, interurban ry. constrn., Ill., 1901-05; chief engr. railroad constrn. in the South and Southwest until 1910; cons. practice on railroad and other projects since 1910; asso. with John F. Wallace (now dec.), offices in New York and Chicago, 1910-21; chief engr. Chicago Ry. Terminal Commn., 1914-21; mem. Chicago Ry. Terminal Commn., 1921-23; consultant to City of Chicago and other cities on ry. terminals since 1923. Mem. Am. Soc. C.E., Western Soc. Engrs., Am. Ry. Engring. Assn., Structural Engrs'. Assn. of Ill., Soc. Terminal Engrs.; fellow Am. Geog. Soc. Clubs: City, Engineers' (Chicago); Transportation (New York). Home: 1400 Lake Shore Drive. Office: 309 W. Jackson Blvd., Chicago IL*‡

NORA, JOSEPH J., physician, surgeon; b. Norway, Mich., Jan. 10, 1901; s. Joseph J. and Mary Ann (Grasse) N.; M.D., U. Geneva, 1936; m. Helen Hills, June 28, 1940; children—James, Lonnie, Ruth, Louise. Intern, Mercy Hosp., Bay City, Mich., 1928; practicing physician, surgeon, Tiskilwa, Ill., 1931-68; farmer; partner Drug Store; dir. Tiskilwa Bank. Ofcl. local hosp.; local health officer. Mem. A.M.A., Mississippi Valley and State med. socs. Author articles in med. jours. Address: Tiskilwa IL Died June 9, 1968; buried St. Mary's Cemetery Tiskilwa IL

NORBECK, KERMIT GEORGE, judge; b. Redfield, S.D., June 18, 1909; s. George and Jane M. (Olson) N.; student S.D. State Coll., 1926-27, U. S.D., 1930-32, LL.B., 1937; m. Winfree Virginia Farmer, Aug. 7, 1935; children—George Philip, Winfree Judith, Mary Virginia. Admitted to S.D. bar, 1937; spl. counsel S.D. Supt. Banks, Pierre, 1937-38; practiced in Redfield, 1939-56; states atty. Spink County, S.D., 1941-44, 51-52; judge 9th Jud. Circuit Ct., Redfield, 1956-70. Served with inf., AUS, 1944-46, as capt. Judge Adv. Gen's Corps., 1952-54. Mem. Am., S.D. bar assns., National Coll. State Trial Judges (faculty 1964). Republican. Lutheran. Mason (Shriner), Elk. Home: Redfield SD Died Dec. 19, 1970.

NORCROSS, FRANK HERBERT, judge; b. Reno, Nev., May 11, 1869; s. Thomas W. and Caroline B. (Sherman) N.; A.B., U. of Nev., 1891, LL.D., 1911; LL.B., Georgetown U., D.C., 1894; m. Adeline L. Morton, July 10, 1895; 1 dau., Adele Cutts (Mrs. Edwin S. Bender). County surveyor, Washoe County, Nev., 1891-92; clerk U.S. Census Office, Washington, 1892-94; admitted to Nev. bar, 1894, Calif. bar, 1903, bar of Supreme Court of U.S., 1922. Dist. atty. Washoe County, 1895-97; mem. Nev. Assembly, 1897-99;

justice Supreme Ct. of Nev., 1904-16 (chief justice, 1909-11, 1915-16); resumed practice at Reno, Nev., 1917; U.S. dist. judge, District of Nevada, 1928-45. Served pvt. to capt. Co. C, Nev. Nat. Guard; U. of Nev. R.O.T.C., Co. A, 1886-91; commd. hon. col., 1941. Mem. Nat. Civic Fedn., Am. Bar Assn., Nev. Bar Assn. (pres. 1920), Am. Inst. Criminal Law and Criminology (v.p. 1913-15). Elector, New York U. Hall of Fame. Chmn. Nev. delegation Rep. Nat. Conv., 1920; mem. council Nat. Econ. League; mem. Phi Kappa Phi. Kiwanian. Grand Master of Masons, Nev., 1909-10; 33 deg.; A.A.S.R. Author: Christianity and Divorce. Contbr. to legal mags., etc. Asso. editor Jour. Am. Inst. Criminal Law and Criminology, 1909-15. Home: Reno NV‡

NORD, WALTER GODFREY, business exec.; b. Denmark, O., Jan. 30, 1884; s. Otto and Mary (Erickson) N.; A.B., Western Res. U., 1908; B.S., Case Institute of Technology, 1909; LL.D., Upsala College, 1954, Oberlin Coll.; Dr. Humanitarian Services, Wilberforce U.; m. Virginia Catherine Grieve, Apr. 2, 1913; children—Mary (Mrs. Joseph Ignat), Eric Thomas, Evan Walter. Steam engr. Youngstown (O.) Sheet & Tube Co., 1909-12; supt. Western Conduit Co., Harvey, Ill., 1912-14; mech. engr. Cleve. Stone Co., 1914-22; organized Am. Specialty Co., Amherst, O., 1919, pres. from 1919; organized Gen. Stone Co., 1922, pres., 1922-35; receiver U.S. Automatic Corp. Amherst, 1929-35, reorganized co. to form U.S. Automatic Corp., 1935, treas., pres. from 1935; chmn. board SuperVision, Inc., Cleveland, Oberlin Savs. Bank, Nordson Corp., Amherst, Ohio. Pres. Am. Swedish Hist. Found. (Phila.); chmn. chmn. exec. com. Lorain County Met. Park Com.; chmn. United Negro Coll. Fund Com., Lorain County; mem. Lorain County Indsl. Devel. Com.; mem. bd. Wilberforce U., Am. Scandinavian Found.; trustee So. Lorain County Hosp. Assn.; trustee, chmn. Lorain county Ohio Information Committee; member citizens committee, Ohio Comprehensive Mental Health Planning; chairman of the board, Lorain County Mental Hygiene Assn.; exec. com. Center for Sightless. Decorated Comdr. Royal Order of Vasa (Sweden); recipient Silver Knight award Nat. Mgmt. Assn., 1960. Mem. Am. Heart Assn., Ohio Mental Health Assn. (pres.), Am. Swedish Inst., Swedish Colonial Soc. (mem. bd.), Am. Soc. Swedish Engrs., Vegetable Growers Assn. Am., Anglican Soc., Adelbert Coll. Alumni Association League O. Sportsmen, Swedish Medical Center, Cleve. Health Museum, Cleveland Art Museum, American Public Health Assn., U.S., Cleveland, Ohio State, New York State, Oberlin, Amherst, Swedish C.'s of C., Am. Soc. Control Cancer, Lorain Co. Tb & Health Assn. (pres.), Small Bus. Mens Assn., Amherst Outdoor Life Assn., Soc. Advancement Scandinavian Studies, Am. Mgmt. Assn., Am. Ordnance Assn., Ohio Future Farmers Assn. Found., Congress Internat. Orgns., Nat. Conf. Christians and Jews, Ohio, Lorain County (trustee) hist. society, Brotherhood St. Andrew, Buckeye State Sheriffs Assn., Navy Industrial Assn., Ohio Forestry Assn., American Swedish Associates, Nat., Ohio associations mfrs., Lorain County Indsl. Council, Alumni Council Case Inst. Tech., Swedish Cultural Soc., Phi Gamma Delta. Republican (exec. com.). Episcopalian (sr. warden). Mason, Eagle. Clubs: Farmer's, Mid Day, Union (Cleve.); Half Century; Oberlin (O.) City, Oberlin Golf; Swedish (Chicago); Rotary (past pres.), Noon Day (past pres.) (Amherst, O.). Owner, operator dairy farm nr. Wellington, O. Home: Oberlin OH Died May 16, 1967; buried Oberlin OH

NORDEN, FRED WASHINGTON, accountant; b. Broseley, Mo., Mar. 5, 1895; s. Ernst and Diza (Williamson) N.; grad. Springfield (Mo.) Bus. Coll., 1913; m. Vida Pearl Davidson, Apr. 19, 1920; 1 dau., Fredda Lee. Tchr. pub. schs., Butler County, Mo., 1914-17; employed with banks, Broseley and Neelyville, Mo., 1920-34; pvt. practice as pub. accountant, Poplar Bluff, Mo., 1934-72. Mem. Mo. Ho. of Reps., 1941-49, chmn. banking com., 1941-43. Served with U.S. Navy, 1918-20, C.P.A., Mo. Mem. Mo. Accountants Assn. (v.p. pub. com. prof. mag. 1962, pres. 1969-71), Am. Legion (post comdr. 1937), 40 and 8. Odd Fellow. Methodist. Address: Poplar Bluff MO Died Mar. 23, 1972.

NORDENHAUG, JOSEF, clergyman, religious orgn. exec.; b. Oslo, Norway, Aug. 2, 1903; s. Johannes Adolf and Elise (Bye) N.; M.Sc., U. Oslo, 1927; Th.M., So. Bapt. Theol. Sem., Louisville, 1930, Ph.D., 1932; LL.D., William Jewell Coll., 1962; H.L.D., Temple U., 1963; m. Helen Bacon Rampp, Aug. 7, 1934; children—Theodore Davis, Karin Elizabeth (Mrs. Paul Ciholas). Came to U.S., 1928, naturalized, 1937. Ordained to ministry Baptist Ch., 1933; asst. pastor First Bapt. Ch., Oslo, Norway, 1932-33; pastor Irene Cole Meml. Bapt. Ch., Prestonburg, Ky., 1933-36, Vinton (Va.) Bapt. Ch., 1936-41, Rivermont Av. Bapt. Ch., Lynchburg, Va., 1941-48; editor The Commission, So. Bapt. Fgn. Mission Bd., Richmond, Va., 1948-50; pres. Bapt. Theol. Sem., Ruschlikon-Zurich, Switzerland, 1950-60; gen. sec. Baptist World Alliance, Washington, 1960-69. So. Bapt. Fgn. Mission Bd. rep. in Europe for relief and rehab., 1954-58; chmn. Bapt. Relief Com. for Hungary, 1956. Contbr. articles various denominational jours. Home: Arlington VA Died Sept. 18, 1969; buried Columbia Gardens, Arlington VA

NORDHOFF, HEINRICH, engr.; b. Hildesheim, Germany, Jan. 6, 1899; s. Johannes and Ottlie (Lauenstein) N.; Diplom-Ingenieur, Technische Hochschule, Berlin-Charlottenburg, 1927; Eng.D. (hon.), Technische Hochschule, Braunschweig, 1950; Dr. rer. pol. h.c., Gottingen U., 1964; hon. doctorate natural sci. Hamburg U., 1964; hon. doctorate commercial science Boston (Mass.) Univ., 1964; m. Charlotte Fassunge, Aug. 12, 1930; children—Barbara, Elisabeth. Bayerische Motoren-Werke A.G. (BMW), Munich; mem. mgmt. A. Opel AG., automobile factory, Ruesselsheim 1936-46; cons. engr., Hamburg, 1946-48; chmn. bd. mgmt. Volkswagenwerk AG, Wolfsburg; prof. Technische Hochschule, Braunschweig, 1955; v.p. Verband der Automobil industrie, Frankfurt; mem. executive com. Prasidium des BDI, Dusseldorf; mem. adv. bd. Allianz-Versicherungs-AG, Munich, Braunschweigische Staatsbank, Braunschweig; mem. bd. August Thyssen-Hutte AG, Duisburg Erste Allgemeine Unfall-und Schadens-Versicherungs-Gesellschaft, Vienna, Berlinsche Feuer-Versicherungs-Anstalt, Munich, Frankfurter Versicherungs-AG, Frankfurt, Dresdner Bank AG, Hamburg, Salzgitter AG., Salzgitter-Drutte, Deutsche Continental Gas-Gesellschaft, Dusseldorf, Frederich Krupp Gmblt, Essen. Mem. governing body German Soc. for Indsl. Mgmt. Hon. freeman Town of Wolfsburg, 1955, Sao Bernardo do Campo, 1960; honorary senator Technische Universitat, Berlin, 1951. Decorated Landesmedaille un Grosses Verdeinstkreuz des Niedersachs Verdienstordens, Knight Order of Holy Sepulchre; also the Southern Cross (Brazil); Comdr. Cross 1st class of Order of Vasa (Sweden); Grand Cross Fed. Order of Merit with Sash and Star, 1964; recipient Elmer A. Sperry award, U.S.A., 1958; Grosskreuzdes Bundesverdienstkreuzes mit Stern, completion millionth Volkswagen, 1955; Daidalos medal, 1967, Wakefield Gold medal, 1967, Amico del Populo Italiano medal, 1967. Mem. World Brotherhood N.Y. Club: Rotary (Braunschweig). Home: Wolfsburg Germany Federal Republic of Germany. Died Apr. 12, 1968.

NORELIUS, ERIC, clergyman, author; ed. Columbus (O.) Univ. (D. D.). Ordained to (Swedish) Lutheran ministry; went to Minn., 1854; founder Gustavus Adolphus Coll., St. Peter, Minn.; pres. Swedish Lutheran Augustana Synod of America. Author: History of the First Swedish Lutheran Congregations in America; Lutheran Tidskrift. Address: Vasa MN‡

NORELL, NORMAN, fashion designer; b. Novelesville, Ind., 1900. Entered career as designer with Hatti Carnegie, 1927; showed 1st collection with mem. firm Traina-Norell, N.Y.C. 1941; Recipient Coty Am. Fashion Critics award (Winnie), 1945, 53, 57, Home: New York City NY Died Oct. 25, 1972.

NORGREN, CARL AUGUST, mfr., engr.; b. Riverside, S.D., Nov. 21, 1890; s. Gustavus and Caroline (Anderson) N.; B.S. in Mech. Engring., U. S.D., 1912; m. Juliet E. Lien, Aug. 24, 1922; children—Carl Neil, Gene Ellen, Leigh Hyatt, Donald Kent, Vanda Caroline. Gen. engring. practice, Yankton, S.D., 1912-13; charge engring. Fairbanks Morse Co., Omaha, Neb., 1913-17; mgr. machinery dept. Salt Lake Hardware Co., Salt Lake City, 1917-18; mgr. N.W. ty. Chgo. Pneumatic Tool Co., Seattle, 1918-19; designer, inventor mech., hydraulic, pneumatic devices; owner, operator ranch at Rifle Colorado 1920-25; organized C. A. Norgren Co., engineers and mfrs., Denver, 1926, pres., 1926-62, chmn. bd., 1962-68; Norgen Farms; with Carl E. Lien organized the Uniited American Life Insurance Company in 1938, president, 1939-43, chairman, from 1943; director First National Bank Englewood, Empire Savings Building and Loan, First Colorado Bankshares, Inc., Denver Realty Assos., Presbyterian Hospital. Member of nat. council Boy Scouts of Am., from 1942, exec. com. Denver, from 1946, past pres. Denver area council. Recipient Silver Beaver, Silver Antelope awards. Licensed mech. engr., Colo. Mem. Am. Soc. Tool Engrs., Am. Soc. M.E., Soc. Automotive Engrs., Am. Soc. Lubrication Engrs., Am. Ordnance Assn., N.A.M. (dir. 1947-49), Izaak Walton League (nat. bd. 1943, 44, 48), Nat. Farm Chemurgic Council, Nat. Western Live Stock Assn., Am., and Colo., Hereford assns., Colo., Denver (dir. 1948-51) C.'s of C., Colo. Com. Indsl. Research and Development, Denver Mus. Natural History (trustee, v.p. 1944-55, pres. 1955-63), Mfrs. Assn. Colo. (v.p. 1944, also dir.), Colo. Engring. Soc., Engring. Soc. Detroit, Denver Civic Symphony Soc. (bd., pres. 1952-53), Nat. Westrn Polled Hereford Assn., (pres. 1955), Mountain State Employers Council, Game and Fish Commn. Colo. (pres. 1945-48), Colo. Farm Bur. Fedn., Denver Zool. Soc., Beta Theta Pi, Sigma Tau, Beta Gamma Sigma. Mason. Clubs: Denver, Athletic, Cherry Hills Country, Kiwanis (v.p. 1943), Saddle and Sirloin, Pinehurst Country, Mile High, Press (Denver). Home: CO Died Aug. 7, 1968; buried Fairmount Cemetery, Denver CO

NORMAN, ANNE, newspaper editor; married. Asso. with Jimmy Fiddler, Hollywood, Cal.; with King Features, N.Y.C., Los Angeles Times, Hartford Times; women's editor Ind. Star-News, Pasadena, Cal., 1960-70. Pasadena CA Died Jan. 31, 1970.

NORMAN-WILCOX, GREGOR, mus. curator; b. Cleve., Sept. 9, 1905; s. Carl Loomis and Eunice (Wilcox) Humphreys; student pub. schs., Cleve. Sch. Art; m. Grace Agusta Steen, Oct. 13, 1934. Curator decorative arts Los Angeles County Museum of Art, 1931-69, on leave as cons.-curator for furnishing of Tryon Palace, New Bern, N.C., 1957-58; writer syndicated series Antiques for Los Angeles Times, 1949-59, nationally syndicated, 1958-69; instr. Am. studies U. Cal. at Los Angeles 1960-62. Mem. Nat. Trust Hist. Preservation, English-Speaking Union, Soc. Preservation New Eng. Antiquities Am. Inst. Interior Designers (hon.). Contbr. articles magazines. Home: Los Angeles CA Died Apr. 26, 1969.

NORRIS, CHARLES CAMBLOS, physician; b. Phila., Pa., June 1, 1876; s. William Pepper and Laura (Camblos) N.; M.D., U. of Pa. Med. Sch., 1898; m. Helen E. Farr, Jan. 12, 1928. Interne, Pa. Hosp., 1898, U. of Pa. Hosp., 1899, Johns Hopkins Hosp., 1900; gynecologic anesthetist, U. of Pa. Hosp., 1900-03; instr. clin. gynecology, U. of Pa. Med. Sch., 1902-11, asst. in gynecologic pathology, 1907-21, instr. gynecology, 1911-22, asst. prof., 1922-27, prof. obstetrics and gynecology and dir. dept., 1927-41; dir. Gynecean Hosp. Inst. Gynecol. Research of U. of Pa., 1926-41; prof. gynecology, U. of Pa. Grad. Sch. Medicine, 1927-41; emeritus prof. obstetrics and gynecology since 1941; attending obstetrician and gynecologist, U. of Pa. Hosp., 1927-41; asso. obstetrician and gynecologist in chief, Pa. Hosp., 1935-41; hon. cons. gynecologist, Phila. Gen. Hosp., 1930-41; formerly cons. obstetrician and gynecologist, Henry Phipps Inst. and Children's Hosp., Phila., retired from active practice, 1941. Served as lt., U.S. Navy, 1916-18. Fellow Am. Coll. Surgs., Phila. Coll. Phys. Mem. Am. Gynecol. Soc. (pres. 1930), Am. Neisserian Med. Soc. (pres. 1937), Am. Bd. Obstetrics and Gynecology, Am. Radium Soc., Am. Gynecol. Club, Am. Soc. for Control of Cancer (dir. 1929-38), A.M.A., Pa. State and Phila. County med. socs., Phila. Obstet. Soc. (pres. 1929-30), Pathol. Soc. of Phila., Delta Psi. Republican. Episcopalian. Club: Philadelphia. Author: Gonorrhea in Women, 1913; Gynecological and Obstetrical Tuberculosis, 1921, rev., 1931; Uterine Tumors, 1930. Co-author (with Dr. John G. Clark). Radium in Gynecology, 1927. Contbr. about 100 articles and papers on obstetrics and gynecology. Home: Bryn Mawr PA‡

NORRIS, EARLE BERTRAM, dean emeritus; born Jamestown, N.Y., Sept. 17, 1882; s. Harry E. and Belle (Barker) N.; B.S. in M.E., Pa. State Coll., 1904, M.E., 1908; M. Faye Hurd, 1905. Designer of spl. machinery, E. Bement's Sons, Lansing, Mich., 1904, cost clk., 1905; asst. supt. Central Implement Co., Standish, Mich., 1905; instr. in mech. engring., Pa. State Coll., 1906-08; asst. prof. mech. engring., U. of Wis., 1908-12, asso. prof., 1912-16; industrial commr. St. Paul (Minn.) Assn. of Commerce, 1916-17; dean of engring, U. of Mont., 1919-28; dean of engring., Va. Poly. Inst., Blacksburg, 1928-52, dean emeritus, 1952, also dir. Engring. Expt. Sta., 1931-52; pres. Va. Poly. Inst. Research Foundation, 1935-53; consulting mechanical engineer. Capt. and maj. Ordnance Dept. U.S. Army, 1917-19; chief engr. Rock Island Arsenal, 1919; lt. col. Ordance Reserve, 1925-40. Cited by General Pershing for eminently meritorious and conspicious services in the A.E.F., 1919; awarded Purple Heart medal. Profl. mech. engr. Va. Mem. So. Assn. Sci. and Industry (trustee), A.S.M.E., Virginia Acad. Science (pres. 1939), Am. Soc. Engring. Education (v.p. 1946-47), Newcomen Soc., Phi Gamma Delta, Tau Beta Pi, Phi Kappa Phi, Sigma Xi, Pi Tau Sigma, Omicron Delta Kappa, Alpha Pi Mu, Scabbard and Blade. Mason. (32 degree). Co-author: Shop Arthmetic (with K.G. Smith), 1912; Advanced Shop Mathematics (with R.T. Craigo), 1913; Gas Engine Ignition (with W.C. Weaver and R.K. Winning), 1916; Heat Power (with Eric Therkelsen), 1931; The Plastic Flow of Metals, 1936; Applied Thermodynamies (with C.E. Trent), 1955. Home: Blacksburg VA Died Oct. 15, 1966.

NORRIS, KENNETH TRUE, mfg. co. exec.; b. East St. Louis, Ill., July 8, 1899; s. William Leroy and Lillian Gertrude (Sharp) N.; ed. pub. schs., Los Angeles; LL.D., Occidental College, Cal., 1965; m. Eileen LaVerne Lunsford, Nov. 30, 1923; 1 son, Kenneth True Jr. With Kittle Mfg. Co., Los Angeles, 1920-30, asst. gen. mgr., 1925-30; founder Norris Stamping & Mfg. Co., 1930, propr., 1930-40, pres., 1940-72, merged to become Norris-Thermador Corporation (name now Norris Industries), 1950, chairman bd., 1959-72; dir. Hoffman Electronics Corp., 1952-67; Crocker-Citizens Nat. Bank, Los Angeles, 1954-58. Mem. bus. adv. com. to Pres. Roosevelt, World War II; chmn. Com. Econ. Devel. Los Angeles and Orange counties, 1944-46; chmn. steel com. Western States Council, 1944-47; mem. War Manpower Com. So. Cal., World War II. Trustee Occidental Coll., from 1951, vice chmn., 1957-59, 62-68, now chmn., chmn. pres.' assos., 1954-63; trustee U. So. Cal., from 1963; chmn. councilors Sch. Medicine, from 1957; bd. dirs. Los Angeles World Affairs Council, 1956-58, and from 1960; trustee Kenneth T. and Eileen L. Norris Found., from 1963. Recipient Navy E, Army-Navy E awards; Presteel award Am. Metal Stamping Assn., 1963; Indsl. award, Am. Soc. Tool & Mfg. Engrs., 1966; named Cal.

Manufacturer of the Year, 1968. Mem. Nat. Security Indsl. Assn. (trustee 1953-56, vice chmn. 1957-58), Am. Ordnance Assn. (regional v.p. 1954-58, chmn. cartridge case com. 1954-58), N.A.M. (dir. 1942-43), Cal. Mfrs. Assn. (pres. 1946-47), Los Angeles C. of C. (dir. 1947-50), Merchants and Mfrs. Assn. Los Angeles (dir. 1942-50). Clubs: California (Los Angeles); San Gabriel (Cal.) Country; Annandale Country (Pasadena, Cal.); Thunderbird Country (Palm Springs, Cal.) Home: San Marion CA Died Mar. 24, 1972.

NORRIS, WILLIAM ARTHUR, JR., mem. Democratic Nat. Com.; b. Cheyenne, Wyo., July 29, 1925; s. William Arthur and Ethel W. (Warlaumont) N.; student Ga. Sch. Tech., 1946-48; B.S., Wyo. U. 1950; m. Jeanette Clark, June 29, 1951; 1 son, William Arthur III. Vice pres. Wortham Machinery Co., Cheyenee, 1948-51, pres., 1951-73; v.p. Timberline Corp., 1961-73; dir. Am. Nat. Bank, Cheyenne. Mem. Wyo. Ho. of Reps. from Laramie County, 1951-52, 55-56, Wyo. Senate from Laramie County, 1957-73; mem. Dem. Nat. Com. for Wyo., 1962-73. Mem. Wyo. Engring. Soc. Club: Cheyenne Rotary. Home: Cheyenne WY Died Feb. 3, 1973.

NORTH, FRANCIS REID, field sec.; b. Peekskill, N.Y., Apr. 19, 1876; s. Charles Randolph and Anna Mary (Haight) N.; A.B., Wesleyan U., Conn., 1897; A.M., Columbia, 1903; m. Helen B. Manning, of Portland, Me., Dec. 29, 1903. Instr., Newark (N.J.) Acad., 1898-06; prin. Portland (Me.) High Sch., 1906-11; field sec. Playground and Recreation Assn. America, 1911—. Methodist. Mem. N.E.A., Phi Nu Theta (Wesleyan U.). Club: Boston City. Home: 43 Summit Av., Brookline. Office: 4 Joy St., Boston MA‡

NORTH, HARRY B., lawyer; b. Rockford, Ill., Dec. 14, 1872; s. Chauncey O. and Martha N.; ed. pub. schs.; m. Bell Pardridge, Nov. 25, 1896; children—Marion Lewin, Frank P., Edna. Admitted to Ill. bar, 1895, and since practiced at Rockford; state's atty. Winnebago County, 1902-12, master in chancery, 1934-45. Republican. Mason (32 deg., Shriner). Address: Central Nat. Bank Bldg., Rockford IL*‡

NORTH, JOHN ALDEN, business exec.; b. North Haven, Conn., Dec. 2, 1901; s. John Richard and Helen Margaret (Alden) N.; grad. Hotchkiss Sch., Lakeville, Conn., 1920; B.S., Yale, 1925; m. Lorene Williams Hoyt, Feb. 6, 1926; 1 son, John Alden. Chmn. The Phoenix of Hartford Ins. Cos., Hartford, ret., 1964; trustee Mechanics Savings Bank, Hartford; trustee Underwriter's Laboratories, Chicago, Illinois, Connecticut Bank and Trust Co.; dir. Sanborn Map Co., Allied Control Co., Conn. Mut. Life Ins. Co., Arrow, Hart & Hegeman Co., Holyoke Water Power Co., Hartford Steam Boiler & Inspection Company. Trustee Hartford YMCA. Life trustee of American Institute for Property and Liability Underwriters, Phila. Mem. Alden Kindred of Am., Mayflower Soc. Am., Berzelius Soc. Republican. Episcopalian. Mason. Clubs: Hartford (Connecticut); Yale (N.Y. City); West Hartford CT Died Oct. 30, 1971.

NORTHCOTE, STAFFORD MANTLE, engraver on wood, artist; b. Brooklyn, July 7, 1869; s. James and Matilda N.; studied engraving with E. Heineman; drawing and painting with Prof. Boyle of the Art Inst., Brooklyn; m. Ida Stephenson, of Brooklyn, 1899. Exhibited at Paris Expn., 1900; hon. mention, Buffalo Expn., 1901; bronze medal, St. Louis Expn., 1904. Home: 283 Carlton Av., Brooklyn NY‡

NORTHROP, EUGENE P(URDY), foundation representative; born Danbury, Connecticut, July 12, 1908; son of Henry Eugene and Lydia (Alvord) N.; student Robert College, Istanbul, 1926-28; B.S., Yale, 1930, M.S., 1932, Ph.D., 1934; m. Marion Wilson Lyon, June 30, 1931;children—David Amos, John Wilson. Instr. mathematics Yale, 1930-35; master mathematics Hotchkiss Sch., Lakeville, Conn., 1935-43; asst. prof. mathematics in coll. U. Chicago, 1943-45, asso. prof., 1945-50, prof., 1950-53, chmn. coll. math. staff, 1943-53, asso. dean of coll., 1946-53; William Rainey Harper professor, 1953-61. Consultant Nat. Sci. Found., 1954-57, Fund for Advancement Education, 1954-55; cons.-rep. in Turkey, Ford Foundation, 1959-61, representative, 1962-69. Trustee Hotchkiss School, 1951-57. Mem. Am. Math. Soc., Math. Assn. Am. Nat. Council Tchrs. Math., Sigma Xi. Club: Quadrangle (Chicago). Author: Riddles in Mathematics, 1944; Fundamental Mathematics, 1944; also articles in profl. jours. Died Jan. 5, 1969.

NORTON, A(RTHUR) WARREN, business exec.; born Meriden, Conn., Dec. 4, 1896; s. Frank Hall and Caroline (Carter) N.; student Browne and Nichols Prep. Sch., Mass., 1915-16; Rose Polytech. Inst., Terre Haute, Ind., 1916-17; S.B., Mass. Inst. Technol., 1921; M. Helen Westfall, 1923; children—Edward Westfall, Warren Stevens. Asst. to works Mgr., Continental Motors Corp., 1921-22; salesman Brooklyn Daily Eagle, 1922-23; partner O'Mara and Ormsbee, Inc., 1923-39; mgr. Christian Sci. Publishing Soc. (and mem. editorial council), 1939-44; chmn. bd., pres., wireless communications system, Press Wireless, Inc., 1944-47; chmn. bd., pres. wireless communications equipment, Press Wireless Mfg. Corp., 1945-48; asst. to Arthur Hays Sulzberger, pub. N.Y. Times. Served in World War I, Naval Aviation. Mem. industry adv. com. and radiocommunications com., Bd. War Communications, World War II; spl. recognition from War Dept. for outstanding civilian service. Mem. Corp. Mass. Inst. Tech. (mem. vis. com. for dept. physics, elec. engring., English and history, food tech.). Trustee World-wide Boradcasting Found. Mem. N.E. Council (dir. aviation com., financial policy com., 1940-44). Asso. press Am. Newspaper Pub. Assn., Boston Com. Econ. Development, New Eng. Shippers (mem. adv. bd. 1942-44). Mass. Inst. Tech. Alumni Assn. (pres. 1945-46), Execs. Club of Boston (mem. 1940-44), Phi Beta Epsilon, Pi Delta Epsilon. Christian Scientist. Mason. Clubs: Union League, M.I.T. (mem. bd. 1945-47) (New York); Westchester Country. Home: White Plains NY Died May 20, 1970; buried Kensico Cemetery, Valhalla NY

NORTON, GRACE FALLOW, author; b. Northfield, Minn., Oct. 29, 1876; d. Willis Herman and Catherine Theresa (Rich) N.; Author: (poems) Little Gray Songs from St. Joseph's, 1912; The Sister of the Wind, 1914; Roads, 1916; What Is Your Legion? 1916; The Miller's Youngest Daughter, 1924. Home: Woodstock, N.Y. Address: 11 Rue Scribe, Paris France‡

NORTON, PATRICK DANIEL, ex-congressman; b. Ishpeming, Mich., May 17, 1876; s. Patrick and Bridget (Dolan) N.; moved with parents to N.D., 1883; B.A., University of N.D., 1897; m. Mary Louise Fitzgerald, of Fargo, N.D., Aug. 22, 1925; children—John Thomas, James Gerald. Admitted to N.D. bar, 1903; county supt. schs., Ramsey County, N.D., 1905-07; chief clerk N.D. House of Representatives, 1907-08; state's atty., Adams Co., 1907-11; sec. of state, N.D., 1911-13; mem. 63d to 65th Congresses (1913-19), 3d N.D. Dist.; del. to Rep. Nat. Conv., 1928. Engaged in farming, livestock raising and law practice. Mem. Am. and N.Dak. bar assns., Phi Delta Theta; Elk, K.C., Forester. Club: Columbia Country (Washington). Office: First National Bank Bldg., Minot ND‡

NORVELL, SAUNDERS, mfr.; b. St. Catharines, Can., Aug. 12, 1864; s. Lewis Conner and Sarah (Saunders) N.; ed. high sch., St. Louis; m. Belle Matthews, Apr. 14, 1886; children—Lucy (Mrs. G. Prather Knapp), Edward Simmons, Mary Spottiswoode (Mrs. Harold W. Jennys), Isabel. Began with The Simmons Hardware Co., St. Louis, 1881, v.p., 1898-1901; pres. The Norvell-Shapleigh Hardware Co., 1901-11; pub. Hardware Reporter several yrs.; chmn. bd. McKesson & Robbins, Inc., mfg. chemists, New York, 1914-26; formerly treas. The Norvell Chem. Corp., Perth Amboy, N.J.; pres. Remington Arms Co., Inc., New York, until 1933, dir. until 1934; chmn. bd. Ingersoll & Norvell, Inc., Hostetter Corp. Mem. Jury of Awards, St. Louis Expn., 1904. Clubs: University, Noonday, Country, St. Louis (St. Louis); Hardware, Lotos, Advertising, Canadian, Amateur Comedy, Drug and Chemical (New York); Bonnie Briar Country, Larchmont Yacht, Horseshoe Harbor, Oak Tennis. Office: 905 West End Av., New York NY‡

NOTESTEIN, WALLACE, educator; b. Wooster, O., Dec. 16, 1878; s. J. O. and Margaret (Wallace) N.; B.A., Wooster, 1900, Litt.D., 1923; Litt.D., Harvard, 1939, Birmingham, 1950, Yale, 1951; LL.D., Glasgow, 1950; D.Litt., Oxford U., 1958; m. Ada Louise Comstock, June 14, 1943. Asst. prof. history U. Kan., 1905-07; instr. history U. Minn., 1908, asst. prof., 1910, asso. prof., 1914, prof., 1917-20; prof. English history Cornell U., 1920-28; Sterling prof. English history, Yale, 1928-47, emeritus, 1947-69; Eastman prof. Oxford U. 1949-50; fellow Balliol Coll., 1949-50. Research asst. Com. Pub. Information, 1917; attached to Dept. of State, 1918, Am. Commn. to Negotiate Peace, Paris, 1919; mem. Brit. com. apptd. by prime minister, House of Commons Records, 1929-32; asso. mem. All Souls Coll., Oxford, 1931-32. Mem. adv. coun. Guggenheim Found., 1939-48. Corr. fellow Brit. Acad.; member American Philosophical Society, Mass. Historical Society, Phi Gamma Delta. Clubs: Century (N.Y.C.); Athenaeum (London, England). Author: History of English Witchcraft, 1913; (with A. B. White) Source Problems in English History, 1915; (with Frances H. Relf) Commons Debates 1629, 1921; D'Ewes Journal of the Long Parliament, 1923; Winning of the Initiative by the House of Commons (Raleigh lecture, Brit. Acad.), 1924; (with F. H. Relf, H. Simpson) Commons Debates 1621, 7 vols., 1935; English Folk, 1938; The Scot in History, 1946; The English People on the Eve of Colonization, 1954; Four Worthies, 1956. Address: New Haven CT Died Feb. 2, 1969; buried Grove Street Cemetery, New Haven CT

NOTHSTEIN, IRA OLIVER, archivist, author; b. Lehighton, Pennsylvania, January 16, 1874; s. Lloyd and Emaline Louisa (Miller) N.; A.B., Muhlenberg Coll., Allentown, Pa., 1897, A.M., 1900, D.D., 1928; grad. Mt. Airy (Phila.) Luth. Theol. Sem., 1900; grad. study U. of Ill., 1919; research work in British Museum, 1932; m. Minnie Louisa Kuhns, Nov. 13, 1900; children—Esther Louisa, Stanley Eugene, Paul Luther, Elizabeth Mathilda, Ruth Dorathea. Ordained ministry Luth. Ch., 1900; home missionary, 1900-07; pastor Grace Ch., Rock Island, Ill., 1907-18; head librarian Denkmann Memorial Library, Augustana Coll., 1918-34, Founder, 1915, editor, 1915-29, Augustana Synod Annual, My Church"; editor Augustana College Library Publications, 1918-34, archivist Augusta College, since 1935; co-editor official hymnal Augustana Synod, 1925. Member A.A.A.S., Lutheran Library Association, Rock Island County Historical Soc., S.A.R. Republican. Author several books since 1917; also compiler, translator and editor of various other publs. Home: 843 22d St., Rock Island IL‡

NOVAK, RALPH B(ERNARD), labor union official; b. Detroit, May 20, 1908; s. John Louis and Anna Catherine (Guentner) N.; ed. St. Joseph's Comml. Coll., Detroit, 1923-27; m. Ida Margaret Burgess, Mar. 2, 1935; children—Elizabeth Ann, Ralph Bernard, Louise Mary, Michael Anthony. Worked for accounting dept. Detroit Times, 1927-47, circulation accountant, 1941-47; pres. Newspaper Guild of Detroit, 1942-43; internat. vice pres. Am. Newspaper Guild, 1945-47, sec.-treas., 1947-51, exec. v.p., 1951-70. Liberal. Roman Catholic. Home: Ossining NY Died June 1971.

NOVARRO, RAMON (REAL NAME RAMON GIL SAMANIEGO), actor; b. Durango, Mexico, Feb. 6, 1899; ed. in Mexico; unmarried. Began as a dancer; debut in Prisoner of Zenda," later starred in Scaramouche, starred in Ben Hur," The Midshipman," The Student Prince," The Barbarian," Son-Daughter," Cat and The Fiddle," Son of India," Mata Hari," Huddle," and many films. Address: Culver City CA Died Oct. 31, 1968; buried Calvary Cemetery, Los Angeles CA

NOVER, BARNET, newspaper corr., columnist, editor, author; b. Feb. 11, 1899; s. Louis and Beulah (Wilk) Nover; B.A., Cornell U., 1919, M.A., 1920; m. Naomi A. Goll, June 28, 1934. Reporter, asso. editor, columnist Buffalo Eve. News, 1920-36; professorial lectr. history and internat. relations U. Buffalo, 1923-36; asso. editor, columnist fgn. affairs Washington Post, 1936-47; chief Washington bur. Denver Post, 1947-72; editor Nover News Service, 1972-73; recorded nat. radio program Washington Views and Interviews, 1944-47; writer weekly article OWI, for shortwave broadcast enemy and neutral countries, also translated 35 langs. for 600 publ. world newspapers World War II; cons. Pres.'s air policy commn., 1947. Mem. standing com. corrs. Congl. Press Galleries, 1964-73, sec.-treas., 1965, chmn., 1965-66. Served with S.A.T.C., U.S. Army, 1917-18. Recipient award of distinction as outstanding former resident of Buffalo, 1955. Mem. Am. Hist. Assn., Council Fgn. Relations, White House Corr. Assn., Phi Beta Kappa, Sigma Delta Chi. Clubs: Nat. Press, Overseas Writers (pres. 1940-43) (Washington). Home: Washington DC Died Apr. 15, 1973.

NOVY, ROBERT LEV, physician; b. Ann Arbor, Mich., Apr. 1, 1892; s. Frederick George and Grace (Garwood) N, M.D., U. Mich., 1919; m. Elsie Lose Backus, Oct. 7, 1916; children—Dorthy N. Wilson, Elsie (Mrs. Henry T. Atkins), Barbara (Mrs. Richard Tabor), Frances (Mrs. John F. Orr), R.L. Robert Lev, Frederick L. Intern Peter Bent Brigham Hosp., Boston, 1919-20; resident Barnes Meml. Hosp., St. Louis, 1920-22; sr. physician, chief cardiology Harper Hosp., Detroit; cons. physician Detroit Receiving Hosp.; cons. Herman Keifer Hosp., Jennings Hosp., Cottage Hosp. Instr. chemistry Ia. U., Iowa City, 1914-15; instr. Washington U., St. Louis, 1920-22; prof. clin. medicine Wayne State U., Detroit, prof. emeritus, 1966-71. Commr. Detroit Bd. Health; pres. emeritus Mich. Med. Service; past pres. Nat. Blue Shield Med. Care Plans. Diplomate Am. Bd. Internal Medicine. Mem. A.M.A. Detroit MI Died May 4, 1971; buried Forest Hills Cemetery, Ann Arbor MI

NOXON, HERBERT RICHARDS, advt. art dir.; b. Wellington, Ont., Can., Dec. 19, 1903; s. Searles and Janet (Jones) N.; student Toronto U., 1920, Ont. Coll. Art, 1921-23, Am. Acad. Art, Chgo., 1925, Grand Central Art Sch., N.Y.C., 1930, Phoenix Art Inst., N.Y.C., 1931; m. Margaret MacDonald Walters, July 15, 1926. Came to U.S., 1923, naturalized, 1938. Illustrator, Meinzinger Studios, Detroit, 1923-24. Mizen-Plumer, Chgo., 1925; creative head W. O. Floing, Detroit, 1926-29; art dir. Campbell-Ewald, Detroit, 1929-30; art dir. A. W. Erickson, N.Y.C., 1930; art dir. McCann-Erickson, N.Y.C., 1931-33, sr. art dir. posters, 1933-64, cons., 1964-70; exhibited at Brit.-Am. Gallery, Am. Water Color Soc., Nat. Acad. Design. Designer, painter War Bond Poster, 1943, other posters Red Cross War Fund Drive, U.S.O., WPB, Petroleum Adminstrn. War; created ofcl. character of Uncle Sam for State Dept., 1951; illustrator ads for Advt. Council's Econ. Ednl. Program; illustrator The Miracle of Am., 1948, Let Freedom Ring, 1952; designed March of Freedom, USIS. Recipient numerous awards for advt. posters nat. competition; citation Nat. War Fund, U.S.O., Treasury Dept., War Savs. Program; award of merit Advt. Fedn. Am., 1961; others. Mem. Nat. Soc. Art Dirs., Colonial Soc. Southampton (L.I.), English Speaking Union. Republican. Presbyn. Clubs: Canoe Brook Country (Summit, N.J.); Art Directors (N.Y.C.). Contbr. articles advt. publs. Home: New York City NY Died Aug. 4, 1971; buried Presbyn. Cemetery, Springfield NJ

NOYES, CHARLES FLOYD, business executive; born in city of Norwich, Conn., July 19, 1878; son Charles Denison and Carrie P. (Crane) N.; ed. Norwich Free Acad.; m. Eleanora S. Halsted (died Mar. 5, 1921); m. 2d, Jessie P. Cooke Smith, Aug. 14, 1926 (died Jan. 1936). Trustee, Title Guarantee Co.; dir. Norwich Daily Bull. Co., adv. bd. Chem. Bank N.Y. Trust Co. Pres. Jessie Smith Noyes Found. Inc. Recipient Horatio Alger award, 1959. Clubs: Union League; Huntington Yacht; Pilgrims. Home: New York City NY Died Sept. 2, 1969.

NOYES, E. LOUISE, educator; b. Mount Sterling, Ill., Dec. 22, 1889; d. Frederick Carter and Lizzie Belle (Curry) Noyes; A.B., Northwestern U., 1911; M.A., Stanford, 1931. Tchr. Highland Park (Ill.) High Sch., 1914-21, Santa Barbara (Cal.) High Sch., 1921-25, head English dept., 1926-54; instr. U. Cal. Santa Barbara Coll., 1954-56. Mem. book selection com. Teen Age Book Club, 1946-68; mem. staff ednl. guide for Coronet Mag., 1946-48; mem. exec. bd. Santa Barbara chpt. Am. Field Service for Internat. Scholarships, 1952-58; mem. Santa Barbara County Com. for Selective Recruitment of Tchrs., sub-chmn. charge work with future tchr. groups, 1959-62. Recipient Lord Balfour Traveling Scholarship, 1930. Mem. Am. Assn. U. Women (mem. exec. bd. Santa Barbara br.), Nat. Council of Tchrs. of English (mem. curriculum commn. 1945-63), Nat. Ret. Tchrs. Assn. Rep. Women, English Speaking Union (sec. 1933-53), Santa Barbara Historical Soc., Santa Barbara Botanical Garden, Phi Beta Kappa, Pi Lambda Theta (editor Women in the News Letter, 1959-64), Delta Kappa Gamma, Alpha Omicron Pi. Episcopalian. Santa Barbara CA

NOYES, GEORGE RAPAIL, univ. prof.; b. Cambridge, Mass., Apr. 2, 1873; s. Charles and Mary Lucretia (Hyde) N.; A.B., Harvard, 1894, A.M., 1895, Ph.D., 1898; U. of St. Petersburg, 1898-1900; Litt.D., U. of Wilno, 1929; LL.D., University of California, 1945; married Florence Augusta Paine, July 31, 1902. Teacher of classics, Browne & Nichols School, Cambridge, Mass., 1894-96; asst. professor English, U. of Wis., 1900-01; teacher, U. of Calif., since 1901, prof. Slavic langs., 1919-43, emeritus since 1943. Mem. Sch. of Slavonic Studies, London; fgn. corr. mem. Polish Acad. of Sciences, Cracow; corr. mem. Slavic Inst. of Prague; fellow of American Academy. Arts and Sciences. Awarded comdrs. Cross Order of Polonia Restituta; Golden Laurel of Polish Academy of Lit. (Warsaw). Clubs: Harvard (San Francisco); Faculty (Berkeley). Author: Tolstoy (in series, Master Spirits of Literature), 1918. Editor: Dryden's Poetical Works, 1909; Selected Dramas of John Dryden, 1910; Hymns Attributed to John Dryden (with G.R. Potter), 1937; Original Poems, together with Translations from the Sanskrit, by A.W. Ryder, 1939. Translator: Pan Tadeusz, by Mickiewicz, 1917; The Religion of Ancient Greece, by Zielinski, 1926; and (with others) Heroic Ballads of Servia, 1913; Plays by Alexander Ostrovsky, 1917; Konrad Wallenrod and Other Writings of Adam Mickiewicz, 1925; Poems by Jan Kochanowski, 1928; Masterpieces of the Russian Drama, 1933; Poems by Adam Mickiewicz, 1944; and various Russian, Polish, Bohemian and Croatian dramas. Am. contributing editor Slavonic Rev., London. Home: 1486 Greenwood Terrace, Berkeley 8 CA‡

NOYES, HARRY ALFRED, research chemist; b. Marlboro, Mass., July 7, 1890; s. Lambert Alfred and Bertha (Keirstead) N.; B.S., Mass. Agrl. Coll., Amherst, Mass., 1912, M.S., 1914; m. Florence Fisherdick, June 25, 1913; children—Mrs. Lorraine Fisherdick Nicholson, Arthur A. (dec.), Carol W. (Mrs. Joseph Graff). Research asst. in chemistry and bacteriology, Purdue U. Exptl. Station, 1913-16; research asso., same, 1916-18; research work with Mellon Inst. Industrial Research and Sch. of Specific Industries, Pittsburgh, Oct. 1918-Mar. 1922; in charge research dept. Welch Grape Juice Co., 1919-22; research chemist Mich. State Dept. Agr., 1922; cereal chemist Mich. Agrl. Expt. Sta., 1922-23; research chemist and food technologist with Dr. Raymond F. Bacon, 1923-32; research chemist for Tex. Gulf Sulphur Co., 1923-32; food technologist having research and production for Foods, Inc., 1933; mng. dir. Applied Sugar Laboratories, Inc., 1934-35; consultant and food technologist with Arthur D. Little, Inc., Dec. 1935 to July 1939. Consultant for food enterprises from 1939; ednl. and training work on nat. defense for Kingsbury Ordnance plant, La Porte, Ind., 1941. Serving as an industrial engr. for Ordnance Dept., U.S. Army, 1942-43. Technologist with Nat. Fireworks, Inc., and asso. companies, 1944; technologist for Noyes Products, Inc. Fellow A.A.A.S., Am. Chem. Soc. (chmn. agrl. and food div. 1922-23); mem. of scientific socs., American Society of Refrigeration Engineers, Beta Kappa Phi, Sigma Xi, Pi Gamma Mu. Lecturer and contbr. to professional jours. on scientific problems, giving emphasis to laboratory orgn. and the problem method" of making industrial research economically practical. Developed processes and procedures for freezing foodstuffs by sugar and sugar-salt solutions based upon taste disired. Inventor of processes using frozen state to produce food conditioning" and producing concentrates from mixtures in the frozen state. Author: Frozen Foods, 1947. Home: Lake Wales FL Died Dec. 22, 1970; buried Wildwood Cemetery Amherst MA

NOYES, MORGAN PHELPS, clergyman; b. Warren, Pa., Mar. 29, 1891; s. Charles Henry and Effie (Morgan) N.; prep. edn., Phillips Exeter (N.H.) Acad.; B.A., Yale, 1914; Union Theol. Seminary, N.Y. City, 1915-17, 1919-20; Columbia University, 1915-17, 1919-20, M.A., 1922; D.D., Yale, 1938; m. Marjorie Bradford Clarke, July 24, 1926; children-Sarah Clarke (Mrs. Sally Mead). William Morgan. Assistant minister of the Madison Av. Presbyn. Ch., New York City, 1919-20; minister Presbyn. Ch., Dobbs Ferry, N.Y., 1920-25, First Presbyn. Ch. Brooklyn, N.Y., 1925-32, Central Presbyterian Ch., Montclair, N.J., 1932-57, emeritus, 1957-72. Vice chmn. dept. worship and the arts, National Council of Churches, 1953-63. Y.M.C.A. work with Russian, Czechoslovak armies, 1917-19. Asso. prof. practical theology, Union Theol. Sem., 1945-51, dir., 1931-45, and from 1951. Fellow corp. Yale, Mem. UN Assn. of U.S.A. (chpt. president from 1966), Psi Upsilon. Club: Century (N.Y.C.). Author: Preaching the Word of God (Lyman Beecher lectures for 1942), 1943; Henry Sloane Coffin: The Man and His Ministry, 1964. Editor: Prayers for Services—a Manual for Leaders of Worship, 1934. Home: Upper Montclair NJ Died June 20, 1972; buried Dorset VT

NUESSLE, FRANCIS E., naval officer; b. Washburn, N. Dak., Jan. 23, 1911; s. William L. and Emma N.; B.S., U.S. Naval Acad. 1932, Air War Coll. 1950, Nat. War Coll., 1955; m. Elizabeth Virginia Hoover, Nov. 4, 1939; children—Warren G., William P., Francis E., Jr., Virginia D. Commd. ensign USN, 1932, advanced through grades to rear adm., 1961; naval aviator, 1935; squadron and ship's officer U.S.S. Saratoga, U.S.S. Lexington, U.S.S. Ranger, U.S.S. Princeton; comdg. officer U.S.S. Gannet until 1942; comdr. bombing Squadron 105 and ASW Group II, 1943; staff, comdr. Naval Task Force for Normandy invasion 1944; successively assigned staffs Chief of Naval Operations, Operational Devel. Force, Naval Striking and Support Force, Southern Europe; commdg. officer U.S.S. Midway, 1957; comdr. Carrier Div. FOURTEEN, 1961-62; comdr. in chief Pacific rep. Joint Strategic Target Planning Staff, 1962-64; chief of staff Naval War College, 1964-66; commander of Fleet Air Norfolk, 1966-67; office of chairman Joint Chiefs of Staff, 1967-70. Clubs: Metropolitan (Washington); N.Y. Yacht, Chevy Chase. Home: Chevy Chase MD Died Nov. 1970.

NUFFER, JOSEPH HENRY, retired; b. Toledo, Jan. 18, 1894; s. Joseph and Anna (Schomburg) N.; student of the public schools; married Hazel Hacker, June 28, 1919 (deceased June 22, 1962); children—Richard, Robert. Various positions Toldeo & Ohio Central R.R., Pa. R.R., 1909-15; clk. Toledo Scale Co., 1915-17, sales dept., 1920-21; sales dept. Willys Farm Lighting Plants, 1921-23; salesman Air-Way Electric Appliance Corp., 1924-25; becoming successively br. mgr., comptroller, asst. sales mgr., and gen. sales mgr., pres., 1936-54, chmn. bd., 1954-55; retired; management consultant, 1956-60. Mem. Toldeo Labor-Mgmt. Citizens Com.; chmn. of board Employees Assn. Toledo. Trustee Toledo Better Bus. Bur. Served as sgt. inf. AEF, 1917-19. Mem. C. of C. (past pres.), Am. Legion, Mason (32 deg.). Clubs: Toledo, Rotary. Home: Toledo OH Died Nov. 11, 1968; buried Woodlawn Cemetery, Toledo OH

NUGENT, WALTER HENRY, clergyman; b. Omemee, Ont., Can., Dec. 20, 1877; s. Henry and Mary Jane (Cork) N.; grad. Albert Coll., Belleville, Ont., 1898; B.C.L., Chicago Law Sch., 1904; B.O., Chicago Conservatory of Music and Dramatic Art, 1904; Ph.D., Midland U., Chicago, 1905; B.D., Chicago Theol. Sem., 1906; D.D., Wheaton Coll., 1918; m. Harriet Louise Whitcomb, Apr. 16, 1907 (dec.); children—Margaret Whitcomb (Mrs. William R. Baker), Gordon Whitcomb; m. 2d, Ruth Eleanore Holmes, June 10, 1951. Entered Canadian Meth. ministry, 1898; minister, Manitoba and N.W. Conf., 1898-1901, M.E. Ch., Lester, Ia., 1901-03; asst. Bishop Samuel Fallows, R.E. Ch., Chicago, 1903-05; minister 5th Av. Congl. Ch., Minneapolis, 1906-10, Cent. Congl. Ch., Newburyport, Massachusetts, 1910-20, Central Presbyterian Church, Portland, Oregon, 1920-29, Austin Presbyterian Church, Chicago, January 1, 1929-Aug. 1948, minister emeritus, 1948-67, new buildings erected for each of the churches and named under his leadership; now president of H.D. Sheldon, Incorporated. Platform lecturer with Winchell Lecture and Entertainment Bureau, Chicago, 1904-05, Eastern Lyceum Bureau, Boston, 1914-20; four-minute speaker during World War I; chmn. hdqrs. com., Ore. Anti-Saloon League, 1920-38. Trustee Albany Coll., Ore., 1921-28, Westminister Foundation, Synod of Ore., 1922-28. Moderator Portland Presbytery, 1923; pres. Portland Ministers' Assn., 1925; sec. Gen. Assembly's Com. on Apportionment, 1925-28. Mem. bd. dirs. Presbyn. Coll. of Christian Edn., Chicago, 1930-49; trustee Chicago Ch. Fedn., 1935-45; mem. bd. dirs. Druce Lake Assn. mem. bd. dirs. Presbyn. Home, Evanston, 1930-59, now hon. dir.; pres. bd. trustees Chgo. Presbytery, 1941-60, then hon. pres. Home: Chicago IL Died Aug. 3, 1967.

NUHN, CLIFFORD JEREMIAH, newspaper editor; b. Poughkeepsie, N.Y., Sept. 23, 1903; s. John and Mary (Clifford) N.; m. Jane M. Worrall, 1925. With Poughkeepsie Newspapers, Inc., 1941-66, pres., 1956-66, publisher, 1952-66; dir. Speidel Newspapers, Incorporated. Member of the American Newspapers Publishers Association, N.Y. State Publishers Assn., N.Y. State Soc. Editors. Home: Millbrook NY Died Jan. 1969.

NUNN, CLEMENT SINGLETON, lawyer; b. Marion, Ky., February 1, 1870; s. Thomas Jefferson and Sallie A. (Clement) N.; student State U. of Ky.; m. Lemah Barnes, of Marion, Ky., Oct. 24, 1894. Admitted to Ky. bar, 1891, and practiced in Marion; also mem. law firm of Nunn & Waller, Paducah. Associate justice Court of Appeals of Ky., Waller, Paducah. Associate justice Court of Appeals of Ky., 1914-16; mem. Ky. Senate, 1918-20. Pres. Ky. State Bar Assn., 1926-27. Democrat. Methodist. Home: Marion, Ky. Office: Paducah KY‡

NUNN, HAROLD FRANCIS, corp. exec.; b. N.Y.C., Feb. 25, 1915; s. Harry J. and Mary A. (Doyle) N.; B.S., Princeton, 1923; m. Marion K. Himmels-May 29, 1941; children—John Hamann, Harold Francis, Marcille Katherine. With Eagle-Picher Co., Cin., 1961-71, exec. v.p. 1965-71, also dir. Home: Cincinnati OH Died Aug. 3, 1971.

NUTT, HUBERT WILBUR, educator; b. Hamilton County, Ind., Aug. 31, 1873; s. John Franklin and Charlotte (Myers) N.; grad. Ind. State Normal Coll., 1907; Ph.B., U. of Chicago, 1914, A.M., 1916, Ph.D., 1923; m. Ella Rigdon, Dec. 22, 1894; children—Hubert Estel, Donald Franklin. Teacher pub. schs., Ind., 1892-1904; prin. high sch., Mitchell, Ind., 1904-07, Somerset, Ky., 1907-09; dean of edn., Marion (Ind.) Normal Coll., 1909-12, Muncie (Ind.) Normal Inst., 1912-13; dir. teacher training U. of Kan., 1914-22, became dir. of teacher training at Ohio Wesleyan Univ., 1922; prof. edn., U. of Texas, summer, 1921, W.Va. Univ., summers, 1925, 26, Kent State Normal Sch., summers, 1927, 28, U. of Ill., summers, 1929, 30. Republican. Presbyterian. Author: The Supervision of Instruction, 1920; Principles of Teaching High School Pupils, 1922; Current Problems in the Supervision of Instruction, 1928. Home: 1638 N. 11th Street, Phoenix AZ‡

NUTTER, EDWARD HOIT, mining engr.; b. Healdsburg, Calif., May 24, 1876; s. Rev. David and Hannah Van Wyck (Hoit) N.; A.B., Stanford, 1902; m. Gertrude Monier Allen, Mar. 7, 1905; children—Edward Allen, Katherine Louise (Mrs. John Prey Tynes), Sheldon Hoit. Mining foremanships, Calif., 1902-03; editor Mineral Wealth, Redding Calif., 1903-04; asst. supt. and supt. Standard Consol. Mining Co., Bodie, Calif., 1904-06; asst. gen. supt. and supt. Liberty Bell Gold Mining Co., Telluride, Colo., 1906-09; engr. Minerals Separation, Ltd., London, 1910; chief engr. Minerals Separation, North Am. Corp. and its predecessor companies in N. America since 1911. Mem. Am. Inst. of Mining and Metall. Engrs., Sigma Xi, Tau Beta Pi, Swedenborgian. Clubs: Commonwealth, Commercial (San Francisco). Known for development and application of flotation process for metalliferous ores in connection with most of the important lead, zinc, copper, silver and molybdenum mines of N. America and many mines abroad; inventor of a number of patented improvements in the process. Orange grower, Redlands dist., Calif. Home: 2834 San Francisco CA‡

NUTTING, MARGARET OGDEN, newspaper pub.; b. Wheeling, W.Va., Feb. 12, 1901; d. Hershel C. and Mary Frances (Moorhouse) Ogden; A.B., Vassar Coll., 1923; m. George Kegley Nutting, Oct. 12, 1926; children—George Ogden, William Courtney. Mgr. Hinton (W.Va.) Daily News, 1923-25; asst. advt. mgr. Evening Jour., Martinsburg, W.Va., 1925-26, pres., 1943—; editorial writer Wheeling Daily News, 1929-33; pres. Parkersburg Sentinel Co., 1943—; Parkersburg Publishing Co., 1943-51, Welch (W.Va.) Daily News; v.p. News Pub. Co., Wheeling, 1943-60, pres., 1960—; pres. of Jamestown Newspaper Corp. (N.Y.), Messenger Printing Company, Fort Dodge, Iowa. Mem. ladies board Garfield Meml. Hosp., Washington, Georgetown U. Hosp. Mem. League Rep. Women. Episcopalian. Club: Vassar. Home: Washington DC Died Oct. 16, 1970.

NUTTLE, HARRY (HOPKINS), business exec.; born Caroline County, Md., Apr. 30, 1885; s. Henry T. and Emma (Hopkins) N.; Ph.B., Dickinson Coll., 1906; m. Zora Joslin, Dec. 5, 1914; children—Harry Joslin, Byron Hopkins. Teacher Dover, Del., Federalsburg, Md., 1906-08; asso. sec. Y.M.C.A., Wilmington, Del., 1908-10; farmer and canner, 1910-73; cannery, Hickman, Md., pres. Peoples Bank of Denton, 1945-73, dir., 1925-73; pres. So. States Cooperative, 1944-47, dir., 1938-68; dir., sec. and treas. Choptank Electric Cooperative, 1938-49. Pres., Maryland Farm Bur., 1935-38; dir., Am. Farm Bureau Fedn., 1937-44. Mem. Md. House of Delegates, 1914-15, Md. Senate, 1918-21. Regent U. of Md., 1935-41, 43-73. Mem. Tri State Packers Assn. (pres. 1939), Sigma Alpha Epsilon. Republican. Methodist. Mason (Shriner), Odd Fellow. Clubs: Rotary, Denton (past pres.). Home: Denton MD Died Feb. 14, 1973.

NUTTMAN, LOUIS MEREDITH, army officer; born Newark, N.J., Jan. 28, 1874; s. George and Louise (Mentz) N.; grad. U.S. Mil. Acad., 1895; m. Mrs. Alice Long Mitchell, Mar. 9, 1909. Commd. 2d lt. inf., U.S. Army, June 12, 1895, and advanced through grades to col., July 1, 1920, brig. gen., May 1, 1932; retired Jan. 31, 1938. Served in Spanish-Am. War, Philippine Insurrection, Boxer Campaign, Mexican Punitive Expdn., World War. Awarded D.S.M., Silver Star Medal (U.S.); Croix de Guerre (France). Club: Army and Navy (Washington). Address: War Dept., Washington DC‡

NUVEEN, JOHN, investment banker; b. Chgo., June 6, 1896; s. John and Ida E. (Strawbridge) N.; Ph.B., U. Chgo., 1919; m. Grace Bennet, June 28, 1927; children—Margaret (Mrs. Rene Beguin), Anna Ridgway (Mrs. Marcus T. Reynolds), John Septimus. With John Nuveen & Co., municipal bonds, Chgo., 1919-68, partner, 1923-36, mng. partner, 1936-53, chmn. bd., 1953-54, vice chmn. bd., 1954-68, also dir.; dir. Interior Design, 1954-68. Founder, chmn. Fgn. Policy Clearing House, 1957-61. With WPB, Region IV, 1942-45, regional dir., 1943-45; minister, chief ECA Mission to Greece, 1948-49, to Belgium and Luxembourg, 1949-50; cons. fgn. investment Dept. Commerce, 1954-56, mem. world trade adv. com., 1957-59; mem. U.S. delegation Atlantic Congress, London, 1959; lectr. fgn. policy Oglethorpe Coll., 1967. Chmn. Ill. Bd. Pub. Welfare Commrs., 1940-41; mem. Chgo. Crime Commn., 1946-66; mem. Fair Campaign Practices Com., 1956-68; mem. Nat. Com. for Effective Congress, 1958-68, vice chmn., 1966-68; vice chmn. World Population Emergency Campaign, 1960-61; mem. Population Crisis Com., 1965-68; mem. Ill. Gov.'s Com. for Distinguished Fgn. Guests, 1962-—. Mem. Kenilworth (Ill.) Bd. Edn., 1934-40, chmn. finance com., 1934, pres., 1937-40. Bd. dirs. Better Govt. Assn., 1926-68, Citizens Assn. Chgo., 1945-52, Am. Friends of Middle East, 1957-68, Fund for Theol. Edn., 1964-68; sec. bd. mgrs. YMCA, Hyde Park, 1922-27, mem. bd. mgrs., adv. bd. Met. Chgo., 1965-68, mem. internat. com., 1932-67, mem. exec. com., 1958-67; trustee U. Chgo., 1938-68, trustee Chgo. Sunday Evening Club, 1934-66, pres., 1945-55; founder Alumni Found., pres., until 1941; trustee Royal Poinciana Chapel, 1938-50, 67-68, Bapt. Theol. Union, 1938-68, Morehouse Coll., 1953-68, Center for Internat. Econ. Growth, 1961-63; Christian Century Found., 1962-68; bd. mgrs. Am. Bapt. Home Missions Soc., 1946-49; trustee Anatolia (Greece) Coll., 1952-65, emeritus, 1965-68; trustee Athens (Greece) Coll., 1961-65, emeritus, 1965-68; trustee, v.p., Ch. Fedn. Greater Chgo., 1946-48; bd. dirs. Citizens Assn. Chgo., 1953-58, v.p., 1953-55; mem. nat. adv. com. CARE, 1954-68, chmn., 1956-68; nat. adv. bd. Am. Found. Continuing Edn., 1955-59; policy com. Am. Inst. Free Labor Devel., 1961-62; bd. dirs. Planned Parenthood Assn., 1962-67, chmn. nationwide campaign com., 1964-66; governing life mem. Art Inst. Chgo., 1951-68; governing mem. Orchestral Assn., 1962-68; founding mem. Citizens Honest Reelection Found., 1962-68; adv. council Am. Farm Sch., Greece, 1959-65, nat. com., 1965-68. Served in Signal Res. Corps., U.S. Army, World War I. Decorated cross comdr. Royal Order Phoenix (Greece); comdr. Order Orange Nassau (Netherlands); recipent citation for pub. service U. Chgo., 1945, Alumni medal, 1963. Mem. Investment Bankers Assn., U.S. (fgn. policy com. 1963-66), Ill. (dir. 1947-48), chambers commerce, Council Fgn. Relations, Council Religion and Internat. Affairs, Nat. Municipal League (council 1941-56, regional v.p. 1950-56), N.C. Municipal Council (pres. 1932-33, chmn. bd. 1933-48, hon. dir. 1948-68), Chgo. Council Fgn. Relations (dir. 1952-63, v.p. 1953-58, mem. speakers bur. 1956-68), Alpha Delta Phi (nat. v.p., exec. council 1963-66, internat. pres. 1965-66). Baptist (trustee 1946-48). Clubs: Bankers Am., University, Quadrangle, Chicago Literary, Commercial, Chicago, Attic, Commonwealth, Mid-Am. (Chgo.); Indian Hill (Winnetka, Ill.); Metropolitan (Washington); Seminole, Golf, Everglades (Palm Beach, Fla.). Home: Winnetka IL Died Aug. 8, 1968.

NYE, GERALD P., ex-senator; b. Hortonville, Wisconsin, Dec. 19, 1892; s. Irwin R. and Phoebe Etta (Prentice) Nye; moved with parents to Wittenberg, Wisconsin at age of 2; grad. high school, Wittenberg, 1911; married Anna Margaret Munch, August 16, 1916; children—Marjorie Eleanor, Robert Gerald, James Prentice; married 2d Arda Marguerite Johnson, December 14, 1940;children—Gerald Prentice, Richard Johnson, Marguerite Deborah. Began as pub. of The Review, Hortonville, 1911; man. and editor of Daily Plain Dealer, Creston, Iowa, 1915; with Des Moines Register and Leader a few months, then moved to N.D. and purchased the Fryburg Pioneer; settled in Cooperstown, N.D., 1919; and became editor and mgr. Griggs Co. Sentinel-Courier; apptd. by Gov. Sorlie to U.S. Senate, Nov. 14, 1925 to fill vacancy caused by death of Hon. Edwin F. Ladd, and elected to same office, Nov. 1926, Nov. 1932 and Nov. 1938, term expired 1945; chmn. of Teapot Dome and Munitions investigating coms.; pres. Records Engring., Inc., 1946-60; spl. asst. for elderly housing FHA, 1960-63; minority staff mem. Senate Com. on Aging, 1963-65; housing cons., legislative rep. David S. Clark, Assos., also Am. Bapt. Service Corp., Washington, 1966-71. Sponsored neutrality legislation and war profit control legislation. Republican. Lutheran. Mason, K.P. Home: Chevy Chase MD Died July 17, 1971; buried Ft. Lincoln Cemetery, Washington DC

NYE, IRENE, educator; b. Eureka, Kan., Nov. 12, 1874; d. Ira Palmer and Esther (Chesebrough) N.; lineal descendant of John Howland of the Mayflower, and of William Chesebrough, first English settler in Stonington, Conn.; prep. edn. Southern Kan. Acad., Eureka; A.B., Washburn Coll., 1895, L.H.D., 1930; Ph.D., Yale, 1911. Teacher Latin and Greek, Southern Kan. Acad., 1895-1901; instr. Latin and history, Washburn Coll., 1905-08; scholar in classics, 1908-09, fellow, 1909-11, Yale; prof. Latin, 1911-12, of classic langs., 1912-15, Washburn Coll.; asst. prof. Greek and Latin, 1915-16, prof. since 1916, dean of faculty since May 19, 1917, Conn. Coll. for Women. Mem. Archaeol. Inst. America, Am. Philol. Assn., N.E. Classical Assn. (v.p. 1938-39); v.p. Classical Assn. Middle West and South, 1911-15; pres. Assn. Classical Teachers of Kan. and Western Mo., 1914-15. Conglist. Author: Sentence Connection, Chiefly Illustrated from Livy, 1911. Contbr. to Classical Jour., Classical Philology and various ednl. jours. Home: 772 Williams St., New London CT‡

NYE, WARD HIGLEY, school supt.; b. Windsor, Ashtabula Co., O., May 24, 1872; s. Frank and Frances (Higley) N.; Adelbert Coll. (Western Reserve U.), Cleveland; A.B., Oberlin, 1901; Harvard, summer, 1903; m. Annie Belle Rathbone, of New Lyme, O., July 2, 1895. Teacher country schs., 5 yrs.; prin. high schs., Bloomfield, Urbana and Oberlin to 1903; supt. schs., Oberlin, 1903-8, Billings, Mont., 1908-—. Mem. Mont. State Textbook Commn., State Bd. of Edn. Democrat. Conglist. Mem. N.E.A., Mont. State Teachers' Assn., Yellowstone Valley Teachers' Assn. Mason (K.T., Shriner). Address: Billings MT‡

NYQUIST, EDNA ELVERA, educator; b. Moundridge, Kan.; d. Gustaf A. and Elvera (Hawkinson) Nyquist; A.B., McPherson Coll., 1931; A.M., U. Kan., 1938; postgrad. U. Ind., 1946-48, Geneva (Switzerland) U., 1952-53, Shakespeare inst., Eng., 1949, 52. With editorial, advt. Ginn & Co. Pubs., Boston, 1944-45; mem. faculty English depts. Ind. U., Bloomington, 1946-48, Ill. State U., 1948-53; asso. prof. Wis. State U., 1955-69. Mem. Modern Lang. Assn., Am. Studies Assn. Author: Pioneer Life and Lore of McPherson County Kansas, 1932. Contbr. articles to profl. jours. Home: Stevens Point WI Died Oct. 12, 1969.

NYSTROM, PAUL HENRY, economist; b. Maiden Rock, Wis., Jan. 25, 1878; s. Andrew and Christine (Westman) N.; graduate New Richmond (Wis.) High School 1902; grad. Superior (Wis.) State Teachers Coll., 1905; Ph.B., U. of Wis., 1909, Ph.M., 1910, Ph.D., 1914; honorary LL.D., Ohio State University, 1950; married Mildred C. Chicker, Aug. 26, 1903; children—Marden Roscoe, Birna Genevieve, Lucile. Worked on farm and clerked in retail stores until 1897; teacher, later principal high schs., and city school, Wisconsin, until 1908; special investigator Wisconsin Tax Commission, summers, 1906, 07, 08; 1st district representative of extension div. U. of Wis., 1909-12; asst. prof. polit. economy, U. of Wis., 1912-13; asso. prof. economics, U. of Minn., 1914-15; dir. trade research, U.S. Rubber Co., New York, 1915-17; sales mgr. Internat. Magazine Co., 1917-21; dir. Retail Research Assn., and Associated Merchandising Corp., 1921-27; prof. marketing Columbia U., 1926-50, professor emeritus and spl. lectr. from 1950; business and marketing consultant from 1927; owner Nystrom's Restaurant, North Hackensack, N.J., 1936-45. Acting chmn. Nat. Retail Code Authority under NRA; pres. Limited Price Variety Stores Assn., 1933-55; pres. Am. Marketing Soc., 1934; editor American Marketing Jour., 1935-36; mem. Fed. Bur. Vocational Edn., 1936-46; chmn. 1937-39, and 1944-46; vice pres. Am. Vocational Assn., 1938-44; chmn. Central Council Nat. Retail Associations, 1942-54, John Ericsson Society (president 1953-58). Clubs: Columbia Faculty, Salesmgrs. (pres. 1925-26), Sales Executives (New York) (pres. 1937-38, 1940-45; chmn. bd. 1945-46). Decorated Order North Star, 1st Class by King of Sweden, 1950; Paul D. Converse Award, U. of Ill., 1949, Charles C. Parlin award, Am. Marketing Assn., 1952. Author: Retail Selling and Store Management, 1913, Economics of Retailing, 1915, 3d edition, 1930; Textiles, 1916; Retail Store Management, 1917; Automobile Selling, 1919; Economies of Fashion, 1928; Economic Principles of Consumption, 1929; Fashion Merchandising, 1932; Elements of Retail Selling, 1936; Retail Store Operation, 1937; Marketing Handbook, 1948; also research and writing on econ. history. Home: Spring Valley NY Died Aug. 17, 1969; buried Maiden Rock WI

NYSTROM, WENDELL CLARENCE, educator; b. Savonburg, Kan., Nov. 30, 1892; s. August and Anna Christine (Ekelund) N.; A.B., Bethany Coll., 1914, Litt.D., (hon.), 1956; A.M., U. Kan., 1934, Ph.D., 1937; m. Persis Ann White, Mar. 15, 1918. High sch. prin., Correctionville, Ia., 1915-17, Norton, Kan., 1921-24, 26-34; spl. rep. Am. Book Co., Chgo., 1920-21; v.p. 1st State Bank, Norton, 1924-25; instr. U. of Kan., 1935-37; asso. prof., head dept. edn. Wittenberg Coll., Springfield, O., 1937-40, prof., from 1940, asst. dean of coll., 1942-46, dean, from 1946, then prof., dean emeritus. Served as 1st lt., 42d Inf., 12th Div., U.S. Army, 1917-19.. Fellow A.A.A.S.; mem. N.E.A. (dept. higher edn.), Am. Assn. Sch. Adminstrs., Nat. Soc. Coll. Teachers Edn., Am. Legion, Ohio Acad. Sci., Phi Delta Kappa, Pi Kappa Delta, Kappa Phi Kappa, Phi Eta Sigma, Delta Sigma Phi. Blue Key, Skull and Chain. Lutheran. Mason (32 deg.). Club: Mens Literary. Author: The selection and Provision of Textbooks with Special Reference to Kansas, 1937. Contbr. profl. mags. Home: Springfield OH Died Mar. 24, 1971.

OAKSEY, GEOFFREY LAWRENCE, Brit. judge; b. London, Eng., Oct. 2, 1880; s. Lord Trevethin and Jessie (Lawrence); student Haileybury Coll., 1894-99; M.A., New College, Oxford, 1903, Hon. Fellow, 1944, Hon. D.C.L., 1947; m. Marjorie Robinson, Dec. 22, 1921;children—Mary Elizabeth, Enid Rosamond, Anne Jennifer, John Geoffrey Tristram. Called to Bar, Jan. 1906; counsel for Canadian Provinces and C.P.R. in Privy Council, 1907-14; counsel for Canada in N. Atlantic Fisheries arbitration, The Hague, 1910; examiner in ecclesiastical causes, 1927-32; atty. gen. to Prince of Wales and Duchy of Cornwall, 1928-32; counsel to Jockey Club, 1922-32; judge High Court, 1932-44; Lord Justice, 1944; British judge internat. military tribunal, Nuremburg, 1945 (president); Lord of Appeal in ordinary since March 1947; vice lieutenant for Wiltshire, 1949. Joined Royal F.A., Essex Brigade, 1914; Herts Brigade, France and Palestine, 1915-18; comd. Herts Yeomanry Brigade, 1919-26, R.A. col. 1926-37. Awarded D.S.O., and T.D., mentioned in dispatches twice. King's Counsel, 1925, created Lord Oaksey Jan. 1, 1947. Chmn. Quarter Sessions Wiltshire, 1945. Mem. Ch. of Eng. Clubs: Brooks', St. James St. (London). Twice pres. English Guernsey Cattle Soc. Home: Oaksey Malmesbury, Wiltshire England Died Aug. 1971.

OBEAR, HUGH HARRIS, lawyer; b. Winnsboro, S.C., Dec. 20, 1882; s. Henry Norwood and Eunice (Harris) O.; B.L., U. of Va., 1906; student U. of Paris (spl. course for officers of U.S. Army), 1919; m. Mildred Fleenor. Admitted to D.C. bar, 1907, practice Wash., 1907-71; sr. partner Douglas, Obear & Campbell, 1939-71. Served as maj. comdg. 1st Batt., 319th Inf., 80th Div., World War I; grad. Army Gen. Staff Coll., Langres, France, 1919. Awarded silver star with oak leaf cluster. Officer Order of Carlos Manuel de Cespedes (Cuba). Former dir. Children's Hosp., Washington; former trustee The Louise Home. Mem. Am., D.C. (pres. 1945) bar assns., Newcomen Soc. N. Am., Thomas Jefferson Soc. Alumni U. Va. (life), Phi Delta Phi. Clubs: Metropolitan (past gov. and v.p.), Army and Navy, Lawyers' (past pres.) (Washington); Chevy Chase (Md.). Home: Washington DC Died Mar. 16, 1971.

OBENSHAIN, WILEY S(HACKFORD), business exec.; b. Bedford County, nr. Roanoke, Va., Oct. 4, 1894; s. David Langburn and Minnie (Oma) O.; dairy course Va. Polytech. Inst., 1914; corr. bus. course, Alexander Hamilton Inst., 1924-25; m. Lela Bell Douglas, July 3, 1919; 1 son, Wiley Shackford. Supt. Purity Ice Cream Co., Jacksonville, Fla., 1915-17, mgr. Charlotte, N.C., 1919-22, zone mgr., 1922-30; zone mgr., dir. Southern Dairies Inc. (formerly Purity Ice Cream Co. and Chapin-Sacks Corp.), Washington, 1930-41, mem. exec. com. from 1941, v.p., 1941-47, exec. v.p., 1947-51, pres., 1951-59, ret., 1959; dir. First Union Nat. Bank, 1953-64, emeritus, 1964-72; pres., dir. Tampa Stock Farms Dairy, Inc.; chmn. bd., Peerless Ice Cream Co., Jersey Ice Cream Co., Inc., Cloverland Dairy Products Corp., Brookhaven Creamery Co., Inc., Magnolia Creamery Co., Inc.; dir. White Ice Cream and Milk Co. Mem. Charlotte Redevel. Com., 1960-67, vice chmn., 1962-67; chmn. bldg. com. A.R.C., Charlotte, 1960-62; chmn. Charlotte Red Cross, 1962-63; mem. adv. bd. Salvation Army, 1962-69. Bd. dirs. Charlotte Community Chest, 1940-41, United Appeal. Served as 1st lieutenant, U.S. Army, San Antonio, Texas, 1917-19; (scientific asst. U.S.P.H.S.). A founder N.C. Dairy Foundation, 1945, dir., from 1945; mem. Internat. Assn. Ice Cream Mfrs. (dir. 1949-51), Charlotte Shippers Mfg. Assn. (dir., 1940-41), N.C. Dairy Products Assn. (pres., 1942-43, dir. 1942-47), C. of C. (dir. 1943-44), N.C. Ice Cream Mfrs. Assn. (dir. 1926-30, pres. 1928), Newcomen Soc. N. Am. Mem. First Christian Church; Mason (32 deg., Shriner). Clubs: Myers Park Country, Charlotte City, Good Fellows, Charlotte Country, Executives, Rotary (pres. 1942-43, dir.) (Charlotte); Columbia Country (Chevy Chase, Md.). Home: Charlotte NC Died Mar. 13, 1972; entombed Forest Lawn Mausoleum, Charlotte NC

OBERLINK, BOYD STEVENSON, mfg. exec.; b. Martinsville, Ill., May 13, 1910; s. Charles and Elsie Grace (Stevenson) O.; student Millikin U., 1928-29; B.S. in Mech. Engring. U. Ill., 1932; m. Alice Jean Jenkins, Nov. 26, 1936; children—Jean, William Boyd. Student engr., tractor div. Allis-Chalmers Mfg. Co., Milw., 1934, asst. mgr. allied equipment, 1937, mgr. Washington office, 1942, asst. indsl. sales mgr., 1943, asst. to exec. v.p., 1945, v.p., 1951-56, group v.p., 1956-59, sr. v.p., 1959-67, also dir.; pres. Canadian Allis Chalmers, 1967-70, ret., 1970. Mem. Navy League

U.S., Soc. Am. Mil. Engrs., Am. Ordnance Assn., Am. Rd. Builders Assn., Soc. Automotive Engineers, YMCA, Pi Tau Sigma. Clubs: Seigniory; Ft. Myers Country. Home: Fort Myers Beach FL Died May 27, 1972.

OBERNDORFER, ANNE SHAW FAULKNER (MRS. MARX E. OBERNDORFER), b. Chicago, Ill., Sept. 26, 1877; d. Samuel and Cornelia Evarts (Smith) Faulkner; ed. Kenwood Inst. Chicago; Chicago Conservatory of Music; Caruthers Normal Sch. of Music; m. Marx E. Oberndorfer, Feb. 12, 1913; 1 dau., Elizabeth Ann. Organizer, 1897, and dir. Program Classes of Chicago Symphony Orchestra; with husband as pianist, official lecturer Chicago Opera Co.; dir. children's concerts, Ravinia Park, Chicago, 4 seasons. Chmn. music div. Gen. Federation Women's Clubs, 1920-26; ednl. dir. Asso. Opera Clubs of Chicago Civic Opera Co. Progressive Republican. Presbyterian. Clubs: Nat. Music Educators, Musicians (hon.). Author: What We Hear in Music, 1915, 13th edit., 1943; Music in the Home, 1916. Compiler: Americanization Songs, 1917; General Federation Song Book, 1921; Best Hymns for Sunday School, 1923; Noels, 1932; The New American Song Book; Opera Librettos for Radio Listeners. Music editor Child Life Mag., 1922-23, Better Homes and Gardens, 1923-24. Home: Webster Hotel, 2150 Lincoln Park W. Studio: 637 Fine Arts Bldg., Chicago IL‡

O'BRIAN, JOHN LORD, lawyer; b. Buffalo, Oct. 14, 1874; s. John and Elizabeth (Lord) O.; A.B., Harvard, 1896; LL.D., 1946; LL.B., U. Buffalo, 1898; LL.D., Hobart Coll., 1916, Syracuse U., 1938, Bklyn. Poly. Inst., 1943, Brown U., 1945, Yale, 1948; m. Alma E. White, Sept. 17, 1902 (dec.); children—Alma (Mrs. Kellog Mann), Janet (Mrs. Winfield L. Butsch), Frances (Mrs. Ames B. Hattrick) (dec.), Alison (Mrs. S. Davis Boylston), Esther (Mrs. Thurston T. Robinson). Admitted to N.Y. bar and in practice at Buffalo, 1898-45; mem. firm Covington and Burling, Washington; mem. N.Y. Assembly, 1907-09; U.S. Atty. Western Dist. N.Y., 1909-14; del.-at-large, N.Y. Constl. Conv., 1915; chmn. draft bd. appeals, Western N.Y., 1917; head War Emergency Div., Dept. of Justice, 1917-19; Buffalo Trustee Albright Art Gallery, 1921-30; community fund, 1923-42; Family Service Soc., 1925-42; vice chmn. N.Y. State Reorgn. Commn., 1925-26; asst. to atty. gen. of U.S., 1929-33; gen. counsel Office of Prodn. Mgmt., Supply Priorities and Allocation Bd., Washington, 1941, and WPB until Dec. 1944; mem. Nat. Adv. Bd. on Mobizn. Policy, 1951-52. Tucker Found. lectr., The Changing Aspects of Freedom, Washington and Lee U., 1952, Godkin Found. lectr., Harvard, 1955. Republican candidate U.S. Senate New York, 1938. Regent University of State of New York, 1931-47; trustee Univ. of Buffalo, 1903-29; overseer Harvard Univ., 1939-45. Pres. Harvard Alumni Assn., 1945, nat. chmn. Endowment Harvard Divinity-sch. 1950-57. Decorated Officer Order of Leopold II (Belgium); recipient Chancellor's Medal, U. Buffalo, 1940, for distinguished pub. service; Presdl. Medal for Merit, 1946, for outstanding service in the war effort; award Nat. Conf. Christians and Jews, for service in field of human relations, 1953; annual medal N.Y. Bar Assn., 1957; ann. award for Fellows Am. Bar Found., 1960. Fellow Am. Acad. Arts and Scis.; mem. Am. Law Inst., various bar assns., Washington Nat. Monument Soc., Washington Lit. Soc., Order Coif, Delta Upsilon, Phi Delta Phi, Phi Beta Kappa (hon.). Republican. Episcopalian (chancellor P.E. Diocese of Western New York, 1932-46). Clubs: Century, Harvard (N.Y.C.); Buffalo (pres. 1940); Metropolitan (pres. 1954-56), Alibi (Washington); Alfalfa (pres. 1952). Home: Washington DC Died Apr. 10, 1973.

O'BRIEN, EDGAR DAVID, banker; b. San Francisco, Apr. 7, 1898; s. George Norton and Florence Rose (McLaughlin) O'B.; B.S. U. Cal. at Berkeley, 1921; m. Mariel Myde, Mar. 21, 1929; 1 dau., Nancy. Agriculturist, 1921-26; with Wells Fargo Bank Am. Trust Company formerly American Trust Co., San Francisco, from 1928, becoming sr. v.p. Mem. Mortgage Bankers Assn. Am., Mortgage Bankers Assn. No. Cal., Cal. Bankers Assn., Rancheros Visitadores, Zeta Psi. Clubs: Pacific-Union, Menlo Country, Merchants Exchange. Home: Woodside CA Died July 18, 1968; inurned Mt. View Columbarium, Oakland CA

O'BRIEN, FRANK CORNELIUS, lawyer; b. Jersey City, N.J., May 15, 1915; s. George J. and Kathryn (Driscoll) O'B.; J.D., John Marshall Coll., Jersey City, 1938; m. Bernice Hoos, Aug. 4, 1945; children—Roger, Frank Cornelius, Edward, Bernice, Dora Jean. Admitted to N.J. bar, 1938, since practiced in Newark; partner firm Pitney, Hardin & Kipp, 1948-70. Served to capt. AUS, 1942-45. Decorated Bronze Star. Mem. Am., N.J., Essex County bar assns. Home: Glen Ridge NJ Died Mar. 1, 1970.

O'BRIEN, HENRY RUST, physician; b. Oberlin, O., July 14, 1891; s. James Putnam and Lizzie (Coffin) O'B.; M.D., U. Mich., 1919; M.P.H., Johns Hopkins U., 1931; m. Mary L. Phillips Carr, Mar. 24, 1926; children—Martha Jane (Mrs. Giles C. Fenn), Susan (Mrs. Susan Bowman), James Putnam.. Intern, Bklyn. Hosp., 1919, U.S. Marine Hosp., Ellis Island, N.Y., 1919-20, Manhattan Maternity Hosp. and Dispensary, 1920; staff mem. Bur. Mines, USPHS, 1920-21; mem. internat. health bd. Rockefeller Found., Thailand, 1921-25; asst. resident in surgery Cin. Gen. Hosp., 1925-26; asso. physician McCormick Hosp., Chiengmai, Thailand, 1926-31; commr. health Lorain County, O., 1931-34, Chattaraugus County, N.Y., 1935-41; asst. dist. state health officer N.Y. State Dept. Health, 1934-35; dir. local health adminstrn. Conn. Dept. Health, 1941-43; commd. lt. col. USPHS, 1943, advanced through grades to col.; assigned to Cairo, Sydney, Manila, Shanghai, Washington, Addis Ababa, 1943-55; dir. profl. edn. Pa. Dept. Health, 1955-64. Guest lectr. Western Res. U., Cornell U., U. Minn. Diplomate Am. Bd. Preventive Medicine. Fellow Am. Pub. Health Assn., A.C.S., Royal Soc. Tropical Medicine and Health, Am. Coll. Preventive Medicine; mem. A.M.A., Am. Soc. Tropical Medicine and Health, Sigma Xi, Alpha Omega Alpha. Home: Camp Hill PA Died Aug. 16, 1970; buried Camp Hill PA

O'BRIEN, JUSTIN MCCORTNEY, educator; b. Chicago, Nov. 26, 1906; s. Quin and Ellen (McCortney) O'B.; student Phillips Exeter Acad., 1921-24; Ph.B., U. Chicago, 1927; A.M., Harvard, 1928, Ph.D., 1936; Doctor of Letters, Wesleyan University, 1966; m. Isabel Ireland, Jan. 24, 1931. Instr. French, Harvard, 1930-31, Columbia, 1931-37, asst. prof., 1937-45, asso. prof., 1945-48, prof. French, 1948-68, Blanche Knopf prof. French, 1968, chairman of the department of French, 1958-63. Board trustees, 2d v.p. French Institute. Served as chief of French sect. with O.S.S., Washington, London, Paris, Washington, Feb. 1943-Oct. 1945; capt. to lt. col., U.S. Army, 1943-45. Decorated Legion of Merit, Croix de Guerre with palm, Chevalier Legion of Honor (France), Order of the British Empire (Great Britain). Awarded Denyse Clairouin prize, 1947; Medalle d'Or du Rayonnement Francais, French Acad., 1965. Fellow John Guggenheim Found., 1943. Mem. Modern Lang. Assn. (exec. council, 1952-55), Societe des Amis d' Andre Gide (v.p. 1968), Phi Beta Kappa, Council on Fgn. Relations. Club: University (N.Y.). Author: The Novel of Adolescence in France, 1937; Portrait of Andre Gide, 1953; Index detaille des Oeuvres completes d' Andre Gide, 1953; French Literary Horizon, 1967. Editor, translator, The Journals of Andre Gide, 4 vols., 1947-51, The Maxims of Marcel Proust, 1948, Madeleine (by Andre Gide), 1952; The Myth of Sisyphus (by Albert Camus), 1955; The Fall (by Albert Camus), 1957; Exile and the Kingdom (by Albert Camus), 1958; From the N.R.F., 1958; So Be It (by Andre Gide), 1959; Pretexts (by Andre Gide), 1959; The Possessed, Caligula (both books by Albert Camus), 1960; Resistance, Rebellion and Death (by Albert Camus), 1961; Altona (by Jean-Paul Sartre), 1961; contributor to the Columbia Dictionary of Modern European Lit., 1947; mem. editorial bd. The Romanic Review (sec. 1937-41; gen. editor, 1954-61, mem. editorial bd.); contbr. articles to various periodicals. Home: New York City NY Died Dec. 7, 1968.

O'BRIEN, LEO FREDERICK, lawyer; b. Galesburg, Ill., June 26, 1924; s. Fred and Charlotte F. (Reavy) O'B.; student Knox Coll., 1943-47, U. Conn., 1943-44, U. Nancy (France), 1946; LL.B., U. Ill., 1950; m. Yvonne B. Uhlman, June 14, 1947; children—Kathleen D., John F., Nancy P., Paula Megan. Admitted to Ill. bar, 1950, since practiced in Galesburg; partner O'Brien & O'Brien, 1950-65; asst. atty. gen. Ill., 1960-64; sr. partner O'Brien & Stoffel, 1965-68; mem. Ill. Ho. of Reps., 1964-68. Knox County supt. Vets. Relief Commn., 1956-57. Served with inf. AUS, 1943-46; ETO. Decorated Combat Inf. Badge. Mem. Am. Legion, V.F.W., Ill., Knox County bar assns. Elk. Home: Galesburg IL Died Mar. 21, 1968.

O'BRIEN, SARA REDEMPTA, teacher; b. at Springfield, Mass.; d. Thomas and Mary Theresa (O'Donnell) O.; grad. Springfield High Sch., 1895, Springfield Normal Training Sch., 1896; studied Columbia. Teacher primary grades since 1896. Took charge of Italian immigrants in pub. evening sch., 1903; introduced and established method of teaching English to foreigners by use of objective illustration. Mem. Springfield Teachers' Club. Roman Catholic. Author: English for Foreigners, 1909. Address: 942 State St., Springfield MA‡

O'BRIEN, THOMAS GEORGE, b. Geneseo, N.Y., Oct. 28, 1874; s. Thomas and Julia (Milan) O'B.; grad. Geneseo Normal Sch., 1908, Rochester (N.Y.) Business Inst., 1901; m. Mary C. Guy, Jan. 4, 1908; children—Guy Edward, Mary Elizabeth, Thomas George. Teacher pub. schs., Cuylerville, N.Y., 1898-1901; mem. faculty Drake Business Coll., Jersey City, N.J., 1901, prin., 1902-05, v.p., 1905-25 (sent to N.Y. City, 1907, to organize Drake Business Sch., of which 8 have been established), pres. since 1925. Pres. Business Edn. Assn. of State of N.Y., 1935-36; treasurer National Association Business Schs., 1943-44. Mem. Gregg Teachers Assn. (pres. 1926). Brooklyn Chamber Commerce. Democrat. Roman Catholic. Clubs: Kiwanis (pres. 1931; lt. gov. div. 1, 1933). Home: 57 Prospect St., Jersey City, N.J. Office: 154 Nassau St., New York NY‡

O'BRIEN, WILLIAM CLAIRE, lawyer; b. Aurora, Ill., Aug. 23, 1904; s. William J. and Mable (Burns) O'B.; A.B., U. Ill., 1926, LL.B., 1927; m. Dorothy Ward, Nov. 26, 1936; children—Ward J., Alberta. Admitted to Ill. bar, 1927, since practiced in Aurora; partner firm O'Brien, Burnell, Puckett and Barnett, 1953-71. Dir. Carl W. Linder Co. Pres. bar officers conf. Ill. Bd. Bar Examiners; vice chmn. Nat. Conf. Bar Examiners; adv. counsel Naval Affairs. Chmn. Aurora chpt. Am. Cancer Soc. Fellow Am. Bar Found.; mem. Am., Ill. (chmn. negligence sect.). Kane County bar assns., Internat. Acad. Trial Lawyers, Am. Coll. Trial Lawyers, Fedn. Ins. Counsel. Republican. Roman Catholic. Elk (past exalted ruler). Club: Aurora Country (pres.). Home: Aurora IL Died Feb. 21, 1971.

O'BRYNE, MICHAEL EDWARD, JR., mfg. co. exec.; b. Baltic, Mich., Nov. 20, 1911; s. Edward and Alice (McKendrick) O'B.; ed. pub. schs.; m. Margaret Turner, June 17, 1936; children—Michael Edward, Edward T. (dec.). Accountant, Mont. Power Co., Butte, 1931-41; with Pacific Car and Foundry Co., Renton, Wash., 1947-72, controller, 1953-72, v.p., 1964-72. dir. several affiliated cos. C.P.A., Wash. Mem. Financial Execs. Inst. (pres. Seattle chpt. 1964), Wash. Soc. C.P.A.'s, Nat. Assn. Accountants (pres. Seattle chpt. 1948, nat. bd. dirs. 1954). Elk. Clubs: Wash. Athletic, Queen City Yacht (Seattle). Home: Seattle WA Died Mar. 27, 1972.

O'BYRNE, JOHN J., clergyman, univ. pres.; b. Germantown, Pa., Jan. 28, 1876; s. John J. and Mary (Kelly) O'B.; grad. St. Vincent's Sem., Germantown, 1896. Ordained priest, R.C. Ch., 1900; prof. Latin, St. John's Coll., Brooklyn, N.Y., 1900-04, St. Vincent's Sem., 1904-06, Niagara U., 1906-20, again at St. John's Coll., 1920-26; pres. St. Joseph's Coll., Princeton, N.J., 1926-29; pres. Niagara U. since 1929. Address: Niagara Univ., Niagara Falls NY‡

OCHS, ARTHUR JR., finance co. exec.; b. N.Y.C., Nov. 9, 1919; s. Arthur and Sue (Bloch) O.; B.S. in Econs., U. Pa., 1939. With United Factors Corp., 1939, v.p., 1954-69; former pres. Fiber Producers Credit Assn.; v.p. United Mchts. & Mfrs., Inc., 1967-69. Former mem. Scarsdale Bd. Edn. Vice chmn. bd. dirs. Surprise Lake Camp. Served with mil. intelligence, AUS, 1942-46. Mem. Tau Epsilon Phi (chmn. bd. trustees). Home: Scarsdale NY Died Apr. 5, 1969.

OCHS, CLARENCE L., bus. exec.; chmn. exec. com., dir. Eaton Mfg. Co.; director Oliver Corporation, Nat. Screw Mfg. Co.; Nat. Acme Co. Home: Cleveland OH Deceased.

OCHTMAN, DOROTHY, artist; b. Riverside, Conn., May 8, 1892; d. Leonard and Mina (Fonda) Ochtman; A.B., Smith Coll., 1914; grad. study Bryn Mawr (Pa.) Coll.; art edn., Nat. Acad. Design, N.Y. City, 1916-19; pupil of father; Guggenheim fellow, European study, 1927-28; m. William A. Del Mar, Jan. 20, 1945. Recipient of numerous awards and prizes, latest being, 1st prize Greenwich Soc. Artists, 1947, 51; Hooker prize and Best in Show, Greenwich Art Soc., 1960. A.N.A., 1929. Mem. Nat. Assn. Women Artists (Medal of Honor, 1952), Allied Artists Am., Grand Central Art Galleries, Audubon Artists, Greenwich Art Society, also Hudson Valley Art Assn. Republican. Conglist. Club: National Arts. Home: Greenwich CT Died Apr. 26, 1971.

O'CONNELL, DESMOND HENRY, mgmt. cons.; b. N.Y.C., Apr. 20, 1906; s. Charles D. and Mary (Grout) O'C.; B.S., U.S. Mil. Acad. 1928; m. Rosemary McGough, May 25, 1935; children—Desmond Henry, Gerald Francis, Timothy Edward. Engr., credit man Gen. Motors Corp., 1929-33; asst. code administr., examiner NRA, NLRB, 1934-38; supr. employee relations S. H. Kress & Co., 1938-47; cons. labor relations, 1947-50; dir. indsl. relations Am. Bakeries Co., Chgo., 1950-56, v.p., 1956-61, dir., 1957-69, exec. v.p., 1961, pres., 1961-68, chmn. bd., chief exec. officer, 1963-68, cons., 1969-73; dir. Upper Av. Nat. Bank, Chgo. Served form 1st lt. to maj., USAAF, 1942-45. Mem. Am. Bakers Assn. (gov.), Mil. Order Loyal Legion, Newcomen Soc., Roman Catholic. Clubs: Westmoreland Country; Chicago Athletic Assn. Home: Hollywood FL Died Feb. 12, 1973.

O'CONNELL, JOHN HENRY, pub. relations exec.; b. Morton, Pa., Feb. 22, 1915; s. Bernard J. and Anne (Donaghy) O'C.; student evening sch. finance, U. Pa.; m. Moira A. Scanlon, Aug. 3, 1940; children—John Henry, Lawrence S., Mark B., Moira A. Various editorial positions Phila. Evening Pub. Ledger, 1934-42; pub. relations exec. Curtiss-Wright Corp., 1942-48; pub. relations dir. Daystrom, Inc., 1948-51; vice pres. Hill & Knowlton, Inc., N.Y.C., 1951-62, sr. v.p., 1962-67, exec. v.p., 1967-71, vice chmn. bd., 1971-72, also dir.; sr. v.p. H&K Marketing Services Corp., 1965-72. Exec. sec. Newsprint Information Com., from 1957. Dir. Summit-Cooper Avenues Association, Montclair, New Jersey, 1956-61, president from 1956-59. Mem. Cardinal's Committee of Laity, N.Y.C., from 1959. Dir. A.R.C., Montclair N.J. chpt., 1956-60, vice chmn., 1959-60. Member Public Relations Soc. of Am. (dir. N.Y. chapter 1959-60), Stockholder Relations Soc.

N.Y. (charter mem.). Club: Glen Ridge Country (N.J.). Home: Upper Montclair NJ Died July 13, 1972; buried Holy Cross Cemetery, Yeadon PA

O'CONNOR, BASIL, lawyer; b. Taunton, Mass., Jan. 8, 1892; s. Daniel B. and Elizabeth A. (O'Gorman) O'C.; B.A., Dartmouth, 1912, LL.D., 1946; LL.B., Harvard, 1915; LL.D., St. John's University, 1941, Blackburn College, 1941, Emory University, 1952, St. Lawrence College, 1954; H.H.D., College of Wooster, 1948, Tuskegee Inst., 1956; LL.D., National U. Ireland, 1958, Baylor U. Coll. Medicine, 1959, U. Mich., 1959, Roosevelt U., 1964; m. Elvira Miller, Aug. 31, 1918 (dec. 1955); children—Bettyann (Mrs. Sidney Culver) (dec.), Sheelagh (dec.); m. 2d, Hazel Royall, 1957. With Cravath & Henderson, New York City, 1915-16; admitted to Massachusetts bar, 1915, New York bar, 1916; with Streeter & Holmes, Boston, Mass., 1916-19; in practice under own name, 1919-24; formed partnership with Franklin D. Roosevelt as Roosevelt & O'Connor, 1925, continuing until Roosevelt assumed office of Pres. of U.S. in 1933; now sr. partner O'Connor & Farber. Pres. Am. Nat. Red Cross, 1944-49; chmn. bd. govs., League of Red Cross Soc., 1946-50; pres. Nat. Found., Ga. Warm Springs Foundation; trustee Salk Inst. Biol. Studies; past chmn. trustees Tuskegee Inst.; hon. trustee Social Legislation Information Service; past pres. Nat. Health Council. Mem. Com. on Character and Fitness, 1st Judicial Dept., New York, 1932-58; president American National Council for Health Edn. Pub., 1957-59. Past president national citizens committee WHO, Inc.; president Internat. Medical Congress. Decorated Medal of Merit (U.S.); Gold Medal National Institute Social Sciences; Grand Cross Order of Honor and Merit Cuban Red Cross Society, Carlos Findlay Decoration (Cuba); Comdr. Legion of Honor, Medal of honor with Palm of Vermeil, Fr. Red Cross Soc. (Fr.); Belgian Red Cross Medal, 1st Class, Comdr. Order of Crown (Belgium); Bulgarian Gold Red Cross Medal; King Christian Red Cross Medal, Comdrs. Cross (Denmark); Silver Medal Greek Red Cross, Cross Grand Comdr. Royal Order of Phoenix; Badge of Honor, Norwegian Red Cross Soc., Comdr. with Star Royal Order St. Olav (Norway); Silver Medal Red Cross (Venezuela); Cross of Merit Italian Red Cross; Grand Officer Order Orange-Nassau (Netherlands); Associate Knight of Venerable Order of Hospital of St. John of Jerusalem; Order of Star (Rumania); Cross of Merit (Finland); Royal Medal of Swedish Red Cross in Gold (only American thus honored); Cross of Distinction, Brazilian Red Cross; Star of Italian Solidarity; Distinguished Service Gold Key of American Congress of Physical Medicine; Lasker award Am. Pub. Health Assn., 1958; Distinguished Service award Internat. Fund Raising Assn., 1965; Silver Buffalo award Boy Scouts of Am., 1966. Fellow American Assn. Advancement of Sci.; mem. (life) Am. bar assns., N.Y. State bar assn., N.Y. Co. Lawyers' Association, Assn. Bar City New York, Harvard Law Sch. Association of N.Y. City, New Eng. Soc., National Inst., Social Scis., Am. Phys. Therapy Assn. (hon.), N.Y. Acad. Scis., Royal Soc. Health, Sigma Phi Epsilon. Democrat. Clubs: Harvard, Bankers, Dartmouth, Lawyers, Cloud, Sky. Home: New York City NY Died Mar. 9, 1972.

O'CONNOR, BERNARD FRANCIS, university prof.; b. ex Lettres, U. of France, 1874; fellow Johns Hopkins, 1880-2, Ph.D., 1883. Instr. French, 1885-91, lecturer Norman French, 1890-1, adj. prof. Romance langs., 1891-4, Columbia. Editor: Choix de Contes Contemporains. Clubs: New York Athletic, Authors, New York Yacht (New York), Manufacturers' (Phila.). Address: 11 Broadway, New York‡

O'CONNOR, DENIS S., physician; b. Biddeford, Me., July 31, 1893; s. Maurice L. and Hanorah M. (Murphy) O'C.; M.D., Bowdoin Coll., 1919; m. Lillian K. Hodson, Oct. 29, 1930. Orthopaedic house officer Mass. Gen. Hosp., Boston, 1924-25; grad. course in orthopaedic surgery Harvard, 1924-26; intern Children's Hosp., Boston, 1925; attending orthopaedic surgeon Yale-New Haven Hosp.; cons. orthopaedic surgeon Griffin Hosp., Derby, Conn., Meriden (Conn.) Hosp., Stamford (Conn.) Hosp., Waterbury (Conn.) Hosp., St. Charles Children's Hosp., Grace-New Haven Community Hosp., New Haven Area Rehab., Inc., Hosp of St. Raphael, New Haven; clin. prof. orthopaedic surgery Yale Med. Sch. Served to capt. M.C., U.S. Navy. Diplomate Am. Bd. Orthopaedic Surgery. Fellow A.C.S.; mem. A.M.A., Am. Acad. Orthopaedic Surgeons, Ar. Rheumatism Assn., Nat. Rehab. Assn. Home: New Haven CT Died May 29, 1971; buried New St. Joseph's Cemetery, Waterbury CT

O'CONNOR, EDWIN, writer; b. Providence, July 29, 1918; s. John Vincent and Mary (Greene) O'C.; A.B., University of Notre Dame, 1939; m. to Veniette Weil, Aug, 1962. Radio broadcaster, Providence, Hartford, Buffalo and West Palm Beach, 1940-42; writer, producer radio sta. WNAC, Boston, 1945-46; free lance writer, 1946-68; author short stories, articles pub. Life, Yale Rev., Atlantic Monthly. Served with USCGR, 1942-45. Author: The Oracle, 1951; The Last Hurrah (Atlantic Monthly prize novel), 1956; The Edge of Sadness (1962 Pulitzer prize), 1961; Official Secret, 1961; I Was Dancing, 1964; All In The Family, 1966. Home: Boston MA Died Mar. 1968.

O'CONNOR, EVANGELINE M., author; b. Rochester, N.Y.; d. Reuben and Almira (Alexander) Johnson; grad. Rochester Free Acad.; m. Rochester, Joseph O'Connor, Nov. 20, 1877; 1 dau., Evelyn. Mgr. State Industrial Sch., Rochester, 1900-09. Translator: Flamini's History of Italian Literature; also other books from German and Italian. Occasional contbr. to periodicals and books of reference, including Famous Names in Fiction, 1908. Home: (summer) Stonington, Conn.; (winter) The Grosvenor, 35 5th Av., New York NY‡

O'CONNOR, JAMES FREDERICK, newspaper exec.; b. Weymouth, Mass., Oct. 1, 1902; s. William F. and Mary (Moore) O'C.; student Boston U., 1920-21, Columbia, 1922-23; m. Betty Louise Allers, Dec. 11, 1951; children—Patricia (Mrs. John H. McLain), Laurie, Margaret. Advt. salesman N.Y. Herald, 1921-28; advt. exec. Buffalo Times, 1928-31; advt. exec. N.Y. World Telegram, 1931-34; advt. exec. Pitts. Post Gazette, 1934-44, circulation dir., 1945-46, bus. mgr., 1948-71, v.p., 1959-71, sec.-treas., 1970-71; dir. P.G. Pub. Co. Bd. dirs. Better Bus. Bur. Mem. exec. bd. Pitts. Conv. Bur. Mem. Pitts. Personnel Assn., Pa. Newspaper Pubs. Assn. Lion. Clubs: Variety, South Hills Country (Pitts.). Home: Pittsburgh PA Died Dec. 11, 1971.

O'CONNOR, JOHN LAWRENCE, educator; b. Troy, N.Y., Sept. 5, 1875; s. John and Mary V. (O'Brien) O'C.; ed. pub. schs.; m. Frances Brazil, Aug. 21, 1908 (dec). Founder, 1902, since 1906 sec. and treas. New York Elec. Trade Sch. Democrat. Catholic. Elk. Author: History of the Kentucky Derby, 1921; Biographical Sketch of John Stuart Skinner, 1924; Breeding and Racing in Provincial Carolina (with Fairfax Harrison), 1931; The DeLancey Stud—Chronicle of Horsebreeding in Northern Colonies (1632-1783), 1932; Racing in America, 1665-1865 (with John L. Hervey); The Western Horseman; also Notes on the Throughbred from Kentucky Newspapers. Contbr. to The Throughbred Record, The Blood Horse, Maryland Horse. Home: Schuylerville, N.Y.; also 1803 Seventh Av., Troy NY‡

O'CONNOR, ROBERT DANIEL, lawyer; b. Renovo, Pa., Aug. 21, 1924; s. William F. and Irene (Graham) O'C.; B.S., Villanova U., 1948; LL.B., Dickinson Sch. Law, 1950; m. Elizabeth J. Deice, Aug. 6, 1948; children—William F., Robert D., Kathleen M. Admitted to Pa. bar, 1951, since practiced in Lock Haven; pvt. practice, 1951-66; sr. partner O'Connor & Saxton, 1966-69. Dist. atty. Clinton County (Pa.), 1956-60. Pres. Clinton County Heart Assn., 1953-56. Served to lt. (j.g.) with USNR, 1943-46. Recipient certificate Merit, Am. Heart Assn. Mem. Clinton County (sec. 1953-67), Am. bar assns., Am. Trial Assn., Am. Judicature Soc., Am. Legion V.F.W. Democrat. Roman Catholic. Elk, Moose, K.C. Home: Lock Haven PA Died Dec. 5, 1969.

O'CONOR, DANIEL JOSEPH, mfg. exec.; b. N.Y. City, Jan. 5, 1882; s. Daniel J. and Katherine (Keller) O.C.; A.B., St. Francis Xavier Coll., N.Y. City, 1903; student Columbia, 1904-06; LL.D., Xavier U., 1955, St. Joseph Coll., married Ruth K. Breuer, 1915 (dec. 1925); children—Daniel J., John F., Mary Helen (Mrs. C.F. Hedges), Gregory T.; m. 2d Rebecca Jane Walker, 1929 (dec. 1945); 1 dau., Rebecca Jane (Mrs. Henry Rollman); m. 3d Dorothy Howland Field, July 28, 1954. Mem. engineering dept. Westinghouse Electric & Mfg. Co., Pittsburgh, 1907-13; co-founder Formica Co., Cincinnati, 1913, pres., gen. mgr., 1934-54; chmn. bd., 1954-56, hon. chmn., from 1956; cons. of laminated plastics, American Cyanamid Co.; dir. emeritus Fifth Third Union Trust Co. Mem. adv. bd. Xavier University, Cincinnati. Club: Queen City (Cin.); Everglades, Bath and Tennis (Palm Beach.). Home: Palm Beach FL Died Dec. 19, 1968; buried Gate of Heaven Cemetery, Hawthorne NY

O'DANIEL, W. LEE, U.S. senator; born at Malta, O., Mar. 11, 1890; s. William Barnes and Alice Ann (Thompson) O'D.; student pub. sch., Arlington, Kan., and business coll., Hutchinson, Kan.; m. Merle Estella Butcher; children—Pat, Mike, Molly. In farming, ranching, flour milling and grain business to 1939; gov. of Tex., 1939-41; elected U.S. Senator from Tex., June 1941 to complete term ending 1943; reelected for term 1943-49. Pres. Ft. Worth C. of C., 1933. Mem. Christian Church (elder Nat. City Christian Ch., Washington, D.C.). Mason (Shriner). Home: Ft Worth TX Died May 1969.

O'DELL, GEORGE EDWARD, lecturer; b. Eng., Nov. 19, 1874; ed. Polytechnic Sch. London; m. Marion M. Chapman. Exec. sec. West London Ethical Society, 1908-13; came to U.S., 1913; field sec. Am. Ethical Union, 1914-17; leader St. Louis Ethical Soc., 1917-18, Grand Rapids (Mich.) Ethical Soc., 1919-23; lecturer for Am. Ethical Union. Founder, 1914, and editor, 1914-17 and since 1927, The Standard. Served with C.E.F. (Toronto Ordnance Depot), 1918-19. Sec. Am. Ethical Union, since 1933. Mem. English Guild Ethical Preachers, Am. Unitarian Assn. (ordained minister), N.Y. Soc. for Ethical Culture (asso. leader since 1944). Author: Public Speaking and Chairmanship, 1911; Some Human Contacts, 1929. Part Author: The Ethical Movement, 1910; Aspects of Ethical Religion, 1926. Home: 1 Clark St., Brooklyn 2, N.Y. Address: 2 W. 64th St., New York NY‡

ODELL, PAUL EDWIN, ry. official; b. Fairhaven, Vt., Apr. 25, 1870; s. Albert and Katherine (McDonough) O.; ed. high sch., Rutland, Vt.; m. Cora I. Baker, of Keene, N.H., Dec. 2, 1891. Began as station helper, Delaware & Hudson Co., at Rutland, 1888; subsequently agt., operator, dispatcher, chief dispatcher, train master, supt., gen. mgr. various rys., U.S. and Mexico; v.p. and gen. mgr. Gulf, Mobile & Northern R.R., 1922-37; retired, 1937. Presbyn. Mason, Elk. Home: 938 17th Av. N., St Petersburg FL‡

ODELL, WILLIAM R., ednl. administrator; b. Brazil, Ind., Aug. 7, 1906; s. Lucien B. and Harriet Emily (DeVol) O.; B.S. U. of Southern Calif., 1927; M.A., Columbia University, 1931, Ph.D.; m. Mildred M. Riffee, Sept. 21, 1927; children—Harriet, William Lucien. Teacher Miami (Ariz.) High Sch., 1927-29; Teachers Coll. fellow, Columbia, 1930-31, instr. and asst. prof., 1931-36; curriculum coordinator, asst. supt. schs. and supt. schs., Oakland (Calif.) Pub. Schs., 1936; prof. edn. Stanford U. Served as lt., C.G. Res., tng. officer Oakland Regt., Port Security Force. Research asst., President Hoover's Nat. Adv. Com. on Edn., 1930. Trustee Mills Coll. and Calif. Soc. Secondary Edn.; dir. Scottish Rite Scaife Scholarship Found.; mem. Citizens' Adv. Com. on Readjustment Edn., State Cal. Mem. Phi Delta Kappa, Kappa Delta Pi, Alpha Kappa Psi. Mason Las Vegas NV Died May 31, 1971; buried Sky Lawn Meml. Park, San Mateo CA

ODENHEIMER, CORDELIA POWELL (MRS. FRANK GILLIAMS ODENHEIMER), b. Leesburg, Loudoun Co., Va.; d. Edward Burr and Cordelia S. (Armstrong) Powell; ed. pvt. schs., Leesburg, Va., and Miss Pegram's and The Misses Hall's schs., Baltimore, Md.; m. Frank Gilliams Odenheimer, of Phila., Pa., Sept. 28, 1887; children—Frank Gilliams, Dorothea Sothoron (dec.). Pres. Md. Div. U.D.C., 7 yrs.; v.p. gen. U.D.C., 1911-13, pres.-gen., 1915-16, reelected, 1916-17; dir. Arlington, Shiloh monuments; mem. Mt. Vernon Chapter D.A.R., Colonial Dames America State of Va., Civil Legion; mem. exec. coop. com. Am. Defense Soc. and woman's sect. of Am. Preparatory Com., also of woman's sect. Navy League; mem. exec. com. Woman's dept. Nat. Civic Federation; mem. com. Nat. Service Sch.; mem. Com. of 100 Women of Nat. Defense World Court League; pres. Polit. Study Club, Washington, 1923-25; pres. Southern Relief Soc., 1925-26. Episcopalian. Author many short stories. Home: The Latrobe. Charles & Read Sts., Baltimore MD‡

ODENWELLER, CHARLES J(OSEPH), JR., govt. ofcl.; b. Cambridge, Mass., Dec. 30, 1903; s. Charles J. and Jennie Elizabeth (Parks) O.; B.S. cum laude, Tufts College, 1926; LL.B., Harvard University, 1929; m. Florence Gosch, May 6, 1933; children—Chariss (Mrs. Harington Southwood-Smith), Parks II, Vicki (Mrs. David R. Millard), Bevan. Admitted Ill. bar, 1929, Ohio bar, 1954, practiced in Chgo., 1929-38; with SEC, 1938-69, head Cleve. office, 1942-61, head corporate reorgn. unit, San Francisco, 1961-69. Mem. Delta Tau Delta. Conglist. Home: Menlo Park CA Died July 25, 1968; buried Alta Mesa Cemetery, Palo Alto CA

ODLAND, MARTIN WENDELL, author, lecturer; b. Meckling, S.D., Jan. 2, 1875; s. Halvor E. and Martha (Dahl) O.; U. of S.D., 1890-96; A.B., U. of Wis., 1898, A.M., 1900; m. Anne S. Nasett, June 22, 1905; 1 son, Wendell A. Teacher pub. schs., Deerfield, De Forest and Madison, Wis., and Minneapolis, Minn., 1898-1904; editor Weekly Wis. State Jour., Madison, 1904-05, Star-Times, Hudson, Wis., 1905-07, Free Press, Fergus Falls, Minn., 1907-21; spl. writer, Minneapolis Tribune and other Minn. newspapers, 1921-28; lecturer, Gen. Extension Div., U. of Minn., 1929-30; exec. sec. to gov. of Minn., 1931-33; investigator for Minn. R.R. and Warehouse Commn., 1933-44. Mem. Minnesota Ho. of Rep., 1917-18. Mem. Minn. Hist. Soc., Norwegian-Am. Hist. Assn. Lutheran. Author: The Saga of the Norsemen in America, 1925; The Life of Knute Nelson, 1926; The Life of Alexander Ramsey, 1927; The New Canaan (hist. novel), 1932; In the Footsteps of Great Americans (lecture and sketches), 1938; Historic Shrines (lecture and sketches), 1942. Lecturer and writer on hist. subjects.*‡

ODLUM, HORTENSE MCQUARRIE, pres. Bonwit Teller; b. St. George, Utah; d. Hector Allen and Ella (Gardner) McQuarrie; ed. public schools, Provo, Utah; m. Floyd B. Odlum, Apr. 1, 1915 (divorced 1935); children—Stanley, Bruce. Began as adviser to owners of Bonwit Teller, women's apparel store, New York, Jan. 1933, becoming pres., 1934, chmn. bd. Office: New York City NY Died Jan. 12, 1970.

ODOM, FREDERICK MARION, judge; b. Union Parish, La., Apr. 4, 1871; s. James Marion and Sarah (Dean) O.; grad. State Normal Coll., Natchitoches, La., 1894; m. Emma Inez Scogin, Dec. 19, 1905; children—Emily Dean, Frederick Marion, Lina Garland, John Scogin. Teacher, pub. schs., Morehouse Parish, La., 1894-99; prin. high sch., Bastrop, La.,

1898-99; admitted to La. bar, 1899, and began practice at Bastrop, 1900; dist. atty. of 6th Judicial Dist. of La., 1908-18; judge Dist. Court, 6th Dist., 1918-24; judge Circuit Court of Appeal, 1924-30; justice Supreme Court of La. since 1930 for term expiring 1944. Democrat. Missionary Bapt. Mason (32 deg.), K.P. Clubs: New Orleans Country, Boston. Home: Bastrop, La. Office: 4 Rosa Park, New Orleans LA‡

O'DONNELL, EMMETT, JR., ret. air force officer; b. Bklyn., Sept. 15, 1906; s. Emmett and Veronica (Tobin) O'D.; B.S., U.S. Mil. Acad., 1928; grad. Air Corps Primary Flying Sch., 1929, Advanced Flying Sch., pursuit course, 1930; Tactical Sch., 1939; m. Lorraine Muller, Dec. 29, 1930; children—Dale Tobin, Patrick Emmett, Terrence. Commd. 2d lt., U.S. Army, 1928, advancing through the grades to general, 1959; dir. of information U.S. Air Forces, 1946-Sept. 29, 1947; dep. dir. pub. relations, Office Sec. Air Force, Sept. 30, 1947-Jan. 1948; steering and coordinating mil. mem. Permanent Joint Bd. on Defense, Can.-U.S. Defense Com., Jan. 1948-Sept. 1948; Air Force mem. Joint Brazil-U.S. Defense Com., Mex.-U.S. Defense Com.; comdg. gen. 15th Air Force, March Air Force Base, 1948-53; also Comdg. Gen. Far East Air Force Bomber Command. Korean Conflict, 1950-51; dep. chief of staff of personnel Hdqrs. USAF, Washington, 1953-59; comdr. in chief Pacific Air Forces, 1959-63, ret.; pres. USO, from 1964; asso. Marx Co. N.Y. Marriott Corp., Washington, Bunker Ramo Corp., Martin Marietta Corp. Member of the board of visitors U.S. Air Force Academy. Decorated D.S.M., D.S.C., Distinguished Flying Cross with 3 oak leaf clusters, Air Medal with oak leaf cluster, Legion of Merit, Presdl. Citation with oak leaf cluster, Silver Star, Korean Service and U.N. medals, Companion of the Bath (Eng.), Asiatic Theatre Ribbon with 4 campaign stars. Clubs: Burning Tree, Army-Navy (Washington), Sky (N.Y.C.). Home: McLean VA Died Dec. 26, 1971; buried U.S. Air Force Acad. Cemetery, Colorado Springs CO

O'DONOGHUE, DANIEL W., judge; b. 1876; LL.D., Georgetown U., 1920. Associate justice Supreme Court Dist. of Columbia. Home: 2303 California St. N.W. Office: Court House, Washington DC*‡

OEHLERT, LEWIS H., lawyer; b. Sheffield, Ia., Aug. 17, 1902; s. Charles and Emma (Nolte) O.; B.A., U. Ia. 1925; LL.B., U. Minn.; 1929; m. Julia T. Gilbertson, Dec. 24, 1929. Admitted to N.D. bar; practice in Fargo, 1929-70; partner firm Nilles, Oehlert, Hansen, Selbo & Magill. Pres. Fargo YMCA, 1937, Greater Fargo Assn., 1946, 47; dir. Florence Crittenton Home. Fellow Am. Bar Found., Am. Coll. Trial Lawyers; mem. Am. Cass County bar assns., State Bar Assn. N.D. (pres. 1961-62), Fargo C. of C. (dir.) Methodist (trustee). Mason (Shriner). Home: Fargo ND Died Dec. 8, 1971; buried Riverside Cemetery, Fargo ND

OERTEL, HORST, pathologist; b. Oberlossnitz by Dresden, Saxony, Jan. 25, 1873; s. Col. Julius and Evelyn (Lossmitzer) O.; ed. gymnasia in Plauen and Meissen, Saxony; M.D., Yale, 1894; univs. of Berlin, Leipzig, and Wurzburg, 1894-98; unmarried. Instr. pathology, New York U., 1898-1903; demonstrator pathol. anatomy, Coll. Phys. and Surgs. (Columbia U.), 1903-07; dir. Russell Sage Inst. Pathology, New York, 1907-12; pathologist to City Hosp., New York, 1903-11; research in Guys Hosp., London, 1913-14; asso. prof. pathology, McGill U., and pathologist to Royal Victoria Hosp., Montreal, 1914-19; Strathcona prof. pathology, dir. Pathol. Inst. McGill U., and pathologist in chief to Royal Victoria Hosp., Montreal, 1919-38. Mem. Soc. Am. Pathologist and Bacteriologists, Pathol. Soc. of Great Britain and Ireland, German Pathol. Soc., Soc. for Exptl. Med. and Biol., New York Pathol. Soc., New York Acad. Medicine, Harvey Soc. Author: The Anatomic Histological Processes of Bright's Disease, 1910; General Pathology, 1921; The Morphological Fluidity of the Human Organism and Its Relation to the Normal Cycle of Human Life and to Disease, 1923; Outlines of Pathology in Their Historical, Philosophical and Scientific Foundations, 1927; The Innervation of Cancers, 4 edits., 1928-31; The Special Pathological Anatomy of the Circulatory, Respiratory, Renal and Digestive Systems, 1938; also many papers on pathol. anatomy, chiefly cancer, diseases of the liver and kidneys, and on the relationship of age period and tissue regression and progression to disease. Address: care Devonshire Club, London England*‡

OFFUTT, THIEMANN SCOTT, judge; b. Montgomery Co., Md., June 12, 1872; s. William Scott and Henrietta I. H. (Baker) O.; University of Virginia, 1891-92; LL.D., St. Johns College; m. Lydia Traill Yellott, of Towson, Maryland, Oct. 20, 1903; children—John Yellott, Thiemann Scott, Mary Traill. Began practice at Towson, 1898; formerly counsel to Bd. of Co. Commrs. of Baltimore Co.; apptd. chief judge 3d Jud. Circuit of Md., and mem. Court of Appeals of Md., for term ending Nov. 30, 1921, elected for term ending Dec. 1, 1936. Formerly mem. Judicial Council of Md. Active in war work; chmn. soldiers and sailors memorial com. of Md. Bar Assn.; mem. advisory com. on selection of legal advisory bds.; etc. Mem. Am. Bar Assn. (pres. of judicial section, 1927-28, also mem. gen.

council same), Md. Bar Assn. (pres. 1923-24), Am. Law Inst., Md. Soc. S.A.R. (pres.), Md. Tercentenary Com. Democrat. Episcopalian. Mason, Elk. Clubs: Lawyers Round Table, Maryland, Elkridge Country. Author: (with Walter L. Clark) Civil Rights of Soldiers and Sailors (pub. by Md. Council of Defense); Offutt's Code of Baltimore Co.; also various published addresses. Compiler Baltimore County Code, 1915. Home: Towson MD‡

O'FLAHERTY, HAL, newspaper corr.; b. What Cheer, Ia., July 8, 1890; s. Peter M. and Lavina (Flathers) O'F.; ed. Des Moines (Ia.) schs.; grad. U.S. School of Military Aeronautics, U. of Ill., 1918; m. Sabine Siebel Smith, May 8, 1919; children—Barry, Sheila. Began as reporter, Des Moines Capital, 1909; bureau mgr. United Press, Omaha, 1912-13; legislative corr., Albany, N.Y., 1915; corr. on Mexican border, 1916; foreign corr. United Press, 1916; London corr. New York Sun, 1917, 19; corr. Chicago Daily News in Scandinavia and the Baltic states, Dec. 1919-22, London corr., 1922, European mgr., 1924, fgn. editor of same, 1926, asst. mng. editor, 1932, managing editor, 1936, then dir. fgn. news service, ret., 1972. War correspondent in Pacific theaters, 1943. Covered Salamaua campaign; Kwajalein, Eniwetok, Emirau landings. Director Foreign Service, 1945. Enlisted in U.S. Air Service, December 1917; trained as pilot at Eberts Field, Lonoke, Ark., and commd. 2d lt.; lt. comdr. U.S.N.R., 1941. Home: Carmell Valley CA Died Dec. 24, 1972.

O'FLANAGAN, DERMOT, bishop; b. Lahinch, Ireland, Mar. 9, 1901; s. Joseph James and Caroline (Coyne) O'F.; student Belvedere Coll., Dublin, Ireland, 1907-17, St. Ignatius Coll., Valkenburg, Holland, 1926-30; LL.D., Carroll College, Helena, Mont., 1960. Came to U.S., 1932, naturalized, 1943. Ordained priest Roman Cath. Ch., 1929; pastor Holy Family Ch., Anchorage, Alaska, 1933-51; apptd. vicar del. Mil. Ordinariate, Ty. Alaska, Yukon, Dist. Mackenzie, 1947-66; apptd. first bishop Diocese of Juneau, 1951. Home: Juneau AK Died Jan. 1973.

O'GARA, ALFRED, investment banker, mfg. exec.; b. Chgo., June 5, 1893; s. Thomas J. and Mae V. (Brady) O'G.; A.B., Yale, 1915; m. Elizabeth Carpenter, May 10, 1933; 1 son, Gordon Carpenter. With O'Gara Coal Co., 1915-17; asso. Thomson & McKinnon, 1920-32; partner Harrison, O'Gara & Co., 1932-38, Alfred O'Gara &Co., 1938-67; chmn., chief executive officer Serrick Corp., 1948-60; director of Defiance Industries, 1960-65. Chairman Chgo. Businessmen's Com., 1946-52; v.p. Rep. Citizens Finance Com., 1947-49, mem. exec. bd., 1947-55; v.p., mem. exec. bd. United Rep. Fund of Illinois, from 1955, gen. campaign chmn. Met. Chgo., 1956; chmn. Cook County Citizens Com. on Financing County Expressways, 1952-54. Trustee Foundation Study of Treaty Law, 1953-54; mem. Nat. Council Metropolitan Opera, N.Y.C., from 1955; bd. dirs., exec. com. Lyric Opera, Chicago, from 1957, chmn. planning com., 1957-60, vice pres., from 1961. Served with M.I., U.S. Army, World War I. Republican. Clubs: Racquet, Saddle and Cycle, Casino, Chicago, Shoreacres (Chgo.); Metropolitan (N.Y.C.). Home: Chicago IL Died Nov. 26, 1968.

O'GARA, CUTHBERT MARTIN, bishop; b. Ottawa, Can., Apr. 1, 1886; s. Martin and Margaret (Bowes) O'G.; M.A., LL.D., Ottawa U.; D.D., St. Michael's Monastery, N.J. Ordained priest Roman Cath. Ch., 1915; lectr. sacred theology, St. Michael's Monastery, Union City, N.J., 1915-24; dir. seminary Shenchow, Hunan, China, 1925-30, prefect apostolic, 1930-34; bishop of Yuanling, Hunan, China, from 1934. Address: Union City NJ Died May 1968.

O'GARA, JOHN EDWARD, govt. official; b. Hanover, N.H., July 8, 1895; s. Edward David and Margaret (Hayes) O'G.; B.S., Dartmouth, 1918; M.C.S., 1920; m. Adele Dreger, Sept. 15, 1925; m. 2d, Lucille Vachon. Prodn. planning, Nashua (N.H.) Gummed & Coated Paper Co., 1920-22; asso. with Macy's New York (unit of R. H. Macy & Co., Inc.) since 1922; management methods dept., 1922-26, delivery supt., 1926-29, asst. personnel dir., 1929-32, asst. gen. mgr., 1932-35, gen. mgr. and exec. vice pres., 1935-42, gen. mgr. and vice pres., 1945-50; numerous posts CIA, 1950-61. Dep. asst. sec. of state for econ. affairs, 1948. Dir. Webster Apts., N.Y., N.Y. Served as ensign (T), U.S. Navy, World War I; as col. U.S. Army, Army Service Force, 1942-44; dep. dir. Office of Strategic Services, 1944-45; col. and comdg. officer 176th Staff and Adminstrn. Group, O.R.C., U.S. Army. Mem. Retail Dry Goods Assn. (mem. exec. com.), Stores Mutual Protective Assn. (pres.), Nat. Urban League (chmn. management adv. com.), Phi Kappa Psi. Clubs: Dartmouth College, Union League (New York); North Hempstead Country, Manhasset Bay Yacht (Long Island, Boca Raton FL Died Mar. 1, 1973.

OGDEN, JAMES MATLOCK, lawyer, university professor; b. Danville, Ind., Apr. 5, 1870; s. Jesse Switzer and Mary Ann (Carter) O.; student Central Normal Coll., Danville, 1890; Ph.B., DePauw U., 1894; LL.B., Harvard, 1899; m. Bess Alice Dean, Nov. 11, 1903; children—Elizabeth Dean (dec.), Mary Ann (Mrs. Ogden Parrish), James M. (deceased), Rural

teacher, 1890-91; prin. Kendallville High Sch., 1894-96; admitted to Ind. bar, 1899, and since practiced at Indianapolis; lectured Ind. Law Sch., 1900-44, pres. 1936-44; prof. Law since Sept. 1944, now in Indianapolis div. of Ind. U. Sch. of Law; city atty., Indianapolis, 1922-24; city corp. counsel, 1924-26; atty. gen. of Indiana for term 1929-33. Supervisor compilation of ordinances City of Indianapolis. Chmn. legislative com. Ind. Municipal League, 1925-26. Mem. exec. com. Indianapolis Ch. Fedn., 1934-38. Chmn. Personnel Bd. of Y.M.C.A. World War. Trustee DePauw U. since 1911; mem. Alumni Bd., De Pauw U., pres., 1918; trustee Y.M.C.A. of Indianapolis (pres. bd. 1920-26; mem. Ind. state com. since 1929). Pres. Nat. Assn. of Attys. Gen., 1933, Internat. Assn. of Attys. Gen., 1933-34. Mem. Am. Bar Assn. (on gen. council 1931-35; v.p. 1934), Ind. State Bar Assn. (pres. 1929-30), Indianapolis Bar Assn. (pres. 1926), Sigma Chi, Delta Chi, Sigma Delta Kappa; honorary member Sigma Phi Kappa Delta. Republican. Methodist (formerly trustee Meridian St. Ch.; state pres. Epworth League (1903). Mason (32 deg.; received Ind. Grand Lodge award 50 yrs. a Mason, 1948). Clubs: Harvard, Lawyers. Author: Ogden's Negotiable Instruments, 1909, 22, 31, 38, 47; Ogden's Manual, 1918, 31; Provision for Atty.'s Fees in Negotiable Instruments, 1942. Contbr. to Cyclo. of Law, Elliott on Evidence, etc.; also articles in legal jours. Portrait presented to Univ. of Ind. on 106th anniversary Ind. Univ. Sch. of Law, by Alumni Assn., 1948. Home: 2801 N. Pennsylvania St. Office: Indiana University School of Law, 102 W. Michigan St., Indianapolis IN‡

OGDEN, ROBERT MORRIS, psychologist; b. Binghamton, N.Y., July 6, 1877; s. James Sherman and Beulah Maria (Carter) O.; B.S., Cornell U., 1901; Ph.D., U. of Wurzburg, 1903; m. Nellie Jouette Dorsey, Sept. 6, 1905; children—Jonathan, Margaret Dorsey, Helen, Mary. Asst. in psychology, U. of Mo., 1903-05; asst. prof. philosophy and psychology, 1905-07, asso. prof., 1907-09, prof., 1909-14, U. of Tenn.; professor psychology, University of Kansas, 1914-16; prof. edn., Cornell University, 1916-39, professor psychology, 1939-45, also dean College of Arts and Sciences, 1923-45, emeritus since 1945. Associate supervisor Summer School of the South, Knoxville, 1911-14; chmn. Cornell summer session, 1919-23. Lecturer on education, Harvard U., 1923. Co-operative editor Psychol. Bull., 1909-29, Am. Jour. of Psychology since 1926. Fellow A.A.A.S. (v.p. Sec. I (psychology), 1936); mem. Am. Psychol. Assn. (sec.-treas. 1913-16, council 1918-20), Southern Soc. Philosophy and Psychology (pres. 1912-13), Assn. Colls. and Univs. of the State of N.Y. (pres. 1938-39), Chi Psi, Sigma Xi, Phi Kappa Phi, Phi Beta Kappa, Phi Delta Kappa. Club: Cornell (New York). Author: An Introduction to General Psychology, 1914; Hearing, 1924; Psychology and Education, 1926, new edit. (with Frank S. Freeman), 1932; The Psychology of Art, 1938. Translator (with Max Meyer): The Problem of Form in Painting and Sculpture (by Adolf Hildebrand), 1907; The Growth of the Mind (by Kurt Koffka), 1924. Contbr. to psychol. and ednl. jours. Address: 215 Dearborn Pl., Ithaca NY‡

OGDON, INA DULEY, writer; b. Rossville, Ill., Apr. 3, 1872; d. William Watson and Lou (Wilson) Duley; student Greer Coll., Hoopeston, Ill., 1892-97; m. James Weston Ogdon, Sept. 2, 1896; 1 son, William Duley. Taught school, 1892-1900; began writing, 1899; has written several hundred texts for hymns, also poems, stories and articles, also literature for girls of high sch. age and articles on the lure of antiques. Republican. Member Disciples of Christ Church. Author of words for Brighten the Corner Where You Are," Jesus Will," You Must Open the Door," Carry Your Cross With a Smile," He Thought of Me,"; series sacred songs and anthems; sacred cantatas The Great Light, " The Christmas Star, " Christ Our Life." Author: (books of verse) A Keepsake from The Old House," Home Woods; Meditations for the Daily Altar; Stories in Rhyme; My Dakota Book. Home: The Old House, R.F.D. 10, West Toledo OH‡

OGILBY, FREDERICK DARLEY, mfg. exec.; b. Elizabeth, N.J., May 20, 1905; s. Frederick Darley and Lena H. (Conover) O.; student Columbia, 1925-26; m. Hilda Daum, Oct. 8, 1938; 1 dau., Margaret Daum. Sales rep. Philco Distbrs., Inc., N.Y. div., 1931-35, sales mgr. Bklyn. div., 1935, N.J. sales mgr., 1936, sales mgr. N.Y. div., 1937, gen. mgr. Phila. div., 1938-45, N.Y. div., 1945-47; sales mgr. radio and television Philco Corp., Phila., 1947-50, v.p., 1950-52, vice president, general manager, 1952, vice president in charge marketing. Member Atlantic Indians Trapshooting Assn. Republican. Lutheran. Clubs: Union League (Phila.); Little Egg Harbor Yacht, Huntingden Valley Country. Home: Rydal PA Died Aug. 1970.

OGLE, ARTHUR HOOK, realtor, banker; b. Belleville, Ill., May 3, 1892; s. Albert Badgley and Ottelia (Rosenbaum) O.; A.B., U. Ill., 1913; m. Ellen Knight, Jan. 30, 1930; children—Jamie (Mrs. Allen Osborne Shafer), Carolyn Bluhm. Editorial staff various St. Louis newspapers, 1913-17; asso. Erwin, Wasey & Co., advt., 1920-24; advt. dir. Wahl Co., 1924-26; mng. dir. Assn. Nat. Advertisers, 1926-29; mdsg. dir. Bauer & Black, 1929-32; partner Needham, Louis & Brorby, 1932-36;

mng. dir. Lauderdale Beach Hotel, 1936-43; v.p., dir. 1st Nat. Bank, Ft. Lauderdale, 1937, then vice chmn.; gen. mgr. Wade Park Manor, Cleve., 1944-46; realtor, Ft. Lauderdale, 1947-72; co-organizer 1st Nat. Bank, Pompano Beach, Fla., pres., dir., 1954-57, chmn., 1957-65; co-organizer, dir. Plantation 1st Nat. Bank, Ft. Lauderdale, Delray Beach Nat. Bank; co-organizer Boca Raton Nat. Bank, dir., 1960-61; co-organizer, dir. 1st Nat. Bank North Broward County, 1962, chmn., 1962-65; pres., dir. Hotel Seacrest Co., Delray Beach, 1954-68. Served as capt. U.S. Army, 1917-19. Mem. C. of C. (past dir.), Ft. Lauderdale Bd. Realtors (past pres.). Rotarian. Clubs: Lauderdale Yacht, 100 Club Broward County. Home: Fort Lauderdale FL Died Sept. 5, 1972.

OGLE, KENNETH NEIL, educator; b. Lake City, Colo., Nov. 27, 1902; s. Wesley Harlan and Luella (Moore) O.; A.B., Colo. Coll., 1925; A.M., Dartmouth, 1927, Ph.D., 1930; Dr. Medicine honoris causa, U. Uppsala, 1962; D.Sc. honoris causa, Colo. Coll., 1963; m. Elizabeth Bartlett, Sept. 18, 1934; children—Betsy (Mrs. Jordan), Nancy (Mrs. Richard F. Brubaker). Teaching fellow U. Minn., 1927-28; research fellow physiol. optics Dartmouth, 1930-34; asst. prof. physiol. optics Dartmouth Eye Inst., 1934-46, prof., 1946-47; staff sect. biophysics Mayo Clinic, Rochester, Minn., 1947-68, research cons. sect. ophthalmology, 1947-68, chmn. sect. biophysics, 1958-68; professor physiol. optics Mayo Grad. Sch. Medicine U. Minn., 1952-68; prof. ophthalmology U. Minn. Med. Sch., 1968; dir. initial phase survey U.S. eye care needs Nat. Inst. Neurol. Diseases and Blindness-Med. Sch. U. Minn., 1968. Member of Am. com. optics and visual physiology A.M.A.; mem. Armed Forces Nat. Research Council vision com.; spl. consultant, U.S. Public Health Service; mem. edn. adv. com. Ednl. Found. in Ophthalmic Optics, Am. Bd. Opticianry; mem. optical aids adv. com. Am. Found. for Blind. Mem. of bd. of directors Rochester Art Center. Recipient Tillyer medal Optical Soc. Am., 1967; Beverly Myers Nelson Achievement award Am. Bd. Opticianry, 1957. Member Biophys. Society, Psychonomic Society, Am. Academy of Ophthalmology and Otolaryngology, Nat. Society Prevention Blindness (mem. com. basic and clin. research), Internat. Acad. of Opticianry (mem. council), A.A.A.S., Am. Assn. for History Medicine, Optical Soc. Am. (asso. editor jour.). Am. Minn. psychol. assns., American Physiological Society, Association for Research Ophthalmology (Proctor medal 1962), Minn. Acad. Sci., Sigma Xi, Pi Kappa Alpha, Gamma Alpha. Rotarian. Author: Researches in Binocular Vision, 1950; Optics-An Introduction for Ophthalmologists, 1961; Oculomoter Imbalance in Binocular Vision and Fixation Disparity, 1967. Asso. editor: Investigative Ophthalmology; hon. editor: Vision Research. Rochester MN Died Feb. 22, 1968; buried Rochester MN

OGLESBY, WILLIAM THOMAS, educator; b. Clarksville, Mo., Sept. 3, 1903; s. Edwin Bright and Frances Lewis (Thomas) O.; B.S., Ore. State U., 1928; D.V.M., Ia. State U., 1931, M.S., 1932; m. Elizabeth Nadene Dreher, June 26, 1932; children—Miriam Elizabeth, Willadene Frances. Teaching fellow vet. physiology, then instr. vet. physiology and anatomy Ia. State U., 1928-32; instr. vet. physiology and pharmacology Mich. State U., 1932-34; faculty La. State U., 1934-67, prof. vet. sci., head dept., 1938-67. Coordinator La. vet. med. tng. program through So. Regional Edn. Bd.; mem. Research Workers Animal Diseases in N.Am. and So. States. Chmn. adv. com. local SSS. Mem. Am. (past chmn. adv. com.), La. vet. med. assns., Assn. Land Grant Colls. and State Univs. (chmn. vet. med. div.), Alpha Zeta, Phi Kappa Phi, Gamma Sigma Delta, Omicron Delta Kappa. Kiwanian. Home: Baton LA Died Apr. 13, 1967; buried Baton Rouge LA

OGOOD, HENRY BROADWELL, b. at Verona, N.Y., Feb. 19, 1869; s. William Broadwell and Martha Ann (Tufts) O.; ed. pub. and pvt. schs., and Eastman Business Coll., Poughkeepsie, N.Y.; m. Jennie E. Beckwith, of Norwich, Conn., June 24, 1896. On father's farm until 1893; with Rau Mfg. Co., Chicago, 1893-7; became identified with the Creamery Package Mfg. Co., 1897, sales mgr., 1903-13, asst. sec. and dir. of sales since 1913. Pres. Bapt. Young People's Union of America since 1916; deacon Englewood Bapt. Ch. Republican. Clubs: Union League, Beverly Country. Home: 9921 Winchester Av. Office: 61-67 Kinzie St., Chicago IL‡

OGSBURY, CHARLES R(EID), mfg. exec.; b. Altamont, N.Y., Feb. 4, 1892; s. Junius D. and Anna (Ostrander) O.; student pub. schs.; m. Mary King; June 2, 1919; 1 dau., Margaret Sothoron (Mrs. MacLester J. Snow). Vice pres. IBM Corp., 1939-41; chmn. dir. Commercial Controls Corp., Rochester, N.Y., 1941-60; vice chmn. bd. Friden, Inc., San Leandro, Cal., from 1956, also dir. Episcopalian. Clubs: Genesee Valley (Rochester, New York). Home: Hillsborough CA Died Aug. 9, 1971; buried Altamont NY

O'HAGAN, ANNE (MISS), journalist; b. Washington, Aug. 8, 1869; d. John and Mary (Fennell) O.; ed. pub. and high schs., Washington; grad. Boston Univ., 1890; active journalist since 1892; did reportorial and editorial work on New York World and Journal, 1892-7. Contb'r fiction, verse and articles since 1897 to mags. Joint Author: Cuba at a Glance, 1898 R7. Address: 158 Waverley Pl., New York‡

O'HANRAHAN, INKA IRENE (MRS. SEAMUS O'HANRAHAN), clin. bioanalyst; b. Warsaw, Poland; d. Hermann and Ala (Eiznerowicz) Winter; student U. Freiburg, Berlin, Germany, 1931-32, U. Berne (Switzerland), 1932; B.A., U. Cal., Berkeley, 1945; m. Seamus O'Hanrahan, 1933; children—Janina (Mrs. Charles Paul), Brigid, Tighe. Came to U.S., 1932, naturalized, 1938. Owner, dir. O'Hanrahan Clin. Lab., San Francisco, 1936-70; lectr. on status of women, 1960-70; vice chmn. bd. dirs. Lab. Services, Inc. Vice chmn. Adv. Commn. on Status of Women, 1965-67. Pres., bd. dirs. Pacific Mus. Soc. Mem. A.A.A.S., U.S. Pub. Health Assn., Soroptimist Fedn. of Americas (pub. affairs chmn.), Nat. Orgn. For Women (nat. sec.-treas.), Bus. and Profl. Women, Am. Assn. U. Women (pres. S.W. chpt.), Guild Psychol. Studies, Cal. Assn. Clin. Labs. (past pres.), Am. Assn. Bionalysts (past nat. bd.), Analytical Psychology Club (past pres.). Club: Soroptimist (past pres. San Francisco). Contbr. articles to profl. jours. Home: San Francisco CA Died Jan. 15, 1970.

O'HARA, BARRATT, congressman; b. St. Joseph, Mich., Apr. 28, 1882; s. Judge Thomas and Mary (Barratt) O'H.; ed. Benton Harbor (Mich.) High Sch., U. of Mo., Northwestern U. Law Sch.; LL.B., Chicago-Kent Coll. of Law, 1912; LL.D., Shorter Coll.-Jackson Seminary, 1962; m. Florence M. Hoffman, Feb. 28, 1906; children—Barratt, Lorence Hoffman, Howard Mears, Florence Frances Louise (dec.). Mem. newspaper editorial staffs, St. Louis and Chicago, 1901-11; lt. gov., Ill., 1913-17 (chmn. Ill. senate vice and wage com. responsible for passage state minimum wage laws, 1913-15); acting gov. at time of S.S. Eastland disaster (Chicago) and as mem. Fed. Bd. of Investigation drafted legislation to prevent similar disasters on Great Lakes; admitted to practice law Supreme Ct. of Ill. and Supreme Ct. of U.S., 1912; spl. asst. corp. counsel in traction reorgn. and subway constrn., 1939-48; mem. 81st to 90th Congresses, 2d Illinois Dist. U.S. delegate 20th General Assembly UN Nightly commentator A.F. of L. radio station, Chicago, 1933-38. Served as corpl., 33d Mich. Vol. Inf., Spanish-Am. War; officer 80th Div., divisional judge adv., 12th and 15th divs., U.S. Army, 1917-18. Awarded medal distinguished mil. service in White, Cuba. Mem. Vets. Fgn. Wars, Am. Legion, United Spanish War Vets. Chgo. Press Vets, Assn., 80th Div. Vets. Assn., Phi Gamma Delta, Phi Delta Phi. Democrat. Author: From Figg to Johnson, 1908; Report of Ill. Senate Vice Commission, 1915; Legislative Compendium (annually), 1925-29; Inside Secrets of Defaulted Real Estate Bonds 1935; Who Made the Constitution? (with Marie Crowe), 1936. Home: Chicago IL Died Aug. 1969.

O'HARA, EDWARD ARTHUR, newspaperman; b. Syracuse, N.Y., Mar. 9, 1888; s. Edward H. and Anna (Hogan) O'H.; student Mercersburg Acad., 1905-07, Princeton U., 1907-11; m. Anna Marie Hannon, Oct. 1, 1913; children—Edward Arthur, Robert George, Mary Grace, Cathaleen Martha (dec.), John Thomas. Successively reporter, editor, advertising solicitor, advertising manager, business manager and gen. mgr. Syracuse Herald, 1911-36, publisher, 1936-39; pub. Syracuse Herald-Journal and Herald-American, 1939-59; pres., dir. Herald Co., 1957-59. Mem. N.Y. State Bd. Mediation. Regent LaMoyne Coll.; chmn. bd. dirs. Sch. Journalism Syracuse U. Mem. Sigma Delta Chi. Republican. Roman Catholic. Clubs: Citizens, Onondaga Golf and Country (Syracuse); Tiger Inn (Princeton U.), Princeton (N.Y.); National Press. Home: Syracuse NY Died May 17, 1972.

O'HARA, ELIOT, painter, author; born Waltham, Mass., June 14, 1890; s. Daniel and Mayfred (Leonard) O'H.; m. Shirley Putnam, Mar. 6, 1924; children—Desmond, Nancy June. Mgr. and pres. O'Hara Dial Co., Waltham, Mass., 1912-28; Guggenheim travel fellow, Europe, Russia, Labrador, 1928-30; founder O'Hara Sch. of Watercolor Painting and Watercolor Gallery, Goose Rocks Beach, Me., 1931; painter in S. America, 1932-33; teacher Telfair Acad., Savannah, Ga., 1933-35, U. of N.C., 1935, Yale Sch. of Architecture, 1935-37, John Herron Inst., Indianapolis, 1937-38, Penn. Mus. Sch. of Indl. Art, Phila., 1938, Norton Sch. of Art, West Palm Beach, 1942, 1945-49; collaborator Ency. Brit. Films, Inc., 1946; producer, dir. many films on painting, from 1949. Served in camouflage sect., United States Navy, 1943-44. Member of the National Academy of Design. Represented in 52 public collections. Author Making Watercolor Behave, 1932; Making the Brush Behave, 1935; Watercolor Fares Forth, 1938; Art Teachers' Primer, 1939; Watercolor at Large, 1946; Water with O'Hara, 1966; co-author: Portraits in the Making, 1948; Watercolor Portraiture, 1949; Watercolor with O'Hara, 1965. Studio: Washington DC Died July 30, 1969.

O'HARA, JOHN (HENRY), author; b. Pottsville, Pa., Jan. 31, 1905; s. Patrick Henry (M.D.) and Katharine Elizabeth (Delaney) O'H.; grad. Niagara Prep. Sch., Niagara Falls, N.Y., 1924; m. Belle Mulford Wylie, Dec. 3, 1937 (dec. Jan. 1954); 1 dau., Wylie Delaney (Mrs. Dennis J. D. Holahan); m. third, Katharine Barnes Bryan, January 31, 1955. Named hon. citizen City of Philadelphia, 1961. Mem. Nat. Inst. Arts and Letters, Loyal Legion (Pa. commandery), The Silurians, Sigma Delta Chi. Clubs: Nat. Golf Links of Am. (Southhampton, L.I., N.Y.); Nassau (Princeton); Field (Quogue, L.I.); Century Assn., The Leash (N.Y.C.); Nat. Press (Washington), Racquet (Phila.); Kew-Teddington Observatory Society, Hessian Relief Society (both Princeton). Author: Appointment in Samarra (novel), 1934; The Doctor's Son and other Stories, 1935; Butterfield 8 (novel), 1935; Hope of Heaven (novel), 1938; Files on Parade (short stories), 1939; Pal Joey (short stories), 1940; Pipe Night (short stories), 1945; Hellbox (short stories), 1947; A Rage to Live (novel), 1949; The Farmers Hotel (novel), 1951; The Searching Sun (play), 1952; Sweet and Sour (essays), 1954; Ten North Frederick (novel), 1955; A Family Party (novella), 1956; From the Terrace (novel), 1958; Ourselves to Know (novel), 1960; Sermons and Soda-Water (3 novellas), 1960; Assembly (short stories), 1961; Five Plays, 1961; The Cape Cod Lighter (short stories), 1962; The Big Laugh (novel), 1962; Elizabeth Appleton (novel), 1963; The Hat on the Bed (short stories), 1963; The Horse Knows the Way (short stories), 1964; The Lockwood Concern (novel), 1965; writer libretto for mus. play Pal Joey, 1940, 52 (winner N.Y. Critics Circle and Donaldson awards, best musical, 1952); (essays) My Turn. 1966; (short stories) Waiting for Winter, 1966; (novel) The Instrument, 1967; And Other Stories (short stories), 1968. Recipient Nat. Book award for Ten North Frederick, 1956; Gold Medal Award of Merit, Am. Acad. Arts and Letters, 1964. Home: Princeton NJ Died Apr. 11, 1970.

O'HARA, WILLIAM L., clergyman, educator; b. New York; grad. Mt. St. Mary's Coll., 1883; entered theol. sem.; ordained priest, 1887; was connected with St. Charles Borromeo's Ch., Brooklyn, N. Y., but in 1888 became prof. logic, Latin and metaphysics at Mt. St. Mary's; elected treas., 1891; v.-p., 1894, and pres., 1897. Address: Emmitsburg MD‡

O'HERN, JENNIE MARGARET (MRS. WILLIAM P. O'HERN), former Dem. Nat. committeewoman; born Chicago, Ill., July 6, 1893; d. Michael Joseph and Jane Francis (Carlin) Keegan; student U. of Chicago, 1912-13; m. William P. O'Hern, Sept. 9, 1914. Stenographer and court reporter for legal firm, Chicago, 1914-16; railroad agent and telegraph operator, Wakpala, S.D., from 1918; Dem. county vice chmn., Corson County, S.D., 1932-36, chmn., 1937-38; S.D. state vice chmn., Dem. State Central Com., 1942; Dem. national committeewoman, 1943-50. Dem. candidate for sec. of state, 1946; del. Dem. Nat. Conv., 1948, 52; sec. S. Dak. Dem. State Cen. Com., 1952. County chmn. Crippled Childrens Hosp. fund drive. State supervisor finance survey Census Bur., 1950-51. Chmn. Indian Welfare of S.D.; chmn. internat. relations, Business and Professional Women's Club, Mobridge, S.D. chapter; mem. National Democratic Woman's Club. Address: Wakpala SD Died Aug. 28, 1970; buried Greenwood Cemetery Mobridge SD

OHL, ROBERT AUSTIN, educator; b. Berwick, Pa., Sept. 17, 1917; s. Ira Franklin and Edna (Cain) O.; B.S., Pa. State Tchrs. Coll., Bloomsburg, 1939; M.A., Columbia, 1947; m. Alice Jean Dallas, Nov. 9, 1945; children—Charles Ira, Robert A. (dec.), Lynn Marie. Tchr. pub. schs., Georgetown, Del., 1947-48, Harrisburg (Pa.) Acad. for Boys, 1948-49; owner photographic studio, Berwick, Pa., 1950-52; indsl. photographer ACF Industries, Inc., 1952-62; asst. prof. Coll. Graphic Arts/Photography, Rochester (N.Y.) Inst. Tech., 1962-67, asso. prof., 1967-70. Vice pres. Greater Rochester Indsl. Photographers, 1968; mem. PSA adv. practices com. to USA Standards Inst. Served with A.C., AUS, 1943-45. Decorated Air medal. Mem. Am. Assn. U. Profs., Profl. Photographers Soc. N.Y., Soc. Reproduction Engrs. Photographic Soc. Am. Republican. Mason. Contbr. articles in field to profl. Rochester NY Died Feb. 23, 1970.

OHLIN, ROY PERCIVAL, lawyer; b. Denver, Mar. 2, 1897; s. Gustave R. and Carolina (Carlson) O.; LL.B., U. Buffalo, 1921; m. Mary E. Martin, Sept. 8, 1926 (dec. Mar. 1960); children—Patricia M. (Mrs. Robert H. Goetz), George R.; m. 2d, Alice M. Ryan, Nov. 8, 1960. Admitted to N.Y. State bar, 1921, since practiced in Buffalo; asst. U.S. atty., 1925-28; sr. partner firm Ohlin, Damon, Morey, Sawyer & Moot, 1963-70. Served with USN, World War I. Fellow Am. Coll. Trial Lawyers, Internat. Acad. Trial Lawyers; mem. Am., N.Y. State, Erie County bar assns., Trial Lawyers Assn. of Erie County (past pres.). La Confrerie de la Chaine des Rotisseurs. Club: Mid-Day. Home: Buffalo NY Deceased.

OHLINGER, GUSTAVUS, lawyer; b. Foochow, China, July 15, 1877; s. Franklin and Bertha S. O. (Am. missionaries); B.A., U. of Mich., 1899, LL.B., 1902, honorary M.A., 1919; Ph.D. (hon.), U. Toledo, 1961; m. to Helen E. Rinehart, 1914; children—John Franklin, Lucy Jane, Mary Alice. Practiced in Shanghai, China, 1903-05, Toledo, O., 1905-62. Captain U.S. Army,

1918, assigned to Military Intelligence Div., Gen. Staff, Washington, D.C. Mem. Toledo Bd. of Edn., 1926-33. Member Phi Beta Kappa fraternity. Unitarian. Contbr. to Atlantic Monthly, Mich. Law Rev., Ency. Americana, etc. Lectr. summer session, Law Sch. U. Mich., 1931-37. Mem. Am. Assn. for UN (bd. govs. 1950-53). Author: Ohlinger's Federal Practice, 8 vols., 1948-54, rev. edit., 1964. Home: Toledo OH Died June 12, 1972; buried Woodlawn Cemetery, Toledo OH

OHLMACHER, JOSEPH CHRISTIAN, pathologist; b. Sycamore, Ill., Oct. 27, 1874; s. Christian John and Gertrude Anna (Sherer) O.; M.D., Rush Med. Coll., Chicago, 1901; m. Florence E. Jayne, Oct. 24, 1910; children—Joseph Philip, William Arthur, Jayne Elizabeth, Gertrude Ann, Albert Edgar. Research student in pathology, Rush Med. Coll., 1899-1901; instr. pathology, Northwestern U. Med. Sch., 1901-02; pathologist and clin. dir. Independence (Ia.) State Hosp., 1902-10; pathologist and asst. supt. Clarinda (Ia.) State Hosp., 1913-18; prof. and head of dept. pathology, Med. Sch., Univ. of S.D. since 1918, dean of Sch. of Med., 1934-46; emeritus prof. since 1948; dir. State Health Lab. of South Dakota since 1918; pathologist Sacred Heart Hosp., Yankton, S.D., since 1923, dir. training med. technologists, since 1948. Member Am. Medical Assn., Am. Public Health Assn., S.D. State Med. Assn., Sioux Valley Med. Soc., S.D. Acad. Science; hon. mem. Woodbury County Med. Assn. Past pres. Sioux Valley Medical Soc., Southwest Iowa Med. Society, Yankton Dist. S.D. State Med. Assn. Republican. Universalist. Mason. Rotarian. Phi Chi. Contbr. on original researches in pathology, bacteriology and serology. Home: 309 Lewis St., Vermilion SD‡

OHLSON, OTTO FREDERICK, ry. official; b. Sperlingsholm, Halland, Sweden, June 6, 1870; s. Otto and Cecelia (Swenson) O.; grad. high sch. in Sweden, 1887; came to America, 1893; m. Marie E. Ricketts, Sept. 1897. Telegraph operator in Sweden, S. America and India, 1887-93; switchman and brakeman Pa. R.R., 1893-1900; with N.P. Ry. as telegraph operator, sta. agent, train dispatcher, chief dispatcher, train master, asst. to gen. supt. and div. supt., 1901-28; gen. mgr. The Alaska R.R. (govt. owned, operated under Dept. of Interior) since 1928. Capt. Engrs., R.C., attending O.T.C., Camp Grant, Ill., 1917; maj. and lt. col. Engr. R.C., A.E.F., Jan. 1918-Dec. 1919; served as terminal supt., div. supt. and gen. supt. in France. Lutheran. Home: Anchorage AK*‡

OHRBACH, NATHAN M., mfg. exec.; b. Vienna, Austria, Aug. 31, 1885; s. Isaac J. and Anna (Dickman) O.; ed. pub. and high schs., New York; m. Mathilda Kane, Feb. 24, 1907; 1 son, Jerome Kane. Began his business career in retail merchandising in 1905; opened his own store in Brooklyn, 1911; est. branch on 14th St., Manhattan, 1923; Newark Store, 1930; Los Angeles Store, 1948; La Mirada, Cal. Store, 1960; chmn. bd. Ohrbach's Inc. until 1965, Ohrtronics, Inc., N.Y.C., 1965-72. Vice pres. Montefiore Hosp.; trustee Fedn. Jewish Charities. Mem. nat. exec. bd. Boy Scouts of Am., general chairman N.Y. annual campaign fund drive, 1945-53. Former mem. Mayor's Mgmt. Survey Com.; former chmn. exec. com. Coop. Retail Tng. Sch. Bus. Civic Adminstrn., City Coll. Decorated Officer French Legion of Honor; Gold Medal of Honor (Republic of Austria); French order of Knight and Companion of Cross of Lorraine; Italian Star of Solidarity; recipient Silver Antelope, Silver Beaver, Silver Buffalo, Boy Scouts Am Eta Mu Pi. Mason. Clubs: Harmonie, City Athletic (N.Y.); Metropolis Country (White Plains, N.Y.). Author: New York City NY Died Nov. 1972.

OJEDA, DON EMILIO DE, Spanish diplomat; began diplomatic career at early age as attache Spanish legation at Peking and later at legation at Rome; apptd. 2d sec. legation in Japan and 3 yrs. later legation at Rome; promoted 1st sec. Spanish Embassy, London, 1880; charge d'affaires in Bolivia and, 1883, minister resident in Montevideo; same to Lima, 1884, and to Athens, 1888; chief polit. sec. foreign office, Madrid, 1889, and chief of the minister's cabinet; promoted minister plenipotentiary in Lima, 1890, to Tangier, 1894; apptd. sec.-gen. to Paris conf. for Treaty of Peace with the U. S.; resumed post in Tangier when treaty was signed; promoted to minister plenipotentiary, 1st class, and apptd. E. E. and M. P. to Washington in June, 1902. Address: Spanish Legation, Washington‡

O'KANE, WALTER COLLINS, entomologist, author; b. Columbus, O., Nov. 10, 1877; s. Henry and Catherine (Van de Water) O'K.; A.B., Ohio State Univ., 1897, A.M., 1909; hon. D.Sc., Ohio State University, 1932; m. Clifford Hetherington, Dec. 30, 1902; children—Elizabeth Wells, Catherine Van de Water, William Henry, Richard Hetherington. In newspaper and mag. work, 1897-1909; circulation mgr. Woman's Home Companion, and Farm and Fireside, Springfield, O., 1900; same, Twentieth Century Farmer, Omaha, Neb., 1901; asst. entomologist, 1909, asso., 1910, entomologist since Sept. 1911, N.H. Exptl. Sta.; prof. of econ. entomology, U. of N.H., 1911-47, prof. emeritus, since 1947. State moth agt., N.H., 1911-13; dep. commr. agr., N.H., 1913-47. Sergt. major, 10th Ohio Regt., Spanish-Am. War. Chairman govs. Crop Protection Inst.; fellow A.A.A.S., Entomol. Soc. America; mem. Am. Assn. Econ. Entomologists (pres. 1919), N.H. Acad. Science (pres. 1924-25), Beta Theta Pi, Sigma Xi, Phi Kappa Phi. Clubs: Authors (New York); Appalachian Mountain; Green Mountain; Authors' (London). Author: Injurious Insects, 1913; Jim and Peggy at Meadowbrook Farm, 1917; Jim and Peggy at Apple-Top Farm, 1923; Trails and Summits of the White Mountains, 1925; Trails and Summits of the Green Mountains, 1926; Trails and Summits of the Adirondacks, 1928. Home: Durham NH‡

O'KEEFE, ANNA (MISS), actress; b. New York; d. Lt.-Col. O'Keefe, 15th N. Y. vol. inf. in Civil war; began career as an amateur in comic opera; joined Casino co. and subsequently sang leading roles with De Wolf Hopper and others.‡

O'KEEFE, DENNIS (EDWARD JAMES FLANAGAN), actor; b. Ft. Madison, Ia., Mar. 29, 1910; s. Edward and Charlotte (Rix) Flanagan; student U. So. Cal., 1932-33; m. Berinde Steffi Duna, Oct. 18, 1940; children—James, Juliana (Mrs. Don Benito). Writer, Our Gang movie series, 1930-31; stunt and doubling actor, 1932-34; bit player, 1933-35; starring appearances in motion pictures; Bad Man of Brimstone, 1937, T-Men, 1947, Story of Doctor Wassell, 1944, Affairs of Susan, 1945, Follow the Sun, 1950, numerous others: TV series, Dennis O'Keefe Show, 1958-59; stock performances in Critics Choice, 1963, The Pleasure of His Company, 1963, That Certain Girl, 1968, others; Broadway appearances in Never Live Over a Pretzel Factory, 1964, Never too Late, 1964-65; author screen plays, screen originals, dir. 3 feature films; dir. films for Pendennis Corp., Europe. Mem. Screen Actors Guild (past dir.). Palm Desert CA Died Aug. 31, 1968; cremated.

OLCOTT, BEN WILSON, ex-governor; b. Keithsburg, Mercer County, Ill., Oct. 15, 1872; s. Hiram Wallace and Mary Jane (Wilson) O.; ed. high sch., Keithsburg; m. Lena O. Hutton, Dec. 25, 1912 (died 1936); children—Chester Wallace (ensign U.S.N., Japanese prisoner since battle of Wake Island), Gordon West (U.S. Army), and Richard Hutton (U.S.A.A.F.) (twins). Went to Ore. at 19, then to B.C., where mined and prospected, later returned to Ill. and was cashier of bank at Keithsburg 6 yrs.; prospector and bank employee in Alaska, 1904-07; returned to Salem, Ore.; apptd. sec. of state by Gov. Oswald West, 1911, and elected to same office, 1912 and 1916; gov. of Ore., 1919-23; pres. Am. Savings Bank, Long Beach, 1923; pres. Union Savings & Loan Assn., Portland, 1927-28; dir. Ore. Mutual Savings Bank. Republican. York Rite Mason, Shriner, Elk. Home: 2610 N.W. Overton St., Portland OR*‡

OLDER, CORA (MIRANDA), author; b. Clyde, N.Y.; d. Peter and Margaret (Sibley) Baggerly; student Syracuse and Stanford univs.; m. Fremont Older, Aug. 22, 1893 (died 1935). Interested in industrial and polit. affairs, prison reform, gardening, and Calif. hist. research. Pres. San Jose Light Opera Company, since 1935. Author: The Socialist and the Prince, 1902; The Giants, 1905; Esther Damon, 1911; When San Jose Was Young, 1916-18; Life of Vasquez, 1919; The Madonna of Monterey (play), 1921; (with Fremont Older) Life of Senator George Hearst; Savages and Saints (novel), 1936; William Randolph Hearst, American (biography), 1936; California Missions and Their Romances, 1938; Love Stories of Old California, 1940. Address: Woodhills Ranch, Cupertino, Santa Clara County CA‡

OLDHAM, LEMUEL E., lawyer; b. Kosciusko, Attala Co., Miss., Feb. 8, 1870; s. Emmett Charles and Malvina Murphy (Doty) O.; ed. U. of Miss. and Eastman Coll. Poughkeepsie, N.Y.; studied law in office of U.S. Dist. Judge H. C. Niles, 1903-06; m. Lida Corinne Allen, of Kosciusko, Miss., June 27, 1895; children—Estelle (wife of Judge C. S. Franklin), Victoria (dec., wife of Paul F. Allen, U.S.A.), Dorothy Zollecoffer, Edward de Graffenried (dec.). Clk. U.S. Circuit Court, Northern Dist. of Miss., 1903-12, and of U.S. Dist. Court, same dist., 1905-18; U.S. commr., 1906-17; U.S. atty., Northern Dist. of Miss., by appmt. of President Harding, since June 23, 1921; mem. law firm of Stone, Oldham, Stone & Stone. Maj. a.d.c. Governor's Staff, Miss. N.G., 1912-16; del. Rep. Nat. Conv., 1920; mem. Rep. Nat. Advisory Com., 1920; mem. Miss. State Rep. Com. Mem. Am., Miss State and Lafayette County bar assns., Miss. Hist. Soc., Sigma Alpha Epsilon. Presbyn. Home: Oxford MS‡

OLEN, WALTER A., truck mfr.; b. nr. Winneconne, Wis., Jan. 31, 1875; s. Andrew and Amelia O.; Teachers Certificate, Oshkosh Normal Sch.; LL.B., Northern Ind. Law Sch., 1900; m. Cora Miller, May 21, 1907; children—Robert A., Donald B., Mildred (Mrs. Dedolph). Tchr. pub. schs. of Winnebago and Shawano (Wis.) Counties; admitted to Wis. bar, 1900, and practiced in Clintonville, 1900-10; aided partners in a machine shop obtain patents on new principle of four wheel drive which they developed; an organizer Four Wheel Drive Auto Co., 1910, pres. and dir. since 1910, gen. mgr., 1913-45, chairman of the board since 1952; director Great Lakes-St. Lawrence Association Member Governors Adv. Com. on Aviation. Mem. Clintonville Park Commn. 30 yrs. Served as mem. Dist. Bd. of Appeal Selective Service, 8th Dist., Wis., Mem. Soc. Automotive Engrs., Am. Road Builders Assn., Wis. Assn. for Disabled, Wis. Hist. Soc., Clintonville County Hosp. Assn. (v.p. and gen. mgr., dir.), C. of C. (an organizer). Mason (32 deg.). Clubs: Rotary, Riverside Golf (Clintonville). Donated personal library of Eben E. Rexford and all the original manuscripts to Public Library of Clintonville. Contbr. technical papers on phases of the automotive industry and on Wis. archaeology in publs. Home: Clintonville, Wis. Office: The Four Wheel Drive Auto Co., Clintonville WI‡

OLIPHANT, CHARLES LAWRENCE, physician; b. Kinsley, Kan., July 30, 1889; s. Hugh Bartus and Alice Mae (Blair) O.; B.S., Valparaiso U., 1913; M.D., St. Louis U., 1917; postgrad. Harvard, 1918, U. Pa., 1929-30; m. Mary Goss Romig, Nov. 29, 1916; children—Charles Romig, M.D., Mary Goss (wife of Robert Fadem, M.D.). Commd. lt. (j.g.), Med. Corps, USN, 1917, promoted through grades to comdr., 1935, retired, 1943, asst. dir. service de-hygiene, Haiti, 1930-34; instr. tropical medicine Women's Med Sch., Phila., 1930-34; instr. hygiene Harvard Med. Sch., 1941; pvt. practice internal medicine, San Diego, Cal., 1943-70; staff Mercy Hosp., Doctor's Hosp., Sharp Meml. Hosp. Fellow Am. Coll. Cardiology; mem. A.M.A., Cal., San Diego County medical societies, Sons Am. Revolution, Nat. Sojourner, Phi Delta, Alpha Epsilon. Republican. Methodist. Mason (32 deg., K.T., Shriner). Charter San Diego CA Died Aug. 8, 1970.

OLIPHANT, HAROLD DUNCAN, newspaper editor; b. Mystic, Conn., Aug. 27, 1882; s. Charles Henry and Sara Curtis (Jennings) O.; prep. edn. Phillips Acad., Andover, Mass., 1896-1900; A.B., Dartmouth Coll., 1907; m. Marjorie Fowler, Sept. 7, 1910; children—Arthur Elwood, Betty. Teacher in private schools, Conn., Pa., Calif., 1907-15; asst. headmaster, Abbott Sch., Farmington, Me., 1915-17; headmaster Portland (Me.) Country Day Sch., 1917-28, St. Luke's Sch., New Canaan, Conn., 1928-29; editor Portland (Me.) Evening News, 1933-35; editorial writer Portland Evening Express, 1935-36; became editor Portland Press-Herald 1936; editor emeritus Guy Gannett Pub. Co. Pres., Portland Players; pres. Council Social Agys., 1933, 54; founder, officer Columbia Concert Series. Bd. dirs. Portland Community Chest, Community Concert Assn.; adv. bd. U. Me.; trustee Waynflete Sch., Portland Jr. Coll.; pres. bd. trustees Portland Public Library. Mem. Am. Soc. Newspaper Editors, English Speaking Union (nat. dir.). Clubs: Fraternity (hon. mem., past pres.), Portland, Portland Country. Independent Republican. Conglist. Contbr. articles and fiction to mags. Home: South Portland ME Died Oct. 18, 1970; buried Methuen MA

OLIVARES, JOSE DE, b. Southern Calif., Nov. 26, 1867; s. Jose and Martha Washington (Gatch) O.; ed. pub. and pvt. schs. of Southern Calif., business coll., Berlitz Sch. of Modern Langs., Liceo de Varones, Guadalajara, Mexico; m. Berta Lillian Owen, Nov. 2, 1896; children—Lenore Constance (dec.), Casper Luis; m. 2d Maria Teresa Ramirez y Jerez, Feb. 15, 1907. Mem. Calif. Nat. Guard, 1884-86; with U.S. Navy, 1886-93; lt. (j.g.) Calif. Naval Reserve, 1894-96; again with U.S. Navy, Spanish-Am. War, 1898, also war corr., Paris Expn. corr., 1900. Official rep. of St. Louis Expn. at Buffalo Expn., 1901; commr. of St. Louis Expn. to Spain, Portugal and Latin-Am. countries, 1902-03; commr. Argentine Republic to St. Louis Expn., 1904. Consul at Managua, Nicaragua, 1906, Madras, India, 1911-14, Hamilton, Ont., 1915-24, Kingston, Jamaica, 1924-29, Leghorn, Italy, 1929-32; retired Nov. 30, 1932. Now private collector fine arts and antiques, specializing in early European masters and meritorious Am. works of past century. Adminstr. Olivares Estate. Mem. Am. Foreign Service Assn., Harding Memorial Assn.; hon. mem. 2d Batt. Green Howards" (A.P.W.O. Yorkshire Regt.), W.I. Reg. and 86th Carnatic Inf. (India) Officers Mess. Two gold medals, St. Louis Expn.; bronze medal for naval service, Spanish-Am. War. Republican. Catholic. Clubs: Giovane Italia, Athletic (Rome). Author: Our Islands and Their People, 1900 (400,000 copies sold 1st 3 yrs.); Parisian Dream City, 1901 (2 edits.). Contbr. short stories and articles to leading publs. Awarded gold medal by U.S. Commn. for his interest and cooperation at Leghorn, in observing the Bicentennial in that city, commemorating the 200th anniversay of the birth of George Washington"; officially commended by Sec. of State Robert Lansing for patriotic spirit, 1917. Home: S. Pasadena, Calif. Address: care Farmers & Merchants National Bank, Main and 4th Sts., Los Angeles CA‡

OLIVE, EDGAR WILLIAM, botanist; b. Lebanon, Ind., Apr. 1, 1870; s. David Henry and Caroline Elizabeth (Lawrence) O.; B.S., Wabash Coll., Crawfordsville, Ind., 1893, M.S., 1895; A.M., Harvard, 1897, Ph.D., 1902; U. of Bonn, Germany, 1903; m. Elizabeth Williams Ristine, of Crawfordsville, Sept. 6, 1898; children—Theodore Ristine, Marian Lawrence. Asst. in botany, Harvard, 1897-98; instr. botany, Harvard and Radcliffe colls., 1898-1903; research asst. of the Carnegie Instn. of Washington at Bonn, 1903-04, U. of Wis., 1904-06; lecturer in botany, U. of Wis., 1905-07; prof. botany, State Coll. of Agr. and Mech.

Arts, Brookings, S.D., and state botanist, 1907-12; curator, Brooklyn Botanic Garden, 1912-20. Fellow A.A.A.S., Bot. Soc. America; mem. Sigma Xi, Phi Beta Kappa, Phi Delta Theta, Am. Phytopathol. Soc. Contbr. chiefly on fungi and fungous diseases of plants. Home: 721 E. 46th St. Office: Chamber of Commerce Bldg., Indianapolis, IN‡

OLIVER, ALLEN LAWS, lawyer; b. Jackson, Mo., Jan. 19, 1886; s. Robert Burett and Marie Elizabeth (Watkins) O.; grad. Southeast Mo. Teachers Coll., summa cum laude, 1901-05; A.B., U. of Mo., 1908, LL.B., 1909; m. Olivia Leachman, Oct. 28, 1913; children—Allen Laws, John Leachman. Admitted to Me. bar, 1909, U.S. Supreme Court bar, 1912; sr. mem. firm Oliver & Oliver, Cape Girardeau, Mo., since 1910; v.p. and treas. Oliver Land & Development Co. Served as major Cadet Corps U. of Mo., 1909; 1st lt. Inf., Mo. Nat. Guard, 1909-13; major Mo. Home Guards, 1917-18; colonel governor's staff, 1937-41; government appeal agent for Cape Girardeau County, World War II. Member State speaker com., Mo. Council of Defense Mo. state v.p. United Service Orgn.; pres. S.E. Mo. Council Boy Scouts Am., 1940-42, trustee of foundation, 1950-—, executive committee, regional representatives national representative, 1952-—, received Silver Beaver award, 1935; president Law Found. Univ. of Mo., 1941-42; pres. Mo. C. of C., 1945-46; mem. com. apptd. by Supreme Ct. of Mo. for adoption of new civil code; appointed by gov., member board visitors, U. of Mo., 1944-45, reapptd., 1946-52 (sec., 1946-52, chmn. bd., 1952-53); bd. of examiners U.S. District Court, Southeastern Division, Eastern District of Mo., 1935-56, mem. bd. dirs. Missouri Good Roads Assn., Inc. Hon. mem. of board Missouri State C. of C. (recipient Distinguished Service plaque 1961). Decorated Red Cross of Constantine; recipient 40 year gold service emblem Boy Scouts Am., 1955; Order of the Coif award U. Mo. Sch. Law, 1959; named Man of the Year S.E. Mo. State Coll., 1962. Fellow Am. Bar Found., Am. Coll. Trial Lawyers; mem. Am. Bar Association (award of merit, 1944) mem. Ho. of Dels. 1945-48 (chmn. com. on unemployment and social security, 1951-57); (committee on drafts), advisory board to Mo. State Resources and Development Commn., 1946-48, Missouri Bar (executive committee 1938-42, president 1943-44, 1952-53, and 59, senior counselor, trustee 1950-—), Cape Girardeau County Bar Assn. (president), American Judicature Society, International Association Insurance Counsel, Missouri Library Association (executive committee 1939-42), S.A.R. (v.p. 1940-41; exec. com. 1941-48; pres. Mo. Soc. 1942-43; pres. gen. nat. soc. 1946-47), U. of Mo. Alumni Assn. (pres. 1940-42; chmn. com. on awards, 1944-48; consulate, 1960; Award of Merit, 1960), Am. Acad. Polit. and Social Sci., Acad. Polit. Science Missouri Bar Foundation (past pres.; trustee). Rotary Internat. (dir. 1938-39; gov. 14th dist. 1935-36; mem. or chmn. various coms. 1936-42), Cape Girardeau. Mo. historical societies, Four Chaplin's Legion of Honor, also Order of Coif, Phi Delta Theta, Phi Delta Phi, Mystical Seven. Mason (K.T.; recipient Certificate of Merit from Grand Commandery, Mo., 1948). Presbyn. Clubs: Rotary (hon.); Cape Girardeau County (trustee 1945-—), Author: The Missouri Bar, 1880-1965, 1965; History of Rotary Club of Cape Girardeau, Missouri 1919-1966. 1967. Home: Cape Girardeau MO Died 1970.

OLIVER, HENRY MADISON, JR., economist; educator; b. Union City, Tenn., Dec. 11, 1912; s. Henry Madison and Agnes (Sullivan) O.; A.B., Southwestern at Memphis, 1934; M.A., Duke, 1936, Ph.D., 1939. Instr. econs. U. Miss., 1937, Duke, 1937-39, Yale, 1939-41; asso. economist Nat. Resources Planning Bd., 1941; Econ. analyst Treasury Dept., 1941-42, 45; asso. prof. econs. U. N.C., 1946-47, Northwestern U., 1947-49; prof. econs. Ind. U., 1949-70; Fulbright lectr. econs. U. Ceylon, 1955-56; adviser Thailand Nat. Inst. Devel. Adminstrn., 1967-70. Served to lt. USNR, 1942-45. Member American, Midwest, Southern economic assns., Ind. Acad. Social Scis., Am. Assn. U. Profs., Phi Beta Kappa, Beta Gamma Sigma. Mem. Unitarian-Universalist Ch. Author: A Critique of Socioeconomic Goals, 1954; Economic Opinion and Policy in Ceylon, 1957; Essays in Economic Analysis, 1970. Home: IN Died Feb. 6, 1970.

OLIVER, WEBSTER J., judge; b. Brooklyn, N.Y., Jan. 14, 1888; s. William P. and Frances L. (Fortune) O.; LL.B., St. Lawrence U. (Brooklyn Law School), 1911; honorary LL.D., from the same university, 1941; m. Genevieve M. Carlin, June 27, 1917 (dec. 1963); 1 son, Robert W. Buyer for Oliver Bros., Inc., hardware, machinery, New York and Pittsburgh, 1902-11; admitted to N.Y. bar, 1911; mem. firm Oliver & McNevin, later Leubuscher, Kayser & Oliver; special U.S. atty., 1935; asst. atty. gen. in Charge of Customs, 1938; presiding judge, U.S. Customs Court, 1940-69, chief judge, until 1965, sr. judge, 1967-69. Served as capt. Ordnance Reserve Corps, 1917-19. Democrat. Roman Catholic. K.C. Home: Brooklyn NY Died Nov. 1969.

OLIVER, WILLIAM F(REDERICK), sugar refining exec.; b. Rutherford, N.J., Sept. 23, 1914; s. William F. and Nellie (Chapman) O.; A.B., Princeton, 1935; m. Doris A. Wheeler, Apr. 20, 1940; children—Dorinda, Susan, Peter. Joined The Am. Sugar Refining Co. (name changed to Amstar Corp.), N.Y.C., 1935, exec. v.p. 1953, pres., dir., mem. exec. com., from 1954, chief exec. officer, from 1955, chmn. bd., 1971; dir., exec. com. Am. Enka Corp.; trust bd. 1st Nat. City Bank; dir. Allegheny Power System, Inc., Monongahela Power Co., Potomac Edison Co., W. Penn Power Co.; trustee, mem. exec. com. Dry Dock Savs. Bank. Trustee also mem. bd. Nutrition Found., Community Service Soc. Mem. Sugar Assn. (dir., mem. exec. com.), Phi Beta Kappa. Episcopalian. Home: New York City NY Died Nov. 4, 1971.

OLMSTED, E. STANLEY, author, pianist; b. Murphy, N.C., Jan. 30, 1877; s. Victor H. and Nancy Elizabeth (Patton) O.; grad. Central High Sch., Washington, 1891; 1 yr. Columbia (now George Washington) Univ.; studied music, languages and aesthetics in Europe; unmarried. Professional pianist, Washington, 1899-1904; dir. of piano, Conservatory Music, Ithaca, N.Y., 1905-07; prof. piano, Crouse Coll., Syracuse Univ., since 1907. Contb'r critical articles and stories to mags. and jours. Club: Town and Gown (Ithaca). Author: Luna (illus. poem), 1903 N3; The Nonchalante, 1906 H4; The Emotionalist, 12. Address: Syracuse NY‡

O'LOUGHLIN, JOHN M(ARTIN), librarian; b. Malden, Mass., Oct. 27, 1895; s. Michael and Alice (O'Connor) O'L.; A.B., Boston Coll., 1918; m. Anna G. O'Connor, Oct. 12, 1927 (dec.); children—Mary Alice, Anne, John S. High sch., librarian Boston Coll. 1925-29, coll. librarian from 1929; trustee Medford Savs. Bank. Mem. spl. commn. to write secret history 1st Naval Dist., World War I; mem. Medford War Price and Rationing Bd., 1942-45. Mem. corp. Lawrence Meml. Hosp.; trustee Medford Pub. Library. Served as chief yeoman, asst. recorder, 1st Naval Dist., World War I. Named Boston Coll. Alumnus of Year, 1961. Mem. Cath. (pres. 1951-53), Am. library associations, Massachusetts Library Trustees Assn. and Spl. Library Assn., Am. Legion, Roman Catholic. K.C. (Past Grand Knight). Editor: Catholic Library World, 1931-37, Reading Medford MA Died June 30, 1964; buried Malden MA

OLSEN, CLARENCE EDWARD, naval officer; b. Aloha, Mich., Oct. 7, 1899; s. Hjalmer Eugene and Anna Gustava (Amundson) O.; B.S., U.S. Naval Acad., 1920; grad. Naval Line Post Grad. Sch., 1928, Naval War Coll., 1929; m. Elisabeth Warren, May 24, 1929 (dec. Dec. 1972); children—Betsey Jane, Charles Frank (adopted). Commd. ensign U.S. Navy, June 1920, and advanced through grades to rear admiral, August 1947; command U.S.S. Arctic, 1941-42, U.S.S. Baltimore, Japanese occupation, 1945-46; comdr. Cruiser Div. Two, since 1950; plans div. of comdr.-in-chief U.S. Fleet, 1942-43; sr. Naval officer in Mil. Mission to Russia, 1943-45; asst. dir. Central Intelligence, 1946-48; comdr. Naval Base, Norfolk, Va., 1948-50; later chief military assistance advisory group, Norway; ret., 1959. Awarded Legion of Merit, Bronze star, Occupation area ribbons. Conglist. Home: Bethesda MD Died Nov. 11, 1971; buried U.S. Naval Acad. Cemetery, Annapolis MD

OLSON, CHARLES, poet; b. Worcester, Mass., Dec. 27, 1910; s. Charles Joseph and Mary Theresa (Hines) O.; B.A., Wesleyan U., 1932, M.A., 1933; postgrad. studies, Harvard, 1939; children—Katherine Mary, Charles Peter. Instr., Clark U., 1934-36; instr., tutor Harvard and Radcliffe Coll., 1936-39; vis. tchr. Black Mountain Coll., 1948-49, tchr. and rector, 1951-56; vis. lectr., prof. State U. of N.Y., Buffalo, 1963-65; vis. prof. U. Conn., 1969-70. Also dir. fgn. langs. OWI, 1942-44; poetry readings at numerous colls., poetry confs., 1957-—. Guggenheim fellow, 1939, 48; Wenner-Gren Found. grant, 1952. Author: Call Me Ishmael, 1947; Y & X, 1948; Projective Verse, 1950; A Letter for Melville, 1951; Apollonius of Tyana, 1951; In Cold Hell in Thicket, 1952; Mayan Letters, 1953, Maximus 1-10, 1953, O'Ryan, 1-10, 1958-65, Maximus 11-12, 1956; The Maximus Poems, 1960; The Distances, 1960; Maximus From Dogtown, 1961; Distances, 1960; Maximus From Dogtown, 1961; Apellez-Moi Ismael, 1962; A Bibliography on America for Ed Dorn, 1964; Gedichte, 1965; Proprioception, 1965; Human Universe, 1965; Maximus Poems IV, V, VI, 1968; Selected Writings, 1967; Letters for Origin, 1969; Special View of History, 1970; Archeologist of Morning, 1970. Address: Gloucester MA Died Jan. 10, 1970; buried Gloucester MA

OLSON, JAMES EDWARD, banker; b. Chgo., Jan. 23, 1914; s. Augustus Edward and Mabel Sara (Carr) O.; A.B., U. Chgo., 1936; m. Helen Ernestine Goodspeed Dudley, Nov. 26, 1949; children—Mary Andrea, James Dudley, Helen Caroline. With S. Shore Securities Co., Chgo., 1947-58, pres., 1952-58; with S. Chgo. Savs. Bank, 1958-68, v.p., 1960-61, v.p., cashier, 1961-62, v.p., 1962-64; pres. 1964-68, also dir. Bd. dirs. S. Chicago Community Hosp., 1967-68. Served with USAAF, 1942-46. Mem. Chi Psi. Mem. Bethany Union Ch. (trustee) Kiwanian (v.p. 1966). Home: Chicago IL Died Sept. 29, 1968; interred Peotone IL

OLSON, JOHN FREDERICK, univ. pres.; b. Highland Park, Mich., Dec. 24, 1919; s. Oscar Thomas and Edith Margaret (Ketcham) O.; A.B., DePauw U., 1941, L.H.D., 1967; S.T.B. summa cum laude. Boston U., 1944, Ph.D., 1949; LL.D., McMurry College, 1966; m. to Jane Elise Pegel, June 22, 1946; children—Margaret Edith, John Frederic, Thomas Albert, Elizabeth Jane, Joanne Ruth. Ordained to ministry Methodist Ch., 1942; asso. pastor, Islington, Mass., 1942-44; interim pastor, Salem, Mass., 1947; mem. staff and faculty Syracuse U., 1948-64, prof. religion, 1961-64, v.p., 1960-64; pres. Oklahoma City U., 1964-69. Director May Avenue Bank, Oklahoma City. Delegate Methodist World Confs., 1951, 56, 61; mem. Meth. World Council, 1956-—; del. World Council Chs., 1957. Bd. dirs. Syracuse and Onondaga County Met. Council Arts and Scis., 1962-64, Okla. Med. Research Found., Okla. County chpt. A.R.C., Frontiers Sci. Found., Central Okla. Mental Health Found., Okalhoma City Symphony Soc.; v.p. Central Okla. Mental Health Assn.; Pres. Assn. Colls. and Univs. Central Okla. Served as chaplain USNR, 1944-46. Recipient Centennial medal Syracuse U., 1967; Distinguished Alumnus award Boston U., 1968. Mem. Am. Soc. Ch. Hist., Acad. Religion, Religious Edn. Assn., Okla. City of C. of C. (dir.), Delta Sigma Pi, Phi Gamma Delta, Alpha Phi Omega, Theta Chi Beta. Rotarian. Clubs: Petroleum, Quail Creek Country. Author: Our Religious Heritage, 1953; also articles. Home: Oklahoma City OK Died June 25, 1969; buried Ann Arbor MI

OLSON, JULIUS JOHANN, judge; b. Dona, Norway, Feb. 22, 1875; s. Carl and Marie Antonette (Beck) O.; grad. Detroit Lakes (Minn.) High Sch., 1897; LL.B., U. of Minn., 1900; m. Caroline Louise Sletten, July 14, 1909; children—Sletten Carl, Katherine Marie. Brought to America, 1883. Admitted to Minn. bar, 1900; practiced at Warren until 1930, when apptd. district judge; elected for term of 6 years, 1932; appointed associate justice Supreme Court of Minnesota, March 1934; elected for term of 6 years, November 1934, reelected 1940 and 1946, retired. Mem. American and Minnesota State bar assns. Lutheran. Democrat. Home: 77 Langford Park Address: 77 Langford Park, St Paul 8‡

OLSON, RALPH J., adjutant gen. Wis.; b. Marinette, Wis., Mar. 3, 1904; s. A.B., Ripon (Wis.) Coll., 1926; attended Res. Officers Sch., Command and Gen. Staff Schs.; married Ruth. Comml. survey supvr., later mgr. Milwaukee pub. office, Wis. Telephone Co., Milwaukee; founded glass company, 1937; apptd. state dir. civil defense, State Wis., Sept. 1950, also The Adjutant General (rank brig. gen., then major gen.), from Oct. 1950; dir. Anchor Savings and Loan Assn. Chmn. Wis. Vets. Bd.; director Rotary Found.; state chairman and member national council U.S.O. Commissioned 2d lt., and entered U.S. Army as capt.; served as regimental adjutant Tank Bn. Comdr.; asst. chief of staff G-1, 11th Armored Div. (part of 3rd Army), E.T.O.; separated as col., 1945; col. Wis. N.G., 1950. Decorated Order of the Fatherland, Order of Valor (Russia); Bronze star. Mem. Am. Legion, Nat. Guard Assn. Mason (Shriner). Elk. Clubs: Rotary, Madison, Maple Bluff Country, Hole-in-One (Golf). Home: Madison WI Died Jan. 29, 1969; buried Forest Hill Cemetery, Madison WI

O'MALLEY, CHARLES P., lawyer; b. Olyphant, Pa., July 16, 1870; s. John and Ann (Gallagher) O'M.; student pub. schs.; studied law in offices of Willard & Warren; m. Myra A. Hill, Jan. 26, 1929. Admitted to Lackawanna County bar, 1894; since in gen. practice of law; mem. law firm O'Malley, Hill, Harris & Harris, Scranton, since 1931. Mem. Pa. Ho. of Reps., 1895. Mem. Lackawanna Bar Assn., Pa. Bar Assn. Republican. Catholic. Club: Scranton (Pa.) Country. Home: 530 Clay Av. Office: Scranton Electric Bldg., Linden St., Scranton PA‡

O'MALLEY, JOHN FRANCIS, univ. dean; b. Emporium, Pa., Oct. 11, 1911; s. Peter J. and Mary (Hayes) O'M.; B.A. summa cum laude, St. Bonaventure, U., 1932, M.A., 1938; Ph.D., U. Pitts., 1953; Commonwealth Pa. grantee Carnegie Inst. Tech., 1934-35; student Harvard, 1941; m. Sarah Alice Felt, June 25, 1938; children—Margaret Aurora (Mrs. Robert B. Marcoux), John F. Social work Commonwealth of Pa., Pitts., 1933-35; tchr., prin. pub. secondary schs., Pa., 1936-46; supervising prin. Emporium (Pa.) Area Joint Schs., 1946-54; supt. Cameron County (Pa.) pub. schs., 1954-60; prof. sch. adminstrn. St. Bonaventure U., 1960-61, dean Sch. Edn., 1961-71. Cons. Olean (N.Y.) pub. schs., 1963-64. Pres. Cameron County Hist. Soc., 1948-59, treas., 1954-60; chmn. SSS Bd. 42, Pa., 1950-52; pres. Emporium Rotary Club, 1951-52. Mem. Am. Assn. Sch. Adminstrs., Am. Assn. Coll. and Univ. Staffing, Nat. Cath. Edn. Assn., Am. Assn. Colls. Tchr. Edn., Collegiate Assn. Devel. Ednl. Adminstrn., Nat. Conf. Profs. Ednl. Adminstrn., Phi Delta Kappa. Home: Olean NY Died Aug. 31, 1971.

O'MALLEY, THOMAS F., lawyer; b. Somerville, Mass., April 5, 1872; s. Patrick and Ellen Brown O'M.; ed. Somerville pub. schools; private instruction and 1 yr. at Boston Coll.; grad. Boston Univ. Law School, 1894;

admitted to Mass. bar, Dec. 12, 1894; married. Mem. Am. Irish-Hist. Soc., Somerville Hist. Soc.; Am. Economic Assn. Has lectured on the Early Irish Settlers in America, and on other hist. subjects before several hist. socs. Author of number of mag. articles on hist. subjects. Address: Somerville MA‡

ONDERDONK, ADRIAN HOLMES, educator; b. St. James School, Washington Co., Md., July 18, 1877; s. Henry and Mary Elizabeth (Latrobe) O.; grad. St. James Sch., 1905 (father headmaster); A.B., Trinity Coll., Connecticut, 1899, A.M. from same college, 1929; m. Evelynne, d. Rev. William C. Richardson, of St. James Church, Philadelphia, Nov. 2, 1912; children—Adrian Holmes, Richardson Latrobe, Henry II. With New York Shipbuilding Co., Camden, N.J., 1899-1900; a master at Gilman Sch., Baltimore, Md., 1900-03; headmaster St. James Sch., 1903-39, now headmaster emeritus and head Latin dept. Senior fellow Trinity College. Member Headmasters' Association, Association Coll. and Prep. Schs. of Middle States and Md., Alpha Delta Phi. Democrat. Episcopalian. Address: St. James School, Washington Co MD‡

O'NEAL, CLAUDE E(DGAR), univ. prof.; b. Coatesville, Ind., Jan. 29, 1884; s. Jacob E(llsworth) and Anna Jane (Harlan) O'N.; grad. Ind. State Normal Sch. (now Ind. State U.), 1910; A.B., Ind. U., 1911, A.M., 1913, Ph.D., 1922; m. Mable Loreen Hostetter, Sept. 8, 1913; children—William B., Anna Josephine (Mrs. Paul V. Wallace). Teacher, prin. Hendricks County (Ind.) schs., 1904-09; head dept. sci. Brazil (Ind.) High Sch., 1911-12; teaching fellow botany, Indiana U., 1912-13; instr. botany Ohio Wesleyan U., 1913-14, asst. prof., 1914-17, asso. prof., 1917-20, prof., 1920-54, head dept. botany; 1922-54. Fellow Ohio Acad. Sci. (pres. 1938-39), A.A.A.S.; mem. Ind. Acad. Sci., Bot. Soc. Am., Phi Beta Kappa, Sigma Xi, Omicron Delta Kappa. Republican. Methodist. Home: Delaware OH Died Feb. 8, 1971; buried Oak Grove Cemetery, Delaware OH

O'NEAL, JAMES, socialist worker; b. Indianapolis, Ind., Mar. 13, 1875; s. John and Clara (Miller) O.; ed. pub. schs.; m. Ella Oswald, of Arlington, N.J., Apr. 24, 1915. Became active in organizing Socialist Party, 1900, and since lectured in 25 states and Can. on socialistic and kindred topics; assistant to nat. sec. Socialist Party 2 yrs.; asso. editor The Worker (weekly), N.Y. City, 1906-8; state sec. Socialist Party for Ind., 1911-13; same for Mass. since Mar., 1915. Unitarian. Author: The Workers in American History, 1911; also numerous booklets on hist. and economic subjects. Home: 19 Helen St. Office: 885 Washington St., Boston‡

O'NEIL, GEORGE F., mfr.; b. Milwaukee, Wis., Sept. 26, 1863; s. Henry Layfield and Elizabeth Jane (May) O'N.; educated public schools; m. Leila Davidson Quinn, Apr. 21, 1886. Chairman bd., O'Neil Duro Co., 1926-41; pres. O'Neil Paint Co., Mil-Wis-Chain Store Properties, Inc., O'Neil Realty Co., Ala. Investment Co., Georgian Court Co.; dir. Fiebing Chem. Co. Mem. Light Battery, F.A., Wis. Nat. Guard, 1885-92. Republican. Episcopalian. Clubs: Milwaukee, Wisconsin Union. Home: 3201 North Lake Drive. Office: 110 E. Wisconsin Av., Milwaukee WI‡

O'NEIL, HUGH ROE, editor; b. Manchester, N.H., Aug. 18, 1909; s. Denis F. and Rose (Mahoney) O'N.; student Manhattan Coll., Boston U.; m. Catherine Thornton, Aug. 24, 1936; children—Mary Alice, Hugh R., Jr., Thomas Thornton. With Manchester Union Leader successively as reporter, state editor, asst. mng. editor, mng. editor, then editor. Mem. Manchester C. of C., Am. Soc. of Newspapers Editors, N.E. Mng. Editors Assn. Club: Calumet, Manchester Press. Home: Manchester NH Died Jan. 3, 1972.

O'NEILL, FRANK J., now retired; b. Syracuse, New York, Mar. 6, 1876; s. James Adam and Margaret (Burns) O'N.; student Manlius Sch., 1896-98; A.B., Williams Coll., 1902; LL.B., Syracuse U., 1904; m. Grace I. Northrup, Sept. 15, 1906; children—Robert J., Emily M. (Mrs. Frank A. Lyons), Frank H., Edward A. Football coach successively at Colgate, Williams, Syracuse, Columbia, 1902-22; lawyer, Syracuse, 1904-15; gen. counsel, Royal Indemnity Co., 1915-22, v.p., 1918-27, pres. since 1927 and Eagle Indemnity Co. (v.p., 1922-27); gen. atty., Royal Ins. Co., Ltd., Liverpool, since 1929 and The Liverpool and London and Glove Ins. Co., Ltd.; also dir. Queens Ins. Co., Star Ins. Co., Newark Fire Ins. Co., Seaboard Ins. Co., Fed. Union Ins. Co., One Hundred Fifty William Street Corp. Received Ahrens medal, Syracuse U., 1940; Order of the Phoenix, The Manlius (N.Y.) Sch., 1931 (ex-trustee). Mem. Ins. Inst. America, Casualty Actuarial Soc., Internat. Assn. Casualty and Surety Underwriters (ex-pres.), Delta Chi. Roman Catholic. Republican. Clubs: Drug and Chemical, Williams (ex-pres.). Home: Colgate Hamilton NY‡

O'NEILL, JAMES MILTON, coll. prof.; b. Victor, N.Y., Dec. 17, 1881; s. John and Margaret (Spellescy) O'N.; B.A., Dartmouth, 1907; post grad. work U. of Chicago, and Harvard; m. Edith Winslow, Sept. 17, 1918; children—John Winslow, James Milton, Margaret Winslow, Hugh Bradley, Richard Winslow, Paul Van Deusen. Teacher dist. school, Vine Valley, N.Y., 1900-01; English master, Hotchkiss Sch., Lakeville, Conn., 1907-09; instr. in English, 1909-11, asst. prof. oratory, 1911-13, Dartmouth Coll.; asso. prof. rhetoric and oratory, 1913-15, prof., 1915-27, U. of Wis.; prof. speech, U. of Mich., 1927-35, Brooklyn (N.Y.) Coll., 1935-70. Mem. Nat. Assn. Teachers of Speech (ex-pres.). Delta Sigma Rho, Pi Epsilon Delta. Former editor Quarterly Jour. of Speech Ed. Catholic. Author: Manual of Debate and Oral Discussion, 1920; Extemporaneous Speaking, 1946; Religion and Educattion Under The Constitution, 1949. Co-Author: Argumentation and Debate, 1917; Purposive Writing and Speaking, 1925; The Elements of Speech, 1926; Debate and Oral Discussion, 1931; Working Principles of Argument, 1932. Compiler of Models of Speech Composition, 1921, Modern Short Speeches, 1923. Co-compiler of Contemporary Speeches, 1930. Editor of Foundations of Speech, 1941. Lecturer on speech education and civil liberties. Home: Brooklyn NY Lakeville CT Died Sept. 20, 1970; buried St. Mary's Cemetery, Salisbury CT

O'NEILL, LEWIS PATRICK, oil co. exec.; b. McAlister, Okla., July 28, 1905; s. Joseph Patrick and Catherine (Maire) O'N.; B.S. in Chem. Engring., Okla. A. and M. Coll., 1927; M.S. in Petroleum Engring., Okla. U., 1928; m. Georgiana Trask, Nov. 11, 1932; children—Patrick Shane, Michael Jerome, Sharon (Mrs. Ronald J. Peebles). Ind. oil and gas chemist, Okmulgee, Okla., 1928; chem. plant operator, Tulsa, 1929-34; engaged in spl. refining projects Phillips Refining Co., Borger, Tex., 1934, Lion Refining Co., Eldorado, Ark., 1935; with Gen. Am. Oil Co. Tex., 1936, v.p. engring. and Prodn., 1957-61, sr. v.p. engring. and prodn., 1961-66, exec. v.p. operations, 1966-69, exec. v.p., 1969-70, cons., 1971, dir., mem. exec. com., 1961-70; v.p. dir. Gen. Am. Oil Ltd.; pres. Gen. Am. Pipeline Co., 1968-70; pres. Premier Petrochem. Co., 1967-70; dir. Gen. Am. Bldg. Corp., Pipeliner Co. Registered professional engrs., Am. Inst. Mining, Metall. and Petroleum Engrs., Ind. Producers Assn., Mid Continent Oil and Gas Assn., Royalty Assn. Clubs: Texas, Engineers (dir.), Petroleum, Petroleum Engrs. Home: Dallas TX Died Dec. 17, 1972; buried Calvary Hill Cemetery, Dallas TX

ONKEN, WILLIAM HENRY, JR., editor; b. Brooklyn, Jan. 16, 1876; s. Capt. William Henry and Elizabeth (Gepfert) O.; B.Sc., Poly. Inst., Brooklyn, 1900; m. Lillian Charlotte Dawe, of Swansea, Wales, Jan. 27, 1904; children—Lillian Catherine, William Henry, Evelyn, George. With New York Evening Post, 1890-94; editor Brooklyn Observer, 1897-99; editor-in-chief The Polytechnic, 1899; asso. editor American Electrician, 1900-06; managing editor Electrical World, 1906-16, editor, 1916-29; v.p. National Association of Owners of Railroad and Public Utility Securities, Inc., 1930-32; pres. Am. Security Owners Assn., 1932—. Episcopalian. Member Internat. Jury Awards, Panama Expn., 1915 (chmn. elec. group dept. machinery). Mem. Am. Inst. Elec. Engrs. Author: Section 18, Standard Handbook for Electrical Engineers, 1906; How to Understand Electrical Work, 1906. Republican. Club: Engineers. President Poly. Alumni Assn., 1919. Home: 96 Remsen St., Brooklyn NY‡

OOSTING, HENRY J., educator; b. Holland, Mich., Mar. 12, 1903; s. John H. and Minnie (Bouwman) O.; A.B., Hope Coll., 1925; M.A., Mich. State U., 1927; Ph.D., U. Minn., 1931; m. Cornelia Ossewaarde, Aug. 17, 1927; children—Jan Kurt, Marta Joy. Instr. botany U. Minn., 1927-32; faculty Duke, from 1932, prof. botany, from 1949, chmn. dept., 1953-63. Mem. A.A.A.S., Am. Inst. Biol. Scis., Bot. Soc. Am. Ecological Soc. Am. (past pres., bus. mgr. from 1950), Assn. Southeastern Biologists, N.C. Acad. Scis. Author: The Study of Plant Communities, 2d edit., 1956. Bot. editor: Ecological Monographs, from 1950. Home: Durham NC Died Oct. 30, 1968; cremated.

OPHEIM, LEONARD BERTINIUS, real estate salesman; b. York, N.D., Mar. 27, 1901; s. Rasmus and Bertha (Lunde) O.; student Concordia Coll., 1915-19, Dakota Bus. Coll., 1920-21; m. Helen Esther Talbot, May 29, 1943. Clerical work Fisk Tire Co., Fargo, N.D., 1921-23, So. Pacific Co., Portland, Ore., 1923-27; farming, 1927-42; baker Franz Bakery, Portland, Ore. 1943-53; realtor, 1953-68. City councilman, 1948-52; mayor Cornelius, 1952-54. Lutheran. Mason. Club: Cornelius Boosters (sec.). Home: Cornelius OR Died May 3, 1968.

OPIE, EUGENE LINDSAY, pathologist; b. Staunton, Va., July 5, 1873; s. Thomas and Sallie (Harman) O.; A.B., Johns Hopkins, 1893, M.D., 1897, LL.D., 1947; Sc.D., Yale, 1930; LL.D., Washington U., 1940; D.Sc. (hon.), Rockefeller University, 1966; m. Gertrude Lovat Simpson, Aug. 6, 1902; children—Thomas Lindsay, Anne Lovat, Helen Lovat, Gertrude Eugenie; m. 2d, Margaret Lovat Simpson, Sept. 16, 1916. Medical house officer Johns Hopkins Hosp., 1897-98; asst. instr., asso. in pathology Johns Hopkins, 1898-1904; mem. Rockefeller Inst. for Med. Research, 1904-10. bd. sci. dirs., 1928-32; vis. pathologist Presbyn. Hosp., N.Y.C., 1907-10; prof. pathology Washington U., St. Louis, 1910-23. dean med. sch., 1912-15; prof. pathology, dir. dept. U. Pa., dir. labs. Henry Phipps Inst., 1923-32, acting dir., 1942-46; prof. pathology Cornell Med. Coll. and pathologist to N.Y. Hosp., 1932-41; sci. dir. Internat. Health Div., Rockefeller Found., 1935-38; vis. prof. Peiping Union Med. Coll., 1939; research Rockefeller Inst. Med. Research, 1941-70. President Nat. Tb. Assn., 1929; research Council Pub. Health Research Inst., N.Y.C. Served from capt. to col. Med. R.C., A.E.F., 1917-19. Awarded Gerhard, Trudeau medals, 1929; medal. Soc. Puertorriquena de Tisologos. 1938; Weber-Parkes Medal and Award of Royal Coll. of Physicians. 1945: Banting Medal, 1946; Jessie Stevenson Kovalenko medal Nat. Acad. Scis., 1959; medal of New York Academy of Medicine, 1960; T. Duckett Jones Memorial award Helen Hays Whitney Found., 1965. Fellow Am. Assn. Advancement Sci.; mem. Nat. Acad. Scis., Assn. Am. Physicians, Am. Assn. of Pathologists and Bacteriologists (pres. 1917). American Association Immunologists (president 1929) Harvey Society (president 1936-38). A.M.A. Episcopalian. Author: Diseases of the Pancreas, 1902; Epidemic Respiratory Disease, 1921. Co-editor of The Jour. Exptl. Medicine, 1904-10. Home: New York City NY Died Mar. 12, 1971; buried Baltimore MD

OPPENHEIMER, FRITZ ERNEST, internat. lawyer; b. Berlin, Germany, Mar. 10, 1898; s. Ernst and Amalie (Friedlander) O.; ed. College Royal Francais, Berlin, 1908-15, Berlin U., 1919-20. Freiburg U., 1920-21; LL.D., Breslau U., 1922; Paris U., 1924-25; London U., 1925; m. Elizabeth Kaulla, Oct. 23, 1927; children—Ellen (Mrs. Paul Handler), Ernest. Mem. Soc. Inner Temple, London, 1938; English barrister-at-law, 1946. Practiced law as mem. German bar, also Paris (France), The Hague (Holland); asso. with solicitors, London, Eng., 1925-35; counselor in chambers of atty. gen. for Eng. and to Brit. Treasury, 1936-40; with law firm Cadwalader, Wickersham & Taft, New York, 1940-43; chief analyst Bd. Econ. Warfare, Washington, 1943; spl. asst. U.S. Mil. Govt. for Germany, Berlin, 1946; spl. asst. for German-Austrian affairs, office of legal adviser, Dept. of State, 1946-48, legal adviser to sec. of State at confs., Council of Fgn. Ministers, Moscow, 1947, London, England, 1947; also Paris, France, 1949; United States deputy fgn. minister on treaty for Austria, 1947; legal adviser to U.S. ambassador at 6-Power Conf. on Germany, London, 1948; pvt. practice, New York, from 1948. Served with the German Army, 1915-18; enlisted as pvt., U.S. army, 1943, advanced through grades to lt. col., 1945; legal staff officer, AUS S.H.A.E.F., London, Versailles, Rheims, Frankfurt, in charge reform of German law and court system, 1944-45; contbd. to preparation of documents and plans in connection with Germany's mil. surrender at Rheims, France, and Berlin, Germany, 1945; participated in drafting mil. govt. and control council legislation for Germany. Mem. Officers Reserve Corps since 1946. Decorated Legion of Merit, Bronze Star Medal. Mem. N.Y. City Bar Assn., Am. Soc. International Law, International Law Association, Council Fgn. Relations. Author various publs. on internat., corporate and tax law in English, French and German. Home: Palo Alto CA Died Feb. 4, 1968.

ORDWAY, SAMUEL HANSON, lawyer, assn. exec.; b. N.Y.C., Jan. 20, 1900; s. Samuel Hanson and Frances Hunt (Throop) O.; A.B., Harvard, 1921, LL.B., 1924; m. Anna Wheatland, June 24, 1924; children—Ellen, Samuel Hanson, Stephen Wheatland (dec.). Admitted to N.Y. bar, 1925; asso. firm Burlingham, Veeder, Master & Fearey, 1924-26; asso. Spencer, Ordway & Wierum, 1926-28, mem. firm, 1928-37, counsel, 1940-58; lectr. Am. U., 1938, Inst. Govt., U. So. Cal., 1939, N.Y.U., 1946; Pres. Nat. Civil Service Reform League, 1940-41; mem. U.S. Council Personnel Adminstrn., 1938-41; cons. Nat. Roster Sci. and Profl. Personnel, 1940-41; mem. U.S. Civil Service Commn., 1937-39, Civil Service Commn. City N.Y., 1934-36; chmn. exec. com. N.Y. Civil Service Reform Assn., 1936; mem. Art Commn. City N.Y., 1937, 41; chmn. N.Y.C. Conf. on Charter Revision, 1934; mem. examining bd. to certify 1st personnel dir. for states R.I., 1939, La., 1944. Vis. com. Littauer Sch. Pub. Adminstrn., Harvard, 1945-57; mem. adv. com. N.Y.U. Div. Tng. for Pub. Service; v.p. Conservation Found., 1948-61, pres., 1961-65, trustee, 1961, chmn. bd., 1969; trustee Am. Constn. Assn. Served from lt. comdr. to capt., USNR, 1941-43. Mem. Assn. Bar City N.Y., Soc. Personnel Adminstrn. (v.p. 1939), Natural Resources Council Am. (chmn. 1954). Republican. Episcopalian. Clubs: Century, University, City, Harvard, Fencers (N.Y.C.); Cosmos (Washington). Author of several books, 1929, including: Resources and American Dream, 1953; Prosperity Beyond Tomorrow, 1956. Home: Yorktown Heights NY Died Nov. 18, 1971.

ORE, OYSTEIN, prof. mathematics; b. Oslo, Norway, Oct. 7, 1899; s. Michal Beer and Christiane Benedicte (Samuelsen) O.; Ph.D., Oslo U., 1924; grad. study, Gottingen (Germany) U.; 1922, Sorbonne, Paris, 1924; fellow Math. Inst. Stockholm, 1923, Rockefeller Internat. Edn., Bd., 1924-25; naturalized citizen, 1934; m. Gudrun Lundevall, Aug. 25, 1930; children—Elisabeth, Berit. Asst. prof. of mathematics, Oslo U., 1925-28; asst. prof. mathematics, Yale, 1927, asso. prof., 1928, prof., 1929-31, Sterling prof. math.,

1931-68, chmn. dept., 1936-45; fellow Branford College since 1933. Mem. Nat. Search Council, 1939-42. Mem. bd. dirs. Norwegian Relief, Inc. (chmn. for Conn. since 1940); Am. Relief for Norway, 1942-47; chairman Relief Mission to Norway, 1945. Decorated Knight, Order of St. Olav (Norwegian), 1947; Guggenheim fellow for hist. studies, Italy, 1954. Member American Mathematics Society (council, 1934-36; colloquium lecturer 1941), American Acad. of Arts and Sciences, also mem. Oslo Academy Science, Sigma Xi; honorary member Gamma Alpha, 1941. Co-editor: Gesammelte Werke of R. Dedekind (with E. Noether), 3 vols., 1930. Author: Les Corps Algebriques et la Theorie des Ideaux, 1934; L'algebre abstraite, 1936; Number Theory and Its History, 1948; Cardano the Gambling Scholar, pub. 1953; Niels Henrik Abel, 1954; Theory of Graphs, 1962; Graphs and Their Uses, 1963; The Four Color Problem, published in 1967. Contributor math. articles to Am., French, German, Norwegian publs. Mem. editorial bd. Annals of Mathematics, 1939-40, Duke Math. Jour., 1935-41, Transactions (Am. Math. Soc.), 1937-44. Am. Jour. Math., 1938-41, Jour. Combinational Math., 1965-68. Home: Hamden CT Died Aug. 13, 1968; buried New Haven CT

O'REAR, EDWARD CLAY, judge; b. Montgomery County, Ky., Feb. 2, 1863; s. Daniel and Sibba O.; ed. pub. schs., Montgomery County, Ky.; studied law in office of Col. John T. Hazelrigg, Morgan County, Ky.; LL.D., Ky. State and Ky. Wesleyan colls.; admitted to bar, 1882; m. Virginia Lee Hazelrigg, Nov. 29, 1882; m. 2d, Mabel Taylor, Nov. 15, 1933. Rep. presdl. elector, 1884; county judge Montgomery County, 1894-98; chief justice Ky. Ct. of Appeals, 7th Dist., 1907-08, and reelected without opposition for term 1909-17; resigned, Dec. 9, 1911, to resume law practice; Rep. nominee for gov. of Ky., 1911. Trustee U. of Ky., 1946. Republican. Episcopalian. Home: Versailles KY‡

O'REILLY, GABRIEL AMBROSE, banker; b. Brandon, Wis., June 22, 1872; s. John and Bridget (Tuite) O'R.; U. of Minn., 1891-94; law, same univ., 1897; m. Carmel Katharine, d. Hon. Maurice F. Egan, of Washington, D.C., Dec. 2, 1910; children—Maurice Francis, John Egan, Carmel Katharine, Gerald Ambrose. Pvt. Co. D, 13th Minn. Vol. Inf., Spanish-Am. War, and Philippine Insurrection; served later as div. supt. schs. Vigan, P.I., supt. schs., Manila, and in charge Govt. Industrial and Commercial Dept.; with Irving Trust Co. since 1916, now v.p. Republican. Catholic. Clubs: India House (New York); Riding and Driving (Brooklyn); University, Manila Polo (Manila). Author of various publs. on trade and banking. Home: 534 3d St., Brooklyn, N.Y. Address: Woolworth Bldg., New York NY‡

ORMSBEE, THOMAS HAMILTON, writer; b. Brooklyn, N.Y., Aug. 25, 1890; s. Hamilton and Agnes (Bailey) O.; A.B., Middlebury (Vt.) Coll., 1915; m. Renee Richmond Huntley, Nov. 16, 1918 (dec.). Reporter Brooklyn Eagle, 1916-17; publicity, editorial work, N.Y. City, 1918-31; free-lance writing, 1932-33; founded Am. Collector, 1933, editor to 1946. Member Chi Psi Frat. Democrat. Episcopalian. Author: Early American Furniture Makers, 1930; The Story of American Furniture, 1934; If you're Going to Live in the Country (with Richmond Huntley), 1937; Collecting Antiques in America, 1940; Furniture of the Walnut Period (with R. W. Symonds), 1947; Prime Antiques and Their Current Prices, 1947; Care and Repair of Antiques, 1949; A Field Guide of American Furniture, 1951; A Field Guide of Victorian Furniture, 1952; Know Your Heirlooms, 1956; English China and Its Marks, 1959; The Windsor Chair, 1960; Writer of the weekly syndicated newspaper feature Know Your Heirlooms," from 1946; columnist on antiques, House & Garden, from 1958. Lectured nationally on American antiques. Contbr. Ency. Americana, 1953-54. Address: Pound Ridge NY Died Aug. 1969.

ORNDOFF, BENJAMIN HARRY, physician; b. Graysville, Pa., Feb. 3, 1881; s. John and Minerva (Roseberry) O.; Ph.G., Valparaiso U., 1905, M.A., 1916; M.D., Loyola U., 1906; Dr. Med. Radiology and Electrology, Cambridge U., Eng., 1926; m. Bernice Harvey, June 29, 1907; children—John Roseberry, Ruth, Jane, Sarah, Harvey Hawkins. Intern Frances Willard Hosp., Chicago, 15 months, 1906-07; pathologist and roentgenologist, same, 1907-21; prof. pathology and roentgenology, Chicago Coll. of Medicine and Surgery, 1910-16; surgeon div. of electrosurgery, Grant Hosp.; med. staff Swedish Covenant Hosp.; sr. staff mem. dept. radiology, Luth. Gen. Hosp., Park Ridge, Ill. prof. and chmn. dept. of radiology, Loyola U. School of Medicine, Chgo. U.S. Navy, 1937-39 (lt. comdr. MC-V), USNR (ret.). Awarded Silver Medal, Western Roentgen Soc., 1916; Gold Medal Radiol. Soc. of N.A., 1927; Gold Medal Am. Coll. of Radiology, 1954; Silver Medal, Swedish delegation, 5th Internat. Congress of Radiology, 1937; Gold Medal, English delegation, 5th Internat. Congress of Radiology, 1950; Citation and Scroll, Radiol. Soc. of N.A., 1954; Stritch gold medal Stritch Sch., Loyola U., 1960; gold medal Centre Antoine Beclere, Paris, 1965. Fellow Am. Coll. of Surgeons, Am. Med. Assn., Am. Coll. of Radiology (treas. 1925-31, exec. sec., 1931-36), Inter Am. Coll. of Radiology, A.C.P.; hon. mem. Italian Soc. of Radiol. Medicine, Columbian Soc. of Radiology, Argentina Assn. of Radiology, Argentina Radiol. Soc., Soc. of Radiology and Physiotherapy of Cuba, Cuban Radiol. Soc.; mem. Radiol. Soc. of N.A. (pres. 1917-18), Am. Roentgen Ray Soc. Soc., Ill. State and Chgo. Med. Socs., British Inst. of Radiology, Rocky Mountain Radiological Soc., (hon. member), Inst. of Medicine of Chgo., Am. Phys. Soc., Am. and Chgo. Heart Assn., Am. Geriatrics Soc., Egon Fischman Meml., S.A.R., Chgo. Art Inst., Chgo. Museum Nat. History, Century of Progress Assn., Chgo. Roentgen Soc. (pres. 1921-23, sec. 1919-21), Physics Club of Chgo., Ill. Acad. of Sci., Chgo. Hist. Soc., A.A.A.S., Sigma Xi, Lambda Rho, Theta Kappa Psi. Del. Internat. Congress of Radiology, Stockholm, 1928, Paris, 1931, pres. of delegates, 4th Congress, Zurich, Switzerland, 1934; del. 2d Inter Am. Congress Radiology, Havana, 1946; chmn. exec. council First Am. Congress of Radiology, 1933; gen. sec. 5th Internat. Congress of Radiology, Chicago, 1937; mem. internat. executive committee 6th International Congress of Radiology, London, 1950; mem. 6th International Congress on Cancer, Paris, 1950. Mason (32 deg., K.T., Shriner). Engaged in research in radiology and electrosurgery. Author of articles in exptl. research and clin. medicine. Address: Park Ridge IL Died Mar. 6, 1971; buried Rogersville PA

ORNDUFF, WILLIAM WILMER, pediatrician; b. Cathage, Mo., Sept. 19, 1910; M.D., U. Ore., 1937. Rotating intern Touro Infirmary, New Orleans, 1937-38; asst. resident pediatrics Bobs Roberts Meml. Hosp., Chgo., 1938-40; resident contagious disease Municipal Contagious Disease Hosp., Chgo.; practice medicine specializing in pediatrics, Portland, Ore. Instr. pediatrics U. Ore., 1959-62, asst. prof., 1962-63. Served to capt. M.C., AUS, 1942-46. Diplomate Am. Bd. Pediatrics. Fellow Am. Acad. Pediatrics; mem. North Pacific, Portland pediatric socs. Research in pediatric neurology. Home: Portland OR Died Oct 5, 1964.

O'ROURKE, FIDELIS (ARTHUR J.), clergyman, univ. adminstr.; b. N.Y.C., Jan. 23, 1902; s. Frank J. and Mary (Walsh) O'R.; student Coll. N.Y.C., 1919-21; LL.B., Fordham U., 1929; B.A., St. Bonaventure U., 1936; postgrad. Holy Name Coll., 1936-40, Columbia, 1941-43. Admitted to N.Y. bar, 1930, D.C. bar, 1938, also U.S. Supreme Ct. bar; with bd. transp. City of N.Y., 1925-34, asst. counsel, 1930-34; joined Franciscan Order, 1934, ordained priest Roman Catholic Ch., 1939; prof. law, chmn. div. bus. St. Bonaventure (N.Y.) coll. (constituted univ. 1950), 1940-66, dean Sch. Bus. Adminstrn., 1940-71, sec. univ., 1955-71. Fellow Am. Geog. Soc.; mem. Am., N.Y. State, Cattaraugus County bar assns., Assn. Colls. Bus. Adminstrn. (pres. N.Y. State, chmn. com. accountancy Middle Atlantic States), Fed. Mediation and Conciliation Service, Am. Arbitration Assn., N.Y. State Council Accountancy (vice-chmn. 1961-71), Am., Cath. econ. assns., Cath. Bus. Edn. Assn. (chmn. planning bd. seaway unit), Nat. Assn. Accountants, Am. Judicature Soc., Am. Irish Hist. Soc., Am. Acad. Polit. Sci., Acad. Polit. and Social Sci., Indsl. Relations Assn. Western N.Y. (exec. bd.). Address: St Bonaventure NY Died Apr. 12, 1971; buried St. Bonaventure Cemetery.

ORR, DOUGLAS WILLIAM, architect; b. Meriden, Conn., Mar. 25, 1892; s. Adam and Mary (Blair) O.; ed. Meriden grammar and high schs.; B.F.A., Yale U., 1919, M.F.A., 1927; m. Helen Merriam Converse, Dec. 22, 1917; 1 dau., Ann (Mrs. John A. Logan, Jr.). Practiced architecture, 1919-66; director of First Nat. Bank & Trust Company, New Haven Gas Light Co.; cons. architect, Princeton U. Served in U.S. Army, 1917-19. Member of the Smithsonian, Art Commission, 1957. Fellow A.I.A. (pres. 1947-49, ex-pres. Conn. chpt.). Academician Nat. Acad. Design; mem. Am. Archtl. Found., Inc.; hon. corr. mem. Royal Inst. British Architects; mem. Phi Gamma Delta. Republican. Conglist. Mason. Clubs: Century (New York City); Lawn (past president), The Quinnipack, Farmington (Charlottesville, Va.). Vice chairman Commn. on Renovation of Executive Mansion, Washington, Fed. Commn. Fine Arts. Home: CT Died July 29, 1966.

ORR, JOHN BOYD (LORD BOYD OF BRECHIN), physiologist; b. Kilmaurs, Scotland, Sept. 23, 1880; s. Robert Clark and Annie (Boyd) O.; M.A., Glasgow Univ., 1902, B.Sc., 1907, M.B., Ch.B., 1913, M.D. cum laude, 1914, D.Sc., 1919; LL.D. (hon.), St. Andrews, 1935, Edinburgh, 1941, Princeton, 1946, univs. Aberdeen, Manchester, Groeningen, Delhi, Santiago, Uppsala, Vollebach (Norway); m. Elizabeth Pearson Callum, 1915; children—Elizabeth Joan, Helen Annie, Donald Noel Boyd (killed in action, World War II). Dir. Rowett Research Inst., Aberdeen, Scotland, 1914-45, dir. Imperial Bur. of Nutrition, 1929-45; prof. agr., Aberdeen Univ., 1942-45, rector Glasgow Univ., 1945, chancellor, 1946; M.P. for Scottish Univs., 1944-47: dir.-gen. FAO, UN, 1945-48. Served as major. med. corps, 1914-18. Decorated D.S.O., Companion of Honour, Papal decoration, Polish Star, Polish Cross, comdr. Legion of Honor (France); created Lord Boyd of Brechin, Mearns, 1949; recipient Nobel prize for peace, 1949, Harben medal Royal Inst. Hygiene, gold medal Internat. Fedn. Agrl. Producers, Nat. Farmers Union of U.S.A., Lasker award, Grocers award of merit, Borden award, Pasteur medal, World Govt. medal. Fellow N.Y. Acad. Medicine (hon.), Royal Soc. (London and Edinburgh), Royal Agrl. Soc. (Sweden); mem. Medical Assn., Physiol. Soc. of U.K., Biochem, Soc. of U.K., Nat. Peace Council (pres.), World Movement for World Govt. (pres.). Author: Scottish Church Crisis, 1905; Minerals in Pastures, 1928; Food, Health and Income, 1935, (with D. H. Lubbock) Feeding the People in Wartime; The White Man's Dilemna. Editor-in-chief Nutrition Abstracts and Reviews, 1929-46. Contbr. sci. articles to various pubs. Home: Angus Scotland Died June 25, 1971.

ORR, LOUIS THOMAS, lawyer, realtor; b. Kankakee, Ill., Nov. 30, 1871; s. James Nicholas and Emma Huntington (Ainsworth) Orr; desc. on both paternal and maternal sides of ancestors who came to America before the Revolutionary War and participated therein; ed. Oberlin Coll., 1889-92; LL.B., U. of Mich., 1895; m. Arabella Ruth Armstrong, of Akron, O., Oct. 15, 1902; children—Louis Thomas, Willard T., Arabella Ruth, Mary Katherine. Admitted to Ill. bar, 1895; mem. firm of H. G. Howard & Co., real estate, until firm incorporated as Howard & Orr Co. in 1922, pres. same since 1924; also intrested in other corpns. Retained 1901, by Women's and Children's Protective Assn. to investigate charges against management of the Eastern Ill. Hosp. for Insane, at Kankakee, resulting in removal of 1 trustee and discharge of many employes; instrumental in starting movement to stop hazing in univs. of U.S., 1922, beginning at U. of Mich.; led in solving coal crises," 1917, by appearing before Interstate Commerce Commn. and Pub. Utilities Commn. of Ill., in argument against the embargo of coal by railroads; successfully opposed laws detrimental to the growth of Chicago which were pending in Ill. legislature, 1922. Lecturer Y.M.C.A. Sch. of Commerce. Mem. Am. and Ill. State bar assns., Chicago Real Estate Bd. (ex-v.p. and chmn. bd. of govs.), Nat. Assn. Real Estate Bds. (chmn. property management div.), Chamber of Commerce U.S.A. Republican. Presbyterian. Mason (K.T., Shriner). Mem. Royal Arcanum, Royal League. Clubs: Hamilton, South Shore Country, Lake Shore Athletic, Collegiate, Midway Athletic, Dixmoor Golf, Hyde Park Men's, Michigan North Woods Club (dir.). Home: 5225 University Av. Office: 82 W. Washington St., Chicago IL‡

ORR, ROBERT HALL, architect; b. Prince Edward Island, Can., 1873; s. James Sample and Mary (Graham) O.; brought to U.S., 1881, naturalized 1894; student of architecture U. of Ill., 1906-08; m. Hilda Letitia Eaton, July 23, 1902; 1 dau., Faith (Mrs. William W. Givens). Draftsman in office of W.H. Weeks, San Francisco, Calif., 1899-1906; in private practice of architecture since 1908. Designer of many chs., Pacific Coast; project engr., insp., F.P.H.A., 1942-45; formed architectural firm, Orr, Strange and Inslee, 1949. President of the Bd. Bldg. and Safety Commissioners, City of Los Angeles, 1930-34. Pres. Architects Bureau, Ltd. Mem. Nat. Guard of Calif., Cav., 1899-1902. Dir. State Assn. of Calif. Architects (past pres. and treas.). Fellow A.I.A. (sponsor of unification of archtl. profession, 1931; nat. policy of A.I.A.). Home: 5022 Marathon St. Office: 3142 Wilshire Blvd., Los Angeles CA‡

ORR, ROBERT WILLIAM, librarian; b. Winterset, Ia., June 9, 1905; s. Maurice J. and Luella (Paullin) O.; B.S., Ia. State Coll., 1930; M.S., Columbia, 1939; m. Elizabeth Strohbehn, Sept. 9, 1939; 1 dau., Gretchen Louise. Order librarian Ia. State Univ. 1930-31, asst. loan dept., 1931-33, asst. reference librarian, 1933-35, reference librarian, 1935-41, asst. librarian in charge pub. services, 1941-43, asst. librarian, 1943-44, asso. librarian, 1944-46, dir. 1946-67, prof. of library sci., 1967-72. Mem. A.L.A., Ia. Library Assn. (pres. 1947-48), Assn. Coll. and Reference Libraries (pres. 1956-57), Phi Lambda Upsilon, Alpha Chi Sigma, Gamma Sigma Delta. Episcopalian. Author library survey reports; contbr. library jours. Home: Ames IA Died Apr. 19, 1972; interred Ia. State U. Cemetery, Ames IA

ORTHWINE, RUDOLF ADOLF, pub., editor; b. Volkmarsen, Germany, Nov. 7, 1893; s. Maximillian and Rosa Louisa (Funke) O.; student pub. schs. and dramatic sch., Germany, City Coll. N.Y., 1913-15; m. Julia Danis, Mar. 7, 1915; 1 dau., Lillian. Came to U.S., 1913. Dramatic actor, Germany, 1910-12; established Accurate Multiple Letter Co., N.Y.C., 1914, later inc. as Rudolf Orthwine Co.; began publ. mag. to which he also contributed, 1925; pub. Pen Zone Sentinel, 1927, also weekly newspapers The Russian Gazette, 1929-34, New America, 1934; pub. Dance Mag., 1941; Am. Dancer mag., 1942; these publs. merged as Dance mag. of which editor, pub., 1942—, Ballroom Dance Mag., 1961—, After Dark, 1968—; pres. Rudolph Orthwine Corp., Chain Store Distbrs., Inc., D.& A. Forwarding Co., Orthwine Mchdse. Assos., Inc., Nationwide Shipping Services, Inc., Rudorlitho Co., Mikhail Mordkin est. small dance group, which appeared in N.Y.C., 1933; with Lucia Chase established Mordkin Ballet, 1936; founded Ballet Theatre, 1939, pres., 1919-41. Founder mem. Ballet Theatre Found. Fellow life mem. Soc. Alumni Am. Acad. Dramatic Arts; mem. Wholesale Stationers Assn., N. Y. Employing Printers Assn., West Side C. of C., Am. Soc. Tchrs. Dancing (hon.), Dance Tchrs. Club Boston, Liederkranz of City N.Y., C. of C. of U.S. Rotarian. Clubs: N.Y. Athletic (life), N.Y. Advertising, Automobile of N.Y. Named Ky. col. Patentee. Home: New York City NY Columbia NJ Died July 13, 1970.

ORTLOFF, HENRY STUART, landscape architect; b. Syracuse, N.Y., Mar. 9, 1896; s. William H. and Anne Gertrude (Pons) O.; student Mass. State Coll., 1916-18. Columbia U., 1919-20; unmarried. Mem. Ortloff and Raymore, Huntington, N.Y. and Arlington, Vt. Author: Garden Bluebook of Annuals and Biennials, 1924; Perennial Gardens, 1931; Garden Maintenance (with H.B. Raymore), 1932; Annuals in the Garden, 1932; Informal Gardens, 1933; New Gardens for Old (with H.B. Raymore), 1934; Color and Succession of Bloom in the Flower Border (with H.B. Raymore), 1935; Garden Planning and Building (with H.B. Raymore); 1939, rev. ed. 1946; Color and Design for Every Garden (with H.B. Raymore), 1951; The Book of Landscape Design (with H.B. Raymore), 1959; Book about Soils (with H.B. Raymore), 1962; Its Your Community (with H.B. Raymore), 1965. Address: Arlington VT Died June 13, 1970; interred Greenfield Cemetery, Hempstead NY

ORTON, DWAYNE, educator, editor; b. Port Hope, Can., May 6, 1903; s. Arthur and Frances May (Nease) O.; (father naturalized U.S. citizen); A.B., Univ. of Redlands, 1926, LL.D., 1944; A.M., Coll. of the Pacific, 1933; grad. studies, Newton-Andover Sem., 1927-28; U. of Calif., 1931, 1939, 1941; U. of So. Calif., 1938; LL.D., Tusculum College, 1948, St. Lawrence University, 1953; L.H.D., Clarkson College of Technology, 1956; D.C.L., Nasson Coll., D.C.S., Pace College, 1958; D.Litt., U. Tampa, 1960, Western New Eng. Coll., 1963; D.H.L., Pratt Inst., 1971; m. Edna Marie Olson, Setpember 11, 1926; children—Jean E. (Hilchey), Nancy M. (Littauer), Lawrence Dwayne. Mech. engring. draftsman, Union Tool Co., 1920-22; instr. Baylor Coll., Belton, Tex., 1926-29; asst. prof. Coll. of the Pacific, Stockton, Calif., 1929-33, asso. prof. and dir. chapel, 1930-35; dir. Junior Coll., Coll. of the Pacific, 1933-34; dean, Gen. Coll., Coll. Pacific, 1934-36; pres. Stockton (Calif.) College, 1936-42; director edn. Internat. Business Machines Corp., 1942-54, educational consultant, editor Think Mag., 1954-64, ednl. cons., chairman editorial board, 1964-71; professorial lecturer Univ. of Santa Clara; national council Student Christian Assn., 1930; asso. Edward W. Hazen Foundation, 1933-39; mem. com. on guidance 1947-50); Calif. State Com. on Needs of Post-High Sch. Youth, 1939-41; mem. State Council N.Y.A. for Calif., 1941; mem. national committee student div., YMCA, 1957-59; N.Y. State Citizens Council, 1944-50; cons. C.A.A., 1941-43, USAF, 1952-53; asst. Adminstr., Fed. Civil Def. Adminstrn., 1951; pres. Council for Internat. Progress in Mgmt., 1957-60, chmn., 1960-63, U.S. rep. to Internat. Mgmt. Council, 1957-71. Mem. Nat. Council Chs. Commn. Ch. and Econ. Life, 1961-71, vice chairman ch. executive devel. bd. Bd. dirs. Freedom House; trustee Pratt Inst., Bklyn., 1947-71; bd. dirs., exec. com. Am. Arbitration Assn.; trustee World Neighbors, 1965-71, U. Redlands, 1968-71; chmn. bd. overseers Johnston Coll., Redlands, Cal., 1968-71. Recipient Distinguished Alumni award U. Redlands, 1962; George Washington Honor medal Freedoms Found., Wallace Clark award in internat. mgmt. Mem. Soc. Advancement Management, A.A.A.S., Phi Delta Kappa, Delta Alpha, Pi Kappa Delta, Pi Gamma Nu. Clubs: Commonwealth (San Francisco); Rotary, Circumnavigators, University (N.Y.C.). Home: New York City NY Died Nov. 22, 1971; buried Forest Lawn Meml. Park, Glendale CA

ORY, EDWARD KID, musician, composer; b. LaPlace, La., Dec. 25, 1886; s. John and Octavie (Denez) O.; student Milesville (La.) Sch.; m. Elizabeth Barbara Lawless, Sept. 15, 1953; 1 dau., Babette Ann. Began profl. career as valve trombonist, leader seven piece band, Milesville, 1896; took up slide trombone, 1900; leader jazz band, New Orleans, 1908-19; recorded 1st phonograph records of Creole jazz band, Ory's Creole Trombone and Soc. Blues, 1921; mem. Joe King Oliver's band, 1925-29. Leon Reney band, 1929-32, recorded with King Oliver, Louis Armstrong, Jelly-Roll Morton, New Orleans Wanderers, New Orleans Bootblacks, other groups, 1925-29; propr. poultry farm, 1932-42; leader 1st jazz band in radio broadcasting on Orson Welles show, 1942-43; leader jazz bands until 1961; star Dixieland at Disneyland, 1961-65; concert tours, Europe, Eng., Scotland, 1956, 1959; star Crescent City's Jazz and Heritage Festival, 1971; Victor, Columbia. Decca, Good Time Jazz, Verve, Crescent records; 1st high fidelity records for Exner Records, 1946; motion picture appearances include New Orleans, 1946, Crossfire, 1947, Mahogany Magic, 1950. Benny Goodman Story, 1956; recorded for Armed Forces Radio Information Recordings, also ednl. jazz film for USIS. Mem. A.S.C.A.P., hot clubs France Grand Prix, 1962, Prix Mondial, 1964, Belgium, Denmark, Holland. So. Cal. Hot Jazz Soc. Composer: Muskrat Ramble, Savoy Blues, Ory's Creole Trombone, The Girl's Go Crazy About the Way IWalk, Blues for Jimmy, Ory's Boogie, Creole Song, Do What Ory Walk, Blues for Jimmy, Ory's Boogie, Creole Song, Do What Ory Say, Sweet Little Papa, Blanche Touquatoux, Booboo's Blue; (lyrics) Eh, La Bas. Address: Honolulu HI Died Jan. 24, 1973; buried Holy Cross Cemetery, Inglewood CA

OSBORN, ALBERT DUNBAR, profl. document examiner; b. Rochester, N.Y., Mar. 2, 1896; s. Albert Sherman and Elizabeth (Dunbar) O.; student Dartmouth, 1916-17; m. Grace Jeannot Ackerman, Oct. 28, 1927; children—Paul A., Russell D. Examination of handwriting, typewriting, ink, erasures, and alterations in documents leading to ct. trials, including N.J. vs. Hauptmann; pioneered use ultra-violet light to observe erased writing; asso. Albert S. Orborn, 1919-46. Treas., Internationality Council N.J. Bd. dirs. Am. Field Service. Served with Am. Field Service in France, 1917, with 27th Div., U.S. Army, 1918-19. Fellow Am. Acad. Forensic Scis.; mem. Am. Soc. Questioned Document Examiners (pres. 1950-51), Delta Kappa Epsilon. Republican. Unitarian. Club: Dartmouth. Author: (with Albert S. Osborn) Questioned Document Problems, 1944. Home: Montclair NJ Died Oct. 27, 1972.

OSBORN, CYRUS RICHARD, executive; b. Dayton, O., Aug. 27, 1897; s. Cyrus and Stella (Hopkins) O.; M.E., U. of Cincinnati, 1921, D.Sc. (hon.), 1948; m. Jeannette Powell, Feb. 20, 1926; children—Sarah Ann, Cyrus William. Tech. engr. Overseas Motor Serv. Corp., 1923-26, gen. mgr., 1926-29; v.p. in charge mfg. Gen. Motors Export Co., 1929-32; mng. dir. Gen. Motors Nordiska, Stockholm, Sweden, 1932-34; asst. to gen. mgr., Gen. Motors Export Div., 1934-36; gen. mgr., Adam Opel, Russelsheim, Germany, 1936-40; asst. to vice pres., Gen. Motors Corp., 1940-41, asst. group exec., 1941-43, vice pres. Gen. Motors Corp., gen. mgr. Electro-Motive div., 1943-50, v.p. in charge engine group Gen. Motors Corp., 1950-59, dir., 1951-63, exec. v.p. engine divs., 1959-63. Served as pvt., U.S. Army, 1918-19. Mem. Soc. Automotive Engrs., Phi Delta Theta, Tau Beta Pi. Republican. Presbyterian. Clubs: Detroit, Bloomfield Hills Country, Economic. Home: Bloomfield Hills MI Died Nov. 15, 1968; buried Dayton OH

OSBORN, FAIRFIELD, naturalist; b. Princeton, N.J., Jan. 15, 1887; s. Henry Fairfield and Lucretia (Perry) O.; grad. Groton Sch., 1905; A.B., Princeton, 1909; grad. work Cambridge U., Eng., 1909-10; D.Sc., N.Y.U., 1955; D.Sc., Princeton, 1957; LL.D., Kenyon College, 1959, Hofstra University, 1966; D.Sc., University of Buffalo, 1962; married Marjorie Mary Lamond, Sept. 8, 1914; children—Nathalie Hazard (Mrs. R. C. Murphy, Jr.), Shirley (Mrs. L. Ayers), Josephine Adams (Mrs. W. M. Roth). Pres. N.Y. Zool. Soc. 1940-69 (mem. exec. com. of bd. trustees 1923-69, sec., 1935-39). Awarded Guttenberg Special Citation; Medal of Honor of the Roosevelt Meml. Assn., St. Nicholas Soc. Distinguished Service Medal. President of the Conservation Foundation, 1948-62, chairman of board, 1962-69; mem. Am. Com. of Internat. Council of Museums; member council of Save The Redwoods League; Member exec. com., adv. bd. Am. Com. Internat. Wild Life Protection; mem. Am. Forestry Assn. (hon. v.p. 1957), Internat. Com. Bird Preservation, Nat. Audubon Soc. Foreign fellow Zoological Society of London. Fellow, N.Y. Acad. Sci. Episcopalian. Clubs: University, Boone & Crockett, Coffee House, Explorers, Century Assn. Editor: The Pacific World (Norton), 1944. Author: Our Plundered Planet, 1948; The Limits of the Earth, 1953. Editor: Our Crowded Planet, 1962. Contbr. articles tech. publs. Home: New York City NY Died Sept. 16, 1969; buried Garrison NY

OSBORN, GEORGE AUGUSTUS, newspaper pub.; born Florence, Wis., Feb. 24, 1884; s. Chase Salmon and Lillian (Jones) O.; A.B., U. Mich., 1907; B.S., Mich. Coll. of Mines, 1910; E.M., 1910; LL.D., Mich. Coll. Mining and Tech., 1961; m. Emma Hannay Dunstan, Sept. 14, 1910 (dec. 1966); children—Helen Dunstan, Ann, George Augustus III (dec.), Janet Mary. Pub., editor Sault Ste Marie (Mich.) News from 1912; became pub., 1915, of Fresno (Calif.) Herald, merged, 1920, with Fresno Republican (Herald sold 1922); pres. Fresno Republican Pub. Co. to 1932 when sold interest; chmn. Sault News Printing Co.; v.p., dir. 1st Nat. Bank, Sault Ste Marie. Del., Rep. Nat. Conv., Kansas City, Mo., 1928; mem. Mich. Unemployment Ins. Study Commn., 1936; dir. Bay Cliff Health Camp; pres. Mich. Merit System Assn., 1936-37; pres. Mich. Press Assn., 1943; pres. Community War Chest, 1943; mem. Straits Mackinac Bridge Authority. Mem. bd. control Mich. Coll. Mining and Tech., 1947-53; mem. bd. control of student publs., U. Mich.; mem. Michigan Civil War Centennial Commission. Mem. Nat. Council from Hiawathaland Council of Boy Scouts Am. Mem. Am. Soc. Newspaper Editors, Hist. Soc. Mich. (pres. 1964-65, trustee 1962-65). Republican. Episcopalian. Mason, Elk, K.P. Clubs: Rotary. U. Mich. Press (pres. 1936). Address: Sault Ste Marie MI Died Jan. 22, 1972; buried Sault Ste Marie MI

OSBORNE, JOHN BALL, consul gen., retired; born Wilkes-Barre, Pa., June 24, 1868; s. Gen. Edwin S. and Ruth (Ball) O.; A.B., Yale, 1889, A.M., 1894; m. Bertha J. Grinnell, Oct. 1, 1891; children—Grace Josephine (Mrs. Cyril Kingenberg), Ruth Elizabeth (Mrs. W. F. Cupples, Jr.), Edwin Grinnell, Bradford Allen. U.S. consul at Ghent, Belgium, 1889-94; studied law in father's office; admitted to bar, Luzerne County, Pa., Jan. 1895, to Phila. bar, Mar. 30, 1895; practiced at Phila. Joint sec. Reciprocity Commn., 1897-1905; chief Bur. Trade Relations, Dept. of State, 1905-12; Am. consul, Havre, France, Aug. 22, 1912, promoted consulgen. at Havre, Sept. 8, 1919; Christiania, Norway, June 30, 1920, Genoa, Italy, supervisory jurisdiction throughout Italy, 1921-26; Stockholm, Sweden, with supervision for all Sweden, 1926-31, Budapest, Hungary, 1931-33, retired, June 30, 1933. Hon. commr.-gen. of U.S. to Universal and Internat. Expn., Brussels, 1910, U.S. del. to Internat. Congress of Chambers of Commerce and Comml. and Indsl. Assn., London, 1910. U.S. del. to Congress of Internat. C. of C., Stockholm, 1927. Lecturer on trade relations, Coll. Polit. Sciences, George Washington U., D.C., 1907-12. Mem. Nat. Geog. Soc., Mil. Order Loyal Legion, Zeta Psi. Republican. Episcopalian. Club: Yale. Author: The Story of Arlington, 1899. Contbr. to mags. and other periodicals on econ. and gen. topics. Address: Westchester Apts., 4000 Cathedral Av. N.W., Washington‡

OSBORNE, MILTON SMITH, architect, consultant; b. Zanesville, O., Mar. 18, 1897; s. Lee and Susanna (Smith) O.; B.Arch., Ohio State U., 1922, Columbia, 1925; M.S., Columbia, 1928; LL.D., U. Man., 1959; m. Sophia May Bookwalter, July 30, 1925; 1 dau. (adopted), Nancy Jean. Dir. U. Man. Sch. Architecture and Fine Arts, 1929-46; prof. architecture, head dept. Pa. State U., 1946-62, prof. architecture emeritus, 1962-72; exhibited drawings of colonial, classic revival bldgs. U.S., Can., Mexico; sketches of European architecture exhibited Nat. Gallery Can., Winnipeg Art Gallery; drawings of colonial, classic revival bldgs. in permanent collection Library Congress, Washington, historic bldgs. of Pa. in permanent collection Pa. Hist. Mus.; designer Gettysburg home Pres. Eisenhower; cons. city planning, rehab. bus. areas. Chmn., Centre Regional Planning Commn.; mem. State College Planning Commn.; mem. Gov.'s Conf. on Natural Beauty, 1966. Dir., v.p. Winnipeg Art Gallery, 1935-46; acting dir. Sch. Architecture U. Toronto, 1957-58. Bd. dirs. Pa. Art Alliance. Practicing registered architect. Fellow Royal Archtl. Inst. Can., Royal Soc. Arts; mem. A.I.A., Man. Assn. Architects (hon. life) Am. Assn. U. Profs., Am. Soc. Engring. Edn., Man. Soc. Artists, Tau Beta Pi, Tau Sigma Delta, Phi Kappa Phi. Rotarian. Club: University. Treatises on early architecture of Ala., Ohio, Man. Home: State College PA Died Nov. 6, 1972; buried Centre County Meml. Park, State College PA

OSBORNE, REGINALD STANLEY, elec. exec.; b. nr. Foxton, N.Z., Feb. 2, 1892; s. Edmund John and Harriet (Nye) B.; student Tech. Coll., Palmerston North, N.Z., 1910; extension courses Columbia, N.Y., William and Mary, Va. univs.; m. Olga Wood, Mar. 25, 1923; children—Jacquelyn Wood (Mrs. William Ross), Geraldyn Frances (Mrs. Robert K. Molloy). Came to the United States, 1912, naturalized, 1924. Gen. superintendent, consulting engineer Acme Bldg. Corp., N.Y. City, 1914-18; orgn. Virginia-Carolina Elec. Works, Inc., Norfolk, Va., 1918, served as pres., 1922-45, director, from 1918, chairman of the board, from 1956; president of Virginia-Carolina Electric Sales, Inc., from 1945, Petroleum Shipping Company, Incorporated, from 1946, Stanart Corporation, from 1954, Electrical Suppliers, Inc., 1936-44, Virginia-Caroline Engineering, Inc., 1930-42. Orgn. received Certificate of Achievement (Navy) for services rendered during World War II. Mem. Am. Orchid Soc., Norfolk Portsmouth Real Estate Board, Y.M.C.A. (director), Society Naval Architects and Marine Engrs., Maritime Assn., Isaac Walton League, C. of C., Nat. Defense Transportation Association (1st v.p.). Presbyn. (deacon). Clubs: Cedar Island Gunning (pres.); Lions; Propeller of U.S. (nat. v.p., mem. bd. govs., Port of Norfolk, com. sponsoring sea scout activities, Norfolk); The Cavalier Yacht and Country, Norfolk Yacht and Country, Virginia (Norfolk). The Osborne Family portrait hangs in the Nat. Archives Gallery, Wellington, N.Z., in recognition of family contribution toward World War I effort. Home: Virginia Beach VA Died Feb. 8, 1967; buried Forest Lawn, Norfolk VA

OSBOURN, SAMUEL EDMUND, educator; b. Shenandoah Junction, W.Va., June 2, 1875; s. James Burr and Nancy Alice (Link) O.; grad. Shepherd Coll. State Normal School, Shepherdstown, W.Va., 1894; A.B. and B.S., Hampden-Sydney (Va.) Coll., 1901, LL.D., 1930; A.M., Princeton, 1904; grad. study, Harvard, summer 1915; hon. A.M., U. of Pa., 1926; m. Mary Day Poore, June 18, 1912; children—James P., Samuel, Jr., Elizabeth (Mrs. R.S. McCoy). Teacher, pub. schs., W.Va., 1894-97; teacher of mathematics, Fredericksburg (Va.) Coll., 1901-03, Lawrenceville (N.J.) Sch., 1904-09, Tome Sch., Port Deposit, Md., 1909-15; headmaster Germantown Acad., 1915-48, ret. 1948; asso. dir. Rittenhouse Coll. since 1948. Mem. Germantown Community Council. Trustee Y.M.C.A., Germantown, Whosoever Gospel Mission, Am. Bible Soc. Mem. Assn. Colls. and Prep. Schs. Middle States and Md., Headmasters Assn. of New Eng.; mem. Phila. Private School Headmasters Assn.; mem. Country Day Schools of Am. Headmasters Assn. (v.p. 1945). Numerous articles and talks on secondary edn. Mem. Kappa Sigma. Democrat. Presbyterian (elder). Clubs: University, Princeton, Philadelphia PA‡

OSGOOD, EDWIN EUGENE, medical educator; b. Fall River, Mass., Jan. 25, 1899; s. William Pleasants and Lydia Lee (Smith) O.; McMinnville (now Linfield) Coll., 1916-18; B.A., U. of Ore., 1923, M.A., M.D., 1924; grad. study, Mayo Clinic, Rochester, Minn., 1923, 26, U. of Vienna, 1927-28. Basel, Freiburg, London, 1928; m. Mable Maru Wilhelm, May 30, 1934; children—Barbara Delight, Beverly Maru, Edwin Boyd, Brenda Gay, Beatrice Joy. Asst. in biochemistry, U. of Ore., 1919-21, instr. in biochemistry, 1921-25, asso. in same, 1925-28, asso. in medicine, 1925-29, asst. prof. biochemistry, 1928-33, asst. prof. medicine, 1929-39, asso. prof., 1939-47, prof. since 1947; director of laboratories, University of Oregon Medical School, 1928-1936; member of staff of Multnomah County and Doernbecher hosps. from 1928, head div. experimental medicine, 1936-64, associate head, 1964-69. Recipient bronze metal sci. exhibit American Medical Association, 1929, hon. mention, 1934, certificate merit, 1938. Distinguished Achievement award, Modern Medicine mag., 1957; U. Ore. Med. School Alumni Assn. meritorious achievement award, 1962; Gov.'s Northwest Scientist award for research in leukemia and Osgood growth prediction charts, 1962; N.W. Sci. award for unraveling human chromosome Ore. Mus. Sci. and Industry, 1963; Robert Roesler de Villiers award for research in leukemia, 1963. Master Am. Coll. Physicians; fellow International Soc. Hematology (councilor U.S. 1950-52), N.Y. Acad. Sci.; mem. Am. Med. Assn., Am. Heart Assn., Pacific Interurban Clin. Club, Ore. State and Portland City and Co. med. socs., Soc. Exptl. Biology and Medicine, N. Pacific Soc. of Internists (pres. 1950-51), Portland Acad. of Medicine (pres. 1952), Society Clinical Investigation, Western Association of Physicians (v.p., 1958-59), American Society of Hematology (vice president, 1958-59), Alpha Kappa Kappa, Alpha Omega Alpha, Sigma Xi. Republican. Club: University. Author: Textbook of Laboratory Diagnosis, 1931 (3d edit. 1940). Co-author of Atlas of Hematology, 1937. Contbr. to Jour. A.M.A., Jour. Lab. and Clin. Medicine, Archives of Internal Medicine, etc. Originator of method of culture of human marrow; developed method to keep human blood cells living over 10 yrs. in culture; Alpha-N concept cell div., cancer and aging. Home: Portland OR Died Oct. 22, 1969; buried Skyline Meml. Gardens, Portland OR

OSGOOD, ELLIS CARLTON, physician; b. Atlantic City, Feb. 27, 1909; s. Ellis S. and Mary (Todd) O.; B.S., Haverford Coll., 1932; M.D., U. Pa., 1938, D.Sc. in Medicine, 1947; m. Katherine Eleanor Wilson, May 23, 1942. Intern, Phila. Gen. Hosp., 1938-40; resident in radiology Episcopal Hosp., Phila., 1940-41, Hosp. of U. Pa., 1941-44; fellow in radiology U. Pa. Grad. Sch. Medicine, 1941-44; instr. radiology U. Pa., 1941-44; radiologist Queen of Angels Hosp., Los Angeles, 1944-46, St. Vincent's Hosp., Los Angeles, 1947-55; asst. clin. prof. radiology U. So. Cal. Sch. Medicine, 1950-52; clin. asso. dept. radiology U. Cal. Hosp., San Francisco, 1953; practice medicine specializing in radiology, Los Angeles, 1955-70; cons. radiology Western Home Office, Prudential Ins. Co. Am., Occidental Ins. Co., Los Angeles. Diplomate Am. Bd. Radiology. Fellow Am. Coll. Radiology; mem. A.M.A., Radio. Soc. N.Am., Pacific Roentgen Ray Soc., Radiol. Soc. So. Cal., Cal., Los Angeles County med. assns., Los Angeles Acad. Medicine. Home: Los Angeles CA Died Jan. 27, 1970; buried Atlantic City Cemetery, Pleasantville NJ

OSKISON, JOHN MILTON, writer; b. Vinita, Ind. Ty., Sept. 21, 1874; s. John and Rachel (Critenden) O.; (mother quarter blood Cherokee Indian); M.L., Willie Halsell Coll., 1894; B.A., Stanford, 1898; studied at Harvard U., 1898-99; m. Florence Ballard Day, of New York, Oct. 21, 1903; children—Helen Day, Oliver Day; m. 2d, Hildegarde Hawthorne, author, of N.Y. City, July 16, 1920. Exchange editor and editorial writer, New York Evening Post, 1903-06; spl. writer on, and asso. editor of Collier's Weekly, 1907-10, financial editor, 1910-12; spl. writer for a syndicate of newspapers on financial topics; spl. writer on Indians for newspapers and mags. Winner Century Magazine's prize competition for coll. grads., 1898, with short story, Only the Master Shall Praise," pub. Jan. 1900; winner of a Black Cat Prize, 1904, with story, The Greater Appeal." Commd. 2d lt. Cav. N.A., Aug. 15, 1917; 1st lt. Inf. N.A., Jan. 3, 1918; served with A.E.F. in France, Apr. 1918-Sept. 23, 1919; discharged, Sept. 23, 1919. Author: Wild Harvest, 1925; Black Jack Davy, 1926; A Texas Titan, 1929; Vision Victorious, 1931; Lone Rider, 1933; Brothers Three, 1935. Contbr. short stories to mags.*‡

OSORIO, OSCAR, pres. El Salvador; b. Sonsomate, El Salvador, 1910. Prominent in revolutionary movement of 1945; forced to leave country, stayed in Mexico; returned to El Salvador, 1948; mem. Revolutionary Council; pres. El Salvador, 1950-56. Home: El Salvador Died Mar. 1969.*

OSTERHAUS, HUGO WILSON, naval officer (ret.); b. Norfolk, Va., Nov. 12, 1878; s. Hugo and Mary Willoughby (Wilson) O.; grad. U.S. Naval Acad., 1900; m. Helen Huntington Downing, Dec. 4, 1913; 1 son, Hugo Wilson. Served with U.S. Navy, 1896-1935, progressing through various grades to rear adm., 1935; served actively in Cuban waters, 1898, Cuban Pacification, 1906, Philippine Insurrection, 1900-04, in European waters during World War; retired, 1935; recalled to active duty as commander Patrol Forces, 12th Naval District, June 1941. Episcopalian. Republican. Clubs: Army and Navy Club, Army and Navy Country Club (Washington); Chevy Chase (Md.) Country; N.Y. Yacht (N.Y. City); Racquet, University (Phila.); Presidio Golf, Bohemian (San Francisco). Address: Saratoga CA Died Sept. 17, 1972; buried Arlington Nat. Cemetery, Arlington VA

OSTERTAG, BLANCHE, artist; b. St. Louis, Mo. Studied under Laurens, L'Hermitte and Delance, Paris. Exhibited in Champ de Mars Salons, 1895, 1896. Mem. Soc. Western Artists. Author: Old Songs for Young America, 1901 D6. Address: Chicago‡

OSTRANDER, DON RICHARD, retired air force officer; b. Stockbridge, Mich., Sept. 24, 1914; s. Wilbur Tindle and Hazel Dell (Hall) O.; student Western State Coll., Kalamazoo, 1931-32; B.S., U.S. Mil. Acad., 1937; grad. Indsl. Coll. Armed Forces, 1947, Advanced Mgmt. Program, Harvard, 1954; m. Frances Ann Dunn, July 6, 1940; children—Mary Frances, Don Richard, Sally Ann. Commd. 2d lt. Cav., U.S. Army, 1937, advanced through grades to maj. gen. USAF, 1958; with Cav., 1938-39; detailed Ordnance Dept., 1939; ordnance, armament officer 8th Fighter Command, ETO, 1942-44; with hdqrs. AAFTAC, Orlando, Fla., 1944-46; armament lab. and chief plans office, engrs. div. Hdqrs. AMC, Dayton, O., 1947-51; dep. comdr., then comdr. Holloman Air Devel. Center, Alamogordo, N.M., 1951-54; assigned hdqrs. ARDC, 1954-58; asst. for guided missiles NATO Internat. Staff, 1958-59; dep. comdr. Advanced Research Projects Agy., 1959; dir. launch vehicle programs NASA, 1960-61; vice comdr. ballistic systems div. Air Force Systems Command, Los Angeles, 1961-62; comdr. Office Aerospace Research, Washington 1962-65, ret., 1965. Decorated Legion of Merit with 2 clusters, D.S.M. Home: Annapolis MD Died Oct. 26, 1972; buried Arlington Nat. Cemetery, Arlington VA

O'SULLIVAN, VINCENT, author; b. N.Y. City, Nov. 28, 1872; s. Eugene and Christine O'S.; ed. grammar sch., New York; Exeter Coll. (Oxford), Eng., and in France; unmarried. Adj. prof. English and Am. literature, Univ. of Rennes, France, 1918-19. Author: A Book of Bargains, 1896; Poems, 1896; The Houses of Sin (poems), 1897; The Green Window, 1899; A Dissertation Upon Second Fiddles, 1902; Human Affairs, 1905; The Good Girl, 1912; Sentiment, 1913; Contes d'Amerique (in French), 1924; (plays) The Hartley Family; The Lighthouse. Translator: Saint Augustine (by L. Bertrand), 1914; Autobiography of Antoine Bourdelle, the Sculptor, 1927; Aspects of Wilde, 1936. Editor of a critical edit. of Ben Johnson's Volpone. Address: care Morgan & Co., Paris France*‡

OTSUKA, RAYMOND M., physician; b. Wailuku, Maui, Hawaii, Deb. 4, 1910; M.D., Rush Med. Coll., Chgo., 1937; m. LaVerne Alice Sauers, Feb. 14, 1940; children—Conrad, Cora, Frank, Anthony, Christine, Dawn and Claudia (twins), Joel. Intern, Cook County Hosp., Chgo., 1940-41, resident in dermatology, 1941-44, resident in radiology, 1944-45, fellow in roentgenology therapy; resident in radiology Ill. Research Hosp., Chgo., 1945-47. Diplomate Am. Bd. Radiology. Mem. A.M.A. Home: Wailuku Maui HI Died Jan. 5, 1965; buried Wailuku Maui HI

OTT, HARVEY NEWTON, designer and mfr. of microscopes and scientific apparatus; b. Walker, Mo., Sept. 18, 1868; s. James Harvey and Mary Sofia (White) O.; grad. high sch., Albion, Mich., 1844; Ph.B., Albion Coll., 1889, hon. D.Sc., 1940; Ph.M., U. of Mich.., 1891; m. Zua Warren Thomas, July 16, 1890; children—Helen Marie (dec.), Harry Glenn; m. 2d, Elizabeth Louise Smith, Oct. 12, 1915. Teacher of biology, Puget Sound Coll., Tacoma, Wash., 1891-93; professor zoology and comparative anatomy, S.D. State Coll., 1893-95; salesman Bausch & Lomb Optical Co., 1896-1903; salesman Spencer Lens Co., mfrs. microscopes and scientific optical instruments, Buffalo, N.Y., 1903-07, gen. mgr., 1907-37, pres. 1919-39, chmn. bd. of dirs., 1939-42, retired Jan. 1, 1942. Trustee Albion Coll. since 1941. Mem. Bd., Buffalo Goodwill Industries. Mem. A.A.A.S., Am. Assn. Scientific Apparatus Makers (ex-pres.), Delta Tau Delta. Republican. Methodist. Clubs: Buffalo Athletic, Buffalo Automobile. Home: 103 Woodbridge Av., Buffalo 14 NY‡

OTTEMILLER, JOHN H(ENRY), librarian, govt. official; b. York, Pa., Sept. 17, 1916; s. Walter Franklin and Maude Estelle (Robey) O.; student, Bread Loaf Sch. of English Middlebury, Vt., 1935-36; A.B., Middlebury (Vt.) Coll., 1938; B.S., Sch. of Library Science, Columbia U., 1940; m. Frances Josephine Thompson, March, 24 1943; children—Joan, John Thompson. Circulation and reference asst., Columbia Coll. Library, 1938-39, 1940-42; asst. preparations div., N.Y. Pub. Library, 1939-40; asst. to librarian Brown U., 1942-44; interdepartmental com. for the acquisition of fgn. publs., Office of Strategic Services, U.S. Govt., 1944-45; acting asst. chief reference div., U.S. Dept. of State, April 1946, acting chief, Aug. 1946, chief, Nov. 1947, acting chief div. of library and reference services, 1948-51; associate librarian, Yale University, 1951-57, associate University librarian, 1957-68; associate in univ. library adminstrn., Simmons Coll. of Library Science, 1953-55. Founder, pres. Shoe String Press, Inc., 1952-68; founder, sec.-treas. Tompsons Malone, Inc., 1957-68. Member of the U.S. Civil Service Com. of Expert Examiners, 1948-51. Chmn. adv. com. of So. Connecticut State Coll. Mem. A.L.A., Conn. Library Assn., Bibliog. Soc. Am., Alpha Sigma Phi. United Brethren religion. Clubs: Groiler; Yale (N.Y.). Author: Index to Plays in Collections, 1900-42, 1943, 4th edit., 1964; Yale's Selective Book Retirement Program. Gen. editor: Who's Who In Library Service, 4th edit. Home: Hamden CT Died July 22, 1968.

OTTO, MAX CARL, prof. philosophy; b. Zwickau (Saxony), Germany, Sept. 28, 1876; s. Carl Friederich and Ernestine (Kunsel) O.; brought to U.S. at age of 5, B.A., U. of Wis., 1906, M.A., 1908, Ph.D., 1911; studied Carroll Coll., U. of Chicago and Heidelberg, Germany; m. Rhoda Owen, June 1920; children—Owen, Mary Ernestine. Mem. faculty U. of Wis. from 1910, prof. philosophy, 1921-47, ret. Mem. Am. Philos. Assn. (pres. Western br. 1929). Author: Things and Ideals, 1924; Natural Laws and Human Hopes, 1926; Is There a God? (with H. N. Wieman and D. C. Macintosh), 1932; The Human Enterprise, 1940. Co-author: Philosophy in American Education, 1945; Religious Liberals Reply, 1947. Contbr. to philos. jours. Home: Madison WI Died Oct. 1968.

OTTOERBOURG, EDWIN M., lawyer; b. N.Y.C., Oct. 1, 1885; s. Eugene and Sarah (Meyerberg) O.; student Coll. City N.Y., 1900-04; LL.B. cum laude, N.Y. Law Sch., 1906. Admitted to N.Y. bar, 1906, since practiced in N.Y.C.; organizer, sr. mem. Otterbourg, Steindler, Houston & Rosen, from 1906. Former chmn. conf. groups Am. Bankers Assn. (trust div.), Nat. Assn. Life Underwriters, Nat. Assn. Real Estate Bds. Mem. Am. Bar Assn. (chmn. com. on unauthorized practice law, 1939-43), N.Y. Co. Lawyers Assn. (v.p. 1950-51; president 1952-54; former del. to Am. Bar Assn. Ho. of Dels.; past chmn. com. on unlawful practice law), Assn. Bar City N.Y. Club: City Athletic. Author: Lost in the Bungle, 1918; A Study of Unauthorized Practice of Law (prepared for Survey of Legal Profession), 1951; other articles and pamphlets relating to bankruptcy and reorgn. Address: New York City NY Died Oct. 17, 1968.

OTTOFY, LOUIS, dental lexicographer, educator; b. Budapest, Oct. 22, 1860; s. Leopold and Louise (Lauffer) O.; came to U.S., 1874; D.D.S., Western Coll. Dental Surgeons, St. Louis, Mo., 1879; hon. M.D., St. Louis Coll. Phys. and Surgs., 1915; LL.D., McKendree Coll., Lebanon, Ill., 1928; m. Nellie Freeman, Dec. 27, 1887; children—Gloria Columbia (dec.), Frederic Freeman. Practiced at Chicago, Yokohama and Manila; prof. physiology, 1890-93, prof. clin. dental therapeutics, 1896-98, Chicago Coll. Dental Surgery; dean and prof. dental pathology, Am. Coll. Dental Surgery, Chicago, 1893-96; resided Japan, 1898-99 and 1920-21, Manila, 1899-1920; dir. Sch. of Dentistry, U. of Philippines, 1915-19; maj. and supervising dental surgeon, Dental Corps, U.S. Army, 1918; ednl. dir. McCarrie Schs. of Mechanical Dentistry, 1926-28, ednl. counselor same since 1928; dean and prof. dental technology, Institute of Dental Science, Oakland, Calif., 1929-30. Made first survey and tabulation of condition of human teeth in the history of dentistry of a group of children in pub. sch., Lebanon, Ill., 1882; made similar surveys in Japan and Philippines, of Chinese, Igorots, Negritos, lepers, etc. Mem. Am. and Ill. (life) dental socs., Chicago Dental Soc. (pres. 1896), Am. Soc. Stomatologists (pres. 1927), Alameda County (Calif.) Dist. Dental Soc., Assn. Mil. Dental Surgeons of U.S.; Mil. Order World War, Delta Sigma Delta, Pi Gamma Mu; founder, fellow and registrar Internat. Coll. of Dentists, 1928; sec. Bd. of Dental Examiners of Philippine Islands, 1914-15. Mason (K.T., Shriner). Club: University (Manila). Author: Outlines of Dental Pathology, 1895; Plantation of Teeth (in Am. Textbook of Operative Dentistry), 1897-1911; All About Your Teeth, Gums and Dentist, 1938; compiler and editor Standard Dental Dictionary, 1923; editor Polk's Dental Register of U.S. and Can., 1925-27 and 1928-30, Internat. Dental Review since 1931. Contbr. over 200 articles on dentistry to jours. Hon. mention and cash prize for essay on Rootfilling and Focal Infection," Internat. Bur. for Protection of Animals, Geneva, 1933. Address: 175 Vernon Terrace, Oakland CA*‡

OVENSHINE, ALEXANDER THOMPSON, army officer; b. Ft. Leavenworth, Kan., June 25, 1873; s. Samuel and Sallie Yeatman (Thompson) O.; student Infantry and Cavalry Sch., 1907, Army Signal Sch., 1908; m. Mary Louise Powell, Dec. 24, 1898; children—Richard Powell, Eugene Samuel, Mary Louise. Enlisted in pvt. 21st Inf., U.S. Army, 1894; commd. 2d lt., 1897; advanced through grades to brig. gen., 1933; retired, June 30, 1937. Awarded D.S.M. and Silver Star (U.S.). Episcopalian. Club: Army and Navy Country (Arlington, Va.). Address: 304 Geneseo Road., San Antonio 9 TX‡

OVERBECK, REYNOLDS COVEL, chemist; b. Hallton, Pa., July 17, 1918; s. Malcolm Thomas and Bessie (Covel) O.; B.A., Wooster Coll., 1940. Chemist, Ohio Agrl. Expt. Sta., Wooster, O., 1938-44; critic prof. edn. Wooster (O.) Coll., 1940-47; chemist Battelle Meml. Inst., Columbus, 1948-51, cons., 1951-71. Fellow Am. Inst. Chemists; mem. Am. Chem. Soc. A.A.A.S., N.Y. Acad. Scis., Ohio Acad. Sci., Nat. Inst. Food Tech. Inventor mercury cathode for chem. analysis, high speed copper analysis apparatus; research trace element analyses, odor and perfume chemistry, nutrition, flavor. Home: Columbus OH Died Nov. 1971.

OVERESCH, HARVEY E., ret. naval officer, ins. exec.; b. Lafayette, Ind., January 20, 1893; s. Henry B. and Anna B. T. (Weil) O.; student Purdue U., 1910; grad. U.S. Naval Acad., 1915; M.S. in Elec. Engring., Columbia, 1922; m. Emily Hodges Forman, Apr. 14, 1917; 1 dau., Emily Hodges (Mrs. James C. Castle). Commd. ensign USN, 1915, advanced through grades to rear adm., 1945; served in U.S.S. South Carolina, World War I; naval attach, Peiping, China, 1937-40; comdr. Destroyer Squadron 5, comdt. Midshipment U.S. Naval Acad.; comdg. officer, Cruiser U.S.S. San Francisco, World War II; ret. as vice adm., 1946; v.p. Hawaiian Pineapple Co., 1946-47; resident v.p., dir. N.Am. Life Ins. Co., Chgo., 1948-67; U.S. Dept. State, attache Am. Embassy, Tokyo, Japan, 1952-55, London, Eng., 1955-57. Clubs: Chevy Chase, Army and Navy (Washington); N.Y. Yacht; Ends of the Earth, St. James (London); Cypress Point (Pebble Beach); Old Capitol (Monterey, Cal.). Home: Pebble Beach CA Died Jan. 19, 1973.

OVERFIELD, CHAUNCEY PERCIVAL, business exec.; b. Brooklyn, Jan. 23, 1872; s. John L. and Olivia M. (Binns) O.; ed. pub. schs.; m. Ione P. Morrison, Oct. 27, 1909; children—Ione (dec.), Janice (Rusack), Muriel (Clark). Pres. Overfield Investment Co., Salt Lake City; v.p. Am. Stoker Co., N.Y.; pres. Kenilworth Mercantile Co.; Commr. Seattle Expn., 1909; del. Dem. Nat. Conv., 1912; treas. Dem. State Com., Utah, many yrs.; former chmn. Rep. Party Finance Com., State of Utah; pres. Hughes Alliance, Utah, 1916. Candidate for Senate, 1930. Mem. Am. Inst. Mining and Metall. Engrs. (life), Soc. Colonial Wars (awarded D.S. certificate by same for work in World War), S.A.R. (citation and gold medal) (ex-pres. Utah soc.; dir. gen. nat. soc., 1925-28). Dir. St. Mark's Hosp.; del. Gen. Conv. P.E. Ch., Washington, D.C., 1928, Denver, Colo., 1931, Atlantic City, 1934, Cincinnati, 1937, Kansas City, 1940. Cleveland, 1943, Phila., 1946; mem. Nat. Com. Washington Cathedral; Utah Commn. N.Y. World's Fair, 1939; chmn. Utah George Washington Bicentennial Commn., 1932 (received thanks joint Session, Utah State Legislature for services in connection therewith 1933); former trustee Rowland Hall, Salt Lake City; hon. v.p. Yorktown Sesquicentennial Celebration, 1932, Clubs: Alta (Salt Lake City); Silver Bow (Butte, Mont.); Bankers, Rocky Mountain (New York). Presented with Commemorative Medal by French Govt. Gold Medal S.A.R.; named first citizen, Salt Lake Tribune, 1949. Home: 88 Virginia St. Office: Dooly Bldg., Salt Lake City‡

OVERFIELD, PETER D., judge; b. at Auburn, Pa., 1875; s. Paul J. and Sarah (Roe) O.; Mansfield (Pa.) State Normal Sch.; A.B., U. of Pa., 1899, LL.B., 1901; m. Virginia Beale Leckie, of Washington, Apr. 28, 1906. Practiced at Pittsburgh, Pa., and Nome, Alaska, 1901-9; U.S. district judge Div. No. 3, Dist. of Alaska, June 16, 1909-Sept., 1913; resumed practice at Los Angeles. Republican. Mem. Battery A, Light Arty., Phila., and with same in service, 1898, Ponce, P.R. Mem. Commn. on Uniform State Laws. Mem. Am. Acad. Polit. and Social Science, Sigma Chi, S.A.R. Mason. Home: Overfield Cotton Co., Casa Grande AZ‡

OVERSTREET, HARRY ALLEN, coll. prof.; b. San Francisco, Oct. 25, 1875; s. William Franklin and Julia (Detje) O.; A.B., U. of Cal., 1899; B.Sc., Oxford U. (Balliol Coll.), 1901; m. Elsie L. Burr, May 18, 1907; children—Edmund William, Robert Howison, Alan Burr; m. 2d, Bonaro Wilkinson Aug. 23, 1932. Instr. and asso. prof. philosophy, U. of Cal., 1901-11; prof. philosophy and head of dept., Coll. City of N.Y., 1911-39, prof. emeritus, 1939-70; research asso. Am. Assn. Adult Edn., 1939-40; extension lecturer U. of Mich., 1945-70, U. of Calif., 1948. Pres. Am. Assn. Adult Edn., 1940-41. Dir. Leadership School, Town Hall, N.Y., 1940-41; Lecturer New Sch. Social Research, 1924-28, Town Hall, N.Y.C., 1938-70, trustee until 1950. Mem. Phi Beta Kappa, Beta Theta Pi. Author: Influencing Human Behavior, 1925; About Ourselves—Psychology for Normal People, 1927; The Enduring Quest, 1931; We Move in New Directions, 1933; A Guide to Civilized Leisure, 1934; A Declaration of Interdependence, 1937; Town Meeting Comes to Town (with Bonaro W. Overstreet), 1938; Let Me Think, 1939; Leaders for Adult-Education (with Bonaro W. Overstreet), 1940; Our Free Minds, 1941; The Mature Mind, 1949; Where Children Come First (with Bonaro W. Overstreet), 1949; The Great Enterprise—Relating Ourselves to Our World, 1952; The Mind Alive (with B. W. Overstreet), 1954; The Mind Goes Forth 1956; (with B. W. Overstreet) What We Must Know About Communism, 1958; (with B. W. Overstreet) The War Called Peace; Krushchev's Communism, 1961, (with B. W. Overstreet) The Iron Curtain, 1963; (with B. W. Overstreet) The Strange Tactics of Extremism, 1964; (with B.W. Overstreet) The FBI In Our Open Society, 1969; numerous monographs and tech. papers. Home: Falls Church VA Died Aug. 17, 1970; buried National Memorial Park, Falls Church VA

OVERTON, GWENDOLEN, author; b. Fort Hays, Kansas, Feb. 19, 1876; d. Capt. Gilbert (U.S.A.) and Jane (Dyson) O.; ed. pub. schs., also pvt. schs. in Paris and Switzerland; unmarried. Author: The Heritage of Unrest, 1901, 1905; Anne Carmel; Golden Chain; Captains of the World. Contbr. to mags. Address: 709 Trust Bldg., Los Angeles CA‡

OVIATT, DELMAR THOMAS, coll. adminstr.; b. Alberta, Can., Nov. 23, 1911; s. John Frederick and Mary (Hatch) O.; student U. Alta., 1937-40; B.A., Stanford, 1949; m. Hazel Hansen, June 28, 1940; children—MarDel, Moyne. Came to U.S., 1949, naturalized, 1955. Tchr. rural schs., Alta., 1931-37; prin. Barnwell Consol. Schs., Alta., 1940-42; supt. schs., Taber, Alta., 1944-47; curriculum dir. Dept. Edn. Alta., 1947-49; asst. prof. edn. Wash. State Coll., 1950, Los Angeles State Coll., 1950-52; prof. edn. U. Utah, 1952-53, Los Angeles State Coll., 1955-62, v.p. acad. affairs, 1962-69. dir. spl. projects, 1969-72. Home: Northridge CA Died Dec. 24, 1971.

OWEN, ARTHUR DAVID KEMP, U.N. official; b. Pontypool, Monmouthshire, U.K., Nov. 26, 1904; s. Rev. Edward and Gertrude (Kemp) O.; M. Com. cum laude, U. of Leeds (Eng.), 1926, LL.D., 1954; LL.D. (honorary), University of Wales, 1969; m. Joyce Morgan (divorced);children—Roger, Gillian; m. 2d, Elisabeth Miller; children—Michael, Hugh. Asst. lectr. econs. Huddersfield (Eng.) Tech. Coll., 1926-29; dir. Social Survey of Sheffield, 1929-33; sec. civil research div. Polit. and Econ. Planning, London, 1933-36; co-dir. Pilgrim Trust Unemployment Survey, London, 1936-37; Stevenson lecturer in citizenship, Univ. of Glasgow, Scotland, 1937-40; gen. sec. Polit. and Econ. Planning, London, 1940-41; personal asst. to Sir Stafford Cripps: Cripps Mission to India, 1942; office of the Lord Privy Seal, 1942; ministry of aircraft prodn., 1942-43; officer in charge of League of Nations Aff. Fgn. Office, 1944-45; Mem. U.K. del. to I.L.O. Conf., 1944, San Francisco Conf., 1945; dep. exec. sec., Prep. Commn. of U.N., London, 1945-46; asst. sec.-gen. for econ. affairs, U.N., N.Y. City, since 1946; chairman, U.N. Tech. Assistance Bd., 1949-52, exec. chmn., 1952-65; co-adminstr. UN Development Programme, 1966-69; sec.-gen. Internat. Planned Parenthood Fedn., 1969-70. Decorated Knight comdr. St. Michael and St. George. Member Royal Inst. of Internat. Affairs, Royal Economic Soc. (London, England). Clubs: Atheneum (London). Author: Social Survey of Sheffield, Reports, 1931-34; British Social Services, The, 1940; Men Without Work: A Study of Unemployment (with others), 1937. Home: N.Y.C. N.Y. Office: United Nations, NYC NY

OWEN, DAVID EDWARD, educator; b. Owatonna, Minn., Dec. 2, 1898; s. Ernest J. and Martha B. (Tuttle) O.; Ph.B., Denison U., 1920, L.H.D., 1955; Ph.D., Yale, 1927; L.H.D., Carnegie Inst. Tech., 1958; m. Louise E. Hamblen, Sept. 12, 1922; 1 dau., Elizabeth B. (Mrs. Robert Shenton), Instr. history Yale, 1923-27, asst. prof., 1927-38; vis. lectr. Harvard, 1937-38, asso. prof., 1938-46 prof., 1946-68; master John Winthrop House, 1957-64, senior fellow Society of Fellows, 1964-68, Gurney professor history, 1958-68. Social Sci. Research Council, fellow 1932-33. Fellow American Academy of Arts and Sciences. Clubs: Harvard (N.Y.C. and Boston); Signet (Cambridge). Author: Imperialism and Nationalism in the Far East, 1929; British Opium Policy in China and India, 1934; English Philanthropy, 1660-1960, pub. 1964. Home: Cambridge MA Died Feb. 13, 1968; buried Mt. Auburn Cemetery, Cambridge MA

OWEN, STEWART DOUGLAS, newspaperman; b. Louisville, Oct. 7, 1898; s. Thomas Baber and Anna (Misomelius) O.; A.B., U. Ill., 1920; m. Garnett Osborn, Oct. 4, 1925; children—Mary Daniel (Mrs. Vincent Rosenthal), Lynne Elizabeth (Mrs. Peter A. Penczer). Worked as a reporter for the Tulsa (Okla.) World, 1919, Beaumont (Texas) reporter for the Tulsa (Okla.) World, 1919, Beaumont (Texas) Jour., 1920; reporter, telegraph editor, city editor Huntington (W. Va.) Advertiser, 1920-23, Huntington Herald-Dispatch, 1923-28; copy reader, rewrite man Chicago Tribune, 1928-30, asst. sports editor, 1930-39, asst. news editor, 1939-41, news editor, 1941-51, city editor, 1951-54, assistant managing editor, 1954-58, night mng. editor, 1958-61, mng. editor 1961-65. Dir. Tribune Co., Ont. Paper Co., Que. & N. Shore Paper Co. Trustee Robert R. McCormick Charitable Trust, Cantigny Memorial Trust, McCormick-Patterson Trust; bd. dirs. Evanston IL Died Oct. 14, 1970; buried Memorial Park, Evanston IL

OWENS, JOHN WHITEFIELD, newspaper editor; b. Anne Arundel County, Md., Nov. 2, 1884; s. Cyrus Whitefield and Eliza Providence (Brashears) O.; ed. pub. schs. and night and summer courses Johns Hopkins; m. Virginia Dashiell, Sept. 16, 1918 (died May 30, 1926); children—Elizabeth Dashiell (Mrs. John E. Semmes, Jr.), John Whitefield (dec.). Began newspaper work with Baltimore Evening Sun, 1911; political reporter Baltimore Sun, 1913-20, mem. Washington bur. of same, 1920-24, London corr., 1924-26, editorial writer, 1926-27, editor, 1927-38; editor-in-chief The Sun and The Evening Sun, 1938-43, contributing editor, 1943. Home: Cockeysville MD Died Apr. 1968.

OYEN, VALBORG HANSINE (MRS. ARNT J. OYEN), librarian; b. Eau Claire, Wis., Dec. 26, 1907; d. Waldemar Theodore and Gurolle (Blestren) Ager; certificate U. Wis. Library Sch., 1928; m. Arnt J. Oyen, June 13, 1942; children—Waldemar Ager, Hildur Marie (Mrs. Stephen Anthony Gleason). Librarian Eau Claire (Wis.) Pub. Library, 1926-41, Poulsbo (Wash.) Pub. Library. Mem. Sons of Norway. Lutheran. Home: Pouisbo WA Died May 26, 1968; interred Poulsbo Cemetery Poulsbo WA

PABST, CHARLES FREDERICK, physician, dermatologist; b. N.Y.C., Dec. 3, 1887; s. Charles and Margaret (Connorton) P.; M.D., L.I. Coll. Hosp., 1909; intern Brooklyn Hosp., 1910-12; unmarried. Student skin diseases in Puerto Rico and Venezuela; conducted clinic for skin diseases at Brooklyn and Greenpoint hosps., 1914-28; attending dermatologist and chief of clinic for skin diseases at Greenpoint Hosp., 1915-57, consultant dermatologist, 1957-71. Commissioned lieutenant (jr. grade), U.S. Navy R.F., Feb. 20, 1918; lt., grade of passed asst. surgeon, Sept. 18, 1918, in charge treatment of skin diseases at U.S. Naval Hosp., Norfolk, Va., until May 1, 1919. Recipient award from Med. Soc. of State N.Y. Fellow A.M.A., Am. Acad. of Dermatology and Syphilology; mem. N.Y. State Med. Soc., Kings County Med. Soc., Alumnus Club L.I. Hosp., Brooklyn Hosp. Presbyn. Mason (32 deg., K.T.). Contbr. numerous articles on skin diseases and regarded as an authority on the subject. An expert swimmer, and saved several persons from drowning, at different times, on L.I. beaches. Gave U.S. Govt., 1934, nonpatented inexpensive formula for fireprofing ships, clothing and other fabrics; called attention to widespread prevalence of ringworm infection of feet, and started health campaign against bare feet; originated term athlete's foot"; secured almost universal adoption of distinctive shape and color for bichloride of mercury tablets; pointed out dangers of overexposure to summer sun and gave the term heliophobe" to individual whose skin will not tan. Address: Brooklyn NY Died Apr. 15, 1971; buried Long Island Cemetery, Farmingdale NY

PACE, FRANK, lawyer; b. Harrison, Ark., July 25, 1872; s. William Fletcher and Sarah Jane (Howell) P.; student University of Arkansas, 1887-89; m. Flora Layton, June 10, 1908 (died September 25, 1940); 1 son, Frank. Admitted to Arkansas bar, 1890, began practice at Harrison, Arkansas; prosecuting atty. 14th Jud. Dist. of Ark., 1894-96; railroad commr., Ark., 6 mos., 1905. Mem. Am. Bar Assn. (gen. council 1918-26; exec. com. 1926-30), Ark. Bar Assn. Democrat. Presbyterian. Club: Country. Home: 2301 Broadway. Office: Pyramid Bldg., Little Rock AR*‡

PACE PEARL CARTER (MRS. STANLEY D. PACE), Republican National committee-woman; born Tompkinsville, Kentucky, January 25, 1896; daughter James C. and Idru (Tucker) Carter; student, Western State Teachers College, Bowling Green, Kentucky, 1917; m. Stanley D. Pace, December 24, 1917; children—Patty (Mrs. Maurice Keen), Stanley Carter, Mary Elizabeth (Mrs. K.M. Carr). Bookkeeper S.D. Pace Co., 1924-31, Cumberland Constrn. Co., both Burkesville, Ky., 1931-40, sec.-treas., 1940-43, pres. from 1943; sheriff, Cumberland Co., Ky., 1937-41. Active Rep. party since 1932, sec. Cumberland Co. exec. com., 1942-44, chmn. exec. com. from 1944; sec. ninth dist. exec. com., 1940-44, vice chmn. exec. com., 1944-48; nat. com. mem. for Ky. 1948-57. Mem. functions and resources com. Ky. State Govt., 1948-51; mem. War Claims Commn., 1953, Fgn. Claims Settlement Commn. U.S., 1954-61. Mem. nat. bd. Woman's Med. Coll. Pa.; dir., from 1948. Mem. Ky. Fedn. Woman's Clubs (coordination chmn. 1953-54), Nat. (dir.), Ky. (dir.; sec. bd., 1948-51) crushed stone assns., Cancer Soc. Ky. (adv. bd.), Crippled Children's Soc. (adv. bd.), D.C. Fedn. Women's Clubs (chmn. Am. fgn. policy div.). Clubs: English Speaking Union, Washington, Executives Wives and Presidential Women, Capitol Speakers (Washington). Home: Burkesville KY Died Jan. 14, 1970.

PACE, THOMAS A(NDREW), lawyer; b. Washington, July 23, 1901; s. Robert Thomas and Mary A. (Mann) P.; certificate Registro Nacional de Contadores, Chile, 1934; certificates Western Res. U.; LL.B., Columbus U., Washington, 1937; LL.M., Cath. U. Am., 1938; m. Zelma Lorraine Steele, June 16, 1928; children—Thomas Steele, Martha Anne (Mrs. Michael Paul Patchan, Jr.). Page, U.S. Senate and Ho. of Reps., 1913-15; with USMC in France, U.S. Govt. in France, Germany, Belgium and Luxemburg, 1917-22; mem. Am. Relief (Herbert Hoover) Adminstrn. in Russia, 1922-23; Am. embassy, Chile, 1928-30; in constrn. bus., also dir. Fred T. Ley Co. in Chile, 1930-34; with U.S.

Govt., Washington, also Cleve., 1935-43, criminal div. Dept. Justice, Washington, 1944-64; spl. asst. to U.S. atty. gen., prosecuting in P.R., 1953-54; later in pvt. practice. Writer legal and econ. articles; collaborator legal texts, bi-lingual and legal dictionaries. Mem. D.C., Va. bars, Nat. Lawyers Club, Am. Legion, V.F.W., S.A.R., Pace Soc. Am. Home: McLean VA Died Jan. 8, 1969; buried Fairfax VA

PACHLER, WILLIAM JOSEPH, labor union ofcl.; b. Thornwood, N.Y., Aug. 20, 1904; s. John A. and Mary (Reilly) P.; student Fordham U., 1922-23; m. Gunhild Swanson, June 17, 1928; children—Virginia, Gloria, Marion, William. With Consol. Edison Co., N.Y.C. until 1939; pres. local Utility Workers Union Am., 1939-46, nat. sec.-treas., 1946-60, nat. pres., 1960-70. Home: Kensington MD Died May 1970.

PACKARD, GEORGE ARTHUR, mining engr.; b. Wakefield, Mass., Apr. 17, 1869; s. George and Marietta Fulton (Swain) P.; desc. Samuel Packard, Hingham, 1638, John Alden and other Mayflower pilgrims, 1620; S.B., Mass. Inst. Tech., 1890; m. Edythe R. Morrill, Apr. 12, 1899 (died Dec. 16, 1929); m. 2d, Myrtle S. Foster, Aug. 27, 1931. Chemist and supt. copper smelting and leaching in Vt. and Ariz., 1890-92; supt. Desloges Consol. Lead Co., Mo., 1893-94; installing cyanide process and supt. gold and silver mines in Mont., Ariz., Utah and Colo., 1895-1900; consulting mining engr. and metallurgist since 1900 (work covering N. and S. America); mgr. Raven Copper Co., Butte, Mont., 1910-13. Acting prof. metallurgy, U. of Mo. Sch. of Mines, 1907. Mem. Alumni Council Mass. Inst. Tech. Mem. Mining and Metall. Soc. America, Am. Inst. Mining Engrs. (chmn. mining methods com. on precious and rare metals, 1923-29; chmn. advisory board 1930; chmn. Boston sect. 1932), Canadian Inst. of Mining and Metallurgy, Geol. Soc. of Boston; Engring. Socs. of New Eng.; former asso. mem. South African Chem., Metall. and Mining Soc. Clubs: Technology Faculty; Mining Club (New York, N.Y.). Contbr. to tech. press and jours. of tech. socs. Contbr. to tech. press and jours. of tech. socs. Home: Wakefield, Mass.; (summer) Westport Point, Massachusetts. Office: 53 State St., Boston 9 MA‡

PACKER, HERBERT LESLIE, edcuator; b. Jersey City, July 24, 1925; s. Abraham and Lillian (Lieberman) P.; B.A., Yale, 1944, LL.B., 1949; m. Nancy Huddleston, Mar. 15, 1958; children—Ann Elizabeth, George Huddleston. Admitted to N.Y. bar, 1950, also U.S. Supreme Ct.; law clk. U.S. circuit judge Swan, 1949-50; practice in Washington, 1950-55; asso. prof. law Stanford Law Sch., 1956-59, prof. law, 1959-72, vice provost 1967-69. Mem. U.S. atty. general's com. poverty and fed. criminal justice, 1961-63; reporter Revision Cal. Penal Code, 1964-69. Served with USNR, 1944-46. Recipient Lloyd W. Dinkelspiel award, 1969, Triennial award Order of Coif, 1970. Mem. Am. Law Inst., Am. Assn. U. Profs., Phi Delta Phi. Club: Elizabethan (New Haven). Author: Ex-Communist Witnesses: Four Studies in Fact-Finding, 1961; The State of Research in Antitrust Law, 1963; The Limits of the Criminal Sanction, 1968; New Directions in Legal Education, 1972; also articles. Address: Stanford CA Died Dec. 6, 1972.

PACKMAN, JAMES JOSEPH, banker, publicist; b. Biala, Poland, May 10, 1907; s. Max and Annie Jennie (Gershberg) P.; student U. So. Cal., 1924-25; m. Lillian Annette Schwartz, June 9, 1929; children—Barbara Ruth, Phyllis Marlene. Came to U.S., 1910, naturalized, 1939. Copy boy Los Angeles Examiner, 1923-25, copyreader, 1925-27; copyreader Chicago Herald-Examiner and Detroit Times and Detroit Free Press, 1927; asst. real estate editor Los Angeles Examiner, 1928; copyreader Los Angeles Express, 1928-30, San Francisco Examiner, 1930-33; copyreader Los Angeles Examiner, 1933-35, telegraph editor, 1935-37, news editor, 1937-39, news editor asst. to mng. editor, 1939-43; mng. editor Milwaukee (Wis.) Sentinel, 1943-52; mng. editor San Francisco Call Bull., 1952-53; asso. editor Newark (N.J.) Star-Ledger, 1957-58; cons. on polit. and fgn. affairs, newspaper operation procedures, 1958—; pvt. finance as Mchts. & Consumers Indsl. Factors; editor San Francisco Progress, 1960-61; dir. pub. relations Golden Gate Nat. Bank, San Francisco, 1961, v.p., 1962-69. Home: San Francisco CA Died Feb. 12, 1969; buried Hills of Eternity.

PADDOCK, WILLARD DRYDEN, sculptor; b. Brooklyn, N.Y., 1873; ed. pub. schs.; studied art, Pratt Inst., Brooklyn, and in France and Italy; married. Has exhibited Nat. Acad. Design, Nat. Sculpture Soc. and Archtl. League America—all N.Y. City; Pa. Acad. Fine Arts, Phila.; Carnegie Inst., Pittsburgh; Corcoran Gallery, Washington; Boston, Providence, etc. A.N.A.; mem. Nat. Sculpture Soc., Artists Fellowship, Inc. Clubs: Century. Home: South Kent CT‡

PADELFORD, SILAS CATCHING, judge, lawyer; A.B., U. of Miss., 1873; served as asso. justice Supreme Court of Tex.; after retiring from the bench resumed practice at Cleburne. Author: Initiative and Referendum. Home: Cleburne TX‡

PADILLA, EZEQUIEL, Mexican fgn. minister; b. Coyuca de Catalan, Mex., Dec. 31, 1890; s. Mariano and Evarista (Penaloza) P.; student Univ. of Mexico and Free Law Sch. (Mexico City), Columbia U. (N.Y. City), Sorbonne (Paris); m. Maria Guadalupe Couttolenc; 2 sons, 3daus. Became prof. law, Univ. of Mexico, 1926; served as Federal dep., 1922-26, 1932-34; Federal senator, 1930, 1934-40; pres. Mex. delegation to Interparliamentary Congress, Washington, 1926; successively atty. gen., sec. of Pub. Edn., minister plenipotentiary to Italy and Hungary; campaigned for election of Avila Camacho and was apptd. fgn. sec., 1940; his effective appearances as Mexican del. at Rio Conference of Am. Fgn. Ministers, Jan. 1942, are said to have greatly furthered U.S. and Pan-Am. interests. Mem. Mexican bar, Am. Inst. of Law and Comparative Legislation, Soc. of Comparative Legislation (Paris). Roman Catholic. Author: In The Tribunal of the Revolution, 1929; The Education of the Common People; The Free Men of America, 1942; En el Frente de la Democracia, 1945; Address: Tacubaya Mexico DF Died Sept. 6, 1971; buried Mexico City.

PAGE, ELIZABETH FRY, author; b. Hillsville, Va.; d. Col. George Thomson and Mary A. A. (Cooley) Fry; revolutionary ancestry; grad. high sch., 1885; pvt. tutors in music, literature and philosophy; m. David Samuel Page, of Nashville, January 12, 1898 (died July 17, 1925). Special writer Chattanooga Times, 1891-1894; editor Southern Florist and Gardener, 1894-1897; asso. editor American Homes, 1895-1896, Taylor-Trotwood Magazine, Nashville, April-September, 1910. Lecturer on lit. and philos. subjects. Mem. Tenn. Woman's Press and Authors' Club (organizer, 1st sec., 4th pres.), Nashville Metaphys. Club (organizer and pres.), D.A.R., U.D.C., U.S. Daughters of 1812. Poet Laureate Tenn. D.A.R., 1912-13; poet laureate Tenn. Div. U.D.C., 1913-14. Pres. Nashville Women's Press and Authors' Club, 1900-19, v.p. since 1920; charter mem. Poetry Soc. of Tenn. Dir. of religious edn., St. Andrew's Parish, Tampa, Fla., 1926-27, St. Peter's Parish, Charlotte, N.C., 1927-28. Club: Writers' (Charlotte, N.C.). Author: Vagabond Victor, 1908; Edward MacDowell—His Work and Ideals, 1910. Home: 813 S. Tyron Charlotte NC‡

PAGE, ELWIN LAWRENCE, judge; b. Concord, N.H., Feb. 22, 1876; s. Charles Tilton and Almira (Booth) P.; A.B., Williams Coll., 1900; student Harvard Law Sch., 1902-04; A.M., Univ. of N.H., 1931; m. Bertha Robertson, June 6, 1910; 1 son, Robertson. Admitted to N.H. bar, 1904; practicing atty. at Concord, 1904-31; city solicitor City of Concord, 1923-31; legislative counsel to gov. of N.H., 1925 and 1931; asso. justice N.H. Superior Court, 1931-34; asso. justice N.H. Supreme Ct., 1934-46; retired. Trustee N.H. Centennial Home for the Aged. Mem. Am., N.H. State bar assns. Republican. Conglist. Author: The Contributions of the Landed Man to Civil Liberty, 1905; Abraham Lincoln in New Hampshire, 1929; George Washington in New Hampshire, 1932. Home: 6 Cambridge St. Office: 77 N. Main St., Concord NH‡

PAGE, FREDERICK HARLAN, clergyman; b. Haverhill, Mass., Dec. 18, 1860; s. Benjamin and Lucy (Barnard) P.; grad. Andover Theol. Sem., 1893; hon. M.A., Dartmouth, 1897, D.D., 1916; m. Grace Wallace Conant, June 11, 1885. One of publishers and editors of the Haverhill Gazette, 1879-81; in newspaper work, Boston, 1881-90; mng. editor Commercial Bulletin, 1886-88; editor Boston Daily Advertiser, 1888-90; ordained Congl. ministry, 1893; asst. pastor Union Ch., Boston, 1893-96; pastor Trinity Ch., Lawrence, Mass., 1896-1906, First Ch., Waltham, 1906-25. Pres. Congl. and Publishing Society, 1910-16; president and chief exec. Mass. Congl. Conf. and Missionary Soc., 1925-34, pres. emeritus since 1934. Trustee Congl. Ch. Union, Boston. Pres. trustees Andover Theol. Sem.; pres. St. Mark Social Centre (Boston); trustee Wheaton Coll. Clubs: Winthrop, Monday, Fortnightly, Boston Veteran Journalists. Home: Waltham, Mass. Office: 14 Beacon St., Boston MA‡

PAGE, ROBERT G(UTHRIE), lawyer, business exec.; b. Columbus, O., July 7, 1901; s. William Herbert and Ruth Gray (Brown) P.; grad. Phillips Acad., 1918; A.B., Yale, 1922; LL.B., Harvard, 1925; m. Marie Jermain T. Walling, June 10, 1931. Admitted to N.Y State bar, 1927, served as sec. to Mr. Justice Louis D. Brandeis, Washington, 1926-27; asso. firm Root, Clark, Buckner & Ballantine, N.Y. City, 1927-34; regional adminstrn. Securities & Exchange Commn. N.Y.C., 1935; mem. firm Debevoise, Stevenson, Plimpton & Page, (all N.Y.C.), 1936-47; pres. Phelps Dodge Corporation, 1947-70, chairman board, from 1967, chairman of the executive committee, also director; bd. directors Chrysler Corp., Bigelow-Sanford Carpet Co., Mfrs. Hanover Trust Co. Trustee Am. Mus. Natural History. Mem. Commerce and Industry Association of New York (dir.), Mining and Metall. Soc. of Am., Am. Inst. Mining and Metall. Engrs., Bar Assn. City of New York. Clubs: River (N.Y. City), Nat. Golf Links (Southampton, L.I.). Home: New York City NY Died Dec. 25, 1970; buried Quogue NY

PAGE, ROBERT M., educator, biologist; b. Pasadena, Cal., Feb. 5, 1919; s. Benjamin Edwin and Marie (Markham) P.; A.B., Harvard, 1941, M.A., 1946, Ph.D., 1948; m. Virginia Michaud, Sept. 7, 1944. Mem. faculty Stanford, 1948-68, prof. biology, 1963-68. Served with AUS, 1942-45. Mem. Bot. Soc. Am., Mycological Soc. Am., Western Soc. Naturalists, Cal. Acad. Scis., Sigma Pi. Home: Palo Alto CA Died May 17, 1968.

PAINE, CLARA AUDREA (MRS. CLARENCE SUMMER PAINE), librarian; b. near Normal, McLean County, Ill., Apr. 5, 1875; d. George Leonard and Elizabeth Ann (Vickery) Sibley; grad. high sch., Jacksonville, Ill., 1893, Brown's Business Coll., 1894; student Ill. Coll., Jacksonville, 1893-94; m. Clarence Sumner Paine (supt. Neb. State Hist. Soc., 1907-16), Dec. 16, 1905 (died 1916); children—Clarence Sibley, Ezra Kempton, Elizabeth Audrea. Librarian Neb. State Hist. Soc., 1916-46; sec.-treas. Miss. Valley Hist. Assn. and business mgr. its Reviews since 1916. State registrar and chmn. Lincoln Borough, Nat. Soc. Colonial Dames in Neb.; Neb. state regent, D.A.R., 1925-27; v.p. gen. Neb. Soc. D.A.R., 1927-30. Mem. Am. Hist. Assn., Miss. Valley Hist. Assn., Kan. State Hist. Soc., Okla. Hist. Soc., Ill. State Hist. Soc., Chicago Hist. Soc., Nat. Soc. Mayflower Descendants (dep. gov. 1925-31), Daughters of Founders and Patriots of America, Soc. of Daughters of Colonial Wars, Sons and Daughters of Pilgrims (gov. for Neb.), Holstein-Friesian Assn. of America. Democrat. Mem. Christian Church. Clubs: Lincoln Woman's, P.E.O. Author: Vickery Family in America. Mem. bd. editors Neb. Geneal. Soc. Contbr. to mags. and newspapers. Home: 1715 S. 20th St., Lincoln NB‡

PAINE, ELLERY BURTON, electrical engr.; b. Willington, Conn., Oct. 9, 1875; s. Albert Aplin and Ellen (Smith) P.; B.S., Worcester Poly. Inst., 1897, M.S., 1898, E.E., 1904; m. Mabel Harriet Hyde, June 6, 1908; 1 dau., Sylvia. With testing dept. Gen. Electric Co., Schenectady, N.Y., 1898-99; elec. engr., Lehigh Valley Coal Co., Wilkes-Barre, Pa., 1899-1902; prof. elec. engring., Stetson U., De Land, Fla., 1902-04, N.C. Coll. Agr. and Engring., Raleigh, N.C., 1904-07, U. of Ill. since 1907, and in charge dept. elec. engring., 1913-44; retired Sept. 1944. Mem. Am. Inst. Elec. Engrs., Soc. for Promotion Engring. Edn., Western Soc. of Engrs., Sigma Xi, Tau Beta Pi, Eta Kappa Nu. Home: 606 Pennsylvania Av., Urbana IL‡

PAINE, HARLAN LLOYD, physician; b. Rockland, Mass., Nov. 3, 1884; s. Ernest M. and Etta J. (Hunt) P.; M.D., Tufts U., 1908; m. Amy M. Yeo, June 10, 1914 (dec.); children—Harlan Lloyd, Dorothy (Mrs. Norton G. Chaucer), Marion (Mrs. Soli Morris), Louis H.; m. 2d, Lucie G. Ratte, May 21, 1949. Intern, Cambridge (Mass.) Hosp., 1908-09; asst. commr. Mass. Dept. Mental Health, 1918-20; chief exec. officer Boston Psychopathic Hosp., 1920-21; supt. Grafton (Mass.) State Hosp., 1921-48, Channing Sanitorium, 1948-51; psychiat. cons. Westborough (Mass.) State Hosp., 1966-71, Westborough and Marlborough Dist. Cts., 1951-71. Trustee, Westborough Savs. Bank, 1934-66, trustee emeritus, 1966-71, mem. investment bd., 1953-66. Mem. Minn. Gov.'s Commn. for Mental Health Survey, 1954; cons. R.I. Devel. Council, 1952-53. Bd. dirs. United Fund Westborough, 1963-71; trustee Grafton Pub. Library, 1929-48; trustee Westborough Pub. Library, 1952-69, treas., 1955-69. Recipient award of merit Tufts U. Sch. Med., 1958. Diplomate Am. Bd. Psychiatry and Neurology. Mem. A.M.A., Am. Psychiat. Assn., New Eng. Soc. Psychiatry, Mass., Worcester Dist. med. socs. Conglist. (trustee until 1948, deacon 1953-56). Mason. Home: Westborough MA Died July 7, 1971; buried RiversideCemetery, Grafton MA

PAINE, HUGH E., business exec.; b. 1905; grad. Williams Coll., 1927;children—Hugh E., Mrs. Thomas James McGreevy. Partner Abbott, Proctor & Paine N.Y.C.; v.p., dir. Commodity Exchange Metal Clearing Assn., Inc.; dir. Commodity Clearing Corp., Essex County-Champlain Nat. Bank, Willsboro, Nypen Co., Inc. Pres. Paine Meml. Free Library; mem. bd. mgrs. Am. Soc. Prevention Cruelty to Animals. Clubs: Harbor View (gov.), Union (gov.). Home: New York City NY Died Mar. 1973.

PAINE, KARL, lawyer; b. Woodstock, Ill., Sept. 27, 1875; s. Waldo W. and Rose (Richards) P.; M.L., George Washington U., 1903; m. Adele M. Carpentier, Dec. 27, 1903; 1 dau., Lexola. Admitted to Ida. bar, 1897; pros. atty., Idaho City, 1897-02, Boise since 1903; atty. Morrison-Knudsen Co., Inc. since 1913. Home: 121 W Jefferson. Office: Boise ID‡

PAINE, ROLAND D., electric co. exec.; b. Burt, Ia., July 6, 1900; s. George Willard and Laura Elizabeth (Stow) P.; student Coe Coll., 1918-20; B.S., Columbia, 1922; m. Elizabeth De Jarnette, Sept. 3, 1923; children—Roland D., George William, Millicent Elizabeth (Mrs. Frederick Thielemann); m. 2d, Virginia Farley Baile, Jan. 30, 1960. With Graybar Electric Co., Inc., N.Y.C., from 1923, dist. operating mgr., Chgo., 1936-58, asst. sec.-asst. comptroller, N.Y.C., 1958-60, sec., comptroller, dir., 1960-62, v.p., 1962-65, mem. exec. com. 1963-65. Mason (Shriner). Home: New Canaan CT Died Mar. 3, 1972; buried Riverview Cemetery, Algona IA

PAINTER, CARL WESLEY, lawyer; b. Martingsburg, O., Oct. 10, 1892; s. David Hugh and Carrie Jeanette (Young) P.; B.A., U. Minn., 1915; LL.B., Harvard, 1920; m. Muriel K. Thayer, June 1917 (div.); 1 dau., Lisa T.; m. 2d, Emily Gail Benjamin, June 1933 (dec. 1961); m. 3d, Therese Toohill Klotz, June 14, 1963. Admitted to N.Y. bar, 1921; asso. Cravath, Swaine & Moore, predecessor firms, 1920-25, mem. firm, 1926-64, of counsel, 1965-71. Chmn. bd. mgrs. vocational service center br. YMCA, N.Y.C., 1946-58, pres. Gen. Assembly, 1952-53; mem. mayor's com. on homeless men, N.Y.C., 1948-52. Dir. Legal Aid Soc. N.Y., 1949-68, mem. exec. com., 1953-68, v.p., 1956-64, pres., 1964-67; dir. Parents' Institute, Inc., 1936-49. Served as 1st lt., Inf., U.S. Army, World War I. Mem. Assn. Bar City N.Y., Am., N.Y. State bar assns., N.Y. Co. Lawyers Assn., Phi Beta Kappa, Delta Sigma Rho, Beta Theta Pi. Clubs: Union, University, Wall Street (N.Y.C.); Ekwanok Country (Manchester, Vt.). Home: New York City NY Died Dec. 30, 1971.

PAINTER, RUSSELL FLOYD, utility exec.; b. Zanesville, O., May 9, 1911; s. Earl Guy and Osie (Fogle) P.; student pub. schs.; m. Dorothy Iona Thomas, Sept. 12, 1934; 1 dau., Dorothy Sue. Salesman Quaker State Oil Corp., Zanesville, O., 1929-36; with Western & So. Life Ins. Co., Newark, O., 1936-38; with Line Material Co., (now McGraw-Edison Co.), Zanesville, 1938-68, 1971-71, foreman 1943-68, safety dir., 1971. Mem. Zanesville City Council, 1966-70, pres., 1968-70; mayor ex-officio, 1968-70; commr. Zane Trace council Boy Scouts Am., 1932-36; pres. Charity Newsies, Zanesville, 1965, chmn. bd.; pres. Pals, Inc., Zanesville, 1964-71. Bd. dirs. county Tb Assn., 1966-71, county chpt. A.R.C., 1965-71; mem. lay adv. bd. Good Samaritan Hosp., Zanesville, 1962-71. Mem. Muskingum County Republican Club, 1962-71, v.p., 1964-65. Eagle (sec. 1955-71), Moose, Elk, Mason Zanesville OH Died Mar. 23, 1971.

PAINTER, THEOPHILUS SHICKEL, zoologist; b. Salem, Va., Aug. 22, 1889; s. Franklin Verzelius Newton and Laura Trimble (Shickel) P.; B.A., Roanoke Coll., Salem. Va., 1908; M.A., Yale, 1909, Ph.D., 1913, hon. Sc.D., 1936; studied U. of Wurtzburg, 1913-14; LL.D., Roanoke Coll., 1942; m. Anna Mary Thomas, Dec. 29, 1917; children—Elizabeth Tyler (Mrs. S.P.R. Hutchins), Anne Trimble (Mrs. Thornton C. Greer), Theophilus S., Joseph Thomas. Instr. in zoology, Yale, 1914-16; adj. prof. zoology, U. Texas, 1916-21, prof., 1922-44, acting pres., 1944-46, pres., 1946-52, distinguished prof., 1952-66, prof. emeritus, 1966-69, also dir. U. Tex. Radiobiol. Lab. Adviser on research Am. Cancer Soc.; bd. dirs. Oak Ridge Inst. Nuclear Studies. Recipient Daniel Giraud medal for sci. research, 1934; 1st Anderson award M.D. Anderson Hosp. and Tumor Inst., 1969. Mem. 10th F.A., Conn. N.G., 1916; 1st lt. S.C., U.S. Army, later capt. A.S., till 1919. Mem. Am. Soc. Zoologists, Nat. Acad. Sci., English Speaking Union, Sigma Xi, Phi Eta Sigma, Alpha Omega Alpha, Phi Kappa Phi, also numerous other sci. socs. Presbyn. Clubs: University, Town and Gown. Am. editor 10th edit. Vade-Mecum. Contbr. numerous sci. articles on cytology, cytogenetics and exptl. zoology. Home: Austin TX Died Oct. 5, 1969; buried Austin Meml. Park, Austin TX

PALAMAR, MICHAEL, physician; b. Little Falls, N.Y., Aug. 6, 1915; s. Nicholas and Titania (Bassey) P.; M.D., Georgetown U., 1942; m. Marjorie White, Jan. 5, 1947; children—Robert Michael, Tanya Lynn. Intern, Gallinger Municipal Hosp., Washington, 1942-43; intern. resident in surgery St. Vincent's Hosp., Jacksonville, Fla., 1946-48; resident Albany (N.Y.) VA Hosp., 1956-58; attending surgeon Nathan Littauer Hosp., Gloversville, N.Y., 1948-70. Served with M.C., AUS, 1943-46. Diplomate Am. Bd. Surgery. Mem. A.M.A., Royal Acad. Medicine and Surgery (London) (hon.). Mason (32 deg., Shriner). Home: Gloversville NY Died Aug. 6, 1970; buried Gloversville NY

PALMARO, MARCEL A., diplomat, investment banker; born in Monaco; the son of Charles L. and Virginia (Cauvin) P.; ed. Univ. Paris (France), 1932; m. Lucile B. Wells, Dec. 21, 1950. Gen. partner Lehman Bros., N.Y.C., 1958—; dir. Unity Fire and Gen. Ins. Co., N.Y.C., Cemento Andino, S.A., Lima, Peru, Corporacion Espanola de Financion Internacional, Sociedad Anonima; consul general Monaco to N.Y.C., from 1950; permanent observer Monaco to UN, from 1955. Mem. bd. Mary Manning Walsh Home, New York City; chmn., pres. Societe des Bains de Mer Monte-Carlo (dir.). Clubs: Knickerbocker (N.Y.C.); Union Interallie (Paris); Seawanhaka Corinthian Yacht (Oyster Bay, N.Y.); Piping Rock (Locust Valley, N.Y.); Racquet and Tennis (N.Y.). Home: New York City NY also Oyster Bay LI NY Died Nov. 21, 1969; buried Menton France

PALMER, AGNES LIZZIE, author; b. London, Eng., July 27, 1874; d. Jesse and Eliza S. (Peake) Page; ed. high sch.; m. William F. Palmer, of N.Y. City, June 29, 1911. Formerly in editorial work, Eng. and Can.; pvt. sec. to Comdr. Eva Booth of the Salvation Army, 1900-11. Author: Guests of Mercy; Salvage of Men, 1913. Home: 3278 Perry Av., New York NY‡

PALMER, BELL ELLIOTT (MRS. JAMES ALLERTON PALMER), author; b. Jacksonville, Ill., Mar. 27, 1873; d. Richard Douglas and Lucy (Twyman) Elliott; ed. Friends' Sch., Phila., and spl. courses, Bryn Mawr Coll. and U. of Chicago; m. James Allerton Palmer, of Jacksonville, Ill., Nov. 1, 1896. Conglist. Author: Peggy, Betty and Mary Ann, 1907; The Single-Code Girl, 1915; also numerous short plays and short stories.*‡

PALMER, CARLETON H., chairman board E. R. Squibb & Sons; born Brooklyn, New York, Mar. 21, 1891; s. Lowell Mason and Grace Humphreys (Foote) P.; ed. Lawrenceville and Pawling Schools and in Europe; m. 2d Winthrop Bushnell Palmer, Dec. 4, 1951. Began with E. R. Squibb Co., 1910, lab. work 2 yrs., became pres., 1915, chmn. bd. since 1941; chmn. bd., dir. E. R. Squibb & Sons of Indiana, Ltd., Jones Estate, Lentheric of Can., Ltd., L.I. R.R., Lentheric, Inc., Lentheric, Ltd. Mem. U.S. com. World Medical Assn.; dir. Nat. Soc. Prevention Blindness; citizens adv. bd. N.Y. Pub. Library. Mem. Am. Drug Mfrs. Assn. (past pres., mem. exec. com.). Club: Metropolitan (N.Y.). Home: New York City NY Died May 1971.

PALMER, CARROLL (EDWARDS), med. research; born Fairmont, Minn., Nov. 3, 1903; s. Roy W. and Grace (Edwards) P.; B.S. Hamline U., 1925, D.Sc., 1959; M.A., U. Minn., 1927, M.D., 1928, Ph.D., 1929; M.D. honoris causa, U. Oslo, Norway, 1956; m. Margaret Michaelson, June 30, 1928; children—Gaela, Richard. Teaching fellow U. Minn., 1926-27, research fellow Inst. of Child Development, 1927-29; asso. in biostatistics Johns Hopkins Sch. of Hygiene and Pub. Health, 1929-36; consultant in child hygiene U.S. P.H.S., 1932-36; statistician and supervisor of med. records Johns Hopkins Hosp., 1935-36; commd. passed asst. surgeon U.S.P.H.S., 1936, medical dir. 1950, dir. of research Child Hygiene Office, 1936-42. Tb research, 1942-67; prof. biostatistics Sch. Pub. Health, U. Cal., Berkeley, 1967-71; spl. projects cons. Mayo Clinic, Rochester, Minn., 1971-72; dir. tuberculosis research office WHO, 1949-55. Recipient Weber-Parkes prize Royal College of Physicians, London, England, 1957; Trudeau medal National Tb Association, 1964. Diplomate of the American Board of Preventive Medicine amd Pub. Health (Founder). Fellow Soc. for Growth and Development; mem. Am. Assn. Anatomists, Soc. Research in Child Development (sec.-treas. 1936-48, chmn. publ. com. 1936-48). Am. Trudeau Soc. Am. Pub. Health Assn., Am. Epidemiol. Soc. Internat. Epidemiol. Assn., Alpha Omega Alpha, Sigma Xi. Club: Cosmos (Washington). Editor: Child Development Abstracts and Bibliography 1933-48. Died Jan. 8, 1972.

PALMER, CHESLEY ROBERT, ex-pres. Cluett, Peabody & Co.; b. Hawkeye, Ia., Aug. 21, 1881; s. Hiram Robert and Sophia Isodene (Chesley) P.; Upper Ia. U.; hon. D.Sc., m. Eleanor Zins, Oct. 31, 1908; children—Robert Louis, Ruth. With Cluett, Peabody & Co. Inc., shirt and collar mfrs., Troy, N.Y., from 1908, salesman, Chicago, 1908-12, asst. mgr., Chicago, 1912-14, mgr., Kansas City, Mo., 1914-22, dir., San Francisco, 1922-25, Chicago, 1925-27, v.p., 1927-29, pres. 1929-48, later director. Member business adv. council Dept. of Commerce. Clubs: Siwanoy Country (gov. and pres.) Union League. Home: Bronxville NY Died Nov. 9, 1968; buried Ferncliff Cemetery, Hartsdale NY

PALMER, EVERETT WALTER, bishop; b. Menomonie, Wis., Jan. 25, 1906; s. John Stephen and May (Sanders) P.; B.A., Dakota Wesleyan U., Mitchell, S.D., 1932, D.D., 1952; B.D., Drew Theol. Sem. 1935, part-time grad. student, 1935-39; grad. student Oxford U., summer 1950; S.T.D., U. Puget Sound, 1961; LL.D., Morningside Coll., 1963; m. Florence Ruth Wales, June 30, 1927; children—Joanne (Mrs. Clifford C. Cate), Elizabeth (Mrs. A. Ross Cash), Ruth (Mrs. John P. McKean). Ordained deacon Methodist Ch., 1934, elder, 1935, consecrated bishop, 1960; pastor in Artesian and Farwell, S.D., 1929-32, Silverton Circuit, N.J., 1933-34, Highland Park, N.J., 1934-42, Camden, N.J. 1942-46, Asbury Park, N.J., 1946-51, Glendale, Cal., 1951-60; bishop Seattle area Meth. Ch., 1960-68, Portland area United Meth. Ch., 1968-71. Mem. gen. bd. edn. Meth. Ch., 1960-71, council of bishops, 1960-71, v.p. com. ecumenical affairs, 1964-71; v.p. com. structure Methodism overseas, 1964-71, chmn. dept. ministerial edn., 1964-71; mem. World, National coun. churches, 1968-71; mem. Meth. World Council; Meth. rep. to Consultation on Ch. Union, 1964-68; mem. bd. nat. missions, bd. Christian social concerns United Meth. Ch.; chmn. Nat. Meth. Urban Life Convocation, 1966. Summer faculty Iliff Sch. Theology, 1964. Garrett Theol. Sem., 1965; Jarrell lectr. Candler Sch. Theology, Emory U., 1967; lectr. Pres. bd. trustees Alaska Methodist University. Decorated Star of Africa (Liberia). Clubs: University (Portland, Oregon); Harbor (Seattle). Author: You Can Have a New Life, 1959; Spiritual Life Through Witnessing, 1955; There is an Answer, 1962; The Glorious Imperative, 1967; Best Sermons 1966-68. Contbr. articles various periodicals. Home: Portland OR Died Jan. 5, 1971; buried Forest Lawn, Los Angeles CA

PALMER, FRANCIS EBER, school supt.; b. Bower Prairie, Ia., Sept. 24, 1863; s. Stephen Alfred an Angeline (Bennett) P.; A.B., Grinnell (Ia.) Coll., 188 hon. LL.D., 1938; m. Mary Lenon, July 5, 189 children—Lorna Angeline (dec.), Eber Lenon. Serve as supt. of schools, Spirit Lake, Ia., 1888-91, Guthri Center, 1891-94, Greenfield, 1894-99, Villisc 1899-1903, Jefferson, 1903-08, Le Mars, 1908-1 Mason City, 1914-18; supt. Ia. Sch. for the Blin Vinton, 1918-39. Mem. Ia. State Teachers Assn. (v.p. Northwestern Ia. Teachers Assn. (pres.), Southwester Ia. Teachers Assn. (pres.). Pres. Am. Assn. Instrs. Blin 1934-36; del. to Gen. Conf. M.E. Ch., Atlantic Cit N.J., 1932. Methodist. Club: Lions Internat. Home: 3 Prospect Av., Batavia NY‡

PALMER, FRANCIS LESEURE, clergyman; b. Fo Wayne, Ind., Aug. 28, 1863; s. William R. and Cla (Skeele) P.; B.A., Amherst, 1885, M.A., 1902; B.D Cambridge Episcopal Theol. Sch., 1892; D.D., Seabur Div. Sch., 1923; m. Elizabeth E. Paine, Oct. 1, 189 children—Georgiana, Theodore. Deacon, 1892, pries 1893, P.E. Ch.; rector St. Paul's Ch., Gardner, Mass 1892-95, St. Paul's Ch., Walla Walla, Wash., 1895-9 Ascension Ch., Stillwater, Minn., 1900-10, 1913-2 instr. Seabury Divinity Sch., 1910-13, prof. divinit 1922-33. Registrar and historiographer Diocese Minn. Canon of Cathedral of Our Merciful Saviou Faribault, Minn. Mem. Theta Delta Chi, Phi Bet Kappa, Am. Dialect Soc., Mediaeval Academy America, Minnesota Historical Society, Churc Historical Society. Mason (Knight Templar). Autho Life of Bishop Gilbert, 1912. Editor The Salt of th Earth, 1921. Asst. editor Webster's Interna Dictionary, 1886-90, 1898-1900. Book reviewer for Th Churchman, The Living Church. Home: 592 Lincol Av., St Paul 2 MN‡

PALMER, FRED CHESTER, lawyer; b. Toppenish Wash., Aug. 4, 1910; s. F. C. and Inez (Faris) P.; LL.B U. Wash., 1935; m. Peggy Hayward, Sept. 10, 193 children—Patricia Helen, Frederick R., Nancy Ine Admitted to Wash. bar, 1936, since practiced i Yakima; with Olson & Palmer, 1946-54, Olson, Palme & McArdie, 1954-57, Palmer, Willis & McArdie 1957-70. Mem. bd. Yakima Valley chpt. A.R.C. Serve as lt. USNR, 1942-45. Mem. Washington State (b govs. 1954-56, president 1958), American College Trial Lawyers, Yakima County (pres. 1949), Am. ba assns., Young Republicans of Yakima County (pre 1940). Episcopalian. Clubs: Yakima Country, Rotar (pres. 1953), Elks. Home: Yakima WA Died Dec. 2 1970; buried Terrace Heights Memorial Park, Yakim WA

PALMER, THOMAS WAVERLY, lawyer; b Tuscaloosa, Ala., Feb. 25, 1891; s. Thomas Waverly an Lulu (Rainer) P.; A.B., U. of Ala., 1910, LL.D (honorary), 1954; LL.B., Harvard University, 191 awarded Sheldon traveling fellowship for legal researc in Spain, 1913-14; married Marguerite Ellen Meeha July 2, 1919;children—Thomas Waverly (dec.), Eleano (dec.), Evelyn (deceased), James, Meehan (killed i action), Richard Rainer, and Marguerite (Mrs. Edwar G. Haladey). In practice Birmingham, Ala., 1914-1 atty. Chile Exploration Co. (Chile Copper Co.), an U.S. consular agt., Chuquicamata, Chile, 1919-21; att for Standard Oil Co. of N.J., 1921-26; exec. rep. an counsel Tropical Oil Co. (Internat. Petroleum Co., Ltd. with temporary residence in Colombia, S.A., 1927-2 counsel Standard Oil Co. (N.J.), 1929-50; pres. and dir Ancon Insurance Co., Balboa-Insurance Co., 1950-5 Dir. The Americas Foundation, Inc., Caribbea Conservation Corps. With Alabama National Guar Mexican border service; capt. 117th F.A., 31st Div. assigned as instr. in reconnaissance, Sch. of Fire fo Field Arty., Ft. Sill, Okla.; maj. F.A., Oct. 191 Counsel Petroleum Supply Committee for Lati American under Petroleum Admn. for War, durin World War II. Decorated Officer Nat. Order of th Southern Cross (Brazil); Commander Order o Liberator (Venezuela); Officer Nat. Order Carlo Manuel de Cespedes (Cuba), 1954. President Pan-Am Soc. U.S. Inc., 1946-49, honorary president (life 1949-68. Pres. N.Y. So. Society, 1938-39; councilo (director) Am. Geographical Soc.; corr. and hon member Instituto da Ordem dos Advogados Brasileiro pres., dir. Venezuelan C. of C. of U.S., Inc. 1942-4 Mem. Am. Bar Assn., S.R., Soc. Colonial Wars, Sigm Alpha Epsilon, Phi Beta Kappa, Pi Gamma Mu Presbyn. (elder). Mason. Clubs: Southern Cross (pa pres.); Pilgrims, Univ., Am. Yacht (Rye, N.Y.); Acaci Army and Navy (Wash.). Author: Guide to Law an Legal Lit. of Spain, 1915; The Law and Legal Literatur of Curacoa (with others), 1934; Gringo Lawyer, 195 Scarsdale NY Died May 28, 1968.

PALMER, WILLIAM SPENCER, ret. investmen exec.; b. Bebington, Eng., May 3, 1906; s. Henry Butle Hardinge and Frances Elizabeth (Johnston) P.; e Birkinhead Sch., 1920-22; m. Elizabeth Sherwood, Jun 27, 1941; 1dau., Frances Peregrine. Came to U.S., 192 naturalized, 1943. dau., Frances Peregrine. Came t U.S., 1923, naturalized, 1943. With Passaic Worste Spinning Co., 1923-28, Panama Pacific Line, 1929-3 v.p., treas., sec. Piling Assos., Inc., N.Y.C., 1938-4 pres. Agnew Accessories, Inc., Englewood, N.J

1946-51; formerly v.p., sec., dir. Templeton, Dobbrow & Vance, Inc., Englewood, Lexington Security Mgrs., Inc., Lexington Research and Mgmt. Corp., Templeton, Liddle & Schroeder Fund; formerly dir. Research Investing Corp., Corporate Leaders Am., Inc., Lexington Corporate Leaders Fund, Inc.; formerly v.p., dir. Templeton Meml. Fund, Inc., Templeton Investment Research Corp.; formerly sec., dir. Quality Data Processing, Inc. Sustaining mem., hist. cons. Maritime Museum Assn. San Diego. Mem. Rancho Santa Fe Assn. Clubs: Rancho Santa Fe Garden; Anglers (N.Y.C.). Home: Santa Fe CA Died Dec. 18, 1972.

PALMQUIST, ELIM ARTHUR EUGENE, clergyman; b. Oakland, Neb., Aug. 16, 1873; s. Andrew and Ellen (Olson) P.; student Morgan Park Acad., 1892-95; A.B., U. of Chicago, 1899; D.B. Grad. Sch. Theol. (U. of Chicago), 1903, Post Grad. Theol. (U. Of Chicago), 1905; D.D., Bucknell U., 1926; married Marie Estelle Coon (died 1905); 2d; Susie Homes Welles, October 9, 1907; children—Mary Estelle (Mrs. Guy Constant Holbrook, Jr.), Charles Welles. Ordained to ministry of Baptist Ch., 1900; pastor First Bapt. Ch., Momence, Ill., 1900-07, Connellsville, Pa., 1907-11, North Av. Bapt. Ch., Cambridge, Mass., 1912-18; dir. New England Area Interchurch World Movement, 1919-20; exec. sec. Phila. Fedn. of Churches, 1920-45; pastor Woodland Baptist Church, Phila., since 1950. Member bd. mgrs. Am. Bapt. Foreign Mission Soc., 1914-17. Served as Y.M.C.A. sec. with A.E.F., 1917-18. Mem. Phila. Mayor's Crime Commn., 1938, Mayor's Commn. on Race, 1944-47; mem. exec. com. Adult Edn. Com.; mem. Com. on State Legislation (Harrisburg, Pa.). Dir. Armstrong Assn. (Phila.). Mem. Delta Tau Delta. Mason. Clubs: Phi Alpha Clergy (Phila.); Merion Narberth PA‡

PANGBORN, GEORGIA WOOD, author; b. Malone, N.Y., Aug. 29, 1872; d. George H. and Mary (Prentice) Wood; ed. Franklin (N.Y.) Acad.; grad. Packer Inst., 1894; m. H.L. Pangborn, of New York, Oct. 3, 1894 (died May 8, 1934); children—Mary Candace, Edgar Wood. Author: Roman Biznet, 1902; Interventions, 1911; Blencka, 1924. Winner of two of the $1,000 prizes offered by Collier's for short stories, 1905-06. Contbr. to Scribner's, Harper's, Collier's Weekly and other mags. Home: 20 Morris St., Albany NY‡

PANNELL, FAYE, nurse educator; b. Red Oak, Tex., July 28, 1912; d. Frank P. and Lillie (Warren) Pannell; diploma Baylor U. Sch. Nursing, 1932; B.S., Columbia Tchrs. Coll., 1939, M.A., 1951. Engaged in pub. health nursing Tex. Health Dept, 1935-42; dir. pub. health nursing Dallas Health Dept., 1946-47; dir. nursing Parkland Meml. Hosp., Dallas, 1947-54; dean Coll. Nursing, Tex. Woman's U., Denton, 1954-69. Profl. nurse traineeship program Dept. Health, Edn. and Welfare; mem. Gov.'s Adv. Com. on Mental Health and Mental Retardation Planning; participant expert adv. com. White House Conf. on Health, 1965. Served to capt. Army Nurse Corps, 1942-46. Named Dallas Woman of Yr., Women's Civic Clubs, 1954. Mem. Am. Nurses Assn., Nat., States (exec. com. So. regional council 1958-62), Tex. (pres. 1954-58, chmn. workshop com. 1958-63) leagues for nursing., So. Regional Edn. Bd. (nursing project adv. com., council on nursing), Tex. Heart Assn. (chmn. nursing com. 1960-64), Am. Assn. U. Women, Delta Kappa Gamma, Phi Lambda Theta. Democrat. Baptist. Club: Altrusa. Home: Denton TX Died Apr. 10, 1969.

PAQUETTE, CHARLES ALFRED, civil engr.; b. Detroit, Mich., Apr. 2, 1872; s. Gervais Paquette de la Vallee and Josephine (L'Etourneau) P.; B.S., U. of Notre Dame, Ind., 1890, C.E., 1891, Litt.B., 1891, M.S., 1896; m. Bertha Mathias, of Elkhart, Ind., Oct. 9, 1894; 1 son, Charles Alfred. Joined engr. corps L.S. & M.S. Ry., 1891; with C.,C.,C. & St.L. Ry. since 1892, as engr. maintenance of way, 1894-99, supt. 1899-1906, asst. chief engr., 1906-12, chief engr. maintenance of way, 1912-15, chief engr., Mar. 1915-Apr. 1, 1924; was also chief engr. Cincinnati Northern R.R., and Evansville, Indianapolis & Terre Haute Ry.; formerly pres. White Construction Co.; pres. Paquette Engring. Corpn.; dir. M.E. White Co. Mem. Am. Soc. Civil Engrs., Am. Ry. Engring. Assn., Western Soc. of Civil Engrs. Republican. Catholic. Home: White Pigeon, Mich. Office: 35 E. Wacker Drive, Chicago IL*‡

PARDEE, HAROLD ENSIGN BENNETT, physician; b. N.Y. City, Dec. 11, 1886; s. Ensign Bennett and Clara (Burton) P.; A.B., Columbia, 1906; M.D., Coll. Physicians and Surgeons (Columbia), 1909; m. Dorothy Dwight Porter, Apr. 15, 1918; children—Althea, Hobart Porter, Pamela. Interne, New York Hosp., 1909-11; in practice in N.Y. City, specializing on diseases of heart and circulation, since 1911; instr. in physiology, Coll. Physicians and Surgeons, 1912-15; instr. in clin. medicine, Cornell U. Med. Sch., 1916-22, asso. in medicine, 1923-27, asso. prof. clin. medicine since 1927; asso. attending physician New York Hospital; attending phys. (cardiac diseases) Polyclinic Hosp.; cons. physician for cardiac disease, Woman's Hosp., M.E. Hosp., N.Y. City. Served as 1st lt. Med. Corps, U.S. Army, July 1917-Jan. 1918; capt. Jan. 1918-Apr. 1919. Mem. A.M.A., Am. Soc. Clin. Investigation, Assn. Am. Physicians, Am. Heart Assn., N.Y. State Med. Soc., New York County Med. Soc. Republican. Conglist. Clubs: Rockaway Hunting (Lawrence, L.I.); Union Club (N.Y. City). Author: Clinical Aspects of the Electrocardiogram, 1924, 4th edit., 1941; What You Should Know About Heart Disease, 1928. Chmn. com. which wrote Criteria for Diagnosis of Heart Disease, 1928, 4th edit., 1939. Many articles on diagnosis and treatment of heart disease in various medical journals. Home: New York City NY Died Feb. 28, 1972.

PARENT, ALPHONSE MARIE, university dean; born St. Jean Chrysostome, P.Q., Can., Apr. 2, 1906; s. Alphonse and Marie (Gosselin) P.; B.A., Laval U., 1925, D.Th., 1929; M.A., U. Louvain (Belgium), 1935, Ph.D., 1936; LL.D. honoris causa, U. Ottawa, 1952, U. Poitiers (France), 1955, McGill U., 1956, University St. Joseph, 1956, Montreal, 1961; LL.D., Univ. Toronto, Can., 1964, Queen's U., 1965, Sir George Williams U., 1965, U. Monitoba, 1966, Western U., 1966, Laurentian U., 1966, U. Windsor, 1967, Royal Canadian Mil. College, 1968. Ordained priest Cath. Ch., 1929, papal chamberlain, 1946, domestic prelate, 1949, protonotary apostolical, 1955; prof. philosophy Sem. of Que. and Faculty Arts Laval U., 1929-44, prof. faculty philosophy, 1936-44, sec. faculty philosophy, 1936-54, founder, 1938, since dir. Summer Sch., sec. gen., registrar, 1944-51, vice rector, 1949-54, 60-69, rector, 1954-60, dean of philosophy, 1969-70; also director of Laval University Press, 1958-70. President National Conf. Canadian Univs., 1955-56, Assn. Canadian Educators of French, 1949-53, Que. Royal Commn. Inquiry on Edn., 1961-66. Decorated companion Order Can., 1967. Fellow Royal Soc. Can.; mem. Am. Cath. Philos. Assn. Home: Quebec City PQ Canada Died Oct. 7, 1970.

PARENTE, PASCAL PROSPER, clergyman, educator; b. S. Giovanni-Benevento, Italy, Sept. 28, 1890; s. John A. and Elizabeth (Lepore) P.; Ph.D., Gregorian U. Rome, 1911, J.C.B., 1914, S.T.D., 1916. Came to U.S., 1920, naturalized, 1930. Ordained priest Roman Cath. Ch., 1915; prof. ascetical and mystical theology Cath. U. Am., 1938-60, emeritus, 1960-71. Dean Sch. Sacred Theology, 1957-59. Mil. chaplain, Italian Army 1916-20. Decorated Medal of Merit. Mem. Gallery of Cath. Living Authors. Author: Studia Mystica, 1941; The Ascetical Life, 1944; The Mystial Life, 1946; The Well of Living Waters, 1948; Spiritual Direction and Susanna Mary Beardsworth, 1950; A City on a Mountain, 1952; Schoolteacher and Saint, 1954; The Angels, 1958; Beyond Space, 1961; The Regimen of Health of the Medical School of Salerno, A.D. 1100, 1967. Home: Cambridge NJ Died Aug. 1971.

PARET, J(AHIAL) PARMLY, editor; b. Bergen Point N. J., Oct. 3, 1870; s. Henry and Anna E. (Parmly) P., nephew Bishop Paret; grad. Grammar Sch. 68, New York, 1886; m. Dec. 26, 1901, Laura Marion Wilson. Made reputation as expert amateur player of lawn tennis having held many championships in U.S. and abroad. Specialized in writing on amateur sports, his articles and books on lawn tennis being recognized as authoritative. Editor Lawn Tennis (official organ U.S. Nat. Lawn Tennis Assn.); edited The Sportsman's Magazine," Oct., 1896, to April, 1897. Author: Lawn Tennis Annual 1897; Spalding's Lawn Tennis Annual, 1900-3; The Woman's Book of Sport, 1901 A2; How to Play Lawn Tennis, 1902; Lawn Tennis—Its Past, Present and Future, 1904 M1. Contb'r to mags. and newspapers on lawn tennis, etc. Now mfg. stationer and printer. Residence: 4 W. 108th St. Office: 32 Broadway New York‡

PARK, EDWARD CAHILL, lawyer; b. Detroit, Apr. 24, 1895; s. Robert Ezra and Clara (Cahill) P.; A.B., Harvard, 1915, LL.B., 1922; postgrad. U. Chgo., 1916-17; m. Fentress Kerlin, Apr. 7, 1917; children—Carla Elizabeth, Darthea Fentress, Edward, George. Admitted to Mass. bar, 1922, practiced in Boston; asso. Sherman L. Whipple, Esq., 1922-30; mem. firm Withington, Cross, Park & Groden; treas., dir. Locke-Ober Co. Mem. Am., Mass., Boston bar assns. Independent. Home: Wollaston MA Died Dec. 22, 1967.

PARK, EDWARDS ALBERT, pediatrician; b. Gloversville, N.Y., Dec. 30, 1877; s. William Edwards and Sara Billings (Edwards) P.; grad. Phillips Acad., Andover, Mass., 1896; A.B., Yale, 1900, hon. A.M., 1922; M.D., Coll. Physicians and Surgeons (Columbia), N.Y. City, 1905; hon. D.Sc., U. of Rochester, 1936; m. Agnes Bevan, Aug. 2, 1913; children—Sara Bevan, Charles Rawlinson, David Chapman. Interne, Roosevelt Hosp., N.Y. City, 1906-08, New York Foundling Hosp., 1908-09; Proudfit fellow in medicine and instr. in medicine, Coll. Physicians and Surgeons, 1909-12; instr. in pediatrics, Johns Hopkins, 1912-15, asso. prof., 1915-21; Sterling prof. pediatrics, Yale Sch. Medicine, 1921-27; prof. pediatrics, Johns Hopkins Sch. of Medicine and pediatrician Johns Hopkins Hosp., 1927-46; prof. pediatrics emeritus, Johns Hopkins School of Medicine, from 1946. Editor Excerpta Medica, Revue Francaise de Pediatrie. Jahrbuch fur Kinderheilkunde, Major Am. Red Cross, World War. Mem. Assn. of Am. Physicians, Am. Pediatric Soc., Acad. of Pediatrics, Soc. Clin. Investigation, A.A.A.S., Am. Soc. Exptl. Pathology, Soc. Exptl. Biology and Medicine, Interurban Clin. Club, Brit. Pediatric Assn., Alpha Delta Phi. Decorated Order of Leopold (Belgium), 1919; Reconnaissance Francaise (France), 1919. Contbr. on rickets, deformities of the skull, physiology of the thymus gland. Home: Garrison MD Died July 11, 1969; buried Margaree Valley, Cape Becton, Nova Scotia Can.

PARK, EDWARDS ALBERT, pediatrician; b. Gloversville, N.Y., Dec. 30, 1877; s. William Edwards and Sara Billings (Edwards) P.; grad. Phillips Acad., Andover, Mass., 1896; A.B., Yale, 1900, hon. A.M., 1922; M.D., Coll. Physicians and Surgeons (Columbia), N.Y. City, 1905; hon. D.Sc., U. of Rochester, 1936; m. Agnes Bevan, Aug. 2, 1913; children—Sara Bevan, Charles Rawlinson, David Chapman. Interne, Roosevelt Hosp., N.Y. City, 1906-08, New York Foundling Hosp., 1908-09; Proudfit fellow in medicine and instr. in medicine, Coll. Physicians and Surgeons, 1909-12; instr. in pediatrics, Johns Hopkins, 1912-15, asso. prof., 1915-21; Sterling prof. pediatrics, Yale Sch. Medicine, 1921-27; prof. pediatrics, Johns Hopkins Sch. of Medicine and pediatrician Johns Hopkins Hosp., 1927-46; prof. pediatrics emeritus, Johns Hopkins School of Medicine, since 1946. Editor Excerpta Medica, Revue Francaise de Pediatrie. Jahrbuch fur Kinderheilkunde. Major Am. Red Cross, World War. Mem. Assn. of Am. Physicians, Am. Pediatric Soc., Acad. of Pediatrics, Soc. Clin. Investigation, A.A.A.S., Am. Soc. Exptl. Pathology, Soc. Exptl. Biology and Medicine, Interurban Clin. Club, Brit. Pediatric Assn., Alpha Delta Phi. Decorated Order of Leopold (Belgium), 1919; Reconnaissance Francaise (France), 1919. Contbr. on rickets, deformities of the skull, physiology of the thymus gland. Home: Birdwood, Garrison, Md. Office: Johns Hopkins Hosp., Baltimore 5, MD‡

PARKE, HENRY WALTER, banker; b. Bay Shore, N. Y., Oct. 12, 1901; s. Walter and Katherine (Novinski) P.; student Marquand Prep. Sch. St. John's Law Sch.; m. Marie C. Hansen Aug. 22, 1920; children—Henry W., Marilyn Anne (Mrs. W. Donald Weir), Wanda Ellen. With Corporation Trust Co., N.Y.C. from 1920, v.p., from 1948; dir. California Packing Corp. Episcopalian (vestryman). Clubs; Bankers of Am. (N.Y.C.); Southward-Ho Country, Bay Shore Yacht (Bay Shore). Home: Bay Shore NY Died June 23, 1970.

PARKER, ALEXANDER WILSON, lawyer; b. Franklin, Va., June 21, 1898; s. John Crafford and Emily Virginia (Norfleet) P.; A.B., Va. Mil. Inst., 1918; LL.B., U. Va., 1923; m. Mary S. McDaniel, June 28, 1924 (dec. June 1959); children—Douglas (Mrs. John Moncure), Emily (Mrs. Edward T. Lemmon, Jr.), Dorothy (Mrs. Robert E. Hale); m. 2d, Elizabeth Taylor Valentine, July 1, 1960; stepchildren—Elizabeth (Mrs. Thomas Wood), Frederick S. Valentine III. Admitted to Va. bar, 1923; counsel Atlantic Life Ins. Co., Richmond, Va., 1925-29; joined firm Christian, Barton, Parker, Epps & Brent, Richmond, 1929, now partner; spl. counsel of Barbara Powers, wife of U-2 pilot Francis Gary Powers at Moscow trial, 1960. Sec., dir., gen. counsel Thalhimer Bros. Inc., Richmond, 1947-72; dir., gen. counsel Broad-Grace Arcade Corp., Richmond, 1946-72; dir. Miller Hofft, Inc. Pres., dir. Richmond War and Community Fund, 1939; v.p. Va. Tb Assn., 1941, Va. Cancer Soc., 1941. Mem. Va. Democratic Central Com. Served as gunnery sgt., U.S. Marine Flying Corps, World War I; lt. comdr., air combat intelligence officer USNR, 1943-45; P.T.O. Mem. Am., Va. (pres. 1951-52), Richmond (past pres.) bar assns., Am. Judicature Soc., Internat. Assn. Ins. Counsel, Soc. Cincinnati, Am. Law Inst., Assn. Life Ins. Counsel, Am. Life Conv., Inst. Jud. Adminstrn., U. Va. Law Sch. Assn. (pres. 1958-59), Navy League U.S. (past pres. Va. council), Va., Richmond chambers commerce, Res. Officers Assn., Mil. Order Caraboa, Soc. Colonial Wars, Sigma Chi. Democrat. Episcopalian (past vestryman). Clubs: Deep Run Hunt (dir.), Commonwealth (past mem. bd. govs.). Home: Richmond VA Died July 11, 1972.

PARKER, BEN HUTCHINSON, bus. exec.; b. Oklahoma City, Nov. 3 1902; s. Milton Edson and Mamie (Newman) P.; E.M., Colo. Sch. of Mines, Golden, Colo., 1924, M.S., 1932, D.Sc., 1934; m. Elizabeth Forwood Thorley, Dec. 26, 1924; one son, Ben Hutchinson. Geologist, Marland Oil Co., 1924-28. Gypsy Oil Co., 1928-29; dist. geologist, E.W. Marland, Inc., 1929-30; reconnaissance geologist, Gypsy Oil Co., 1930-31; instr. in geology, Colo. Sch. of Mines, 1932-35; asst. prof., 1936-39, asso. prof., 1940-42, pres. 1946-50; institutional rep. in War Program of U.S. Office of Edn., 1940-44; research geologist, Gulf Oil Corp., 1935-36; asst. chief geologist, Argentine govt. oil fields, 1939-40; v.p., Frontier Refining Co., from 1942; pres. Gold Crest Mining Co., 1939-49; sec. dir. Uranium Prospectors Co., 1954-55; pres., dir. Gold Hill Mining and Milling Company, Golden Investment Company; director Golden State Bank; secretary Colo. Geol. Survey, 1946-50. Member of Colorado Board Examiners for Profl. Engrs., Land Surveyors, 1952-60. Ofcl. U.S. del. 21st Internat. Geol. Congress, 1960.

Mem. Mining and Metall. Soc. Am., Geol. Soc. Am., Am. Petroleum Inst., Am. Institute Mining and Metall. Engrs., Am. Assn. Petroleum Geologists (pres. 1960-61). Rocky Mountain Assn. Petroleum Geologists, Tau Beta Pi. Sigma Gamma Epsilon, Kappa Sigma. Mason. Clubs: University, Denver, Petroleum (Denver). Home: Mining Golden CO Died July 31, 1969.

PARKER, CHAUNCEY DAVID, banking; b. Boston, Mass., Jan. 18, 1873; s. Gustavus D. and Garafeia (Tucker) P.; A.B., Harvard, 1895; unmarried. Pres. C.D. Parker & Co., bankers; pres. Seaboard Utilities Shares Corpn., Utilities Hydro & Rails Shares Corpn., Railroad Shares Corpn.; also trustee or director many other companies. Clubs: Exchange, Harvard, University, The Country, Longwood Cricket. Home: Osterville, Mass., and 173 Bay State Rd., Boston. Office: 150 Congress St., Boston MA‡

PARKER, FRANCES, author; b. at Deerfield, Mich., Jan. 17, 1875; d. Dayton and Idalia Estelle (Cogswell) P.; ed. Blissfield pub. schs. and Detroit Seminary. Lived on a Montana ranch, 1891-1905. Author: Marjie of the Lower Ranch, 1903; Hope Hathaway, 1904; Winding Waters, 1909. Address: Bradentown FL‡

PARKER, FRANCIS LEJAU, army officer; b. Abbeville, S.C., June 24, 1873; s. William H. and Lucia G. P.; grad. U.S. Mil. Acad., 1894; honor grad. Army Sch. of the Line, 1908; grad. Army Staff Coll., 1909, Army War Coll., 1920; unmarried. Commd. 2d lt. 5th Cav., U.S. Army, 1894; advanced through grades to brig. gen., 1933; col. and brig. gen. Nat. Army, 1917-19. Instr., U.S. Mil. Acad., 1897-98, and Gen. Service Schs., 1904-07; duty in Cuba, 1898-99, Puerto Rico, 1899-1900, Philippine Islands, 1901, 1903-04, 1910-12, 1931 and 1934-36, China, 1912, and Colo. coal strike, 1914-15; mem. bd. to revise cav. drill regulations, 1915-16; a.-d.-c. to Brig. Gen. L.H. Carpenter, to Brig Gen. George W. Davis, and to Gov. Gen. W. Cameron Forbes, P.I.; Gen. Staff Corps, 1915-17 and 1920-21; mil. observer with Roumanian armies, 1916-17; mil. attache, Petrograd. and mil. observer with Russian armies, June-Aug. 1917. Comdr. 119th Inf., 30th Div., Jan.-Apr. 1918, 312th Cav., Apr.-May 1918, 171st Inf. Brigade, A.E.F., Aug.-Nov. 1918; with 2d sect. Gen. Staff, Hdqrs. A.E.F., Nov. 1918-June 1919; comdr. 1st Cav., 1920-21; chief of staff 6th Division, Jan.-July, 1921; mil. attache, Mexico, 1921-23; detailed in F.A., 1923-26; comdr. 12th F.A., July-Nov. 1924; with U.S.-Mexico Mixed Claims Commn., Dec. 1924-Dec. 1925; with Tacna-Arica Arbitration Commn., Dec. 1925-June 1926; in Inspr. Gen.'s Dept., Oct. 1926-Dec. 1927; vice-chmn. Nat. Bd. of Elections, Nicaragua, 1928; chief of Bur. Insular Affairs, with rank of brig. gen., Jan. 1929-Jan. 1933, continuing as acting chief to Aug. 1933; comdr. 2d F.A. Brig., Oct. 1933-May 1934; comdr. Ft. Stotsenberg, P.I., 1934-36; comdr. 1st Cav. Div., Sept. 1936; retired from active service, 1936. Clubs: Army and Navy, Army and Navy Country (Washington, D.C.); Army and Navy (Manila); Charleston. Home: 14 Lamboll St., Charleston 2 SC‡

PARKER, FRANKLIN NUTTING, theologian, educator; b. New Orleans, La., May 20, 1867; s. Linus and Ellen Katharine (Burruss) P.; Centenary Coll. of La., Jackson, 1883-84; Tulane U., 1885; Vanderbilt U., 1885; D.D., Centenary, 1901, Trinity, 1916; m. Minnie Greves Jones, Dec. 20, 1899. Ordained deacon M.E. Ch., S., 1888, elder, 1889; pastor Patterson, La., 1886, Carrollton Av. Ch., New Orleans, 1888-90, Parker Chapel, 1891-92, Rayne Memorial Ch., New Orleans, 1893-96, First Ch., Baton Rouge, 1897-99, Carondelet St. Ch., New Orleans, 1900-02; presiding elder Baton Rouge Dist., 1903-04; pastor First Ch., Monroe, La., 1905; presiding elder New Orleans Dist., 1907-10; prof. Bibl. lit., Trinity Coll., Durham, N.C., 1911-15; prof. systematic theology, Emory U., 1915-42, former dean Candler School Theology; retired since 1941. Delegate General Conference M.E. Church, S., 7 times; delegate Ecumenical Methodist Conference, London, 1901, Toronto, 1911. Elected bishop M.E. Ch., S., at Atlanta, Ga., May 1918, but declined. Mem. Uniting Conf. Mem. Chi Phi. Mason. Home: 1969 N. Decatur Rd. Address: Emory University GA*‡

PARKER, FREDERIC, JR., physician; b. Boston, Sept. 20, 1890; s. Frederic P.; M.D., Harvard, 1916; m. Marie Custler. Asst. prof. bacteriology Columbia Coll. Phys. and Surg., N.Y.C., 1922-23; asst. pathologist Boston City Hosp., 1923-32, dir. Mallory Inst. Pathology, 1932-51; asst. prof. pathology Harvard, Boston, 1928-34, asso. prof. pathology, 1934-51. Served to 1st lt., M.C., U.S. Army, World war I. Diplomate Am. Bd. Pathology. Mem. Am. Assn. Pathologists and Bacteriologists, A.A.A.S., New Eng. Soc. Pathologists (past pres.), Mass. Med. Soc. Author: (monograph) Hodgkins Disease and Allied Disorders. Asst. editor: Am. Jour. Pathology, 1933-40. Contbr. articles to med. jours. Home: Newton Centre MA Died Oct. 25, 1969; buried Bedford MA

PARKER, GRADY P., educator; b. Winfield, Tex., Mar. 30, 1903; s. Dr. Joseph J. and Exa Lee (O'Dea) P.; B.A., N. Tex. State U., Denton, 1929; M.A., So. Meth. U., 1935; Ed.D., U. Tex., Austin, 1942; m. Bernice Greathouse, May 6, 1925; children—Mary Ann (Mrs. Mary Ann Bankston), Margie Nell (Mrs. Richard L. Goodwin). Prin. pub. schs., Winfield, 1924-26, Jefferson, 1926-29; supt. pub. schs., Hughes Springs, 1929-35, Jefferson, 1935-39; research fellow curriculum and instrn. U. Tex., 1939-40; asso. prof. chemistry Tex. A. and M. Coll., 1940-45, adminstrv. asst. dept. chemistry, 1945-47, planned orgn. and adminstrn. Tex. A. and M. Coll. System, 1947-48, asso. prof. edn. and psychology, 1947-52, prof. edn. and psychology, 1952-54, head dept. edn. and psychology, 1954-61, prof. edn., chmn. math.-sci. edn. com. and programs, 1961-72. Mem. bd. judges for research sci. edn. U. Colo., 1953-54; vis. prof. dept. edn. Sam Houston State Coll., Huntsville, Tex. Served with N.G., 1921-23. Fellow Tex. Acad. Sci. (v.p., sec.-treas., bd. dirs.), A.A.A.S.; mem. Nat. Sci. Tchrs. (state dir. 1952-55; life), Am. Assn. U. Profs. (chpt. pres. 1959), Tex. Assn. Instrn. Suprs. (exec. chmn., dir. programs 1954-61), Tex. Assn. County Supts. (exec. chmn., coordinator projects 1954-61), Tex. Assn. Sci. Adminstrs. (exec. chmn., sec. 1954-61), N.E.A. (life), Tex. Tchrs. Assn. (life), Assn. for Edn. Tchrs. Sci. Episcopalian. Mason (32, K.T., Shriner), Rotarian. Author: Guidebook for Secondary School Science, Experiments for Life Science, Experiments for Earth Science, Experiments for Physical Science. Home: College Station TX Died Feb. 3, 1972; buried College Station City Cemetery, College Station TX

PARKER, H. WAYNE, govt. ofcl.; b. Newago County, Mich., Dec. 3, 1904; s. Ernest E. and Ella M. (Stevens) P.; grad. high sch.; m. Marjorie Rice, Mar. 15, 1947; children—Elaine (Mrs. Frank Shaw). John Wayne, James Edward, Thomas Jethro. Asst. paymaster Bissell Carpet Sweeper Co., Grand Rapids, Mich., 1922-46, asst. traffic mgr., 1923-46; life ins. agt. Mut. Benefit Life Ins. Co. of Newark, Grand Rapids, 1946-54; postmaster Grand Rapids Post Office, 1954-67; mem. Gent County Bd. Suprs., Grand Rapids, 1952-54. Pres., Union High Sch. Community Council, Grand Rapids, 1937-38; mem. traffic squad Grand Rapids, 1940-61, capt., 1948-49; mem. Grand Rapids Pub. Recreation Bd., 1938-48; chmn. Individual Gifts div. Grand Rapids Community Chest, 1935-40; chmn. individual gifts A.R.C., 1946; team capt. U.S.O. fund drive, 1940-41; team capt., joint YWCA-YMCA drive, 1951; co-chmn. individual 1941; chmn. membership campaign Grand Rapids Civic Theater, 1940, 46, 65; Kent County chmn. Mich. Week, 1965, 66; mem. exec. bd. Kent County Tb Soc. Campaign chmn. Harry Kelly for Gov., Kent County, 1950, Fred Alger for Gov., Kent County, 1952; campaign exec. Republican campaign for Eisenhower, 1952. Bd. dirs. Grand Rapids Community Concert Assn., pres., 1952-53; adv. bd. Grand Rapids Citizens for Decent Literature; mem. adv. com. Aquinas Coll. Served from specialist 1st class to chief specialist, USNR, 1942-45. Recipient Distinguished Service award Grand Rapids Jr. C. of C., 1940. Mem. Nat. Assn. Postmasters (past pres., past sec.-treas.), Am. Bus. Club (past pres., dist. gov. Grand Rapids chpt.), Am. Legion, Grand Rapids Assn. Life Underwriters (past treas., past sec., past v.p. past pres.), Grand Rapids Jr. C. of C. (past 2d v.p., past 1st v.p., past chmn. Cheers for Victory" program). Conglist. (past deacon, past pres. men's club). Mason (Shriner, Scottish Rite). Clubs: Rotarian (past v.p., past program chmn. Grand Rapids), Grand Rapids Breakfast (sec.). Home: Grand Rapids MI Died June 4, 1967.

PARKER, JAMESON, b. Balt., Jan. 13, 1909; s. Summer Abrahams and Grace Dudres (Wagner) P.; student U. Vienna, 1929; A.B., Johns Hopkins, 1930; grad. student Harvard, 1931-32; m. Sydney Buchanan Sullivan, June 8, 1933; children—Judith Armistead, Francis Jameson. Vice pres., treas. structural steel firm Parker & Derby, Inc., Balt., 1933-36; investment analyst Trail & Middendorf, Inc., 1936-40; research, pub. relations dir. Md. Pub. Expenditure Council, Balt., 1940-42; exec. officer transp. br. Office Sec. Navy, 1942-45; asst. to Mark Sullivan, N.Y. Herald Tribune, 1945-50; mem. Econ. Mission to P.I., 1950; information and editorial specialist Office Pub. Affairs, Dept. of State, 1950-52, staff news div. Dept. State, 1953-55; spl. asst. to Am. ambassador, Brussels, 1952-53; mem. U.S. delegation 10th Inter-Am. Conf., Caracas, Venezuela, 1954, Inter-Am. Econ. Conf., 1954; spl. asst. Asst. Sec. State for Pub. Affairs, 1955-59; econ. officer, 1st sec. Am. embassy, Bonn, Germany, 1959-65; dir. Gunston Hall, Lorton, Va. Address: Lorton VA Died Jan. 6, 1972; buried Pohick Church Graveyard, Lorton VA

PARKER, JO A., manufacturer; b. at Cambridge City, Ind., July 28, 1869; s. William Franklin and Mary F. (Callender) P.; ed. Forestville Acad., N.Y., and graded schs. of Indianapolis; unmarried. Went into newspaper business at age of 16; now engaged in mfg. timber products and in land and timber brokerage. Entered politics during the Farmers' Alliance agitation; joined People's party, 1892; was nominated, 1897, for clerk of Court of Appeals in Ky. and made notable campaign; 5 yrs. sec. Nat. Reform Press Assn.; chmn. Nat. Com. People's Party, 1900-4; mem. Exec. Com. since 1896; chmn. Ky. State Com. since 1895. Writer and lecturer on economic questions. Address: Louisville KY‡

PARKER, ROBERT HUNT, justice; b. Enfield, N.C., Feb. 15, 1892; s. R.B. and Victoria C. (Hunt) P.; A.B., U. Va., 1912, LL.B., 1915; LL.D., University of North Carolina, 1958; married Rie W. Rand, Nov. 28, 1925. Admitted to N.C. bar, 1914; practice of law, Enfield, and Roanoke Rapids, N.C., 1915-32; solicitor Third Jud. Dist. N.C., 1924-32, judge Superior Ct., 1932-52; asso. justice N.C. Supreme Ct., 1952-67, chief justice, 1967-69. Mem. house of representatives North Carolina General Assembly, 1923-24; mem. commn. to study improvements, adminstrn. justice in N.C., 1947-49, mem. Jud. Council, 1949-51. Served with F.A., U.S. Army, 1917-19. Mem. Am. Legion, 40 et 8, Vets. Fgn. Wars. Democrat. Episcopalian. Home: Roanoke Rapids NC Died Nov. 1969.

PARKER, STANLEY V., officer U.S. Coast Guard; b. Cincinnati, O., Oct. 26, 1885; s. Samuel Boardman and Elizabeth Helen (Chappell) P.; student Tech. Sch. of Cincinnati, 1901-04; grad. Coast Guard Acad., 1906; m. Doris Devereux, Aug. 24, 1916; children—Stanley Devereux, Robert Devereux. Commd. 3d lt. (now ensign), U.S. Coast Guard, Oct. 1906, and advanced through the grades to rear adm., 1942; served as comdr. Naval Air Stations, Key West, Fla., and Rockaway, N.Y., 1917-19; admitted to Calif. bar, 1934. Capt. of Port, N.Y. City, 1942-45; Comdr. Western Area, U.S. Coast Guard, 1946-47; ret. 1947. Decorated Victory and Defense medals, Legion of Merit. Mason. Author: Coast Guard Boarding Manual, Maual for U.S. Commissioners in Alaska, 1937. Home: Oakland CA Died Jan. 1968.

PARKER, WALTER HUNTINGTON, mining co. exec.; b. Stillwater, Minn., Aug. 1 1884; s. Reuben S. and Jennie Annette (Huntington) P.; E.M., U. of Minn., 1907; hon. grad. Sch. of Fire, Field Arty., Fort Sill, 1917; m. Veola Fourrell, Aug. 16, 1921. With Pa. Mining Co., Argentine, Colo., 1905, Bingham, Utah, 1906; mgr. Fairview Mining Co., Berlin, Wash., 1907; chief engr. Internat. Coal Co. and Mont. Coal & Iron Co., 1908-12; cons. city engr. Bearcreek, Mont., 1909; cons. structural and mining engr., Vancouver, B.C., Can., 1913-14, Mont., Colo., Minn., and Alberta, 1914-17; asso. prof. mining and head of dept. Sch. of Mines and Metallurgy, U. of Minn., 1919-23; prof. mining and head of dept., 1923-49, prof. of mining emeritus from 1949; cons. mining engr.; president San Juan Mining and Exploration Company. Mem. Minn. Nat. Guard, 1903-07; captain C.A.C., U.S. Army, World War; mem. Gen. Court Martial, 1917; mem. staff Sch. of Fire, Fort Sill, 1917; overseas, 12 mos., as bn. comdr. 69th Arty., C.A.C., and camp adjt. Romagne, France. Fellow A.A.A.S.; mem. Am. Inst. Mining and Metall. Engrs., Soc. for Promotion Engring. Edn. Am. Soc. Civil Engrs., Gen. Alumni Assn. U. of Minn. (dir.). Veterans of Foreign Wars, American Legion, Order of Founders and Patriots of America, Soc. of Colonial Wars, Engineers Club of Minneapolis, Soc. Westcott Descendants, Huntington Family Assn., Minn. Fed. Engr. Soc., New England Hist.-Geneal. Soc. Minn. Hist. Soc., Inst. of Mining and Metallurgy (England), Mining and Metall. Soc. Am., Am. Forestry Assn., Am. Mus. Natural Hist., Forty and Eight, Theta Tau. Republican. Episcopalian, Scottish Rite Mason. (K.T., Shriner). Clubs: Lions, Campus. Editor: Bluebooks. Sch. of Mines, 1922-50. Home: Phoenix AZ Died Jan. 25, 1968.

PARKER, WILLIAM GORDON, artist, author; b. Clifton, N.J., June 12, 1875; s. Elijah S. and Sarah E. P.; ed. Brooklyn Poly. Inst.; grad. Art Students' League; m. Verna E. Clark, of Arkansas City, Kan., Aug. 3, 1905. Illustrates his own books and contributes illustrations and stories to mags.; mem. editorial staff Wichita Eagle. Author: Grant Burton, the Runaway, 1899; Six Young Hunters, 1898; Rival Boy Sportsmen, 1900; Two Boys in the Blue Ridge, 1901. Address: Wichita KS‡

PARKER, WILLIAM HENRY, law enforcement officer; b. Lead, S.D., June 21, 1902; s. William H. and Mary (Moore) P.; LL.B., Los Angeles Coll. Law, 1930; postgrad. Northwestern U., 1940-41; m. Amelia H. Schultz, May 6, 1928. With Los Angeles Police Dept., from 1927, chief police, from 1950. Chmn. Gov.'s Law Enforcement Adv. Com., 1957-58, Los Angeles Civil Def. Disaster Bd., 1962-63. Pres. Los Angeles Area council Boy Scouts Am., 1962; mem. adv. bd. Bd. Deliquency Control Inst. U. So. Cal. Served to capt. AUS, 1943-45; ETO. Decorated Purple Heart; Croix de Guerre; Star of Solidarity; named Hon. Chief Nat. Police, Korea, 1952, Citizen of Year, Los Angeles C. of C., 1953; recipient B'nai B'rith Merit award, 1953, Sylvania award, 1954, James Madison award Los Angeles Freedom Club, 1959, Freedom award Immaculate Heart Coll., 1960, Service Mankind award Los Angeles Sertoma Club: Catholic Big Brothers (Dir.). Mem. Peace Officer's Assn. Cal., Internat. Assn. Chiefs Police, Am. Legion, Sigma Delta Kappa. Club: Catholic Big Brothers (dir.). Home: Los Angeles CA Died July 16, 1966.

PARKER, WILLIAM RILEY, educator; b. Roanoke, Va., Aug. 17, 1906; s. Frank Benjamin and Bertha Ladow (Riley) P.; student, Roanoke Coll. (Salem, Va.), 1923-27, A.B., 1927; M.A., Princeton, 1928; B. Litt., Oxford, 1934; D.Litt., Middlebury College, 1953;

LL.D., U. Mich., 1956; L.H.D., Roanoke Coll., 1962, Miami U., 1962; m. Mary Ann Blakesley, Sept. 20, 1932; children—Pamela, Robin. Instr. English, Northwestern U., 1928-32; research in Eng., 1934-35; instructor, Ohio State Univ., 1935-36; asst. prof., 1936-41; visiting prof., Johns Hopkins Univ., 1937; visiting prof., Duke Univ., summer 1938 and 1941; research in England, autumn 1938; asso. prof., Ohio State Univ., 1941-43; prof., 1943-46; visiting prof., U. of Southern Calif., summer 1946; prof. New York U., 1946-56; prof. English, Ind. U., 1956-58, Distinguished Service professor of English, 1958-68, chmn. department of English, 1966-68; chief lang. development program U.S. Office Edn., 1958-59, mem. nat. adv. com., lang. devel., 1959-64. Mem. Fulbright Internat. Exchange Persons, 1950-54, U.S. nat. commn. UNESCO, exec. com., 1954-58, vice chmn., 1957-58; mem. Nat. Council Humanities, 1968. Recipient Guggenheim fellow, Fulbright research award, 1962-63; Gold medal Goethe Inst. Munich, 1966; Distinguished Nat. Service award N.Y. State Fedn. Fgn. Lang. Tchrs., 1967. Mem. Modern Humanities Research Association, American Council of Learned Societies (secretary of the bd. dirs., 1950-56), Modern Lang. Assn. (exec. sec. 1947-56, dir. fgn. lang. program 1952-56, pres. 1959), Coll. English Assn., Nat. Council Teachers of English, Am. Assn. Tchrs., French, Bibliog. Soc. (London), Phi Beta Kappa (mem. senate 1961-68). Clubs: Century, Andiron. Author: Milton's Debt to Greek Tragedy in Samson Agonistes, 1937; Milton's Contemporary Reputation, 1940; The National Interest and Foreign Languages, 1954, rev. edit., 1962; The Language Curtain and Other Essays on American Education, 1966. Editor: The Dignity of Kingship Asserted (by G. S.), 1942; publs. of Modern Lang. Assn., 1948-56, compiler style sheet, 1951; William Winstanley's Lives of the Most Famous English Poets, 1963; Milton: A Biography, 2 vols., 1966; author articles, revs. Home: Bloomington IN Died Oct. 28, 1968.

PARKER, WILLIAM STANLEY, architect; b. Boston, Mass., Oct. 28, 1877; s. Charles E. and Mary Tilden (Phillips) P.; S.B., Harvard, 1899; m. Elizabeth S. Porter, Mar. 18, 1920. Practiced architecture at Boston since 1902; mem. State Planning Bd., 1935-38, Boston City Planning Bd., terms, 1933-48 (chmn. 1940-43). Mem. Am. Inst. Architects (sec. 1917-23; 2d v.p. 1923-24), Boston Soc. Architects (pres. 1930-32). Republican. Unitarian. Clubs: Footlight, Tavern (Boston); Harvard (N.Y. City). Home: 148 Mt. Vernon St. Office: 120 Boylston St., Boston MA‡

PARKES, CHARLES HERBERT, surgeon; b. Chicago, Ill., Oct. 15, 1872; s. Charles Theodore and Isabella Jane (Gonterman) P.; grad. Lake View High Sch., Chicago; student Northwestern U.; M.D., Rush Med. Coll., 1897; m. Edna Bigelow, of Toronto, Can., Sept. 21, 1916. Practiced at Chicago since 1897; attending surgeon Illinois Masonic Hospital. Mem. Ill. National Guard, 1899-1910; member M.C., U.S.A., July 1917-Aug. 1919; served with A.E.F. in France; hon. discharged as maj. Fellow Am. Coll. Surgeons, A.M.A., Chicago Med. Soc. (sec. 1913-14). Republican. Mason. Home: 1910 Lincoln Av., Chicago IL*‡

PARKES, HENRY BAMFORD, author; b. Sheffield, Eng., Nov. 13 1904; s. James Frederick and Rosa (Burrows) P.; B.A., Oxford, 1927; Ph.D., U. of Mich., 1929; m. Mollie Brown, 1931; children—Nancy, Alison; m. 2d, Ruth Monroe Mittelmann, 1961; m. 3d, Lauretta Bender, 1967. Came to U.S., 1927; naturalized, 1940. Instr. history dept. N.Y. U., 1930-41; asst. prof., 1941-45, asso. prof., 1945-49, prof. since 1949; chmn. grad. div, Am. Civilization, 1944-68; lecturer at the New School, 1946-50; member of the editorial staff of the Baltimore Sun, 1943; visiting professor of Barnard College, 1954-55; Fulbright prof. Am. Civilization, U. Athens, 1956-57. Democrat. Author: Jonathan Edwards, 1930; A History of Mexico, 1938; Marxism: An Autopsy, 1939; Recent America, 1941; The Pragmatic Test, 1941; The World After War, 1942; The American Experience, 1947; The United States of America, 1953; Gods and Men, 1959; The Divine Order, 1969. Contbr. to mags. Home: New York City NY Died Jan. 7, 1972; cremated.

PARKES, WILLIAM ROSS, surgeon; b. Milwaukee, Wis., June 14, 1869; s. William Beckley and Mary J. (McNickle) P.; Ph.M., Northwestern U., 1893; M.D., Rush Med. Coll., 1893; m. Emma R. Miller, June 3, 1897; 1 son, William M. Intern Presbyn. Hosp., Chicago, 1893-95; health commr. of Evanston, 1901-09; attending surgeon Evanston Hosp., 1907-27, chief of surg. dept., 1927-33, chief emeritus since 1933; asso. prof. surgery, Northwestern U. Med. Sch.; chief of med. staff Presbyn. Old People's Home. Fellow A.M.A., Am. Coll. Surgeons; mem. Ill. State and Chicago med. socs., Assn. Am. Physicians. Republican. Presbyterian. Clubs: University (Chicago and Evanston); Glenview (Glenview). Home: 1835 Chicago Av., Evanston IL‡

PARKHURST, FREDERIC AUGUSTUS, organizing engr.; b. Woburn, Mass., Aug. 11, 1877; s. George Ezekiel and Sarah Frances (Turner) P.; ed. Woburn High Sch., by pvt. study and 2 yrs.' course of lectures on advanced steam engring., Mass. Inst. Tech.; m. Abby Joanna Glidden, Feb. 3, 1904; children—Anna Glidden, Walter Glidden. Began as spl. apprentice, Vaughn Machine Co., Peabody, Mass., 1895, advancing to asst. supt., organization work, same place, 1902; with Portland Co. 2 yrs., associated with Harrington Emerson as chief of staff; gen. mgr. Pacific Iron Works, Bridgeport, Conn., 1905-07; organizing engr. with Ferracute Machine Co., Bridgeton, N.J., 1907-12; organizing engr. Aluminum Castings Co. plants in Detroit, Cleveland, Buffalo, etc., 1912-18; became organizing engr., New York, since 1919; cons. expert in orgn. management and process development; with tank sect., Ordnance Dept., 1918. Republican. Conglist. Author: Applied Methods of Scientific Management, 1912; Scientific Management in the Foundry, 1914; The Predetermination of True Costs and Relatively True Selling Prices, 1916; Symbols, 1917; Lectures, The Science of Management, 1917; also booklets, lectures and articles in mags., etc. Home: Russell Av., Suffield, Conn. Office: Suffield CT‡

PARKINSON, BURNEY LYNCH, educator; b. Lincoln County, Tenn., Jan. 1, 1887; s. Samuel Moore and Adelia (Jamison) P.; B.S., Erskine Coll., S.C., 1909; Litt.D., 1939; grad. study U. of S.C., Columbia; M.A., George Peabody Coll., Nashville, Tenn., 1920, Ph.D., 1926; m. Belvidera Ashleigh Dry, June 30, 1914. Teacher of English and prin. high sch., Laurens, S.C., 1909-11; supt. graded sch., Albemarle, 1911-14; supt. city schs., Laurens, 1914-18; state high sch. supervisor, S.C., 1920-23; prof. sch. adminstrn. and dir. of extension, U. of S.C., 1923-27; pres. Presbyn. Coll. of S.C., 1927-28; mem. faculty summer sch., Furman U., 1928, U. of Ala., 1929, 30, 31; dir. teacher training certification and elementary edn., State of Ala., 1928-32; pres. Miss. State Coll. for Women, 1932-52; prof. edn. Mary Washington Coll., U. Va., 1952-56; vis. prof. Wm. Carey Coll. Miss., 1957-64. Asso. mgr. Southern Div. Am. Red Cross, World War. Mem. Nat. Edn. Assn., S.C. Teachers' Association (ex-pres.), Assn. of Colleges and Secondary Schs. of Southern States (v.p. 1940-41), Phi Beta Kappa, Phi Delta Kappa, Omicron Delta Kappa. Democrat. Presbyterian (commr. to Gen. Assembly 1939). Clubs: Kiwanis (pres.), 13 Club, Forum, Drama. Author: High School Manual for South Carolina, 1922; A History of Columbia, S.C., Schools, 1925; The Professional Preparation and Certification of Public School Teachers in South Carolina, 1926. Editor South Carolina Education (mag.), 1923-26. Home: Albemarle NC Died Dec. 7, 1972; buried Albemarle Cemetery, Albemarle NC

PARKINSON, WILLIAM NIMON, surgeon; b. Philadelphia, Pa., Sept. 17, 1886; s. Walter and Sarah (Nimon) P.; B.S., Villanova (Pa.) Coll., 1907, LL.D., 1932; M.D., Temple U., 1911; M.S., U. of Pa., 1925; D.Sc., Pa. Mil. Coll., 1949, Ed.D. (honorary), Dickinson College, 1951, L.H.D. Hahnemann Medical College, 1955; LL.D., Jefferson Medical College, Phila., 1957; Dr. Med. Sci., Woman's Medical College, Phila., 1959. Assistant surgeon Joseph Price Hosp., Phila., 1912-17; surg. Montgomery Hosp., Norristown, Pa., 1922-25; chief surg. Fla. East Coast Hosp., St. Augustine, Fla., 1926-28; prof. clin. surgery, Temple U., 1928-71, dean sch. medicine, 1929-59, dean emeritus, 1961-71; v.p. in charge med. center, 1953-61, med. director Temple U. Hosps., 1929-61. Trustee Magee Hosp. for Convalescents, Skin and Cancer Hosp., Philadelphia. Served as captain M.C., U.S. Army, World War I, Fellow Am. Coll. Surgeons; mem. A.M.A., Pa. State Medical Society, Philadelphia Medical Society, Phi Chi, Alpha Omega Alpha. Republican. Baptist. Clubs: Medical, Philadelphia Country, Union League, Rotary. Address: Philadelphia PA Died Apr. 19, 1971.

PARKS, EDD WINFIELD, writer, univ. prof.; born Newbern, Tenn., Feb. 25, 1906; s. Edward Winfield and Emma (Wallis) P.; student U. of Tenn., 1922-23, Occidental Coll., 1923-24; A.B., Harvard, 1927; A.M., Vanderbilt University, 1929, Ph.D., 1933; married Aileen, Wells, November 3d, 1933. Fellow and instr. English, Vanderbilt U., 1928-33; prof. English, Cumberland U., 1933-35; asst. prof. advancing to prof. English, U. of Ga., 1935-64, Alumni Found. Distinguished prof. English, 1964-68; vis. prof. Duke U., summers 1936, 38, 39, U. N.C., 1953; Fulbright lectr. Am. Literature, U. Copenhagen, 1955; vis. prof. Am. Lit., U. Brazil, 1949, Fulbright prof., 1958; Carnegie fellow, 1948, 52. Served as 2d lt., later capt., Mil. Intelligence, U.S.A., 1943-46; spl. mission to England, spring, 1945. Awarded Army Commendation Ribbon. Mem. Am. (executive council), Southeastern (pres. 1961-62) studies assns., So. Humanities Conf. (chairman 1962-63), Modern Lang. Assn. (chmn. So. lit. discussion group 1960) and South Atlantic Modern Lang. Assn. (pres. 1958-59). Author, co-author or editor books, 1933—, including: Safe on Second, 1953; Backwater, 1957; William Gilmore Simms as a Literary Critic, 1960; Ante-Bellum Southern Literary Critics, 1962; Nashoba, pub. 1963; Henry Timrod, 1963; Edgar Allan Poe as Literary Critic, 1964; Sidney Lanier, The Man, the Poet, the Critic, 1968; Hints to the Gentle Reader, 1969; (with Aileen Wells Parks) The Collected Poems of Henry Timrod, 1966. Thomas MacDonagh The Man-The Patriot-The Writer. 1967. Mem. editorial bd. Am. Quar., 1957-58, Miss., Quar. Contbr. articles to symposia, anthologies and mags. Address: Athens GA Died May 7, 1968.

PARKS, JOHN LOUIS, univ. dean, physician; b. Muskogee, Okla., Jan. 4, 1908; s. John S. and Della N. (Northcutt) P.; B.A., U. Wis., 1930, M.S., 1932, M.D., 1934, tng. obstetrics, gynecology, 1935-37; m. Mary Dean Scott, Aug. 31, 1930; 1 son, John Scott. Intern U. Cin., 1934-35; instr. U. Cin., 1934-35; instr. pathology U. Wis., 1937-38; chief med. officer obstetrics and gynecology Gallinger Municipal Hosp., 1938-44; prof. obstetrics and gynecology George Washington University, from 1944, dean Sch. Medicine, 1957-67, dean University Medical Center, from 1967, v.p. for med. affairs, 1972; medical dir. hosp., 1957-65; cons. D.C. Gen. Hosp., Walter Reed Med. Center, Nat. Insts. Health. Exec. com. Gorgas Meml. Inst. Trustee Greater Washington Ednl. TV, Inc. Decorated Eloy Alfaro Fundacion Internacional (Panama). Diplomate Am. Bd. Obstetrics, Gynecology (past dir.). Fellow A.C.S. (bd. govs. 1956-59). Royal College of Obstetricians and Gynaecologists; hon. fellow Bklyn. Gynecol. Soc., Central, S. Atlantic assns. obstetricians and gynecologists, S.W., Fla., Wash., Miami, Panama obstet. and gynecol. soc., Obstet. Soc. Phila., Soc. Obstetricians and Gynaecologists Can., La Societa Triventa di Ostetricia e Ginecologia; mem. American College of Obstetrics and Gynecology (v.p. 1957), Assn. Am. Med. Colls. (pres. 1967-68, mem. exec. council), Nat. Bd. Med. Examiners (exec. com., pres.), Interstate Postgrad. Med. Association (president 1966), Med. Soc. D.C., Washington Gynecol. Soc., Smith-Reed-Russell Soc., Am. Gyneocology Soc. (treas. 1955-59, pres. elect 1972-73), American Assn. Obstetrics and Gynecology (pres. 1961), So. Medical Association, Am. Medical Assn., Sigma Xi, Osler Soc., Alpha Omega Alpha, Nu Sigma Nu, Alpha Delta Phi. Contbr. med. jours. Home: Annapolis MD Died July 5, 1972.

PARKS, JOHN SHIELDS, retired; b. Hackettstown, N.J., Jan. 16, 1870; s. Irving William and Ann Elizabeth (Shields) P.; student Illinois Coll., Jacksonville; LL.D., U. of Ark., 1934; m. Grace Whittlesey, Dec. 16, 1888; children—Meryl Anarie, Ann Elizabeth. Formerly pres. The Times Record Co., pubs. Fort Smith (Ark.) Times Record, Southwest Times Record, Southwest American; also formerly pres. Shreveport (La.) Lamp Chimney Co., Radiant Glass Co., The Garrison Co., Fort Smith Engraving Co., Southern Chem. Co.; v.p. Old Home Investment Co.; receiver Ft. Smith & Western R.R. State printer of Kansas 2 yrs.; mem. Idaho House of Representatives 2 years. Democrat. Episcopalian. Mason (32 deg., K.T., Shriner), Elk. Home: 221 N. 16th St. Office: First Nat. Bank Bldg., Fort Smith AR‡

PARRISH, JOHN BERTRAND, railroad exec.; b. New Kent County, Va., 1877; vice pres. Chesapeake & Ohio Ry., Richmond, Va.; pres. Lexington (Ky.) Union Station Co.; dir. State Planters Bank & Trust Co., Richmond. Home: 6303 Towana Rd. Office: care Chesapeake & Ohio Railway, Richmond VA*‡

PARRY, SIDNEY LOREN, stock broker; b. Worthington, Minn., Aug. 4 1902; s. William John and Katherine (Prideaux) P.; student Yankton (S.D.) Coll., 1922-24; B.S., Northwestern, 1926; m. Elizabeth Beckwith, Sept. 1, 1928; 1 dau. Elizabeth Jane (Mrs. Duane Miller). Private secretary to the Public Service Company of Northern Illinois, Chicago, Ill., 1926-28; asst. to pres. Chicago Stock Exchange, 1928-39, vice pres., 1939-45; exec. vice pres. Assn. Stock Exchange Firms, 1945-50; director public relations and advertising, Charles W. Scranton & Co., New Haven, 1951-53; partner DeCoppet and Doremus, from 1956, members N.Y. Stock Exchange. Chmn. bd. trustees Yankton Coll. Served in USNR, 1942-45; active duty as lt. comdr. Mem. Sigma Chi, Delta Sigma Pi. Republican. Presbyn. Clubs: Union League, New York Stock Exchange Luncheon, City Midday (N.Y.C.); Wee Westport CT Died Nov. 10, 1968; buried Evergreen Cemetery, Westport CT

PARSONS, DONALD JOHNSON, corp. exec.; b. Washington, May 21, 1909; s. Frank T. and Margaret Nancy (Johnson) P.; B.S., George Washington U., 1935; m. Sarah Frances Powell, Nov. 12, 1935; children—Ellen Powell, Donald Douglas. Spl. agt. F.B.I., 1936-42, cons. engr. lab., 1942-47, sci. chief, 1947-54, asst. dir. charge lab., 1954-61; exec. v.p. Frank Parsons Paper Company, Inc., 1961-65, president, treasurer, 1965-69; dir. Prudential Savs. & Loan Assn.; mem. mchts. adv. council Internat. Paper Co., Mead Corp. Bd. dirs., v.p. Edgar Hoover Found. Mem. Paper Distbn. Council, Nat. Paper Trade Association, American Chem. Society, Chem. Soc. Washington, Alpha Chi Sigma. Home: Lorton VA Died July 13, 1969; buried Cedar Hill Cemetery, Washington DC

PARSONS, EMMA FOLLIN (MRS. CLIFFORD W. PARSONS), Rep. Nat. committeewoman; b. Fairport, Mo.; d. James Madison and Prudence Louise (Norman) Follin; ed. Baldwin City (Kan.) pub. and high schs.; Ph.B., Baker U., Baldwin City, Kan., 1898-1902; B.S., Kan. State Agrl. Coll., Manhattan, Kan., 1910-11; m. Clifford W. Parsons, June 12, 1912. Asst. postmaster, Baldwin City, Kan., 1902-06; sch. teacher, Hutchinson, Kan., 1906-08, Wichita, Kan., 1908-10, Argentine High Sch., Kansas City, Kan., 1911-12; spl. teacher, Tucson, Ariz., 1920-24; supervisor of the Census, Ariz., 1930.

Republican National committeewoman for Ariz., 1940-48; vice chmn. Rep. State Com., 1938-40. Mem. Pima County Women's Republican Club (pres.), D.A.R. (vice regent Tucson chap.), Delta Delta Delta, Ariz. Fedn. Women's Republican Clubs (pres. 1933-35), Am. Assn. of U. Women. Home: 405 Granada St., Tucson AZ‡

PARSONS, ERNEST WILLIAM, educator; b. Wellington, Somersetshire, Eng., Apr. 20, 1873; s. William Agley and Harriet (Howe) P.; came to Can., 1883, to U.S., 1913; A.B., McMaster U., 1899, Th.B., 1901, D.B., 1902, A.M., 1903, DD., 1923; Ph.D., U. of Chicago, 1912; m. Frances Lyda Paisley, Nov. 4, 1912. Ordained Bapt. ministry, 1901; pastor First Ch., Port Arthur, Ont., Can., 1901-08; prof. mathematics and science, Port Arthur Collegiate Inst., 1908; prof. English and sociology, Brandon (Man.) Coll., 1912-13; prof. N.T. Interpretation, Pacific Sch. of Religion, Berkeley, Calif., 1913-14; prof. English Bible and Bibl. langs., 1914-18, N.T. interpretation, 1918-28, Rochester Theol. Sem.; prof. N.T. interpretation, Colgate-Rochester Div. Sch., 1928-41, emeritus; lecturer, U. of Chicago, summers 1925, 30, 31; visiting prof. New Testament interpretation, McMaster U., 1932-43. Mem. Phi Beta Kappa. Clubs: Alpha Chi, Automobile. Author: An Historical Examination of Some Non-Markan Elements in Luke, 1914; Religion of the New Testament, 1939. Part author of Studies in Early Christianity, 1928; The Process of Religion, 1933; Environmental Factors in Christian History, 1939; Christian Leadership in a World Society, 1945. Editor and contributor Anniversary Volume, Rochester Theol. Sem., 1925. Editor Rochester Theol. Sem. Bulletin, 1924-28. Home: 253 Alexander St., Rochester 7 NY‡

PARSONS, J(AMES) RUSSELL, ins. exec.; b. Albany, N.Y., Dec. 27, 1896; s. James Russell and Frances Theodora (Smith) P.; A.B., Harvard, 1919; m. Margaret Chubb, June 4, 1921; children—James Russell (killed in action over Italy, 1943), Frances Dorothea (Mrs. Rene Pingeon), Victoria Lee (Mrs. Robert M. Pennoyer), Margaret Hendon (now Mrs. Franklin E. Parker). Joined Chubb and Son, 1920, partner, 1925-59; hon. dir. Associated Aviation Underwriters; dir. Vigilant Ins. Co., N.Y.C., Federal Insurance Co. of N.J. Mem. Ins. Soc. N.Y. Home: West Orange NJ Died June 9, 1970.

PARSONS, JAMES KELLY, army officer (ret.); b. Rockford, Ala., Feb. 11, 1877; s. Lewis E. and Catherine (Kelly) P.; prep. edn., pub. and pvt. schs., Birmingham, Ala.; grad. Inf. and Cav. Sch., Fort Leavenworth, Kan., 1904, Command and Staff Sch., Fort Leavenworth, 1923, Army War Coll., Washington, 1924, Navy War Coll., Newport, R.I., 1925; m. Volinda Henderson, July 23, 1904. Commd. 1st lt., 3d Ala. Vol. Inf., 1898; commd. 2d lt., inf., U.S. Army, 1899, and advanced through grades to maj. gen. 1936; served in Spanish-Am. War; with inf. and Castner's Native Scouts, Philippine Insurrection, 1899-1901; co. comdr. and bn. adj., 20th Inf., 1904-09, post q.m., Monterey, Calif., 1909, regtl. q.m., 1909-11; insp. instr. N.Y.N.G., 1916-17; served on Gen. Staff, Tours, France, World War I; participated St. Mihiel and Meuse-Argonne offensives; comdr. Embarkation Camp, St. Nazaire, 1918-19, gassed, 1919; duty with N.Y.N.G., 1919-20; officer in charge Nat. Guard affairs, 5th Corps Area, 1920-22; with Office of Chief of Inf., 1925-26, War Dept. Gen. Staff, 1926-29; comdt. Tank Sch. and comdg. officer Ft. George G. Meade, 1929-30; comd. 9th C.A. Dist., 1931, 23d Inf. Brigade, 1931-33, 5th Brigade and Vancouver (Wash.) Barracks, 1933-36, 2d Div. and Ft. Sam Houston, Tex., 1936-38, 3d Corps Area, Baltimore, 1938-40, ret. 1941. Decorated D.S.C., D.S.M., Purple Heart. Club: Army-Navy (Washington). Home: 1661 Crescent Pl., Washington 9‡

PARSONS JOHN CALVIN, physician; b. Elmira, Ill., Jan. 6, 1897; s. Arthur and Martha (Sizemore) P.; M.D., U. Ia., 1920; m. Dorothy Honnold Hull, July 23, 1921; 1 son, John Calvin. Intern, U. Cal., 1920-21; house officer in medicine and Tb Stanford, 1921-22; former chief medicine VA Hosp., Des Moines; practice medicine specializing in internal medicine, Des Moines. Diplomate Am. Bd. Internal Medicine. Fellow A.C.P., Am. Soc. Clin. Pathologists; mem. A.M.A., World Heart Soc., Alpha Omega Alpha, Phi Gamma. Republican. Presbyn. Home: Leon IA Died May 28, 1968; buried Des Moines IA

PARSONS, JOHN FREDERICK, aero. research sci.; b. Joliet, Ill., May 10, 1908; s. John Francis and Cora Belle (Lingle) P.; student San Diego State Coll., 1924-26; A.B., Stanford, 1928, Engr. in Mech. Engring. Aero., 1930; m. Evalyn Katharine Hughes, June 19, 1937; children—Patricia Jean (Mrs. Dennis I. Winsten), John Fredrick, Richard Alan. Aeronautical research engineer for the Langley Aero. Lab., NACA, 1931-40; aero. research sci. Ames Aero. Lab., NACA, 1940-48, asst. to dir., 1948-50, asso. dir. (became Ames Research Center NASA, 1958), 1952-69, chief unitary plan wind tunnel program NACA, 1950-56. Fellow Am. Inst. Aeros. and Astronautics; mem. Sigma Xi. Home: Palo Alto CA Died Mar. 2, 1969.

PARSONS, LEWIS MORGAN, bus. exec.; b. Phila., Pa., Jan. 9, 1898; s. Alonzo and Romelia (Morgan) P.; student William Penn Charter Sch., Phila., 1905-15, U. of Pa., 1915-17, Mass. Inst. Tech., 1918; pilot, U.S. Navy Air Corps, 1917-19; m. Marion Park, Nov. 8, 1921; 1 dau., Marion. With Bethlehem Steel Corp., 1919-38, Phila., mgr. sales, 1936-38; vice pres., gen. mgr. sales, Jones & Laughlin Steel Corp., Pittsburgh, 1938, dir. 1938-44; asst. to vice pres., U.S. Steel Corp. of Del., 1944-50, v.p., mem. bd. dirs., mem. exec. com., 1950; vice president United States Steel Company, 1950; v.p. Washington and Phila. U.S. Steel Corp., 1954-1970. Republican. Baptist. Clubs: Duquesne (Pittsburgh); Union League, Racquet (Phila.); Madison Square Garden, Twenty-Nine (N.Y.); Metropolitan, Burning Tree, Carlton (Washington, Dist. Columbia); Pine Valley Golf (Clementon, N.J.); Rolling Rock (Ligonier, Pa.); Pacific Union (San Francisco). Home: Washington DC

PARSONS, LLEWELLYN B(RADLEY), chemist; b. Saginaw, Mich., Feb. 28 1897; s. Edward L. and Maude Winifred (Morey) P.; B.S., Syracuse U., 1919, M.S., U. Wis., 1921, Ph.D., 1923; m. Edna Marcia Claflin, June 15, 1921. Research chemist Cudahy Packing Co., Omaha, 1923-24, supervising chemist, 1924-33, research dir., 1933-39; research supervisor Lever Bros. Co., Cambridge, Mass., 1939-41, chief chemist, 1941-48, mgr. basic research labs., 1948-50, asst. dir. research and development, 1950-51, dir. research and development, 1951-54, v.p. research development, 1954-60, v.p., from 1960 also dir. Mem. Am. Chem. Soc., Am. Oil Chemists Soc., A.A.A.S., Am. Soc. for Testing Materials, Sigma Xi, Sigma Chi, Alpha Chi Sigma, Phi Lambda Upsilon. Phi Kappa Alpha. Home: Ridgewood NJ Died Feb. 28, 1968.

PARSONS, LOUELLA O., former motion picture columnist; b. Freeport, Ill.; d. Joshua and Helen (Wilcox) Oettinger; grad. Dixon (Ill.) High Sch.; student Dixon Coll.; Litt.D., Quincy Coll., 1959; m. Harry Watson Martin, Jan. 4, 1930 (dec.); 1 dau. (by previous marriage), Harriet Parsons. Began career with Essanay Studios, Chgo., reading and writing motion picture scripts; later started first motion picture column for Chgo. Herald, then worked on Morning Telegraph, N.Y.C. for 5 years; with Hearst publs. 1922-65; went to Cal., 1925; has covered many motion picture events; formerly editor motion picture dept. Internat. News Service; appeared on radio programs. Awarded Med. Center Aides award, City of Hope, Heart of Gold award, Mt. Sinai Hosp., Masquers award; Golden Flame award Cal. Assn. Press Women, 1958. Clubs: Women's Nat. Press, New York Women's Press; Hollywood Women's Press; Greater Los Angeles Women's Press. Author: How to Write for the Movies, 1914; The Gay Illiterate, 1944; Tell It to Louella, 1961 Roman Catholic. Home: Beverly Hills CA Died Dec. 9, 1972; buried Holy Cross Cemetery.

PARSONS, WILLARD H., surgeon; b. Brookhaven, Miss., May 3, 1898; s. William F. and Ophelia (Herring) P.; student Tulane U., 1914-17; M.D. Jefferson Med., Edna Earl Sparks, Oct. 23, 1922; children—Edna Earl (Mrs. H. Thurston Whitaker), Ruth Lee (Mrs. Emmett C. Neil). Practice of medicine, Vicksburg, Miss., 1922; chief staff and dir. surgery Vicksburg Clinic, 1929-62; dir. surgery Vicksburg Hosp., Inc., 1929-62; civilian cons. surgery to surgeon-General Army U.S. Far Eastern Theatre, 1962-63, to Surgeon Gen. of U.S.A., Dept. of Defense, 1964-69; emeritus cons. surgery to surgeon gen. of Army, 1967-69; former cons. thoracis surgery U.S. Vets Hosp., Jackson; prof. clinical surgery emeritus U. of Miss. Medical Sch.; past dir. grad. tng. in surgery Vicksburg Hosp. and Vicksburg Clinic. Diplomate Am. Bd. Surgery Founders Group. Fellow A.C.S. (chmn. bd. govs. 1953-56, regent 1956-65, vice chmn. bd. regents 1963-65, 1st v.p. 1965-66), Internat. Cardiovascular Soc.; mem. Soc. Surgery Alimentary Tract, Am. Cancer Soc. (Miss. Cancer pres. 1955-57, nat. dir.), Southeastern Surg. Congress (pres. 1960-61), Pan-Pacific Surgical Soc., Royal Soc. Medicine (affiliate), Southern Soc., Clin. Surgeons (pres. 1950-51), So. (v.p. 1950-51), Western, Am. surg. assns., New Orleans Surg. Soc., Societe Internationale de Chirurgie, Issaquena-Sharkey-Warren Counties Med. Soc. (past pres.), Miss. State Med. Assn. (past chmn. surgery sect.). Sigma Alpha Epsilon, Alpha Omega Alpha, Alpha Kappa Kappa. Presbyn. Club: Vicksburg Country. Author: Cancer of Breast, 1960; also surg. publs. Adv. editorial bd. Cancer. Contbr. books and numerous clin. papers. Home: Vicksburg MS Died Mar. 9, 1969.

PARSONS, WILLIAM BARCLAY, surgeon; born N.Y. City, May 22, 1888; s. William Barclay and Anna DeWitt (Reed) P.; grad. St. Mark's Sch., 1906; A.B., Harvard, 1910; M.D., Coll. Physicians and Surgs., Columbia U., 1914; m. Rose Saltonstall Peabody, Mar. 22, 1919; children—William Barclay, Jr., Rose Peabody (Mrs. Russell Vincent Lynch), Anne Barclay (now Mrs. Harold A. Priest, Jr.). Member of the faculty of medicine, Coll. Phys. and Surgs, Columbia U., 1935-39, and 1945-53, attending surg. Presbyn. Hosp., Vanderbilt Clinic, 1939-52, mem. med. bd., from 1945; prof. clin. surgery, Coll. of Phys. and Surg., 1949-53, professor emeritus clinical surgery, 1953-73; director of surgery, first surg. div. Welfare Hosp.; cons. in surg., N.Y Orthopedic Hosp., from 1946. Served as lt., later capt Am. Ambulance Field Service, France, 1916. Presbyn Hosp. Unit, France, Mobile Hosp., Champagne Aisne-Marne, St. Mihiel, Meuse Argonne offensives Army Occupation, 1916-19; served as lt. col. to col chief surg. service and unit dir. 2d Gen. Hosp., chie surg. cons. Southwest Pacific area; chief surg. cons., 6t Service Command. Awarded Legion of Merit, 1945 Trustee N.Y. Inst. for Edn. of the Blind, and St. Mark' School. Fellow Am. Coll. Surgeons; fellow Sec Surgery, N.Y. Acad. Medicine; mem. Am. Surg. Assn Am. Bd. Surg. (founders' group), Soc. clin. Surg. (sec 1934-35), Med. and Surg. Soc., New York Surg. Soc New York Acad. Med. (chmn. com. on professiona standards, 1932-42, com. on med. information, pres 1951-52), A.M.A. (vice-chmn. sect. on surg., gen. an abdominal, 1940), Soc. Clin. Research, Harvey Society Nat. Bd. Med. Examiners (2d term of 6 yrs. 1947), Soc Med. Consultant to the Armed Forces (councilor 1946), Societe Internationale de Chirurgie (sec. Am. br 1947-49), Century Assn., Soc. of The Cincinnati, New Hampshire Br. Chmn. coms. on radioactive research and blood bank, Presbyn. Hosp. Republican Episcopalian. Clubs: Harvard (New York and Boston) Author: Sections in Surgical Clinics of North America vol. 16, 1936, vol. 19, 1939, 1947; sect. in Operative Surgery, 1941; sect. in Surgical Treatment, 1947; also numerous papers on surg. Home: Darien CT Died Jan 2, 1973; buried Wilton CT

PARSONS, WILLIAM LEWIS, lawyer; b. New Portland, Me., Nov. 11, 1884; s. Albert S. and Rhoda F (Abbott) P.; A.B., Bates Coll., 1905, LLD., 1971; J.B. Boston U. Sch. Law, 1907; m. Rae Bryant, Oct. 14, 1908 (dec. 1916); 1 dau., Dorothy P. Whitten; m. 2d, Helen Sutherland, Mar. 23, 1918 (dec. 1960). Admitted to Mass. bar, 1907, since practiced in Boston; admitted U.S. Supreme Ct. bar, 1919; asso. law dept. Boston & Albany R.R., Boston, 1908-16, asst. counsel, 1916-39, asst. counsel New York Central System, 1940-50; gen. atty. charge Boston & Albany R.R. Law Dept., 1950-52; chmn. Conf. of Trunk Line Counsel, 1943-44; dir. Winchester Trust Co., 1921-63, pres., 1933-55, chmn. bd., 1955-63. Selectman, Winchester, Mass., 1920-21, mem. Planning Bd., 1924-49, chmn. 1925-49. Pres. Bates Coll. Alumni Assn., 1937-39, mem. bd. of overseers 1939-44, mem. bd. of fellows, 1944, chmn bd., 1964-70. Mem. Mass. State Bar Assn., Phi Beta Kappa, Delta Sigma Rho. Republican. Conglist. Home: Kingfield ME Died Oct. 28, 1972.

PARTIPILO, ANTHONY VICTOR, surgeon; b. Bari, Italy, Sept. 1900; s. Victor and Claudia (Mazzone) P.; student Northwestern U., 1918-19, DePaul U., 1919-20; M.D., Loyola U., Chgo., 1924; m. Marion Webber Killeen, Apr. 24, 1926 (dec.); 1 dau., Marion (Mrs. Stuart A. Helffrich). Naturalized, 1927. Intern St. Mary's of Nazareth Hosp., Chgo., 1924-26; sr. attending surgeon St. Mary's Hosp., 1925-46; pvt. practice of medicine, 1925-66; house surgeon Lakeview Hosp., 1925-26; asso. anatomy Stritch Sch. Medicine, Loyola U., 1925-28, instr. surgery, 1928-31, clin. asso. surgery, 1931-33, asst. prof., 1933-38, asso. prof. surgery, 1938-57, clin. prof. surgery, 1957-66; attending surgeon Mercy Hosp., 1928-46; dir. Chgo. Postgrad. Sch. Surgery, 1936-42; sr. attending surgeon Columbus Hosp., 1946-66; chief surg. staff Mother Cabrini Hosp., 1950-66; cons. surgeon Ill. Pub. Welfare Dept., Cuneo Meml. Hosp. Served as lt. col. AUS, 1942-46. Decorated Cavallieri Ufficiale (Republic Italy), 1959. Fellow A.M.A., A.C.S., Internat. Coll. Surgs.; mem. Ill., Chgo. med. socs., Phi Beta Phi. Roman Catholic. Club: Lake Shore (Chgo.). Author: Surgical Technique and Principles of Operative Surgery, 6th edit., 1957. Contbr. to Treatment of Cancer and Allied Diseases (Pack and Ariel), 1958. Died Jan. 6, 1966.

PARTLOW, WILLIAM DEMPSEY, psychiatrist; b. Ashville, St. Clair County, Ala., Feb. 4, 1877; s. David A. and Catherine (Beason) P.; student St. Clair Coll. and State Normal Sch., Florence, Ala.; M.D., U. of Alabama, 1901, hon. LL.D., 1921; M. Margaret Nixon, Apr. 26, 1905; children—Wm. Dempsey, Margaret Cummings, Nixon Beason (dec.), Kathleen, David Beason. Intern Bryce Hosp., Tuscaloosa, Ala., 1901-02; asst. phys. same, 1902-08, asst. supt., 1908-19; supt. Ala. State Hospitals since July 1, 1919. Chmn. Medical Advisory Board, West Alabama counties, in draft, World War I, and World War II. Member State Board of Health, Alabama, 1918-47; member State Board Medical Examiners, 1918-47; member State Bd. Examiners for Registration of Nurses. 1919-27. Fellow Southern Psychiatric Assn. (pres. 1936-37), Am. Psychiatric Assn.; mem. A.M.A., Ala. State Med. Assn. (pres. 1917-18), Am. Pub. Health Assn. Democrat. Methodist. Rotarian. Partlow State School for Mental Defectives named in his honor, also supt. same. Home: Tuscaloosa AL*‡

PARTRIDGE, EVERETT P(ERCY), chem. engr.; b. Edinburg, N.Y., Dec. 15, 1902; s. Edward Everett and Minnie Amelia (Wood) P.; B.S., Syracuse University, Syracuse, New York, 1925; M.S., University of Michigan, 1926, Ph.D., 1928; m. Jane Harris Hazard, June 20, 1925; 1 son, Everett George. Asso. editor Indsl. and Engring. Chemistry, 1928-31; supervising ngr. Nonmetallic Minerals Expt. Sta., U.S. Bur. Mines, 931-35; dir. research Hall Labs. div. Calgon Corp., 935-60, dir. labs., 1960-66, corporate v.p., 1966-67, dir., 1950-67, cons., 1967-69. Mem. exec. com. div. ngring. and indsl. research NRC, chmn. Internat. Water Conf.; mem. Nat. Tech. Adv. Com. on Water Quality Requirements. Pres. Beaver area Community Chest; chmn. local unit Am. Cancer Soc.; dist. chmn. Boy Scouts Am. Named Engr. of Year, Beaver County Chpt. Pa. Soc. Profl. Engrs., 1967. Fellow A.A.A.S., Am. Soc. M.E., mem. Am. Chem. Soc., Am. Inst. Chem. Engrs., Am. Soc. Testing and Materials, Newcomen Soc., Delta Upsilon. Clubs: University (Pitts.); Beaver Valley Country. Home: Beaver PA Died Apr. 1969.

PATCHEN, KENNETH, author, poet, artist; b. Niles, O., Dec. 13 1911; s. Wayne and Eva (McQuade) P.; student U. Wis., 1929-30; m. Miriam Oikemus, June 28, 1934. Guggenheim fellow. 1936. Exhibited paintings various cities and univs., one-man show San Francisco Art Inst., 1972. Originator painted covers limited editions books, including Dark Kingdom, Sleepers Awake, Panels for the Walls of Heaven, Red Wine and Yellow Hair. Author: Before the Brave (poetry), 1936; First Will and Testament (poetry), 1939; The Journal of Albion Moonlight, 1941; The Dark Kingdom (poetry) 1942; The Teeth of the Lion (poetry), 1942; Cloth of the Tempest (poetry) 1943; Memoirs of a Shy Pornographer, 1945; An Astonished Eye Looks Out of The Air (poetry), 1945; Sleepers Awake, 1946; Panels For The Walls of Heaven (poems in prose), 1947; The Selected Poems of Kenneth Patchen, 1947; Pictures of Life and of Death, 1947; They Keep Riding Down All The Time, 1947; See You In The Morning, 1948; Red Wine and Yellow Hair (poetry), 1949; To Say If You Love Someone (poetry) 1949; Orchards, Thrones and Caravans (poetry), 1952; The Famous Boating Party (poems in prose), 1953; Fables and Other Little Tales (prose), 1953; Poemscapes (songs and proverbs), 1955; Glory Never Guesses (poems and paintings), 1955; Surprise for the Bagpipe Player (silkscreen reprodns. and poems), 1956; Hurrah for Anything (poems and drawings), 1957; When We Were Here Together (poems), 1957; Because It Is (poems and drawings), 1959; Don't Look Now (drama), 1959: But Even So (poems and drawings), 1963; There's Love All Day (poems), 1970; AFlame and AFun of Walking/Faces (fables and drawings), 1970; Wonderings (picture-poems, drawing-poems), 1971; In Quest of Candle-Lighters (poetry, prose, drawings), 1972: exptl. radio play The City Wears A Slouch Hat, Columbia Workshop, N.Y.C., 1942; pub. numerous anthologies. Appeared radio, TV, nightclubs, concert stage with jazz groups, 1957-58. Recorded Kenneth Patchen Reads with The Chamber Jazz Sextet, 1957, Selected Poems of Kenneth Patchen, Read by Himself, Kenneth Patchen Reads with Jazzing Canada; Kenneth Patchen Reads His Love Poems, 1961; The Love Poems of Kenneth Patchen, 1960; Kenneth Patchen Reads His Funny Fables, 1973; Kenneth Patchen Reads From the Journal of Albion Moonlight, 1973; Doubleheader (poems-drawings), 1966; Hallelujah Anyway (picture-poems), published in 1967; Collected Poems, published in 1968. Recipient Shelly Memorial award, 1954; 10,000 award for life-long contbn. to Am. letters Nat. Found. Arts and Humanities, 1967. Home: Palo Alto CA Died Jan. 8, 1972; cremated.

PATE, WALTER ROMNY, educator; b. near Madison, Jefferson County, Ind., Nov. 26, 1877; s. Randel Ross and Eliza Ellen (Buchanan) P.; A.B., Univ. of Neb., 1917; A.M., Columbia, 1929; m. Gertrude Louisa Sewell, Apr. 21, 1900; children—Neva Beatrice, Leonard Leroy, Mildred Ellen, Robert Sewell. Successively supt. schs., Danbury, Trenton, Grafton, Sidney, Neb., 1896-1910; supt. schs., Alliance, 1910-23; prof. in edn., dept. State Teachers Coll., Chadron, 6 summers, 1918-23; pres. State Normal Sch. and Teachers Coll., Peru, Aug. 1, 1923-Sept. 1, 1947, president emeritus since Sept. 1, 1947. Mem. N.E.A., Neb. State Teachers' Assn. (pres. 1923), Neb. Schoolmasters' Club, Phi Delta Kappa, Kappa Delta Pi, Kiwanis Club. Democrat. Methodist. Mason (K.T., 32 deg., Shriner). Lecturer teachers' institutes. Home: Peru NE‡

PATENAUDE, ESIOFF LEON, lawyer; b. St. Isidore, Laprairie, P.Q., Can., Feb. 12, 1875; s. Hilaire and Angele (Trudeau) P.; hon. LL.D., Laval U., 1934, Montreal U., 1923, McGill U., 1935, Bishop's Coll., 1937; m. Georgianna Deniger, May 8, 1900; children—Alphonse, Rose (Mrs. Hubert Prevost). Admitted to bar P.Q., 1899; elected to P.Q. Legislature for Laprairie, 1908-12, 1912-15, 1923-25; apptd. minister Inland Revenue for Can., Borden Cabinet, 1915; elected to House of Commons for Hochelaga, 1915-17, 1925; apptd. Sec. of State, 1917; Minister of Justice, Meighen Cabinet, 1926; lt. gov. P.Q., 1934-40. Pres. Alliance Nat. Mutual Life Ins. Co.; chmn. bd. Adminstrn. & Trust Co.; v.p. Credit Foncier Franco-Canadien; dir. Provincial Bank of Can., McColl Frontenac Oil Co. Ltd., Commerce Mutual Fire Ins. Co., Canadian Merc. Ins. Co. Home: 1321 Sherbrooke St. W., Apt. 80A. Office: 680 Sherbrooke St. W., Montreal PQ‡

PATENOTRE, ELEANOR ELVERSON, newspaper pub.; b. Phila., Pa., June 22, 1870; d. James and Sallio (Duval) E.; ed. pvt. schs.; m. Jules Patenotre (former French ambassador to Washington and Madrid), of Baye, France, Mar. 27, 1894 (died Dec. 1925); children—Constance Yvonne (Countess de Castellane), Raymond. Pres. and pub. The Philadelphia Inquirer since 1929. Mem. Acad. Natural Sciences Phila., Associated Press. Clubs: Civic, Acorn. Address: Elverson Bldg., Philadelphia PA‡

PATERSON, WILLIAM TAIT, clergyman; b. Glasgow, Scotland, Apr. 30 1884; s. William Tait and Annie (Small) P.; student Manitoba Coll., Winnipeg, 1906-09; B.Th., Lane Theol. Sem., 1913, Auburn Theol. Sem., 1929; D.D., Wooster Coll., 1927; m. Wanda Chase Carey, Dec. 3, 1913; children—William Tait, James Carey, Samuel Doak, Esther Lowry, Donald Goerge. Came to U.S., 1910, naturalized 1920. Student-missionary in Saskatchewan, Manitoba, Nova Scotia, and Ohio, 1906-13; ordained to Presbyterian ministry, 1913; pastor Cumberland, O., 1913, Norwood, O., 1920-47, Batavia, O., 1947-57; ret.; spl. lecturer homiletics McCormick Theol. Sem. Chgo., 1932-34. Moderator Presbytery of Cincinnati, O., 1925 (pres. Bd. Nat. Missions, 1940-41; Com. Ministerial Relations); stated clerk pro tem, 1946-47; moderator Synod of O., 1926-27, mem. Gen. Coun.; Judicial Commn., 1935-41; chairman Com. United Promotion; commr. General Assembly, Presbyterian Church, U.S. of America, 1922, 32, 43; delegate Pan-Presbyterian Alliance, Aberdeen, Scotland, 1913; mem. Gen. Council Presbyn. Gen. Assembly, 1934-40. Served with Y.M.C.A., A.E.F., World War, Pres. and sec. Lane Theological Seminary, Cincinnati; dir. McCormick Theol. Sem. (Chicago), Norwood Service League; pres., Council Chs. (Cincinnati, 1944-46); mem. War Chest Bd. (Cin.); mem. adv. bd. Cincinnati DeMolay; chmn. Management Com. Norwood Y.M.C.A., 1946. Dir. Y.M.C.A., Hamilton County; dir. and sec. Western Educational Society. Mem. Pi Gamma Mu, Caledonian Soc. of Cincinnati (former pres. and chaplain). Republican, Mason (32 degree, K.T.). Clubs: Clergy, Cosmic, Rotary; Norwood Kiwanis. Contributor to the Minister's Annual, also articles to magazines; contri Cincinnati OH Died Oct. 12, 1970; buried Linwood Cemetery, Russellville OH

PATRICK, DAVID LYALL, research adminstr.; b. Iowa City, Oct. 25, 1899; s. George Thomas White and Maude (Lyall) P.; A.B., State U. Ia., 1922; A.M., Stanford U., 1926, Ph.D. (Royall Victor fellow, 1928-30), 1934; m. Alice Ruth Steininger, Sept. 4, 1926. Instr. in Eng., U. of Ia., 1926-28, Stanford U., 1931-34; asst. prof. of Eng., U. of Ariz., 1934-37, asso. prof., 1938-47, dean of grad. coll. and prof. of English, 1947-57, coordinator research, from 1955, v.p. of academic affairs, 1957-60. Mem. A.A.A.S., Beta Theta Pi. Author: The Textual History of Shakespeare's Richard III", 1936; Recent Literature of the English Renaissance (with Hardin Craig and others), Studies in Philology, 1935-40; College Composition (with Richard Summers), 1946. Address: Tucson AZ Died Mar. 14, 1969.

PATRICK, JOHN HAYWARD, wholesale heating, plumbing and elec. co. exec.; b. Burlington, Vt., July 29, 1901; s. Roy L. and Harriet E. (Stone) P.; B.S., U. Vt., 1923; M.B.A., Harvard, 1925; m. Elizabeth H. Booth, Oct. 17, 1925; children—David K., Mary E. Treas., dir. Blodgett Supply Co., Incorporated, Burlington, Vermont, 1926-—, president, 1953-67, chairman, 1967-—; director of G. S. Blodgett Co., Inc., Burlington, 1927-—, v.p., 1940-—; v.p., dir. Swanton Co., Inc., Burlington, 1950-—; clk. (sec.) Eastern Magnesia Talc Co., Inc., Burlington, 1926-53, dir., 1929-—, chmn. bd., 1953-64; vice president, 1953-—; director National Life Insurance Company (Montpelier, Vermont), Rock of Ages Corp. (Barre, Vt.), Chittenden Trust Co. (Burlington). Alderman, City of Burlington, 1930-32; mem. Vt. Senate, 1943-45, 45-46. Mem. Plumbing and Heating Wholesalers N.E. (pres. 1945), Phi Delta Theta. Trustee U. Vt., 1950-56. Republican. Conglist. (trustee). Mason. Clubs: Tobique Salmon (sec.-treas. 1952-—) (New Brunswick, Can.); Ethan Allen (past gov.), Burlington Country (life) (Burlington). Home: VT Deceased.

PATRICK, RANSOM RATHBONE, educator, artist; b. Santa Barbara, Cal., July 28, 1906; s. Daniel John and Pearl Ethel (Lawrence) P.; B.A., U. Wash., 1944; M.F.A., Princeton, 1947, Ph.D., 1959; m. Dorothy Mae Thompson, Mar. 2, 1940. Asso. prof. art Oberlin Coll., 1947-48; asst. prof. U. Minn., 1948-49; asso. prof. Western Res. U., 1949-50, prof., 1950-54, chmn. div. art, 1950-52, dir. div. art and architecture, 1952-54; prof. aesthetics and art Duke, from 1954, chmn. dept. aesthetics, art and music, 1954-60, chmn. dept. art from 1960; exhibited paintings annually Pacific N.W. Annual Exhbn., Seattle, 1931-43; mural painting in Officer's Club. Sandpoint Naval Air Sta., Seattle; marketing and design cons. Found. Accounts, Inc. Mem. Am. Soc. Aesthetics (trustee 1955-58, sec.-treas. 1950-55), Southeastern Art Assn., Coll. Art Assn., Am. Assn. U. Profs., Delta Tau Delta. Club: Princeton (N.Y.C.), Author articles. Bus. mgr. Jour. Aesthetics Durham NC Died Apr. 27, 1971.

PATRICK, ROBERT F., corp. exec.; b. Burlington, Vt., 1903; grad. U. Vt., 1925; M.B.A., Harvard, 1927. Pres., treas., dir. G.S. Blodgett Co., Burlington; chmn. bd., mem. exec. com. Rock of Ages Corp.; dir. Blodgett Supply Co. Pres., dir. Mary Fletcher Hosp.; trustee U. Vt. Home: Burlington VT Died Nov. 30, 1967; interred family mausoleum, Lakeview Cemetery, Burlington VT

PATT, JOHN FRANCIS, ret. radio exec.; b. Shenandoah, Ia., Oct. 14, 1905; s. Ralph Haven and Mabel (Mentzer) P.; A.B., U. Kan., 1926; m. Ruth Richardson, June 7, 1927; children—Martha Ruth (Mrs. W. Hayden Thompson), Patricia Lee (Mrs. Robert L. Cloutier), Joan Frances (Mrs. Christopher L. Kincade). Engaged as asst. radio editor Kansas City Star, 1922-26; v.p., gen. mgr. radio sta. WGAR, Cleve., 1930-50; asst. gen. mgr. radio sta. WJR, Detroit, 1926-30; pres. The Good Will Station, Inc., Detroit, 1950-60, chmn. bd., 1960-64. Campaign chmn. Cleve. War Chest, 1943. Mem. Broadcast Pioneers Soc. (pres. 1957-58), Sigma Delta Chi, Beta Theta Pi. Episcopalian. Clubs: Advertising (pres. 1928-40), Rotary (past pres.), Hermit, Cleve. Country (past pres.), Union (Cleve.); Detroit Athletic, Detroit Adcraft. Home: Cleveland OH Died Nov. 19, 1972.

PATTEN, BRADLEY MERRILL, embryologist; b. Milwaukee, Wis., June 14 1889; s. William and Mary Elizabeth (Merrill) P.; A.B., Dartmouth Coll., 1911, Chamberlin fellow 1911-12; A.M., Harvard, 1912. Ph.D., 1914; m. Barbara Standish, June 13, 1914; 1 daughter, Elizabeth (Mrs. Walter E. Garrey). Assistant in zoology Harvard University, 1912-14; instructor in histology and embryology, Western Reserve U. Med. Sch., Cleveland, O., 1914-16, sr. instr., 1916-18, asst. prof., 1918-21, asso. prof., 1921-34; asst. dir. for med. sciences. Rockfeller Found., 1934-36; prof., head dept. anatomy, med. sch. U. Mich., 1936-59, emeritus, 1959-71; U.S. hydrographer Internat. Ice Patrol, 1914; visiting investigator, Carnegie Embryological Inst., Baltimore, Md., 1925, Pathol. Inst., Vienna, 1927. Nat. Sigma Xi lecturer, 1949-50; vis. prof. U. P.R., 1952, U. Otago Medical School, New Zealand., 1954, Medical School, Univ. Buenos Aires, 1958. U. Miami, 1959; U. Adelaide, Australia, 1961. Contributing mem. White House Conf. on Child Health and Protection, 1930. Fellow A.A.A.S., Ohio Acad. Science; mem. Am. Naturalists, Am. Soc. Zoologists, Am. Assn. Anatomists (2d v.p. 1934-36), Marine Biological Lab., Woods Hole, Massachusetts, Michigan Medical Society (honorary life), Phi Beta Kappa, Phi Sigma Kappa, Sigma Xi, Alpha Omega Alpha. Author: The Early Embryology of the Chick, 1920; The Embryology of the Pig. 1927; The Cardiovascular System, in Morris' Anatomy, 1942; Human Embryology, 1946; Heart Development, in Gould's Pathology of the Heart, 1953; Foundations of Embryology, 1958. Micro-moving picture methods of recording activities of living embryos. Asso., editor Am. Jour. Anatomy, 1941-58. Contbr. to zool., med. jours. Home: Ann Arbor MI Died Nov. 8, 1971; buried Woods Hole MA

PATTEN, CHARLES HARRELD, banker; b. Edmond, Oka., 1909; ed. U. Okla., 1930. Sr. v.p., dir. Valley Nat. Bank, Phoenix; dir. Beatrice Foods Co. Home: Phoenix AZ

PATTERSON, DAVID H., JR., business exec.; b. South Windsor, Conn., 1875. Pres. and dir. Fibreboard Products, Inc., Independent Paper Stock Co., Precision Electrotype Co., San Francisco, Federal Container Co., Phila., Pa., Maryland Container Co., Baltimore, Glass Containers, Inc., Los Angeles, Calif. Mason (Shriner). Home: 2950 Lake St. Office: Russ Bldg., San Francisco CA*‡

PATTERSON, EDWIN WILHITE, prof. law; b. Kansas City, Mo., Jan. 1 1899; s. Louis Lee and Roberta Ann (Wilhite) P.; grad. Central High Sch., Kansas City, Mo., 1906; A.B., U. of Mo., 1909, LL.B., 1911, LL.D., 1936; S.J.D., Harvard, 1920; m. Dorothy Madison Thomson, Dec. 28, 1915; children—Clifton Connell (dec.), Edwin Wilhite, Penelope. Began practice at Kansas City, 1911; with Holmes, Holmes & Page until 1913; practiced alone, 1913-15; adj. prof. law, U. of Tex., 1915-17; asst. prof. law, U. of Colo., 1917-18, prof., 1918-20; prof. law, State U. of Ia., 1920-22; editor Ia. Law Review, 1922; asso. prof. law, Columbia, 1922-24, prof., 1924-45; Cardozo professor jurisprudence, 1945-57, emeritus, 1957-65; Nelson Meml. lectr. U. Missouri, 1954; acting professor law, Stanford University, summer 1933; visiting prof. law University of Texas, 1943, U. of Va., 1957-58, U. of Southern Cal., 1958-59. Member joint committee Ency. of Social Sciences; adviser Restatement of Restitution (Am. Law Inst.), 1933-37. Dep. supt. of ins., State of N.Y., 1936; in charge Revision of New York Ins. Law, 1935-39; cons. proposed comml. code Law Revision Commn. N.Y. Mem. Mo. and Ia. State Bar, Am. Bar Assn. (chmn. com. on qualification and regulation of ins. cos. 1935-40; council sect. ins. law 1940-45), Academia Colombiana de Jurisprudencia (1941), Phi Delta Phi, Phi Beta Kappa, Order of Coif, QEBH (sr. soc. Univ. of Mo.). Democrat. Author: The Insurance Commissioner in the Unites States, 1927; Cases and Materials on Insurance, 1932; 3d edit., 1955; Essentials of Insurance Law, 1935, 2d edit., 1957; Cases on

Contracts, 1935; Cases on Contracts (with others), 1941, 4th edition, 1957; Materials for Legal Method (with N.T. Dowling and R.R. Powell); 1946; Jurisprudence: Men and Ideas of the Law, 1953; Legal Protection of Private Pension Expectations, 1960. Contbr. on legal subjects. Home: Charlottesville VA Died Dec. 23, 1965.

PATTERSON, ERNEST MINOR, economics; b. Cincinnati, O., July 17, 1870; s. John Paul and Henrietta Frances (Jackman) P.; A.B., Park Coll., Parkville, Mo., 1902, A.M., 1904, LL.D., 1936; grad. study U. Chgo., 1909-10; Ph.D., U. Pa., 1912, LL.D., 1950; LL.D., Occidental Coll., 1946; married Elsie Davis Reynolds, July 3, 1906; 1 daughter, Grace Frances. Prof. Latin, Henry Kendall Coll., Muskogee, Okla., 1902-05; prin. Wasatch Acad., Mt. Pleasant, Utah, 1905-08; dean, Washington College, Tennessee, 1908-09; instructor in finance, U. of Pa., 1910-15, asst. prof. econs., 1915-19, prof. 1919-50, emeritus; visiting prof. Institut Universitaire de Hautes Etude Internationales, Geneva, Switzerland, 1929; lecturer Academy Internat. Law, The Hague, 1931. Member Am. Acad. Polit. Social Science (president 1930-53, pres. emeritus 1953-69), Am. Econ. Assn. (vice pres. 1936), Am. Philos. Soc. (ex-sec.), Delta Sigma Phi, Beta Gamma Sigma, Pi Gamma Mu, Phi Beta Kappa. Author or co-author of numerous books relating to field; latest publ.: An Introduction to World Economics, 1947. Contbr. to profl. jours. Home: Philadelphia PA Died Nov. 9, 1969.

PATTERSON, ERNEST ODELL, lawyer; b. Greenfield, Adair County, Ia., Oct. 5, 1874; s. Daniel A. and Margaret (Priddy) P.; student State U. of Ia., 1892-95; LL.B., Nat. Univ. Law Sch., Washington, D.C., 1903, LL.D., 1904; M. Dawn Smith, Aug. 30, 1912; 1 son, Ernest Odell. Admitted to D.C. bar, 1906; asst. atty. Interior Dept., Washington, D.C., 1906-08; moved to S.D., 1908; v.p., gen. counsel Western Townsite Co., 1910-25; mayor of Dallas, S.D., 6 yrs.; mem. S.D. Senate, 1913-15 (chmn. judiciary com.); gen. counsel, Royal Mut. Union Life Ins. Co. of Des Moines, at Dallas, for states of S.D. and Neb., 1915-25; circuit judge, 11th Jud. Circuit of S.D., by apptmt. of Gov. Gunderson, July 1, 1925-Jan. 1926 (resigned); solicitor Interior Dept., by apptmt. of President Coolidge, 1926-29. Served as pvt. Co. G, 51st Ia. Inf. Vols., Spanish-Am. War. Mem. Am. and S.D. bar assns. Republican. Mason (32 deg., K.T., Shriner). Home: 2704 E. 13th Pl., Tulsa OK‡

PATTERSON, FREDERICK BECK, b. Dayton, O., June 22, 1892; s. John Henry and Katherine Dudley (Beck) Patterson; educated in public and private schools, Dayton, O.; preparatory sch., Chatham House, Ramsgate, England, 2 years; m. 2d, Armenal W. Gorman, Oct. 25, 1928. Began as helper in foundry of Cash Register Co. (founded by father) and advanced through various depts. to sec. and 3d v.p., pres. 1921-35, vice-pres. and dir., 1935-36, dir., 1937-41. Volunteered as private, World War; served as lt. commanding 15th Photographic A.S., in France. Called a meeting of citizens, 1923, and in 2 days raised $400,000 to purchase 5,000 acres of land required for U.S. Air Service at Dayton, presenting same to Govt. Mem. Nat. Aeronautic Assn., Ohio Soc. of N.Y. Chevalier Legion of Honor (France). Republican. Episcopalian. Mason. Clubs: Dayton Country, Miami Valley Hunt. Made a five months' hunting expedition through British East Africa in 1927, and brought back many specimens to Dayton Museum of Natural History, also 8,000 feet of motion picture film. Home: Delray Beach FL Died June 1, 1971.

PATTERSON, GEORGE FRANCIS, clergyman; b. Stockton, Ill., Oct. 20, 1874; s. Edward Sheffield and Ella Nancy (Harrison) P.; D.D., Lombard Coll., 1928; m. Helen Mary Pierce, Aug. 24, 1905; children—Lillian Elizabeth, Jean Hubbell (dec.). Ordained ministry Universalist Ch., 1904; minister, Rochester, Minn., 1904-09, Tuttle Memorial Ch., Minneapolis, 1909-11, People's Unitarian Ch., Kalamazoo, Mich., 1911-17, First Unitarian Ch., Peterborough, N.H., 1917-19, Second Congl. Soc. Unitarian Ch., Concord, N.H., 1919-23; field sec. Am. Unitarian Assn., 1923-28, became administrative v.p., 1928, dir. dept. of ministry, 1937-39; minister All Souls Unitarian Ch., Tulsa, Okla., 1939-44; minister First Parish of Framingham, 1944-47; acting dean, Starr King Sch. for Ministry, Berkeley, Calif., since 1947. Mem. Boston Assn. of Ministers, Sigma Nu. Republican. Unitarian. Mason. Club: Unitarian (Boston). Home: 2441 Le Conte Av., Berkeley CA‡

PATTERSON, GRAHAM CREIGHTON, publisher; b. Pittsburgh, Pa., Dec. 25, 1881; s. John Mitchell and Margaret Laird (Macfarlane) P.; A.B., Cornell U., 1904; m. Maude Dewar, May 5, 1909; children—Maude Elizabeth (Mrs. Sheldon Lee), John Graham. Gen. sec. Cornell U. Christian Assn., 1904-05; advertising mgr. Federal Elec. Co., Chicago, 1905-07; advertising rep. for mags., 1907-18; pres. Union Electrotype Co., Chicago 1917-18; pub. and pres. Christian Herald, 1918-35; chmn. bd. Farm Jour., Phila., 1935-66, pub., 1935-62; pub. Pathfinder-Town Jour., Wash., 1943-69. Ex-pres. Christian Herald Children's Home, Nyack, N.Y., Mayesville (S.C.) Ednl. and Industrial Inst., Christian Herald Industrial Missions, China, Bowery Mission of New York City; vice-chmn. Am. Com. China Famine; member agr. committee Nat. Assn. Mfrs.; chmn. bd., Met. Phila. Soc. for Crippled Children and Adults; vice chairman of Phila. Area United Negro College Fund; chairman Advertising Fedn. of Am., 1950-51; dir. Freedom's Found., Found. for American Agr. Mem. Rural Research Institute (president), Magazine Publishers' Assn. (exec. com.; dir.), Delta Upsilon. Rep. Presbyn. Clubs: University (Chicago); University (Cleveland); University (New York City, N.Y.); Detroit Athletic, Recess (Detroit); Merion Cricket, Merion Golf, Poor Richard (pres. 1944-45), Racquet; Downtown. Home: Evanston IL Died Nov. 23, 1969.

PATTERSON, JAMES, actor in Birthday Party. Address: Los Angeles CA Died Aug. 1972.

PATTERSON, JOHN NEVILLE, real estate investor; b. Phila., July 20, 1910; s. Thomas Austin and Josephine Marie (Neville) P.; B.S., U. Pa., 1932, M.A., 1933; m. Anne M. Calhoun, Nov. 25, 1936; children—Joan, John S., Sue Anne. Sch. tchr., Del., Pa., 1933-35; engaged in pub. bus., also govt. service, 1936-42; regional dir. NYA, Pa., N.J., Del., 1939-40; dir. tng. War Manpower Commn., region 3, 1941, area manpower dir. for Phila., 1942-43; partner Patterson-Korchin and Co., mgmt. cons., Phila., 1946-50; with Penn Fruit Co., Phila., 1950-62, exec. v.p., 1959-61, pres., 1961-62; pres. Andorra Homes, Inc., Phila., 1964-70; dir. Phila. Transp. Co., 1960-62, Commonwealth Realty Trust, 1961-70, Comast Corp., 1964-70. Mem. Adv. Commn. City County Consol. Phila., 1950; mem. Mayor Phila. Commn. Transit Labor Relations, 1959-60; mem. Phila. Com. City Policy, 1937-63; exec. com. Phila. Council Community Advancement, 1962; vice chmn. Citizens Com. Pub. Edn., 1960-65; chmn. S.E. Pa. Ams. for Democratic Action, 1954-55; chmn. Phila. Adv. Council Vocational Edn., 1969-70; dir. Phila. Bd. Edn. Task Forces, 1965. Co-chmn. Clark Dilworth Mayorial Campaign, 1949. Trustee Phila. Gen. Hosp., 1957-60; bd. dirs. Schuylkill Valley Nature Center, 1969-70. Served to lt. (s.g.) USNR, 1944-46. Mem. Phila. Food Distbrs. Assn. (pres. 1962). Home: Philadelphia PA Died Oct. 7, 1970.

PATTERSON, JOSEPH T., lawyer, state govt. ofcl.; b. Eupora, Miss., July 10, 1907; s. Albert Thomas and Mae V. (Harpole) P.; student Miss. State Coll., Miss. Coll.; LL.B., Cumberland U.; m. Margaret D. Steadman, Dec. 22, 1944; children—Joe Steadman, William Albert. Admitted to Miss. bar, 1929; practice of law, Calhoun City, Miss.; city atty. Town of Calhoun City; atty. Calhoun County Bd. Suprs.; asst. atty. gen. State of Miss., 1947-55, atty. gen., 1956-69. Rep. Miss. Legislature, 1932-36, 40-44; clk. Office of Senator Pat. Harrison, 1935. Mem. Am., Miss. bar assns., Lambda Chi Alpha. Baptist. Home: Jackson MS Died Apr. 1969.

PATTERSON, MRS. LINDSAY (LUCY BRAMLETTE PATTERSON), b. Castle Rock, Tazewell, Tenn.; d. William Houston and Cornelia Humes (Graham) P.; grad. Salem Coll., Winston-Salem, N.C., 1882; M. Lindsay Patterson, of Winston-Salem, Sept. 6, 1888. Founder and 1st pres. N.C. Federation of Women's Clubs; pres. N.C. Hist. Soc., Salem Alumnae Assn.; v.p. gen. D.A.R. for N.C.; chmn. Jamestown Hist. Commn. for N.C.; served as state chmn. (N.C.) for Relief in Belgium. Republican nominee for Congress, 1922. Decorated by King Alexander of Jugo-Slavia for work in Serbia; hon. mem. Kola Sestara of Jugo-Slavia; mem. Y.W.C.A., Authors' League of America. Republican Nat. Committeewoman for North Carolina. Clubs: Acorn (Phila.); Colony. Donor Patterson Cup for writers. Presbyn. Lecturer in Internat. relations. Contbr. to mags. and newspapers on spl. research lines. Home: Bramlette," Winston-Salem, N.C.; (summer) Long Hope Hill, Russellville, TN‡

PATTERSON, OTTO, ins. co. exec.; b. Mt. Vernon, Ill., 1890; m. Edith Bradbury, Nov. 26, 1918; children—Theodore, Thomas Otto. Retired chmn. Am. Automobile Ins. Co.; dir. Am. Ins. Co., Am. Automobile Ins. Co., Asso. Indemnity Corp. Contributed to modernization auto liability ins. rating formulae. Clubs: University, the Missouri Athletic (St. Louis). Home: University City MO Died Mar. 24, 1967.

PATTERSON, RALPH MORRIS, ret. physician; b. Morning Sun, O., Nov. 26, 1904; s. Charles Epley and Elizabeth (Merryman) P.; B.S., U. Mich., 1926, M.D., 1930, M.S., 1939; m. Sophie Tammason, Apr. 26, 1929. Physician Ypsilanti (Mich) State Hosp., 1931-35; asst. surgeon U.S. Med. Center, 1935-36; prof. psychiatry U. Mich., staff physician Neuropsychiat. Inst., Ann Arbor, Mich., 1937-51, also cons. psychiatry Mich. Children's Inst. and Girls Tng. Sch. and VA; dir. Columbus Psychiatric Inst. and Hosp.; prof. chmn. psychiatry Coll. Medicine Ohio State U., 1951-65, prof. psychiatry, 1965-71. Fellow Am. Coll. Psychiatrists, Am. Psychiat. Assn.; mem. Assn. Research Neuropsychiatry and Mental Diseases, Central Neuropsychiat. Assn. Author: (with R. Kaelbling) Eclectric Psychiatry, 1966. Address: Columbus OH Died Apr. 4, 1972.

PATTERSON, ROBERT FOSTER, coll. dean; b. Pottsville, Ark., Oct. 14, 1905; s. Samuel Jasper and Lily Margaret (Davis) P.; A.B., Tarkio (Mo.) Coll., 1927 A.M., Univ. Neb., 1932; Ph.D., Univ. Colo., 1940; m Garnet Jorgensen, July 17, 1929; children—Samuel Charles, Mary Margaret. Prin. Plattsmouth (Neb.) High Sch., 1927-35; prof. govt. and history Tarkio Coll. 1935-42; asst. prof. history, Univ. S.D., 1942-44, prof of govt., dir. of research, 1944-46, dean, sch. bus. 1946—; pres. Council Profl. Edn. Bus. U.S., 1965. Dir. Citizens Bank. Mayor Vermillion, 1956-60. Recipient medal honor Am. Edn. Assn., 1963. Vice pres. Am. Assn. Collegiate Schs. Bus., 1962-63, president 1963-64. Mem. Economic History Assn., C. of C. (pres. 1947), Phi Beta Kappa, Delta Sigma Pi, Beta Gamma Sigma. Republican. Methodist. Mason (K.T., Red Cross of Constantine, Shriner). Home: Vermillion Died Mar. 27, 1969.

PATTERSON, WILLIAM LESLIE, physician; b. Amherst, N.S., Can., Dec. 25, 1879; student Acadia Coll., Wolfville, Yale; M.D., Boston U., 1909; m. Marguerit Rosin. Intern, Mass. Meml. Hosp., Boston, 1909-11; mem. med. staff Westboro (Mass.) State Hosp., until 1912; 3d asst. physician Fergus Falls (Minn.) State Hosp., from 1912, supt., 1927-61, med. dir., 1962-69, also staff cons. Diplomate Am. Bd. Psychiatry and Neurology. Mem. A.M.A., Am. Psychiat. Assn. Rotarian. Home: Fergus Falls MN Died Dec. 13, 1969; buried Cannon Falls MN

PATTISON, HAROLD, clergyman; b. Newcastle-on-Tyne, Eng., Sept. 16, 1869; s. T. Harwood (D.D.) and Emily A. (Bainbridge) P.; brought to America, 1874; B.S., Rochester U., 1891, D.D., 1912; studied abroad, 1892-93; Rochester Theol. Sem., 1893-95; m. Mary B. Sperry, Oct. 11, 1898; children—Eric H., Kenneth B., Mrs. Barbara L. Crawford, Harwood; m. 2d, Marguerite O. Woike, Jan. 17, 1927; 1 dau., Ottilie Marguerite. Missionary, Bozeman, Mont., 1891-92; ordained Baptist Ministry, 1896; pastor Hartford, Conn., 1896-1909, St. Paul, Minn., 1909-11, Washington Heights Church, New York, Dec. 1911-25; ordained deacon, 1930, priest, 1931. P.E. Ch.; minister Community Ch., Little Neck, L.I., N.Y., 1926-30; rector Christ Ch., Oyster Bay, L.I., 1934-40; retired. Served with Y.M.C.A. in France during World War I. Mem. Sigma Chi (sec.), Delta Kappa Epsilon. Author of For the Work of the Ministry. Home: 43-20 Morgan St., Little Neck LI NY‡

PATTON, DAVID HUBERT, ednl. cons., author; b. Mount Orab, Ohio, Nov. 2 1894 s. M. Roy and Rachel L. (Stratton) P.; A.B., Wilmington (O.) Coll., 1923; A.M., Cincinnati Univ., 1931; student Ohio State U., 1932, 1944; Litt.D., Wilmington College, Ohio, 1962; married Gladys W. Knight, June 19, 1915; 1 dau., Violet L. Elementary teacher, Mount Orab, O., 1914-16; supt. village schs. Ohio, 1918-22, county supt. Ohio Schools, 1922-31; supt. Bellevue (O.) pub. schs., 1931-37; asst. supt. Toledo pub. schs., 1937-45; supt. Syracuse (N.Y.) city schs., 1945-55; ednl. cons. dept. sch. services and publs. Wesleyan U., Middletown, (Conn) 1955-59. Instr. Toledo U., summer sessions. Served as head accounting div. 6th dist. ordnance, World War I. Mem. New York State Regents' Examination Bd., 1946-55; mem. bd. YMCA. Mem. N.E.A. (life), N.Y. State Tchrs. Assn., N.Y. State Supts. Council, Child Guidance Clinic, Inc., Syracuse Ednl. and Cultural Planning Council, Chamber of Commerce, Phi Delta Kappa, Kappa Delta Pi (hon. mem.). Mem. Soc. of Friends. Clubs: Rotary (past pres); Torch, Kiwanis (past pres.; nat. hon. award for distinguished service, 1935). Methodist. Author: Personal Efficiency and Citizenship, 1935; Building Correct English, grades 2-6, 1939; Work Mastery Spelling Series, grades 1-8, 1949; Common Words for High School, 1943, 70; Work Study for High School, 1945; Arithmetic, grades 1 and 2, 1949; New Standard Arithmetic, grades 3-8, 1947; General Mathematics for Jr. High School, grades 7-8-9, 1947; Arithmetic, Numbers at Work Series, grades 2-9, 1957; English Using our Language, grades 3-8, 1953; Common Words for Secondary Schools, 1958; New Webster Language, grade 2, 1961; Spelling for Word Mastery, grades 1-8, 1963; Language Mastery Speller, grades 1-8, 1968. Home: La Jolla CA Died Mar. 8, 1968; entombed El Camino Meml. Park, San Diego CA

PATTON, ODIS KNIGHT, prof. law; b. Zearing, Ia., July 24, 1889; s. William H. and Cora Esther (Barnes) P.; B.A., State U. of Ia., 1912, M.A., 1913, Ph.D., 1916, LL.B., 1917; S.J.D., Harvard, 1923; m. Mary Orvilla Orton, Aug. 4, 1926. Instr. polit. science, State U. of Ia., 1914-17; mem. research staff Ia. State Hist. Soc., summers 1913-16; practiced law in Sioux City, Ia., 1917-18; asst. code commr. and legislative draftsman for State of Ia., 1918-19; Ia. code annotator, 1920-22; asso. code editor State of Ia., 1922-24; asso. prof. law, State U. of Ia., 1923-27, prof. since 1927; cons. editor and legislative draftsman N.J. code revision, summers 1928-30; faculty editor Ia. Law Review, 1924-26; vis. professor law Ohio State U., 1958-59, 61-62. West Virginia University, 1965-66. Entered the regular U.S. Army as pvt., 1917; discharged as 1st lt., Dec. 1918. Mem. Am. and Ia. State bar assns., State Hist. Soc. of Iowa, Order of Coif, Delta Chi, Delta Sigma Rho.

Author: Iowa Annotations to the Restatement of the Law of Contracts as Adopted by the American Law Institute, 1934; (with F. A. Daum) Iowa Annotations to the Restatement of the Law of Conflict of Laws as Adopted by the American Law Institute, 1935; also co-author of other legal works. Editor: (with U. G. Whitney) Code of Iowa, 1924; Legislative Procedure and Practice in Iowa, 1940; also other legal works. Contbr. to legal periodicals. Home: Iowa City IA Died July 18, 1967; buried Adel IA

PAUL, CHARLES EDWARD, mech. engr., educator; b. Belfast, Me., Dec. 6, 1876; s. Jesse Granville and Annie Julia (Leach) P.; grad. Chauncy Hall Sch., Boston, 1895-96; S.B. in Mech. Engring., Mass. Inst. of Tech., 1900; m. Mary E. Yenawine, June 14, 1905. Began as designer and sales engr. James W. Tufts Co., Boston, 1900; asst. prof. mech. engring., Kan. State Coll., 1903-05; prof. mech. engring., N.M. Coll. Agr. and Mech. Arts, 1905-07; prof. mechanics Pa. State College, 1907-08; with Armour Institute of Technology (now Ill. Inst. Tech.) since 1908, successively asso. prof. mechanics until 1914, professor mechanics in charge dept., 1914-41; dir. dept. engring. science, 1933-41, chairman department mathematics, 1934-37, retired as prof. emeritus of mechanics, 1941; consulting practice, specializing in industrial construction and materials since 1908; asso. editor Am. Builder and of Cement World, 1910-15; constrn. engr. Nat. Lumber Mfrs. Assn., 1915-21. Mem. Am. Soc. for Testing Materials (member sub-com. on timber specifications), American Soc. for Engring. Education, Western Soc. Engrs., Tau Beta Pi, Theta Xi, Sphinx. Republican. Club: University of Chicago. Author of booklets and tech. articles relating to building constrn., concrete, lumber, estimating and contracting. Home: 1528 Farwell Av., Chicago IL‡

PAUL, J. GILMAN D'ARCY, exec.; b. Baltimore, Md., Jan. 31, 1887; s. D'Arcy and Charlotte Abbott (Gilman) P.; A.B., magna cum laude, Harvard, 1908, A.M., 1914, unmarried. Pvt. sec. to U.S. ambassador to Argentina, 1912; spl. asst., U.S. Embassy, Paris, 1914-15; asst. editor, Atlantic Monthly Mag., 1916-17; spl. asst., U.S. Legation, The Hague, 1917-18; mem. U.S. delegation to Peace Conf., Paris, 1918-19; mem. secretariat-general, Naval Disarmament Conf., Washington, D.C., 1921-22; with Office of Strategic Services, Washington, D.C., 1944-46; owner and operator of large farm in Maryland. Pres. bd. trustees Baltimore Museum of Art; trustee Peabody Inst., Johns Hopkins U., Peale Mus. Mem. Md. Hist. Soc. (v.p.), Walpole Soc., Alpha Delta Phi. Clubs: Hamilton St., Bachelors Cotillion, Harvard (Baltimore); Harvard (New York); 1925 F Street (Washington). Translator and editor: Pribram, The Secret Treaties of Austria-Hungary; Les Diverses Familles Spirituelles de la France (Maurice Barres). Author: The Maryland Palatinate; also numerous articles and reviews. Home: Baltimore MD Died Jan. 12, 1972; buried Greenmount Cemetery, Baltimore MD

PAUL, JOHN HAYWOOD, clergyman, educator; b. Rapides Parish, La., Sept. 23, 1877; s. John T. and Lurany Madison (Watkins) P.; ed. under pvt. tutors and spl. courses at the U. of Chicago and at Meridian (Miss.) College; D.D., Meridian Coll., 1914, Asbury, 1921; m. Effie Richardson, Sept. 22, 1898 (deceased); children—Cyrus Foss, Wilson Benton, Victorine, John Marcus; m. 2d, Corey Agnes Stephens, 1946. Rural pastor M.E. churches, Texas and Miss., until 1903; city editor Pentecostal Herald, Louisville, Ky., 1904-08; prof. philosophy, Meridian Coll., 1909-13; editor The Way of Faith, Columbia, S.C., 1914-15, 1922-23; v.p. Asbury Coll., Wilmore, Ky., 1916-22; lecturer Interdenom. Conv., Japan, 1917; pres. Taylor U., Upland, Ind., 1922-31; pres. John Fletcher Coll., University Park, Ia., 1934-37. Dir. Applied Theol. Asbury Sem., 1941-46. Editor The Christian Witness, 1923-46. Author: Silver Keys, 1907; The Hereafter, 1909; The Way of Power, 1917; What Is New Theology?, 1921; Life and Times of Bishop William Taylor, 1927. Winner Christian Advocate gold prize for Meth. doctrinal statement, Francis Asbury Centenary, Louisville‡

PAUL, JOHN R., physician; b. Phila., Pa., Apr. 18, 1893; s. Henry Neill and Margaret Crosby (Butler) P.; A.B., Princeton, 1915; M.D., Johns Hopkins Med. Sch., 1919; honorary Master of Arts, Yale University, 1940; D.Sc. (honorary), University of Chicago, 1956; married Mary Leita Harlan, Sept. 30, 1922. Asst. pathologist, Johns Hopkins Med. Sch., 1919-20; intern, Pa. Hosp., Phila., 1920-22; dir., Ayer Clinical Lab., Phila., 1922-28; asst. asso. prof. internal med., Yale U. Med. Sch., 1928-40; prof. preventive medicine, 1940-61, emeritus prof. epidemiology and preventive medicine, 1961-71; dir. regional serum bank World Health Orgn., 1961-66; mem. coms. virus research, Nat. Found. Infantile Paralysis, 1940-48; cons. sec. of War, 1941-46; dir. neurotropic Virus Disease Com., Army Epidemiol. Bd., 1941-46, dir. com., virus, rickettsial diseases, 1946-56; chmn. virus and rickettsial study sect. research grants div. USPHS, 1946-51; govt. service in Middle East, 1943-44, Japan, 1946, Korea, 1953, Med. Mission to Soviet Union, 1956; mem. live poliovirus vaccine com. Nat. Insts. Health, 1958-71, sr. cons. internat. fellowship program, 1957-62; mem. com. investigate U.S. Food and Drug Adminstrn., Nat. Research Council, 1960. Recipient Alvarenga prize, Coll. Physicians, Phila., 1928; John Phillips Meml., A.C.P., 1942; Medal of Freedom U.S.A., 1946; Howard T. Ricketts award, U. Chgo., 1954; Charles V. Chapin award, R.I. Med. Society, 1959; Kober medal Association American Physicians, 1963. Mem. subcom. cardiovascular disease NRC, 1946-53. Fellow A.C.P., Royal College Physicians, Royal Soc. Health (Eng.); mem. Assn. Am. physicians (pres. 1956), Am. Soc. Clin. Investigation (pres. 1938), Nat. Acad. Sci., Am. Acad. Arts and Scis., Royal Soc. Medicine London (hon.), World Health Organization (past member of the expert committee on viruses 1952-66). Clubs: Graduate (New Haven); Ivy (Princeton); Century, Yale (N.Y.); Authors (London). Author: The Epidemiology of Rheumatic Fever, 1942; Clinical Epidemiology, 1958, 2d edit., 1966; A History of Guilford CT Died May 6, 1971; buried Grove Street Cemetery, New Haven CT

PAULEN, BEN SANFORD, ex-gov.; b. De Witt Co., Ill., July 14, 1869; s. Jacob Walter and Lucy Belle (Johnson) P.; ed. high sch., Fredonia, Kan.; U. of Kan. 1 term; Bryant & Stratton Business Coll., St. Louis; m. Barbara Ellis, of Holton, Kan., Feb. 14, 1900. In mercantile business, Fredonia, 1890-1919; pres. Wilson County Bank, since 1918; pres. Security Nat. Bank, Independence, Kan. Mayor of Fredonia, 1900-04; mem. Kan. State Senate, 1913-21; lt. gov. of Kan., 1921-23; gov. of Kan., term 1925-29. Republican. Christian Scientist. Mason. Rotarian. Home: Independence KS‡

PAULEY, SCOTT SAMUEL, forest geneticist; b. Sault Ste. Marie, Mich., Dec. 21, 1910; s. John Livingood and Flossa Viola (Scott) P.; B.S., U. Minn., 1939; M.S., Mich. State Coll., 1942; Ph. D., Harvard, 1947; m. Fritzi Klawans, Dec. 28, 1937; 1 dau., Nan Fritzi. Forest ranger Wis. Conservation Dept., 1939-40; instr. forestry Mich. State Coll., 1942-43; asst. prof. Harvard, 1947-52; lectr. forest genetics, geneticist Maria Moors Cabot Found. Bot. Research, Harvard, 1952-55; asso. prof. University Minn., 1955-57, prof., 1957-70. Vice pres., dir. Forest Genetics Research Found. Served as lt. USNR, 1943-45. Mem. Soc. Am. Foresters, A.A.A.S., Am. Inst. Biol. Sci., Genetics Soc. Am., Soc. Study Evolution, Sigma Xi, Alpha Zeta, Gamma Sigma Delta, Xi Sigma Pi. Author articles in field. Home: Mahtomedi MN Died Apr. 18, 1970; cremated.

PAULI, HERTHA, author; b. Vienna, Austria, Sept. 4, 1909; d. Wolfgang and Bertha (Schuetz) Pauli; came to U.S., 1940, naturalized, 1952; student Gymnasium and Acad. Dramatic Arts, Vienna; m. E.B. Ashton, Jan. 5, 1951. Actress, Breslau and Max Reinhardt Theatres, Germany, 1927-33; writer stories, radio plays, 1929, books after return to Veinna, 1933; lit. agt., Vienna, 1934-38; pubs. rep., Paris, 1938-40; on screen writer's team, Hollywood, Cal., 1941-42; author Alfred Nobel, 1942; Silent Night, 1943; The Story of the Christmas Tree, 1944; St. Nicholas' Travels, 1945; I Lift My Lamp (with E. B. Ashton), 1948; The Most Beautiful House, 1949; The Golden Door, 1949; Lincoln's Little Correspondent, 1952; Three is a Family, 1955; Bernadette and the Lady, 1956; Christmas and the Saints, 1956; Cry of the Heart, 1957; The First Easter Rabbit, 1961; The Trumpeters of Vienna, 1961; The First Christmas Tree, 1961; Her Name was Sojourner Truth, 1962; America's First Christmas, 1962; Little Town of Bethlehem, 1963; The First Christmas Gifts, 1965; Gateway to America, 1966; The Secret of Sarajevo, 1965; Handel and the Messiah Story, 1968; Toward Peace, 1969; Pietro and Brother Frances, 1971; Break of Time, 1962. Decorated Silver Medal of Honor (Austria). Club: P.E.N. Home: Huntington NY Died Feb. 1973.

PAUMGARTNER, BERNHARD, conductor, composer; b. Vienna, Austria, Nov. 14, 1887; s. Johann Nepomuk and Rosa (Papier) P.; J. Theresianum Vienna, U. Vienna, 1911; pupil of Bruno Walter; Dr. jur., Dr. n.c. phil.; m. to Inge Handl, in September 1956; two children by previous marriage—Peterhans, Rosanna. Conductor, Vienna Musicians Orch.; dir. Mozarteum Salzburg, 1917; pres. Mozarteum Acad.; guest conductor Salzburg Festival, 1960, also throughout Europe; founder Mozart Chamber Orch., Salzburg; lectr. musicology on radio; pres. Salzburger Festspiele, 1960-71. Recipient Austrian Medal Art and Sci. Lion. Author: Mozart; Bach; Schubert; Beethoven; Salzburg; Erinnerungen. Composer operas, stage music, songs, choruses. Home: Salzburg Austria Died July 27, 1971; buried Petersfriedhof Salzburg.

PAUST, ELNAR BERNHARDT, lawyer; b. Bklyn., May 6, 1907; s. John H. and Letty (Bernhardt) P.; A.B., Columbia, 1929, LL.B., 1932; m. Mary Ellen Riber, Sept. 9, 1934; children—John R., Barbara Ellen. Admitted to N.Y. bar, 1932; counsel Milbank Tween Hope & Hadley, 1933-46; counsel Esso Standard Oil Co., N.Y.C., 1946-51, asso. gen. counsel, 1951-54, gen. counsel, 1954-60; asst. gen. counsel Standard Oil Co. (N.J.), 1960-63, asso. gen. counsel, 1963-68, gen. counsel, 1968-73. Research fellow Southwestern Legal Found. Mem. Am. Soc. Internat. Law, Am. Bar Assn., Assn. Bar City N.Y., Am. Petroleum Inst., Beta Theta Pi. Clubs: University (N.Y.C.); Knickerbocker Country (Tenafly, N.J.); Englewood (N.J.); North Fork Country, Old Cove Yacht (L.I., N.Y.). Home: Englewood NJ Died April 10, 1973.

PAUSTOVSKY, KONSTANTIN GEORGIEVICH, writer; b. 1892. Author: Kara Bugaz, 1932; Kolchida, 1934; The Romantics, 1935; Black Sea, 1936; Northern Tales, 1939; Distant Years, 1946; Tale of the Forests, 1948; Birth of the Sea, 1952; Restless Youth, 1955; The Golden Rose, 1956; The Beginning of the Unknown Age, 1958; The Time of Great Expectations, 1959; A Jump to the South, 1960; The Best Novels, 1962; Selections, 1961; Story of a Life, 1964; Zolotoi Lin'. Address: Moscow USSR Died July 14, 1968.

PAXTON, EDWIN JOHN, edit., pub.; Paducah, Ky., July 10, 1877; s. William Francis and Frederica (Fisher) P.; ed. pub. schs. and St. Mary's Acad., Paducah; m. Florence Brown, of Paducah, June 19, 1924; children—Edwin J., Marie Louise, Francis Robert. Editor and pub. Paducah Sun since 1900; dir. Southern Textile Machinery Co. Mem. Paducah Bd. of Trade. Elk, K.C. Rotarian. Home: Paducah KY‡

PAXTON, JOHN RICHARD, surgeon; b. Topeka, Kan., Dec. 4, 1906; s. Frank McAfee and Anna (Fox) P.; A.B., U. So. Cal., 1932, M.D., 1936; m. Janet Hall, Jan. 28, 1937; children—John Richard II, David Michael, Julie Meredith. Intern San Bernardino County Hosp., 1935-36; med. resident Olive View Sanitarium, 1936, resident chest surgery, 1936-39; fellow gen. surgery Cleve. Clinic, 1939-41; pvt. practice gen. surgery, Glendale, Cal., 1941-68; clin. professor surgery U. So. Cal.; sr. attending surgeon Los Angeles Gen. Hosp.; dir. Glendale Memorial Hospital (past president board of trustees). Asso. chief examiner Los Angeles subsidiary Nat. Bd. Med. Examiners, 1946-52; mem. med. adv. bd. Cancer Prevention Soc., 1946-49. Diplomate Am. Bd. Surgery. Fellow A.C.S.; mem. Los Angeles County (past pres. Glendale br.), Cal. (ho. dels. 1947-48, 50-52) med. assns., Internat. Acad. Medicine, U. So. Cal. Med. Alumni Assn. (past pres.), U. So. Cal. Gen. Alumni Assn. (exec. bd.), U. So. Cal. Med. Faculty Club (past pres.), A.A.A.S., Los Angeles Acad. Medicine, Los Angeles Surgical Society (president 1963, mem. bd. dirs. 1963-68), Los Angeles Co. Physicians' Aid Soc., Paxton Med. Group Assn. (past president), Pacific Coast Surgical Association, Alpha Omega Alpha. Club: Lions (past pres.) (San Fernando). Contributor articles in field to medical journals. Home: Glendale CA Died Nov. 2, 1968.

PAXTON, KENNETH T., corp. exec.; b. 1906; married. With G.C. Murphy Co., 1928-71, v.p. personnel, 1947-71, chmn. bd., dir., 1968-71. Address: McKeesport PA Died July 16, 1971; buried Jefferson Memorial Park.

PAYNE, ANTHONY MONCK-MASON, epidemiologist, educator; b. London, Eng., Aug. 10, 1911; s. John Ernest and Sylvia May (Moore) P.; B.A. with honours, Trinity Coll., Cambridge U., 1933; M.B., B.Ch., Cambridge U. and St. Bartholomews Hosp., London, 1936; M.R.C.P., London, 1941; M.D., Cambridge U., 1946; M.A. (hon.), Yale, 1960; m. Margaret Catherine Smith, Aug. 15, 1941. Came to U.S., 1960. Successively house physician, casualty officer, sr. resident med. officer, med. supt. emergency med. service Royal Free Hosp., London, 1937-41, sr. med. registrar, 1946; sr. epidemiologist Central Virus Reference Lab. and Oxford Regional Lab., Pub. Health Lab. Service, Med. Research Council, 1947-51; med. officer WHO, Geneva, Switzerland, 1952-55, chief med. officer charge endemo-epidemic diseases and virus diseases, 1955-60; Anna M.R. Lauder prof. epidemiology and pub. health, chmn. dept. Yale Sch. Medicine, 1960-66; asst. dir.-gen. WHO, Geneva. 1966-70. Secretary expert adv. panel virus diseases, expert coms. hepatitis, influenza, poliomyelitis and respiratory virus diseases WHO, 1952-60, mem. expert adv. panel virus diseases, 1960-70; sci. group virus research, 1960-70; adv. com. med. research Pan-Am. Health Orgn., 1962-70; asso. mem. commn. immunization. Armed Forces Epidemiological Bd., 1961-70; sub-com. geographic pathology Nat. Acad. Scis., 1962-70. Bd. dirs. Conn. Health League. Served to lt. col. Royal Army Medical Corps, 1941-45. Fellow Royal College of Physicians; member American Public Health Association, Assn. Tchrs. Preventive Medicine, N.Y. Acad. Scis., Am., Internat. epidemiological socs., Sigma Xi. Author numerous articles in field. Home: Geneva Switzerland Died Oct. 14, 1970.

PAYNE, F(ANNY) URSULA, teacher, playwright; b. Lynn, Mass.; d. Alfred Rickman and Annie Maria (Mitchell) P.; desc. of Diggory Priest, of the Mayflower; grad. Girls' High Sch., Brooklyn, N.Y., 1894; grad. Brooklyn Training Sch. for Teachers, 1895; studied Cornell, Columbia and Harvard; B.S., New York U., 1908, M.A., 1930; spl. courses in drama, pageantry and sociology, at Columbia, Dartmouth and New York U. Teacher, elementary schs., Brooklyn, 1895-1900; model teacher, Maxwell Training Sch. for Teachers (formerly Brooklyn Tr. Sch. for Teachers), 1900-1921; teacher of history and pageantry, Maxwell Teachers Tr. Coll., 1921-—; now assigned to Egasmus Hall (High Sch), Brooklyn. Episcopalian. Republican. Author (plays): The Parted Sisters, 1914; Winning an Heiress, 1915; Two War Plays for Schools, 1918; Plays for Anychild, 1918; Plays and Pageants of Democracy, 1919; Plays and Pageants of Citizenship, 1920; The Child at the

Crossroads, 1921; God's Creatures (drama), 1922; Up from Barbarism (drama), 1925; My Lady's Furs (poem), 1928. Home: 498 Westminister Rd., Brooklyn NY‡

PAYNE, FRANKLIN STOREY, publisher; b. Ia., Jan. 5, 1896; s. Jesse David and Edith (Storey) P.; student pub. schs., Chgo.; m. Lucile Lisette Hopp, Oct. 10, 1921; children—Betty Lucile (wife of Dr. Craig Williamson), Shirley Louise (Mrs. Dan Boone). With Hearst Newspapers, 1919-70; pub. Los Angeles Examiner, 1955-70. Served as 2d lt., U.S. Army, 1918-19. Club: Rotary. Home: Los Angeles CA Died Aug. 1970.

PAYNE, LEON MATHER, lawyer; b. Pitts., June 3, 1915; s. Leon Frank and Sarah Brownson (Mather) P.; A.B. cum laude, Brown U., 1936; LL.B., U. Tex., 1939; m. Carolyn Lelia Wilson, 1951; children—Leon Mather, Miriam Wilson. Lawyer, Andrews, Kurth, Campbell and Jones, Houston, 1939, partner, 1947-72; gen. counsel. sec., dir. Fla. Gas Transmission Co., Fla. Gas Co.; dir. El Paso Natural Gas Co., El Paso Products Co., Wilson Industries, Inc. Adv. dir. Mus. of Fine Arts; trustee emeritus Brown U. Served as maj. USAAF, 1942-45. Decorated D.F.C. (2), Air Medal (6). Mem. Am., Fed. Power, Houston bar assns., State Bar Tex., Am. Judicature Soc., Phi Beta Kappa, Phi Delta Phi. Presbyn. Bd. student editors Tex. Law Review. Home: Houston TX Died May 24, 1972.

PAYNE, MONTGOMERY ASHBY, forester; b. Winterville, Miss., July 28, 1906; s. Beckwith Benjamin and Frances Cameron (Montgomery) P.; B.S., U. of the South, 1927; M.F., Yale, 1929; grad. student Tulane U., 1938-39; m. Ivy Elizabeth Cunningham, June 7, 1941. Lecturer Southern Forestry Edn. Project, Am. Forestry Assn., 1929-30; helped organize Forest Service of Brazil, 1930-31, extension forester Miss. Agrl. Extension Service, Miss. State Coll., 1939-44; regional cons. Forest Resource Appraisal, Am. Forestry Assn., 1944; prof. forestry and head dept. Miss. State College, 1945-50; cotton planter, cons. forester from 1951. Member Society American Foresters (past chmn. Gulf States sect.), Forest Products Research Soc., Assn. So. Agrl. Workers (past chmn. forestry sect.), Miss. Forestry Assn. (mem. exec. com.), Delta Council (forestry com.), Kappa Alpha. Presbyn. Mason. Winterville MS Died Feb. 14, 1970.

PEABODY, GEORGE HARMAN, art writer, philanthropist; b. Baltimore (nephew of the late George Peabody, philanthropist); 4 yrs. art writer on old New York Express; 8 yrs. art editor New York Commercial Advertiser; chief founder Free and Unsectarian Peabody Home for Aged and Indigent Women.‡

PEACE, ROGER CRAFT, newspaper pub.; b. Greenville, S.C., May 19, 1899; s. Bony Hampton and Laura Estelle (Chandler) P.; A.B., Furman U., Greenville, 1919; hon. degrees U. S.C., Furman U.; m. Etca Tindal Walker, May 31, 1920 (dec. June 21, 1965); children—Roger Craft (dec. July 1951), Dorothy Ann (Mrs. Edmund A. Ramsaur); m. 2d, Amy Newgren Schwartzenberg, Apr. 9, 1966 (dec. Sept. 1967). Reporter Greenville News, 1914-19, sports editor, 1919-20, editor, 1920-24, bus. mgr., 1924-34, pub., 1934-66; chmn. bd. Multimedia, Inc., Multimedia Broadcasting Co., Greenville News-Piedmont Co., Asheville (N.C.) Citizen Times Pub. Co.; dir. Peoples Nat. Bank, Piedmont & No. Ry.; pres. C. of C., 1934-35; chmn. Community Chest, 1936; col. on governor's staff, 1930-34. Appointed U.S. Senator from South Carolina to fill vacancy James F. Byrnes, Aug.-Nov. 1941; mem. S.C. Preparedness for Peace Commn. (chmn. exec. committee) 1942; mem. Bd. S.C. Research, Planning and Development, 1946-56. Trustee S.C. Found. Independent Colls. Entered R.O.T.C., Plattsburg, 1918; served as instructor, U.S. Army, Camp Perry, 1919. Member Southern Newspaper Pubs. Assn. (dir. 1935), S.C. Press Association (president 1938-39), Furman U. Alumni Assn. (pres. 1944-45). Baptist. Elk. Clubs: National Press (Washington, D.C.); Biltmore Forest (Biltmore, N.C.); Greenville Country, Poinsett, Green Valley (Greenville, S.C.). Home: Greenville SC also Cedar Mountain, N.C., and Hollywood FL Died Aug. 21, 1968.

PEACH, ROBERT ENGLISH, airlines exec.; b. Syracuse, N.Y., Mar. 9, 1920; s. John Clayton and Emily (Kelley) P.; B.A., Hamilton Coll., 1941; student U. Chgo., 1941, Cornell U., 1945-47; m. Martha Minge Clarke. Aug. 8, 1944 (div.); children—Robert English John Minge, Timothy English, David, Martha; m. 2d, Ann C. Tarbania, June 6, 1960; 1 son, Ryan English. Asst. to pres. Hamilton Coll., 1941; flight capt. Robinson Airlines (now Mohawk Airlines, Inc.), 1946, traffic mgr., 1947, gen. mgr., exec. v.p., 1948-54, pres., dir., 1954-68, chmn. bd., 1968-71; dir. Homestead Sav. & Loan Assn., Hayes Nat. Bank First Trust & Depository Co., Syracuse, Lab. for Electronics, Waltham, Mass., Oneida County Indsl. Devel. Corp. Trustee Hamilton Coll., N.Y. State Regional Hosp. Rev. and Planning Council; pres. bd. mgrs. Faxton Hosp. Served as lt. comdr. USNR, 1942-45. Mem. Empire State (chmn. bd.), Utica chambers commerce, Nat. Alliance Businessmen (past chmn.). Clubs: Kiwanis, Yahnundasis Golf, Fort Schuyler (Utica); Wings (N.Y.C.); Sadaquada (New Hartford, N.Y.); Nat. Aviation (Wash.); Century (Syracuse, N.Y.). Home: Clinton NY Died Apr. 20, 1971; buried Hamilton College Cemetery.

PEACOCK, VIRGINIA TATNALL, journalist; b. Phila., Pa., Jan. 7, 1873; d. John Brooks and Virginia Tatnall (Marshall) P.; descendant 1st Quaker settlers of Phila. and Burlington, N.J.; ed. Eden Hall, Torresdale, Pa. (Convent of the Sacred Heart.) Commenced journalistic work on Washington staff, Philadeplhia Times, 1897; society editor Washington Post since July, 1907. Traveled extensively in U.S., Mex., and Europe. Mem. Nat. Soc. D.A.R., Columbia Hist. Soc. Author: Famous American Belles of the Nineteenth Century, 1900. Address: 2466 Ontario Rd., Washington‡

PEAKE, ELMORE ELLIOTT, author; b. Decatur, O., Mar. 25, 1871; s. Thomas DeWitt and Lida (Vail) P.; ed. at various places in Ohio, and at Janesville, Wis.; m. Bonnie Grace Thompson, of Lake Geneva, Wis., Oct. 8, 1907. Private sec. to M. H. McCord, M.C., 1890-2; same to supt. telegraph, Richmond & Danville R.R. (now Southern), 1892-3; later with Central of Ga. R.R., in similar capacity. Has been writing fiction since Jan., 1896. Author: The Darlingtons, 1900; The Pride of Tellfair, 1903; The House of Hawley, 1905; The Little King of Angel's Landing, 1906. Editorial writer Chicago Evening Post, 1917-—. Home: 221 N. Kensington Av., La Grange IL‡

PEARCE, CHARLES A., publisher; b. Chicago, July 21, 1906; s. William Clark and Alice (Paxton) P.; A.B., Hobart Coll., 1927; married Margaret Edwards, 1931 (div. 1936); 1 dau., Katharine Ann (Mrs. James H. Allen); m. 2d, Clara Kent, 1936; children—Sally (Mrs. Merle Cox), Ellen. Asst. editor D. Appleton & Co., N.Y. City, 1927-29; editor Harcourt, Brace & Co., 1929-39; a founder of Duell, Sloan & Pearce, Inc., 1939, editor in chief, 1939-61, v.p., 1945-61; exec. editor Meredith Press, 1961-63; executive v.p. Cue Ventures, Inc., 1963-66; publisher Abercrombie & Fitch, 1966-70; editorial cons. Winchester Press. Served armed forces, assigned O.S.S., 1944, Air Force, Jan.-June 1945. Mem. Am. Assn. for World Press (secretary, dir.), Merc. Library Assn. (dir.), Phi Beta Kappa, Sigma Phi. Clubs: Dutch Treat, P.E.N. Editor: The New Yorker Book of Verse; editorial adv. bd. Tarrytown NY Died Feb. 1, 1970.

PEARCE, CHARLES SIDNEY, orgn. exec.; b. Wichita, Kan., Aug. 28 1808; s. Samuel Warwick and Elizabeth Wilson (Martin) P.; ed. Carnegie Inst. Tech., 1920; B.S., Ohio State U., 1924; m. Lucile Willard Martin, Sept. 16, 1925; children—William David, Ruth Ellen. With Weirton Steel Co., 1919-20, Tenn. Furniture Corp., Chattanooga, Tenn., 1924-26; estimator, Frigidaire div. Gen. Motors Corp., Dayton, O., 1926-29, gen. foreman, 1929-30, supr. porcelain enameling, 1930-35; with Resettlement Adminstrn., U.S. Dept. of Agr., 1935-38; mng. dir. Porcelain Enamel Inst., 1938-44; with American Ceramic Soc., from 1944, gen. sec., from 1946. Trustee Ed. Orton, Jr. Ceramic Found.; pres. Ceramic Development Co. Fellow Am. Ceramic Soc., Am. Soc. Assn. Execs., Lambda Chi Alpha, Beta Gamma Sigma. Clubs: Rotary (Columbus); Faculty (Ohio State U.). Home: Columbus OH Died May 15, 1972; buried Union Cemetery Columbus OH

PEARCE, EVA F., coll. dean; b. Georgetown, Ga., Oct. 27, 1876; d. James Wright and Sarah (Carswell) Pearce; A.B., Brenau Coll., 1896; A.M., Columbia, 1912; unmarried. Prof. of English, Brenau Coll., since 1909, dean since 1920; condr. student groups for study in literary centers of Eng. and Italy, 1920-28. Mem. bd. trustees, Brenau Coll. Democrat. Methodist. Home: 623 E. Spring, Gainesville GA*‡

PEARL, MARY JEANETTE, coll. dean; b. nr. St. Johns, Mich., July 16, 1900; d. Orsamus Merrill and Margaret (Armour) Pearl; B.A., U. Toronto, 1922; M.A., U. Mich., 1923, Ph.D., 1937; postgrad. Am. Acad. in Rome, 1924-27, 30-31. Mem. faculty Sweet Briar Coll., 1928-65, prof. Greek and Latin, 1943-65, acting dean, 1948-49, dean, 1950-65. Reader fgn. lang. publs. Survey of OSS, 1942-45. Mem. Archaeol. Inst. Am., Am. Philol. Assn., Classical Assn. Middle West and South, Phi Beta Kappa. Address: Sweet Briar VA Died Feb. 16, 1966; buried St. Johns MI

PEARSON, DREW (ANDREW RUSSELL), newspaper corr.; b. Evanston, Ill., Dec. 13, 1897; s. Paul Martin and Edna (Wolfe) P.; ed. Phillips Acad., Exeter, N.H., 1915; A.B., Swarthmore Coll., 1919; m. Countess Felicia Gizycka, Mar. 12, 1925; 1 dau., Ellen Cameron, III; married 2d, Luvie Moore, November 12, 1936. Director of the American Friends Service Committee in Serbia, Montenegro and Albania, 1919-21; instr. in industrial geography, U. of Pa., 1921-22; lectured on Am., Australian and New Zealand chautauquas, 1921-23; visited Japan, China and Siberia, reporting results of Washington Arms Conference for newspaper syndicate, 1922; interviewed Europe's Twelve Greatest Men" for newspaper syndicate, 1923; lecturer in commercial geography, Columbia U., 1924; reported anti-foreign strikes in China, 1925; reported Geneva Naval Conf. for Consol. Press, 1927; staff United States Daily, 1926-33, Baltimore Sun, 1929-32; reported 6th Pan-Am. Conf., Havana, 1928; accompanied Secretary of State Kellogg to Paris to sign Anti-war Treaty, 1928; reported London Naval Conference, 1930, Cuban revolution, 1931; reported Rio de Janeiro (Brazil) Conf., 1942; UN Conf., San Francisco, 1945; Paris Peace Conf., 1946, Summit Conf., Geneva, 1955, proposed conf., 1960; U.S. del. Atlantic Conf., London, 1959; pres. Food for Peace Com., from 1961; sec. America's Conscience Fund, from 1963; visited and interviewed Premier Khrushchev, President Tito, King and Queen of Greece, Premier Fanfani; Organized Friendship Train to Europe, 1947-48. President of Big Brothers of Nat. Capital Area. Recipient Sigma Delta Chi Nat. Award for best Washington journalism of 1942. Decorated: French Legion of Honor; First Order Star of Solidarity (new Italian Republic); Knights of Columbus Internat. Gold Medal for 1948. Named Father of the Year, 1948. Served in A.U.S., 1918. Pres. International Platform Association, 1950. Founder Intercollegiate Newspaper Association, 1919; member Kappa Sigma, Delta Sigma Rho, Phi Beta Kappa. Quaker. Clubs: Overseas Writers, National Press, Cosmos (Washington, D.C.); Circus Fans of America. Co-Author: Washington Merry-Go-Round; More Merry-Go-Round; The American Diplomatic Game; The Nine Old Men; USA—2nd Class Power?; Will Khrushchev Bury Us?, 1962; The Senator; c-author: Case Against Congress, 1968; author of the newspaper column Daily Washington Merry-Go-Round", 1931-69. Contbr. to mags. Home: Washington DC and Rockville, Md. Died Sept. 1, 1969; buried Potomac MD

PEARSON, GERALD H(AMILTON) J(EFFREY), physician; b. Key West, Fla., Sept. 21, 1893; s. George Lloyd and Frances Hancock (Baxter) P.; A.B., U. of Western Ont., 1915, M.D., 1915; D.Sc., U. of Pa., 1930; m. Mary Agnes Mackenzie, July 3, 1916; children—Frances P. (Mrs. Samuel E. Bucher), Lesley P. (Mrs. Louis J. Fridenberg), George R. M. Intern Ontario Hosp. for Insane, Mimico, Ont., 1915-16; pvt. practice psychiatry Phila., from 1930; asso. prof. child psychiatry Temple U. Med. Sch., 1940-48; dean Inst. Phila. Assn. for Psychoanalysis, 1950-58; asso. in psychiatry U. of Pa. Grad. Sch. from 1930. Served as capt., M.C., Canadian Army, 1916-19. Mem. Am. Psychoanalytic Soc., Am. Psychiatric Assn., Am. Orthopsychiatric Soc., Am. Group Therapy Assn., Am. Soc. Psychosomatic Med., A.M.A., Phila. Pediatric Soc., Phila. Pschiat. Soc., Phila. Neurol. Soc., Phila. Assn. for Psychoanalysis. Author: Common Neuroses of Children and Adults (with Dr. O. S. English), 1937; Emotional Problems of Living (with Dr. O. S. English), 1945; Emotional Disorders of Children, 1949; Psychoanalysis and the Education of the Child, 1954; Adolescence and the Conflict of Generations, 1958. Address: Philadelphia PA Died July 2, 1969.

PEARSON, HENRY CARR, educator; b. East Saugus, Mass., Aug. 23, 1871; s. George Henry and Sara Lucasta (Dearborn) P.; A.B., Harvard, 1892; post-grad. work, Clark U., 1898, Columbia, 1901; m. Lillian White Allen, July 28, 1896. Prin. Horace Mann Sch. of Columbia U., and prof. edn., Teachers Coll., Columbia, 1903-28. Fellow A.A.A.S.; mem. N.E.A., Headmasters Assn. Republican. Unitarian. Clubs: Rotary, Fort Lauderdale Country. Author: Greek Prose Composition, 1897; Latin Prose Composition, 1903; Essentials of Latin, 1905. Co-author; Essentials of English, 1914; Essentials of Spelling, 1919; Everyday Reading, 1927; Latin I, 1929; Latin II, 1930; Everyday Spelling, 1931. Contbr. on ednl. topics. Home: 1700 N.E. 3d Court, Fort Lauderdale FL‡

PEARSON, JOSEPHINE ANDERSON, educator; b. nr. Gallatin, Tenn., June 30, 1870; desc. of Colonial ancestry; d. Rev. Philip Anderson, (D.D.) and Amanda Caroline (Roscoe) P.; A.B., Irving Coll., 1890; A.M., Cumberland Coll., 1896; studied Vanderbilt and U. of Mo. Principal high sch., McMinnville, Tenn., 1900-04; served as prin. and teacher Nashville Coll. for Young Ladies, and on faculty Winthrop State Normal Coll., and as dean Higbee Sem., Memphis; dean and prof. philosophy and history, Woman's Coll., Columbia, Mo., 1909-15; dean and prof. philosophy, Southern Sem., Buena Vista, Va., 1922-27; later dean of faculty, Manch Coll. (Stauton, Va.); served as prof. English and philosophy, St. Agnes Coll. and Conservatory; lecturer on literature, travel and art. Was a prominent speaker and writer against woman suffrage; a leader in advocating Dixie Highway. Mem. numerous socs. and clubs. Contbr. series of historical articles on Tenn. women, etc. Address: 2817 West End Av., Nashville TN‡

PEARSON, LESTER BOWLES, former prime minister Can.; b. Ont., Can., Apr. 23, 1897; s. Edwin Arthur and Annie Sarah (Bowles) P.; B.A., U. Toronto, 1919; M.A., Oxford U. (Eng.), 1925; 50 hon. degrees; m. Maryon Elspeth Moody, Aug. 22, 1925; children—Geoffrey Arthur Holland, Patricia Lillian. Served as pfc. with U. Toronto hosp. unit, Salonika, 1915-16; comd. lt. Canadian Army, 1917, trans. as pilot, with rank of flight lt. Royal Flying Corps, World War 1. Lectr. history, later asst. prof., U. Toronto, 1923-25; 1st sec. Dept. External Affairs, Ottawa, Ont., 1928-35; with rank of counsellor Office of High Commr. for Can.,

›ndon, 1935-41; asst. under-sec. of state for external ‹airs, 1941; minister counsellor Canadian legation, 'ashington, 1942-44, E.E. and M.P., 1944, ambassador U.S., 1945-46; under-sec. of state for external affairs, ›46-48, sec. 1948-57; elected mem. House of ›ommons, for Algoma East, Ont., Can., 1948, 49, 53, ', 58, 62, 63, 65, leader of Liberal Party of Can. and pposition in House of Commons, 1958-63; prime inister of Can., 1963-68; chmn. Commn. on Internat. evel., World Bank, 1968-69; chancellor, prof. Sch. ternat. Affairs Carleton U., Ottawa, 1969-72. Hon. :es. Montreal Expos Baseball Club, Canadian Council ›r Internat. Cooperation, World Federalists of Can., ›n. chmn. Canadian Council Christians and Jews, anadian nat. com. United World Colls., Children's osp. Eastern Ont. Internat. exec. chmn. Council 'orld Tensions, 1960, internat. co-chmn., 1963. Mem. anadian delegation League Nations, Food and Agr. rgn. of U.N., and UNRRA; rep. of Canadian prime inister at meeting of Commonwealth Prime Ministers, ondon, 1949, head Canadian delegation, 1964, 65, 66; ımn. delegation Commonwealth Meeting on Fgn. ffairs, Colombo, Ceylon, 1950, Japanese Peace Treaty onf., San Francisco, 1951; an adviser Canadian elegation Conf. for UN Charter, San Francisco, 1945; ead delegation 3d-11th Gen. Assemblies, UN, pres. :h session, 1952-53; rep. of Can. at signing North tlantic Treaty, Washington, 1949, and at subsequent ATO council meetings, chmn. council, 1951; chmn. anadian delegation, 9-power Conf. on German earmament, London, 1954. Chancellor or Victoria U., oronto. 1951-58. Chmn. bd. govs. Internat. Devel. esearch Centre, 1970; mem. internat. hon. com. Dag ammarskjold Found.; adv. com. Woodrow Wilson nternat. Center for Scholars, Washington. Decorated fficer Order Brit. Empire; named hon. freeman City of ondon, 1967; hon. fellow Weizmann Inst. Sci., Israel, 968; companion Order of Can.; recipient Nobel peace rize, 1957; Family of Man award, 1965; Atlantic Union ioneer award, 1966. Hon. fellow Toronto Acad. Aedicine; hon. mem. Royal Archtl. Inst. Can., Royal oc. Can., Internat. Inst. for Strategic Studies (pres. 968), Canadian Inst. for Internat. Affairs (chmn. nat. dv. com. 1968-72), Vanier Inst. Family (life), Acad. olit. Sci. of Columbia U. Mem. Liberal Party. Author:)emocracy in World Politics, 1955; Diplomacy in the Juclear Age, 1959; The Four Faces of Peace, 1964; 'eace in the Family of Man (Reith Lectures), 1968; The :risis of Development, 1970; Words and Occasions, 970; Mike, Volume I of the Memoirs of The Right Ionourable L.B. Pearson, 1972. Home: Ontario Canada)ied Dec. 27, 1972.

'EARSON, WILLIAM NORMAN, educator; b. Butler, N.J., Jan. 5, 1924; s. William and Amelia (Smith) '.; B.A., Tusculum Coll., 1947; Ph.D., Vanderbilt U., 951; m. Patricia C. Weiss, June 18, 1950; hildren—Catherine W., Christopher W., Mark P. nstr., dept. biochemistry Vanderbilt U. Med. Sch., 950-54, asst. prof., 1954-60, asso. prof., 1960-67, prof., 967-68, asso. dir. div. nutrition, 1960-68. Cons. utrition program Nat. Center for Chronic Diseases, 959-68, Nat. Research Council, A.M.A. Served with AUS, 1943-46. Recipient Mead-Johnson Award, 1967. Mem. A.A.A.S., Am. Inst. Nutrition (sec. 1966-68), Am. Pub. Health Assn., Sigma Xi. Home: Nashville TN Died Nov. 28, 1968.

PEASE, KINGSLEY EUGENE, educator; b. Hartville, Mo., June 20, 1875; s. George A. and Susan Jane (Carson) P.; B.S., Northwestern Univ., 1901; m. Taipeng, Perak, F.M.S., July 27, 1905, Florence Emily Archer. Teacher, Anglo-Chinese High Sch., 1901-3; prin. Anglo-Chinese Boarding Sch., 1903-5, also prin. both schools since 1905; local treas. Bd. Foreign Missions, M.E. Ch. Address: Anglo-Chinese School, Singapore, Straits Settlements.‡

PEASE, LUCIUS CURTIS (LUTE PEASE), cartoonist, painter; b. Winnemucca, Nev., Mar. 27, 1869; s. Lucius Curtis and Mary Isabel (Hutton) P.; grad. Malone (N.Y.) Acad., 1887; m. Nell Christmas McMullin, June 22, 1905. Began as rancher, Santa Barbara County, Calif., 1887; prospector and gold miner including 5 yrs. in Alaska; Yukon-Nome corr. Seattle-Post-Intelligencer, 1897-1901; U.S. commr. Kotzebue Sound-Point Hope Dist., Alaska, 1901-02; political cartoonist and reporter Portland Oregonian, 1902-05; editor in chief Pacific Monthly, Portland, Ore., 1906-13; political cartoonist Newark (N.J.) Evening News, 1914-1954; painter of portraits and landscapes. Exhibited at Nat. Acad., Nat. Arts Club, New York. Winner of Pulitzer prize for cartoons, 1949. Clubs: Newark Art; Art Center of the Oranges, N.J. Contbr. articles and short stories to mags. Home: 105 Durand Rd., Maplewood NJ‡

PEASLEE, AMOS JENKINS, retired ambassador, born at Clarksboro, New Jersey on March 24, 1887; son of Gideon and Emma (Waddington) P.; A.B., Swarthmore (Pennsylvania) Coll., 1907; studied Birmingham U., Eng.; LL.B., Columbia, 1911; LL.D., Swarthmore College, Earlham College and State University N.J.; married Dorothy K. Quimby, Feb. 12, 1920; children—Dorothy Waddington, Amos Jenkins, Lucy Raynes, Richard Cutts. International lawyer; U.S. ambassador to Australia, 1953-56; dep. spl. asst. to President, 1956-59. Dep. chmn. U.S. delegation UN Disarmament Conf., London, 1957. Director Am. Courier Serv., World War I, with rank of major attached to General Pershing's headquarters, France; chairman New York-European Election Commission which held election in Army and Navy in Europe, 1917; judge advocate of Gen. Court Martial in France, 1918; represented U.S. at Liabach conference, 1919, Penal Law Soc. conf. at Geneva, 1947, German dept. settlement conf. at London, 1952; rep. U.S. as adviser U.S. delegation UN General Assembly, 1957, UN Disarmament Commn., 1957; attached to American Commission to Negotiate Peace, Paris, France, 1919; chmn. Appeals Board Washington, D.C., 1933-34; commander U.S. Coast Guard, World War II. National commander U.S. Coast Guard League, 1947. Mem. U.S. Council of Def., 1947. Rep. Am. Soc. Internat. Law at San Francisco Conference, 1945. Hon. president bd. trustees Friends Central Sch., Phila.; trustee Underwood Hosp., Bryn Mawr Coll. Decorated D.S.M., Panama. President Swarthmore Coll. Alumni Association, 1941. Member American Bar Assn., Inter-Am. Bar Assn. (del. Rio and Mexican confs.), Assn. Bar of City of N.Y., Am. Soc. Internat. Law, Internat. Law Assn. (pres. Am. br. 1928-29); Internat. Bar Assn. (sec. gen. 1947-53), Am. Council Learned Socs., Delta Upsilon, Phi Beta Kappa, Delta Sigma Rho. Republican. Quaker. Clubs: Metropolitan, Army and Navy also the Capitol Hill (Washington); University, Columbia University (N.Y.C.); Union League (Phila.); Mantoloking, Bay Head Yacht. Author: Proposed Amendments to Judiciary Articles of the Covenant of the League of Nations, 1918; a Permanent U.N., 1942; Three Wars with Germany, 1944; U.N. Govt., 1945; Constitutions of Nations, 3 vols., 1950, 56, 65; Constitutional Documents of International Governmental Organizations, 2 vols.; also internat. law, world order, and other legal topics. Home: Clarksboro NJ Died Aug. 29, 1969.

PECK, HENRY AUSTIN, ednl. adminstr., author; b. Somerville, Mass., Apr. 6, 1921; s. Clarence Barnard and Ruth (Frazee) P.; A.B. summa cum laude, Tufts Coll., 1942; M.A., Fletcher Sch. Law and Diplomacy, 1947, Ph.D., 1952; Doctor of Humane Letters, Tufts Univ., 1963; m. Janet Emerson, July 3, 1948; children—Susan P., John E., Christopher A. Instr. econs. Tufts Coll., 1947-48; prof. econs. U. Me., 1948-68, dir. Sch. of Bus. Adminstrn., 1959-61, vice president for academic affairs, 1961-68; president State U. Coll. at Potsdam, N.Y., 1968-70. Member of board of trustees of Dean Junior College. Served as technician, Signal Corps, AUS, World War II. Mem. Am. Econ. Assn., Phi Beta Kappa, Phi Kappa Phi. Author: Seaports In Maine, 1953; International Economics, 1957; Financing Unemployment Compensation in Maine, 1958. Home: Potsdam NY Died Feb. 10, 1970.

PECK, JOHN SEDGWICK, electrical engr.; b. New Haven, Conn., Nov. 20, 1871; s. Henry Dwight and Jennie M. (Tucker) P.; prep. edn. Staunton Mil. Acad., Va.; M.E., Cornell, 1892; m. Josephine H. Arnold, of Boston, 1900. Began work in shops of Eddy Electric Co., Hartford, 1892; entered students' course, 1893, Westinghouse Electric & Mfg. Co., finally being placed in charge of the designing and constrn. of transformers; appointed acting chief elec. engr. British Westinghouse Elec. & Mfg. Co., Oct. 1, 1904, chief elec. engr., Oct. 1, 1905, consulting elec. engr., July 1906; chief elec. engr., Metropolitan-Vickers Elec. Co., Ltd., 1919-—. Fellow Am. Inst. E.E.; mem. Inst. Elec. Engrs. Gt. Britain, Manchester Assn. Engrs., A.A.A.S. Clubs: Engineers (London and Manchester). Address: Schenley, Bentinck Rd., Altrincham England‡

PECK, MORTON EATON, prof. botany; b. La Porte City, Ia., Mar. 12, 1871; s. Geo. D. and Clara (Eaton) P.; A.B., Cornell Coll., Mt. Vernon, Ia., 1895, A.M., 1911, hon. Sc.D., 1940; m. Jessie Grant, May 15, 1905. Instr. biology, Marionville, Mo., 1896-97; prof. biology, Ellsworth (Ia.) Coll., 1897-1905; professor botany, Ia. Wesleyan Coll., 1907-08, Willamette U., since 1908. Made bot. collection in Brit. Honduras, 1905-07. Mem. Bot. Soc. America, Phi Beta Kappa, Sigma Xi. Republican. Methodist. Author: The Book of the Bardons and Other Poems, 1925; also A Manual of the Higher Plants of Oregon. Contbr. on distribution of seed plants and many taxonomic papers. Home: Salem OR‡

PECK, STAUNTON BLOODGOOD, civil and mech. engr.; b. N.Y. City, Oct. 20, 1864; s. Thomas Bloodgood and Mary Frances (Staunton) P.; student Columbia, 1882-86, fellow in engring., 1886-87, M.E., 1886, C.E., 1887; m. Clarabelle Moberly, 1893 (died 1910); m. 2d, Lola Maurene Downin, 1914. Mech. engr. with Burr & Dodge, Phila., 1887-88; asst. chief engr., Link-Belt Engring. Co., Phila., 1881-91; chief engr., Link-Belt Machinery Co., 1891-1906; v.p. Link-Belt Company, 1906-28, served as president during World War; retired 1928. Member Alpha Delta Phi. Republican. Episcopalian. Clubs: Union League, Rittenhouse, Sunnybrook Golf (Phila.); University (New York). Home: Montgomery Av., Chestnut Hill, Philadelphia PA‡

PECKHAM, HOWARD LOUIS, army officer; b. Norwich, Conn., May 29, 1897; s. Frank E. and Frances E. (Beckwith) P.; B.S., U.S. Mil. Acad., 1918; grad. Inf. Sch., 1926, Command and Gen. Staff Sch., 1940; m. Marion Davis Shaw, June 16, 1925; children—Howard Louis, Jean Anne. Commd. 2d lt., Corps of Engrs., Nov. 1, 1918, and advanced through the grades to maj. gen., U.S. Army, April 1952; chief of staff, 8th Armored Div., Ft. Knox, Ky., April-July 1942; combat comdr., 12th Armored Div., Aug. 1942-Oct. 1943; dir. fuels and lubricants div., Office Q.M. Gen., Oct. 1943-March 1946; dir. procurement div., Office Q.M. Gen., Jan.-June 1946; air Q.M., Hq. Army Air Forces, June 1946-Apr. 1947; comdg. gen., Am. Graves Registration Comd., European Area, Paris, 1947-49; comdg. gen. N.Y. Q.M. Procurement Agency, 1950-51; acting dep. Q.M. gen., 1951-52; comdg. gen. Ft. Lee, Va., 1952-54; chief Army & Air Force Exchange Service, 1954-72. Decorated D.S.M., U.S. Army. Club: Army and Navy (Washington. Died Oct. 1972.

PECORA, FERDINAND, judge; b. Nicosia, Italy, Jan. 6, 1882; s. Louis and Rose (Messina) P.; brought to U.S. in 1887, naturalized citizen; student St. Stevens Coll. and Coll. City of New York; LL.B., N.Y. Law Sch., 1906; LL.D., John Marshall Coll. of Law, 1940; LL.D., St. Lawrence U. (Brooklyn Law Sch.), 1942; married Florence Louise Waterman, Nov. 30, 1910 (dec. Sept. 1970); 1 son, Louis Wellington. Admitted to N.Y. bar 1911; asst. dist. atty. N.Y. County, 1918-22, chief asst. dist. atty., 1922-30; as counsel to U.S. Senate Com. on Banking and Currency, Jan. 1933-June 1934, conducted investigation into banking and stock market practices, and helped draft laws passed by Congress in 1933-34, creating Securities and Exchange Commn. to regulate stock exchanges and the issue and sale of securities; apptd. one of original members of Securities and Exchange Commn. by President Franklin D. Roosevelt, July 1, 1934; resigned Jan. 21, 1935, to accept apptmt. by Governor Lehman as justice of Supreme Court of N.Y. State to fill vacancy; nominated by both Dem. and Rep. parties for full 14 yr. term as Supreme Court justice, and elected Nov. 5, 1935; reelected 1949 as nominee of Democratic, Republican, Liberal and City Fusion parties, resigned to be candidate of Democratic, Liberal and City Fusion parties for mayor, 1950; counsel to law firm Schwartz & Frolich. Director of the Freedom House, New York City. Trustee of New York Law School. Designated by the governor to preside over an extraordinary special and trial term of the Supreme Court for trial of indictments for racketeering" crimes, 1936. Vice chairman of National Progressive Party, New York, 1915-16. Mem. Assn. Bar City of N.Y., N.Y. County Lawyers Assn. Democrat. Episcopalian. Mason, Elk, K.P. Clubs: Manhattan, Nat. Democratic (N.Y.C.). Author: Wall Street Under Oath. Home: New York City NY Died Dec. 7, 1971.

PECORA, WILLIAM THOMAS, govt. ofcl.; b. Belleville, N.J., Feb. 1, 1913; s. Cono and Anna (Amabile) P.; B.S., Princeton, 1933; Ph.D. in Geology, Harvard, 1940; D. Sc., Franklin and Marshall Coll., 1969; D. Eng., Colo. Sch. Mines, 1970; m. Ethelwyn Elizabeth Carter, Apr. 7, 1947; children—William C., Ann S. With Geol. Survey, Dept. Interior, 1939-71, chief br. geochemistry and petrology, 1957-61, research geologist 1961-64, chief geologist, 1964-65, dir., 1965-71, undersec. Dept. Interior, 1971-72; field geological investigations nickel deposits in the United States, Alaska, Brazil and Venezuela, 1939-42, mica deposits and also associated pegmatite deposits in Brazil, 1943-46, also alkalic igneous rocks, related carbonatite deposits, phosphate minerals. Mem. U.S. Civil Service Commn. Bd. Examiners, 1947-67; adv. panel earth scis. NSF, 1950-55; adv. com. geology Ednl. Testing Service, from 1950; adv. council dept. geology Princeton, 1946-72, div. earth scis. NRC-Nat. Acad. Scis., 1962-65; mem. standing com. Fed. Council Sci. and Tech., 1965-72; mem. adv. bd. for research and grad. edn. Rutgers U., 1965-68; mem. council for arts and scis. George Washington U., 1967-72; mem. vis. com for geol. scis. Cal. Inst. Tech., 1968-72; mem. earth scis. adv. bd. Stanford U., 1971-72; mem. com. to visit dept. geol. scis. Harvard, 1966-71; mem. adv. com. dept. mineral scis. Mus. Natural History, Smithsonian Instn., 1966-72; mem. Pres.'s Distinguished Service Awards Bd., 1972. Recipient Rockefeller Pub. Service award, 1969; Distinguished Service award Dept. Interior, 1968, NASA, posthumously, 1972. Fellow Geol. Soc. Am. (councilor 1957-60), Am. Acad. Arts and Scis., Mineral, Soc. Am. (councilor 1964-66); mem. Brazilian Academy of Sciences (fgn. mem.), Nat. Acad. Scis., Am. Philos. Soc., Geol. Soc. Washington (pres. 1964). Club: Cosmos (Washington). Contbr. profl. jours. Home: Washington DC Died July 19, 1972.

PEDIGO, JOHN HARDIN, lawyer; b. Henry County, Va., Dec. 31, 1872; s. John Hardin and Ellen Cornelia (Davison) P.; ed. under pvt. tutor and in pub. schs.; m. Clara Harris, Jan. 2, 1902 (dec.). Admitted to Wash. bar, 1895, and since practiced at Walla Walla; mem. Pedigo, Watson & Gose; pres. Hylu Corp.; v.p. and gen. atty. Walla Walla Valley Ry. Co.; v.p. and atty. Wahluke Investment Co.; dir. and atty. First Nat. Bank of Walla Walla, Security Service Corp., Robison Land & Livestock Co., Inc.; atty. N.P. Ry. Co., Touchet (Wash.) State Bank, Prescott (Wash.) State Bank. Republican. Home: Walla Walla, Wash. Office: First Nat. Bank Bldg., Walla Walla WA‡

PEEBLES, ANNA DAVIS, educator; b. Douglassville, Tex., Oct. 9, 1904; d. Archie Mitchel and Mattie (Davis) Peebles; grad. Sam Houston State Tchrs. Coll., Huntsville, Tex. Tchr. Marshall (Tex.) pub. schs., 1927-39, 43-46, Baytown pub. schs., 1939-43, Houston pub. schs., 1946-69. Mem. Tex. Tchrs. Assn., Houston Tchrs., Classroom Tchrs. Methodist. Mem. Order of Eastern Star. Club: University Women's. Home: Houston TX Died Oct. 4, 1969.

PEEBLES, FLORENCE, biologist; b. Pewee Valley, Ky., June 3, 1874; d. Thomas Chalmers and Elizabeth Southgate (Cummins) P.; A.B., Goucher Coll., Baltimore, Md., 1895; Mary E. Garrett scholar in biology, Bryn Mawr Coll., 1895-96; Mary E. Garrett fellow, student U. of Munich and U. of Halle, 1899; Ph.D., Bryn Mawr Coll., 1900; grad. study univs. of Bonn, 1905, Wurzburg, 1911, Freiburg, 1913; unmarried. Demonstrator in biology, Bryn Mawr Coll., 1897-98; instr. in biology, Goucher Coll., 1899-1902, asso. prof., 1902-06; instr. in science, Miss Wright's Sch., Bryn Mawr, Pa., 1906-12; European fellow Assn. Coll. Alumni, 1912-13; acting head of dept. biology, Bryn Mawr Coll., 1913; head of dept. biology, Sophie Newcomb Coll., Tulane U., 1915-17; asso. prof. biology, Bryn Mawr, 1917-19; prof. biol. sciences, Calif. Christian (now Chapman) Coll., since 1928; extension lecturer, U. of Calif., since 1927. Research worker, Marine Biol. Lab., Woods Hole, Mass., 10 times between 1895 and 1924; holder Am. Woman's Table at Naples Zool. Station, Italy, 5 times between 1898 and 1927. Fellow A.A.A.S.; mem. Am. Soc. times between 1898 and 1927. Fellow A.A.A.S.; mem. Am. Soc. Naturalists, Corpn. Marine Biol. Lab., Phi Beta Kappa. Episcopalian. Contbr. to Biol. Bull., Jour. Exptl. Zoology, etc. Home: Altadena CA‡

PEELER, WINSTON SNIDER, oil company executive b. Dallas, May 16, 1912; s. Cletus Ewing and Cleo (Snider) P.; B.S. in Chem. Engring., Rice U., 1933; m. Mary Frances Blaylock, Jan. 5, 1952; children—Sue (Mrs. John R. Newell), Lee C. Chem. engr. Pan Am. Refining Corp., Texas City, Tex., 1934-57, gen. supt., 1955-57; gen. mgr. mfg. Am. Oil Co., N.Y.C., 1957, v.p, dir., 1958-60, gen. mgr. employee and pub. relations, dir., Chgo., 1961-62; exec. v.p., dir. Service Pipe Line Co., Tulsa, 1962-64, pres., dir., 1964-67; v.p. mfg. and transp. Am. Oil Co., 1967-71. Registered profl. engr., Tex. Mem. Am. Inst. Chem. Engrs., Am. Petroleum Inst., Nat. Petroleum Refiners Assn. (dir., mem. exec. com.). Assn. Oil Pipe Lines (chmn. exec. com.), Newcomen Soc. N.Am., Engrs. Soc. Republican. Baptist. Club: University (Chgo.). Home: Chicago IL Died Oct. 1971.

PEERY, JOHN CARNAHAN, college pres.; b. Burkes Garden, Va., Feb. 24, 1876; s. Thomas and Sarah Henrietta (Repass) P.; A.B., Roanoke Coll., Salem, Va., 1900, A.M., 1902; graduate Southern Luth. Theol. Sem., Columbia, S.C., 1905; (D.D., Lenoir Coll., 1919); m. Pearle Miller Powlas, of Hickory, N.C., Aug. 4, 1920. Ordained Luth. ministry, 1905; pastor Lynchburg, Va., 1905-11; pres. Elizabeth Coll., Salem, Va., 1911-17; pastor College Ch., Hickory, 1917-19; pres. Lenoir Coll., 1919—. Democrat. Club: Kiwanis. Home: Hickory NC‡

PEET, ELIZABETH, coll. prof.; b. N.Y. City, Mar. 26, 1874; d. Isaac Lewis (LL.D.) and Mary (Toles) Peet; g.d. Harvey Prindle Peet, both father and g.-father having served as prin. New York Instn. for Instruction of the Deaf; B.A., George Washington U., 1918, Pd.D., 1937; M.A., Gallaudet College, 1923, hon. L.H.D., 1950. Teacher R.I. Sch. for the Deaf, 1899-1900; with Gallaudet Coll. (only coll. for deaf in the world), 1900-50, as prof. langs. and dean of women. Mem. Conv. Am. Instrs. of the Deaf, Am. Assn. Univ. Women, Columbian Women of George Washington U., (past president 3 terms), D.A.R., Assn. of Deans of Women. Presbyterian. Member League Republican Women. Address: 1801 Clydesdale PL., Washington DC‡

PEET, ROY WILLIAM, assn. mgr.; born Kansas City, Mo., Feb. 22, 1898; s. William James and Catherine Agnes (Shannon) P.; student U. Mo., 1915, Harvard, 1916-17; m. Helen Elizabeth Adair, Apr. 23, 1919; children—Suzanne Catherine (Mrs. Poillon), William James. Engaged in soap mfg. bus. from 1918; sales dept. Colgate-Palmolive-Peet Co., 1922-26, dir. advt., 1937-40, asst. to pres., 1940-44, v.p., 1944-48; sec.-mgr. The Soap and Detergent Association from 1948. Chairman American Fat Salvage Committee, 1942-48; pres. East Amwell Taxpayers Association, 1958-59; mem. exec. com., bd. dirs. N.J. Taxpayers Assn., 1959-62, pres., 1961-62; exec. com., bd. dirs. Brand Names Found., 1949-62. Former committeeman East Amwell Twp.; former mayor East Amwell; mem. Hunterdon County Bd. Chosen Freeholders, 1965-67, dir. bd., 1967. Served as 2d lt. A.S., 1918. Bd. gov. Sigma Chi Found. 1946-49. Mem. Sigma Chi. Clubs: Union League (N.Y.C.); Copper Hill Golf (Flemington). Home: Ringoes NJ Died Feb. 22, 1969.

PEGLER, WESTBROOK JAMES, journalist; born Mpls., Minn., Aug. 2, 1894; s. Arthur James and Frances (Nicholson) P.; ed. Lane Tech. Sch., Loyola Acad., Chgo., 1911-12; hon. LL.D., Knox Coll., 1943; m. Julia Harpman, Aug. 28, 1922 (dec. 1955); m. 2d, Pearl Doane, 1959 (div. 1961 m. 3d, Maud Towart, 1961. Corr. European Staff U.P., 1916-18; corr. same with A.E.F., 1917-1918; served in U.S. Navy, 1918-19; sports editor United News, New York, 1919-25; Eastern sports corr. Chicago Tribune, 1925-33; with New York World-Telegram. Chicago Daily News and other papers, 1933-44; with King Features Syndicate, New York City, 1944-62; free-lance writer, journalist, 1962-69. Received Pulitzer award for reporting, 1941; Gold Medal, Nassau County Bar Association, 1944; Am. Legion Award; Nat. Headlines Club Award (twice) for achievement in journalism. Clubs: Jonathan (Los Angeles); Nat. Press (Washington). Author: Tain't Right, 1936; Dissenting Opinions of Mister Westbrook Pegler, 1938; George Spelvin, American, 1942. Address: Tucson AZ Died June 24, 1969.

PEGRAM, ROBERT BAKER, III, ry. official; b. Marion, Ala., Aug. 22, 1874; s. Robert Baker and Ella Goodwin (Wyatt) P.; ed. pub. and pvt. schs., Memphis; m. Susan Mary Wright, July 14, 1897. Began, 1890, as clerk Memphis & Charleston Ry., later with Memphis Freight Bur. and I.C. R.R.; connected with Southern Ry. since 1897; soliciting freight agt., later commercial agt. at Birmingham, Ala., 1904-05; chief clerk to v.p., St. Louis, 1905; asst. gen. freight agt., Nashville, Tenn., 1905-07; gen. freight agt., Nashville, 1907-08, Charleston, S.C., 1908-10; gen. agt. exec. dept., Charleston, S.C., 1910-17, Memphis, 1917-18; gen. purchasing agt. Southern R.R. Lines, 1918-20; v.p. Southern Ry. System since Mar. 1, 1920; pres. Atlanta Terminal Co. and Tallulah Falls Ry.; retired from active business, Jan. 1945. Episcopalian. Clubs: Piedmont Driving, Capital City. Home: Biltmore Apts. Office: Southern Ry. Bldg., Atlanta GA‡

PEGUES, ALBERT SHIPP, college prof.; b. Cheraw, S.C., Feb. 19, 1872; s. Rev. Wesley Leatherwood and Amanda Olivia (Dickinson) P.; A.B., Wofford Coll., S.C., 1892, A.M., 1895; studied Cornell Univ. and Univ. of Chicago; (Litt.D., Wofford College, 1915); m. Pearl Irene Lockett, of Georgetown, Tex., June 6, 1899. Began as instr., 1893, asso. prof. English lit., 1903-06, prof. and head English dept., 1906-19, dean of faculty College of Liberal Arts, 1915-19, Southwestern U., Georgetown, Tex.; dean Coll. Liberal Arts and prof. English, Southern Methodist U., Dallas, Tex., 1919—. Prog. Democrat. Mem. Chi Psi. Address: 3413 Harvard Av., Dallas TX‡

PEGUES, BOYKIN WITHERSPOON, prof. civil engring.; b. Stonewall, La., Oct. 1, 1874; s. Thomas Godfrey and Rebecca (Witherspoon) P.; B.S. in Civil Engring., La. State U., 1895; grad. work, Cornell U., summers, 1905-22; M.S. in Civil Engring., U. of Wis., 1928; m. Mable Chapman, June 17, 1923. Chainman, transitman, U.S. govt. Engrs., 1895-99; with La. State U. since 1899, as asst. prof. civil engring., 1899-1901, prof., 1901-26, acting dean coll. of engring., 1926-31, head dept. of civil engring. since 1931. Mem. La. State Bd. Engring. Examiners. Life mem. La. Engring. Soc.; mem. Am. Soc. Civil Engrs., Phi Kappa Phi, Tau Beta Pi. Home: 3804 Perkins Road, Baton Rouge LA*‡

PEIRCE, WALDO, artist; b. Bangor, Me., 1884; s. Mellen C. and Anna (Hayford) P.; prep. edn. Phillips Acad., Mass.; A.B., Harvard, 1908; art edn. Julian Academy, Paris, and various European countries, especially Spain; Dr. Fine Arts, Colby College Maine, 1957; married third Alzira Boehm, 1930; children—Chamberlain, Michael (twins), Anna Gabrielle; married 4th, Ellen Larsen, 1946; children—Jonathan Waldo, Karen Julia. Ambulance driver with French Army, 1915-17 (received Croix de Guerre); later with American Intelligence Department, Madrid; lived in Paris, southern France and Tunis after the war; traveled in Spain with Ernest Hemingway; secured material for his paintings of bulls in Pamplona; returned to U.S., 1930. Paintings have been shown at all important nat. and internat. exhbns. in U.S., also Wildenstein Galleries, London, and Museum of Modern Art, Paris. Represented in Met. Museum, Whitney Museum, Pa. Acad. Fine Arts, Addison Gallery of Am. Art (Andover, Mass.), Brooklyn Museum; also murals in several public bldgs. Awarded 1st prize, Artists for Victory, 1944; purchase prize, Paintings of the Year, 1948. Member Phi Beta Kappa. Club: Harvard (N.Y.C.). Home: Searsport ME Died Mar. 8, 1970.

PELL, JOHN L. E., screen scenario writer, author; b. New York, N.Y., Nov. 16, 1876; s. Thomas Jefferson and Emily Josephine (Everitt) P.; ed. Graham Sch., N.Y. City, Sedgwick Prep. Sch., Great Barrington, Mass.; m. Ella Gretchen Tefft, Apr. 30, 1901; 1 son, Everitt Hamilton. Broker on N.Y. Produce Exchange, 1897; later, mem. Bertine & Co., interior decorators; still later asst. sales mgr. Gryphon Tire & Rubber Co., and dir. Tenn. Electric Steel Co.; retired from business to follow writing. Authority on Colonial and Revolutionary periods. Mem. S.R. Independent Republican. Episcopalian. Club: Wyantenuck Country. Began writing for moving pictures, 1908; wrote scenarios for Down to the Sea in Ships," 1923, Nathan Hale," D. W. Griffith's America" (with Robert W. Chambers), and other silent screen dramas; als dramatic sketches for Nat. Broadcasting Co., includin Forty Fathom Trawlers," George Washington," Th Cross of Christ," etc. Formerly broadcast hist. featur programs, WEAF (Red Network), and WJZ (Blu network). Author: (with Clay Perry) The Canad Doctor, 1932; Sheffield MA‡

PELL, WILLIAMSON, JR., lawyer; b. N.Y.C., Dec 5, 1911; s. Williamson and Vida (Kneeland) P.; grac Hotchkiss Sch., 1929; A.B., Princeton, 1933; LL.B Harvard, 1936; m. Elizabeth Ullman, Apr. 11, 196 children by previous marriage—Mary (Mrs. Scott Hil Jr.), Angelene P., Frederick Wagner III, Tria (Mrs. Gu O. Dove II), Gladys Williamson. Admitted to N.Y. ba 1936, since practiced in N.Y.C.; partner firm Iacrs Nash, Brophy, Barringer & Brooks, 1953-72. Truste Union Sq. Savs. Bank; dir. W.L. Crown Constrn. Co Trustee Madison Sq. Boys Club. Mem. Am. Col Probate Counsel, Phi Beta Kappa. Home: Bernardsvill NJ Died Feb. 1972.

PENDLETON, ALBERT HUNTINGTON, lawyer; b Lebanon, Conn., Mar. 15, 1901; s. Frank Story an Gertrude Hortense (Huntington) P.; B.S. in Elec Engring., Worcester Poly. Inst., 1923; LL.B., Duquesn U., 1927; m. Esther Carman, Nov. 20, 192 children—Frank Carman, Richard Wesley, Charle Brian, Marcia Starkweather (Mrs. Edmund Jane Doering III). Admitted to Pa. and Ill. bars, 192 practice in Chgo., 1927; mem. firm Pendleton, Neuman Williams & Anderson, and predecessors, 1933. Fellov Am. Coll. Trial Lawyers; mem. Am., Chgo. bar assns Bar Assn. 7th Fed. Circuit, Patent Law Assn. Chgo (pres. 1957), Am. Judicature Soc., Am. Patent Lav Assn. Clubs: Union League (Chgo.); Kenilworth (Ill.) Home: Kenilworth IL Died Oct. 1972.

PENDRAY, LEATRICE M., newspaper columnist; b Colorado City, Texas, Oct. 1, 1905; d. Homer Alonz and Lena Rivers (Jones) Gregory; A.B., U. of Wyo 1927; m. G. Edward Pendray, June 27, 192 children—Guenever Lee (Mrs. Barton W. Knapp) Elaine Louise (Mrs. William Jennings), Lynnette An (Mrs. Chester Wertsch). Editorial assistant, late entertainment editor, Delineator Magazine, 1927-2 researcher, Scripps-Howard Newspaper Alliance, 192 woman's page columnist (writing under pen name o Jacqueline Hunt and Judith Wilson), food editor an beauty editor, United Feature Syndicate, 1929-4 organizer Am. Features Syndicate, 1930; partne Pendray & Co., N.Y.C., 1959-71. Active Crestwoo (N.Y.) P.T.A.; commr. Crestwood Girl Scouts, 1950-52 pub. relations dir., 1950; pub. relations chmn Westchester County Girl Scouts and Rock Hill Cam Com. Mem. American Rocket Soc. (a founder, mem exptl. com., librarian, asst. editor Astronautics), So Women Engrs. (asst. sec. 1957-62). Club: Crestwoo Women's (pres. garden dept. 1953-55, 58-60, di 1955-56, v.p., program chmn. 1963-66). Episcopalian Author: Win Him If You Want Him, 1937; Be Lovelie and Be Loved, 1943. Contbr. to mags. Home Crestwood NY Died Oct. 7, 1971; buried Greenhil Cemetery, Laramie WY

PENICK, ISSAC NEWTON, clergyman, educator; b Carroll County, Tenn., Oct. 9, 1859; s. Elijah Warre and Mary Jane (Rowland) P.; ed. U. of Tenn.; A.B. Southwestern Bapt. U., 1896, Th.M., 1922; studie medicine and law; m. Josephine Shankle, 1881 children—Lillian Alverder, Lellie Jane, Mittie Dove Margrete Jesephine, Ruby Blond, John Newton Marion Warren, Albert Kay. Ordained Bapt. ministry 1889; pastor Second Ch., Jackson, Tenn.; 2 yrs., Firs Ch., Martin, Tenn., 22 yrs.; prof. of Union U., 1918 largely instrumental in building Hall-Moody Coll., an pres. of bd. trustees over 20 years; formerly dean Unior U., Jackson; prof. evangelism, Summer Sch. Southwestern Bapt. U., 4 summers; held over 50 debate on religious questions and over 400 evangelisti meetings. Editor Baptist Builder 16 yrs. Truste Southern Bapt. Theol. Sem., Louisville, an Southwestern Bapt. Theol. Sem., Ft. Worth. Mem. Am Research Soc., Southern Sociol. Congress. Home: 43 E. College St., Jackson TN*‡

PENNELL, WALTER OTIS, electrical engr.; b Exeter, N.H., Jan. 13, 1875; s. Robert Franklin an Martha Morgan (Otis) P.; B.S., Mass. Inst. Tech., 1896 m. Sarah M. Corson, of Phila., June 8, 1903 children—Dorothy, Ford; m. 2d, Elizabeth H. Kimball of Exeter, N.H., July 11, 1936; 1 daughter, Martha Teacher electrical engineering Lafayette College Pennsylvania, 1896-98; asst. engr. Bell Telephone Co. o Phila., 1898-1902; engr. Am. Telephone & Telegrap Co., Boston, 1902-03; chief engr. Mo. & Kan Telephone Co., Kansas City, Mo., 1903-12; bldg. an equipment engr., 1912-16, acting chief engr., 1916-17 chief engr., 1918-36, Southwestern Bell Telephon System, St. Louis; retired, 1936. Planned and supervise erection of telephone plants in many states of the Union originator of several patents of widely-used telephon devices. Mem. N.H. Ho. of Reps., 1939-40; v.p. Exete Hosp. Corporation; director Exeter News Letter director New England Council. Past president St. Loui Electrical Board of Trade, Engineers Club of St. Louis Fellow Am. Inst. E.E.; mem. Math. Assn. America

Order Founders and Patriots of America, N.H. Seacoast Regional Development Assn. (dir.). Republican. Conglist. Club: Exeter Country. Author of papers on engineering and mathematics. Home: Exeter NH‡

PENNEWELL, ALMER MITCHELL, clergyman; b. Middletown, Mo., June 23, 1876; s. William Thomas and Ann M. (Parkey) P.; B.A., Central Wesleyan Coll., Warrenton, Mo., 1905; B.D., Garrett Bibl. Inst., 1908, D.D., 1925; m. Claudia B. Daniel, Dec. 20, 1900; children—Marian Frances, Charles Stuart. Ordained Meth. ministry, 1900; pastor St. Catherine, Mo., 1900-01, Warrenton, Mo., 1901-05, Congress Park, Ill., 1905-06, Bethel Ch., Chicago, 1906-08, Wanakena, N.Y., 1908-10, Maywood, Ill., 1910-12, Oak Park, Ill., 1912-15, Morris, Ill., 1915-19, Convenant Ch., Evanston, Ill., 1919-25, Wheaton, 1925-28, Ravenswood, 1928-33, St. John's Ch., Chicago, 1933-47; retired, now Midwest dir. Spiritual Mobilization Office, Chicago. Republican. Author: Old Carson's Christmas, 1924; Miscellaneous Poems, 1935; The Methodist Movement in Northern Illinois, 1942; Poems: Come Christmas," 1943; Sing,Parson, Sing," 1947; A Voice in the Wilderness"; Biography of Rev. Jesse Walker, 1947. Address: 1243 First Nat. Bank Bldg., 33 S. Clark St., Chicago IL‡

PENNEY, JAMES CASH, merchant; b. Hamilton, Mo., Sept. 16, 1875; s. James C. and Mary Frances (Paxton) P.; ed. high sch.; hon. Dr. Business Adminstrn., Kan. Wesleyan U., 1925, Bryant Coll., 1953; D.C.S. (hon.), Boston U., 1927, Drexel Inst. Tech., 1954; LL.D., Rollins Coll., 1928, U. Wyo., 1945, Westminster Coll., 1949, Shurtleff Coll., 1951, U. Mo., 1954, Ia. Wesleyan U., 1958, Baylor U., 1959; L.H.D. (hon.), Hastings Coll., 1951, Coe Coll., 1955, Carson-Newman Coll., 1957, Taylor Univ., 1957; L.H.D. (hon.), Long Island U., 1966; D. of Public Service, Brigham Young Univ., 1968; m. Berta A. Hess, Aug. 24, 1899 (dec. 1910); children—Roswell Kemper (dec.) James Cash (dec.); m. Mary Kimball, July 29, 1919 (dec. 1923); 1 son, Kimball; m. Caroline Autenreith, Aug. 10, 1926; children—Mary Frances (Mrs. P. F. Wagley), Carol (Mrs. D. L. Guyer). Founder, 1902, J.C. Penney Co., Inc., operating more than 2,000 domestic and fgn. retail units, including 1700 in U.S., president, until 1917, chmn. board, 1917-58, dir., 1958-71; pres., dir. Sterling Industries, James C. Penney Found., Inc.; founder Penney Retirement Community, Penney Farms, Fla.; trustee Eastern States Expn., Allied Youth; dir. Am. Royal Live Stock Expn. and Horse Show, Kansas City, Mo., Agrl. Hall of Fame; hon. chmn. bd. dirs. Laymen's Movement; com. mem. Chapel of Four Chaplains; hon. life mem. Distributive Edn. Clubs Am.; mem. edn. com. Horatio Alger Awards Com.; hon. co-chmn. adv. council National 4-H Foundation. Named to Hall of Fame in Distbn., State Okla. Hall of Fame; recipient Tobe award for distinguished contbn. to Am. retailing, 1953, Horatio Alger award, Am. Schs. and Colls. Assn., 1953, Scroll of Honor, Mayor of N.Y.C., 1965, Am. Mothers Com. citation, 1967, named Layman Extraordinary, Laymen's Movement Bd. Dirs., 1967; Partner in 4-H Nat. Citation, 1969. Mem. Nat. Inst. Social Scis., Missouri, N.Y. State chambers commerce, Mo. Guernsey breeders assns., Am. Guernsey Cattle Club, Dairy Shrine Club, English Guernsey Cattle Soc. (hon. life), Royal Agrl. Soc. Eng. (hon. life), Newcomen Soc. N. Am., Aberdeen Angus Assn., N.Y. Farmers Assn. Mason (33 deg. Shriner, K.T.). Clubs: Everglades (Palm Beach, Fla.); Rotary, Union League (N.Y.C.); Fairfield (Conn.) Country; Pequot Yacht (Southport, Conn.); Fairfield County Hunt Club (Westport, Conn.). Author of: Fifty Years With The Golden Rule; Lines of a Layman; View From The Ninth Decade; collaborator J.C. Penney: The Man with a Thousand Partners; Main Street Merchant; J.C. Penney, Merchant Prince. Home: New York City NY and Green Farms, Conn. Died Feb. 12, 1971; buried Woodlawn Cemetery, New York City NY

PENNEY, MINNIE FREEMAN (MRS. EDGAR B. PENNEY), b. Pa.; d. William E. and Sarah (Cushing) Freeman; ed. York (Neb.) Meth. Coll.; business course, Lincoln Business Coll.; m. Edgar B. Penney, of Lexington, Neb., Apr. 22, 1891; children—Freeman Seth, Frederic Doyle. Charter mem. Pawnee Chapter D.A.R., Neb. Federation Women's Clubs, Neb. Dept. Am. Legion Auxiliary (1st pres.); served as mem. bd. dirs. Gen. Federation Women's Clubs; mem. League Am. Pen Women, Pi Beta Phi Sorority; hon. mem. Nat. Camp Fire Orgn. Committee woman from Neb. of Rep. Nat. Com., term 1924-28. Episcopalian. Club: Omaha College. Home: Fullerton NB‡

PENNINGTON, LEVI TALBOTT, coll. pres. emeritus; b. Amo, Hendricks County, Ind., Aug. 29, 1875; s. Josiah and Mary Furnas (Cook) P.; A.B., Earlham Coll., Richmond, Ind., 1910; corr. work, Armour Inst. Sacred Lit.; A.M., U. of Ore., 1922; D.D., Linfield Coll., 1923; m. Bertha May Waters, June 1, 1898 (died June 28, 1903); children—Mrs. Mary Esther Pearson, Bertha May; m. 2d, Florence Rebecca Kidd, Feb. 28, 1905. Teacher country and graded schs., Mich., and newspaper work until 1904; pastor Friends chs. in Ind., 1904-11; pres. Pacific Coll., Newberg, Ore., 1911-41, except 2 yrs., 1919-21, as head of Forward Movement of Friends in America, and 1 year, 1930-31, spent in travel and speaking tour of eastern United States and British Isles; pres. emeritus Pacific College since 1941; public speaking tour of U.S., 1945-46. Mem. Society of Friends (Orthodox). Mem. N.E.A., Assn. Oregon Colleges, Ore. Ednl. Assn., etc. Won state and interstate oratorical honors while in coll.; widely known as pub. speaker. Author (poems); All Kinds of Weather. Contbr. on religious and ednl. subjects, also short stories, poems, etc. Newberg OR‡

PENNOYER, FREDERICK WILLIAM, JR., naval officer; b. East Orange, N.J.; s. Frederick William and Huldah (Palmer) P.; student Stevens Inst. Tech., 1910-11; B.S., U.S. Naval Acad., 1915; M.S., Mass. Inst. Tech., 1920; naval aviator, Flight Training Naval Air Station, Pensacola, Fla., 1923; m. Margarette W. Bispham, Apr. 6, 1918; 1 son, Frederick William III (capt. USN ret.). Commd. ensign, U.S. Navy, 1915, and advanced through the grades to vice adm., 1950; specialized in aeronautical engineering since 1921; Bureau of Aeronautics general representative, Wright Field, Dayton, Ohio; ret. comdr. Naval Air Material Center, U.S. Naval Base, Phila. Decorated Legion of Merit (Gold Star), Air Medal, Commendation ribbon. Fellow Inst. Aeronautical Sciences. Address: Coronado CA Died Jan. 21, 1971; buried Mt. Rosecrans Cemetery, San Diego CA

PENNOYER, PAUL GEDDES, lawyer; b. Oakland, Cal., Oct. 30, 1890; s. Albert Adams and Virginia (Edmands) P.; student U. Cal. at Berkeley, 1907-08; A.B., Harvard, 1914, LL.B., 1917; m. Frances Tracy Morgan, June 16, 1917; children—Virginia (Mrs. Norman B. Livermore, Jr.), Paul G., F. Tracy (Mrs. August H. Schilling), Robert M., Katherine (Mrs. Eugene E. O'Donnell), Jessie (Mrs. Frank V. Snyder). Admitted to N.Y. bar, 1919; asso. White & Case, N.Y.C., 1920, partner, 1928-71; partner A. Iselin & Co., 1929-33. Rep. State Dept. UN, San Francisco Conf. on Internat. Orgn., 1945; secretariat State-War-Navy Coordinating Com., 1945. Mem. United Republican Finance Com. N.Y. Hon. gov. N.Y. Hosp.; chmn. Riverside Found.; dir., trustee N.Y. Philharmonic, N.Y.C.; trustee, and former secretary of the Pierpont Morgan Library, N.Y.C. Served as capt., F.A., AEF, U.S. Army, World War I, as col. GSC, World War II. Decorated Legion of Merit; chevalier Legion d'Honneur. Mem. Police Relief Assn. Nassau County (trustee), Locust Valley Cemetery Assn. (dir.), Assn. Bar N.Y.C., Am., N.Y., Internat. bar assns., N.Y. County Lawyers Assn., Bar Assn. Nassau County, Soc. Mayflower Descendents, France Am. Soc., Inc. (dir., mem. exec. com.), Fedn. des Alliances Francaises aux Etats-Unis (trustee). Episcopalian. Clubs: Down Town Association, Recess Board Room, Harvard, Links, Brook, Century (N.Y.C.), Travellers (Paris), Bohemian (San Francisco), Piping Rock, Creek (bd. govs.) (Locust Valley). Home: Locust Valley NY Died June 30, 1971; buried Locust Valley (N.Y.) Cemetery.

PENROSE, LIONEL SHARPLES, educator; b. June 11, 1898; M.A., M.D., St. John's Coll., Cambridge U.; D.Sc., McGill U., 1958; m. Margaret Leathes; 4 children. Research dir. Royal Eastern Counties Inst., Colchester, 1930; dir. psychiatric research, Ont., Can., 1939; Galton prof. eugenics University Coll., London, 1945-65; research dir. Kennedy-Galton Centre Harperbury Hosp., St. Albans, Eng., 1965-72. Recipient Albert Lasker award for med. research, 1960; J. P. Kennedy, Jr. award for research in mental retardation, 1964. Fellow Royal Soc. Author: The Influence of Heredity on Disease, 1934; The Biology of Mental Defect, rev. edit., 1963. Home: London England Died May 12, 1972.

PENZOLDT, PETER JOHN, educator; b. Munich, Germany, Jan. 18, 1925; s. Fritz and Lilly (Hoffmann) P.; Licence es Lettres, U. Geneva (Switzerland), 1947, Certificat de Pedagogie, Doctorat es Lettres, 1950; m. Rachel Lea Vallette, June 17, 1950; 1 dau., Sylviane Elizabeth. Came to U.S., 1950, naturalized, 1956. Tchr., Ecole de Hautes Etudes Sociales, Geneva, 1949-50; asst. prof. humanities San Francisco State Coll., 1950-52; mem. faculty Sweet Briar Coll., 1952-69, prof. French and comparative lit., 1962-69, chmn. dept. modern langs., 1959-61. Mem. Am. Assn. U. Profs. (v.p. Sweet Briar chpt. 1954-55), Modern Lang. Assn., Am. Assn. Tchrs. French, Am. Assn. Tchrs. German, Nat. Wildlife Fedn., Isaak Walton League, Nat. Rifle Assn. Author: The Supernatural in Fiction, 1952; also articles. Address: Sweet Briar VA Died Aug. 21, 1969; buried Geneva Switzerland.

PEO, RALPH FREDERICK, mfr. constrn. materials; b. Rochester, N.Y., May 3, 1897; s. Juilian F. and Flora (Van Schaick) P.; M.E., Rochester Inst. Tech., 1917; m. Magdalene Heath, Jan. 1, 1918 (dec.); children—Jack H.; m. 2d, Ethelmay Brent, Dec. 4, 1943; children—Elizabeth Forbes, Barbara Brent. Engring. dept. various automobile mfrs.; asst. chief engr. Am. Radiator Co., 1923-24, chief engr., 1925-27; v.p., Houdaille-Hershey Corp., 1935-45; v.p., gen. mgr. Houde Engring. Co., 1927-45; pres., chmn. Frontier Industries, Inc., 1946-55; chmn., chief exec. officer, dir. Houdaille Industries Inc. (merger Frontier Industries, Inc., Houdaille-Hershey), from 1955; dir. Marine Trust Co. Western N.Y., DuBois Chems., Inc., Am. Bosch Arma Corp. Named outstanding businessman Niagara Frontier, U. Buffalo, 1955, Sylvania, 1955. Mem. Am. Ordnance Assn. C. of C. (past v.p., dir.), Soc. Automotive Engrs., Newcomen Soc. N.A. Mason. Clubs: Automobile, Canoe, Buffalo Yacht, Buffalo (Buffalo); Cherry Hill Country (Ridgeway, Ontario). Patentee. Home: Buffalo NY Died Nov. 28, 1966.

PEOPLES, JAMES ALEXANDER, educator; b. Columbia, Tenn., Feb. 5, 1877; s. James Harvey and Margaret (Douglass) P.; grad. Webb Sch., Bell Buckle, Tenn., 1895; LL.B., Vanderbilt, 1902; m. Emma Clary Webb, of Nashville, Tenn., Oct. 15, 1903; children—Ruth, Joe Webb, Marjorie, Jas. A., Clary Webb. Founder and headmaster Peoples Sch., Franklin, Tenn., 1902-05, Peoples-Tucker Sch., Springfield, Tenn., 1908-25, Lee Sch., Blue Ridge, N.C., since 1925. Mem. Assn. Colls. and Secondary Schs. of Southern States, Sigma Chi, Pi Gamma Mu. Democrat. Methodist. Kiwanian. Home: Blue Ridge NC‡

PEOPLES, RICHARD GRIER, educator; b. nr. Columbia, Tenn., Mar. 8, 1869; s. James Harvey and Margaret Simonton (Douglass) P.; B.A., Erskine Coll., Due West, S.C., 1886, LL.D., 1917; m. Alla Clary, of Bell Buckle, Tenn., Nov. 28, 1900. Prin. pub. schs., Leeville, Tenn., 1886-87; asst. Webb Sch., Bell Buckle, 1887-91; prin. high sch., Gleason, Tenn., 1891-92; asst. Webb Sch., 1892-99; co-prin. McTyeire Inst., McKenzie, Tenn., 1899-1902; prin. Wartrace (Tenn.) Training Sch., 1902-03; prin. Peoples Sch., Franklin, Tenn., 1903-25; prof. Latin and Greek, Westminster Coll., Fulton, Mo., since 1925; chmn. Regional Com. of the South, Am. Classical League Investigation, 1921-24. Trustee Webb Sch., Martin Coll. (Pulaski, Tenn.). Democrat. Mem. M.E. Ch., S. Kiwanian. Home: Fulton MO‡

PEPPER, BAILEY B(REAZEALE), entomologist; b. Easley, S.C., Mar. 20, 1906; s. Bailey B. and Eugenia (Sheriff) O.; B.S., Clemson Coll., 1929; M.S., Ohio State U., 1931; Ph.D., Rutgers, 1934; m. Margaret M. Forgham, Oct. 9, 1937; children—James Bailey, Carl Forgham. Mem. faculty Rutgers U., from 1935, prof. entomology, from 1945; staff N.J. Agrl. Expt. Sta. since 1935, research specialist, chmn., from 1945. Mem. Middlesex Co. Mosquito Extermination Commn., 1946-70; sec. State Mosquito Control Commn. Mgr. Marlboro State Hosp. Mem. Am. Assn. Econ. Entomologists, Entomological Society of Am. (chmn. Eastern br. 1963-64; pres. 1968), A.A.A.S., New Jersey State Hort. Soc., N.J. Health and San. Assn., Am. Mosquito Control Assn., N.J. Mosquito Extermination Assn. (sec.), Sigma Xi. Contbr. articles sci. jours. Home: Edison NJ Died Dec. 22, 1970.

PEPPER, STEPHEN COBURN, univ. prof.; b. Newark, N.J., Apr. 29, 1891; s. Charles Hovey and Frances (Coburn) P.; student Browne and Nichols Sch., 1908-09; A.B., Harvard, 1913, A.M., 1914, Ph.D., 1916; L.H.D., Colby College, 1950, Tulane U., 1961; LL.D., University of California, 1960; married Ellen Hoar, February 12, 1914; children—Sherman Hoar (dec.), Elizabeth Hoar (Mrs. F. B. Wood), Frances Coburn. Instructor in philosophy and psychology, Wellesley Coll., 1916-17; with U. of Calif. since 1919, as asst. in philosophy, 1919-20, instr., 1920-23, asst. prof., 1923-27, asso. prof., 1927-30, prof. philosohpy, 1930-58, prof. emeritus, 1958-72, chmn. philosophy, 1953-58, chmn. art dept., 1938-52, asst. dean College Letters and Science, 1939-47; faculty mem. Hamline U., Macalester Coll., 1958-59, Colby Coll., 1959; faculty mem. Carus lecturer Tulane Univ., 1961. Pvt. U.S. Army, 1918. Member Philos. Assn., American Association for Aesthetics, Coll. Art Assn., Am. Acad. Arts and Scis., Internat. Inst. Philosophy, Pi Eta (Harvard), Phi Beta Kappa. Author: Modern Color, 1919; Aesthetic Quality, 1938; Knowledge and Society, 1938; World Hypotheses, 1942; The Basis of Criticism in the Arts, 1945; A Digest of Purposive Values, 1947; Principles of Art Appreciation, 1950; The Work of Art, 1956; The Sources of Value, 1958; Ethics, 1960. Contributor Psychological Review, Jour. of Philosophy, Philosophical Review, Jour. of Aesthetics. Home: Berkeley CA Died May 1972.

PEPPERMAN, W(ALTER) LEON, street ry. official; b. Lowndes Co., Ala., 1876; ed. pub. schs.; unmarried. Began, 1894, in office of Theodore Roosevelt, U.S. civil service commr., and was later civil service examiner in U.S. and mem. first Civil Service Commn. in Philippines; asst. to chief of Bur. of Insular Affairs, Washington, 1902-5; chief of office of administration, Panama Canal, 1905-7; now v.p. Interborough Rapid Transit Co., Rapid Transit Subway Constrn. Co., N.Y. & Queens County R.R. Co., New York Rys. Co.; dir. Fifth Av. Coach Co., New York Transportation Co., Interborough Consolidated Corpn., etc. Clubs: Calumet, St. Nicholas, Sleepy Hollow (New York); Chevy Chase (Washington). Author: Who Built the Panama Canal? 1915. Home: 30 W. 59th St. Office: 165 Broadway New York‡

PEPPLER, CHARLES WILLIAM, univ. prof.; b. Baltimore, Jan. 16, 1872; s. Charles and Laura Virginia (Godman) P.; grad. Baltimore City Coll., 1889; A.B.,

Johns Hopkins, 1892, fellow, 1895-96, Ph.D., 1898; student, University of Berlin, 1902; married Edith Virginia Adams, June 11, 1902. Prof. Greek lang. and lit., Emory Coll., Oxford, Ga., 1898-1912; prof. Greek, Trinity Coll. and Duke Univ., 1912-44, now emeritus. Mem. mng. com. Am. Sch. Classical Studies, Athens; mem. Am. Philol. Assn., Am. Assn. Univ. Profs., Phi Beta Kappa. Methodist. Author: Comic Terminations in Aristophanes and the Comic Fragments, Parts I-V, 1902-21; Durative and Aoristic, 1933, 39; articles and book revs. in classical and philol. jours. Home: 406 Buchanan Rd., Durham NC‡

PEREIRA, I(RENE) RICE, artist; b. Boston, Aug. 5, 1907; d. Emanuel Rice and Hilda (Vanderbilt) Rice; student Art Students League, New York City, 1928-31, worked in Paris, Italy, N. Africa and Eng.; Ph.D. (hon). Universite Libre and Internat. Fedn. Sci. Research Socs. of Europe, Asia, Africa, 1969. Instructor of painting and composition Design Lab., New York City, 1935-39, Pratt Inst., 1942, Ball State Tchrs. Coll., summer 1951; lecr. various schs., museums, art groups; several radio appearances. One-man shows A.C.A. Gallery (3 shows), 1933-35, (2 shows) 46, 49, Howard U., Washington, 1938, East River Gallery, 1939, Julien Levy Gallery, 1939, Art of the Century, 1944, Arts Club Chgo., 1945, Mus. Modern Art (14 Americans), 1946, San Francisco Mus. Art, 1947, Barnett Aden Gallery, Washington, 1948, Phillips Andover Acad., 1949, Santa Barbara Mus. Art, Portland Mus. Art, M. H. De Young Meml. Mus., San Francisco, 1950, Memphis Acad., U. Syracuse, Balt. Mus., Ball State Tchrs. College, Duriacher Bros., N.Y.C., 1951, 54, Phillips Meml., Washington, Dayton Art Inst., 1952, U. Mich., 1954, Phila. Art Alliance, 1955, Corcoran Gallery, Washington, 1956, Wellons Gallery, N.Y.C., 1956, Nordness Gallery, N.Y.C., 1958, Rome-N.Y. Founds., Italy, Amel Gallery, N.Y., Agra Gallery, Washington, 1965, Weatherspoon Gallery, Greensboro, 1968, Mint Museum, Charlotte, N.C., 1968, Wilmington College, 1968; one-man retrospective exhibition Whitney Museum American Art, 1953, also circulated by museum to Des Moines Art Cen., San Francisco Mus., Dallas Mus. Represented in permanent collections Met. Mus. Art, Whitney Mus. Am. Art, Mus. Modern Art, N.Y.C., Chgo. Art Inst., Wadsworth Atheneum, Hartford, museums of Toledo, San Francisco, Balt., Newark, Detroit, and Delgado Mus., New Orleans, Worcester (Mass.) Mus., Norton Gallery, Palm Beach, Boston Mus., Corcoran Gallery, Washington, Norfolk Mus., Guggenheim Mus., N.Y., Finch Coll. Museum, New York, Smith College Museum, Phoenix Museum, Bklyn. Mus., Dallas Mus., Kansas City Mus., Milw. Art Center, Phillips Meml. Mus., also various colleges, foundations, public and private collections. Exhibited major exhbns. of U.S. including Corcoran, Carnegie, Pa. Acad., Art Inst. Chgo., Masterpieces 20th Century Mus. Modern Art, also Venice Biennials, other European and fgn. exhbns. Recipient Pepsi Cola Co. Paintings of the Year award, 1947; Greatness and Leadership award UN Day, Philippines, 1968; hon. philosopher poet laureate United Poets Laureate International, 1969; recipient of numerous honorable mentions. Life fellow of the Internat. Inst. Arts and Letters; mem. United Poets Laureate Internat. (hon.), Internat. Platform Assn., Centro Sudi E Scambi Internazionali. Author: Light and the New Reality, 1952; The Transformation of Nothing and the Paradox of Space, 1956; The Nature of Space, 1956; The Lapis, 1957; Crystal of the Rose, 1959; The Simultaneous Ever-Coming To Be', 1961; The Finite Versus The Infinite, 1962; The Transcendental Formal Logic of the Infinite; The Evolution of Cultural Forms, 1966; also biographies, articles on works, various publs. Home: New York City NY Died Jan. 1971.

PERIN, FLORENCE HOBART, author; b. Brooklyn, N.H., Aug. 17, 1869; d. George W. L. and Lydia Maria (Sawtelle) Hobart; State Normal Sch., Salem, Mass.; m. Rev. George Landor Perin, of Brookline, Mass., Nov. 6, 1901; 1 son, George Landor. Author: The Optimist's Good Morning, 1907; The Optimist's Good Night, 1910; Sunlet Days, 1915; The Heart of an Optimist, 1925. Home: 23 Naples Rd., Brookline MA‡

PERINI, LOUIS ROBERT, JR., pres. Perini Corp. Address: West Palm Beach FL Died Apr. 16, 1972.

PERKIN, RICHARD SCOTT, sci. instrument mfr.; b. N.Y.C., Oct. 17, 1906; s. Richard William and Mary Harriet (Malone) P.; student Pratt Inst., 1924-25; LL.D., University of Bridgeport, 1963; D.Sc. (hon.), Rensselaer Poly. Inst. 1963, Bowdoin Coll., 1966, Poly. Inst. Bklyn., 1966, Wesleyan U., 1966; m. Gladys Frelinghuysen Talmage, Apr. 29, 1930; children—Richard Talmage, John Thorne, Winifred Hume, Robert Suydam. Asst. investment adviser Am. Trust Co., Bklyn., 1926-27; customers broker E. W. Clucas & Co., N.Y.C., 1927-29; partner George H. Prentiss & Co., 1929-33; customers broker Chisholm & Chapman, 1933-34, H. N. Whitney & Sons, 1934-37; pres. Perkin-Elmer Corp., Norwalk, Conn., 1937-60, chmn. bd., 1937-69; dir. New Canaan Co., New Canaan Water Co., So. New Eng. Telephone Co., Aetna Life & Casualty; trustee U.S. Trust Co. of New York. Mem. vis. coms. depts. chemistry, astronomy Harvard Coll. Bd. dirs. Rehab. Center So. Fairfield County; trustee Am. Mus. Natural History, Columbia-Presbyn. Med. Center, Pratt Institute. Fellow Am. Optical Soc., Am. Acad. of Arts and Scis.; member Am. Astron. Soc., Am. Phys. Soc. Clubs: Broad Street, Links, River, Harvard (N.Y.C.); Country (New Canaan); Harvard Faculty (Cambridge, Mass.); Mastigouche Fish and Game (Que.); Metropolitan (Washington); Noroton (Conn.) Yacht; White's (London); Travellers (Paris); Tabusintac (New Brunswick, Conn.). Home: New Canaan CT Died May 22, 1969.

PERKINS, AGNES FRANCES, prof. English; b. Oxford, N.Y., Oct. 20, 1875; d. Gerritt Henry and Frances (Wilcox) Perkins; student Oxford (N.Y.) Acad.; A.B., Bryn Mawr Coll., 1898; A.M., 1899; grad. student Columbia U., 1929-31, M.S., 1930. Engaged as teacher, Baldwin Sch., Bryn Mawr, Pa., 1898-1901; reader in English, Bryn Mawr Coll., 1899-1900; teacher, Holman Sch., Phila., 1902-06; instr., Wellesley Coll., 1906-11; asso. prof. English, 1911-26, prof. English since 1926, chmn. department English composition, 1935-42 (prof. emeritus since 1944); professor English, Constantinople Coll., 1912-14. Member Modern Language Assn. America, N.E. Association of Teachers of English, American Assn. University Women, Am. Assn. Univ. Profs. Episcopalian. Clubs: Bryn Mawr (N.Y. City); Bryn Mawr (Boston). Author: Introduction to the Study of Rhetoric, 1903, 1907, 1926; Vocations for the Trained Woman, 1910. Home: 15 Roanoke Rd., Wellesley MA‡

PERKINS, BERTRAM LUCIUS, constrn. and engring. co. exec.; b. Schenectady, Oct. 4, 1922; s. Lucius Junius and Edwinna (Reed) P.; B.S. in Indsl. Mgmt., U. Cal. at Los Angeles, 1947; m. Janet MacQueen Bledsoe, Apr. 17, 1943; children—Richard Clement, Katherine Ann (Mrs. Vaughan Olson), John Stewart, Nancy Jean, Dorothy Lynn. Foreman, Morrison-Knudsen Co., Inc., Los Angeles area, 1947, supt., 1948-50, 51-53, gen. supt., also project mgr., 1953-58, dist. gen. supt. for Los Angeles, 1958-60, dist. mgr., 1960-64, v.p. of corp., 1961-68, dir., 1962-72; resident partner RMK-BRJ constrn. program, South Vietnam, 1965-67, v.p. operations, Boise, Ida., 1967, exec. v.p., 1968-69, pres., chmn., 1969-72. Served with USMCR, 1942-46, 50-51. Mem. Am. Soc. Mil. Engrs., Phi Delta Theta. Republican. Roman Catholic. Clubs: Jonathan; Houston; Club de Caza y Pesca Las Cruces; Hillcrest Country, Boise ID Died June 3, 1972.

PERKINS, CHARLES EDWIN, ry. official; b. Chicago, Ill., Mar. 31, 1871; s. William Wirt and Belle M. (Parry) P.; student Amherst Coll., 1890-91; m. Georgia Atherton Townsend, Sept. 10, 1902; children—Ralph C., William R. Began as office boy, K.C., F.S.&M. Ry., 1891; chief clk. to gen. agt., St.L.&S.F. R.R., at Kansas City, 1896-97; successively chief tariff clk., chief clk. and asst. gen. freight agt., K.C., P.&G. Ry. (now K.C.S. Ry.), 1897-1901; assy. gen. freight agt., K.C.S. and gen. freight agt. Texarkana &Ft. Smith rys., 1901-06; asst. gen. freight agt. K.C.S. Ry., at Kansas City, 1906-09; asst. gen. freight agt. and gen. freight agt. St.L., I.M.&S. Ry. (now M.P. R.R.), at St. Louis, 1910-13; with M.P. R.R. since 1913, successively as asst. gen. traffic mgr., 1913-18, freight traffic mgr. during federal control, gen. traffic mgr., 1919-20, became v.p. in charge of traffic, Mar. 1, 1920, now chief traffic officer. Methodist. Mason (32 deg., Shriner). Clubs: Noonday, Mo. Athletic, Glen Echo Country; Union League (Chicago); Amherst (New York). Home: 625 S. Skinker Blvd. Office: Missouri Pacific Bldg., St Louis MO*‡

PERKINS, ELIZABETH WARD (MRS. CHARLES BRUEN PERKINS), author; b. N.Y. City, Aug. 7, 1873; d. Thomas Wren and Sophia Howard Ward; prep. edn., Brearley Sch., N.Y. City; took entrance exam., Bryn Mawr; student music in Europe 2 yrs.; studied art under Charles H. Woodbury, N.A., of Boston; m. Charles Bruen Perkins, of Boston, Sept. 8, 1896; children—Francis D., Dr. Anna W., Elinor C. (Mrs. Lewis P. Mansfield), Mary E. Collaborated with Charles H. Woodbury in originating a course in observation—mental training through drawing; initiated application of the system in kindergartens, schs., museums, etc.; a founder Woodbury Training Sch. in Applied Observation, 1928; lecturer on ednl. subjects. Chmn. women's war socs. for Brookline and Suffolk County, World War; pres. Children's Art Centre, Boston; trustee Children's Mus., Boston; mem. corpn. Perkins Inst. for the Blind, Watertown, Mass.; mem. Am. Federation of Arts, Guild of Boston Artists. Catholic. Club: Women's City (Boston). Author: Observation, 1919; The Art of Seeing (with Charles H. Woodbury), 1925; also articles in mags. and transls. from the French and German. Home: 231 Boston MA‡

PERKINS, FRANCIS DAVENPORT, music critic, editor; b. Boston, Nov. 18, 1897; s. Charles Bruen and Elizabeth Howard (Ward) P.; ed. Country Day sch. for Boys, Boston, 1908-14, N.E. Conservatory of Music, 1908-14, Trinity Coll. Cantab., 1914-15; A.B., Harvard, 1919; m. Joan Lloyd, Sept. 12, 1945. Exchange editor N.Y. Tribune, 1919-22, asso. music critic, since 1922, acting music critic N.Y. Herald Tribune (formerly N.Y. Tribune), 1939-40, music editor 1950-52, associate music critic, 1952-70. Served with United States Army, France, 1918-19; with anti-aircraft artillery, 1942-44; transferred to mobile radio broadcasting co., 1944, overseas, 1944-45. Mem. N.Y. Music Critics Circle (chmn. 1959-60), Am. Newspaper Guild. Roman Catholic. Club: Harvard, (N.Y.C.). Contbr. mus. mags.; ann. article on music for New Internat. Year Book, 1931-42, Collier's Year Book, 1955-58; articles Grove's Dictionary of Music and Musicians, various other anns., mags.; sketches Dict. Am. Biography. Home: New York City NY Died Oct. 9, 1970; buried Forest Hills, Boston MA

PERKINS, FRED BARTLETT, judge; b. Burrillville, R.I., Feb. 16, 1897; s. Fred William and Sophia Louise (Bartlett) P.; A.B., Brown U., 1919; LL.B., Harvard, 1922; m. Mildred G. Randall. Admitted to R.I. bar, 1922, practiced law in Providence, 1922-52; first asst. U.S. atty. Dist. of R.I., 1926-29; asso. justice R.I. Superior Ct., 1952-69. Mem. Bd. of Bar Examiners of R.I., 1930-56; chmn., 1949-56. Hon. trustee R.I. Hosp. Instr. mil. sci. and tactics Brown U., 1917; pvt., Coast Arty. Corps, U.S. Army, 1918; commd. 2d lt., 1918; overseas, 1918-19, v.p. Gladdings, Inc.; chmn. Pub. Utility Hearing Bd. (R.I.), 1939-48. Moderator, Town of Barrington, R.I., 1944-52. Past sec. of Corp., Brown U., also bd. fellows. Dir., Home for Aged Men and Aged Couples Chmn. Central Fellowship Com. Universalist Ch. Am., 1946-52; pres. R.I. Universalist Conv., 1939-46; pres. First Universalist Ch. of Providence, 1929-64. Republican State Central Com. (R.I.), 1946-50. Mem. R.I. (past pres.), Am. bar assns., Phi Beta Kappa, Delta Sigma Rho, Delta Upsilon. Clubs: Rhode Island Country (Barrington); Hope, University (Providence); Clambake (Newport). Home: West Barrington RI Died Mar. 30, 1969.

PERKINS, HENRY FARNHAM, zoologist; b. Burlington, Vt., May 10, 1877; s. George H. and Mary Judd (Farnham) P.; A.B., U. of Vt., 1898; Ph.D., Johns Hopkins, 1902; m. Mary Keyser Edmunds, June 11, 1903. Instr. biology, 1902-06, asst. prof. zoology, 1906-11, prof. zoology, 1911-45; emeritus since 1945, University of Vermont; curator University Museum, 1926-31, director Robert Hull Fleming Museum, U. of Vermont, 1931-45; research assistant Carnegie Institution, 1903-05; assistant in fish investigation, Bur. of Fisheries, 1906, 08, 13. Fellow Johns Hopkins, 1916-17. Dir. Eugenics Survey of Vt., 1925-37; sec. Vt. Commission on Country Life, 1928-31, exec. v.p., 1932-44; chmn. Interstate Commn. on Lake Champlain Fishing since 1936. Republican. Conglist. Fellow A.A.A.S.; mem. American Society Zoologists, American Eugenics Society (president 1931-34, director, 1934-47), Champlain Valley Archaeol. Society (v.p. since 1937), Life Extension Inst., Delta Psi, Phi Beta Kappa. Clubs: Ethan Allen, Vt. Bird (pres. 1922-23), Chittenden County Fish and Game (dir.). Contbr. numerous papers on invertebrates, birds, heredity and eugenics. Lecturer on zoology, museum adminstrn., archaeology and eugenics. Address: 205 S. Prospect St., Burlington VT‡

PERKINS, MILO RANDOLPH, foreign investment consultant; b. Milwaukee, Wis., Jan. 28, 1900; s. Walton Asher and Gail Miriam (Randolph) P.; grad. Riverside High School, Milwaukee, Wis., 1916; LL.D., (hon.), U. of Arizona, 1964; m. Tharon Kidd, Aug. 21, 1919; children—Milo Randolph (dec.), George Kidd (2d lieut. U.S.M.C.R.; dec.). Salesman Bemis Brothers Bag Co., Houston, Texas, 1919-23, sales mgr., 1923-26; partner King-Perkins Bag Co., Houston, 1926-35; asst. to U.S. sec. of Agr., Washington, D.C., 1935-37; asst. adminstr. Farm Security Adminstrn., 1937-39; asso. adminstr. A.A.A. and pres. Federal Surplus Commodities Corp., 1939-41; dir. of Marketing, U.S. Dept. of Agriculture, 1940-41, and became administrator Surplus Marketing Adminstrn., July 1940; chmn. U.S. Sect. Joint War Prodn. Com., U.S. and Canada, Nov. 1943-July 1942, Washington, D.C., exec. head Economic Defense Bd., 1941; became exec. dir. Bd. of Econ. Warfare, 1941; fgn. investment cons.; owner Turfgrass Farm, Tucson. Decorated So. Cross (Brazil). Democrat. Clubs: Metropolitan (Washington, D.C.); Tucson Country, Metropolitan. Contbr. Atlantic, Harpers, Reader's Digest. Home: Tucson AZ Died Oct. 26, 1972.

PERKINS, NATHANIEL JAMES, educator; b. Carysbrook, Va., May 31, 1877; s. Isaac Otey and Margaret Lelia (Hughes) P.; grad. Doane Acad., Granville, Ohio, 1898; A.B., Denison Univ., Granville, 1902; m. Ethel Vernon Beard, Sept. 1, 1904 (died Jan. 19, 1934); 1 dau., Ethel Goodwin; m. 2d, Elda Wright Hare, June 3, 1939. Assistant principal high sch., Nashville, Ill., 1902-03; prin. city high schs., Aspen, Colo., 1903-04; prin. high sch., Sanford, Fla., 1904-08, supt. schs., 1908-14; prin. high sch., Carysbrook, Va., 1914-16; instr., Fork Union (Va.) Mil. Acad., 1916-17, president, 1917-30, headmaster since 1930, ret. 1950; mem. Va. Legislature, 1936-41; mem. bd. Va. dept. Insts. and Pub. Welfare. Col. R.O.T.C. Mem. Fluvanna County, Fluvanna County Fair Assn. (dir.), S.A.R., Beta Theta Pi. Baptist. Mason (K.T., Shriner). Chmn. Local Bd., Selective Service. Home: Carysbrook VA‡

PERKINS, THOMAS CLARK, trucking co. exec.; b. N.Y.C., Nov. 3, 1919; s. Joseph L. and Elisa Jane (Ditty) P.; student N.Y.U., 1939, Pa. State U., 1957; m.

Margaret Flanagan, Jan. 15, 1938; children—Thomas Randolph, Richard Brian, Pamela Elizabeth. Sec., treas. Perkins Warehouses, Inc., Long Island City, N.Y., 1946-69; pres. Perkins Motor Express, West Haven, Conn., 1961-69; exec. v.p. Perkins Trucking Co., Inc., Long Island City, 1962-69, also dir. Served to 1st lt., AUS, 1944-46. Mem. Am. Trucking Assn., New Haven Traffic Assn., N.Y. State New Eng. Motor Carrier Council (operations council), Conn. Motor Truck Assn., Quarter Century Traffic Club, Queens County Traffic Club. Clubs: Madison Winter. Mason. Home: Madison CT Died Nov. 17, 1969.

PERKINS, WALTER EUGENE, actor; b. at Biddeford, Me.; s. Jotham and Ruth B. P.;unmarried. Began stage career at Boston Museum, 1885; later with Electrical Doll Stock Co. in Winnipeg, and repertoire with John Jack, Maggie Mitchell, Held by the Enemy, with Jas. A. Herne in Drifting Apart, with Chas. Frohman's stock co. in Lost Paradise and Men and Women; The County Fair, Barrel of Money, All the Comforts of Home, Charley's Aunt, The New Boy, 1896-1900; My Friend from India, My Wife's Step-Husband, The Man from Mexico; starred in Jerome, a Poor Man, season 1902-3; stock star, 1903-4; starred in Who Goes There?, 1904-5. Residence: 138 W. 22d St. Address: Actor's Fund, New York NY‡

PERLEA, IONEL, conductor; b. Ograda, Roumania, Dec. 13, 1900; s. Victor and Margarete (Linch) P.; student piano, cello, composition in Munich (Germany) under Anton B. Wallbrunn; student Leipzig (Germany) Conservatory, 1920; m. Lisette Cottescu, Dec. 3, 1932; 1 son, Ion. Came to U.S., 1949, naturalized, 1960. Conductor, Leipzig Opera, 1921-22, Rostock (Germany) Opera, 1923; gen. mgr., mus. dir. Bucharest (Roumania) Opera, 1930; quest conductor throughout Europe, 1936-44; conductor La Scala, Milan, Italy, also other prin. opera houses in Italy, 1938-60; debut Met. Opera, 1949; conductor San Francisco, 1951, Los Angeles, 1951, NBC Symphony, 1950-57, Chgo., 1953, Cleve., 1954, Detroit, 1952, San Antonio, 1953, also European festivals; permanent conductor Fairfield County (Conn.) Symphony, 1955-70; prof. conducting Manhattan Sch. Music, 1952-70, permanent conductor, 1952-70; recording artist for RCA Victor, Vox and Remington records. Composer: String Quartet, 1921; Variations, 1930; Don Quichotte, 1946; Sinfonia concertante for Violin and Orchestra; Sinfonia in do. Address: New York City NY Died July 29, 1970.

PERLMAN, JACOB, economist; b. Byelostock, Poland, May 10, 1898; s. Mark and Pauline (Blankstein) P.; came to U.S., 1912, naturalized, 1918; B.A., U. Wis., 1919, M.A., 1922, Ph.D., 1926; m. Helen Aronson, Apr. 3, 1935; children—Matthew S., Judith S. (Mrs. Robert G. Martin). Statistician, N.Y. State Dept. Labor, 1919-21; instr. U. Wis., 1921-26; asst. prof. Northwestern U., 1926-27; asso. prof. U. N.D., 1928-33; staff mem. com. govt. statistics and adv. com. to sec. labor, 1933-34; chief hour and wage statistics div. Bur. Labor Statistics, 1934-40; chief economist, asst. dir. bur. old age and survivors ins. Social Security Adminstr., 1940-49, liaison officer, 1949-51; UN adviser Govt. Colombia and Central Bank Colombia, 1951-52, Govt. Greece, 1952-54; internat. economist FOA, 1954-55; UN adviser Govt. Bolivia, 1955, Govt. Philippines, 1956; dir. surveys NSF, 1956-57, head Office Econ. and Manpower Studies, 1956-65; cons. economist in sci. and tech., 1965-68; lectr. Am. U., 1940-49, Cath. U. Am., 1940-51, Johns Hopkins, 1948-51; vis. prof. U. Philippines, 1956; professorial lectr. Am. U., 1966-67; prof. U. Conn., 1967. Fellow Social Sci. Research Council, 1927-28. Author numerous articles, monographs. Address: Washington DC Died Apr. 8, 1968.

PERLSTEIN, MEYER AARON, pediatrician; b. Chgo., Apr. 6 1902; s. Moses Aaron and Rose (Silverman) P. B.S., U. Chgo., 1924, M.D., 1928; m. Minnie Oboler, May 7, 1928; children—Lee R. (wife of Dr. Bernard J. Axelrad), Ruth N. (wife of Dr. Michel Stein), Paul. Intern Cook County Hosp., Chgo., 1927-28, chief children's neurology service, attending staff; pvt. practice pediatrics, Chgo., 1929-69, San Jose, Cal., 1969; attending staff pediatrics Michael Reese Hosp., Chgo.; chief med. staff Ill. Children's Hosp. Sch.; prof. pediatrics Cook County Postgrad. Sch. Medicine; asso. prof. pediatrics Northwestern U. Med. Sch.; cons. neuropediatrics dept. phys. medicine U. P.R. Mem. adv. panel Cerebral Palsy project Nat. Inst. Neurologic Diseases and Blindness; adv. com. cerebral palsy Am. Pub. Health Assn.; adv. com. neuropediatrics U. P.R.; research adv. bd. United Cerebral Palsy, 1955; sci. council Brain Research Found.; bd. govs. Ill. Assn. Crippled; mem. Acad. Dentistry for Handicapped; med. adviser Ill. Epilepsy League, Chgo. Club Crippled Children, Spastic Children's Center, United Cerebral Palsy Chgo., Julian D. Levinson Research Foundation, Chicago; professional advisory council National Soc. Crippled Children and Adults, 1957; neuropediatric cons. Jewish Children's Bur., Chgo. cerebral palsy cons. Nat., Mich., socs. crippled children and adults, Crippled Children's Sch., Jamestown, N.D. Recipient citation Illinois Council Exceptional Children, 1964; U.S. Com. award distinguished internat. service rehab. disabled, 1965. Diplomate American Bd. Pediatrics. Mem. A.M.A., Ill., Chgo. med. socs., Chgo. Pediatric Soc., Chgo. Diabetes Assn., Inst. Medicine Chgo., Am. Acad. Neurology, Am. Acad. Pediatrics. Am. Acad. Cerebral Palsy (past pres.), Internat. Council Exceptional Children, Am. League Against Epilepsy, A.A.A.S., Ill. Epilepsy League, Am. Assn. Mental Deficiency, Am., Ill. pub. health assns., Israel Med. Assn. (Am. physicians fellowship com.), Nat. Geographic Soc., Phi Beta Delta, Alpha Omega Alpha. Mem. B'nai B'rith. Author numerous articles, papers in field. Asso. editor Cerebral Palsy Rev., Digest of Pediatrics. Address: San Jose CA Died Oct. 29, 1969; interred San Jose CA

PERRIN, FRANK L., editor; b. Kinnickinnic, St. Croix County, Wis., Dec. 22, 1862; s. William Louis and Julia Frances (Loring) P.; LL.B., University of Wisconsin, 1886; married Fannie Warfield Ball, 1887 (died 1917); m. 2d, Alice Wells Buttles, 1920. Practiced in Pierce and St. Croix counties, Wis.; editor Herald, Chippewa Falls, Wis., with St. Louis Globe-Democrat, Times, and The Star; editor and mgr. Gazette, Reno, Nev., 1912, Christian Science Monitor since 1916, as chief editorial writer, exec. editor, 1929-34, asso. editor and contbg. editor. Mason. Home: 1001 Third St., Santa Monica, Calif. Office: 1 Norway St., Boston‡

PERRY, BEN EDWIN, educator, author; b. Fayette, O., Feb. 21, 1892; s. Edwin Stuart and Delle (Wickizer) P.; B.A., U. Mich., 1915, M.A., 1916; Ph.D., Princeton, 1919; m. Lillian M. Pierce, July 19, 1922. Instr. Urbana (O.) U. Sch., 1919-20; instr. Latin Dartmouth, 1920-22, Western Res. U., 1922-24; asst. prof. classics U. Ill., 1924-28, asso. prof., 1928-41; prof., 1941-60, emeritus prof., 1960-68; Sather prof. classical lit. U. Cal., 1951; vis. prof. classics U. Mich., winter 1967. Member advisory council Am. Acad. in Rome; mng. com. Am. Sch. Classical Studies at Athens. Served in U.S. Army, 1918-19. Fellow Guggenheim Found., 1930-31, 1954-55; recipient Award of Merit, Am. Philol. Assn., 1955; Festscrift in his honor Classical Studies Presented to Ben Edwin Perry by his students and Colleagues at Univ. of Ill. 1924-60, 1969. Mem. Am. Philol. Assn. (dir. 1943-47, 51-53, vice president 1951-53), Am. Oriental Society, International Society for Folk-Narrative Research, Classical Association of Middle West and South, Soc. Byzantine Research in Athens, Phi Beta Kappa. Author: The Metamorphoses Ascribed to Lucius of Patrae, 1920; Studies in the Text History of the Life and Fables of Aesop, 1936; Aesopica (volume 1), 1952; The Origin of the Book of Sindbad, 1959; Secundus the Silent Philosopher, 1964; Babrius and Phaedrus (Loeb Library series), 1964; The Ancient Romances, a Literary-Historical Account of Their Origins, 1967. Co-author: Index Apuleianus, 1934. Asso. editor: Classical Philology, 1948-51. Contbr. philol. publs. Home: Urbana IL Died Nov. 1, 1968; interred Mt. Hope Mausoleum, Urbana IL

PERRY, CLAY LAMONT, mathematician, educator; b. San Francisco, Feb. 26, 1920; s. Clay Lamont and Matie V. (Bishofberger) P.; A.B. (La Verne Noyes scholar), U. Cal. at Los Angeles, 1942; Ph.D. (NRC fellow), U. Mich., 1949; m. Kathleen Kelly, Sept. 6, 1946; children—Virginia, Carol. Sr. mathematician Oak Ridge Nat. Lab., 1950-53; dir. Computer Center, prof. U.S. Naval Postgrad. Sch., Monterey, Cal., 1953-55; mgr. math. scis. dept. Stanford Research Inst., Menlo Park, Cal., 1955-60, cons., from 1960; dir. Computer Center, prof. math. U. Cal. at San Diego, La Jolla, from 1960. Served to 1st lt. USAAF, 1942-46. Mem. Assn. for Computing Machinery, Am. Math. Soc., Math. Assn. Am., Soc. Indsl. and Applied Math., Sigma Xi. Author: Programming and Coding for Digital Computers, 1961. Office: San Diego CA

PERRY, HECTOR H., lawyer; b. New London, Wis., Aug. 20, 1876; s. Ebenezer P. and Caroline J.P.; studied law in father's office; m. Jennie H. Monty, Dec. 1900. Practiced at Ellendale since 1902; mem. Whipple & Perry, law and real estate; clk. Dist. Court of Dickey County, N.D., 4 yrs.; mem. Dem. State Com., N.D., 1912-16 (chmn. last 2 yrs.), also mem. since 1928 and again chmn., 1928, 30; mem. Dem. Nat. Com., 1916-24 and 1932; Dem. candidate for U.S. senator, 1920; apptd. collector of internal revenue for N.D., 1933. Trustee N.D. State Normal and Industrial Sch. 4 yrs. Home: 1516 S. 8th St. Address: Federal Bldg., Fargo ND*‡

PERRY, JOHN, naval officer; b. Enoree, S.C., July 29, 1897; s. William Gregory and Frederica (Mc Kenzie) P.; student, Clemson (S.C.) Coll., 1914-16; B.S., U.S. Naval Acad., 1919; m. Madeline Gleason, July 15, 1921; children—John (dec.), Madeline. Commd. ensign U.S. Navy, 1919, and advanced through grades to vice adm.; served in U.S.S. New York and Dorsey, 1919-23; flight training, Pensacola Naval Air Sta., 1923, received wings, June 1923; served in various Pacific aircraft squadrons, 1923-26, piloted plane in 1st squadron west coast to Hawaii flight, 1934; commd. and comdr. Naval Base, Kodiak, 1941-42; chief of staff, Fleet Air, West Coast, 1942-43; comdr. U.S.S. Belleau Wood, participating in Hollandia, Mariannas and Philippine campaigns, 1944; comdr. Fleet Air Wing 1, Okinawa, 1945-46; chief of staff, Air Force Atlantic, div. comdr. Essex type carriers, Atlantic, 1946-48; comdr. Fleet Air Wing 4, operating in N.W. and Alaska, and comdr. Fleet Air, Seattle, Wash., 1948-50; comdr. NAAT, Corpus Christi, Tex., 1950-51, cardivs. land 5, 1951-52, Alaskan Sea Frontier, also COM 17, 1952-54, Com FAIR, Jacksonville, Fla., 1954-55, Com FAIR, Whidbey, Wash., 1955-59, ret., 1959. Decorated Distinguished Service medal, Silver Star, Combat Legion of Merit, Presidential unit citation (2); various campaign, area and fgn. medals. Episcopalian. Home: Greenville SC Died Aug. 7, 1972; buried Washelli Cemetery, Seattle WA

PERRY, LEWIS, academy prin.; b. Williamstown, Mass., Jan. 3, 1877; s. Arthur Latham (D.D., LL.D.) and Mary Brown (Smedley) P.; grad. Lawrenceville (N.J.) Sch., 1894; B.A., Williams Coll., 1898; L.H.D., 1920; M.A., Princeton, 1899; Litt.D., Dartmouth Coll., 1915; M.A., Yale Univ., 1916; L.H.D., Amherst Coll., 1928, Univ. of N.H., 1932; LL.D., Harvard Univ., 1932; m. Margaret Lawrie Hubbell, Nov. 11, 1911 (died Dec. 23, 1928); children—Lewis, Emily Ruth; m. 2d, Juliette Adams, June 25, 1935. Teacher Princeton Prep. Sch., 1898-99; master Lawrenceville Sch., 1899-1901; instr. English, 1901-04, asst. prof., 1904-11, prof. English lit., May 1911-14, Williams College; prin. Phillips Exeter Academy 1914-46. Mem. N.H. Hist. Soc., Am. Philol. Assn., Alpha Delta Phi (nat. pres. 1931-33). Conglist. Mason (K.T.). Clubs: Alpha Delta Phi, Williams, Century Assn. (New York); Harvard, Tavern (Boston). Editor: Marlowe's Jew of Malta," 1908. Address: Boston MA Died Mar. 1970.

PERRY, MIDDLETON LEE, physician; b. Lancaster, Tex., Aug. 15, 1868; s. Middleton and Ellen (Ellis) P.; student U. of Tex., 1888-89; M.D., U. of Tenn., 1892; grad. study U. of Va., U. of Vienna, Austria; m. Jamie Wimberly, Jan. 16, 1902 (now dec.); children—Middleton Lee, Wimberly Raymond. Asst. physician N.J. State Hosp., Morris Plains, 1894-98; pathologist Ga. State Sanitarium, Milledgeville, 1899-1903; supt. State Hosp. for Epileptics, Parsons, Kan., 1903-18; supt. Topeka (Kan.) State Hosp. since 1918. Mem. Am. and Kan. State med. assns., Shawnee County Med. Soc., Am. Psychiatric Assn., Central Neuropsychiatric Assn. Democrat. Address: State Hospital, Topeka KS‡

PERRY, RICHARD ROSS, JR., lawyer; b. Washington, D.C., Sept. 4, 1871; s. Richard Ross and Callie (Thaw) P.; A.B., Harvard, 1892; LL.B., Georgetown U., 1894, LL.M., 1895; unmarried. Mem. R. Ross Perry & Son, 1895 until death of father, 1915, since alone, at Washington. Mem. Phi Beta Kappa (Harvard), Delta Chi (Georgetown U.). Republican. Episcopalian. Clubs: Metropolitan (Washington, D.C.); Chevy Chase (Md.); Harvard (New York). Home: 1635 Massachusetts Av. Office: Union Trust Bldg., Washington DC‡

PERRY, WILLIAM L., tobacco co. exec.; b. Osceola, Ann (Motley) P.; student Trinity Coll. (now Duke U.), 1918-19; m. Alice Lee Barbee, Oct. 11, 1919. Joined Liggett & Myers Tobacco Co., N.Y.C., 1920, assistant secretary treasurer, 1946-50, treasurer, director, 1950-54, vice president and director, 1954-61, chairman of executive committee, from 1959. Methodist. Clubs: Hudson River Country (Yonkers, N.Y.); Rockefeller Center Luncheon, Union League (N.Y.C.). Home: Cumberland House New York City NY Died Feb. 18, 1967.

PERSON, JOHN L., assn. exec.; b. Attleboro, Mass., Dec. 16, 1907; s. Axel and Grace (Woodbury) P.; B.S., U.S. Mil. Acad., 1929; B.S. in Civil Engring., Mass. Inst. Tech., 1932; postgrad. Berlin Tech. Inst., 1938-39, Nat. War Coll., 1947-48; m. Beth Christian, Aug. 26, 1932; 1 son, John L. Commd. 2d lt. U.S. Army, 1929, advanced through grades to brig. gen.; comdg. officer Mil. Pipeline Service, dep. chief engr. ETO, 1944-45; mem. Miss River Commn., 1954-56; mem. bd. engring. for rivers and harbors, 1954-56; dir. civil works Office Chief Engrs., 1956-59; ret., 1959; exec. cons., 1959-65; exec. v.p. Nat. Rivers and Harbors Congress, Washington, 1965-69. Decorated D.S.M., Legion of Merit with oak leaf cluster, Medailee de Reconnaissance. Fellow Am. Soc. C.E.; mem. Permanent Internat. Assn. Navigation Congresses (past chmn. Am. sect.), Soc. Am. Kensington MD Died Oct. 3, 1969; buried Arlington Nat. Cemetery, Arlington VA

PERSONS, JOHN WILLIAMS, air force officer; b. Montgomery, Ala., Sept. 19, 1899; s. Frank Stanford and Kate Minnis (Abrams) P.; grad. Gulf Coast Mil. Acad., Gulfport, Miss., 1915; student Ala. Poly. Inst.; grad. AC Tactical Sch., Maxwell Field, Ala., 1939; m. Juliette Florence McLendon, Mar. 19, 1927; 1 dau., Juliette (Mrs. Charles S. Doster, Jr.). Served as 2d lt. Royal Flying Corps, Can., 1917-19; commd. 2d lt. AC, U.S. Army, 1929, advanced through grades to maj. gen. USAAF, 1953; flying instr. AC Advanced Flying Sch., Kelly Field, Tex., 1939; comdr. 54th Bomb Squadron, Maxwell Field, 1939; chief test Eglin AFB, Fla., 1941; dir. tng. AC Advanced Flying Sch., Moody Field, Ga., 1942; comdr. Marianna Army Air Field, Fla., 1942; comdr. Atsugi Army Air Field, Japan, 1945-46; chief USAF Flying Safety Service, Langley Field, Va., 1946, insp. gen. 1st Region, Langley AFB, 1948-50; comdr. Alaska AF Depot, 1953; dep. comdr. Alaskan Air Command, 1953; dep. dir. personnel procurement and tng., Hdqrs. AF, Washington, 1953-54; comdr. 3510th Flying Tng. Wing, Randolph AFB, Tex., 1954-57; comdr. 14th Air Force, Robins AFB, Ga., 1957-72. Decorated Legion of Merit with cluster. Mem. Phi Delta Theta. Address: Robins AFB GA Died Jan. 1972.

PETEET, WALTON, agricultural economist; b. Pelham, Ala., Nov. 6, 1869; s. William Young and Nancy (Young) P.; ed. Livingston (Ala.) Acad.; m. Carrie Cleere, of Russellville, Ala., Mar. 31, 1897; children—George Walton, Walton, Harrington. Originator, 1913, and organizer rural credit system in Tex., and author original cooperative law of Tex.; dir. commodity orgn. Tex. Farm Bur. Federation, 1920-23; dir. cooperative marketing for Am. Farm Bur. Federation, Chicago, Ill., Feb. 1-Dec. 12, 1923; sec. Nat. Council Farmers' Cooperative Marketing assns., Washington, D.C. since Jan. 1, 1924. Ex-pres. bd. dirs. Agrl. and Mech. Coll. of Tex. Democrat. Methodist. Mason (32 deg.). Author of the first child labor law in Tex., and many bulls. on cooperative marketing. Home: Dallas, Tex. Address: Burlington Hotel, Washington DC‡

PETER, MARC, diplomat; b. Geneva, Switerland, Dec. 21, 1873; Coll. and U. of Geneva, Licence en droit, 1895, Doctorat en droit, 1897; m. Jeanne Lachenal, of Geneva, Apr. 27, 1901; children—T. Georges, Marc. Judge in Geneva, 1898-1901; practiced law, 1901-19; mem. Swiss Parliament, 1911-19; E.E. and M.P. from Switzerland to U.S., Nov. 1919—. Author: Le Syndic Butin et la reunion de Geneve a la France, 1914; Geneve et la Revolution, 1921; Une amie de Voltaire, Madame Gallatin, 1925. Contbr. to various hist. publs. Home: 6 Kalorama Circle. Office: 2419 Massachusetts Av., Washington DC‡

PETERMAN, MYNIE GUSTAV, pediatrist; b. Merrill, Wis., Mar. 5, 1896; s. Albert Frederick and Ida (Braatz) P.; Sc.B., U. of Wis., 1918; A.M., Washington U., St. Louis, 1920; M.D., Washington U. Sch. of Medicine, 1921 (fellowship, scholarship, 1920-21); m. Mildred Mackenzie, Sept. 29, 1924; children—Albert Frederick, Mary Jean. Practiced as physician in Milwaukee since 1925; introduced new treatment for epilepsy in childhood, 1924, new test for syphilis, 1927, classification for convulsions, 1933; chief resident physician City and County Hosp., St. Paul, 1921-22; fellow, 1st asst. and asso. in pediatrics, Mayo Foundation and Clinic, 1922-25; dir. laboratories and research, Milwaukee Children's Hosp., 1925-33; former chief staff Milwaukee County Hospital; med. dir. Nat. Children's Rehab. Center, 1967-68; cons. USPHS Bur. Indian Affairs; cons. Bur. Medicine, FDA, med. staff drug surveillance br., 1964-67; cons. staff Columbia Hosp., Milw. In Chem. Warfare Div. U. Wis., 1917-18; 1st sgt. S.A.T.C., 1918, World War; 1st lt. Med. R.C., 1924, col., 1950. Diplomate Am. Bd. Pediatrics. Fellow Am. Acad. Neurology; mem. A.M.A., Internat. Congress Pediatrics, Am. Academy of Pediatrics, Central Soc. Clin. Research, American Association for research Nervous and Mental Diseases, Wis. State and Milwaukee Co. med. soc., Am. Epilepsy Soc., Milw. Pediatric Soc., Osler Soc., Madrid Pediatric Society, Sigma Xi, Phi Sigma. Clubs: Army and Navy, Torch (Washington). Author chpts. in med. works and research articles in med. publs. Editor English transl. Diseases of Children (5 vols.), 1935. Home: Milwaukee WI Died Oct. 14, 1971.

PETERS, HEBER WALLACE, executive; born at New Bedford, Massachusetts, December 13, 1892; s. Heber Cushing and Agnes Winonah (Thurber) P.; A.B., Cornell U., 1914; m. Elsie Frieda Germain, Sept. 1, 1922; children—Wallace Cushing, Joy Germain. Sec., Cornell U., 1914-16; asst. to pres. Packard Motor Co., Detroit, Mich., 1916-18, office mgr., 1919-21, gen. mgr. Detroit Br., 1921-24, Packard Motor Co. of Chicago, 1924-28; v.p. of distribution Packard Motor Co., 1928-32; asst. gen. sales mgr. Cadillac Motor Car Co., 1934-36; investment counselor, Detroit, 1936-38; provost, Cornell U., 1938-43; executive Edward G. Budd Mfg. Co., 1943-45; vice president, John Price Jones Corp., 1946-51, G.A. Brakeley & Co., 1962-65. Devel. cons. Bowdoin Coll., 1958-61. Woods Hole Oceanographic Instn., 1959-64. Trustee Air Force Museum Foundation. Chairman of the Tompkins County chapter, Am. Red Cross, 1941-43. Served as pursuit pilot, 1st lt. Air Service, U.S. Army, and officer in charge of flying, Field No. 9, 3d Aviation Instrn. Center, Issoudun, France, 1918-19; cited for exceptionally meritorious service. Mem. Foreign Policy Assn., Phi Delta Theta. Republican. Clubs: Cornell of Mich., Cornell, University (N.Y.C.). Home: Summit NJ Died Dec. 27, 1971.

PETERS, JAMES, educator; b. Sheridan, Wyo., May 1, 1909; s. George E. and Dora (Starr) P.; grad. high sch.; m. Jacqueline J. Johnston, Nov. 23, 1932; children—Karolee K. (Mrs. Roderick Downing), Ronald J. Partner, A.W. Johnston Sch. Bus., Billings, Mont., 1932-42, also mgr. advt. sheet Billings Reminder; pub. accountant San Francisco area, 1946-51; tchr. Heald Coll., Sacramento, San Jose Cal., 1952-56, prin. Sacramento, 1954-55; pres. Stenotype Schs. for Bus. and Reporting, San Francisco, Sacramento, Carmichael, Redwood City, Cal., 1956-66. Mem. San Francisco, Sacramento, U.S. chambers commerce, Better Bus. Bur. San Francisco, Sacramento. Arranged carrying of class in stenotype in various Cal. prisons. Home: San Diego CA Died Apr. 9, 1967.

PETERS, JAMES ARTHUR, biologist; b. Durant, Ia., July 13, 1922; s. Arthur J. and Jane Terrell (Pascoe) P.; student U. Ill., 1941-42; B.S., U. Mich., 1948, M.A., 1950, Ph.D., 1952; postgrad. student U. Tex., 1950; m. Beatriz Moisset de Espanes, June 18, 1964; 1 son, Steven; children by previous marriage—Jane, Arthur James, Jennifer Laura, Druscilla Anne, Jeffrey Edward. Mem. faculty Brown U., 1952-58, asst. prof. biology, 1955-58; Fulbright prof., Quito, Ecuador, 1958-59; asso. prof., then prof. biology San Fernando Valley State Coll., Northridge, Cal., 1959-64; asso. curator Smithsonian Instn., Washington, 1964-66, curator and supr., 1966-72. Served with USAAF, 1942-45. Fellow Herpetologists League; mem. Am. Soc. Ichtyologists and Herpetologists (pres. 1970), Soc. Study Evolution, Soc. Systematic Zoology, Brit. Herpetological Soc. Herpetological Assn. Africa, Assn. Tropical Biology (asso. editor 1969-70), Biol. Soc. Washington, S. Cal. Acad. Scis. Author: Snakes of the Subfamily Dipsadinae, 1960; (with others) Catalogue of Neotropical Squamata, 1970. Editor: Classic Papers in Genetics, 1959. Compiler: Dictionary of Herpetology, 1964. Cons. Am. Heritage Dictionary, Ency. Brit. Home: Rockville MD Died Dec. 18, 1972; buried Greenup IL

PETERS, JOHN RUSSELL, physician, educator; b. Cin., Oct. 4, 1896; s. Ezra and Lillian (Hodge) P.; B.S., M.D., Ohio State U., 1928; m. Gertrude Elvina Mann, Dec. 24, 1918; 1 dau., Gwendolyn Carol (Mrs. Robert A. Jasperson). Intern St. Francis Hosp., Columbus, O., 1928; mem. staff VA Hosp., Chillicothe, O., 1929-34; asst. to asst. prof. psychiatry, U. Louisville, 1934-50; asst. supt. Dayton (O.) State Hosp., 1950-51; asso. prof., then prof. psychiatry, now emeritus Loma Linda U.; sr. attending psychiatrist Los Angeles County Gen. Hosp., 1951-68; dir. Glendale (Cal.) Mental Health Service, 1956-59, Los Angeles County Assn. Mental Health, 1956-58; dir. out-patient dept. White Meml. Hosp., Los Angeles, 1952-60; sr. cons. Armed Forces Examining St., Los Angeles, 1952-68. Mem. bd. dirs. Asheville Rural Sch. and Sanitarium, 1953-68. Served from lt. comdr. to capt., USNR, 1940-47. Diplomate Am. Bd. Psychiatry and Neurology. Fellow Am. Psychiat. Assn., A.A.A.S., A.M.A.; mem. Cal., Los Angeles County med. socs., Los Angeles Assn. Neurology and Psychiatry. Address: Glendale CA Died Feb. 20, 1968.

PETERS, RAYMOND ELMER, judge; b. Oakland, Cal., Apr. 17, 1903; s. Frank J. and Mabel C. (Whitaker) P.; A.B., U. Cal. at Berkeley, 1925, J.D., 1927; m. Marion Estabrook, July 23, 1928; children—Janet (Mrs. Arthur Garrison), Douglas Kirk (dec.). Admitted to Cal. bar, 1927; asso. Garret W. McEnerny, San Francisco, 1927-29; partner Louis R. Deadrich, Oakland, Cal., 1929-30; chief law sect. Cal. Supreme Ct., 1930-39, asso. justice, 1959-73; presiding justice Dist. Ct. Appeal, 1st Appellate Dist., San Francisco, 1939-59; instr. law. Oakland Coll. Law, 1927-39. Vice pres. Cal. League Am. Indians, 1957-73; dir. San Francisco Law Sch.; trustee Franklin Hosp., 1956-59; pres. Intertribal Friendship House, Oakland. Mem. Cal. Conf. Judges (pres. 1948-49), No. Cal. Service League (pres. bd. dirs. 1948-60), Alumni Assn. Sch. Law U. Cal. (pres. 1954-55), Am. Friends Service Com. (chmn. Indian com. East Bay), Cal. Heritage Council (bd. trustees 1961-73), Order of Coif. Club: Commonwealth (San Francisco). Contbr. articles law jours. Home: Berkeley CA Died Jan. 2, 1973.

PETERSEN, ANDREW N., congressman; b. in Denmark, Mar. 10, 1870; s. Tyler and Hansina (Furst) P.; brought to U.S. in infancy; ed. pub. schs., Boston, Mass. and Brooklyn, N.Y.; m. Olga E. Holch, of Brooklyn, 1896. Learned pattern maker's trade, and began on own account, 1893; started foundry, 1900, now pres. and treas. Brooklyn Foundry Co. Mem. 67th Congress (1921-23), 9th N.Y. Dist. Republican. Mason (K.T.). Home: 319 Highland Blvd., Brooklyn NY‡

PETERSEN, HJALMAR, gov. Minn.; b. Eskildstrup, near Svendborg, Denmark, Jan. 2, 1890; s. Lauritz and Anna (Hansen) P.; m. Rigmor Wosgaard, Aug. 5, 1914 (died 1930); 1 dau., Evelyn; m. 2d, Medora Belle Grandprey, June 28, 1934; 1 dau., Karla Jeannette. Came to U.S., 1891, naturalized through father's papers. Worked as printer on Minn. and S.D. newspapers, 1904-14; established Askov (Minn.) American, editor and pub. Served as member Minn. State House of Representatives, 1931-35; elected lt. gov. of Minn., 1934, and succeeded to office of gov., 1936, to fill unexpired term, 1935-37; elected to R.R. and Warehouse Commn., 1936; candidate for nomination for gov., primary election, June 1938; nominee for gov., general election, Nov. 1940 and 1942, on Farmer-Labor ticket; candidate for nomination for gov., primary election, July, 1946, on Republican ticket; elected railroad and warehouse commr., 1954, 60; ret., 1967. Pres. Am. Pub. Co. Lutheran. Home: Askov MN Died Mar. 29, 1968; buried Askov Cemetery, Askov MN

PETERSEN, WILLIAM EARL, educator; b. Pine City, Minn., Feb. 3, 1892; s. Matz and Mary Kathryn (Sorensen) P.; B.S., U. Minn., 1916, M.S., 1917, Ph.D., 1928; D.Sc. (honorary), University of Vermont, 1956; married Alma Agnes Lindstrom, Aug. 24, 1917; children—Dorothy May (Mrs. John F. Grimmel), William Earl, Allan Donald, Raymond George, Joanne Marlene. Dairy extension specialist Kan. State Coll., 1917-20; field sec. Holstein Frierian Assn., Minn., 1920-21; mem. faculty U. Minn. from 1921, prof. dairy husbandry, from 1943; hon. prof. Peru Agricultural Coll., LaMolina, Peru. Decorated Knight Cross Order of Danneborg (Denmark); recipient Borden award, 1942; Morrison award, Am. Soc. Animal Prodn., 1956; listed One Hundred Living Great in Minnesota, 1949. Foreign honorary member Royal Academy Agr., Sweden, 1945. Member New York Academy Science, Society Exptl. Biology and Medicino, Am. Chem. Soc., A.A.A.S., Am. Genetic Assn., Am. Soc. Animal Prodn., Am. Physiol. Soc., Am. Dairy Sci. Assn. (pres. 1949-50), Sigma Xi (state pres. 1951), Gamma Alpha (nat. treas. 1932-40), Alpha Zeta, Alpha Gamma Rho. Unitarian. Producer tech. motion picture in color, The Science of Milk Production, 1945, No Hand Stripping (in 7 langs.), 1947. Author: Dairy Science, 1939 (1950); American Agriculture (with A. Boss, H. K. Wilson), 4 vols., 1939-46. Contbr. articles sci. jours. Home: St Paul MN Died Mar. 15, 1971.

PETERSON, ELMER THEODORE, editor; b. Algona, Ia., June 23, 1884; s. Sven Peter and Emma Christina (Runbeck) P.; B.A., Bethany Coll. (Kan.), 1906, Litt.D., 1928; m. Ora Webster, June 11, 1907; children—Webster Theodore, Edwin Paul, Philip Erik. Began as editor Lindsborg Record, 1905; became editor and owner Cimarron (Kan.) Jacksonian, 1907; telegraph editor Wichita Eagle, 1916; reporter Kansas City Star, 1917; with Wichita Beacon, 1917-27, resigning as editor; editor Better Homes and Gardens magazine, 1927-37; later asso. editor Daily Oklahoman, Oklahoma City. Mem. City Planning Commn., Oklahoma City; bd. dirs. Okla. chpt. Arthritis and Rheumatism Found. Winner of Editor and Publisher" war editorial contest, October 1918. One of first promoters of transcontinental highway movement; promoter for soil conservation. Mem. Friends of the Land (mem. Nat. bd. of dirs.; mem. bd. dirs. Oklahoma City chpt.), Sigma Delta Chi. Republican. Meth. Mason. Clubs: Men's Dinner (Oklahoma City); Rotary Club. Author: Trumpets West, 1934; Forward to the Land, 1941; Cities Are Abnormal, 1945. Contbr. to mags. Address: Oklahoma City OK Died May 1969.

PETERSON, JOHN VALDEMAR, retired naval officer; b. Harlan, Ia., Dec. 22, 1898; s. Paul and Emma (Jorgensen) P.; B.S., U.S. Naval Acad., 1923; m. Elizabeth Greene, Feb. 28, 1931; 1 dau., Marcia St. John. Commd. ensign, U.S.N., 1923, served in fleet, 1923-25, naval aviator, on U.S. Saratoga and U.S.S. Ranger, 1926-52, retired as rear adm., 1952; prof. naval sic. U. Kan., 1946-48, U. Cal. at Berkeley, 1951-53. Decorated Distinguished Flying Cross, Legion of Merit, Presidential Unit Citation, Netherlands Distinguished Service Medal. Mem. Delta Upsilon. Club: San Diego Country (Chula Vista, Cal.). Home: Coronado CA Died May 1968.

PETERSON, MELL ANDREW, orgn. exec.; born Algona, Ia., Sept. 7, 1908; s. Albert Leroy and Viva Beatrice (Norton) P.; B.S., U.S. Naval Acad., 1930; student ordnance engring., Naval Postgrad Sch., 1936-39; m. Ann M. Murtagh, Sept. 17, 1931; children—Mell, Charles A., Elizabeth Ann. Commd. ensign, USN, 1930, advanced through grades to rear adm., 1959; indsl. control and mfg. officer Naval Weapons Plant, Washington, 1951-52; comdg. officer Naval Ordnance Plant, Indpls., 1952-54; asst. chief Bur. Ordnance, Navy Dept., 1957-58; comdr. Naval Ordnance Lab., White Oaks, Silver Spring, Md., 1958-59, ret.; exec. v.p., dir. Bulova Research & Development Labs., Inc., Woodside, N.Y., 1959-61; corporate devel. planning, Northrop Corp., Beverly Hills, Cal., 1962-63; Western rep., exec. dir. Los Angeles Post Am. Ordnance Assn., 1963—. Profl. engr., D.C. Decorated Silver Star, Bronze Star. Mason. Clubs: Kiwanis (Indpls.); N.Y. Yacht. Home: Los Angeles CA Died Dec. 1970.

PETTEGREW, MARION EDGAR, mgmt. cons.; b. Danville, Ill., Mar. 19, 1908; s. Parke and Emma Eleanor (Price) P.; student Ohio State U., 1925-31; m. Louise Faber Johnson, Aug. 23, 1928; 1 son, Robert Parke. Partner, Parke Pettegrew & Son Co., Columbus, O., 1932-42; mfg. supt., personnel dir. Chase Brass & Copper Co., Cleve., 1942-45; mgr. employee relations Ethyl Corp., Baton Rouge, also N.Y.C., 1945-49; dir. pub. and employee relations Swank, Inc., Attleboro, Mass., 1949-51, v.p. mfg., 1951-53; gen. mgr. parts div. Sylvania Elec. Products, Inc., Warren, Pa., 1953-56 v.p. operations, 1956-58, sr. v.p., 1958-62; pres., dir. Erie Resistor Corp., Erie Resistor of Can., Ltd., Fryling Mfg. Co., Fryling Electric Products, Inc., Electron Research, Inc., Elgin Labs., Inc., until 1964; now mgmt. cons. Dir. Shelmark Industries, Inc. Trustee, Ohio Real Estate Investment Co. Mem. Worthington OH Died Oct. 17, 1972.

PETTERSON, LEROY DAVID, mining exec., pharm. chemist; b. Lee, Nev., June 28, 1885; s. Niles Fredrick and Elizabeth B. (Ogilvie) P.; Pharm. Chemist, U. Cal. Coll. Pharmacy, 1910; m. Lillian L. Abbee, Dec. 8, 1913 (div. 1924); children—Carmon E. (Mrs. Russel Clardy), Le Roy Hampton; m. Laura Powers, Apr. 8, 1928; 1 dau., Georgia Lou (Mrs. Grant W. Trimlett). Pharmacist, Palace Hotel Pharmacy, San Francisco, 1909-11; asst. adv. mgr. Owl Drug Co., San Francisco, 1912-13; mgr. ranch, 1913-15; druggist Kimberlin Drug Co., Kingsburg, Cal., 1915-16; raisin farmer, nr. Selma, Cal., 1916; wheat farmer, nr. Lincoln, Cal., 1916-19; druggist J. A. Riley Co., Chico, Cal., 1919-20; pharm. chemist Napa (Cal.) State Hosp., 1922-25, Patton State Hosp., 1925-32; mgr. Petterson Titus Labs., 1932-38; druggist Thrifty Drug Co., San Bernardino, Cal., 1939-40, Arcade Drug Co., Colton, Cal., 1940-45, Sav on Drugs, San Bernardino, 1945-59. Gen. mgr. Shiffer Mining Syndicate, Los Angeles, 1958-70; pres. LeRoy D. Petterson & Assos., San Bernardino, 1958-70. Bd. dirs. Shiffer Assos. Sci. Found., 1960-70, pres., 1963-70; bd. dirs. mem. exec. council Thinking Unlimited, Inc. Recipient certificate of appreciation Cal. Bd. Pharmacy, 1965. Mem. Cal. Pharm. Assn., Cal. Alumni Assn. (life), Pharmacy Alumni Assn. (life), Nev. Mining Assn. (asso.), Retail Clks. Internat. Assn. (life), Phi Delta Chi. Presbyn. (deacon). Mason (K.T.); member Order Eastern Star. Research in earth metals. Home: San Bernardino CA Died Apr. 9, 1970.

PETTEYS, ALONZO, banker; b. Wilcox, Neb., Nov. 25, 1887; s. Willard Alonzo and Cora (Swain) P.; A.B., Grinnell Coll., 1911; Doctor of Laws, Grinnell College, 1961; married Anna C. Feddersen, May 6, 1914; children—Helen C. (Mrs. Warren M. Watrous), Anne Mae (Mrs. Lyle Pattee), Robert Alonzo. Cashier Weldon Valley Bank, Weldona, Colo., 1912-20, Farmers State Bank, Brush, 1920-35, vice pres., 1935-61, president, from 1961, director, from 1920; pres., director Equitable Savings & Loan Assn., Brush, Colo., Farmers Realty. Co., Brush; chmn. bd., director Denver Basin Oil Company, Brush; dir. N.W. Airlines. Pub. Service Co., Colorado. Awarded Colo. U. Sch. of Bus. award for Outstanding Colo. Businessman for 1945. Mem. Am. Bankers Assn. (mem. exec. council, 1930-33, Country Bank Operations Commn., 1948-49, mem. pub. relations council, 1948-49), Colo. Bankers Assn. (pres. 1929-30), Newcomen Soc. North America. Republican. Elk. Mason (Shriner). Clubs: Denver, Denver Press (Denver). Home: Boulder City NV Died Mar. 21, 1968; buried Brush Meml. Cemetery, Brush CO

PETTIS, CHARLES EMERSON, cons. civil engr.; b. Salem, O., July 16, 1901; s. Charles Willis and Cora (Norris) P.; student Mt. Union Coll., 1918-20; B.C.E., Ohio State U., 1923, C.E., 1933; m. Genevieve Marie Kenyon, Dec. 11, 1923; 1 dau., Marilyn Joyce (Mrs. Lisle E. Nied). Instrumentman, N.Y.C. R.R., Toledo, 1923-27, asst. supr. bldgs., 1927-31, asst. engr., 1931-32; asst. engr. Champe, Finkbeiner & Assos., Toledo, 1932-40; partner Finkbeiner, Pettis & Strout, Toledo, 1940-64, mng. partner, 1965-70, cons.; cons. civil engring. Named Toledo Area Engr. of the Year, 1969. Registered profl. engr., Ohio, Mich., Ind., Ill., Ga., Ky., Tenn., S.C., Va., W.Va.; certified Am. San. Engring. Intersoc. Bd. Mem. Tech. Soc. Toledo, Nat., Ohio, Toledo socs. profl. engrs., Am. Soc. C.E., Cons. Engrs. of Ohio (recipient Distinguished Cons. award 1970), Mich. Engring. Soc., Ohio Water Pollution Control Conf., Water Pollution Control Fedn., Am. Waterworks Assn., Am. Acad. San. Engrs., Ohio State U. Assn., Sigma Nu. Presbyn. Kiwanian. Club: Toledo. Address: Toledo OH Died May 22, 1972.

PETTITT, BYRON BUCK, oil co. exec.; b. De-Ridder, La., Oct. 2, 1910; s. Bernard Montgomery and Minnie Green (Robertson) P.; student Houston Law Sch., 1932-33; grad. mgmt. problems for execs. course, U. Pitts., 1953; m. Dorothy Ann Morcock, Jan. 13, 1934 (dec. Feb. 1944); children—Julia Ann, Byron Buck; m. 2d, Jymme Nowlan, Dec. 19, 1946; 1 son, Bernard Montgomery III. With Gulf Oil Corp., 1929-68, div. gen. mgr. Chgo. div., 1958-60, Houston div., 1960, v.p. charge S.W. marketing region, 1960-63; adminstr. sales level. domestic marketing hdqrs., 1963-68; exec. v.p. Gulf Tire & Supply Co., 1965-68. Active Houston United Fund. Mem. Texas Mfrs. Assn. (dir.-at-large; life mem.), Am. Petroleum Inst., Houston C. of C. (life), Houston Better Bus. Bur. (life). Methodist. Mason. Clubs: Houston, Internat. (Houston). Home: Houston TX Died Feb. 25, 1969; buried Memorial Oaks Cemetery, Houston TX

PETTUS, JAMES THOMAS, shoe company exec.; b. Davidson Co., Tenn., Jan. 31, 1874; s. Joseph A. and Mary Alice (Roberts) P.; A.B., South Ky. Coll., 1892; m. May Watkins, Mar. 7, 1914; children—Irene (Mrs. Philip Kingsland Crowe), James Thomas. Stock Clk. Rice Stix & Co., St.L., 1892-98; with Roberts, Johnson & Rand Shoe Co., 1898-1911; v.p. Internat. Shoe Co., 1911-48, dir. since 1911. Democrat. Mem. Christian Ch. Home: 23 Braeburn Dr., Country Club Grounds, Clayton, Mo. Office: 1509 Washington Av., St Louis 3‡

PETTUS, WILLIAM JERDONE, M.D.; b. Va., Sept. 5, 1862; M.D., Med. Coll. of Va., Richmond, 1884; m. Daisy Caden. Asst. surgeon, U.S. Pub. Health Service, 1886-90, passed asst. surgeon, 1890-99, surgeon, 1899-1917, sr. surgeon since 1917. Fellow Am. Coll. of Surgeons, A.M.A.; mem. S.C. Med. Assn. Office: 68 S. Battery, Charleston SC*‡

PEW, J(OHN) HOWARD, industrialist; born Bradford, Pa., Jan. 27, 1882; son of Joseph Newton and Mary Catherine (Anderson) P.; ed. Shadyside Acad., Pitts., Grove City (Pa.) Coll., Mass. Inst. Tech.; m. Helen Jennings Thompson, Jan. 3, 1907 (dec. 1963). Engr. Marcus Hook Refinery, Sun Oil Co., 1901, and successively asst. supt., supt., vice pres., then president, 1912-47; chmn. bd. Sun Oil Company; director Sun Shipbuilding & Dry Dock Company. President bd. of trustees Grove City College. President bd. trustees United Presbyterian Found. Republican. Presbyterian. Clubs: Union League (Phila.); Merion Golf, Merion Cricket (Haverford, Pa.). Home: Ardmore PA Died Nov. 27, 1971.

PEYTON, GARLAND, geologist; b. Mt. Airy, Ga., Oct. 2, 1892; s. John Thomas and Emma Jane (Ayers) P.; B.S., E.M., Sch. Mines N. Ga. Agrl. Coll., 1914; student, Ohio State U., 1926, U. Minn., 1930; m. Martha Gara Griswold, Aug. 28, 1918; children—Garland, Martha Ann, Barbara Jane. Mining engr. U.S. Smelting, Refining & Mining Co., 1914-17; dir. Sch. Mines N. Ga. Agrl. Coll., 1919-29; research engr. Tenn. Copper Co., 1929-31; state mining engr. Ga. Dept. Mines and Geology, 1937-38; dir., state geologist Ga. Dept. Mines, Mining and Geology, from 1938. Served as 1st lt., inf., U.S. Army, 1917-19, as capt., 1933-37. Mem. Geol. Soc. Am., Am. Assn. Petroleum Geologist, Am. Inst. Mining and Metall. Engrs., Soc. Econ. Geologists, Assn. Am. State Geologist (pres. 1948), Pi Kappa Alpha, Sigma Gamma Epsilon. Democrat. Baptist. Mason, Elk. Home: Decatur GA Died Oct. 18, 1964.

PFEIFFER, TIMOTHY NEWELL, lawyer; b. Camden, N.J., Nov. 3, 1886; s. George and Adaline (Adams) P.; grad. William Penn Charter Sch., Phila., Pa., 1904; A.B., Princeton, 1908; LL.B., Harvard, 1912; m. Eleanor Knox Wheeler, June 10, 1914; children—Egbert Wheeler, Timothy Adams, Katharine Bradford, Eleanor Knox. Admitted to N.Y. bar, 1912, practicing at N.Y. City; dep. asst. dist. atty. N.Y. County, 1913-15; counsel Am. Social Hygiene Association, 1915-17, former treas.; spl. dep. atty. gen. N.Y., in prosecutions under Anti-Trust Act, 1921-22, in Nassau County Investigations, 1923; mem. Milbank, Tweed, Hadley & McCloy. Chief counsel N.Y. State Temp. Commn. Courts, 1956-57; vice chmn. N.Y. State Temp. Commn. on Revision Penal Law, 1961-71. Trustee Teachers Coll. Columbia University, Woodrow Wilson Found. (v.p.). Served as capt. Sanitary Corps, U.S. Army; War Dept. Commn. on Training Camp Activities, later transferred to F.A. Camp Taylor, World War. Organizer, 1917, Voluntary Defenders Com. for Criminal Courts. Mem. Am. Bar Assn., Am. Law Inst. (mem. council, adv. drafting code of criminal procedure), N.Y. State, N.Y. City (v.p.) bar assns., Legal Aid Society N.Y. (pres., 1950-55, dir.), Nat. Health Council (treas., 1937-48), Nat. Probation and Parole Assn. (pres., 1937-41); The Youth House (v.p. and dir. 1944-55), N.Y. City Mission Society (director). Presbyn. Clubs: Century, University. Home: New York City NY Died Feb. 12, 1971.

PFEIL, JOHN SIMON, corp. exec.; born Wertheim, Baden, Germany, Aug. 24, 1889; s. Simon and Elizabeth (von Oberndorff) vonP.; ed. schs. of Heidelberg, Germany; grad. Harvard, 1913; m. Marie deCoen, Oct. 31, 1922; children—Theodor, John S. New England mgr. Frigidaire Div., Gen. Motors Corp., Boston, 1913-41; v.p. Stone & Webster, Inc., N.Y.C., 1946-56, ret.; v.p. Am. Ordnance Assn.; treas. and director of Associated Industries of Massachusetts. Commissioner Massachusetts Port Authority. Served as col., ordnance dist. chief, Boston Ordnance Dist., U.S. Army, 1941-46. Decorated Legion of Merit. Received Gold Medal of Am. Ordnance Assn., 1954. Mem. Benjamin Franklin Found., Franklin Inst. (v.p.). Republican. Clubs: Down Town, Harvard. Home: Wellesley Hills MA Died June 1967; buried Newton MA

PFEILER, WILLIAM KARL, univ. prof.; b. Braunschweig, Germany, Dec. 7, 1897; s. Robert and Sophie (Lismann) P.; certificate of maturity, Realgymnasium, 1920; student U. of Bonn, 1920-21; Ph.D., U. of Cologne, 1924; student Stanborough Coll., Eng., summer 1925, U. of Mich., summer 1928; m. Mildred Corinne Erickson, June 20, 1928; children—Robert Charles, William Lawrence. Came to U.S., 1926, naturalized, 1932. Instr. Neanderthal Sem., Germany, 1924-26; asso. prof. history and German, Union Coll., Neb., 1926-28; instr. U. of Neb., Lincoln, 1928-31, asst. prof., 1931-36, asso. prof., 1936-43, prof. German language and literature 1943-67, professor emeritus, 1967-70, chmn. dept., 1950-63; visiting professor, Germany, 1958. Served with German army, 1916-19; in employ of U.S. War Dept., 1944. Mem. Mod. Lang. Assn. Am., Mod. Humanities Research Assn., Raabe-Gesellschaft (Germany), Phi Beta Kappa. Democrat. Presbyterian. Club: Pen (German sect. London). Author: In Deutschland (with J. E. A. Alexis), 1930, rev. edit., 1937, Faust als repräsentativer Mensch (Germanic Rev. VI, 1, 1931), Uncle Sam and his English (with E. Wittmann) (Berlin, 1932), Coleridge and Schelling's Treatise on the Samothracian Deities (Modern Languages Notes, March 1937), War and the German Mind (Columbia U. Press, 1941); German for Children (with Carter and Dolezal), 1956; German Literature in Exile, 1957. Contbr. to Columbia Dictionary of Modern European Literature, N.Y., 1947, Ency. Americana, 1955. Home: Lincoln NE Died Jan. 31, 1970; buried Lincoln (Neb.) Meml. Cemetery.

PFISTERER, HENRY ALBERT, educator, cons. engr.; b. Hyde Park, N.Y., June 11, 1908; s. Albert G. and Louise (Beck) P.; C.E., Cornell U., 1929; M.A. (hon.), Yale, 1957; m. Hortense Marchessault, Aug. 26, 1939; children—Carole E., Charles H. A. Engr., H. G. Balcom, 1929-30; instr. engring. Cornell U., 1930-33; engr. Nat. Park Service, 1934-38, Wilcox & Erickson, 1939-41; asst. prof. architecture Yale, 1941-46, asso. prof., 1946-56, prof., 1956-72; cons. engr., New Haven, 1941-72; partner Wilcox, Erickson & Pfisterer, 1941-50; owner Henry A. Pfisterer, cons. engr., 1951-72; dir. New Haven Trap Rock Co. Mem. Hamden Zoning and Planning Commn.; pres. Conn. Bldg. Congress, 1955-56, Conn. Fedn. Planning and Zoning Agencies, 1958. Mem. Conn. (past dir.), Nat. socs. profl. engrs., Am. Soc. C.E., Am. Concrete Inst., Conn. Soc. Civil Engrs. Clubs: Quinnipiack; Faculty (Yale); Cornell (N.Y.C.). Author: (with Harold Dana Hauf) Design of Steel Buildings, 1949. Home: Hamden CT Died May 26, 1972.

PFLAGER, HENRY BARBER, lawyer; b. Chgo., Sept. 22, 1903; s. Harry Miller and Alyce (Barber) P.; B.A., Princeton, 1926; LL.B., Harvard, 1934; LL.D., MacMurray Coll., 1960; m. Dorothy Holloway, Jan. 12, 1931 (dec. Dec. 1963); children—Henry Barber II, Godfrey Holterhoff; m. 2d, Katherine King, Feb. 25, 1967. Admitted to Mo. bar, 1934, practiced in St. Louis; partner firm Orr, Pflager & Andreas, 1939-70. Dir. St. Louis Union Trust Co. Pres. adminstrv. bd. control, trustee City Art Museum St. Louis; mem. adv. bd. Washington U. Law School, St. Louis U. Law Sch.; pres. trustees Met. YMCA Endowment Fund; dir. Barnard Free Skin and Cancer Hosp. Mem. Am. Bar Assn. (chmn. real property, probate and trust law sect. 1952), Am. Law Inst., Mo., St. Louis bar assns. Methodist. Clubs: Noonday, St. Louis Country, University (St. Louis); Princeton (N.Y.C.). Address: MO Died Apr. 1, 1972.

PHAIR, JOHN J(OSEPH), physician; b. Cin., Sept. 10, 1904; s. Robert J. and Barbara (Arns) P.; B.S., U. Cin., 1926, M.B., 1928, M.D., 1929, M.S., 1931; M.P.H., Johns Hopkins, 1933, Dr.P.H., 1938; m. Phyllis E. Wolfe, Mar. 20, 1930; 1 son, John P. Intern resident Cin. Gen. Hosp., 1928-31; instr. medicine Coll. of Medicine, Cin., 1931-32; fellow Rockefeller Found., 1932-33, mem. field staff, 1933-36; asso. prof. Sch. Hygiene Johns Hopkins, 1936-46; prof. preventive medicine U. Louisville, 1946-49, U. Cin., 1949-70; cons. to coordinator Inter Am. Affairs, 1943, sec. of war, 1942-46, U.S. Group Control Council, 1945, USPHS, 1946-70, FCDA, 1952-70; advisory fellow Mellon Inst., Pitts., 1966. Fellow Am. Pub. Health Assn. Ohio Academy. Sci., A.A.A.S., A.C.P., Indsl. Med. Assn.; mem. A.M.A., Am. Indsl. Hygiene Assn., Soc. Exptl. Medicine and Biology, Am. Epidemiol. Soc., Sigma Xi, Delta Omega. Clubs: Pendennis (Louisville); Cosmos (Washington); Hopkins (Balt.); Cincinnati (Cin.). Home: Cincinnati OH Died Aug. 10, 1970; buried Spring Grove Cemetery, Cincinnati OH

PHARR, HURIEOSCO AUSTILL, banker; b. Buena Vista, Ala., Sept. 23, 1891; s. John Wales and Mattie (Ervin) P.; A.B., B.S., Marion Mil. Inst., 1910; m. Sue Coleman Ranier, Apr. 24, 1917. Runner Bank of Mobile, N.B.A., 1910, later asst. cashier; cashier Consol. Peoples Bank of Mobile, 1918-24; v.p., trust officer First Nat. Bank of Mobile, 1924-47, pres., 1947-67, chmn., from 1967. Baptist (deacon). Mason. Kiwanian. Home: Mobile AL

PHELPS, ISAAC KING, chemist; b. Enfield, Conn., Feb. 16, 1872; s. John and Corintha Jane (King) P.; B.A., Yale, 1894, Ph.D., 1897; A.M., Harvard U., 1898; studied U. of Heidelberg; m. Martha Austin, June 27, 1904 (died Mar. 15, 1933). Asst. in chemistry, Yale, 1894-97, also Silliman fellow same period; Thayer scholar Harvard, 1897-98; instr. in chemistry, Yale, 1899-1908; asst. prof. physiol. chemistry, George Washington U., 1909-10; jr. organic chemist Bur. Chemistry, Washington, D.C., 1910-12; organic chemist Bur. of Mines, 1912-13, chemist, Bur. of Chemistry, 1913-23; chem. dir. Wamesit Chem. Co., Lowell, Mass., 1923-25; consultant in chemistry and in food production and distribution; biochemical work, staff of the Connecticut State Hosp., retired 1942; teaching and chem. research, Wesleyan U., 1942-44. Professor of Chemistry, Rollins College, 1944-48, Bethune-Cookman Coll. since 1948. Mem. Joint Com. of Definitions and Standards of foods and drugs, U.S. Dept. Agr., 1914-21; collaborator in preparation of U.S. Pharmacopaea X. Mem. A.A.A.S. Club: University

(Winter Park). Republican. Conglist. Contbr. research papers in chem. jours. Address: Bethune-Cookman College, Daytona Beach FL‡

PHELPS, J(AMES) MANLEY, teacher and lecturer; b. Malta, Ill., Jan. 24, 1891; s. James Manley and Olive (Billig) P.; A.B., Northwestern U., 1912; grad. Cumnock Sch. of Oratory (Northwestern U.), 1913; M.A., U. of Ill., 1916; m. Mary Catherine Denny, Feb. 7, 1931. Prof. of speech, Dakota Wesleyan Univ., 1913-14, Univ. of Ill., 1914-18, Univ. Sch. of Music and Other Fine Arts, Lincoln, Neb., 1919-24; asst. prof. literary interpretarion, Sch. of Speech, Northwestern Univ., 1924-30; prof. English and Speech, De Paul Univ., from 1932. Pres. and dir. Phelps School of Speech. Creator of Phelps Plan of Visual Edn. known as Better English and Better Speech." Lecturer and reader Redpath Chautauqua. Radio features, Your Speech," Your English" and Let's Talk"; lecturer before women's clubs and business organizations; commercial records and talking motion pictures for business houses and A Century of Progress Expn. Served as jr. petty officer instr. U.S. Naval Res. Force, World War I. Mem. Am. Legion, Speech Assn. Am. (founder), Am. Assn. Univ. Profs., Nat. Council Tchrs. of English, Delta Sigma Rho, Pi Kappa Delta, Beta Theta Pi, Delta Epsilon, Elks. Author, educator, radio artist, sales expert and business adviser, national authority in English and speech. Home: Chicago IL Died Oct. 12, 1971; buried North Shore Garden of Memories.

PHELPS, JOHN NOBLE, mfg. co. exec.; b. Cleve., Aug. 22, 1912; s. James Arthur and Edna (Crofoot) P.; B.B.A., Western Res. U., 1942; m. Vivian Kinsel, Apr. 2, 1946; 1 son, John Charles, Jr. Insp. wage and hour div. U.S. Dept. Labor, Cleve., 1942, dir. labor relations Cleve. Crane Co., Wickliffe, O., 1943-44; indsl. relations cons., Cleve., 1944-48; pres. PEC Corp., Richmond, Cal., 1949-68. Rotarian. Home: Anselmo CA Died Sept. 27, 1968.

PHELPS, RUTH SHEPARD, writer; b. Aurora, Ill., June 18, 1876; d. Edmund Joseph and Louise (Richardson) P.; B.L., Smith Coll., 1899; M.A., Columbia, 1910; studied Radcliffe Coll., 1914-15; Ph.D., U. of Chicago, 1924; m. Paul Morand, Jan. 9, 1929. Instr. Romance langs., 1910, asst. prof., 1916, asso. prof., 1919, prof., 1926-28, U. of Minn. Mem. Modern Lang. Assn. America, Soc. Colonial Dames, Dante Soc., Phi Beta Kappa. Author: Skies Italian (London), 1910; An Italian Grammar, 1917; Italian Silhouettes, 1924; The Earlier and Later Forms of Petrarch's Canzoniere, 1925. Editor: Lyrics and Sonnets (by Arthur Upson) in The Bibelot for Mar. 1908, 2d edit., 1909; Sonnets and Songs (by same), 1911; Glacosa's Partita a Scacchi, 1921; Sybil (in collaboration with Paul Morand, pseud., Phelps Morane), 1931 (issued in Paris). Contbr. essays and verse to mags.*‡

PHILBIN, PHILIP J., congressman; b. Clinton, Mass., May 29, 1898; s. John Henry and Delia (Gormley) P.; A.B., Harvard, 1920; LL.B., Columbia, 1924; m. Lillan Sundberg, June 15, 1929 (dec. 1953); children—Mary Ellen Bamby, Ann Blenda. Admitted to Mass. bar. 1924; in gen. practice in own name at Clinton, Mass.; counsel and mem. of firm Philbin Bros., Clinton, Mass.; mem. 78th to 91st Congresses Third Massachusetts District. Member Boston, Mass. State and Worcester County bar assns., Harvard Alumni and Columbia Alumni assns. Democrat. Home: Clinton MA Died June 14, 1972.

PHILIP, ANDRE, politician; b. Pont-Saint-Esprit, France, June 28, 1902; s. Louis and Gilberte (Vincent) P.; LL.D., 1929; m. M. Coreman, October 3, 1924; children—Olivier, Jean, Christiane, Nicole, Loic. Prof. econs. U. Lyon, 1926; elected dep. from the Rhone since 1936; resistance movement Liberation in S-E of France, 1941-42; Minister Interior Algier's Govt., 1942-44; pres. commn. Constitution, 1946; Minister Finances and Nat. Economy, 1946-47; French rep. to U.N. European Econ. Commn., Gen. Agreement Tariff Trade, Internat. Trade Orgn., 1946-70; mem. cons. assembly Strasbourg, 1949-51; del. gen. European Movement, 1949-71; pres. Mouvement Democratique et Socialiste pour les Etats-Unis d'Europe, 1949-70; delegate general Campagne Europeene de la Jeunesse; prof. laws U. Paris, 1956-67; dir. OCDE, 1967-70. Author: Guild-Socialism and Trade-Unionism, 1923; Le recours pour exces de pouvoir et l'activite corporative, 1923; l'Angleterre Moderne, 1924; Le probleme ouvrier aux Etats-Unis, 1926; Modern India, 1929; Henri de Man, Au dela du Marxisme, 1930; La Crise de L'Economie Dirigee, 1930; Trade Unionism and Syndicalism, 1936. l'Europe Unie et se place dans l'Economie Intenationale, 1953; others. Home: Saint Cloud Paris France Died July 5, 1970; buried Les Houches, Savoie France.

PHILIPPE, ROBERT RENE, engr.; b. Boston, Mar. 17, 1906; s. Rene Edward and Anna F. (Robert) P.; S.B., Mass. Inst. Tech., 1929; student Carnegie Inst. Tech., 1938-39; m. Mary Alice Allen, June 15, 1935; children—Allen R., Catherine R., Sharon Y. Constrn. worker Compressed Air Tunnel, N.Y.C., 1929-32; asst. soils mechanics lab. Mass. Inst. Tech., 1932-34; chief soils mechanics lab. Muskingum Dams, O., 1934-37; chief soils mechanics lab. Corps. Engrs., Pitts., 1937-41, dir. Ohio River div. labs., 1941-51, chief spl. engring. br. research and development Office Chief Engrs., from 1951; cons. engr. dams, airfields, foundations; lectr. soil mechanics Carnegie Inst. Tech., 1938-39; guest lectr. U. Ill., from 1949; lectr. prof. George Washington U., 1955. Mem. Am. Soc. C.E., Internat. Soc. Soil Mechanics and Found. Engring., Soc. Am. Mil. Engrs. Home: Alexandria VA Died June 29, 1968; buried Ivy Hill Cemetery Alexandria VA

PHILIPS, CARLIN, physician; b. Kenton, O., Dec. 17, 1871; s. William Hunter (M.D.) and Harriet (Carlin) P.; B.S. U. of Mich., 1894. M.D., 1897; m. Emma English of Birmingham, Ala. Feb. 19, 1905. Practiced New York, 1897-—; instr. nervous and mental diseases, also in pathology of nervous system, New York Post Grad. Med. Sch., 1899-1903; asso. pathologist, Bellevue Hosp., 1897-1903; visiting phys. prison, alcoholic and psycopathic wards, and asst. visiting phys. med. wards, same; 1st lt. Med. Reserve Corps, 1917; later maj. M.C. U.S.A. and in service 25 months. Democrat. Episcopalian. Mem. A.M.A., N.Y. State and New York County med. socs., New York Path. Soc., Phi Kappa Psi. Home: 2025 Broadway, New York‡

PHILLIPPE, GERALD LLOYD, business exec.; b. Ute, Ia., Sept. 27, 1909; s. Charles Crockett and Alice (Hitchens) P.; B.B.A., U. Neb., 1932, M.A., 1933, LL.D., 1960; LL.D., U. Akron, 1965; m. Jean Reese, August 4, 1937; children—Carol Jean, Miriam Sue, John Richard. With General Electric Company since 1933, traveling aduitor, 1935-42, statistician, 1942-47, auditor apparatus dept., 1947-50, comptroller apparatus dept., 1950-51, mgr. finance, apparatus sales div., 1951-53, comptroller, 1953-61, pres., 1961-63, chmn. bd., 1963-68. Chmn. Council for Financial Aid to Edn. Trustee Nat. Safety Council, Presbyn. Hosp. of City of N.Y. Mem. Nat. Indsl. Conf. Bd. (trustee) Financial Execs. Inst. (pres. N.Y. City Control, 1958-68), Phi Beta Kappa, Chi Phi, Beta Gamma Sigma. Clubs: Mohawk (Schenectady); Scarsdale (N.Y.) Golf; Laurel Valley Golf (Ligonier, Pa.); Augusta (Ga.) Nat. Golf; Sea View Country (Absecon, N.J.); University (N.Y.C.). Home: Greenwich CT Died Oct. 17, 1968.

PHILLIPPI, STANLEY ISAAC, fgn. service officer; b. Elberta, Utah, Apr. 29, 1900; s. Wesley Martin and Amanda (Brubaker) P.; student U. Ida., 1919-23, Stanford, 1944-45; m. Ofa Estella Ott, Mar. 25, 1926; children—Ralph Edwin, Mona Lois (Mrs. William K. Kelley), Stanley Robert. Engring. Asst. irrigation, Ida., Tex., 1922-26; draftsman, asst. engr., engr., chief engr. Middle Rio Grande Conservancy Dist., Albuquerque, 1926-42; irrigation adviser Mil. Govt. Korea, 1945-48, ECA, Korea, 1949-51, Thailand, 1951-56; chief natural resources div. ICA, Ceylon, 1956-61; water resources engr. AID, Accra, Ghana, from 1961. Served to maj. AUS, 1942-46. Mem. Phi Gamma Delta. Home: Farmington NM Died Jan. 14, 1971.

PHILLIPS, ALBANUS, JR., business exec.; born Cambridge, Md., Oct. 8, 1902; s. Albanus and Daisy (Lewis) P.; student Cambridge (Md.) High Sch., 1914-17, Tome Sch., Port Deposit, Md., 1918-21; m. Anita Applegarth Spedden, Nov. 20, 1929; children—Anita Spedden, Jr., Albanus, III, Douglas Howard. Began as employee Phillips Packing Co., Cambridge, Md., 1921, v.p., 1929-47, pres., 1947-57; v.p. p. Phillips Hardware Co., Inc., Cambrdige, 1929-70. Republican. Methodist. Mason (Shriner), Elk. Clubs: Cambridge Country, Cambridge Yacht. Home: Cambridge MD Died Dec. 16, 1970; buried Dorchester Meml. Park.

PHILLIPS, ALFRED NOROTON, ex-congressman; b. Darien, Conn., Apr. 23, 1894; s. (the late) Dr. Alfred Noroton and Elizabeth Marriner (Plumley) P.; student Darien and Stamford pub. schs.; Betts Acad. and Hotchkiss Sch.; A.B., Yale, 1917; m. Mary Gaines Smith, May 2, 1918; children—Elizabeth Haskings (Mrs. Ronald T. Speers), Laura Louise (Mrs. Stanley P. Gosnay). Manufacturer, also pub. real estate broker, farmer; active in farmers' cooperatives in Maryland; mayor Stamford, Conn., 1923-24, 1927-28 and 1935-36; mem. 75th Congress (1937-39), 4th Conn. Dist.; newspaper and broadcast columnist; owner Fairfield Co. Agency, Darien; mem. bd. of dir. and exec. v. pres., Greater Weaklies Assos. of N.Y. City; former publisher Darien (Connecticut) Review, pres. Phillips Pharmaceutical Products, Inc.; owner and operator of farm at Cecilton, Maryland. Major, Conn. Nat. Guard, 1923-33; served with A.E.F., World War I; volunteer, World War II (commd. over age) capt. Organized American Legion (except for one county) in Connecticut. Pres. Conn. League of Municipal Execs., 1935-36; held office and active in many local orgns. Pres. Conn. Editorial Association, 1942; v.p. Old Bohemia Hist. Soc., Elkton, Md. Mem. Conn. Editorial Assn., Yale Alumni Assn., Darien, Zeta Psi, S.A.R. Democrat. Presbyterian. Clubs: Stamford (Conn.) Yacht; Nat. Press (Washington). Home: DarienCT also Cecilton MD Died Jan. 18, 1970; buried St. Stephens Episcopal Ch. Cemetery, Earleville MD

PHILLIPS, BENJAMIN DWIGHT, president T. W. Phillips Gas & Oil Co.; b. New Castle, Pa., Nov. 20 1885; s. Thomas W. and Pamphila (Hardman) P.; ed Hiram (O.) College; m. Undine Conant, Apr. 6, 1909 children—Stella (Mrs. Rolland L. Ehrman), Clarinda (Mrs. J. F. Sprankle, Jr.), Undine (Mrs. Frank L Wiegand, Jr.), Benjamin Dwight, Victor Karl, Donald Conant; m. 2d, Mildred Welshimer, July 11, 1963 Began in the natural gas and oil business, 1906, with T W. Phillips Gas & Oil Co., pres.; pres., dir. Pa Investment & Real Estate Corp., Anderson Gas Co.; dir Citizens Nat. Bank (New Castle, Pa.), Butler Consol Coal Co., Thorofare Markets, Inc. Vice pres. N.Am Conv. Christian Chs. Trustee Butler YMCA Republican. Mem. Christian (Disciples) Ch. Clubs Butler Country; Duquesne, Pittsburgh Athletic Assn (Pitts.); Youngstown (O.). Home: Butler PA Died Oct 23, 1968; buried North Cemetery, Butler PA

PHILLIPS, BERT GEER, artist; b. Hudson, N.Y. July 15, 1868; s. William J. and Elizabeth (Jessup) P.; ar edn., Nat. Acad. Design and Art Students League of New York, Julian Acad., Paris; m. Rose H. Martin, Oct 1899; children—Ralph Jessup, Margaret Elizabeth Specialist on murals and Indian subjects. Prin. works (mural decorations); Polk County Court House, Des Moines, Ia., Capitol Bldg., Jefferson City, Mo.; San Marcos Hotel, Chandler, Ariz.; Taos County Court House, N.M. Rep. Thomas Gilcrease Foundn. Mus. Philbrook Mus., Tulsa, Okla.; Woolaroc Mus. Bartlesville, Okla.; permanent collection State Mus. Santa Fe, N.M. Founder of Taos (N.M.) Art Colony Mem. Am. Art Assn., Paris. Club: Salmagundi (New York). Home: Taos NM‡

PHILLIPS, CHARLES GORDON, clergyman; b. St Neot, Cornwall, Eng., Oct. 24, 1892; s. William Charles Lansdowne and Mary Jane (Hosken) P.; brought to U.S., 1910, naturalized, 1920; grad. Ferris Inst., 1916 A.B., Albion Coll., 1920, hon. D.D., 1946; B.D., Garrett Bibl. Inst., 1922; M.A., Northwestern, 1923; m. Alice F Stanton, June 11, 1921; children—Mary Alice (Mrs James Ragland), Gordon Wesley. Ordained to ministry Meth. Ch., 1921; minister Sherwood Meth. Ch., Mich. 1917-20, Arnold Meml. Ch., Chicago, 1920-23, St Luke's Ch., 1923-31, Wesley Meth. Ch., 1931-33 (both Detroit), Trenton, Mich., 1933-34, First Meth. Ch. Dearborn, Mich., 1934-42; supt. Port Huron dist. 1942-48; exec. sec. Meth. Union of Greater Detroit 1948-58, ret.; pres. Mich. Christian Advocate Publishing Co., ret. Mem. Meth. Conf. Bd. Edn. 1930-56. Bd. Ministerial Tng., 1925-42; asst. treas Detroit Annual Conf., 1931-32; mem. Camp Commn from 1945; 1st v.p. Mich. State Epworth League 1927-31, state pres., 1931-34. Candidate for Congress Mich. 7th Dist., 1944; candidate for gov. of Mich. 1946, 48. Trustee Mich. Christian Advocate, 1933-58 Bronson Hosp., 1945-48, Northwestern, 1934-42 1950-64, Adrian Coll., 1946-53, Meth. Found. of Mich. 1948-64; mem. Mich. Youth Comm., 1933-38. Served as sgt., 1st Platoon, Co. A, R.O.T.C., Albion Coll. 1917-18. Recipient Distinguished Alumnus award Ferris State Coll., 1965. Mem. Seminar Twelve (1927-52), Le Cercle Francais. Clubs: Contributor (pres., 1919-20); Rotary (1934-41, Dearborn, Mich.) Home: Detroit MI Died May 8, 1970; buried Grand Lawn Cemetery Detroit MI

PHILLIPS, EDNA M., minister; b. Chgo.; d. Ivar O and Rosa (Messick) Phillips; A.B., U. So. Cal., 1917 M.A., 1918, Ph.D., 1935; student Columbia. Minister 1916-68. Pres. Los Angeles br. Nat. League Am Penwomen, 1954-56, 58-60; v.p. Hollywood-Wilshire Symphony. Mem. Am. Inst. Fine Arts, Beverly Hill Pen Women (founder, pres. 1962-68). Clubs: San Souce Celebrity, Hollywood Bridge (pres.); So. Cal Culture (devotional chmn. 1968). Editor: Anthology fo Nat. League Am. Penwomen. Home: Hollywood CA Died Apr. 8, 1970.

PHILLIPS, EVERETT FRANKLIN, apiculturist; b Hannibal, O., Nov. 14, 1878; s. Taylor Franklin and Belle (Hofer) P.; A.B., Allegheny Coll., Pa., 1899, D.Sc 1929; Ph.D., U. of Pa., 1904; m. Mary Hibbs Geisler Oct. 27, 1906; children—Everett Franklin, William Taylor, Howard Geisler. Acting in charge of apiculture U.S. Bur. of Entomology, 1905-07, and in charge same 1907-24; prof. apiculture, Cornell U., 1924-46, emeritu since 1946. Fellow A.A.A.S.; pres. (1925-26) and fellow Apis Club (internat.); fellow Entomol. Soc. America mem. Ithaca Council of Social Agencies since 1941 mem. bd. Tompkins Co. Memorial Hosp. and othe local agencies; mem. Academy of Natural Science (Phila.), American Society Zoologists, American Assn Econ. Entomologists (pres. 1933-34), Phi Delta Theta Phi Eta, Phi Beta Kappa, Sigma Xi, Pi Gamma Mu Ecologists' Soc. Author: Bee-keeping, 1915, revised edit., 1928; also various Govt. publs. on bee-keeping and the diseases of bees. Gov. 28th dist., Rotary Internat 1935-36, chmn. Internat. Service Com. and mem. Aim and Objects Com., 1936-37, 3d, v.p., 1939-40 nominating com. for pres. 1939-42 (chmn. 1941-42) Home: 508 Stewart Av., Ithaca NY‡

PHILLIPS, FRANK MCGINLEY, statistician; b Knox County, O., July 30, 1874; s. Deroy Elwood and Julia (Beard) P.; grad. Kellogg (Ia.) High Sch., 189

B.Di., Newton (Ia.) Coll., 1896; M.D.I., Ia. State Normal Sch., 1907; A.B., Ia. State Teachers Coll., 1911; M.A., State U. of Ia., 1915; Ph.D., George Washington U., 1919; m. Carrie Marie Ervin, Mar. 24, 1897; children—Anna Marie, Ruth Reona, Beryl (dec.), Russie Dale, Eileen Halcyon, Wayne (dec.), Jack Wendell. City supt. schs., Ia. and Minn., 1903-14; registrar and head Dept. Edn., Central Coll., Pella, Ia., 1914-17; head Dept. Mathematics, Ia. Wesleyan Coll., 1917-18; asso. prof. statistics, George Washington U., 1918-30; statistician War Dept., Washington, 1918-19; dir. Washington office Fed. Bd. Vocational Edn., 1919-20; statistician, scientific research, U.S.P.H.S., 1920-23; chief Div. of Statistics, U.S. Bur. Edn., 1923-30; actuary and chief Div. of Statistics, Fed. Employees Compensation Commn., 1930-43; asst. prof. mathematics Western Md. Coll., 1943-44; acting director research and statistics, Nat. Cath. Comm. Serv., U.S.O. 1944-47; visiting prof. of statistics and math. at Stetson University since 1947. Member American Statistical Assn., Am. Pub. Health Assn., Am. Meteorol. Soc., A.A.A.S., N.E.A., Nat. Assn. Pub. Sch. Business Officers, Nat. League Compulsory Attendance Officers, Phi Delta Kappa, Pi Gamma Mu. Methodist. Made with others, sch. building survey for Portland, Ore., and outlined 15-yr. program for 1922-37; finance survey of Huntington, W.Va., 1929; bldg. survey of Arlington County, Va., 1930. Author: Educational Ranking of States, 1924, 30; (booklets) Graphic View of Our Schools, of Education in Our States, of Recent Trends in Our Schools; bulls. U.S. Pub. Health Service and U.S. Bur. Edn. Contbr. to mags. Home: 645 W. Minnesota Av., Deland FL‡

PHILLIPS, GEORGE FELTER, lawyer; b. Davenport, Ia., Mar. 5, 1892; s. Charles J. and Emma (Felter) P.; A.B., Princeton, 1914; LL.B., Columbia, 1917; m. Mary Weston, June 2, 1921 (dec. Aug. 1958); children—Lydia (Mrs. David J. Laub), Charles Weston, George Felter; m. 2d, Gwen Irwin Wheeler, Sept. 24, 1959. Admitted to N.Y. State bar, 1917, since practiced in Buffalo; partner Phillips, Lytle, Hitchcock, Blaine & Huber, and predecessors, 1928-1971. Dir. emeritus Marine Midland Banks, Inc., Marine Midland Trust Co. Western N.Y.; dir. Dunlop Tire & Rubber Corp., cpl., Spl. asst. Office Chief Ordnance, U.S. Army, 1942-45. Bd. dirs., past pres. Children's Aid Soc. Buffalo; dir. Buffalo Mus. Natural Sci. Served as maj., F.A., U.S. Army, 1917-18. Mem. Buffalo and Erie County Hist. Soc. (dir., past pres.). Clubs: Buffalo, Saturn (Buffalo); The Brook (N.Y.C.); Cottage, Nassau Buffalo NY Died Feb. 14, 1971.

PHILLIPS, GLENN RANDALL, bishop; b. Paulding County, O., May 21, 1894; s. Samuel Kepler and Iva Evelyn (Randall) P.; A.B., Ohio Wesleyan U., 1915, D.D., 1932; student Drew Sem., Madison, N.J., 1915-16; S.T.B., Garrett Bibl. Inst., Evanston, Ill., 1917, D.D., 1933; L.H.D., Coll. of Osteopathic Physicians and Surgeons; LL.D., University of Southern Cal., 1950; married Ruth Estella Clinger, Dec. 31, 1918; 1 son, Randall Clinger. Ordanied to ministry of M.E. Ch., 1920; pastor Southern Calif.-Ariz. Conf., Moorpark, Calif., 1919, Santa Maria, Calif., 1920-25, North Hollywood, 1925-29. Phoenix, Ariz., 1929-30, First Methodist Church, Hollywood, California, 1930-48; resident bishop Denver area, 1948-68, Portland, Ore. area, 1968-70. Mission visitations to Africa, Asia, Europe and India. Served as YMCA war work sec., England, 1918. Special lecturer Kokokahi Christian Life Conf., Honolulu, 1937, Sch. of Relgion, U. of Southern Calif., 1940-48. Official visit to Meth. mission projects India, 1950. Director Los Angeles City Missionary Soc., Plaza Community Center. Pres. Los Angeles Ministerial Assn., 1934; v.p. Los Angeles Ch. Fedn., 1941; chmn. dept. ministerial life and relations, 1941 and 1945. Registrar Bd. of Ministerial Training, Southern Calif.-Ariz. Conf., 1936-48. Delegate 1st Western Jurisdictional Conf., Meth. Ch., 1940, Gen. Conf. Meth. Ch., 1944, 48, and Western Jurisdictional Conf., 1944, 48. Trustee U. So. Cal. to 1950, University of Denver, Iliff School of Theology. Member Alpha Sigma Phi, Delta Sigma Rho, Phi Kappa Phi, Phi Beta Kappa. Republican. Mason (grand prelate Grand Commandery of Calif., K.T., 1934-35). Club: Lions (Denver). Contbr. sermons to Ministers Annual, articles to religious jours. Directed party through Japan, China and Philippines, 1935. Home: San Diego CA Died Oct. 6, 1970; buried Forest Lawn, Glendale CA

PHILLIPS, HARRY HUNGERFORD SPOONER, JR., pub. exec.; b. Maplewood, N.J., Aug. 17, 1901; s. Harry Hungerford Spooner and Olga Antonia (Karcher) P.; student Wesleyan U., 1921-23; m. Eleanor Augusta Hackett, June 27, 1927 (dec. Feb. 22, 1952); children—Eleanor P. White, Harry Hungerford Spooner, III; married 2d, Martha Potter Munson, Jan. 13, 1954. Acct. exec. N. W. Ayer & Son, Inc., 1923-28, advt. sales The New Yorker, 1928-36; with Time, Inc., 1936-60, advt. mgr. Time, 1943-44, advt. dir., 1944-53; pub. Sports Illustrated, 1954-59; v.p. McCann-Erickson Advertising, 1960-61; dir. Patent Trader, Inc. Pres. Wesleyan U. Press, Inc., chmn. dept. sch. services and publs., Wesleyan U., 1961-65; pres. Am. Edn. Publs., 1965-68; chmn. bd. dirs. Everyweek Ednl. Press, Ltd., U.K., 1966-68. Vice pres. bd. trustees Nat. Art Mus. Sport, 1959-66; bd. dirs. Mt. Kisco Boys' Club, 1948-50, Spence-Chapin Adoption Service, 1949-52; trustee Wesleyan U., 1952-61. Mem. Phi Nu Theta. Clubs: River, Bedford Golf and Tennis, Stanwich, Gulf Stream Bath and Tennis. Home: Mt Kisco NY Died Aug. 21, 1968; buried St. Matthews Church Yard, Bedford NY

PHILLIPS, JAMES DAVID, b. Chicago, Ill., June 1, 1868; s. James Mill and Ellen (Stewart) P.; B.S. in Architecture, U. of Ill., 1893; Master of Architecture, University of Ill., 1943; m. Clara Moore, M.D., June 17, 1916. Instr. shop work and machine design, U. of Ill., 1892-93, in gen. engring. drawing, 1893-1902; asst. prof. drawing, U. of Wis., 1902-09, asst. dean Coll. of Engineering, 1909-20, business mgr. 1920-38; retired July 1, 1938, Dir. Army Vocational Sch., U. of Wis., 1918-19. Inventor (with Carl Hambenchen) electrolytic method for removing oxides from silver and other metals. Mem. Soc. Promotion Engring. Edn., A.A.A.S., Wis. Acad. Sciences, Arts and Letters, Tau Beta Pi, Sigma Xi, Pi Tau Sigma, Theta Xi, Phi Kappa Phi. Club: University. Author: Free-hand Lettering, 1902; Essentials of Descriptive Geometry (with A.V. Millar), 1909; Mechanical Drawing for Colleges and Universities (with H.D. Orth), 1915; Mechanical Drawing for Secondary Schools (with F.D. Crawshaw), 1916; also numerous articles relating to university financing; Graphical Analysis of Price-Time Changes. Investment analyst. Home: 2015 Los Angeles CA‡

PHILLIPS, JAMES FREDERICK, ret. USAF officer; b. Cambridge, Ida., Feb. 25, 1900; s. Nelson George and Laura (Bender) P.; B.S., U. Ia., 1922; grad. Engr. Sch., 1924, Army Flying Sch., 1928, Chem. Warfare Sch., 1935, Army Air Forces Tactical Sch., 1939; m. Marcella Lindeman, June 27, 1927; children—Laura Marley, Frederica Lindeman. Commd. 2d lt. U.S. Army, 1923 and advanced through the grades to maj. gen., 1950; exptl. devel. work in aerial photography and mapping, Wright Field, Ohio, 1929-35; staff work on aero. research, devel. and prodn. aircraft, 1940-45; chief materiel div. Office Asst. Chief of Staff, Materiel and Services; Cambridge Research Center, 1951-52, Hdqrs. AAF, 1944-45; fgn. service, 1945-46; A.F. sec. Research and Devel. Bd., 1947-50; staff asst. Aircraft Industries Assn.; dir. Guided Missile Council Aerospace Industries Assn.; cons. missiles and space vehicles. Distinguished marksman, and mem. 3 Internat. Rifle Teams, 1923, 24, 25. Mem. Tau Beta Pi, Sigma Xi, Theta Tau. Clubs: Cosmos, Army and Navy (Washington). Home: Mount Vernon VA Died Feb. 5, 1973.

PHILLIPS, KATHRYN SISSON (MRS. ELLIS L. PHILLIPS), educator; b. Eureka, Kan., Mar. 16, 1879; d. Fletcher Marion and Sarah Elizabeth (Whitson) Sisson; B.Lit., Ohio Wesleyan, 1901, LL.D., 1956; M.A., Columbia, 1919; Humane Letters, Keuka Coll., 1959, U. Cin., 1964; m. Ellis Laurimore Phillips in September 19, 1919; children—Jean McLean (Mrs. John E. Burri), Ellis L. Dean of women Chadron State Tchrs. Coll., Neb., 1913-15, Ohio Wesleyan, Delaware, 1915-19; organized, pres. Nat. Assn. Dean of Women, 1916-20. Trustee Isabella Thorburn Coll., Lucknow, India, Finch Coll., N.Y.C., Ohio Wesleyan U., Del., Santiago Coll., Chile; v.p. Ellis L. Phillips Found. Mem. Nat. Soc. Colonial Dames, P.E.O. Methodist. Club: Colony. Author: My Room in the World, 1964. Home: New York City NY Died Jan. 11, 1970.

PHILLIPS, LEROY, publisher; b. Columbus, O., May 28, 1870; s. George Whitefield and Sarah Elizabeth (Ball) P.; grad. Worcester (Mass.) Acad., 1888; A.B., Amherst, 1892, A.M., 1907; M. Caroline Sherman King, May 3, 1899 (died 1939). Mgr. New Eng. edit., The Youth's Companion, 1892-96; foreign rep. Illustrated American, 1897-98; mgr. trade dept. Ginn & Co., publishers, Boston, 1899-1918; in pub. business in own name since 1910; with Baker International Play Bureau since 1925. With Foyer du Soldat, attached to 8th French Army, 1918-19. Member Psi Upsilon. Author: Bibliography of the Writings of Henry James, 1906, revised, 1930. Editor: Views and Reviews by Henry James, 1908; Types of Modern Dramatic Composition, 1927. Home: 21 Chauncy St., Cambridge, Mass. Office: 569 Boylston St., Boston 16‡

PHILLIPS, MARIE TELLO (MRS. CHARLES J. YAEGLE), writer; b. Louisville, Ky., Feb. 23, 1874; d. Manly and Rowena Lucinda (Seales) Tello; ed. Ursuline Coll., Nottingham, O.; A.B., Western Res. U.; m. Watson P. Phillips, Aug. 28, 1912 (dec.); m. 2d, Charles J. Yaegle, Aug. 3, 1929. Founder, 1923, and pres. Pittsburgh branch and Pa. State League of Am. Pen Women; nat. pres. Bookfellows Library Guild; pres.-gen. Pittsburgh chapter Poetry Soc. of Great Britain and America. Received citation for literary attainments as hon. corr. mem. Inst. Litteraire et Artistique de France; mem. Authors League, Authors Guild, Poetry Soc. of America, Nat. League of Am. Pen Women, Sigma Tau Delta, Eugene Field Soc., Am. Acad. of Poets; hon. mem. Mark Twain Soc., 1945. Awarded Sigma Tau Delta Diamond Torch, 1927, Bookfellows Silver Torch, 1927; certificate of merit in genealogy, Inst. of Am. Genealogy, 1939; Nat. League Am. Pen Women award, 1945; Citations, war work, 1943-45. Democrat. Catholic. Clubs: Congress of Clubs (Pittsburgh); Surf (Miami Beach, Fla.). Author: (verse) Book of Verse, 1922; A Voice from the Stars, 1929; Greetings from Father Pitt, 1929; Ten Thousand Candles, 1931; The Honeysuckle and the Rose, 1933; Mary of Scotland, and, Once Upon Time, 1937; (novels) Stella Marvin, 1928; Bound in Shallows, 1930, 2d edit., 1932; There's A Divinity, 1937; (essays) More Truth Than Poetry, 1934; Boruquet's Victory, 1948; contbr. to mags., newspapers, club and radio programs. Has written words and melody of numerous songs. Home: 6427 Darlington Rd., Pittsburgh 17. Office: Box 598, Pittsburgh PA‡

PHILLIPS, MICHAEL JAMES, author; b. Owosso, Mich., Nov. 8, 1876; s. Michael and Annie (O'Toole) P.; ed. pub. schs., Owosso; m. Nina Jeanette Robinson, of Grayling, Mich., May 14, 1902. City editor Owosso Daily Press-American, 1900-9; editor rifle practice dept., National Guard Mag., Columbus, O. Served in Mich. N.G., Dec. 1, 1896-—, pvt. to maj. and insp. small arms practice; enlisted in Co. G, 33d Mich. Vol. Inf., Apr. 26, 1898; hon. discharged, Dec. 18, 1898; with Gen. Shafter's Army, and participated in Battle of Santiago, July, 1898. Democrat. Catholic. Mem. Spanish War Vets., U.S. Inf. Assn., Mich. Authors' Assn. Author: In Our Country's Service, 1909; Bunty Prescott at Englishman's Camp, 1912. Address: Owosso MI‡

PHILLIPS, PERCY WILSON, lawyer; b. Southampton, N.Y., June 2, 1892; s. Wilson Edwards and Katharine (Baird) P.; LL.B., Cornell U., 1915; married Margaret Richards Terrell, Aug. 14, 1920 (died 1943); children—Margaret Terrell Bontempo, Janice Terrell Hormes, Alan Terrell (died 1944), Barbara Gaddis; married second, Betty R. Darter, 1952. Admitted to New York bar, 1915, and began practice of law with Sackett, Chapman, Brown & Cross, N.Y. City; mem. U.S. Bd. Tax Appeals, 1925-31; resigned to enter law practice in Washington, D.C.; mem. firm of Ivins, Phillips & Barker, Lecturer, University of N.C., 1929-31, Cornell University, 1937. Served as 1st lt., Field Arty., U.S. Army, World War. Mem. Am. Bar Assn. (chmn. sect. taxation, 1944-46, Ho. of Dels., 1947-48), District of Columbia, N.Y. State bar assns., Cornell Law Assn. (past vice pres.). Republican. Methodist. Mason. Clubs: Cornell (N.Y.C.); Cornell (ex-pres.), University (Washington); Columbia Country (Chevy Chase); Lake Placid (N.Y.). Joint Author: The Federal Gift Tax, and Taxation Under the A.A.A. Contbr. numerous articles on fed. taxation. Chevy Chase MD Died May 15, 1969.

PHILLIPS, ROGER SHERMAN, publisher; b. Butler, Pa., Oct. 27, 1922; s. Thomas W. and Alma (Sherman) P.; grad. Phillips Acad., 1940; student Yale, 1940-41; m. Virginia Dickson, Mar. 27, 1943 (div. 1951); 1 dau., Virginia Sherman; m. 2d, E. Michele Baldauf, June 8, 1951 (div. 1962); son (adopted) Richard Kevin; children—Sherman, Roger Sherman; m. 3d, Jeannine Kay DeKlyn, Apr. 21, 1962. V.P. T. W. Phillips Gas & Oil Co., Butler, Pa., 1949-51; pres., pub. UN World, 1950-53, World, Am. mag. of world events, 1953-55; dir. T. W. Phillips Gas & Oil Co., Pa. Real Estate Investment Co.; dir., asst. treas. All State Venture Capital Corp. (Bridgeport, Conn.); dir., mem. finance com. Am. Heritage Pub. Co. Trustee, v.p. Nat. Art Museum of Sport, Inc.; trustee, 1st v.p. finance Mid Fairfield County Youth Mus., Westport, Conn. Mem. Nat. Planning Assn. (nat. council), St. Hubert Soc. Republican. Mem. Disciples of Christ. Mason (32 deg., Shriner, Jester). Clubs: Duquesne (Pitts.); Coral Harbour Yacht (Bahamas); Campfire of Am.; Coral Reef Yacht (Miami, Fla.); Adventures; Club Limited. Home: South Norwalk CT Died Feb. 12, 1969.

PHIPPS, DON HOLCOMB, fruit cooperative mgmt.; b. Wenatchee, Wash., Aug. 30, 1906; s. John R. and Nettie (Holcomb) P.; B.S., Washington State U., 1929; m. Pearl M. Torrence Smallidge, July 13, 1929; children—Jack R., Don E. Sales, First Nat. Bank, Wenatchee, Wash., 1924; fruit rancher-owner Wenatchee, Wash., 1929-38; with Union Oil Co., 1931-41; with Northwest Wholesale, Inc., 1941-70; dir. Farm Credit Banks Spokane Bd., 1960-70. Active YMCA. First United Ch. Methodist. Home: Wenatchee WA Died July 10, 1970; buried Wenatchee WA

PHIPPS, MICHAEL GRACE, business exec.; b. Little Daly, Eng., Jan. 10, 1910; s. John Shaffer and Margarita (Grace) P.; grad. St. Paul's Sch., Concord, N.H., 1928; B.A., Yale, 1932; m. Muriel Pillans Lane, Apr. 10, 1936; children—Elaine Lane, Susan Grace. Pres. Bessemer Properties, Inc., Palm Beach, Fla.; dir. W. R. Grace & Co., N.Y.C. Served as lt. col. USAAF, 1942-45. Decorated Air Medal. Home: Palm Beach FL Died Mar. 13, 1973.

PHOENIX, CHARLES E., mining engr.; b. in Wisconsin, Mar. 26, 1871; s. Ludger and Eliza Ann (Lutz) P.; student U. of Wis., 1893; Law Dept., U. of Wis., 1894, and 1902; m. Olla May Johnson, June 19, 1909. Began engring. work with C. & N.W. Ry., 1897; with W. G. Kirchoffer, Baraboo, Wis., 1898-01; removed to Whatcom (now Bellingham), Wash., 1903; with Alaska Central Ry., summer, 1904; U.S. deputy mineral surveyor since 1907; surveyed the Skagit Queen Group Wash., embracing 36 locations and 4 millsites; Republican. Mem. Am. Inst. Mining Engrs. Mason. Address: Bellingham Washington DC‡

PIASECKI, PETER F., postmaster; b. Milwaukee, Wis., May 30, 1876; s. Theophil and Catharine (Inda) P.; ed. pub. schs.; m. Emily Sonnenberg, of Milwaukee, Oct. 25, 1899; 1 son, Peter F. Postmaster of Milwaukee since 1923. Served as lt. 1st Wis. Vols., U.S. Vols., Spanish-Am. War; lt. col. 1st Wis. Inf., on Mexican border, 1916; col. inf., U.S.A., World War; with 32d Div., A.E.F., occupation sector in Alsace, Aisne Marne, Oise Aisne and Meuse Argonne offensives, march to the Rhine, and with Army of Occupation; col. O.R.C. Mem. Nat. Aeronautic Assn., Izaak Walton League, Spanish War Vets., Mil. Order Foreign Wars, Mexican Border Vets. Assn., Am. Legion, Milwaukee Assn. Commerce (air service com.), Rotary Internat., Milwaukee Advertising Club. Elk. Club: Milwaukee Yacht. Home: 3046 S. Superior St. Office: Main Post Office, Milwaukee WI‡

PIASTRO, MISHEL, violinst; b. Kertz, Russia, June 1892; s. Boris and Maria (Sengin) P.; student Petrograd (Leningrad) Conservatory under Leopold Auer, 1902-10; grad. (with highest honors), 1910; married (wife deceased); 3 children; m. 2d, Joan Scardon, 1941; came to U.S., 1920, naturalized, 1927. Began career as violinist, 1910; won annual 1,000 ruble prize, Russia, 1911; concertized throughout Russia, Scandinavia, Poland, etc., 1910-13; appeared as soloist at Koussevitsky's symphony concerts, Moscow and Petrograd, 1914, introducing Glazounoff's violin concerto in several cities; made tour of 500 concerts, visiting Siberia, China, Japan, Siam, Sumatra, Java, Singapore, British India, Philippine Islands, Australia, New Zealand, etc., and giving command performance before King of Siam in Bangkok, 1915-20; debut in Carnegie Hall, N.Y. City, 1920; concert tour throughout U.S., 1920-25; solo violinist, concertmaster and asst. condr., San Francisco Symphony Orchestra, 1925-30; concertmaster N.Y. Philharmonic Orchestra, 1931-43, and asst. condr. Philharmonic Symphony Society of New York, 1941. Muscial dir. Longines Symphonette radio program; 1st time recs. for Decca. Recipient Pushpa Malla Medal, King of Siam. Address: New York City NY Died Apr. 10, 1970.

PIAZZA, FERDINAND, hosp. adminstr.; b. Burgio, Italy, Nov. 15, 1902; s. Joseph and Antionette (Serra) P.; came to U.S., 1909, naturalized, 1925; B.S., City Coll. N.Y., 1925; M.D., George Washington U., 1929; m. Connie Lavoti, Sept. 6, 1936; 1 son, Frederick; m. 2d, Marjorie Ruggieri, Nov. 27, 1966; adopted son, Frank Daniel. Intern Met. Hosp., N.Y.C., 1929-30, admitting physician, 1930-31, resident surgery, 1931-32, vis. surgeon, 1933-38; pvt. practice, 1933-38; exec. physician Harlem Hosp., N.Y.C., 1938-40; dep. med. supt. Fordham Hosp., N.Y.C., 1940-42; gen. med. supt. Met. Hosp., N.Y.C., 1954-57, med. supt., 1948-54, 57-67; med. supt. Sydenham Hosp., N.Y.C., 1946-48; asst. clin. prof. preventive medicine N.Y. Med. Coll., 1958-67. Served to lt. col., M.C., AUS, 1942-46. Decorated Order Merit (Republic Italy), 1965. Fellow Am. Coll. Hosp. Administrs.; mem. Am. Great Neck NY Died Apr. 21, 1968.

PIAZZONI, GOTTARDO, artist; b. Intragna, Switzerland, Apr. 14, 1872; s. Paolo and Teresa (Cavalli) P.; prep. edn., grammar sch., Intragna, and Ginnasio, Locarno, Switzerland; art edn., Calif. Sch. of Design, Julian Acad. and Ecole des Beaux Arts, Paris; m. Beatrice Delmue, Dec. 5, 1905; children—Romy, Mireille. Condr. pvt. art sch., San Francisco, 1901-05, 1907-12; instr. landscape painting, Calif. Sch. Fine Arts, 1918-29, and since 1935; exhibited St. Louis, New York, Chicago, Corcoran Gallery, Wash., D.C., Rome, Paris. Rep. in Golden Gate Park Memorial Mus. Calif. Palace of Legion of Honor, Mills, Coll. Art Gallery, Municipal Collection, Phoenix, Ariz. and S.F. Museum of Art., Art Institute Chicago, Chicago Society, Etchers. Awarded gold medal, Calif. Sch. of Design, 1904; Emanuel Walter fund purchase prize, 1919; San Francisco Art Assn., 1924; medal of first award for sculpture, San Francisco Art Assn. Ann. Exhbn., 1927, Hon. mem. San Francisco Art Assn. (dir. 15 yrs.), Calif. Soc. Etchers (ex-pres.), Chicago Soc. Etchers, Calif. Soc. Mural Artists. Executed murals, Land and Sea, San San Francisco CA‡

PICASSO, PABLO RUIZ, painter, sculptor, ceramits; b. Malaga, Spain, Oct. 25, 1881; s. Jose Ruiz Blasco and Maria Picasso Lopez b.; ed. in Barcelona, Madrid; m. 2d, Jacqueline Boque, Mar. 2, 1961; 2 sons, 2 daus. by previous marriage. Founder and leader cubist sch., later in surrealism in France, 1900-73; designer for Diaghilev Ballet, 1917-27; dir. Prado Gallery, Madrid, 1936-39; works include; (murals) Spanish Pavilion, Paris Exhbn., 1937; (paintings) Les Arlequins, L'Aveugle, La famille de singe, Femme a la mandoline, Guernica; (portraits) Stravinsky, J. Couteau, G. Appollinaire, Max Jacob; (still-lifes) In Paris, Berlin, London, Phila., galleries; sculpture design for Civic Center, Chgo., 1966; (decorations for Russian Ballets) Parade, 1917, Tricorne, 1918; Pulcinella, 1919. Recipient Pennell Meml. medal for achievement in graphic arts Pa. Acad. Fine Arts, 1949; Lenin prize, 1962; named honorary citizen of Antibes. Published series of etchings (with text) entitled Songe et Mensonge de Franco, 1937. Author: Le Desir attrape par la quene (play), 1943. Address: Par Mougins AM France Died April 9, 1973

PICKARD, SAMUEL NELSON, banker; b. Neenah, Wis., Dec. 3, 1897; s. Herman W. and Lulu (Nelson) P.; student Wayland Acad. (Beaver Dam, Wis.), 1912-13, high sch. grad., Ripon, Wis., 1913-16; m. Dorothea Wilgus, Sept. 1, 1924; children—James Curtis, Julia, Judith, Thomas Nelson, Samuel Wilgus. Messenger, First Nat. Bank, Ripon, 1916, bookkeeper, 1917, teller, 1918-22, asst. cashier, 1923, cashier, 1925, v.p., 1930, dir., 1926-73; exec. v.p. Marine Nat. Bank of Neenah (formerly Nat. Mfrs. Bank), Neenah, Wis., 1932-37, pres., 1937-67, chmn. bd., 1967-73; treas., dir. Oshkosh B'Gosh, Inc., 1934-73; dir. Marine Corp. of Milw., Miles Kimball Co. Served with U.S. Marine Corps, 1918-19. Trustee Ripon Coll. Wayland Acad. Wis. Taxpayers Alliance. Mem. Am. Bankers Assn., Wis. Bankers Assn. (pres. 1938-39), Am. Legion, Phi Delta Theta. Republican. Presbyn. Mason. Rotarian (pres. Ripon 1928-29, pres. Neenah 1937-38). Clubs: North Shore Golf (Neenah); Chicago Athletic. Home: Neenah WI Died Jan. 17, 1973.

PICKELLS, CHARLES WILLIAM, organist; b. Looe, Cornwall, Eng., Oct. 4, 1874; s. Charles (D.D.) and Marguerite Eleanora (Robinson) P.; ed. Bristol (Eng.) Grammar Sch., De Garmo Inst., Fishkill-on-Hudson, N.Y., Harvard Univ. (spl. student music), 1904; m. Mary Hamilton Farley, of New York, Apr. 28, 1899. Organist and choirmaster, House of Prayer, Newark, N.J., 1895-7, St. Andrew's Episcopal Ch., St. Johnsbury, Vt., 1898-1900, (also supervisor music, city schs., St. Johnsbury), St. Mary's, Burlington, N.Y., 1899-1901, St. Stephen's, Boston, 1901-4, Christ Ch., Elizabeth, N.J., 1904-9; instr. music in pub. schs., Roselle, N.J., 1905-8, and Somerville, 1906-8; supervisor of music pub. schs. of New York, Sept., 1908-Mar. 1912, dept. music, Flushing High School, 1912-13, Brooklyn Training Sch. for Teachers, 1913-—. Organist and choirmaster St. George's Episcopal Church, Flushing, N.Y., Nov. 1, 1909-—. Address: Flushing NY‡

PICKENS, JAMES MADISON, editor; b. Eutaw, Ala., Dec. 2, 1872; s. James Madison and Mary Catherine (Williams) P.; ed. pub. schs. and under pvt. tutors; studied at George Washington U., U. of Besancon (France), and spl. courses at U.S. Dept. of Agr.; m. Mary Evans Drown, Nov. 22, 1899; 1 dau. Marjorie (Mrs. Reid T. Milner). Entered Service of U.S. Dept. of Agr. as stenographer, 1897; editor publs. of Bur. of Animal Industry, 18 yrs.; editor publs. of Bur. of Plant Industry, 1926-42; retired Dec. 31, 1942. With Y.M.C.A. with French Army, 10 months, 1918-29. Mem. Botanical Soc. Washington. Club: National Press. Home: 417 Dorset Av., Chevy Chase 15 MD‡

PICKLESIMER, HAYES, banker; b. nr. Hager, Ky., Jan. 25, 1899; s. Boyd and Mary (Williams) P.; student Magoffin Inst., Salyersville, Ky., 1914-16, Eastern Kentucky State Normal School, Richmond, 1917; Doctor of Laws (honorary), Bethany College, Bethany, West Virginia, 1963; married Sara Ruth Matthews, Jan. 8, 1919; children—Mary Janice, John. With Salyersville Nat. Bank, 1917, Kanawha Valley Bank, Charleston, W.Va., in various capacities, 1918-23; cashier Bank of Wyoming, Mullens, W.Va., 1923-24; dep. commr. of banking, W.Va., 1924-26; pub. accountant, offices at Charleston and Huntington, 1926-28; asst. cashier, Kanawha Valley Bank, Charleston, 1928-29, cashier, 1929-35, v.p., 1935, dir., 1936, exec. v.p., 1940-49, president, 1949-66, chairman board, 1967-69. Member board trustees Morris Harvey College, Meml. Hosp., Charleston. Mem. Small Bus. Credit Commn., 1943-46. Member West Virginia Bankers Assn. (past pres.), American Bankers Assn. (chmn. com. on state legislation 1948-50), W.Va. C. of C. (treas., since 1938). Republican. Presbyn. Mason. Clubs: Rotary, Edgewood Country, Berry Hills Country. Home: Charleston WV Died Dec. 11, 1969; buried Charleston WV

PICKRELL, HOMER P., newspaper editor; b. Oskaloosa, Ia., July 28, 1885; s. Willet H. and Anna (McCracken) P.; ed. Friends' University, Wichita, Kansas; married Marie Griffin, August 14, 1913 (deceased, July 24, 1958); 1 son, Donald Griffin; married 2d, Jewel Street, September 2, 1960. Began as reporter Wichita (Kan.) Beacon, 1907; with Chicago Record Herald, 1909-11, St. Louis Post Dispatch, 1912-18; editor Albuquerque Journal, 1927-64; editor Albuquerque Herald, 1919-25. Republican. Mason. Home: Albuquerque NM Died Aug. 1971.

PIERCE, ALFRED MANN, clergyman, editor; b. Union Point, Ga., Sept. 28, 1874; s. Thomas Foster and Susan (Sinquefield) P.; A.B., Emory Coll. (now Univ.), 1895, D.D., 1927; m. Bessie John Almand, of Conyers, Ga., Nov. 29, 1899; children—Carolyn Virginia (Mrs. Fielding Dillard), Susan Lovick, Mary Milton. Ordained ministry M.E. Ch., S., 1897; among pastoral charges served are Cedartown, Ga., Carrollton, St. James, Augusta, First Ch., Griffin, Druid Hills, Atlanta; editor Wesleyan Christian Advocate since 1923. Del. to Gen. Conf. of M.E. Ch., S., 1930. Trustee Wesleyan Coll., Macon, Ga. Mem. Pi Gamma Mu, Kappa Alpha. Democrat. Mason. Home: 1446 Ponce de Leon Av. N.E. Office: Wesley Memorial Bldg., Atlanta GA‡

PIERCE, CARLETON CUSTER, former dir. select. serv. W.Va.; b. Rowlesburg, W.Va., Oct. 19, 1877; s. John Franklin and Amanda Elizabeth (Moore) P.; student Franklin Coll., New Athens, O., 1896-97; diploma in law, West Virginia U., Morgantown, W.Va., 1901; m. Mary May Buckner, Nov. 28, 1902; children—Carleton Custer (officer U.S.N.R.), Oscar Buckner (U.S. Army). Began as school teacher, 1895; engaged in various businesses, including fruit growing, coal mining and public utilities, and holding official positions in corporations, which relinqushed when apptd. dir. selective service for West Virginia, 1941; now dir. office selective service records. Served as 1st lt., U.S. Vols., during Spanish-Am. War; mem. W.Va. Nat. Guard, advancing through the grades to brig. gen., 1929; called to Federal duty, 1940, retired for age, 1941, continuing to serve as acting adj. and dir. of selective service; brig. gen. hon. ret. list. A.U.S. Presdl. Medal for Merit; decorated Spanish-Am. War and Good Conduct medals. Former mem. legislature, W.Va., past pres. bd. of edn., and pros. atty., Preston County, W.Va. Mem. Sigma Chi. Mason, K.P. Club: Preston Country (Kingwood, W.Va.) Home: 112 Morgantown St., Kingwood, W.Va. Office: 513 1/2 Capitol Street, Charleston WV‡

PIERCE, CLAY ARTHUR, corpn. exec.; b. Cote Brilliant, Mo., Dec. 25, 1873; s. Henry Clay and Minnie (Finlay) P.; ed. St. Paul's Sch., Concord, N.H.; Harvard, class of 96; m. Irene Tewksbury, of Chicago, Oct. 15, 1898; children—Irene (Mrs. Norvin H. Green), H. C., E. E. (dec.). Became connected with the Waters-Pierce Oil Co., 1899, pres., June 1905; pres. Pierce Oil Corpn. from 1913 until retired; pres. Pierce Petroleum Corpn., 1923-26 (voluntarily resigned); dir. Brier Hill Collieries; sole administrator of H. C. Pierce Estate. Republican. Episcopalian. Club: Rumson Country. Home: Rumson NJ‡

PIERCE, DANIEL THOMPSON, corpn. official; b. Washington, D.C., March 22, 1875; s. Daniel Thompson and Anne M. (Pitcher) P.; studied law Columbian (now George Washington) U.; m. Hadassah Hellen, of Washington, D.C., Nov. 21, 1897. Editor Public Opinion, 1895-1905; contbr. on polit., sociol. and ry. subjects to newspapers and mags. Vice chmn. Anthracite Operators Conf., 1926-30; asst. to chmn. Consol. Oil Corpn. since 1930. Clubs: American Yacht, Metropolitan, Regency, etc. Home: 277 Park Av. Office: 630 5th Av., New York NY‡

PIERCE, EARLE VAYDOR, clergyman; b. Portage, Mich., July 23, 1869; s. Dwight Clark and Mary Ellen (McEldowney) P.; student Sioux Falls (S. Dak.) Coll., 1887-92; A.B., U. of Chicago, 1894; student Crozer Bapt. Theol. Sem., Chester, Pa., 1900-01; D.D., Sioux Falls Coll., 1916; m. Elinore Mapes, Oct. 16, 1918. Ordained Bapt. ministry, 1894; pastor First Ch., Ironton, O., 1894-1900, First Ch., Ipswich, S.D., 1906-10, Central Ch., Minneapolis, 1910-18, First Ch., Brookings, S.D., 1918-24, Lake Harriet Ch., Minneapolis, 1924-39, pastor emeritus, 1939-44; leader of fundamentalists of Northern Bapt. Conv., 1928-44, leader emeritus since 1944. Editor The Ironton Register (daily and weekly), 1903. Trustee Twin City Bapt. Union, Watchman-Examiner Foundation, Sioux Falls Coll., N.W. Bapt. Hops. Association, (v.p.), N.W. Theological Seminary and Bible Training Sch., Eastern Bapt. Theol. Sem., Central Bapt. Theol. Sem., Northern Bapt. Theol. Sem.; mem. bd. mgrs. Am. Bapt. Fgn. Mission Soc., 1930-37, and 1938-48; member Council Finance and Promotion of Northern Baptist Convention, 1932-37; president Northern Baptist Convention, 1937. Mem. Gen. Council, 1938. Pres. Bapt. Hosp. Fund, Inc. Republican. Author of The Conflict Within My Self; The Church and World Conditions; The Supreme Beatitude; also several religious pamphlets. Home: 10 Red Cedar Lane, Minneapolis MN‡

PIERCE, MARVIN, corporation exec.; b. Sharpsville, Pa., June 17, 1893; s. Scott and Mabel (Marvin) P.; B.A. Miami U., 1916, LL.D., 1950; B.S., M.I.T., 1918; B.S., Harvard, 1918; m. Pauline Robinson, Aug., 1918 (dec. 1949); children—Martha Ann (Mrs. W. G. Rafferty), James, Barbara (Mrs. G. W. Bush), Scott; m. 2d, Willa Gray Martin, June 28, 1952. Started as engr. Lord Construction Co., N.Y. City, 1919-21; asst. to pres. McCall Corp., N.Y. City, 1921-36, vice president 1936-45, pres., 1946-57; chmn. bd. dirs., 1957-58; Time Mag., 1958-60, Cowles Pub., 1960-63; mem. staff Internat. Exec. Service Corps., 1966-69, serving in Brazil and Argentina, 1968. Named M-Man of Year, Miami U., 1968. Mem. U.S. Seniors Golf Assn., Phi Beta Kappa, Beta Theta Pi. Republican. Presbyterian. Clubs: Apawamis, Manursing Island, Am. Yacht University. Home: Rye NY Died July 17, 1969.

PIERCE, OLIVER WILLARD, pianist; b. Hillsdale Mich., 1869; A.B., Hillsdale Coll., 1891, A.M., 1894 student N.E. Conservatory of Music, 1888, 1889 Konigliche Hochschule fur Musik, Berlin, 1891-2, and of Moritz Moskowzski, Berlin, 1892, 1893; m. Grace Estelle Clarke, of San Francisco, Sept. 2, 1903. Head pianoforte teacher, Ohio Wesleyan U. Conservatory of Music, 1890-1, 1893-4; a founder, 1894, pres., 1901-7 Met. Sch. of Music, Indianapolis; founded, 1907, and ınce pres. Coll. of Mus. Art, Indianapolis. Has ppeared as soloist with Theodore Thomas Orchestra nd Cincinnati, Detroit and Indianapolis Symphony rchestras, etc. Mem. Ind. Music Teachers' Assn. ex-pres.). Mason (32 deg.); Past Comdr. Raper 'ommandery, K.T. Clubs: Columbia University charter mem.), Athenaeum. Honorary Mus.D., Iillsdale Coll., 1919. Home: 1745 N. Pennsylvania St., ndianapolis IN‡

IERPONT, HENRY EDWARDS, railway official; b. wo Rivers, Wis.; s. Henry S. and Lydia (Gardner) P.; d. pub. schs.; m. Mrs. Mattie K. Simpson, of Lexington, Io., Dec. 18, 1894 (she died November 19, 1933). egan as telegraph operator with C.,M. & St. P. Ry., 883, successively in station and auditing departments nd freight agt. at Kansas City, Mo., until 1892, div. frt. nd passenger agt., La Crosse, Wis., 1892-96, asst. gen. t. agt., Chicago, 1896-1907, gen. frt. agt., 1907-13, frt. affic mgr., 1913-20, traffic mgr., 1920-26, v.p., 926-38; retired, Nov. 1, 1938. Mem. Wis. Soc. of 'hicago, Chicago Assn. Commerce. Clubs: Union eague, South Shore Country. Home: 1660 Hyde Park oul., Chicago IL ‡

IERSON, COEN GALLATIN, educator; b. Dubois 'ounty, Ind., Mar. 7, 1901; s. John B. and Ellen McBride) P.; B.A., DePauw U., 1922; M.A., U. Ill., 924; Ph.D., U. Wis., 1932; m. Viva Bolin, June 18, 919 (dec. May 1926); children—John, Robert; m. 2d, lizabeth P. O'Neal, November 29, 1963. Faculty ePauw U., from 1925, prof. history from 1945, head ept., 1960-66, John Clark Ridpath prof., 1960-66, prof. meritus, 1966-72; vis. professor Ind. University, ummers 1939-51, 66; exchange lectr. U. Exter (Eng.), 953-54; vis. prof. English, Illinois State Univ., 1966-68. 'ellow Royal Hist. Soc.; mem. Am. Assn. U. Profs., Am. Iists. Assn., Conf. British Studies, Phi Beta Kappa. uthor: Canada and the Privy Council, 1960; also rticles. Home: Greencastle IN Died May 18, 1972; uried Greencastle, Ind.

'IFER, DRURY AUGUSTUS, engr., educator; born 'harleston, S.C., Mar. 18, 1905; s. Drury Fair and lizabeth Chalmers (Tarrant) P.; B.S., U. of Vashington, 1930, M.S., 1931; m. Patricia Martincevic, ept. 21, 1929 (dec.); children—Drury Louis, Patricia lizabeth (Mrs. Dimitri Papahadjopoulos); m. 2d irginia Senner nee Davis, July 7, 1951; hildren—David Senner, Barbara Senner (Mrs. Thomas orson), John Senner. Mine ofcl. Sub Nigel Ltd., Nigel, ransvaal, S. Africa, 1932-37; mine ofcl. DeBeers onsolidated Mines Ltd., Kimberley, S. Africa, 937-45; mgr. seconded to Cape Coast Exploration td., 1937-39; mgr. seconded to Consol. Diamond Iines S.W. Africa, 1939-42; mgr. Dutoitspan and ultfontein Mining Cos. 1942-45; prof. mining engring. . Washington, 1947-71, emeritus, 1971, director of chool of Mineral Engineering, 1947-69; director of the IcGregor Mus., Kimberley, 1942-45. Mem. Wash. tate Indsl. Com., Mining Sect., 1950-52, Wash. State d. Registration Profl. Engrs., 1951-56, South African iovt. Mining Engrs. Commn. Examiners, Diamond Iines, 1943-45; mem. Wash. State Govs. Forest Area se Council, 1963-65. Awarded Union S. Africa Mine Igr's. Certificate of Competency, 1935. Mem. Am. ıst. Mining and Metall Engrs. (vice chmn. indsl. inerals div. 1948, chmn. North Pacific sect. 1950-51), ssn. Mine Mgrs. South Am. Mining Congress, 'orthwest Mining Assn. (trustee 1958-61), W. Coast Iineral Assn., Loyal Knights Round Table (pres. eattle table 1955-56), Sigma Xi. Home: Seattle WA ied Oct. 18, 1971; buried Seattle WA

IGEON RICHARD, investment banking; b. East oston, Mass., Apr. 25, 1882; s. William Broadhead and lemmie E. (Gardner) P.; grad. Boston Latin Sch., 900; m. Emma R. Kelley, Feb. 20, 1911; hildren—Mary (Mrs. Robert H. Pelletreau), Judith Mrs. Lyman B. Brainerd), Ruth (Mrs. Welles T. Seller). 'ith Estabrook & Co., Boston, 1901-70, mem. firm, 916-70; Maritime Corp. Served as member First Corps adets, Boston, 1907-10, First Motor Corps, Boston, 916-18. Treas. Boston Latin Sch. Assn. Clubs: lgonquin (Boston); Woods Hole Golf (Woods Hole); ountry (Wellesley). Home: Wellesley Hills MA Died Iov. 5, 1970.*

IGOTT, JAMES M., investment banker; b. Bethel prings, Tenn., Sept. 12, 1894; s. John T. and Dona Hendrix) P.; student schs. of Jackson, Tenn.; m. rredericka Blankenship, Sept. 26, 1925; 1 dau., Mary redericka (Mrs. Joseph O. Kostner, Jr.). With Central epublic Company, Chicago, 1926-57, successively ond salesman, sales mgr., v.p., 1926-52, exec. v.p., 952-54, pres., 1954-57, dir., 1949-57, Central Republic o. consolidated with Dean Witter & Co., became ltd. artner; treas., dir. Ins. Exchange Bldg. Corp. Trustee raham Found. Advanced Studies in Fine Arts. Clubs: hicago Athletic Association, Bond (Chgo.). Home: hicago IL Died June 23, 1969; buried Calvary emetery, Chicago IL

IKE, HARRY HALE, voice teacher; b. Dubury, Iass., Jan. 27, 1874; s. Theodore Lyman and Martha Iaria (Hale) P.; ed. pub. schs., and pvt. teachers; mus. In. in Boston under George L. Osgood, voice, Fred Field Bullard, composition, and J. Wallace Goodrich, organ; m. Marion Wharton Corrie, June 5, 1906. Began mus. work in boy choir under Warren Locke at Appleton Chapel, Harvard U.; later took charge of chorus choirs in Boston and Newburyport; sang under Walter Spalding, in Cambridge and Boston, Mass.; established as voice teacher in Atlanta, Ga., 1903; now choir dir. and organist Central Presbyn. Ch. First published compositions, 1899, and has since published part songs, ch. anthems and solo songs, etc. Contbr. to mus. mags. Home: 663 Washington St. Studio: Lowndes Bldg., Atlanta GA‡

PIKE, JAMES ALBERT, clergyman; b. Oklahoma City, Feb. 14, 1913; s. James Albert and Pearl Agatha (Wimsatt) P.; student U. Santa Clara, 1930-32, U. Cal. at Los Angeles, 1932-33; A.B., U. So. Cal., 1934, LL.B., 1936; J.S.D., Yale (Sterling fellow 1936-37), 1938; student Va. Theol. Sem., 1945-46; student Union Theol. Sem., 1946-47, B.D. magna cum laude, 1951; S.T.D. (hon.), Trinity Coll., Hartford, Conn., 1953, U. King's Coll., Halifax, N.S., 1954; J.U.D. (hon.), Dickinson Coll., 1954; Litt.D. (honorary), Alfred U., 1955, Lewis and Clark Coll., 1963; D.D. (hon.), Grinnell Coll., 1957, Va. Theol. Sem., 1959; LL.D., U. So. Cal., 1960; H.H.D., Westminster College, 1962; L.H.D., Hebrew Union College, 1962; D.C.L. (hon.), Wilmington Coll., 1967; m. Esther Yanovsky, Jan. 29, 1942 (div. July 1968); children—Catherine, James Albert, Constance, Christopher; m. 2d, Diane Kennedy, Dec. 20, 1968. Admitted to the California bar, 1936; assistant to reporter American Lau-Inst., 1937; atty. SEC, 1938-42; lectr. Cath. U. Am., 1938-39, George Washington U., 1938-42; ordained deacon Protestant Episcopal Ch., 1944, priest, 1946; curate St. John's Ch., Washington, and chaplain George Washington U., 1944-46; fellow, tutor Gen. Theol. Sem., 1946-47; rector Christ Ch., Poughkeepsie, N.Y., Epis. chaplain Vassar Coll., 1947-49; head dept. religion and chaplain Columbia, 1949-52, asso. religion and law, 1952-53, adj. professor, 1953-58; dean Cathedral St. John the Divine, N.Y.C., 1952-58; bishop co-adjutor Diocese of Cal., 1958, bishop of Cal., 1958-66; sr. fellow Center for Study of Democratic Instns., Santa Barbara, 1966-69; lectr. law U. Cal., Berkeley, 1966-67; adj. prof. Grad. Theol. Union, Berkeley, 1966; founding pres. Found. for Religious Transition, 1969. Mem. standing committee Protestant Episcopal Ch., 68, Diocese N.Y., 1952-58, pres., 1955; deputy to the general conventions, 1952, 55; delegate at large Anglican Congress, 1954. Chmn. Cal. adv. com. to U.S. Commn. on Civil Rights, 1959-69. Trustee Gen. Theol. Sem., N.Y.C., Virginia Theol. Seminary, 1955-60, Church Divinity School of Pacific. Served as ensign, Lieutenant (j.g.) with USNR, 1943-45. Hon. fellow U. Tel-Aviv, 1956; post-doctoral fellow Soc. for Religion and Higher Edn.; recipient Medallion of Valor, State of Israel, 1961. Mem. Fed., San Francisco bar assn., American Academy of Political and Social Sci., Council for Middle Eastern Affairs (dir.), Order Coif. Clubs: Century Assn. (N.Y.C.); Pacific Union (San Francisco); Authors' (London). Author: Cases and Other Materials on the New Federal and Code Procedure, 1938; Beyond Anxiety, 1953; If You Marry Outside Your Faith, 1954; Doing the Truth, 1956; The Next Day, 1957; Our Christmas Challenge, 1961; Beyond the Law, 1963; A Time for Christian Candor, 1964; Teenagers and Sex, 1965; What Is This Treasure, 1966; You and The New Morality, 1967; If This Be Heresy, 1967. Co-Author: The Faith of the Church, 1951; Road Blocks to Faith, 1954; The Church, Politics and Society, 1955; Man in the Middle, 1956; A Roman Catholic in the White House, 1960; The Other Side, 1968. Editor: Modern Canterbury Pilgrims, 1956. Editor-at-large The Christian Century. Home: Santa Barbara CA Died Sept. 2, 1969; buried St. Peter's Protestant Cemetery, Jaffa Israel

PILAT, CARL FRANCIS, landscape architect; b. Ossining, N.Y., Aug. 19, 1876; s. Carl Francis and Anna (Enzinger) P.; grad. Ossining High Sch., 1893; Mt. Pleasant Mil. Acad., 1894; New York U., 1894-96; B.S. in Agr., Cornell U., 1900; travel and study in Eng., Germany, France and Italy, 10 months; m. Aloysia A. Cavanagh; 1 dau., Mary Olive. Asst. landscape architect to Charles W. Leavitt, Jr., New York, 1901-06; mem. firm of Hinchman, Pilat & Tooker, 1906-10, Hinchman & Pilat, architects and landscape engrs., 1910—. Landscape architect, Dept. of Parks of Greater New York. Asso. Technical Advisory Corpn. Mem. Nat. City Planning Conf., Am. City Planning Inst., Architectural League of New York, Am. Soc. Landscape Architects, Am. Civic Assn., Phi Gamma Delta. Clubs: City, Phi Gamma Delta. Home: 106 W. 56th St. Office: 15 Park Row, New York NY*‡

PILLSBURY, ELEANOR BELLOWS (MRS. PHILIP WINSTON PILLSBURY), assn. exec.; b. Minneapolis, Jan. 16, 1913; d. Henry Adams and Mary (Sanger) Bellows; brad. Northrup Collegiate Sch., Minneapolis, 1930; stu. Smith Coll., 1930-31; m. Philip Winston Pillsbury, July 5, 1934; children—Philip Winston, Henry Adams. Vice chmn. Hennepin Co. A.R.C., 1948-54, Nat. Fund Raising Campaign, A.R.C., 1951-53; secretary American Red Cross National Convention, 1950, member Mid-Western advisory council, 1950-54; director Minnesota research Council, National Health Council, 1950-53; exec. vice chmn. Planned Parenthood, Minn. League, 1947-48, pres., 1948-50; pres. Planned Parenthood Fedn. Am., 1950-53, chmn. exec. com., 1953-54, v.p., 1960-71, dir.; v.p. Internat. Planned Parenthood, 1953-56, regional steering com., 1953-55, chmn. spl. gifts, 1954-55, 1st v.p. Western Hemisphere regional council, 1955-65; president Service League to Hennepin County General Hospital, 1960-64, vice president, 1967-71. Recipient of Lasker award, 1953; Margaret Sanger award, 1966. Member of Colonial Dames of America, Minneapolis Junior League, National Council Chs. (women's com.). Club: Cosmopolitan (N.Y.). Episcopalian. Home: Wayzata MN Died Aug. 27, 1971.

PILLSBURY, GEORGE BIGELOW, army engr.; b. Lowell, Mass., Dec. 19, 1876; s. George Harlin and Mary Augusta (Boyden) P.; student Mass. Inst. Tech., 1894-96; grad. U.S. Mil. Acad., 1900; m. Bertha Eldredge Smith, June 22, 1909; children—George Harlin, Elizabeth Eldredge (Mrs. William B. Pringle, Jr.), Philip Lansdale, Thomas Sidney. Commd. 2d lt. Engr. Corps, U.S. Army, June 13, 1900, and advanced through grades to col., Nov. 30, 1928; engr. Alaska Rd. Commn., 1904-08; asso. prof. mathematics, U.S. Mil. Acad., 1908-12; dist. engr., New London (Conn.) Dist., 1912-16, Los Angeles (Calif.) Dist., 1916-17; comdr. 115th Engrs., 1917-18, 102d Engrs., 1918; corps engr., 2d Corps, A.E.F., 1918-19; mem. joint bd. of engrs., St. Lawrence Waterway, 1923-26; dist. engr., Phila. Dist., 1928-30; asst. to chief of engrs. U.S. Army, with rank of brig. gen., June 27, 1930, to Dec. 31, 1937; retired from active service, on own request. Awarded Distinguished Service Medal (U.S.). Clubs: Rittenhouse (Philadelphia); Bohemian (San Francisco). Home: Ross CA‡

PILLSBURY, JOHN SARGENT, flour mfr.; b. Minneapolis, Minn., Dec. 6, 1878; s. Charles Alfred and Mary Ann (Stinson) P.; B.S., U. of Minn., 1900; m. Eleanor J. Lawler, Dec. 5, 1911; children—John Sargent, Edmund Pennington, Ella Sturgis, Charles Alfred, Jane Lawler, George Sturgis. Learned flour milling business by working in all depts. of Pillsbury Mills, Inc., 1900-06, traveled 2 yrs., sales mgr., sec., treas., 1909-13, v.p., 1913-32, became chmn. bd., 1932, later honorary chairman board Pillsbury Company; dir. Northwestern Nat. Bank, Northwest Bancorporation. Served as battalion adjutant with the rank of 1st lt., Minn. N.G., until 1904, trustee Pillsbury Settlement House, Mpls. Mem. Chi Psi. Republican. Conglist. Clubs: Minneapolis; River, Links (N.Y.C.); Gulf Stream, Bath and Tennis (Palm Beach, Fla.). Home: Crystal Bay MN Died Jan. 31, 1968; buried Lakewood Cemetery, Minneapolis MN

PILLSBURY, WALTER BOWERS, psychologist; b. Burlington, Ia., July 21, 1872; s. William Henry Harrison and Eliza Crabtree (Bowers) P.; student Penn Coll., Oskaloosa, Ia., 1888-90; A.B., U. of Neb., 1892; Ph.D., Cornell, 1896; LL.D., U. of Neb., 1934; m. Margaret M. Milbank, June 16, 1905; children—Margaret Elizabeth, Walter Milbank. Asst. in psychology, Cornell U., 1895-97; instr., U. of Mich., 1897-1900, asst. prof., 1900-05, jr. prof. philosophy and dir. psychol. lab., 1905-10, prof. since 1910, chmn. dept. of psychology, 1929-42; emeritus since 1932; Henry Russel lecturer, University of Michigan, 1933. Lecturer in psychology, Columbia University, 1908-09; exchange professor Sorbonne, 1923. Chairman editorial com. Studies in Psychology (in honor of Prof. Titchener), 1917. Pres. Am. Psychol. Assn., 1910-11, Western Philos. Assn., 1907; v.p., and chmn. sect. H, A.A.A.S., 1913; mem. Nat. Research Council, 1921, 1931-34, Linguistic Soc. of America, Nat. Acad. Science, 1925, Associe Etranger de la societe francaise de psychologie, 1925. Contbr. to Am. Jour. of Psychology, Philos. Review, Scientia, etc. Author: L'Attention, 1906; Attention, 1908 (Spanish transl. 1910); Psychology of Reasoning, 1910; Essentials of Psychology, 1911, 20, 30; Fundamentals of Psychology, 1916, revised edit., 1934; Psychology of Nationality and Internationalism, 1919; Education as the Psychologist Sees It, 1925; Psychology of Language (with C.L. Meader), 1928; History of Psychology, 1929, 1936. An Elementary Psychology of the Abnormal, 1932; Psychology of Memory, 1938; Handbook of Psychology (with L.A. Pennington), 1942. Translated (with Prof. Titchener) Kulpe Introduction to Philosophy, 1897. Address: 1811 Hermitage Rd., Ann Arbor MI‡

PINANSKI, SAMUEL, theatre exec.; b. Boston, Mass., June 7, 1893; s. Nathan and Ida (Ginsberg) P.; student Boston Latin Sch., 1908, Volkman Cch. (now Nobel & Greenenough), 1910; grad. Lowell Textile Inst., 1913, M.S. and title Hon. Prof., (hon.), 1950; Doctor of Oratory (hon.), Staley Coll., 1950; m. Ann Green, June 17, 1915; children—Ruth (Mrs. Green), Doris (Mrs. Dunne). Pres. Am. Theatres Corp.; dir. John Hancock Mutual Life Ins. Co.; mem. bd. dirs., Theatre Owners of Am. (pres. 1949-50, 1951-52). Nat. chmn. motion picture industry, U.S. Savings Bond Drive, of Seventh War Loan. Trustee Museum of Science, E.E. chap. of Arthritis and Rheumatism Foundn., Lowell Textile Inst. (pres. bldg. assn., vice chmn., bd. trustees), Children's Hosp., Children's Cancer Research, Cambridge Sch. of Design. Mem. exec. bd. Boston council Boy Scounts of Am.; mem. bd.

overseers, Boys' Clubs of Boston; mem. adv. com., Mass. Sch. of Art. Chmn. Menorah Institute. Pres. Hebrew Free Loan Soc. Club: Variety of New England (trustee, chief barker for 1951). Home: Brookline MA Died Feb. 8, 1972.

PINCKARD, HAROLD RECENUS, editor; b. Monticello, Ill., Oct. 20, 1897; s. Lynne Recenus and Pernia Grace (Wollington) P.; student U. Ill., 1917-20; A.B., Marshall Coll., 1939; m. Mary Augusta King, Nov. 13, 1925; 1 dau., Joanne Mary (Mrs. Salvatore). Staff Chicago Evening Jour., 1920-21, Danville (Ill.) Comml.-News, 1921-22, Huntington Advertiser, 1922-23, Huntington Hearld-Dispatch, 1923-27; editor Huntington Hearld-Advertiser, 1927-72; tchr. book reviewing, editorial writing Marshall Coll. Sch. Journalism, 1932-42. Bd. dirs. Y.M.C.A., TB Assn., Symphony Assn., Automobile Club, 'Community Players; pres. Huntington community chest, 1937-38. Mem. Sigma Delta Chi, Pi Delta Epsilon, Psi Upsilon. Republican. Methodist. Author articles on coal industry. Home: Huntington WV Died Jan. 1972.

PINCKNEY, JOHN ADAMS, bishop; b. Mt. Pleasant, S.C., Mar. 8, 1905; s. Francis Douglas and Mary Lee (Adams) P.; student Coll. of Charleston, 1925-26, DuBose Meml. Sch., 1926-28; B.D., U. South, 1931, D.D., 1964; m. Hilda W. Emerson, Oct. 8, 1931; children—Hilda Emerson (Mrs. William C. Ross), John Adams, Francis Douglas. Ordained to ministry Episcopal Ch., 1931; minister Diocese of S.C., 1931-37, Ch. of Holy Cross, Tyron, N.C., 1937-39; rector St. Paul's Ch., Charleston, S.C., 1939-41; minister Holy Trinity Ch., Clemson, S.C., also chaplain Episcopal students Clemson Coll., 1941-48; rector St. James' Ch., Greenville, S.C., 1948-59; archdeacon Diocese of Upper S.C., 1959-63, bishop, 1963-72. Dir. youth confs. Kanuga Confs., Hendersonville, N.C., 1932-42, dir. confs. program, 1942-50, v.p. confs., 1967, pres. bd. trustee confs., 1971-72; sec. Diocese of Upper S.C., also sec. Diocesan Exec. Council, 1954-63; dep. to Gen. Convs. and Provincial Synods. Pres. bd. trustee Porter Acad., Charleston, S.C.; trustee Episcopal Radio-TV Found. Mem. Newcomen Soc. Home: Pacolet SC Died Dec. 7, 1972; buried Churchyard of Trinity Ch., Columbia SC

PINE, DAVID ANDREW, judge; b. Washington, D.C., Sept. 22, 1891; s. David Emory and Charlotte (McCormick) P.; LL.B., Georgetown University, 1913; honorary Doctor of Laws, 1954; graduate work at Georgetown U., 1913-14; m. Elizabeth Bradshaw, Aug. 23, 1916 (dec.); 1 dau., Elizabeth Pine Dayton; m. 2d, Elenore E. Townsend, July 8, 1959. Admitted to D.C. bar, 1913; with Dept. of Justice as confidential clerk to United States attorney general, 1914-16, law clerk, 1916-17, asst. attorney, 1919; special assistant to United States atty. gen. in Western States, 1919-21; private practive of law, Washington, D.C., 1921-34; mem. of firm of Easby-Smith, Pine & Hill, 1925-29; chief asst. U.S. atty., Dist. of Columbia, 1934-37; U.S. atty. for D.C., 1938-40; judge U.S. Dist. Ct. for D.C., 1940-70, chief judge, 1959-61, sr. judge, 1965. Served as 1st lt., later capt. inf., assigned to Provost Marshal Gen., World War I. Mem. Am. Bar Assn., Bar Assn. D.C. Democrat. Episcopalian. Clubs: Lawyers (past pres.), Barristers (past pres.); Metropolitan (Washington); Chevy Chase (Md.). Home: Washington DC Died June 11, 1970.

PINESS, GEORGE, physician; b. Odessa, Russia, Oct. 16, 1891; s. Louis and Sara (Roussel) P.; naturalized Am. citizen since 1914; M.D., U. of Maryland, 1913; Doctor Humane Letters, Hebrew Union Coll., 1959; Doctor of Laws, Loyola U. of Los Angeles, 1964; m. Hortense Weil, Apr. 6, 1898; children—Maxine Louise (wife of Ralph Bookman, M.D.), George, Jr. Intern. Passaic (N.J.) Gen. Hosp., 1913-14; resident physician, Hosp. of Good Samaritan, Los Angeles, 1916-18; grad. work in allergy, Peter Bent Brigham Hosp., Boston, Mass., 1918; in practice of medicine, Los Angeles, Calif., 1918-70; sr. attending in medicine, Cedar of Lebanon Hosp., 1918, attending in medicine, Hosp. of Good Samaritan; chief allergy clinic, Good Hope Hosp. Assn., Childrens Hosp. Soc. (all Los Angeles); consultant in allergy, Barlow Sanatorium, Los Angeles, 1920, St. Anne's Maternity Hosp., 1944, Long Beach V.A. Hosp., 1946; lecturer in pediatrics (allergy), U. of Calif., San Francisco, 1945, Bishop Johnson Sch. of Nursing; asso. prof. medicine U. So. Cal., 1944-48; chief of allergy, chmn. med. adv. bd. City of Hope Med. Center; past chmn. bd. St. Anne's Maternity Hosp. Sr. surg. USPHS Res. Member board directors Union Bank, Los Angeles. Dir. Los Angeles Convalescent Home, (asso.) Los Angeles Physicians Aid Assn. Director Los Angeles Convalescent Home; pres. Wilshire Blvd. Temple; pres. Fedn. Jewish Welfare Orgns., Holy Family Adoption Service; trustee Asso.-In-Group Donors; Union Am. Hebrew Congregations; v.p. Los Angeles Welfare Fedn.; dir. Council of Fedn. and Welfare Funds; adv. bd. So. California Symphony Association. Mem. bd. trustees Reed College, Portland, Oregon; regent of Immaculate Heart College, Los Angeles. Recipient gold feather Community Chest, 1955; merit award Los Angeles Jr. C. of C., 1965. Mem. adv. bd. allergy Am. Bd. Internal Medicine. Fellow A.C.P., Am. Acad. Allergy; mem. Am. Acad. Applied Nutrition, Cal., Los Angeles acads. medicine Am. Found. for Allergic Diseases (trustee), Los Angeles Physician Aid. Mason (Shriner). Clubs: Los Angeles, Los Angeles CA Died Dec. 26, 1970.

PINNELL, EMMETT LOUIS, educator; b. Oak Hill, Mo., Oct. 10, 1915; s. Louis David and Celia Mae (Wright) P.; B.S., U. Mo., 1940; M.S., U. Minn., 1942, Ph.D., 1948; m. Agnes Joan Moonan, June 19, 1948; children—Patrick, Linda, Robert, Peter, Anthony, Margaret, Mary. Research asst. U. Minn., 1940-41, research fellow, 1941-43, instr., 1943-48, asst. prof., 1948-52, asso. prof., 1952-57; prof., chmn. dept. of field crops U. Mo. Served with A.C., AUS, 1943-45. Mem. A.A.A.S., Am. Soc. Agronomy, Genetics Soc., Alpha Zeta, Gamma Alpha, Sigma Xi. Home: Columbia MO

PINNELL, LEROY KENNETH, univ. dean; B.S., Daniel Baker Coll.; M.A., W. Tex. State U.; Ed.D., U. Tex. Dean, prof. coll. edn. Eastern N.M. U., Portales. Home: Portales NM Died Oct. 25, 1972.

PINNEY, HARRY BOWMAN, dentist; b. Joliet, Ill., Apr. 18, 1875; s. Daniel H. and Mary (Bowman) P.; D.D.S., Chicago Coll. Dental Surgery, 1900; m. Mary Watt Skinner, Dec. 7, 1910. Began practice at Chicago, 1900; practiced at Nevins & Pinney, 1920-22, Pinney & Hodgman since 1922; specialist in extraction and X-ray work; prof. exodontia, Chicago Coll. Dental Surgery, since 1927. Mem. Am. Dental Assn. (sec.), Ill. State Dental Soc., Chicago Dental Soc., Xi Psi Phi. Republican. Presbyterian. Mason (32 deg., Shriner). Clubs: Rotary, Medical and Dental Arts. Home: 930 Columbian Av., Oak Park, Ill. Office: 55 E. Washington St., Chicago IL‡

PINSKI, DAVID, author; b. in Russia, Apr. 5, 1872; s. Isaac Mordecai and Sarah (Mardfin) P.; ed. U. of Berlin, 1897-99, Columbia, 1903-04; m. Adele Kaufman, of Bessarabia, Russia, May 21, 1897. Came to U.S., 1899; served as editor (weeklies) Der Arbeiter, Der Kaempfer, Die Wochenschrift, Daily Socialist-Zionist Die Zeit. Pres. Jewish Nat. Workers' Alliance, Jewish Theatre Soc. of New York. Socialist-Zionist. Author: The Treasure (comedy), 1916 (prod., 1920, by Theatre Guild, at Garrick Theatre, New York); Three Plays, 1918; Temptations (short stories), 1919; Ten Plays, 1919; King David and His Wives (drama), 1923; The Final Balance (prod., 1928, at Provincetown Playhouse, New York); Arnold Levenberg (novel), 1928; The Generations of Noah Edon (novel), 1931; also 6 vols. of dramas and 14 vols. of stories in Yiddish. Mem. Authors' League America, Dramatists' League America; pres. Jewish P.E.N. Club. Home: 2178 Broadway, New York NY*‡

PIPER, WILLIAM THOMAS, airplane manufacturer; b. Knapps Creek, N.Y., Jan. 8, 1881; s. Thomas and Sarah (Maltby) P.; B.S., Harvard Univ., 1903; m. Marie Vandewater, July 30, 1910 (dec.); children—William Thomas, Jr., Mary Vandewater (Mrs. John Savage Bolles), Thomas Francis, Howard, Elizabeth Maltby (Mrs. Thomas Hartford); m. 2d, Clara S. Taber, Dec. 22, 1943. Employed as construction supt., 1903-14; oil producer, Bradford, Pa., since 1914; pres. and dir. Piper Aircraft Corp., mfg. airplanes, 1929-70; mem. firm Dallas Oil Company. Served as private Pennsylvania Volunteer Inf., 1898; capt., engrs., U.S. Army, 1918-19. Mem. Pa. C. of C. (dir.). Republican. Rotarian. Home: Lock Haven PA Died Jan. 1970.

PIPES, LOUIS A(LBERT), scientist; b. Mexico City, Mexico, Oct. 22, 1910; s. David F. and Nela (de la Garza) P.; B.S., Cal. Inst. Tech., 1933, M.S., 1934, Ph.D., 1936; m. Johanna Woelfl. Teaching fellow Cal. Inst. Tech., 1934-36; instr. Rice Inst., 1936-37; postdoctoral fellow U. Wis., 1937-38; asst. prof. Harvard, 1938-46; prof. U. Cal. at Los Angeles, 1947-71, also research engr.; cons. Aerospace Corp., El Segundo, Cal., U.S. Naval Ordnance Test Sta., China Lake, Cal. Fellow I.E.E.E.; asso. fellow Inst. Aero. and Space Sics.; mem. Am. Math. Soc., Operations Research Soc. Author: Applied Mathematics for Engineers, 1946; Matrix Methods for Engineering, 1963; Operational Methods in Non Linear Mechanics, 1965; Computational Methods in Engineering; Marix-Computer Methods in Engineering, 1969; Digital Computer Methods in Engineering, 1969. Mem. bd. editors Jour. Applied Physics, 1952-71; asso. editor Jour. of Franklin Inst., Transp. Sci. Home: Playa del Rey CA Died Jan. 17, 1971; buried Westwood Memorial Chapel, Los Angeles CA

PIRE, DOMINIQUE GEORGES, clergyman, Nobel prize winner; born in Dinant, Belgium, February 10, 1910; the son of Georges and Bertha (Ravet); student philosophy Studium de la Sarte-Huy, Belgium, 1929-32; Doctorate Theology, U. Angelicum, Rome, Italy, 1936; student sociology U. Louvain, Belgium, 1936-37. Tchr. moral philosophy and sociology Studium de la Sarte-Huy, 1937-47; founder Huy Open Air Stations, 1938, Family Aid Service, 1940; founder of the international organization Aid to Displaced Persons, 1949, with affiliates in Germany Austria, Belgium, France, Luxembourg, Switzerland, also regional offices Denmark, Italy, Norway and Holland; founder many homes for displaced persons in Europe, and Europe villages; founder (association) The Heart Open to t World; founder of U. of Peace, Huy, Belgium, 196 founder of pilot-village Island of Peace, East Pakista 1962, a PIRE2d Island of Peace, in Madras State, Ind 1967. Decorated Croix de Guerre with palms, Cro d'Honneur du Merite Civique Francais, Resistan Medal with crossed swords, Medal of World War Legion of Honor; Cross of Merit Order of Me (Germany); recipient Nobel Peace prize, 1958, Sonni prize, Denmark, 1964. Author: Batir la Paix, 196 Vivre ou mourir ensemble, 1969. Address: Huy Belgiu Died Jan. 30, 1969; buried Cemetery of the Sarte, H Belgium

PIRELLI ALBERTO, rubber co. exec.; b. Milan, Ita Apr. 28, 1882; s. Giovanni B. and Maria (Sormani) grad. Sch. Econs., Milan; student Poly. Inst. Mila Faculty of Law U. Genoa; m. Ludovica Zambellet July 11, 1914; children—Giovanna Maria, Elen Giovanbattista, Leopoldo. Former pres., now honora chmn. Pirelli Societa per Azioni, Milan, Italy; chm Pirelli S.p.A., Industrie Pirelli S.p.A. (both Milan partner Pirelli & C., Milan; dir. Societe Internationa Pirelli, Basle, Switzerland, Dunlop Holdings Ltc Dunlop Ltd. (both London), G.I.M., Florence, Ita Mediobanca, Riunione Adriatica di Sicurta (bo Milan). Honorary Plenipotentiary Minister. Minister State, Italy, 1938. Mem. Internat. C. of C. (past pres Home: Milan Italy Died Oct. 19, 1971.

PIRQUET, CLEMENS FREIHERR VON, universi prof.; b. Vienna, Austria, May 12, 1874; s. Pet Freiherr and Flora Frelin (von Pereira) von P.; Ph.B., of Louvain, 1894; univs. of Vienna, Konigsberg ar Graz; N.D., Graz U., 1900; m. Maria van Husen, Borbeck, Germany, Sept. 1, 1904. Asst. to Pro Escherich, Vienna, 1901-9; privat docent, Vienna, 190 prof. pediatrics, Johns Hopkins U., and dir. Harri Lane Home for Children since Feb. 1, 1909. Roma Catholic. Author: Die Serumkrankheit, 1905; Klinisch Studien uber Vakzination und vakzinale Allergie, 190 Studied the symptomatical effects of injection of hor serum in man, as it is used in diphtheria antitoxin, ar wrote, with Dr. Schick, a monograph on this morb entity under the name of Serumdisease"; in exa studies of the symptoms of cowpox vaccination, formed a new theory as to the incubation time infectious diseases, and the immunity in sam attributing it to the accelerated reaction at a secor infection. Gave the name allergy" to the changed kir of reaction of the organism, which had been in tou with a disease; on the basis of these theoretical and cli studies, devised a new means of cutaneous diagnos which proved practical in tuberculosis, and is applie especially to children (cutaneous tuberculin test" of vo Pirquet test"). Address: 118 W. Franklin St., Baltimor

PISHTEY, JOSEPH JOSEPHSON, clergyman; Bridgeport, Conn., Apr. 6, 1899; s. Joseph and Ma (Haimilla) P.; grad. St. Platons Russian Orthodox Theo Sem., Tenafly, N.J., 1921; m. Susanna Padick, June 1922; children—Joseph, Wallace, Sonya (Mrs. Joh Perich). Ordained to ministry Russian Orthodox Ch 1924; pastor in Terryville, Conn., 1924-33, Old Forg Pa., 1933-35, Olyphant, Pa., 1935-40, Holy Trini Russian Orthodox Ch., Yonkers, N.Y., 1940-7 chancellor Russian Orthodox Ch. Am., 1963-72; chm adminstrv. com. Russian Orthodox Procathedra 1945-72. Chmn. Orthodox Clergy Fellowsh Westchester County, 1966-72. Spiritual advis Federated Russian Orthodox Clubs, Russian Orthodo Catholic Mut. Aid Soc. Trustee Russian Children Home, 1937-72; bd. dirs. St. Tikhon's Orthodox Sem South Canaan, Pa., St. Vladimir's Orthodox Theo Sem., Crestwood, N.Y. Author: The Divine Liturgy the Russian Orthodox Church, 1940; The Sacraments Confession and Communion, 1943; The Passions of O Lord, 1944. Address: Yonkers NY Died Nov. 2, 197 buried St. Tikhon's Monastery, South Canaan PA

PITCHER, CHARLES SIDNEY, hosp. ar institutional consultant; b. Rome, Pa., Oct. 13, 1874; Sidney Dunham and Kate Jane (Allen) P.; stude Orwell (Pa.) Acad., 1887-88, Rome (Pa.) Acad 1889-90, Eastman Business Coll., Poughkeepsie, N.Y 1893-94, extension dept., Indianapolis (Ind.) Coll. Law, 1900-03, N.Y. Sch. of Social Work, Columbi 1913-14, Teachers Coll., Columbia University, 1916-1 B.Sc., Eastern Coll., Manassas, Va., 1921; La Sa Extension U. (Chicago) Depart. of Law, 1941-44; Mamie Ann Birs, June 12, 1894 (died Nov. 18, 193 children—Charles Winfield, Mamie Elizabeth; m. 2 Harriet Elliott (Ferguson) Mitchell, June 14, 193 Clerk Hudson River State Hosp., Poughkeepsie, N.Y 1892-93, asst. storekeeper, 1893-96, storekeepe 1896-1900; resident steward Manhattan State Hosp East, New York, N.Y., 1900-01; resident steward, Kin Park (N.Y.) State Hosp., 1901-06, resident steward ar dep. treas., 1906-11, steward and dep. treas., 1911-2 sec. to com. on dietary and food supplies of all hosps. Dept. of Mental Hygiene (formerly State Hos Commn.), Albany, N.Y., 1916-20; mem. purchasi com., N.Y. State Hosps., Albany, N.Y., 1913-16; mer legislative com. on budget, chmn. sub-com. in charge statistics, Dept. of Mental Hygiene, Albany, N.Y 1916-18; supt., Presbyn. Hosp., Phila., 1920-33, se orp., 1931-32, chmn. corp., 1933; dir. course in hosp. nd institutional management, Temple U., Phila., 924-28; consultant and administrator, Hollywood Calif.) Hosp., 1937; consultant and administrator, resbyn. Hosp. Olmsted Memorial; Lessee Hollywood Hosp., Hollywood, Calif., 1937-38, consultant, 1938-41. erved as 1st lt., S.C., Surgeon Gen.'s. Office, 1918. Dir. nstitutional div. U.S. Food Adminstrn., 1918; mem. oint conf. com. Hosp. Assn. of Pa. and State med. socs., 928-29; mem. survey com. Phila. Hosp. and Health urvey, 1929; mem. Mayor Moore's Com. to study osp. situation in Phila., 1932; expert examiner, N.Y. Civil Service Commn., Municipal Civil Service Commn. f N.Y. City, 1914-31. Charter hon. fellow Am. Coll. of Hosp. Adminstrs.; life mem. Am. Hosp. Assn. (mem. om. on training hosp. execs. 1923-24; mem. com. on ublic edn. 1932-33); mem. Joint Com. Nat. Hosp. Assns., 1933-37; charter life mem. and trustee Am. Protestant Hosp. Assn. (mem. exec. com.; chmn. com. n publicity; chmn. legislative-com., chmn. com. on raining hosp. exec.; v.p. 1931-32; pres. elect 1932-33; res. 1933-34; chmn. trustees sect. 1940-41); charter nem. Pa. Hosp. Assn. (v.p.; chmn. legislative com.; nem. public relations com.; trustee 1930-33); mem. Hosp. Assn. of Phila. (v.p.; trustee, mem. exec. com.; chmn. legislative com. 1923-37); mem. Internat. Hosp. Assn., Coll. of Hosp. Management (Marquette U., Milwaukee, Wis.; mem. advisory bd. 1923-24), Quartermaster's Assn. (Washington, D.C.), Pa. Soc. Mayflower Descendants. Awarded Charter Hon. Fellowship by American College of Hospital Adminstrators, 1934. Presbyn. Mason (Royal Arch.; K.T.; Scottish Rite). Member of Orwell (Pa.) Grange treasurer). Clubs: Yorktown (Virginia) Country (Life mem.); Arrowhead Alpine (Alpine Glens Park, Cal.; Asso. life mem.); Union Masonic (Towanda, Pa.). Author: Hospital Management, 1940; also articles on osp. management to The Modern Hospital, Hospital Management, and other hosp. publs.; article Do Hospitals Lose Money Through Associated or Group Hospital Plans?"; addresses before Am. Coll. of urgeons, 1923; Kitchen Organization and Administration (pamphlet), 1914. Prepared reports of Com. on Dietary and Food Supplies for N.Y. State Hosps., 1916-20. Editorial supervisor, Basic Quantity ood Tables (book), 1917. Author of pamphlet nstitutional Food Conservation" printed and istributed in 1918 by the United States Food Adminstration. Address: Rome PA‡

ITFIELD, ROBERT LUCAS, physician; b. at Germantown, Pa., Feb. 28, 1870; s. Benjamin H. and rances (Pleasants) P.; prep. edn. Friends' Sch., Germantown, Westtown Sch., Chester Co., Pa.; M.D., . of Pa., 1892; m. Georgiana G. Starin, of Phila., 1894. esident phys. German Hosp., 1892-3; demonstrator in acteriology, Medico-Chirurg. Coll., 1902-4; visiting hys. St. Timothy's Hosp., 1908—, and to Germantown Hosp. Fellow Coll. Physicians of Phila. epublican. Mem. Soc. of Friends. Club: Germantown ricket. Author: Bacteriology, 1906; also essays, etc. ddress: 5211 Wayne Av., Germantown Philadelphia‡

ITKIN, FRANCIS ALEXANDER, planning cons.; ormer state ofcl., b. Akron, O., June 2, 1899; s. Stephen Henderson and Bessie Hamilton (Alexander) P.; B.S. in E.E., Case Inst. Tech., 1922; m. Ruth Elizabeth Mason, Mar. 17, 1928; 1 son, Stephen Henderson. Asso. with everal engring. cos., Pitts. and Phila., 1923-30; chief ngr. and constrn. supt. water supply and sewage system evel., 1930-34; mem. staff Nat. Resources Com., oaned to Pa. to assist in establishment state planning ctivities, 1934-35; asst. dir. Pa. State Planning Bd., 934, exec. dir., 1936-55, 59-64; dir. community devel. a. Dept. Commerce, 1955-59; adminstr. Pa. Housing nd Redevel. Program, 1949-59; chmn. Interstate Commn. on Delaware River, 1948-62; mem. exec. com. Gt. Lakes Commn., 1956-69, chmn. Pa. delegation, 961-69; 1st chmn. Interstate Conf. on Water Problems, 958-60; sec.-treas. Pa. Planning Assn.; mem. various ch. coms. Interstate Commn. on Potomac River Basin, nterstate Com. Postwar Reconstrn. and Devel. Council tate Govts., 1943-44; mem. bd. Pa. Roadside Council, a. Forestry Assn. (past v.p., dir.); chmn. Pa. Pub. ervice Inst. Bd., 1951-61, sec. Pa. Recreation Council, 952-55; past v.p., bd. Harrisburg Symphony Soc.; nat. r. Nat. Rivers and Harbors Congress, 1949-69, mem. xec. com., 1961-69; mem. adv. bd. Harrisburg Hosp.; ustee Harrisburg Pub. Library, pres. bd., 1948-62. erved in heavy arty. Officers Tng. Sch., Ft. Monroe, a., World War I; served in USCGR, World War II. ecipient silver medal meritorious award Am. Soc. lanning Ofcls., 1961; Breidenthal Distinguished ervice medal Nat. Rivers and Harbors Congress, 1964; Distinguished Service award Am. Inst. Planners, 1964. Mem. Am. Soc. Planning Ofcls. (pres. 1953-54), Nat. Assn. State Planning and Devel. Agys. (past pres.), Am. nst. Planners, Am. Planning and Civic Assn., Pa. Soc. N.Y., Engrs. Soc. Pa., Phi Delta Theta. Methodist chmn. ch. bldg. com., past pres. bd. trustees, past pres. fcl. bd.). Clubs: Eclectic, Torch (past pres.). Author rticles in field. Contbg. editor Planning and Civic omment. Lectr., cons. state, regional and community lanning. Address: Camp Hill PA Died May 27, 1969.

PITTMAN, ERNEST WETMORE, chem. corp. exec.; born Detroit, Michigan, Dec. 19, 1889; s. Lansing Mizner and Annette Phelps (Steuart) P.; grad. Phillips Andover Acad., 1909; Ph.B., Sheffiedl Scientific Sch. (Yale), 1912; m. Estelle Young Romeyn, Oct. 23, 1915; children—Estelle Patricia, Steuart Lansing, Annetae Romeyn (dec.). Engr. apprentice, 1912; engr. Niles, Bement Pond Co., 1912-14, New England Westinghouse Co., 1914-17, Nat. Commerical Bank, Albany, 1919-22; pres. Rathbone Sard & Co., 1922-26; engr. Dillon Read & Co., 1926-31; former pres., chmn. exec. com. Interchem. Corp., also dir. Mem. board managers Memorial Hosp., N.Y. City; chief Rubber and Chemical Section, U.S. Strategic Bombing Survey, Chief of Am. Rubber Mission to Soviet Union, 1942. Served as capt. Ordnance Dept., Watervliet Arsenal, U.S. Army, 1917-19. Mem. Chi Phi, Aurelian. Clubs: Union, University (New York). Home: Washington DC Died Apr. 1970.

PITTMAN, HOBSON, artist; b. Epworth, N.C., Jan. 14, 1899; s. Biscoe and Alice (Walston) P.; editor Pa. State U., Columbia and Carnegie Inst. Tech.; student Rouse Art Sch., Tarboro, N.C., 1912-16. Dir. art Friends Central Country Day Sch., 1931-58; instr. criticism and painting Pa. Acad. Fine Arts; lectr. Phila. Mus. Art. Exhibited in large museums of U.S., Paris, London and Venice; had one-man shows in large Am. cities, including Milch Galleries, N.Y.C., Babcock Galleries, N.Y.C., McCleaf Galleries, Phila., Erdman Hall of Bryn Mawr Coll, 1971, David, David, Inc., Phila., 1972; retrospective exhbn. N.C. Mus. Art; exhbns. at Ackland Mus., Chapel Hill, N.C., Richmond (Va.) Mus. Art, 1966, Pa. Acad. Fine Arts, 1966; retrospective at Mus. Art of Pa. State U., 1972, Pa. Acad. Fine Arts, 1973; represented Met. Mus. Art, Whitney Mus., N.Y.C., Pa. Acad. Fine Arts, Phila. Mus. Art, Phillips Meml. Gallery, Washington, Va. Mus. Fine Arts, Richmond, Neb. Art Assn., Lincoln, Butler Art Inst., Youngstown, O., Carnegie Inst., Pitts., Brooks Meml. Gallery, Memphis, Addison Gallery Am. Art, Andover, Mass., John Heron Art Mus., Indpls., Wilmington (Del.) Soc. Artists, IBM, Pa. State U., Florence (S.C.) Mus., Ency. Brit., N.A.D., N.C. State Art Gallery collections; art museums Bklyn., Cleve., Toledo, Montclair, Phoenix, Santa Barbara. Recipient numerous honors and awards including: 1st prize Butler Mus. Am. Art, 1955; John S. Guggenheim Grant, 1956; Columbia U. Painting Prize, 1960; Pa. State U. medal of honor; State of N.C. award, 1967; N.C. award in fine arts, 1968. Fellow Phila. Mus. Art; mem. Pa. Acad. Fine Arts, Internat. Platform Assn., Internat. Inst. Arts and Letters (hon.), N.A.D., Phila. Watercolor Club. Home: Bryn Mawr PA Died May 5, 1972.

PITTS, LLEWELLYN WILLIAM, architect; b. Uniontown, Ala., Sept. 10, 1906; s. William Llewellyn and Mattie (Harwood) P.; B.S., Ga. Inst. Tech., 1927; m. Garnette Northcott, June 5, 1935; 1 dau., Sally (Mrs. James M. Stokes). With Robert & Company and Felch & Southwell, architects, Atlanta, Georgia, 1927-30; member of firm Stone & Pitts, architects and engrs., Beaumont, Tex., 1930-57; sr. partner Pitts, Mebane & Phelps, architects and engrs., Beaumont, 1957-64, Pitts, Mebane, Phelps and White, 1964-67; principal works include 19 Coca-Cola bottling plants (first honor award indsl. architecture Houston plant, A.I.A. 1951), 1940-60, master plan and 35 bldgs. Lamar State Coll. Tech., Beaumont (medal of honor S.E. Tex. chpt. A.I.A. 1955), numerous bldgs. for Gulf Oil Co., Port Arthur, Tex., 1952-60, Socony Mobil Oil Co. bldgs., Beaumont, 1952, Shell Oil Lab., New Orleans, 1958, library bldg. Tex. Tech. Coll., Lubbock, 1960, Texaco Research Center, Port Arthur, 1960, also university buildings, schools and hosps. in Texas; co-designer State Office Bldg., 1957, Tex. Employment Commn. Bldg. (both Austin), 1958, U.S. Embassy Office Building, Mexico City, 1959, Labor Dept. Building, Washington; consultant Beaumont Planning Commn., 1953; chmn. archtl. adv. com. Tex. Bldg. Commission, 1958-61. Member of board of directors First Security National Bank (Beaumont, Texas). A.I.A. del. to Union Internat. Architects, 1963. Gen. chmn. Beaumont United Appeals fund campaign, 1954. Served to lt. comdr. USNR, 1942-45. Fellow A.I.A. (nominating committee 1961; member nat. bd. dirs. 1963-66, chmn. com. on future of the profession 1966-67); member of the Texas Soc. Architects (pres. 1961), Sociedad de Arquitectos Mexicanos (hon.), Alpha Tau Omega, Phi Kappa Phi, Tau Beta Pi, Pi Delta Epsilon. Episcopalian. Clubs: Beaumont Country (pres. 1953), Rotary (pres. 1956), Round Table (pres. 1952), Beaumont Downtown (Beaumont); The Citadel, Headliners (Austin, Tex.). Home: Beaumont TX Died June 23, 1967; buried Magnolia Cemetery, Beaumont TX

PITTS, MARY HELEN MCCREA WEAVER, lawyer, law librarian; b. Spokane, Wash., Mar. 20, 1898; d. William Stone and Kate Wordly (Brook) McCrea; student Whitman College, 1916-17, Wellesley College, 1917-18; A.B., U. Washington, 1920; diploma U. So. Cal. Library Sch., 1924; A.M., Gonzaga U., 1930, LL.B., 1955, J.D., 1967; postgrad. U. Chgo., 1933, Stanford, 1950-51, U. Ida., 1951, U. Utah, 1954; m. Samuel Pool Weaver, Jan. 1, 1957; m. 2d, Herbert Ryder Pitts, Mar. 27, 1967. Asst. librarian Lewis and Clark High Sch., 1921-22, 26-28, head librarian 1929-40; library asst. Seattle Pub. Library, 1922-23, Los Angeles Pub. Library, 1923-24; sec. Wash. Edn. Bur., 1924-26; librarian Libby Jr. High Sch., 1928-29; instr. library sci. Wash. State Coll., 1937-40; librarian 14th Naval Dist., Pearl Harbor, 1941-43; admitted to Hawaii bar, 1955; law librarian Supreme Ct., Hawaii 1943-61; law library cons., 1963-69. Del. 2d Internat. Library Congress, Madrid, Spain, 1935; del. World Sunday Sch. Congress, Rio de Janeiro, 1932, Oslo, Norway, 1936. Bd. dirs. Honolulu Community Theater, 1958-60; mem. bd. dirs. Honolulu Theatre for Youth, 1959, 61. Member Miami Heart Inst. Women's Auxillary, Nat. League of Am. Pen Women (br. pres. 1966-68, state pres. 1968-70), Am., Hawaii library assns., Am. Assn. Law Libraries, Am. Assn. U. Women, Honolulu Acad. Arts, Bishop Mus. Assn., Am., Hawaii bar assns., Composers Artists and Authors Am. (state pres. 1959-63), Internat. Platform Assn., Internat. Fedn. U. Women, Archaeol. Inst. Am., Pioneer Assn. State of Wash., Waiki Bus. and Profl. Women's Club, Nat. Assn. Women Lawyers, Internat. Fedn. Women Lawyers, YWCA (life), Eastern Washington State Hist. Soc. (life), Delta Delta Delta, Phi Delta Delta. Episcopalian. Mem. Order Eastern Star, Daus. of Nile. Clubs: Wellesley; Altrusa. Co-editor; Significance of the School Library, 1937. Contbr. articles, childrens poems to mags. Home: Spokane WA Died Sept. 5, 1969; buried Fairmount Meml. Park Spokane WA

PIVER, SARA ELIZABETH EARLY (MRS. SARA EARLY PIVER), nurse; b. Charlottesville, Va.; d. Fred Roy and Annie (Fansler) Early; diploma U. Va. Hosp. Tng. Sch. for Nurses, 1931, Woman's Hosp., 1933; B.S., U. Va., 1936; m. William C. Piver, Aug. 31, 1940 (div. Oct. 1963); children—William C., Sandra Roy. Asst. night supr. Siani Hosp., Balt., 1936-37; obstetric, gynecology supr. Belview Hosp., Camden, N.J., 1938; asst. dir. nurses, instr. Woman's Homeopathic Hosp., Phila., 1938-40; sci. instr. Luth. Hosp., Cleve., 1940-41; dir. nurses, instr. Bapt. Hosp., Alexandria, La., 1941-42; asst. dir., instr. Tayloe Hosp., Washington, N.C., 1946-47; instr. State Dept. Edn., Beaufort County Hosp., Washington, N.C., 1962-63; pub. health nursing Beaufort County Health Dept., 1965-69, program coordinator, discussion leader continuing edn. program, 1968. Mem. P.T.A., 1953-67, v.p., 1958-59; mem. Washington Safety Council, 1957-60, sec.-treas., 1957-59; organizer, president of the Aux. Beaufort County Medical Society, 1953-55; state chmn. Jane Todd Meml. Fund, 1954-56; organizing mem. Little Tar Heel League, 1957, sec.-treas., 1958-60, recipient Meritorious Civic Service certificate, 1962; mem. Washington Woman's Club, 1955-59, bd. dirs. 1958-59. Bd. dirs. Civil Def., A.R.C., Tideland Mental Health Assn. Recipient Community Service certificate Aux. Med. Soc. N.C., 1963. Mem. Am., N.C., Dist. 20 (past pres.) nurses assns., N.C. Pub. Health Assn., Registered Nurses Club (past pres.), U.D.C. (pres. 1965-67), D.A.R. (neighborhood study com. Econ. Opportunity Act 1965-66). Democrat. Episcopalian. Home: Washington DC Died Aug. 7, 1969.

PLACHY, FRED JOSEPH, coll. pres.; b. Ponca, Neb., Apr. 19, 1901; s. Joseph and Rose (Washiecek) P.; B.S., Huron (S.D.) Coll., 1927; M.A., U. Neb., 1931; Ed.D., Colo. State Coll., 1951; m. Margaret Rich, Jan. 1, 1927; children—Shirley Rose (Mrs. Robert W. Dunn), Fredric Rich, Jon Milton. Faculty Colegio Americano Para Varones, Barranquilla, Colombia, S.A., 1927-36; tchr., dir. Presbyn. Boys Sch., 1927-36; supt. pub. schs., Colome, S.D., 1936-39, Tyndall, 1939-43; dean Huron Coll., 1943-47; supt. pub. schs., Wilmot, S.D., 1947-49; asst. prof. edn. Colo. State Coll. Edn., 1949-51; prof. edn., dir. extension Black Hills Tchrs. Coll., Spearfish, S.D., 1951-52; pres. Adams State Coll., Alamosa, Colo., from 1952. Mem. Alamosa C. of C. (pres.), Nat., Colo. edn. assns., S.D. Edn. Assn. (pres. Southeast dist. 1947), Am. Assn. Sch. Adminstrs., Newcomen Soc., Phi Delta Kappa. Republican. Presbyn. (elder). Rotarian (dist. gov. 1962-63). Home: Denver CO Died Dec. 21, 1972; buried Fairmont Cemtery, Denver CO

PLANT, MARION BORCHERS, lawyer; b. Davis, Cal., July 30, 1907; s. Albert June and Mary (Borchers) P.; A.B., U. Cal. at Berkeley, 1929, LL.B., 1933; m. Frances Bernice Boone, Apr. 23, 1936; children—Brenda (Mrs. Jerry Lee Taylor), Alison (Mrs. William Leslie Portello). Admitted to Cal. bar, 1933, since practiced in San Francisco; asso. Brobeck, Phleger & Harrison, 1933-46, partner, 1946-68. Mem. Am. (mem. council; chmn. sect. labor relations law 1965-66), Cal., San Francisco bar assns. Clubs: Bohemian, Pacific Union. Home: San Francisco CA Died 1968.

PLASTER, JERRY GLEN, hosp. adminstr.; b. Sapulpa, Okla., Nov. 3, 1935; s. Glen E. and Florine (Vanderburg) P.; B.S., U. Denver, 1957; m. Dorothy J. Schmunk, Feb. 5, 1956; children—Craig, Cinthia, Bradley, Polly. Accountant, Alexander J. Lindsay & Co., 1957-60, Lenhart & Plaster, C.P.A.s, Scottsbluff, Neb., 1960-65; asst. adminstr. W. Neb. Gen. Hosp., Scottsbluff, 1965-70. Pres. Mormon Trail Dist., Boy Scouts of Am., 1967-70; chmn. Zoning Bd. of Adjustment, 1966-67. Mem. Scotts Bluff County Assn. Pub. Accountants (pres. 1962-63), Am. Inst. C.P.A.'s, Neb. Soc. C.P.A.'s, Am. Assn. Hosp. Accountants, Scottsbluff Jr. C. of C. (pres. 1963-64), Neb. Jr. C. of C.

(v.p. 1964-65), Sigma Chi. Republican. Methodist. Home: Scottsbluff NE Died Feb. 12, 1970; interred Fairview Cemetery Scottsbluff NB

PLATE WALTER, artist; b. Woodhaven, L.I., N.Y., June 9, 1925; s. Oscar Herman and Loretta (Finnell) P.; student Grand Central Sch. Art, N.Y.C., 1942-43, Ecole des Beaux Arts, also La Grande Chaomiere Leger, Paris, France, 1947-50; m. Gladys Brodsky, July 2, 1953; children—Marc, Daniel. Tchr., Art Students League, Woodstock, N.Y., summers 1959-62; asso. prof. art Rensselear Polytech. Inst., 1964; distinguished vis. critic art U. So. Ill., spring 1962; one man show Ganso Gallery, N.Y.C., 1954, Stable Gallery, N.Y.C., 1958-60; group exhbns. include Purchase Exhbn. of Kresge Art Center, Mich. State U., 1959, Whitney annuals, 1957-61, Young Am., 1957, Nature in Abstraction, 1958, 63 Annual at Denver Art Mus., 1957, Contemporary Paintings and Sculpture at U. Ill., 1959, biennials Am. painting and sculpture Detroit Inst. Art, 1960, biennials exhbns. Pa. Acad. Fine Arts, 1955, 60, Abstract Expressionist Painting and Sculpture of the Fifties at Walker Art Center, Mpls., 1960, Pitts. Internat., 1955, 26th and 27th biennial exhbns. Art Inst. Chgo., 1959, 61, Am. abstract show Tate Gallery, London, Eng., 1959, Internat. Art Exhbn. Abstract Artists, Tokyo, Japan, 1959; rep. permanent collections Corcoran Gallery, Whitney Mus., Johnson Found. Co., also pvt. collections. Recipient Woodstock Found. award, 1953, 1st prize Corcoran Biennial, 1959. Address: Woodstock NY Died Aug. 6, 1972.

PLATOU, RALPH VICTOR, physician; b. Valley City, N.D., Jan. 20, 1909; s. Ludwig Stoud and Martha (Schoyen) P.; B.S., U. Minn., 1932, M.B., 1935, M.D., 1936, M.S. in Pediatrics, 1941; m. Joanne Pierson, Jan. 23, 1942; children—Peter, Thomas, Mary Kirk. Intern and resident physician Babies' Hosp., N.Y.C., 1936-38; resident physician and instr., dept. pediatrics U. Minn., 1938-41; asso. prof., acting head dept. pediatrics Tulane U. Med. Sch., 1942-43, prof., chmn. dept. pediatrics., 1944-67; prof. pediatrics, chmn. dept. pediatrics U. Hawaii, 1967-68; medical director Kaui-Keolani Children's Hospital, Honolulu, Hawaii; cons. USAF; cons. to surgeon-gen. U.S. Army (Europe), 1962; chmn. Fulbright Com. in med. and biol. scis., 1964-68. Diplomate Am. Bd. Pediatrics (dir.; exec. sec. 1968). Mem. Am. Acad. Pediatrics (cons. com. med. edn.), Am. (v.p. 1962-63), La. pediatric socs., Soc. Pediatric Research, Am., La. med. assns., Soc. Clin. Investigation, Alpha Omega Alpha, Phi Gamma Delta, Nu Sigma Nu, Delta Omega. Contbr. profl. jours. and texts. Former editor Pediatrics. Office: Honolulu HI Died Sept. 15, 1968.

PLATT, LIVINGSTON, lawyer; b. N.Y. City, March 7, 1885; s. Frank H. and Caroline Elizabeth (Livingston) P.; grad. Phillips-Andover Acad., 1903; A.B., Yale, 1907; LL.B. cum laude, N.Y. Law Sch., 1909; m. Agnes Booth, June 28, 1909; children—Frank H., William V., Livingston, Priscilla Lester (Mrs. Albert B. Hooke). Admitted to N.Y. State bar, 1909, since practiced in N.Y.C. and White Plains with Bleakley, Platt, Schmidt, Hart & Fritz and predecessor firms; chmn. bd., dir. T. Hogan & Sons, Incorporated, R.A.C. Corporation; director of National Bank of Westchester. Trustee of the Village of Rye, 1925-29, mayor, 1930-41, mayor City of Rye, 1942-43. Del. N.Y. State Constitutional Conv. 1938. 1st lt., Air Service, U.S. Army, 1917-18. Trustee Miriam Osborn Meml. Home. Mem. Am. Legion, U.S. Seniors Golf Assn. (pres. 1950-52, honorary president 1961-63), National Tb Assn. (past director, treasurer 1942-45), Soc. Cincinnati. Rep. (chmn. Westchester County com., 1943-51, chmn. exec. com., 1951-53; mem. N.Y. Rep. State Com. and executive committee 1943-53. Mason. Clubs: Blind Brook, American Yacht, Apawamis (pres. 1927-38) (Rye); The Links, Univ., Yale (pres. 1929-31), Down Town Assn. (N.Y.C.). Home: Rye NY Died Nov. 1968.

PLATT, SAMUEL, lawyer; b. Carson City, Nev., Nov. 17, 1874; s. Joseph and Malvina (Bash) P.; Stanford U., Calif.; LL.B., Columbian (now George Washington) U., 1897; married. Began practice, Carson City 1896; identified with important mining suits; ex-pres. of Reno Evening Gazette. Rep. candidate dist. atty., Ormsby County, Nev., 1897, atty.-gen. of Nev., 1899; apptd. asst. sec. of state, Nev., 1900; elected mem. Nev. Ho. of Rep., 1903; reelected, 1905, and elected speaker of House; apptd. U.S. atty. Dist. of Nev., by President Roosevelt, 1906, reapptd. by President Taft, 1910; apptd. spl. asst. to atty.-gen. of U.S., May 24, 1910; del. 4 Rep. state convs. Rep. nominee for U.S. senator, 1914 (defeated in statewide vote by 38 votes); del.-at-large to Rep. Nat. Conv., 1916, 20, 28; nominee for U.S. senator, 1928 and 1940; apptd. Nev. counsel for Reconstruction Finance Corp., and Defense Plant Corporation, 1914; director Pacific Nat. Life Assurance Co. Mem. Am. Bar Assn., Washoe County Bar Assn. (pres.), Roosevelt Memorial Assn. (state chmn.), Nev. Community Concert Assn. (pres.), Delta Upsilon. Mason, K.P., Elk, Eagle. Club: Rotary. Home: 1000 Plumas St.

PLAUT, EDWARD, merchant; b. New York, N.Y., Nov. 9, 1891; s. Albert and Bertha (Berns) P.; A.B., Princeton, 1912; A.M., Columbia, 1913, Ph.D., 1916; m. Edith Newman, Feb. 2, 1916; children—Albert, Walter, Edward; m. 2d, Alexandra Stewart Plankinton, April 4, 1933; m. 3d, Yvonne Mavet, December 20, 1938. Past pres. Lehn and Fink Products Co., and subsidiary cos. Served during World War as lt. Sanitary Corps. Mem. bd. trustees Coll. of Pharmacy, Columbia; trustee Central Presbyterian Church, N.Y. City. Member Am. Chem. Soc., Am. Pharm. Assn., Soc. Chem. Industry, A.A.A.S. Democrat. Presbyterian. Mason (Shriner). Clubs: Princeton (New York); St. Cloud Country, Polo, Cercle Interallie (Paris). Home: Carefree AZ Died Mar. 1972.

PLAYTER, HAROLD, consular service; b. Girard, Kan., Oct. 19, 1877; s. Joseph H. and Eva M. (Dodds) P.; grad. Collegiate Sch., Santa Barbara, Calif., 1897; student U. of Calif., 1897-98; m. Jess Hale Houston, Oct. 4, 1909; children—Virginia Eva (dec.), Carmelita Patricia, Jane Houston. Mill man, clerk and supt. mines, 1899-1907; with cyanide plant, Mexico, 1909-14; farmer and writer of short stories, 1914-16; apptd. consul, Saltillo, Mexico, 1919, Corinto, Nicaragua, 1921, Seville, Spain, 1926-28, Lille, France, 1928-33, St. Michael's, Azores, 1933-36, Newcastle-on-Tyne, England, since Sept. 1936. Mem. Kappa Alpha. Address: Dept. of State, Washington DC‡

PLUMMER, JOHN WATROUS, lawyer; b. Newton, Kan., Aug. 16, 1924; s. Bernard W. and Laura E. (Hackney) P.; student Colo. U., 1942; A.B., Bethel Coll., 1951; LL.B., Washburn U., Topeka, Kan., 1954; m. Evelyn M. Pierce, Dec. 23, 1951; children—Douglas W., Richard W., Dale W., Barbara Jo. Admitted to Kan. bar, 1954; partner Peterson & Plummer, Newton, 1955-68; county atty. Harvey County, Kan., 1956-61; assistant city attorney, Newton, 1967-68. Active Community Chest. Mem. Harvey County Republican Control Com. Served to cpl. AUS, 1942-46. Mem. Am. Kan., Central Kan. (sec., treas.), Harvey County (v.p. 1966-67, pres. 1967-68) bar assns., Am. Legion, Nat. Dist. (state dir. 1961, v.p.) Kan. County (v.p. 1959, pres. 1960, chmn., 1959). Republican. Episcopalian (vestryman). Elk, Lion. Home: Newton KS Died Sept. 1, 1968.

PLUMMER, RALPH WALTER, physician; b. Chicago, Ill., Oct. 18, 1874; s. George Washington and Emily Elvira (McClintock) P.; student Allegheny Coll., 1890-94; M.D., U. of Chicago, 1897; student Naval War Coll., 1921-22; H.M.D., Hahnemann Med. Coll., 1935; m. Lillian Cecile Butts, Oct. 19, 1899. Began as physician, U.S. Navy, 1897; served with U.S. Navy Med. Corps, 1899-1929, retiring with rank of capt.; med. dir. Hahnemann Hosp., Phila., since 1930. Awarded citations in Philippine Insurrection and World War. Fellow Am. Coll. of Surgeons, A.M.A.; mem. Phi Kappa Psi. Republican. Methodist. Mason (32 deg., Shriner). Club: Union League (Phila.). Home: 4224 Pine St. Office: Hahnemann Hospital, Philadelphia PA*‡

PLUMMER, SAMUEL C., retired surgeon; b. Rock Island, Ill., Apr. 27, 1865; s. Samuel C. and Julia (Hayes) P.; desc. Francis Plummer, Newburyport, Mass., 1633; A.B., Augustana Coll., 1883, A.M., 1886, Ph.D., 1900; M.D., Chicago Medical College, 1886; Sc.D., Northwestern U., 1940; m. Mary Louise Middleton, March 18, 1903; children—Susan M., William M. (dec.), Samuel C, III. Practiced surgery, Chicago, 1891-1936; successively prof. anatomy, operative surgery and clin. surgery Northwestern U. Med. Sch., 1891-1908; hon. staff surgeon to St. Luke's Hosp.; chief surgeon, C., R.I.&P. Ry., 1902-36; retired, 1936. Apptd. 1st lt. Med. Reserve Corps, U.S. Army, 1911; served 16 mos. in World War (8 mos. in France) as maj. Med. Corps, U.S. Army. Fellow Am. Coll. Surgeons; mem. Am. and Western surg. assns., Chicago Surg. Soc., A.M.A., Ill. State and Chicago med. socs., Inst. of Medicine Chicago. Home: 914 Thirteenth St., Boulder CO‡

PLYLER, ALVA WASHINGTON, clergyman, editor; b. Iredell County, N.C., Sept. 14, 1867; s. Robert Conrad and Mary Lunda (Kimball) P.; A.B., Trinity Coll. (now Duke U.), Durham, N.C.; grad. study U. of Chicago, 1909; D.D., Asbury Coll., 1932; D.D., Duke U., 1937; m. Grace Davis Barnhardt, July 20, 1911; children—Mary Barnhardt (dec.), Helen Davidson. Ordained ministry M.E. Ch., S., 1892; pastor successively Hot Springs, Pineville, Winston, Waxhaw, Asheboro and Weaverville (all of N.C.) until 1904; presiding elder Asheville dist., 1905-07, Salisbury dist., 1908; pastor Trinity Ch., Charlotte, 1910-11, First Ch., Lexington, 1912-15, Wadesboro, 1916-17, Centenary Ch., Greensboro, 1918-20; presiding elder, Greensboro dist., 1921; editor N.C. Christian Advocate, 1921-45. Member Editorial Council of Religious Press of America; mem. Joint Bd. of Sesquicentennial Celebration of Am. Methodism; member of 6 General Confs. M.E. Ch., S.; mem. 6th Ecumenical Conf., Atlanta, Ga., 1931, Uniting Conf., Kansas City, 1939. Trustee Meth. Assembly, Brevard Coll. Mem. Southern Meth. Press. Assn. (pres.), Omicron Delta Kappa, Phi Beta Kappa Associates. Democrat. Club: Varsity (Duke U.). Author: The Iron Duke of the Methodist Itinerancy, 1925. Joint Author: Men of the Burning Heart; Letters of Travel in the Arctic, Scandinavia, Russia and Germany, 1935. Home: 1009 W. Market St., Greensboro NC‡

PLYLER, MARION TIMOTHY, clergyman, edito b. Iredell County, N.C., Sept. 14, 1867; s. Robe Conrad and Mary Lunda (Kimball) P.; A.B., Trini Coll. (now Duke U.), 1892, A.M., 1897, D.D., 193 grad. study U. of Chicago, 1898; A.M., U. of N.C., 190 D.D., 1931; M. Epia Duncan Smith, June 20, 190 children—Leroy Smith, Epia Duncan, Marion Timoth Conrad Norfleet, Mern, Grace, Eleanor Kimba Ordained ministry M.E. Ch., S., 1892; pastc successively Wilmington, Murfreesboro, Plymoutl Louisburg, Chapel Hill, Greenville, and Washington (a in N.C.), 1892-1910; presiding elder Elizabeth Cit (N.C.) dist., 1911-14, Raleigh dist., 1915; pastor Grac Ch., Wilmington, N.C., 1916-19; presiding elde Durham (N.C.) dist., 1920-23, Raleigh Dist., 1924-2 asso. editor, mgr. N.C. Christian Advocate, 1928-3 editor and mgr. 1920-46. Trustee Greensboro Co Mem. Gen. Conf. M.E. Ch., S., 1914, 18, 22, 34; men spl. session on Methodist unification, 1924; mem. Met Ecumenical Conf., London, 1921, Atlanta, 1931; men of Uniting Conf. in Kansas City, 1939; men Southeastern Jurisdictional Conf., Asheville, N.C 1940; mem. Gen. Centenary Commn., 1918-2 alternate del. Gen. Conf., 1926, 30, 38 and 40; chmı Joint Com. on Building Univ. Ch. at Chapel Hill, N.C 1918-35; chmn. Joint Commn. on Meth. Union in N.C chmn. bd. mgrs. N.C. Pastors School at Duk University since 1918; mem. Rural Ch. Inst. at Duke U chmn. Wesley Foundation at Univ. of N.C. Men Southern Methodist Press Assn., S.A.R. (chaplai General National Congress), Phi Beta Kappa, Omicro Delta Kappa. Democrat. Club: Varisty. All-Sta All-time Football Team." Duke U. Author: Leroy Le Smith—Lawyer of the Old School, 1916; Bethel Amor the Oaks, 1925; Thomas Neal Ivey—Golden Hearte Gentleman, 1925. Co-author: Men of the Burnir Heart, 1918. Contbr. letters of travel in America an Europe; contbr. to South Atlantic Quarterly. Hom 1415 Gregson St., Durham NC‡

PLYMIRE, REGINALD FLOYD, electric utilit exec.; b. Vallejo, Cal., Aug. 22, 1909; s. Jessie B. an Marian L. (Jones) P., B.S. in Elec. Engring., U. Wash 1930; m. Inga M. Jensen, July 27, 1934; children—Jer B., Julie E. With Puget Sound Power & Light Co Bellevue, Wash., 1930, v.p., 1957-65, sr. v.p., 196 Mem. Am. Inst. Electronic and Elec. Engrs., Edisc Electric Inst., Nat. Sales Execs. Conf., N.W. Electr Light and Power Assn. (past pres.), Seattle, Bellevu chambers commerce, Municipal League Great Seattle, Phi Beta Kappa, Tau Beta Pi, Zeta Mu Ta Home: Bellevue WA Died May 1, 1972.

PO-CHEDLEY, DONALD STEPHEN, educator; Buffalo, Aug. 30, 1917; s. Stephen and Agn (Wallenhorst) Po-C.; B.S., Canisius Coll., 1942; M.A U. Buffalo, 1949; Ph.D., Fordham U., 1956; m. Grac Erskine Phillips, Oct. 6, 1945; children—Donal Kevin, Pamela, Judith, David, Patrice. Instr. biolog D'Youville Coll., Buffalo, 1948-52, chmn. biology dep 1956-69; grad. asst. biology Fordham U., 1952-55, inst biology Coll. Pharmacy, 1955-56. Served with AU 1942-45. Mem. A.A.A.S., N.Y. Acad. Sci., An Entomol. Soc., Am. Legion, Sigma Xi. Roman Catholi Home: Buffalo NY Died Apr. 1, 1969.

POE, FLOYD, clergyman; b. Daisy, Tenn., Dec. 1877; s. John H. and Sarah Louise (Bean) P.; desc. c maternal side of Wm. H. Bean, first white settler Tenn.; A.B., Cumberland U., Lebanon, Tenn., 190 A.M., 1909; B.D., Cumberland Theol. Sem., 1904; B.D Lane Theol. Sem., Cincinnati, O., 1907; voice stud Ohio Conservatory, Cincinnati, 1907-09; D.D Lebanon (O.) U., 1910; LL.D., Cumberland U., 193 m. Glenna Ruhl, June 28, 1905; 1 dau., Helen Louis Pastor Main St. Presbyn. Ch., Lebanon, O., and pre Lebanon U., 1904-11; pastor First Presbyn. Ch Independence, Kan., 1911-18, El Paso, Tex., 1918-2 City Temple, Dallas, Tex., 1928-47. Trustee ar moderator Synod of Tex., 1930-31; mem. judici commn., Presbyn. Ch. U.S.A.; mem. staff nat. missio of Presbyn. Ch., U.S.A. Chmn. Com. on Christian Edr Synod of Tex., 1929-32; trustee Trinity U., Sa Antonio, Tex. Member com. on Camp and Churc Activities, Presbyterian Church, U.S.A., special lectur on preaching, Perkins School of Theology. Mem. Ch Alpha, Pi Kappa Alpha. Democrat. Mason. Club Rotary, Town and Gown. Editor Cumberland Annual, The Phoenix, 1903. Contbr. to Presby Advance, Presbyn. Banner, Presbyn. Tribune, Tex Scrap Book, Southwest Quarterly Review, etc. Hom 4409 Westway, Dallas TX‡

POEHLER, W(ILLIAM A(UGUST), colleg president; b. Courtland, Minn., July 9, 1904; s. Herma Fred and Mary (Havemeier) P.; B.D., Concordia Sen 1929; M.A., University of Minnesota, 1945, Ph.D 1954; D.D., Concordia Seminary, Springfield, 196 married Justine Schneidmiller, July 16, 192 children—Bernardine (Mrs. Keith Graham), Zo (Mrs. Donald Lusk), Elizabeth (Mrs. Robe Trembath), Theodora (Mrs. Robert Koeppe Ordained to ministry Lutheran Church, 1930; pastc Woodlake, Minn., 1930-35, Morristown, 1935-4 Mpls., 1940-46; pres. Concordia Coll., 1946-71. Mer St. Paul Civil and Human Rights Commn., Commn. Tchr. Edn. Objectives; mem. curriculum commn. Lut

Ch.-Mo. Synod, 1953-65; bd. dirs. Luth. Edn. Conf. N.A.m., 1966-69. Mem. History of Edn. Soc., C. of C., Comparative Education Soc., Religious Edn. Assn., Nat. Ednl. Philosophy Soc., N.E.A., Phi Delta Kappa, Alpha Lambda Phi. Author: God Goes to Golgotha; Progress Tests for Luther's Catechism; Three's In Our Lord's Passion; Evaluation of Australian and New Zealand Luterhan Educational System, 1959; Planning and Promoting the Parish Educational Agencies, 1960; A Brief History of Religious Education, 1964; What Then Was Man?, 1969. Home: St Paul MN Died Dec. 9, 1971.

POILLON, WILLIAM CLARK, banker; b. New York, Nov. 19, 1872; s. William and Clara (Wilson) P.; ed. Coll. City of New York, 1887-9; m. Cora Clark, of Leavenworth, Kan., June 5, 1905. Asst. treas., treas., v.-p. and pres., Mercantile Trust Co., New York, 1889, until merger of co. with Bankers Trust Co., 1911; v.-p., mem. exec. com. Bankers Trust Co.; dir. U.S. Realty & Improvement Co.; mem. firm Tucker, Anthony & Co., bankers. Clubs: Metropolitan, Recess, Sleepy Hollow Country. Home: 353 Riverside Drive. Office: 60 Broadway, New York NY‡

POINTS, ARTHUR JONES, oil co. exec.; b. Salt Lick, Ky., July 19, 1904; s. Allen H. and Jesse Irene (Jones) P.; A.B., Georgetown Coll., Ky., 1925; m. Lucille E. Ashworth, Oct. 7, 1928; children—John Thomas, Carolyn L. (Mrs. Tommy L. Preston), Nancy Marie, Steven Arthur. Banker, 1925-31; joined Ashland Oil & Refining Co., 1931, auditor, 1939-43, asst. to pres., 1943-45, controller from 1945. Member of Ashland (Ky.) School Board, 1967-69. Trustee Georgetown Coll. Mem. Ohio Valley Accountants Assn., Am. Petroleum Inst., Kappa Alpha. Home: Ashland KY Died May 11, 1969; buried Ashland Cemetery, Ashland KY

POLDERVAART ARIE, law librarian; b. Vierpolders, Netherlands, Oct. 21, 1909; s. Arie and Heiltje (Huisman) P.; brought to U.S., 1914, derivative citizenship; A.B. summa cum laude, Coe Coll., Cedar Rapids, Ia., 1931; A.M., Univ. of Ia., 1934; student Coll. of Law, Univ. of Ia., 1931-32, 1933-34; Doctor of Jurisprudence, University of Iowa, 1953; studied law library sci. under Helen S. Moylan; m. Edna Beryl Kerchmar, Mar. 20, 1936; children—Arie William, Patricia Ann. Grad. 45th Nat. Training Sch. for scout execs., Mendham, N.J., 1935; asst. boy scout exec., Northern N.M. Council, 1935-37; advt. mgr. Santa Fe (N.M.) Daily Sun, 1937; admitted to N.M. bar, Aug. 17, 1939; apptd. state librarian and law librarian of New Mexico by state Supreme Court, Jan., 1938; law librarian, Coll. of Law, U. of N.M., 1947-63. Nat. commr. on Uniform State Laws, 1957-69. Awarded Silver Beaver award Boy Scouts of Am., 1940. Mem. New Mexico State Library Assn. (pres. 1941-42, 1942-43), Am. Assn. Law Libraries (pres.-elect 1946-47, pres. 1947-48), N.M. State Library Commission, American Bar Association, The Order of the Coif, American Library Assn., Phi Kappa Phi, Pi Delta Epsilon. Methodist. Club: Santa Fe 20-30 (charter mem., pres. 1940). Author: Legislative Drafting in New Mexico, 1942; Black Robed Justice, 1948; New Mexico Practice Manual, 1949; Manual for Effective Legal Research, 1955; Justice of the Peace Manual, 1958; Probate Manual, 1961; New Mexico Notary Register, 1963; New Mexico Probate System, pub. 1965. Member of the editorial staff of the New Mexico Statutes, 1941, 6 vols., asso editor, 1953, 12 vols. Contbr. to library, legal and religious publs. Home: Albuquerque NM Died June 3, 1969; buried Fairview Meml. Park Cemetery, Albuquerque NM

POLHAMUS, JOSE NELSON, journalist; b. Puerto Principe, Cuba, June 14, 1871; s. Gen. Mariano E. P., Cuban patriot, (sec. of war of insurgent govt. in war of 1868-70); father killed by Spaniards; ed. in New York, including 3 yrs. at Coll. City of New York; m. at New Orleans, May 6, 1895, Miss Amparo de Miranda, of Havana, Cuba. Reported Blaine's Pan-Am. Conf. for New York Herald; afterward was on New York World; later editor El Universal, City of Mexico; then sp'l writer New Orleans Picayune; has been local agt. and later gen. agt. of govt. of Republic of Cuba for States of La., Miss., Ala., Ga. and Tenn.; Spanish stenographer Havana Custom House, Jan. 3, 1899; chief Protest Bd., Mar., 1899; sec. Seizure Comm'n Cuban Customs Service, May, 1899; chief div. customs and revenue cutter service Cuban Republic, May 20, 1902; apptd. Feb., 1903, on sp'l service as Sec. Comm'n of Treaty of Reciprocity between the U.S. and Cuba. Address: Havana Cuba‡

POLING, DANIEL ALFRED, clergyman, editor, author; b. Portland, Ore., Nov. 30, 1884; s. Charles C. and Savilla (Kring) P.; A.B., Dallas (Ore.) Coll., 1904, A.M., 1906; student Lafayette (Ore.) Sem.; grad work, Ohio State U., 1907-09; LL.D., Albright Coll., 1916; Litt.D., Defiance Coll., 1921, Norwich University, 1952; D.D., Hope College, 1925; S.T.D., Syracuse U., 1927; D.D., U. of Vt., 1934; LL.D., Temple U., 1937; D.D., Phillips U., 1939; L.H.D., Bucknell U., 1946, Bates Coll., 1952, Clarkson Coll.; H.H.D., Huntington Coll.; D.D., William Jewell Coll., 1960; m. Susan Vandersall, Sept. 25, 1906 (died July 1918); m. 2d, Lillian Diebold Heingartner, Aug. 11, 1919; 8 children. Prohibition candidate for governor of Ohio, 1912. Pastor of the Marble Collegiate-Dutch Reformed Ch., N.Y., 1922-30, Bapt. Temple, Phila., 1936-48. Chaplain, Chapel of Four Chaplains, 1948 (Inter-faith Shrine). Honorary life pres. World's Christian Endeavor Union; chmn. bd., editorial cons. Christain Herald; corporator Presbyn. Ministers Life Insurance Fund. Trustee Bucknell U.; mem. General War-Time Commission of the Churches; maj. Chaplain Officers' Reserve. Received Silver Buffalo award, Boy Scouts of America; humanitarian award, Welcome Chapter, Pa. Eastern Star, 1940; War Dept. award for conspicuous service as accredited war corr. overseas theater of combat, 1946; Medal of Merit, United States Government, 1947; Benjamin Franklin award 1961; Order of Lafayette, 1961; Clergyman of the Year, Religious Heritage Assn., 1963; Ten Commandments award Order of Eagles, 1964; citation from the Government of Israel, 1965. President of the Greater New York Federation of Chs., 1926-27. Gen. Synod Reformed Ch. Am., 1929-30. Mem. Am. Legion, Military Order Fgn. Wars, Newcomen Soc. Mason (33 deg.). Clubs: Nat. Press (Washington); Explorers (New York City); Overseas Press (New York City); Union League (N.Y.C.). Author: Mothers of Men, 1914; Huts in Hell, 1918; Learn to Live, 1923; What Men Need Most, 1923; An Adventure in Evangelism, 1925; The Furnace (novel), 1925; John of Oregon (novel), 1926; Radio Talks to Young People, 1926; Dr. Poling's Radio Talks, 1927; The Heretic (novel), 1928; Youth and Life, 1929; Between Two Worlds (novel), 1930; John Barleycorn His Life and Letters (novel), 1933; Youth Marches, 1937; Fifty-two Story Sermons for Children, 1940; Opportunity Is Yours, 1946; A Treasury of Best-Loved Hymns, 1942; A Preacher Looks at War, 1943; Your Daddy Did Not Die, 1944; A Treasury of Great Sermons, 1944 Faith is Power for You, 1950; Prayers for the Armed Forces, 1950; The Glory and Wonder of the Bibel (with Dr. Henry Thomas); Your Questions Answered with Conforting Counsel; Mine Eyes Have Seen, 1959; Jesus Says To You, 1961; He Came from Galilee, 1965. Home: Philadelphia PA Died Feb. 7, 1968.

POLK, ALBERT FAWCETT, ex-congressman; b. Frederica, Del., Oct. 11, 1869; s. Theodore A. and Sarah E. (Fawcett) P.; B.A., Delaware Coll., Newark, Del., 1889, M.A., 1892; m. Martilla Evans, December 29, 1897 (died March 5, 1938). Began in the practice of law at Georgetown, Del., 1892; formerly chmn. Dem. County Com., Sussex Co., and mem. Dem. State Com.; counsel for Del. Senate, 1899; a legislative atty. for Del. legislature, 1905; mem. Bd. of Edn., Georgetown 7 yrs.; mem. Town Council, 1915; mem. and sec. Sussex Co. Bd. Law Examiners; mem. 65th Congress (1917-19), Del.-at-large; U.S. commr. Dist. of Del. since 1930. Presbyn. Mason (K.T.); Grand High Priest Grand Chapter R.A.M. of Del., 1911. Home: 812 N. Adams St. Office: P.O. Bldg., Wilmington DE‡

POLLACK, ERVIN HAROLD, educator; b. St. Louis, Apr. 19, 1913; s. Jacob Morris and Tillie (Padratzik) P.; student St. Louis U., 1932-35; J.D., Washington U., 1939; postgrad., Columbia, 1939-41; m. Lydia Irene Weiss, June 12, 1940; children—Jay Robert, Joan Nancy. Admitted to Mo. bar, 1939; asst. to librarian Columbia, 1939-41; librarian Hays, Podell & Shulman, N.Y.C., 1942; asst. prof. law, law librarian Ohio State U., 1947-50, asso. prof. law, law librarian, 1950-54, prof. law, law librarian, 1954-59, prof. law, dir. research services, 1959—. Sec. OPA, 1942-47; cons. Office Econ. Stblzn., 1951, Library of Congress, 1959-64, State Dept., 1966-72; cons. Orgn. Central Am. States, 1970-72; recipient certificate merit, 1969. Trustee, Ohio Legal Center; bd. dirs. Ohio Library Found. Fellow Ohio Bar Found.; mem. Internat. Assn. Philosophy of Law and Social Philosophy, Am. Arbitration Assn. (nat. panel of arbitrators), Ohio Assn. Law Libraries (pres. 1949-51), Am., Ohio bar assns., Am. Soc. Polit. and Legal Philosophy, Am. Assn. Law Libraries (pres. 1958-59), Ohio Library Assn., Am. Assn. U. Profs. (sec. Ohio chpt. 1953-55), Order of Coif. Author: Legal Research and Materials, 1950, Fundamentals of Legal Research, 1967. Editor: Ohio Court Rules Annotated, 1949; Ohio Unreported Judicial Decisions Prior to 1823, 1952; Brandeis Reader, 1956; Human Rights (Amintaphali), 1971. Home: Columbus OH Died June 9, 1972.

POLLACK, LOUIS, art dealer; b. N.Y.C., May 21, 1921; s. Samuel and Gussie (Pollack) P.; student of public schools; married Laure Garner, May 29, 1952; children—Claude V. and Sabine L. Study of art history, trends in U.S., Eng., France, Italy; founder, dir. Peridot Gallery, N.Y.C., 1948-70; Pres. Collectors Graphics, Inc., 1961-70. Mem. Art Dealers Assn. Am. Inc. Home: New York City NY Died Aug. 18, 1970; buried Cimetiere de Bagneux, Paris France

POLLAK ROBERT, broker; born Cleveland, June 24, 1903; s. Herman and Luella (Cohn) P.; Ph.B., U. of Chicago, 1924; m. Janet Spitzer, May 7, 1929; 1 son, Richard. Stock and commodity broker, Chicago, since 1924; music critic The Chicagoan, 1929-33, Chicago Daily Times, 1933-41; drama critic Chicago Daily Times, 1941-47, Chicago Sun and Times (upon merger of two separate papers), 1947-52; part-time columnist Lerner-Sagan neighborhood papers, 1960; partner of H. Hentz & Co. (brokers), Chgo. Pres. Immigrants Service League, 1961-63, dir., 1958-71. Clubs: Quadrangle (U. Chgo.), Tavern (Chgo.). Home: Chicago IL Died May 4, 1971.

POLLARD, CLAUDE, lawyer; b. Carthage, Tex., Feb. 14, 1874; s. Hamilton and Sarah Jane (Davis) P.; ed. pub. schs., Panola Co., Tex.; m. Julia S. Newton, of Bonham, Tex., Dec. 27, 1897; children—Lorraine, Claude. Began practice at Carthage, 1895; county atty., Panola Co., 1895-98; district atty., 4th Texas Dist., 1900-05; asst. atty. gen. of Tex., 1905-09, atty. gen. of Texas, 1927-30. Counsel Railway General Managers Association of Texas since 1930. Mem. Texas Bar Association (pres. 1921-22), American Judicature Society. Democrat. Methodist. Mason (32 deg.), K.P., Odd Fellow. Clubs: Houston; Austin. Wrote pamphlets; Beginnings of Texas History; Life of David Crockett; Life of Randolph of Roanoke; Great Light in Masonry. Home: 2310 Windsor Rd. Office: Norwood Bldg., Austin TX‡

POLLARD, ERNEST MARK, ex-congressman; b. Nehawka, Neb., Apr. 15, 1869; s. Isaac and Viola (Welsh) P.; B.A., U. of Neb., 1893; m. Maud Rose, 1896 (died 1903); 2d, Gertrude Waterman, 1895. Mgr. Isaac Pollard & Son, fruit growers, since 1899. Mem. Neb. Legislature, 1896-1900; elected to 59th Congress, 1905, for unexpired term (1905-7) of E. J. Burkett, elected to U.S. Senate; re-elected to 60th Congress (1907-9), 1st Neb. Dist. Pres. Neb. Rep. League, 1900. Address: Nehawka NB‡

POLLARD, HARRY STRANGE, univ. prof.; b. Lansing, Mich., Oct. 18, 1900; s. Walter Punchard and Ella Laura (Strange) P.; A.B., Olivet Coll., 1922; M.S., U. of Ia., 1924; Ph.D., U. of Wis., 1933; m. Edwina Obenauer, Jan. 2, 1925; 1 dau., Patricia. Mathematics dept., Miami U., 1927-71, prof., head dept., 1946-71. Mem. Am. Math. Soc., Math. Assn. of Am., Inst. of Math. Statistics. Presbyn. Home: Oxford OH Died 1971.

POLLARD, JOHN WILLIAM HOBBS, N.D.; b. Brentwood, N.H., Feb. 22, 1872; s. Francis Dow and Mary Jane (Gray) P.; B.L., Dartmouth, 1895; M.D., with honors, U. of Vt., 1901; student in physical culture, Harvard, summer semesters, 1896, 1902; post-grad. work in medicine, Harvard, 1905-06; student in biology, Harvard, summer semesters, 1910, 11; m. Kate Marion Blunt, of Haverhill, Mass., Dec. 28, 1898. Physical director and instr. physiology, Union Coll., Schenectady, N.Y., 1897-1900, phys. dir. Lehigh U., 1901-02, dir. dept. physical edn., U. of Rochester, 1902-05, prof. physical edn. and lecturer on hygiene, U. of Ala., 1906-10; prof. physical edn. and asso. prof. biology, Washington and Lee U., 1910-15; prof. hygiene and physical edn., same, 1915-21, health commissioner, Quincy (Illinois) Public Health District, 1921-24. In practice of medicine 1924, dist. health supt. of Ill. State Dept. Pub. Health, 1925; commr. of health, Evanston, Illinois, since 1926. President S. Atlantic Intercollegiate Athletic Assn., 1913—, Va. State Public Health Assn., 1914—; mem. Am. Pub. Health Assn., International Soc. of Medical Health Officers, American Micros. Soc., Am. Assn. Advancement Physical Edn., Soc. Coll. Gymnasium Dirs., Theta Delta Chi, Alpha Kappa Kappa. Mason (32 deg., K.T.). Mem. Soc. of the Genessee (Rochester, N.Y.), N.H. Hist. Soc. Commd. 1st lt. Med. R.C., May 19, 1917; post surgeon, Coast Defenses of New Bedford, July 4, 1917-July 26, 1918; capt. Med. R.C., Dec. 31, 1917; maj., Med. Corps U.S.A., July 27, 1918; attending surgeon for the army, Phila., July 26, 1918-May 31, 1919; hon. discharged, May 31, 1919; commd. lt. col. Med. R.C., June 4, 1919, col., 1924; recommissioned col. Med. Res., 1929; now comdg. officer 119th Gen. Hosp. Home: 919 Washington St., Evanston IL‡

POLLITT, LEVIN IRVING, b. Salisbury, Md. Apr. 28, 1866; s. Levin Irving and Anne Maria (Ralph) P.; A.B., Western Md. Coll., Wesminster, 1889, A.M., 1892, hon. A.M., 1926, LL.D., 1939; m. Fanny L. Bertron, Dec. 27, 1894; children—Pauline Frances (Mrs. Douglas R. Morrison), Levin Irving. Teacher Western Md. Coll., 1889-90, Chamberlain-Hunt Acad., Port Gibson, Miss., 1890-98, also editor Port Gibson (Miss.) Reveille, 1895-98; gen. mgr. Natchez (Miss.) Water & Sewer Co., 1898-1901, Pine Bluff (Ark.) Water & Light Co., 1901-04; pres. Suffolk (Va.) Gas-Electric Co., 1909-24, Bluefield (Va.) Gas & Power Co., 1911-24, Henrico County (Va.) Gas Co., 1912-20, Sumter (S.C.) Gas & Power Co., 1912-24, Gas Light Co. of Augusta, Ga., 1914-24, Husband Flint Products Co., 1918-20; v.p. and gen. mgr. Southern Gas & Electric Corp., 1909-23, pres. 1923-45. Editor and historian, Presbytery of Baltimore. Mem. Presbytery of Baltimore (moderator 1927-28); v.-moderator Presbyterian Church in U.S.A., 1933-34; moderator of Synod of Baltimore, 1935. Member American Gas Association, Md. Hist. Society, St. Andrew's Society, Eastern Shore Society of Baltimore (president 1925), S.A.R. Democrat. Helped establish 1st full time course of gas engring., Johns Hopkins U., 1924. Author: History of Brown Memorial Church, 1945. Contbr. chapter to Colonial Eastern Shore, 1918. Home: 1715 Park Av. Office: 808 Park Av., Baltimore MD‡

POLTORATZKY, MARIANNA A., educator; b. St. Petersburg, Russia, Nov. 24, 1906; d. Artemy I. and Anna P. (Ivanitzky) Poltoratzky; M.A., Leningrad (Russia) U., 1929, D.Phil., 1937; Ph.D., U. Graz (Austria), 1947. Came to U.S., 1950, naturalized, 1955. Dozent, Leningrad U., 1933-36; dozent, chmn. Slavic dept. Rostov-on-Don (Russia) U., 1936-42; prof. Slavistics, U. Graz, 1945-50; lectr. Columbia, 1950; sr. instr. Army Lang. Sch., Presidio, Monterey, Cal., 1950-57; prof. Russian Summer Sch., Middlebury (Vt.) Coll., 1951, 53-59; asso. prof. Russian, acting chmn. dept. Georgetown U., 1957-61; dir., prof. Summer Inst. Critical Langs., Putney, Vt., from 1960; prof. Russian, chmn. dept. Vassar Coll., 1961-66; prof. State U. N.Y., Albany, 1966-68; vis. prof. N.Y.U., 1963; founder Russian Summer Sch., Norwich (Vt.) U., dir., 1968. Trustee N.Y. Inst. Slavistics, 1964-68. Mem. Modern Lan. Assn., Am. Assn. U. Profs., Learned Soc., Am. Assn. Tchrs. Slavic and E. European Langs. Author: (with C. Wolkonsky) Handbook of Russian Roots, 1961; Russian Folklore, 1964; Russian Culture; 1965; Comparative English-Russian Grammar, 1966; Russian Lexicology and Lexicography, 1967. Translator lit. in time of Peter I, also Survey Russian Linguistics, Russian Historical Grammar, others. Office: Albany NY Died Sept. 7, 1968.

POLYZOIDES, ADAMANTIOS THEOPHILUS, internat. politics; b. Greece, Sept. 9, 1885; s. Dr. Theophilus and Elizabeth P.; studied law, Nat. Univ., Athens, 1903-08; m. Aglaia Armodios, Feb. 15, 1908; children—Theophilus Achilles, Elizabeth Zoe. Came to U.S., 1908, naturalized citizen, 1921. Became editor Atlantis (Greek daily), New York, also monthly mag., 1908; elected pres. Atlantis, Inc., 1927, resigned Mar. 1933; pres. New Generation Publishing Co., Inc.; pub. NEON BHMA-The New Tribune, Independent Greek Am. Daily, 1933-34; lecturer in internat. relations and internat. journalism, also mng. editor World Affairs Interpreter," U. of Southern Calif.; mem. editorial staff Los Angeles Times; writer for San Francisco Argonaut; radio commentator, war analyst, lecturer on post-war reconstruction; spoke or wrote several langs. Active member Williamstown Inst. and Round Table conferences pertaining to internat. affairs; has lectured widely before colleges on international topics; lecturer and speaker on democracy versus dictatorship. Mem. Inst. of World Affairs, U. of Southern Calif., since 1931. Member Academy Political Science, American Acad. Political and Social Science, Am. Political Science Assn., Am. Economic Assn., Am. Social Soc., Am. Soc. Internat. Law. Am. Peace Soc., League for Am. Citizenship, Am. Hist. Assn., Royal Economic Soc. (London); mem. Conf. on Immigration Policy of New York. Grand Comdr. Order of the Holy Sepulchre (Orthodox), Jerusalem; Knight Comdr. Order of the Redeemer (Greece); Comdr. Order of the Phoenix (Hellenic Republic). Republican. Member Eastern Greek Orthodox Ch. Clubs: New York Press, Town Hall; Nat. Press (Washington, D.C.); Commonwealth (San Francisco); Authors, Scribes (Los Angeles). Home: Los Angeles CA Died June 1969.*

POND, FRANCIS JONES, prof. chemistry; b. Holliston, Mass., Apr. 8, 1871; s. Abel and Lucy A. (Jones) P.; B.S., Pa. State Coll., 1892; M.A., Ph.D., U. of Gottingen, Germany, 1896; m. Nellie Olds, of Circleville, O., June 10, 1902; children—Catherine Olds (dec.), Elizabeth Olds, Nathan Jones. Instr. chemistry and assaying Pa. State Coll., 1896-1901, asst. prof. chemistry and metallurgy, 1901-03; asst. prof. engring. chemistry Stevens Inst. Tech., 1903-06; asso. prof. chemistry, 1906-09, prof. chemistry since 1909, dean freshmen since 1907. Mem. Sigma Chi, Tau Beta Pi, Phi Kappa Phi; fellow A.A.A.S., Am. Chem. Soc. Conglist. Club: Commonwealth (Upper Montclair). Author: The Chemistry of the Terpenes, 1902. Contbr. to chem. jours. Home: 167 Summit Av., Upper Montclair NJ*‡

POND, JOHN ALLAN, coll. adminstr.; b. Toronto, Ont., Can., Aug. 2, 1914; s. Allan Merle and Daisy Blanche (Hodgson) P.; student Shaw's Bus. Coll., 1930-37, Boston U., 1938-39; B.B.A., Northeastern U., 1942; postgrad. Springfield Coll., 1942; M.B.A., U. Chgo., 1950; m. Barbara Olive Curtis, Oct. 28, 1939; children—Robert Allan, Jeffrey Craig. Asst. bus. mgr., purchasing agt., supt. bldgs. and grounds Springfield (Mass.) Coll., 1937-44; procurement chief U.S. Army C.E., Manhattan Project U. Chgo., 1944-46; asst. purchasing agt. U. Chgo., 1946-50; dir. purchasing N.Y.U., Bellevue Med. Center, N.Y.C., 1950-53, U. Colo., Boulder, 1953-59; exec. dir. U. Chgo. Alumni Found., 1959-60; v.p. bus. affairs, asso. sec.-treas. to trustees William Jewell Coll., Liberty, Mo., 1960-71, exec. v.p., 1971-73. Dir., treas. Gold Hill Assn. Mgmt. analyst, cons. Bd. County Commrs. for Larimer County Hosp., Ft. Collins, Colo., 1953-60; cons., mgmt. and financial analyst, vol. and pub. hosps., 1953-73; lectr. service clubs, community, coll. and univ. groups, 1938-73. Mem. Long-Range Finance Planning Com., Liberty, 1965-67, Carnegie Found. Research grantee, 1955. Mem. Nat., Central assns. coll. and univ. bus. officers assns., Am. Mgmt. Assn., Internat. Platform Assn., Nat. Peace Officers Assn., Acad. Polit. Sci., Am. Acad. Polit. and Social Scis., Nat. Assn. Ednl. Buyers (pres. 1968-69). Mason, Rotarian. Clubs: Executive Program (Chgo.). Contbr. articles to profl. jours. Home: Liberty MO Died Jan. 3, 1973.

POND, ROBERT ANDREW, business exec.; b. Syracuse, N.Y., Sept. 25, 1892; s. Andrew Herbert and Harriet (Beadel) P.; student Syracuse U., 1910-12, U. Pa., 1912-13; m. Winifred Smith, Oct. 25, 1921; 1 dau., Harriet. Became president of A. H. Pond Co., Inc. (Keepsake Diamond Rings), Syracuse, 1938, chmn. board; member board directors Marine Midland Trust Co., Windle Co. (Fla. hotels); trustee Syracuse Savs. Bank. Mem. adv. bd. Salvation Army. Trustee YMCA. Republican. Methodist. Home: Syracuse NY Died Mar. 7, 1970; buried Oakwood Cemetery, Syracuse NY.

POOL, DAVID DE SOLA, rabbi; b. London, Eng., May 16, 1885; s. Eleazar Solomon and Abigail (Davis) P.; B.A., 1st class honors, U. of London, 1903; studied univs. of Berlin and Heidelberg; Ph.D., summa cum laude, Heidelberg; Rabbinerseminar, Berlin; hon. degrees Columbia, N.Y. U., Jewish Theol. Sem. Am., Hebrew Theol. Coll., Chgo., Chgo. Coll. Jewish Studies; m. Tamar Hirschenson, February 6, 1917; children—Prof. Ithiel de Sola, Dr. Naomi de Sola. Minister Spanish and Portuguese Synagogue, Shearith Israel, N.Y.C., 1907-70. One of the three Jewish representatives appointed to serve on Herbert Hoover's food conservation staff, 1917; co-founder, v.p. Jewish Welfare Board; field organizer of army welfare work, 1917-18, and chairman Committee Army and Navy Religious Activities of J.W.B. 1940-47; appointed one of three Am. representatives on Zionist Commission to Palestine, 1919; regional dir. for Palestine and Syria of Am. Joint Distribution Com. War Relief and Reconstrn., 1920, 21. A founder Palestine Lighthouse, Am.-Israel Cultural Found., Am. Friends of Alliance Israelite Universelle, U.S.O., Conf. Christians and Jews. Dir. Jewish Edn. Assn., N.Y.; president Young Judea of America, 1915-19, 24, 25; pres. N.Y. Bd. Jewish Mins., 1916-17; founder, pres. Union Sephardic Congregarions, 1928-67, hon. pres., 1967-70; co-founder, pres. Synagogue Council Am., 1938-40; mem. Pres.'s Advisory Com. National Youth Adminstrn.; rep. of Jewish Army and Navy chaplains to Chief of Chaplains. U.S. del. NATO Parliamentary Congress, London, 1959; lectr. Jewish music; organizer Am. Jewish Tercentenary. Author: The Kaddish, 1909; Hebrew Learning Among the Puritans of New England, 1911; Capital Punishment in Jewish Literature, 1916; Portraits Etched in Stone, published in 1952; (with Tamar de Sola Pool) An Old Faith in the New World, 1955; Why I Am a Jew, 1957; (with Tamar de Sola Pool) Is There An Answer? An Inquiry Into Some Human Dilemmas, 1966. Editor, translator numerous volumes Hebrew liturgy, Spanish, Jewry, pamphlets; reviews. Home: New York City NY Died Dec. 1, 1970; buried Congregation Shearith Israel Cemetery, Cypress Hills.

POOL, JOE, congressman; b. Tarrant County, Tex., Feb. 18, 1911; s. William Wesley and Bonnie Jean (King) P.; student Tex. U., 1929-33; LL.B., So. Meth. U., 1937; m. Elizabeth Chambless, Apr. 21, 1940; children—Richard, Wesley, John, Joe. Admitted to Tex. bar, 1937; engaged in practice law with J. Frank Wilson, 1937-40, 46-47; mem. Tex. Ho. of Reps. from Dallas County, 1952-58, chmn. investigating com., 1953-54, chmn. motor traffic com., 1957-58; mem. 88th to 90th Congresses, at-large Tex. Mem. Interstate Coop. Commn., 1952-56. Served with AUS, 1943-45. Life mem. Dallas C. of C. Democrat. Office: Washington DC Died July 1968.

POOLE, JOHN, realtor; b. Parkersburg, W.Va., May 17, 1875; s. Nathan Algernon and Lillian Agnes (DeCamp) P.; ed. commercial coll. and Am. Inst. of Banking, Washington, D.C.; m. Frances Barber, July 12, 1921; children—Marjorie Ann, (by previous marriage) John L., Nathan and Thomas S. Clerk and cashier United States Express Co., Washington, 1890-98; mem. Reeves, Poole & Co., 1898-1900; with Washington Loan & Trust Co., 1900-08; asst. cashier Nat. City Bank, 1908-09; cashier Commercial Nat. Bank, 1909-13; pres. Federal Nat. Bank, 1913-22; pres. Federal-Am. Nat. Bank, 1922-33, and past pres. Stockholders' Assn., Federal Reserve Bank of Richmond; mem. Federal Advisory Council, representing Fifth Federal Reserve Dist., 1929-31; now pres. The American Co., realtors; mem. bd. dirs. Chesapeake & Potomac Telephone Co. Chmn. Liberty Loan Com., Washington, 5 campaigns; former treas. Dist. Council of Defense, Roosevelt Memorial Assn. (for Washington), European Relief Council; chmn. Nat. Budget Com. for D.C.; treas. Columbia Instn. for the Deaf, D.C. Memorial Commn., Southeastern U., Y.M.C.A.; trustee American U., Washington, D.C.; ex-pres. D.C. Bankers Assn., Washington Chapter Am. Inst. Banking. Pres. Internat. Assn. Rotary Clubs, 1918-19. Republican. Episcopalian. Mason (32 deg., Shriner), Odd Fellow. Clubs: Rotary (ex-pres.), Columbia Country. Home: 17 E. Woodbine St., Chevy Chase, Md. Office: 807 15th St. N.W., Washington DC*‡

POOLE, LYNN D., writer, photographer, artist; b. Eagle Grove, Iowa, August 11, 1910; the son of Harry George and Laura Jane (Buellis) P.; A.B., Western Res. U., 1936, M.A., 1937; m. Gray Johnson, Jan. 1, 1941. Organized dept. edn. Walters Art Gallery, Balt., 1938-42; organized dept. pub. relations Johns Hopkins, 1946, Baltimore, in charge dept., 1946-65, assistant to the president, 1965-67, originated Johns Hopkins Sci. Review, weekly TV program, 1948-55, 2d weekly TV program Tomorrow's Careers, 1955, 3d weekly TV program, Johns Hopkins File 7, 1956; lectr. John Hopkins Sch. Med., from 1959; visiting lecturer at Immaculate Heart College; consultant public relations 1946-69; consultant ednl. television B.B.C., 1952 exhibited photographs, U.S. and Eng.; exhibited one man show SculptoGraphs, Balt., 1968, N.Y.C., 1968 Founding mem. Balt. Pub. Relations Council, pres 1952-53. Major public relations officer P.T.O. U.S.A.A.F., 1942-46. Recipient 19 awards for Johns Hopkins Sci. Review program, including George Peabody awards, 1950, 52; five awards for Tomorrow's Careers; American Coll. Pub. Relations Assn. ann award for outstanding achievement, 1951. Mem. Am Soc. Aesthetics (founding mem., sec.-treas. 1947-51) Am. Coll. Pub. Relations Assn. (bd. dirs., 1949-53 sec.-treas. 1952-53, exec. com. 1953-57, pres. 1956-57) Am. Heart Assn. (pub. relations council), Pub. Relations Soc. Am., Nat. Assn. Edn. Broadcasters, Photog. Soc Am., Royal Photog. Soc. Gt. Britain. Episcopalian Author: Science Via Television, 1950; Today's Science and You, 1952; Your Trip Into Space, 1953; Science The Super Sleuth, 1954; Diving for Science, 1955 Frontiers of Science, 1958; Ballooning in the Space Age 1958; (with Gray Poole) Ballons Fly High in the Sky 1960, Dated by Science, 1961, Scientists Who Changed the World, 1960, The Story of Icebergs, 1961 Carbon-14 Dating, 1962, Volcanoes in Action, 1962 Deep in Caves and Caverns, 1962, Weird and Wonderful Ants, 1962, Scientists Who Work Outdoors 1963, History of Olympic Games, 1963, Insect Eating Plants, 1963, Scientists Who Work With Astronauts 1964, Electronics in Medicine, 1964, I Am a Chronic Cardiac, 1964, Scientists Who Work with Cameras 1965, Birds Who Board At Our House, 1965, Fireflies in Nature and Laboratory, 1965, Doctors Who Saved Lives, 1966, One Passion, Two Loves, 1966, The Magnificent Traitor, 1967, Men Who Dig Up History 1967; Men Who Pioneered Inventions, 1968. Writer weekly nationally syndicated column, 1958-65. Home Baltimore MD Died Apr. 14, 1969.

POOLE, RUFUS GILBERT, lawyer; b. Ipswich, S.D. Dec. 14, 1902; s. Floyd and Marva (Evans) P.; student No. State Tchrs. Coll., Aberdeen, S.D., 1921-24; LL.B. U. Chicago, 1927; m. Hellene Roosevelt, Aug. 5, 1936 (div. Aug. 1955); 1 son, Rufus Gilbert; m. 2d, Suzanne Hanson, Sept. 10, 1955. Admitted N.M. bar, 1957 counsel Ill. Legislative Reference Bur., 1928-33; asst. solicitor Dept. Interior, and chmn. legislative com. for Dept. Interior and Fed. Emergency Adminstr. of Pub Works, 1933-37; asso. solicitor Dept. Labor, 1938-39 asso. gen. counel Wage and Hour Div., 1939-40 admitted to D.C. bar, 1942, practiced in Washington 1942-57, Albuquerque, New Mexico, 1957-68. Member American (chmn. section of administrative law 1955-56), Fed. bar assns., Am. Judicature Soc., N.M Bar Assn. Phi Delta Phi. Clubs: Cosmos, Metropolitan (Washington). Republican. Author Albuquerque NM Died Nov. 23, 1968; buried Blue Lake, Taos Indian Reservation.

POOLER, CHARLES ALFRED, advt. exec.; b Boston, Feb. 17, 1909; s. Charles Alfred and Elizabeth O. (Johnson) P.; A.B., Dartmouth, 1930; m. Helen Mustonen, July 16, 1938; children—Pamela, Charles Priscilla, William. Advt. dept. Lever Bros. Co., 1930-40 with Benton & Bowles, Inc., since 1941, sr. v.p. and dir. 1952—. Dir. Advt. Research Found. Mem. Copy Research Council, Market Research Council N.Y. American Marketing Assn. Club: University. Home West Redding CT Died Feb. 24, 1972.

POOLEY, EDWARD MURRAY, editor; b. Milton Fla., Feb. 4, 1898; s. Edward Murray and Annie Olivia (Nelson) P.; student U. of the South, Sewanee, Tenn. 1915-17; m. Ruth Underwood, Oct. 21, 1928; 1 dau. Ann. Reporter, advancing to mng. editor Houston Press, 1926-37; editor El Paso Herald-Post, 1927-63 Served as 2d lt., pilot, U.S. Army Air Service, 1917-20 Mem. Kappa Sigma, Sigma Delta Chi. Democrat Episcopalian. Club: El Paso Country. Home: El Paso TX Died June 4, 1969; interred Restlawn Mausoleum El Paso TX

POOR, CHARLES MARSHALL, educator; b Manchester, N.H., Oct. 4, 1872; s. Joseph A. and Mary V. P.; A.B., Brown U., 1893; Ph.D., 1896; A.M. Stanford, 1894; m. Helen L. Given, of Auburn, R.I., July 9, 1901; children—Eleanor L., Marion D. Instr. in German, Brown U., 1895-1900; prin. high schs. Cranston, R.I., 1900-07; instr. in German, U. of Ill. 1907-15; prof. German, Lombard Coll., Galesburg, Ill. 1915-30, also dean, 1916-30; became dean Knox Coll. 1930, resigned Apr. 1, 1933. Mem. Phi Gamma Delta Phi Beta Kappa. Congregationalist. Editor: Iwan der Schreckliche (Oxford Univ. Press), 1912; Zwei Marchen (same), 1914. Home: Clermont, Fla., and Onekama MI‡

POOR, HENRY VARNUM, III, potter, painter; b Chapman, Kan., Sept. 30, 1888; s. Alfred James and Josephine (Graham) P.; A.B., Stanford, 1910; art edn. Slade Sch., London, and Julian Acad., Paris; m Elizabeth Breuer; children—Josephine Lydia, Anne K. Peter Varnum. Resident artist American Academy in

Rome, 1950; professor of painting Columbia University, 1952. Specialist in pottery and tile decoration; designer of tile ceiling, Union Dime Savings Bank, N.Y. City. Paintings on permanent exhbn. in Rehn Gallery, Metropolitan Museum and Whitney Museum, N.Y. City, Art Inst. Chicago, Newark (N.J.) Museum, San Francisco (Calif.) Museum, Cleveland Museum, Addison Memorial Museum, Andover, Mass.; 12 mural panels completed in true fresco for Dept. of Justice Bldg., Washington, D.C.; large mural, Conservation of American Wild Life," for Dept. of Interior Bldg., Washington, D.C.; large fresco, The Land Grant Mural," for Penn State Coll., 1941; Fresco, New Courier-Jour. Bldg., Louisville, others. Pres. Skowhegan (Me.) School Painting and Sculpture. Landscape prize, Art Inst., Chicago; 3d prize, Carnegie Internat., 1933. Mem. Jury of Award, San Francisco Internat. Expn., 1939. Received presdl. appointment as mem. Commn. of Fine Arts, Washington, 1944-45. Mem. Art Advisory Com. to the State Dept. Unit of Artists, Alaska Theatre of War. Mem. Nat. Inst. Arts and Letters, Artists Equity Association (1st vice president 1953). Author and illustrator: An Artist Sees Alaska; A Book of Pottery-from Mud into Immortality. Home: New City NY Died Dec. 8, 1970; buried Mt. Repose, Haverstraw NY

POOR, RUSSELL SPURGEON, govt. ofcl.; b. Cowgill, Mo., Mar. 10, 1899; s. Alvin Eustace and Mollie (Petty) P.; student Mo. Wesleyan, Cameron, Mo., 1917-19; B.S., U. of Ill., 1923, M.S., 1925, Ph.D., 1927; D.Sc., Birmingham-Southern College, 1955; married Cleta Viola Price, June 17, 1927 (dec.); children—William Russell, Robert Clair; m. 2d, Edna G. Ketchum, Nov. 18, 1967. Asst. chemistry Mo. Weslyan Coll., 1918; asst. city chemist, Kansas City, Mo., 1919; prin. Brookfield (Mo.) High Sch., 1920; asst. geology, U. of Ill., 1923-27, fellow in geology, 1927; jr. geol. Ill. Geol. Survey, summers 1923-24, 26, Ky. Geol. Survey, summer 1925; asso. prof. geol. Birmingham-Southern Coll., Birmingham, Ala., 1927-28, prof. geol. and head geol. dept., 1928-43, dir. extension dept., 1936-39, chmn. div. of natural scis., 1937-43, adminstrative asst. to the pres., 1943-44; dean grad. Sch. and dir. Auburn Research Foundation, Ala. Polytech. Inst., Auburn, 1944-49; chmn. Univ. Relations Div. Oak Ridge Inst. of Nuclear Studies, 1949-53; administrator for 32 Southern univs. in making research facilities of Oak Ridge Nat. Lab. available to scientists of the country; Nat. Sci. Found., Washington, 1952; dir. med. center study, U. Fla., 1952-53; became provost Univ. Fla., 1953; then dir. div. nuclear edn. and tng. U.S. AEC. Mem. Pres.'s Com. on Employment of the Handicapped, 1956-62; asso. chmn. com. on dental health Commn. on the Survey of Dentistry in the U.S., American Council on education, 1958-60. Fellow Society of Economic Geologists, Geological Society of Am., American College of Dentists (hon.); mem. Am. Inst. Mining, Metall. and Petroleum Engineers (chmn., southeast sect. 1943), Ala. Acad. Sci. (pres. 1935); mem. adv. council So. Research Inst.: mem. Conf. Deans So. Grad. Schs. (sec.-treas., 1940-49), Nat. Insts. Health (nat. adv. council dental research), Newcomen Soc., Sigma Xi, Phi Beta Kappa, Phi Kappa Phi, Omicron Delta Kappa. Clubs: Engineers (Birmingham); Kiwanis (Gainsville); Cosmos (Washington). Contbr. sci. publs. Home: Bethesda MD Died Feb. 17, 1972.

POORE CHARLES GRAYDON, writer; b. Monterrey, Mexico, Aug. 20, 1902; s. Charles Graydon and Anne Elizabeth (Lynch) P.; Ph.B., Yale, 1926; m. Mary Elizabeth Carter, Jan. 11, 1930; children—Charles Graydon (dec.), Susan C. (Mrs. Thaddeus Brys). Writer various depts. N.Y. Times, 1929-71, asst. editor N.Y. Times Book Review, 1934-41, co-editor and daily book critic, 1945-71; panelist Invitation to Learning, CBS. Served from capt. to maj., Gen. Staff Corps, AUS, 1942-45. Decorated Croix de Guerre (France). Mem. N.Y. Newspaper Guild (mem. rep. assembly), Yale Library Assos., Authors League. Clubs: Elizabethan (New Haven, Connecticut); Century Association (N.Y.C.). Author: Goya, A Biography, 1938. Editor The Hemingway Reader, 1953. Home: New York City NY Died July 26, 1971.

POPE, AMY ELIZABETH, b. Quebec, Can., June 30, 1869; d. Alexander and Mary (Bonham) P.; came to U.S., 1892; diploma, Sch. of Nursing, Presbyn. Hosp., New York, 1894; diploma Teachers Coll. (Columbia), 1913. Instr. Sch. of Nursing, Presbyn. Hosp., New York, 1906-10, 1911-13; supt. Insular Sch. of Nursing, San Juan, P.R., 1910-11; instr. Sch. of Nursing, St. Luke's Hosp., San Francisco, 1914-20. Author: Practical Nursing, 1907; Essentials of Dietetics, 1908; Anatomy and Physiology for Nurses, 1913; Physics and Chemistry for Nurses, 1916; Dietary Computer, 1917; Pope's Manual of Nursing Procedure, 1919; A Text-Book of Simple Nursing Procedures for High Schools; Materia Medica, Pharmacology and Therapeutics for Nurses, 1921. Address: St. Luke's Hospital, San Francisco CA‡

POPE, ARTHUR UPHAM, Persian art; b. Phoenix, R.I., Feb. 7, 1881; s. Louis Atherton and Imogene (Titus) P.; B.A., Brown U., 1904, M.A., 1905; Ph.D. (honorary), University of Teheran; married Phyllis

Ackerman. Instr. dept. of philosophy, Brown U., 1904-06, 1908-10; asst. prof. same dept., U. of Calif., 1911-17; asso. prof., Amherst Coll., 1917-18; dir. Calif. Art Museum, San Francisco, 1923-24; advisory curator Muhammadan art, Art Inst. Chicago, 1925-35; hon. art adviser to Persian Govt. since 1925; hon. prof. history of Iranian art, U. of Teheran, from 1936; 19 research expdns. to Persia from 1929; trustee and adviser Textile Museum of D.C., 1925-30; adviser Persian Art, Pa. Mus., from 1928. Special commr. of Persian Govt. to Sesquicentennial Expn., Phila., 1926; dir. Persian sect. Dept. of Fine Arts, same, 1926; organizer Exhibition of Persian Art, Pa. Museum, 1926, also joint organizer 1st Internat. Conf. Persian Art, Phila., 1926; consultant San Francisco Opera House, 1927-28; organizer and dir. Internat. Exhibition Persian Art, Royal Acad., London, 1931, and co-dir. 2d Internat. Congress for Persian Art, London, 1931; dir. Am. Inst. Persian Art and Archeology since 1930. Lecturer in various museums in America. With personnel br., attached to Gen. Staff, U.S. Army, Washington, D.C., World War I. Decorated Order of Elmi, 1st Class; Danash Order of Humayun, 1st Class, 1964. Comdr. Order of the Crown. Exec. sec. Internat. Assn. for Iranian Art and Archeol., since 1930; dir. Iranian Institute's Archtl. Survey of Iran; dir. Asia Inst.'s Sch. for Asiatic Studies; asso. dir. 3d Internat. Exhbn. of Iranian Art, Leningrad, 1935; co-dir. 3d Internat. Congress for Iranian Art and Archeol., Leningrad, Moscow, 1935; chancellor, Asia Inst., 1947-53, chancellor emeritus from 1953; organizer, dir., editor-in-chief proceedings 4th Internat. Congress Iranian Art, N.Y., Washington, 1960; pres. Institute Archael. Studies Teheran. Mem. India Soc., Royal Central Asian Soc., Royal Asiatic Soc. (London), Internat. Assn. Iranian Art and Archeology (pres. 1960), Iranian Acad. Organizer, dir. Com. Nat. Morale, 1940-46; organizer Internat. Conf. Asian Problems, N.Y., 1952. Delegate 220th Anniversary Celebration of Russian Academy of Sciences, Moscow, 1945. Author several books, also numerous articles Am. and fgn. jours.; organizer, financed contbd. to text, Survey of Persian Art, 3000 pages text, 5000 illustrations; editor of Bulletin, Iranian Inst. Lectr. Dir. Exhbn. of Persian Art, New York, 1940, 1949. Home: Warren CT Died Sept. 1969.

POPE, BAYARD FOSTER, banker; b. Hingham, Mass., Oct. 5, 1887; s. William Carroll and Mabel Richmond (Downer) P.; prep. edn., Prince Sch. and Nobles Pvt. Sch., Boston; A.B., Harvard Univ., 1909; m. Elma Marguerite Neergaard, Sept. 17, 1910; children—Bayard Foster, Alan Neergaard. Began as salesman Mason, Lewis & Co., Boston, 1908; with Blodget & Co., Boston, 1909-27, partner, 1920-27; pres. Stone & Webster and Blodget, 1927-Mar. 1932, then vice chmn., 1932; exec. v.p., later chmn. bd. to 1955, then dir., mem. exec. com. Marine Midland Corp.; dir., cons. The Marine Midland Trust Company of New York; director, member executive com. Union Service Corp.; chmn. retirement board of Remington Rand division of Sperry Rand Corp.; mem. sr. adv. bd. The Marine Trust Co. of Western N.Y.; dir. Howes Leather Co., Tri-Continental Corp., Tri-Continental Financial Corp., Sperry Rand Corp. Hon. chmn. bd. trustees Community Service Soc.; chmn. mems. council, dir. Greater N.Y. Fund; Commr. Port of N.Y. Authority; dir. Port Authority Trans Hudson Corp. Trustee N.Y.U.-Bellevue Med. Center, Tuskegee Inst., Peoples Symphony Concerts, Grand Central Art Galleries. Republican. Episcopalian. Clubs: Harvard, Recess, Links (N.Y.C.). Home: New York City NY Died Nov. 1968.

POPE, FRANCIS HORTON, army officer; b. Fort Leavenworth, Kan., May 7, 1876; s. John (maj. gen., U.S. Army) and Clara Pomeroy (Horton) P.; grad. U.S. Mil. Acad., 1897; grad. Ecole de l'Intendance, Paris, 1914, Army War Coll., 1924; m. Harriet Ankeny, Oct. 20, 1908; 1 dau., Mary Ankeny. m. 2d, Blanche Wilson Hampson, Sept. 27, 1924. Commd. 2d lt. Cav., U.S. Army, 1897; promoted through grades to col., July 1, 1920; apptd. asst. q.m. gen., Jan. 24, 1927, with rank of brig. gen., term of 4 yrs.; served in Cuba, Spanish-Am. War; with Army of Cuban Occupation, 1899; instr. mathematics, U.S. Mil. Acad., 1899-1903; Philippine campaigns, 1903-05; Mexican Punitive Expdn., 1916; lt. col. and col. (temp.) in France, World War, 1917-19; dir. Motor Transport Service, A.E.F., Feb.-Aug. 1918; dep. dir. Motor Transport Corps, Aug. 1918-Aug. 1919; retired from active service by operation of law, May 31, 1940, brig. gen. U.S. Army (retired); on active duty to December 31, 1943. Mem. Mil. Order World War, Soc. Army of Santiago de Cuba, Soc. Moro Campaigns, Mil. Order Loyal Legion, Am. Legion. Decorated D.S.M. (U.S.); Officer Legion of Honor (Franch). Episcopalian. Clubs: Army and Navy, Chevy Chase. Home: Washington DC Died June 1971.

POPE, FREDERICK, corp. official; b. Boston, Mass., Nov. 20, 1877; s. Eugene Alexander and Ella M. (Brown) P.; S.B., Lawrence Scientific Sch. (Harvard), 1901; m. Mary Stockton McLaughlin, Apr. 8, 1912; children—Frederick, Richard Stockton. Cons. engr., 1912; organized the Standard Aniline Products Co. and built the first dye plant to start in U.S. after beginning of World War; cons. engr. Newport Chem. Works, 1915-17; refinanced New York Steam Corp., 1920, 1st

v.p. in charge operations, 1920-23; dir. Fiduciary Trust Co., Salvage Process Corp. (N.Y.), Rio Grande Gateway Bridge Corp. (Brownsville, Tex.). Served as major and assistant chief of Chemical Warfare Service in A.E.F., 1917-19; reorganized Chem. Warfare Service for A.E.F. Consultant to War Dept. since 1942, to Office War Mobilization since 1943. At request of Gen. Lucius Clay went to Germany for Survey of German chem. plants, chem. industry, 1948; at request of Gen. MacArthur went to Japan for survey of Japanese chem. plants, chem. industry, 1949. Trustee Lingnan U.; member Overseer's Com. to Visit Grad. School Engring. and Physics Dept., Harvard. Mem. Council of Fgn. Relations. Decorated Officier d'Academie (French). Republican. Episcopalian. Clubs: Century, Union, Harvard, New York Yacht, Traveller's (Paris). Home: 969 Fifth Avenue, New York, N.Y.; and Little River Farm," Wilton, Conn. Office: 30 Rockefeller Plaza, New York NY‡

POPE, WALTER LYNDON, judge; b. Valparaiso, Ind., Jan. 26, 1889; s. Carey Joseph and Margaret (Lyndon) P.; A.B., U. of Neb., 1909; J.D., U. of Chicago, 1912; Doctor of Laws, University of Montana; married Evangeline Bash Long, June 15, 1915 (died May 24, 1921); children—Richard Lyndon, Judith Evangeline, Margaret Jane; m. 2d, Frances Housel, Nov. 30, 1922 (divorced 1926); m. 3d, Luella Bash Platt, Aug. 11, 1926. Practiced law Lincoln, Neb., 1912-16, Missoula, Mont., 1917-49; asst. prof. law (part time), U. of Neb., 1913-16; prof. law (part time), Law Sch., U. of Mont., 1916-48; spl. asst. to atty. gen. of U.S., 1937-41, in connection with Northern Pacific Land Grant litigation. Mem. Mont. Ho. of Rep., 1923. Apptd. Judge, U.S. Court of Appeals for the Ninth Circuit, 1949, chief judge U.S. Court of Appeals, 1959, chairman advisory committee Admiralty Rules, 1960-69; senior circuit judge, 1961-69. Member of the Montana State Bar Association (president 1929-30), Phi Alpha Delta, Order of Coif. Baptist. Kiwanian. Home: Missoula MT also San Mateo CA Died Mar. 27, 1969; buried Missoula MT

POPOVIC, VLADIMIR, govt. ofcl. Yugoslavia; born Cetinje, Montenegro, Yugoslavia, Jan. 27, 1914; s. Luka and Stana (Jovanovic) P.; student U. Belgrade, 1932-37; m. Vjera Radimir, Sept. 1946. Del. students Belgrade U. to World Students Congress, Paris, 1937; leader Peoples Liberation Movement, Croatia, Yugoslavia, and mem. Supreme Hdqrs. Peoples Liberation Army and Partisans Units of Yugoslavia, 1941-45; polit. and mil. rep. Yugoslavia to Bulgaria, 1945; Yugoslavian ambassador to U.S.S.R., 1945-48; del. to Paris-Peace Conf., 1946; regular sessions, U.N. Gen. Assembly, N.Y., 1946-53; 1st dep. minster fgn. affairs, Belgrade, 1948-50; ambassador to U.S., 1950-54; chmn. Fgn. Relations Com. of Nat. Assembly, 1954-56; ambassador to China, 1955-58; mem. Fed. Exec. Council of F.P.R. of Yugoslavia, mem. coordination com.; pres. Orgn. Com. and Econ. Fgn. Relations Com. Served as capt., Rep. Army Spain, 1937-39; maj. gen. 3d Army Corps, Peoples Liberation Army, 1944. Address: Belgrade Yugoslavia Died Apr. 1, 1972.

PORTER, ARTHUR LE MOYNE, lumberman; b. Muscatine, Ia., July 14, 1873; s. George William and Laura A. (Van Buren) P.; ed. high sch.; m. Alma Francis, of Dallas, Tex., Apr. 16, 1917. Organized, 1902, and sec-treas. Western Retail Lumbermen's Assn.; organized, 1903, Lumbermen's Mutual Soc., of which is sec.-treas.; organized, 1916, Nat. Builders' Bureau, of which is pres. Mem. Ia. N.G. 5 yrs. Trustee Spokane Chamber of Commerce. Mem. Hoo Hoo. Republican. Baptist. Mason. Clubs: City, Advertising, Athletic, Transportation, Country. Home: 725 W. 20th St. Office: Columbia Bldg., Spokane WA‡

PORTER, BRUCE, artist; b. San Francisco, Feb. 23, 1865; s. Charles Bruce and Annie (Williamson) P.; ed. in Calif., Eng., and France; m. Margaret Mary, d. late William James, Oct. 6, 1917; children—Robert Bruce, Annie Mary (dec.), Catherine James. Engaged in stained glass and mural painting work since 1891. Designer of R. L. Stevenson Monument, San Francisco; mural decoration, numerous church windows at San Francisco, Monterey, Stockton, San Mateo, etc.; gardens at Burlingame, San Francisco, etc. Originator with Gelett Burgess, of the Lark (bibelot); writer poems and criticism. Founder, with Joseph Worcester, of endowed Society for Helping Boys. Decorated Chevalier Legion of Honor; Order of King Leopold. Mem. Am. Painters and Sculptors. Home: 3234 Pacific Av., San Francisco CA‡

PORTER, ERNEST WARREN, lawyer; b. Boston, Oct. 30, 1873; s. James E. and Annie M. (Dickie) P.; ed. Y.M.C.A. Sch. Modern Langs., Boston, 1893; Law Sch., Boston, 1894-5; Kent Coll. Law, 1895-6; LL.B., Chicago Law Sch., 1897, D.C.L., 1898; Ph.B. Taylor U., Upland, Ind., 1899; M.A., Amity Coll., 1909; LL.D., Western Ia. Coll., 1909); m. Winifred May Taylor, of Auburn, N.S., Sept. 7, 1898. Admitted to bar, Ill., 1896, D.C., 1905; instr. Ill. Coll. Law, Chicago, 1897-8; instr. polit. and social science, history, pvt. sch., Boston, 1900-3; pres. and prof. economics and law, Potomac U., Washington, since 1904. Republican. Baptist. Address: 1881 3d St. N.W., Washington DC‡

PORTER, FRED THOMAS, lawyer; b. Terrell, Tex., Mar. 10, 1904; s. Fred Thomas and Mary Womack (Dashiell) P.; J.D., U. Tex., 1926; m. Margaret Tugwell, June 9, 1932; children—Fred Thomas III, Lucinda Ann (Mrs. R. L. McRoberts). Admitted to Tex. bar, 1926; practice in Dallas, 1943-71; asst. dist. atty., Kaufman County, 1927-35, dist. atty., 1939-43; asso. Robertson, Leachman, Payne, Gardere &Lancaster, Dallas, 1943-47; mem. firm Leachman, Matthews & Gardere, 1947-54, Leachman, Gardere, Akin & Porter, 1954-65; partner Gardere, Porter & DeHay, 1965-71. Pres. Delta Theta Phi Ednl. Found.; mem. chancellors U. Tex. Law Sch. Fellow Am. Coll. Trial Lawyers, Internat. Acad. Trial Lawyers; mem. Am., Dallas (pres., chmn. bd. dirs.) bar assns., State Bar of Texas (dir. 1965-68, chmn. bd. dirs. 1967-68), Internat. Assn. Ins. Counsel, Tex. Assn. Def. Counsel, Delta Theta Phi. Methodist Dallas TX Died Nov. 5, 1971; buried Terrell TX

PORTER, HENRY (HARRY) ALANSON, graphic arts exec.; b. Warren, O., Oct. 12, 1886; s. Alanson Chauncy and Lucy (Zellers) P.; LL.D., Webster U., 1940; m. Harriet Jane Dailey, Oct. 30, 1912 (dec.); 1 dau., Ruth (Mrs. Jack W. Woodburn). Successivley sales mgr., v.p. in charge sales, sr. v.p. Harris-Seybold Co., Cleve., 1906-56. Exec. v.p. edn. council Graphic Arts Industry, 1956-66. Chmn. bd. Brentwood Hosp., Cleve. Named Graphic Arts man-of-the-year, 1955; recipient president's medal Internat. Graphic Arts Edn. Assn. Mem. Internat. Printing Pressmen's and Asst.'s Union (hon.), Direct Mail Advt. Assn. (pres. 1949-50). Author articles, pamphlets. Home: Cleveland OH Died Dec. 22, 1968; buried Knollwood Cemetery, Cleveland OH

PORTER, J(AMES) SHERMAN, editor; b. Bladen, Gallia Co., O., July 11, 1872; s. Daniel Thomas and Nancy (Wilson) P.; ed. pub. schs.; m. Rowena Viola Booton, of Gallipolis, O., Sept. 9, 1893; children—Stella Pauline (dec.), Mary Dorothy, James Sherman. Teacher and ins. business till 1905; entered newspaper work as editor Gallipolis Journal, 1905; mng. editor Lexington Herald, 1908-16; admitted to bar and licensed to practice law in Ky., 1911; probation officer, pub. schs., Lexington, 1916-20; chief federal prohibition insp., Ky., Nov. 1920-Aug. 1921; editor Burley Tobacco Grower and publicity dir. Burley Tobacco Growers' Cooperative Assn., 1921-27; mgr. Lexington Automobile Club, 1928-32; in unemployment relief work, Fayette Co., Ky., 1933-35; editor Daily Independent, Maysville, Ky., since 1935. Democrat. Methodist. K.P. (Grand Chancellor, State of Ky., 1931-32), Woodman, Odd Fellow; mem. Jr. Order United Am. Mechanics, daughters of America, Pythian Sisters. Home: 478 W. 2d St. Office: 43 W. 2d St., Maysville KY‡

PORTER, JAMES A., prof. art, chmn. dept. Howard U. Home: Washington DC Died Feb. 28, 1970.*

PORTER, JAMES DUNLOP, lawyer; b. Milwaukee, May 24, 1909; s. Paul James and Lila (Dunlop) P.; LL.B., U. Wis., 1933; m. Elizabeth Smith Swensen, Apr. 7, 1934; children—William Swensen, James Dunlop, Jr. Admitted to Wis. bar, 1933, practiced in Milwaukee. Dir. A. O. Smith Corp., others. Episcopalian. Clubs: University, Milwaukee. Office: Milwaukee WI Died Oct. 1, 1969.

PORTER, KIRK HAROLD, univ. prof.; b. Waukegan, Ill., Apr. 7, 1891; s. Jeremiah Merchant and Alice (Kirk) P.; A.B., U. of Mich., 1914, M.A., 1916; Ph.D., U. of Chicago, 1918; m. Irene Gray, June 12, 1923; children—Carolyn Alice, Marjorie Jean. Asso. prof., Polit. Science, Kansas State Teachers Coll., 1918-19; asst. prof. Polit. Science, U. of Ia., 1919-25, asso. prof., 1925-28, prof., 1928-40, head and prof., Polit. Science Dept. from 1940. Member Nat. Municipal League, Am. Polit. Science Assn., Am. Assn. Univ. Profs., Am. Soc. Internat. Law, Am. Acad. Polit. and Social Sciences, Am. Soc. for Pub. Adminstrn., Alpha Tau Omega. Republican. Clubs: Iowa City Country, Rotary, Triangle (Iowa City). Author: History of Suffrage in the United States, 1918; County and Township Government in the United States, 1922; National Party Platforms, 1924; State Administration, Iowa City IA Died May 2, 1972.

PORTER, L(ESTER) G(ILBERT), corp. exec.; b. Peotone, Ill., Feb. 19, 1903; s. Edgar Ross and Rosa J. (Lasche) P.; student U. Ill., 1921-25; m. Dorothy E. Graham, June 15, 1929. Joined Borg Warner Corp., Chgo., 1934, treas., 1951, formerly president, chmn. finance committee and dir.; mem. board of directors Szabo Food Service, also Borg Warner Acceptance Corp., Ball Corporation, LaSalle Nat. Bank, Chgo. Mem. Ill. Mfrs. Assn. Clubs: Commercial, Chicago, Chicago Athletic (Chicago); Flossmoor (Ill.) Country. Home: Chicago IL Died Aug. 19, 1970; buried Peotone IL

PORTER, ROYAL A(RTHUR), physicist; born Adair, Ill., Feb. 8, 1877; s. George E. and Mary (Ritter) P.; B.S., Northwestern, 1901, M.S., 1902; Ph.D., Gottingen Univ., 1912; m. Eleanore Lukens, June 22, 1914. Fellow in physics, Northwestern, 1901-02; instr. Syracuse U., 1902-05, asst. prof., 1905-06, asso. prof., 1906-12, prof. physics, 1912-47, chmn. dept., 1919-39, prof. emeritus since 1947. Fellow Am. Physical Soc., A.A.A.S.; mem. Am. Inst. E.E., Soc. Engring. Edn., Am. Assn. Univ. Profs., Phi Beta Kappa, Sigma Xi, Acacia. Republican. Methodist. Mason. Home: 861 Ostrom Av., Syracuse 10 NY‡

PORTER, WHITNEY CLAIR, physician; b. Indpls., Aug. 19, 1897; s. Harry Alfred and Daisy (White) P.; M.D., U. Colo., 1926; m. Sarah Jane Hunter, Aug. 27, 1928; children—Whitney Allen, Catherine (Mrs. William Stevens Cole). Intern, Denver Gen. Hosp., 1926-27, cons. ophthalmologist, until 1970; postgrad. in phys. ophthalmology U. Pa. Grad. Sch. Medicine, 1929-30; resident in ophthalmology U. Ia., 1931-33, asst. in ophthalmology, 1932; hon. staff Mercy, Childrens hosps.; cons. staff St. Lukes Hosp.; ophthlmology staff Colo. Gen. Hosp.; asso. clin. prof. ophthalmology U. Colo. Sch. Medicine, Denver. Served to lt. col., M.C., AUS. Diplomate Am. Bd. Opthalmology. Mem. A.M.A., Am. Acad. Ophthalmology and Otolaryngology. Home: Denver CO Died Aug. 25, 1970; buried Denver CO

PORTER, WILLIAM N(ICHOLS), ret. army officer, business exec.; b. Lima, O., Mar. 15, 1886; s. William Harley and Ilva (Nichols) P.; B.S., U.S. Naval Acad., 1909; grad. Army Indsl. Coll., Washington, 1926, Command and Gen. Staff Sch., Ft. Leavenworth, Kan., 1927, Chem. Warfare Sch., Edgewood, Md., 1931, Air Corps Tactical Sch., Maxwell Field, Ala., 1937, Army War Coll., Washington, 1938; m. Gladys Baxter, July 20, 1910; children—William Baxter (U.S.N.), John Harley (dec.), Margaret Baxter (wife L.M. Stevens, Jr., U.S.N.). Commd. ensign, U.S.N., 1909, resigned, 1910; commd. 2d lt., U.S. Army, 1910, advanced through grades to maj. gen., 1941; comd. 30th Arty. C.A.C., 1918-19; transferred to C.W.S., 1920, chief, 1941-45; ret. 1945; pres. Chem. Constrn. Corp., 1947-53; chmn. bd. 1953-54; chemical consultant American Cyanamid Company; cons. Byrne Assos., N.Y., profl. engr. N.Y., O. Awarded Distinguished Service Medal, Comdr. Order Brit. Empire, Order of Leopold (Belgium). Past mem. Nat. Research Council. Mem. Am.-Arab Assn. for Commerce and Industry (pres.). Epis. Clubs: Army and Navy, Army-Navy Country (Washington). Home: Key West FL Died Feb. 1973.

PORTER, WILLIAM WALLACE, Christian Science lecturer; b. Crown Point, N.Y., Jan. 6, 1864; s. Rev. G.W.S. and Jennie (Stickles) P.; ed. pub. schs. of N.Y. State; m. Alice E. Brown, 1886; children—Allene M. (Mrs. Emory J. Douglas), Irene E.; m. 2d, Mrs. Lillie May De Nio, 1905; children—Margaret (Mrs. Edward Jefferies), and stepdaughters, Louise (Mrs. George E. Quigley), Lillie (Mrs. Fitz Herbert Delisser). Stenographer A.T.. F. Ry., 1884-89; gen. supply agt. Pueblo Smelting & Refining Co., 1889-1902; sec.-dir. Guggenheim Bros., 1903-06; connected with Christian Science Ch. in 1903; Christian Science practitioner since 1906; degree C.S.B. conferred by Bd. of Edn., 1st Ch. of Christ, Scientist, of Boston, Mass., 1910; 1st reader, 2d Ch. of Christ Scientist, New York City, 1908-11; mem. Bd. of Lectureship, 1916-32; mem. Christian Science Com. on Publication for State of New York, 1932-35. Mason (32 deg.). Address: 20 Park Av., New York NY*‡

PORTERFIELD, ROBERT HUFFARD, producer, director, actor; b. Austinville, Va., Dec. 21, 1905; s. William Breckenridge and Daisy (Huffard) Porterfield; student U. Va., Am. Acad. Dramatic Arts, 1929; Litt.D., Hampden-Sydney Coll., 1948. Founder, mng. dir. Barter Theatre of Va., Abingdon, 1932; pres. Martha Washington Inn Corp., Abingdon, from 1955; dairy farm mgr., owner, Glade Spring, Va.; broadway plays include Ivory Door, 1929, Dagger and the Rose, 1929, Mina, 1930, Blind Windows, 1931, The Blue Ghost, 1932, Cyrano de Bergerac, 1932, Bury the Dead, Let Freedom Ring, 1936, Petrified Forest, 1937; producer The Hill Between, 1938; motion pictures include Seargeant York, 1941, Army Chaplain, 1942, The Yearling, 1946, Thunder Road, 1958; commd. to conduct, produce playwriting contest Woodrow Wilson Centennial Celebration Com., 1956; founder Washington County Pub. Library; commd. to produce The Tempest, Virginia 350th Anniversary Commn., Jamestown Festival, 1957; founder, producer The Playhouse, Abingdon, Va.; nat. lectr. Established Barter Theatre of Va. award for outstanding contbn. current N.Y. season, 1939; founder ANTA; trustee Nat. Theatre Conf., officer Southeastern Theatre Conf. Chmn. Va. Cancer Crusade, 1957-58; officer Va. Care Com., 1958-59; state flying Santa Clause for Tb Assn.; active promotion Va. Travel Council, Va. Conservation Com.; dir. Am. Nat. Theatre Academy, from 1962; president, founder Barter Found., Inc., from 1962. Served as pvt. motion picture unit, USAAF, 1943-46. Recipient Antoinette Perry award for outstanding contbn. to theatre, 1948; named first citizen of Abingdon, 1957; Medal of Honor, Virginians of Md., Inc., 1962. Mem. Nat. Trust for Hist. Preservation U.S., Washington County (Va.) Hist. Soc., Old Abingdon Assn., Va. Highlands Cotillion Soc., First Families of Va. Soc., Kappa Alpha, Omega Delta Kappa. Presbyn. Address: Abingdon VA Died Oct. 28, 1971; buried Abingdon VA

PORTMAN, ERIC, actor; b. Halifax, Yorkshire, Eng., July 13, 1908; s. Matthew and Alice (Harrison) P.; student Rishworth Sch., Yorkshire. Debut appearance on London State in Comedy of Errors, 1924; joined Old Vic company, 1927; Broadway debut in role of Oliver Farrant in I Have Been Here Before, 1938; appeared numerous plays including Major Barbara, Master Builder, Misalliance, Desire Under the Elms, 1931, Masque of Kings, 1938, The Browning Version, Harlequinade, 1948, Separate Tables, 1955, also A Passage to India, in 1962; the motion pictures include Murder in the Red Barn, 1934, Moonlight Sonata, 49th Parallel (The Invaders), One of Our Aircraft is Missing, We Dive at Dawn, Uncensored, Deep Blue Sea, Freud, 1962, The Man Who Finally Died, West Eleven, The Belford Incident. TV debut in A Double Life, Alcoa Hour, 1956, British TV in Medea, also Helen of Troy. Mem. Ch. of Eng. Home: Cornwall England Died Dec. 7, 1969.*

POSEY, CHESTER ALFRED, advt. exec.; b. Peekskill, N.Y., Jan. 14, 1896; s. Alfred and Christine Eliza (Cooke) P.; A.B., Yale, 1917; m. Olive Clarke Lewis, Sept. 14, 1921; children—Chester Lewis, Priscilla. Copy editor J. Walter Thompson Co., N.Y.C., 1919-25; established firm Olmstead, Perrin & Leffingwell, advt., N.Y.C., 1925, merged with H.K. McCann Co., 1929; v.p., dir. McCann-Erickson, Inc., 1929-58, sr. v.p. Captain, 30th F.A., U.S. Army, World War I. Home: Scarsdale Manor S., Scarsdale, NY; also Candlewood Lake Club, Brookfield, CT Home: Pompano Beach FL Died Feb. 11, 1971.

POSNER, EDWIN, securities broker; b. Balt., Nov. 22, 1890; s. Samuel and Henrietta (Ehrlich) P.; grad. Lawrenceville (N.J.) Sch., 1908; m. Florine R. Weil, Oct. 17, 1917 (dec.); children—Evelyn (Mrs. Harry F. Weber, Jr.), Joan (Mrs. Richard J. Koshland). Engaged in securities bus., 1908-69; partner Andrews, Posner & Rothschild, N.Y.C., 1928-69. Former mem. and chmn. bd. govs. Am. Stock Exchange. Clubs: Lawyers; Sunningdale Country. Home: New York City NY Died Oct. 4, 1969.

POSNER, LOUIS SAMUEL, lawyer; b. London, England; s. Samuel and Anna (Cohen) P.; 1 son, David L. Came to U.S., 1884, citizen through father's naturalization. Admitted to bar and in practice at New York since 1902; mem. Dos Passos Bros., 1910-17, Jonas & Neuberger, 1922-33; practicing alone. Del. to World Zionist Conv., London, 1920; president New Era Club for Boys since 1906; director and chairman law com., Jewish Child Care Assn. of New York; mem. N.Y. advisory com. of Federal Housing Administration; member Board of Edn., New York, term 1931-35; mem. N.Y. State Mortgage Commn., 1935-37; chmn. Teacher's Retirement Bd.; former gen. chmn. of Municipal Com. for Relief of Home Owners; former impartial chmn. Painting Industry in N.Y. City; trustee of Law Review of St. John's Coll. Mem. Assn. Bar of City of N.Y., N.Y. County Lawyers Assn., Am. and N.Y. State bar assns. founder member, Zeta Beta Tau fraternity. Member Liberal Party. Jewish religion. Mem. Spanish and Portuguese Temple. Clubs: City, Metropolis, City College. Contbr. articles to numerous law jours. Home: 2 E. 61st St. Office: 170 Broadway, NY City ‡

POSSE, ROSE (BARONESS); ALSO KNOWN AS ROSE MOORE STRONG., Ex-pres. Posse Normal Sch. Gymnastics; b. Newburyport, Mass.; d. Foster Waldo and Catherine Moore (Ballou) Smith; m. Newburyport, Mass., Baron Nils Posse, of Stockholm, Sweden, June 29, 1887 (died Dec. 1895); m. 2d, William T. Strong, of Boston, July 6, 1904 (died Apr. 22, 1919). Founder Posse Gymnasium Journal, 1892; dir. Posse Gymnasium, 1896-1911; pres. Posse Normal Sch. of Gymnastics, 1911-15; hon. pres. Posse Sch., Inc., Kendal Green, Mass. V.p. Boston Physical Edn. Soc., 1899-1901; pres. physical training dept., N.E.A., 1914, 15; pres. Congress Physical Edn., Panama P.I. Expn., 1915; v.p. Mass. Med. Gymnastic Assn., 1904-05; rec. sec. Am. Assn. Adv. Physical Edn., 1899-1901; v.p. Am. Physical Edn. Assn., 1906-—; pres. Therapeutic Gymnastic Soc., 1907-16. Editor: Medical Gymnastics, by Baron Nils Posse, 1896. Pres. N.E. Women's Press Assn., 1919-21; v.p. Arts and Letters Club, 1919; v.p. Bacon Soc. of America, 1929; mem. Poetry Soc. America; pres. N.Y. Poetry Group since 1934. Home: The Shelton, 48th St. and Lexington Av., New York NY‡

POST, LEVI ARNOLD, prof. Greek; b. Stanfordville, N.Y., July 8, 1889; s. Isaac Rushmore and Mary Lydia (Arnold) P.; prep. edn., Oakwood Sem., Union Springs, N.Y., 1903-07; A.B., A.M., Haverford (Pa.) Coll., 1911; A.M., Harvard, 1912; A.B., Rhodes Scholar, New Coll., Oxford U., Eng., 1916, A.M., 1922; grad. study U. of Caen, France, 1919; m. Grace Hutcheson Lickely, Oct. 4, 1919; children—Robert Lickely, Arnold Rae, Jennifer Anne. Teacher mathematics, Moses Brown School, Providence, R.I., 1912-13; with Ambulance Americaine, Neuilly-sur-Seine, France, 1915; sec. Y.M.C.A. with B.E.F., Mesopotamia, 1916-17; instr. in French and German, Haverford Coll., 1917-18; served as pvt., corpl. and sergt. inf., later with Censor and Press Co., sch. detachment, Caen, May 1918-July 1919; instr.

in Greek, Haverford Coll., 1919-22, asst. prof., 1922-28, asso. prof., 1928-33, prof. Guggenheim fellow, 1932; Sather professor of classics, University of Calif., 1947-48. Member American Philological Assn. (sec.-treas. 1935-39; editor 1935-38, v.p., 1944-45; pres. 1945-46), Archaeological Inst. of America, Phi Beta Kappa. Democrat. Quaker, Translator: Thirteen Epistles of Plato, 1925; Menander-Three Plays, 1929. Contbr. to Quarterly Rev., Hibbert Jour. Classical Quarterly, Classical Philology, Am. Journal of Philology, etc. Author: The Vatican Plato and its Relations, 1934. Editor, Loeb Classical Library since 1940. Home: Haverford PA Died May 26, 1971.

POSTLETHWAITE, WILLIAM WALLACE;, b. Harrisburg, Pa., Nov. 17, 1870; s. Edward Thomas and Eliza Francis (Denning) P.; ed. pvt. and pub. schs., Phila.; hon. A.M., Colorado Coll., 1928; m. Lucile Hood Newman, Oct. 15, 1902; children—Isabel (Mrs. Perry P. Greiner), Constance (Mrs. J. Harley Murray), Treas. Claridge Coal Co., Greensburg, Pa., 1893-96; asso. with Gen. Wm. J. Palmer, founder of Colorado Springs, Colo., also sec. Antlers Hotel Co., Colorado Springs Co. and Nat. Land & Improvement Co., 1897-1911; treas. Colorado Coll., 1911-40; dir. Colorado Coll. Museum since 1940. Mem. Bd. of Park Commrs., Colorado Springs, 1923-47; Dir. Colorado Coll. Archeol. Inst. America, 1928, 29, 33; asst. in excavation of Chetro Ketl. Chaco Canyon, N.M., for Sch. of Am. Research, 1931-37. Mem. bd. of dirs. of Sch. of Am. Research (Santa Fe, N.M.), president Colo. Springs Chapter Archeol. Inst. America, 1930-37; dir. Colo. Springs Fine Arts Center, 1931-38, sec. since 1938. Mem. A.A.A.S., Am. Assn. Museums, State History Soc. of Colo., New Mexico Archeol. Society, Colorado-Wyoming Academy Sci., Colorado Archeol. Soc. (pres. 1939), Delta Epsilon (pres. 1939-40). Presbyterian. Clubs: Winter Night (sec.-treas., 1907-32; pres., 1933). Home: 1319 N. Wahsatch Av. Address: Colorado College, Colorado Springs CO‡

POSTNIKOV, FEDOR ALEXIS (F. A. POST), engineer, aeronaut; b. Kovno, Russia, Feb. 29, 1872; s. Alexis Semen and Mary Fedor (Radchenko) P.; grad. 1st Imperial Mil. Sch. (Petrograd), 1891, with rank 2d lt. of Ussuri Cossack Army; Officers' Aeronautical Sch., St. Petersburg, 1897; grad. as mil. engr., St. Petersburg, 1899; capt., mil. engr., 1901; lt. col. Russian Admiralty (Navy Dept.), 1905; M.S. in C.E., U. of Calif., 1907; m. Mary Nicolas Smirnov, of St. Petersburg, Aug. 9, 1895. Cossacks scout comdr., 1892-4; sr. engr. Yards and Docks Dept., under Russian Govt., 1899-1906; officer-aeronaut in Russian Army, 1898; as head Navy Aero Detachment took part in defense of Vladivostok, and in raids with cruisers during Russo-Japanese War, in capacity as organizer and comdr. Navy Aero Detachment, 1904-5; commd. 1st lt. Aviation Sect. Signal Corps, U.S.A., Mar. 27, 1917; capt. jr. mil. aviator, July 24, 1917, at Ft. Omaha, Neb.; asst. aero engr., experimental work and designing dirigibles, with Good year Co., Akron, O., Jan.-May 1918; designing engr., with dock and terminal sect. Constrn. Corps, U.S. Army, Washington, D.C., until June 1919. Has designed and built numerous buildings, dams, harbors, etc. Internat. balloon pilot certificate No. 77. Mem. Russian Tech. Soc. (life), Aero Club of America, Internat. Esperanto Assn., etc. Author: Siberian Cossack Cousin, 1916. Writer on tech. subjects in English, Russian and Esperanto langs. Home: 1633 Dwight Way, Berkeley CA‡

POTTER, CHARLES, physician; b. Providence, Nov. 13, 1908; s. Max and Bessie (Chernoff) P.; M.D., Columbia, 1935; m. Lillian Kelman, June 8, 1941; children—Eleanor Jean, Deborah Ruth (Mrs. Elliot Brener), Elizabeth Ann. Intern, Michael Reese Hosp., Chgo., 1936-38; house surgeon Providence Lying-In Hosp., 1939, later dir. family planning clinic and sr. obstetrician; gynecologist R.I. Hosp., Providence; dir. div. obstetrics and gynecology Miriam Hosp., Providence, 1958-68, pres. staff, 1960; clin. instr. obstetrics Harvard Med. Sch., Boston, Tufts, Boston. Chmn. med. adv. bd. Planned Parenthood of R.I., 1941-70; v.p., chmn. adoption com. Jewish Family and Children's Service, 1960-64, hon. pres., 1970. Recipient Margaret Sanger award. Diplomate Am. Bd. Obstetrics and Gynecology. Fellow A.C.S., Boston Obstet. Soc. (sr.); mem. A.M.A., Am. Coll. Obstetricians and Gynecologists, Am. Assn. Planned Parenthood Physicians, New Eng. Obstet. and Gynecol. Soc. Home: Providence RI Died Dec. 10, 1970; buried Sharon Meml. Park, Sharon MA

POTTER, DAVID, naval officer; b. Bridgeton, N.J., 1874; s. William Elmer and Alice (Eddy) P.; B.A., Princeton, 1896; admitted to N.J. bar, 1897; m. Jane, d. late Vice Chancellor Martin Philip Grey, 1904. Entered U.S. Navy 1898; served at sea during war with Spain and Philippine campaign; fiscal officer of customs, Vera Cruz, Mexico, during Am. occupation, 1914; mem. Navy Compensation Board, 1917-19; fleet paymaster Atlantic Fleet, 1919-21; paymaster gen. of Navy and chief Bur. of Supplies and Accounts, with rank of rear adm., 1921-25; mem. bd. for settlement of claims arising from treaty limiting naval armament, 1923; mem. Naval War Claims Bd., 1926-30; gen. insp., Supply Corps, West Coast, 1930-34; in charge Naval Finance and Supply Sch., 1934-38; promoted rear adm. Supply Corps, Nov. 14, 1927; retired Jan. 1, 1939. Author: (novels) The Lost Goddess, 1908; The Eleventh Hour, 1910; The Lady of the Spur, 1910; I Fasten a Bracelet, 1911; An Accidental Honeymoon, 1911; The Unspeakable Turke, 1912; The Streak, 1913; Diane of Star Hollow, 1918; The Marshes, 1919; (memoirs) Sailing The Sulu Sea, 1940, also monographs on financial and business affairs of the Navy, and has lectured on such subjects. Address: 2999 Pacific Av., San Francisco CA‡

POTTER, DAVID MORRIS, educator; b. Augusta, Ga., Dec. 6, 1910; s. David Morris and Katie (Brown) P.; A.B., Emory U., 1932, Litt.D., 1957; M.A., Yale, 1933, Ph.D., 1940; M.A., Oxford, 1947; LL.D., U. Wyoming, 1955; married to Ethelyn E. Henry, 1939 (divorced 1945); m. 2d, Dilys Mary Roberts, July 18, 1948; 1 dau., Catherine Mary. Instr. history U. Miss., 1936-38, Rice Inst., Houston, 1938-42; Harmsworth prof. Am. history and Fellow of Queen's Coll., Oxford, 1947-48; mem. faculty Yale, 1942-61, asst. prof., 1942-47, asso. prof., 1947-49, prof., 1949-50, Coe prof. Am. history, 1950-61, editor Yale Rev., 1949-51; fellow Timothy Dwight Coll., 1942-61; Coe prof. Am. history Stanford U., 1961-71; Walgreen lecturer U. of Chicago, 1950; Commonwealth Fund lectr. U. Coll., London, Eng., 1963; Walter L. Fleming lectr. La. State University, 1968; vis. prof. summer sessions Conn. College, 1947, U. Delaware, 1954, Univ. of Wyo., 1952, 55, Stanford U., 1957, 58, Stetson U., 1959, State U. N.Y., 1966. Fellow American Academy Arts and Sciences; member American Philosophical Society, Phi Beta Kappa, Omicron Delta Kappa. Author or editor: Lincoln and His Party in the Secession Crisis, 1942; Trail to California: The Overland Diary of Vincent Geiger and Wakeman Bryarly, 1945; A Union Officer in the Reconstruction (with J. H. Croushore), 1948; Nationalism and Sectionalism in America (with T. G. Manning), 1949; Government and the American Economy (with T. G. Manning), 1949; People of Plenty: Economic Abundance and the American Character, 1954; The South and the Sectional Conflict, pub. 1968. Home: Los Altos Hills CA Died Feb. 1971.

POTTER, DELBERT MAXWELL, mining man; b. Canton, O.; s. Hiram B. and Arminda E. (Carter) P.; ed. grammar and high schs., Canton; m. Lizzie S. Dorsey, of Paola, Kan., Oct. 31, 1882. Began mining in New Mexico, 1882; was one of discovers of the Telegraph and Bald Mountain mining districts in N.M.; operated mines extensively in Colo., Cal., Ariz. and Mexico; now sec. and gen. mgr. of the Home Stake Gold Mining and Milling Company; pres. Ariz. Power & Water Co.; v.p. Ariz. Gold Mining & Milling Co.; builder and dir. Clifton Northern R.R.; prin. owner Morenci Inspiration Copper Co.; largely interested in irrigation projects and cattle ranching. Served as guide and scout in expdns. against Apache Indians and in Geronimo campaign; dep. U.S. marshal for Southern N.M. under Marshal Romero; chief dep. sheriff in Grant Co., N.M., under Sheriff Whitehill; p.m. gen. with rank of col., Ariz. N.G., on staff of Gov. R.E. Sloan. Originator, 1906, of movement to unite the states in behalf of good roads; pres. Southern Nat. Highways Assn. since 1912; v.p. Robert E. Lee Nat. Highways Assn. Pres. and gen. mgr. Morenci-Inspiration‡

POTTER, FRANK B(ELL), U.S. atty.; b. Smithville, Tenn., June 6, 1891; s. Leroy Jackson and Mary Eliza (Whaley) P.; student Alden Rives Coll., 1906, Chattanooga (Tenn.) Bus. Coll., 1908-09; LL.B., Cumberland U., 1912; m. Birdie Lucile Blow, Dec. 24, 1912; children—Geraldine Lucile (Mrs. Earl A. Schneider), Frank Bee, William Beverly. Admitted to Texas bar, 1912, and practied in Ft. Worth, 1912-33; appted. asst. U.S. atty., July 1, 1933, served until 1945; acting U.S. atty., 1945-47; U.S. atty. 1947-53; later in pvt. practice. Member Tex. legislature, 1923. Mem. Am., Fed., Ft. Worth bar assns., State Bar Tex., Tarrant County Hist. Soc. Democrat. Methodist. Mason (33 deg., K.T., Shriner). Clubs: Kiwanis, Ft. Worth, El Club Saxino-Latino (past pres.). Home: Fort Worth TX Died Nov. 3, 1970.

POTTER, GEORGE MILTON, educator; b. Marion Co., Mo., Oct. 12, 1875; s. James Irving and Emily Frances (Bibb) P.; A.B., La Grange (Mo.) Coll., 1895, A.M., 1899; student Harvard Univ., 1897-98; A.M., University of Chicago, 1912, LL.D., Shurtleff College, 1927; Hillsdale Coll., 1933; m. Vashti Chandler of Chicago, Aug. 14, 1901. Prof. La Grange (Mo.) Coll., 1898-1902; prin. Tabor (Ia.) Coll. Acad., 1902-05 Cedar Valley Sem. Osage, Ia., 1905-11; pres. Shurtleff Coll., Alton, Ill., 1912-33; chief dep. treas. Madison Co., Ill., since 1934. Dir. Ill. Bapt. State Conv., 1913-29 (pres. 1920-22). Mem. Phi Delta Kappa. Democrat. Mason. Speaker and writer on ednl. and religious topics. Home: 1914 Washington Av., Alton IL‡

POTTER, HARRY S., illustrator; b. Detroit, Dec. 29, 1869; s. Henry Z. and Emma (Baker) P.; ed. Museum of Art Sch., Detroit, 1891-4; pupil of Jean Paul Laurens and Benjamin Constant, Academie Julian, Paris, 1894-5, and Jules Simon, Raphael Collin and Gustave Courtois, later; m. Detroit, July 9, 1896, Lilian Webster. Illustrative artist, Detroit Free Press, 1890-4, New York Journal, 1896-1903; illustrator for leading mags., since 1903. Mem. Am. Artists' Assn. (Paris), Alliance Francaise. Address: Van Dyck Studios, 939 8th Av., New York NY‡

POTTER, HENRY NOEL, research engr.; b. at Rochester, N.Y., Jan. 20, 1869; s. Charles Barton and Sarah Jane (Weaver) P.; B.S., Amherst, 1891; student course of Westinghouse Electric Co., 1892-3; Berlin and Gottingen, Germany, 1894-8; (Sc.D., honoris causa, Amherst, 1905); m. Lilian Heron, of Allegheny, Pa., Oct. 15, 1894. With Westinghouse Electric & Mfg. Co., Pittsburgh, 1891-4; asst. to Prof. Walter Nernst, Gottingen, 1898; with George Westinghouse as spl. engr., 1898-07 (in charge pvt. research lab., 1903-7); engring. expert Sawyer-Mann Electric Co., 1904-7; pvt. work, and gold mining, Raw hide, Nev., 1908; development of electrolytic amalgamation machinery, 1909-—; president of Potter Engineering Company, Los Angeles. Brought Nernst Lamp to America; discovered silicon monoxide; has taken out over 100 patents for processes and devices, in U.S. and Europe. Mem. Am. Chem. Soc., Delta Kappa Epsilon (Ahmerst). Club: Chemists (New York). Republican. Address: 7032 Hawthorn Av., Hollywood, Los Angeles CA‡

POTTER, MARY ROSS, educator; b. Bloomington, Ill., Jan. 30, 1871; d. Bradford Simmons and Mary Adelaide (Farrington) P.; Ill. Wesleyan U., 1887-91; Litt.D., Ill. Wesleyan U., Bloomington, 1935; grad. Ill. Wesleyan Conservatory of Music, 1888; A.B., Northwestern U., 1892; N.A., Boston U., 1897; Am. Sch. for Classical Studies, Rome, 1904-05; Univ. of Geneva, Switzerland, 1912-13; unmarried. Teacher of langs., Ill. State Normal Sch., Normal, 1892-99; prof. langs., Northern Ill. State Normal Sch., DeKalb, 1899-1905; dean of women, Northwestern U., 1905-24; counselor for women, 1924-1929; dean of women, Monmouth College, 1929-1935. Instrumental, with others, in organizing, 1912, Chicago Collegiate Bur. of Occupations, whose work is opening vocational opportunity to coll. trained women. Methodist. Mem. Am. Assn. Univ. Women, Phi Beta Kappa, Kappa Alpha Theta. Clubs: Woman's Club, Woman's University Guild (Evanston). Address: Pentwater MI‡

POTTER, NATHANIEL BOWDITCH, physician; b. Keeseville, N.Y., Dec. 25, 1869; s. George Sabine and Mary Gill (Powell) P.; brother of Mary Knight P. (q.v.); A.B., Coll. City of New York, 1888; A.B., Harvard, 1890, M.D., 1896; m. Mary Sargent, of Brookline, Mass., Jan. 25, 1908. Med. interne Mass. Gen. Hosp., 1896-8; visiting phys. New York City, Ruptured and Crippled, and French hosps.; consulting phys. Manhattan State Hosp. for the Insane at Central Islip; asso. in medicine, Columbia Univ. Mem. N.Y. Co. Med. Soc., New York Pathol. Soc., N.Y. Acad. Sciences, Harvard Med. Soc. Editor of English transl., Sahli's Clinical Diagnosis (with Francis P. Kennicutt, q.v.), 1905; Ortner's Therapeutics, 1908. Address: 48 W. 35th St., New York‡

POTTER, STEPHEN, author; b. London, Eng., Feb. 1, 1900; s. Frank Collard and Elizabeth (Reynolds) P.; B.A. in English Lang. and Lit., Merton Coll., Oxford U., 1923; m. Mary Attenborough, 1927 (div. 1955); children—Andrew, Julian; m. 2d, Heather Lyon, 1955; 1 son, Luke. Sec. to Henry Arthur Jones, dramatist, 1925-26; lectr. English lit. London U., 1926-38; writer-producer BBC, 1938-48, editor lit. features and poetry, 1942-45, chmn. lit. com., 1943-44; dramatic critic New Statesman, 1945-46; book critic News Chronicle, 1946-47; editor Leader mag., 1949-51; lectr. in Am., 1952-58. Author: (novel) The Young Man, 1929; D. H. Lawrence, A First Study, 1939; Minnow among Tritons (letters of Mrs. Coleridge), 1934; Coleridge and S.T.C., 1935; The Muse in Chains, A Study in Education, 1937; Gamesmanship, 1947; Lifemanship, 1950; One-Upmanship, 1952; Humour Anthology, 1954; Potter in America, 1956; (autobiography) Steps to Immaturity, first volume published in 1959; Squawky, 1965; Anti-Woo, 1965. Editor: The Nonesuch Coleridge, 1934. Clubs: Athenaeum, Savile, Garrick (London); Royal and Ancient (St. Andrews, Scotland); Edinburgh (Scotland) Croquet; Leander (Henley, Eng.). Home: London England Died Dec. 2, 1969

POTTER, THOMAS PAINE, clergyman; b. Blairstown, Ia., Oct. 27, 1875; s. Ellis Wilson and Susannah Maria (Jackson) P.; A.B., Cornell Coll., Mt. Vernon, Ia., 1905, Doctor of Divinity, 1942; m. Alma H. Burlingame, June 27, 1900 (died Apr. 3, 1914); children—Ruth Hannah, Paul Burlingame; m. 2d, Gertrude May Campbell, May 3, 1916; 1 son, Thomas Paine, Jr. Ordained ministry Meth. Episcopal Ch., 1899; various pastorates, 1899-1914; field sec. Ia. Meth. Hosp., Des Moines, 1914-16; pastor, 1916-19; with apportionment dept. World Service Com., M.E. Ch., 1919-25; asst. editor Gen. Minutes of M.E. Ch., 1925-41; sec. Statistical Office of Methodist Ch., 1941-44, Methodist Membership Studies since 1944; historian Upper Iowa Conf. of M.E. Church since 1933, statistician, 1909-44, statistician emeritus since 1944, delegate to Gen. Conf., 1928, and an asst. sec.; 1st reserve del. from Upper Iowa Conf. to same, 1936; reserve del. (seated), 1st gen. conf. of the Meth. Church,

1940; mem. North Central Jurisdictional Conf., 1940; mem. Bd. Edn., Teaneck, N.J., 1934-37, vice-pres., 1936-37; trustee Baxter (Tennessee) Seminary; secretary Methodist Historical Society of City of N.Y., 1933-39; treas. Nat. Assn. of Ch. Statisticians, Am. European Fellowship (treas.). Mem. King of Kings" com. Republican. Contbg. editor Am. Ency. Supplement; contbr. Internat. Ency. Supplement, Ency. Britannica Year Book, Paebar Anthology of Verse, also on religious, historical and statistical subjects, prose and verse. Home: 1359 N. Hudson Av., Chicago 10 IL‡

POTTER, WILLIAM W., judge; b. Maple Grove Twp., Barry Co., Mich., Aug. 1, 1869; s. Lucien B. and Clarinda L. (Trimmer) P.; grad. high sch., Nashville, Mich., 1891; student Summer Sch., Ypsilanti State Normal Coll.; LL.B., University of Mich., 1895; LL.D., University of Detroit, 1930; m. Margaret D. Richardson, of Harrison, Mich., April 5, 1894; children—Louise, Doreen (Mrs. J. E. Hanna), Philip R., Charles W., Marguerite, Elizabeth (Mrs. E. C. Starr). Superintendent of schools, Harrison, Michigan, 1891-94; admitted to Michigan bar, 1894, and began practice at Hastings; member of firm of Barrell & Potter, 1895-96, Colgrove & Potter, 1896-1919; served as city atty. Hastings; pros. atty. Barry Co., 2 terms; mem. Mich. State Senate, 1899-1900; mem. Mich. Pub. Utilities Commn., 1919-27; atty. gen. of Mich., term 1927-28 inclusive; apptd. justice Supreme Court of Mich., and elected to same office, term beginning Jan. 1, 1928, reelected 1935 for term beginning Jan. 1, 1936. Mem. Am. and Mich. State bar assns. Republican. Mason (K.T.), Odd Fellow, K.P. Author: History of Barry County, 1912; The Law of Interest, 1910; Michigan Evidence, Civil and Criminal, 1920. Home: 334 Evergreen Av., East Lansing, Mich. Address: Capitol Bldg., Lansing MI‡

POTTS, WILLIS JOHN, surgeon; b. Sheboygan, Wis., Mar. 22, 1895; s. Horace and Hannah (Boeyink) P.; A.B., Hope Coll., Holland, Mich., 1918; S.B., U. of Chicago, 1920; M.D., Rush Med. Coll., 1924; interne Presbyn. Hosp., Chicago; Logan fellowship in surg. Rush Med. Coll., 1925-26; post grad. work, Frankfort, Germany, 1930-31; m. Henrietta Neerken, July 7, 1922; children—Willis John, Edward Eugene, Judith Eleanor. Began gen. practice, Oak Park, Ill., 1925; specialized in surgery, 1931-65, ret.; author syndicated newspaper column, 1965-68; professor of emeritus surgery Northwestern U. Med. sch., 1960-68; cons. surgery, Children's Memorial Hospital, Chicago. Sergt. Chem. Warfare Service, 1917-18; 1 year in U.S. and 1 year in France; lt. col. &colonel A.U.S., serving in Southwest Pacific with 25th Evacuation Hosp., 1942-45. Fellow Am. Coll. Surgeons; certified by Am. Bd. of Surgery; mem. Am. Med. Assn., Ill. and Chicago Med. Socs., Chicago Surg. Soc., Western Surg. Soc., Inst. Med. of Chicago, Am. Assn. Thoracic Surgery, Am. Surg. Assn., Central Surg. Assn. Am. Heart Assn. (pres. Chgo. 1960-61). Unitarian. Author: The Surgeon and The Child, 1959; Your Wonderful Baby, 1966. Contbr. to med. jours. Home: Sarasota FL Died May 5, 1968.

POTTS, WYLODINE GABBERT (MRS. THOMAS C. POTTS), oil co. exec., planter; b. Senatobia, Miss., Apr. 11, 1898; d. James Tate and Mildred (Merriwether) Gabbert; student Miss. State Coll. for Women, 1916-18; m. Thomas Coleman Potts, Dec. 22, 1920; children—Wylodine (Mrs. Walter Francis Dilatush), Iley (Mrs. Joseph Patterson George). Sec. Crenshaw Oil Co. (Miss.), 1926-40, v.p., dir. Operator 600 acre plantation Quitman and Tunica counties, Miss. Mem. Am. Shorthorn Assn. Methodist (trustee, pres. Women's Soc. Christian Service 1950). Home: Crenshaw MS

POUND, EZRA, poet; b. Hailey, Ida., Oct. 30, 1885; s. Homer Loomis and Isabel (Weston) P.; Ph.B., Hamilton Coll., 1905; M.A., U. Pa., 1906; m. Dorothy Shakespear, 1917; children—Homar Shakespear. Mary (de Rachewiltz). Instr., Wabash Coll., 1906; traveled in Spain, Italy, Provence; pub. 1st vol. poetry, Venice, 1908; lived in London, 1908-20; fgn. corr. Poetry Mag., 1912-19; founded (with Wyndham Lewis) mag. Blast, 1914; London editor Little Rev., 1917-19; lived in Paris, 1920-24; Paris corr. for Dial, 1922; lived in Rapallo, Italy, 1924-45; founded The Exile (pub. only 4 issues), 1927; broadcast over Italian radio to U.S., from 1941; arrested by Americans, 1945, interned nr. Pisa, Italy; brought to U.S. to be tried for treason, declared psychologically unfit to stand trial, 1946; committed to St. Elizabeth's Hosp., Washington, released, 1958; returned to live in Italy; considered a prin. founder and moving spirit of modern poetry in English; engaged in lifetime project of composing the Cantos (106 poetic syntheses of virtually whole of world cultural history). Recipient award for distinguished service to Am. letters Dial Mag., 1928; Bollingen award for poetry for Pisan Cantos, Library of Congress, 1949. Fellow Acad. Am. Poets. Author numberous works including: A Lume Spento, 1908; Personae, 1909; The Spirit of Romance, 1910; Canzoni, 1911; Ripostes, 1912; Gaudier-Brzeska, a memoir, 1916; revised edit., 1960; Pavannes and divagations, 1918; (musical score for opera) Le Testament, 1919-21; Hugh Selwyn Mauberly, 1920; The Cantos. 1925, 28, 30, 34, 37, 40, 48, 50, 55, 59, 65; How to Read, 1931: Homage to Sextux Propertius, 1934; Make it New, 1934; The ABC of Reading, 1934: Guide to Kulchur, 1938; Letters, 1907-41 (edited by D. D. Paige), 1950; Literary Essays, 1954; Brancusi, 1957; Impact: Essays on Ignorance and the Decline of American Civilization, 1960. Editor works including: (anthology) Des Imagistes, 1914; The Chinese Written Character as a Medium for Poetry (Ernest Fenollosa), 1935; (anthology, with Marcella Spann) Confucius to Cummings, 1964. Translator many works including: Sonnets and Ballate (Guido Cavalcanti), 1912; Certain Noble Plays of Japan, 1916; Confucius: The Unwobbling Pivot and the Great Digest, 1947; Women of Trachis (Sophocles), 1957; (with Noel Stock), Love Poems of Ancient Egypt, 1962; The Translations of Ezra Pound (edited by Hugs Kenner), 1963. Address: Merano Italy Died Nov. 1, 1972. buried Isola Sam Wichele, Venice Italy

POUND, G(RELLET) C., corp. exec.; b. Chicago, June 8, 1891; s. Ernest G. and Minnie (Campbell) P.; student pub. schs.; m. Dorothy Sonwell, May 7, 1922. Salesman, MacLaren's Imperial Cheese Co., Chicago, 1910-12; with Kraft Foods Co. since 1912, general sales manager, 1931-34; vice president, 1934-44, exec. v.p., 1944-51, pres., 1951-56, chmn. bd., 1956-58, also dir., mem. exec. com.; pres., dir. Nat. Dairy Products Corp.; dir. Grocery Mfrs. of Am., Inc. (dir. 1942-48, v.p. 1942-45). Clubs: Lake Shore (Chicago); Sunset Ridge Country (Winnetka). Home: Chicago, IL Died Sept. 1968.

POWDERMAKER, HORTENSE, educator, author; b. Phila., Dec. 24, 1900; d. Louis and Minnie (Jacoby) Powdermaker; B.A., Goucher Coll., 1920, Sc.D. (hon.), 1957; Ph.D., U. London (Eng.), 1928. Research asso. Inst. Human Relations, Yale, 1934-37; faculty Queens Coll., 1938-68, prof. anthropology, 1954-68, prof. emeritus, 1968-70; organized dept. anthropology and sociology, 1938, research associate anthropology University of California at Berkeley, 1968-71; vis. prof. or lectr. Columbia, U. Cal. at Los Angeles, U. Minn., ASTP program at Yale. Trustee Goucher Coll., 1958-61. Grantee Australian Nat. Research Council, 1929-30, NRC, 1930-31, Social Sci. Research Council, 1933-34, 68-70, Wenner-Gren Found. Anthrop. Research, 1947-48, 68-70, Guggenheim Found., 1953-54. Mem. N.Y. Acad. Scis. (chmn. anthropology sect., v.p. acad. 1944-46), Am. Ethnol. Soc. (pres. 1946-47), Am. Anthrop. Soc. (council 1938-70), Am. Sociol. Soc. (rep. to Am. Council Learned Socs. 1950-53). Author: Life in Lesu: The Study of a Melanesian Society in New Ireland, 1933; After Freedom: A Cultural Study in the Deep South, 1939; Probing our Prejudicies, 1944; Hollywood, the Dream Factory, 1950; Copper Town: Changing Africa, The Human Situation of the Rhodesian Copperbelt, 1962; Stranger and Friend, the Way of an Anthropologist, 1966; also papers in science jours. Home: Berkeley CA Died June 15, 1970.

POWELL, ADAM CLAYTON, JR., congressman, clergyman, author; b. New Haven, Conn., Nov. 29, 1908; s. Adam Clayton and Mattie Fletcher (Schafer) P.; A.B., Colgate U., 1930; M.A., Columbia U., 1932, D.D., Shaw U., 1935; LL.D., Va. Union U., 1947; m. Isabel Geraldine Washington, Mar. 8, 1933 (div. 1943); m. 2d, Hazel Scott, Aug. 1945 (div.); 1 son, Adam Clayton III; m. 3d, Yvette Diago; 1 son, Adam Diago. Minister, Abyssinian Baptist Ch., 1937-60; elected to City Council of New York, 1941; founder People's Voice, editor in chief, co-publisher, 1942; elected to Congress Nov. 1945; mem. 79th-87th Congresses from New York 16th District; member 88th-91st Congresses, N.Y. 18th Dist., chmn. com. edn. and labor, until 1967. Del. Parliamentary World Govt. Conf., London, 1951-52, ILO Conf. Geneva, Switzerland, 1961, 63, 64. Decorated Knight of Golden Cross, Ethiopia, 1954. Mem. World Assn. Parliamentarians on World Govt. (v.p.). Author: Is This a White Man's War? 1942; Stage Door Canteen, 1944; Marching Blacks, 1945, Adam Clayton Powell, 1960. Died Apr. 4, 1972.

POWELL, CAROLINE AMELIA, engraver on wood; b. Dublin, Ireland; pupil of W. J. Linton and Timothy Cole; studied drawing at the Cooper Union and the Nat. Acad. Design, New York; engraving under W. J. Linton and Timothy Cole. Engraved for the Century Magazine, 1880-95; only woman in America who practices wood engraving as an art in the style of the famous revival of about 1880. Exhibited at Berlin, Munich, Paris, etc.; medal, Chicago Expn., 1893; silver medal, Buffalo Expn., 1901. Mem. Soc. Am. Wood Engravers. Home: 1762 N St. N.W., Washington DC‡

POWELL, CECIL FRANK, physicist, educator; b. Tonbridge, Eng., Dec. 5, 1903; s. Frank and Elizabeth (Bisacre) P.; M.A., Ph.D., Cambridge U., 1928; Sc.D. (hon.), univs. Dublin, 1950, Bordeaux, 1952, Warsaw, 1959, Berlin, 1960, Padua, 1964, Moscow, 1966; m. Isobel T. Artner, 1932; children—Ann E., Jane Phyllis. Research asst. to Prof. A.M. Tyndall, Bristol, 1928; Melville Wills prof. physics U. Bristol 1948-64, Henry Overton Wills prof., 1964-69. Past chmn. sci. policy com. European Center Nuclear Research, Geneva; past chmn. cosmic ray commn. Internatl. Union of Pure and Applied Physics, mem. Sci. Research Council U.K., chmn. nuclear physics bd. Vernon Boys prizeman Phys. Soc. London, 1947; Hughes medal Royal Soc. 1949. Royal medal, 1961; Nobel prize physics, 1950; Lomonosov Gold medal Acad. Scis. USSR, 1968; Guthrie medal Inst. Physics and Phys. Soc., 1969. Fellow Royal Soc., Phys. Soc. London (hon.); fgn. mem. Royal Irish Acad. (hon.), Acad. Scis. USSR. Author: Nuclear Physics in Photographs (with G.P.S. Occhialini), 1947; Study of Elementary Particles by the Photographic Method (with P. Fowler Bristol England Died Aug. 9, 1969.

POWELL, DONALD ADAMS, ry. exec.; b. Fair Haven, Vt., Sept. 17, 1900; s. John Thomas and Stella (Adams) P.; student Dartmouth; LL.B., Boston U., 1923; m. Agnes Blair, Mar. 21, 1930 (dec. 1967); 1 son, Blair Adams; m. Alice Marvin Schofield, June 3, 1968. Admitted to N.Y. bar, 1925; with law firm Clark, Carr & Ellis, 1923-53; asst. to gen. counsel U.P. R.R. Co., 1946-53, treas., 1954-65. Mem. Lambda Chi Alpha. Clubs: Lake Placid (N.Y.); Rock Spring Country (West Orange, N.J.). Home: New York City NY Died Feb. 7, 1972; buried Gate of Heaven Cemetery, Hanover NJ

POWELL, EDWARD THOMSON, lawyer; b. at Delaware, O., Apr. 2, 1874; s. Thomas Edward and Eliza (Thomson) P.; A.B., Ohio Wesleyan U., 1894; LL.B., Ohio State U., 1896; unmarried. Mem. firm Powell & Powell since 1898; dir. Delaware Chair Co. Mem. Sigma Chi, Phi Beta Phi. Democrat. Methodist. Mason. Clubs: Columbus, Athletic, Scioto Country, Arlington Country. Home: 518 E. Broad St. Office: Spahr Bldg., Columbus OH‡

POWELL, G. THOMAS, banker; b. Glen Head, N.Y., Sept. 21, 1874; s. George S. and Hannah J. Powell; m. Elsie Mershon, Oct. 5, 1898; 1 son, George Alfred; m. 2d, Grace Thomas Austin, Feb. 27, 1909; children—Elizabeth Underhill (Mrs. A. Dudley Harrison), Grace Thomas. Pres. First Nat. Bank of Glen Head, N.Y., since 1927. A founder of Nassau County (N.Y.) Farm Bureau and dir. 23 yrs., also served as chmn.; a founder Long Island Research Exptl. Farm, Riverhead, N.Y.; pres. and mgr. Nassau County Co-operative Assn. for 6 yrs.; a founder N.Y. City Market Growers Assn. and treas. 8 yrs.; pres. Non-Partisan Taxpayers Assn., Glen Cove, N.Y., since 1933; trustee State Sch. Applied Agr., Farmingdale, N.Y., for 7 yrs.; mem. Mayor's Economic Commn. City of Glen Cove; dir. Nassau Taxpayers League. Mem. Soc. of Friends. Address: 93 Walnut Road, Glen Cove NY‡

POWELL, NATHAN, teacher; b. Mexia, Tex., Aug. 19, 1869; s. William Henry and Emily Isabel (Wood) P.; Trinity U., Tehuacana, Tex., until 1889; B.A., Vanderbilt, 1894; B.D., Yale, 1896; studied Gottingen and U. of Chicago; m. Minnie E. Keiser, of Union City, Tenn., July 7, 1896; children—Florence Lee, Isabel Frances, Julia Alice, Lois Elizabeth, Mary Ann. Teacher San Antonio (Tex.) Female Coll., 1902-03; teacher modern langs., Agrl. and Mech. Coll. of Texas, 1907-09; originated and organized movement that resulted in founding Southern Meth. U., Dallas, Tex., 1910-13; founder, 1915, and pres. Powell Univ. Training Sch., Dallas. Trustee Southwestern Univ., Georgetown, Tex. Mem. M.E. Ch., S. Mason (32 deg.). Clubs: Kiwanis, Dallas Athletic, Dallas Automobile, Glennhaven Country. Home: 6201 Hillcrest Av. Address: Powell University Training Sch., Dallas TX‡

POWELL, NOBLE CILLEY, bishop; b. Lowndesboro, Ala., Oct. 27, 1891; s. Benjamin Shelley and Mary Irving (Whitman) P.; ed. Ala. Poly. Inst., 1911-15, U. of Va., 1915-17, Va. Theol. Sem., 1917-20, D.D. (hon.), 1930; D.D., Univ. of the South, 1942; D.D. (honorary), Washington College, 1957; m. Mary Wilkins Rustin, Apr. 21, 1924; children—Philip Noble C., Thomas Hooker. Ordained to ministry of Episcopal Ch., 1920; rector St. Paul's Memorial Ch., U. of Va., 1920-31, Emmanuel Ch., Baltimore, Md., 1931-37; dean Washington Cathedral and Warden Coll. of the Preachers, 1937-41; bishop coadjutor Diocese of Maryland, 1941; bishop of Maryland, 1943-63. Mem. bd. trustees, Gen. Theol. Seminary, New York. Trustee Va. Theological Seminary Church Pension Fund, Ch. Life Ins. Corp. Mem. Seven Soc. of U. Va., Bachelors Cotillion (Balt.), Raven Soc., Phi Beta Kappa, Theta Chi. Clubs: Baltimore MD Died Nov. 28, 1968; buried St. Thomas' Churchyard, Garrison Forest MD

POWELL, PAUL, sec. state Ill.; b. Vienna, Ill.; ed. high sch., Vienna. Mayor of Vienna; mem. Ill. Gen. Assembly, 1934-64, speaker 3 sessions, minority leader 4 sessions; downstate dir. Democratic Central Com., 1945-53; mem. Dem. Com. Johnson County; sec. state Ill., 1965-70. Dir. Ill. Assn. Agrl. Fairs; sec. Massac County Fair; past dir. Vienna Twp. High Sch. Voted outstanding legislator of Ill. by the Press, 1951, 55. Democrat. Mason, Elk, Eagle. Home: Vienna IL Died Oct. 10, 1970.

POWELL, RICHARD STERLING, banker; b. Chicago, Ill., May 27, 1876; s. Adolphus H. and Bell M. (Matteson) P.; ed. pub. schs.; m. Marinette Lombard, May 1906. Began as messenger Bankers Nat. Bank, Chicago, 1894, teller, 1901; cashier, First Nat. Bank, Iron Mountain, Mich., 1901-19; pres. First Nat. Bank, Appleton, since 1919; pres. First Nat. Bank, Niagara,

Wis.; dir. Marine Nat. Exchange Bank, Milwaukee. Home: 508 N. Vine St. Office: First Nat. Bank, Appleton WI‡

POWELSON, WILFRID VAN NEST, lieutenant U.S.N.; b. Middletown, N.Y., Sept. 15, 1872; grad. U.S. Naval Acad., 1893; m. Margaret Olivia Miller, of Cincinnati, 1898. After being grad. at head of his class from Naval Acad., was sent by Govt. for spl. course in naval architecture at U. of Glasgow, where he grad. with honor; attached to flagship New York," on staff of admiral, 2 yrs.; while attached to Fern" at Key West was ordered to make examinations in reference to the destruction of the Maine" at Havana; his testimony before the court of inquiry, proving the Maine" was blown up by a mine, was widely and favorably commented on by scientific jours.; was in command of the gun on St. Paul" which sunk the Terror" nr. Porto Rico; 2 days before the St. Paul" went out of commission he fell 72 feet, with elevator, to hold of vessel, receiving serious injuries; obtained 6 months' leave of absence; promoted from ensign to jr. lt., and, Mar. 6, 1901, to lt.; retired, July 3, 1902. Elec. expert, N.Am. Co., 1902-3; with Union Electric Light & Power Co., St. Louis, 1903, becoming gen. mgr., 1904, pres., treas. and gen. mgr., 1906-08; mem. firm Cooper & Powelson, engrs., and mgrs. pub. utilities corpns., New York, 1908-—. Clubs: New York Yacht, University, Bankers. Address: 60 Wall St., New York NY‡

POWER, CHARLES GAVAN, Canadian government official; born Sillery, P.Q., Canada, January 18, 1888; son William and Susan (Rockett) Power; B.A., Loyola Coll., Montreal, 1907; LL.L., Laval U., Quebec, 1910; m. Rosemary Pendleton, Sept. 18, 1912; children—William Pendleton, Francis Gavan, Rosemary (wife of Lt. Lewis Cannon). Enlisted in Canadian Army, Jan. 1915; served overseas, twice wounded, invalided from service, 1918; held rank of capt. and acting major. Elected to House of Commons, 1917, re-elected 1921, 25, 26, 30, 35 and 40; sworn of the Privy Council and apptd. minister of pensions and nat. health, Oct. 23, 1935; apptd. postmaster gen., Sept. 19, 1939; served several times as acting minister of nat. defense; minister of Dept. of Nat. Defense for Air, 1940-45; asso. minister of nat. defense, 1940-45. Liberal. Catholic. Home: Ottawa ON Canada Died May 1968.*

POWER, JAMES EDWARD, postmaster; b. San Francisco, Calif., Apr. 29, 1876; s. James Edward and Hanorah (Ryan) P.; ed. high sch.; studied law 1 yr.; m. Winifred Foster, of San Francisco, Nov. 26, 1900. Began yr.; m. Winifred Foster, of San Francisco, Nov. 26, 1900. Began as distributor automobile tires, 1915; pres. Power Rubber Co. since 1916. Mem. Bd. of Edn., San Francisco, 1911-13 inclusive; mem. Bd. of Supervisors, 1914-21; apptd. postmaster of San Francisco, 1922. Mem. Calif. Acad. Science. Republican. K.C. Clubs: Olympic, Union League, Commonwealth. Established school children's savings bank system in San Francisco. Home: 1378 Portola Drive. Office: 7th and Mission Sts., San Francisco CA‡

POWER, JOHN JOSEPH, JR., corp. exec.; b. Worcester, Mass., Apr. 18, 1911; s. John Joseph and Anna (Kehoe) P.; B.A., Georgetown U., 1933; B.S., Worcester Poly Inst., 1935; m. Agnes Coakley, Nov. 28, 1935; children—John Joseph III, Kathleen (Mrs. F. William Sullivan), Marie, Shelia, David, Suzanne, Eileen. With Automatic Sprinkler Corp. of Am., 1936-68, successively mgr. Pitts. office, 1939-43, asst. to pres., Youngstown, O., 1943, v.p., 1943-50, exec. v.p., 1950-65, pres., 1965-68; pres. Automatic Sprinkler of Can. Ltd., 1950-63. Dir. Ann. Giving, Georgetown U., 1961-62, devel. fund Trinity Coll. Library, Washington, 1958-60. Mem. Nat. Automatic Sprinkler Fire Control Assn. (pres. 1955-56, chmn. pension com. 1963-68), Sigma Alpha Epsilon. Club: Chesterton. Home: Youngstown OH Died Aug. 27, 1968.

POWERS, EUGENE PAUL, coll. pres.; b. Pitts., May 5, 1913; s. Frank H. and Mary (Crawford) P.; B.S., U. Pitts., 1938, M.Ed., 1942; Ed.D., Temple U., 1954; m. Margaret J. Paul, Aug. 5, 1939; 1 son, Eugene P. Dean evening div. Villanova (Pa.) U., 1949-55; head, dept. edn. and psychology East Stroudsburg (Pa.) State Coll., 1959-66; pres. Kansas City (Mo.) Coll. Osteopathy and Surgery, 1966-68. Guest lectr. St. Joseph's Coll. (Pa.), LaSalle Coll. (Pa.), Scranton U. (Pa.), Johns Hopkins. Vice pres. Delaware County (Pa.) Bd. Ednl. Television, 1955; pres. Pa. Audio-Visual Assn. Tchr. Edn., 1956-58; mem. ednl. council St. Joseph's Hosp., Reading, Pa., 1954-59; mem. Met. Kansas City Coordinating Com. for Regional Med. Programs, 1966-68. Served to capt. USNR, 1942-45, 47-48. Mem. Kappa Phi Kappa, Kappa Sigma, Phi Delta Kappa, Alpha Sigma Lambda. Rotarian, K.C. Club: Kansas City. Contbr. articles to ednl. and naval jours. Home: Kansas City MO Died July 19, 1968.

POWERS, GROVER FRANCIS, pediatrician; b. Colfax, Ind., Aug. 12, 1887; s. Francis William and Elizabeth Catherine (Shobe) P.; B.S., Purdue U., 1908, Sc.D., 1935; M.D., Johns Hopkins U., 1913; M.A., Yale U., 1927; honorary Sc.D., Indiana University, 1949; married Beatrice Farnsworth, Aug. 21, 1916; 1 son, Ross Farnsworth. Laboratory assistant in biology, Purdue University, 1908-09; interne and assistant resident in pediatric Johns Hopkins Hospital, Baltimore, 1913-16, physician in charge pediatrics, out-patient department, 1916-21; instructor and asso. in clin. pediatrics, Johns Hopkins U., 1916-21; med. dir. Babies Milk Fund Assn., Baltimore, 1916-21; asst. later asso. prof. pediatrics, Yale U., 1921-27, prof. pediatrics, 1927-52, prof. emeritus, 1952-68; cons. pediatrician Grace-New Haven Community Hosp., pediatrician in chief Henry Ford Hosp., Detroit, 1927; New Haven Hosp. from 1927; former consultant Mental Hygiene Division, USPHS; hon. chmn. sci. research adv. bd. Nat. Assn. of Retarded Children. Trustee of the Southbury Training School; mem. of editorial board. Pediatrics. Recipient Borden Award, Am. Acad. Pediatrics, 1947, John Howland award Am. Pediatric Soc., 1953; Jos. P. Kennedy Jr. award; 2d International award. Certified by Am. Bd. Pediatrics. Fellow A.M.A., Am. Acad. Pediatrics; mem. Am. Pediatric Soc. (p. pres.), Soc. for Pediatric Rsrch., Am. Soc. for Clin. Investigation, Inter-urban Clin. Club, National Association for Retarded Children (chmn. sci. research adv. bd.), Brit. Pediatric Soc. (corr.), Sigma Xi, Alpha Omega Alpha. Episcopalian. Club. Faculty (new Haven). Home: New Haven CT Died Apr. 18, 1968.

POWERS, JOSEPH HARRELL, clergyman; b. Houston, Jan. 9, 1910; s. Charles Joseph and Willie Armelia (Rush) P.; student pub. schs., pvt. tutors; m. Helen Ann Crabb, Dec. 17, 1940; children—Anita Joyce, Joseph Harrell, James Douglas, John Robert, Jordan Glenn, Jathan Paul (dec.), Joel Edward Thurman Thomas Jefferson Eugene. Mining trapper Gauley River Mining Co., Gauley Bridge, W.Va., 1925-27; office boy Dockman Candy Co., Balt., 1927-28, asst. candy maker 1928; floorman Charlotte Cotton Mills (N.C.), 1928-29; shrimper, crabber, oysterman Sea Food Industries Biloxie, Miss., 1930-33; salesman, Colo., 1933; with circulation dept. Mil. Sentinel, 1933-34; ordained to ministry Nat. Council of Full Gospel Assemblies, 1934; pastor Old Ashbury Ch., Mil., 1934-38; evangelistic field and youth work, 1938-42; gen. camp dir. Treasure Island Children's Camp, N. Woods, Wis., 1938; camp dir. Camp Robinhood, No. Minn., 1940; nat. dir. Nat. Youth Council Milw., 1938-40; def. work, other endeavors, 1942-46; Salvation Army campaigner, 1946-50; evanglist work, 1950-51; founder Ch. of Faith, Kansas City, Kan., 1952, since gen. pastor; founder Ch. Maid Industries, St. Louis, Okla., 1955, since pres.; dir. Harvest Time Broadcast, Tecumseh, Okla., 1956-67. Mem. ministerial body Ch. of God of Firstborn, Newton, Kan.; active reform sch. work, Okla., 1957-61; exec. officer, World-wide Missionary Endeavor. Mem. Nat. Council Full Gospel Assemblies, Am. Ch. Assn. (pres. 1939-67). Fundamental Ministerial and Layman's Assn., Am. Mgmt. Assn. (mem. pres's council). Author: This is the Way. Editor, Harvester Magazine, Kansas City, 1954-67. Home: Kansas City KS Died Apr. 10, 1967; interred Highland Park Cemetery Kansas City KS

POWERS, RALPH AVERILL, container mfr.; b. Houlton, Me., Sept. 24, 1893; s. Llewellyn and Martha (Averill) P.; student Volkmann Sch., Boston, also Bowdoin Coll., Harvard; m. Bernice Taylor, Nov. 3, 1915; children—Nancy P. (Mrs. C. M. LaCour), Joan (Mrs. N. E. Humphreville), Susan; m. 2d, Katharine Parker Francis, Aug. 31, 1934; 1 s., Ralph Averill. Pres., dir. Robertson Paper Box Co., Inc. and predecessor Robertson Paper Co., Montville, Conn., 1921; exec. v.p., dir. Am. Agrl. Chemical Co., 1929-33; dir. Hartford Electric Light Company; corporator Savs. Bank of New London; mem. Conn. adv. bd. Liberty Mut. Ins. Co. Dir. paperboard div. WPB, Washington, 1944-45; mem. Conn. Development Commn., 1946-53; v.p., dir. New Eng. Council, 1946-52. Vice pres., trustee Conn. Hosp. Assn.; pres., trustee Lawrence and Meml. Assn. Hosps., 1947-56; trustee Pequot Chapel, New London; v.p., director American Found. Religion and Psychiatry, N.Y.C. Served as ensign (aviator) USN, World War I. Mem. N.A.M. (dir. 1952-55), Nat. Paperboard Assn. (v.p., dir. 1951-55), Folding Paper Box Assn. Am. (pres. 1947-49, dir.), Marine Hist. Assn. Inc., Mystic (trustee), New London (dir.), Conn. (dir.) chambers commerce, U.S. (pres. 1929-32), Mass. (pres. 1927), Conn., Western Mass. squash racquet assns., Conn. Sr.'s Golf Assn., Newcomen Soc. Eng., Delta Kappa Epsilon. Clubs: Harvard, Racquet and Tennis, Canadian (N.Y.C.); Harvard Tennis and Racquet, Madison Square Garden (Boston); The Country (Brookline, Mass.); New Haven Lawn; Dauntless (Essex, Conn.); New London Country, Thames (New London, Conn.). Canadian Squash Racquets champion, 1925, U.S. Vets Squash Racquets champion, 1936. Home: New London CT Died Aug. 1, 1971; buried Gardner Cemetery, New London CT

POWERS, ROBERT DAVIS, JR., naval officer; b. Gloucester County, Va., Mar. 21, 1908; s. Robert Davis and Hattye Ruth (Lewis) P.; LL.B., Washington and Lee U., 1929, LL.D., 1962; m. Mary Kathryn Carney, Oct. 15, 1937; children—Robert Carney, David Lewis, Mary Kathryn. Admitted to Va. bar, 1929; practice in Norfolk and Portsmouth, 1929-41; asst. city atty., Portsmouth, 1941; commd. lt. (j.g.) USNR, 1937, advanced through grades to rear adm., USN, 1961; counsel Judge Advocate Navy Ct. Inquiry Japanese Attack on Pearl Harbor, 1944; fleet legal officer Atlantic Fleet, 1947-50; asst. judge adv. gen. internat. and adminstrv. law U.S. Navy, 1956-58; dir. W. Coast Office Judge Advocate Gen., 1958-60; dep. judge advocate gen. U.S. Navy, 1960-64; practice law, Portsmouth, Va., 1964-71; asso. judge Portsmouth Juvenile and Domestic Relations Ct., 1971; lectr. internat. law. Mem. Am., Fed., Va. bar assns., Judge Advocates Assn., Am. Soc. Internat. Law, Pi Kappa Phi, Omicron Delta Kappa, Phi Alpha Delta. Methodist. Home: Portsmouth VA Died Dec. 1971.

POWERS, SAMUEL RALPH, univ. prof.; b. Petersburg, Ill., May 16, 1887; s. John William and Nancy Temperance (Erwin) P.; grad. Ill. Normal U., 1910; B.A., Illinois U., 1912; M.A., Minn. U., 1919, Ph.D., 1923; m. Eda May Olds, Oct. 10, 1910 (dec. Feb. 1972); children—Philip Nathan, Merrill E., Samuel Ralph, Karol R. (dec.). Teacher rural schs. Menard County, Ill., 1905-08; Garfield High, Terre Haute, Ind., 1912-16; Univ. High Sch., U. of Minn., 1916-20; prof. edn., U. of Ark., 1920-21; instr. edn., U. of Minn., 1921-23; asso. prof. natural sciences, Teachers College, Columbia U., 1923, prof., 1927-52, emeritus, 1952-70, head dept. teaching of natural scis., 1928-52; edn. cons. Bur. of Medicine, U.S.N., 1952-53; visiting prof. Abbassia Men's Tchr. College, 1954-55, St. Paul's Coll., Lawrenceville, Va., 1959-62; specialist sci. adult edn. sect. Office of Edn., 1960. U.S. Educational Foundation in Egypt., 1954-55; adminstr. ofcr. Tchrs. Coll. Bur. Ednl. Rsrch. in Science (supported by Gen. Education Board), 1935-43. Expert Industrial Personnel Division, Army Service Forces, War Dept., 1942-44. Presented with Outstanding Achievement Award, U. of Minn., 1951; Fulbright Award, visiting prof., Cairo, Egypt 1954-55. Mem. Assn. for Edn. Sci. Teachers (hon. member), National Sci. Tchrs. Assn. (commn. edn. basic scis., 1957-58), Nat. Soc. Study Edn. (chmn. com. sci. teaching, 1932), Am. Ednl. Research Assn. (chmn. com. research teaching sci. and math., 1941-42, 1947-48), Nat. Assn. Research in Science Teaching (pres. 1938), Nat. Council Sci. Teachers (chmn. com. teacher edn., 1938-42), N.E.A., A.A.A.S. (fellow), Phi Delta Kappa, Tau Kappa Epsilon. Author of research papers in the teaching of natural sciences, and numerous articles in educational jours. Co-author of textbooks for high schs. and colleges. Editor: Science in Modern Living Series, 1935-42; mem. editorial bd. World Book Ency., 1936-52; editor: Science Education mag., 1944-45. Home: Haworth NJ Died Aug. 26, 1970; buried Rosehill Cemetery, Petersburg IL

POWERS, THOMAS JEFFERSON, author; b. at Phila., Sept. 2, 1875; s. Thomas Joseph and Jennie (Ross) P.; cadet U.S. Mil. Acad., July 5-Dec. 31, 1892; m. Jane Masten Ewell, of San Francisco, Dec. 27, 1910. Actor, with Girard Ave. Stock Co., Forepaugh Stock Co., Phila., and Murry Hill Stock Co., New York, and in vaudeville, 1893-8. Commd. 2d lt. 25th U.S. Inf. July 9, 1898; 1st lt. 20th Inf., Sept. 8, 1899; capt. 13th Inf., July 28, 1905. Author: The Garden of the Sun, 1911. Address: War Dept., Washington‡

PRAHL, AUGUSTUS JOHN, educator; b. Lingenau, Germany, Oct. 18 1901; s. Anton and Maria Barbara (Saalmann) P.; student U. Koenigsberg, Germany, 1923-25; M.A., Washington U., St. Louis, 1928; Ph.D., John Hopkins, 1933; m. Hermine Eleanor Rickl, Mar. 13, 1939. Came to U.S., 1925, naturalized, 1932. Instr. German, Ind. U., 1928-30, Johns Hopkins, 1933-36; asst. prof. U. Md., 1936-39, asso. prof., 1939-45, prof. fgn. langs. since 1945, resident dean grad. year abroad, Zurich, Switzerland, 1949-50, asso. dir. overseas program, 1952-53, dir., 1953-54, dir. Far East Program, 1956-57, asso. dean grad. sch., 1957-66. In charge of naval document section U.S.N., Bremen, Germany, 1947-48; mem. bd. ednl. advisors U.S. Army in Europe, 1952. Mem. Modern Lang. Assn. Am., American Association of University Professors, Goethe Soc. Md. and D.C., Delta Sigma Phi, Phi Kappa Phi. Author: Gerstaecker und die Probleme seiner Zeit, 1938. The Forty-Eighters (with A.E. Zucker) 1950. Home: College Park MD Died Oct. 29, 1970; buried Cedar Hill Cemetery, Suitland MD

PRATT, ARTHUR PEABODY, clergyman; b. Dorchester, Mass., June 27, 1872; s. Charles O. and Sarah S. (Peabody) P.; A.B., Boston U., 1896, S.T.B., 1901, A.M., 1902, Ph.D., 1909; post-grad. work, Harvard U. and Andover Theol. Sem.; D.D., Middlebury Coll., 1915; married Helen Maud Armstrong, June 8, 1904; 1 son, Robert Armstrong. Acting pastor, Berlin, Mass., 1898-1903; ordained Conglist ministry, 1901; pastor 1st (united 1st and 3d) Ch., Chelsea, 1903-06, 1st Church, Bellows Falls, Vermont, 1906-16, Greenfield, Mass., 1916-1941; preacher, Community Ch., Mt. Dora, Fla., 1947-48. Member International Congl. Council, Bournemouth, Eng., 1930. Mem. Mass. Soc. S.A.R., Phi Beta Kappa, Beta Theta Pi. Mason (32 deg.). Lecturer, and author of essays on English poets and mysticism; also author of Good Cheer," a devotional book for use in hospitals. Address: Mount Dora, Fla.; (summer) Friendship ME‡

PRATT, AUGUSTE G., chmn. emeritus Babcock & Wilcox Co.; b. Bklyn., Mar. 31, 1881; s. Nat. W. and Carrie V (Deudney) P.; M.E., Stevens Institute

Technology, Hoboken, N.J., 1903, D.E. (hon.), 1953; m. Ruth Nesmith, Jan. 5, 1905 (dec. Dec. 1962); children—Mrs. E. P. Meier, Mrs. D. N. Fisher, Mrs. J. P. Naramore, Mrs. J. W. Todd. With Babcock & Wilcox Co., mfrs. water tube steam boilers, etc., 1903-—, pres. 1924-48, chmn. bd., 1948-65, chmn. emeritus. Mem. Nat. Indsl. Conf. Bd. Trustee Stevens Inst. Tech. Mem. Am. Soc. M.E., Chi Psi. Clubs: University (N.Y.) Knickerbocker Country (Englewood, N.J.). Home: Englewood NJ Died Jan. 22, 1970.

PRATT, CHARLES DUDLEY, lawyer; b. Honolulu, Mar. 24, 1900; s. John Scott Boyd and Sarah Catharine (Dickson) P.; A.B., Yale, 1922, LL.B., 1924; m. Dora Marion Broadbent, Mar. 24, 1925; children—Charles Dudley, Joan Catharine, Barbara Marie, David Walton. Admitted to Hawaii bar, 1924, 9th Circuit Ct. Appeals, 1936, U.S. Supreme Ct., 1945; practice of law, Honolulu, 1924-70; mem. firm Pratt, Tavares & Cassidy, 1947-60, Pratt, Moore, Bortz & Vitousek, 1960-67, Pratt, Moore, Bortz & Case, 1967-70; lectr. business law U. Hawaii extension; mem. Supreme Ct. Legal Ethics Com., 1942-64. Pres. Palama Settlement, 1941-46; 1st pres. Hawaii Estate Planning Council, 1955-56. Trustee Punahou Sch., 1933, sec., 1952-56, vice chairman, 1956-63, chairman, 1963-70; trustee of the Honolulu Art Acad., 1957-61, 63-70. Fellow American College of Probate Counsel; member of Am. Bar Assn., Bar Assn. Hawaii (mem. bar. exam. com. 1943-46, vice president 1966, president 1967), Phi Delta Phi. Rotarian (president 1957-58, dist. gov. 1960-61). Home: Honolulu HI Died Apr. 17, 1970; buried Oahu Cemetery, Honolulu HI

PRATT, CHARLES STEBBINGS, lawyer; b. Oak Park, Ill., Sept. 27, 1901; s. Charles Alpheus and Julia (Stebbings) P.; A.B., U. Mich., 1923; J.D., U. Chicago, 1927; m. Grace Goodman, Feb. 20, 1932; 1 dau., Carolyn Starbuck. Admitted to Ill. bar, 1927; counsel Lord, Bissell & Brook; dir. Geo. W. Brady & Co., Mangood Corp. (formerly Goodman Mfg. Corp.); dir. Arens Control, Inc. Mem. Am., Ill., Chgo bar assns., Phi Gamma Delta, Phi Delta Phi. Rep. Conglist. Clubs: Indian Hill (Winnetka); Chicago Law, Union League. Home: Winnetka IL Died Jan. 26, 1970.

PRATT, FREDERICK SANFORD, b. Newton Mass., Aug. 27, 1872; s. Lucius G. and Ellen E. (Plimpton) P.; A.B., Harvard, 1894, B.S., 1895; m. Ella Winifred Nickerson, June 10, 1897; children—Frederick T., Henry N., Laurence O., Albert. Mem. firm Stone & Webster, Inc., 1895-1929, v.p. 1917-29. Republican. Clubs: Algonquin, Harvard (Boston). Home: Duxbury MA Died May 30, 1968.

PRATT, GEORGE COLLINS, lawyer; b. Flandreau, S.D., Nov. 20, 1882; s. Collins and Sarah (Daley) P.; student U. of S.D., 1900-03; LL.B., Chicago Kent Coll. Law, 1905; married Alice Chambers, 1916 (died 1945); m. 2d, Marcella Morin, 1946. Admitted to Ill. bar, 1905, N.Y. bar, 1909, Calif. bar, 1931; began practice at Chicago; sec. Western Electric Co., 1908-25, gen. atty., 1919-27, v.p. and gen. counsel, 1927-30; dir. and gen. counsel Graybar Electric Co., 1925-28, Elec. Research Products, Inc., 1926-30, (v.p., 1930-39), Los Angeles counsel, Western Electric Co. Mem. Squadron A Cav., N.G.N.Y., 1913-16, serving on Mexican Border, 1916; served as capt. Signal Corps, U.S. Army, 1917-19, with 319th Field Signal Batt., A.E.F., later radio officer 1st Army. Mem. Am. and Los Angeles bar assns., Assn. Bar City New York, State Bar of Calif., S.R. Republican. Clubs: Jonathan, Shadow Palm Desert CA Died Mar. 23, 1968.

PRATT, JAMES ALFRED, mechanical engr.; b. Chelsea, Mass., Apr. 6, 1873; s. James Woodman and Clara (Noble) P.; ed. pub. schs., Providence, R.I.; studied mech. engring. as cadet engr. under G. W. Bartlett, in shops, Providence; pedagogy, New York U., 1908; m. Edith I. Harris, of Providence, Aug. 4, 1902. Instr. Sockanosset Sch. and asst. to consulting engr., 1901-6; instr. Pratt Inst., Brooklyn, and acting head, machine dept., 1907-8; instr., now dir. Williamson Free Sch. Mech. Trades. Methodist. Mem. Soc. Promotion Engring. Edn., Am. Soc. Mech. Engrs., etc. Author: Materials and Construction, 1912. Address: Williamson School P.O., PA‡

PRATT, JOHN LOWELL, book publisher; b. Montclair, N.J., Feb. 22, 1906; s. John Barnes and Mabel Clara (Dodge) P.; A.B., Dartmouth Coll., 1929; m. Katharine Warren Jennison, Aug. 15, 1931; children—John Clark, Nancy Jennison, Anthony Barnes; m. 2d, Elizabeth Richmond Parker, Nov. 27, 1952. Salesman advancing to pres., A. S. Barnes & Co., publishers, N.Y.C., 1929-58; pres. Am. Sports Pub. Co., Inc., 1958-60; v.p. Thomas Nelson and Sons, 1960-62; pres. J. Lowell Pratt & Co., Inc., 1962-68, also American Sports Publishing Company, Inc.; director of Summerville Mfg. Co., Ga.; v.p., dir. Arlington Cemetery Co., N.J. Lt. comdr., USNR. Republican. Mem. Christian Ch. Clubs: Coffee House (N.Y.); Dutch Treat. Editor: Sport Sport, Sport, More Sport, Sport, Sport, Pro Pro Pro. Author: (with Jim Benagh) The Official Encyclopedia of Sports, 1964. Home: New York City Died Dec. 25, 1968.

PRATT, LUCY, author; b. Deerfield, Mass., July 29, 1874; d. James Clay and Sarah Anne (Smith) P.; ed. acad. and pvt. schs. Instr. in Hampton Inst., Va., 1897-1904. Author: Ezekiel Stories—Ezekiel, 1909; Ezekiel Expands, 1914; Felix Tells It, 1915. Contbr. to mags. Home: Deerfield MA‡

PREGEANT, VICTOR EUGENE, III, banker, lawyer; b. Thibodaux, La., June 22, 1922; s. Victor Eugene, Jr. and Odessa (Riche) P.; B.A., U. Richmond, 1943, J.D., 1948; grad. Rutgers U. Grad. Sch. Banking, 1956; m. Lucile Edwards Guthrie, June 1, 1946; 1 dau., Michele Rene. Admitted to Va. bar, 1948; asst. city atty., Richmond, 1948-50; with Fed. Res. Bank, Richmond, 1950, asst. v.p., sec. to bd., 1961-72; instr. comml. law U. Richmond, 1949-50; counsel Monumental Floral Gardens Civic Assn., 1952-72. Bd. dirs. William Byrd br. Assn. Preservation Va. Antiquities, 1952-72, pres., 1957-58. Served to 1st lt. USAAF, 1943-45. Mem. Am., Va. bar assns., Am. Judicature Soc., Bar Assn. City Richmond, Internat. Platform Assn., Smithsonian Instn., Va. Mus. Fine Arts, McNeill Hon. Scholastic Law Soc., Sigma Phi Epsilon, Delta Theta Phi. Presbyn. Club: Westwood Racquet (past bd. Richmond VA Died Dec. 22, 1972.

PRENTICE, JAMES STUART, economist, educator; b. Toronto, Ont., Can., July 1, 1889; s. Alexander and Helen (Lunan) P.; B.A., Queen's U., 1914, M.A., 1927; Ph.D., U. Chgo., 1931; m. Margaret Gibson MacDonald, Dec. 12, 1921; children—W. Neil, Helen A., Margaret J., Robert Alexander. Came to U.S., 1928, naturalized, 1942. Prof. econs. Hislop Coll., Nagpur, India, 1920-26, also lectr. U. Nagpur; economist Dept. of Labor, Ottawa, Can., 1927-28; prof. econs. Defiance (O.) Coll., 1928-30; asst. prof. Middlebury (Vt.) Coll., 1931-37, asso. prof., 1937-49, Hepburn Chair prof. econs., 1949-56, chmn. dept. econs., 1950-56, chmn. social scis. div., 1952-56; vis. prof. Dickinson Coll., Carlisle, Pa., 1956-72. Mem. Council for Social Action Congl. Chs. in U.S., 1938-44. Served with Canadian Army, France, 1914-19. Mem. Am. Econs. Assn., Am. Econ. History Assn., Econ. Carlisle PA Died July 26, 1972.

PRESBY, CHARLOTTE SULLEY, reader, teacher; b. Troy, N.Y.; d. E. Pennistone and Jennie Elizabeth Sulley; grad. New York Sch. of Expression, 1895; studied in London and Paris; m. Edwin O. Presby, of N.Y. City, 1896. Began as asst., 1895, later co-prin., pres. since 1907, New York Sch. of Expression; specialist in voice training for speech and the curing of defective speech. Episcopalian. Studio: 332 W. 56th St., New York NY‡

PRESCOTT, ANSON WARD, b. Clearwater, Minn., Mar. 5, 1873; s. Harrison Whittier and Sarah L. (Tenney) P.; Willamette U., Salem, Ore., 1890-93; LL.B., Willamette Coll. of Law, 1896; m. Maud M. West, of Clatsop, Ore., Nov. 14, 1896. Law practice, 1896-99; news and editorial writer, Portland Oregonian, 1900-09; clk. U.S. Senate committees, 1909-13; sec. Joint Com. Federal Aid to Good Roads, 1913-14; sec. Nat. Progressive Rep. League, 1910-12; sec. Rep. Publicity Assn. since 1915. Mason (32 deg., Shriner). Office: Continental Trust Bldg., Washington DC‡

PRESCOTT, ARTHUR TAYLOR, univ. prof., dean; b. Mansfield, La., June 11, 1863; s. Ben and Kate Eggleston (Taylor) P.; B.S., La. State U., 1884, M.A., 1885; also studied U. of La. (now Tulane U.), U. of Va. and U. of Chicago; m. Katherine Eleanor Dougherty, Jan. 4, 1888. Prin. high sch., Marshall, Tex., 1886-87, Baton Rouge, 1893-94; organizer and 1st pres. La. Poly. Inst., 1894-99; became head dept. of govt. (polit. science), La. State U., 1899, also 1st dean of men, La. State U., and later dean Coll. Arts and Sciences, now emeritus. Mem. commn. created by legislative act, 1906, to revise taxing system of La.; mem. building com. in charge of construction of $5,000,000 plant for La. State U., and chmn. of its exec. com., 1922-27. Mem. Am. Polit. Science Assn., Nat. Municipal League. Formerly editor University Quarterly. Address: 741 North St., Baton Rogue LA*‡

PRESCOTT, DANIEL ALFRED, prof. edn.; b. Manassas, Va., Mar. 18, 1898; s. Daniel Howard and Eva Mary (Foote) P.; B.S., Tufts Coll., 1920; Ed.M. and Ed.D., Harvard, 1923; m. Eleanor Richardson, June 25, 1920 (divorced); m. 2d, Ruth Sharrett, Nov. 26, 1934 (div. 1949); m. 3d Annalise Boehmer Wagner, January 3, 1950. Professor science La Grange College, 1920-21; instructor Graduate School of Education (Harvard), 1923-24, faculty instructor, 1924-27; research in Europe for Harvard U., 1926-27; lecturer Institut J. J. Rousseau, Geneva, Switzerland, 1927-28; prof. edn., Rutgers U., 1928-31 and 1932-39; prof. edn., U. of Chicago, 1939-47; became prof. education, dir. Inst. for Child Study, U. of Md., 1947, prof. and dir. emeritus Inst. Child Study, ret., 1968. Fulbright lectr., Australia, 1962-63, Chulalongkorn U., Bangkok, Thailand, 1963; cons. tchr. edn. U.S. Dept. of State, Malaysia, 1963; lecturer on teacher edn., India, Nepal, Thailand, 1960-61; also lecturer at the World Congress on Early Childhood Edn., Athens, Greece, 1956; staff Internat. Workshop on Ednl. Psychology, Frankfurt, Germany, 1952; research investigator Gen. Edn. Bd., New York, 1931-32; research asso. Inst. Child Welfare, lecturer Sch. Edn., U. of Calif., during leave of absence from Rutgers, 1937-38. Mem. Internat. Congress on Peace through Edn., Prague, 1927, Internat. Congress on Bilingualism, Luxembourg, 1928. Mem. Am. Council on Edn.; chmn. com. on emotion and the educative process, 1934-38; 1st vice-chmn., 1938; coordinator of div. on child development and teacher personnel, commn. on teacher edn., 1938-44. Expert cons. on teacher edn., mil. govt. in Germany, Mar.-June 1948; staff, UNESCO Seminar on Childhood Edn., Podebrady, Czechoslovakia, July-Sept., 1948. Served in Am. Field Service with French Army, World War; S.A.T.C., 1918. Awarded medal Am. Field Service (Fr.); Dupont prize, Tufts Coll., 1920; Phi Delta Kappa award, Harvard, 1922; A. Bruce Greig award Drexel Inst. Tech., 1968. Mem. N.E.A., Am. Assn. Univ. Professors, Am. Psychol. Assn., Soc. for Research in Child Development, A.A.A.S., Md. Soc. Mental Hygiene (v.p. 1953), Phi Beta Kappa, Delta Tau Delta, Phi Delta Kappa. Presbyn. Club: Manor Country (Norbeck, Md.). Author: The Determination of Anatomical Age in School Children, 1923; Le Vocabulaire des Enfants et Les Livres de Lecture, 1928; Education and International Relations, 1930; The Training of Teachers, 1933; Emotion and the Educative Process, 1938; Helping Teachers Understand Children, 1945; The Child in the Educative Process, 1957; Factors That Influence Learning, published 1958; co-author The Emergent Middle School, 1969. Contributor to jours. Home: Silver Springs MD Died May 7, 1970; buried Waldfriedhof Berlin-Dahlem Germany.

PRESCOTT, EDWARD PURCELL, investment banker; b. Cleve., Apr. 1, 1904; s. William Howard and Margaret (Purcell) P.; grad. Taft Sch., Watertown, Conn., 1921, Williams Coll., 1925; m. Carolyn Brayton, Sept. 11, 1926; children—Charleen, Edward P., Joanne (Mrs. Lovett P. Baker); m. 2d, Beverly McClelland, Mar. 7, 1947; children—Susan M., Thomas M. (dec.), Pamela H. With Otis & Co., Cleve., 1925-31, Lamson Bros. & Co., Chgo., 1932-34; sr. partner Prescott, Merrill, Turben and Company, mem. N.Y. Stock Exchange, 1934-70, limited partner, 1970-73; chmn. Curtis Noll Corp.; dir. Specialty Converters, Inc. Served to col. AUS, 1942-45; chief requirements and distbn. div. Transp. Corps. Decorated Legion of Merit; Order Brit. Empire. Home: Willoughby OH Died Jan. 30, 1973.

PRESCOTT, STEDMAN, judge; born Norbeck, Maryland, August 30, 1896; s. Alexander F. and Edith Stanley (Kellogg) P.; LL.B., Georgetown U., 1919; m. E. Callender Minnick, July 14, 1917; children—Calia P. Belt, Stedman, Mary P. Rosenberger, Anne P. Brandau. Admitted to Md. bar, 1924; practice of law, Rockville, 1924-38; state's attorney Montgomery County, 1930; judge 6th Jud. Circuit of Md., Rockville, 1938-55, chief judge, 1955-56, asso. judge Court Appeals, Md., judge, 1956-66, chief judge, 1964-66. Dir. Bank of Bethesda. Mem. city council, Rockville, 1924-30; state senator, 1934. Served as 1st lt. U.S. Army, World War I. Fellow Am. Bar Assn. (del.); mem. Md. Bar Assn. (pres. 1954), Delta Theta Phi. Clubs: Lions, Rotary (Rockville). Home: Rockville MD Died Nov. 13, 1968; entombed Rockville Cemetery, Rockville MD

PRESS, SAMUEL DAVID, theologian; b. Cambria, Wis., May 24, 1875; s. Rev. G. and Julia (Guenther) P.; grad. Elmhurst (Ill.) Coll., 1893; grad. Eden Theol. Sem., Webster Groves, Mo., 1896; student U. of Berlin, U. of Chicago; Dr. Theol., U. of Halle, 1925; m. Elise Scheef, Jan. 15, 1907; children—Walter, Elsie, Reinhold, Doris. Ordained to ministry Evang. Synod of N.A., 1896; pastor successively Marlin, Gay Hill, again at Marlin, Houston (all of Tex.), until 1908; prof. theology Eden Theol. Sem., 1908-19, pres., 1919-41, prof. since 1941. Home: 7535 Carondelet Av., St. Louis 5. Office: 475 E. Lockwood Av., Webster Groves MO‡

PRESSEY, HENRY ALBERT, engineer; b. Lewiston, Me., Sept. 24, 1873; s. Warren E. and Annie R. (Irish) P.; B.S., Columbian (now George Washington) U., 1893, Ph.D., 1906; B.S., Mass. Inst. Tech., 1896; m. Perley Fitch, of Washingtonville, Orange Co., N.Y., Oct. 18, 1899; children—Henry Albert, Warren Fitch. Engr. on Met. Water Works, Boston, 1897; engr. with U.S. War Dept., 1898; hydrographer U.S. Geol. Survey and prof. civil engring., Columbian U., from 1899; in pvt. practice since 1903; v.p. Spencer Water Company; also director of the Southern Pub. Service Corpn., Oxford Water & Electric Co., Graham Water & Electric Co., Morgantown Water Co. Consulting engr. N.Y. State Water Supply Commn., 1909. Dir. Am. Forestry Assn.; mem. Am. Soc. C.E., American Institute of Electrical Engineers, Washington Society Engineers. Comd. Engr. Co. D.C. N.G. Presbyterian. Clubs: University, Washington Country. Author: Hydrography of Southern Appalacian Region, Parts I and II, 1902; Water Powers of the State of Maine, 1902; Flow of Rivers in the Vicinity of the City of New York, 1903; Hydrography of Cecil County, Md., 1903. Home: Mt. Vernon, N.Y. Office: 350 Madison Av., New York NY‡

PREST, WILLIAM MORTON, judge; b. Blackburn, England, Feb. 22, 1862; s. William and Rebecca (Morton) P.; on paternal side descendant of French

Huguenot family, and, on maternal side, of old Scotch family; brought to America when 2 yrs. of age; student Wesleyan Acad., 1882-84; A.B., Amherst Coll., 1888, A.M., 1891; LL.B., Boston U. Sch. of Law, 1891; m. Emma A. Day, July 9, 1880 (died 1881); 1dau., Alice E.; m. 2d, Bertha F. Sias, Jan. 10, 1912; m. 3d, Katharine Grinnell, Apr. 15, 1933. Admitted to Mass. bar, 1891; practiced at Boston; pres. Paul Revere Trust Co., 1913-17; judge of Probate Ct., Boston, since 1918; dir. State St. Trust Co. Mem. Boston Licensing Bd., 1916-18, Judicial Council, Mass., 1924-28, administrative Com. Probate Courts, 1931-32. Served as capt. Co. M, Mass. Volunteer Militia. Trustee Wesleyan Acad., 1920-25. Mem. Am. Acad. Arts and Sciences, Delta Kappa Epsilon. Republican. Clubs: Union, Curtis, Law, Lawyers (Boston). Home: 165 Bay State Rd., Boston MA*‡

PRESTON, ADELAIDE B., educator; b. Torrington, Conn., Nov. 18, 1871; d. James Hubert and Elizabeth (Van Volkenburg) P.; prep. edn. Winsted (Conn.) High Sch. and Robbins Sch., Norfolk, Conn.; B.L., Smith Coll., 1895. Teacher Morgan Sch., Portsmouth, N.H., 1895-96; teacher mathematics and Latin, Hillman Coll., Clinton, Miss., 1896-1900, Leache Wood Sem., Norfolk, Va., 1900; teacher Latin, St. Katharine's Sch., Davenport, Ia., 1905-09; head teacher St. Mary's Hall, Burlington, N.J., 1911-13; prin. Annie Wright Sem., Tacoma, Wash., 1913-29; founder of Miss Preston's Outdoor School, Phoenix, Ariz., 1929. Mem. Am. Assn. Univ. Women, N.E.A. Republican. Episcopalian. Club: Smith College. Address: 3d Av. and Virginia St., Phoenix AZ‡

PRESTON, ARTHUR MURRAY, banker; b. Washington, Nov. 1, 1913; s. Ord and Carolyn M. (Murray) P.; grad. Phillips Acad., Andover, Mass., 1931; B.S., Yale, 1935; LL.B., U. Va., 1938; m. Elizabeth P. McBride, Mar. 17, 1941; children—Peter M., Lewis McBride, Julia P., Eleanor O. Admitted to Va. bar, 1937, D.C. bar, 1938, Md. bar, 1950; with firm McKenney, Flannery & Craighill, Washington, 1938-40; sr. partner firm Craighill, Aiello & Preston, Washington, 1945-59; v.p. Am. Security and Trust Co., Washington, 1959-68; v.p. Am. Security Corp., Washington, 1960-68; dir. Acacia Mut. Life Ins. Co. Gen. chmn. Washington United Givers Fund campaign, 1964. Trustee Group Hospitalization from 1962; bd. dirs. Washington Hosp. Center, from 1949; pres., 1961-65. Served with USNR, 1940-45. Decorated Congl Medal Honor, Silver Star. Mem. D.C. Bankers Assn. (pres. 1965-66), D.C. Bar Assn. Clubs: Chevy Chase; Metropolitan (Washington); Yale (N.Y.C.). Chevy Chase MD Died Jan. 7, 1968; buried Arlington Nat. Cemetery Arlington VA

PRESTON, GEORGE H., physician; b. Baltimore, Md., May 10, 1890; s. George Junkin (M.D.) and Emma (Heinrichs) P.; A.B., John Hopkins U., 1911, M.D., 1915; M. Alice Dorough, Sept. 6, 1919 (dec. 1951); m. 2d, Ellen J. H. Macduff, 1952. Supt. Ga. Training Sch. for Mental Defectives, 1921-24; psychiatrist, Children's Memorial Clinic, Richmond, Va., 1924-28; commr. mental hygiene, Md., 1928-49. Clin. adminstr. Chestnut Lodge, Inc., 1952-56; clin. dir. Child Guidance Clinic, Atlanta, from 1956; frequent internat. lecture trips, from 1956. Fellow American Orthopsychiatric Assn. (president 1944), Am. Psychiat. Assn.; mem. Ga., S.E. psychiat. socs., Am. Assn. on Mental Defiency. Author: Psychiatry for Curious, 1940; The Substance of Mental Health, 1943; Should I Retire?, 1952. Home: Atlanta GA Died Mar. 6, 1972; buried Arlington Meml. Cemetery Atlanta GA

PRESTON, JOHN FISHER, army officer; b. Baltimore, Md., Nov. 5, 1872; s. John Fisher and Eliza (Thomas) P.; A.B., Baltimore City Coll., 1890; B.S., U.S. Mil. Acad., 1894; distinguished grad. Sch. of the Line, 1920; grad. Gen. Staff Sch., 1921. Army War Coll., 1923; mem. General Staff Corps eligible list; m. Meeta Campbell Graham, Dec. 23, 1896. Commd. 2d lt. 16th U.S Inf., 1894; promoted through grades to col., July 1, 1920. Served in Santiago Campaign, Spanish-Am. War, 1898; participated in 5 engagements, Philippine Insurrection; apptd. col. 303d Inf., 76th Div., 1917; served in France, 1918, 19; col. 63d Inf., Madison Barracks, N.Y., July 1919; chief of staff, 8th Corps Area, U.S., 1923-26; col. 1st U.S. Inf., 1926-28; assigned to Command 4th Brig., 2d Div., June 20, 1927; detailed to Insp. Gen.'s Dept., 1928; apptd. insp. gen., rank of maj. gen. for 4 years. from Dec. 1, 1931; retired Nov. 30, 1936 with rank of maj. gen. U.S. Army. Awarded Silver Star and cited for gallantry in action"; nominated for brevet capt., Santiago, 1898. Dir. Nat. Bank of Fort Sam Houston, San Antonio, Tex. Episcopalian. Clubs: Army and Navy (Washington); Army-Navy Country (Arlington, Va.). Home: Baltimore, Md. Address: 149 Davis Court, San Antonio TX‡

PRESTON, JOHN WHITE, judge; b. Woodbury, Cannon County, Tenn., May 14, 1877; s. Hugh Lawson and Thankful Caroline (Doak) P.; A.B., Burritt Coll., Spencer, Tenn.; post-grad. work Bethan (W.Va.) Coll.; m. Sara Rucker, Jan. 8, 1902; children—Mrs. Elizabeth P. Genesy, John White, Jr. Admitted to Tenn. bar, 1897, and practiced in Woodbury; removed to Calif., 1902; mem. Preston & Preston, Ukiah and San Francisco; pres. Preston Loan & Investment Co.; dir. Ft. Bragg (Calif.) Commercial Bank. Chmn. Mendocino County Dem. Central Com., 1904-08; mem. Calif. Ho. of Rep., 1908; renominated, 1910 (declined); U.S. atty. Northern Dist. of Calif., Dec. 23, 1913-July 24, 1918, resigned; spl. asst. U.S. atty. gen. for war work, July 24, 1918-May 15, 1919, resigned; practiced in San Francisco; asso. justice of Supreme Court of State of Calif., 1926-35, reelected, 1930, without opposition, to 12-year term; resigned and resumed pvt. practice, Oct. 1935. Apptd. by the President as spl. counsel for U.S. Govt. to prosecute Elk Hills Oil litigation; also spl. asst. to atty. gen. of U.S. in charge tideland eminent domain proceedings at Terminal Island. Pres. Lawyers Club of Los Angeles, 1940. Mem. Am., Calif. State, Los Angeles and San Francisco bar assns. Clubs: Commonwealth, Press (San Francisco); Stock Exchange (Los Angeles); Los Angeles Country. Home: 166 Av. 64, Pasadena 2, Calif. Office: Rowan Bldg., Los Angeles‡

PRESTON, MALCOLM GREENHOUGH, educator; b. Phila., Dec. 29, 1905; s. Benjamin and Mary Ann (Walker) P.; student Girard Coll., 1923; B.S. in Econs., U. Pa., 1927, M.A., 1932, Ph.D., 1955; LL.D., Phila. College Textiles and Science, 1967; m. Hazel Nina Sturgeon, Oct. 4, 1929; children—Malcolm Sturgeon, Ross Sturgeon, Mary Anne. Asst. instr. psychology U. Pa., 1931-36, instr. psychology, 1936-39, asst. prof., 1939-46, asso. prof., 1946-52, professor in psychology, 1952-71, also co-director educational survey, 1954-60; general manager Phila. Belt Line R.R. Co., 1935, v.p., 1952-67, pres.. 1967-71; research cons. Franklin Inst., 1943-56, Marriage Council of Phila., 1946-56. Mem. Nat. Research Council adv. com. to Q.M. Gen., 1949-53. Fellow Am. (chmn. com. on relations with social work profession 1951-52), Eastern (chmn. program com.) psychol. associations, A.A.A.S.; member of Comml. Exchange of Phila., Sigma Xi. Unitarian. Clubs: Downtown, Franklin Inn, Traffic. Home: Bala-Cynwyd PA Died Sept. 13, 1971.

PRESTON, ROBERT J., chief police Oakland, Cal. Address: Oakland CA Died Sept. 1967.

PRETTYMAN, E(LIJAH) BARRETT, judge; b. Lexington, Va., Aug. 23, 1891; s. Forrest Johnston and Elizabeth Rebecca (Stonestreet) P.; A.B., Randolph-Macon Coll., 1910, A.M., 1911, LL.D., 1961; LL.B., Georgetown U., 1915, LL.D., 1946; LL.D., Wm. Mitchell Coll. Law, 1961; m. Lucy C. Hill, Sept. 15, 1917; children—Elizabeth Courtney, Elijah Barrett. Admitted to Va. bar, 1915; mem. Potter, Prettyman & Fisher, Hopewell, Va., 1915-17; spl. atty. Internal Revenue Dept., Washington, D.C., and N.Y. City, 1919-20; asso. and mem. firm Butler, Lamb, Foster and Pope, Chicago, and Washington, D.C., 1920-33; gen. counsel Bur. Internal Revenue, Washington, 1933-34; corporation counsel of D.C., 1934-36; mem. Hewes, Prettyman and Awalt, Washington, D.C., and Hartford, Conn., 1936-45; professor of taxation, Georgetown University Law Sch.; judge United States Court of Appeals for D.C., from 1945, chief judge, 1958-60, later senior circuit judge. Chairman of the President's Conference on Adminstrv. Procedure, 1953-54; chmn. Adminstrv. Conf. of U.S., 1961-62; chmn. Pres.'s Adv. Commn. Narcotics and Drug Abuse, Jud. Conf. U.S. Adv. Com. Appellate Rules. Served U.S. Army, 1917-19, advancing to capt. inf. Trustee Randolph-Macon Coll., Am. U. Mem. Am., Fed. D.C. (past pres.) bar associations, Washington Board of Trade (past president), Phi Beta Kappa, Order of Coif, Sigma Upsilon, Kappa Sigma, Gamma Eta Gamma, Omicron Delta Kappa. Democrat. Methodist. Clubs: Civitan Internat., Burning Tree, Metropolitan. Chevy Chase, Lawyers. Author articles on taxation and administrative practice of law. Home: Washington DC Died Aug. 4, 1971.

PRETTYMAN, VIRGIL, educator; b. Townsend, Del., Mar. 13, 1874; s. Cornelius Wiltbank and Emily Elizabeth (Gooding) P.; A.B., Dickinson Coll., 1892, A.M., 1895, Pd.D., 1905; student Harvard and Columbia, 1894-97; m. Lulu Reedy, Mar. 23, 1897; children—Lambert, Virgil. Instr. in secondary schs., 1892-94; prin. Horace Mann High Sch., New York, 1894-1914; headmaster Horace Mann School for Boys, 1914-20; pres. Prettyman & McFarlane, Inc., New York. Dir. Camp Moosilauke, summer sch. for boys, Pike, N.H., 1900-20. Mem. N.E.A.; pres. New York Schoolmasters' Assn., 1904-05, Principals' Athletic Council, N.Y., 1905-10, Private Schools Athletic Assn. of New York City, 1915-18, Assn. of Colls. and Schools Middle States and Md., 1918-19; financial adviser to pres. of Robert Coll. and Am. Coll. for Girls, Istanbul, Turkey, since 1932; mem. adv. bd. of Horace Mann Sch., since 1945. Mem. Phi Beta Kappa, Beta Theta Pi. Author: (Inglis and Prettyman) First Book in Latin, 1906; Easy First Lessons in Turkish. Home: 2522 Castilla Island, Ft Lauderdale FL‡

PREYER, WILLIAM YOST, chem. co. exec; b. Cleveland, O., June 4, 1888; s. Robert and Ellen Janet (Yost) P.; student private and pub. schs. Elizabeth City, Cuyahoga Falls, O. and Greensboro, N.C.; m. Mary Norris Richardson, June 15, 1916; children—William Yost, Lunsford Richardson, Robert Otto, Norris Watson, Frederick Lynn. Yard salesman, shipping clk., outside foreman Guilford Lumber Co., Greensboro, N.C., 1905-16; with Vick Chem. Co., 1916-58, sec., treas. and purchasing and prodn. mgr., Greensboro, N.C., Phila., Pa., and New York City, 1919-26, 2d v.p., 1926, 1st v.p., 1929-33, v.p. and treas., 1933-37, exec. v.p., 1937-38, pres., 1938-48, chmn. auditing com., mem. exec. com., 1948-58; pres. Nat. Amusement Corp., Greensboro, N.C., 1932-45, Vick Financial Corp., N.Y.C., 1933-36; an incorporator Reins. Corp. N.Y., pres., 1936-47, chmn. bd., 1947-56; v.p., dir. Piedmont Financial Co. N.Y., 1928-57, dir. Piedmont Life Ins. Co., Atlanta, Wachovia Bank & Trust Co., Winston-Salem, N.C., Security Life & Trust Co., Winston-Salem, Am. Ins. Co., Newark. Mem. exec. com. Presbyn. Home, Inc., 1949-70; life trustee Childrens Home Soc. N.C., Inc., pres., 1949-52; pres. Carolinas Red Feather Services, 1955-56; mem. gen. bd. Nat. Conf. Christians and Jews, 1962-65; pres. Gen. Greene council Boy Scouts Am., 1923-25; trustee, mem. exec. and finance com. Greensboro Coll., 1938-70. Mem. Greensboro C. of C. (pres. 1925-26, 49-50), O.D.K. Dem. Presbyterian (elder, First Ch., Greensboro). Clubs: Advertising, Athletic, Cloud, Rockfeller Center, Metropolitan (N.Y. City); Golf, Greensboro Country. Home: Greensboro NC Died Dec. 8, 1970; buried Green Hill Cemetery, Greensboro NC

PRICE, HANNIBAL, diplomat; b. Cape Haitien, July 9, 1875; s. Hannibal and Josephine (Curet) P.; classical studies, Coll. of Beauvais, France; grad. Nat. Law Sch. Port-au-Prince, Hayti; m. Amelie Lizaire, of Port-au-Prince, July 9, 1902; 1 dau., Germaine. Practiced law in Port-au-Prince; apptd. sec. to Pres. Hyppolite, 1893, later sec. to Pres. Sam; sec. Haitian Legation, Washington, D.C., 1911-13; mem. Nat. Bureau du Contentieux, Haiti, later counselor of state; E.E. and M.P. from Haiti to U.S. since Jan. 1925. Mem. Societe Francaise de Legislation Comparee (life). Catholic. Author of various legal works and a dictionary of Haitian laws. Address: 1730 Connecticut Av. N.W., Washington DC‡

PRICE, JOSEPH LINDON, physician; b. Davenport, Okla., Mar. 22, 1911; s. Thomas E. and Florence (Elliott) P.; M.D., U. Ia., 1937; m. Edna Henrie, June 1, 1940, (div.); children—Michael, Patrick, Sally. Intern, Salt Lake County Gen. Hosp., Salt Lake City, 1937-39; asst. to Dr. E.R. Dumke, Ogden, Utah, 1940-41; gen. practice medicine and surgery, Redding, Cal., 1946-68; mem. staff Meml. Hosp., Redding, 1946-68, bd. dirs., 1963-68, pres. bd., 1963-68. Cattle rancher, 1951-68; almond rancher, 1953-68. Mem. Shasta County, Cal. Republican Central Com., 1951-59, chmn., 1957-59; mem. Cal. Rep. Central Com. Served to capt., M.C., AUS, 1941-46. Mem. Am., Cal. med. assns., Shasta County Med. Soc., Am. Hereford Assn. Republican. Elk. Developer almond tree; inventor vet. instrument. Home: Cottonwood CA Died Sept. 17, 1968.

PRICE, MARGARET (MRS. HICKMAN PRICE, JR.), Vice chmn. Democratic Nat. Com.; b. N.Y.C., Oct. 15, 1912; d. George Henry and Ruth (Miller) Bayne; ed. Bryn Mawr Coll.; m. Hickman Price Jr., Nov. 22, 1941; 1 son, Marston. Dem. candidate for state auditor gen. of Mich., 1948, 50; mem. Dem. Nat. Com., 1952-61, founder, mem. adv. council, 1956-60, vice chmn., dir. women's activities, 1960-68, mem. exec. com., 1956-68; chmn. (1st woman) com. permanent orgn. Dem. Nat. Conv., 1960. Chmn. YWCA World Emergency Fund, 1941-42; del. White House Conf. Children and Youth, 1950, 60; mem. U.S. com. UN Internat. Children's Emergency Fund, 1951-55; spl. ambassador, personal rep. of Pres. John F. Kennedy to Inauguration Pres. of Paraguay, 1963. Chmn. Mich. Youth Commn., 1949-56; bd. commrs. Mackinac Island State Park, 1949-56; mem. Gov.'s Commn. on Inter-govt. Relations, 1954, Gov.'s Commn. Pub. Health Study, 1956; mem. Def. Adv. Com. Women in Services, Bd. dirs. Brazilian Am. Cultural Inst. Recipient Nat. Order of So. Cross (Brazil), 1965. Mem. Nat. Capital Dem. Club, Am. Newspaper Women's Club, League Women Voters. Home: Washington DC Died July 23, 1968.

PRICE, MARGARET WRIGHT, orgn. exec. b. Lebanon, Mo., May 13, 1910; d. James Harvey and Julia (Clark) Wright; m. Holton R. Price, Jr., Nov. 2, 1929; children—Julia (Mrs. J. T. Johnstone), Sally (Mrs. Theodore Simpson). Leader, trainer, officer Girl. Scout council Greater St. Louis, 1940-63, mem. regional com. Girl Scouts U.S.A., 1949-60, chmn., 1954-60, mem. field com., 1954-60, finance com., 1960-63, chmn. nat. devel. com., 1960-63, dir., 1954-73, exec., 1960-69, 1960-69. v.p., 1960-63, nat. pres., 1963-69, life mem. hon. pres. bd. dirs., ofcl. visitor 16th world conf. World Assn. Girl Guides and Girl Scouts, Brazil, 1957, del. 18th world conf., Denmark, 1963, Conf. coordinator, chmn. adv. com. Mo. Youth for Environmental Quality 1969—. Bd. dirs. Nat. Center Vol. Action, St. Louis Mental Health Assn., Mo. Assn. Mental Health. Named St. Louis Woman of achievement, St Louis MO Died Mar. 1973.

PRICE, MILES OSCAR, librarian; b. Plymouth, Ind., July 31, 1890; s. Emanuel and Mary Jane (Dickson) P.;

B.S., U. of Chicago, 1914; B.L.S., U. of Ill., 1922; LL.B., Columbia University, 1938; LL.D., Temple University, 1954; married Fannie Elliott, Jan. 3, 1915; children—Miles Macy (died 1937), Mary Dunsdon (Mrs. Peter J. Franco). Assistant with the University of Chicago Library, 1910-14; dept. chief, U. of Ill. Library, 1914-22; librarian Patent Office Scientific Library, Washington, D.C., 1922-29; librarian law library, Columbia U., from 1929, prof. law emeritus, 1962-68; instr. Columbia Sch. of Library Service, summers, from 1937; cons. Library of Congress, 1962-64; dir. libraries study project Assn. Am. Law Schs., 1964-67. Mem. A.L.A. (council 1924-25 and 1933-37). Spl. Library Assn. N.Y. (exec. bd. 1930-31), D.C. Library Assn. (pres. 1924-25), Am. Assn. Law Libraries (pres. 1945-46). Mem. bar of State of N.Y. Methodist. Mason. Editor: Brief and Specifications for Library Service in the Fed. Govt., 1923. Compiler: (with Dorsey W. Hyde, Jr.) Directory of Informational Resources of District of Columbia, 1926; Introduction to Legal Bibliography and Brief Making for First Year Law Students, 1932; Syllabus in Law Library Administration, 1937, 1946; Subject Headings in Am. and English Law, 1939; Orderwork in a Law Library, 1941; Catalog for law library of 15,000 vols. (photog. reprint), 1942; Manual of Standard Legal Citations, 1950. Author: (with Harry Bitner) Effective Legal Research, 1953, rev. edit., 1963. Contbr. to Jour. of Patent Office Soc. and Am. Polit. Science Rev., and various library publs. Address: Washington DC Died Aug. 18, 1968; buried Wilmington IL

PRICE, ORE LEE, pub., lawyer; b. Champaign, County, Ill., Apr. 25, 1877; s. James Parker and Mary (Long) P.; B.S., Pacific Coll., Newberg, Ore., 1897; LL.B., U. of Ore., 1900; m. Margaret L. Beharrell, June 1903; children—Margaret Hazelmary, Barbara Lee. Admitted to Ore. bar, 1900, and began practice at Portland; pres., treas. and mgr. Oregonian Pub. Co. until Jan. 1939; now in practice of law; dir. Portland Traction Co. Mem. Sigma Delta Chi, Phi Delta Phi. Mason, K.P. Republican. Presbyterian. Home: 2681 S.W. Buena Vista Drive. Office: Pacific Bldg., Portland OR‡

PRICE, RAYMOND B., mfr.; b. Newark, N.J., Dec. 4, 1872; s. David Frank and Margaretta Beach (Crowell) P.; S.B., Mass. Inst. Tech., 1894; m. Helene Morton Keane, of Chicago, Ill., Feb. 28, 1906. Chemist, Boston Rubber Hose & Rubber Co., 1894-8; supt. Calumet Tire & Rubber Co., Chicago, 1899-1905; pres. Rubber Regenerating Co., since 1905; dir. U.S. Rubber Co., 1917-—, and other rubber corpns. Ranch owner and operator, Calif. Office: 1133 Broadway, New York NY‡

PRICE, RICHARD REES, educator; b. Hafod, Wales, May 23, 1875; s. John Rees and Sarah Ann (Evans) P.; B.A., U. of Kan., 1897; B.A., Harvard, 1900, M.A., 1901, Ed.D., 1923; m. Louise Snow Wood, Aug. 28, 1901; 1 dau., Sarah. Teacher high sch., Hutchinson, 1897-99, prin., 1901-02; supt. city schs., Hutchinson, 1902-09; dir. univ. extension, U. of Kan., 1909-13; director university extension and professor, University of Minn., since 1913, professor emeritus since 1943; exec. sec. Minn. Assn. Professional Engrs. since 1944. Editor Interstate Schoolman, 1904-09. Mem. Kan. State Text Book Commission, 1907-09; sec.-treas. and executive, League of Kan. Municipalities, 1910-13; sec.-treas. League of Minn. Municipalities since 1913, honorary president since 1943; president National University Extension Association, 1923. Member National Edn. Assn., Minn. Edn. Assn., Phi Beta Kappa, Phi Delta Kappa. Republican. Presbyterian. Club: University. Author: The Financial Support of the University of Michigan, 1923; The Financial Support of State Universities, 1924; also chapter XII in Kent's Higher Education in America, 1930; The Center for Continuation Study at the University of Minnesota, 1943. Home: 73 Arthur Av. S.E., Minneapolis 14 MN‡

PRICE, WILLIAM GRAY, JR., maj. gen., retired; b. Chester, Pa., Mar. 23, 1869; s. Wm. Gray and Jane Elizabeth (Campbell) P.; ed. pub. and private schs.; hon. Doctor Mil. Sci., Pa. Mil. Coll.; m. Sallie Pennell Eyre, June 1, 1893. Entered Nat. Guard of Pa., April 1886; promoted through grades to brig. gen. N.G. Pa., 1910; brig. gen. N.A., Aug. 5, 1917; maj. gen. Pa. N.G., May 16, 1919; maj. gen. U.S.R.C., Apr. 9, 1921. Served as lt. col. 3d Pa. Vols., Spanish-Am. War; apptd. comdr. 53d Arty. Brig., Camp Hancock, Ga., Aug. 5, 1917, and comdr. same throughout its service in Europe; participated in Marne, Vesle, Argonne, Leys-Scheldt operations, Fr. and Belgium; apptd. comdg. gen. Pa. N.G. on return from France, May 15, 1919; retired Mar. 23, 1933. Awarded D.S.M. (U.S.); Croix de Guerre (Belgium and France); Comdr. Legion of Honor (France). Republican. Episcopalian. Clubs: Union League, Corinthian Yacht (Phila.); Chester (Chester); Army and Navy (Washington). Home: 24 W. Sellers Av., Ridley Park PA‡

PRICE, WILLIAM HUNDLEY, JR., lawyer; b. Grundy Center, Ia., Aug. 7, 1926; s. William H. and Henriette (Engelkes) P.; LL.B., J.D., Drake U., 1950; m. Mona Jeanne Branley, Aug. 30, 1950; children—Virginia Lee, William Hundley III, Thomas Edward, Stephen Richard, Sara Jeanne. Admitted to Ia. bar, 1951, Minn. bar 1957; mem. firm Christie & Price, Davenport, Ia., 1951-55, Streiff & Price, Rochester, Minn., 1955-62, Price & Dunlap, Rochester, 1962-72. Dir., sec. Am. Premier Ins. Co., 1961-65. Bd. dirs. Greater Rochester United Fund, 1963-72, pres. 1968, gen. campaign chmn. 1964. Served with USMCR, 1944-46. Mem. Am., Ia., Minn., 3d Jud. Dist., Olmsted County bar assns., Am. Judicature Soc., Delta Theta Phi. Republican. Club: Sertoma (charter pres. 1960. Minn. dist. gov. 1962). Rochester Golf and Country (dir.). Home: Rochester MN Died Apr. 23, 1972.

PRICE, WILLIAM WIGHTMAN, educator, naturalist, author; b. Milwaukee, Jan. 20, 1871; s. Robert Martin and Harriet (Wightman) P.; removed to Calif., 1880; ed. pub. schs. of Riverside and Oakland, Calif.; grad. Stanford Univ., 1897, M.A., 1899; teacher in Thacher Sch., Nordhoff, Calif., 1899-1900; m. June 6, 1900, Bertha de Laguna. At age of 16 explored the deserts and mountains of Ariz., discovering new and little-known birds, mammals and reptiles. Author of scientific papers; contb'r to Overland Monthly and Sunset mags. Mem. Beta Theta Pi, Calif. Acad. Sciences, Am. Ornithologists' Union, Am. Hist. Assn., Sierra Club, Cooper Club. Founder of Agassiz Hall, school for boys, and Camp Agassiz, a summer school of nature study in the Sierras. Address: Alta Placer Co CA‡

PRIDE, FREDERICK W.R., lawyer; b. Portsmouth, O., June 8, 1904; s. Frederick M. and Grace (Stokley) P.; A.B., Ohio State U., 1926; LL.B., Harvard, 1929; m. Margaret Armstrong, Dec. 29, 1930; children—Patricia, Margaret, Penelope. Admitted to N.Y. bar, 1930; asso. with Hughes, Schurman and Dwight, 1929-37; mem. firm Royall, Koegel & Rogers, N.Y.C., 1937-72; justice Ct. of Spl. Sessions, Bronxville, N.Y., 1955-72, gen. counsel War Contracts, also gen. counsel U.S. Navy, Price Adjustment Bd., 1943-45. Board trustees Finch Coll., 1967-72. Mem. Am., N.Y. State bar assns., Assn. Bar City N.Y., Ohio Soc. N.Y., Ohio State U. Alumni Assn. (nat. pres. 1951-53), Sigma Chi. Presbyn. Clubs: Siwanoy Country (Bronxville); Chevy Chase (Md.); Metropolitan (Washington); Lawyers, Sky (N.Y.C.); Nat. Golf Links (Southampton). Asso. editor Harvard Law Rev. Contbr. articles Bronxville NY Died Aug. 1972.

PRIEST, ALAN, archaeologist; born at Fitchburg, Mass., Jan. 31, 1898; s. Gen. George Herbert and Marian Louise (Works) P.; B.A., Harvard, 1920, grad. student, 1921-24; unmarried. Asst. in Fine Arts, Harvard, 1921, asst. and tutor, 1922-23; mem. 2d Fogg Expdn. to China, 1924-25; Carnegie fellow, China, 1925; Sachs fellow, China, 1926-27; curator Dept. Far Eastern Art, Met. Museum of Art, 1928-63, curator emeritus, 1963-69. Author: Aspects of Chinese Painting, 1954. Address: New York City NY Died Jan. 21, 1969

PRIMS, JAMES EDWIN, steel co. exec.; b. Evanston, Ill., Feb. 8, 1931; s. Edwin M. and Charlotte (Klock) P.; B.S., Lawrence Coll., Appleton, Wis., 1952; M.B.A. with distinction, Northwestern U., 1964; m. Joan Munson, Dec. 26, 1952; children—Cathryn, Peter, Leslie. Personnel adminstr. Honeywell, Inc., 1956-60; cons. Booz, Allen &Hamilton, Inc., Chgo., 1960-62; financial exec. Interlake Steel, Inc., Chgo., 1962-—. Served to lt. USNR, 1952-55. Home: Hinsdale IL Died Jan. 26, 1969.

PRINCE, LEON NATHANIEL, physician; b. Phila., Dec. 8, 1906; s. Nathaniel and Elizabeth N. Prince; B.S., William and Mary Coll.; M.D., Jefferson Med. Coll., 1933; m. Marie J. De Prisco, Nov. 12, 1931; children—Robert Leon, Patricia Marie, Barbara Elizabeth (Mrs. Paul Cirilis). Asso. prof. obstetrics and gynecology Jefferson Med. Coll., Phila.; chief obstet. ward St. Vincent's Hosp. Mem. med. com. Southeastern Pa. Planned Parenthood Assn. Served with USCGR, World War II. Diplomate Am. Bd. Obstetrics and Gynecology. Fellow A.C.S., Am. Coll. Obstetricians and Gynecologists (founder); mem. A.M.A. Contbr. numerous articles on perinatal mortality and morbidity to med. jours. Home: Philadelphia PA Died Jan. 27, 1970; buried Laurel Hill Cemetery.

PRINGSHEIM, NEENA HAMILTON (MRS.), writer and lecturer on art; b. Hamilton, O.; d. Prof. Edward John (D.D.) and Eliza (Cleland) Hamilton; ed. Hanover Coll., Ind., A.M., 1896; Univ. of Heidelberg, Germany, in dept. art and archaeology, Ph.D., 1901; studied at univs. of Berlin, Hahe, Munich, Paris, and Heidelberg; m. Toronto, Can., Jan. 31, 1903, Hans Hugo Pringsheim, Ph.D. Prof. in Elmira (N.Y.) Coll., 1902-5. Lecturer on Greek, Flemish and German Art, and upon the Italian Renaissance. Author: Die Anbetung der Konige in der Italienischen Malerei, 1901 G15; also mag. articles on art topics. Address: 13 1/2 Hilliard St., Cambridge MA‡

PRINOSCH, FRANCIS J., rwy. co. exec.; b. 1909; married. With Atlantic Coast Line R.R. Co., 1929-67, asst. sec., 1943-45, asst. sec., asst. treas., 1945-60, asst. v.p., sec., asst. treas., 1960-67; asst. v.p., asst. sec., asst. treas. Seaboard Coast Line R.R. Co., Jacksonville, Fla., 1967-68, asst. v.p., sec., asst. treas., 1968-71. Address: Jacksonville FL Died July 23, 1971.

PRINZMETAL, ISADORE HARRY, lawyer, painter; b. Buffalo, Jan. 21, 1906; s. Harry and Anna (Stein) P.; B.A. with honors, U. Cal. at Los Angeles, 1927, J.D., 1930; m. Nancy Kaufman, Apr. 16, 1942; children—Michael, Karen, Debbie, Jan, Donna, Mark. Admitted to Cal. bar, 1930; asso. firm Lissner, Roth & Gunter, Los Angeles, 1930-36; resident counsel Metro-Goldwyn-Mayer Studios, 1936-42; practice in Beverly Hills, Cal., Los Angeles, 1942-69. Mem. faculty dept. econs. U. Cal. at Berkeley, 1928-30; inheritance tax appraiser State of Cal., 1963-—; one-man show Gallerie de Ville, Beverly Hills, 1963-64, Frank Lang Gallery, Los Angeles, 1966; rep. permanent collections Los Angeles County Mus., U. Cal. at Los Angeles, U. Cal. at Berkeley, other museums, pvt. collections. Vice pres. Jewish Fedn. Council Greater Los Angeles, Am. Jewish Congress; pres. Los Angeles Hillel Council; founding mem. Center for Study Democratic Instns. Bd. dirs. Cal. Assn. for Health and Welfare, Cedars-Sinai Med. Center; bd. overseers U. Judaism. Mem. Am. (bd. dels.), Los Angeles County, Beverly Hills (pres.) bar assns., State Bar Cal. (disciplinary bd., vice chmn. corps. com., chmn. pub. relations com.), Order of Coif. Mem. B'nai B'rith (v.p. So. Cal. Anti-Defamation League). Editor: Cal. Law Rev., 1928-30. Home: Los Angeles CA Died Mar. 19, 1970.

PRITCHARD, HARRY N., partner McCormick & Co., investment bankers. Address: Chicago IL Deceased.*

PRITCHETT, JOSEPH JOHNSTON, clergyman M.E. Ch., South; b. Hannibal, Mo., Feb. 18, 1872; s. Rev. J. H. P. (D. D., gen. missionary sec. M. E. Ch., South); attended Central Coll., Fayette, Mo., and grad. Emory and Henry Coll., Va., 1889 (A. M., A. B. and A. M., Univ. of Va.); m. 1897, C. Evangeline Shackelford. Pres. Hiwassee Coll., 1891-3; prin. public schools, Moberly, Mo., 1893-5; pres. Methodist Coll., Clarence, Mo., 1895-8; pres. Morrisville Coll., Mo., 1898-1900; lecturer. Active in politics as advocate of free coinage of silver. Address: Lebanon MO‡

PRITZKER, DONALD NICHOLAS, hotel, co. exec.; b. Chgo., Oct. 31, 1932; s. Abram N. and Fanny (Doppelt) P.; A.B. cum laude, Harvard. 1954; J.D., U. Chgo., 1959; m. Sue Sandel, June 10, 1958; children—Penny, Tony, J.B. Admitted to Ill. bar, 1959; exec. v.p. Hyatt Corp., 1960-63, pres., 1963-72; pres. Hyatt Internat., 1968-72. Bd. dirs. Jewish Welfare Fedn. San Francisco, Mt. Zion Hosp., San Francisco; mem. adv. council Sch. Bus., U. Cal. at Berkeley. Served to lt. (j.g.) USNR, 1954-56. Home: Atherton CA Died May 6, 1972

PROBST, MARVIN, pres., chmn. bd. dirs. Graham, Anderson, Probst & White, Architects. Home: River Forest IL Died Mar. 1970.*

PROBST, NATHAN, lawyer; b. New York, N.Y., June 21, 1897; s. Nathan and Clara (Roth) P.; A.B., Columbia, 1918, LL.B., 1920. Admitted to N.Y. bar, 1920; asso. with Curtis, Mallet-Prevost & Colt, New York, 1920-21; asst. U.S. atty. Southern Dist. N.Y., 1921-22; spl. asst. U.S. atty. gen. 1922-24; engaged in the private practice of law, 1924-66; professor at St. Johns University Law Sch., Brooklyn, 1925-50; co-adjutor in preparation of constitution for Virgin Islands. Major, A.U.S.; in mil. service, 1942-46. Jewish religion. Address: Brooklyn Heights NY Died Dec. 30, 1966.

PROCTOR, CARROLL LEIGH, public utilities; b. Charlotte County, Va., Feb. 1, 1880; s. Thomas A. and Margaret (Skidmore) P.; B.S., in M.E., Va. Polytechnic Institute, 1902, M.E., 1903; married Ruth Scott. With General Electric Company, 1903-08; general superintendent Athens Ry. & Electric Co., 1908-15; sales mgr. Empire Dist. Electric co., 1915-18; vice-pres. and gen. mgr. Danbury & Bethel Gas & Electric Co., 1918-19; vice pres. and gen. mgr. Empire Dist. Electric Co., Joplin, Mo., 1919-25; vice president and general manager Toledo Edison Co., 1925-28, pres. 1938-49, chmn. bd., 1949-60. Trustee, Young Men's Christian Association, Toledo Newsboys' Association; dir. Toledo Museum of Art; director (life) O. Chamber of Commerce. Toledo Zoological Soc. Mem. Am. Inst. Elec. Engrs. Clubs: Toledo Country, Inverness Golf, Toledo, Rotary (past pres.). Home: Toledo OH Died Jan. 2, 1969; buried Toledo OH

PROCTOR, MORTIMER ROBINSON, gov. Vt.; b. Proctor, Vt., May 30, 1889; s. Fletcher Dutton and Minnie Euretta (Robinson) P.; A.B., Yale, 1912; LL.D., Norwich U., U. Vt., 1945; m. Lillian Washburn Bryan, Nov. 14, 1942 (dec. 1961); 1 son, Mortimer Robinson. With Vermont Marble Co. since 1912; v.p., 1935-52, president, 1952-63, director, 1912-68; pres. White Pigment Corp., 1948-52; dir. Vt. Mut. Fire Ins. Co. Mem. Vt. Legislature, 1933-39, speaker of House of Reps., 1937, lt. gov. of Vt., 1941-45, gov., 1945-47, presidential elector Vermont, 1956. Dir., past v.p. Vt. Children's Aid Society; member board of curators Vermont Historical Society, 1941-59; mem. exec. bd. Green Mt. council Boy Scouts Am. Served as lt, 71st Regt., C.A.C., U.S. Army, France, 1918. Dir. N.E. Council, 1935-43. Mem. Grange, Am. Legion, Vets.

Fgn. Wars, Psi Upsilon, Scroll and Key. Eagle, Elk. Mason. Clubs: Vt. Automobile (dir. 1949-68). Tobique Proctor VT Died Apr. 28, 1968.

PROCTOR, ROBERT, lawyer; b. Newton Centre, Mass., Dec. 1, 1898; s. Thomas W. and Anne Louise (White) P.; student Country Day Sch., Newton, Mass., 1909-15; A.B., Dartmouth, 1919; LL.B., Harvard, 1924; m. Nathalie H. Bishop, May 20, 1939. Admitted to Mass. bar, 1924, practiced as asso. firm of Choate, Hall & Stewart, Boston, 1924-27, mem. firm, 1927-42 and from 1946; admitted to D.C. bar, 1946, also mem. firm Douglas Proctor, MacIntyre & Gates, Washington, 1946-48; asst. to pres. Lockheed Aircraft Corp., Burbank, Calif., 1942-43; dir., mem. exec. com. State Street Bank and Trust Co.; trustee Am. Optical Co.; dir. OK Tool Company, Lockheed Aircraft Corporation. Member of Procurement Task Force, Second Hoover Commn., 1953-55. Served as 2d lieutenant, infantry, U.S. Army, 1918; spl. cons. to sec. of War, Aug.-Dec. 1940; commd. lt. col., A.A.F., Aug 1943, and advanced to col., Sept. 1944; served as exec. asst. and exec. to comdg. gen., A.A.F., Aug. 1943-Feb. 1946, Washington. Awarded Legion of Merit. Mem. Air Force Assn. (director 1947-51), American Massachusetts, Essex County, Salem, Boston (member of the council, 1929-35, mem. grievance com., 1929-35) bar assns., Phi Beta Kappa, Alpha Delta Phi. Clubs: Somerset Tavern (Boston); Myopia Hunt (Hamilton). Home: Manchester MA Died Sept. 25, 1967; buried Newton Cemetery, Newton MA

PROFFITT, HENRY WALTON, lawyer; b. N.Y.C., July 30, 1898; s. Charles Calvin and Lucy Grace (Mooney) P.; A.B., Columbia, 1919, LL.B., 1921. Admitted to N.Y. bar, 1922; partner Barry, Wainwright, Thacher & Symmers, 1928-52; sr. partner Thacher Proffitt, Prizer, Crawley &Wood (successor firm) 1952-69; trustee Empire Savs. Bank; trustee Leonard Wood Meml.; title adv. com. Title Guarantee Co. Trustee Columbia U., 1955-59, Gen. Theol. Sem. Mem. Assn. Bar City N.Y., Am., N.Y. State bar assns., Columbia Law Sch. Alumni Assn., Inc. (pres. 1951-53). Episcopalian. Clubs: University, Church, Down Town Assn., Columbia University (N.Y.C.); The Creek (Locust Valley, N.Y.); Union. Home: New York City NY Died Nov. 1, 1969.

PROHASKA, JOHN VAN, surgeon, educator; b. Bohemia, Sept. 6, 1904; s. Anthony and Teresa (Hambacher) P.; came to U.S., 1920, naturalized, 1926; B.S., U. Chgo., 1928, research Grad. Sch., 1928-30, M.D., 1933; m. Astrid Paulson, Nov. 27, 1929; 1 son, Peter Van. Intern surgery U. Chgo. Clinics, 1934, Douglas-Smith research fellow, 1935-36, asst. resident surgery, 1936-38, chief resident surgeon, 1939; prof. surgery U. Chgo. Med. Sch., 1954-69. Diplomate Am. Bd. Surgery. Fellow A.C.S. (award for motion pictues); mem. Am., Western, Central surg. assns., Soc. Univ. Surgeons, Soc. Internat. de Chirurgie, Chgo. Surg. Soc. (pres. 1962-63), A.M.A. (certificate of merit for exhibit), Soc. Surgery Alimentary Tract (a founder, sec. 1965-69), Am. Assn. Cancer Research, Chgo. Med. Soc. (council 1951-54), Inst. Medicine Chgo., Am. Geriatrics Soc., A.A.A.S. (bd. rep. for Soc. Surgery Alimentary Tract), Ill. Assn. Advancement Sci., Czechoslovak Med. Soc. (hon.), Order Purknje Soc., Sigma Xi, Alpha Omega Alpha. Clubs: University, Chicago Literary. Home: Chicago IL Died June 12, 1969.

PROPPER DE CALLEJON, DON EDUARDO, ret. govt. ofcl.; b. Madrid, Spain, Apr. 9, 1896; s. Maximiliano Propper and Juana de Callejon; Barister in law, Univ. of Madrid, 1917; m. Elena Fould-Springler, Dec. 28, 1929; children—Felipe, Elena. Entered the Diplomatic Corps, Spanish Govt., 1918, and served as diplomatic attache, Spanish Legation in Belgium, 1918-22; 3d Sec., Ministry of Fgn. Affairs, 1922-24; 2d sec., Spanish Embassy in Lisbon, 1924-26, in Vienna, 1926-29, in Cairo, 1929-30; 1st sec., charge div. of coding and registry, Ministry of Fgn. Affairs, 1930, ret. from active service, 1931-36; returned and served as 1st sec., Embassy of Spain in Paris, 1936, 1939; 1941; Spanish consulate in Larache, 1941-42; M.P., Consulate Gen. at Rabat, 1943-44; head of diplomatic cabinet, Ministry Fgn. Affairs, 1944-49; M.P. consul gen. of Spain in Zurich, 1945; Minister Counselor in Spanish Embassy, Washington, 1949, Charge d'Affairs Spain, 1949-50; E.E. and M.P. United States, 1943-55; Spanish ambassador to Canada, 1955, Spanish ambassador to Norway. Decorations: Grand Cross of Civil Merit, Knight of the Order of Charles III, Medal of Moroccan Peace, Grand Officer of the Khaliffan Order of Nixan el Alauita, Morocco, Comdr. of the Austrian Legion of Honor (gold), Officer of the French Legion of Honor; Knight of the Order of Saint Maurice and St. Lazarus, Italy, of the Crown of Italy, of Pius, Holy See, of the Crown of Belgium, of St. Olaf, Norway; officer of the Cuban Red Cross, Officer of the Order of Christ, Portugal, Grand Cross of Italy. Home: Chateau de Royamont Norvege par Asniere loise (SO) France Died Jan. 11, 1972.

PROSKAUER, JOSEPH M., lawyer; b. Mobile, Aug. 6, 1877; A.B., Columbia Coll., 1896; LL.B., Columbia, 1899, LL.D., 1929; LL.D., Dartmouth, 1953, Brandeis U., 1955, L.I.U., 1956, N.Y.U., 1956, Colgate University, Hamilton, N.Y., 1957, Fordham University, 1967; D.H.L., Hebrew Union Coll., 1946. Admitted to N.Y. bar, 1899, and practiced in N.Y.C. until 1923; justice Supreme Ct. of N.Y., appellate div., 1st dept., 1923-30; resumed practice of law, 1930; sr. mem. Proskauer, Rose, Goetz & Mendelsohn, N.Y.C. Cons. Am. delegation UN Conf., San Francisco, 1945. Mem. N.Y. City Charter Revision Co., 1935; chmn. N.Y. State Crime Commn., 1951-53. Past. pres., hon. pres. Am. Jewish Com.; past pres. YWHA of N.Y.; trustee, past pres. Fedn. Jewish Philanthropies. Mem. Am., N.Y. State bar assns., Assn. Bar City N.Y. (past v.p.), N.Y. County Lawyers Assn. (past pres.), Lotos, Manhattan, Lawyers, City, Columbia University (N.Y.C.). Home: New York City NY Died Sept. 10, 1971.

PROSSER, CHARLES ALLEN, educator; b. New Albany, Ind., Sept. 20, 1871; s. Reese William and Sarah Emma P.; B.S., De Pauw, 1897, A.M., 1906, Ph.D., 1919; LL.B., U. of Louisville, 1898; grad. student Columbia, 1908-10, Ph.D., 1915; hon. A.M. Hanover Coll., 1903; LL.D., Alfred U., 1919; D.Sc., Stout Inst., Menomonie, Wis., 1925; m. Zerelda A. Huckeby, Dec. 30, 1896; 1 son, William L. Began as instr. elementary schs., instr. science and English lit., New Albany High Sch.; supt. New Albany, 1900-08; supt. Children's Aid Soc., New York, 1909-10; asst. commr. edn. for Mass., 1910-12; dir. William Hood Dunwoody Indusl. Inst., (Minneapolis) 1915-45; dir., Fed. Bd. for Vocational Edn., 1917-19; sec., Nat. Soc. for Vocational Edn., 1923; editor, Century Co. since 1923; mem. consultant editorial bd., The Nation's Schools; trustee, James J. Hill Technical Library, St. Paul since 1925. Mem., Minn. Crime Comm., 1926; chmn., com. on Adult Edn., Am. Vocational Assn., 1927; mem., legislative com. Am. Vocational Assn., 1928; dir., survey of employment possibilities for the handicapped, 1929; dir., Survey of Vocational Edn., Philippine Islands, 1930, Hawaiian Islands, 1931; chmn. nat. commn. on Tech. Employment, 1931; mem. nat. com. on occupations, Am. Council on Edn., 1933; chmn. Minneapolis Local N.R.A. compliance bd., 1933-34; mem., nat. com. on apprenticeship regulations for N.R.A. codes, 1934; chmn., com. on employer-employee relations, Minneapolis Civic & Commerce Assn., 1934; mem., Lumber Code Authority, 1934; chmn. Minneapolis Employer-Employee Bd., 1935; mem. bd. dirs. Inst. for Research; mem. adv. com., Mooseheart Lab. of Child Research; mem. adv. council, Yenching U., nat. adv. com. on Revision of Am. Vocational Assn. constitution, 1937-39; chmn. Minn. Apprenticeship Council, 1939-40; Nat. Youth Adminstrn. cons. (Washington, D.C.), 1940; mem. adv. council for Minn., Northern Wis., N.D., S.D., and Iowa on Training Within Industry, 1940; arbitrator, Minn. War Emergency Arbitration Panel, 1941; mem. State adv. com. for Vocational Training of War Prod. Workers, 1941; mem. com. on human resources and skills, 1942; mem. Private Comml. Trade Sch. Com. for Minn., 1942; chmn. com. on rehabilitation through vocational edn. for the Minn. Range, 1942; council mem.-at-large, Boy Scouts of Am.; mem. adv. com. for Minn. War Manpower Commn. (Minneapolis) since 1943; spec. cons. Kamehameha Schs., Honolulu, 1943-44; mem. on panel for training within industry sect. of War Prodn. Bd., 1944; spl. cons., Edn. Div., Office Coordinator of Inter-Am. Affairs (Washington, D.C.), 1944; arbitrator, Am. Arbitration Assn., 1944-45. Author: New Harmony Movement, 1903; The Teacher and Old Age, 1913; Vocational Education in a Democracy, 1925; Have We Kept the Faith, 1929; Adult Education—The Evening Industrial School, 1929; Vocational Education and Changing Conditions, U.S. Bulletin, 1934; Life Adjustment Series, 1936-37; Secondary Education and Life (Inglis Lecture), 1939. Editor: Shop Training Manual, 1941 (Nat. Youth Adminstrn), Machine Shop Training 1943, Welding Training Units, 1942; Vocational Education Series for Am. Tech. Soc., 1944. Home: 2824 Irving Av. S., Minneapolis MN‡

PROUT, HENRY GOSLEE, engineer; b. Fairfax Co., Va.; s. William and Amanda (Goslee) P.; served in Army of the Potomac, 1863-5; C.E., University of Mich., 1871; (hon. A.M., Yale, 1902; LL.D, University of Mich., 1911); m. Gabriella Perin, Dec. 19, 1877. Maj. of engrs., and later col. of gen. staff, army of the Khedive of Egypt, 1873-8; comd. expdn. in the Soudan and was gov. of the Provinces of the Equator; editor Railroad Gazette, 16 yrs.; v.-p. and gen. mgr. Union Switch & Signal Co., 1903-14; retired. Mem. Am. Soc. C.E., Am. Geog. Soc. Clubs: Century, Railroad (New York); University (Pittsburgh); Yountakah (Nutley). Home: Nutley NJ‡

PROUTY, WINSTON LEWIS, U.S. senator; b. Newport, Vt., Sept. 1, 1906; student Bordentown Mil. Acad., also Lafayette Coll., Easton, Pa.; m. Frances C. Hearle (dec. 1960); m. 2d, Jennette Herbert Hall, 1962. President of Prouty & Miller; member of the board of dirs. Chittenden Trust Co., Asso. Industries of Vt. Mayor, Newport, 1938-41; mem. Vt. Ho. of Reps., 1941, 45, 47, speaker, 1947; candidate lt. gov., 1948; chmn. Vt. Water Conservation Bd., 1948-50; mem. 82d to 85th congresses, Vt. rep.-at-large, mem. Vets. Affairs Com., 1951-56, Fgn. Affairs Com., 1953; mem. U.S. Senate, from Vt., 1959-71, mem. Com. on Small Bus., Spl. Com. on Unemployment Problems; Com. on Commerce, labor and public welfare committee; member of the U.S. commn UNESCO, 1959. Republican. Conglist. Home: Newport VT and Washington DC. Died Sept. 10, 1971; buried Newport VT

PROVENCE, HERBERT WINSTON, clergyman, educator; b. Greenville, S.C., Nov. 2, 1873; s. Rev. Samuel Moore and Indie Mayo (Watkins) P.; M.A., Richmond (Va.) Coll., 1894; Th.M., Southern Bapt. Theol. Sem., Louisville, Ky., 1897, Th.D., 1898; m. Mary Hall, of Richmond, Va., Nov. 16, 1898; children—Herbert Hall, Effie Ruth. Ordained Bapt. ministry, 1893; pastor Montgomery, Ala., 1898-1902, Ensley, Birmingham, Ala., 1902-04; missionary, Shanghai, China, 1904-12; pastor Clinton, Miss., 1912-13; prof. Bible and philosophy, Miss. Coll., 1913-14; prof. English, Furman U., 1914-20, prof. Christianity, 1920-31; pres. Greenville Woman's Coll., 1931-33; now treas. Provence-Jarrard Company, printers. Mem. editorial staff Sunday School Bd., Southern Bapt. Conv., 1928-30. A founder Ala. Bapt. Ministers' Benefit Soc. Democrat. Home: Greenville SC‡

PROWSE, ROBERT JOHN, bridge engr.; b. Concord, N.H., Sept. 4, 1906; s. John Thomas and Ruth (Potter) P.; B.S.C.E., Northeastern U., 1928; postgrad. Carnegie Inst. Tech., 1942; m. Mildred Katherine Veino, June 1, 1934; children—John James, Joan Mary (Mrs. Irving Richard Gourley), Kathryn (Mrs. Hugh Goodwin Butterfield). Draftsman, Hamilton (Ont., Can.) Bridge Co. Ltd., 1929-34; designer N.H. Hwy. Dept., Concord, 1934-41; designer Koppers Co., Pitts., 1942-43; chief bridge designer N.H. dept. of pub. works and hwys., Concord, 1947-56, asst. bridge engr., 1957-68, bridge engr., 1968-69; cons. engr. David B. Steinman, Concord, 1956-57. Spl. lectr. Northeastern U. grad. sch., Boston, 1956-57; instr. New Eng. Coll., Henniker, N.H., 1957-59. Served to lt. with USNR, 1943-46. Recipient Bridge Design Award, Lincoln Arc Welding Found., 1958, 61, 64. Registered profl. engr., N.H. Fellow Am. Soc. C.E.; mem. Am. Legion (comdr. 1948). Home: Concord NH Died Dec. 20, 1969.

PRUDDEN, RUSSELL FIELD, investment adviser; b. Lockport, N.Y., Oct. 4, 1893; s. Walter Lewis and Estelle (Field) P.; B.S., Wharton Sch. Finance, U. Pa., 1916. Bond investment man Nat. City Co., Phila., 1916-19; credit dept. Nat. Bank Commerce, 1919-20, Chem. Bank, N.Y.C., 1920-23; bank examiner N.Y. State, 1923-25; asso. Tucker Anthony & Co., N.Y.C., Boston, 1925-30; sr. bank examiner charge investment adv. sect. N.Y. State Banking Dept., 1930-33; investment adviser, 1933-64; pub., editor weekly Prudden's Digest of Investment and Banking Opinions, 1938-64. Served as ensign U.S. N.R.F., 1917-19. Mem. Analysts Soc., Soc. Colonial Wars, Newcomen, St. Nicholas Soc. Clubs: Watch Hill (R.I.) Yacht; The Creek (Locust Valley, N.Y.). Author: The Bank Credit Investigator, 1922. Home: New York City NY Died Aug. 1969.

PRUNTY, MERLE CHARLES, educator; b. Wellington, Kan., Jan. 31, 1888; s. Alonzo Leonard and Vinettie (Mounce) P.; A.B., Kan. State U., 1909; M.A., U. of Chicago, 1927; student Columbia, 1920; Colo. State Teachers' Coll., 1933; LL.D., Tulsa U., 1928; Ph.D., Colorado State Coll. of Education, 1934; m. Emma Mae Holliday, Aug. 25, 1910 (dec.); 1 son, Merle Charles; m. 2d, Grace Echo Moulton, June 25, 1921; children—Lon Moulton, Mary Lee, Elouise, Roma Josephine, Virginia Grace. Prin. high schs., Kan. and Mo., 1909-18; prin. Tulsa (Okla.) Central High School, 1918-29; supt. Tulsa public schools, 1929-34; dir. personnel and head of extra-class division Stephens Coll., Columbia, Mo., since 1934. Summer lecturer various universities and colleges and frequent contbr. to state and nat. edn. assn. programs, Hon. mem. North Central Assn. Secondary Schs., Colls. and Univs. (pres. 1929-30); pres. Nat. Assn. Secondary School Principals, 1922; pres. Nat. Platoon Orgn., 1934-35; mem. N.E.A. (legislative and resolutions coms. 1930-38), Phi Delta Kappa, Sigma Nu. Republican. Episcopalian. Rotarian. Mem. advisor bd. Sch. Acitivities Mag. Contbr. numerous ednl. articles to professional mags. Home: Columbia MO Died Feb. 9, 1972.

PRUTTON, CARL FREDERICK, chem. engr.; b. Cleve., July 30, 1898; s. Daniel J. and Julia (Seelbach) P.; B.S., Case Inst. Tech., 1920, M.S., 1923, D.Eng. (hon.), 1955; Ph.D., from Western Res. U., 1928, D.Sc., 1963; D.Eng. (hon.), Clarkson Coll. Tech., 1960, Manhattan Coll., 1960, Marietta Coll., 1962; m. to Marie A. Saunders, June 2, 1919; children—Carl F., Dorothy E. (Mrs. Jose Castillo), Carolyn A. (Mrs. J.R. Small), Mary L. (Mrs. R.L. Sutherland), John R., Helen M. (Mrs. G.L. Conrad). Instr. Case Inst. Tech., 1920-26, asst. prof., 1926-28, asso. prof., 1928-35, prof., 1935-36, head dept. chemistry and chem. engring., 1936-48; v.p. Mathieson Chem. Corp., 1948-53; v.p. and tech. director Food Machinery and Chemical Corporation, N.Y.C., 1954-56, executive vice pres., 1956-60, dir., 1960-70; mem. bd. dirs. Commercial Solvents Corp. Head process development br. Rubber Dir.'s Office, U.S. Government, 1942-44. Trustee

Clarkson Institute of Technology, 1960-70. Received Nat. Assn. Mfrs. Modern Pioneer Award, 1938, Perkin Medal, 1961. Member of the American Institute of Chemical Engrs., Am. Chem. Soc., Soc. Automotive Engrs., Am. Petroleum Inst., Petroleum Inst. Britain, Sigma Xi, Tau Beta Pi. Author: Physical Chemistry (with Dr. S. H. Maron), 1944. Author articles tech. jours. Issued about 100 patents chem. field. Home: Oklawaha FL Died July 1970.

PRUYN H. SEWALL, banker; b. Glens Falls, N.Y., July 21, 1904; s. Howard H. and Elizabeth (Dempster) P.; student Glens Falls Acad., 1923; B.A., Williams Coll.,. 1927; M.B.A., Harvard, 1929; m. Carolyn Decker, June 2, 1930; children—Carolyn (Mrs. Kirk A. Hudson), Hendrik H., Sarah E. (Mrs. Richard M. Somers, Jr.), Martha S. (Mrs. Alan D. Judson). With Chem. Bank & Trust Co., N.Y.C., 1930-33; with State Bank of Albany, from 1933, asst. v.p., 1936-38, v.p., 1938-64, sr. v.p., 1964-68; dir. Central Savs. & Loan Assn., Albany. Past bd. dirs. Albany Boys Club. Mem. C. of C., N.Y. State Bankers Assn., Am. Inst. Banking, Phi Delta Theta. Clubs: William (N.Y.C.); Lake Placid (conf. adv. com.); Schuyler Meadows Country; Fort Orange. Home: Loudonville NY Died Mar. 14, 1968; buried Pineview Cemetery, Glens Falls NY

PRYOR, RALPH H(UNTINGTON), coll prof.; born Montrose, Minn., Feb. 18, 1898; s. Leonard Henry and Carolyn (McLeod) P.; B.S., U. of Minn., 1922; A.M., U. of So. Calif., 1931, Ed.D., 1939; m. Alice Marjorie Dailey, June 8, 1925; children—Marycarol Bazacos, Virginia Lovett, Robert. Supt. of schs. Chokio, Minn., 1923-25, Plainview, Minn., 1925-30; head dept. commerce and prin. Citrus Evening High Sch. and Jr. Coll., Azusa, Calif., 1930-42; head dept. of economics and commerce, Ariz. State Coll., Flagstaff, 1942-47; head dept. economics and bus. administrn. Willamette U., Salem, Ore., 1947-48; prof. bus. adminstrn. Chico (Calif.) State Coll., from 1948; visiting professor Whittier Collge, summer 1949, New Mexico Highlands U., summer 1950, 51. President Teachers Assn., Flagstaff, Ariz.; chmn. curriculum com., dir. student activities, Ariz. State Coll.; pres. Civitan Service Club, Azusa, California, 1940; chmn. Am. Red Cross, Flagstaff, Ariz. Served in U.S. Army, World War I. Mem. Am. Assn. Univ. Profs., United Business Edn. Assn., Calif. Bus. Educators Assn., Phi Delta Kappa, Pi Omega Pi, Delta Epsilon. Republican. Methodist. Mason (32 deg.), O.E.S. Club: Lions. Home: Chico CA Died Sept. 23, 1969.

PUCHNER, IRVING A., lawyer; b. Wausau, Wis., Sept. 13, 1899; s. Alfred W. and Arminda (Panabaker) P.; student, Lawrence Coll., 1916, U. of Chgo. 1926-28; A.B., U. Wis., 1921, LL.B., 1930; m. Helen H. Sisson, June 12, 1922; children—Judith Ann, Alfred Irving. Reporter Wis. State Jour., Madison, 1924; salesman Hibbard-Spencer Bartlett & Co., Chicago, 1923-26; admitted to Wis. bar, 1930; practiced law, Milw., 1930-68; gen. counsel Wis. Fund, Inc., Milw. Painting and Decorating Contractors Assn.; village attorney Greendale, Wis. Served as ensign, USNRF, 1918-19. Mem. Am. Legion (past county comdr.), Am., Wis., Milw. bar assns., Order of Coif. Clubs: Milw. Athletic, Wis. Amateur Field Trial (past pres.). Author several law review articles. Home: Fox Point Died Aug. 6, 1968.

PUCKETT, CHARLES ALEXANDER, educator; b. Gainesville, Texas, Oct. 24, 1889; s. John William and Stella Viola (Meachum) P.; A.B., U. of Tex., 1911; M.A., Harvard, 1916; m. Fidelia Miller, Oct. 6, 1920. Prin., Huntsville and Waco, Tex., 1911-20; supt. pub. schs., Gainesville, 1920-23, Mexia, Texas, 1923-26; dean arts and scis. Tex. Western Coll., 1927-34, from 1935, acting pres., 1934-35. Served as capt., inf. U.S. Army, 1917-19. Mem. Tex. State Teachers Assn., Kappa Delta Pi, Phi Delta Kappa. Home: El Paso TX Died Feb. 1, 1970.

PUCKETT, WILLIAM OLIN, educator; b. Cornelius, N.C., May 3, 1906; s. William Lawrence and Mary (Washam) P.; A.B.,, Davidson Coll., 1927; M.A., U. N.C., 1931; Ph.D., Princeton, 1934; m. Virginia Lewis House, June 18, 1942; children—Virginia Northington, John Lawrence, James Butler. Asst. prof. biology Southwestern Coll., Memphis, 1935; instr. biology Princeton, 1935-38, asst. prof., 1939-46; research investigator OSRD, 1943-45; prof. biology Davidson Coll., from 1946, chmn. pre-med. studies, chmn. biology dept., 1946-70. Recipient Thomas Jefferson award. Mem. N.C. Acad. Sci. (pres. 1954), Am. Soc. Zoologists, Am. Assn. Anatomists, Sigma Xi, Gamma Sigma Epsilon, Omicron Delta Kappa, Sigma Chi. Presbyn. (ruling elder 1958-72). Mason. Home: Davidson NC Died June 3, 1972; buried Mimosa Cemetery, Davidson NC

PUGH, GRIFFITH THOMPSON, college pres.; b. Newberry Co., S.C., Apr. 3, 1874; s. William Pearson and Caroline Thompson (Moore) P.; B.A., Wofford Coll., Spartanburg, S.C., 1897, M.A., 1901; studied Vanderbilt U., 1902-5, Ph.D., 1906; m. Lila Wayne Epps, of Williamsburg Co., S.C., Sept. 14, 1905. Prin. and supt. graded high schs., S.C., 1897-1902; teaching fellow, Vanderbilt U., 1903-5; prof. mathematics and astronomy, 1905-16, pres. since Oct. 26, 1916, Columbia (S.C.) Coll. Mem. State Teachers' Assn., S.C. Democrat. Mem. M.E. Ch., S. Wrote: (brochure) The Pleistocene Deposits of South Carolina. Address: Columbia College, Columbia SC‡

PUGH, WILLIAM LEONARD, prof. English; b. Lenox, Ia., Oct. 1, 1874; s. John and Ruth M. (Daniels) P.; grad. Corning (Ia.) Acad., 1893; A.B., Parsons Coll., Fairfield, Ia., 1897, A.M., 1901, Litt.D., 1930; A.M., Northwestern U., 1908; Ph.D., Harvard, 1911; m. Nattie Esther Armstrong, June 9, 1902 (died 1933); 1 daughter, Helen Henrietta (Mrs. Harvey Warnock Daniell), married 2d, Dr. Ruth J. Frank, December 23, 1935. Instructor in Greek, Latin and German, Corning Acad., 1899-1901; prin. high sch., Corydon, Ia., 1902-03, supt. schs., 1903-07; with Wofford Coll. since 1911, prof. English, 1912-47, emeritus since 1947, mem. extension and summer sch. faculties, 1922-31, summer sch. Mich. State Normal Coll., 1932, Asheville Normal and Teachers Coll., 1933. Member Modern Lang. Assn. America, Mediaeval Acad. Am., Pi Gamma Mu, Phi Kappa Phi, Phi Beta Kappa. Presbyterian. Author: Studies in the Vocabulary of the Middle English Romance of Sir Perceval of Galles, 1908; The Strong Verb in Chaucer, 1911. Home: 1052 Otis Blvd., Spartanburg SC‡

PULIDO, AUGUSTO F., charge d'affaires Venezuela to U.S. since 1899; b. Caracas, Venezuela, S.A., Sept. 10, 1873; s. Dr. Lucio P., diplomatist and statesman; ed. Caracas, Venezuela, and Paris, France; grad. Caracas, Ph.B.; unmarried. Entered diplomatic career, 1890, as attache to Court of St. James; transferred to Paris, France, 1891; attache to Venezuelan legation in Washington, 1895; charge d'affaires in Washington, 1899; previously was chief clerk in the House of Deputies, Venezuela, 1899; Liberal in politics. Address: 2007 O St., Washington DC‡

PULLEN, ELISABETH, author; b. at Portland, Me.; d. Charles and Anna T. (Daveis) Jones; received thorough edn. in pianoforte, singing and theory of music; m. Stanley T. Pullen, of Portland, Me., Sept. 8, 1894. Reviewer and mus. critic Portland Daily Press several yrs; editorial contbr. to Literary World, Boston. Speaking from childhood both Italian and English, has chosen in fiction to illustrate especially the manners and customs of Calabria and Sicily. Author: (over signature of E. Cavazza) Don Finimondone (collection short stories); The Man from Aidone; Rocco and Sidora; (under own name) Mr. Whitman, 1902. Contbr. to mags. of short stories, critiques, verses and transls. from Italian and French. Since marriage signs work, Elisabeth Pullen." Mem. Soc. Colonial Dames of America. Residence: Portland ME‡

PULLEY, FREDERICK, artist; b. Union City, Ind., Aug. 15, 1875; s. Jacob and Matilda (Wiley) P.; student Corcoran Sch. of Art (Washington), John Herron Art Sch. (Indianapolis), 1903-05; extension student Ind. U., 1918-22, Purdue U., 1923-35; m. Cora May Mansfield, Aug. 6, 1898; children—Pearl May (wife of Rev. Eugene Bushong), Amber Matilda (Mrs. Wayne Winchester). Editor and pub. Union City (Ind.) News, 1897-99; free lance commercial artist, 1910-16; draftsman U.S. Topographical Bur., 1906-09; instr. Indianapolis pub. schs. since 1917; head of dept. of graphic arts, Arsenal Tech. Schs., 1933-41. Represented at Phila. Sesqui-Centennial, 1926; Century of Progress Expn., 1933; Nat. Gallery of Art, John Herron Art Mus.; U. of Pittsburgh (15 original drawings); Indiana U.; Purdue U.; Ball Teachers Coll.; Culver Mil. Acad.; Earlham Coll.; Manchester Coll., Ia. State U. Awarded 1st prize for etchings Hoosier Salon, 1925, 30, 32 and Summer Salon, 1936; 1st hon. mention John Herron Art Mus., 1934; 1st prize for etchings Ind. State Fair, 1917-31, Ayres Purchase prize, Ind. Artists Club, 1943; New Orleans Art League War Bond Prize, 1943, Elliott Memorial prize, Hoosier Salon, 1944, Indiana Fed. Art Clubs prize, Hoosier Salon, 1945, Indiana U. Purchase Prize, Indiana Artists Club, 1950. Mem. Chicago Soc. of Etchers, Ind. Soc. of Print Makers, New Orleans Art League, Brown County Art Gallery Assn., Hoosier Salon Patrons Assn., Ind. Hist. Soc. Mem. Christian Ch. Clubs: Salmagundi (New York); Portfolio (Indianapolis); Indiana Artists. Illustrator of books. Contbr. to Indianapolis Sunday Star, 1924-47; author-illustrator of syndicated newspaper feature, Our America." Home: E. 75th St. and Sargent Rd., Indianapolis IN‡

PULLMAN, JOHN, lawyer; b. Bklyn., Dec. 16, 1912; s. James and Mable (Brazier) P.; B.A., Wesleyan U., Middletown, Conn., 1934; LL.B., St. Lawrence U., 1938; m. Janet Esterbrook, Sept. 7, 1940; children—Susan, Nancy, Wesley, Cynthia. Admitted to N.Y. bar, 1938, since practiced privately in N.Y.C.; asso. police justice, Garden City, L.I., from 1962; mem. faculty Bklyn. Law Sch., 1938-41, and from 1957, St. Lawrence U., 1938-41. Trustee Wesleyan U., from 1963, gen. chmn. alumni fund, 1960-62; mem. bd., sec. Alpha Delta Phi Found. Mem. N.Y. N.G., 1937-45. Mem. N.Y. County Bar Assn., Alpha Delta Phi. Mem. Community Ch. Club: Faculty (Wesleyan U.). Home: Garden City LI NY Died June 26, 1971.

PULLY, BERNARD SHAW, actor; b. Newark, May 14, 1910; s. Joseph and Sarah Lerman; student pub. schs., N.Y.C.; m. Hope Stone Feb. 1, 1947; 1 son, Steven Alan. Appeared in numerous motion pictures, 1944-72, including Eve of St. Mark, 1944, Pin Up Girl, 1944, Wing and a Prayer, 1944, Something for the Boys, 1944, Greenwich Village, 1944, Tree Grows in Brooklyn, 1945, Don Juan Quilligan, 1945, Do You Love Me, 1946, Nob Hill, 1945, Lady in Cement, 1966, Taxi, 1953, Myra Breckinridge, 1970, Bell Boy, 1960, Hole in the Head, 1959, Guys and Dolls, 1955, The Love God, 1968; mem. original cast Guys & Dolls, N.Y.C., 1950; appeared in summer stock, radio and television shows, night clubs. Appeared for Bonds for Israel in hosps. and charities. Recipient Antoinette Perry award N.Y. Drama Critics Circle, 1957, Donaldson award, 1952. Mem. Screen Actors Guild, Am. Guild Variety Artists, Los Angeles CA Died Jan. 6, 1972.

PULTZ, LEON M(ERLE), horticulturist; born Lake Preston, S.D., July 6, 1904; s. Andrew Miller and Caroline (Hintz) P.; B.S., S.D. State Coll., 1925, M.S., 1927; Ph.D., U. of Chicago, 1929; m. Mary Ora Halfhill, June 4, 1926; children—Patricia Ann (Mrs. John H. Bolinger, Jr.), Mary Caroline (Mrs. Charles A. Magee). Agricultural research on sugar beets Department of Agriculture, Salt Lake City, 1929-36, agrl. research on weed control, Ames, Ia., 1938-40, prin. horticulturist Beltsville, Md., 1949-57, chief oilseeds and indsl. corps br., 1957-70; asst. prof. botany U. of Ariz., 1936-38, head dept. botany and range ecology, 1940-47, head dept. horticulture, 1947-49. Fellow A.A.A.S., mem. Am. Soc. Agronomy, Botanical Soc. of Washington, Sigma Xi, Phi Kappa Phi. Mason. Home: Hyattsville MD Died Feb. 7, 1970; buried San Diego CA

PURCELL, FRANCIS ANDREW, clergyman; b. Chicago, Ill., Mar. 17, 1872; s. James and Johanna (Brazil) P.; grad. St. Benedict's Coll., Atchison, Kan., 1893; theol. studies at St. Mary's Sem., Baltimore, 1893-98; and U. of Minerva, Rome, 1903-05; ordained R.C. priest, 1898; asst. pastor St. Anne's Ch., Chicago, 1898-1903; apptd. rector Cathedral Coll. of the Sacred Heart, now Quigley Preparatory Seminary, 1905; now pastor St. Mel's Ch., Chicago. One of examiners of clergy of Archdiocese of Chicago. Address: 22 N. Kildare Av., Chicago IL*‡

PURDON, ALEXANDER, shipping co. exec.; M.S. in Edn., Boston U.; student Harvard, Yale; m. Margaret Baird, June 22, 1934; children—Gail B., Joan R. With Com. Am. Steamship Lines, until 1959, exec. dir., 1954-59; pres., chief exec. officer U.S. Lines Co., N.Y.C. Bd. dirs. Am. Mcht. Marine Inst., Nat. Fgn. Trade Council. Mem. Soc. Naval Architects and Marine Engrs. (mem. council 1961-70, exec. com.), U.S. C. of C., Transp. Assn. Am. (dir.), Nat. Def. Transp. Assn. Clubs: Congressional Country, University (Washington); Maplewood (N.J.) Country; India House, Downtown Athletic (N.Y.C.). Home: Berkeley Heights NJ Died Jan. 4, 1970; buried Fairview Cemetery, Westfield NJ

PURDY, GEORGE FLINT, librarian; b. Mason City, Ia., Sept. 2, 1905; s. George Hartley and Hattie (Flint) P.; A.B., Ia. State Tchrs. Coll., 1925; B.L.S., Columbia, 1933; Ph.D., U. Chgo., 1936; m. Anna Breidinger, Aug. 3, 1927; children—Robert Edward, Anne Marie. Tchr., Kelley, Ia., 1925-27, Calumet, Ia., 1927-32; librarian Wayne State U., 1936-70, lectr. librarianship, 1936-49; lectr. librarianship U. Ill., summers 1943, 45, 47, 57. Initiator, contbr. Detroit Met. Project of U.S. Office of Edn. Mem. Mich. Bd. Libraries, 1961-69. Mem. A.L.A. (pres. library edn. div. 1949-50, mem. council 1941-43, 46-50, 67-69), Assn. Coll. and Research Libraries, Mich. Library Assn. (pres. 1962-63, Librarian of Yr. 1968). Home: Detroit MI Died Sept. 24, 1969; buried Detroit MI

PURDY, KEN WILLIAM, editor, writer; b. Chgo., Apr. 28, 1913; s. William and Mary H. (Buggy) P.; student U. Wis., 1931-35; m. Lucille von Urff, Jan. 6, 1946; children—Geoffrey, Tabitha. Reporter Athol (Mass.) Daily News, 1934; editor The Free Press, Oshkosh, Wis., 1935; asso. editor Radio Guide, Chgo., 1936-37, Click, Phila., 1938; mng. editor Radio Digest, 1939; asso. editor Look, 1939-41; editor Victory, 1941-45; cons. Crowell-Collier, 1945; editor Parade, 1946-49, True, 1949-54, Argosy, 1954-55; editorial chmn. Ziff-Davis Pub. Co., 1955-56; contbg. editor HMH Publishing Co., from 1956; contributor to numerous U.S. and foreign magazines. Member of Delta Kappa Epsilon. Clubs: Sports Car Am., Antique Automobile Am.; Bugatti Owners, Vintage Sports Car (Eng.); Century (N.Y.C.). Author: Kings of the Road, 1952; Bright Wheels Rolling (with James Melton), 1954; The Wonderful World of the Automobile, 1960; (with Stirling Moss) All But My Life, 1963; (with Horst Baumann) The New Matadors, 1965; (with Thomas Burnside) Motorcars of the Golden Age, 1966; The Ken Purdy Book of Automobiles, 1972. Home: Wilton CT Died June 7, 1972.

PURDY, RICHARD TOWNSEND, automotive exec.; b. Caro, Mich., Oct. 11, 1906; s. Fred Joseph and Carrie (Townsend) P.; A.B., U. Mich., 1929; m. Daisy

Charron, Sept. 1, 1934; children—Jill Ann, James Clark, Mary Jane, Richard Townsend. Security officer Detroit Trust Co., 1929-33; mgr. municipal buying dept. First of Mich. Corp., 1933-42; administrv. asst. Automotive Council for War Prodn., 1942-46; sales rep. Budd Co., 1946-50; Washington rep. Nash-Kelvinator Corp., 1950-53; pres. Am. Motors (Can.), Limited, 1955; vice president, treasurer American Motors Corporation, Detroit, 1956-67. Mem. Beta Theta Pi. Home: Phoenix AZ Died Nov. 11, 1972; buried Caro MI

PURIN, CHARLES MALTADOR, univ. prof.; b. Riga, Russia (now Latvia) Aug. 14, 1872; s. Martin and Ama Andrevna (Veetols) P.; grad. Nat. German-Am. Teachers' Sem., Milwaukee, 1898; A.B., U. of Wis., 1907, M.A., 1908, Ph.D., 1913; postgrad. studies, Univ. of Leipzig, Germany, 1914; m. Hedwig Hermione Reinsch, Dec. 25, 1899;children—Carl Ferdinand, Alexander Richard. Came to U.S., 1894, naturalized, 1899. Teacher pub. schs. in Chicago and Milwaukee, 1898-1903; head modern language dept., E. Division High Sch., Milwaukee, 1907-10; successively instr., asst. prof., asso. prof. of German, U. of Wis., 1910-15; head Coll. Dept., Milwaukee State Normal Sch. (now Milwaukee State Teachers Coll.), 1915-23; on leave as asso. prof. of German, U. of Tex., 1916-17; lecturer in German, Hunter Coll., New York, 1923-27; mem. Spl. Investigating Com. of Three of Modern Fgn. Lang. Study sponsored by Am. Council on Edn. (Carnegie Foundation), New York, 1924-27; dir. U. of Wis. Extension Div., Milwaukee Center, and prof. of German, 1927-42; guest prof., summers, Western Reserve U., Columbia Teachers' Coll., Northwestern U., U. of Wis. Capt. Castle Heights Mil. Acad., Lebanon, Tenn., 1942-50. Associate editor Monatshefte, 1928-41. Member N.E.A., Horace Mann League, National Federation Modern Foreign Language Teachers of the Central West and South (past pres.), Nat. Fedn. Modern Lang. Teachers Assns. (pres. 1949-52), Am. Assn. Teachers of Ger. (pres. 1948; sec. nat. soc.; past pres. Wis. chap.). Author: Latvian Lyrics, 1889; The Training of Modern Foreign Language Teachers in the U.S., 1929; A Standard German Vocabularly, 1931; (with Kind and Reinsch) Conversational Approach to German, 1947; (with Keil) Lernund Lesenbuch. Editor of various German texts. Address: 3059 N. Maryland Av., Milwaukee 77‡

PURKISS, ALBERT C., stockbroker; b. Betteravia, Cal., Oct. 16, 1907; s. Myrton M. and Huldah A. (Glines) P.; B.A., Stanford, 1929; m. Helen D. Fitch, Dec. 15, 1931; children—Durinda (Mrs. Leslie G. Brownlee), Marily (Mrs. John M. Wilson), Richard A. So. Cal. mgr. Walston & Co., Inc., N.Y.C., 1946-50, Eastern Div. Mgr., 1950-55, sr. v.p., dir., 1955-64, vice chmn. bd., 1964-67. Clubs: Bond, Stock Exchange Luncheon (N.Y.C.); Wee Burn Country (Darien, Conn.); Harbor View (N.Y.). Home: Greenwich CT Died June 9, 1967.

PURNELL, WILLIAM C(HILDS), lawyer; b. Elkton, Md., Sept. 14, 1903; s. William Greenbury and Matilda (Childs) P.; B.S., St. John's Coll., Annapolis, Md., 1923; LL.B., Harvard, 1927; m. Charlotte M. Thilo, Feb. 4, 1928; children—George W.T., Charlotte E. Admitted to Md. bar, 1926, since practiced in Baltimore; asst. U.S. atty., Md., 1928-30; asst. gen. atty. Western Md. Ry. Co., 1931-34, gen. atty., 1934-48, gen. counsel, 1948, v.p., gen. counsel, 1948-71, also dir.; director Union Trust Company of Maryland. Chairman Baltimore chapter of A.R.C., 1962-65, mem. nat. bd. govs., 1965-68. Mem. bd. election supervisors, Balt., 1938-39, bd. zoning appeals, 1939-41, Civil Service Commn., 1947-66; chmn. Balt. City Hosps. Commn., 1966-68. Bd. visitors and govs. St. John's Coll., Annapolis, 1947-59; dir. S. Balt. Gen. Hosp. Commd. capt., U.S. Army, 1941; served as maj., lt. col. and col. 175th Inf. Regt., 29th Inf. Div., E.T.O., 1944-46; brig. gen., 29th Inf. Div., Md. N.G., 1947-57, major general, 1957-62. Member of American Bar Assn., Maryland, Baltimore (v.p. 1950) bar assns., Gamma Eta Gamma, Phi Sigma Kappa. Republican. Episcopalian. Clubs: Merchants (pres. 1959-62), University (pres. 1960-65), Green Spring Valley Hunt, Center, Maryland. Home: Towson MD Died Jan. 1971.

PUSEY, EDWIN DAVIS, educator; b. Princess Anne, Md., Jan. 6, 1870; s. Edwin and Katharine Ellen (Davis) P.; A.B., St. John's (Md.) Coll., 1889, LL.D., 1919; A.M., Columbia, 1924; m. Anita Mary Southgate, Jan. 31, 1894 (dec.); 1 dau., Frances Southgate (Mrs. Herbert Ruhrman); m. 2d, Bessie H. Payne, Aug. 26, 1926. Instr. Yates Inst., Lancaster, Pa., 1889-90; same, St. John's Coll., 1892-94, asst. prof. Latin, 1894-1902; prin. high sch., Roberdel, N.C., 1907-09; supt. schs., Laurinburg, N.C., 1909-12, Goldsboro, N.C., 1912-14, Durham, N.C., 1914-23; prof. edn., Winthrop Coll., Rock Hill, S.C., 1924-25; prof. edn., U. of Ga. 1925-44, dean Coll. of Edn. 1941-44; retired Jan. 1945. Captain infantry, U.S. Volunteers, 1898-99. Author: Per Pupil Costs in Georgia Schools, 1931. Editor: Proceedings of Assn. Colls. and Secondary Schs. of Southern States, 1922, 23; editor of High School Quarterly, 1933-36, School and College, 1936-37. Home: 387 Milledge Av., Athens GA‡

PUTHUFF, HANSON DUVALL, artist; b. Waverly, Mo., Aug. 21, 1875; s. Alonzo Augustus Duvall and Mary (Lee) P.; grad. Univ. Art Sch., Denver, Colo., 1893; m. May Percival Longest, Oct. 4, 1910; children—Duvall Joseph Percival, Lee Churchhill, Robert Hanson, Paul Meredith, Mathilda Latham. Recipient many prizes and honors since 1909. Commd. to paint 3 backgrounds in Theodore Roosevelt Memorial Hall, Am. Museum of Natural History, N.Y. City, 1937; backgrounds for five habitat groups, North Am. Hall, Los Angeles Museum, 1938. Mason, Modern Woodman. Home: 1361 Journey's End Dr., La Canada CA‡

PUZINAS, PAUL PETER, artist, educator; b. Riga, Latvia, Aug. 3 1907; s. Peter Paul and Anna (Rackovska) P.; M.A., Latvian State Art Acad., 1932; academican, Lithuania, 1938. Came to U.S., 1947, naturalized, 1953. Prof. arts Lithuanian State Art Acad., Kavnas, 1938-40; instr. Art League L.I., 1956, Jackson Heights Art Club, N.Y.C., 1959-—; art dir. Lithuanian Days mag., 1949-57; painting demonstrations TV, art centers U.S., 1950-60; established Paul Puzinas Art Sch., Little Neck, L.I., N.Y., 1961. Served with Lithuanian Underground Army, 1940-45. Recipient medal for best painting of yr. and outstanding achievement in art, Los Angeles, 1950; first award Sixth Internat. Madonna Art Festival, 1951; Grand Nat. award Am. Artists Profl. League, 1956; Emily Lowe award Allied Artists Am., 1957; gold medal honor Hudson Valley Art Association, 1959; Andrew Carnegie award, 1964. Member Allied Artists of America, Soc., Am. Artists Profl. League, Hudson Valley Art Assn., Art League L.I. Inc. Reconstructed Panevezys Cathedral, including paintings and murals, 1938. Home: New York City NY Deceased.

PYLE, HELEN MARY, librarian; b. Chester Springs, Pa., June 25, 1908; d. DeWitt Clinton and Sara (Sheneman) Pyle; B.S. in Secondary Edn. with honors, West Chester State Tchrs. Coll., 1931; B.S. in Library Sci., Drexel Inst. Tech., 1944. Tchr., librarian Marcus Hook (Pa.) Sch. Dist., Jr. High Sch., 1931-43; librarian Wyeth Inst. Applied Biochemistry, Phila., 1944-48; librarian Sun Oil Co., pub. relations dept., 1948-63, general office library, 1964-70. Mem. American Library Assn., Pa. Library Assn. (chmn. Phila. dist. 1948-50), Spl. Libraries Assn. (dir. 1952-55; pres. Phila. chpt. 1946-48), Chester County Hist. Soc. Author articles in field. Home: Devon PA Died Jan. 9, 1970.

PYRE, GEORGE JOHN, mfg. co. exec.; b. Chgo., Nov. 27, 1912; s. John George and Estelle (Gregory) P.; M. Ronelva Patricia Patterson, July 10, 1937; 1 dau., Johanna. With Ford Motor Co., 1928-30, U.S. Steel Co., 1930-33, John Sexton & Co., 1933-39, Gen. Motors Corp., 1942-44, Dormeyer Co., 1944-53; organizer, chmn. bd. Peer Cartage Co., Chgo., 1952-62; pres. Dormeyer-Webcor, Co., Chgo., 1962; vice pres., dir. Webcor, Inc., Chicago; executive v.p. Bon Voyage Travel Co., Chgo., from 1959. Bd. dirs. Chgo. Boys Club. Mem. Am.-Hellenic Assn. Advanced Edn. (exec. v.p.). Greek Orthodox (trustee). Moose, Elk, Home: Skokie IL Died May 7, 1967.

PYRTLE, E. RUTH, principal of public schools; b. at Charleston, West Virginia; d. Jame Allen and Elizabeth Sarah (Davis) P.; grad. high sch., Lexington, Neb., 1891; A.B., U. of Neb., 1904, A.M., 1907; studied Columbia and U. of Neb. Prin. pub. sch., Lincoln, Neb., since 1902 (leave of absence 1 yr., 1918-19, for Y.W.C.A. war work, at Des Moines, Ia.); mem. State Bd. Edn., Neb., 1923-29. Pres. N.E.A., 1929-30, also served as pres. dept. of elementary principals N.E.A., 1927-28, and chmn. com. on teachers' retirement allowances, 1925-29; mem. Neb. Parent Teachers' Assn. (state bd.), Am. Assn. Univ. Women, League of Women Voters, Neb. Women's Edn. Club, Neb. Writers' Guild, D.A.R., Pi Gamma Mu. Methodist. Author: Early Virginia Families, 1930; History of Lincoln, Neb., Public Schools (Vol 1, 1864-1907), 1933. Home: 1711 D St., Lincoln NE‡

PYUN, YUNG-TAI, Korean diplomat; b. Seoul, Korea, Dec. 15 1892; s. Jung-sang and Gang; student Union Coll., Pei Tung Chow, China, 1915; m. Chai Moon-gyung, Mar. 1, 1904 (dec. 1937); four daus., four sons; m. 2d, Lee Hyo-yim. Feb. 18, 1940; 1 son. Tchr. English. Choong-ang Middle Sch., Seoul, Korea, 1920-43; tchr. English. lit., U. Korea, 1945-48; presdl. envoy P.I., 1949; head Korean delegation ECAFE, Lahore, Pakistan, 1951; minister fgn. affairs, Korea, 1951-54, prime minister, 1954-55; head Korean delegation 7th, 8th, 9th sessions UN Gen. Assembly. Author: Tales from Korea, 1946; Songs from Korea, 1948; Korea my Country, 1954. Home: Seoul Korea Died Mar. 1969.

QUAIL, FRANK ADGATE, lawyer; b. nr. Canonsburg, Pa., June 18, 1865; s. William and Phoebe D. (Lipscomb) Q.; A.B., Washburn Coll., Topeka, Kan., 1887; LL.B., U. of Mich., 1889; LL.D., Washburn Coll. (Kan.), 1937; unmarried. Admitted to Ohio bar, 1889; asso. Henderson, Kline & Tolles, Cleveland, 1889-95; mem. firm Henderson, Quail, Schneider & Peirce. Mem. Bd. of Appeals, U.S. Selective Service, Northern Ohio Dist., 1917-18. Trustee of Case Sch. of Applied Science (pres. bd. since 1924), Washburn Coll., Cleveland Clinic Foundation; one of organizers and 1st trustees Cleveland Coll. Member of Cleveland C. of C. (past dir. and v.p.); mem. Cleveland Bar Association (pres. 1946), S.A.R. Presbyterian (president of board Calvary Church). Clubs: Union, University, Mid-Day, City (Cleveland).*‡

QUAIN, ERIC P., surgeon; b. Sorsjon, Dalecarlia, Sweden, Aug. 22, 1870; s. Per H. and Margaret (Ericson) Q.; M.D., U. of Minn., 1898; m. Fannie A. Dunn, 1903; children—Marion Margaret, Buell Halvor (dec.); m. 2d, Hilda Gustafson, 1940. Came to United States, 1888, became a naturalized citizen, 1895. Began practice at Bismarck, N.Dak., 1899; organized the Quain & Ramstad Clinic (20 members), 1910, and served as chief of staff until 1939; now retired except as surgical consultant; former coroner and health officer, Bismarck; served as lt. col. M.C., U.S. Army, with A.E.F., World War I; organized med. unit known as Base Hosp. No. 60, A.E.F.; now col. med., inactive. Fellow Am. Coll. Surgeons; mem. Founders Group, Am. Bd. of Surgery; mem. A.M.A., N.D. State Med. Assn. (ex-pres.), Western Surg. Assn., Soo Line Ry. Surgeons' Assn. (ex-pres.), Alpha Kappa Kappa, Pi Gamma Mu. Republican. Mason. Retired. Author numerous med. and surgical articles; travelogues from fgn. lands. Home: 2075 Raynor St., Salem OR‡

QUAINTANCE, ALTUS LACY, entomologist; b. New Sharon, Ia., Dec. 19, 1870; s. Greenberry Plumley and Sarah Jane Q.; B.S.A., Fla. Agrl. Coll. (U. of Fla.), 1893; M.S., Ala. Poly. Inst., 1894, Sc.D., 1915; m. Nellie M. Yocum, of Lake City, Fla., Dec. 12, 1895;children—Leeland Charles, Howard Wilbur. Entomologist with Ala. Poly. Inst., 1894, Fla. Agrl. Coll. and Expt. Sta., 1895-98, Ga. Agrl. Expt. Sta., 1899-1901; with Md. Agrl. Coll. and Expt. Sta, and state entomologist of Md., 1901-03; spl. agt. Bur. Entomology, U.S. Dept. Agr., 1903-—; entomologist in charge deciduous fruit insect investigations, 1905-—; asso. chief of bur. in charge research work, 1923-31. Fellow Entomol. Soc. America, A.A.A.S.; pres. Assn. Econ. Entomologists, 1904, Entom. Soc. Washington, 1912; sec. Md. State Hort. Soc., 1902-03; chmn. sect. entomology Assn. Agrl. Colls. and Expt. Stas., 1903. Has written numerous expt. sta. bulls. and contributed to publs. U.S. Dept. Agr.; joint author Coccidae Americanae. Home: Silver Spring MD‡

QUARLES, CHARLES BULLEN, lawyer; b. Kenosha, Wis., Apr. 7 1884; s. Charles and Emma (Thiers) Q.; A.B., U. Wis., 1907; m. Elisabeth McKay, Sept. 4, 1909; children—Mary (Mrs. Michael O'Hara), Elisabeth (Mrs. Robert Hagge). Admitted to Wis. bar, 1909; practiced in Milw.; mem. Quarles, Herriott & Clemons. Mem. Am. (past mem. ho. dels.) Wis., Milw. bar assns., Milw. Legal Aid Soc. (past pres.), Wis. Service Assn. (past pres.), Milw. Civic Alliance (past pres.). Mason, Home: Milwaukee WI Died June 27, 1968; buried Green Ridge Cemetery Kenosha WI

QUARLES, JAMES THOMAS, organist, music educator; b. St. Louis, Mo., Nov. 7, 1877; s. Dr. Ralph Augustus and Elizabeth Emily (Howard) Q.; grad. St. Louis High Sch., 1897; studied piano with Vieh, Galloway and Ehling; organ with Charles Galloway and later with Charles M. Widor, of Paris, France; harmony, counterpoint, fugue, composition, with Ernest R. Kroeger, of St. Louis; Mus.Doc., Denver (Colo.) College of Music, 1931. Mus.Doc., Chicago Musical College, 1938; m. Gertrude Dunning, July 29, 1903; 1 dau., Gertrude Elizabeth (Betty). Organist West Presbyn. Ch., St. Louis, 1897-1900; organist and choirmaster Lindell Av. M.E. Ch., 1900-13, Scottish Rite Cathedral, 1904-13; dean dept. arts, Lindenwood Coll., 1903-13; organist St. Louis Symphony Orchestra, 1907-13; dir. Moolah Chanters (Shrine), 1906-13; condr. St. Louis Choral Art Soc., 1908-10; organist Cornell U., 1913-16, asst. prof. music, 1916-23, acting head music dept., 1921-23; organist and choirmaster St. John's P.E. Ch., Ithaca, 1918-23; prof. music, Univ. of Missouri, 1923-48, professor emeritus since 1948; visiting professor music, University of New Mexico, 1948-49; organized, 1924, and dean Sch. of Fine Arts, 1924-35. Organist and choirmaster of Mo. M.E. Church. Recitals, St. Louis Expn., 1905, San Francisco Expn., 1915, and throughout U.S. Asso. of Am. Guild Organists; mem. Am. Musicological Society, Music Library Association, Music Teachers' National Association, (chmn. of com. on library 1928-43, pres. 1943-46), National Assn. of Schs. of Music (chmn. com. on library), Am. Assn. Univ. Profs., Assn. Music Executives in State Univ. (pres. 1932), Mo. Music Teachers Association (pres. 1912-13, 1925 and 1933), Phi Mu Alpha (supreme v.p. 1926-31, supreme pres. 1932-36, member nat. exec. com. 1936-42). Democrat. Episcopalian. Mason (32 deg., K.C.C.H., Shriner). Composer anthems, songs and organ pieces. Home: 300 Westmount Av., Columbia MO‡

QUARLES, LOUIS, lawyer; b. Kenosha, Wis., Jan. 15, 1883; s. Charles and Emma Walden (Thiers) Q.; A.B., U. Mich., 1905; LL.D., Lawrence Coll., 1952, Marquette U., 1961; m. Inez Boardman French, June 30, 1908 (dec. 1968); children—Louise Inez (Mrs. Will C. Huggins), Ruth French (dec.), Charles Samuel.

Admitted to Wis. bar, 1908; with Quarles, Spence & Quarles, 1908-10; now mem. Quarles, Herriott, Clemons, Teschner & Noelke; mem. Bd. Law Examiners, 1918-22; mem. exec., finance coms., Northwestern Mutual Life Ins. Co., 1929-61, ret.; sec., dir., mem. exec. com. Allen Bradley Co.; dir., mem. exec. com. Ozite Corp.; bd. dirs. Peter Cooper Corp., Oilgear Co., Kimberly-Clark Corp., Oilgear Co., C., M., St. P. & P. R.R., Miller Brewing Co. Pres. bd. Village of Fox Point, 1931-36, trustee, 1926-31; pres., dir. Mil. Community Devel. Corp., 1952-64; chmn. bd. trustees Milw.-Downer Coll., 1930-49; pres. Marquette U. Sch. Medicine Inc.; dir. Milw. Country-Day Sch. (hon.), Allen Bradley Found. Recipient Centennial Award, Northwestern U., 1951. Mem. Am. Bar Assn., Am. Patent Bar Assn., Milwaukee County Bar Assn. (past pres.), Patent Law Assn. Milwaukee (pres. 1934-35), Am. Patent Law Assn., Psi Upsilon, Phi Beta Kappa, Phi Delta Phi (hon.), Alpha Sigma Nu (hon.). Republican. Mason. Clubs: Milwaukee, University, City, Yacht (Milw.); Chemists (N.Y.). Home: Milwaukee WI Died Feb. 7, 1972.

QUASIMODO, SALVATORE, Italian poet; b. 1901; 2 children. Asst. editor Tempo, 1938-40, now dramatic critic; prof. Italian lit. Giuseppe Verdi Conservatory, Milan, Italy, from 1941; contbr. prin. Italian, fgn. reviews; works on classical Greek and Italian culture, alsp contemporary events. Recipient (Dylan Thomas), Etna-Taormina internat. prize, 1953; Nobel prize in lit., 1959. Laurea honoris causa, Oxford U., 1967. Author: (verse) Acque e terre, 1930; Oboe Sommerso, 1932; Odore Di Eucaliptus ed altri versi, 1933; Poesie, 1938; Giorno dopo giorno, 1946; La vita non e sogno, 1949; Il falso e Vero Verde, 1953; La terra impareggiabile (collection), 1958; Tutte le poesie, 1960; Il poets e il politico e altri saggi, 1960; Scritti sul Teatro, 1961; Dare e avere, 1966. Translations of Greek lyric and dramatic poets, Shakespeare, Moliere, Neruda, Eluard, Arghedi, Milan Italy Died June 14, 1968; buried Famedio, Milan Italy

QUAYLE, HENRY JOSEPH, entomologist; b. Isle of Man, Eng., Apr. 29, 1876; s. John and Jane (Skinner) Q.; A.B., U. of Ill., 1903; M.S., U. of Calif., 1911; m. Mary Elizabeth Reed, July 7, 1915. Came to U.S., 1880. Nursery insp., Ill., 1903; asst. in entomology, U. of Calif., 1903-05; instr. zoology, Ia. State Coll., 1905-06; asst. prof. entomology and asst. entomologist, Agr. Expt. Sta., U. of Calif., 1906-12, asso. prof. and asso. entomologist, 1912-15; now prof. entomology, U. of Calif. Citrus Expt. Sta.; conducted 1st large scale mosquito campaign in west, 1904-06; collaborator Federal Hort. Bd. on Mediterranean fruit fly study, Spain, Italy, Egypt, Palestine, and general citrus insects in India, Japan, and Hawaii; studied citrus insects in Australia, Spain, and Italy, 1923; introduced cyanide fumigation methods, particularly calcium cyanide, in Australia; introduced liquid hydrocyanic acid and dust method of fumigation in Spain, dust cyanide method of controlling rabbits in Australia. Del. Pan-Pacific Scientific Congress, Sidney and Melbourne, Australia; del. 4th Internat. Entomol. Congress, Ithaca, N.Y., 1928; in charge federal govt. fruit fly survey, Bermuda, Azores, Mediterranean region and S.Africa, 1929-30; mem. com. to advise on fruit fly campaign in Fla., 1930. Twice pres. Am. Assn. Econ. Entomologists (Pacific slope br.); 1st pres. Entomol. Club of Southern Calif.; fellow A.A.A.S.; mem. Sigma Xi, Alpha Zeta. Author: Citrus and Other Subtropical Fruit Insects, 1938; also numerous bulls., report and papers, chiefly on subtropical fruit insects. Address: U. of Calif. Citrus Experiment Station, Riverside CA‡

QUEENY, EDGAR MONSANTO, business exec.; b. St. Louis, Missouri, September 29, 1897; s. John Francis and Olga (Monsanto) Q.; A.B., Cornell, 1919; m. Ethel Schneider, Nov. 10, 1919. With Monsanto Chem. Co. from 1919, as sec., 1920-24, v.p., 1924-28, pres., 1928-43, chmn. board 1943-60; chairman finance com., 1960-65, dir.; dir. Am. Airlines, Inc. Grad. mem. Bus. Council Washington; trustee Nat. Indsl. Conf. Bd., 1938-63, later sr. mem. Dir. United Fund of Greater St. Louis, St. Louis Symphony Society; field asso. trustee of American Museum Natural History. Enlisted as seaman 2d Class, United States serving overseas, later lieutenant jr. l. during World War i. Trustee Herbert Hoover Found.; chmn. bd. trustees Barnes Hosp., St. Louis; dir. Am.-Korean Found., World Rehab. Fund. Mem. Ducks Unlimited (U.S., Can.) (bd. trustees), Am. (dir.), Miramichi (dir.) salmon assns., Alpha Delta Phi. Republican. Clubs: Racquet, St. Louis Country, Cuivre, Log Cabin, St. Louis (St. Louis); Boone & Crockett, Links, Explorers (N.Y.C.). Author: Cheechako, 1941; Spirit of Enterprise, 1943; Prairie Wings, 1946. Home: St Louis MO Died July 7, 1968; buried Bellefontaine Cemetery, St Louis MO

QUERY, WALTER GRAHAM, tax commr.; b. Lancaster, S.C., May 4, 1877; s. Rev. James Walter and Lucy Ellen (Graham) Q.; ed. pub. schs., Wellford, S.C.; LL.D., U. of S.C., 1938; m. Minnie Osceola Coan, Nov. 23, 1899; children—Lois, Walter Graham, James Ernest, Dorothy Vernon. Began as clk. in store, at Wellford, S.C., Oct. 1893; clk., later mgr. Tucapau Mills (S.C.) Store, 1897-1905; in gen. mercantile business, 1905-25; mem. S.C. Tax Commn., 1915-21, chmn. since 1922. Mem. S.C. Ho. of Rep., 1915. Chmn. bd. trustees Wellford Sch. Dist., and W-L-T High Sch., 1919-35; pres. bd. trustees Chicora Coll. for Women, Columbia, S.C., 1923-31. Sec. Nat. Tax Assn., 1927-41; editor Proceedings, 1928-41. Democrat. Presbyn. Mason. Home: Wellford, S.C. Office: Columbia SC*‡

QUESADA, MANUEL CASTRO, diplomat; b. San Jose, Costa Rica, Dec. 24, 1877; s. Florencio and Dolores (Quesada) Castro; ed. Liceo de Costa Rica and Escuela de Derecho del Colegio de Aboga dos de Costa Rica, M.L., 1904; unmarried. Judge Criminal Court, San Jose, 1903; elected mem. Constl. Congress of Costa Rica, 1904, reelected, 1908; minister foreign affairs of Costa Rica, 1910-15; spl. minister to republics of Guatemala and Salvador, Nov. and Dec., 1911; E.E. and M.P. of Costa Rica to U.S. since Aug. 31, 1915. Roman Catholic. Clubs: Internacional (San Jose); Metropolitan (Washington, D.C.). Address: Legation of Costa Rica, 1501 16th St., Washington DC‡

QUIAT, IRA L(OUIS), lawyer; b. Weld County, Colo., Nov. 1, 1891; s. Philip and Anna (Shames) Q.; LL.B., Denver U., 1913; m. Esther Greenblatt, June 15, 1921; children—Marshall, Gerald M., Carole (wife of Dr. Harold C. Leight). Admitted to Colo. bar, 1913; practice in Denver, from 1919; state counsel HOLC, 1933-36. Dir. Guaranty Bank & Trust Co. Mem. Colo. Senate, 1927-33. Vice pres., dir. Gen. Rose Meml. Hosp., Am. Med. Center; mem. exec. com., mem. bd. Eleanor Roosevelt Cancer Found. First lt., F.A., U.S. Army, 1917-19. Mem. Am., Colo., Denver (pres. 1958-59) bar assns. Mason. Clubs: Green Gables Country; The 26. Home: Denver CO Died Jan. 2, 1967.

QUILICI, GEORGE L., Judge; b. Chicago, Ill.; s. Henry and Anna (Martinelli) Q.; LL.B., De Paul U.; graduate work, Northwestern U.; J.D., John Marshall Law Sch.; m. Virginia Iralson (artist). Admitted to Ill. bar; elected judge of the Municipal Court, Chicago, 1940; reelected, 1942, 1948, 54, 60; Judge Circuit Court, State of Illinois, 1962-69; apptd. spl. prosecutor of election fraud cases in County Court of Cook County (Ill.), on recommendation of Citizens Assn., 1935-38; apptd. com. on character and fitness of Supreme Court of State of Ill., reappointed 1938, 39. Served with signal corps in France, formerly major, United States Army (Res.) Mem. nat. panel Am. Arbitration Assn.; past chmn. bd. Nat. Pub. Housing Conf., past pres. Pub. Housing Assn. Chicago; treas. Citizens Com. for Better Music; chmn. com. on Awards of Chicago Commn. on Human Relations, 1946-55. Recipient 1950 community services award, Chgo. Indsl. Union Council; Star of Solidarity (Italy); Commendatore Al Merito (Republic of Italy); Citation of Merit, Am. Legion. Mem. Am., Ill., Chgo. bar assns., Am. Legion, Am. Contract Bridge Assn., Am. Civil Liberties Union, Res. Officers Assn., Vets. Fgn. Wars, Chgo. Contract Bridge Assn. (pres. 1956-58), Phi Alpha Delta. Clubs: City (bd. govs.), Chicago Literary (v.p.). Home: Chicago IL Died May 6, 1969; buried Rose Hill Cemetery, Chicago IL

QUIMBY, (FRANK) BROOKS, coll. prof.; b. Turner, Me., Feb. 18, 1897; s. J. Frank and Althea (Coffin) Q.; A.B., Bates Coll., 1918; Ed. M., Harvard, 1930; m. Inez Robinson, Aug. 22, 1923; 1 son, Laurence H. Teacher Hartford (Conn.) High Sch., 1919; Dean Acad., 1920; Deering High Sch., Portland, Me., 1922-27; dir. debating, Bates Coll., 1927; prof. argumentation and head dept. speech, 1938-67. Served as 2d lt. F.A. (res.), U.S. Army, 1918; 1st lt. F.A., Res. Corps. Recipient Distinguished Alumnus award from Delta Sigma Rho-Tau Kappa Alpha in 1964. President of the New England Speech Conf., 1947; mem. Speech Assn. Am. (mem. com. internat. debating), Delta Sigma Rho (nat. officer), Phi Beta Kappa, Tau Kappa Alpha. Republican. Methodist. Club: Kiwanis. Author: Manual for Directors of High School Debating, 1930, rev., 1934; Medical Economics, 1935; Analysis for the Debate Handbook, 1938; So You Want to Debate, 1948; So You Are Directing Debating, 1948; So You Want to Debate International Organization, 1952; So You Want to Discuss and Debate, 1954, rev., 1962. Contbr. articles on debate to profl. jours. Address: Lewiston ME Died Dec. 1968.

QUIN, CHARLES KENNON, judge; b. Tangipahoa, La., March 24, 1877; s. Henry Columbus and Cora Rosalee (Kennon) Q.; ed. pub. schs., Colorado County, Tex.; m. Elizabeth Rebecca Townsend-Marston, July 27, 1904. Was city supt. Columbus (Tex.) pub. schs. and supt. Colo. County pub. schs.; admitted to Tex. bar, 1908; in practice at Columbus; judge 25th Jud. Dist., Tex., 1922-23; in practice at San Antonio since 1923; atty. for city of San Antonio, 1929-32, mayor of San Antonio, 1933-39, reelected May 1941, resigned Jan. 1943, to take office as judge 57th Judicial Dist. of Tex., to which was elected Nov. 1942. Commissioned major infantry, Texas National Guard, 1918. Member San Antonio Chamber of Commerce, Junior Chamber of Commerce (honorary). Democrat. Methodist. Mason; mem. Eagles, Modern Woodmen of America, Praetorians, Lions, Elks, Herman Sons, Sojourners, Texas Pioneers. Clubs: Optimists, Breakfast, Advertising (hon.). Home: 1041 Mistletoe Av., San Antonio TX‡

QUINBY, WILLIAM CARTER, physician; b. Worcester, Mass., May 26, 1877; s. Hosea Mason and Sarah Rumford Pierce (Carter) Q.; A.B., Harvard U., 1899; M.D., Harvard Med. Sch., 1902; m. Marguerite E. Thayer, Jan. 29, 1910; children—John Thayer, William Carter, Jr. House pupil Mass. Gen. Hosp., 1902-03; asst. genito-urinary surgeon Boston Dispensary, 1907-09; asst. surgeon New England Baptist Hospital, Boston, 1908-14; in charge experimental surgery Brady Clinic, Johns Hopkins Hospital; asso. in urology same, 1915-16; asst. in surgery, Harvard, 1916, instr., 1917, asst. prof. genito-urinary surgery, 1921-27, clin. prof., 1927-41, emeritus 1941, emeritus, active service, 1942-45; urologist Peter Bent Brigham Hosp., 1916-45, urol. surg. emeritus, 1946, Brigham Hosp., 1916-45, urol. surg. emeritus, 1946; acting surg.-in-chief, Peter Bent Brigham Hospital, 1947-48. Fellow Am. Coll. Surgeons, A.A.A.S.; mem. Am Assn. Genito-Urinary Surg., A.M.A., Am. Urol. Assn., Am. Physiol. Soc., Am. Soc. Clin. Investigation, Clin. Soc. Genito-Urinary Surgeons, Surgical Research Soc., New England Surg. Soc., Boston Surg. Soc., Am. Acad. Arts and Sciences, Brit. Assn. Urol. Surgeons (hon.). Clubs: Harvard, The Country. Home: 83 Penniman Rd., Brookline, Mass. Office: 1101 Beacon St., Brookline MA‡

QUINN, CHARLES HENRY, elec. engr.; b. Sacramento, Calif., Oct. 7, 1876; s. John and Harriet H. (Owner) Q.; grad. West Tex. Mil. Acad., San Antonio, 1896; B.S., Purdue U., 1899; m. Florence M. Letts, Dec. 11, 1944 (dec.). Chief elec. engr. Norfolk & Western Ry. Co., 1901-23; vice pres. and dir. Basin Oil Co., Los Angeles, since 1942; chmn. bd. Elec. Products Corp. since 1946; mem. adv. com. to bd. dirs. Bank of America Nat. Trust & Savings Assn. since 1942; dir. Blue Diamond Corp., Pacific Finance Corp., So. Calif. Edison Co. Mem. Franklin Inst., Phila. Republican. Home: 727 S. Beverly Glen Blvd., Los Angeles 24. Office: Pacific Mutual Bldg., 523 W. 6th St., Los Angeles‡

QUINN, JAMES LELAND, ex-congressman; b. Venango County, Pa., Sept. 8, 1875; s. Mark and Margaret (Gorham) Q.; student St. Thomas Sch., Braddock, Pa., 1881-88; m. Clara Elizabeth Kramer, May 24, 1900; children—James Leland, Margaret, Ruth, Clara. Began as reporter, 1891; owner and pub. The Journal, Braddock, Pa.; mem. Pa. State Legislature, 1933-35; mem. 74th and 75th Congresses (1935-39), 31st Pa. Dist. Democrat. Catholic. K.C., Elk, Eagle. Home: Braddock PA*‡

QUINN, JOHN FRANCIS, coll. dean; b. Aurora, Ill., June 30, 1888; s. John Francis and Mary Ann (Downey) Q.; A.B., Loyola U., Chicago, 1909, A.M., St. Louis U., 1917, grad. study, 1920-24. Teacher, Latin and English, Loyola Univ. High Sch., Chicago, 1913-14, St. Ignatius High Sch., 1917-20; prin., Marquette Univ. High Sch., Milwaukee, Wis., 1925-27; prin., St. Ignatius High Sch., Chicago, 1927-34; dean, liberal arts coll., U. of Detroit, 1934-49, rector of U. and chmn. bd. trustees 1949-57; rector St. Stanislaus Novitiate, Cleve., 1957-71. Trustee University of Detroit, 1934-71. Compiled and edited Loyola Book of Verse, 1920. Home: Cleveland OH Died June 22, 1971.

QUINTON, HAROLD, utilities exec.; b. Topeka, Kan., Jan. 20 1899; s. Frank C. and Nena (Hoffman) Q.; student Washburn Acad., 1912-15, Northwestern, 1927; Doctor of Laws, University of So. California; m. Grace Walker, Feb. 7, 1921; one dau., Jacqueline (Mrs. Charles H. Reed). Sec. Precision Machine Co., Washington, 1920-21; auditor income tax unit Treasury Dept., 1921-23, tech. advisor, 1924-25; tax specialist Arthur Andersen & Co., C.P.A., Chicago, 1925-27, mgr., partner, Los Angeles office, 1928-42; v.p. So. Calif. Edison Co., Los Angeles, 1942, exec. v.p., 1948-54, mem. bd. dirs., exec. com., 1945-69, pres., 1954-59, chmn. bd., 1959-69, chief exec. officer, 1954-65; dir. Edison Elec. Inst., 1948-57, mem. adv. com., 1958-69; dir., mem. exec. com. Pacific Mut. Life Ins. Co.; pres. Calabasas Developers, Ind.; dir. Kaiser Industries Corp., Kaiser Steel Corp., Buffums', Western Bancorp.; dir., mem. Los Angeles adminstry. com. United Cal. Bank. Trustee U. So. Cal., vice chmn., treas., 1965-69; bd. dirs. Los Angeles chpt. A.R.C., Stanford Research Inst. Served from pvt. to sgt. maj., 1st U.S. Cavalry, 83d and 5th F.A., U.S. Army, 1917-20, AEF, France, 1918-19. Recipient Town Hall Civic Achievement award, 1967; Cal. Industrialist of the Year, by California Museum of Science and Industry, 1967. Member of Pacific Coast Elec. Assn. (past director, v.p.), Nat. Assn. Elec. Cos. (past dir., v.p. and chmn.), Cal. C. of C. (dir.), Nat. Indsl. Conf. Bd. (sr. mem.), Beta Gamma Sigma. Clubs: Los Angeles Country, California, University. Home: Santa Monica CA Died Apr. 29, 1969; buried Court of Freedom, Forest Lawn Meml. Park, Los Angeles CA

QUIRK, JAMES THOMAS, magazine publisher; b. Phila., Mar. 13, 1911; s. John J. and Katherine (McAvoy) Q.; A.B., Villanova U.; m. Elizabeth Wolstenoroft (dec.); 1 son, Rory J.; m. 2d, Mary Louise Connolly, Feb. 1, 1964; stepchildren—J. Thomas Connolly, A. Jerome Connolly, Richard Connolly. With Triangle Publs., Inc., 1940-69, pub. TV Guide, 1953-69.

Served with AUS, World War II NATOUSA, ETO. Decorated Bronze Star with two clusters, Legion of Merit with cluster. Mem. Advt. Council) dir.), Mag. Pubs. Assn. (dir.). Address: Berwyn PA Died Jan. 1969.*

QUYNN, ALLEN GEORGE, naval officer; b. Baltimore, Md., June 16, 1894; s. Daniel Hauer and Mary (Whiting) Q.; grad. U.S. Naval Acad., 1915; m. Rachel Motter, Sept. 14, 1918; children—Allen George, Serene Kunkel, Margaret Motter. Commd. ensign, U.S. Navy, 1915, and advanced through the grades to commodore, 1944; served in ocean escort duty, World War I; placed U.S.S. Tennessee in commn.; comd. U.S.S. Mindanao and U.S.S. Asheville, China Station, 1936-38; present during Japanese attack, Pearl Harbor, 1941; dep. comdr. and chief of staff Service Force, Pacific Fleet, 1943-49; ret. as rear adm., 1949. Rep. of U.S. Navy in logistic matters, Trident Quebec Conf., 1943. Decorated D.S.M., Legion of Merit; recipient letters of commendation from Comdr. in Chief Asiatic Fleet, U.S. State Dept. and Foreign Missionary Soc. Mason. Home: Frederick MD Died June 17, 1971; buried Mt. Olivet Cemetery, Frederick MD

RAAB, WILHELM, physician and univ. prof.; b. Vienna, Austria, Jan. 14, 1895; s. Dr. Richard and Rosa (Gerenyi) R.; grad. cum laude, Schotten-Gymnasium, Vienna, 1913; M.D., Med. Faculty, U. of Vienna, 1920; 'M.d., German U. of Prague (Czechoslovakia), 1926; research fellow, Harvard Med. Sch., 1920-30; m. Olga Elizabeth Palmborg, June 17, 1930; children—Karl-Herbert, Fredrik-Holger; m. 2d, Helen Hubaczek, May 26, 1970; came to U.S. to reside, 1939. Began as med. house officer, Vienna, 1920; first asst. to Clin. Prof. Biedl, German U., Prague, 1921-26, privat-dozent in pathol. physiology, 1926-35; asst. and first asst., First Med. Clinic, U. of Vienna, 1926-36, privat-dozent in internal medicine, 1935-39; ofcl. examiner in internal medicine, U. of Vienna, 1936; physician in chief, Krankenhaus d. Kaufmannschaft, Vienna, 1936-39; asst. prof. clin. medicine, U. of Vt., 1939-45; prof. experimental medicine, since 1945; cons. specialist Mary Fletcher Hosp., Placid Meml. Hosp.; attending physician and head cardiovascular research unit, DeGoesbriand Meml. Hops., Burlington, Vt.; founder Preventive Heart Reconditioning Found., 1963. Cons. High Commrs. Office, Germany, 1950; Fulbright research prof. U. of Innsbruck, Austria, 1957-58. Mem. Pres.' Citizens' Com. on Fitness of Am. Youth, 1959. Served as lt. Med. Corps., Austro-Hungarian Army and German Army, 1916-18, 1938. Awarded 2 Austrian war medals for bravery (silver 1st class and bronze), other Austrian and Hungarian war decorations. Diplomate Am. Bd. Internal Medicine. Fellow Am. Coll. Physicians, Am. Coll. Cardiology, Am. Coll. Chest Physicians, Am. Coll. Sports Medicine, Life mem. Austro-Am. Inst. of Edn.; mem. A.M.A., New York Acad. Sciences, Soc. Exptl. Biology and Medicine, Vt. State Med. Soc., Chittenden Co. Med. Soc., Am. Physiol. Soc., Endocrine Soc., Soc. Internal Medicine, American Heart Association, Society of Gerontology, Society Study Arteriosclerosis, N.E. Cardiovascular Soc.; corr. mem. Gesellschaft d. Aerzte, Vienna; mem. Sigma Xi. Unitarian. Clubs: Research, Faculty, Layman's League. Author: Hormone und Stoffwechsel, 1926; Innersekretorische Storungen und Organotherapie, 1932; Hormonal and Neurogenic Cardiovascular Disorders, 1952; (with Hans Kraus) Hypokinetic Disease, 1961; Preventive Myocardiology, 1970; also numerous sci. articles and monographs. Editor: Prevention of Ischemic Heart Disease, 1966. Home: Burlington VT Died Sept. 21, 1970.

RABEL, ERNST, scholar in comparative law, ancient and modern; b. Vienna, Austria, Jan. 28, 1874; s. Albert and Berta (Ettinger) R.; J.D., U. of Vienna, 1895; student in Paris, 1896, Leipzig, 1899; Dr. honoris causa, Athens, 1937; m. Anny Weber, April 9, 1912; children—Lili Elizabeth, Frederick Karl. Came to U.S., 1939, naturalized, 1945. Practiced in Vienna courts; asst. prof., U. of Leipzig, 1902, asso. prof., 1904; prof. law, U. of Basle, Switzerland, 1906, U. of Kiel, 1910; U. of Gottingen, 1911, U. of Munich, 1916, U. of Berlin, 1926-35; dir. Inst. for Comparative Law, Munich, 1916-26, Inst. for Foreign and Internat. Private Law (Kaiser Wilhelm Soc. for Promotion of Science), 1926-37; judge Appellate Court, Basle, Switzerland, 1907-10, Munich, 1920-25; judge Mixed Tribunal between Germany and Italy, 1921-27; judge and hoc. Permanent Court of Internat. Justice (World Court), The Hague, 1925-27; mem. exec. council League of Nations Internat. Inst. for Unification of Private Law in Rome, 1927-34. Mem. permanent conciliation commns. between Germany and Italy, 1928-35, Italy and Norway, 1929-36. With Am. Law Inst., 1939-42; engaged in research work for U. of Mich. since 1942. Corr. mem. academies of science in Bologna and Turin. Author books pub. in German and English since 1915; latest publ.: The Conflict of Laws: A Comparative Study, Vol. I, 1945, Vol. II, 1947. Vol. III, 1950. Editor or co-editor publs. relating to law. Address: Law Research Bldg., Ann Arbor MI‡

RABIN, MICHAEL, concert violinist; b. N.Y.C., May 2, 1936; s. George and Jeanne (Seidman) R.; student Juilliard Sch. Music, 1947-52. Ann. coast to coast concert tours, U.S., Can. and Europe, also S.Am., S.Africa, Israel, Australia, 1952-72; recitals, 1950-72; soloist with maj. symphony orchs., 1951-72; radio and TV appearances, 1950-72; recording artist for Columbia, Capitol and Angel records. Named One of Outstanding Young Men of Am., 1965; Ford fellow, 1959. Mem. Phi Beta (patron). World premiere Richard Mohaupt Violin Concerto, 1954, Paul Creston Violin Concerto, 1961. Address: New York City NY Died Jan. 19, 1972.

RACHMIEL, JEAN, painter; b. Haverstraw-on-Hudson, N.Y., May 10, 1871; s. Alexandre and Sarah R.; pub. sch. edn., New York; art pupil 1st under his father, later under George de Forest Brush, New York; went to Paris, 1890; 3 yrs. under Jules Lefebvre; entered Ecole des Beaux Arts and studied 8 yrs. with Leon Bonnat. Exhibitor Paris Salon annually since 1898. Mem. Assn. des Anciens eleves de l'Atelier Bonnat. Distinguished as a realist in art.*‡

RACKEMANN, FRANCIS MINOT, physician; b. Milton, Mass., June 4, 1887; s. Felix and Julia (Minot) R.; A.B., Harvard, 1909, M.D., 1912; m. Dorothy Mandell, Apr. 28, 1917; children—Dorothy, Francis M., Elizabeth, William M. Research fellow in medicine, Presbyterian Hosp., 1914-16; resident in medicine, Mass. Gen. Hosp., 1916-17; asst. in medicine, Harvard Med. Sch., 1916-25, instr., 1925-35, lecturer in medicine, 1935-73; physician Mass. Gen. Hosp., 1918-48, consultant. First lt., Med. Corps, U.S. Army, 1918-19; dist. Med. Officer for Civilian Defense, 1942-45; civ. expert consultant to the Surgeon Gen., 1946-73. Chmn. bd. trustees Boston State Hosp.; sec. Harvard Med. Sch. Dormitory Fund, 1923-27. Mem. Am. and Mass. med. assns., Assn. American physicians, Am. Society Clinic Investigation, American Assn. Study of Allergy (pres. 1925), American Academy Allergy, American Academy Arts and Sciences, Harvey Society, American Society Study of Asthma and Allied Conditions (pres. 1917), Am. Clin. and Climatol. Assn. (sec. 1933-41, pres. 1948), Harvard Med. Sch. Alumni Assn. (sec. and treas. 1923-27, pres. 1929). Clubs: Harvard, Union Boat (Boston); Country (Brookline); Harvard (New York). Author: Clinical Allergy; Asthma and Hay Fever, 1931. Home: Boston MA Died Mar. 1973.

RACKLEY, JOHN RALPH, educator; b. Lambert, Okla., Aug. 29, 1907; s. John William and Mertie (Hammer) R.; A.B., U. of Okla., 1931, A.M., 1935; grad. work, Yale, Vanderbilt U.; Ph.D., George Peabody Coll., 1940; m. Virginia Douthit Mills, Feb. 4, 1937; 1 son, Gordon Mills. High sch. teacher of social science, Oklahoma City, Okla., 1930-39; (leaves of absence for grad. study, 1933-34, 1937-38); mem. faculty, Teachers Coll. of Com., 1939-49, prof. of social science and dean of college, 1946-49; prof. of edn. and dean, Coll. of Edn., U. of Okla., 1949-55; deputy United States commissioner of education, 1955-56; prof. edn. and dean coll. edn. Pa. State U., 1956-62, v.p. resident instrn., professor of education, 1962-65, provost of the university, 1967-69; supt. pub. instrn. Commonwealth, Pa., 1965-67. Chmn. of Gov's Adv. Com. Pub. Edn. Pa., 1957-58. Mem. Nat. Council Accreditation of Tchr. Edn., 1957-60; mem. Middle States Assn. Commn. on Instns. Higher Edn., 1962-65; Chmn. Cornell U. Adv. Council for Edn., 1962-67; mem. adv. com. on education in armed forces Dept. Def., 1957-60; member adv. com. on edn. of deaf Dept. Health, Edn. and Welfare, 1964-65. Served with Signal Corps, U.S. Army, 1943-46, now lt. col. Res. ret. Pres. Am. Assn. Colls. for Tchr. Edn., 1961-62. Mem. Alpha Tau Omega. Home: State College PA Died Dec. 24, 1969; buried Centre County Memorial Park, State College PA

RADEMACHER, HANS, mathematician; b. Hamburg, Germany, Apr. 3, 1892; s. Henry Adolph and Emma Friderike (Weinhover) R.; Ph.D., U. Gottingen, 1917; Doctor of Science, University of Pa., 1962; m. Susanne Gaspary, Apr. 1921; m. 3d, Irma Schoenberg Wolpe, Sept. 10, 1949. Privatdocent U. Berlin, 1919-22; prof. extraordinarius U. Hamburg, 1922-25; prof. ordinarius U. Breslau, 1925-34, dismissed by Nazis, 1934; with U. Pa., 1934-69, successively vis. prof., asst. prof., prof. mathematics, 1939-62, prof. emeritus, 1962-69; mem. Inst. for Advanced Study, Princeton, 1953, 60-61; vis. prof., Guggenheim fellow Tata Inst. Fundamental Research, Bombay, India, 1954-55; vis. prof. N.Y.U., 1962-64; visiting professor Rockefeller Inst., N.Y.C., 1964-66; affiliate Rockefeller University, 1966-69. Mem. Am., London math. socs., Math. Assn. Am., Soc. Indsl. and Applied Mathematics, Societe Mathematique de France, Sigma Xi. Author articles math. jours. Home: Philadelphia PA Died Feb. 7, 1969.

RADO, SANDOR, psychiatrist; b. Hungary, Jan. 8, 1890; s. Adolph and Cornelia (Rado) R.; grad. Humanistic Gymnasium, 1907; Dr. Polit. Sci., U. Budapest, 1911, M.D., 1915; m. Emmy Krissler, Dec. 1, 1926 (dec.); children—George, Peter. Came to U.S., 1931, naturalized, 1937. Intern Zeitschrisft fur Psychoanalyse, Imago, 1925-34; dozent Berlin (Germany) Psychoanalytic Inst., 1923-31; dir. N.Y. Psychoanalytic Inst., 1931-41; clin. prof. psychiatry, dir. Psychoanalytic clinic Columbia, 1944-55; prof. psychiatry and dir. Grad. Sch. Psychiatry State U. N.Y. College of Medicine N.Y.C., 1956-58; pres., prof. at New York School of Psychiatry, 1958-67, dean emeritus, 1968-72; attending psychiatrist N.Y. State Psychiatric Inst. and Hosp., Army Med. Center, Walter Reed Hosp., 1946-52; cons. Manhattan State Hosp. Cons. Army Induction Center, 1942-45; examiner S.S.S., 1943-47; mem. N.Y. State Mental Hygiene Council, 1956-68. Recipient Samuel W. Hamilton award, Am. Psychopathological Assn., 1956. Fellow N.Y. Acad. Medicine, Am. Psychiatric Assn., A.A.A.S., mem. Internat. Psychoanalytic Assn., Am. Orthopsychiatric Assn., Am. Psychopathological Association, Society for Human Genetics, American Medical Assn., N.Y. Acad. Sciences, Assn. for Psychoanalytic Medicine, Am. Psychoanalytic Association, Assn. for Research Nervous and Mental Diseases. Author Psychoanalysis of Behavior, Collected Papers, Vol. I, 1956, Vol. II, 1962. Editor: Changing Concepts of Psychoanalytic Medicine, 1956. Author articles sci. publs. U.S. and Germany, and others. Home: New York City NY Died May 14, 1972.

RAEMER, CLIFFORD M., lawyer; b. Fairmont, Okla., 1903; A.B., U. Okla., 1927; LL.B., U. Ill., 1932; m. Ruby M. Raemer; 1 dau., Karen Raemer. Admitted to Ill. bar, 1934; atty. Marion County Housing Authority, 1947-53, 53-66; U.S. dist. atty. Eastern Dist. Ill. 1953-61; lawyer Salem, Ill., 1961-67; attorney Salem Airport Authority, 1961-67. Served as lt. comdr. USNR, 1945. Mem. Marion County, Fed., Am. bar assns., Phi Delta Phi. Home: Salem IL Died Nov. 10, 1967.

RAGAN, FRANK XAVIER, wholesale merchandising exec.; b. Phila., Sept. 14, 1897; s. James J. and Mary (Cheeseman) R.; student LaSalle Prep. Sch., 1911-15, St. Joseph's Coll., Phila., 1915-19; m. Eleanore C. Murray, July 7, 1920; children—Frank Xavier, Marie Louise (Mrs. R. J. McCormick, Jr.). With Anheuser-Busch, Inc., 1925-46, with Standard Brands, Inc., from 1946, v.p., from 1957. Home: New York City NY Died Apr. 3, 1972; buried Calvery Cemetery, Gulph Mills PA

RAGEN, JOSEPH EDWARD, ofcl.; b. Trenton, Ill., Nov. 22, 1896; s. William and Mollie (Rinesmith) R.; ed. in parochial pub. schs of Carlyle, Ill.; m. Loretta Heyer, Nov. 25, 1926; children—Jane L., William J. Dep. sheriff, Clinton County, Ill., 1922-26, sheriff, 1926-30, county treas., 1930-33; warden, Ill. State penitentiary, Menard, 1933-35; warden and supt. all prisons, Joliet, 1935-41; with U.S. Dept. of Justice, 1941-42; warden, Ill. State penitentiary, Joliet, 1942-61; dir. Ill. Dept. Pub. Safety, 1961-65; v.p. Louis Joliet Bank, 1965-71. Served in U.S. Navy, 1918-19. Recipient citation OSRD, 1945, D.A.V., 1949; recipient nat. award Garden Clubs Am., 1954. Past pres. Warden's Assn., Am. Correctional Assn.; life mem. Post Comdrs. Club Am. Legion. Roman Catholic. Rotarian (hon. life mem.). Address: Springfield IL Died Sept. 22, 1971; buried Carlyle IL

RAGLAND, WILLIAM T., judge; b. Marion County, Mo., Oct. 5, 1866; s. John T. and Mary E. (Jackson) R.; student State Teachers Coll., Kirksville, Mo.; spl. course, Washington U., 1 yr., and student law dept. 1 yr.; LL.D., U. of Mo., 1930; m. Mary E. Watson, Oct. 7, 1890: children—Harold P., Mrs. Marie McHenry, Reginald W. Admitted to Mo. bar, 1889, and began practice at Paris; pros. atty. Monroe County, Mo., 1893-97; chmn. Mo. State Bd. Law Examiners, 1905-11; asso. with Frank W. McAllister 5 yrs.; judge 10th Jud. Circuit, 1911-19; commr. Supreme Court of Mo., 1919-23; asso. justice Supreme Court of Mo., term 1923-33; mem. Ragland, Otto & Potter; now retired. Mason, Odd Fellow, Democrat. Mem. Potter; now retired. Mason, Odd Fellow, Democrat. Mem. Christian (Disciples) Ch. Home: 1440 E. Chapman Av. Orange CA‡

RAGO, HENRY ANTHONY, poet, editor, educator; born in Chicago, October 5, 1915; the son of Louis and Theresa (Argenzio) R.; LL.B., DePaul U., 1937, Litt.D. honoris causa, 1965; M.A. magna cum laude, U. Notre Dame, 1939, Ph.D. magnu cum laude, 1941; m. Juliet Maggio, Oct. 7, 1950; children—Maria Christina, Maria Carmela, Anthony Pascal, Maria Martha. Teaching fellow U. Notre Dame, 1939-41; instr. English, DePaul U., 1941-42; lectr. philosophy Barat Coll. of Sacred Heart, 1941-42; asst. prof. humanities U. Chgo., 1947-54; prof. humanities St. Xavier Coll. Women, 1954-56; asso. editor Poetry mag., 1954-55, editor, 1955-69; staff Bread Loaf Writers Conf., Middlebury, Coll., Vt., 1965-69; fellow Sch. Letters, Ind. U., 1965-69; Isabelle Kellogg Thomas lectr. Goucher Coll., 1965; Gertrude Clarke Whittall lectr. Library Congress, 1966; vis. prof. theology and lit. U. Chgo. Div. Sch., 1965-66; vis. prof. humanities and religion New Collegeiate div. U. Chgo., 1966-67, professor of theology and literature, 1967-69. Mem. nat. poetry council Rockefeller Found., 1960-66; panelist Nat. Council Arts, Nat. Found. Arts and Humanities, 1966-69. Served to 1st lt. AUS, 1942-46. Decorated Bronze Star; Rockefeller Found. travel grantee, 1960-61; Ford Found. study and travel grantee, 1969-70. Recipient Clarence B. Randall award for poetry Soc. Midland Authors, 1965, D. H. Lawrence fellowship, 1967. Mem. Modern Poetry Assn. (trustee). Author: The Philosophy of Esthetic Individualism, 1941; The Travelers, 1949; Conoscenza della Luce, 1959; A Sky of Late Summer, 1963; Praise of Comedy: ADiscourse, 1963. Editor: (with Stanley Kunitz, Richard Wilbur, Poems in Folio, 1956-57, Contbg. editor New City, 1960-69. Home: Chicago IL Died May 26, 1969; buried Calvary Cemetery, Evanston IL

RAGOZIN, ZENAIDE ALEXEIEVNA, author; b. in Russia; she traveled extensively in Europe; came to U.S., 1874, and became naturalized citizen. Mem. Royal Asiatic Soc. of Great Britain and Ireland; Am. Oriental Soc.; Societe Ethnologique of Paris; Athenee Oriental, Paris; Anglo-Russian Literary Soc., London; Hist. Soc. of Texas Univ., etc. Author: Story of Chaldea; Story of Assyria; Story of Media, Babylon and Persia; Story of Vedic India (in the Stories of the Nations series); History of the World, (1st and 2d parts: Earliest Peoples and Early Egypt); Siegfried, the Hero of the Netherlands; Beowulf, the Hero of the Anglo-Saxons; Frithjof, the Viking of Norway; Roland, the Paladin of France; Salammbo, the Maid of Carthage (in Tales of Heroic Ages series). Translated from French Anatole Leroy Beaulieu's The Empire of the Tsars and the Russians. Address: 82 Park St., Orange NJ‡

RAGSDALE, EDWARD TILLOTTSON, automotive mfr.; b. Hopkinsville, Ky., May 15, 1897; s. Roy Cleveland and Emma Mae (Coleman) R.; student Ind. State Normal, 1916-17; m. Sarah Gertrude Judd, Oct. 30, 1920; children—Helen Florence (Mrs. Frank Worack), Mildred Francis. Various positions Maxwell Motor, Midwest Engine Co., Pres-O-Lite Co., Pierce Arrow; draftsman Buick Motor div. Gen. Motors Corp., Flint, Mich., 1923-39, asst. chief engr., 1939-49; gen. mfg. mgr., 1949-56, gen. mgr., 1956-59; v.p. Gen. Motors Corp., 1956-59; dir. Indsl. Mut. Assn. Mem. exec. bd. Boy Scouts Am.; dir. A.R.C., Child Guidance; mental bd. regents Gen. Motors Inst. Dir. Plant City Com. Trustee United Fund; chmn. archtl. and bldg. com. Flint Coll. and Cultural Mus.; bd. dirs. Flint Osteo. Hosp. Served as 1st sgt. AAC, 1917-19, liaison officer Brit. Flying Corps. Mem. Soc. Automotive Engrs., Am. Legion, C. of C. (past pres., dir.), Mfrs. Assn. (dir.). Mason (32 deg.), Elk. Clubs: Kiwanis, Flint Golf, City (dir.) (Flint). Patentee automotive field. Home: Flint MI Died June 17, 1971.

RAHMN, ELZA LOTHNER, musician; b. in Koping, Sweden, June 21, 1872; d. Axel and Alice L'Orange Lothner; grad. Royal Conservatory, Stockholm, 1889; Virgil Piano Sch., New York, 1897; m. Boston, July 17, 1900, Capt. Magnus A. Rahmn. Has been organist of several chs., Europe and U.S. Composer works for piano; pianist; teacher. Founder of The Lothner Music Sch., Worcester, Mass.; mem. Internat. Soc. Pianoforte Teachers and Players. Address: 663 Flatbush Av., Brooklyn‡

RAINES, JOHN MARLIN, educator; b. Tarkio, Mo., Sept. 8, 1907; s. E.N. and Anna Grace (Marlin) R.; A.B., Mus. B., Tarkio Coll., 1928; A.M., Cornell U., 1929, Ph.D., 1935; m. Ann Herrick, Dec. 26, 1935; 1 dau., Margaret. Instr. English, Muskingum Coll., New Concord, O., 1929-31; prof. English, Mo. Valley Coll., Marshall, 1935-39; instr. English, Woodrow Wilson Jr. Coll., Chgo., 1939-43, Cornell U., 1945-46; asst. prof. U. Okla., 1946-50, prof. English, 1950, 1951-71, David R. Boyd prof., chmn. dept., 1951-53; vis. asso. prof. English, U. Cal., Davis, 1957. Served from lt. (j.g.) to lt. USNR, 1943-45, lt. comdr. Res. Mem. Modern Lang. Assn., Am. Assn. U. Profs., Phi Kappa Phi. Episcopalian. Contbr. articles profl. jours. Home: Norman OK Died July 24, 1971.

RAINEY, LILIUS BRATTON, ex-congressman; b. Dadeville, Ala., July 21, 1876; s. Samuel Laurence and Elizabeth (Bass) R.; student Ala. Tech. Inst., Auburn, Ala., 1896-99; LL.B., U. of Ala., 1902; m. Julia La Coste Smith, of Gadsden, Ala., July 18, 1911; children—Audrey, Lilius B., Laurence, Kenneth. Began practice at Gadsden, 1902; solicitor, Gadsden, 1911-17; mem. 66th and 67th Congresses (1919-23), 7th Ala. Dist. Democrat. Capt. Ala. N.G., 1903-07. Mason (Shriner), Odd Fellow, K.P., Elk. Home: Gadsden AL‡

RAJAGOPALACHARYA, CHAKRAVARTI, chief minister government of Madras; b. Hosur, Salem Dist., India, 1879; s. Chakravarti Venkatarya and Singaramma; student Central Coll., Bangalore; Presidency Coll. and Law Coll., Madras; m. Alamelamangamma, 1899; children—C. R. Krishnaswami, C. R. Rasmaswami (dec.), Namagiri, C. R. Narasimhan, Lakshmi (Mrs. D. M. Gandhi). Joined bar, 1900; practiced at Salem, India, 1900-15; joined Mahatma Gandhi's Satyagraha campaign and non-cooperation movement, 1919-20; general secretary Indian National Congress, 1921-22 (member working committee 1922-42, 1946-47); secretary Prohibition League of India, 1930; Prime Minister, Madras, 1937-39; asso. with Indian freedom movement since 1906; induced All India Congress Com. to offer cooperation in war effort, 1940; imprisoned in connection with Indian freedom movement 5 times, 1921-42; asst. to Mahatma Gandi in Gandhi-Jinnah talks, 1944; mem. Interim Govt. of Gandhi 1946-47; gov. West Bengal, Aug. 1947-June 1948; acted as gov. gen., India, Nov. 1947; gov. gen. India, 1948-50, cabinet minister, 1950-72; chief minister Madras, 1952-54. Author: Fatal Cart and other stories, Prohibition Manual, 1935; Way Out (booklet), 1942. Reconciliation (booklet), 1942; Marcus Aurelius and Socrates in Tamil, Tamil Essays, Tamil Mahabharat stories, Upanishads for lay readers, Bhagavat Gita selections and notes, 1923-42. Edited Mahatma Gandhi's Young India during Gandhi's incarceration. Home: Tyagarayanagar, Madras Died Dec. 27, 1972.

RAKOTOMALALA, LOUIS, diplomat of Madagascar; b. Tananarive, Madagascar, Sept. 11, 1901; m. Alice Rabakovelo, 1925. Mem. local assemblies in Madagascar, 1944-58; mem. Nat. Assembly Madagascar, 1958-60; minister fgn. affairs, 1960; ambassador to U.S., also permanent rep. Madagascar to UN, 1960-68. Formerly mgr. export firms in Madagascar; dir. Banque de Madagascarl hon. mgr. Banque Nationale Pour Le Commerce et L'industrie. Mem. Malagasy Acad. Home: Tananarive Madagascar Died July 1, 1968; buried Tenanarive Madagascar

RALEY, JOHN WESLEY, univ. chancellor; b. Rosebud, Tex., Aug. 15, 1902; s. Leonidas Washington and Margaret Frances (Duncan) R.; A.B., Baylor U., 1923, LL.D., 1949; Th.M., Southwestern Bapt. Theol. Sem., Ft. Worth, 1927; Th.D., Eastern Bapt. Theol. Sem., Phila., Pa., 1933; D.D., Okla. Bapt. U., Shawnee, 1935; m. Helen Wilma Thames, June 23, 1929; children—John Wesley, Helen Thames. Served as pastor of small churches while student; principal rural school, Chilton, Texas, 1922-23; teacher American history Carlsbad (N.M.) High Sch., 1923-24; ordained Bapt. ministry, 1921; pastor First Ch., Smithville, Tex., 1927-30. First Ch., Bartlesville, Okla., 1931-34; pres. Okla. Bapt. U. 1934-61, chancellor, 1961-68. Pres. bd. trustees, Okla. Bapt. U., 1933-34; past pres. Okla. Ind. Coll. Found., Inc. Named to Okla. Hall of Fame, 1958. Fellow Royal Soc. Arts Eng.; mem. So. Bapt. Edn. Assn., C. of C. Democrat. Mason. Rotarian (past pres. Shawnee). Home: Shawnee OK Died May 19, 1968; buried University Garden, Resthaven Memorial Park, Shawnee OK

RALL, EDWARD EVERETT, coll. pres. (emeritus); b. Van Horn, Ia., Feb. 11, 1876; s. Otto and Anna (Steiner) R.; grad. Ia. State Teachers' Coll., 1895; B.A., State U. of Ia., 1900; Ph.D., Yale, 1903; Teachers Coll., Columbia, 1904-05; m. Nell Hardy Platt, July 17, 1917; children—Joseph Edward, David P. Asso. prin. pub. sch., Hawarden, Ia., 1895-98; prin. high sch., Red Oak, Ia., 1903-04; instr. in edn., U. of Tex., 1905-11; prof. edn. U. of Tenn., 1911-16, also supervisor Summer Sch. of the South; pres. North Central (formerly North-Western) Coll., Naperville, Ill., 1916-46. Mem. Phi Beta Kappa. Home: Sherman Garden Apts., 1862 Sherman St., Evanston IL‡

RALLI, ELAINE PANDIA, educator, physician; b. N.Y.C., May 13, 1894; d. Pandia Constantine and Daisy (Wehle) Ralli; A.B., Vassar Coll., 1916; M.D., N.Y.U., 1925. Instr. medicine N.Y.U., 1929-32, asst. prof., 1932-39, asso. prof., 1939-68; vis. physician Bellevue Hosp., N.Y.C., 1941-68; attending physician Lenox Hill Hosp., now chief metabolism service; dir. out patient services Dept. of Hospitals City of N.Y., 1950-68; att. physician U. Hosp., 1948-68, St. Joseph's Hospital, Stamford, Conn.; consultant to Surgeon General, 1952-54. Mem. N.Y. Acad. Medicine, Soc. Exptl. Biology and Medicine, Am. Physiol. Soc., Am. Inst. Nutrition, Harvey Cushing Soc., Assn. Study Secretion. Author: The Management of the Diabetic Patient, 1965. Contbr. articles profl. jours. Home: Stamford CT Died Oct. 6, 1968.

RALSTON, BURRELL OTTO, physician; b. Jefferson City, Tenn., Jan. 28, 1887; s. William Oscar and Martha E. (Mitchell) R.; A.B., Maryville (Tenn.) Coll., 1909; M.D., Rush Med. Coll., Chicago, 1915; student University of Berne, Switzerland, 1925-26, Stanford Univ. Sch. of Medicine, 1929-30; m. Marion Churchill McCartney, May 12, 1925. Resident pathologist Presbyn. Hosp., Chicago, 1916-21; instr. in pathology, Rush Med. Coll., 1916-21, instr. and asst. clin. prof. in medicine, 1921-24; prof. medicine, Sch. Medicine, U. So. Cal., 1929-43, dean, 1943-54, emeritus, 1954. Served as 1st lt. Med. Corps, U.S. Army, 1917. Mem. A.M.A., Inst. of Medicine Chicago, Pacific Clin. Interurban Soc., Calif. State Med. Assn., Assn. Am. Physicians, Los Angeles Co. Med. Soc., Los Angeles Acad. Medicine. Republican. Clubs: California, Los Angeles Country, Bohemian. Contbr. Los Angeles CA Died May 1970.

RALSTON, BYRON BROWN, lawyer; b. Fostoria, O., Sept. 26, 1890; s. William McCamus and Wealtha Jane (Brown) R.; B.S., U.S. Naval Acad., 1914; M.S., Columbia, 1921; J.D., N.Y.U., 1931; m. Lucy Virginia Gordon, June 4, 1919; 1 dau., Lucy Virginia. Commd. ensign U.S.N., 1914, advanced through grades to lt. comdr., 1921, ret. 1928; trust dept. Chem. Bank & Trust Co., N.Y.C., 1928, legal staff trust dept., 1933-71, co. merged with Corn Exchange Bank Trust Co., to form Chem. Corn Exchange Bank, 1954; admitted to New York bar, 1932; dir. Internat. Minerals & Chem. Corp. Dir. John Jay and Eliza J. Watson Found. Served with U.S.N., 1940-45. Profl. engr., N.Y.; licensed ship engr. Protestant Episcopal. Mason. Clubs: Pelham Country; Lawyers, Yacht (N.Y.C.); Army and Navy (Washington). Home: Pelham NY Died Apr. 9, 1971.

RALSTON, WILLIAM CHAPMAN, b. San Francisco, Apr. 25, 1863; s. William Chapman and Lizzie (Fry) R.; ed. various pvt. schs., and colls.; spl. course in mining, U. of Cal., class of 1889; m. Georgia Grayson, of Oakland, Cal., June 7, 1889. Successively mine foreman, supt., mgr. and pres., Fulton Iron Works, 1882-06; pres. Humboldt Land & Cattle Co., 1911-—; pres. W. C. Ralston Brokerage Corpn., Burlington Gold Mining Co., Julia Consolidated Mining Co., etc. U.S. appraiser, Port of San Francisco, 1891-3; mem. Cal. Ho. of Rep., 1901 (speaker of House, pro tem.), State Senate 2 terms, 1903-5; asst. treas. U.S., at San Francisco, 1907-—; Republican. Bahaist. Mem. Am. Inst. Mining Engrs. (ex-v.-p.), Cal. Miners' Assn. (ex-pres.), Zeta Psi (Iota Chapter). Mason, K.T. Home: 2101 Van Ness St. Office: 315 Bush St., San Francisco‡

RAMANI, RADHAKRISHNA, diplomat of Malaysia; b. S. India, Oct. 21, 1901; s. Radhakrishna Iyer and Kamalambal; B.A., in Philosophy, U. Madras, 1921, M.A. in English Lang. and Lit., 1924, B.Law, 1927; Barrister-at-Law, Middle Temple, London, Eng., 1929; m. June Janaki, 1924. Lectr. English lit., also examiner U. Madras, 1926-27; practice law specializing advocacy and court work, 1928-70; advocate High Ct. Judicature, Madras, 1920-29; English barrister, Kuala Lumpur, 1929-70; counsel for govt. numerous occasions; rep. behalf Govt. India polit. prisoners taken into custody as wartime collaborators with Japanese occupation authorities and secured their releases, World War II; adminstr. fund for relief of Indians during occupation of Malaya, 1946-50; chmn. Malaysian Bar Council, 1950-63, Income Tax Bd. Rev., 1950-54; chmn. Malaysian br. Internat. Commn. Jurists; mem. exec. com. World Peace through Law Orgn., 1961-70; concillor Municipality Kuala Lumpur, 1946-54; mem. Fed. Legislative Council Malaya, 1948-55; chmn. exec. com. Malaysian Red Cross, 1955-63; permanent rep. Malaysia to UN, 1963-70. Mem. Internat. Bar Assn. Author: Studies in Shakespeare: Merchant of Venice, Macbeth, others, 1924-25. Editor: (English poetry) Flowers of Eden, 1928. Collaborator: Indian Princes Under British Protection, 1928. Home: Kuala Lumpur Malaysia Died Sept. 1970.

RAMBAUD, GEORGE GIBIER, physician; b. in France, 1875; M.S., U. of France, 1892; M.D., Coll. Phys. and Surg. (Columbia), 1899. Dir. New York Pasteur inst. since 1900. Mem. A.M.A., Med. Soc. State of N.Y., etc. Officier d'Academie, 1909, Chevalier de la Legion d'Honneur, France, 1912. Club: New York Athletic. Address: 361 W. 23d St., New York NY‡

RAMBEAU, MORJORIE, actress; b. San Francisco, Calif., 1889; d. Marcel and Lillian Burnette (Kindelberger) R.; ed. pub. schs.; m. Willard Mack (marriage dissolved); m. 2d, Hugh Dillman, Mar. 8, 1919 (divorced Sept. 13, 1923). First appeared on the stage as a child, at the Alcazar Theatre, San Francisco, 1901; played with stock companies in Calif., later as lead"; starred in Merely Mary Ann," 1911-12; appeared as Minnie in The Girl of the Golden West," at Columbus, O., 1912, as Nelly in Kick-In," Proctor's Fifth Av. Theatre, New York, 1913; played in So Much for So Much," Kindling," Eyes of Youth," The Sign on the Door," etc. Home: Palm Springs CA Died July 7, 1970.

RAMSEY, JAMES BASIL, banker; b. Hopkins Co., Ky., Feb. 15, 1893; s. William Wallace and Ella (Gilmore) R.; grad. high sch., Madisonville, Ky.; m. Villa Sisk, of Earlington, Ky., Oct. 18, 1916;children—Julia Gilmore, James Basil. Began as bookeeper, Farmers Nat. Bank, Madisonville, 1911; cashier Farmers Merchants Bank, Slaughters, Ky., 1916-17; mgr. F.D. Ramsey estate, 1917-20; pres. Hopkins County Bank, Madisonville, 1920-26; cashier Third Nat. Bank, Knoxville, Tenn., 1926; 1st v.p. Holston Nat. Bank, 1927; pres. Holston-Union Nat. Bank, 1927-69; pres. Holston Trust Co.; dir. Nashville br. Federal Reserve Bank of Atlanta, Nashville br. Knoxville Power & Light Co., Inter-Southern Life Ins. Co. Dmocrat. Baptist. Mason (Shriner), Elk. Home: Knoxville TN Died Aug. 1969.

RAMSEYER, JOHN ALVIN, educator; b. Husson, Ill., Apr. 13, 1908; s. Louis and Iva (Mohr) R.; A.B., Bluffton Coll., 1929; M.A., Ohio State U., 1934, Ph.D., 1948; m. Zoa Manges, Aug. 1931; children—John A., Elinor Jeanne ((Mrs. John Stuart Allen). High sch. tchr., Sulphur Springs, O., 1929-31, Dover, O., 1935-38; high sch. tchr., prin., Genoa, O., 1931-35; tchr., U. Sch., Ohio State U., 1938-46, asst. dir., 1943-46, dir., 1946-51; summer teaching U. N.C., U. Va., Emory U., Ohio State U., 1938-51; dir. Sch-Community Devel. Study, Ohio State U., 1951-56, prof. ednl. adminstrn; 1951-68, dir. Sch. Edn., 1965-68; prof. ednl. adminstrn., Washington State U., summer, 1958; interim dir. U. Council Ednl. Adminstrn., summer 1959; special cons.

com. for advancement sch. adminstrn., Am. Assn. Sch. Adminstrs., Washington, 1962; cons. Ednl. Adminstrn. Project New Eng. Bd. Higher Edn., 1962 U. Hawaii, 1965, Pa. Dept. Edn., 1965, U. Pa., 1966. Bd. govs. Phi Delta Kappa Ednl. Found. Mem. U. Council Ednl. Adminstrn. (trustee, 1956-62, treas. 1962-68), Ohio Assn. Sch. Adminstrs., Nat. Assn. Secondary Sch. Prins., N.E.A., Am. Assn. Sch. Adminstrs., Com. for Advancement Sch. Adminstrn., Nat. Council Accreditation Tchr. Edn., Nat. Assn. Profs. Sch. Adminstrn., (mem. planning com. 1967-68), Internat. Platform Assn., Ohio Edn. Assn., Phi Delta Kappa, Phi Kappa Delta. Author: Supervised Correspondence Study Series in Mathematics, 1940-41; (with Margaret Willis, Gene Oppy, Harold Reynard) Secondary Education for Veterans of World War II, 1945; Aviation Education in Ohio, 1946; (with Lewis Harris, Millard Pond, Howard Wakefield) Factors Affecting Educational Administration, 1955; (with Roald F. Campbell) The Dynamics of School-Community Relationships, 1955; (with Campbell,, Corbally, Jr.) Introduction to Educational Administration, 1958, rev., 1962, 1966; (with others) Leadership for the Improvement of Instruction, 1960; (with others) Educational Administration: Selected Readings, 1965 (with Glenn Immegart) A Rondo of Discord, 1962. Contbr. articles profl. jours. Home: OH Died Aug. 20, 1968.

RAMSPECK, ROBERT, ex-congressman; b. Decatur, Ga., Sept. 5, 1890; s. Theodore R. and Ida (Word) R.; LL.B., Atlanta Law Sch., 1920, LL.D. (hon.), 1940; LL.D., Ohio Wesleyan U., 1951; m. Nobie Clay, Oct. 18, 1916; children—Dorothy (Mrs. Dorothy R. Dunson), Betty (Mrs. T. D. Webb, Jr.). Deputy clerk, Superior Court of Georgia, 1907-11; chief clerk of post office, United States House of Rep., 1911; sec. to Congressman William S. Howard, 1912; sec. Decatur Chamber Commerce, 1912-14; office dep. U.S. marshal, Northern Georgia Dist., 1914-16, chief deputy, 1917-19; ins. and real estate business, 1919-21, newspaper business, 1922; solicitor City Court, Decatur, 1923-27; practice of law, Decatur, 1927-29; mem. Ga. Ho. of Rep., 1929; mem. 71st to 79th Congresses (1929-47), 5th Ga. Dist. Resigned Jan. 1946 to become v.p. Air Transport Association of America; chmn. U.S. Civil Service Commn., 1951-52; vice president Eastern Air Lines, 1953-62. Democratic Whip. Chairman Speakers Bureau, Democratic National Com., 1944. Member Dem. Congl. Campaign Com. Mem. Delta Theta Phi. Democrat. Presbyterian. Mason (Shriner), Elk. Home: Kensington MD Died Sept. 10, 1972; buried Decatur GA

RAMSTAD, N(ILES) OLIVER, surgeon; born Meridian, Wis.; Mar. 22, 1875; s. John O. and Karen (Narveson) R.; M.D., University of Minn., 1899; grad. work Vienna, 1902-03, Harvard U., 1905-08; m. Edna Winchester, June 20, 1906; 1 dau., Edith Winchester (Mrs. William H. Hughes). Interne St. Barnabas Hosp., Minneapolis, 1899-1900; practice in Bismarck, N.D., since 1900-49; co-founder Quain & Ramstad Clinic, 1903; dir. Provident Life Ins. Co. Former health officer, City of Bismarck. Fellow Am. Coll. Surgeons (governor 1938-39), A.M.A.; mem. N.D. State Med. Assn. (pres. 1927; chmn. council, 1937-46). Am. Bd. Surgery (founder group), Southern Minn. Med. Assn. (hon.), Am. Goiter Assn., Alpha Kappa Kappa. Clubs: Kiwanis, Executive (dir.), Bismarck Medical. Home: 824 4th St. Office: 221 5th St., Bismarck ND‡

RAMUS, CARL, surgeon U.S.P.H.S.; b. Chicago, Ill., Oct. 1, 1872; s. Christian Emil and Sybla (Faulds) R.; student under mother and tutors; M.D., Rush Med. Coll., 1897 (De Laskee Miller prize for best essay on obstetrics and gynecology); m. Anna Tucker, of Sacramento, Calif., and Honolulu, Sept. 27, 1912; children—Michael, Francesca. Commd. asst. surg. U.S.P.H.S., Mar. 9, 1899; passed asst. surgeon, Mar. 20, 1904; surgeon Mar. 3, 1913. Quarantine duty, Havana, 1899-1900; asst. med. officer, Ft. Stanton (N.M.) Sanatorium, 1900-02; chief quarantine officer, Hawaiian Islands, 1909-12; med. examiner, Ellis Island, N.Y., 1912-16; med. attache Am. Consulate, Naples, 1916-20; in charge First Aid Sta., Naples, during World War; apptd. surgeon in charge U.S. Marine Hosp., Evansville, Ind., 1920. Del. Office Internationale d'Hygiene Publique, Paris, 1919; Internat. Conf. on Care of Wounded Soldiers, Rome, 1920. Student of Oriental philosophy. Mem. A.M.A., Astron. Soc. of Pacific, Am. Legion, Vets. of Foreign Wars. Decorated for war service by Italian Govt. Author: Marriage and Efficiency, 1922; Outwitting Middle Age, 1926; Behind the Scenes with Ourselves, 1931; also articles in jours. Address: U.S. Public Health Service, Washington DC*‡

RANCK, CLAYTON HAVERSTICK, clergyman; b. nr. Lancaster, Pa., Jan. 14, 1876; s. Jacob Eby and Martha Bausman (Haverstick) R.; prep. edn. Franklin and Marshall Acad., Lancaster, and Deichmann's Prep. Sch., Baltimore, Md.; A.B., Franklin and Marshall Coll., Lancaster, 1898; student Union Theol. Sem., 1900-01; grad. Theol. Sem. of Ref. Ch., Lancaster, 1903; post-grad. work, Columbia and Johns Hopkins Univs.; m. Kate Ernst (A.B., Goucher Coll., 1910), June 4, 1914; children—Kathryn Ernst, Clayton Ernst. Teacher mathematics, Franklin and Marshall Acad., 1898-1900; ordained ministry Ref. Ch. in U.S., 1904; pastor Mercersburg Acad., 1903-05, 3d Ref. Ch., Baltimore, 1905-16; gen. sec. Assn. Schs., Colls. and Seminaries of Ref. Ch. in U.S., 1916-18; pastor St. John's Ref. Ch., Harrisburg, Pa., 1918-22; pastor Reformed Ch. of Oak Lane, Pa., and of the students of the U. of Pa. belonging to the Ref. Ch., 1923-28; pastor to students of Phila. belonging to the Evang. and Reformed Ch., 1928-49 and of students belonging to Congl. Christian Ch., 1945-49. Editor social service dept. Ref. Ch. Messenger, 1912-14. Contbr. to Easton MD‡

RAND, ARTHUR HENRY, JR., investment banker; b. Mpls., Aug. 24, 1915; s. Arthur Henry and Roberta (Rae) R.; grad. Hill Sch., Pottstown, Pa., 1935; student U. Va., 1939; m. Irene Marquardt, Mar. 27, 1945 (div. Jan. 1971); children—Suzanne M., Katharine Roberta, Arthur Henry III. With Woodard-Elwood & Co., Mpls., 1936-42, 46-72, treas., dir., 1960, v.p., treas., dir., 1962-64, senior v.p. dir., 1964-72; v.p., dir. Ford Aviation Co. Dir. Upper Tonka Council Community Chest Agy., 1948-55, pres., 1951-55; bd. dirs. Animal Humane Soc., Hennepin County, 1950-72, treas., 1953-57, pres., 1957-66, chmn. spl. gifts div. Hennepin County chpt. A.R.C., 1951, bd. dirs., 1952-58, mem. Sch. Bd., Mound., Minn., 1954-57; chmn. Hennepin County Sch., Survey Com., 1957; chmn. Invest-in-Am. Week, 1959; vice chmn. Spl. Gifts div. United Fund, 1962. Justice of peace, Orono, 1952-66; pres. bd. dirs. Minn. Crippled Children and Adults Camp Courage Found. Served with AUS, 1942-46. Mem. Investment Bankers Assn. Am. (gov.), Twin City Securities Traders Assn. (pres.), Twin City Bond Club (past dir.), Min. Field Trial Assn. (v.p.). Mason (Shriner). Clubs: Minneapolis, Minneapolis Hockey (past dir.), Lafayette (gov., past pres.) (Mpls.); Belle Aire Yacht (Excelsior, Minn.); Riviera (Chan Hassen, Minn.); Desert Valley Golf (Carefree, Ariz.) Home: Carefree AZ Died Jan. 27, 1972; buried Lakewood Cemetery, Minneapolis MN

RAND, CHRISTOPHER, writer; b. N.Y.C., Feb. 14, 1912; s. William Blanchard and Ellen (Emmet) R.; B.A., Yale, 1934; divorced; children—Christopher T., Mary, Richard A., Peter, Diana. Editor, Coast mag., San Francisco, 1937-39; editorial writer San Francisco Chronicle, 1939-42; with OWI, 1942-46; corr. N.Y. Herald Tribune, 1946-51; writer New Yorker mag., 1951—. Nieman fellow Harvard, 1948-49. Author: Hong Kong, 1952; A Nostalgia for Camels, 1957; The Puerto Ricans, 1958; Grecian Calendar, 1962; Christmas in Bethlehem, 1963; Cambridge U.S.A., 1964; Mountains and Water, 1965; Los Angeles, 1967; The Changing Landscape - Salisbury, Connecticut, 1968. Home: Salisbury CT Died Sept. 5, 1968.

RAND, CLAYTON THOMAS, pub., lecturer; b. Onalaska, Wis., May 25, 1891; s. Artemus Reed and Cora Jessie (Shaul) R.; B.S., Miss. A. and M. Coll., 1911; B.S., Harvard, 1913; m. May Ella Smylie, July 30, 1914; 1 son, Clayton Thomas. Admitted to bar, 1917; in law practice, Jackson and Philadelphia, Miss., 1917-25; owner, editor and publisher Neshoba (Miss.) Democrat, 1919, The Dixie Press (Gulfport, Miss.), 1925-71; pub. lecturer, 1920-71. Mem. Alumni Assn. Miss. State (formerly Miss. A. and M. Coll.) (pres. 1931-32), Nat. Editorial Assn. (pres. 1936-37), Clubs: Rotary of Gulfport (dist. gov. La. and Miss., 1934-35); Boston, International House (New Orleans). Author: Abracadabra or One Democrat to Another, 1936; Men of Spine in Mississippi, 1940; Ink on My Hands, 1940; Stars in Their Eyes, Dreamers and Builders, 1954; pamphlets: The New Deal and Diocletian; At 42, I Confess; He Could Take It; co-author with R. L. Smitley: The World Is Mine, Appolonius, Philosopher and Financer, 1958; Sons of the South, 1961, 67. Home: Gulfport MS Died Feb. 26, 1971.

RAND, FRANK PRENTICE, author; b. Worcester, Mass., Nov. 8, 1889; s. John Prentice and Harriet M. (Anderson) R.; grad. Cushing Acad., 1908; B.A. Williams Coll., 1912; M.A., Amherst, 1915; L.H.D., U. Mass., 1955, Williams Coll., 1956; m. Margarita Sutherland Hopkins, Aug. 17, 1916. Instr. English, U. of Me., 1913-14, same, Univ. of Mass., 1914-21, assistant prof., 1921-27, asso. prof., 1927-33, professor, 1933-60, head of dept., 1933-55; general manager academic activities, and dramatic coach, 1920-47; acting dean, Sch. Liberal Arts, 1948-55. Lecturer University of Oregon Summer School, 1929. Trustee Cushing Academy, since 1944. Sergeant 1st class, M.C., United States Army, 1918-19. Mem. Shakespeare Assn. America, Modern Lang. Assn., Coll. English Assn. (dir. 1939-40), Phi Sigma Kappa (editor Signet, 1914-29; sec. 1919-22), Delta Sigma Rho, Phi Kappa Phi. Conglist. Author verse, plays, local history, from 1917; translator: (with Dan F. Waugh) Crumpled Leaves of Old Japan, 1922. Home: Amherst MA Died Feb. 8, 1971; buried Wildwood Cemetery Amherst MA

RAND, GERTRUDE, psychologist; b. New York, N.Y., Oct. 29, 1886; d. Lyman Fiske and Mary Catherine (Moench) Rand; B.A., Cornell U., 1908; M.A., and Ph.D., Bryn Mawr, 1911; Sc.D., Wilson College, Pa., 1943; m. Clarence Errol Ferree, Sept. 28, 1918 (died 1942). Research fellow Bryn Mawr, 1911-12, Sarah Berliner research fellow, 1912-13; demonstrator and reader in experimental and ednl. psychology, same Coll., 1913-14, and asso. in exptl. and applied psychology, 1914-25; demonstrator in exptl. psychology and research asst., Nat. research Council's Com. on Industrial Lighting, 1925-27; asso. prof. of research ophthalmology, Johns Hopkins U. Sch. Medicine, 1928-32, asso. prof. physiol. optics, 1932-36; asso. dir. Research Lab. of Physiol. Optics, Baltimore, Md., 1936-43; research asso. in ophthalmology on Knapp Foundation, Coll. Phys. and Surg., Columbia U., 1943-57; cons. Knapp Memorial Laboratory, College of Physcians and Surgeons, Columbia University, 1957-70. Mem. Armed Forces NRC Vision Com., subcom. on Color Vision and Illumination Standards. Recipient Edgar D. Tillyer Medal, Optical Soc. Am., 1959. Fellow A.A.A.S., Am. Psychol. Assn., Illuminating Engineering Society (Gold medal 1963), Optical Soc. of Am., American Acad. of Ophthalmology and Otolaryngology (hon.); mem. N.Y. State Psychol. Assn., Am. Inst. Physics, University Profs., American Assn. University Women, Inter Society Color Council (color blindness com.), Internat. Council Women Psychologists; mem. adv. com. and com. on Vision Testing Procedures, Nat. Society for Prevention Blindness. Republican. Presbyterian. Clubs: Cosmopolitan (N.Y.) Oldfield (L.I.), Women's Faculty (Columbia); Cornell Women's (New York). Author: the Factors Which Influence the Sesitivity of the Retina to Color, 1913; Radiometric Apparatus for Use in Psychological and Physiological Optics, 1917, Studies in Physiological Optics, 2 vols., 1934 (with C. E. Ferree). Co-inventor Ferree-Rand perimeter, light-sense tester, acuity projecter, multiple-exposure tachistoscope, variable illuminator, and other optical and ophthalmol. instruments. Inventor Rand Anomalscope; co-inventor Hardy-Rand-Rittler Pseudoisochromatic Plates. Contbr. mags. Home: Stony Brook LI NY Died June 30, 1970; buried Baltimore MD

RAND, JAMES HENRY, mfr. office supplies and equipment; b. North Tonawanda, N.Y., Nov. 18, 1886; s. James Henry and Mary (Scribner) R.; Class of 1908, Harvard; m. Evelyn Greely, May 3, 1929; children by previous marriage—Miriam R. Boxwell, James Henry III and Marcell N. (twins). Founder Remington Rank Inc., mfrs. office supplies and equipment, 1926, president, 1926-55, vice chairman of Sperry Rand Corp. (merger of Remington Rand Inc., and Sperry Corporation), 1955-68. Clubs: Fishers Island (N.Y.) Country; Harvard (New Canaan, Conn.); Norwalk (Conn.) Yacht; Saturn (Buffalo); Metropolitan, Union League, University (N.Y. City); Tokeneke, Wee Burn Country (Darien, Conn.); Turf & Field (N.Y.); Everglades (Palm Beach, Fla.). Home: Darien CT Died June, 1968.

RANDALL, CLYDE NATHANIEL, coll. dean; b. N. Ogden, Utah, Apr. 4, 1906; s. Heber J. and Mary L. (Montgomery) R.; A.B., U. Utah, 1932, J.D., 1953; M.B.A., Stanford, 1944, Ph.D., 1946; m. Florence M. Grix, Sept. 19, 1937; children—Reed Heber, Boyd Clyde, Florence Elaine, Dale Samuel. Asst. comptroller U. Utah, 1934-47, head dept. accounting, 1947-58, dean Coll. Bus., 1958-70, also prof. accounting; admitted to Utah bar, 1953. C.P.A., Utah. Rotarian. Home: Salt Lake City UT Died Dec. 13, 1970.

RANDALL, LAWRENCE MERRILL, physician; b. LaMoille, Ia., Aug. 12, 1895; s. Addison J. and Edith (Cox) R.; M.D., U. Ia., 1921; M.S., U. Minn., 1931; m. Faith Meek, Mar. 29, 1923; children-Robert Lawrence, Mary Virginia (Mrs. Douglas Fulton), David Addison. Intern U. Ia., 1921-22, resident obstetrics and gynecology, 1922-24; 1st asst. obstetrics and gynecology U. Minn., Mayo Found., 1925, asst. prof., 1932-35, asso. prof., 1936-46, prof., 1946-60, emeritus prof., 1960-69; head sect. obstetrics and gynecology Mayo Clinic, 1937, chmn. sections, 1949, mem. bd. govs., 1948-55. Diplomate Am. Bd. Obstetrics and Gynecology (chmn.). Mem. A.M.A., Am. Coll. Obstetricians, Am. Assn. Obstetricians and Gynecologists, Central Assn. Obstetricians and Gynecologists, Minn. Soc. Obstetricians and Gynecologists, Alumni Assn. Mayo Found. Med. Edn. and Research, Societe Royale Belge de Gynecologie et d'Obstetrique (fgn. corr.) Am., Chgo. gynecol. socs., Sigma Xi, Phi Kappa Sigma, Nu Sigma Nu. Republican. Episcopalian. Contbr. med. articles profl. jours. Home: Rochester MN Died Jan. 11, 1969.

RANDALL, PAUL KING, JR., advt. agy. exec.; b. Irvington, N.Y., Dec. 1, 1928; s. Paul King and Katharine (Patteson) R.; grad. Hackley Sch., 1946; A.B., Hamilton Coll., 1950. Sales and advt. mgr. Mfrs. Marketing Co., N.Y.C., 1950-56; account exec. Batten, Barton, Durstine & Osborn, Inc., N.Y.C., San Francisco, Chgo., Dallas, 1956-65, v.p., regional mgr., Dallas, 1965-71. Mem. exec. com. Dallas council Boy Scouts Am. Served with N.Y. N.G., 1951-53. Mem. Assn. Broadcast Execs. Tex. (past dir.), Dallas Advt. League, Dallas Tennis Assn. (dir.), Am. (vice chmn. S.W. Council), S.W. (past v.p., dir.) assns. advt. agys., Dallas C. of C. (chmn. communications com.), Chi Psi. Republican. Clubs: Dallas Racquet (dir., past pres.), Dallas 500. Home: Dallas TX Died Dec. 27, 1971; buried Sleepy Hollow Cemetery, Tarrytown NY

RANDALL, RUTH PAINTER, author; b. Salem, Va. Nov. 1, 1892; d. Franklin V. N. and Laura Trimble (Shickel) Painter; A.B., Roanoke Coll., 1913, Litt.D., 1958; A.M., Ind. U., 1914; Litt.D., MacMurray Coll., 1954, Bradley U., 1960; LL.D., Knox College, 1958; m. James Garfield Randall, Aug. 21, 1917 (dec. 1953). Collaborator with J. G. Randall on biog. research life of Lincoln; author: Mary Lincoln: Biography of a Marriage, 1953; Lincoln's Sons, 1956; The Courtship of Mr. Lincoln, 1957; Lincoln's Animal Friends (juvenile book), 1958; I Mary, 1959; Colonel Elmer Ellsworth, 1960; I Varina, 1962; I Jessie, 1963; I Elizabeth, 1966; I Ruth: Autobiography of a Marriage, publ. 1968. Recipient Woman Achievement award, Altrusa Club, Urbana, 1961. Mem. Illinois Hist. Society, Nat. League Am. Pen Women, Soc. Midland Authors. Club: University of Illinois. Contbr. newspaper mags., lit. Urbana IL Died Jan. 22, 1971; buried Mt. Hope Cemetery, Champaign IL

RANDEGGER, GIUSEPPE ALDO, pianist, composer, teacher; b. Naples, Italy, Feb. 17, 1874; s. Edoardo and Emmelina (Orefici) R.; ed. schs. in Naples; entered Royal Conservatory of Music at 14, and 2 yrs. later won scholarship, and continued until received degree of Maestro di Musica, Pianoforte and Organ, with highest honors; m. Henriette Brinker, of Cleveland, O., June 20, 1907. Located at Atlanta, Ga., 1893; taught piano 4 yrs. and concertized through the South; dean Sch. of Music, Hamilton Coll., Lexington, Ky., 1906-07; taught music at Bellmont College, Nashville, Tenn., The Castle," and the Irving Sch., Tarrytown, N.Y.; was dir. mus. faculty Belmont Coll., Nashville, Tenn.; toured principal cities of U.S. and Can., Italy and England; Concert Chorale Ensemble, Randegger Societa per la Musica Italiana. Founded Randegger Conservatory of Music, N.Y. City, and dir. and teacher same; also founded the Randegger Trio, conducts summer session at Luzerne, in Adirondacks. Recognized as a leading exponent of Italian music in America; has served as judge New York Music Week Assn. contests for piano and other branches; soloist lecturer over radio. Naturalized Am. citizen. Composer: (operas) The Promise of Medea (libretto by Henriette Brinker Randegger); Via Pacis, art message for world peace, with vocal solos, ensembles (libretto by same), etc.; for orchestra, Death and the Soul, Valse and Sacrificial Dances of the Virgins; also many piano pieces, songs, etc. Address: 13 W. 88th St., New York NY‡

RANDLES, ANDREW J., clergyman; b. Waterman, Ill., Dec. 15, 1877; s. William John and Emily (White) R.; B.A., Monmouth (Ill.) Coll., 1902; grad. Pittsburgh Theol. Sem., 1905; D.D., Westminster Coll., New Wilmington, Pa., 1927; m. Myrtle E. Beitel, June 7, 1905; children—Emily (dec.), Elizabeth, Janet, Martha. Ordained ministry U.P. Ch., 1905; pastor New Athens, O., 1905-09, Vandergrift, Pa., 1909-15, Second Ch., New Castle, Pa., 1915-32; corr. editor The United Presbyterian, 1925-33; sec. Bible sch. work, U.P. Ch., 1932-45; mem. exec. com. Internat. Council of Religious Edn., 1932-45. Dir. and mem. bd. management Pittsburgh-Xenia Theol. Sem., 1916-33; mem. United Staff Pa. State S.S. Assn.; mem. Council Christian Edn. United Presbyn. Ch.; mem. bd. dirs. Allegheny County Sunday Sch. Orgn.; mem. edn. com. Pa. State Council Christian Edn., 1933-45; pastor, Liberty United Presbyn. Ch., Youngstown, O., since 1945. Pres. bd. adminstrn. U.P. Ch., 1931-41; chmn. com. on pastoral settlements, Gen. Assembly, 1931-32; mem. Pittsburgh Council of Week-Day Religious Education, 1940-45. Youngstown OH‡

RANEY, MCKENDREE LLEWELLYN, librarian; b. Stanford, Ky., Feb. 28, 1877; s. William Gabriel and Anne Josephine (Jones) R.; A.B., Centre Coll., Ky., 1897, LL.D., 1927; Ph.D., Johns Hopkins, 1904; m. Catharine Placide Coulehan, Nov. 6, 1903; children—Llewellyn, Ruth. Instr. Latin, Centre Coll., 1897-98; instr. classics, Hogsett Mil. Acad., Danville, Ky., 1898-99; fellow in Greek, Johns Hopkins, 1901-03; asst. librarian, 1903-08, librarian, 1908-27, Johns Hopkins Univ.; dir. U. of Chicago Libraries, 1927-42. Member Am. Library Assn., Bibliog. Soc. America, Phi Beta Kappa. Organizer of A.L.A. overseas war service, 1918; mgr. it's importation service under Dept. of State, War Trade and Censorship bds. Dec. 1917-July 1919; chairman A.L.A. book buying committee, 1920-29 and chairman committee on photographic reproduction of library materials, 1936-1937; manager A.L.A. microphotography demonstration, with United States Navy Dept. aid, Paris Exposition 1937; organizer of similar program Rome (1938), Zurich (1939), and often in the United States. Trustee, Biological Abstracts, 1938-43. Author: Maryland's Stock of Wild Life, 1916; The University Libraries (University of Chicago Survey, Volume VII), 1933; (with others) If Lincoln Had Lived, 1935; (with Harold L. Leupp); The H.W. Wilson Company's System of Scale Pricing, 1941. Editor: The Courier, 1934-42; Microphotography for Libraries, 1936, 37; also numerous contributions to professional jours. Home: 3732 Beech Av., Baltimore 11 MD‡

RANK, JOSEPH ARTHUR, (1st Baron Rank of Sutton Scotney), motion picture circuit exec., prod. exec.; b. Hull, Yorkshire, Eng., Dec. 23, 1888; s. Joseph and Emily (Voase) R.; ed. Leys Sch., Cambridge, Eng.; LL.D., Boston U., 1948; m. Honorable Laura Ellen Marshall; children—Ursula Helen (Mrs. Lance R. Newton), Shelagh Mary (Mrs. Robin Cowen). Pres. Rank-Hovis-McDougall, Ltd. (flour milling); pres. Rank Orgn., Ltd., 1962-72; dir. Gaumont Brit., Ltd. Rank TV and Gen. Trust, Ltd., Odeon Asso. Theatres, Ltd., Odeon Properties, Ltd.; founder Religious Film Soc., later expanding to include comml. motion pictures; with C.M. Woolf formed G.F.D., 1935; formed Eagle-Lion Distbrs., Ltd.; formed co-ordinating unit for interests, J. Arthur Rank Orgn. (Mgmt.), Ltd., 1946, Circuits Mgmt. Assn., Ltd., 1948. Recipient 4 Motion Picture Academy Awards for art and art direction in black and white and colour film prodn., 1948. Methodist. Club: Bath (London). Home: Sutton Scotney Hants England Died Mar. 29, 1972.

RANKIN, JEANNETTE, former congresswoman; b. ranch nr. Missoula, Mont., June 11, 1880; d. John and Olive (Pickering) R.; lived on ranch until 15; B.S., U. Mont., 1902; student sch. Philanthropy, N.Y., 1908-09. Social worker, Seattle, 1909; active in woman suffrage work in Wash., 1910, Cal., 1911, Mont., 1912-14; field sec. Nat. Am. Woman Suffrage Assn.; chmn. Mont. State Suffrage Com. in successful campaign, 1914; visited New Zealand, 1915, and worked as a seamstress in order to gain personal knowledge of social conditions; mem. 65th Congress (1917-19), Mont. at large, being first woman ever elected to U.S. Congress. Republican. Mem. Nat. Women's Trade Union League Am. Club: Missoula Woman's. Address: Missoula MT Died May 18, 1973.

RANKIN, JOHN WATKINS, hosp. adminstr.; b. Concord, N.C., May 11, 1919; s. Samuel Wharton and Louise Evans (Watkins) R.; A.B., U. N.C., 1939; certificate hosp. adminstrn., Duke, 1941; fellow hosp. adminstrn., W. K. Kellogg Found., 1942; m. June Williamson, Apr. 20, 1967; children—John Robert, Samuel Martin, Juliann, Louise Watkins, John Watkins. Regional hosp. officer Office Civilian Def., USPHS, Atlanta, 1942-43; supt. Tuomey Hosp., Sumter, S.C., 1943-46; dir. James Walker Meml. Hosp., Wilmington, N.C., 1946-52, Milwaukee County Instns. and Depts., 1952-61, Charlotte (N.C.) Meml. Hosp., 1961-72. Pres. Medi-Data, Inc. Pres. Greater Milw. Hosp. Council, 1955, S.C. Hosp. Assn., 1946, Wis. Hosp. Assn., 1958, Tri-State Hosp. Assembly, 1959. Fellow Am. Coll. Hosp. Adminstrs.; mem. Am. Hosp. Assn. (past del.), Am. Pub. Welfare Assn., Am. Pub. Charlotte NC Died June 24, 1972; buried Oakwood Cemetery, Concord NC

RANSFORD, CHARLES ORRIN, editor; b. St. Joseph, Mo., Apr. 6, 1868; s. Charles Orrin, Sr., and Elizabeth (Abbott) R.; ed. Central Coll., Fayette, Mo., and Vanderbilt U. (non-grad); D.D., Central Coll.; m. Maude Blackburn, Nov. 25, 1897; children—Charles Orrin, Willie Elizabeth (dec.), William Blackburn, Mrs. Mary Catherine Rist., Paul. Ordained ministry M.E. Ch., S., 1893; minister Mo. Conf. M.E. Ch. S.; presiding elder St. Charles Dist., 1907-08, and Fayette Dist., 1916-20; editor St. Louis Christian Advocate, 1921-28; corr. Christian Century, 1929-34; asso. editor Christian Advocate, Nashville, 1934-40, asst. editor Christian Advocate, Chicago, 1941-42; sec. Mo. Conf. M.E. Ch., S. since 1901; trustee Conf. Trust Fund, Mo. Conf., M.S. Ch., S. Odd Fellow. Contbr. articles on Mo. Meth. history. Home: Shelbina MO‡

RANSON, ARTHUR JONES, clergyman; b. Huntersville, N.C., Aug. 26, 1873; s. John James and Rose Elizabeth (Hunter) R.; A.B., Erskine Coll., Due West, S.C., 1893, A.M., 1918, D.D., 1926; student Erskine Theol. Sem., 1895, Princeton Sem., 1900; m. Julia E. Cowan, June 23, 1897 (died Aug. 8, 1902); m. 2d, Kate P. Walker, Dec. 21, 1903; children—Mary (Mrs. Frank L. Woodruff), John Walker (dec.), Arthur Jones. Ordained ministry Asso. Ref. Presbyn. Ch., 1895; pastor Prosperity, Tenn., 1895-1901, Corsicana, Tex., 1901-05, Spartanburg, S.C., 1905-10; missionary, India, 1910-24; pastor Newbury, S.C., 1927; pres. Bryson Coll., Fayetteville, Tenn., 1927-29; pastor New Albany, Miss., Aug. 1929-Sept. 1945; pastor Shiloh Ch., Lancaster, S.C., since Sept. 1, 1945. Moderator Asso. Ref. Presbyn. Synod, 1926; fraternal delegate to United Presbyterian Assembly, 1926, 1945. Clubs: Kiwanis, Lions. Home: 103 W. Hood St., Lancaster SC*‡

RAO, K. KIRSHNA, govt. ofcl. India; b. Masulipatam, India, Dec. 23, 1924; s. Kunapareddi Achayya and Seethamma Rao; B.A., in Econs., Madras (India) U., 1943; LL.B., Bombay (India) U., 1945; barrister-at-law, Inner Temple, London, Eng., 1948; LL.M., London U., 1949; J.S.D., Columbia, 1955, N.Y.U. (Founders Day certificate), 1955; m. Bhanumathi Menon, Mar. 17, 1962;children—Maya, Tara. Practice law with P. Lingayya Chowdary, Masulipatam, then P.V. Subba Rao, 1947-49, and Sir Walter Monckton, 1948-50; legal adviser, legal dept. UN, 1950-57; legal adviser, dept. sec. charge legal and treaties div. Indian Ministry External Affairs, 1957-62, legal adviser, dir. legal and treaties div., 1962-70, joint sec., legal adviser, 1965-70; participant numerous internat. confs., also UN assemblies. Sec. UN Lawyers Assn.; founder mem., sec. gen. Maritime Law Assn. India; mem. editorial bd. Indian Year Book Maritime Law; founder mem. Indian Soc. Internat. Law, 1959, then exec. pres., and editor-in-chief jour.; mem. gov. body Indian Acad. Internat. Law and Diplomacy, also mem. faculty; lectr. Nat. Acad. Adminstrn., Mussoorie, India, Indian Council World Affairs. New Delhi; examiner internat. law various univs., also Union Pub. Service Commn. India Author numerous articles in field. Home: New Delhi India Died Nov. 1970.

RAPACKI, ADAM, Polish govt. ofcl.; b. Lvov, Poland, Dec. 24, 1909; grad. Higher Sch. Commerce, Warsaw, Poland, 1932. Active socialist student movement, 1929-32, research worker Coop. Science Institute, Institute for Research Market Conditions and Prices; while in German prison organized anti-fascist movement, 1939-45; deputy of Parliament, 1947; minister of navigation, 1947-50; member supreme board of Central Com. of Polish Socialist Party, mem. polit. com., 1948; mem. Central Com. of Polish United Workers Party, 1948, mem. polit. bur., 1956-70; dep. chmn. Polish Peace Com., 1949; minister higher edn. Govt. Poland, 1950-56, minister fgn. affairs, 1956-70; dep. to the Seym, 1947-70. Author plan to set up de-nuclearized zone in Central Europe. Address: Warsaw Poland Died Oct. 1970.

RAPEE, LEON ANDRE, realtor; b. Moscow, Russia, Dec. 25, 1903; s. Simon A. and Sophia (Courant) R.; B.A., Conservatoire de Paris, 1930; student U. Sorbonne, 1930-32, Alliance Francaise, 1930-31, LaSalle U. Law Sch., 1951-54; m. Eleanor Altman, Sept. 30, 1933; children—Stuart Michael, Bruce Elliott. First violinist NBC, 1928-30; tchr. beauty culture, Chgo. and Rockford, Ill., 1936-39; pres. Am. TV Co., Inc., 1954-69, Rapee Co., Inc., Realtors, 1942-69; exec. dir. Normandy Isle Improvement Assn., 1946-69; pres., chmn. bd. Stubru Land Devel., Inc.; pres. Stubru Syndicated Investments, Inc., Lenel, Inc., of Miami; real estate investments. Pres., chmn. bd. Free Enterprise Assn. Fla., Inc. Chmn. orgns. and extension Miami dist. Boy Scouts Am., 1953-69. Certified property mgr. Recipient Humanitarian award, Govt. Equador. Mem. Am. Fedn. Musicians, Nat. Cosmetologist Assn., N.O. Shore Bus. Assn. (dir., treas.), Greater Miami Cosmetologists Assn., (treas.), Miami Beach Taxpayers Assn., Nat. Inst. Real Estate Mgmt. Elk. Clubs: Haylof: (pres.), Silver Spurs.

RAPIER, THOMAS GWYNN, newspaper man; business mgr., 1879-96, gen. mgr., 1896-14, New Orleans Picayune; now retired. Pres. People's Homestead Assn. Home: 1836 Baronne St. Office: 327 St. Charles Av., New Orleans LA‡

RAPPAPORT, PERCY, govt. ofcl.; b. N.Y.C., Mar. 2, 1895; s. Jacob and Minnie (Scher) R.; B.C.S., N.Y.U., 1916; m. Regina Youle, Sept. 30, 1925; children—Donald, Susan. With Price, Waterhouse & Co., N.Y.C., 1917-55, mgr., 1922-37, partner, 1937-55; asst. dir. U.S. Bur. of Budget, 1955-58. Mem. Am. Inst. Accountants, N.Y. State Soc. C.P.A.'s. Clubs: Lotos (N.Y.C.); New York University Men in Finance (dir.). Home: Upper Montclair NJ Died Aug. 21, 1971.

RAPPORT, DAVID, physiologist; b. Pitts., Aug. 29, 1891; s. John and Fannie (Binder) R.; A.B., Harvard, 1912, M.D., 1916; m. Jean DeWilde Simpson, June 18, 1931; children—Elizabeth, Nancy. Austin teaching fellow in physiology, Harvard, 1919, instr., 1920-21; research fellow, Cornell Med. Sch., 1921-24; instr. and sr. instr., Western Res. Med. Sch., 1925-29; prof. physiology, Tufts U. Med. Sch., 1929-70. Served as 1st lt. med. corps, A.E.F., 1917-19. Fellow Am. Acad. Arts and Sciences, A.A.A.S.; mem. Am. Physiol. Soc., Soc. Exptl. Biology and Medicine, Radiation Research Soc., Alpha Omega Alpha, Sigma Xi. Clubs: Harvard (Boston), Faculty (Cambridge). Contbr. articles on circulation, metabolism, endocrines, cellular respiration. Home: Cambridge MA Died Oct. 1970.

RASMUSSEN, ALBERT TERRILL, clergyman, educator, social researcher; b. Regina, Sask., Can., Oct. 20, 1911; s. James Peter and Altha (Stone) R.; brought to U.S., 1920; A.B., Whitworth Coll., 1934; B.D., Chgo. Theol. Sem., 1937; Ph.D., U. Chgo., 1943; m. Marion F. Kirkland, Dec. 24, 1936; children—Terrill Ann, Linda Kirkland. Ordained to ministry of Congl. Ch., 1938; research asso. Chgo. Theol. Sem., 1938-40; dir. survey Congl. Chs. So. Cal., 1940; dir. research Washington Fedn. Chs., 1942-43; dir. field and research Chgo. Congl. Union, 1943-46; Arthur J. Gosnell prof. social ethics and sociology of religion Colgate Rochester Div. Sch., 1946-57, director dept. religious community research, 1946-57; professor of religion and society Pacific Sch. Religion, Berkeley, California, 1957-69, also director Bureau of Community Research; faculty Graduate Theol. Union, Berkeley; vis. lectr. social ethics Yale Div. School, 1954-55; visiting professor at Union Theological Seminary, N.Y.C., summer 1960; research cons., lectr., writer on Christian ethics and religion in urban soc. Mem. Am., Rural sociol. socs., Religious Research Assos., Assn. Christian Social Ethics Profs., Nat. Council Chs. (com. ch. and econ. life, dept. internat. relations). Author: The Field and Strategy of Congreagtionalism in Southern California, 1940; A Comparative Study of Congregational and Other Protestant Churches in Chicago, 1946; Christian

Social Ethics, 1956; Christian Responsibility in Economic Life, 1965. Contbr. periodicals. Mem. editorial com. Social Action. Home: El Cerrito CA Died Mar. 15, 1969.

RASMUSSEN, MARIUS PETER, educator; b. Bennington, Vt., Oct. 1, 1893; s. Christian II. and Anna M. (Jensen) R.; B.S., Cornell, 1919; Doctor of Philosophy, 1924; married Else M. Jacobsen, Mar. 25, 1920 (died October 8, 1957); children—Allan Eric, Kenneth Edgar; m. 2d, Dr. Ellen S. C. Nelson, August 27, 1960. With Nat. Fertilizer Association, Balt., 1919-20; agrl. economist U. Vt., 1920-21; prof. marketing Cornell, 1924-58, emeritus; free lance writer and consultant; investigator in marketing N.Y. State Agrl. Expt. Sta., Ithaca, since 1924; research agt. in marketing Bur. Agrl. Econs., Dept. of Agr., Washington, 1922-24; agrl. economist, 1927-28, sr. agrl. economist, 1929-30; prin. econ. expert in marketing Fed. Farm Bd., Washington, 1933; expert marketing specialist Farm Credit Adminstrn., 1934-41; econ. cons., fruit and vegetable com. Am. Farm Bur. Fedn., Chg., 1933-41; research cons. Fla. Citrus Commn., Lakeland, 1941; head cons. W.P.B., Washington, 1942-43; cons. economist Farm Credit Adminstrn., 1949-52; advisor, cons. Am. Nat. Coop. Exchange, Inc., N.Y.C., 1933-54; econ. cons. United Fresh Fruit and Vegetable Assn., 1935-50; advisor, cons. Am. Nat. Foods, Inc., 1954-58; dir. market research N.Y. State Commn. Agr., 1953-59, cons. editor Comml. Vegetable Grower, 1952, Am. Vegetable Grower, 1953-70. Mem. Am. Marketing Association, American Farm Economic Assn., International Conference Agricultural Economists, Sigma Xi, Phi Kappa Phi, Alpha Zeta. Republican. Lutheran. Mason. Author state and fed. publs., articles on marketing and agrl. econs. Home: Middlebush NJ Winter Largo FL Died Jan. 18, 1970; buried Troy NY

RATH, HOWARD HARBIN, business exec.; b. Waterloo, Ia., May 7, 1898; s. John W. and Maude (Harbin) R.; B.S., U. Ill., 1921; m. Mary Brown, Feb. 3, 1927; children—Betty Jane (Mrs. Donald R. Reichert), Marilyn (Mrs. John H. Dempster). Asst. treas. The Rath Packing Co., Waterloo, 1922-26, treas., 1926-43, v.p., treas., 1943-48, 1st v.p. treas., 1948-50, president, 1950-56, chmn. bd., 1956-65, chairman of the executive committee, also dir.; dir. Nat. Bank of Waterloo, I.C. R.R. Dir. National Live Stock and Meat Board. Member American Meat Inst. (dir. and mem. exec. com.), Ia. Mfrs. Assn. (director), N.A.M., U.S., Waterloo C.'s of C., Phi Kappa Sigma. Presbyn. Clubs: Elks, University (Chgo.); Rotary. Home: Waterloo IA Died Jan. 25, 1971; buried Waterloo IA

RATHER, JOHN THOMAS, JR., architect; b. Copperas Cove, Tex., Sept. 8, 1896; s. John Thomas and Nettie Roach (Box) R.; A.B., Rice Inst., 1919, B.S., 1920; m. Mary Lyda Stokes, 1926. Practice of architecture, Tex., 1920-68; partner Staub, Rather & Howze, Houston, 1935-68. Former chmn. Tex. State Bd. Archtl. Examiners. Fellow A.I.A. Methodist. Home: Houston TX Died Jan. 10, 1968.

RATHVON, NATHANIEL PETER, corporation exec.; b. Denver, Colo., Apr. 26, 1891; s. Samuel Forney and Emily (Magraw) R.; student Culver Mil. Acad., 1907-09; B.A., U. of Colo., 1913, LL.B., 1915; m. Helen Hall, Sept. 18, 1917; children—Nathaniel Peter, Joan Frances, Judith Hall. Admitted to Colorado bar, 1915; practiced law, Denver, 1915-16; practiced abroad, principally in China, 1916-22; treas. Theadore Schulze & Co., N.Y. City, 1923-31; partner brokerage firm Munds, Winslow, N.Y. City, 1931-33; pres. Pacific Eastern Corp., N.Y. City, 1933-36; v.p. Atlas Corp., Jersey City, N.J., 1936; pres. Rathvon & Co., investments, N.Y. City, 1937-42; pres. Radio Keith Orpheum Corp., June 1942-Sept. 1948; pres. Motion Picture Capital Corp., 1949-53; ind. motion picture producer, from 1953. pres. R. K. Tompkins y Asociados S.A. de C.V., Mexico. Served as pvt. F.A., 1918. Recipient Mexico DF Mexico Died May 26, 1972.

RAUCH, GEORGE W., ex-congressman; b. Warren, Ind., Feb. 22, 1876; s. Philip and Martha (Jones) R.; ed. Valparaiso Normal Sch. (now univ.); grad. Northern Ind. Law School, 1902; m. Emma Asenath Nolen, July 10, 1918; children—George Washington, Martha Ellen, Richard Andrew. Admitted to bar, 1902, and since in practice at Marion, Ind. Mem. 60th to 64th Congresses (1907-17), 11th Ind. Dist.; Democrat. Home: Marion IN‡

RAUCH, RUDOLPH STEWART, business exec.; born N.Y. City, Feb. 21, 1892; s. William and Susan Spring (Paton) R.; student St. Pauls Sch., Concord, N.H., 1903-09; Litt.B., Princeton, 1913; m. Mary Banks French, Oct. 11, 1913; children—Rudolph Stewart, Mary Paton (Mrs. Henry B. Roberts), Thomas Morton. Pres. Winchester Simmons Co., Phila., 1922-24; vice pres. Phila. Rubber Works Co., 1924-29; dir. B. F. Goodrich Co. from 1932, mem. exec. com., 1935-60; pres. North Bros. Mfg. Co., 1939-46. Trustee St. Pauls Sch., 1933-36; mem. indsl. adv. bd., Nat. Recovery Adminstrn., 1934-35; member of board of trustees Trudeau Sanatorium; 1947-52; and manager of the Overbrook School for the Blind. Served as capt., U.S. Army, 1917-19. Mem. Soc. of the Cincinnati, Vets. Foreign Wars. Episcopalian. Clubs: Philadelphia; Racquet and Tennis (N.Y. City). Home: Villa Nova PA Died Oct. 13, 1971.

RAUDENBUSH, DAVID WEBB, lawyer; b. Washington, Dec. 17, 1906; s. Webb Russell and Florence (Miller) R.; grad. St. Paul Acad., A.B., Princeton, 1928; LL.B., Harvard, 1931; m. Agnes Patton Woodhull, June 30, 1934; children—Peter Vroom, Brenda, Hilary, Lucy. Admitted to Minn. bar, 1931, since practiced in St. Paul; asso. Kellogg, Morgan, Chase, Carter & Headley, 1931-35, partner various successor firms, 1936-69, now Briggs & Morgan. Member board of directors Family Service of St. Paul, 1936-56, pres., 1953-54; dir. St. Paul Community Chest, 1948-51, 59-62, v.p., 1959-62. Civilian operations analyst USAAF, Orlando, Fla., India China, 1942-45. Mem. Am., Minn., Ramsey County bar assns., Am. Judicature Soc., Phi Beta Kappa. Author: Democratic Capitalism, 1946. Home: St Paul MN Died Nov. 12, 1969.

RAUH, BERTHA FLOERSHEIM (MRS. ENOCH RAUH), welfare worker; b. Pittsburgh, Pa., June 16, 1865; d. Samuel and Pauline (Wertheimer) Floersheim; ed. high sch., Pittsburgh; m. Enoch Rauh, Dec. 5, 1888 (now dec.); children—Helen Blanche, Richard Solomon. Dir. dept. pub. welfare, Pittsburgh, 1922-34 (said to be the first woman in U.S. to be apptd. mem. mayor's cabinet). Pres. Milk & Ice Assn. for 38 yrs. Mem. bd. Animal Rescue League; mem. auxiliary bd. Pittsburgh branch, Pa. Assn. for Blind; mem. Nat. Anti-syphilis Com. for Pittsburgh; mem. Pan-Am. Cooperative Foundation for Pittsburgh; mem. adv. bd. League for Hard of Hearing; mem. adv. bd. Pittsburgh Nat. Guard; mem. bd. Girl Scouts, Travelers Aid Soc., Family Society; mem. Civic Club of Allegheny County (mem. of bd. 38 yrs.), Historical Soc. of Allegheny County, Urban League, Academy Science and Arts, Pittsburgh Symphony Society (founder with son), Congress of Women's Clubs. Republican. Ref. Jewish religion. Clubs: Concordia, Civic, Republican Woman's Club of Pa., Westmoreland Country, Business and Professional Woman's. Home: 5837 Bartlett St., Pittsburgh PA‡

RAVDIN, ISIDOR SCHWANER, phys. and surg.; b. Evansville, Ind., Oct. 10, 1894; s. Marcus and Wilhelmina (Jacobson) R.; B.S., Ind. U., 1916; M.D., U. Pa., 1918; L.H.D. (hon.); LL.D., Sc.D.; m. Elizabeth Glenn, June 2, 1921; children—Robert Glenn (dec. 1972), Elizabeth, William Dickie. Intern U. Pa. Hosp., 1918-19, chief resident phys., 1919-20; instr. surgery U. Pa., 1920, asso. in surgery, 1922-27, asst. prof. surg. research, 1927, prof., 1928-35, Harrison prof. surgery, 1935-45, John Rhea Barton prof. surgery, 1944-59, dir. Harrison Dept. Surg. Research, 1944-59, prof. surgery, v.p. for med. affairs University Pennsylvania, 1959-65, vice chmn. medical devel., from 1965; surgeon in chief U. Pa. Hosp., 1945-59. Dir. Mead Johnson & Co., 1962-68. Pres. American Cancer Society, 1962-63; mem. Nat. Adv. Health Council; alternate mem. Civilian Advisory Council to Sec. of Def.; sr. civilian cons. surgeon Surgeon Gen. of the Army. Chmn. clin. studies panel Cancer Chemotherapy Nat. Service Center, Nat. Insts. Health. Member board of trustees Phila. Mus. Art, Rosenbach Mus. Phila. Served as brig. gen. M.C., AUS, 1942-45; maj. gen. ret. Decorated Legion of Merit with oak leaf cluster; Olaf of Acrel medal (Sweden); recipient Phila. award. Diplomate of American Board of Surgery. Hon. fellow England, Scotland, Canada royal colls. surgeons; mem. Internat. Fedn. Surg. Colleges and Societies (vice president), Am. Surgical Association (pres. 1958-59), A.C.S. (pres. 1960), International Blood Transfusion Soc. (past president), Pan-Pacific Surg. Assn. (ex-pres.), Phila. Acad. Surgery (ex-pres.), Am. Assn. Surgery Trauma, A.M.A., Am. Soc. Exptl. Pathology, Societe Internat. de Chirurgie, Internat. Soc. Surgery, Am. Physiol. Soc. Editor: Kirschner Surgery (3 vols.), 1932-36. Home: Philadelphia PA Died Aug. 27, 1972; buried West Laurel Hill Cemetery

RAVEL, VINCENT MARVIN, physician; b. El Paso, Tex., Jan. 22, 1914; s. Joseph B. and Theresa (Hurwitz) R.; M.D., Baylor U., 1937; postgrad. U. Pa., 1945-46; m. Annette Kluger, Mar. 30, 1941; children—Rita L., Jerrold M., Benita, Elsie F. Intern, R. E. Thomason Gen. Hosp., El Paso; resident Albert Einstein Hosps.; dir. dept. radiology Providence Meml. Hosp., El Paso, R.E. Thomas Gen. Hosp., 1952-69; sr. El Paso Radiol. Group, 1960-69. Vice pres. El Paso Symphony Orch. Assn.; vice chmn. Liberty Hall and Coliseum Bd., 1962; pres. Jewish Community Council. Served to comdr. USNR, 1940-46. Diplomate Am. Bd. Radiology. Fellow Am. Coll. Angiology, A.A.A.S., Am. Coll. Radiology, Acad. Internat. Medicine, Am., Tex. med. assns., Radiol. Soc. N.Am., Soc. Nuclear Medicine. Mem. B'nai B'rith. Clubs: Coronado Country, El Paso. Contbr. articles profl. jours. Home: El Paso TX Died Feb. 13, 1969.

RAWLEIGH, WILLIAM THOMAS, mfr.; b. on farm nr. Mineral Point, Wis., Dec. 3, 1870; s. Charles David and Sarah Malinda (Babcock) R.; ed. rural schs.; m. Minnie B. Trevillian of Mineral Point, Wis., Nov. 16, 1890; children—Anna May (Mrs. Robert F. Koenig), Wilbur T. (dec.), Lucille (Mrs. Quentin R. Smith); m. 2d, M. Marguerite Schneider, of Freeport, Ill., Mar. 14, 1923. Began as retailer of proprietary products, 1889, later mfr. and wholesaler; incorporated as W. T. Rawleigh Co., 1895, since pres.; editor Freeport Daily Standard, 1909; pres. Rawleigh-Schryer Co., 1911-17; pres. W.T. Rawleigh Co., Ltd. Mem. city council, Freeport, 1906-07; mayor of Freeport, 1909-11; mem. Ill. Ho. of Rep., 1910-12. Chmn. Freeport-Hughes Alliance, 1911; Prog. presdl. elector, 1911; chmn. La Follette-for-President com., treas. Nat. Joint La Follette-Wheeler Com. and del. to Cleveland (O.) Conf., 1924. Founder and pres. Rawleigh Foundation for Pub. Service. Republican. Methodist. Mason, Odd Fellow. Club: Hamilton (Chicago). Donor of statue, Lincoln the Debater," to Stephenson Co., Ill., 1929. Address: IL‡

RAWLINGS, NORBORNE L., naval officer, corp. exec.; born Lawrenceville, Va., June 18, 1894; s. James and Jane Gee (Meredith) R.; B.S., U.S. Naval Acad., 1917; M.S., Mass. Inst. Tech., 1921; m. Lucy Dabney Hix, June 8, 1921; children—Dabney Hix (Mrs. J. L. Holloway III), Norborne. Commd. ensign U.S.N., 1917 and advanced through grades to rear admiral, Feb. 22, 1943; naval architect, June 1921; served on U.S. Destroyer based on Queenstown, Ireland, World War I; head of shipbuilding div. Bur. of Ships, Navy Dept., Washington, D.C., 1939-42; in command of U.S. Naval Drydocks, in charge of constrn. and expansion of ship repair yard and operations, Hunters Point, San Francisco, 1943-45; work in navy related to designing, constrn., and maintenance of naval vessels and operation of naval shipyards; vice chief, material div. office asst. sec. of Navy, Navy Department, Washington, until retirement, 1947; spl. rep. Newport News Shipbuilding and Dry Dock Co., 1947-49, asst. gen. mgr., 1949-50, gen. mgr., from 1950, v.p., 1952-53, exec. v.p., 1953-60, v.p. nuclear power activities, 1960, ret., then dir., chmn. exec. com. Recipient 2 Legion of Merit awards. Mem. U.S. Naval Inst., Soc. Naval Architects, Marine Engrs., Soc. Naval Engrs. Clubs: James River Country; India House, University (N.Y.C.). Presbyn. Home: Newport News VA Died May 2, 1972; buried Arlington Nat. Cemetery, Arlington VA

RAWSON, CARL WENDELL, artist; b. Van Meter, Ia., Jan. 28, 1884; s. Charles David and Olive Permelia (Ridgway) R.; ed. Cumming Sch. of Art (Des Moines), Minneapolis Sch. of Art, Nat. Acad. Design (N.Y.C.); m. Luella Willis Pattee, Oct. 7, 1906 (dec. May 1958); children—Wendell Pattee, Suzanne Pattee; m. 2d, Marjorie B. Webster, May 2, 1959, Cartoonist Minneapolis Tribune, 1906-15; portrait and landscape painter, specializing in north woods country. Represented by portraits in numerous public and private collections. Mem. Am. Artists Profl. League, Iowa Author, Republican. Protestant. Clubs: Rotary, Minneapolis Automobile, Country. Home: Minneapolis MN Died Dec. 4, 1970.

RAY, FREDERICK AUGUSTUS, JR., author; b. Maryland, N.Y., Apr. 5, 1871; s. Frederick A. and Mary Elizabeth (Larkin) R.; ed. pub. schs. and Hartwick Sem.; m. Ethel Elizabeth Tubbs, of Maryland, N.Y., Dec. 21, 1897. Teacher, life ins. agt., and traveling salesman, since 1890. Mem. Dutch Reformed Ch. Democrat. Author: Maid of the Mohawk, 1906; The Devil Worshiper, 1908. Address: Herkimer NY‡

RAY, HERBERT JAMES, naval officer; b. Feb. 1, 1893; entered U.S. Navy, 1910, and advanced through the grades to commodore, 1945. Decorated Silver Star, Distinguished Flying Cross (both Army). Address: Washington DC Died Dec. 1970.

RAY, MARLE BEYNON, author; b. Phila.; d. Honore Briece and Catharine (Kenny) Lyons; B.A., Adelphi Coll.; postgrad. Columbia; m. Oscar Willard Ray, Sept. 7, 1917; 1 dau., Ruth (Mrs. John Graham). Mng. editor Vogue mag., N.Y.C., 1911-21; asso. editor Harper's Bazaar, N.Y.C., 1921-26; v.p. Woodworth Cosmetic Co., N.Y.C., 1928-29; cons. in advt. and fashion, 1929-31, Author: How Never To Be Tired, 1938; Doctors of the Mind, 1942; How to Conquer Your Handicaps, 1948; The Best Years of Your Life, 1952; The Importance of Feeling Inferior, 1957; The Five-Minute Dessert, 1961; You and the Seven Arts, 1966; also fiction and articles appearing in Sat. Eve. Post, Cosmopolitan, Am., McCall's, Harper's Bazaar, Reader's Digest, Ladies' Home Jour., others. Mem. P.E.N., Kappa Kappa Gamma. Home: New York City NY Died Feb. 8, 1969; buried Long Ridge Cemetery, Stamford CT

RAY, P(ERLEY) ORMAN, college prof.; b. Colchester, Vt., Dec. 11, 1875; s. Orman P. and Mary Isadore (Williams) R.; A.B., U. of Vt., 1898; A.M., 1902, LL.D., 1931; post-grad. Cornell U., 1901-03, U. of Wis., 1907; Ph.D., Cornell, 1909; m. Florence E. Nelson, August 9, 1905; children—Rosalind, Joyzelle Firenze. Admitted to Vt. bar, 1900; fellow in Am. history, Cornell U., 1901-02, asst., 1902-03; prof. Am. history and govt., Pa. State Coll., 1903-14; Northam prof. history and polit. science Trinity Coll., 1914-15; prof.

polit. science, Northwestern U., 1915-26; prof. polit. science, U. of Calif., 1926-46, emeritus since 1946. Member American Political Science Assn., Nat. Municipal League, Phi Delta Theta, Phi Beta Kappa, Phi Kappa Phi. Clubs: Faculty (Berkeley); Commonwealth (San Francisco). Author: The Repeal of the Missouri Compromise, 1909; An Introduction to Political Parties and Practical Politics, 1913; The Convention That Nominated Lincoln, 1916; (with F.A. Ogg) Introduction to American Government, 1922; Major European Governments, 1931; (with F.A. Ogg) Essentials of American Government, 1932. Berkeley 7 CA‡

RAY, PHILIP ALEXANDER, lawyer, author; born in the city of Salt Lake City, Utah, on May 27, 1911; son of William W. and Leda (Rawlins) R.; student U. Utah; B.A. (cum laude), Stanford, 1932, LL.B., 1935; m. Denece Sanford, Sept. 12, 1935. Admitted to Cal. bar, 1935; asso. partner McCutchen, Olney, Mannon & Greene, and successor firms, San Francisco, 1935-54, 46-54, 57-58; gen. counsel Dept. of Commerce, 1954-56, under-sec., 1959-61. Vice pres., dir. J. H. Pomeroy & Co., Incorporated, San Francisco, 1958-59; senior research asso. Hoover Inst., Stanford; partner law firm Kelso, Cotton, Seligman & Ray, San Francisco, Cal., 1967-70. Trustee, San Francisco Symphony, also trustee Am. Enterprise Inst. for Pub. Policy Research. Served as combat intelligence officer USNR, World War II, lt. comdr. Decorated Bronze Star. Mem. Am., Cal. bar assns., Am. Law Inst., World Affairs Council No. Cal. (trustee). Clubs: Burlingame Country; Cypress Point (Cal.); Pacific Union (San Francisco). Author: South Wind Red, 1962. Home: Hillsborough CA Died July 16, 1970.

RAY, S(ILVEY) J(ACKSON), editorial cartoonist; b. near Marceline, Mo., Mar. 15, 1891; s. Lewis Franklin and Sarilda Ann (Jackson) R.; student Art Students League of New York, 1919-20; m. Claird Mary Sohns, Nov. 14, 1921. Illustrator and advt. artist, Kansas City Journal, 1913-15, Kansas City Star, 1915-31, editorial cartoonist, Kan. City Star since 1931. Rep. in Huntington Library, San Marino, Calif. Recipient citation from U.S. Treasury Dept. for Distinguished Services rendered in behalf of Nat. War Savs. Program, 1942; medal from Freedoms Found., Valley Forge, Pa., for outstanding achievement in bringing about a better understanding of the Am. way of life, 1951. Home: Gashland MO Died Feb. 1970.

RAYMOND, FREDERICK WINGATE, college pres.; b. Weymouth, Mass., Oct. 14, 1874; s. John Alcyon and Enna Alberta (Waldron) R.; A.B., Amherst Coll., 1899; B.D., Divinity Sch. (Yale), 1902; student Chicago Theol. Sem., summer 1930; m. Clara A. Brockett, of New Haven, Conn., July 1, 1903; children—Helen Wingate (Mrs. William S. Davis), Alice Brockett (dec.), Elizabeth Waldron (dec.), Ruth Beatrice (dec.), Frederick Wingate, Virginia Brockett (dec.). Ordained ministry Congl. Ch., 1902; successively pastor at Bridgewater, Conn., 1901-02, Anderson, Ind., 1902-03, Hamilton, N.Y., 1903-07, Proctor, Vt., 1908-16, Glastonbury, Conn., 1916-23, Oak Park, Ill., 1924-31; asst. supt. Congl. Christian Conf. of Ill., 1931-34; pres. Defiance Coll. since 1934. With Y.M.C.A., Camp Lee, Va., and with Speakers' Bur., 1917-18. Mem. Phi Delta Theta. Republican. Clubs: Apollos (Chicago); Rotary (Defiance). Contbr. articles to mags. Home: 809 N. Clinton St., Defiance OH‡

RAYMOND, JOSEPHINE HUNT (MRS. JEROME HALL RAYMOND), lecturer; b. Kaneville, Ill.; d. Rev. Eli Lester and Deborah (Mead) Hunt; Litt.B., Northwestern U., 1892; grad. student, U. of Wis., 1895-97, Litt.M., 1897; U. of Chicago, 1901-06; m. Jerome Hall Raymond, Aug. 15, 1895 (died, 1928). Teacher State Normal Sch., Oshkosh, Wis., 1893-95; lecturer on gen. lit., U. of Chicago, 1908-09; prof. comparative lit., Toledo (O.) U., 1909-10. Lecturer for women's clubs, univ. extension socs. and similar orgns., 1905—. Mem. Kappa Kappa Gamma, Phi Beta Kappa, D.A.R. Contbr. to mags. Has traveled extensively in Europe and Can., U.S. and Mexico. Home: 748 Judson Av., Evanston IL‡

RAYNOLDS, HERBERT F., judge; b. Central City, Colo., Nov. 28, 1874; s. Joshua Saxton and Sarah (Robbins) R.; A.B., Harvard, 1897; LL.B., Columbia, 1901. Began practice at Albuquerque, N.M., 1901; became judge 2d Jud. Dist. of N.M., 1912; asso. justice Supreme Court of N.M., 1919-22, chief justice, 1922, resigned Dec. 28, 1922. Republican. Club: Lawyers. Compiler: Digest of New Mexico Reports, Vols. 1-28, 1925. Home: El Paso TX*‡

REA, MRS. HENRY R., b. Pittsburgh, Pa., Nov. 17, 1865; d. Henry W. and Edith Anne (Cassidy) Oliver; ed. Charbonnier's and Anne Brown Sch., New York, N.Y.; m. Henry Robinson Rea, Apr. 23, 1889; children—Edith Anne, Henry Oliver. Mem. central com. Am. Red Cross, hon. mem.; mem. Com. of Eleven appointed by Pres. Harding to investigate soldier's relief, 1921; mem. Wilmer Foundation Com. Republican. Clubs: Colony (New York); Sulgrave (Washington); Rolling Rock (Pa.); Allegheny Country (Sewickley, Pa.); Pittsburgh (Pa.) Golf; Everglades, Bath and Tennis, Gulf Stream (Palm Beach). Home: Farmhill," Sewickley, Pa.; also Lagomar," Palm Beach FL Office: Henry W. Oliver Bldg., Pittsburgh PA‡

REA, ROBERT, librarian; b. San Francisco, Calif., 1877. Asst. librarian, San Francisco Public Library, 1905-12, librarian since 1912. Sec. Bd. of Library Examiners of Calif. Mem. A.L.A., Calif. Library Assn. (pres. 1936-37). Address: Public Library, San Francisco CA‡

READ, CECIL BYRON, educator; b. Lewis, Ia., Jan. 11, 1901; s. Byron Justus and Mattie (Burns) R.; A.B., Colo. Coll., 1927; A.M., Princeton, 1928; M.S., Colo. U., 1935; Ph.D., Colo. State Coll. Edn. 1938; m. Mabel Marie Culbert, Dec. 25, 1928 (dec. Dec. 1931); 1 son, Byron Joseph; m. 2d, Janet Marguerite Williams, Apr. 20, 1935; children—Barbara Janet, Beverly Jean. Instr. in math. Princeton, 1928-29; master in math. Taft Sch., Watertown, Conn., 1929-31; head math. dept. Genessee Wesleyan Jr. Coll., Lima, N.Y., 1931-32; asst. prof. math. U. Wichita (Kan.), 1932-39, asso. prof., 1939-40, prof., 1940-62, head dept. math., 1940-60; vis. prof. Central Mich. Coll. Edn., summers 1941, 49, Baylor U., summer 1962; prof. Central Mich. U., Mt. Pleasant, 1962-64, prof. history of math., 1964-72; vis. prof. Western Mich. U., summer 1966. Active Boy Scouts Am. Mem. Nat., Mich. councils tchrs. math., Mich. Edn. Assn., Indian Math. Soc., Math. Assn. Am., Am. Math. Soc., Central Assn. Sci. Math. Tchrs. (pres. 1960-61), Phi Beta Kappa, Alpha Phi Omega, Pi Mu Epsilon, Phi Delta Kappa, Kappa Delta Pi, Delta Epsilon, Tau Kappa Alpha, Kappa Mu Epsilon, Phi Kappa Phi (pres. Central Mich. U. Chpt. 1971-72). Methodist. Kiwanian (became lt. gov. 1968). Writer of articles on math. history, and teaching of math., rev. of math. books. Math. editor School Science and Mathematics. Home: Mount Pleasant MI Died June 5, 1972; buried Evergreen Cemetery, Colorado Springs CO

READ, HERBERT, author; b. Kirbymoorside, Yorkshire, Eng., Dec. 4, 1893; s. Herbert and Eliza (Strickland) R.; student Crossley's Sch., Halifax, U. Leeds, 1912-14; fellow U. London, 1940-42; hon. degrees univs. Leeds, York, Buffalo, Boston; m. Evelyn Roff, 1919; 1 son, John; m. 2d, Margaret Ludwig, 1935; children—Thomas, Sophia, Piers Paul, Benedict. Asst. prin. H. M. Treasury, 1919-22; asst. keeper Victoria and Albert Mus., 1922-31; Watson Gordon prof. fine arts, U. Edinburgh, 1931-33; editor Burlington Mag., 1933-39; dir. George Routledge & Sons, publishers, 1939-64. Served as capt. Yorkshire Regt., Brit. Army, 1915-18. Decorated Mil. Cross, Distinguished Service Order. Was created Knight, 1953. Recipient Erasmus prize, 1967. Fellow Society of Industrial Artists; mem. Am. Academy Arts and Letters (honorary), National Institute Arts and Letters (honorary), Society Edn. in Art (pres.). Author: The Innocent Eye, 1933; In Defence of Shelley, 1935; Poetry and Anarchism; 1938; The Knapsack, 1939; The Politics of the Unpolitical, 1943; Education Through Art, 1943; Collected Poems, 1945; (essays) A Coat of Many Colours, 1945; Collected Essays in Literary Criticism, 1949; The Philosophy of Modern Art, 1952; The True Voice of Feeling, 1953; Art and Industry, 1954; Icon and Idea, 1955; The Art of Sculpture, 1956; A Concise History of Modern Painting, 1959; The Forms of Things Unknown, 1960; The Contrary Experience (autobiography), 1963; Concise History of Modern Sculpture, 1964; Origins of Form in Art, 1965; Art and Alienation: The Role of the Artist in Society, 1967; others. Home: York England Died June 12, 1968.

READ, OLIVER MIDDLETON, naval officer; b. Hobonny Plantation, S.C., Jan. 12, 1889; s. Oliver Middleton and Mary Louise (Gregory) R.; student Virginia Mil. Inst., 1905-06; B.S., U.S. Naval Acad., Annapolis, Md., 1911; m. Constance Sears, Dec. 18, 1918;children—Mary Louise, Oliver Middleton, III. Commd. ensign. U.S. Navy, 1911, promoted through grades to rear adm.; served in various types of ships, U.S. Navy, at Vera Cruz, Mexico, 1914, submarine service, World War, 1917-18, in Chinese waters and at Shanghai, 1932; became first U.S. naval attache and U.S. naval attache for air, U.S. Legation, Ottawa, Can., Aug., 1940; on duty as staff comdr. in chief, U.S. Fleet until Mar. 1942, on sea duty, 1942-46; deputy commander of the Atlantic Reserve Fleet, 1946-51; promoted rear adm., Oct. 1942. Awarded Navy Cross for submarine service during World War; Mexican Service medal, Victory medal (with one star), Yangtze Service medal, Legion of Merit, gold star in lieu of second Legion of Merit, Combat Distinguishing Device (for actual combat with the enemy for which first Legion of Merit was awarded), Am. Defense Service Medal, Asiatic-Pacific Area Campaign Medal, Am. Area Campaign Medal, European-African-Middle Eastern Area Campaign Medal, Victory Medal (World War II), Cruzeiro do Sul (Order of the Southern Cross—Brazil), War Service Medal, Diploma, and Citation (Brazil), Comdr. of British Empire. Mem. Soc. of Cincinnati in State of S.C., Hero of Washington chapter of Heroes of 76. Mason (K.T.), Sojourners. Episcopalian. Club: Soc of the Cincinnati in State of S.C. Home: MA Died Mar. 1972.

REALS, WILLIS H(OWARD), educator; b. Fayetteville, N.Y., Apr. 3, 1892; s. Jacob and Amelia (Wright) R.; A.B., Syracuse U., 1916, M.A., 1921; Ph.D., Columbia U., 1928; m. Mary Louise McCarthy, July 26, 1922; 1 son Willis McCarthy. High sch. prin., Vernon, N.Y., 1916-17, Clark's Summit, Pa., 1918-21, Ithaca, N.Y., 1921-27; asso. prof., later prof. edn. Washington U., St. Louis, 1928-60, asst. dean U. Coll., 1940-42, dean, 1942-54, dean and prof. emeritus, 1960-67. Instr. Signal Corps, 1917-18. Pres. sch. bd., University City, Mo., 1942-52. Recipient Mex. Gerontol. Soc. award, 1956. Fellow Nat. Gerontol. Soc.; mem. N.E.A., Am. Assn. Sch. Adminstrs., Adult Edn. Assn. U.S., Mo. Assn. Social Welfare, Extension Assn., Assn. U. Evening Colls. (pres.), Mo. State Tchrs. Assn., Nat. Soc. Study Edn., Am. Edn. Research Assn., Phi Beta Kappa, Phi Delta Kappa, Kappa Delta Pi, Republican. Mason. Club: University. Author: A Study of the Summer High School, 1928; Planning a Successful Retirement, 1961. Contbr. to ednl. jours. Home: St Louis MO Died Oct. 6, 1967; buried Oak Grove Cemetery St Louis MO

REAMS, FRAZIER, congressman; b. Franklin, Tenn, Jan. 15, 1897; s. Herschel Burger and Tabitha (Frazier) R.; A.B., U. of Tenn., 1919; LL.B., Vanderbilt U., 1922; m. Crystal Petree, June 27, 1924; children—Martha Lee, Frazier. Admitted to Ohio bar 1922, and since practiced law in Toledo; sr. mem. firm Reams, Bretherton & Neipp since 1937; pres. and dir. The Community Broadcasting Co. Neipp since 1937; pres. and dir. The Community Broadcasting Co. (operating sta. WTOL) since 1937, Am. Bank, Port Clinton, O., 1947-48; trust officer and v.p. The Comml. Savs. Bank & Trust Co., Toledo, 1924-29; dir. Lucas Co. Bank. Pros. atty. Lucas Co., 1933-37; U.S. collector of internal revenue, 1942-43; dir. pub. welfare, State O., 1945-46; mem. 82d and 83d Congresses, from Ninth Ohio Dist.; member Toledo Port Commn., 1938-42; chmn. Greater Toledo Community Chest campaign, 1947; chmn. Nat. War Fund Campaign for Ohio, 1946. Trustee Bowling Green State U. Served as pvt. to lt. F.A., U.S. Army, World War I. Recipient Silver Beaver award Boy Scouts Am. Mem. Am., Ohio, Toledo bar assns., Am. Legion (v. comdr. Dept. Ohio, 1927-28, comdr. Toledo post 1925-26), Toledo Soc. for Crippled Children (bd. trustees), Phi Gamma Delta, Phi Delta Phi. Meth. Mason (Shriner). Home: Toledo OH Died Sept. 15, 1971; buried Woodlawn Cemetery, Toledo OH

REAVIS, JAMES OVERTON, clergyman; b. Monroe Co., Mo., Dec. 8, 1872; s. James Overton and Ellen (Roselle) R.; A.B., Westminster Coll., Mo., 1896, A.M., 1897; B.D., Presbyterian Theological Seminary, Louisville, Ky., 1899; M.A., New York University, 1901; B.D., Princeton Theological Seminary, 1901; LL.B., University of S.C., 1914; mem. S.C., bar D.D., Austin Coll. Tex., 1908; m. Eva Fulton Witherspoon, of Louisville, Dec. 18, 1902. Ordained Presbyn. ministry, 1899, pastor 1st Ch., Dallas, 1902-05; sec. Foreign Missions Presbyn. Ch. of U.S., office at Nashville, Tenn., 1905-11; pastor 1st Ch., Columbia, S.C., 1911-14; prof. English Bible, homiletics and pastoral theology, Columbia (S.C.) Presbyn. Theol. Sem., 1914-20; sec. of foreign missions, Presbyn. Ch. of U.S., since 1920; visited missions in Congo, Africa, 1910, Japan and Korea, 1918.*‡

REBER, SAMUEL, foreign service officer; b. Easthampton, N.Y., July 15, 1903; s. Samuel and Cecilia Sherman (Miles) R.; student Groton Sch., Groton, Mass., 1916-21; A.B., Harvard U., 1925; unmarried. Foreign service officer since Oct. 1, 1926; vice consul, Callao, Lima, Peru, 1927-29; charge d'affaires, U.S. legation, Monrovia, Liberia, 1930-31; U.S. mem. League of Nations Com. on Libera, 1931-32; sec. U.S. delegation, Gen. Disarmament Conf., Geneva, 1932-35; tech. adviser, U.S. delegation, London Naval Conf., 1935-36; sec. of Embassy, Rome, 1936-39; assigned to Dept. of State, 1939-42; spl. mission to Martinique, 1942; asst. to President's special rep. in N. Africa, 1943; mem. of Allied Mil. Mission to Italy, 1943; dep. vice-pres., Allied Control Commn., Italy; Political Officer, S.H.A.E.F., 1944-45; polit. adviser U.S. delegation Council of Fgn. Ministers Conf., Paris, 1946; dep. dir. Office European Affairs, State Dept., 1947; U.S. dep., Council Fgn. Minsters for Austria, 1948; political adviser U.S. High Commission for Germany; now deputy U.S. High Commissioner for Germany. Clubs: Washington DC Died Dec. 25, 1971.

REDIGER, MICHEL JON, physicist; b. Humbolt, Neb., Nov. 13, 1939; s. Lavern Chester and Dorothy (Swanson) R.; B.S., U. Neb., 1961, M.S., 1964; postgrad. U. Minn., 1964-66; m. Leila Beverly Ammon, Sept. 10, 1966. Grad. teaching asst. physics dept. U. Neb., 1961-64; grad. teaching asst. physics dept. U. Minn., 1964-65, research asst., 1966, research asso., 1966; physicist Los Alamos Sci. Lab., 1965; physicist Goodyear Atomic Corp., Piketon, O., 1966-69; predoctoral fellow Summer Inst. Theoretical Physics, Physics Dept. U. Colo., 1964. Nat. Defense Edn. Act fellow, 1965-66. Mem. Am. Phys. Soc., Waverly Jr. C. of C. Republican. Methodist. Home: Waverly OH Died May 29, 1969; buried Milford NB

REDMAN, HARRY NEWTON, composer, artist; b. Mount Carmel, Ill., Dec. 26, 1869; s. Charles and Lucy Newton (Hunnewell) R.; began musical edn. N.E. Conservatory of Music, 1885; later became pupil in composition and organ of George W. Chadwick. Condr., organist and choirmaster, Erie, Pa., 1891-97; charge of music for Erie Centennial, 1895, and directed Living Am. Flag, composed of school girls and believed first of its kind in U.S.; mem. faculty New Eng. Conservatory of Music since 1897. Compositions include many songs, 2 sonatas for violin and piano, 4 string quartets, pieces for piano, suite for organ (prelude, pastoral, fugue); music section of Boston Pub. Library has most important works, fine arts section has painting sketch book; self-educated in art; started painting, 1922; art works include oil and water color both landscape and figure; first exhibited at Pa. Acad. of Fine Arts, 1926; also at Carnegie Internat., Museums of Fine Arts, Boston, Cincinnati; his painting The Ridge" is included in the permanent collection of the Boston Museum of Fine Arts.*‡

REDMAN, JOSEPH REASOR, naval officer; b. Grass Valley, Calif., Apr. 17, 1891; s. Joseph Reasor and Katherine (Dwight) R.; B.S., U.S. Naval Acad., 1914; M.S., Columbia, 1921; m. Marion Smith, 1932. Commd. ensign, U.S. Navy, 1914, and advanced through the grades to rear adm., 1943; comd. U.S.S. C-5 on submarine duty during World War I; radio duty fleet, 1921-24; bureau engring., 1924-27, fleet 1927-30; chief of frequencies sect., naval communications, 1930-33, 1937-39; tech. adviser to U.S. delegation Internat. Radio Telegraphy Conf., Madrid, 1932, Cairo, 1938; comd. U.S.S. Canopus, 1934-36, Henderson, 1939-41, Phoenix, 1942-43; dep. dir. naval communications, 1942, dir. since 1943; mem. Bd. of War Communications, Joint Communications Bd. and Combined Communications Bd., State Dept. special com. on communications. Home: Bethesda MD Died Sept. 1968.

REECE, MRS. CARROLL (LOUISE GOFF), ex-congresswoman; b. Milw., Nov. 6, 1898; d. Guy Despard and Louise (Van Nortwick) Goff; grad. Miss Spence Sch., N.Y.C.; m. Carroll Reece, Oct. 30, 1923; 1 dau., Louise Goff (Mrs. George W. Marthens II). Propr., Mgr. Goff Properties, Clarksburg, W.Va., chmn. bd. dirs. 1st Peoples Bank, Johnson City, Tenn., Carter County Bank, Elizabethton, Tenn.; dir. Southeastern Security Life Ins. Co.; mem. 87th Congress (1st Dist. from Tenn.). Del. Republican Nat. Conv., 1956, 60; Rep. nat. committeewoman for Tenn. Trustee Robert A. Taft Found., Institute Fiscal and Polit. Edn. Mem. Tenn. Hist. Soc., Bus. and Profl. Women's Club, D.A.R., Colonial Dames, Daus. of 1912. Clubs: Monday, Johnson City Country; Chevy Chase, Sulgrave (Washington). Home: Johnson City TN Died Mar 14, 1970; buried Monta Vista, Johnson City TN

REED, ALBERT AUGUSTUS, lawyer, b. Sharon, Conn., Feb. 6, 1868; s. Elias Baldwin and Miranda (Candee) R.; U. City of N.Y.; LL.B., Columbia, 1887; LL.B., U. of Colo., 1894; LL.D., 1927; m. Lydia Howell, Aug. 7, 1889; children—Margaret Howell, Charlotte Baldwin, Esther Candee, Frances du Bois. Began practice, Poughkeepsie, 1889; removed to Boulder, Colo., 1891; gen. counsel Mercantile Bank & Trust Co., Boulder Nat. Bank, 1904-16, and Boulder Bldg. &Loan Assn.; sec. Northern Colo. Investment Co.; pres. Mercantile Bank & Trust Co., 1904-12; removed to Denver, 1916. Prof. of law, U. of Colo., 1895-1916. City atty. Boulder, 1907-10; del. Rep. Nat. Conv., 1908; candidate for state senator, 1908. Mem. Judicial Commn. Presbyn. Ch., U.S.A., 1931-39; now retired. Mem. Am. Colo., and Denver bar assns., Phi Delta Phi. Home: 670 Marion St., Denver CO‡

REED, ANNA YEOMANS (MRS. JOSEPH AMBROSE REED), professor of education; born in Walworth, N.Y., Sept. 23, 1871; d. Lucien Theron and Susan Sophia (Cleveland) Yeomans; A.B., U. of Neb., 1899, M.A., 1900; Ph.D., U. of Wis., 1902; m. Joseph Ambrose Reed, of Seattle, Wash., June 10, 1890; 1 son, Albert Cleveland. Instr. in history, U. of Neb., 1899-1901; dir. guidance and placement pub. schs., Seattle, Wash., 1913-17; dir. jr. div. U.S. employment service, 1918-21; asst. prof. edn., U. of Chicago, 1922-24; asso. prof. edn., New York U., 1924-25, asso. prof. personnel administration, 1925-26, prof. since 1926; mng. dir. The Nat. Personnel Service, Inc. Mem. Phi Beta Kappa, Kappa Alpha Theta, Pi Gamma Mu. Author: Seattle Children in School and Industry, 1915; Newsboy Service, 1917; Junior Wage Earners, 1920; Human Waste in Education, 1927; The Effective and the ineffective College Teacher, 1935. Home: Fifth Av. Hotel, New York NY‡

REED, CLARE OSBORNE (MRS. CHARLES B. REED), musician; b. Plymouth, Ind.; d. John G. and Marilda (Boyd) Osborne; grad. pub. schs., Chicago; B.A., Chicago Musical Coll., also post-grad. course; studied in Europe 2 yrs., under Leschetizky and Oscar Raif, composition under Karl Nawratil; m. Dr. Charles Bert Reed, of Chicago, June 23, 1892. Founder, 1901, Columbia Sch. of Music, Chicago, pres. and dir., 1901-30. Mem. Soc. Am. Musicians, Ill. Music Teachers Assn., Lake View Musical Soc. (hon.). Clubs: Chicago Woman's, The Cordon (charter mem.), Woman's City. Mem. Mu Iota Chapter of Mu Phi Epsilon. Home: 4629 Dover St. Studio: 410 S. Michigan Av., Chicago IL‡

REED, DONALD ROSS, physician; b. Eldora, Ia., July 25, 1906; s. John Daniel and Bertha May (Baker) R.; M.D., U. Ia., 1929; m. Isabelle Evelyn Preston, Oct. 12, 1936; 1 dau., Janet (Mrs. Eric Walter Anderson). Intern, L.I. Coll. Hosp., Bklyn., 1929-31, asst. resident in pediatrics, 1931-32, resident, 1932-33; resident Charles V. Chapin Hosp., Providence, 1932; asst. pediatrician Presbyn-Babies Hosp., N.Y.C.; attending pediatrician Phelps Meml. Hosp., Grasslands Hosp., Valhalla, N.Y.; courtesy staff Dobbs Ferry (N.Y.) Hosp.; instr. pediatrics Columbia Coll. Phys. and Surg.; pediatrician St. Faith's House, Tarrytown, N.Y., St. Christopher's Sch., Dobbs Ferry; founder, med. dir. Hudson River-No. Westchester Speech Center, Inc. (name now Donald R. Reed Speech Center). Mem. med. adv. bd. Children's Village, Dobbs Ferry; pres. Westchester County Bd. Health, 1966-71. Diplomate Am. Bd. Pediatrics. Fellow Am. Acad. Pediatrics; mem. A.M.A., Westchester County Med. Soc. (pres. 1959-60), Westchester County Acad. Medicine (pres. 1962-63). Home: Irvington-on-Hudson NY died Jan. 9, 1971.

REED, EDWIN CLARENCE, writer; b. at Cambridge, Mass., Aug. 17, 1877; s. Clarence Gilman and Emma Ritchie (Foster) R.; Somerville (Mass.) Latin Sch.; commercial coll.; Berlitz Sch. of Langs.; Harvard Med. Sch.; LL.B., Washington College of Law, 1913; A.M., George Washington Univ., 1919; m. Ivy Kellerman, Oct. 4, 1909. Left med. sch., 1902, to take charge of affairs of father, bldg. contr., Boston, disposing of business, 1906; in gen. ins. business, Rockford, Ill., 1906-08; gen. sec.-treas. Esperanto Assn. of N. America, 1908-13. U.S. rep. 5th International Esperanto Congress, Barcelona, Spain, 1909, and 7th Congress, Antwerp, Belgium, 1911. Am. mem. Internat. Esperato Konstanta Komitaro de la Kongreso and Lingva Komitato, Washington Chamber of Commerce. Club: Nat. Press (Washington). Author of articles relating to Esperanto, internationalism, world-peace, etc. Spl. legal and economic work at Washington, 1915—. With economic div., Federal Trade Commn., Oct. 1917-Aug. 1919. Home: 2518 17th St., N.W., Washington DC‡

REED, FRANK LEFEVRE, musician; b. Richmond, Ind., July 17, 1871; s. Albert Samuel and Ellen Maria (LeFevre) R.; student Wabash Coll. (Crawfordsville, Ind.), Ithaca (N.Y.) Conservatory of Music, Cincinnati Coll. of Music; pupil of Dr. Percy Goetschius, New York, in theory and composition; m. Marion Courtney Mohler, 1905; children—Mignon India, Egmont Mohler. Prof. piano and musical theory, Pa. Coll. of Music, Meadville, 1906-13; prof. music, U. of Tex., 1913-25; director Univ. Conservatory of Music since 1925. Fellow Am. Coll. Musicians (U. State of N.Y.), 1902. Composer of symphonic pieces (orchestra) for Pageant of Austin; 4 symphonic pieces (orchestra) for Pageant of Auburn Theol. Sem.; Inauguration Processional (orchestra); piano pieces, songs, cantata, etc. Home: 2508 Guadalupe St., Austin TX‡

REED, GEORGE LETCHWORTH, housing cons.; b. Olean, N.Y., Oct. 14, 1900; s. Newton Luther and Ella Letchworth (Smith) R.; B.S. in Civil Engring., U. Wis., 1924; m. Reese Louise Cofer, Aug. 31, 1927; children—Charlotte Hampton (Mrs. Keith E. Hall), George Letchworth, structural engr.; Boston, Fla. and Atlanta, 1925-35; with U.S. Pub. Housing Authority, Washington, 1935-38, planner in P.R., 1938-42; engaged in war workers housing, Hampton Roads, Va., 1942-43; housing attache embassy, London, Eng., 1946; housing adviser FOA mission to Greece, 1947-51, Burma, 1953-55; pvt. cons. practice, 1956-62; cons. Dominican Republic, 1955-57, P.R. Urban Renewal and Housing Corp., 1958-61, World Bank, Govt. Chile, Interam. Bank on Housing and Urban Growth, 1961-62; housing cons. Alliance for Progress, 1962-63; housing finance cons. UN, 1963-64; tech. adviser W. Africa Operations Office, AID, 1964-67. Bd. directors St. Johns Sch., San Juan, P.R., 1939, Anglo-Am. Sch., Athens, Greece, 1948; bd. govs. Rangoon (Burma) Sailing Club, 1951. Served with U.S. Navy, 1918-19; to lt. col. AUS, 1943-45; ETO. Decorated Royal Order St. George (Greece), 1951. Registered profl. engr., Fla., 1928, P.R. Coll. Engrs., 1961. Life mem. Chilean Soc. Planning and Devel.; mem. Am. Soc. C.E. (pres. Ga. 1930), Interam. Planning Soc. (founder mem. 1946), Am. Fgn. Service Assn., Am. Soc. Pub. Adminstrn., Internat. Fedn. Housing and Planning, Nat. Assn. Housing and Redevel. Ofcls., Res. Officers Assn., Pro-Arte (Santo Domingo), Acacia, Theta Tau. Presbyn. Clubs: Royal Hellenic Yacht (Athens); West River Sailing (Galesville, Md.). Home: Kensington MD Died Aug. 11, 1970.

REED, HARLOW JOHN, chem. co. exec.; b. Wakefield, Mich., May 5, 1918; s. John Frederick and Irene Maud (Baker) R.; S.B. in Electrochem. Engring., Mass. Inst. Tech., 1939; children—Candace, Jamison, Jennifer. Engr., Phelps Dodge Refining Corp., 1939-40; smelter supt. Chile Exploration Co., 1940-43; engr., later partner Singmaster & Breyer, cons. engrs., N.Y.C., 1946-60; v.p. prodn. and engineering Olin Mathieson Chemical Corporation (name changed to Olin Corporation), 1960-65, exec. v.p. metals, 1965-68, exec. v.p., chief operating officer, 1968-71; dir. Somers Thin Strip, Inc., Olinkraft, Inc., FRIA, Ormet Corp. Served with AUS, 1943-46. Mem. Am. Inst. Mining Engrs. Clubs: Century, Chemists' N.Y. Yacht (N.Y.C.); Storm Trisail, Aspetuck Valley Country. Larchmont (N.Y.) Yacht. Home: Weston CT Died Apr. 30, 1971.

REED, HELEN LEAH, author; b. St. John, N.B.; d. Guilford Shaw and Ella (Berryman) R.; English, Huguenot and Colonial ancestry; parents went to Boston, 1865; grad. Radcliffe Coll., 1890; first winner of Sargent prize (Harvard), 1890, for metrical translation from Horace. Mem. Am. Folk-Lore Soc. (sec. Boston branch), Circolo Italiano, Woman's Auxiliary Civ. Service Reform Assn., Collegiate Alumnae, Woman's Edn. Assn., Poetry Society (London), Mass. League of Women Voters, and Authors' League of America. Clubs: College, Authors (Boston); Lyceum (London, England). Author: Miss Theodora, 1898; Brenda, Her School and Her Club, 1900; Brenda's Summer at Rockley, 1901; Brenda's Cousin at Radcliffe, 1902; Brenda's Bargain, 1903; Irma and Nap, 1904; Amy in Acadia, 1905; Brenda's Ward, 1906; Napoleon's Young Neighbor, 1907; Irma in Italy, 1908; Serbia, a Sketch, 1916; Memorial Day and Other Verse, 1917. Contbr. to periodicals. Address: Riverbank Ct., Cambridge MA*‡

REED, HENRY CLAY, educator; b. Tyrone, Pa., May 15, 1899; s. William Watson and Marian Amanda (Rothrock) R.; A.B., Bucknell U., 1922; A.M., Pa. State Coll., 1929; Ph.D., Princeton, 1939; m. Marion L. Bjornson, Apr. 2, 1927. High Sch. teacher, Pa., 1919-24; mem. faculty, U. of Del., from 1924, prof. history, from 1947, then prof. emeritus, chmn. dept., 1944-52. Mem. Del. Tercentenary Commn., 1937-38. Mem. Am. Hist. Assn., Am. Assn. Univ. Profs., Newcomen Soc., Am. Soc. of Ch. History, Am. Assn. for State and Local History, Middle States Council for Social Studies, Archaeol. Soc. of Del., Natural Hist. Soc. of Del., N.J. Hist. Soc., Sigma Alpha Epsilon, Phi Kappa Phi. Editor: The Burlington Court Book, 1944; Delaware, A History of the First State, 1947. Contbr. articles on Delaware history in profl. jours. Home: Newark DE Died July 29, 1972.

REED, HERBERT, newspaper man; b. New York, Oct. 19, 1876; s. John Herbert and Anna (Bard) R.; grad. Peekskill (N.Y.) Mil. Acad., 1894, Cascadilla Sch., Ithaca, N.Y., 1895; matriculated in Cornell U.; student New York U. Law Sch.; m. Mary Everett Jennings, of East Orange, N.J., Jan. 28, 1905. Began as reporter, Evening Sun, New York, 1896; various positions to asst. city editor, Evening Telegram, 1896-03; writer on baseball and amatuer sports, later asst. Sunday editor, to 1908, New York Herald; became specialist in amateur sport, writing under pseudonym Right Wing." Went to England, 1912, to study English sport, especially football; now independent writer on amateur sport. Mem. Alpha Chi Sigma, Chi Psi. Author: Football for Public and Player, 1913. Home: East Orange, N.J. Office: Fifth Av. Bldg. New York‡

REED, HORACE, business exec.; b. Mansfield, O., Feb. 8, 1870; s. Horace L. and Jane (Wasson) R.; student pub. schs.; m. Mary L. McWilliams, Oct. 2, 1894; children—John McWilliams, Horace W., Carl N. Est. Niagara Lithograph Co., Buffalo, N.Y., pres. since 1896; pres. H. L. Reed Co., Mansfield, O.; pres. Buffalo Savings Bank since 1948; dir. Mfrs. & Traders Trust Co., Barcalo Mfg. Co. Mem. Buffalo Historical Soc., Buffalo Soc. Natural Sciences, Lithographers Nat. Assn. Republican. Presbyterian. Clubs: Buffalo, Rotary, Wanakah Country (Buffalo). Office: 1050 Niagara St., Buffalo NY‡

REED, IVY KELLERMAN, editor; b. at Oshkosh, Wis., July 8, 1877; d. of William Ashbrook and Stella V. (Dennis) Kellerman; sister of Karl Frederic K. (q.v.); A.B., Ohio State U., 1898; A.M., Cornell U., 1899; Ph.D., magna cum laude, U. of Chicago, 1904; U. of Berlin; LL.B., Washington Coll. of Law, 1913; m. Edwin C. Reed, of Washington, Oct. 4, 1909. Instructor Greek, Iowa (now Grinnell) Coll., 1907; instr. Latin, Toledo Central High Sch., 1908; dir. Am. Sch. of Esperanto, 1909-19; editor Amerika Esperantisto, 1911-14. Mem. Phi Beta Kappa, Delta Delta Delta, Internat. Esperanto Lingva Komitato. Author: A Complete Grammar of Esperanto, 1910; Kiel Placas Al Vi, 1910; La Rego de la Ora Rivero, 1911; Practical Grammar of Esperanto, 1915. Contbr. articles, short stories and verse to mags. Address: 2518 17th St N.W., Washington DC‡

REED, IVY KELLERMAN, editor; b. at Oshkosh, Wis., July 8, 1877; d. of William Ashbrook and Stella V. (Dennis) Kellerman; sister of Karl Frederic K. (q.v.); A.B., Ohio State U., 1898; A.M., Cornell U., 1899; Ph.D., magna cum laude, U. of Chicago, 1904; U. of Berlin; LL.B., Washington Coll. of Law, 1913; m. Edwin C. Reed, of Washington, Oct. 4, 1909. Instructor Greek, Iowa (now Grinnell) Coll., 1907; instr. Latin, Toledo Central High Sch., 1908; dir. Am. Sch. of Esperanto, 1909-19; editor Amerika Esperantisto, 1911-14. Mem. Phi Beta Kappa, Delta Delta Delta, Internat. Esperanto

Lingva Komitato. Author: A Complete Grammar of Esperanto, 1910; Kiel Placas Al Vi, 1910; La Rego de la Ora Rivero, 1911; Practical Grammar of Esperanto, 1915. Contbr. articles, short stories and verse to mags. Address: 2518 17th St. N.W., Washington DC‡

REED, LUTHER DOTTERER, clergyman, educator; b. N. Wales, Pa., Mar 21, 1873; s. Rev. Ezra L. and Annie (Linley) R.; A.B., Franklin and Marshall Coll., 1892, A.M., 1897; grad. Luth. Theol. Sem., Phila., 1895; student U. of Leipzig, 1902; D.D., Thiel, 1912, Muhlenberg, 1912; A.E.D. (Doctor of Fine Arts), Muhlenberg, 1936; m. Catherine S. Ashbridge, June 2, 1906. Pastor Allegheny, Pa., 1895-1903, Jeanette, Pa., 1903-04; dir. Krauth Memorial Library, Lutheran Theological Seminary, Mt. Airy, Phila., 1906-50; professor liturgics and church art, same, 1911-45; president of the Seminary, 1939-45; pres. emeritus, 1945-72. President Church Music and Liturgical Art Soc., 1907-36; pres. and editor Memoirs, Luth. Liturgical Assn., 1898-1906; pres. Associated Bureaus of Church Architecture of the U.S. and Can., 1930-40; sec., later chmn. joint com. which prepared text and music of the Common Service Book and other hymnals and liturgical books of United Luth. Ch.; conducted confs. on the liturgy, ch. architecture and ch. music in many states; archivist of ministerium of Pa., 1909-39, United Luth. Ch. since 1919. Clubs: University, Art Alliance (Phila.); Lake Placid. Author: (with Harry G. Archer) Psalter and Canticles Pointed for Chanting, 1897; Choral Service Book, 1901; Music of the Responses, 1903; Season Vespers, 1905; The Lutheran Liturgy, 1947; also numerous articles on church music, worship, church art, etc. Editor: History of the First English Evangelical Lutheran Church in Pittsburgh, 1909; Philadelphia Seminary Biographical Record, 1923. Co-editor: Philadelphia Seminary Bulletin, 1916-33, Lutheran Church Review, 1920-28. Chmn. United Luth. Ch. com. on Common Service Book; chmn. joint coms. on liturgy and on the hymnal now preparing common Liturgy and Hymnal for all Luth. Chs. in U.S. and Can. of Nat. Luth. Council; charter mem. Fed. Council's Com. on Worship; mem. dept. worship and fine arts Nat. Council Chs. Hon. asso. Am. Guild of Organists; hon. mem. Church Architectural Guild; vice pres. Hymn Soc. of America; mem. Faith and Order Cons. on Intercommunion, and Ways of Worship. Del. United Luth. Ch., 3d Philadelphia PA. Died Apr. 3, 1972.

REED, MARY DEAN (MRS. VERNER Z. REED), b. Columbus, O., Oct. 8, 1875; d. Silas Dean and Eunice Carrie (Dawson) Johnson; ed. pub. and pvt. schs.; m. Verner Z. Reed, July 18, 1893 (died 1919); children—Margery Verner (Mrs. Paul T. Mayo, dec.), Verner Z., Joseph Verner. Pres. Reed Partnership. Trustee U. of Denver, Colo. Mus. Natural History. Republican. Episcopalian. Clubs: Denver Country, Cherry Hills Country. Home: 475 Circle Drive, Denver CO‡

REED, MARY WILLIAMS (KATE CAREW), artist, journalist; b. San Francisco, Calif., June 27, 1872; d. Robert Neil and Virginia (Gluyas) Williams; ed. San Francisco Art Assn. (gold medal) and Academie Colarossi, Paris; m. H. Kellett Chambers, dramatist, of Sydney, Australia, Apr. 29, 1897; 1 son, Colin Chambers-Reed; m. 2d, John A. Reed, of London, Eng., and New York, Dec. 3, 1916. Interviewer and caricaturist with New York World and New York Tribune until 1913; later with London Tatler, Patrician and Eve mags. Exhibited at Chicago Expn. (silver medal); Grand Salon, Paris, 1924 and 1928. Address: Lyceum Club, 138 Piccadilly, London England‡

REED, PERLEY ISAAC, journalism; b. Lowell, O., Sept. 28, 1887; s. Benjamin and Nellie (Hall) R.; Ph.B., Nat. Normal U., 1908; A.B., magna cum laude, Marietta Coll., 1912, A.M., 1914; fellow in English, Ohio State U., 1914-16, Ph.D., 1916; spl. work, Columbia, 1924; m. Aldia Barnett, 1909; children—Judson Wardlaw, Gloria; m. 2d, Elizabeth Frost, 1922. Teacher, principal and supt. schs. until 1911; prof. English, Ogden Coll., Bowling Green, Ky., 1912-14; asso. prof. English, Md. State Coll., College Park, 1916-17; prof. and head dept. of English, U. of Md., 1917-20; spl. examiner U.S. Civil Service Commn., Washington, D.C., summer 1918; asst. prof. English, W.Va. Univ., 1920-22, asso. prof., 1922-24, prof., 1924-27, prof. and head dept. of journalism, 1927-39, dir. Sch. of Journalism, 1939-58, director emeritus School of Journalism, 1958. Exec. sec. W.Va. State Journalism Conf., 1922-53; dir. W.Va. Competition of High Sch. Periodicals 1922-58; sponsor W.Va. State Inst. of Sch. Journalism 1932-58; lecturer W.Va. county teachers institutes, 1922-31. Mem. Am. Assn. Univ. Profs., Assn. for Edn. in Journalism, Am. Soc. of Journalism School Adminstrs. (nat. pres. 1944-47), Kappa Tau Alpha (nat. pres. 1944-46), Phi Beta Kappa. Presbyterian. Club: XX Club (Morgantown). Author: Am. Characters in Am. Plays, 1918; Applied Writing by the Journalistic Method, 1929; Writing Journalistic Features, 1931; Applied Composition (with Elizabeth Frost Reed), 1936; The Quality Newspaper, 1942; The Modern Newspaper as a Social Instrument, 1942. Editor: West Virginia Fourth Estatesman, 1941-58. Contributor to professional magazines. Home: Morgantown WV Died Apr. 1973.

REED, THOMAS HARRISON, municipal consultant; b. Boston, July 29, 1881; s. Eugene Austinella and Julia Ann (Mathews) R.; A.B., Harvard, 1901, LL.B., 1904; postgrad. Columbia, 1908-09; LL.D., U. Brussels, 1930; m. Julia Russell, June 29, 1904; children—Howard Russell, Thomas Harrison, Eugene Marshall; m. 2d, Doris Darmstadter, May 19, 1937. Admitted to N.Y. bar, 1906, Cal. bar, 1913; asso. prof. govt. U. Cal., 1909-19, prof. municipal govt., 1919-22; prof. polit. sci. U. Mich., 1922-36; dir. consultant service Nat. Municipal League, 1933-38; dir. of studies, Rep. Program Com., 1938-39; exec. sec. to Gov. Hiram Johnson, Jan.-Aug. 1911; city mgr., San Jose, Calif., July 1, 1916-Aug. 1, 1918; dir. of research, Pa. Commn. to Study Municipal Consolidation in Allegheny County, 1928-29; also dir. research, City and County Met. Devel. Com., St. Louis, 1929-30. Lectr. municipal govt., Harvard, 1929-30; local govt. counsellor, Connecticut Public Expenditure Council 1943-47; cons. on charter commns., Nassau Co., N.Y., 1935-36, Hartford, Conn., 1946, Richmond, Va., and Baton Rouge 1947, Shreveport, 1949. Decorated officer Order of Leopold (Belgium). Mem. Am. Polit. Sci. Assn., Nat. Municipal League, Internat. City Mgrs. Assn. (hon.), Govtl. Research Assn. (hon.), Delta Chi, Beta Gamma Sigma, Republican. Conglist. Clubs: Harvard (New York), Hartford (Hartford, Conn.). Author: Government for the People,, 1915; Forms and Functions of American Government, 1916; Loyal Citizenship, 1919; Government and Politics of Belgium, 1924; Municipal Government in the United States, 1926; (with Paul Webbink) Documents Illustrative of American Municipal Governemnt, 1926; Essentials of Loyal Citizenship, 1929; Oakland County—A Survey of County and Township Administration and Finance, 1932; (with A. W. Bromage) Organization and Cost of County and Township Government, 1933; The Government of Nassau County, N.Y., 1934; Twenty Years of Government in Essex County, 1937; The Government of Atlanta and Fulton County, 1938; Municipal Management, 1941; (with Doris Reed) The Government of Cincinnati, 1924-44, 1944, Report to the Citizens of Augusta, Ga., 1945, Evaluation of Citizenship Training and Incentive in American Colleges and Universities, 1950, Preparing College Men and Women for Politics, 1952, The Cincinnati Area Must Solve its Metropolitan Problems, 1953, The Niagara Falls Industrial Community, 1953. Editor: Government in a Depression, 1933; Legislatures and Legislative Problems, 1933. Translator (with H. Russell Reed); Leopold of the Belgians, 1929; Leopold First, 1930. Contbr. on city govt., city charters, etc. Address: Wethersfield CT Died Dec. 6, 1971; buried Forest Hills Cemetery, Boston MA

REED, VICTOR JOSEPH, bishop; b. Montpelier, Ind., Dec. 23, 1905; s. Victor L. and Henrietta M. (Collins) R.; S.T.L., No. Am. Coll., Rome, Italy, 1930; Ph.D., U. Louvain (Belgium), 1939. Ordained priest Roman Catholic Ch., 1929; asst. chancellor Oklahoma City-Tulsa Diocese, 1939-40, bishop, 1958-71; pastor St. Francis Xavier Ch., Stillwater, Okla., 1940-47; rector Holy Family Cathedral, Tulsa, 1947-57. Address: Oklahoma City OK Died Sept. 8 1971.

REED, WILLIAM REYNOLDS, commr. coll. athletics b. Oxford, Mich., Nov. 28, 1915; s. William and Mary Ann (Pritchard) R.; A.B., U. Mich., 1936; m. Frances Haigh, Feb. 10, 1940; children—Patricia, Linda, Rosemary. Asst. athletic publicity dir. U. Mich., 1936-39; dir. Service Bur., Big-Ten Conf., 1939-42, 45-47, asst. commr., 1951-61, commr., 1961-71; exec. asst. Nat. Collegiate Athletic Assn., 1946-47; adminstrv. asst. U.S. Sen. Homer Ferguson, 1947-51. Dir. Chgo. Tube & Iron Co. Director United States Olympic Committee. Dir. National Football Found, Athletic Inst. Served to lt., USNR, 1942-45. Republican. Conglist. Clubs: Executives, Tavern (Chgo.); Valley Lo Country. Home: Glenview IL Died May 20, 1971.

REEDER, CHARLES LEONARD, consulting eng'r; b. Baltimore, Oct., 1876; s. Andrew J. and Anna E. R.; prep. ed'n Baltimore City Coll.; grad. Johns Hopkins, 1896; sp'l studies in elec. and mech. engineering; married. In eng'ring Gen. Elec. Co., 1896-7; City Passenger Ry. System, Baltimore, 1897-8; began individual practice, Apr., 1897. Residence: Arundel Apartments. Office: Equitable Bldg., Baltimore‡

REEDER, GLEZEN ASBURY, JR., university pres.; b. Cleveland; s. Glezen Asbury and Amelia S. (Ward) R.; A.B., and A.M., Baldwin U., Berea, O. (D.D.); B.D., Boston U.; m. Lucy May Spencer, of Adelphi, O., Nov. 27, 1890. Ordained M.E. ministry; began as pastor, Le Roy O., 1882; now pres. Baldwin U. Thrice mem. Gen. Conf. M.E. Ch.; mem. Commn. on Federation and Union. Address: Berea OH‡

REEDY, ROSE STROMAN (MRS. F. C. REEDY), banker; b. Springfield, S.C., Apr. 22, 1904; d. Charles Benjamin and Eugenia (Porter) Stroman; B.A., Columbia, 1925; m. F.C. Reedy, Oct. 7, 1933; 1 dau., Frances Rose (Mrs. William O. Buyck). Tchr. English, Pickens (S.C.) High Sch., Belhaven (N.C.) High Sch., 1925-32; dir. Bank of Clarendon, Manning, S.C., 1957-69. Pres., Civic League, 1936-38; chmn. U.S. Savs. Bonds, 1948-69; pres. Cancer Soc., 1956-69; sec., treas Beautification Com., 1948-53. Mem. Am. Legion Aux (pres. Manning 1961-62), D.A.R., Am., S.C. rose socs. Am. S.C. camellia socs., Nat. Council of Garden Clubs (life), Garden Club of S.C. (eleven year history chmn 1962-69, rec. sec. 1965-67, treas. 1967-69), S.C. Landscape Critics Council (v.p. 1963-65). Clubs: Camellia Garden (pres. 1951-54, 59), National Accredited Judges (sec. 1959-61); Garden (dir. E. Low Country 1956-59, state bd. 1956-59 Camellia Garden (pres. 1959-61, Manning SC Died Oct. 17, 1969.

REEP, SAMUEL AUSTEN, educator; b. Mpls., May 8, 1912; s. Samuel Nicholas and Grace Ann (Austen) R.; B.B.A., U. Minn., 1935, M.A., 1940; Ph.D., U. Chgo., 1948; m. Margaret E. Allan, Dec. 26, 1947; children—James Allan, Thomas Austen, Carolyn Frances. Instr., U. San Antonio, 1939; asst. prof. Ga. State Coll., 1940-42, U. So. Cal., 1947; asso. prof. Drake U., 1948-49; faculty Cal. State Coll., Long Beach, 1953-70, prof. finance, 1960-70, chmn. div. bus. adminstrn., 1960-65. Mem. Am. Assn. U. Profs., Am. Finance Assn., California State College Professors, Alpha Kappa Psi, Beta Gamma Sigma, Phi Kappa Phi, Pi Gamma Mu, Sigma Delta Psi. Home: Los Alamitos CA Died Apr. 2, 1970; buried Lakewood Cemetery, Minneapolis MN

REES, ALBERT WILLIAM, clergyman, educator; b. Muscogee Co., Ga., Nov. 30, 1877; s. Thomas Clopton and Martha Olivia (Kimbrough) R.; A.B., Emory Coll., Oxford, Ga., 1903; m. Gussie Alexander Lee, of Dawson, Ga., Dec. 7, 1905; children—Mary Olivia (dec.), Willa Frances, Gussie Lee, Elinor Louise. Ordained ministry M.E. Ch., S., 1905; prin. high sch., Brewton, Ga., 1903-06; pastor Vidalia, Ga., 1905-09; pres. Sparks (Ga.) Coll., 1909-17; pastor Moultrie, Ga., 1917-20; presiding elder, Cordele Dist., South, Ga., 1921-22; prin. Emory U. Acad., Oxford, Ga., 1922-29; pastor Camilla, Ga., 1929-—. Kiwanian. Home: Camilla GA‡

REES, EDWARD H., congressman; b. Emporia, Kan., June 1886; s. John J. and Martha S. (Evans) R.; student Kan. State Teachers Coll., Emporia, 1907-13; m. Margaret Agnes Antle, June 21, 1926; 1 son, John Edward. Sch. teacher, 1909-11; clerk of court, Lyon County, 1912-18; admitted to Kan. bar, 1915; mem. Kan. Ho. of Rep., 1925-31, Kan. Senate, 1933-35; mem. 75th to 86th Congresses, from 4th Kan. Dist.; v.p., dir. Citizens Nat. Bank, Emporia. Mem. Am. Legion. Republican. Conglist. Mason (33 deg., K. T., Shriner). Clubs: Lions, Forum (Emporia). Home: Emporia KS Died Oct. 25, 1969.

REESE, CHARLES H., paper co. exec.; b. W. Pittston, Pa., 1895; ed. Cornell U., 1924. Vice pres., dir. Nekoosa-Edwards Paper Co. Pres., dir. Nekoosa-Edwards Found. Home: Port Edwards WI Died May 20, 1968.

REESE, GEORGE LEE, lawyer; b. Fort Payne, Ala., Jan. 11, 1872; s. John W. and Nancy Ann Reese; ed. pub. school and law offices Lindsey & Goodsell, Comanche, Tex.; m. Ru'Blanche Freeman, Apr. 16, 1898 (died 1907); children—Maude Amy, George L.; m. 2d, Jim Jackson, Sept. 4, 1910; children—Randolph, Annette. Admitted to bar at Comanche, Tex., and to Supreme Court of Tex.; 1898, to state bar of N.M., 1905; admitted to Okla. and Colo. State Bars; engaged in practice of law since 1898. Pres. N.M. State Bar Assn., 1941. Chairman Roosevelt County (N.M.) Council of Defense, 1918-19; govt. appeal agent Selective Service Bd., Chaves County, N.M., 1942-43. Democrat. Presbyterian. Mason (Shriner), Elk. Home: 712 W. Alameda, Av. Office: 424 White Bldg., Roswell NM*‡

REESE, JOSEPH HAMMOND, life ins. exec.; b. Phila., Nov. 13, 1896; s. Joseph and Anna (Hammond) R.; student pub. schs. Phila.; Chartered Life Underwriter designation, 1930, Agy. Management Certificate, 1933; m. Ethel Allen, June 30, 1921; children—Robert A., Jay R., Joseph Hammond. Bank teller Nat. Bank of Germantown, Phila., 1921-25; rep. Equitable Life Ins. Co. of Ia., 1925-28; unit mgr. home office agy. Penn. Mut. Life Ins. Co., Philadelphia, 1928-35, gen. agt. in charge 1936-60; owner Reese Cons. Services, Rydal, Pa., from 1960. Served as 1st lt. U.S. Army, World War I. Mem. Am. Soc. Chartered Life Underwriters (pres. 1938, organizer, pres. Phila. chpt. 1930-32) Am. Coll. Life Underwriters (sec. from 1949, mem. registration bd. since 1945, exec. com. from 1949), Nat. Assn. Life Underwriters (life mem. Million Dollar Round Table), Phila. Assn. Life Underwriters (dir. 1942-45). Recipient pres. cup award of Phil. Assn. 1949. Republican. Episcopalian. Clubs: Skytop (Pa.) Lodge; Union League (Phila.); Country, Huntington Valley Hunt (Huntington Valley, Pa.). Author articles profl. jours. Address: Rydal PA Died Oct. 9, 1968.

REESE, SCOTT CHARLES, mfg. co. exec.; b. Wood County, O., May 31, 1903; s. George W. and Amanda (Mosser) R.; student East Liverpool (O.) Bus. Coll.; m. Gertrude Pearl Starr, Apr. 23, 1928; children—Richard S., Donna. With Scio Pottery Co., 1933-66, pres., 1952-66, also treas., personnel dir., dir.; pres. and dir.

cio Bank Co., 1952-66; dir. Nolan Co., Bowerston, O. Mem. Am. Ceramic Soc., Ohio C. of C., N.A.M., Nat. Small Businessmens Assn. Home: Scio OH Died Mar. 2, 1966.

REESE, WILBUR FORD, lawyer; b. Nashville, Oct. 1, 1917; s. Ralph Byrne and Bessie (Ford) R.; B.A., Tulane U., 1939, LL.B., 1941; m. Beverly Hess, Jan. 20, 1942; children—Thomas Ford, Beverly (Mrs. John Church, Jr.), Linda Louise, Marianne. Admitted to La. bar, 1941; mem. firm St. Clair Adams & Son, 1941; partner firm Adams & Reese, New Orleans, 1945-71. Dir. George Engine Co., Inc., Harvey, La., Frierson Realty Corp., Harvey, Libco, Inc., New Orleans, Mid-States Constructors, Inc., New Orleans. Adviser to staff So. Bapt. Hosp., New Orleans, 1961-71. Served to lt. comdr. USNR, 1942-45. Fellow Am. Coll. Trial Lawyers; mem. Am. Judicature Soc., Am., La. (sec.-treas. 1950-51, 59-60), New Orleans (pres. 1953-54) bar assns., Internat. Assn. Ins. Counsel (exec. com. 1965-71, pres. 1969-70), Fedn. Ins. Counsel, Def. Research Inst. (dir. 1968-70), New Orleans C. of C., Beta Theta Pi, Omicron Delta Kappa, Phi Delta Phi, Kappa Delta Phi. Methodist. Home: New Orleans LA Died Aug. 2, 1971; buried Metairie Cemetery, New Orleans LA

REESER, EDWIN B., former pres. Barnsdall Oil Co.; b. New Ringgold, Pa., July 15, 1873; s. John F. and Elizabeth (Mintzer) R.; ed. pub. schs., New Ringgold; m. Mary E. Isherwood, Nov. 11, 1897; children—Edwin Isherwood, Harry Courtney. Former president Barnsdall Oil Co. and of Am. Petroleum Institute. Republican. Mason. Club: Bankers Club. Home: 7 E. Woodward Blvd., Tulsa OK Office: 120 Broadway, New York NY also Petroleum Bldg., Tulsa OK*‡

REESMAN, BUDD AARON, advt. exec.; b. Highland Park, Ill., May 26, 1907; s. John Samuel and Minnie (Haungs) R.; student DePauw U., 1924-27; B.S., Northwestern U., 1928; Indsl. Engr., Northwestern Tech., 1942; m. Elizabeth Austin Ling, Sept. 1, 1928; children—Clifford John, Budd Aaron. Advt. mgr. North Shore Pub. Co., 1930-42; tng. dir. J. I. Case Co., 1942-43; engr. Sundstrand Corp., 1943-45; pres. Display Craft, Ind., Rockford, Ill., 1945-48; sec., account exec. E. R. Hollingsworth & Assos., Rockford, Ill., 1948-59; advt. mgr. Greenlee Bros. & Co., Rockford, Ill., 1959-68; pres. Traffic Engring., Inc.; instr. supervisory mgmt. foremanship tng. courses Ill. Univ. Extension Div. (Rockford). Comdg. officer Rockford sqdn., group operations officer Civil Air Patrol, 1949-57; auditor Owen Twp., 1961-68; pres. Winnebago County Dep. Sheriffs Assn., 1961-65. Mem. Rockford Advt. Club, Indsl. Advt. Research Inst. Mason (Shriner). Clubs: Pleasant Valley Hunt (past pres.), University, Elks, Mauh-Nah-Tee-See Country. Home: Rockford IL Died Nov. 22, 1968.

REEVE, WILLIAM FOSTER, III, educator; b. Camden, N.J., July 25, 1892; s. William Foster and Mary Joy (Grey) R.; prep. edn. Episcopal Acad., Phila., 1905-08, Gunnery Sch., Washington, Conn., 1908-10; Litt.B., Princeton, 1914; LL.B., U. of Pa., 1917; m. Kathleen Helen Wilson, Sept. 3, 1919; children—William Foster Wilson, Mark. Admitted to Pa. bar, 1919, N.J. bar, 1920; began practice in Phila., with firm Bell, Kendrick, Trinkle & Deeter, 1919-22; lecturer in law, U. of Pa. Law Sch., 1920-22, asst. prof. of law, 1922-24, prof. from 1924, Ferdinand Wakeman Hubbell prof. of law, 1938-50, Algernon Sidney Biddle professor of law, 1950-63, professor emeritus, 1963-72; visiting professor summers, Cornell Law School, 1930, Columbia Law Sch., 1931. Served in M.C., U.S. Army, 1917-19; with Base Hosp. No. 10 attached to B.E.F., Le Treport, France. Dir. Newton Twp. Sch. Dist., 1934-48, pres., 1945-48, 61-63; mem. Marple-Newtown Jr. High Sch. Authority; mem. Newtown Twp. Sch. Authority, 1955-61. Adviser on trusts Am. Law Inst. Mem. Am. Bar Assn., Pa. Bar Assn., Sharswood Law Club, Dial Lodge, Sons of the Revolution. Republican. Clubs: Rose Tree Fox Hunting (Media, Pa.); Princeton, Rittenhouse (Phila.). Author of Pa. Annotations to the Restatement of the Law of Trusts (under auspices of Pa. State Bar Assn.). Home: Newtown Square PA Died Jan. 27, 1972.

REEVES, ALEC HARLEY, scientist; b. Redhill, Eng., Mar. 10, 1902; s. Edward Ayearst and Grace (Harley) R.; B.S. in Engring., Imperial Coll. Sci., London, 1923. Research engr. Internat. Western Electric Co., London, 1923; project leader Paris (Eng. and France) lab. Internat. Tel. & Tel. Co., 1924-40; prin. sci. officer Royal Aircraft Establishment, 1940-45; divisional head Standard Telecommunications Labs., Ltd., Harlow, Eng., 1945-60, senior scientist, 1964-70, sr. prin. research engr.; head Reeves Telecommunications Labs., London, 1970-71. Boy Scout leader, 1918-29, 35-40; vol. probation officer, Surrey and London, 1950-71. Mem. Outward Bound Trust of Eng., 1950-71; bd. govs. Royal Hosp. Incurables, London, 1952-71. Served to wing comdr. RAF, World War II. Decorated officer British Empire, 1965, also Commander Order of British Empire, 1969; recipient Ballantine Gold medal Franklin Inst., Phila., 1965; City of Columbus award Internat. Communications Inst., Genoa, Italy, 1966. Fellow Radar and Electronics Assn., Instn. Elec. Engrs. Club: Ski of Great Britain. Inventor pulse code modulation, 1937; co-inventor, oboe system bombing through overcast, 1941. Home: Harlow Essex England Died Oct. 13, 1971.

REEVES, ARCHIE R., state ofcl., prodn. supt.; b. Mo., Oct. 28, 1898; s. David and Ida (Hoover) R.; student pub. sch., m. Lucie Jahn, Apr. 16, 1918; children—Ruth (Mrs. Howard Hoffmann), Roy F., James A. Sales mgr. Capitol Life Ins. Co., Canon City, Colo., 1935-37; owner Silver State Feed & Produce, Canon City, 1938-51; supt. prodn. Colonna & Co. of Colo., Canon City. Mayor, Canon City, 1949-55; mem. Colo. Parole Bd. Chmn. adv. bd. Order of De Molay, 1935-45. Methodist. Mason (Shriner). Home: Canon City CO Deceased.

REEVES, DANIEL F., pres., gen. mgr. Los Angeles Rams Profl. Football Team. Address: Los Angeles CA Died Apr. 15, 1971.

REEVES, FRANK DANIEL, mem. Democratic Nat. Com.; b. Montreal, Can., Mar. 23, 1916; s. Frederick Barrow and Sarah Marie (Crutchfield) R.; came to U.S., 1922, naturalized, 1943; A.B. cum laude, Howard U., 1936, LL.B., 1939; m. Elizabeth Dolores Walker, Dec. 29, 1939 (div.); children—Deborah Elizabeth, Daniel Robert; m. 2d, Senora M. Wood, 1967. Admitted to D.C. bar, 1943; asst. to Thurgood Marshall, spl. counsel N.A.A.C.P., 1940-42; adminstrv. asst. Washington bar, N.A.A.C.P., 1942; faculty Howard U. Law Sch., 1942-43; trial atty. President's Com. Fair Employment Practice, 1943-45; atty. OPA, 1945-46; pvt. practice, Washington, 1946-73; sr. partner firm Reeves, Robinson & Duncan, 1954-61, Reeves, Robinson, Rosenberg, Sherry & Hamlin, 1961-73. Vice chairman District of Columbia primary campaign organization for Averill Harriman, 1952; campaign staff Adlai Stevenson presidential campaign, 1952; spl. asst. to gen. chmn. Estes Kefauver campaign com., 1956; mem. Dem. Nat. Com. for D.C., 1960-73; mem. Dem. Central Com. D.C., 1952-60. Bd. dirs. United Givers Fund. Mem. Am., Nat., D.C., Washington bar assns., N.A.A.C.P. (exec. com. D.C. br., nat. legal com.), Americans for Dem. Action (exec. bd. D.C.), Kappa Alpha Psi. Elk. Club: Nat. Capital Democratic. Home: Washington DC Died Apr. 8, 1973.

REEVES, GEORGE CURTIS, advt. exec.; b. Cin., Jan. 28, 1905; s. George A. and Mabel F. (Curtis) R.; student U. Cin., 1924-28; m. Margaret Ellen Fitzgerald, Nov. 28, 1931; 1 dau., Ellen Fitzgerald (Mrs. Wolcott H. Johnson). With J. Walter Thompson Co., advt. agy., 1929—, beginning as copy writer, successively copy group head, copy dir., v.p., 1944-60, exec. vice pres., 1960-65, vice chairman of board, 1965-67, dir., 1950-69; former mgr. Chgo. office; dir. Nat. Boulevard Bank of Chgo. Mem. Chgo. Crime Commn. Dir. Lake Forest Hosp.; trustee Chgo. Hort. Society. Member of Am. Assn. Advt. Agencies (vice chairman 1958). Clubs: Chicago; Exmoor Country (Highland Park, Ill.). Home: Lake Forest IL Died Nov. 1969.

REEVES, JAMES HAYNES, army officer; b. Centre, Ala., Sept. 20, 1870; s. James A. and Mary E. (Haynes) R.; grad. U.S. Mil. Acad., 1892; grad. Inf.-Cav. Sch., 1897, Gen. Staff Sch., 1920, Army War Coll., 1921; m. Katharine V. S. Richardson, 1914; 5 children. Commd. 2d lt., cav., June 11, 1892; advanced through grades to brig. gen., Oct. 2, 1927. Served as aide to Maj. Gen. Joseph Wheeler, May-Oct. 1898, Spanish-Am. War; participated in Santiago campaign and recommended for brevet of 1st lt. for conduct at Battle of Santiago; with China Relief Expdn., 1900; in Phillippines, 1903-06; mil. attache Am. Legation, Pekin, China, 1901-03 and 1907-12; organized 353d Inf., N.A., and served as col. World War I, participating in St. Mihiel and Meuse-Argonne offensives; with Army of Occupation, Germany, 1918-May 1919; comdr. 8th Cav., 1921-23; mem. Gen. Staff, 1923; asst. chief of staff (Mil. Intelligence), 1924-27; comdr. Vancouver Barracks, 1928-Sept. 1929, 21st Inf. Brigade, Schofield Barracks, Hawaii, 1929-31, 9th Coast Arty. Dist., Fort Winfield Scott, Calif., 1931-32, 4th Coast Arty. Dist., Fort McPherson, Ga., 1932-34; retired, Sept. 30, 1934. Awarded D.S.C. (U.S.) for exceptional heroism in action near St. Mihiel, Sept. 12-13 1918; D.S.M. for exceptionally meritorious and distinguished services; 2 Silver Star citations; Croix de Guerre and Officer de l'Ordre de l'Etoile Noire (France); Order of Double Dragon (China). Chmn. Atlanta chapter Am. Red Cross, 1934-37, exec. dir., 1938-46. Club: Army and Navy (Washington). Home: 307 2d Av. S.E., Atlanta GA‡

REEVES, JOHN RICHARD THOMAS, JR., chief counsel Indian Service; b. Chaptico, Md., Sept. 15, 1877; s. John Richard Thomas and Elizabeth Eleanor (Hayden) R.; LL.B., Georgetown Law Sch., 1905; m. Nettie Estelle Rule, Mar. 5, 1907; children—Richard Rule, George William. Entered Indian field service, U.S. Dept. of Interior, 1906, trans. to hdqrs. in Washington as clerk, 1908, later serving as asst. div. chief, asst. law clerk, 1908-21, atty. on solicitors staff, 1921-29, chief counsel since 1929. Mem. Am. Bar Assn. Episcopalian. Home: DeWitt Hotel, 244 E. Pearson St. Office: Merchandise Mart, Chicago, IL‡

REEVES, WINONA EVANS, corr., editor, writer; b. Big Mound, Ia., Aug. 14, 1871; d. James McFarland (M.D.) and Helen Isabel (Lusk) Evans; prep. education Whittier Academy, Salem, Iowa; B.S., Ia. Wesleyan College, 1891, M.S., 1896, L.H.D., 1942; married Harry J. Reeves, December 23, 1897 (died Oct. 17, 1945); children—Helen Lusk (Mrs. Robert Sabert Casey), Mrs. Agnes Reeves-Colville. Society and club editor, Keokuk (Ia.) Daily Gate City, 1912-20; editor Blue Book of Iowa Women and Blue Book of Nebraska Women, 1914-16; editor P.E.O. Record since 1918; fgn. corr. Bd. Fgr. Missions Presbyn. Ch. since 1923. Del. to Women's Internat. Week, Budapest, 1938, Paris, 1939; v.p. from U.S.A. since 1938. Mem. Nat. Fedn. of Press Women (v.p. 1939-41), Am. Assn. Univ. Women, P.E.O. Sisterhood (nat. pres. 1909-11), Ill. Woman's Press Assn. (v.p. 1940-41), Cordon, D.A.R. Republican. Presbyterian. Author: The Story of P.E.O., 1919, vol. II, 1935; As We Were Saying, 1944. Lecturer. Home: 2842 Sheridan Rd., Chicago IL‡

REGAN, BEN, investment banker; b. Big Rapids, Mich., Dec. 23, 1910; s. John Michael and Mary Angela (Jeffs) R.; attended Loyola University, 1928; LL.D., Marquette University, 1960; m. Doris Barnett, July 29, 1936; children—Royal J. B., Ben. Asso. Hornblower & Weeks, Chgo., 1928-42; pres. Nationwide Food Service, Inc., Chgo., 1957-60; now gen. partner Hornblower & Weeks-Hemphill, Noyes, N.Y.C.; chmn. Frontier Airlines; dir. 21 Brands, Inc., Am. Decalcomania Co., AVEMCO Corp., Columbia Pictures Corporation, AMK Corporation, Roman Corporation, Screens, Incorporated, Multicolor, Incorporated, H. C. Bohack Co., Inc. Chairman Ill. Aeronautics Commission, 1941-45; commissioner Port of New York Authority; director N.Y. Bd. Trade. Chmn. bd. trustees Mundelein Coll.; bd. regents Marquette U.; bd. trustees Fordham U., Marymount Manhattan Coll., Oblate Coll.; member of the board of trustee of the Henrotin Hospital; board advisers St. Joseph's Hospital; advisory board University Illinois, 1942-70, Loyola University. Decorated Knight of Malta, Knight Holy Sepulchre, Chevalier Grand Duche of Luxembourg, Cavalier Republic of Italy. Mem. Nat. Aero. Assn. (dir. 1948-—), Inst. Food Tech., Wine and Food Soc. Clubs: Economic, Chicago Athletic Assn., Yacht (Chgo.); Recess, Sky, Turf and Field, Manhattan, Union League (N.Y.C.); Nat. Aviation, Capitol Hill, Nat. Press (Washington); Deepdale (L.I.); Canadian (Toronto, Ont.). Sponsor Who's Who in Aviation, 1942, 43. Home: Rye NY also Westport, CT Died 1970.

REGISTER, GEORGE SCOTT, U.S. judge; b. Bismarck, N.D., Nov. 27, 1901; s. George M. and Minnie (Scott) R.; A.B., Jamestown Coll., 1923, LL.D. (hon.), 1960; J.D., U. Mich., 1926; LL.D., Wesley Coll., 1951; m. Grace C. Cummins, Sept. 21, 1934; children—Joanne C., George Robert. Admitted to N.D. bar, 1928; spl. asst. atty. gen., N.D., 1928-29; states atty. Burleigh County, N.D., 1929-53; mem. firm Register & Thompson, Bismarck, 1953-55; chief judge Dist. Ct. N.D., 1955-72. Mem. 4th Jud. (past pres.), Am., N.D., bar assns., S.A.R. Methodist. Mason (32, Shriner). Club: Bismarck Kiwanis (past pres.). Home: Bismarck ND Died Mar. 18, 1972.

REICHERT, MOTHER THOMAS, superior of Ursuline Convent; b. Cumberland, Md., Nov. 11, 1868; d. Francis and Teresa (Wirtman) Reichert; A.B., Pittsburg, Kan., 1920. M.A., Notre Dame Univ., 1927. Teacher, Louisville, Ky., 12 years; co-founder, Ursuline Acad., Paola, Kan., 1895, prin., 1895-1924; dean Coll. of Paola, 1924-41, superior-general, 1941-44; supervisor of education for the schools of the Ursuline community of Paola, Kansas. Address: Ursuline Convent, Paola KS‡

REICHMANN, DONALD AUGUST, librarian; b. Centralia, Ill., Dec. 12, 1919; s. August C. and Anna (Reichmann) R.; A.B., Elmhurst Coll., 1942; B.S. in L.S., U. Chgo., 1947; m. Ruth Elizabeth Koenig, Apr. 7, 1956. Asst. exec. sec. A.L.A.A., Chgo., 1947-48; exec. asst. dir. Enoch Pratt Free Library, Balt., 1948-50, gen. reference, 1950-51; dir. Hazleton (Pa.) Pub. Library, 1951-53; head merc. br. Free Library Phila., 1953-63, coordinator dist. services, 1963-66; dir. Albuquerque Pub. Library, 1966-71. Part-time instr. Drexel Inst. Tech. Library Sch., 1961-66. Served with AUS, 1942-46. Mem. A.L.A. (reference services div. com.), Spl. Libraries Assn. Editor: Between Librarians, 1948-51; Pa. Library Assn. Bull., 1952-57. Home: Albuquerque NM Died Nov. 3, 1971.

REID, ALBERTA BANCROFT (MRS.), author; b. San Francisco, Mar. 2, 1873; d. Albert Little and Fannie (Watts) Bancroft; early ed'n in Miss West's Sch., San Francisco, the Sophienstift at Weimar, Germany, and privately by German governess; then at Ogontz Sch., Pa., 1891-3, grad. 1893; m. Walnut Creek, Calif., July 24, 1901, James Steel Reid, lawyer. Mem. Calif. Chapter D.A.R. Presbyterian. Republican. Clubs: Century, Fortnightly (hon.), Town and Country. Author: Royal Rogues, 1901 P2. Contb'r verses and sketches to Sunset. Address: 2943 Broderick St., San Francisco CA‡

REID, DELAFAYETTE, librarian; b. Alton, Ill., Apr. 18, 1915; s. deLafayette and Florence (Miller) R.;

student Shurtleff Coll., 1932-35; B.J., U. Mo., 1938; B.S. in Library Sci., U. Ill., 1940, M.S., 1948; m. Mildred Joyce Weaks, Apr. 18, 1936; children—Sherrill Jean, deLafayette III. Reporter, Democrat-Argus, Caruthersville, Mo., 1938-39; asst. circulation dept. U. Ill. Library, Urbana, 1940-41, asst. acquisition dept., 1941-42, bibliographer, acquisition dept., 1945-46, librarian, undergrad. div. Galesburg, 1946-49; asst. dir. U. Kan. Libraries, Lawrence, Kan., 1949-51; chief of pub. services Ill. State Library, Springfield, 1951-54, asst. state librarian, 1954-65, dep. state librarian, 1965-70. Served with USNR, 1942-45. Mem. Am., Ill. library assns., Am. Assn. State Librarians, Adult Edn. Assn. U.S., Ill. Adult Edn. Assn. (past pres.), N.E.A. (dept. audio visual instrn.), Ill. Audio Visual Assn. Bapt. Rotary. Co-prod., editor U. Ill. Library Orientation film Contact with Books, 1942. Home: Rochester IL Died Oct. 1, 1970.

REID, ELLIOTT GRAY, aero. engr.; b. Sycamore, O., May 29, 1900; s. J. Nelson and Etta A. (Bennington) R.; B.S., U. Mich., 1922, M.S., 1923, Aero. Engr., 1938; m. Charlotte Katherine Jenkins, May 15, 1926; 1 dau., Margaret Anne (Mrs. T. j. Fogel). Jr. aero. engr., NACA Langley Field, Va., 1922, asst., 1924, associate, 1927, exptl. and theoretical aerodynamics; prof. aerodynamics, Stanford; cons. engrs., 1927-68; currently aerodynamic cons. Hdqrs. USAF. Private S.A.T.C., U. Mich. Oct.-Dec. 1918. Recipient citation Distinguished Alumnus, Engring. Centennial, U. Mich., 1953. Fellow Royal Aero. Soc. (Gt. Britain), Am. Inst. Aero. and Astronautics; member of Sigma Xi, Tau Beta Pi. Author: Applied Wing Theory, 1932; also tech. reports and notes NACA. Contbr. to tech. journals. Home: Menlo Park CA Died Sept. 24, 1968.

REID, HELEN ROGERS (MRS. OGDEN MILLS REID), b. Appleton, Wis., Nov. 23, 1882; d. Benjamin Talbot and Sarah Louise (Johnson) Rogers; student, Grafton Hall, Wis., 1893-99; A.B., Barnard Coll., 1903; Litt.D., Miami U., 1931, Columbia, 1949, Bates Coll., 1951, Manhattanville College of the Sacred Heart, 1953; Dr. Hum., Rollins College, 1933; L.H.D., Syracuse Univ., 1941, Lafayette College, 1941, N.Y.U., 1944, Yale, 1950, C. W. Post College, Long Island University, 1964; LL.D., Oglethorpe Univ., 1935, University of Toronto, Canada, 1947, Smith College, 1948, University of Wisconsin, 1953, Temple University, 1953, Mt. Holyoke College, 1954; married Ogden Mills Reid. Mar. 14, 1911 (died Jan. 3, 1947);children—Whitelaw, Elisabeth (dec.), Ogden Rogers. Newspaper work with New York Herald Tribune, 1918-58; vice president N.Y. Tribune, Inc., 1922-47, pres., 1947-53, chmn. bd., 1953-55. Treas., N.Y. State Campaign Com. for Woman Suffrage, until 1917; mem. U.S. Govt. Contract Com., 1953-61. Trustee Metropolitan Museum of Art, Herald Tribune Fresh Air Fund, New York City; trustee Barnard Coll., chmn. bd., 1947-56. Republican. Episcopalian. Clubs: Colony, Women's University. Women's City. Home: New York City NY Died July 27, 1970; buried Sleepy Hollow Cemetery, Tarrytown NY

REID, HENRY JOHN EDWARD, aeronautical engr.; b. Springfield, Mass., Aug. 20, 1895; s. Henry and Sophia (Mowle) R.; B.S. in E.E., Worcester Poly. Inst., 1919, Dr. Engring. (hon.), 1946; married Mildred J. Woods, June 26, 1920; children—Phyllis Virginia, Henry J. E. Began as student research engineer, Westinghouse Company (East Pittsburgh), 1919; in charge of maintenance and millwrighting Noiseless Typewriter Company, Middletown, Conn., 1920-21; jr. mech. engr. Nat. Advisory Com. for Aeronautics, Langley Field, Va., 1921-26, engr. in charge laboratories and director, 1926-60. Served as private, Engineers Reserve, United States Army, 1918; member ALSOS mission to Europe, 1944-45. Member board of directors, Hampton-Elizabeth City County Community Chest, 1943-45, pres. 1946. Fellow Inst. of Aeronautical Sciences; mem. Soc. Automotive Engrs., Nat. Rifle Assn. (life), A.A.A.S., Tau Beta Pi, Sigma Alpha Epsilon. Conglist. Mason. Clubs: Rotary (Hampton); Engineers Club of Va., Peninsula. Author of Tech. Notes, Nat. Adv. Com. on Aeronautics. Office: Landley Field VA Died July 30, 1968.

REID, IRA DE AUGUSTINE, educator; b. Clifton Forge, Va., July 2, 1901; s. Daniel A. and Willie R. (James) R.; A.B., Morehouse Coll., 1922, LL.D., 1953; M.A., U. Pitts., 1925; Ph.D., Columbia, 1939; Doctor of Laws, Haverford College, 1967; m. to Gladys Russell Scott, Oct. 15, 1925 (dec. June 1956); 1 dau., Enid Harriett; m. 2d, Anne M. Cooke, Aug. 12, 1958. Indsl. sec. N.Y. Urban League, 1924-28; dir. research Nat. Urban League, N.Y.C., 1928-34; prof. sociology Atlanta U., 1934-46; prof. ednl. sociology Sch. Edn., N.Y.U., 1946-47; vis. prof. sociology N.Y. Sch. Social Work, Columbia, 1951-54; prof. sociology, chmn. 'dept. sociology and anthropology Haverford (Pa.) Coll., 1947-66, professor emeritus, 1966-68; also visiting prof. sociology Pa. State U., summer 1958, Harvard. Summer 1963; vis. dir. dept. extra-mural studies Univ. Coll., Ibadan, Nigeria, 1962; Danforth distinguished prof. sociology Internat. Christian Univ., Tokyo, Japan, 1962-63. Sr. cons. study of the aged, Pa. Dept. Welfare; co-dir. study social and med. services for the elderly, Phila. Geriatric Center. Member advisory council teacher grants Danforth Foundation. Consultant on the minorities War Manpower Commission, 1940-42; advisory com. U.S. Dept. Labor, 1946-48; cons. higher edn. trusteeship div. UN, 1949; mem. governor's commn. on higher edn., Pa., 1956-68; mem. commn. on higher edn., Phila., 1958-68; cons. Am. Council on Edn., 1964; mem. Gov.'s Commn. Police Brutality, 1964. Bd. dirs. Met. YMCA; mem. bd. trustees Nat. Child Labor Com. Bd. overseers Wm. Penn Charter Sch., Phila. Fellow A.A.A.S., Am. Sociol. Assn. (v.p. 1954); mem. Eastern Sociol. Soc. (pres. 1955), Urban League Phila. (pres.), Phi Beta Kappa. Democrat. Mem. Soc. Friends. Author: The Negro Immigrant, 1939; In a Minor Key, 1940; (with Arthur F. Raper) Sharecroppers All, 1941. Editor: Racial Desegregation and Integration, 1956; editor of Phylon, jour. race and culture, 1943-47. Home: Haverford PA Died Aug. 15, 1968.

REID, LOUDON CORSAN, physician; b. North Bay, Ont., Can., Oct. 13, 1893; s. Herbert Gates and Mary Fisher (Ferguson) R.; M.D., McGill U., 1916, C.M., 1916; m. Grace A. Lodge, Feb. 12, 1925; children—H. G., Martha. Came to U.S., 1924, naturalized, 1944. Intern Royal Victoria Hosp., 1920-25; pvt. practice surgery, Detroit, 1925-30; asso. prof. pathology N.Y. Med. Coll., 1930-39; prof. physiology N.Y.U. Sch. Medicine, 1939-69, Rush H. Kress prof. research surgery, 1950-69. Served with Canadian Army, 1915-19, with AUS, 1942-46. Home: Bronxville NY Died July 15, 1969.

REID, O. L., educator; b. Xenia, O., July 18, 1875; s. John William Henry and Ruth Allan (John) R.; A.B., Ind. U., 1898; LL.B., U. of Louisville, 1905; post-grad. work, summers, Indiana U., U. of Chicago and New York U.; A.M., New York U., 1922; m. Helen Florence Kelley, July 8, 1902; children—Janet (dec.), Jane, Robert Chase (dec.). Teacher, Rensselaer, 1898-1900; reporter Chicago Record, 1900-01; teacher Commercial High Sch., 1901-02, Boys' High Sch., 1902-11, both in Louisville; prin. Girls' High Sch., Louisville, 1911-16; supt. schs., Louisville, 1916-20; supt. schs. Youngstown, O., July 12, 1920-1926; pres. Yale Private School, 1926-42; head of department of English, Youngstown College, 1935-45, head division social sciences since 1945. Member National Com. to Defend America by Aiding the Allies; Mem. N.E.A. (life), Am. Hist. Assn., Acad. of Polit. Science, Beta Theta Pi, Youngstown Chamber of Commerce (pres. 1925), Mahoning Chapter Am. Red Cross. Presbyn. Mason. Editor: Lockhart's Life of Scott, and Franklin's Autobiography. Home: Poland OH Office: 410 Wick Av., Youngstown 2 OH‡

REID, ROBERT HALEY, business exec.; b. London, Ont., Can., Jan. 17, 1906; s. Edward E. and Ethel E. (Jeffery) R.; student U. Toronto, 1924-28; m. Jannaca van Nostrand, Nov. 11, 1929 (dec.); children—Terrence, Susan, Jane; m. 2d, Adele Saunders White, Mar. 24, 1952 (dec.). With Wood, Gundy & Co., Ltd., Toronto, 1928-32; office mgr. Harrison & Co., 1932; investment dept. London Life Ins. Co., 1933-36, exec. asst., 1936-38, dir., mem. exec. com., 1938, mng. dir., 1941-72, v.p., 1946-53, exec. v.p., 1953-58, pres. 1958; dir. Huron & Erie Mortgage Corp., Can. Trust Co., Abitibi Paper Co., Ltd., Interprovincial Pipe Line Co., Lakehead Pipe Line Co. Mem. Canadian Life Ins. Assn. (past pres.), Canadian Health Ins. Assn. (past pres.). Home: London Ontario Canada Died Nov. 1972.

REID, T. ROY, govt. ofcl.; b. Gowensville, S.C., Aug. 26, 1889; s. Stafford and Mary Tallulah (Foster) R.; S.B., Clemson Coll., 1912; S.M., U. Wis., 1926, Sc.D., 1937; LL.D., University of Arkansas, 1956; married Bertha B. Smith, December 22, 1912 (dec. Oct. 1939); 1 son, Thomas R.; m. 2d, Kate Fulton, Mar. 18, 1942. Teacher gen. sci., Clinton Coll., Clinton, Ky., 1912-13; tchr. agrl. chemistry, Agrl. and Mech. Coll., Monticello, Ark., 1913-17; county agrl. agent, Monticello, 1918; asst. 4-H Club Agent, Extension Service, Little Rock, Ark., 1919, agent in marketing, 1920-23; asst. dir. Agrl. Extension, Coll. of Agr., U. Ark., 1923-35; regional dir. Resettlement and Farm Security Adminstrn., Little Rock, 1935-41; asst. to Sec. of Agr., Dept. Agr., 1941, dir. personnel, 1942-54, dir. U.S. Dept. Agr. Grad. Sch., 1954-58; cons. ICA, 1958-69. Mem. Soc. for Personnel Adminstrn., Epsilon Sigma Phi. Baptist. Home: Tallahassee FL Died June 16, 1969; buried Roselawn Cemetery, Tallahassee FL

REID, WILLIAM ALFRED, univ. lecturer; b. Page County, Va., June 16, 1871; s. Joseph Henry and Ann Sarah (Watson) R.; ed. acads. and under pvt. tutors; LL.B., Columbian (now George Washington) U., 1900; LL.M., Southern Normal U., 1901; summer course in economics, Harvard; m. Helen Gibson. Spl. rep. George Washington U., 1907-11, presenting its work in foreign countries; has served as spl. agt. U.S. Dept. Commerce; rep. Am. commercial interests in India, China, Egypt and European countries; rep. Pan-Am. Union in S. and Central America, retired from Union, 1937; now lecturing on internat. topics at various universities; specializing in Inter-American Workshops", summers 1943-45; lecturer on Econ. Survey of Latin Am. nations at Sch. of Foreign Service, Georgetown Univ. Spl. commercial-industrial investigations in countries of the Caribbean, 1925, and in Hudson Bay regions, Canada, 1927; in Central America and Northern S. America 1929; in S. America, 1937-38; loaned to State of Calif 1930. Del. to 1st Pan Am. Scientific Congress, Santiago Chile, 1908. Mem. Societe Academique d'Histoir Internationale, France. Author: Seeing South America Seeing Latin Republics of North America; Ports an Harbors of South America; etc. Author-editor of Am Nation Series (more than 80 booklets), pub. by Pan-Am Union, also other pamphlets. Home:The Ontario Washington DC‡

REIDY, PETER J., cons. engr.; b. Long Island City Mar. 15, 1900; s. Maurice Alphonse and Mary Agne (Hession) R.; student Bklyn. Polytech. Inst., 1922; m Alby Eugenia Cobb, July 22, 1947. Engr., Purdy & Henderson Co., N.Y.C., 1922-32; mem. firm Purdy & Henderson Assos., Inc., cons. engrs., N.Y.C., 1933-42 pres., chmn. bd., 1943-58; v.p., dir. Purdy & Henderso Co., N.Y.C. and Havana, Cuba, 1942-52; commnr. dep bldgs., N.Y.C., 1958-62, comdr. dept. pub. works 1962-63; exec. dir. Triborough Bridge and Tunne Authority, 1963-71; dir. General Analine & Film Corp Ninth Federal Savings and Loan Association. Bd. govs N.Y. Bldg. Congress, Inc. Mem. Mayor N.Y.C. Slum Clearance Com.; mem. Grand Jury Assn. N.Y. County chmn. constrn. div. Greater N.Y. council Boy Scout Am. Fellow Am. Soc. Cons. Engrs.; mem. N.Y. Assn Cons. Engrs. (pres. 1957-58). Home: New York Cit Died June 4, 1971; buried Gate of Heaven, Mt. Pleasan NY

REIF, HERBERT R., lawyer; b. Pitts., July 29, 1898 LL.B., Cornell U., 1923. Admitted to N.Y. bar, 1924; s partner firm Johnson, Reif & Mullen, Rochester, N.Y Mem. Am., N.Y. State, Monroe County bar assns., Ph Delta Phi. Address: Rochester NY Died Jan. 15, 1971

REIGER, SIEGFRIED HEINRICH communications co. exec.; b. Lindau, Germany, Ma 28, 1920; s. Heinrich L. and Mathilda (Barthel) R.; B.S in Physics, Tech. U., Munich, Germany, 1940, M.S. i Physics, 1948; m. Irmgard H. Tanzer, Oct. 13, 1945; son, Peter H. Came to U.S., 1947, naturalized, 1955; s staff mem., also project leader communications satellit studies RAND Corp., Santa Monica, Cal., 1959-63 chief date transmission projects Air Force Cambridg (Mass.) Research Center, 1952-56, asst. chi communications lab., 1956-59; v.p. tech Communications Satellite Corp., Washington, 1964-70 Cons. Presidential Sci. Adv. Com., 1961-70. Sr. mem I.E.E.E. Home: Bethesda MD Died July 14, 1970.

REIK, THEODOR, psychologist, author; b. Vienna Austria, May 12, 1888; s. Max and Caroline (Trebitsch R.; Ph.D., U. Vienna, 1912; m. Marla Cubelic, 193 children—Arthur, Theodora, Miriam. Came to U.S 1938, naturalized, 1944. Asso. Sigmund Freud, U Vienna, 1910-38; lectr. Psychoanalytic Inst., Vienna Berlin, Germany, The Hague, Netherlands, N.Y.C 1912-44; dir. Soc. for Psychoanalytic Psychology N.Y.C., 1941-70; also professor of psychology Adelph University. Recipient 1st prize for psychoanalyti paper, 1915. Diplomate Am. Psychol. Assn. Autho Ritual (preface by Sigmund Freud), 1931; Th Unknown Murder, 1936; Surprise and th Psychoanalyst, 1937; From Thirty Years With Freud 1940; Masochism in Modern Man, 1941; A Psychologist Looks at Love, 1944; Psychology of Se Relations, 1945; Listening With the Third Ear, 1948 Fragment of a Great Confession, 1948; The Secret Sel 1952; The Haunting Melody, 1953; The Search Within 1956; Myth and Guilt, 1957; On Love and Lust, 1957 A Mystery on the Mountain, 1959; The Compulsion t Confess, 1959; The Creation of Woman, 1960; Sex i Man and Woman, 1960; The Temptation, 1961; Jewis Wit, 1961; The Need to be Loved, 1963; Curiosities o the Self, 1965; The Many Faces of Sex, 1966; 1 psychol. books in German. Contbr. to English, German Dutch, Spanish psychol. publs. Address: New York Cit NY Died Dec. 31, 1969.

REILAND, KARL, clergyman; b. Brooklyn, N.Y., Oc 23, 1871; s. George M. and Katherine (Gilcher) R prep. edn., Cheshire (Conn.) Mil. Acad. and Hotchkis Sch., Lakeside, Conn; M.A., Trinity Coll., Conn., 189 student P.E. Theol. Sem., Alexandria, Va., 189 Berkeley Div. Sch., Middletown, Conn., 1901; D.D Trinity, 1915, LL.D., Hobart College, 1914; D.D Wesleyan U., Middletown, 1927; L.H.D., Rollin College, Winter Park, Fla., 1935; m. Elizabeth Burwel June 20, 1901; 1 dau., Virginia Field (Mrs. George W Cobb, Jr.). Deacon, 1901, priest, 1902, P.E. Ch.; recto Trinity Ch., Wethersfield, Conn., 1901-04; asst. Grac Ch., N.Y. City, 1904-10; rector St. Andrew's Ch Yonkers, N.Y., 1910-12, St. George's Ch., New York 1912-36; now rector emeritus also writing an broadcasting. Trustee Post-Graduate Hosp., Columbi U., Berkeley Divinity Sch.; dir. Inst. Marital Relation vice-pres. Modern Churchmen's Union (Eng.). Mem Churchman's Assn., Delta Kappa Epsilon. Mason (3 degrees). Clubs: The Club, Players, Century. Autho The World's Miracle and Other Observations, 192 Address: CT‡

REILLY, JOHN DAVID, shipbuilder; b. Yonker N.Y., Aug. 1, 1888; s. James and Mary J. (Collier) R grad. high sch., Yonkers, N.Y., 1907; LL.D. (honorary

Georgetown University, 1951; m. Mary F. Murray, June 17, 1914; children—John David and Mary Agnes. Began as shipbuilder with Robins Dry Dock and Repair Co., Bklyn., 1907; with Todd Shipyards Corp., N.Y.C., 1916-71, dir., 1920-71, pres., 1932-53, chmn. bd., 1953. Comdr. USNR, ret. Member Am. Com. Lloyd's Register of Shipping; member board of managers American Bureau of Shipping. Member Am. Soc. Naval Architects North East Coast Instn. Engrs. and Shipbuilders. Roman Catholic. Knight of Columbus, Elk. Clubs: India House Club, New York Athletic, Hudson River Country, Westchester Country, Seaview, N.Y. Yacht, Lake Placid, Midocean (Bermuda); Bohemian. Home: Yonkers NY Died Amy 30, 1971.

REILLY, WILLIAM JOHN, educator, business consultant; b. Pittsburgh, Pa., Mar. 6, 1899; s. William John and Anna Jean (Kelly) R.; B.S., Carnegie Inst. Tech., 1921, M.S., 1923; Ph.D., U. of Chicago, 1927; m. Gladys Margaret Bogue, May 1, 1926; children—Ann Bogue, Myrtle Jean, Norman Bogue. Mem. research staff, Carnegie Inst. Tech., 1922-23; U. of Chicago, 1923-25; mem. sales research staff Procter & Gamble Co., 1925-27; originated miniature sample theory for testing accuracy and reliability of market information, 1927; asso. prof. marketing in charge of market studies, U. of Tex., 1927-29; dir. of research Erickson Co., 1929-32; founder, 1932, and since dir. Nat. Inst. for Straight Thinking; mgr. St. Louis Div. of Am. Weekly, 1933-36; v.p. and gen. mgr. Townsend & Townsend, Inc., and chmn. bd. Townsend Advertising Research Inst., 1937-39; account exec. Lennen & Mitchell, 1939-41; consultant on personnel research and employment Vick Chem. Co., 1942; personnel consultant, Sales Affiliates, Inc., 1942-54, many corps., from 1954. Recipient Paul D. Converse award for outstanding contbrs. advancement of sci. in marketing, 1959. Mem. Inst. Mgmt., Am. Mgmt. Association, Phi Eta, Acacia. United Presbyterian. Club: Columbia University. Mason (K.T., Shriner). Author: What Place Has the Advertising Agency in Market Research?, 1929; Marketing Investigations, 1929; Methods for the Study of Retail Relationships, 1929; Methods for the Measurement of Retail Trade Territories, 1929; Sales Quota Procedure, 1930; The Law of Retail Gravitation, 1931; Straight Thinking, 1935; How to Find and Follow Your Career, 1936; How to Use Your Head, 1938; How to Improve Your Human Relations, 1942; The Law of Intelligent Action, 1945; The Twelve Rules for Straight Thinking, 1947; How to Avoid Work, 1948; Career Planning for High School Students, 1952; Successful Human Relations, 1952, Life Planning for College Students, 1954; How to Make Your Living in Four Hours A Day, 1955; How to Get What You Want Out of Life, 1957; In Search of a Working Philosophy of Life, 1959; Opening Closed Minds, 1964. Home: Radburn NJ Died Nov. 17, 1970.

REIMER, MARIE, chemist; b. Sunbury, Pa.; d. David and Cornelia (Collins) R.; A.B., Vassar, 1897; Ph.D., Bryn Mawr, 1904; Univ. of Berlin, 1902-3. Asso. prof. chemistry, Barnard Coll. (Columbia), 1903—. Protestant. Member Am. Chem. Soc., Deutsche Chemische Gesellschaft. Contbr. articles to Am. Chem. Journal, etc. Address: 604 W. 112th St., New York NY‡

REIMERT, WILLIAM DANIEL, newspaper exec.; b. Summit Hill, Pa., Aug. 14, 1902; s. William A. and Mary (Snyder) R.; grad. Mercersburg Acad., 1920; A.B., Ursinus Coll., 1924, LL.D., 1956; Litt.D., Cedar Crest Coll., 1967; m. Martha Virginia Moorman, July 30, 1932. With sales dept. Lehigh Portland Cement Co., 1924-25; asst. mgr. Allentown (Pa.) C. of C., 1928-30; editor Allentown Evening Chronicles, 1930-36; exec. editor, dir. Allentown Call Chronicle Newspapers, 1936-71, v.p., 1966, pres., 1967-71; mem. bd. publ. United Ch. Herald. Past pres. Lehigh Valley Tb. Soc.; v.p. Allentown Art Mus.; pres. bd. Salvation Army; bd. dirs. Good Shepherd Home, Allentown Indsl. Devel. Corp., Lehigh Valley Safety Council, Home Ministries United Ch. of Christ; chmn. trustees Ursinus Coll., Collegeville, Pa. Hon. citizen Allentown and Macungie. Mem. Am., Pa. socs. newspaper editors, A.P. Mng. Editors Assn., (life) Allentown C. of C. (rec. sec., past v.p.), Tunkhannock Creek Assn., Tunkhanna Fishing Assn., Sigma Delta Chi. Republican. Clubs: Livingston, Lehigh Valley, Lehigh Country (Allentown). Home: Macungie PA Died Oct. 1, 1971; buried St. Peters Cemetery, Lynnville PA

REINHARD, ADOLPH EARL, steel co. exec.; b. Terre Haute, Ind., Dec. 20, 1895; s. Herman A. and Nettie M. (Solomon) R.; B.S., Rose Poly, 1919; m. Helen K. Landahl, Dec. 29, 1925; children—Norma J. (Mrs. Thomas Koch), Richard E. (M.D.). Supt. open hearth and Bessemer plant, Youngstown Sheet & Tube Co. (O.), 1919-43; asst. gen. supt., v.p. Great Lakes Steel Corp., Ecorse, Mich., 1943-54; v.p. in charge Portsmouth operations, gen. mgr. Detroit Steel Corp., Portsmouth, O., 1955-68; cons. Koppers Internat., Concepcion, Chile, 1962. Mem. Am. Inst. Mining Metall., and Petroleum Engrs., Am. Iron and Steel Inst., Assn. Iron and Steel Engrs. Mason (32 deg.), Elk, Kiwanian. Home: Wyandotte MI Died Nov. 25, 1968; buried Mich. Memorial Cemetery, Flatrock MI

REINHARDT, EMIL FRED, army officer; b. Bay City, Mich., Oct. 27, 1888; s. C. H. and Sybilla (Tomhafe) R.; B.S., U.S. Mil. Acad., West Point, N.Y., 1910; grad., Command and Gen. Staff Sch., 1923, Army War Coll., 1931; m. Laura Bishop, Oct. 2, 1919; children—Laura Jane (Mrs. Robert E. Smock), Ann Sybil (Mrs. William G. Stevenson). Commd. 2d lt., U.S. Army, 1910, advanced through ranks to maj. gen., Apr. 1942. Comd. 69th Div. in action (European Theater) which made initial contact with Soviet Army on the Elbe River; ret. Sept. 30, 1946. Home: San Antonio TX Died July 24, 1969; buried Ft. Sam Houston Nat. Cemetery.

REINHARDT, G(EORGE) FREDERICK, inst. adminstr.; b. Berkeley, Cal., Oct. 21, 1911; s. George Frederick and Aurelia Isabel (Henry) R.; A.B., U. of Calif., 1933; A.M., Cornell U., 1935; diploma, Cesare Alfieri Inst., Florence, Italy, 1937; LL.D. honoris causa, Mills College, 1962, University of California, 1963, Gonzaga U., 1964; m. Lillian Larke Tootle, Sept. 10, 1949; children—George Frederick, III, Anna Aurelia, Charles Henry, Catherine Jane. Andrew D. White fellow in political science Cornell University, 1936; with International Boundary Commn., U.S. AND Mexico, 1935-36; fgn. service officer, 1937-68, served in Vienna, Tallinn, Riga, Moscow, Algiers, Naples, Paris, Frankfurt, and duty with Dept. of state, Washington; consul gen., 1947; chief, Div. of Eastern European Affairs, Dept. of State, 1948, dir. Office of Eastern European Affairs, 1950; counselor of Embassy, Paris, 1951-55; U.S. ambassador to Viet Nam, 1955-56; counselor Dept. of State, 1957-60; U.S. ambassador to United Arab Republic, U.S. minister to Kingdom of Yemen, 1960-61; ambassador to Italy, 1961-68; sr. dir. Stanford Research Inst. Internat., 1968-71. Served as ensign, USNR, 1932-37. Mem. Am. Fgn. Service Assn. (pres. 1959-60), Zeta Psi. Clubs: Bohemian (San Francisco); Metropolitan (Washington); Brook (N.Y.C.); Caccia (Rome). Address: Zurich Switzerland Died Feb. 22, 1971; buried Protestant Cemetery, Rome, Italy

REINHARDT, GUENTHER, writer, public relations cons.; b. Mannheim, Germany, Dec. 13, 1904; s. Dr. Philipp Victor and Lilli Johanna (Zimmern) R.; A.B., Royal Coll., Mannheim, 1922; B.S., State U. Economics, Mannheim, 1925; A.M., Heidelberg, 1925; postgrad. research, Columbia, N.Y., 1925-27; m. Helen I. Williams, Aug. 5, 1937 (dec.). Statistician Ladenburg, Thalmann & Co., N.Y.C., 1926-29; chief statistician Toerge & Schiffer, 1929-30; mgr. investment dept. Amalgamated Bank, 1930-32; contbr. Swiss newspapers, 1925-45; spl. corr. Europe and Washington, McClure Newspaper Syndicate, 1932-38; mem. staff N.Y. Daily News, 1939-40; contbr. leading newspaper syndicates and nat. mags., 1932-68; corr. (Berlin) Internat. News Service, 1946; cons. U.S. House of Rep. spl. com. on Un-American activities, 1934-35, spl. employee F.B.I., 1936-43; research cons. Rep. Nat. Com., 1943-44; cons. Office U.S. Co-ordinator of Inter-Am. Affairs, 1944-45, with Counter Intelligence Corps, U.S. Forces, ETO, 1946-47; expert cons. sec. of army, 1947-48; pub. relations cons., 1949-68. Mem. Fgn. Press Assn. (mem. sec., mem. exec. com., 1936-42). Club: Nat. Press (Washington). Author: The Organization of the German Steel Trust (German), 1925; The Jews in Nazi Germany, 1933; Fish and Torpedoes (Jap espionage), 1938; You Americans (with B. P. Adams), 1939; Source Materials for Psychological Warfare, 1944; Investigative Procedures, 1948; Evaluation Criteria on Nazi Party Membership, 1950, Crime Without Punishment, 1952. Home: New York City NY And Reno, Nev. Died Dec. 2, 1968.

REINHARDT, RALPH HOMER, indsl. engr.; b. Chgo., Dec. 1, 1907; s. Homer Lewis and Grace (Gibbs) R.; student Northwestern U., 1931-33; m. Virginia Ruth Benz, Mar. 30, 1934; children—Arden Georgiana (Mrs. Daniel H. Thompson), John Allen. Bonus clk. R. R. Donnelley & Sons, Chgo., 1926-28, time study man, 1928-32, efficiency man, 1932-42; mgmt. engr. Stevenson, Jordan & Harrison, Inc., N.Y.C., 1942-43, mgmt. engrng. supr., 1943-47; plant mgr. Richardson Co., Melrose Park, Ill., 1947-52, indsl. engrng. mgr., 1952-68. Mem. Soc. Packaging and Handling Engrs., Industrial Management Soc., Indsl. Engrng. Group, Rubber Mfrs. Assn., Tau Delta Kappa. Episcopalian. Home: Lombard IL Died Apr. 29, 1968.

REINICKE, FREDERICK GEORGE, naval officer; b. Tripoli, Ia., Apr. 8, 1888; s. Rev. Joseph and Katherine (Forler) R.; grad. U.S. Naval Acad., 1910; m. Nan Chadwick, Aug. 22, 1921; children—Ann Chadwick, Frederick Rogers. Commd. ensign, U.S. Navy, 1912, and advanced through the grades to commodore, 1943; served in U.S.S. Va., 1910-13, U.S.S. Galveston, 1913-16; comd. U.S.S. Aylevin in Eng. Channel and North Sea; gunnery officer U.S.S. Miss., 1921-24; comdr. U.S.S. Osborne and U.S.S. Paulding, 1926-29, U.S.S. Tulsa, 1932-35; exec. officer U.S.S. Tenn., 1937-38; served ashore, instr. U.S.N.A. 1919-21, Training Sta., Newport, 1924-26; grad. mgr. athletics, U.S.N.A., 1929-31; sr. course Naval War Coll., 1931-32; in charge pub. relations, office Naval Operations, Navy Dept., 1935-37; naval director, Port of New York, 1939-45; commissioner, Marine and Aviation City of New York and mem. N.Y. Air Authority, 1946-47; advisor to the government of Thailand, 1950-51. President, Am. Asiatic Assn.; hon. mem. Maritime Assn. Decorated Navy Cross, Second Nicaraguan Campaign, Yangtze Service, Victory and Defense medals, Legion of Merit medal, Commander Order of the British Empire; Order of Orange and Nassau with Swords (Netherlands). Clubs: New York Yacht, Tuxedo, Leash. Home: New York City NY Died Nov. 1969.

REISER, ARMAND EDOUARD, air force officer; b. Hollidaysburg, Pa., Jan. 5, 1924; s. Frank Joseph and Jane (Rollet) R.; B.S. in Fgn. Service, Georgetown U., 1948; M.A. in Govt., George Washington U., 1951; grad. Air War Coll., 1966; m. Neva Louise Curtis, Mar. 6, 1947; children—Armand Edouard, Jane Curtis, Nancy Jo, Martha Ann. Statistician, WPA, 1940-41, OPA, 1941-43; commd. 2d lt. USAAF, 1944, advanced through grades to lt. col. USAF, 1963; pilot in CBI, World War II; chief analysis div. and operations statistics div. Hdqrs. SAC, 1946-49; chief program control dr., directorate mil. personnel Hdqrs. USAF, 1951-55; asst. U.S. air attache designate to Cambodia, Laos and S. Viet Nam, 1959-61; assigned Hdqrs. Pacific Air Forces, 1961-63; dir., prof. aerospace studies George Washington U., 1963-65; U.S. air attache to Lebanon, Jordan and Cyprus, 1966-68. Decorated D.F.C. with 3 oak leaf clusters, Air medal with 3 oak leaf clusters, Air Force Commendation medal. Mem. Air Force Assn., Arnold Air Soc. Republican. Catholic. Author: Career Development for Military Controllership, 1951; Counterinsurgency, A Case Study: Southeast Asia, 1965. Co-author: The Role of Military Intelligence in National Security Policy Formulation, 1966. Home: Arlington VA Died Apr. 30, 1968.

REISMAN, MORTON, ednl. adminstr.; b. Chgo., Aug. 10, 1907; s. Louis and Ida (Krone) R.; student Crane Jr. Coll., 1925-27; Ph.B., U. Chgo., 1931; M.A., Northwestern U., 1940; m. Zelda Kane, June 30, 1935; 1 son, Arthur Lee. Tchr. Cook County (Ill.) dist. schs., 1935-36, prin., 1936-40, supt., 1940-49; exec. dir. Congregation B'nai Zion, Chgo., 1949-51; dir. Anshe Emet Day Sch., Chgo., 1951-67. Mem. Am. Assn. Sch. Adminstrs., N.E.A., Supts. Round Table No. Ill., New Edn. Fellowship (v.p. 1960-65), Internat. Reading Assn., Ind. Schs. Assn. Greater Chgo. (pres. 1966-68), Phi Delta Kappa. Jewish religion. Home: Chicago IL Died July 13, 1967.

REISSNER, ALBERT, psychoanalyst and research in organo-therapy; born in Chemnitz, Germany, Mar. 5, 1883; s. Falk and Helen (Fuchs) R.; student psychiatry, psychology, medicine, biology, oral surgery, univs. of Berlin, Munich, Tuebingen, Phila., Cairo, Naples, Florence, London, Paris, New York; Dr. Med. Faculty summa cum laude, Tuebingen; B.A. (hon.), Oriental U., Alexandria; married Johanna Krafft; children—Dr. Fritz A., Helga Karker. Came to the United States, 1940, naturalized, 1946. Research worker Polyclinic Royal University Munich, 1905-22; certified specialist to royal family; served as head various hosps. during World War I; formerly prof. materia medica, comparative medicine; affiliated with Columbia, N.Y.U., L.I. Coll. Medicine, New Sch. Social Research, Alfred Adler Inst. for Individual Psychology, Mental Hygiene Service at Community Ch., N.Y.; mem. of staff Alfred Adler Consultation Center, New York; consultant and lecturer at Pastors' Clinic, Methodist Hospital, Brooklyn; mem. psychiat. forum Bklyn. State Hosp. First v.p. Community Mental Health Council. Recipient 7 honors and medals. Fellow Assn. Advancement Psychotherapy; mem. Rudolph Virchow Med. Soc., Am. Soc. Sci. Study of Religion, American Academy Psychotherapists, Order St. Luke the Physician, Institute Individual Psychology, New York State, Brooklyn psychol. assns., Association for Scientific Study Sex, American Assn. Religious Psychotherapy, American Assn. Alfred Adler Psychology, New York Acad. Sci., A.A.A.S. Episcopalian. Author many publs. Discoverer Reissner-Rhodan-Reaction (new method for diagnostic purposes), Vaduril Organo-therapeutic, and other discoveries relating to field. Address: Brooklyn NY Died Jan. 23, 1970.

REITER, BERNARD L., treas. Tenneco Chemicals, Inc., also dir.; dir. Muodex Products of Can. Ltd. Home: New York City NY Died Apr. 22, 1968.

REMARQUE, ERICH MARIA, author; b. Osnabruck, Westphalia, Germany, June 22, 1898; s. Peter Maria and Anne Maria Remarque; French descent; student Gymnasium and Seminar at Osnabruck and Univ. of Munster; m. Ilse Intta Zambona (div.); m. 2d, Paulette Goddard, Feb. 25, 1958. Served on Western Front during World War I; after the war was successively teacher, race driver, test driver, sport editor, dramatic critic and writer. Came to U.S., 1939, naturalized, 1947. Decorated Grand Cross Merit (Germany). Mem. German Acad. Speech and Poetry. Roman Catholic. Author: All Quiet on the Western Front, 1929; The Road Back, 1931; Three Comrades, 1937; Flotsam, 1941; Arch of Triumph, 1946; Spark of Life, 1951; A Time to Love and A Time to Die, 1954; The Black

Obelisk, 1957; Heaven Has No Favorites, 1961; The Night in Lisbon, 1964. Address: Locarno Switzerland Died Sept. 25, 1970.

REMER, CHARLES FREDERICK, univ. prof.; b. Young America, Minn., June 16, 1889; s. Frederick and Rachel Elizabeth (Thomas) R.; A.B., U. of Minn., 1908; A.M., Harvard, 1917, Ph.D., 1923; m. Alice Winter, July 19, 1911. Served in Bur. of Edn. P.I., 1910-12; instr. economics, St. John's U., Shanghai, China, 1912-15, prof., 1917-22; tutor div. history, govt. and economics, Harvard, 1923-24; Orrin Sage prof. economics, Williams Coll., Williamstown, Mass., 1924-28; prof. economics, U. of Mich., from 1928, emeritus; on leave as dir. Geneva Research Center, 1938-39; on leave as chief Far Eastern Section, Office of Coordinator of Information, 1941-42; chief Far Eastern Division, Office of Strategic Services, 1942-44; adviser on Far Eastern investment and finance in the Dept. of State, 1944-45; dir. study of internat. econ. relations of China, Social Science Research Council of New York, 1928-31; asso. mem. Page Sch., Johns Hopkins U., 1932-33; mem. Am. Econ. Mission to the Far East, 1935. Member American Econ. Assn., Am. Association University Professors, Far Eastern Assn., Phi Kappa Phi. Episcopalian. Clubs: Research (U. of Mich.), American (Shanghai, China), Cosmos, Washington. Compiler: Readings in Economics for China, 1922. Author: The Foreign Trade of China, 1926, Japanese translation, 1930; American Investments in China, 1929; Foreign Investments in China, 1933 (Japanese transl. 1935); (with W. B. Palmer) A Study of Chinese Boycotts, 1933. Contbr. articles on Far East and on econ. problems to Quar. Jour. of Economics, Chinese Social and Polit. Science Rev. Home: Ann Arbor MI Died July 2, 1972.

REMICK, GRACE MAY, author; b. Chelsea, Mass.; d. William Barker and Sarah Baker (Thompson) R.; ed. Chelsea High Sch., Boston Normal Sch. and under tutors; studied English at Oxford, Eng., 1889-90, French, in Switzerland and Paris, German, in Germany; unmarried. Began as writer, at Boston, 1897. Author: Glenloch Girls, 1909; Glenloch Girls Abroad, 1910; Glenloch Girls' Club, 1911; Glenloch Girls at Camp West, 1912; Jane Stuart—Twin, 1913; Jane Stuart's Chum, 1914; Jane Stuart at Rivercroft, 1915; Jane Stuart—Comrade, 1916; The Sheldon Six Series. Home: Sharon MA‡

REMY, CHARLES FREDERICK, judge; b. near Town of Hope, Bartholomew County, Ind., Feb. 25, 1860; s. Calvin Jones and Miranda (Essex) R.; A.B., Franklin (Ind.) Coll., 1884, LL.D., 1905; LL.B., U. of Mich., 1888; m. Deborah Henderson, Nov. 25, 1891; 1 son, William Henderson. Practiced at Columbus, firm of Hacker & Remy, 1888-96; mem. Ind. Ho. of Rep., 1895; reporter Supreme Court of Ind.; 2 terms, 1896-1904; practiced at Indianapolis with James M. Berryhill, 1905-19; judge Appellate Court of Ind., 1919-31; resumed practice as mem. of Remy & Remy. Trustee Franklin Coll. Mem. Am., Ind. State and Indianapolis bar assns., S.A.R., Indiana Pioneer Soc. Republican. Baptist. Clubs: Columbia, Century Literary. Home: 44 E. 54th St. Office: 424 Circle Tower Indianapolis IN‡

RENNEBOHM, OSCAR, ex-gov.; b. near Leeds, Columbia County, Wis., May 25, 1889; s. William Carl and Julia (Brandt) R.; Ph.G., Univ. of Wisconsin, 1911, LL.D. (honorary), 1962; m. Mary Fowler, September 8, 1920; 1 daughter, Carol Ann. Manager drug store, Madison, Wis., 1911; purchased drug stores, 1912, 1920, eleven stores between 1920-28, pres. 17 Rennebohm Drug Stores, Inc., 1929, now hon. chmn. bd.; lt. gov. State of Wis., 1944, re-elected, 1946, became gov. (to fill unexpired term of Walter S. Goodland, deceased), March 13, 1947, elected gov., 1948, was not a candidate for re-election, returned to bus. director First Nat. Bank, Wis. Life Ins. Co. (emeritus); hon. chairman board Rennebohm Drug Stores, Inc. Pres., Oscar Rennebohm Found., Inc. Trustee, Meml. Union; regent U. Wis., 1952-61; dir., v.p., exec. committee University of Wisconsin Foundation. Established 10 general scholarships for high school graduates University of Wis., 1944. Recipient of Am. Druggist citation for outstanding community service, 1947, citation U. Wis. Coll. Pharmacy, 1953, Foremost Citizen award City of Madison, 1954; named Alumnus of Year, U. Wis. Alumni Assn., 1959. Volunteered as able-bodied seaman, World War I; disch. rank of ensign. Active in Red Cross and Community Union work. Mem. State Bd. of Pharmacy 20 yrs. Mem. Am. Pharm. Assn. (past v.p., hon. pres.), Nat. Assn. Retail Druggists (past treas.), Nat. Assn. Chain Drug Stores (dir.), Nat. Assn. Bds. Pharmacy (hon. pres.), Wis. Pharm. Assn. (past pres.), Am. Legion, 40 and 8. Republican. Lutheran. Mason (33 deg.), Eagle, Mouse, K.P. Clubs: Kiwanis, Madison. Home: Madison WI Died Oct. 15, 1968; buried Forest Hill Cemetery, Madison WI

RENNIE, SYLVESTER WILDING, physician; b. Montreal, Que., Can., July 25, 1903; s. John Ingraham and Frances Agnes (Neville) R.; brought to U.S., 1913, naturalized, 1919; M.D., U. Pa., 1930; m. Margaret Carolyn Valentine, Sept. 29, 1934. Intern, Abington (Pa.) Meml. Hosp., 1930-31, clin. tng. in surgery, 1931-32; clin. tng. in obstetrics and gynecology Womans Hosp., N.Y.C., 1932-34; chief obstetrics and gynecology dept. Del. Hosp., Wilmington; chief obstetrics and gynecology Del. State Hosp., Gov. Bacon Health Center. Turstee, Brandywine Coll., 1968-71. Served to maj., M.C., AUS, 1942-44; PTO. Diplomate Am. Bd. Obstetrics and Gynecology. Fellow A.C.S., Internat. Coll. Surgeons, Am. Coll. Obstetrics and Gynecology; mem. A.M.A., Am. Fertility Soc., Internat. Fertility Assn., Del. (pres. 1961-62), New Castle County (pres. 1953-54) med. socs., U. Pa. Alumni Assn. (past pres. Del.). Coub: University (pres.) 62-64 (Wilmington). Home: Wilmington DE Died Feb. 20, 1971; buried Riverview Cemetery, Wilmington DE

RENO, DORIS SMITH (MRS. PAUL HALVOR RENO), newspaper exec.; b. Aurora, Ind., Jan. 15, 1907; d. George Richard and Blanche (Shutts) Smith; A.B., DePauw U., 1928; M.A., Mills Coll., 1931, postgrad., 1940; m. Paul Halvor Reno, Oct. 15, 1932; children—Elisabeth Margret (Mrs. John V. Hardeman, Jr.), Susanna Clare (Mrs. Larry Barthelmas). Music-dance editor, critic Miami (Fla.) Herald, 1940-72. Mem. Poetry Soc. Am., Phi Beta Kappa, Theta Sigma Phi. Home: Miami FL Died Apr. 18, 1973.

RENO, GUY BENJAMIN, lawyer; b. Browning, Ill., June 30, 1892; s. Benjamin Franklin and Emma (Workman) R.; A.B., U. Ill., 1915, LL.B., 1917; d. Hazel Kinnear, Sept. 2, 1919; children—Ben (dec.), Roger. Admitted to Ill. bar, 1917; asst. state's atty. Winnebago County, Ill., 1919-23; partner firm Large & Reno, Rockford, Ill., 1925-58, Reno, Zahm, Folgate & Skolrood, 1958-70; chmn. bd. Am. Nat. Bank and Trust Co., Rockford, 1941-72. Pres. Rockford Community Chest, 1958-59, Rockford Community Trust, 1966-68. Bd. dirs. Boys Farm Sch., Winnebago County, Ill., mem. adv. bd. Rockford Salvation Army, Rockford YWCA; counsellor Rockford Coll.; trustee Swedish-Am. Hosp. Assn., Rockford, 1946-67, hon. trustee 1967-72. Served to 2d lt., F.A., AUS, 1918. Mem. Am., Ill., Winnebago County bar assns., Am. Judicature Soc., Pi Kappa Alpha, Phi Alpha Delta. Republican. Methodist. Mason. Clubs: Midday, Forest Hills (Rockford). Home: Rockford IL Died Nov. 18, 1972; buried Greenwood Cemetery, Rockford IL

RENTSCHLER, GEORGE ADAM, machinery mfr.; b. Fairfield, O., Nov. 14, 1892; s. George Adam and Phoebe (Schwab) R.; Litt.B., Princeton U., 1915; m. Rita Rend Mitchell, Nov. 11, 1936; children—George A., Charles E. M., Frederick B. II. Began as machinist with Hooven, Owens, Rentschler Co., Hamilton, O., 1915; organized Gen. Machinery Corp. by merging H.O.R. with Niles Tool Works Co., 1928, merged Gen. Machinery Corp. with Lima Locomotive Works to create Lima Hamilton Corp., 1948, merged this with Baldwin Locomotive Works to form Baldwin-Lima Corp., mfrs. heavy machinery, Eddystone, Pa., 1950, chmn. exec. com., 1950-65; organized and controlled def. plants during World War II, including Am. Oerlikon Co., Charleston Shipbldg. & Dry Dock Co., Gen. Machinery Ordnance Co., Southeastern Shipbldg. Co. (built 88 Liberty ships at Savannah); dir. Armour & Co., Barber Oil Corp., Bendix Aviation, Cin. & Suburban Bell Telephone Co., Cin. Gas & Electric Co., Fifth Third Union Trust Co., Cin., Motor Wheel Corp., Philip Carey Mfg. Co. (chmn.), U.S. Lines, William Powell Mfg. Co., Cin. Served in Air Service, U.S. Army, World War I. Recipient certificate of Commendation for wartime services Sec. Navy, World War II. Clubs: Chicago; Camargo (Cin.); National (Southampton); Brook, Twenty-Nine, Lambs, Links (N.Y.). Address: New York City NY Died May 22, 1972; buried Sacred Heart Cemetery, Southampton NY

REQUA, EARL FRANCIS, railroad exec.; b. Everett, Wash., July 26, 1904; s. Walter James and Minnie (Sheehan) R.; LL.B., U. Wash., 1930; m. Othelia Aadsen, July 28, 1931; 1 dau., Patricia Claire (Mrs. August S. Caron). Admitted to Wash. bar, 1930; with firm Padden &Moriarty, Seattle, 1930-37; with N.P. Ry., 1937-70, gen. solicitor, 1949-61, v.p., gen. counsel, 1961-68, senior vice president, 1968-70. Member Chi Phi, Phi Delta Phi. Home: St Paul MN Died Apr. 1, 1970.

RESNICK, JOSEPH YALE, congressman; b. Ellenville, N.Y., July 13, 1924; s. Morris and Anna (Zaida) R.; ed. pub. schs.; m. Ruth Lehrer, June 14, 1947; children—Jeffrey, Deborah, Todd, David. Founder, 1947, chmn. bd. Channel Master Corp., mfrs. TV equipment, Ellenville, 1947-69. founder Dynafoam Corp., 1959; founder, 1961, since pres. Questron Am., Inc., plastic processing equipment; mem. 89th Congress 28th Dist. N.Y. Charter founder Eleanor Roosevelt Meml. Found., Boys Town Jerusalem; bd. dirs. St. Cabrini Home, Inc. Served with U.S. Merchant Marine, 1942-44. Democrat. Home: Ellenville NY Died Oct. 6, 1969.

RETTGER, LEO FREDERICK, bacteriologist; b. Huntingburg, Ind., Mar. 17, 1874; s. John Henry and Mary Catherine (Woellner), R.; grad. Ind. State Teachers Coll., 1894; B.A., U. of Ind., 1896, M.A., 1897, LL.D., 1931; Ph.D., Yale, 1902; student U. of Strassburg; m. Clara V. Snyder, June 9, 1903; 1 son, James Frederick. Asst. in bacteriology and chem. U. of Ind., 1897-1900; instr. bacteriology, Yale, 1902-06, assistant professor, 1906-19, professor, 1910-42, professor emeritus since June 1942. Research fellow Rockefeller Institute for Med. Research, 1903-06; part time bacteriologist in charge, department of animal diseases, Storrs Agrl. Expt. Sta., 1908-46; lecturer in bacteriology, Wesleyan Univ., 1916-17. Mem. Soc. Am. Bacteriologists (pres. 1916), A.A.A.S., North-Am. Conf. of Research Workers in Animal Diseases (pres. 1932), Sigma Xi, Delta Omega, Phi Gamma Delta. Republican. Conglist. Author: Intestinal Flora; Animal Diseases; contbr. to various scientific and med. jours. Home: 340 Ogden St., New Haven CT‡

RETTIG, H. EARL, broadcasting exec.; b. Chgo., June 4, 1903; s. Henry G. and Elizabeth M. (Karker) R.; m. Rosalie Castner, Dec. 2, 1934;children—H. Earl, Richard C. and Ronald M. (twins). Various positions Halsey Stuart & Co., 1921-28, Fox Film Corp., 1928-35, Wagner Prodns., 1935-36, Major Pictures, 1936-38, Hal Roach Studio, 1938-39, Walt Disney Prdns., 1940-41; asst. treas., studio treas. RKO-Radio Pictures, Inc., 1941-44; sec., treas., dir. Rainbow Prodns., Inc., 1945-49; with NBC, 1950-63, successively dir. finance and operations, v.p. prodn. and bus. affairs, v.p. TV network services, v.p., treas.; pres., dir. Cal. Nat. Prodns., Inc., 1950-63; sec. Hope Enterprises, 1963-69; pres. Living Music, Inc., Spectacular Music, Inc.; v.p., dir. Figaro, Inc.; v.p., gen. mgr. RTRA Charities, Inc., 1963-69. Home: North Hollywood CA Died Apr. 17, 1969.

REUBEN, ODELL RICHARDSON, coll. pres.; b. Silverstreet, S.C., June 18, 1918; s. James J. and Matilda (Stewart) R.; A.B., Benedict Coll., Columbia, South Carolina, 1942, B.D., 1945, Doctor of Pedagogy, 1961; B.D., Oberlin (O.) College, 1946, S.T.M., 1947; Ph.D., Duke, 1970; Doctor of Laws (honorary), Allen University, Columbia, 1955; m. Anna Mays Daniels, Sept. 20, 1945; children—Wilhelmenia Matilda, Lucy Jeanette, Anna Marie, Odell Richardson, Jayne and Janice Reuben (twins). Ordained to the ministry of the Baptist Ch., 1943; pastor in Allendale, S.C., 1943-48, Ware Shoals, S.C., 1946-49; instr. theology and social studies Morris Coll., Sumter, S.C., 1947-48, pres., 1948-70. Bd. dirs. Community Hosp., Sumter, S.C. Council Human Relations. Mem. N.E.A., Am. Tchrs. Assn., S.C. Palmetto Assn., S.C. Christian Action Council, N.A.A.C.P., Am. Acad. Polit. Sci. Mason. Address: Sumter SC Died Oct. 5, 1970.

REUTER, IRVING JACOB, b. Indianapolis, Ind., Feb. 26, 1885; s. Jacob and Wilhelmina (Mottery) R.; grad. Emmerich Manual Training High Sch., Indianapolis, 1903; B.S., Purdue, 1907; m. Jeanette M. Graham, Feb. 24, 1909; 1 dau., Wilma Pearl (dec.). Asst. engr. Overland Motor Co., 1909; chief engr., factory mgr. and gen. mgr. Remy Electric Co., 1909-25; pres. and gen. mgr. Olds Motor Works, 1925-29; pres. and gen. mgr. Oakland Motor Car Co., 1930-31; pres. and gen. mgr. Olds Motor Works and Buick Motor Co., 1931-33; also mng. dir. Opel Motor Works, Germany, 1930. Mem. Delta Tau Delta. Presbyterian. Mason. Clubs: Biltmore Country (Biltmore, N.C.); Asheville Country, Everglades; Bath and Tennis (Palm Beach, Fla.). Home: Asheville NC Died Apr. 21, 1972.

REUTER, RUDOLPH ERNST, pianist; b. New York, N.Y.; s. Gustave and Marguerite (Grill) R.; studied music under masters in New York, Royal (State) Academy, Berlin, Germany; Dr. causa honoris, Capital U., Columbus, O., 1953; m. Elizabeth Ann Tinker, 1939; 1 dau., Anna Margaret. Received Mendelssohn prize, Berlin; debut Hamburg Symphony Orchestra; prof. Imperial Acad. Music, Tokyo (reorganized on modern plan); concert tour Europe, 1922-24; later faculty mem. and mus. dir. Am. Conservatory of Music; annual concert tours of U.S., soloist with orchestras of New York, Chicago, Minneapolis, St. Louis, Indpls., Detroit, Los Angeles, San Francisco, etc. Pres. Soc. Am. Musicians (2 yrs.). Republican. Clubs: Arts, Cliff Dwellers, Bohemians. Home: Chicago IL Died Jan. 4, 1973.

REUTHER, WALTER PHILIP, labor leader; b. Wheeling, W.Va., Sept. 1, 1907; s. Valentine and Anna (Stoker) R.; student Wayne U., 3 yrs.; recipient of numerous honorary degrees; m. to May Wolf, Mar. 13, 1936. Began as apprentice tool and die maker Wheeling (W.Va.) Steel Corp., 1924; employed by Briggs Mfg. Co., Gen. Motors Co. and Ford Motor Co., Detroit, 1927-32, foreman of latter, 1931-32; traveled by bicycle through Europe and the Orient, observing auto plants and machine shops, 3 yrs.; returned to U.S. to organize auto workers, 1935; established and became pres. Local 174, United Automobile Workers, Congress Industrial Orgns.; hon. pres. West Side Local; v.p. Internat. Union, United Automobile, Aircraft and Agrl. Workers of America, CIO, 1946 has been president since 1946; director International Union Skilled Trades Dept., and of Consumer's Division; director General Motors Department UAW, 1939; pres. CIO from 1952; pres. CIO Div. of new combined orgn., the Am. Fedn. of Labor and the Congress of Indsl. Orgns., 1955-70, also president of industrial union department. Proposed plan to produce defense aircraft by mass production methods in automobile plants; mem. labor management policy com. War Manpower Commn.; mem. labor management policy com., Labor Prodn. Div., W.P.B.; labor mem. Mobilization Adv. Bd. Mem. bd. trustees Roosevelt Coll. Led 113-day strike Gen. Motors workers, Nov. 21, 1945 to Mar. 13, 1946, winning wage increase and improved working conditions; focussed natl. attention on union demand of wage increases without price increases." Vice pres., exec. bd. Internat. Confedn. Free Trade Table Unions; v.p., exec. bd., pres. automotive div. Internat. Metalworkers Fedn. Mem. numerous govt. coms. and commns. Bd. dirs., trustee, or officer UN Assn. U.S.A., Eleanor Roosevelt Cancer Found., Am. Cancer Soc., United Found. of Detroit, NAACP, Religion and Labor Found., Nat. Housing Conf., Detroit Symphony Orch., Nat. Sr. Citizens Edn. and Research Center, Inc.; nat. chmn. Citizens Crusade Against Poverty; chmn. bd. Met. Detroit Citizens Devel. Authority. Author: Selected Papers of Walter P. Reuther, 1961; (with Edith Green) Education and the Public Good, 1963. Contbr. to New Horizons of Economic Progress, 1964, other publs. on labor, econs., polit. and social problems. Home: Detroit MI Died May 9, 1970.

REVELL, FLEMING H., JR., publisher; b. Chicago, Ill., Nov. 29, 1882; s. Fleming H. and Josephine (Barbour) R.; ed. Lawrenceville Sch. and Yale; m. Marion Cornell, Aug. 15, 1911 (died Sept. 1, 1941); 1 dau., Muriel (Mrs. Charles E. Marshall, now deceased); married Carolyn Conner, January 27, 1949. Entered publishing company, Fleming H. Revell Company, New York, N.Y., 1907, chairman board. Mem. Alpha Delta Phi. Clubs: Yale (New York); Los Angeles Country, Riviera Equestrian, Los Angeles Athletic, (Los Angeles). Home: Los Angeles CA Deceased.

REYERSON, LLOYD HILTON, univ. prof.; b. Dawson, Minn., May 1, 1893; s. John Emil and Lydia (Hilton) R.; Bachelor of Arts, Carleton College, 1915, D.Sc., 1956; Master of Arts degree, U. of Ill., 1917; Ph.D., Johns Hopkins U., 1920; m. Nelle Nickell, Mar. 7, 1918; children—Jean Elizabeth (Mrs. A. H. Moseman), James Hilton (killed in action March 5, 1945). Instr. in chemistry, U. of Minn., 1919-21, assistant prof., 1921-26, asso. prof., 1926-30, prof. since 1930; dir. Northwest Research Inst., U. of Minn., 1934-60, administrative asst. in charge of chemistry, 1937; assistant dean, 1945-54, prof. phys. chemistry emeritus, 1961-69; mem. New Eng. Inst. for Med. Research, 1962-69. Welsh Foundation lectr. in chemistry, 1962. Chmn. sci. adv. com. Minn. War Industries, 1942-45. Apptd. chmn., canvassing com. for Am. Chem. Soc. Award in Pure Chemistry, 1944-45. Served as 2d lt., Chemical Warfare Service, 1918-19. Fellow John Simon Guggenheim Found., 1927-28, 58. U.S. del. to Internat. Union of Pure and Applied Chemistry, Warsaw, Poland, 1927, The Hague, The Netherlands, 1928, Stockholm, Sweden, 1953. Scientific consultant to the Royal Norwegian government, summer, 1946. Chmn. fgn. research scientists program, Nat. Acad. Scis. Knight 1st class Royal Order St. Olav (Norway), 1950; Distinguished Alumni Award, Carleton Coll., 1955. Fellow A.A.A.S., Am. Inst. Chemists (councillor at large 1958-60, president 1965-66), Faraday Society, member of American Chem. Soc. (sec. colloid div., 1937, chmn., 1939, counselor, 1943-44, 50-51, 55-57, mem. council policy com., 1952-54, 1956-61, chmn. nat. meeting, Mpls., 1955, councillor from Colloid Div., 1952-53, chmn. Minn. Sect., 1952, apptd. to Manpower Commn., 1952), Am. Phys. Soc. (chmn. bd. 1966-67), Minnesota Academy Science, American Association University Professors, American Inst. of Chemists (honorary, councillor at large 1958-63), Sigma Xi (president of the Minn. chapter 1956-57, Distinguished Service award Minn. chpt. 1962), Phi Beta Kappa (pres. Minn. Alpha. 1943-44), Phi Lambda Upsilon, Alpha Chi Sigma. Rep. Conglist. Mason. Clubs: Tonskeklubben (Minneapolis); Chemists (N.Y.C.); Cosmos (Washington). Author articles professional jours. Asso. editor Jour. of Phys. Chemistry, 1937-38. Home: Ridgefield CT Died Sept. 7, 1969.

REYNAL, EUGENE, publisher; b. New York, N.Y., Mar. 31, 1902; s. Eugene Sugny and Adele (Fitzgerald) R.; student St. George's Sch., Newport, R.I., 1915-20; A.B., Harvard, 1924; M.A., Oxford U., Eng., 1926; m. Elizabeth Young, June 21, 1938; children—Eric Young, Anthony; m. Katherine Beall, June 12, 1947. Began with Harper & Brothers, 1926, advertising mgr. and asst. to pres. until 1930; organized and managed Blue Ribbon Books, Inc., 1930; pres., 1934-39; founded with Curtice N. Hitchcock, Reynal &Hitchcock, Inc., pubs., 1934, chmn. bd., pres. and dir.; joined Harcourt, Brace & Co. with which Reynal & Hitchcock was merged in 1948, v.p., dir. charge trade dept., 1948-55; resigned to reorganize own firm Reynal & Co., pres. 1955-68; mng. dir. U.S. Internat. Book Assn., 1945-46 (on leave of absence from Reynal & Hitchcock, Inc.). Commd. capt., Air Corps, Army of the U.S., Aug. 8, 1942., maj., 1944, inactive duty, 1945. Democrat. Clubs: Century, Coffee House, Dutch Treat. P.E.N. (N.Y.C.). Home: New York City NY Died Mar. 20, 1968.

REYNARD, GRANT, artist; b. Grand Island, Neb., Oct. 20, 1887; s. Stephen Blackstone and Jennie Lynd (Bacon) R.; student Chicago Art Inst., 1906-07, Chicago Acad. Fine Arts, 1908-11; L.H.D., Baldwin-Wallace College, 1955; married Gwendolen Smythe Crawford, Sept. 22, 1917; children—Barbara Ann (Mrs. Donald Addison Dey), Mary Tyson. Illustrator, 1915-26; etching and painting since 1926. Represented in Metropolitan Museum, New York Fogg Museum; Newark Museum; Addison Museum; Library of Congress; N.Y. Pub. Library. One-man shows: Addison Mus.; Montclair Art Mus.; Andover, Kennedy & Company, N.Y.; Grand Central Galleries; Clayton Gallery, Asso. Am. Artists, N.Y. Taught Grand Central School, Millbrook Sch.; artist in residence S.D. State Coll.; lectr. art; pres. Montclair Art Museum, 1955-65, also art chmn., 1950-55. Recipient Carrigan prize, Salmagundi Club, Nat. Acad. Prize, 1951. Member N.A.D., N.J. Water Color Soc., Asso. Artists N.J., Society American Graphic Artists, Am. Water Color Soc., Audubon Artists, Am. Artists Group. Home: Leonia NJ Died Aug. 13, 1968; buried George Washington Meml. Park, Paramus NJ

REYNOLDS, CARL VERNON, physician; b. Asheville, N.C., June 13, 1872; s. John Daniel and Theresa Elmire (Shepherd) R.; student Asheville Mil. Acad., Wofford Coll., Spartansburg, S.C., 1889-91; M.D., U. City of New York, 1895; post grad. course Bromnton Hosp., London; m. Nellie Alyne Cocke, Apr. 1, 1896; 1 child, Alyne Johnston; m. 2d, Edith Holland Randolph. Practiced medicine, specializing in tuberculosis, Asheville, N.C., 1895-1934; altruistic city health officer, Asheville, part-time, 1898-1910, 1914-23; mem. med. staff of Mission, Biltmore and French Broad Hosps.; chief med. examiner Prudential Life Ins. Co. (uninterrupted service for 30 yrs. receiving bronze, silver, gold and locket medal for service); examiner New Eng. Mutual Security Life Ins. Cos.; State Health Officer, 1934-47, re-elected for 4 yr. term, 1947; retired July 1948. Mem. teaching staff Sch. of Pub. Health, Chapel Hill, N.C., 1936; Officer and dir. Blue Ridge Nat. Bank; dir. Am. Nat. Bank of Commerce, Asheville. Pres. Certified Milk Commn. Consultant in War Manpower Comm., Procurement and Assignment Service for Physicians, July 1942; chmn. subcom. on Pub. Health, Procurement and Assignment Service, Office of Defense Health and Welfare Services, Nov., 1941; mem. Nat. Com. of Malaria Prevention Activities, 1942, 43, 44, 45; mem. nat. com. for Celebration of Pres. birthday for Nat. Foundation for Infantile Paralysis; chmn. State Nutrition com.; mem. com. on Health and Pub. Welfare Planning Bd.; mem. and sec. N.C. Hosp. and Med. Care Commn., 1944; mem. State Stream Sanitation and Conservation com., 1945-46; mem. N.C. Resource-Use Edn. Commn. of the State Planning Bd.; mem. exec. com. of N.C. State Planning Bd. com. on Services for Children and Youth, 1946; Fellow Am. Pub. Health Assn. (1st vice pres. southern br. 1939). Mem. Buncombe County Med. Soc. (pres.-sec. 1904), Tri-State Med. Soc. (exec. council, 1911, vice pres. council, 1916), N.C. Med. Soc. (pres. 1920, mem. med. preparedness com. 1944-45), Miss. Valley Med. Assn., Southern Med. Assn., A.M.A., Nat. Assn. for Prevention of Tuberculosis, Bd. of Trade, Good Rd. Assn. (past pres.), N.C. State Bd. of Health (pres. 1933), Raleigh Acad. of Medicine, 1935, Health Officers Qualifying Bd. of U.S. Conf. of Mayors, 1937, State and Terr. Health Officers' Assn. (chmn. subcom. of Fed. Relations com. for securing seriologic tests among registered men in U.S.), State, Terr. and Provincial Health Authorities of N.Am. (vice pres., 1941-42, pres. 1942-43), Internat. Soc. of Med. Health Officers (vice pres. 1942), N.C. Mental Hygiene Soc. (mem. exec. com. 1943-46), Calhoun Literary Soc., Kappa Alpha. Methodist. Clubs: Asheville Country (pres.), Biltmore Forest Country (mem. bd.), Rotary. Home: 1100 New York Drive, Altadena CA‡

REYNOLDS, CHARLES LEE, clergyman; b. De Graff, O., May 10, 1874; s. James Irwin and Julia Elvira (Reeves) R.; A.B., Washington and Jefferson Coll., 1896; grad. McCormick Theol. Sem., 1899; D.D., Coe Coll., Cedar Rapids, Iowa, 1906; m. Agnes Bush Pearson, Nov. 11, 1902 (died Aug. 12, 1938); children—Mrs. Eleanor Pearson McConnell, Margaret Pearson (Mrs. J. W. Gibson). Ordained Presbyn. ministry, 1899; pastor Cottage Grove Av. Ch., Des Moines, Ia., 1899-1906, 2d Ch. Lexington, Ky., 1906-16, Park Ch., Newark, N.J., 1916-28; supt. ch. extension, Newark Presbytery, 1928-46; retired former recording sec. Ch. Extension Bd. Newark Presbytery, now supt. emeritus. Moderator, Synod of Ky., 1915. Dir. N.J. Temperance Soc. (sec.), Goodwill Home and Rescue Mission. V.p. Presbyterian Hosp. Mem. Nat. Inst. Social Sciences; chmn. Christian Conf. on Legislation of N.J. Mem. Robert Treat Council, Boy Scouts. Mem. The Temperance League of N.J., Kappa Chi, Phi Delta Theta. Club; Rotary. Author of church dramas, articles and poems. Contributed a weekly sermon to Kentucky newspapers for 3-1/2 years. Gov. 3d dist., Internat. Assn. Rotary Clubs, 1920-21. Exchange preacher in Europe, summer 1936. Home: 420 Clifton Av., Newark NJ‡

REYNOLDS, CHARLES RANSOM, former surgeon gen., U.S. Army; b. Elmira, N.Y., July 28, 1877; s. George Gardiner and Lucy (Pratt) R.; student Elmira (N.Y.) Acad., 1895, U. of Mich., 1895-97; M.D., Univ. of Pa., 1899; Sc.D., Dickinson Coll., Carlisle, Pa.; m. Jane Boyd Hurd, Dec. 26, 1910; children—Charles Ransom, Hebe Louise. Mem. Med. Corps, U.S. Army, 1900-39; surgeon gen. with rank of maj. gen., 1935-39; retired. Served in Philippine Insurrection; surgeon 77th Div., chief surgeon 6th Corps, chief surgeon 2d Army, A.E.F., World War I; comdt. Med. Field Service Sch., Carlisle, Pa., 1923-31. Decorated Legion of Honor (France), 1919; Silver Star for gallantry while aiding wounded," in Philippines, 1906, also D.S.M., World War (both U.S.). Comdr. Order Public Health, France. President 10th Internat. Congress of Military Medicine and Pharmacy. Dir. Am. Trudeau Soc. Fellow Am. Coll. Surgeons, Am. Coll. Physicians; mem. A.M.A., Am. Acad. of Medicine, Assn. of Military Surgeons of Am. (past pres.); bd. dirs. Gorgas Memorial Inst., Walter Reed Memorial Assn.; mem. Nu Sigma Nu, Alpha Omega Alpha. Presbyn. Clubs: Army and Navy Keene Valley NY‡

REYNOLDS, CONGER, public affairs counselor; b. Dexter, Iowa, March 23, 1891; son of John Quincy and Sarah Emily (Pugh) R.; student Drake University, Des Moines, 1908-09; A.B., University of Iowa, 1912; LL.D. (honorary), Carthage College, 1952; m. Daphne Goodenough, December 25, 1917; children—Conger, Dawn M. Reporter Des Moines Register and Leader, 1912-15; dir. journalism, publicity U. Ia., 1915-17; night editor, then mng. editor Paris edition, Chicago Tribune, 1919-20; writer N.Y. Daily News, 1922; vice consul, consul, fgn. service officer U.S., in Halifax, N.S. and Stuttgart, Germany, 1922-29; dir. pub. relations Standard Oil Co. of Ind., Chgo., 1929-55; dir. Office of Pvt. Coop., U.S. Information Agy., Washington, 1956-61. Chmn. Oil Industry Information Com., 1949. Served as press officer G.H.Q., A.E.F., U.S. Army, 1917-19. Mem. Public Relations Society of America, Public Relations Clinic Chgo. (past pres.), Press Vets. Chgo., Phi Beta Kappa, Sigma Delta Chi. Republican. Episcopalian. Clubs: Dacor (Washington); Lake Shore (Chgo.). Contbr. articles profl. jours. Home: La Jolla CA Died Feb. 17, 1971; buried El Camino Meml. Park, San Diego CA

REYNOLDS, FRANK WILLIAM, plastics engr.; b. Scotia, N.Y., Nov. 11, 1901; s. Herbert Caleb and Lizzie (Betts) R.; grad. tech. course, Gen. Electric Co., 1922; m. Anne Winkler, Aug. 9, 1931; children—Patricia (Mrs. Alexander Wilson II), Shirley (Mrs. Robert C. Beaty), Mark, Nancy (Mrs. David A. Davenport), Phyllis (Mrs. Bradford G. Weekes III). With Internat. Bus. Machines Corporation, from 1931, mgr. plastics research lab., Endicott, N.Y., from 1951. Mem. Soc. Plastics Industry (founder, 1st pres. Binghamton sect. 1957, nat. council from 1957), Internat. Soc. Plastics Engrs. (pres. 1961-62, exec. com. 1961-63). Home: Binghamton NY Died Nov. 17, 1971; buried Vestal Hills Meml. Park Vestal NY

REYNOLDS, HERBERT BYRON, mech. engr.; b. Baltimore, Md., Apr. 8, 1888; s. Byron and Ulyssa Irene (Williamson) R.; grad. Baltimore Poly. Inst., 1908; M.E., Cornell U., 1911, M.M.E., 1915; m. Sarah Genet Haswell, June 22, 1914 (died Oct. 6, 1918); m. 2d, Ruth Herlong, Jan. 21, 1922. Apprentice, Westinghouse Electric & Mfg. Co., 1911-12, inspector, 1912; turbine tester, Gen. Electric Co., 1913; asst. engr. Interborough Rapid Transit Co., N.Y. City, 1913-17; mech. asst. to supt. of motive power, United Railways & Electric Co., Baltimore, Md., 1917-18; fuel engr., U.S. Govt. Bureau of Mines, 1918; mech. research engr., Interborough Rapid Transit Co., N.Y. City, 1919, mech. engr. 1919-41 (Interborough Rapid Transit Co. became part of N.Y. City Transit System, 1940), supt. of motive power, IRT div. 1941-44, supt. of power generation, the entire system, 1944-49; engr. J. G. White Engring. Corp., 1949-53; cons. engr., 1953-68. Member trustees Garden School. Fellow A.S.M.E., Am. Inst. Elec. and Electronic Engrs.; mem. Sigma Xi. Club: Engineers (N.Y.C.). Contbr. articles to mags.; also papers delivered before A.S.M.E. Home: Jackson Heights NY Died Oct. 10, 1968.

REYNOLDS, JACKSON ELI, retired; b. Woodstock, Ill., Jan. 20, 1873; s. James N. and Myra H. (Giddings) R.; A.B., Stanford U., 1896; LL.B., Columbia, 1899; LL.D., Colgate Univ., 1930; Honorary Fellow, Stanford University, 1941; m. Marion D. Taylor, May 21, 1903. Asst. prof. law, Stanford U., 1899-1901; practiced at N.Y. City, 1901-18; lecturer and asso. prof. law, Columbia 1903-06 and 1913-17; gen. atty. Central R.R. Co. of N.J., 1906-17; pres. First Nat. Bank of City of N.Y., 1922-37, chmn. bd. First Nat. Bank, July 1937-Jan. 1939, chmn. orgn. com. Bank for Internat. Settlements under the Young Plan. Home: Locust Valley NY ‡

REYNOLDS, JOHN HENRY, savs. and loan assn. exec.; b. Erie, Pa., Oct. 6, 1900; s. William Wallace and Nell (Henry) R.; m. Ethel Valentine, July 13, 1937; children—John Wilson, James Moore. Dir. Lawrence-Cedarhurst Fed. Savs. & Loan Assn., Cedarhurst, L.I., N.Y., 1938-68, pres., 1954-68, chmn. bd., 1963-68. Home: Atlantic Beach NY Died Aug. 29, 1968; buried Trinity Churchyard, Hewlett NY

REYNOLDS, WILLIAM HOWARD, univ. dean; b. Herrin, Ill., Sept. 8, 1922; s. Herbert Emuel and Ruby (Hood) R.; B.Ed., So. Ill. U., 1943; Ph.D., U. Chgo., 1951; m. Harriet A. Ravnahrib, June 9, 1949; children—Margaret Jean, William George. Prof. polit. sci. Ill. Inst. Tech., 1948-52; regional dir. case analysis Office Salary Stblzn., Chgo., 1952-53; with Ford Motor Co., 1953-63; prof. marketing U. So. Cal., 1963-67, U. Ill., Chgo. Circle, 1967-68; dean, prof. bus. adminstrn. Sch. Bus. Adminstrn., Wayne State U., 1968-72. Dir. Inst. Advanced Advt. Studies, Los Angeles, 1965-67; research dir. Mgmt. Council Merit Employment, Tng. and Research, 1965-67. Served to capt. USMCR, 1943-46. Decorated Purple Heart. Mem. Am. Marketing Assn. (chmn. travel and transp. sect. 1965-67, book and monograph editor 1967-68), Econ. Club Detroit, Beta Gamma Sigma. Author: (with J.H. Myers) Consumer Behavior and Marketing Management, 1967; Products and Markets, 1969. Home: Birmingham MI Died Nov. 12, 1972.

RHAESA, WILLIAM A., gas co. exec.; b. 1909. With Mich. Consol. Gas Co., 1927—, asst. treas., 1945-49, treas., 1949-53, v.p. and treas., 1953—. Home: Detroit MI Died Nov. 1970.*

RHEEM, RICHARD SCOFFIELD, business exec.; b. Oakland, Calif., Dec. 24, 1903; s. William Sponsler and Helena (Stratton) R.; student Univ. of Calif., Berkeley, 1921-22; m. Constance Patterson, Oct. 29, 1923; children—William Sponsler, Robert Scofield, Constance De'Armand. Formed (with brothers), The Pacific Galvanizing Co., Emeryville, Calif., 1926, successor firm, Rheem Mfg. Co. incorporated Jan. 22, 1930, pres. and dir., 1930-58, retired 1958; pres. Rheem California Land Company; dir. Hongkong-Shanghai Banking Corp. of Cal. Trustee De Young Meml. Mus., San Francisco, pres., 1963-71. Mem. Pilgrims of Am., Soc. Colonial Wars, Cal. C. of C. (dir.). Republican. Presbyterian. Mason. Clubs: Pacific-Union, Bohemian, English Speaking Union (dir.) (San Francisco): The California (Los Angeles): Burlingame Country (Hillsborough, Cal.); Saint Francis Yacht (San Francisco). Home: San Francisco CA Died Dec. 1971.

RHETTS, CHARLES EDWARD, lawyer; b. Columbus, Ind., May 21, 1910; s. John Edward and Effie (Maupin) R.; A.B., Dartmouth Coll., 1931, LL.B., Harvard, 1934; LL.D., Cuttington College (Liberia), 1963; m. Ruth Fisher, Apr. 9, 1938; children—John Edward, Paul, Abigail. Counsel, NRA, 1934-35, Resettlement Adminstrn., 1935-37; private practice, Chicago, 1937-38; counsel, power div., Fed. Emergency Adminstrn. Public Works, 1938-39; asso. solicitor, U.S. Dept. Labor, 1939-41; exec. asst., dir. of materials, War Production Bd., 1941-42, dir. foreign div., 1942; spl. asst. to atty. gen., U.S. Dept. Justice, 1942-44; 1st asst. War Div., U.S. Dept. Justice, 1944-46; dir. U.S. Dept. of Justice Mission in Europe, 1946; acting asst. atty. gen., 1945; gen. practice law, Washington, 1946-56, 60-62, 64-71, Salem, Ind., 1956-60; U.S. ambassador to Liberia, 1962-64. Served as lt. (j.g.) USNR, 1944. Mem. Phi Beta Kappa. Home: Washington DC Died 1971.

RHOADES, MABEL CARTER, economist; b. at Syracuse, N.Y., Nov. 12, 1875; d. D. Prentice and Isablla (Carter) R.; Ph.B., Syracuse U., 1898, Ph.M., 1903; student U. of Halle, Germany, 1903-4; Ph.D., U. of Chicago, 1906. Asst. sec. Bur. of Charity, Syracuse, 1898-9; teacher Syracuse High Sch., 1900-2; fellow in sociology, Syracuse U., 1902-3, and fellow from Syracuse, at U. of Halle, 1903-4; field research for Russell Sage Foundation, under Boston Sch. for Social Workers, 1907-10; prof. economics and sociology, Wells Coll., Aurora, N.Y., since 1910. Mem. Am. Sociol. Soc., Am. Assn. for Labor Legislation, Nat. Child Labor Com., Consumers League America, Phi Beta Kappa, Alpha Phi. Unitarian. Home: Aurora NY‡

RHOADS, SAMUEL NICHOLSON;, b. Philadelphia, Pa., Apr. 30, 1862; s. Charles and Anna (Nicholson) R.; ed. Friends' Sch.; spl. course in journalism, Harvard; studies in natural science, Acad. Natural Sciences and Museum Science and Art, Phila., and Carnegie Museum, Pittsburgh; m. Mary A. Cawley, Apr. 5, 1898; 1 son, Evan L. Since 1893 has collected museum specimens of natural history in nearly every state in the Union, Can., B.C., Cuba, Mex., Central and S. America. Life mem. Acad. Natural Sciences, Phila.; mem. Am. Philos. Soc., Am. Ornithologists' Union. Mem. of Society of Friends, Orthodox branch. Edited reprint of Ord's Zoology, 1894; Facsimile Reprint of Young's Catalogue of American Plants of Paris (1783). Author: The Mammals of Pennsylvania and New Jersey, 1903. Contbr. many papers on Am. and African mammals and on Am. birds, reptiles and molluscs to zool. jours. describing about 100 new species and races of mammals and birds. Home: Haddonfield NJ‡

RHODES, FOSTER TWICHELL, pottery co. exec.; b. Glens Falls, N.Y., May 16, 1906; s. Charles F. and Grace E. (Twichell) R.; M.E., Cornell U., 1928; m. Josephine B. Williams, Sept. 2, 1933; children—Ellen B., Stanley W. With Onondaga Pottery Co. (co. name changed to Syracuse China Corp.), Syracuse, N.Y., 1928-67, exec. v.p., 1956-58, president, 1958-63, chairman of board, 1963-67, also dir.; pres., dir. Vandesca-Syracuse, Ltd., Joliette, Can., 1959-63, chairman board, 1963-67; dir. Pass & Seymour, Incorporated, Solvay, New York, First Trust & Deposit Company, Syracuse, 1959-67. Trustee, v.p. Everson Mus. Art, Syracuse; bd. dirs. United Community Services Syracuse. Mem. Mfrs. Assn. Syracuse (dir.), U.S. Potters Assn. (past pres.). Am. Restaurant China Mfrs. Assn. (dir., past pres.), Am. Ceramic Soc., Better Bus. Bur. (dir.), C. of C. (dir.), Tau Beta Pi, Phi Kappa Phi, Tau kappa Epsilon. Clubs: Cornell, Technology, Century (Syracuse). Home: Fayetteville NY Died Sept. 18, 1967; buried Pine View Cemetery, Glens Falls NY

RHODES, WILLARD E., grocery co. exec.; b. Granada, Colo., 1912. Pres. Associated Grocers, Inc., Thriftway Stores, Inc.; pres., dir. Coop. Food Distbrs. Am.; chmn. bd. Western Family Foods, Inc.; dir. Pacific Mercantile Co. Home: Seattle WA Died Dec. 10, 1968; buried Wash. Meml. Park, Seattle WA

RHYNE, BRICE WILSON, lawyer; b. Charlotte, N.C., Mar. 9, 1917; s. Sydneyham Sylvanus and Mary (Wilson) R.; student Elon (N.C.) Coll., 1938-39; A.A., George Washington U., 1947, J.D., 1951; m. Thelma Campbell, May 29, 1948; children—Brice Wilson, Paul Henry, Patricia, Theresa. Admitted D.C. bar, 1951, U.S. Supreme Ct., 1955; partner law firm Rhyne & Rhyne, Washington, 1951-72; asso. gen. counsel Nat. Inst. Municipal Law Officers. Served with AUS, 1942-45. Decorated Bronze Star, Purple Heart, Presdl. Unit citation with oak leaf cluster. Mem. Bar Assn. D.C. (chmn. com. on atomic energy law 1957-58, elections bd. 1968), Fed. Communications Bar Assn., Am. Bar Assn. (D.C. chmn. sect. local govt. law 1962, chmn. com. on transp., traffic and parking 1957-69, mem. council 1966-70). World Peace Through Law Center, Am. Judicature Soc., 22d Inf. Assn. (treas. 1959-72), Nat. 4th Inf. Div. Assn. (pres. 1968-70, chmn. monument com. 1957-72), Delta Theta Phi. Co-editor: The Municipal Attorney, 1959-72; NIMLO Municipal Law Review, 1953-72; Federal Money for Cities, 1966. Home: Alexandria VA Died June 24, 1972; buried Ivy Hill Cemetery, Alexandria VA

RIBAR, IVAN, Yugoslav politician; b. 1884; became mem. Nat. Council, 1918; pres. Constituent Assembly, 1921; pres. Presidium of Yugoslav Rep., 1945-68. Address: Belgrade Jugoslavia Died Feb. 1968.

RIBBLE, FREDERICK D. G., univ. prof.; b. Culpeper, Va., Jan. 14, 1898; s. Frederick Goodwin and Caroline Stribling (Marshall) R.; A.B., William and Mary Coll., 1916; M.A., U. of Va., 1917, LL.B., 1921; LL.M., Columbia U., 1932; Jur. ScD., Columbia, 1937; LL.D., Washington and Lee U., 1949, William and Mary College, 1952, Northwestern University, 1960; married to Mary Mason Anderson, December 18, 1940; 1 son, Frederick Goodwin. Instructor law U. Va., 1920-21; asst. prof. law, 1921-24, associate prof., 1924-27, prof. since 1927, acting dean, law dept., 1937-39, dean, 1939-63, emeritus, 1963-71; asso. Sands, Williams and Lightfoot, Richmond, Va., 1928. Alternate member board of Appeals in Visa Cases, 1942-44, mem. 1944-45. Served as pvt., F.A., U.S. Army, 1918. Mem. U.S. Nat. Commn. for UNESCO, 1946-51. Pres. Assn. of Am. Law Schs., 1951. Mem. council Am. Law Inst.; mem. Am., Va. (pres. 1955-56) bar assns., Kappa Sigma, Phi Delta Phi, Omicron Delta Kappa, Phi Beta Kappa. Episcopalian. Clubs: Colonnade, Cosmos (Washington). Author: State and National Power Over Commerce, 1937. Editor: Minor on Real Property, 2d edit., 1928. Home: VA Died Dec. 1, 1971.

RIBNER, IRVING, educator; b. Bklyn., Aug. 29, 1921; s. Adolph and Helen (Dangler) R.; B.A., Bklyn. Coll., 1941; M.A., U. N.C., 1947, Ph.D., 1949; m. Roslyn Greenblatt, Sept. 11, 1943; children—Clifford Neil, Jonathan Paul. Instr., U. N.C., 1946-49; instr. Ohio State U., 1949-52; instr. Queens Coll., 1952-53; asst. prof. to prof. Tulane U., 1953-64; H. Rodney Sharp prof. English, U. Del., Newark, 1964-68; prof., chmn. English dept. State U. N.Y., Stony Brook, 1968-70, prof., 1970-72. Served with Signal Corps, AUS, 1942-46. Guggenheim fellow, 1957-58; Fulbright fellow, 1958-59; Huntington Library fellow, summer 1961; Am. Council Learned Socs. fellow, 1961-62; Mem. Modern Lang. Assn. Am., Shakespeare Assn. Am., Renaissance Soc. Am. Author: The English History Play in the Age of Shakespeare, 1957, rev. 1965; Patterns in Shakespearian Tragedy, 1960; Jacobean Tragedy, 1962. Editor: The Complete Plays of Christopher Marlowe, 1963; The Atheist's Tragedy, 1964; The Complete Works of Shakespeare (Revised Kittredge edition), 1971. Home: Belle Terre NY Died July 2, 1972.

RICE, ABIGAIL RUTH BURTON (MRS. CARL V. RICE), club woman; b. Oswego, Kan., Nov. 19, 1895; d. Ellsworth L. and Abigail Ruth (Thomas) Burton; ed. St. Teresa's Acad. Kansas City, Mo.; m. Carl V. Rice, Nov. 13, 1919; children—Ruth Isabell (Mrs. Jefferson W. Mitchell, Jr.) Carlene Virginia (Mrs. George I. Lind), Mary Elizabeth (Mrs. Samuel J. Wells), Grace Lucille (Mrs. John A. Muder, Jr.). Vice pres. Rupert Diecasting Co., Kansas City, Mo., 1941-60, Rice Investment, Inc., Kansas City, Mo., C & R Investments, Inc., Kansas City, Mo., Midwest Pump Co., Kansas City, Mo., Adv. council Kan. Dept. Practical Nurse Edn., Kansas City, 1959-61, Kansas City Hosp. Nurse Endowment Assn., 1959-61; mem. Wyandotte County Com. for Aged, Kansas City. Vice chmn. Kan. Dem. Com., 1928, chmn., 1930. Mem. Friends of Art, Kansas City Art Inst. Assn., Women's Kansas City Philharmonic, Wyandotte County Hist. Soc., Wyandotte County Rose Soc., Women's Aux Wyandotte County Bar Assn., Am. Legion Aux. (mem. exec. com. Kan. 1929), Civic Music Assn., Daus. Colonists, Internat., Am. harpists socs., D.A.R., P.E.O. Presbyn. Clubs: Pelican Yacht (Ft. Pierce, Fla.); Chi Omega Mothers, (Kansas City, Mo. and Kansas City, Kan.); Kansas City Garden, Music (pres. 1946-48) Mozart, History, Fortnightly, (Kansas City, Kan.). Home: Kansas City KS Died Nov. 15, 1968.

RICE, CHARLES A., educator; b. Rankin, Ill., June 5, 1873; s. John Milton and Delilah (Clapp) R.; B.S., Ill Wesleyan U., Bloomington, Ill., 1899; M.A., University of Ore., 1923; LL.D., from Willamette University, 1931, m. Frances Mary Iliff, of Normal, Ill., June 30, 1902; children—Charlotte (Mrs. Walter J. Widmer), Milton William. Teacher, Ill., until 1903; prin. training dept. Ore. State Normal, 1903-1907; prin. pub. schs., Portland, Ore., 1907-11, advanced through various positions, to supt., 1925-37, retired, 1937. Mem. Ore. State Teachers' Assn. (ex-president), Nat. Society for Study of Platoon Schs. (pres.), Ore. State S.S. Assn (ex-pres.), Portland Chamber Commerce, Sigma Chi, Phi Kappa Phi. Republican. Methodist. Mason (Shriner). Clubs: City, Rotary, Multnomah Amateur Athletic. Author of Ore. supplements to Frye and Atwood Geography, 1920, and to Hughes Elementary Community Civics, 1923. Home: 1656 S.E. 25th Av. Portland OR‡

RICE, CLATON SILAS, clergyman; b. Magnolia, Ia. Nov. 30, 1883; s. Eugene Taylor and Fannie Maria (Dalton) R.; B.S., Bellevue Coll., 1905; grad. Princeton Theol. Sem., 1908; M.A., Princeton, 1908; postgrad McCormick Theol. Sem., 1909; D.D., Pacific Sch Religion, 1935; m. Esther Wood, Dec. 17, 1913, children—Carol, Glen Griffith, Jean, Mary Eleanor. Served as home missionary in St. George, Myton, and Cedar City (all Utah); pastor in New Plymouth, Ida., 1919-23; asst. supt. So. Idaho Congl. Conf., 1923-25, supt. So. Ida. and Utah Congl. Conf., 1925-29; supt. Mont. Congl. Conf., 1929-34; supt. Wash. Congl. Conf., 1934-46, now supt. emeritus. With Japanese chs. in Hawaii under Hawaiian Evang. Assn., 1955-56. Mason (Shriner). Club: China (Seattle). Author: The Morman Way; Songs of the Mormon Way (verse); We Sought the Wilderness (a geneal. story), 1949; Ambassador to the Saints, 1965; also several booklets of verse including Out West Where I Come From; That Slender Tree, and Midmorn. Contbr. to religious mags. Home: San Rafael CA Died Nov. 7, 1972.

RICE, HARMON HOWARD, author; b. Washington Ia., Apr. 6, 1870; s. John Smith and Delia Ann (Stone) R.; ed. Ia. Wesleyan U. and Denver Law Sch.; m. Mattie Ethel Edwards, of Denver, June 4, 1896. In various business positions until 1902; sec. Am. Hydraulic Stone Co., 1902-12; comptroller Goldsborough Engrng. Co., 1913—. Mem. Phi Delta Theta. Methodist Republican. Author: Concrete Block Manufacture Processes and Machines, 1906; The Life That Now Is 1907; Brothers (pub. in Chicago Record-Herald, Mgr. 1913). Contbr. to tech. mags. upon blocks, etc. Home 1341 York St. Office: Bank Bldg., Denver‡

RICE JAMES EDWARD, farmer, educator; b. Aurora Ill., Mar. 12, 1865; s. James R. and Emeline (Wing) R. grad. Granville Mil. Acad., N. Granville, N.Y., 1885 B.S. in agr., Cornell, 1890; m. Elsie Van Buren, Sept. 14 1898 (dec.); m. 2d, Louise E. Dawley, Oct. 31, 1936 Asst. in Coll. of Agr., Cornell, 1891-92; farmer in Bucks County, Pa., 1892-93; partner firm White & Rice operating Fernwood Fruit & Poultry Farm, at Yorktown, N.Y., 1893-1903. Lecturer in farmers' insts in states of N.Y., N.J., Md. and Minn., 1893-1903 (winters); prof. poultry husbandry, Cornell, 1903-34 prof. emeritus since July 1, 1934; member of Egg and Apple Farm; Trumansburg, New York, and Appledale Orchards, Mexico, New York. President Yorktown Telephone Co., 1901-03; pres. Tompkins County Improvement Assn. Chmn. Nat. Breeder and Hatchery Fair Trade Practice Com.; pres. N. Eastern Poultry Producers Council; chmn. 1st and 7th U.S. World's Poultry Congress Com. Fellow Poultry Science Assn. life mem. N.Y. State Fruit Growers Assn., New York State Agricultural Society, Ithaca Automobile Association (v.p.), American Poultry Assn. (chmn committee on protection of poultry industry), World's Poultry Science Assn. (president), Poultry Science Assn. (pres.), N.Y. State Grange, Sigma Xi; hon. mem Alpha Zeta, Helios Soc., Ho-Nun-De-Ka Soc. Mem council Nat. Boy Scouts of America. Chmn. U.S. Com of 1st World's Poultry Congress, 1921; president of 8th World's Poultry Congress, 1939-48; pres. Trumansburg Rotary Club, 1927, 28. Co-Author: Practical Poultry Management (textbook); Judging Poultry for Production. Editor Poultry Science series of textbooks Presbyterian. Progressive Republican. Home: 536 N. E 62d St., Miami 38 FL‡

RICE, JOHN, chmn. bd. Gen. Crushed Stone Co.; b. Pottstown, Pa., Oct. 10, 1866; s. George and Isabelle Hitner (Potts) R.; prep. edn. Hill Sch., Pottstown, Pa., 1876-82; Ph.B., Sheffield Sci. Sch., Yale, 1885; m. Carrie Arndt Drake, Jan. 5, 1898; children—Virginia R. Love, John. Draftsman Cofrode & Saylor Bridge Works, Pottstown, 1885-89; asst. engr. in constrn. cable and elec. rys., Pittsburgh, 1889-92; v.p. and gen. supt. Lehigh Constrn. Co., Bethlehem, Pa., 1893-98; engr. Broadhead Contracting Co., Easton, Pa., 1898-1900; with Gen. Crushed Stone Co., Easton, Pa., since 1900, successively as gen. supt., v.p. and pres. to 1938, chmn. of bd. since 1938; pres. Easton Trust Co., Hotel Easton Co.; pres. Bd. of Trade, 1915; mem. City Council, 1910-12; chmn. Emer. Relief Commn., Northampton County, Pa., 1932-36; Rep. presidential elector, 1912. Served as county fuel chmn. during World War. Mem. Nat. Crushed Stone Assn. (dir. past pres.), Pa. Crushed Stone Assn. (1st pres.), N.Y. Stone Assn. (1st pres.), Delta Psi. Republican. Club: Yale, University (Phila.); Pomfret, Northampton County of Easton (pres.); Graduates (New Haven); Easton Anglers Assn. (v.p.). Home: 426 Clinton Terrace. Office: Drake Bldg., Easton PA*‡

RICE, JOHN ANDREW, writer; b. Lynchburg, S.C., Feb. 1, 1888; s. John Andrew and Anna Bell (Smith) R.; B.A., Tulane, 1911; Rhodes scholar from Louisiana at Oxford University, Eng., 1911-14, B.A., 1914; studied University of Chicago, 1916-18; m. Nell Aydelotte, Dec. 28, 1914; children—Frank Aydelotte, Mary Aydelotte; m. 2d, Caroline Dikka Moen, 1942; children—Peter Nicolai, Elizabeth Didrikke. Instructor Webb Sch., Bellbuckle, Tenn., 1914-16; with Mil. Intelligence Div., U.S. Army, Washington, D.C., 1918-19; asso. prof. classics, U. of Neb., 1919-26, chmn. dept., 1926-28; prof. classics, Rutgers, 1928-30, also head dept. of classics N.J. Coll. for Women; prof. classics, Rollins Coll., 1930-33; a founder Black Mountain (N.C.) Coll., 1933, prof. classics, 1933-39, rector, 1934-39; writer, 1939-68. Guggenheim fellow for research in Europe, 1929-30. Mem. Am. Assn. Rhodes Scholars, Sigma Alpha Epsilon. Recognized as an authority on writings of Dean Swift. Author: I Came Out of the Eighteenth Century, 1942. Co-winner of Harpers 125th Anniversary Prize, 1942. Contbr. to periodicals. Home: NY Died Nov. 17, 1968.

RICE, JOHN WINTER, bacteriologist; b. Williamsport, Pa., July 4, 1891; s. William and Margaret Christiana (Winter) R.; B.S., Bucknell U., 1914, M.S., 1915; A.M., Columbia, 1918, Ph.D., 1922; m. Edna Amelia Miller, Aug. 21, 1918 (died 1921); children—John Miller, Martha Jane; m. 2d, Ruth Miriam (Hoffa) Frantz Aug. 6, 1922;children—Jasper Hoffa Frantz (stepson), Andrew Cyrus, William Floyd, Ruth Eleanor. Teacher of biology, high sch., Hazleton, Pa., 1915-16; instr. of biology, Bucknell U., 1916-18, asst. prof., 1918-23, asso. prof., 1923-24, prof. of bacteriology 1924-59, professor emeritus 1959-71; chmn. dept. biology, 1939-42, 44-58; dir. Health Service, from 1950; instr. bacteriology, Yale Army Laboratory Sch., 1918, Columbia, summer 1922; special investigator on bacteriology of paper milk containers, N.Y. State Agrl. Exp. Station, Geneva, N.Y., summers 1938 and 39. Consultant bacteriologist, Geisinger Memorial Hosp. Pres. Lewisburg, Bd. of Health, 1924-47; pres. Milk Control Dist. 4 of Pa. since 1927; pres. Pa. Assn. of Dairy and Milk Inspectors, 1927-28. Chmn. com. of Pa. Dept. of Health to study York plate pasteurizer, 1931, Union County (Pa.) Nutrition Council, 1942-43. Served as 2d lieutenant Sanitary Corps, U.S. Army, during World War. Mem. Am. Pub. Health Assn., Am. Social Hygiene Assn., A.A.A.S., Soc. Am. Bacteriologists (pres. Central Pa. br. 1935-36), Inst. Food Technologists, Am. Forestry Assn., Am. Soc. Quality Control, Delta Upsilon, Omicron Delta Kappa. Republican. Methodist. Mason. Home: Lewisburg PA Died Jan. 29, 1971; buried Lewisburg Cemetery.

RICE, LABAN LACY, educator; b. Dixon, Ky., Oct. 14, 1870; s. Laban Marchbanks and Martha (Lacy) R.; A.B. Cumberland U., 1891, M.A., 1892, Ph.D., 1894; m. Blanche Alexander Buchanan, Nov. 23, 1892; children—Katharine (wife of Dr. James H. Shaw), Annie Hays (Mrs. Perry O'Neil). Prof. English lang. and lit., Cumberland U., 1894-97; asso. editor, The Cumberland Presbyterian, 1897-99; prof. English lang. and lit., Cumberland U., 1899-1904; headmaster The Castle Heights Mil. Acad., 1904-13, pres. and sole owner same, 1913-21; pres. Junior Mil. Acad., 1920-29; owner and dir. Camp Kawasawa, for boys, 1919-22, and the Nakanawa Camps, for girls, since 1920; part owner and asso. dir. Camp Sequoyah for Boys, Asheville, N.C., 1929-36; chancellor of Cumberland University, Lebanon, Tenn., 1939-40, president, 1941-46; professor English, Peabody Summer Sch., 1904; editor, Cumberland Presbyn. Review, 1902-04. Mem. State Exec. Com. Y.M.C.A., 1895-1920. V.p. Southern Appalachian Sect. of Camp Dirs. Assn. of America, 1929; mem. Southern Assn. for the Advancement of Science, Am. Academy Political and Social Sci., American Assn. for Advancement of Science, Kappa Sigma. Author: A Mountain Idyll," 1921; Sonnets to B.B.R.," 1922; The Madonna of the Slate," 1923; Three Minute Lay Sermons," 1937; A Woman's Answer and Other Verse, 1946; Relativity for the Man in the Street, 1948. Democrat. Presbyterian. Address: Ware Neck VA‡

RICE, M. WILFRED, banker; b. Newark, Feb. 26, 1909; s. Abraham and Anna (Hausner) R.; B.S., N.Y.U., 1934, M.B.A. cum laude, 1935; m. Betty Ann Stern, Oct. 4, 1940; children—Frederick A., Margaret Louise, William Lawrence. With Nat. State Bank, Newark, 1926-65, vice chmn., 1961-65; pres., dir. First Small Bus. Investment Corp., N.J., 1960-68, Carteret Savs. & Loan Association, 1965-68; mem. board dirs. Resistoflex Corporation, Mem. Essex County (N.J.) Park Commn., 1961-68, treas., 1965. Mem. N.Y.U. Alumni Fedn. Clubs: Down Town, 744 (Newark); Mountain Ridge Country (W. Caldwell, N.J.); New York Univ. (N.Y.C.). Home: South Orange NJ Died Mar. 6, 1968.

RICE, ROBERT, ry. official; b. Galesburg, Ill., Oct. 13, 1874; s. F. C. R.; A.B., Knox Coll., Galesburg, 1896; studied Harvard, 1896-98; m. Lillian Pierce, Nov. 11, 1904. Began as sect. laborer C., B.&Q. R.R., 1898, successively trainmaster and asst. supt. Galesburg div., asst. supt. Ottumwa div., 1905-06, supt. Hannibal div., 1906-08, St. Joseph's div., 1908-12, Aurora div., Jan.-Sept. 1912; gen. supt. Ia. dist., 1912-16, Mo. dist., at St. Louis, 1916-18; federal mgr. C.&S. Ry., Denver, Colo., 1918-20, v.p. and general mgr., 1920-39, v.p., 1939-47, retired Nov. 1, 1947. Home: 155 Gilpin St. Office: C. A. Johnson Bldg. Denver CO‡

RICE, STUART ARTHUR, sociologist, statistician; b. Wadena, Minn., Nov. 21, 1889; s. Edward Myron and Ida Emelin (Hicks) R.; A.B., U. of Wash., 1912, A.M., 1915; Ph.D., Columbia U., 1924; m. Chineta Williamson, 1914; m. 2d, Sarah Alice Mayfield, May 29, 1934; 1 son, Stuart Arthur. Sec. Industrial Welfare Commn., Wash., 1913; confidential insp. Dept. of Pub. Charities, New York, 1914-15; supt. New York Municipal Lodging House, 1916-17; field rep. War Camp Community Service, 1918; ednl. dir. N.W. Div. Am. Red Cross, 1919-20; instr. and asst. prof. sociology, Dartmouth, 1923-26; prof. sociology, later prof. sociology and statistics, U. of Pa., 1926-40; research sec. for social statistics, Social Science Research Council, 1931-32; prof. sociology, U. of Chicago, 1932-33; acting chmn. Com. on Govt. Statistics and Information Services, 1933; asst. dir. of Census, 1933-36; chmn. Central Statis. Bd., 1936-40; asst. dir. Bur. of Budget for Statis. Standards Exec. Office of President, 1940-55; president Surveys & Research Corporation, Washington, 1955-65, adviser-consultant, 1965-69. Mem. of the staff Social Sci. Research Council, 1931-32, pres. research com. on social trends, 1931-32. Decorated Order of Rising Sun, 2d class (Japan). Mem. Internat. Statis. Inst. (hon. pres. 1953-69), Inter Am. Statis. Inst. (chmn. organizing com., 1st v.p., 1941-50); Internat. Union for Scientific Study of Population, Econometric Soc.; Am. Sociol. Soc., Am. Statis. Assn. (pres. 1933), Am. Council of Learned Socs., 1928-32, Social Science Research Council, 1937-42; fellow A.A.A.S. (v.p. 1937, 57); mem. exec. com. establishment of Franklin D. Roosevelt Library, 1938-39; Mem. organizing com. and chmn. statistics sect. 8th Am. Scientific Congress, Washington, 1940; chmn. arrangements com. Internat. Statis. Confs., Washington, 1947; chmn. U.N. Nuclear Statis. Commn., 1946; contributions com. U.N. Gen. Assembly, 1951-56; U.S. rep. UN Statis. Commission, 1947-55; mem. U.S. rep. com. on improvement of nat. statistics (inter-Am.), 1950-55; statis. missions to London, the Hague, Brussels, 1945, Japan, 1946-47, 1951, 1952; statis. adviser to Govt. of Republic of Korea, 1958-64; U.S. del. to internat. statis. conf., Athens, 1936, Rome, 1936, Prague, 1938, Rio, 1945, 55, Mex. City, 1948, Berne, 1949, Bogota, 1950, New Delhi and Calcutta, 1951, Bangkok, 1952, Ottawa, 1952, Rome, 1953, Stockholm, 1957, Tokyo, 1960, Belgrade, 1965; pres. Fed. Statis. Users Conf., 1957-58. Numerous publs. in field. Home: Washington DC Died June 4, 1969; buried Nat. Meml. Park, Falls Church VA

RICH, ARNOLD RICE, pathologist; b. Birmingham, Ala., Mar. 28, 1893; s. Samuel and Hattie (Rice) R.; A.B., U. of Va., 1914, M.A., 1915; M.D., Johns Hopkins University, 1919; M.D. (honorary) University Zurich; married Helen Elizabeth Jones, June 3, 1925; children—Adrienne Cecile, Cynthia Marshall Asst. in pathology, Johns Hopkins U., 1919-20, instr., 1920-21, asso., 1921-23, asso. prof., 1923-44, prof., 1944-47, Baxley prof., dir. dept., 1947-58, Baxley professor emeritus, 1958-68; resident pathologist, Johns Hopkins Hosp., 1920-26, asso. pathologist, 1929-44, pathol.-in-chief, 1947-58, now hon. cons.; expert cons. to the Surg. Gen., U.S. Army; mem. sci. adv. bd. Armed Forces Inst. of Pathology (chmn. 1951); special cons. USPHS; consultant in pathology Veterans Administration; consultant in med. research, Chem. Warfare Service, since 1943; adv. consultant Tuberculosis Control Div., U.S.P.H.S.; Nat. Research Council (com. on pathol., 1947-52). U.S. State Dept. del., 1st Internat. Allergy Congress, 1951; mem. Comite d'Honneur, 50th anniversary celebration of discovery of anaphylaxis, Paris, 1952. Served with U.S. Army, 1917-18; lt. commander USNR, ret. Decorated Chevalier Legion of Honor (France); awarded Charles Mickle hon. fellowship, U. Toronto Faculty of Medicine, 1956; Kober medal, Assn. of Am. Physicians, 1958; Gordon Wilson medal, Am. Clin. and Climatol. Assn., 1960; Trudeau medal, Nat. Tb Assn., 1960; Gairdner Found. (Can.) Internat. award, 1960; honorary Plaque, Japanese Soc. for Tb, 1960; medal A.C.P., 1963; Seaman award Assn. Mil. Surgeons U.S., 1963. Trustee Roland Park Co. Sch., 1944-51. Fellow A.A.A.S., Internat. Assn. Allergists, Royal Soc. Medicine London (hon.); honorary member Pathological Society of Great Britain and Ireland, Am. Clin. and Climatol. Assn., Harvey Soc., Soc. Francaise d'Allergie; fgn. corr. mem. Soc. Med. des Hopitaux de Paris; fgn. mem. Soc. Aregentina de Anat. Norm. y Patc'; corr. mem. Soc. Brasileria de Tuberc., Tb Soc. of Scotland; asso. mem. Soc. Anat. de Paris. Dir. Md. Tb Assn., 1947-51. Mem. Nat. Acad. Scis., Assn. Am. Physicians, Soc. Exptl. Biology and Medicine (editorial bd. Proc. 1943-47), Soc. Exptl. Pathology, Am. Assn. Pathologists and Bacteriologists, Phi Beta Kappa, Sigma Xi, Alpha Omega Alpha. Club: 14 W. Hamilton St. Author: The Pathogenesis of Tuberculosis 1944, rev. 1951, Spanish edit., 1946, Japanese edit., 1954. Mem. editorial bd. Bull. of the Johns Hopkins Hosp., 1925-63, Internat. Archives Allergy and Immunology, Internat. Review Experimental Pathology. Contributor articles in field. Home: Baltimore MD Died Apr. 17, 1968; buried Baltimore Nat. Cemetery, Baltimore MD

RICH, CARL W., congressman; b. Cin., Sept. 12, 1898; s. David William and Rosa (West) R.; A.B., U. Cin., 1922, LL.B., 1924, LL.D., 1959; m. Frances Ivins, Sept. 8, 1926. Admitted to Ohio bar; asst. city solicitor, asst. city pros., Cin.; judge Common Pleas Ct. of Hamilton County; mem. 88th U.S. Congress 1st Ohio Dist. Pres., chmn. bd. Cin. Royals, profl. basketball team; pres. Kennedy Savs. & Loan Co.; v.p. Central Hyde Park Savs. & Loan Co.; dir. First Nat. Bank, Morrow, O., Grand Central Savs. & Loan Co., Home State Savs. & Loan Co., Hamilton Mut. Ins. Co.; legal counsel bldg. and loan cos. Mem. adv. bd. Greater Cin. unit Salvation Army. Mem. city council, Cin., then mayor. Trustee Cin. Zool. Soc. Served with U.S. Army, World War I; served to col., CWS, AUS, World War II. Recipient Nat. Distinguished Alumni award Tau Kappa Alpha; 1961. Mem. Lambda Chi Alpha, Phi Alpha Delta, Omicron Delta Kappa, Tau Kappa Alpha. Republican. Mason (33 degree, Shriner), Moose, Eagle. Club: Cincinnati (past v.p.). Home: Cincinnati OH Died June 26, 1972; interred Spring Grove Mausoleum, Spring Grove Cemetery, Cincinnati OH

RICH, EDNAH ANNE, technical normal school pres.; b. Santa Barbara, Cal., Mar. 16, 1871; d. Joseph Addison and Pluma Estelle (Holcomb) R.; grad. Sloyd Training Sch., Boston, 1895; studied in Sweden and Leipzig, Germany, also Harvard Summer Sch. Prin. Anna S.C. Blake Manual Training Sch. and supervisor domestic science, and manual training in pub. schs., Santa Barbara, 1892-1913; pres. State Normal Sch. of Manual Arts and Home Economics, Santa Barbara, 1909-—. Mem. Cal. State Bd. Edn., 1906-10; mem. Internat. Com. Art and Industrial Assn., London, 1908, Dresden, 1912; mem. Cal. State Teachers' Assn. (council of edn.), Southern Cal. Teachers' Assn., etc. Author: Paper Sloyd for Primary Grades, 1905. Address: Arlington Hotel, Santa Barbara CA‡

RICH, ROBERT FLEMING, ex-congressman; b. Woolrich, Pa., June 23, 1883; s. Michael B. and Ida B. R.; grad. Mercersburg Acad., 1902; B.S. (hon.) Dickinson Coll., Class 1907; m. Julia Trump, June 10, 1911; children—Elizabeth Margaret Shaw, Catharine Ann, Julia Trump. Vice pres., treas. and gen. mgr., Woolrich Woolen Mills, pres. State Bank of Avis (Pa.); dir., sec., treas., Chatham Water Co.; dir., treas., Pierce Mfg. Co.; dir., sec., Oak Grove Improvement Co.; dir., Lock Haven Trust Co.; del. Rep. Nat. Conv., 1924; mem. 71st to 77th Congresses, 1930-43, 15th Pa., Dist.; re-elected 79th, 80th and 81st Congresses, 1944-51. Pres. bd. trustees, Williamsport-Dickinson Sem., (now Lycoming College) trustee Dickinson Coll., Lock Haven Hosp.; dir. State Y.M.C.A., Lock Haven Y.M.C.A. mem. alumni council Mercersburg Acad., Phi Kappa Psi. Methodist. Mason (33 deg.). Clubs: Ross (Williamsport, Pa.); Clinton Country (Lock Haven, Pa.); Williamsport Country; Burning Tree, Chevy Chase (Washington, D.C.). Home: Woolrich PA Died Apr. 1968.

RICH, THADDEUS, musical dir., violinist; b. Indianapolis, Ind., Mar. 21, 1885; s. William Shipman and Susan Blanche (Slager) R.; studied violin under Richard Schliewen and Hugh McGibney (U.S.); pupil of Arno Hilf, violin, Wendling and Von Bose, piano, Quasdorf and Jadassohn, composition, Reinicke and Hermann, ensemble, Leipzig Conservatory of Music, 1897-1902; mem. Leipzig Gewandhaus Orchestra under Arthur Nikisch, 1901-02; student Royal Hochschule der Musik, Berlin, under Josef Joachim, 1902-03; Mus.D., Temple U., 1913; m. Almyra Chandler Williams, Oct. 1, 1910; children—Louise Chandler (wife of Dr. Blanchard William Means), Thaddeus. Concert-master Berlin-Charlottenburg opera, 1903-04; tour of Germany and Austria, 1904-05; returned to U.S. and appeared on tour, 1905-06; concert master and asso. condr. Phila. Orchestra, 1906-26; dean Coll. of Music, Temple U. since 1913; founded Rich Quartette, 1908; conducted Phila. Festival Orchestra, 1915-26; asso. with Leopold Stokowski at Curtis Inst. of Music (Phila.), 1925-26; asso. with Nikolai Sokoloff as asst. dir. of Federal Music Project since 1935. Owner of collection of rare stringed instruments. Decorated with Order of the Crown by King Ferdinand of Rumania, 1922. Home: Philadelphia PA Died Apr. 1969.*

RICHARDS, BERNARD GERSON, author and journalist; b. Keidan, Lithuania, March 9, 1877; s. Alexis and Chana (Sirk) R.; educated Hebrew schs. and under pvt. instruction, also night sch. in U.S.; m. Gertrude Gerzunskie, Feb. 8, 1903; children—David H., Ruth Z., Joseph W., Judah A. Came to U.S. with parents, 1886; served as reporter Boston Post; became editor New Era Mag.; corr. and editor various Jewish newspapers and mags., and feature writer Boston Evening Transcript, New York Globe, Tribune, etc.; sec. for five years of Jewish Community (Kehillah), N.Y. City; a founder, and exec. dir. Am. Jewish Congress, 1915-32; sec. Am. Jewish delegation to Peace Conf., Paris, 1919. Mem. exec. com. Zionist Orgn. of America; chmn. exec. com. Jewish Council of Greater New York; dir. Jewish Information Bur.; on staff Nat. Emer. Council, Washington, D.C., 1935-36; with U.S. Immigration and Naturalization Service, 1939-40; became asso. with Dem. Nat. Com., Washington, D.C., 1932, now exec. asst. Independent Democrat. Jewish religion. Author: The Discourses of Keidnasky, 1903; Home: 310 W. 106th St. Office: 103 Park Av., New York‡

RICHARDS, CHARLES GORMAN, clergyman; b. Pittsburgh, Pa., June 28, 1872; s. Peter K. and Rosina (Corselius) R.; grad. Susquehanna Collegiate Inst., 1893; A.B., Princeton, 1897; grad. McCormick Theol. Sem., Chicago, 1901; D.D., Dubuque (Ia.) Coll., 1912; m. Mary Louise McKnight, June 26, 1902; children—Alexander M., Louise (Mrs. Robt. N. Marshall). Ordained Presbyterian ministry, 1901; pastor First Ch., Columbus, Ind., 1901-06, Sterling, Ill., 1906-11, First Ch., Auburn, N.Y., 1911-19; exec. sec. dept. of kingdom extension in New Era Movement of Presbyn. Ch., 1919-21; pastor Rogers Park Ch., 1921-29, First Ch., Verona, N.J., 1929-46. Trustee Hanover Coll., 1902-05, Cayuga Presbytery, 1912-19. Mem. Nat. Service Commn.; sec. and mem. exec. com. Social Service Commn. of Presbyn. Ch., U.S.A., 1917-19. Mason (K.T.). Contbr. to religious and social periodicals. Clubs: Princeton, Rotary. Home: 331 S. 6th St., Chambersburg PA‡

RICHARDS, CHARLES LENMORE, ex-congressman; b. Austin, Nev., Oct. 3, 1877; s. Charles Alexander and Letitia Stone (Bonner) R.; A.B., Stanford, 1901; m. Elizabeth Hoffman, Jan. 6, 1909. Began practice at Tonopah, Nev., 1901; dist. atty. Nye County, Nev., 1903-04; mem. Nev. Ho. of Rep., 1919; moved to Reno, 1919; chairman Dem. State Committee, 1920; member 68th Congress (1923-25), Nevada at large. Mem. Am., Nev. State, Washoe and Nye County bar assns. Mason, Elk, Eagle. Club: Kiwanis (pres.). Home: 1207 Riverside Drive. Office: Waldorf Bldg., Reno NV‡

RICHARDS, CHARLES MALONE, clergyman, educator; b. Liberty Hill, S.C., Feb. 1, 1871; s. Rev. John Gardiner and Sophia (Smith) R.; A.B., Davidson (N.C.) Coll., 1892, D.D., 1906; grad. Columbia (S.C.) Theol. Sem., 1895; LL.D., Hampden-Sidney Coll., 1938; m. Jane Leighton McDowell, Dec. 31, 1896; children—Mary James, Charles M. (dec.), James McDowell, Sophia, Jane Leighton. Instr. Hebrew and Greek, Columbia Theol. Sem., 1896; ordained ministry Presbyn. Ch. in U.S., 1896; pastor successively Mechanicsville, S.C., Statesville, N.C., and Davidson Coll., until 1926; prof. Bible. Davidson Coll., since 1926. Moderator Synod of N.C., 1907. Trustee Gen. Assembly of Presbyn. Ch. (U.S.) and Foundation, Inc.; trustee Davidson Coll., Union Theol. Sem. in Va., Mitchell Coll., Statesville. Mem. Phi Beta Kappa, Omicron Delta Kappa, Kappa Alpha, Eta Sigma Phi. Democrat. Mason, K.P. Home: Davidson NC‡

RICHARDS, DICKINSON W., physician; b. Orange, N.J., Oct. 30, 1895; s. Dickinson W. and Sally (Lambert) W.; A.B., Yale, 1917, D.Sc., 1957; A.M., Columbia, 1922, M.D., 1923, D.Sc., 1966; m. Constance B. Riley, Sept. 19, 1931; children—Ida E., Gertrude W., Ann H., Constance L. Research fellow Nat. Inst. for Med. Research, London, Eng., 1927-28; research on problems of pulmonary and cardiac physiology Coll. Phys. and Surg., Columbia, 1928-73, Lambert prof. medicine, 1947-61, emeritus, 1961-73, dir. 1st med. div. Bellevue Hosp., N.Y.C., 1945-61. Served as 1st lt. U.S. Army, 1917-18, A.E.F., 1918. Decorated chevalier Legion of Honor (France); recipient Nobel Prize in medicine and physiology (with others), 1956. Fellow Am. Acad. Arts and Scis.; mem. Assn. Am. Physicians (pres. 1962), Nat. Acad. Scis. Presbyn. Club: Century Assn. (N.Y.C.). Editor: (with A. P. Fishman) Lakeville CT Died Feb. 23, 1973.

RICHARDS, GEORGE HUNTINGTON, lawyer; b. Bath. Me., Aug. 1, 1882; s. William R. and Charlotte B. (Blodget) R.; A.B., Yale, 1903; LL.B., N.Y. Law Sch., 1907; m. Marianna M. Middlebrook, May 25, 1910; children—Marianna (Mrs. Max Bovarnick), Sarah H. (Mrs. Gifford B. Pinchot), Frederic M. Tchr., Phillips Andover Acad., 1903-05; admitted to N.Y. bar, 1907; asso. Miller, King, Lane & Trafford, 1907-11; partner Reynolds, Richards & McCutcheon, 1911-49; partner Reynolds, Richards, Ely & LaVenture, 1949-69, sr. partner. Dir. Overseas Securities Corp. Mem. exec. com. Civil Service Reform Assn., 1945-69. Mem. Woods Hole Oceanographic Inst., Yale Assn. of Class Secs. (pres. 1920), Am. Bar Assn., Bar Assn. City N.Y. Club: Cruising of Am. Home: New York City NY Died Oct. 20, 1969.

RICHARDS, HERBERT MONTAGUE, corp. exec., mem. Rep. Nat. Com.; b. Honolulu, Hawaii, Oct. 2, 1904; s. Theodore and Mary Cushing (Atherton) R.; A.B., Wesleyan U., Middletown, Conn., 1926; m. Logan Mary Shepherd, Aug. 5, 1927 (dec. Jan. 1934); m. 2d, Leilani Rohrig, May 31, 1935; children—Herbert Montague, James A., G. Manning, Mary L. Overseer Ewa Plantation Co., 1926-28; sec., asst. mgr. Kahua Ranch, Ltd., 1928-30; contract dept. Hawaiian Electric Co., Ltd., 1930-34; with Castle & Cooke, Ltd., Honolulu, from 1934, asst. sec., from 1941; assistant secretary Waialua Agricultural Company, Ltd.; asst. sec., dir. Ewa Plantation Co., Kohala Ditch Company, Limited, Kahala Sugar Company; secretary, treasurer, director of Kahua Ranch, Ltd.; dir. Hawaiian Telephone Co., Hawaiian Electric Co., Ltd., Hawaiian Trust Co., Ltd., Home Ins. Co. of Hawaii, Ltd.; spl. partner Weaver Motors. Pres., dir. Honolulu Meml. Park, Inc. Mem., past. pres. of Aloha council Boy Scouts of America. Member Republican National Com. from Hawaii, from 1955; mem. Honolulu Bd. Supvrs., 1945-46; del. Hawaii Statehood Constitutional Convention, 1956; hon. consul Fed. Republic of Germany in Honolulu. Mem. Hawaii Conference United Church of Christ (pres. bd. 1950-53, treas., chmn. bd. trustees), Psi Upsilon. Home: Honolulu HA Died Mar. 7, 1970.

RICHARDS, JEAN MARIE, educator; b. Petersburg, Va., Nov. 10, 1872; d. George S. and Mary (Nichols) R.; B.L., Smith Coll., Northampton, Mass., 1895; post-grad. work, Syracuse U., Litt.D. Apptd. first dean of women, also prof. English, Syracuse U., 1908, and organized self-govt. among women students there; now head of Katharine Gibbs School, Boston, Mass. Mem. Phi Beta Kappa, Phi Kappa Phi. Episcopalian. Home: 90 Marlborough St., Boston MA‡

RICHARDS, JOSEPH H., lawyer; b. nr. Spencer, Ind. Asst. atty., 1880-3, gen. atty., 1883, St. Louis, Fort Scott & Wichita R.R.; gen. atty. Wichita & Colo. R.R. since 1884; later asst. to pres. and v.-p. same cos.; receiver St. Louis, Fort Scott & Wichita R.R., 1887; v.-p. and gen. atty. Wichita & Western Ry., July, 1887; now gen. atty. Mo. Pacific system for lines in Southern Kan. Address: Ft Scott KS‡

RICHARDS, LELA HORN (PSEUDONYM LEE NEVILLE), author; b. Junction City, Kan., 1870; d. Dr. Thomas G. and Emily (Shannon) Horn; student Denver U. and in N.Y. City; married Charles E. Richards, 1892; children—Mrs. Catherine Howell, Eleanor Schneider. Episcopalian. Club: Ladies Literary. Author: Blue Bonnet in Boston, 1915; Blue Bonnet Keeps House, 1916; Blue Bonnet Debutante, 1917; Only Henrietta, 1919; Blue Bonnet of the Seven Stars, 1920; Then Came Caroline, 1921; Henrietta's Inheritance, 1920; Caroline at College, 1922; Caroline's Career, 1923; Blue Bonnet's Family, 1929; Poplars Across the Moon (under the name of Lee Neville), 1937. Home: 217 S. 11th East St., Salt Lake City UT‡

RICHARDS, LOUISE, indsl. interior designer; b. Washington; d. Hugh M. and Bessie (Hodges) Beville; student Traphagen Sch. Design, N.Y.C., Ziegler Acadamie, Paris, France; m. Harper Richards, June 10, 1941; children—Holly, Wynn. Designer, Mable McIlvain Downs, 1937-38. 39-41; free lance fashion artist and designer, Paris, 1939-41; partner, indsl. designer and architect Harper Richards Assos., 1943-66. Regional dir. Fashion Group of Chgo., 1956, mem. council, 1957-66; chmn. costume collection Chgo. Hist. Soc. Mem. women's bd. Greater North Michigan Avenue Assn., Traveler's Aid Society; member of the board of Margaret Etter Creche Day Nursery, Chgo.; active Am. Cancer Soc., Seeing Eye orgn.; pres. N. Dearborn Assn., 1958, exec. com., 1959-66. Cited as one of 12 leading career women in Chgo., Chgo. Tribune, 1959. Member of Art Institute of Chicago, also Women's Archtl. League, Am. Inst. Interior Designers. Clubs: Saddle and Cycle, Arts (Chgo.). Home: Chesterton IN Died Nov. 27, 1966; buried Greenville MS

RICHARDS, PAUL STANLEY, ranchman; b. at Madison, Wis., Aug. 3, 1870; s. Charles Herbert and Marie (Miner) R.; A.B., Yale, 1892; LL.B., U. of Pa., 1895; m. Mary Black, of Willow, Wyo., Sept. 14, 1910. Admitted to Pa. bar, 1895, and practiced in Phila.; removed to Wyo., 1901, and engaged in sheep raising; mgr. Niobrara Sheep Co., Gordon, Neb., 1903-5; mgr. and prin. owner Walker Creek Sheep Co., Douglas, Wyo., since 1907; pres. and mgr. Western Ranch Exchange, land and live stock, Douglas. Republican. Conglist. Home: Pueblo CO

RICHARDS, RALPH H(ARE), real estate and mortgage broker; born New Matamoras, Ohio, November 9, 1892; son of John Alfred and Jennie C. (Hare) R.; B.S. in Business Administration, Ohio State U., 1922, M.A., 1924, grad. student 1925-27, student Columbia U., 1927-30; m. Charlotte Rushford, Sept. 14, 1929; 1 dau. (by previous marriage), Mrs. Floyd Herren. Instr. in finance, Ohio State U., 1922-24; asst. prof., 1924-27; instr., Am. Inst. of Banking, N.Y. City, 1927-31; asst. prof. of finance, Columbia U., summer 1928; v.p. Edgar Higgins, Inc., investment counsel, 1929-31; dir. field service, U.S. Savings and Loan League, Chicago, 1931-33; exec. vice pres. Fed. Home Loan Bank, Pittsburgh, 1933-34, pres., 1934-48; organized Richards, Carroll & Assos., home protection insurance, on instructional staff, Am. Savings and Loan Inst., Grad. Sch. Northwestern U., 1939-41; acting gov. Fed. Home Loan Bank System, 1946; later chmn. investment com. and mem. exec. com. Fed. Home Loan Bank System Retirement Fund; real estate and mortgage broker representing various lenders in home finance. Member of the Academy of Political Science, also Beta Gamma Sigma, Alpha Kappa Psi, Tau Kappa Epsilon. Republican. Presbyn. Elk. Moose. Club: Magnolia Yacht. Author articles in field. Address: New Martinsville WV Died Jan. 21, 1967.

RICHARDS, ROGER G., corp. exec.; b. Holyoke, Mass., 1925; B.S. in Chemistry, U. Mass., 1946; married. With Monsanto Chem. Co., 1947-52, Diamond Alkali Co., 1952-64; with Celanese Corp., from 1964, v.p., from 1967; chmn. bd. Celanese Coatings Co., Brit. Paints (Australia) Pty. Ltd.; pres. Celanese Plastics Co.; dep. chmn. Brit. Paints Ltd.; v.p., dir. Polyplastics Co. Ltd.; dir. Icatal Plastics Ltd. Home: Madison NJ

RICHARDS, ROSALIND (MISS), author; b. S. Boston, Mass., 1874; d. Henry and Laura Elizabeth (Howe) R.; ed. at home and at The Shaw Sch., Boston. Author: The Nursery Fire, 1904 L6; Two Children in the Woods, 1907 E3. Address: Gardiner ME‡

RICHARDSON, ALEXANDER HENDERSON, co. dir.; b. Charles Town, W.Va., Aug. 23, 1872; s. Charles Taylor and Jennie Love (Forrest) R.; ed. pub. schs.; m. Anna Bourke, Nov. 1, 1922. Bookkeeper, Standard Oil Co., St. Paul, 1897-1906, treasurer Standard Oil Co. (Neb.), 1906-11, v.p., 1911-17, pres., 1917-37; sec. bd. dirs. Northwestern Bell Telephone Co., Omaha. Home: 104 S. 38th Av. Office: 118 S. 19th St., Omaha‡

RICHARDSON, EDWARD H(ENDERSON), surgeon; b. Farmville, Va., Nov. 13, 1877; s. Hilary Goode and Mary (Perkins) R.; master accounts, Eastman Business Coll., Poughkeepsie, N.Y., 1894; student Va. Poly. Inst., 1896-97; A.B., Hampden-Sydney Coll., 1900, LL.D., 1921; grad. study Johns Hopkins U., 1900-01, M.D., 1905, surg. apprentice, 1905-10; m. Emily Gould, June 27, 1905; children—Mary Gould (Mrs. W. A. Horsley Gantt), Edward H., Jr. Resident house officer, assistant resident gynecologist and resident gynecologist, Johns Hopkins Hosp., 1905-10, asst. visiting gynecologist since 1912; instr. in gynecology, Johns Hopkins U., 1910-12, asso. in clin. gynecology, 1912-34, asso. prof. gynecology, 1934-47, now emeritus; vis. gynecologist Union Memorial Hosp., Woman's Hosp., Church Home and Hospital, Sinai Hosp., Sheppard and Enoch Pratt Hosp. Fellow Am. Coll. Surgeons; mem. A.M.A., Southern Med. Assn., Southern Surg. Assn., Am. Gynecol. Soc. (v.p. 1934-35), Baltimore City Med. Soc. (pres. 1926, 27), Kappa Sigma, Omicron Delta Kappa, Phi Beta Kappa. Presbyterian. Clubs: Johns Hopkins, Elkridge. Home: 3RICHARDSON Baltimore MD‡

RICHARDSON, FREDERICK ALBERT, editor The Internat. Quarterly; b. Burlington, Vt., Aug. 31, 1873; s. Albert E. and Frances A. R.; ed. Burlington high school; grad. Univ. of Vt., A.B., Harvard; m. June 11, 1895, Harriette B. Taber. Address: 27 W. 67th St., New York‡

RICHARDSON, GEORGE BURR, geologist; b. New York, Aug. 21, 1872; s. George Wentworth and Emma (Breck) R.; grad. Harvard, S.B., 1895, S.M., 1898; Ph.D., Johns Hopkins, 1901; unmarried. Has done geol. work for U.S. Geol. Survey in different parts of the U.S. since 1896; asst. geologist same since 1900. Author: Reconnaissance in the Cape Nome Region, Alaska (assisting Alfred H. Brooks), 1901 U6; Indiana Folio, Geologic Atlas of the United States, 1903 U6. Address: U.S. Geol. Survey, Washington‡

RICHARDSON, H. GEORGE, cable mfg. exec.; b. Clifton Heights, Pa., May 3, 1901; s. Robert J. and Florence E. (Herdman) R.; m. Mary Lucille Yeatman, Jan. 17, 1931; children—H. George, William, Robert, Mary Lucille. Vice pres. Gen. Cable Corp. Clubs: Lotos (N.Y.C.); Manor Country (Norbeck, Md.); Indian Lake (Indian Lake Estates, Fla.). Home: Rye NY Died July 6, 1971; buried Gate of Heaven Cemetery, Valhalla NY

RICHARDSON, HENRY SMITH, mfg. chemist; b. Greensboro, N.C., July 19, 1885; s. Lunsford and Mary Lynn (Smith) R.; Davidson (N.C.) Coll., 1906; student U.S. Naval Acad.; m. Grace Stuart Jones, Dec. 16, 1914; children—Grace Stuart, Mary Keene, Henry Smith, Robert Randolph, John Page. Salesman, Vick Chem. Co., 1907-15, gen. mgr., 1915-19, pres., 1919-29, chmn. bd., 1929-38, chmn. exec. com., 1938-53, chmn. bd., 1953-57, hon. chmn., 1957-72 (name changed to Richardson-Merrell, Inc. 1962). Founder L. Richardson Meml. Hosp. for Negroes, Greensboro, and donor (with L. Richardson, Jr.) Richardson Field at Davidson Coll.; founder, trustee, chmn. bd. Smith Richardson Found.; exec. bd. Boy Scouts Am., 1942-72; a leader in effecting passage of legislation for state commn. for conservation of wild life in N.C. Mem. Kappa Sigma, Omicron Delta Kappa. Democrat. Presbyn. Home: Greens Farms CT Died Feb. 11, 1972; buried Green Hill Cemetery Greensboro NC

RICHARDSON, HILARY GOODE, clergyman; b. Prince Edward County, Va., Mar. 17, 1874; s. Hilary Goode and Mary Anne (Perkins) R.; A.B., Hampden Sidney Coll., 1894; student U. of Va., 1894-95; grad. Union Theol. Sem., Richmond, Va., 1898; grad. student in Semitic langs., Johns Hopkins, 1908-10; m. Anna Holmes Davis, Dec. 3, 1901 (died June 14, 1945). Ordained to the ministry of the Presbyterian Church, 1898; pastor Central Ch., Clarksburg, West Virginia, 1898-1908; divested of office of minister of Presbyn. Ch. because of inability to subscribe to doctrines of same, 1915; entered ministry of Unitarian Ch.; minister 1st Unitarian Congl. Ch., Yonkers, N.Y., since 1917. Asso. mem. Am. Schs. of Oriental Research. Mem. Soc. Bibl. Lit. and Exegesis, Am. Oriental Soc., Palestine Oriental Soc. Contbr. to Harvard Theol. Rev., Am. Jour. Semitic Langs., and other jours.; wrote Life and the Book. Home: 147 N. Broadway, Yonkers NY‡

RICHARDSON, HUGH, capitalist; b. Vicksburg, Miss., Nov. 4, 1869; s. Lee and Louise (French) R.; Southwestern Presbyn. U., 1882-87; Princeton Univ., 1894; m. Josephine Inman, of Atlanta, Ga., June 24, 1896; children—Hugh Inman, Lee, Josephine Inman, Louise. Formerly mem. Inman, Smith & Co., Atlanta; in realty and investment business since 1907. Served as Ga. dir. War Savings Com. during war period. Trustee Princeton U., 1918-24; mem. bd. dirs. Oglethorpe U. Democrat. Presbyn. Clubs: Capital City, Brookhaven Golf, Piedmont Driving (Atlanta); Princeton (New York). Home: Broadlands," Paces Ferry Rd., Atlanta; (summer) Lake Toxaway, N.C. Office: 160 Peachtree St., Atlanta GA‡

RICHARDSON, JOHN S(ANFORD), educator; b. Darke County, O., Dec. 14, 1908; s. Cary Lincoln and Luella (Deeter) R.; B.S., Miami U., 1933, M.A., 1936; Ph.D., Ohio State U., 1942; m. Helen Kathryn Ryan, Feb. 20, 1937; children—Alan Ralph, Neil Ryan, Lynne Elizabeth. Elementary, high sch. tchr.; prin. McGuffey Sch.; instr. Miami U., 1936-39, asst. prof., 1939-42, asso. prof., 1942-47; asso. prof. Ohio State U., 1948-53, prof., 1953-69; vis. prof. Northwestern U., 1953, Ore. State Coll., 1956. Dir. Nat. Sci. Found Academic Year Inst., Ohio State U., 1957-69; sci. edn. cons. Grolier, Inc.; dir. ERIC Information Analysis Center for Sci. Edn.; editorial dir. Compton's Illustrated Sci. Dictionary; dir. Sci. Edn. Centers for Research and Development. Member U.S. national commission for UNESCO. Member President's Com. on Scientists and Engrs. Fellow A.A.A.S.; mem. Nat. Sci. Tchrs. Assn. (pres. 1956-57), N.E.A., Phi Beta Kappa, Phi Delta Kappa. Presbyn. Author: (with G. P. Cahoon) Methods and Material for Teaching General and Physical Science, 1951; Science Teaching in Secondary Schools, 1957; (with A.B. Garrett and Earl J. Montague) Chemistry, A First Course in Modern Chemistry, 1966; (with S. E. Williamson and Donald W. Stotler) The Education of Science Teachers, The Supervision of School Science Programs. Editor: School Facilities for Science Instruction, 1961. Resource Literature for Sci. Teachers, 1966. Contbr. ednl. jours., publs. Home: Columbus OH Died May 22, 1969.

RICHARDSON, M. S., banker; b. Holgate, O., 1895; grad. U. Akron, 1917; LL.B., Western Res. U., 1924. Chmn. bd., chief exec. officer, dir. Akron Nat. Bank & Trust Co. (O.); dir. Joseph Dyson & Sons, Inc., Akron Coca-Cola Bottling Co. Trustee emeritus, past pres. Akron Gen. Hosp.; trustee Edwin Shaw Hosp., Akron Clinic Found., Mental Hygiene Clinic, Akron Community Trusts; trustee, past chmn. bd. Summit County chpt. A.R.C.; life trustee, past pres. Summit County Rehab. Center; exec. com. Akron Area Devel. Com.; permanent mem. adv. com. Jr. League; mem. adv. com. Coll. Bus. Adminstrn., U. Akron. Mem. Summit County Republican Exec. Com. Mem. Phi Delta Phi, Lone Star. Mason, Rotarian (past pres. Akron). Clubs: City, University (Akron). Home: Cuyahoga Falls OH Died Apr. 24, 1971.

RICHARDSON, MARK E(DWIN), assn. official; b. Phila., Oct. 17, 1905; s. James Archibald and Lillian K. (Bradshaw) R.; grad. Girard Coll., 1922; m. Adelaide E. Wright, June 22, 1927; children—Mark Edwin, Joanne A. (Mrs. Robert C. Maddox). Staff Lybrand, Ross Bros. & Montgomery, N.Y.C., 1922-44, partner, 1944-63; exec. v.p. N.Y. C. of C., 1963-66. Mem. Am. Inst. C.P.A.'s, (past v.p.), Nat. Assn. Accountants, Am. Accounting Assn., Nat. Tax Assn. Home: Mountainside NJ Died Aug. 22, 1972; cremated.

RICHARDSON, ROBERT PRICE, clergyman, ch. adminstr. b. Memphis, Mar. 8, 1896; s. Edgar Morrison and Anna Black (Price) R.; A.B., Southwestern Presbyn. U., 1917; student sch. mil. aeros. U. Tex., 1918; B.D., Union Theol. Sem., 1923; studied lang. U. Nanking, 1923-24; D.D. (hon.), Southwestern at Memphis, 1938; m. Agnes Davidson Rowland, June 13, 1923; children—Susan, Robert Price, William R., Edgar M. Tchr., coach Chamberlain-Hunt Acad., Port Gibson, Miss., 1917-18; dir. athletics Southwest. U., 1919-20; ordained to ministry Presbyn. Ch., 1923; missionary to China under Bd. World Missions, Presbyn. Ch., U.S., 1923-51; also clergyman, Taichow, Kiangsu, China; prisoner of Japanese, 1941-42, repatriated, 1942; regional dir. Kiangsu Province, China, UNRRA, 1946-47; detained by Communists in China, 1950-51; v.p. in charge development Southwestern at Memphis, 1951-61; minister of adminstrn. First Presbyn. Ch., Pine Bluff, Ark., 1961-66. Served as cadet, U.S. Army A.C., 1918. Mem. Kappa Sigma, Omicron Delta Kappa. Clubs: Executive, Kiwanis (Memphis). Home: Pine Bluff AR Died Apr. 23, 1967; buried Memphis TN

RICHARDSON, ROY MUNDY DAVIDSON, lawyer; b. Martinsville, N.J., June 19, 1895; s. James Davidson and Sarah Evaline (Mundy) R.; A.B., Rutgers U., 1915, LL.D., 1951; B.A., M.A., Oxford U., 1921, Rhodes Scholar; m. Claire Mae Gano, Jan. 24, 1925; children—James Donald Davidson, Lois (Mrs. William Burdick), Janet Jill (Mrs. Eugene Britton III). Admitted to New York State bar, 1923; with legal department of W. R. Grace & Co., 1921-24; lectr. internat. law Bklyn. Law Sch., 1924-25; asso. Dewey, Ballantine, Bushby, Palmer & Wood, and predecessor firms, N.Y.C., 1925-68, partner, 1934-68, head Paris office, 1931-34; surrogate Kings Co., 1950; trustee, vice pres. Union Sq. Savs. Bank, 1940-68. Mem. Mayor's Com. on the Judiciary. Rep. candidate for Congress, 1944, 46; mem. N.Y. Electoral College, 1956, 1960. Chairman trustees Rutgers U., 1958-64, bd. govs., 1964-68; trustee Packer Collegiate Inst., Bklyn. Hosp., Bklyn. Bur. Social Service and Childrens Aid Soc.; sec. N.Y. State Rhodes Scholar Selection Com., 1947-56. Served as ensign USNR, 1917-19. Mem. Am., N.Y., Bklyn. (pres. 1962-63), bar assns., Assn. Bar City N.Y. (chmn. exec. com. 1954-55, vice pres. 1955-56), N.Y. Co. Lawyers Assn., Phi Beta Kappa, Phi Delta Phi, Delta Upsilon. Republican (treas. Kings Co. com.). Presbyn. (pres., trustee, elder). Mason. Clubs: University, Down Town Assn. (N.Y.C.); Somerset Hills Country (Bernardsville, N.J.); Brooklyn, Heights Casino, Rembrandt (Bklyn.); Country (Far Hills, N.J.). Home: Brooklyn NY Died Dec. 31, 1968; buried Mt. Horeb Methodist Episcopal Cemetery, Martinsville NJ

RICHARDSON, WILLIAM EDWIN, educator; born nr. Mt. Olive, Miss., Dec. 17, 1900; s. William Napolean and Bernelia (Dearman) R.; A.B., Miss. Coll., 1923; Th.M., So. Bapt. Theol. Sem., 1932, Ph.D., 1939; D.D., Cumberland U., 1946; m. Elizabeth Ferguson, June 29, 1933; children—Jane, June. Prin., Lebanon Consol. Sch., Raymond, Miss., 1923-26; coach and tchr. Plaquemine (La.) High Sch., 1926-27; tchr. DuPont Manual High Sch., Louisville, 1928-30; ordained to ministry of Bapt. Ch., 1927; pastor Hopewell Ch., New Castle, Ky., 1928-35, First Ch., Columbia, Ky., 1935-39, First Ch., Columbia, Tenn., 1939-46; prof. religion Cumberland U., 1946-49, pres. univ., 1949-51, pres. bd. trustees, 1946; pres. Bethel Coll., Hopkinsville, Ky., 1951-60; head of religion dept. Carson-Newman Coll., Jefferson City, Tenn., 1960-68, prof. religion, 1960-69. Mem. edn. commn. So. Bapt. Conv. 1946-53. Mem. So. Assn. Jr. Colls. (pres. 1960), Assn. Bapt. Profs. Religion. Mason. Club: Rotary International. Address: Jefferson City TN Died Sept. 1, 1971; buried Westview Cemetery Jefferson City TN

RICHARDSON, WILLIAM KING, lawyer; b. Boston, Mass., June 27, 1859; s. Henry L. and Frances M. (Lincoln) R.; A.B., Harvard, 1880, A.M., 1886; B.A., Oxford U., Eng., 1884. Admitted to bar, 1887; now mem. firm of Fish, Richardson & Neave, and specializing in patent law. Episcopalian. Mem. Mass. Soc. of the Cincinnati, Phi Beta Kappa. Clubs: Harvard (New York), Somerset. Home: 306 Beacon St. Office: 84 State St., Boston MA‡

RICHARDSON, WILLIAM LLOYD, AF officer, ret.; b. Saginaw, Mich., Dec. 14, 1901; grad. U.S. Mil. Acad., 1924; m. Georgia Richardson; children—Patricia, Janet. commd. 2d lt. Coast Arty., June 1924, advanced through the grades to maj. gen., July 28, 1950; became comdg. officer, Company of Cadets, and instr., U.S. Mil. Acad., June 1939; on duty in the Operations and Training Div., War. Dept. Gen. Staff, Washington, D.C., 1941-42; assigned to 8th Air Force overseas, July 1942; returned to this country to command the 51st Coast Arty. Brigade (Antiaircraft), Fort Bliss, Tex., Feb. 1943; comdg. IX Air Defense Command Ninth Air Force, Europe, Dec. 1943; chief, guided missiles group, Hdqrs. U.S. Air Forces, 1946-50; comdg. Air Force Missile Test Center, Patrick Air Force Base, Cocoa, Fla., 1950-54, (ret.); asst., Defense Electronic Products Div., Radio Corp., Am. Home: VA Died Mar. 21, 1973.

RICHEL, GEORGE WILLIAM, mfg. co. exec.; b. Alpena, Mich., Dec. 2, 1905; s. Charles A. and Helena (Bloom) R.; B.S. in Elec. Engring., U. Mich., 1927; m. Lucile M. Rice, June 17, 1930; children—Ann Elizabeth (Mrs. Wayne Schuh), Priscilla Perry (now Mrs. David Sliwa). Employed with the Electrical Specialties Company, Detroit, 1927-33; with Consumers Power Co., 1934-55, div. mgr., Grand Rapids, Mich., 1949-55; exec. v.p., dir. Wolverine Brass Works, Grand Rapids, 1955-61, pres., 1961-66, chmn. bd. and chief executive officer, 1967-70; dir. Grand Rapids City Coach Lines, Muskegon City Coach Lines, Mfrs. Supply Co. Trustee Blodgett Meml. Hosp. Mem. Mich. Mfrs. Assn. (dir.). Home: Grand Rapids MI Died Mar. 7, 1970.

RICHESON, JOHN JACOB, educator; b. St. Paris, O., Feb. 7, 1874; s. Samuel Deaton and Mary Elizabeth (Strasburg) R.; student Ohio Northern U., Ada, O.; Pd.B., Ohio U., 1910; Pd.D., Miami U., 1915; M.A., Teachers' Coll. (Columbia); m. Clara Viola Cromwell, of Westville, O., Feb. 1895; 1 dau., Mrs. Marian Lycan. Formerly teacher and supt. schs., Champaign Co., O.; organized centralized sch. in Mad River Tp., Champaign Co., also in Wayne Tp., Clinton Co., O.; head Rural Training Dept. and instr. in geography, Ohio U., 1910-14; dean State Normal Coll. of Ohio U., 1914-20; supt. of schs., Decatur, Ill., 1921-26, of Youngstown, O., 1926-31; mgr. Security Mutual Life Ins. Co., Youngstown. Mem. N.E.A., Ohio State Teachers' Assn., Southeastern Ohio Teachers' Assn. (pres.), Ohio Edn. Assn. (pres.), Phi Delta Kappa. Baptist. Mason (32 deg.). Clubs: Cosmopolitan, Tawse. Home: 171 W. Marion Av., Youngstown OH‡

RICHLING, DON JOSE, diplomat; b. Montevideo, Uruguay, July 8, 1874; s. Edward W. and Rosa (Pereira) R.; student in Uruguay, Germany and Austria, 1887-95; m. Jeanne Fleury. Began as consul gen. to S. Africa, 1906, at New York, 1910-12; insp. of consulates in N. and C. America and the West Indies, 1912-20; in charge consul gen's. office, New York, 1920-28, dean of consular corps, 1928-33; E.E. and M.P. from Uruguay to U.S., 1934-41; during his pub. career has been apptd. to spl. and confidential missions of his govt. to Eng., Germany, Austria-Hungary, Italy, Poland, Russia, Can. and Cuba. Decorated Comdr. Order of Carlos Manuel de Cespedes (Cuba); Merit Order, Grand Official (Ecuador). Clubs: Lawyers, Whitehall (New York); Metropolitan, Racquet, Chevy Chase (Washington). Home: The Shoreham Hotel, Washington DC Office: 44 Wall St., New York NY*‡

RICHMOND, CHARLES BLAIR, educator; b. Ewing, Lee County, Va., Mar. 13, 1893; s. James Samuel Benton and Adelia Anne (McLin) R.; A.B.; Hampden-Sydney (Va.) College, 1916, Litt.D. (hon.); m. Dorothy Dixon, Nov. 10, 1925; 1 dau., Diane Dixon (Mrs. Diane Simpson). Instr. Latin and athletics coach, Greenbrier Mil. Sch., Lewisburg, W.Va., 1916-25, also commandant, 1917-25; director Camp Greenbrier, Alderson, W.Va., 1916-25; pres. Ky. Mil. Institute, Lyndon, Kentucky, 1925-66, chairman of the board, 1965-68. Member of the civilian advisory board 2nd Army, U.S. Army. Sec.-treas. Assn. of Mil Colls. and Schs. of the U.S., 1934-35, pres., 1939-40, exec. com., 1953-68; joint com. on R.O.T.C., 1954; adv. panel R.O.T.C. affairs to reserve forces policy bd. Dept. Army, 1960-62; chairman Kentucky State Commn. Pvt. Schs., 1953. Mem. So. Assn. Colls. and Secondary Schs. (Ky. State com. since 1941), Phi Kappa Alpha, Presbyn. Mason. Clubs: Rotary, Pendennis, Venice Yacht, Owl Creek. Home: Louisville KY Died Dec. 23, 1968; buried Cave Hill Cemetery, Louisville KY

RICHMOND, GEORGE CHALMERS, clergyman; b. Springfield, Mass., Apr. 10, 1870; s. William Lockhart and Elizabeth (Chalmers) R.; A.B., Yale, 1895; Yale Theol. Sch., 2 yrs.; B.D., Hartford Theol. Sem., 1898; unmarried. Deacon, 1902, priest, 1903, P.E. Church; asst. to Bishop Huntington, 1901-04; asst. Ch. of Holy Trinity, New York, 1904-05; rector St. George's Ch., Rochester, N.Y., 1905-08, old St. John's Church, Phila., 1908-18; renounced Episcopal orders, Dec. 24, 1918, and became independent minister Calvary Ch., N.Y. City; minister Central Ch., St. Louis, 1920-21; minister Community Ch., Los Angeles, 1922-24; in Eng., 1924-25, preaching, lecturing and studying social conditions. While in Eng. his case was reviewed by the authorities of the Established Ch. and they unanimously requested the Bishop of Pa. to reopen the case and restore him to priestly office; was presented for trial in ecclesiastical court of Diocese of Pa., under 127 charges for defiance of Bishop P.M. Rhinelander; pleaded own case and was acquitted of 124 and found guilty on 3 charges; was suspended for 2 yrs., but immediately restored; rector Webster Hall Religious Forum, Detroit, 1926; later preached in England and Scotland; acting rector All Saints Parish and Christ Ch., Brooklyn, N.Y.; 1931-32; lecturer San Francisco Religious Forum and spl. preacher under bishop of Calif., 1933. Mem. Am. Acad. Polit. and Social Science, Fabian Soc. (London). Mason (32 deg.); official speaker for Masonic Ednl. Com. of Grand Lodge of Mich. Author: The Pulpit and the Revolution, 1920; Memorial of F.D. Huntington. Address: 7212 Tabor Rd., Philadelphia PA‡

RICHMOND, HAROLD BOURS, mfr.; b. Medford, Mass., Mar. 22, 1892; s. Benjamin and Effie Louise (Libby) R.; S.B., Mass. Institute Tech., 1914; D.Eng. (hon.), Norwich U., 1947; m. Florence Hoefler, Oct. 5,

1921; children—Robert Bours, Priscilla (Mrs. Raymond V. Randall). Elec. engr. with Stone & Webster Management Assn., 1914-15, Gen. Vehicle Co., 1915-16; instr. in elec. engring., Mass. Inst. Tech., 1916-19; with Gen. Radio Co., mfrs. elec. and radio laboratory apparatus, since 1919, director, 1922, treasurer 1926-44, chairman board and management committee, 1914-70; dir., member investment com. Liberty Mutual Ins. Co., Liberty Mutual Fire Insurance Company. Corporator Home Savings Bank, Boston, 1941-70, trustee 1945. Chief Guided Missiles Division of Nat. Defense Research Com., Wash., D.C., 1942-45. Chmn. Nat. Acad. of Science Adv. Com. to Army Ord. Dept. on Guided Missiles 1945-48. Commissioned first lieutenant Coast Artillery Res. Corps, May 15, 1917; served Coast Defenses, Chesapeake Bay and Coast Defenses, Boston, May 1917-July 1918; comdr. supply co., 45th Arty., C.A.C., service in U.S. and France, July 1918-Feb. 1919. Awarded Presidential Medal for Merit for defense work; recipient award Scientific Apparatus Makers, 1956. Town Meeting rep., Arlington, Mass., 1925-29; mem. aviation com. N.E. Regional Planning Commn., 1935-45; mem. corp., Mass. Inst. Tech., 1932-44, since 1952; pres. Alumni Assn., 1938-39; mem. Corp. Northeastern U., 1943-70, trustee, 1944-70; trustee Norwich U., 1946-70; trustee, American Child Guidance Foundation, 1953-70. Member adv. com. James Jackson Cabot Foundation (Norwich U.). Fellow Inst. Radio Engrs., Am. Inst. Elec. Engrs.; mem. Radio Mfrs. Assn. of Washington, D.C. (dir. 1926-32; pres. 1929-30). Dir., pres., chmn. Scientific Apparatus Makers Assn., 1938-52; treas. and trustee New England Industrial Research Found., Incorporated, 1938-51. Vestryman Church of Epiphany, Winchester, Massachusetts, 1933-36. Clubs: Winchester Country (Winchester); Arlington Rifle (Woburn, Mass.); Technology (New York); Commercial (Boston); Kennebunk Winchester MA Died May 1970.

RICHMOND, KENNETH CALVIN, corporate exec.; b. Marion, N.Y., Apr. 23, 1894; s. John E. and Julia (Goodrich) R.; ed. Univ. of Rochester; B.S., Mass. Inst. Tech., 1917; m. Frances N. Comstock, Apr. 23, 1921;children—Gail E. (Mrs. Victor Matthews), Kenneth C., Patricia Ann (Mrs. Thomas J. Gorman) Nancy Hanks (Mrs Henry Mueller, Jr.). Industrial engr. Miller, Franklin, Bassett & Co., N.Y. City, 1920-22; controller The Stein-Bloch Co., Rochester, N.Y., 1923-27; v.p. and treas. Abraham & Straus, Inc., dept. store, Bklyn., 1928-64, exec. v.p., 1964-69; v.p. Federated Dept. Stores, Inc. Mem. exec. com. mchts. Inst. Retail Mgmt., N.Y.U.; chmn. Nat. Controllers Congress; founder, chmn. bd. N.Y. State Council Retail Mchts., 17 years; officer U.S. C. of C.; mem. Citizens Adv. Com. to Gov. Harriman; 1st sponsor, chmn. Asso. Merchandising Controllers Group. Served in World War I, lt (j.g.) USNR. Awarded Navy Cross, Legion of Honor. Mem. Eta Mu Pi, Alpha Delta Phi. Home: Garden City NY Died Jan. 20, 1969; buried Woodlawn Cemetery, Wellsville NY

RICHTER, CONRAD MICHAEL, author; b. Pine Grove, Pa., Oct. 13, 1890; s. John Absalom and Charlotte Esther (Henry) R.; educated Susquehanna Acad. and High Sch.; Litt.D., Susquehanna U., 1944, U. N.M., 1958, Lafayette Coll., 1966; LL.D., Temple Univ., 1966; L.H.D., Lebanon Valley Coll., Annville, Pa., 1966; m. Harvena Achenbach, Mar. 24, 1915; 1 dau., Harvena. Editor Patton (Pa.) Weekly Courier, 1910; reporter for Johnstown (Pa.) and Pittsburgh papers, began contributing to Mitchell Kennerly's Forum and other periodicals, then to general magazines; short story, Brothers of No Kin, selected by Edward O'Brien as his choice for 1914. Member National Institute of Arts and Letters. P.E.N., Authors' League. Recipient gold medal for literature from Soc. of Librarians of N.Y. U., 1942, for Sea of Grass, and The Trees; received Pulitzer prize for fiction for The Town, 1951; Nat. Book award for The Waters of Kronos, 1961. Author: Early Americana and Other Stories, 1936; Sea of Grass, 1937; The Trees, 1940; Tacey Cromwell, 1942; The Free Man, 1943; The Fields, 1946; Always Young and Fair, 1947; The Town, 1950; The Light in the Forest, 1953; The Mountain on the Desert, 1955; The Lady, 1957; The Waters of Kronos, 1960; A Simple Honorable Man, 1962; The Grandfathers, 1964; Individualists Under the Shade Trees in A Vanishing America, 1964; A Country of Strangers, 1966; The Awakening Land, 1966; Over the Blue Mountain, 1967; The Aristocrat, 1968. Collector early Am. life and speech. Home: Pine Grove PA Died Oct. 30, 1968.

RICHTER, EMIL HEINRICH;, b. Leobschutz, Germany, Jan. 2, 1869; s. of Max and Emily (Waagen) R.; ed. largely under pvt. tuition, in Switzerland; unmarried. Came to America, 1888; studied painting and sculpture; worked at World's Fair decorations, Chicago, 1892; with Mus. Fine Arts, Boston, since 1899, asso. in the print dept., Sept. 1918-—. Contbr. on art topics. Home: Santa Barbara CA‡

RICHTER, GISELA MARIE AUGUSTA, archaeologist; b. Aug. 15, 1882; ed. Girton Coll., Cambridge U., Eng., Brit. Sch. Archaeology, Athens; Litt.D., Cambridge U. and Trinity Coll., Dublin, Ireland; L.H.D. (hon.), Smith Coll.; D.F.A., Rochester U.; Ph.D., (hon.), U. Basel (Switzerland); Litt.D. (hon.), Oxford (Eng.) U. Asst. dept. Greek and Roman art N.Y. Met. Mus. Art, N.Y.C., 1906-20, asst. curator, asso. curator, 1920-25, curator, 1925-48, hon. curator, curator emeritus, 1948-72. Recipient Achievement award Am. Assn. U. Womens, 1944; medal Am. Acad. Rome, 1955; Isabella d'Este award, 1965; Gold medal Am. Archaeol. Inst., 1968. Life fellow Met. Mus. Art; mem. Soc. Antiquaries (London), Am. Philos. Soc., Brit. Acad. Acad. Nazionale dei Lincei, Acad. di Archeologia Naples, Acad. Pontificia di Archeologia (Rome). Author: The Craft of Athenian Pottery, 1923; Ancient Furniture, 1926; The Sculpture and Sculptors of the Greeks, 1929, 4th edit., 1970; Animals in Greek Sculpture, 1930; Kouroi, 1942, 3d edit., 1970; Archaic Attic Gravestones, 1944; Greek Painting, 1944; Roman Portraits, 1949; Archaic Greek Art, 1949; Three Critical Periods in Greek Sculpture, 1952; Greek Portraits I, 1955; Ancient Italy, 1955; Handbook of Greek Art, 1959, 6th edit., 1969; Greek Portraits II, 1959; Greek Portraits III, 1960; The Archaic Gravestones of Attica, 1961; Greek Portraits IV, 1962, Greek Portraits V, 1964; The Portraits of the Greek, 3 vols., 1965; The Furniture of the Greeks, Etrsucans and Romans, vols., 1965; The Furniture of the Greeks, Etrsucans and Romans, 1966; Korai, Archaic Greek Maidens, 1968; The Engraved Gems of the Greeks, Etruscans and Romans, Part I, 1968, Part II, 1971. Asso. editor: The Am. Jour. of Archaeology. Address: Rome Italy Died Dec. 24, 1972.

RICHTER, RICHARD BIDDLE, physician; b. La Porte, Ind., May 9, 1901; s. Harry Walter and Elizabeth (Biddle) R.; S.B., U. Chicago, 1922; M.D., Rush Medical Coll., 1925; m. Gudrun Anderson, Jan. 27, 1926;children—Tor, Anders. Interne Presbyn. Hosp., Chicago, 1924-25; grad. work in neurology, Rush Med. Coll., 1925-30, asst. clin. prof. neurology, 1932-39; asst. prof. medicine, U. of Chicago, 1936-45, asso. prof. of medicine, 1945-46, prof. of neurology, 1946-71; attending neurologist, Albert Merritt Billings Hosp., 1936-71, Cook County Hosp., 1934-38. Mem. American Neurological Assn. (pres. 1963), Am. Association of Neuropathologists (president 1960-61), Assn. for Research Nervous and Mental Diseases, Am. Acad. Neurology, American Association for Advancement of Sci., A.M.A., Chicago Neurol. Soc. (past pres.), Chicago Med. Soc., Phi Beta Kappa, Alpha Omega Alpha, Sigma Xi. Clubs: Quadrangle, Chicago Literary (Chicago). Mem. editorial adv. bd., Jour. of Neuropathology and Experimental Neurology since 1950, and Neurology, 1950-71. Home: Chesterton IN Died Apr. 6, 1971.

RICKARD, THOMAS ARTHUR, mining engr.; b. Pertusola, Italy, Aug. 29, 1864; s. Thomas and Octavia Rachel (Forbes) R. (both English); early edn. in Russia and at Queen's Coll., Taunton, Eng.; U. of London, 1881; asso., Royal Sch. of Mines, London, 1885; Sc.D., Colo. Sch. Mines, 1927; came to U.S., 1885; m. Marguerite Lydia Rickard, Dec. 20, 1898. Assayer and surveyor, Colo., 1885-87; mine mgr., Calif., 1887-89; travel and examination of mines in Australia and New Zealand, 1889-91; mine mgr., France, 1891-91; state geologist of Colo., 1895-1901; examining mines in Can. and W. Australia, 1896-98; consulting mining engr. at Denver, during intervals. Editor Engineering and Mining Journal, 1903-05; editor Mining and Scientific Press. San Francisco, 1906-09, The Mining Magazine, London, 1909-15, Mining and Scientific Press, San Francisco, 1915-22; contbg. editor Engring. and Mining Jour.-Press, 1922-29. Lecturer, mining geology, Harvard, 1912-15. Fellow Royal Anthrop. Inst.; mem. Am. Inst. Mining and Metall. Engrs. (hon.), Instn. Mining and Metallurgy, London (gold medalist 1932). Pres. Calif. branch English-Speaking Union, 1926-32. Club: Union (Victoria, B.C.). Author: Stamp-Milling of Gold Ores, 1897; Across the San Juan Mountains, 1903; The Sampling and Estimation of Ore in a Mine, 1904; The Copper Mines of Lake Superior, 1905; Journeys of Observation, 1908; Through the Yukon and Alaska, 1909; Flotation Process, 1916; Technical Writing, 1919; Man and Metals, 1932; A History of American Mining, 1932, Retrospect, 1937; The Romance of Mining, 1944. Home: 33 Sylvan Lane, Victoria BC‡

RICKENBACKER, EDWARD VERNON (EDDIE"), aviator; b. Columbus, O., Oct. 8, 1890; s. William and Elizabeth R.; Dr. Aeronautical Sci., Pa. Mil. Coll., 1938, Brown U., Siloam Springs, 1940 U. of Miami, 1941; D.Sc., U. of Tampa (Fla.), 1942; L.H.D., U. Founds. and Am. Theol. Sem., Wilmington, Del., 1943; Sc. D., Westminster Coll., New Wilmington, Pa., 1944; LL.D., Okla. City U., 1944, Capital U., Columbus, O., 1945, Coll. of South Jersey, 1948, Hamilton Coll., 1956, William Jewell Coll., 1962; Dr. Eng., Lehigh U., 1948; Sc.D. (hon.), Lafayette Coll., Easton, Pa., 1952; Sc. D., The Citadel, Charleston, S.C., 1954, Ohio State U., 1957; graduate Internat. Correspondence Sch.; m. Mrs. Adelaide F. Durant, Sept. 16, 1922; children—David E., William F. Became widely known as auto-racer and won championships at nat. and internat. meets; accompanied Gen. Pershing to France as mem. Motor Car Staff, June 1917; trans. to Air Service at own request, Aug. 25, 1917, and assigned as engr. officer to Issoudon Tng. Field; became comdg. officer 94th Aero Pursuit Squadron, the first Am. aero unit to participate actively on the Western front (this unit was credited with 69 victories-the largest number of victories of any Am. unit-Rickenbacker heading the list with 26 victories to his credit); was the first comdg. officer to conduct his own squadron into Coblenz; retired at close of war with rank of capt. World War II activities included; spl. mission for sec. of War to England, So. Pacific, N. Africa, Iran, India, China, Russia, Iceland, Greenland and Aleutians. Awarded Medal of Merit, 1947; awarded D.S.C. with 9 oak leaves, Congressional Medal of Honor (U.S.); Legion of Honor, Croix de Guerre with 4 palms (French). Silver Buffalo Boy Scouts Am., 1944, Big Brother of the Year, 1953. V.p. Am. Airways, Inc., asst. to pres. Aviation Corp., 1932-33; v.O. North Am. Aviation, Inc., 1933-34; gen. mgr. Eastern Air Lines, Inc., 1935; pres., gen. mgr., director, 1938-53, chairman bd., 1954-63; director Wackenhut Corp., Fla. Press. Air Force Aid Soc. Mem. exec. bd. Boy Scouts Am.; dir. Boys' Clubs of Am. Forced down while on a Pacific flight, 1942, rescued after 24 days at sea on a life raft. Author: Fighting the Flying Circus, 1919; Seven Came Through, 1943; Rickenbacker An Autobiography, 1967. Home: New York City NY Died July 23, 1973.

RICKERBY, ARTHUR BURROUGHS, photographer; b. N.Y.C., Mar. 15, 1921; s. Frank and Charlotte (Burroughs) R.; B.A., Duke; m. Wanda A. Pfrinder, Oct. 30, 1956; children—Arthur Burroughs, Bradford Emil, David Grady. With U.P; free-lance photographer; staff photographer Life mag., until 1972. Photographs rep. permanent collection Mus. Modern art, N.Y.C. Served with photog. unit USNR, World War II. Recipient photog. citation U.S. Navy; one of 10 photographers featured in Men and Sport, Gallery Modern Art, N.Y.C., 1968. Home: Bethel CT Died 1972.

RIDABOCK, RAYMOND BUDD, artist; b. Stamford, Conn., Feb. 16, 1904; s. Harvey Millington and Alice (Budd) R.; student Williams Coll., 1922-24, Columbia U. Extension, 1928-29; m. Nancy Hough, Feb. 17, 1943; 1 dau., Joan (Mrs. George Crossman II). Exhibited Am. Water Color Soc., Art U.S.A., Audubon Artists; Balt. Mus., Boston Arts Festival, Butler Inst., Berlin Acad. Art, Pa. Acad., Inst. Contemporary Art, Boston, Wadsworth Atheneum, IBM Galleries, Lever House, N.Y. World's Fair, Watercolor U.S.A., U.S. Embassy, Lima, U.S. Mission, Geneva, Williams Coll., Munson-Williams-Proctor Inst., Norfolk Mus., Va., Del. Art Center and others; traveling shows Am. Watercolor Soc. Instr. Silvermine Coll. Art, 1958-70, Greenwich Art Center, 1962-70. Vice pres. Danbury area Tb and Health Assn. (1959-62, pres. 1962-65). Recipient 55 art awards including Audubon Artists medal honor, Williams Coll. Purchase award. Fellow Silvermine Guild (bd. dirs. 1958-65, 67-70); mem. Am. Watercolor Soc., Audubon Artists, Casein Soc., Conn. Acad., Conn. Watercolor Soc., Delta Psi. Club: St. Anthony (N.Y.C.). Episcopalian. Home: Redding Ridge CT Died 9, 1970.

RIDDER, HERMAN HENRY, publisher; b. New York, N.Y., June 25, 1908 s. Bernard Herman and Hilda (Luyties) R.; student, Blessed Sacrament Acad., All Hallows Inst., student, Columbia; m. Virginia Randolph, Feb. 11, 1938 (divorced); 1 dau., Marsha Randolph; m. 2d, Florence Murphy Pearson, April 18, 1953; one adopted son, Thomas P. LeBosquet. Publisher St. Paul (Minn.) Daily News, 1937; publisher, St. Paul Dispatch and Pioneer Press, 1945-69; v.p. Northwest Publs.; pres. and dir. Ridder Publications publisher of Independent-Press-Telegram, Long Beach, Cal., 1952-69. Served with U.S. Marine Corps, disch. as maj. Group Intelligence Officer, Okinawa, World War II. Awarded Bronze Star. Mem. Reserve Officers of the Naval Services, Marine Corps Reserve Officers Assn., C. of C. Clubs: Long Beach Yacht; Racquet, Thunderbird Country (Palm Springs). Home: Long Beach CA Died Sept. 15, 1969; buried Rye Beach NH

RIDDICK, CARL W., ex-congressman; b. Wells, Minn., Feb. 25, 1872; s. Isaac Hancock and Alice (Wood) R.; student Lawrence U., Appleton, Wis., and Albion (Mich.) Coll. Owner and publisher White Pigeon (Mich.) Journal, 1897-99, Winamac (Ind.) Republican, 1899-1910; sec. Rep. Ind. State Central Com., campaigns 1906, 08; settled on Govt. homestead in Mont., 1910; county assessor Fergus Co., Mont., 2 terms, 1915-18 inclusive; mem. 66th and 67th Congresses (1919-23), 2d Mont. Dist.; Rep. nominee for U.S. senator, 1924. Home: Riva MD‡

RIDDLE, JAMES MARION, JR., corp. exec.; b. Nashville, Nov. 18, 1913; s. James Marion and Clymetra (Boykin) R.; E.E., Ill. Inst. Tech., 1934; m. Grace Colbert Graver, Apr. 15, 1943; children—Beth Graver, Virginia Boykin. Engr., RCA Corp., 1935-45; pres. Narco Sci. Industries, Ft. Washington, Pa., 1945-65, chmn., chief exec. officer, from 1965; adv. bd. Girard Trust Bank, Phila., OTC Securities Fund. Chmn. spl. com. Radio Tech. Commn. Aeros., Washington, from 1960. Member vis. com. Drexel Inst. Tech. Served with USAAF, World War II. Mem. Aviation Distbrs.-Mfrs. Assn. (pres. 1955-56), Sportsmens Pilot Assn., Soc. Quiet Birdmen, Alpha Tau Omega. Clubs: Cricket, Aviation (bd. govs.), Peale (Phila.); Mantoloking (N.J.) Yacht (bd. govs.). Home: Ambler PA Died Feb. 15, 1970; buried Philadelphia PA

RIDDLE, OSCAR, biologist; b. Cincinnati, Ind., Sept. 27, 1877; s. Jonathan and Amanda Emiline (Carmichael) R.; A.B., Ind. U., 1902, LL.D., 1933; Ph.D., U. Chgo., 1907; D.H.C., Cath. U. of Chile, 1946; m. Leona Lewis, June 3, 1937. Tchr. biology Model and Tng. Sch., San Juan, P.R., 1899-1901; mem. natural history expdn. to Orinoco River, 1901, Cuba, 1902; tchr. physiology Central High Sch., St. Louis, 1903-05; asst. in zoology U. Chgo., 1904-07, asso. in zoology and exptl. therapeutics, 1908, instr., 1908-11; travel and study in Europe, 1910-11; research asso. at Chicago and Cold Spring Harbor, Carnegie Instn., 1912-14; research staff Carnegie Sta. for Exptl. Evolution, 1914-45; lectr. S.A. and Mexico, 1945-47. Chmn. Am. delegations 2d Internat. Congress for Sex Research, London, 1930; del. Carnegie Instn. to 2d Pan-Am. Congress of Endocrinology, Montevideo, 1941. Capt. with U.S. Army, 1918-19. Recipient humanist of yr. award Am. Humanist Assn., 1958, distinguished service certificate award National Association of Biology Teachers, 1958. Fellow of the A.A.A.S. (vice pres. 1935), American Acad. Arts and Scis., fgn. corr. Academia Nacional de Medicina, Buenos Aires, Soc. de Patologia Clinica, Brazil, Soc. de Biologia, Montevideo and Santiago, Physiological Soc. of India, Facultad de Ciencias Biologicas y Medicas, Santiago; hon. mem. Societa Italiana di Endocrinologia, Royal Soc. Arts London; mem. Soc. Linneenne de Lyon, Am. Philos. Soc., Nat. Acad. Scis., Am. Soc. Zoologists, Am. Physiol. Soc., Genetics Soc. Am., Am. Soc. Naturalists, Washington Acad. Scis., Soc. for Study of Evolution, Assn. for Study of Internal Secretions (pres. 1928-29), Soc. Exptl. Biology and Medicine, Harvey Soc., Nat. Inst. Social Scis., American Rationalist Fedn. (president 1959-60), Am. Inst. City N.Y. (trustee, v.p.; gold medal 1934), Sigma Xi, Pi Gamma Mu, Phi Delta Theta, Gamma Alpha. Author: The Unleashing of Evolutionary Thought (awarded 2 first prizes), 1955. Contbr. papers on physiology of development and reproduction, physiol. and chem. basis of sex, heredity, endocrinology. Sect. editor Biol. Abstracts, 1926-46; Excerpta Medica, 1946-68; mem. publ. bd. Endocrinology, 1931-34, 39-42. Home: Plant City FL Died Nov. 29, 1968; buried Grandview Cemetery, Bloomfield IN

RIDGELY, HILLIARD SAMUEL, lawyer; b. at Siam, Ia., Oct. 16, 1874; s. Eli and Olive Marie (Allen) R.; grad. North Platte (Neb.) High Sch.; LL.B., U. of Neb., 1897; m. Evea J. Fenwick, of North Platte, June 21, 1899. Began practice at North Platte, Neb., 1897; co. atty., Lincoln Co., Neb., 1899-1902; city atty., North Platte, 1902; city atty., Cody, Wyo., 1903, Basin, Wyo., 1906; U.S. dist. atty., Dist. of Wyo., by appmt. of President Taft, Jan. 15, 1912; Republican. Presbyn. Mason (32 deg.). Club: Industrial. Address: Cheyenne WY‡

RIDGES, ROBERT PAUL, business exec.; b. Chgo., Oct. 13, 1903; s. Robert Alexander and Agnes M. (Dillon) R.; student U. Denver, 1922-23; B.S. Northwestern U., 1926; m. Margaret Elder Wilson, Aug. 8, 1925 (dec.); 1 dau., Jane Wilson (Mrs. William Reed Olsen). Pub. accountant Lybrand, Ross Bros. & Montgomery, Chgo., 1926-32, N.Y.C., 1933-36; gen. mgr. Ill. Watch Case Co. Elgin, 1932-33; with Alexander Smith & Sons Carpet Co., Yonkers, N.Y., 1936-52; asst. to treas., 1937, sec., controller and vice pres., 1948-52; treas. Quitman Mills, Inc. (Ga.), 1947-52; v.p. finance. S.B. Penick & Co., 1953-67, also dir., mem. exec. com., until 1967. Mem. Yonker Mayor's Adv. Com. on Revenues. 1949-50. C.P.A., N.Y. State. Mem. Am. Inst. C.P.A.'s. Republican. Contbr. articles to profl. publs. Home: Lyme CT Died Nov. 29, 1972; interred Lyme CT

RIDGEWAY, GEORGE L., bus. cons.; b. Bridgeville, N.Y., Sept. 17, 1901; s. Willis Everett and Chloe (Loveland) R.; A.B., Princeton University, 1923; B.Litt., Queens College, Oxford University, 1928; married to Florence Grey Fowler, June 19, 1930; children—James Robin, George David, Christopher Worth (deceased). Master, Lake Placid (New York) Sch. for Boys, 1923-24, Riverdale Country Sch., 1924-26; asso. prof. history, Hamilton Coll., Clinton, N.Y., 1929-30, asso. prof. govt., 1930-31; asst. prof. history, Wells Coll., Aurora, N.Y., 1933-34, asso. prof. history, 1934-39, prof. and chmn. dept. of history and govt., 1939-46; asst. in U.S. Dept. of State, 1942-46, specialist in United Kingdom Div. of Commercial Policy, 1945-46; dir. econ. research, Internat. Bus. Machines Corp., 1946-55; cons. pub. affairs, 1955-61; ofcl. Internat. Labour Office, Geneva, Switzerland, 1961-63; cons. international affairs IBM, 1963-68. Rep. Internat. C. of C. to Statis. Commn. of UN Econ., Social Council, 1947-61; mem. com. bus. statistics U.S. C. of C. Democrat. Episcopalian. Clubs: Princeton (N.Y.); Highlands Country (Garrison, N.Y.); Mecox Yacht (Bridgehampton, N.Y.). Author: Merchants of Peace (for Carnegie Endownment for Internat. Peace), 1938, rev. 1959. Contbr. to The Dictionary of Am. Biography. Home: Garrison-on-Hudson NY Died May 11, 1968.

RIDGWAY, GRANT, mfg. exec.; b. Shawneetown, Ill., May 19, 1868; s. Thomas S. and Jane (Docker) R.; student Lafayette Coll., Easton, Pa., 1887-91; m. Ethel Saunders, Nov. 11, 1897; children—Virginia (Mrs. L. T. Ellis), Harriette (Mrs. Samuel Clark), Jane (Mrs. W. B. Plumer). Started as office boy Northwestern Yeast Co., 1895, now pres. Republican. Presbyterian. Home: 207 Cumberland Av., Kenilworth IL Office: 1750 N. Ashland Av., Chicago IL*‡

RIDINGS, EUGENE WARE, army officer; b. Grant County, Okla., Jan. 9, 1899; s. Samuel P. and Nettie (Lewis) R.; student Oklahoma U., 1917-18, Marion (Ala.) Mil. Inst., 1918-19; B.S., U.S. Mil. Acad., 1923; grad. Inf. Sch., 1931, Command and Gen. Staff Sch., 1937, Army War Coll., 1940; m. Vera Bernhard, Oct. 3, 1928; 1 son, Eugene Ware. Commd. 2d lt., U.S. Army, 1923, and advanced through the grades to brig. gen., Jan. 1945. Decorated Bronze Star, Silver Star with oak leaf cluster, Legion of Merit with oak leaf cluster. Home: Staunton VA Died 1969.

RIDLEY, CLARENCE SELF, army officer; b. Corydon, Ind., June 22, 1883; s. William and Margaret (Inman) R.; B.S., U.S. Mil. Acad., 1905; m. Bessie Thomson, July 10, 1907; m. Gladys Peard Kay, July 21, 1965. Commd. 2d lt. Corps of Engrs., U.S. Army, 1905, advanced through the grades to col., 1935, brig. gen., 1938, maj. gen., 1941; gov. Panama Canal and pres. and dir. Panama R.R. Co., 1936-40; duty with 3d Div., Fort Lewis, Wash., 1940-41; comdg. gen. 6th Div., Fort Snelling, Jan. 1941; chief military mission to Iran, 1942-46; ret. 1947. Decorated D.S.M., 1946; Order of Hamayoun, 2d Class of Iran, 1947; Officer Order of Leopold by King of Belgium. Address: Carmel CA Died July 26, 1969; buried U.S. Military Academy Cemetery West Point NY

RIEBEL, FRANK A., physician; b. Columbus, O., Oct. 28, 1903; s. John Augustus and Mabel (Kiner) R.; B.S., Ohio State U., 1923, M.D., 1925; postgrad. U. Vienna, 1925; m. 2d. Violet Miller, Nov. 8, 1943; children—Michael Stuart, Linda, Frank; (by previous marriage) Barbara Jeanne, Nancy Ann. Radiologist, Met. Hosp., N.Y.C., 1926; resident radiotherapist, Montefiore Hosp., N.Y.C., 1927; fencing coach Ohio State U., Columbus, 1928-47, now asso. prof. dept. radiology. Chmn. fencing com. Nat. Coll. Athletic Assn., 1944-48; mem. Olympic Com., 1948. Fellow Am. Coll. Radiology; mem. Radiol. Soc. N.A. Office: Columbus OH Died June 6, 1972.

RIEBER, TORKILD, oil executive; b. Voss, Norway, Mar. 13, 1882; s. Hans and Kristie (Helland) R.; ed. high sch. and nautical acad. in Norway; m. Miriam Marbe, Sept. 26, 1909; children—Ruth, Harold. Came to U.S., 1898, naturalized, 1904. Went to sea, 1897, serving in various capacities on sailing and steam vessels, finally as master of one of the first tankers to load oil from the Spindletop Field in Tex.; tanker purchased by The Texas Co., 1905; served in marine and refining depts. of Texas Co., ashore in various capacities, until 1919; with J. S. Cullinan interests, 1919-27, becoming in 1926 v.p. Am. Republics Corp.; elected v.p. The Texas Co. in charge export and marine depts., 1927, dir. and mem. exec. com., 1928, chmn. bd., 1935-40; pres. Barber Oil Corp. and its predecessor Barber Asphalt Corp. 1942-56, chairman of the board, 1956-68; chairman American Gilsonite Company, Salt Lake City, 1946-68; dir. Hotel Waldorf-Astoria Corp., N.Y.C., U.S. Lines Co., Am. Steamship Owners Mut. Protection & Indemnity Assn., Inc. (both N.Y.C.). Mem. Am. Petroleum Inst. (dir.). Home: New York City NY Died Aug. 10, 1968.

RIEMAN, CHARLES ELLET, banker; b. Baltimore, Md., Dec. 4, 1870; s. Joseph Henry and Anne (Lowe) R.; A.B., Princeton, 1892; m. Elizabeth Taylor Goodwin, Feb. 8, 1899. Began in banking with Comml. and Farmers Nat. Bank, 1894; became pres. Western Nat. Bank of Baltimore, 1906, now chmn. bd.; dir. Fifth Dist. Federal Res. Bd., Md. Life Ins. Co., Baltimore Equitable Soc., Eutaw Savings Bank, Safe Deposit & Trust Co. Pres. Presbyn. Eye, Ear and Throat Charity Hosp., 30 yrs.; trustee Peabody Inst., 27 yrs. Presbyterian. Clubs: Merchants, Maryland (Baltimore); Ivy, Nassau (Princeton). Home: 10 E. Mt. Vervon Pl. Office: 14 N. Eutaw St., Baltimore MD*‡

RIEMER, GUIDO CARL LEO, educator; b. Munchenbernsdorf, Germany, Aug. 27, 1873; s. Karl Titus and Agnes (Heussler) R.; A.B., Bucknell U., Pa., 1895, A.M., 1896, LL.D., 1926; A.M. Harvard, 1900; univs. of Leipzig and Berlin, 1903-05; Ph.D., Leipzig, 1905; m. Mary Grier Youngman, of Danville, Pa., Dec. 23, 1901; children—Karl, Grier, Hugo, George, Isabel, Hans. Came to U.S., 1882. Prof. German, Bucknell U., 1901-18; mem. Dept. of Public Instruction of Pa., 1918-23; pres. State Normal Sch., Bloomsburg, Pa., 1923-27; pres. State Teachers Coll., Clarion, Pa., 1928-37; prof. of speech, State Teachers Coll., Kutztown, Pa., since 1937. Mem. N.E.A., Nat. Assn. of Teachers of Speech, Pa. State Ednl. Assn., Phi Gamma Delta, Phi Delta Kappa. Rotarian. Author: Die Adjektiva bei Wolfram von Eschenbach, 1906; Worterbuch und Reimverzeichnis zu dem Armen Heinrich Hartmanns von Aue, 1912. Translator; G. Freytag's Doctor Luther, 1916. Contbr. articles on education. Home: Kutztown PA‡

RIEPE, CARL CHRISTOPH, lawyer; b. Burlington, Ia., Mar. 9, 1885; s. Fred and Sophie (Frewert) R.; A.B., State U. Ia., 1910, LL.B., 1912; m. Dorothy I. Ripley, Feb. 20, 1915; 1 son, Carl R. Admitted to Ia. bar, 1912; since practiced in Burlington; mem. firm Hirsch, Riepe & Wright, and predecessor firm, 1913-69; atty. Des Moines County, 1919-20. Mem. Ia. Hwy. Commn., 1926-35; U.S. commr., 1917-20, referee in bankruptcy, 1925-26. Mem. Am., Ia. bar assns., Internat. Assn. Ins. Counsel, Am. Counsel Assn., Burlington C. of C. (past pres.), Phi Delta Phi, Sigma Alpha Epsilon. Mason, Elk. Home: Burlington IA Died Jan. 18, 1969.

RIETMULDER, JAMES, pub. exec.; b. Paterson, N.J., Jan. 20, 1915; s. James and Dora (Harding) R.; student N.J. State Tchrs. Coll., 1933-36, B.S., N.Y. U., 1942; m. Jean Waddle, July 8, 1950; children—Joy, Jill, James, Jay, Jon, Joseph. Asst. editor World Affairs Books, 1936-37, lit. sec. Nat. Peace Conf., 1937-39; asst. asso. dir. Assn. Press, 1937-51, dir., 1952-64; exec. v.p. Stackpole Books, 1964-67, pres., 1968-72. Served to 2d lt. AUS, 1943-45. Mem. Nat. Assn. Social Workers, Direct Mail Advt. Assn. Club: Advertising (N.Y.). Home: Lewisberry PA Died July 27, 1942.

RIFE JOHN MAYNARD, real estate co. exec.; b. West Milton, O., July 22, 1917; s. Carl S. and Elizabeth (Spencer) R.; student Columbia, 1936-37, Pace Inst. 1938; m. Mary Knox Elliott, Apr. 6, 1943; children—John M. Guerin DuBose. Pub. relations and sales Gen. Motors Corp., 1936-52; sales gen. agt. sales mgr. Life Ins. Co. Ala., Gadsden, 1952-58; v.p. Seaboard Properties, Ocean Reef, N. Key Largo Fla., 1958-69; dir. First Nat. Bank Tavernier, First Nat. Bank, Upper Keys, Keys Investment Corp. Served with AUS, 1942-45; ETO. Republican. Episcopalian. Clubs: Ocean Reef, Racquet, Coral Reef Yacht, Miami, Palm Bay. Address: North Key Largo FL Died Aug. 7, 1969.

RIGDON, CHARLES LOAMMI, lawyer; b. Jasper Co., Ill., Mar. 2, 1876; s. David Baker and Mary Eliza (Coan) R.; A.B., U. of Wyo., 1902; LL.B., U. of Kan., 1904; m. Etta Goodrich Lund, of Dell Rapids, S.Dak., June 12, 1907. Began practice at Wheatland, Wyo., 1904; county and pros. atty., Laramie Co., Wyo., 1908-12; U.S. atty., Dist. of Wyo., 1914-21. Democrat. Baptist. Mason (32 deg.), Elk. Home: 2323 Carey Av., Cheyenne WY‡

RIGGINS, H. MCLEOD, physician; b. Charlotte, N.C., Nov. 30, 1900; s. Charles Robert and Eleanor (De Armond) R.; B.S., U. of N.C., 1922; M.D., Jefferson Med. Coll., 1924; m. Mildred Kimberly, November 16, 1929; children—Robert C.K., Anne Kimberly. Intern. Phila. Gen. Hosp., 1924; asst. physician Loomis Sanatorium, Loomis, N.Y., 1926-29; resident physician Bellevue Hosp., Chest Service, N.Y. City, 1929; chief resident physician Bellevue Hosp. Chest Service, 1931, 1932; vis. physician Columbia U. Div. Bellevue Hosp.; attending physician N.Y. Eye and Ear Infirmary; formerly asso. clin. prof. medicine Coll. Physicians and Surgeons, Columbia U.; med. dir. N.Y. Cancer Research Inst., 1959-68. Head U.S. delegation XVI Conf. Internat. Union Against Tb, Istanbul, Turkey, 1959; del. Nat. Health Council. Fellow N.Y. Acad. Medicine (chmn. hist. and cultural sect. 1959-61); mem. Am. Thoracic Soc. (past v.p. and pres.), New York Soc. for Thoracic Surgery (past sec.-treas., v.p. and pres.), New York Tb. and Health Assn. (mem. bd. dirs.), Nat. Tb. Assn. (pres. 1959-60), Am. Assn. for Thoracic Surgery, N.Y. County Med. Soc., N.Y. State Med. Soc., Am. Med. Assn., Am. Coll. Physicians, Am. Clin. and Climatol. Assn., N.Y. Acad. Medicine, Bellevue Alumni Assn., Kappa Psi. Presbyterian. Club: University, River (New York City). Co-editor of Streptomycin and Dihydrostreptomycin in Tb., 1949. Author numerous papers and articles in various med. and sci. jours. Home: Mercer Island WA Died Apr. 1973.

RIGGS, ROBERT, artist; b. Decatur, Ill., Feb. 5, 1896; s. Frank O. and Alice M. Riggs; student Art Students League, N.Y.C., and Academie Julien, Paris. Travel in Europe, Africa, China, Siam, West Indies; works as commercial and non-commercial artist. Represented in Whitney Mus., Mus. Modern Art, Bklyn. Mus., Met. Mus., N.Y. Pub. Library, Pa. Museum, U.S. Library of Congress, Art Inst. Chgo., Copenhagen Mus., Los Angeles Mus., collection of King of Italy; life's work in lithography by Library of Congress Pennell Fund. Recipient Logan medal for water colors, Chicago Art Institute, 1926; recipient of the Logan medal for lithography, 1934; Eyre medal, 1932, Pennell medal, 1934; also Gribel medal and Championship prize, Art Directors medal 3 times; Art Dirs. medal for color, twice; for black and white, 7 times. Served as pvt. Base Hosp. 48, World War I. Collects Am. Indian and African material, including phonograph records of their music. Mem. N.A.D., Phila. Zool. Soc. Home: Philadelphia PA Died Apr. 15, 1970.

RIGGS, THEODORE FOSTER, surgeon; b. Hope Station, Dak. Ty., July 7, 1874; s. Thomas Lawrence and Cornelia Margaret (Foster) R.; B.A., Beloit (Wis.) College, 1898, LL.D., 1946; M.D., Johns Hopkins, 1903; house officer Johns Hopkins Hospital, 1903-04, Union Protestant Infirmary, Baltimore, 1904-07; studied Berlin and Berne, 1908; married Ida R. Smith, Chester, N.S., January 1, 1914 (died Feb. 5, 1915);

married 2d, Katharine Z. Cugle, Baltimore, Sept. 3, 1916; children—Thomas Lawrence II, Foster Logie. Pvt. asst. to Dr. Arthur W. Elting, Albany, N.Y., 1908; in practice at Pierre, S.D., since 1909. Fellow Am. Coll. Surgeons, Western Surg. Assn., Am. Bd. of Surgery; mem. S.D. State Med. Assn., A.M.A., Newcomen Soc., Sigma Chi. Republican. Conglist. Mason (K.T., Shriner), Elk. Home: Pierre SD‡

RIGGS, THEODORE SCOTT, ret. army officer; b. Ft. Leavenworth, Kan., Apr. 1, 1907; s. Kerr Tunis and Mary Virginia (Fosdick) R.; grad. Phillips Acad., Andover, Mass., 1924; B.S., U.S. Mil. Acad., 1928; student Imperial Defence Coll., London, Eng., 1951; m. Phillis Wey Symmonds, Jan. 11, 1930; children—Theodore Scott (U.S. Army), Robert M., Goerge T., David K. Commd. 2d lt., U.S. Army, 1928, advanced through grades to maj. gen., 1953, ret.; instr. U.S. Mil. Acad., 1934-38; chief staff U.S. Army Forces Middle East, 1942; dep. chief of staff Allied Land Forces So. Europe, 1952-53; chief information and edn., U.S. Army, 1955-56; comdg. gen. VI U.S. Army Corps, 1958-59; chief staff Combined Mil. Planning Staff, Central Treaty Orgn., Ankara, Turkey, 1959-60, ret., 1960. Decorated Legion of Merit with cluster; Order Brit. Empire. Mem. Assn. Grads. U.S. Mil. Acad., Andover Alumni Assn. Washington DC Died Aug. 10, 1970; buried Arlington Nat. Cemetery, Arlington VA

RIGSBEE, ALBERT VINSON, life ins. co. exec.; b. Durham, N.C., Mar. 26, 1925; s. Hubert Alexander and Annie (Crabtree) R.; M.D., U. Va., 1949; m. Patricia Moore, Nov. 24, 1949; children—Douglas Craig, Patricia Ann, Mark Allen. Asst. med. dir. Acacia Life Ins. Co., Washington, 1952-61, med. dir., 1961-69; postgrad. tng. Charlotte (N.C.) Meml. Hosp., also Harvard Med. Sch., Cambridge, Mass., 1962. Pres., Heart Assn. No. Va., 1966-67; chmn. Sci. Fair Judges, Va., 1955-65. Served to ensign USNR, World War II; to 1st lt. AUS, 1947-50; to capt. USAF, Korean War. Recipient Welburn award Arlington County Med. Soc., 1959. Mem. Assn. Med. Dirs. Home: Alexandria VA Died May 6, 1969.

RIHBANY, ABRAHAM MITRIE, clergyman; b. El-Shiweir, Lebanon, Syria, Aug. 27, 1869; s. Mitrie and Marsha (Mutter) R.; ed. Am. Boarding Sch., Suk El Gharb, Lebanon, 1886-88; came to U.S., 1891, landing in N.Y. City, with 9 cents; student Ohio Wesleyan U., Delaware, O., 1895-96; D.D., Meadville (Pa.) Theological Sem., 1922; m. Alice May Siegle, of Wauseon, O., Nov. 15, 1894; children—Marguerite R. (dec.), Edward H. Began preaching in Congl. Ch., Morenci, Mich., 1896; ordained Unitarian ministry, 1900; pastor 1st Ch., Toledo, 1902-11, Ch. of the Disciples (Unitarian) Boston, 1911-38, emeritus. Rep. Syrian socs. in America at Peace Conf., Paris, 1919. Club: Authors' (Boston). Author: A Far Journey, 1914; The Syrian Christ, 1916; Militant America and Jesus Christ, 1917; America, Save the Near East, 1918; The Hidden Treasure of Rasmola, 1920; Wise Men from the East and from the West, 1922; The Christ Story for Boys and Girls, 1923; Seven Days with God, 1926; The Five Titles of Jesus, 1940. Widely known as lecturer on contrasts and harmonies between Eastern and Western civilizations. Republican. Contbr. to mags. Home: Brookline MA‡

RIKER, IRVING, lawyer; b. Newark, N.J., May 7, 1896; s. Adrian and Louise C. (Dawson) R.; student Newark Acad., Lawrenceville Sch.; A.B., Princeton, 1917; law sch., Columbia, 1919-21; m. 1st Elizabeth A.M. Cumming, Oct. 27, 1921; children—William I., Robert A.; m. 2d Eleanor White, Aug. 11, 1941. Admitted to N.J. bar, 1921, practiced in Newark; mem. firm Riker, Danzig, Scherer & Brown. Chmn. bd. Fidelity Union Trust Co.; dir. Thomas & Betts Co., Inc., Hoffman-La Roche, Inc., Mutual Benefit Life Ins. Co. Trustee Point Pleasant (N.J.) Hosp. Served as 1st Lieutenant, Infantry, U.S. Army attached 316th Inf., assigned 2d Pioneer Inf., 1917-19. Mem. Am., N.J. State and Essex County (president 1943-44) bar assns. Clubs: Essex, Down Town (Newark, N.J.); Manasquan River Golf (N.J.); Cap and Gown (Princeton, N.J.). Home: Mantoloking NJ Died Dec. 1970.

RILEY, HENRY ALSOP, physician; b. New York, N.Y., July 23, 1887; s. Henry Augustus and Marianna (Littlefield) R.; ed. Collegiate Sch., N.Y., 1904; B.A., Yale, 1908; A.M., Columbia, 1912, M.D., 1912; Sc.D. (honorary), Columbia University, 1959; m. Mary Chapman Edgar, Oct. 6, 1917 (dec.); children—Edgar Alsop, Mary (Mrs. Herbert McCoy Patton, Jr.); m. 2d, Mrs. Sidney P. Henshaw, July 8, 1954. Interne, Presbyterian Hospital, 1913; hosp. appts. at Presbyterian, N.Y. Nursery and Child's, Volunteer, Vanderbilt Clinic, Neurol. Inst., N.Y. Orthopaedic, Post-Graduate, Englewood, Greenwich; pvt. practice in neurology and psychiatry, N.Y. City, 1916-63. Consulting neurologist, Neurol. Inst. of N.Y.; prof. emeritus clin. neurology Coll. of Phys. & Surg., Columbia U.; cons. neurologist, Presbyterian Hospital, N.Y.C. Served with the 105th Machine Gun Bn., Med. Corps. 1917-18; adjutant, N.Y. Neurosurg. Sch., War Dept., 1918. Mem. Med. Adv. Bd., Selective Service System, 1941-45. Decorated Chevalier, Legion of Honor (France), 1949. Honorary mem. Spanish Neurological Society, Italian Neurol. Soc.; corr. mem. Paris Neurol. Soc.; hon. mem. Soc. Neurology and Psychiatry of Rosario, Argentina; corr. mem. Acad. Medicine, Paris; mem. American Neurological Association, Am. Psychiatric Association, Am. Assn. Anatomists, Association Research in Nervous and Mental Disease, N.Y. Acad. of Medicine, Alpha Delta Phi, Sigma Xi, Alpha Omega Alpha. Clubs: University, Union (N.Y.C.). Author of books, including: (with F. Tilney) Form and Functions of the Central Nervous System, 1938; Atlas of the Basal Ganglia, Brain Stem and Spinal Cord, 1943. Home: New York City NY Died Nov. 1, 1966.

RILEY, HERBERT DOUGLAS, naval officer; b. Balt., Dec. 24, 1904; s. Marion Herbert and Sarah Maud (Mealy) R.; grad. Balt. Polytech. Inst., 1923; B.S., U.S. Naval Acad., 1927; grad. Nat. War Coll., 1950; divorced; 1 dau., Lynne Lovelace. Commd. ensign U.S. Navy, 1927, advanced through grades to vice adm., 1958; designated naval aviator, 1930; served in various aviation squadrons, 1929-41; operations officer patrol wings, Pacific, 1942, dep. comdg. naval officer (air), 1933-44; comdg. officer U.S.S. Makassar Strait, 1944-45; operations officer 1st Carrier Task Force, 1945; dep. airborne comdr. Bikini atomic bomb tests, 1946; strategic planner Office Chief Naval Operations, Navy Dept., 1946-47; naval asst. to sec. def. Forrestal, 1948-49, asst. chief staff plans Atlantic Fleet, 1950-51; dep. chief staff SACLANT, NATO, 1951-52; comdg. officer U.S.S. Coral Sea, 1952-53; chief staff Carrier Div. 2, 1953-54; dir. politico-mil. policy Office Chief Naval Operations, 1955-56; comdr. Carrier Div. 1, also attack carrier task force, 7th Fleet, 1957; chief staff U.S. Pacific Command, 1958-61; dep. chief naval operations, 1961-62; dir. Joint Staff, Joint Chiefs of Staff, 1962-64. Decorated D.F.C., also Bronze Star medal with combat V, Navy and Air Force Commendation medal (3) (U.S.); comdr. Order British Empire; Peruvian Air Cross 1st class. Mem. Md. Hist. Soc., S.A.R. Clubs: Chevy Chase (Md.); Army and Navy (Washington); Queen Anne (Md.). Home: Kent Island MD Died Jan. 17, 1973.

RILEY, THOMAS JOSEPH, editor; b. New Bedford, Mass., Mar. 10, 1908; s. Peter Joseph and Mary Alice Clementine (Murphy) R.; student Georgetown U., 1926-28; B.Lit., Columbia, 1930; m. Hilda Jean Sylvia, Nov. 28, 1935; children—Thomas Joseph, Jean (Mrs. Paul Murray), Rosemary (Mrs. Thomas E. Leen). Reporter for New York Am., 1930; reporter, feature writer, columnist New Bedford Evening Standard and Standard Times, 1931-32; news commentator radio sta. WNBH, New Bedford, 1933; mng. editor New Bedford News, 1934; asso. news editor news and spl. events dept. NBC, 1935-39; advt. specialist def. savs. staff Treasury Dept., 1941-42; rewrite man, feature writer Boston Am., 1943-59; editor editorial page, chief editorial writer Boston Record American Sunday Advertiser, 1960-70. Mem. International Association of Laryngectomees (member board directors). Clubs: Boston Cured Cancer (president 1967); Catholic Press (president 1961) (Boston). Home: Milton MA Died June 20, 1970; buried Milton Cemetery.

RINEHART, STANLEY MARSHALL, JR., publisher; b. Pittsburgh, Pa., Aug. 18, 1897; s. Dr. Stanley Marshall and Mary (Roberts) R.; student Harvard U., 1915-17; m. Mary Noble Doran, May 25, 1919 (divorced, 1929); children—Mary Roberts, II, George H. Doran; m. 2d, Frances A. Yeatman, July 28, 1933; 1 son, Stanley Marshall, III. Advertising mgr., v.p., G. H. Doran Co., N.Y. City, 1919-27; dir., Doubleday, Doran & Co., 1927-29; pres. and dir. Rinehart & Co., Inc. 1929-60; sr. v.p., dir. Holt, Rinehart and Winston, Co., Inc. 1929-60; sr. v.p., dir. Holt, Rinehart and Winston, Inc., 1960-69. Pvt., 2d lt., 83d Div., A.E.F., 1917-19. Republican. Episcopalian. Club: Harvard (N.Y.C.). Home: New York City NY Died Apr. 26, 1969.

RINGLAND, ADAM WEIR, clergyman; b. at Amity, Pa.; s. John Newton and Jane Bane (Weir) R.; B.A. and M.A., Centre Coll., Danville, Ky., 1872; grad. McCormick Theol. Sem., Chicago, 1875; (D.D., Otterbein, 1887); m. Elena H. Potter, of Mt. Pleasant, Ia., Apr. 29, 1875. Ordained Presbyn. ministry, 1875; pastor 1st Ch., Dubuque, Ia., 1875-6, Tuscola, Ill., 1877-8, Bement, Ill., 1878-84, 1st Ch., Duluth, Minn., 1884-93; pres. Macalester Coll., St. Paul, 1893-4; pastor Collingwood Ch., Toledo, O., 1894-6, 2d Ch., Evanston, Ill., 1896-8, 60th St. Ch., Chicago, 1898-1900, Berwyn, Ill., 1901-5; in pvt. business, McAlester, Okla., 1906-11; pastor 1st Ch., Denison, Tex., Nov. 19, 1911—. Dir. Dubuque Theol. Sch., 1875-98, McCormick Theol. Sem., 1888-98; corporator Presbyn. Ministers' Fund. Phila., 1889—. Republican. Mem. Phi Delta Theta (Ky. Alpha). Mason. Address: Denison TX‡

RINGSTAD, EDWARD OLSON, prof. psychology; b. Trondhjem, Norway, Oct. 18, 1871; s. Ole Johannesen and Randi (Tiller) R.; came to U.S., 1888; grad. Red Wing (Minn.) Sem., 1894; B.L., U. of Minn., 1898, M.L., 1899; studied U. of Wis.; m. Aagot Helland, Oct. 6, 1901. Teacher Red Wing Sem., college dept., 1899-1917; prof. psychology, St. Olaf Coll., since 1917. Mem. Pub. Bd. Norwegian Luth Ch. (former sec.); mem. Luth. Brotherhood America. Has specialized in problems of consciousness and human personality. Home: Northfield MN‡

RINGWALT, RALPH CURTIS, lawyer, author; b. Mt. Vernon, O., Feb. 19, 1874; s. John Shaffer and Julia Chamberlain (Curtis) R.; A.B., Harvard, 1895, LL.B., 1901; m. Harriet Stockbridge, of New York, Oct. 7, 1909. Instr. in argumentation and debating, 1895-8, lecturer in pub. speaking, 1901-4, Columbia Coll. Author: Briefs for Debate, 1896; Modern American Oratory, 1898; Briefs on Public Questions, 1905. Editor: American Public Problems Series. Contbr. to newspapers and mags. Address: 16 Gramercy Park, New York NY‡

RINSLAND, HENRY DANIEL, educator; Charlottesville, Va., Sept. 8, 1889; s. Louis and Lucinda (Hartman) R.; A.B., U. Okla., 1920, A.M., 1923; Ph.D., Columbia, 1935; m. Martha A. O'Daniel, July 7, 1918; 1 dau., Almeda. Tchr. and supt. schs., 1912-17; dir. guidance Ardmore City Schs., 1918-24; instr. advancing to prof. edn. U. Okla. since 1924, dir. ednl. research, 1930-48. Served as capt. and maj. Adj. Gen.'s Office, 1940-46. Fellow A.A.A.S.; mem. N.E.A., Am. Ednl. Research Assn., Nat. Soc. Study Edn., Am. Council on Measurements (pres., 1950-52), Am. Assn. Univ. Prof., Acacia (life), Phi Delta Kappa, Kappa Delta Pi. Episcopalian. Mason, Rotarian. Author: Analysis of Completion Sentences and Arithmetical Problems as Items for Intelligence Tests, 1935; Test Construction and Grading, 1937; A Basic Vocabulary for Elementary School Children, 1944; The Pupils Own Vocabulary Spellers, 1945; A Clinical Method of Grading, 1947 and 1949; several standardized tests; numerous articles. Editor Rinsland Teaching Tests for Oklahoma, since 1931; asso. editor Jour. of Exptl. Edn.; adv. editor Dictionary Educational Terms. Patents: Normal Curve Template and Rinsland's Rapid Scorer. Home: Norman OK Died Apr. 19, 1971.

RIPLEY, ALDEN LASSELL, artist; b. Wakefield, Mass., Dec. 31, 1896; s. Aiden P. and Inez (Lassell) R.; student Fenway Sch. Illustration, Boston, Sch. Mus. Fine Arts, Boston; Paige traveling fellow, 1924-25; married to Doris Verne, 1920. Painter 1926—; works represented Chgo. Art Inst., Boston Mus. Fine Arts, Municipal Art Gallery, Davenport, Ia., High Mus. of Art, Atlanta, Beaverbrook Art Gallery, Fredericton, N.B., Can.; mural works include Purchase of Land from Indians, Winchester (Mass.) Pub. Library, Paul Revere's Ride, Lexington (Mass.) Post Office, Paul Revere: The Events of his Life, 14 paintings, 1959-65. Awards and prizes include: Logan Prize, Internat. Water Color Exhbn., Chgo., 1928; 1st prize and purchase, Contemporary Water Color Exhbn., Boston, 1929; Obrig prize N.Y. Water Color Club, 1933; Blair Purchase Prize, Chgo., 1936; Am. Watercolor Soc. medal, 1945, Osborne purchase prize, 1947, Harriet Sanford Stuart Meml. purchase prize, N.Y.C., 1952, Hans Obst prize, N.Y.C., 1954; Ranger Fund purchase prize, Nat. Acad., 1953; Am. Artists Profl. League, Gold Medal, Grand Nat. Exhbn., N.Y.C., 1954, Hon. Mention, 1955, prize and gold medal, 1965; B. L. Makepeace Award of Merit, Boston Soc. Water Color Painters, 1955; George S. Keyes Prize and Gold Medal. Concord Art Association, 1955; first prize American Artists Profl. League, 1955, watercolor award, 1964, 66; asso. mems. award Allied Artists Exhibition, 1957; Richard Mitton Memorial award, Gold Medal Jordan Marsh Exhibition, 1958, 61, 65; award excellence Boston Watercolor Soc., 1960; Lena A. Mason prize N.A.D., 1964; award Acad. Artists Assn., 1966; other honorable mentions and local prizes. Mem. of Nat. Soc. of Mural Painters, Guild of Boston Artists. Am. Soc. Water Color Painters, Audubon Artists, Nat. Acad. Design, Allied Artists of Am., Am. Artists Profl. League, Boston Soc. Water Color Painters. Home: Lexington MA Died Aug. 29, 1969; buried Westview Cemetery, Lexington MA

RISLEY, PAUL L(EMUEL), zoologist; b. Elk Rapids, Mich., May 28, 1906; s. Carl Shugart (Rev.) and Laura Maude (Gray) R.; A.B., Albion (Mich.) Coll., 1927; M.S., U. of Mich., 1929, Ph.D., 1931; m. Louise Evelyn Clark, Dec. 31, 1931; children—Barbara Gray, Carolyn Clark. Instr. zoology, U. of Mich., 1930-31; asso., zoology, State U. of Ia., 1931-37, asst. prof., 1937-42, asso. prof., 1942-45; prof. biology, University of Oregon from 1945, chmn. dept. biology, 1945-53. Spl. research fellow Karolinska Inst., Sweden, 1965-66; participant 5th World Congress Fertility and Sterility, Stockholm, 1966, 9th World Congress of Anatomists, Leningrad, USSR, 1970. Mem. Am. Assn. Advancement of Science, Soc. of Reprodn., American Soc. Zoologists, Am. Assn. Anatomists, Am. Soc. Naturalists, Am. Assn. U. Profs., Ore. Acad. Sci., Sigma Xi, Sigma Nu, Phi Sigma, Gamma Alpha. Contbr. articles on embryology, cytology, histology, endocrinology, sex and reproduction in animals in scientific publs. Home: Eugene OR Died May 10, 1971.

RITTENBERG, DAVID, educator; b. N.Y.C., Nov. 11, 1906; s. Joseph and Sadie (Bloch) R.; B.A., Coll. City N.Y., 1929; Ph.D., Columbia, 1934; m. Sara Merson, June 30, 1930; 1 son, Stephen. Prof. biochemistry Coll. Physicians and Surgeons, Columbia, 1934-56, exec.

officer dept. biochemistry, 1956-64, chmn. dept. biochemistry, 1956-69. Bd. govs. Weizmann Inst. Sci., Rehovoth, Israel, hon. fellow. Member Nat. Acad. Scis., Am. Acad. Arts and Scis. Home: New York City NY Died Jan. 24, 1970.

RITTENBERG, HENRY H., portrait painter; b. Libau, Russia, Oct. 2, 1879; s. Morris and Esther (Kramer) R.; brought to U.S., 1885; ed. N.E. Manual Training High Sch., Phila., Pa.; ed. in art, Pa. Acad. Fine Arts, under Wm. M. Chase, 1897-1900, Bavarian Acad., Munich, 1902; m. Rachel Sachs, Dec. 26, 1905; 1 dau., Caroline Augusta (Mrs. B. Albert Stern). Exhibited widely in U.S.; awarded 1st Cresson traveling scholarship, Pa. Acad. of Fine Arts, 1904; honorable mention Philadelphia Art Club, 1906; Maynard portrait prize, N.A.D., 1920; Norman Waite Harris prize, Art Institute Chicago, 1925; Proctor portrait prize, N.A.D., 1926; portrait prize Nat. Arts Club, New York, 1938. Served as instr. Beaux Arts Inst. of Design, Art Students' League, and in charge spl. portrait classes of N.A.D. (all N.Y. City). Active in Liberty Loan drives and in Div. of Publicity, World War. Represented in Hall Am. Artists N.Y.U., Am. Acad. Arts and Letters, Federal Court (Phila.), U. of Pa., Phila. Art Club, Coll. of Physicians, Hahnemann Med. Coll., Jefferson Med. Coll., Phila. Bar Assn., Phila. Pub. Library; State Capitol, Harrisburg, Pa.; Columbia U., New York; New York Produce Exchange; U. of Panama; N.Y. C. of C.; Pub. Library, Greenville, S.C.; Dept. of Justice, Washington; N.Y. Academy Medicine; U. Va.; Oberlin Coll.; Franklin and Marshall Coll.; Skidmore Coll.; N.Y. Hist. Soc. and in many art collections. Sec. and treas. Gainsborough Studios Corp. A.N.A., 1921, N.A., 1927; sec. Allied Artists of America; treas. Nat. Commn. to Advance Am. Art.; mem. council Nat. Acad. Design, 1933-39; hon. mem. Beaux Arts Inst. Design. Life mem., fellow Pa. Acad. Fine Arts; mem. Art Alliance of America, Allied Artists of America, Painters and Sculptors Assn. (New York), Artists Profl. League, N.Y. Soc. of Painters, Artists Fund Soc., N.Y. Fine Arts Assn. (sec.), Artists Fellowship. Clubs: Salmagundi, MacDowell, Artists Life, Nat. Arts (New York); Washington Arts (Washington, D.C.). Home: New York City NY Died 1969.

RITTER, HOWARD L(ESTER), educator; b. Washington, Feb. 12, 1916; s. George Howard and Ruby (MacFarlane) R.; B.S., U.S. Naval Acad., 1938; Ph.D., Pa. State U., 1943; m. Marie Louise Kruecke, July 12, 1941; children—Howard Lester, Carl Peter, Mary Ann, Margaret Jo, Mark MacFarlane. Research chemist Socony-Vacuum Oil Co., 1943-46; instructor, asst. prof. chemistry U. Wis., 1946-52; professor, head dept. chemistry Miami U., 1952-62, research professor, 1962-67. Recipient Eminent Chemist award Cin. sect. Am. Chem. Soc., 1962. Member Am. Chem. Soc., Am. Phys. Soc., Pi Kappa Phi, Pi Mu Epsilon, Phi Lambda Upsilon, Sigma Pi Sigma, Sigma Xi. Author: An Introduction to Chemistry, 1955; also articles chem. jours. Home: Oxford OH Died Nov. 21, 1967.

RITTER, THELMA, actress; b. Bklyn., Feb. 14, 1905; d. Charles Ritter; student Am. Acad. Dramatic Arts; m. Joseph Moran, Apr. 2, 1927; children—Joseph Anthony, Monica Ann. Appeared various parts stock company Poli Theatre, Elizabeth, N.J.; various roles radio programs including Theatre Guild of the Air, Mr. District Atty., Big Town, Aldrich Family, others, 1945-46; motion picture roles include Miracle on 34th Street, 1946, Letter to Three Wives, 1949, Father was a Fullback, 1949, The Mating Season, 1951, The Model and the Marriage Broker, 1952, Titanic, 1953. The Farmer Takes a Wife, 1953, Lucy Gallant, 1955, Daddy Long Legs, 1955, The Proud and the Profane, 1956, A Hole in the Head, 1959, Pillow Talk, 1958, The Misfits, 1960, Birdman of Alcatraz, 1961, How the West Was Won, 1961, Second Time Around, 1962, For Love or Money, 1962, New Kind of Love, 1963, Move Over Darling, Boeing, Boeing, 1965, TV debut, 1955; TV appearances, U.S. Steel Hour, The Catered Affair, The Late Christopher Bean, The Show-Off, others; Broadway plays include New Girl in Town, also, UTBU, 1966. Co-winner Antoinette Perry, Best Musical Actress, 1957. Active Girl Scout orgn., Am. Cancer Soc. fund-raising campaigns. Home: Forest Hills NY Died Feb. 5, 1969.

RITTER, WILLIAM LEONARD, army officer; b. Hartford City, Ind., Jan. 12, 1898; s. Charles E. and Sara M. (Hess) R.; grad. Inf. Sch., company officers course, 1923, advanced course, 1931; m. Grace E. Moore, Sept. 27, 1924; 1 dau., Anne Slocum. Commd. 2d lt., U.S. Army, 1917, advancing through the grades to brig. gen., 1944; served with 4th Div. during World War I; participated in Tunisian, Sicilian and Italian campaigns during World War II; chief of staff and dep. comdr. U.S. Army Forces in Africa and the Middle East, 1944-46; prof. mil. science and tactics U. of Calif., Berkeley, 1946-50. Decorated Distinguished Service Medal, Bronze Star Medal with Oak Leaf Cluster, Purple Heart with oak leaf cluster; Order British Empire. Home: St Petersburg FL Died July 6, 1971.

RITTMASTER, ALEXANDER III, investment counselor, business analyst; b. N.Y.C., Nov. 19, 1916; s. Arthur and Jeanette (Newman) R.; student Columbia, 1935-36; grad. N.Y. Stock Exchange Inst., 1939; m. Sylvian Goodkind. Feb. 23, 1939; children—Peter Alan, Ronnie Ann, Toni Lynn, Laura. Owner Thompson & Rittmaster, N.Y.C., 1946-56; pres. Rittsmaster & Co., Inc., 1957-69; dir., chmn. exec. com., financial cons., chmn. bd. Dolly Madison Industries, Inc. Home: New York City NY Died June 27, 1969.

RIVAS, DAMASO DE, pathologist, parasitologist; b. Diria, Granada, Nicaragua, Dec. 11, 1874; s. Mauricio and Carmen (Aleman) R.; B.S., U. of Pa., 1908, M.S., 1909, M.D., and Ph.D., 1910; m. Rosa Reinish, Jan. 23, 1904; children—Carlos Theodore, Ana Rosa, Maria Luisa. Bacteriologist to filtration bur. of Phila., 1904-06, state health dept., Pa., 1907-10, pathologist since 1917; research fellow in biology, U. of Pa., 1910, asst. dir. dept. of comparative pathology and Sch. of Tropical Medicine since 1910, asst. prof. parasitology, 1917-22, prof. since 1922; pathologist to Friend's Hosp., Frankford, Pa., since 1916; also pathologist Skin and Cancer Hosp., Phila.; dir. and pathologist Pan-Am. Hosp., New York, 1927. Formerly co-worker at Pasteur Inst.; asst. Koch Inst., Berlin, and student at univs. of Paris, Lille, and Heidelberg; has been mem. of scientific excursions for study of tropical diseases of Africa. Awarded medal of Inst. Pasteur, Paris. Mem. Internat. Council of World Court League and rep. to the Peace Conf. in Paris. Pa. del. to 2d Internat. Congress of Tuberculosis, Washington, D.C., 1908; pres. Nicaraguan delegation of 2d Scientific Pan-Am. Congress, Washington, D.C., 1916-17; delegate from Nicaragua to Sexto Mexico Latino-Americo, Havana, 1922; mem. A.M.A., Am. Soc. of Tropical Medicine; Coll. of Physicians (Phila.), Pan-Am. Med. Assn., Societe de Pathologie Exotique of Paris (corr.), Alpha Kappa Kappa. Roman Catholic. Author: Human Parasitology, 1920; Clinical Parasitology and Tropical Medicine, 1935. Contbr. to med. journals. Home: Villa Rosa, Lansdowne PA‡

RIVERA, JOSE GARIBI, clergyman; b. Guadalajara, Jan. 30, 1889; s. Miguel and Joaquina (Rivera) G.; grad. Guadalajara Sem.; D.D., Gregorian U., Rome, Italy, 1916. Ordained priest, Roman Catholic Ch., 1912, consecrated bishop, 1930; aptd. bishop titular of Rhosus and Auxiliary of Guadalajara, 1929; aptd. titular archbishop of Bizya and coadjutor of Guadalajara, 1934, archbishop of Guadalajara 1936-71; created cardinal, 1958. Address: Guadalajara Mexico Died May 27, 1972; interred crypt Cathedral of Guadalajara, Mexico

RIVERS, L. MENDEL, congressman; b. Berkeley County, S.C., Sept. 28, 1905; s. Lucius Hampton and Henrietta Marion (McCay) R.; student College of Charleston, 1926-29, U. of S.C. Law Sch., 1929-31; m. Margaret Middleton, Sept. 1, 1938; children—Margaret Middleton (Mrs. Robert Eastman), Lois Marion (Mrs. Rene Ravenel), Lucius Mendel, Jr. Admitted S.C. bar, 1932; served in State Legislature of South Carolina, 1933-36; chmn. Charleston County house delegation, State Legislature, 1934-36; spl. atty. Dept. of Justice, 1936-40; mem. 77th to 91st Congresses, 1st Dist. S.C., chmn. armed services com. Episcopalian. Mason, Elk. Home: Charleston SC Died Dec. 28, 1970; buried St. Stephen's Episcopal Ch., St. Stephen SC

RIVES, ZENO J., congressman, lawyer; b. in Hancock Co., Ind., Feb. 22, 1874; s. Alfred J. and Lettice S. (Heath) R.; ed. pub. schs., Litchfield, Ill.; read law in office; m. St. Louis, Jan. 31, 1905, Effie A. Karns. Admitted to bar, Oct. 12, 1901, and engaged in practice. Mem. Congress, 21st Ill. dist., 1905-7. Presby'n. Republican. Address: Litchfield IL‡

ROACH, ABBY MEGUIRE, author; b. Phila.; d. Charles Atkinson and Emma E. (Geiselman) Meguire; student Wellesley Coll.; 1893-4; m. Louisville, Neill Roach, June 1, 1899. Contbr. to mags.; wrote a number of short stories as Abby Swain Meguire. Clubs: Woman's, Authors, Fortnightly, Art, Musical, Woman's Suffrage. Author: Some Successful Marriages, 1906. Home: 105 W. Hill St., Louisville KY‡

ROACH, SIDNEY C., ex-congressman; b. Linn Creek, Mo., July 25, 1876; s. Littleberry J. and Frances M. (Crain) R.; ed. pub. schs. and St. Louis Law Sch.; m. Edith King, of Osage Co., Mo., Oct. 1899. Began practice at Linn Creek, 1897; county atty. Camden Co., Mo., 4 terms; mem. Mo. Ho. of Rep., 1909-13; mem. 67th and 68th Congresses (1921-25), 8th Mo. Dist. Dir. 1st Nat. Bank, Linn Creek. Republican. Methodist. Mason, Odd Fellow. Home: Linn Creek MO‡

ROADHOUSE, CHESTER LINWOOD, univ. prof.; b. Watsonville, Calif., Jan. 5, 1881; s. John James and Imogene (Kimberlin) R.; student, U. of Calif., 1902-03; D.V.M., Cornell U., 1906; student, U. of Bern, Bern, Switzerland, 1927-28; m. Christine Judah, Dec. 2, 1910; children—Katharine (Mrs. Robert F. Black), Frances (dec.), Donald (dec.). Vet. insp., U.S. Dept. Agr., 1906-09; chief dairy insp., Dept. of Health, San Francisco, 1909-10; chief veterinarian, Dept. of Health, Berkeley, 1910-11; asso. prof., vet. science, U. of Calif., 1911-17; veterinarian and bacteriologist, San Francisco and Alameda Counties Med. Milk Commns., 1911-17; prof. Dairy Industry, Univ. of Calif., 1917-69; inaugurated supervision city milk, San Francisco, city dairy and milk, Berkeley; director California Dairy Council; U.S. del. to World's Dairy Congress, Berlin, Germany, 1937. Mem. Internat. Assn. Milk Sanatarians (pres. 1921), Am. Dairy Science Assn. (pres., 1934-35); Pacific Slope Dairy Assn. (pres. and dir., 1922-47), A.A.A.S., Theta Delta Chi, Sigma Xi, Alpha Zeta. Republican. Mason. Clubs: Davis Rotary (pres. 1931). Author: (textbook) The Market Milk Industry (with Dr. J. Lloyd Henderson), 1941; Lab. Manual for Market Milk, 1947. Contbr. circulars and bulletins on dairy science. Home: Santa Rosa CA Died Sept. 23, 1969; buried Santa Clara (Cal.) City Cemetery.

ROBB ELISE DE LA FONTAINE (MRS. ROBERT CUMMING ROBB), social worker; b. Lille, France; d. Fred and Mia (Bourgignonde Colette) de la Fontaine; came to U.S., 1914, naturalized 1921; B.A., Barnard Coll., 1920; M.A., Columbia, 1944, diploma Sch. Social Work, 1931; postgrad. U. Chgo., summers 1937, 38, Harvard, summer 1944, Columbia, 1944-46; m. Robert Cumming Robb, Aug. 25, 1949. Asst. supt. Dutchess County Bd. Child Welfare, Poughkeepsie, N.Y., 1921-24; chief probation officer Dutchess County Children's Ct., Buffalo Children's Aid Soc., 1924; dir. Children's Bur. Memphis and Shelby County, 1924-28; dir. home finding Children's Aid Soc., Pitts., 1928-29; dir. child-placing dept. DePalchin Faith Home, Houston, 1929-30; intern Inst. for Child Guidance, Commonwealth N.Y.C., 1930-31; dist. sec. Yorkville dist. Community Service Soc., N.Y.C., 1931-48; dir. Family Service, Pasadena, 1948-54; pvt. practice as social case worker, Pasadena, 1954-61, part-time, Laguna Beach Cal., 1961-69. Part-time faculty mem. N.Y. U., 1932-36, Sch. Social Work, Columbia, 1934-48, U. Chgo., summer 1939, U. Cal. at Los Angeles, 1948-49. Active Aux. S. Coast Community Hosp., South Laguna. Bd. mem. South Coast Child Guidance Clinic, 1961-69, Pasadena Com. on Alcholism, 1958-69, Las Madrecitas Aux. Holy Family Adoption Agy., Los Angeles, Laguna Civic Ballet, Laguna Beach; mem. Orange County Philharmonic Soc. Mem. Nat. Assn. Social Workers, Am. Assn. Psychiat. Social Workers (charter), Acad. Certified Social Workers, Alumnae of Columbia Sch. Social Work (past mem. bd.), League Women Voters, Alumnae Assn. Barnard Coll., Alumnae Assn. Columbia U. of So. Cal., Aux. County Med. Assn. Recipient Community Service award Alhambra Episcopal Ch. Home for Children, 1961. Clubs: Columbia University (So. Cal.); Cosmopolitan (N.Y.C.); Town and Gown (Irvine, Cal.); Dana Strand (Dana Point, Cal.). Contbr. to various profl. publs. Home: Dana Point CA Died Jan. 4, 1969; interred Pacific View Meml. Park Newport Beach CA

ROBB, EUGENE SPIVEY, publisher; b. Lincoln, Neb., Jan. 9, 1910; s. Andrew Jefferson Christy and Alice May (Spivey) R.; A.B., U. Neb., 1930; grad. student Princeton, 1933; J.D., George Washington U., 1939; L.H.D. (honorary), Siena College, 1961; m. Lillemor Taylor, June 20, 1936; children—Peter Berlet, Victoria Alice, Christina Emma, Deborah Mary. Reporter Lincoln (Neb.) Star, 1926-32; editor Advt. Almanac, 1933-34; Washington rep. Hearst publs., 1935-45, asst. mgr., dir. Hearst Newspapers. 1946-52; pub. Albany (N.Y.) Times Union, 1953-69, Knickerbocker News, Albany, 1960-69; v.p., dir. Hearst Corp.; director Asso. Press. Mem. Pulitzer Prize jury, 1965-66. President Saratoga Performing Arts Center, 1966-68; board trustees Russell Sage College bd. dirs. Nat. Urban League, Albany Hosp., Albany Boys Club. Mem. newspaper adv. com. N.P.A., 1951-53; chmn. newspaper central committee Audit Bureau Circulations, 1951-53. Mem. Am. Newspaper Pubs. Assn. (1964-66), Fedn. Internat. Editors Jours. (v.p. 1964-69), N.Y. State Publs. Assn. (pres. 1959), D.C. Bar Assn., Phi Beta Kappa, Sigma Delta Chi, Phi Delta Phi, Delta Upsilon. Clubs: Nat. Press (Washington); University, Fort Orange (Albany); Riverside (Conn.) Yacht; Schuyler Meadows (Loudonville). Home: Loudonville NY Died Aug. 18, 1969; buried Albany Rural Cemetery, Menands NY

ROBB, RICHARD ALEXANDER, lawyer; b. Ithaca, Mich., June 2, 1909; s. Alexander W. and Ida (Kinkerter) R.; A.B., Eastern Mich. U., 1931; J.D., Detroit Coll. Law, 1942; m. Ann Louise Monroe, Aug. 7, 1935; 1 dau., Diane Louise (Mrs. Phillip Kary). Tchr. Ferndale (Mich.) High Sch., 1931-42; admitted to Mich. bar, 1942; asst. exec. sec. Muskegon (Mich.) Mfrs. Assn., 1942-52; partner firm Landman, Hathaway, Latimer, Clink & Robb, Muskegon, 1952-71. Mem. Industry panel WLB, 1943-45. Mem. Am., Mich., Muskegon County (pres. 1961-62) bar assns., Greater Muskegon C. of C. (dir. 1957-60), Pi Kappa Delta, Kappa Delta Pi, Presbyn. Mason, Lion (pres. 1952-53). Club: Century (Muskegon). Contbr. articles to legal jours. Home: Muskegon MI Died July 28, 1971.

ROBBINS, EDWARD RUTLEDGE, educator, author; b. Somerset County, N.J., Dec. 5, 1870; s. Sylvester and Sarah Isabella (Bird) R.; A.B., Princeton, 1894 (Phi Beta Kappa; winner sophomore math. prize, math. fellowship); m. Helen Carrell, of Hatboro, Pa., Apr. 30, 1919. Taught Lawrenceville Sch., 1894-99, Wm. Penn Charter Sch., 1899-1914; with ednl. dept. John Wanamaker Store, Phila., 1918-22; supt. schs., Jenkintown, Pa., 1922-26; v.p. Darlington Jr. Coll.,

West Chester, Pa. Mem. Phila. Headmasters' Assn. Republican. Presbyn. Author: Algebra, 1897; Complete Arithmetic, 1901; New Plane Geometry, 1906; New Solid Geometry, 1907; Plane Trigonometry, 1909; Exercises in Algebra, 1910. Home: Hatboro PA‡

ROBBINS, FRANKLIN G., ry. official; b. La Crosse, Wis., Feb. 15, 1876; s. Edwin G. and Alice N. Stafford R.; ed. pub. schs., Minneapolis, and Shattuck Sch., Faribault, Minn.; m. Alice R. Rexroat, of Concord, Ill., June 2, 1906. Messenger, rodman and telegraph operator M., St.P. and S. Ste. Marie Ry.; with C.B. & Q. Ry. Co., 1906-13, advancing to div. supt.; supt. Erie R.R., Buffalo, N.Y., 1913-16; gen. supt. Erie R.R. at Chicago 1917; dir. Bur. of Service, Interstate Commerce Commn., Washington, D.C., 1920-22; v.p. Chicago region, Erie R.R., since 1922; dir. C. & W.I. R.R., Belt Line Ry. Co. of Chicago. Entered U.S. Army as maj., Dec. 1917, later lt. col.; served as aide to S. M. Felton, dir. gen. of rys.; asst. gen. mgr. railroads in France; hon. discharged, June 1919. Mem. Old Time Telegraphers' Assn. Republican. Christian Scientist. Mason. Clubs: Union League, Traffic (Chicago); Army and Navy (Washington, D.C.). Home: 4828 Dorchester Av. Office: 1303 Transportation Bldg., Chicago IL‡

ROBBINS, GASTON A., congressman; b. in Ala., Sept. 26, 1869; grad. Univ. of N.C., 1879; admitted to N.C. bar, 1880; returned to Ala.; practiced at Selma; member Congress, 1891-5; elected for term 1899-1901; Democrat. Address: Selma AL‡

ROBBINS, JOSEPH CHANDLER, missionary sec.; b. Rodan, N.S., Mar. 20, 1874; s. Joseph Henry and Mary Gauld (Scott) R.; Ph.B., Brown U., 1897, D.D., 1919, also D.D. from Acadia University, 1931; grad. Newton Theological Instn., 1902; D.D., Franklin College, 1919; m. Effie B. Starkey, of Troy, N.H., June 7, 1902. Ordained Bapt. ministry, 1902; missionary Philippine Islands, 1902-09; foreign sec. Am. Bapt. Foreign Missionary Society, 1926-40. Trustee Brown U. Mem. 1st N.H. Vols., Spanish-Am. War. Trustee Newton Theol. Instn. Mem. Alpha Tau Omega, Phi Beta Kappa (Brown). Republican. Author: Appeal of India, 1919; Following the Pioneers, 1922. Home: White Plains, N.Y. Office: 152 Madison Av., New York NY‡

ROBBINS, MILTON HERBERT, physician; b. N.Y.C., May 23, 1903; s. Abraham Elliot and Rebecca Robbins; M.D., George Washington U., 1928; m. Alice Robbins, Sept. 16, 1933; children—Dolores (Mrs. Donald Jacobsen), Paul. Intern, Hosp for Joint Disease, N.Y.C., 1928-30, adj. in medicine and cardiology, 1934-50, asso. in medicine and cardiology, 1950-71; intern Jewish Maternity Hosp., 1930; asso. physician Fordham Hosp., N.Y.C., 1950, attending physician 1951; asso. in medicine Bronx (N.Y.) Municipal Hosp. Center, 1955-71; attending physician Lincoln Hosp.; asso. attending Peninsula Gen Hosp., Far Rockaway, N.Y., St. Joseph's Hosp., Far Rockaway; physician, staff in internal medicine Nassau Communities Hosp., Oceanside, N.Y., Franklin Gen. Hosp., Valley Stream, N.Y. Served to capt. M.C., AUS, 1942-46. Diplomate Am. Bd. Internal Medicine. Fellow A.C.P., Am. Coll. Cardiology; mem. A.M.A., Am. Heart Assn., Bronx County, Nassau County med. socs. Home: North Woodmere NY Died Feb. 8, 1971; buried Beth David Cemetery.

ROBBINS, MILTON HOLLEY, JR., business man; b. Lakeville, Conn., Jan. 27, 1871; s. Milton Holley and Anna E. (Bostwick) R.; Ph.B., Sheffield Scientific Sch. (Yale), 1891; m. Annie E. Stayner, of Staten Island, N.Y., Aug. 24, 1895. With Otis Elevator Co. for 14 yrs., representing the co. in every state and ty. of the Union except Mont.; v.-p. Union Ice Co. Pres. San Francisco Chamber of Commerce, 1911 and 1912; pres. Merchants' Assn. of San Francisco, 1910-11; dir. Home Industry League of Cal. Republican. Congregationalist. Mem. Theta Delta Chi. Clubs: Pacific Union, Union League. Commercial (v.-p.). Home: Alameda CA Office: 354 Pine St., San Francisco CA‡

ROBBINS, RICHARD WHITFIELD, business exec., livestock farmer; b. Norwich, Kan., Mar. 24, 1892; s. William Webster and Grace Hazel (Doorley) R.; A.B., Yale, 1913; m. Mary A. Lightner, Jan. 25, 1941 (div. 1952); children—Richard, William; m. 2d, Opal Teeter, 1967. Investment banker, N.Y., N.Y., 1913-17; sec.-treas., John B. Semple & Co., Sewickley, Pa., 1917-19; pres. Inland Mfg. Co., nr. Coraopolis, Pa., 1917-21; practising indsl. engr., Pitts, 1921-29; pres. Pa. Airlines, now Capitol Airlines, 1930-31; pres. Transcontinental and Western Airlines, 1931-35; member board dirs. A.T. & S.F. Ry., First Nat. Bank of Kansas City, Kan. Power and Light Co. Livestock farmer, cattle rancher, Belvidere, Kansas 1935-71. Pres. Kansas Live Stock Assn., 1957-58; mem. Kansas Industrial Development Commission, chairman, 1939-45. Trustee Eisenhower Found., Abilene, Kan., Sterling (Kansas) College, College of Emporia, Kansas, Menninger Found. Chmn. Pratt and Kiowa Cos., Kansas Rep. Central Com., 1935-47; del. Rep. Nat. Conv. Phila., 1940. Presbyn. Elk Mason (32 deg.). Clubs: University (New York City); Park Hill Country (Pratt, Kan.); Wichita (Kan.); Chicago. Address: Pratt KS also Belvidere KS Died June 29, 1971; buried Harper KS

ROBBINS, SAMUEL DOWSE, speech pathologist; b. Belmont, Mass., Dec. 28, 1887; s. Chandler and Maria Wellington (Mead) R.; A.B., Harvard, 1911, A.M., 1919; L.H.D. (honorary), Emerson College, 1955; married Rosa Margaret Seymour, July 10, 1917; children—Chandler Seymour, Roger Wellington, Samuel Dowse, Jr. Established sch. for correction of stammering, 1914-15; conducted research in speech pathology, Harvard, 1918-19, resulting in discovery of some changes in cerebral circulation in stammering and fright; instituted plan for systematic classification of speech disorders, adopted by Am. Speech Correction Assn., 1930; dir. of Boston Stammerers' Inst., 1916-40; in charge speech correction Mass. Gen. Hosp., 1920-43; speech therapist, Mass. Div. Mental Hygiene, 1927-57; later prof. emeritus speech therapy Emerson Coll. and mng. trustee of Inst. of Speech Correction, Inc.; lecturer Tufts Coll. Dental Sch., 1948-52; awarded research grant under Pub. Health Service Act, 1961. Mem. Belmont Town Meeting since 1926. Trustee Belmont Savings Bank. Fellow A.A.A.S., Am. Speech and Hearing Assn. (permanent sec. 1931-40, pres. 1941-42, chmn. Terminology Committee 1929-54), American Psychol. Assn. Republican. Conglist. Author: Stammering and Its Treatment, 1926; A Dictionary of Terms Dealing with Disorders of Speech (with Sara M. Stinchfield), 1931; Correction of Speech Defects of Early Childhood (with Rosa S. Robbins), 1937; A Dictionary of Speech Pathology and Therapy, 1951. Contbr. to scientific jours. Home: Belmont MA Died Jan. 28, 1968; buried Mt. Auburn Cemetery Cambridge MA

ROBBINS, THOMAS HINCKLEY, JR., naval officer; b. Paris, France, of Am. parents, May 11, 1900; s. Thomas Hinckley and Alice Bradford (Ames) R.; ed. Gilman Country Sch., Baltimore, Md., 1914; B.S. (distinguished grad.) U.S. Naval Acad., 1919; m. Barbara Little, Nov. 19, 1930; 1 dau., Barbara. Commd. ensign, 1919 and advanced through the grades to rear admiral, 1945; with naval forces Europe, 1920-24; command U.S.S. SC96, 1923; naval aviator since 1927; continued through grades on aviation duties in various squadrons; command U.S.S. Sandpiper, 1934-35; VS Squadron 4, U.S.S. Langley, 1935-36; student Naval War Coll., 1936-37; aviation officer, staff Naval War Coll., Newport, R.I., 1937-39; navigator U.S.S. Lexington, 1939-40; aviation officer, staff Scouting Force, 1941; aviation plans officer, hdqrs. Cominch, Washington, D.C., 1942; chief of staff, Fleet Air Quonset, 1943; staff, Army-Navy Staff Coll., Washington, D.C., 1943-44; command U.S.S. Lexington, 1945; Office of the Sec. of Navy, Washington, D.C., 1946-47; Commander Carrier Div. 17, 1948-49; joint strategic survey com. of Joint Chiefs of Staff, 1949-52; commander carrier division 2 1952-53; Chief of Staff, Naval War Coll., 1953-56, pres., 1944, 56-57; with Office of Sec. of Navy, Washington, 1957-60; commandant Potomac River Naval Command, 1960-62, ret., 1962. Decorated Legion of Merit with comabt surharge, Sec. of War Commendation ribbon, Presidential Unit Citation (2 stars); World War I Victory medal (1 star, Atlantic fleet), Defense ribbon (1 star, Pacific fleet), Am. Theatre medal, Pacific theatre medal (3 campaign stars), World War II Victory medal, Philippine Liberation medal (1 campaign star). Clubs: N.Y. Yacht; Army and Navy (Washington); Exploreres. Home: Stonington CT Died Dec. 12, 1972.

ROBERT, SARAH EMILY CORBIN, teacher, lecturer; b. Williamsport, Pa., Aug. 26, 1886; d. William Wallace and Emma Flora (Hamilton) Corbin; A.B., Syracuse (N.Y.) U., 1909; student Columbia U., summers 1925, 29; hon. Litt.D., Lincoln Mem. Univ. 1940; m. Henry Martyn Robert, Jr., Aug. 26, 1919; 1 son, Henry Martyn, 3d. Taught history in pub. schs. of Brocton, N.Y., 1909-11, Rome, N.Y., 1911-14, Atlantic City, N.J., 1914-19; conducted spl. courses in parliamentary law, summers, U. of Md. and Columbia; lectured on parliamentary law before women's clubs and societies; speaker on Americanism and Am. citizenship in every state of the Union and has given radio broadcasts on same subjects frequently, 1935-41. Exec. dir. Annapolis' 300th Anniversary Celebration, 1949. Mem. Nat. Soc. Daughters Am. Revolution (treas. gen., 1935-38; pres. gen., 1938-41), Daughters of Founders and Patriots of Am. (nat. v.p. and recording sec., 1931-37), Colonial Dames of Am., Daughters of Colonial Wars, Alpha Phi. Lectured widely on adjusting meetings to the needs of war, 1942-45. Decorated Huguenot Cross (Huguenot Soc. Pa.), B.F. Goodrich award for distinguished public service." Clubs: Arundel (Baltimore, Md.), Colonial Dames (Washington, D.C.). Author of articles on history research and parliamentary law. Home: Annapolis MD Died May 3, 1972.

ROBERTS, ANNE MASON, govt. ofcl.; b. Cin.; B.A., U. Cin., 1928, M.A. in Psychology, 1936; m. Stanley Roberts; 3 daus. Tchr., Cin. Pub. Schs., until 1945; consumer relations officer OPA, 1945-46; racial relations officer HHFA, 1946-48; housing economist, div. slum clearance and urban redevel., 1950, later field rep. for Area IV, relocation adviser to Region I, N.Y.C., then regional relocation officer, asst. regional dir. for urban renewal, became dep. regional dir. for Region I (New Eng. and N.Y. State), 1961, dep. regional

adminstr. Region I, 1962, now dep. regional adminstr. Dept. Housing and Urban Devel., 1966-—; former exec. dir. N.Y.C. anti-poverty program. Mem. nat. adv. com. on internat. housing AID. Recipient Fed. Woman's award, 1967. Mem. Nat. Urban League, Nat. Council Negro Women. Address: New York City NY Died Oct. 1971.*

ROBERTS, (HENRY) CHALMES, editor; b. Austin, Tex., July 31, 1870; s. Maj.-Gen. A.S. and Fanny (Chalmers) R.; ed. in pvt. schs. and univs. of Va. and Tex.; unmarried. Was attached to U.S. Legation, Constantinople, during 2d Cleveland administration; went to Turko-Grecian War as corr. London Daily News; went to Spanish-Am. War, corr. London Daily Mail and Brooklyn Eagle; sent by Harper's to Egypt in 1899, editor and mng. dir. of World Today (English edit. of World's Work), 1906-32; dir. Heinemann Holdings, Ltd. Contributor to Harper's Magazine, Atlantic Monthly, Harper's Weekly, Everybody's, etc. Clubs: Metropolitan (Washington); White's, St. James (London); Travellers (Paris). Home: 25 Jermyn St., S.W., London England‡

ROBERTS, COLETTE JACQUELINE, art critic; b. Paris, France, Sept. 16, 1910; d. Alfred Cami and Juliette Emilie Rothschild (de Mulhouse) Levy; B.A., Latin-Langues Philosophie, 1928; student La Sorbonne Institut d'Art et Archeologie, Ecole du Louvre, 1928-37, and Academie Ranson, 1925-31; pupil Henri Focillon and Bissiere; m. Edward Sherrill Roberts, Sept. 12, 1934 (div. 1948); 1 son, Richard Barclay. Came to U.S. 1939, naturalized, 1943. Researcher, lectr. writer French Press and Information Service and France Forever, N.Y.C., 1940-46; pub. relations, 1947-71; gallery dir. Nat. Assn. Women Artists, N.Y.C. 1947-49; sec. to curator Far Eastern art, Met. Mus. Art, 1950-51; gallery dir. Grand Central Moderns, N.Y.C., specializing in modern Am. Art, 1952-68; associate director A.M. Sachs Gallery, 1968-71; free lance interviewer for Archives American Art. Organized exchange cultural exhbns. sponsored by American and French embassies; chmn. French sect. A.R.C., 1947, 48, 49; team coordinator advanced gift com. French sect. A.R.C. 1950-71; v.p. Friends of A.D.I.R., Inc. (Charity) 1951-71; art critic for France Amerique, 1953-71. Aujourd'hui, Art et Architecture, 1960-68, Queens Coll., 1960-61; adj. professor history of art New York U., 1957-71. Exhibited Salon d'Automne, Paris, 1928-30, Gallery Barreiro, Paris, 1928. Decorated Chevalier Order des Palmes Academiques (France). McDowell, 1960. Contbr. articles Modern Am. Art. Author 2 monographs on Mark Tobey, 1959, 60; Louise Nevelson, 1964. Home: New York City NY Died Aug. 9, 1971.

ROBERTS, EDWARD DODSON, educator; b. Cincinnati, O., Aug. 31, 1877; s. Harry Clay and Amelia (Dodson) R.; B.A., U. of Cincinnati, 1899, M.A., 1907; M.A., Columbia, 1908; LL.D., Coll. of Wooster, 1932; m. Florence Marshall, June 26, 1915 (died July 10, 1920); 1 son, Edward Marshall; m. 2d, Rosabelle Mitchell, June 14, 1924; 1 dau., Ruth Mitchell. Teacher and prin. Cincinnati pub. schs., 1899-1912, asst. supt. schs., 1912-27, asso. supt., 1927-29, supt., 1929-37; asso. supt., 1937-38; teacher English, Holmes High Sch., Covington, Ky., 1938-48. Acting prof. edn., University of Nevada, 1922; instr., Coll. of Edn., Ohio State U., summers, 1924-26, U. of Cincinnati, 1926-29, Syracuse U., summer, 1939. Dir. English, ednl. bur., Nat. War Work Council, Y.M.C.A., during World War I. Mem. Gen. Council Presbyn. Ch., 1930-33; mem. Commn. on Marriage, Divorce and Remarriage, Presbyn. Ch., 1930-31; moderator Presbytery of Cincinnati, 1927-29; mem. Bd. Nat. Missions and Ch. Extension, Presbytery of Cincinnati since 1929 (pres., 1929-40). Trustee Lane Theol. Sem., Coll. of Wooster; dir. Heart Council, Central Clinic, 1927-38; dir. Citizenship Council of Cincinnati Community Chest; vice chmn. Citizenship Council since 1942; pres. Teachers Annuity and Aid Assn. of Hamilton County, O., 1913-38; mem. exec. committee Cincinnati Employment Center and Four Point Program, 1937-38. Member N.E.A., American Assn. Sch. Adminstrs. (life), Soc. for Study of Edn., Ohio Edn. Assn., Southwestern Ohio Teachers Assn. (ex-pres.), Cincinnati Schoolmasters Club (charter mem., ex-pres.), Ky. Edn. Assn., Covington Schoolmasters Club, Phi Beta Kappa, Phi Delta Kappa. Presbyterian (elder and clk. session, Seventh Ch., Cincinnati). Mason (32 deg.). Home: 3533 Burch Av., Cincinnati 8 OH‡

ROBERTS, ERNEST PORTER, banking; b. Brunswick, Me., Feb. 18, 1869; s. John and Lydia S. (Porter) R.; ed. Concord pub. schs.; m. Esther B. Jackman, Sept. 14, 1899; children—Porter, John Harland, Mary Elizabeth. Employed as clk. with railroad companies, 1885-99; with N.H. Savings Bank since 1899, treas. 1914-38, pres. since 1938; pres. Concord Housing Co.; dir. First Nat. Bank, Eagle Phenix Hotel Co., New Industries Co. (all of Concord). Republican. Conglist. Club: Concord Country. Home: 4 Wilson Av. Office: 97 N. Main St., Concord NH‡

ROBERTS, FRANK HUBERT, gas pipeline co. exec.; b. nr. Nettleton, Kan., Jan. 6, 1916; s. Blaine and Emma (Carlson) R.; B.S., U. Kan., 1938, M.B.A., 1940; m.

Marjorie Veta Dillon, Mar. 5, 1943; children—Barry, Janet, Craig. Asst. instr. U. Kan., 1938-39; staff accountant Arthur Anderson & Co., Kansas City, 1939-45; accountant No. Natural Gas Co., Omaha, 1945-50, asst. controller, 1950-58, chief accounting officer, 1958-63, controller, 1963-72, v.p., 1969-72. Trustee Arthritis Found. Mem. Ind. Natural Gas Assn., Am., So., Midwest gas assns., Financial Execs. Inst., Nat. Accountants Assn. Home: Omaha NB Died Oct. 20, 1972; buried Omaha NE

ROBERTS, GEORGE, lawyer; b. Bklyn., July 3, 1884; s. George H. and Maria (Pettit) R.; B.A., Yale, 1905; LL.B. cum laude, Harvard, 1908; m. Grace Lee Middleton, Apr. 27, 1918; children—Constance (Mrs. Robert L. Hoguet, Jr.), Rosamond G. (Mrs. Donald Arthur, Jr.). Admitted to N.Y. bar, 1908, since practiced in N.Y.C.; mem. firm Winthrop & Stimson, 1912-14; partner Winthrop, Stimson, Putnam & Roberts, 1914-68. Special consultant to Committee on Organization of Exec. Br. Govt., 1954-68; spl. com. on Fed. Loyalty Security Program; mem. working group Pres. com. on Transport Policy and Orgn.; spl. counsel R.F.C., 1932-33; adv. bd. Sec. of War's Bd. on Non-Appropriated Funds, 1945-46. Chmn. trustees Army Relief Soc.; trustee, chmn. bd. Roosevelt Hosp., N.Y.C., 1956. Fellow American Bar Assn.; member Am. Law Inst., Assn. Bar City N.Y. (mem. exec. com. 1933-37, v.p. 1941-43, chmn. com. bill of rights 1942-46), Am. (chmn. spl. com. retirement benefits 1951-56), N.Y. State bar assns., Council Foreign Relations. Clubs: University, Downtown, Century Assn., Links, River (N.Y.C.); Ausable (St. Hubert's, N.Y.); Maidstone (Easthampton, N.Y.); Chevy Chase (Washington). Home: New York City NY Died Aug. 8, 1968; buried Green-Wood Cemetery, Brooklyn NY

ROBERTS, GEORGE EDWARD THEODORE, author; b. Fredericton, N.B., July, 1877; s. Rev. George Goodridge (M.A., LL.D.) and Emma Wetmore (Bliss) R.; ed. Fredericton Collegiate Sch., and partial course in Univ. of New Brunswick, 1897; m. Elgin, N.B., 1903, Frances Seymour, d. Rev. Thomas Allen. Sub-editor New York Independent, winter of 1897-8; sp'l corr. The Independent in Tampa and Cuba during Spanish-Am. War, 1898, and in Newfoundland, 1899; editor Newfoundland Mag., 1900; since then in gen. lit. work. Contb'r to Am. and Canadian mags. Traveler in out-of-the-way places. Member Union Club, Bridgetown, Barbadoes, B. W. I. Mem. Ch. of England. Conservative. Author: Northland Lyrics (part author), 1899 S9; Hemming, the Adventurer, 1904 P3; Brothers of Peril, 1905 P3. Residence: Fredericton, N.B., Can. Address: Care L. C. Page & Co., Boston‡

ROBERTS, HENRY LITHGOW, historian; b. Denver, Sept. 27, 1916; s. Griffith Henry and Myra (Sowles) R.; B.A., Yale, 1938, Ph.D., 1942; D.Phil., Oxford, 1948; m. Deborah Hathaway Calkins, Nov. 10, 1945;children—John Griffith, Deborah Hathaway, Hugh David. Research analyst OSS, 1942-45, Dept. State, 1946; asst. prof. history Columbia, 1948-54, asso. prof., 1954-56, dir. program on East Central Europe, 1954-67, prof. history, 1956-67, dir. Russian Inst., 1956-62; prof. history Dartmouth, 1967-72. Served from ensign to lt. USNR, 1943-46. Author: Rumania, 1951; Britain and the United States, 1953; Russia and America, 1956; Eastern Europe, 1970. Editor: Slavic Rev., 1965-67. Home: Rochester VT Died Oct. 17, 1972.

ROBERTS, INA BREVOORT, author; b. Yonkers, N.Y., May 21, 1874; d. Willard and Fannie J. (Hawkins) Deane; ed. Maplewood Inst., Concordville, Pa., 1882-6, high sch., Newark, N.J., 1889-90; m. J. Edwards Roberts, of New York, Aug. 28, 1895. In lit. work since 1897; editor The Club Woman's Weekly" and Club Women of New York." Clubs: Rainy Day, Pen and Brush, William Lloyd Garrison Equal Rights Assn., Woman's Republican, Minerva Past Parliament, New Yorkers, New York State Federation. Author: The Lifting of a Finger, 1901. Address: Hotel Astor NY‡

ROBERTS, LLOYD SHERWOOD, lawyer; b. Winfield, Kan., March 14, 1900; s. Charles Willis and Mabel (Hutchinson) R.; A.B., Kan. U., 1925; LL.B., Washburn Coll., 1927; m. LaVerne Snyder, Aug. 9, 1928; 1 dau., Kay Frances. Admitted to Kan. bar, 1927; partner law firm Roberts & Roberts, 1927-68; engaged in oil and gas and mineral operations, extensive farming. Trustee William Newton Meml. Hosp., 1941-59. Mem. Kan. Bar Assn., Am. Judicature Soc. Kan.-Okla. Secondary Recovery Assn., Delta Upsilon, Phi Alpha Delta. Lion. Home: Winfield KS Died Oct. 11, 1968.

ROBERTS, MALCOLM FERGUSON, investment banker; b. Attleboro, Mass., Sept. 11, 1894; s. Frances Donaldson, Apr. 9, 1970. With James N. Wright & Co., investment bankers, 1915-18; v.p., sec. Sidlo Simons Roberts & Co., from 1918, later pres.; mgr. Hornblower & Week-Hemphill, Noyes, Denver, from 1961, later cons. Chmn. budget commn. United Fund; active A.R.C. Mem. Nat. Assn. Security Dealers (gov. 1963-66), Investment Bankers Assn. Am. (gov., dir.). Home: Denver CO Died Nov. 26, 1971.

ROBERTS, SAMUEL JENNINGS, physician; b. DeKalb, Mo., Sept. 21, 1897; s. James William and May (Gore) R.; M.D., Washington U., St. Louis, 1925; m. Eunice Kirby Stacy, July 29, 1954. Tchr., prin. Platte County Pub. Schs., De Kalb, 1915-18; intern U.S. Naval Hosp., Mare Island, Cal., 1925-26; chief resident physician Jackson Meml. Hosp., Miami, Fla., 1926-27, staff pediatrician, 1932-62; asst. resident in pediatrics Strong Meml. Hosp., Rochester, N.Y., 1929; sr. house physician Childrens Hosp., Detroit, 1930, chief resident physician, 1931-32; practice medicine specializing in pediatrics, Miami, 1932-62. Diplomate Am. Bd. Pediatrics. Mem. A.M.A., So. Med. Assn., Am. Acad. Pediatrics, Phi Beta Pi. Democrat. Methodist. Mason. Contbr. articles on children's allergies to med. jours. Home: Marion NC Died May 23, 1971; buried Ballew Meml. Cemetery, Nebo NC

ROBERTS, STEPHEN W(ILBUR), educator; b. Middlebourne, W.Va., July 29, 1902; s. Joshua Sheridan and Flora (Ankrom) R.; student Bethany Prep. Sch., 1922; A.B., Broaddus Acad. and Coll., 1927; student U. Chgo., 1927; B.S. in edn., Bucknell U., 1932; M.A., N.Y.U., 1935; LL.D. (hon.), Alderson-Broaddus College, 1957; married to Eleanore Weddell, Dec. 21, 1926; children—Margaret Suzanne, John Sheridan. Tchr., coach high schs., Bridgeport, W.Va., Muncy, Pa., 1927-36; scout, asst. coach Bucknell U., 1932; mgr. baseball Susquehanna League, Muncy, Pa., 1932-35; prof., coach East Stroudsburg (Pa.) State Tchrs. Coll., 1936-42; dir. admissions, pub. relations Wayland Acad., Beaver Dam, Wis., 1942-51; headmaster Perkiomen Sch. Boys, 1951-66, headmaster emeritus, 1966-70; asst. to pres. Alderson Broaddus Coll., 1967, dir. admissions, 1967-70. Mem. Service Acad. Selection Board, 1957-70. Board of directors Upper Perkiomen Planning Commission, Perkiomen Valley Boy Scouts; bd. trustees Montgomery County Community College. Mem. Perkiomen Valley Community Concerts Assn. (pres.), Am. Assn. Sch. Adminstrs., Am. Coll. Pub. Relations Assn., N.E.A., Boarding Sch. Assn. of Phila. Region (pres. 1962-63), Upper Perkiomen Valley C. of C. (pres. 1961-62, dir.). Baptist. Mason. Clubs: Toastmasters, Rotary (pres. Beaver Dam 1949-50). Address: Philippi WV Died Sept. 12, 1970.

ROBERTS, TARLTON TAYLOR, clergyman, educator; b. Hume, Ill., Aug. 11, 1874; s. John Samuel and Mary E. (Taylor) R.; grad. high sch., Hume, 1894; student Ky. U., Lexington, Ky., 1898-1902; A.B., Phillips U., Enid, Okla., 1923; D.D., Christian Coll., Auburn, Ga., 1922; m. Phoebe Allen of Lexington, Jan. 1, 1903; children—David Allen, Gordon Strobridge, Nina Dorthy, Margaret Evelyn. Ordained ministry Christian (Disciples) Ch.; successively pastor Gratz, Mt. Moriah, Fairview and Morganfield, Ky., until 1907; financial sec. MacLane Coll., Hopkinsville, Ky., 1909-13; sec. and business executive Phillips U., Enid, Okla., 1914-24; solicitor for endowment, Nat. Bd. of Edn., Disciples of Christ, Indianapolis, 1924; pres. Randolph Coll., Cisco, Tex., 1925-31; asso. dir. Nat. City Christian Ch., Washington, D.C., 1931; exec. v.p. Am. Temperance Life Ins. Co. since Jan. 1932; also rep. Equitable Life Assurance Soc. of U.S., 1934; promotional sec. Nat. Temperance Bur. Mason (32 deg., K.T.). Clubs: Rotary, Country. Author: Ever-Increasing Endowment. Promoting $1,000,000 campaign to found Amarillo Coll. Address: Woodard Washington DC‡

ROBERTS, THOMAS REASER, physicist; b. Mpls., Mar. 13, 1923; s. Thomas Cleveland and Dorothy (Reaser) R.; A.B. cum laude, Harvard, 1943; M.A., U. Minn., 1949, Ph.D., 1950; m. Carol Naus, May 2, 1942; children—Thomas Naus, Margaret Elizabeth, Shelley. Research chemist Shell Oil Co., Wood River, Ill., 1943; tchr., research asst. U. Minn., 1946-50; research physicist aero. research div. Mpls. Honeywell Regulator Co., 1950-51; staff mem. Los Alamos Sci. Lab., 1951-68. Chmn. Republican Party, Los Alamos County, 1956, mem. N.M. Central Com., 1957-68; mem. N.M. Ho. of Reps., 1957-60. Pres., bd. dirs. Mesa Pub. Library; mem. bd. of regents U. of New Mexico, 1961-68 pres., 1967-68. Served to lt. (j.g.) USNR, 1944-46. Mem. Am. Phys. Soc., Sigma Xi. Unitarian. Home: Los Alamos NM Died Feb. 24, 1968.

ROBERTS, WILLIAM ALLERTON, lawyer; b. Brooklyn, N.Y., July 16, 1900; s. William Allerton and Helen Elizabeth (O'Sullivan) R.; C.E., Tufts Coll., 1918; LL.B., Georgetown U., 1925; m. Caro-Margaret Chenay, December 15, 1923; children—William Allerton, Jr. (killed in action 1944), Helen Emily Shields, John Arthur (dec.), Martha Alice (Mrs. Creath). C.E. various construction companies, 1920-22. Transit Commissioner, Boston, 1922-23, Interstate Commerce Commn., 1923-26; began practice law, 1926; sr. atty. examiner Interstate Commerce Commn., 1927-30; spl. asst. corp. counsel for D.C. and counsel of Pub. Utilities Commission, D.C., 1930-34; people's counsel, Washington, 1934-36; sr. partner Roberts & McInnis, 1936-65; chmn., dir. Nat. Film Studios, Inc.; pres., dir. South Fla. Broadcasting Co.; Roberts Bros. Co., Big Horn Powder River Co.; pres. Fla. Air-Power, Inc. Nat. treas. Kefauver Com. Served as 2d lt. Signal Corps, 1918; 1st lt. Mass. Nat. Guard, 101st F.A., 1923; col. Air Corps, on active duty including South Pacific theatre, 1941-44, on inactive duty since Aug. 1944, USAF Ret. Res. Mem. Inter-Am. (chmn. transportation and communications com.), Am. bar assns., D.C. Bar Assn., Fed. Bar Assn. (ex-pres.; dir. Fed. Bar Bldg. Corp.), Interstate Commerce Practitioners Assn., Fed. Communications Bar Assn., Am. Vets. World War II, Sigma Delta Kappa. Democrat. Catholic. Mem. K.C. Clubs: Cosmos (Washington), Congressional Country, Capitol Yacht; Nat. Lawyers. Author: Valuation of Public Utilities, 1934. Home: Washington DC Died Apr. 8, 1968; buried Arlington Nat. Cemetery, Arlington VA

ROBERTSON, A. JAMES, astronomer; b. Rockford, Ill., May 1, 1867; s. Charles A. and Henriette G. (Ward) R.; B.S., U. of Mich., 1891; D.Sc., U. of Georgetown, 1933; m. Carolina Ancona, Oct. 8, 1903;children—Armand J., Marie Ancona, John Ancona; m. 2d, Martha P. Worthington, Sept. 21, 1911; children—Arabella Piatt, Charles Worthington. Asst. Nautical Almanac Office of U.S. Naval Observatory, 1893-1908, prin. asst., 1908-24, astronomer, 1924-27, sr. astronomer, 1927-30, head astronomer since 1930, asst. dir., 1927-29, and dir., 1929-39; professional consultant of Navy Dept. Math. Astonomy, and allied subjects since 1930. Derived the elements of the orbit of the fifth satellite of Jupiter now in use by internat. agreement in all important almanac offices; derived method for computing eclipses now in general use; also new method for computing occulations. Mem. Am. Astron. Union, Internat. Astron. Union, Astronomischer Gesellschaft, Societe Astronomique de France. Contbr. to astron. jours. and monthly notices of R.A.S. Pub., 1940, a zodiacal catalogue of 3539 stars for equinox 1950, under auspices of Nautical Almanac Office. Home: Box 3642, Georgetown Station, Washington DC‡

ROBERTSON, A. WILLIS, former United States senator; born at Martinsburg, West Virginia, May 27, 1887; son of Franklin Pierce and Josephine Ragland (Willis) R.; B.A., Univ. of Richmond, 1907, LL.B., 1908, LL.D., 1945; LL.D., Washington & Lee, U., 1949, Coll. of William and Mary, 1956; m. Gladys C. Willis, October 19, 1920; children—A. Willis, Marion Gordon. Admitted to Va. bar and began practice at Buena Vista, Va., 1908; mem. firm Willis & Robertson, 1908-10; mem. Va. State Senate, 2 terms, 1916-22 (resigned); commonwealth's atty., Rockbridge County, 1922-28; chmn. Va. Com. Game and Inland Fisheries, 1926-32; mem. 73d Congress 1933-35), Va. at large; 74th to 79th Congresses (1935-47), 7th Va. Dist.; elected to U.S. Senate, Nov. 5, 1946, for unexpired term of Carter Glass, dec.; relected U.S. Senate, 1948, 54, 60, chmn. com. banking and currency, also joint com. def. production; consultant International Bank for Reconstruction and Devel., from 1966. Served as first lieutenant, captain, and major, inf., U.S. Army, 1917-19. Mem. Jamestown Soc., S.A.R., Soc. Cin., Sons Confederate Vets., Phi Alpha Delta, Pi Kappa Alpha, Omicron Delta Kappa, Phi Beta Kappa. Democrat. Baptist. Home: Lexington VA Died Nov. 1, 1971.

ROBERTSON, FRED, lawyer; b. Craigville, N.Y., July 2, 1871; s. John M. and Nancy J. (Haley) R.; ed. common schs.; m. Luella J. Hotchkiss, May 15, 1900 (died Mar. 20, 1937); 1 dau., Agnes (Mrs. Eugene S. Gosney); m. 2d, Nelle Numbers James, June 18, 1938. Admitted to Kan. bar, 1897, mem. several bars, including Supreme Court of U.S. and U.S. Circuit Court of Appeals for 8th and 10th Circuits; pros. atty. Rawlins County, Kan., 1899-1903; member State Senate from 39th District, 1909-13; chairman Board Education at Atwood; U.S. district attorney, 1913-21; former mem. firm of Robertson, Boddington & Emerson. Prosecuted I.W.W. case in which 27 men were sent to prison on one verdict. Member Kansas State Bd. Law Examiners, 1924-48. Chairman Dem. State Com. of Kansas, 1924-46; del. to Dem. Nat. Conv., New York, 1924, Chicago, 1932. Mem. Am., Kan. and Wyandotte County bar assns., Phi Alpha Delta. Democrat. Episcopalian. Dir. in various corporations and financial interests. Home: 2219 Washington Blvd. Office: 2219 Washington Blvd., Kansas City KS‡

ROBERTSON, HOLCOMBE MCGAVOCK, physician; b. Max Meadows, Wythe County, Va., Oct. 24, 1874; s. Walter Henderson and Sallie (McGavock) R.; A.B., Hampden-Sydney (Va.) Coll., 1896; M.D., U. of Va., 1900; m. Sarah Irvine Curtis, June 2, 1903; children—Holcombe McGavock (dec.), Virginia Keith, Randal McGavock. Interne, St. Vincent's Hosp., 1900-01 (Norfolk); gen. practice Wythe County, 1901-02; U.S. Pub. Health Service, 1902-38, becoming med. dir. Mem. A.M.A., Med. Soc. Va., Sigma Chi, Alpha Omega Alpha. Presbyterian. Home: 3912 Seminary Av., Richmond VA‡

ROBERTSON, LAWRENCE VERNON, lawyer; b. Rockbridge County, Va., July 4, 1906; s. John Thomas and Theresa Beatrice (Campbell) R.; student U. W.Va., 1926-30; LL.B., U. Ariz., 1931; m. Lemma Withers Starling, Nov. 1, 1934; 1 son, Lawrence Vernon. Admitted to Ariz. bar, 1931, practiced in Tucson; sr. mem. firm Robertson & Fickett, 1967-71. Mem. Bd. Ariz. Bar Examiners, 1948-52; adv. counsel ethics Supreme Ct. Ariz., 1945-52. Chmn. trustees Bank Tucson; gen. counsel So. Ariz. Bank & Trust Co. Past pres., dir. Tucson Little Theatre, S.W. chpt. Arthritis and Rheumatism Found; founder Tucson Med. Center, 1948-50; mem. Gov. Ariz. Adv. Com., from 1969. Co-chmn. Ariz. Americans for Goldwater, 1964. Bd. dirs. Rheumatism and Arthritis Found., 1948-52; nat. adv. bd. Scripps Clinic and Research Found., from 1965. Recipient medallion of honor U. Ariz. President's Club, 1962. Mem. Am., Ariz., Pima County bar assns., Internat. Assn. Ins. Counsel, Am. Counsel Assn., Tucson C. of C. (past v.p., dir.), Phi Delta Phi. Sigma Nu. Clubs: Old Pueblo (past pres., dir.); Tucson Country, Mountain Oyster (Tucson); San Diego Yacht; La Jolla (Cal.) Country. Home: Tucson AZ Died Nov. 5, 1971.

ROBERTSON, LEROY J., composer; b. Fountain Green, Utah, Dec. 21, 1896; s. Jasper Heber and Alice (Adams) R.; diploma, N.E. Conservatory of Music, Boston (studied under Chadwick), 1923; student of Carl Busch, 1925, Ernest Bloch, 1930, 32, Hugo Leichtentritt, 1933; A.M., Brighman Young U., 1932; Ph.D., U. of Southern California, 1954; Naomi Nelson, Sept. 1, 1925; children—Alice Marian, Renee, Karen Naomi, James Leroy Prof. and head music dept. Brigham Young U., 1925-48; prof. head music dept. U. of Utah, 1948-62; chamber music played by Chgo., Walden, W.Q.X.R. (N.Y.), N.B.C., Hart House, Lener, San Francisco, Roth, Paganini and other string quartets; orchestral works performed by Brigham Young U., Utah, Houston, C.B.S., N.B.C., Los Angeles, Pittsburgh, Athens, Detroit, Phila., Toronto symphony orchs., N.Y., Berlin, Israeli philharmonics; performances throughout the Americas, Europe, Africa, Orient and Australia; works recorded by Columbia, Vanguard, Soc. for Preservation Am. Musical Heritage. Chmn. exec. music com. Latter Day Saints Ch., 1963-69, cons. to gen. music com. until 1971. Awarded Endicott prize for Overture Emin, Boston, 1923; 1st place for Quintet for Piano and Strings, Soc. for Pub. of Am. Music, New York, 1936; $350.00 prize for Rhapsody for Piano and Orchestra, Utah Inst. of Fine Arts, 1945; Reichhold award of $25,000.00 for Trilogy, 1947; N.Y. Critics Circle award for String Quartet in E Minor, 1941. Mem. Phi Beta Kappa, Kappa Gamma Psi, A.S.C.A.P. Minor, 1941. Mem. Phi Beta Kappa, Kappa Gamma Psi, A.S.C.A.P. Fellow Utah Acad. of Sciences, Arts and Letters. Compositions include: (chamber music) Quintet for Piano and Strings in A Minor, String Quartet in E Minor, American Serenade for String Quartet; (orchestral works) Trilogy, Passacaglia, Endicott Overture, Saguara Overture, Festival Overture, Concerto for Violin and Orch., Concerto for Violincello and Orch., Rhapsody for Piano and Orch.; (choral works) Oratorio from the Book of Mormon, Alleluiah and Chorale for Symphonic Band and Chorus; (solo piano) Three Etudes, Novelette. Home: Salt Lake City UT Died July 25, 1971; buried Salt Lake City UT

ROBERTSON, MILES E., business exec.; b. Canastota, N.Y., Nov. 14, 1889; s. Robert Duncan and Frances A. (Greenfield) R.; Syracuse U., 1912; m. Constance Pierrepont Noyes, Aug. 24, 1918. Various positions Oneida (N.Y.), Ltd., 1913-22, asst. sales mgr., 1922-24, dir., from 1923, asst. gen. mgr., 1925, gen. mgr. from 1926, pres., 1950-60, chmn. bd., 1955-67, ret., 1964, hon. chmn., from 1967, later chmn. exec. com. Mem. Am. Mgmt. Assn. (dir. 1935-37), Asso. Industries N.Y. State (dir., from 1947), Beta Theta Pi. Elk. Home: Kenwood Station, Oneida NY Died Oct. 6, 1972.

ROBERTSON, NORMAN A(LEXANDER), ednl. adminstr.; b. Vancouver, B.C., Mar. 4, 1904; s. L. F. and F. (MacLeod) R.; B.A., Univ. of Brit. Columbia, 1923; LL.D.; student Balliol Coll., Oxford U., 1923-26; LL.D., Cambridge U.; m. H. J. Welling, 1928; children—Alix, Judith. Third sec., Can. External Affairs, Service, Ottawa, 1929; under sec. of State for External Affairs, 1941-46; high commr. for Canada in the United Kingdom, London, Eng., 1946-49, 1952-57; clerk of Privy Council and sec. to Cabinet, Ottawa, 1949-52; ambassador from Can. to U.S., Washington, 1957-58; under-sec. for external affairs Canadian govt., 1958-64; chief negotiator for Can. in Geneva, chmn. Canadian Tariffs and Trade Com., 1964-67; dir. grad. Sch. Internat. Affairs, Carleton U., Ottawa, Ont., Can., 1965-68. Home: Ottawa ON Canada Died July 16, 1968.

ROBERTSON, REUBEN BUCK, corp. exec.; b. Cin., June 11, 1879; s. Charles Dumbreck and Cynthia (Buck) R.; A.B., Yale, 1900; postgrad. U. Cin. Law Sch., 1900-03; D.Sc., N.C. State Coll., 1932; LL.D., Western Carolina Coll., 1956; m. Hope Thomson, June 7, 1905; children—Hope (Mrs. Russell Norburn), Reuben Buck (dec.), Laura Thomson (dec.), Logan Thomson. Admitted to bar, 1903; mem. firm Robertson and Buchwalter, 1903-06; spl. assignments in mfg., 1907-12; gen. mgr. Champion Fibre Co., 1912-18, v.p., 1918-25, pres., 1925-35; exec. v.p. Champion Papers, Inc., 1935-46, pres., 1946-50, 55-62, chmn. bd., 1950-60. hon. chmn. bd. dirs., until 1972. Past pres. N.C. Forestry Assn.; past chmn. So. Conf. Human Relations in Industry; past mem. adv. bd., N.C. sect. R.F. Corp.; past chmn. Asheville Community Chest, 1933; past chmn. bd. trustees Western Carolina Teachers Coll.; ex-trustee U. N.C., Asheville Sch.; past mem. State Planning Bd.; past chmn. N.C. Wood Utilization Com. Dept. Commerce; past mem. So. Appalachian Research Council; past chmn. City-County Dept. Com., Asheville; mem. Pres's. Labor Industry Con., 1942; mem. bus. adv. council Dept. Commerce; past mem. Nat. War Labor Bd.; past trustee Com. Econ. Devel., Jr. Achievement. Inst. Paper Chemistry. Past dir. N.A.M.; past pres. Am. Paper and Pulp Assn. Named Man of South for 1950; Conservation award Am. Forestry Assn., 1954, Human Relations award Soc. Advancement Mgmt., 1957. Mem. Zeta Psi, Phi Delta Phi. Democrat. Presbyn. Mason (32). Clubs: Pen and Plate (past pres.); Yale of Asheville; Canton Civitan (ex-pres.); Biltmore Forest Country. Home: Asheville NC Died Dec. 26, 1972.

ROBERTSON, ROBERT CRAWFORD, orthopedic surgeon; b. Coulterville, Ill., July 29, 1899; s. John Wylie and Mary Elizabeth (Crawford) R.; A.B., U. Ill., 1921, B.S., 1922, M.S., 1924, M.D., 1925; m. Frankie Marion Condray, Sept. 7, 1925; children—Elizabeth Eugenia (Mrs. Stephen Tripp Smith), Mary Louise (Mrs. Thomas Burke Hodgson). Intern, resident St. Luke's Hosp., Chgo., 1924-26; fellow Willis C. Campbell Clinic, Memphis, 1926-27; practice medicine, specializing in orthopedic surgery, Chattanooga, 1927-69; founder, chief orthopedic services Baroness Erlanger Hosp., T.C. Thompson's Childrens Hosp.; mem. staff Meml. Hosp., Tenn. State Tb. Hosp., past chief of staff Pine Breeze Sanitorium; cons. Hamilton Meml. Hosp., Dalton, Ga., Copper Basin Gen. Hosp., Copper Hill, Tenn., Emerald-Hodgson Hosp., Sewanee, Tenn.; designated orthopedic surgeon U.S. Employees Compensation Commn., Tenn. Crippled Children's Service Bd. dirs. Little Theater, Meml. Hosp., Chattanooga. Served to 2d lt. with inf., U.S. Army, 1918-19, to col. with M.C., AUS, 1942-45, 51-55. Decorated Legion of Merit, Bronze Star medal, Purple Heart; recipient Arrowhead award. Diplomate Am. Bd. Orthopedic Surgery. Fellow A.C.S., Am. Acad. Orthopedic Surgeons, Internat. Acad. Medicine, Am. Geriatric Soc.; mem. A.M.A., So. Tenn. med. assns., Hamilton County (past pres.), Chattanooga med. socs., Chattanooga Acad. Surgery (past pres.), Clin. Orthopedic Soc. (past v.p.), Internat. Soc. Orthopedic Surgery and Traumatology, Soc. Med. Cons. to Armed Forces, Sigma Xi, Alpha Omega Alpha, Zeta Psi, Phi Beta Pi. Rotarian. Clubs: Chattanooga Golf and Country, Lookout Mountain Fairyland. Contbr. articles to profl. jours. Home: Chattanooga TN Died Jan. 15, 1969; buried National Cemetery Chattanooga TN

ROBERTSON, ROBERT SPELMAN, chief justice of Ont.; b. Goderich, Ont., Dec. 11, 1870; s. William Roderick and Fanny Augusta (Smith) R.; LL.D., U. of Toronto, 1943; m. Laura Gertrude Segsworth, June 1, 1900; 4 sons, 1 dau. Called to Ont. bar, 1894; practiced law, Stratford, 1898-1916, Toronto, 1917-38; chief justice of Ont. since 1938. Mem. bd. govs., Upper Can. Coll., Toronto Western Hosp. Clubs: York, Royal Canadian Yacht. Mem. United Ch. of Can. Home: 53 Castle Frank Rd. Address: Osgoode Hall, Toronto Canada‡

ROBERTSON, THOMAS ERNEST, patent lawyer; b. Washington, D.C., May 7, 1871; s. Thomas J. W. and Jane M. (Turner) R.; LL.B., National Univ., Washington, 1906, LL.D., 1926; LL.D., Bates Coll., 1930; m. Mary Brackett, June 29, 1897; children—Thomas Brackett, Nathan Wood, Louis. Practiced patent law in Washington, D.C., 1906-20, as sr. mem. Robertson & Johnson; commr. of patents, by apptmt. of Presidents Harding, Coolidge and Hoover, 1921-33. Apptd. by President Coolidge chmn. Am. delegation to negotiate treaty concerning indsl. property, The Hague, Oct. 8-Nov. 6, 1925 (duty ratified by U.S. Senate); del. to Pan-Am. Trade Mark Conv., Washington, 1929; prof. patent law, Nat. Univ. Law Sch., 1926-42. Trustee Storer Coll. (Harpers Ferry). Chairman Patent Section, Am. Bar Assn., 1939; hon. mem. Am. Patent Law Assn. (pres. 1918-19), Gamma Eta Gamma. Republican. Episcopalian (deputy to General Conventions of Episcopal Ch., 1931-46). Club: Cosmos. Home: 6902 Piney Branch Rd., Washington 12 DC‡

ROBERTSON, WALTER SPENCER, business executive; b. Nottoway Co. Va., Dec. 7, 1893; s. William Henry and Anne M. (Robinson) R.; student Hoge Military Acad., 1907-09, Coll. of William and Mary, 1910-11, Davidson College, 1911-12; LL.D., Davidson Coll., 1955, U. Richmond, 1955, Hampden-Sydney Coll., 1958, Univ. S.C., 1959, Coll. William and Mary, 1960; m. Mary Dade Taylor, Nov. 4, 1925; children—Walter Spencer, Jr., Catherine Taylor (Mrs. Herbert A. Claiborne, Jr.), and Jaquelin Taylor. Partner of Scott & Stringfellow, Richmond, Va., 1925-42, 46-65. Chief United States Lend-Lease Mission to Australia, 1943-44; econ. adviser to U.S. Dept. of State, 1945; minister and counselor econ. affairs U.S. Embassy, Chungking, 1945-46; charge d'affaires, Sept. 1945-July 1946; U.S. Commr., Peiping Exec. Hdqrs. (Marshall Truce Commn.), 1946; mem. pub. adv. com. to E.C.A. China Aid Program, 1948; asst. sec. state for Far East Affairs, 1953-59. Mem. U.S. delegation Geneva Conf., 1954, Manila Pact Conf., Bangkok, 1955, ministerial meeting North Atlantic Council, Paris, France, 1955, SEATO Fgn. Ministers Conf., Karachi, 1956, Canberra, 1957, Manila, 1958; chmn. U.S. delegation Colombo Plan Conf. Wellington, New Zealand, 1956; U.S. delegate 14th United Nations Gen. Assembly. V.p. State and City (now State-Planters) Bank & Trust Co. 1922-25; pres. Richmond Stock Exchange, 1930-33 governor New York Stock Exchange, 1961-64; pres. Robertson Investment Corp.; trustee Geo. C. Marshall Found.; mem. adv. bd. Robert E. Lee Meml. Found. Hoover Instn. War, Revolution and Peace Stanford Dulles oral history project Princeton. Trustee Va. Hist. Soc., Richmond Meml. Hosp.; bd. visitors Coll. William and Mary; pres. Va. Mus. Fine Arts, 1959-67, Richmond Community Council, 1940-43; past mem. bd. govs. Assn. of N.Y. Stock Exchange Firms, Invstmnts. Bankers Assn. Am. Served in U.S. Air Corps (pilot), 2d lt., World War I. Mem. English Speaking Union, Soc. of Cinn., Soc. Colonial Wars, Phi Beta Kappa, also member Omicron Delta Kappa. Decorated: Medal for Merit (1946); Grand Cordon of the Order of Propitious Cloud (Chinese); Knight Grand Cross Most Exalted Order of the White Elephant (Thailand); Republic of Korea Medal; Philippine Legion of Honor (comdr.). Episcopalian. Clubs: Metropolitan, Alibi (Washington); Brook (N.Y.C.); Commonwealth (Richmond). Home: Richmond VA Died Jan. 18, 1970; buried Hollywood Cemetery, Richmond VA

ROBEY, LOUIS W., financial counsellor; b. Balt., Apr. 10, 1883; s. William W. and Anna V. (Plecker) R.; A.B., Bucknell U., 1904; LL.B., U. Pa., 1909; LL.D., Alderson-Broaddus College, 1954, Bucknell Univ., Lewisburg, Pa., 1959; married Effie Jane Derr, Sept. 7, 1912. Instr. Latin, Greek, Bucknell U., 1904-06; instr. comml. law U. Pa., 1909-11; admitted to Pa. bar, 1910, practiced in Phila., 1909-31; real estate law, finance Temple U., 1913-29; dir. Marts & Lundy, financial counsellors, N.Y.C., 1932-68, vice president, 1932-56, vice chairman, 1956-58, sr. cons., hon. vice chmn., 1958-68; pub. relations counsellor Am. Bapt. Bd. Edn., 1942-68. Mem. Phi Beta Kappa, Delta Upsilon, Order of Coif, Phi Delta Phi. Republican. Baptist. Clubs: Advertising (New York City); The Merion Golf (Ardmore, Pa.). Author: Outlines of Real Estate Law and Finance, 1924; Check Lists of Fund Raising Essentials, 1954; and, Outline of Fund-Raising Procedures, 1962; also monographs in field. Home: New York City NY Died June 28, 1968; buried Muncy PA

ROBEY, RALPH WEST, economist, journalist; b. Masontown, W.Va., Aug. 29, 1899; s. John Calvin and Joan (West) R.; A.B., Indiana U., 1920; A.M. Columbia U., 1923, Ph.D., 1938; m. Kathleen Moran, Jan. 28, 1941. Clerk in Nat. City Bank, New York, 1918-21; with Federal Reserve Bd., 1921-22; instr., U. of Rochester (N.Y.), 1923-25; lecturer on banking, Columbia U., 1925-38, asst. prof. 1938-46, financial editor New York Evening Post, 1931-33; contbg. editor Washington, (D.C.) Post, 1933-35; asso. editor Newsweek Mag., 1937-38, writer column Business Tides" 1938-46; editorial work Nat. Assn. Mfrs., 1941-46; chief economist, v.p. 1946-53; economist Wertheim & Co., N.Y.C., 1953-54; prof. banking U.S.C., 1954-57; econ. adv. N.A.M., 1956-63; adj. prof. Am. U., from 1953; cons. Mem. Bus. Research Adv. Council, 1957-66, Nat. Labor Mgmt. Manpower Policy Com., 1957-63. Pres. Council Applied Econs., 1936-39; mem. Rep. candidate Alf. M. Landon's personal staff, 1936, pres. camp. Mem. Conf. Business, Economists, Am. Econ. Assn., Sigma Alpha Epsilon, Beta Gamma Sigma, Alpha Kappa Psi, Phi Chi Theta (hon.) Clubs The City Tavern Association, also mem. The Cosmos (Washington, D.C.); Century, Neronians (N.Y.C.). Editor: The Monetary Problems, 1936. Author: Fundamentals in Real Estate (with Blake Snyder), 1927; Contemporary Banking (with H. P. Willis and J. M. Chapman), 1933; Roosevelt vs Recovery, 1934 Purchasing Power, 1938. Home: Washington DC Died July 5, 1972; buried Forest Hills Cemetery Boston MA

ROBINS, CHARLES A., past gov. of Ida.; b. Defiance, Ia., Dec. 8, 1884; s. Charles Macalester and Rebecca Jane (Burke) R.; A.B., William Jewell Coll., Liberty, Mo., 1907; M.D., U. Chgo., 1917; m. Patricia Simpson, Nov. 15, 1939; children—Patricia A., Paula J., Rebecca J. In gen. med. prac., St. Maries, Ida., 1919-46; mgr. St. Maries Hosp., St. Maries, Ida., 1939-46; dist. surgeon, C.M. & St.P.R.R., 1939-46; state senator, 1938,40, 42, 44, pres. pro-tem of senate, 1943-44; gov. of Ida., 1947-51; medical dir. North Idaho Med. Service Bureau. Awarded nat. honors for 1st prize, post history, Am. Legion. Mem. A.M.A., Phi Gamma Delta, Nu Sigma Nu. Republican. Episcopalian. Mason, Elk, Eagle, Eastern Star. Club: Kiwanis. Home: Lewiston ID Died Sept. 20, 1970; buried Lewis Clark Meml. Gardens, Lewiston ID

ROBINS, ELIZABETH, (MRS. GEORGE RICHMOND PARKS) (PSEUD. C.E. RAIMOND), author; b. Louisville, Ky.; d. Charles E. and Hannah M. R.; ed. Putnam Female Sem., Zanesville, O.; m. George Richmond Parks, of Boston, Jan. 12, 1885 (dec.). Author: George Mandeville's Husband, 1894; The New Moon, 1895; Below the Salt, 1896; The Open Question, 1898; The Magnetic North, 1904; A Dark Lantern, 1905; (play) Votes for Women; The Convert, 1907; Come and Find Me, 1908; The Florentine France, 1909;

Where Are You Going To?, 1912; Way Stations, 1913; Camilla, 1918; The Messenger, 1920; Time Is Whispering, 1923; Secret That Was Kept, 1926; Ibsen and the Actress, 1928; Prudence and Peter and Their Adventure with Pots and Pans, 1928; Florentine Frame, 1929; Secret That Was Kept, 1930; Theatre and Friendship, 1932. Address: Backset Town, Henfield, Sussex England*‡

ROBINSON, B(RITTAIN) B(RAGUNLER), agronomist; b. Topeka, Kan., Dec. 4, 1899; s. Harold and Nettie Maude (Bragunier) R.; B.S., Tex. A. and M. Coll., 1922; M.S., Mich. Agr. Coll., 1924; Ph.D., Mich. State Coll., 1932; m. Lois Chamberlin, 1923; children—Nancy June, Thomas Wood; m. 2d, Clara Mildred Green, Dec. 28, 1932; 1 dau., Alice Roxana. Asst., Mich. State Coll., 1922-24; jr. and asst. plant breeder U.S. Dept. Agr., East Lansing, Mich., 1924-31, asst. and asso. plant breeder, Corvallis, Ore., 1932-35, agronomist, sr. agronomist, Washington, 1936-50, charge fiber plants other than cotton, ARA, 1946-50, prin. agronomist charge abaca prodn. Central Am., Inter-Am. Inst. Agrl. Scis., Turrialba, Costa Rica, 1950-52; research agronomist RFC, then U.S. Gen. Services Administrn. charge abaca prodn. C.A., 1953-57; research adviser crops ICA, Beirut, Lebanon, 1958, Dacca, East Pakistan, from 1959. Field exploratory survey fiber plants, Haiti, 1941, 55; fiber cons., Peru, Chile, Ecuador, 1941; textile cons. Tech. Indsl. Intelligence Com., U.S. Army, Germany and Italy, 1945; fiber cons. Pan Am. Union, 1947, 49; del. Seed Conf., Ankara, Turkey, 1959. Mem. Sigma Xi, Gamma Sigma Delta, Phi Sigma. Episcopalian. Mason. Club: Dacca (East Pakistan). Author: The Braqunier Family in America, 1969; also numerous tech. articles. Home: Lake Worth FL Died Dec. 10, 1969; buried Oakwood IL

ROBINSON, BARCLAY, lawyer; born at Hartford, Conn., June 6, 1897; s. Lucius F. and Elinor (Cooke) R.; A.B., Yale, 1919, law student, 1922-23; law student Harvard University, Cambridge, Mass., 1920-22; m. Mary Parsons, Nov. 29, 1930; children—Barclay, Betsy Alden (Mrs. Betsy Taylor). Admitted to Conn. bar, 1923, practiced in Hartford, member firm, Robinson, Robinson & Cole, 1926-50, counsel, from 1962; senior vice president in charge trust department Hartford National Bank and Trust Co., 1950-61, vice-chmn. charge trust dept., 1961-62, also dir.; dir. Dime Savs. Bank Hartford, Aetna Life Ins. Co., Aetna Casualty & Surety Co., Avon Water Co., The Ensign-Bickford Company, Smyth Mfg. Co., Standard Fire Ins. Co. Alderman, Hartford, 1927-33, pros. atty., 1927-30, corp. counsel, 1934-36, also mem. bd. finance; probate judge Dist. Avon, 1936-57. Member board dirs., president Hartford. Hosp.; director Castine (Maine) Community Hospital; v.p., dir. Conn. Humane Society; trustee Horace Bushnell Meml. Hall Corp., McLean Fund. Mem. Am., Conn., Hartford Co. bar associations, Conn. State Bank Assn. Conglist. Clubs: Hartford, Farmington Valley Polo. Home: Avon CT Died Sept. 24, 1971; buried Cedar Hill Cemetery Hartford CT

ROBINSON, CHARLES ALEXANDER, educator; b. W. Hebron, Washington Co., N.Y., Feb. 22, 1871; s. William and Mary Elizabeth (Archibald) R.; grad. Phillips Acad., Andover, Mass. (high honors), 1890; A.B., Princeton (Latin salutatorian), 1894, A.M. (classical fellow), 1895, Ph.D., 1901; traveled and studied in England, Germany, Italy, and Greece, 1895-96; attended Johns Hopkins, 1896-97; m. Sarah Sharpe Westcott, of Camden, N.J., June 16, 1898. Instr. Greek, 1897-98, Latin, 1898-1903, Princeton; head of Latin dept., John C. Green Sch. of Science of Princeton, 1900-03; prin. Peekskill Mil. Acad. since Dec. 1903. Mem. Am. Philol. Assn. Presbyterian. Republican. Author: Outlines of Latin Prose Syntax, 1899 (Princeton); The Tropes and Figures of Isaeus (Ph.D. thesis), 1901 (Princeton). Assisted Prof. A. F. West in publication of West's Latin Grammar, 1902. Address: Peekskill NY‡

ROBINSON, EDWARD G., actor; b. Bucharest, Romania, Dec. 12, 1893; s. Morris and Sarah Goldenberg; brought to U.S., 1903; ed. Townsend Harris Hall, N.Y., 1907-10, Coll. City N.Y. 1910-12, Columbia U. Am. Acad. Dramatic Arts N.Y.C.; m. Gladys Lloyd Cassell, Jan. 21, 1927 (div. Aug. 1956); 1 son, Edward G.; m. 2d, Jane Bodenheimer, Jan. 16, 1958. Made First profl. appearance as Satan in Paid in Full, Binghamton, N.Y., 1913; first N.Y.C. appearance as the Frenchman and Andre Lemair in Under Fire; appeared in numerous other important roles, 1916; appeared in Middle of the Night, 1956; toured in Darkness at Noon, 1951-52; made film debut in the Bright Shawl (silent), 1923; played leading roles in films including Little Caesar, 1930, The Little Giant, 1933, Dark Hazard, 1934, Barbary Coast, 1935, Kid Galahad, 1937, Unholy Partners, 1941, The Sea Wolf, 1941, Double Indemnity, 1944, Our Vines Have Tender Grapes, 1945, All My Sons, 1948, Key Largo, 1948, Operation X, 1951, Illegal, 1955, Actors and Sin, 1952, Hell on Frisco Bay, 1955, Ten Commandments, 1956, Hole in the Head, 1959, 1959, My Geisha, Seven Thieves, Pepe, 1959-60, Sammy Going South, The Prize, The Outrage, Cheyenne Autumn, Good Neighbour Sam, Boy Ten Feet Tall, Robin and the Seven Hoods, Biggest Bundle, Never a Dull Moment, Peking Blonde, Grand Slam, Operation St. Peter, Cincinnati Kid, MacKenna's Gold, Song of Norway, The Ole Man Who Cried Wolf, also on radio programs and television programs. Served with U.S. Navy during World War I, with O.W.I., World War II. Recipient Townsen Harris medal Alumni Assn. Coll. City N.Y., 1936, Eleanor Roosevelt Humanitarian award, 1963. Decorated chevalier Legion de'Honneur, France, 1952; officer de l'Instruction Publique. Mem. Actors Equity Assn. Clubs: Lambs (N.Y.); Masquers (Hollywood, Cal.). Author: The Kibitzer (with J. Swerling), 1929. Home: Beverly Hills CA Died Jan. 26, 1973.

ROBINSON, FANNIE RUTH, educator; b. Carbondale, Pa.; d. Charles A. and Mary (Frothingham) R.; A.B., Rutgers Coll., 1871, A.M., 1873; Ph.D., Lake Forest U., 1894. Preceptress Ferry Hall, Lake Forest Univ., several yrs.; dean and pres. 7 yrs., Oxford (O.) Coll.; now head Miss Robinson's Sch., Boston. Contbr. of prose and verse to mags.; represented in Crandall's Representative American Sonnets. Address: 46 Chestnut St., Boston‡

ROBINSON, FRED J(AMES), lumberman; b. Detroit, Mich., Sept. 1, 1870; s. Thomas and Sarah (Wilkinson) R.; ed. pub. schs.; m. Nelly Hendricks, Dec. 10, 1891; children—Ethel, W. Dean, Edith. Pres. Fred. J. Robinson Lumber Co. Dist. chief of ord. Mich. World War; adjusted all uncompleted contracts in Mich. for Ordnance Dept. after close of war. Awarded D.S.M. (U.S.). Republican. Clubs: Detroit, Bloomfield Hills Golf. Home: Bloomfield Hills MI Office: 11300 E 8 Mile Rd., Detroit MI‡

ROBINSON, GEROLD TANQUARY, univ. prof.; b. Chase City, Va., June 21, 1892; s. George Benson and Anna May (Hervey) R.; A.B., Stanford U.; A.M., Columbia U., 1922, Ph.D., 1930; m. Clemens Tanquary, Mar. 4, 1921. Mem. editorial bd. The Dial, 1919, The Freeman, 1920-24; teacher of history, Columbia Univ. since 1924, mem. faculty of polit. sci. since 1931, dir. Russian Inst., 1946-51, Seth Low professor history since 1950; research in Russia studying agrarian history of country, 1925-27 and 1937; corr. mem. Sch. Slavonic Studies, U. of London (England) since 1927; mem. adv. com., Russian lang. sect., Harvard U., 1934, Columbia U., 1935, U. of Calif., 1936, 37; chief, USSR Division, Research and Analysis Branch, Office of Strategic Services, U.S. Government, 1941-45; same, Department of State, 1945. Awarded Medal of Freedom by War Department, 1947. Served as 1st lieut., United States Army, 1917-19. Mem. Com. on Slavic Studies of Am. Council of Learned Socs. 1937-48; com. World Area Research, Social Sci. Research Council, 1946-51; joint com. Slavic studies Am. Council Learned Socs. and Social Sci. Research Council, 1948-51; trustee Institute of Current World Affairs, 1939-43; Council on Foreign Relations, American Hist. Association, Am. Philos. Soc. (received Lewis prize, 1956), Sigma Delta Chi, Phi Beta Kappa. Club: Century (N.Y. City). Author: Rural Russia Under the Old Regime, 1932. Contbr. to Persistent Questions in Public Discussion, 1924; Civilization in the United States, 1922; Nationalism and Internationalism, 1950; Foundations of National Power, 1951; also articles on Russian history and other subjects to books and jours.; editorial adviser to Encyclopedia of Social Sciences, Social Science Abstracts; mem. editorial bd. of Jour. of Modern History, 1937-39, Am. Slavic and East European Review. Home: New York City NY Died Apr. 1971.

ROBINSON, GUSTAVUS HILL, lawyer, educator; b. Whitestone, N.Y., Jan. 11, 1881; s. Gustavus Hawes and Margaret (Hill) R.; grad. Mt. Hermon (Mass.) Sch., 1901; A.B. summa cum laude, Harvard U., 1905, LL.B., cum laude, 1909, S.J.D., 1916; m. Sarah Fuller Anderson, Aug. 15, 1916; children—Douglas Hill Robinson, M.D., Margaret Hill Robinson (Mrs. Frederick L. Olmsted). Admitted to Mass. and N.Y. State bar, 1910; asso. firm Burlingham, Montgomery and Beecher, N.Y.C., 1909-12; prof. law. Tulane U., 1912-15, U. Mo., 1916-18, U. Cal., 1919-22, Boston U., 1922-29, Cornell U., Ithaca, N.Y., from 1929, William Nelson Cromwell prof. internat. law, emeritus, until 1972. Lectr. admiralty law U. Cal., 1949; vis. prof. U. Leiden, Netherlands, spring 1959; cons. N.Y. State Law Revision Commn.; admiralty cons. Lend-Lease Adminstrn., Washington; cons. Comml. Code for U.S. Served as capt., San. Corps, AUS, 1918-19. Mem. Phi Beta Kappa, Phi Delta Phi, also various prof. assns. Episcopalian. Clubs: Savage, Cornell (N.Y.). Author: Cases and Authorities in Public Utilities, 1926, 2d edit., 1935; Admiralty Law in the U.S., 1939. (U.S. Maritime Commn. placed a copy on each ship, 1944). Mem. bd. editors, Harvard Law Rev., 1907. Contbr. to law revs. Home: Ithaca NY Died Sept. 11, 1972.

ROBINSON, HOWARD LEE, lawyer; b. near Clarksburg, W.Va., Nov. 21, 1887; s. Joseph Blackwell and Martha Evelyn (Fox) R.; LL.B., Washington and Lee, 1913; m. Katherine Ernst, Jan. 14, 1926. Admitted to W.Va. bar, 1913, in practice at Clarksburg; mem. Robinson & Robinson, 1921-34; mem. Robinson & Stump since 1934; U.S. atty. Northern Dist. of W.Va., 1934-38. Served as pvt. U.S. Army, 1917-19. Chmn. Harrison County Dem. Exec. Com., 1930-32; del. to Dem. Nat. Conv., Chgo., 1940. Mem. Am. Law Inst., Am. Bar Association, W.Va. State and Harrison Co. (pres., 1940) bar assns., Am. Judicature Soc., Internat. Assn. Ins. Counsel, Acad. Polit. Sci. Democrat. Baptist. Mason. Clubs: Kiwanis, also Clarksburg Country. Home: Clarksburg WV Died Nov. 3, 1963; buried Benedum Cemetery Bridgeport WV

ROBINSON, HOWARD WEST, educator; b. Phila., Apr. 20, 1896; s. William John and Jennie (Scott) R.; B.S., U. Pa., 1921, M.S., 1925; Ph.D., Vanderbilt U., 1929; m. Corinne G. Hogden, Sept. 9, 1944; 1 son, Glenn Adrian. Instr., research medicine U. Pa., 1923-25; instr., asst. prof. biochemistry Vanderbilt U. Med. Sch., 1925-31; fellow Children's Hosp. Research Found., Cin., 1931-41; sect. editor Chem. Abstracts since 1940; research chemist dept. pediatrics Temple U. Med. Sch., 1941-44, prof. physiol. chemistry since 1944. Mem. Am. Chem. Soc., Am. Assn. Biol. Chemists, A.A.A.S., Franklin Inst., Phila. Physiol. Soc., Sigma Xi (chpt. pres. 1951-52). Protestant Episcopal. Co-author: Approved Laboratory Technic (rev. edit.), 1951. Contbr. med. articles profl. publs. Home: Lansdowne PA Died Mar. 1971.

ROBINSON, JACK ROOSEVELT, athlete, business exec.; b. Cairo, Ga., Jan. 31, 1919; s. Jerry and Mallie (McGriff) R.; student U. Cal. at Los Angeles, 1939-41; LL.D., Berthune Cookman Coll., Daytona Beach, Fla., 1951, Howard U., 1957; m. Rachel A. Isum, Feb. 10, 1946;children—Jack Roosevelt (dec.), Sharon A., David R. First negro to enter profl. baseball, 1946; played with Bklyn. Dodgers, 1946-56; retired, 1956; former v.p. Chock Full O'Nuts Co., N.Y.C. Chmn. N.A.A.C.P. Fight for Freedom Fund, 1957. Mem. bd. parole Conn. State Prison; board of directors, aldo cons. A.T.I.; dir. YMCA Greater N.Y.C., board mgrs. Harlem br. Served as 2d lt., cav., AUS, 1941-44. Recipient Spingarn medal, 1956. Mem. N.A.A.C.P., Nat. Conf. Christians and Jews. Home: Stamford CT Died Oct. 24, 1972.

ROBINSON LYDIA GILLINGHAM, translator; b. Geneva, Ill., Nov. 12, 1875; d. James C. and Emma J. (Gillingham) R.; A.B., Rockford (Ill.) Coll., 1896. Asst., Chicago Pub. Library, 1898-1905; asst. editor The Monist and The Open Court, 1907-17; editor of publs., Chicago Pub. Library, since 1919. Translator: Babel Bible, Third Lecture (Delitzsch), 1906; Music in the Old Testament (Cornill), 1909; Akbar, Emperior of India (Garbe), 1909; Geometrical Solutions Derived from Mechanics (from Heiberg's German translation of Archimedes), 1909; Has the Psychological Laboratory Proved Helpful? (Billia), 1909; Spinoza's Short Treatise on God, Man and Human Welfare (from Dutch), 1909; The Algebra of Logic (Couturat), 1914; What is Dogma? (Le Roy), 1918; also numerous scientific and philos. articles from the French and German. Trustee Rockford Coll. Mem. A.L.A., Ill. Library Assn. Clubs: Library, College. Home: Versailles Hotel. Address: Public Library, Chicago IL‡

ROBINSON, MARY DUMMETT NAUMAN, author; b. Hancock Barracks, Houlton, Me.; d. Col. George Nauman, U.S.A.; ed. Charleston, S.C.; m. Lancaster, Pa., Frederick Robinson, U.S.A., 1875. Author: Sidney Elliott; Twisted Threads; Clyde Wardleigh's Promise; Eva's Adventures in Shadowland; The Enchanted Princess; Colonel Robinson's Boys. Address: 223 E. King St., Lancaster PA‡

ROBINSON, REMUS GRANT, surgeon; b. Birmingham, Ala., Dec. 15, 1904; s. Remus G. and Lily (Hill) R.; B.S., U. Mich., 1927, M.D., 1930; M. Marybodine Busey, Dec. 28, 1933; children—Carole Y., Ilene E., Frederick E. Intern Homer G. Phillips Hosp., St. Louis, 1930-31, resident, 1931-34; practice medicine specializing in gen. surgery, Detroit, 1934-70; mem. staff Providence Hosp., 1953-70, sr. attending surgeon, 1957-70; mem. staff Sinai Hosp., 1955-70. Mem. med. hosp. study com. Detroit Commn. Community Relations, 1957-70; mem. Boys Com. Detroit, 1960-70; co-chmn. United Negro Coll. Fund, 1952; mem. Detroit Met. Regional Planning Commn., 1955-70; mem. diocesan com. on Christian social relations Episcopal Ch., 1961-62. Mem. Detroit Bd. Edn., 1955-70, pres., 1958-59, and 1965-66. Trustee Citizens Redevel. Corp. Detroit; chmn. bd. govs. Wayne State U., 1958-59. Named hon. alumnus Wayne State U., 1959; recipient numerous awards for public service, including those from Urban League, 1952, Booker T. Washington Trade Assn., 1950, N.A.A.C.P., 1956, Wayne State U., 1956; Lamp of Learning award Mich. Fedn. Tchrs., 1965. Diplomate Am. Bd. Surgery, Internat. Bd. Surgeons. F. A.C.S., Internat. Coll. Surgeons; mem. Wayne County, Nat., Mich., Detroit (Physician of Year 1961) med. socs., A.M.A., Am. Fracture Soc., Internat. Soc. Proctology, Greater Detroit Bd. Commerce, Alpha Phi Alpha, Sigma Pi Phi. Episcopalian. Club: Detroit Economic. Home: Detroit MI Died June 14, 1970.

ROBINSON, SAMUEL MURRAY, naval officer; b. Eulogy, Tex., Aug. 13, 1882; s. Michael and Susan Sinai (Linebarger) R.; grad. U.S. Naval Acad., 1903; post grad. in elec. engring.; hon. Dr. Science, Union Coll., Schenectady, N.Y.; Dr. of Engring., Stevens Inst.,

Hoboken, N.J.; m. Emma Mary Burnham, Mar. 1, 1909; children—James Burnham (comdr. U.S.N.), Murray. Served 11 years at sea; manager Puget Sound Navy Yard, 1925; promoted through grades to rear admiral, 1931, and apptd. chief of Bureau of Engring. and engr. in chief of Navy; inspector of machinery, Schenectady, N.Y., 1935; head of Compensation Bd., 1938; chief of Bureau of Engring. and Coordinator of Shipbuilding, 1939; chief of Bureau of Ships and coordinator of shipbuilding, 1940; promoted to vice admiral, 1942, and apptd. chief of Office of Procurement and Material; promoted to admiral 1945; adminstr. Webb Inst. Naval Architecture, 1949-52; ret., 1952. Decorated D.S.M.; Order British Empire; Officer de l'Ordre de la Couroune (Belgium); Order Southern Cross (Brazil). Mem. Am. Soc. Naval Engrs., U.S. Naval Inst.; hon. mem. Soc. of Mech. Engrs. Clubs: University (Washington, D.C.); New York Yacht, Nassau (New York). Author: Electric Ship Propulsion. Home: Houston TX Died Nov. 11, 1972; buried Houston TX

ROBINSON, WILFREID, editor; b. Makanda, Ill., May 14, 1871; s. Alvin and Minerva (Price) R.; self-ed.; m. Mary Meeks of Roswell, N.M., May 16, 1900; 1 dau., Mary Jane. Began with Danville (Ill.) Leader, 1886; editor Danville Daily Press, 1889-90, Paris (Ill.) Gazette, 1891-92; reporter Chicago News, 1893-94, Rocky Mountain News, Denver, 1895-96, Roswell (N.M.) Record, 1900-03; founded, 1904, and served as editor Roswell Register-Tribune, later editor Roswell Despatch; now editor Calsbad Chronicle. Offered governorship of N.M., November 1909, but declined. Pres. Pecos Valley Editorial Assn., 1907; del. Nat. Editorial Assn., 1910. Contbr. to mags.; wrote serial, Travels on the South Seas; (novelettes) Undine; The John Dean Letters; Impressions of a Tenderfoot; The Bread War; David Galliene; etc. Pub. speaker and lecturer. Democrat. Home: Carlsbad NM‡

ROBINSON, WILLIAM EDWARD, business executive; b. Providence, R.I., June 27, 1900; s. William and Elizabeth L. (Mahoney) R.; grad. La Salle Acad., 1918; B.S., New York U., 1923; m. Marguerite Luddy, June 30, 1929; 1 dau., Wilma (Mrs. A. C. Ewert, Jr.); m. 2d, Ellan Reid Paddock, Aug. 17, 1961; step-dau., Margaret Paddock (Mrs. Derek A. Lee, Jr.). Local advt. mgr. World Telegram, 1930-32, asst. to gen. mgr. Hearst newspapers and advt. dir. N.Y. Evening Journal, 1933-36; advt. dir., 2d vice pres. and corp. dir. N.Y. Herald Tribune, 1936-45, bus. mgr., 2d v.p. and corp. dir., 1945-47, exec. v.p. and corp. dir. 1948-54, pub., 1954; chmn. bd., chief exec. officer Robinson-Hannagan Assos., Inc., 1954-55; pres. Coca Cola Co., 1955-58, chmn. bd., chief exec. officer, 1958-61, dir., chmn. exec. com., chmn. adv. com., 1961-69; mem. board of directors of Trans World Airlines, also Mfrs. Trust Co., Coca-Cola Co., Coca-Cola Export Corp., Libby-Owens-Ford Glass Co.; trustee Harlem Savs. Bank. Mem. exec. com. New York World's Fair 1964-65. Mem. Nat. Fund Med. Edn.; dir. Boys' Clubs Am.; finance com. chmn. Eisenhower Exchange Fellowships, 1960; vice chmn. United Community Campaigns, 1960; mem. Eisenhower Library Commn. Mem. bus. adv. council Dept. Commerce. Trustee, Am. Heritage Found. Mem. Delta Upsilon, Alpha Delta Sigma. Clubs: Union League, Dutch Treat; Blind Brook; Augusta Nat. Golf (gov.); Overseas Press, Links, Stanwich; Cotton Bay; Lost Tree. Home: Lost Tree Village North Palm Beach FL Died June 6, 1969; buried Putnam Cemetery, Greenwich CT

ROBINSON, WILLIAM H., county ofcl.; b. White Stone, Va., May 1, 1909; s. William H. and Mary E. (Gaskins) R.; A.B., Va. U., 1930; M.A., U. Chgo., 1945; m. Kitty Kidd, Jan. 13, 1960. Parole officer Ill. Dept. Pub. Safety, 1930-41, 45-48; dir. Youth Service Bur. Ch. Fedn. Greater Chgo., 1948-55; field work instr. sch. Social Adminstrn. U. Chgo., Baptist Missionary Tng. Sch. Chgo., 1948-55; rep. Gen. Assembly Ill., 1955-65; asst. exec. sec. social welfare dept. Ch. Fedn. Greater Chgo., 1965-67; dir. Cook County Dept. Pub. Aid, Chgo., 1967-73. Served with AUS, 1943-45. Recipient Distinguished Service Award in welfare and govt. Chgo. chpt. Frontiers Internat., 1958. Distinguished Service Award Ill, Welfare Assn., 1961, Service Recognition award Ill. Youth Commn., 1963, Ode to Excellence award Omega Psi Phi, 1963, Dorothy Wrigley Offield award for distinguished leadership in planned parenthood, 1964, Clarence Darrow Humanitarian award, 1965; named Outstanding Freshman Legislator Newspaper Corrs. in Springfield, 1955, Layman of Year Greater Chgo. Churchmen, 1958. Home: Chicago IL Died Mar. 24, 1973.

ROBSON, MARTIN CECIL, glass co. exec.; b. Coxhoe, Eng., Nov. 3, 1908; s. William and Isabel (Atkinson) R.; ed. pub. schs.; m. Agnes Jean Spears, June 26, 1929; children—William S., Carolyn J. (Mrs. Russell W. Schwem), Martin C. Came to U.S., 1919, naturalized, 1940. Accountant, Turner Glass Co., Terre Haute, Ind., 1928-31; office mgr. Hocking Glass Co., Lancaster, O., 1931-38; gen. offices mgr. Anchor Hocking Glass Corp., Lancaster, 1938-55, treas., 1955-62, sec.-treas., 1962-65, v.p., treas., 1965-71; asst. treasurer, director Anchor Corporation & Closure, Ltd., Toronto, Ontario, Canada, 1958-71; treas. The Standard Glass Mfg. Co., Lancaster, O., 1958-71; asst. treasurer Plastics, Incorporated, 1968-71; v.p., dir. GlassCrafters, Inc., 1965-71; director Hocking Valley Nat. Bank & Hotel, Lancaster. Dir. Fairfield County chpt. A.R.C. Mem. Am. Mgmt. Assn., Am. Soc. Lancaster OH Died Mar. 10, 1971; buried Maple Grove Cemetery.

ROCHE, FREDERICK W., lawyer; b. Boston, July 23, 1914; s. David F. and Gertrude (Kelley) R.; A.B., Boston Coll., 1936; LL.B., 1939; m. Nancy N. Coffin, June 28, 1947; children—Frederick C., Thomas N., David W. Admitted to Mass. bar, 1939; law clk. Supreme Jud. Ct., 1939-40; asst. corp. counsel City Boston, 1940-41; legal counsel to gov. of Mass., 1946; mem. firm Roche, Carens & De Giacomo, Boston, 1947-71. Mem. Finance Commn. Boston, 1946-48; chmn. Mass. Housing Bd., 1949-50; judge adv. Mass. N.G., 1948-64. Bd. dirs. Ford Found. Program for Bonding Minority Contractors, Boston; mem. president's council Boston Coll, 1969-71. Served to maj. AUS, 1941-46. Fellow Boston Coll. Law Sch, 1969-71. Mem. Mass., Boston bar assns. Club: Engineers (Boston). Home: Belmont MA Died July 13, 1971; buried Belmont MA

ROCHLEN, AVA MICHAEL, aircraft, pub. relations exec.; b. Odessa, Russia, June 16, 1891; s. Michael and Pauline (Tchudnowsky) R.; student pvt. tutoring and high schs., Russia, student eve. and corr. courses, journalism-liberal arts home studies, and spl. sci. studies in U.S.; m. Marguerite Jennison, Sept. 16, 1914 (div. 1928); children—Mary Audre (wife of Dr. Sidney S. Greenberg), Hartwell Porter, Donald H., Miriam Kendis (Mrs. Ned Moss), David Yale, Martha Gail (Mrs. Robert Kelly, Jr.); m. 2d, Margaret Norma Taylor, Mar. 16, 1936. With Los Angeles Express-Tribune, 1919-17; reporter, feature writer Los Angeles Times, 1917-27; feature writer, by-line reporter Hearts Newspapers-Universal News Service, Los Angeles Examiner, 1927-37; aviation editor Universal News Service, 1928-37; dir. pub. relations Douglas Aircraft Co., Santa Monica, Cal., 1937-69, v.p. pub. relations, 1954-61, mgmt. cons., 1960-69; vice chmn. exec. com. Hill & Knowlton, Inc., Los Angeles, Cal., 1960-69; commr. Department of Airports, Los Angeles, 1961-69; pub. relations cons. Volunteers of Am., 1961-69. Member Aircraft War Prodn. Council, 1939-46; mem. West coast com. Nat. Labor Bd., 1939-41; industry mem. metal working com. ILO, 1946-47, Am. del. ILO for Industry, Stockholm, Sweden, 1947. Decorated Legion of Honor (French), 1957. Member Aviation C. of C. of Am. (chmn. pub. relations com. 1949-51), Pub. Relations Soc. Am., Am. Rocket Soc., Aircraft Industries Assn. (past chmn. nat. pub. relations adv. com.), A.I.M. Clubs: Nat. Press, Overseas Press; Greater Los Angeles Press, Los Angeles City Commissioners (v.p.). Home: Los Angeles CA Died Aug. 1969.

ROCKEFELLER, LEWIS KIRBY, ex-congressman; b. Schenectady, N.Y., Nov. 25, 1877; s. Spencer and Nettie (Kirby) R.; Ph.B., N.Y. State Coll. for Teachers, Albany, 1898; m. Clara Bain, Jan. 25, 1899; children—John J., Elizabeth (Mrs. Louis Potter). Employed in Finance Bur., N.Y. State Dept. Pub. Instrn., 1898-1904; chief accountant Municipal Accounts Bur., State Comptroller's Office, 1905-15; dep. state tax commr. and later asst. to pres. N.Y. State Tax Commn., 1915-33; acounting and auditing, 1933-37; elected 75th Congress, 27th N.Y. Dist., Nov. 2, 1937, to fill term of Philip A. Goodwin (deceased); mem. 76th and 77th Congresses (1939-43), same district. Chmn. Columbia County Rep. Com., 7 yrs. Former pres. Columbia County Agrl. Soc.; past pres. Columbia County Soc. of New York; past pres. N.Y. State Assn. Fair Socs.; sec.-treas. N.Y. State Tax Assn. Republican. Presbyterian. Mason, Elk. Club: National Republican (New York). Home: Chatham NY*‡

ROCKEFELLER, WINTHROP, former gov. Ark.; b. N.Y.C., May 1, 1912; s. John D. Jr. and Abby Greene (Aldrich) R.; ed. Lincoln Sch., N.Y.C., Loomis Sch. Windsor, Conn., 1928-31, Yale, 1931-34; LL.D., U. Ark., Hendrix Coll., Coll. William and Mary, Coll. Ozarks; L.H.D., N.Y.U.; H.H.D., U. San Francis Xavier, Sucre Bolivia; D.C.L., Southwestern at Memphis; m. Barbara Sears, Feb. 14, 1948 (div. 1954); 1 son, Winthrop; m. 2d, Jeannette Edris, June 11, 1956 (div. 1971). With Humble Oil & Refining Co. (Tex.), 1934-37, Chase Nat. Bank, 1937-38; exec. v.p. Greater N.Y. Fund, 1938; fgn. dept. Socony-Vacuum Oil Co., 1939-51; trustee Rockefeller Brothers Fund, dir. Rockefeller Center, Inc. Chmn. bd. Colonial Williamsburg Found. Republican Nat. Committeeman, Ark., 1961-—, gov. Ark., 1967-70. Chmn. Ark. Indsl. Devel. Commn., 1955-64; mem. nat. adv. health manpower council NIH. Trustee Nat. Urban League, 1940-64, Loomis Sch., Nat. 4-H Club Found., Vanderbilt U. Served from pvt. to lt. col. U.S. Army, 1941-46; with 77th Inf., invasion Guam, Leyte, Okinawa. Recipient Bronze Star medal with oak leaf cluster, Purple Heart. Mem. Santa Gertrudis Breeders Internat. Assn. (pres., dir.), Delta Kappa Epsilon, Kappa Delta Pi. (hon.) Baptist. Clubs: Yale, Links (N.Y.C.); Little Rock Country; Pleasant Valley Country. Home: Morrilton AR Died Feb. 1973.

ROCKEY, KELLER E., marine corps officer; b. Columbia City, Ind., Sept. 27, 1888; s. Charles Henry and Florence Ida (Emrich) R.; grad. Mercersburg Acad., 1905, B.S., Gettysburg Coll., 1909; student Yale Univ. Forest Sch., 1910-11, Marine Corps Sch., 1924-25, Command and Gen. Staff Sch., 1925-26; Mil. Science Dr. (hon.), Gettysburg College, 1947; m. Frances Maria Masury, June 1, 1916 (dec.); children—Martha Maria, William Keller; married 2d, to Susan McGee, August 4, 1948. Commissioned second lt., Marine Corps, 1913 and advanced through the grades to lt. gen. (temp.); capt. and major 5th Marines, 2d Div., A.E.F.; major, Gendarmerie d'Haiti, 1919-22, battn. comdr. in Nicaragua, 1928-29; instr. Marine Corps Sch., 1926-28; staff, Marine Corps Hdqrs., 1922-24, 1934-37; staff, Comdr. Battle Force, U.S. Fleet, 1937-39; Office, Chief of Naval Operations, 1939-41; chief of staff, 2d Marine Div., 1941-42; dir., Div. of Plans and Policies, Marine Corps Hdqrs., 1942-43; asst. comdt. U.S. Marine Corps, 1943-44; comdg. gen. 5th Marine Div., 1944; comdg. 5th Div. U.S. Marines, at Iwo Jima, 1945; comdg. 3d Amphibious Corps, Northern China, 1945-46. Comdg. F.M.F. Atlantic, 1947-49, ret. 1950. Awarded Navy Cross, with Star (two citations), D.S.C. (Army); Distinguished Service Medal (Navy); Distinguished Service Medal (Army), Expeditionary medal (navy and marine corps), Victory medal, Medale Merite (Nicaragua); Cloud and Banner (China). Mem. Sigma Chi, Theta Nu Epsilon. Clubs: Army-Navy, Army-Navy Country. Address: Washington DC Died June 1970.

ROCKWELL, DAVID LADD, b. Akron, O., Aug. 11, 1877; s. David Ladd and Mary Elizabeth (Metlin) R.; pub. schs., Ravenna, O., Western Reserve Acad., Hudson, O., Kenyon Coll., Gambier, O., 1897-99; m. Katherine Arighi, of Kent, O., Oct. 1900; 1 dau., Mary Katharine. Elected mayor of Kent, 1900, reelected, 1902 (resigned Jan. 1903); elected probate judge Portage Co., 1902, reelected, 1905 (resigned Oct. 1908); apptd. by Gov. Harmon supt. Ohio State Building & Loan Assn., 1911 (resigned Oct. 1912). Del. Dem. Nat. Conv., 1900, 20, 28; mem. Dem. State Central Com., also exec. com., 20 yrs., and chmn. Dem. Exec. Com. Portage Co. practically same period; Dem. candidate for lt. gov. of Ohio, 1908; apptd. mem. bd. trustees Kent State Coll. by Gov. Cox, 1919, reapptd. by Gov. Donahey, 1925, and by Gov. White, 1931 (pres. of bd., 1925-29); nat. mgr. campaign for nomination of Wm. G. McAdoo for President of U.S., 1923, 24. Home: Ravenna OH*‡

ROCKWELL, FLETCHER WEBSTER, chmn. Nat. Lead Co.; b. St. Louis, Mo., Feb. 28, 1877; s. Fletcher W. and Mary (Robinson) R.; ed. East Orange, N.J., pub. schs., 1889-93, and Chicago Manual Training Sch., 1894-96; m. Emeline Hauk, Oct. 26, 1901 (died Apr. 13, 1933); children—Mary Elizabeth (Mrs. James Brett McKinney), Ann Carolyn (Mrs. Harry W. Anderson); m. 2d, Mrs. Alexander Grosset, Feb. 1, 1936; stepchildren—Alexandra Grosset (Mrs. Albert B. Diss, Jr.), Janet Graham Grosset (Mrs. Dorsey Yearley), Barbara Bobbs Grosset (Mrs. Stuart Douglas). Supt. White Lead Works, 1896; gen. supt. consol. Southern and Shipment Lead Works, 1906, Chicago; prodn. mgr. Nat. Lead Co., 1920, mem. bd. dirs., 1926, and mem. exec. com., 1927, v.p., 1937, pres. since Jan. 1938; dir. Irving Trust Company, Excess Insurance Co. of America. Republican. Episcopalian. Clubs: Lawyers, Bankers, Economic (New York); Round Hill (Greenwich, Conn.). Home: Winding Lane, Greenwich CT‡

ROCKWELL, HOMER, advertising dir.; b. N.Y.C., July 2, 1902; s. George Dennis and Adele (Stein) R.; ed. pub. schs. and high sch.; New York, and Columbia U.; m. Ethel Virginia Matthews, Dec. 1, 1927; children—Homer Matthew, Paul Hunter; married 2d, Anne Stuart Carr, October 27, 1951. Advertising copywriter, Stanley E. Gunnison, Inc., 1923-1926, account executive, 1926-30, vice president, 1931-34; advt. sales rep., Screenland Mag., Inc., 1935-36, Macfadden Publs., 1937-42; successively eastern advt. mgr., vice pres. and advt. mgr., exec. vice pres. Hunter Publs., 1942-44; vice pres. and advt. dir. Liberty Mag., Inc. (which purchased Hunter Publs.), 1944-48, dir. 1947; with Esquire mag., 1949-50, Better Living mag. 1950-71. Club: Wee Burn (Darien, Conn.). Home: Darien CT Died May, 1971.

ROCKWELL, MARYELDA, physician; b. Cedar Rapids, Neb., Aug. 9, 1909; d. Marshall J. and Emily L. Rockwell; M.D., Loma Linda U., 1937. Intern, Los Angeles County Gen. Hosp., 1936-37; intern in pediatrics Bellevue Hosp., N.Y.C., 1937-39; resident Children's Hosp., Columbus, O., 1939-40; mem. pediatric cons. staff City Hosp., Savanna, Ill.; staff Jane Lamb Hosp., Clinton, Ia., Mercy Hosp. Diplomate Am. Bd. Pediatrics, Nat. Bd. Med. Examiners. Mem. A.M.A., Am. Acad. Pediatrics, Am. Assn. U. Women, Clinton C. of C., World Problems Study Group. Home: Clinton IA Died Nov. 9, 1970; buried Clinton Meml. Park, Clinton IA

ROCKWOOD, GEORGE I., engr., mfr.; b. Boston, Mass., Jan. 13, 1868; s. Edward Otis and Caroline

(Washburn) R.; descendant of Gov. William Bradford, of Plymouth, Mass., 1620; ed. Phillips Acad. and Worcester Poly. Inst.; Dr.Engring. from the latter in 1929; m. Ellen T. Cheever, Nov. 13, 1890 (died Apr. 6, 1933); m. 2d, Anna V. Outhouse, May 12, 1933; children—George I., Ellen V. With Wheelcock Engine Co., Worcester, 1888-1892; consulting engr., Worcester, 1893-1905; pres. and treas. Rockwood Sprinkler Co., 25 yrs.; dir. Worcester Bank & Trust Co. Prof. thermodynamics, 1907, 08; life trustee Worcester Poly. Inst., pres. ad interim since 1939; pres. bd. trustees Rural Cemetery, Worcester. Hon. mem. Am. Soc. M.E. (v.p.); mem. Am. Antiquarian Soc. Founder the Alexander Lyman Holley Gold Medal for Great Achievement, administered by The Am. Soc. of Mechanical Engineers, New York. Pres. bd. trustees, Home Aged Females, Worcester. Republican. Conglist. Clubs: Worcester, Tatnuck. Author: Cheever, Lincoln and the Causes of the Civil War. Home: 2Military Rd., Worcester MA Military Rd., Worcester MA‡

RODALE, JEROME IRVING, editor, pub.; b. N.Y.C., Aug. 16, 1898; s. Michael and Bertha (Rouda) R.; student N.Y.U., 1916-17, Columbia, 1917; m. Anna Andrews, Dec. 1, 1917; children—Robert, Ruth, Nina. Acct., N.Y.C., 1916-19, Washington, 1919-23; chmn. bd. Rodale Mfg. Co., Inc., Rodale Press, Lutron Electronics Co.; editor, pub. Organic Gardening and Farming mag., Prevention mag., Quinto Lingo mag.; pub. Health Bulletin; associate editor of Theatre Crafts magazine; editor and publisher of Rodale's New York; mem. bd. dirs. Rodale Theatre, Rodale Saturday Night Showcase Theatre, New York City. President Soil and Health Found., Allentown, Pa. Author: Strengthening Your Memory, 1938; Cross-Word Puzzle Word-Finder, 1938; Sleep and Rheumatism, 1938; Pay Dirt, published 1945; The Glossaries, published in 1946; The Word-Finder, pub. 1947; The Healthy Hunzas, 1948; Stone-Mulching in the Garden, 1948; The Organic Front, 1948; The Phrase Finder, 1954; The Health Finder, 1954; Stones of Jehoshaphat, 1954; How to Eat for a Healthy Heart, 1954; This Pace Is Not Killing Us, 1954; Twenty Ways to Stop Smoking, 1954; The Nutritional Way to Stop Smoking, 1954; Ophelia The Cat, 1954; Organic Merry-Go-Round, 1954; Organic Trip to England, 1954; Organic Gardening, 1955; Poison in Your Pots and Pans, 1955; Is Our Intelligence Declining?, 1955; Bone Meal for Good Teeth, 1955; Are We Really Living Longer?, 1955; The Health Builder, 1957; Skits and Conversations Toward Better Health, 1958; The Girl and the Teenager (play), 1958; Mr. Mother Goose (play), 1959; The Skyscraper (play), 1959; The Goose (play), 1960; Encyclopedia of Organic Gardening, 1958; The Complete Book of Composting, 1960; The Prevention Method for Better Health, 1950; The Encyclopedia for Healthful Living, 1960; How to Grow Vegetables and Fruits by the Organic Method, 1961; The Synonym Finder, 1961; The Complete Book of Food and Nutrition, 1961; Toinette (musical comedy), 1961; The Encyclopedia of Common Diseases, 1962; The Unpublished Story (play), published 1962; The Vanity of Nothing (dramatic composition), 1963; The Health Seeker, 1963; Moon over Taurus (play), 1963; Mary Contrary (children's mus. comedy), 1963; Streets of Confusion, The Devil and the Nails (2 one-act plays), 1963; How to Landscape Your Own Home, 1963; (play) It Happens Every Day, 1963; (play) Man on the Bridge, 1963; (play) The Yugoslav Medical Mystery, 1963; (play) The Stones of Jehoshaphat, 1963; Our Poisoned Earth and Sky, 1964; (play) The Hairy Falsetto, 1964; The Padlock (play), 1965; The Moon is in Tsoris (play), 1965; The Complete Book of Vitamins, 1966; (play) A Fluoridation Comedary Dromedary, 1966; (plays) Streets of Confusion, The Man on the Bridge, 1966; Rodale's Revue (comedy skits), 1966; The Organic Way to Plant Protection, 1966; The Prostate, 1967; Smoke and Die, Quit and LiveSome Versions of Moliere's School for Wives, 1968; numerous others. Home: Allentown PA Died June 7, 1971; buried Northwood Cemetery, Emmaus PA

RODDY, GILBERT MORGAN, ins. co. exec.; b. Bellevue, Pa., Oct. 17, 1910; s. Edward Grieves and Alice (Morgan) R.; S.B., Mass. Inst. Tech., 1931, S.M., 1932; m. Frances Kellogg Newbury, Apr. 27, 1942; 1 son, Gilbert Morgan. With Arkwright-Boston Ins. Co., also Mut. Boiler and Machinery Ins. Co., Waltham, Mass., 1934-72, successively security analyst, asst. treas., treas., v.p., exec. v.p., 1934-58, pres., dir., 1958-65, chmn., pres., dir., 1965-72; dir. New Eng. Mchts. Nat. Bank, Am. Mut. Reins. Co., Chgo., W.H. Nichols Co., Waltham, FM Ins. Co. Ltd. (London). Pres. Emerson Hosp., Concord, 1952-57; life mem. corp. Mass. Inst. Tech.; trustee Wheaton Coll., 1951-57, Fenn Sch., Concord, Mass., 1967-70, Boston Mus. Sci. Served to col. AUS, 1941-46. Mem. Mass. Inst. Tech. Alumni Assn. (pres. 1957-58). Home: Concord MA Died Oct. 15, 1972; buried Sleepy Hollow, Concord MA

RODE, ALFRED, ins. exec.; b. Bellingham, Wash., Aug. 11, 1895; s. Charles and Lena (Wahl) R.; LL.B., U. Wash., 1921; m. Cora Louise Gardiner, Nov. 30, 1922; children—Coral Ann (Mrs. Harlan K. Veal), Helen Virginia (Mrs. Halden L. Conrad, Jr.), Alfred Gardiner. Admitted to Wash. bar, 1921; with Shank, Belt & Fairbrook, then Shank, Rode, Cook & Watkins, Seattle, 1921-47; asst. gen. counsel Northwestern Mut. Fire Assn. and Northwest Casualty Co. (later merged as Northwestern Mut. Ins. Co.), Seattle, 1937-45, dir., 1943-69, gen. counsel, vice chmn. bd., 1945-54, chmn., 1954-69. Served as ensign USN, World War I. Mem. Am., Wash. bar assns. Republican. Episcopalian. Clubs: Rainier, Washington Athletic. Home: Seattle WA Died Jan. 7, 1969.

RODGERS, DAVID JOHN, assn. exec.; b. Vancouver, B.C., Can., Feb. 6, 1912; s. Vincent Uriah and Grace (Sater) R.; came to U.S., 1913; B.A., Pomona Coll., 1933; postgrad. U. Cal. at Berkeley, 1933-34; m. Helen M. Holtham, Nov. 22, 1939; children—John David, Mark Brian. Sales, accounting Nat. Cash Register Co., also Charles R. Hadley Co., Los Angeles, 1948-52; asst. exec. sec. systems and machines Cal. Osteo. Assn., also exec. sec. Cal. Osteo. Hosp. Assn., Los Angeles, 1952-58; adminstrn. Arcade Hosp., Sacramento, 1959-61; exec. sec. Osteo. Physicians and Surgeons Cal., Sacramento, 1961-68. Home: Sacramento CA Died Sept. 24, 1968.

RODGERS, RAYMOND, educator, business cons.; b. Jackson, Ky., Sept. 28, 1899; s. James L. and Lacy (Haight) R.; A.B., U. Ky., 1921; M.B.A., N.Y.U., 1925; m. Anna Vogt, June 10, 1921; children—June A., Dianne. Instr. banking Sch. Commerce, Accounts and Finance, also Grad. Sch. Bus. Adminstrn., New York University, 1925, prof. banking, 1937-68; lecturer at Graduate School of Credit and Financial Mgmt. of Dartmouth, also other ednl. instns. and orgns.; former asst. advt. mgr. Alexander Taylor & Co., N.Y.C.; former asst. underwriter Nat. Surety Co.; former fgn. corr. Nat. City Bank; former office mgr., staff mem. Inst. Internat. Finance; former cons. economist State St. Trust Co., Boston, Socony-Vacuum Oil Co. Served with U.S. Navy, World War I. Mem. Arch and Square, Sphinx, Beta Gamma Sigma, Alpha Phi Sigma, Delta Sigma Pi, Sigma Sigma Sigma. Club: Lawyers (N.Y.C.). Author: (with Hardy) Consumer Credit and Its Uses, 1932: (also editor) (with Foster) Money and Banking, 1936; Banking, 1961. Contbg. editor Financial Handbook, Bankers Monthly, Ency. Americana. Home: Weston CT Died Dec. 23, 1968; buried Willowbrook Cemetery, Westport CT

RODGERS, WILLIAM, corp. exec.; b. Pitts., Oct. 22, 1903; s. Joseph H. and Alzona (Finley) R.; grad. Mercersburg Acad., 1922; student Lehigh U.; m. Dorothy Taylor, June 11, 1929. With Rodgers Sand Co., Pitts., 1926-29, (became McCrady-Rodgers Co.), v.p., 1929-48; prin. owner Moore Flesher Hauling Co., Inc., Pitts., 1938-72, chmn. bd., 1953-72; gen. sales mgr. Blaw-Knox Co., Pitts., 1953, v.p., gen. sales mgr., 1953-59, sr. v.p., gen. sales mgr., 1959-64, dir.; dir. Heppenstall Co., Pitts.; White Cross Stores, Inc., Monroeville, Pa., Pitts. Brewing Co. Bd. dirs. Boys Club Western Pa., Vocational Rehab. Center Pitts.; bd. mgrs. Western Pa.-Humane Soc. Served from lt. to lt. col., AUS, 1942-45; Italy, Africa. Decorated Legion of Merit. Mem. Pitts. Athletic Assn., Sigma Nu. Republican. Presbyn. Clubs: Rolling Rock (Ligonier, Pa.); Pittsburgh Athletic Assn. Pittsburgh Golf, Duquesne (Pitts.); Internat., Army and Navy (Washington); Pike Run Country (Jones Mills, Pa.). Home: Pittsburgh PA Died June 10, 1972.

RODMAN, CLARENCE JAMES, business exec.; b. Milw., July 10, 1891; s. Henry Herman and Lillian Matilda (Schiek) R.; B.A., Ripon Coll., 1913; M.S., U. Wis., 1914, D.Sc., 1947; student Grad. Sch., Yale, U. Pitts.; LL.D., Mt. Union Coll., 1948; D. Bus. Adminstrn., D.C.S., Parsons Coll., 1955; H.H.D., (hon.), Coll. Wooster; m. Hazel Purcell, Nov. 19, 1925; children—James Purcell, Robert Ladd. Research chemist Eastman Kodak Co., 1916-17, Westinghouse Electric Co., 1917-25, cons. engr., 1925; dist. mgr. Reisert Automatic Water Purifying Co., 1925-27; v.p., sec., dir. Alliance Mfg. Co., 1925-44; pres., treas., dir. Steel San. Co., 1927-34; chmn. bd., treas., dir. Alliance Porcelain Products Co., 1934-44; pres., dir. treas. Alliance Ware, Inc., 1944-57, v.p., dir. Alliance Ware, Ltd., Vancouver, B.C., Can., 1945; pres., dir. Vit-Steel Co., Burlington, Ia., 1945; v.p., dir. Crane Steelware, Quebec, 1947-57; pres., dir. George Lumber Co., Bergholz, O., 1946-72, S.T.D., Inc., Alliance O., 1946-51, Allen Box Co., 1951-72; exec. com. Alliance Devel. Corp., 1956-72; pres. Carnation City Devel. Corp., 1958-72; chmn. bd. Vitri Finish, Inc., City of Industry, Cal., 1958-72; chmn., dir. Gen. Implement Corp., Clearwater Internat. Airport, Fla., 1959; pres., treas., owner Alliance Tool Co., 1959-72; pres., sec. Hiltop Farms, Bergholz, 1959-72; dir. Mt. Union Bank, Alliance, Oak Rubber Co., Midland Buckeye Savs. & Loan Assn. Mem.-at-large Nat. council Boy Scouts Am.; organizer, sponsor Alliance Area Youth Center. Mem. Alliance Sch. Bd., v.p., 1929-30; chmn. task com. steel plumbing fixtures NSRB, Washington, 1948-52; mem. industry adv. com. Munitions Bd. Indsl. councilor Ohio Research Found., 1951-61; dir. Rodman Research Center, Mt. Union Coll.; donor to libraries. Recipient Navy Bur. Ordnance award for outstanding research and devel. spl. anti-submarine device, World War II; First Citizen of Alliance award, 1956; named Hon. Texan by Gov. of Texas, 1956; Hon. Rotarian, 1957; Book of Golden Deeds award Exchange Club, 1960, Citizen's award Ohio Library Assn., 1962, Silver Beaver award Boy Scouts Am. Donor Alliance Public Library, 1956-61, Camp Rodman, Boy Scouts Am.; Rodman Playhouse, Mt. Union Coll. Lilly M. Rodman Presbyn. Ch. Camp. Mem. Nat. Assn. Formed Metal Plumbing Ware (pres.), Am. Ceramic Soc., Porcelain Enamel Inst., Tax Found., Indsl. Conf. Bd. (asso.), Wildlife Found., Am. Home Laundry and Machine Assn. (asso.), Pressed Metal Inst., Engring. Soc., Am. Photog. Soc., Am. Soc. Testing Materials, A.A.A.S., A.E.S., Nat. Rifle Assn., Am. Inst. Chemistry, Tri-Country Outdoor League (past pres.), U.S., Ohio, Alliance chambers commerce, Am. Inst. Aeros. and Astronautics, Fraternal Order Police, N.A.M., Nat. Small Bus. Men's Assn., Ohio Assn. Chiefs Police, Am. Ordnance Assn., Indsl. Information Inst., Psi Kappa Omega, Alpha Chi Sigma. Republican. Presbyn. Mason (32 degree, Shriner), Elk. Clubs: Lake Shore (Chgo.); Congress Lake (Hartville, O.); Union, Al Koran (Cleve.); Rotary (Alliance, hon. mem.), Exchange (hon.), Lions (hon.), Kiwanis (hon.). Contbr. numerous articles to sci. jours. Holder numerous patents U.S. and fgn. countries. Home: Alliance OH Died Jan. 30, 1972.

RODRIGUEZ-SERRA, MANUEL, lawyer; b. at Sabana Grande, P.R., Sept. 15, 1871; s. Manuel and Isabel (Serra) Rodriguez; ed. Coll. of the Jesuits, Santurce, P.R.; Instn. de Ensenanza Superior, San Juan; admitted bar Sup. Ct. of U.S., Sup. Ct. of N.Y., and Sup. Ct. of P.R.; m. Encarnacion Molina y Cifredo, of San Juan, Sept. 18, 1897. Served as capt. of vols., Spanish Army; in command of troop when Admiral Sampson's fleet bombarded San Juan; an atty. in cases brought by Catholic Ch. of P.R. to recover properties, and moneys, 1904; mem. firm of Hartzell & Rodriguez-Serra, San Juan. Mem. Municipal Council, San Juan, 1905-6; mem. Rep. Exec. Com. of P.R., 1905-6. Trustee Insular Library of P.R.; an incorporator, and sec. Porto Rican Civic Assn., 1912—; commr. from P.R. on Uniform State Laws. Member Am. Bar Assn. (gen. council), Assn. Bar City of New York, and of Porto Rico. Clubs: City (New York), Country, Casino de Puerto Rico, Casino Espanol. Home: Santurce, P.R. Office: Telephone Bldg., San Juan PR*‡

ROE, FREDERICK WILLIAM, univ. prof.; b. Wolcott, N.Y., Apr. 3, 1874; s. William and Sarah Jane (Dill) R.; grad. Cazenovia Sem., 1893; B.A., Wesleyan U., Conn., 1897; M.A., Columbia, 1904, Ph.D., 1909; hon. Litt.D., Beloit Coll., 1922; m. Lucy May Lewis, Jan. 2, 1901 (died Nov. 22, 1934); m. 2d, Nancy Roberts, June 28, 1937. Teacher of English, successively Duluth High Sch., Mt. Hermon Sch. for Boys, Allegehny Preparatory Sch., 1897-1903; instr. English University of Wisconsin, 1905-09, associate professor, assistant and junior dean, 1909-27, professor, 1927-44, emeritus prof., since 1944. Member Phi Beta Kappa, Alpha Delta Phi. Congregationalist. Club: University. Author: Carlyle as a Critic of Literature, 1910; Social Philosophy of Carlyle and Ruskin, 1921; Early Essayists, 1922. Editor: Nineteenth Century English Prose (joint editor), 1908; Dickens' Tale of Two Cities, 1910; English Prose (joint editor), 1913; Ruskin—Selections and Essays, 1918; Carlyle— Sartor Resartus, 1927; Arnold—Essays and Poems, 1928; Victorian Prose, 1947. Home: 2015 Van Hise Av., Madison WI‡

ROE, JOSEPH HYRAM, biochemist, educator; b. Winchester, Va., Dec. 27, 1892 s. Joseph Ashby and Julia Abbott (Winkfield) A.B., Roanoke Coll., 1916; A.M., Princeton, 1917; Ph.D., George Washington Univ., 1923; Ph.D., Yale, 1934; m. Clara Grace Lauck, Aug. 19, 1922; 1 son, Joseph Hyram. Instr. biochemistry, George Washington Univ. Sch. of Medicine, Washington, D.C., 1919, asso. prof., 1919-22, prof., 1922-67, head of department, 1922-32, 1938-59, sabbatical leave, 1932-33; visiting prof. U. So. Cal., summer 1951. Served as pvt. F.A., World War I; 2d lt. F.A. Res., 1918-23; capt. to maj. San. Corps Res., 1925-42; cons. War Dept. selection med. trainees, 1944-45; cons., com. on food composition, Nat. Research Council, on vitamin C assay of foods, 1943-46; regional gas officer Office Civil Def., Washington Region, 1943-45; mem. Sci. Manpower Commn., 1952-54; biochemistry com. Nat. Bd. Med. Examiners, 1958-62, Am. Bd. Clin. Chemistry, 1959-67; cons. med. research VA Center at Martinsburg, W.Va., 1956-60, 64-67. Recipient award of merit George Washington U. Med. Soc., 1954; Alumni achievement award George Washington U., 1955; Ernest Bischoff award Am. Assn. Clin. Chemists, 1956, Eloy Alfaro award, 1961. Fellow A.A.A.S. (council 1953-56, 61-63); mem. Cosmotographers (pres. 1962-63), Am. Soc. Biol. Chem., Am. Chem. Soc., Am. Inst. Nutrition (sec. 1948-51, mem. council 1958-61), Am. Assn. Clin. Chemists (chmn. of the Capital section 1963-64), Soc. Exptl. Biology and Medicine (chmn. D.C. sect. 1944-45), A.M.A. (affiliate), Am. Assn. U. Professors, Washington Academy Medicine (pres. 1960-62), George Washington Univ. Alumni Assn. (v.p. 1940-44, 54-56), Smith-Reed-Russell Soc., Alpha Omega Alpha, Alpha Chi Sigma, Sigma Xi. Lutheran. Club: Cosmos (Washington). Author: Principles of Chemistry, 9th edition, 1963; A Laboratory Guide in Chemistry, 4th edition, 1963; A Laboratory Manual of Biochemistry (with C. R. Treadwell), 6th edition, 1959; sect. Chemical Determination of Vitamin C in Methods of Biochemical Analysis, 1953. Contbr. articles to biochem. and med. jours., Washington DC Died May 18, 1967.

ROEBUCK, JOHN RANSOM, physicist; b. London, Ont., Can., Sept. 23, 1876; s. Henry Simpson and Lydia Abigail (Macklem) R.; A.B., Toronto U., 1902, Ph.D., 1906; m. Margaret Hilda Kittson, Montreal, Can., Sept. 29, 1906. Demonstrator in physics McGill U., 1902-5, lecturer, 1905-7; instr. physics, 1907, asst. prof., 1913, asso. prof. since June 1919, U. of Wis. Mem. Am. Chem. Soc., Am. Physical Soc., A.A.A.S. Author: The Science and Practice of Photography, 1917. Home: 2210 Hollister Av., Madison WI‡

ROEDER, BERNARD FRANKLIN, ret. naval officer; b. Cumberland, Md. Feb. 4, 1911; s. William Phillip and Anna (Ritter) R.; B.S., U.S. Naval Acad., 1931; student U.S. Naval War Coll., 1949-50; m. Kathleen Fitch, July 11, 1936; children—Bernard Franklin, Franke (Mrs. Hans G. Haimberger), Anne, Kathleen. Commd. ensign U.S. Navy 1931, advanced through grades to vice adm., 1965; various assignments in cruisers, destroyers, also aircraft carriers, prior to 1941; mem. staff U.S. Naval Forces in Philippines, Java and Australia, 1941-42; assigned Navy Dpet., 1943; at sea, 1945-49; comdr. destroyers off Korea, 1950-51; dir. naval communications U.S. Navy, 1961-65; comdr. amphibious force Pacific Fleet, 1965-66, 1st Fleet, 1966-69; ret., 1969. Bd. dirs. San Diego Opera Guild, San Diego A.R.C. Decorated D.S.M., Legion of Merit with 4 oak leaf clusters, Navy Commendation medal, various campaign and unit ribbons; Philippine Presdl. citation; Korean Presdl. citation. Mem. Vets. Wireless Assn. (hon.), I.E.E.E. (sr.), Armed Forces Communications and Electronics Assn. (dir.), U.S. Srs. Golf Assn. Home: Coronado CA Died Sept. 3, 1971.

ROEDER, FRED VINCENT, educator; b. E. Greenville, Pa., Oct. 18, 1904; s. Preston Thomas and Clara Amelia (Krull) R.; A.B., Ursinus Coll., 1925; M.S. in Edn., U. Pa., 1941, Ed. D., 1949; m. Arline M. Albitz, Aug. 30, 1933; 1 son, Edward Arlen. Tchr., dean Perkiomen Sch., Pennsburg, Pa., 1925-43; coordinator area 3 Pa. Area Coll. Program, 1946-48; mem. faculty Lafayette Coll., 1943-46, 48-67, prof. edn., head dept., 1957-67, dir. summer session, 1954-67. Mem. N.E.A., Am. Assn. U. Profs., Phi Delta Kappa. Lutheran. Mason. Home: Bethlehem PA Died Sept. 24, 1967; buried Bethlehem PA

ROEMER, HENRY A., steel exec.; b. Struthers, O.; s. Henry and Margaret (Hill) R.; ed. pub. schs.; m. May Ethel Sahli, 1905 (deceased January 1960); children—James, Henry, Margaret (Mrs. Blair), Jack J., Gretchen (Mrs. Gayton.). Employed as superintendent Am. Sheet Steel Co., 1906-07; asst. supt. Youngstown Sheet & Tube Co., 1907-13; gen. supt. Canton Sheet Steel Co., 1913-16, asst. gen. mgr., 1916-19; gen. mgr. Hydraulic Steel Co., Canton, 1919; v.p., gen. mgr. Superior Sheet Steel Co., Canton, 1919-22, pres., 1922-27; pres. Continental Steel Corp., 1927-31; pres. Youngstown Pressed Steel Co., 1931-33; became chmn. and pres. Sharon Steel Corp., 1931, chmn. and pres., 1955-57, chmn. executive com., dir.; dir. Union Nat. Bank, Youngstown, O.; dir. Waynesburg & Washington R.R.; cons. Sharon Steel Corp., 1964-69. Trustee Youngstown (O.) Coll. Republican. Clubs: Youngstown, Youngstown Country (pres.); Duquesne (Pittsburgh); Union (Cleveland); Woodmont Rod and Gun (pres.) (Berkeley Springs, W.Va.); Sharon Country (pres.). Home: Brookfield OH Died Nov. 13, 1969; buried Brookfield Cemetery, Brookfield OH

ROEMERSHAUSER, ALVIN E(ARL), banker; b. St. John Parish, La., Dec. 23, 1907; s. Phillip and Virginia (Keller) R.; student Soule Coll., Loyola U. of the South, New Orleans; grad. Am. Inst. Banking, 1929; m. Evelyn V. de Gruy, Sept. 16, 1936; children—Alvin Earl, Ralph Phillip, Ronald Joseph. With Whitney Nat. Bank of New Orleans, 1925-68, asst. cashier, 1946-48, asst. v.p., 1948-55, v.p., 1955-68. Mem. Am. Inst. Banking (exec. council, pres.), Am. Bankers Assn., C. of C. Club: Internat. House. Home: New Orleans LA Died Sept. 7, 1968; buried Saint-Louis Cemeterie.

ROESCH, KARL ALEXANDER, motor co. exec.; b. Cleve., Dec. 14, 1903; s. Herman G. and Josephine E. (Wolf) R.; B.Sc., Ohio State U., 1926; m. Estelle C. Droeger, Nov. 9, 1929 (dec. Aug. 1955); children—Janet E. (Mrs. Frank A. Frauenfelder), Robert C., Lynne C., John B.; m. 2d, Catherine H. Beltaire, Mar. 17, 1956. With White Motor Co., Cleve., from 1929, beginning as salesman, successively br. mgr., asst. to v.p. sales, gen. mgr. coach div., dir. service, 1929-55, v.p. Autocar div., from 1956; pres. Autocar Sales & Service Co. Mem. Soc. Automotive Engrs., Beta Theta Pi. Mason. Clubs: University (Cleve.); Arnomink (Phila.). Home: Ithan-Villanova PO PA Died July 7, 1969.

ROESSNER, ELMER (STIRLING), editor, writer; b. Oakland, Cal., May 1, 1900; s. Harry William and Anne (Stirling) R.; student pub. schs., Cal.; m. Irma Jeanette Lott, Sept. 2, 1920; children—Eugene, Donald. Reporter, San Francisco News, 1918-20, city editor, 1921; mng. editor NEA Service, 1923, editor Internat. Illustrated News, 1926; asst. city editor Los Angeles Herald, 1927-30; feature editor N.Y. Telegram and World-Telegram, 1930-40; asst. mng. editor PM, 1941; information specialist OWI, 1942; civilian cons. Stars & Stripes, 1945; editor McClure Newspaper Syndicate, 1946-51, bus. news columnist, 1951-72; editor-in-chief Bell-McClure Syndicate, North American Newspaper Alliance, New York City, 1960-71. Mem. Sigma Delta Chi. Clubs: The National Press (Washington); Late Watch (San Francisco); Silurians, Dutch Treat (N.Y.C.). Author articles. Jamaica LI NY Died Apr. 28, 1972; buried Pinelawn Meml. Park, Pinelawn LI NY

ROGERS, BERNARD, composer; b. N.Y. City, Feb. 4, 1893; s. Solomon and Jeannette (Schalk) R.; student Inst. Mus. Art, N.Y. City, 1919-21; Mus.D. (hon.), Valparaiso University, 1959; H.H.D. (honorary), Wayne State University, 1962; m. Lillian Soskin, 1913 (div. 1933); m. 2d, Anne Thacher, June 1934 (died Oct. 1935); 1 dau., Anne Thacher; m. 3d, Elizabeth Mary Clark, Aug. 27, 1938. Mem. faculty, chmn. composition dept. Eastman Sch. Music, Rochester U., 1929-67. Composer: compositions include The Passion, 1944; The Raising of Lazarus, 1929; The Exodus, 1933; The Warrior, 1947; Elegy for F. D. Roosevelt, 1948; Five Fairy Tales, 1935; A Letter from Pete, 1950; The Prophet Isaiah, 1950; Portrait, 1952. Recipient Loeb prize, Inst. Mus. Art, 1920; Pulitzer traveling scholarship (Columbia Univ.), 1921; Guggenheim fellowship, 1927-29; Ditson prize, (Met. Opera), 1946; Juilliard Commn., 1947; Koussevitzky Found. Commn., Louisville Orchestra Commn.; Fulbright Grant, 1953; commn. from Ford Found., 1960; Lillian B. Fairchild award, 1962; Meth. Youth Conference commn., 1963; American Wind Symphony commn., 1964. Mem. of A.S.C.A.P., Nat. Inst. Arts and Letters, Pi Kappa Lambda, Phi Mu Alpha. Author: The Art of Orchestration, 1950. Mem. editorial staff, critic Musical America, 1913-24. Home: Rochester NY Died May 24, 1968.

ROGERS, DONALD AQUILLA, judge; b. Evansville, Ind., Feb. 17, 1901; s. Lon D. and Florence (Barnhill) R.; J.D., Ind. U., 1927; m. Marie Woolery, Aug. 20, 1924; children—Barbara (Mrs. John H. Houseworth), Jack, David. Admitted to Ind. bar, 1924; dep. clk. Monroe County, 1923-27; pros. atty. 10th Jud. Circuit Ind., 1928-29; with firm Rogers & Steckley, 1928-30, Blair & Rogers, 1930-33; judge 10th Jud. Circuit Ind., 1933-43; pvt. practice, Bloomington, 1946-55, partner with son, 1955-65; judge Monroe Superior Court, Bloomington, from 1965. Dir. Monroe County State Bank, Bloomington, Workingmens Fed. Savs. and Loan Assn., Bloomington. Chmn. Monroe County UN Com., 1951-52; pres. White River council Boy Scouts Am., 1942-43. Mem. Ind. Ho. of Reps. from Monroe County, 1949-50; chmn. Monroe County Central Democratic Com., 1960-62. Trustee Ind. U., 1963-66; bd. dirs. Ind. Sch. Religion, from 1955. Served to maj. AUS, 1943-46, ETO. Mem. Am. Judicature Soc., Am. Law Inst., Ind. Hist. Soc., Ind. Bar Assn. (bd. mgrs. 1936-38), Phi Delta Phi, Phi Delta Theta, Order of Coif. Mem. Christian Ch. (past chmn. ofcl. bd., elder). Kiwanian (past pres. Bloomington) Mason. Home: Bloomington IN Died Oct. 19, 1969.

ROGERS, ERNEST ALBERT, univ. prof.; b. Vinton, Ia., Aug. 10, 1866; s. Richard and Ann (Cannon) R.; grad. Tilford Acad., 1889; student Ia. State Teachers Coll., 1889-90; D.D.S., State U. of Ia., 1892, M.D., 1904, post-grad. work in bacteriology; m. Adelaide F. Joy, January 4, 1901. With State University of Iowa since 1892, as assistant demonstrator in laboratory, 1892-95, lecturer on dental anatomy, and demonstrator dental technology, 1895-98, lecturer regional anatomy and clin. dentistry, 1899-1904, prof. and head of dept. of clin. dentistry, supt. of clinics, 1904-16, asst. chair of oral surgery, lecturer dental jurisprudence, 1910-15, lecturer gen. hygiene, 1913-43, prof. and head dental econ. and roentgenology, and dir. dental infirmary, 1916-40, prof. roentgenology and dental econs., 1940-43, prof. of dentistry (emeritus) since 1943. Has done pioneer work in arousing interest in oral hygiene, lecturing and conducting examinations in schools throughout Iowa. Major, Dental Reserve, (inactive). Fellow Am. College Dentists; member American Dental Assn., Iowa State Dental Soc., Radiol. Soc. of N.A., Omicron Kappa Upsilon Xi, Psi Phi. Republican. Presbyterian. Contbr. on dental subjects. Club: Triangle. Home: Fort Collins CO‡

ROGERS, FREDERICK MORRIS, clergyman, educator; b. Salem, Marion Co., Ill., Dec. 13, 1872; s. Oliver Jasper and Martha Angelina (Morris) R.; A.B., Marlonville (Mo.) Coll., 1890; student Coll. of the Bible, Transylvania Coll., Culver-Stockton Coll.; D.D.; m. Emma Wilson Hawkins, of Canton, Mo., Sept. 9, 1896. Ordained ministry Christian (Disciples of Christ) Ch., 1894; pastor chs. in Mo., Ill. and at Long Beach, Calif., till 1915; supt. missions, Christian Missionary Soc. of Southern Calif., 1915-20; a founder, 1920, and chancellor Calif. Christian Coll., 1920-26; field sec. United Christian Missionary Soc., 1927-29; head of dept. of benevolence same, 1929-—; gen. sec. Nat. Benevolent Assn. of the Christian Ch., 1929-—. Home: 605 S. Mariposa Av., Los Angeles, Calif. Office: 618 Paul Brown Bldg., St Louis MO*‡

ROGERS, HARRY CLAYTON, clergyman; b. Mt. Sterling, Ky., Sept. 6, 1877; s. Thomas F. and Sally Anne (Smith) R.; grad. high sch., Mt. Sterling; student Ky. Mil. Inst.; A.B., Centre Coll., Danville, Ky., 1899; grad. McCormick Theol. Sem., 1902; D.D., Centre College, also Park College, 1912; m. Fannie Alexander Andrews, Oct. 15, 1902; children—Elizabeth, Sarah. Ordained Presbyn. ministry, 1902; pastor, Hinsdale, Ill., 1902-04, Ft. Madison, Ia., 1904-07, Linwood Blvd. Ch., Kansas City, Mo., 1907-41, College City Ch., San Francisco, since Sept. 1, 1941. Y.M.C.A. worker, Camp Funston, Kansas, and in France, World War. Trustee Presbyn. Theol. Sem., Park Coll. (Parksville, Mo.); mem. Gen. Council Presbyterian Church in U.S.A. Mem. Kappa Alpha. Author: Seven Candies of the Lord, 1908; With the Cross and the Flag in France, 1918; The Mind of Christ in the Winning of Souls, 1922; Evangelism for This Day; Walking with God. Home: 6 Diaz Av., San Francisco CA‡

ROGERS, JAMES GRAFTON, lawyer, educator; b. Denver, Colo., Jan. 13, 1883; s. Edmund J. A. and Maria Georgina D. (Burrell) R.; St. Paul's Sch., Concord, N.H., 1899-1901; A.B., Yale, 1905, hon. M.A., 1931; LL.B., Denver U., 1908. LL.D., 1930; LL.D., U. of Colo., 1935, U. of Pa., 1936; Litt.D., Colorado Coll., 1937; m. Cora May Peabody, May 24, 1910; children—Ranger, Lorna (Mrs. S. H. Hart), Hamilton. Reporter N.Y. Sun, 1905-06; asst. gen. of Colo., 1909-10; jr. mem. Rogers, Shafroth & Rogers, 1911-19, Hodges, Wilson & Rogers, Denver, 1923-28; prof. Denver U. Law Sch., 1910-27, dean, June-Dec, 1927; dean of law, U. of Colo., 1928-35 (on leave 1931-33); asst. U.S. Sec. of State, 1931-33; master Timothy Dwight College and prof. law, Yale, 1935-42; in Office of Strategic Services, Washington, D.C., 1942-44 (deputy dir.); chairman Strategic Planning Group; pres. Fgn. Bondholders Protective Council, 1943-53 (chmn. exec. com. 1953-55); mayor Georgetown 1953-55, 57-59; chmn. Am. Fund Free Jurists of N.Y., 1952-57. Mem. (rank of minister) Allied Electoral Mission to Greece, 1946; mem. fgn. affairs section Hoover Commn., 1948; pres. State Hist. Soc. Colo., 1950-59, chmn., 1959-71. Served AUS, July 1918, disch. as 1st lt., Dec. 1918. Founder, 1912, and pres. Civic League of Denver; pres. Denver Council Boy Scouts Am., 1920-21; pres. Mayor's Adv. Council, Denver, 1923. Trustee World Peace Foundation (Boston), 1937-53; trustee St. Paul's School, Concord, 1941-45; also Conn. College, 1939-43. Member American Bar Assn. (exec. com. 1927-28; council on legal edn., term 1929-37, chmn. 1934-37; chmn. com. on international law 1931-33); member Association of Bar, N.Y., Colorado State Bar Assn. (pres. 1925-26), Council on Foreign Relations, Foreign Assn. (dir. in exec. charge 1946), Authors League, 1946), Psi Upsilon, Elihu, St. Elmo, Aurelian, Elizabethan (Yale), Phi Delta Phi; mem. council Nat. Conf. Bar Assn. Delegates, term 1926-28 (chairman 1928-29). Clubs: Colorado Mountain (founder and 1st pres.), City (pres. 1920), University (president 1922-24), Cactus (pres. 1920-21), (Denver); Cosmos, (Washington); Century, American Alpine (president, 1938-41), Yale (New York City, N.Y.). Author of books, The Fire of Romance, 1919; The Goldenrod Lode, 1920; The Third Day, 1922; American Bar Leaders, 1932; Judicial Assistance (with A. H. Feller), 1939; World Policing and the Constitution, the Rockies, 1958; My Rocky Mountain Valley, 1968; also author of numerous published papers and addresses. Home: Denver CO Died Apr. 23, 1971.

ROGERS, JAMES STERLING, church official; b. Mayfield, Ky., Mar. 3, 1871; s. James Thomas and Martha Ann (Sawyer) R.; student Clinton (Ky.) Coll.; A.B., Ouachita Coll., Arkadelphia, Ark., 1901, D.D., 1911; M.Th., Southern Bapt. Theol. Sem., Louisville, Ky., 1904; Th.D., Southwestern Bapt. Seminary, 1914; studied University of Chicago and Moody Bible Institute, Chicago; m. Sallie Curry, of Paragould, Arkansas, December 23, 1893; children—Velne Lee (Mrs. E. S. Campbell), James Sterling, Martha Jean (Mrs. Frank Nunnalley), Mary Louise. Began ministry Southern Bapt. Ch., 1897; pastor successively Claredon, Searcy, Ohio Street Ch., Pine Bluff, Ark., until 1908; sec. Ark. Bapt. State Conv., 1908-11; prof. of Bible, Ouachita Coll., 1911-12, 1914-15; again sec. Ark. Bapt. State Conv., 1915-19; prof. of New Testament, Southwestern Bapt. Sem., 1919-21; gen. sec. Ark. Bapt. State Conv., 1922-29; pres. Central Coll., Conway, Ark., since 1929. Democrat. Home: Conway AR‡

ROGERS, LESTER BURTON, coll. dean; near Commiskey, Ind., Nov. 4, 1875; s. John Hamilton and Ruth (Morin) R.; B.S., Moores Hill (Ind.) Coll., 1899; studied U. of Chicago, 1902-03, Teachers Coll. (Columbia), 1906-07, 1910-11, A.M., 1907, Ph.D., 1915; m. Nettie Mae Hopkins, Sept. 25, 1902; children—Mary Jean, Elizabeth. Teacher rural schs., Ind., 3 yrs., supt. schs., 3 yrs.; teacher high sch., Spokane, Wash., 1903-06; head dept. of philosophy and edn., Tri-State Coll., Angola, Ind., 1907-10; prof. edn., Lawrence Coll., Appleton, Wis., 1911-19; research scholar, Teachers Coll. (Columbia U.), 1910-11; prof. secondary edn., Ind. U., summer session, 1911; lecturer teachers insts., etc.; spl. lecturer on edn., U. of Southern Calif., 1919-20, asst. to pres. and dean Sch. of Edn., 1921-22, dean Sch. of Edn. 1922-45, dean summer session, 1921-45, dean emeritus, Sch. Edn., and Summer Session since 1945. Mem. N.E.A., Soc. Coll. Teachers of Edn. (pres. 1931-32), Nat. Soc. for Study of Edn., Am. Assn. Univ. Profs., Phi Delta Kappa, Phi Kappa Phi, Alpha Pi Zeta, Gamma Rho Tau, Skull and Dagger. Methodist. Mason. Author: Comparative Study of Township, District, Consolidated, Town and City Schools of Indiana, 1915; Story of Nations (in collaboration), 1934. Contbr. ednl. jours. Home: 2726 Cuesta Rd., Santa Barbara CA‡

ROGERS, LESTER CUSHING, constrn. exec.; b. Elgin, Ill., Sept. 26, 1893; s. Walter A. and Julia M. (Cushing) R.; B.S. in Civil Engring., U. Wis., 1915; LL.D. (honorary), George Williams College; m. Lucile Pritchard, Apr. 17, 1917 (dec. Mar. 1962); children—Nancy (Mrs. V. J. Sala), Lucile (Mrs. F. H. Orbison), Barbara (Mrs. H. W. Stinson), Lester Cushing; m. 2d, Genevieve Fox, Jan. 10, 1963. Engr. Bates & Rogers Constrn. Co., Chgo., 1915-17, successively supt., dist. mgr., v.p., dir., 1917-37; pres., dir. Bates & Rogers Constrn. Corp., Chgo., 1937-61, chmn. bd. and director, from 1961. Trustee George Williams Coll. Served as lt., F.A., AUS, 1918-19; AEF. Mem. Am. Soc. C.E. (life member), Western Soc. Engrs., Am. Concrete Inst., Asso. Gen. Contractors Am. (p.p.), Tau Beta Pi. Republican. Conglist. Clubs: Union League (Chgo.); Indian Hill (Winnetka, Ill.). Home: Winnetka IL Died Feb. 1972.

ROGERS, LORE ALFORD, bacteriologist; b. Patten, Me., Feb. 7, 1875; s. Luther B. and Mary E. (Barker) R.; B.S., U. of Me., 1896; U. of Wis. 1 yr.; D.Sc., U. of Md. 1923, U. of Me., 1925; m. Beatrice C. Oberly Oct. 3, 1906; 1 son, John Oberly. Asst. bacteriologist, N.Y. Expt. Sta., Geneva, N.Y., 1899-1902; dairy bacteriologist, U.S. Dept. Agr. since 1902, in charge research laboratories, Bureau Dairy Industry (retired 1942); chairman program committee World's Dairy Congress, 1923; Borden Award, 1937. Member Society American Bacteriologists (president 1923), Dairy Science Association, Washington Acad. Sciences, Washington Acad. Medicine, Kappa Sigma. Home: 3635 S. St. N.W., Washington DC; also from May to Oct., Patten ME‡

ROGERS, MALCOLM JOSEPH, cotton broker; b. New Iberia, La., Apr. 29, 1905; s. Elias C. and Laura (Orgeron) R.; student pub. schs.; m. Inez A. Harang, Nov. 10, 1928; children—Malcolm Joseph, Noel B. Page boy New Orleans Cotton Exchange, 1919-23, mem., 1931; with cotton brokerage firm, 1923-31; mem. N.Y. Cotton Exchange, 1933-69, mem. bd. mgrs., 1944-62, pres., 1956-58. Home: South Orange NJ Died July 28, 1972; buried Gate of Heaven Cemetery Hanover NJ

ROGERS, MARVIN CARSON, chem. engr.; b. North St. Paul, Minn., May 13, 1904; s. Charles Wesley and Marie (Rufenacht) R.; B.S., U. Minn., 1926; M.S., U. Mich., 1927, Ph.D. 1929; m. Evelyn Beatrice Zehner, June 11, 1932; children—John William, Marvin Carson. Engr., Whiting-Swenson Co., Ann Arbor, Mich., 1929-32; group leader research Standard Oil Co. (Ind.), Whiting, 1932-37; asst. prof. chem. engring. U. Minn., 1938-40; dir. research R. R. Donnelley &Sons Co., Chgo., 1940-57; exec. dir. Photoengravers Research Inst., Chgo. and Park Forest, Ill., 1957-68; cons., dir. Chgo. Paper Testing Lab., 1957-68; corp. dir. Printing Plate Supply Co., Chgo.; mem. adv. bd. ABC Industries, Inc., Paterson, N.J. Mem. exec. bd. Calumet Council, Boy Scouts of Am., 1952-68, Silver Beaver award, 1954, nat. council rep., Cal. Council, 1959-64. Mem. graphic arts adv. com. Carnegie Inst. Tech., 1959-68. Served to lt. col. Chem. Corps, AUS, 1943-45. Fellow Inst. of Printing; mem. T.A.P.P.I., Am. Chem. Soc. (dir., chmn. 1946-60), A.A.A.S., Am. Inst. Chem. Engrs., Tech. Assn. for Graphic Arts (pres. 1950-51). Mason. Home: Flossmoor IL Died Mar. 13, 1968.

ROGERS, MARY COCHRANE, writer; b. Derry, N.H., May 28, 1869; d. James and Abigail Smith (Hall) R.; ed. State Normal Sch. (Salem, Mass.), Radcliffe Coll., and under pvt. teachers; unmarried. Teacher in N.H., Mass., R.I., Southern Calif. and Winnipeg, Can.; writer since 1908. Mem. Authors' League America, N.H. Hist. Soc., Daughters of N.H. Episcopalian. Wrote: Rogers Rock, Lake George, Mar. 13, 1758, A Battle Fought on Snow Shoes, 1917. Home: Derry, N.H. Address: Hotel Oxford, Copley Square, Boston MA‡

ROGERS, ROBERT SAMUEL, univ. prof.; b. Madison, N.J., Dec. 5, 1900; s. Robert William and Ida Virginia (Ziegler) R.; A.B., U. of Pa., 1920; A.M., Columbia, 1922; A.M., Princeton, 1921, Ph.D., 1923; Carter Memorial Fellow, Am. Acad. in Rome, 1923-24; m. Dorothy Elizabeth Taylor, June 17, 1926; children—Robert Taylor, David Taylor. Instr. in classics, Princeton, 1924-28, Columbia, summers 1926 and 1927; asst. prof. classics, Western Reserve U., 1928-37; prof. of Latin and Roman studies, Duke U. since 1937, chmn. dept., 1940-62, chmn. classical studies, 1962-66; lectr. Latin, Johns Hopkins, 1939-40; vis. prof. Latin, U. N.C., 1961-62, 64-65, summers, 1947, 48, 54, 62. Mem. Am. Philol. Assn. (2d v.p. 1959, pres. 1961), Am. Numismatic Society, Classical Assn. Middle West and South, Phi Beta Kappa. Author: Criminal Trials and Criminal Legislation under Tiberius, 1935; Studies in the Reign of Tiberius, 1943. Editor: (with Kenneth Scott and Margaret M. Ward) Caesaris Augusti Res Gestae et Fragmenta, 1935. Consulting editor: The Corpus of Roman Law. Home: Durham NC Died Jan. 2, 1968.

ROGERS, SAMPSON, JR., partner McMaster, Hutchinson & Co., Chgo.; dir. Avenue State Nat. Bank, Oak Park. Home: Oak Park IL Died Aug. 3, 1972.

ROGERS, SAMUEL H., banker; b. Windom, Minn., Mar. 11, 1907; s. Samuel L. and Elizabeth (Holler) R.; A.B., U. Minn., 1928; m. Margaret Pinger, May 16, 1931; children—Margaret L., Samuel H., Elizabeth A. With Northwestern Nat. Bank, Mpls., since 1929, v.p. 1943-59, sr. v.p., exec. trust officer, 1959-68; dir., exec. com. Archer Daniels Midland; dir. Northwestern Nat. Bank Mpls., Kamloops Lumber Co., Ltd., Revelstoke Bldg. Materials Ltd., Lithium Corp. Am.; chmn. bd. Blandin Paper Co.; dir. Mpls. Northfield & So. Railway, Pence Realty Co., Pence Automobile Co.; mem. adv. com. Northwestern Bancorporation. Trustee Mpls. Found.; pres. board of trustees St. Barnabas Hospital; trustee of the YWCA (mem. finance committee, chmn. investment com.), Bishop Seabury Mission, Charles K. Blandin Found.; adv. com. The Sheltering Arms. Mem. Minn. Hist. Soc. (treas., exec. com.), Minn. Orchestral Association (investment com.), Phi Beta Kappa, Phi Delta Theta. Episcopalian. Clubs: Minneapolis (mem. finance com.), Minikahda. Home: Minneapolis MN Died Oct. 1, 1968; buried Lakewood Cemetery, Minneapolis MN

ROGERS, WILLIAM LOVELAND, air force officer; b. Larchwood, Ia., Dec. 29, 1911; s. William B. and Olivia B. (Loveland) R.; student U. S.D., 1929-30; B.S., U.S. Mil. Acad., 1934; M.S. in Engring., Cornell U., 1939; m. Dolores Stack, Mar. 15, 1947; children—Jonathan S., Martha O., James B., Genevieve L. Commd. 2d lt. U.S. Army, 1934, advanced through grades to maj. gen. USAF, 1961; comdr. 1141st Engr. Combat Group, 1943-46, 347th Engr. Gen. Service Regt., 1946-47; engr. 10th Air Force, 1947-49; student Air War Coll., 1949-50; chief air installations div., D/Mat. Hdqrs. Mil. Air Transp. Service, 1950-51, dep. dir. materials Hdqrs., 1951-52; dir. air installations Air Research and Devel. Command, 1952-54, asst. dep. comdr., supr. operations, 1954; asst. devel. programming Hdqrs. USAF, 1954-58; vice comdr. Air Force Missile Test Center, Cape Canaveral, Florida, 1958-61; commander Arnold Engring. Devel. Center, Air Force Systems Command, 1961-68. Decorated Silver Star, Legion of Merit with oak leaf cluster, Commendation ribbon with oak leaf cluster. Mem. Am. Rocket Soc., Soc. Am. Mil. Engrs., Beta Theta Pi. Club: N.Y. Athletic Club. Home: Tullahoma TN Died Sept. 1968.

ROGOSIN, I., business exec.; b. Vilna, Russia (formerly Lithuania), Feb. 16, 1887; s. Samuel and Hannah (Meltzer) R.; ed. pub. schs.; m. Evelyn Vogedes, Feb. 1923; 1 son, Lionel. Began in knit goods bus., Brooklyn, N.Y., 1905; pres., Hudson Knitting Mills, Union City, N.J., 1907-10; with Am. Knitting Mills, Brooklyn, 1910-12; pres., Atlas Knitting Mills, 1912-25, Art Silk Knitting Mills, 1919-25, Crystal Mills, 1919-25, and Varynit Mills, 1921-25, Knitted Textiles, 1920-25 (these mills were merged into Am. Rayon Products Corp., pres. until resignation, 1927); pres., dir. and chmn. bd. of Beaunit Mills, Inc., 1927-61, ret., chmn. exec. com.; pres. chmn. bd. Nat. Weaving Co., Inc.; pres. Skenandoa Rayon Corp., chmn. bd., 1953-71; pres., chmn. bd. N. Am. Rayon Corp., Am. Bemberg Co.; pres. Rogosin Industries, Ltd., Israel, 1956-71. Mem. North Hudson Jewish Center and Synagogue, Brooklyn Jewish Center. Club: Preakness Hills Country, Paterson, N.J. Home: Weehawken NJ Died May 1971.

ROHRBACH, JOHN FRANCIS DEEMS, business exec.; b. N.Y.C., 1889; N.Y.U., 1911. Chmn. Raybestos-Manhattan, Inc., Passaic, N.J.; dir. Milford Rivet & Machine Co. (Milford, Conn.), New Jersey Bank and Trust Co.; dir. Passaic-Clifton Y.M.C.A.; gov. Passaic Gen. Hosp. Home: Montclair NJ Died Dec. 25, 1968; buried New Haven CT

ROIG, HAROLD JOSEPH, lawyer, bus. exec.; b. Poughkeepsie, N.Y., July 7, 1885; s. Adolphus S. and Josephine (Cope) R.; A.B., Cornell U., 1907; LL.B., Columbia, 1909; m. Henrietta Havens, Jan. 10, 1917; children—Jean (Mrs. J. T. Ross), Carol (Mrs. David G. Watrous), Leila, Josephine (Mrs. G. W. Humphrey). Admitted N.Y. bar, 1909, practiced firm Byrne & Cutcheon, later Ivins, Wolf & Hoguet, N.Y. City, 1909-15; counsel W.R. Grace & Co., 1915, secretary, 1916-42, director, 1929-59, director emeritus, 1959, vice president, 1927-45, vice chmn., 1945-50, dir. and officer affiliated cos.; dir. Pan American Grace Airways, 1929-55, pres., 1939-49; member of the advisory board Marine Midland Grace Trust Company N.Y.; former dir., pres., chmn. Naco Fertilizer Co. Mem., sec. nitrate com. U.S., World War I. Police judge Village of Kings Point, L.I., 1928-39, trustee, 1939-44; past commr. Town Gulf Stream, Fla. Hon. life trustee Lenox Hill (N.Y.) Hosp.; former trustee and pres. Buckley Country Day Sch. Decorated El Sol del Peru; Orden Nacional al Merito (Ecuador); El Condor de los Andes (Bolivia). Former mem. N.Y. Cotton Exchange, Liverpool Cotton Exchange, N.Y. Commodity Exchange, N.Y. Coffee & Sugar Exchange; mem. Assn. of Bar of City of N.Y., Phi Beta Kappa. Episcopalian. Clubs: Church, Univ., India House (N.Y.C.); Gulf Stream Golf, Gulf Stream Bath and Tennis (gov., past pres.); Gardiners Bay Country (Shelter Island, N.Y.); Piping Rock (Locust Valley, L.I., N.Y.); Mashomack Fish and Game Preserve (Shelter Island, N.Y.). Editor: Columbia Law Rev., 1909. Home: New York City NY Died July 4, 1972; buried St. Mary's Churchyard Shelter Island NY

ROJANKOVSKY, FEODOR S., painter; b. Mitava, Russia, Dec. 24, 1891; s. Stephan and Lydia (Kordasevich) R.; student Acad. Fine Arts, Moscow, Russia; m. Nina G. Fedotov, Apr. 12, 1946; 1 dau., Tatiana. Pub. sketches and drawings various lit. mags., Russia, 1915-17; illustrator books, Poltava, Russia, 1918-19; stage designer Poznan Opera House, Poland, 1920-22; art dir. publishing firm, Poland, 1922-25; illustrator books, Paris, London, also asso. movie, advt. firms, Paris, 1926-40; illustrator children's books, 1941-70. Served with Russian Army, World War I. Recipient gold medal Art Directors Club, 1948; Silver Jubilee award Limited Editions Club, 1954; Children's Book Festival award N.Y. Herald Tribune, 1955; Caldecott award, 1956. Home: Bronxville NY Died Oct. 12, 1970; buried Woodlawn Cemetery, Bronx NY

ROLFE, DANIEL THOMAS, physician, coll. dean; b. Tampa, Fla., Mar. 1, 1902; s. Everett R. and Carrie Lee (Thomas) R.; B.S., Fla. A. and M. Coll., 1922; M.D. with honors, Meharry Med. Coll., 1927; grad. study U. Chgo., 1928-30; m. Birdie Lucile Scott, Aug. 9, 1952. Intern George W. Hubbard Hosp., Nashville, 1927-28, now mem. adv. com.; instr. Meharry Med. Coll., 1927-28, prof. physiology, 1930-38, chmn. dept. physiology and pharmacology, 1938-52, acting chairman dept. anatomy, 1950-52, chmn. dept. physiology, dean Sch. Medicine, 1952-66, dean student affairs, 1966-68; guest dept. physiology Cornell U. Med. Coll., 1943-44; mem. med. adv. com. VA Hosp., Tuskegee, Ala. Diplomate Nat. Bd. Med. Examiners, 1935. Recipient Tolbert Anatomy prize Meharry Med. College, 1927; Distinguished Service plaque Fla. A. and M. Coll., 1953; Distinguished Service medal Nat. Med. Assn., 1956. Fellow A.A.A.S.; member World, Am., Nat., Tenn., Nashville, Volunteer State med. assns., Am. Physiol. Soc., Assn. Am. Med. Colls., Nat. Soc. Med. Research, Tenn. Acad. Sci., Nashville Acad. Medicine, Tenn. Council Human Relations, Nashville Symphony Assn., Nashville Community Relations Council, Homer G. Phillips Interns Alumni Assn., Meharry Alumni Assn. (exec. sec. 1939-59), Nashville Arts Council, Assn. UN, Alpha Omega Alpha (chpt. counselor), Kappa Alpha Psi. Mason. Author profl. articles. Home: Nashville TN Died May 26, 1968; buried Greenwood Cemetery, Nashville TN

ROLFS, FRED MAAS, botanist, plant pathologist; b. Le Claire, Ia., Mar. 5, 1875; s. Maas Peter and Maria C. (Neimeier) R.; B.S., Ia. State Coll. Agr. and Mechanic Arts, 1897; M.S., Colo. State Agrl. Coll., 1903; grad. student Columbia, 1907; Ph.D., Cornell U., 1913; m. Adeline D. Evans, Aug. 23, 1903. Asst. prof. botany and horticulture, Colo. State Agr. Coll., 1899-1903; prof. botany and horticulture, U. of Fla., 1903-06; plant pathologist, Mo. Fruit Expt. Sta., 1906-10; asso. prof. botany, plant pathology and bacteriology, Clemson Agrl. Coll., of S.C., 1913-15; prof. horticulture, Okla. Agrl. and Mech. Coll., 1916-23, prof. botany and plant pathology 1923-38. Fellow A.A.A.S.; mem. Bot. Soc. America, Am. Path. Soc., Ecol. Soc. America, Okla. Acad. Science, Okla. Pecan Growers Assn., Sigma Xi, Phi Kappa Phi, Pi Gamma Mu. Episcopalian. Author of experiment sta. bulletins on diseases of plants. Home: 510 W. Maple. Stillwater OK‡

ROLLERT, EDWARD DUMAS, automobile mfg. co. exec.; b. Crete, Ill., Mar. 16, 1912; s. Edward Andrew and Rose May (Dumas) R.; B.S. in Chem. Engring., Purdue U., 1933, M.S. in Engring., 1934, D. Indsl. Mgmt. (hon.), 1960; m. Helen I. Rorabeck, July 13, 1935; children—Edward David, John Michael. With Gen. Motors Corp., 1934-69, gen. mgr. Harrison radiator, div., 1955-59, v.p., 1959-69, gen. mgr. Buick motor div., 1959-65, exec. v.p., div., 1965-66, exec. v.p. car and truck body and assembly group, 1966-68, dir., member executive com. corp., car and truck group exec., 1965-66, exec. v.p. overseas non-automotive and def. divs., 1968-69. Chmn. Radio Free Europe for Mich., 1969. Chmn. bd. regents Gen. Motors Inst.; Bd. dirs. Albion Coll.; bd. dirs. Asso. Industries N.Y., 1956-59, chmn. bus. climate com., 1958-59. Chmn. advanced gifts Community Fund, Lockport, N.Y., 1958; chmn Explorer Post, Boy Scouts Am., 1954-55. Mem. research adv. bd. Purdue U. Mem. Am. Soc. Metals, Am. Soc. M.E., Soc. Automotive Engrs., Sigma Xi, Tau Beta Pi. Methodist. Home: Bloomfield Hills MI Died Nov. 27, 1969.

ROLLINS, CLARA SHERWOOD (MRS.), b. St. Louis, Feb. 28, 1874; Author: A Burne-Jones Head; Threads of Life; various short stories in magazines and poems; also 4 farces for amateurs, published under maiden name, Clara Harriot Sherwood. Address: Care Lamson, Wolffe & Co., Boston MA‡

ROLZ-BENNETT, JOSE, UN ofcl.; b. Quetzaltenango, Guatemala, Aug. 9, 1918; s. Federico Rolz and Maria Cristina Bennett; degree in law and social scis. Faculty of Law, U. Guatemala, 1941; m. Julieta Castro de Rolz Bennett, June 15, 1941; children—Jose Rafael, Maria Cristina, Julieta, Patricia. Hon. prof. law U. Costa Rica and Guatemala, 1944, 62; hon. prof. humanities U. Guatemala, 1965, prof. faculties law and humanities, 1945-55, dean Faculty Humanities, 1945-54; mem. Nat. Constituent Assembly and Assembly Com. which drafted Guatemala's Constn., 1945; pres. bd. dirs. Guatemalan Social Security Inst., 1946-48; mem. Guatemalan delegation 10th-12th sessions, also 1st-3d emergency spl. sessions UN Gen. Assembly; mem. Guatemalan delegation 17th-22d sessions, also 6th-7th spl. session UN Trusteeship Council; mem. UN vis. mission to Trust Terrs. Pacific, 1956; Guatemalan rep. Conf. on Statute of Internat. Atomic Energy Agy., 1956; mem. UN Commn. to Togoland under French administrn., 1957; ambassador, permanent rep. Guatemala to UN, 1958, acting dir. UN div. trusteeship, 1958-61; chief UN rep. in Katanga, Congo, 1962; personal rep. of sec.-gen. and temporary UN adminstr. of W. New Guinea, 1962; dep. chef de cabinet to sec.-gen. UN, 1962-64; undersec. spl. polit. affairs UN, 1965-68, also charge Office Pub. Information, 1965-68, under sec. gen. for spl. polit. affairs, 1968-71, also charge div. human rights, 1968-71. Decorated Order of Merit (Ecuador). Author: El Problema de la Seguridad en la Estimativa Juridica, 1941; Co-legislacion Constitucional Centroamericana, 1949; Carta de las Universidades Lationamericanas, 1949; Digesto Constitucional Guatemalteco, 1945; Guatemala: Realities and Problems, 1953. Home: Guatemala City Guatemala Died Dec. 1972.

ROMAINS, JULES, author; b. Saint-Julien-Chateuil, Velay, France, Aug. 26, 1885; s. Henri and Marie (Richier) Farigoule; Ph.D. in Philosophy; Masters Degree in Humanities and Scis.; m. Lise Dreyfus, Dec. 18, 1936. Prof. philosophy lycees Brest, Laon, Paris and Nice, 1909-19; lit. career, 1904-72; interested in Abbey Group (with Arcos, Vildrac and Duhamel), then met Moreas, Paul Fort, Apollinaire, Max Jacob, Picasso and Modigliani; travelled through Europe; pres., then pres. honor French Pen-Club, then internat. pres. Pen-Clubs, 1936-41; left France for U.S., then for Mexico, 1940-45; creator with Henri Bonnet of Assembly of Havana, 1941; editorial writer for L'Aurore, 1953-72. Pres. Nat. Found. Zellidja Scholarships. Mem. French Acad., Men of Letters (superior council), Theater Universal Assn. (pres.), French Poets Assn. (pres. 1967-72). Author: (play) Knock, or the Triumph of Medicine; The Soul of Men, 1904; The Unanimous Life, 1908; Genoese Ode, 1925; The White Man, 1936; The Erected Stones, 1945; Choice of Poems, 1948; Houses, 1953; (novels) The Regenerated Borough, 1906; Paris' Powers, 1911; Death of a Nobody, 1911; The Boys in the Backroom, 1913; Donogoo-Tonka, 1920; The Body's Rapture, 3 vols., 1922-29; Men of Good Will, 27 vols., 1932-45; Salsette Discovers America, 1942; Jerphanion's Son, 1956; A Singular Woman, 1957; The Need to See, 1958; Un Grand Honnete Homme, 1961. Home: Paris France Died Aug. 14, 1972; buried Cemetery Pere-Lachaise.

ROMANOWITZ, HARRY ALEX, educator; b. Covington, Ky., Jan. 8, 1901; s. Harry Jacob and Essie May (Marks) R.; E.E., U. Cin., 1924, M.S., 1939; Ph.D., U. Mich., 1948; m. Mildred Edna Foster, Sept. 18, 1926; children—Byron F., Lois J. Engr. sales rep. Kelley-Koett Mfg. Company, Covington, Ky., 1925-30; instr. Ohio Mechanics Inst., 1930-41; asst. prof., asso. prof., prof. elec. engring., U. Ky., 1942—, head dept. 1952-66. Recipient Distinguished Alumnus award U. Cin., 1969. Registered engr., Ky. Fellow I.E.E.E.; mem. Am. Soc. Engring. Edn., Sigma Pi Sigma, Sigma Xi. Tau Beta Pi, Eta Kappa Nu. Author text books including (with Russell E. Puckett) Introduction to Electronics, 1968; Introduction to Electric Circuits, 1971; also manuals on electronics and circuits. Home: Lexington KY Died Mar. 17, 1971; buried Highland Cemetery Fort Mitchell KY

ROMUALDEZ, NORBERTO, judge; b. Burawen, Leyte, P.I., June 6, 1875; s. Daniel and Trinidad (Lopez) R.; A.B., 1897, D.C.L., 1921; m. Beatrice D. Buz, Oct. 27, 1907. Admitted to P.I. bar, 1903, clk. Court of First Instance, Leyte, 1901-03; pros. atty. (fiscal), Leyte, 1906-10; asst. city atty., Manila, 1910-11; asso. judge Court of Land Registration, 1911-13; judge Court of First Instance, 15th Dist., 1913-14, 22d Dist., 1914-19; del. to Postal Conv., Madrid, Spain, 1920; asso. justice Supreme Court of Philippines since 1921. K.C. Author: A Bisayan Grammar, 1908; The Tagbanwa Alphabet, 1914; Philippine Orthography, 1918; The Psychology of the Filipino, 1924. Home: 302 A. Mabini. Address: Arellano Bldg., Manila PI*‡

RONAN, DANIEL JOHN, congressman; b. Chgo., July 13, 1914; s. Daniel J. and Justina (McKenzie) R.; B.A., Loyola U., Chgo., 1938, postgrad., 1939-41, 47-48. Mem. Ill. Ho. of Reps., 1948-50; alderman City of Chgo., 1951-64; mem. 89th Congress 6th Dist. Ill. Served with USAAF, 1943-46; CBI. Mem. Am. Legion, V.F.W., Am. Vets. Democrat. K.C. Home: Chicago IL Died Aug. 1969.

RONNEBERG, EARL FRIDTHJOV, architect, structural engr.; b. Chgo., May 15, 1905; s. Nathal T. and Hedvig (Jensen) R.; B.S., U. Ill., 1929; m. Bertha J. Cohn, Oct. 7, 1929; children—Jenny L. (Mrs. Laude E. Hartrum), Earl Fridthjov, Ronnie N., Peter L. Supt., Ronneberg Engring. Co., Chgo., 1929-31; spl. field agt. U.S. Govt., 1931-39; propr. N. Ronneberg Co., Chgo., 1939-72. Dist. chmn. Chgo. Area council Boy Scouts Am., 1952-54, cubmaster, 1940-57. Recipient Silver Beaver, Boy Scouts Am., 1954. Mem. Ill. Soc. Architects, Am. Assn. Engrs., Structural Engrs. Soc. Ill., Am. Soc. C.E. Home: Chicago IL Died Feb. 12, 1972.

ROOK, GUSTAV S., educator; b. Westfalia, Germany, Dec. 19, 1915; s. Gustav H. and Anna E. (Pichler) R.; came to U.S., 1923, naturalized, 1928; B.S., Northeastern U., 1939, Ed. M., 1959; m. Audrey G. Gallant, Nov. 26, 1942 (dec. June 1971); children—Janice V., Robert G., Gary S., Richard C., Susan M. Prof., chmn. dept. graphic sci. Coll. of Engineering, Northeastern University, Boston, dean of Lincoln College, 1964-70. Committeeman local Boy Scouts Am.; mem. Manatiquot Sch. Bldg. Com., Braintree, Mass., East Braintree Library Building Committee. Member Am. Soc. Engring. Edn., New Eng. Engring. Graphics Assn., Mass. Tech. Drawing Tchrs. Assn. Author: (with A. E. Sanderson) Graphic Representation, 1952. Home: Braintree MA Died June 12, 1970; buried New Calvary Cemetery, Boston MA

ROOME, KENNETH ANDREW, stock broker; b. Tenafly, N.J., May 27, 1901; s. James and Lizzie (Westervelt) R.; student pub. schs.; m. Catherine Wilcox, June 1, 1925 (dec. Jan. 1945); 1 dau., Elizabeth Westervelt (Mrs. Gordon Logan); m. 2d, Rheba Shain, Feb. 16, 1946 (deceased). With the firm of Parkinson and Burr, brokers, 1916; became partner in firm of Hardy & Company in 1925, now sr. partner; former vice chmn. bd. Hudson & Manhattan R.R. Served with Squadron A, N.Y. N.G., 1920-25. Mem. Holland Soc. (v.p.). Clubs: Union League, Knickerbocker Country (N.Y.C.); Englewood (N.J.). Home: Tenafly NJ Died Dec. 4, 1967; buried Brookside Cemetery, Englewood NJ

ROOP, JAMES CLAWSON, b. Upland, Pa., Oct. 3, 1888; s. Albert A. and Mary (Clawson) R.; grad. Blight School, Phila., Pa., 1905; B.S. in E.E., U. of Pa., 1909; m. Rebecca Haigh, Mar. 7, 1929. Instr. in elec. engring., U. of Pa., 1909-10; with Phila. and West Chester Traction Co., 1910-15; cons. work under Prof. G. F. Sever, N.Y. City, 1915-16; in charge constrn. and testing work, J. G. White Management Corp., 1916-17, gen. supervision and spl. reporting on pub. utilities, 1919-21; with Bur. of Budget, Washington, D.C., June 1921-June 1922, asst. dir., Jan.-June 1922; with Woods Bros. Constrn. Co., Lincoln, Neb., 1922-25; pres. Monomarks, Inc., May 1925-Oct. 1926; with Dawes Bros., Inc., Chicago, 1926-29; mem. Dominican Econ. Commn., Apr.-July 1929; dir. U.S. budget, Aug. 1929-Mar. 1933; with Pan-Am. Airways, Inc., 1935-49; consultant to chmn. munitions bd., 1949, retired. Vice president and treas. Pan-Am. Airways Corp. and its principal subsidiaries. Served as captain, major and lt. col. Engr. Corps, U.S. Army, World War I; in Engr. Supply Office, Sept.-Dec. 1917, Office of Gen. Purchasing Agt., A.E.F., Dec. 1917-Sept. 1919; mem. staff Mil. Bd. of Allied Supply, July-Nov. 1918; served as col., brig. gen. U.S. Army, 1942; gen. purchasing agt. U.S. Army Forces in Australia and U.S. Mem. of Allied Supply Council in Australia. Decorated D.S.M. (U.S.); Legion of Honor (France); Order Crown of Italy. Republican. Episcopalian. Clubs: Army and Navy (Washington); University (New York). Home: New Canaan CT Died Jan. 23, 1972; buried New Canaan CT

ROOS, EDWIN G., mfg. exec.; b. St. Louis, Oct. 5, 1894; s. Henry and Elizabeth (Roeder) R.; A.B., U. Ill., 1917; m. Frances Wendl, Oct. 3, 1922; 1 son, Peter. Vice pres. charge sales Certainteed Products Corp., 1936-39; v.p., sales dir. Plymouth Cordage Co., 1939-51, pres., 1951-72; president, dir. Plymouth Cordage Co. Canada, Ltd., Plymouth Cordage Industries, Incorporated; director of Plymouth National Bank; trustee Plymouth Five Cents Savs. Bank. Dir., exec. com. Jordan Hosp. Home: Plymouth MA Died June 17, 1971; buried St Louis MO

ROOS, WALTER L., lawyer; b. St. Louis, Nov. 18, 1890; s. Henry and Elizabeth (Roeder) R.; A.B., U. Mo., 1913; LL.B., Washington U., St. Louis, 1915; m. Hazel M. Walker, Nov. 14, 1935; children—Elizabeth (Mrs. Richard H. Beuthel), Virginia Lee (Mrs. Frank Clayton Stiers), Carolyn Frances (Mrs. James R. Brandie). Admitted to Mo. bar; practiced in St. Louis; mem. firm Armstrong, Teasdale, Roos, Kramer & Vaughan, St. Louis; ret. Mem. Phi Delta Phi, Kappa Alpha. Mason (33 deg.). Home: St Louis MO Died Aug. 29, 1972; interred Oak Grove Mausoleum, St Louis County MO

ROOT, EDWARD CLARY, author; b. Bloomfield, N.J., Jan. 6, 1877; s. Joseph Henry and Jean (Christie) R.; A.B., Yale, 1900; student Harvard Law Sch., 1900-02; admitted to Mass. bar, 1902; m. Louise Bass, of Rome, Ga., Aug. 31, 1907 (died Mar. 21, 1914). Vice pres. Justice-Hawley Co., New York. Club: Yale (New York). Author: Huntington, Jr., 1906; The Unseen Jury, 1907. Also writer of advertising literature. Address: 111 Waverly Pl., New York NY‡

ROOT, ERNEST ROB, editor; b. Medina, O., June 23, 1862; s. Amos Ives and Susan (Hall) R.; Oberlin Coll., 1881-86; awarded degree LL.D. by Ohio State U., June 3, 1944; m. Elizabeth M. Humphrey, Dec. 15, 1885; 1 son, Alan I. In business with father, mfg. beekeepers' supplies and pub. bee culture lit. since 1885, chmn. bd. of dirs., The A. I. Root Company since 1941. Editor Gleanings in Bee Culture (monthly). Vice-pres. Savings Deposit Bank, Medina, since 1905. Vice-president Ohio Commission to Jamestown (Va.) Exposition. Republican. Congregationalist. Mason. Author numerous books relating to field since 1905. Lectr. Redpath Chautauquas, 1924-28. Home: Medina OH‡

ROOT, WALTER STANTON, educator; b. Buffalo, Sept. 18, 1902; s. William Francis Stanton and Leontine Margaret (Root) R.; student Rutgers Coll., 1920-21; B.Sc. cum. laude, Wesleyan U., 1922-24; postgrad. Univ. and Bellevue Hosp. Med. Sch., 1925-27; Ph.D., U. Pa. 1930; m. Elizabeth Wigfall, Jan. 26, 1928 (dec.); 1 son, Richard Wigfall; m. 2d, Pauline Elizabeth Warner, Nov. 4, 1961. Asst. in biology Wesleyan U., 1924-25; asst. physiologist U.S. Army Sch. Aviation Medicine, summer 1925; asst. instr. physiology U. Pa. Med. Sch., 1927-29; asst. prof. physiology Syracuse Med. Sch., 1929-31, asso. prof., 1931-36; asso. prof. U. Md. Med. Sch., 1936-37; asso. prof. Coll. Physicians and Surgeons Columbia, 1937-48, prof. physiology, 1948-68, emeritus, 1968-72. Spl. field staffs, cons. Rockefeller Found., Mahidol U., Bangkok, Thailand, 1968-69; Woods Hole scholar (Wesleyan U.), Marine Biol. Lab., summer 1924; investigator Marine Biol. Lab., summers 1928-36, mem. corp.; group research program Am. Bur. Med. Aid to China, Nanking, summer 1948; dir. Am. Bur. for Med. Aid to China, 1949-61, v.p., 1951-61; mem. 18th Internat. Physiol. Congress, Copenhagen, 1950. Research asso. med. physics. U. Cal., fall 1952; mem. physiology test com. Nat. Bd. Med. Examiners, 1957-61; mem. med. scis. screening com. Conf. Bd. Asso. Research Councils (Fulbright awards), 1957-62, chmn., 1962-64; com. nomenclature for randombred animals Inst. Lab. Animal Resources Nat. Acad. Scis.-NRC, 1964-70. Decorated Armed Forces medal (China). Fellow N.Y. Acad. Scis. (council 1949-50, v.p. 1951, pres. 1956), N.Y. Acad. Medicine (asso.); mem. Assn. Research Nervous and Mental Disease (asso.), Research Def. Soc. Eng. (life), S.A.R., Nat. Resuscitation Soc. (adv. bd.), Am. Physiol. Soc., Soc. Exptl. Biology and Medicine (sec.-treas. 1958-67), Order of Founders and Patriots, N.Y. State Soc. Med. Research (pres. 1954-55), Am. Heart Assn. (sci. council), A.A.A.S. (council 1964), Harvey Soc., Sigma Xi (chpt. pres. 1962-63), Nu Sigma Nu. Republican. Episcopalian. Cons. editor Hematopoietic Mechanisms, N.Y. Acad. Scis., 1959; mng. editor: Proc. Soc. Exptl. Biol. and Med., 1958-67; editor Life History of the Erythrouyte in Methods in Medical Research. Vol. 8, 1960; co-editor Physiol. Pharmacology, Vol. I, 1962, II, 1965, III, IV, 1967; hon. mem. editorial adv. board Jour. Photochemistry and Photobiology, 1962-66. Contbr. Am. Jour. Physiol., Macleod's Physiol. in Modern Medicine, 1941; Jour. Applied Physiology, Jour. Biological Chemistry. Bard's Med. Physiology, 1956, 61, Handbook of Physiology, 1963, 65, Mountcastle, Med. Physiology, 1968. Home: Woods Hole MA Died Mar. 30, 1972; buried Kensington CT

ROOT, WILLIAM CAMPBELL, educator; b. Grass Valley, Cal., Oct. 26, 1903; s. Orville Hurd and Jean Marion (Campbell) R.; B.S., U. Cal., 1925; A.M., Harvard, 1927, Ph.D., 1932; m. Pauline Dikeman, Apr. 16, 1932. Research asso. Harvard, 1930-32; instr. chemistry Bowdoin Coll., 1932-34, asst. prof., 1934-39, asso. prof., 1939-46, chmn. dept., 1941-66, prof. from 1946, Charles W. Pickard prof. chemistry, 1952-69. Recipient James Norris Flack award for outstanding achievement in teaching in chemistry. Fellow Royal Anthrop. Inst. of Gt. Britain and Ireland; mem. Am. Chem. Soc., Am. Anthrop. Assn., Soc. Am. Archeology, Phi Beta Kappa, Sigma Xi, Phi Lambda Upsilon, Alpha Chi Sigma, Theta Delta Chi. Democrat. Episcopalian. Contbr. tech. articles sci. jours. Home: Brunswick ME Died June 13, 1969.

ROOTH, IVAR, banker; b. Sweden, Nov. 2, 1888; s. Otto and Ellen (Hertzman) R.; student U. Upsala, 1906-11, U. Berlin, 1911-12; 3 children by first marriage; m. 2d Ingrid Soderlind, July 19, 1931; 1 child. Solicitor Stockholm (Sweden) Handelsbank, 1914-15, head comml. credit dept., 1915-16; asst. mgr. Stockholm Mortgage Bank, 1920-29; gov. Central Bank of Sweden, 1929-48; dir. Bank for Internat. Settlements, 1931-33, 37-49; headed mission to Iraq for Internat. Bank Recovery and Development, 1951; chmn. bd., mng. dir. Internat. Monetary Fund, 1951-56. Home: Stockholm Sweden Died Feb. 1972.

ROPERS, HAROLD, lawyer; b. San Francisco, Aug. 15, 1904; s. August Paul and Julia (Crowley) R.; student Hastings Coll. Law, San Francisco, 1931; m. Rolyne

Belluomini, May 16, 1931; children—Michael, Mark. Admitted to Cal. bar, 1931; mem. legal dept. Pacific States Savs. & Loan, San Francisco, 1929-37; asso. Thomas L. Chamberlain, Auburn, Cal., 1937-40; partner Bronson, Bronson & McKinnon, San Francisco, 1940-50; partner Eugene J. Majeski, Redwood City, Cal., 1951; practice law, Redwood City, 1937-66. Instr. comml. law Am. Inst. Banking, 1942-50. Mem. Republican Central County Com., 1942-50. Mem. Am. Coll. Trial Lawyers, Internat. Assn. Ins. Counsel, R.R. Trial Assn., State Bar Cal., Am., San Mateo bar assns. Home: Menlo Park CA Died Oct. 12, 1966.

RORABAUGH, GUY OSCAR, sugar co. exec.; b. Salida, Colo., May 20, 1911; s. Oscar Guy and Florence (Morris) R.; student Colo. State U., 1929-32; B.A., U. Colo., 1935; m. Clare L. Canning, May 5, 1934 children—Rosemary (Mrs. Walter E. Burkitt), Thomas G., Diane (Mrs. C.E. Baker). With Holly Sugar Corp., Colorado Springs, Colo., 1935-70, mgr. research lab., 1952-56, dir. research, 1956-62, gen. supt., 1962-64, v.p. operations, 1964-70; v.p. Big Horn Limestone Co., Billings, Mont., 1962-70, also dir. Mem. adv. bd. Agrl. Research Service, U.S. Dept. Agr., Washington, 1960-70; mem. industry adv. bd. Sugar Research Found., N.Y.C., 1955-70; v.p. Beet Sugar Devel. Found., Ft. Collins, Colo., 1965-70, also dir. Mem. Am. Chem. Soc., Inst. Food Technologists, Am. Soc. Sugar Beet Technologists (Meritorious Service award 1964), Acacia Frat. Conglist. Colorado Springs CO Died May 3, 1970; interred Evergreen Shrine of Rest Mausoleum Colorado Springs CO

RORER, JAMES BIRCH, plant pathologist; b. Ogontz, Pa., Dec. 29, 1876; s. William A. and Sarah Tyson (Heston) R.; B.A., Harvard, 1899, M.A., 1902; m. Ethel Stuart Wimer, of Washington, D.C., Feb. 10, 1909. Asst. in botany, Harvard, 1899-1902; scientific asst. U.S. Dept. Agr., 1902-05; asst. pathologist same, 1906-08; mycologist Bd. of Agr., Trinidad, B.W.I., 1909-18; dir. Dept. of Agr., Associacion de Agricultores del Ecuador, and plant pathologist, 1919-22; agr. adviser and mgr. of Hacienda Panigon. Fellow A.A.A.S.; mem. Bot. Soc. America, Am. Phytopathol. Soc. Contbr. papers dealing with diseases of peaches and apples, sugar cane, cocoanuts, cacao and other tropical crops. Has specialized in tropical agr. Address: Casilla de correo X", Guayaquil Ecuador‡

ROSE, BENJAMIN MORRIS, merchant; b. Warsaw, Poland, May 6, 1898; s. Hyman and Yetta (Bernstein) R.; came to U.S., 1903, naturalized, 1908; C.E., Coll. City N.Y., 1920; m. Bessie O. Ox, Aug. 15, 1920; children—Barbara (Mrs. Lawrence Bensman), Eloise (Mrs. Selwyn Blumberg), Hermina (Mrs. Joseph Shugol), Gilbert E. Exec., Samuel Stores, N.Y.C., 1920-38; mgr. Star Clothing, Detroit, 1938-43; pres. Chelsea Clothes, Wyandotte, Mich., 1943-69. Chmn., Mich. Anti-Defamation League, 1956-69; mem. Mich. Bd. Vocational Edn., Lansing, 1958-63; pres. Jamestown Gen. Hosp., 1934-35; v.p. Wyandotte Gen. Hosp., 1953-57. Gov., Wayne State U., co-chmn. bd. govs., 1969. Served to 2d lt. U.S. Army, 1918. Mem. Am. Arbitration Assn., Zionist Orgn. (dir. Detroit 1967-69). Lion (pres. 1937-38). Home: Allen Park MI Died Apr. 24, 1969.

ROSE, CARLTON RAYMOND, chemist, metallurgist; b. Ann Arbor, Mich., June 16, 1873; s. Preston B. and Cornelia (Robinson) R.; Ph.B., U. of Mich., 1894, A.M., 1896; Mass. Inst. Tech., 1900-1; m. Winifred Higbee, of Buchanan, Mich., Aug. 12, 1897. Instr. chemistry, U. of Ill., 1896-1900; prof. metallurgy, Colo. Sch. of Mines, 1901-03; supt. smelters, U.S. Zinc Co., Pueblo, Colo., 1903—. Mem. Am. Inst. Mining Engrs., Colo. Scientific Soc., Delta Upsilon. Mason (K.T.). Clubs: Pueblo Commerce, Minnequa Country. Address: Box 860 Pueblo CO‡

ROSE, DANA, utility exec.; b. Chgo.; s. Frank Lisle and Jessie (Allen) R.; A.B., Hillsdale Coll.; m. Elinor Kiess, Dec. 25, 1935; children—Stuart Rex, Douglas Dana, Bruce Geoffrey. With Mich. Bell Telephone Co., 1938-68, successively mgr., Kalamazoo, mgr., Grand Rapids, dir. customer relations, pub. relations dept., Detroit, 1938-55, asst. v.p., Detroit, 1955-68. Mem. bd. advisers Wayne State U. Press. Mem. Pub. Relations Soc. Am., Nat. Society for Study of Communication, Delta Sigma Phi, Theta Alpha Phi, Epsilon Delta Alpha. Republican. Methodist. Home: Royal Oak MI Died Dec. 23, 1968.

ROSE, DWIGHT CHAPPELL, investment counsel; b. Waterford, Conn., Sept. 7, 1897; s. Frank Bowen and Nellie Avery (Chappell) R.; grad. Bulkeley Sch., New London, Conn., 1915; student U. of Mich., 1915-16; B.S., Harvard, 1919; student Harvard Law Sch., 1920-21; unmarried. Bond salesman Lee, Higginson & Co., 1919-20; asso. with Scudder, Stevens & Clark, investment counsel, 1922-31, gen. economist and mgr. instns. dept., 1927-31; gen. partner Brundage, Story & Rose, investment counsel, 1931-56, ret., now cons. Served in Officers' Training Corps of the United States Army, Plattsburg, and Camp Lee, Va., Feb.-Nov. 1918. On active duty as lt. comdr. U.S.N.R., May 29, 1942 to October 15, 1945, commander (inactive) since 1945. Mem. Investment Counsel Assn. of Am. (pres. 1937-48), American Econ. Assn., Am. Statis. Assn., Acad. Polit. Sci., Fed. Grand Jury Assn. So. Dist. N.Y. Republican. Unitarian. Club: Harvard, U. Mich. Author: A Scientific Approach to Investment Management, 1928; The Practical Application of Investment Management, 1933; The Policyholders' Interest in Equity Investment, 1939. Home: Waterford CT Died Oct. 2, 1969.

ROSE, E(RNEST) H(ERBERT), metall. engr.; b. Kinsley, Kan., July 6, 1897; s. George Alonzo and Bertha (Ginn) R.; B.S. in Chem. Engring., U. Kan., 1920; m. Lucile Collins, Sept. 25, 1919; children—Miriam (Mrs. M. MacAskill), George H. Mill supt. Patino Mines, Bolivia, 1925-27; mill supt. Moctezuma Copper Co., Mexico, 1928-30; asst. mill supt. Internat. Nickel Co. of Can., 1930-36, mill supt., 1936-45; cons. metallurgist Copper Range Co., Mich. 1946-47; research engr. Tenn. Coal and Iron div. U.S. Steel Corp., 1947-54; project dir. metallurgy, materials adv. bd. Nat. Acad. Scis., 1954-56; chief beneficiation engr. Koppers Co., Pitts., from 1957. Mem. raw materials adv. com. AEC, 1949-59. Mem. Am. Inst. Mining, Metall. and Petroleum Engrs. (dir.), Mining and Metall. Soc. Am., A.A.A.S., Tau Beta Pi. Author articles, holder patents on utilization low grade Pittsburgh PA Died May 27, 1968; buried Mt. Hope Cemetery Penn Hills PA

ROSE, FORREST HOBART, coll. dean; b. Lewis Center, O., Dec. 23, 1899; s. Charles and Mary (Collier) R.; A.B., Ohio Wesleyan U., 1922, A.M., 1929; Ph.D., U. Wis., 1938; m. Ruth Esther Smith, Aug. 23, 1924; children—Barbara Lee, Mary Lou. Prof. speech Kan. Wesleyan U., Salina, 1925-27, Park Coll., Parkville, Mo., 1927-30, Southeast Mo. State Coll., 1930-45, dean since 1945. Specialist speakers sect. Office Civilian Def., Washington, 1942. Vice chmn. state advisory com., Salvation Army. Mem. Speech Assn. Am., Mo. Debate Assn. (sec., treas. 1929-32, pres. 1932-34), Mo. State Speech Assn., N.E.A., Mo. State Teachers Association, Pi Kappa Delta (nat. pres. 1938-40), Delta Sigma Rho, Theta Alpha Phi, Alpha Psi Omega, Kappa Delta Pi, Chi Phi. Methodist. Mason, Lion. Home: Cape Girardeau MO Died Dec. 20, 1969; buried Meml. Park, Cape Girardeau MO

ROSE, FRANK WATSON, contracting co. exec.; b. Cohutta, Ga., Sept. 3, 1917; s. Frank Watson and Bonnie (Rollins) R.; B.S. in Civil Engring., Ga. Inst. Tech., 1943; m. Ellen Radcliff Nooe, Mar. 15, 1944; children—Georgann (Mrs. Charles B. Cunningham III), Frank Watson III, Margaret, Richard. With Richards & Assos., Inc., Carrollton, Ga., 1946-69, exec. v.p., 1946-69; dir. Southwire Co., Carrollton. Pres., Carroll Service Council, Carrollton, 1946. Trustee W. Ga. Coll. Found., Carrollton. Served to capt. AUS, 1943-46. Mem. Power and Communication Contractors Assn. (pres. 1961, dir.), V.F.W., Am. Legion, Carrollton C. of C. (v.p. 1965). Episcopalian (sr. warden 1968-69). Mason. Clubs: Lions International, Sunset Hills Country (pres. 1956). Home: Carrollton GA Died Jan. 20, 1969.

ROSE, HELOISE DURANT (MRS. C. H. M. ROSE), author, lecturer and dramatist; b. Brooklyn, N.Y.; d. Thomas Clark (M.D.) and Heloise (Timbrell) Durant; ed. in Eng., Italy, Germany; m. Arthur Frethey, of London, 1890 (died 6 weeks after marraige); m. 2d, Charles H. M. Rose, of New York, 1895; 1 son, Durant Timbrell. Mem. Dante League of America (founder), Dante Society (Cambridge, Mass.), Am. League Penwomen; founder Rockland Co. Welfare Assn.; founder President Claudel Circle (French lit. soc.), St. Petersburg Players. Active in war work and mission nursing. Club: Nat. Arts. Author: Pine Needles (poems); A Ducal Skelton (novel); Dante (dramatic poem), 4th edit., 1921 (trans. into Italian, staged by Novelli and acted in Italy with music by Mascagni; said to have been the first Am. play prod. on Italian stage); Un Heros de la Vendee; The Great Consolidated; Our Family Motto; Raoul Coquelin (drama); one act plays At the Well; Kidnapped; Scrambled Eggs Overthere; On a Green Bench; Unsolved Problem; The Gods Pay a Visit; Mrs. Titcomb's Breach of Promise Case; By the King's Command. Also short stories, spl. articles, etc. Home: St Petersburg FL‡

ROSE, RAY CLARKE, author; b. Oxford, Chenango Co., N.Y., Mar. 21, 1870; s. William John and Mary Elizabeth (Clarke) R.; ed. pub. schs., Mich.; m. Marguerite Aline Bright, of Chicago,‡

ROSE, ROBERT HUGH, M.D., writer b. Carthage, Mo., Jan. 24, 1876; s. Reginald Heber and Doshea (Early) R.; prep. edn., high sch. and Carthage Collegiate Inst.; A.B., DePauw, 1898; M.D., Coll. Physicians and Surgeons (Columbia), 1902; m. Lesa LaBagh Sage, Sept. 11, 1918 (died June 6, 1938); 1 son, Robert Hugh. Practiced at New York City since 1904; instr. in gastro-enterology, Post-Grad. Med. Sch., 1914-24, Mem. Draft Bd. No. 145, World War. Fellow A.M.A.; mem. Am. Med. Editors' Assn., Med. Soc. State of N.Y., New York County Med. Soc., Greater N.Y. Med. Soc., Am. Stomatol. Assn. (treas. 1925), Soc. Med. Jurisprudence, Washington Heights Med. Soc. (ex-pres.), Authors Guild of America, Phi Kappa Psi; life mem. Midyork Club. Republican. Epsicopalian. Author: Eat Your Way to Health, 1915-24; How to Stay Young, 1933; also numerous articles on weight control, blood pressure, etc., in med. and popular mags. Home: 20 W. 83d St.

ROSE, S. BRANDT, physician, pathologist; b. London, Eng., June 22, 1901; s. A. and Y. (Brandt) Rose; M.D., McGill U., 1925, M.S., 1926; D.Sc., U. Pa., 1930; m. Florence DeBring, Oct. 9, 1937;children—John, Robert. Intern Univ. Hosp., Ann Arbor, Mich., 1926-27; asso. immunology U. Pa., 1930-32; prof. bacteriology and immunology Woman's Med. Coll. of Pa., Phila., 1929-36; dir. Coll. Hospital Laboratory, 1930-32; chief division of bacteriology Philadelphia General Hospital, 1936-48, chief div. med. microbiology, 1967-71; dir. lab. Chestnut Hill Hosp., 1948-66. Diplomate Am. Bd. Pathology in clinic pathology (trustee). Fellow Coll. Am. Pathologists; mem. A.M.A., Am. Soc. Clin. Pathologists, Soc. Am. Bacteriologists. Editorial bd. biol. abstracts Am. Jour. Clin. Pathology. Home: Cynwyd PA Died Aug. 25, 1971; buried West Laurel Hill Cemetery, Bala-Cynwyd PA

ROSECRANS, WILLIAM STARKE;, b. Los Angeles, Calif., Mar. 13, 1889; s. Carl Frederic and Lillian (McManman) R.; B.A., M.A., LL.D., Loyola U. (St. Vincent's Coll.), Los Angeles, Claremont College; married Elisabeth Helm, 1916. President W. S. Rosecrans, Inc., Rosecrans Farms; past chairman bd. Los Angeles Br. Fed. Res. Bank of San Francisco. Director Crocker-Citizens National Bank. Past president Am. Forestry Assn.; president Conservation Assn. of Southern Calif.; past president Los Angeles Chamber of Commerce; director Los Angeles County Farm Bur. (past v.p. Calif.); past v.p. C. of C. of U.S. Chairman of the bd. of fellows, Claremont Grad. Sch. and University Center; past chairman bd. regents, Loyola U. of Los Angeles; past chmn. Cal. Bd. of Forestry; pres. Southern Calif. Council for Inter-Am. Affairs; mem. adv. council U.S. Forest Service; mem. exec. com. Cal. Water Conf.; past member agrl. adv. council, U. Cal.; past mem. advisory com. U.S. Dept. Agriculture on Soil & Water Conservation. Formerly coordinator for Defense Contract Service and Priorities for Dist. of Southern Calif., and Ariz., Office of Prodn. Management; formerly chmn. study com. Conservation and Natural Resources, U.S. Commn. Intergovernmental Relations; formerly coordinator for victory gardens and home food prodn., Los Angeles County. Decorated Chevalier Confrerie des Chevaliers du Tastevin, Command de Grand Conseil de Bordeaux; awarded Bronze Plaque, Los Angeles C. of C.; Am. Forestry Assn. Bronze Plaque, 1952; Most Useful Citizen Service Watch, Los Angeles Realty Board, 1957; National Brotherhood award, National Conference of Christians and Jews, 1960. Member of the American Forestry Assn. (dir.), Ecol. Soc. Am., S.W. Mus.; A.A.A.S., Delta Phi Epsilon. Rotary. Clubs: California (Los Angeles); Bohemian (San Francisco); also member of Wine and Food Society of London (Los Angeles); Valley (Montecito); Los Angeles Men's Garden. Home: Los Angeles CA Died July 28, 1965; buried Calvary Cemetery, Los Angeles CA

ROSEN, CHARLES F., cons.; b. Cleve., Aug. 5, 1910; s. Moses and Mary (Woldman) R.; B.A., Ohio State U., 1932; M.A., 1933; m. Eleanor Steinberg, Nov. 23, 1939; children—Robert S., Donald B. Pres. Charles F. Rosen Co.; exec. v.p. W. B. Doner & Co., 1943-62, Revco, D.S., 1962-68. Clubs: Adcraft, Standard-City, Franklin Hills Country. Author: Use Your Own Couch, 1957. Home: Southfield MI Died Dec. 25, 1970; buried Beth-El Meml. Park.

ROSEN, JULIUS JACK, corp. exec.; b. Balt., Jan. 15, 1919; s. Abraham and Fannie (Ruben) R.; grad. Talmudical Acad., Balt.; student Balt. City Coll.; Md. Inst.; Johns Hopkins; m. Claire Aileen Bloom, May 27, 1952; children—Ede A., Amy S., Lisa B., Judy E. Co-founder, exec. v.p. Rosens Inc., mercantile bus., 1940-44, pres., 1944-49; co-founder, exec. v.p. Charles Antell Inc., toiletries and cosmetics, 1950-55, pres., 1955-59; co-founder, v.p., dir. Gulf Guarantee Land & Title Co. (Fla.), 1959-64; pres. Gulf Am. Corp., Balt., 1964-69, Rosen Investment Corp., Balt., 1959-69, Guild Life Ins. Co., 1965-69, Fenestra, Inc., 1967-69; dir. Modern Air Transp., 1966-69. Bd. dirs. Fannie Rosen Found., Balt. Symphony Soc., Boys Town of Jerusalem, Gulf Am. Found., Robert Linder Found.; chmn. bldg. com., bd. dirs. Talmudical Acad.; founder, mem. Harry Truman Peace Center; founder Garden of Patriots, Cape Coral, Fla., Gulf Am. Art Gallery, Miami, Fla.; chmn. nat. guardians Nat. Hebrew Day Schs. Served with AUS, 1941. Recipient Louis Brandeis award; Man of Year award Talmudical Acad.; Humanitarian award B'nai B'rith, also Kether Shem Tov award, 1969. Home: Baltimore MD Died Nov. 22, 1969; buried Baltimore MD

ROSEN, SAMUEL, motion picture theater exec.; b. N.Y.C., Oct. 23, 1898; s. Charles and Lillie (Diamondstone) R.; attended U. Pa.; m. Eleanor Fabian, June 15, 1926; children—Arthur M., Helen N. (Mrs. Jacob L. Yellin), Charles T., E. David. Vice chmn. Stanley Warner Corp., Stanley Warner Cinerama Corp.;

sec., treas. Fabian Theatres. Trustee Yeshiva U., Beth Israel Hosp.; a founder Albert Einstein Coll. Medicine, N.Y.C.; nat. vice chmn. founder Albert Einstein Coll. Medicine, N.Y.C.; nat. vice chmn. B'nai B'rith Found.; dir., asso. treas. Will Rogers Meml. Fund, Will Rogers Hosp. mem. exec. com. American-Jewish Com.; bd. dirs. N.Y. chpt. Nat. Assn. Visually Handicapped, Retina Found. Mem. Nat. Theatre Owners Am. (exec. com.). Jewish. Clubs: Inwood Country (L.I.); City Athletic, Harmonic (N.Y.C.). Home: New York City NY Died July, 1969.

ROSEN, VICTOR HUGO, psychoanalyst; b. N.Y.C., Nov. 21, 1911; s. Alexander and Mary (Schwartzman) R.; A.B., Columbia, 1932, M.D., 1936; m. Elizabeth Ruskay, June 7, 1936 (div. June 1965); children—Barbara (Mrs. Norton Garber), Winifred; m. 2d, Elise Snyder, Dec. 15, 1965. Intern pathology Mt. Sinai Hosp., N.Y.C., 1936-37; rotating intern Bklyn. Jewish Hosp., 1937-38; resident neurology Montifiore Hosp., N.Y.C., 1938-39; fellow psychiatry Johns Hopkins Hosp., 1939-41, N.Y. Psychoanalytic Inst. 1946-51, asst. attending psychiatrist, 1950-55; attending psychiatrist Bronx VA Hosp., 1948-52; med. dir. treatment center N.Y. Psychoanalytic Inst., 1955-62, mem. faculty, 1956-66; clin. prof. psychiatry Albert Einstein Coll. Medicine, Yeshiva U., 1967-73; attending psychiatrist Bronx Municipal Hosp., 1967-73; pvt. practice, N.Y.C., 1946-73. Served to maj. M.C., AUS, 1941-45; ETO. Fellow Am. Psychiat. Assn.; mem. Acad. Neurology, Am. Psychoanalytic Assn. (pres. elect 1964-65, pres. 1965-66, mem. editorial bd. jour. 1960-73), A.M.A., A.A.A.S. Editorial bd. Psychoanalysis and Contemporary Science, 1969-73. Contbr. articles to profl. jours. Home: Deep River CT Died Feb. 5, 1973.

ROSENBAUM, OTHO BANE, army officer; b. Marion, Va., Aug. 26, 1871; s. Thomas Marion and Nannie Victoria (Bane) R.; grad. U.S. Mil. Acad., 1894, Gen. Staff Sch., 1923, Army War Coll., 1924; hon. grad. Sch. of the Line, 1922; m. Katherine Marie Rawolle, Aug. 26, 1895 (now deceased); children—Frederick Buchanan, Elizabeth Carlotta (wife of Col. John Adams Ballard, U.S. Army), Otho Bane (dec.), William Lockridge (dec.). Commd. 2d lt. inf., U.S. Army, June 12, 1894; advanced through grades to brig. gen., Nov. 6, 1927; retired Aug. 31, 1935. Served in Cuban Campaign, Spanish-Am. War, Philippine Insurrection, World War. Given distinguished service citation for gallantry in action," at Santiago, Cuba, 1898. Lutheran. Clubs: Army and Navy, Army and Navy Country (Washington). Home: 2115 P St. N.W., Washington 7 DC Address: War Dept., Washington 25 DC‡

ROSENBAUM, SAMUEL RAWLINS, lawyer; b. Phila., Pa., Sept. 28, 1888; s. Morris and Hannah (Rottenburg) R.; B.A., Central High Sch., Phila., 1906; B.S., U. Pa., 1910, LL.B., 1913, LL.M., 1917; LL.D., Wesleyan U., 1962; Mus.D., Phila. Mus. Acad., 1967; student Inns of Ct., London, 1913-16; m. Rosamond May Rawlins, 1913 (dec. 1924); children—Jack Rawlins (dec.), Rosamond Margaret (Mrs. Rosamond Bernier), Hugh Samuel (dec.), Heather May (Mrs. Manuel de Jimenez); m. 2d, Edna Phillips, 1933; children—Joan Davies (Mrs. Mauricio Solaun), David Hugh. Admitted to Pa. bar, 1913, practiced in Phila., 1913-72. Vice pres. Albert M. Greenfield & Co., Bankers Securities Corp., 1926-43; pres. WFIL Broadcasting Co., 1932-43. Impartial trustee, Music Performance Trust Fund of Am. Phonograph Industry, 1949-69; chmn. Independent Radio Network Affiliates, 1937-40. Asst. city solicitor, 1920-24. Vice pres. Phila. Orch. Bd.; pres. Robin Hood Dell Concerts, 1938-41; trustee Phila. Coll. Art; chmn. Phila. Council for Performing Arts, 1964-65; mem. music adv. panel USIA, 1965-72; trustee Phila. Mus. Art, 1962, 66. Legislative draftsman Judge Adv. Gen., U.S. Army, 1917; spl. asst. U.S. atty. East Dist. Pa. 1918-19. Served to col. AUS, World War II; comdg. Officer Radio, Luxembourg. Decorated Legion of Merit (U.S.), Legion of Honor (France), also decorations from Luxembourg, Czechoslovakia, Italy, Poland, Belgium and China: recipient Am. Composers Alliane Laurel Leaf award, 1962; Nat. Assn. Composers and Conductors award, 1962; Distinguished Service award Wayne State U. Mem. Am., Pa., Phila., Phila., FCC bar assns., Order of Coif., Phi Beta Kappa, Sigma Delta Chi. Author: The English County Courts, 1916; Commercial Arbitration in England, 1916; The Rule-Making Authority in the English Supreme Court, 1917; Henry S. Drinker, a biographical memoir. Translator numerous works. Home: Philadelphia PA Died Nov. 9, 1972.

ROSENBERG, JAMES N., lawyer, painter; b. Allegheny City, Pa., 1874; A.B., Columbia, 1895. LL.B., 1898; D.H.C., University of Santo Domingo; D.H.L., Hebrew Union College; m. Bessie Herman, 1905; children—Dr. Elizabeth Zetzel, Mrs. Maxwell Geismar, Robert. Paintings in major museums. Hon. chmn. Am. Jewish Joint Distbn. Com., Dominican Republic Settlement Assn., Jewish Heritage Found.; hon. chmn. Nat. Art in Jewish Life, Am. Jewish Congress. Founder Pathways to Peace seminars State U. Coll., Plattsburgh, N.Y., 1965. Mem. Am., N.Y. State bar assns., Assn. Bar City of N.Y. (founder Hammarskjokl Forums 1962). Clubs: Nat. Arts, Lotos; Quaker Ridge Golf; Town Hall (Scarsdale). Jewish religion. Author: Corporate Reorganization and the Federal Courts, 1924; On the Steppes, 1927; Painter's Self-Portrait, 1958; 50 Lithographs, 1964; A Step Toward World Peace Through Law Which Precludes Resort to Force, 1965; Unfinished Business, 1967; others. Home: Scarsdale NY Died July 21, 1970.

ROSENBERG, SAMUEL, artist, educator; b. Phila., June 28, 1896; s. Solomon and Anna (Dickstein) R.; A.B., Carnegie Inst. Tech., 1926; m. Libbie Levin, Dec. 24, 1922; 1 son, Murray Z. Dir. art Irene Kaufmann Settlement, 1917-28, YM and YWHA, 1926-64, Pa. Coll. Women, 1937-44; prof. art Carnegie Inst. Tech., from 1926; works exhibited in insts. and mus. Chgo., Cin., Cleve., Detroit, Des Moines, Indpls., Kansas City, Milw., Mpls., St. Louis, Springfield, Syracuse, Toledo, Carnegie Internat., Herron Institute (Indianapolis), New York City, Philadelphia, San Francisco, Los Angeles, New Haven, Columbia, and others; represented Carnegie Inst., Ency. Brittanica, Butler Art Inst., Pa. State U., Pitts. Ct. House, Pitts. Bd. Edn., U. Pitts., Baltimore Mus., Westmoreland County (Pa.) Mus., and several others; one man shows from 1922, Carnegie Inst., 1922, 37, 56, 58, Greensburg, 1940 60, Bucknell U., 1948, 60, U. Tenn., 1948, Cleve., 1951, Indiana State Teachers College, 1955, Baltimore Museum of Art, 1959, Asso. Artists Pitts., Hewlett Gallery, 1965, and several others; exhibited Carnegie Paintings in the U.S., 1945, 47, 49; 16 exhbns. Pittsburgh Internat. (formerly Carnegie Internat.). Recipient awards Asso. Artists Pittsburgh, intermittently from 1917, Butler Art Inst., citation of achievement Hadassah, 1954; Merit award Alumni Assn. Carnegie Inst. Tech. (now Carnegie Mellon U.), 1961; Ryan award for meritorious teaching Carnegie Inst. Tech., 1963; Gov. Scranton award for achievement in fine arts, 1965; Myrtle award Pitts. chpt. Hadassah, 1965; artist of yr. City of Pittsburgh Arts and Crafts Center, 1950; artist of year, Junior C. of C., 1948. Member Pitts. Art Commn., Am. Assn. of Univ. Profs., Asso. Artists Pitts. (hon. life mem. 1965, honored 50-year exhibitor 1966), Marquis Biog. Library Soc. (adv.), Abstract Art of Pittsburgh, Phi Kappa Phi, Delta Phi Delta. Home: Pittsburgh PA Died July 23, 1972.

ROSENBERRY, LOIS CARTER KIMBALL MATHEWS (MRS. MARVIN BRISTOL ROSENBERRY), educator; b. Cresco, Ia., Jan. 30, 1873; d. Aaron and Emma Wilhelmina (Laird) Kimball; grad. State Normal Sch., Winona, Minn., 1890; A.B., Stanford, 1903, A.M., 1904; Ph.D., Radcliffe Coll., 1906; Litt.D., Lawrence Coll., Appleton, Wis., 1930; m. George Raynolds Mathews, June 9, 1897 (died Dec. 10, 1899); m. 2d, Marvin Bristol Rosenberry, June 24, 1918. Teacher pub. schs., 1890-97; instr. Vassar Coll., 1906-10; asso. prof. history, Wellesley Coll., 1910-11; dean of women, 1911-18, asso. prof. history, 1911-19, Univ. of Wis.; acting prin. Nat. Cathedral Sch. for Girls, Washington, D.C., 1928-29. Mem. Am. Assn. Univ. Women (pres. of its predecessor, Assn. Collegiate Alumnae, 1917-21), Madison Coll. Women's Club (pres. 1923-25), Delta Gamma, Phi Beta Kappa. Episcopalian. Author: Expansion of New England, 1909; The Dean of Women, 1915; (with Marion Talbot) History of the American Association of University Women, 1931. Contbr. Dictionary Am. Biography, Conn. Tercentenary Hist. Pamphlets. Home: 81 Cambridge Rd., Maple Madison WI‡

ROSENBLATT, SOL A(RIAH), lawyer; b. Omaha, Neb., Dec. 11, 1900; s. Morris M. and Mollie R.; A.B. cum laude, Harvard, 1922 (awarded Harvard scholarships and Coolidge medal), LL.B., 1924; married to Elizabeth Block, 1927 (divorced 1946); children—Robert Alan, Richard Lee; married second, Estrella Carroll Boissevain, August 19, 1946. Admitted to New York bar, 1925; gen. counsel Dem. Nat. Com., 1936-42; apptd. div. administrator under NRA, 1933; appointed national director of compliance and enforcement, NRA, 1934; apptd. impartial chmn. under collective agreements of Coat and Suit Industry, 1935-40, reapptd. 1947-54, 1954-68; mem. N.Y. State commn. Uniform State Laws, 1956-62; adv. bd. High Sch. Fashion Industries, N.Y. Apptd. capt. Specialist Res., U.S. Army, 1934, maj., 1940, on active duty, 1942-45, col., Air Corps. Charter mem. Air Force Association, Incorporated. Member of the American, New York State, N.Y. County bar assns., Assn. Bar City of N.Y., Delta Sigma Rho, Am. Legion. Club: Sands Point, L.I., N.Y. Home: New York City NY Died May 4, 1968.

ROSENBLUETH, ARTURO STEARNS, physiologist; b. Chihuahua, Mexico, Oct. 2, 1900; s. Julio G. and Maria (Stearns) R.; student Nat. Sch. Medicine, Mexico City, Mexico, 1918-21, Sch. Medizin, Berlin, Germany, 1923; M.D., Ecole de Medecine, Paris, France, 1924-27; m. Virginia Thompson, Sept. 5, 1931. Faculty, U. Mexico, 1928-30, prof., 1929-30; J.S. Guggenheim Found. fellow Harvard, 1930-32, fellow in physiology, 1932-33, asst. prof., 1934-44; head dept. physiology Nat. Inst. Cardiology, Mexico City, 1944-60; head dept. physiology, dir. Center for Research and Advanced Studies, Nat. Poly. Inst., Mexico City, 1960-70. Mem. El Colegio Nacional, Instituto Nacional de La Investigacion Cientifica. Author: (with W. B. Cannon) Autonomic Neuroeffector Systems, 1937, The Supersensitivity of Denervated Structures, A Law of Denervation, 1949; Transmission of Nerve Impulses at Neuroeffector Junctions and Peripheral Synapses, 1950; Mind and Brain, A Philosophy of Science, 1970; also numerous articles. Research on transmission nervous impulses in autonomic and synaptic junctions, physiology central nervous system and of heart. Home: Mexico City Mexico Died Sept. 20, 1970.

ROSENBLUM, FRANK, labor leader; b. N.Y.C., May 15, 1888; s. Louis and Ann (Karna) R.; ed. pub. schs.; m. Ida Beispil, Sept. 19, 1924; children—Beaty, Leigh, Howard. Leader in Hart Schaffner and Marx clothing strike, 1910; led revolt of insurgent workers at United Garment Workers' Conv., Nashville, Tenn., which led to formation of Amalgamated Clothing Workers of Am., 1914 (a founder), v.p., dir. Western orgn. dept., 1914-72; exec. v.p. A.C.W.A. (AFL-CIO), 1940-72, gen. sec.-treas., July 1946-72; mem. CIO Internat. Affairs Com., 1950-72. Dir. Amalgamated Trust & Savings Bank, Chgo., Amalgamated Bank of N.Y., Amalgamated Life Ins. Co., Inc.; chmn. bd. Amalgamated Ins. Co. Chgo. Trustee Amalgamated Ins. Fund Amalgamated Cotton Garment & Allied Industries Ins. Fund. Mem. Congress of Indsl. Orgns. Allied Industries Ins. Fund. Mem. Congress of Indsl. Orgns. (v.p. 1940-72), Bur. World Fedn. of Trade Unions (mem. exec. Chicago IL Died Feb. 9, 1973.

ROSENBLUM, HERMAN, shirt mfg. co. exec.; b. Springfield, Tenn., Dec. 28, 1887; s. Nathan and Fanny (Stern) R.; ed. pub. schs., Springfield; m. Erma Moses, Dec. 12, 1925; 1 son, James M. Sec.-treas. N. Rosenblum and Sons, womens wear mfrs., 1909-19; pres. Enro Shirt Co., Louisville. Mem. local council Boys Club; active Louisville Salvation Army. Club: Standard Country. Home: Louisville KY

ROSENBLUM, JACOB JOSEPH, lawyer; b. New York, N.Y., Nov. 15, 1897; s. Hyman and Mary (Levy) R.; graduate Townsend Harris Hall High School, 1915; B.S., College City of New York, 1919; J.D., New York Univ., 1923; m. Evelyn Harriet Levinsohn, Dec. 17, 1939; children—Michael Frank, Helen Jane. Admitted to New York bar, 1924; associated with George Z. Medalie, 1923-31; special deputy asst. atty. gen. N.Y. State in investigation and prosecution of election frauds, 1926-30, serving without compensation; asst. U.S. atty., Southern Dist. of N.Y., 1931-35; spl. asst. U.S. atty. for Nev., 1934; spl. asst. to atty. gen. of U.S. Dept. of Justice, Northern Dist. of N.Y., 1935, in prosecution of Arthur Flegenheimer, alias Dutch Schultz"; deputy asst. dist. atty. of New York County, as chief asst. to Thomas E. Dewey in racket and vice investigation, 1935-37; asst. dist. atty., New York County, chief Homicide Bureau, 1938-42; pvt. practice as sr. mem. firm Garey & Garey; ret., 1966. Vice pres. United Hebrew Immigrant Soc. Spl. counsel N.Y. State Joint Legislative Com. to investigate communism in children's camps. Hon. pres. East Bronx Y.M. and Y.W.H.A.; founder, pres. emeritus Civic Center Synagogue, N.Y.; mem. Honor Legion, and Detective Endowment Association, Police Department, City of New York; former hon. dep. police commr., fire commr., N.Y.C., Mem. N.Y.U. Law Sch. Alumni Assn. (dir. 1963-66), Am. Legion (past commander Post 1025). Republican. Home: New York City NY Died Jan. 23, 1971; buried Union Field Cemetery, Long Island NY

ROSENMAN, SAMUEL IRVING, lawyer; b. San Antonio, Feb. 13, 1896; s. Sol and Ethel (Paler) R.; A.B., Columbia, 1915, LL.B., 1919; m. Dorothy Reuben, Sept. 15, 1924; children—James Sol, Robert. Admitted to N.Y. bar, 1920; mem. N.Y. State Legislature, 1922-26, bill drafting commr. 1926-28; counsel to Gov. Franklin Delano Roosevelt, 1929-32; apptd. justice N.Y. Supreme Ct., 1932, re-apptd., 1933, later elected for 14-year term; resigned to become spl. counsel to Pres. Roosevelt, 1943; spl. counsel to Pres. Truman, 1945-46; mem. steel industry fact finding bd. 1949; chmn. ry. labor emergency bd., 1963. Recipient Pres.'s Medal for Merit; Legion of Honor. Mem. Am., N.Y. State Bar Assns., Assn. Bar City N.Y. (pres. 1964-66), Phi Beta Kappa, Delta Sigma Rho, Phi Epsilon Pi. Democrat. Jewish religion. Author: Working With Roosevelt, 1952. Editor: Public Papers and Addresses of Franklin D. Roosevelt, 1928-45. Home: New York City NY Died June 24, 1973.

ROSENSON, ALEXANDER MOSES, economist, govt. ofcl.; b. N.Y. City, June 4, 1900; s. Seidel and Yetta (Osmansky) R.; M.A., U. Cal., 1938; Ph.D., U. Chicago, 1953; married Miriam Shapiro, May 31, 1925; children—Vivian, Leon. Member of staff Brookings Inst., Washington, 1940; economist Dept. of State, 1942, chief Monetary Affairs Staff 1951; alternate U.S. exec. dir. Inter-Am. Devel. Bank, 1961-67, deputy administrative manager, 1967-69; mem. U.S. delegation Allied Reparations Commission, 1945, to Contracting Parties of General Agreement on Tariffs and Trade, 1953; mem. U.S. delegation to Econ. Commn. for Latin Am., 1955. Mem. Am. Econ. Assn., Phi Beta Kappa. Contbr. profl. jours. Home: Washington DC Died June 28, 1969.

ROSENSTOCK-HUESSY, EUGEN, educator; b. Berlin, Germany, July 5, 1888; s. Carl Theodor and Paula (Rosenstock) R.; ed. unvis. of Zurich, Berlin; J.D., Heidelberg U., 1909, Ph.D., 1923; D.D., Munster U., 1958; LL.D. (hon.), U. of Cal., 1967; m. Margrit Huessy 1915 (dec. 1959); 1 son, Johannes. Privatdozent der Rechte, law faculty, U. Leipzig, 1912-19; editor Daimler Werkzeitung, Stuttgart, 1919-20; 1st head Acad. Labor, Frankfurt- am-Main, 1921-22; head Inst. Psychology, Karlsruhe, Tech. Hochschule, 1922-23; prof. history of law, sociology U. Breslau, 1923-33, prof. emeritus, 1934; lectr., Oxford, Eng., 1927. Harvard 1933-36; prof. social philosophy Dartmouth Coll., Hanover, N.H., 1935-57, prof. emeritus, 1957; guest prof., Cologne U., 1961-62; vis. expert adult edn., Bavaria, 1952; vis. prof. theology (Fulbright), Munster U., 1957, 58; vis. prof. Am. history U. Cal. at Los Agneles, 1959; head of Amerika-Institut, U. Koln, 1961-62; Regents' prof. U. Cal. at Santa Barbara and Santa Cruz, 1965-66; vis. prof. U. of Cal. at Santa Cruz, 1966; U.S. del., internat. conf. The University Today, 1958. Initiated German Work Camps, 1925-33; vice chmn. World Assn. Adult Edn., London, 1929-33; co-founder Camp William James, 1940. Decorated Comdr. Great Cross, West Germany, 1960. Member Am. Goethe Soc. (hon.). Conglist. Author: Out of Revolution, Autobiography of Western Man, 1938; The Christian Future, 1946, rev. edit., 1966; The Multiformity of Man, 1949; Biblionomics, 1959; The Generations of the Faith; Die Sprache des Menschengeschlechts, 2 vols., 1963-65; Judaism Despite Christianity, 1968. Eugen Rosenstock-Huessy Soc. founded Bielefeld, Germany, 1963. Home: Norwich VT Died Feb. 24, 1973.

ROSENTHAL, DORIS, artist; b. Riverside, Calif.; d. Emil J. and Ann (Unruh) Rosenthal; student Columbia U., 1912-13; Art Students League, 1918-19, in Paris, Berlin, Munich, Rome, 1920-21; m. Jack Charash, Dec. 2, 1922. Exhibited in all important nat. and internat. shows since 1934; biennial exhbns. Midtown Galleries, N.Y. City, 1936, 37, 39, 41, 42, 43, one-man shows 1946, 52, 55; had one-man show Dayton (O.) Mus., 1943, Balt. Mus., Springfield (Mass.) Mus., Midtown galleries, 1957, 65. Represented in Metropolitan Mus., Museum of Modern Art (N.Y.), Toledo (O.), Rochester (N.Y.), San Diego (California), Colorado Springs (Colorado), Brooklyn and Cranbrook museums, Addison Gallery of American Art (Andover, Massachusetts), U. of Arizona, Okla. State U. Mus. Natural and Cultural History, and Ency. Britannica collections. Included in the Modern Museum Paris show of Century of Am. Art in U.S., 1938. One of 10 representative Am. artists with 5 pictures at Detroit Mus., Mar. 1943. Awarded Gugenheim fellowships for painting in Mexico, 1931-32, 1936-37; grant from Am. Acad. Arts and Letters, 1952; Thomas B. Clark award, 1952. Fellow International Institute Arts and Letters; mem. Audubon Artists (bd. dirs.). Articles and illustrations of her work appear in The New Yorker, Life, Art News, and other nat. mags. Home: Profirio Diaz, Oaxaca Mexico Died Nov. 1971.

ROSENTHAL, IDA, mfg. exec.; b. Minsk, Russia, Jan. 9, 1886; d. Abraham and Sarah (Shapiro) Cohen; student schs. in Poland; extension studies Columbia; m. William Rosenthal, June 10, 1906; 1 dau., Beatrice (wife of Dr. Joseph A. Coleman). Came to U.S., 1905, naturalized, 1912. Wholesale, retail dress bus. 1920; co-founder Maidenform, Inc. (formerly Maiden Form Brassiere Co., Inc.), N.Y.C., 1922, treas., 1922-73, pres., 1958-73, chmn. of bd., 1959-73, also trustee; dir. A. Cohen & Sons, Inc., jobbers, distbrs. Co-founder Camp Lewis, Boy Scouts Am.; co-founder Judaica and Hebraica Library, N.Y.U.; founder Albert Einstein Coll. Medicine; dir. Bronx Hosp., Bayonne Indsl. YMCA. Home: New York City NY Died Mar. 1973.

ROSENTHAL, JEAN, lighting and prodn. designer, theatre cons.; b. N.Y.C., Mar. 16, 1912; d. Dr. Morris and Dr. Pauline (Scharfmann) Rosenthal; student Friends Sem., 1926-28, Neighborhood Playhouse, 1928-30, Yale Drama Sch., 1931-34. Tech. dir. W.P.A. Fed. Theatre Productions, including Caesar, Shoemaker's Holiday, Native Son, Five Kings, 1937-39, for N.Y.C. Opera prodns., including Wozzeck, Bluebeard, Cenerentola, Falstaff, Hansel and Gretel, The Trial, 1945-51, for Ballet Soc., 1946-50, N.Y.C. Ballet, 1949-57, Martha Graham Prodns., 1938-69; prodn. and lighting Am. Shakespeare Festival Theatre, 1954-59, Dallas Civic Opera, 1957-69; lighting designer for Broadway prodns., including West Side Story, Jamaica, Dark at the Top of the Stairs, Becket, Taste of Honey, A Funny Thing Happened on the Way to the Forum, The Disenchanted, Redhead, Dear Liar, Hello Dolly, Fiddler on the Roof, Luv, Baker Street, Odd Couple, and others; cons., designer for numerous theatre bldgs., throughout U.S. Pres. Theatre Prodn. Service, 1937. Mem. United Scenic Artists, Actors Equity, Am. Ednl. Theatre Assn. Home: New York City NY Died May 1, 1969.

ROSENTHAL, SARAH G(ERTRUDE), lawyer, b. N.Y.C., d. Robert L. and Rose (Kossoff) Rosenthal; B.A., Barnard College; also LL.B., Yale; m. July 4, 1931 (div. June, 1939). Admitted to Ariz. bar, 1930; practice Phoenix, 1930-39; dir. Center Sch. Adult Edn., N.Y.C., 1941-42; wage and hour insp. Wages and Hour div. U.S. Dept. Labor, N.Y.C., 1943-44, field rep. Bur. Labor Statistics, N.Y.C., 1944; rulings and enforcement atty. War Labor Bd., N.Y.C., 1944-47; pres. Rose St. Devel. Corp., Branford, Conn., 1955-70; exec. sec. Branford Housing Authority 1950-70. Mem. Branford Bd. Finance 1956-66; member of the board of directors for the New Haven area Mental Council; corr. sec. Conn. Council Human Rights; chmn. Conn. Commn. Civil Rights, 1960—; mem. sec. Conn. adv. com. to U.S. Commn. Civil Rights; bd. dirs. Conn. Assn. Mental Health, New Haven Human Relations Council; adv. bd. Conn. Child Study and Treatment Home; bd. dirs., pres. New Haven Family Service; bd. dirs., South Central Conn. Regional Mental Health Plan Council, New Haven Fedn. Dem. Clubs, Branford Women's Dem. Club. Mem. Women's Aux. Brandeis U., League Women Voters, Ariz. Bar Assn., Municipal Finance Officers Assn., C. of C. Clubs: Federated Democratic Women's (dir.). Barnard College. Home: Branford CT Died June 2, 1970.

ROSLING, GEORGE, U.S. judge; b. N.Y.C., Dec. 22, 1900; A.B., Columbia, 1920; LL.B., St. Lawrence U., 1923; m. Sadie Spolan; children—Judith, Joan. Admitted to N.Y. bar, 1924, also Dist. Cts. Eastern and So. Dist. N.Y., 2d Circuit Ct. Appeals; justice City Ct., City N.Y., 1960-61; U.S. dist. judge Eastern Dist. N.Y., 1961-73. Chmn. Tchrs. Retirement Bd. City N.Y., 1955-59. Home: Brooklyn NY Died Apr. 16, 1973.

ROSS, ALFRED JOSEPH, investment banker; b. N.Y.C., Apr. 13, 1906; s. Andrew and Delia (Collopy) R.; student N.Y.U., 1923-29; m. Annette Collins, Sept. 7, 1935; children—Richard, Alfred, Peter, David, Mary Louise, Donald. Clk. N.Y. Stock Exchange, 1923-29; trader Roosevelt & Son, 1930-34; joined Dick & Merle-Smith, N.Y.C., 1934, became partner, 1938, name changed to Roosevelt & Son, 1971, chmn. bd., 1971. Club: Nassau Country. Home: Manhasset NY Died Dec. 30, 1971; buried Holy Rood Cemetery, Westbury LI NY

ROSS, ALLAN CHARLES, editor; b. Auburn, N.Y., Apr. 8, 1870; s. Charles Humphrey and Louise (Stoutenburgh) R.; ed. pub. schs.; m. Mabel Smith Putnam, Nov. 14, 1895; children—Allan Kendrick, Mabel Ross Southgate. With Democrat and Chronicle, Rochester, N.Y., since 1903, editor 1925-36, retired with title editor emeritus, Apr. 1, 1936. Mem. Rochester Chamber Commerce. Republican. Presbyterian. Club: Rochester Automobile. Home: 133 Castlebar Rd., Rochester NY‡

ROSS, ARTHUR M(AX), univ. ofcl.; b. Rochester N.Y., May 1, 1916; s. S. H. and Arline (Myers) R.; A.B., Harvard, 1937; Ph.D., U. Cal. at Berkeley, 1941; m. Jane D. Noble, Sept. 11, 1942; children—Audrey, Marilyn, Richard, Leslie. Lectr. econs. Mich. State Coll., 1946; with U. Cal. at Berkeley, 1946-66, lectr. and research asso. Inst. Indsl. Relations, 1946-48, asso. prof. indsl. relations, 1948-53, prof., 1953-66, dir. Inst. Indsl. Relations, 1954-63; commr. labor statistics. U.S. Dept. Labor, 1965-68; v.p. state relations and planning U. Mich., 1968-70; asso. umpire Gen. Motors Corp. and UAW-CIO, 1949-50; permanent arbitrator Convair and Internat. Assn. Machinists, 1955-60; impartial umpire North Am. Aviation and United Auto Workers, 1960-65; arbitrator for East Bay Drayage Industry, 1959-65. Assistant program Dir. of the War Manpower Commn., 1942-44; hearing officer and arbitrator War Labor Bd., Detroit, 1944, vice chmn. war shipping panel, Washington, 1944-45; regional chmn. WBS, San Francisco, 1951-52, nat. pub. mem., 1952; chmn. Minimum Wage Board, State of California; mem. President's Atomic Energy Labor-Mgmt. Panel, 1953-58; mem. fed. fact finding bds. on atomic energy, 1952, on nonferrous metals industry, 1954; cons. Cal. Dept. Employment, Inst. Internat. Edn., President's Commn. Migratory Labor, WSB; served various Presdl. emergency bds., 1961-64; mem. Nat. Manpower Task Force, 1964-70; chmn. conf. indsl. relations and economic devel. I.L.O., 1964. Chmn. central adjustment bd. No. Cal. Cannery Industry. Guggenheim fellow, 1960. Mem. Nat. Acad. Arbitrators (past gov. v.p., 1957-59); Indsl. Relations Research Assn. (mem. exec. bd. 1953-56, pres. 1965-66), Phi Beta Kappa. Club: Harvard (San Francisco, California). Author: Trade Union Wage Policy, 1948; (with Arthur Kornhauser and Robert Dubin) Industrial Conflict, 1954; New Concepts in Wage Determination (with George W. Taylor), 1957; (with Paul Hartman) Changing Patterns of Industrial Conflict, 1960, (with others) Unemployment and the American Economy, 1964; (with others) Unemployment and Labor Market Policy, 1964, Industrial Relations and Economic Development, 1966; Employment, Race and Poverty, 1966. Contbr. articles profl. jours. Home: Ann Arbor MI Died June 5, 1970; buried Lake George, High Sierras CA

ROSS, EARLE D(UDLEY), coll. prof.; b. Ross Hill, N.Y., Dec. 20, 1885; s. John Warren and Fanny Jane (Coleman) R.; Ph.B., Syracuse U., 1909, Ph.M., 1910; A.M., Cornell, 1912, Ph.D., 1915; student University of Wisconsin, 1913-14; married Ethel Eileen Newbecker, June 27, 1917; children—Ronald Dudley, Bruce Mitchell, Betsy Georgene (Mrs. Jack E. Bayha). Instructor history, Missouri Wesleyan College, 1915-17, Simpson Coll., 1917-18, Ill. Wesleyan U., 1918-19; prof. and head history dept., N.D. Agrl. Coll., 1919-23; asso. prof. history, Ia. State Coll., 1923-43, prof. econ. history and coll. historian, 1943-73; research asso., Ia. State Hist. Soc., 1941-42. Mem. Am. Hist. Assn., Miss. Valley Hist. Assn., Agr. Hist. Soc. (pres. 1947), Econ. Hist. Assn., Ia. State Hist. Soc., S.A.R., Phi Beta Kappa, Phi Kappa Phi, Pi Gamma Mu. Democrat. Methodist. Author books relating to field; latest publ.; Iowa Agriculture: An Historical Survey, 1951. Editor: A Century of Farming in Iowa, 1946. Asso. editor Social Science Mag., 1925-73. Home: Ames IA Died Mar. 22, 1973.

ROSS, EDWARD ALSWORTH, sociologist; b. Virden, Ill., Dec. 12, 1866; s. William Carpenter and Rachel (Alsworth) R.; A.B., Coe Coll., Ia., 1886; U. of Berlin, 1888-89; Ph.D., Johns Hopkins, 1891; LL.D., Coe, 1911; m. Rosamond C. Simons, June 16, 1892; children—Frank Alsworth, Gilbert, Lester Ward; m. 2d, Helen Forbes, Sept. 29, 1940. Prof. economics, Ind. U., 1891-92; asso. prof. polit. economy and finance, Cornell, 1892-93; prof. sociology. Stanford, 1893-1900, U. of Neb., 1901-06, U. of Wis., 1906-37. Lecturer on sociology Harvard, 1902, U. of Chicago, 1896, 1905; dir. of edn., The Floating University," 1928-29, Northwestern U., 1939. Pres. Am. Sociol. Soc., 1914 and 1915; sec. Am. Econ. Assn., 1892-93; advisory editor Am. Journal of Sociology, since 1895; mem. Institut International de Sociologie, Phi Beta Kappa. Author: Honest Dollars, 1896; Social Control, 1901; The Foundations of Sociology, 1905; Sin and Society, 1907; Social Psychology, 1908; Latter Day Sinners and Saints, 1910; The Changing Chinese, 1911; Changing America, 1912; The Old World in the New, 1914; South of Panama, 1915; Russia in Upheaval, 1918; What is America?, 1919, The Principles of Sociology, 1920, 30, 38; The Russian Bolshevik Revolution, 1921; The Social Trend, 1922; The Social Revolution in Mexico, 1923; The Outlines of Sociology, 1923; The Russian Soviet Republic, 1923; Roads to Social Peace, 1924, Reports on the Employment of Native Labor in Portuguese Africa, 1925; Civic Sociology, 1925, 33. Standing Room Only?, 1927; World Drift, 1928; Seventy Years of It, 1936; New Age Sociology, 1940. Part author: Changes in the Size of American Families in One Generation, 1924; Readings in Civic Sociology, 1926. Contbr. of numerous articles to econ. and sociol. jours. and lit. periodicals. Home: 3545 Topping Rd., Shorewood, Madison WI‡

ROSS, EMORY, ret. missionary; b. Kendallville, Ind., July 28, 1887; s. Allison Troy and Elizabeth (Williams) R.; A.B., Eureka Coll., 1908, D.D., 1939; L.H.D., Tougaloo So. Christian Coll., 1961; postgrad. U. Chgo., U. Wis., Coll. Missions, Indpls.; m. Myrta M. Pearson, June 15, 1917; children—Frances Elizabeth (Mrs. E. Cummings), Roger Pearson, Rachel Ann (Mrs. William K. Parmenter). Sec.-treas., So. Christian Inst., Edwards, Miss., 1908-10; tchr. Eureka Coll., 1910-12; ordained to ministry Disciples of Christ Ch., 1912; missionary Disciples of Christ Ch., Republic of Liberia, 1912-16; missionary Belgian Congo, gen. sec. Congo Protestant Council, 1917-33; mem. Belgian Royal Commn. for Protection of Natives, 1928-33; bd. dirs. Am. Leprosy Missions, Inc., N.Y.C., 1936—, gen. sec., 1937-40, v.p., 1940-48, chmn., 1948-59; sec. Am. Com. Ethiopian Crisis, 1935; exec. sec. African com. Nat. Council Chs., N.Y.C., 1935-53; v.p. Am. Aid for Ethiopia, Inc., 1936-37; acting asso. sec. M.E. Bd. Fgn. Missions, 1936-37; gen. sec. Fgn. Missions Conf. N.Am., 1940-45. Bd. dirs. Albert Schweitzer Fellowship, Inc., N.Y.C., 1945-73, treas., 1945-62, pres. 1962-65, hon. pres., 1965-73; chmn. Com. for African Students in N.Am., 1947-52; v.p. Internat. Inst. Differing Civilizations, Brussels, 1949-73, exec. com., 1958-60; cons. Bd. for Fundamental Edn., 1952-61; counsellor Cancer Internat. Research Co-op., 1962-67; adv. com. U.S.-S. African, Leader Exchange Program, 1957-67; adv. com. Operation Crossroads Africa, N.Y.C., 1961-64. Trustee Phelps Stokes Fund, 1941-69, chmn., 1950-61, now chmn. emeritus; trustee Booker Washington Agr. and Indsl. Inst. Liberia, 1939-50, Liberian Found., N.Y.C., 1948-57, N.Y. State Colonization Soc., 1950-68, Internat. Devel. Services, Inc., N.Y.C. 1956-64, Mills Coll. Edn., N.Y.C., 1958-60, Tougaloo So. Christian Coll., 1958-68, African-Am. Inst., Inc., Washington, N.Y.C., 1955-67 (pres. 1957-61), Am. Health Edn. for African Devel., 1962-73; bd. dirs. Grant Found., Inc., Pitts., 1953-73, African Med. and Research Found., Inc., N.Y.C., 1959-73, Binder Schweitzer Amazonian Hosp. Found., Inc., N.Y.C., 1960-65, Agrl. Tech. Assistance, Los Angeles, 1961-65. Decorated chevalier del'Ordre Royal du Lion (Belgium). Fellow Royal Geog. Soc. London (life), Am. Geog. Soc.; mem. Royal African Soc. London (life), South African Inst. Race Relations of Johannesburg (council 1954-69), Council Fgn. Relations, Tau Kappa Epsilon. Mem. Christian Ch. Author: Out of Africa 1936; African Heritage, 1952; (with Gene Phillips) New Hearts—New Faces 1954; (with Myrta P. Ross) Africa Disturbed, 1959. Co-author: World Faith in Action, 1951. Home: New York City NY Died Mar. 1973.

ROSS, FRANK ALEXANDER, educator, statistician; b. N.Y. City, Jan. 23, 1888; s. James Alexander and

Elizabeth Wordin (Naramore) R.; Ph.B., Yale, 1908, grad. study, 1909-11; M.A., Columbia, 1913, Ph.D., 1924; m. Dorothy Gere Reddy, Nov. 24, 1926; 1 dau., Elizabeth Gere. Civil engr. in Calif., 1908-09; teacher sociology and statistics, Columbia, 1914-17, 1919-26; asst. prof. sociology, 1926-37; prof. sociology and chmn. dept. Syracuse Univ., 1937-41; dir. survey of Near East for Near East Relief and other philanthropies, 1926; dir. research and surveys on Negro since 1926; various connections with Federal Govt. since 1917, Federal Emergency Relief Administrn., 1934-35. Editor Jour. Am. Statis. Assn., 1925-34 and 1941-45 (originator Procs. same 1928); sec.-treas. Social Science Abstracts, 1928-34; editor of History, Economics and Public Law (Columbia), 1934-37. Mem. bd. of trustees and treas. Thetford Acad., 1942-48. Served as 1st lt., capt., maj. San. Corps, U.S. Army, chief surgeon's office, A.E.F., 1917-19; maj. San. R.C., 1919-33. Fellow Am. Statis. Asso.; mem. Inst. of Mathematical Statistics, Sociol. Research Assn., A.A.A.S., Sigma Xi, Alpha Kappa Delta. Republican. Mason. Author: School Attendance in the U.S., 1920 (census monograph), 1924; Near East and American Philanthropy (with C. L. Fry and E. Sibley), 1927; Bibliography of Negro Migration (with L. V. Kennedy), 1934. Contbr. to sociol. publs. Home: Thetford VT Died Jan. 30, 1968; buried North Thetford (Vt.) Cemetery.

ROSS, FRANK MACKENZIE, cement co. exec.; b. Galsgow, Scotland, Apr. 14, 1891; s. David and Grace (Archibald) R.; ed. Royal Acad., Tain, Scotland; hon. degrees U. N.B., 1956, U. B.C., 1958, St. Francis Xavier U. N.S., 1961, U. Abereden (Scotland), 1961; m. Phyllis Gregory Turner, 1946. Hon. co-chmn., hon. dir. Canadian Cement Lafarge Ltd.; chmn. Internat. Paints (Can.) Ltd., Grosvenor-Laing (B.C.) Ltd., Grosvenor-Laing (Langley Park) Ltd., Grosvenor-Internat. Ltd. (all Vancouver), pres., dir. West Coast Shipbuilders Ltd., Vancouver; dir. Can. Wire & Cable Co., Ltd., De Laval Turbine Co. Ltd. (both Toronto), RCA Victor Ltd. (Montreal), McCord St. Sites Ltd., Redhill Investment Corp. Ltd., Westcoast Transmission Co. Ltd., McDonald Buchanan Properties Ltd. (all Vancouver), Langley Greenhouses Ltd. (B.C.), Grosvenor Estates Adv. Bd., London, Eng. Lt. gov. B.C., 1955-60. Served with Canadian Army, World War I. Decorated Mil. Cross; created companion on St. Michael and St. George; knight St. John Jerusalem. Clubs: St. James's (Montreal) Vancouver, B.C. Turf and Country Ltd. (dir.), University, Faculty Terminal City (Vancouver). Home: British Columbia Canada Died Dec. 11, 1971.

ROSS, JULIAN LENHART, educator; b. Meadville, Pa., Feb. 11, 1903; s. Clarence Frisbee and Etta (Lenhart) Ross; A.B., Allegheny Coll., 1923, Litt.D., 1964; A.M., Harvard, 1924, Ph.D., 1927; m. Carol E. Moodey, July 16, 1929; children—Peter M., Stephen M. Instr. English Allegheny Coll., Meadville, 1927-28, asst. prof., 1928-36, asso. prof., 1936-44, prof., 1944-70, dean instrn., 1949-66. Mem. Nat. Council Tchrs. English, Am. Assn. U. Profs., Phi Beta Kappa, Phi Delta Theta, Delta Sigma Rho. Author: Philosophy in Literature, 1949. Home: Meadville PA Died Jan. 25, 1972.

ROSS, OGDEN, army officer; b. Troy, N.Y., Apr. 6, 1893; s. E. Ogden and Jean (Neely) R.; LL.B., Albany Law Sch., Union Univ., 1915; m. Elizabeth W. Cheney, Feb. 17, 1920; children—Ogden Cheney, Cynthia. Enlisted, 105th Inf., N.Y. Nat. Guard, 1910, and advanced through the grades to brig. gen., 1940; served on Mexican Border, 1916; with 27th Div., A.E.F., France and Belgium, World War I; asst. div. comdr. 27th Div., Pacific Area, 1940-44, comdr. Marshall-Gilbert Islands, 1944-45, World War II. City Treasurer, Troy, 1920-25; assistant to v.p. and gen. mgr., D.&H. R.R., 1924-38; N.Y. State senator, 1933-37; mem. N.Y. Constitutional Conv., 1938; N.Y. State tax commr., 1939-45; called into active service, Oct. 1940, on duty in the Pacific Area for four years. Pub. relations dir. Troy (N.Y.) Savings Bank. Awarded Legion of Merit, Silver Star, Purple Troy NY Died Oct. 27, 1968; buried Oakwood Cemetery, Troy NY

ROSS, SAMUEL LOUIS, investment co. exec.; b. Waterbury, Conn., Aug. 14, 1892; s. David Bernard and Victoria (Pelkus) R.; A.B., Cornell U., 1915; m. Helen Brandt, Oct. 18, 1925; children—Anne R. Sheppard, David Brandt. With D. B. Ross Shoe Mfg. Co., Bklyn., 1915-22; dir. radio program dept. Am. Tel. & Tel. Co., 1922-26; mgr. artists bur. NBC, 1926-45; with Renyx Field & Co., mutual funds, N.Y.C., from 1945, pres., 1958-59, chmn. bd., from 1960; v.p., dir. Corp. Leaders of Am., Inc., from 1958, Lexington Fund, Inc., N.Y.C., from 1958; trustee Lexington Income Trust. Mem. Radio and Television Execs. Soc., Radio Pioneers, Phi Beta Kappa, Beta Sigma Rho. Club: Cornell (N.Y.C.). Home: Hartsdale NY Died Feb. 23, 1970.

ROSSELLE, WILLIAM QUAY, clergyman; b. Dawson, Pa., Oct. 12, 1869; s. John Van Meter and Sarah Belle (Snyder) R.; ed. Teachers' Training Sch., Normalville, Pa.; Ohio Normal U., Ada, O.; Ph.D., Waynesburg (Pa.) Coll., 1897, D.D., 1911; m. Gail Scott, of Waynesburg, July 15, 1895; 1 dau., Mary. Ordained Bapt. ministry, 1895; pastor First Ch., Homestead, Pa., 1895-1903, First Ch., Williamsport, 1903-08, 5th Ch., Phila., 1908-19; became pastor First Ch., Malden, Mass., 1919, now retired. Now lecturing at large. Member board American Bapt. Publication Soc., Missionary Corpn. of Northern Bapt. Conv.; mem. bd. dirs. Mass. Bapt. State Conv. Mem. Am. Forestry Assn., Am. Geog. Soc. Republican. Clubs: Boston City, University. Mason (K.T.). Lecturer. Home: Malden MA‡

ROSSETER, JOHN HENRY, merchant; b. N.Y. City, Aug. 6, 1869; s. John H. and Winifred (Commin) R.; ed. St. Ignatius Coll., San Francisco, Calif.; m. Jane Gilchrist, of Berkeley, Calif., June 6, 1906 (died Aug. 29, 1913); m. 2d, Alice Gertrude May, of San Francisco, Sept. 7, 1916. Sec.-mgr. Pacific Coastwise Conf., Pacific Coastwise Lumber Conf. Dir. of operations U.S. Shipping Board, 1918-19. Clubs: Pacific Union (San Francisco); India House (New York); Chevy Chase (Washington). Home: 945 Green St., San Francisco; (country) Rancho Wikiup, nr. Santa Rosa, Calif. Office: 311 California St., San Francisco CA‡

ROSSI, LUIS BANCHERO, Peruvian business exec.; b. 1930; Degree in Chem. Engring., La. Libertad U., 1951. Owner an import agy., 1951-55, bonita cannery, 1955-58; in fish meal prodn. bus., Chimbote, Peru, 1958; pres. Consorcio Pesquero del Peru, a joint marketing agy., 1961-72, also owner newspaper chain. Address: Lima Peru Died 1972.

ROSSITER, CLINTON, educator; b. Phila., Sept. 18, 1917; s. Winton Goodrich and Dorothy (Shaw) R.; A.B., Cornell U., 1939; A.M. Princeton, 1941, Ph.D., 1942; LL.D., Kenyon Coll., 1956; M.A., Cambridge U., 1960, Litt.D., 1965; Litt.D., Franklin and Marshall, 1961; L.H.D., Alfred U., 1961; m. Mary Crane, Sept. 5, 1947;children—David, Caleb, Winton. Instr. polit. sci. U. Mich., 1946; instr. govt. Cornell U., 1946-47, asst. prof., 1947-49, asso. prof., 1949-54, prof. govt., chmn. dept., 1956-59, Senior Univ. prof. of Am. instns., 1959—; Pitt professor American history and fellow Selwyn College, Cambridge University (England), 1960-61; visiting professor of politics Princeton, 1958; faculty Claremont (California) Summer Sch., 1950, Salzburg (Austria) seminar in Am. studies, 1953; Johnson lectr. Pomona Coll., 1955; Walgreen lectr. U. Chgo., 1956; Bacon lecturer Boston University, 1962; Fitzpatrick lectr. Canisius College, 1963; others. Chmn. council Inst. Early Am. History and Culture. Cons. Fund for Republic, Rockefeller Found., Ford Found.; mem. bd. dirs. Woodrow Wilson Found., 1959-63. Served as lt. USNR, 1942-46, Guggenheim fellow, 1953-54; Fulbright scholar U. London, 1968; Fulbright lectr. Hebrew U. and U. of Tel Aviv, 1968; recipient Bancroft, Woodrow Wilson Found., Inst. Early Am. History prizes, 1953. Fellow American Academy Arts and Sciences, American Society of Historians; member of the American, N.Y. (pres. 1951-53) polit. sci. assns., Am. Studies Assn. (pres. N.Y. chpt. 1955-56), Am. Hist. Assn., Am. Antiquarian Soc. (hon. life), Phi Beta Kappa, Sigma Phi. Club: Century Assn. (N.Y.C.). Author: Constitutional Dictatorship, 1948; The Supreme Court and the Commander in Chief, 1951; Seedtime of the Republic published, 1953; Conservatism in America, 1955, revised edition published, 1962; The First American Revolution, 1956; The American Presidency, 1956, rev. edit. 1960; Parties and Politics in America, 1960; Marxism: The View from America, 1960; The Political Thought of the American Revolution, 1963; Six Characters in Search of a Republic, 1964, Alexander Hamilton and the Constitution, 1964. 1787: The Grand Convention, 1966; The American Quest, 1971. Editor: Aspects of Liberty, 1958; The Federalist, 1961; The Essential Lippman, 1963. Writer, Pres.'s Commn. on Nat. Goals, 1960. Home: Ithaca NY Died July 10, 1970.

ROSSITER, FREDERICK MCGEE, author; b. Elmore, O., Mar. 12, 1870; s. Samuel G. and Jennie (McGee) R.; B.S., Battle Creek (Mich.) Coll., 1893; M.D., Rush Med. Coll., 1896, U. of Pa., 1897; L.R.C.P. and M.R.C.S., London U., 1920; m. Mary Henry, Dec. 29, 1897 (now dec.); children—Henry, Margaret (Mrs. J. H. White). Mem. staff Battle Creek Sanitarium, 1897-1902; gen. practice, 1902-28; prof. medicine, Coll. of Med. Evangelists, Los Angeles, Calif., 1922-26. Author: Practical Guide to Health, 1909; The Romance of a Living Temple, 1924; The Torch of Life or Key to Sex Harmony, 1932; The Doctor Goes to See; Health for Today. Contbr. to mags. Home: 956 Muirfield Rd., Los Angeles CA‡

ROSSITER, PERCEVAL SHERER, surgeon general U.S. Navy; b. Shepherdstown, W.Va., Nov. 30, 1874; s. Joel Tomkins and Benetta (Sherer) R.; student U. of Md.; m. Isabel P. Jacobi, July 25, 1898; 1 dau., Ernestine Sherer. Capt. asst. surgeon, U.S.V., Spanish-Am. War, 1898; entered Med. Corps of the Navy, 1903; mem. U.S. Naval Mission to Brazil, 1922-26; comdg. officer Brooklyn (N.Y.) Naval Hosp., 1929-32, Washington (D.C.) Naval Hosp., 1932-33; became surgeon gen. U.S. Navy, 1933; retired Dec. 1, 1938; chief of staff Gallinger Municipal Hosp., Washington, D.C. Fellow Am. Coll. Surgeons, Am. Coll. Physicians, A.M.A.; mem. Assn. Mil. Surgeons (pres. 1936-37). Home: 111 N. Alfred St., Alexandria, Va. Office: Gallinger Hospital, Washington DC‡

ROSSMAN, JOSEPH, patent atty., author; b. Philadelphia, Pa. Oct. 5, 1899; s. Louis and Rebecca (Freeman) R.; B.S. in Chem. Engring., U. of Pa., 1922; A.M., George Washington U., 1927, LL.B., 1927; M.P.L., Washington Coll. of Law, 1927; Ph.D., American U., 1930; m. Mildred Katzmann, July 1, 1927; 1 son, Ronald Eugene. Patent examiner U.S. Patent Office, 1923-35; patent counsel Marathon div., Am. Can. Co., from 1935; research staff of Patent Foundation, George Washington University, from 1954; admitted to D.C. bar, 1927, Pennsylvania bar, 1948, bar U.S. Ct. Customs and Patents Appeals, 1930, U.S. Supreme Ct., 1930; lecturer Patent Law Grad. Sch., U.S. Dept. Agr., 1934-35; mem. Nat. Inventors Council, U.S. Dept. Commerce. Fellow American Inst. of Chemists, Franklin Institute, A.A.A.S. (chmn. com. patents, trademarks, etc.); mem. Am. Chem. Soc., Tech. Assn. of Pulp and Paper Industry, Am. and Phila. patent law assns., American, Phila. bar assns., Patent Office Soc., Sigma Xi. Mason. Author: The Psychology of the Inventor, 1931, 2d edit., 1932, Swedish translation, 1935; The Law of Patents for Chemists, 1932, 2d edit., 1935; The Protection by Patents of Scientific Discoveries, 1934; Industrial Creativity, 1964. Editor of the Journal of Patent Office Society, 1931-35. Co-editor: Patents, Research and Management, 1961; The Law of Chemical, Metallurgical and Pharmaceutical Patents, 1967. Contbr. numerous articles on legal and tech. subjects to mags. and jours. Home: Philadelphia PA Died Jan. 29, 1972.

ROSSMAN, SAMUEL S., pub. accountant; b. Atwood, Colo., Nov. 5, 1896; s. Harris and Rose (Heller) R.; grad. Park's Bus. Coll., Denver, 1911; grad. in higher accountancy, LaSalle Extension U., 1922; graduate personal investment Dun & Bradstreet, Chgo., 1961; m. Pauline May Miller, Oct. 23, 1918 (dec.); children—Dorothy (Mrs. F. Pomerleau), Ruth (Mrs. David Ansuriza), Helen (Mrs. Leon Bonfadini); m. 2d, Ethel Richards Godsell, Apr. 5, 1954 (dec. June 1956); m. 3d Clare Kathleen Kelly, July 12, 1958. Travelling auditor Utah Oil Refining Co., 1920-24; pvt. accountant to D. C. Jackling, San Francisco, 1928-42; supr. Wayne Mayhew & Co., C.P.A.'s, San Francisco, 1942-43; comptroller Rudiger, Lang Co., Berkeley, 1943-45, Neon Maintenance Co., San Francisco, 1946-49; self-employed, San Francisco and Grass Valley, Cal., 1949-55; accountant for estates of Daniel C. and Virginia Jackling, San Francisco, 1956-65, tchr. higher accounting and math., McGill, Nev., 1926-28. Recipient Army and Navy E" award, 1945. Mem. Nat. Soc. Pub. Accountants, Am. Accounting Assn., Nat. Soc. Tax Cons., Transp. Club San Francisco. Elk. Home: Napa CA Died July 2, 1971.

ROTCHFORD, HUGH BABB, lawyer; b. Keokuk, Ia., Apr. 5, 1905; s. Michael Hugh and Ann Catherine (Babb) R.; A.B., Loyola U., Los Angeles, 1925, also LL.B.; m. Caroline L. Morris, June 14, 1913. Admitted to Cal. bar, 1926, since practiced in Los Angeles; sr. partner Chase, Rotchford, Downen & Drukker; lectr. law U. So. Cal., 1952-54; spl. asst. U.S. atty. gen., 1954-55; spl. hearing officer Dept. Justice, 1956-59. Lectr. state bar program for continuing edn., Cal., 1949-50; mem. Cal. Medical-Legal Com., Med. Malpractice Def. Lawyers Group. Mem. Am. Fed., Los Angeles bar assns., State Bar Cal., Town Hall Am. Judicature Soc., Internat. Assn. Ins. Counsel, Casualty Ins. Adjusters Assn., Delta Sigma Phi. Home: Los Angeles CA Died 1969.

ROTH, FERI, violinist; b. Zolyom, Hungary, July 18, 1899; s. Martin and Carolina (Jakobovits) R.; diploma Budapest Royal Acad. Music, 1917; Mus.D., 1949; m. Elisabeth Acht-Aknai, Jan. 4, 1931. Debut as child in Budapest; 1st violinist Budapest Opera, 1919-20; concertmaster Berlin Volksoper, 1922-25; established Roth Quartet, 1926; quartet made U.S. debut, 1928; numerous recordings; prof. U. Cal. at Los Angeles. Author: How Many Are in Your Quartet (memoirs).

ROTHBERG, SIDNEY, pharmacologist; b. Bklyn., Apr. 17, 1914; s. Harry and Sarah (Horowitz) R.; B.S., Bklyn. Coll., 1939; postgrad N.Y.U., 1947-48, U. Md., 1956-60; m. Dorothy Schaffel, Oct. 15, 1939 (dec. Apr. 1959); children—David Michael, Frances B., Eric Joseph, Cathy Ann. Research asso. Jewish Hosp., Bklyn., 1930-33; biochemist Cumberland Hosp., Bklyn., 1933-43; research pharmacologist, directorate med. research Med. Research Lab., Edgewood Arsenal, Md., 1954-70. Served with AUS, 1943-54, now lt. col. Res. Mem. Armed Forces Chem. Assn., Soc. Exptl. Biology and Medicine, Soc. Am. Microbiologists, Sci. Research Soc. Am., A.A.A.S. Contbr. articles in field to sci. jours. Patentee in field. Home: Edgewood MD Died July 26, 1970.

ROTHENBERG, MILTON, tobacco co. exec.; b. Chgo., Dec. 23, 1916; s. Samuel and Grace (Saltzman) R.; student Northwestern U., 1937-38; diploma Harvard Grad. Sch. Bus. Adminstrn., 1965; m. Gertrude Cohen, Feb. 21, 1942; children—Debra Lyn, Robert David, Arden Joy. With U.S. Tobacco Co., 1942-72, v.p., 1965-72, also dir.; dir., product mgr. Tuchersharpe Pen Co., Inc., 1962-68, nat. sales mgr., 1968-72. Mem. Assn. Help Retarded Children. Named Favorite Exec., Ill. Assn. Tobacco Distbrs., 1964. Mem. Nat. Assn. Tobacco Distbrs., Am. Mgmt. Assn. Mem. B'nai B'rith. Home: Stamford CT Died Mar. 4, 1973.

ROTHENBURGER, WILLIAM FREDERIC, clergyman; b. Holgate, O., Mar. 5, 1874; s. Christian William and Catherine Jane (Leonhart) R.; A.B., Ohio Normal U., 1898, Hiram Coll., 1900; B.D., U. of Chicago, 1907; D.D., Spokane U., 1932; m. Kate Parmly Teachout, June 27, 1906; 1 dau., Ruth Mae Ferguson; m. 2d, Leila Covert Avery, Aug. 9, 1913; children—Ada Jane Rogers, Wilma; married 3d, Arlene Dux Scoville, Aug. 2, 1943. Ordained to the ministry of the Disciples of Christ Church, 1900; pastor Ashtabula, Ohio, 1900-05; pastor Irving Park Church, Chicago, 1906-07; pastor Franklin Circle Ch., Cleveland, 1908-18, First Ch., Springfield, Illinois, 1918-27, Third Church, Indianapolis, 1927-43; minister-at-large. Executive director Conference on The Church and the New World Mind, 1944. Made tour of mission fields of Orient, 1924; study tour of Europe, 1911. Pres. Disciples Internat. Conv., 1934; pres. Disciples Congress. Mem. United Christian Missionary Soc. (chmn. bd. mgrs. and committee foreign missions; dir. Pension Fund; chairman Commn. Missionary Policy and Relationships; sec. Commn. on Restudy of Disciples of Christ; fraternal del. to Conf. of Chs. of Christ in Great Britain, 1936; pres. bd. trustees, Flanner House, Indianapolis, Ind.; mem. bd. trustees Ward College, Buenos Aires, Argentina; mem. Good Will Seminar to South Am., 1940; mem. Assn. for Promotion of Christian Unity; mem. Bd. of Church Extension; del. Fed. Council of Churches. Mem. Theta Phi. Mason. Author: The Cross in Symbol, Spirit and Worship, 1930; also wrote many tracts; contbr. various religious publns. Home: 3751 Central Av., Indianapolis IN‡

ROTHIER, LEON, basso; b. Rheims, France, Dec. 26, 1874; s. Francois and Antoinette (Caoussin) R.; ed. High Sch., for Commerce and Industry; musical training at Nat. Conservatory of Music, Paris, winning 3 first prizes, 1897, 98, 99; m. Simone Charpy de Mauborget, of Paris, May 17, 1905. Began with Nat. Opera, Paris; first basso Metropolitan Opera Co., New York, since 1910. Prin. roles: Mephisto, in Faust," the father in Louise," Count des Grieux in Mason," Orkel in Pelleas and Melisande," Rejoined regt. 1st day of mobilization for World War, Aug. 2, 1914. Decorated Officier Instruction Publique (France); Chevalier Legion of Honor (France); Chevalier Ordre de Leopold II (Belgium). Mason. Address: Metropolitan Opera House, New York NY*‡

ROTHKO, MARK, artist; b. Dvinsk, Russia, Sept. 25, 1903; s. Jacob and Kate (Goldin) Rothkovich; brought to U.S., 1913; student Yale, 1925; m. Mary Alice Beistle, Mar. 31, 1945 (dec. 1970). One man exhbns. Contemporary Arts Gallery, N.Y.C., 1933, J. B. Neumann Galleries, N.Y.C., 1939, Art of this Century Galleries, N.Y.C., 1945, Betty Parsons Gallery, N.Y.C., 1946, 47, San Francisco and Santa Barbara museums art, 1946; rep. collections Whitney Mus., Mus. Modern Art, N.Y.C., San Francisco Mus., Bklyn. Mus., Edward Root Collection, Clinton, N.Y., numerous pvt. collections. Recipient Creative Arts award Brandeis U., 1964, 65. Mem. Fedn. Modern Painters and Sculptors. Specializes in abstract, surrealist art. Home: New York City NY Died Mar. 1970.

ROTHROCK, ADDISON M(AY), physicist; b. West Chester, Pa., May 12, 1908; s. Henry Abraham and Eleanor (Cleves) R.; B.S., Pa. State Coll., 1925; D.Sc., Ashland College, 1964; married to Elizabeth Thomas Bland, Jan. 5, 1929; 1 son, Richard Cleves. Grad. asst. Pa. State Coll., 1925-26; head fuel injection section, Langley Lab., Nat. Adv. Com. for Aeronautics, 1926, chief fuels and lubricants div., Lewis Lab., 1942, chief research, 1945, assistant director NACA, 1947-58; assistant director of NASA, 1958, scientist for propulsion NASA, 1959-61, asso. dir. Office of Plans, 1961-63, dir., 1963; prof. applied sci. George Washington U., 1964-68. Mem. AEC Lexingon Project, 1948. Served on various coms. Co-ordinating Research Council, NASA, Dept. Def. Fellow Inst. Aero. Sci., Am. Inst. Aeros. and Astronautics; mem. Am. Rocket Soc. (sr. mem.), Sigma Xi, Sigma Alexandria VA Died June 21, 1971.

ROTHSCHILD, KARL, physician; b. Kirchberg, Germany, Nov. 29, 1897; s. Julius and Albertina (Salomon) R.; student U. Frankfurt, 1916-19, U. Koln, 1919-20; M.D., U. Heidelberg (Germany), 1921; m. Emilie M. Zemo, Apr. 28, 1956. Came to U.S. 1924, naturalized, 1929. Asst., U. Heidelberg, 1921-22, Brain Disease Hosp., Frankfurt, Germany, 1922-23; asst. Mercy Hosp., Wilkes Barre, Pa., 1924-25; resident physician State Hosp., Kings Park, N.Y., 1926; practice medicine specializing in neuropsychiatry, New Brunswick, N.J., 1925-56, Plainfield, N.J., 1956-69; hon. staff mem. Middlesex Gen. Hosp., New Brunswick, 1956-69; hon. neuropsychiatrist St. Peter's Gen. Hosp., New Brunswick, 1956-69; cons. neurologist Roosevelt Hosp., Menlo Park, N.J., 1930-69. Recipient SS medal, 1944. Fellow A.C.P., Am. Psychiatric Association (life mem.), A.A.A.S., N.Y. Acad. Scis.; mem. Sons. Union Vets. Civil War (dep. comdr. N.J., 1954-55). Contbr. numerous articles to med. jours. Home: Plainfield NJ Died Aug. 29, 1969; buried Hillside Cemetery Plainfield NJ

ROTHSTEIN, IRMA, sculptor; b. Rostov, Russia; d. Emil and Josephine (Horowitz) Rothstein; student Women's Acad., Vienna, 1921-22, Art Sch. Prof. Anton Hanak, 1922-29, Sch. For Woodcarving, Hallstadt, Austria, 1923-24. Came to U.S., 1938, naturalized, 1944. Exhibited in one man shows at Gallery Neumann & Salzer, Vienna, 1934, Artists Gallery, N.Y.C., 1940, 43, New Sch. Social Research, N.Y.C., 1941, 61, Bonestell Gallery, N.Y.C., 1944, 47, Galerie St. Etienne, N.Y.C., 1954, 56, Coronet Gallery, N.Y.C., 1960, La Boetie Gallery, N.Y.C., 1965; exhibited in group shows at N.Y. Worlds Fair, 1940, 65, Met. Mus., 1942, 58, Phila. Acad., 1954, Syracuse Mus., 1946, 49, 51, 58; rep. permanent collections Newark Mus., Syracuse Mus. Fine Art, George Walter Vincent Smith Mus., Springfield, Mass. Recip. 1st prize Mint Mus., 1946, Am. Artists Profl. League award, 1946, 2d prize Painters and Sculptors Soc., 1949, 1st prizes Springfield Art Mus., 1951, 58. Allen Ross Meml. prize, 1964; 1st prize Composers, Authors and Artists Soc., 1968. Mem. Nat. Sculpture Soc., Archtl. League, Springfield Art League, New York City NY Died May 1971.

ROTNEM, RALPH ARTHUR, broker; b. Mabel, Minn., Nov. 8, 1903; s. Arne and Minnie (Tollefson) R.; B.S., U. Minn., 1925; M.B.A., Harvard, 1929; m. Alma E. Martin, July 22, 1939; 1 son, Richard. Partner, Harris, Upham & Co., N.Y.C., 1929-65; sr. v.p. Harris, Upham & Co., Inc., 1965-69, cons., 1969-73; past mem. adv. com. Bankers Trust Co. Bd. dirs. Nelson Fund; bd. dirs., treas. Princeton County Day Sch., 1956-57. Mem. Nat. Fedn. Financial Analysts (v.p. 1958-59), N.Y. Soc. Security Analysts (pres. 1958-59), Assn. Customers Brokers (bd. dirs., sec. 1942-43), Wall St. Forum, The Forum, Chi Phi, Alpha Kappa Psi. Republican. Presbyn. Clubs: Harvard (N.Y.C. and Boston), Singing Beach (Manchester, Mass.). Asso. editor Financial Analysts Jour., 1958-66. Home: Prides Crossing MA Died Feb. 8, 1973.

ROUCOLLE, ADRIENNE (MISS), author; b. Toulouse, France, June 14, 1875; brought by parents to U.S., 1878, settling in Denver; removed, 1880 to Fort Collins, Colo.; ed. in public schools and State Agr'l Coll.; began writing at 14, her first sketches being published in the Ft. Collins Courier. Author: His Aunt's Fortune; Child of the Sun; Not Like Other Girls; The Flood of Toulouse; Her Wedding Morn; The Gypsy; The Kingdom of the Good Fairies. Address: Fort Collins CO‡

ROULSTON, MARJORIE HILLIS, author; Peoria, Ill., May 25, 1890; d. Newell Dwight and Annie (Patrick) Hillis; ed. Miss Dana's Sch., Morristown, N.J.; m. Thomas H. Roulston, Aug. 1, 1939. Mem. editorial staff Vogue mag., 1918-36, exec. editor, 1932-36. Turstee Bklyn. Inst. Arts and Scis.; governing com. Bklyn. Botanic Garden. Mem. Authors Guild Am. (council). Republican. Conglist. Author: Live Alone and Like It, 1936; Orchids on Your Budget, 1937; Work Ends at Nightfall, 1938; New York, Fair or No Fair, 1939; You Can Start All Over, 1951; Keep Going and Like It, 1967. Address: New York City NY Died Nov. 1971.

ROUS, (FRANCIS) PEYTON, pathologist; b. Baltimore, Md., Oct. 5, 1879; s. Charles and Frances Anderson (Wood) R.; B.A., Johns Hopkins, 1900, M.D., 1905; (hon.) Sc.D., Cambridge Univ., U. of Mich., 1938. Yale, U. of Birmingham, McGill U., 1949, U. Chgo., 1954, Rockefeller Inst., 1959, Jefferson Univ., 1966, U. of Hartford, 1967; M.D. (hon.), U. Zurich, 1946, Jefferson Med. Coll., 1966; LL.D., St. Lawrence Univ., 1963; m. Marion Eckford de Kay, June 15, 1915; children—Marion (Mrs. Alan Hodgkin), Ellen deKay, Phoebe (Mrs. Thomas J. Wilson). Resident house officer, Johns Hopkins Hosp., 1904-06; instr. in pathology, U. of Mich., 1906-08; asst., asso., asso. mem., Rockefeller Inst. for Med. Research, 1909-20, mem. in pathology and bacteriology, 1920-45, mem. emeritus 1945; mem. bd. scientific consultants Sloan-Kettering Inst. Cancer Research, New York City, 1957-70; Linacre Lecturer Cambridge U., 1929, honorary fellow Trinity Hall, same. Fellow A.A.A.S.; mem. Nat. Acad. Sciences, Am. Philos. Soc., Assn. Am. Physicians, Am. Assn. Pathologists and Bacteriologists, Am. Soc. for Exptl. Pathology, Soc. for Experimental Biology and Medicine, Harvey Soc., N.Y. Pathological Soc., N.Y. Acad. Medicine, Am. Assn. for Cancer Research, Phi Beta Kappa, Alpha Omega Alpha, Sigma Xi. Foreign mem. Royal Society; hon. fellow Royal Soc. Medicine and Coll. Pathologists, London, Weizmann Inst. Science, Israel; hon. mem. British Physiol. Soc., Pathol. Soc. of Great Britain and Ireland, American Society for Microbiology, New York Path. Soc., Conn. Med. Soc.; fgn. corr. mem. British Med. Association, Academie de Medecine, Paris; mem. Royal Acad. Sciences of Denmark, Norwegian Academy of Science and Letters. Awarded John Scott medal and award, 1927; Walker prize, Royal Coll. Surgeons, England, 1941; Anna Fuller Award, 1952; Kober Medal, Assn. Am. Physicians, 1953; Bertner medal and award, U. Tex., 1954; Kovalenko Medal, Nat. Acad. Scis., 1956; distinguished service award Am. Cancer Soc., 1957; Lasker award Am. Pub. Health Assn., 1958; Landsteiner award, Am. Assn. Blood Banks, 1958; N.Y. Acad. Medicine medal, 1959; Judd award, Memorial Center for Cancer, 1959; Gold Medal, Royal Soc. of Medicine (London), 1962, United Nations Prize for cancer research, 1962; Gold-headed Cane award American Assn. of Pathologists and Bacteriologists, 1964; Cleveland medal Am. Cancer Soc., 1966; Nat. Medal of Sci., 1966; Paul Ehrlich award, Germany, 1966; Nobel prize in medicine, 1966. Co-editor Jour. Exptl. Medicine. Contbr. researches on cancer and viruses. Club: Century. Home: New York City NY Died Feb. 16, 1970.

ROUSE, ARTHUR B., ex-congressman; b. Burlington, Ky., June 20, 1874; s. Dudley and Eliza B.; B.S., A.M., Hanover (Ind.) Coll., 1896; LL.B., Louisville (Ky.) Law Sch., 1900; m. Minnie Elizabeth Kelly, of Westwood, O., Dec. 14, 1910; children—Arthur B., Robert K. Admitted to bar, 1900, and since in practice at Erlanger. Mem. Dem. State Exec. Com., 1903-10; mem. 62d to 69th Congresses (1911-27), 6th Ky. Dist.; chmn. Nat. Dem. Congressional Com. Home: Erlanger KY‡

ROUSH, OLIVER EUGENE, sr. v.p., cashier First Nat. Bank of Miami; dir. Coral Way Nat. Bank, Miami. Mem. exec. com., treas. Dade County unit Am. Cancer Soc.; mem. community devel. adv. bd. City of Coral Gables; past dir. Dade County chpt. A.R.C.; past pres. Greater Miami Clearing Assn. Mem. Miami-Dade County C. of C., Better Bus. Bur. So. Fla. (dir.), Ursinus Coll. Alumni Assn., Am. Inst. Banking, Fla., Am. bankers assns. Kiwanian (past pres. S.W. Miami). Clubs: Coral Reef Yacht, Coral Gables Country. Home: Coral Gables FL Died Sept. 16, 1970; buried Mifflintown PA

ROUTH, EUGENE COKE, clergyman, editor; b. Legrange, Tex., Nov. 26, 1874; s. Joseph Edward and Mary Ellen (Stramler) R.; A.B., U. of Tex., 1897; D.D., Baylor U., 1919; m. Mary M. Wroe, Dec. 20, 1897 (died June 21, 1925); children—Mary Lucile (Mrs. Clinton E. Burnett), Ross Holland, Alice Elizabeth (Mrs. J. Christopher Pool), Porter Wroe, Eugene Copass, Leila Katherine (Mrs. Wendell Arnett); m. 2d, Alice Routh, July 7, 1926. Teacher high sch., San Saba, Texas, 1898-1901; ordained to ministry of Baptist ch., 1901; evangelist, 1901-03; pastor Lockhart, Tex., 1903-07; editor South Tex. Baptist, San Antonio, 1907-12; asso. editor Baptist Standard, Dallas, Tex., 1912-14, editor, 1914-28; editor Baptist Messenger, Oklahoma City, 1928-43; editor and mgr. The Commission, Foreign Mission Bd., Southern Bapt. Conv., Richmond, Va., 1943-48; retired. Mem. Texas State Hist. Assn., Oklahoma State Hist. Soc. Author: Life Story of Dr. J. B. Gambrell, 1929; The Story of Oklahoma Baptists, 1932; Reading the Bible, 1934; Are All Roads the Same?, 1941; The Word Overcoming the World, 1941; Evening and Morning in China, 1950; Adventures in Christian Journalism, 1950; Who Are They?, 1951; Scattered Abroad, 1952; Baptists on the March, 1952; According to the Scriptures, 1955. Home: Lockhart TX‡

ROWAN, THOMAS LESLIE, corp. exec.; b. Feb. 22, 1908; s. Thomas and Hannah Josephine (Birrel) R.; ed. Panchgani, India; Tonbridge; Queens Coll., Cambridge U.; m. Catherine Patricia Love, 1944; 2 sons, 2 daus. Joined Colonial Office, 1930; with Treasury, 1933; asst. daus. Joined Colonial Office, 1930; with Treasury, 1933; asst. pvt. sec. to chancellor of Exchequer, 1934-37; asst., then prin. pvt. sec. to Prime Minister Churchill, 1941-45, to Prime Minister Attiee, 1945-47; permanent sec. Office of Minister for Econ. Affairs, 1947; 2d sec. H.M. Treasury, 1947-49, 51-58; econ. minister in Embassy, Washington, 1949-51; mng. dir. Vickers, Ltd., 1962-72, dep. chmn., 1966-67, chmn., 1967-71; dep. chmn., dir. Brit. Aircraft Corp., 1962-71; vice chmn. Legal and Gen. Assurance; dir. Barclays Bank, Ltd. Chmn. Brit. Council, 1971-72; pres. Overseas Devel. Inst., 1967-72, chmn., 1960-67. Clubs: Senior United Service; Hawks (Cambridge). Chelsea England Died Apr. 29, 1972.

ROWE, ALBERT HOLMES, physician; b. Oakland, Cal., Sept. 15, 1889; s. Albert and Susan Abbie (Holmes) R.; B.S., U. Cal. at San Francisco, 1911, M.S., 1912, M.D., 1914; m. Mildred E. Porter, 1915; children—Albert Porter, Charles Adams, Edward Holmes, Robert Nelson. Intern, U. Cal. at San Francisco Hosp., 1914-15, allergist, until 1970; asst. in medicine Mass. Gen. Hosp., Boston, 1915-16; practice medicine specializing in internal medicine and allergy, Oakland, San Francisco, 1916-70; allergist Cowell Infirmary, U. Cal. at Berkeley; cons. in allergy and metabolic diseases Highland Alameda County Hosp., Oakland; lectr. medicine U. Cal. Med. Sch., San Francisco, 30 years, lectr. meritus, until 1970; founder allergy clinic Children's Hosp. of East Bay, Oakland; cons. in allergy Merritt Hosp., Oakland. Diplomate Am. Bd. Internal Medicine. Mem. Am. Assn. for Study Allergy (pres. 1928), Allergy Found. Am. (past chmn. No. Cal. sect.). Republican. Conglist. Mason (Shriner). Author: Handbook for Diabetics, 1928; Food Allergy, 1931; Clinical Allergy, 1937; Elimination Diets and the Patient's Allergies, 1941, 43; Food Allergy and the Elimination Diet, 1971. Mem. editorial staff Jour. Allergy. Founder 1st allergy soc. in Am. Home: Oakland CA Died Oct. 29, 1970; buried Oakland CA

ROWE, CLIFFORD PAUL, educator; b. Anderson, Ind., May 21, 1905; s. Robert M. and Victoria V. (Wells) R.; B.A., Pacific U., 1929; student U. Ida., 1933; M.Ed., U. Ore., 1943; m. Alice Louise Watson, July 28, 1936; children—Clifford Gwynne, Helen Kathleen (Mrs. Frank Imbrie). Instr., English Kimberly (Ida.) High Sch., 1929-32, Grass Valley (Ore.) High Sch., 1933-38, Klamath Falls (Ore.) High Sch., 1939-45; asst. prof. journalism Pacific U., Forest Grove, Ore., 1945-52, asso. prof., 1952-59, prof., 1959-68, chmn. journalism dept., 1945-68. Councilman, City of Forest Grove, 1946-50, mayor, 1954-64; chmn. Ore. Sister City Program, 1962-63. Trustee Am. Coll. Pub. Relations Assn., 1954-55, pres. N.W. Dist., 1953-54. Mem. Am. Assn. U. Profs., Assn. Edn. Journalism, Portland Art Assn., Blue Key, Pi Delta Epsilon (nat. merit medal 1957, pres. 1963), Sigma Delta Chi. Mem. Christian Ch. Rotarian, K.P. Columnist weekly newspapers, 1951-58. Home: Forest Grove OR Died Sept. 29, 1968.

ROWE, GUY, artist; b. Salt Lake City, Utah, July 20, 1894; s. Edward Everett and Gertrude (Dewey) R.; ed. Detroit Sch. of Fine Arts, 1913-19; m. Corinne Finsterwald, June 1, 1919; 1 son, Charles Everett. Former miner, cowhand, mechanic, bill collector, acrobat, and lumberjack; began career as artist drawing chalk portraits in a Detroit vaudeville prior to art sch.; became commercial artist, noted for still life portraits and covers for Time; painter of many portraits of leading figures in Roosevelt adminstrn. for pvt. collectors; rediscovered ancient method of painting in wax; paintings signed Giro. Recipient Christopher award for Bible portraits. Mem. Detroit Soc. of Independent Artists (charter), Artists Equity, Am. Designers. Club: Scarab. Home: Huntington Station NY Died Aug. 25, 1969.

ROWE, JESSE PERRY, geologist; b. Salem Centre, Mich., May 5, 1871; s. Perry and Lydia Louise (Weed) R.; student U. of Ore., 1893; B.S., U. of Neb., 1897; fellow in dept. of geology, U. of Neb., 1897-98, M.A., 1903, Ph.D., 1906, hon. Sc.D., 1935; student U. of Calif., summer, 1901, U. of Chicago, summer, 1905; m. Anna Elizabeth Richards, June 11, 1901 (died Oct. 5, 1939);children—Helen Elizabeth, John Philip, Thomas Dudley. Asst. prin. and head science dept., Butte High Sch., 1898-99; prin. Lincoln Sch., Butte, 1899-1900; instr. physics and geology, U. of Mont., 1900-01, prof. since 1901. Asst. U.S. Geol. Survey, 1906-07; dir. 5 summer sessions, U. of Mont.; prof. geology, U. of Mich., 1921-22; prof. geology, Columbia, summer 1922; in charge geology dept., U. of Mich., summer 1923; prof. geology, Columbia, summers 1925, 26; prof. geology, Cornell U., Ithaca, summer 1927, 28; visiting prof. geology, Princeton, 1928; prof. geology and geography, The Floating Univ.," 1928-29; prof. geology, U. of Mich., summer 1929. U. of Southern Calif., summer 1930, U. of Calif., Berkeley, summer 1936; visiting prof. geology U. of North Carolina, 1942-45. Fellow A.A.A.S., Geol. Soc. America; mem. Am. Forestry Assn., Am. Inst. Mining and Metall. Engrs., Am. Assn. Petroleum Geologists, Mont. Acad. Science, Arts and Letters, Pan Hellenic Soc. Mont. (pres. 1907), Mont. State Teachers Assn. (pres. 1908), State Assn. of School Trustees (pres. 1915), Mont. Geog. Soc. (pres. 1915-16), Elisha Mitchell Scientific Soc. (U. of N.C.). Mem. State Text Book Commn. Exec. and community organizer War Camp Community Service, in charge of work in Los Angeles and surrounding cities, 1918-19. Mem. Phi Kappa Psi, Sigma Xi. Clubs: Missoula, Missoula Country (sec.-treas.), Elks. Author of bulletins and books on Some Volcanic Ash Beds of Montana," Montana Coal and Lignite Deposits," Some Economic Geology of Montana," Practical Mineralogy Simplified," Essentials of Miner-alogy," Geography of Montana," and many articles on econ. geology, in leading geol., scientific, and mining publs. Home: Missoula MT; Carolina Inn, Chapel Hill NC‡

ROWE, ROBERT G., security dealer; b. Phila., 1895. Exec. v.p., dir. Stroud & Co., Phila.; v.p., dir. Federal United Corp.; dir. Eastern Lime Corp., Baederwood Center, Inc., Wilbur Chocolate Co., Ritter Finance Co. Mem. Phila.-Baltimore Stock Exchange. Trustee Pennsylvania Real Estate Investment Trust. Home: Villanova PA Deceased.

ROWE, STUART HENRY, educator; b. New Haven, Conn., May 24, 1869; s. Henry B. and Celia (Stuart) R.; A.B., Yale, 1890; fellow in pedagogy, Columbia, 1892-94; Ph.D., U. of Jena, 1895; m. Agnes Helen Ford, of Syracuse, N.Y., June 4, 1897; 1 dau., Constance. Began as instr. Pennington (N.J.) Sem., 1890; with State Normal Sch. (Mankato, Minn.), 1895-98, Lovel Sch. Dist. (New Haven, Conn.), 1898-1904; lecturer Yale, 1901-04; head dept. pedagogy, Brooklyn Teachers' Training Sch., 1904-10; lecturer Brooklyn Inst. Arts and Sciences, 1908-09, Adelphi Coll., 1909-10; prin. Wadleigh High School, New York, 1910-—. Mem. N.E.A. and kindred orgns. Conglist. Republican. Author: Physical Nature of the Child, 1899; The Lighting of School Rooms, 1904; Habit-Formation and Its Science of Teaching, 1909. Address: 104 Hillcrest Av., Yonkers NY‡

ROWLAND, BENJAMIN, JR., educator; b. Overbrook, Pa., Dec. 2, 1904; s. Benjamin Sr., and Louise Clem (Lennig) R.; student St. Paul's Sch., Concord, N.H., 1918-24; S.B., Harvard, 1928, Ph.D., 1930; m. Lucy Thomas, Nov. 19, 1941; children—Lucy Rowland (Mrs. Allan Baer), Virginia, Sarah and Elise (twins), Margaret. Mem. faculty Harvard, 1930-72, prof. fine arts, 1950-60, Gleason prof. fine arts, 1960-72. U.S. del. UNESCO Kushan Congress, Kabul, Afghanistan 1970; paintings exhibited Stuart Gallery, Boston, 1948, Doll & Richards, 1949, 50, 51, 52, 54, 63, Obelisk Gallery, Washington, 1955, Boston Painting, Whitney Mus., 1949, 50; rep. permanent collections Fogg Mus., Boston Mus. Fine Arts, Detroit Inst. Arts, City Art Mus. St. Louis; lectr. U. Rome, 1958. Fulbright and Guggenheim fellow, 1957-58. Fellow Royal Soc. Arts (London); mem. Cambridge Art Assn., Archaeol. Inst. Am., Am. Acad. Arts and Scis., Chinese Art Soc. Am., Boston Soc. Watercolor Painters. Author: Jaume Huguet, 1932; Wall-paintings of India, Central Asia and Ceylon, 1938; The Wall-paintings of Horyuji (trans. and edited with W.R.B. Acker), 1943; Outline and Bibliographies of Oriental Art, 1938, 40, 45, 52, 58, 68; Art and Architecture of India, 3d edit., 1967; Art in East and West, 1954, 66 (also Russian, Japanese edits.); Gandhara Art from Pakistan, 1960; the Evolution of the Buddha Image, 1963; The Classical Tradition in Western Art, 1963; From Cave to Renaissance, 1965; Ancient Art from Afghanistan, 1966; Zentral Asien, 1970 Editor: J.J. Jarves, The Art Idea, 1960; mem. editorial staff Art Quar. Home: Cambridge MA Died Oct. 3, 1972; Philadelphia PA

ROWLAND, CLARENCE H., baseball exec. Professional baseball player (catcher), Dubuque (Ia.), Three-I League, 1903-05, mgr., 1905-08, owner, mgr., 1911-13; mgr., Aberdeen (Wash.), Northwestern League, 1909; mgr., Peoria, Three-I League, 1914; mgr., Chicago White Sox, Am. League, 1915-18, winning Am. League pennant and World Series over N.Y. Giants, 1917; owner, Milwaukee Club, Am. Assn., 1919; scout, Detroit Tigers, Am. League, 1920, Cincinnati Reds, Nat. League, 1923-27; mgr. Nashville, Southern Assn., 1929-30; pres., mgr., Reading, Internat. League, 1931-32; head of farm system, Chicago Cubs, Nat. League, 1933-40; pres., Los Angeles, Pacific Coast League, 1942-43; pres., Pacific Coast League 1947-69. Home: Chicago IL Died May 17, 1969.

ROY, FRANCIS ALBERT, coll. dean; b. Cambridge, Mass., Nov. 3, 1907; s. Benjamin L. and Elisabeth (Leblanc) R.; A.B., St. Anne U., N.S., 1926; L. as L., U. Paris, 1930; Ph.D., University of Wisconsin, 1934; m. Dorothy Orme Thomas, November 25, 1935 (deceased March 31, 1964); children—Thomas Orme, Catherine Elisabeth, Mary Frances; m. 2d, Suzanne R. Sprinkle, 1965. Instructor of French, U. of Wis., 1930-34; instr. French and humanities U. Ariz., 1934-35, asst. prof., 1935-44, asso. prof., 1944-50, prof., 1950-51, dean Coll. Liberal Arts, 1951-70; vis. prof. Mills Coll., summers 1937, 39, Laval U., Que., summer 1950. Mem. bd. examiners basic scis. State Ariz. Mem. North Central Assn. (commn. on colls., univs.) Delta Upsilon, Phi Kappa Phi, Pi Delta Phi. Roman Catholic. K.C. Home: Tucson AZ Died Oct. 5, 1970; buried Holy Hope Cemetery, Tucson AZ

ROY, VICTOR LEANDER, SR., educator; b. Mansura, La., June 18, 1871; s. Leander Francois and Adelina (Cailleteau) R.; B.S., La. State U., 1890; Univ. of Chicago, 1894; student Tulane U., 1894-96, M.A., 1925; m. Josie Sanford, Aug. 6, 1896; children—Lucile Mary, Reuben Sanford, John Overton, Victor L. Jr. Teacher, Southwestern La. Indsl. Inst.; parish supt. schools, Avoyelles Parish, 1904-09, pres. La. State Normal Coll., 1911-29; bursar La. State U., 1931-33, sec. of faculty, 1933-34; pres. emeritus, La. State Normal College, since 1940. Pres. Louisiana Teachers Association, 1910. Mem. Kappa Sigma (Gamma Chapter). Mason. Democrat. Baptist. Home: Baton Rouge LA‡

ROYALL, KENNETH CLAIBORNE, former sec. of war, lawyer; b. Goldsboro, N.C., July 24, 1894; s. George and Clara Howard (Jones) R.; A.B., U. of N.C., 1914; LL.B., Harvard, 1917; m. Margaret Best, Aug. 18, 1917; children—Kenneth Claiborne, Jr., Margaret (Mrs. James Evans Davis). Admitted to the North Carolina bar, 1916; private law practice, Goldsboro, North Carolina, 1919-30, Raleigh and Goldsboro, N.C., 1931-42; law practice as Dwight, Royall, Harris, Koegel & Caskey, New York City and Washington, 1949-57; Royall, Koegel, Harris & Caskey, 1958-61, Royall, Koegel and Rogers, 1961-—. State senator of North Carolina in 1927 (author North Carolina Bank Liquidation Statute); Presidential elector (N.C.), 1940. Served as 2d lt. F.A., 1917-18, 1st lt. overseas, 1918-19; col. Army U.S., 1942-43, brigadier general, 1943-45; special assistant to Secretary of War, service overseas, 1944, 45. Counsel in sabateur case before special session of U.S. Supreme Court, 1942, appointed under secretary of war, November 1945; apptd. Sec. of War, July 1947, Sec. of Army, 1947-49. Del.-at-large Democratic Nat. Conv., 1964. Mem. Presidential Racial Com., Birmingham, 1963; nat. chmn. Lawyers Com. for Johnson and Humphrey, 1964. Trustee John Fitzgerald Kennedy Library. Decorated D.S.M. Mem. Gen. Alumni Assn. of Univ. of N.C. (president 1959-60), Am., N.C. (pres. 1929-30), New York bar associations, American Law Institute, Phi Beta Kappa, Delta Kappa Epsilon (hon. nat. pres. 1948). Episcopalian. Clubs: Carolina Country (Raleigh, N.C.); Metropolitan (Washington). Asso. editor of Harvard Law Review, 1915-17. Home: Raleigh NC Died May 27, 1971.

ROYCE, DONALD, investment banker; b. Crestline, O., Feb. 7, 1900; s. Luman Herbert and Mayme (Gardner) R.; student Pa. State Coll., 1918-19, Centre Coll., 1920; m. Laura Roberts, Sept. 10, 1923; children—Donald, Suzanne (Mrs. Charles F. O'Connor), Sally (Mrs. Richard G. Thorpe); m. 2d, Jean Reeve, December 9, 1966. Engaged as salesman with National City Company, New York City, 1920-27; v.p. Nat. City Co. of Cal., 1927-32; v.p., dir. Blyth & Co., Inc., 1932-47; pres. William R. Staats Co., Los Angeles, Co., Inc., 1932-47; pres. William R. Staats Co., Los Angeles, 1947-51, sr. partner, 1951-65, chmn. bd., 1965-69; vice chmn. Glore Forgan William R. Staats, Inc., 1965-69; dir. Norris-Thermador Corp., Purex Corp., Ltd., Lear Siegler Corp., U.S. Leasing Corp. Trustee Centre Coll. Republican. Conglist. Home: Santa Monica CA Died July 16, 1969; buried Forest Lawn Cemetery, Glendale CA

ROYCE, ROBERT RUSSEL, architect; b. Stryker, O., May 22, 1902; s. Clarence Theodor and Sarah (Henning) R.; B.Arch., Ohio State U., 1926; m. Helen E. Smith, Mar. 7, 1928; 1 son, Robert Richard. Pianist, Ted Weems Orch., 1923-27; architect R.R. Royce & Assos., Columbus, O., 1928-46, Ft. Lauderdale, Fla., from 1946. Mem. A.I.A., Sigma Chi. Club: Scioto Country (Columbus). Principal works include luxury homes, apts., theatre and bank bldgs. Home: Columbus OH

ROYER, ARNOLD LENNEL, newspaper exec.; b. Indpls., Apr. 13, 1912; s. Lennel O. and Grace (Woodard) R.; m. Mary Edna Buckler, July 31, 1936; 1 son, Thomas Robert. Advt. rep. Indpls. Times, 1934-42; adv. dir. Birmingham (Ala.) Post, 1943-50; mgr. gen. advt., also mgr. Retail Advt. Press, Cleve., 1950-67; bus. mgr. Cin. Post & Times-Star, 1967-71. Served with AUS, 1943-46; PTO. Decorated Bronze Star. Mem. Ohio Newspaper Assn. (dir.). Clubs: Queen City, Cincinnati. Home: Cincinnati OH Died Sept. 26, 1971.

ROYSTER, HUBERT ASHLEY, surgeon; b. Raleigh, N.C., Nov. 19, 1871; s. Dr. W. I. and Mary (Finch) R.; A.B., Wake Forest Coll., 1891, hon. Sc.D., 1931; M.D., U. of Pa., 1894; m. Louise Page, Nov. 6, 1901; children—Mrs. Virginia Page Oxnard, Dr. Hubert Ashley, Jr., Dr. Henry Page. Intern Mercy Hosp., Pittsburgh, 1894-95; surgeon in chief (emeritus) St. Agnes Hosp.; hon. chief surg. service Rex Hosp.; Southern Surg. Assn. (sec. 1916-25; pres. 1926), fellow Am. Surg. Assn., Am. Bd. Surgery; pres. N.C. Lit. and Hist. Assn., 1941-42. Author: Appendicitis, 1927; Medical Morals and Manners, 1937. Home: 2318 Beechridge Rd., Raleigh NC‡

ROYSTER, LAWRENCE THOMAS, physician; b. Norfolk, Va., Aug. 18, 1874; s. Lawrence and Alice Josephine (Ridley) R.; Norfolk Acad., 1884-92; student U. of Va., 1892-97, M.D., 1897; post-grad work in hosps. and clinics of New York, Boston, Baltimore, etc.; m. Ola Park, Dec. 9, 1903 (dec.). Practiced at Norfolk, 1900-23; prof. and head dept. pediatrics, U. of Va., 1923-42. Mem. State Bd. of Health, Va.; mem. Sch. Bd. of Norfolk, 11 yrs.; mem. Children's Code Commn. of Va.; founder and ex-pres. Norfolk Soc. for Prevention of Cruelty to Children; ex-pres. Norfolk Assn. Philanthropics, Bonney Home for Girls; was founder and chief of staff, King's Daughters Clinic; active in promoting med. exam. of school children in the South. Mem. A.M.A. (ex-chmn. pediatric sect.), Southern Med. Assn. (ex-chmn. pediatric sect.), Am. Pediatric Soc., Am. Anthropol. Soc., Am. Assn. of Physical Anthropologists, Va. Soc. of the Cincinnati, Phi Beta Kappa, Alpha Omega Alpha, Sigma Chi, Sigma Xi; fellow Am. Acad. Pediatrics, A.A.A.S. Democrat. Baptist. Author: Nutrition and Development. Part Author: (Chapin and Royster) Diseases of Children. Speaker and writer on med. and sociol. topics, especially pertaining to children. Retired. Home: University Station, Charlottesville VA‡

RUBIN, WILLIAM BENJAMIN, lawyer; b. Russia, Sept., 1873; s. Henry and Bessie (Bernstein) R.; Litt.B., U. of Mich., 1895, LL.B., 1896; m. Sonia Mesirow, 1898 (died 1915); 1 son, Abner Jay Rubien: m. 2d, Josephine Geraghty, of Milwaukee, Wis., June 29, 1935. Came to U.S., 1882, naturalized through father's papers. Admitted to N.Y. bar, 1896; mem. firm of Rubin, Zabel & Ruppa; trial counsel of nat. prominence. Elk. Liberal Democrat. Club: Milwaukee Athletic. Author: The Toiler in Europe, 1916; The Bolshevist, 1919; The Constitution and Democracy, 1937. Home: 1830 E. Kane Place. Office: Mariner Tower, Milwaukee WI‡

RUBIN DE LA BORBOLLA, DANIEL FERNANDO, anthropologist, mus. dir.; b. Puebla, Puebla, Mex., May 20, 1907; s. Dr. Juan Rubin de la Borbolla and Trinidad Cedillo; grad. high sch., Evanston, Ill.; student State Coll., Puebla, Mex.; grad. U. Mexico, 1930; Ph.D., Northwestern U.; m. Sol Arguedas, Oct. 1944; children—Daniel, Sol, Maria de la

Paz. Chief anthropologist Nat. Mus. Anthropology, 1931-36; prof. human biology Nat. Prep. Sch., U. Mexico, 1931-36, prof. faculty philosophy and letters at univ., 1931-37; explored Monte Alban, Oaxaca, other anthrop. research Tzintzuntzan, Michoacan, Teotihuacan, Chupicuaro, Guanajuato, also Tiatilco, Mexico, 1933-53; founder, dean Nat. Sch. Anthropology and History, Mexico City, 1940-45; dir.-gen. Nat. Mus. Anthropology, 1947-53; chmn. U. Museum, Nat. Autonomous U. of Mexico, counselor for rector, dir. gen. of univ., from 1951; dir. Univ. Mus. Science and Art, Nat. U.; dir. Nat. Mus. Popular Arts and Crafts, from 1949; exec. sec. Nat. Council Arts and Crafts, from 1951; tech. adviser cultural matters Ministry Fgn. Relations, from 1950. Trustee arts, crafts Nat. Coop. Bank Mex. Mem. Mexican, Royal, Am. anthrop. socs., Mexican Folklore Soc., Am. Acad. Natural Scis., Am. Assn. Phys. Anthropologists, Am. Museum Assn. Contbr. articles anthrop. publs. Home: Mexico City Mexico Deceased.

RUBINOVITZ, GEORGE, b. 1914; B.B.A., City Coll. N.Y.; LL.B., Bklyn. Law Sch.; married. With Witco Chem. Co., Inc., 1942-71, sec., 1958-71. Address: New York City NY Died Dec. 17, 1971.

RUBY, EDWARD ERNEST, editor; b. Cambridge, Ind., Feb. 25, 1874; s. James Tate and Sarah Helen (Aikin) R.; A.B., Indiana University, 1897, A.M., 1901; m. Blanche Blynn, of Fort Wayne, Ind., Dec. 6, 1899; children—James Tate, Katherine Elizabeth (Mrs. Henry Taylor), Edward Ernest, David Blynn (dec.). Instructor in Romance languages, Indiana University, 1900-02; prof. of Latin, Illinois Coll., Jacksonville, Ill., 1902-04; same, Whitman Coll., 1904-30, also dean, 1911-30; head of editorial dept. George Banta Pub. Co. (Collegiate Press), 1930—. Librarian, Camp Lewis, 1917-19; supervisor A.L.A. work in mil. and naval stas. Pacific Northwest, May 1918-Jan. 1919; dir. A.L.A. work, Army of Occupation, Germany, Jan.-June 1919. Mem. Archaeol. Inst. America, Phi Delta Theta, Phi Beta Kappa. Democrat. Conglist. Home: Menasha WI‡

RUBY, LIONEL, educator; b. Chgo., Aug. 24, 1899; s. Sebastian and Anna (Kanter) R.; Ph.B., U. Chgo., 1921, J.D., 1923, Ph.D., 1930; m. Violet Pritzker, Jan. 10, 1928 (div.); 1 son, Norman; m. 2d, Louise Ramis Landes, July 25, 1954; 1 son, Roy. Admitted to Ill. bar, 1923, practiced in Chgo., 1926-28; lectr. U. Chgo., 1931-33; instr., asst. prof. Ind. U., 1934-43, 46-49; prof. philosophy Roosevelt U., 1949-69, chmn. dept., 1954-60; prof. philosophy Cal. State Coll., Hayward, 1969-72. Hearing officer War Labor Bd., 1943-44, vice chmn. trucking panel, 1944-45, chmn., 1945; arbitrator panels Fed. Mediation and Conciliation Service, Am. Arbitration Assn. Mem. Am. Soc. Aesthetics, Am. Philos. Assn. (chmn. com. on information service 1961-67), Internat. Assn. Philosophy Law and Social Philosophy, Am. Soc. for Polit. and Legal Philosophy. Author: Logic: An Introduction, 1950; The Art of Making Sense, 1954; Logic and Critical Thinking, 1970. Home: Los Angeles CA Died Mar. 1972.

RUDD, JUDSON ARCHER, educator; b. Belpre, Kan., Nov. 28, 1902; s. Guy Verne and Mary Jane (Archer) R.; A.B., Ottawa (Kan.) U., 1925; M.A., U. Kan., 1926; LL.D., Wheaton Coll., 1943; m. Lucile Searcy, Sept. 7, 1927; 1 dau., Mary Frances. Instr. commerce and mathematics Austin Coll., 1926-27; instr. U. Ala. Sch. Commerce and Bus. Adminstrn., 1927-30; prof. mathematics William Jennings Bryan Coll., 1931-56, treas., 1932-40, v.p., 1932-33, acting pres., 1933-36, pres., 1936-55, pres. emeritus, 1955-70, professor of business, from 1956. Mem. adv. council Internat. Child Evangelism Fellowship; mem. Friends of Higher Edn. Named Man of the Year, Dayton Lions Club, 1952. Mem. N.E.A., Nat. Assn. Evangs. Baptist. Club: Lions. Home: Dayton TN Died Oct. 6, 1970; buried Dayton TN

RUDDER, JAMES EARL, educational administrator and reserve army officer; born at Eden, Texas, May 6, 1910; son of Dee Forest and Annie (Powell) R.; student John Tarleton Agrl. Coll., Texas, 1927-30; Indsl. Edn. degree, Tex. A. and M. Coll., 1932; grad. study Tex. Chirstian U., 1939; LL.D., Baylor University, Waco, 1960; married to Margaret E. Williamson, June 12, 1937; children—James Earl, Margaret Anne, Linda, Jane, Robert. Tchr., football coach Brady High Sch., 1933-38, John Tarleton Coll., Stephenville, 1938-41; operator Brady Drug Store, 1935-49; rancher, businessman, Brady, Tex., 1946—; v.p., pub. relations counsellor Brady Aviation Corp., 1953-55; commr. Gen. Land Office State Tex., 1955-58; v.p. Tex. A. & M. U., 1958-59, pres., 1959-70; pres. Texas A. & M. U. System, 1965-70. Member of the executive committee of the Tenneco, Incorporated. Mayor of Brady, 1946-52; mem. State Bd. Pub. Welfare, 1953-55; chmn. Vets. Land Bd., 1955-58; mem. Inf. Adv. Bd.; mem. Tex. Governor's Commission on Education Beyond High School, 1966; member National Advertising Commission on Rural Poverty, 1966-67; state chmn. March of Dimes, 1966. Hon., vice pres. State Fair of Texas; member council and exec. bd. Tex. A. and M. Coll. Trustee Research Analysis Corp., Southwest Research Institute; member of the board of directors Texas United Fund, Sam Houston area council Boy Scouts Am., Nat. Space Hall of Fame Found., 1968; bd. visitors U.S. Mil. Acad. 1st lieutenant to colonel AUS, 1941-46; commanded Provisional Ranger Force at Normandy, 109th Inf. Regt., 28th Div. in Battle of Bulge, and liberation of Colmar; comdg. gen. 90th Inf. Div. Res., 4th Army, Austin, Tex., 1955-65; asst. dep. comdg. gen. for moblzn. Continental Army Command, 1965-67. Decorated D.S.C., Legion of Merit, Silver Star, Bronze Star with oak cluster, Purple Heart with oak-leaf clusters (U.S.); Legion of Honor with Croix de Guerre and palm (France); Order of Leopold with Croix de Guerre and palm (Belgium); recipient gold citizenship award V.F.W., 1965; Army and Navy Legion of Valor, 1965; Outstanding Citizenship award Tex. Dist. Exchange Clubs, 1967; Distinguished Service Medal. Mem. Res. Officers Assn., Am. Legion (post comdr. 1949), Vets. Fgn. Wars (nat. security com.), Land-Grant Assn. (nat. def. com.), Assn. U.S. Army (adv. bd.), Assn. Tex. Colls. and Univs. (commn. ednl. policy), Am. Council Edn. (commn. adminstrv. affairs), Asso. Western Univs., Inc. (exec. com.). Mason (33 deg.). Home: College Station TX Died Mar. 23, 1970; buried College Station City Cemetery, College Station TX

RUDDIMAN, EDSEL ALEXANDER, chemist; b. Dearborn, Mich., Dec. 27, 1864; s. William and Catherine (Noble) R.; grad. Detroit High Sch., 1884; Pharm. Chemist, U. of Mich., 1886; M.Pharm., 1887; M.D., Vanderbilt U., 1893; m. Jennie Evelyn Perry, July 29, 1889; children—Stanley Perry, Edith Helen. Chemist in charge mfg. lab. of Milburn & Williamson, 1887-90; chemist to Tenn. Bd. Pharmacy, 1897-1920; food and drug inspection chemist, 1907-14; prof. pharmacy and materia medica, in dept. of pharmacy, 1890-1920, dean Sch. of Pharmacy, 1919-20, Vanderbilt U.; chief chemist John T. Milliken & Co., pharmaceutical chemists, 1921-26; research chemist with Ford Motor Co., 1926-42. Author: Incompatibilities in Prescriptions, 1897; Whys in Pharmacy, 1906; Manual of Materia Medica, 1907; Theoretical and Practical Pharmacy, 1917. Home: 22179 Long Blvd., Dearnborn MI‡

RUDDY, EDWARD MICHAEL, judge; b. St. Louis, June 20, 1899; s. Michael John and Sarah Elizabeth (Carrick) R.; student Benton Coll. Law, 1920-21; LL.B., City Coll. Law, 1925; m. Elsie Frankey, Sept. 6, 1923; children—Kenneth Edward, Edward Neal, Vincent James. Admitted to Missouri bar, 1925; jr. accountant Price Waterhouse &Co., 1922; with Shell Oil Co., 1923-25; pvt. gen. practice law, St. Louis, 1925-39; Judge City Ct., St. Louis, 1936-38; circuit judge Judicial Circuit, 1939-51; judge St. Louis Ct. Appeals, 1951-69; lectr. Recipient Award of Honor, 1961. Mem. Am. Bar Assn., Am. Judicature Soc., Mo. Bar Integrated, St. Louis Bar Assn., Lawyers Assn. St. Louis (award of honor 1961), Phi Delta Phi. Roman Catholic. K.C. Clubs: Serra of St. Louis. Kiwanis. Home: St Louis MO Died Mar. 18, 1969.

RUDINGER, ELLEN ECKSTEIN (MRS. GEORGE RUDINGER), physician; b. Jena, Germany, Jan. 5, 1915; d. Ignaz and Hilde (Sachs) Eckstein; M.D., State U. N.Y., Buffalo, 1939; m. George Rudinger, Aug. 16, 1947; children—David J., Ann N. Came to U.S., 1937, naturalized, 1943. Intern, Buffalo Gen. Hosp., 1939-40, resident in medicine, 1940-42, asso. physician, until 1971; cons. internist Rosa Coplon Jewish Home and Infirmary, Buffalo, until 1971; asst. clin. prof. medicine State U. N.Y., Buffalo, until 1971. Diplomate Am. Bd. Internal Medicine. Mem. A.M.A., Am. Soc. Internal Medicine. Club: Zonta (2d v.p., program chmn. Buffalo 1960). Home: Buffalo NY Died July 22, 1971; buried Forest Lawn Cemetery, Buffalo NY

RUE, MILTON, ex-mem. Rep. Nat. Com.; b. Red Lake Falls, Minn., Sept. 28, 1899; s. John J. and Christine Amelia (Johnson) R.; student Valley City (N.D.) Normal, 1916-19, Interstate Bus. Coll., Fargo, N.D.; m. Norma Craven, Sept. 27, 1924; children—Beverly Norma (Mrs. Lynwood Wellington), Milton Llewellyn, Mary Barbara, (Mrs. Dan Dahl). Propr. Rue Constrn. Co., Bismarck, North Dakota, 1932-69; president The Milton Rue Company; dir. Provident Life Ins. Co., Bismarck, Bismarck Building and Loan Association, First National Bank of Bismarck. Member House of Reps., N.D., 1933-35, Senate, 1941-56; chairman Rep. Party, N.D. 1946-52, member Rep. Nat. Com., 1952-58. Mem. exec. bd. Bismarck Hosp.; trustee Bismarck Jr. Coll. Served with F.A., U.S. Army, World War I. Mem. Am. Legion, Vets. Fgn. Wars, 40 et 8. Mason (Shriner). Elk. Eagle. Home: Bismarck ND Died May 29, 1968; buried Fairview Cemetery, Bismarck ND

RUFF, G. ELSON, clergyman; b. Dunkirk, N.Y., Feb. 9, 1904; s. George Grant and Martha Ellen (Elson) R.; student U. of Pittsburgh, 1922; Phila. Lutheran Theol. Sem., 1923-26; A.B., Thiel Coll., 1923, Litt.D., 1943; A.M., University of Pennsylvania, 1928; L.H.D. (honorary), Wagner Coll., 1956; m. to Thelma Suttles; children—George Elson, Jan Alan, Joan Elsa. Began as newspaperman with Phila. (Pennsylvania); Inquirer; ordained to ministry of Evangelical Lutheran Ch., 1926; pastor St. Paul's Ch., Shavertown, Pa., 1926-37, Christ Ch., Schuykill Haven, Pa., 1937-40; book editor United Lutheran Publ. House, Phila., 1940-45; editor in chief, 1946-62; editor The Lutheran, 1945-72. President Asso. Ch. Press, 1953-55. Author: The Dilemma of Church and State, 1954. Home: Philadelphia PA Died Jan. 1972.

RUFFIN, MARGARET ELLEN HENRY, author, lecturer; b. Daphne, Baldwin County, Ala.; d. Thomas and Mary (Nugent) Henry; grad. St. Joseph's Coll., Emmitsburg, Md., 1877; (L.H.D. first woman in Ala., U. of Paris, 1907, also U. of Dublin); m. Mobile, Ala., 1887, Francis Gildart Ruffin, Jr., of Richmond, Va. (now deceased) Student of and lecturer on languages, music and literature, especially Celtic history and antiquities. Active worker in Gaelic revival. Author (poems); Drifting Leaves, 1884; John Gildart, 1900; The North Star, 1904; also Eden on the James, The Sphinx, and mag. articles on Gaelic subjects. Received letter from King and Queen, and minister of edn. of Norway on publishing The North Star; request for picture from Societie des Gens de Lettres and Bibliotheque Nationale of Paris, to be placed among writers of eminent distinction. Address: 404 Church St., Mobile Al‡

RUFFINI, ELISE ERNA, educator, lectr.; b. Austin, Tex.; d. Ernst F. and Elise (Weitz) Ruffini; B.S., Columbia, 1947, M.A. Asso. prof. fine arts Columbia U., 1944-49, acting head fine arts dept. Tchrs. Coll., 1943-49; lectr. art, art edn. Co-author: series of 8 books New Art Education, for pub. schs. first grade through eight, 1944. Mem. Am. Assn. U. Women. Home: San Angelo TX Died June 30, 1970.

RUGGLES, CARL, composer; b. Marion, Mass., Mar. 11, 1876; s. Nathaniel Sprague and Josephine (Hodge) R.; m. Charlotte Snell, Apr. 27, 1908; 1 son, Micah Haskell. Founder and conductor, Winona Symphony Orchestra, 1908; instr. and inaugurator, seminar in modern composition, U. of Miami, Fla., from 1939. Painter in oils and water colors; exhbns., galleries in Chicago, Detroit, Addison, Brooklyn, also Bennington Coll. Mem. Southern Vt. Artists, Nat. Assn. Composers and Conductors, Nat. Institute Arts and Letters. Protestant. Composer: Men and Mountains, Portals, Suntreader, Organum, (chamber music), Angels Vox Clamans, In Deserto, Toys, Evocations. Represented U.S. at Venice Festival and Barcelona Festival, Internat. Soc. for Contemporary Misic. Home: Arlington VT Died Oct. 24, 1971; buried Evergreen Cemetery, Arlington VT

RUGGLES, CHARLES, actor; b. Los Angeles, Feb. 8, 1892; s. Charles Sherman and Maria Theresa (Heinsch) R.; ed. pub. schs., Los Angeles and San Francisco; married. Made first theatrical appearance in stock co. at Alcazar Theatre, San Francisco, 1908; now appearing in motion pictures; played in Friendly Enemies, New York stage, 1942. Member Catholic Actors Guild, Episcopal Actors Guild, Actors Equity Assn. Clubs: Lambs, New York Athletic (New York); Los Angeles Athletic. Home: Los Angeles CA Died Dec. 1970.

RUHL, ARTHUR BROWN, author; b. Rockford, Ill., Oct. 1, 1876; s. Antes Schoch and Nellie (Brown) R.; A.B., Harvard University, 1899; m. Zinaida Yakovnchikoff, of Berlin, Germany, June 11, 1926; 1 son, Arthur Paul. Member of staff of New York Evening Sun, 1899-1904; with Collier's Weekly, 1904-13; dramatic critic, New York Tribune, 1913-14; corr. for Collier's in France and Belgium, 1914, Central Europe, 1915, Russia, 1916-17, France, 1918, in Baltic States, 1919; corr. N.Y. Evening Post in Baltic States and Poland, 1920; Berlin corr. New York Herald-Tribune, 1925-26. Club: Harvard (New York). Author: A History of Track Athletics in America (Sportsman's Library Series), 1905; A Break in Training, 1906; The Other Americans, 1908; Second Nights, 1914; Antwerp to Gallipoli, 1916; White Nights, 1917; New Masters of the Baltic, 1921; The Central Americans, 1928. With American Relief Administration in Russia, 1922-23. Home: 45 W. 11th St., New York NY‡

RULON, PHILLIP JUSTIN, prof. edn.; b. Keokuk, Ia., Mar. 11, 1900; s. William Edgar and Alberta Edna (Ruckman) R.; A.B., Stanford U., 1926, A.M., 1928; Ph.D., U. of Minn., 1932; A.M. (hon.). Harvard U., 1942; m. Dorothy Louise Overfelt, Mar. 11, 1927; children—Phillip Justin, Dorothy Elizabeth Rose. Teacher, Peninsula Sch., Menlo Park, Calif., 1925-28; instr. ednl. psychology, U. of Minn., 1928-30; instr. Grad. Sch. Edn., Harvard U., 1930-34; asst. prof., 1934-40; asso. prof., 1940-44, prof. since 1944; acting dean, Grad. Sch. of Edn., 1943-48. Research assoc. math., Tufts Coll. (Navy research project), 1942-46; spl. cons. to sec. of War, 1940-48. Sec., Ednl. Research Corp., 1938-50, treas., 1948-54, pres., 1954-58, treas., 1958-68. Regents Dis. Achievement award U. Minn., 1963. Fellow A.A.A.S., Am. Psychol. Assn., Am. Statis. Assn. Author: The Earth and Its Life (with E.E. Cureton), 1932; The Sound Motion Picture in Science Teaching, 1933; An Experimental Comparison of Two Shorthand Systems (with Walter Deemer), 1942; (with others) Multivariate Statistics for Personnel Classification, 1967; numerous publs. on internat. lang. for aviation, related subjects. Home: Cambridge MA Died Aug. 1968.

RUMPF, ARTHUR NEWELL, banker; b. South Bend Ind., Feb. 8, 1908; s. Arthur George and Lois (Newell) R.; A.B., Dartmouth, 1930; student Rutgers U. Grad. Sch. Banking, 1945, Northwestern U. Inst. for Mgmt., 1955; m. Mary S. Bleuler, June 22, 1932; children—Norman A., Karen. With Harris Trust & Savs. Bank, Chgo., 1930-68, successively asst. cashier, asst. v.p., v.p., 1930-61, senior vice president, 1961-63, president, director, 1963-68; dir. Clark Equipment Co. Treas., trustee Chgo. Wesley Meml. Hosp.; trustee Meth. Old Peoples Home, Keep Am. Beautiful; bd. dirs. Community Fund of Chgo. Inc.; treas. Citizens Traffic Safety Board. Mem. Chgo. Assn. Commerce and Industry (dir.), Chicago Clearing House Assn. (pres.). Clubs: University, Westmoreland Country, Commercial, Chicago (Chgo.); University (Milw.). Home: Evanston IL Died Feb. 3, 1968.

RUNDQUIST, GEORGE E., organization executive; b. New York, N.Y., July 6, 1896; s. Ernest F. and Emily (Olson) R.; student New York Univ., 1937, Harvard 1936; m. Alice Louise Perinchief, Mar. 14, 1932. Salesman Lewis Pub. Co., New York, N.Y., 1916-18; asso. editor Lewis Pub. Co., 1919-23; investment securities bus., Los Angeles, 1923-26; asso. editor Am. Hist. Soc., New York, engaged in genealogical research and pub., 1926-39; asso. editor James T. White & Co., New York, N.Y., 1939-41; asso. sec. Am. Friends Service Com. (Quakers), New York office, Feb.-Oct. 1942; asso. sec. Fgn. Service sect., Phila., 1945-47; exec. sec. Com. on Resettlement of Japanese Americans (organized by Fed. Council of Chs. of Christ in Am. and Home Mission Council of N.Am. in cooperation with Fgn. Missions Conf. of N. Am.), 1942-45. Asst. dir. Am. Civil Liberties Union, 1948-51, field dir., 1951-54; exec. dir. N.Y. union, 1951-65, now dir. Upper Pinellas chpt., Fla. Served in 332 Bn., Tank Corps, France, 1918-19. Mem. Soc. of Friends. Home: Dunedin FL Died May 27, 1969.

RUNGE, EDITH AMELIE, educator; b. Leverkusen, Rhein, Germany, Feb. 24, 1916; d. Otto and Cornelia (Steinam) Runge; came to U.S., 1921, naturalized, 1926; A.B., summa cum laude, Swarthmore Coll., 1938; Ph.D., Johns Hopkins, 1942. Head English dept. Averett Coll., Danville, Va., 1942-43; mem. faculty Mt. Holyoke Coll., 1943-71, prof. German, 1961-71, chmn. dept., 1948-54, 60-67; prof. German, Middlebury (Vt.) German Sch., summers 1951-53, 60. Mem. Am. Assn. U. Profs. (sec. Mt. Holyoke 1944-46, exec. council 1959-60), Modern Lang. Assn. Am., Am. Assn. Univ. Women, New Eng. Modern Lang. Assn., Am. Assn. Tchrs. German (pres. Conn. Valley chpt. 1961-62), The Brandywiners Ltd. (charter), Phi Beta Kappa (pres. Theta of Mass. 71). Author: Primitivism and Related Ideas in Sturm and Drang Literature, published in 1946; also articles, papers. Home: South Hadley Died Aug. 19, 1971; buried Lower Brandywine Cemetery, Wilmington DE

RUNNING, THEODORE RUDOLPH, prof. mathematics; b. Colfax, Wis., Dec. 14, 1866; s. Ole Aslaksen and Birgit (Sletveit) R.; B.S., U. of Wis., 1892, M.S., 1896; Ph.D., 1899; m. Clara Bertine Anderson, Sept. 21, 1898 (died February 7, 1942). Professor mathematics, chemistry and physics, St. Olaf College, Northfield, Minnesota, 1893-95, 1900-03; fellow in mathematics, Univ. of Wisconsin, 1895-97; instr. in mathematics, U. of Wis., 1897-1900; instr. mathematics, U. of Mich., 1903-07, asst. prof., 1907-13, junior prof., 1913-15, asso. prof., 1915-20, prof., 1920-37, prof. emeritus since 1937; acting asst. dean Coll. Engring. and Architecture, U. of Mich., 1924-25. Fellow A.A.A.S.; mem. Am. Math. Soc., Math. Assn. of America, Soc. for Promotion Engring. Edn., Am. Soc. Univ. Profs., Mich. Acad. Science, Arts and Letters, Sigma Xi. Democrat. Presbyterian. Author: Empirical Formulas (translated into French and Japanese), 1917; Graphical Mathematics (translated into Japanese), 1927; Graphical Calculus, 1937; First Year College Mathematics (with L. C. Plant), 1939. Co-editor of chapter on mathematics in Chemical Ann Arbor MI‡

RUPE, DALLAS GORDON, investment banker; b. Dallas, Aug. 11, 1902; s. Dallas Guy and Gretchen (Irvine) R.; student pub. schs., Dallas; m. Ruby Landers, Mar. 30, 1921; children—Paula Dallas (Mrs. Robert E. Dennard), Dallas Gordon III. Chmn. bd. Dallas Rupe & Son, Inc., Dallas Rupe & Co., pres. dir. Rupe Investment Corp., Dallas, Rupe & Son Properties Corp., Dallas, Thurman Randle & Co., Dallas; v.p., dir. Enid Hotel Co. (Okla.), Wallace Development Co., Wallace Realty Co. (all Enid); chmn. bd. Baker Hotel, Inc., Hutchinson, Ka., also Hoosier Gas Corp., Vincennes, Ind., Moore Investment Co., Parker Oil Corp., Dallas, Big D Prodns., Inc. Dallas, Hutchinson Baker Hotel Co., Inc., Wabash Properties Corp.; partner Dallas and Gordon Rupe Partnership, Dallas; voting trustee Manchester Terminal Corp., Houston; mem. N.Y. Stock Exchange; dir. A. H. Belo Corp. (Dallas Morning News, Radio-TV Sta. WFAA), Lone Star Steel Co., Dallas. Mem. devel. com. Bishop Coll.; exec. com. Dallas Grand Opera Assn.; mem. com. Nat. Council on Crime and Delinquency. Pres., trustee Bexar Found., Rupe Found.; trustee Nat. Jewish Hosp., Denver, Dallas Natural Sci. Assn.; adv. trustee Episcopal Extension Found.; bd. devel. Bapt. Coll.; devel. council Baylor U. Med. Center, Callier Hearing and Speech Center, Tex. Hosp. Assn. Health Careers; mem. Tex. Research Found., S.W. Legal Found.; So. Meth. U. Arts Found.; bd. dirs. State Fair Tex., Greater Dallas Planning Council, Dallas Zool. Soc., Thanks-Giving Sq. Mem. Dallas C. of C., Dallas (trustee), Tex. hist. socs., Dallas Fedn. Music Clubs, Def. Orientation Conf. Assn., Navy League U.S., Anglo-Texan Soc., Ducks Unltd., English Speaking Union, Tex. Rifle Assn., Dallas Civic Music Assn., Newcomen Soc. Clubs: City, Dallas, Dallas Country, Imperial, Terpsichorean, Dallas Gun, Texas Game Fishing, Dallas Woods and Waters (Dallas); Koon Kreek (Athens, Tex.); Sportsmen's Clubs of Tex., St. Charles Bay Hunting (Rockport, Tex.); Yale Fishing (hon.); Admirals: Fishing of Am. Home: Dallas TX Died Mar. 4, 1970; buried Dallas TX

RUPEL, I(SAAC) WALKER, educator; b. Walkerton, Ind., May 3, 1900; s. David Edmund and Daisie Flora (Snethen) R.; B.S., U. Ill., 1923; M.S., U. Wis., 1924, Ph.D., 1932; m. Ruth Mabel Peterson, Sept. 6, 1924 (dec. 1956); children—John W., Joan (Mrs. Don P. Hegi); m. 2d, Cora Bradley Davies, Aug. 17, 1957. Tchr. rural sch., Wyatt, Ind., 1917-18; dairy herdsman, also test supr. in Ill., 1918-19; instr. dairy husbandry U. Wis., 1924-28, asst., then asso. prof., 1929-45; exchange prof. agr. U. Hawaii, 1930; prof. dairy sci., head dept. A. and M. Coll. Tex., College Station, from 1945. Ofcl. type classification judge Am. Jersey Cattle Club, from 1945; ofcl. judge livestock Nat. Fair Guatemala, 1941, Brown Swiss Cattle XIII Exposition, Girardot, Colombia, 1961; mem. U.S. delegation XVth World's Dairy Congress, London, 1959, XVIth Congress, Copenhagen, 1962. Dir. Lilly Ice Cream Co., Byran, Tex. Pres. Brazos County chpt. Nat. Found., 1959-61. Fellow A.A.A.S., Tex. Acad. Sci.; mem. Am. Dairy Sci. Assn. (exec. bd. 1955-58, pres. 1962), Am. Dairy Assn. Tex (dir., 1945-60), Tex. Jersey Cattle Club (dir. 1950-53), Am. Soc. Animal Sci., Am. Soc. Exptl. Biology and Medicine, Am. Assn. U. Profs., Sigma Xi, Phi Kappa Phi Phi Sigma, Alpha Zeta. Methodist. Rotarian (dir. Bryan 1957-59). Author, co-author research and extension bulls. Asso. editor Jour. Dairy Sci. 1944-51; editorial bd. Jour. Animal Sci., 1951-54. Home: Bryan TX Died May 28, 1971.

RUPLEY, JOSEPH WILLIAM, corporation exec.; b. Denver, Feb. 11, 1902; s. William C. and Orpha O. (Baldwin) R.; student Stanford, 1919-20; B.S., Whitman Coll., 1923; m. Janet Allyn McCorskey, May 27, 1936; children—William Houston, Joseph R. (dec.). Reporter, financial editor, Wash. corr. Spokane Daily Chronicle, 1923-34; asst. gen. agt., personnel officer Farm Credit Administration of Spokane, 1934-43; director personnel, acting executive officer O.W.I., Washington, 1943; chief field representative United States Bureau Budget, San Francisco, 1943-53; mgmt., financial cons., 1928-68; lectr. mgmt. and govt., Stanford, 1947-52, U. Cal., Berkeley, 1950-54; treas. Safeway Stores, Inc., Oakland, Cal., 1953-67, cons., 1967-68; chmn. bd., chief financial officer Tinsley Labs., Inc., Berkeley, Cal., 1967-68. Mem. bd. regents U. of Pacific, Stockton, Cal. Member American Society Pub. Adminstrn., Am. Mgmt. Assn., Pacific Northwest Personnel Mgmt. Assn. (co-founder, past pres.), Pacific Coast Bd. Intergovtl. Relations (co-founder, chmn. agenda, exec. com. 1945-53). Clubs: Stock Exchange, (San Francisco); The Orinda (California) Country. Contbr. articles on mgmt. and govt., various profl. publs. Home: Orinda CA Died Apr. 8, 1968.

RUPP, CHARLES, JR., physician; b. Phila., Oct. 12, 1908; s. Charles and Helena C. (Bauer) R.; grad. Wm. Penn Charter Sch., 1925; A.B., Harvard, 1929, M.D., 1933; m. Marjorie Drew, 1937 (dec. Nov. 2, 1950); m. 2d, Jane M. Dubbs, 1954. Neurologist Phila. Gen. Hosp., 1944-68, chmn. dept. neurology U. Pa. division, 1960-68, consultant since 1968-70; associate professor of neurology U. Pa. and Graduate School, 1946-70, neurologist, psychiatrist in chief, Lankenau Hosp.; pres. med. bd. Phila. Gen. Hosp., 1954-57; cons. neurology VA Hosp., Coatesville, Pa. Diplomate Am. bd. Psychiatry and Neurology, dir., 1961-69, pres., 1969. Fellow Am. Psychiat. Assn. (life), Coll. Physicians of Phila.; mem. A.M.A., Am. Assn. Neuropathologists, Soc. Biol. Psychiatry, Phila. Neurological Soc. (sec. 1944-54, pres. 1954-55), Am. Neurological Assn. (assistant secretary 1948-55, sec. 1955-59, first vice pres. 1959-60), A.A.A.S., Am. Academy Neurology, Assn. Research Nervous and Mental Diseases. Club: Harvard (Phila.); University (N.Y.C.). Contbr. articles med. publs. Home: Philadelphia PA Died Sept. 1, 1970; buried West Laurel Hill Cemetery, Philadelphia PA

RUSHING, JAMES ANDREW, singer; b. Oklahoma City, Aug. 26, 1903. Singer, Walter Page's Blue Devils, Bennie Moten, 1920-30; with Count Basie band, 1935-50; with own group, 1950-52; singer, 1952-72; appeared at major festivals and on fgn. tours, 1957-72; played at clubs, N.Y.C. Address: Philadelphia PA Died June 8, 1972.

RUSHMORE, STEPHEN, gynec.-obstet. (retired); b. Rochester, N.Y., Oct. 19, 1875; s. Edward (M.D.) and Clara Sidney (Riley) R.; A.B., Amherst Coll., 1897, D.Sc., 1937; M.D., Johns Hopkins U., 1902; m. Alice Dammann, Oct. 29, 1910; 1 dau., Alice Stephanie. Resident in gynecology, Johns Hopkins Hospital, 1905-06; practiced in Boston since 1907; professor gynecology, Tufts College Medical School, 1907-27, also dean of same, 1922-27; secretary State Board of Registration in Medicine, 1931-42; dean of Middlesex Univ. School of Med., 1942-45. Fellow Am. Coll. Surg.; mem. Am. Gynecol. Soc., A.A.A.S., N.E. Obstet. and Gynecol. Soc., Obstet. Soc. of Boston, N.E. Surg. Soc., Boston Surg. Soc., Phi Beta Kappa, Delta Phi, Alpha Kappa Kappa. Democrat. Quaker. Home: 853 W. University Pkway, Baltimore 10 MD‡

RUSKIN, JERROLD HAROLD, mfg. co. exec.; b. New Rochelle, N.Y., Sept. 2, 1912; s. Jacob S. and Irma (Loevin) R.; A.B., Harvard, 1933; LL.B., Yale, 1936; m. Catherine Bahr, May 11, 1946. Admitted to N.Y. bar, 1936; atty. Texas Co., 1936-46; with Am. Cyanamid Co., 1947-68, gen. mgr. indsl. chem. div., 1961-65, v.p. company, 1965-68; vice president, director Formica Corp., Cincinnati; dir. Formica Internat. Ltd., London, England. Served to lt. comdr. USNR, 1942-46. Mem. Assn., Bar City N.Y., Pulp Chems. Assn. (exec. com. 1959-61), Mfg. Chemists Assn., Soc. Plastics Industry Yale Law Sch. Assn., Society of the Chemical Industry (London). Mason. Clubs: Harvard (N.Y. and N.J.); Yale (Montclair). Editor Yale Law Rev., 1934-36. Home: Montclair NJ Died June 30, 1968.

RUSS, HUGH MCMASTER, lawyer; b. Buffalo, Jan. 2, 1900; s. Harvey Wheeler and Daisy Madeleine (Brown) R.; student Kent (Conn.) Sch., 1911-17; A.B., Lafayette Coll., 1922; LL.B., Harvard, 1925; m. Anne L. Humphreys, Mar. 26, 1927 (divorced 1939); m. 2d Lavinia Faxon, May 4, 1941 (div. 1958); children—Hugh McMaster, Jr., Margaret Askew; m. 3d, Frances L. Barrell, Mar. 17, 1961. Admitted to N.Y. bar, 1925, later practiced in Buffalo, mem. Hodgson, Russ, Andrews, Woods & Goodyear 1946-71; instr. law Millard Fillmore Coll., U. Buffalo, 1928-42, lectr. fire ins., 1935-40; v.p., dir. Truscott-Woodward Elec. Co., Inc.; sec., dir. Richard L. Wood & Co.; dir. Armstrong-Roth-Cady Co., South Buffalo Railway Company, Conemaugh & Black Lick R.R. Co., Patapsco & Back Rivers R.R. Co., Phila., Bethlehem & New Eng. R.R. Co., Steelton & Highspire Railroad Co. Mem. appellate div. 4th dept. com. on character and fitness Supreme Ct. Town bd. Town Genesee Falls, N.Y.; mem. Genesee State Park Commission. Bd. dirs. Boys Club of Buffalo, Buffalo Better Bus. Bur., Buffalo Legal Aid Soc., Inc.; exec. com., dir. Buffalo chpt. Am. Red Cross; pres. Letchworth Tourist Assn.; chmn. special gifts div., Sister Kenny Found. of Buffalo, Inc., 1947, 1948. Served as pvt. U.S.M.C., 1918-19. Fellow Am. Coll. of Trial Lawyers, Am. Bar Found. Am. Judicature Soc.; mem. Internat. Assn. Arson Investigators, Am., N.Y. State and Erie Co. (past pres.) bar assns., Buffalo Council World Affairs (exec. com., pres.), Newcomen Soc., Chi Phi. Rep. (committeeman). Episcopalian. Mason. Clubs: Lawyers (past pres.), Insurance Field (past pres.). Rotary (dir.), Saturn (dean, dir.), Midday (Buffalo). Home: Buffalo NY Died Nov. 14, 1971.

RUSS, JOHN MEGGINSON, educator; b. Mitchell, S.D., Oct. 18, 1891; s. William Cyrus and Lila Elnora (Megginson) R.; grad. Ohio Mil. Inst., Cin., 1912; student Ohio Mechanics Inst., Cin., 1913-15; B.S. in Indsl. Engring., Ohio State U., 1929, M.S., 1930; m. Virginia Grace Smith, Sept. 2, 1934. Instr. English and mathematics Ohio Mil. Inst., 1912-13; instr. engring. drawing, machine design, mathematics Ohio Mechanics Inst., 1915-23; various engring. positions Lodge & Shipley Machine Tool Co., Toledo Electric Welder Co., Cincinnati Milling Machine Co. (all Cin.), 1915-23; asst. to cons. engr., 1923; asst. prof. engring. drawing Ohio State U., 1923-30, asso. prof., 1930-35; exchange prof. Purdue U., 1932-33; guest prof. Carnegie Inst. Tech., 1933-34; vis. instr. engring. drawing U. Ia., 1935-36, asso. prof., 1936-45, prof., 1945-51, prof., head dept., from 1952. Profl. engr., Ia. Mem. Am. Soc. M.E., Am. Soc. Engring. Edn., Iowa City Engrs. Club, Am. Inst. Indsl. Engrs., Nat. Soc. Profl. Engrs., Sigma Xi, Tau Beta Pi, Pi Tau Sigma, Theta Xi. Presbyn. Mason. Author: (with F. G. Higbee) Engineering Drawing Problems, 1940. Contbr. profl. publs. Home: Iowa City IA Died July 4, 1969; buried Bellevue OH

RUSSELL, BERTRAND, EARL RUSSELL, author; b. Eng., May 18, 1872; s. John (Viscount Amberley) and Katherine (Stanley) R.; M.A., Trinity Coll., Cambridge University; m. Alys W. Smith, 1894 (div.); m. 2d, Dora Winifred Black, 1921 (div.); children—John Conrad, Katharine Jane; m. 3d, Patricia Helen Spence, 1936 (div.); 1 son, Conrad Sebastian Robert; m. 4th, Edith Finch, 1952. Began as fellow and lecturer Trinity College, Cambridge; temporary professor Harvard University, Lowell lecturer, 1914; professor philosophy, National Univ. of Peking, 1920-21; lecturer, U. of Chicago, 1938; professor philosophy, University of California at Los Angeles, 1939. Awarded Nicholas Murray Butler medal, 1915; Sylvester medal of Royal Society, England, 1934; received Order of Merit, 1949; recipient of the Nobel Prize for literature, 1950. Fellow Royal Society; fellow Trinity College. Author Proposed Roads to Freedom, 1918; Introduction to Mathematical Philosophy, 1919; The Analysis of Mind, 1921; The ABC of Atoms, 1923; The ABC of Relativity, 1925; Philosophy, 1927; Sceptical Essays, 1928; Marriage and

Morals, 1929; Mysticism and Logic, 1918; Our Knowledge of the External World as a Field for Scientific Method in Philosophy, 1915; Principia Mathematica (with Dr. A. N. Whitehead), 1910-13; The Conquest of Happiness, 1930; The Scientific Outlook, 1931; Education and the Good Life, 1926; Education and the Social Order, 1932; In Praise of Idleness, 1935; Which Way to Peace?, 1936; The Amberley Papers (with Patricia Russell), 1937; Power, 1938; An Inquiry Into Meaning and Truth, 1940; A History of Western Philosophy, 1946; Human Knowledge, its Scope and Limits, 1948; Authority and the Individual, 1949; Unpopular Essays, 1950; New Hopes for a Changing World, 1951; The Impact of Science on Society, 1952; Satan in the Suburbs, 1953; Nightmares on Eminent Persons, 1954; Human Society in Ethics and Politics, 1954; Portraits from Memory, 1956; Why I Am Not A Christian, 1957; Common Sense and Nuclear Warfare, 1958; Wisdom of the West, 1959; My Philosophical Development, 1959; Fact and Fiction, 1961; Has Man a Future?, 1961; Unarmed Victory, 1963; Autobiography, Vol. I, 1967; Vol. II, 1968; War Crimes in Vietnam, 1967. Home: Merioneth Wales Died Feb. 2, 1970.

RUSSELL, EDWARD HUTSON, educator; b. Petersburg, Va., Nov. 26, 1869; s. Warren and Susan (Vincent) R.; grad. Va. Mil. Inst., 1891; course in law, Richmond (Va.) Coll.; m. Lillian Watson Whitehead, of Farmville, Va., Sept. 12, 1895. Prin. schs., Pulaski, Va., 1892-4; commandant Fishburne Mil. Sch., Waynesboro, Va., 1894-6; prin. pvt. sch., Glade Spring, Va., 1896-7; supt. pub. schs., Bristol, Va., 1897-05; mem. and sec. State Bd. Sch. Examiners, eastern section of Va., 1905-10; president State Normal School for Women, Fredericksburg, Va., Aug. 1, 1910—. President Va. State Teachers' Assn., 1914; member N.E.A., Southern Ednl. Assn., Nat. Soc. Promotion Industrial Edn., Kappa Alpha, etc. Mason (K.T.). Address: Fredericksburg VA‡

RUSSELL, FARIS R., banking co. exec.; b. Franklin, Tenn., Feb. 6, 1883; s. Rev. George Alexander and Felicia (Putnam) R.; grad. Gainesville, Tex., high sch., 1899; m. Mary Clayton Martin, Dec. 7, 1909. With Ralli Bros. of London, cotton buying agency, Gainesville, Tex., 1899; office man and cotton buyer Western Cotton Co., Oklahoma City, 1900-01; messenger Western Nat. Bank of City of New York, 1901; served in various other minor capacities until 1903; with Nat. Bank of Commerce in New York, 1903-28, as loan clk., 1904-07, asst. cashier, 1907-15, cashier, 1915-18, v.p., 1918-28; gen. partner White, Weld & Co., 1928-40; chairman executive committee, chmn. bd. Ward Baking Co. 1941-57. Mayor Mill Neck, L.I., N.Y., 1929-34. Clubs: Piping Rock Country; Creek. Home: Locust Valley NY Died Sept. 9, 1969.

RUSSELL, FRANCIS WAYLAND, clergyman; b. Fairport, N.Y., Sept. 21, 1865; s. Byron P. and Betsy (Pitman) R.; B.Sc., U. of Neb., 1890; grad. McCormick Theol. Sem., 1894; D.D., Coe Coll., 1903; m. Lucile Cross, Oct. 1897 (died Sept. 6, 1940); m. 2d, Margaret H. Kirton, 1941. Ordained Presbyn. ministry, 1894; Fairbury, 1894-97, Marshalltown, Ia., 1897-1903, Boulder, Colo., 1903-04, West Presbyn. Ch., St. Louis, 1904-19, St. John's Ch., Berkeley, Calif., 1919-23; pres. Mt. Hermon (Calif.) Assn., Inc. Moderator Synod of Mo., 1915; chmn. foreign missions work for Mo. and Calif. Mem. Loyal Legion, S.A.R., Sigma Chi, Pi Gamma Mu. V.p. Magna Charta Day Assn. Kiwanian. Home: 1133 Hamilton Av., Palo Alto CA‡

RUSSELL, FRANK F., bus. exec.; b. Grand Mere, P.Q., Can., Aug. 9, 1904; s. Frank Henry and Marietta (Ford) R.; ed. Milton Acad.; B.A., Yale, 1926; m. Alice Russell; 1 stepdau., Louise Masri. Salesman, Guaranty Co. of New York, 1928; employed by Nat. Aviation Corp., 1928, v.p., 1929, sec., 1932, dir., 1937, pres., 1939, chmn. exec. com., 1954—; past chmn., dir. Cerro Corp., N.Y.C.; dir. Chase Manhattan Bank, Otis Elevator Co., Nat. Aviation Corporation, Worthington Corp. Mem. Am. Inst. Mechanical Engineers, Pan Am. Soc. U.S., Peruvian Am. Assn. Clubs: Yale, Downtown Association, Canadian (New York City); Metropolitan (Washington); Nacional (Lima, Peru). Home: Newtown PA Died Mar. 1969.

RUSSELL, FRANK MARION, bus. consultant; b. Lohrville, Ia., June 23, 1895; s. Fred and Amanda (Moore) R.; student Ia. State Coll., Ames, 1915-19; m. Phebe Gale, Sept. 15, 1940; children—Gale, Morgan Niles. Spl. asst. to asst. sec. U.S. Dept. Agr., 1922-23, asst. to sec. agr., 1924-29; v.p. NBC, 1929-58; bus. cons., 1958-72. Served as sgt. U.S. Army, World War I. Mem. Phi Delta Theta, Sigma Delta Chi. Clubs: Nat. Press, Metropolitan (Washington). Home: Chevy Chase MD Died Nov. 11, 1972.

RUSSELL, H(ARRY) EARLE, fgn. service officer; b. Kalamazoo, Mich., Sept. 16, 1889; s. Charles Fremont and Edna Ella (Pratt) R.; A.B., U. of Mich., 1913, J.D., 1915; m. Josephine D. Lewis, July 2, 1919; 1 son, Harry Earle. Vice consul at Saloniki, Greece, 1916-19, Smyrna, Turkey, 1919-21, Rome, Italy, 1921-22; consul at Rome, 1922-24, Casablanca, Morocco, 1924-30, Alexandria, Egypt, 1930-34; consul gen., Alexandria, 1934-36; consul gen. Johannesburg, South Africa and 1st sec. of Am. Legation, Pretoria, 1936-41; consul gen., Casablanca, 1941-44, Capetown, South Africa, 1944-46, Sydney, Australia, 1946; counselor, Am. Embassy, Canberra, Australia, 1946-47; fgn. service officer, attached to staff of U.S. polit. adviser to Supreme Comdr. Allied Forces, Tokyo, Japan, 1947-48; consul gen., Toronto, Ont., Can., 1948-50. Decorated Comdr. Order of Oudom Alouite by Sultan of Morocco, 1930; Medal of Freedom, 1947. Mem. Diplomatic and Fgn. Officers Ret. (past treas.). Home: Takoma Park MD Died Nov. 3, 1971; buried Rock Creek Cemetery Washington DC

RUSSELL, HARRY LUMAN, research; b. Poynette, Wis., Mar. 12, 1866; s. E. Fred (M.D.) and Lucinda Estella (Waldron) R.; B.S., U. of Wis., 1888, M.S., 1890; post-grad. studies U. of Berlin, Pasteur Inst., Paris, Zool. Sta., Naples; Ph.D., Johns Hopkins U., 1892; hon. Sc.D., U. of Wis., 1934; m. H. May Delany, Dec. 20, 1893 (dec.); children—Gertrude E. (dec.), Eldon Babcock; m. 2d, Susanna Cocroft Headington, July 27, 1932 (dec.). Assistant prof. bacteriology, 1893-97, prof., 1897-1907, dean College Agriculture, director Experimental Station, 1907-31, U. of Wisconsin; dir. Wis. Alumni Research Foundation since 1931. Dir. Wis. State Hygiene Lab., 1903-08; pres. advisory board Wis. Tuberculosis Sanatorium; mem. Wis. com. U.S. War Finance Corp.; apptd. mem. staff U.S. Food Adminstrn., Jan. 1918; mem. agrl. advisory com. Am. Bankers Assn., 1922-40; rep. Internat. Edn. Bd. in making survey of ednl. instns. of Far East, 1925-26 (leave of absence from coll.). Republican. Author: Outlines of Dairy Bacteriology, 1894-1905; Agricultural Bacteriology, 1898; Public Water Supplies (with Prof. F. E. Turneaure), 1939; Experimental Dairy Bacteriology (with Prof. E. G. Hastings), 1909; Agricultural Bacteriology (with same), 1921; Dairy Bacteriology (with same), 1919; also reports and bulls. Wis. Expt. Sta., 1893-1930. Home: 1 Langdon St., Madison WI‡

RUSSELL, HELEN GERTRUDE, educator; b. Gorham, Me., Sept. 28, 1901; d. Walter Earle and Winifred (Stone) Russell; A.B., Wellesley Coll., 1921; A.M., Columbia, 1924; Ph.D., Radcliffe Coll., 1932. Tchr. high sch., Mt. Holly, N.J., 1921-23, Horace Mann Sch. for Girls, N.Y.C., 1923-27; instr. mathematics Wellesley Coll., 1928-29, 32-36, asst. prof., 1936-45, asso. prof., 1945-51, prof., 1951-68, also Helen Day Gould prof. mathematics. Mem. Am. Math. Soc., Am. Assn. Mathematics, Assn. Tchrs. Mathematics in N.E., Sigma Xi, Phi Beta Kappa. Methodist. Home: Gorham ME Died Oct. 24, 1968; buried Gorham ME

RUSSELL, HENRY DOZIER, lawyer; b. McDonnough, Ga., Dec. 28, 1889; s. Henry McDowell and Molly (Kelley) R.; A.B., U. of Ga., 1912, B.L., 1914; m. Carolyn Crawley, Feb. 18, 1921. Admitted to Ga. bar, 1914, practiced in Macon; city atty., Macon, Ga., 1924-25. Mem. Nat. Guard 33 yrs.; active service World War I and II; comdg. gen. 30th Div., 1932-42; comdg. gen. 48th Div., 1946-52. Mem. Phi Beta Kappa. Home: Macon GA Died Dec. 31, 1972; buried Riverside Cemetery, Macon GA

RUSSELL, L(ULU) CASE, writer; b. Yankton, S.D., Apr. 3, 1876; d. Lucien William and Agnes Maria (Rounds) Case; grad. Yankton High Sch.; m. John Lowell Russell, of Yankton, Oct. 5, 1901; children—Evangeline, John Lowell. Writer of verse and short articles for mags., 1901-10; began writing for the screen, 1911, and has produced several hundred photoplays. Author: (books) Here Lies, 1914; Photoplaywrights' Primer, 1916. Now writing for mags. and radio, ghost writing autobiographies. Home: 12535 Kling St., North Hollywood CA‡

RUSSELL, MANLEY HOLLAND, coll. pres.; b. Star City, Ark., Mar. 23, 1908; s. Manley Holland and Alma (Ligon) R.; student Ark. Poly. Coll., 1927-29; B.A., Ark. A. and M. Coll., 1938; M.S., Okla. State U., 1942; LL.D., Hendrix Coll., 1965; m. Lillian Irene Croom, Aug. 2, 1930; children—Rita Lee (Mrs. Benjamin Serebrenni). Head tchr., Selma, Ark., 1929-33; prin. Tillar (Ark.) High Sch., 1933-35; supt. Tillar pub. schs., 1935-43; supt. schs., Lake Village, Ark., 1943-47, Star City, Ark., 1947-49; supt. Lake Village pub. schs., 1949-53, Crossett (Ark.) pub. schs., 1953-63; pres. Henderson State Tchrs. Coll., Arkadelphia, Ark., 1963-69; vice chmn. Educators Investment Co.; dir., vice chmn. exec. com. Educators and Profl. Life Ins. Co. Pres. Ark. Athletic Assn., 1952-54, Ark. Council Econ. Edn., 1963-65. Arkadelphia C. of C., Ark. Ednl. Assn., (pres. 1952-53), Ark. Sch. Adminstrs. Assn., Phi Delta Kappa. Democrat. Methodist. Mason, Rotarian. Home: Arkadelphia AR Died Dec. 1969.

RUSSELL, RICHARD BREVARD, senator; b. Winier, Ga., Nov. 2, 1897; s. Richard Brevard and Ina (Dillard) R.; grad. Gordon Inst., Barnesville, Ga., 1915; B.L., U. of Ga., 1918; LL.D., Mercer U., 1957, The Citadel. Engaged in law practice in Winder, Georgia, 1919; formerly county attorney, Barrow County, Ga.; mem. Georgia Ho. of Rep., 1921-31, speaker of Ho., 1927-31; elected gov. Ga. for term, 1931-33; elected to U.S. Senate, Nov. 1932, to fill vacancy; assumed duties as senator, Jan. 1933, senator 1933-71; pres. pro tem, in 91st Congress, mem. and former chmn. Senate Armed Services com.; chmn. Senate Appropriations committee, member committee Space Aeronautics Sciences, Joint Committee Atomic Engery. Mem. Mem. Presdl. commn. Investigate Assassination Pres. Kennedy. Served USNRE, 1918. Recipient Minute Man of Year in National Defense award, Reserve Officers Association, 1959. Member of the American and Georgia State bar assns., Am. Legion, Forty and Eight, Sphinx, Sigma Alpha Epsilon. Demo. Mason, Elk, Odd Fellow. Club: Burns (Atlanta). Home: Winder GA Died Jan. 1971.

RUSSELL, RICHARD JOEL, educator; b. Hayward, Cal., Nov. 16, 1895; s. Frederick James and Nellie Potter (Brennan) R.; A.B., U. Cal., 1920, Ph.D., 1926; m. Dorothy King, 1924 (dec. 1936); 1 son, Benjamin James; m. 2d, Josephine Burke, 1940; children—Robert Burke, Charles Douglas, John Walter, Thomas William. Teaching fellow U. Cal., 192-22, asso. in geography, 1923-25, Hitchcock prof., 1965; asso. prof. geology Tex. Technol. Coll., 1926-27; asso. prof. geography La. State U., Baton Rouge, 1928-29, prof. phys. geography, 1930-71, head dept., 1936-49, asst. dir. Sch. Geology, 1944-49, dean grad. sch., 1949-51, dir. Coastal Studies Inst., 1953-66; lectr. geography, summers, U. Cal., Harvard, Clark U.; collaborator Soil Conservation Service, 1935-71; geologist La. Geol. Survey, 1935-40. NSF cons. adv. govt. Indonesia, 1959-60; mem. panel of scientists adv. Ho. Reps. Com. on Sci. Astronautics, 1960-71; U.S. del. Internat. Geog. Congress, Amsterdam, 1938, Stockholm, 1960, U. Cal.; La. State U. del. to Internat. Geog. Congress, Paris, 1931, Rio de Janeiro, 1956, to Internat. Geol. Congress, Moscow, 1937, to Internat. Geol. Congress, London, 1948, Algiers, 1952; mem. coastal geomorphology commn. Internat. Geog. Union, 1952-69; council Internat. Assn. Sedimentologists, 1952-58; pres. conf. deans So. Grad. Schs., 1952; mem. U.S. Mil. Establishment Research and Devel. Bd., Com. Geophys. and Geog., 1948-56, panel on Gen. Scis., 1956-61. Served to ensign, USNRF, 1918-19. Recipient 1st W.W. atwood award for studies in phys. geography Assn. Am. Geographers, 1937. Vega medalist Royal Swedish Soc. Anthropology and Geography, 1961; USN Distinguished Pub. Service award, 1967. Fellow A.A.A.S., Am. Geog. Soc. (Cullum Geog. medal 1962), Geol. Soc. Am. (pres. 1957; chmn. S.E. div. 1970); mem. Assn. Am. Geog. (council 1937-39, pres. 1948, Outstanding Achievement award 1960), NRC (rep. 1941-41; mem. exec. com. div. geol. and geog., 1942-44, com. on high level waste disposal 1954-62, chmn. earth scis. div. 1954-55), So. Assn. Land Grant Colls and Univs. (sec. 1954-59), Am. Assn. Petroleum Geologists (Distinguished lectr. 1943), Am. Geophys. Union, Nat. Acad. Scis., Acad. Scis. Gottingen (corr.), Royal Danish Acad. Sci. and Letters (corr.), Geol. and Mineral Soc. Am. Univs. (hon.), So Belge Geol. Paleo et Hydrologie, 1948; Royal Geography Soc. Netherlands (hon.), Sigma Xi, Phi Sigma Kappa, Theta Tau (nat. pres. 1928-32), Gamma Alpha, Phi Sigma, Phi Kappa Phi. Democrat. Mason. Clubs: Faculty (La. State U., pres. 1946); Cosmos (Washington). Author: River Plains and Sea Coasts, 1967; co-author Culture Worlds. Asso. editor Geologie der. Meere and Binnengewasser (Berlin), 1939-41; Zeitschrift fur Geomorphologie, 1957-71. Contbr. numerous articles to sci. jours. Home: Baton Rouge LA Died Sept. 17, 1971.

RUSSELL, SAMUEL, JR., farmer; b. Camden, S.C., Jan. 14, 1873; s. Samuel and Lucy MacDonough (Hubbard) R.; Harvard, 1892-93; m. Julia Palmer Webster, of Brooklyn, N.Y., June 22, 1898. Began farming 1900, breeder Hereford cattle; now retired. Former Conn. state v.p. Am. Saddle Horse Breeders' Assn.; mem. Middletown Bd. of Edn. 15 yrs. Mem. Conn. Ho. of Rep. 5 terms; mem. Governor Holcomb's staff 6 yrs., rank of maj. Republican. Home: Camden SC‡

RUSSELL, WILLIAM LOGIE, psychiatrist; b. New Brunswick, Can., July 24, 1863; s. William and Jane (Logie) R.; student U. of N.B., 1879-81; M.D., Univ. Med., Coll. (New York U.), 1885; m. Addie Lena Lewis, Feb. 15, 1888. Hosp. work, N.J., 1885-87; pvt. practice, N.Y. City, 1888-97; 1st asst. physician Willard State Hosp., N.Y., 1897-1903; med. insp. N.Y. State Hosp. Commn., 1903-10; med. supt. L.I. State Hosp., 1910-11; med. dir. Bloomingdale Hosp., 1911-26; psychiatric dir. Soc. New York Hosp., 1926-36; cons. psychiatrist New York Hospital and Grasslands Hospital; emeritus professor psychiatry, Cornell Univ. Medical Sch. Mem. A.M.A., Am. Psychiatric Assn. (ex-pres.), Nat. Com. for Mental Hygiene (v.p.), N.Y. Psychiatric Soc. (ex-pres.), New York Soc. Clin. Psychiatry, Med. Soc. State of N.Y., Westchester County Med. Soc. (ex-pres.), Assn. for Research Nervous and Mental Diseases, New York Acad. Medicine, A.A.A.S. Republican. Episcopalian. Club: Nat. Arts (New York). Home: Heathcote Inn, Scarsdale, N.Y. Office: 515 E. 68th St., New York NY‡

RUSSUM, SARAH ELIZABETH, state supt. schs.; b. Carthage, Mo., July 27, 1877; d. Isaac Fisher and Sarah Amanda (Caldwell) R.; B.E., Southwest Mo. Teachers Coll., Springfield, Mo., 1909; student U. of Wash.; B.S. U. of Ida., 1922; student Sch. of Edn., U. of Chicago.

Began as teacher pub. schs. at Carthage, Mo., 1896; settled in Ida.; formerly state supt. public instrn., Ida.; state dir. elementary edn., Wash. Mem. N.E.A., A.A.A.S., Pi Lambda Theta. Republican. Conglist. Clubs: College Women's, Business and Professional Women's. Home: 1103 Maxwell St., Spokane WA*‡

RUTH, JOHN A., lawyer; b. Dover, Okla., May 21, 1918; s. August Herman and Myrtle (Spindle) R.; B.A., Okla. State U., 1939; LL.B., U. Okla., 1941; m. Murrow E. Hilbish, Aug. 12, 1942; children—John Alan H., Deborah, Margaret. Admitted to Okla. bar, 1941; practiced in Hennessey, 1941-42, 46-47, Kingfisher, 1947-72; partner firm Reilly & Ruth, 1947-54, Ruth & Beall, 1966-72; spl. Justice Okla. Supreme Ct., 1968. Founder, dir., gen. counsel Kingfisher Bank & Trust Co. Chmn. Kingfisher County chpt. A.R.C., 1956-58, Kingfisher County March of Dimes, 1953-54; pres. Kingfisher Pub. Schs. Bd. Edn.; 1st v.p. Okla. Assn. Christian Chs.; founder, sec., bd. dirs., gen. counsel Kingfisher County Devel. Found. Chmn. Kingfisher County Republican Com., 1954-56. Served with AUS, 1942-46. Named Nat. Father of Year and Okla. Father of Year, Am. Nat. CowBelles, 1958. Mem. Am., Okla. (past sect. chmn.), Kingfisher County (past pres.) bar assns., Xi Mu. Mem. Christian Ch. (elder). Mason, Rotarian. Home: Kingfisher OK Died Nov. 27, 1972.

RUTH, JOHN P(ILLING), business exec.; b. Wilmington, Del., May 3, 1895; s. William and Louisa (Arrants) R.; B.S., Drexel Tech., Phila., 1926; B. A., Purdue U., 1938; m. Edna V. Wyman, May 6, 1916; 1 dau., Evelyn C. (Mrs. David White). Vice pres. and dir., The Glidden Co., Cleveland, 1947-71; dir. Zinc Chem. Co. Treas., City Newport, Del., 1922-23. Mem. Lead Industries Assn. (dir.). Mason (past master; R.A.M., past high priest; K.T.). Home: Shaker Heights OH Died Feb. 27, 1971.

RUTHERFORD, MARGARET, actress; b. London, Eng., May 11, 1892; d. William Rutherford and Florence (Nicholson) Benn; m. J. B. Stringer Davis, Mar. 26, 1945. First stage appearance Old Vic, 1925; appeared numerous plays West End theatres, 1933-72; performed Importance of Being Ernest, Dublin, 1957; on tour Australia for Elizabethan Theatre, in Time Remembered, also Happiest Days of Your Life, 1957-58; performed in Farewell, Farewell, Eugene, Garrick Theatre, London, N.Y.C., 1959-60; appeared Manoel Theatre, Malta, 1961, Haymarket Theatre, 1962, 67, The Saville Theatre, London, 1965; appeared in numerous pictures, the latest being V.I.P., Murder at the Gallop, On the Double, Murder She Said, Chimes at Midnight, Murder Ahoy, The Countess from Hong Kong, Arabella, 1967; TV productions, including Day After Tomorrow, Two Wise Virgins from Hove, 1961; TV in The Kidnapping of Mary Smith, 1963; poetry readings various theatres London, Malta, Croydon, Stratford-on-Avon, Coventry Cathedral, Royal Festival Hall. Decorated Order Brit. Empire, 1961; Medal Ingenio et Arte, King of Denmark; recipient Acad. award for best supporting actress of 1963 for The V.I.P.'s; named best supporting actress Fgn. Press Assn. Mem. English-Speaking Union. Home: Chalfont St Peter England Died May 22, 1972.

RUTHVEN, ALEXANDER G(RANT), univ. pres.; b. Hull, Ia., Apr. 1, 1882; s. John and Katherine (Rombough) R.; B.S., Morningside Coll., 1903; U. of Chicago, summer quarter, 1902; Ph.D., U. of Mich., 1906; Sc.D., Kalamazoo Coll., 1931, Mich. Coll. of Mining and Technology, 1937; LL.D., Albion Coll., 1930, Northwestern U., 1930, Morningside Coll., 1931, Denison U., 1933, Tulane U., 1938, U. of Calif., 1938, U. of N.M., 1944, Wayne U., 1950; Dr. Honoris Causa, Catholic University of Chile, 1944; m. Florence Hagle, September, 1907; children—Katherine Lenora, Alexander Peter, Bryant Walker. With Univ. of Michigan since 1906; successively instr. zoology and curator Museum of Zoology, 1906-11, asst. prof. and curator Museum of Zoology, 1911-13, asst. prof. and dir. Museum of Zoology, 1913-15, prof. and dir. Museum of Zoology, 1915-29, dir. univ. museums, 1922-36, chmn. dept. of zoology and dir. Zool. Labs., 1927-29, dean adminstrn., 1928-29, pres., 1929-51, emeritus since 1951. Chief field naturalist, Mich. Geol., Biol. Survey, 1908-12. Dir. various sci. expeditions, in North, South and Central America. Awarded Blue Grand Cordon of the Order of the Brilliant Jade, 1938. Fellow A.A.A.S., Am. Acad. Arts and Sciences; mem. Am. Soc. Zoologists, Am. Soc. Naturalists, Mich. Acad. Science, Arts and Letters (pres. 1913-15), Am. Philos. Soc., Am. Soc. Ichthyologists and Herpetologists, Assn. Am. Geographers, Phi Sigma, Gamma Alpha, Sigma Xi, Phi Beta Kappa, Phi Kappa Phi; corr. mem. London Zool. Soc. Author of numerous papers on zool. subjects. Home: Ann Arbor MI Died Jan. 18, 1971; buried Ann Arbor MI

RYAN, ARTHUR, newspaperman; b. Hadley, Mass., Nov. 28, 1884; s. Patrick and Catherine (Reilly) R.; grad. Williston Acad., 1904; Litt.B., Princeton, 1908; L.H.D. (honorary), Mt. Holyoke Coll., 1961; m. Mary E. O'Connell, Oct. 3, 1911; children—James A., Elizabeth, Catherine (Mrs. Leonard Wasselle), Mary. Staff Holyoke (Mass.) Transcript-Telegram, 1908-61, successively reporter, city editor, bus. mgr., mng. editor,

1930-56, editor, 1957-61; treas. Holyoke Transcript Pub. Co., Valley Photo Engraving Co., WHYN Radio-TV Corp., Trustee, v.p. Holyoke Pub. Library. Mass. mem. adv. com. press censhorship, World War II. Mem. Izaak Walton League (pres. Mass. br.), Holyoke C. of C. (dir.), New Eng. Soc. Newspaper Editors. Republican. Roman Catholic. Author articles on outdoor life, Arbitrator labor disputes. Home: South Hadley MA Died Apr. 26, 1972.

RYAN, CORNELIUS EDWARD, army officer; b. Boston, May 12, 1896; s. Thomas Joseph and Julia Elizabeth (Driscoll) R.; B.S., U. Conn., 1918; student Mass. Inst. Tech., 1924-25; grad. French Tank Sch., Versailles, France, 1928; grad. Command and Gen. Staff Coll., Ft. Leavenworth, Kan., 1939; m. Inez Marie Brown, May 18, 1931; children—Walter Joseph, Edward Francis, Elizabeth Anne. Commd. 2d lt. U.S. Army, 1917, advanced through grades to maj. gen., 1952; with AEF, World War I; assigned European campaigns, World War II; comdr. U.S. garrison, Berlin, Germany, 1946-47; rep. U.S. to Berlin Allied Kommandatura; comdr. Camp Breckinridge, Ky., 1949-51, Pa. Mil. Dist., 1949-50, Ft. Dix, N.J., 1953-55; comdg. gen. 101st Airborne div., 9th Inf. Div., then 69th Inf. Div.; chief Korean Mil. Adv. Group, 1951-53; chief Mil. Assistance Adv. Group to France, 1956, 57; exec. vice chmn. President's Com. on Govt. Contracts, 1957; now dir. multilateral finance div. U.S. Mission to NATO, also U.S. rep. infrastructure com. NATO. Recipient D.S.M. with oak leaf cluster, Legion of Merit, Bronze Star medal (U.S.); Order of Leopold II, Croix de Guerre with palm (Belgium); Mil. Cross (Czechoslovakia); Legion of Honor, Croix de Guerre with palm (France); Ulchi Distinguished Mil. Service medal with gold star, Presidential Unit citation, Taekuk Distinguished Mil. Service medal with silver star (Korea); Order of Merit of Adolphe de Nassau (Luxembourg); Order Orange Nassau (Netherlands); Commemorative Cross (Poland); Comdr. Brit. Empire. Mem. Am. Legion, Mil. Order World Wars, Phi Kappa Tau, Eta Lambda Sigma, Phi Phi. Roman Catholic. Home: Paris France Died 1972.

RYAN, JOHN WILLIAM, telephone co. exec.; b. Newton, Mass., June 3, 1919; s. George B. and Mary (Dinegan) R.; B.A., U. N.C., 1941; grad. Advanced Mgmt. Program, Harvard, 1961; m. Helen Perot Walker, Feb. 23, 1952; children—Elizabeth Perot, John Walker, Mary Webb, Nancy Morris. With New Eng. Telephone Co., 1946-56, Am. Tel. & Tel. Co., 1956-58; asst. comptroller, then gen. accounting mgr. Bell Telephone Co. Pa., 1958-59; asst. comptroller Am. Tel. & Tel. Co., 1959; with Northwestern Bell Telephone Co., 1959-70, v.p., gen. mgr. Neb. area, 1963-64, v.p. pub. relations, 1964-70. Mem. Central Omaha Study Com., 1962-70; dir. devel. Econ. Devel. Council Omaha, 1965-70; trustee Omaha Indsl. Found., 1963-70; adv. com. econ. edn. Omaha pub. schs., 1963-70. Bd. govs., mem. pub. relations com. Boys Clubs Omaha, 1963-70; adv. bd. Duchesne Coll., 1963-70; devel. bd. Duchesne Acad., 1963-70, also mem. exec. com., chmn. finance and scholarship com.; trustee, mem. exec. and membership coms. Neb. Council Econ. Edn., 1964-70; bd. dirs., v.p. Omaha Civic Music Assn., 1962-70; bd. dirs. Omaha Civic Opera Assn., 1960-70, Omaha United Community Services, 1963-70, Omaha Sister City Assn., 1964-70; adv. council nursing Creighton Meml. St. Joseph's Hosp., Omaha, 1964-70. Served with British Am. Ambulance Corps, 1941; to lt. USNR, 1941-46; ETO, PTO. Mem. Omaha C. of C. (bd. dirs., v.p., mem. exec. com.). Clubs: Omaha, Omaha Country; St. Anthony (N.Y.C.). Home: Omaha NE Died Aug. 18, 1970.

RYAN, PATRICK L., clergyman; b. Limerick, Ireland, Apr. 29, 1876; s. Thomas and Mary Creagh R.; ed. St. Patrick's Coll., Carlow, and St. Paul's Seminary, St. Paul, Minn. Came to U.S., 1898, naturalized citizen, 1915. Ordained priest R.C. Ch., 1899; apptd. curate Holy Cross Ch., San Francisco, Calif., 1899; gen. dir. Affiliated Cath. Charities, 1911-16; pastor St. Edward's Ch., San Francisco, 1916; vicar gen. Archdiocese of San Francisco, 1917; pastor Star of the Sea Ch., San Francisco, 1920. Home: 4420 Geary St., San Francisco*‡

RYAN, ROBERT, actor; b. Chgo., Nov. 11, 1913; s. Timothy A. and Mabel (Bushnell) R.; A.B., Dartmouth, 1932; m. Jessica Cadwalader, Mar. 11, 1939; children—Timothy, Cheyney, Lisa. Theatrical appearances include Clash by Night, N.Y.C., 1941, Coriolanus, N.Y.C., 1955, Anthony and Cleopatra, 1960, Mr. President, 1962; motion pictures include Set-Up, 1948 (Cannes award 1948), Crossfire, 1949, Bad Day at Black Rock, 1955, About Mrs. Leslie, 1956, Clash by Night, 1951, Men in War, 1957, God's Little Acre, 1958, Ice Palace, 1959, King of Kings, 1960, Billy Budd, The Longest Day, 1962, The Professionals, 1966; TV spls. include The Great Gatsby, 1958, The Snows of Kilimanjaro, 1960. Pres. theatre group U. Cal. at Los Angeles, 1959-73; dir. Westwood Internat. Center, 1950-73; co-chmn. Hollywood br. Nat. Com. Sane Nuclear Policy, 1959-73. Pres. Oakwood Sch., N. Hollywood, 1950-73. Served with USMCR, 1942-45. Mem. Motion Picture Acad. Arts and Scis., Psi Upsilon. Home: New York City NY Died July 11, 1973.

RYAN, WILL CARSON, educator; b. New York, N.Y., Mar. 4, 1885; s. Will Carson and Sarah Anne (Hobby) R.; A.B., Harvard, 1907; studied Columbia, 1907-10; Ph.D., George Washington U., 1918, LL.D., 1932; m. Isabel Van Dewater, June 20, 1908; children—Carson Van Dewater, Carl Schurz, Isabel Edith, John Walker, Flora Ruby, Chester Maupin. Inst. French and German, high sch., 1909-10; Carl Schurz fellow, Columbia, 1910-11; instr. in German, U. of Wis., 1911-12; asst. editor, 1912-14, editor, 1915-17; dir. information service, U.S. Bur. Edn., 1917-20; ednl. editor N.Y. Evening Post, 1920-21; prof. of edn., Swarthmore Coll., 1921-30; dir. of edn., U.S. Indian Service, 1930-34, dir. planning and research, 1934-35; mem. ednl. staff Commonwealth Fund, 1935-36; staff asso. Carnegie Foundation for the Advancement of Teaching, 1936-40; Kenan prof. of edn., U. of North Carolina, 1940-68; cons. U.S. Dept. Health, Edn. and Welfare, 1950-68; secretary British Educational Mission to U.S., 1918; asso. editor School and Soc., 1921-27; editor Progressive Edn., 1939-40, High Sch. Journal, 1940-51, Understanding the Child, 1942-57. Child welfare consultant, United Service to China, 1945-47, sch. mental health cons., World Fed. Mental Health, 1958; Fulbright programs officer U.S. Department of State, Europe and Near East, 1949-50. Educational surveys, Saskatchewan, 1918. Santo Domingo, 1924, Porto Rico, 1925, Friends' Schs., 1924-27, Indian Schools, 1927, Virgin Islands, 1928; Methodist Secondary Schools, 1930; child welfare in China, 1945-46. Mem. N.E.A., National Vocational Guidance Assn. (pres. 1926-27), Progressive Edn. Assn. (pres. 1937-39), Child Study Assn. of America, Am. Pub. Health Assn., American Assn. Advancement Scis., Nat. Congress Parents and Tchrs. (chmn. mental health 1955-58), Phi Beta Kappa Assos., New Edn. Fellowship, Phi Beta Kappa, Phi Delta Kappa. Clubs: Cosmos (Washington); Harvard (New York). Author: The Literature of American School and College Athletics; Mental Health Through Education; Studies in Graduate Education; Essentials of Educational Psychology; also bulls. pub. by U.S. Bur. Edn. Home: Chapel Hill NC Died May 28, 1968.

RYAN, WILLIAM FITTS, congressman; b. Albion, N.Y., June 28, 1922; s. Bernard and Harriet (Fitts) R.; A.B., Princeton, 1944; LL.B., Columbia, 1949; m. Priscilla Marbury; children—William, Priscilla, Virginia, Catherine. Admitted to N.Y. State bar, 1949; asso. firm Hatch, Wolfe, Nash & Teneyck, N.Y.C., 1949-50; asst. dist. atty. N.Y. County, 1950-57; mem. 87th-92d congresses from 20th Dist. N.Y. Pres., N.Y. Young Democrats Club, 1955-56; founding mem. Riverside Dems., Inc., N.Y. Reform Dem. Movement; Democratic leader 7th Assembly Dist., N.Y. County, 1957-61; Reform Dem. candidate for mayor of N.Y.C., 1965; del. Dem. Nat. Conv., 1968. Served to 1st lt. F.A., AUS, World War II; PTO. Home: New York City NY Died Sept. 17, 1972; buried St. Thomas Ch., Croom MD

RYDER, OSCAR BAXTER, economist; b. Pamlico County, N.C., Feb. 9, 1885; s. Oliver and Martha Allison (Russell) R.; A.B., U. of Richmond, Va., 1908, A.M., 1909; A.M., Harvard U., 1915, grad. student, 1914-17; m. Gilby Nanine Kelly, Nov. 30, 1918. Prin. pub. high sch., Sussex County, Va., 1909; instr. in English, John Marshall High Sch., Richmond, 1911-14; asst. in econ. history, Harvard, 1915-17; asst. prof. economics, U. of Louisville, Ky., 1918; mem. staff planning and statistics, U.S. Shipping Bd., 1918; mem. staff price sect., War Industries Bd., 1918-19; economist U.S. Tariff Commn., 1919-33; asst. chief economics div. and mem. planning com. of U.S. Tariff Commn., 1933; chief imports div. NRA and rep. of NRA on exec. com. for coordination of commerical policies, 1933-34; commr. U.S. Tariff Commn., 1934-55 (vice-chmn. 1939-42; chmn. com. for reciprocity information, 1939-42; chmn. of Tariff Commn. 1942-53), ret., 1955; writer and cons. internat. trade policies and problems. Mem. Joint Com. of League of Nations on Clearing Agreements, 1934-35. Mem. Trade Agreements Com., 1934-47; del. Conf. on Trade and Employment, Havana, 1947-48. Mem. Am. Econ. Assn., Phi Beta Kappa. Author: Broad Silk Manufacture and the Tariff, 1925; various mag. articles. Clubs: Cosmos, Harvard (Washington). Home: Alexandria VA Died Sept. 21, 1972.

RYERSON, EDWARD LARNED, b. Chgo., Dec. 3, 1886; s. Edward Larned and Mary (Mitchell) R.; Ph.B., Yale, 1908, M.A. (hon.), 1932, LL.D. (hon.), 1962; student Mass. Inst. Tech., 1909; LL.D., Kenyon Coll., 1947, Williams Coll., 1952, U. Chgo., 1956; D.C.L., Ripon Coll., 1948; m. Nora Butler, Oct. 6, 1914 (dec. Dec. 1971); children—Nora (Mrs. George A. Ranney), Edward, Morton (killed in action USAAF 1944). Formerly chmn., then hon. dir. Inland Steel Co., Joseph T. Ryerson & Son, Inc. Hon. v.p. Am. Iron and Steel Inst., mem. bd., 1939-53, chmn. com. pub. relations, 1946-53. Chief delegation U.S. steel and iron ore mining reps. to USSR, 1958; lectr. Fulbright exchange program Australian univs., 1958. Hon. chmn. Chgo. Ednl. TV Assn., founding chmn., 1953, pres., 1953-67; pres. emeritus Hosp. Planning Council Met. Chgo., 1962; chmn. Ill. Pub. Aid Commn., 1932-33, 41-48; pres. Community Fund Chgo., 1931-38, 42-44, Chgo. Commons, 1941-45, Community Chests and Councils,

Inc., 1947-50. Bd. dirs. Council on Foundations, Inc., pres., 1949-62; bd. dirs. Epsicopal Ch. Found., 1949-70; dir. John Crerar Library, 1933-64, pres., 1953-54; trustee Orch. Assn. Chgo., 1930-57, pres., 1938-52, hon. trustee, 1957-71; trustee U. Chgo., 1923-56, chmn. trustees, 1953-56, life trustee, 1956-71; trustee Chgo. Community Trust, 1931-58, Chmn. exec. com., 1944-56; trustee Carnegie Endowment Internat. Peace, 1933, hon., 1956; fellow Yale Corp., 1932-44. Recipient numerous medals and awards, including Elbert H. Gary Meml. award Am. Iron and Steel Inst., 1951, Centennial award Northwestern U., 1951, Emmy award Acad. TV Arts and Scis., 1962, Damen award Loyola University, Chicago, Ill., 1963; Alexis de Tocqueville service award Welfare Council of Metropolitan Chicago, 1965. Republican. Episcopalian. Clubs: Attic, Chicago, Commerical, Mid-America, Old Elm, Union League, Cliff Dwellers (Chgo.); Yale (N.Y.C.). Home: Chicago IL Died Aug. 2, 1971.

RYERSON, WILLIAM NEWTON, engineer; b. in New York, Dec. 7, 1874; s. William Tunis and Julia H. (Newton) R.; E.E., Sch. of Mines (Columbia), 1896; m. Martha Taft, of Brooklyn, Oct. 31, 1900. With operating dept., Met. St. Ry. Co., New York, 4 yrs., Manhattan Ry. Co., 4 yrs., Interborough Rapid Transit Co., 1 yr.; supt. Ont. Power Co., Niagara Falls, Ont., 1905-9; gen. mgr., and chief engineer, Great Northern Power Co., Duluth, 1909-22; pub. utilities management dept. Day & Zimmermann, Inc., Phila., Aug. 1, 1922—. Fellow Am. Inst. E.E.; mem. Am. Soc. M.E., Engring. Institute of Can., Nat. Elec. Light Assn., Delta Kappa Epsilon. Episcopalian. Club: Engineers. Contbr. to engring. socs. Home: 255 W. Tulpehocken St. Office: 1600 Walnut St., Philadelphia PA‡

RYON, HARRISON, lawyer; born New Hampton, Ia., Feb. 14, 1892; s. John A. and Mary Emily (Fitch) R.; student Beloit (Wis.) Coll., 1911-13; A.B., Leland Stanford, Jr., U., 1915; J.D. cum laude, U. of Chicago, 1917; m. Elizabeth Edwards, June 22, 1917 (divorced June 9, 1925); 1 dau., Patricia (Mrs. Eugene F. Foubert); m. 2d, Hazel Cowan, June 24, 1926. Consulting engr. in indsl., personnel and labor relations as associate, later partner, The Scott Co., Phila., 1919-20; mng. indsl. relations, Chicago and South Bend factories, Wilson Bros., Chicago, 1920-22; admitted to Calif. bar, 1922; Nev. bar, 1930; mem. Schauer, Ryon & McIntyre, Santa Barbara, 1922-70; specializes trial practice, trust, probate law. Attended 2d O.T.C., Fort Sheridan, Ill., and commd. 2d lt. Inf., 1917; attached to 86th Div. staff; later with Adj. General's Dept., Newark, N.J.; assigned to standardizing trade tests for Army; capt. Adj. General's Reserve Corps to 1934. Pres. Santa Barbara County Bar Assn., 1934-35; vice chmn. Cal. State Bar Conf. of Bar Assn. Dels., 1936-37, chmn. 1937-38. Fellow Am. Coll. Probate Counsel; mem. Assn. Bar City of N.Y., State Bar of Cal. (mem. legislative com., 1938-39, chmn., 1939-41; member board of governors, 1939-42; vice president, 1940-42); mem. Am. Bar Assn., Am. Law Inst. (Calif. rep., 1940, 42, 45), State Bar of Calif., Nev. State Bar, Sigma Chi. Active in establishment of Pub. Relations Dept., Calif. State Bar; chmn. nat. defense and pub. relations com., same 1941, 42; war service commn. same, 1945; pres. Santa Barbara Museum of Art, 1945-49, first vice president, 1950. Republican. Presbyn. Clubs: Montecito Country, University (Santa Barbara.) Home: Santa Barbara CA Died Dec. 22, 1970; buried Santa Barbara Cemetery.

RYUS, CELESTE NELLIS, pianist; b. Ft. Hays, Kan., Feb. 7, 1877; d. De Witt C. and Emma Virginia (McAfee) Nellis; ed. pub. schs., Ft. Hays and Topeka, Kan., and 2 yrs. at Topeka High Sch.; grad. in music at Topeka, Kan., 1892, at Chicago Conservatory of Music, 1895; taught there 2 terms till June, 1897; grad. Royal Hochschule of Music, Berlin, 1899, under Prof. Barth; studied repertoire with Moszkowski, Paris, 1900; m. Capt. Harmon David Ryus, June 2, 1906. Appeared in concerts at Chicago Expn., 1893, Paris Expn., 1900, receiving medals and diplomas; has made concert tours in Europe and America. Lutheran. Address: 703 Valencia St., Los Angeles CA‡

SAALFIELD, ADA LOUISE (ADA LOUISE SUTTON), author; b. Brooklyn; d. George D. and Amanda Elizabeth (Adams) Sutton; direct descendant of John Quincy Adams and Sir John Sutton, Essex, England, 1336; graduate of Hunter College, New York; m. Arthur James Saalfield, August 1, 1885; children—Albert George, Arthur James, Mrs. Edith Maud Laird, Robert Sutton, Mrs. Alice Consuelo Handy. Author: Drummond Year Book; Mr. Bunny, His Book, 1902; Seeds of April's Sowing, 1902; Sweeter Still Than This, 1905; Teddy Bears, 1906; Baby Dear, 1907; Little Maid in Toyland, 1908; Peter Rabbit Series; Friendship Series, 1908; Billy Possum; Blossom Babies; Cycle of Gems; Mushroom Fairies. Mem. Authors' League America, Portage Country, Woman's City Club, Federation of Women's Clubs (Akron), Protective Animal League, Anti-Vivisection League, Humane Assn., Better Akron Federation, Cleveland Red Cross, Akron Y.W.C.A. Home: Hotel Portage, Akron OH‡

SAARINEN, ALINE BERNSTEIN, art critic; b. N.Y.C., Mar. 25, 1914; d. Allen Milton and Irma (Lewyn) Bernstein; B.A., Vassar Coll., 1935; M.A., Inst. Fine Arts, N.Y.U., 1940; L.H.D. (honorary) University of Michigan, 1964; D.Lit. (honorary) Russell Sage College; married Joseph H. Louchheim, June 1935 (div. June 1951); children—Donald, Hal; m. 2d, Eero Saarinen, Dec. 26, 1953 (dec.); 1 son, Eames. Asst. editor Art News mag., 1945-46, mng. editor, 1947-48; asso. art editor and critic N.Y. Times, 1948-53, asso. art critic, 1954-58; correspondent NBC, 1964-72; mem. American, Revolution Bicentenary Commission, Commission Fine Arts New York State Council on Arts. Recipient award for best fgn. art criticism Venice Biennale, 1950, award for newspaper art criticism Am. Fedn. Arts, 1953. Frank Jewett Mather award, 1953; Guggenheim fellow, 1957. Mem. Internat. Assn. Art Critics, Phi Beta Kappa. Author: The Proud Possessors, 1958. Contbr. articles nat. mags. Address: New York City NY Died July 1972.

SABIN, EDWIN LEGRAND, author; b. Rockford, Ill., Dec. 23, 1870; s. Henry and Esther F. (Hotchkiss) S.; bro. of Elbridge Hosmer S. (dec.); A.B., State U. of Ia., 1892; m. Mary Caroline Nash, Oct. 7, 1896. Mem. Phi Beta Kappa, Beta Theta Pi. Author: The Making of Iowa, 1900; The Magic Mashie, 1902; Beaufort Chums, 1905; When You Were a Boy, 1905; Bar B Boys, 1909; Range and Trail, 1910; Circle K, 1911; Kit Carson Days, 1914, 35; Pluck on the Long Trail, 1912; Old Four Toes, 1912; With Carson and Freemont, 1912; Treasure Mountain, 1913; On the Plains with Custer, 1913; Scarface Ranch, 1914; Buffalo Bill and the Overland Trail, 1914; Gold Seekers of '49, 1915; With Sam Houston in Texas, 1916; The Boy Settler, 1916; Opening of the West with Lewis and Clark, 1917; The Great Pikes Peak Rush, 1917; How Are You Feeling Now?, 1917; On the Overland Stage, 1918; General Crook and the Fighting Apaches, 1918; Boys' Book of Indian Warriors, 1918; Opening the Iron Trail, 1919; Lost with Lieutenant Pike, 1919; Boys' Book of Frontier Fighters, 1919; Building the Pacific Railway, 1919; Into Mexico with General Scott, 1920; Boys' Book of Border Battles, 1920; Desert Dust, 1922; The Rose of Santa Fe, 1923; The City of the Sun, 1924; With George Washington into the Wilderness, 1924; White Indian, 1925; Rio Bravo, 1926; In the Banks of Old Hickory, 1927; Old Jim Bridger on the Moccasin Trail, 1928; Gold1929; Wild Men of the Wild West, 1929; Mississippi River Boy, 1932; Pirate Waters, 1941. Contbr. to mags. Lit. critic. Address: Hemet CA‡

SACHS, HOWARD JOSEPH, investment banker; b. New York, N.Y., Jan. 23, 1891; s. Harry and Nellie (Lorsch) S.; A.B. cum laude, Harvard U., 1911; m. Eleanor B. Saxe, Sept. 18, 1928; 1 son, Peter Griggs. Partner of the firm of Goldman, Sachs & Company, 1915-63, limited partner, 1963-69. Directors Gimbel Brothers, Inc. Dir., pres. Stamford Hospital. Clubs: Grolier, Recess, Harvard (New York City); Stanwich (Greenwich, Conn.). Home: Stamford CT Died Dec. 7, 1969.

SACHS, JAMES HENRY, entrepreneur; b. N.Y.C., Nov. 17, 1907; s. Arthur and Alice (Goldschmidt); S.; grad. Middlesex Sch., 1925; A.B., Harvard, 1929, student Bus. Sch., 1931; student Trinity Coll., Cambridge U., 1930; m. Margery Fay, Feb. 8, 1932; children—Samuel II, Cecily, Arthur Gordon, Stephen Fay. A founder Newsweek mag., 1933; editor, pub. Nashville Times, 1939-40; with OWI overseas, 1941-45; gen. mgr., dir. Young Am. Mags., Young Am. Films, 1946-47; dir. N.Y. Water Service Corp., Western N.Y. Water Corp., Rochester & Lake Ontario Water Corp., 1948-51; dir., mem. finance com. Am. Heritage Pub Corp., pubs. Am. Heritage and Horizon mags., 1954-69; co-owner David White, Inc., book pubs. Former vice chmn. Mianus River Gorge Conservation Com., function of Nature Conservancy. Mem. zoning bd. appeals, Pound Ridge, N.Y., 1948-58, planning bd., 1955-58, town supr., 1959-67; legislator Westchester County, Dist. 3, 1969-71, chmn. com. on legislation. Trustee Hiram Halle Meml. Library, Pound Ridge, 1952-56; mem. 250 assos. Harvard Bus. Sch.; an organizer Nat. Jr. Achievement. Clubs: Harvard, Players (N.Y.C.). Home: Pound Ridge NY Died Apr. 21, 1971.

SACHS, NELLY, poet, dramatist; b. 1891; ed. U. Berlin. Refugee in Sweden, 1940. Recipient Swedish Lyric prize, Jahresring Lit. prize, Annette Droste prize, Dortmund prize, Nobel prize for lit., 1966. Author: Wohnungen des Todes, 1947; Sternverdunkelung, 1949; Und Niemand weiss weiter, 1957; Flucht und Verwandlung, 1959; Gesammelte Lyrik, 1961; Gesammelte Dramatik. Translator Swedish poetry: Von Welle und Granit, 1947; Aber auch diese Sonne ist heimatios, 1958; Ausgewahite Gedichte, 1963; Vom Leiden Israels, 1964. Address: Stockholm Sweden Died June 1970.*

SACHSE, HELENA V. (MRS. SADTLER), authority on cooking for sick; b. Phila., Nov. 30, 1875; d. Julius Frederick (Litt.D.) and Emma Caroline (Lange) Sachse; ed. Girton Sch., Haverford, Pa., and grad. Phila. Cooking Sch., 1899; m. Phila., June 3, 1901, Samuel S. Sadtler. Lecturer on cooking for the sick at Lackawanna and Hahnemann hosps., Scranton, Pa., Norristown (Pa.) Hosp., Pottsville (Pa.) Hosp., and Germantown (Pa.) Hosp. Author: How to Cook for the Sick and Convalescent, 4 edits., 1901-5 L5. Address: Bethlehem Pike, Flourtown PA‡

SACK, HENRI S(AMUEL), educator; b. Davos, Switzerland, Nov. 25, 1903; s. Hermann and Isabelle (Pohli) S.; diploma math. and physics Tech. Hochschule (Zurich, Switzerland), 1925, D.Sc. in Math., 1927; m. Charlotte Fein, Aug. 30, 1933; children—Renee A., Claudia M. Came to U.S., 1940, naturalized, 1946. Asst., Eidg. Tech. Hochschule, Zurich, 1925-27; asst. U. Leipzig, 1927-33; asst. U. Brussels, 1933-37, chef de travaux, 1937-40; research asso. Cornell U., 1940-44, asso. prof. engring. physics, 1944-49, prof., 1949-64, Walter S. Carpenter Jr. prof., 1964-72, dir. Materials Sci. Center, 1963-68; asst. editor Physikal Zeitscr, 1929-33; indsl. cons. Mem. Am. Phys. Soc., Swiss Phys. Soc., Sigma Xi, Gamma Alpha (hon.). Author: (with P. Debye) Theorie der elektr. Molecular Eigenschaften, 1934; also publs. field dielectric properties, electrolytes, supersonics. Home: NY Died Mar. 16, 1972.

SACKETT, CARL LEROY, lawyer; b. Driftwood, Neb., Feb. 27, 1876; s. John Henry and Martha Ann (Burd) S.; LL.B., Ohio State U., 1901; m. Margaret Woods, May 1, 1914; 1 son, Carl Leroy (U.S. Air Force). Admitted to Ohio bar, 1901, practicing in Sheridan, Wyo., since 1902; city atty., 1905-06, 1910-11; mem. Wyo. Ho. of Rep., 1919-20 (Dem. floor leader); U.S. dist. atty., Wyo., 1933-49. Mem. legal advisory bd., Sheridan County, Wyo., World War. Mason, Elk, Odd Fellow. Stockman. Resident of Wyo. since 1879. Address: 2715 Evans Av., Cheyenne WY‡

SACKETT, EARL L., naval officer (ret.); b. Bancroft, Neb., Mar. 29, 1897; s. Samuel Lazier and Minnie Estelle (Armstrong) S.; B.S., U.S. Naval Acad., 1919; M.S., U. Cal., 1934; m. Elizabeth Louise Stanford, June 1, 1921; 1 dau., Maidie Mason (wife of Lt. Col. ret. H. R. Barr, U.S.M.C.). Commd. ensign U.S. Navy, 1919, and advanced through grades to rear adm., 1947; submarine or engring. duty, 1924-42; assisted raising U.S.S. Squalus, 1939; comdr. sub-tender, Canopus, 1940-42 (scuttled at Corregidor to avoid capture); mem. staff of Am. Nimitz, 1944-46; ret. from active service, Jan. 1, 1947. Awarded Navy Cross, Army Distinguished unit badge, Bronze Star, Navy commendation ribbon, various area and service medals and ribbons. Republican. Episcopalian. Clubs: Yacht (Coronado), Margate (Md.) Yacht, Annapolis (Md.) Yacht; Army-Navy (Manila, P.I.). Home: CA Died Oct. 7, 1970; buried Arlington National Cemetery, Arlington VA

SACKETT, SHELDON F(RED), newspaper and radio exec.; b. Jefferson, Ore., Aug. 2, 1902; s. Fred Brown and Harriet Elizabeth (Schenck) S.; A.B., Willamette Univ., 1922; grad. student, Univ. of Ore., 1923, grad. asst., Columbia (Teachers' Coll.), 1924; m. Sara Elizabeth Pratt, June 3, 1925 (div. June 10, 1930); m. 2d, Beatrice Walton, Dec. 31, 1931 (dec. May 17, 1947); m. 3d, Evelyn Zinglemann Schwabe, Aug. 2, 1948 (div. Oct. 3, 1949); m. 4th, Elizabeth Worthington, Jan. 30, 1950; children—David Schuyler, Marcia Anne, John Walton, Schuyler Worthington. Editor and publisher, McMinnville (Oregon) Telephone Register, 1925-28; managing editor and co-publisher, Oregon Statesman, 1928-39; editor and pub. Coos Bay (Ore.) Times, 1930-68; pres., radio stas. KVAN, Inc., 1937-68, KOOS, Inc., 1936-68, KROW, Inc., Oakland, California, 1945-68, V, Inc., 1952, California Labor Press, Incorporated, 1955; owner Portsmouth (Va.) Times, 1957-68; pres., pub. World Newspapers, Inc., San Francisco. Mem. Sigma Delta Chi, Sigma Tau, Alpha Kappa Nu. Democrat. Methodist. Elk. Clubs: Commonwealth, Press (San Francisco); University, Press (Portland, Ore.). Home: San Francisco CA Died Sept. 1, 1968.

SADACCA, HENRI, mfg. exec.; b. 1894. Chmn. dir. Noma Lites Inc., N.Y.C. Home: New York City NY Died May, 1969.

SADD, WALTER ALLEN, banker; b. Wapping, S. Windsor, Conn., Mar. 29, 1863; s. Henry Wells and Abigail (Avery) S.; Ph.B., Yale, 1884; m. Carolyn Terry, Oct. 1, 1889. Moved to Chattanooga, Tenn., 1889; pres. Chattanooga Savings Bank since 1908; chmn. bd. First Nat. Bank of Chattanooga, 1929-32; chmn. bd. Signal Mountain Portland Cement Co.; dir. Title Guaranty & Trust Co. Served as alderman and mem. Sch. Bd. Republican. Episcopalian. Mason (K.T.). Clubs: Mountain City (Chattanooga); New York, Yale (New York). Home: 840 Vine St. Office: 8th and Broad Sts., Chattanooga TN*‡

SADLAK, ANTONI NICHOLAS, congressman; b. Rockville, Conn., June 13, 1908; ed. St. Joseph's Parochial Sch., George Sykes Manual Training and High Sch.; student Georgetown Coll.; LL.B., Georgetown U.; m. Alfreda Janina Zalewska, May 30, 1939; children—Antoni, Alita. Former asst. sec.-treas. Hartford Prodn. Credit Assn.; spl. inspector, Spl. Inspections Div., U.S. Dept. of Justice, 1941-42; formerly exec. sec. to B. J. Monkiewicz, congressman-at-large, edn. supervisor, Conn. Dept. Edn., 1946; mem. 80th to 85th Congresses, congressman-at-large, Conn.; probate judge, Vernon, until 1969. Commd. lt. U.S.N.R., 1944, assigned to staff Adm. Thomas C. Kincaid; duty in New Guinea, Philippines and China. Home: Rockville CT Died Oct. 18, 1969.

SAERCHINGER, CESAR (VICTOR CHARLES), writer, lecturer, broadcaster; b. Aix-la-Chapelle, Oct. 23, 1884; s. Victor and Anna (Lange) S.; came to U.S., 1898, naturalized, 1910; ed. Realgymnasium. Halle, Germany, and pub. schs., New York, N.Y.; studied music with pvt. teachers; traveled in England and France for study, 1910; m. Marion Wilson Ballin. March 30, 1915 (deceased); children—Dagmar (Mrs. Christopher Wilson), Eugene Henry Benjamin. Editorial assistant National Cyclopedia of American Biography, 1908-10; contributor to musical magazines since 1912; edited (under supervision of Daniel Gregory Mason) The Art of Music (14 vols.), 1913-17; on editorial staff Current Opinion. 1917-18; fgn. corr. New York Evening Post at Berlin, 1919-24, Phila. Ledger at London, 1925-26, Curtis-Martin Newspapers at London, 1926-30; European editor Musical Courier, 1920-30; European dir. Columbia Broadcasting System, organizing first regular transatlantic service, 1930-37; broadcasting The Story Behind the Headlines," N.B.C., 1938-48. Decorated Silver Cross of Honor (Austria), 1934. Co-founder Modern Music Soc. of N.Y., 1913; Internat. Soc. for Contemporary Music (Salzburg), 1922; Artur Schnabel Meml. Com. (first pres.), 1952. Pres. The Friedberg Management, 1952-57; adminstr. Martha Baird Rockefeller Aid to Music Program, 1956-60. Mem. Assn. of Radio and Television News Analysts, Overseas Press Club of America. Author: A Narrative History of Music (with Leland Hall), 1915; The Opera, 1916; Hello, AmericaSchnabel: a Biography, 1956. Editor: International Who's Who in Music, 1918; The Art of Music (14 vols.), 1915-17; Rendezvous with Destiny (NBC recordings), 1946. Contbr. to mags. Contbg. editor Am. Edn. Press, 1940-50. Home: Bedford Village NY Died Oct. 1971.

SAGENDORPH, ROBB, pub.; b. Newton Center, Mass., Nov. 20, 1900; s. George and Jane Cooper (Hansell) S.; grad. Noble and Greenough Sch., Harvard, 1922; Litt.D. (hon.), New England College, 1959; m. Beatrix Thorne, October 27, 1928; children—Jane Thorne, Lorna. Dir. Penn Metal Co., 1942-67; founded Yankee Mag., pres. and dir. Yankee, Inc., 1935-70; pub. Old Farmer's Almanack; resident analyst, Office of Censorship, 1942-45. Moderator, selectman, Dublin, N.H. Chmn. board Monadnoch Region Assn., 1966-68. Recipient annual award N.E. Soc. of N.Y., 1961. Mem. Nat. Grange, American Meteorological Society, Harvard Alumni Association (director 1962-65). Republican. Clubs: Country (Brookline); Century Association, Harvard (N.Y.C.). Compiler: The Old Farmer's Almanac Sampler. Co-author: Rain, Hail, and Baked Beans. Editor: New England, 1962; That New England, 1966. Dublin NH Died July 4, 1970; buried Dublin NH

SAHLGREN, G. F. JORAN, educator; b. Aspo, Sweden, Apr. 8, 1884; s. Dean Alb and Jenny (Goransson) S.; Ph.D., U. Uppsala (Sweden), 1912-16. Lectr. Swedish lang. U. Uppsala, 1912-16; lectr. U. Lund, 1916-29, prof., 1929-71; mgr. Swedish Place Names Archives, Uppsala, 1928-50; collaborator SAOB; 1913-20; co-founder VSL, 1920, sec., 1920-27; pub. Arv, 1945-51; insp. Sobermanland-Nerikes, Uppsala, 1931-42. Mem. English Place Name Soc., Swedish Lit. Soc. Finland, K. Vlaamse Acad voor Taalen Letterkunde, GAA (chmn. 1965-71), Royal Acad. Letters Barcelona. Author: The Nature Name Skagerhult Paris, 1912, 35; Scandinavian Place Names in linguistic and Real Light, 1924-27; Eddica et scaldica, 1927-28; Swedish Fair Tales and Legends, 1937-53; Swedish Name Book, 1939-40; Swedish Folk Tales, 1939-47; Swedish Fairy Tales, 1943-45; Swedish Folk Books, 1946-56; Joy-bringers, 1956; Swedish Folk Songs, 1957-58. Address: Uppsala Sweden Died Aug. 28, 1971.

SAINT, PERCY, lawyer; b. Franklin, La., May 8, 1870; s. John David and Ellen Jane (DuBose) S.; student U. of Ala., 1888-90, and Tulane Law Sch.; m. Cora Lee McCardell, Dec. 7, 1903; children—Isabelle Mary (Mrs. James Oniell), Percy DuBose. Admitted to La. bar, 1893, and began practice at Franklin; mem. La. Ho. of Rep., 1916; dist. atty. 23d Jud. Dist. of La., 1917-20; dist. judge 23d Jud. Dist., 1920-24; atty. gen. of La. 2 terms, 1924-32. Democrat. Methodist. Mason, Elk. Home: 1310 Leontine St. Office: 2104 Am. Bank Bldg., New Orleans LA*‡

SAINT-DENIS, MICHEL JACQUES, drama dir., educator; b. 1897; ed. Coll. Rollin, Paris, France, also Lycee de Versailles. First theatre work at Vieux Colombier; founder, producer, actor Compagnie des Quinze, 1930; founder London Theatre Studio, 1935; head French sect. BBC (pseudonym Jaques Duchesne), 1940-44; founder English service of Radio-Diffusion Francaise, 1944; co-founder, dir.-gen. Old Vic Theatre Center and Old Vic Sch., 1946-52; dir. Centre Nat. Dramatique de l'Est, also founder, dir.-gen. Ecole Superieure d'Art Dramatique, Strasbourg, 1952-57; adviser found. Nat. Theatre Sch. Can., Montreal; cons. drama div. Juilliard Sch., Lincoln Center, N.Y.C., 1959; insp.-gen. theatre Ministry Cultural Affairs, Paris, 1959-71; gen. artistic adviser Royal Shakespeare Theatre, Stratford-on-Avon and London, 1962-71; co-dir. drama div. Juilliard Sch., N.Y.C., 1968-71; co-dir. Royal Shakespeare Theatre, 1965; prodns. include The Witch of Edmonton, 1937; Three Sisters, 1938; Twelfth Night, 1939; (play) Oedipus, 1945; (opera) Oedipus Rex, 1962; The Cherry Orchard, 1962. Author: The Rediscovery of Style, 1960. Home: London England Died July 31, 1971.

ST. DENIS, RUTH, dancer, head of own school; b. Newark, N.J., Jan. 20, 1879; d. Thomas L. and Ruth Emma (Hull) St. Denis; ed. district sch.; m. Ted Shawn, Aug. 13, 1914. Began as professional dancer, 1906, and went to Europe same yr.; continued there 2 yrs., appearing principally in Germany; toured U.S., 1910; founded, with husband, the Denishawn Sch. in Los Angeles; toured the Orient, 1925-26, and has made many tours of U.S. with husband; moved school to N.Y. City, 1920, and built Denishawn House, Van Cortlandt Park, 1929; left Denishawn House and now producing religious pageants; lecturing since 1931; revised Radha (dance which made her famous), summer 1941; inc. Soc. of Spiritual Arts and Ch. of Divine Dance, Calif.; inc. Ruth St. Denis Found., 1948; has theatre and monthly ch. services. Author: Lotus Lights (verse), 1932; Ruth St. Denis: Unfinished Life. Hollywood CA Died July 21, 1968; buried Forest Lawn Cemetery, Hollywood CA

ST. JOHN, CHARLES GRIFFIN, state supt. schs.; b. Sparta, Wis., Feb. 6, 1873; s. Levi and Jane (Jones) J.; prep. edn. high sch., Clear Lake, S. Dak.; student State Teachers Coll., Madison, Wis., 1897 to 1901; m. Pearl Ida Borne, of Clear Lake, Dec. 27, 1906; 1 dau., Nina Marie. Began teaching in Deuel Co., S.Dak., 1895; county supt. Deuel Co., 1913-17 and 1920-25; state supt. schs., 1925-28; pres. Clear Lake Farmers' Elevator, 1901-27. Founder of Young Citizens' League for School Children in S.Dak., 1925. Republican. Baptist. Mason. Home: Pierre SD‡

ST. JOHN, FRANCIS R., librarian; b. Northampton, Mass., June 16, 1908; s. Edward B. and Mary (Shaughnessy) St. J.; A.B., Amherst Coll., 1931; B.L.S., Columbia Sch. Library Service, 1932; m. Helen McLeod, Dec. 26, 1931. Asst., reference dept., N.Y. Pub. Library, 1931-39; asst. librarian Enoch Pratt Free Library, Baltimore, 1939-41; chief, circulation dept., N.Y. Pub. Library, 1941-47; dir. library service Veterans Adminstrn., 1947-49; acting librarian Army Med. Library, U.S. Army, Washington, 1943-45; chief librarian Brooklyn Pub. Library 1949-63, Franklin Publs.; cons. on library mgmt. and bldgs., 1947—; pres. Francis R. St. John Library Consultants, 1964-67; trustee Flatbush Savs. Bank. Mem. N.Y. Commr. Edn.'s com. on reference and research library resources, 1960-62. Served with U.S. Army, 1943-45; commd. 1st lt., 1944, disch. as capt., 1945. Decorated Legion of Merit. Mem. Am. (exec. bd. 1950-54, chmn. adv. com. library tech. project 1962), N.Y. library assns., Am. Acad. Polit. Sci., Archons of Colophon, Delta Upsilon, Alpha Beta Alpha. Author: Internship in the Library Profession, 1938; also articles New York City NY Died July 19, 1971.

ST. JOHN, THOMAS RAYMOND, mgmt. cons.; b. Chgo., Jan. 16, 1911; s. Raymond G. and Minerva M. (Hall) St. J.; m. Virginia H. Sullivan, July 1, 1929; children—Thomas J., Donald R., Virginia M., Robert D. Salesman wholesale paper Beaver Paper Co., Chgo., 1928; constrn. survey work Turner Constrn. Co., Chgo., 1929-30; with Armour & Co., Chgo., 1931-62, beginning as student salesman, successively gen. line salesman, sr. salesman, div. mgr. Cin., div. mgr. Cleve., asst. mgr. direct sales dept., mgr. direct sales dept., asst. sales mgr. beef div., asst. mgr. beef div., mem. president's office staff, asst. gen. mgr. beef div., gen. mgr. beef div., 1931-55, v.p., gen. mgr. beef, lamb and veal divs., Chgo., 1955-58, v.p.-southwest area mgr. Armour Foods, 1958-62; exec. v.p. Braun & Co., Troy, O., 1962-64; mgmt. cons. 1964-70. Address: Winnetka IL Died Dec. 18, 1970; buried Holy Sepulchre Cemetery, Chicago IL

ST. LAURENT, LOUIS STEPHEN, Canadian govt. ofcl.; b. Compton, Quebec, Can., 1882; ed. St. Charles Coll., Sherbrooke, Quebec, Laval Univ., Quebec City, grad. in law; LL.D., Laval, 1915; Queen's Univ., 1930, U. of Manitoba, 1935, Montreal Univ., 1943, Bishop's Coll., 1943, Dalhousie Univ., 1947, Ottawa U., 1947, Dartmouth, 1948, McGill, 1949, Rensselaer, Institute, N.Y., 1949, St. Louis, 1950, St. Lawrence, 1950, U. Toronto, 1950, U. Western Ontario, 1951, Northwestern U., 1951, U.B.C., 1952, U. of London, 1952, St. Francis Xavier U., Antigonish, 1953, U. of Delhi, Peshawar U., 1954, McMaster U., 1955, Sherbrooke University, 1956; D.C.L. (hon.), Mount Allison U., Sackville, New Brunswick, 1952; Oxford, 1953; married Jeanne Renault, May 19, 1908;children—Marthe (wife of Dr. Mathieu Samson), Renault, Jean-Paul, Therese (Mrs. G. F. Lafferty), Madeleine (Mrs. Hugh O'Donnell). Served as batonnier local Quebec City bar, batonnier-gen. of Quebec Province bar; hon. life pres. Canadian Bar Assn. Pleaded many cases before the Supreme Court of Canada and before the Judicial Com. of the British Privy Council. Deputy chmn. Canadian delegation, Gen. Assembly, London. Acting prime minister, summer 1946. Apptd. mem. Imperial Privy Council, Jan. 1946; minister of justice, atty. gen., Dec. 1941-Dec. 10, 1946; Canadian Sec. of State for External Affairs, 1946-48; Prime Minister of Can., 1948-57, resigned. Home: Quebec Quebec Canada Died July 25, 1973.

ST. LEWIS, ROY, lawyer; b. Sharon, Pa., Sept. 27, 1891; s. John Griffith and Mary Ann (Davis) St. L.; prep. edn., high sch., Sharon, Pa., 1906-10; LL.B., U. of Okla., 1915; m. 2d, Peggy Hammond Taylor, July 29, 1943. Practiced at Holdenville, Okla., 1915-17, 1919-20; assistant attorney for Okla. of Chicago, Rock Island & Pacific Railway Company, with hdqrs. at El Reno, Okla., 1920-22; asst. U.S. atty. Western Dist. of Okla., 1922-24; gen. practice at Oklahoma City, 1925; U.S., atty. Western Dist. of Okla., 1925-28; apptd. spl. asst. to atty. gen. of U.S., 1928, in prosecution of W. K. Hale and John Ramsey for murder of Osage Indians in Okla.; reapptd. U.S. atty., 1929, resigned Aug. 1931; asst. atty. gen. U.S., 1931-33; ex-mem. Long. St. Lewis & Nyce, Washington; president Rocky Mountain Fuel Co., Denver, 1951-69; president, publisher The Diplomate Magazine; apptd. general counsel with rank of col. Civil Air Patrol, auxilliary U.S.A.F., 1952. Served overseas regimental sergeant major, 345th Infantry, 87th Division, U.S. Army, 1917-19. Am. Legion del. to Fidac Congress, Morocco, Africa, Sept. 1933, London, Eng., 1934, Brussels, Belgium, 1935; commander National Press Club Post, 1943. Mem. American Bar Association (v.p. 1930-32), Okla. State and Okla. County, District of Columbia bar assns.; Kappa Sigma, Phi Alpha Delta. Pres. Okla. State Soc. in Washington, D.C., 1938-41. Republican. Baptist. Mason (32 deg., Shriner), Moose. Clubs: Oklahoma City; National Press (Washington, D.C.). Home: Washington DC Died Nov. 1, 1969.

ST. ONGE, WILLIAM LEON, congressman; b. Putnam, Conn., Oct. 9, 1914; s. William A. and Alma (Desautels) St. O.; B.A., Tufts Coll., 1941; LL.B., U. Conn., 1948; Dr. Law and Culture, Mex. Acad. Internat. Law, 1963; LL.D., St. Michael's Coll., Vermont, 1966; m. Dorothy Hughes, Sept. 15, 1945; children—William H., Mary, Susanne, Constance, Anne. Admitted to Conn. bar, 1948, since practiced in Putnam; probate judge Putnam, 1948-62; pros. atty. Putnam City Ct., 1949-51; mayor of Putnam, 1961-62; mem. 88th-91st Congresses, 2d Dist. Conn., mem. jud. com., mecht. marine and fisheries com. Instr. U. Conn. Coll. Pharmacy and Sch. Bus. Adminstrn., 1948-52. Chmn. Putnam Housing Authority, 1948-56; dir. Putnam Redevel. Agency, 1956-58. Mem. Putnam Bd. Edn., 1940-41; mem. Conn. Ho. of Reps. from Windham County, 1940-41; Democratic candidate for U.S. Ho. of Reps., 1960. Bd. dids., v.p. Conn. Urban Renewal Assn.; adviser-trustee Annhurst Coll., Woodstock, Conn.; member congl. bd. visitors U.S. Coast Guard Acad. Served with USAAF, 1942-45. Mem. Am., Conn. Windham County bar assns., U. Conn. Law Sch. Alumni Assn. (trustee), V.F.W., Am. Legion, K.C. Home: Putnam CT Died May 1, 1970; buried St. Mary's Cemetery, Putnam CT

SALANT, WILLIAM, pharmacologist; b. Courland, Russia, Feb. 2, 1870; s. Solomon and Theresa (Geffen) S.; came to America, 1884; B.S., Cornell U., 1894; grad. student in biology, Columbia, 1894-5; M.D., Coll. Phys. and Surg. (Columbia), 1899; studied Sch. of Biology and Sch. of Mines, Columbia; m. Annie Oser, of Waterbury, Conn., 1899. Fellow Rockefeller Inst., 1899-07; asst. Cornell Med. Sch., 1902-3, Coll. Phys. and Surg., 1905-7; adj. prof. pharmacology and physiol. chemistry, U. of Ala., 1907-8; chief Pharmacol. Lab., Bur. of Chemistry, U.S. Dept. Agr., since June, 1908. Mem. Am. Soc. Pharmacology and Exptl. Therapeutics, Am. Physiol. Soc., Am. Soc. Biol. Chemists, Soc. Exptl. Biology and Medicine, Am. Chem. Soc., A.M.A., Sigma Xi. Author of numerous publs. in pharmacology, physiology and pathology, in various scientific jours.; also monographs pub. by Bur. of Chemistry, U.S. Dept. Agr. Home: 3429 34th St., Washington DC‡

SALAZAR, ONTONIO DE OLIVEIRA, former prime minister Portugal; b. Apr. 29, 1880; s. Ontonio de Oliveira and Maria do Resgate Salazar; ed. Coimbra U.; D.C.L., hon., Oxford U., 1941; LL.D., hon. Fordham U.; unmarried. Prof. of econ. sciences Coimbra U., 1918; mem. of parliament; minister of finance, 1926 and 1928-40; minister for colonies, ad interim, 1930; prime minister 1932-68 (presented to a nat. plebiscite the new political constitution of Portuguese Republic that was in force); minister of war, ad interim, 1936-44; minister for foreign affairs, 1936-47; minister of defense, 1961-62; ex-officio member of the Council of State. President of National Union. Decorated with Grand Cross of following orders: Torre e Espada, Sao Tiago da Espada, Imperio Colonial Portugues (Portugal), St. Michael and St. George (Gt. Britain), Leopold (Belgium), Polonia Restituta (Poland), St. Mauricio e St. Lazaro (Italy), Boyaca (Colombia), Manhauia (Morocco), Merito (Chile), Service Fidele (Roumania), Isabel a Catolica (Spain), Cruzeiro do Sul (Brazil), Merito Militar (Brazil), Merito (Dominican Republic). Author books including: O agio do ouro, 1916; Questao cerealifera do trigo, 1916; Alguns aspectos da crise das subsistencias, 1918; A minha resposta, 1919; O Centro Catolico Portugues, 1922; Reducao das despesas publicas, 1923; Discursos e notas politicas (6 vols. 1926-66) (translations into French, English, Spanish, German, Polish, Italian, Bulgarian, Rumanian and Hungarian. Home: Lisbon Portugal Died July 28, 1970.

SALAZAR, RUBEN, journalist; b. Chihuahua, Mexico, Mar. 3, 1928; s. Salvador and Luz (Chavez) S.; B.A., U. Tex. at El Paso, 1954; m. Sally Robare, May 15, 1960; children—Lisa Marie, Stephanie Ann, John Kenneth. Came to U.S., 1929, naturalized, 1949. With El Paso Herald-Post, 1952-54, Santa Rosa Press Democrat, 1954-56, San Francisco News, 1957-59; with Los Angeles Times, 1959-70, assigned Vietnam, 1965-66, bur. chief, Mexico City, 1966-69, columnist, 1969-70; news dir. KMEX-TV, Los Angeles, until 1970. Served with AUS, 1950-52. Home: Santa Ana CA Died Aug. 29, 1970; buried Pacific View Memorial Park, Newport Beach CA

SALAZAR ARGUMEDO, CARLOS, Guatemalan lawyer, engineer, and public man; b. Guatemala, 1863; s. Federico Salazar and Josefa Argumedo; ed. Polytechnic School; U. of Guatemala; m. Sofia Gatica; children—Carlos, Federico, Enrique, Oscar, Margarita, Jose. Military Inspector, 1884; sec. of Supreme Court, 1886; prof. of constl. law, U. of Guatemala, 1886-1905; judge of primary court, 1892-95; magistrate, Court of Justice, 1895-1908; Guatemalan representative before Central Am. International Court of Justice, 1908; mem. Hague Tribunal since 1909, dean of Faculty of Law, 1909. Guatemalan del. to Pan-Am. Conf., Havana and Montevideo, 1928-33, one time fgn. minister of affairs, prof. civil law, U. of Guatemala. Address: Callejon de Cordova 2, Guatemala City*‡

SALERNO, GEORGE FRED, baking co. exec.; b. Chgo., July 22, 1909; s. Fred G. and Frances (Noto) S.; B.S. in Commerce, Loyola U., Chgo., 1933; m. Sylvia Stoerk, Jan. 11, 1936; children—Gaye, Judith A., Lynn. With Salerno-Megowen Biscuit Co., Chgo., 1933-70, various assignments including v.p., exec. v.p., 1933-52, pres., 1952-70; vice chairman, mem. exec. committee, dir. Pabst Brewing Company. Dir., Biscuit and Cracker Mfrs. Assn. Home: Wilmette IL Died Dec. 27, 1970; buried All Saints Cemetery, Des Plaines IL

SALERNO, VITO LORENZO, cons. engr.; b. N.Y.C., May 16, 1915; s. Vincenzo and Vincenzo (Gatti) S.; B. Civil Engring. cum laude, Coll. City N.Y., 1939, M. Civil Engring. (Grad. Study award 1939), 1939; D. Aero. Engring., Poly. Inst. Bklyn., 1947; m. Carmela Gravina, July 18, 1942; children—Vivian, Valerie. Naval architect Bur. Ships, Navy Dept., 1939-46; mem. faculty Poly. Inst. Bklyn., 1946-51, asso. prof. aero. engring., asso. dir. aero. and submarine structures, 1948-51; prof. aero. engring. Rensselaer Poly. Inst., 1951-52; from cons. to tech. dir. nuclear components div. Combustion Engring., Inc., 1953-57; cons. research Grumman Aircraft Engring. Corp., 1957-58; dean Coll. Sci. and Engring. Fairleigh Dickinson U., 1958-62; cons. engr. aero-space and nuclear power companies, 1958-62; dir. Applied Technology Assos., Incorporated, Ramsey, N.J., 1962-66, president, tech. dir., 1966-71. Recipient Community Service award Bergen County (N.J.) Soc. Profl. Engrs., 1961, Alumni Achievement award Stuyvesant High Sch., N.Y.C., 1961. Registered prof. engr., N.Y., N.J. Asso. fellow Inst. Aero-Space Scis.; mem. Am. Soc. M. E., Pressure Vessel Research Council. (chmn. design div.), N.Y. State Soc. Profl. Engrs. (president New York City chapter 1968-69), Sigma Xi, Tau Beta Pi, Sigma Gamma Tau. Home: Bronx NY Died July 24, 1971; buried Woodlawn Cemetery, Bronx NJ

SALLEY, ALEXANDER SAMUEL, JR., author; b. Orangeburg Co., S.C., June 16, 1871; s. Alexander McQueen and Sarah (McMichael) S.; grad. S.C. Mil. Acad., 1892; m. Harriet G. Milledge, of Atlanta, Ga., July 11, 1918. Admitted to bar, 1889. Secretary Hist. Commn. of S.C., Apr. 1, 1905—. Has written, compiled or edited a number of works on S.C. history. Democrat. Contbr. of hist. and biog. and bibliog. articles to various publs. Home: 901 Laurens St. Office: State House, Columbia SC‡

SALLEY, NATHANIEL MOSS, educator; b. Orangeburg, County, S.C., Nov. 12, 1876; s. George Lawrence and Martha Susan (Stokes) S.; student S.C. Mil. Acad., Charleston, 1892-93; A.B., Wofford Coll., Spartanburg, S.C., 1897, Litt.D., 1933; grad. study summers, Columbia, 1902, U. of Chicago, 1907, U. of Wis., 1913, 20, 22; m. Margaret Cooper, Nov. 12, 1901; children—Samuel Marion, Mary Julia (deceased), Dorothy Stokes (Mrs. F. B. Clements, Jr.), George Lawrence, Margaret (Mrs. A. E. Swenson). Teacher rural schs., S.C., 1897-99; instr. in English and history, Carlisle Fitting Sch., Bamberg, S.C., 1899-1903; prin. grade schs., Bamberg, 1903-05; supt. city schs., Laurens, S.C., 1905-06; supt. pub. schs., Greenwood, S.C., 1906-10; prof. edn. and dean Sch. of Edn., Fla. State Coll. for Women (name changed to Fla. State Univ., 1947), 1910-37 (dean emeritus since). Mem. Fla. Edn. Assn., N.E.A., Kappa Delta Pi, Phi Kappa Phi, Kappa Sigma Fraternity. Democrat. Methodist. Mason. Home: 211 S. Copeland St., Tallahassee FL‡

SALPETER, HARRY, art dealer, writer; b. Lemberg, Austria, Aug. 16, 1895; s. Louis and Ethel (Schaumann) S.; brought to U.S., 1899, naturalized, 1926; student pub. schs. N.Y.C.; m. Betty Berkowitz, Mar. 23, 1919. Reporter Harlem Home News, 1914-21; telegraph editor Oklahoma Leader, 1921-24; asst. and asso. lit. editor N.Y. World, 1924-31; contbr. articles on art and artists to Coronet and Esquire mags., 1936-49; owner, Harry Salpeter Gallery, Inc., N.Y.C., 1947-67; also Provincetown (Mass.) br., 1954-55. Member Am. Fedn. Arts, Mus. Modern Art, Am. Friends Hebrew U., Archives Am. Art. Author: Doctor Johnson and Mr. Boswell, 1928; preface to Modern Library edit. of Gerhardt Hauptmann's Heretic of Soana, 1928. Contbr. popular mags., newspapers. Home: New York City NY Died Nov. 13, 1967; buried Mt. Hebron Cemetery, Flushing NY

SALPETER, HIGH, assn. exec.; b. Passaic, N.J., Dec. 28, 1911; s. Benjamin and Anna (Udelsman) S.; student N.Y.U., 1930-31; B.A., Bklyn. Coll., 1935; postgrad. Sch. for Social Work, N.C.U., 1936; m. Bernice Franklin, Sept. 8, 1935; 1 son, Richard, Dir. Intergovt. Refugee Commn., N.Y.C., Washington, Geneva, 1936-39; Am. sec. Hebrew U. Jerusalem (Israel), 1948-50; exec. asst. to pres. United Mchts. and Mfrs., N.Y.C., 1951-52; dir. Police Athletic League, N.Y.C., 1962-65; exec. dir. Met. Taxicab Bd. Trade, Inc., N.Y.C., 1965; vice president, secretary Woolman Systems, Inc. affiliate of Corn Products Company. Vice-pres. Internat. Cultural Centers for Youth, Inc., N.Y.C., Interfaith Group, N.Y.C.; hon. pres. Am. Jewish Congress, 1962; mem. N.Y.C. mayor's Task Force; chmn. Fedn. Jewish Philanthropies, 1946-66; adviser Cath. Charities, Co-chmn. Am. Israel Cultural Found., 1962-66; bd. dirs. Am. Israel Soc. Recipient numerous Man of Year awards including, Fedn. Jewish Philanthorpies, 1955, N.A.A.C.P., 1959, Queens Council Chs., 1946, A.R.C., 1966. Founding mem. Am. Soc. Community Relations Execs. Author: (play), Baruch, 1937. Home: Forest Hills NY Died Feb. 15, 1969.

SALSBURG, ZEVI WALTER, educator, phys. chemist; b. Wilkes-Barre, Pa., Aug. 9, 1928; s. Theodore and Frances (Shinkman) S.; B.S. in Chemistry, U. Rochester, 1950; student Cal. Inst. Tech., 1950-51; Ph.D. in Chemistry, Yale, 1953; m. Bertha Rosen, Dec. 21, 1958;children—Alan Israel, Linda Sydel. Mem. faculty Rice U., 1954-70, prof. chemistry, 1962-70; cons. Los Alamos Sci. Lab., 1955-70, Lawrence Radiation Lab., Livermore, Cal., 1957-70, Bell Telephone Labs, 1964; FMC lectr. Princeton, 1964. Chmn. panel chemistry for evaluating nat. NSF grad-fellowship application, NRC., 1965-67, Grantee NSF, 1952-53; NRC fellow, 1953-54; Guggenheim fellow, 1961-62; recipient Teaching Excellence award Brown Coll., Rice U., 1968. Mem. Am. Chem. Soc. (tour lectr. 1961), Am. Math. Soc., Phi Beta Kappa, Sigma Xi. Distinguished guest prof. La. State U., 1967. Editor: Solution Theory Section of the Collected Works of J.G. Kirkwood; (with J. Poirer) Simple Dense Fluids: Data and Theory, 1968. Home: Houston TX Died June 20, 1970.

SALTER, RICHARD GENE, county ofcl.; b. Salt Lake City, Aug. 31, 1926; s. Priscilla M. (Cox) S.; B.S., U. Utah, 1952, M.S., 1953; m. Elizabeth Bates, Sept. 18, 1948; 1 dau., Hollis. Asst. planner Salt Lake County Planning Commn., Salt Lake City, 1953-55; asso. market analysis Nat. Planning and Research, Inc., Salt Lake City, 1955-56; dir. planning San Joaquin County Planning Commn., Stockton, Cal. Served with USNR, 1944-46. Mem. Am. Inst. Planners, Am. Soc. Planning Ofcls., San Joaquin County Planning Assn., Gamma Theta Upsilon, Sigma Gamma Epsilon. Home: Stockton CA Deceased.

SALTONSTALL, NATHANIEL, architect; born in Milton, Mass., Apr. 24, 1903; s. Philip L. and Frances A. F. (Sherwood) S.; student Harvard, 1928, Mass. Inst. Tech., 1931. Architect, Boston, 1945-71. Mem. nat. council Archtl. Registration Board. Pres. Wellfleet, Cape Code, Mass.; hon. pres. Inst. Contemporary Art, Boston; v.p., adv. bd. of Skowhegan (Me.) Sch. Painting and Sculpture; trustee Mus. Fine Arts, Boston, vis. com. School of Museum of Fine Arts, Boston, chmn. vis. com. textile dept.; bd. dirs. Boston Archtl. Center; mem. nat. com. Am. Ballet Soc.; adv. council Friends of Art at Colby Coll., Waterville, Me. Registered architect, Mass., Va., N.Y. Member of the Boston Soc. Architects, Mass. State Assn. Architects, Am. Arbitration Assn., A.I.A. Club: Harvard (Boston). Home: Boston MA Died 1971.

SAMFORD, JOHN A., air force officer; b. Hagerman, N.M., Aug. 29, 1905; s. Charles MacDanial and Adline Williams (Shepperson) S.; student N.M. Normal U., Las Vegas, N.M., 1919-23, Columbia U., 1923-24; B.S., U.S. Mil. Acad., 1928; grad. Air Corps Primary Flying Sch., 1929. Advanced Flying Sch., attack course, 1929, Air Corps Tech. Sch., engr.-armament course, 1935, Air Corps Tactical Sch., 1939; m. Elizabeth Baylor Illg, July 18, 1929; 1 son, John Alexander. Commd. 2d lieut., F.A., 1928, transferred to Air Corps, 1929, advancing through the grades to lt. gen., 1956; dep. chief of staff 8th Air Force, Eng., 1944; comdt. Air Command and Staff Sch., 1949-50, Air War Coll., 1950-51; dir. intelligence USAF, 1952-56; dir. Nat. Security Agy., 1956-69. Home: Washington DC Died Nov. 20, 1968; buried Arlington Nat. Cemetery Arlington VA

SAMMARCO, G. MARIO, operatic baritone; b. Palermo, Sicily, Dec. 13, 1873; studied under Antonio Cantelli. Debut at Milan, 1894, and was at once engaged for Giordano's opera, Andrea Chenier, at La Scala, Milan; sang in all the musical centres of Europe; came to Manhattan Opera House, New York, for its first season; later with Chicago-Phila. Opera Co.‡

SAMMIS, ARTHUR MAXWELL, coll. dean; b. Bridgeport, Conn., Sept. 23, 1911; s. Louis Benedict and Miriam Frances (Stern) S.; student Coll. Pacific, 1929-30; student U. Cal. at Berkeley, 1931-32; J.D., Hastings Coll. Law, 1939; m. Eugenia Louise Rutherford, Apr. 25, 1936; children—Ian Michael, Theodore Wallace, Robert Jeffrey. Admitted to Cal. bar, 1939, also U.S. Supreme Court; with Bank Am., San Francisco, 1940-42; sec. Com. Bar Examiners, State Bar of Cal., 1942-43; atty. Regional War Labor Bd., San Francisco, 1943-44; mem. firm Athearn, Chandler & Farmer, Hoffman & Angell, San Francisco, 1944-47; mem. faculty Hastings Coll. Law, 1944-70, instr. law, 1944-46, asst. prof., 1946-47, prof. law, registrar, 1947-63, asso. dean, 1953-63, dean 1963-70. Mem. adv. com. Office Pub. Defender, City and County San Francisco, 1964-70. Served to lt. comdr., USNR, World War II. Mem. Am., San Francisco bar assns., Am. Law Inst., State Bar of Cal., Am. Arbitration Assn. (mem. No. Cal. adv. council), Continuing Edn. Bar (deans adv. com.). Rotarian. Author: (with Verrall) Cases on California Community Property, 1966, rev. edit., 1971. Home: Tiburon CA Died Oct. 29, 1970.

SAMMOND, HERBERT STAVELY, musician; b. Milwaukee, Dec. 4, 1871; s. Charles Frederick and Elizabeth (Saul) S.; ed. pub. schs.; m. Lina Doane, of Brooklyn, N.Y., July 19, 1899; children—Harry Alfred, William Arthur, Marjorie Isabel. Organist Middle Collegiate Ch., N.Y. City; condr., founder of the Morning Choral of Brooklyn, N.Y.; song leader New York Coast Artillery, stationed in forts around N.Y. City, World War. Judge for Nat. Music League of America, New York Music Ednl. League. Mem. Am. Guild Organists. First pres. L.I. Music Festival Assn., Inc. Conglist. Mason. Clubs: Twelve-forty-five, St. Wilfrid. Home: 725 Argyle Rd., Brooklyn NY‡

SAMPEY, JOHN RICHARD, JR., educator; b. Louisville, Aug. 5, 1896; s. John Richard and Annie (Renfroe) S.; student U. Louisville, 1919; S.B., U. Chgo., 1920, S.M., 1921, Ph.D., 1923; post doctorate research, Johns Hopkins, 1923-24, 30-31; m. Jewell Cheatham, Sept. 4, 1925; children—John, Richard III, Jane Renfroe. Grafflin scholar Johns Hopkins, 1923-24; asso. prof. chemistry Howard Coll., 1924-26, prof., 1926-34; prof. chemistry Furman U., 1934-67. Served from pvt. to 2d lt., inf., U.S. Army, 1918-19; AEF in France; as lt. col., inf., AUS, 1941-45; ETO, PTO. Decorated various service medals. Recipient coll. chemistry teacher award, Manufacturing Chemists Association, 1961. Fellow A.A.A.S.; member American Chemical Society (chmn. Ala. and S.C. sects; Charles H. Herty medal 1954), Ala. (past pres.), S.C. (pres. 1940) acads. scis., So. Assn. Sci. and Industry (trustee). Res. Officers Assn., Am. Legion. Baptist (deacon, Sunday sch. tchr.). Contbr. numerous articles profl. jours. Home: Greenville SC Died 1967.

SAMPLE, JOHN GLEN, exec.; born Lutesville, Mo., July 3, 1891; s. William W. and Mattie (Glen) S.; B.S., Will Mayfield Coll., Marble Hill, Mo., 1909; m. Helen M. Scanlon, Nov. 1, 1921; children—Joseph, Sally (Mrs. Sally S. Aall). Co-founder of Blackett-Sample-Hummert, Inc. (later Dancer-Fitzgerald-Sample, Inc.), 1923, ret. 1948; pres. Port Royal, Inc., Naples, Fla. Capt. Inf., 89th Div., U.S. Army, World War I. Comdr. U.S.N.R., with 7th Amphibious Force, Pacific, World War II. Decorated Bronze Star medal (Navy), Navy Commendation medal, Purple Heart (Army), World Wars I and II medals; also campaign badges and Philippine Liberation ribbon. Presbyterian. Clubs: Chicago, Racquet (Chicago); Onwentsia (Lake Forest, Ill.); Yacht, Hole-in-the-Wall Golf (Naples, Fla.); Delray Beach (Fla.) Yacht. Home: Naples FL Died Nov. 25, 1971.

SAMPSELL, MARSHALL EMMETT, public utilities official; b. Marshall, Tex., Feb. 28, 1874; s. Joseph Benjamin and Fannie (Allnut) S.; A.B., U. of Chicago, 1896; LL.B., Chicago Coll. of Law, 1901; m. Edna Florence Smith, of Chicago, July 25, 1900; children—Marshall G., David S., Joseph C., Bruce E. Clk. U.S. Circuit Court, Northern Dist. of Ill., 1902-07; was receiver Chicago Union Traction Co. and North and West Chicago St. R.R. cos.; now pres. Central Ill. Public Service Co., Super Power Co. of Ill.; dir. various pub. utility cos. Republican. Mem. Royal League. Clubs: Chicago, Old Elm. Exmoor. Home: Highland Park, Ill. Office: 20 Wacker Drive Bldg., Chicago IL‡

SAMPSON, WILLIAM JAMES, JR., mfg. exec.; b. Youngstown, O., Nov. 8, 1896; s. William James and Florence (Wick) S.; grad. Choate Sch., 1916; student Yale, 1920; m. Elizabeth Crawford, Apr. 23, 1950; children—Margaret (Mrs. Gordon P. Wills), Mary (Mrs. Darrell A. Block), William James III (dec.). With Elyria Iron & Steel Company, Elyria, Ohio, also Cleveland, 1920-27; with Steel & Tubes, Incorporated,

Cleveland, Toledo, 1927-29, president, 1930-32; vice president in charge sales Steel and Tubes div. Republic Steel, 1933-37, gen. mgr. sales, 1941-42; asst. gen. sales mgr. Republic Steel Corp., 1937-41; pres. Am. Welding & Mfg. Co., Warren, 1942-60, chairman of the board, 1960-68; dir. Union Savs. & Trust Co., Albee Homes, Inc. Mem. bd. govs. Smaller War Plants Corp., Region V, World War II; mem. tubular adv. com. iron and steel br. WPB; pres. Indsl. Information, Inc., 1947-56, trustee, 1947-61. Chmn. Trumbull County and Region 10, Ohio Republican Finance Com., 1948-58. Regional, nat. bd. dirs. Jr. Achievement Econ. and Bus. Found., New Wilmington, Pa.; member adv. bd. St. Joseph's Riverside Hospital, Warren. Trustee Youngstown U., Thiel College, Greenville, Pa. Served as sgt., U.S. Army, 1917-19. Member Chamber of Commerce, American Legion, Am. Ordnance Assn. (dir. Cleve. 1957-64). Clubs: Union (Cleve.); Youngstown Country, Youngstown (Youngstown, O.); Yale (N.Y.C.). 40 Redfern Dr. Home: Youngstown OH Office: Dietz Rd., Warren OH Died June 5, 1969.

SAMS, JAMES HAGOOD JR., orgn. exec.; b. Columbia, S.C., Apr. 26, 1903; s. James Hagood and Caroline (Earle) S.; B.S., Clemson Coll., 1924; E.E., Cornell U., 1926; M.S., U. of Mich., 1931, Ph.D., 1937; m. Elizabeth Dargan, Aug. 26, 1931; children—James Hagood, III, Frank Dargan. Test engr. Gen. Electric Co., 1926-27; instr. engring. Clemson (S.C.) Coll., 1927-31, asst. prof. mech. engring., 1931-34; U. of Mich., 1934-36; asso. prof. mech. engring. Clemson (S.C.) Coll., 1936-41, prof. mech. engring. 1946-60, vice dean of engineering, 1947-50, acting dean of engring., 1950-51, dean, 1951-60; exec. sec. Nat. Council Engring. Examiners, 1967-70, dir. 1970. Mem. sci. adv. com. S.C. SSS, 1955-57. Served in research and devel. Power Plant Lab., Air Material Command, 1941-43, chief engring., liaison office Bur. Aeronautics, United States Navy, 1944-45; colonel USAF Reserve, 1945-63, retired. Decorated with Victory Medal, and War Department Commendation Medal. Chmn. S.C. State Bd. Engring. Examiners, 1951-54, v. chmn., 1967-—; dir. so. zone Nat. Council State Boards of Engring. Examiners, 1951-54, executive secretary, 1960-67. Mem. Nat. Soc. Profl. Engrs. (named S.C. engr. of year 1968), Am. Soc. M.E. (v.p., 1956-58; representative to Engrs. Joint Council, 1958-60; chmn. sects. com. region IV 1951), Am. Soc. Engring. Edn. (chmn. degree designations com., 1954-58), S.C. Soc. Engrs. (pres. 1952), Engrs. Council for Profl. Development (mem. council 1954-59, exec. com., 1955-57, 58-59), Newcomen Soc., Air Force Assn., Nat. Sojourners, Tau Beta Pi, Phi Kappa Phi. Mason (past master). Clubs: Rotary (charter pres. 1956-57, dist gov. 1966-67), Clemson Fellowship (pres. 1948-49). Home: Clemson SC Died Nov. 10, 1970.

SAMS, ROBERT SHIELDS, lawyer; b. Atlanta, Apr. 16, 1905; s. Richard Fuller and Elizabeth (Jones) S.; B.S., Princeton, 1925; B.A. in Jurisprudence, Oxford U., 1927; m. Mary Blair Armstrong, Oct. 15, 1930; children—Robert S., Mary Blair (Mrs. Richard Edelman). Admitted to Ga. bar, 1928, practiced in Atlanta; asso. Troutman & Troutman, 1928-30, Colquitt, Parker, Troutman & Arkwright, 1930-35, Colquitt, MacDougald, Troutman & Arkwright, 1935-37; partner MacDougald, Troutman & Arkwright, 1937-47, MacDougald, Troutman, Sams & Branch, 1947-49, MacDougald, Troutman, Sams & Schroder, 1949-53, now Troutman, Sams, Schroder & Lockerman; hon. Belgium consul, Atlanta, 1949-59. Dir. Munich Am. Reassurance Company, Nat. Bank of Georgia. Former vice chairman planning div. Met. Atlanta Community Services, Incorporated. Decorated chevalier de L'Ordre de la Couronne. Mem. Am., Ga., Atlanta bar assns., Princeton Alumni Assn. Ga., English-speaking Union (chmn. Atlanta branch), Phi Beta Kappa, Delta Sigma Rho. Episcopalian. Clubs: Piedmont Driving, Capital City, Commerce, Lawyers (Atlanta). Home: Atlanta GA Died Dec. 13, 1969; buried Westview Cemetery, Atlanta GA

SAMUEL, MAURICE, author, translator, lectr.; b. Macin, Roumania, Feb. 8, 1895; s. Isaac and Fanny (Acker) S.; student Manchester Secondary Sch., Eng., 1907-11, Victoria Univ., Manchester, Eng., 1911-14; D.H.L., Brandeis U., 1964; m. Gertrude Kahn, Sept. 17, 1921 (div. 1961), children—Eva (Mrs. Chester Rapkin), Gershon; m. 2d, Edith Brodsky, Jan. 29, 1962. Came to U.S., 1914, naturalized 1921. Author: The Outsider, 1921; Whatever Gods, 1923; You Gentiles, 1924; I, The Jew, 1927; What Happened in Palestine, 1929; King Mob, (under pseudonym Frank K. Notch), 1930; On the Rim of Wilderness, 1931; Jews on Approval, 1932; Beyond Woman, 1934; The Great Hatred, 1940; The World of Sholom Aleichem, 1943; Harvest in the Desert, 1944; Web of Lucifer, 1946; Prince of the Ghetto, 1948; The Gentleman and the Jew, 1950; The Devil that Failed, 1952; Level Sunlight, 1953; Certain People of the Book, 1955; The Professor and the Fossil, 1956; The Second Crucifixion, 1960; Little Did I Know, 1963; Blood Accusation 1967; Light on Israel, 1968; In Praise of Yiddish, 1971. Editor, translator: The Ten Commandments (Solomon Goldman), 1956; Forward from Exile, autobiography of Shmarya Levin, 1967. Translator: The Jewish Anthology (Edmond Fleg), 1925; Selected Poems (C.N. Bialik), 1926; The World in the Making, 1927, Europe, 1928 (both by Count Hermann Keyserling); The Sinner (retitled Yoshe Kalb), 1933, The Brothers Ashkenazi, 1936, The River Breaks Up, 1938, East of Eden, 1939 (all I.J. Singer); Haggadah of Passover, 1942; The Lights Go Down (Erika Mann), 1940; Heil Hunger (Martin Gumpert), 1940; Theodor Herzl (Alex Bein), 1941; The Nazarene, 1939, What I Believe, 1941, Children of Abraham, 1942, The Apostle, 1943, Moses, 1945 (all Sholom Asch). Broadcast ann. NBC summer radio series with Mark Van Doren, 1953-72; public lectr. Served as sgt., U.S. Army, 1917-19. Recipient of Sat. Rev. Lit. award, 1943, Stephen Wise award, 1956, B'nai B'rith Heritage award, 1967, Manger award, 1972. Home: New York City NY Died May 4, 1972; buried Mount Hebron Cemetery New York City NY

SANBORN, JOHN CARFIELD, ex-congressman; b. Chenoa, Ill., Sept. 28, 1885; s. Orville D. and Frances (Carfield) S.; A.B., Oberlin (O.) Coll., 1908; LL.B., Columbia, 1912, A.M. in Political Science, 1912; m. Jessie Margaret McNabb, November 6, 1912 (deceased November 1955). Idaho State representative from Gooding County, 1921, 23, 25, 27, 29, state senator, 1939, 41, majority floor leader in Ida. House Rep., 1927, 29; Rep. floor leader in Ida. senate. 1941; mem. 80th and 81st Congresses, 1947-50, 2d Dist. of Ida.; farmer Hagerman, Ida. since 1913. Alternate del. Rep. Nat. Conv., 1952; presdl. elector, 1960. Mem. Nat., Ida. State and Hagerman Grange, Farm Bur. (state dir. Ida. fedn. 1954, 60-68, legislative rep. 1959, 61, 63). Methodist (trustee). Mason (Shriner). Home: Hagerman ID Died May 16, 1968.

SANCHEZ, ALLAN JUAN, corp. exec.; b. Garyville, La., Nov. 30, 1908; s. Anatole J. and Alcidie (Chapron) S.; student Tulane U., 1935-41; m. Gladys Barbara Scott, May 9, 1935; 1 dau., Emily Elizabeth. Accountant, Fed. Land Bank of New Orleans, 1932-38, City of New Orleans, 1938-40; state auditor La. Hwys. Dept., 1940-42; v.p. finance, sec. Lykes Bros. S.S. Co., Inc., New Orleans, 1946; v.p. finance, sec., comptroller Lykes Corp., New Orleans; v.p., controller, sec. Lykes-Youngstown Corp.; sec.-treas. Lykes Financial Corp., 1966-70. Served to maj. AUS, 1942-46; lt. col. Res. ret. Mem. Assn. Waterline Accounting Ofcrs., Data Processing Assn. (past dir.), Mil. Order of World Wars, Res. Officers Assn. Roman Catholic. Club: Propellar. Home: New Orleans LA Died June 5, 1970; buried Lakelawn Mausoleum.

SANDALL, CHARLES EDWARD, lawyer; b. York, Neb., Jan. 13, 1876; s. Andrew L. and Matilda (Kaliff) S.; York (Neb.) Coll., 1897-1901; LL.B., U. of Mich., 1904; m. Marie E. Romsdal, June 28, 1905 (died Dec. 11, 1939); children—Mildred Marie (Mrs. Homer A. Scott), Ruth Eileen (Mrs. Clyde E. Bolton), Esther Del (Mrs. Herman Frerichs), Marian Elizabeth (Mrs. Leo Sonderegger), Charles Edward, John Chester (killed in action, Germany, July 19, 1944), Jerrol Genieve, James Lawrence; m. 2d, Marion Davis Moore, Nov. 17, 1942. Began practice, York, Neb., 1904; county atty., York County, Neb., 3 terms, 1906-12; mem. Neb. State Senate, 2 terms, 1915-17; mem. Supreme Ct. Commn., Neb., 1925-26; U.S. atty. for Neb., 1930-35; del. at large, Rep. Nat. Conv., 1920, 28. Mem. Am. and Neb. State bar assns., and York County Bar Assn., York Chamber Commerce. Republican. Presbyterian. K.P., Elk. Home: 3007 P St., Lincoln. Office: First National Bank Bldg., York, Neb.; and First Nat. Bank Bldg., Lincoln NE‡

SANDER, JOHN FERDINAND, physician; b. Mt. Vernon, Ind., 1898; s. Charles H. and Emily (Koerner) S.; M.D., U. Mich., 1923; m. Elizabeth Isabel Cogan, Nov. 1929; children—John Egan, Charles H. Intern, Univ. Hosp., Ann Arbor, Mich., 1923-25; asst. pediatrician Harvard, 1925-26; asst. resident Children's Hosp., Boston, 1925-26; instr. pediatrics U. Mich., 1926-27, later extracurricular lectr.; sr. attending pediatrician St. Lawrence Hosp.; sr. attending pediatrician, dir. outpatient clinics Edward W. Sparrow Hosp.; sr. attending Ingham Med. Hosp.; asst. clin. prof. dept. human devel. Mich. State U. Served to comdr., M.C., USNR, 1942-45. Diplomate Am. Bd. Pediatrics. Mem. A.M.A., Am. Acad. Pediatrics, Ingham County Med. Soc. (pres. 1949). Home: Okemos MI Died Dec. 3, 1969; buried Evergreen Cemetery, Lansing MI

SANDERS, GEORGE, actor; b. St. Petersburg, Russia, July 3, 1906; ed. in Eng.; m. 2d, Zsa Zsa Gabor (div.); m. 3d Benita Hume Colman, Feb. 10, 1959 (dec.); m. Magda Gabor (div.). Early career, textile industry; 1st motion picture Lloyds of London, others include The Whole Truth, Dorian Gray, Death of a Scoundrel, The Lodger, Forever Amber, All About Eve, Ivanhoe, Moonfleet, Scarlet Coat, Hangover Square, Ghost and Mrs. Muir, Solomon & Sheba, The Last Voyage, A Touch of Larceny, Jungle Book, 1968, numerous others. Recipient Oscar award for supporting role in All About Eve, 1950. Author: Memoirs of a Professional Cad, 1960. Address: Lausanne Switzerland Died Apr. 25, 1972.

SANDERS, HENRY NEVILL, prof. Greek; b. at Edinburgh, Scotland, 1869; s. William Rutherford and Georgiana Bridget (Woodrow) S.; studet Edinburgh U., 1887; B.A., Trinity U., Toronto, Can., 1894, M.A 1897; studied Gottingen U.; Ph.D., Johns Hopkir 1903; m. Lilian M. Caulfeild, of Toronto, Can., June 2 1894. Fellow in Greek, Johns Hopkins, 1897-8; lectur in Greek, McGill U., 1898-1902; prof. Greek, Bry Mawr Coll., since 1902, also sec. of faculty. Home: Bry Mawr PA‡

SANDERS, LEE STANLEY, lawyer, engr.; b. Chgo Sept. 25, 1913; s. Walter and Valentine (Zolock) S.; B.S Northwestern U., 1935; J.D., Loyola U., 1938; m Rosemary T. Shea, July 13, 1940; children—Lee S Melissa R. Admitted to Ill. bar, 1938, Cal. bar, 1948; di endowment funds, Real estate Northwestern U 1935-43; v.p., sec. Roadmaster Products Co., Lo Angeles, 1946-51; sec., dir. Dist. Bond Co., 1946-5 sec. Indsl. Mgmt. Corp., 1946-51, Gross, Rogers & Co 1946-51, Tetco Co., 1946-51; exec. v.p. Los Angele Orthopaedic Found. and Orthopaedic Hosp., 1951-7 Served as officer USNR, 1943-46. Home: Pasadena C Died Apr. 14, 1970.

SANDERS, WALTER BENJAMIN, educator; b. Ar Arbor, Mich., July 30, 1906; s. Chauncey K. and Ma B. (Paine) S.; B.S. in Architecture, U. Ill., 1929; M Architecture, U. Pa., 1930; m. Carroll Thompson, Au 25, 1935. Instr. architecture Columbia, 1930-36; ass editor Am. Architect mag., 1937-38, Archtl. Foru mag., 1938-39; vis. lectr. Pratt Inst., 1939-40, Columbi 1946-49, U. Mich., 1947-49; prof. architecture U Mich., 1949-72, chmn. dept., 1954-64; partner Sande & Breck, Architects, N.Y.C., 1938-42, Sanders Malsin, N.Y.C., 1946-50; prin. Walter Sander Architects, Ann Arbor, 1950-72; design cons. Albe Kahn Asso. Architects & Engrs., Detroit, 1955-7 Cons. community facilities div. FHA, 1952. Serve from lt. to lt. col., USAAF, 1942-46. Decorated Bron Star medal, Legion of Merit; recipient hon. mentic Smithsonian Gallery of Art, 1940, spl. commendatic N.Y. chpt. A.I.A. House awards, 1940, 2d and 3d priz Bloomingdale's House Competition, N.Y.C., 1946, go medal Mich. Soc. Architects, 1964. Fellow A.I.A. (di 1968-72); mem. Assn. Collegiate Schs. Architectu (dir. 1963-65, pres. 1965-67), Mich. Soc. Architec (dir. 1968-72), Congresses Internationeau d'Architecture Moderne, Bldg. Research Inst. (di 1959-67), Mich. Acad. Sci., Arts and Letters, Sigma N Phi Kappa Phi, Alpha Rho Chi, Tau Sigma Delt Scarab. Contbr. articles profl. jours. Home: Ann Arbo MI Died Mar. 19, 1972.

SANDERSON, EDWARD FREDERICK, Cleveland, Ohio, March 16, 1874; s. of Frederic Milton and Harriet (White) S.; A.B., Amherst, 189 B.D., Hartford Theol. Sem., 1899; m. Ethel Eame Brooklyn, June 29, 1912 (died 1917); 1 son, Davi Eames; m. 2d, Grace Jarvis Schauffler, Sept. 19, 193 Ordained Congregational ministry, 1899; past Washington St. Ch., Beverly, Mass., 1899-1903, Centr Ch., Providence, R.I., 1903-08, Ch. of the Pilgrim Brooklyn, 1909-14; Goodwill Industries, Brookly 1915-16; dir. The People's Inst., N.Y. City, 1916-2 Served as mem. 1st Conn. Vol. Inf., Spanish-America War, 1898. Address: Nantucket MA‡

SANDERSON, SAMUEL GILBERT, oil co. exec.; Saxton, Pa., May 9, 1895; s. Samuel Knight and Ma Elizabeth Sanderson; m. Virginia Roth Jackso children—Samuel Gilbert, Mrs. John Frost. With Gu Oil Co., Houston, 1913-61, from supt. natural gas pla to v.p., Tulsa, 1919-61. Home: Tulsa OK Died Apr. 1969.

SANDERSON, WALTER W., sr. v.p. Nat. Bank Washington. Office: Washington DC Died Jan. 2 1973.

SANDLIN, JOHN NICHOLAS, ex-congressman; Minden, La., Feb. 24, 1872; s. Nicholas J. & Iren (McIntyre) S.; ed. pub. schs.; m. Ruth Reame, Minden, 1899 (now dec.); m. 2d, Emma Lou Palm Crichton, of Minden, 1913. Began practice at Minde 1896; dist. atty., 6 yrs.; judge 2d Jud. Dist. of La. 10 yrs mem. 67th to 74th Congresses (1921-37), 4th La. Dis Democrat. Methodist. Mason (32 deg., Shriner), K.P Woodman. Home: Minden LA‡

SANDOR, PAL, educator; b. Szolnok, Hungary, Ap 1, 1901; s. Maximilien and Hermine (Kahn) S.; Ph.D. Sci., U. Vienna (Austria), 1926; m. Julie Szerenyi, De 23, 1925. Writer fine arts, philosophy, sociolog translator, Vienna, 1920-27 Budapest, 1927-45; Hungarian govt. service, 1945-57; prof. philosophy U Budapest (Hungary), 1957-72. Decorated Order Libery, Order Socialist Fatherland, Order Labor. Me Assn. Dissemination Sci. (pres. dept. philosoph 1957-72), Hungarian Acad. Scis. Internat. Hegel Soc PEN Club. Mem. Hungarian Socialist and Labor Part Author: Fascist Labor Codes, 1934; Marx or Hendrik d Man, 1934; History of Dialectics, 1942; Engels, th Philosopher, 1945; Planning and Capitalism, 1948; Th Logic of Aristotle, 1958; History of Philosophy, 196 Nicolaus Cusanus, 1965; The Philosophy of Hen Bergson, 1967, Against the Flood, 1970; Abo Ideology, 1972; Two Frankfurt Schools, 1972; Th History of Hungarian Philosophy, 1900-1945, 197 and others. Home: Budapest Hungary Died Feb. 2 1972; buried Kerepesi Street Cemetery, Budape Hungary

SANDROK, EDWARD GEORGE, comptroller; b. Chicago, May 5, 1913; s. Edward G. and Grace May (Neil) S.; student Northwestern U., 1933-43; m. Gertrude J. Van Stright, Nov. 28, 1934; children—Robert Edward, Richard William. Auditor, Continental Ill. Nat. Bank and Trust Co., Chicago, 1934-40, sr. investment analyst, 1940-45, asst. dir., comptroller, A.C.S., Chgo. since 1945; sec. treas., Franklin H. Martin Memorial Found., Surg. Pub. Co. Chicago; bus. mgr. Annual Clin. Congress. Dir. Evang. Child Welfare Agy. Distinguished Service award A.C.S., 1966. Mem Profl. Conv. Mgmt. Assn. (pres.), Medical Society Execs. Conf., American Conv. and Travel Institute, Chicago Assn. of Commerce, Indsl. Relations Assn. Chgo., Investment Analyst Soc. Christian and Missionary Alliance. Clubs: Town Executives, Economic. Home: Chicago IL Died July 19, 1967; buried Chapel Hills Garden South, Chicago IL

SANDS, THOMAS EDMUND, railway official; b. Albany, N.Y., Jan. 1, 1869; s. George and Katherine (Sheridan) S.; ed. pub. and high schs., Albany; m. Katherine Hurley, of St. Paul, Minn., June 30, 1898. Began as tally boy" with J. Rathbun & Co., lumber dealers, Albany, 1881; later with Durant & Elmore, grain dealers; with Chicago, St. Paul, Minneapolis & Omaha Ry., 1886-8; entered employ of Minneapolis, St. Paul & Sault Ste. Marie R.R. (Soo Line), 1888; successively contracting and traveling freight agt., chief clerk, asst. gen. freight agt. and gen. freight agt., Apr. 15, 1909-16, freight traffic mgr. since Apr. 1, 1916, same rd. Catholic. Clubs: Athletic, Rotary, Traffic. Home: 3748 Park Av., Minneapolis MN‡

SANDY, WILLIAM CHARLES, psychiatrist; b. Troy, N.Y., Sept. 9, 1876; s. William Charles and Eliza (Rounsavell) S.; A.B., Columbia, 1898, M.D., Coll. Physicians and Surgeons, 1901; m. Vida Dowers, Dec. 30, 1905; children—Elizabeth, William Charles. Intern, Newark (N.J.) City Hosp., 1902-03; asst. physician N.J. State Hosp., Trenton, 1905-13, Kings Park State Hosp., N.Y., 1913-15; med. dir. S.C. State Hosp., Columbia, 1915-17; asst. supt. Conn. State Hosp., Middletown, 1917-18; psychiatrist State Com. for Mental Defectives, N.Y., 1919-21; dir. Bur. of Mental Health, State Dept. of Welfare, Pa., 1921-44 (retired). Served with Med. Corps, U.S. Army, 1918-19; lt. col. Med. Res. Corps to Nov. 1945. Diplomate, Am. Bd. of Psychiatry and Neurology, Mem. Am. Med. Assn. N.Y. and Seneca County medical societies, Am. Psychiatric Assn. (sec.-treas., 1933-38, pres., 1939-40), Pa. Psychiatric Soc. (pres., 1939-40). Asso. editor Am. Jour. of Psychiatry. Episcopalian. Mason. Contbr. articles to med. jours. Home: Sandynook, Sheldrake-on-Cayuga, Ovid NY (winter) 310 N. Geneva St., Ithaca NY‡

SANFORD, FRANK GOODWIN, art instr., b. Medford, Mass., Mar. 3, 1874; s. Daniel and Maria Simpson (Preble) S.; ed. Canton, Mass., pub. schs., Cargill's Bus. Coll., New Haven, Conn., C. L. Fox Art Sch., Portland, Me., 1889-1900, Pratt Inst., Brooklyn, 1900-2; unmarried. Taught cast drawing and sketching from life, and lecturer on art anatomy, 1894-1900; teacher of design, Chautauqua (N.Y.) Inst., summers 1902, 1903; in Sept., 1902, began teaching manual training Oak Park (Ill.) pub. schs.; teacher of drawing and manual arts, Allendale Farm Sch. for Boys, Lake Villa, Ill., since 1903. Dir. dept. Arts and Crafts, Chautauqua (N.Y.) Inst., since 1904. Unitarian. Author: Arts and Crafts for Beginners, 1904 C2. Home: 180 Oxford St., Portland ME Address: Lake Villa IL‡

SANFORD, JOHN B., editor; b. Mulberry, Tenn., May 17, 1869; s. Samuel L. and Jane (Kennedy) S.; ed. pub. schs., and San Jose (Cal.). State Normal Sch.; m. Nina B. Hughes, of Ukiah, Cal., Dec. 25, 1898. Editor and propr. Dispatch-Democrat. Ukiah, 1898-—; mem. Cal. Ho. of Rep. 1895, 97, 99, Senate, 1903, 05, 07, 09, 11, 13; chmn. Dem. legislative caucus, 1897-13; chmn. Dem. State Conv., 1908; vice-chmn. Dem. State Com., 1908-10; mem. Dem. Nat. Com., 1912-16; Register U.S. Land Office, San Francisco, 1913-—. Baptist. Mason. Club: Iroquois. Home: Ukiah CA‡

SANFORD, ROLLIN B., lawyer; b. Nicholville, St. Lawrence County, N.Y., May 18, 1874; s. Henry T. and Louise (Brewster) S.; A.B., Tufts Coll., 1897; LL.B., Union U., 1899; m. Harriet Keeler, Apr. 4, 1904; children—Jane, William Keeler, Kate. Admitted to N.Y. bar, 1899, and practiced in Albany. Dist. atty., Albany County, 1908-14; mem. 64th to 66th Congresses (1915-21), 28th N.Y. Dist.; then mem. N.Y. State Bd. Law Examiners. Republican. Episcopalian. Mem. Theta Delta Chi. Mason. Club: Fort Orange. Home: Loundonville NY Office: 120 State St., Albany NY*‡

SANGER, PAUL WELDON, surgeon; b. Minco, Okla., Sept. 17, 1906; s. Paul and Frances (Jones) S.; grad. Webb Sch., Bell Buckle, Tenn., 1924; B.A., U. Okla., 1928; M.D., Vanderbilt U., 1931; m. Mary Ann Carr, Dec. 30, 1936; children—Paul Weldon, Ann, Frances Bailey. Intern Duke Hosp., 1931-32, resident, 1932-37; pvt. practice thoracic and cardiovascular surgery, Charlotte, N.C., 1938-68; dir. Heineman Research Lab., Charlotte Meml. Hosp., 1946-68, dir. Hartford Research Lab., 1959-68. Dir. Consol. Credit Co., Builders Life Ins. Co. Mem. med. adv. com. Duke, 1965-68; mem. Presidents' Commn. Heart Disease, Cancer and Stroke; exec. com. United Med. Research N.C., 1956-68; mem. Nat. Heart Council, NIH, 1963-68. Trustee Charlotte Country Day Sch., Webb-Bell Buckle Sch.; mem. central com. Morehead Scholarship Fund. Served to col., M.C., AUS, 1942-45. Decorated Legion of Merit. Mem. A.C.S., A.M.A., So. Surg. Club, Am. Thoracic Assn. (exam. bd. 1961-67), Am. Assn. Thoracic Surgery, Soc. Vascular Surgeons, N.C. Med. Soc., Excelsior Surg. Soc., Internat. Cardiovascular Soc., Med. Assn. Vanderbilt U. (pres. 1967). Episcopalian. Author articles synthetic fibers for artery replacement, pulmonary vascular and cardiac problems. Home: Charlotte NC Died Sept. 8, 1968; buried Yokon OK

SANGER, WINNIE MONRONEY (MRS. FENTON M. SANGER), M.D., b. Jefferson, ILL., Feb. 2, 1874; d. Sylvester L. (M.D.) and Elizabeth (Buckles) Monroney; grad. high sch., Carmi, Ill., 1890; Ph.B., Scarritt Coll., Neosho, Mo., 1900; M.D., Washburn Coll. (now part of U. of Kan.), 1904; m. Fenton Mercer Sanger, M.D., Apr. 30, 1897; children—Fenton Almer (M.D.), Winifred M. (dec.). Teacher, Carmi, 1891-94; teacher high sch., Oklahoma City, 1894-97; practiced medicine since 1904, now associated in practice with husband and son. Med. insp. pub. schs., Oklahoma City, 1918-23; med. adviser women of Okla. State U., 1924-28. Mem. Am. and Okla. County and State med. assns., Gen. Federation Woman's Clubs (dir. 1926-28), State Fed. Woman's Clubs (ex-pres.), Okla. City Fed. Woman's Clubs (parl.), Nat. League Am. Pen Women (pres. Okla. City br. 1932-34), Am. Assn. Univ. Women, Okla. Nat. Consumer's Tax Commn., Inc. (chmn.), O.E.S., D.A.R., Chi Omega Epsilon. Democrat. Methodist. Clubs: Cosmopolitan, State Writers. Home: 1430 Sherwood Lane. Office: Key Bldg., Oklahoma City OK‡

SANNER, SYDNEY, lawyer; b. Baltimore, Oct. 16, 1873; s. James Biscoe and Ann Maria (Beetly) S.; grad. Helena (Mont.) High Sch., 1892; m. Kirtlye Hill, of Miles City, Mont., Dec. 11, 1901. Admitted to Mont. bar, 1894; practiced in Helena until Apr., 1895. Bigtimber, 1895-9, Miles City, 1899-08; judge 7th Jud. Dist. of Mont., 1909-13; asso. justice Supreme Ct. of Mont., term 1903-19. Democrat. Unitarian. Mem. Am. Bar Assn., Mont. Bar Assn. Mason. Clubs: Montana, Lambs (Helena); Miles City (Miles City). Home: Helena MT‡

SANTE, CHRISTOPHER ALFRED, market research exec.; b. N.Y., Oct. 12, 1919; s. Alfred and Elizabeth M. (Meertens) S.; B.A., N.Y. U.; m. Louise Brown, Sept. 11, 1943; children—Lucinda J., Chandler A. From trainee to research dir. William Esty Co., 1941-52; v.p., dir. research Lennen & Newell, Inc., N.Y.C., 1952-57, sr. v.p. research and market planning, 1957-68; v.p. O'Brien Sherwood Assos., 1968-72. Active Boy Scouts Am. Served from pvt. to 1st lt., AUS, 1942-46. Mem. Am. Marketing Assn., Nat. Campfire Club Am. Am. Mgmt. Assn., Advt. Research Found., A.I.M. Home: Forest Hills NY Died Oct. 9, 1972; buried Princeton ME

SANTE, HANS HEINRICH, govt. ofcl.; b. Wuppertal, Germany, Mar. 3, 1908; s. Karl B. and Hildehard (Hagemann) S.; ed. Grosse Juristische Staatspruefung; m. Eva M. Kempf, Mar. 14, 1949; children—Hans-Georg, Ulrich Andreas, Thomas-Wilhelm, Viktoria-Maria. Joined German Fgn. Service, 1950; counselor embassy, Ottawa, Can., 1956-59; minister embassy, Moscow, USSR, 1963-68; consul gen. in Boston, 1968-71. Home: Boston MA Died Sept. 17, 1971.

SARBACHER, GEORGE W(ILLIAM), JR., former congressman; b. Phila., Pa., Sept. 30, 1919; s. George W. and Martha (Hunter) S.; B.S. in Commerce, Temple U., 1942; m. Florence Wintz Forsyth, Aug. 15, 1942; children—Susan Pence, Sandra Ann, George William III. Enlisted in U.S. Marine Corps, commd 2d lt., June 13, 1942; served 2 1/2 yrs. S.W. Pacific on Guadalcanal, Bougainville, and Guam; received permanent capt. commn. regular U.S. Marine Corps, 1946; mem. 80th U.S. Congress (1947-49), 5th Dist. Pa. (N.E. Phila.); dep. dir. revenue for Pa.; dir. field engring., sec., v.p., pres., chmn. bd. Nat. Sci. Labs., Inc., 1950-69; chmn. mgmt. adv. team U.S. Postal Service, 1970-73. Mem. I.E.E.E., U.S. Navy League. Republican. Methodist. Mason (32 deg.). Club: Army-Navy. Home: Bethesda MD Died Mar. 4, 1973.

SARCHET, CORBIN MARQUAND, newspaperman; b. Charleston, Ill., Jan. 23, 1871; s. Solomon Bichard and Rose Ann (Hutchinson) S.; grad. high sch., Charleston; student Campbell U., Holton, Kan., 2 yrs.; m. Stella Montgomery Huggins, of Petersburg, Ill., Sept. 1, 1900; children—Rebecca (Mrs. Orville E. Bedelf), Corbin Marquand. City editor Charleston Daily Plaindealer, 1896-98; Okla. State Capital, Guthrie, 1900-03; newspaper corr. and spl. writer since 1903; sec. Chamber Commerce, Ponca City, Okla., since 1919. Mem. Rep. State Central Com. of Okla. 4 yrs.; publicity dir. same com. 8 yrs. Mem. World's Press Congress, Nat. Editorial Assn., Nat. Assn. Commercial Secs. Republican. Presbyn. Club: Rock Cliff Country. Home: 914 E. Broadway. Office: Chamber of Commerce, Ponca City OK‡

SARDEAU, HELENE (MRS. GEORGE BIDDLE), sculptor; b. Antwerp, Belgium, July 7, 1899; d. John and Caroline (Weiner) Silberfeld; came to U.S., 1914, naturalized, 1933; ed. Barnard Coll., 1919-20, Cooper Union, 1920-21, Art Students League, 1921-22, Sch. of Am. Sculpture, 1924-25; m. George Biddle, Apr. 17, 1931; 1 son, Michael John. One-man exhibitions: Arden Galleries, New York, 1924; Chicago Art Inst., 1925; Ehric Galleries, New York, 1929; Galeria di Roma, 1932; Boyer Galleries, Phila., 1933; Julien Levy Gallery, New York, 1934; Santa Barbara Mus., 1943; Asso. Am. Artists, 1944, Dintenfas Gallery, N.Y.C., 1964, Works in permenent collections: Whitney Mus., Met. Mus., Smithsonian Instn., Pa. Acad., Phila. Mus., Tel Aviv Mus., Palestine, Croton (N.Y.) High Sch., Greenfield (Mass.) Post Office. Executed masks for Delphic Festival, Greece, 1927; bronze reliefs for Nat. Library, Rio de Janeiro, 1942; also works in Fairmont Park, Phila.; bronze fountain in entrance plaza, Phila. Museum. Commnd. by Mexican Govt. to execute reliefs for the Supreme Court Bldg., Mexico City, 1945 and by Liturgical Arts Soc. to execute figure of St. Joan of Arc, 1949. Awarded Avery prize for sculpture, 1934. Mem. Sculptors Guild, Artists Equity Assn. Democrat. Home: Croton-on-Hudson NY Died Mar. 23, 1969.

SARGEANT, FRANK WADLEIGH, ins. official; b. Candia, N.H., Mar. 7, 1860; s. Jesse W. and Lydia A. (Emerson) S.; ed. Phillips Exeter Acad.; m. Lizzie A. French, Oct. 14, 1885. Employed for a time by mercantile firm in Boston and in office N.Y.&N.E. R.R.; entered service of N.H. Fire Ins. Co., 1882, became pres. Aug. 1905, now chmn. of board. Mason. Democrat. Conglist. Rotarian. Home: Manchester NH*‡

SARGENT, AMOR HARTLEY, lawyer; b. Felicity, O., Mar. 18, 1876; s. Elbert Marion and Mary Elizabeth (Hartley) S.; Ph.B., Grinnell Coll., 1897; LL.B., U. of Ia., 1899; m. Grace C. Witwer, Sept. 22, 1903, children—Harriet (Mrs. Harry B. Graefe), Mary (Mrs. George F. Karch). Admitted to Iowa bar, 1899; in claim dept. Burlington, Cedar Rapids & Northern R.R., Cedar Rapids, Ia., 1899-1900; in office of Hubbard, Dawley & Wheeler, Cedar Rapids, 1900-03; mem. of firm Crissman & Sargent, Cedar Rapids, 1903-08, Deacon, Good, Sargent & Spangler, 1908-21, Deacon, Sargent & Spangler, 1921-41, Sargent, Spangler & Hines since 1941; counsel Universal Engring Corporation; director and vice pres. Lefebure Corp. Mem. Bd. of Edn., Cedar Rapids, 1910-22 (pres., 1915-22). Mem. Am., Iowa State and Linn County bar assns., Beta Theta Pi, Phi Delta Phi. Republican. Presbyterian. Mason (hon. 33 deg.), Elk. Club: Cedar Rapids (Ia.) Country. Home: 2237 Washington Av., S.E. Office: 915 Merchants National Bank Bldg., Cedar Rapids IA‡

SARGENT, ARCHER DOWNING, lead co. exec.; b. Bklyn., May 20, 1906; s. Olin Archer and Elizabeth (Downing) S.; B.S., Columbia, 1927; m. Margaret Etta Banks, Sept. 16, 1939; children—Malcolm Banks, Bruce Downing. With Haskins & Sells, C.P.A.'s, N.Y.C., 1927-34; with Nat. Lead Co., 1934-71, treas., 1968-71. Mem. Westfield (N.J.) Town Council, 1964-69. C.P.A., N.Y. Mem. Am. Inst. C.P.A.'s, N.Y. State Soc. C.P.A.'s, Westfield Sch. Boosters Assn., Beta Gamma Sigma. Clubs: Westfield Tennis (past pres., bd. govs.); Echo Lake Country (Westfield); Whitehall, Columbia Varsity C. (N.Y.C.). Home: Westfield NJ Died July 29, 1971; buried Fairview Cemetery Westfield NJ

SARGENT, CHRISTOPHER GILBERT, coll. prof.; b. Vincennes, Lee County, Ia., Mar. 25, 1872; s. Stephen and Mary M. (Noel) S.; A.B., Parsons Coll., Fairfield, Ia., 1899, M.A., 1920; Pd.M., Colo. State Teachers Coll., Greeley, Colo, 1912; B.S.A. Colo. Agrl. Coll., Ft. Collins, Colo., 1919; M.A. in Education, Columbia, 1926; m. Marie L. Bandy, Sept. 27, 1899; children—Cecil Gilbert, Helen Marie, Roger Browning, Homer Bandy and Howard Benoit (twins). Teacher rural schs., Ia. and Colo., 1899-1904; owned and conducted farm nr. Grand Junction, Colo., 1904-08; county supt. schs., Mesa County, Colo., 1908-12; specialist in rural edn., Colo. Agrl. Coll., 1912-15; prof. rural edn., same, 1915-32, also state dir. of vocational edn., Colo., 1917-32; prof. rural edn. New Mexico Normal Univ., Las Vegas, summers, 1933, 34, 35. Granted life state teachers' certificate, Colo., for eminent service in rural edn.," 1912. Member N.E.A., Am. Vocational Assn., Colo. State Teachers' Assn., Colo. Schoolmasters' Club. Presbyterian. Mason. Advocate of rual sch. improvement by consolidation of schs. Writer and lecturer on rural and vocational education. Employed in war work. E. I. du Pont de Nemours & Company at Lowell, Mass., 1943-45, also at Pasco, Washington. Author articles for mags. Home: 1059 White Av., Grand Junction CO‡

SARGENT, EDWARD, merchant, banker; b. Janesville, Wis., Apr. 1, 1877; s. John Henry and Margerete (Burns) S.; ed. pub. schs.; m. Estelle Beal, of Edina, Mo., Nov. 13, 1904; children—Elizabeth E., Virginia. Began in mercantile business with Sargent

Bros., El Rito, N.M., 1892; dealer in sheep and wool; pres. Rio Arriba State Bank, Chama Merchandise Co.; dir. Bond Sargent Co., Bond Baker Co., Denver Union Stock Yards Co. State auditor, N.M., 1918; county commr., Rio Arriba Co., 1920; lt. gov., N.M., 1924, 26; mem. Rep. Nat. Com. 1924-32. Catholic. Home: Chama NM*‡

SARGENT, NOEL GHARRETT, economist; b. Bellingham, Wash., May 22, 1894; s. John Herod and Carrie (Gharrett) S.; A.B., U. Wash., 1915; A.M., U. Minn., 1916; postgrad. U. Chgo. 1916-17 U. Minn., 1919-20; LL.D., Whitman Coll., 1948; m. Margorie Dean Way, Feb. 20, 1918; children—John Norwood, Mary Jane (Mrs. Lee Donnelly), Martha (Mrs. Charles Reinhart). Prof. econs., St. Thomas Coll., St. Paul, 1917-19; instr. finance, U. Minn., Extension Div., 1917-19; acting editor Am. Econ., summer 1918; lectr. Mpls. Am. Com. and Minn. Sound Govt. Assn., 1919-20; chief econ. N.A.M., 1920-46, sec., 1933-55, hon. sec. rep. to ILO Conf., San Francisco, June-July 1948, cons. 7th session Econ. and Social Council, Geneva, 1948; organizer and dir. Indsl. Relations Dept., 1920-39; acting chief exec. officer, 1932-34, 1947-48; mem. adv. com. on comml. activities in fgn. services of State Dept., 1945-53. Mem. U.S. Adv. Com. on Unemployment, 1930; hon. mem. Conf. Nat. Orgns. (sec. 1944-50); sec. U.S. Inter-Am. Council, 1950; exec. dir. U.S. Inter-Am. Council, 1950; exec. dir. U.S. Inter-Am. Council, 1960; adv. U.S. delegate, London Conf. Internat. C. of C., 1945; represented Internat. Orgn. Of Indsl. Employers at UN Conf., 1947, Inter-Am. Council of Commerce and Production, Orgn. Am. States, 1951; mem. Export Adv. Com. U.S. Dept. Commerce, 1946-53; represented AID in Pakistan, Korea, 1957-58; Taiwan, 1960, Costa Rica, 1961, Honduras, 1962; spl. cons. NASA, 1964. Past pres. Half Hollows (L.I., N.Y.) Sch. Bd. Dir. Nat. Council Chs., 1955-58. Decorated French Legion of Honor; recipient Freedom Found. award, 1950. Mem. Am. Econ. Assn., Conf. Bus. Economists, S.R., Lambda Chi Alpha (nat. Sec. 1926-32; nat. pres., 1938-42). Organizer of Internat. Bus. Conf., 1944. Republican. Episcopalian (rep. at Conf. on Ch. and Econ. Life, 1947, 1950, Constituting Conv., Nat. Council Chs., 1951); bd. dirs. Westminster Choir Coll., N.J., acting pres., 1961-62. Author articles employment relations, taxation, etc. Compiler (with John Scoville) of Fact and Fancy in T.N.E.C. Monographs, 1942. Organizer and contbr. to 2 vol. reference book The American Individual Enterprise System. Home: Jamesburg NJ

SARGENT, PAUL DUDLEY, civil engr.; b. Machias, Me., May 8, 1873; s. Ignatius Manlius and Helen Maria (Campbell) S.; B.C.E., U. of Me., 1896; m. Sarah Sawyer McAllister, of Calais, Me., June 6, 1900. Asst. engr., Washington Co. R.R., Me., during construction, 1897-98, and same position, maintenance of way dept., 1899-1903; register of deeds, Washington Co., 1903-05; state highway commr., Me., 1905-11; asst. dir. Office of Pub. Rds., U.S. Dept. Agr., Feb. 15, 1911-Sept. 1, 1913; chief engr. State Highway Commn. Me., since Sept. 1, 1913. Mem. Me. N.G., 1896-99. Mem. Am. Soc. C.E., Am. Soc. for Testing Materials, Me. Soc. C.E., S.A.R., Mass. Highway Assn., Am. Rd. Builders' Assn., Phi Gamma Delta. Mem. exec. com. Federal Highway Council; mem. Am. Assn. State Highway Officials (pres. 1920). Republican. Universalist. Mason (K.T., Shriner). Clubs: Abnaki, Augusta Rotary (pres. 1923-24), Augusta Country. Home: 83 Western Av., Augusta ME‡

SARGENT, PORTER, publisher; b. Brooklyn, June 6, 1872; s. Francis Porter and Roselyn (Hitchcock) S.; A.B., Harvard U., 1896, and A.M., 1897; m. at Rome, Italy, Margaret Upham, of Boston, Mar. 9, 1907; children—Upham (deceased), Porter. Assistant in botany, later in zoology, Harvard; master of science, Browne and Nichols Sch., Cambridge, Mass., 1896-1904; engaged in research in comparative neurology, Harvard, 1897-1901, and independently with grants from Carnegie Inst., 1902-04; dir. of science, Nautical Preparatory School, 1903-04; founder, 1904, and for 10 yrs. dir., Sargent's Travel Sch. for Boys (5 times round the world); organizer and dir. Sargent School Service. Organizer, with W. P. Everet, of Boston, Harvard Liberal Club. Club: Harvard (Boston). Editor and pub. Sargent's Handbooks; Handbook of New England, 3 edits.; Private Schools, 22 edits.; Summer Camps, 12 edits.; Handbook for Private School Teachers; editor Elihu Vedder's Poems, Edgar Waterman Anthony's A History of Mosaics, etc. Author: Spoils: Poems From a Crowded Life, 1935; Our Poesy Is as a Gum, 1935; The New Immoralities; Clearing the Way for a New Ethics, 1935; also numerous mag. articles, etc. Home: 26 Weybrdige Rd., Brookline. Office: 11 Beacon St., Boston MA‡

SARNOFF, DAVID, chmn. RCA; b. Uzlian, Minsk, Russia, Feb. 27, 1891; s. Abraham and Lena (Privin) S.; brought to U.S., 1900; ed. pub. schs. and spl. course in elec. engring. Pratt Inst., Brooklyn, N.Y.; D.Sc., St. Lawrence U., 1927; D.Sc., Marietta College, 1935, Suffolk Univ., 1939, Suffolk Univ., 1939, Pa. Mil. College, 1952; D.Litt., Norwich U., 1935; D.C.S., Oglethorpe U., 1938, Boston U., 1948; LL.D., Jewish Theol. Sem. of Am., 1946, Bethany Coll., 1946, John Carroll U., 1950, University Pa., 1952, Fairleigh Dickinson Coll., 1953, U. So. Cal. Pratt Inst., 1954; L.H.D., U. Louisville, 1950; D.Eng., Drexel Inst. Tech., 1953; D.Sc., U. Notre Dame, 1955, Temple U., 1958; LL.D., Fordham U., 1955, Dropsie Coll., 1957, U.R.I., 1957; m. Lizette Hermant, July 4, 1917; children—Robert William, Edward, Thomas Warren. Messenger boy with Comml. Cable Co., 1906; same yr. became office boy Marconi Wireless Telegraph Co.; promoted to mgr. Marconi Sta., Sea Gate, N.Y., 1909; wireless operator on S.S. Beothic, Newfoundland, and equipped vessel and made trip as operator to Arctic ice fields on sealfishing expdn., 1911; wireless operator on S.S. Harvard, 1910, later at John Wanamaker's, N.Y., 1911-12; radio insp. Marconi Co. and instr. Marconi Inst., 1912; chief radio insp. and asst. chief engr., Marconi Co., 1913; successively contract mgr., asst. traffic mgr. and commercial mgr. same co., until 1919, and upon absorption of Marconi Co., by Radio Corp. of America, 1919, was taken over as commercial mgr. of latter, then elected gen. mgr., 1921, v.p. and gen. mgr., 1922, exec. v.p., 1929, pres., 1930, chmn. bd., 1947-69, hon. chmn., 1970-71; chmn. bd. dir. RCA Communications Inc.; dir. NBC, Chatham Square Music School. Trustee American Heritage Found., Ednl. Alliance, Thomas A. Edison Found., Nat. Found. Infantile Paralysis, United Seamen's Service, Inc., U.S. Council Internat. C. of C., Pratt Inst., N.Y. U. Dir. Armed Forces Communications Assn.; councillor N.Y.U. Nat. chmn. A.R.C. Fund Campaign, 1954. Chmn. Nat. Security Training Commission, 1955. Commd. lieut. col., S.C. Res., U.S. Army, 1924, col., 1931, brig. gen., 1944, brig. gen. Army of the U.S. Hon. Reserve. Decorated Officer Polonia Restituta (Poland), Chevalier Legion of Honor, Officer Legion of Honor, Comdr. Legion of Honor (France), Officer Order Oaken Crown (Luxembourg), Legion of Merit, Medal for Merit, U.S. Treasury's Silver Medal, Richard J. H. Gettheil Medal; recipient Horatio Alger award, 1951; Gold Citizenship Medal and Citation of Vets. Fgn. Wars, 1950; Pub. Service Award of Merit presented by Civil Service Leader, 1951; Annual award from Radio-Television Mfrs. Assn., 1952; founder award Inst. Radio Engrs., 1953; first ann. Keynoter award Nat. Assn. Radio and Television Broadcasters, 1953; Engring and Science award Drexel Institute of Technology, 1953, numerous others. Fellow I.E.E.E., Royal Soc. Arts (London); hon. fellow Weizmann Inst. Sci.; hon. mem. Brit. Instn. Radio Engrs.; mem. Academy of Political Science, Armed Forces Advisory Com., N.Y. State C. of C., Council Fgn. Relations, Mil. Govt. Assn., Mil. Order World Wars, Nat. Aero Assn., Nat. Inst. Social Scis., N.Y. Soc. Mil. and Naval Officers World Wars, Grant Monument Assn. (trustee), Naval Order U.S. (life mem.), U.S. Naval Inst., Am. Shakespeare Festival Found., Crusade for Freedom (chmn. Greater N.Y. com. 1951). Newcomen Soc. Eng., Res Officers Assn., Radio Pioneers, Vet. Wireless Operators Association, honorary mem. Brit. Instn. Radio Engrs., Radio Club America, Beta Gamma Sigma, Tau Delta Phi. Clubs: India House, Century Country, Lotos, Rockefeller Center Luncheon (New York City); Army-Navy, Metropolitan, Federal City (Washington). Author: Looking Ahead, 1968. Office: New York City NY Died Dec. 12, 1971; buried Valhalla Cemetery Valhalla NY

SARPER, SELIM, former minister fgn. affairs of Turkey; b. 1899; ed. U. Ankara. Officer fgn. service, Turkey, 1927-68; served in Odessa, Moscow, Berlin, Bucharest; press officer to prime minister, 1940-44; ambassador to Moscow, 1944-46, Rome, 1946-47; permanent rep. UN, 1947-57; Turkish minister fgn. affairs, 1960-62. Home: Ankara Turkey Died Oct. 1968.

SATENSTEIN, EDWARD, pres. Am. Book-Stratford Press, 1961-65, chmn. bd., 1965-—. Home: New York City NY Died June 1968.*

SATTER, MARK J., lawyer; b. Chgo., Feb. 22, 1916; s. Isaac and Yetta (Dunkleman) S.; grad. Peoples Jr. Coll., 1935; LL.B., De Paul U., 1939; m. Clarice Komsky, Oct. 22, 1939; children—David, Paul, Julietta, Susan, Beryl. Admitted to Ill. bar, 1939; practiced in Chgo., 1939-65. Mem. Housing Advisory Com. Chgo., 1963-64, Commn. on Human Relations, Chgo., 1963-64; counsel Nat. Cath. Council for Inter-racial Justice. Mem. Chgo., Ill. bar assns. Spl. work includes authorship Chgo. Bar Record, Ill. Bar Jour., Personal Finance Law Quar., numerous articles on consumer problems. Address: Chesterton IN Died July 12, 1965; buried Waldheim Cemetery.

SATTERFIELD, JOHN VINES, JR., banker; born Marion, Ark., May 14, 1902; s. John Vines and Mary L. (Marshall) S.; attended Earle High Sch.; m. Thelma Holt, June 26, 1928; children—John Vines III, William Walter, Hammond Holt. Chairman of the board, chief executive officer First National Bank of Little Rock, Arkansas. Mayor, City of Little Rock, 1939-41. Commd. maj., Army Air Forces, Feb. 13, 1942, lt. col., June 1943; col. Dec. 30, 1944. Democrat. Presbyterian. Clubs: Country, Pulaski Heights Lions (past pres.). Home: Little Rock AR Died Mar. 6, 1966.

SATTLER, WILLIAM MARTIN, educator; b. Tyndall, S.D., Oct. 31, 1910; s. John Jacob and Paulina (Max) S.; B.A., Yankton Coll., 1932; M.A., U. Mich., 1934; Ph.D., Northwestern U., 1941; m. Dorothy Ogborn Sept. 3, 1939; children—Richard W., Robert J. Tchr. pub. high schs., S.D., 1932-37; teaching fellow Northwestern U., 1937-38; teaching asst. U. Ill., 1938-39; instr. English, U. N.H., 1939-40; asst. prof. speech U. Okla., 1940-43, asso. prof., 1943-48; asst. prof. speech U. Mich., 1948-51, asso. prof., 1951-57, prof., 1957-69, chmn. dept., 1960-69. Served from lt. (j.g.) to lt. (s.g.), USNR, 1944-46. Mem. Speech Assn. Am. (chmn. com. on publs. 1953-57), Central States Speech Assn. (pres. 1950-51, exec. sec. 1947-50), Nat. Soc. Study Communication, Internat. Soc. Study Gen. Semantics. Co-author: Discussion and Conference, 1954, 2d edit., 1968. Contbr. to Ann Arbor MI Died Apr. 4, 1969.

SAUERWEIN, ALLAN, lawyer; b. Baltimore, Nov. 29, 1875; ed. pub., pvt. schs. of Baltimore; LL.B., U. Md., 1896. Admitted to Md. bar, 1896, since practiced in Baltimore; partner firm Tydings, Sauerwein, Benson and Boyd. Mem. Am., Md., Baltimore bar assns. Office: Davison Bldg., Charles and Fayette Sts., Balt 1‡

SAUND, DALIP S(INGH), congressman; b. Amritsar, India, Sept. 20, 1899; s. Natha Singh and Jeoni (Kaur) S.; B.A. with honors, U. Punjab, India, 1919; M.A., U. Cal., 1922, Ph.D., 1924; m. Marian Z. Kosa, July 21, 1928; children—Dalip S., Julie G., Eleanor B. Came to U.S., 1920, naturalized, 1949. Farmer, 1930-53; judge justice Ct. of Westmorland, Cal., 1953-57; propr. D.S. Saund Fertilizers, Westmoreland, 1953-73; mem. 85th-87th congresses, 29th Dist. Mem. Am. Math. Soc., Math. Assn. Am., India Assn. Am. (past pres.), Sigma Psi. Democrat. Clubs: Toastmasters (past dist. gov.), Lions (Westmoreland). Author: My Mother India, 1930; Congressman from India, 1960. Home: Hollywood CA Died Apr. 22, 1973.

SAUNDERS, CHARLES W., restaurateur; b. Oct. 8, 1902. Propr. Charlie's Cafe Exceptionalle, Mpls. Address: Minneapolis MN Died Mar. 29, 1964.

SAUNDERS, DEALTON, botanist, S. Dak. Agr'l Coll. Expt. Sta. since 1897; b. Alfred, N.Y., 1869; grad. Univ. of Neb., 1893 (A.M., 1894); m. Dec. 29, 1897, Eva Merritt, Wellsville, N.Y. Instr. in biology, Lincoln High School, 1895-6; specialist on the algae (phycology). Address: Brookings SD‡

SAUNDERS, EUGENE DAVIS, lawyer; b. Evington, Va., Jan. 9, 1898; s. Eugene Davis and Laura (Barelli) S.; LL.B., Tulane U., 1918; m. Mae Mayo East, Dec. 12, 1924; children—Sylvia Mae (Mrs. William D. Davis, Jr.), Carol Alice (Mrs. George B. Harrison III). Admitted to La. bar, 1919, also U.S. Supreme Ct.; practice in New Orleans, 1919-69; mem. firm Milling, Saal, Saunders, Benson & Woodward, 1949-69. Dir. J. Ray McDermott & Co., Inc., Jahncke Service, Inc. Mem. New Orleans (pres. 1960-61), Am., La. bar assns. Home: New Orleans LA Died May 8, 1969.

SAUNDERS, LAWRENCE, medical pub.; b. Phila., Pa., June 17, 1890; s. Walter Burns and Frances (Baugh) S.; B.S., Wharton Sch., U. of Pa., 1914; m. Dorothy Love, Feb. 2, 1924; children—Martha Randolph (Mrs. James J. Ferguson), Walter Grier, Morton Trebel, Nancy Gayle Wynne, Sally Love. With W.B. Saunders Co., med. pubs., 1914-68, treas. and dir., 1916-36, president, 1936-56, chairman, 1956-68; dir. Fidelity-Phila. Trust Co. Served as lieutenant (j.g.) Pay Corps, USNRF, World War I. Dir. Phila. Council Internat. Vistors; mem. George S. Cox Med. Research Inst.; mem. Marine Biol. Lab., Woods Hole. Mem. bd. dirs. Internat. House Phila.; bd. corporators Women's Med. Coll., Marriage Council. Member Nat. Book League (London), S.A.R., Zeta Psi. Episcopalian. Clubs: Rittenhouse, Franklin Inn (Phila.); Cosmos (Washington). Merion Cricket. Home: Bryn PA Died Aug. 22, 1968; buried Church of the Messiah, Woods Hole MA

SAVAGE, ALFRED ORVILLE, oil co. exec.; b. Blackwell, Okla., Oct. 2, 1911; s. Clifford Clarence and Lida (Ruggs) S.; B.S., Okla. State U., 1936; student Advanced Mgmt. Program, Harvard, 1949; m. Jene Allen, July 10, 1933; children—Allen, Gary, Kay. Sr accountant Standard Oil Co. (N.J.), 1936-48, asst comptroller, 1949-55, dep. comptroller, 1956 comptroller, 1957-68. Finance com. Girl Scouts Am. chmn. Citizens Com. Promoting Recreational Facilities for Children. Mem. adv. Com. Advanced Mgmt Program, Harvard, Adelphi Coll. Mem. Am. Petroleum Inst., Controllers Inst. Am. (nat. com. on edn.) Protestant. Home: Garden City NY Died Nov. 1, 1968 buried Blackwell OK

SAVAGE, CHARLES WINFRED, physical edn.; b. Churchville, N.Y., Aug. 9, 1869; s. George and Emma E. (Brooks) S.; A.B., Oberlin (O.) Coll., 1893; A.M. Harvard, 1898; hon. M.P.E., Springfield (Mass.) Coll. 1927; m. Elizabeth K. Pelton, Aug. 24, 1898 children—Doris (Mrs. R. A. Ride), Ruth (Mrs. C. J Mefort). Instr. in Latin, Oberlin Acad., 1893-96 Shadyside Acad., Pittsburgh, Pa., 1898-1904; prof physical edn. and dir. athletics, Oberlin (Ohio) Coll. 1906-36, head of dept. of physical edn. for men

1922-36, now emeritus; dir. Chautauqua Sch. of Phys. Education, 1917-27. Member Am. Intercollegiate Football Rules Committee, 1905-28, U.S. Olympic Games Com., 1924, 28. Mem. President's Com. of 50 on Social Hygiene since 1920; mem. White House Conf. on Child Health and Protection since 1929. Fellow Am. Physical Edn. Assn. (president 1926-28); mem. American Acad. Physical Education (historian since 1941), College Dirs. Soc. Physical Education (pres. 1914-15), Midwest Soc. Physical Edn. (pres. 1920-21), Ohio Coll. Assn. (chmn. com. on athletics), North Central Assn. Colls. and Secondary Schs. (mem. com. on athletics and phys. edn.), Ohio Conf. Mgrs. Assn. (pres. 1929-32); pres. Ohio Athletic Conf., 1933-35. Voted hon. life mem. Coll. Physical Edn. Assn., Am. Assn. for Health, Phys. Education and Recreation. Awarded Oberlin Alumni Assn. medal, 1938, for notable service to Alma Mater," Meritorious Award of the Ohio Assn. for Health, P.E. and Recreation, 1944. Progressive Republican. Conglist. Contbr. on physical edn. to mags., etc. Apptd. expert consultant information branch, Spl. Service Div., Army Service Forces, 1943. Home: 310 Reamer Pl., Oberlin OH‡

SAVAGE, JAMES EDWIN, educator; b. Nowata, Okla., Oct. 13, 1903; s. William Currens and Myrtle (Arnold) S.; B.A., Coll. of Emporia, 1928; M.A., U. Ark., 1937; Ph.D., U. Chgo., 1942; m. Mary Kathryn Johnston, Aug. 13, 1935; children—Margaret Louise, Kathryn Mary (dec.). Coach, prin. twp. high sch., Kirkwood, Ill., 1930-39; instr. English, Cornell U., 1942-43, 1945-46; prof. English, U. Miss., 1946-72, chmn. dept., 1953-60. Served from lt. to lt. comdr. USNR, 1943-45. Recipient Henry E. Huntington Library research grant, summer 1954. Mem. Modern Lang. Assn., The Malone Soc., Am. Assn. U. Profs. Presbyn. Author articles in field. Home: Oxford MS Died June 5, 1972.

SAVAGE, LEONARD JIMMIE, educator, statistician; b. Detroit, Nov. 20, 1917; s. Louis and Mae (Rugawitz) S.; B.S., U. Mich., 1938, Ph.D. in Math., 1941; D.Sc. (hon.), U. Rochester; m. Jean Strickland, July 10, 1964; children by previous marriage—Sam Linton, Frank Albert. Rackham fellow Inst. Advanced Study, Princeton, 1941-42; instr. math. Cornell U., 1942-43; research mathematician Brown U., 1943; research asso. Columbia, 1944-45, N.Y.U., 1945-46; Rockefeller fellow Marine Biol. Lab., Woods Hole, Mass. and U. Chgo., 1946-47; research asso. U. Chgo., 1947-49, mem. faculty, 1949-50, prof., 1954-60, chmn. dept., 1956-59; prof. U. Mich., 1960-64; Eugene Higgins prof. statistics Yale, 1964-71. Guggenheim fellow Paris, France and Cambridge, Eng., 1951-52, Rome, Italy, 1968; Fulbright grantee, France, 1951-52; fellow Center Advanced Study Behavioral Sci., 1963-64. Fellow Inst. Math. Statistics (pres. 1957-58), Am. Statis. Assn., A.A.A.S.; mem. Internat. Statis. Inst., Am. Math. Soc. Author: Foundations of Statistics, 1954; (with L. E. Dubins) How to Gamble If You Must, 1965. Home: New Haven CT Died Nov. 2, 1971.

SAVILLE, CALEB MILLS, hydraulic engr.; b. Melrose, Mass., May 27, 1865; s. George W. W. and Helen (Mills) S.; A.B., Harvard, 1889; post-grad. work Lawrence Scientific Sch. 1 yr.; m. Elizabeth Thorndike, Oct. 1891; 1 son, Thorndike. Div. engr. Met. Water Bd., Boston, 1895-1905; hydraulic specialist with French & Bryant, Brookline, 1905-07; engr. in charge 3d div., Isthmian Canal, 1907-12, conducting investigations on foundations, etc., of Gatun Dam, resulting in construction of the dam at that locality; also investigations in hydrology and meteorology of Panama Canal, triangulation survey of Canal Zone, etc.; mgr. and chief engr. Bureau of Water, Metropolitan Dist., Hartford, Conn., for installation and operation of new water supply for Hartford costing about $40,000,000; consulting engineer The Water Bureau since 1948; mem. Com. on Regional Planning, Metropolitan Dist. Awarded Norman medal, Am. Soc. C.E., 1914, Brackett Memorial medal, N.E. Water Works Assn., 1917, 27 and 34; President's Premium, Inst. of Water Engrs. (Eng.), 1931; prize of Conn. Soc. Civil Engrs., 1945. Honorary mem. New England Water Works Assn. (past pres.), Connecticut Soc. Civil Engrs.; mem. Institute of Water Engrs. (England), Am. Water Works Assn., Am. Soc. C.E.; Boston Soc. C.E., Harvard Engring. Soc., Am. Meteorol. Soc., Royal Meteorol. Soc. (Eng.), Am. Geophysical Union, Soc. Mayflower Descendants, Soc. Colonial Wars. Club: Harvard (Boston). Writer on water supply subjects. Cons. editor Water Works Engineering. Home: 53 N. Beacon St.

SAVILLE, THORNDIKE, cons. engr.; b. Malden, Mass., Oct. 3, 1892; s. Caleb Mills and Elizabeth (Thorndike) S.; A.B., Harvard, 1914, M.S., 1917; B.S., Dartmouth, 1914, C.E., 1915; M.S., Mass. Inst. Tech., 1917; E.D. (hon.), Clarkson Coll., 1944, Syracuse University, 1951; D.Sc., New York University, 1957; m. Edith Stedman Wilson, Sept. 10, 1921; 1 son, Thorndike. Sheldon traveling fellow, Harvard, 1919; asso. prof., later prof. hydraulic and sanitary engring., U. of N.C., 1919-32, also chief engr. N.C. Dept. of Conservation and Development, 1920-32; prof. hydraulic and sanitary engring., New York U., 1932-57, emeritus, 1957-69, asso. dean Coll. of Engring., 1935, dean, 1936-57, now emeritus; vis. prof. in hydraulics, U. Cal. at Berkeley, 1956; director Science and Engring. Center Study, University of Florida, 1958-60, consultant, 1960-66; chmn. Cons. Panel on Water Supply, N.Y.C., 1950-51; engr. mem. N.Y. State Pub. Health Council, 1947-58; rep. N.Y. State to Del. River Adv. Com., 1956-58; cons. Water Resources, N.Y. State Commn. Revision Constrn., 1957-58; cons. engr. Rockefeller Found. to govt. of Venezuela on water supply for Caracas, leave of absence, 1926-27. Student O.T.C., Plattsburg and Ft. Monroe, Aug.-Nov. 1917; commd. 2d lt. C.A.C., 8th Co.; transferred to Signal Corps, Dec. 12, 1917; promoted 1st lt. and detailed to Langley Field, Va., as sanitary engr.; mem. Beach Erosion Bd., Office of Chief Engr. U.S. Army, 1930-63, Coastal Engineering Research Board, 1963-69; exec. engr. water resources sect. of Nat. Resources Bd., 1934-35; mem. water resources com. of Nat. Resources Planning Bd., 1935-43, chairman project review com., 1940-43; cons. engr. on water resources and coastal engring. Mem. adv. council USPHS, 1949-52. Recipient jubilee medal Am. Soc. Mech. Engineers. Del. engring. socs. U.S. to Conf. Engring. Edn., London, 1953, Zurich, 1954; chmn. U.S. delegation, Paris, 1957, London, 1962; pres-gen. 5th Internat. Congress Coastal Engring., 5th, 1954, 6th, Fla., 1957. Fellow Am. Pub. Health Assn., A.A.A.S., Am. Soc. C.E. (hon. mem.; pres. met. sect. 1942-43, dir. 1945-48); mem. Water Pollution Control Fedn., Engrs. Joint Council (pres. 1954-55), Engrs. Council for Profl. Devel. (pres. 1955-56), Am. Soc. Engring. Edn. (hon.), Am. Water Works Assn., N.E. Water Works Assn., N.Y. Sewage Works Assn., Boston Soc. C.E., Am. Soc. Engring. Edn. (v.p. 1948-49, pres. 1949-50; Lamme award 1954), Harvard Engring. Soc. (pres. 1948), Mayflower Descs., Am. Inst. Cons. Engrs., Am. Meteorol. Soc., Am. Geophys. Union, Am. Acad. San. Engrs., Nat. Soc. Professional Engineers, International Association Hydraulic Research, Phi Beta Kappa, Sigma Xi, Tau Beta Pi. Clubs: Harvard (New York City). Author reports and articles on hydrology, water power, water supply, sewage and coastal engring. Home: Gainesville FL Died Gainesville FA Died Feb. 21, 1969; buried Chapel Hill NC

SAVORGNAN, ALESSANDRO, Italian diplomat; b. Trieste, Oct. 10, 1908; s. Franco Rodolfo and Giulia (Monti) S.; D. Jurisprudence, U. Rome, 1930; m. Rosette Andrus Sorge, Dec. 26, 1940; children—Roderic, Alessandro. Joined Italian Fgn. Service, 1934; vice consul, Lyons, France, 1935-36; vice consul, chief office, St. Louis, 1936-41; assigned Ministry Fgn. Affairs, Rome, 1941-43, 44-46; consul in Salzburg, Germany, 1943; 1st sec. legation, Caracas, Venezuela, 1947-48, counsellor embassy, 1948-50; dep. consul gen. in N.Y.C., 1950-53; assigned Ministry Fgn. Affairs, 1953-55; consul gen. in Algiers, Algeria, 1955-59, in San Francisco 1959-67; with Ministry of Fgn. Affairs, Rome, 1967, ambassador to Uruguay, Montevideo, until 1973. Decorated officer Order of Merit of Italian Republic; officer Legion of Honor (France). Clubs: Sci. 18 (charter, dir.) (Rome); Bohemian (San Francisco). Home: Died Mar. 1973.

SAWADA, KYOICHI, photographer; b. Aomori, Japan, Feb. 22, 1936; s. Naoyoshi and Maki (Aoyama S.; grad. Aomori High Sch., 1954; m. Sata Tazawa, June 18, 1956. With U.P.I., 1961-70, staff photographer Saigon (Vietnam) bur., 1965-70. Recipient 1st prize news photography and grand prize 10th annual World Press Photo Exhbn., 1965, Overseas Press Club Am. award, 1966, 67, Pulitzer prize in journalism for news photography, 1966, U.S. Camera Achievement award, 1966, 1st and 2d prizes newsphotography and grand prize World Press Photo Exhbn., 1966. Home: Hong Kong Died Oct. 1970.

SAWYER, BONNER DUPREE, lawyer; b. Grantsboro, N.C., Dec. 22, 1902; s. Walter Britton and Effie (Brinson) S.; student U. N.C.; m. Lethea Gaskins, Oct. 31, 1926; 1 son, William Britton. Admitted to N.C. bar, 1924; practice in Hillsboro, 1930-—; partner firm Sawyer & Loftin, 1959-—. Mem. N.C. Jud. Council, 1960-65; permanent mem. Jud. Conf. U.S. 4th Circuit Ct. Appeals, 1962-72. Vice pres., dir. Hillsboro Savs. & Loan Assn. Mem. Nat. council Boy Scouts Am., 1950, recipient Silver Beaver award, 1948. Trustee Johnston-New Hope Trust Fund, James M. Johnston Trust Charitable and Ednl. Purposes, Mt. Olive (N.C.) Coll., 1967-72. Fellow Am. Coll. Trial Lawyers; mem. Am., N.C., Orange County (pres. 1946), 15th Jud. (pres. 1952) bar assns., N.C. State Bar (pres. 1963-64), Delta Theta Phi. Baptist. Mason, Lion (charter mem., past pres. Hillsboro). Home: NC Died Jan. 25, 1972; buried Hillsborough Town Cemetery, Hillsborough NC

SAWYER, HAROLD EVERETT, clergyman; b. Clinton, Conn., Dec. 15, 1889; s. Enoch Augustus and Matella Julia (Waterhouse) S.; A.B., Trinity Coll., Hartford, Conn., 1913; A.M., Columbia, 1920; grad. Gen. Theol. Seminary, 1916, S.T.D., 1947; D.D., Trinity College, 1947; unmarried. Ordanied to ministry Episcopal Ch., 1916; curate Ch. of Redeemer, Morristown, N.J., 1916-17, St. Agnes' Chapel, Trinity Parish, N.Y. City, 1917-24; rector Grace Ch., Utica, N.Y., 1924-46; sec. dept. of social service, chmn. for examining chaplains; mem. Diocesan Council, Diocese of central N.Y., 1924-38; pres. Standing Com., 1940-46; dep. to Gen. Conv. P.E. Ch., 1931, 34, 37, 40, 43 (provisional dept., 1934-37). Consecrated bishop of Erie, Utica, N.Y., Nov. 6, 1946. Pres. St. Margaret's Corp. (Utica); v.p. English Clerical Union; mem. Newcomen Soc. of Eng., Erie Social Hygiene Assn., Erie County Health and Tuberculosis Assn. dir. Family Welfare Assn., 1924-46. Hon. asso. Am. Guild of Organists. Republican. Club: Ft. Schuyler (Utica). Home: Old Saybrook CT Died Jan. 1969.

SAWYER, HENRY BUCKLAND, b. Lowell, Mass., Apr. 28, 1871; s. Jacob Herbert and Mary Elizabeth (Wentworth) S.; ed. private schs., traveled extensively; m. Georgia W. Pope, Apr. 28, 1906; children—Henry B., Jr., Avery, Elizabeth W. Began with Chicopee Mfg. Co., Chicopee Falls, Mass., 1888; with Stone & Webster, engrs. and mgrs. pub. service cos., 1890, later becoming member of firm and then v.p. of corporation (retired, Apr. 30, 1931; formerly president and dir. New England Transportation Co.; mem. advisory board Mass. Investors Trust; trustee New York, N.H.&H. R.R. Co., Old Colony R.R. Co., Providence, Warren & Bristol R.R. Co., Hartford & Conn. Western R.R. Company, The Boston Terminal Company, Suffolk Savings Bank. Mem. Board of Finance of City of Fall River, 1932-36. Served with Battery A, Field Arty., Mass. Vols., from 1896 until resignation as lt. comdg., 1906. Trustee Boston Symphony Orchestra, Incorporated; trustee New England Conservatory of Music; mem. Franklin Foundation; dir. Home for Aged Men. Life member New England Historic Geneal. Society. Republican. Unitarian. Clubs: Union (Boston); Harvard Travellers; Country (Brookline). Home: 274 Beacon St., Boston 16‡

SAWYER, RUTH (MRS. ALBERT C. DURAND), author; b. Boston, Aug. 5, 1880; d. Francis Milton and Ethelind J. Sawyer; grad. Garland-Kindergarten Normal Sch., Boston, 1900; B.S., Columbia, 1904; m. Albert C. Durand (M.D.), June 4, 1911; children—David, Margaret. Took up professional story-telling, 1908; began writing short stories for mags., specializing in Irish folk stories. Unitarian. Author numerous books since 1915; latest publs.: The Little Red Horse, 1950; Maggie Rose, 1952; Journey Cake, Ho1953; A Cottage for Betsy, 1954; The Enchanted Schoolhouse, 1956; The Year of the Christmas Dragon, 1960; Dietrich of Berne; Daddles, 1963; Joy To the World, 1966; My Spain, 1967. Recipient Newberry medal for most distinguished contbn. to Am. lit. for children, 1937; Regina medal, 1965; Laura Ingalls Wilder medal. Home: Lexington MA Died June 3, 1970.

SAWYER, WELLS M(OSES), painter; b. farm in Ia., Jan. 31, 1863; s. Moses Calvin and Helen Jane (Cass) S.; studied law with William T. Rankin, also U.S. Judge Frank Allyn, 1879-82; art education, pupil of John O. Anderson, 1882-85, Chicago Art Institute, 1885-86, Corcoran School of Art, 1891-92, Washington Art Students League, 1893-97; private pupil of Howard Helmick; m. Kathleen Alton Bailey, June 8, 1896; children—Helen Alton (Mrs. Jerry Farnsworth), Bailey M. (Australian Air Force; killed in line of duty, 1941). Painted and illustrated in Chicago, 1886-90; with div. of illustrations, U.S. Geol. Survey and Bureau Am. Ethnology, Washington, D.C., 1891-97; prepared exhibit for Bur. of Animal Industry for Chicago World's Fair, 1893; artist to Pepper-Hearst expedition to Florida Keys (under Frank Hamilton Cushing), 1896-97; Office of Secretary of Treasury in charge design and inspection of furnishings for federal bldgs., 1897-1906; sec. holding co.; with Nat. City Bank of New York (pres. City Bank Club, 1914-15); retired because of poor health, 1926; lived in Spain until the war, pictures painted there in 30 one man shows, nat. and other galleries, colls., clubs in Spain and U.S.A.; spent much time in Mexico and Fla. Had one-man shows in large galleries of U.S. and abroad since 1898; works shown in exhibitions in U.S. and England. Represented in the permanent collections of large museums and galleries throughout U.S. Asso. mem. Chicago Soc. of Artists, 1889; mem. Am. Water Color Soc., Allied Artists of Am. Soc. Washington Artists (since 1892), Studio Guild (life); mem. Yonkers Art Assn. since 1915 (hon. pres.); mem. Provincetown and Sarasota Art Assns. Club: Salmagundi (life). Forwarding address: 47 Fifth Av., NYC 3 NY; (winter) Mira Mar Apt. K Sarasota FL‡

SAXMAN, M(ARCUS) W(ILSON), steel mfg.; b. Latrobe, Pa., Dec. 9, 1895; s. M. W. and Anna Frances (Suydam) S.; E.M., Lehigh U., 1918; m. Eleanor Elizabeth Bernheim, Nov. 10, 1920; children—Marcus Wilson, III, Virginia Clayton (Mrs. John Wandrisco). Gen. mgr. Derry Glass Co., 1919-24, Bradenville Coal & Coke Co., 1920-24; sec. Latrobe Steel Co., 1924-38, vice president, 1935-40, president, 1940-60, chairman of the board, 1960-68; pres. Unity Land Co. 1940-68. Treas. Latrobe Hosp. Pres. Latrobe Found. Home: Latrobe PA Died Sept. 13, 1968.

SAYERS, REAGAN, lawyer; b. Lufkin, Tex., June 21, 1914; s. Sam R. and Clyde (Philen) S.; student Tex. Christian U., 1930-32; LL.B., U. Tex., 1936; m. Katherine O'Brien. Admitted to Tex. bar, 1936, since practiced in Ft. Worth; partner Rawlings, Sayers &

Scurlock, 1936-69. Dir. Tex.-Okla. Express, Inc., Hood Rentals, Inc., C & J Leasing Co., Cherokee Terminal Co., Bonded Safeway Van Lines, Inc., Merchants Fast Motor Lines, Inc., Gem Storage & Terminal Co. Served from pvt. to capt., AUS, 1942-46. Decorated Croix de Guerre avec palme, Medal of Metz (France). Mem. Am., Ft. Worth bar assns., State Bar Tex., Motor Carrier Lawyers Assn. (pres. 1954-55), ICC Practitioners Assn., Phi Kappa Psi. Methodist. Mason. Clubs: Rivercrest Country, Forth Worth (Ft. Worth); Nat. Lawyers (Washington); Austin, Headliners (Austin, Tex.); Imperial (Dallas). Home: Ft Worth TX Died Oct. 27, 1969.

SAYRE, A(LBERT) NELSON, geologist; b. Granville, O., Jan. 28, 1901; s. Albert Thomas and Ida (Clouse) S.; B.S., Denison U., 1923, D.Sc., 1949; postgrad. U. Kan., 1923-24; Ph.D., U. Chgo., 1928; m. May Harriet Ludenslager, June 25, 1927 (dec. 1955); 1 dau., Elizabeth May (Mrs. Frank U. Naughton III); m. 2d, Elizabeth Dyer Gregg, Feb. 8, 1958. Geologist, Indian Terr. Oil & Illuminating Gas Co., Bartlesville, Okla., 1924; instr. U. Pa., 1926-29; geologist Ground Water div. U.S. Geol. Survey, Washington, 1929-46, chief of div., 1946-59, staff scientist, 1959-62; cons. ground water geologist, Washington, 1962-67; asso. Behre, Dolbear & Co. N.Y.C.; geologic adviser Office Inter-Am. Affairs, 1943; adviser U.S. Army, S.W. Pacific Area, 1944-45; rep. Dept. Interior on panels of Research and Devel. Bd., Munitions Bd. Dept. Def., 1946-52; del. Nat. Acad. Sci. to assemblies of Internat. Union Geodesy and Geophysics, 1948-67; cons. State N.C., Southampton Assn. (N.Y.). Recipient Medal of Freedom, 1946, Erasmus Haworth Distinguished Alumnus award, 1952, Distinguished Service award Dept. Interior, 1959. Fellow Geol. Soc. Am., A.A.A.S., Am. Geophys. Union (gen. sec.), Internat. Commn. on Subterranean Waters (past pres.); mem. Washington Acad. Sci. (past pres.), Am. Assn. Petroleum Geologists, Soc. Econ. Geologists, Am. Water Works Assn. Episcopalian. Club: Cosmos. Contbr. sci. jours. Home: Washington DC Died Oct. 12, 1967.

SAYRE, FRANCIS BOWES, diplomat; born South Bethlehem, Pennsylvania, April 30, 1885; son of Robert Heysham and Martha Finley (Nevin) S.; A.B., Williams Coll., 1909, LL.B., Harvard Univ., 1912, S.J.D., 1918; LL.D., Ursinus Coll., 1934; D.C.L., University of the South (Sewanee), 1938; L.H.D., Williams College, 1937; Litt. D., Bucknell College, 1942; LL.D., Rollins College, 1943; LL.D., Bowdoin College, 1944, U. of Rochester, 1949, Park College, Mo., 1950; m. Jessie Woodrow, d. President Woodrow Wilson, November 25, 1913 (died Jan. 15, 1933); children—Francis Bowes, Eleanor Axson, Woodrow Wilson; m. 2d, Elizabeth Evans Graves, June 28, 1937. Dep. assistant district attorney New York County, New York, 1912-13; assistant to president of Williams College and instructor in government in the college, 1914-17; Thayer teaching fellow, Harvard Law Sch., 1917-18, asst. prof. law Harvard U., 1919-24, prof., 1924-34; leave of absence, 1923-25; lecturer U. of Southern Calif., summer, 1923; adviser in foreign affairs to Siamese govt., 1923-25; apptd. E.E. and M.P. from Siam, 1925; jurisconsult to Ministry of Foreign Affairs, Siamese govt., 1925-30; negotiated on behalf of Siam new polit. and commercial treaties with France, Great Britain, The Netherlands, Spain, Portugal, Denmark and Sweden, 1925, Norway and Italy, 1926, abolishing extraterritoriality in Siam, also treaty of arbitration with Great Britain, 1925; dir. Harvard Inst. of Criminal Law, 1929-34; trustee Mass. State Training Schs., with supervision of juvenile delinquents of state, 1932-33; state commr. of correction, Mass., 1933; asst. Sec. of State (U.S.), by appmt. of President Franklin D. Roosevelt, 1933-39, in charge negotiation of Am. trade agreements under Sec. of State; chmn. Exec. Com. on Commercial Policy, U.S. Govt., 1933-39; chmn. U.S. Interdepartmental Com. on Philippines, 1934-39; mem. Board of Foreign Service Personnel, 1937-39; mem. Board of Examiners for the Foreign Service, U.S. State Department, 1937-39; U.S. High Commr. to the Philippines, 1939-42; escaped from Corregidor by submarine, Feb. 1942; special assistant to secretary of state and dep. dir. Foreign Relief and Rehabilitation Operations, 1943; diplomatic adviser, United Nations Relief and Rehabilitation Administration, 1944-47; headed UNRRA missions to Egypt, India, South Africa, Southern Rhodesia, Iraq, Iran, Cuba, Colombia and Dominican Republic, 1945; Denmark, Brazil, Uruguay, Argentina, Chile, Ecuador, Panama, Mexico, Portugal, Belgium, Peru, Bolivia and Venezuela, 1946; Guatemala, 1947; negotiating for relief supplies and funds for destitute war victims in Europe and Asia; U.S. Rep. in Trusteeship Council of United Nations with rank of ambassador, 1947-52, pres. Trusteeship Council, 1947-48, headed Trusteeship Council mission to president, 1947-48; headed Trusteeship Council mission to Western Samoa, 1947; member United States del. to 2d, 2d Special and 3d Sessions, Gen. Assembly of U.N., 1947-48, personal rep. in Japan of presiding bishop of Protestant Episcopal Ch. U.S.A., 1952-53. Trustee Woodrow Wilson Found. Created Phya Kalyan Maitri by King of Siam, 1924; awarded Grand Cross Crown of Siam, 1924; Grand Cross of White Elephant (Siam), 1925; Siamese decoration, 1953; Grand Officier Order of Orange-Nassau (Netherlands), 1925; Knight Grand Comdr., Chula Chom Klao (Siam), 1926; Comdr. Order of the Dannebrog, 1st Class (Denmark), 1926; Grand Cross Royal Order of Isabel la Catolica (Spain), 1926; Grand Cross Order of Christ (Portugal), 1926; Comdr. Order of Saint Olav, 1st Class (Norway), 1927; Grand Officier de la Legion d'Honneur (France), 1969 Grand Order Sacred Treasury (Japan). Mem. representing Siam, Permanent Court of Arbitration at The Hague, 1925-34. Fellow, Am. Acad. Arts and Sciences; member Internat. Inst. Polit. and Social Sciences (Belgium), Academie Diplomatique Internationale, Phi Beta Kappa, Sigma Phi. Democrat. Epsicopalian. Club: Cosmos (Washington). Author: Experiments in International Administration, 1919; Cases on Labor Law, 1922; Cases on Criminal Law, 1927, abridged edition, 1930; Siam Treaties with Foreign Powers, 1920-27, 28; Cases on the Law of Admiralty, 1929; Am. Must Act, 1935; The Way Forward; The American Trade Agreements Program, 1939; The Protection of American Export Trade, 1939; Glad Adventure (autobiography), 1957. Home: Washington DC Died Mar. 29, 1972; interred National Cathedral Washington DC

SAYRE, WALLACE STANLEY, polit. scientist; b. nr. Pt. Pleasant, W.Va., June 24, 1905; s. Alford and Cornelia (Tucker) S.; A.B., Marshall Coll., 1927; A.M., N.Y.U., 1928, Ph.D., 1930; LL.D., 1954; m. Kathryn McKnight, June 20, 1929; children—Alison, Linda. Asst. polit. sci. Marshall Coll., 1926-27; teaching fellow govt. N.Y.U., 1929. mem. faculty, 1929-40, asst. prof., 1934-40, adminstrv. asst. charge Pub. Service Tng. Program, 1937-38; sec. N.Y.C. Civil Service Commn., 1937-38, commr., 1938-42; prin. personnel cons. OPA, 1942, asst. dir. fuel rationing div., 1942-44, dir. personnel, 1944-46; prof. adminstrn. Cornell Sch. Bus. and Pub. Adminstrn., 1946-49; prof. govt. City Coll. N.Y., 1949-54, chmn. dept., 1951-54; vis. prof. pub. adminstrn. Columbia, 1950-52, prof. pub. adminstrn., Columbia 1954-59, Eaton professor of public administration, 1959, chmn. dept. public law and government, 1963-69; consultant Ford Foundation, 1952-53; research director N.Y. State Commn. on Govt. of N.Y.C., 1953. Mem. Mayor's Adv. Council, N.Y.C., 1954-61; vice chmn. Temporary Commn. N.Y.C. Finances, 1965-67; Member Commission Model Civil Service Law, 1938-39; adv. com. personnel management AEC 1948-53; exec. com. Citizens Union of N.Y., 1935-38, 50-67; mem. bd. dirs. Regional Plan Assn. of N.Y., from 1960. Mem. Am. Acad. Arts and Sciences, National Academy of Public Administration, Club: Cosmos. Author: Your Government, 1932; Outline of American Government, 1933; Charter Revision for the City of New York (with Russell Forbes and others), 1934; Education and the Civil Service in New York City (with Milton Mandel), 1937; The U.N. Secretariat, 1950; Personnel Administration in the Government of New York City (with Herbert Kaufman), 1952; Training for Specialized Mission Personnel (with Clarence Thurber), 1952. Editor Federal Government Service, published 1954, revised edit., 1965; Four Steps to Better Government of N.Y.C., 1954; (with Herbert Kaufman) Governing New York City, 1960, rev. edit., 1965. Contbr. books: Our Racial and National Minorities, 1937; The American Politician, 1939; Public Management in the New Democracy, 1941; Elements of Public Administration, 1946; The Administration of Foreign Affairs and Overseas Operations, 1951; (with Judith H. Parsis) Voting for President, 1970. Contbr. to Great Cities of the World, 1968; Congress and Urban Problems; Government, Technology and Social Problems; also encys., jours. Home: New York City NY Died May 18, 1972.

SBARBORO, ALFRED ENRICO, banker; b. San Francisco, Aug. 25, 1875; s. Andrea and Romilda (Botto) S.; student Heald's Bus. Coll., 1890; m. Ersilia Sartori, June 11, 1904; 1 dau., Alfreda (Mrs. Mathew Cullinan). Pres. Italian Am. Bank, 1922-27; exec. v.p. Bank of Am., S.F., 1927-40, ret. 1940, dir. since 1927; dir. Pacific Nat. Fire Ins. Co. since 1927, Di Giorgio Fruit Corp. since 1946, Di Giorgio Wine Co., since 1946, Western Mdse. Mart since 1929, Mchts. Nat. Realty Co. since 1932. Club: Commonwealth (S.F.). Address: 1201 California St., SF 9‡

SCAIFE, LAURISTON LIVINGSTON, bishop; b. Milton, Mass., Oct. 17, 1907; s. Roger L. and Ethel May (Bryant) S.; student Milton Acad., 1926; A.B., Trinity Coll, 1931; S.T.B., Gen. Theol. Sem., 1938; S.T.D., Gen. Theol. Sem., 1948, Hobart and William Smith Colls., 1949; D.D., Trinity College, 1948; LL.D., Alfred U., 1952; D.D., Trinity Coll. (Toronto), 1952; D.Th., St. Sergius Theol. Sem. Paris, 1953; m. Eleanor Morris Carnochan, October 19, 1939; children—Sibyll Grosvenor, Cynthia Lincoln. Master classical languages, St. Paul's Sch., Concord, N.H., 1937-38; curate, St. Thomas Episcopal Ch., N.Y. City, 1938-42; rector, Trinity Episcopal Ch., Newport, R.I., 1942-45; rector, Calvary Episcopal Ch., Pittsburgh, 1945-48; consecrated 7th bishop of Diocese of Western N.Y., 1948. Served as chaplain, Naval Res., 1944-46. Trustee St. Vladimir's Theol. Seminary, N.Y. City, 1941-70, Gen. Theol. Sem., N.Y.C., Hobart and William Smith colls., Nichols Sch.; chmn. trustees DeVeaux Sch.; dir. Buffalo Mus. Science. Member Society Mayflower Descendants, Pilgrim Soc., Signet Soc. of Cambridge Alpha Delta Phi. Clubs: University, Union, Century Association (New York City); Pundit (Buffalo); Buffalo Athletic, Buffalo, Buffalo Tennis and Squash, Saturn Union (Boston). Editor: The Russian Priests o Tomorrow, 1939. Home: Buffalo NY Died Sept. 19 1970; buried Hingham MA

SCANDRETT, RICHARD B., JR., lawyer; b Pittsburgh, Pa., Apr. 12, 1891; s. Richard B. and Agnes (Morrow) S.; A.B., Amherst, 1911; LL.B., Columbia Univ., 1916, Univ. of Colorado, 1916; Litt.D., Bethany 1944; m. Mary Emma Landenberger, October 4, 1930 children—Nancy (Mrs. Robert Ross), Dwight Morrow Eugenia (Mrs. Daniel Robbins), Alexander. Instructor Allegheny High Sch., 1911; admitted to Colorado bar 1916, New York bar, 1922, U.S. Supreme Court bar 1930; law clk. with William V. Hodges, Denver 1916-17; prof. law, U. of Colo., 1917; with Simpson Thacher & Bartlett, N.Y. City, 1919-23; chmn treasurer's advisory bd., Rep. Nat. Com., 1924; treas N.Y. County Rep. Com., 1928-32; legal and financia adviser to chmn. bd. Am. Gas &Electric Co., 1924-25 v.p., 1925-29; mem. law firm Scandrett & Chalaire 1930-60; mem. Allied Commn. on Reparations, 1945 pres. Survey Assos., Inc., 1935-49. Mem. of the board of directors Grenfell Assn. of America, chief UNRRA Mission to Byelorussia, 1946. Treas. Rep. Co. Com. of Orange Co., 1934-39; del. Rep. Nat. Conv., 1936; del. Rep. State Conv., 1930-36, 38; del., permanent chmn Rep. Judicial Conv., 9th Dist., 1937; received 1,998,628 votes as Rep. candidate for congressman-at-large from N.Y., 1938. Trustee Kiskiminetas Springs School; mem. bd. Calvin Coolidge Meml. Found. Served with Aviation Divison, U.S.N.R.F., advancing to ensign (naval aviator), 1918-19. Awarded Amherst Coll. medal for eminent service," 1936. Mem. Am., Orange County bar assns., Soc. of Military and Naval Officers, Fgn. Policy Association, Orange Co. Soc. (pres. 1935-36), The Society of Friendly Sons of St. Patrick, Pilgrims Acad. Polit. Sci. (life), New Eng. Soc., Beta Theta Pi, Phi Delta Phi, Delta Sigma Rho. Conglist. Mason, K.T. Clubs: Metropolitan Opera, University, Players. Author: Divided They Fall, 1941. Contbr. to mags. Home: Cornwall NY Died Dec. 15, 1969; cremated.

SCANLAN, JOHN JEROME;, business exec.; b. New York, N.Y., Oct. 1, 1909; s. Jeremiah and Ellen L (Dennin) S.; stud. Am. Inst. of Banking, New York U.; m. Dorothea O'Callaghan, Oct. 12, 1935. With Nat. City Bank of N.Y. and its trust affiliate, City Bank Farmers Trust Co., successively as page, messenger, clerk, sr. clerk handling investments, 1924-45; sec. and asst. to pres. N.Y. Cotton Exchange, 1947, sec., 1946, pres. N.Y. Merc. Exchange, 1960-70; exec. v.p. Nat. Stock Exchange, 1964-70; dir. Hamilton Fed. Savs. and Loan Assn.; mem. adv. com. Food Industry N.Y. Pres. City Bank Club (employee orgn.), 1942. Knight of Malta, K.C. Republican. Roman Catholic (mem. Cardinal's commn. laity). Clubs: Arkwright (dir.), Merchants (dir.), Commodity (v.p.). Home: Brooklyn NY Died June 11, 1970; buried St. Charles Cemetery, Farmingdale NY

SCANNELL, DAVID D., surgeon; b. Boston, Mass. June 24, 1874; s. Daniel and Joanna (Lyons) S.; grad. Boston Latin Sch., 1893; A.B., Harvard, 1897, M.D., 1900; m. Elizabeth A. Macdonald, Feb. 14, 1912; children—David D., John Gordon. Began practice at Boston, 1900; interne Boston City Hosp., 1900-02, Boston Lying-In Hosp., 1902; instr. in anatomy, Harvard Med. Sch., 1903-08, in surgery, 1908-11; asst. prof. clin. surgery, Tufts Coll. Med. Sch., 1911-12; lecturer on surgery, Grad. Sch. of Medicine, Harvard, 1912-15; cons. surgeon Boston City Hosp. and Quincy City Hosp.; cons. surgeon, U.S.P.H.S.; surgeon-in-chief Whidden Hosp., Everett, Mass.; trustee Home Savings Bank. Del. from Mass. to A.M.A. House of Delegates. Served as 1st lt., advancing to col., Med. Corps, U.S. Army, 18 months, World War. Mem. Boston Sch. Com. 11 yrs., chmn. twice. Member Mass. State Board Education, since 1947. Fellow Am. Coll. Surgeons mem. A.M.A., Mass. Med. Soc. Democrat. Catholic. Clubs: Harvard. Home: 489 Walnut Av., Jamaica Plain Boston. Office: 475 Commonwealth Av., Boston MA‡

SCARBOROUGH, (WILLIAM) BYRON, lawyer; b Ft. Worth, Oct. 6, 1912; s. L.R. and Neppie (Warren) S.; A.B., Baylor U., 1933, LL.B., 1935; m. Joyce Cole; children—Karen, William Byron. Admitted to Tex. bar, 1935; partner firm Cantey, Hanger, Gooch, Cravens & Scarborough, Ft. Worth. Cons. edn., mem. adv. com. local pub. schs. Served to lt. USNR, World War II; PTO Mem. Am., Tex., Ft. Worth bar assns. Baptist (deacon) Mason, Lion (past pres.). Clubs: River Crest Country, Shady Oaks Country, Ridglea Country, Fort Worth, Petroleum, Fort Worth Boat. Home: Fort Worth TX Died June 6, 1968; buried Greenwood Cemetery, Fort Worth TX

SCARBOROUGH, GEORGE MOORE, playwright; b. Mt. Carmel, Tex., June 3, 1875; s. Judge John B. and Mary Adelaide (Ellison) S.; student Baylor U. and U. of Tex.; LL.B., U. of Tex., 1897; m. Annie Saunders, 1899. Practiced law in Tex., 1897-1905; reporter New York American, 1906-09; with U.S. Dept. Justice, 1909-14. Author: The Lure, 1913; At Bay, 1913; The Court of

Last Resort, 1913; What is Love? 1914; The Heart of Wetona, 1916; Moonlight and Honeysuckle, 1918; The Son-Daughter, 1919; Bluebonnet, 1920; The Mad Dog, 1921; Mrs. Hope's Husband, 1921; The Grail, 1922. Co-Author: (with Annette A. Westbay) The Girl I Loved; The Moon of Honey; It. Home: 626 St. Paul Av., Los Angeles CA‡

SCARLETT, FRANK M., federal judge; b. Brunswick, Ga., June 9, 1891; s. Frank M. and Bessie Brailsford (Bailey) S.; student Glynn Acad., Brunswick, 1898-1908, Gordon Coll., Barnesville, Ga., 1908-10; LL.B., U. of Ga., Athens, Ga., 1913; m. Mary Louisea Morgan, June 15, 1923 (dec. Oct. 1962); children—Mary Louise (Mrs. L. G. Crowe), Frank M., Richard; m. 2d, Mary Roberta Waller, May 29, 1965. Admitted Ga. bar, 1913; practiced law in Brunswick under name Courtland Symmes and Scarlett, 1913-15, pvt. practice, 1915-29; apptd. solicitor fo city court of Brunswick, 1919-29; enetered partnership under name of Reese, Scarlett, Bennett and Highsmith, 1929-37, with Reese, Scarlett, Bennett and Gilbert, 1937-46; U.S. So. Dist. judge, Feb. 14, 1946. Former dir. Am. Nat. Bank Brunswick, Sea Island Co., Sea Island Beach, Ga. Chmn. Dem. exec. com. 1925-45. Pres. Brunswick C. of C., 1936-38; mem. Alpha Tau Omega. Presbyterian (elder). Mason (Shriner). Elk. Clubs: Capitol City (Atlanta); Oglethorpe (Savannah, Ga.). Home: Brunswick GA Died Nov 19, 1971.

SCARLETT, WILLIAM, retired bishop; b. Columbus, O., Oct. 3, 1883; s. William and Myra (Siebert) S.; A.B., Harvard, 1905; D.D., (hon.), 1950; B.D., Episcopal Theol. Sch., 1909, D.D., 1967; LL.D., U. Ariz., 1922, Washington U., 1932; D.D., U. of South, 1932; m. Leah Van Riper Oliver, Sept. 2, 1941. Deacon, 1909, priest, 1910, P.E. Ch.; asst. St. George's Ch., N.Y., 1909-11; dean Trinity Cathedral, Phoenix, 1911-22; dean Christ Ch. Cathedral, St. Louis, 1922-30; elected bishop co-adjutor, P.E. Ch., 1930; bishop of Mo., 1935-53, ret.; chmn. Joint Commn. on Social Reconstrn. P.E. Ch., 1940-52; chmn. dept. Internat. Justice and Goodwill, Nat. Council Chs. Christ in Am., 1948-52. Mem. Sec. Navy's Civilian Adv. Commn. Regent U. Ariz., 1913-21; mem. Am. Council Race Relations; mem. nat. com. Am. Civil Liberties Union, 1930-55. Member Delta Tau Delta. Mason. Clubs: Harvard (N.Y.C. and Boston). Contbr. Best Sermons, 1926; What Are We Fighting For?, and other volumes. Editor: Christianity Takes a Stand; Christian Demand for Social Justice; Phillips Brook's Selected Sermons; To Will One Thing; mem. editorial bd. Christianity and Crisis, 1954-56. Contbr. to Interpreters Bible. Home: Castine ME Died Mar. 28, 1973.

SCATES, DOUGLAS EDGAR, educator; b. San Diego, Calif., Dec. 11, 1898; s. Walter Bennett and Leona Louise (Roberts) S.; A.B., Whitworth Coll, Spokane, Wash., 1922; Ph.D., U. of Chicago, 1926; m. Marjorie Lee Baldwin, Dec. 26, 1922 (div. 1950); children—Charmain Lathrope, Marian Lee; m. 2d, Alice Virginia Yeomans, July 4, 1952 (div. Apr. 1955); m. 3d, Eleanor Virginia Robertson, Aug. 26, 1955. Asst. to examiner U. Chgo., 1923-24, instr. in dept. of edn., 1924-26; asst. prof. of edn. Indiana U., 1926-29; dir. bur. of research, Cin. Pub. Schs., 1929-39; associate professor education, Duke University, 1939-46; professor, 1946-48; summer school instr. in univs. of Chicago, 1925, 27, Loyola, 1926, Ind., 1928, 29, Cincinnati, 1930. Duke, 1931-48, Redlands, 1958, Fla., 1956, 1957, 1959-66; with Office of Secretary of War, Personnel Research Section, 1946-47. Dir. research in scientific personnel, for the American Council on Edn., on projects sponsored by the Office of Naval Research, 1948-50: vis. prof. edn. Queens Coll., City of N.Y. 1950-52; asst. to the dean tchr. edn. City Univ. of N.Y., 1952; cons. Office Naval Research, also Human Resources Research Inst., U.S.A.F., 1950-52; engaged in writing Washington, 1952-53; prof. edn. U. Fla. 1953-67, cons. statis. lab., 1955-62; research specialist, American Social Health Assn., N.Y.C., 1954-55. Military service, Wash. N.G., May-Oct. 1918; and S.A.T.C., Oct.-Dec., 1918. Fellow A.A.A.S. (member council 1947-55), Am. Psychol. Assn.; mem. N.E.A., Am. Ednl. Research Assn. (exec. com., 1937-43, 46-49; v.p. 1946-47; pres. 1947-48; chmn. com. to revise constn. 1949-51; chmn. com. research promotion 1952-56). American Association School Administrators, Am. Statis. Assn. (v.p. 1941, field rep., Cincinnati, 1937-39; pres. N.C. chapter, 1941-42, field epresentative, North Carolina. 1945-48), Psychometric Society, National Council on Measurement in Education, Phi Delta Kappa (chmn., commn. on Research and Program, 1946-50). Am. Assn. Univ. Profs. Vice pres. Ohio Conf. Statisticians, 1932, pres. 933; pres. Ednl. Research Dept. Ohio Edn. Assn., 934, 1935. Presbyterian. Author: The Methodology of Educational Research (with C. V. Good, A. S. Barr), 936; Methods of Research (with C. V. Good), 1954. Chairman editorial board and editor, Review of Ednl. Research of Ednl. Research 1937-43; asso. editor Journal of Educational Research, 1930-39, mem. editorial bd., 1939-48; contbg. editor Journal of Experimental Education, 1932-48; mem. bd. of editors. ncy. of Educational Research, 1939-41, 1946-50; assoc. editor, Jour. Am. Statis. Assn., 1948-50; editor esearch sect. Jour. Teacher Edn. 1950-59. Home: Gainesville FL Died Nov. 16, 1967; buried Hillcrest emetery, Gainesville FL

SCHAAF, ANTON, sculptor; b. Milwuakee, Wis., Feb. 22, 1869; s. Karl and Florentina (Bee) S.; studied art at Cooper Union, New York, under Shirlaw, Cox and Beckwith, at Charcoal Club under St. Gaudens and Dewing and at Nat. Acad. Design under Ward; m. Grace Androvette, of Brooklyn, N.Y., Apr. 17, 1912. Principal works: Shaw memorial, Woodlawn Cemetery, N.Y.; statue of Gen. Ord, Vicksburg Nat. Mil. Park, also a number of busts and reliefs in same park; Meredith portrait tablet, at Tomkins Avenue Church, Brooklyn; war memorial, Central Congl. Ch., Brooklyn; Prudential Ins. Co. war memorial, Newark, N.J., Ridgewood war memorial, and 14th Inf. soldiers monument, Brooklyn; Benjamin Franklin statue, Sesquicentennial Expn., Phila.; Haym Salomon monument, N.Y. City, soldier called Armistice"; War Memorial, Glendale, Brooklyn, N.Y.; Relief, J. Temple Gwathmey, New York Cotton Exchange; Relief, J. Waldo Smith, Ashokan Dam, New York; Capt. Ericsson & Monitor Relief, New York City; Portrait Wm. H. Todd, New York City; Parks S. Cadman memorial, Central Congl. Ch., Brooklyn, N.Y. Mem. Nat. Sculpture Soc., Archtl. League, New York. Home: 397 E. 17th St., Brooklyn NY Studio: 1931 Broadway, New York NY‡

SCHAEFER, BERTHA, gallery dir., interior designer; b. Yazoo City, Miss.; d. Emil and Julia (Marx) Schaefer; B.A., Miss. State Coll. for Women; diploma, Parsons Sch. Design, 1922. Owner Bertha Schaefer Interiors, N.Y.C., 1924-71; gallery dir. Bertha Schaefer Gallery of Contemporary Art, N.Y.C., featuring Am. and European painting and sculpture, 1944-71; designer furniture for Modern by Singer, M. Singer & Sons, N.Y.C., 1950-61; interior designer for pvt. homes, apts., hotel lobbies, and restaurants. First decorative showing Regency, Antiques' Exhbn., Grand Central Palace, 1928; installed pioneer decorative interior application of flourescent lighting, 1939; created The Modern House Comes Alive, exhbn. furnished models of architects advanced designs, 1947-49; furnished gallery exhibition of interior design in Fine Arts, Phila. Art Alliance, 1952; designed Gen. Electric Bathroom, 1953; created color layout for auditorium of new temple, Washington Hebrew Congregation, 1954. Recipient Good Design award, Mus. Modern Art, 1952; award Decorators' Club of New York, 1959. Member American Inst. Decorators, Home Lighting Forum, Illuminating Engring. Soc., Archtl. League of N.Y., Decorators' Club of N.Y. (pres. 1947-48, 55-57), Am. Fedn. Arts, Art Dealers Assn. Am., Inc. Home: New York City NY Died May 24, 1971.

SCHAEFER, MILNER BAILY, oceanographer; b. Cheyenne, Wyo., Dec. 14, 1912; s. Heinrich Gottlieb and Kate Rosse (Baily) S.; B.S. magna cum laude, U. Wash., 1935; Ph.D., 1950; m. Isabella Long, May 4, 1949; children—Kate Baily, Kurt Milner, Patrick Joseph. Sci. asst. Internat. Fisheries Commn., 1934-35; asst. biologist, then biologist Wash. Dept. Fisheries, 1935-39; scientist Internat. Pacific Salmon Fisheries Commn., 1939-42; instr. Sch. Fisheries, U. Wash., 1946; with U.S. Fish and Wildlife Service, 1946-50, chief research and devel. Pacific Oceanic fishery investigation, Honolulu, 1948-50; dir. investigations Inter-Am. Tropical Tuna Commn., La Jolla, Cal., 1951-63, sci. cons., 1963-70; mem. staff Scripps Instn. Oceanography, La Jolla, 1951-70, prof. oceanography, dir. Inst. Marine Resources, 1962-70. Mem. com. effects atomic radiation oceanography and fisheries, Nat. Acad. Scis.-NRC, 1956-63, com. oceanography, 1957-68, chmn., 1964-67, mem. Latin Am. sci. bd., 1963-68; sci. adv. com. marine protein resources devel., 1963-70; expert fisheries, secretariat Internat. Conf. Law of Sea, Geneva, Switzerland, 1958; cons. spl. fund UN, 1960-65; chmn. standing com. marine sci. Pacific Sci. Assn., 1962-66; mem. expert panel tuna research FAO, 1964-69, chmn. 1964-66, mem. IWP working group marine resources appraisal, 1966-70; mem. Gov. Cal. Adv. Council Marine Resources, 1965-70, chmn., 1965-66; adv. com. fisheries and oceanography State Dept., 1965-65; adv. com. marine resources devel. Dept. Interior, 1967, science adviser, since 1967-69, consultant National Council Marine Resources and Engring. Devel., 1967-70. Served as officer USNR, 1942-46. Recipient Diploma de Reconocimienta (Costa Rica), 1967. Founding fellow Am. Inst. Fishery Research Biologists; fellow of the California Academy of Sciences, mem. Am. Soc. Icthyologists and Herpetologists, Nat. Oceanography Assn. (bd. dirs. 1966-67), Pacific Fishery Biologists (pres. 1939-40), Am. Fisheries Soc., Am. Geophys. Union, Am. Statis. Assn., Biometrics Soc., Am. Soc. Limnology and Oceanography (pres. Western div. 1956-57), Marine Tech. Soc., Phi Beta Kappa, Sigma Xi. Home: San Diego CA Died July 27, 1970.

SCHAEFFER, CHARLES EDMUND, general sec.; b. near Fleetwood, Pa., Dec. 26, 1867; s. John S. and Magdalena (Peters) S.; Keystone State Normal Sch., Kutztown, Pa.; A.B., Franklin and Marshall Coll., 1889; grad. Theol. Sem. Reformed Ch. in U.S., Lancaster, Pa., 1892; D.D., Heidelberg U., Tiffin, O., 1910; S.T.D., U. of Hungary, 1929; m. Carrie S. Leinbach, Nov. 1, 1892; m. 2d, Alice Naomi Quillman, Nov. 9, 1927. Ordained Reformed Ch. ministry, 1892; pastor Macungie, Pa., 1892-96, Ch. of the Ascension, Norristown, Pa., 1896-98, St. Mark's Ch., Reading, Pa., 1898-1909; gen. sec. Bd. of Home Missions Ref. Ch. in U.S., since 1908; pres. Gen. Synod Ref. Ch., 1929-32. Mem. Fed. Council Churches of Christ in America; sec. Commn. on Evangelism; pres. Phila. Fedn. of Chs., 1932-35; pres. Home Missions Council, New York 1933-35; pres. Western Sect. Alliance of Ref. Chs., 1933-35. Author: Our Home Mission Work; Glimpses Into Hungarian Life; Beside All Waters—A Study in Home Missions; The Man From Oregon, 1944. Home: 124 S. 50th St. Address: 1505 Race St., Philadelphia PA‡

SCHAEFFER, ROBERT E., poet, educator; b. May 27, 1929; E.A., Eastern Mich. U. With U. Cal. Student Bookstore, Los Angeles; tchr. arts and humanities extension U. Cal. at Los Angeles. Mem. Hist. Poetry Soc. So. Cal., Santa Monica Writers Club, (chmn. poetry 1965). Author: Saturday Poems, 1964; The Farm and Its Seasons, 1965; A Single Breath, 1969; Go Wrestle with the Wind, 1969. Address: Inglewood CA Died Oct. 11, 1972.

SCHAEFFER, ROBERT L., surgeon; b. Fleetwood, Berks County, Pa., Dec. 23, 1881; s. George S. and Catharine M. (Leibelsberger) S.; ed. Keystone State Normal Sch., 1898-1901; A.B., Franklin and Marshall College, 1904, D.Sc., 1943; M.D, University of Pennsylvania, 1908; D.Sc., Muhlenberg College, Allentown, Pennsylvania, 1947; married Millie Louise Ochs, November 30, 1914; children—Frances Clara, Robert L., Charles David. Began as interne Allentown (Pa.) Hosp., 1908, anesthetist, 1909-14, asst. surgeon, 1914-23, surgeon in chief, 1923-60, chief of staff; surgeon for Central R.R. Co., Reading R.R. Co.; dir. First Nat. Bank, Allentown, Trustee Allentown Hosp.; Franklin and Marshall College, Cedar Crest Coll. Fellow Am. Coll. Surgeons; mem. A.M.A., Medical Soc. of State of Pa. (president 1955-56), Am. Bd. of Surgery, C. of C. (vice president). Democrat. Mem. Allentown PA Died Jan. 11, 1965; buried Fairview Cemetery Allentown PA

SCHAFFER, OTTO GEORGE, educator; b. Lake Geneva, Wis., Feb. 25, 1886; s. Gottlieb George and Wilhelmina (Meister) S.; student Lake Forest Coll., 1909-10; B.S., U. of Ill., 1914; m. Anne Caspersen, Feb. 17, 1917. Began as landscape architect, 1914; private practice landscape architecture, Lake Forest, Ill., 1915-20; instr. landscape architecture, U. of Ill., 1920-54, prof., 1930, head dept., 1931-54, emeritus, 1954. Chmn. Zoning Commn., Urbana, 1940. Fellow Am. Soc. Landscape Architects (trustee 1944-46); mem. Ill. State Bd. Art Advisors. Unitarian. Club: University. Contbr. articles to mags. Home: Urbana IL Died Apr. 21, 1970.

SCHAFFER, WILLIAM I., lawyer; b. Phila., Pa., Feb. 11, 1867; s. George A. and Mary H. (Irwin) S.; pub. sch. edn.; LL.D., Lafayette Coll., 1920, University of Pennsylvania, 1939; Villanova College, 1940; married Susan A. Cross. Admitted to Pennsylvania bar, 1888; dist. atty. Delaware County, Pa., 1893-1900; state reporter of Pa., 1900-19; atty. gen. of Pa., 1919-21; justice Supreme Court of Pa., 1921-40, chief justice, 1940-Jan. 4, 1943. Republican. Clubs: Union League, Rittenhouse, Philadelphia (Phila.). Home: Haverford PA Office: 2610 Girard Trust Bldg., Philadelphia PA‡

SCHAIRER, JOHN FRANK, research scientist; b. Rochester, N.Y., Apr. 13, 1904; s. John George and Josephine Marie (Frank) S.; B.S. in Chemistry, Yale, 1925, M.S. in Geology, 1926, Ph.D. in Chemistry, 1928; m. Ruth Naylor, July 20, 1940; children—John Everett and Jeanne Evelyn (twins). Physical chemist, geophysical lab. Carnegie Instn. of Washington, 1927-69, research asso., 1969-70; spl. asst. div. one Nat. Def. Research Com., 1942-45. Recipient Hillebrand award, Chem. Soc. Washington, 1942; President's Certificate of Merit, 1948; Medal of Honor (Eng.), 1948, Arthur L. Day medal, Geol. Soc. Am., 1953. Mem. Nat. Acad. Scis., Mineral. Soc. Am. (pres. 1943, recipient Roebling medal 1963), Geological Soc. Am. (v.p. 1944), Am. Chem. Society, Am. Geophys. Union, Nat. Capital Orchid Soc. (pres. 1949-50, 63-64, editor bull. 1951-70), Geochem. Soc. (p.p.), Internat. Assn. Volcanology (v.p. 1957-60), Sigma Xi, Gamma Alpha, Alpha Chi Sigma. Clubs: Cosmos (Washington); Men's Garden of Montgomery County. The mineral Schairerite named in his honor, 1931; The Schairer Vol. of Am. Jour. Sci., 1969. Home: Chevy Chase MD Died Sept. 26, 1970; buried Rock Creek Cemetery, Washington DC

SCHAPER, WILLIAM AUGUST, univ. prof.; b. La Crosse, Wis., Apr. 17, 1869; s. Henry and Elizabeth (Otte) S.; grad. State Normal Sch., River Falls, Wis., 1891; B.Litt., U. of Wis., 1895; M.A., Columbia, 1898, Ph.D., 1901; U. of Berlin, Germany, 1900-01; m. Harriett E. McKowen, Dec. 25, 1907. Prin. Alma (Wis.) High Sch., 1891-93; instr. in polit. science and history, Duquesne (Ia.) High Sch., 1898-1900; instr. polit. science, U. of Minn., 1900-01, asst. prof., 1901-04, prof, 1904-17; prof. finance, Sch. of Business, Univ. of Okla., 1925-38; reinstated by U. of Minn. as prof. of polit. science, emeritus, Jan. 1938. Mem. Phi Beta Kappa. Author: Sectionalism and Representation in South Carolina, 1901; also various repts. and articles in polit. science publs. Regular contbr. to Tax systems of the

World since 1929. Winner of Justin Winsor Prize in Am. history, 1900. Home: 808 S. Flood Av., Norman OK‡

SCHARFF, MAURICE ROOS, cons. engr.; b. Natchez, Miss., Apr. 14, 1888; s. Monroe and Rosa (Roos) S.; prep. edn., Phillips Exeter Acad., Exeter, N.H.; B.S., Mass. Inst. Tech., 1909, M.S., 1911; m. Jeanne Adler, Apr. 30, 1919; 1 son, Samuel Adler. Asst. engr., Morris Knowles, cons. engr., Pittsburgh, Pa., 1911-14, prin. engr., 1914-16, asst. chief engr. and v.p., 1916-21; valuation engr., Phila. Co. and affiliated corps, 1921-25, chief engr., 1925-27; chief engr., Pittsburgh br. Byllesby Engring. and Management Corp., 1927-28; cons. engr., Pittsburgh, 1928-32, N.Y.C., 1932-42, 1946-67; director Duquesne Light Company (Pittsburgh). Consultant to Task Force on Water Resources, Commn. on Orgn. Exec. Branch of Govt., 1954-55; cons. ICA and govts. Viet Nam, Laos, 1956-58. 1st lt. to capt. C.E., U.S. Army, 1918-19. Maj. to col., Corps of Engrs., U.S. Army, 1942-46. Mem. Am. Inst. Cons. Engrs., Am. Soc. C.E.; asso. mem. Am. Inst. E.E., Soc. Am. Military Engrs., Military Order World War. Republican. Clubs: City, Technology (New York); Cosmos (Washington, D.C.). Author: Electrical Utilities (with W. E. Mosher and others), 1929; Depreciation of Public Utility Property, 1940. Home: New York City NY Died Apr. 6, 1967; buried Arlington Nat. Cemetery Arlington VA

SCHARPS, ANDREW, banker; b. N.Y.C., Dec. 22, 1905; s. Albert Turner and Jeanette (Korn) S.; A.B., Princeton, 1926; student Harvard Bus. Sch., 1927-28; m. Kathryn Frank, June 3, 1931; children—Elizabeth (Mrs. John L. E. Griffith), Andrew. With Mfrs. Trust Co., 1926-46, 52-61, v.p., 1952-61; with Wertheim & Co., 1947-51; with Mfrs. Hanover Trust Co., 1961-70, vice pres., treas., 1963-66, sr. v.p., 1967-70. Mem. N.Y. Soc. Security Analysts. Clubs: Pinceton of N.Y.; Quaker Ridge Golf (Scarsdale). Home: Scarsdale NY Died May 29, 1971.

SCHATTSCHNEIDER, ELMER ERIC, univ. prof.; b. Bethany, Minn., Aug. 11, 1892; s. Julius John and Clara (Volkmann) S.; A.B., U. Wis., 1915; A.M., U. Pitts., 1927; Ph.D., Columbia, 1935; LL.D., Moravian Coll., 1960; m. Florence Adeline Walker, June 16, 1917; 1 son, Frank Walker. Y.M.C.A. sec., Butler, Pa., 1915; teacher, Butler (Pa.) Sr. High Sch., 1919-27; instr. govt., Columbia, 1927-30; asst. prof. polit. science, N.J. Coll. for Women, New Brunswick, N.J., 1929-30; asst. prof. govt., Wesleyan U., Middletown, Connecticut, 1930-35, associate professor, 1935-38, John E. Andrus professor, 1939-60, emeritus professor, 1960-71, chmn. Pub. Affairs Center, 1955-61. Mem. Conn. Bd. Mediation and Arbitration, Conn. Bd. Pardons. Bd. dirs. Citizenship Clearing House, chmn., 1957-61. Served with USNRF, 1918-19. Mem. Am. Polit. Science Assn. (pres. 1956-57), Phi Beta Kappa. Author: Politics, Pressures, and the Tariff, 1935; Party Government, 1940; The Struggle for Party Government, 1948; The Semisovereign People: A Realist's View of Democracy in America, 1960; Two Hundred Million Americans in Search of a Government, 1969. Co-author: Guide to the Study of Public Affairs; Local Political Surveys, 1962. Home: Old Saybrook CT Died Mar. 4, 1971.

SCHATZ, CARL F., corp. exec.; b. 1906; student U. Pitts. With G.C. Murphy Co., from 1937, v.p. finance, from 1968, also dir. C.P.A., Pa. Address: McKeesport PA Died June 29, 1970.

SCHAUB, IRA OBED, dir. agrl. extension; b. Stokes County, N.C., Sept. 28, 1880; s. William Henry and Mary Laura (Grabs) S.; B.S., North Carolina State Coll. of Agr. and Engring., 1900; student Johns Hopkins U., 1900-03; D.Sc., Clemson Coll., 1937; m. Maud Kennedy, July 27, 1910; children—Maud Kennedy, Ira Obed, Jr. Asst. chemist, Ill. Exptl. Sta., 1903-05; asst. prof. Soils, Iowa State Coll., 1905-09; Boys and Girls Club agt., North Carolina State Coll., 1909-13; farm supt., demonstration work, Frisco R.R., 1913-18; field agt., extension service, U.S. Dept. of Agr., 1919-24; dean, Sch. Agric., 1926-45; dir. Experiment Station, 1937-39; dir. Agricultural Extension Service 1924-50 (on leave since Oct. 1948) agricultural expert to Germany, under United States Office Military Government. Member Pine Burr Farm Bur., Assn. Southern Agrl. Workers (pres. 1940), Acacia, Epsilon Sigma Phi (Distinguished Service Ruby 1940), Kappa Sigma, Phi Kappa Phi, Alpha Zeta, Gamma Sigma Epsilon, Lambda Gamma Delta. Mason, Grange. Co-author Soil Physics Lab. Guide. Home: Raleigh NC Died Sept. 13, 1971; buried Mt. Pleasant Methodist Church, King NC

SCHAUFFLER, RACHEL CAPEN, writer; b. at Brunn, Austria, Mar. 9, 1876; d. Henry Albert (D.D.) and Clara Eastham (Gray) S.; brought to America, 1881; grad. Central High Sch., Cleveland, 1893; A.B., Vassar, 1897; unmarried. Teacher in Miss Frazer's Sch. for Girls, Lakewood, N.J., 1903-5; head of English Dept. Lakewood Sch. for Girls, 1910-12; teacher and welfare worker, N.J. State Hosp. for Insane, Trenton, 1912-13. Presbyn. Mem. Phi Beta Kappa. Club: Women's University (New York). Author: The Goodly Fellowship, 1912. Home: 645 Esplanade, Pelham Manor NY‡

SCHEDLER, DEAN L., govt. ofcl.; b. Stillwater, Okla., Sept. 10, 1914; s. Frank Carl and Ethel Lillian (Smith) S.; student Okla. A. and M. Coll., 1931-34; A.B., George Washington U., 1935; m. Jacquette Kilness, May 22, 1946. Mem. editorial staff, Manila (Philippines) Daily Bulletin, 1938-40; fgn. corr., Associated Press, 1940-46, war corr., Bataan, Dec. 7, 1941 and throughout Pacific area until conclusion of hostilities; dir. public relations, U.S. Dept. of Justice, Washington, 1947-70. Mem. Kappa Alpha, Sigma Delta Chi. Clubs: Overseas (N.Y. City); National Press (Washington). Home: McLean VA Died Aug. 1970.

SCHEETZ, FRANCIS HARLEY, lawyer; b. Norristown, Pa., Sept. 30, 1894; s. Remandus and Elizabeth (Harley) S.; B.A., Cornell U., 1915, B.Chem., 1916; LL.B., Harvard, 1921; m. Virginia DeMorat Smith, May 27, 1926. Admitted to Pa. bar, 1922, U.S. Supreme Ct., 1940; asso. Evans, Bayard & Frick, Phila., 1921-28, partner, 1928-54; partner Pepper, Hamilton & Scheetz and predecessor, Phila., 1954-68. Trustee emeritus, presdl. councillor Cornell U.; asso. trustee U. Pa. Am. Field Service, French Army, 1917; served 2d lt. to capt., U.S. Army, 1918; AEF. Mem. Am., Pa., Phila. bar assns., Bar Assn. City N.Y., Juristic Soc., Theta Delta Chi. Clubs: Merion Cricket, Midday, Racquet; Century Assn.; Union League. (N.Y.C.). Home: Villanova PA Died Sept. 25, 1968; buried Riverside Cemetery, Norristown PA

SCHEFFEY, LEWIS CASS, gynecologist; b. Stamford, Conn., Sept. 21, 1893; s. Lewis Cass and Esther Mary (Werner) S.; P.D., Phila. Coll. of Pharmacy and Science, 1915; M.D., Jefferson Med. Coll., 1920, D.H.L., 1959; D.Sc., Ursinus U., 1943; married Anna Catherine Thun, December 12, 1922; children—Lewis Cass, III, Julia Westkott, Andrew Jackson Werner, Hildegarde Thun, Cornelia Anne. Pharmacist, Jefferson Hosp., Philadelphia, 1915-20; resident physician Jefferson Med. Coll. Hosp., Phila., 1920-22, formerly assistant gynecologist; also with dept. of gynecology, Jefferson Med. Coll., 1923-69, successively as instr., asst. prof. and asso. prof., clin. professor, professor of obstetrics and gynecology, head dept., dir. div. gynecology, 1946-55, prof. emeritus, 1955-69. Served as private Med. Reserve Corps, 1917, S.A.T.C., 1918. V.p. Carl Schurz Meml. Found. Diplomate Am. Bd. Obstetrics and Gynecology. Fellow A.C.S., Coll. Physicians Philadelphia, Pitts. Obstet. and Gynecol. Soc. (hon.); mem. Am. Gynecological Society (president 1959), Obstet. Soc. Phila. (past pres.), A.M.A., Pa. Med. Soc., Phila. County Med. Soc. (past pres.), Pan Pacific Surg. Assn., Am. Acad. Obstetrics and Gynecology, Intersociety Cytology Council (pres. 1956), American Radium Society, American Association for Cancer Research, Am. Cancer Soc. (mem. exec. committees Pennsylvania and Philadelphia divisions; president 1957-58); Jefferson Society Phila., Acad. Natural Sciences of Phila., Am. Acad. Polit. and Social Science, Pa. Museum of Art, Pa. Acad. Fine Arts, German Soc. Pa., Pa.-German Folklore Soc. (pres. 1938-40), Hist. Soc. of Berks Co. (Pa.), Alumni Assn. of Phila. Coll. of Pharmacy and Sci. (past pres.), Jefferson Med. Coll. Alumni Assn. (past pres.), Am. Huguenot Soc., Sydenham Med. Coterie, Phi Delta Chi, Phi Alpha Sigma (past nat. pres.), Alpha Omega Alpha (hon.). Episcopalian. Clubs: Art Alliance, Racquet (Phila.). Home: Haverford PA Died Mar. 13, 1969; buried St. Mary's Ch., Ardmore PA

SCHEIBERLING, EDWARD NICHOLAS, lawyer; b. Albany, N.Y., Dec. 2, 1888; s. Martin and Mary (Schneider) S.; LL.B., Union U., 1912; m. Ethel F. Fitzpatrick, Nov. 11, 1939; 1 son, Edward N. (died 1948). Engaged in practice of law, Albany, N.Y., since 1912; sr. mem. firm of Scheiberling & Schneider, later Scheiberling, Rogan & Maney; justice, City Ct., Albany, 1924-29; admitted to practice before U.S. Supreme Ct., 1940. Served with inf., U.S. Army, 1916-19; 2d lt., 312th Inf., 78th (Lightning) Div., 1917; promoted 1st lt., Dec. 1917; with A.E.F., France, 1918; participated in offensives St. Mihiel and Meuse-Argonne; promoted capt., Oct. 1918; hon. disch. June 1919. Awarded Legion d'Honneur by Govt. of France, 1945. National commander American Legion, 1944 (New York department commander, 1935-36; charter member 40 and 8 (Albany); v.p. and dir. Nat. Conv., N.Y. City, 1937, 1947; mem. nat. legislative com., 1939, 1940, 1941, vice chmn. 1943-44). Dir. Albany County Am. Red Cross; chmn. Community Chest Campaign, 1939; gen. chmn. Albany U.S.O. campaign, 1941; mem. nat. council Boy Scouts of Am. (v.p. Ft. Orange Council); official consultant to American delegation, San Francisco Conf., 1945; chmn. N.Y. State World War Memorial Authority, 1935-41. Director Catholic Charities, Albany Diocese. Trustee State University of New York, 1948. Member American Bar Association, N.Y. State Bar Assn., Albany County Bar Assn. (past pres.), 312th U.S. Inf. Assn., 78th Div. Assn., Military Order of the World Wars. Democrat. Roman Catholic. Elks. Clubs: Albany (N.Y.), Manhattan, Military-Naval (N.Y. City). Home: Albany NY Died Sept. 10, 1967; buried Lady Help of Christians Cemetery Glenmont NY

SCHEIN, ERNEST, lawyer; b. Chicago, Aug. 4, 1899; s. Louis and Frances (Langer) S.; student U. Chicago, 1915; A.B., Harvard, 1919, LL.B., 1922; m. Elizabeth Weston Cain, Dec. 27, 1930; children—Robert, Linda, Ann. Admitted to Ill. bar, 1922, D.C. bar, 1942; practicing lawyer, Chicago, 1922-67, Washington, 1942-67. Active participation in representation claims arising out of war damage to U.S., fgn. govts. President of the Legal Aid Society of D.C. Candidate from Illinois to U.S. Ho. of Reps., 1930. Mem. Ill. Commn. Sesquicentennial N.W. Ty., 1937; member of D.C. Election Board. Chief of the Philippines division U.S. Comml. Co. in Fgn. Econ. Adminstrn. and R.F.C., 1944-46; head pub. and pvt. claims settlement Philippine War Damage Comn, Washington and Manila, 1947-48; counsel for Philippine religious instns. in recovery war claims. Served in USN, World War I. Mem. Washington Performing Arts Soc. (dir.), Fed., Am. (chmn. com. war claims), mem. of council of section on internat. law), D.C. (chmn. com. Internat. Law, 1956-57), Chgo. bar assns., Am. Law Inst., Am. Soc. Internat. Law, Am. Acad. Polit. and Social Sci., Legal Aid Bur. (pres.), Fgn. Law Soc. (president). Clubs: Cosmos, Nat. Press, Harvard (pres.) (Washington); Harvard (Philippines); Lambs, Harvard, Bohemians (N.Y.C.); Tavern, Cliff Dwellers (Chgo.). Home: Washington DC Died June 10, 1967; buried Rosehill Cemetery, Chicago, IL

SCHELDRUP, NICOLAY HILMAR, surgeon retired; b. Tovik, Norway, Sept. 1, 1873; s. Andrew Martin and Hannah (Wanvig) S.; came to U.S., 1891; M.D., Rush Med. Coll., 1897; m. Eva Dunsmoor, Aug. 5, 1897; children—Alfred H., Sylvia Louise (wife of Dr. Harold R. Leland), Eugene W., Robert D. Began practice, Granite Falls, Minn., 1897; associated in surgery with Prof. Frederick A. Dunsmoor, Minneapolis, 1906-14; founder, 1925, and pres. Med. and Surg. Clinic; dir. Perfection Mfg. Co.; retired. Served as capt. Med. Corps, U.S. Army, 1918-19. Decorated Knight Order of St. Olaf, first class (Norway). Republican. Lutheran. Home: Miami FL Died 1968.

SCHENCK, HASSIL ELI, univ. trustee, farmer; b. Boone County, Ind., Apr. 25, 1893; s. Ethan Allen and Mary Elizabeth (Smith) S.; student Central Normal Coll., Danville, Ind., 1911, Ind. State Normal Coll., Terre Haute, 1912; m. Izella Craig, Feb. 10, 1916; 1 dau., Rosemary (Mrs. Cary' R. Kern). Pres. Ind. Farm Bur., Inc., 1936-58, Farm Bur. Mut. Ins. Co., Ind., 1937-58, Hoosier Farm Bur. Life Ins. Co., Inc., 1937-58, Rural Acceptance Corp., 1952-58; v.p., dir. Beech Grove State Bank, 1950-55; v.p. Am. Agrl. Ins. Co., 1950-58. Trustee Purdue U., from 1959. Mem. Am. Farm Bur. Fedn. (dir. 1938-58), Indpls. Producers Marketing Assn. (dir. 1948-54), Columbus (O.); Livestock Marketing Assn. (dir. 1948-54). Methodist. Mason. Kiwanian; mem. Order Eastern Star. Address: Lebanon IN Died Nov. 24, 1971; buried Mt. Tabor Cemetery, Fayette IN

SCHENCK, NICHOLAS, theatre exec.; b. Russia. Connected with entertainment field many years; pres. and dir. Loew's Inc., Loew's Boston Theatres Co.; pres. Midland Investment Corp., Kansas City, Mo. Home: Miami Beach FL Died Mar. 1969.*

SCHENCK, PAUL F., congressman; b. Miamisburg, O., Apr. 19, 1899; s. James B. and Amanda Jane (Fornshell) S.; student U. Wis.; m. Charlotte Rairdon, Nov. 21, 1921; children—Richard R., Thomas F. Tchr. high sch.; dir. recreation, 1929-35; real estate, mortgage loans, ins. bus., 1935 (all Dayton, O.); mem. 82d-88th congresses, 3d Dist. Ohio. Bd. edn. Dayton Sch. Dist., 1941-50, also pres.; pres. Dayton Real Estate Bd., 1947-49. Mason (K.T., Shriner). Republican. Home: Dayton OH Died Nov. 30, 1968; buried Woodland Cemetery, Dayton OH

SCHENCK, PAUL WADSWORTH, lawyer; b. Albion, Mich., Aug. 18, 1874; s. Alonzo and Amanda (Wadsworth) S.; night course, Lake Forest (Ill.) U., 1898. Began practice of criminal law at Chicago about 1898; moved to Los Angeles, Calif., 1901; retired 1927. Mem. Los Angeles Acad. Criminology. Elk. Home: La Manana, Lake Hughes P.O., Los Angeles CA‡

SCHENK, FRANCIS JOSEPH, bishop; b. Superior, Wis., Apr. 1, 1901; s. Nicholas and Frances (Fischer) S.; A.B., Coll. of St. Thomas, St. Paul, Minn., 1922; student St. Paul Sem., 1920-26; ordained June 13, 1926; S.T.B., Catholic U. of America, Washington, D.C., 1926. J.C.D., 1929. Sec. to Archbishop Dowling, 1928; vice chancellor Archdiocese of St. Paul, 1928-34; prof. moral theology, St. Paul Sem., 1934, prof. canon law, 1935; censor of books, 1935, defender of the marriage bond, 1935; pastor, Cathedral of St. Paul, St. Paul, Minn., 1942; vicar general, Archdiocese of St. Paul, 1942; bishop Diocese of Crookston, Minn., 1945-61, Diocese of Duluth, 1961-69; consecrated 1945. K.C. Author Mixed Religion and Disparity of Cult, 1929. Home Duluth MN Died Oct. 28, 1969.

SCHENK, HENRY L., banker; b. N.Y.C., 1898; m BeSchenk; 1 dau., Mrs. Sy Berman. Pres., Trade Bank and Trust Co. (merger Nat. Bank N. Am. 1970) 1924-70; vice chmn. Nat. Bank N. Am., N.Y.C.; dir Internat. Stretch Products, Inc. Mason. Home: Miami Beach FL Died Mar. 10, 1973.

SCHERCHEN, HERMANN, musician; b. Berlin, Germany, June 21, 1891; s. Carl Hermann and Berta (Burke) S.; Dr. Honoris Causa, U. Koenigsberg (Germany), 1928; autodidact/prof., U. Santiago (Chile), 1949; m. Pia Andronescu, Sept. 1954; children—Myriam, David, Esther, Nathan, Alexandra. Mem. Berlin Philharmonic Orch., 1906-11; with Schoenberg's Pierrot Lunaire and Kammersinfonie, Berlin, 1911-14; conductor in Russia, later civil prisoner, 1914-19; conductor in Berlin, 1919-22, in Frankfurt, 1922-26, over German radio, 1926-28; gen. music dir., Koenigsberg, 1928-30; chief Musikkollegium, Winterthur, Switzerland, 1944-50; musical dir. Radio Beromuenster, Gravesand, Switzerland, 1954-—, Westminster Records, 1950-—, Fondation of Gravesano Electroacoustical Experimentals Studios, Switzerland, 1954-—; condr. Loata Theatre, Milan, also Phila. Orch., 1964. Author: Hand-book of Conducting, 1928; Vom Wesen der Musik (The Nature of Music in U.S.), 1949; Musik fuer Jedermann, 1950. Editor: Gravesano(Tessin) Switzerland Died June 12, 1966.

SCHERCK, GORDON, corp. exec.; b. St. Louis, 1903; student Washington U., 1922, St. Louis U., 1927; m. Marjorie Lesser; children—Gordon, Roger. Chmn. bd. Scherck Richter Co., St. Louis; dir. Am. Self Service Stores. Vice pres. Jewish Hosp. St. Louis, Jewish Community Center St. Louis. Home: Clayton MO Died Nov. 20, 1967.

SCHERER, PAUL EHRMAN, clergyman; b. Mt. Holly Springs, Pennsylvania, June 22, 1892; s. Melanchton Gideon Groseclose and Alice Melvina Catherine (Ehrman) S.; B.A., College of Charleston (S.C.), 1911, M.A. magna cum laude, 1913; B.D., Lutheran Theological Seminary, Mt. Airy, Philadelphia, 1916; D.D., Roanoke Coll., Salem, Virginia, 1923; LL.D., College of Charleston, 1935; Litt.D., Wittenberg Coll., 1936; L.H.D., Gettysburg Coll., 1939; m. Lilie Fry Benbow, Sept. 4, 1919; children—Barbara Benbow (Mrs. Martin van Buren Sargent), Pamela Benbow (Mrs. Chalmers Coe). Ordained ministry Luth. Ch., 1916, asst. pastor Holy Trinity Ch., Buffalo, N.Y., 1918-19; instr. Mt. Airy Theol. Sem., 1919-20; pastor Holy Trinity Ch., New York, 1920-45; Brown professor of homiletics, Union Theological Seminary, New York City, 1945-60; vis. prof. Union Theological Sem., Richmond, Va., 1960-61, Francis Landey Patton visiting prof. homiletics Princeton (N.J.) Theol. Sem., 1961-68. Radio preacher, Sunday Vespers, 1932-45; asso. editor, The Interpreter's Bible, 1942-57. Lyman Beecher lecturer, 1943; Jarrell Found. lecturer, 1944; Cole lecturer, Vanderbilt University, 1945, Perkins lecturer, 1955, Mullins lecturer, 1957; Earl lectr., 1964. Member Pi Kappa Phi. Author: (sermons and lectures) When God Hides, 1934; Facts that Undergird Life, 1938; The Place Where Thou Standest, 1942; For We Have This Treasure; Event in Eternity; Plight of Freedom; Love is a Spendthrift, 1961; The Word God Sent, 1965. Home: Princeton NJ Died Mar. 26, 1969; buried Princeton Cemetery, Princeton NJ

SCHERER, TILDEN, clergyman, educator; b. Independence Co., Ark., Dec. 24, 1876; s. Michael M. and Edgefield (Morgan) S.; A.B., A.M., King Coll., Tenn., 1902; B.D., Union Theol. Sem. in Va., 1906; D.D., Austin Coll., Sherman, Tex., 1913; m. Eugenia Brogdon, of Richmond, Va., Aug. 31, 1904; children—Brogdon Morgan, Wallace Brown, Iverson Britton, Michael Stuart. Ordained ministry Presbyn. Ch. in U.S., 1906; pastor Hoge Memorial Ch., Richmond, Va., 1906-09; editor Onward," with Southern Presbyn. Com. of Publn., Richmond, 1909-11; pres. and financial agt. King Coll. since 1911, also trustee. Democrat. Mason, Kiwanian. Asso. editor Centennial Gen. Catalogue of Union Theological Seminary in Virignia, 1907. Home: Bristol TN‡

SCHERESCHEWSKY, JOHN FORBY, dir. Rumsey Hall Boys School; b. Baltimore, Md., Dec. 2, 1909; s. Joseph Williams and Bessie Berry (Conklin) S.; A.B., Harvard, 1932; m. Elizabeth Wass Foster, Jan. 20, 1933; children—John Forby, Michael Foster, Elizabeth, Deborah. Teacher Brown and Nichols School, Cambridge, Massachusetts, 1932-33, Fessenden Sch., West Newton, 1933-35; head jr. sch., Suffield Acad., Connecticut, 1935-39, entire school, 1939-41; president, director Rumsey Hall School., Inc., Cornwall, Conn., 1941-69; panelist on TV program, What in the World. Commd. lt. (j.g.) USNR, June 15, 1943, lt. U.S.N.R., 1944. Apptd. Naval Aide to Gov., 1947, with rank of comdr. Elected Representative to State Legislature, 1946. Awarded Bronze Star with combat V. Republican. Clubs: Trident, Harvard Varsity; Harvard (Boston, New York, Conn.); Sandy Bay Yacht. Author and commentator of radio program, and newspaper column You and Your Child. Home: CT Died Feb. 9, 1969; buried Gloucester MA

SCHERMAN, HARRY, chmn. Book-of-the-Month Club, author; b. Montreal, Can., Feb. 1, 1887; s. Jacob and Katharine (Harris) S.; ed. Phila. pub. schs.; student Wharton School of Finance and Law School, U. of Pa., 1906-07; m. Bernardine Kielty, June 3, 1914; children—Katharine Whitney, Thomas Kielty. Journalism, N.Y. City, 1907-12; advertising work with Ruthrauff & Ryan, J. Walter Thompson Co. and others, 1912-16; one of organizers Little Leather Library Corp., pubs. of 10-cent classics, 1916 (pres. 7 years); partner Sackheim & Scherman, Inc., advt. agency, specializing in books, 1921-26; originated Book-of-the-Month Club, 1926, pres. 1931-50, chmn. bd., 1950-69. Chairman board National Bureau Econ. Research, 1952-56, dir.-at-large, 1957-66, director emeritus, 1967-69. Honorary trustee Committee Economic Development. Author: The Promises Men Live By: A New Approach to Economics, 1937; The Real Danger in Our Gold, 1940; The Last Best Hope of Earth, 1942. Contbr. numerous articles on economics to mags. Home: New York City NY Died Nov. 12, 1969.

SCHERMERHORN, RICHARD, JR., landscape architect and city planner; b. Brooklyn, N.Y., Oct. 17, 1877; s. Richard and Jane Agnes (Fiske) Schermerhorn; educated Brooklyn Poly. Prep. Sch. and Inst., 1888-94, Rensselaer Poly. Inst., 1894-97; m. Margaret Medbury Doane, June 2, 1930; 1 son, Derick Doane. Began as landscape architect, 1900, in pvt. practice since 1909; engaged on over 100 private estates, also parks, cemeteries, country clubs, subdivisions, college campuses; consultant Allegany and Taconic state parks; designed master plans for Great Neck, Huntington, Lawrence, in N.Y., Newark, N.J., etc.; lecturer on landscape architecture, Columbia, 1935-39; landscape architect and site planner, Elizabeth (N.J.) Housing Authority; consultant landscape architect, Hudson River Conservation Society; landscape architect and planner for U.S. Army (Fort Hamilton), 1941. Cons. Architects Def. Housing Projects, Bound Brook, N.J., 1942; cons., planner projects of housing developments since 1942. Served as capt. engring. sect. Sanitary Corps, U.S. Army, 1917-19; with A.E.F. 8 mos., participated St. Mihiel offensive; assignment with Engring. Dept. on Commn. to Negotiate Peace. Fellow Am. Soc. Landscape Architects (former nat. trustee, ex-pres. N.Y. Chapter); mem. Am. Soc. Civil Engrs. (life), Holland Society New York (ex-trustee), N.Y. State Historical Assn., Dutch Settlers Soc. of Albany, N.J. Society Architects (asso.), Chi Phi. Licensed professional engr., N.Y. and N.J. Author: Schermerhorn Genealogy and Family Chronicles, 1914. Contbr. to jours. on landscape architecture, city planning, etc., and genealogy. Home: 173 Orange Road, Montclair NJ Office: 342 Madison Av., New York 17 NY‡

SCHERR, HARRY, JR., lawyer; b. Cin., Feb. 23, 1915; s. Harry and Rosa Lee (Wall) S.; grad. Woodberry Forest Sch., Va., 1932; A.B., Yale, 1936; LL.B., W.Va. U., 1939; m. Marguerite LeCron Thompson, May 8, 1943; children—Harry 3d, Herbert Thompson, Leslie LeCron. Admitted to W.Va. bar, 1939, practiced in Huntington, 1939-72. Pres., dir. Dacon Constructors; dir. Thomas Co. Mem. Nat. Conf. on Continuing Edn. of the Bar, Arden House, 1958; mem. W.Va. Gov.'s Commn. on Water Resources, 1968-72. Served as comdr. United States Navy, 1941-46, captain USNR. Member of American, W.Va. (exec. council 1953-56, 57-58, pres. 1958-59), Cabell County bar assns., W.Va. State Bar, W.Va. (pres. 1950-51), Huntington Chambers Commerce Beta Theta Pi, Phi Alpha Delta. Republican (vice chmn. Cabel County exec. com. 1939-40). Episcopalian (vestryman 1949-52, chmn. W.Va. Conf. Episcopal Laymen 1951-53). Elk. Clubs: Engineers, City (Huntington); Guyan Golf and Country; Press (Charleston, W.Va.). Home: Huntington WV Died Apr. 19, 1972.

SCHERTZ, HELEN PITKIN, author; b. at New Orleans, Aug. 8, 1877; d. John Robert Graham F. (U.S. minister to Argentine Republic under Harrison) and Helen Fearing (Fuller) Pitkin; ed. pvt. sch., governesses and Newcomb Coll., New Orleans; m. Christian d'Augstburg Schertz, of Lorraine, Germany, Apr. 29, 1909; was on staff New Orleans Democrat. State pres. La. Branch Internat. Sunshine Society; King's Daughter; mem. Charity Organization Soc., Soc. Prevention Cruelty to Animals, Soc. Prevention Cruelty to Children, New Orleans Choral Symphony Soc., D.A.R., U.S. Daughters 1776-1812; hon. La. v.-p. Old Northwest Geneal. Soc. of Ohio (Columbus). Episcopalian. Author: Over the Hills (long poem), 1903; An Angel by Brevet, 1904. Home: Bayou St. John, New Orleans‡

SCHEUCH, FREDERICK CHARLES, univ. prof.; b. Lafayette, Ind., Mar. 29, 1871; s. Frederick Herman and Elizabeth Catharine (Lahr) S.; ed. Gymnasium, Frankfort-on-the-Main, Germany, 1882-88; Colegio Santo Tomas, Barcelona, Spain, 1888-89; B.M.E., Purdue U., 1893, A.C., 1894; LL.D., U. of Mont., 1938; attended univs. of Vienna, Paris, Madrid, 1923-24; m. Jimmie D. Straughn, Dec. 24, 1898; children—Straughn Frederick (dec.), Natalia Miriam; m. 2d, Mrs. Nelle Zinn Burt, June 29, 1936. Instr. French, Purdue U., 1893-94; prof. mech. engring. and modern langs., U. of Mont., 1895-98, prof. French, German and Spanish, 1895-1936, sec. of faculty, 1895-1908, acting pres., June 1915-Sept. 1917, and May 1935-Jan. 1936, became vice-pres., 1917, pres. emeritus since Sept. 1937. Sec. Am. Consulate, Barcelona, Spain, under father, who was consul there. Consultant to fraternities, Purdue U., since Jan. 1939. Mem. Sons American Revolution, Sigma Chi (grand consul 1939-41). Clubs: Athelstan (Battle Creek); University (Chicago). Republican. Episcopalian. Life mem. Societe Academique d'histoire Internationale, Paris; hon. asso. Franco-Am. Com. Alliance Sociale et Civique, Paris. Home: Battle Creek, Mich. Address: Saint Mary's Lake, Battle Creek, Mich; (summer) Frankfort MI‡

SCHICKHAUS, EDWARD, banker; b. Newark, Apr. 17, 1898; s. Edward and Josephine (Miller) S.; student Newark Acad.; A.B., Princeton, 1920; LL.B., N.J. Law Sch., 1924; spl. studies money and banking N.Y.U. Grad. Sch.; m. Louise M. Dixon, Mar. 20, 1930; 1 dau., Ann Dixon. With Fidelity Union Trust Co., Newark, 1920-63, v.p., 1939-60, sr. v.p., 1960-63; v.p., dir. William Dixon, Inc.; dir. Driver-Harris Co., Amerace-Esna, First Nat. Iron Bank of Morristown, N.J. Chmn. capital loan fund committee Diocese of Newark. Served with USNR. World War I. Republican. Episcopalian. Clubs: Essex, (Newark); Essex Country (West Orange); Nantucket (Mass.) Yacht. Prepared revisions of certain statutes on banking. Home: West Orange NJ Died Jan. 30, 1969.

SCHIEDT, RICHARD CONRAD FRANCIS, coll. prof.; b. Weissenfels, Prussia, Sept. 21, 1859; s. Francis and Julia (Jansen) S.; grad. Gymnasium, Zeitz, Prussia, 1878; student in mathematics, zoology, chemistry, univs. of Erlangen and Berlin, 1878-81; theology at Lancaster, Pa., 1885-87; post-grad. work, U. of Pa. and Harvard; Ph.D., U. of Pa., 1899, hon. Sc.D., 1910; m. Sophie E. Gantenbein, Aug. 23, 1888; children—Mary Madeleine Julia, Norma Ruth (Mrs. Persifor H. Smith), Richard Conrad Francis. Prof. biology and geology, Franklin and Marshall Coll., Pa., 1887-1918; prof. anatomy and embryology, U. of Tenn. 1919; professor biology emeritus, Franklin and Marshall Coll., since 1927; retired, 1919. Research chemist for Armstrong Cork Company (linoleum division), 1924-28; entomologist Pa. State Board Agr., 1893-1900. Mem. academic council Carl Schurz Memorial Foundation. One of first members Woods Hole (Mass.) Marine Biol. Orgn. Fellow A.A.A.S.; mem. Am. Chem. Soc., Soc. Am. Zoologists, Soc. Old German Students in American, Societe Jean Jacques Rousseau, Geneva, Deutsche Philos. Gesellschaft, Euckenbund, Steuben Society, Concord Soc. of America, Phi Beta Kappa, Phi Kappa Sigma. Min. of Reformed Ch. in U.S. Author: Principles of Zoology, 1893; Laboratory Guide in Zoology, 1898; Plant Morphology, 1900; On the Threshold of a New Century, 1900; Glimpses into the Growth of America's Art Life, 1909; American Art in the Making, 1926; The Verdict of History-a Plea for Peace, 1940. Contbr. on scientific and ednl. subjects. Address: 1043 Wheatland Av., Lancaster PA*‡

SCHIERBERG, GEORGE BERNARD, steel exec.; b. St. Louis, Mar. 5, 1892; s. John Henry and Frances Josephine (Murphy) S.; ed. pub. schs., night and extension courses; m. Evelyn Sanders, Aug. 15, 1942. Asst. to pres. Miss. Valley Trust Co., St. Louis, 1910-24; treas. Walsh Fire Clay Products Co., St. Louis, 1924-27, Robertson Aircraft Corp. and successor Universal Aviation Corp., St. Louis, 1927-30; sec.-treas. Granite City Steel Co. (Ill.), 1930-49, exec. v.p., treas., dir., exec. com., 1949-56, pres., treas., 1956-57, chmn. finance com., dir.; dir. Consol. Freightways, Inc., Menlo Park, Cal., St. Louis Shipbldg. Fed. Barge Lines, Inc.; dir., exec. com. First Granite City Nat. Bank, Granite City, Ill. Mem. Am. Iron and Steel Inst., Mo. Hist. Soc., Am. Mgmt. Assn. Clubs: Union League (N.Y.C.); Algonquin Golf, Missouri Athletic (St. Louis). Home: St Louis MO Died Dec. 31, 1967; buried St Louis MO

SCHIFF, LEONARD ISAAC, physicist; b. Fall River, Mass., Mar. 29, 1915; s. Edward Ephraim and Matilda (Brodsky) S.; B.E., Ohio State U., 1933, M.S., 1934; Ph.D., Mass. Inst. Tech., 1937; m. Frances Margaret Ballard, Aug. 25, 1941; children—Ellen Margaret, Leonard Ballard. Research physicist Gen. Electric Co., summer 1937; Nat. Research Council fellow, research asso. U. Cal., Cal. Inst. Tech., 1937-40; instr. U. Pa., 1940-42, asst. prof., 1942-44, asso. prof., 1944-47, acting chmn. physics dept., 1942-45; research physicist Nat. Def. Research Com., Columbia, 1941-45, U. Cal., 1944-45; mem. anti-submarine warfare operation research group, 1943-45; staff Los Alamos Sci. Lab., N.M., 1945-46; asso. prof. Stanford, 1947-48, prof., 1948-71, exec. head physics dept., 1948-66; dir. Varian Assos., 1948-53; vis. prof. Ia. State Coll., 1952, U. Paris, 1956-57, Univ. Madras and Bombay (India), 1963; Guggenheim fellow, 1956-57; vis. com. physics dept. Mass. Inst. Tech., 1954-56, 68-71; cons. editor McGraw Hill Book Co., 1954-71; dir. Annual Reviews, Inc., 1969-71; Stewart lectr. U. Mo., 1955; Phillips lectr. Haverford, 1963; Tektronix Found. lectr. Ore., 1964. Vice president and director of the Varian Found., 1961-71, mem. phys. scis. program com. Alfred P. Sloan Found., 1961-66, chmn., 1965-66. Chmn. adv. com. physics div. Office Sci. Research, Air Research and Devel. Command USAF, 1955-65; sci. adv. group Office Aerospace Research, USAF, 1963-71; mem. consultative group Com. on Space Research, Internat. Council Sci. Unions, 1968-71; cons. ad hoc com. on phys. scis. NRC, 1968-70. Recipient Lamme medal Ohio State U., 1959; Oersted medal Am. Assn. Physics Tchrs., 1966; Dinkelspiel award Stanford U., 1966;

award for outstanding contributions to research Office Aerospace Research, 1970. Mem. Internat. Conf. Theoretical Physics, Tokyo, also Kyoto, Japan, 1953. Fellow Am. Phys. Soc. (councillor 1953-57, chmn. nuclear physics div. 1967-68), Am. Acad. Arts and Scis., A.A.A.S., (mem. coun. 1966-69), California Acad. of Sci.; mem. Am. Assn. Physics Tchrs., Fedn. Am. Scientists (council del.), American Assn. Univ. Professors, National Acad. Sciences (mem. space science board 1965-70, chmn. sect. physics 1969-71), Sigma Xi, Tau Beta Phi. Club: Cosmos (Washington). Author: Quantum Mechanics, 3d edition, 1968. Author science research and review articles. Associate editor Review Sci. Instruments, 1943-45, Phys. Rev., 1945-47, 63-65, Physics Today, 1950-56, Rev. of Modern Physics, 1951-54, Ann. Rev. Nuclear Sci., 1952-63, Journal of Mathematical Physics, 1960-62. Home: Menlo Park CA Died Jan. 19, 1971; buried Alta Mesa Cemetery, Palo Alto CA

SCHIFF, ROBERT WILLIAM, shoe mfr.; born Leizevo, Lithuania, July 4, 1886; s. Chaim Hirsh and Ethel (Schleszinger) S.; ed. Talmudic Coll., Tolsai, Lithuania, 1902-05; m. Rebacca Lurie, 1912 (died 1927); children—Saralyn L. (Mrs. Jos. S. Blatt) (dec.), Mrs. Fredi Levin, Herbert H. Mildred (Mrs. Herbert Lee); m. 2d, Mrs. Ann Rose Neff, Oct. 21, 1930; step-daughter, Margy Neff (Mrs. Arnold Newman). Came to United States, 1905; naturalized citizen, 1919. Began as clerk in shoe store, 1911, mgr. shoe dept., 1912; opened store with partner, at Marion, O., 1913; sold interest in chain of 12 stores to partner, 1919; organizer, 1920, pres., treas. Shoe Corp. Am., 1920-65, chmn., 1965, dir. Dir. Am. Joint Distbn. Com., Inc.; trade and industry chmn. United Jewish Appeal. Hebrew religion. Mason. Club: Lions. Home: Columbus OH Died 1971.

SCHIFFELER, CURT CONRAD, hotel exec.; b. Kaiserslautern, The Palatinate, June 5, 1892; s. Carl and Marie (Seitz) S.; m. Mary Wood Stasel, Feb. 24, 1923; children—Melody, Carl. Began as apprentice Carlton Hotel, Frankfurt-on-Main, 1909; later asso. with The Ritz, Paris, Trianon Palace Hotel, Versailles, Carlton, London, Ritz Carlton, Montreal, Ritz Carlton, N.Y.C., 1914, Chase Hotel, St. Louis; built Ft. Hayes Hotel, Columbus, O., 1922, Hotel Van Cleve, Dayton, O., 1926; mng. dir. Hotel Gibson Cin., 1929-34; v.p., gen. mgr. Hotel Raleigh, Washington, 1936-56. Club: Press (Washington). Home: Chevy Chase MD Died Jan. 22, 1969.

SCHILLING, WILLIAM FRANK, farmer; b. Hutchinson, Minn., Nov. 11, 1872; s. William and Mary Catherine (Lallier) S.; ed. high sch., Hutchinson, 2 yrs.; m. Margaret D. Hannemann, of Northfield, Minn., Aug. 22, 1900; children—Mary Catherine, Charlotte Bertha, Margaret Jeannette, Dorothy Cecelia, William Frank, Louis Patrick, Joel Heatwole, Ruth Elizabeth. Learned printer's trade; city editor Appleton (Minn.) Press, then editor Northfield News 13 yrs.; farming and raising pure-bred Holstein cattle since 1900. Member of Federal Farm Board since 1929. Widely known as advocate of cooperation in dairying among farmers; has addressed meetings of farmers in all states of U.S.; pres. since 1917, of Twin City Milk Producers' Assn. (over 8,500 members); mem. governing bd. Minn. Farmers' Institutes. Formerly capt. Minn. N.G. Republican. K.C. Home: Northfield MN‡

SCHINDLER, RUDOLF, physician; born Berlin, Germany, May 10, 1888; s. Richard I. and Martha (Simon) S.; student U. of Freiburg (Germany), 1905-07; M.D., U. of Berlin, 1912; m. Gabriele Winkler, 1922 (dec. 1964); children—Richard Rudolf, Peter (dec.), Wolfgang (dec.), Ursula (Mrs. James B. Gibson); m. 2d, Marie Koch. Came to U.S., 1934, naturalized, 1940. Asst. in path. dept. Hosp. Schwabing, Munich, Germany, 1913-14, asst. in med. dept., 1919-23; engaged in pvt. practice of medicine, specializing in gastroenterology, Munich, 1923-34, Chicago, 1934-43, Los Angeles since 1943; visiting prof. medicine, U. of Chicago, 1934-36, asso. clinical prof. medicine, 1936-37, asso. prof. medicine, 1937-43; attending gastroscopist Michael Reese Hosp., 1936-37; cons. gastroscopist Cook County Hosp., 1936-37; clinical prof. of medicine, Coll. Med. Evangelists, 1943-68; sr. attending staff mem. Los Angeles County Gen. Hosp. Consulting gastroenterologist, Veterans Administration, Midway Hosp., Los Angeles, Long Beach Veterans Hospital, Temple Hosp., Los Angeles. Served as military surgeon Bavarian Inf. Regt. and pathologist 6th German Army, 1914-18. Decorated Iron Cross; Bavarian Mil. Service Order with swords; German Cross for Trench Soldiers. Awarded gold medal, Am. Med. Assn., 1936. Author: Lehrbuch d. Gastroskopie, 1923; Nervensystem u. spontane Blutungen, 1927; Gastroscopy, 1937 (2d edit., 1950); Gastritis, 1947; numerous publications on stomach diseases. Invented rigid gastroscope, 1922; flexible gastroscope, 1932; optical diagnostic esophagoscope, 1948. Mem. Inst. Medicine Chicago, Am. Gastro-Enterological Assn., Internat. Gastro-Enterological Association, American Gastroscopic Society (1st. Pres.), A.A.A.S., A.M.A., Calif. Soc. Int. Med., Sigma Xi. Roman Catholic. Home: Los Angeles CA Died Sept. 1968.

SCHINE, J. MYER, hotels and theaters; b. Russia, 1892; ed. Jamestown (N.Y.) High Sch. and private tutoring; m. Hildegarde Feldman, Aug. 30, 1925; children—Doris June, G(erard) David, Renne (Mrs. Lester Crown), C(arles) Richard. President of Schine Enterprises, Gloversville, N.Y., 1920-57, chmn. bd., pres., 1957-71; owner Schine Inn (Chiconee, Mass., Massena, N.Y.), Shine Airport Hotel, Bradley Airfield, Conn., Ambassador Hotel (Los Angeles) Hotel Northampton and Wiggins Tavern (Northampton, Mass.), St. Regis Motor Inn; treas. SKIDEK Corp., Electronic Recreations Corp.; developed chain candy stores (Mrs. Wiggins); dir. First Bank & Trust Co., Boca Raton, Florida, Trust Company of Fulton Co. Bank, Gloversville, N.Y. Dir. Nathan Littauer Hosp. Mason (Shriner), Elk, Odd Fellow, K.P. Club: Lotos (N.Y.C.). Home: New York City NY Died May, 1971.

SCHIRER, GEORGE, exec.; b. Reading, Pa., 1885. Chmn. board dirs., Sperry & Hutchinson Co., 1960-66. Home: Sands Point NY Died Feb. 1970.

SCHLAIKJER, ERICH MAREN, cons. geologist, engineer; b. Newton, O., Nov. 22, 1905; s. Erich and Clara (Ryser) S.; B.S., Harvard, 1929, M.A., Columbia, 1931, Ph.D., 1935; m. Jospehine Ayres, Apr. 28, 1951; children—Maren, Michael, Patrecia Jo. In charge, 10 geol. and paleontol. expedn., Gt. Plains Area of U.S. for Harvard U., 1925-34, Yukon Terr. Alaska Expdn. for Am. Museum of Nat. History, 1936, with Barnum Brown, Am. Museum-Sinclair Expdn., southwestern Wyo., 1937; Am. Museum-Sweet Expdns., Big Bend Area, Tex., 1939-40, Comml. Petroleum and Mining Geology, Rocky Mountain Area, 1946-49, Tutor of geology, Bklyn. Coll., 1932-34, instr., 1935-39, asst. prof., 1940-47, prof., 1948-50; pres. Lakota Petroleum Corp., 1950-67. Served in U.S. Air Force, 1st lt., 1942, active duty, advanced to lt. col., 1945. Awarded Bronze Star Medal, Army Commendation Ribbon, seven campaign stars to the Asiatic Pacific Theatre Ribbon. Awarded (with Barnum Brown) Cressy Morrison prize, N.Y. Acad. Sci., 1939. University fellow Columbia U. Fellow Geol. Soc. Am., Paleontol. Soc. Am., A.A.A.S.; mem. Am. Assn. Petroleum Geologists, Nat. Soc. Profl. Engrs., Am. Geophys. Union, Soc. for the Study of Evolution, Am. Inst. Profl. Geologists (charter), Sigma Xi. Clubs: Explorer's (dir., 1942-43, sec., 1947-49 and various coms.), Harvard (N.Y.C.); Petroleum, Columbine Country (Denver). Author articles on geology and paleontology profl. jours. Home: Littleton CO Died Nov. 5, 1972; buried Tower of Memories, Denver CO

SCHLANGER, BEN, architect; b. N.Y.C., Nov. 20, 1904; s. Louis and Esther (Komito) S.; student Columbia, 1923-25; grad. Nat. Inst. Archtl. Edn., 1932; m.; 1 dau., Dorothy (Mrs. Warren Isman); m. 2d, Marion Friedberg, Apr. 12, 1967. Practicing, consulting architect for theatre bldgs., N.Y.C., 1931-71; works include UN Assembly Bldgs., Lincoln Center Bldgs., Met. Opera House, N.Y. State Theatre, Philharmonic Hall, New Madison Sq. Garden, World Fair (all N.Y.C.), Colonial Williamsburg (Va.), Tacna Theatre, Lima, Peru, Olympic Theatre, Bogota, Colombia, Los Angeles Civic Cultural Center, Place Des Arts Cultural Center, Montreal, Clowes Hall, Indpls., U. Ill. Basketball Arena, John F. Kennedy Cultural Center, Washington, Ruben Dario Nat. Theatre, Managua, Nicaragua, Nat. Arts Center, Ottawa, Man. Theatre Center, Winnipeg, Honolulu Theatre for Youth; also lectr. Columbia, Yale, Pratt Inst. Mem. Bldg. Code Revision Com. theatre bldgs., N.Y.C., 1951; consulting architect Sydney (Australia) Opera House, Powell Symphony Hall, St. Louis. Trustee Nat. Inst. Archtl. Edn.; mem. exec. bd. U.S. Inst. Theatre Tech. Recipient Municipal Art Soc. award, 1963, Ford Found. grants, 1960-64, Albert S. Bard Archtl. award, 1964. Fellow Soc. Motion Picture and TV Engrs.; mem. ANTA, U.S. Inst. Theatre Tech. (past v.p., Annual Achievement award 1968), A.I.A. (chmn. com. auditorium and theatre architecture, chmn. awards com. N.Y. chpt.). Contbr. articles to profl. jours. Pioneer TCA Synchro-Screen for motion pictures. Home: New York City NY Died May 3, 1971; buried Sharon Gardens, Valhalla NY

SCHLENZ, HARRY EDWARD, civil engr.; b. Denver, Nov. 1, 1905; s. Edward and Viola G. (Harder) S.; B.S., U. Ill., 1927, M.S., 1929, C.E., 1933; m. Norma B. Addison, Aug. 4, 1942; children—Susan (Mrs. Robert L. Moran), Dianne, Deborah, Harry A. Research grad. asst. U. Ill. Engring. Expt. Sta., 1927-29, instr. water supply and sewage treatment, 1929-30; v.p., sales mgr. Pacific Flush Tank Co., 1930-54, pres., 1954-69, dir., 1933-69. Pres. Water Pollution Control Fedn. 1961-62, adv. com. to asst. sec. interior Frank DiLuzio, commr. Fed. Water Pollution Control Adminstrn. Trustee U. Ill. Athletic Assn., 1949-53, pres., 1953; trustee U. Ill., 1953-58. mem. Lake Geneva com. George Williams Coll. Recipient gold medal Camp Custer; William J. Orchard award for distinguished service to water pollution control field, 1968. Fellow Am. Soc. C.E.; mem. Ill. Soc. Engrs., Am. Pub. Works Assn., Am. Acad. San. Engrs., Water and Sewage Works Mfrs. Assn. (pres. 1957), Central States Water Pollution Control Assn., Sigma Xi, Alpha Kappa Lambda, Tau Beta Pi, Chi Epsilon, Scabbard and Blade. Clubs: Barrington Hills Country; Army and Navy (Chgo.); Engineers (N.Y.C.). Home: Barrington IL Died 1969.

SCHLIEDER, FREDERICK (WILLIAM), organist, composer; b. Foreston, Ill., Jan. 22 1873; s. Frederick Ernst and Mary Christine (Lohr) S.; ed. high sch.; Mus.B., Syracuse U., 1895, Mus.M., 1915, Mus.Doc., 1932; pupil of Alexander Guilmant and Henri Dallier, Paris, France, 1900-01; m. Mabel Sarah Price, Nov. 14, 1900; 1 dau., Dorothy Muriel. Dir. music, Centenary Coll. Inst., Hackettstown, N.J., 1897-1903, 1901-03; organist Mt. Morris (N.Y.) Bapt. Ch., 1903-08, First M.E. Ch., Montclair, N.J., 1908-10, Collegiate Ch. of St. Nicholas, New York, 1910-23; improvisation. Sch. of Sacred Music, Union Theol. Sem.; dept. theory, Trenton (N.J.) Conservatory. Fellow American Guild Organists; member Nat. Assn. Organists (pres. 1918, 19, 20), Am. Guild Organists (council), N.Y. State Music Teachers Assn. (ex-pres.), Delta Kappa Epsilon. Republican. Episcopalian. Club: St. Wilfrid. Author: Lyric Composition Through Improvisation; Creative Harmony; Creative Music Education; Fundamentals of Music, Beyond the Tonal Horizon. Lecturer and writer on musical law and practice; composer of sacred and secular music. Home: The New York 19‡

SCHLING, MAX, JR., florist; b. Yonkers, N.Y., July 21, 1914; s. Max and Louise W. (Schneider) S.; student Riverdale Country Sch., 1928-32, Sheffield Sci. Sch., Yale, 1932-35; m. Dorothy Russell Tomy, Apr. 11, 1942; children—Max III, Wallace Crane. With Max Schling, Inc., florists, N.Y. City, 1935-71, chmn. bd., 1969-71; with Max Schling Seedsman, 1935-63, pres., 1942-63; v.p. Constance Spry Inc., 1949-68; sec. George Carson Boyd, Wilmington, Del., 1959-61; dir. Scott-Fanton Museum and Hist. Soc., Danbury, Conn., 1970-71. Served as sgt., U.S. Army, 1943-46. Member National Retail Florists Assn. (dir. 1947-48, 1948-49), Hort. Soc. N.Y. Clubs: Florists (trustee 1948-50). Rotary (N.Y.C.). Home: Brookfield CT Died Mar. 16, 1971.

SCHLOSSBERG, JOSEPH, labor exec.; b. Russia, 1875; s. Max and Bessie (Feldman) S.; student Columbia Coll., New York, 1905-07; m. Anna Grossman, Sept. 5, 1905; children—Ruth, David Mathias. Gen. sec.-treas Amalgamated Clothing Workers of Am., N.Y.C., 1914-40, gen. sec.-treas. emeritus, 1940-71. Trustee Coll. City N.Y. Home: New York City NY Died Jan. 15, 1971; buried Old Montefiore Cemetery, Laurelton NY

SCHMEISSER, HARRY CHRISTIAN, physician; b. Balt., 1885; M.D., Johns Hopkins U., 1912, Ph.D. in Pathology, 1914. Fellow, asst. instr., asso. pathologist Johns Hopkins U., Balt., 1912-19; chief labs., mem. med. bd. John Gaston Hosp.; cons. Baptist Meml. Hosp., Methodist Hosp.; chief div. pathology, and bacteriology, prof., dir. Pathol. Inst., U. Tenn., Memphis. Diplomate Am. Bd. Pathology. Fellow A.C.P.; mem A.M.A., Am. Assn. Pathologists and Bacteriologists, Am. Soc. Exptl. Pathology, So. Med. Assn. Home: Memphis TN

SCHMIDT, ALFRED FRANCIS WILLIAM, educator and librarian; b. Glenbeulah, Wis., Jan. 31, 1873; s. Heinrich E. and Anna W. (Herrling) S.; student Mt. Angel (Ore.) Coll., 1889-91 (A.M., 1898); A.B., Leland Stanford Jr. U., 1895; m. Cornelia May Jones, Oct. 5, 1904 (dec. 1962); children—Engelbert, Martha, Alfred Robinson, Walter Theodore. Asst. in library, Stanford U., 1894-97, asst. and instr. Anglo-Saxon, 1896-97, instr. German, 1897-1900, head classifier in library, 1900-01, asst. librarian, 1901; asst. in classification, Library of Congress, 1902-06; instr. German, 1905-06, asst. prof., 1906-11, prof., 1911-38, prof. library science 1925-38, dir. Div. of library science, 1927, prof. of library science emeritus since 1938, George Washington U., also librarian, 1906-33. Acting prof. German, Howard U., 1909-13, prof., and supervisor of courses in German, 1913-14; classifier of philosophy,auxiliary sciences of history and universal and Old World history, Library of Congress, 1913-25. Republican. Unitarian. Mem. Am. Hist. Assn., A.L.A., D.C. Library Assn., Am. Mus. Natural History, Am. Assn. University Professors, Bibliographical Society of America, National Geog. Soc., Nat. Travel Club, Kappa Sigma, Pi Gamma Mu; fellow A.A.A.S., Acad. of Polit. Science. Club: Cosmos. Collaborator of Library of Congress schemes of classification for polygraphy, education, auxiliary sciences of history and universal and Old World history and European war; also occasional articles and addresses. Home: Annapolis MD Died Feb. 5, 1966; buried Glenwood Cemetery Washington DC

SCHMIDT, ARTHUR ALEXANDER, pub. relations counsel; b. Indpls., May 6, 1901; s. Benjamin F. and Evelyn (Benner) S.; B.S., U.S. Naval Acad., 1922; m. Vella Griffith Brittein, Feb. 1930; 1 dau., Nancy (Mrs. Richard Sherman); m. 2d, Valerie Bettis, 1959. Resigned USN, 1922; advt. and promotion exec. Paramount Theatres, Detroit, 1928-32; advt. mgr. Loew's Theatres and Metro-Goldwyn-Mayer, N.Y.C., 1932-41; asst. to pres. Columbia Pictures, Los Angeles, 1946-48, dir. advt. and publicity, 1948-52; mng. dir.

Pub. Relations Mgmt. Corp., 1952-54; now chmn. Arthur Schmidt & Assos., N.Y.C. Served from lt. comdr. to comdr., USNR, 1941-46; dep. dir. Naval Photog. Services, 1943-45. Mem. Pub. Relations Soc. Am. Clubs: Army and Navy (Washington); New York Yacht, Union League (N.Y.C.). Home: New York City NY Died June 7, 1969.

SCHMIDT, ERNEST R., mfg. exec.; b. Phila., 1895. Exec. v.p., dir. Budd Co.; dir. Am. Pulley Co. Home: Abington PA Died 1971.

SCHMIDT, FRANK HENRY, lawyer; b. Dixon, Ill., July 1900; s. Henry F. and Martha (Kessler) S.; student Midland Coll., 1919-20, U. Neb., 1920-21; A.B., U. So. Cal., 1931, J.D., 1931; m. Helen Sweet Emley, June 18, 1924; children—Helen Lee, Betty Faye. Clk., First Nat. Bank, Omaha, 1916-17; chief clk. Peters Nat. Bank, Omaha, 1921-25; br. mgr. Cal. Bank, Los Angeles, 1925-26, v.p., exec. trust officer, 1955-58, sr. v.p., 1958-64, exec. v.p., 1964-65; cashier, v.p. Cal. Trust Co., Los Angeles, 1926-46, exec. v.p., 1946-50, pres., 1950-55; dir. Santa Monica Comml. Co., Fontana Ranchos Water Co., Spring Street Realty Co., Pond Land Co.; partner firm Hill, Farrer & Burrill, Los Angeles, from 1965. Mem. Am. Cal., Los Angeles bar assns., Los Angeles C. of C., Am., Cal. bankers assns. Clubs: California (Los Angeles); Bel-Air Bay. Author legal and trust articles. Home: Los CA Deceased.

SCHMIDT, ORVIS ADRIAN, banker; born Gresham, Wis., Jan. 28, 1912; s. Walter Anthony and Elise (Rockman) S.; A.B., Lawrence Coll., Appleton, Wis., 1933; A.M., Tufts Coll., Medford, Mass., 1935; student U. of Chicago, 1935-36; m. Elizabeth Merriam, Nov. 14, 1936; children—Roger Merriam, Brian Kirkwood. Research asst., office of sec., U.S. Treasury Dept., 1936-37; U.S. Treasury rep., Am. Embassy, Brazil, S.A., 1937-38; mem. div. Monetary Research, 1938-40; asst. dir., Fgn. Funds Control, 1941, dir., 1944-47; asso. dir. div. Monetary Research, Mar.-Nov. 1947; staff loan dept. Internat. Bank of Reconstruction and Development, Washington, D.C., 1947, asst. to loan dir., 1949-51, asst. dir. dept. operations, Western Hemisphere, 1952-56, dir., 1956-64; spl. adviser to the Pres., 1964-67; liaison with Inter-Am. Com. for Alliance with Progress, 1964-67. Mem. Am. Econ. Assn., Phi Chevy Chase MD Died Nov. 20, 1967; buried Gresham WI

SCHMIDT PETER PAUL, physician; b. Phila., Apr. 26, 1912; s. Joseph M. and Anna (Skafarek) S.; B.A., N.Y.U., 1933; M.D., L.I. Coll. Medicine, 1937; m. Mary Ann Campanaro, Oct. 1, 1939; children—Cristina, Lucy, Victoria. Intern at Kings County Hospital, 1937-38; resident pulmonary diseases Riverside Hosp., N.Y.C., 1938-40; resident internal medicine Kennedy Gen. Hosp., 1947-49; with VA, 1941-42, 46-49, cardiologist, clin. dir., chief of medicine, 1946-47, 49-50, part time pulmonary clinic. Served from 1st lt. to maj., M.C., AUS, 1942-46; ETO. Mem. Am., N.Y. State, Nassau County med. assns., Am. Fedn. Clin. Research, Nassau Soc. Internal Medicine. Diplomate Am. Bd. Internal Medicine. Address: Merrick NY Died Sept. 11, 1969; interred Calvary Cemetery Woodside NY

SCHMITT, ARTHUR J., mfg. exec.; b. Chgo., June 14, 1893; s. Henry W. and Barbara Elizabeth (Schneider) S. Pres. Walnart Electric Mfg. Co., 1921-29; dist. mgr. Continental Fibre Co., 1929-32; pres. Am. Pnenolic Corporation, Chgo., 1932-60; founder-chmn. Amphenol Corp. Founder Fournier Inst. Tech., 1940; trustee De Paul U., Ill. Inst. Tech. Club: Union League (Chgo.). Home: Lemont IL Died Mar. 29, 1971; buried Hillside IL

SCHMITT, GLADYS, author; b. Pitts., May 31, 1909; d. Henry H. and Leonore (Link) Schmitt; A.B. magna cum laude, U. Pitts., 1932, grad. work, 1932-33, Litt.D. (hon.), 1961; m. Simon Goldfield, Nov. 27, 1939. With Scholastic (mag.), 1933-42, beginning in Pitts. office, transferred to N.Y.C. office, 1939; prof. English Carnegie Inst. Tech., Pitts., 1942-72. Won 3d prize in Scholastic high school poetry contest, 1929; 1st prize Witter Bynner Coll. awards, 1931. Endowed with Thomas S. Baker chair in English Lit. Carnegie-Mellon U., Pitts., 1970. Author: Gates of Aulis (novel), 1942; David the King, 1946; Alexandra, 1947; Confessors of the Name, 1952; the Persistent Image, 1955; A Small Fire, 1957; Rembrandt, 1961; Electra, 1965; The God-forgotten, 1972; Sonnets for an Analyst, 1973. Contbr. poetry and short stories to mags. Home: Pittsburgh PA Died Oct. 3, 1972.

SCHMITZ, DIETRICH, banker; b. Seattle, Wash., Oct. 25, 1890; s. Ferdinand and Emma (Althof) S.; ed. public schools, Seattle, Wash., student University of Wisconsin, 1913-14; m. Margaret Huteson, October 20, 1920; children—Gloria Gretchen, Alan Frederic, Margaret Ann. With Union Savings & Trust Co., Seattle, 1907-14, William A. Read & Co., Chicago, 1915-16, Union Nat. Bank, Seattle, 1916-24 (v.p. 1921-24); v.p. Nat. Bank of Commerce, Seattle, 1924-28, Pacific Nat. Bank, 1928-34; pres. Pacific Nat. Co., 1928-34; pres. and trustee Wash. Mutual Savings Bank, Seattle, Washington, 1934-57, chairman of the board and trustee, 1958-68, honorary chairman and trustee, 1968-70; exec. com., dir. Pacific Nat. Bank; dir., chmn. finance com. Gen. Ins. Co. Am., 1929-66; trustee No. Life Ins. Co.; treas. Seattle Found. Served as ensign, later lt. (j.g.) U.S. Navy, overseas duty with Atlantic Cruiser and Transport Force, 1917-19. Mem. Seattle Bd. Edn., 1928-61 (pres. 1932, 36, 37, 42, 46, 51, 53, 60); mem. coun. of adminstrn. Nat. Assn. of Mut. Savs. Banks, 1934-56; adv. com. Children's Orthopedic Hosp.; chairman King County War Finance (now Savs. Bonds) coms., 1941-70. Mem. Wash. Bankers Assn. (v.p. 1953-54, pres. 1954-55), Am. Bankers Assn. (state v.p. 1952-53), Phi Gamma Delta. Republican. Clubs: Rainier, University, Washington Athletic, Seattle Yacht. Home: Seattle WA Died Apr. 11, 1970; buried Acacia WA

SCHMUCKER, SAMUEL CHRISTIAN, biologist; b. Allentown, Pa., Dec. 18, 1860; s. Beale Melancthon and Christiana Marie (Pretz) S.; A.B., Muhlenberg Coll., 1882, A.M., 1885, M.S., 1891; Sc.D., 1913; Ph.D., U. of Pa., 1893, hon. fellow in botany, same, 1899; m. Katherine Elizabeth Weaver, Dec. 29, 1885; children—Beale M., Dorothy M. Prof. natural science, Carthage (Ill.) Coll., 1883-84, Boys High Sch., Reading, Pa., 1884-89, State Normal Sch., Indiana, Pa., 1889-95; biology, State Teachers Coll., West Chester, 1895-1923, emeritus since 1923. Lecturer on biology, Phila. Cooking Sch., 1898-1902; dean of faculty and prof. zoology, Wagner Inst., Phila., since 1907; also popular lecturer to schools, teachers' gatherings and chautauquas. Mem. N.E.A. Episcopalian. Independent Republican. Author: The Study of Nature, 1907; Columbia Elementary Georgraphy, 1909; Under the Open Sky, 1910; The Meaning of Evolution, 1913; Man's Life on Earth, 1925; Heredity and Parenthood, 1929. Club: Rotary. Home: West Chester PA‡

SCHNABEL, TRUMAN GROSS, physician, educator; b. Georgetown, Pa., Feb. 7, 1886; s. Edwin Daniel and Emeline (Woodring) S.; A.B., Lehigh U., 1907; M.D., U. Pa., 1911; m. Hildegard Rohner, Oct. 21, 1916;children—Truman Gross, Elizabeth S. (Mrs. Chamblin). Intern Hosp. U. Pa., 1911-13; practice internal medicine, Phila., since 1913; tchr. med. sch. U. Pa., 1913-51, emeritus prof. medicine, 1951-71; former staff mem. Howard Hosp.; dir. out-patient dept. medicine Hosp. U. Pa.; cons. Phila. Gen., Presbyn., Rush, Kensington and Nazareth hosps. Mem. com. Am. Found. Studies in Govt. since 1934. Recipient of Strittmatter award, Philadelphia County Medical Society, 1960; also Shaffrey award from St. Joseph's College in 1963. Served as major M.C., Army of the U.S., 1917-19. Diplomate Am. Bd. Internal Medicine (chmn. 1949-50). Fellow A.C.P. (v.p. 1956-57), Phila. Coll. Physicians; mem. Am. (chmn. sect. internal medicine 1953), Pa. (speaker 1940-44), Phila. Co. (pres. 1953) med. socs., Am. Gastro Enterological Assn., Am. Clin. and Climatol. Assn., Phila. Pathol. Soc., S.R., Sigma Nu, Alpha Omega Alpha, Phi Alpha Sigma Sigma Xi. Author articles in med. jours. Home: Wynnewood PA Died Aug. 27, 1971.

SCHNACKENBERG, ELMER JACOB, judge; b. Indpls., Aug. 22, 1889; s. Jacob and Anna (Farley) S.; LL.B., U. Chgo., 1912; m. Hazel E. Bard, May 15, 1916; children—Jeanne (Mrs. Lyman Cherry), Elmer, Frank, George, Paul, Roy. Stenographer Reliance Mfg. Co. also Pullman Co., 1906-08, law office, 1908-10; tchr. pub. sch., 1910-12; admitted to Ill. bar, 1912, practiced in Chgo., 1912-45; gen. atty. South Park Commrs., 1925-30; dir. South Chgo. Savings Bank, 1927-68; judge Circuit Ct. Cook Co., Chgo., 1945-54, U.S. Ct. Appeals, 7th Circuit, 1954-68. Mem. Ill. Legislature, 1912-13, 22-44, speaker Ho. of Reps., 1941-44; treas. Ill. Def. Council, 1941-44. Mem. Chgo. Bar Assn. Clubs: Chicago Athletic, South Shore Country. Home: Chicago IL Died Sept. 15, 1968; buried Oak Woods Cemetery, Chicago IL

SCHNADER, WILLIAM A(BRAHAM), lawyer; b. Bowmansville, Pa., Oct. 5, 1886; s. Charles B. and Elizabeth (Renninger) S.; A.B., Franklin and Marshall Coll., 1908, LL.D., 1931; LL.B., U. of Pa., 1912, LL.D., 1963; LL.D., Temple University, 1952; married Ethel K. Heinitsh, June 9, 1915. Began practice of law at Phila., Pa., 1913; mem. firm of Schnader, Harrison, Segal & Lewis; special dep. atty. gen. of Pa., 1923-30, attorney general, 1930-35. Chmn. Gov.'s Com. on Constitutional Revision, 1963-68. Mem. Nat. Conf. Commnrs. on Uniform State Laws (pres. 1939-42); pres. Nat. Assn. Attorneys General, 1933; first vice president, Am. Law Inst. Chmn. bd. trustees Franklin and Marshall Coll. (Lancaster, Pa.); trustee Cedar Crest Coll. (Allentown, Pa.), Temple U. Recipient gold medal for distinguished service to Am. jurisprudence Am. Bar Assn., 1960. Mem. Pa. Bar Assn. (pres. 1962-63). Mem. Phi Beta Kappa, Chi Phi, Phi Delta Phi, Order of the Coif. Republican. Mem. United Ch. of Christ. Mason. Clubs: Union League, Philadelphia Cricket, Rittenhouse. Home: Philadelphia PA Died Mar. 18, 1968.

SCHNAKENBERG, HENRY, artist; b. New Brighton, N.Y., 1892; student Art Students League, N.Y.C.; hon. degree, U. Vt. Elected mem. Nat. Inst. of Arts and Letters, 1952. Represented in Met. Mus. Art, Whitney Mus. Am. Art, Art Inst. Chgo., Bklyn. Mus., Pa. Acad. Fine Arts, Mpls. Art Inst., U. Neb. Mus., also art museums in San Francisco, Springfield (Mass.), Wichita. Home: Newton CT Died Oct. 13, 1970.

SCHNEIDER, CLEMENT JOSEPH, educator; b. New Franken, Wis., Nov. 21, 1927; s. Clem A. and Florence (Dantinne) S.; B.A., St. Louis U., 1952, Licentiate in Philosophy, 1953 S.T.L., 1960; Ph.D., Cornell U., 1964. Joined Soc. of Jesus, 1945, ordained priest Roman Catholic Ch., 1958; asst. prof. sociology Creighton U., 1965-72, acad. v.p., 1968-72, acting pres., 1969-70, also dir. Mem. A.A.A.S., Am. Cath. Sociol. Assn., Am. Assn. Higher Edn., Midwest, Am. sociol. assns., Soc. Sci. Study Religion, Gerontol. Soc. Author: (with Gordon Streib) Retirement in American Society: The Cornell Longitudinal Study, 1971; Impact and Process, 1971. Home: Omaha NE Died Oct. 20, 1972; buried Holy Sepulchre Cemetery, Omaha NE

SCHNEIDER, EDWARD ALEXANDER, banker; b. N.Y.C., Nov. 30, 1901; s. Edward J. and Julia A. (Distlehurst) S.; ed. pub. schs., also spl. banking courses; m. Genevieve A. Eifen, Oct. 17, 1928. With Bank of Am., Nat. Trust &Savs. Assn., San Francisco, 1926-48; with Bank of Hawaii, Honolulu, from 1948, sr. v.p., 1958-62, pres., 1963-66. Dir. Pacific Coast Banking Sch., Oahu Devel. Conf., Honolulu Community Chest, Honolulu council Navy League U.S. Mem. Hawaii Bankers Assn. (pres. 1963), Honolulu C. of C. Clubs: Oahu Country, Outrigger Canoe, Pacific (Honolulu). Home: Honolulu HI Died May 8, 1972.

SCHNEIDER, ERICH, educator; b. Siegen, Westfalia, Germany, Dec. 14, 1900; s. Wilhelm and Marie (Weber) S.; student univs. Frankfurt (Main), Gottingen, Munster, 1918-24; Dr. rer.pol., U. Frankfurt, 1922; Dr.rer.pol. (hon.), Free U. Berlin, 1957; Dr.econ. (hon.), Comml. Acad. Stockholm, 1959; hon. doctorates U. Paris, 1960, U. Louvain, 1963, U. Rennes, 1966; Dr.oec. (hon.), Comml. Acad. Helsinki, 1961; m. Erna Daub, Apr. 4, 1930. Tchr. math. and physics, Dortmund and Koblenz, 1925-36; habilitation for econs. U. Bonn, 1932; prof. U. Aarhus (Denmark), 1936-46; prof. U. Kiel (Germany), 1946-70, dir. Inst. for World Econs., 1961-69. Pres., Gesellschaft fur Wirtschafts-und Sozialwissenschaften (verein fur Socialpolitik), 1963-66. Recipient Gold medal Bundesverband Deutscher Volks-und Betriebswirte, 1965, Grosses Verdienstkreuz des Verdienstordens der Bundesrepublik Deutschland, 1968. Fellow Econometric Soc., Royal Econ. Soc. London; mem. Danish Acad. Tech. Scis., Internat. Statis. Inst., Institut International des Finances Publiques, Am. Econ. Assn. (hon.), Sci. Acad. U. Lund, Finnish Acad. Scis., Internat. Assn. for Research in Income and Wealth, Instituto Lombardo, Accademia di Scienze e Lettere Milano. Author books (in several edits. and translated into various langs.) including: Theorie der Produktion, 1934, Einfuhrung in die Wirtschaftstheorie, 1947-62, 4 vols., Wirtschaftlichkeitsrechnung, 1951; Industrielles Rechnungswesen, 1954; Volkswirtschaft und Betriebswirtschaft, 1964; Aufgaben und Ubungen zur Wirtschaftstheorie, 1965; Zahlungsbilanz und Wechselkurs, 1968. Home: Kiel Federal Republic of Germany Died Dec. 5, 1970.

SCHNEIDER, GEORGE, chemist, textile co. exec.; b. Bklyn., Mar. 28, 1897; s. Peter and Rose (Gelden) S.; grad. U. Buffalo, 1918; m. Gladys Bower, Jan. 1, 1919; 1 dau., Dorothy (Mrs. Henry Staehling); m. 2d, Hazel McIntyre, Sept. 4, 1956. Chemist, Celanese Corp. of Am., 1920-45, v.p., dir., 1945-50, sr. v.p., 1950-59, vice chmn., 1959-71; dir. Canadian Chem. Co., Celanese Mexicana, Celanese Colombiana, Celanese Venezolana. Served as lt., C.W.S., U.S. Army, 1917-18. Fellow Am. Inst. Chemists; mem. Am. Inst. Chem. Engrs., Soc. Chem. Industry. Clubs: Chemists (N.Y.C.); Rock Spring (N.J.). Home: Short Hills NJ Died Nov. 1971.

SCHNEIDERS, ALEXANDER A(LOYSIUS), educator; b. Sioux City, Ia., Feb. 2, 1909; s. Mathias and Mary Anne (Mootz) S.; Ph.B., Creighton U., 1930; M.A., Georgetown U., 1931, Ph.D., 1934; m. Glen Ogle, August 11, 1934; children—Ronald, Sandra, Anne, Paul, Mary, Eileen, Gregory. Fellow in philosophy and psychology, Georgetown U., 1930-34; asst. to dir. personnel, Nat. Archives, Washington, D.C., 1935-36; instr. psychology, Loyola U., Chicago, 1936-39, asst. prof. psychology and dir. student personnel, 1939-45; asso. prof. psychology and dir. dept. of psychology, U. of Detroit, Mich., 1945-48, prof. and dir. dept. of psychology, 1948-53; prof. director psychol. services Fordham U., N.Y., 1953-61; prof. psychology Boston Coll., 1961-68. Fellow Mass. Psychol. Assn.; mem. New Eng., Am., Am. Catholic (pres. 1952-53, dir.), psychol. assns., Sigma Xi. Democrat. Roman Catholic. Author: Outline of Rational Psychology, 1941; Introductory Psychology, 1951; Psychology of Adolescence, 1951; Personal Adjustment and Mental Health, 1955; Adolescence and the Challenge of Maturity, 1965; The Anarchy of Feeling, 1963; Personality Dynamics and Mental Health, 1965; Counseling the Adolescent, 1967. Co-editor Proc. of Inst. for the Clergy, 1957; editor: Proc. Am. Cath. Psychol. Assn., 1962; co-editor: Personality Development and Adjustment in

Adolescence, 1960. Editor: The Catholic Psychological Record. Home: Newtonville MA Died Sept. 30, 1968.

SCHNEIDEWIND, RICHARD, educator; b. Manila, P.I., Dec. 16, 1900; s. Richard and Gabina (Gabriel) S.; student Detroit Jr. Coll., 1918-19, U. Chicago, 1918; B.S., U. Mich., 1923, M.S., 1928, Ph.D., 1933; m. Jane Morris, Feb., 1943. Mem. Univ. Mich. dept. engring. research, 1924-37, mem. faculty U. Mich., 1937-70, prof. metallurgical engring., 1945-70, cons. cast metal field since 1935 (research in electroplating field, 1924-30, in cast metals field, 1930-70); dir. Sparton Corporation. Recipient William H. McFadden gold medal of Am. Foundrymen's Soc. for contributions to knowledge of malleable irons, 1950. Mem. Am. Foundrymen's Soc., Soc. Automotive Engrs., Am. Soc. Metals, Am. Soc. Testing Materials, Am. Soc. Engring. Edn. Author: Unit Operations (with G. G. Brown and assos.), 1950. Contbr. articles engring. pubs. Holder patents methods of chromium plating. Home: Ypsilanti Died Feb. 21, 1970.

SCHNEIRLA, THEODORE CHRISTIAN, animal psychologist; b. Ray City, Mich., July 23, 1902; s. Christian and Mary Emily (Badger) S.; A.B., U. Mich., 1924, M.Sc., 1925, Sc.D., 1928; m. Leone Margaretta Warner, June 12, 1926; children—Lois Janet, Donn (dec.). Instr. psychology N.Y.U., 1928-30, asst. prof., 1931-41, asso. prof., 1941-45, adj. prof., 1947-68; adjunct prof. biology City U. of N.Y., 1965-68; asso. curator dept. animal behavior Am. Mus. Natural History, 1942-47, curator, 1947-68. Fellow NRC. Fellow John Simon Guggenheim Meml. Found., 1944-46. Fellow A.A.A.S., Am. Psychol. Assn., N.Y. Zool. Soc., American Academy of Arts and Sciences; mem. Explorers Club, Am. Zool. Soc., Am. Soc. Naturalists, Ecol. Soc. Am., Internat. Union Study Soc. Insects (pres. N.A. sect. 1952-55), N.Y. Entomol. Soc. (pres. 1949), Sigma Xi, Phi Sigma, Gamma Alpha. Democrat. Author: Learning and Orientation in Ants, 1928; (with N. R. F. Maier) Principles of Animal Psychology, 1935; Recent Experiments in Psychology, 1938. Contbr. articles profl. publs. Home: New York City NY Died Aug. 20, 1968.

SCHOCH, EUGENE PAUL, chemist; b. Berlin, Germany, Oct. 16, 1871; s. Oscar and Jenny (Finck) S.; C.E., U. of Tex., 1894, A.M., 1896; Ph.D., U. of Chicago, 1902; m. Clara L. Gerhard, June 14, 1902; children—Arthur Gerhard, Margaret Magdalene, Eugene Paul. Fellow, U. of Tex., 1893-94, tutor chemistry, 1894-96, instr., 1897-1905, adj. professor, 1905-08, asso. prof., 1908-11, prof. phys. chemistry, 1911-40, prof. chem. engring. since 1938; dir. Bur. Indsl. Chemistry, 1928-42. Asso. editor Jour. of Physical Chem., 1909-23, Sch. Sc. and Mathematics (Chicago), 1905-10. Fellow A.A.A.S., Tex. Acad. Sc. (pres., 1908-09); mem. Am. Chem. Soc., Am. Inst. Chem. Engrs., Phi Beta Kappa, Sigma Nu. Democrat. Conglist. Author: (with W. A. Felsing) General Chemistry, 1938; also papers on research on reactions by electric discharges through gases, producing dry lump lignite, potassium sulfate from polyhalite, high strength gypsum plaster. Home: 2212 Nueces St., Austin TX‡

SCHODER, ERNEST WILLIAM, educator, hydraulic engr.; b. Dewey, Fidalgo Island, Wash., Aug. 17, 1879; s. Herman and Sophia (Huntemann) S.; B.S. and B.S. in Mining, U. of Washington, 1900; Ph.D., Cornell U., 1903; unmarried. In charge Hydraulic Lab., Cornell U., Sch. of Civil Engring., 1904; asst. prof. exper. hydraulics, Cornell U., 1904-19, prof. 1919-47, emeritus, 1947-68. Was hydraulic expert for U.S., State of N.Y., municipal and corporate interests; consultant for Army Engrs. on river models, 1937-38. Commd. capt. engrs., U.S. Army, Aug. 1917; instr. and engr. officer Camp Lee, Petersburg, Va.; asst. dir. of training, Camp Humphreys, Va.; spl. duty in Office of Chief of Engrs., Washington. Fellow A.A.A.S., Am. Soc. C.E.; mem. Soc. Am. Mil. Engrs., Phi Gamma Delta, Sigma Xi, Phi Beta Kappa. Author: Hydraulics Section, Marks' Mechanical Engrs'. Handbook (1st 4 edits.); Hydraulics (with F. M. Dawson), also author of papers on exptl. studies of pipes and wires in Trans. Am. Soc. C.E. and M.E. since 1902. Home: Seattle WA Died May 16, 1968; buried Lakeview Cemetery, Seattle WA

SCHOELLKOPF, J. FRED IV, corp. exec.; b. Buffalo, Oct. 1, 1910; s. Jacob Frederick Jr. and Olive C. (Abbott) S.; B.A., Cornell U., 1935; m. Patricia Calkins, Aug. 28, 1935; children—J. Fred, V. Marion, Sandra, Phoebe, Patricia. Gen. sales mgr., asst. sec. Bell Aircraft Corp., 1935-42; dir., chmn. exec. com. Crescent Niagara Corp., 1960-68; sr. and ltd. partner Schoellkopf & Co., 1947-50; pres., dir. Niagara Share Corp., Buffalo, 1950-61, chmn. bd., dir., 1961-69; pres., dir. Marine Midland Corp., 1966-68; chmn. bd., dir. Marine Midland Banks, Inc.; v.p., dir. Marine Midland Bldgs. Corp., Marine Midland Properties Corp.; director Gen. Signal Co., Marine Midland Trust Co., Western N.Y., Seventy Niagara Services, Incorporated Ont. Marine, Inc., Carborundum Company, Buffalo Ins. Corp. (Chgo.), Dunlop Tire & Rubber Corp., Umont Mining, Inc., N.Y. Telephone Co., Marine Midland Internat. Corp., Baseball Holding Corp. Dir. mem. finance com. Buffalo Soc. Natural scis.; trustee YMCA Buffalo; bd. trustees, dirs., United Fund Buffalo and Erie County, Dir. Buffalo Fine Arts Acad., Albright-Knox Art Gallery, Greater Buffalo Development Foundation; trustee Berkshire Sch. Served as lt. col. USAAF, 1942-45, inactive Res., 1945-69. Decorated Distinguished Flying Cross, Air Medal with 6 oak leaf clusters. Mem. Buffalo Hist. Soc. (life), Am. Inst. Banking, Navy League (dir. Niagara Frontier council), Newcomen Soc. Clubs: Mid-Day, Buffalo, Bond, Pack, Buffalo Athletic, Thursday, Chairman's (Buffalo); Lunch, Fifth Avenue, Governor's (N.Y.C.); Wanakah Country (Hamburg, N.Y.); Metropolitan (Washington). Home: Lake View NY Died Dec. 7, 1969.

SCHOEN, JOHN EDMUND, educator; born Milwaukee, Mar. 6, 1898; s. Anthony George and Barbara (Kasseckert) S.; B.S., Marquette U., 1919; M.S., U. Wis., 1929; m. Anna Jirikowic, Aug. 18, 1923; children—John R., William A., Mary Ann. Part time engineer, Power and Mining Company, Milwaukee, 1916-17, Cutler Hammer Co., 1917-18, Portland Cement Assn., 1918-19; coll. apprentice Allis Chalmers Mfg. Co., Milwaukee, 1919, Feed Water Heater Co., 1920-22; mem. faculty Marquette U., 1922-67, prof. mech. and metall. engring., 1929-67, formerly head dept. mech. and metall. engring., also director department mechanical engineering; consulting engineer in heat power, mechanical design, and metallurgy since 1930; also cons. to many cos. on fire and explosion. Mem. Mayors adv. com. City Milw. Bldg. Code deviations. Mem. A.S.M.E., Am. Soc. Metals, Am. Soc. Engring. Edn., Engrs. Soc. Milwaukee. Rep. Roman Cath. Contbr. articles in engring. jours. Home: Milwaukee WI Died Mar. 30, 1967; buried Holy Cross Cemetery Milwaukee WI

SCHOENECK, EDWARD, lawyer; b. Syracuse, N.Y., Aug. 6, 1875; s. Henry and Elvina (Heindorf) S.; LL.B., Syracuse U., 1903; m. Katherine Hart, July 20, 1908. Admitted to N.Y. bar, 1903, and practiced in Syracuse; mem. Bond, Schoeneck & King. Mem. Bd. Supervisors, Onodaga County, 1902, 03; mem. N.Y. Assembly, 1904-07; mayor of Syracuse, 1910-13; lt. gov. of N.Y., 1915-16, 1917-18. Mem. N.Y. State Liquor Authority since 1933. Republican. Lutheran. Home: 500 N. McBride St. Office: State Tower Bldg., Syracuse NY*‡

SCHOFIELD, ALBERT GEORGE, civil engr.; b. Berkeley, Cal., June 10, 1912; s. Albert Edward and Lena May (Lovie) S.; student San Jose State, 1929-31, Stanford, 1931-32, U. Cal., Fresno State; m. Eunice A. Bannon, May 21, 1935 (dec. Jan. 1969); children—Bonnie Elizabeth (Mrs. James McDaniel), Toni Jean (Mrs. Bruce A. Blackledge); m. 2d, Cuma Riggs, Feb. 1970. Engr., U.S. Bur. Pub. Rds., 1931, U.S. Forest Service, 1932-41, Lockheed Aircraft Corp., 1941-46, Pacific Gas & Electric Co., 1947-51; asso. hwy. engr. Cal. Div. Hwys., 1951-60; gen. practice civil engr., Fresno, 1960-70; pres., dir. A. G. Schofield, Inc.; part-time asst. prof. math., engring. Fresno State Coll. Mem. Am. Soc. C.E., Nat. Soc. Profl. Engrs. Home: Fresno CA Died May 6, 1970; buried Fresno Meml. Gardens Fresno CA

SCHOLER, WALTER, architect; b. Portland, Ind., May 8, 1890; s. Henry and Anna (Weuthrich) S.; student Columbia, 1913-14; m. Alice Caster, Oct. 20, 1911; children—Walter, Emerson Caster, Charles Edward. Mem. archtl. firm Nicol, Scholar and Hoffman, Lafayette, Ind., 1920-25; pvt. practice, Lafayette, 1925-45; partner firm Walter Scholar & Assos., Lafayette, 1945-72; prin. works include bldgs. for Purdue U., Ball State Tchrs. Coll., Franklin Coll., Wabash Coll. Mem. Ind. Bd. Registration Architects, 1946-68. Fellow A.I.A. Home: Lafayette IN Died Jan. 29, 1972.

SCHOLL, WILLIAM M., physician, business exec.; b. La Porte, Ind., June 22, 1882; s. Peter and Clara (Hana) S.; M.D., Ill. Med. Coll., 1904, Chgo. Med. Sch., 1922. Pvt. practice medicine, Chgo., 1905-49; founder, pres. Scholl Mfg. Co., Inc., Chgo., 1904-68, Scholl Mfg. Co., Ltd., Toronto, 1908-68, Scholl Mfg. Co., Ltd., London, Eng., 1910-68; Foot Specialist Pub. Co., Chgo., 1917-68, Foot Comfort Shops, Inc., since 1924, Dr. Scholl's Foot Comfort Shop, Inc., since 1933, Med. & Surg. Pub. Co. since 1928, Chgo. Plastic Products Co. since 1942; v.p. Arno Adhesive Tapes, Inc., since 1929, Foot Clinics of Chgo. since 1912; dir. Cia. Dr. Scholl. Founder, v.p., trustee Illinois College of Podiatry since 1912. Mem. Am. Sch. Practipedics. Clubs: Ill. Athletic, South Shore Country, Germania, Swedish (Chgo.). Home: Chicago IL Died Mar. 29, 1968.

SCHOLLE, HARDINGE, retired cons.; b. St. Paul, Minnesota, Apr. 30, 1896; s. Gustave and Lillian (Jones) S.; ed. La Villa, Switzerland, 1909-12; Coite School, Munich, 1912-14; A.B., Harvard, 1918; m. Elizabeth Klapp, Apr. 10, 1917; children—Margaret Lillian (Mrs. Nicholas Forell), Oliver Coleman; m. 2d, Eleanor Peabody, Apr. 24, 1930. Asst., decorative arts dept., Metropolitan Museum of Art, N.Y. City, 1921-23; asst., curator decorative arts dept., Chicago Art Inst., 1923-26; dir. Museum of the City of N.Y., 1926-51; cons. Nat. Trust for Historic Preservation in U.S., Washington, 1951-63. Corpl. 437th engineer detachment, 2d lt. Mil. Intelligence Div., 1918. Clubs: Harvard, Grolier (New York City). Home: San Mateo CA Died May 1969.

SCHOLTZ, JOSEPH D., govt. ofcl.; b. Louisville, Jan 16, 1890; s. Charles and Hermine S.; student Cornell Univ., Class of 1912; m. Ann Louise Cassilly, Oct. 24 1914; children—Joseph D., Phillip H., Robert L., Anne Q. Began as exec. Denunzio Fruit Co., Louisville, 1910 advancing to vice-pres.; pres. Bd. of Park Comrs. Louisville, 1933-35; pres. Louisville Water Co. 1935-37; mayor of Louisville, 1937-41; regional dir. Omaha, Neb., Office of Civilian Defense, 1942-72 Served in O.T.S., Camp Zachary Taylor, during World War. Pres. Ky. Municipal League 1939-40; chmn advisory com. U.S. Conf. of Mayors 1937-72; dir Louisville Y.M.C.A., Louisville Library Bd. Mem Kappa Sigma, Am. Legion, Forty and Eight. Democrat Episcopalian. Clubs: Pendennis, Rotary, 235, Big Springs, Audubon Country (Louisville). Home: Omaha NB Died Sept. 1972.

SCHONBERGER, E(MANUEL) D(EO), educator; b Blue River, Wis., Dec. 25, 1875; s. Francis M. and Marie (Vopalensky) S.; A.B., Yankton (S.D.) Coll., 1901; M.E., Columbia Coll. of Expression, 1904; student U. of Chicago, 1912; m. Sara L. Wallace, Aug. 19, 1908; children—Clinton, Robert, Mary (Mrs. L. M. Landgraf), Marguerite (Mrs. F. P. LaMontagne). Teller, Bank of Chamberlain, S.D., 1901-03; entertainer and talent salesman, Slayton Lyceum Bur., 1905-07; asst. prof. English, Olivet (Mich.) Coll., 1907-09; asst. prof. public speaking, Washburn Coll., Topeka, Kan., 1911-23; instr. Colo. U., summers 1917-18; asso. in English, U. of N.D., 1923-26, asso. prof. pub. speaking, 1926-34, prof. and head of dept., 1934-48, retired Aug. 1948. Dir. Dakota Playmakers, 1923-48. Served as 4-minute speaker, World War I. Mem. Am. Assn. U. Profs., Nat. Assn. Teachers of Speech, Am. Ednl. Theatre, Delta Sigma Rho, Pi Epsilon Delta. Democrat. Conglist. Mason (32 deg., Shriner). Clubs: Lyons, Franklin, Fortnightly. Author: Play Production for Amateurs, 1939; Pistol of the Beg and Solstice (plays translated from Czech-Poet Lore), 1924-25; Fundamentals of Play Production, 1949; mag. articles. Home: 1918-1/2 6th Av., Los Angeles 16‡

SCHONFELD, WILLIAM A., child psychiatrist; b. Nuremberg, Germany, Aug. 12, 1906; s. Martin and Helen (Spitzer) S.; brought to U.S., 1907; B.S., N.Y.U., 1928, M.D., 1931; m. Louise R. Rost, June 30, 1935; 1 son, William Rost. Intern Morrisania City Hosp., 1931-32, resident pediatrics and psychiatry, 1932-34; pediatric-psychiatry Bellevue Hosp. Psychiat. Inst., 1931, Mt. Sinai Hosp., 1942; pvt. practice, 1934-70; specialist in child and adolescent psychiatry; asst. attending psychiatrist, div. child psychiatry Presbyn. Hosp.; vis. pediatric-psychiatry, Morrisania City Hosp.; asst. clin. prof. child psychiatry Coll. Phys. and Surgs., Columbia; asso. attending Children Service, N.Y. Psychiat. Inst. & Hosp.; asso. clin. prof. pediatric-psychiatry, N.Y. Med. Coll., 1948-59. Chmn. Westchester's Multidisplinery Conf. Problems Adolescence, 1962-70. White House Conf. Children and Youth (tech. cons. 1950, 60, 70). Served as maj. M.C., AUS, 1942-46. Awarded Commendation Medal for Psychiatric Rehab. Diplomate Am. Bd. Pediatrics; Am. Bd. Psychiatry and Neurology in psychiatry; American Board Psychiatry and Neurology in child psychiatry. Fellow Am. Psychiat. Assn. (com. psychiatry childhood and adolescence and chairman of subcommittee on adolescence); mem. Westchester County Psychiat. Society (vice president 1956, 60), American Society for Adolescent Psychology (president since 1967-69), New York Academy Medicine, Soc. Research Child Devel., Am. Acad. Pediatrics (chairman of area Committee on Youth), Internat. Assn. Child Psychiatry, Am. Assn. U. Profs., Am. Ortho-Psychiat. Assn., Soc. Adolescent Psychiatry (pres. 1961-62), Westchester Mental Health Association (board directors, chairman committee on edn.). Mason (past master). Contbr. numerous articles devel. and psychiatry in adolescence to med. jours. Home: Mamaroneck NY Died Sept. 21, 1970.

SCHOONOVER, FRANK EARLE, illustrator; b. Oxford, N.J., Aug. 19, 1877; s. John and Elizabeth (LeBar) S.; ed. 9 yrs. at Model School, Trenton, N.J., 4 yrs. art dept. Drexel Inst., Phila., under Howard Pyle; m. Martha Culbertson, Jan. 18, 1911; children—Cortlandt, Elizabeth, Louise. Has illustrated for national mags., also for several publishing houses; muralist; portrait painter. Mem. Soc. of Illustrators. Club: The Players. Author, having written articles on life of the Canadian trapper of the Far North in Scribner's mag., etc. Home: Willmington DE Died Sept. 1, 1972; buried Old St. Anne's Church, Middletown DE

SCHORGER, ARLIE WILLIAM, chemist; b. Republic, O., Sept. 6, 1884; s. John Valentine and Cora Ellen (Meyers) S.; Ph.B., Wooster (O.) Coll., 1906; M.A., Ohio State University, 1908; Ph.D., University of Wisconsin, 1916, D.Sc. (honorary), 1961; D.Sc. (honorary), Lawrence College, 1955; married William Davison, John Rodger. Asst. chemist Bur. Standards, Washington, 1908, Bur. Internal Revenue, 1909; research chemist U.S. Forest Service, 1909-17; dir. chem. research C. F. Burgess Labs., 1917-31; president of the Burgess Cellulose Company, Freeport, Illinois, 1931-50; professor wildlife management U. Wis., 1951-55, emeritus, 1955-72; dir. Research Products

Corporation, Burgess Cellulose Company. Member of Wisconsin Conservation Commn., 1953-60. Recipient Brewster award, 1958. Fellow Am. Ornithol. Union; mem. Am. Chem. Soc., Nat. Audubon Soc. (dir. 1957-59), Am. Soc. Mammalogy, Cooper, Wilson, Wis. ornithol. socs., Wis. Hist. Soc., Wis. Archeol. Soc., Wis. Acad. Scis. (pres. 1942-43), Phi Beta Kappa, Sigma Xi, Delta Upsilon. Republican. Presbyn. Club: Madison. Author: Chemistry of Cellulose and Wood, 1926; The Passenger Pigeon, 1955; The Wild Turkey, 1966. Author articles on chemistry, ornithology. Holder numerous chem. patents. Home: Madison WI Died May 26, 1972.

SCHRADE, LEO FRANZ, musicologist; b. Allenstein, Germany, Dec. 13, 1903; s. Franz and Margarethe (Hoppe) S.; Dr.phil., U. Leipzig (Germany), 1927; m. Els Jacob, Apr. 13, 1929; 1 dau., Lavinia (Mrs. Jean Bruneau). Came to U.S., 1938, naturalized, 1944. Privatdozent, U. Koenigsberg (Germany); 1929-32, U. Bonn (Germany), 1932-37; mem. faculty Yale, 1938-58, prof. history music, 1948-58, dir. grad. studies dept. music, 1940-58; prof. U. Basel (Switzerland), dir. Musikwissenschaftliches Inst. der Universitat, 1958-64; Charles Eliot Norton prof. poetry Harvard, 1962-63. Mem. Am. Musicol. Soc., Mediaeval Acad. Am., Internat. Musicol. Soc., Internat. Soc. Mus. Libraries, Vereniging voor Nederlandse Muziekgeschiedenis, Societe Francaise de Musicologie, Societe Belge de Musicologie, Schweizerische Musikforschende Gesellschaft. Author: Die Handschriftliche Ueberlieferung der altesten Instrumentalmusik, 1931; Beethoven in France, 1942; Monteverdi, 3d edit., 1964; Bach, The Conflict between the Sacred and the Secular, 1954; La representation d'Edipo Tiranno au Teatro Olimpico, 1960; L. Milan, Libro de Musica de Vihuela de Mano, 1927; Polyphonic Music of the 14th Century, 4 vols., 1956-64; Tragedy in the Art of Music, 1963; W. A. Mozart, 1964; also numerous articles. Editor: Yale Studies in the History of Music, 1946-58, Collegium Musicum, 1950-58; co-editor Jour. Renaissance and Baroque Music, 1946-47, Annales Musicologiques, 1953-63, Archiv fur Musikwissenschaft, 1958-64. Home: Basel Switzerland Died Sept. 21, 1964.

SCHRADER, CHARLES E., univ. dean; b. Toledo, O., Apr. 19, 1890; s. Charles Joseph and Anna E. (Caldwell) S.; student St. John's Coll., 1910-12, St. Stanislaus Sem., 1912-16; A.B., A.M., Gonzaga U., 1919; student St. Louis U., 1923-27, Columbia U., 1927, Ludwig-Maximillian Universitat, Munich, Germany, 1930-32; Ph.D., St. Louis U., 1933. Entered Jesuit Order, 1912; ordained priest Roman Catholic Church, 1926; instructor Loyola Academy, Chicago, 1919-23, professor history Loyola University, Chicago, 1928-30; professor and head of dept. of history, St. John's College, Toledo, 1933-34; prof. of history and head dept., U. of Detroit, 1934-50, dean grad. div., 1937-50. Mem. Am. Hist. Assn., Medieval Acad. of Am., Am. Cath. Hist. Assn., Nat. Cath. Edn. Assn., Mich. Acad. Science, Art and Letters, Pi Gamma Mu. Home: Clarkston MI Died Nov. 1, 1969.

SCHRADER, GEORGE H., humanitarian. Entered mfg. business founded by father, 1844; invented disappearing window, and the air valve used in bicycle and automobile tires; retired from active business. Built Hub House for social workers of New York, the Caroline Rest Home for Mothers (Hartsdale, N.Y.), Sea Breeze Hosp. for tuberculous children (Coney Island), and a hall of the Roman Catholic Cancer Home, Hawthorne, N.Y. Home: Hartsdale NY‡

SCHRAKAMP, JOSEPHA, author; b. in Germany; d. Edward S.; ed. in Germany. Taught in New York schs. Author: Das Deutsche Buch, 1887, 1904; (with Professor Wenckebach) Deutsche Grammatik fur Amerikaner, 1887; Erzahlungen aus der deutschen Geschichte, 1888; Sagen und Mythen, 1893; Beruhmte Deutsche, 1894; Grammatical Drill, 1898; Conversational Exercises, 1898; Le livre Francais, 1905. Address: 29 E. 29th St., New York NY‡

SCHREINER, GEORGE ABEL, author; b. Germany, Aug. 21, 1875; s. Johannes H. and Anna Elizabeth (Apel) S.; ed. mil. acads.; Europe and South Africa; B.F.S. from Georgetown University in 1927; m. Marie Anna Elizabeth Richter, of Danbury, Conn., October 26, 1902. Officer of arty. on Boer side Boer War. Mng. editor San Antonio (Tex.) Light-Gazette, 1912-13; war corr. Associated Press in Mexico, Dardanelles, Poland, Macedonia, West Front (France), etc.; polit. corr. in various European countries; negotiator between Am. Embassy and Austro-Hungarian Govt., at Vienna, Mar.-Apr. 1917. Came to U.S., 1900, naturalized citizen, 1906. Author: The Iron Ration, 1918; La Detresse Allemande, 1918; From Berlin to Bagdad, 1918; The Craft Sinister, 1920; Entente Diplomacy and the World (with B. de Siebert), 1921; Cables and Wireless, 1924. Address: Club de Corresponsales Extranjeros, Calle San Juan de Letran 31, Mexico City Mexico‡

SCHREINER, OSWALD, chemist; b. Nassau, Germany, May 29, 1875; s. Louis and Susanne (Volkert) S.; grad. Baltimore Poly. Inst., 1892; Ph.G., U. of Md., 1894; Johns Hopkins, 1894-95; B.S., U. of Wis., 1897, M.S., 1899, Ph.D., 1902; m. Frances Rector, Oct. 11, 1902; children—Louis Rector, Oswald. U.S. Pharmacopeia research fellow, U. of Wis., 1895-96, asst. in pharm. technique, 1896-97, instr., 1897-1902, instr. phys. chemistry, 1902-03, expert phys. chemist, Bureau of Soils, U.S. Dept. Agr., summer 1902, chemist, 1903-06, chief Div. Soil Fertility Investigations, 1906-40; asst. to chief, Bur. of Plant Industry, 1940-44; collaborator since 1944; counseling professor chemistry, American University, 1914-34. United States delegate 1st International Congress of Soil Science, Washington, D.C., 1927, chmn. exec. com. same; U.S. del. 4th Pacific Science Congress, Java, 1929 and Congress Internat. Sugar Cane Technologists, Java, 1929; cons. del. Inter-Am. Conf. on Agr., 1930; U.S. del. 3d Internat. Congress Soil science, Oxford, Eng., 1935; del. 8th Am. Scientific Congress, Washington, 1939. Fellow A.A.A.S., Am. Society Agronomy; mem. American Chemical Society, American Soc. Biol. Chemists, Assn. of Agrl. Chemists (pres. 1928), Washington Acad. Science, Bot. Soc. America, Soil Sci. Soc. of America, Internat. Soil Sci. Soc., Internat. Sugar Cane Technologists, Sigma Xi, Phi Beta Kappa. Club: Cosmos. Author: The Sesquiterpenes, 1904; Colorimetric, Turbidity, and Titration Methods Used in Soil Investigations, 1906; The Chemistry of Soil Organic Matter, 1910, Lawn Soils, 1911; Nitrogenous Soil Constituents, 1913. Home: 21 Primrose St., Chevy Chase 15 MD‡

SCHRODER, WILLIAM HENRY, lawyer; b. Atlanta, Mar. 20, 1914; s. William Henry and Suzanne (Spalding) S.; A.B. cum laude, U. Notre Dame, 1935; LL.B. summa cum laude, U. Ga., 1938; m. Mary Elizabeth Barge, Sept. 19, 1939; children—William Henry, Mary Barge (Mrs. Archie J. Baker, Jr.), John Timothy, Belle Spalding. Admitted to Ga. bar, 1938, practiced in Atlanta; partner firm Troutman, Sams, Schroder & Lockerman, 1942-70. Dir. Nat. Bank of Ga., Dinkler Hotels Corp. Served to lt. USNR, 1943-45. Mem. Am., Ga., Atlanta (exec. com.) bar assns., Am. Judicature Soc., Atlanta Lawyers Club, Mil. Order World Wars, Am. Legion, Am. Coll. Trial Lawyers, Nat. Assn. Ry. Trial Counsel (exec. com.), U. Notre Dame (1st pres. Atlanta), U. Ga. (treas.) alumni assns., Phi Beta Kappa, Phi Delta Phi, Chi Phi. Catholic. Clubs: Gridiron, Atlanta Country, Capital City (bd. govs.), Commerce, Peachtree Golf, Piedmont Driving, Peachtree Racket (pres.) (Atlanta). Home: Atlanta GA Died May 25, 1970; buried Westview Cemetery, Atlanta GA

SCHROEDER, JOSEPH EDWIN, lawyer; b. Wyandotte County, Kan., May 22, 1905; s. Joseph and Mora (Dillon) S.; LL.B., U. Kansas City, 1929; m. Alice Virginia Hutton, June 17, 1926; children—Marvalee (Mrs. Charles A. Roath), Joseph Edwin, Mora Alice (Mrs. Glenn G. Buchanan). Admitted to Kan. bar, 1929; pvt. practice, Kansas City, Kan., 1929-40; judge div. 4, Dist. Ct. Wyandotte County, 1940-41; county counsellor Wyandotte County, 1941-48; pvt. practice, Kansas City, Kan., 1941-67; sr. partner firm Stanley, Schroeder, Weeks, Thomas & Lysaught, 1949-67. Dir. Home State Bank, Republic Mut. Fire Ins. Co., Larson Bros. Co., Inc. Bd. advisers Donnelly Coll., 1958-67, chmn., 1960, bd. dirs. Assn. Conquest Blindness, 1950-67. Mem. Am., Kan., Wyandotte bar assns., Am. Judicature Soc. Republican. Clubs: Kansas City, Milburn Golf and Country, Terrace (Kansas City, Kan.). Home: KS Died Oct. 8, 1967; buried Meml. Park, Kansas City KS

SCHUCK, ARTHUR FREDERICK, govt. ofcl.; b. Washington, Ind., May 11, 1896; s. Peter F. and Wilhelmina Sophia (Beckeneyer) S.; student U. Ill., 1915-17, Kent Coll. Law, 1922; m. Cleopha A. Bessmer, Feb. 21, 1927 (dec. Aug. 1954); children—Arthur Frederick, Dorothy Ann; married 2d, Elizabeth Berg, Mar. 10, 1955; 1 son, Neil R. Sandberg. With U.S. Treasury Dept., 1919-21, Snyder, Hay & Garfield, bus. cons., 1921-26 Sears Roebuck & Co. and subsidiaries, 1927-39; partner McClure, Hadden & Ortman, bus. cons., 1940-42; financial assignments for Stewart Warner Corp., 1942-44; controller, treas. Joseph N. Eisendrath & Co., 1944-45; cons. Advance Mortgage Co., 1945; treas. Ill. Agr. Assn. and subsidiaries, 1945-50; exec. v.p., chief adminstrv. officer George Getz Corp. and subsidiaries, 1950-54; ind. cons. bus., 1954-57; financial adv. ICA-U.S. Operations Mission to Ecuador, 1957-71. Served with U.S. Army, 1917-19. Mem. Controllers Inst., Am. Legion. Mason (32 degree, Shriner). Club: University (Chgo.). Home: Rolling Prairie IN Died Dec. 6, 1971.

SCHUELEIN, HERMANN, (shoe line), brewery exec.; b. Munich, Germany, Jan. 24, 1884; s. Josef and Ida (Baer) S.; student U. Munich, U. Berlin; J.D., Ph.D., U. Erlangen, Germany, 1909; m. Luise Fanny Levi, Apr. 15, 1913 (dec. June 1950); 1 dau., Annemarie (Mrs. Samuel Anatole Lourie). Came to U.S., 1936, naturalized, 1944. Pres. Munich Loewenbraeu, Bavaria, Germany, 1911-35; cons. Liebmann-Rheingold Brewers, Bklyn., 1936-37, mng. dir., 1937-50, chmn. bd., mng. dir., 1950-54, chmn. bd., from 1954. Decorated Grand Cross Order of Merit (West German Republic). Home: New York City NY Deceased.

SCHUIRMANN, ROSCOE ERNEST, naval officer; b. Chenoa, Ill., Dec. 17, 1890; grad. U.S. Naval Acad., 1912; m. Hardinia Taylor; 1 dau., Hardy. Entered U.S. Navy, 1908, and advanced through the grades to rear adm., 1942; ret., 1951. Home: Washington DC Died July 1971; buried Arlington Nat. Cemetery.

SCHULE, JAMES RAYMOND, advt. exec., lawyer; b. Bklyn., Jan. 2, 1920; s. John Joseph and Katherine (Tormey) S.; B.A., St. John's Coll., 1941, LL.B. cum laude, 1948; m. Dorothea Tresham, May 28, 1949; children—Jane, Katherine, James Raymond. Admitted to N.Y. bar, 1948; partner firm Tompkins, Boal & McQuade, N.Y.C., 1948-57; with Batten, Barton, Durstine & Osborn, Inc., N.Y.C., 1957-70, v.p., 1957-65, exec. v.p., 1965-70, sec., 1960-70, also dir., mem. exec com. Pres., Cath. Apostolate of Radio, TV and Advt. Recipient Pietas medal St. John's U., 1967. Knight of Malta, Knight Holy Sepulchre. Home: Westbury NY Died Mar. 1970.

SCHULER, LORING ASHLEY, editor; b. New Bedford, Mass., Aug. 24, 1886; s. Jacques and Emma Loring (Ashley) S.; spl. student, Harvard, 1908-10; m. to Myra V. Blake, September 30, 1913 (deceased January 13, 1967); children—Stanley Carter, Benson Blake (dec.). Newspaper work, New Bedford (Mass.) Standard, 1904-09, Boston Herald, 1910, New York Evening World, 1910-13; asso. editor, later art editor, Country Gentleman, 1913-20; mng. editor Ladies' Home Jour., 1920-24; editor The Country Gentleman, 1924-27; editor Ladies' Home Journal, 1927-35; contbr. articles to nat. magazines. Episcopalian. Field rep. War Prodn. Bd., salvage and smaller war plants, 1942-44; partner Vernon Scott and Loring Schuler, orgn. and industry counselors, 1944-65. Home: Greenwich CT Died June 4, 1968; buried St. Asaph's Church Yard, Bala-Cynwyd PA

SCHULHOFF, HENRY BERNARD, army engr.; b. Keyport, N.J., Oct. 30, 1904; s. Adolph and Amalia (Feuerlicht) S.; B.S., Rutgers U., 1930, M.S., 1936; M. Esther Graham Bell, May 8, 1938; 1 son, Kenneth Bell. San. engr. Hdqrs. 1st U.S. Army Engrs., 1942-55; v.p. Lanning San. Engring. Co., 1955-58; san. engr. Hdqrs. 1st U.S. Army Engrs., 1958-61, Hdqrs. Eastern Transport Air Force, 1961-64; civil engr. (san.) Office of Post Engr., Ft. Dix. N.J., 1964-68. Fellow Am. Inst. Chemists; mem. Soc. Am. Mil. Engrs. Republican. Presbyn. Home: Yardville NJ Died Mar. 20, 1968.

SCHULL, HERMAN WALTER, army officer; b. Liverpool, Eng., May 30, 1875; s. of Ludolph Morris and Anne Jane (Johnson) S.; brought to U.S., 1880; grad. U.S. Mil. Acad., 1899, Army War Coll., 1923; m. Loraine Edson, Jan. 26, 1901; children—Marion (dec.), Herman Walter, Edson. Commd. 2d lt. 6th Arty., Feb. 15, 1899; promoted through grades to brig. gen., June 3, 1934. Served in artillery in Cuba, 1899-1902; detailed in Ordnance Dept., 1902; served Sandy Hook Proving Ground, N.J., 1902-03, Frankford Arsenal Phila., 1903-06; comdg. officer 73d Co., Coast Artillery, Fort Monroe, Va., also mem. Arty. Bd., 1906-07; duty in Office of Chief of Ordnance, Washington, D.C., 1907-09; asst. to comdg. officer Watertown Arsenal, 1909-10; served Manila (P.I.) Ornance Depot, 1910-13; officer in charge of shops, Springfield Armory, 1914-15; comdg. officer Benicia Arsenal. Calif., 1915-17; acting chief inspection div. Ordnance Dept., 1917-19; comdg. officer, Aberdeen Proving Ground, 1919-22; student Army War Coll., 1922-23; mem. tech. staff, Washington, D.C., 1923-24; comdg. officer, Springfield Armory, Mass., 1924-29, Watervliet Arsenal, N.Y., 1929-32, Rock Island Arsenal, Ill., 1932-34; became chief of mfg. service Ordnance Dept., Washington, with rank of brig. gen., 1934; retired May 31, 1938; recalled to active duty Jan. 26, 1942, relieved Nov. 23, 1943. Awarded D.S.M. (U.S.). Episcopalian. Clubs: Army and Navy, Army-Navy Country (Washington); Rotary of Rock Island Ill. (hon.) Address: Box 2097, Carmel CA‡

SCHULLINGER, RUDOLPH NICHOLAS, surgeon; b. N.Y.C., Mar. 11, 1896; s. Julius and Alexandrina (Sorg) S.; grad. Lawrenceville Sch., 1913; B.S., Princeton, 1917; M.D., Columbia, 1923; m. Audrey Poole Bender, Mar. 8, 1926; children—John Nicholas (M.D.), Joan S. (Mrs. DeLacy H. Seabrook). Intern Roosevelt Hosp., N.Y.C., 1923-26; practice surgery, N.Y.C., 1926-68; professor clin. surgery Columbia, 1958-61, prof. emeritus clin. surgery, 1961-69; consultant in surgery Presbyterian Hosp., N.Y.C. Charter trustee emeritus of Princeton; trustee of the Brook Found. Served as col., M.C., AUS, World War II; surg. dir. Gen. Hosp. No. 2, 1942-45. Decorated Legion of Merit, 1945. Fellow Am. Surg. Assn., N.Y. Surg. Soc., N.Y. Acad. Medicine; mem. N.Y. Acad. Scis., Alumni Assn. Coll. Physicians and Surgeons, Columbia U. (pres. 1959-60), Alpha Omega Alpha. Presbyn. Clubs: Woodstock VT Died June 27, 1969; buried Woodlawn Cemetery, New York City NY

SCHULTZ, EDWARD WATERS, forester; b. Junction City, Kan., Jan. 13, 1919; s. Elmer Houser and Mary (Waters) S.; student U. Cal. at Los Angeles, 1936-38, Ore. State U., 1938-41; B.S. in Forestry, Columbia, 1963; m. Elinor Ruth Kesler, July 3, 1938; children—Nedra Anne (Mrs. John B. Gallahan), Kurt

Edward, Lynn Ellen Wri[illegible]. Dist. ranger U.S. Dept. Agr. Forest Service, Escondido, Cal., 1948-52; forest supr. San Isabel Nat. Forest, Pueblo, Colo., 1953-56, mgmt. analyst, 1956-60, dir. adminstrv. mgmt., 1961-64, asso. dep. chief. Washington, 1964-66, regional forester, Atlanta, 1966-68, dep. chief, Washington, 1968-71; dep. chief for Nat. Forest Systems, 1971-72. Recipient certificate of merit U.S. Dept. Agr. Forest Service, 1950. Mem. Soc. Am. Foresters, Am. Soc. Range Mgmt., Am. Forestry Assn., Exec. Assn. Clumbia U., Lambda Chi Alpha. Methodist. Mason. Springfield VA Died Dec. 30, 1972.

SCHULTZ, GEORGE F., artist; b. Chicago, 1869; self-taught in art. Landscape and marine painter. Mem. Chicago Water Color Club (pres.), Chicago Soc. Artists (sec.). Club: Cliff Dwellers. Represented in collections of Union League Club, Archie Club, Cliff Dwellers Club (all of Chicago). Home: 4003 Greenview Av. Office: Schiller Bldg., Chicago IL‡

SCHULTZ, LOUIS, oral surgeon; b. Bischwiller, Bas-Rhin. France, Apr. 15, 1867; s. Charles and Louise (Ostertag) S.; ed. Gymnasium; D.D.S., Chicago Coll. Dental Surgery, 1901; M.D., U. of Ill., 1905; m. Sophie Degel, May 22, 1892 (dec.); children—Dr. Carl Emil, Dr. Louis William, Louise (dec.), John (dec.). Came to U.S., 1884, naturalized, 1890. Practiced at Chicago since 1905; attending physician and surgeon Cook County Hosp., 1918-22; prof. oral surgery and pathology, University of Illinois, 1919-32, professor emeritus of oral surgery and pathology, 1932; rhinologist and laryngologist. Fellow A.M.A.; mem. Am. Bd. Plastic Surgery, Ill. State and Chicago dental and med. socs., Delta Sigma Delta. Mason (K.T.). Contbr. to Dental Rev., Jour. Am. Dental Assn., Surgerv, Gynecology and Obstet., Archives of Pathology and Lab. Medicine; various tech. papers before med. and dental assns. Retired. Home: 617 William St., River Forest IL*‡

SCHUMACHER, ANTON HERBERT, indsl. engr.; b. Kansas City, Mo., May 3, 1908; s. Frank A. and Mary M. (Carey) S.; B.S., U. Kan., 1929; m. Winnifred E. S[illegible]holer, Aug. 30, 1929; 1 dau., Mary Winnifred (wife of Mr. D.M. Hawkins). Valuation engr. Mo. Pub. Service Commn., 1929-42; instr., prodn. engr., quality control engr. Pratt & Whitney Aircraft Corp. Mo., Kansas City, 1942-46; cost estimator J. F. Pritchard & Co., Kansas City, 1946-47; utilities engr., City of Kansas City, 1947-60; chief rate engr. Gas Service Co., Kansas City, Mo., 1960-68. Mem. Engrs. Club Kansas Cith, Native Sons Kansas City, Sigma Phi Epsilon. Club: Hillcrest Country. Home: Kansas City MO Died Aug. 12, 1968.

SCHUMACHER, HENRY CYRIL, psychiatrist; b. Humphrey, Neb., July 6, 1893; s. Christian and Helena (Schmitt) S.; B.S., St. Louis U., 1917, M.D., 1919; LL.D., St. Benedict's Coll., Atchison, Kan., 1938; grad. student Sch. of Hygiene and Pub. Health, and Phipps Psychiatric Clinic, Johns Hopkins U., 1924-25; m. Rita Eisenmenger, Sept. 26, 1922; 1 dau., Jane; m. 2d, Audrey Sims, June 4, 1943. Assistant psychiatrist, Yankton State Hospital, 1920-22, psychiatrist, All-Phila. Child Guidance Clinic, 1926; instr. psychiatry, Grad. Sch. of Med., U. of Pa., 1926; asst. prof. mental hygiene, Sch. of Applied Social Sciences, Western Reserve U., 1927-29, asso. prof., 1929-42; asso. in pediatrics, Sch. of Med., Western Reserve U., 1933-47; lecturer, psychiatry, St. Vincents Charity Hosp., Sch., of Nursing, 1934-41; visiting lecturer, sociology and edn., John Carroll U., summers, 1939, 40, 41; lecturer in psychiatry, Lucas County Hosp. School of Nursing, 1940-46, Bolton School of Nursing, Western Res. U., 1936-47; lectr. in psychology, Grad. School Western Res. U., 1945-47; cons. psychiatrist, St. Ann's Hosp., 1928-47; commd. officer rank of med. dir. U.S.P.H.S., 1947-57; cons. in mental health activities and acting regional med. dir., San Francisco, 1949-50; lectr. in psychiatry, Sch. of Social Welfare, U. Cal., summer 1948, lectr. public health 1952-56; area cons. VA, 1953-56; cons. mental health USPHS, region IV Atlanta, Ga., 1956-57; retired USPHS, 1957; univ. psychiatrist, U. Fla., 1957-62, associate professor psychiatry, 1959-71. Served with U.S. Army, Jefferson Barracks, 1917. Fellow in psychiatry, National Committee for Mental Hygiene, 1925-26; diplomate in Psychiatry, Am. Bd. Psychiatry and Neurology, Inc., 1939. Diplomate Bd. of Preventive Medicine and Pub. Health, 1949. Fellow A.M.A., Am. Psychiatric Assn., Am. Orthopsychiatric Assn. (v.p. 1936-37, pres. 1943), Soc. for Research in Child Development, National Research Council, A.A.A.S., Am. Acad. Child Psychiatry, Am. Assn. Mental Deficiency; mem. Am. Coll. Preventive Medicine, American Assn. of Public Health Physicians, Am. Sociol. Society, Rorschach Inst., Inc., Ohio Mental Hygiene Soc. (pres. 1931, med. dir., 1944-47), Cleveland Neurol. Soc. (sec. treas., 1938-39; chairman 1939-40), Ohio State Medical Soc., (past sec. chmn. sec. on nervous and mental diseases), Am. Pub. Health Assn., Nat. Conf. on Social Work (past chmn. mental hygiene div.), Phi Beta Pi, Alpha Omega Alpha. Author: The Adolescent, 1938. Contbr. to scholarly jours. Home: Gainesville FL Died Feb. 14, 1971; buried Barrancas Nat. Cemetery Pensacola FL

SCHUMANN, EDWARD ARMIN, surgeon; b. Washington, D.C., July 9, 1879; s. Francis and Augusta (Jung) S.; A.B., Central High Sch., Phila., 1897; M.D., U. of Pa., 1901; m. Hazel Prince, June 8, 1910; children—Edward Armin, Francis, Robert. Practiced in Phila., 1901-70, limiting to obstetrics and gynecology; intern Phila. General Hosp., 1901-03; surgeon Gynecean Hosp., 1906-10; dir. obstetrics and gynecology Frankford Hosp., gynecologist and obstetrician Phila. Gen. Hosp., 1916-44; obstetrician Chestnut Hill Hosp., 1919-70; lecturer obstetrics Jefferson Med. Coll., 1916-24; surgeon-in-chief Kensington Hosp. for Women, 1931-44; chief of service, obstetrics and gynecology, Protestant-Episcopal Hosp.; prof. obstetrics, U. of Pa., 1935-39; cons. gynecologist, Jewish, Burlington County, Misericordia and Meml. hosps.; civilian coms. USN Hosp. Phila. Lt. comdr. U.S. Naval R.C., A.E.F. Hon. fellow Am. Assn. Obstetricians, Gynecologists and Abdominal Surgeons; fellow A.C.S.; mem. Am. Bd. Obstetrics and Gynecology (charter mem., v.p.), Am. Gynecol. Soc. (pres. 1945), Coll. of Physicians in Phila., Delta Upsilon, Alpha Mu, Pi Omega, Alpha Omega Alpha. Honorary member Central Association Obstetricians and Gynecologists. Republican. Clubs: Gynecologists, Cricket, Franklin Inn (Phila.). Author: Ectopic Pregnancy, 1921; Gonorrhea in Women, 1928; Text Book of Obstetrics, 1936; also 5 chapters in Curtis' Obstetrics and Gynecology, 1933. Contbr. profl. articles. Home: Lafayette Hill PA Died Oct. 18, 1970.

SCHUNK, ARTHUR JOHN, former postmaster; b. Hay Creek Twp., Goodhue County, Minn., Oct. 25, 1876; s. Jacob Daniel and Sarah Phylis (Saunders) S.; ed. high sch., Red Wing, Minn.; student Fort Worth (Tex.) U.; studied in law office, Red Wing; m. Melissa Olive Russell, (deceased); children—Russell J., Dorothy P.; m. 2d, Sarah Constance Breun, Nov. 18, 1911 (now dec.); m. 3d, Alice W. Tracy, Aug. 11, 1945. Organizer and lecturer Improved Order Red Men, 1902-09; superintendents of agents, Northern Accident Insurance Company, Aberdeen, S.D., 1909-10, president, 1910-11; president Northern Casualty Co., 1910-14; Northwest mgr. Lion Bonding & Surety Co., Minneapolis, 1914-18; with A.J. Schunk Co., gen. ins. agts. and surety bonds, Minneapolis, since 1918, owner and pres. same. Postmaster of Minneapolis, 1929-33. Mem. Hennepin County Rep. Com. 12 yrs.; mem. Rep. State Central Com. (exec. com.). Episcopalian. Mason (32 deg., Shriner), Elk. Clubs: Minneapolis Athletic, Minneapolis Automobile. Home: 3217 Bryant Av. S. Office: New York Life Bldg., Minneapolis 2 MN‡

SCHUTZER, PAUL GEORGE, photojournalist; b. Bklyn., July 11, 1930; s. Hyman B. and Ruth (Schwartz) S.; student Cooper Union, 1949, L.I. U., 1951, Bklyn. Law Sch., 1953; m. Bernice Berlin, July 15, 1951;children—Dena Anne, David Avrum. With Time-Life, 1956-67. Recipient award Art Directors Club, N.Y.C., 1954; award for excellance Am. Inst. Graphic Arts, 1956; George Polk Meml. award, 1958; Grand prize White House News Photographers Assn., 1959; award spot news Washington Newspaper Assn., 1959; First prize mag. picture story Nat. Press Photographers Assn., Mo. U. and Ency. Britannica, 1959; Best Mag. reporting from abroad award Overseas Press Club, 1965. Home: New Rochelle NY Died June 5, 1967.

SCHWAB, ROBERT SIDNEY, physician; b. St. Louis, Oct. 6, 1903; s. Sidney Isaac and Helen Dorothy (Stix) S.; A.B., Harvard, 1926, M.D., 1931; B.A., St. Johns Coll., Cambridge, 1928, M.A. Physiology, honors part II, Tripos, 1929; m. Dorothy Smith Miller, Aug. 26, 1932 (dec. May 1971); m. 2d, Joan Sheahan, Oct. 15, 1971. Intern medicine and neurology Boston City Hosp., 1931-34; resident neurology Mass. Gen. Hosp., Boston, 1935, established electroencephalographic lab., dir., neurologist, 1937-72; resident psychiatry Boston Psychopathic Hosp., 1936; asso. prof. neurology Harvard Med. Sch., now prof. emeritus; cons. neurologist Cape Cod Hosp., Mass. Eye and Ear Infirmary. Met. State Hosp., Br. Office Vets. Bur.; U.S. Naval Hosp., Chelsea, Mass. Mem. med. adv. bd. Parkinson's Disease Found.; chmn. med. adv. bd. Myasthenia Gravis Found. Am. Fulbright lectr. U. Munich, Germany, 1957. Served to comdr. USN, 1941-46. Diplomate Am. Bd. Neurology and Psychiatry. Fellow Am. Acad. Neurology; mem. Am. Neurol. Assn. (v.p.), Am. Psychol. Assn., Eastern Assn. Electroencephalographers (pres. 1946), Am. (sec. 1947-49, pres. 1950-51), Brit., French Italian electroencephalographic socs., Boston Soc. Neurology and Psychiatry, Assn. for Research in Nervous and Mental Disease, Internat. Fedn. Electroencephalographic Socs. (v.p.), Ergonomics Research Soc. Eng. Clubs: Cambridge Cruising (Eng.); Harvard (Boston). Author: Electroencephalography in General Practice, 1951. Editor: Electroencephalography and Clin. Neurophysiology. Contbr. articles to profl. jours. Home: Boston MA Died Apr. 6, 1972; buried Mt. Wollaston Cemetery, Quincy MA

SCHWAB, ROY VALENTINE, wholesale drug exec.; b. Los Angeles, July 31, 1902; s. Gottfried F. and Margaret (Baumgartner) S.; grad. pub. schs.; m. Dorothy S. Hayslip, June 12, 1926. With Brunswig Drug Co., Los Angeles, 1918-68, director, 1941-68, president, 1943-68, chairman of the board, 1962-68. Club: California (Los Angeles). Home: Pasadena CA Died Dec. 14, 1968.

SCHWALM, VERNON FRANKLIN, coll. pres.; b. Mishawaka, Ind., Apr. 10, 1887; s. Harrison M. and Margaret (Spohn) S.; prep. edn., Manchester Acad.; A.B., Manchester Coll., North Manchester, Ind., 1913; A.M., U. of Chicago, 1916, Ph.D., 1926; m. Florence R. Studebaker, Oct. 17, 1914; 1 dau., Edith Elizabeth. Teacher pub. schs., Ind., 1904-11; tutor Manchester Acad., 1911-13; prof. history, Manchester Coll., 1913-27, dean 1918-27; pres. McPherson (Kan.) Coll., 1927-41; pres. Manchester Coll., from 1941. Mem. State Bd. Edn., Kan., 1937-41; moderator Nat. Conf. Ch. of Brethren, 1938, 1952, mem. Gen. Brotherhood Bd. Mem. Kan. Sch. Masters Club. Mem. Ch. of Brethren. Kiwanian. Author: Otho Winger, 1952; My Educational Pilgrimage (autobiography). Home: North Manchester IN Died May 10, 1972.

SCHWARTZ, B. DAVIS, oil co. exec.; b. N.Y.C., Sept. 18, 1902; s. Samuel and Lena (Davison) S.; student pub. schs., N.Y.C.; m. Rose Gale, Mar. 29, 1929; children—Barbara, Bette Jane (Mrs. Peter Nelson), Linda (Mrs. Allan Eisinger), Louise (now Mrs. Robert Datilla and Sanford L. Secretary-treasurer Paragon Oil Co. div. Texaco Inc., N.Y.C., 1955-66. Asso. treas., L.I. Jewish Hosp.; treas., chmn. executive committee Brotherhood-in-Action, Incorporated; sec. treas. Brookdale Foundation; co-chmn. adv. bd. Happy Landing Fund; exec. com. Community Council of N.Y. Bd. Rabbis; nat. commn. Anti-Defamation League, B'nai B'rith; leader Mt. Sinai Hosp., School for Schizophrenic Children, Guild for Blind; sec.-treas., trustee Brookdale Found.; v.p., treas. Paragon Fund; sec.-treas. Bros. Assos. Board assos. C. W. Post Coll. Long Island U. Recipient Brandeis Gold medal for service to humanity, 1960, Human Relation medal Joint Def. Appeal, 1961; received Man of Year award Happy Landing Fund, in 1964. Mason, Elk. Clubs: Overseas Press of Am. (N.Y.C.); Fresh Meadow (Gt. Neck, L.I.); Unity (Bklyn.). Contbr. articles to indsl. publs. Home: Kings Point NY Died July 5, 1969.

SCHWARTZ, CHARLES, lawyer; grad. Coll. City N.Y., 1913; LL.B., N.Y. U., 1915; m. Bertie Grad; children—Stuart, Ernest, Louise (Mrs. Horowitz). Admitted to N.Y. bar, 1916; sr. partner firm Schwartz & Frohlich; sec. Columbia Pictures Corp., 1936-68. Mem. A.S.C.A.P. Author: (with Louis Frohlich) The Law of Motion Pictures; (with Mrs. Schwartz) Faith Through Reason. Home: New York City NY Died Nov. 4, 1969; buried Washington Cemetery, brooklyn NY

SCHWARTZ, ISAAC HILLSON, physician; b. Somerville, Mass., Mar. 25, 1912; s. Edward Elias and Ida (Hillson) S.; M.D., U. Basle (Switzerland); m. Caroline Lewis Mekelburg, Oct. 17, 1937; children—Miriam (Mrs. Michael Jay Salkind), Jane, Jonathan. Pediatric house officer Boston City Hosp., 1940-41; intern St. Lukes Hosp., New Bedford, Mass., 1941-42, chief pediatric dept., chief electronencephlography, until 1970; resident in pediatrics U.S. Naval Hosp., Phila.; postgrad. in neuropsychiatry Hosp. of U. Pa.; pediatrician New Bedford Child and Family Service; med. dir. Dartmouth (Mass.) Well-Child Clinic, New Bedford Cerebral Palsy Unit; alternate electroencephlographer Truesdales Hosp., Fall River, Mass.; med. officer New Bedford Health Dept.; mem. neurology dept. seizure unit Boston Children's Med. Center. Corporator, New Bedford Five Cents Savs. Bank. Bd. dirs. Opportunity Center. Served to comdr., M.C., USNR, 1942-46. PTO. Diplomate Am. Bd. Pediatrics. Fellow Am. Acad. Pediatrics; mem. A.M.A., Am. Acad. Child Psychiatry, New Eng. Pediatric Soc., Mass. Med. Soc., Pi Lambda Phi. Democrat. Jewish religion. Research on electroencephalography. Home: Dartmouth MA Died Mar. 20, 1970; buried Tifereth Israel Cemetery, New Bedford MA

SCHWARTZ, JACK WILLIAM, army officer; b. Ft. Worth, Dec. 12, 1905; s. Abraham Benjamin and Lena (Halpern) S.; student Texas Christian U., 1922-23; B.S., U. Tex., 1926, M.D., 1928; m. Jessie Augusta Wickham, June 1, 1937; children—Jean Anne, William Wickham. Intern, Fitzsimons Gen. Hosp., Denver, 1928-29; commd. 1st lt., M.C., U.S. Army, 1929, advanced through grades to maj. gen., 1959; various assignments Army gen. hosps.; chief surgery Bataan Gen. Hosp., World War II; Japanese prisoner, 1942-45; chmn. urol. Service Letterman Gen. Hosp., 1946-53, Walter Reed Gen. Hosp., 1953-56; comdg. gen. Madigan Gen. Hosp., 1956-58; comdg. gen. Tripler Army Hosp., Hawaii, also chief surgeon U.S. Army Pacific, 1958-60; comdg. gen. Letterman Gen. Hosp., San Francisco, 1960-68. Decorated Legion of Merit with oak leaf cluster. Fellow A.C.S.; mem. A.M.A., Am. Urol. Assn., Pan Pacific Surg. Assn., Alpha Omega Alpha. Mason (32 deg.). Home: San Francisco CA Died May 1968.

SCHWARTZ, JULIA AUGUSTA, author; b. Albany, N.Y., Feb. 3, 1873; d. George and Emma G. (Young) S.; A.B., Vassar Coll., 1896, A.M., 1897. Mem. Phi Beta

Kappa. Author: Vassar Studies, 1899; Five Little Strangers, 1904; Wilderness Babies, 1905; Elinor's College Career, 1906; Famous Pictures of Children, 1907; Beatrice Leigh at College, 1907; Wonderful Little Lives, 1909; Little Star-Gazers, 1917; When Jean and I Were Sophomores, 1918; A Friend Indeed, 1923; Northward Ho, (with Vilhjalmur Stefansson), 1925; From Then Till Now, 1929. Address: La Jolla CA‡

SCHWARTZ, LEW, publisher, editor; b. Montreal, Can., May 5, 1907; s. Elie and Rose (Rosen) S.; B.A., McGill U., 1927; grad. study U. Montreal; m. Frances Bell, May 3, 1935; 1 son, Edward. Came to U.S., 1934, naturalized, 1953. Reporter, Montreal Star; pub. Canadian Mercury; with N.Y. World-Telegram, 1935, Fairchild Publs., 1935-36; editor Am. Wine and Liquor Jour., Wine and Liquor Retailer, 1936-42, pres., owner Liquor Publs., Inc., 1942; owner Spirits mag., Mida's Criterion, 1942-44; organized Hudson Valley Printing Corp., Milton, N.Y., 1943, propr. Hudson Valley Newspapers, Inc.; organized Ellis Publs., publishers Jewelry mag., 1944-53, Nat. Jeweler, 1953; organizer, pres. Abelard-Press, Inc., N.Y.C., gen. trade publishers, 1948, pub. Spot mag., 1950-71; propr. Henry Schuman, Inc. (became Abelard-Schuman, Ltd.), 1953; organized Abelard-Schuman, Ltd., London, Eng., 1954, now pres.; organized Abelard-Schuman, Canada, Ltd., 1959, owner Creition Books, Inc., 1960. Active Fedn. Jewish Philanthropies. Mem. McGill Graduate Society (v.p. Eastern U.S.), McGill Soc. N.Y. (pres. 1960), McGill U. Alumni Orgn. Jewish religion. Club: Lotos (N.Y.C.). Home: Scarsdale NY Died Sept. 12, 1971; buried Sharon Gardens, Kensico Cemetery, Valhalla NY

SCHWARTZ, MILTON HENRY, advt. exec.; b. Chgo., Apr. 24, 1905; s. Max and Sarah (Smith) S.; student U. Ill., 1921-24; m. Lillian Zolla, Sept. 24, 1927; children—Stuart E., William A. Various advt. positions Lord & Thomas, Chgo., 1924-27, 32-42; advt. mgr. Foreman Nat. Bank, Chgo., 1927-31; with Foote, Cone & Belding, Chgo., 1942-70, v.p., 1947-56, sr. v.p., 1956-70, dir., 1953-70. Home: Highland Park IL Died Aug. 31, 1970.

SCHWARTZ, SAMUEL D., social service; b. N.Y. City, Aug. 11, 1890; s. Moritz and Bertha (Salmon) S.; graduate Joseph Medill High Sch., Chicago, 1909; Ph.B., University of Chicago, 1912, M.A., 1913; married Roey Cowen, June 18, 1924; children—Marjorie (Mrs. Elmer S. Eppstein), Rabbi Frederick C. Dir. of clubs, Chicago Hebrew Inst., 1911-14; asst. supt. Sinai Social Center, 1914-16; exec. dir. Emil G. Hirsch Center (formerly Sinai Social Center) since 1916; secretary, trustee Sinai Temple, 1917-68. organized and founded Sinai Temple Forum, one of the great forum organizations in America, exec. dir., 1914-64; hon. life trustee, hon. life exec. dir. Chgo. Sinai Congregation. Director Am. Platform Guild; past member board directors Bd. of Jewish Edn. Recipient citation from Hebrew Union College and Jewish Inst. Religion, 1954; citation U. Chgo. Alumni Association, 1960; citation Natl. Assn. Temple Adminstrs., 1963, City of Hope, 1966. Mem. Nat. Forum Assn. (past pres.), Nat. Assn. Community Center Secs., Nat. Conf. Social Work, Nat. Conf. Jewish Social Service, Chicago Council Social Agencies, League for Industrial Democracy, Am. Assn. Social Workers (dir.), Nat. Assn. Temple Adminstrs. (sec., dean), Am. Civil Liberties Union, Am. Friends Hebrew U., U. Chgo. Alumni Association, Jewish Chautauqua Society (life mem.), American Association for Adult Education. Jewish religion. Member B'nai B'rith (former pres. Adolf Kraus Lodge). Clubs: City (mem. edn. com.; race relations com.), Covenant (hon. dir.), Men's Club of Sinai. Home: Chicago IL Died Mar. 20, 1968; buried Rosehill Cemetery, Chicago IL

SCHWARTZ, WALTER MARSHALL, SR., machinery mfr.; b. Phila., June 22, 1877; s. Charles Wheeler and Sarah (Preston) S.; student Germantown Acad., Phillips (Andover) Acad.; m. Lillian O. Hamilton, Apr. 30, 1904; children—Olivia, Walter Marshall, P. Kay, Lillian; married 2d, Catharine D. Ford, June 7th, 1956. With Proctor & Schwartz, Inc., Phila. (formerly Phila. Textile Machinery Co.), 1896-—, successively machine shop apprentice, erector, salesman, gen. mgr., v.p., pres., chmn. bd., 1942-—. Home: 502 W. Allen Lane, Mt. Airy, Philadelphia PA Office: Seventh St. and Tabor Rd., Philadelphia PA‡

SCHWARTZ, WILLIAM SPENCER, physician; b. Portsmouth, O., Aug. 21, 1904; s. William Henry and Ethel (Cotton) S.; student Ohio State U., 1923-24; B.S., U. Cin., 1926, M.S., 1929, M.D., 1930; m. Helena Salmon Peebles, July 24, 1930. Intern, Trudeau Sanatorium, 1929-30, resident physician, 1933-46; practice medicine specializing in internal medicine and pulmonary disease, N.Y., O., 1930-33, Saranac Lake, N.Y., 1933-46, Brecksville, O., 1946-48, Oteen, N.C., 1948-71; instr. Trudeau Sch. Tb, Saranac Lake, 1930-46; chief Tb service VA Hosp., Brecksville, 1946-48; chief staff VA Hosp., Oteen, 1948-71. Cons. Tv div. FSA, USPHS, Washington; mem. exec. com. VA-Armed Forces Chemotherapy Study. Diplomate Am. Bd. Internal Medicine. Mem. A.M.A., Buncombe County Med. Soc., Nat. Tb Assn., Am. (pres.-elect, past v.p.), So. (past pres.), N.C. thoracic socs., Alpha Omega Alpha, Phi Chi, Chi Asheville NC Died Aug. 14, 1971; buried Portsmouth OH

SCHWARZ, BERTHOLD THEODORE DOMINIC, physician; b. Jersey City, Aug. 21, 1899; s. Wladyslaw J. A. and Virginia Jadwiga (von Tobolewski) S.; student St. Johns Coll., 1918-20; M.D., N.Y.U., 1924; m. Thyra Ericson, Jan. 1, 1924; children—Berthold Eric, Eric Berthold (dec.), Virginia Karen (Mrs. George Pickering Balz). Intern Jersey City Hosp., 1924-25; pvt. practice specializing in internal medicine, Jersey City, 1925-69; asst. med. dir. Bankers Nat. Life Ins. Co., N.J., 1928-30, med. dir. 1930, v.p. 1943-63, sr. v.p., 1963-65; dir. The Trust Co. N.J. (Jersey City), also member exec. com. Trustee Hudson County unit American Cancer Society; trustee Memorial Organ Fund N.J. State Coll. Served with U.S. Army, 1918. Decorated Gen. Haller Mil. Cross (Poland). Certified Specialist Life Ins. Medicine. Fellow Am. Pub. Health Assn., Acad. Medicine N.J., Royal Society Health (London), Am. Med. Soc. of Vienna (Austria), Royal Soc. Health (London); mem. Assn. Life Ins. Med. Dirs. Am. (hon. emeritus life), Am. Physicians and Surgeons, Soc. for Relief of Widows and Orphans of Med. Men (vice pres. and chmn. of investment funds), A.M.A., Am. Heart Assn., Am. Legion. Republican. Roman Catholic. Author profl. articles. Home: Upper Montclair NJ Died June 20, 1969.

SCHWARZ, HENRY FREDERICK;, b. Greenwich, Conn., Sept. 3, 1906; s. Henry Frederick and Irma (Hemmer) S.; A.B., Harvard, 1929, Ph.D., 1938; Litt.B., Oxford U., 1937; m. Marialisa Gutherz, Apr. 18, 1931; children—Anne Elizabeth (Mrs. James E. Wing, Jr.), Caroline, Henry F. Asst. history Harvard, 1931-34, 37-39, instr. and tutor, 1940-42; asst. prof. Wellesley Coll., 1942-46, asso. prof., 1946-51, prof., 1952-71, Elisabeth Hodder prof. history, 1955-71; preceptor Princeton, 1939-40. Author: The Imperial Privy Council in the 17th Century, 1943; Genealogical Tables To Illustrate the History of Western Europe, 1948. Editor: Matternich the Coachman of Europe, Statesman or Evil Genius, 1962. Contbr. Bohemia Under the Habsburgs in Handbook of Slavic Studies (ed. L.I. Strakhovsky), 1949. Died Jan. 4, 1971.

SCHWARZENBACH, ERNEST BLACKBROOK, distbng co. exec.; b. Rueschlikon-Zurich, Switzerland, May 24, 1898; s. Herman and Emily (Bauman) S.; came to U.S., 1922, naturalized, 1929; Baccalaureate, Zurich State Coll., 1917; student Columbia, 1924-25; M.B.A., N.Y.U., 1927; m. Marcelle Guignard, July 16, 1929; children—Colette (Mrs. Marshall D. Shulman), Robert B. With Guaranty Trust Co. N.Y., and subsidiary, 1922-36; partner, then v.p., dir. Smith, Barney &Co., N.Y.C., 1936-65; pres. Sony Corp. Am., Long Island City, 1966-68. Dep. mayor, then mayor Village of Great Neck Estates, L.I., N.Y., 1949-62. Home: Great Neck Estates NY Died Sept. 1968.

SCHWEINHAUT, HENRY ALBERT, judge; b. Washington, D.C., Feb. 9, 1902; s. Peter and Anne (Leavy) S.; LL.B., National U., Washington, D.C., 1924; m. Margaret M. Collins, July 27th, 1928; children—Joan Catherine (Mrs. Michael Delehanty), Mary Ann (Mrs. Wm. Thebus). Admitted to bar, 1924, gen. practice law, Washington, D.C., 1924-34; asst. U.S. atty., Washington, D.C., 1934-36; special asst. to attorney general, 1936-45; judge U.S. Dist. Court for District of Columbia, 1945-56, ret. Lecturer on evidence and agency, Washington Coll. of Law (D.C.), 1932-39; lecturer on evidence, Catholic Univ. of Am., Washington, D.C., 1944-48. Member Dist. of Columbia Bar Assn. (past vice president), Sigma Delta Kappa. Clubs: The Barristers, Lawyers, Nat. Lawyers (Washington). Home: Kensington MD Died June 22, 1970.

SCHWEITER, LEO HENRY, army officer; b. Wichita, Kan., Apr. 16, 1917; s. Otto T. and Bertha (Schmid) S.; student U. Wichita, 1935-36; B.S., Kan. State Coll., 1939; M.A., U. Mo., 1940; m. Virginia Van Pflaum, July 24, 1954; children—Henry J., Gail A., Mary Jean, Caroline V. Commd. 2d lt., U.S. Army, 1941, advanced through grades to maj. gen., 1968; comdg. officer 5th Spl. Airborne Force Group, 1st Spl. Forces, 1961-62; with Office Spl. Asst. for Counterinsurgency and Spl. Activities, Joint Chief Staff, Washington, 1962-64, with Office Dep. Chief Staff for Operations, 1964-66; assigned to Ft. Campbell, Ky. and Vietnam, 1966-69; dep. comdg. gen. U.S. Army Combat Devel. Command, Ft. Belvoir, Va., 1969-71; chief of staff U.S. Army Vietnam, 1971-72; ret., 1972. Decorated D.S.M., Silver Star with oak leaf cluster, D.F.C., Legion of Merit with oak leaf cluster, Bronze Star with three oak leaf clusters, Air medal with 24 oak leaf clusters, Purple Heart with two oak leaf clusters. Mem. De Molay, Phi Kappa Phi, Alpha Zeta. Home: Carlisle PA Died Aug. 23, 1972.

SCHWEIZER, J. OTTO, sculptor; b. Zurich, Switzerland, Mar. 27, 1863; s. Jacob and Carolina Elisabeth (Labhardt) S.; ed. Art Sch., Zurich; Royal Acad., Dresden; under Dr. J. Schilling, Dresden, and at Florence, Italy; m. Bertha Maria Meynen, 1902; 1 son, Antonin. Came to U.S., 1894, naturalized, 1904. Exhibited at Nat. Acad. Design, New York; Nat. Sculpture Soc., New York; Acad. Fine Arts, Phila.; etc. Principal works; statue, General Peter Muhlenberg, Rayburn Plaza, North Side City Hall, Phila.; Angel of Peace," Pittsburgh; statues of Abraham Lincoln, Gen. M. Gregg, Gens. Pleasanton, Humphrey, Geary, Hays, Gettysburg, Pa.; Pa. State memorial and Gen. Wells, Vermont memorial, Gettysburg, Pa.; Molly Pitcher, Carlisle, Pa. (all state memorials); statue of Abraham Lincoln, and portrait medallions of Gen. U.S. Grant and 7 other gens., Lincoln Memorial Room, Union League, Phila.; equestrian statue, Frederick W. von Steuben, Sherman Blvd., Milwaukee, Wis.; Steuben statues, Valley Forge, Pa., and Utica, N.Y.; Melchior Muhlenberg, bronze groups, Germantown, Pa.; James J. Davis group, Mooseheart, Ill.; statues of Adj. Gen. Stewart and Senator G. Oliver, Capitol Bldg., Harrisburg, Pa.; statue of James B. Nicholson, Phila., Senator Clay, Marietta, Ga.; Mother of the South," Little Rock, Ark.; Colored Soliders State Memorial, Fairmont Park, Phila., Pa.; East Germantown war memorial; Central High School war memorial; E. M. Schell memorial; Preston Retreat; Apotheosis of Emanuel Swedenborg; marble busts of F. D. Pastorius and Carl Schurz (Old Custom House), The Lord's Supper, high relief in bronze, all in Phila.; bronze group Christward, Vista, Calif.; also numerous ideal groups, portrait medallions, busts, medals, plaquettes; Statue Blessing of Christ," Phila., etc. Fellow Nat. Sculpture Soc. Home and studio: 2215 W. Venango St., Philadelphia PA‡

SCHWINGEL, VINCENT JOHN, mfg. co. exec.; b. Dansville, N.Y., May 17, 1903; s. John A. and Mary (Goodwin) S.; A.B., Cornell U., 1925; m. Margaret V. O'Herron, July 11, 1931; children—Mary Ellen (Mrs. Arthur Skove), Margaret Ann (Mrs. Rodolph A. Kraft), Katherine (Mrs. George Bacon), Elizabeth M. (Mrs. John Sullivan) Salesman, Blum Shoe Mfg. Co., Dansville, N.Y., 1925-26; with Foster Wheeler Corp., N.Y.C., 1926-67, sec.-treas., 1956-62, sec., 1962-67. Active local Boy Scouts Am. Mem. Am. Soc. Corp. Secretaries, Alpha Sigma Phi. Republican. Roman Cath. K.C. Home: Basking Ridge NJ Died Oct. 14, 1967; buried Dansville NY

SCHWINN, FREDERICK SIEVERS, civil engr.; b. Ft. Scott, Kan., June 20, 1889; s. Benjamin Franklin and Lillie (Sievers) S.; ed. Lewis Inst. and Armour Inst. Tech., Chicago; m. Beatrice Sanford Barnes, Dec. 25, 1912; children—Frederick Seamans, Elizabeth Caroline, David Sanford. Rodman, instrumentman and asst. engr. S.P. Co., Sacramento, 1908-13; asst. engr. and asst. supt. S.P. Lines, Lafayette, La., 1913-17; asst. div. supt. I.. N. Ry., Palestine, Tex., 1917-18; engr. for receiver, 1918-20, chief engr. for receiver, 1920-22; chief engr. Internat. G.N. R.R. Co., Dec. 1, 1922-June 1, 1925; asst. chief engr. Gulf Coast Lines and Internat. G.N. R.R., 1925-27; asst. chief engr. M.P. Lines, 1927-56; engring. cons. and analyst, 1956-68. Registered professional engineer, civil. Member of American Railway Engineering Association (director 1941-45; v.p., 1947-48, pres. 1949), Am. Soc. Testing Materials, Soc. Am. Mil. Engrs., Am. Soc. C.E., Tex. Soc. Profl. Engrs., Houston Engring. and Scientific Soc. Republican. Episcopalian. Home: Houston TX Died Dec. 2, 1968; interred Meml. Mission Mausoleum, Forest Park's Calvary Cemetery Houston TX

SCIPIO, LYNN A., mech. engr., educator; b. White County, Ind., Oct. 20, 1876; s. Adolphus and Evaline (Mahiu) S.; A.B., Tri-State Coll., Angola, Ind., 1902; student Armour Inst. Tech., Chicago, 1903; B.S. in Mech. Engring., Purdue U., 1908; M.E., 1911, Ph.D., 1931; m. Margaret Booher, Aug. 27, 1908; 1 dau., Elizabeth E. Teacher, pub. schs., Ind. advancing to prin. and supt.; asst. prof. mech. engring., U. of Neb., 1908-12; dean Robert Coll. Engring. Sch., Constantinople, and cons. engr., 1912-20; dir. Am. Soc. Heating and Ventilating Engrs. Research Lab., U.S. Bur. Mines, Pittsburgh, 1920-21; dean Robert Coll. Engring. Sch., 1921-43; head engineer, War Production Board, 1943-44; industrial Rehabilitation Specialist for U.N.R.R.A., 1945-47; mem. Am. Soc. Mech. Engrs., Am. Soc. Heating and Ventilating Engrs., Nat. Research Council, Sigma Xi, Pi Tau Mu. Methodist. Mason. Author: English-Turkish Technical Dictionary, 1939; Elements of Machine Design, 1928. Home: 525 Hartford St., Worthington OH‡

SCOON, ROBERT, philosophy; b. Geneva, N.Y., Sept. 21, 1886; s. Charles Kelsey and Caroline (Maxwell) S.; B.A., Hamilton Coll., 1907; apptd. Rhodes scholar from State of N.Y., 1907; B.A., Merton Coll. (Oxford U.), 1910; Ph.D., Columbia, 1916; L.H.D., Hamilton, 1939; m. Elizabeth Grier Hibben, Nov. 23, 1915; 1 son, John Grier Hibben. Instr. classics, Princeton, 1911-14; asst. prof. classics, Washington U., 1914-15; asst. prof. classics, Princeton, 1915-23, asso. prof. philosophy, 1923-28, prof. since 1928, chairman dept. of philosophy, 1934-52, Stuart professor of philosophy, from 1936. Served as 2d lt. inf., U.S. Army, 1918. Mem. Am. Philos. Assn., Acad. Polit. Sci., Chi Psi, Phi Beta Kappa (pres. Princeton U. chapter, 1939-47), pres. Princeton Branch English Speaking Union, 1944-46. Republican. Presbyterian. Clubs: Nassau (Princeton); Princeton (New York). Author: Greek Philosophy Before Plato, 1928. Compiler and Editor: Selections from Roman Historical Literature (with C. H. Jones and C. C. Mierow), 1915. Home: Princeton NJ Deceased.

SCOPES, JOHN T., author; co-author: Center of the Storm, 1966. Home: Shreveport LA Died Oct. 21, 1970; buried Paducah KY*

SCOTT, ALBERT WOODBURN, JR., merchant, lawyer; b. San Francisco, Calif., Nov. 6, 1869; s. Albert Woodburn and Georgiana (Smith) S.; A.B., U. of Calif., 1891; m. Ruth Pearl Van Vactor, June 1907. With Scott & McCord. mchts., San Francisco, 1892-95; practiced law, San Francisco, 1895-99; mem. Scott & Magner, wholesale grain and forage, 1899-1909; sec. and treas. Scott, Magner & Miller, 1909-20; succeeded by A. W. Scott & Co., of which was prop., 1920-22, and pres. of successor, A. W. Scott Co., 1922-30; practicing law since 1930. Formerly mem. bd. of dirs. West Coast-San Francisco Life Ins. Co., Panama-P.I. Expn.; pres. San Francisco Street Repair Assn., 1906-07, Civic League of Improvement Clubs, 1907-09; mem. exec. com. Citizens' Health Campaign, 1908-09. Mem. Acad. Science (San Francisco). Republican. Presbyterian. Mason, Odd Fellow, Elk. Clubs: Bohemian, Union League, Press, Commonwealth, Commercial, Merchants' Exchange. Home: 78 Buchanan St., San Francisco CA*‡

SCOTT, ARTHUR CURTIS, consulting engr.; b. Belmont, N.Y., Aug. 31, 1873; s. John Harrison and Mary A. (Kinney) S.; B.S. in M.E., R.I. State Coll., Kingston, R.I., 1895; post-grad. work, summers, Harvard, Brown, Cornell U., Mass. Inst. Tech., Clark U. and U. of Wis.; grad. student, U. of Wis., 1901-2, Ph.D., 1902; m. Alice Elizabeth Clarke, of Albany, N.Y., June 23, 1901. Instr. in physics, 1895-7, prof., 1897-01, prof. physics and elec. engring., 1902-3, R.I. State Coll.; prof. elec. engring., U. of Tex., 1903-11; consulting practice, 1911-—; pres. Scott Consulting Engring. Co.; consulting engr., Austin, Tex., in rebuilding dam across Colo. River and hydro-electric installation, 1912, etc. Conglist. Mem. Am. Soc. Mech. Engrs., Am. Inst. Elec. Engrs., Soc. for Promotion of Engring. Edn.; hon. mem. Southwestern Elec. and Gas Assn. Home: 1420 Sanger Av. Office: 632 Wilson Bldg., Dallas TX‡

SCOTT, CHARLES HERRINGTON, business man; b. Montgomery, Ala., Dec. 27, 1870; s. Thomas Jefferson and Mary A. (Taylor) S.; ed. Montgomery High Sch., U. of Ala., 1887 (left in jr. year), Howard Coll., 1888 (left in sr. yr.); m. Josephine Bennett, of Jefferson, Ga., Aug. 22, 1900. Since 1890 engaged in mineral and timber land business in firm of T. J. Scott & Son, of which is now sr. mem.; v.-p. and treas. Pacific Co.; dir. Empire Land Co. and Peru cos., Ala. Marble Quarries, Scott Investment Co., Ala. Colony Co. Civ. engr. Capt. 3d Ala. Vol. Inf. Spanish-Am. War, detailed as a.-a.-g., 1st div., 3d Army Corps, Camp Shipp. Apptd. Rep. referee by Pres. Roosevelt, 1903; Ala. mem. Rep. Nat. Com., 1904-—. Progressive Rep. candidate for gov. of Ala., 1910. Baptist. Clubs: Lawyers, Republican, New York Athletic (New York). Home: Sycamore, Ala. Address: Montgomery, AL and 54 W. 40th St., New York NY

SCOTT, ERNEST DARIUS, army officer; born Petrolia, Ont., Can., Sept. 6, 1872; s. Alexander Bruce and Margaret (Tweedy) S.; student U. of Neb., 1892-94; B.S., U.S. Mil. Acad., 1898; also grad. Army Sch. of the Line, Army Staff Coll., Field Arty. Sch. of Fire, Army War Coll., Navy War Coll., at various dates, 1908-29; m. Ella von Gerichten, Oct. 8, 1903 (dec. Sept. 12, 1943); children—Florence-May (Mrs. Robert C. Cameron) (dec.), Bruce von Gerichten, Ernest Darius (deceased); m. 2d, Mrs. William S. Baer, May 1, 1944. Came to U.S., 1884, naturalized, 1889. Cadet U.S. Mil. Acad., June 15, 1894; promoted through grades to brig. gen., Dec. 1, 1931; ret. from mil. serivce Sept. 30, 1936. Served in Spanish-Am. War and Philippines, 1898-1901; col. (temp.) in France and Germany, 1917-19; participated in Einville sector, Toul sector, Marne defensive, Marne offensive, St. Mihiel and Meuse Argonne offensives. Awarded D.S.M. and three silver star citations. Mem. Assn. Grads. U.S. Mil. Acad., Mil. Order of the Carabao, Mil. Order of World War, Nat. Sojourners, Heroes of '76. Mason (32 deg.). Club: Army and Navy (Washington); Bath, Committee of One Hundred (Miami Beach, Fla.). Co-author: Studies in Minor Tactics, 1915; Troop Leading, Division, 1916. Home: 590 Melaleuca Lane, Bay Pt., Miami 38 FL‡

SCOTT, EUGENE CRAMPTON, clergyman; b. Columbus, Miss., July 24, 1889; s. Eugene Claudius and Rachel (Pierce) S.; student, Chamberlain-Hunt Acad., Port Gibson, Miss., 1906-07, B.A., Southwestern Presbyn. Univ., 1911; B.D., Union Theol. Sem., 1916; hon. D.D., Austin Coll., 1934; m. Emma Elizabeth Foust, June 28, 1916; children—Lucille Foust (Mrs. Lucile S. Hicks), Rachael Pierce (Mrs. J. Harvey Glass), Emily Wynne (Mrs. Robert L. Cowan, Jr.). Cashier Mobile & Ohio R.R., freight office, Columbus, Miss., 1911-13; ordained to ministry, Presbyn. Ch., U.S. (South), 1916; pastor Aberdeen, Miss., 1916-18 (also Amory and Hamilton), First Presbyn. Ch., Gadsden, Ala., 1918-21; supt. Home Missions, Nashville Presbytery, Clarksville, Tenn., 1921-22; pastor First Presbyn. Ch., Ensley, Ala., 1923-26; asst. stated clerk, Gen. Assembly, Presbyn. Ch., U.S., 1926-35; stated clerk (exec. sec.) and treas., Dallas, 1935-50, Atlanta, 1950-59. Mem. Pi Kappa Alpha. Mason. Compiler: The Ministerial Directory, The Presbyterian Church in the U.S., 1861-1941, rev. ed. 1951. Home: Atlanta GA Died Mar. 19, 1972; buried Westview Cemetery Atlanta GA

SCOTT, GEORGE GILMORE, biologist; b. Geneseo, N.Y., May 3, 1873; s. John Laughlin and Mary (Jameson) S.; A.B., Williams Coll., 1898; A.M., 1899; Ph.D., Columbia, 1913; m. Phebe Tomkins Persons, 1902;children—Robert Townley, Richard Persons. Associated with College of the City of New York since 1901, as tutor, instructor, assistant professor, asso. prof., prof., and since 1936, emeritus prof. of biology; investigator U.S. Bur. Fisheries, 1913, 14, 18; consultant in zoology, Rollins Coll.; mem. exec. com. Thomas R. Baker Museum, Rollins Coll. Fellow A.A.A.S., N.Y. Zool. Soc.; mem. Am. Soc. of Zoologist, Am. Soc. of Naturalists, Fla. Acad. Sciences (chmn. sect. of biol. sciences, 1939), Fla. Audubon Soc. (exec. com. 1944-45), Asso. Physicians of Long Island (hon.), Phi Beta Kappa, Club: University (Winter Park, Fla.; pres. 1941-42). Author: Science of Biology, 1930; Microscopic Anatomy of Vertebrates (with J. I. Kendall), 1935. Home: 460 Henkel Circle, Winter Park FL‡

SCOTT, GORDON HATLER, educator; born Winfield, Kan., Apr. 10, 1901; s. John Hart and Grace (Hatler) S.; A.B., Southwestern Coll., 1922, Sc.D. (hon.), 1960; student Johns Hopkins U., 1922-23; A.M., U. of Minn., 1925; Ph.D., 1926; student Universite de Lyons, France, 1930; m. Luella Marguerite Smith, Dec. 25, 1923; children—Gordon Hatler Smith, John Edward Smith. Asst. in biology Southwestern Coll., 1920-22; asst. in zoology Johns Hopkins, 1922-23; teaching fellow in anatomy U. Minn., 1923-26; asst. prof. anatomy Loyola U., Chicago, Ill., 1926-27; asst. Rockefeller Inst. for Med. Research, 1927-28; asst. prof. cytology Washington U., 1928-31; asso. prof., 1931-42; prof. anatomy and head of dept. U. So. Cal., 1942-45; prof. anatomy and head of dept. Wayne State U., 1945-50, acting dean, 1948-50, prof. anatomy, 1950-70, dean Coll. Medicine 1950-63, v.p. med. sch. devel., 1961-68; vis. prof. anatomy Univ. B.C., 1968-69, Stanford University, 1969. Mem. White House Conf. on Child Health and Protection, 1930; mem. com. on electron microscopy NRC, 1941-43; mem. project com. neurology program Nat. Adv. Neurol. Diseases and Blindness Council, NIH. Trustee of Detroit Inst. Cancer Research, Kresge Eye Inst., Leukemia Found., Child Research Center Mich. (pres.); Mich. State Pub. Health Adv. Council, Detroit Med. Center Devel. Corp., Rehab. Inst.; pres. bd. trustees Mich. Health Council. Recipient Outstanding Achievement medal U. Minn. Bd. Regents, 1958; Distinguished Service award Wayne State U. Sch. Medicine, 1964. Fellow Johnson Found. Med. Physics, 1939. Fellow A.A.A.S.; mem. Am. Assn. Anatomists (past v.p.), Assn. Am. Med. Colls. (v.p. 1956-57, mem. exec. council 1957-59), Am. Soc. Zoologists, Soc. Exptl. Biology and Medicine, Alpha Omega Alpha. Gamma Alpha, Sigma Xi, Alpha Epsilon Delta. Contributor numerous articles to medical and sci. jours. Past mem. editorial bd. Anat. Record. Home: Pleasant Ridge MI Died Jan. 30, 1970.

SCOTT, HAROLD WILSON, banker; b. Summit Hill, Pa., Jan. 29, 1896; s. Wilson and Elizabeth (Walker) S.; student Drexel Inst. Tech., 1910-12, U. Pa., 1920-21, Am. Inst. Banking, 1914-30; LL.D. (hon.), Beaver College, 1963; m. Sara Boyd Christine, June 10, 1922; children—Ronald C., H. Wilson. With First Pa. Banking & Trust Co., Phila. (and predecessor Bank of North Am.), from 1914, successively clk., asst. treas., treas., asst. to exec. v.p., v.p., 1914-55, sr. v.p., 1955-61; chairman, dir. Commonwealth Realty Trust, from 1961; director Peirce-Phelps, Inc., Reilly-Whiteman-Walton Co., Bright Stores, Inc., Lansford & Lehighton, Commonwealth Telephone Co. (Dallas, Pa.), Food Fair Stores, Inc., McCloskey Varnish Co., George D. Wetherill & Company, Inc., Phila. Sheraton Corporation (Phila.). Republican. Presbyterian. Home: Merion Station PA

SCOTT, HERBERT, clergyman; b. Athens, O., June 28, 1872; s. William Henry and Sarah (Felton) S.; B.Sc., Ohio State U., 1893; student Yale Div. Sch., 1895-97; D.D., Ohio Wesleyan U., 1909; m. Clara Esther Luse, Oct. 14, 1897; children—John Luse, Alford Herbert. Ordained ministry M.E. Ch., 1897; pastor, Alexandria, O., 1897-99, North Ch., Columbus, 1899-1901, First Ch., Marietta, 1901-06; Spencer Chapel, Ironton, 1906-08; supt. Columbus Dist., 1908-12; pastor Trinity Ch., Portsmouth, O., 1912-14, Grace Ch., Zanesville, O., 1914-20, First Ch., Des Moines, Ia., 1920-26, First Ch., Salina, Kan., 1926-28, First Ch., Rochester, N.Y., 1928-35, Dormont Ch., Pittsburgh, Pa., 1935-36, Mary S. Brown Memorial Ch., Pittsburgh, 1936-41, retired. Mem. Gen. Conf. M.E. Ch., 1912, 20; mem. bd. mgrs. Meth. Brotherhood, 1908-12; mem. Freedmen's Aid Bd., 1910-20; mem. Book Com. M.E. Ch., 1912-20. Home: 725 Hinman Av., Evanston IL‡

SCOTT, JAMES EDWARD, clergyman; b. Plymouth Eng., Dec. 14, 1874; s. James and Emma (Brannon) S.; student Rutherford Coll., Newcastle-on-Tyne, Eng.; A.B., Grove City (Pa.) Coll., Ph.D.; D.D., W.Va. Wesleyan Coll.; m. Harriet Randall, 1896 (now dec.); children—Lawrence Albert; married 2d, Wilhelmena Ortland, Apr. 5, 1934. Came to United States, 1903, naturalized, 1917. Ordained M.E. ministry, 1903; pastor successively Benwood, W.Va., St. Paul's Ch., Grafton, 1915-17, St. Andrews Ch., Parkersburg, 1917-22, First Ch., Moundsville, 1922-26; supt. Parkersburg Dist., M.E. Ch., 1926-31; pastor First Ch., Fairmont, 1931-35, Thomson Ch., Wheeling, 1935-41, Central Church, Charleston, W.Va., since Oct. 1, 1941. Trustee W.Va. Wesleyan Coll. Republican. Mason. Kiwanian. Clubs: Meadowbrook Country, Kiwanis. Home: Charleston WV‡

SCOTT, JOHN MARCY, coal co. exec.; b. Peoria, Ill., Feb. 12, 1902; s. Walter Dill and Anna (Miller) S.; B.S.C., Northwestern U., 1924; m. Mary Louise Gent, Sept. 16, 1926; children—John Marcy, Walter Dill. With Republic Coal & Coke Co., Chgo., 1941-68, pres., 1967-68. Home: Wilmette IL Died Dec. 31, 1968.

SCOTT, JOHN REED, author; b. Gettysburg, Pa., Sept. 8, 1869; s. of Hugh Daniel and Mary (Harris) S.; A.B., Pa. Coll., Gettysburg, 1889, A.M., 1892, Litt.D., 1915; m. Frances White, Oct. 20, 1898. Began practice of law at Gettysburg, 1891; county solicitor, Adams County, Pa., 1894-98; removed to Pittsburgh, 1898; mem. law firm of White, Childs & Scott. Spl. counsel, Treas. Dept., Washington, D.C., 1921-23; resumed practice in Washington before state and federal courts of Pa., Md. and D.C. Commd. capt. a.d.c., Nat. Guard Pa., July 16, 1898; judge advocate U.S. Army, June 29, 1918, duty in office of Judge Advocate Gen., Washington; lt. col., Apr. 22, 1919; hon. discharged, Dec. 31, 1920; lt. col. Judge Advocate Gen., Res., U.S. Army, Mar. 4, 1921; col., Mar. 7, 1925; col. of auxiliary reserves, June 19, 1934, col. Inactive-Reserves, U.S. Army, June 19, 1939. Mem. Pa. Soc. of the Cincinnati, Pa. Soc. Colonial Wars, Sigma Chi. Clubs: Metropolitan, Army and Navy (Washington). Author: The Colonel of the Red Huzzars, 1906; Beatrix of Clare, 1907; The Princess Dehra, 1908; The Woman in Question, 1909; The Impostor, 1910; In Her Own Right, 1911; The Last Try, 1912; The First Hurdle, 1912; The Unforgiving Offender, 1913; The Red Emerald, 1914; The Duke of Oblivion, 1915; The Cab of the Sleeping Horse, 1916; The Man in Evening Clothes, 1917. Address: care Metropolitan Club. Washington DC*‡

SCOTT, NORMAN, opera, concert singer; b. N.Y.C., Nov. 30, 1928; s. Maurice and Flora (Silvern) S.; B.B.A., City College of New York; married Erica Glanz; 1 dau., Monika. Sang with N.Y.C. Opera Co., 1948-51, Vienna State Opera, Sept.-Oct., 1956, Metropolitan Opera Co. (bass singer), 1951-68; has appeared with leading opera cos., Pitts., New Orleans, Phila., San Antonio, Havana, Cuba, etc., 1949-51; with Symphony orchestras. N.B.C. Symphony (under Toscanini) in Beethoven 9th (twice), Verdi Requiem, Aida, Falstaff; concertized throughout U.S.; guest artist TV shows; in 1st Am. performances of Christopher Columbus, N.Y. Philharmonic, 1952, The Rake's Progress, with Met. Opera, 1953; guest appearance, Chile, 1959, Argentina, 1960. Commd. ensign, USN, 1943, served South Pacific, disch. lt., 1946. Recipient Presdl. Citation. Mem. Am. Guild Mus. Artists. Recorded with M.G.M., R.C.A. Victor, Columbia, and Remington records; recorded Boris Godunov with Met. Opera. Home: New York City NY Died Sept. 22, 1968; buried Ferncliff Cemetery NY

SCOTT, ROGER BURDETTE, physician, educator; b. Moundsvillw, W.Va., Feb. 3, 1913; s. Albert B. and Edith (Parry) S.; A.B., W.Va., U., 1934, B.S., 1936; M.D., Johns Hopkins, 1938; m. Martha Gooding Fitts, Aug. 10, 1940; children—Sandra H. (Mrs. Theodore C. Morehouse), Bryant M., R. Parry. House officer medicine Johns Hopkins Hosp., Balt., 1938-39, house officer gynecology, asst. resident, resident in gynecology, 1939-44; instr. gynecology Johns Hopkins Sch. Medicine, Balt., 1946-50; asso. prof. obstetrics and gynecology Western Res. U. Sch. Medicine, Cleve., 1950-62, prof., 1962-68. Mem. adv. com. Maternal Health Assn., Cleve., 1951-68, pres., 1960; mem. adv. com. on obstetrics and gynecology FDA, Bur. Medicine, Dept. Health, Edn. and Welfare, 1965-68. Served to lt., M.C., USNR, 1944-46. Diplomate Am. Bd. Obstetrics and Gynecology (asso. examiner 1952-68). Mem. A.M.A., Am. Gynecol. Soc., Am. Gynecol. Club (pres. 1964), Soc. for Gynecologic Investigation (pres. 1964), Am. Coll. Obstetricians and Gynecologists, Am. Assn. Obstetrics and gynecology, Am. Soc. Cytology, Phi Beta Kappa, Alpha Omega Alpha, Delta Tau Delta. Contbr. numerous articles on endometriosis and gynecologic cancer to med. jours., also chpts. to med. books. Home: Cleveland OH Died Dec. 16, 1968.

SCOTT, RUSSELL B(URTON), physicist; b. Ludlow, Ky., Apr. 17, 1902; s. Burton W. and Carrie May (Riggs) S.; B.S. cum laude, U. Ky., 1926, M.S., 1928; m. Leonora Downing, June 13, 1928; children—Marion Lee (Mrs. William F. Kenkel), Burton W. Instr. physics U. Ky., 1927-28; mem. staff Nat. Bur. Standards, 1928-67, chief cyrogenic engring. lab., Boulder, Colo., 1953-62, acting dir. Boulder labs., 1962-63, mgr., 1963-67. Mem. U.S. nat. com. Internat. Inst. Refrigeration, 1957-60, mem. ad hoc. com. establish U.S. membership, 1956-57, mem. commn. I, 1959-67.

Fellow Am. Phys. Soc., A.A.A.S.; mem. Research Soc. Am. (pres. Boulder chpt. 1961), Phi Beta Kappa, Sigma Pi Sigma. Author: Cryogenic Engineering, 1959; also numerous articles. Am. editor, contbr.; Technology and Uses of Liquid Hydrogen, 1964, Am. editor Jour. Cyrogenics, 1960-67. Home: Boulder CO Died Sept. 24, 1967.

SCOTT, S. SPENCER, publishing exec.; born Elizabeth, N.J., June 21, 1892; s. Sylvester M. and Mary Catharine (Hamilton) S.; grad. Mercersburg Acad., 1910, U. of Mich., 1914, Columbia U. Grad. Sch., 1919; married Edna Minsinger, 1919; children—Carolyn (now Mrs. Dimitri Dejanikus), and S. Spencer, Junior. Began with Henry Holt and Company, N.Y. City, 1914-20; asso. with Harcourt Brace Co., pubs., 1920, vice pres. 1922-41, v.p., gen. mgr., 1942-48, pres., 1948-55, retired, continued as dir. and consultant. President Scarsdale Library Bd., 1941-53; vice chmn. and treas. Council on Books in Wartime, Inc., Armed Services Editions, Incorporated; director of Community Service Society of New York, 1946-59 (general chairman of 101st Year Fund Drive; chmn. pub. interest com.); trustee Scarsdale Found. (pres. since 1953); president Point O'Woods Assn., 1953-55; chmn. citizens adv. com. Scarsdale, N.Y. Bd. Edn., 1956; founder, pres. Friends of Scarsdale Parks, 1956-62, honorary pres., dir., 1963-71; gov. Clements Library Associates University Mich., 1956-71; dir.-at-large U. Mich. Alumni Assn., 1956, v.p., 1957. Recipient Regents citation U. Mich., 1959, Distinguished Alumni Service medal, 1960. Democrat. Clubs: Town, Scarsdale (past pres.); Boulder Brook Riding; Century Assn., Dutch Treat, Coffee House, Publishers Lunch (pres. 1947-48) (N.Y.C.). Home: Scarsdale NY Died Jan. 1, 1971.

SCOTT, WENDELL G(ARRISON), physician; b. Boulder, Colo., July 19, 1905; s. Ira Dudley and Callie (Soper) S.; A.B., U. Colo., 1928, Sc.D. (honoris causa), 1954; M.D., Washington U., 1932; m. Ella Johnson, June 29, 1929; children—Horace Wendell, Ann (Mrs. Michel TerPogossian), Sarah Jane (Mrs. C. H. Wallace). Served his internship at the Barnes Hosp., St. Louis, 1933-34, asso. radiologist, 1938; instr. sch. medicine Washington U., St. Louis, 1934-38, asst. prof. radiology, 1938-40, asst. prof. clin. radiology, 1940-41, asso. professor, 1941-56, prof., 1956-72; mem. alumni rep., dir. Washington U., 1954-58. Cons. radiology Oak Ridge Inst. Nuclear Studies, 1955-62, mem. cancer control com. Nat. Cancer Inst. USPHS, 1958-60, 66-70, mem. nat. radiation adv. com., 1960-64; mem. dependents med. care adv. com. Dept. of Defense, 1958-67; mem. com. radiol. NRC., 1947-52, 54, chmn. 1955-64; cons. spl. med. adv. bd. Vets. Administration, 1952-57, chmn. 1954-56, area cons. radiol., 1957-72; cons. radiol., pathology, Armed Forces Inst. Pathology, 1953-58. Served as lt. to capt., med. corps USNR, 1942-46; rear adm. Med. R.C., 1958-65; res. consultant radiology Bur. Medicine and Surgery, Navy Dept., 1946-72; mem. adv. commn. cancer control br. U.S.P.H.S., Health, Edn., Welfare, Chmn. Genitourinary Task Force; mem. adv. bd. for conquest cancer U.S. Senate, 1970-71; mem. Nat. Cancer Adv. Bd., 1971-72, President's Nat. Cancer Adv. Bd. Dir. Am. Cancer Soc., 1957-72, pres., 1963-64. Recip. numerous awards, citations for sci. contbns. by med. socs. Diplomate Am. Bd. Radiology. Fellow Am. Coll. Radiology (chmn. commn. on pub. relations 1950-60, chancellor 1960-64, recipient gold medal 1965, chmn. com. mammography); mem. A.M.A. (chmn. section radiology 1958, del. 1966-72), Mo., So. med. assns., Detroit Medical Soc. (honorary), St. Louis Soc. Radiologists (pres. 1946-48), Am. Radium Soc. (v.p.), Am. Roentgen Ray Soc. (treas. 1947-56, pres. 1958-59), Radiol. Soc. N.A. (vice president 1944), U.S. Assn. Mil. Surgeons (exec. council 1946), Med. Cons. World War II, Tex., Rocky Mountain radiol. socs. (hon.), Washington U. Sch. Medicine Alumni Assn. (pres. 1954). Sociedad de Cancerologia de Guadalajara (hon.), also fraternities of Sigma Xi and Alpha Omega Alpha. Clubs: University, Bellerive Country, Racquet, St. Louis, Clayton, (St. Louis). Author articles medical journals. Editor: Genetics, Radiobiology, and Radiology (Charles C. Thomas), 1959; Planning Guide for Radiologic Installations; associate editor American Journal. Roentgenology and Radium Therapy, 1949-66. Editor Your Radiologist, 1956-68, Cancer, 1964-72. Home: St Louis MO Died May 4, 1972; buried Oak Grove Cemetery St Louis MO

SCOTT, WINFIELD TOWNLEY, writer; b. Haverhill, Mass., Apr. 30, 1910; s. Douglas Winfield and Bessie Irving (Townley) S.; A.B., Brown U., 1931; Ed.D. (hon.), R.I. Coll.; Litt.D. (hon.), U. N.M.; m. Savila B. Harvey, May 22, 1933 (div. 1946); 1 son, Lindsay Bothwell; m. 2d, Eleanor Metcalf, Apr. 26, 1946; children—Joel Townley, Susan, Jeannette, Douglas Herrick. Began as member of the staff of the Providence Jour., 1931-51, lit. editor, 1941-51. Trustee Providence Pub. Library, 1941-51. Received Guarantor's award for poetry, 1935, Shelley Meml. award, 1940; Harriet Monroe prize, 1966; named Phi Beta Kappa poet Brown U., Tufts Coll., Harvard. Member of P.E.N., Phi Beta Kappa. Author (verse): Elegy for Robinson, 1936; Biography for Traman, 1937; Wind the Clock, 1941; The Sword on the Table, 1942; To Marry Strangers, 1945; Mr. Whittier and Other Poems, 1948; Three Self-Evaluations (with others), 1953; The Dark Sister, 1958; Scrimshaw, 1959; Exiles and Fabrications, 1961; Collected Poems 1937-1962, 1962; Change of Weather, 1964; New and Selected Poems, 1967; A Dirty Hand, Literary Notebooks, 1969; Alpha Omega, A Newport Childhood and Last Poems, 1971. Lit. editor; New Mexican, 1961-64. Editor: The Man with the Calabash Pipe (by Oliver La Farge), 1966; The Poems of Robert Herrick, 1967; Judge Tenderly of Me, The Poems of Emily Dickinson, 1968. Home: Santa Fe NM Died Apr. 28, 1968; buried Santa Fe (N.M.) Meml. Gardens.

SCOTTEN, ROBERT MCGREGOR, diplomatic service; b. Detroit, Mich., Aug. 18, 1891; s. Oren and Mary Clarke (McGregor) S.; A.B., Yale U., 1914; Harvard Grad. Sch., 1915-16; m. Ann Boyd, Dec. 3, 1929. Athletic instr., Yale-in-China, Changsha, 1914-15; apptd. sec. of legation, U.S. Dept. of State, 1916; assigned to Berlin, Germany, 1916-17, Madrid, Spain, 1917-19, Guatemala, C.A., 1919-20, Paris, France, 1921-22, Berlin, Jan.-May 1922, Constantinople, Turkey, 1922-24; foreign service officer assigned as 1st sec., Rio de Janeiro, Brazil, 1924-25, Asuncion, Paraguay, 1925-26; consul, Asuncion, 1926-27; asst. chief Div. Current Information, 1927-30; press liaison officer, Commn. of Inquiry and Conciliation, Bolivia and Paraguay, Washington, D.C., 1929; 1st sec., Paris, 1930-31; counsellor of embassy, Santiago, Chile, 1934-35, Rio de Janeiro, Santiago, 1935-36, Rio de Janeiro, 1936-39, Madrid, 1939-40; envoy extraordinary and minister plenipotentiary, Dominican Republic, 1940-42, Costa Rica, 1942; ambassador to Ecuador, 1943-47; ambassador to New Zealand, 1952-56. Mem. Zeta Psi. Clubs: Barbados WI

SCOTT-HUNTER, GEORGE, prof. music; b. Stirling, Scotland, Mar. 19, 1874; s. George Hunter and Elizabeth Clarke Scott; ed. Royal High Sch., Stirling, and Stanley House, Bridge of Allan; studied as articled student in music, 1888-93, under late Dr. Charles E. Allum, organist and condr. Holy Trinity Cathedral Ch., Stirling, and became his first asst.; m. Kathryn Hynson Bush, of St. Louis, Mo., Dec. 27, 1911. Organist, choirmaster and condr. in Scotland; came to U.S., 1910; with Skidmore Sch. of Arts, Saratoga, N.Y., 1911-12; head of dept. of organ and composition, North Carolina Coll. for Women (state), 1914-23. Head of dept. of harmony and mus. appreciation, Chautauqua Instn., N.Y., 1917. Organist Holy Trinity P.E. Ch., Greensboro; dir. Salisbury Oratorio Soc. Mem. Am. Guild Organists, Concert organist, composer, lecturer. Episcopalian. Clubs: Kiwanis, Greensboro Country. Address: Greensboro NC‡

SCOVILLE, ANNIE BEECHER, teacher, lecturer; b. Norwich, N.Y.; d. Samuel and Harriet E. (Beecher) S.; ed. Dana Hall Sch., Wellesley, Mass., 1883-85; Wellesley Coll., 1885-88; Oxford U., England, 1890-91; unmarried. Teacher Hampton Inst., Va., 6 yrs., also making trips in various capacities to Dakotah, Omaha and Winnebago Indians; teacher, Catherine Aiken Sch., Stamford, Conn., 10 yrs.; in charge of Negro Orphanage connected with Johns Hopkins Hospital, Baltimore, 1912-13; connected with Hampton Inst. as student of situation in the South and lecturer before Northern schs. and colls. Conglist. Editing letters of Henry Ward Beecher and acting as lit. executor for his family. Home: Stamford CT‡

SCRANTON, CASSIUS A., lawyer; b. Goodwine, Ill., Apr. 4, 1885; s. Hiram J. and Sarah A. (Gillette) S.; student Grand Prairie Seminary, Onarga, Ill., 1904-05; LL.B., John Marshall Law Sch., 1912; m. Nelle B. Ducey; children—Kenneth E., Mary Eileen (Mrs. Richard T. McHugh). Examiner of titles, Chicago Title and Trust Co., 1912-19, asst. sec., 1919, mem. law dept., 1925-35, vice pres., 1936, head legal div. of title dept., 1936-49, sr. v.p., 1949. Taught post-grad. course, Loyola U. Law School, 1925-26, real property course, John Marshall Law Sch., 1925-28. Mem. Chicago, Ill., Am. bar assns., Chicago Law Inst. Republican. Clubs: Union League, Twenty, LaGrange Country. Contbr. articles to various legal jours. Home: Oak Park IL Died Jan. 1970.

SCREWS, WILLIAM PRESTON, army officer; b. Montgomery, Ala., Jan. 1, 1875; s. Henry Preston and Nora (Canty) S.; student Savage Sch., Starke's Univ. Sch., Montgomery, Ala., Marion (Ala.) Mil. Inst., Infantry Sch., Ft. Benning, Ga., 1925, Army War Coll., Washington, 1929; m. Josephine W. Lahey, Nov. 17, 1901; 1 son, James Lahey. Commd. as 2d lt., 1899, advanced through grades to brig. gen., 1940: asst. gov. Mindinao, 1905-07; comd. 167 Inf., 84 Inf. Brig., 42 Div. (Rainbow) World War I; ret., June 1940. Awarded D.S.M.; mem. French Legion of Honor; Citation Comdr. in Chief, A.E.F. City commr. Montgomery, Ala., 1931-47; mem. Ala. Alcoholic Beverage Control Bd. since 1948. Mem. Am. Legion, Rainbow Veterans, Vets. Fgn. Wars, Spanish Am. Vets. Democrat. Presbyterian. Mason (K.T., Shriners, 33 deg., Scottish Rite). Clubs: Rotary (hon.), Army-Navy (Washington), Beauvoir Country. Home: 208 Fairview Av., Montgomery AL‡

SCRIBNER, GILBERT HILTON, corp. exec.; b. New Rochelle, N.Y., Oct. 17, 1890; s. Gilbert Hilton and Josephine Romeyn (Brown) S.; Ph.B., Yale U. Sci. Sch., 1912; LL.D., U. Kansas City; m. Nancy D. Van Dyke, May 7, 1917 (dec. 1962); children—Gilbert Hilton, William V. D. (U.S. Army; killed in action in Germany), Gertrude Hunter (Mrs. Robert S. Smith), Nancy Brown (Mrs. William T. Kirk, Jr.), Mary (Mrs. Robert D. Judson). Engaged in central bus. real estate and bldg. mgmt., from 1912; chmn. Scribner & Co.; dir. Wm. Wrigley, Jr., Co., IBM Corp., First Nat. Bank of Chgo., Clearing Indsl. Dist., Midland Warehouses, Inc., Abercrombie & Fitch; trustee Mut. Life Ins. Co. of N.Y., Estate of Jonathan Clark. Commd. capt. 41st Brigade Army Arty., World War I; 1st Ill. F.A., 1914-16. Republican. Episcopalian. Clubs: Commercial, Chicago, University, Indian Hill, Old Elm. Home: Winnetka IL

SCRUGGS, LOYD, inventor, mfr.; b. Willisburg, Ky., Mar. 11, 1875; s. Sabritt and Margaret Jane (DeBaun) S.; ed common schs. until 11; studied mechanics pvtly.; m. Edith B. Sims, Nov. 16, 1909. Pres. Copper Clad Malleable Range Co., prop. The Loyd Scruggs Co. Has taken out numerous patents covering improvements in cooking ranges, theatre ventilation, electric motors, electric razors, etc.; designer of apparatus for production of stage illusions, in collaboration with the late Howard Thurston, magician. Member Academy of Science of St. Louis, Mo. Member Christian (Disciples) Church. Clubs: Missouri Athletic, Contemporary Club. Contbr. on merchandising and business administration. Home: 7469 Washington Blvd. Office: Missouri Insurance Bldg., St Louis 1 MO‡

SCUDDER, HUBERT B., congressman; b. Sebastopol, Calif., Nov. 5, 1888; grad. pub. schools; m. Helen B. Norton, June 18, 1924. Supt. of utilities, City of Sebastopol, 1912-20; entered ins. and real estate bus., 1920; councilman, Sebastopol, 1924, mayor, 1926; mem. Calif. State Legislature, 1925-40; elected vice chmn. Republican State Cent. Com., 1940, sec., 1942; real estate commr. and mem. gov.'s council, 1943-48; mem. 81st to 85th Congresses, 1st Cal. Dist. Served with Coast Arty., World War I. Home: Sebastopol CA Died July 1968.

SCULLEN, ANTHONY JAMES, civil engr.; b. Little Falls, N.Y., Sept. 4, 1889; s. Thomas and Catherine (Fikely) S.; C.E., Rensselaer Poly. Inst., 1911; hon. D.Engr., Columbus U., 1930; m. Elizabeth Helen Moore, Dec. 31, 1912; children—Elizabeth Mary, Anthony James, Edward Joseph. Asst. city engr., Little Falls, N.Y., 1911-12; instr. civil engring., Catholic Univ., 1912-18, asso. prof., 1918-23, prof., 1923-70, dean, sch. engring. and architecture, 1937-70; chief engr., bldg. div., Dist. Columbia, 1924-34, consulting engr. since 1934. Papal decoration, Medale Benemarinte, 1938. Member Am. Soc. of C.E. K.C. Club: Cosmopolitan (Washington, D.C.). Home: Washington DC Died July 8, 1970; buried Gate of Heaven Cemetery, Silver Spring MD

SCULLY, HUGH DAY, ex-consul gen. of Canada; b. Toronto, Can., Aug. 27, 1883; s. William and Lydia E. (Day) S.; grad. U. of Toronto, 1906; m. Edith Louise Ballard, Nov. 3, 1909; children—Hugh B., George W. Asst. sec., Canadian Mfrs. Assn., Toronto, 1907-11; sec. Canadian Home Market Assn., Toronto, 1911-16; asst. gen. mgr. and dir., Russell Motor Car Co., 1916-22; vice pres. and mgr., Stewart, Scully Co., Ltd., investment bankers, Toronto, 1922-32; commr. excise, Dept. Nat. Revenue, Ottawa, 1932-33, commr. customs, 1934, 43; consul gen. of Canada at New York City, 1943-50; advisor to Fedn. of British Industries, 1950-68. Mem. Pilgrims of United States, Newcomen Society, Canadian Society of New York, St. George's Soc. of N.Y., Soc. Fgn. Consuls, English Speaking Union of U.S. Clubs: Royal Ottawa Golf; Univ. (Toronto and New York); Canadian (New York). Home: Toronto ON Canada Died Apr. 10, 1968.

SCULLY, WILLIAM A., bishop; b. N.Y. City, Aug. 6, 1894; s. William T. and Mary (McCarthy) S.; grad. St. Joseph's Sem., Yonkers, N.Y.; LL.D., Fordham U., 1942. Ordained to ministry Roman Cath. Ch., 1919; studied at Cath. U., Washington, 1919-20; asst., and in 1936 pastor, Ch. of the Sacred Heart of Jesus, N.Y. City, also mem. Cath. Sch. Bd.; dir. religious edn. N.Y. Archdiocese, 1940; monsignor, 1941; asst. exec. dir. N.Y. Cath. Charities, 1945; became bishop coadjutor Albany (N.Y.) diocese, 1945-69; pastor St. Mary's Ch., Troy, N.Y., 1945-69. Province chaplain Newman Clubs of N.Y. Prov. Fedn. since 1940. Trustee Troy Pub. Library. Address: Troy NY Died Jan. 1969.

SCUPHAM, GEORGE WILLIAM, physician; b. Chicago, Ill., July 4, 1889; s. William C. and Johanna (Doepp) S.; U. of Mich., 1912; M.D., Northwestern U., 1916; m. Estelle Kent, Jan. 15, 1920; children—William Kent, Jean Elizabeth, George Robert, Joanne. Interne Cook County Hosp., Chicago, 1916; private practice of medicine since 1919, practice limited to internal medicine; clin. asst. in medicine, Northwestern University Med. Sch., 1921-24, associate professor medicine, 1937-69; senior attending physician St. Lukes Hospital; former attending physician Cook County hosps. Commd. 1st lt., U.S. Army Med. Corps, Feb. 1918, later serving as major in U.S. and France; hon. discharged Sept. 1919. Mem. A.M.A., Chicago Soc. Internal Medicine, Chicago Inst. Medicine, Central Soc. Clin. Research, Sigma Xi, Alpha Omega Alpha, Alpha Tau Omega. Republican. Presbyn. Home: Homewood IL Died Mar. 20, 1969.

SCUPIN, CARL ALBERT, utility co. exec.; b. Junction City, Kan., July 15, 1901; s. Waldemar and Elizabeth (Kummer) S.; widower; 1 dau., Jean Ann (Mrs. Jack M. Mohler). With United Utilities, Inc., Abilene, Kansas, from 1926, pres., chief exec. officer, 1959-64, chairman of board, 1964-67, also dir.; pres., dir. subsidiaries; dir. City Nat. Bank and Trust Co., Kansas City, Mo., The J. B. Ehrsam & Sons Mfg. Co., Enterprise, Kan., Kansas Power and Light Co., Topeka. Trustee Eisenhower Found.; mem. Kansas Eisenhower Library Commn. Mem. Kansas C. of C. (director), Armed Forces Communications and Electronics Assn., Ind. Pioneer Telephone Assn. Republican. Presbyn. Club: Kansas City (Mo.). Home: Abilene KS Died Nov. 22, 1972.

SEACREST, FREDERICK SNIVELY, newspaper pub.; b. Lincoln, Neb., July 17, 1894; s. Joseph Claggett and Jessie E. (Snively) S.; student Univ. of Neb., 1913-14; student of journalism, Columbia, 1916-17; m. Dorris Tilton, July 15, 1919 (divorced 1930); children—Mark T., Ann (Mrs. Wayne O. Southwick); married 2d, Mildred Ellis Potter, April 22, 1940. Pres., director of Journal-Star Printing Company. Lincoln Journal, Sunday Journal and Star, Lincoln Morning Star, Lincoln, Neb., 1951-71; v.p., dir. State Jour. Co., 1930-71; pres. Jacob North Printing Co., Lincoln Envelope Co., Jacob North & Co., 1957-58; v.p., dir. KFAB Broadcasting Co., Omaha. Trustee J. C. Seacrest Trust, 1935-71; trustee Neb. Wesleyan, 1958-71, chmn. investments dept., 1959-71, bd. govs., 1964-71; mem. Lincoln Foundation; trustee U. Neb. Foundation, Paine Meml. Fund, 1958-71, Lincoln Manor Sr. Citizens Home; mem. bd. dirs. Lincoln Council on Alcoholism. Served aviation div., World War I. Mem. Lincoln Symphony Bd., 1946-48. Mem. Asso. Press, Internat. Circulation Mgrs. Assn., Inland Daily Press Assn., Midwest Circulation Mgrs. Assn., Neb. Art Assn., C. of C. (dir. 1944), Neb. Reclamation Assn., Newcomen Soc., Am. Legion, YMCA, S.A.R., Internat. Platform Assn., Delta Upsilon, Sigma Delta Chi. Republican. Meth. (chairman board trustees; director ch. meml. fund). Mason (32 deg., Shriner), Modern Woodman, Royal Arcanum, Elk. Clubs: Rotary, University, Country (Lincoln). Home: Lincoln NB Died Sept. 1971.

SEAGER, ALLAN, author, educator; b. Adrian, Mich., Feb. 5, 1906; s. Arch and Emma (Allan) S.; A.B., U. Mich., 1930; B.A., Oxford (Eng.) U., 1933, M.A., 1947; m. Barbara Jane Watson, Nov. 10, 1938 (dec. Dec. 1966); children—Mary Vincent, Laura Allan; m. 2d, Joan Rambo, Mar. 25, 1968. Member faculty of University of Michigan, 1935-68, professor of English, 1958-68. Guggenheim fellow, 1965. Author (novels) Equinox, 1943, The Inheritance, 1948, Amos Berry, 1953, Hilda Manning, 1956, Death of Anger, 1960; (short story collections) The Old Man of the Mountain, 1950, A Fieze of Girls, 1964; (trans. from French) (Stendhal) Memoirs of a Tourist by Henri Beyle, 1962. Home: Tecumseh MI Died May 10, 1968.

SEAGO, ERWIN, lawyer, ex-govt. ofcl.; b. Jersey County, Ill., Sept. 16, 1902; s. Charles T. and Pearl (Erwin) S.; student U. Colo., 1925; B.A., Millikin U., 1926; J.D., U. Chgo., 1930; m. Nell M. Penick. Admitted to Ill. bar, 1930, Va. bar, 1952; sr. partner firm Seago, Pipin, Bradley & Vetter, Chgo., 1934-54; v.p., gen. counsel, dir. Deerfield State Bank (Ill.), 1934-48; gen. counsel Deerfield Savs. & Loan Assn., 1934-52; corp. counsel Village of Northbrook, Ill., 1942-52, Village of Deerfield, 1943-52; Chgo. counsel Pan Am. World Airways, 1946-52; lectr. aviation law U. Va. Law Sch., 1952-61; spl. asst. to sec. commerce, also dir. Office Strategic Information, 1955-57; chief atty. airports FAA, 1959-65, cons., 1965-68; general counsel Commonwealth Transportation Consultants, Inc., Washington, D.C. Advisor to Ethiopian delegation to Chgo. Internat. Civil Aviation Conf., 1944; chmn. draft bd., Buckingham County, Va., 1953-55; cons. to Va. Commn. on Airports Authority, 1957; mem. Va. Airports Authority, 1958. Trustee Sarah Hackett Stevenson Meml., 1932-52, chmn. bd., 1950; trustee Olivet Inst., Chgo., 1936-52, vice chmn. bd., 1942-52. Recipient Merit award for distinguished service in law Millikin U., 1956. Mem. Am., Ill. (vice chmn. aviation com. 1948-50). Chgo. (chmn. aviation com. 1943-50), Fed., Va. State bar assns., Chgo. Assn. Commerce and Industry (chmn. aviation com. 1949-50), Law Club, Phi Delta Phi, Sigma Alpha Epsilon. Clubs: National Lawyers, Cosmos (Washington); Va.-Carolinas Morgan Horse (pres.), also Farmington Country. Co-author: Partners and Partnerships—Law and Taxation, 1956; also numerous articles, book revs. Mem. editorial adv. bd. Jour. Air Law and Commerce, 1953-57. Home: Dillwyn VA Died Oct. 23, 1968; buried Chellowe, Buckingham County VA

SEALS, JOHN H., founder and editor of The Sunny South, a family paper; b. Warren Co., Ga.; grad. Mercer Univ. with high honors (A.M.). Was prin. Lee High School and Cuthbert Male High School; founder and editor Georgia Literary Crusader; the 1st and only man who has succeeded in establishing a literary weekly in the South. Unmarried. Address: Atlanta GA‡

SEARCY, MRS. EARLE BENJAMIN, state ofcl.; b. Shelbyville, Ill.; d. James Bonnell and Mollie (Parker) Isenberg; student Monticello Coll., 1910-11, Oberlin Coll., 1912-13; grad. Beethoven Conservatory Music, St. Louis, 1916; student Hinshaw Conservatory Music, Chgo., 1916-17; m. Earle Benjamin Searcy, Jan. 27, 1917; children—Barbara Jane (Mrs. Kenneth Welles Damewood), Earle Benjamin. Clk., Supreme Ct., State of Ill., Springfield. Active in A.R.C., War Camp Community Service. Recipient citation for meritorious service Govt. Salute to Women. Mem. Ill. Fedn. Republican Women, Am. Legion Aux. Mem. Christian Ch. Clubs: Amateur Musical, Zonta. Home: Springfield IL Died Mar. 23, 1968.

SEARCY, HUBERT FLOYD, college official; born Skipperville, Ala., July 2, 1908; s. Duncan Alexander and Susan Elizabeth (Hulon) S.; A.B., Birmingham-Southern Coll., 1929, LL.D., 1942; A.M., Duke U., 1933, Ph.D., 1937; married Christine Mason Quillian, December 22, 1934; children—Jane Quillian, Susan Elizabeth, Hubert Floyd, Jr. Assistant registrar, Birmingham-Southern College, 1929-30, alumni secretary, 1930-32, assistant prof. polit. science, 1934-36, asso. prof. and pub. relations dir., 1937-38; summer sch. faculty, Duke U., 1936, 37; pres. Huntingdon Coll., 1938-68, chancellor, 1968-71. Past pres. Montgomery Civic Music Assn., Ala. Colleges, 1943-44; Montgomery Council on Foreign Relations, 1942-43; mem. commn. on Institutions of Higher Edn., Southern Assn. of Colleges and Secondary Schs., Commn. on Citizenship, Assn. of American Colleges, 1944-48; chmn. Ednl. Survey Commn. Apptd. by Gov. of Ala. to study public schs. and instns. of higher learning, 1943-45. Mem. bd. vistors Air University, Maxwell Air Force Base, Ala.; mem. Univ. Senate of Meth. Ch., National Commn. on Accrediting; Nat. Com. for Accreditation of Teacher Education; chmn. Ala. Com. on Selection Rhodes Scholars 1962. Mem. Am. Soc. Internat. Law, Nat. Assn. Schs. and Colls. of Meth. Ch. (pres. 1957-58), Pi Kappa Alpha, Phi Beta Kappa, Omicron Delta Kappa, Kappa Phi Kappa, Pi Gamma Mu. Democrat. Clubs: Beauvoir Country, Lay rep. Ala. Conf. Meth. Ch. to Uniting Conf., 1939, Southeastern Jurisdictional Conf., 1940, 44, 48, 52, 56, Gen. Conf. 1944, 56. Methodist. Contbr. profl. jours. Address: Montgomery AL Died April, 1971.

SEARER, JAY CHARLES, chem. co. executive; born Tremont, Pa., May 31, 1914; s. George F. and Maude M. (Fegley) S.; B.S., Franklin and Marshall Coll., 1937; Ph.D., Northwestern U., 1941; M. B.A., U. Buffalo, 1959; m. Mercedes L. Bohren, June 14, 1940; children—Deborah A., Jeffrey C. Asst. chemistry Franklin and Marshall Coll., 1936-37, Northwestern U., 1937-41; instr. chemistry Lake Forest Coll., 1940-41; research chemist Durez Plastics & Chems. Co., N. Tonawanda, N.Y., 1941-45, dir. resin research, 1945-56; with Durez plastics div. Hooker Chem. Corp., 1956, general manager, 1958-62, vice president, 1962-67, group vice president, 1965-67. Member N.Y. C. of C. (dir. 1958-67), Soc. Plastics Industry, Am. Chem. Soc., Mfg. Chemists Assn., Am. Assn. Corrosion Engrs., Am. Mgmt. Assn., Phi Beta Kappa, Sigma Xi, Beta Gamma Sigma. Home: Darien CT Died June 25, 1967; buried Lake View Cemetery, New Canaan CT

SEARLE, HARRIET RICHARDSON (MRS. WILLIAM D. SEARLE), carcinologist; b. Washington; d. Charles F. E. and Charlotte Ann (Williamson) Richardson; A.B., Vassar, 1896, A.M., 1901; Ph.D., Columbian, 1903; m. William D. Searle, 1913. Collaborator Smithsonian Instn. Mem. Biol. Society, Washington, Washington Acad. Sciences; fellow A.A.A.S. Has contributed to Proceedings of United States National Museum and other publs.; monograph on the Isopods of North America, Bull. 54, U.S. Nat. Mus., 1905. Home: 1810 Wyoming Av., Washington DC‡

SEARLE, ROBERT WYCKOFF, clergyman; b. New Brunswick, N.Y., May 25, 1894; s. Rev. John Preston and Susan (Bovey) S.; A.B., Rutgers U., New Brunswick, N.J., 1915, D.D., 1929; student New Brunswick Theol. Sem., 1916-17, 1920-21; m. Helen Loraine Menzies, June 2, 1923; 1son, Raymond Preston. Master Kingsley Sch., Essex Fells, N.J., 1915-16; asst. minister Ft. Washington Collegiate Ch., 1921-23; minister First Reformed Ch., Albany, N.Y., 1923-30; asso. pastor Madison Av. Presbyn. Ch., N.Y. City, 1930-34; gen. secretary Greater New York Federation Churches, 1934-48. Director Community Relations, Protestant Council of the City of New York, 1948-50; editor of The Protestant World, 1950-53; exec. dir. Home Advisory Council, Inc., serving Home Term Ct., 1953-67; chairman Mayors Com. on Probation, N.Y.C.; mem. Mayors Committee on the Courts, N.Y. City. Del. Universal Christian Council, Oxford, 1937; N. Am. Ecumenical Conf., Toronto, 1941. Pvt. U.S. Ambulance Service, 1917; sgt. maj. 303d F.A., 1917-19, World War I. Mem. Delta Upsilon, Phi Beta Kappa. Independent Democrat. Author: Contemporary Religious Thinking, 1933; City Shadows, 1938; Author of Liberty, 1941; Tell It to the Padre, 1943. Home: Scarborough-on-Hudson NY Died June 16, 1967.

SEARLES, COLBERT, coll. prof.; b. Wilton, Me., Aug. 15, 1873; s. David C. and Nancy (Weich) S.; A.B., Wesleyan U., Conn., 1895; Ph.D., U. of Leipzig, 1899; m. Beatrice Thomson, Mar. 28, 1900; children—Bert, Janet. Instr. in French and Italian, Ind. U., 1899-1900; asso. prof. English and modern langs., U. of Ark., 1900-01; asso. prof. Romance langs., Stanford, 1901-14; prof. Romance langs., U. of Minn. since 1914. Mem. Modern Lang. Assn. America (exec. council and editorial staff since 1927; pres. 1935), Am. Council Learned Socs. (com. on grants and fellowships), Philol. Assn. of Pacific Coast (pres. 1913-14). Editor: Catalogue de tous les Livres de feu M. Chapelain, 1912; Le Cid of Pierre Corneille, 1912; Andromaque of Racine, 1914; Francois le Champi of George Sand, 1914; Les Sentiments de l'Academie Francaise sur le Cid (U. of Minn. Publs.); Fables of La Fontaine, 1930; Anthology of Modern French Literature (with Prof. I. C. Lecompte), 1931; 7 French plays. Contbr. to mags. and philol. jours. Home: 2417 Emerson Av. S., Minneapolis MN‡

SEARLS, CARROLL, lawyer; b. Nevada City, Cal., June 9, 1894; s. Fred and Helen (Pond) S.; A.B., U. Cal., 1915; m. Elise M. Myers, Sept. 20, 1919. Admitted to Cal. bar, 1916, practiced law, Nevada City, 1916-23, Pasadena, Cal., 1923-26; atty. Newmont Mining Corp., N.Y.C., 1926-70, sec., 1948-70, dir., 1935-70, gen. counsel, 1947-70. Mem. Am. Bar Assn., Assn. Bar City N.Y. Club: Lawyers (N.Y.C.). Home: New Rochelle NY Died Nov. 4, 1970.

SEARLS, DAVID THOMAS, lawyer; b. Sulphur Springs, Tex., June 30, 1905; s. Robert E. Lee and Lutie (Smith) S.; A.B. cum laude, Southwestern U., 1925, LL.D. (hon.), 1960; LL.B., U. of Tex., Austin, 1929; m. Catherine Montgomery, May 1, 1934; children—Susan (Mrs. McMahon), Cathey (Mrs. Johnson), David Thomas. Mem. faculty Southwestern U., 1925-26, U. Tex., 1926-29; admitted to Tex. bar, 1929, practiced in Houston; asso., firm Robertson, Robertson & Payne, Dallas, 1929-30, Vinson, Elkins, Sweeton & Weems, Houston, 1930-72, partner, 1939-53, sr. partner Vinson, Elkins, Searls & Connally, 1953-72; gen. counsel, v.p. Gulf Oil Corp., 1958-61; dir. 1st City Nat. Bank Houston, Kaneb Pipe Line Co., Murphy Oil Corp., G.W. Murphy Industries, Inc. Mem. Am. (chmn. antitrust sect. Am., 1954, mem. atty. gen. nat. com. to study antitrust laws), Tex., Houston (pres. 1958-59) bar assns., Am. Coll. Trial Lawyers, Phi Delta Phi, Kappa Sigma. Clubs: Houston Country, Ramada. Home: Houston TX Died Oct. 1972.

SEARS, FRANCIS PHILIP, lawyer, ins. exec.; b. Waltham, Mass., Oct. 30, 1869; s. Philip Howes and Sarah Pratt (Lyman) S.; student Nobles Sch., 1886; spl. course Mass. Inst. Tech., 1886-87; A.B. cum laude, Harvard, 1891, LL.B., 1895; m. Marie Musgrave Merrill, Mar. 27, 1915; children—Francis Philip, Elizabeth Merrill (Mrs. Benjamin O. Gardiner), Sarah Lyman (Mrs. R.H. Dulany Randolph). Admitted to Mass. bar, 1895; atty. B.&M. R.R. and Travelers Ins. Co., 1895-98; pvt. law practice, Boston, 1899-1902; incorporator Columbian Nat. Life Ins. Co., Boston, 1902, treas., 1902, v.p., 1905, comptroller, 1906, pres., 1933, chmn. bd. dirs., 1947; pres. Dixmont Co., T.D. & R.D. Merrill, Inc.; v.p., dir. Merrill & Ring Lumber Co., Ltd. Dist. treas. Family Welfare Soc. of Boston, 1903-05; social service dept. treas. Mass. Gen. Hosp., 1912-33. Mem. bd. aldermen, Waltham, 1900-03. Trustee Kings Chapel. Mem. Boston C. of C., Boston Atheneum, Boston Young Men's Christian Union, Essex Inst. of Salem, Soc. Promoting Theol. Edn., Soc. Propagating Gospel Among Indians. Clubs: Somerset, Union (Boston); Myopia Hunt (Hamilton). Home: Boston MA‡

SEARS, HESS THATCHER, life ins. co. exec., orgn. ofcl.; b. Ames, Ia., Oct. 20, 1912; s. Charles T. and Olga (Hess) S.; grad. Mercersburg (Pa.) Acad., 1930; A.B., Princeton, 1934; C.L.U., 1946; m. Betty Harper, Mar. 21, 1942; children—Elizabeth (Mrs. Dennis S. Hager), Susan (Mrs. John Spence, Jr.). With Equitable Life Ins. Co. Ia., Des Moines, 1934-73, sec., mem. exec. com., 1963-73. Pres., United Fund Ia., 1955-57, United Community Services Des Moines, 1958-60; mem. Gov. Ia. Commn. on Human Rights, 1959-62; chmn. tech. com. Spiritual Well Being; mem. planning adv. bd. White Ho. Conf. on Aging, 1970-73. Bd. dirs. United Community Funds and Councils Am., 1961-73, chmn. adv. council, 1962-63, v.p., 1963-67, chmn. exec. com., 1964-66, recipient Nat. Community Service award, 1966. Served with AUS, 1941-43. Decorated Legion of Merit. Recipient Community Service award Des Moines Tribune, 1959. Mem. Life Office Mgmt. Assn. (pres. 1962-63). Episcopalian. Home: Des Moines IA Died Jan. 13, 1973.

SEARS, JESSE BRUNDAGE, author, educator; b. Kidder, Mo., Sept. 25, 1876; s. William Wallace and Angeline Augusta (Johnson) S.; A.B., Stanford, 1909; student U. of Wis., 1909-10, U. of Chicago, 1910,

Columbia, 1910-11, Ph.D., 1920; m. Stella Louise Richardson, June 22, 1904; children—Robert Richardson, William Norman. Instr. in edn., U. of Wis., 1909; instr. in edn., Stanford U., 1911, asst. prof., 1912-16, associate professor, 1917-21, professor, 1922-42, professor emeritus since 1942; visiting associate prof. edn., University of Minn., 1920-21, summer 1921; prof. edn., U. of Pa., summer of 1927; lecturer U. of Pittsburgh, summer 1930; visiting prof. U. of Southern Calif., summer, 1936; spl. consultant Ednl. Policies Commn., 1937; with Am. Council on Edn., 1937. Fellow A.A.A.S.; mem. N.A.S.A., National Society College Teachers of Edn., Nat. Soc. for Study of Edn., American Educational Research Association, Phi Beta Kappa, Phi Delta Kappa. Rep. Conglist. Author: Spelling Efficiency in the Oakland Schools, 1915; Classroom Organization and Control, 1918; The Arlington Sch. Survey, 1921; Report of Survey Commn., Univ. of Minn. (Vols. IV and V), 1922; Philanthropy in the History of American Higher Education, 1922; The School Survey, 1925; Marysville (Calif.) Union High School Survey, 1925; Berkeley School Properties Survey, 1926; The Napa School Survey, 1927; Sutter County Instructional Survey, 1929; Modesto Junior College Survey, 1932; Research Mem. on Education in the Depression, 1937; City School Administrative Control, 1938; The Administrative Organization of Sacramento's School System, 1940; Public School Administration, 1947; The Nature of the Administrative Process, 1950. Joint Author: Report of School Survey of Salt Lake City Schools, 1916; The Boise Survey, 1920; The Cost of Education in California, 1924; Twenty-five Years of American Education, 1924; Sacramento School Survey, 1928; Modern School Administration, 1933; Tracy Union High Sch. Survey, 1935; The Challenge of Education, 1937; Stockton School Survey, 1938; Education in War Time and After, 1943; other school surveys, also numerous papers in professional jours. Editor: School Administration in the Twentieth Century, 1934. Home: 40 Tevis Pl., Palo Alto CA‡

SEARS, JULIAN D(UCKER), geologist; born Baltimore, Maryland, June 3, 1891; the son of Dr. Thomas Edward and Julia (Ducker) S.; A.B., Johns Hopkins, 1913, Ph.D., 1919; m. Elizabeth T. Lamdin, June 16, 1919 (dec. 1969); children—William Brewster, Richard Sherwood. Geologist, U.S. Geol. Survey, 1915-16. Sinclair Central Am. Oil Corp., 1917-18; rejoined staff, U.S. Geol. Survey, geologist, 1918-23, administrative geologist, 1924-48, staff geologist 1948-61. Recipient Distinguished Service medal Dept. Interior. Mem. Geol. Soc. of Am., Am. Assn. of Petroleum Geologists, Soc. of the Cincinnati of Md., Phi Gamma Delta, Phi Beta Kappa. Club: Kenwood Golf and Country (Bethesda, Md.). Contbr. numerous articles and reports to tech. jours. and U.S. Geol. Survey publs. Home: Chevy Chase MD Died May 1970.

SEARS, WILLIS G., judge; b. Willoughby, Ohio, Aug. 16, 1860; s. Stephen S. and Mary S.; student law, U. of Kan.; m. Belle V. Hoadly, May 1887 (died). Admitted to Neb. bar, 1884; mem. law firm Sears, Horn & Sears, Omaha. County atty. Burt County, Neb., 1895-1901; mem. Neb. Ho. of Rep., 1901-04 (speaker); judge 4th District of Neb., 1904-23; mem. 68th to 71st Congresses (1923-31) 2d Neb. Dist.; judge 4th Dist. of Neb. since 1933. Republican. Mason, Odd Fellow. Address: District Court, 4th District, Omaha NB*‡

SEATON, JOHN LAWRENCE, clergyman, coll. pres.; b. Manchester, Ia., Jan. 25, 1873; s. Milon D. and Mary (Riley) S.; grad. Epworth (Ia.) Sem., 1895; A.B., Upper Ia. U., 1898; S.T.B., Boston U. Sch. of Theology, 1901; Ph.D., Boston U., 1905; Williams scholar, Harvard, 1913-14; D.D., Upper Ia. U.; Litt.D., Dakota Wesleyan U.; LL.D., W.Va. Wesleyan U. and Boston U.; L.H.D., Principia College and Albion College; married Jessie Evans Davis, Aug. 27, 1900; children—William Davis, Mary Wells. Ordained M.E. ministry, 1897; asso. pastor Morgan Memorial Institutional Ch., Boston, 1898-1900; pastor Norwood, Mass., 1901, Grandview Av. Ch., Dubuque, Ia., 1901-04; prof. psychology and Bible, Dak. Wesleyan U., Mitchell, S.D., 1904-14; pres. Coll. of the Pacific, San Jose, Calif., 1914-19; coll. sec. Bd. of Edn., M.E. Ch., New York, Apr. 1919-24; president Albion College, 1925-45; retired Sept. 1945. College and university consultant since 1945. President of the University Senate, M.E. Church since 1925 and secretary Educational Assn., 1925-34; president Assn. of American Colls., 1938-39. Mem. Commn. on Public Relations of Assn. of Am. Colls., Am. Council on Edn.; chmn. Commn. on Higher Edn. and Bd. of Review, N. Central Assn. Colls. and Secondary Schools. Del. to Gen. Conf. M.E. Ch., 1932, 36; Uniting Conf., Methodist Ch., 1939. Mem. N.E.A., Phi Beta Kappa. Mason. Clubs: Rotary, Torch. Contbr. numerous articles on religious and ednl. topics. Address: 35-45 81st St., Jackson Heights NY‡

SEATON, ROY ANDREW, educator, engineer; b. Glasco, Kan., Apr. 17, 1884; s. Oren Andrew and Sarah Elizabeth (Bartley) S.; B.S. in Mech. Engring., Kan. State Coll., 1904, M.S., 1910; studied U. of Wis., summer 1908; S.B. in Mech. Engring., Mass. Inst. Tech., 1911; Sc.D., honorary, Northeastern University, 1942; m. Gay Perry, June 26, 1913 (died Oct. 4, 1918); 1 son, James Newell; m. 2d, Elnora Wanamaker, June 14, 1921; children—Sarah Frances, Robert Wanamaker, Elnora Margaret, Roy Andrew, II. With Kan. State Coll. most of time, 1904-70, instr. asst. prof. of mathematics, 1904-06, instr. and asst. prof. mech. engring., 1906-10, prof. applied mechanics and machine design, 1910-20, dean school of engring. and architecture and director Engineering Experimental Station, 1920-49; prof. applied mechanics Kan. State Coll., 1949-70; on leave of absence as director of Engineering, Science and Management Defense Training, U.S. Office of Edn., 1940-42; acad. dir. Air Force Inst. Tech., Wright-Patterson AFB, O., 1953-57; designing draftsman steam turbine dept. Gen. Electric Co., 1911-12. Served as capt. engring. div. Ordnance Office, U.S. Army, Washington, D.C., designing arty. ammunition Jan.-Dec. 1918. Chmn. Kan. Registration Bd. for Professional Engrs., 1931-47; chmn. Kansas Bd. Engring. Examienrs since 1947; director Nat. Council of State Bds. of Engring. Examiners, 1935-37; rep. of Soc. for Promotion Engring. Edn. on Engrs. Council for Professional Development, 1937-42; mem. Com. on Professional Training, Engrs. Council for Professional Development, 1933-38. Mem. Am. Soc. Mech. Engrs. (past vice chmn. Mid-Continent sect.), Soc. for Promotion Engring. Edn. (pres. Neb.-Kan. Sect. 1923-24; mem. council 1926-29; v.p. 1930-31; pres. 1932-33; awarded Lamme medal, 1942), Kan. Engring. Soc. (v.p. and acting pres. 1929-30; pres. 1930-31), Engring. Sect. Assn. Land Grant Colls. and Univs. (sec. 1925-29; chmn. 1929-30), Am. Assn. U. Profs. (hon.), Phi Kappa Phi, Sigma Xi, Sigma Tau, Acacia. Mason. Clubs: Manhattan Country, Rotary. Author: Concrete Construction for Rural Communities, 1916; also bulletins, arts. in tech. press, etc. Editor Engring. Expt. Sta. Record Quarterly, 1925-29, Engring. Expt. Sta. Record Summary, 1929. Home: Manhattan KS Died May 23, 1970; buried Sunset Cemetery Manhattan KS

SEAVER, FRED JAY, mycologist; b. Webster County, Ia., Mar. 14, 1877; s. Joshua Marshall and Guhelma M. (Sturtevant) S.; B.S., Morningside Coll., Sioux City, Ia., 1902, Sc.D., 1931; M.S., State U. of Ia., 1904, Ph.D., 1912; student Columbia, 1906-07; m. Hortense Adelaide Schnebly, June 14, 1905 (died July 25, 1940); children—Bernice, Hortense Eloise (Mrs. Albert Cullen Hewitt, Jr.); m. 2d, Mrs. Finetta A. Fry Heller, Sept. 23, 1941; 1 stepson, Robert A. Heller. Instr. in biology, Iowa Wesleyan Coll., 1905-06, prof., 1906; asst. prof. botany, N.D. Agrl. Coll., mycologist to expt. station, 1907-08; dir. labs. N.Y. Bot. Gardens, 1908-11, curator 1912-43, head curator 1943-49, mem. board mgrs. 1947-49; ret.; asso. prof. biology Fla. Southern College, 1949-50. Received certificate of Accomplishment from State University of Iowa, 1947. Bot. explorations for New York Botanical Gardens in Bermuda, Trinidad and Puerto Rico for the government. Member Mycological Society America (editor Mycologia, official organ), Bot. Soc. America (chmn. mycol. sect., 1932), Nat. Geog. Soc., Torney Bot. Club (treas. 1921-22; v.p., 1943, pres. 1945), Sigma Xi; fellow A.A.A.S. Republican. Methodist. Author: The North American Cup-fungi (operaculates), 1928, supplemented edit., 1941; also many tech. papers. Home: Winter Park FL Died Dec. 21, 1970.

SEAVER, KENNETH, business exec.; born Woodstock, Vt., Aug. 26, 1877; s. Thomas O. and Nancy Jane (Spalding) S.; ed. Phillips Andover; Mass. Inst. Tech., 1900; m. Mabel Bright, June 2, 1903;children—Ethel S. Verner, Mary S. Hewitt, Virginia S. Ritter, Tom (died in U.S. Armed Services). Dir. Harbison-Walker Refractories Co., Pittsburgh, Pa., since 1918, v.p. since 1929, retired 1947. Chmn. bd., treas., dir. Pittsburgh Metall. Inc. Clubs: Duquesne, Oakmont Country. Home: 5831 Walnut St., Pittsburgh 32. Office: Oliver Bldg., Pittsburgh 22‡

SEAWELL, HERBERT FLOYD, lawyer; b. Duplin Co., N.C., Aug. 8, 1869; s. Virgil Newton and Ellen (Croom) S.; student, Wake Forest Coll., 1890-91; grad. Law Dept., U. of N.C., 1892; m. Ella McNeill, of Carthage, N.C., July 30, 1895; children—Herbert F., Henry, Ella Meade. In practice law, Carthage, since 1892; state's atty. 7th N.C. Jud. Dist., 1894-98; U.S. atty., Eastern Dist., N.C., 1910-14; mem. U.S. Bd. of Tax Appeals, term 1929-36. Rep. candidate for judge Superior Ct., 1898, for gov. of N.C., 1928; apptd. judge U.S. Dist. Ct., 1909, not confirmed by senate; qualified as Republican candidate for associate justice North Carolina Supreme Court. Member Federal, American and North Carolina State bar assns. Baptist (trustee 1st Ch.). Mason. Home: Carthage NC‡

SEAY, WILLIAM ALBERT, coll. dean; b. Charleston, Mo., Sept. 12, 1920; s. William Arthur and Rui (Brooks) S.; B.S.A., U. Ky., 1942, M.S., 1948; Ph.D. in Soils, U. Wis., 1950; m. Lyda Maxine Short, June 27, 1943; children—Edward Allen, Sally Brooks, Jeffrey Short. Asst. prof. agr. U. Ky., 1949-52, asso. prof., 1952-54, prof., 1954-56, adminstrv. asst. to dean, 1956-57, vice dir. Agrl. Expt. Sta., Lexington, 1957, acting dean Coll. Agr. and Home Econs., also acting dir. Ky. Extension Service and Ky. Agr. Expt. Sta., 1958-59, 61-62, dean and dir., 1962-69. Served to lt. col. AUS, 1942-46. Mem. A.A.A.S., Am. Soc. Agronomy, Internat. Soil Sci. Soc., Soil Sci. Soc. Am., Association Southern Agrl. Workers (pres. 1967), Ky. Acad. Sci., Sigma Ki, Alpha Zeta, Gamma Sigma Delta. Contbr. articles profl. jours. Home: Lexington KY Died Feb. 1, 1969.

SEBRING, HAROLD LEON, univ. dean; b. Olathe, Kan., Mar. 9, 1898; s. John Thomas and Anna Lee (Hayden) S.; B.S., Kansas State Coll., 1923; LL.B., University of Florida, 1928; LL.D., Kansas State University, 1963; m. Elise Bishop, Oct. 25, 1928; 1 son, Harold Leon. Admitted to Fla. bar, 1928; in practice of law, Gainesville, Miami and Jacksonville, Fla., 1928-34; circuit judge 8th Judicial Circuit of Fla., 1934-43; justice Supreme Court of Fla., 1943-55, ret. on call; chief justice Florida Supreme Court, 1951-53; dean, prof. law Coll. of Law, Stetson Univ., St. Petersburg, Florida, 1955-68; director Florida Hospital Service Corporation; mem. Florida Motion Picture Industry Com., 1945. Member Florida Constitution Revision Commission. Director Stetson Law Center Foundation. Served with 15th F.A., 2d Div., U.S. Army during World War I; participated in all major U.S. offensives; with Army of Occupation in Germany, 9 mos.; overseas 22 mos. Under designation from Pres. of the U.S., served as judge, U.S. Military Tribunal, Germany, Oct. 25, 1946-Aug. 20, 1947, in trial of Nazi war criminals. Decorated Silver Star with oak leaf (U.S.), Croix de Guerre with silver star, Cord de Fourragere (France). Member of the awards jury, Freedoms Found.; mem. of Children's Home Soc. of Fla. (dir.), Fla. Probation and Parole Assn. (exec. com.). Mem. Am., Fla., St. Petersburg bar assns., Southeastern Regional Conference of Law Teachers (chairman 1958-63), Alumni Association College of Law (U. of Fla.), Phi Delta Phi, Blue Key, Acacia. Baptist. Clubs: Tallahassee Rotary (dir.), Tallahassee Golf and Country, St. Petersburg Yacht. Home: St Petersburg FL Died July 1968.

SEDER, ARTHUR RAYMOND, railroad exec.; b. Minneapolis, Minn., Sept. 25, 1889; s. James I. and Minnie (Kiekhofer) S.; student North Central Coll., Naperville, Ill., 1907-09; B.S., Univ. of N.M., 1911; m. Aline Grantham, Dec. 24, 1913 (dec. Dec. 1944); children—Margaret (Mrs. Robert Briggs Selover), Edwin, Arthur, Alan, Mary Lynn; m. 2d, Dorothea Zehnder, Aug. 1, 1946. Prin. high schs., Carlsbad and Clovis, N.M., 1911-18; various positions, including comptroller C.&N.W. Ry. system, St. Paul, Minn., 1918-38, asst. comptroller, gen. auditor, Chicago, 1938-45, vice president, 1945-52; vice president, comptroller, dir. C., St.P., M.&O. Ry. Co., 1945-52; v.p. Assn. Am. R.R.'s, 1952-69. Mem. Controllers Inst. of Am., Sigma Chi. Republican. Methodist. Mason. Clubs: Union League (Chicago); St. Paul Athletic. Home: Naperville IL Died July 24, 1969; buried Acacia Park Cemetery, Pilot Knob, Mendota MN

SEDGWICK, FRANCIS MINTURN, sculptor; b. N.Y.C., Mar. 13, 1904; s. Henry Dwight and Sarah (Minturn) S.; student Groton Sch., 1917-20; A.B., Harvard, 1926, grad. student, 1930-31; student Cambridge U., Eng., 1926-27; pvt. student sculpture, 1933-37; m. Alice de Forest, May 8, 1929; children—Alice (Mrs. John Atherton), Robert M. II, Pamela (Mrs. Jerome R. Dwight), F. Minturn, Henry de Froest M., Katherine, Edith, Susanna. Sculpture and paintings one-man show, N.Y.C., 1937, Phila., Boston, Cambridge, Mass., Rockland, Me., 1956, Santa Barbara, Cal., 1957; several exhibits Nat. Acad., N.Y.C.; sculptor of Laurel Hill Memorial Monument, San Francisco, 1955, Dumbarton Oaks Pan, 1916, Am. Field Service Monument, London, Eng., 1962; portrait busts of James B. Conant, Judge Learned Hand; also raising comml. cattle, Santa Ynez Valley, Cal. Life mem. Met. Mus. Art, N.Y.; mem. bd. Santa Barbara Symphony Orchestra; steering com. Affiliates U. Cal. at Santa Barbara; v.p. Asso. Harvard Clubs, 1953-57. Clubs: Knickerbocker, Harvard (N.Y.C.); Century River; University (San Francisco); Somerset (Boston). Author: The Rim, 1945; Power and Purity, 1961. Home: Olivos CA Died Oct. 27, 1967.

SEE, HAROLD PHILIP, broadcasting co. exec.; b. Bklyn., Sept. 3, 1907; s. Henry Philip and Gracia (Lamphear) S.; student pub. schs.; m. Evelyn Whitermore, Aug. 30, 1930; children—Evelyn (Mrs. James L. Cooper), Audrey (Mrs. Herman Bitter). Newspaper reporter Bklyn. dailies, 1926-28; radio operator U.S. Mcht. Marine, 1928-30; engring. technician-supr. NBC, 1930-41, TV research and devel., 1945-57; dir. TV Hearst Radio, Inc., Balt., 1947-49; gen. mgr. Chronicle Pub. Co., KRON-TV and KRON-FM, San Francisco, 1949-72, v.p. for television, 1960-71, pres., 1971-72 (name changed to Broadcast div. Chronicle Pub. Co. 1964); pres. Chronicle Broadcasting Co., 1966-71, chmn. bd., 1971-72; pres. Western Communications, Inc., Sierra TV Co.; pres., dir. Bakersfield Broadcasting Co. (Cal.), 1954-60. Research devel. and flight testing of guided missiles NDRC, 1941-45. Employer mem. wage bd. Cal. Indsl. Welfare Commn., 1962. Adv. bd. San Francisco Area Sci. Fair, 1962-63; bus. edn. adv. com. City Coll. San Francisco; adv. com. Coll. of San Mateo, 1966; pub. information com. No. Cal. Industry-Edn. Council, 1966; exec. mem. FCC Spl. Nat. Indsl. Adv. Com.; vice chmn. NBC-TV Affiliates Com., 1966. Mem. Nat. Assn. Broadcasters (TV code rev. bd. 1965-72, dir. 1956, mem. joint comml. and ednl. broadcasters com.), Cal. Broadcasters Assn.

(v.p. 1955, dir. 1963), Television Bur. Advt. (dir. 1960-62), Soc. Radio and Television Pioneers, No. Cal. Acad. Arts and Scis. (past pres.), Acad. Television Arts and Scis. San Francisco (1st v.p. 1963-65), San Francisco Down Town Assn. (dir. 1966). Patentee automatic sequential TV broadcast operating equipment. Office: San Francisco CA Died Sept. 21, 1972.

SEEGAL, DAVID, educator, clin. investigator; b. Chelsea, Mass., June 23, 1899; s. Morris and Rose (Beerman) S.; student Harvard, M.D., 1928; m. Emily Beatrice Carrier, July 8, 1925. Intern, asst. resident physician, resident physician Presbyn. Hosp. N.Y.C., 1928-32; asst. in medicine, instr. Columbia, 1930-35, asso. prof. medicine, 1942-47; dir. research, div. chronic diseases, Welfare Island, 1936-42; dir. research service 1st div. Goldwater Meml. Hosp., 1942-47, 51-64; prof. medicine L.I. Coll. Medicine, 1947-48; prof. medicine Columbia, 1951-64, prof. emeritus, 1964-72; prof. medicine State U. Med. Center, Bklyn., 1950-51, asso. attending physician, Presbyn. Hosp., 1945-47, 1952-56, attending physician, 1956-72; dir. med. service Maimonides Hosp., Bklyn., 1947-51. Cons. epidemic diseases U.S. Sec. War, 1942-45. Del., Nat. Conf. on Chronic Disease (chmn. com. on practice), Chgo., 1951; mem. N.Y. Com. on Study Hosp. Internships and Residencies; med. adv. com. Unitarian Service Com.; med. adv. council Masonic Found. Med. Research and Human Welfare, Assn. Am. Physicians, Assn. Am. Med. Colls. Recipient Army and Navy certificate of appreciation, 1948. Fellow A.M.A.; mem. Am. Soc. Clin. Investigation, Am. Assn. Immunologists, Soc. for Exptl. Biology and Medicine, Harvey Soc., A.A.A.S., Alpha Omega Alpha (mem. editorial bd. Pharos). Jewish religion. Club: Omega. Co-editor: Jour. Chronic Diseases, 1955. Contbr. chpt. on allgery (with E.B.C. Seegal) in Agents of Disease and Host Resistance (Frederick P. Gay), 1935; chpt. (study on hosp. internships and residencies in Trends in Medical Edn., 1947; chpt. Methuselah: Myth or Promise, in Frontiers in Medicine, 1950; contbr. articles to med. jours., poems to med., alumni, poetry mags. Mem. adv. bd. Familiar Medical Quotations; editorial adv. bd. Jour. Chronic Diseases. Home: New York City NY Died July 24, 1972.

SEEGER, WALTER G., business exec.; born St. Paul, Minn., Mar. 8, 1886; s. John A. and Elvina (Yoerg) S.; student U. of Minn., 1905-07; m. Nellie Ienza Luse, Apr. 14, 1909; children—Dorothea, Miriam, Helen; married second to Florence N. Carlton, 1959. With Seeger Refrigeration Co., St. Paul, since 1907, beginning as metal worker and advanced through various depts.; sales dept. and exec. div., pres., 1936-50, chmn. bd., 1950-55; chmn. bd. Whirlpool-Seeger Corp. (merger Whirlpool Corp., Seeger Refrigerator Co. and Delaware Appliance Corp.), 1953-58; dir.; trustee Minn. Mutual Life Insurance Co., St. Paul; director of Great Northern Railway Company. Trustee of the Shriners Hospital for Crippled Children. President St. Paul Association of Commerce, 1940. Member Delta Upsilon. Republican. Episcopalian. Clubs: Rotary, Minnesota, St. Paul Athletic. St Paul MN Died Jan. 6, 1969; buried Acacia Park Cemetery.

SEELBACH, LOUIS, lawyer; b. Louisville, Mar. 29, 1890; s. Louis and Marie Helen (Durbeck) S.; student Louisville Male High Sch., 1903-07; A.B. Centre Coll., Danville, Ky., 1910; LL.B., Harvard, 1914; m. Daisy A. Peck, Oct. 5, 1916; children—Harriet B. (Mrs. Warner L. Jones, Jr.), Helen L. (Mrs. Lewis R. Hardy, Jr.), Louis, Albert P. Admitted to Ky. bar, 1914 and since practiced in Louisville; mem. Middleton, Seelbach, Wolford, Willis & Cochran; gen. counsel Standard Oil Co. (Kentucky), 1956-63; pres. Bourbon Stock Yard Co., 1950-69, chairman of the board, 1969-71; division counsel Southern Ry. Company, from 1949. Mem. Louisville and Jefferson Co. Air Bd., 1930-41. Mem. bd. of trustees Center College, Ky., 1952-56. Served as 2d lieutenant F.A., U.S. Army, 1918. Mem. Am., Ky. and Louisville bar assns., Sigma Alpha Epsilon. Mason. Clubs: Pendennis, Louisville Louisville KY Died May 24, 1971; buried Cave Hill Cemetery Louisville KY

SEELIG, M. G., surgeon; b. Helena, Ark., Feb. 19, 1874; s. Simon and Vera (Cohen) S.; grad. high sch., St. Louis, Mo., 1892; A.B., Harvard, 1896; M.D., Columbia, 1900; m. Clover Althea Hartz, Jan. 10, 1906; children—Clover Marjorie (Mrs. Edwin Fleischmann), Frank Hartz, Vera Marjorie (deceased). Intern and resident surgeon, Mt. Sinai Hospital, New York City, 1900-03; University of Berlin, Germany, 1903-04; in surgical practice, St. Louis, Mo., 1904-32; professor surgery, St. Louis University, 1905-16; professor clinical surgery, Washington University Sch. of Medicine, 1916-48; surgeon Jewish Hospital, 1917-31; asso. surgeon Barnes Hosp.; director pathology, Barnard Free Skin and Cancer Hosp., 1940-48; ret. 1948. Served as lt. col. Med. Res. Corps, World War. Fellow A.M.A., American College Surgeons, American Surgical Association, Western Surgical Assn. Author: History of Medicine, 1925. Contbr. articles to med. jours. Home: 54 Belleau Av., Atherton CA‡

SEFERIADES, GEORGE, Greek diplomat, writer; b. Feb. 29, 1900; student Athens, Paris; Litt.D. (hon.), Cambridge (Eng.) U.; Dr. Philosophy (hon.) Thessaloniki; Litt.D. (honorary), Oxford U. Princeton U.; m. Maria Zannos, 1941. Entered Greek Fgn. Service, 1926; vice consul, London, 1931-34, Athens, 1934-36; consul, Albania, 1936-38, Athens, 1938-41; staff Greek Fgn. Office, Egypt, South Africa, 1941-44; chef de cabinet to Regent, 1945-46, counselor of embassy, Ankara, 1948-50, London, 1951-52; ambassador to Lebanon, minister to Syria, Iraq and Jórdan to 1956; ambassador to Great Britan, 1957-62. Recipient Nobel prize fot lit., 1963. Fellow Am. Acad. Arts and Scis. (hon. fgn.), Modern Lang. Assn. (hon.). Author (pseudonym George Seferis): The Turning Point, 1931, Mythistorema, 1935; Gynmopedia, 1936, Esseys, 1962, Poems 1924-46, 1950, Log Book III, 1955, Three Secret Poems, 1966, others; (English translation) The King of Asine and Other Poems, 1948, Poems, 1960, Collected Poems, 1924-55, others. Address: Athens Greece Died Sept. 20, 1971; buried Athens Greece

SEGAL, PAUL MOSES, lawyer; b. Denver, Colo., Dec. 8, 1899; s. Sol and Susie (Freud) S.; A.B., Columbia, 1920; LL.B., U. Denver, 1922; LL.D., Loyola University (New Orleans), 1957; m. Rena Greenblatt, Aug. 21, 1921; children—Ruth (Mrs. Maurice Gurin) and Paul F., Jane (Mrs. Wirt Harris, Jr.), Susan (Mrs. Robert Jacobi), David, Daniel. Admitted to Colorado bar, 1922, and practiced in Denver, 1922-29, deputy dist. atty., 1924-29; admitted to D.C. bar, 1929; asst. gen. counsel, Fed. Radio Commn., Mar.-Dec. 1929; formed firm of Segal, Smith & Hennessey, Mar. 1942, dissolved, 1957; formed firm Segal & Marmet, 1959; gen. counsel Am. Radio Relay League since 1924. Tech. advisor, Am. delegation Internat. Telecommunications Confs., Madrid, 1932, Cairo, 1938, Washington, 1947. Served as pvt. U.S. Army, 1918; with U.S.N.R., active duty, 1942-45; sea duty, Central Pacific, 1944; disch. to inactive duty rank of commdr. Mem. Inst. Radio Engrs. (sr. mem.), Am., Colo., Denver and D.C. bar assns., Phi Sigma Delta, Delta Sigma Rho, Tau Epsilon Rho. Clubs: National Press, Engineers. Home: Washington DC Died May 24, 1968.

SEGEL, DAVID, educational psychologist; b. Marion County, Kan., Apr. 12, 1894; s. Carl John and Clara Marie (Gran) S.; B.A., U. of Calif., 1917; A.M., Teachers Coll. (Columbia), 1922; Ph.D., Stanford, 1931; m. Naomi Elvira Claes, Aug. 10, 1919. Asst. dir. research, city schs., Long Beach, Calif., 1924-31; ednl. cons. Office of Edn., Dept. Health Edn. and Welfare, Washington, 1931-58; dir. bur. Measurement, sch. edn., Ind. U., 1958-59; director Lincoln Guidance Research Project Albuquerque (New Mexico) Pub. Schools, 1959-72; prof. edn. Mich. State U., summer, 1941; mem. of the extension div. U.Va., 1952-54; personnel analyst, Civilian Personnel Div., Sec. of War's Office, Washington, 1944. Cons. to War Dept., 1947, AAF, Randolf Field, Tex., 1951. Developed method of differential prediction. Diplomate in Psychology Am. Psychol. Assn. Mem. Am. Ednl. Research Assn. (sec.-treas., 1943-46), Am. Psychol. Assn., Phi Delta Kappa. Author: Differential Diagnosis of Ability in School Children, 1934; The Scientific Aptitude Test; (with others) The Victory Corps Aeronautics Aptitude Test; Multiple Aptitude Tests; (with others) The Lincoln Project, 1962; also bulletins and contbr. to ednl. and psychol. jours. Home: Los Altos CA Died Jan. 21, 1972; buried Alta Mesa Cemetery Palo Alto CA

SEGNI, ANTONIO, former pres. of Italian Republic; b. Sassari, Feb. 2, 1891; Degree Agrl. and Comml. Law; m. Laura Segni; children—Mario, Giuseppe, Celestino, Paolo. Teacher agrarian law universities Pavia, Perugia, Cagliari; rector Sassari U.; under-sec. Ministry Agr. 2d Bonomi Govt., 1944-45, Parri Govt., 1945, 1st De Gasperi Govt., 1945-46; minister agr., 1946-51, chmn. com. for reform agrarian coops., 1946-48; prepared, put into practice Land Reform Bill; minister pub. instrn., 1951-54; prime minister Republic of Italy, 1955-57, 59-60; foreign minister of Italy, 1960-62; pres. Italian Republic, 1962-64. Decorated Cavaliere della Milizia Aurata and the Gran Croce dell 'Ordine Piano (Holy See). Member of the Academia dei Lincei. Member Christian Democratic Party. Author: L'intervento Adesivo; L'Intervento in Apello; II Processo Monitorio; La Rome Italy Died Dec. 1, 1972.

SEIBEL, FREDERICK OTTO, cartoonist; b. Durhamville, Oneida County, N.Y., Oct. 8, 1886; s. Carl Theodore and Clara Dorothy (Felter) S.; ed. high sch., Oneida, N.Y., 1902-05, Art Students' League, N.Y. City, 1905-07; studied under Kenyon Cox, Howard Pyle, Frank Vincent DuMond, Albert Sterner; m. Edna M. Anderson, Jan. 21, 1914. Began as commercial artist, 1911; with advertising agency, Utica, N.Y., 1912-15; cartoonist with Utica Herald-Dispatch, 1915; staff cartoonist Albany Knickerbocker Press, 1916-26; news cartoonist Richmond (Va.) Times-Dispatch, 1926-68. Received Harmon award for cartoons, 1928. Mem. Nat. Cartoonist Soc. (charter), Assn. Am. Editorial Cartoonist's (charter), Pi Delta Epsilon. Episciopalian. Mason (32 deg., Shriner). Club: Va. Press (charter). Home: Richmond VA Died June 18, 1969.

SEIBELS, GEORGE GOLDTHWAITE, naval officer; b. Montgomery, Ala., Jan. 4, 1872; s. Emmet and Anne (Goldthwaite) S.; ed. Coll. Prep. Sch., Culpeper County, Va., 1886-88, Starke Univ. Sch., Montgomery, Ala., to 1896; m. Aileen Pettit, May 7, 1907; children—Mabel Pettit, Emmet, George Goldthwaite. Asst. paymaster U.S. Navy, 1896; advanced through grades to highest grade of Supply Corps and commd. pay dir. with rank of rear adm., Sept. 1933; retired from active service, Feb. 1, 1936. Decorated Dewey medal (Battle of Manila Bay), Spanish-Am. War, Philippine Campaign, Mexican Campaign and World War medals. Episcopalian. Home: 711 S. Perry St., Montgomery AL‡

SEIBOLD, MYRON JAMES, lawyer; b. Mt. Vernon, O., June 20, 1908; s. Frederick C. and Caroline (Fehr) S.; B.S. in Elec. Engring., Carnegie Inst. Tech., 1929; LL.B., George Washington U., 1933; m. Alma M. Winterbottom, July 29, 1932; children—Myron James, Suzanne Carol, Daryl Alma. Jr. examiner U.S. Patent Office, 1929-34; admitted to D.C. bar, 1933, Mich. bar, 1937, Cal. bar, 1960; practiced in Detroit, 1957-59; patent counsel Square D Co., Detroit, 1934-57; patent atty. Garrett Corp., Los Angeles, 1959-60; asso. firm Fulwider, Patton, Rieber, Lee & Utecht, Los Angeles, 1960-66, partner, 1967-70. Mem. Am., Fed., Los Angeles County, Santa Monica Bay Dist. bar assns., Am., Los Angeles patent law assns., State Bar Cal., Mich., Bar Assn. D.C., U.S. Supreme Ct., Eta Kappa Nu. Home: Los Angeles CA Died Dec. 17, 1970.

SEIDNER, HOWARD MAYO, physician; b. Chgo., July 23, 1921; s. Maurice P. and Bertha (Reisman) S.; B.S., Northwestern U., 1941; M.D., U. Ill., 1944; m. Rosalind S. Pearlman, Apr. 4, 1953; children—Ruth, Linda, Ann. Intern, Michael Reese Hosp., 1944-45, resident, 1945-47; practice medicine specializing in obstetrics and gynecology, Chgo., 1947-68; chief dept. obstetrics and gynecology Bethany Hosp., Chgo., 1956-68; obsete. cons. Chicago Board of Health, 1955-68. Diplomate Am. Bd. Obstetrics and Gynecology. Fellow Am. Coll. Obstetrics and Gynecology; mem. World, Am., Pan Am. med. assns., American Soc. Abdominal Surgeons, Ill., Chgo. med. socs., Ill. Soc. Med. Research, Am. Geriatrics Soc., Am. Writers Assn., Royal Society Health (Great Britain). Contributed articles in field to med. jours. Research in method of stabilizing aspirin in aqueous solution. Home: IL Died May 31, 1968.

SEIGLE, JOHN SANDERS, telephone co. exec.; b. Americus, Kan., Oct. 4, 1914; s. Andrew Jackson and Nellie (Sanders) S.; B.S. in Elec. Engring., U. Kan., 1937; m. Elizabeth Cornelia Cummings Hughes, Jan. 14, 1967; children by former marriage—John Michael, Elizabeth Ann, Barbara Lynn, Mary Kathleen; stepchildren—Gwen Hughes, Norman Hughes. With So. Bell Tel. & Tel. Co., 1936-73, v.p., gen. mgr., 1957-64, v.p., comptroller, 1964-73. Pres. Atlanta Jr. Achievement, 1965-67; chmn. bd. So. area Jr. Achievement, 1968. Mem. Armed Forces Communications and Electronics Assn., Alpha Tau Omega. Rotarian. Home: Atlanta GA Died 1973.

SEITZ, CHARLES EDWARD, agrl. engr.; b. Reno, Nov. 6, 1890; s. Edward Lewis and Fannie Harvey (Leonard) S.; student U. Nev., 1911-12; asso. degree, Ont. Agrl. Coll., 1914; student Ia. State Coll., 1917, also corr. studies in engring., architecture, bus.; m. Nancy Dove Hughes, Jan. 23, 1918; children—Martha Leonard (Mrs. John David Wey), Charles Edward. Drainage engr. Va. Agrl. Extension Service, 1914-16, agrl. engr., 1916-19; asso. prof., head agrl. engring. dept. Va. Poly. Inst., 1919-22, prof., head dept., dir. extension, research and resident teaching, 1922-54, ret. Mem. Va. Planning Bd., 1930-38; chmn. Va. Com. on Relation of Electricity to Agr., 1924-34; chmn. Va. Farm Electric Council, 1945-52; pres., chmn. bd. dirs. Va. Tech. Athletic, Council, 1949-53; chmn. Va. Tech.-Blacksburg-Christianburg Water Authority, 1954-72. Served with 1st Va. Cav., Mexican Border Service, 1916-17, as cadet pilot, USAAF, 1917-18. Recipient Cyrus Hall McCormick Gold Medal, 1951; selected Man of the Year in Service to Agr., 1954. Fellow Am. Soc. Agrl. Engrs. (pres. 1932-33); mem. Soc. Promotion Engring. Edn., Sigma Alpha Epsilon, Epsilon, Sigma Phi, Alpha Zeta. Club: University (Blacksburg). Agrl. Engring. bldg. named Seitz Bldg. in his honor, Va. Polytech. Inst. Address: Blacksburg VA Died Aug. 20, 1972; buried Westview Cemetery, Blacksburg, VA

SEITZ, FRANK NOAH, gas co. exec.; b. St. Louis County, Mo., Sept. 25, 1909; s. Frank Lee and Catherine (Felchlin) S.; B.S. in Civil Engring., Washington U., St. Louis, 1933; m. Caroline Ruth Garrell, May 5, 1937. With So. Cal. Gas Co., 1939-50; with So. Counties Gas Co., Los Angeles, 1950-69, vice president, 1955-63, senior vice president, 1963-69, also director. Div. leader campaigns Santa Monica chpt. A.R.C., Los Angeles chpts. Am. Heart Assn. and Community Chest. Mem. Cal. Republican Central Com., 1958-69. Served to lt. col. AUS, 1940-46. Mem. Am., Pacific Coast gas assns., Am. Mgmt. Assn., Sales and Marketing Assn. Los Angeles (past dir.), U.S., Cal. chambers commerce, Sigma Xi. Presbyn. (past chmn. trustees). Mason. Home: Santa Monica CA Died Nov. 7, 1969.

SEITZ, IRA JAMES, physician; b. Mandan, N.D., Apr. 30, 1898; s. William H. and Fannie M. (Robbins) S.; student Hedding Coll., 1917-19; A.B., Asbury Coll., 1922; M.S., Northwestern U., Chgo., 1927, M.D., 1930; m. Jennie S. Garvey, June 26, 1922. Intern Wesley Meml. Hosp., Chgo., 1930-31; pvt. practice medicine, Roseburg, Ore., 1931-71; mem. officer VA, 1931-64; cons. gen. surgery urology, med. adminstrn. VA Hosp., Roseburg, 1964-71; mem. staffs Wahoe County, St. Mary's hosps., 1942-48. Served with AUS, 1918; served to lt. col., M.C., AUS, 1944-46. Recipient citation V.F.W. for work with Cal. vets. at VA Hosp., Fresno, 1952. Fellow A.C.S.; mem. A.M.A., Cal. Med. Soc., S.A.R., Mayflower Soc., Am. Legion, D.A.V., Sigma Xi. Methodist. Mason (Shriner), Kiwanian. Author: Studies in Avian Diabetes Mellitus, 1927. Home: Roseburg OR Died Sept. 3, 1971.

SEKERA, ZDENEK, educator; b. Tabor, Czechoslovakia, July 3, 1905; s. Emil and Marie (Zizkova) S.; B.A., M.A. in Math. and Physics, Masaryk U., Brno, Czechoslovakia, 1928; R.N.Dr. in Theoretical Physics, Charles U., Prague, Czechoslovakia, 1931, Ph.D. in Meteorology and Dynamic Oceanography, 1939; m. Gabriela Sterbova, Jan. 7, 1943; 1 son, Michael. Came to U.S., 1946, naturalized, 1953. Pvt. dozent meteorology Charles U., 1939, 45-47; sr. theoretical meteorologist U. Chgo., 1947-48; vis. asso. prof. U. Cal. at Los Angeles, 1948-49, mem. faculty, 1949-73, prof. meteorology, 1955-73, chmn. dept., 1962-67, mem. Inst. Geophysics, 1969-73. Cons. physics of planetary atmospheres to industry, 1957-73; mem. aerological commn. Internat. Meteorol. Orgn., 1945-49; mem. radiation commn. Internat. Assn. Meteorology and Atmospheric Physics, 1957-73. Recipient C.G. Rossby Research Medal Am. Meteorol. Soc., 1966. Guggenheim fellow, 1956, 61; NSF sr. post-doctoral fellow, 1957, 61. Mem. Am., Royal meteorol. socs., Am. Geophys. Union, Am. Optical Soc., A.A.A.S. Asso. editor Geophys. Research, 1968-70. Contbr. to Atmospheric Physics, 1969-73. Home: Los Angeles CA Died Jan. 1, 1973.

SEKERS, NICHOLAS THOMAS, silk mfg. co. exec., designer; b. Sopron, Hungary, Dec. 15, 1910; s. Leopold Paul and Jolan (Krausz) S.; student Acad. Commerce, Budapest, Textile Tech. Coll., Krefeld; M.A. (hon.), U. Manchester, 1963; m. Agota Anna Balkanyi, Dec. 12, 1941; children—Christine Ann (Mrs. Jean Raymond Roger Baudrand), David Nicholas Oliver, Alan Peter John. Dir., Adria Silk Mills Ltd., Budapest, 1931-37; mng. dir. West Cumberland Silk Mills Ltd., Whitehaven, 1938-72; chmn. Sekers Fabrics, Ltd., Whitehaven, 1966-72; mem. Council Indsl. Design, 1966-72. Mem. council Soc. Royal Opera House, 1962-72, Shakespeare Theatre Trust, 1967-72; freeman Worshipful Co. Musicians, 1966-72; chmn. London Mozart Players, 1962-67, vice chmn., 1967-72; chmn. council London Philharmonic Orchestra, 1965-67, vice chmn., 1967-72. Trustee Glyndebourne Arts Trust, Rosehill Arts Trust, Whitehaven, Chichester Festival Theatre; bd. govs. Yehudi Menuhin Sch., Stoke d'Abernon. Created knight bachelor, 1965; decorated mem. Order Brit. Empire; hon. asso. Manchester Coll. Art and Design, 1963; recipient Duke Edinburgh prize for elegant design, 1962, Harper's Bazaar trophy for creative design, 1962. Fellow soc. Indsl. Artists, Royal Soc. Arts (v.p.). Home: London England Died June 23, 1972.

SELBY, MARK WEBSTER, shoe mfr.; b. Portsmouth, O., Aug. 14, 1876; s. George Dyar and Lydia Verlinda (Webster) S.; student Ohio Wesleyan U., 1894-97; m. Maude Odgan Grimes, June 9, 1898 (died Jan. 17, 1904); 1 dau., Alice Christine (Mrs. Edward M. Cobb); m. 2d, Adelaide Hare, Jan. 20, 1912. With Selby Shoe Co., 1897-1928, becoming v.p. and treas., now dir., retired; pres. Mitchellace, Inc., Standard Supply Co.; dir. Hurth Hotel Co., Citizen's Budget Co.; v.p. and trust officer Security Central Nat. Bank (mem. exec. com.). Trustee Ohio Wesleyan U. Mem. Phi Kappa Psi. Mason. Methodist. Clubs: Rotary, Country (Portsmouth); Cincinnati Club. Home: 1321 4th St. Office: National Bank Bldg., Portsmouth OH‡

SELDEN, CHARLES A(LBERT), newspaper corr., retired; b. Nantucket, Mass., Oct. 10, 1870; s. Charles and Lydia C. (Hodges) S.; A.B., Brown U., 1893, hon. M.A. from same university, 1933; m. Grace, d. Rev. John A. Savage, Oct. 13, 1895; children—Eva (Mrs. C. Everett Banks), John Charles. On staffs Providence Journal and New York Sun, 1893-1904, New York Evening Post, 1904-16; traveling corr. New York Times Mag., 1916-17; Paris corr. New York Times, 1918-19; European corr. N.Y. Evening Post, 1920; mag. writer in Asia, Europe and America, 1921-28; then London correspondent New York Times until Dec. 31, 1936. Clubs: Overseas Writers (Washington); Pacific Club (Nantucket); National Liberal (London). Home: 29 Liberty St., Nantucket MA‡

SELDEN, LYNDE, express exec.; b. Duluth, Minn., Nov. 10, 1891; s. Stephen L. and Florence L. (Dickinson) S.; B.A., Yale, 1913; m. Muriel Wiggin, May 15, 1917; children—Muriel, Joan, Albert Wiggin. With Guaranty Trust Co., 1913-14, 1916, Engring. Securities Corp., N.Y. City, 1918, Am. Sugar Refining Co., N.Y. City, 1919-27, sec., 1926-27; v.p. Chase Nat. Bank, 1928-36; with Am. Express Co. from 1936, vice chmn., 1941-56, now dir.; former director Otis Elevator Co. Served as 2d lt. AS Aircraft Prodn., 1917-18. Member Squadron A Ex-members Assn., N.Y. Soc. Mil. and Naval Officers World Wars, Inc. Republican. Episcopalian. Clubs: N.Y. Yacht (N.Y.); Round Hill Country; Belle Haven: Indian Harbor Yacht. Home: Greenwich CT Died Sept. 26, 1972; buried Putnam Cemetery, Greenwich CT

SELDES, GILBERT (VIVIAN), author, critic, ret. ednl. administrator; born in Alliance, New Jersey, January 3, 1893; s. George S. and Anna (Saphro) S.; prep. edn. Central High Sch., Phila. Pa.; A.B., Harvard, 1914; m. Alice Wadhams Hall, June 21, 1924 (dec.); children—Timothy, Marian. Music critic, Phila. Evening Ledger, 1914-16; newspaper corr. abroad during World War; polit. corr. in Washington, D.C., of L'Echo de Paris, 1918; asso. editor Colliers, 1919; asso., later mng. editor, The Dial, 1920-23; dramatic critic of Dial, of N.Y. Evening Graphic, 1929; columnist, N.Y. Journal, 1931-37; dir. television programs CBS, 1937-45; prof., also dean The Annenberg School of Communications, U. of Pa., 1959-63. Served as sergt. U.S. Army, 1918. Mem. National Institute of Arts and Letters, also Phi Beta Kappa. Author: Seven Lively Arts, 1924; The Stammering Century, 1928; The Movies and the Talkies, 1929; The Wings of the Eagle, 1929; The Years of the Locust, 1933; Mainland, 1936; Movies for the Millions, 1937; Your Money and Your Life, 1938; Proclaim Liberty, 1942; The Great Audience, 1950; Writing for Television, 1952; The Public Arts, 1956; also play: adaptation of Lysistrata, 1930; historial motion picture: This Is America, 1933; also murder mysteries under pseudonym Foster Johns. Co-author: (play) Swingin' the Dream, 1939. Editor: Portable Ring Lardner, 1946. Home: New York City NY Died Sept. 28, 1970.

SELIG, LESTER NORTH, ofcl. Gen. Am. Transportation Corp.; b. Brooklyn, N.Y., Sept. 10, 1893; s. Louis N. and Bertha (Norden) S.; prep. edn. Boys' High Sch., Brooklyn; grad. Brooklyn Law Sch., 1914; m. Helen Montgomery, Mar. 8, 1925; 1 dau., Shirley Selig Frey; m. 2d, Vera Sellwood, Oct. 11, 1946; children—Leslie Veva, Louis North. Began as workman in shops of Gen. Am. Tank Car Corp., Chgo., 1914; now chmn. exec. com. Gen. Transp. Co., Chgo.; dir. Gen. Am. Transp. Company. Chmn. bd. trustees Chgo. Med. School, 1948-56. mem. Palm Springs Airport Commn. Mem. Palm Springs City Council, 1966-68. Served as enlisted man, advancing to 2d lt., 1st lt. and capt., engrs., U.S. Army, 1917-18; with A.E.F., May 1918-June 1919. With W.P.B., 1942-45; mem. tech. adv. com. Q.M.C., 1943-45. Decorated Legion of Honor (France). Mem.Am.-Ry. Car Inst. (pres. 1954-56), Art Inst. Chicago (life), Phi Alpha. Republican. Jewish. Clubs: Standard, Tavern, Cloud; Tamarisk County (Palm Springs, Cal.); Palette. Home: Palm Springs CA Died Nov. 23, 1968; buried San Gorgonio Meml. Park, Banning CA

SELIGMAN, BEN B(ARUCH), educator, economist; b. Newark, Nov. 20, 1912; s. Reuben and Toby (Carlson) S.; A.B. cum laude, Bklyn. Coll., 1934; M.S., Columbia, 1936; m. Libby Contract, Oct. 1, 1938;children—Robert Eli, Ruth Miriam. Econs. tchr., N.Y.C. high schs., 1940-41; commodity analyst OPA, 1942-45; mng. editor Labor and Nation, 1945-46; lectr. econs. Bklyn. Coll., 1947-49; economist Council Jewish Fedns., 1946-53; dir. community services Jewish Labor Com., 1953-55; dir. Washington office Am. Jewish Com., 1955-56; internat. affairs analyst United Auto Workers, 1956-57; dir. research Retail Clerks Internat. Assn., 1957-65; prof. econs., dir. Labor Center, U. Mass., 1965-70. Acting dir. Office Jewish Population Research, 1949-50; asso. fellow Inst. Policy Studies, 1963-65; cons. in field, 1945-70; trustee Fed. Statistics Users Conf., 1959-65, joint Council Econ. Edn., 1962-65; reader U.S. Office Edn., 1966—. A Barton Hepburn fellow, 1935; recipient Philip Sterm Fund award, 1964; Guggenheim fellow, 1967-68; receipient Distinguished Alumnus award of honor Bklyn. Coll., 1968. Mem. Assn. Evolutionary Econs. (v.p. 1969), Indsl. Relations Research Assn. (bd. dirs. 1969—), Am. Econ. Assn., Assn. Evolutionary Econs., Adult Edn. Assn. Author: Main Currents in Modern Economics, 1962; Most Notorious Victory; Man in an Age of Automation, 1966; Permanent Poverty, An American Syndrome, 1968. Editor: Poverty as a Public Issue, 1965; Aspects of Poverty, 1968; Economics of Dissent, 1968. Home: Amherst MA Died Oct. 23, 1972.

SELIGMAN, SELIG JACOB, TV prod.; b. N.Y.C., Jan. 24, 1918; s. Jacob and Bella (Nemenoff) S.; B.A., N.Y.U., 1937; LL.B., Harvard, 1940, LL.M., 1941; m. Muriel Bienstock, Mar. 28, 1948; children—Joel, Brad, Dale, Lucy, Adam. Admitted to N.Y. bar, 1941; staff office gen. counsel Securities and Exchange Commission, 1941; branch counsel, consumers durable goods div. WPB, 1941-43; staff theatre dept. Paramount Pictures, assigned legal aspects U.S. versus Paramount litigation, 1946; asst. to v.p. United Paramount Theatres, 1948-50; v.p. Northio Theatres Corp., 1951; prod., writer ABC Western div., 1953; sta. mgr. KABC-TV, Los Angeles, 1953; v.p. ABC, 1958, exec. prod. Combat, Day in Court, Accused, Dr. I.Q., Shindig, Mickey, Gen. Hosp., The Young Marrieds, Charley, Candy, Hell in the Pacific, The High Commissioner, Midas Run, Cop-Out, Smashing Time, ABC-TV Network; pres. Am. Broadcasting-Paramount Theatres, Inc., subsidiary Selmur Prodns., Inc., 1960-69. Served with signal intelligence, AUS, 1943-45; U.S. pros., Nuremburg War Trials, 1945; staff Solicitor's Office, State Dept., 1945. Mem. Phi Beta Kappa. Author: Honey on the Hill, 1953, also numerous short stories. Home: Los Angeles CA Died June 20, 1969.

SELKE, GEORGE ALBERT, educator, govt. ofcl.; b. LaCrosse, Wis., June 28, 1888; s. Albert and Wilhelmina (Wokkenfus) S.; grad. State Tchrs. Coll., St. Cloud, Minn., 1913; A.B., U. Minn., 1916; A.M., Columbia, 1926; honorary degree University of Vienna, 1946; LL.D. (honorary), University of North Dakota, 1947; married Eda Carol Ehri, 1920. Teacher rural schs., S.D., 1907-08; prin. village sch., Sartell, Minn., 1908-10; county supt. schs., Benton County, 1910-13; supt. schs., Mabel and Chokio, 1913-18; dir. elementary and high schs., Minn. State Dept. Edn., 1920-24; successively assistant professor, lecturer, U. of Minn., 1924-27; pres. State Teachers Coll., St. Cloud, 1927-46; chancellor U. of Montana 1946-51; deputy chief edn. and cultural relations div., High Commn. for Germany, 1951, chief div. of cultural affairs, office of public affairs, 1952-70. Private, depot brigade, United States Army, 1918; maj., U.S. Army, Military Government, England, Italy and Austria, 1943-46; cultural and educational dir. Salzburg, Austria, 1945; endl. mission to Korea for U.S. War Dept., 1948. Director Nat. Youth Admn. for Minn., 1935-39, Minn. State dir. War Manpower Commn., 1943. Gov. Minn-Dakotas Dist. of Kiwanis International, 1941 (chairman. Internat. Com. on Boys and Girls Work, 1942); pres. Am. Assn. of Teachers Colls., 1941-42; mem. Nat. Commn. on Colleges and Civilian Defense. Mem. N.E.A., Phi Delta Kappa, Kappa Delta Pi. Presbyn. Author: (with Julius Boraas) Rural School of Administration and Supervision, 1926; Handbook for County Superintendents of Schools (with C. B. Lund), 1935. Home: Bad Godesberg Germany Died Oct. 1970.

SELKE, W(ILHELM) ERICH (CHRISTIAN), univ. prof.; b. La Crosse, Wis., Nov. 9, 1885; s. Albert and Wilhelmina (Wokkenfusz) S.; standard diploma Minn. State Teachers Coll., St. Cloud, 1911; A.B., U. of Minn., 1916, A.M., 1922, Ph.D., 1933; m. Lulu Mabel Elliott, July 25, 1917 (dec.); children—Albert George (deceased), Elizabeth, Janet. Rural sch. teacher Bon Homme Co., S.D., 1908-10; prin. graded sch., Kinney, Minn., 1911-13; St. Paul Park, 1913-15; supt. schs. Atwater, 1916-17, Paynesville, 1917-19, Wayzata, 1922-25; sec. Com. Recommendations, U. of Minn., 1919-22; dir. teacher training and placement N.D. State Teachers Coll. Mayville, 1925-36; prof. edn. U. of N.D., 1936-66. Alderman City of Grand Forks, 1940-49, pres. city council, 1946-48. Pres. Lake Agassiz Boy Scouts of Am., 1947-48, nat. council rep. 1946-51, mem. exec. bd. since 1938. Mem. N.E.A., N.D. Edn. Assn. (cons. mem. legislative com., 1948-53, pres. 1952-53; past dir., past mem. welfare com.). Mem. bd. dirs. Grand Forks Co. Red Cross, 1938-40, N.D. Sch. Adminstrs. Assn., Assn. Supervision and Curriculum Development, Nat. Council Teachers English, Nat. Soc. Study of Edn., Phi Delta Kappa, Alpha Phi Omega. Conglist. Mason. Recipient Silver Beaver award, 1947. Author: Our Government in North Dakota, 1931. Adv. editor Educational Leadership, 1948-49. Contbr. numerous articles to profl. mags. Home: Grand Fork ND Died Sept. 26, 1966; buried Meml. Park Cemetery Grand Forks ND

SELLARDS, ELIAS HOWARD, geologist; b. Carter City, Ky., May 2, 1875; s. Wiley W. and Sarah (Menach) S.; B.A., University of Kansas, 1899, M.A., 1901; Ph.D., Yale University, 1903; married Anna Mary Alford, September 4, 1907; children—Helen Alford, Daphne Alford. Asst. Kansas State Geological Survey, 1900-01, Carnegie Museum, Pittsburgh, summer, 1903; instr. geology and mineralogy, Rutgers Coll., 1903-04; prof. geology and zoology, U. of Fla., 1904-07; state geologist of Fla., 1907-18; geologist, Bur. of Economic Geology, U. of Texas, 1918-22, chief geologist, 1922-25, associate director, 1925-32, director, 1932-45; director emeritus since 1945; director Texas Memorial Museum, Austin, since 1938; expert geologist Tex.-Okla. boundary dispute, 1921. Mem. first Conf. for Conservation of Natural Resources, Washington, 1908. Mem. Geol. Soc. of America (councillor 1938-40, 1943; v.p. 1943), Paleontological Society (president 1942), Society Econ. Paleontologists and Mineralogists (president 1938), Am. Assn. Petroleum Geologists, (hon. mem. since 1946). Author of reports and papers in Bulletin, Geol. Soc. of America, Am. Jour. of Science, Jour. of Geology, Kan. State Geol. Survey. State Geol. Survey of Fla. and Bur. of Economic Geology, U. of Tex. Home: 2525 Jarratt Av., Austin 21 TX‡

SELLS, CATO, b. Vinton, Ia.; s. George Washington and Elizabeth Catherine (Hedden) S.; ed. pub. schs., LaPorte City, Ia.; A.M. and hon. LL.D., Cornell Coll., Mt. Vernon, Ia.; hon. LL.D., Baylor U., Waco, Tex.; m. Lola Abbott McDaniel, June 30, 1891;

children—Dorothy M., Donald D., Mrs. H.C. Burke, Jr. Admitted to bar, 1889 and practiced at LaPorte City and Vinton; served as city atty., later mayor of LaPorte City; elected state's atty., 1891, and re-elected, 1893; U.S. dist. atty. by apptmt. Pres. Cleveland, 1894-99; (successfully prosecuted the noted Van Luven conspiracy pension fraud cases); moved to Texas, 1907; pres. Tex. State Bank & Trust Co., Cleburne; commr. Indian Affairs, by apptmt. of President Wilson, 1913-21. First state chmn. orgn. promoting Texas Centennial Exposition, 1924-25; chmn. program com. and toastmaster on The All Texas Special Good Will Tour," 1927. Democrat (former Dem. nat. committeeman for Texas; del.-at-large to Dem. Nat. Conv. at Kansas City, Baltimore, and New York). Presbyn. Mason, Odd Fellow. Hon. mem. Rotary and Lions clubs. Home: 2016 Windsor Pl., Fort Worth TX‡

SELMER, ERNST WESTERLUND, educator; b. Halmbyboda, Uppsala, Sweden, Apr. 23, 1890; s. Ludwig Marius and Nina Maria Mathilda (Westerlund) S.; grad. in philology, U. Oslo (Norway), 1913, Ph.D., 1918; m. Ella Sejersted, Sept. 27, 1968. Univ. fellow German lang. U. Oslo, 1917, lectr. German philology and gen. phonetics, 1924, lectr. German, 1918-60, apptd. to U. Phonetics Inst., 1918-60. Mem. Vidensk. Akad., Frisian Acad. (Netherlands), Royal Danish Soc. Sci. and Lang., Sci. Soc. Uppsala. Author: Haandbok i elementaer Fonetikk, 5th edit., 1958; Apokope und Zirkumflex, 1930; Experimentelle Beitrage zur Zulu Phonetik, 1935; Sunnmorestudier, 1948; Tysk lydlaere, 1936, others. Editor: last 6 edits. Aschehougs Fremmedorbok, also Opuscula Phonetica; Norwegian editor: Nordist Laerebok for Talepaedagoger, vol. 1, 1954, vol. 2, 1955. Address: Oslo Norway Died 1971.

SELVAGE, WATSON, college prof.; b. at New York, June 19, 1873; s. Capt. John T. Watson and Annie Marie (Bartemus) S.; B.A., St. Stephen's Coll., Annandale, N.Y., 1898, M.A., 1904; A.B., Cornell U., 1902; M.A., U. of Pa., 1904; Harvard, 1904-5; Columbia; B.A., M.A., King's Coll., Royal U. of Windsor, N.S., 1905; fellow Owens Coll., Manchester U., Eng.; unmarried. Lecturer on philosophy, Coll. City of New York, 1905-11, Manchester U., 1908-9; prof. ethics and apologetics, U. of South, 1911. Pres. Alumni of St. Stephen's Coll. Episcopalian. Mem. Sigma Alpha Epsilon, Phi Eta. Club: Graduates (New York). Address: Sewanee TN‡

SEMANS, EDWIN WALKER, lawyer; b. Uniontown, Pa., Dec. 4, 1901; s. Thomas Breckenridge and Virginia Belle (Smith) S.; student Lawrenceville Sch.; B.S., Princeton, 1924; LL.B., U. Pa., 1928; m. Mary Stark, May 2, 1931; children—Edwin Walker, Harold Stark. Admitted to Pa. bar, 1928, U.S. Supreme Ct. bar, 1938; associated with MacCoy, Evans & Lewis, 1968-71. Mem. bd. mgrs. Armed Services br. YMCA. Mem. Am., Pa., Phila. bar assns., Phi Delta Phi. Presbyn. Clubs: Union League (Philadelphia); Merion Cricket (Haverford, Pa.); Merion Golf (Ardmore, Pa.). Home: Narberth PA Died Mar. 18, 1971; buried West Laurel Hill Cemetery.

SEMANS, HARRY MERRICK, dental surgeon; b. Delaware, O., Oct. 1, 1867; s. William Oliver and Abigail (Merrick) S.; B.A., Ohio Wesleyan U., 1890, M.A., 1897; student Phila. Dental Coll., 1894-95; D.D.S., New York Coll. of Dentistry, 1897; studied Starling-Ohio Med. Coll., Columbus, O., 1912-14; m. Besse Ann Merrick-Bell, Oct. 8, 1901; children—Frank Merrick, Ruth Ellen. Practiced at Columbus, 1897-1915; instr. dental technic, 1898-1901, dental anatomy and anesthesia, 1901-03, prof. operative dentistry, 1903-07, dental dept. Ohio Med. U.; prof. operative dentistry and dean dental dept. Starling-Ohio Med. Coll., 1907-14; prof. operative dentistry and dean Coll. of Dentristry, Ohio State U., 1914-38, dean emeritus since July 1, 1938. Member Signal Corps, 14th Regt., Ohio Nat. Guard, 1889-92. Pres. Am. Assn. Dental Schools, 1937-38. Fellow Am. Coll. of Dentists; mem. Am. Dental Assn., Ohio State Dental Soc. (pres. 1920-21), Columbus Dental Soc. (ex-pres.), Am. Inst. Dental Teachers (ex-pres.), Phi Kappa Psi, Psi Omega, Omicron Kappa Upsilon (hon.), S.A.R. Democrat. Mem. 1st Community Ch. Mason (32 deg., Shriner). Colorado Springs CO‡

SEMBOWER, CHARLES JACOB, professor English; b. Newburg, W.Va., Apr. 3, 1871; s. Henry Frank and Sarah Ann (Lackey) S.; A.B., Ind. U., 1892; Harrison fellow, U. of Pa., 1907-9, Ph.D., 1909; m. Lois Alta Brunt, June 26, 1901. Instr. in English, Ind. U., 1892; asst. in English, Cornell U., 1895-7; asst. prof. English, 1897-03, asso. prof., 1903-9, prof., 1909-—, Ind. U. Conglist. Mem. Modern Lang Assn. America, Am. Acad. Polit. and Social Science, Sigma Chi, Phi Beta Kappa. Author: The Life and Poetry of Charles Cotton, 1911. Address: Bloomington IN‡

SEMMANN, LIBORIUS, music teacher; b. Grafton, Wis., Oct. 30, 1873; s. Hermann Gottlieb and Johanna (Vocket) S.; student harmony, counterpoint, composition and orchestration under Hugo Kann, Milwaukee, piano under William Boeppler, Milwaukee; Mus. Doc., Marquette Univ., Milwaukee, 1930; m. Luise Damm, of Niederdorla, Thuringen, Germany, August 7, 1900; children—Armin, Waldemar. Teacher Boeppler Sch. of Music, 1897-99; with Wis. Conservatory of Music, 1899-1910; dean Coll. of Music, Marquette Univ., 1911-30; with Musical Art Studios and Shorewood Opportunity School, Milwaukee, since 1930. Member Music Teachers' National Association, Music Supervisors' Nat. Conf., Wis. State Teachers' Assn., Wis. Music Teachers' Assn. (pres. 1931), Assn. Presidents and Past Presidents of State Music Teachers' Assns. (organizer and pres. 3 terms, now hon. pres.), Milwaukee Civic Music Assn. (pres. 1927-29, 1933-34), Wis. Music Teachers Assn. (pres. 1932-34), Am. Interprofessional Inst. Lutheran. Composer piano pieces, male, female and mixed choruses, sacred, secular, and patriotic songs, etc. Author of book of poetry, Priase Ye the Lord. Home: 3523 N. 23d St., Milwaukee WI‡

SEMSCH, OTTO FRANCIS, architect, cons. engr.; b. Milwaukee, Wis., Sept. 26, 1872; s. Francis and Aurelia (Sieber) S.; student Tech. U., Karlsruhe, Germany, 1891-92, Tech. U., Charlottenburg-Berlin, Germany, 1892-94; m. Gertrude Luedeke (died Nov. 15, 1935); 1 dau., Gertrude May. Began as archtl. engr., 1894; designer of foundations, structural and mechanical engring. of Mills Hotel, Singer, Bourne, Scribner, Furness-Withy and Internat. Merchantile Marine office bldgs., New York, Gwynne Bldg., Cincinnati, O., First Nat. Bank, Conn. Mutual Life Ins. Bldg., Hartford, Conn., U.S. Naval Acad., Annapolis, Md., St. Luke's Hosp., New York, St. Margaret's Memorial Hosp., Pittsburgh, Pa., Naval Hosp., Washington, D.C.; architect Montclair (N.J.) Municipal Bldg.; designer of wind-bracing of the Singer Tower. Registered architect N.Y. and N.J.; licensed professional engr., N.Y. Mem. bd. of edn., Montclair, N.J.; mem. Soc. Am. Mil. Engrs. Republican. Congregationalist. Contbr. archtl. articles to jours. Home: 143 E. 39th St. Office: 111 E. 40th St., New York NY*‡

SENANAYAKE, DUDLEY SHELTON, former prime minister Ceylon (name now Sri Lanka); b. Colombo, Ceylon, June 19, 1911; s. Don Stephen and Emily Maud (Dunuwille) S.; ed. St. Thomas' Coll., Mt. Lavinia; natural sci. tripos, M.A., Corpus Christi Coll. (fellow), Cambridge (Eng.) U.; barrister-at-law. Engaged in practice of law, Ceylon; mem. State Council under Donoughmore Constn. to rep. Dedigama Constituency, 1936; minister agr. and lands in first cabinet after independence, 1947; prime minister, minister def. and external affairs, 1952-54; resigned as prime minister, 1953; prime minister, minister def. and external affairs, mem. Parliament for Dedigama, 1960-73; prime minister, 1965-70. Pres. United Nat. Party. Home: Colombo Sri Lanka Died Apr. 12, 1973.

SENGSTACK, JOHN F(REDERICK), management cons., accountant; b. N.Y. City, Apr. 28, 1893; s. John and Katherine (Damke) S.; student N.Y.U.; m. Mildren Myers, 1938; children—Ruth, David. Management cons., indsl. engr., accountant; ret. partner Lybrand Ross Bros & Montgomery, N.Y. City, N.Y.; dir. Summy Birchard Pub. Co., music publs., Chicago, Ill.; dir. Doubleday & Co.; exec., trustee several estates and trusts. C.P.A., N.Y. Mem. Am. Inst. Accountants, Music Pubs. Assn. Am. (past pres.). Clubs: Downtown Athletic (N.Y.C.); Cliff Dwellers (Chgo.); Pine Valley (N.J.) Golf; Baltusrol Golf (Springfield, N.J.). Home: New York City NY Died Oct. 1970.

SENIOR, JOSEPH HOWE, retired corp. exec.; b. Philadelphia, Mar. 21, 1870; s. William Taylor and Sally (Howe) S.; ed. high sch., Philadelphia; m. Lily M. Mullikin, Aug. 18, 1890; children—Lillian Mae (Mrs. William M. Grover), Adele Gertrude. Dir. Am. Ins. Co., Bankers Indemnity Ins. Co., Foreign Vintages, Inc. Republican. Presbyn. Mason (32 deg., Shriner). Clubs: India House, Masonic (New York); Quogue County. Home: Maplewood NJ Miami FL Shadowlawn," Quogue, LI NY Office: Rockefeller Plaza, New York NY‡

SENTNER, RICHARD FAULKNER, steel co. exec.; b. N.Y.C., Sept. 28, 1902; s. Joseph and Juanita M. (Brandon) S.; student Columbia, 1918-19; m. Jessie H. Paull, Aug. 14, 1939; children—Richard Faulkner, Mary J.P., Edward H. With A. G. de Sherbinen & Co., N.Y.C., 1919-22, Jones &Laughlin Steel Corp., 1922-23, Anderson Meyer & Co., N.Y.C., 1923-26; salesman, sales mgr., Wheeling Steel Corp., 1926-47; with U.S. Steel Corp., Pitts., from 1948, asst. v.p., 1948-50, asst. exec. v.p., 1951-56, exec. v.p., from 1957; dir. Hoosier Crown Crop.; chmn. bd. Hoosin Crown Corp., Wheeling Stamping Co. Dir. U.S. Steel and Carnegie Pension Fund. Mem. Am. Iron and Steel Inst., Farm Equipment Inst., Am. Ordnance Assn. Republican. Episcopalian. Clubs: Duquesne (Pitts.); Pinnacle, Cloud (N.Y.C.); Carlton (Washington); Ligonier-Allegheny Country, Edgeworth (Sewickley, Pa.); Rolling Rock (Ligonier, Sewickley PA Died Dec. 26, 1971.

SERAKOFF, LEONARD, stock broker; b. St. Louis, Feb. 13, 1921; s. Morris and Anna (Zlotnikov) S.; B.A., U. Mo., 1942; m. Peggy Barbarash, Jan. 8, 1950; children—Charlene (Mrs. Teifeld), Betty Ann, Diane Lynn. Gen. partner Friedman, Brokaw & Co., St. Louis, 1950-61; v.p., dir. Semple, Jacobs & Co., Inc., St. Louis, 1961-65; gen. partner Kohlmeyer & Co., Chgo., 1965-66; asst. v.p. A. G. Becker & Co., Inc., Chgo., 1967. Bd. dirs., mem. exec. com. Midwest Stock Clearing Corp., Chgo., 1961-67; bd. govs. Midwest Stock Exchange, 1961-67, chmn. com. floor procedure, 1964-67; allied mem. N.Y. Stock Exchange, 1951-67; mem. Chgo. Bd. Trade, 1951-61. Mem. Chgo. Natural History Museum. Served to capt. AUS, 1942-46. Home: Wilmette IL Died Feb. 19, 1967.

SERLIN, OSCAR, theatrical producer; b. Yalowka, Grodnow, Russia, Jan. 30, 1901; s. Max and Fania Serlin; came to U.S., 1910; student Waller High Sch., Chicago, De Paul Acad., De Paul Univ., Chicago; married Jane Udell, 1932 (divorded); children—Michael David, Dorothy Fortune; married 2d, Babette de Sheim, August 9, 1942; 1 son, Anthony Block. First theatrical job, doorman Victoria Theatre, Chicago; later assistant manager, Olympic Theatre, Chicago; became author of vaudeville acts, then director of amateur shows and wrestling promoter; successively co-producer of The Guinea Pig (by Preston Sturges), Broken Dishes (by Martin Flavin), Lost Sheep (by Belford Forrest); was head of Eastern talent department for Paramount Pictures for 3 years; later assistant producer, Paramount Pictures; talent scout and assistant to David Selznick for Gone with the Wind, Tom Sawyer and Nothing Sacred; presented the Russian film, The New Gulliver, in U.S.; produced The City, Carnegie Foundation documentary film; adapted The Singer of Sorrow, Russian play and The King's Maid (by Ferenc Molnar); produced Life With Father (by Lindsay and Crouse), The Moon Is Down (by Steinbeck), The Family (by Victor Wolfson); Beggars Are Coming to Town (by Theodore Reeves); Life With Mother; Strip for Action (producer with co-authors Lindsay and Crouse); Washington Square (by Ruth Goodman and Augustus Goetz); first Anta Album, 1948. Sylvania TV awards com., 1951-54. Home: West Cornwall CT Died Feb. 27, 1971.

SETZER, RICHARD WOODROW, coll. ofcl.; b. Williamsburg, Va., Nov. 8, 1918; s. Richard Thomas and Evelyn (Poovey) S.; A.B., Lenior Rhyne Coll., 1939; M.A., George Peabody Coll., 1947, Ph.D. 1951; m. Joan Bliss, Jan. 10, 1942; children—Joan Marion, Jean Ree. High sch. tchr. and coach, N.C., 1939-42; asso. prof. econs. Catawba Coll., 1947-49; dean Sch. Bus., Lamar State Coll. Tech., 1951-61, dean coll., 1961-64, v.p. acad. affairs, 1964-69. Dir. Gateway Nat. Bank, Beaumont. Chmn. Beaumont Com. Employ Physically Handicapped, 1957-59, Beaumont Community Study Family and Children Problems, 1959-69. Bd. dirs. Beaumont Community Council. Served with AUS, 1942-46; ETO. Recipient Presdl. citation for meritorius ser. Com. Employment Physically Handicapped, 1959. Mem. Southwestern Social Sci. Assn., Phi Delta Kappa, Kappa Delta Pi, Alpha Tau Omega. Lutheran. Beaumont TX Died Mar. 9, 1969.

SEVIER, JOSEPH RAMSEY, clergyman, educator; b. Greeneville, Tenn., Dec. 18, 1877; s. Charles Lyman and Julia Elizabeth (Brown) S.; prep. edn., Randolph-Macon Acad., Front Royal, Virginia; A.B., King Coll., Bristol, Tenn., 1898, D.D. from same coll., 1914; studied Union Theol. Sem. of Va., 1900, 03; m. Edith Rogers Love, of St. Louis, Mo., Oct. 26, 1904; children—Virginia Love (Mrs. Edwin Langdon Hanna), John Love. Prin. high sch., Ellendale, Va., 1898-1900; ordained Presbyn. ministry, 1903; pastor 3d Ch., Lynchburg, Va., 1903-07, 2d Ch., Alexandria, 1907-11, 1st Ch., Augusta, Ga., 1911-25; pres. Fassifern Sch. for Girls, Hendersonville, N.C., since 1925. Charter mem. Schoolmasters' Club, Asheville, N.C.; mem. Camp Directors' Assn. America. Dir. and Owner Camp Greystone for Girls, Tuxedo, N.C. since 1920. Mason. Kiwanian (past gov. Carolinas Dist. Kiwanis Internat.). Home: Hendersonville NC‡

SEWALL, LEE GOODRICH, hosp. adminstr.; b. Marlin, Tex., Aug. 25, 1907; s. Francis Bates and Mary (Goodrich) S.; B.A., U. Tex., 1927, M.D., 1931; M.S. in Hosp. Adminstrn., Northwestern U., 1954; m. Mary Eleanor Andrews, Mar. 9, 1940; children—Murphy Andrews, Frank Bates. Intern Cleve. City Hosp., 1931-32; resident Deaconess Hosp., Cleve., 1932-33, Lakeside Hosp., Cleve., 1933-34; gen. practice medicine, Waco, Tex., 1934-38; med. officer VA Hosp., North Little Rock, Ark., 1938-42; sr. med. officer VA Hosp., Ft. Custer, Mich., 1942-44; clin. dir. VA Hosp., Lyons, N.J., 1944-46; chief psychiatry and neurology service VA br. office, St. Louis, 1946-47; dir. profl. services VA Hosp., Roanoke, Va., 1947-51; mgr. VA Hosp., Downey, Ill., 1951-55, Leech Farm, Pitts., 1955-57; hosp. dir. VA Hosp., Perry Point, Md., 1957-65, Consol. VA Hosp., Little Rock, 1965-71; director med. audit research project VA Hosp., Perry Point, 1948-64; assistant prof. public health administration School Hygiene and Public Health, Johns Hopkins, 1958-65; clin. prof. psychiatry Arkansas School Medicine, 1966-71. Served from major to lieutenant colonel, M.C., AUS, 1944-46. Diplomate Am. Bd. Psychiatry and Neurology. Fel. Am. Psychiat. Assn.; mem. A.M.A., Group For Advancement Psychiatry, Am. Coll. Hosp. Adminstrs., North Lake County Mental Health Soc. (past pres., dir.), Western Pa. Mental Health Assn. (dir.), Alpha Omega Alpha. Home: Little Rock AR Died Feb. 12, 1971.

SEWARD, ALLIN CAREY, JR., lawyer, UN ofcl.; b. Balt., May 5, 1909; s. Allin Carey and Helen E. (Parrott) S.; A.B., Johns Hopkins, 1931; student law sch., Georgetown U., 1930-42; student law sch. Temple U., 1944-45; m. Helen Dawkins, July 16, 1934; 1 son, Allin Carey; m. 2d, Lelia R. Pearson, Oct. 12, 1968. School tchr., social worker, 1931-37; with U.S.D.A., 1937-41; established system for purchase, allocation and distribution of fire-defense equipment Office Civilian Def. Dec. 1941-Mar. 1942; chief management engring. staff Fgn. Econ. Adminstrn., 1942-Oct. 1943; asst. to dir. dept. conf. and gen. services, U.N., Mar. 1946-June 1948, adminstrv. officer U.N. mediator in Palestine, June 1948-Jan. 1949; deputy dir. conf. div., U.N., Jan. 1949-Feb. 1950, chief U.N. field operations service, 1950-55, 60-64, dir. UN Purchasing and Transp. Div., 1955-60, deputy director Office of Gen. Services, 1964-chief Adminstrv. officer, Congo, in charge liquiddation of Operations des Nations Unies au Congo, disposal officer Emergency Force, Gaza, 1967. Entered USN, 1943; assistant to supply officer. Mem. Kappa Alpha. Democrat. Clubs: Manursing Island, Tudor and Stuart. Home: Georgetown CT Died May 19, 1971.

SEWELL, JESSE PARKER, clergyman; b. Viola, Tenn., Jan. 21, 1876; s. William Alexander and Nancy Tennessee (Barry) S.; prep. edn., Viola Normal Coll.; Nashville Bible School (now David Lipscomb Coll.); LL.D., Harding Coll., Searcy, Ark., 1933; m. Daisy Elizabeth McQuigg, June 1, 1899; 1 son, Jesse McQuigg; married 2d, Mrs. J. A. Rummells, April 1, 1948. Ordained to Ministry Ch. of Christ, 1895; pastor Houston Street Ch., Sherman, Tex., 1900-02 and 1905-06, First Ch., Dallas, 1902-05, San Angelo, 1906-12, Coll. Ch., Abilene, 1912-17, also pres. Abilene Christian Coll., 1912-24; built up coll. from non-accredited acad. to standard coll. with more than 700 students, now president emeritus; pastor of the South Side Church, Fort Worth, Tex., 1924, Fifth Avnue Church, Corsicana, Texas, 1925-27, Grove Avenue Church, San Antonio, 1927-46; special lecturer, Harding College, since 1949. Has conducted evangelistic campaigns in 25 states and in Washington, D.C.; a leader in prohibition campaign in Tex. for 25 yrs.; mem. state bd. mgrs. and nat. bd. dirs. Anti-Saloon League. Served as chmn. Am. Red Cross, Taylor County, Tex.; in charge S.A.T.C., Abilene Christian Coll., World War; active in Liberty Loan drives, etc. Mem. Tex. State Teachers' Assn. (life); exec. sec. Assn. of Tex. Colleges, 6 yrs. Author: The Bible in One Hundred Lessons, 1921; New Testament Outlines, Vol. I, 1922, Vol. II, 1923; Bible Lectures (3 vols.), 1919-23; The Church and the Ideal Educational Situation, 1931. Editor in chief Bible School Quarterly Series and Christian Education Training Series since 1932. Home: Sewell Hall, Harding College, Searcy AR‡

SEXTON, HAROLD EUSTACE, archbishop of B.C.; born at Adelaide, South Australia on May 14, 1888; son of Richard J. and Lucy (Sexton) S.; student St. Peter's Coll., Adelaide, Keble Coll., Oxford U., Trinity Coll., Toronto. Ordained deacon Ch. of England, 1911, priest, 1912; curate St. Paul's Ch., Port Adelaide, 1911-14, All Saints' Ch., Hindmarsh, 1915-16; vicar St. Martin's Ch., Hawksburn, Melbourne, 1920-23; S.P.G., preacher, 1923-24; curate St. Margaret's Ch., Westminster, 1925-27; vicar All Saints' Ch., Upper Norwood, 1927-35; bishop co-adjutor B.C., 1935-36, bishop of diocese, 1936, archbishop and metropolitan B.C., 1952-72. Served as chaplain BEF, 1916-1918. Home: Victoria BC Canada. Died Mar. 29, 1972.

SEXTON, JOHN MOODY, educator; b. Albia, Ia., Aug. 15, 1909; s. John Peter and Myrtle May (Moody) S.; B.S. in Edn., De Paul U., 1934; M.S. in Edn., Drake U., 1949; m. Betty Jane Scott, Dec. 5, 1937; children—Suzanne, John Dennis. Tchr., coach, Albia, 1936-38, W. Des Moines, Ia., 1938-43, St. Petersburg, Fla., 1943-48; Prin. South Side Jr. High Sch., St. Petersburg, 1948-54, Northeast Sr. High Sch., 1954-65; dir. Pinellas County pub. schs., Clearwater, Fla., 1965-67. Mem. Fla. com. So. Assn. Colls. and Schs., 1956-61. Served with AUS, 1944-45. Mem. Fla. Prins. Assn. (pres. 1955-56), Nat. Assn. Secondary School Prins. (pres. 1964-65). Rotarian (pres. St. Petersburg 1956-57). Home: St Petersburg FL Died July 4, 1967.

SEXTON, THOMAS SCOTT, life ins. co. exec.; b. Sistersville, W.Va., May 5, 1913; s. Michael P. and Josephine (Scott) S.; A.B., U. W.Va., 1935; M.D. (certificate of honor), U. Md., 1939; m. Elizabeth Ann Johnson, Nov. 23, 1940; 1 dau., Deborah Dudley (Mrs. James P. O'Callaghan). Intern Mercy Hosp., Balt., 1939-40; fellow Mayo Found., 1941, 45-47; asst. med. dir. Mass. Mut. Life Ins. Co., Springfield, 1947-51, asso. med. dir., 1951-56, med. dir., 1956-59, v.p., 1959-62, v.p., chief med. dir., 1962-68, sr. v.p., 1968-73, dir., 1965-73. Served to maj., M.C., USAAF, 1941-45. Mem. Assn. Life Ins. Med. Dirs. Am. (v.p., pres. 1969-70), Am. Life Conv., New Eng. Med. Dirs. Group, Home Office Life Underwriters Assn., Mayo Found. Alumni Assn., Kappa Alpha (So.). Home: Granby MA Died Jan. 9, 1973; buried Springfield MA

SEYMOUR, HAROLD J., consultant on unconstitutional finance and public relations; born in St. Paul, Minnesota, August 24, 1894; son of Frederick and Bessie (Townsend) Seymour; B.S., Harvard, 1916; m. Martha M. Andrews, April 10, 1920; children—Martha B. (Mrs. M. K. Smith), Mary Madison (Mrs. Sidney H. Paige), John Andrews. Vice president and director of the John Price Jones Corporation, New York, New York, 1919-43. Served as ensign, U.S. Naval Air Service, 1917-19. Campaign manager, U.S.O., 1941, 1942; campaign manager National War Fund, 1943, general manager, 1944-46; dir. Northern Valley Savings & Loan Association. Past pres. Tenafly (N.J.) Community Chest; past vice pres. Englewood (N.J.) Hosp. Mem. Am. Assn. Fund Raising Counsel (past pres.). Republican. Episcopalian. Clubs: Harvard (N.Y.). Knickerbocker Country. Author: Design for Giving, 1947; Tenafly NJ Died Apr. 10, 1968.

SHACKFORD, MARTHA HALE, coll. prof.; b. Dover, N.H., Aug. 25, 1875; d. Charles Burnham and Caroline (Cartland) Shackford; B.A., Wellesley Coll., 1896; critic in English, Vassar Coll., 1898-99; studied in Italy, 1899-1900; Ph.D., Yale, 1901. Instr. English lit., 1901-06, asso. prof., 1906-18, prof., 1918-43, prof. emeritus since 1943, Wellesley Coll. Mem. Modern Lang. Assn. America, Shakespeare Assn. (New York), The Friends of Lafayette, N.E. Poetry Society, N.E. Hist.-Geneal. Soc., N.H. Hist. Soc., Norfolk Record Soc. (Eng.), Phi Beta Kappa. Author: A First Book of Poetics, 1906; Masterpieces of European Literature, 1906; English Masterpieces of the Nineteenth Century, 1906; (with Margaret Judson) Composition-Rhetoric-Literature, 1908, 1917; Shakespeare in London, 1926; Plutarch in the English Renaissance, 1929; E. B. Browning, R. H. Horne-Two Studies, 1935; Wordsworth's Interest in Painters and Pictures, 1945; Studies of Certain Nineteenth Century Poets, 1946. Editor: Spenser's Faerie Queene, Book I, 1905, Macaulay's Lays of Ancient Rome, 1907, 13; Shakespeare's As You Like It, 1911; Chaucer—Selected References, 1911, 18; Legends and Satires from Mediaeval Literature, 1913; Wellesley Verse (1875-1925), 1925; Letters from Elizabeth Barrett to B. R. Haydon, 1939. Contbr. to ednl. and other publs. Home: 7 Midland Rd., Wellesley MA‡

SHACKLEFORD, THOMAS MITCHELL, JR., lawyer; b. Brooksville, Fla., June 26, 1884; s. Thomas Mitchell and Nannie Clopton (Rhea) S.; ed. pub. and pvt. schs., Fla., until 1900; student Jesuit High School, Tampa, Fla., 1900-01; John B. Stetson U., 1901-02; B.A., U. Fla., 1905; LL.B., U. Va., 1907; m. Mary Baird, June 23, 1915 (dec.);children—Mary Baird (Mrs. Norman S. Brown), Thomas Mitchell III (dec.), Nan Rhea (Owen), Frederick T. Admitted Fla. bar, 1907, practiced in Tampa, 1907-73; of counsel Shackleford, Farrior, Shannon & Stallings, now named Shackleford, Farrior, Stallings, &Evans; vice counsul of Honduras at Tampa, 1909-14; referee in Evans; vice counsul of Honduras at Tampa, 1909-14; referee in bankruptcy, 1914-18; county atty. Hillsborough County, 1923-29; commr. on Uniform State Laws, 1933-35; atty. State Road Dept., 1941-45; chmn. bd. emeritus of Tampa Fed. Savs. and Loan Assn. Pres. emeritus, fellow U. Fla. Found., Inc.; hon. mem. Children's Home (Tampa). Mem. Am. Bar Assn., Fla. State Bar Assn. (past pres.), Hillsborough County Bar Assn. (past pres.), Am. Law Inst., Am. Judicature Soc., Kappa Alpha, Phi Beta Kappa, Blue Key. Mason (32 deg., K.T., Shriner). Elk. Democrat. Episcopalian. Clubs: Mystic Krewe of Gasparilla, Palma Ceia Golf, University, Tampa Yacht and Country. Home: Tampa FL Died Jan. 10, 1973.

SHAFER, MORRIS LUTHER, lawyer, educator; born Weatherly, Pa., Aug. 8, 1903; s. Elmer George Ellsworth and Mary Ann (McCarter) S.; student Temple U., 1921-22; Ph.B. with honors, Muhlenberg Coll., 1925, LL.D., 1958; M.A., Lafayette Coll., 1929; student U. Pa., 1933, LL.D., 1947; Ph.D., N.Y.U., 1934; LL.D. (hon.), Dickinson College, Carlisle, Pa., 1959; L.H.D., Elizabethtown (Pa.) College, 1960; married Mary Abigail Walker, June 24, 1939. Adminstrv. and teaching staff, div. gen. edn. N.Y.U., 1934-43, adminstrv. asst. to dean, 1939-43; lectr. Wharton Sch. U. Pa., 1946; adjunct staff econs. Rutgers U., 1947-50; admitted to Pa. bar, 1947; practiced Lehigh County, Pa., 1947-54, 56-68; mem. firm Snyder, Wert, Wilcox, Shafer & Doll, Allentown, Pa., 1954-56; solicitor to register of wills, polit. subdivisions, Lehigh County; dean, profl. law Dickinson Sch. Law, 1956-65; asst. dir. com. on continuing legal edn. Pa. Bar, 1965-66. Adviser Joint-State Govt. Commn., 1956. Mem. Am., Pa., Lehigh County bar assns., Am. Judicature Soc. Home: Wynnewood PA Died Oct. 11, 1968; buried Grandview Cemetery, Allentown PA

SHAFFER, JOHN CHARLES, newspaper publisher; b. Baltimore, Md., June 5, 1853; s. James and Ann (Crout) S.; ed. pub. schs. of Baltimore; m. Virginia Conser, Dec. 23, 1878. Head of J. C. Shaffer & Co., grain merchants, Chicago, 1904-20; head of J. C. Shaffer Grain Co., 1920-34; pres. Richmond (Ind.) St. Ry. Co., 1888-93; organized syndicate and purchased all the st. rys. of Indianapolis, and was pres., 1889-93; pres. Asbury Park St. Ry. Co., 1892; built Chicago & Englewood Electric Ry., 1893; pres. and pub. Chicago Evening Post, 1901-31; pres. and publisher Indianapolis Star, Muncie Star; owner and pub. Louisville Herald 14 yrs., also Rocky Mountain News and Denver Times. Methodist. Clubs: American (London); Denver (Denver); Chicago, Union League, Press (pres. 1910), Glen View, Congressional Golf. Office: 111 W. Jackson Blvd., Chicago IL‡

SHAFFER, LEWIS, container mfg. co. exec. Admitted to Ill. bar; mem. firm Shaffer, Seelig, Mandel & Shapiro, Chgo.; sec. Stone Container Corp., Chgo. Office: Chicago IL Died Mar. 29, 1973.

SHAHN, BEN, artist; b. Russia, Sept. 12, 1898; s. Hessel and Gittel (Lieberman) S.; brought to U.S., 1906, naturalized, 1918; student N.Y.U., Coll. City of N.Y., Nat. Acad. Design, Art Students League; hon. degrees Princeton, 1962, Rutgers U., Hebrew Union Coll., 1964, Harvard, 1967; m. Tillie Goldstein, 1922 (dec.); children—Judith, Ezra; m. 2d, Bernarda Bryson, 1935; children—Susanna, Jonathan, Abigail. One man shows Mus. Modern Art, 1947, Venice Biennale, 1954; works exhibited many museums, galleries and univs. throughout U.S., including Art Inst. Chgo., Detroit Inst. Arts, Newark Mus. Assn., Met. Mus. Art, N.Y.C., Mus. Modern Art, N.Y.C., Mus. City of N.Y., Phillips Gallery, Washington; murals in Fed. Security Bldg., Washington, Bronx (N.Y.) Central Annex P.O., William Grady Technical High School, Brooklyn, N.J. State Mus., Trenton, Peabody Coll., Nashville, others; retrospective exhbns., Amsterdam, 1961, Rome Vienna, others; exhbn. prints, graphics Germany Sweden, Eng., others; mosaic murals; portrait of Dag Hammarskjold commd. by Nat. Mus., Stockhold; lecturer colls. and univs.; Charles Eliot Norton prof., Harvard U., 1956-57. With O.W.I., World War II. Recipient Pennell Medal, Pa. Acad., 1939, Graphics Medal, 1953, Art Dirs. Medal, 1949, 55, Brazil award, St. Paulo Biennale, 1953; Temple Gold Medal, Pa. Acad. Exhbn., 1956; Gold Medal, Am. Inst. Graphic Arts Soc.; 4th prize with copper medal, Corcoran Biennial, 1961. Mem. Artists Equity, Academia de Artes y Ciencias de Puerto Rico, Acadamia dell'Arte e del Desegno (Florence, Italy), American Academy of Arts and Letter, National Institute of Arts and Letters. Author: Shape of Content; The Alphabet of Creation; Love and Joy About Letters. Designer, illustrator numerous books. Home: Roosevelt NJ Died Mar. 14, 1969.

SHAMBAUGH, BERTHA M. H. (MRS. BENJAMIN F. SHAMBAUGH), author; b. Cedar Rapids, Ia., Feb. 12, 1871; d. Frank J. (lawyer) and Katharine (Mosnat) Horack; grad. Iowa City High Sch., 1889; student State U. of Ia., 1889-92; m. Benjamin F. Shambaugh, of Iowa City, Aug. 11, 1897. Teacher (natural science) pub. schs., Iowa City, 1892-97. Mem. Ia. Fed. of Women's Clubs (adv. bd. Ia. history), Pi Beta Phi. Unitarian. Clubs: Iowa Authors, University (charter mem., ex-historian). Author: Amana—The Community of True Inspiration, 1908; Amana That Was and Amana That Is, 1932; Amana in Transition. Contbr. to Hasting's Encyclopedia of Religion and Ethics, Dictionary of Am. Biography, Dictionary of Am. History, also to the World Today, The Outlook, The Palimpsest, etc. Designer Iowa Corn Folk, Sesqui Centennial Expn., Phila., 1926; mem. Iowa Women's Advisory Committee, New York World's Fair, 1939. Home: 219 N. Clinton St., Iowa City IA‡

SHAMBAUGH, GEORGE ELMER, M.D.; b. in Clinton Co., Ia., Nov. 15, 1869; s. John and Eva Ann (Ressler) S.; Ph.B., State U. of Ia., 1892; M.D., U. of Pa., 1895; studied U. of Berlin, 1895-96, U. of Vienna, 1896-97; m. Edith Capps, of Jacksonville, Ill., May 2, 1901. Specialist in diseases of the ear, nose and throat; prof. otolaryngology and head of dept., Rush Med. Coll., 1916-35; clinical prof. emeritus since 1935; instr. anatomy of the ear, nose and throat, U. of Chicago, 1900-35; otologist and laryngologist Presbyn. Hosp., 1902-35. Fellow Am. Otol. Society (ex-pres.), Am. Laryngol. Assn. (ex-pres.); mem. A.M.A., Chicago Med. Soc., Chicago Laryngological and Otological Soc. (ex-pres.). Awarded Lenval prize (international prize in otology) for research on the internal ear, 1912. Club: University. Contbr. to Journal of the Am. Med. Assn., Annals of Otology, Rhinology and Laryngology, Laryngoscope; editor Archives of Otolaryngology, 1923-37; has written chapters on the ear and nasal sinuses for several textbooks. Home: 5625 University Av. Office: Peoples Gas Bldg., Chicago IL‡

SHAMBURGER, CARL SHUFORD, nurseryman, b. Smith County, Tex., Oct. 27, 1903; s. Matthew Shuford and Margaret Ann (Morgan) S.; m. Ruth Shank, Oct. 10, 1924 (dec. 1935); children—Peggy (Mrs. George Hendricks), Patsy (Mrs. J. B. McKenzie); m. 2d, Anne Dudley Killam, June 9, 1937; 1 son, Carl Shuford. Owner Carl Shamburger Nursery, Phoenix, also cattle ranch. Palo Pinto County, Tex., 1959-67; pres. Carl Shamburger & Co., oil interests, oil prodn., Tex., La., Miss., Ark., Okla. Mem. Am. Assn. Nurserymen, Am. Rose Soc. Democrat. Mem. Disciples of Christ Ch. Mason (Shriner). Address: Tyler TX Died Aug. 22, 1967; buried Tyler TX

SHANDS, COURTNEY, ret. naval ofcr.; b. Ferguson, Mo., Dec. 1, 1905; s. Claire Walton and Carey Jacqueline (Risque) S.; B.S., U.S. Naval Acad., 1927; student Nat. War Coll., 1951-52; m. Elizabeth Worthen Jones, June 6, 1927; children—Courtney, Carey (Mrs.

Richard Lane). Commd. ensign U.S. Navy, 1927, advanced through grades to rear adm., 1955; naval aviator, 1929; participated Atlantic operations, including Malta, 1942, invasion Guadalcanal, 1942; comdr. aircraft carrier U.S. Oriskany, 1952-53; commander Carrier Division 18, 1957-58; director atomic energy div. Navy Dept., 1954-57; dep. comdr. Field Command Armed Forces, Spl. Weapons Project, Sandia Base, Albuquerque, N.M., 1958-61, dep. comdr. Def. Atomic Support Agy., 1961-62; ret., 1962. Decorated Navy Cross, Legion of Merit, Bronze Star, Presidential Unit Citation, Air Medal; Alexandria VA Died Nov. 21, 1968; buried Arlington Nat. Cemetery, Arlington VA

SHANE, GEORGE (WALKER), newspaperman, artist; b. Eldon, Ia., Dec. 8, 1906; s. Frank and Abigail (Walker) S.; student, U. of Ky., 1925-26, Art Inst., Chicago, 1927; m. Florence Holmes, Jan. 20, 1933; children—Felicia, Katherine, Mary. Newspaper work since 1928; editor weekly newspaper, 1930-35; art critic Des Moines Register and Tribune, 1938-69; paintings in permanent collections Des Moines Art Center, Davenport, Iowa Municipal Art Gallery, Joslyn Memorial Museum, Omaha, Neb., Ia. State, Mulvane Art Center of Topeka, Kansas, also in Blanden Memorial Art Gallery, Fort Dodge, Iowa and pvt. collections. Pres. Des Moines Art Forum, 1952. Served with U.S. Army, 1944-45. Recipient of purchase award Ia. Art Salon, 1947. Member of Ia. Civil Liberties Union, Sigma Chi. Unitarian. Contbr. articles on minority group problems. Home: Des Moines IA Died Mar. 1, 1969; buried Glendale Cemetery, Des Moines IA

SHANK, SAMUEL HERBERT, consul; b. Indianapolis, Ind., Feb. 4, 1871; s. William Henry Harrison and Mary Elmira (Kuhn) S.; A.B., Butler Coll., Irvington, Ind., 1892; LL.B., Ind. Law Sch., 1897; m. Norma Frances Bradt, of Flint, Mich., Feb. 28, 1907. Deputy clk., Co. Ct., Marion Co., Ind., 4 yrs.; in law practice, 1901-3; vice and deputy consul, Winnipeg, Can., Nov. 7, 1903; consul, Winnipeg, Can., Mar. 30, 1904, Mannheim, Germany, Mar. 30, 1907, Sherbrooke, Can., Mar. 21, 1912, Fiume, Hungary, August 20, 1912, Palermo, Italy, Apr. 24, 1914—. Republican. Mem. Disciples of Christ. Club: Marion (Indianapolis). Home: Indianapolis IN Address: American Consulate Palermo Italy‡

SHANNON, FREDERICK FRANKLIN, clergyman; b. Morris County, Kan., Feb. 11, 1877; s. James W. and Kate P. (Sullivan) S.; ed. Webb Sch., Bell Buckle, Tenn.; Harvard, 1898-99; Litt. D., Syracuse U., 1924; LL.D., Lincoln Memorial U., 1929; m. Effie Grace Myers, May 3, 1903; 1 son, Frederick Nighbert. Ordained Methodist Episcopal Church, South, 1899; pastor Logan, W.Va., 1899-1900, Grace Ch., Brooklyn, 1904-12. Ref. Ch. on Heights, Brooklyn, 1912-19, Central Ch., Chicago, 1920-39. Author: The Soul's Atlas and Other Sermons, 1911; The New Personality, 1915; The Enchanted Universe, 1916; The Breath in the Winds, 1918; God's Faith in Man, 1919; The Economic Eden; The Land of Beginning Again; The Infinite Artist; The Country Faith; A Moneyless Magnate; The New Greatness; The Unfathomable Christ; Doors of God; The Universe Within; Christ Eternal; The Supreme Court of the Soul; Why God Made Flowers; The Christian God; The Poet Eternal, 1945. Lecturer, colleges, universities and clubs. Home: 6933 Oglesby Av., Chicago*‡

SHAPIRO, JOSEPH M., business exec.; b. Borisov, Russia, Sept. 25, 1888; m. Edna Root; children—James J., Edward A., Robert M. Organized Simplicity Pattern Co., N.Y.C., 1927, pres., dir., treas., 1927-49, chmn. bd., 1949-68; dir. Dominion Simplicity Patterns, Ltd., Toronto, Simplicity Patterns, Ltd., London, Eng., Pictorial Patterns Pty., Ltd., Sydney, Australia. Home: New York City NY Died July 29, 1968.

SHAPLEY, HARLOW, astronomer; b. Nashville, Mo., Nov. 2, 1885; s. Willis Harlow and Sarah (Stowell) S.; A.B., U. Mo., 1910, A.M., 1911, LL.D., 1927; Ph.D., Princeton, 1913, Sc.D., 1933; Sc.D., U. Pitts., 1931, U. Pa., 1932, Brown U., Harvard 1933, U. Toronto (Can.), 1935, N.Y. U., U. Copenhagen, 1946, U. Delhi, U. Hawaii, 1947, U. Ireland, 1959, St. Lawrence U., 1963; D.D., U. Chgo., 1969; LL.D., Oglethorpe U., 1931; Dr. Honoris causa, U. Michocan (Mex.), U. Mexico, 1951; Litt.D., Bates Coll., 1942; m. Martha Betz, Apr. 15, 1914; children—Mildred (Mrs. Ralph Matthews), Willis, Alan Lloyd, Carl. Astronomer, Mount Wilson Obs., Cal., 1914-21; dir. obs. Harvard, 1921-52, Paine prof. astronomy, 1922-56, emeritus, 1956-72; Wm. A. Neilsen research prof. Smith Coll., 1956-57; Phi Beta Kappa resident lectr. various Am. Colls., 1957-58. Lectr., Lowell Inst., 1922; exchange lectr. Belgian univs., 1926; Halley lectr., Oxford, 1928; Harry Todd lectr. State of Mass., 1929; lectr. Jayne Found., Phila., 1930; Darwin lectr. Royal Astron. Soc., 1934; lectr. several fgn. univs., 1951-72. Life mem. corp. Mass. Inst. Tech. Researches in photometry, cosmogony. Trustee Worcester Found. Exptl. Biology, pres., 1942-48; trustee Sci. Service, Institut Reserche Scientifique D'Afrique Central (Africa), Woods Hole Oceanographic Inst. Recipient numerous sci. awards including Pope Pius XI prize, 1941; Calcutta Sci. Soc. Medal, 1947; Gold medal Indian Assn. for Cultivation Sci., 1947; Order of Aztec Eagle (Mexico), Crux de Honor (Puebla). Fellow Am. Acad. Arts and Sci. (pres. 1939-44); mem. A.A.A.S. (pres. 1949), Indian (hon.), Nat. acad. scis., various other fgn. sci. assns., exec. officer of several. Author: The Inner Metagalaxy, 1957; Of Stars and Men, 1958; The View from a Distant Star, 1964; Beyond the Observatory; Through Rugged Ways to the Stars, 1969. Address: Cambridge MA Died Oct. 1972.

SHARKEY, JOSEPH EDWARD, journalist; b. Cambridge, Mass., Mar. 13, 1877; s. James and Margaret (Bradley) S.; ed. Harvard, 1895-99; m. Beatrice Laurans, June 14, 1913. Reporter and editorial writer, Boston Traveler; reporter Boston Transcript, 1895-98; with Associated Press since 1898, reporter and editor Boston office, 1898-1907, asst. corr. in Paris, France, 1907-13, chief of Japanese bureau, 1913-Oct. 1921, chief of Paris bureau, 1929-33, Geneva bureau, 1933-37. Served as corr. on missions, European and Asiatic countries. Went to Omsk, Siberia, winter of 1918, to report the expedition of Admiral Kolchak against Russian Soviet Army, and to Korea, 1918-19; also to China and Philippines; called to Washington, 1921, by Associated Press, to report Conf. on Limitation of Armament and Far Eastern Affairs; reported internat. polit. confs. at Genoa, The Hague, Lausanne, and European Security Conf., at Locarno, Oct. 1925, which adopted the Rhine Pact and other machinery for the permanent pacification of Europe; also covered the Irish rebellion, Greek revolution and Three-Power Naval Conf., Geneva, 1927, Stresa Polit. Conf., 1935, the League of Nations sessions, levying sanctions against Italy, 1935, and the 9 Power conference at Brussels of 1937, convoked to consider Japan's military activities in China. Asso. Press corr. at Geneva, 1923-29. Retired Decmeber 31, 1937, after 40 consecutive years of service in the Associated Press; volunteered as spl. Asso. Press corr. at Geneva at outbreak of World War II; returned to U.S., 1940. Member City Council, Cambridge, Mass., 1899-1902, Bd. of Edn., 1902-05. Sec. Harvard Club, Paris, 1911-12; sec. U.S. sect. Franco-Am. Com., 1912; pres. Anglo-Am. Press Assn., Paris, 1912; mem. exec. council Am. Assn. of Tokyo, 1918-19. Mem. Am. Acad. Polit. and Social Science. Vice-pres. Internat. Assn. of Journalists accredited to the League of Nations, 1933-34. Clubs: Harvard of Tokyo (v.p. 1921-22); Harvard of Geneva; American of Paris (member of the executive com., 1933-34). Author: The Ethics of Journalism, The Great Century of French Literature, The Centennial of Cambridge. Has lectured before Greater Boston organizations on war, particularly Japan's war on U.S. Appt'd historian of World War II by Cambridge (Mass.) Com. on Pub. Safety; historian Washington Elm Memorial Com.; member State Hist. Com. for World War II; apptd. chmn. hist. com. by Mass. Com. Pub. Safety. Decorated: Officer, Legion of Honor (France); Knight, Order of Holy Sepulchre (Greece); Chevalier, Order of Crown (Belgium). Address: 10 Rue Ernest Deloison, Neuilly-Sur-Seine France‡

SHARP, CARL J., business exec.; b. Chicago, Aug. 7, 1893; s. Eugene Vallentine and Mary (Baker) S.; ed. pub. schs. of Chicago; m. Hattie Sonne, Nov. 6, 1915 (dec. 1968). Salesman real estate, 1909-15; vice-pres. of sales, Tempco Mfg. Co., 1915-17; sales mgr. Cornell Wood Products Co., 1917-25; pres. Acme Steel Co. 1927-52, chmn. exec. com., 1959-60; dir. B. & O.T.C. R.R., Northern Ill. Gas Co., Ill. Inst. Gas Tech. Pres. Glenwood Sch. for Boys; trustee Illinois Inst. of Tech. Recipient Horatio Alger award, 1954. Mem. Chicago Chamber of Commerce (dir.). Republican. Clubs: Union League, Chicago, Commercial (Chgo.); Flossmoor Country. Home: Flossmoor IL Died Sept. 27, 1968.

SHARP, GEORGE CLOUGH, lawyer; b. Flyria, O., Sept. 19, 1897; s. William Graves and Hallie (Clough) S.; diploma, Ecole libre des Sciences Politiques, 1918; LL.B., Columbia, 1922; m. Ruth Baldwin, Apr. 30, 1936; children—Anna, George. Pvt. sec. to U.S. ambassador to France, 1914-19; admitted to N.Y. bar, 1923, since practiced in N.Y.C.; partner firm Sullivan & Cromwell, 1929-71. Trustee French Inst.; bd. dirs., v.p. Am. Friends of France, Inc. Served as lt. col. AUS, OSS, 1943; legal adv. SHAEF Mission to France, 1944-45. Decorated Order of Pologna Restituta (Poland); Legion of Honor, Croix de Guerre (France). Mem. Assn. Bar City of N.Y., N.Y. County Lawyers Assn., Am., N.Y. State bar assns., Am. Judicature Soc., Council Fgn. Relations, Inc., Sigma Chi. Clubs: Knickerbocker, Downtown Assn. (N.Y.C.); Bedford (N.Y.) Golf and Tennis. Home: Katonah NY Died Dec. 31, 1972.

SHARP, HENRY STAATS, educator; b. Stuyvesant Falls, N.Y., Mar. 26, 1902; s. Isaac and Clara (van Alstyne) S.; A.B., Cornell U., 1924; A.M., Columbia, 1926, Ph.D., 1929; m. Gertrude Schuyler Hargrave, June 6, 1928; children—John Van Alstyne, Schuyler, Katherine E. Asst. prof. geology, Denison U., 1930-32; instr. geology Columbia, 1932-37, asst. prof., 1937-45, asso. prof., 1945-49, prof., 1949-67, prof. emeritus, 1967-69, exec. officer, dept. geology and geography Barnard Coll., 1941-64; geologist Mil. Geology Unit, U.S. Geol. Survey, 1947-49. Fellow Geol. Soc. Am.; mem. Assn. Am. Geographers. Mng. editor, Jour. of Geomorphology, 1938-42. Home: Southbury CT Died Oct. 20, 1969.

SHARP, JOHN H., judge; b. Robertson County, Tex., Apr. 25, 1874; s. Andrew Jackson and Mollie (Brown) S.; A.B., D.C.L., Southwestern U.; m. Eula King, June 6, 1906; children—Lucille, Helen. Mem. commn. appeals Tex. Supreme Court, 1929-35; asso. justice Tex. Supreme Court since 1935. Democrat. Mason, K.P. Home: 9 Niles Rd. Address: State Capitol Austin TX‡

SHARP, JOSEPH LESSIL, judge, b. Logan, Utah, Oct. 8, 1914; s. Joseph Lessil and Helga (Larsen) S.; student U. Ida., 1937-38, 1945; B.S. in Edn., Utah State Coll., 1941; m. Elsie Joyce Fox, Feb. 16, 1941; children—William D., Jacqueline Elsie. Farmer, Hagerman, Ida., 1929-34; constrn. worker, 1935; with fire control U.S. Forest Service, summers, 1936-42; tchr. high sch., Mackay, Ida., 1940-41, prin., 1941-44; prin., Salmon, Ida., 1944-47, Nezperce, Ida., 1947-49; supt. pub. instrn. Custer County, 1949-51; Justice of the Peace, Challis precinct, 1951-53; probate judge, Custer County, 1953-71; pres. Custer County Abstract Co., Ltd. (name changed Custer County Title, Inc., 1959), 1947-71; owner Challis Ins. Agy. Finance chmn. Custer County central com., Republican Party, 1956-64; Rep. precinct committeeman Challis, 1964-71. Mem. Ida. Probate Judges' Assn. (pres. 1962-64). Lion (charter; pres. Challis 1965-66), Mason. Challis ID Died Apr. 11, 1971; buried Challis Cemetery Challis ID

SHARPLESS, FREDERIC COPE, physician; born Haverford, Pa., Oct. 1, 1880; s. Isaac and Lydia Trimble (Cope) S.; A.B., Haverford Coll., 1900, LL.D. (hon.), 1970; M.D., U. Pa., 1903; m. Louise Sangree, Oct. 26, 1909. Intern Pa. Hosp., Phila., 1904-96; gen. practitioner, Rosemont, Pa., 1906-47; dir. med. services Bryn Mawr Hosp., 1938-47; gen. couns. Bryn Mawr Coll., 1932-47; physician, Shipley Sch., 1932-47; practiced medicine, Greensboro, Vt., 1951-55. Mem. bd. mgrs. Haverford Coll.; mem. bd. trustees Bryn Mawr Coll.; trustee Dunwoody Home, Newtown Square, Pa., 1924-47. Fellow Phila. Coll Physicians; mem. A.M.A. Home: Haverford PA Died Nov. 16, 1971; buried Haverford Friends Meeting Graveyard Haverford PA

SHARTS, JOSEPH WILLIAM, author, lawyer; b. Hamilton, O., Sept. 14, 1875; s. Joseph William and Sarah Belle (Ealy) S.; A.B., magna cum laude, Harvard, 1897; m. Ruth, d. Rev. S. Q. Helfenstein, July 7, 1915; 1 son, Joseph William. Admitted to Ohio bar, 1899; atty. for Eugene V. Debs at his Cleveland (O.) trial, 1918; atty. for Bishop William Mantgomery Brown at heresy trial, 1924, 25. Served as corpl. Co. C, 1st Ohio Inf., Spanish-Am. War. Member United Spanish War Veterans, Dayton and Montgomery County Historical Society. Mason. Author: Ezra Caine, 1900, The Romance of a Rogue, 1902; The Hills of Freedom, 1904; The Black Sheep, 1909; The Vintage, 1911; The King Who Came, 1913; Biography of Dayton, 1922. Home: 1230 Phillips Av., Dayton 10 OH Office: 527 W. 2d St., Dayton 2 OH‡

SHATTUCK, GEORGE CHEEVER, physician; b. Boston, Mass., Oct. 12, 1879; s. Frederick Cheever and Elizabeth Perkins (Lee) S.; Noble and Greenough School, 1892-97; A.B., Harvard University, 1901, honorary A.M., 1919; M.D., Harvard University Medical Sch., 1905; med. study in Vienna, 1907-08; m. Virginia Grigsby Chandler (Peabody), July 9, 1932; step-sons, Francis W. Peabody, Grigsby C. Peabody. physician to out-patients, later assistant visiting physician Mass. Gen. Hosp., 1912-21; mem. Am. Red Cross Commn. to Serbia (combating typhus fever), 1915; maj. med. service, Harvard Surgical Unit, B.E.F., 1916; temp. hon. major, Royal Army Med. Corps, Harvard Unit, 1917-19; gen. med. sec. League of Red Cross Societies, Geneva, 1919-21; mem. visiting staff Boston City Hosp., 1921-41; attending specialist in tropical medicine, U.S. Marine Hosp., Brighton, Mass., 1923; mem. Hamilton Rice 7th Expedition to Amazon, 1924-25; consultant tropical diseases, Mass. General Hosp. since 1928; mem. faculty Museum of Comparative Zoology, Harvard, 1933-62; clinical prof. tropical medicine, Harvard School of Public Health, 1938-47; emeritus; consultant tropical diseases Boston City Hosp., from 1941; consultant to secretary of war on tropical medicine, 1941-44; cons. in tropical diseases, Peter Bent Brigham Hospital, Boston, emeritus, also V.A., West Roxbury, Mass., 1945-52, V.A. Boston and Farmingham since 1952; adviser to Resources Div., Office of Quartermaster Gen., War Dept., 1942. Pres. Boston Health League, Inc., 1939-49; pres. Mass. Central Health Council, 1938-48; chmn. Health Council United Community Services, Boston, 1950-53; pres. Brookline Citizens Committee, 1941. Awarded Serbia Order of St. Sava of III Class, 1918; Distinguished Service Order (Great Britain), 1919; Theobold Smith Medal, Am. Acad. Tropical Medicine, 1954; Orden Nacional de Merito Commendador, Carlos J. Findlay, Cuba, 1950; Orden Nacional do Cruzeiro do Sul, Oficial, Brazil, 1958; Prof. Honorario, Universidad de San Carlos, Guatemala, 1956; Richard Pearson Strong medal Am. Found. Tropical Medicine; bronze medal New England Wild Flower Soc., 1965. Mem. Mass. Med. Soc., Am. Pub. Health Assn., A.A.A.S., Am.

Acad. Arts and Scis., Am. Acad. Tropical Medicine (pres. 1947-48), Am. Society Tropical Medicine, Royal Soc. Tropical Medicine and Hygiene (local sec. for U.S., 1939-49), Nature Conservancy (gov. 1956-62, Mass. rep. 1957-70; hon. mem.), Pan. Am. Soc. New Eng. (gov. 1941-65). Mem. Hon. Pub. Health Soc., Sigma Xi, Delta Omega, Beta Chapter. Author: Principles of Medical Treatment, 6th rev. edit., 1926; The Peninsula of Yucatan, 1933; Medical Survey of the Republic of Guatemala, 1938; Handbook of Health for Overseas Service (with Wm. Jason Mixter), 2d rev. edit., 1943; Diseases of the Tropic, 1950; A Memoir of Frederick Cheever Shattuck, M.D., 1967. Home: Brookline MA Died June 12, 1972.

SHATTUCK, HENRY LEE, lawyer and trustee; b. Boston, Mass., Oct. 12, 1879; s. Frederick Cheever and Elizabeth Perkins (Lee) S.; grad. Noble and Greenough Sch., Boston, 1897; A.B., Harvard, 1901, LL.B., 1904; LL.D., Williams Coll., 1936, Nat. U. Ireland, 1950, Harvard Coll., 1952, LL.D. (honorary), Trinity College, Dublin, Ireland, 1955; unmarried. Admitted to Mass. bar, 1904, and began practice with Ropes, Gray & Gorham, Boston; mem. firm, 1909-19; mem. firm Shattuck & Gray, 1922-28; treas. Harvard Coll., 1929-38; mem. firm Shattuck & Brooks, trustees, 1941-68; senior fellow of President and Fellows of Harvard Coll., 1938-52, Harvard Soc. of Fellows 1944-45; honorary dir. New Eng. Mchts. Nat. Bank; hon. dir. Cabot Corp., Fiduciary Trust Co. N.Y.; dir. Gualey Coal Land Co.; past trustee Mut. Life Insurance Co., N.Y., Nat. Municipal League (council). Chmn. Boston Municipal Research Bur., 1947-59. Chmn. local bd., Selective Draft, Boston, 1918-19; mem. Loyalty Rev. Bd., Civil Service Commn., 1947-53; chairman Interim Mixed Parole and Clemency Board for German War Criminals, 1953-54. Mem. Mass. House of Representatives, 1920-30 and 1943-48; chmn. Com. on Ways and Means, 1923-29; House chmn. Joint Com. on Public Service 1943-47; mem. Commn. on Interstate Cooperation, 1947-48. Mem. Boston City Council, 1934-41. Hon. pres. North Bennet St. Indsl. Sch.; treas. The Charitable Irish Soc., 1946-59; past trustee Boston Mus. Fine Arts; trustee (hon.) Woods Hole Oceanographic Instn.; past trustee Noble and Greenough Sch. Mem. American, Mass. State and Boston bar assns., Am. Acad. Polit. and Social Sci., Mass. Hist. Soc., Am. Acad. Arts and Sciences. Republican. Clubs: Harvard, Somerset, Union, Tavern, Brookline Country (Boston); Harvard (N.Y.); Cosmos (Washington). Home: Boston MA Died Feb. 2, 1971; buried Mt. Auburn Cemetery Cambridge MA

SHATTUCK, HOWARD FRANCIS, physician; b. Clinton, Wis., Dec. 19, 1887; s. Edward Albert and Florence Viola (Shepard) S.; A.B., Yale, 1911; M.D., Coll. of Physicians and Surgeons (Columbia), 1913; m. Elizabeth Colt, May 10, 1919; children—Howard Francis, Jr., Roger Whitney. Intern Presbyterian Hospital, N.Y. City, 1914-15; physician Presbyn. Hosp. Dispensary N.Y. City, 1916-21; asst. attending physician Post-Grad. Hosp., 1919-28, attending physician 1928-36; attending physician Roosevelt Hospital, 1936-52, chief 1st medical division, 1944-52, consulting physician, from 1952; instructor in medicine, Post-Grad. Med. Sch. (Columbia), 1917-23, asst. prof., 1923-30, prof. clin. medicine, 1930-36; clin. prof. medicine, Columbia U. Coll. Phys. and Surgs., 1936-52. Commd. 1st lt. Med. Corps, U.S. Army, in France, 1917-18. Fellow Am. Coll. Physicians; mem. A.M.A., N.Y. Acad. Medicine, N.Y. State Med Soc., Am. Gastro-Enterol. Assn. (pres. 1935-36), Hosp. Graduates Club, Clin. Research Soc., Phi Beta Kappa, Sigma Xi, Psi Upsilon, Elihu Club. Episcopalian. Club: Century. Contbr. to med. jours. Home: New York City NY Died Jan. 6, 1972.

SHAUGHNESSY, CLARK DANIEL, football coach; b. St. Cloud, Minn., Mar. 6, 1892; s. Edward and Lucy Ann (Foster) S.; A.B., U. of Minn., 1918; m. Louvania Mae Hamilton, Dec. 5, 1917; children—Clark Daniel, Marcia Mae, Janice Beryl. Dir. of athletics and football coach, Tulane U., New Orleans, 1915-20, head football coach, 1921-28; dir. of athletics and football coach, Loyola Univ., New Orleans, 1928-33; head football coach and prof. of phys. edn., U. of Chicago, 1933-40, Stanford U., 1940-41; athletic dir., head football coach, U. of Md., 1943; prof. physical edn. and head football coach, U. of Pittsburgh, 1943-46; U. of Md., 1946; v.p. and tech. adviser Chicago Bears football team. Mem. American Football Coaches Assn., Delta Theta Phi, Sigma Chi. Author: Modern T Formation with Man in Motion; Football in War Santa Monica CA Died May 15, 1970.

SHAW, ESMOND, architect, educator; b. Saba, Dutch West Indies, July 30, 1902; s. Carl Addison and Elizabeth Anne (Pike) S., student McGill U., 1920-22, Art Student's League N.Y.C., 1922-24, N.Y.U., 1936; m. Enid Mary Cruickshank, Dec. 3, 1924; children—Jean (Mrs. John O. Sheehan), Faith (Mrs. Peter Harrison); m. 2d, Sybil Cahoon Jacobsen, June 16, 1967. Draftsman, designer Am. Bapt. Home Mission Soc., N.Y.C., 1923-24, Hobart Upjohn, N.Y.C., 1924-30, Eric Gugler, N.Y.C., 1930-31; supervising park designer Dept. Parks N.Y.C., 1934-35; pvt. archtl. practice, 1939-59; gen. drafting, detail design, preliminary studies Ralph S. Gerganoff, Ypsilanti, Mich., 1945-46; prof. architecture, asst. dean Cooper Union Art Sch., 1935-56, prof. architecture, head dept., asst. dean Sch. Art and Architecture, 1956-63, dean, head dept. architecture, 1963-64, dean, 1965-68, dean emeritus, 1968-72. Mem. architect's selection com. N.Y.C. Bd. Edn., 1966-70; mem. citizens tech. adv. com. Rye (N.Y.) Planning Commn., 1945-46; art cons. N.Y. State Div. Vocational Rehab., 1947-70; mem. lower middle income housing subcom. Westchester County (N.Y.) Council Social Agys., 1957-58; chmn. Rye Bd. Archtl. Rev., 1951-61; mem. activities com. Beaux Arts Inst. Design, 1955-56. Trustee Nat. Inst. Archtl. Edn., 1956-59, chmn. bd., 1959-61; trustee Rye Pub. Schs., 1941-48, v.p. sch. bd., 1946-48. Recipient Gov. Gen.'s medal Can., 1920. Arnold W. Brunner fellow, 1951. Fellow A.I.A (chmn. adv. com. edn. com. 1961-65, chmn. LeBrun fellowship com. N.Y. chpt. 1966-68. mem. other coms.); mem. Am. Arbitration Assn. (nat. panel arbitrators). Contbr. numerous articles, reports to profl. lit. Co-editor: Planning and Community Appearance, 1958. Home: New York City NY Died Nov. 13, 1972; buried Ferncliff Cemetery Mausoleum, Hartsdale NY

SHAW, FREDERICK BENJAMIN, army officer; b. Burlington, Pa., June 24, 1869; s. Charles D. and Margaret H. (Dickinson) S.; m. Mary B. Davis, July 8, 1908 (died May 1, 1946); children—Marion (wife of Brig. Gen. H. L. Peckham), Barbara (wife of Lt. Col. F. M. Hinshaw), Frederick B., Robert C., Daniel J. Enlisted in U.S. Army, 1892, commd. 2d lt., and advanced through grades to brig. gen.; retired as brig. gen., 1933; served in Puerto Rica, Cuba, Philippine Islands, Mexican Border and World War I. Author: History of the 2d Infantry U.S. Army (genealogy). Record of the descendants of Anthony Shaw, Boston, 1653. Home: 1920 Queen's Lane, Arlington VA‡

SHAW, QUINCY A., mining exec.; b. Boston, July 30, 1869; s. Quincy A. and Pauline E. A. (Agassiz) S.; B.A., Harvard, 1891; m. Sarah W. Pemberton, May 12, 1896. With Calumet & Hecla Mining Co., 1891-1916, auditor, 1894-1904, second v.p., 1904-10, pres., 1910-16; Calumet & Hecla Mining Co. merged with other cos. to form present Calumet & Hecla Consol. Copper Co., now dir.; pres. North Am. Mines, Inc., since 1929. Clubs: Somerset, Tennis and Racquet (Boston); Myopia Hunt (Wenham); The Country (Brookline); Racquet and Tennis (New York). Home: 11 Exeter St. Office: 209 Washington St., Boston MA‡

SHAW, RALPH ROBERT, research exec.; b. Detroit, May 18, 1907; s. Max and Pauline (Sandburg) S.; A.B., Western Res. U., 1928; B.S., Columbia, 1929, M.S., 1931; Ph.D., U. Chgo., 1950; m. Viola Susan Leff, Nov. 27, 1929 (dec. Mar. 1968); m. 2d, Mary McChesney Andrews, Feb. 5, 1969. Asst., Cleve. Pub. Library, 1923-28, N.Y. Pub. Library, 1928-29; sr. asst., chief bibliographer Engring. Socs. Library, N.Y., 1929-36; chief librarian Gary (Ind.) Pub. Library, 1936-40; dir. libraries U.S. Dept. Agr., Washington, 1940-54, instr. sci. mgmt. Grad. Sch., 1946; prof. Grad. Sch. Library Service Rutgers U., 1954-64, dean, 1959-61, Distinguished prof., 1961-64; dean library activities U. Hawaii, Honolulu, 1964-68, prof., 1968-69, prof. emeritus, 1969-72. Instr., Columbia Sch. Library Service summers 1936-37, 51; v.p. Mini-print, Scarecrow Press, Inc., Scarecrow Reprint (all Metuchen, N.J.); pres. Nokaoi Press, Honolulu; dir. research and devel. Grolier-Ednl. Corp., N.Y.C., 1970-72; dir. Franklin Publs., Inc.; adv. com. Handbook of Latin Am. Studies, 1944-54, U.S. Quar. Booklist, 1944-54. Cons. prep. commn. for UNESCO, 1945; adviser FAO, 1945, cons., 1947; cons. ICA, India, 1957; bd. expert examiners U.S. Civil Service Commn., 1946-61; mem. U.S. nat. com. Internat. Fedn. Documentation, 1960-72; cons. UN mgmt. survey, 1947, sci. cons., gen. hdqrs. Tokyo, 1947; U.S. del. Royal Soc. Sci. Information Conf., London, 1948; mem. internat. adv. com. on bibliography UNESCO, 1954-61; mem. sci. information council NSF, 1964-68. Served with Med. Dept., USAAF, 1944-45. Recipient Dist. Service award Gary (Ind.) Jr. C. of C., 1938; Superior Service award U.S. Dept. Agr., 1951; Dewey medal, 1953. Mem. A.L.A. (hon. pres. 1956-57), A.A.A.S. (publs. com.), Spl. Libraries Assn., Ind. (past pres.), D.C., N.J. (pres. 1962-63) library assns., Nat. Book Com. Democrat. Mem. Soc. of Friends. Clubs: Oahu (Hawaii) Country; Cosmos. Author: Theory and History of Bibliography, 1934; Engineering Book Available in America Prior to 1830, 1933; International Activities of the American Library Assn., 1946; Literary Property in the U.S., 1951; Use of Photography for Clerical Routines, 1953; American Bibliography 1801-1819, 19 vols.; Libraries of Metropolitan Toronto, 1960. Contbr. articles to profl. jours. Patentee in field. Home: Honolulu HI Died Oct. 14, 1972; buried Nat. Meml. Cemetery of the Pacific, Honolulu HI

SHAW, ROBERT, U.S. judge; b. Jersey City, May 22, 1907; s. Andrew and Mary (Smith) S.; LL.B., Rutgers U., 1932; m. Jeanette E. Van Houten, Oct. 14, 1943. Admitted to N.J. bar, 1935; practice in Newark, 1935-62; sr. mem. firm Shaw, Pindar, McElroy, Connell & Foley, 1962; U.S. dist. judge Dist. N.J., 1962-72. Mem. N.J. Legislature from Essex County, 1937-38; mayor Township of Caldwell, 1955-61. Served with AUS, 1943-45. Mem. Am., N.J., Essex County bar assns., Nat. Lawyers Club. Club: Essex Fells (N.J.) Country. Home: Caldwell RD NJ Died July 9, 1972; buried Prospect Hill Cemetery, Caldwell NJ

SHAW, ROBERT KENDALL, b. Worcester, Mass., July 18, 1871; son of Joseph Alden and Eliza Antoinette (Thompson) S.; A.B., Harvard, 1894; studied N.Y. State Library Sch., 1897-99, B.L.S., 1901; m. Bertha Mower Brown, of Eau Claire, Wis., Sept. 20, 1902. Teacher, Highland Mil. Acad., Worcester, Mass., 1894-97; on staff N.Y. State Library, 1898-1901, Library of Congress, 1901-04; librarian Brockton (Mass.) Pub. Library, 1904-05; asst. librarian, 1905-09, librarian, 1909-39, now emeritus Worcester Free Pub. Library. Mem. Am. Lib. Assn., Mass. Library Club, Bay Path Library Club, Am. Antiquarian Soc., Worcester Hist. Soc., Phi Beta Kappa. Republican. Episcopalian. Clubs: Worcester Rotary, Worcester Shakespear, Worcester Harvard, Bohemian. Author: Samuel Swett Green, 1926; All Saints Church Centennial, 1935. Home: 38 Monadnock Rd., Worcester MA‡

SHAW, WILLIAM FREDERICK, educator; b. Tifton, Ga., Feb. 26, 1910; s. Matthew Sylvester and Edna (Cox) S.; student Mercer U., 1927-30; A.B., Furman U., Greenville, S.C., 1931; M.A., U. Tex., 1936; m. Margaret Willis Williford, Aug. 1, 1934; children—William Frederick, John Williford, Caroline Eljean, Edna Eljean. Prin., Pearson (Ga.) High Sch., 1933-35; supt. Pearson Pub. Schs., 1935-37; instr. English, Auburn U., 1937-39; asst. prof. English, N.M. State U., 1939-44; asso. editor N.M. Extension Service, 1944-46; asst. prof. English, U. Miami, Fla., 1946-47, asso. prof., 1947-65, asst. dir. guided studies, 1957-58, dir., 1958-64, chmn. humanities div., 1964-65; dr. humanities div. Miami-Dade Jr. Coll. South, 1965-67, dean acad. affairs, 1967-70, v.p. devel., 1970-72, distinguished service prof., 1969; freelance writer, lectr., cons. on edn. and writing; lit. columnist Miami News, 1956-65; book columnist Miami Herald, 1966-72. Co-dir. Southeastern Writers Conf. Mem. Met. Dade County Study Commn., 1970. Mem. Hist. Assn. So. Fla. (pres.), Mercer Alumni Assn. S.E. Fla. (pres.), South Dade C. of C. (chmn. edn. com.), Blue Key Iron Arrow, Pi Kappa Alpha, Omicron Delta Kappa, Sigma Upsilon. Democrat. Home: Miami FL Died Jan. 1972.

SHAWHAN, NARCISSA TAYLOE MAUPIN (MRS. CHARLES S.), parliamentarian; b. Gallion, Ala.; d. Judge Robert Lemon and Anne Ogle (Tayloe) Maupin; ed. Barton Acad. and Miss Lesesne's Select Sch. for Girls, Mobile, Ala.; m. Charles Shrader Shawhan, of Mobile, Oct. 14, 1891. Parliamentarian, Woman's Summer Sch. of Missions, (Montreat, N.C.), Virginia Sch. of Missions, W.Va. Sch. of Missions, Tex. Sch. of Missions; instr. in parliamentary law, Ala. State Coll. for Women, Montevallo, Ala. Founder and ex-pres. of Mobile Br. League of Am. Pen Women. Parliamentarian for Nat. Conv. League of Am. Pen Women, Washington, D.C., 1924. Pres. Mobile Presbyterial Auxiliary. Charter mem. Colonial Dames of Ala., Mobile Chapter D.A.R. (ex-regent), Octagon House Chapter U.S. Daughters of 1812 (ex-regent); past pres. Woman's Auxiliary, Government Street Presbyn. Ch.; mem. Order of Colonial Governors. Author: The New Parliamentary Law Library (textbook). Home: 254 N. Conception St., Mobile AL‡

SHAWN, EDWIN M. (TED SHAWN), b. Kansas City, Mo., Oct. 21, 1891; s. Elmer Ellsworth and Mary Lee (Booth) S.; student U. of Denver; hon. M.P.E., Springfield (Mass.) Coll., 1936; m. Ruth St. Denis, Aug. 13, 1914. Began as teacher and professional dancer, Los Angeles, Calif., 1912; founded, with Ruth St. Denis, the Denishawn Sch., Los Angeles, 1915, later moved to N.Y. City; toured U.S. and England with Denishawn Dancers, 1922-25, the Orient, 1925-26, toured America, 1931, 32; appeared alone in Germany and Switzerland, 1930, 31; formed 1st company of men dancers, 1933, since toured America with same, also showed in London, 1935; seventh consecutive season with men dancers, 1930-40; dir. Summer School of Dance, Graduate School of Physical Edn., George Peabody Coll. for Teachers, Nashville, Tenn.; managing dir. of Jacob's Pillow Dance Festival, Inc., and University of the Dance, from Oct. 1941. Built and operated first theatre in U.S. designed and used exclusively for art of the dance. Decorated Cross of Dannebrog (Denmark); recipient of Capezio Dance award, 1956; citation Men's Garden Clubs Am., 1964, New Eng. Regional Theatre Conf., 1964, Nat. Fedn. Music Clubs, 1965; medal Nat. Soc. Arts and Letters, 1965. Served as second lieutenant, Company I, 32d Infantry, U.S. Army, 1918. Mem. National Society of Arts and Letters (adv. board), Sigma Phi Epsilon. Author: Ruth St. Denis, Pioneer and Prophet, 1920; The American Ballet, 1926; Gods Who Dance, 1929; Fundamentals of a Dance Education, 1937; Dance We Must, 1940; How Beautiful Upon the Mountain, 1943; Every Little Movement: A Treatise on Francois Delsarte, 1954; 16 Dances in 16 Rhythms, 1956; Thirty Three Years of American Dance, 1959. One Thousand and One Night Stands, 1960. Address: Lee MA also Eustis, Fla. Died Jan. 9, 1972; buried Jacob's Pillow Becket MA

SHEA, ANDREW BERNARD, corp. exec.; b. Riverdale, N.Y., Feb. 21, 1903; s. Patrick and Teresa (Mulgrew) S.; student Fordham Prep. Sch., 1916-20, LL.B., Fordham U., 1924; m. Constance Green, Oct. 22, 1931; children—Andrew P., Donald, Michael. Joined W.R. Grace & Co., 1920, mem. legal dept., 1923-32, sub-mgr. import trading dept., 1932-34, in Peru, 1934-36, mgr. Peruvian bus., 1936-39, v.p., 1939-49, dir. 1946-70; 1st. v.p. W.R. Grace & Co., 1950-55, exec. v.p., 1955-70, dir, emeritus, 1970-72; pres. dir. Pan Am.-Grace Airways, Inc., 1949-67; chmn. bd. Grace Line, Inc., 1967-68. Mem. Peruvian-Am. Assn. (dir.), Colombia-Am. C. of C., Fgn. Policy Assn., Ecuadorean-Am. Assn.; Pan Am. Soc. hon. v.p., Bar Assn. City N.Y. Roman Catholic, Knight of Malta. Clubs: India House, Pinnacle, Wings, Economic (N.Y.C.); Metropolitan (Washington); Piping Rock. Home: Great Neck NY Died Nov. 15, 1972; buried Holy Rood Cemetery, Westbury NY

SHEA, EDMUND BURKE, lawyer; b. Ashland, Wis., Mar. 24, 1892; s. William F. and Nora (Madden) S.; A.B., U. of Wis., 1913; LL.B., Harvard, 1916; m. Dorothy Thigpen, Nov. 3, 1920; children—Charles T., Elizabeth, Sheila, Dorothy. In practice of law, Milwaukee, Wis., 1920-69; mem. firm Shea, Hoyt, Greene, Randall & Meissner. Home: Milwaukee WI Died May 18, 1969.

SHEA, JOHN JOSEPH, state ofcl.; b. Worcester, Mass., June 1, 1922; s. Cornelius Humphrey and Anne (Mahoney) S.; A.B., Holy Cross Coll., 1943; M.S. in Social Work, Boston U., 1950; m. Mary Agnes Daly, Aug. 22, 1953; children—John Michael, Robert Thomas, James, William. Trainee probation officer Boston Juvenile Ct., 1947-48; probation officer Municipal and Dist. Ct. Probation Dept., Milw., 1948-54; juvenile probation officer, Portland Me., 1954-57; dir. State Probation and Parole Dept., Augusta, Me., 1957-68, sec. State Probation and Parole Bd., adminstr. Interstate Compact for Parole Supervision, 1958-68; adminstr. Interstate Compact on Juveniles, 1958-68. Mem. Me. Com. on Problems of Mentally Retarded, 1959-68; mem. state com. 1960 White House Conf. on Youth. Dir. Androscoggin Valley Mental Health Clinic. Served as pfc AUS, 1943-46; ETO. Mem. Nat. Probation and Parole Assn. (mem. profl. council 1958-68), New Eng. Conf. Crime and Deliquency (treas. 1960), Assn. Juvenile Compact Adminstrs. (pres. 1963-64), Assn. Paroling Authorities (exec. com. 1962-64, 66-68), Parole and Probation Compact Adminstrs. (exec. com. 1963-64 65-66, 66-67). Am. Legion. Roman Catholic. Home: Portland ME Died Dec. 16, 1968.

SHEA, LEWIS ANTHONY, banker; Bklyn., Dec. 19, 1899; s. John Edward and Elizabeth (Bible) S.; student Pace Inst., 1919-21, N.Y.U., 1922-24; m. Janice M. Slaughter, Oct. 23, 1923; children—Jeanne A., Lewis A. With Bank of L.I., 1915-16, Nat. Butchers and Drovers Bank, 1920-21; asst. nat. bank examiner, 1921-27, bank examiner, 1927-31; v.p. First Nat. Bank & Trust Co. (name changed to Conn. Nat. Bank), Bridgeport, 1931-35, exec. v.p., 1935-43, pres., 1943-67, chmn. bd., 1967-71; dir. Conn. Ry. & Lighting Co. Life mem. Robert Morris Associates. Mem. of executive bd. Pomperaug council Boy Scouts Am.; mem. Community Chest; mem. financial adv. bd., Bridgeport. Dir. Bridgeport Hosp., American Red Cross. Member of Civil Defense Council. Served in U.S. Army, 1917-19, lt. USNR, 1937-46; naval aide Gov. Conn., 1939-41, 43-46. Mem. Am. Legion, C. of C., Vets. Fgn. Wars, Navy League of U.S. (bd. mem.), Am. Inst. Banking. Clubs: Rotary, Algonquin, Brooklawn Country (Bridgeport); Bankers of Am., Union League (N.Y.C.); Hartford, Fairfield Beach (Conn.). Home: Fairfield CT Died June 7, 1971; buried Mountain Grove Cemetery, Bridgeport CT

SHEARER, TOM ELLAS, educator; b. Cumerland, Ia., Oct. 14, 1906; s. Charles Perry and Edna (Thompson) S.; A.B., U. Ia., 1927, J.D., 1929; student New Sch. for Social Research, 1938; m. Vesper N. Spencer, Dec. 25, 1929; 1 son, Cyrus Thompson. File clerk Cleve. Trust Co., 1929; admitted to Ia. State bar, 1929; practiced in Eldon, 1929-30; asst. prof. polit. sci. Pa. State Coll., 1930-34; editor Tax Services, Prentice-Hall, Inc., N.Y.C., 1934-37, mng. editor, 1937-38, ednl. dir., 1938-39; salesman, Des Moines, 1939-41, mid-west mgr., 1941-42, asst. v.p. Prentice-Hall, Inc., 1945-46; pub. Iowa Today mag., 1939; asso. prof. econs. Parsons Coll., Fairfield, Ia., 1946, exec. v.p. 1946-47, acting pres., 1947-48, pres., 1948-54; pres. Coll. of Ida., 1954-64; dir. devel. Center for Study Democratic Instns., from 1964. Served with USAAF, 1943-45. mem. Iowa Bar Assn., Am. Acad. Polit. and Social Sci., Ia. Hist. Soc., Delta Theta Phi, Pi Gamma Mu, Phi Kappa Phi. Republican. Presbyn. (elder). Clubs: Rotary, Fairfield Golf. Author monographs. Contbr. articles to tech. and profl. mags. Office: Santa CA

SHEEHAN, PERLEY POORE, editor, author; b. Cincinnati, O., June 11, 1875; s. David Este and Alfarata (Winder) S.; Ph.B., Union Coll., Schenectady, N.Y., 1898; m. Virginie Pont, of Paris, France, 1902. Newspaper corr. New York, London and Paris, until 1908; editor in charge Paris Hearld, 1905-07; asso. editor Munsey publs., 1908-10. Author: The Seer, 1913; Those Who Walk in Darkness, 1915; The Passport Invisible, 1916; If You Believe It, It's So, 1919; Apache Gold (pseud. White Birch"), 1919; The House with a Bad Name, 1921; Hollywood as a World Center, 1924; The Whispering Chorus, 1927; The Bayou Shrine, 1928; Three Sevens, 1928. Co-Author: We Are French (with Robert H. Davis), 1914; Efficiency (one-act play), 1916. Writer for Famous Players Lasky, Goldwyn and other film producers; motion picture director, Adapted and supervised Universal's production, The Hunchback of Notre Dame." Made unique collection of Seminole medicinal plants from Big Cypress Swamp, Fla., for N.Y. Bot. Garden, 1920. Mem. Alpha Delta Phi. Address: American Express Co., Nice France‡

SHEEHAN, ROBERT WADE, mag. editor, writer; b. Wallingford, Conn., Mar. 20, 1903; s. Jeremiah Edward and Mary Anne (Coughlin) S.; student N.Y. Prep. Sch., 1922, Trinity Coll., Hartford, Conn., 1923-25; m. Dorothy Laden, Apr. 4, 1929. Coll. corr. Hartford Times, 1925; asst. editor, The Spectator, ins. periodical, 1926-29, asso. editor, 1929-35, mng. editor, 1935-40; dir. publs. and pub. relations Nat. Assn. Ins. Agts., 1940-42; asso. editor War Progress, confidential report of W.P.B., 1942-43; Washington staff corr. Time mag., 1943-45; asso. editor Fortune mag., 1945-59, mem. bd. editors 1959-68; contbr. articles to Fortune and other periodicals. Recipient Alumni medal of excellence Trinity Coll., 1967. Mem. Delta Kappa Epsilon. Home: New York City NY Died July 23, 1971; buried St. Peter's Cemetery, Troy NY

SHEEHY, MAURICE S(TEPHEN), clergyman; b. Irwin, Ill., Apr. 26, 1898; s. Maurice J. and Ellen (O'Connor) S.; A.B., Loras Coll., Dubuque, Ia.; grad. St. Paul Seminary, Minn., 1922; S.T.B., Catholic U. of Am.; A.M., Ph.D., LL.D., Laval University; LL.D., St. Norbert's College, 1963. Professor and athletic dir. Loras Coll., 1922-27; instr. religion Catholic U., 1927, asst. to rector, 1931-36, asso. professor and head department religion, 1936-58. Domestic prelate to Pope Pius XII; name prothonotary apostolic by Pope John XXIII. Served as captain, chaplain, Naval Air Station, Jacksonville, Fla., U.S.S. Miss, and U.S.S. Saratoga, dist. chaplain 14, Naval Dist.; rear admiral U.S. Naval Reserve, ret. vice admiral, 1958; pastor St. Pius X Church, Cedar Rapids, Iowa, from 1958; dean of Cedar Rapids (Iowa) Catholic Church, from 1958, Decorated: Bronze star and six battle stars. Mem. Nat. Catholic Edn. Assn. (chmn. personnel com. 1929, chmn. finance com., coll. sect. 1934); mem. Eastern Assn. Coll. Deans (pres. 1937); mem. bd. visitors, Naval Acad., 1937; mem. Catholic Anthropol. Assn., Mil. Chaplains Assn. (pres.), Pi Gamma Nu, Phi Kappa. Author: Christ and the Catholic Coll., 1926; Problems of Student Guidance, 1929; College Men, 1936; Head Over Heels, 1951; Six O'Clock Mass, 1952; The Priestly Heart, 1956; Communist War on God, 1956; Father Nick of Hickory Creek, 1966. Home: Dubuque IA Died Feb. 10, 1972; buried Mt. Olivet Cemetery Dubuque IA

SHEELY, WILLIAM CLARENCE, judge; b. Gettysburg, Pa., Mar. 28, 1902; s. William and Eugenia (Hanna) S.; B.S., Gettysburg Coll., 1923; LL.B., M.A., Dickinson Sch. Law, Carlisle, Pa., 1926, LL.D., 1952, D.C.L., 1960; LL.D., Gettysburg College, 1959; m. Dorothy Bushnell, Feb. 12, 1930. Admitted to Pa. bar, 1926, Pa. Supreme Ct., 1926, Superior Ct., Dist. Cts., U.S. Supreme Ct.; asso. Keith & Sheely, Gettysburg, 1926-35; presiding judge 51st Jud. Dist., Adams and Fulton cos., from 1935; pres. Dicksinson Sch. Law, 1939-59. Mem. Am., Pa. (pres.), bar assns., Sigma Chi. Democrat. Presbyn. Mason (K.T., 33 degree), Elk, Odd Fellow. Home: Gettysburg PA Deceased.

SHEETS, HAROLD F., business exec.; b. Rochelle, Ill., May 2, 1883; s. Frank D. and Mary (Ellinwood) S.; A.B., Yale, 1903; m. Margaret Prentiss Austin, Sept., 1907 (dec. 1948); children—Harold Frank, Emily (Mrs. Teachout), Elizabeth (Mrs. Coach), Suzanne (Mrs. Emrich); m. 2d, Ruth Wilmot Cawlishaw, June 1950 (dec. Jan. 1955); m. 3d, Frances Gooding Twyeffort, Aug. 1955. Former chmn. bd. and dir. Socony-Vacuum Oil Co., Inc.; dir. Crocker-Citizens Nat. Bank. With War Dept., Washington, 1949; econ. adviser to Gen. Douglas MacArthur, Japan, 1949. Mem. Santa Barbara Found.; v.p. Cottage Hosp., Santa Barbara; bd. dirs., past pres. Santa Barbara Boys Club. Mem. U.S. C. of C. (past dir.), Council Fgn. Relations. Clubs: Interallied Club of Paris; University (N.Y.C., Santa Barbara); Valley (Montecito, Cal.); Santa Barbara; Coral Casino. Home: Santa Barbara CA Died May 29, 1969; inurnment Santa Barbara Cemetery, Santa Barbara CA

SHEFFIELD, FREDERICK, lawyer; b. N.Y.C., Feb. 26, 1902; s. James Rockwell and Edith (Tod) S.; student Groton, 1915-20; A.B., Yale, 1924, LL.B., 1927; m. Carolyn Cornell Blair, Nov. 22, 1935; children—James Rockwell, Margaret Blair, Ann Cornell. Admitted to N.Y. bar, 1928, practiced in N.Y.C., 1928-71; mem. Webster, Sheffield, Fleischmann, Hitchcock & Brookfield, N.Y.C., 1961-71; asst. U.S. commr. U.S. World's Fair Commn., 1940-41; director of American Sugar Co., Liggett & Myers. Trustee Carnegie Corporation N.Y., also chmn. exec. com., 1959-71, chmn. bd., 1966-71; trustee Smith Coll., Northampton, Mass.; dir. St. Luke's Hosp., Trudeau Inst.; dir., past chmn. N.Y. Sch. Social Work; fellow Pierson Coll. of Yale U. Mem. Yale Athletic Assn. (bd. control 1927-32 48-52). Clubs: Downtown Assn., Yale, Century Assn., Coffee, University (N.Y.C.); Wilton New York City NY Died May 1971.

SHEIL, BERNARD J(AMES), archbishop; born Chicago, Ill.; ed. St. Viator's Coll., Bourbonnais, Ill. Ordained priest R.C. Ch., 1910; asst. pastor St. Mel's Ch., Chicago, 1910-17; chaplain Great Lakes Naval Tng. Sta., 1918-19, Cook Co. Jail, 1919-23; asst. pastor Holy Name Cathedral, spiritual director Quigley Prep. Sem., 1919-23; asst. chancellor Archdiocese of Chgo., 1923-24, chancellor, 1924-28; auxiliary bishop, 1928-69, vicar gen. 1928-39, Adminstr. 1939-40, pastor of St. Andrew's Ch.; named titular archbishop of Selge, 1959. Treas. Internat. Eucharastic Congress, 1926. Founder, past dir. Cath. Youth Orgn. Founder, pres. Bishop Sheil Found. Home: Tucson AZ Died Sept. 13, 1969.

SHEININ, JOHN J(ACOBI), former coll pres.; b. Bobruysk, Russia, Mar. 21 1900; s. Jacob and Chernia (Rosenhaus) S.; naturalized citizen; B.S., U. Ala., 1928; M.S., Northwestern, 1929. Ph.D., 1932, M.B., 1932, M.D., 1933; Sc.D. (hon.), The Chicago Med. Sch., 1949; m. Ruth Aaron, Sept. 3, 1932; 1 son, James Charles. Instr., dept. anatomy, U. Ala., 1925-27; fellow in anatomy, dept. anatomy, med. sch., Northwestern University, 1927-32; prof. anatomy, The Chicago Med. Sch., 1932-66, prof. emeritus, 1967-72, chmn. dept. anatomy, 1932-57, dean, 1935-62, pres., 1950-66, pres. emeritus, 1967-72. Recipient Gold medal award Phi Lambda Kappa, 1952; Merit award Northwestern U., 1956; Horatio Alger award Am. Schs. and Colls. Assn., 1957; Jesuit Centennial citation, 1957; Edn. award Immigrants' Protective League, 1958; Founders' Day award Loyola U., 1962; Service to Youth award YMCA, 1964; Achievement award Phi Epsilon Pi, 1966; Merit award U.S. Navy and 9th Naval Dist., 1966; named to Hall Fame, City Chgo., 1967, Wisdom Hall Fame, 1970. Fellow Institute of Medicine of Chgo., Am. Acad. Gen. Practice, Am. Geriatrics Soc., Royal Soc. Health; mem. Assn. Am. Med. Colleges (emeritus), American Assn. Anatomists, Soc. for Exptl. Biology and Medicine, A.A.A.S., Am. Assn. U. Profs., Ill. Acad. Sci., Ill. Med. Soc., A.M.A., Fedn. State Bds., Chicago Med. Soc., Phi Delta Epsilon, Sigma Xi, Phi Epsilon Pi, Alpha Omega Alpha. Jewish religion. Clubs: Executives, Standard. Contbr. articles med. jours. Home: Chicago IL Died Jan. 9, 1972; buried Memorial Park Cemetery Skokie IL

SHELDON, G. L., banker; b. Jay, Vt., July 8, 1909; s. H. L. and Madge (Lucier) S.; student Columbia, 1931; m. Merna Russell, June 9, 1930; 1 son, Donald R. With Bank of N.Y. from 1926, became comptroller and exec. v.p., prin. organizer, treas. Bank of N.Y. Co. Mem. Financial Execs. Inst. Home: Garden City NY Died Aug. 5, 1970; buried Pinelawn Memorial Park Long Island NY

SHELDON, GRACE CAREW, journalist, author; b. Buffalo, N.Y.; d. Judge James and Sarah (Carew) S.; prep. ed'n Buffalo Sem.; grad. Wells Coll., 1875; had advanced ed'n in music, including vocal, instrumental and thorough-bass. Founded May 1, 1886, and pres. of Internat. Woman's Exchange of Buffalo, which accents work only from self-supporting women in U.S.; originated drawing-room talks in Buffalo and other Am. and European cities on Scott and his novels; delegate to Internat. Press Congress, Bordeaux, Sept. 1895; corr. Buffalo Courier while in France; on staff Buffalo Courier, 1890-1900; sent to S. America, Feb., 1896, to write regarding gold mine controversy; visited the Orinoco, Northern Venezuela, Curacao, Hayti and the West Indies, writing specials for New York and Buffalo papers; now has syndicate of her own which she supplies weekly as she travels. Charter mem. Scribblers' Club, Buffalo; corr. mem. Nat. Geog. Soc., Washington; active mem. League of American Pen-women. Author: As We Saw It in '90, 1891; From Pluckemin to Paris, 1899. Founder Internat. Progressive Thought League, 1906. Residence: Buffalo NY‡

SHELDON, ROY HORTON, life ins. exec.; b. Sutherland, Ia., Aug. 6, 1894; s. Daniel Marion and Catherine Elizabeth (Davis) S.; student pub. schs.; m. Irene Waybright, Oct. 19, 1916; children—Barbara S. (Mrs. Glenn G. Whitaker), Dorothy S. (Mrs. James C. Humphries), Rogr H., Patricia S. (Mrs. J. Thiel Sullivan). Salesman, Equitable Life Ins. Co. of Ia., Los Angeles, 1917-19, gen. agt., 1919-34, spl. rep., 1934-70. Los Angeles Fire Commn., 1955-61. Treas., H E A R Found., 1957-60. Mem. Million Dollar Round Table Nat. Assn. Life Underwriters, Life Underwriters Assn. Los Angeles (past pres., past dir.), Los Angeles C. of C. Republican. Presbyn. Mason, Kiwanian. Clubs: Jonathan, Wilshire Country. Home: Los Angeles CA Died Oct. 1970.

SHELDON, WILMON HENRY, college prof.; b. Newton, Mass., Apr. 4, 1875; s. Henry Newton and Clara Phelps (Morse) S.; A.B., Harvard, 1895, A.M., 1896, Ph.D., 1899; m. Elisabeth Franc Dunham, of Richmond, Ind., June 12, 1903. Prof. philosophy,

Dartmouth, since 1909. Mem. Am. Philos. Assn. Democrat. Contbr. to philos. jours. Home: Hanover NH‡

SHELFORD, VICTOR E(RNEST), zoologist; b. Chemung, N.Y., Sept. 22, 1877; s. Alexander Hamilton and Sarah Ellen (Rumsey) S.; student W. Va. University, 1899-1901; University of Chicago, 1901-07, S.B., 1903, Ph.D., 1907; m. Mary Mabel Brown, June 12, 1907 (deceased August 17, 1940); children—Lois F. (Mrs. E. H. Bennett), John V. Teacher, pub. schs., Chemung County, N.Y., 1895-97; tutor in zoology, W.Va. U., 1901; asst. and inst. dept. of zoology, U. of Chicago, 1903-14; research work in European museums, 1908; in charge marine ecology, Puget Sound Biol. Sta., alternate summers, 1914-30, editorial bd. publs., 1921-30; asst. and asso. prof. zoology, U. of Ill., 1914-27, prof. 1927-46, acting head of dept., 1939-40; chmn. of dept., 1940-41, prof. emeritus, 1946; biologist in charge Research Labs., Ill. State Natural History Survey, 1914-29. Chmn. Nat. Research Council Com. on Grassland, 1932-39, mem. com. on Wild Life, 1931-35; founder, Grassland Research Foundation, 1939, pres., 1958, chmn. scientific adv. bd., 1959-68, Ecologists' Union (now Nature Conservancy), 1946; lecturer Purdue University Science Institute, 1935, Stone Laboratory, Ohio State University, 1937. Recipient Nash Conservation Award, 1953. Fellow Entomol. Society America, A.A.A.S.; member American Society Zoologist, Ecol. Society America (1st pres. 1916, chmn. com. on preserves 1917-19, sr. chmn. 1921-23 and 1930-36, editorial bd. Ecology 1920-28, chmn. com. for study of communities, 1931-37), Philadelphia Acad. Natural Scis. (corr.), Soc. Liminology and Oceanography, Am. Soc. Naturalists, National Association American Geographers, Illinois Academy of Sciences, Sociedad Mexicana de Historia Natural, Phi Beta Kappa, Sigma Xi, Phi Sigma. Author: Animal Communities in Temperate America, 1913; Laboratory and Field Ecology, 1929; Animal Ecology and Taxonomy (with Allee and Park), 1937; Bio-Ecology (F. E. Clements), 1939. Compiler: Naturalist's Guide to the Americas, 1925. Contbr. scientific jours. and publs. Home: Urbana IL Died Dec. 27, 1968.

SHELLEY, HENRY CHARLES, author; b. Sussex, Eng.; m. Kathleen Ethel Rogers. Corr. Westminster Gazette during Boer War; editor Weekly Mail, Johannesburg, S. Africa, 1902-8; London editor Rand Daily Mail, 1903-4; lit. and dramatic editor, Boston Herald, since 1906. Author: The Story of Dumbarton Castle, 1895; The Story of Bothwell Castle, 1895; The Homes and Haunts of Thomas Carlyle, 1895; The Songs of Burns, 1896; The Ayrshire Homes and Haunts of Burns, 1897; Chats About the Microscope, 1899; How to Buy a Camera, 1902; Literary By-Paths in Old England, 1906; John Harvard and His Times, 1907; Untrodden English Ways, 1908; Inns and Taverns of Old London, 1909; Gilbert, White and Selborne, 1909. Address: The Herald Boston‡

SHELTON, JANE DE FOREST, author; b. at Derby, Conn.; d. Edward Nelson and Mary Jane (de Forest) S. Author: By the Way, or an Idler's Diary, 1887; The Salt Box House, 1900. Contbr. to mags. Address: Derby CT‡

SHELTON, WILLARD ELLINGTON, newspaperman; b. St. Louis, Oct. 2, 1905; s. William Price and Mattie (Griffin) S.; A.B., Eureka Coll., 1927; grad. work Washington Univ. (St. Louis), 1930-31; m. Marie Price, Oct. 14, 1928; 1 dau., Mary Sue; m. 2d, Isabelle Graham, Feb. 14, 1948; 1 dau., Gale. High sch. teacher, 1927-28; mem. editorial staff Christian Evangelist, 1928-35, editor, 1935-38; editorial writer St. Louis Star-Times, 1938, editor of editorial page, 1939-43; editorial writer and columnist, The Chicago Sun, 1943-46; Wash. bureau, PM, N.Y. Star, 1946-49; Washington editor The Nation, 1949-53; polit. columnist CIO News; asst. editor AFL-CIO News, 1955-58, mng. editor, 1958-68. Mem. Lambda Chi Alpha, Pi Kappa Delta, Sigma Delta Chi. Contbr., Am. Mercury, Nation, New Republic. Home: Arlington VA Died Dec. 1, 1970.

SHELTON, WILLIAM ARTHUR, clergyman, educator; b. Azusa, Calif., Sept. 6, 1875; s. Leroy and Sarah Elizabeth (Rogers) S.; B.A., Hargrove Coll., Ardmore, Okla., 1905; M.A., Yale, 1908, B.D., 1908; studied U. of Chicago, six semesters; D.D., Emory, 1914; m. Viola W. Davis, Sept. 25, 1900; children—Mildred, Arthur Leroy, Curtis Yeomans (dec.), Frederick Davis, John Hadley, Eleanor Ruth (dec.). Ordained ministry M.E. Ch., S., 1899; pastor in Okla., 1899-1905, 1908-11; pres. Okla. Wesleyan Coll., 1911-14; prof. O.T. and Semitic langs., Emory U., 1914-30; pastor Mt. Vernon Place M.E. Ch., S., Washington, D.C., 1930-32, Grace Ch., Atlanta, 1932-38, dist. supt., Birmingham Dist., Meth. Church, 1938-41; now pastor Highlands Meth. Church, Birmingham; head dept. of religion Birmingham-So. Coll. since 1949. Mem. General Bd. of Education, M.E. Ch., S., 1914-18. In Egypt and Western Asia, 1920, as mem. U. of Chicago Oriental Expdn. for archeol. research. Member Oriental Soc. Palestine, Archeol. Inst. America, Soc. Bibl. Lit. and Exegesis, Ga. Acad. Sciences, Linguistic Soc. America; fellow Royal Geog. Soc. of Gt. Britain. Fraternal del. from M.E. Ch., S., to M.E. Ch., Springfield, Mass., 1924; mem. Gen. Conf. M.E. Ch., S., 1914, 22, 26, 30, 34, 38; mem. Uniting Conf., Kansas City, 1939, Gen. Conf., Atlantic City, 1940. Pres. Christian Council of Atlanta, 1935-38. Mem. Ga. State Bd. Edn., 1937-38. Mason (32 deg.). Address: 1427 33rd St., Birmingham AL‡

SHENEMAN, HESTER MARY DICKERSON (MRS. MCKINLEY SHENEMAN), social worker exec.; b. Tina, Mo.; d. John L. and Laura (Boley) Dickerson; B.S., State Tchrs. Coll., Maryville, Mo., 1924; M.S.W., Chgo. U., 1940; m. McKinley Sheneman, Nov. 30, 1950. Tchr. high sch. Gallatin, Mo., 1924-33; caseworker Jackson County Relief, Kansas City, Mo., 1933-38, Child Guidance Clinic, Kansas City, Mo., 1939-44; exec. Spofford Home, 1944-69; exec. Assn. Children's Agys., 1959-60. Mem. Woman's C. of C. Kansas City, Am. Assn. Social Work, Mo. Assn. Social Welfare, Orthopsychiat. Assn., Assn. Psychiat. Social Workers. Clubs: Altrusa. Woman's City, Presidents and Past Presidents. Home: Shawnee Mission KS Died Nov. 14, 1969.

SHEPARD, EARL DORMAN, clergyman, educator; b. LeRoy, Genesee Co., N.Y., Jan. 21, 1870; s. Edwin Dorman and Mary Elizabeth (Heddon) S.; A.B., Syracuse U., 1892, A.M., 1895 (D.D., 1913); m. Kate Leora Abbott, of Syracuse, June 29, 1893. Ordained M.E. ministry, 1894; pastor Eden, N.Y., 1894, Honeoye Falls, 1899-1904, Grace Ch., Rochester, N.Y., 1905-14; pres. Genesee Wesleyan Sem., since 1914. Mem. Gen. Conf. M.E. Ch., Minneapolis, Minn., 1912; del. same, Saratoga Springs, N.Y., 1916. Mem. Delta Upsilon, Phi Beta Kappa. Home: Lima NY‡

SHEPHERD, GRACE M., state supt. schs.; b. Ottumwa, Ia.; d. Thomas K. and Melissa (Whitcomb) S.; A.B., Hastings (Neb.) Coll., 1894; grad. Kan. State Normal Sch., 1895; post-grad. work, U. of Chicago; unmarried. Teacher high sch. (Hiawatha, Kan.), State Normal School (Lewiston, Ida.), high sch. (Boise, Ida.); state supt. pub. instrn., Ida., since Jan. 1, 1911. Republican. Club: Columbian. Home: 602 Washington St. S., Boise ID‡

SHEPHERD, HAROLD, legal educator; b. Paris, Ida., Nov. 28, 1897; s. Joseph Russell and Rose (Budge) S.; A.B., Stanford University, 1919, J.D., 1922; LL.D., Tulane University, 1946; m. Eleanor Stahman, June 9, 1921 (dec.); m. 2d, Marian Graham McCracken, Feb. 18, 1959. Prof. of law and dean, Law Sch., U. of Wyoming, 1922-23; asso. prof. law, Stanford, 1923-26, prof., 1926-30; prof. law, U. of Chicago, 1930-31; prof. law and dean, Law Sch., U. of Wash., 1931-36; Wald prof. of contracts, U. of Cincinnati, 1936-39; professor law, Duke University 1940-42, dean law sch., 1947-49; William Nelson Cromwell Prof. law Stanford U.; also visiting prof. of law, Columbia Univ., summer 1929, Univ. of Chicago, 1929-30, U. of Minn., summer 1930, Stanford, summer 1932; visiting prof. Duke U., 1939-40; professor law Stanford U., 1949-61, prof. law emeritus, 1961-71; vis. prof. law U. Utah, 1961-62. Secretary Assn. of Am. Law Schools, 1937-40; pres., 1941. Second lt., U.S. Army, World War I. Serving as major, lt. col. and col., Army of U.S., World War II; chief Contract Termination Br., later of Legal Div., Office Chief of Ordnance. Mem. Am., Wyo., Wash. and Ohio bar associations, Phi Beta Kappa, Order of Coif (national president 1959-61), Phi Alpha Delta, Theta Chi. Author: Cases and Materials on Contracts; Contracts and Contract Remedies (with H. Wellington), 1957; Introduction to Freedom of Contract (with B. Sher), 1960. Home: Santa Cruz CA Died Oct. 2, 1971; buried Oakwood Cemetery Santa Cruz CA

SHEPHERD, PATRICIA DRAKE (MRS. JAMES LEFTWICH SHEPHERD III), educator; b. Waco. Tex.; d. Paul Jewett and Ione (Johnston) Drake; A.B., M.A., Baylor U.; Ph.D., U. Pa., 1949; m. James Leftwich Shepherd III, Sept. 10, 1953. Instr. German, U. Tex., 1942-49; prof. German, Baylor U., 1949-72, chmn. dept., 1958-70. Mem. Modern Lang. Assn., Am. Assn. Tchrs. German, South Central Modern Lang. Assn., Am. Assn. U. Women. Presbyn. Author: Grillparzer and Biedermeier, 1953; also articles on German lit. Home: Waco TX Died Apr. 10, 1972.

SHEPHERD, PEARCE, actuary; b. Chicago, Dec. 3, 1901; s. Edwin S. and Alice Mary (Pearce) S.; student Western State Normal Sch., Kalamazoo, Mich., 1916-20; Ph.B., U. of Chicago, 1924; m. Margaret Doheny, Nov. 25, 1919. Clk., Marcus Gunn & Lynn A. Glover, Chicago, 1921-25, North Am. Reassurance Co., N.Y. City, 1925-28, asst. actuary and asst. sec., 1928-32; mathematician Prudential Ins. Co., Newark, 1932-35, asst. actuary, 1935-42, asso. actuary, 1942-43, 2d v.p., 1943-47, v.p. and asso. actuary, 1947-54, v.p. and actuary, 1954-59, v.p., chief actuary, 1959-62, sr. v.p. and chief actuary, 1962-66. Chmn. exec. com. Med. Information Bur., 1963; chmn. Health Ins. Council, 1965; sec. U.S. sect., permanent committee for International Congresses Actuaries. Fellow Soc. Actuaries (pres. 1958-59); mem. Home Office Life Underwriters Assn. (pres. 1946), Phi Beta Kappa, East Orange NJ Died Sept. 5, 1969.

SHEPPARD, HARRY R., congressman; b. Mobile, Ala., Jan. 10, 1885; studied law for 3 years; m. Kay O'Keefe Olson, May 24, 1933. Began with Santa Fe R.R. in transportation dept.; then engaged in copper business; traveled on 3 continents for business interests; developed King's Beverage and King's Labs. and was pres. and gen. mgr. to 1934. Mem. 75th to 77th Congresses (1937-43), 19th Dist. and 78th to 82d Congresses, 21st Dist., 83d-87th Congresses, 27th Dist., 88th Congress, 33rd Dist.; dean Cal. Congl. Delegation; mem. Def. Appropriations Com.; chmn. sub-com. mil. constrn. Democrat. Home: Yucaina CA

SHEPPARD, LAWRENCE BAKER, business exec.; born Baltimore, Md., Dec. 13, 1897; s. Harper Donelson and Henrietta Dawson (Ayres) S.; grad., Haverford Sch., 1917; LL.B., U. of Va., 1921; m. Charlotte Newton, June 12, 1919; children—Charlotte Newton (Mrs. William Todd DeVan), Lawrence Baker (deceased), Alma (Mrs. Lorne Tolhurst), Patricia Anne (Mrs. William J. Winder). With Hanover (Pa.) Shoe, Inc., 1921-68, v.p., gen. mgr., dir., pres., then chmn. bd.; chmn. bd., dir. Sheppard and Myers, Incorporated; chmn. bd. Nat. Bank & Trust Company of Central Pa.; president, general manager Hanover Shoe Farms; president Standardbred Horse Sales Co., Harrisburg, Pa. Mem. Albemarle County bar. V.p. Nat. Footwear Mfrs. Assn.; mem. exec. committee, U.S. Trotting Association; v.p., Hambletonian Soc.; steward, Trotting Horse Club of America, Incorporated; director Hanover Gen. Hosp. Served as cons., Leather and Shoe Sec., W.P.B., dept. chief of div., asst. dir. Textile, Clothing and Leather Bur., World War II. Served as ensign in the U.S. Navy, World War I. Recieved Medal of Freedom, hdqrs. U.S. Forces European Theatre, 1945; certificate of appreciation from War Dept., 1946; T. Kenyon Holly Memorial Award by Philanthropic Foundn. of Shoe and Leather Industry, 1948. Republican. Mem. Pa. State Chamber of Commerce (director), American Legion. Phi Gamma Delta. Mason (K.T., Shriner), Elk. Clubs: Country, Arcadian, Republican (Hanover); Army and Navy (Washington, D.C.). Home: Hanover PA Died Feb. 26, 1968.

SHERE, LEWIS, corp. exec.; b. Oxbow, Saskatchewan, Can., Sept. 8, 1895; s. Joshua and Anna (Kohen) S.; B.S., U. Minn. 1920; m. Esther Sharlitt, June 14, 1931; children—Madelon (Mrs. Donald Wittenberg), Joshua. Bacteriologist, chemist Minn. State Health Dept., 1920-26; milk sanitarian Ill. Dept. Pub. Health, 1926; dir. city div. dairy products Chgo. Health Dept., 1926-28; dir. research and publicity Diversey Corp., Chgo., 1928-32, sec., 1932-34, v.p., 1934-43, pres., from 1943. Mem. Am. Pub. Health Assn., Inst. Food Technologists, Am. Dairy Sci. Assn., Chgo. Dairy Tech. Soc., Nat. Assn. Sanitarians. Internat. Assn. Milk and Food Sanitarians, Dairy Industries Supply Assn., Am. Chem. Soc. Home: Chicago IL Died Jan. 29, 1971; buried Shalom Meml. Park.

SHERER, REX W., educator; b. Scranton, Pa., Jan. 10, 1876; s. William and Mary J. (Herrmanns) von Scherer; Ph.B., U. of Calif., 1898; m. Angelita L. Hohwiesner, of San Rafael, Calif., Oct. 8, 1904; 1 dau., Louise Angelita. Instr. science and mathematics, Selborne Sch., San Rafael, Calif., 1898-1901; master English and mathematics, St. Mathews Sch., Burlingame, Calif., 1901-04; mgr. edn. dept. D. Appleton & Co. on Pacific Coast, 1904-08; mgr. fire ins. dept. Voss, Conrad & Co., San Francisco, 1908-11; pres. and mgr. Hitchcock Mil. Acad., 1911-25; comptroller Tamalpais Sch. since 1925; mem. advisory bd. Mercantile Trust Co. of Calif. since 1924; sec. Richard Diener Co. since 1925. Maj. N.G.C., 1901-04. Mason. Clubs: University, Marin Golf and Country. Home: San Rafael CA‡

SHERIDAN, LAWRENCE VINNEDGE, landscape architect, consultant on city and regional planning; b. Frankfort, Ind., July 8, 1887; s. Harry C. and Margaret (Vinnedge) S.; B.S. in C.E., Purdue U., 1909, C.E., 1912; student Harvard Sch. of Landscape Architecture, 1916-17; m. Grace Emmel, Dec. 15, 1919; children—Roger Williams, Roderick Kessler, Harry C. II, Philip. Transitman, insp., chief insp., Bd. of Park Commrs., Indianapolis, 1911-14; Bureau Municipal Research, N.Y., 1914-16; planner Camp Pike, Ark., 1917; engr. Dallas Property Owners Assn., 1919-21; exec. sec. City Plan Commn., Indianapolis, 1921-23; private practice in landscape architecture and city planning since 1923; pres. Met. Planners, Inc., 1953-56, planning counselor, 1956-72; tchr. history of landscape architecture Purdue U.; cons. planning and zoning USAF, 1955-72; cons. landscape architect for Purdue U., Crown Hill Cemetery, Indpls.; cons. to Ind. and Ky. State Planning Bds., 1934-37; regional counselor Nat. Resources Planning Bd. for Ind., Ill., Ohio, Wis., Mich., Ky., and W.Va., 1937-41; redesigned Camp Robinson, Ark., on site of Camp Pike, 1940; camp development or site plans for Ft. Eustis, Va., Billings Gen. Hosp., Ft. Benjamin Harrison, Ind., Camp Chaffee, Ark., and Camp Atterbury, Ind., 1940-41. Served as 2d lt., F.A., A.E.F., 1918-19; commd. 2d lt. Coast Arty. Reserve, 1923, and advanced to grade of lt. col., Construction Div., Q.M. General's Office, 1941; Deputy Service Command Engr., 9th Service Command, 1942-45; colonel, Corps Engrs., Army U.S., August 1942-46;

resumed practice city and regional planning, and landscape architecture. Recipient of the Distinguished Service award by the American Institute of Planners, 1957. Fellow American Society of Landscape Architects, American Soc. of Civil Engineers (life); mem. American Inst. of Planners (pres. 1940), Ind. Engring. Soc. (past pres.), Indiana Society of Pioneers, Sigma Phi Epsilon. Christian Scientist. Club: Service (Indpls.). Home: Indianapolis IN Died Jan. 26, 1972.

SHERIDAN, SARAH M., business executive; b. Detroit, Mich., Sept. 10, 1876; d. Thomas Sarsfield and Eva Ernestine (Porter) S.; ed. high sch., Detroit. Began with the Peninsular Electric Light Co., 1893, and after it was merged with the Detroit Edison Co., continued with the latter, of which was made sales mgr., 1910, v.p. 1921. Mem. Arts and Crafts Soc., Detroit. Episcopalian. Clubs: Woman's City, Detroit Athletic. Home: 120 Virginia Park. Office: 2000 Second Av., Detroit MI‡

SHERK, KENNETH WAYNE, educator; b. Cottage Grove, Ore., Mar. 29, 1907; s. Alvin Lloyd and Florence Ethel (Bisbey) S.; A.B., Reed Coll., 1928; Ph.D. (Pfister research fellow) Cornell U., 1934; m. Dorothy Lucille Blacking, June 7, 1930; children—Larry Wayne, Lida Dee, Betty Blacking, Kenneth Lloyd, Marjorie Joy, Jerome Ray. Asst. chemistry Cornell, 1928-30, 31-33; teaching fellow Rice Inst., Houston, 1930-31; asst. prof. chemistry Smith Coll., 1935-43, asso. prof., 1943-51, prof., 1951-72, chmn. dept. chemistry, 1951-58, dir. grad. study, 1959-68, dir. Clark Sci. Center, 1969-72, dir. NSF In-Service Inst., 1960-61, 63-64, 66-67, 69-70. Asso. prof. U. Hawaii, 1949-50. Chmn. Williamsburg (Mass.) Bd. Health, 1946-48, Williamsburg Sch. Bd., 1954-68; dir. Region II Mass. Com. Pub. Safety, 1942-43; Mass. adv. council for univ. extension and corr. courses, 1959-65. Mem. A.A.A.S., Am. Chem. Soc. (sect. chmn. 1964), Sigma Xi, Acacia. Republican. Mason. Contbr. sci. articles to chem. jours. Home: Williamsburg MA Died Aug. 11, 1972.

SHERMAN, CHARLES LAWRENCE, tool mfr.; b. Rockford, Ill., Mar. 28, 1905; s. Robert H. and Winifred M. (Lawrence) S.; student Beloit Coll., 1923 U. Ill., 1924; m. Genevieve A. Johnson, Mar. 6, 1929; children—Ronald Dwight, Leigh Lawrence. Elec. contractor, 1925-28; farmer, 1929-30; truck owner hwy. constrn., 1931-33; set up man presses Nat. Lock Co., Rockford, Ill., 1933-40; electrician, traveling sales and service, 1942-55; asst. supt. Whitney Metal Tool Co., Rockford, 1955-56, supt., 1956-59, gen. mgr., 1959-61, v.p., 1961-65, exec. v.p., 1965-68, pres., 1966-67. Mem. adv. bd. Precision Sheet Metal Inst. Chgo. Mem. Rockford C. of C. Eagle. Club: One-a-Month. Patentee wire loop former. Home: Rockford IL Died June 29, 1968.

SHERMAN, JOHN K(URTZ), journalist, critic; b. Sioux City, Ia., Apr. 19, 1898; s. Valentine Christophe and Leora Melissa (Chase) S.; student, Univ. of Minn., 1917-18; m. Jane Chase, Sept. 16, 1929;children—Janet, John Kurtz, Willis. Joined staff of Minneapolis (Minn.) Daily Star, 1925 (later Minneapolis Star-Journal, then Minneapolis Star and Tribune), music critic, 1926-69, art, drama and book critic, 1928-69, arts editor and columnist, 1935-69; lecturer on arts; has conducted various radio programs over Mpls. stations. Granted regional writing scholarship by Rockefeller Found., 1946, for the writing of Music and Maestros: The Story of the Minneapolis Symphony Orchestra, 1952. Member Phi Mu Alpha, Sinfonia. Author: Music and Theater in Minnesota History, 1958; Sunday Best, Collected Essays, 1963. Home: Minneapolis MN Died Apr. 18, 1969.

SHERMAN, LAWRENCE WILLIAM, JR., coll. pres.; b. Sidney, O., July 12, 1928; s. Lawrence William and LaDonna (Motsinger) S.; B.S., B.A., Miami U., Oxford, O., 1951; M.B.A., Ind. U., 1952; m. Alice Pool, June 12, 1951; children—Ann Elizabeth, Susan Elaine, Stephen Charles, Mark Jeffrey. Instr., A. and M. Coll. Tex., 1952-54; asst. prof. U. Mass., 1954-56; faculty asso. Ind. U., 1956-57; sr. operations analyst Ford Motor Co., Detroit, Syracuse, N.Y., 1957-58; instr. Syracuse U., evenings 1957-58; cons. Smith-Corona, Syracuse, 1958; asst. to dean Grad. Sch. Retailing, U. Pitts., 1958-61, asst. to dean Grad. Sch. Bus., asst. dir. mgmt. program for execs., 1961-62; dean Sch. Bus. Adminstrn, and Div. Liberal Arts, Robert Morris Jr. Coll., Pitts., 1961-65; pres. Robert Morris Coll., Carthage, Ill., 1965-69. Mem. Am. Marketing Assn., Am. Econs. Assn., Eta Mu Pi, Cathage IL Died Feb. 26, 1969.

SHERMAN, THOMAS B., editor; b. Augusta, Ga., Sept. 4, 1891; s. Albert G. and Annie Lee (Hood) S.; student Acad. of Richmond County, Ga., 1902-06; Univ. Ga., 1907-09; m. Chloe Wachmann, Nov. 20, 1928; 1 s., William C. Reporter, rewrite man, Music Critic Atlanta Constitution, 1909-11, Birmingham News8 1911-16, Atlanta Journal, 1916-17. Mag. editor, King Features, hdqrs. New York, 1920-26; music critic St. Louis Post-Dispatch, 1926-65, editor Sunday mag., 1926-38, editor Pictures, 1938-44, editor editorial title page, 1944-47, contbg. editor and music critic, 1965-68, literary editor and editor Post-Disptach Sunday book page, 1947-68, also music and arts editor, 1956-68, also was editor Post Dispatch 75th Anniversary Supplement. Mem. Washington University adv. council, 1958-59. Served as capt., Arty., AUS, 1917-19; overseas, 1918. Recipient Gold medal from chpt. A, Daus. of Confederacy, 1906; gold medal St. Louis chpt. Nat. Soc. Arts and Letters, 1967. Former v.p. Am. Newspaper Guild. Mem. Am. Music Critics Association (pres. 1960-62), Sigma Alpha Epsilon. Democrat. Home: Clayton MO Died Sept. 28, 1968.

SHERMAN, WILLIAM BOWEN, physician, educator; b. Providence, Oct. 17, 1907; s. Henry Clapp and Cora Aldrich (Bowen) S.; A.B., Columbia, 1926, A.M., 1927, M.D., 1931; m. Catherine B. McKecknie, Sept. 20, 1941; children—Phoebe, Martha (dec.), John William. Intern Presbyn. Hosp., N.Y. City, 1931-33, asst. physician, 1936-47, asst. attending physician, 1947-55, associate attending physician, 1955-71; assistant resident physician, assistant medicine Johns Hopkins Hosp., 1933-35; clin. asst. Roosevelt Hosp., N.Y. City, 1936-41, asst. attending physician, 1941-46, attending physician, 1947-71, director of the Institute of Allergy, 1960-71; asst. medicine Columbia, 1936-47, associate, 1947-50, assistant clinical professor, 1950-52, asso. clin. prof. since 1952; pvt. practice medicine, N.Y.C. since 1935; cons. Halloran V.A. Hosp., 1948-51, Area Office, V.A. since 1946; civilian cons. to Surgeon Gen. of Army, 1947-71, cons. USPHS, 1956-71, National Advisory Council of Allergy and Infectious Diseases, 1959-63. Chmn. organizing com. 4th Internat. Congress Allergology, 1961; hon. pres. 6th Internat. Congress on Allergology, 1967; chairman board Allergy Found. Am., 1967-71; exec. com. Am. Found. Allergic Diseases. Served as capt. to lieutenant colonel, U.S. Army, 1942-46. Recipient Robert Chobot award, 1964; Distinguished Service award Am. Acad. Allergy, 1965. Diplomate in allergy Am. Bd. Internal Medicine (chairman of sub specialty board of allergy 1957). Fellow A.C.P., Am. Acad. Allergy (pres. 1957-58), N.Y. Acad. Med.; mem. Soc. Exptl. Biol. and Med., Am. Clin. and Climatol. Assn., American Medical Association, N.Y. Acad. Sci., Phi Beta Kappa, Phi Gamma Delta. Clubs: Century Association, University (N.Y.C.). Author: Hypersensitivity Mechanics and Management, 1968; asthma sect. Musser's Internal Medicine, 1951, sect. allergy in Sodeman's Pathologic Physiology, 1950; Allergy in Pediatric Practice (with W. K. Kessler), 1957; sects. on asthma and hay fever in Cecil-Loeb Textbook of Medicine, 1963; sect. on atopic diseases in Santer and Alexander's Immunologic Diseases, 1965; tech. New York City NY Died Mar. 1, 1971; buried Sleepy Hollow Cemetery, Tarrytown NY

SHERO, LUCIUS ROGERS, prof. Greek; b. Smethport, Pa., Apr. 5, 1891; s. William Francis and Lucy Sophronia (Rogers) S.; Franklin and Marshall Coll., Lancaster, Pa., 1906-07; B.A., Haverford Coll., 1911; M.A., U. of Wis., 1912, Ph.D., 1920; B.A., 3d class, Lit.Hum., Oxford, U., 1917; m. Julia Adrienne Doe, June 20, 1918 (dec. 1951); children—Gertrude Caroline, Lucy Adrienne, Frances Livia. Fellow Univ. Wis., 1912-14; Rhodes scholar from Wis., at Oxford U., 1914-17; asso. prof. Latin, 1917-19, prof. Latin, 1919-20, Macalester Coll.; Hoffman prof. Greek, St. Stephen's Coll., Annandale, N.Y., 1920-28; prof. Greek, Swarthmore Coll., 1928-59, emeritus 1959-68, registrar, 1944-48, chmn. div. humanities, 1951-54. Visiting professor, Stanford University, 1932; annual professor, American School of Classical Studies at Athens, 1936-37; mem. mng. com. American Sch. Classical Studies. Mem. Am. Philol. Assn. (sec.-treas. 1939-44, dir. 1947-49, pres. 1949-50), American Guild of Organists, Classical Association Atlantic States, Archaeol. Inst. Am., Am. Assn. Univ. Profs., Hymn Soc. of America, Phi Beta Kappa. Episcopalian. Home: Swarthmore PA Died May 31, 1968.

SHERRILL, CLARENCE OSBORNE, born in Newton, N.C., May 24, 1876; son of Miles Osborne and Sarah Rosanna (Bost) S.; student Trinity Coll. (Duke U.), 1895-97; honor grad. U.S. Mil. Acad., 1901, Army Sch. of Line, Fort Leavenworth, Kan., 1906; grad. Army War Coll., 1907; m. Geraldine Caldwell Taylor, Nov. 30, 1905; children—Clarence Caldwell, Minnie Elizabeth. Commd. 2d lt., Corps Engrs., U.S. Army, Feb. 18, 1901; advanced through grades to col., Engrs., N.A., Aug. 5, 1917; lt. col., U.S. Army, July 1, 1920; resigned, Dec. 31, 1925; col. U.S. Engr. Reserve Corps, 1926-49; colonel Honorary Reserve U.S. Army since 1950. City manager, Cincinnati, 1926-30 and 1937-44; now retired. Vice pres. Kroger Grocery & Baking Co., 1930-35; pres. Am. Retail Fedn., 1935-37. Served in Philippine Insurrection, 1901-03; col. engrs., chief of staff, 77th Div., France, World War. Awarded D.S.M. (U.S.); Croix de Guerre with Palm (France). Service in Army also included mil. and engring. assignments; in charge river and harbor improvements, flood control, levee constrn., bridge bldg.; dir. pub. bldgs. and parks, Washington, D.C., 1921-25; mil. aid to Presidents Harding and Coolidge; etc. Chmn. Cincinnati Com. on Co-ordination and Cooperation; chmn. Cincinnati Employment Advisory Council, 1928-32; mem. City Planning Commn., Cincinnati, 1926-30 and 1937-44. Mem. Am. Soc. C.E., Cincinnati Chamber of Commerce (hon. life mem.), Am. Mil. Engrs. Methodist. Clubs: Commonwealth, Cincinnati Country, Engineers (Cincinnati); Army and Navy, Chevy Chase (Washington, D.C.). Author: Military Map Reading, 1910; Topographical Surveying, 1910; Rapid Sketching, 1910. Home: 2211 E. Hill Av., Hyde Park, Cincinnati 8 OH‡

SHERRILL, SAMUEL WELLS, educator; b. at Maryville, Tenn., Sept. 7, 1869; s. James Houston and Mary Texanna (Wells) S.; A.B., Maryville (Tenn.) Coll., 1892, A.M., 1895; m. Lucie Minnis, of New Market, Tenn., June 18, 1893. Supt. schs., Jonesboro, Tenn., 1892-1900, Carthage, Tenn., 1900-3, Trenton, 1903-5, Paris, 1906-11; head of dept. of psychology and methods, State Normal Sch., Johnson City, Tenn., 1911-15; state supt. pub. instrn., Tenn., since Apr. 9, 1915. Trustee U. of Tenn. Democrat. Presbyn. K.P. Wrote: Heroes in Gray, 1910; Handbook for Teachers, 1913. Home: 1517 Hawkins St. Address: State Capitol, Nashville TN‡

SHERRILL, WILLIAM LANDER, clergyman; b. Lincolnton, N.C., Feb. 9, 1860; s. Samuel Pinckney and Sarah Catherine (Lander) S.; ed. Lincolnton (N.C.) Acad.; m. Luetta Connor, May 21, 1884; 1 son, Henry Connor. Began as pharmacist, Dallas, N.C., 1879; mayor of Dallas, 1884; ordained ministry M.E. Ch., S., 1890; pastor successively Morganton, Connelly Springs, Elkin, Hickory, Lenoir, Mocksville, Asheboro, Murphy, Pineville, Leaksville, until 1924; asso. editor N.C. Christian Advocate, 1906-11. Sec. Western N.C. Conf. M.E. Ch., S., 1894-1938; sec.-treas. Bd. of Edn., same conf., 1925-29; mem. Gen. Conf., M.E. Ch., S., 1910, Gen. Bd. Ch. Extension, 1910-14. Mem. Mecklenburg County (N.C.) Chapter S.A.R., chaplain N.C. State Chapter, 1930-31, historian, 1931-32; charter mem. N.C. Pharmaceutical Assn., 1880. Author: The Annals of Lincoln County, N.C.; A Brief History of the Lander Family; A Brief Biography of Gen. Matthew Locke, of Rowan County, N.C. (1730-1801); A Brief Biography of Peter Cartwright, the pioneer Methodist Preacher of the Middle West; A Brief Biography of General James Pinckney Henderson of Charlotte NC‡

SHERWOOD, ARNOLD COOPER, railroad exec.; b. Patterson, N.J., Aug. 5, 1892; s. Clarence and Hulda Doty (Drew) S.; student pub. schs. and bus. coll; m. Margaret Holmes, Oct. 28, 1914; 1 son, Robert James. With U.P. R.R., N.Y.C., 1908-60, asst. sec., 1946-52, sec. 1952-60. Home: Paterson NJ Died Oct. 29, 1970; buried George Washington Meml. Park.

SHERWOOD, CARLTON MONTGOMERY, counsellor institutional financing; b. Buffalo, N.Y., Apr. 12, 1895; s. William Burt and Gertrude (Kring) S.; m. Ann Glover, Apr. 22, 1926; children—Hugh Clements, Elizabeth Ann. Sec. Y.M.C.A., Buffalo, 1915-17; enlisted Hdqrs. Troop, 78th Div., A.E.F., 1917, serving in Argonne and St. Mihiel engagements and on British front; after Armistice served as asso. dir. Flag Hut, Army Y.M.C.A., Brest, France; gen. sec. N.Y. State Christian Endeavor Union, 1919-27; exec. sec. Citizen's Com. of 1000, 1926-36; extension sec. Internat. Soc. Christian Endeavor, 1927-31, gen. sec., 1931-34; also editor The Christian Endeavor World, 1930-34 and sec. The World's Christian Endeavor Union, 1931-34; pres. Interdenom. Young People's Commn., 1932-33; exec. dir. Asso. Bds. for Christian Coll. in China, 1934-36. Dir. Congl. Nat. Pension campaign, 1937-38; now president and mem. firm Pierre, Hedrick & Sherwood, Inc., instnl. financing. Pres. Deering (N.H.) Community Center, Inc.; dir. N.H. Children's Aid Soc. Pres. Am. Assn. Fund Raising Counsel, 1945-47. Trustee N.Y. Theol. Sem., chmn. trustees 1964-66; trustee Wainwright House, Rye, New York; member of exec. council Found. Integrative Edn.; mem. commn. on religion and health Nat. Council Chs., chmn. commn., 1956-59. Recipient Vetus Maister Honoris Causa nat. award Am. Assn. Fund Raising Counsel, 1964. Mem. Am. Soc. Psychical Research (trustee), S.A.R. Mason. Home: Pleasantville NY Died Sept. 14, 1970; buried Forest Lawn Cemetery, Buffalo NY

SHERWOOD-DUNN, BERKELEY, M.D., banker; b. Rushford, N.Y.; s. William Erwin and Harriet Elizabeth (Peterson) Dunn; M.D., New York U., 1884; Bach. es lettres, U. of Paris, France, 1884, Dr. of Medecine, 1889; m. at Nice, France, Louise Lacy, d. Royal C. Knapp, of Rochester, N.Y., 1892; children—Gladys (dec.), Yerkes and Hamilton (twins), Dorothy; m. 2d, Princess Guerke, 1923. Practiced at Paris, 1888-97; asst. prof. gynecology, Tufts Coll. Med. Sch., Boston, 1900; surgeon to Cushing Hosp., Boston; joint owner and editor Annals of Gynecology and Pediatrics, Boston, 1900; between 1902-14, was sec. Century Trust Co. and dir. Bankers Life Ins. Co.; pres. European-Am. Bk., Del. & Northampton Ry., N.Y. & Del. Riv. Ry., and was officer or dir. numerous other corpns. and banks at New York and in S.C. Author of numerous med. papers and books. Nat. committeeman for S.C. Progressive Party, 1912. Apptd. dir. A.R.C. Hosp., Amiens, France, 1915; French Army med. service, front line, title benevole, grade of col., Oct. 1915; wounded, Nov. 1915; service at Paris, 1916-19; asst. to l'Hopital Cochin, Paris, 1916-18. Awarded eight decorations, including Legion of Honor. Founder and pres. Washington-Lafayette Com. Mem. various Am. and European med. socs., Soc. Alliance Francaise; v.p. Am. Civic Alliance.

Episcopalian. Clubs: Automobile, Athletic, Lawyers' (New York); Aiken (S.C.) Gun; American (founder and pres.), Nice Golf (France). Home: Waldorf Hotel, New York NY Office: 54 Boul. Victor Hugo, Nice France‡

SHIDEHARA, BARON KIJURO, Japanese premier; b. Aug. 11, 1872, Osaku-fu; s. of Shinjiro S.; grad. Tokyo Imperial Univ., law, 1895; became consul Chemupolo, 1899; London, 1899; consul, Antwerp, 1900; Fusan, 1901; councillor of embassy, Washington, D.C., 1912; transferred to London, Eng., 1914; vice minister foreign affairs, Tokyo, 1915-19; A.E. and P. to U.S., 1919-22; created baron, 1920; foreign minister, Tokyo, 1929; premier of Japanese govt., Oct. 1945. Decorated Grand Cordon. Imperial Order of the Sacred Treasure. Address: 562 Sendagaya 1-chome, Shibuya-ku, Tokyo Japan*‡

SHIELS, JAMES, mail order co. exec.; b. Edinburgh, Scotland, Jan. 7, 1902; s. George and Helen (Baird) S.; student Leith Acad., 1907-17; m. Alice Mary Wright, June 27, 1928; 1 dau., Norma Jean (Mrs. Paul Joseph Dias). Came to U.S., 1924, naturalized, 1940. Store mgr. R. & J. Farquhar Co., Boston, 1924-32; with Joseph Breck & Sons, Boston, 1932-68, v.p., 1952-64, dir., sec., 1960-68, sr. v.p., 1964-68. Mem. Am. Seed Trade Assn. (past dir.), Atlantic Seedsmens Assn. Republican. Mason (K.T., Shriner), Rotarian. Home: Milton MA Died Apr. 15, 1968; buried Blue Hills Cemetery, Braintree MA

SHILLADY, JOHN R., social worker; b. County Down, Ireland, Nov. 1, 1875; s. William and Sarah Ann (McGaffin) S.; brought to U.S., 1880; ed. pub. schs., Detroit, Mich.; m. Etta May Rohde, of Detroit, Mich., Nov. 24, 1902. Exec. sec. Buffalo Assn. for Relief and Control of Tuberculosis, 1909-13; sec. Industrial Bd. of N.Y. State Dept. of Labor, 1913-14; exec. sec. Hospitals Com. of N.Y. State Charities Aid Assn., Apr.-Dec. 1914; dir., later sec., New York Mayor's Com. on Unemployment, 1914-17; dir. Dept. of Prevention, Office of the Commr. Charities and Corrections, Westchester Co., N.Y., 1917-18; sec. Nat. Assn. for Advancement of Colored People, Feb. 1918-Aug. 1920; exec. dir. Nat. Consumers' League, 1920-22; gen. dir. Nat. Assn. Travelers Aid Socs., 1922-24; dir. Shillady and Stuart, Inc., social organization service, 1925-28; administrative sec. 1st Internat. Congress on Mental Hygiene, 1928-30. Mem. Nat. Conf. Social Work, Am. Assn. Social Workers. Club: City. Home: 317 S. 2d Av., Mt Vernon NY‡

SHIPPEY, (HENRY) LEE, newspaper man; b. Memphis, Tenn., Feb. 26, 1884; s. William Francis and Elizabeth Kerr (Freleigh) S.; ed. pub. schs., Kansas City, Mo.; m. Madeleine Babin; children—Henry, Charles, John, Frank, Sylvia. Columnist Kansas City Star, 1916, feature writer, 1917, corr. in France, 1918-19, corr. in Mexico, 1920; editor Tampico Press, 1921-22; editor Lee Side O' L.A." column, Los Angeles Times, 1927-50. Mem. Calif. Writers Guild (pres.), Sigma Delta Chi, Epsilon Phi, Alpha Phi Gamma, and Alpha Eta Rho. Club: Authors of Hollywood (vice-pres.). Author: The Testing Ground, 1926; Personal Glimpses, 1929; Folks You Should Know, 1930; Where Nothing Ever Happens, 1935; California Progress, 1936; The Girl Who Wanted Experience, 1937; The Great American Family, 1938; Play, The Great American Family (with R. F. Chapin and Charley King); If We Only Had Money, 1939; It's an Old California Custom, 1948; The Los Angeles Book, 1950. Sierra Madre CA Died Dec. 1969.

SHIVE, JOHN W(ESLEY), plant physiologist; born Halifax, Pa., Feb. 13, 1877; s. Daniel Aaron and Jane (Shoop) S.; Ph.B., Dickenson, 1906, A.M., 1907; Ph.D., Johns Hopkins, 1915; Sc.D., Rutgers, 1946; m. Kate Northrop, Aug. 27, 1907; children—John Northrop, Scott Lee. Asst. desert bot. lab., Carnegie Inst., summer 1913; plant physiologist, expt. sta., Rutgers U., 1915; asso. prof. plant physiol., 1921-23, prof. since 1923, emeritus prof. since 1946; collaborator U.S. Dept. of Ag. Regional Lab., 1939-46; asso. editor Soil Science, Bull. Torey Bot. Club. Fellow A.A.A.S., 1921 (rep. in council, 1944); mem. Bot. Soc. Am., Soc. Exp. Biol., Am. Chem. Soc., Am. Soc. Plant Physiologists (pres. 1939-40, Stephen Hales Prize Award, 1938). Mem. Royal Academy Agr. of Sweden, 1939. Mem. Sigma Xi, Phi Beta Kappa, Gamma Alpha. Contbr. articles to prof. jours. Home: 1 Rutgers St., New Brunswick NJ‡

SHLENKER, IRVIN MORRIS, banker; b. Natchez, Miss., Apr. 12, 1905; s. Simon and Hannah (Wexler) S.; student La. State U.; m. Bertha Alyce Masur, Dec. 30, 1934; children—Sidney Leo, Gay (Mrs. Gus Block). Sec.-treas. F. Strauss & Son, Inc., wholesale grocers, Monroe, La., 1927-37; pres. Gulftex Drug Co., Houston, 1937-50, Terratex Corp., real estate and investments, Houston, 1937-50, Gulf Inland Corp., real estate and investments, Houston, 1937-50; vice chmn. Houston Nat. Bank; chmn. bd. Internat. Bank, Houston, 1962-71; dir. Highlands State Bank (Tex.). Mem. WPB, World War II. Pres. United Fund Houston and Harris County, 1964-71, Jewish Inst. Med. Research, Tex. Med. Center, 1959-71, Houston Jewish Home Aged, 1954-60, Jewish Community Council Houston, 1948-52, also Houston Vocational Guidance Service; chmn. United Jewish Appeal Harris County, 1963. Bd. dirs., exec. com. Am. Hebrew Congregations, 1954-71; bd. dirs. Nat. Conf. Christians and Jews, 1950-71. Recipient Brotherhood citation Nat. Conf. Christians and Jews, 1957. Mem. Am. Bankers Assn., Zeta Beta Tau. Jewish religion (past pres. congregation). Clubs: Petroleum, Houston, Westwood Country (past pres.) (Houston). Home: Houston TX Died Dec. 29, 1971; buried Beth Israel Cemetery Houston TX

SHOCKLEY, M. AUGUSTUS WROTEN, med. officer, U.S. Army; b. Ft. Scott, Kan., May 13, 1874; s. William Bridges and Anna Gertrude (Alexander) S.; student U. of Kan., 1892-93, U.S. Naval Acad., 1894-95; M.D., Kan. City Med. Coll. (U. of Kan.), 1898; grad. Gen. Staff Sch., 1922; m. Irene Brown, 1948. Began as 1st lt., asst. surgeon, 7th U.S. Volunteer Inf., 1898, and promoted through grades to brig. gen., regular army, 1935; dir. Field Service and Corr. Sch. for Med. Officers, U.S. Army, 1915-17; instr. Sch. of the Line and Staff Coll., U.S. Army, 1919-22; prof. mil. hygiene, U.S. Mil. Acad., 1927-31. Fellow Am. Coll. Surgeons; mem. Assn. Mil. Surgeons, A.M.A., Sigma Chi. Awarded D.S.M. (U.S.); Officer Legion of Honor (France). Author: Outline of the Medical Service of the Theatre of Operations, 1922. Home: 2035 W. Olive Av., Fresno CA‡

SHOEMAKER, DANIEL NAYLOR, plant breeder; b. Fair Haven, O., Nov. 16, 1869; s. Abraham and Mary (Kindley) S.; B.S., Earlham Coll., Richmond, Ind., 1894; teacher, Fair Haven High Sch., 1895-99; student Cold Springs Harbor Summer Sch., 1899, 1900; fellow in botany and asst. in zoology, Johns Hopkins, 1902-03, Ph.D., 1903; m. Frances E. Hartley, of Baltimore, July 15, 1903; 1 dau., Dorothy. Teacher, Welch Neck High Sch., Hartville, S.C., 1902-03, at same time engaging in cotton breeding work; became connected with U.S. Dept. of Agr., 1904; stationed at Waco, and engaged in cotton breeding, 1904-07; in charge cotton breeding investigation, 1907-10; plant breeder, hort. investigations, 1910-31 (retired). Mem. Bot. Soc. Washington (pres. 1925-26), Washington Acad. Sciences, Phi Beta Kappa. Mem. Soc. of Friends. Home: 6800 Eastern Av., Takoma Park DC‡

SHOEMAKER, JOSEPH ADDISON, b. Biggsville, Henderson County, Ill., Aug. 23, 1872; s. Adam Clark and Drusilla (Harrell) S.; ed. pub. schs. and business coll.; m. Frances Esther Warrick, Feb. 14, 1900; 1 dau., Gertrude Josephine (Mrs. Dudley F. Estes). In real estate office, Council Bluffs, Ia., 1891-92; with C., B & Q. R.R. Co., Council Bluffs, 1892-96; in supt.'s office C.&N. Ry. Co., Norfolk, Neb., 1896-99, D.&R.G.W. R.R. Co., Salida, Colo., 1899-1902; with Armour & Co., South Omaha and Chicago, 1902-08; general mgr.'s asst. and traffic manager Union Stock Yard Co., South Omaha, 1908-13; with Denver Union Stock Yards Co. since Jan. 1913, as gen. mgr. until 1926, pres. and gen. mgr., 1926-39, pres., 1939-41, chmn. bd. since 1941; pres. and dir. Gen. Stock Yards Corp. (holding large interests at St. Paul, Sioux City, Fort Worth, Louisville, East St. Louis and Toronto), 1927-35, Ogden (Utah) Union Stockyards Co., 1936-41; vice pres. and dir. Northern Okla. Gas Co., Ponca City, Okla., 1936-44. Formerly dir. Stockyards Nat. Bank, Denver Cattle Loan Co., Union Rendering Co., Record-Stockman Pub. Co. (also v.p.). Formerly dir. Denver Chamber of Commerce, Denver Convention and Tourist Bureau. Now retired from active business. Republican. Methodist. Mason. Clubs: Denver (Colo.) Athletic. Home: 1280 Albion St., Denver CO‡

SHOEMAKER, RICHARD HESTON, educator; b. Cynwyd, Pa., Apr. 5, 1907; s. Richard Martin and Susan E. L. (Heston) S.; grad. William Penn Charter Sch., 1925; A.B. U. Pa., 1935; B.S., Columbia, 1938; M.A., Washington and Lee U., 1941; m. Helen Louise Rose, Nov. 23, 1936; 1 son, Richard Martin. Clk., Girard Trust Co., Phila., also Merion Title & Trust Co., Ardmore, Pa., 1928-33; asst. librarian, later univ. librarian Washington and Lee U., 1939-47; librarian Newark Colls., Rutgers U., 1947-59, prof. library service Rutgers Grad. Sch. Library Service, New Brunswick, N.J., 1959-70. Carnegie fellow, 1958. Mem. A.L.A., bibliog. socs. Am., U. Va. Club: Archons of Colophon. Author: (with Ralph R. Shaw) American Bibliography, 1801-1819, 22 vols., 1958-66; American Imprints, 1820-30, 11 vols., 1964-72. Home: New Brunswick NJ Died Mar. 3, 1970.

SHOHL, WALTER MAX, lawyer; b. Cincinnati, July 12, 1885; s. Charles and Annie (Thurnauer) S.; A.B., Harvard, 1906; LL.B., 1908; unmarried. Admitted to Ohio bar, 1908, and since practiced in Cincinnati; mem. firm Dinsmore, Shohl, Barrett, Coates & Deupree, and predecessor firms, 1912-61, counsel, 1961-70, professor law U. Cincinnati, 1921-27, bd. dirs., 1941-70. Mem. Ohio Senate, 1917-18; judge, Court of Appeals of Ohio, 1918-21. Mem. bd. of Ohio State Bar Examiners, 1931-35, chmn., 1935. Mem. Regional Loyalty bd., Sixth Region, 1950-52. Mem. Am., Ohio bar assns., Cincinnati Bar Assn. (pres. 1933-34), Legal Aid Society of Cin. (pres. 1955-56). Clubs: University, Queen City (Cin.), Losantiville Country. Home: Cincinnati OH Died Feb. 5, 1970; buried United Jewish Cemetery, Cincinnati OH

SHOMO, E. H., communications exec.; b. Chgo., 1907; ed. Northwestern U.; m. Lorraine E. Becker; children—Albert, Mrs. Richard McCauley; 1 stepson, James Hamilton. Successively Midwest Salesman Macfadden Publs.; advt. mgr. Chgo. Herald-Examiner; mgr. classified advt. Chgo. Tribune, with CBS, from 1936, mgr. sta. KMOX, St. Louis; mgr. WBBM radio, Chgo., 1950-59, gen. mgr., from 1959, also v.p. parent co., later pres. Field Communications Corp., also gen. mgr. WFLD-TV. Bd. dirs. Boy Scouts Am., John Howard Assn.; bd. dirs., mem. edn. com. Better Bus. Bur. Mem. Ill. C. of C. (law and order com.), Broadcast Advt. Club Chgo., Chgo. Press Club. Clubs: Tavern, Executive, Sky-Line Corp., also chief officer sta. WFLD. Address: Chicago IL Died Apr. 15, 1972.

SHOOK, EDGAR, lawyer; b. Niangua, Mo., Dec. 21, 1894; s. Lafayette Franklin and Mary R. (Hoover) S.; A.B., Scarrit-Morrisville Coll., 1915; postgrad. Drury Coll., 1916; LL.B., U. Mo., 1922; m. Elizabeth Stone Harwood, July 21, 1928; children—Charles H., Susan (Mrs. Frank Williams), Edgar. Admitted to Mo. bar, 1922, also U.S. Supreme Ct.; practice in Kansas City, Mo., 1929-70; mem. firm Shook, Hardy, Ottman, Mitchell & Bacon and predecessors, 1934-70. Bd. dirs. United Funds, Inc. Mem. Am. Bar Assn. Mo. Bar, Lawyers Assn. Kansas City. Home: Kansas City MO Died Aug. 25, 1970.

SHOR, GEORGE GERSHON, editor; b. Vienna, Austria, Sept. 1, 1884; s. Elias Philip and Helen Fannie (Weirauch) S.; came to U.S., 1893; A.B., Brown U., 1906; m. Lelah Luther, Mar. 25, 1913; 1 son, Francis Marion Luther; married 2d Dorothy Williston, September 8, 1917 (dec. Nov. 1971); children—Samuel Wendell Williston, Dorothy Hathaway (Mrs. Philip D. Thompson), George G. Jr. Began as reporter for Providence Journal, Boston Herald, Boston American, 1906-09; news editor and acting mng. editor Boston American, 1913; mng. editor Phila. Evening Times, 1914; with Chicago Herald until 1917; editor and mgr. Internat. News Service, Inc., and Cosmopolitan News Service, 1921-27; managing editor Philadelphia Record, 1928-29, American Weekly, 1929-53, retired. First lt. U.S. Army, Aug. 15, 1917; assigned adjutant's office, 33d Div., Camp Logan, Tex.; capt. Jan. 1918; went to France with 33d Div.; trans. to 1st A.C., A.E.F.; organized personnel adjutant's sect. First Am. Field Army and personnel adj. with rank of maj.; commd. maj. Army of U.S., Mar. 11, 1943; assigned to Office Strategic Services, Washington, D.C.; promoted to lieut. col., Feb. 11, 1944; ret. Oct. 1, 1944. Member of the Society of American Legion Founders, Phi Beta Kappa, Phi Sigma Kappa. Mason. Club: Overseas Press of Am. Address: Cold Spring NY Died June 20, 1967; buried Arlington Nat. Cemetery, Arlington VA

SHORIKI, MATSUTARO, Japanese govt. ofcl.; b. Dalmon-Machi, Honshu Island, Japan, Apr. 11, 1885; s. Shojiro Shoriki; grad. Sch. Law, Tokyo Imperial U., 1911. Police insp., then charge dist. station houses Met. Police Bd., Tokyo, Japan, 1913-21; dir. secretariat, 1921-23; pub. Yomiuri Shimbun; organized Great Japan Tokyo Baseball Club, 1934, on tour U.S., 1935; established TV network, 1951; assisted establishment Japan Atoms-for-Peace Council, 1955; rep. Etchu to Diet, nat. legislative assembly, 1955, minister, without portfolio, dir. Hakkaido Development Bd., Japanese cabinet, 1955; chmn. Nat. Safety Commn., dir. Sci. and Tech. Bd.; chmn. Japanese Atomic Energy Commn., 1956-69. Home: Kanagawa Japan Died Oct. 1969.*

SHORT, ALBERT, insurance; b. Sussex County, Del., 1866; ed. commercial sch. and Central High Sch., Phila. Formerly cashier Berkshire Life Ins. Co., Phila.; organizer Girard Life Ins. Co., and pres. 1927-44, now chmn. bd. Home: 558 Beverly Blvd., Beverly Hills, Pa. Office: 529 Chestnut St., Philadelphia 6 PA‡

SHORT, WALLACE MERTIN, clergyman; b. on farm near College Springs, Ia., June 28, 1866; s. James Black and Eugenia (Noe) S.; grad. Amity College, Iowa, 1887; B.A., Beloit College, Wisconsin, 1893, M.A., 1896; B.D., Yale Divinity School, 1896; m. Mary Eliza Morse, July 8, 1896; children—Emily Vesta, Burton Harrison, John Wallace. Ordained Congl. ministry, 1896; pastor Evansville, Wis., 1896-1903, Beacon Hill Ch., Kansas City, Mo., 1903-10, 1st Ch., Sioux City, Ia., 1910-14; was founder and pastor Central Ch. (independent), Sioux City, Ia., Sept. 1, 1914-Dec. 31, 1918. Editor The Unionist and Public Forum. Moderator Congl. Assn. of Missouri, 1905-06; mem. industrial com. Nat. Council Congl. Chs. of U.S., 1907-10. Mayor of Sioux City, commn. form of government, 1918-24; mem. Iowa State Legislature, 1931-32; helped to found Farmer-Labor Party and was the party's candidate for governor of Ia., 1934, 36, 38. Mem. Phi Beta Kappa. Author: The Deeper Meaning of the Temperance Question, 1915; Let There Be Light, 1916; Can We Live Together in Peace?, 1921; also published sermons and addresses; contbr. to mags. Home: 1524 Isabella St. 410 Jennings St., Sioux City IA‡

SHORT, ZUBER NATHANIEL, physician; b. Buena Vista, Ga., Aug. 5, 1873; s. John Robert and Elizabeth Jane (Zuber) S.; U. of Ga., 1889-91; M.D., Hahnemann Med. Coll., Phila., 1895; m. Daisy Mary Young, Mar.

23, 1910 (died Jan. 1915); m. 2d, Julia Goodyear Mullarky, Sept. 19, 1917; 1 son, James Edward. Practiced Hot Springs, Ark., 1895; asso. with brother, as Drs. Short & Short, 1898-1905, since alone; specializes in diseases of eye, ear, nose and throat. Fellow Am. Coll. Surgeons. Mem. A.M.A., Ark. State Med. Assn., Pi Gamma Mu, etc. Ind. Democrat. Episcopalian. Mason (Past Grand High Priest, R.A. Chapter of Ark.; Past Grand Comdr. K.T., Ark.); chmn. K.T. Ednl. Foundation of Ark. Clubs: Hot Springs Country, Rotary (past pres.), Recipient of Beaver Scout award, 1932. Office: Medical Arts Bldg., Hot Springs National Park AR‡

SHOUP, GUY V., lawyer; b. Bedford, Ia., Feb. 7, 1872; s. Timothy Van Scoyoc and Sarah (Sumner) S.; ed. pub. schs., Ia.; m. M. Adell Colliver, June 5, 1906; 1 dau., Frances E. Admitted to Calif. bar, 1894, and began practice at San Bernardino; practiced at Boise, Ia., 1894-96; with S. P. Co. since 1896, successively atty. claims dept., San Francisco, until 1901, asst. land atty., 1901-06, atty. at Reno, Nev., 1907-09, with law dept., San Francisco, 1909-18, gen. solicitor, same co. and Western Pacific R.R. Co. during federal control, 1918-20, and gen. solicitor S. P. Co. since 1927; pres. First National Bank of Los Altos; dir. Ariz. Eastern R.R. Co., Central Pacific Ry. Co., North Western Pacific R.R. Co., Southern Pacific Equipment Co.; Southern Pacific Land Co., Southern Pacific R.R. Co., East Coast Oil Co., Wells, Fargo Bank and Union Trust Co. of San Francisco, First Nat. Bank of Los Altos. Retired from service of Southern Pac. Co. as general solicitor at his own request, May 1, 1939, after nearly 43 years service. Mem. Am. and Calif. State bar assns. Republican. Clubs: Union League, Commonwealth, Los Altos CA‡

SHREVE, CHARLES EVERETT, lawyer; b. Washington, Apr. 3, 1905; s. Charles S. and Adrienne (VonEzdorf) S.; J.D. with honors, George Washington U., 1928; m. Catharine Beavers, June 18, 1927; 1 dau., Linda A. (Mrs. Ronald K. Harris). Admitted to D.C. bar, 1928; mem. firm Shreve & Shreve, Washington, 1930-34; atty. mixed claims commn. State Dept., 1929-30, Lumber Code Authority, 1934-35; with SEC, 1935-72, exec. asst. dir., 1962-68, dir. div. corp. finance, 1968-70; counsel law firm Hogan & Hartson, Washington, 1970-72. Lectr., panelist groups such as Practising Law Inst., Southwestern Legal Found., Am., Fed. bar forums. Recipient Distinguished Service award SEC, 1968. Mem. Fed. Bar Assn. Contbr. articles to profl. jours. Home: Rockville MD Died Nov. 7, 1972.

SHRINER, HERB, radio, TV humorist; b. Toledo, O., May 29, 1918; student pub. schs., Ft. Wayne, Ind.; m. Eileen Joy (dec. Apr. 1970); children—Indy, Will and Kim (twins). Organized harmonica quintet; solo engagement Oriental Theater, Chgo.; toured Australia as humorist, harmonica player until 1940; feature role Broadway Revue, Inside U.S.A.; 15 minute radio comedy program also TV shows; formerly host, chief interrogator comedy quiz program Two for the Money, CBS radio, TV. Served with U.S. Army, World War II. Home: Ft Lauderdale FL Died Apr. 1970.

SHRYOCK, BURNETT HENRY, SR., univ. dean; b. Carbondale, Ill., Feb. 4, 1904; s. Henry William and Jessie (Burnett) S.; student So. Ill. Normal; A.B., U. Ill., 1925; A.M., Columbia Tchrs. Coll., 1940; m. Mary Ann Hewitt, Aug. 5, 1940; children—Mary Ann, Burnett Henry, William Hewitt. Student painting Chgo. Art Inst., Am. Acad. Art in Chgo., 1925-26; advt. illustrator, 1926-32, portrait painter, from 1932; chmn. art dept. U. Kansas City, 1944-47; chmn. art dept. So. Ill. U., 1950-55, dean Sch. Fine Arts, from 1955; one man show landscapes and figure paintings Quest Galleries, Chgo., 1939, paintings William Rockhill Nelson Gallery, Kansas City, Mo., 1946; exhibited Am. Show and Internat. Water Color Exhbn., Chgo. Art Inst.; one-man pvt. showing of portraits, murals Washington Park Race Track, Chgo.; traveling exhbn. Am. Water Color Show, Chgo. Art Inst., 1944-45; traveling exhbn. Ala. Water Color Show, 1944-45; rep. pvt. and pub. collections, including St. Louis City Art Mus., So. Ill. U., U. Kansas City, Helen Hayes collection, Earle Ludgin collection; portraits of Helen Hayes, Frank Mandel, Mrs. Clarence Decker, Andre Maurois, Delyte Wesley Morris, Roscoe Pulliam, William Henry Shryock, others. Dir. New Orleans Acad. Art; mem. Ill. Arts Council; vice chairman art committee Illinois Sesquicentennial Commission. Recipient of anonymous purchase prize Third Ann. Mo. Exhbn., 1943, 3d prize Ala. Water Color Show, 1944; hon. mention Central Ill. Exhbn., 1944. Mem. Nat. Art Edn. Assn., Coll. Art Assn., Nat. Council Deans Fine Arts (original mem.), Arts Club Chgo., Kappa Delta Pi, Delta Tau Delta. Episcopalian. Home: Carbondale IL Died Jan. 13, 1971; buried Oakland Cemetery, Carbondale IL

SHRYOCK, RICHARD HARRISON, educator; b. Phila., Mar. 29, 1893; s. George Augustus and Mary Harrison (Chipman) S.; B.S., Central High Sch., Phila., 1911; student Phila. Sch. Pedagogy, 1911-13; B.S. in Edn., U. Pa., 1917, Ph.D., 1924; LL.D., Duke, 1962; m. Rheva Ott, Sept. 10, 1921; children—Barbara Ott, Richard Wallace. Tchr. pub. schs., Phila., 1913-16; Harrison fellow, U. Pa., 1919-20; instr. history, Ohio State U., 1921-24, U. Pa., 1924-25; asso. prof. history, Duke, 1925-31, prof., 1931-38; prof. Am. history, U. Pa., 1938-49, prof. history, 1958-63, professor medical history, 1948-49; on leave as fellowship secretary Social Sci. Research Council, N.Y.C., 1935, 36; lectr. med. history Women's Med. Coll. Pa., 1944-49; dir. Inst. Hist. Med. Johns Hopkins, 1949-58, prof. emeritus, 1958; librarian Am. Philos. Soc., 1958-65. Mem. bd. Russel Sage Found., 1956-65; mem. Nat. Hist. Publs. Commn., 1950-53, Nat. Portrait Gallery Commn., 1965-67. Served as pvt. Field Ambulance Corps, U.S. Army, 1917-18; student U.S. Army Med. Sch., 1918. Served as lt. (T), USCG Res., 1943-45, lt. comdr. (T), 1945. Mem. Am. Philos. Soc., Internat. Assn. U. Profs. (pres. 1958), Internat. Union History Sci. (v.p. 1958), Am. Assn. U. Profs. (pres. 1950), History Sci. Soc. (pres. 1941-42), Am. Council Learned Socs. (acting dir., 1946-47), Am. Assn. Med. History (pres. 1946-47), Am. Hist. Assn. (chmn. exec. com. 1956), Internat. Acad. History of Medicine (honorary president 1964-72), also Phi Beta Kappa, Delta Tau Delta. Clubs: Franklin Inn, Rittenhouse (Phila.), Cosmos (Washington); Hamilton Street (Balt.). Author: Georgia and the Union in 1850, 1926; The Development of Modern Medicine, 1936; American Medical Research: Past and Present, 1947; Unique Influence of the Johns Hopkins University on American Medicine, 1953; (with O. T. Beale) Cotton Mather: First Significant Figure in American Medicine, 1954; The National Tuberculosis Association, 1904-54, 1957; The University of Pennsylvania Faculty: A Study in American Higher Education, 1959; The History of Nursing; An Interpretation of the Social and Medical Factors Involved, 1959; Medicine and Society in America, 1660-1860, 1960; Medicine in America; Historical Essays, 1966; Medical Licensing in America, 1650-1965, 1967. Editor: The Letters of Richard D. Arnold, M.D., 1929; Pa. Mag. History and Biography, 1940, 41-46. Contbr. hist. subjects. Home: Philadelphia PA Died Jan. 30, 1972.

SHUFF, JOHN A., union ofcl. Sec.-treas. Internat. Alliance Theatrical State Employees and Moving Picture Machine Operators U.S. and Can., AFL-CIO. Office: New York City NY Died Feb. 16, 1970.

SHUFORD, A. ALEX, JR., textile mfr.; b. Hickory, N.C., Apr. 2, 1905; s. A. Alex and Maude (Ferguson) S.; A.B., U. N.C., 1926; M.B.A., Harvard, 1928; LL.D., Lenoir Rhyne Coll., 1950; D.Bus. Adminstrn., Catawba Coll., 1960; m. Alice Gibbon, Apr. 25, 1929; 1 dau., Margery. Errand boy Shuford Mills, Inc., 1929, pres., 1947-71; treas. Hickory Spinners, Inc., Lavonia Mfg. Co. Trustee Catawba Coll., U. N..C. Mem. Evang. and Reformed Ch. Home: Hickory NC Died Dec 25, 1971.

SHULL, FRANK LESLIE, b. Springfield, Ill., Feb. 11, 1869; s. Edward S. and Martha (Summer) S.; A.B., Wabash Coll., Crawfordsville, Ind., 1891; m. Florence A. Nutt, July 2, 1902; children—Martha A., Frank L., Florence N. Became pres. Benjamin Franklin Savings & Loan Assn., 1926. County commr., Multnomah County, Ore., since 1931; former pres. Bd. of Edn., Portland. Mem. Portland Chamber Commerce (ex-pres.), Beta Theta Pi; former dir. Chamber Commerce of U.S. Republican. Presbyterian. Home: 2686 Overton St. Office: Court House, Portland OR‡

SHULMAN, CHARLES E., clergyman; b. Ukraine, July 25, 1900; s. Maurice and Rachel S.; ed. Ohio Northern U., 1916-20 (LL.B.), LL.D., 1954; student U. Cin., 1922-23, U. Chgo., 1923-24 (Ph.B.), 1924-27 (A.M.), Hebrew Union Coll., 1922-27 (ordained rabbi, 1927); D.D., Hebrew Union Coll.-Jewish Inst. Religion, 1956; D.D., Boston U., 1967; m. Avis Clamitz, June 27, 1929; 1 dau., Deborah Louise. Admitted Ohio bar, 1920; worked in law dept. N.Y. Central R.R., Cleve., 1920, Santa Fe R.R. Albuquerque, N.M., 1921; rabbi, Johnstown Pa., 1926-27, Wheeling, W.Va., 1927-31, North Shore Congregation Israel, Glencoe, Ill., 1931-47, Riverdale Temple, N.Y.C., Sept. 1, 1947-68. Chaplain with rank of lt. comdr., USN, 1943; active duty, naval training stations at Bainbridge, Md., Newport, R.I.; on staff comdr. Seventh Fleet as Jewish chaplain, in Southwest Pacific. Pres. Chgo. Rabbinical Assn., 1942; mem. nat. adv. bd. Anti-Defamation League of B'nai B'rith; mem. exec. bd. Mt. Council N.Y. Anti-Defamation League; mem. nat. adminstrv. com. Am. Jewish Congress; mem. nat. adv. council Jewish Nat. Fund. Chmn. com. on pub. schs. N.Y. Bd. of Rabbis; mem. exec. bd. Henry Hudson Sch. for Brain Injured Children, N.Y.C. Lect. on Jewish Theology, Oberlin Coll. Grad. Sch., 1953. Trustee Hadley Corr. Sch. for the Blind. Mem. USO Council of Chgo.; mem. Nat. Jewish Welfare Bd. (com. on Army-Navy Religious Activities). Traveling rep. United Jewish Appeal to Europe, N. Africa, Israel, 1952-53. Chmn. Bronx Urban League; mem. exec. bd. Urban League Greater New York, Boy Scouts of Bronx; exec. bd. Bronx sect. Nat. Conf. Christians and Jews. Recip. Geo. Washington medal Freedoms Found., 1953, 54, 55, 61, 63, 65, 66. Author: Problems of Jews in the Contemporary World, 1934; Europe's Conscience in Decline, 1939; Religion's Message to a War-torn World, 1942; The Test of a Civilization, 1947; On Being a Jew, 1954; A People That Did Not Die, 1956; The Best Years of Our Lives, 1958; What it Means to be a Jew, 1960; Humanity's Unfinished Business, published, 1964. Member of the editorial board Reconstructionis chairman editorial board The American Zionis Contributor to religious journals. Home: New York Cit NY Died June 2, 1968.

SHULTZ WILLIAM JOHN, economist; bor Brooklyn, N.Y., Apr. 25, 1902; s. William and Ma (Eastman) S.; A.B., Columbia, 1922, A.M., 1922, Ph.D 1924; LL.B., New York Law Sch., 1930; m. Luis Viggiani, Mar. 9, 1923. Lecturer in history, Columbia 1921-23; instr. in history, Coll. City New York 1922-23; instr. in social science, Hunter Coll., 1924-25 asst. prof. economics, U. of Chicago, 1926; financia economist, Nat. Industrial Conf. Bd., 1926-30 professor business adminstrn., Bernard M. Baruch Sch Bus. and Pub. Adminstrn., Coll. Univ. N.Y., 1932-64 ret.; cons. New York, U.S. Treasury, 1942, N.Y. Stat Tax Commn., 1943. Prentice-Hall Inc., 1944; president Am. Management Counsel Co., 1946-48. Marketin and management cons. Mem. Am. Marketing Assn Beta Gamma Sigma, Phi Beta Kappa, Torch and Scrol Author books in field; latest: American Marketing 1961. Contbr. fiction, articles to mags. Home: Nev Harbor ME Died May 23, 1970.

SHUPING, CLARENCE LEROY, lawyer; b. Rowa County, N.C., Feb. 1, 1886; s. Adam Dolphus and Juli Maria (Honeycutt) S.; ed. Salisbury pub. schs. an private study; m. Ruth Hampton, June 1 1916;children—C. Leroy Jr., Hampton, J. Brooks Admitted to N.C. bar, 1912, U.S. Dist. Ct. for N.C. 1913, U.S. Ct. Appeals for 4th Circuit, U.S. Suprem Ct., 1935; engaged in gen. civil practice, Greensboro exec. sec. Nat. Fuel Adminstrn. for N.C., 1917-19 founder, organizer 1st Young Dem. Club in N.C., 1928 chmn. Guilford County Demo. Exec. Com., 1927-30 managed state campaign U.S. Senator Josiah W. Bailey 1930; chmn. finance com. Dem. Nat. Com. for N.C. 1931-33; del.-at-large Dem. Nat. Conv., Chgo., 1932 mem. com. permanent orgn.; managed Roosevelt's campaign in N.C. for nomination for pres., 1932; chmn N.C. Com. for Adminstrn. NRA, 1933-34; adv. com N.C. Dem. Exec. Com., 1932-38; chmn. Dem. Nat Committeeman for N.C., 1934-36; mem. state campaign com. U.S. Senator Willis Smith, 1950. Mem. Am. Ba Assn. (chmn. N.C. adv. com. simplification an improvement of appellate practice, in fed. cts.; mem N.C. Com. on Procedural Reform, 1938, also N.C. com for improving adminstrn. of justice 1938-47), N.C. Ba Assn. (v.p. 1932-33), N.C. State Bar, Greensboro Ba Assn. (pres. 1950). Democrat. Methodist. Home Greensboro NC Died Mar. 24, 1971; buried Green Hil Cemetery Greensboro NC

SHURLY, BURT RUSSELL, laryngologist, otologist b. Chicago, Ill., July 4, 1871; s. Col. Edmund R. P. an Augusta (Godwin) S.; B.S., U. of Wis., 1894; M.D. Detroit Coll. of Medicine, 1895; post-grad. course, U. o Vienna; m. Viola Palms, June 28, 1905; children—Mari G., Beatrice A., Burt Russell, Edmund R. P., Fredricka P. Practiced, Detroit, since 1895; prof. laryngology and medicine, Detroit Coll. Med.; cons. laryngologist Harper Hosp.; chief of staff Shurly Hosp.; laryngologist and otologist Woman's Hosp.; pres. Detroit Tuberculosis Sanatorium. Actg. asst. surgeon U.S Army and U.S. Navy, Spanish-Am. War; passed asst surgeon, chief surgeon Mich. Naval Brig.; lieut. col. M.R.C.; med. dir. comdg. Detroit Coll. of Medicine and Surgery Base Hosp. No. 36, service in France, 1917-19; col. Med. R.C. Mem. Bd. of Edn., Detroit (pres.). Fellow Am. Coll. Surgeons, Am. Coll. Physicians, Am. Acad. Medicine; mem. A.M.A., Mich. State Med. Soc. Am. Laryngol. Assn. (pres. 1935), Am. Otol. Soc., Am. Climatol. and Clin. Assn. (ex-pres.), Am. Acad. of Ophthalmology and Otolaryngology (ex-pres.), Am. Assn. Rhinology, Laryngology and Otology, American Rhinol., Laryngol. and Otol. Assn. (ex-pres.); v.p. Am. Board of Otolaryngology. Republican. Episcopalian. Mason. Member Loyal Legion, Am. Legion, Military Order World War (former surgeon-general; comdr. Detroit Chapter). Clubs: Detroit, Detroit Athletic, University, Intercollegiate Alumni, Country, Grosse Pointe, Grosse Ile Country, Prismatic, Grist Mill. Mem Order of Purple Heart. Home: 1027 Seminole Av. Office: 62 Adams Av. W., Detroit MI*‡

SHVERNIK, NIKOLA (MIKHALLVICH), govt. ofcl. USSR; b. nr. St. Petersburg, Russia, May 19, 1888. Became worker in the elec. machine plant, and joined underground revolutionary movement, 1902; frequently imprisoned or exiled for polit. activities; head commissariat of Workers and Peasants Inspection, Council of Peoples Commissars, 1922-25; also mem. Presidium Central Control Com. of Communist Party from 1925, became mem. its secretariat, 1926; became mem. central com. Metals Workers Union, 1929, also mem. All-Russian Central Exec. Com., and mem. Presidium of All-Union Central Exec. Com.; sec.-gen. All-Union Central Council of Trade Unions, 1930-44; mem. Anglo-Soviet Trade Union Com., 1941, serving as head of union delegation to inspect war factories in Eng., 1942, and mem. Russian delegation Brit. Trade Union Congress, 1943; elected dep. Council of Nationalities (lower chamber Supreme Soviet, which is the two chamber parliament), 1937, chmn., 1938; chief authority on labor unions politburo of Communists Party, 1939-70; 1st vice chmn. Presidium of Supreme ɔviet of U.S.S.R., 1944, also chmn. Presidium of ıpreme Soviet of Russian Soviet Federated Socialist epublic (elected for second 4 yr. term, 1950); this ɔsition is frequently referred to as pres. of the Soviet nion. Chmn. All-Union Central Council of Trade nions, 1953-57; alternate chmn. party control com. .P.S.U. Central Com., 1956-70, chmn., 1962-66; mem. residium Cent. Com. C.P.S.U., 1957-61; mem. Central om. C.P.S.U. Decorated Oredr of Lenin (3), others. ddress: Moscow USSR Died Dec. 1970.

IBERELL, LLOYD E., railroad exec., writer; b. ingston, O., Sept. 18, 1905; s. Albert and Henrietta 1arjorie (Davis) S.; ed. Chillicothe Bus. Coll., 1923, U. in., Ohio State U.; m. Sarah Alma Keefer, 1940; ıildren—Lloyd Emerson, Jr., Thomas Elbert. With .&W. Ry., 1924-68, various positions freight stas. and affic depts., Norwood, Clare (both O.), Kenova, W. a., also Cin., Winston-Salem, N.C., 1924-27, agt. 'orwood (Cin.), 1947-48, Columbus, O., 1949-68; chief roperty and transp. Cin. Ordnance Dist., Army Service orces, also transp. specialist U.S. Army Transp. Corps, in., World War II. Registered transp. legislative agt. hio Legislature, 1949-57; chmn. Columbus Area ouncil Transp. Orgns., 1959, press agt., 1960-61; ımn. r.r. service com. Columbus area Eastern R.R. residents Conf., 1954-56. Chmn. r.r. com., transp. div. saster preparedness Franklin Co. chpt. A.R.C.; chief ansp. services Columbus and Franklin County Civil ef., 1954-60; pres. founder, Christian Youth Center, c., Central O., 1953-58, adviser to pres. and chmn. bd. ustees. Mem. Columbus R.R. Freight Agts. Assn. res. 1961-62), Soc. for Preservation Memory of Steam ocomotives, Assn. Am. R.R.'s, Ohio R.R. Assn. (vice ımn. Franklin County com.), Norfolk and Western ets.' Assn., Q.M. Assn., Def. Supply Assn., Nat. Def. ransp. Assn. (pres. Columbus 1955-56, nat. dir. 955-56), Ohio, Columbus Area chambers commerce, hio Hist. Soc. (r.r. and agrl. archives com.), Upper hio Valley Assn., Fortean Soc., Ohioana Library Assn. :o-editor Ohioana Mag. 1958-68), Soc. of Over a housand, Soc. Bibliosophers (a founder, corr. sec.), nglo-Am. Powyseana Soc. (founder, internat. sec.), m. Mus. Natural History. Clubs: Transportation (pres. 952-53, editor News 1950-52, hon. life mem. 954-68), Export-Import (Columbus); Rounce and offin (Los Angeles); Rowfant (Cleve.); Ohio Coal; ue Field Hunting; Ohio Railway Museum. Author: A bliography of the First Editions of John Cowper owys, 1934; Dard Hunter, The Mountain House and hillicothe, 1935; At the Beams of Peace, Poems from e Valley of Legend, 1936; Burton Stevenson of Home ook Fame, 1937; Miniatures to Murals, 1943; ecumseh, The Man, His Career and His Chillicothe ortrait, 1944; also numerous book intros., articles, ook revs. Editor and pub.: Imprimatur, A Folio of ersonalities, Impressions, and Observations, Cin., 941-45; editor: The Book Collector's Packet, 1945-46. ome: Gibralter House Columbus OH Died Dec. 22, 968; cremated Green Lawn Columbus OH

IBLEY, CLYDE LAWSON, assn. executive; b. ussellville, Ala., Aug. 7, 1899; s. Thomas Pinkney and mma (Berryhill) S.; student U. Ala., 1920; m. Grace eele, Dec. 23, 1919. Staff Birmingham Bapt. Hosps., 929-65, adminstr., 1933-65; mem. exec. com., bd. ustees Blue-Cross Blue-Shield of Ala., from 1936, sec., 947-57, pres., 1957-60, chmn. bd., from 1960. Adv. bd. osp. Licensing Commn. Ala., 1949-53; mem. com. on ırsing edn. bd. control So. Regional Edn., 1950-59; dv. council hosp. constrn., hosp. planning div. Ala. ept. Health, 1947-57. Bd. trustees Jefferson County b San., 1951-53, 55-57; past pres. Birmingham Hosp. ouncil; mem. med. adv. com. Jefferson County chpt. .R.C. Recipient Distinguished Service award Ala. osp. Assn., 1962. Fellow Am. Coll. Hosp. Adminstrs. .p. 1949-50; bd. regents 1955-61, bd. awards and stimonials 1962); mem. Am. (v.p. 1941-42, chmn. ouncil govt. relations 1961-62, bd. trustees 1962-64). la. (pres. 1939-41, trustee, from 1938, sec. 1942-52), ɔuthwide Bapt. (pres. 1955-56) hosp. assns., Vis. urses Assn. (dir. 1949-59, pres. bd. 1954-56), S.E. osp. Conf. (pres. 1937-38, chmn. nominating com. 955-56), Birmingham Regional Hosp. Council (pres. 945-46, 56-57, sec.-treas. 1962-63, v.p. 1963-64). aptist. Kiwanian. Home: Birmingham AL Died Mar. 9, 1968; buried Elmwood Cemetery, Birmingham AL

IBLEY, JOSIAH, clergyman; b. Augusta, Ga., May 2, 1877; s. Robert Pendleton and Susie (Bolling) S.; 'ebb Sch., Bellbuckle, Tenn.; B.A., Pomona Coll., alif., 1899; B.D., Yale, 1902; successful Yale U. ebater against Princeton, 1901; D.D., King, 1911, omona, 1922; LL.D., Tusculum, 1935; m. Adeline 'ebb, Sept. 4, 1906; children—Lois (Mrs. James W. utton), Peyton, Josiah. Ordained Presbyterian ministry y Presbytery of Los Angeles, Calif., 1902; pastor 1st h., Azusa, Calif., 1902-05, 1st Ch., Long Beach, Calif., 905-09, 1st Ch., Knoxville, Tenn., 1909-14, Calvary h., San Francisco, 1914-20, 2d Presbyn. Ch., Chicago, 920-26; pastor Westminster Presbyn. Ch., Pasadena, alif., 1926-33 (half million dollar ch. erected 1928); astor Lindsay Memorial Church, Memphis, Tenn., 933-44; Jan. 1944, retired; interim pastor Presbyterian hurch, Ojai, Calif., Dec. 1944-July 1945; preached at arious chs. since 1945; for 3 yrs. has preached niversity of Tenn., Univ. of Chicago, Univ. of Ill., Stanford U., Pomona Coll., etc.; acting pastor Calvary Presbyn. Ch., Apr.-June 1951. Mem. Nat. Service Commission and mem. committee on men's work of General Assembly Presbyn. Ch. U.S.A., 1916-20; pres. San Francisco Ch. Federation, 1918-20; del. Gen. Assembly Presbyn. Ch., 1908, 23, 29, 39, moderator Presbytery of Los Angeles, 1932, W. Tenn. Presbytery, 1935-36; vice moderator Synod of Tenn., 1937, chmn. edn. and action. Chmn. religious group Memphis China Relief Com. Dir. Memphis Pub. Affairs Forum, Synod of Tenn. Westminster Foundation. Dir. Dubuque (Iowa) College and Seminary; trustee Pomona College; trustee Chicago Church Federation, 1920-26. Chaplain Democratic National Convention, San Francisco. Mem. Public Affairs Forum, Illinois Society Mayflower Descendants, S.A.R., Pasadena Pastor's Union (pres.), Phi Beta Kappa (pres. Assn. of Memphis Area. 1937-40). Pres. Memphis Ministerial Assn. (all denoms.), 1937-38; dir. and organizing pres. Memphis Peace Action Council; del. internat. com. and mem. nat. com. Am. Christian German Refugees. Was chmn. exec. com., Ill. edn. campaign for $3,000,000. Mem. Chi Alpha. Mason. Clubs: Memphis Country, Cross Cut, Civitan (life mem., dir., 1943-44). Executives (Memphis), Oceanside Toast Masters. Author: Pathfinders of the Soul Country, and Other Sermons for Today. Contbr. The Music of the Gospel; Contribution of Sidney Lanier and Joseph Le Conte to Religious Thought of 20th Century. Address: R. 2, Box 205, Vista CA‡

SIEDER, OTTO F., constrn. engr.; b. Newark, N.J., Jan. 23, 1881; s. August and Sophia (Schalle) S.; B.S., Lafayette Coll., 1902, D.Sc., (hon.), 1952; m. Mary Elvina Gradwohl, Sept. 4, 1906 (dec.); children—Violet Mariot, Roswell Gilbert, Marion Janet (Mrs. Nils Ohlson); m. 2d, Viola Bicknell Lounsbury, Dec. 27, 1952. Design engr. Purdy & Henderson, N.Y.C., 1902-04; design engr., squad leader Am. Bridge Co., N.Y.C., 1904-06; design and constrn. engr. Westinghouse, Church, Kerr & Co., N.Y.C., 1906-09; fgn. rep. charge office Milliken Bros., Buenos Aires, 1909-12; chief engr. Levering & Garrigues Co., N.Y.C., 1912-21, v.p., chief engr., 1921-31; cons. engr. Marc Eidlitz & Sons, N.Y.C., 1931-33; pvt. practice, N.Y.C., also Maplewood, N.J., 1933-40; supervisor engring. and constrn. War Dept., Washington, 1940-42; chief Indsl. Constrn. Div., Office Chief of Engrs., Washington, 1942-45; exec. v.p., gen. mgr. The H. K. Ferguson Co., Cleve., 1945-53, pres., 1953-55, vice chmn. bd., 1955, retired; former chmn. bd. Central Pipe Fabrication & Supply Co. Chmn. adv. bd. Utilization Govt. Indsl. Plants, Washington. Pres. Bernardsville (N.J.) Civic Assn. Registered profl. engr., Ohio, Mich., N.Y. Mem. Nat. Constructors Assn., C. of C., Alpha Chi Rho. Presbyn. Club: Chagrin Valley Country (Cleve.). Home: Bernardsville NJ Died Oct. 17, 1969; buried Somerset Hills Meml. Park, Basking Ridge NJ

SIEFF, ISRAEL MOSES, mgmt. exec.; b. Manchester, Eng., Apr. 5, 1889; s. Ephraim S.; ed. Manchester U., LL.D. (hon.); m. Rebecca Doro, 1910 (dec.); children—Michael David, Marcus Joseph, Daniel (dec.), Judith Hannah (Mrs. Schechterman). With Marks and Spencer, Ltd., London, Eng., 1915, vice-chmn., joint mng. dir., 1926-64, chmn., joint mng. dir. 1964-67, pres., 1967-72; farmer; founder Daniel Sieff Research Inst., Rehovoth, Israel, 1934. Sec., Zionist Commn., 1918; hon. pres. Joint Palestine Appeal. Chmn. bd. govs. Carmel Coll.; hon. fellow, bd. govs. Weizmann Inst. Sci., Rehovoth. Created baron and life peer of Brimpton (Eng.), 1966. Hon. fellow, mem. Ct. of Patrons Royal Coll. Surgeons Eng.; fellow Royal Anthrop. Inst., Royal Geog. Soc., Brit. Inst. Mgmt. (all Eng.); mem. World Jewish Congress (v.p. chmn. European exec.), Zionist Fedn. Great Britain and Ireland (hon. pres.), Anglo-Israel C. of C. (chmn. 1950-65, pres.), Polit. and Econ. Planning (chmn. 1931-39, vice-chmn. 1939-64, now pres.), Multiple Shops Fedn. (v.p. 1946-61). Address: London England Died 1972.

SIEGEL, IRWIN, physician; b. Cleve., Sept. 13, 1924; s. Morris and Molly (Binder) S.; M.D., Western Res. U., 1947; m. Jean Marie Lafaye, June 24, 1952; children—Suzanne Lynn, Judith Ann, Laurel Alice. Intern, Michael Reese Hosp., Chgo., 1947-48; postgrad. dept. biochemistry Western Res. U., Cleve., 1948-50; resident in medicine Crile VA Hosp., Cleve., 1950-52, staff physician dept. medicine, 1955-56; asst. physician outpatient clinic Mr. Sinai Hosp., Cleve., 1955; asso. attending physician Central Dispensary and Emergency Hosp., 1957; mem. staff Washington Hosp. Center, 1958-60; asst. dir. new drug br. FDA, Washington, 1959, asso. dir., 1960, dep. med. dir. 1961-63; asst. chief Psychopharmacology Service Center, Nat. Inst. Mental Health, NIH, Bethesda, Md., 1963-65, asst. chief artificial kidney and chronic uremia program Nat. Inst. Arthritis and Metabolic Disease, 1965-70. Served from 1st lt. to capt., M.C., AUS, 1952-54. Diplomate Am. Bd. Internal Medicine. Fellow A.C.P.; mem. A.M.A., A.A.A.S., Am. Soc. for Artificial Internal Organs. Home: Bethesda MD Died Feb. 28, 1970; buried Washington DC

SIEGEL, LESTER, corp. exec.; b. Chgo., 1893; grad. Cornell U. Chmn. bd. Harzfeld's Inc., Kansas City Mo. Home: Kansas City MO Died June 9, 1971.

SIKES, CLARENCE S., ry. official; b. Augusta, Ga., Feb. 14, 1869; s. Robert H. and Eva (Ingalls) S.; student Richmond Mil. Acad., Augusta, 1879-83; m. Medora Rhodes, of Edinburg, Ind., Sept. 14, 1887; children—Chase B., Alvin R., Mabel H. In accounting dept., Georgia R.R., Augusta, 1883-95; with Great Northern Ry., at St. Paul, Minn., 1895-1902, C., H.&D. R.R., 1902-04; became connected with Pere Marquette R.R., as auditor traffic accounts and gen. auditor, 1904, v.p. and gen. auditor, 1918-30; retired. Republican. Christian. Clubs: Detroit Athletic, Augusta Country. Home: 2353 Walton Way, Augusta GA‡

SIKORSKY, IGOR I., aero. engr.; b. Kiev., Russia, May 25, 1889; s. John S.; grad. Naval Coll., St. Petersburg, 1906; grad. Inst. Tech. Kiev, 1908; M.S. (hon.), Yale, 1935; hon. degrees Wesleyan and Lehigh U., Fla. So. Coll., R.I. State Coll., Northeastern U., U. Pa., U. Bridgeport (Conn.), Yale; D.Sc., Colby Coll., 1955, Trinity Coll., 1965, Fairfield U., 1966; m. Elizabeth A. Semion, Jan. 27, 1924; 1 dau., 4 sons. Came to U.S., 1919, naturalized, 1928. Designed and built flying machines on own account, 1908-11; with Russo-Baltic Railroad Car Works, 1912-18, as head of engring. dept. of its aviation factory; built and flew the first multimotored airplane, 1913; designed and built 75 large four-motored bombers used by Russian Army; went to France, 1918, and was commd. by French govt. to build the Sikorsky plane for mil. use, but prodn. cut short by armistice; organized Sikorsky Aero Engring. Corp., 1923, Sikorsky Mfg. Corp., 1925, and in 1928, Sikorsky Aviation Corp., United Aircraft Corp.; engring. mgr. Sikorsky Aircraft div. until 1957, ret., but continued as adviser and cons. Has developed several types of planes, among them the first 4-engine plane, 1913, 1st successful, long-range clippers, which pioneered transoceanic air service; developed first successful helicopter produced in Western Hemisphere, 1939. Recipient Potts medal Franklin Inst., 1933; hon. fellow Rochester Mus. Arts and Scis., 1943; hon. fellow Am. Helicopter Soc. 1944, Gen. W.E. Mitchell award, 1944; Copernican citation, 1943; Benjamin Franklin fellow Royal Soc. for Encouragement Arts, Manufactures and Commerce, London, 1960; First Fawcett Aviation award, 1944; Warner medal Am. Soc. M.E., 1944; Hawks Meml. Trophy, 1947; Gold medal Fed. Aeronautique Internat., 1947; Presdl. certificate Merit, 1948; Silver medal Royal Aero. Soc., Eng., 1949; Alexander Klemin award Am. Helicopter Soc., 1950; Collier Trophy, 1950; Daniel Gugenheim medal 1951; Nat. Def. Transp. award, 1952; Godfrey Lowell Cabot award N.E. Aero Club; one of 50 Americans chosen for Popular Mechanics Hall of Fame; John Scott medal City of Phila., 1955; James Watt Internat. gold medal (London, Eng.), 1955; United Aircraft Corp. established trophy in his honor, 1961; Engr. of Year, Conn. Soc. Profl. Engrs., 1962; Grover E. Bell award Am. Helicopter Soc., 1960; Cross of Chevalier Legion of Honor, France, 1960; Elmer A. Sperry award, 1964; Modern Pioneers Creative Industry medal N.A.M., 1965; award of honor Wisdom Soc., 1966; Hall of Fame award Internat. Aerospace Hall of Fame, 1966; Nat. Medal of Sci., 1967; Wright Brothers trophy, 1967; John Fritz medal, 1968, numerous other awards. Hon. fellow Royal Aero. Soc.; mem. Nat. Acad. Engring., Soc. Automotive Engrs., Am. Soc. M.E., Nat. Aero. Assn., Aero. C. of C., Am. Helicopter Soc., Am. Inst. Aeros. and Astronautics (Sylvanus A. Reed award 1942), Am. Soc. French Legion of Honor, Order of Daedalions, Soc. Exptl. Test Pilots, Aerospace Industries Assn. Am., Aircraft Owners and Pilots Assn., U.S. Naval Inst., Navy League U.S., Early Birds Aviation, Profl. Engrs. State Conn., Royal Soc. Arts (Eng.); Royal Aero. Soc. (Eng.). Mem. Russian Orthodox Ch. Clubs: OX5 of Am.; Quiet Birdmen; Wings; Nat. Aviation. Author: Winged Message of the Stratford CT Died Oct. 26, 1972; buried Stratford CT

SILER, VINTON EARNEST, physician, educator; b. West Manchester, O., June 25, 1909; s. Raymond Henry and Mary Catherine (Brown) S.; B.A., Miami U., Oxford, O., 1931; B.M., U. Cin., 1934, M.D., 1935; m. Marjorie R. Hall, Sept. 12, 1941. Research asst. dept. pediatrics Research Found. U. Cin., 1931-34, instr. surgery, 1941-43, asst. prof., 1943-53, asso. prof., 1953-61, prof., 1961-71; intern Cin. Gen. Hosp., 1934-35, asst. resident in surgery, 1935-37, 38-40, resident in surgery, 1940-41, attending surgeon gen. surg. div., clinician out-patient dispensary, 1948-71, dir. Surg. Chem. Lab., 1941-71, founder, dir. hand clinic, until 1971; asst. resident in surgery U. Cal. Med. Sch., at San Francisco, 1937-38; attending surgeon Children's Hosp of U. Cin., 1948-71, Christian R. Holmes Hosp., 1948-71, Jewish Hosp., 1945-71; cons. surgeon Bethesda Hosp., 1943-71, VA Hosp., 1942-71; dir. laser surgery U. Cin. Med Center, 1965-71. Mem. exec. council Cin. Area council Boy Scouts Am.; chmn. devel. council Miami U., 1955-60, trustee, 1957-66. Recipient Alumni award Miami U., 1961. Diplomate Am. Bd. Surgery. Fellow Am. Assn. for Surgery of Trauma, Soc. for Surgery Alimentary Tract; mem. A.M.A., Am., Ohio, Mont Reid (pres. 1962), Cin. surg. socs., Internat. Soc. Surgery, A.C.S., Pan-Pacific, Western, Central surg. assns., Halsted Soc., Soc. Univ. Surgeons, Am. Soc. for Surgery Hand (pres. 1968-69), A.A.A.S., Ohio Med. Assn., Cin. Acad. Medicine, N.Y. Acad. Scis., Am. Soc. U. Profs., Hist. and Philos. Soc. Ohio,

Endowment Fund Assn. U. Cin., Rookwood Philos. and Lit. Soc. Cin., Cin. Rose Soc. (pres. 1959-60), Phi Beta Kappa, Sigma Xi, Alpha Omega Alpha (pres. Cin. chpt. 1964-71), Pi Kappa Epsilon, Phi Sigma, Nu Sigma Nu, Theta Chi. Clubs: Commercial, Commonwealth (pres. 1959-60), Torch, Cincinnati Country, Camargo, Queen City, Faculty, University (Cin.); Recess; Stumps Boat. Contbr. articles to med. jours. Home: Cincinnati OH Died Oct. 27, 1971; buried Spring Grove Meml. Mausoleum, Cincinnati OH

SILKETT, ALBERT FRANK, educator; b. Red Oak, Ia., Dec. 24, 1904; s. Albert Carroll and Sylvia Delilah (Silkett) S.; A.B., Simpson Coll., 1925; summer, part-time student U. Neb., 1926-33, Ia. State Coll., 1938, U. Chgo., 1945-46, DePaul U., Chgo., 1947-48; student Ind. U. 1953-54; m. Mildred R. Turnbaugh, June 9, 1940;children—David Edward, James E. Tchr., prin., supt. schs., Ia., 1925-29, 37-38; interviewer Ia. State Employment Service, 1938-39; observer U.S. Weather Bur., 1939-42; head dept. mathematics and physics, dean of men Cotner Coll., 1930-33; agrl. agt. Dept. of Agr., also Neb. Extension Service, 1933-36; head dept. meteorology Rankin Aero. Acad., 1942-44; instr. physics U. Notre Dame, 1944; instr. mathematics and physics Purdue U., 1946; instr., asst. prof. physics U. Ill., Chgo., 1946-69, acting chmn. dept., 1947-48, 49-50. Past pres. Green Lake Community Assn., Calumet City, Ill., 1957-61. Active in Boy Scouts, sci. fairs in Ill., Ind., mem. Lansing Sci. Fair Council. Recipient citations for judging Chgo. Pub. Sch. Sci. Fair, 1966, N.W. Ind. Sci. Fair, 1966; plaque Chgo. Pub. Sch. Sci. Fair, 1967; award for service to education and youth Lansing Classroom Teachers Assn., 1967. Mem. Ill. Acad. Sci. (membership com.), Am. Meteorol. Soc., NRA, Am. Soc. Engring. Edn., A.A.A.S., Chgo. Area Tchrs. Sci. Assn. (pres.), Psi Chi. Home: Lansing IL Died Feb. 7, 1969.

SILLEN, LARS GUNNAR, chemist, educator; b. Stockholm, Sweden, July 11, 1916; s. Oskar and Brita (Gentele) S.; fil kand, U. Stockholm, 1934, fil mag. 1936, fil lic (Ph.D.), 1937, fil dr. 1940; m. Birgit Bjernekull, Apr. 9, 1939; children—Gunnar, Bo, Birgitta, Lars. Asso. prof. chemistry Stockholm U., 1941-48; prof. inorganic chemistry Chalmers' Inst. Tech., Goteborg, 1948-50; prof. inorganic chemistry Royal Inst. Tech., Stockholm, 1950-70, dean chemistry dept., 1956-60; Arthur D. Little vis. prof. chemistry Massachusettes Institute Technology, spring 1957; visiting professor geochemistry U. Cal., San Diego, 1966; Hill Foundation visiting prof. U. of Minnesota, 1967; vis. prof. U. Central Venezuela, 1968. Consultant Swedish Research Inst. National Defence, 1942-68; president commn. equilibrium data analytical sect., Internat. Union Pure and Applied Chemistry, 1953-59; chmn. exec. com. 7th Internat. Conf. Coordination Chemistry, Stockholm-Uppsala, 1962. Mem. vis. com. Woods Hole Oceanographic Instrn., 1962-65. Member Swedish Chem. Soc. (bd.), Swedenborg Inst., Swedish Numismatic Soc., Swedish Motordrivers Temperance Soc., Royal Swedish Acad. Scis., Royal Swedish Acad. Engring. Scis., Deutsche Akademie der Naturforscher Leopoldina. Author: (with others) Problems in Physical Chemistry, 1952; Stability Constants, Vol. I, 1956, Vol. II, 1957, 2d edit., 1964. Editor Svensk Kemisk Tidskrift, 1955-62. Mem. adv. bd. Acta Chem Scand, others. Home: Djursholm Sweden Died July 23, 1970.

SILLIMAN, HARRY INNESS, editor, pub.; b. Mahanoy Plane, Pa., Dec. 15, 1876; s. John H. and Hannah (Rhoads) S.; ed. pub. schs.; m. Argenta Fay Jones, May 10, 1913; 1 dau., Edna Kathryn. Owned Tamaqua Herald at 19; with Tamaqua Courier since 1899, now asso. editor; owner and editor Pottsville Journal; pres. Miners' Journal Newspaper Co. Corporal Co. B, 8th Pa. Vol. Inf., Spanish-Am. War. Mem. Planning Commn., Pottsville. Mem. bd. dirs. Pottsville Hosp., Y.W.C.A. Republican. Presbyterian. Clubs: Pottsville, Schuylkill Country. Home: 1101 Mahantonga St. Office: 213 S. Center St., Pottsville PA*‡

SILVER, JESSE FORREST, clergyman; b. nr. Canton, O., Aug. 8, 1872; s. John B. and Anna Elizabeth (Baer) S.; prep. edn., pub. schs. and Deerfield, O., select sch.; student Mt. Union Coll., Alliance, O., 1891-94, Pittsburgh Bible Inst., 1916-17; m. Margaret J. George, of Indiana Co., Pa., Apr. 28, 1897; children—Mrs. Anna G. Sedwick, Raymond G., Helen N., Marian. Ordained Free Meth. ministry, 1897; pastor Indiana, Pa. (on trial), 1896-97, Greensburg, 1898-1900, Tarentum, 1901-03; district elder (supt.) Rochester (Pa.) dist., 1904-07, Butler dist., 1908-11; pastor Butler, 1912-14, East End, Pittsburgh, 1915; dist. elder Pittsburgh district, 1915-16; asso. pastor Gospel Tabernacle, Pittsburgh, 1917-19; writing and evangelism, 1920-28. Sec. Pittsburgh Conf. Free Meth. Ch., 1900-15; del. and asst. sec. Gen. Conf., Chicago, 1911, 15; editor Providence Mission Tidings (monthly), 1907-16; Bible teacher Toccoa Falls Inst., Toccoa, Ga., 1929-31. Mem. Southern Calif. Premillennial Assn. Republican. Author: The Lord's Return, 1914, 7th edit., 1922; Will Hell Be Vacated? 1918; The Rapture, 1919. Address: 162 W. Los Angeles CA‡

SILVERA, FRANK ALVIN, actor, dir., prod.; b. Kingston, Jamaica, W.I., July 24, 1914; s. Alfred Neville and Gertrude Louise (Bell) S.; student Northeastern U. Law Sch., 1934-36; m. Anna Lillian Quarles, Oct. 3, 1942 (div. Dec. 1964); children—Frank Alvin, Linda Ann. Profl. debut, 1934; Broadway debut as Anna's father in Anna Lucasta, 1945, later played same role in London prodn. His Majesty's Theatre, and on tour; created Broadway roles of Guttman, Tennessee Williams' Camino Real, John Pope Sr. in Hatful of Rain; other roles in Broadway plays include Deschamps in Mademoiselle Colombe, M. Duval in Lady of the Camellias; off-Broadway roles include Nat Turner in Black Moses, role of Irish Seaman Maguire in Longitude 49, also King Lear for N.Y. Shakespeare Festival; screen roles in Fear and Desire, Viva Zapata, 1951, Killer's Kiss, The Fighter, Crime and Punishment, Key Witness, Mountain Road, Mutiny on the Bounty, Greatest Story Ever Told, Apaloosa, 1966, Hombre, 1967; appeared on recordings of poetry selections; Hollywood stage roles in View from the Bridge (also dir.), Am Enemy of the People, Three Sisters, Blues for Mr. Charlie; mem. Actor's Studio, 1950-70, condr. workshops, N.Y.C. and Hollywood; prod., dir., role in Broadway presentation The Amen Corner, 1965-70; mem. cast TV show High Chapparal; dir. Hatful of Rain, Metro Theatre; founder Am. Theatre of Being, Hollywood, Cal; Home: Pasadena CA Died June 1970.

SILVERMAN, IRVING, educator; b. Boston, Dec. 17, 1912; A.B., Coll. William and Mary, 1934, A.M., 1936; Univ. fellow U. Wash., 1936-38; Ph.D. in Philosophy, 1946; married; 1 child. Instr. Classics, Coll. William and Mary, 1934-36; prof. fgn. langs. Radford Coll., Va. Poly. Inst., 1938-73, also dean div. humanities. Served with AUS, 1942-46. Rockefeller fellow, 1941-42. Mem. Am. Philol. Assn. Author: Augustus and the Opposition. Address: Radford VA Died Feb. 5, 1973.

SILVERMAN, MORRIS, rabbi; b. Newburgh, N.Y., Nov. 19, 1894; s. Simon and Lena (Friedland) S.; A.B., Ohio State U., 1916; A.M., Columbia, 1917; grad. Jewish Theol. Sem. Am., 1922, M.H.L., 1947, D.H.L., 1952, D.D., 1956; D.H.L., Ohio State U., 1965; m. Althea H. Osber, June 29, 1919; children—Ben Ami (dec.), Hiliel E., Arthur B., Elihu O. (dec.). Rabbi Mt. Sinai Temple, Bklyn., 1917-20; chaplain city prison, 1917-20; rabbi Temple Israel, Washington Heights, N.Y.C., 1920-23; Emanuel Synagogue, Hartford, Conn., 1923-61, rabbi emeritus, 1961-72; chaplain Conn. Constnl. Conv., 1965; instr. Jewish history Conn. State Coll., 1934-38. Mem. Hartford Def. Council, 1942; dir. Hartford Jewish Fedn., 1940-43, clergy co-chmn. Clergy Mgmt. Conf., 1942. Pres. Conn. br. United Synagogue of Am., 1929-36, mem. exec. com., 1934, hon. pres. Connecticut Valley, 1963-72; exec. com. Rabbinical Assembly Am., 1929-32, pres. Conn. br., 1947; chmn. World Jewish Commn., 1963. Mem. Hartford War Council, War Records Com., Red Cross. Adv. Council, 1943-72; mem. Conn. Commn. Civil Rights, 1943, chmn., 1946-54; mem. adv. com. Bur. of War Records of Nat. Jewish Welfare Bd., 1944; dir. North End Community Center, 1944; apptd. reemployment committeeman by Dir. Selective Service, 1944. Bd. mgrs. Service Canteen, 1944-45; sec. Ministers Assn., Bklyn., 1919-20; pres. Hartford Assn. Ministers and Rabbis, 1934-35. Chmn. Rabbinical com. on seminary affairs for Conn., 1943, Conn. State Commn. on Civil Rights, 1943-72; bd. overseers Jewish Theol. Sem. Am., 1946; mem. nat. com. on Leaders Tng. Fellowship of Jewish Theol. Sem., 1946; Hartford rep. to Am.-Jewish Conf., 1943; chmn. Nat. Conf. of State and City Commns. Against Discrimination and of Civil Rights, 1958, Trustee Mt. Sinai Hosp., United Jewish Social Service, Old Peoples Home, Hartford Zionist Dist., Jewish Congress; mem. Conn. State Adv. Council Mental Health, 1964. Cited by Am. Hebrew for good will work between Jew and Christian, 1943; recipient Greater Hartford Citizens award, 1950, Freedoms Found. medal and prize, 1951-52; hon. pres. Young Peoples League in Hartford. Mem. Am. Acad. Jewish Research, Jewish Publ. Soc., Rabbinical Assembly Am., Nat. Conf. Jews and Christians, Zionist Orgn., Hartford Citizens Com. for Civic Progress, Phi Beta Kappa. Mem. B'nai B'rith: hon. mem. K. P. Club: Tumble Brook Country (hon. mem.) (Bloomfield, Conn.). Author: Hartford Jews, 1959-1970, 1970. Editor: Junior Prayer Book, Vol. I, 1933, Vol. II, 1937; Sabbath and Festival Prayer Book, 1936; High Holiday Prayer Book, 1939; New Sabbath and Festival Prayer Book, 1945; co-editor Prayer Book for Summer Camps, 1954; editor Selihot Service, 1954, Our Prayer Book, 1961; editor and compiler: Simhas Torch Service, 1941; Purim Service, 1947; Torah Readings for the Festivals, 1949; Prayers of Consolation, 1952; Weekday Prayer Book, 1956; editor: Healing Cometh from the Lord, 1961; Israeli Edit. High Holiday Prayer Book, 1964; Heaven on Your Head (comments on the Bible). Editor for Joint Prayer Book Commn., Rabbinical Assembly of Am., United Synagogue Am.; Passover Haggadah, 1959. Contbr. to yearbooks and jours. Founder Prayer Book Press, 1936. Home: Hartford CT Died Mar. 3, 1972; buried Emanuel Synagogue, Hartford CT

SILVEUS, WILLIAM ARENTS, lawyer, author; b. Waynesburg, Greene County, Pa., Nov. 6, 1875; s. David Moredock and Euphen May (Ely) S.; B.A., Waynesburg Coll., 1901; LL.B., U. of Tex., 1906; m Jessie Shriver, July 15, 1902; adopted son, Willian Isaac. Began general practice at San Antonio, Tex. 1906, later also engaged in real estate investmen business and making loans on own account. Mem. bd dirs. Tex. Children's Finding Assn., Tax-Payers Defens League of Bexar County, Tex. Mem. Am. Assn. for th Advancement of Science, Acad. Science of Tex. Botanical Soc. of America, Am. Soc. Plan Taxonomists, Scientific Soc. of San Antonio, Tex Democrat. Presbyterian. Author: Texas Grasses, 1933 Paspalum and Panicum, 1942; Nature's Way, 1942 assisted in revising First Book of Grasses by Agne Chase, also pub. Has traveled over 160,000 mile collecting grasses, 60,000 miles in last 2 yrs.; ha mounted 1000 specimens. Home: 832 Cambridge Oval San Antonio TX‡

SIMIC, STANOJE, minister of fgn. affairs of th Federated People's Rep. of Yugoslavia; b. Belgrade 1893. Graduated from the law faculty of the Univ. o Belgrade and has been in the diplomatic service o Yugoslavia since 1919. Served as Sec. in Yugosla legations in Budapest, Brussels, and Tirana; as consul i Korea, Albania and Zadar; counselor of the Yugosla Legation, Paris. Ambassador of the Yugosla Govt-in-Exile to Moscow, 1942-Mar., 1944, bu resigned to join Marshall Tito who reapptd. him to thi post. In April, 1945 he was apptd. Yugosla Ambassador to the U.S. and remained in this positio until he was given his present portfolio. Del. of hi country to the San Francisco Conf., 1945; vice chmn. o the Yugoslav delegation to the Paris Conf., July-Oct. 1946. Vice pres. of the Presidium of the Republic o Serbia; pres. of the Nat. Popular Front of Serbia. Home Belgrade Yugoslavia Died Feb. 26, 1970.*

SIMLER, GEORGE BRENNER, air force officer; b Johnstown, Pa., Feb. 16, 1921; s. George Brenner an Katharine (Taggart) S.; B.S., U. Md., 1948; grad. Na War Coll., 1961; m. Eleanor Bergeron, Nov. 15, 1942 children—George B., Pierre, Catherine, Eleanor Michael. Commd. 2d lt. USAF, 1942, advanced throug grades to gen.., 1972; stationed ETO, 1943-44, Hdgrs. Washington, 1948-51, U.S. Air Force Acad., 1957-60 S.E. Asia, 1965-66; vice comdr. in chief U.S. Air Force Europe, 1969-70; comdr. Air Tng. Command Randolph AFB, Tex., 1970-72, sr. mil. rep. permanen joint bd. for def. Can./U.S., 1967-72. Decorate D.S.M., with two oak leaf clusters, D.F.C., Air medal Purple Heart, Legion of Merit. Mem. Phi Delta Theta Home: Colorado Springs CO Died Sept. 9, 1972; burie U.S. Air Force Academy CO

SIMLEY, IRVIN T., business cons.; born Portland N.D., Nov. 8, 1887; s. Thrond O. and Gertrude (Linn S.; B.A., Luther Coll., 1911; M.A., Columbia, 1927; m Agnes Pauline Stadheim, Dec. 27, 1914 (dec. Jan 1956); children—Gretchen Bernice (Mrs. A. W Ostberg), Agnes Ingrid (Mrs. K. O. Monge), Doroth Helen (Mrs. H. C. Steffens). Tchr. Luther Acad., Aber Lea, Minn., 1911-14; supt. schs. Rolette (N.D.) Consol Schs., 1914-17, Rugby, N.D., 1917-21, Thief Rive Falls, Minn., 1921-26, South St. Paul, Minn., 1926-57 edn. cons., 1957-59, cons. United Fed. Savs. & Loan 1959-67. Pres. Dakota County Tb and Health Assn Mem. Nat., Minn. edn. assns., State Bd. Control Minn High Sch. League (past pres.), Phi Delta Kappa Kiwanian. Author: High School and You, 1937 Assignment and Guide Book, 1940; also articles on edn I. T. Simley High Sch., South St. Paul, named for him Home: South St Paul MN Died June 10, 1967.

SIMMILL, ELVIN RAYMOND, state judge; b Newark, Feb. 4, 1906; s. Herbert G. and Clara Elis (Schroedter) S.; m. Sylvia Bowermaste children—Elaine Polhemus, Carolyn Cameron, Joa Thiers. Admitted to N.J. bar, 1930; judge Monmout County Ct., 1953-64, Superior Ct. N.J., 1964-7 Trustee Monmouth Coll., West Long Branch, N.J 1954-67, chmn. bd., 1959-67. Home: Belmar NJ Die July 19, 1971.

SIMMONDS, FRANK WILLIAM, educator, banke b. nr. Cedar, Kan., Mar. 16, 1876; s. Angus MacDonal and Christina (Tillman) S.; B.Sc., Salina U., 190 M.Sc., 1903; grad. work U. Kan.; studied law; m Margaret Dale Boughman, June 3, 1900 (died 1922) children—Dale (Mrs. D. Howard Moreau), Helen (Mrs Williams R. Kuhns), Christine (Mrs. Wm. J Kinnamon); m. 2d, Clara Blanche Burns, June 8, 192 (died 1938). Teacher of rural schools, supt. schs Mankato, Kan., 1902-13, Lewiston, Ida., 1913-20; pioneer in developing Junior-Senior High School on th 6-3-3 basis at Lewiston, Ida.; condr. numerous count teachers institutes in Kan. and Ida.; mgr. Eastern dis C. C. of U.S., 1920-23; also federated work of r presidents with Nat. Chamber; sr. dep. mgr., Am Bankers Assn., 1923-44; retired Jan. 1, 1944. Develope and organized system of regional bank managemer conferences throughout the U.S., and regional clearin house associations. Sec. National Banking Cod Authority under NRA. Mem. Kan. State Bd. of Edn 1910-13; organized and managed circuit of summe chautauquas, 1906-13. Dir. N.E.A., 1917-20; pres. Ida State Teachers' Assn., 1919. Mem. exec. com. Stat Council of Defense, and federal food administrato during World War I; appointed col. on staff Gov. Ky., 1933. Mem. Acad. Polit. Science, S.R., Inst. Am. Genealogy (life), Pioneer Trails Assn. (dir.), Pi Gamma Mu. Rep. Mason (32 deg., Shriner). Author of Genealogy of the Simmonds Family of Nova Scotia and the United States; several textbooks; brochures on Cooperative Farm Marketing, Relationship State Bank and Federal Reserve System, Uniform State Banking Laws, Better Understanding of Economic Conditions, Inter-Bank Relationship Essential, Interest Rates on Deposits, etc. Edited Volume of Commercial Bank Management Studies, also Volume of Proceedings of Bank Management Conferences. Home: Flemington NJ Died Aug. 6, 1971.

SIMMONS, DANIEL AUGUSTUS, judge; b. Coffee Co., Ala., Jan. 18, 1873; s. Mason and Nancy A. (Fort) S.; ed. high sch., and under pvt. tutors in chemistry, physics, psychology and biology; m. Rose Ella Burleson, of Mary Esther, Santa Rosa Co., Fla., June 4, 1896. Practiced in Westville and Chipley, Fla., 1903-7; sec. to Governor Broward, 1907-9; removed to Jacksonville, 1910; circuit judge Duval Co., terms 1913-19, 1919-25. V.p. Our Home Life Ins. Co. Asso. Soc. for Psychical Research, Eng. Democrat. Conglist. Mason, K.P. Author: The Science of Religion, 1916. Home: 2206 Laura St. Office: County Bldg., Jacksonville FL‡

SIMMONS, DAYTON COOPER, banker; born Utica, Miss., May 20, 1877; s. George Whitfield and Sarah Lucinda (Cooper) S.; student pub. schs., Copiah Co., Miss.; m. Annie Belle Ferguson, Nov. 1, 1904; children—Sarah Carolyn (Mrs. Lawson), William James, Dayton Cooper. Pres. D. C. Simmons, Inc., Utica, Mississippi, Utica Lumber and Gin Co., Utica Cotton Growers Warehouse Co.; pres., dir. Bank of Utica; v.p. Utica Box Co.; dir., chmn. exec. com., loan, trust, investment coms. Deposit Guaranty Bank & Trust Co., Jackson, Miss.; dir., mem. exec., finance coms. Standard Life Ins. Co., Jackson, Miss. Member bd. S.S.S., World War I, chmn. bd. 3 Hinds Co., Miss., World War II; mem. adv. council War Assets Adminstrn., Zone V. Chmn. bd. trustees Utica High Sch., Miss. Bapt. Hosp., Jackson; bd. trustees Hinds Co. Agrl. High Sch., Jr. Coll. Mem. Jackson C. of C. (board dirs.). Baptist (deacon, chmn. finance com.). Mason. New addition to Miss. Bapt. Hosp. named in his honor. Home: 734 Fairview St. Office: Deposit Guaranty Bank & Trust Co., Jackson MS‡

SIMMONS, DWIGHT LANE, lawyer; b. Hillsboro, Tex., Dec. 7, 1898; s. Harland H. and Edith M. (Porter) S.; A.B. Southwestern U., 1921; M.A., Columbia, 1922; LL.B., U. Tex., 1926; m. Loraine Marshall, Sept. 15, 1921; 1 son, Marshall. Admitted to Tex. bar, 1926; asso. with firm Thompson, Knight, Baker & Harris, Dallas, 1926-34; mem. firm Thompson, Knight, Simmons & Bullion, Dallas Press. Dallas Legal Aid Society, Incorporated, 1957; president board trustees Highland Park Ind. School Dist., 1948-50; trustee Community Guidance Service; chmn. adv. com., 1956-57, also trustee Southwestern Legal Found. Mem. Am., Tex. Dallas (dir. 1953-54, pres. 1956) bar assns. Fellows Am. Bar Found., Dallas County Campaign Screening Com., Inc. Dallas Air Power Council, Phi Delta Phi, Kappa Sigma. Methodist (ofcl. bd.). Mason. Clubs: Dallas (sec. 1956-57), Dallas Country, Insurance, Dallas TX Died Nov. 11, 1970.

SIMMONS, ERNEST J., author, lectr.; b. Lawrence, Mass., Dec. 8, 1903; s. Mark and Annie (McKinnon) S.; A.B., Harvard, 1925, A.M., 1926, Ph.D., 1928; L.H.D. degree, Northwestern University, 1968; m. Winifred McNamara, June 20, 1940; 1 son, Richard D. Instr., then asst. prof. Harvard, 1929-40; asso. prof., then professor and chmn. dept. Slavic langs. Cornell U., 1941-45; prof. Slavic langs., chmn. dept., also prof. Russian lit. Columbia, 1946-59; acting dir. Center Advanced Studies, Wesleyan U., 1967. Mem. cultural mission to USSR for Am. Council Learned Societies, 1947; mem. joint com. Slavic studies Am. Council Learned Societies and Social Sci. Research Council, 1947-58; pres. Com. Ednl. Future Columbia, 1957-58; Phi Beta Kappa vis. scholar 1959-61, 64-65; Danforth vis. lectr., 1961-63, cons. Ford Found., 1961-63; sr. fellow Center for Advanced Studies, Wesleyan U., Middletown Conn., 1963-64, acting dir., spring 1967; Patten Found. lectr. Ind. U., 1964. Bd. trustees Sarah Lawrence Coll., 1956-58; bd. dirs. Monadnock Community Coll., 1967-72. Mem. Modern Lang. Assn. (exec. com. 1956-57), Am. Civil Liberties Union (acad. freedom com. 1957-58). Clubs: Harvard, Century Assn. (N.Y.C.). Author: English Literature and Culture in Russia, 1932; Pushkin, 1937; Dostovesky, the Making of a Novelist, 1940; Tolstoy, 1946; Russian Fiction and Soviet Ideology, 1958; Chekhov, a biography, 1962; Introduction to Russian Realism, 1965; Introduction to Tolstoy's Writings, 1968. Address: Dublin NH Died May 3, 1972.

SIMMONS, GEORGE E(VANS), univ. prof.; b. Gates, Tenn., June 28, 1898; s. John Richard and Senthia Elizabeth (Kirksey) S.; diploma, W. Tenn. State Normal (now Memphis State Univ.), 1917; B.J., Univ. of Mo., 1921; A.M., Vanderbilt U., 1926; m. Mabel Clarke, June 25, 1921; children—George Clarke, Kirksey. Reporter, telegraph editor, Nashville (Tenn.) Tennessean, 1921-22; telegraph editor, Tampa (Fla.) Tribune, 1922-23; copyreader, Kansas City (Mo.) Journal, also reporter, Kansas City Times, 1923; sports editor, Tampa Tribune, 1923-24; city editor, Nashville Tennessean, 1924-26; asst. prof. journalism, Tulane Univ., 1926-34, asso. prof., 1934-37, prof., 1937-64, prof. emeritus, 1964, asst. dean of arts and sciences, 1939-44, acting dean, 1944-47, asso. dean, 1961-64; vis. prof. journalism U.S.C., 1964-66; lectr. journalism No. Ill. U., 1966-67; vis. prof. journalism Univ. of Alabama, 1967-68. Mem. Assn. Edn. in Journalism (pres. 1954), Phi Beta Kappa, Kappa Tau Alpha (nat. pres. 1948-50), Sigma Delta Chi. Democrat. Home: New Orleans LA Died Mar. 16, 1972; buried New Orleans LA

SIMMONS, JAMES HENRY, prof. English; b. Wake Forest, N.C., May 29, 1867; s. William G. and Mary Elizabeth (Foote) S.; A.B., Wake Forest Coll., 1888, A.M., 1889; Litt.D., U. of Ga., 1925; studied U. of Chicago and Columbia Univ., Harvard, Johns Hopkins Univ.; m. Mary Lillian White, June 15, 1892; children—William G., Thomas C., James H., Mrs. Kate Lide, Mrs. Mary F. Paris, Mrs. Lessie S. Lide and Mrs. Lillie Palmour. Professor at Carson and Newman Coll., Tenn., 1889-91; head Dept. English, William Jewell Coll., Mo., 1891-98; prof. English and sec. of faculty, Shorter Coll., Rome, Ga., 1898-1910; prof. English, Brenau Coll., 1910-47; professor English, summer sessions, University of Ga., 1923-38. Mem. Phi Beta Kappa (hon.). Baptist. Author: The Place of English in the College Course; A Guide to Systematic Reading; Errors in the Use of English. Address: 202 N. Prior St., Gainesville GA‡

SIMMONS, JAMES WILLIAM, mfr. cottonseed products; b. Dallas, Tex., Aug. 11, 1885; s. James William and Mary Phillippa (Barry) S.; student St. Edward's U., Austin, Tex., 1901-02; m. Rebekah Baggett, Apr. 7, 1910 (dec. 1950); 1 son, James William; m. 2d, Blanche Washington, Jan. 30, 1954. Chmn. bd. Lubbock Cotton Oil Co., Quanah Cotton Oil Co.; pres. Sweet Water Cotton Oil Co. (Tex.); dir. Rep. Nat. Bank Dallas, Employers Casualty Co., Employers Nat. Ins. Co., Employers Nat. Life Ins. Co. Dir. Tex. Employers Ins. Assn. Trustee Tex. Research Found.; adv. bd. St. Paul Hosp. Democrat. K.C. Clubs: Chaparral, Dallas Country, Dallas. Home: Dallas TX Died Apr. 22, 1969; entombed Cherry Hill Mausoleum, Dallas TX

SIMON, ANDRE LOUIS, wine and food authority, author; b. Paris, France, Feb. 28, 1877; s. Ernest Constant and Jeanne (Dardoize) S.; student Ecole Bossuet and Petit Seminaire N.D. des Champs, Paris; m. Edith Winifred Symons, Oct. 17, 1900; children—Jeanne, Marcelle, Andre, Peter, Madeleine. Founder Wine and Food Soc., London, Eng., with chpts. in United Kingdom, U.S., Australia, Africa, Far East. pres., 1933-70. Author: History of the Wine Trade in England 3 vols. 1906-09; A Dictionary of Wines, 1935; A Concise Encyclopedia of Gastronomy, 9 vols., 1939-46; We Shall Eat and Drink Again, 1944; Vintagewise, 1946; A Wine Primer, 1946; Andre Simon's French Cookbook: The Noble Grapes and Great Wines of France, 1957; Wine in Shakespeare's Days and Shakespeare's Plays, 1964; others. Home: London England Died Sept. 5, 1970.

SIMON, CLARENCE TURKLE, educator; b. Newton, Ia., May 13, 1897; B.A., Wittenberg Coll., Springfield, O., 1919; grad. Northwestern U. Sch. of Speech, 1920; M.A., Northwestern, 1922; Ph.D., State U. of Ia., 1924; Doctor of Science, Wittenberg Coll., 1954; m. Dorothy Will, 1936 (dec. 1965); children—Lee Will, John Turkle. Professor of speech re-education, Northwestern University, 1924-47, also director speech and hearing clinic, 1928-47, professor psychology of speech, also coordinator grad. studies in speech, 1949-65, professor emeritus, 1965-67; lectr. and consultant in psychology; visiting professor U. Hawaii, 1947-49, University of Washington, 1957-58; cons. prof. in logopedics Wichita State U., 1958-67; asst. editor Quarterly Journal of Speech Education, 1925-30; consulting editor for speech McGraw-Hill Book Company. Served as acting sergeant United States Army, July-Dec. 1918. Diplomate in clin. psychology Am. Bd. Examiners. Mem. American Speech Association (pres. 1930-31), Am. Psychol. Assn., American Speech and Hearing Assn. (v.p. 1938-40); pres. 1946; recipient honors 1950), Illinois Psychological Assn., Sigma Xi, Pi Kappa Delta, Beta Theta Pi. Editor Speech Monographs, 1932-41. Home: Wichita KS Died Dec. 30, 1967.

SIMON, GRANT MILES, architect; b. Phila., Pa., Oct. 2, 1887; s. Frederick Paul and Mary Ann S.; student Sch. Industrial Art., 1905-06; B.S., U. of Pa., 1911, M.S., 1911; ed. T Square Atelier, 1907-09, Acad. of Fine Arts, 1907-08, Ecole des Beaux Arts, Paris, France, 1914-15; m. Jamie Holcombe Hearin, Apr. 13, 1923 (divorced 1940); 1 dau., Jane Holcombe; m. 2d, Georgette Archer, June 14, 1941, 3 sons, Adrian, John, Philip. Architect for Meade Memorial, Washington, Municipal Stadium, Phila., Fidelity-Phila. Bank and Office Bldg., and University Club, both Phila. also various banking, office, and instnl. bldgs., and residences; architect for restoration various houses, Phila.; cons. on city and town planning; in governmental work, 1942-44; advisory architect Phila. Nat. Shrines Park Commn., 1947; exec. architect, U. of Pa. plan of development, from 1948; painter pvt. and public collections. Chairman Philadelphia Historical Commission. Served on Committee of American Embassy, Paris, France, 1914-15. American Com. for Relief of French Students, 1914-18. Recipient Freedoms Foundation Award, 1958; Colonial Philadelphia Historical Society Award, 1961. Fellow Am. Inst. Architects; mem. Soc. Beaux Arts Architects. Club: Union League. Lithographer and painter; represented in Pennell Collections, Library of Congress, Acad. Fine Arts (Phila.), Bklyn. Mus. Art. Author: Historic Germantown (with H. M. and M. B. Tinkcom), 1954; The Beginnings of Philadelphia, 1957. Address: Philadelphia PA Died May 4, 1967.

SIMON, HENRY WILLIAM, editor; b. N.Y.C., Oct. 9, 1901; s. Leo L. and Anna (Mayer) S.; A.B., Columbia, 1923, M.A., 1927, Ph.D., 1933; student New Coll., Oxford U., 1925-26; m. Margaret Halsey, 1935 (div.); m. 2d, Rosalind Kunstler, Dec. 15, 1951. Tchr. English, Fieldston Sch., U. Tenn., 1923-32; head lit. div. New Coll., Columbia, 1932-38, asst. prof. edn. Columbia Tchrs. Coll., 1934-41; vis. prof. edn. Univ. Coll. of Southwest, Exeter, Eng., 1936-37; music critic PM, 1940-44; editor Simon & Schuster, New York City, 1944-70, v.p., and dep. editor-in-chief, 1957-62, executive editor, 1962-67, editorial cons., 1967-70; chmn. Music Critics Circle of N.Y., 1944. Mem. of P.E.N. Author: The Teaching of Poetry Appreciation, 1932; The Reading of Shakespeare, 1933; Preface to Teaching, 1938; A Treasury of Grand Opera, 1946, rev. 1965; Pocket Book of Great Operas (with Abraham Veinus), 1949; Festival of Opera, 1957; What Is a Teacher?, 1964; An Audio-Visual History of Music, Published 1968. Editor of following: Five Great Comedies by Shakespeare, 1939; Five Great Comedies by Shakespeare, 1943; The Sonnets, Songs and Poems of Shakespeare, 1950; Four Great Historical Plays by Shakespeare, 1951; A Treasury of Hymns (with Maria Leiper), 1953; A Treasury of Christmas Songs and Carols, 1955; Victor Book of the Opera, 1967. Home: New York City NY Died Oct. 1, 1970.

SIMON, NAIF LOUIS, anesthesiologist; b. Quincy, Mass., Oct. 31, 1914; s. Louis P. and Latifa (Boulus) S.; B.S., Boston U., 1937, M.D., 1942; m. Beverly Mary Dorley, Sept. 22, 1949; 1 dau., Lynne Marie. Intern, Lynn (Mass.) Hosp., 1942-45; resident during mil. service, 1942-46; with Quincy City Hosp., 1946-68, dir. anesthesiology dept., 1946-68, dir. inhalational therapy, 1946-68, founder, dir. Sch. Nurse Anesthetists, 1947-68, med. dir. intravenous therapy dept., 1946-68, lectr. Sch. Nursing, 1946; anesthesia privileges Milton (Mass.) Hosp., Cape Cod Hosp., Hyannis, Mass. Served to capt. M.C., AUS, 1943-46. Fellow Am. Coll. Anesthesiology, Internat. Coll. Surgeons, Am. Geriatrics Soc.; mem. Am., Mass. (cons. hypnosis 1960) med. assns., Norfolk S. Dist., Pan-Am. med. socs., Am., New Eng., Mass. socs. anesthesiology, Am. Soc. Clin. Hypnosis, Internat. Anesthesia Research Soc., Sons of Lebanon, Boston U. Alumni Assn., Phi Chi. K.C. Home: Quincy MA Died Nov. 26, 1968; buried Blue Hill Cemetery Braintree MA

SIMONS, AMORY COFFIN, artist; b. Charleston, S.C., Apr. 6, 1869; s. John and Mary Hume S.; pupil Pa. Acad. Fine Arts, and of Dampt and Peuch, Paris. Received 3 prizes at Am. Art Assn. of Paris; hon. mention, Paris Expn., 1900. Address: 17, bis, Rue Campagne-Premiere, Paris France‡

SIMONS, HANS, educator, author; b. Velbert, Germany, July 1, 1893; s. Walter and Erna (Ruehle) S.; Dr. jur. et rer. pol., Koenigsberg (Germany); L. H.D., New School of Social Research; married to Eva Haym, June 14, 1924; children—Regula, Ursula. Teacher, educational administration, government adminstrator; executive director League of Nations Assn., 1919-25; dir. Institute of Political Science, Berlin, 1925-29; District Governor, Lower Silesia, 1930-32; prof. internat. relations, Grad. Faculty, Polit. and Social Sci., New School for Social Research, N.Y. City, since 1935; dean Sch. of Politics, 1943-50, Pres. Sch. 1950-60; cons. general education, Ford Found., India, 1960-72; cons. Office of Strategic Services, 1944; Chief, Governmental Structures Branch, Civil Affairs Division, OMGUS, 1947-49. Mem. Fgn. Policy Assn., Polit. Sci. Association, Council Foreign Relations. Member commn. to study the orgn. of peace, Nat. Planning Assn. Author: Preamble to the League of Nations Covenant, 1919; Political Education and Universities, 1925. Contbr. of articles to Social Research, Journal of Adult Edn., Am. Scholar, Christianity and Crisis, Polit. and Econ. Democracy, Canada, The Empire and the League, World Currents and Canada's Course, Mexico and the United States, War in Our Time, Proceedings of the Inst. of Public Affairs. Home: New Delhi India Died Mar. 28, 1972.

SIMONS, HOWARD PERRY, engring. educator; b. Canton, O., July 14, 1907; s. Laird Perry and Elizabeth Josephine (Eierman) S.; B.A., Ohio State U., 1928, M.Sc., 1930, Ph.D. (Univ. fellow 1938-39), 1940; student Phila. Textile Sch., 1929-30, U. Pa., part-time 1930-33; m. Dorothy May Weber, June 1, 1935;

children—Martin Perry, Donald Laird. Instr. chemistry Drexel Inst., 1930-32; dir. research Phoenix Hosiery Co., 1933-37; mem. faculty W.Va. U., 1939-72, prof. chem. engring., 1947-72, chmn. dept., 1959-69. Registered profl. engr., W.Va. Fellow Am. Inst. Chemists; mem. Am. Inst. Chem. Engrs., Am. Chem. Soc. (past chmn. No. W.Va. sect.), Am. Soc. Engring. Edn. (past chmn. chem. engring. div.), Nat., W.Va. (past pres. Morgantown) socs. profl. engrs., Morgantown C. of C., Sigma Xi (past pres. W.Va. U.), Tau Beta Pi, Phi Lambda Upsilon, Sigma Gamma Epsilon, Morgantown WV Died June 3, 1972; cremated.

SIMPSON, CLARENCE L(ORENZO), diplomat; born Royesville, Liberia, Oct. 28, 1896; s. Alpha Douglas and Flora (North) S.; student Coll. West Africa, 1915-16; LL.D., Liberia Coll., 1920; m. Abrahametta Benedicia, Sept. 8, 1931; children—Clarice, Clarence, Amanda. Collector of customs, 1924-26; mem. law firm Simpson & Simpson since 1933, co. atty., 1926-28; sec. Gen. Post Office, 1928-31, acting postmaster gen., 1931; speaker Ho. Reps., 1931-34; sec. state for fgn. affairs, 1934-44; del. League Nations, 1934; v.p. Liberia, 1944-52; chmn. Liberian delegation Conf. Internat. Orgn., U.N., 1945; ambassador to U.S. 1952-56, to U.K., from 1956; ret.; practiced in Liberia; mem. Internat. Deiplomatic Acad.; vice chmn. ad hoc polit. com 7th session Gen. Assembly, U.N., 1952. Chmn. adv. board Y.M.C.A. Vice president trustee Liberia Coll., 1944; pres., trustee U. Liberia. Decorated Knight of Grand Band, Order Star of Africa. Mem. Nat. Bar Assn. (past sec.). True Whig Party (sec.-gen.). Mason (past grand master). Home: Monrovia Liberia Died Jan. 1969.

SIMPSON, CUTHBERT AIKMAN, clergyman; b. Charlottetown, P.E.I., Can., May 24, 1892; s. James and Alice Maude Susan (Des Brisay) S.; student St. Peter's Sch., Charlottetown; B.A., Kings Coll., Nova Scotia, 1915, M.A., 1918, D.D. (hon.), 1939; B.A., Christ Church, Oxford, 1921, Diploma in Theology, 1922, M.A., 1939, B.D. and D.D., 1945; S.T.B., Gen. Theol. Sem., N.Y. City, 1929, S.T.M., 1932, D.Th., 1935; D.C.L. (hon.), Bishops Coll., Lennoxville, 1947; L.H.D., Simpson College, Indianola, Iowa, 1962; Doctor of Divinity, St. Andrews College, 1967; m. Jessie Katherine Matheson Kemp, September 24, 1918 (deceased April 1961). Came to the United States, 1927, naturalized, 1937. Ordained deacon in the Church of England (Protestant Episcopal Ch.), 1920, priest, 1921; rector, St. Alban's Ch., Woodside, N.S., 1922-28; tutor Gen. Theol. Sem., 1928-30, instr. in Old Testament, 1930-34, assistant prof., 1934-40, professor, 1940-54, Bishop Paddock lecturer, 1946, Regius professor of Hebrew and Canon of Christ Church, Oxford, 1954-59, dean of Christ Church, Oxford, 1959-69; William C. Winslow lecturer, Seabury-Western Theological Seminary, Evanston, Illinois, 1947. Capt., pay corps. Canadian Army, 1916-19. Rhodes scholar, P.E.I., 1916. Mem. Soc. for O.T. Study, Soc. of Bibl. Lit. and Exegesis, Am. Oriental Soc. Author: Revelation and Response in the Old Testament, 1947; Jeremiah, The Prophey of My People," 1947; The Early Traditions of Israel, 1948; The Composition of the Book of the Judges, 1958. Course on Old Testament in The St. James Lession series (with Bernard Iddings Bell), 1944. Contbr. to Liberal Catholicism and the Modern World, edited by Frank Gavin, 1934; Interpreter's Bible, 1952. Address: Oxford England Died June 30, 1969; buried Christ Church, Oxford England

SIMPSON, FRANK LESLIE, univ. prof.; b. South Barnstead, N.H., Mar. 19, 1875; s. Charles Edward and Sarah Abbie (Clark) S.; A.B., Boston U., 1898, LL.B., summa cum laude, 1903, LL.M., 1910; fellow of Boston University Law School, 1903-04; J.D., Suffolk University, 1943; m. Mabel Elizabeth White, Sept. 20, 1905; 1 son, Donald Robert. General practice since 1903; librarian and instr., Boston Univ. Law Sch., 1904-07, asst. prof. law, 1907-10, prof., 1910-43; dean, Suffolk University Law School, since 1942. Member American, Massachusetts State and Boston bar associations, American Law Inst., Mass. Law Society, Phi Beta Kappa, Gamma Eta Gamma and Theta Delta Chi. Grand Master of Masons in Mass., 1926-28; pres. Masonic Edn. and Charity Trust, 1926-28; chmn. Special Crime Commission, Mass., 1933. Author: Bigelow's Cases on Bills and Notes, 1905; Simpson's Cases on Torts, 1908; Massachusetts Law (6 edits.), 1915-44. Home: 11 Millett Rd., Swampscott MA Office: 20 Derne St., Boston MA‡

SIMPSON, HARTLEY, univ. dean; b. Tilton, N.H., 1900; s. Hartley F. and Una G. (Bushman) S.; A.B., Bowdoin College, 1922, LL.D. (honorary), 1956. student Cornell University, 1923-26. Instructor of history Cornell Univ., 1923-26; asst. prof. history U. Pitts., 1926-29; research asst. history Yale, 1930-42, research asso., 1942-46, asso. prof., 1947-67, asst. dean Grad. Sch., 1942-47, asso. dean, 1947-56, dean, 1956-61, ret., 1962. Mem. Am. Hist. Assn., Phi Beta Kappa. Author hist. articles. Address: Franklin NH Died Oct. 4, 1967; buried Park Cemetery, Tilton NH

SIMPSON, HERMAN, writer; b. Kalvaria, Russian Poland, Dec. 10, 1873; s. Jeroham H. and Yetta (Volkovski) S.; came to America, 1886; B.A., New York U., 1894; Columbia U. Sch. of Polit. Science, 1894-7; unmarried. Was teacher history, Coll. City of New York; later on editorial staffs, Historians' History, Internat. Ency., Internat. Year Book; editor in chief New York Call, 1909-11; founder New Review (now defunct), of which was editor, 1913-14. Contbr. numerous articles on economic, polit. and lit. topics to Standard Ency., The Independent, The Bookman. Club: Liberal. Home: 170 W. 121st St., New York NY‡

SIMPSON, JOHN R., banker; b. Scranton, Pa., Dec. 10, 1907; s. Harry and Josephine (Ramsey) S.; Ph.B., Brown U., 1933; m. Elizabeth Edwards, Apr. 7, 1934; children—Susannah S., John R., Jr. With Sibley, Lindsay & Curr Co., Rochester, N.Y., 1933-34; with Cleland Simpson Co., Scranton, Pa., 1934-69, became v.p., 1937, pres. 1947, then chmn. bd.; pres. Third Nat. Bank & Trust Co., 1949-69; chmn. bd. Simpson Real Estate Corp. Trustee Hahnemann Hosp., Scranton Pub. Library, Keystone Coll.; v.p. Community Chest. Mem. Pa. C. of C. (bd. dirs.). Home: Waverly PA Died Dec. 18, 1969.

SIMPSON, KEMPER, economist; b. Chattanooga, Tenn., Apr. 7, 1893; s. Solomon and Flora (Kemper) S.; student Baltimore City Coll., 1907-10; A.B., Johns Hopkins, 1914, Ph.D., 1917; unmarried. Lecturer Johns Hopkins U., 1917; economist Federal Trade Commn., 1918-21; asst. prof., Princeton, 1923; economist U.S. Tariff Commn. (advisor abroad), 1924-29; prof. of economics, U. of Cincinnati, 1927; special advisor to group of Rep. senators opposing Hawley-Smoot tariff, 1929; economist Goldman Sachs Trading Corp., 1929-31; cons. economist for banks, importers, and foreign industries, 1931-34; econ. advisor Securities and Exchange Commn., 1934-37; member of original Roosevelt Brain Trust, 1932, conducted research for the Temporary Nat. Econ. Com. in the Federal Trade Commission; chief of Iberian section Board of Economic Warfare; economist United States Tariff Commn.; tariff adviser, Economic Co-operation Adminstrn., Am. Embassy, Athens, Greece. Author: The Capitalization of Good Will, 1921; Economics for the Accountant, 1921; Introduction to World Economics, 1934; The Margin Trader, 1938; Big Business, Efficiency, and Facism, 1941. Editor and compiler of a number of government reports. Contbr. to econ. jours. Home: Alexandria VA Died June 29, 1970.

SIMPSON, KIRKE LARUE, newspaper man; b. San Francisco, Calif., Aug. 14, 1881; s. Sylvester C. and Frances Marion (McFarland) S.; ed. pub. schs.; m. Ella May Field, Apr. 6, 1945 (dec. Oct. 1952); m. 2d, Irene L., Oct. 1953. Began newspaper work in Tonopol, Nev. and San Francisco, 1906; with Associated Press, Washington, 1908-45. Served in 1st Calif. Vol. Inf., Philippine campaigns, during Spanish-Am. War and Philippine Insurrection, 1898-99; commd. maj. Mil. Intelligence O.R.C., U.S. Army, 1921. Club: Nat. Press, The Gridiron. Awarded Pulitzer prize, 1921, for article on the Unknown Soldier." Home: Los Gatos CA Died June 16, 1972; cremated, ashes interred Los Gatos Memorial Park Los Gatos CA

SIMPSON, RICHARD LEE, dentist; b. Fincastle, Va., Apr. 21, 1873; s. John Charlton and Sarah Elizabeth (Backenstoe) S.; student Washington and Lee U., 1891-92; D.D.S., U. of Md., 1896, hon. A.M., 1907; m. Elma Walker, 1901; 1 adopted dau., Virginia Jaqueline (Mrs. Leslie Reid Jones). Practiced dentistry, Fincastle, Va., 1896-1904, Richmond, Va., since 1904; prof. of operative dentistry, crown and bridge work and dean of dept., Univ. Coll. of Medicine, Richmond, 1905-13; prof., dean dental dept., Med. Coll. Va., 1913-15, now emeritus prof. clin. practice. Mem. Va. State Bd. Dental Examiners, 1903-05. Fellow Am. Coll. Dentists; mem. Nat. Dental Assn., Va. Dental Assn. (ex-pres.), Richmond Dental Soc. (past pres.), Xi Psi Phi, Omicron Kappa Upsilon. Democrat. Presbyterian (elder). Mason. Club: Hermitage Golf (Richmond). Inventor of several dental appliances; has lectured and given clinics before state and nat. socs., also Internat. Dental Congress, St. Louis, 1904, and Chicago Centennial Dental Congress, 1933. Originated the securing of the Betty Davis Wood $1,200,000 endowment for the Med. Coll. of Va. Recipient of testimonial banquet and gold medallion from the Richmond Dental Soc., Sept. 24, 1938. Home: 2913 Hawthorne Av. Office: 301 E. Franklin St., Richmond VA‡

SIMPSON, ROBERT EDWARD, ry. official; b. Glen Alpine, N.C., Oct. 20, 1869; s. James Locke and Hattie E. (Tate) S.; ed. common schs.; m. Annie Ellis, of Hickory, N.C., Dec. 10, 1902. With Western N. Carolina Ry. and its successor, the Southern Ry., since Apr. 13, 1882; began as water boy, and successively section foreman, extra gang foreman, work train conductor, track supervisor, freight and passenger conductor, roadmaster, trainmaster, asst. supt., 1906-07, supt., 1907-14, gen. supt., 1914-20, gen. mgr. Lines East, since Oct. 16, 1920, gen. mgr. Lines West, since Oct. 1, 1927. Democrat. Episcopalian. Mason (33 deg., Scottish Rite, Grand Cross Court of Honor, Shriner). Clubs: Red Fez (Charlotte, N.C.); Hickory Country (Hickory, N.C.); Bannockburn Club (Washington, N.C.); Queen City, Cincinnati (both of Cincinnati). Home: Hickory NC Address: Cincinnati OH*‡

SIMPSON, SLOAN, b. Weatherford, Tex., Oct. 25, 1876; s. John Nicholas and Susan Elizabeth (Sloan) S.; A.B., Harvard, 1899; m. Eleanora Laurenson Myer, of Baltimore, Md., Jan. 11, 1911; 1 dau., Elizabeth Laurenson. Left college junior year to join 1st U.S. Vol. Cav. (Rough Riders"); served as pvt. and corpl. participated in battles of Las Guasimas and San Juan, Cuba; transferred to regular army as 2d lt. 10th Inf. resigned Oct. 13, 1898, and returned to college. Commissioned maj. and asst. insp. Tex. N.G., 1900; also served as capt. and adj. 4th Inf. Tex. N.G., until retirement, 1913; commd. maj. 133d F.A., 1917 promoted lt. col. and assigned to 133d F.A.; served in France as lt. col. and chief of staff of 61st F.A. Brig. Mgr. Bailey County Cattle Co., Tex., 1900-07 postmaster of Dallas, Tex., 1907-12; partner with William Pagen and Son, cotton exporters, 1913-17, now mem. Sloan Simpson & Co., bankers, brokers. Republican. Catholic. Mason (32 deg.). Clubs: Harvard (New York), Dallas, Dallas Country, Brook Hollow Golf. Home: 4605 Abbott Av. Office: First Nat. Bank Bldg., Dallas TX‡

SIMS, CECIL, lawyer; b. Atlanta, Ga., June 20, 1893; s. Charles Milton and Moselle (Park) S.; LL.B. Vanderbilt Univ., 1914; m. Grace Wilson, Sept. 21, 1921; children—Cecil (killed in action, Germany, Nov. 21, 1944), Wilson, Grace, Betty. Admitted to Tenn. bar 1914, practiced in Tenn., 1914-68; partner firm Bass, Berry & Sims, Nashville, Tenn. Dir. Nat. Life and Accident Insurance Co., Spur Distributing Co., Inc. Capt., 322d Inf., 81st Div., U.S. Army, World War I. Mem. bd. trustees, Vanderbilt U.; mem. bd. edn. Davidson County, Tenn. Mem. exec. com. Bd. of Control for So. Regional Edn. Mem. Tenn. State Senate 1925. Received Founder's Medal, Law Dept. Vanderbilt U., 1914. Mem. Phi Beta Kappa (mem. exec. com.) Alpha Tau Omega. Meth. Clubs: Coffee House, Belle Meade Country (Nashville). Home: Nashville TN Died June 22, 1968.

SINCERBEAUX, FRANK H., lawyer; b. Kelloggsville N.Y., July 12, 1874; s. Edward M. and Mary E. (Rooks) S.; Certificate, State Normal and Training Sch. Oneonta, N.Y., 1890-93; A.B. (salutatorian), Yale 1902; LL.B., Columbia, 1905; m. Jessie Marion Batterson, June 30, 1903 (deceased Sept. 1962); children—Helen (Mrs. Arlington W. Clark), Robert, Barbara; m. 2d, Jean Mason Newman, Feb. 6, 1963. Tchr. dist. sch., Cayuga County, N.Y., 1891-92; prin. Union Sch., Port Jefferson, N.Y., 1893-98, placing it under supervision of N.Y. State Bd. of Regents; admitted to N.Y. State bar, 1904; active in procuring repeal of annual N.Y. State Mortgate Tax Law 1905-06; in gen. practice since 1906, specializing in wills, trusts and savings bank law; assn. with Bowers & Sands, 1906-14, mem. Bowers & Sands, 1914-17, Middlebrook & Borland, 1917-26, Middlebrook & Sincerbeaux, 1926-44, Sincerbeaux & Shrewsbury 1944-69; trustee, The Greenwich Savings Bank since 1930. Dir. Estate Eugene A. Hoffman, Inc., 1917-69, Forest Hills Gardens, Inc., 1937-55 (v.p. 1945-54), N.Y. Sch. for the Deaf, 1937-69 (president 1947-54), mem. exec. com., 1941-69; v.p. Eva Gebhard-Gourgaud Found., 1947-59, trustee 1947-69; exec. bd. 1935-69 Greater N.Y. Councils Boy Scouts Am. (gen. counsel 1947-60, finance com., 1943-67), Queens Council Boy Scouts Am. (v.p. 1932-43); awarded Silver Beaver by Queens Council and Silver Antelope by Region II, Boy Scouts of Am. for distinguished service to boyhood; Veterans award, Nat. Council Boy Scouts Am., 1964. Episcopalian (ch. adv. Diocese L.I., 1944-58; warden Ch. Resurrection, Kew Gardens, N.Y., 1939-69 vestryman, 1926-39, Distinguished Service Cross of Diocese 1951). Mem. Assn. Bar City of N.Y., N.Y. State and Am. bar assns. S.A.R., Phi Beta Kappa, Skull and Bones, Psi Upsilon, Phi Delta Phi. Club: Down Town. Contbr. articles to law reviews. Home: Forest Hills NY Died May 10, 1969; buried Indian Mound Cemetery, Moravia NY

SINCLAIR, JOHN STEPHENS, corp. dir.; b. Bklyn. Apr. 6, 1897; s. David Macowan and Alice Elizabeth (Stephens) S.; grad. Boys High Sch., Bklyn., 1915; A.B. Columbia, 1920; LL.B., 1922; m. Mary Hewes Biddle Mar. 27, 1924 (div. 1948); children—Mary (Mrs. C. Douglas Buck, Jr.), David, Sylvia Buell (Mrs. Stephen K. Carr), John Biddle; m. 2d, Barbro Johnson, Dec. 30 1961. Admitted to Pa. bar; practiced in Phila., until 1936; pres. Fed. Res. Bank of Phila., 1936-41; v.p. N.Y. Life Ins. Co., 1941-42, exec. v.p., dir., from 1942; pres. Nat. Industrial Conf. Bd., 1948-63; dir. Union Pacific R.R. (N.Y.), Oregon Short Line R.R. (Utah) Oregon-Washington R.R. and Navigation Co. (Oregon), Los Angeles and Salt Lake R.R. Co. (Utah) Fund-raising chmn. N.Y. Chpt. A.R.C., 1950-51, chpt. chmn., 1952-57, nat. fund-raising chmn., 1952. Served as 2d lt., inf., U.S. Army, 1918-19. Republican. Wilton CT Died Oct. 29, 1972.

SINCLAIR, PETER THOMAS, pulp and paper co. exec.; b. Portland, Ore., Dec. 25, 1906; s. A. C. and Mary (Brasel) S.; B.S. in Elec. Engring., Ore. State Coll. 1928; m. Kathryn Ludington, Dec. 12, 1931;children—Janet (Mrs. Roland F. Banks, Jr.), Katharine A. (Mrs. John Timothy Collins, Jr.), Employed with Crown Zellerbach Corporation

1928-70, v.p. indsl. relations, 1953-54, v.p. mfg. and converting, 1954-56, pres., chief exec. officer Crown Zellerbach Can., 1956-59, exec. v.p. corp., 1959-63, pres., 1963-69, chairman board, 1969-70, also dir.; dir. Zellerbach Paper Co., Wells Fargo Bank, St. Francisville Paper Co., Pacific Indemnity Group The Clorox Company, Crown Simpson Pulp Co. Mem. bd. trustees Institute of Paper Chemistry. Mem. N.A.M. (dir.), Am. Paper Inst. (dir.). Clubs: Stock Exchange (San Francisco); Vancouver (B.C., Can.). Home: San Francisco CA Died Apr. 7, 1970.

SINDEBAND, MAURICE LEONARD, elec. engring. exec.; b. Russia, Apr. 14, 1887; s. Simon and Ida (Jabelow) S.; brought to U.S., 1890, derivative citizen; E.E., Columbia, 1907; m. Lyllian Levy, Feb. 26, 1914; children—Seymour J., Allan L. Asst. elec. engr. N.Y.C. R.R.; v.p. Am. Electric Power Co. (formerly) Am. Gas & Electric Co., 1914-28, Am. Brown Boveri Electric Corp., 1929-32; receiver Insull Elec. Properties in Ohio; vice chmn. Ogden Corp., dir.; v.p., sec. dir. Mt. Olive & Staunton Coal Co.; director American Bosch Arma Corp., Syntex Corporation, S.A., Avondale Shipyards, Incorporated. Profl. engr., N.Y. Fellow Am. Inst. E.E. Inventor electric automatic train control, automatic reactor for power circuits, electronic voltage regulator for generators, carrier telephony system using high-voltage power conductors, method for prevention electric power arcs from New York City NY Died Dec. 5, 1971.

SINGER, BERTHOLD, consul gen.; b. Jaszbereny, Hungary, Nov. 23, 1860; s. Maximilian and Fanny (Kopper) S.; U. of Budapest, 1880-82, U. of Berlin, 1882-84; LL.D., Chicago Law Sch., 1918; m. Anna Ebner, July 16, 1885 (died 1937); children—Fay (Mrs. M. H. Ehlert), Albert, Alexander, Ada (dec.). Came to U.S., 1884, and to Chicago, 1889; consul-gen. Turkey; consul Costa Rica; mem. advisory board De Paul U., also lecturer on internat. law. Knight and Comdr. Order of Isabella the Catholic. Author: United States and Foreign Copyright Laws, 1907; Patents, Trade-Marks, Designs, Copyrights, 1909; Patent and Trade-Mark Laws of the World, 1911; Trade-Mark Laws of the World and Unfair Trade, 1913; International Law, 1918; Patent Laws of the World, 1930. Home: Barrington, Ill. Office: Steger Bldg., Chicago IL‡

SINGER, FREDERICK GEORGE, ret. bus. exec.; b. Paignton, South Devonshire, Eng., June 20, 1897 (parent U.S. citizens); s. Franklin Morse and Blanche Vanderbilt (Marcelin) S.; student Lycee Janson de Sailly, Paris, France, 1904-07, Praetoria House, Folkestone, Kent, Eng., 1907-11, Ecole de l'Ile de France, Liancourt, France, 1911-14; B.A., Sorbonne U., Paris, 1914; m. Simone Raunay, Aug. 12, 1919; 1 son, Alain Frederick Raunay. X-ray asst. Am. Women's War Hosp., Eng., 1914-15; civilian employee office naval attache, U.S. Embassy, Paris, France, 1918, asst. trade commr., 1920-23; importer Am. mdse. to France, 1919-20; exec. E.I. duPont de Nemours & Co., Inc., 1924-58. Dir. Mental Health Assn. Del., pres., 1956-63. Served as 1st lt. Norton-Harjes Ambulance Service, French Army, 1916-17; cpl. 24th Arty., C.A.C., U.S. Army, 1918. Decorated Knight Legion of Honor, Croix de Guerre (twice), Croix du Combatant Engage Volontaire, medal Verdun, Palmes Academiques (France). Member of the American Ordnance Association. Member Protestant Episcopal Church. Clubs: Barnacle (Vineyard Haven, Mass.); Capitol Hill (Washington); Travellers, American (Paris); Am. Vols. French Army (pres. 1935-36); Royal Automobile (London, Eng.); Wilmington, Wilmington Country; Vicmead Hunt; Greenville Country. Home: Greenville DE Died Feb. 1, 1971.

SINGER, WILLARD EDISON, educator, physicist; b. Bexley, O., May 2, 1904; s. Simon A. and Grace G. (Cromwell) S.; A.B., Capital U., 1925; B.E.E., Ohio State U., 1926, M.A., 1927, Ph.D., 1951; m. Irene K. Vogel, Dec. 25, 1932. Grad. asst. Ohio State U., 1927-28, 1930-31; instr. physics Bowling Green State U., 1927-34, asst. prof., 1934-43, asso. prof., 1943-51, prof. since 1951, chmn. dept, 1947-1967. Mem. A.A.A.S., Am. Assn. Physics Tchrs., Am. Phys. Soc., Ohio Acad. Sci. Lutheran (mem. ofcl. bds.) Home: Bowling Green OH Died Mar. 18, 1972; buried Fish Cemetery near Bowling Green OH

SINGLETON, WILLIAM DANIEL, auto mfg. exec.; b. Dallas, Feb. 7, 1908; s. John B. and Martha (Stollie) S.; B.S., Tex. A. and M. Coll., 1929; m. Sara Z. Bowers, Feb. 16, 1949; children—William Daniel, Sally (Mrs. Sally Bowers MacDonald). Asst. gen. mfg. mgr. Ford div. Ford Motor Co., 1951-55, mgr. def. prodn. operations, 1952-55, gen. mfg. mgr. Lincoln div., 1955-57, plant mgr. Lincoln plant, 1958-63, regional operations mgr., Automotive Assembly div., 1963-65, spl. asst. to gen. mgr. automotive assembly div., 1965-69. Served as lt. col. AUS Res., 1941-46. Decorated Purple Heart. Mem. Soc. Automotive Engrs., Tau Beta Pi. Home: Bloomfield Hills MI Died July 29, 1969.

SINK, CHARLES ALBERT, past pres. Univ. Mus. Soc., U. Mich.; b. Westernville, N.Y., July 4, 1879; s. Herman and Caroline (Gleasman) S.; A.B., U. Mich., 1904; M.Ed. (hon.) Mich. State Normal Coll., 1929; LL.D., Battle Creek (Mich.) Coll., 1930; H.H.D., Wayne State U., 1957; m. Alva Joanna Gordon, June 18, 1923; Sec., Univ. Sch. Music. U. Mich., 1904-07, sec. and bus. mgr., 1907-27, pres. 1927-40; v.p., dir. Mich. Life Ins. Co. Mem. City Council, Ann Arbor, Mich., 1912-18; mem. Mich. Ho. of Reps., 1919-20, 1925-26, Senate, 1921-22, 1927-28, 1929-30; candidate for lt. gov. Mich. Rep. primaries, 1932; mem. Rep. State Central Com., Mich., 1929-36; del. or guest at most Rep. State convs., 1912-72, Rep. Nat. convs., 1920-72. Chmn. Mich. State Tchrs. Retirement Fund Commn., Mich. Hist. Commn.; mem. Mackinac Island State Park Commn., George Washington Bicentennial Commn., Ann Arbor Hist. Commn. Past mem. numerous civic orgns. and coms. Co-founder Acacia (Mich.), 1904, now hon. nat. pres. Recipient King Albert medal for services in connection with starving Belgian children, World War. Mem. Internat. Assn. Concert Mfrs. (chmn. bd. 1962; hon. chmn.), Phi Kappa Phi, Phi Mu Alpha Sinfonia, Alpha Epsilon Mu, numerous orgns. for promotion of music. Conglist. Mason, Rotarian. Clubs: Michigan Union, Ann Arbor, University of Michigan, Presidents of University Michigan. Author of pamphlets, Music in Our Colleges and Universities, Michigan's Teacher's Retirement Law. Home: Ann Arbor MI Died Dec. 17, 1972.

SINSEL, RUPERT ALSTON, lawyer; b. Gafton, W.Va., Dec. 19, 1904; s. Charles Arthur and May (Davidson) S.; student U. W.Va., 1922-26; LL.B., George Washington U., 1929; m. Elizabeth Reppert Putnam, Dec. 23, 1932; children—Charles Arthur III, Douglas Putnam. Admitted to W.Va. bar, 1929; practiced in Clarksburg, W.Va., 1936; asso. firm Ira E. Robinson, 1936-51; mem. firm Sinsel & Sinsel. Dir. Empire Nat. Bank of Clarksburg; pres. Clarksburg Indsl. Devel. Corp., 1963-71. Asst. land purchasing officer Nat. Capital Park and Planning Commn., Washington, 1926-32; spl. agt. FBI, N.Y. div. office, 1932-35; govt. appeal agt. SSS; mem. W.Va. Commn. on Constl. Revision. Mem. W.Va. Senate rep. 13th dist., 1949-50; del. 3d dist. Republican Nat. Conv., 1952. Bd. dirs. Ednl. Found., Inc.; co-trustee W.Va. Bapt. Edn. Soc.; bd. govs. Alderson-Broaddus Coll.; mem. Daywood Art Gallery, 1950-69. Fellow Am. Bar Found.; mem. Am. Judicature Soc., Am., Harrison County (pres. 1950), W.Va. bar assns., W.Va. State Bar (pres. 1960, past bd. govs.), Clarksburg C. of C. (dir.), Phi Kappa Sigma, Phi Delta Phi. Mason (32 deg., Shriner), Kiwanian. Clubs: Clarksburg Country, Oral Fishing. Home: Clarksburg WV Died Apr. 10, 1972.

SIODMAK, ROBERT, bus. exec., director; b. Memphis; ed. U. Marbourg (Germany). Formerly engaged in banking in Europe; film editor and writer, Ufa, Berlin, Germany, 1929; dir. films The Tempest, Tumult, The Slump is Over, The Burning Secret, Hatred, Personal Column, West Point Widow, Fly By Night, Night Before the Divorce, Christmas Holiday, The Suspect, The Strange Affair of Uncle Harry, The Spiral Staircase, Dark Mirror, The Killers, Great Sinner, Time Out of Mind, Cry of the City, Thelma Jordan; collaborator original Conflict; producer, dir. Rats, My Father the Actor, The Devil Strikes at Night, The Rough and the Smooth, Katya, My School Friend, Affaire Nina B, Tunnel 28 Shoot, Custer Goes West. Address: Ascona Switzerland Died Mar. 1973.

SIPLE, PAUL ALLMAN, explorer, author, geographer; b. Montpelier, O., Dec. 18, 1908; s. Clyde L. and Fannie Hope (Allman) Siple; B.S., Allegheny College, 1932, D.Sc. (honorary), 1942; Ph.D. (Geography), Clark U., 1939; D.Sc., U. Mass., 1958, Boston U., 1958, Clark U., 1958, Bowling Green State U., 1959, Kent State Coll., 1968; hon. grad. Phila. Textile Inst., 1946; LL.D., Gannon Coll., 1958; married Ruth I. Johannesmeyer, Dec. 1936; children—Ann Byrd, Jane Paulette (Mrs. Wertime), Mary Cathrin (Mrs. Remmington). Youngest mem. Admiral Byrd's Antarctic Expdn., chosen after tests among 600,000 Boy Scouts of America; in charge of biol. and zool. work of expdn., bringing back specimens of penguins, seals for Am. Museum of Natural History, 1928-30, head of biological dept. Adm. Byrd's 2d expdn., 1933-35, and mem. Byrd's personal staff; in charge erecting and equipping the base in which Byrd lived alone 4 1/2 mos. in 1934; leader Marie Byrd sledging party into newly discovered land; toured Europe, Asia Minor and N. Africa, off the beaten paths, 1932-33; geographer Div. Territories and Island Possessions, Dept. of Interior, assigned to U.S. Antarctic Expdn. as leader of West Base, Little America, 1939-41; geographer and tech. supervisor of supplies and equipment; on furlough, 1941, from U.S. Antarc. Expdn. and employed by the War Dept. as a civilian expert on design of cold climate clothing and equipment; head research and map projects for U.S. Antarctic Service, 1941-42; commd. capt. Q.M. Corps, AUS, July 1942; discharged as lt. col., Aug. 1946. Mil. Geographer, sci. adviser Office Chief of Research and Devel., Dept. Army Gen. Staff, 1946-63, leader winter environmental teams, 1951-53; sci. attache for Australia, New Zealand, Am. embassy, Canberra, Australia, 1963-66; spl. sci. adviser U.S. Army Research Office, Arlington, Va., 1967-68. Sr. war dept. rep. Navy Antarctic Expdn. Highjump, 1946-47; dep. to Admiral Byrd, U.S. Antarctic Programs, sci. adviser Operation Deep Freeze I, 1955-56; sci. leader U.S. IGY Amundsen-Scott South Pole Sta., 1956-57; mem. numerous arctic, sci. coms. Mem. nat. council and camping com. of Boy Scouts of Am. Awarded Congl. medals, 1930, 37, 46; Heckel sci. prize, Hatfield award, 1931, Legion of Merit Award, 1946; exceptional civilian service award, Dept. Army, 1957; David Livingstone Centenary medal, Am. Geog. Soc., 1958; Hubbard medal, Nat. Geog. Soc., 1958; Distinguished Civilian Service award, Dept. Def., 1958; Patron's medal, Royal Geog. Soc. 1958; Hans Egede medal, Royal Danish Geographical Society, 1960, numerous other medals and awards; Mt. Siple and Siple Island named for him by New Zealand govt. Fellow Arctic Institute of America, American Geographic Society; mem. Antarctican Soc. (past pres.), Australian Antarctic Club, A.A.A.S., Am. Polar Soc. (1st pres.), Assn. Am. Geographers (v.p. 1958, pres. 1959), Am. Geophys. Union, International Geophysical Year (U.S. com.), Vets. Fgn. Wars (hon.), Clark University Geography Society numerous other arctic and sci. socs., Phi Beta Kappa, Sigma Xi, Alpha Chi Rho, Omicron Delta Kappa, Phi Beta Phi, Alpha Phi Omega. Methodist. Clubs: Exchange (Erie, Pa.); Kiwanis (Bloomington, Ill.); Explorers. Lecturer. Author: A Boy Scout with Byrd, 1931, Exploring at Home, 1932; Scout to Explorer, 1936; The Second Byrd Antarctic Expedition—Botany Report, 1938; Adaptations of the Explorer to the Climate of Antarctica, 1939; 90 deg. South, 1959. Originator Wind-Chill Index; co-designer principles leading to devel. thermal boot; researcher design climate controlled housing; patentee in field. Home: Arlington VA Died Nov. 25, 1968; buried Nat. Meml. Park, Falls Church VA

SIPPEL, BETTIE MANROE, club woman; b. Baltimore, Md.; d. William Wesley and Melcena Elizabeth (Talbott) Oursler; ed. pub. schs. and under pvt. tutors; m. John F. Sippel, of Baltimore, Mar. 7, 1890; 1 dau., Dorothy (Mrs. Wm. H. Maltbie). Active in club work since 1903; served as v.p. and pres. Md. State Federation of Women's Clubs and as pres. Sorosis Club; also served as dir. of Md. for Gen. Fed. Women's Clubs, and as chmn. Finance Com. G.F.W.C.; elected pres. G.F.W.C., June 1928. Regent Baltimore Chapter D.A.R.; pres. Woman's Missionary Society of Brown Memorial Presbyn. Ch. Widely recognized as conductor of classes on current events. Mem. exec. com. President's Conf. on Home Building and Home Ownership; adviser, President's Orgn. on Unemployment Relief; mem. advisory com. Campaign Against Hoarding; mem. nat. council Inter-Am. Inst. of Intellectual Cooperation. Home: 307 St. Dunstan's Rd., Baltimore MD‡

SIRES, RONALD VERNON, educator; b. Osakis, Minn., Sept. 27, 1901; s. Alvin and Sarah (Blake) S.; B.A. magna cum laude, Ohio Wesleyan U., 1923; Ph.D., U. Wis., 1936; divorced; children—Justine Claire, David Vernon. Tchr. history Ishpeming (Mich.) High Sch., 1923-25; asso. prof. Ball State Tchrs. Coll., 1930-43; mem. faculty Whitman Coll., 1943-70, prof. history, 1947-67, prof. emeritus, 1967-70. tchr. summers Ohio Wesleyan U., 1946, U. Puget Sound, 1956; Fulbright lectr. U. West Indies, 1953-54; research in London, Eng., 1951-52. Mem. Wash. bd. Am. Civil Liberties Union, 1962-64. Research grantee Social Sci. Research Council, 1952, 56. Mem. Am., Pacific hist. assns., Am. Assn. U. Profs. (council 1959-62), Phi Beta Kappa. Contbr. profl. jours. Home: Washington DC Died Nov. 24, 1970; buried Superior WI

SIROKY, VILLEM, dep. prime minister Czechoslovakia; b. Slovakia, 1902. Elected mem. parliament, Communist Party, Prague, 1935; during World War II was arrested and interned; escaped and remained in U.S.S.R. until 1945; vice premier Czechoslovakia, 1945; dep. prime minister, also minister fgn. affairs, 1948-71; chmn. delegation to 5th Gen. Assembly, U.N., 1950. Address: Prague Czechoslovakia Died Oct. 1971.*

SIRRINE, JOSEPH EMORY, industrial engring.; b. Americus, Ga., Dec. 9, 1872; s. George William and Sarah Euodias (Rylander) S.; Greenville Mil. Inst., 1883-86; B.S., Furman, 1890; hon. M.E., Clemson (S.C.) Agricultural College, 1928; LL.D., Presbyterian College, 1941; m. Jane Pinckney Henry, Nov. 8, 1898. Gen. engr. work, 1890-95; southern mgr. Lockwood, Green & Co., Greenville, S.C., 1895-1902; organizer, 1902, and since head of J. E. Sirrine & Co., designers of industrial and power plants, steam and hydro-electric; chairman board of directors Brandon Mills (Greenville, S.C.), vice president Dunean Mills, Industrial Cotton Mills, Chiquola Mfg. Co. all in S.C.; director Arcade Cotton Mills, Aragon Baldwin Mills, Watts Mills, Wallace Mills, Judson Mills, Piedmont Mfg. Co., The Florence Mills, Piedmont Plush Mills, F. W. Poe Mfg. Co., Union Bleachery, First Nat. Bank, Liberty Life Ins. Co., Greenville News-Piedmont Co. (all in Greenville), Ware Shoals Mfg. Co., Graniteville Mfg. Co., Woodside Cotton Mills, Easley Cotton Mills (all of S.C.), Marion Mfg. Co. (N.C.), Camperdown Mill, Norris Cotton Mills, Riverdale Mills, Inman Mills, Union-Buffalo Mills (all of South Carolina), J. P. Stephens & Co. (N.Y.). Life trustee Clemson College. Mem. American Soc. C.E., Am. Soc. Mech. Engrs., Am. Inst. E.E. Ind.

Democrat. Episcopalian. Mason. Clubs: Greenville Country; Biltmore Forest Country (N.C.); Merchants (New York). Home: 210 Pettigrue St. Office: 215 S. Main St., Greenville SC*‡

SISCOE, FRANK GOTCH, fgn. service officer; b. Swoyerville, Pa., Dec. 3, 1913; s. Floyd Benjamin and Jennie (Huber) S.; A.B., Rutgers U., 1934, LL.B., 1938; m. Anne Pinkerton, Oct. 23, 1946; 1 son, John Pinkerton. Admitted to N.J. bar, 1939; atty., attache Mexico, Paraguay, Argentina and Spain, Dept. Justice, 1941-47; 2d sec., counsel career Dept. State, 1947; assigned Prague, Czechoslovakia, 1947-50, Rome, Italy, 1950-52, 1st sec., 1952; with Dept. State, 1952; assigned Moscow, U.S.S.R., 1953-55; with Dept. of State, 1955-57; counselor Am. Embassy, Warsaw, Poland, 1957-59; assigned Dept. of State, Washington, 1960-65; counselor Am. Embassy, Copenhagen, Denmark, 1965-68. Mem. Phi Beta Kappa. Home: Plainfield NJ Died Feb. 1971.

SISSON, JEAN, lawyer; b. Boston, May 14, 1892; A.B., Harvard, 1914, LL.B., 1917. Admitted to Mass. bar, 1919; mem. firm Friedman & Atherton, Boston. Mem. Am., Mass. bar assns. Office: Boston MA

SISTO, LOUIS STANLEY, banker; b. Boston, May 11, 1899; s. Michael A. and Anna Maria (Astrella) S.; ed. pub. schs. of Boston; m. Hazel Mendez, Feb. 15, 1921; children—John A., Gerard W. Jr. clk., United Fruit Co., 1918, comptroller, 1944-67, v.p., 1957-58, v.p. finance, 1958-59, exec. v.p., 1959-62, cons., dir., 1962-67; chmn. bd., dir. Republic Nat. Bank Miami (Fla.), 1967—. Mem. Inst. Am., A.I.M. Home: Miami FL Died Feb 1972.

SITWELL, (SIR) OSBERT, author; b. London, Eng.; s. Sir George R. and Lady Ida (Denison) S.; ed. Eton. Served as officer in Brigade of Guards, 1912-19. Succeeded his father as 5th baronet, July 1943. Chmn. mgmt. com. Inc. Soc. Authors, 1944-48, 51-52 (London); fellow Royal Society Lit., and on council of Sheffield University. Author: Twentieth Century Harlequinade and other Poems, 1916; Argonaut and Juggernaut, 1919; The Winstonbourg Line, 1919; Who Killed Cock Robin?, 1921; Out of the Flame, 1923; Triple Fugue and other Stories, 1924; Discursions on Travel, Art and Life, 1925; Before the Bombardment, 1926; England Reclaimed, 1927; All at Sea (play, with Sacheverell Sitwell), 1927; The People's Album of London Statues (illustrated by Nina Hamnett), 1928; The Man Who Lost Himself, 1929; Sober Truth (with Margaret Barton), 1931; Collected Poems and Satires, 1931; Winters of Content, 1932; Dickens, 1932; Miracle on Sinai, 1933; Brighton (With Margaret Barton), 1935; Penny Foolish, 1935; Those Were the Days, 1938; Trio (with Edith and Sacheverell Sitwell), 1938; Escape With Me, 1939; Two Generations, 1940; Open the Door, 1941; Gentle Caesar (play, with R. J. Minney), 1942; A Place of One's Own, 1942; Sing High, Sing Low, 1944; Left Hand, Right Hand, 1944; The Scarlet Tree, 1946; Great Morning, 1948; Laughter in the Next Room, 1949; Noble Essences, 1950; Wreck at Tidesend, 1952; The Four Continents, 1954; On the Continent (poems), 1957; Fee Fi Fo Fum, 1959; Tales My Father Taught Me, 1962; Pound Wise, 1963; Poems about People or England Reclaimed, 1965. Created comdr. Order British Empire, Companion of Honor, 1958; companion of lit. Royal Soc. Lit., 1967. Hon. asso. Am. Inst. Arts and Letters. Home: Florence Italy Died May 4, 1969; inurned Cemetery of the Allori, Florence Italy

SIZER, LAWRENCE BRADFORD, pub. relations; b. Oak Park, Ill., May 24, 1902; s. Wells Bradford and Mary (Howes) S.; student Olivet (Mich.) Coll., 1923-26; m. Catharine L. Wheeler, Aug. 24, 1927; children—Suzanne (Mrs. Albert S. Chapman), Stephen Randall, Mary Catharine. With Marshall Field & Co., 1940-57, successively advt. mgr., sales promotion mgr., v.p. pub. relations, 1951-57; pub. relations dir. Field Enterprizes, Inc. and others; v.p., dir. Chgo. Shopping News, Newsprint Engraving, Chgo. Engraving Co.; dir. Fidelity Health & Accident Ins. Co. (Benton Harbor, Mich.), Bank of Three Oaks (Mich.). Dir. Mercy Hosp., Benton Harbor, Mich. Mem. State Street Council of Chgo. (dir.). Home: Benton Harbor MI Died Oct. 23, 1972.

SKAPSKI, ADAM STANISLAS, fgn. service office; b. Krakow, Poland, May 21, 1902; s. Stanislas and Helen (Gostwicka) S.; Diploma Engring., Polytechnic Warsaw, 1922; M.Sc., Jagellonian U., Cracow, 1924, certificate to teach secondary schs., 1925, Ph.D. Phys. Chemistry and Philosophy, 1927, Degree of Docent, 1931; postdoctoral metall. research Metallografiska Inst., Stockholm, 1933-34; m. Mary Alice King. Tchr. tech. secondary sch., univ. asst., 1922-31; lect. U. Cracow, 1931-32; prof., 1932-34; prof. Acad. Mining and Metallurgy, Cracow, 1934-39; imprisoned USSR for refusal of collaboration, 1939-42; sec. for edn. Polish Govt. in Exile, 1942-45; asst. prof. U. Chgo., 1946-48; prof. U. Neb., 1948-53, U. Vt., 1953-60; technical cooperation adviser Agency for International Development to Nigeria, 1960. Tech. cons. to Polish steel cos., 1934-39; dir. Inst. Metals, Mining Acad. Cracow, 1935-39; adviser Polish Ministry Nat. Def., 1936-39, Polish Ministry Edn., 1938-39; chmn. Polish Corrosion Com., 1937-39; cons. Ford Found., 1958-60, Nat. Sci. Found., 1960-68. Decorated Polish Golden Cross of Merit, Polish Commandership Polonia Restituta. Mem. Assn. Polish Chem. Engrs. (pres. 1937-39), Iron and Steel Inst., Am. Inst. Mining and Metall. Engrs., Am. Soc. U. Profs., Am. Phys. Soc. Contbr. articles tech. and ednl. jours., Poland, Germany, Britain, Sweden, U.S.; also short stories. Home: Milton VT Died Aug. 24, 1968; buried Western Nigeria.

SKEEL, ADELAIDE, author; b. Newburgh, N.Y.; d. Rufus Reed and Sarah Patten (Henry) S.; A.B., Vassar, 1873. Contbr. and illustrator for photographic publs. Lecturer on hist. subjects. Mem. D.A.R. Author: An After Christmas Thought, 1879; My Three-Legged Story Teller, 1892; King Washington (with William H. Brearley), 1897. Home: Newburgh NY‡

SKEELS, WINES HARRIS, clergyman; b. Watertown, N.Y., Oct. 16, 1876; s. Wines Richardson and Amy Fidell (Chapin) S.; Tufts Coll., 1898-9; B.D., St. Lawrence U. Theol. Sch., Canton, N.Y., 1903; m. Lena L. Dunlap, of Fitchburg, Mass., June 26, 1902. Ordained Universalist ministry, 1903; pastor Santa Paula, Cal., 1903-5, Victor, N.Y., 1905-8, Little Falls, N.Y., 1908-10; state supt. chs. (Universalist Gen. Conv., 1911-20; pastor, Denver, Colo., Dec. 1, 1920-23; now headmaster, Monte Vista Sch., Riverside, Calif. Chmn. trustees Nathaniel Stacy Memorial Assn.; sec. Bd. Fgn. Missions Universalist Ch., 1917-19; trustee Clinton Liberal Inst., Canton, N.Y., 1910-20. Mem. N.G.N.Y., 1899-1900. Republican. Lecturer on Universalist denominational work. Home: 370 New Magnolia Av., Riverside CA‡

SKERPAN, ALFRED ANDREW, historian, educator; b. Rochester, N.Y., Mar. 21, 1914; s. Alfred and Mary (Hoscoe) S.; A.B., Harvard, 1935; M.A., Yale, 1937, Ph.D., 1943; postgrad. Columbia U., 1947-48; m. Ruth Elizabeth Penley, Nov. 26, 1951; children—Elizabeth Penley, Alfred Lindsay. Instr. history Norwich U., 1937-38, Coll. City N.Y., 1941-42; analyst OSS, Washington, 1942-43, intelligence and liaison officer, chief of mission, London, 1943-45; intelligence research analyst U.S. Dept. of State, 1945-46; asst. prof. to prof. history Kent (O.) State U., 1946-67. Dir. NDEA Inst. on World Communism, 1967. Served to lt. (j.g.) USNR, 1943-46. Recipient Fulbright Research scholarship to Helsinki, Finland, 1954-55. Mem. Am. Assn. U. Profs. (past state pres.), Ohio Hist. Soc., Ohio Acad. History (sec.-treas. 1963-67; citation for distinguished service 1967), Am. Hist. Assn., A.A.A.S., Phi Alpha Theta. Conglist. Contbr. articles to profl. jours; monographs. Home: Kent OH Died Dec. 5, 1967; buried Standing Rock Cemetery Kent OH

SKIDMORE, CHARLES H., state supt. public instruction, Utah; b. Richmond, Utah, July 23, 1875; s. William Lobark and Sarah Armina (Knapp) S.; student, Brigham Young Coll., Logan, Utah, 1891-1901, U. of Chicago, 1901-02, Teachers Coll., Columbia U., 1922-26, U. of Calif., U. of Utah, Utah State Agrl. Coll.; m. Louise Wangsgard, June 3, 1903; children—Anna, Irl, Leone (dec.), Demoivre Ray, Loraine, Zella (Mrs. Eldon Taylor McEntire), Rex Austin, Charles Jay, Mary Louise. Elementary school teacher, 1893-97; prof. math. and English, Brigham Young Coll., 1902-12; supt. Granite Sch. Dist., Salt Lake County, Utah, 1912-17; Boxelder Sch. Dist., Brigham City, Utah, 1917-32; elected for three four-year terms as state supt. of public instr. 1933-45. Pres. Nat. Council of Chief State Sch. Officers, 1943. Mem. Nat. Edn. Assn. (state dir.), Utah Edn. Assn. (pres.), Soc. of Superintendents (pres.), Brigham Coll. Alumni (pres.), Vocational Edn. (Utah State Dir.). Club: Rotary (Salt Lake).‡

SKIDMORE, LOUIS, architect; b. Lawrenceburg, Ind., Apr. 8, 1897; postgrad., Mass. Inst. Tech., 1921-24; LL.D., Bradley U., 1952. Designer, Maginnius & Walsh, 1923-26; asst. to gen. mgr., chief of design Chgo. World's Fair, 1929-35; with firm Skidmore, Owings & Merrill, 1935-62 (name changed to Skidmore, Owings & Merrill, 1936), ret., 1955, cons. Served with U.S. Army, 1918-19. Recipient Distinguished Nat. Alumni award Bradley U., 1952; Rotch Traveling fellow, 1926-29; vis. scholar Am. Acad. Rome, 1927. Mem. Am. Inst. Architects (medal N.Y. chpt. 1949, Gold medal 1957). Author: Tudor in Arch; (with Samuel Chamberlain) B. Prin. works include: Atomic Energy Commn. town site, Oak Ridge, 1945; Creole Petroleum town site, Amuay Bay, Venezuela, Terrace Plaza Hotel, Cin., both 1948; Mfrs. Hanover Trust Co., N.Y.C., 1954; USAF Acad., Colo. Springs, Colo., 1960; various facilities and locations H. J. Heinz Co., Pitts. Home: Winter Haven FL Died Sept. 27, 1962.

SKILLING, DAVID MILLER, clergyman; b. Lonaconing, Md., Oct. 4, 1868; s. John D. (M.D.) and Mary (Quail) S.; A.B., Washington and Jefferson Coll., 1888, A.M., 1891, D.D., 1902; student Western Theol. Sem., Pittsburgh, 1888-91; m. Virginia Sinclair, Apr. 19, 1899 (died Apr. 17, 1941); children—Dr. David Miller, Mary Virginia (wife of Rev. H. Ganse Little). Ordained ministry Presbyn. Ch., 1891; asst. pastor Market Square Ch., Harrisburg, Pa., 1891-94; pastor Central Ch., Allegheny, Pa., 1895-1902, Presbyn. Ch., Webster Groves, Mo., 1902-37, now pastor emeritus; moderator Synod of Mo., 1925, 26; member Board of Pensions of Presbyterian Church in U.S. of America; mem. Alliance of Reformed Chs. throughout the World holding the Presbyterian System; del. to Councils, Pittsburgh, 1921, Cardiff, Wales, 1925, Boston, 1929, Montreal, 1937. Dir. Presbyn. Theol. Sem. (Chicago), Lindenwood Coll. (St. Charles, Mo.); trustee Mo. Valley Coll. (Marshall). Mem. Phi Delta Theta. Republican. Mason, Lion. Club: Missouri Athletic (St. Louis). Has written A Great Gospel for To-day," Biography of Rosanna Hull" Webster Groves MO‡

SKILLING, WILLIAM THOMPSON, teacher and science writer; b. Winchester, Ill., Dec. 6, 1866; s. Josiah Hamilton (M.D.) and Margaret Lucy (Thompson) S.; student State Normal Sch., Los Angeles, Calif., 1888-1891, Stanford Univ., 1892-93; B.S., U. of Calif., 1900, M.S., 1901; m. Bird Hildreth, June 22, 1903; 1 son, Hugh Hildreth. Began as teacher public schs., 1893; teacher of sciences and prof. of astronomy, San Diego State Normal Sch. and San Diego State Coll., 1901-37; retired since 1937. Mem. Astronomical Soc. of the Pacific, San Diego Astronomical Soc., Natural History Soc. of San Diego (fellow). Club: Scholia (San Diego, Calif.). Author: Nature-Study Agriculture (elementary sch. textbook), 1920; Tours Through the World of Science (textbook for high sch.), 1933; Astronomy (with R. S. Richardson) (textbook for colleges), 1939, rev. edit., 1947; Pre-Training Navigation (with R. S. Richardson), 1942; Sun, Moon and Stars (with R. S. Richardson), 1946; science bulletins for the Calif. State Dept. of Education and magazine articles on science. Home: 3140 Sixth Av., San Diego 3 CA‡

SKINNER, ALBURN EDWARD, business exec.; b. Westfield, N.Y., Feb. 3, 1872; s. Charles Patterson and Sarah (Jernegan) S.; student Phillips Andover Acad., 1889-91; A.B., Yale, 1895; A.M., Harvard, 1896, Grad. Sch., 1895-97; m. Elizabeth Mary Howard, Aug. 31, 1899; children—Mary Alethea (Mrs. Alden W. Boyd), Laura Elizabeth (Mrs. Day Tuttle Jr.). Dir. and vice pres. 1st Nat. Bank, Ottawa, Kan., 1898-1908; dir. 1st Mortgage Investment Co., Kansas City, Mo.; dir. and vice pres. Nat. Bank of Westfield (N.Y.), State Bank of Mayville (N.Y.), 1st Nat. Bank of Ripley (N.Y.), 1908-28; dir., vice pres. and treas. Warren Nash Motor Corp., New York, asso. Nash Cos. in Buffalo, Syracuse and Newark, 1920-36; dir., treas., pres. Warren Service Corp., New York, N.Y., 1923-46; dir. and treas. Citrus Concentrates, Inc. (now Juice Industries, Inc.), 1936-48, ret. Joint receiver Chautauqua Inst. U.S. Dist. Court for Western Dist. of N.Y., 1934-37. Trustee Chautauqua (N.Y.) Inst. since 1908, chmn. bd. 1946. Mem. Phi Beta Kappa, Beta Theta Pi. Liberal. Protestant Episcopal Ch. Clubs: Yale, Lake Placid. Home: 54 Walbrooke Rd., Scarsdale NY‡

SKINNER, BEVERLY ODEN, educator; b. Redfield, O., Feb. 16, 1875; s. Thomas P. and Harriet Newell (Brown) S.; student Ohio U., 1896-98; Ph.B., U. of Chicago, 1905; M.S. in Edn., Ohio U., 1912; m. Ada Chalfant, of Streator, Ill., Dec. 28, 1904; children—Chads Oden, Harriet Finley, Beverly Chalfant. Teacher, country schs. of Perry County, O., 1893-96; teacher high sch., Chillicothe, O., and Streator, Ill., 1898-1907; supt. city schs., Athens, O., 1907-16, Marietta, 1916-28; instr. Ohio U., summers, 1908-18, Fairmount (W.Va.) State Normal Sch., summers, 1923-27; pres. Wilmington Coll., 1928-31; became state dir. edn., O., 1931; now retired. Mem. N.E.A., Ohio State Teachers Assn., Beta Theta Pi. Democrat. Presbyn. Mason. Home: R.F.D. 2, Marysville OH‡

SKINNER, CLARENCE AURELIUS, physicist; b. Loudoun Co., Va., Jan. 6, 1871; s. John Thomas and Susanne (Tinsman) S.; B.Sc., U. of Neb., 1893, grad. student and fellow in physics, 1893-96; U. of Berlin, 1896-99, Ph.D., 1899; m. Christabel Ditchburn, 1916; 1 son, John William. Demonstrator physics, 1899-1901, adj. prof., 1901-03, asst. prof., 1903-06, prof. and head dept. physics, 1906-19, U. of Neb. Chief, optical div. U.S. Bur. of Standards, 1919—. Baptist. Mem. Am. Phys. Soc. Home: Kensington MD‡

SKINNER, DAVID A., gen. mgr. S.C. Chamber of Commerce; b. St. Mary's, Ont., Can., June 26, 1877; s. William and Helen (MacDonald) S.; ed. high sch., St. Mary's; Ph.G., Detroit Coll. of Pharmacy, 1898; m. Edna Waitt, Oct. 9, 1900 (dec.); married 2d Mayme Smith Wickham, Aug. 16, 1944. Came to U.S. 1894, naturalized citizen, 1902; went to Puerto Rico, 1898, and continued there in various positions under the govt. and with U.S. Treasury Dept. until 1909; apptd. spl. agt. Bur. of Census, 1909, later supervisor of census of Puerto Rico; asst. chief Bur. of Mfrs., U.S. Dept. of Commerce and Labor, 1911-12; asst. sec. Chamber Commerce U.S.A., 1912-20, sec., 1920-38, counselor since 1938; asst. to pres. C. of C. Charleston, S.C., 1939-40; gen. mgr. S.C. State Chamber of Commerce, of S.C., 1940-50. Home: 294 Granada Rd., West Palm Beach FL‡

SKINNER, ERNEST M., organ builder; b. Clarion, Pa., Jan. 15, 1866; s. Washington Martin and Alice (Francis) S.; ed. pub. schs.; m. Mabel Hastings, Mar. 29, 1893; children—Eugenie (Mrs. Ernest Shorrock), Richmond, Ruth (Mrs. George C. Scott). Mechanic, tuner, draughtsman, George S. Hutchings, 1890-1901; in organ building business alone, 1901, inc. as Ernest M. Skinner Co., 1905, pres., 1905-17; v.p. and tech. dir. Skinner Organ Co. since 1917. Mem. Am. Guild Organists, Nat. Assn. Organists, Harvard Musical Soc. Inventor Pitman wind chest; inventor of Themodist, device which accents notes on player piano; developed about 33 new organ voices, especially reproductions of orchestral colors; developed player instruments; builder of organ in Nat. Cathedral, Washington, D.C. Republican. Author: The Modern Organ, 1915; The Composition of the Organ, 1947. Contbr. to various pubs. in music. Home: 30 Prospect St., Reading MA‡

SKINNER, HOWARD K., opera co. exec.; b. San Francisco. Rancher, Colo., Cal., Mexico; miner, Nev.; mcht. seaman; worker in lumber camp; sec. San Francisco Symphony, 1936-39, mgr., 1939-64; mgr. San Francisco Opera, 1951-71. Active Stage Door Canteen, U.S.O., World War II. Served with U.S. Army A.C., World War I. Address: War Memorial Opera House, San Francisco Died Feb. 1971.*

SKINNER, LEWIS BAILEY, engr.; b. Cincinnati, O., July 8, 1874; s. John Calvin and Mary Jane (Bailey) S.; student Case Sch. Applied Science, Cleveland, O.; B.S., Colo. Sch. of Mines, 1895; m. Olive Anne Webb, Aug. 23, 1898. Metallurgist Standard Smelting & Refining Co., Durango, Colo., 1895-96; research chemist Anaconda (Mont.) Copper Mining Co., 1896-98; supt. chemically pure depts. Western Chem. Mfg. Co., Denver, 1898-1900; supt. U.S. Reduction &Refining Co., Colorado Springs, Colo., 1900-03; gen. supt. Portland Mill, Colorado Springs, 1903; treas. and gen. supt. Western Chem. Mfg. Co., 1903-10, v.p. and gen. mgr., 1910-20, now pres. and dir.; mgr. research dept. Midwest Refining Co., 1920-21; now cons. chem. and metall. engr., Denver, Colo. Inventor Skinner roasting furnace, muriatic and salt cake furnace, reverberatory volatilization process for complex zinc ores, process and apparatus for treating phosphate rock. Trustee Colo. Sch. Mines, 1919-23 (ex-pres. bd.). Mem. Am. Inst. Mining and Metall. Engrs., Colo. Scientific Soc. (ex-pres), Am. Chem. Soc.; Colo. Chemists Assn. (pres. 1935). Republican. Conglist. Mason (32 deg., K.T., Shriner). Clubs: Teknik, Denver Country, Denver Motor. Home: 1705 Franklin St., Denver CO*‡

SKINNER, PAUL BUTLER, investment banker; b. Wichita, Kan., Dec. 20, 1885; s. Lysander D. and Margaret (Butler) S.; m. Virginia Hughes; 1 dau., Virginia (Mrs. Louis J. Fellenz). Gen. and ltd. partner Hornblower & Weeks, Chicago, retired. Clubs: Mid-Day, Athletic (Chicago). Home: Palm Beach FL Died Aug. 22, 1969.*

SKINNER, WILLIAM WOOLFORD, chemist; b. Baltimore, Md., Mar. 28, 1874; s. Levin Phillips and Mary (Willis) S.; B.S., Md. Agr. Coll., 1895, M.S., Columbian U., 1897, Sc.D. (hon.), U. of Md.; m. Georgia Mitchell, Aug. 24, 1899; 1 child, Jean. Chemist, U. of Md., 1895-99; asst. chemist Agr. Exp. Sta., U. of Ariz., 1899-1902; asso. chemist, U. of Ariz., 1902-04; asst. chemist Bur. of Chemistry, U.S. Dept. of Agr., 1904-14; chief Water & Beverage Lab., Bur. of Chemistry, 1914-21; asst. chief Bur. of Chemistry, 1921-27; asst. chief chem. and tech. res., Bur. of Chemistry and Soils, 1927-35, asst. chief, 1935-39; asso. chief Bur. of Agrl. Chemistry and Engring., 1939-42; chief Bur. of Agrl. and Indsl. Chem., 1942-44; director Nat. Tech. Advisory Inst., since 1944. Member and chairman Board of Regents, U. of Md., 1916-42; chmn. Md. State Board Agr., 1935-42. Fellow A.A.A.S.; mem. Am. Chem. Soc., Assn. Official Agrl. Chemists (pres.), Washington Chem. Soc. (pres.), Kappa Alpha, Alpha Chi Sigma, Sigma Xi. Mason. Club: Cosmos (Washington, D.C.). Editor: Book of Methods. Joint author: Food Sanitation and Health, Chemistry in Industry, numerous technical bulletins and papers. Home: 6 Knowles Av., Kensington, Md. Office: Union Trust Bldg., Washington‡

SKOOG, ANDREW LEONARD, neurologist; b. Carver, Minn., Jan. 10, 1877; s. John and Augusta (Borg) S.; student U. of Colo.; M.D., Northwestern U., 1902; post-grad. work, U. of Vienna, U. of Paris and Nat. Hosp., London, 3 yrs.; m. Anna Belle Gordon, Dec. 21, 1910; 1 dau., Lura Marie. Asst. supt. Kan. State Hosp. for Epileptics, at Parsons, Kan., 1904-06; phys. Woodcroft Hosp., at Pueblo, Colo., 1906-08; instr. and asso. prof. nervous and mental diseases, U. of Kan., 1910-14, prof. and dept. head, 1914-28; consultant in psychiatry U.S. courts; lectr. history of medicine U. of Kan. Med. Sch. Member American Association of the History of Medicine, Am. Med. Assn., Jackson County Med. Soc., Am. Psychiatric Assn., Assn. for Research in Nervous and Mental Diseases, Central Neuropsychiatric Soc., Southern Med. Assn., Kansas City Acad. Medicine, Phi Beta Pi. Democrat. Presbyterian. Clubs: City, Mission Hills Country. Contbr. on nervous and mental diseases to tech. publs. in U.S., Paris and Berlin. Home: 5425 Mission Drive. Office: 904 Grand Av., Kansas City MO‡

SKOURAS, SPYROS P., motion pictures; b. Skourohorion, Greece, Mar. 28, 1893; m. Saroula Bruiglia; children—Daphne Dolores, Spyros, Dianna, Plato. Became naturalized citizen of United States, 1913. Began as busboy in St. Louis hotels; organized chain of theatres, St. Louis (sold to Warner Bros.); successively gen. mgr. Warner Bros. circuit; asso. with Paramount Pictures; pres. Nat. Theatres Amusement Co. and pres. Twentieth Century-Fox Film Corp., 1942-62, chmn. bd., until 1969; chmn. bd. Prudential Lines, Inc. 1969-71, Skouras Lines. Home: Rye NY Died Aug. 16, 1971.

SKULNIK, MENASHA, actor; b. Warsaw, Poland, 1894; s. Morris and Ida Skulnik; came to U.S., 1913, naturalized, 1920; m. Sarah Kutner, May 1912; children—Hannah (Mrs. Wilson), Maya; m. 2d Anna Drucker, June 1948. Appeared as starring commedian on 2d Av., N.Y.C., 1920-50; Broadway appearances include The 5th Season, 1952, The Flowering Peach, 1955, Uncle Willie, 1957, The Law and Mr. Simon, 1960, The 49th Cousin, 1961, Come Blow Your Horn, 1963. Mem. Actors Equity Assn. Club: Friars (N.Y.C.). Home: New York City NY Died June 4, 1970.

SLABAUGH, HAROLD WATSON, lawyer; b. Akron, O., Sept. 10, 1896; s. Watson Ellsworth and Jessie Maude (Gongwer) S.; A.B., Dartmouth, 1918; student U. Mich. Law Sch., 1919-22; m. Thelma Lewis, Oct. 24, 1923; children—Thelma (Mrs. William E. Osgood), Juliann (Mrs. Hutchinson). Admitted to the Ohio bar, 1922, since practiced in Akron, mem. firm Slabaugh, Walker, Pfleuger, Roderick & Myers, and predecessor firms, 1925-70; director, mem. exec. com., chmn. trust com. Akron Nat. Bank & Trust Co., chmn. Summit Properties. Trustee Akron YMCA, 1935-41; trustee Akron Gen. Hosp., 1931-65, pres., 1957-62. Served with the Marine Flying Corps., World War I. Member S.A.R., Sigma Nu. Republican. Member Disciples of Christ Church. Clubs: Dartmouth (New York City, Cleve.); University, Akron City (Akron). Home: Akron OH Died Sept. 30, 1970.

SLACK, CHARLES MORSE, physicist; b. Marietta, O., Dec. 4, 1901; s. William Henry and Enid (Warner) S.; B.S., U. of Ga., 1922; M.A., Columbia U., 1923, Ph.D., 1926; m. Evelyn Francis, May 31, 1926; children—Charles William, Winifred Evelyn, Warner Vincent. Instr. in physics, Columbia U., 1926-27; research physicist, lamp div. Westinghouse Electric Corp., Bloomfield, N.J., 1927-43, asst. dir. research, 1943-46, dir., 1946-49, tech. dir. atomic power div., Pitts., 1949-50, asst. mgr., 1950, dir. engring. and research, lamp div., 1953. Mem. A.A.A.S., Am. Inst. E.E., Am. Phys. Soc. Author papers on X-rays and electronics. Home: Upper Montclair NJ Died Dec. 1971.

SLACK, L(EMUEL) ERT(US), judge; b. Johnson County, Ind., Oct. 8, 1874; s. Elisha O. and Nancy A. (Teeters) S.; LL.B., Ind. Law Sch., Indianapolis, 1897; m. Mayme Shields, Oct. 31, 1897. Began practice at Franklin, Ind., 1897; dep. pros. atty. Johnson County, 1897-98; county atty., 1899-1905; mem. Ind. Ho. of Rep., 1901-03, Senate, 1905-07; candidate in Dem. State Conv. for nomination as gov. of Ind., 1908 (defeated by 30 votes by Thomas R. Marshall); U.S. atty. for Ind. by appmt. of Pres. Wilson, Jan. 16, 1916-Jan. 11, 1920; apptd. spl. asst. atty. gen., Jan. 11, 1920; mayor of Indianapolis, 1928-29; apptd. judge Superior Court by Gov. McNutt, Nov. 6, 1936. Christian Scientist. Mason (32 deg., Shriner), Odd Fellow, K.P. Clubs: Ind. Democratic, Lawyers, Hoosier Motor, Highland Golf and Country (Indianapolis); Hillview Country (Franklin, Ind). Author: Golf Putting (booklet), 1936. Home: Valley Mills. Address: Security Trust Bldg., Indianapolis IN*‡

SLADE, ALBERT ARTHUR, supt. schs.; b. Bridport, Eng., Mar. 6, 1876; s. Henry Peach and Harriet Wheeler (Russell) S.; brought to U.S. in infancy; grad. Ia. City Acad., 1897; B.A., State U. of Ia., 1911; m. Nellie Katherine Hall, Oct. 30, 1901; children—Thora Fern, Ruth Meriam. Teacher rural, village and city schs. until 1902; prin. Iowa City Grammar Sch., 1902-10; supt. schs., Iowa City, 1912-14, Cody, Wyo., 1915-19; state commr. edn., Wyo., 1919-20; supt. schs., Casper, Wyo., 1920-27; supt. schs., Laramie, Wyo., 1927-45; retired, Aug. 1945. Mem. Wyo. State Bd. of Edn. Mem. N.E.A. (mem. Nat. Council of Teacher Retirement). Dept. Superintendence N.E.A. (mem. advisory council), Wyo. State Teachers' Assn. (pres. 1920-21), Phi Delta Kappa, Pi Gamma Mu, Kappa Delta Pi. Republican. Presbyterian. Mason. Rotarian. Home: Fort Collins CO‡

SLADE, ARTHUR JOSEPH, management cons.; b. Toronto, Ont., Feb. 20, 1893; s. Joseph and Eva K. (Worsley) S.; extension student Queens U., 1913-14; m. Kathleen M. Morrison, Dec. 29, 1919. Came to U.S., 1923, naturalized, 1953. Clk. Mchts. Bank of Can., 1911-15, br. mgr., 1919-20; exec. v.p., gen. mgr. Slade Mfg. Co., Ltd., 1920-23; salesman, sales mgr. automobiles, hardware, advt. and indsl. service firms, 1923-25; sales mgr., dir. Am. Dist. Steam Co., 1923-25; v.p., gen. mgr., dir. Canadian Dist. Steam Co., Ltd., 1928-35, Northeastern Piping & Constrn. Corp., 1929-35; operator Thermalite Insulation Co., 1935-37; spl. assignment Robert Gair Corp., 1937-39; partner Rogers & Slade, 1939-51, Rogers, Slade & Hill, 1951-63. Past pres. YMCA, Community Chest. Pres. Carlton Found., Inc. Served as maj. Canadian Army, World War I. Decorated Distinguished Service Order, Mil. Cross. Mem. C. of C. (past pres.), Am. Mgmt. Assn., N.A.M., Nat. Indsl. Conf. Bd., Assn. Consulting Mgmt. Engrs. Clubs: Canadian (N.Y.C.); Monticeto Country; Channel City; Cosmopolitan. Home: Santa Barbara CA Died June 6, 1971.

SLATER, DENNISTON LYON, investor; b. Locust Valley, L.I., N.Y., July 26, 1927; s. Horatio Nelson and Martha Byers (Lyon) S.; grad. Hotchkiss Sch., Lakeville, Conn., 1945; B.A., Yale, 1951; m. Anne Doris Kerr, May 7, 1959. Pres., partner Slater Bros. Co., Inc., 1954-71, chairman board Fanny Farmer Candy Shops, Inc., 1962-71, exec. com.; member bd. directors Warner Bros.-Seven Arts Ltd. Member bd. of overseers Grenville K. Baker Boys Club, Locust Valley, N.Y. Served with USNR, 1945-46, AUS, 1951-53. Clubs: Piping Rock (Locust Valley); Racquet and Tennis, Madison Square Garden (N.Y.C.); Traveler's (Paris, France); Everglades (Palm Beach, Fla.); Philadelphia Gun. Home: Locust Valley LI NY Died Aug. 26, 1971.

SLATER, HARRY GEORGE, utility exec.; b. Boston, May 20, 1908; s. Henry and Jennie (Blotcher) S.; A.B., Harvard, 1929, LL.B., 1932; m. Charlotte Moskow, Aug. 6, 1933; children—Barbara Jean, Gerald Erwin, Harvey Michael. Admitted to Mass. bar, 1932, U.S. Supreme Ct., 1948, N.Y. bar, 1952; practice in Boston, 1932-39; spl. asst. atty. gen. U.S., 1939-40; atty. SEC, 1940-45, chief counsel, 1945-50; sr. v.p., dir. Niagara Mohawk Power Corp., Syracues, N.Y., 1951-70; vice chmn. Empire State Atomic Devel. Associates; trustee Onondaga County Savings Bank. Pres., Syracuse Community Housing Development Corporation; vice president Jewish Home Central N.Y., Syracuse. Member Am., N.Y. State, Onondago County bar assns. Jewish religion (v.p., trustee temple). Club: Lafayette Country (past pres.) (Jamesville, N.Y.). Home: Syracuse NY Died Dec. 28, 1970; buried Syracuse NY

SLATER, HUGHES DE COURCY, newspaper man; b. Marion, Smythe Co., Va., Apr. 12, 1874; s. John S. and Anna Maria (Rothwell) S.; grad. Central High Sch., Washington, D.C., 1891; student Columbian (now George Washington) U., 1891-92; European travel and study, 1919-20; m. Elsie Pomeroy, d. John McElroy, of Washington, D.C., Mar. 30, 1899; children—Elsie McElroy (dec.), John McElroy. Editor Public Opinion (now merged with Literary Digest), 1894-96; civ. engr. and railroad reconnoissance, Northern Mexico, 1897; editcr and pub. El Paso Hearld (evening), 1898-1929, and of The El Paso Times (morning and Sunday), 1925-29. Served as capt. inf., 90th Div., U.S.A., A.E.F., France and Germany, 1917-19. Independent Republican. Author of treaty of 1906 with Mexico by which long-standing Rio Grande claims were adjusted. Home: El Paso TX‡

SLATER, WILLIAM KERSHAW, scientist, writer; b. Oldham, Eng., Oct. 19, 1893; s. James and Mary Ann (Kershaw) S.; B.Sc. with 1st honours in Chemistry, Manchester U., 1914, D.Sc., 1926; D.Sc. (hon.), Belfast U., 1952; m. Hilda Whittenbury, Apr. 6, 1921; children—James Keith, Evelyn Whittenbury (Mrs. Kendall Cork), John Michael. Lectr. chemistry Manchester U., 1917-20; Beit Med. Research fellow Univ. Coll., London, 1923-28; dir. research Dartington Hall, Devon, Eng., 1928-42; sr. advisory officer Ministry Agr., 1943-49; sec. Agrl. Research Council, 1949-60; cons., lectr., writer, 1961-70. Member scientific CENTO; vice president of the United Nationa Conference Application Science and Tech. for Benefit Less Developed Areas. Chmn. projects com. Freedom from Hunger Campaign. Decorated knight Order British Empire. Fellow Royal Inst. Chemistry (pres. 1961-63), Royal Soc.; mem. Brit. Assn. (hon. sec. 1962-66). Author: Man Must Eat, 1963. Address: Pulborough Sussex England Died Apr. 19, 1970.

SLAUGHTER, DANELY PHILIP, surgeon; b. Paris, Ill., June 1, 1911; s. Albert W. and Mary Golden (Danely) S.; B.S., U. Ill., Urbana, 1932, M.D., Chgo., 1936; m. Mary Elizabeth Whitney, Jan. 7, 1938; children—John W., Mary Golden. Served internship at Research and Educational Hospitals, Chgo., 1935-36, resident internal medicine, 1937 resident gen. surgery, 1937-39, attending surgeon, dir. Tumor Clinic, 1942-70; asst. resident Meml. Hosp., N.Y.C., 1939, fellow Nat. Cancer Inst., 1940-41, resident surgery, 1941-42; practice medicine specializing in gen. surgery, oncology, Chgo., 1942-70; clin. prof. surgery Coll. Medicine U. Ill., 1952-70; chief dept. surgery, dir. Tumor Clinic St. Francis Hosp., Evanston, Ill., 1946-70; attending surgeon Presbyn-St. Lukes Hosp., Chgo., 1942-70; mem. cancer control com. NIH, 1950-55; mem. com. cancer therapy and diagnosis NRC, 1951-56; mem. clin. studies panel on adjuvant chemotherapy of cancer, mem. sub-com. on breast cancer protocol Nat. Cancer Inst., 1950-55. Recipient Distinguished Service award Ill. div. Am. Cancer Soc., 1964; Danely Philip Slaughter ann. lecture established in his honor, 1969. Diplomate Am. Bd. Surgery. Mem.

A.M.A., Chgo. Med. Soc., Chgo. Surg. Soc., A.C.S. (past com. chmn.), Soc. Head and Neck Surgeons (past pres.), James Ewing Soc. (past pres.), Am., Central surg. assns., Internat. Soc. Surgeons, Soc. U. Surgeons, Am. Thyroid Assn., Pan Am. Med. Assn., Am. Cancer Soc. (past pres., vice chmn. bd. dirs. Ill. div.), Inst. Medicine, Sigma Xi, Alpha Omega Alpha, Nu Sigma Nu, Sigma Chi. Clubs: University (Chgo.), Westmoreland Country (Wilmette, Ill.). Contbr. articles med. jours., chpts. to books. Home: Northfield IL Died Apr. 11, 1970.

SLAUGHTER, SETH WARREN, clergyman, educator; b. Raytown, Mo., Nov. 23, 1893; s. Orlando V. and Elizabeth (Havron) S.; student U. Mo., 1912-13, Culver Stockton Coll., 1913-14; A.B., Drake U., 1916, D.D., 1955; M.A., 1918; B.D. U. Chgo., 1922; D.D., Culver Stockton, Coll., 1955; m. Cora Louise Hamil, July 23, 1918; children—Mary Elizabeth, Seth Warren. Ordained ministry of Disciples of Christ, 1913; pastor, Waukegan, Ill., 1918-20; camp pastor, Great Lakes, Ill., 1918-19; pastor, Roanoke Christian Ch., Kansas City, Mo., 1923-30, First Christian Ch., Lawrence, Kan., 1930-37; dean Kansas Bible Coll., Lawrence, 1933-37, Drake U. Bible Coll. 1937-49; dean Missouri School of Religion, Columbia, 1949-58, dean emeritus, 1958-70, prof. applied Christianity, 1958-70; pastor University Church of Christ, Des Moines, Ia., 1938-39. Mem. Lawrence Library Board; pres. Lawrence Relief Assn.; mem. Bd. of Education, Disciples of Christ, president of Missouri Convention, 1952-53; mem. exec. com. Ia. Council Christian Edn., worship com. Fed. Council of Chs. of Christ in America. Mem. Religious Edn. Assn. America, Delta Theta Chi. Club: University (Des Moines). Contbr. articles to Christian Evangelist, World Call, others. Editor: Drake U. Bull. on Religion, 1937-49. Home: Columbia MO Died Mar. 12, 1970.

SLEMONS, CLYDE C., health officer; b. Cedar Springs, Mich., Dec. 31, 1874; s. James and Mary E. (Countryman) S.; M.D., Detroit Coll. of Medicine, 1905, Dr.P.H., 1931; m. Myrtle E. Gilbert, of Sherman, Mich., Jan. 4, 1899 (died, 1914); 1 dau., Marion; m. 2d, Isabelle Campbell, of Saulte Ste Marie, Mich., June 28, 1919; 1 dau., Anne. Commr. of schs., Wexford Co., 1899-1903; health officer Grand Rapids, 1909-1930; commr. of health, Mich., 1930-38. Mem. Am. Med. Assn., Mich. State and Ingham Co. med. socs., Am. Pub. Health Assn., Internat. Soc. Med. Health Officers (pres. 1937). Republican. Mason. Home: 1324 Logan S.E., Grand Rapids MI‡

SLEPIAN, JOSEPH, research engr.; b. Boston, Mass., Feb. 11, 1891; s. Barnett and Anne (Bantick) S.; A.B., Harvard, 1911, A.M., 1912, Ph.D., 1913; grad. study Gottingen, Germany, 1913-14, Sorbonne, Paris, 1914; D. Engring., Case Inst. Tech., 1949; D.Sc., Leeds, England, 1955; m. Rose Grace Myerson, Nov. 11, 1918; children—Robert Myer, David. Instr. mathematics, Cornell U., 1914-15; engr. Westinghouse Electric & Mfg. Co., East Pittsburgh, 1918-56, former asso. dir. research; developed auto-valve lightning arrester to protect cross country transmission lines, generating stas. and substas., the de-ion principle of de-energizing destructive arc of interrupted electric circuit and control of huge currents in electric arcs with current in pencil lead; inventor of Ignitron mercury arc retifier. Mem. Nat. Academy of Sciences, Am. Inst. E.E., Am. Phys. Soc., Am. Electrochem. Soc., Am. Math. Soc., Phi Beta Kappa. John Scott medal, 1932, Westinghouse Order of Merit; Lamme, Edison medals by Am. Inst. E.E. Author: Conduction of Electricity in Gases; also numerous technical papers. Home: Pittsburgh PA Died Dec. 19, 1969.

SLICHTER, WALTER IRVINE, electrician; b. St. Paul, Minn., May 7, 1873; s. Henry Clay and Lettie (Irvine) S.; Coll. City of New York, 2 yrs.; in Europe 2 yrs.; E.E., Columbia, 1896; m. Mabel Ostrom, 1903; 1 dau., Margaret. Entered employ Gen. Electric Co., Schenectady, 1896; asst. to Dr. Charles Proteus Steinmetz, 1897-1904; mem. ry. dept. of co., 1904-09, and asst. to v.p. and chief engr. and mem. staff consulting engrs., 1909-10; prof. elec. engring. and head dept., Columbia U., 1910-41, professor emeritus since 1941. Republican. Episcopalian. Fellow Am. Inst. Elec. Engrs. (v.p. 1922-24; treas. since 1930); fellow Am. Soc. Mech. Engrs., Engring. Foundation (chmn. engring. library bd.), N.Y. Acad. Science, Am. Assn. Advancement of Sciences; member Society for Promotion of Engineering Education, Sigma Xi, Theta Delta Chi and Tau Beta Pi fraternities, etc. Club: Columbia University (New York). Author: Principles Underlying the Design of Electrical Machinery, 1926; also writer of technical articles read before engineering societies. Associate editor American Handbook of Elec. Engring., Am. Pocketbook of Mining Engring., Internat. Ency. Civilian dir. U.S. Air Service Sch. for Radio Officers, Columbia U., 1917-18. Address: care Dept. Electrical Engineering, Columbia Univ., Morningside Heights, New York 27 NY‡

SLIM, MONGI, Tunisian diplomat; b. Tunis, Tunisia, Sept. 15, 1908; s. Abed and Habiba (Beyram) S.; Degree in Math., Lycee Saint-Louis, Paris, France, 1929; Degree in Law, Faculte de Droit, Paris, 1932. Engaged in practice of law, Tunis, 1936-join Neo Destourien Party, 1936, permanent sec. nat. counsel of party, 1937, dir. of party, 1945-55; Minister of state, 1954-55, minister of interior, 1955-56, minister of state, 1956; ambassador of Tunisia to U.S. and head Tunisian delegation to UN, 1956-61; consul gen. for U.S. and U.S. Territories, Washington, 1957-61, formerly pres. Gen. Assembly; ambassador to UN, 1961-62; sec. of state for fgn. affairs; personal rep. Paris Bourguiba; sec. of state for justice, 1966-69. Gov. Islamic Center, Washington. Address: Tunis Tunisia Died Oct. 23, 1969.

SLIM, WILLIAM, gov. gen., comdr.-in-chief Commonwealth of Australia; b. at Bristol, England, Aug. 6, 1891; s. John and Charlotte (Tucker) S.; ed. King Edward's Sch.; LL.D. (hon.), Cambridge University, 1946, also Leeds, Birmingham, Sydney, Adelaide, Melbourne; D.Litt. (hon.), New England (Australia); Dr. Common Law (hon.), Oxford U., 1948; m. Aileen Robertson, Jan. 1, 1926; children—John (Brit. Army), Una (Mrs. Nigel Frazer). Active service, Gallipoli, France, Mesopotamia, 1914-18; with 10th Indian Brigade, Brit. Army, E. Africa, 1940; maj. gen. comdr. 10th Indian Div., Iraq, Syria, Persia, 1941; lt. gen. comdr. 15th Corps, 1942, 14th Army, 1943-44; comdr.-in-chief Allied Land Forces, S.E. Asia, 1945; comdt. Imperial Defence College, London, 1946-47; dep. chmn. Brit. Rys., 1947-48; chief Imperial Gen. Staff, 1948-52; field marshall, 1949; governor general and also the comdr.-in-chief Commonwealth of Australia from 1953. Decorated: Knight Grand Cross of the Bath; Knight Grand Cross of St. Michael and St. George; Knight Grand Cross of Royal Victorian Order; and Knight Grand Cross Order of Brit. Empire; Companion Distinguished Service Order; Mil. Cross (all Eng.); Chief Comdr. Legion of Merit (U.S.).Author: Defeat into Victory, 1955. Home: London England Died Dec. 14, 1970.

SLIPHER, VESTO MELVIN, astronomer; b. on farm, Clinton County, Ind., Nov. 11, 1875; s. David Clark and Hannah (App) S.; A.B., Ind. U., 1901; A.M., 1903, Ph.D., 1909, LL.D., 1929; hon. Sc.D., U. of Ariz., 1923, U. of Toronto, Canada, 1935; m. Emma Rosalie Munger, Jan. 1, 1904; children—Marcia Frances, David Clark. Astromer, Lowell Obs., 1901-15, asst. dir., 1915-17, dir. 1917-52; in charge Lowell solar eclipse expdn. to Syracuse, Kan., June 1918, and to Ensenada, Mexico, 1923. Awarded the Lalande prize and gold medal, Paris Acad. Sciences, 1919; Henry Draper gold medal of Nat. Acad. Sciences for discoveries in astron. physics, 1932; gold medal of Royal Astron. Soc., 1933, George Darwin lecturer, same society, 1933; awarded the Catherine Wolfe Bruce gold by Astronomical Soc. of the Pacific, 1935. Mem. Nat. Acad. of Sciences, Am. Philos. Soc.; asso. Royal Astron. Soc. (London); fellow Am. Acad. Arts and Sciences, A.A.A.S. (v.p. 1933); mem. Internat. Astron. Union, Am. Astron. Soc. (v.p. 1931), Societe Astronomique de France, Phi Beta Kappa, Sigma Xi fraternities. Extensive investigations in astronomical spectroscopy; studies on the rotations and atmosphere of the planets; directed search that led to finding Lowell's trans-Neptunian planet—the new planet, Pluto. Discovered the rapid rotation and enormous space velocities of the nebulae, which furnished the observational basis for the expansion of the universe theory, that has grown out of Einstein's theory; high velocities of the star clusters; the cosmic radiations of the night sky; etc. Contributed numerous papers to astronom. publs. on the planets, nebulae, clusters, comets, stars and aurora. Address: Flagstaff AZ Died Nov. 8, 1969.*

SLOAN, DUNCAN LINDLEY, judge; b. Pekin, Allegany County, Md., Apr. 3, 1874; s. James Muir and Ella (Frederick) S.; A.B., Washington and Jefferson Coll., 1892; studied law with Judge David W. Sloan, Cumberland, Md.; m. Marion DeWitt, Feb. 22, 1917; 1 son, James DeWitt. Admitted to Md. bar, 1895, and began practice at Cumberland; city atty. Cumberland, 1910-14; chief judge 4th Jud. Circuit, Md., and asso. judge Md. Court of Appeals, 1926-41, re-elected, 1942; apptd. by gov. as chief judge Court of Appeals, 1943; retired, 1944. Mem. Am. Bar Assn., Md. State Bar Assn. (pres. 1931-32), Bar Assn. Allegany County (ex-sec.). Republican. Presbyterian. Elk. Clubs: Kiwanis (ex-pres.), Cumberland Country. Home: Dingle, Cumberland MD*‡

SLOANE, JOSEPH CURTIS, educator; b. Allegheny City, Pa., Oct. 22, 1873; s. James Renwick and Frances Brard (Swanwick) S.; Geneva Coll., Beaver Falls, Pa., 1889-91; A.B., Princeton, 1895; m. Julia Larned, d. Jesse Lathrop and Fanny (Larned) Moss, of Lake Forest, Ill., June 25, 1904. Teacher, DeLancey Sch., Phila., 1895-9; asst. head master, 1899-01, head master, Lake Forest (Ill.) Sch., 1901-5; teacher Hill Sch., Pottstown, Pa., 1905-10; head master, Berkeley Sch., New York, since Sept. 25, 1910. Mem. Phi Beta Kappa. Presbyn. Address: 270 W. 72d St., New York NY‡

SLOANE, RUSH RICHARD, lawyer, capitalist; b. Sandusky, O.; s. John Nelson and Cynthia (Strong) S.; m. Elyria O., Helen F. Hall. City clerk 2 terms; probate judge 2 terms; apptd. by President Lincoln gen. agt., Postoffice Dept., March, 1861. Was delegate to Pittsburg Conv., 1856, which organized the Rep. party, and was invited guest at Phila. Rep. Nat. Conv., June, 1900. Aided in organizing the Cassius M. Clay brigade," April, 1861, to protect City of Washington, was a mem. of the brigade; chmn. Rep. State Com. of Ohio, 1865-6; candidate of Liberal (Greeley) party for Congress, 1872; mayor Sandusky, 1879-81. In 1852 was sued for $6,000 damages in U.S. court for professional services as a lawyer in defending 6 slaves, escaping to Canada, under the Fugitive Slave Act of 1850; was mulcted in damages and paid the judgment. Was railroad pres. 10 yrs. Built the Big Four" R.R. between Springfield and Columbus, O. Owned much valuable real estate in Chicago, Ind., Mass., Toledo and Sandusky, O., where he has built the largest hotel (Sloane House) and block and dwelling house in the city; pres. The Firelands Hist. Soc. Mem. S.A.R.; life mem. Ohio State Archaeol. and Hist. Soc.; mem. Ohio State Centennial Comm'n; one of the speakers at Ohio Centennial Celebration, May, 1903, at Chillicothe, O. Address: Sandusky OH‡

SLOCUM, STEPHEN ELMER, cons. engineer; b. Glenville, N.Y., June 5, 1875; s. William Warren and Mary E. (Conde) S.; B.E., Union Coll., N.Y., 1897; scholar and fellow, Clark U., 1897-1900. Ph.D. in mathematics and physics, 1900; m. Anna Jeannette Ware, June 25, 1902; children—Dorothy Jeannette, Walter Ware, Marianna Conde, Stephen Elmer. Instr. in civ. engring., U. of Cincinnati, 1900-01, in applied mathematics, 1901-04, asst. prof., 1904-05; asst. prof. mathematics, U. of Ill., 1905-06; prof. applied mathematics, U. of Cincinnati, 1906-20; cons. engr., Phila. and Ardmore, Pa., since 1920; specialist in marine propulsion and in noise and vibration engring. Former mem. Am. Soc. C.E.; mem. Am. Soc. Naval Engrs. (hon. life), S.R. Awarded gold medal by Am. Soc. Naval Engineers, 1927, for original research in modern hydrodynamics. Presbyn. elder since 1905. Author: Strength of Materials, 1906, 11; Theory and Practice of Mechanics, 1913; Resistance of Materials, 1914; Hydraulics, 1915; Beggars of the Sea (hist. novel), 1928; Noise and Vibration Engineering, 1931; also many monographs and articles in scientific, popular and Ardmore PA‡

SMALL, BENJAMIN FRANCIS, lawyer, corporate exec.; b. Terre Haute, Ind., Nov. 18, 1919; s. Benjamin F. and Rose (MacFall) S.; A.B., Ind. State U., 1941, LL.D., 1969; J.D. with distinction, Ind., U., 1943; m. Dorothy Burget, May 2, 1943; children—Ben Francis III, Mary Ellen. Admitted to Ind. bar, 1943, U.S. Supreme Ct., 1948; asst. prof. law U. Kansas City, 1943-44; vis. prof. U. N.C., summers 1944, 55, asst. prof., 1944-45; vis. prof. Ind. U., summer 1944, asst. prof., 1945-47, asso. prof., 1947-51, prof., 1951-67, acting asso. dean charge Indpls. div., 1952, asso. dean Sch. Law, 1960-64; dean Indpls. div. Sch. Law, 1964-67; faculty U. Tex., summer 1955, N.Y. U., summer 1960; vis. prof. constl. law Washington U., 1958-59; exec. v.p. Life Ins. Assn. Am. (merged with Am. Life Conv. 1973, name now Am. Life Ins. Assn.), 1967-69, pres., 1969-73. Mem. Am., Ind. bar assns., Am. Law Inst., Assn. Life Ins. Counsel, Am. Acad. Forensic Sics., Am. Arbitration Assn., Indpls. Bar Assn., Order of Coif, Phi Delta Phi (nat. pres.) Republican. Clubs: Indianapolis Athletic; Canadian University (N.Y.); Scarsdale Golf, Scarsdale, Town. Author: Workmen's Compensation Law of Indiana, 1950. Home: Potomac MD Died Feb. 16, 1973.

SMALL, CHARLES C., business executive; b. Kennebunkport, Me., Oct. 1, 1876; s. Joseph C. and Sarah Ann (Whitehouse) S.; student public schools; m. Kathleen T. Powers, Dec. 29, 1897; children—June L., Sarah Ann. President Knickerbocker Ice Co., since January 1921; pres. American Ice Co., Feb. 1927-May 1945; chmn. bd. since May 22, 1945; pres. and dir. Knickerbocker Laundry Co., Inc., since Aug. 1932; chairman of board, Ice Refrigeration Co., Inc.; vice pres. and dir., Nat. Ice Advt. Co., Knickerbocker Ice Co.; dir. Coca-Cola Bottling Co. of N.Y., Inc. Dir. Nat. Assn. of Ice Industries. Mem. of Nat. Ice Code Authority. Mem. N.Y. State C. of C.; Am. Soc. of Refrigerating Engrs. Clubs: Metropolitan (New York City); Pomonok Country (Flushing, New York); Arundel Golf (Kennebunkport, Me.). Home: 156-11 Oak Av., Flushing NY Office: 535 Fifth Av., New York NY‡

SMALL, JOHN CLAY, editor; b. Palestine, Tex., Apr. 10, 1873; s. William Davis and Eliza Cathrine (Moore) S.; ed. pub. schs. and country printing office; m. Maude Edmondson Hughes, of Kansas City, Mo., Nov. 5, 1902. Telegraph editor Kansas City Times, 1899-01; with St. Louis Republic, 1901-4; asst. to gen. mgr. of press bur. St. Louis Expn., 1904; editor The New Southwest, St. Louis, 1905-10; sec. and mgr. Arkansas Farmer & Homestead Co., pubs., Arkansas Homestead, 1910-13; now editor The Pulaskian (weekly). Mem. Ark. Press Assn.; 1st pres. Little Rock Press Club; sec. Little Rock Fair. Dep. state commr. mines, mfrs. and agr. Democrat. Methodist. Address: Little Rock AR‡

SMALL, SIDNEY AYLMER, author; b. Brooklyn, N.Y., Aug. 20, 1876; s. Charles Sidney and Martha A. (Elmer) S.; grad. Trinity Sch., New York, 1895; E.E., Columbia, 1899; m. Margaret D. Haberlin, of Brooklyn, N.Y., Mar. 28, 1910; children—Charles Sidney, Edward Haberlin. Asst. in elec. engring., Columbia, 1899-1901; science teacher, Trinity Sch., since 1901.

Episcopalian. Author: Electrical Railroading, 1908; The Boy's Book of Physics, 1922; The Boy's Book of Electricity, 1923; The Boys' Book of the Earth, 1924. Home: 1076 Nelson Av., New York NY‡

SMALLENS, ALEXANDER, musical dir.; b. St. Petersburg, Russia, Jan. 1, 1889; s. Pantaleimon Ossipowitch and Anna (Rosovski) S.; brought to U.S. 1890, naturalized, 1919; A.B., Coll. of City New York, 1909; student Inst. Musical Art, New York, 1905-09, Conservatoire Nationale, Paris, 1909-11; m. Ruth White May 15, 1935; 1 son, Alexander. Asst. condr. Boston Opera Co., 1911-14; condr. Century Opera Co., 1914, Boston Nat. Opera, 1915-17, Anna Pavlowa South Am. tour, 1917-19, Chicago Opera Co., 1919-22; condr. Berlin and Madrid operas, 1923; musical dir. Phila. Civic Opera Co., 1923-30; condr. Phila. Orchestra, 1928-34; condr. Robin Hood Dell, Phila., since 1930; condr. Lewissohn Stadium, New York, since 1934; has conducted premieres of Am. operas, Rip van Winkle", Four Saints in Three Acts", Porgy and Bess"; conducted revival of Porgy and Bess", also made guest appearances with Chicago Civic Opera, the Watergate Concerts in Washington, D.C., the 26th season at Lewisohn Stadium, N.Y.C., and Hollywood Bowl Concerts, Los Angeles, 1943; guest conductor Netherlands Opera, 1956-57. Musical dir. Internat. Ballet, 1944; appointed music dir. Radio City Music Hall Symphony Orch., 1947. Radio conductor for Atwater Kent, Ford Sunday Evening Hour, Sealtest, N.B.C. Orchestra, etc. Mus. dir. European tour of Am. Nat. Ballet Theatre. Dir. world tour Porgy and Bess, 1953-56. Received Townsend Harris medal and hon. Phi Beta Kappa from Coll. of the City of New York. Home: Tucson AZ Died Nov. 24, 1972.

SMALLWOOD, DELLA GRAEME, seminary prin.; b. Lawrence, Mass.; d. Richard W. and Phoebe Robinson; ed. Boston Normal Sch., Emerson Sch. of Oratory; in music by Julius Eichberg, Luther Mason; in art by Fraulein Hentz; in elocution by Dean Southwick; in natural science under Prof. Agassiz; m. George T. Smallwood, of Boston. Prin. Washington Sem., since Oct. 1, 1893. Episcopalian. Mem. D.A.R. (vice-pres. gen.), Daughters of 1812. Y.W.C.A. (v.-p.), W.C.T.U. (life.) Club: Twentieth Century. Address: 3520 16th St. N.W., Washington DC‡

SMART, JACKSON WYMAN, pub. accountant; b. Chicago, June 10, 1898; s. Allen R. and Anna (Rightmyer) S.; grad. U. Mich., 1920; m. Dorothy Brynes, Aug. 30, 1929; children—Jackson Wyman, Dorothy Delle (Mrs. John R. Montgomery III), Allen Rich. Partner Touche, Ross, Bailey & Smart, 1947-71; director Uptown Nat. Bank, Thomas Industries, Inc. Mem. Palm Springs Com. of 25. Bd. dirs., v.p. Boys Club of Palm Springs, 1968-71. Served in naval aviation, U.S. Navy, 1918. Mem. Am. Inst. Accountant, Ill. Soc. C.P.A.'s (pres. 1945), Psi Upsilon. Republican. Presbyterian. Clubs: Mid-Day (Chgo.); Exmoor Country (pres. 1950-51, Highland Park, Ill.); Thunderbird Country, Racquet (Palm Springs, Cal.). Home: Wilmette IL Died Jan. 8, 1971; buried Winnetka Congregational Church Cemetery, Winnetka IL

SMART, JOHN STUART, JR., metall. engr.; b. Des Moines, Mar. 24, 1913; s. John Stuart and Blanche (Senft) S.; B.S. in Chem. Engring., U. Mich., 1934; m. Lily Hindley, Mar. 6, 1937; children—John S., William F., Susan L. Metallurgist, Ford Motor Co., 1934-35, Detroit Lubricator Co., 1935-36; with Am. Smelting & Refining Co., N.Y.C., 1936-69, asst. to v.p., dir. research, 1953-56, asst. dir. research, 1956-58, gen. sales mgr., 1958-69; president Asarco Intermetallics, Incorporated. Mem. bd. United Engring. Trustees, 1962-69, treas., 1965-69; bd. Engring. Found., 1962-69. Recipient Mathewson medal Am. Inst. Mining and Metall Engrs., 1948. Mem. Internat. Lead-Zinc Research Organization, Inc. (vice pres. 1966-69), Am. Inst. Mining and Metall. and Petroleum Engrs. (v.p. 1961-62; pres. Metall. Soc. 1961), Am. Soc. Metals, Research Soc. Am., Metall. Soc. (pres. 1961), Lead Industries Assn. (v.p. 1962-63), Am. Zinc Inst. (dir. 1960-69, v.p. 1965), Mining and Metall. Soc. Am., Delta Upsilon. Episcopalian. Clubs: Bankers Am., Mining (N.Y.C.). Home: Westfield NJ Died Dec. 7, 1969.

SMART, RICHARD ADDISON, mech. eng'r; b. Fort Wayne, Ind., Nov. 18, 1872; s. Hon. James H. and Mary H. (Swan) S.; ed. pub. schs., Indianapolis; grad. Purdue Univ., M.E., 1892; m. La Fayette, Ind., June 12, 1901, Elsie Douglas Moore. Asso. prof. experimental eng'ring, Purdue Univ., 1899-1901; experimental eng'r for B. F. Sturtevant Co., Boston, 1901-3; now asst. to supt. of production, Westinghouse Electric & Mfg. Co., Pittsburg. Mem. Am. Soc. Mech. Eng'rs; asso. mem. Am. Ry. Master Mechanics' Assn. Author: Handbook of Engineering Laboratory Practice, 1898 W9. Address: Westinghouse Electric & Mfg. Co., East Pittsburg PA‡

SMEDLEY, M(ARTIN) HARVEY, lawyer; b. Long Island City, N.Y., Oct. 5, 1902; s. Mason O. and Josephine M. (Shelsey) S.; student Columbia, 1919-21; A.B., Princeton, 1924; LL.B., Fordham U., 1928; m. Marjorie Jean Middleton, Feb. 7, 1934 (dec. Aug. 27, 1935); 1 dau., Mary Jane. Admitted to N.Y. bar, 1929; practice of law, Jamaica, N.Y., 1930-35; asso. with Roberts B. Thomas, New York, 1935-45; private practice of law, New York, 1945-68, specializing in trade assn. work and labor-management relations, particularly in structural steel industry; sec. and gen. counsel Am. Inst. of Steel Constrn., the Iron League of New York, Inc., and Steel Painting Contractors Assn.; dir. and gen. counsel Quigley Co., Inc.; pres. The Malba Assn., 1949-52, dir., 1942-55; trustee Flatbush Savings Bank, Brooklyn. Served as government appeal agent SSS, 1940-47. Mem. Tax Inst., Inc., Am. Judicature Soc., Am., N.Y. State, Queens County (bd. mgrs. 1940-50, pres. 1946-47) bar assns., N.Y. Bldg. Congress. Republican. Roman Catholic. Clubs: Garden City Golf (pres., gov.); Cherry Valley Country; Princeton (N.Y.C.); Lawrence Beach. Home: Garden City NY Died Nov. 27, 1968; buried Mt. St. Mary's Cemetery, Flushing NY

SMELTZER, CLARENCE HARRY, univ. prof.; b. Bellefonte, Pa., Sept. 4, 1900; s. William C. and Sallie A. (Garbrick) S.; B.S., Columbia, 1922, A.M., 1923; Ph.D., Ohio State U., 1931; m. Margaret W. Mussina, June 22, 1927; 1 dau., Kay (Mrs. Martin Ewer). Tchr., & asst. prin., McBurney Jr. Sch., N.Y.C., 1920-24; instr. in psychology, Temple U., Phila., 1924-29, Ohio State U., 1929-31; asst. prof. psychology, Temple U., 1931-34, asso. prof. 1934-41, prof., chmn. dept., 1941-62, Thadeus L. Bolton prof. of psychology, 1961-67, professor emeritus of psychology, from 1967; teacher summer sessions, Pa. State Coll., Temple U., Ohio State U., Miami U. Consultant on personnel State Emergency Relief Adminstrn., Harrisburg, Pa., 1935-37; tech. consultant on civil service Dept. of Labor and Industry (Pa.), 1937-39; consultant on civil service, employment bd., Dept. Pub. Assistance (Pa.), 1939-42, Pa. State Civil Service Commn. from 1942, N.J. Civil Service Commn., from 1937, Veterans Administration, from 1958; consultant for Craig & Gravatt, personnel specialists, Philadelphia, from 1942. Member A.A.A.S., Am. Assn. Univ. Profs., Am., Eastern and Pa. psychol. assns., Am. Assn. Applied Psychologists, Southeastern Pa. League for Nursing (director), Nat. Soc. Coll. Teachers of Edn., Pa. Conf. on Family Relations, Indsl. Relations Assn. of Phila, Alpha Psi Delta, Phi Delta Kappa, Sigma Phi Epsilon, Blue Key. Author: Handling Test Scores, 1933; Psychology for Student Nurses, 1962; Psychological Evaluations in Nursing Education, 1965; The Interview in Student Nurse Selection, 1967; also articles profl. jours. Home: Glenside PA

SMERTENKO, CLARA MILLERD, coll. prof.; b. Benton Harbor, Mich., Sept. 14, 1873; d. Norman Alling and Clara Elizabeth (Church) Millerd; grad. Acad., Grinnell Coll., Ia., 1889; A.B., Ia. (now Grinnell) Coll., 1893, A.M., 1894; Ph.D., U. of Chicago, 1900; U. of Berlin, 1905, 06; m. Johan J. Smertenko, Dec. 26, 1919. Preceptress, Grinnell Acad., 1894-98; so. prof. Greek and philosophy, 1898-1906, prof. Greek lit. and philosophy, 1906-12, prof. history of thought, 1912-21, Grinnell Coll.; lecturer history of edn., Teachers' Coll. (Columbia U.), and history of philosophy, Hunter Coll., 1921-23; prof. English Lang. and lit., Skidmore Coll., 1923-25; asst. prof. Greek and Latin, U. of Ore., 1927—. Mem. Am. Philol. Assn., Western Philos. Assn., Classical Assn. of Middle West, Phi Beta Kappa. Conglist. Author: On the Interpretation of Empedocles, 1908. Contbr. to jours. and periodicals. Y.M.C.A. hosp. service, with 1st Div. A.E.F. in France, Dec. 1917-Oct. 1918. Home: Saratoga Springs NY Address: Eugene OR‡

SMILEY, DEAN FRANKLIN, physician, educator; b. Cheyenne, Wyo., July 7, 1894; s. Elmer Ellsworth and Edith Constance (House) S.; A.B., Cornell, 1916, M.D., 1919; m. Alice Dimon, Sept. 10, 1919; children—Jane Constance (Mrs. Parker Hart), Beth Anne (Mrs. Henry Borst). Interne N.Y. Hosp., 1919-20; mem. faculty, student Health Service Cornell U. 1920-42, prof. dept. hygiene and preventive medicine, 1928-42; cons. in health and fitness, A.M.A., Chicago, 1946-48; sec. Assn. Am. Med. Colleges, Chicago, 1948-57; exec. dir. Edn. Council Fgn. Med. Grads., 1957-63. Served as comdr. M.C., U.S. Navy, 1942-46. Diplomate Am. Bd. Preventive Medicine. Fellow Am. Pub. Health Assn. (mem. com. on survey med. edn.); mem. Am. Med. Writers Assn. (pres. 1956-57), Sigma Xi, Alpha Omega Alpha. Editor Jour. of Med. Edn., 1951-57. Pub. (with A. G. Gould) Your Health, 1951; Your Evanston IL Died Nov. 20, 1969; cremated.

SMILLIE, WILSON GEORGE, pub. health adminstrn.; b. Eaton, Colo., Nov. 2, 1886; s. John Wilson and Christina (Trenholme) S.; A.B., Colo. Coll., 1908; M.D., Harvard Univ., 1912, D.P.H., 1916; hon. D.Sc., Colorado Coll., 1939; honorary D.Sc., University of Sao Paulo, Brazil, 1950; m. Faye Anderson, Sept. 2, 1914 (died Oct. 11, 1918); children—John Wilson, Faye Anderson; m. 2d, Octavia Hall, Feb. 16, 1923 (dec. 1970); children—Addie Louise, Ann Dickson. Intern and asst. resident physician, Peter Bent Brigham Hosp., Boston, 1912-14; instr. Harvard Med. Sch., 1914-16; fellow Rockefeller Inst., 1917; mem. staff Internat. Health Div., Rockefeller Foundation, 1917-27; dir. Instituto de Hygiene, Sao Paulo, Brazil (lent by Rockefeller Foundation), 1919-21; prof. pub. health administration, Harvard Sch. Pub. Health, 1927-37; prof. pub. health and preventive medicine, Cornell U. Med. College, 1937-55. Fellow N.Y. Acad. Medicine; mem. Assn. Am. Physicians, Am. Pub. Health Assn., Sigma Chi, Alpha Omega Alpha, Delta Omega, Sigma Xi. Conglist. Mason. Author: Pub. Health Adminstrn. in the United States, 1935, 40, 47. Preventive Medicine and Pub. Health, 1946; The History of Public Health in America, 1953. Co-Author: Problems of the New Cuba, 1935. Also writer many papers on med. subjects. Home: Newfane VT Died Aug. 1971.

SMITH, ALBERT CHARLES, educator; b. Monroeville, O., Nov. 10, 1906; s. Louis E. and Christine A. (Ryf) S.; B.S., Ohio State U., 1929, M.S., 1931, Ph.D., 1942; m. Edith M. Norman, June 16, 1932; one daughter, Joy Darlene (Mrs. James West). Student assistant Ohio State University, Columbus, 1927-29; grad. asst. pharmacy Purdue, 1929-33; pharmacology dept. U. Tenn. 1934-35; pharmacist profl. store Wells Yeager, Best, Lafayette, Ind., 1935-36; prof. pharmacy Ferris, Inst., 1936-44, Ohio No. U., 1944-71, acting dean, 1950, dean coll. pharmacy, 1951-63, professor of pharmaceutical chemistry, 1963-71; part-time lab. technician. Big Rapids, Mich., 1938-44. Registered pharmacist, Ohio, Ind. Mem. Am. Pharm. Assn., Am. Chem. Soc., Am. Assn. Advancement Sci., Northwestern Ohio Druggists Assn., Nat. Education Association, Am. Association Coll. Pharmacy (co-chairman), National Association Pharmacy (co-chairman), Sigma Xi, Kappa Alpha Phi, Phi Rho Alpha, Kappa Psi. Methodist. Kiwanian. Home: Ada OH Died Aug. 12, 1972; buried Riverside Cemetery Monroeville OH

SMITH, ALFRED FRANKLIN, clergyman; b. Charleston, Mo., Mar. 28, 1869; s. James Washington and Martha Alberta (English) S.; A.B., Central Coll., Fayette, Mo., 1891, D.D., 1912; studied Vanderbilt University, 1891-92; Litt.D., Birmingham Southern Coll., 1929; m. Lucy Maude Cunningham, of Medicine Lodge, Kan., Sept. 20, 1893; children—Lucy Hortense (Mrs. Amos Mansfield Kidder, dec.), Mildred K. (Mrs. Archibald C. Loud, dec.). Ordained ministry M.E. Ch., S., 1892; pastor Centralia, Mo., 1892-93, Montgomery, 1893-1896, Moberly, 1896-98, Hannibal, 1898-1901, Kirkwood, 1901-03; pres. Central Coll. for Women, Lexington, Mo., 1903-08; pastor Tulsa, Okla., 1908-10, Galloway Memorial Ch., Jackson, Miss., 1910-13, St. Paul's Ch., St. Louis, Mo., 1914-17, Centenary Ch., St. Louis, 1917-18; editor St. Louis Christian Advocate, Nov. 1918-Sept. 1921; chaplain Barnes Hosp., St. Louis, 1921-23; editor Christian Advocate, Nashville, 1923-32; book editor and publishing agt., July 1932—. Mem. Gen. Conf. M.E. Ch., S., 1930; mem. Methodist Ecumenical Conf., 1931. Mem. World Confs., Oxford and Edinburgh, 1937. Mem. S.A.R., Chi Phi. Clubs: Round Table, Belle Meade Country. Editor Talking with God. Address: 810 Broadway Nashville TN‡

SMITH, ALICE RAVENEL HUGER, artist; b. Charleston, S.C., July 14, 1876; d. Daniel Elliott Huger and Caroline (Ravenel) Smith; ed. pvt. sch. and Carolina Art Assn.; hon. Dr.Litt., Mount Holyoke College, 1937. Exhibited water colors, Water Color Club (New York), Am. Water Color Soc., Pa. Acad. Fine Arts, Art Inst. Chicago, and wood block prints at Chicago Soc. of Etchers, Cincinnati Museum, Print Makers of Los Angeles, etc. Mem. Southern States Art League, Carolina Art Assn., Charleston Museum. Episcopalian. Author: (with D. E. Huger Smith) Life of Charles Fraser (miniature painter). Illustrator: Twenty Drawings of the Pringle House, 1914; The Dwelling Houses of Charleston, S.C. (by Alice R. H. Smith and D.E. Huger Smith), 1917; A Woman Rice-Planter (by Patience Pennington); Adventures in Green Places (Herbert Ravenel Sass), 1935; A Carolina Rice Plantation of the Fifties (with Herbert Ravenel Sass and D. E. Huger Smith), 1936; Historical notes to a Charleston Sketch Book (by Charles Fraser). Home: -Studio: 69 Church St., Charleston SC*‡

SMITH, ALSON JESSE, clergyman, author; b. Danbury, Conn., Aug. 12, 1908; s. Gifford Alson and Josephine Louise (Hull) S.; A.B., Dickinson Coll., 1930; B.D., Garrett Bibl. Inst., 1933; student Yale Grad. Sch., 1936-37; m. Florence McLeod, Mar. 20, 1932; children—Stephen Hull, Philip Alson. Ordained to ministry, Meth. Ch., 1934; minister Philipsburg, Mont., 1933-35, Waterbury, Conn., 1935-40, Bayport, L.I., 1941-45, Bklyn. 1945-47, Stamford, Conn., 1947-50; exec. dir. Temperance and Tolerance Assn., 1950-51; lectr. Columbia Lecture Bur., 1950-51. Mem. Author's League Am., Friends of Lit., Research Council on Problems of Alcohol. K.P. Republican. Author: Brother Van, 1947; Faith to Live By, 1948; Religion and the New Psychology, 1951; The Psychic Sourcebook, 1951; Chicago's Left Bank, 1953; Syndicate City, 1954; Immortality; The Scientific Evidence, 1954; Live All Your Life, 1955; A View of the Spree, 1961; Primer for the Perplexed, 1963. Home: Canaan CT Died May 17, 1965.

SMITH, ARTHUR A., rancher; b. Marion County, O., Oct. 7, 1875; s. Seneca A. and Nancy Ellen (West) S.; ed. pub. schs. of Cardington, O.; m. Martha Blanche Haley, May 24, 1905; children—Nancy (Mrs. Horace M. Gaims), Barbara (Mrs. Pedro E. Guerrero). Teacher,

Cardington, Ohio, 1896-99; warehouseman, Colo. Fuel & Iron Co., Laramie, Wyo., 1901-04; clerk and bookkeeper, W. H. Holliday Co., Laramie, 1905-08; mgr. Fall Creek Sheep Co., American Falls, Ida., 1908-14; rancher Sterling, Colo. since 1914, mgr. and partner A. A. Smith & Co. since 1942, pres. Haley-Smith Cattle Co. since 1938; formerly sec.-treas. Plains Motor Co., Sterling, Colo. Mem. Sterling Park Bd.; past pres. Sterling Sch. Bd. Mem. Colo. Livestock Prodn. Credit Assn. (pres.), Am. National Livestock Assn. (president), Colo. Stockgrowers and Feeders Assn. (past pres.). Republican. Episcopalian. Mason (past master). Elk. Clubs: Country (Sterling); Rotary (Sterling, Colo.). Home: 914 S. Division Av., Sterling CO‡

SMITH, ARTHUR MUMFORD, U.S. judge; b. Scott, Ind., Sept. 19, 1903; s. Ora Lynn and Genevieve (Mumford) S.; A.B., U. Mich., 1924, J.D., 1926; m. Elizabeth Barbara Allan, June 14, 1926; children—Carrol Jean (Mrs. Dwight A. Lewis), Arthur Allan. Admitted to Mich. and Ill. bars, 1926; pvt. practice patent law, Chgo., 1926-29, patent law, Detroit, 1929-33, patent law, Detroit and Dearborn, Mich., 1933-59; also. judge U.S. Ct. Customs and Patent Appeals, 1959-68; lectr. patent law U. Mich. Law Sch., 1952-59; panelist patent law sect., summer patent session, Practicing Law Inst., N.Y.C., 1958. Mem. Detroit Olympic Games Com., 1958-59; pres. Abraham Lincoln Civil War Round Table Mich., 1956-57; speakers bur. Lincoln Sesquicentennial Commn., 1958-68. Mem. mgmt. com. Detroit YMCA, 1948-59; trustee Methodist Union Greater Detroit, 1957-59; chmn. Detroit area com. Patents, Trademark and Copywright Found., George Washington U., 1959. Mem. Am. Bar Assn. (speaker patents nat. speakers bur.), State Bar Mich., Am., Mich. (pres. 1939; life mem.), patent law associations, American Judicature Society, and Gamma Eta Gamma. Methodist (past trustee). Rotarian (pres. Dearborn 1953-54). Author: Supplementary Materials in Patent Law, 1953; Patent, Law, Cases, Comments and Materials, 1 vol., 1954, rev., 1964; The Art of Writing Readable Patents, 1958; also articles, reports. Participating editor Patent Licensing, 1959. Home: Washington DC Died Nov. 20, 1968; buried Dearborn MI

SMITH, BETTY, novelist; b. Bklyn.; Dec. 15, 1896; d. John and Catherine (Hummel) Wehner; grad. U. Mich., 1930; spl. student Yale Drama Sch., 1930-34. Tchr. creative writing U. N.C., 1963-65. Recipient Alumni award U. N.C., 1964; Certificate of Merit for accurate portrayal contemporary Am. life in novels, N.Y. Mus. Sci. and Industry. Mem. Author's League, Dramatists Guild, Matrix (hon.). Author: A Tree Grows in Brooklyn, 1943; Tomorrow Will be Better, 1948; Maggie Now, 1958; Joy in the Morning, 1963. Home: Chapel Hill NC Died Jan. 17, 1972.

SMITH, BEVERLY WAUGH, JR., writer and lawyer; b. Balt., Aug. 9, 1898; s. Beverly Waugh and Eleanor (Euker) S.; A.B., Johns Hopkins, 1919; postgrad. Harvard Law Sch., 1919-20; grad. final honours Sch. of Jurisprudence, Oxford U. (Rhodes scholar 1920), 1922; M.A., 1968; M. Grace Cutler, May 21, 1926. Admitted to N.Y. State bar; practiced in N.Y.C., 1923-26; reporter, later fgn. corr. and columnist, N.Y. Herald Tribune, 1926-31; with American Mag., staff writer and asso. editor, 1931-46; Washington editor, senior contbg. editor Sat. Eve. Post, 1946-64, contbg. writer, 1964-69; admitted to D.C. bar, 1964. Served as 2d lt., arty., U.S. Army, 1918. Mem. Phi Beta Kappa, Omicron Delta Kappa, Alpha Delta Phi. Clubs: Nat. Press, Cosmos (Washington). Author: (with Grace Cutler Smith) Through the Kitchen Door, 1938. Contbr. articles and fiction to Am. Mag., Reader's Baltimore MD Died Oct. 22, 1972.

SMITH, CHARLES EDWARD, critic-historian and musicologist; b. Thomaston, Conn., June 8, 1904; s. Walter Richard and Lulu Jane (Whiteman) S.; m. Louise Miller, Nov. 22, 1933 (div.). Critic-historian of jazz, 1930-70; helped create network radio jazz series CBS, 1930's; music script editor OWI, 1942-45; inaugurator reissue programs and jazz records, supr. Jelly Roll Morton's album, New Orleans Memories; now mem. Internat. Adv. Council and critic Jazz Magazine, N.Y.C. Founding mem. Hot Record Soc., 1930's, also Inst. for Jazz Studies. Recipient Silver Medal award for contribution to jazz growth and understanding, Down Beat, 1959. Author: The Symposium, 1930. Editor: (with another) Jazzmen, 1939; The Jazz Record Book, 1942; contbr. to The Jazz Makers, 1957, Jazz, 1959, Big Bill Blues, 1964, Art Voices; also contbr. numerous articles in field of jazz to mags. and record New York City NY Died Dec. 1970.

SMITH, CHARLES GROVER, physicist; born Waco, Tex., Oct. 27, 1888; s. Sam Houston and Bell (McGaughy) S.; A.B., U. of Tex., 1911; Ph.D. in physics, Harvard, 1936; m. Aurelia Mayer Vick, Sept. 29, 1919; children—William Vick, Mary Elizabeth, Helen Aurelia. Research engr. Am.-Radio & Research Corp., Medford, Mass., 1919-22; research engr. Raytheon Mfg. Co. 1922-59 (a founder and dir. 1922-28); dir. Cambridge Labs., 1926-28, Thenos Corp., 1933-38. Mem. A.A.A.S., Am. Phys. Soc., Am. Inst. Elec. Engrs., Sigma Xi. Research in field of gaseous conduction; holds patents on rectifiers, oscillators, gaseous lamps, control devices. Home: Medford MA Died June 1969.

SMITH, CHARLES LYSLE, lawyer; b. Chgo., Jan. 13, 1895; s. Charles George and Alta (Williams) S.; B.S., Northwestern U., 1917, LL.B., 1920; m. Ruth Graves, Aug. 26, 1924; 1 dau., Ellen Graves (Mrs. Smith Simmons). Admitted to Illinois bar, 1920, practiced in Chgo., asso. Wilson, McIlvaine, Hale & Templeton, 1920-24, pvt. practice, from 1925; sr. partner firm Winston Strawn, 1967. Trustee Village of Glencoe, 1940-48. Trustee Northwestern U., 1956-60. Lt. (j.g.), USN, World War I. Recipient Norman Waite Harris polit. sci. prize, 1917. Mem. Northwestern U. Associates, Soc. Mayflower Descs. (gov. Ill. soc. 1963-66), Phi Delta Theta, Phi Delta Phi. Clubs: University, Legal, Law, Mid-day (Chgo.); Skokie Country; Lake Zurich (Ill.) Golf. Home: Glencoe IL Died May 8, 1972; buried Memorial Park Skokie IL

SMITH, CLARENCE BEAMAN, agriculturist; b. Howardsville, Mich., Sept. 21, 1870; s. Alonzo and Harriett (Maybee) S.; B.S., Mich. Agrl. Coll., 1894, M.S., 1895, D.Sc., 1917; univs. Halle and Bonn, Germany, 1898-99; m. Lottie Lee Smith, of Lansing, Mich., Oct. 2, 1901; children—Helen, Herbert, Beaman, Roger, Huron, June. With U.S. Dept. of Agr. since 1896; hort. editor, Experiment Station Record, 1897-1906; agriculturist in the office of Farm Management, 1906-12; in charge farm management field studies and demonstrations, 1912-14; chief of Office Extension Work North and West, 1915-21; chief, Office Extension Work, U.S. Dept. Agr., 1921-38; retired. Democrat. Protestant. Author: Farmer's Cyclopedia of Agriculture (with E. V. Wilcox), 1904; Farmer's Cyclopedia of Livestock (with same), 1907; The Agricultural Extension System of the U.S. (with M. C. Wilson), 1930. Home: 1 Montgomery Av., Takoma Park DC (summers) Atlanta MI‡

SMITH, COURTLAND, b. New York, N.Y., Mar. 7, 1884; s. Orlando Jay and Evelyn V. (Brady) S.; U. of Wis., 1907; m. Elinor Cary, 1912 (divorced); children—Evelyn, Orlando Jay (dec.), Archie B. (dec.); m. 2d, Mary Stuart Kernochan, 1929 (dec.). Pres. Am. Press Assn., 1908-21; asst. to Postmaster Gen. Hays, 1921-22; sec. Motion Picture Producers and Distributors of America, Inc., 1922-26; v.p. and gen. mgr. Fox Hearst Corp., 1926-30; produced first sound news reel for Fox Movietone; opened first news reel theatre in the world, 1929; pres. Pathe News, Inc., 1930-37; now pres. I-R System, Inc. Mem. Loyal Legion, Phi Gamma Delta. Home: Santa Fe NM Died Aug. 1970.

SMITH, COURTNEY CRAIG, coll. pres.; b. Winterset, Ia., Dec. 20, 1916; s. Samuel Craig and Myrtle (Dabney) S.; A.B., Harvard, 1938, A.M., 1941, Ph.D., 1944; student (Rhodes Scholar), Oxford U., 1938-39; LL.D., U. Pa., 1958, Temple U., 1959, U. Pitts., 1960; L.H.D., Bucknell U., 1958; D.Litt., W.Va. University, 1959; Doctor of Laws, La Salle College, 1967; m. Elizabeth Bowden Proctor, Oct. 12, 1939; children—Courtney Craig Jr., Elizabeth Bowden (Mrs. Gregory K. Ingram), and Carol Dabney. Teaching fellow, tutor of English, Harvard, 1939-43; instr. English, Princeton, 1946-48, asst. prof., 1948-53, bicentennial preceptor, 1951-53; nat. dir. Nat. Woodrow Wilson Fellowship Program, 1952-53; Am. sec. Rhodes Scholarships 1953-69, pres. Swarthmore Coll., 1953-69; bd. dirs. Phila. Sav. Fund Soc.; bd. electors George Eastman vis. professorship, Oxford U. Mem. bd. Pa.-N.J.-Del. Met. Project, Inc., 1958-65. Trustee Eisenhower Exchange Fellowships, Inc.; mem. bd. overseers Harvard, 1955-61, now mem. vis. com. dept. English; vis. com. for humanities Johns Hopkins; commn. internat. edn. Am. Council on Edn., 1962-65; dir. Markle Found.; dir. Assn. Am. Colls., 1957-61. Served ensign to lt. (j.g.), USNR, 1944-46. Decorated Hon. Officer Order British Empire. Mem. Modern Lang. Assn., Am. Assn. U. Profs. (asso.). Assn. Am. Rhodes Scholars (bd. dirs.), Phi Beta Kappa. Mem. Soc. of Friends. Clubs: University, Century (N.Y.C.); Rolling Green Golf; Harvard, Sunday Breakfast, Ozone (Phila.). Home: Swarthmore PA Died Jan. 16, 1969.

SMITH, DANIEL FLETCHER, JR., naval officer; b. Pittsburgh, Tex., Mar. 31, 1910; s. Daniel Fletcher and Nannie Lou (Hightower) S.; B.S., U.S. Naval Acad., 1932; grad. Nat. War Coll., 1953; m. Virginia Griggs, Apr. 16, 1947; stepchildren—Stephen Griggs Mace, Barbara Virginia (Mrs. Byron C. Campbell). Commd. ensign U.S. Navy, 1932, advanced through grades to rear adm., 1960; service in Pacific Fleet, 1932-35; designated naval aviator, 1936; service aboard carriers U.S.S. Enterprise, Lexington and Independence, World War II; comdr. U.S.S. Randolph, 1956-57; chief navy information, Navy Dept., 1960-62; comdr. Carrier Div. 3, U.S. Pacific Fleet, 1962-64; chief naval air base tng., Pensacola Fla., 1964-67; comdr. Naval Air Test Center, Patuxent River, Md., 1967-71. Decorated D.F.C. with 3 gold stars, Air medal with 1 gold star. Home: Jacksonville FL Died Oct. 5, 1971.

SMITH, DENA (MRS. WARREN R. SMITH), state ofcl., b. Kewaunee, Wis., Oct. 19, 1899; attended bus. schs., Milw.; m. Warren R. Smith (dec., 1957). Mgr. music depts. stores Milw. until 1949; sec., asst. to state treas. Wis.; state treas. Wis., from 1957. Vice-chmn. 4th congressional dist. Nat. Com. Republican Party, 3 terms; mem. Electoral College, 1960. Mem. Commrs. Pub. Lands, Wis., State (Wis.) Bd. Canvassers. Trustee Conservation Wardens Pension Fund, Wis. Mem. Internat., Nat., Wis. fedns. bus. and profl. women's clubs. Home: Milwaukee WI

SMITH, DILMAN M. K., pub. opinion research exec.; b. Olewein, Ia., Oct. 29, 1902; s. Dilman and Maud (McKean) S.; A.B., Drake U., 1924; grad. study Columbia (fellowship) 1925-26; m. Helen Buell, Apr. 23, 1927; 1 dau., Mary Jo. Mem. market research and sales promotion staff Standard Oil Co. of Ind., 1930-37; developed new techniques in automobile accessory and style mdse. fields, 1937-38; v.p. Opinion Research Corp., Princeton, N.J., since 1939, vice chairman of the board, 1957-63; currently research cons. to mfrs. automobiles, elec. appliances and home furnishing; lectr. on indsl. relations; dir. Princeton Research Park, Inc. Director Retirement Council, Incorporated New York City. Member American Statistical Assn., Nat. Assn. Pub. Relations Counsel, American Marketing Association (vice president), Phi Beta Kappa. Methodist. Mason. Clubs: Nassau, Rotary (Princeton, N.J.). Author reports bus. conditions. Home: Scottsdale AZ Died.

SMITH, DOUGLAS FORREST, lawyer; b. Council Bluffs, Ia., 1893; LL.B., U. Mich., 1917; m. Josephine Land, 1920. Admitted to Neb. bar, 1919; lawyer for U.P. R.R., Omaha, 1920-35; practice in Chgo., 1935-73; mem. firm Sidley & Smith. Served in U.S. Army, 32d F.A., 1917-18. Office: Chicago IL Died May 15, 1973.

SMITH, E(LMER) BOYD, author, illustrator; b. St. John, N.B., Can., May 31, 1860; studied art in Paris. Author: My Village, 1896; The Story of Noah's Ark, 1905; The Story of Pocahontas and Capt. John Smith, 1906; Santa Claus and All About Him, 1908; The Circus and All About It, 1909; The Chicken World, 1910; The Farm Book, 1910; Seashore Book, 1912; Railroad Book, 1913; The Early Life of Mr. Man, 1914; In the Land of Make Believe, 1915; After They Came Out of the Ark, 1918; The Story of Our Country, 1920; The Country Book, 1924; Lions 'n' Elephants 'n' Everything, 1929. Home: Wilton CT*‡

SMITH, E(DMUND) HOWARD, paper mfr.; b. Montreal, Can., Dec. 28, 1895; s. Charles Howard and Alice Y. (Day) S.; student Westmount Acad.; B.Sc., McGill U., 1920; m. Vera V. Gardner, Apr. 23, 1918; children—Gardner Howard, Robert Howard. With Howard Smith Paper Mills, Ltd., Montreal, Can., 1920-70, beginning as clk., successively resident mgr. in Cornwall, sec.-treas., mng. dir., v.p. and mng. dir., v.p., 1920-46, pres., 1946-70, dir., 1928-70, chmn., 1956-70; pres. Can. Paper Co.; dir. Alliance Paper Mills, Ltd. Mem. Canadian Pulp and Paper Assn. (past pres.), Canadian Mfrs. Assn. Home: Westmount Que Canada. Died Jan. 5, 1970.

SMITH, EDWARD DEVEREUX, b. Livingston, Ala., Sept. 5, 1876; s. Addison Gillespie and Florence Devereux (Hopkins) S.; A.B., U. of Ala., 1896; LL.B., Georgetown U., D.C., 1898; studied Summer Law Sch., U. of Va., 1904; m. Florida Whiting Graves, Mar. 24, 1904; children—Addison, Edward. Practiced in Birmingham, Ala., 1898-1919; apptd. gen. solicitor Southern Group Bell telephone cos., at Atlanta, 1919; gen. counsel Southern Bell Tel. and Tel. Co., Mar. 1929-July 1941, v.p., 1935-41; v.p. and dir. Coca Cola Bottling Co. of Laconia, N.H.; v.p. in charge Trust Dept., Fulton National Bank, Atlanta, Ga., 1941-47; retired. Democratic national committeeman for Ala., 1916-19. Mem. Phi Beta Kappa, Phi Delta Theta. Clubs: Piedmont Driving. Author: A Telephone Rate Case, 1941. Home: 134 W. Pace's Ferry Rd., Atlanta GA‡

SMITH, EDWARD EVERETT, clergyman; b. Audrain County, Mo., Feb. 5, 1861; s. George and Melvina (Coons) S.; student U. of Mo., 1887; B.A., Westminster Coll., Fulton, Mo., 1890, M.A., 1893; B.D., McCormick Theol. Sem., 1893; D.D., Washington and Lee U., 1926; m. Anne Primrose, Jan. 23, 1896. Ordained ministry Presbyn. Ch. in U.S., 1894; pastor Brownwood, Tex., 1894-96, Fourth Av. Ch., Owensboro, Ky., since 1898. Awarded U.S. medal for home work, World War. Democrat. Mason (K.T.). Home: 417 Daviess St., Owensboro KY*‡

SMITH, EDWARD WILLIS, judge; b. Smith Co., Tex., Mar. 8, 1872; s. Edward Willis and Jonnie (Robertson) S.; ed. common schs.; m. Helen Kennedy, of Colorado, Tex., Dec. 17, 1902. Began practice at Colorado, Tex., 1904; moved to Sweetwater, 1910, to San Antonio, 1914; asso. justice Court of Civil Appeals, term Nov. 24, 1920-Jan. 1, 1923. First sergt. Co. K, 4th Tex. Vol. Inf., Spanish-Am. War. Democrat. Presbyn. Mason, K.P., Woodman. Club: Lions. Home: San Antonio TX‡

SMITH, ELMO, publisher; b. Grand Junction, Colo., Nov. 19, 1909; s. Wilmer and Katie (Mohler) S.; B.A., Coll. Ida., 1932, LL.D., 1956; m. Dorothy Leininger, Oct. 8, 1933; children—Dennis, Janice. Editor, pub. Ont. Argus Observer, 1933-46, Blue Mountain Eagle, 1946-68, Madras Pioneer, 1949-68, Hood River News, 1961-68, Dallas Itemizer-Observer, 1964-68; senator State of Ore., 1949-56, gov., 1956-57; pub. Albany (Ore.) Democrat Herald, 1957-68. Chmn. Ore. div. Am. Cancer Soc., 1962, chmn. Western div., 1963. Home: Albany OR Died July 15, 1968.

SMITH, ELVA SOPHRONIA, b. Burke, Vt., 1871; d. Franklin Horatio and Hattie Lovisa (Powers) Smith; grad. Lyndon Inst., 1888; grad. Vt. State Normal Sch., 1890; grad. Carnegie Library Sch., Pittsburgh, Pa., 1902. Teacher pub. schs., Vt. and Calif., until 1901; mem. staff Carnegie Library, Pittsburgh, since 1902, head of children's dept., 1925-44; instr., later asso. prof. library science, Carnegie Library Sch., 1904-44; instr. extension div., Pa. State Coll., 1922-25, summer library sch., 1945; instr. N.H. State Library Inst., summer, 1946. Asso. chmn. of home edn., Nat. Congress of Parents and Teachers, 1934-38. Mem. A.L.A. (exec. bd. and council, 1926-30; chmn. children's noranan's sect. 1923, chmn. book production com., 1924-29), mem. other coms. at various times, Pa. Library Assn., Carnegie Library School Assn. (pres. 1921-28), Fgn. Policy Assn.; hon. mem. of Eugene Field Soc. Unitarian Church. Clubs: Library (Pittsburgh); Woman's (Concord, N.H.); National Travel. Editor or co-editor numerous books since 1915; editor (with Alice I. Hazeltine) Stories of Love, 1951. Compiler annotated catalogs Concord NH‡

SMITH, F. JANNEY, physician; b. Baltimore, Md., Nov. 18, 1888; s. Dr. B. and Frances Gist (Hopkins) S.; A.B., Johns Hopkins, 1909, M.D., 1913; special course Rockefeller Inst., 1917; m. Jeanie Wilmer Smart, Feb. 14, 1917 (dec.); children—Martha Janney (Mrs. Charles A. McGowan), Virginia Carter, F. Janney (deceased), Robert Gibbons; m. 2d, Colleen F. Forney, May 22, 1948; children—Steven, Holly. Medical House office, Johns Hopkins Hospital, 1913-14; assistant resident physician and instructor in medicine in Johns Hopkins Medical School, 1914-15; first resident physician Henry Ford Hospital at its opening in 1915, physician in charge of cardio-respiratory division, 1919-66, senior consultant in cardiology, 1953-66; private practice of cardiology, 1959-66. Diplomate American Board of Internal Medicine, 1937. 1st lt., captain, M.C., U.S. Army, 1917-19. Fellow American Coll. of Physicians; mem. Am. Clin. and Climatol. Assn., Central Soc. for Clin. Research, Am. Trudeau Soc., Mich. Trudeau Soc., Am. Heart Assn., Wayne County Med. Soc., A.M.A., Johns Hopkins Med. and Surg. Assn., Pithotomy Club, Phi Gamma Delta, Phi Beta Kappa, Alpha Omega Alpha. Clubs: Detroit Boat; Country (Grosse Pointe, Michigan); Witenagemote. Contbr. numerous articles to med. jours. Home: Grosse Pointe Farms MI Died Nov. 9, 1966; buried Woodlawn Cemetery Detroit MI

SMITH, FITZ-HENRY, JR., lawyer; b. Boston, Nov. 20, 1873; s. Fitz-Henry and Maria K. (Longley) S.; A.B., Harvard, 1896; LL.B., Harvard Law Sch., 1899; unmarried. Practiced, Boston, 1899—; mem. Gen. Court of Mass., 1914-19. Mem. Am. Bar Assn., Maritime Law Assn. of U.S., Massachusetts Bar Association, Bar Assn. City of Boston, Soc. for Preservation of N.E. Antiquities, Massachusetts Historical Soc., Bostonian Soc. (dir.), Boston Chamber of Commerce. Clubs: St. Botolph, Union, Harvard, Massachusetts, Nisi Prius, Republican, Press. Contbr. on maritime law and hist. subjects. Home: 132 Newbury St. Office: 35 Congress St., Boston MA‡

SMITH, FRANCES STANTON, writer; b. Buffalo, N.Y., June 21, 1871; grad. Acad. of the Holy Angels, Buffalo, 1889; m. Charles Bennett Smith (q.v.), June 10, 1902. Writer for mags., 1890-4; in charge musical dept., Buffalo Express, 1895; musical editor Buffalo Courier, and editor women's page Buffalo Enquirer, 1897-1902; mem. Woman's Bd. Mgrs., and sec. com. on publicity and promotion same, Pan-Am. Expn., 1901; active worker in ednl. movements and mus. enterprises, Buffalo and elsewhere. Mem. bd. regents Trinity Coll., Washington. Apptd. first woman mem. N.Y. State Civil Service Commn., Apr. 2, 1919. Club: Congressional (Washington). Home: 392 Porter Av., Buffalo NY Official Address: Drawer 5, Capitol, Albany NY‡

SMITH, FRANCIS EDWIN, Pension Fund of Disciples of Christ; born Cedar Rapids, Iowa, September 18, 1877; s. Geroge Washington and Mary Matilda (Fosdick) S.; A.B., Eureka Coll., 1904; student Drake U., 1905-06, U. of Chicago, 1916; hon. D.D., Butler U., 1937; m. Inez Stewart, July 12, 1904; children—Frances Ewing (Mrs. Edward P. King), Stewart R. (U.S. aviation medicine), Emily Ruth, Mary Pauline (dec.). Served Second Christian Ch., Cedar Rapids, Ia., 1906-12; minister, Jackson St. Christian Ch., Muncie, Ind., 1912-19; sec. Bd. Ministerial Relief, Indianapolis, Ind., 1919-28; sec. Pension Fund of Disciples of Christ, 1928-45. Home: 530 West 44th St., Office: 800 Test Bldg., Indianapolis 4 IN‡

SMITH, FRANK C., business exec.; b. Hickman, Ky., Sept. 9, 1892; s. Chesley Chambers and Frances (Duncan) S.; student Vanderbilt U., 1911-15; m. Elizabeth Hall, Oct. 26, 1920; children—Frank Chesley, Jr., Elizabeth Avon. In real estate, mortgage and banking bus., 1919-33; pres. Houston Natural Gas Corporation, 1933-55, chairman board of directors, 1955, then hon. chmn. bd.; mem. bd. dirs. Houston Bank & Trust Co.; pres. So. Gas Assn., 1943. Pres. Tex. div. Am. Cancer Soc., 1946-52, chmn. bd. dirs., 1952-55; dir. Tex. Coll. Arts and Industries, 1939-55, chmn., 1941-52; bd. govs. Univ. Houston, 1958-63; chmn. bd. govs. S.W. Research Inst., 1954; chmn. bd. trustees Inst. Gas Tech., Chgo., 1941-43, 56-57, trustee, 1941—; pres., trustee Univ. of Houston Foundation. Served with U.S. Army, 1917-19. Mem. Am. Gas Assn. (dir. 1947-54; pres. 1953) Delta Kappa Epsilon. Methodist. Clubs: Houston, Tejas, Bayou, Kiwanis (pres. 1924; trustee Internat. 1927-29). Home: Houston TX Died Jan. 1971.

SMITH, FRANKLIN G., mfg. exec.; b. Bellevue, O., Oct. 23, 1867; s. Albert B. and Elizabeth Anne (Lewis) S.; student pub. schs., Bellevue; m. Ada M. Richards, Oct. 18, 1892 (died June 1941); children—Phillip F. (dec.), Norman F., Robertson F.; m. 2d, Elsie M. Bohuslav, Oct. 3, 1950. Pres. Osborn Mfg. Co., 1892-68. now hon. chmn. Life trustee Cleve. YMCA. Baptist (life trustee). Clubs: Union, Mid-Day (Cleve.); Chagrin Valley Hunt (Gates Mills, O.). Home: Cleveland OH Died May 13, 1968; buried Lake View Cemetery, Cleveland OH

SMITH, FRED ANDREW, lawyer; b. Columbus, O., Nov. 19, 1907; Fred H. and Helen (Biehl) S.; A.B., Ohio State U., 1930, J.D., 1931; m. Thelma Hewitt, Jan. 12, 1928; children—Fred Hewitt, Diana Lynn (Mrs. Newman). Admitted to Ohio bar, 1931, practiced in Toledo, 1931-72; asso. firm Tracy, Chapman & Welles, 1931-35, successor firm Welles, Kelsey & Cobourn, 1935-44; labor adviser Northwestern Ohio, 1945-46; mem. firm Lord, Hayward, Smith & Notnagel, 1946-50, Cobourn, Smith, Rohrbacker and Gibson, until 1972. Fellow Am., Ohio (pres. 1961-70) bar assn. founds.; mem. Am. (Ohio del.), Ohio (pres. 1955-56). Toledo (pres. 1952-53) bar assns., Am. Judicature Soc., Order of Coif, Phi Delta Phi. Home: Toledo OH Died Dec. 21, 1972.

SMITH, FREDERICK ARTHUR, newspaper corr.; b. Mendota, Ill., July 22, 1875; s. William Hutchinson and Mary Elizabeth (St. John) S.; student Northwestern U. 2 yrs.; m. Marie Beauvais, of St. Louis, Mo., June 2, 1911; children—Arthur B., Mary Elizabeth. Began with Chicago Journal, 1898; later with Chicago Daily News, Chicago Examiner, Chicago Inter-Ocean, St. Louis Post Despatch, New York American, New York Press, New York News; joined staff of Chicago Tribune as night editor, June 1914, and became city editor, 1917; war corr. Tribune, 1918; foreign corr. same, in Far East, 1919, 20. Was in France when Armistice was signed, Nov. 1918, and made way through retreating German armies; wore first Am. uniform into Berlin, arriving there Nov. 24, 1918; last 400 miles was covered in German battle plane, with German ace as pilot. Writer, publicist and lecturer on Oriental situation, 1921-22. Mem. Sigma Alpha Epsilon. Methodist. Address: 510 Rhode Island Av. N.W., Washington DC*‡

SMITH, FREDERICK MILLER, writer, coll. prof.; b. Richmond, Ind., June 16, 1870; s. James W. and Abbie F. (Miller) S.; A.B., Ind. U., 1899; unmarried. Asst. editor Woman's Home Companion, 1900-05. Instr. English, 1910-18, asst. prof., 1918-31, prof. 1931-37, Cornell U. Author: The Stolen Signet, 1909; Eight Essays, 1927; Some Friends of Doctor Johnson, 1931. Editor: Essays and Studies, 1922. Contbr. to mags. Home: 3 Reservoir Av., Ithaca NY‡

SMITH, GEORGE ALBERT, JR., educator; b. Salt Lake City, Sept. 10, 1905; s. George Albert and Lucy E. (Woodruff) S.; A.B., U. Utah, 1926; M.B.A., Harvard, 1934, D.C.S., 1937; m. Ruth H. Nowell, July 6, 1935; children—George Albert, III, Samuel N., Robert N. Missionary, adminstrv. officer Swiss-German Mission Ch. Jesus Christ of Latter-day Saints, Basel, Switzerland, 1926-29; in business, 1929-32; mem. faculty, grad. sch. bus. adminstrn. Harvard, 1934-69, prof. bus. adminstrn., 1945-69, sr. asst. dean, 1939-45; vis. instr. bus. adminstrn. Yale Law Sch., 1937-38; visiting professor Stanford University, 1954; vis. professor University Hawaii, summer 1964; special cons. business orgns., ednl. instns. and U.S. Government Depts. and agencies, 1936-69. Served as capt., chaplain corps, 222 F.A., Utah, N.G., 1930-33; asst. dir., dir. Spl. Navy Supply Corps O.T.S., 1942-46. Mem. Am. Econ. Assn., Am. Acad. Polit. Sci., Am. Soc. Pub. Admintrn. Am. Petroleum Inst., Sigma Chi, Phi Kappa Phi. Author: Policy Formulation and Administration, 1950. Co-author rev. editions 1955, 59, 62; Managing Geographically Decentralized Companies, 1958; Business, Society & the Invididual, 1962. Home: Belmont MA Died Oct. 12, 1969; buried Salt Lake City Cemetery.

SMITH, GEORGE EDSON PHILIP, civil engr.; b. Lyndonville, Vt., Dec. 29, 1873; s. Franklin Horatio and Hattie Lovisa (Powers) S.; B.S. in C.E., Univ. of Vt., 1897, C.E., 1899, Dr.Engring. from same, 1929; studied U. of Wis., 1910-11; m. Maude North, Oct. 1, 1904; 1 son, George Edson Philip. Instr. civil engring., Univ. of Vermont, 1897-1900; professor civil engineering, University of Arizona, 1900-06, prof. irrigation engring. since 1906. Consulting engr. Agrl. Products Corp., 1916-19; also served as Ariz. land planning consultant, Nat. Resources Bd., 1934-35; mem. Tucson City Planning Commn., 1937-46. Introduced caisson well; wrote water code for Ariz.; assisted in development of pump irrigation; researcher in soil temperature control; irrigation econs.; etc. Fellow A.A.A.S.; life member American Geophysical Union; mem. Am. Soc. C.E. (formerly pres. Ariz. sect.), Am. Assn. Engrs., Am. Soc. Agrl. Engrs. (ex-chmn. Pacific Coast Sect.), Western Irrigation and Drainage Research Assn., Sigma Xi, Kappa Sigma, Phi Beta Kappa, Phi Kappa Phi, Phi Beta Kappa Assos. Conglist. Mason (K.T., Shriner). Author of papers and bulletins pertaining irrigation and ground water supplies in the Southwest, and to engring. and polit. problems of Colorado River and to relation of ground water supplies to the physiography. Home: 1195 Speedway, Tucson AZ‡

SMITH, GRAFTON ADRIAN, physician; b. Des Moines, Feb. 13, 1925; s. Grafton Allen and Dorothy Adrienne (Porter) S.; M.D., Washington U., St. Louis, 1948; Ph.D. in Surgery, U. Minn., 1956; m. Mary Louise Matthews, June 18, 1948; children—Stephen Norval, Michael Scott, Susan Diane, John Kevin. Surg. intern, Mpls., 1948-49; resident U. Minn., Mpls., 1949-51, 53-55; practice medicine specializing in surgery and thoracic surgery, Columbia, Mo., 1958-70; instr. surgery U. Mo., Columbia, 1954-56, clin. asst prof., 1961-70; a founder intensive care unit Boone County Hosp., Columbia, 1968. Real estate developer, Columbia. Served with M.C., USNR, 1951-53. Diplomate Am. Bd. Surgery, Am. Bd. Thoracic Surgery. Mem. A.M.A., A.C.S., Am. Coll. Chest Physicians, Mo. Med. Assn., Boone County Med. Soc., Mo. Surg. Soc. (pres. 1968), So. Thoracic Surg. Assn., Navy League, Am. Columbia MO Died Oct. 19, 1970; buried Mo. Meml. Park Cemetery, Columbia MO

SMITH, GUY LINCOLN, editor; b. Johnson City, Tenn., Sept. 30, 1898; s. Guy Lincoln and Mary (Johnston) S.; A.B., Princeton, 1919; m. Thelma McNab, June 4, 1921; children—Guy L. III, Shirley Lu, Reuben McN. Editorial writer The Knoxville (Tenn.) Journal, 1920; founder, 1921, Johnson City (Tenn.) Chronicle, pub. same until 1935; pub. Johnson City (Tenn.) Staff News, 1924-35; founder Bristol (Tenn.) Bulletin, 1925. Editor The Knoxville (Tenn.) Journal, 1937-68; dir. Roy N. Lotspeich Publishing Co. Mem. Republican State Exec. Com., 1944-52, chmn., 1948-58; del. Rep. Nat. Conv., 1944, 48, 52, 56, 60, 64; Tenn. mgr. Eisenhower-Nixon campaign, 1952, 56; mem. Rep. Nat. Com., 1953-58. Mem. C.O.T.S., Camp Lee, 1918. Mem. Am. Soc. Newspaper Editors, S.R. Republican. Presbyn. Clubs: Cherokee Country; City. Home: Knoxville TN Died Nov. 21, 1968; buried Johnson City TN

SMITH, HAL HORACE, JR., investment banker; b. Ionia, Mich., Nov. 14, 1903; s. Hal Horace and Bell (Yales) S.; grad. Taft Sch., 1923; B.A., Yale, 1927; m. Margaret Wheeler, June 14, 1930; children—Hal Horace III, Leonard. Sec., treas. Central West Caualty Co., 1928-31; partner Smith, McRae & Co., trust investments, 1931-36; mng. partner Smith, Hague & Co., mems. N.Y. Stock Exchange, 1936-73; dir. Modern Materials, Prophet Co. Pres. Detroit Stock Exchange, 1943-44. Councilman, City of Grosse Pointe, Mich. Dir., trustee Leader Dogs for the Blind. Mem. U.S. (sec., v.p. 1942), Western (pres. 1939), Mich. (pres. 1936-40) squash rackets assns., Alpha Delta Psi. Home: Grosse Pointe Farms MI Died 1973.

SMITH, HAROLD LEONARD, lawyer; b. Shelton, Conn., Dec. 30, 1896; s. Leonard Charles and Elizabeth Evalena (Burke) S.; Bachelor Arts, Trinity College, 1922, Doctor of Laws (honorary), 1958; LL.B., Harvard, 1925; m. Emma Marie Teitscheid, July 30, 1927; 1 son, Harold Leonard. Newspaper reporter Eve. Sentinel, Derby, Conn., 1915-17; admitted to N.Y. bar, 1926, Conn., 1927; in gen. practice law, N.Y. City, 1926-71; asso. Hughes, Schurman & Dwight, 1925-34, mem. firm. 1934-37; mem. of law firm Hughes, Hubbard and Reed, 1937-71. Mem. bd. trustees Scarsdale (N.Y.) Sch. Dist., No. 2, 1940-43; bd. sch. dirs., 2d Supervisory Sch. Dist., Westchester Co., N.Y., 1941-48; mem. bd. trustees Village of Scarsdale, 1948-51, mayor of village, 1951-53. Alumni mem. bd. trustees Trinity Coll., 1947-53. Served as 2d lt., F.A., U.S. Army, World War I; mem. Squadron A, N.Y. N.G., 1926-30. Mem. Am. and N.Y. State bar assns., Assn. Bar City of N.Y., N.Y. Co. Lawers Assn., Am. Legion, Phi Beta Kappa, Sigma Nu. Republican. Presbyn. Clubs: Downtown Athletic, Down Town Assn., Squadron A Ex-Members Association (N.Y.C.); Skytop (Pa.). Home: Edmonds WA Died Aug. 17, 1971.

SMITH, HAROLD STEPHEN, paper mfr.; b. New York, N.Y., Sept. 2, 1893; s. Harry and Lillian (Wustlich) S.; m. Irene Hunt, Apr. 29, 1916; children—Donald, Doris (Mrs. Burd Edwards Smyth);

m. 2d, Mrs. Bunne Lee Locy, May 5, 1953. Started in business for self at age 23 (1917) organized The Wright Co., 1919; pres. and dir. The Wright Co., Inc., newsprint, N.Y.C., 1919-70; pres. Me. Seaboard Paper Co., 1945-70, Crofton Paper Co. and The Alberni Paper Company, 475 Park Avenue Corporation; chairman of the board Wood Flong Co.; dir. New England Pub. Service Co., New England Industries; trustee Northern New England Co. Pres. U.S. Newsprint Mfrs. Assn. Chmn. newsprint advisory com. O.P.A.; mem. overall paper advisory com. O.P.A., internat. newsprint com. W.P.B., newsprint advisory com. W.P.B., overall paper advisory com. W.P.B. Clubs: Westchester Country; Manhattan, New York City NY Died June 3, 1970.

SMITH, HARRISON, editor, pub.; b. Hartford, Conn., Aug. 4, 1888; s. Oliver Cotton (M.D.) and Claribel (Waterman) S.; A.B., Yale, 1911, M.A., 1914; m. Claire Spencer, Oct. 22, 1918; children—Harrison Venture, Patricia. Mem. editorial dept., Century Mag., 1911-13; ednl. book salesman Century Co., 1913-15; reporter N.Y. Tribune, 1915-17; newspaper corr. Japan and Russia, 1917-18; editor Harcourt Brace & Co., 1919-28; v.p. Cape & Smith, 1929-31; pres. Harrison Smith & Robert Haas, Inc., 1931-36; editor Doubleday Doran & Co., 1936-38; vice president Durrell & Co.; asso. editor Saturday Rev. Trustee Carnegie Fund for Authors. Mem. Psi Upsilon. Republican. Conglist. Clubs: Yale, Overseas, City Island Yacht, Grolier, Lambs (N.Y.C.); Farmington (Conn.) Country. Author: From Main Street to Stockholm. Editor: From Main Street to Stockholm, Letters of New York City NY Died Jan. 1971.

SMITH, HARRY DE FOREST, prof. Greek; b. Gardiner, Me., Jan. 22, 1869; s. Charles James and Sarah Elizabeth (Hildreth) S.; B.A., Bowdoin, 1891, M.A., 1894; M.A., Harvard, 1896; U. of Berlin, Germany, 1896-97; M.A., Amherst, 1912; m. Adela Hills Wood, of Rockland, Me., June 19, 1895; 1 dau., Barbara. Teacher in city schs., Rockland, 1891-95; instr. Greek, U. of Pa., 1897-98; instr. ancient langs., 1898-99, asst. prof. Greek, 1899-1901, Bowdoin; asso. prof. Greek, 1901-03, prof., 1903-39, prof. emeritus since 1939, Amherst. Dir. Converse Memorial Library since 1935, now emeritus, Mem. Am. Philol. Assn., N.E. Classical Assn., Am. Assn. Univ. Profs., Delta Kappa Epsilon, Phi Beta Kappa. Home: Amherst MA‡

SMITH, HAVILAND, record co. exec.; b. N.Y.C., June 2, 1905; s. Julian Pearce and Helen (Holbrook) S.; student David Mannes Sch. Music, 1924-25; U. Pa.; children—Haviland, Michael Haviland, Carolyn Haviland; m. 2d, Louise Hopkins Feb. 17, 1965. Runner, Remick, Hodges & Co., N.Y.C., 1926-27; sec. Joseph Heinrichs Corp., Long Island City, N.Y., 1927-30, Smith & Mossi Corp., 1928-30; owner, photographer Haviland Smith Studio, comml. photography, N.Y.C., 1930-37, Charlotte, N.C., from 1937; owner, rec. engr. Haviland Smith Rec. Studio; pres. Dixie Record Co., Inc.; owner Haviland Smith Galleries; pres. Mi'Lyn, Inc.; v.p. Hypo Music, Inc. Active United Appeal, Heart Fund, United Arts Fund drives. Mem. U.S. Power Squadrons, Profl. Photographers Am., Profl. Photographers N.C., C. of C. Episcopalian. Clubs: Charlotte Civitan, Commodore Yacht. Charlotte NC

SMITH, HENRY ERSKINE, author; b. New York. Officer 7th Regt., N.G. N.Y.; vet. same. Mem. St. Nicholas Soc., N.E. Soc., Soc. Colonial Wars, Soc. War of 1812, S.R.; treas. and dir. Soc. Am. Dramatists and Composers. Playwright since 1907. Clubs: New York Yacht, Union League, Authors. Author: On and Off the Saddle, Characteristic Sights and Scenes from the Great Northwest to the Antilles, 1894; Love's Diplomacy, 1899; Circumstantial Evidence; also other stories; (plays): Pride of the Rancho (also book, 1910); Descriptive Evidence; Desperate Chance; The Pearl Necklace; The Pink Letter; The Willed Away Widow; An Actor's Love; Diplomacy Wins Over Recklessness; Battle of Wits; A Romance of the Plains.*‡

SMITH, HENRY LEE, JR., educator; b. Morristown, N.J., July 11, 1913; s. Henry Lee and Elise Garr (Henry) S.; A.B. summa cum laude, Princeton, 1935, M.A., 1937, Ph.D., 1938; Litt.D., Wagner Coll., S.I., 1961; m. Virginia von Wodtke, Aug. 10, 1946; children—Heather, Marshall, Randolph, Letitia. Lectr. English, Barnard Coll., Columbia, 1938-40; instr. English, Brown U., 1940-42; condr. program Where Are You From, radio sta. WOR, 1939-41; asst. chief div. tng. service Dept. State, 1946-47, asst. dir. Fgn. Service Inst., dir., prof. linguistics sch. langs. and linguistics Fgn. Service Inst., 1947-53, dean sch. langs., 1955-56, prof. linguistics and English, State U. N.Y. at Buffalo, 1956, acting dir. program in linguistics, 1967-68, chmn. dept. anthropology, 1956-65; vis. prof. linguistics U. State N.Y., 1949, 61, dir. communications workshop, 1950, 61; vis. prof. Linguistic Inst., Ind. U., 1951; vis. prof. linguistics U. Pa., 1965-66; adv. com. Fulbright and Smith-Mundt applicants English, 1953-57; Inglis lectr. Harvard, 1954. Mem. grad. adv. council Princeton U. Dept. Oriental Studies, 1961-70; cons. Ford Found., 1960-61. Served as maj., edn. br., information and edn. div., AUS, 1942-45; with Office Provost Marshal Gen., 1945-46. Fellow A.A.A.S. (mem. council), Am. Anthrop. Assn. (del. to div. anthropology and psychology NRC and Nat. Acad. Sci. 1960-63); mem. Washington Acad. Sci., Linguistic Soc. Am. (exec. com. 1960-63, 69), N.Y. Council Tchrs. English (chmn. com. linguistics 1961-66), Soc. Gen. Semantics, Anthrop. Soc. Washington, Am. Council Learned Socs. (com. lang. program 1946-59), Soc. Colonial Wars, S.R., Phi Beta Kappa. Clubs: Saturn, Buffalo Canoe (Buffalo); Princeton University Elm; Princeton (N.Y.C.); Cosmos (Washington). Author: An Outline of English Structure (with George L. Trager), 1951; Linguistic Science and the Teaching of English, 1956; Linguistic Readers series, 1963-67; English Morphophonics; Implications for the Teaching of Literacy, 1968; also numerous ednl. TV films on lang. and linguistics, 1959. Contbr. profl. publs; linguistic adv. panel Am. Heritage Dictionaries, 1966-69. Del. 3d, 4th UNESCO Nat. Confs., 1951, 53, Home: Buffalo NY Died Dec. 13, 1972.

SMITH, HERBERT EDWARD, ret. chmn. U.S. Rubber Co.; b. San Jose, Calif., Aug. 16, 1889; s. Sandford Edward and Kate (Cortelyou) S.; ed. Washburn Boys Prep. Sch., U. of Calif., Class of 1911; m. Alice Crocheron, Jan. 20, 1913; children—Herbert DeWitt, Sandford Cortelyou, Janet Alice (Mrs. Gerald H. Phipps). Salesman Gorham-Revere Co., 1913-15. Revere Rubber Co., N.Y. City, 1915-18; branch mgr., U.S. Rubber Co., New York, 1918-24; gen. mgr. U.S. Rubbert Export Co., Ltd., 1924-25; gen. mgr. gen. div. U.S. Rubber Co., 1925-26, 2d v.p., 1926-27; v.p. U.S. Rubber Export Co., Ltd., 1927-29, pres. 1929, now chmn.; v.p. U.S. Rubber Co., 1929-42; v.p., vice chmn. exec. com., 1942, pres., chmn. exec. com. and member of the finance committee, 1942-49, chmn. bd., 1949-51, retired 1951, then dir., mem. finance com.; dir., mem. finance com. Carrier Corp. Dir. of National Safety Foundation; trustee of Automotive Safety Found., Consol. Edison Co. Mem. Sigma Alpha Epsilon. Republican. Episcopalian. Clubs: Metropolitan, The Links; University of Calif., Pacific-Union Club Calif. Home: New York City NY Died Jan. 1968.

SMITH, HERBERT WILSON, lawyer; b. Edison, O., July 9, 1888; s. Franklin (educator) and Luella (Wilson) S. (newspaper writer); A.B., B.Sc., U. of Mich., 1910; student law dept. same univ.; m. Mary Isabel Buchanan, 1913; m. 2d, Clare M. Goodyear, 1936. Admitted to D.C. bar and to bar Supreme Court of U.S.; pres. Standard Gas Co. (Ohio), 1913-17; mining operator in N.M., 1917-19; chief div. war minerals relief, div. mineral tariffs, div. research Am. Mining Congress, 1919-25, Union Carbide & Carbon Corp., 1925-51; pres., Lancaster, Fraser, Smith Corporation, 1952-55, Strategic Minerals Corp., 1955-57; chmn. Dominion Resources Corp., 1957-70. Member Am. Judicature Soc., Am. Bar Association, Am. Society International Law, International Law Assn., Am. Inst. Mining and Metall. Engineers, Am. Chem. Society, Society Am. Mil. Engrs., Army Ordnance Assn., Am. Mining Congress, S.A.R., Phi Gamma Delta (past pres. nat. frat.). Republican. Episcopalian. Mason (32 deg.). Clubs: University, National Press (Washington); University, Phi Gamma Delta (pres. 1940-43) (New York); Lawyers (Michigan). Contbr. mags. and syndicates, on Government and Business," Reciprocal Trade Agreements and the Mining Industry," etc. Home: Washington DC Died Oct. 18, 1970.

SMITH, HOWARD REMUS, live stock commr.; b. Somerset, Hillsdale County, Mich., Apr. 16, 1872; s. Frederick Hart and Mary Selina (Burr) S.; B.S., Mich. Agrl. Coll., 1895; m. Hazel Ruth Neu, Apr. 3, 1912; children—Genevieve Louie, Frederick Hart. Boyhood on farm devoted largely to live stock operations; asst. prof. animal husbandry, 1900-01, asso. prof., 1901-02, prof., 1902-12, U. of Neb.; prof. animal husbandry, U. of Minn., 1912-15; livestock specialist for First Nat. Bank, St. Paul, and Great Northern Ry., 1915-17; live stock commr., Chicago Live Stock Exchange, 1917-21, Nat. Live Stock Exchange since July 1, 1921; gen. mgr. Nat. Live Stock Loss Prevention Bd., 1934-51. Apptd. member U.S. Live Stock Industry Com., 1917. President National Agricultural Society; member American Society Promotion Agricultural Science, etc. Republican. Conglist. Club: Saddle and Sirloin. Home: Somerset MI‡

SMITH, HUBERT WINSTON, educator; born Tex., May 18, 1907; s. Thomas and Myrtle (Hawkins) S.; A.B., U. Tex., 1927, M.B.A., 1931; student U. Edinburgh, 1936-38; LL.B., Harvard (Faculty scholarship), 1930, M.D. (Henry Cabot Jackson fellow 1939-41), 1941; m. Catherine Hall McKinley, Aug. 26, 1936; children—Charles McKinley, Alan Winston, Stephen Hall, James Jackson. Asso. Price Waterhouse & Co., accts., Boston, 1928-29; admitted to Tex. bar, 1930; asso. Thompson, Knight, Baker & Harris, Dallas, 1930-34; partner Smith & Carter, 1934-36; prof. law Jefferson U., eves. 1930-35; demonstrator anatomy, med. sch. U. Edinburgh, 1936-37; Research fellow Rockefeller Found., asso. med.-legal research, law and med. schs. Harvard, 1941-44, prof. legal medicine U. Ill., 1945-49; research prof. law and medicine, prof. law and legal medicine, dir. law-sci. program Tulane U., 1949-52; lecturer legal medicine, med. school La. State U., 1951-52; professor law, sch. law, prof. legal medicine, sch. medicine (Galveston), and dir. law-sci. inst. U. Tex., 1952-67; chancellor of Law-Science Acad., 1967-71; dir. inter-profl. studies Coll. Law U. Okla., Norman, also cons. prof. dept. psychiatry and behavioral scis., U. Okla. Med. Center, Oklahoma City, 1968-71; lectr. legal aspects of psychiatry Menninger Clinic and Found. Member Nat. Bd. Med. Examiners. Cons. legal medicine V.A. Hosp., Houston; sometime cons. forensic psychiatry U.S. Pub. Health Hosp., Ft. Worth and V.A. Hosp., Gulfport, Tex. Mem. Coroner's Commn., Orleans Parish. Nat. adv. Am. Assn. Psychiatric Treatment Criminal Offenders; founder Law-Sci. Movement, Law-Sci. Short Course for trial lawyers; chmn. com. mental states and law La. State Inst., 1951-52. Mem. White House Conf. Problems Children and Youth, 1951; mem. com. on reform of Law of Evidence (Tex.); com. on cooperation of Tex. State Bar with med. profession. Served as lt. officer charge legal med. br. Bur. Medicine and Surgery, U.S.N., 1944-45. Awarded Sir Wright Smith prize in med. botany, 1937; Foster award, med. sch. Harvard, 1938; Milton award in sci. research, 1942-43; Gold medal, citation Law-Science Academy, 1959. Research fellow Rockefeller Found., 1941-44; fellow and chancellor Law Sci. Acad. Am.; pres. Law Sci. Found. Am. Mem. Nat. Bd. Med. Examiners. Fellow Internat.Academy Trial Lawyers and the New York Academy of Medicine; member Am. Soc. Science, Research, Mass. Soc. C.P.A. (hon.), Law-Sci. Acad. Am., Law-Sci. Found. Am. (pres.), Scribes, Phi Beta Kappa, Beta Alpha Psi, Beta Gamma Sigma, Order of Coif, Phi Delta Phi. Episcopalian. Author numerous monographs and articles in medico-legal field. Editor: National Symposia on Scientific Proof and Relations of Law and Medicine, 1941, 46; asso. editor Jour. Criminal Law and Criminology, 1946-60. Editor-in-chief, coordinator, contbr. Symposium on Law and Science, 1969. Home: Norman OK Died July 9, 1971; buried Sparkman-Hillcrest Meml. Park, Dallas TX

SMITH, HUGH ALLISON, coll. prof.; b. Henry County, Mo., May 8, 1873; s. Joseph H. and Ellen (Nichols) S.; A.B., U. of Mo., 1897, A.M., 1898; U. of Paris, 1902, 1907-08; Harvard, 1904-05; m. Edna Carpenter, June 12, 1899; children—Frances Eugenia, Edna Louise, Alison. Teaching fellow, U. of Mo., 1897-98; asst. prof. modern langs., 1899, asso. prof., 1901, prof. French, 1903, Colorado Coll., Colorado Springs, Colo.; prof. of French and chmn. of dept. of French and Italian, U. of Wis., 1905-48, emeritus. Mem. exec. council Alliance Francaise; mem. bd. Am. Univ. Union; lecturer, The Sorbonne, Paris, 1922, 30; dir. Am. University Union, Paris, 1929-30. Mem. Modern Lang. Assn. America, Soc. Amicale Gaston Paris, Soc. des anciens Textes, Paris, Phi Beta Kappa. Chevalier Legion of Honor (France). Asso. editor Romanic Review. Democrat. Presbyterian. Club: University. Author: Main Currents of the Modern French Drama, 1925. Editor: Les Sept Sages de Rome, 1911; French texts, Pierrille, 1909; Smith and Greenleaf French Reader, 1920; Dumas' Demi-monde, 1921, Fils Naturel, 1923, and Dame aux Camelias, 1924; Brieux's Blanchette, 1923; Curel's la Nouvelle Idole; Maeterlinck's Pelleas et Melisande, 1924. Contbr. to Romance philology and lit. jours. Home: Madison 5 WI‡

SMITH, J. EMIL, newspaper editor and publisher; b. Springfield, Ill., Sept. 1, 1880; s. John S. and Anna C. (Carlson) S.; ed. Springfield pub. schs.; m. Lyda M. Mockhee, July 9, 1900 (dev. Nov. 1955); children—Emil Griffiths (dec.), Mayme Jeannette (Mrs. C. A. Schryver). Reporter Springfield News, 1896; later with Morning Monitor and Ill. State Register; became editor Ill. State Journal, 1930; publisher Ill. State Jour. and Register, 1942-55, pub. emeritus, 1955-69; v.p., dir. Copley Press, Inc., 1953-69; columnist Making Conversation, Ill. State Jour., 1931-59; dir. Security Fed. Savs. & Loan Assn. Clk., City of Springfield, 1907-11, commr. of finance, 1915-27, mayor, 1927-30. Mem. Ill. Def. Council, Ill. Planning Commn. Republican. Presbyterian. Elk, Eagle, Rotarian. Club: Sangamo. Home: Springfield IL Died Apr. 14, 1969; buried Oak Ridge Abbey, Springfield IL

SMITH, J. NEIL, investment co. exec.; b. Pleasant Hill, Mo., Jan. 30, 1895; s. Granville Moody and Annie Bell (Pinnell) S.; grad. Phillips Andover Acad.; Ph.B., Yale Sheffield Sch., 1916; m. Frances Bachman, Sept. 22, 1946; children—J. Neil, Deborah (Mrs. John Lieper Allen), Melissa (Mrs. Max LaPrelle Elliott), Ronald N. Vice president of the United Funds, Inc., Kansas City, Mo., vice pres., dir. Continental Research Corp., Kansas City, Mo.; vice pres. of Waddell and Reed, Inc.; mem. bd. dirs. Employers Reins. Corp., Washington Water Power Co. Trustee William Jewell Coll.; bd. dirs. Helping Hand Inst. Clubs: Kansas City Country; University. Home: Kansas City MO Died Nov. 30, 1971.

SMITH, JOHN ELIJAH, church official; b. Jefferson Twp., Hillsdale County, Mich., Aug. 9, 1871; s. Charles Henry and Amelia (Barbour) S.; student Alma Coll., 1889-90; A.B., Kalamazoo Coll., 1894; D.D., 1921; grad. Newton Theol. Instn., 1897; m. Lotta Blanche Kroll, Aug. 13, 1897; children—Priscilla Margaret (Mrs. Arthur J. Hutton), Gordon Kroll, Arthur Barbour. Ordained ministry Bapt. Ch., 1897; pastor Keene, N.H., 1897-1902, Kalamazoo, 1902-13; in business, Spokane,

Wash., 1913-16; pastor First Ch., Spokane, 1916-23; exec. sec. Mich. Bapt. Conv., 1923-28; editor Mich. Baptist, 1923-28; exec. sec. N.Y. Bapt. State Conv., 1928-36; editor Baptist New Yorker, 1928-36. Mem. bd. mgrs. E. Wash. and N. Idaho Bapt. Conv., 1917-23; mem. bd. promotion Northern Bapt. Conv., 1919; mem. bd. missionary corp., 1927-28; mem. survey com. Northern Bapt. Conv., 1927-29. Trustee Kalamazoo Coll., 1923-28, Hillsdale Coll., 1927, Keuka Coll, 1932-40. Republican. Kiwanian. Home: 106 DeWitt Road, Syracuse NY‡

SMITH, JOHN JOSEPH, banker; b. Bklyn., Feb. 11, 1896; s. William L. and Ellen A. (Burke) S.; student Alexander Hamilton Inst., N.Y. Inst. Banking; Bachelor Comml. Science, St. Johns Univ., 1960; m. Charlotte E. Peterson, Dec. 29, 1920. With Chem. Nat. Bank, N.Y.C., 1919-26; v.p. Citizens Bank of Bklyn., 1926-28; successively asst. v.p., v.p., regional v.p. for Bklyn. and Queens, Chem. Corn Exchange Bank, N.Y.C., 1928-56, chmn. adv. bd. for Bklyn., 1956-68; pres., trustee E. New York Savs. Bank, Bklyn., 1956-68. Treas. Democratic Exec. Com. Kings County, N.Y. Bd. dirs. Bklyn. Pub. Library. Served with inf. U.S. Army, World War I. Decorated Silver Star; recipient Conspicious Service Cross, State N.Y.; Silver Beaver award Boy Scouts Am. Mem. Bklyn. C. of C. (dir.). Club: Brooklyn (dir.). Home: Brooklyn NY Died Oct. 8, 1968.

SMITH, JOHN SLOAN, transp. co. exec.; b. Marion County, Ind., Jan. 20, 1907; s. Lynn Burnside and Marie (Sloan) S.; student John B. Stetson U., 1925-26, U. Cin., 1927; m. Joan L. Wall, June 4, 1930; children—John Burnside, Nancy Ann. Engr., Noblitt Sparks Industries, 1927-29; v.p. charge engring. Aero Mayflower Transit Co., 1929-45, v.p., gen. mgr., 1945-54, pres., gen. mgr., from 1954; pres. Hogan Transfer & Storage Corp., Aero Mayflower Transit Co., Ltd. Can.; v.p. Ind. Ins. Co., Cooling Grumme Memford Co. (both Indpls.); dir. Advisors Fund, Inc. (N.Y.C.), Central Adjusting Co., Consol. Ins. Co., Premium Finance Co. Mem. Am. Trucking Assn. (com. of 100), Household Goods Carriers Bur. (past pres., dir.), Nat. Def. Transp. Assn. (life), Sigma Nu. Mason (Shriner). Clubs: Rotary, Columbia, Indianapolis Athletic, Athenaeum Turners, Meridian Hills Indianapolis IN Died Apr. 1969.

SMITH, JOHN WALTER, railway exec.; b. Balt., July 20, 1900; s. James Goldfinch and Christina (Reif-Schneider) S.; B.S., C.E., U. Maryland, 1921; married May Elizabeth Appel, September 4, 1926; children—Anne (Mrs. John Westcott Stewart), John Walter. Engring. insp., constrn. work S.A.L. Ry. Co., 1924, maintenance of way dept., 1925, div. engr., 1932, operating and engring. dept., 1936-44, asst. chief engr., asst. gen. supt., 1944-46; asst. to pres. S.A.L. R.R. Co., 1946-50, v.p. in charge adminstrn., 1950-52, became pres. dir., 1952, also mem. exec. com., now chmn. Seaboard Coast Line R.R. Co.; chmn. exec. bd. Cinchfield R.R. Co.; chmn., dir. Gainesville Midland R.R. Co., Tavares & Gulf R.R. Co.; pres., dir. Southeastern Investment Co., Duval Connecting R.R. Co.; dir., mem. exec. com. Jacksonville Terminal Co. (Fla.), Louisville & Nashville R.R. Co.; dir. Richmond, Fredericksburg & Potomac R.R. Co., Richmond-Washington Co., Richmond Terminal Co., State Planters Bank of Commerce and Trusts, Tampa & Gulf Coasts R.R. Co. Trustee Richmond Meml. Hosp. Mem. Am. Ry. Engring. Assn., Nat. Defense Transp. Assn. Episcopalian. Clubs: University, Traffic, Links (N.Y.C.); Princess Anne Country (Virginia Beach, Va.); Country of Virginia, Commonwealth, Forum (Richmond, Va.); Metropolitan (Washington); Burning Tree (Bethesda, Md.); Deerwood, Hidden Hills (Jacksonville, Fla.); Oglethorpe (Savannah, Ga.); Pinehurst (N.C.) Country. Home: Richmond VA Died May 3, 1972; buried Westhampton Meml. Park, Richmond VA

SMITH, JOSEPH EARL, economist; b. Howard, Kan., Sept. 23, 1888; s. Henry L. and Anna Dilla (Raper) S.; A.B., Cotner Coll., Neb., 1908; B.A. (Rhodes scholar from Neb.), Oxford Univ., 1911; A.M., U. of Neb., 1914; Ph.D., Wallas Coll. England, 1930; m. Mary E. Boyer, Nov. 22, 1939. Prof. of economics, Hiram Coll., Ohio, 1920-37; prof. economics, Youngstown (O.) Coll., 1937-48, dean, 1949-70. Served at lt., inf., U.S. Army, World War I; area dir., War Manpower Commn., World War II. Mem. Am. Econ. Assn. Home: North Jackson OH Died Aug. 28, 1970; buried Hillside Cemetery Cortland OH

SMITH, JOSEPH FIELDING, church ofcl.; b. Salt Lake City, July 19, 1876; s. Joseph Fielding and Julina (Lambson) S.; grad. Latter-day Saints Coll., 1897; m. Louie Shurtliff, Apr. 26, 1898 (dec.); children—Josephine, Julina; m. 2d, Ethel Reynolds, Nov. 2, 1908 (dec.); children—Emily, Naomi, Lois, Joseph Fielding, Amelia, Lewis W., George R., Douglas A., Milton E.; m. 3d, Jessie Evans, Apr. 12, 1938 (dec. 1971). Counselor in the first presidency and pres. Council of the Twelve, Ch. Jesus Christ Latter-day Saints, 1951-72, mem. church bd. edn., 1918. Dir. Zion's First National Bank, Beneficial Life Ins. Co. Mem. loan com., mem. bd. Brigham Young U. Mem. Geneal. Soc. Author: Essential in Church History, 1922; The Way to Perfection, 1931; The Progress of Man, 1936; Life of Joseph F. Smith, 1938; Signs of the Times, 1942; Restoration of All Things, 1945; Church History and Modern Revelations (2 vols.), 1947-50; Man: His Origin and Destiny, 1954; Doctrines of Salvation (3 vols.), 1954; Answers to Gospel Questions (5 vols.), 1957; Take Heed to Yourself, 1966. Home: Salt Lake City UT Died July 2, 1972.

SMITH, JULIUS CLARENCE, lawyer; b. Greenville, S.C., Dec. 17, 1889; s. Clarence A. and Belle (Willingham) S.; A.B., Wake Forest (N.C.) Coll., 1911, LL.B., 1915; m. Lila Keith, Oct. 26, 1916 (dec.);children—Julius Clarence III, Keith; married 2d, Pattie Mae Hardson, March 5, 1958. Admitted to N.C. bar, 1915, and in practice, Greensboro; mem. Smith, Moore, Smith, Schell & Hunter; specializes ins. law and adminstrv. law; v.p., gen. counsel, dir., mem. exec. and finance coms. Jefferson Standard Life Ins. Co., 1933-55, ret., dir., mem. exec. com. Pres. C. of C., 1934-35; life mem. N.C. Federal Judicial Conf. Mem. Am. Bar Assn. (mem. ho. of delegates, 1936-39; mem. special com. on administrative law, 1935-46; mem. Council, Sect. Administrative law, 1946-50), N.C. State Bar (pres. 1935-37), Assn. Life Ins. Counsel, Am. Life Conv. (legal sect.), Am. Coll. Trial Lawyers, S.A.R. Democrat. Presbyn. Clubs: Linville (N.C.) Country; Port Royal Beach (Naples, Fla.); Rotary, Greensboro Country. Author articles on ins. and adminstrv. law. Home: Greensboro NC Died June 18, 1968.

SMITH, LEONA JONES (MRS. ROBERT JAMES SMITH), research psychologist; b. Granville, N.Y., Nov. 28, 1912; d. Owen P. and Katherine (Owen) Jones; B.E., State U. N.Y., Albany, 1948; M.S., Union Coll., 1957; Ph.D., N.Y. U., 1963; m. Robert James Smith, Aug. 1, 1936; children—Robert W., Sally E. (Mrs. James D. McNeill). Tchr., Castleton Union Sch., Castleton-on-Hudson, N.Y., 1933-36; research asst. Union Coll. Character Research Project, Schenectady, 1947-57; research psychologist, 1957-69; research cons. YMCA, religious denominations. Program writer Young Mothers' Council Am. Mothers, 1964-69. Mem. Am. Psychol. Assn., Nat. Council on Family Relations, Sociedad Interamerican de Psicologia, Soc. for Sci. Study of Religion, Religious Edn. Assn., Sigma Xi. Author: Dynamic Luxuries of Great Homes, 1961; Let Your Husband Be a Man, Your Wife a Woman, 1961; (with Ernest M. Ligon) The Marriage Climate, 1963; Guiding the Character Development of the Preschool Child, 1968. Home: Albany NY Died Dec. 29, 1969; buried Ilion Cemetery Ilion NY

SMITH, LEVI PEASE, banker; b. Burlington, Vt., Aug. 30, 1885; s. Charles P. and Anna (Pease) S.; Bachelor of Arts, University of Vermont, LL.D., 1950; LL.B., Harvard University; m. Julia Pease, June 20, 1914; children—Frederick Plimpton, Robert Pease, Levi Pease, Jr. v.p. Burlington Savings Bank, 1917-34, pres., 1935-58, chmn. board, 1959-70; director Vermont Broadcasting Corp. Mem. Vt. House of Reps., 1923-24; state senator, Vt., 1925-26, 1927-28, 1929-30. Chmn. Vt. State Banking Advisory Bd., 1935-39. Mem. Administrative Council Nat. Assn. Mut. Savs. Banks, 1934-42, pres., 1942-43, mem. com. fed. taxation. State chmn. U.S. Savs. Bonds Div.; pres. Vt. State Bankers Assn., 1929. Mem. exec. council Am. Bankers Assn., 1930-33, 1943-44, administrative com., 1943-44; econ. policy commn., 1944-50. Pres., dir. Converse Home (Burlington, Vt.), Club: St. Botolph Burlington VT Died June 18, 1970.

SMITH, LLOYD DEWITT, designing engr.; b. Howell, Mich., Aug. 14, 1873; s. George Augustus and Henrietta Elizabeth (Savery) S.; ed. pub. schs. of Detroit, Mich.; m. Bessie King, Jan. 31, 1900 (divorced 1903); children—Lloyd Harold (dec.), Kenneth Homer; m. 2d Mabel E. Gale, May 8, 1915. Designing engineer, Murphy Iron Works, Detroit, 1893-1907; pres. Smith Chandelier Co.; established own bus. under name of Smith Chandelier Co., Detroit, Mich., 1907, ret. 1920. Mem. Gen. Soc. Mayflower Des. (dep. gov. gen.), S.A.R. (vice pres. general Nat. Soc., 1946-48), Soc. War of 1812 (pres. Mich. chapter 1946), Detroit Hist. Soc. Episcopalian. Mason (32 deg.), Home: 731 Grand Marais Blvd., Grosse Pointe 30 MI‡

SMITH, LLOYD WADDELL, investment securities; b. Florham Park, N.J., May 18, 1870; s. George Washington and Susan Alice (Waddell) S.; prep. edn., Morris Acad., Morristown, N.J., and Phillips Andover (Mass.) Acad.; Ph.B., Yale, 1895; LL.B., Harvard, 1898; m. Helen S. Norton, Feb. 15, 1917. Began as jr. clk., N. W. Harris Co., Chicago, 1898, became partner, 1909; pres. and chmn. bd. Harris, Forbes & Co., N.Y. City, 1923-31; became dir. and chmn. governing bd. Chase, Harris, Forbes Corpn., 1931. Trustee Washington Assn. of N.J. Mem. Phi Delta Phi, Book and Snake. Republican. Presbyn. Clubs: University, Yale, Recess, Bankers, Broad Street, Braidburn Country. Collector of Americana and Washingtoniana. Home: Madison NJ Office: 60 Cedar St., New York NY*‡

SMITH, LOUIE HENRIE, chief in charge publications of Ill. Soil Survey; b. Crystal Lake, Ill., Apr. 15, 1872; s. Charles Watson and Ann (Robinson) S.; B.S., U. of Illinois, 1897, M.S., 1899; Ph.D., U. of Halle, Germany, 1907; m. Bessie I. Morgan, June 18, 1914. Assistant chemist, 1899-1903, chief asst. chemist, 1903-05, Ill. Agrl. Expt. Station (U. of Ill.); asst. prof. plant breeding, U. of Ill., 1905-11, prof., 1911-20, chief in charge of publications of Soil Survey since 1920, and acting head agronomy dept., 1913-14, 1918-19, emeritus prof. since 1940. Mem. Am. Chem. Soc., A.A.A.S., Am. Genetic Assn., Am. Soc. Agronomy, Ill. Acad. Science, Sigma Xi, Gamma Alpha, Phi Lambda Epsilon, Alpha Zeta, Gamma Sigma Delta. Universalist. Author of bulls. and other scientific contbns. along the lines of plant breeding and soil survey. Address: Rural Route No. 2 Urbana IL*‡

SMITH, LUTHER WESLEY, clergyman; b. Melrose, Mass., Apr. 19, 1897; s. Wesley Lorenzo and Harriet (Swan) S.; A.B., Harvard, 1920, B.D., Newton Theol. Instn., 1923; D.D., Syracuse Univ., 1938; Dr. Humanities, Keuka Coll., Keuka Park, N.Y., 1947; LL.D., Franklin College, Franklin, Indiana, 1948; honorary D.D., Denison University, 1950; married Harriet Vaughan, June 15, 1928; children—Luther Wesley, Harriet Ann, Laura Vaughan. Ordained ministry, Bapt. Ch., 1923; pastor First Church, Columbia, Mo., 1923-34, First Ch., Syracuse, N.Y., 1934-38. Pres. Mo. Bapt. Ministers' Conf., 1933-34; exec. sec. Am. Bapt. Pub. Soc., 1938-56; exec. sec. Am. Bapt. Bd. Edn., 1941-56; cons. sec. Am. Bapt. Bd. Edn. and Publ., 1956-63; founder, exec. sec. Am. Bapt. Assembly Green Lake, Wis., 1944-56, adviser bd. trustees, 1956-71. Hon. dir. Am. Bapt. Christian Higher Edn. Challenge Program, 1959-60; hon. chmn. Am. Bapt. Conv., Phila., 1962; member executive com. Baptist World Alliance, 1939-55; mem. exec. com. Gen. Commn. Chaplains Armed Service Personnel U.S.A., 1941-54; chmn. Bd. of Trustees of the Internat. Council Religious Edn., 1942-50; chmn. exec. bd. div. of Christian edn. Nat. Council Chs. of Christ in U.S.A., 1950-54; nat. dir. Am. Bapt. World Mission Crusade, 1945-47. Trustee Atlanta U., Spelman College, Benedict Coll., 1938-67. Served as ensign USNRF, World War I. Member of Phi Beta Kappa. Club: Rotary. Author: And So I Preached This, 1936. Contbg. author: Christian Journalism Today; various nat. religious mags. Nat. Religious Weekly Radio speaker Blue network 1942 Series Christian Edn. and Our Nat. Morale; speaker Am.'s Town Meeting of the Air, 1948; nat. radio preacher Columbia's Ch. of Air, 1950, 51. Home: St Petersburg FL Died Mar. 27, 1971; buried Green Lake WI

SMITH, MARJORIE C., educator; b. Troy, N.Y., Feb. 3, 1903; d. Seth William and Emma (Shook) Smith; A.B., (Albany) N.Y. State Coll.; A.M., Columbia. Mem. faculty Syracuse (N.Y.) U., asst. prof. edn., dean of women, 1949-69. Bd. dirs. Cazenovia Jr. Coll. Mem. American Penwomen (N.Y. br.), Nat. Assn. Deans of Women, Am. Assn. U. Women, N.Y. State Assn. Deans, Eastern N.Y. Assn. Tchrs. English (past pres.), Prof. Women's League of Syracuse, Am. Personnel and Guidance Assn., Eta Pi Upsilon, Pi Lambda Theta, Sigma Alpha Iota. Clubs: Corinthian (Syracuse); Zonta, Business and Professional Women's. Home: Syracuse NY Died Aug. 3, 1972.

SMITH, MARTHA ROSE KAPANTAES (MRS. ROBERT CLIFFORD SMITH), assn. exec.; b. Alexandria, Pa., Jan. 9, 1927; d. Nicholas Angelo and Odessa Mae (Wible) Kapantaes; student Flore Inst. Beautology and Cosmotology, 1943-44; m. Robert Clifford Smith, Mar. 21, 1945 (dec. Sept. 1962). Tchr., Flore Inst. Beautology and Cosmology, 1944-45; erec. sec. Southampton (N.Y.) C. of C., 1964-70. Asst. to pres. Hampton Animal Shelter, Southampton, 1954-63, dir. animal shelter projects, 1954-63. Methodist (pres. Woman's Soc. Christian Service 1952-54, mem. ofcl. bd. 1952-70, mem. pastoral relations com. 1966-70). Home: Southampton NY Died Feb. 13, 1970.

SMITH, (THOMAS) MAX, musical critic; b. at New York, Dec. 26, 1874; s. Normand and Elena (Imhof) S.; A.B., Yale, 1898; student Columbia Law Sch.; admitted to N.Y. bar, 1901, but never practiced. Mus. edn. begun at age of 8; among teachers were Eugene Meyer and Peter Schnecker, of New York, Tivendell, of Cassell, Germany, Richard Buchmayer, Stenz and Schoepfer, of Dresden, Prof. Samuel Sanford and Horatio W. Parker (q.v.), of Yale U., and Ernst Catenhusen, formerly of New York; in addition to theoretical studies has studied piano, violin, cello and singing; m. Seattle, Wash., Mary Hardy, May 15, 1909. Mus. editor and critic New York Press, 1903-16, New York American, 1916-19, 23. Republican. Conglist. Contbr. to mags. Clubs: Press (New York), Graduates (New Haven, Conn.). Home: Keene Valley Essex Co NY‡

SMITH, MCGREGOR, utilities exec.; born at Cooksville, Tennessee, June 5, 1899; son of Mary Rutledge and Graeme (McGregor) S.; B.S. in C.E., U. of Tenn., 1921; student Vanderbilt U., Nashville, 1926-27; m. Elizabeth Wilson, Nov. 12, 1924; children—McGregor, Wilson. Assistant engr. Tenn. R.R. & Pub. Utilities Commn., 1921-22, engr., 1922-26; mgr. South New Orleans Light & Tracton Co., 1926-27; v.p. and gen. mgr. La. Power & Light Co., Algiers, La., 1928-36, pres. and gen. mgr., 1936-39; v.p. and gen. mgr. Fla. Power & Light Co., 1939, pres., 1939-54, chmn. bd., 1954-72. Mem. Phi Gamma Delta. Presbyn. Mason. Clubs: County (Coral Gables); Biscayne Yacht (Miami). Home: Coral Gables FL Died June 1972.

SMITH, MERLE NEGLEY, clergyman; b. Lake City, Ia., Dec. 11, 1872; s. William Thompson and Amelia (Jack) S.; grad. Epworth (Ia.) Sem., 1888; A.B., Cornell Coll., Mt. Vernon, Ia., 1894, D.D., 1906, LL.D., 1924; B.D., Drew Theol. Sem., Madison, N.J., 1898; LL.D., U. of Southern Calif., 1929; m. Mae Wolfe, July 19, 1898 (deceased, 1945); children—Mae Isobel, Esther-Merle. Teacher and registrar, Drew Theological Seminary, 1898-1902; ordained ministry M.E. Ch., 1900; pastor Ackley, Ia., 1902-05, Marshalltown, 1905-09, Colorado Springs, Colo., 1909-16, Pasadena, Calif., 1916-37. Served with Y.M.C.A. at Presidio, San Francisco, and overseas, 1917-18. Trustee U. of Southern Calif. Director of the North American Holding Corporation. Del. to five gen. confs. Meth. Ch. Mem. Sigma Nu, Phi Beta Kappa. Mason, K.P. Clubs: New Century, Twilight. Home: 1680 E. California St., Pasadena 5 CA‡

SMITH, MERRIMAN, newspaper corr.; b. Savannah, Ga., Feb. 10, 1913; s. Albert C. and Juliet Worth (Merriman) S.; student Oglethorpe U., 1931-34, L.H.D., 1964; LL.D., Knox Coll. 1968; m. Eleanor Doyle Brill, 1937 (div. 1966); children—Merriman, Timothy, Allison; m. Gailey L. Johnson, 1966; 1 dau., Gillean. Sports writer Atlanta Georgia-American, 1932-33; staff Sunday mag. Atlanta Jour., 1934-35; mng. editor Athens (Ga.) Daily Times, 1935-36; staff correspondent UPI, 1936-70, White House Corr. since 1941; accompanied Pres. Roosevelt on wartime trips in and out of U.S. with Pres. Truman at Potsdam Conf.; was at Warm Springs, Ga. at time of Roosevelt's death and received Nat. Headliners award for coverage of story, 1945; with Pres.-elect Eisenhower in Korea, 1952; with Pres. Eisenhower at Bermuda Big Three conf., 1953, also Paris NATO Council meeting, 1957, 1959 Asian tour, 1960 Summit in Paris; with President Kennedy to DeGaulle and Khrushchev meetings, 1961, Pres. Johnson on all major foreign meetings, with President in Europe and Asia. Appeared TV panelist on Jack Parr Show, Who Said That?, Meet The Press, Face the Nation, Reporters' Roundup; Merv Griffin Show, 1965-66, 69, A View from the White House, 1966-67, 69. Recipient award distinguished service journalism, U. Mo., 1963, U. Cal. at Los Angeles, 1964; Pulitizer prize journalism, 1964, Presdl. Medal of Freedom, 1969. Mem. White House Corrs. Assn. (pres. 1944-45), Pi Kappa Phi. Club: National Press (Washington). Author: Thank You, Mr. President, 1946; A President Is Many Men, 1948; Meet Mister Eisenhower, 1955; A President's Odyssey, 1961; The Good New Days, 1962. Contbr. N.Y. Times, Sunday mag., This Week mag., Holiday, Life mags. Home: Washington DC Died Apr. 13, 1970; buried Arlington Nat. Cemetery, Arlington VA

SMITH, NATHANIEL WAITE, lawyer; b. Providence, R.I., Nov. 18, 1873; s. Nathaniel Waite and Emily Frances (Cole) S.; A.B., Yale, 1896; LL.B., New York Law Sch., 1898; m. Ellen Howard Weeden, Sept. 23, 1905; children—Mary Weeden (Mrs. Rockwell King Du Moulin), Nathaniel W., Jr. Began practice at Providence, 1899; asst. atty., atty. and counsel for R.I. of N.Y., N.H.&H. R.R. Co., 1903-18, gen. atty., 1918-20; gen. counsel R.I. Co., 1907-14; mem. Swan, Keeney & Smith since 1920. Asst. judge adv. general R.I. Militia and R.I. N.G., 1905-17; lt. gov. of R.I., 1925-27. Mem. Am. and R.I. State bar assns., R.I. Hist. Soc., Alpha Delta Phi. Republican. Unitarian. Mason (K.T.). Clubs: Providence Art, Turks Head, Hope, Agawam Hunt (Providence). Home: South Kingstown, R.I. Office: 911 Turks Head Bldg., Providence 3 RI‡

SMITH, NICOL HAMILTON, chemist; b. Phila., Pa., Apr. 20, 1899; s. Frank G. and Jeannie M. (McPherson) S.; B.S., U. of Pa., 1923, M.S., 1924, Ph.D., 1927; m. Agnes Morton, December 31, 1927; 1 dau., Isabelle M. Instr. U. of Pa., 1924-27; chief chemist Solidon Products, Inc., Phila., 1927-32; with Franklin Inst. Phila., 1932-70, asso. dir., 1932-50, exec. director labs., 1950-53, dir., 1953-70. Sr. tech. aide, N.D.R.C., 1942-44. Presdl. Certificate of Merit, World War II. Mem. Am. Chem. Soc., Am. Physical Soc., Phi Beta Kappa, Sigma Xi, Tau Beta Pi. Mason. Home: Huntingdon Valley PA Died Aug. 21, 1970.

SMITH, NORMAN KEMP, college prof.; b. at Dundee, Scotland, 1872; M.A., U. of St. Andrews, Scotland, 1893, D.Phil., 1901; studied univs. of Jena, Berlin and Paris. Lecturer in philosophy, U. of Glasgow, 1895-06; Stuart prof. psychology, 1906-13. McCosh prof. philosophy, 1913—. Princeton U. Author: Studies in the Cartesian Philosophy, 1901. Address: Broadmead, Princeton NJ‡

SMITH, NORMAN MURRAY, educational adminstrator; born Williston, S.C., November 16, 1883; son Dr. Winchester C. and Eugenia Kanapau (Murray) S.; graduate U.S. Naval Academy, 1906; C.E., Rensselaer Poly. Inst., 1909; grad. Naval War Coll., 1926; hon. Dr. Eng. Rensselaer Poly. Inst., 1939; m. Genevieve Thompson, June 11, 1921. Around the world as midshipman on U.S.S. Colorado, transferred as jr. lieut. Civ. Engr. Corps, Apr. 20, 1907; promoted through grades to rear adm., Dec. 3, 1933; chief of Bur. of Yards and Docks and chief civil engr. of the Navy, 1933-38. Engaged on constrn. and maintenance of Training Sta. (Great Lakes, Ill.), Navy Yards of Puget Sound and Mare Island; built naval base, Pearl Harbor, 1914-17; built plants, hospitals, dredged harbors and developed waterfronts in 6th and 11th Naval Dists., World War I; duty in naval dists. and Bur. Yards and Docks, at San Diego, Norfolk, Washington, and Boston, 1913-33; built air sta. and all naval establishments within San Diego Naval Base, 1918-23; adminstr. Works Progress Adminstrn., 1935-38; retired Dec., 1937; returned to active duty with Naval Constrn. Battalions, Camp Parks, Calif., 1942; ret., 1945; pres. Univ. of South Carolina, 1946-52. Mem. Am. Soc. C.E., Am. Mil. Engineers, Nat. Soc. Professional Engrs., Mil. Order of the Carabao, Theta Xi. Democrat. Mason, K.T. Clubs: Athenian (Oakland, Calif.); Union (Boston); Arlington (Portland, Ore.); Army and Navy, Army-Navy Country (Washington); Chevy Chase, Cuyamaca (San Diego, Calif.). Home: Williston SC Died Nov. 1968.

SMITH, PAUL EDWARD, educator; b. Altoona, Pa., June 20, 1908; s. Thomas Paul and Eva Rachel (Brumbaugh) S.; B.A., Dickinson Coll., 1930; M.A., Am. U., 1937; Ph.D., Cath. U., 1942; m. Lucile Merritt Blackwell, June 12, 1935; children—Paul Edward, Charles Merritt. Instr. English and Latin, Dickinson Jr. Coll., 1930-34; instr. English, Am. U., 1934-38; fellow Folger Shakespeare Library, Washington, 1934-36; instr., then asst. prof. English, U. Md., 1938-43; successively specialist, asst. dir., then dir., div. internat. ednl. relations, U.S. Office Edn., 1943-52; successively asst. dir., program officer, Iraq, regional tng. officer Near East and Africa, Beirut, ICA Dept. State, 1952-56; sec. com. internat. relations N.E.A., 1956-68. Del., sec. N.E.A. delegation World Confedn. Orgns. Teaching Profession, Manila, 1956, Frankfurt, 1957, Rome, 1958, Washington, 1959, Amsterdam, 1960, New Delhi, 1961, Stockholm, Sweden, 1962, Rio de Janeiro, 1963, Paris, 1964, Addis Ababa, 1965, Seoul, Korea, 1966; mem. exec. committee UN Association, 1964; member corporation United States Com. UNICEF, 1959-68; chmn. U.S. Com. Interchange Tchrs., 1945-52; sec. U.S. Selection Com. for Buenos Aires Conv. Students, 1943-49. Bd. dirs. Washington Fgn. Student Service, Am. Community Sch., Beirut. Mem. National Education Association, English Speaking Union (bd. govs. Washington), Am. Friends of Middle East, Omicron Delta Kappa, Phi Delta Kappa; honorary member All-Indonesian Teachers Union, Jamaica Union Tchrs., Union Panamanian Tchrs., Nat. Union Educators Ecuador, Trinidad-Tobago Teachers Union, Cuban Educational Association, Kenya National Union of Teachers, Phi Kappa Psi. Club: Cosmos (Washington). Author books and articles internat. ednl. relations. Home: Washington DC Died Mar. 15, 1968; buried Rock Creek Cemetery, Washington DC

SMITH, PAUL JORDAN, author; b. Wytheville, Va., Apr. 19, 1885; s. Rev. J. Wesley and Lucy (Jordan) S.; student Emory and Henry Coll., 1903-04; B.A., U. of Chattanooga, 1906, Litt. D., 1946; studied Lombard Coll., Galesburg, Ill., 1907-08, U. of Chicago, 1912, U. of Calif., 1914-15; m. Ethel Sloan Park, 1904 (dec.); m. 2d, Sarah Bixby, Mar. 30, 1916 (dec.); children—Isabel Jordan, Wilbur Jordan, Ralph Wendell; m. 3d, Dorothy Eads Wysor, June 26, 1934. Instr. in English, U. of Calif., 1914-16, instr. in English novel, extension liv., 1918-20; literary ed. of the Los Angeles Times, 1933-58; lectr. on American hist. novel, U. Cal., from 1958. Adv. bd. Huntington Hartford Found., 1950-65. Mem. Authors' League Am., Oxford Bibliog. Soc. Episcopalian. Clubs: Zamorano (Los Angeles); Authors' (London). Author books, latest being: Burton's of Melancholy and Burtoniana, 1959; The Road I Came, 1960; Poetry from Hidden Springs, 1962; also editor or compiler several books; contbr. to newspapers and mags. Home: Los Angeles CA Died June 17, 1971; buried Newbern VA

SMITH, PHILIP E., anatomist; b. De Smet, S.D., Jan. 1, 1884; s. John E. and Elmira (Stratton) S.; B.S., Pomona Coll., 1908; M.S., Cornell U., 1910, Ph.D., 1912; Sc.D., Princeton, 1948, Pomona Coll., 1950, Columbia, 1954; m. Irene Patchett, 1913; children—Frederika Patchett, Philip Bartlett. Asst. instr. in anatomy Cornell U., 1910-11, instr., 1911-12; instr. in anatomy, U. Cal., 1912-17, asst. prof., 1917-21, asso. prof., 1921-26; asso. prof. anatomy, Stanford, 1926-27; prof. anatomy, Columbia, 1927-52, prof. emeritus, 1952-70; research associate Stanford University, 1956-70. Recipient Charles Mickle fellowship, 1940, E. R. Squibb award, 1942. Mem. Am. Assn. Anatomist (pres. 1940-42), Am. Physiol. Soc., Soc. Exptl. Biology and Medicine (pres. 1937-38), Assn. Study Endocrina Glands (pres. 1939-40), Harvey Soc. (pres. 1938-40), French Legion of Honor, Nat. Acad. Sci., Sigma Xi. Democrat. Co-author Florence MA Died Dec. 1970.

SMITH, R(OBERT) BLACKWELL, JR., educator, pharmacologist; b. Petersburg, Va., Nov. 2, 1915; s. Robert Blackwell and Mary Lavinia (Ridout) S.; S.B., Med. Coll. of Va., 1937; S.M., U. of Fla., 1938; Ph.D., University of Chicago, 1941; LL.D., Hampden Sydney College, 1966; m. to Esther Bergliot Ostrem, Sept. 6, 1942; children—Peter Blackwell, Susan (Mrs. George Cabell III), Nan. Grad. scholar U. of Fla., 1937-38; univ. fellow in pharmacol., U. of Chgo., 1938-41; pharmacol., div. pharm., U.S. Food and Drug Adminstrn., Washington, 1941-45, acting chief, 1945; lectr. to full prof. pharmacology Med. Coll. Va., 1945-57, dean sch. of pharmacy 1947-56, asst. pres., 1954-56, pres., 1956-68; 1st provost Med. Coll. Va., health scis. div. Va. Commonwealth U., 1968-69, prof. pharmacology, 1969-71; cons. pharmacol., 1947-71; nat. cons. pharmacology surg. gen. USAF, 1956-62. Dir., treas. U. Center in Va., 1960-71. Mem. com. food protection NRC, 1950-71; chmn. pres.'s coun. Va. State Instns. of Higher Edn. 1959-62; chmn. joint WHO-FOA expert com. on food additives, Geneva, 1957; member WHO expert adv. panel on health lab. methods, 1958-71. Mem. Am. Soc. for Pharmacol. and Exptl. Therapeutics, A.A.A.S., Sigma Xi, Phi Kappa Phi, Rho Chi. Democrat. Baptist. Researcher in toxicology and biol. assay. Clubs: Torch, Commonwealth. Rotary; Country. Home: Richmond VA Died Oct 8, 1971.

SMITH, RALPH ELIOT, plant pathologist; b. Boston, Mass., Jan. 9, 1874; s. Obed F. and Emily M. (Simpson) S.; B.S., Mass. Agrl. Coll., 1894; U. of Munich, Germany, 1898; m. Jessie A. Carroll, of Wilmington, O., June 28, 1896; 1 son, William Carroll (dec.). Instr. in botany, 1894-96, asst. prof., 1896-1903, Mass. Agrl. Coll.; asst. prof. plant pathology, 1903-08, asso. prof., 1908-11, prof. since July 1, 1911, U. of Calif. Republican. Mem. Am. Phytopathol. Soc., Societe Mycologique de France, A.A.A.S., Phi Sigma Kappa, Alpha Zeta, Sigma Chi, Phi Sigma. Club: Faculty (U. of Calif.) Home: 2721 Hillegass Av., Berkeley CA‡

SMITH, RALPH TYLER, senator; b. Granite City, Oct. 6, 1915; s. Alfred Thomas and Clara (Slattery) S.; A.B., Ill. Coll., 1937; J.D., Washington U., St. Louis, 1940; m. Mary Elizabeth Anderson, Oct. 23, 1942; 1 dau., Sharon Lynne. Dir. Greater Alton (Ill.) Assn. Commerce, 1964-66; chmn. bd. Bank of Alton, 1969-72; del. Ill. Republican Conv., 1954-69; mem. Ill. Ho. of Reps., 1955-69, majority whip, 1963, speaker of house, 1967-69; del., parliamentarian Ill. Rep. Conf., 1966; del. Rep. Nat. Conv., 1968; downstate campaign mgr. Carpentier for gov. Ill., 1964, Ogilvie for gov. Ill., 1968; mem. U.S. Senate from Ill., 1969-70. Served with USNR, 1942-46. Mem. Am., Ill., Madison County Alton, Wood River bar assns., V.F.W., Am. Legion. Presbyn. Elk, Eagle, Moose, Mason (Shriner), Optimist. Home: Alton IL Died Aug. 13, 1972; buried Edwardsville IL

SMITH, RALPH WINFIELD, insurance and investments; b. near Chicago, Ill., June 29, 1871; s. Charles D. and Jennie (Paddock) S.; student Ohio Wesleyan U.; m. Katherine Donovan, Mar. 25, 1903; 1 dau., Mrs. Alaine Claire Burr. Studied law while acting as confidential messenger-clerk for Gov. William McKinley of Ohio; admitted to the bar in Ohio, 1893, Ill., 1893, Colo., 1897, also U.S. Courts; practiced law until early in 1897, then apptd. mgr. and attorney of Colorado of American Bonding Co. of Baltimore; vice-pres. and mgr. western dept. same company, 1899-1904; vice-pres. Nat. Surety Corporation's Western Exec. Dept. with headquarters in Denver since 1904; underwriting and claim mgr. Employers Mutual Ins. Co. of Colo., 1915-39; retired. Mem. Bd. Pardons, Colo., 1903-10; alternate del. Rep. Nat. Conv., 1908, 12; del. Rep. Nat. Conv., 1916. Mem. State Bd. Capital Mgrs. of Colo., 1915-19; pres. and dir. Denver Motor Club, 1908-22; v.p. Am. Automobile Assn., 1908-16. During World War I served as U.S. Food Adminstr. for Denver; mem. Citizen's Recruiting Com. of Colo.; exec. chmn. League for Nat. Defense for Colo.; state inspector Am. Protective League of U.S. Dept. of Justice in charge of espionage activities; pres. One Hundred Percent Am. Loyalty Club of Colo. (1917-18). Life mem. U.S. Civil Legion; mem. Colo. and Denver bar assns., Sons of Revolution. Republican. Mason (K.T., 32 deg., Shriner). Clubs: Denver (life), Denver Press (life), Denver Country (charter member). Home: 1305 E. 7th Av. Office: Railway Exchange Bldg., Denver CO‡

SMITH, RAYMOND ABNER, coll. prof.; b. Gibson County, Ind., Jan. 14, 1875; s. William Franklin and Rosa Frances (Williams) S.; A.B., Butler U., Indianapolis, 1900, A.M., 1904; grad. student U. of Pa., 1902-03; B.D., Yale University, 1905; LL.D., Texas Christian University, 1944; m. Grace Jean Clifford, Dec. 27, 1905; children—Raymond Clifford, Marian Frances, Ralph Emerson. Prof. edn., Atlantic Christian Coll., Wilson, N.C., 1905-06, pres., 1916-20; mfg. business, 1906-13; supt. Beckley (W.Va.) Inst., 1913-16; prof. edn., Tex. Christian U., Fort Worth, since 1920, dir. sch. of edn. since 1923, dean since 1943. First sergeant, later 2d lieut., 159th Indiana Volunteer Infantry, Spanish-American War. Member A.A.A.S., N.E.A., Progressive Education Assn., Am. Assn. Univ. Profs., Nat. Soc. for Study of Edn., Nat. Soc. College Teachers of Edn., Nat. Soc. for Curriculum Study, Pi Gamma Mu. Club: Torch. Home: 2625 Cockrell Av., Fort Worth 9 TX‡

SMITH, REUBEN ROBERT, distillery co. exec.; b. N.Y.C., Oct. 17, 1900; s. Morris and Sadie (Getlar) S.; ed. pub. schs., N.Y.C.; m. Reda Garfield, June 23, 1929; 1 dau., Margot Jennifer. Advt. dir. Freed Eisman Radio

Corp., N.Y.C., 1923-27; with A. H. Geuting Co., Phila., 1928-31, dir., 1950-51; with A. S. Beck Shoe Corp., N.Y.C., 1932-33; staff Continental Distilling Corp., Phila., 1934-39, v.p., 1942-69; gen. mgr. Hanscom Baking Corp., N.Y.C., 1940-41; v.p. Publicker Distillers Products, Inc., marketing orgn. Old Hickory, Kinsey, W. A. Haller Distilleries, Phila., 1959-69, dir., 1960-69, v.p. J.A. Dougherty's Sons, Inc., Phila., 1963-69. One man show Phila. Art Alliance, 1957, Butler Inst. Am. Art, Youngstown, O., 1958, Pyramid Club, Phila., 1958, Art Found., Long Beach, N.J., 1960; dir. publicity Photog. Soc. Am. Silver Anniversary Convention, Phila., 1958; contbr. photographs numerous publs., including Photo Maxima, Internat. Ann., Popular Photography mag., art portfolio Galerie de France. Dir. Stevens Sch. for Girls, Chestnut Hill, Pa., 1953-55. Recipient prize for direct mail advt. Postage mag., 1927; gold medal merit for outstanding advt. Nat. Shoe Retailers Assn., 1928; honors for journalistic achievement Photog. Soc. Am., 1958, recipient photographic awards, 1957 and 1962. Mem. Contemporary Art Assn. (founder, exec. dir. 1948-50). Home: Philadelphia PA Died Mar. 27, 1969.

SMITH, ROBERT HAYS, b. at Oakville, Pa., January 13, 1877; s. of William and Charlotte Matilda (Gelvin) S.; Ph.B., Dickinson Coll., Carlisle, Pa., 1898, A.M. and LL.B., 1900; m. Susan Nicol, of Stockton, Calif., June 24, 1908; 1 son, (Francis) Nicol. Admitted to Pa. bar, 1902, and began practice at Carlisle; moved to Coalinga, California, 1903, and practiced until 1907; pres. Bank of Coalinga, 1907-10; pres. Freehold Realty Co., Huntington Park Realty Co., Coalinga-Pacific Oil & Gas Co., Carson Patents Co., Ltd. Lt. col. on staff of Gov. James N. Gillett, 1906-11; in charge of refugees of San Francisco fire, Golden Gate Park, 1906. Trustee, incorporator, 1911, Sch. of Law, Dickinson Coll. Mem. Calif. Petroleum Miners' Assn. (an organizer; dir.), Am. Bar Assn., Calif. Bar Assn., Astron. Soc. of Pacific, Calif. Hist. Soc., Alumni Assn. of Dickinson Sch. of Law (v.p.). Republican. Presbyn. Clubs: Bohemian, Olympic (San Francisco); Burlingame Country, San Mateo-Burlingame Polo, Monterey Bay Golf Club (ex-pres.). Home: Burlingame CA Office: Mills Towers, San Francisco CA‡

SMITH, ROBERT PATERSON, oil co. exec.; b. Jan. 20, 1903; ed. The Ewart, Newton Stewart; m. Joyce Mary Whinney, 1935; 2 daus. With Asiatic Petroleum Co., Calcutta, India, 1926-27; with Burmah-Shell, India, 1928-52; with The Burmah Oil Co. Ltd., London, Eng., 1952-71, dir., 1955-71, asst. mng. dir., 1956, mng. dir., 1957-64, chmn., 1965-71. Home: Glasgow Scotland Died May 28, 1971.

SMITH, ROBERT SIDNEY, economist, educator; b. Waterbury, Conn., June 13, 1904; s. Leslie James and Laura (Rouse) S.; A.B., Amherst Coll., 1927, A.M., 1928; Ph.D. (Amherst Meml. fellow), Duke, 1932; m. Lucille Mulholland, Aug. 2, 1932; children—Frances (Mrs. James W. Vaughan, Jr.), Laurence. Instr., asst. prof., asso. prof., prof. econs. Duke, Durham, N.C., 1932-69, chmn. dept. econs., 1964-68, James B. Duke distinguished prof. econs., 1964-69; vis. prof. N.C. Coll., 1940, U. Costa Rica, 1945, U. San Carlos (Guatemala), 1949, Northwestern U., 1947, U. N.C., 1955-56, U. Buenos Aires, 1956, U. de Valle, Cali, Colombia, 1968; State Dept. lectr. 1955, 56, 57; Fulbright lectr., Chile, 1965. Latin Am. specialist Dept. State, 1955-57; mem. Nat. Def. Exec. Res., 1957-69. Hon. consul, Guatemala, 1955-63; recipient James Alexander Robertson Meml. prize Conf. Latin Am. History, 1963. Guggenheim Meml. fellow, 1942, Ford Found. Faculty Research fellow, 1959-60. Mem. Am., So. (pres. elect 1968-69) econ. assns., Econ. History Soc., Royal Econ. Soc., Inter-Am. Statis. Assn., Phi Beta Kappa, Alpha Kappa Psi. Author: The Spanish Guild Merchant: A History of the Consulado, 1250-1700, 1940; Mill on the Dan: A History of Dan River Mills, 1882-1950, 1960; contbg. author other books. Mem. editorial bd. Hispanic Am. Hist. Review, 1947-53, So. Econ. Jour., 1959-62, Atlantic Quar., 1960-68. Bus. History Rev., 1966-69; founder, editor History of Political Economy, 1967-69. Contbr. Ency. Brit., Ency. Social Sci., articles to profl. publs. Home: Durham NC Died Mar. 23, 1969; buried Maplewood Cemetery, Durham NC

SMITH, ROBINSON, author; b. Hartford, Conn., Dec. 27, 1876; s. James Allwood and Caroline Elizabeth (Robinson) S.; A.B., Yale, 1898, A.M., 1901; post-grad. work, Harvard, 1900; m. Martha Butler, of San Francisco, June 6, 1905 (died 1910); 1 dau., Lucinda Noble. Episcopalian. Author: The Soul-at-Arms and Other Poems, 1900; Dream and Drama (poems); 1910; Life of Cervantes, 1914; Food Values and the Rationing of a Country, 1918; Solution of the Synoptic Problem, 1920, 22; The Solution of the Homeric Question, 1923. Compiler: English Quotations, 1907; The Children's Bible, 1911; A Consecutive Life of Christ, 1911; The Flower of English Poetry, 1912; The Original Iliad, 1930. Translator: The Earliest Lives of Dante, 1901; Don Quijote, 1910, 14, 32. Working on Belgian relief com. in Belgium and France, 1914-19; maj. Am. Red Cross, 1919-20, service in Russia. Home: 31 bis rue de France, Nice France‡

SMITH, RUTH ANN COOK, book dealer, author; b. New York, Nov. 20, 1869; d. William and Augusta (Story) Cook; grad. Fremont (Neb.) Normal Sch., 1888, Central City (Neb.) M. E. Coll., 1890; m. May 29, 1907, H.A. Hammond Smith, artist. Teacher Neb. pub. schs., 1885-7, Beatrice, Neb., 1890-3; lecturer for New York Bd. Ed'n, 1903-7; prop'r of Knickerbocker Book Shop; dealer and publisher of natural history books. Contb'r to edn'l publs., mags. and newspapers. Author: Along Four-Footed Trails, 1904 P12. Residence: 212 E. 15th St. Office: 106 E 23d St New York NY‡

SMITH, S(AMUEL) L(EONARD), educator; b. McEwen, Tenn., Oct. 10, 1875; s. John Marshall and Ida Penelope (James) S.; A.B., Southwestern, Memphis, 1907, Ed.D., 1932; M.A., George Peabody Coll., Nashville, 1918; attended summer schs., U. of Chicago, 1906, Harvard, 1918; m. Rosa Reasley, Oct. 9, 1895; children—Ida Marie (Mrs. John Egbert Crain), John Beasley, Samuel Lisbeth (Mrs. Fred Murff). Began as rural school teacher in Tennessee, 1894-1900; co-principal McEwen Normal School, 1900-01; teacher of Latin and Greek, Elizabeth Training School, 1901-02; admitted to Tenn. bar, 1902; prin. Montgomery Acad., Clarksville, 1902-07; prin. high school and supt. Clarksville schs., 1907-14; state rural school supervisor and state agent of rural schools, 1914-20; dir. southern office, Julius Rosenwald Fund, Nashville, 1920-38; dir. pub. relations, George Peabody College, 1938-46, Provost, 1946-47, emeritus; chmn. Peabody Vet. Housing and Facilities Com., 1946-47; hon. president Tennessee Association Relief of Ex-Convicts; president Davidson County Anti-Tuberculosis Association; president Tennessee Tuberculosis Association; president Inter-State School Building Service; mem. of President's Conf. on The Economic Conditions of the South. Mem. N.E.A., Nat. Council on Schoolhouse Construction (former pres.). Nashville Chamber Commerce, American Bar Association, American Judicature Society, Phi Delta Kappa. Chief consultant Tennessee Civil Service Commission. Save the Children Federation. Democrat. Member Church of Disciples of Christ. Odd Fellow, K.P. Clubs: University, Commercial, Civitan. Contributor articles, Negro Public Schools in the South," in Southern Workman, July 1927, and Nov. 1928; Development of Health Education for Negro Teachers," Passing of Hampton Library School, " Library Facilities in Negro Secondary Schools," in Jour. of Negro Education, July 1937, Jan. 1940 and July 1940, respectively; also author Community School Plans" (for rural schs. in South); co-author Suggestions for Improvement and Beautification of School Plants"; (with Dr. Ray Hamon) School Plant Workshop Bulletin, 1945; Suggestions for Landscaping Rural Schs."; History of Tennessee Tuberculosis Association. Directed building of 5000 rural schs. in Southern states through aid of Julius Rosenwald Fund, the last being the Eleanor Roosevelt School at Warm Springs, Ga., dedicated by President Roosevelt, Nov. 18, 1937. Home: 1218 17th Av. S. Office: George Peabody College, Nashville 4 TN‡

SMITH, SAMRAY, editor; b. Crystal Lake, Mich., Sept. 28, 1914; s. Samra and Pearl Anne (Keicher) S.; A.B., Guilford Coll., 1934; M.A., Haverford Coll., 1935; A.B. in L.S., U. of N.C., 1939; m. Evelyn A. Zahig, Sept. 19, 1960. Instructor English, asst. to librarian Guilford Coll., 1936-38; asst. reference librarian Emory U. Library, 1940-41; librarian Inst. of Govt., U. N.C., 1941-42, mng. editor Popular Govt., 1942; head order sect. Va. State Library, 1946-49; librarian Gen. Library, Stephens Coll., 1949-52, acting librarian of coll., 1950-52; staff A.L.A., 1951-68, editor of publs., publishing dept., 1951-54, publications officer Assn. Coll. and Ref. Libraries, 1954-56, editor A.L.A. Bull., 1956-68, dir. information dept., 1963-68. Served as 1st Lt. USMCR, 1943-45. Mem. A.L.A. Club: Chicago Press. Home: Chicago IL Died Apr. 1968.

SMITH, THOMAS JEFFERSON, clergyman, educator; b. Omaha, Neb., May 2, 1877; s. Andrew and Ellen (Brady) S.; A.B., Creighton U., 1896; entered Soc. of Jesus, 1896; studied asceticism, St. Stanislaus Sem., Florissant, Mo., 1896-8, belles lettres, at same, 1898-1900, post-grad. philosophy and sciences, St. Louis U., 1900-3, A.M., 1902, divinity, at same, 1907-11. Prof. classics, St. Louis U., 1903-7; ordained R.C. priest, 1910; v.-p. St. Louis U., and dean Coll. of Arts, 1913-16; v.-p. St. Ignatius Coll., Cleveland, O., 1916-19, pres. since July 1919. Address: 1911 W. 30th St., Cleveland OH‡

SMITH, THOMAS NEWILL, educator; b. Trafford, Pa., Oct. 17, 1909; s. Dallas M. and Cynthia (Newill) S.; B.S., Juniata Coll., 1932; M.S., U. Pitts., 1938; m. Helen E. Holman, Jan. 27, 1946; children—Cynthia Sue, Bonnie Jean. Owner operator Smith Hat Shop and Smith Paint Co., Pitts., 1932-37; tchr., Greenburg (Pa.) High School, 1937-39; coordinator distributive edn., Sharon, Pa., 1940-41; personnel dir. North Africa and Italy, also regional dir. North Italy for A.R.C., 1942-46; asst. prof. Mich. Tech. U., Houghton, Mich., 1947-49; supt. bus. edn. W.Va., 1949-51; prof., head Sch. Bus. Adminstrs. Mich. Tech. U., from 1951. Adv. council Econ-Soc. Mich. Pres. Upper Mich. Tourist Assn. Decorated Medal of Freedom. Rotarian. Home: Dollar Bay MI Deceased.

SMITH, THOMAS WILLIAM, clergyman; b. Jacksonville, Ill., Dec. 8, 1865; s. Thomas William and Annie Eliza (Sisson) S.; A.B., Illinois Coll., 1887; Yale U., 1887-88; grad. Union Theol. Sem., New York, 1894; D.D., Ill. Coll., 1908; m. Jane L. Russel, Sept. 15, 1904 (died 1906); m. 2d, Grace Millard French, Aug. 31, 1911;children—(by 1st marriage) Jane Russel; (by 2d marriage) William Thomas. Taught in Ill. Coll., 1888-90; ordained Presbyn. ministry, 1894; pastor Lenox (later St. Nicholas Av.) Ch., New York, 1894-1914, Arlington Av. Ch., E. Orange, N.J., 1914-18; Y.M.C.A. service overseas, 1918-19; minister, Westminster Presbyn. Ch., Jacksonville, Ill., 1920-24, First Presbyn. Ch., Hibbing, Minn., 1925-36; pastor First Presbyn. Ch., Northville, 1936-41; now living in St. Petersburg, Fla., serving as supply. Moderator Presbytery of Duluth, 1931-32. Mem. Phi Beta Kappa. Home: St. Petersburg FL‡

SMITH, VINCENT E., educator; A.B., Xavier U.; M.A., Ph.D., Cath. U. Am.; LL.D., St. Mary's Coll., Cal. Prof. philosophy Sarah Lawrence Coll., 1968-72. Address: Bronxville NY Died May 18, 1972.

SMITH, VINE HAROLD, lawyer; b. Hanover, Conn., Dec. 30, 1874; s. Norman and Lucinda Maria (Cutler) S.; A.B., Harvard, 1898, LL.B., 1903; m. Harriet G. Leach, Mar. 4, 1905 (died Oct. 28, 1937); m. 2d, Ruby Bickford Farnham, Oct. 4, 1938; children—Grace Cutler, Vine Harold, Jr., Wayne J. Farnham (stepson). Teacher gram. sch., Canterbury, Conn., 1893-94; teacher preparatory sch., Howe Military Sch., Lima, Ind., 1899-1900; admitted to N.Y. bar, Apr. 1904, and began practice in N.Y. City; asst. U.S. atty., Eastern Dist. N.Y., 1915-19; asst. corp. counsel, N.Y. City, 1927-34; asst. U.S. atty., Eastern Dist. of N.Y., 1934-39; U.S. atty., Jan.-Sept. 1939; asst. U.S. atty., 1939-47, practice of law since 1947. Mem. Brooklyn Bar Assn., Federal Bar Assn. of N.Y., New Jersey and Conn., Norwich (Conn.) Soc. of N.Y. City, New Eng. Soc. of Brooklyn, N.Y. Democrat. Mason. Home: 610 Carlton Av. Office: Federal Bldg., Brooklyn NY‡

SMITH, WADE COTHRAN, evangelist; b. Rome, Ga., June 1, 1869; s. Edward Reed and Susan (Cothran) S.; ed. grammar sch. until 12 yrs. of age, later by pvt. study; m. Zaidee Lapsley, Jan. 26, 1897;children—Cothran Godden, James Lapsley, Zaidee Lapsley, Elizabeth Cothran. Cotton exporting business, 1892-1912; editor Missionary Survey (now Presbyn. Survey), Richmond, Va., 1912-21; called as pastor to The Church by-the-Side-of-the-Road, Greensboro, N.C., 1921; licensed to preach and ordained, under extraordinary process," by Presbytery of Orange; field worker for extension dept. of Gen. Assembly's Training Sch., Richmond, Va., 1925-29; specializes in training for evangelism; held evangelistic meetings in schools, colleges and churches throughout United States and Can., 1931-49; pastor Fontana Community Ch., 1948-53; asso. editor So. Presbyn. Jour., Weaverville, since 1953. Lesson writer, staff Sunday Sch. Times, Phila., since 1917, conducting Say, Fellows" column for boys, and Little Jetts" cartoons column. Independent. Author: The Little Jetts Telling Bible Stories, 1916; Say, Fellows, 1923; On The Mark, 1925; The Testament for Fishers of Men, 1925; Come and See, 1927; Get Set, 1930; Come and See, the Second Bringing Forward the Days of the Acts, 1930; New Testament Evangelism, 1930. Come and See" transl. into French, 1931; rewrote, "The Pilgrims Progress" in modern language issued 1931 (revised and illustrated by The Little Jetts), 1950; The Little Jetts Bible (Old Testament), 1942; The Little Jetts Bible (Vol. II, New Testament), 1944; You Can, 1949; Little Jetts Youth Talks, 1953. Home: Weaverville, N.C. Address: care The Sunday School Times, Phila PA‡

SMITH, WALT ALLEN, sculptor; b. Wellington, Kan., Mar. 1, 1910; s. James Allen and Lotta (Sears) S.; student U. Cal. at Los Angeles, 1937; Master's Degree, Strutz Acad., 1947; graduated The Otis Art Institute, in 1950; student Los Angeles City Coll., 1958; m. Helen Frances Baker, Feb. 15, 1935. Exhibited one-man shows, 3d St. Gallery, 1950, Cal. Exhibitors, 1951, Florentine Gallery, 1958, Tandy Art Gallery, 1963, Guardian Bank of Hollywood, Cal., 1964-65; exhibited two-man show Engrs. Credit Union Bldg., 1962, others; exhibited group shows, Nat. Orange Show, 1948, 50, 59, Los Angeles County Mus., 1957-59, International Madonna Festival, 1960-66, Santa Barbara (Cal.) Art Festival, 1960-62, Duncan Vail Gallery, 1956-66, Pasadina (Cal.) Art Festival, 1960-61, Smithsonian Institution, Miniature Painters and Sculptors Association Am., many others; work represented in numerous pvt. collections; important works include Fishel Mural, Sherlock Sculptured Wall (Cal.), Electronic Engrs. Cal., Meml. for Hungarian Revolution of 1956, Cole of Cal.; instr. jewelry design Strutz Acad., 1948; sculpture judge Cal. State Fair and Expn., Sacramento, 1962, 64, judge Hollywood Bowl, 1966. Chmn. Artists Adv. Bd., So. Sect., 1966-67. Served with AUS, 1942-45. Recipient art awards. Fellow Internat. Inst. Arts and Letters; mem. Cal. Art Club, Alumni Assn. Otis Art Inst. (pres. 1951-62), Miniature Painters Sculptors Gravers Soc. Home: Los Angeles CA Died Apr. 5, 1971.

SMITH, WARREN LOUNSBURY, educator, economist; b. Watertown, N.Y., Mar. 23, 1914; s. Burt W. and Fannie Sylvia (Allen) S.; B.A., U. Mich., 1947, M.A., 1949, Ph.D., 1952; m. Ann Elizabeth Schwartz, Aug. 27, 1943; children—Andrew L., Samuel W., Catherine A. Instr. econs. U. Mich., 1952-53; asst. prof. U. Va., 1953-56; asso. prof. Ohio State U., 1956-57; mem. faculty U. Mich., 1957-72, prof. econs., 1959-72, chmn. dept., 1963-68, 70-71; vis. lectr. Harvard, 1958-59; member Council of Econ. Advisers, 1968-69; cons. to govt. agencies, from 1958. Mem. Am. Econ. Assn., Econometric Soc., Am. Finance Assn., Am. Assn. U. Profs., Phi Beta Kappa. Author: Debt Management in the United States, 1960; Reserve Requirements in the American Monetary System, 1963; (with Ronald L. Teigen) Readings in Money, National Income and Stabilization Policy, rev. edit., 1970; Macroeconomics, 1970; Ann Arbor MI Died Apr. 23, 1972.

SMITH, WENDELL, news and sports reporter; b. Detroit, June 27, 1914; s. John Henry and Gertrude (Thompson) S.; B.S. in Edn., W.Va. State Coll.; m. Wyonella Delores Hicks, Nov. 25, 1949. Sports and city editor Pitts. Courier, 1937-49; sports writer Chgo.'s Am., 1947-63; news-sports reporter WBBM-TV, 1963-64, WGN-TV, 1964-72 (both Chgo.); writer sports column Chgo. Sun-Times, 1969-72; talent scout Bklyn. Dodgers, 1947-50. Mem. Chgo. Press Club (gov. 1964), Nat. Acad Television Arts and Scis. (gov. 1965), Chgo. Headline Club (gov. 1964), Chgo. Sportscasters Assn. (pres. 1969—). Club: Chicago Press (pres. 1972). Author: (with Jackie Robinson) The Jackie Robinson Story, 1947. Home: Chicago IL Died Nov. 26, 1972; buried Chicago IL

SMITH, WILLIAM ROY, prof. history; b. Bluff Springs, Tex., Nov. 16, 1876; s. Wade Morris and Alice (Davidson) S.; B.A., U. of Tex., 1897, M.A., 1898; Ph.D., Columbia, 1903; m. Marion Parris, of N.Y. City, June 11, 1912. Actg. prof. history, U. of Colo., 1900-01; lecturer in history, Columbia, 1901-02; asso. in history, 1902-07, asso. prof., 1907-14, prof. since 1914, Bryn Mawr Coll. Mem. Am. Hist. Assn., Phi Beta Kappa (U. of Tex.); fellow Tex. State Hist. Soc. Democrat. Episcopalian. Author: South Carolina as a Royal Province, 1903; also (brochures) The Quarrel Between Governor Smith and the Provisional Council of Texas, 1904; Sectionalism in Pennsylvania During the Revolution, 1910; British Imperial Federation, 1921. Home: Byrn Mawr PA‡

SMITH, WILLIAM STEVENSON, archaeologist; b. Indianapolis, Feb. 7, 1907; s. Louis Ferdinand and Edna Wirth (Stevenson) S.; student U. Chicago, 1924-26; A.B., Harvard, 1928, Ph.D., 1940. Asst. to George A. Reisner, Harvard, 1889; with Egyptian Expdn., Giza Pyramids, 1930-39, 46-47; asst. curator, department of Egyptian art. Museum of Fine Arts, Boston, 1941-54, asso. curator, 1954-56, curator, 1956-69; lecturer in Egyptian art Harvard, 1948-69; director American Research Center in Egypt, Cairo, 1951. Served as lieutenant commander U.S.N.R., active duty 1942-46. Fellow American Acad. Arts. and Scis.; mem. Archeol. Inst. Am., German Archaeological Institute, American Oriental Soc. Author: Ancient Egypt as represented in the Museum of Fine Arts, 1942; A History of Egyptian Sculpture and Painting in the Old Kingdom, 1946; A History of the Giza Necropolis, Vol. 2 (with George A. Reisner), 1955; The Art and Architecture of Ancient Egypt, 1958; Interconnections in the Ancient Near East, 1965. Home: Cambridge MA Died Jan. 13, 1969.

SMITH, WILLIS, JR., lawyer; b. Raleigh, N.C., July 11, 1921; s. Willis and Anna (Lee) S.; A.B., Duke, 1942, LL.B., 1947; m. Vernon Hope Fountain, Mar. 4, 1944; children—Vernon Fountain, Dolly Lee, Anne Creecy. Admitted to N.C. bar, 1947, practiced in Raleigh, 1947-71; partner firm Smith, Leach, Anderson & Dorsett, 1950-71. Sec., dir. Royal Cotton Mill Co., 1946-64, Blendspun, Inc. Pres., Def. Research Inst., 1971, also bd. dirs.; pres. regional chmn. Angier-Duke Scholarship Com., 1954-55; chmn. local Salvation Army, 1961, Wake County March of Dimes, 1951. Co-chmn. N.C. Campaign for Nixon, 1968. Served with USNR, 1942-45. Mem. Am. (chmn. standing com. legal assistance to servicemen 1946-66), N.C. bar assns., N.C. State Bar (council), Internat. Assn. Ins. Counsel (dir., exec. com.), Phi Delta Phi, Kappa Alpha. Methodist (past chmn. bd.). Clubs: Carolina Country, Sphinx (Raleigh). Home: Raleigh NC Died Dec. 4, 1971.

SMITHEY, WILLIAM ROYALL, univ. prof.; b. Morven, Amelia County, Va., Aug. 24, 1881; s. William Rosser and Nannie Jane (Greene) S.; B.A., Randolph-Macon Coll., Va., 1902, M.A., 1903; grad. work, U. of Chicago, 1917; Ph.D., U. of Wis., 1918; m. Margaret Diana Logan, May 28, 1918; children—William Royall, Hamilton. Teacher high sch., Richmond, Va., 1903-07; prin. high sch., Petersburg, Va., 1907-13; prof. and dir. summer quarter, Madison Coll., Harrisonburg, 1913-16; asst. in edn., Univ. of Wis., 1916-18; sec. Va. State Bd. of Edn., 1918-19; prof. secondary edn., U. of Va., 1919-52; visiting prof. (summers) Duke U., 1932, 35, U. of Mich., 1936. Mem. Va. State Edn. Assn. (ex-pres.), Phi Beta Kappa, Phi Delta Kappa, Pi Gamma Mu, Kappa Delta Pi. Mem. exec. com. Southern Assn. Coll. and Secondary Schs., 1940-47, pres. 1946. Democrat. Methodist. Club: Colonnade (U. of Va.). Editor Charlottesville VA Died Oct. 21, 1967; buried University Cemetery Charlottesville VA

SMOCK, P(ETER) MONROE, editor; b. Geneva, Pa., Feb. 27, 1874; s. William and Susanna (Anderson) S.; grad. Edinboro (Pa.) State Normal Sch., 1892; m. Agnes M. Lias, of Payette, Idaho, Feb. 2, 1919;children—(by first marriage) Carlyle Hamilton, Mrs. Margaret Lucile Owens, Everett Monroe; (by 2d marriage) Frances Susannah, Robert Burns, William Wilson. Ordained Bapt. ministry, 1896; pastor 1st Ch., Waverly, Ia., 1899-1902; dir. Hot Springs (S.D.) Nat. Bank, 1903-07; pastor 1st Ch., Boise, Ida., 1907-09; admitted to bar, 1910; candidate for Congress on Progressive ticket, 1912; mem. Progressive Nat. Com. for Ida., 1912-16. Owner and editor Vashon Island News-Record; Commr. Vashon Water Dist.; sec. Good-Will Farm. Pros. atty. Payette Co., Ida., 1917—. Mem. Henry Ford's peace expdn., winter 1915-16. Commr pub. welfare, King Co., Wash., 1922-25. Mem. Am. Lit. Assn., Seattle Geneal Soc., S.A.R. Mason (32 deg.) Clubs: Caledonian, Vashon-Mawry Burns Club (sec.) Popular lecturer. Home: Vashon WA‡

SMYTH, FRANCIS SCOTT, educator; b. Oregon City, Oregon, October 7, 1895; s. Sidney and Bessie (McGaw) S.; student Reed Coll., Portland, Ore., 1913-14; A.B., Univ. of Calif., 1917, A.M., 1919, M.D., 1922; D.M.S., University of Indonesia, 1959; married Elizabeth Burket, September 13, 1924; children—Elizabeth Ann, Francis Scott. Interne and asst. resident Children's Hosp., Boston, 1922-23; 2d resident New York Nursery and Child's Hosp., 1924; asst. resident St. Louis Children's Hosp., Jan.-June 1925; instr. pediatrics Univ. of Calif. Med. Sch., San Francisco, 1925-26, asst. prof., 1926-28; asst. prof. pediatrics Washington Univ. Sch. of Medicine, 1928-30; asso. prof. Univ. of Calif. Medical Sch., 1930-32, prof., 1936-64, prof. emeritus, 1964-72, dean 1942-54, coordinator U. Indonesia project, 1954-60, coordinator Airlangga University project, 1959-72; director Indonesian Projects, Djakarta and Surabaja, 1959-65. Member American Pediatric Soc., American Medical Assn., Soc. Pediatric Research (hon.), Am. Acad. Pediatrics. Phi Chi, Sigma Pi. Republican. Presbyn. Author: Handbook of Pediatric Procedures, 1930. Contbr. studies on allergy, diabetes, renal rickets, etc. to pediatric and med. jours. Home: San Mateo CA Died Feb. 6, 1972.

SMYTH, MARGARITA PUMPELLY, artist; b. at Newburgh, N.Y., Aug. 6, 1873; d. Raphael and Eliza (Shepard) Pumpelly; pupil of Abbott H. Thayer; m. at Brighton, Eng., Henry Lloyd Smyth (q.v.), Nov. 8, 1894. Address: Belmont St., Watertown MA‡

SMYTH, WILMA LOUISE, state ofcl.; b. Bay Point, Cal., Dec. 26, 1915; d. William T. and Florence (Collins) Smyth; A.B., U. Cal. at Berkeley, 1936; M.S.W., U. Denver, 1955. Caseworker, Pub. Welfare in Cal., 1937-42; casework supr., adminstr. Cowlitz County Welfare Dept., Kelso, Wash., 1942-46; child welfare cons. Mont. Dept. Pub. Welfare, Helena, 1946-53, field supr., Great Falls, 1955-57; med. social cons. Mont. State Bd. of Health, Helena, 1958-69. Beef cattle rancher, White Sulphur Springs, Mont., 1961-69. Mem. Nat. Assn. Social Workers, Mont. Pub. Health Assn., Acad. Certified Social Workers, Mont., Meagher County Stockgrowers assns. Contbr. articles to profl. jours. Home: Helena MT Died Sept. 21, 1969.

SMYTHE, GEORGE WINFRED, army officer; b. Norristown, Pa., Aug. 4, 1899; s. David N. and Laura Virginia (Brooks) S.; student West Chester Normal Sch., 1918, Muhlenberg Coll.; Allentown, Pa., 1919-20; B.S., U.S. Mil. Acad., 1924; Inf. Sch., Fort Benning, Ga., 1927-28; Command and Gen. Staff Sch., Fort Leavenworth, Kan., 1935-36; m. Susie Hubbell Coley, Aug. 12, 1924; children—George W., John David. Commd. 2d lt., U.S. Army, June 12, 1924, and advanced through grades to maj. gen.; served as company officer 29th inf., Fort Benning, Ga., 1924-27; prof. Mil. Science and Tactics. Staunton (Va.) Mil. Acad., 1928-32; co. officer 33d inf., Fort Clayton, Canal Zone, 1932-34, 4th inf., Fort George Wright, Spokane, Wash., 1934-35; dir. phys. edn., U.S. Mil. Acad., 1936-40; staff officer 27th inf., Hawaiian dept., Schofield Barracks, T.H., 1940-42; mem. gen. staff Army Service Force Mil. Lend Lease, Washington, D.C., 1942-43; comdg. officer 47th Inf., 9th Inf. Div., North Africa, Sicily, Eng., France, Belgium and Germany, 1943-44; asst. div. comdr., 80th Div., Germany, 1945; with hdqrs. Army Ground Forces, Fort Monroe, Va., 1945; chief of staff 3d Army, Ft. McPherson, 1947; asst. division comdr. 1st Inf. Division, 1949. Decorated Purple Heart with cluster, Silver Star Medal (cluster 1945), Distinguished Service Cross, 1944, Bronze Star (U.S.); Chevalier Legion of Honor, Cross of War with palm, 1945 (France); Russian Medal of Bravery, 1945; O.B.E. (Eng.), 1946; Office Order of Leopold, with palm, Cross of War, 1940 (palm, 1946) (Belgium). Mem. Alpha Tau Omega. Mason. Awarded Edgerton Sabre by U.S. Mil. Acad. for best all round athlete, class 1924. Home: Arlington VA Died Jan. 1969.

SNEATH, MRS. SAMUEL B. (LAURA S SNEATH), b. Martinsburg, Knox Co., Ohio; d. William and Mary Ann (Anderson) Stephenson; ed. high sch. normal sch. and under pvt. tutors; passed State Bd Examiners, receiving 3-yr. certificate at age of 20; m Samuel B. Sneath, of Tiffin, O., Nov. 5, 1879. Civic and philanthropic worker; assisted in establishing City Library, at Tiffin, and mem. bd. trustees 30 yrs.; has served as mem. local and State charity bds., local and State missionary socs. Presbyn. Woman suffragist. Pres Ohio State Federation of Women's Clubs, 1902-4; 2d and 1st v.-p. Gen. Federation of Women's Clubs 1912-16, and chmn. program com., 1912-14. Mem Colonial Dames of America, D.A.R. Unanimously endorsed by Ohio State Federation of Women's Clubs Oct., 1915, as candidate for presidency of Gen Federation. Has served as del. many convs., State and Nat.; del. of Gen. Federation to Pan-Am. Congress Washington, D.C., 1915. Has maintained summer home at Port Colborne, Can., for the last 17 yrs. and a winter home in New Orleans since 1900. Address: Tiffin OH‡

SNEDDEN, DAVID, writer, lecturer; b. Havilah Calif., Nov. 19, 1868; s. Samuel and Anna (O'Keefe) S. A.B., St. Vincent's Coll., Los Angeles, Calif., 1889 A.B., Leland Stanford Jr. U., 1897; A.M., Columbia 1901, Ph.D., 1907; m. Genevra Sisson, June 30, 1898 children—Hope, Donald (dec.), Ruth, Pauline, Janet Robert. Prin. schs., Santa Paula, Calif., 1892-95; supt schs., Paso Robles, Calif., 1897-1900; asst. prof. edn. Leland Stanford Jr. U., 1901-05; adj. prof. edn. Columbia, 1905-09; state commr. edn. of Mass. 1909-16; prof. edn. Columbia, 1916-35; prof. emeritus since July 1, 1935. Mem. N.E.A., A.A.A.S., Phi Beta Kappa, Phi Delta Kappa (Columbia). Pres. Nat. Soc. for Vocational Edn., 1918-20. Author: Administration of Education for Juvenile Delinquents, 1906; School Reports and School Efficiency (Snedden and Allen) 1907; Educational Administration in the United States (Dutton and Snedden), 1908; Problems of Vocational Education, 1911; Problems of Educational Readjustment, 1914; Problems of Secondary Education. 1917; Vocational Education, 1920; Sociological Determination of Objectives in Education, 1921. Educational Sociology, 1922; What's Wrong with American Education?, 1927; Educational Sociology for Beginners, 1928; School Educations, 1930; Cultural Education and Common Sense, 1931; Secondary Schools in 1960, 1931; Towards Better Education. 1931; Educations for Political Citizenship, 1934. Introductory Sociology for Teachers, 1935. Home: 440 Amherst St., Palo Alto CA‡

SNELL, JOHN LESLIE, educator, historian; b. Plymouth, N.C., June 2, 1923; s. John Leslie and Lessie Ann (McLamb) S.; A.B., U. N.C., 1946, A.M., 1947, Ph.D., 1950; m. Maxine Pybas, Dec. 18, 1943; children—Marcia Ruth, John McCullough, Leslie Ann. Instr. history U. N.C., 1946-49; asst. prof. history U. Wichita, 1949-51; faculty history Tulane U., 1953-66 prof., 1959-66, dean of Grad. Sch., 1963-66; prof history University Pennsylvania, 1966-68; Univ Distinguished prof. U. N.C., Chapel Hill, 1968-72, summer tchr. U. Tenn., U. Mich., Vanderbilt U., Standford U. Mem. Friends of Library, U. N.C. Served to 1st lt. USAAF, 1943-45; ETO. Decorated Air medal, Distinguished Flying Cross. Scholar for hist. research Am. Council Learned Socities, 1951-53. Mem. Am (dir. study grad. edn. history 1958-60), So. hist. assns., Am. Assn. U. Profs., U. N.C. Alumni Assn., Omicron Delta Kappa, Phi Alpha Theta. Methodist. Author Wartime Origins of the East-West Dilemma Over Germany, 1959; Illusion and Necessity; The Diplomacy of Global War, 1939-1945, 1963. Co-author, editor: The Meaning of Yalta, 1956; The Nazi Revolution, 1959; The Education of Historians in the United States, 1961; The Outbreak of the Second World War; Design or Blunder, published in 1962; Critical Issues in History, 1967. Editor: European History in the South, 1959 Contbr. Ency. Americana, numerous articles profl jours. Home: Chapel Hill NC Died May 27, 1972.

SNIDER, CLYDE FRANK, educator; b. Allen Co., Kan., Mar. 5, 1904; s. James Isaac and Jessie Marian (Hubbard) S.; A.B., U. Kan., 1928, A.M., 1930; Ph.D. U. Ill., 1936; m. Lois Lucille Riley, July 15, 1930 (died Mar. 1970); one daughter, Betty Marie (Mrs. James E. Needham); m. 2d, Ruth Mary Weeks, Jan. 9, 1971 Bank clk., Savonburg, Kansas, 1920-23; teacher in the summer session Washburn Coll., Topeka, 1929; asst instr. polit. sci. U. Kan., 1928-30, asst. sec. Bur. Govt Research, 1929-30; instr. govt. Ind. U., 1930-34; asst. U Ill., 1934-36, instr., 1936-39, asso., 1939-41, asst. prof., 1941-43, asso. prof. 1943-49, prof. polit. sci., 1949-71, chmn. dept. polit. sci., 1957-61, chmn. div. social scis., 1958-60; cons., research Ind. Com. Govtl. Econ., 1934, Ill. Legislative Council, 1940, Ill. Tax Commn., 1940, Ill. Dept. Revenue, 1943, Illinois Revenue Laws Commn., 1948-71, Ill. Commn. to Study State Govt., 1950; research Ill. Constitution Study Commn., 1966. Mem. Am. Polit. Sci. Assn., Nat. Municipal League, Alpha Kappa Lambda, Phi Beta Kappa, Phi Delta Kappa, Pi Sigma Alpha, Square and Compass, Presbn Mason. Author: Legislative Procedure in Kansas (with F. H. Guild), 1930; Township Government in Indiana 1932; County Government in Illinois, 1943; American State and Local Government, 1950, (with Samuel K

Gove) revised edition 1965; Local Govt. in Rural America, 1957; (with Irving Howards) County Government in Illinois, 1960; (with Roy Anderson) Local Taxing Units: The Illinois Experience, 1968. Dept. editor Nat. Municipal Rev., 1958-61. Mem. bd. editors Am. Polit. Sci. Rev., 1941-44. Contbr. profl. jours. Home: Urbana IL Died July 17, 1971.

SNODGRASS, ROBERT EVANS, entomologist; b. St. Louis, Mo., July 5, 1875; s. James Cathcart and Annie Elizabeth (Evans) S.; ed. Stanford U.; m. Ruth Mae Hansford, Sept. 18, 1924; children—Ruth Maye, Eleanor Hansford. Began teaching at Wash. State Coll., 1901; with Bur. of Entomology and Plant Quarantine, U.S. Dept. Agr., since 1918. Mem. Entomol. Soc. America, Washington Entomol. Soc.; hon. mem. Royal Entomol. Soc. of London, Societe Entomologique de Belgique, New York Entomol. Society, Societe Entomologique de France. Author: Anatomy and Physiology of the Honeybee, 1925; Insects, Their Ways and Means of Living, 1930; Principles of Insect Morphology, 1935; also technical papers on anatomy, metamorphosis and feeding apparatus of insects. Home: 3706 13th St. N.W., Washington DC‡

SNODGRASS, ROBERT RICHARD, b. Dow, Indian Territory, Okla., 1902; law degree, U. Mich., 1925. Chmn., pres. Atlas Finance Co. Home: Atlanta GA Deceased.

SNOOK, JOHN S., ex-congressman; b. near Antwerp, O., Dec. 18, 1862; s. Col. W. N. and Martha (Snook) S.; 1st grad. of Antwerp schs.; student Ohio Wesleyan U. 3 yrs.; studied law 2 yrs. under Judge Wilson H. Snook; LL.B., Cincinnati Coll. Law Sch., 1887; m. Edith May Wells, Aug. 3, 1891; 1 son, Jean D. Practiced law, Antwerp, O., 1887-90, since at Paulding; Dem. nominee for presdl. elector, 1892; nominee for Congress, 1894; mem. 57th and 58th Congresses (1901-05) and 65th Congress (1917-19), 5th Ohio Dist.; judge Court of Common Pleas, 1915-17 and 1930-39. Del. to Nat. Dem. Conv., 1912, 32. Presbyterian. Home: Paulding OH‡

SNOOK, JOHN WILSON, prison warden; b. Salmon, Ida., Oct., 20, 1876; s. John Walls and Emily C. (Ellis) S.; ed. pub. schs. and prep. yr., Utah Agrl. Coll.; m. Charlotte Louise Clayson, Jan. 27, 1903; children—John Clayson, Fred Richard, Quinton. Dep. U.S. Marshal, Alaska, 1898-1904; mem. Ida. Ho. of Rep., 2 terms, 1909 and 1921 (chmn. state affairs com.); warden Ida. State Penitentiary, 1909-17 and 1924; warden U.S. Prison, Atlanta, Ga., 1925-29 (resigned). Elected pres. Warden's Assn. America, 1929. Republican nominee for Idaho State Senate, Lemhi County, 1934. Episcopalian. Ex-pres. Sea Breeze Beach Club; No. 1 mem. and 1st exalted ruler Salmon Lodge, No. 1620 B.P.O. Elks; pres. Ida. State Elks Assn. Passed as number one among 47 others taking civil service examination for prison warden, N.Y. State. Home: Baker ID‡

SNOW, EDGAR PARKS, author and lecturer; born Kansas City, Mo., July 19, 1905; s. James Edgar and Anna (Edelmann) S.; ed. Kansas City Coll., U. Mo.; m. Lois Wheeler, 1949; children—David C., Sian. Began newspaper work with Kansas City Star; assistant editor China Weekly Review (Shanghai), 1929-30, and correspondent for the Chicago Tribune, 1929; corr. Consol. Press. Association India, China and Manchuria, 1930-34; spl. corr. N.Y. Sun, 1934-37, London Daily Herald, 1932-41; lecturer Yenching Univ., Peiping, 1934-35; first newspaper corr. to enter Soviet China and interview and photograph its leaders during Chinese civil war; co-author of plan for Chinese Indsl. Cooperatives, 1938; covered Sino-Jap war 1931-33 and 1937-41; returned to U.S., 1941 and was assigned overseas to Africa, India, Iran, China, Soviet Russia, Great Britain, France, Germany, Austria as accredited war corr. Saturday Evening Post, 1942-46; associate editor Saturday Evening Post, 1943-51; special research consultant Harvard, 1956; corr. Look mag., China, 1960-61; corr. Le Nouveau Candide of Paris, in China, 1964-65; lectr. Recipient Army citation, 1947; Lawrence S. Mayers Peace award, 1956. Mem. World Academy of Art and Science, Beta Theta Pi. Clubs: Overseas Press, National Press (Washington); Foreign Correspondents (founder-mem.) (Japan). Author: Far Eastern Front, 1934; Impressions of the Northwest (in Chinese only), 1936; Red Star Over China, 1937; The Battle for Asia, 1941; Smash Hitler's International (with others), 1941; People on Our Side, 1944; Bondage and Glory, Eng., 1945; Pattern of Soviet Power, 1945; Stalin Must Have Peace, 1947; Random Notes on Red China (monograph), 1957; Journey to the Beginning, 1958; The Other Side of the River: Red China Today, 1962; Washington-Tokyo-Peking, 1969; photographed and produced documentary film One Fourth of Humanity—The China Story, 1968. Editor and compiler of Living China, 1936. Pub. 4-hour interview with Mao Tse-tung, 1965. Died Feb. 15, 1972.

SNOW, FRANCIS, editor; b. Boston, Mass., Nov. 17, 1876; s. Charles B. and Jennie M. S.; A.B., Harvard, 1903; Ph.D., Columbia, 1910; studied U. of Berlin, The Sorbonne, univs. of St. Petersburg, Kharkov, etc. Instr. Romance langs., Harvard, 1903-05; prof. Romance langs. and univ. extension lecturer, U. of Toronto, Can., 1910-14; head Russian Bur. (U.S.) Com. on Pub. Information, World War; with Current History (mag.), New York, since 1919, mng. editor since 1923. Mem. Authors' League America, Soc. of Authors and Producers (London); corr. mem. Royal Spanish Acad. Arts and Sciences, 1929. Recommended for decorations by two foreign govts. Club: Authors, Among his writings are the following: Light Symbolism in the Medieval Religious Lyric; Alba, Aube and Tagelied in the Light of the History of Culture; Red Flowers (novel of Russia, issued in U.S. and Eng.); Sweden (1907-26); Ten Centuries of Russian Art; Izaak Levitan, Painter of the Russian Soul; The Seasons in Russian Painting; also other studies in Russian art and numerous articles on internat. affairs in mags. and newspapers. Translator: The Cabin (La Barraca, of Blasco Ibaniez), 1917. Speaks, writes and reads 32 langs. Address: care New York Times, 229 W. 43d St., New York NY‡

SNOW, JOHN BEN, corp. ofcl.; b. Pulaski, N.Y., June 16, 1883; s. Benjamin and Mary (Watson) S.; student Mt. Hermon Sch., Sch., 1902; B.C.S., N.Y.U., 1904, Jr. accountant Haskins & Sells, 1905; clk. F. W. Woolworth Co., N.Y.C., 1906, store mgr., Port Jervis, N.Y., 1907, N.Y.C., 1908-10; corp. exec. F. W. Woolworth & Co. Ltd., Liverpool, Eng., 1910-37, dist. supt., 1910-14, buyer, 1915-19, supt. of buyers in charge of mdse. also dir., 1920-37; chmn. Speidel Newspapers Inc. and affiliates, Colorado Springs, Colo., 1937-73; owner Western Horseman mag., Colorado Springs, 1943-73. Pres. John Ben Snow Found.; trustee Rancheros Visitadores; founder N.Y.U. Med. Center, N.Y.U. Law Sch. Mem. Nat. Cowboy Hall of Fame, Oklahoma City. Mem. Am. C. of C. in London, Country Gentlemen's Assn., Colorado Springs Fine Arts Center, Salinas (Cal.) Rodeo Assn., Pikes Peak (Colo.) or Bust Rodeo Assn., Phi Gamma Delta, Alpha Kappa Psi. Republican. Baptist. Mason. Clubs: American (gov.), Pilgrims (Eng.); Pilgrims, National Press (Washington); Press and Union League (San Francisco); New York Athletic (N.Y.C.); Rotary. El Paso (Colorado Springs); Royal Automobile (Eng.). Home: Reno NV

SNOWDEN, R(OBERT) BRINKLEY, banking; b. Memphis, Tenn., Mar. 19, 1869; s. Robert Bogardus and Annie Overton (Brinkley) S.; student U. of the South, Sewanee, Tenn., 1884-88, Princeton, 1888-90; m. Sara E. Day, of Bayonne, N.J., Nov. 16, 1892; children—Annie Dorothy Huetta (Mrs. Stanley M. Rowe), Robert Bogardus, Thomas Day, Brinkley S., John Bayard. Mem. firm Snowden & Snowden, real estate, since 1890; v.p. Bank of Commerce & Trust Co. since 1908; v.p. Tenn. Joint Stock Land Bank, Miss. Joint Stock Land Bank; dir. Memphis Br. Federal Reserve Bank of St. Louis. Gen. chmn. Memphis Red Cross drives, World War. Dir. Tenn. Home for Incurables. Mem. Delta Tau Delta. Democrat. Episcopalian. Clubs: Tennessee, Waponaca Outing, Prickly Heat, Memphis Country. Home: 1397 Central Av. Office: Commerce Title Bldg., Memphis TN‡

SNYDER, ALBAN GOSHORN, consul-gen.; b. Charleston, W.Va., Nov. 5, 1877; s. Charles Philip and Jane Adelia (Goshorn) S.; B.A., Washington and Lee U., 1898; studied law, W.Va. U., 1902; m. Evelyn Schuber, of Ancon, Canal Zone, Sept. 16, 1911; children—Evelyn Troy, Mary Jane. Am. vice-consul at Diaz, Mex., 1899-1901; sec. legation and consul-gen. at Bogota, Colombia, 1903-06 (charge d'affaires, Dec. 18, 1903-Dec. 6, 1905); consul-gen. at Buenos Ayres, 1906-09, at Panama, Panama, Jan. 11, 1909-Oct. 20, 1920; consul-gen. at Christiania (now Oslo), Norway, Feb. 9, 1921-—. Address: Am. Consulate-General, Oslo Norway‡

SNYDER, FREDERIC SYLVESTER, merchant; b. Huntington, Vt., Jan. 13, 1868; s. Orvis Wellington and Ellen M. (Stockwell) S.; ed. pub. and pvt. schs.; m. Anne Thompson Wills, Apr. 19, 1909; children—Leonard Wellington, Charlotte, Margaret. President Batchelder & Snyder Co. and predecessors (wholesale foods), Boston, 1906-31; chmn. nat. bd. dirs. Inst. of Am. Meat Packers, 1906-31, pres., 1921-24; pres. Atlantic Brick & Tile Co. and predecessor, 1936-40; presdient Ocean Crest Corporation of New Jersey; trustee Winchester Savings Bank; incorporator Charlestown Five Cents Savings Bank. Served as mem. U.S. Food Purchase Bd., World War; chief Div. Coordination of Purchase, also Meat Div., Cold Storage Plants Div., U.S. Food Administrn. Trustee Boston Chamber of Commerce Realty Trust. Pres. Boston Chamber of Commerce, 1922-23, 1931, 32, 33. Home: Winchester MA‡

SNYDER, HOWARD MCC., army med. officer; b. Cheyenne, Wyo., Feb. 7, 1881; s. Albert Campbell and Priscilla McClelland (McCrum) S.; student U. Colo., 1899-1901; M.D., Jefferson Med. Coll.; hon. grad. Army Med. Coll., 1908; hon. grad. U.S. Mil. Acad., 1929; Research Bd. Tropical Medicine, P.I., 1909-11; grad. study Mayo Clinic, 1924, Sch. Tropical Medicine, San Juan, P.R., 1930-32, N.Y.U. and Bellevue Hosp., 1934; grad. Army Med. Field Service Sch., 1932; m. Alice Elizabeth Concklin, July 12, 1910; children—Howard McCrum, Richard Concklin. Intern Presbyn. Hosp., Phila., 1905-06; commd. 1st lt. M.C., U.S. Army, 1908, advancing through grades to maj. gen., 1943; sr. med. advisor N.G. of U.S., 1936-40; asst. insp. gen. War Dept., 1940-46; mem. com. to Pres. of U.S. on Integration and Improvement of U.S. med. and Hosp. Services, 1946; mem. Chief of Staff's adv. Group, 1946-48; research asso., conservation of human Resources Project and Manpower Council, Columbia U., N.Y.C., 1948-50; sr. med. officer S.H.A.P.E., 1951-52; physician to Pres. of U.S., 1953-61. Recipient Fed. Hosp. Certificate of Recognition, Am. Hosp. Assn., 1958, U.S. Health award, Met. Washington Bd. Trade and Med. Soc. D.C., 1960; decorated D.S.M.; Grand Comdr. Order Ouissam Alouite (Morocco); Grand Comdr. Order of So. Cross (Brazil). Fellow A.C.S., A.P.A. (hon.); mem. A.M.A., N.Y. Soc. Mil. and Naval Ofcrs. of World War, Mil. Order of Carabao, Assn. Mil. Surgeons of U.S. Home: Washington DC Died Sept. 22, 1970; buried U.S. Mil. Acad., West Point NY

SNYDER, JOHN OTTERBEIN, zoology; b. Butler, Ind., Aug. 14, 1867; s. James D. and Maria Adeline (Kiser) S.; A.B., Stanford U., 1897, A.M., 1899; m. Frances Arle Hamilton, June 2, 1901; children—Evelyn Hamilton, Cedric Otterbein. Asst. U.S. Fish Commn. large part of time, 1907-16; naturalist on U.S. Albatross, deep sea investigations, 1902, 06; expert ichthyologist U.S. Nat. Museum, 1914; fisheries expert Calif. Div. of Fish and Game, 1909-30; dir. U.S. Bur. of Fisheries Marine Lab., Woods Hole, Mass., 1926; exec. head dept. of zoology, Stanford U., 1926-32, emeritus prof. since 1932; in charge Bur. of Fish Conservation Division of Fish and Game of Calif., 1931-37. Fellow A.A.A.S., Calif. Acad. Science; mem. Sigma Xi, Cooper Ornithol. Club. Author of numerous papers and monographs on the geog. distribution and speciation of fishes of West America, Mexico, Hawaii, Japan and Okinawa; also Life History of Salmon. Home: Stanford University CA‡

SNYDER, MURRAY, public relations executive; born in Brooklyn, New York, June 20, 1911; the son of Edward and Ida (Schneider) S.; student pub. schs., San Antonio Jr. Coll., Columbia U.; m. Betty Gathings, Jan. 3, 1943; children—Susan, Diana. Reporter San Antonio Light, 1928-29; polit. writer Albany and Washington corr. Bklyn. Eagle, 1931-37; press aide Borough Pres. of Bklyn., 1938-39; polit. writer N.Y. Post, 1940-41; polit. writer N.Y. Herald Tribune, 1946-52, Albany corr., 1951-52; asst. press sec. White House, 1953-57; Asst. Sec. of Def. for Public Affairs, 1957-61; pres. Murray Snyder Assos., pub. relations, 1962-69; asst. adminstr. for pub. affairs FAA, Washington, 1969. Served as pvt. to capt. Inf., U.S. Army, 1942-46. Mem. Silurians, Sigma Delta Chi. Club: Nat. Press. Home: Washington DC Died Nov. 2, 1969; buried Rock Creek Cemetery, Washington DC

SOARES, THEODORE GERALD, clergyman, educator; b. Abridge, Eng., Oct. 1, 1869; s. Augusto and Kathleen Mary (Carbery) S.; came to America, 1886; A.B., U. of Minn., 1891, A.M., 1892; Ph.D., U. of Chicago, 1894, D.B., 1897; D.D., Knox Coll., Ill., 1901; D.D., Meadville Theol. Sch., Chicago, Ill., 1938; m. Lilian May Martin, July 10, 1894; 1 dau., Geraldine (Mrs. Bayne B. Blankenship). Ordained Bapt. ministry, 1894; pastor Rockford, Ill., 1894-99, Galesburg, 1899-1902, Oak Park, 1902-05; univ. extension lecturer on Bibl. lit., U. of Chicago, 1899-1905, prof. homiletics, 1906-08, homiletics and religious edn., 1908-26, religious edn., 1926-30, also head dept. of practical theology; Earl lectures, Pacific Sch. of Religion, 1927; guest prof., Calif. Inst. Tech., winters 1928-30, prof. ethics, 1930-45, emeritus since 1945; preacher Hyde Park Congl. Ch., Chicago, 1919-25; minister Neighborhood Ch. (Unitarian and Congregational), Pasadena, Calif., 1930-45, emeritus since 1945. Pres. Council Religious Education Association, 1914-16; pres. Religious Edn. Association, 1921-24; mem. Bd. of Preachers, Harvard Univ., 1922-30, 1931-39. In France for Y.M.C.A., speaking at Am. camps, 1918. Mem. Am. Philos. Assn., Phi Kappa Psi, Phi Beta Kappa. Clubs: Athenaeum, Twilight, Annandale Country, University, Pasadena Athletic. Author: The Supreme Miracle, and Other Sermons, 1904; His Life Series, 1905; Heroes of Israel, 1909; Lessons from the Great Teachers (with Lillian M. Soares), 1911; A Baptist Manual, 1911; The Social Institutions and Ideals of the Bible, 1915; Practical Theology (in Smith, Guide to the Study of the Christian Religion), 1917; Studies in Comradeship (for A.E.F.), 1919; A Study of Adult Life, 1923; How to Enjoy the Bible, 1924; Religious Education, 1928; The Story of Paul, 1930; Three Typical Beliefs, 1937; The Origins of the Bible, 1941; The Growing Concept of God in the Bible, 1943. Editor: University of Chicago Sermons, 1915; (with Shailer Mathews, and W. C. Bower) Publications in Religious Education of University of Chicago, 1914-31. Contbr. to Biblical and educational dictionaries. Home: La Casita d'Ancede Dana Point CA‡

SOBILOFF, HYMAN JORDAN, industrialist; b. Fall River, Mass., Dec. 16, 1912; s. Israel and Fannie (Gollub) S.; student U. Ariz., 1929-32, Boston U., 1932-33, N.Y.U., 1943-44; Doctor of Laws, Fla. So. College, 1956; m. Adelaide Goldstein, July 9, 1933; 1 son, Stephen. Chmn. bd., dir. Larchfield Corp., Marshall-Wells Internat., Nassau, Bahamas, Johnson

Stores, Inc., Raleigh, N.C., Auto-Lec Stores, Inc., New Orleans. Founder, trustee Nat. Found. Research Allergies, Boston; mem. Funk Found. Med. Research, Inc., Edward Adaskin Ednl. Found., Inc. Hon. chancellor Fla. So. Coll., 1955. Founder Albert Einstein Coll. Medicine, Technion-Israel Inst. Tech. Clubs: Ledgemont Country (Providence); Lotos, New York University (N.Y.C.); Montauk Yacht (L.I., N.Y.). Author: Dinosaurs and Violins, 1954; In the Deepest Aquarium, 1959; Breathing of First Things, 1962. Home: New York City NY Died Aug. 10, 1970.

SOCKMAN, RALPH WASHINGTON, clergyman; b. Mt. Vernon, O., Oct. 1, 1889; s. Rigdon Potter and Harriet O. (Ash) S.; B.A., Ohio Wesleyan, 1911; D.D., 1923; M.A., Columbia, 1913; Ph.D., 1917; S.T.D., 1954; grad. Union Theol. Sem., 1916; LL.D., Dickinson Coll., Carlisle, Pa., 1930; D.D., N.Y. U., 1932, Wesleyan U., 1934; L.H.D., Rollins Coll., 1937; Litt.D., Fla. Southern, 1937; L.H.D., Washington and Jefferson Coll., 1942; S.T.D., Northwestern U., 1947, Syracuse U., 1962; D.C.L., Miami U., 1952; D.D., Oberlin Coll., 1954; L.H.D., U. Tampa, 1954, Bloomfield Coll. and Sem., 1955; Litt.D., Duke, 1954; LL.D., Ohio U., 1954, Lehigh U., 1959, Ricker Coll., 1960, U. of Pacific, 1961, Carroll Coll., 1962, Morningside Coll., 1965; m. Zellah Widmer Endly, June 15, 1916; 1 dau., Elizabeth Ash. Intercollegiate sec. Y.M.C.A., 1911-13; asso. minister Madison Av. M.E. Ch., now Christ Ch. N.Y.C., 1916, minister, 1917-61, emeritus, 1961-70; dir. of Hall of Fame for Great Americans, N.Y.C., 1961-70; Lyman Beecher lectr., Yale, 1941; asso. prof. practical theology Union Theol. Sem., Harry Emerson Fosdick vis. prof., 1963-64. With Army YMCA, 1918. Pres. Fedn. of Chs., 1927-29; dir. Union Theol. Sem., N.Y. U., dir. Hall of Fame; trustee N.Y.U., Ohio Wesleyan U., Drew U. Pres. Ohio Soc. of N.Y., 1940-43, Chmn. World Peace Com. Methodist Ch., since 1928; chaplain, N.Y.U.; elected mem. Harvard Bd. of Preachers, 1944. Vice pres. Ch. Peace Union, 1944, pres., 1947. Visiting professorship homiletics, Yale, 1947-48. Chmn. Interfaith Com., Am. Soc. for Russian Relief; del. to Russia, 1947. Trustee Syracue U. Recipient 1st annual award by World Com. for Christian Broadcasting for service to America's religious life, 1958, Gold Medal award Nat. Inst. Social Scis., 1968. Mem. Phi Beta Kappa, Delta Sigma Rho, Phi Delta Theta, Sigma Chi. Clubs: Century, Metropolitan, Monday, Quill. Author numerous books; latest publ.: The Higher Happiness, 1950; How to Believe, 1953; The Whole Armor of God, 1955; A Lift for Living, 1956; Man's First Love, 1958; The Meaning of Suffering, 1961; The Lord's Prayer; Who Christ Commended. Contbr. Interpreters Bible, 1954. Address: New York City NY Died Aug. 29, 1970; buried Mt Vernon OH

SOHON, FREDERICK WYATT, seismologist; b. South Bethlehem, Pa., June 3, 1894; s. Michael Druck and Sarah Harrisonia (Marsteller) S.; Chem.E., Columbia, 1915; student St. Andrew-on-Hudson, Poughkeepsie, 1916-20; A.B., Woodstock (Md.) Coll., 1922, A.M., 1923; student Ignatuiskolleg, Valkenburg, Holland, 1924-28; Ph.D., Goergetown U., 1933. Entered Society of Jesus, 1916; ordained priest R.C. Ch., Holland, 1927. Instr. in mathematics, Coll. of Holy Cross, Worcester, Mass., 1915-16; prof. of chemistry and dir. seismic station, Fordham U., 1923-24; prof. of astronomy and asst. dir. Georgetown Astron. Observatory, 1928-30; dir. Seismol. Observatory, Georgetown U., from 1930, head of dept. and prof. of math. physics, from 1932, dean of Grad. Sch., 1934-36. Mem. A.A.A.S., Math. Assn. America, Am. Math. Soc., Am. Geophys. Union, Seismol. Soc. Am., Astronomische Gesellschaft, Washington Philos. Soc., Phi Lambda Upsilon, Tau Beta Pi, Sigma Xi. Democrat. Mem. K. of C. Author: Theoretical Seismology, Part I, 1936, Part II, 1932; The Stereographic Projection, 1941. Contbr. to professional jours. Died July 1972.

SOLF Y MURO, ALFREDO, Peruvian foreign minister; b. Lambayegue, Peru, May 16, 1878; s. Alfredo Solf and Ricardina Muro; graduate (as lawyer) Univ. San Marcos, Lima, Peru. Became prof. law, San Marcos Univ., then rector; minister for fgn. relations since 1939; represented Peru at Rio Conference for American Foreign Ministers. Roman Catholic. Address: Ministerio de Relaciones Exteriores, Azangaro 655 Lima Peru*‡

SOLHEIM, ARTHUR OLIVER, supt. schs.; b. Valley City, N.D., Oct. 6, 1921; s. Elling S. and Helen (Sogaardon) S.; B.A., Concordia Coll., 1947; M.Ed., U. N.D., 1954; m. Phyllis A. Johnson, Nov. 26, 1948; children—William, Edward, Donald. Tchr., coach high sch., Marietta, Minn., 1948-50, Plentywood, Mont., 1950-51, Carrington, N.D., 1951-53, Lanesboro, Minn., 1953-57; supt. schs., Lake Bronson, Minn., 1957-62, Minneota, Minn., 1962-66, Lakefield, Minn., 1966-68. Served with AUS, 1942-45. Mem. N.E.A., Minn. Edn. Assn., Am., Minn. assns. sch. adminstrs. Lutheran. Kiwanian. Home: Lakefield MN Died Dec. 24, 1968.

SOLIDAY, DAVID SHRIVER, investment banker; b. Hanover, Pa., Dec. 11, 1895; s. William R. and Martha Katherine (Winebrenner) S.; grad. Andover Sch., 1913; B.A., Amherst Coll., 1919; m. Louise Huntington Kondolf, May 8, 1920. Engaged in security bus. with Graham, Parsons & Co., Phila., 1920-22; partner Hopper, Soliday & Co., Phila., 1922-66; hon. chmn. Hopper, Soliday, Brooke, Sheridan, Inc., 1966-9; pres., dir. Ekco Oil Co., 1950-61; dir. Peoples Light & Power Co., 1937-40, Tex. Pub. Service Co., 1937-40, Mountain State Power Co., 1940-54, Smith & Wesson Co., McDavid & Co., Inc., 1946-53, Pacific Power & Light Co., 1954-69. Mem. Phila.-Balt.-Wash. Stock Exchange. Bd. dirs. Merion Civic Assn., 1926-59, Merion Community Assn., 1928-69. Served with U.S. Army, 1918. Mem. Psi Upsilon. Clubs: Phila. Country, Racquet (Phila.). Home: Merion Station PA Died June 19, 1969.

SOLON, HARRY, portrait painter; b. San Francisco, June 5, 1873; s. Meyer and Bertha (Goodman) S.; ed. Calif. Sch. of Design, 1889-91, Art Inst. Chicago, 1895-98, Academie Julian, Paris, 1910-12; unmarried. Works: portrait of Dr. Bennett Mitchell, Capitol Bldg., Des Moines, Ia.; Hon. Edwin Morgan, U.S. Ambassador to Rio Janeiro; Hon. Leland Harrison, U.S. diplomatic service; etc. Address: Florida 935, Buenos Aires Argentina‡

SOLON, LEON VICTOR, artist, writer; b. Stoke-on-Trent, England, 1872; s. Louis M. (artist, author, collector) and Laura (Arnoux) S.; ed. under tutelage; studied art Royal Coll. of Art, London (nat. scholarship and Royal Exhbn. medalist); m. Marjorie Anderson of Dundee, Scotland. Formerly frequent exhibitor at Paris Salon, Royal Acad. London, and at internat. and other art exhbns. Came to U.S., 1909, and engaged in decoration and art direction of various industries; made polychromatic decorations of architecture and sculpture for Museum of Fine Arts, Phila.; coloring of exterior sculpture, Rockefeller Centre. Awarded Brunner prize for research into science of design and color composition, its educational application, 1940. Pres. bd. trustees New York Sch. of Applied Design for Women. Mem. Nat. Sculpture Soc. (treas. and mem. council), Archtl. League of New York (successively treas., sec., v.p.), Nat. Soc. Mural Painters, Hellenic Soc. (London). Awarded Friedsam gold medal, 1924; gold medal, Am. Inst. Architects, 1931; gold medal citation, Architectural League of New York, 1932; Binns medal Am. Ceramic Soc.; President's medal, Archtl. League, 1935; international gold and silver medals for decorative painting. Author: Polychromy, Architectural and Sculptural. Contbr. to architectural and other publs. Address: Palm View Guest Home, 4204 Manatee Av., W., Brandenton FL‡

SOMERVILLE, FREDERICK HOWLAND, educator, author; b. Northfield, Vt., Apr. 7, 1872; s. Josiah G. and Florence (Brown) S.; B.S., in C.E., Worcester Poly. Inst., 1895; m. Eleanor C. Stacey, of Phila., Pa., Apr. 8, 1909. Master of mathematics, Lawrenceville (N.J.) Sch., 1895-1903, William Penn Charter Sch., Phila., 1903-14, also spl. examiner Civ. Service Commn., Phila., 1912-13; headmaster Wilkes-Barre Acad., 1914-18; gen. editor and Eastern mgr. for W.H. Wheeler & Co., pubs., Chicago, since 1918. Republican. Conglist. Author: First Year in Algebra, 1905; Elementary Algebra, 1908; Exercises in Algebra (with E. R. Robbins), 1905; (series of arithmetics) Primary, Intermediate, Advanced (with E. U. Graff), 1919. Home: 38 S. Ashmead Pl., Germantown PA Address: 201 N. Broad St., Philadelphia PA‡

SOMMER, MARTIN S., clergyman, educator; b. Baltimore County, Md., Mar. 31, 1869; s. William M. C. and Emily (Fritsche) S.; A.B., Baltimore City Coll., 1889; grad. Concordia Sem., St. Louis, 1892; hon. Litt.D., Valparaiso U., 1937; m. Laura Brinkmeyer (died 1916); m. 2d, Mary E. Kohne, July 15, 1918; children—Martin W. H., Roger Llewellyn. Ordained Evang. Luth. ministry, 1892; pastor Grace Ch., St. Louis, 1892-1920; built new church and started 5 congregations; prof. homiletics. Concordia Theol. Sem., 1920-46. Republican. Author: Prayer Book, 1902; Life of Luther, 1910; The Voice of History, 1913; The Truth Which Makes Us Free. Editor of The Lutheran Witness since 1914.‡

SOMMERS, CHARLES LEISSRING, merchant; b. Green Bay, Wis., Feb. 14, 1870; s. George and Amalie (Stern) S.; B.A., U. of Minn., 1890; m. Rosa Davidson, May 3, 1904; children—Davidson, Elinor Julia. Trustee G. Sommers & Co. (est. 1881, as B. Sommers Co.); wholesale gen. mdse. Regent U. of Minn., 1910-23; pres. St. Paul Bur. Research, 1932-34; chmn. City and Co. Bd. Pub. Welfare, St. Paul, 1928-35; chmn. Minn. Sanitorium Commn., 1918-19; mem. St. Paul Charter Commn. since 1947. Selected One of 100 Living Greats of Minn., 1950; Distinguished Service award University Minn., 1951; Silver Beaver, Silver Antelope and Silver Buffalo, Boy Scouts Am. President Ramsey Co. Sanitarium; dir. Children's Hosp., Nat. Council Christians and Jews. Hon. life mem. St. Paul Community Chest, Nat. Exec. Bd. Boy Scouts Am. Mem. Phi Beta Kappa, Pi Beta Nu, Beta Theta Pi. Clubs: Rotary, St. Paul Assn., St. Paul Athletic. Minn. Rep. Unitarian. Home: 7 Crocus Hill. Office: 315 Newton Bldg., St Paul MN‡

SONDERN, FREDERIC EWALD, pathologist; b. Stuttgart, Germany, Mar. 30, 1867; s. Charles F. and Augusta (Bever) S.; brought to U.S., 1871; ed. under tutors; M.D., Coll. Physicians and Surgeons (Columbia), 1889; m. Elsa M. Ottmann, Apr. 30, 1895. Began practice at N.Y. City, 1889; former pres. N.Y. Post-Grad. Med. Sch. and Hosp. Member Am. Assn. Pathologists and Bacteriologists, N.Y. Pathol. Soc., N.Y. Acad. Medicine. Republican. Episcopalian. Club: University. Home: 180 W. 58th St., New York City*‡

SONFIELD, ROBERT LEON, lawyer, assn. ofcl.; b. Nacogdoches, Tex., Mar. 6, 1893; s. Leon and Martha (Chapman) S.; LL.B., U. Tex., 1915; grad. student, Columbia, 1915-16; m. Dorothy Huber, Sept. 15, 1927 (dec. Dec. 1949); children—Robert Leon, Richard Huber; m. 2d, Margie Whitson Erwin, Aug. 24, 1952; 1 stepson, Thomas Sidney Erwin. Admitted Tex. bar, 1915; practice in Beaumont, 1916-17, in Houston, 1921-70; mem. firm Sonfield & Sonfield, 1958-70, Sonfield & Hasse, Brownsville, Tex., 1970-72; pres. Republic Title Company Houston (Texas); chmn. legal research group Houston Commn. Zoning, 1961-62. Mem. S.A.R., 1918-72, pres. Tex., 1960-61, nat. trustee for Tex., 1959-60, chancellor gen., 1961-63, pres. gen., 1963-64. Independent candidate for justice Tex. Ct. Civil Appeals, 1948. Served with 36th Div., U.S. Army, 1917-21; AEF in Germany; served to lt. col. AUS, 1942-47. Mem. State Bar Tex., Cameron County Bar Assn., Sons Confederate Vets., Am. Legion (dist. comdr. 1940-41), Freedom's Found. Valley Forge, Am. Judicature Soc., Patriotic Edn., Inc. Methodist. Club: Knife and Fork (Houston), Houston Turn-Verein (life). Valley Inn and Country (Brownsville). Home: Brownsville TX Died June 24, 1972.

SONNETT, JOHN FRANCIS, lawyer; b. Throgs Neck, N.Y., July 14, 1912; s. John A. and Margaret (McLaughlin) S.; B.S., Fordham U., 1933, LL.B., 1936; m. Monya Karpeshuk, June 24, 1939; children—John Peter, Stephen Franklin. Admitted to N.Y. bar, 1936; asso. firm Cotton, Franklin, Wright & Gordon, N.Y.C., 1936-41; exec. asst. to U.S. atty. So. Dist. N.Y., 1941-43; chief asst. U.S. atty., 1943; civilian spl. asst. to sec. navy, 1945; asst. U.S. atty. gen. charge claims div. Dept. Justice, 1945-47, asst. U.S. atty. gen. charge anti-trust div., 1947-48; partner firm Cahill, Gordon, Sonnett Reindel & Ohl, N.Y.C., 1948-66, sr. partner, 1967-69. Dir. Perkins Services N.V., Massey Ferguson Services N.V., FOSECO, Inc. Served to lt. comdr. USNR, 1943-45. Clubs: University, India House (N.Y.C.); Army and Navy Nat. Lawyers (Washington); Coral Ridge Yacht (Ft. Launderdale, Fla.). Home: New York City NY Died July 31, 1969.

SONNEYSYN, H. O. (SONNY), editor; b. Granite Falls, Minn., Mar. 23, 1900; s. T. and Anne (Olson) S.; student Park Region Luther Coll., Fergus Falls, Minn., 1918-19, St. Olaf Coll., Northfield, Minn., 1919-20; m. Margaret E. Stussy, Sept. 17, 1955. Printer's devil Clarissa (Minn.) Ind., 1912-17; reporter Fergus Falls Free Press, 1919-20; mem. editorial staff Ironwood (Mich.) Daily Globe, 1924-27, city editor, 1928-30; mgr. area office, 1930-35; reporter Duluth (Minn.) Free Press, 1935-37; owner, pub. Bertha (Minn.) Herald, 1927-28; editor North Hennepin Post, Robbinsdale, Minn., 1937-40; editor Ironwood (Mich.) Times, 1940-45; exec. editor four Post publs., v.p. of co., Robbinsdale, Minn., 1945-69. Bd. dirs. YMCA. Recipient 1st place for editorial page excellence and Herman Roe Meml. award Minn. Newspaper Assn., 1965. Mem. Minn. Newspaper Assn., Sigma Delta Chi. Mason, Lion. Clubs: Half Century; Minnesota Press. Home: Robbinsdale MN Died Dec. 20, 1969.

SONTAG, RAYMOND JAMES, prof. of history; b. Chgo., Oct. 2, 1897; s. Anthony Charles and Mary Elizabeth (Walsh) S.; B.S., U. Ill.; 1920, A.M., 1921; Ph.D., U. Pa., 1924; Litt.D., Marquette U., 1959; LL.D., Notre Dame, 1960, U. Cal., 1966; m. Dorothea Agar, June 17, 1927 (dec. Apr. 1965); children—John Philip, Mary Agnes (Mrs. R.E. Johnson), William Robert, James. Instr., U. Iowa, 1921-22; instr. history Princeton U., 1924-25, asst. prof., 1925-30, asso. prof., 1930-39, Henry Charles Lea prof. and chmn. dept. history, 1939-41; Sidney Hellman Ehrman prof. European history U. Cal. at Berkeley, 1941-65, emeritus, 1965-72. Chief of German War Documents Project. Dept. State, 1946-49. Served as 2d lt. inf., U.S. Army, 1918. Mem. Am. Philos. Soc., Am. Catholic Hist. Assn. (pres. 1952), Am. Hist. Assn. (pres. Pacific Coach br. 1959). Council on Fgn. Relations. Author: (with D. C. Munro) The Middle Ages, 1928; European Diplomatic History, 1871-1932, 1933; Germany and England-Background of Conflict, 1938; A Broken World, 1919-1939, 1971. Editor: Documents on German Foreign Policy, 1918-45, (Am. editor-in-chief), 1949; Nazi-Soviet Relations (with J. S. Beddie), 1948. Address: Berkeley CA Died Oct. 27, 1972; buried St. Joseph's Cemetery, San Pablo CA

SOONG, T.V., pres. Bank of China, former minister of finance, pres. Exec. Yuan; b. 1891; s. Charles Jones (Charlie) Soong; member of Soong family ruling China today; brother of Madame Chiang Kai-shek; student St. John's Shanghai; A.B., Harvard, 1915; Ph.D., Columbia. Sec. Canton Govt., 1923; pres. Canton Central Bank, then Shanghai Central Bank, 1924; state councilor Nat. Chinese Govt., 1928; minister of finance of Nat. Govt., 1928-33 (resigned); vice pres. Exec. Yuan, later acting pres., 1930, became pres. 1939; mem. Nat. Econ. Council of China from 1932; founder Bank of China and chmn. from 1936; chmn. of bd. Bank of Canton from 1936; minister of finance from 1939; negotiated large U.S. loan to China; became China's rep. on Pacific War Council, Mar. 1942, replaced Generalissimo Chiang Kai-shek as acting pres. of Chinese Cabinet, Dec. 1944; resigned as Premier of China, Feb. 1947; mem. State Council of China. Considered best financier ever produced by China" (John Gunther); established Chinese finance on Western system, and world-renowned as a financier. Died April 25, 1971.*

SOPER, HORACE WENDELL, physician; b. Hillsboro, Ill., Aug. 25, 1867; s. William Leroy and Sarah D. (Homrighaus) S.; grad. high sch., Ramsey, Ill.; M.D., Washington U., St. Louis, Mo., 1894; m. Mary Reynolds Holcombe, Aug. 12, 1908. Practice at St. Louis since 1894; specializes in diseases of digestive system. Member A.M.A. (chmn. and sec. gastro-enterology and proctology sect.), Am. Gastro-Enterol. Assn. Clubs: University, St. Louis Country. Author: Clinical Gastro-Enterology, and Health Essays. Home: 4731 Westminster Pl. Office: Wall Bldg., Vandeventer and Olive Sts., St Louis MO‡

SORDONI, ANDREW JOHN, JR., bldg. and electric line constrn. co. exec.; b. Forty Fort, Pa., Dec. 29, 1916; s. Andrew John and Ruth (Speece) S.; student U. Pa., 1935-38; m. Margaret Barnard, July 26, 1941; children—Andrew John III, William, George, Stephen. Founder, 1946, now chmn. bd. Sterling Products Co., Kingston, Pa.; founder, 1947, now chmn. bd., dir. Sterling Truck Sales; chmn. bd., pres., dir. Commonwealth Telephone Co., Dallas, Pa., 1964-67; pres. Harvey's Lake Light Co., Dallas, Pa., 1948-67, Sterling Engring. & Mfg. Co., Wilkes-Barre, Pa., 1949-67, Sordoni Constrn. Co., Forty Fort, 1955-67, Sterling Hotels System, Wilkes Barre, 1958-67, pres., dir. Nat. Tree Surgeons, Inc., Forty Fort, Pub. Service Enterprises of Pa., Inc., Sordoni Enterprises, Inc.; gen. mgr. Lacy, Atherton & Davis, Wilkes-Barre, Sterling Farms, Alderson; dir. Pa. Mfrs. Assn. Ins. Co., United Gas Improvement Co. Pres. Andrew J. Sordoni Found., Inc.; dir., exec. com., finance com. Samuel H. Kress Found., N.Y.C. Trustee, past pres. Wyo. Valley Hosp. Wilkes-Barre. Served to capt. USAF, 1942-46. Mem. Pa. C. of C. (past pres., dir.), Pa. Ind. Telephone Assn. (dir.), Luzerne County (v.p.), Pa. (gov.) mfrs. assns., Navy League U.S. (charter) V.F.W., Am. Legion, Beta Theta Pi. Republican. Mason (Shriner, Jester), Rotarian. Clubs: Marco Polo; Union League (Phila.); Westmoreland. Home: Forty Fort PA Died July 9, 1967.

SORENSEN, CHARLES E., automobile executive; b. Copenhagen, Denmark, Sept. 7, 1881; s. Soren and Eva Christine (Abrahamson) S.; brought to U.S., 1885; naturalized through father's citizenship; ed. Buffalo, N.Y. pub. schools; m. Helen E. Mitchell, June 30, 1904; 1 son, Clifford M.; m. 2d, Edith Thompson Montgomery, Jan., 1960; Began as apprentice in pattern dept., Jewett Stove Works, Buffalo, N.Y., 1895, later worked in tool room, foundry, machine shop and drafting room; pattern-maker Art Stove Works, Detroit, 1900, and later Mich. Stove Works; as pattern-maker with Bryant & Berry, machinists and foundrymen, Detroit, met Henry Ford, then engaged in exptl. work; with Ford Motor Co. 1904-44, beginning as pattern-maker, later in charge of dept., advanced to asst. supt., gen. supt., vice-president and director; resigned Mar. 13, 1944. Elected pres. and dir. Willys-Overland Motors, Inc., July 12, 1944, vice chmn. bd. dirs., Jan. 15, 1946; dir. Miami Beach First Nat. Bank. Pres. Miami Heart Inst. Decorated by Denmark, Norway, Czechoslovakia. Clubs: LaGprce Country, Committee of 100, Bath (Miami Beach, Fla.); Estate Carlton Golf, HaPenny Bay, St. Croix Tennis, St. Croix Country (St. Croix, Virgin Islands). Home: St Croix VI Died Aug. 13, 1968.

SORENSEN, JOHN HJELMHOF, advt. exec., cartoonist; b. Copenhagen, Denmark, Nov. 22, 1923; s. Paul Albertus and Elly (Hjelmhof) S.; student N. Copenhagen, 1941-43; m. Elizabeth Lucille Hunter, June 25, 1949; children—Karen, Lise, Erik. Came to U.S., 1946, naturalized, 1951. Accountant, Copenhagen, 1941-45, N.Y.C., 1946-47, 49-50; art and creative director with various advertising agencies, 1955-69; pres. John Sorensen & Associates, Inc., advt. agency, Little Rock, 1959-69. Cartoonist, 1953-69, for popular mags. in U.S., book selections, also publs. in Can., Eng., France, Italy, Scandinavia, Germany, Spain, S.A., Orient. Bd. dirs. Goodwill Industries, Performing Arts Council; chmn. bd. dirs. Ark. Arts Festival; trustee Ark. State Sanatorium. Served with Danish Army, 1945-46. Recipient 1st awards Outdoor Advt. Assn. Am. for best outdoor campaign of yr., 1956-59; John Sorensen Permanent Collection established in library Syracuse U., 1966. Mem. Nat. Cartoonists Soc. Clubs: Little Rock, Top of Rock, Hardscrabble Country, Little Rock Racquet. Home: Little Rock AR Died Apr. 6, 1969; buried Pine Crest Meml. Park Little Rock AR

SORENSON, ROY, assn. exec.; b. Milw., June 17, 1900; s. Peter C. and Hannah (Peterson) S.; Ph.B., U. Wis., 1922; grad. study U. Chgo., 1932; LL.D., Golden Gate Coll., 1960; m. Pearl Lichtfeldt, June 23, 1925; 1 son, Glenn. Sec. boys' work Milw. YMCA, 1922-27; program staff Nat. Council YMCA's, Chgo., 1927-36; mem. nat. bd. YMCA's; instr. boys' work, spring terms George Williams Coll., Chgo., 1928-35; asso. exec. Nat. Council, 1936-46, gen. sec. YMCA of San Francisco, 1946-66. Chmn. Gov.'s Commn. on Met. Problems, 1959; mem. Cal. Commn. State Govt. orgn and Economy, 1962; mem. nat. exec. com. 1960 White House Conf. on Children and Youth, 1959; mem. Nat. Com. Children and Youth, 1960, chmn., 1964; chairman California Coordinating Council for Urban Policy, 1964; chairman California Inter-Govtl. Council on Urban Growth, 1965. Dir. Community Research Assos., N.Y. Past pres., trustee Rosenberg Found., San Francisco. Club: Rotary. Author: Community Survey of Social and Health Work, Kansas City, Mo., 1939; The Art of Board Membership, 1950; Designing Education for Values; A Case Study in Institutional Change, 1955. Contbr. numerous articles profl. jours. Home: Sausalito CA Died Dec. 12, 1966; buried Mt. Tamalpais Cemetery, San Rafael CA

SOSMAN, ROBERT BROWNING, chemist; b. Chillicothe, O., Mar. 17, 1881; s. Francis A. and Mary R. (Browning) S.; B.Sc., Ohio State U., 1903, hon. Sc.D., 1938; S.B., Mass. Inst. Tech., 1904, Ph.D., 1907; Sc.D., Alfred U., 1953, U. Toledo, 1954; m. Sarah Gibson Noble, September 30, 1911; children—Robert Noble, George Gibson, Esther Browning, Edward Carey. In lab. of A. D. Little, Boston, 1906-08; physicist, asst. dir., Geophysical Lab., Carnegie Inst., 1908-28; phys. chemist, asst. dir. Research Lab., U.S. Steel Corp., 1928-47; prof., Dept. Ceramics, Rutgers University, 1947-62. Consulting chemist, Ordnance Dept., U.S. Army, 1918; lecturer on geophysics, Mass. Inst. Tech., 1925-26; nat. councilor, Ohio State University Research Foundation, 1937-45. Chmn. com. C-8 on refractories, Am. Soc. Testing Materials, 1948-56. Mem. Am. Chem. Soc., Am. Phys. Soc., Am. Ceramic Soc. (pres. 1937, Orton Meml. lectr., hon. mem. 1952, Bleininger Award, 1953, Purdy Award, 1957, Jeppson award 1960), Am. Assn. U. Profs., Am. Geophys. Union, Am. Inst. Mining and Metall. Engrs. (Howe Meml. Lectr., 1948), Geol. Soc. Am., N.Y., N.J. mineral. clubs, Brit. (hon.), German ceramic socs., Appalachian Mt. Club (chairman N.Y. chpt., 1942-44), Sigma Xi; past president, Philos. Society Washington (1920), Washington Academy Sciences (1928). Club: Delta Upsilon. Author of The Properties of Silica, 1927; Pyrometry of Solids and Surfaces, 1940; and papers in scientific periodicals on high-temperature thermometry, refractories, and mineral chemistry and physics. Home: Westfield NJ Died Oct. 30, 1967.

SOUERS, SIDNEY WILLIAM, business exec.; b. Dayton, O., Mar. 30, 1892; s. Edgar D. and Catherine (Rieker) S.; student Purdue U., 1911-12; A.B., Miami U., 1914, LL.D., 1953; LL.D., Lindenwood Coll., 1966; m. Sylvia Mettell, May 28, 1943. Pres. Mortgage & Securities Co., New Orleans, 1920-25, Piggly Wiggly Stories, Memphis, Mar. 1925-Oct. 1926; exec. v.p. Canal Bank & Trust Co., New Orleans, La., 1925-30; financial v.p. Mo. State Life Ins. Co., St. Louis, 1930-33; v.p. General Am. Life Ins. Co., 1933-37, dir., exec. com., 1936-73, exec. v.p., 1937-41, chmn. exec. com., 1953-54, chmn. bd., 1954-57, pres., chmn. 1957-58, chmn., chief exec. officer, 1958-65, chmn. bd., chmn. exec. com., 1965-69, chmn. emeritus, dir., exec. com., 1969-73; dir., past chmn. bd. Nat. Service Industries, Inc., Atlanta; dir. Volkswagan Ins. Co., Transit Casualty Co., hon. dir. McDonnell Douglas Corp. Commr., treas., chmn. finance com. Bi-State Devel. Agy. Trustee Jefferson Nat. Expansion Meml. Assn.; bd. dirs. United Fund of Greater St. Louis. Dir. emeritus Lindenwood College, St. Charles, Mo.; trustee Westminster Coll., Govtl. Research Inst.; hon. trustee George Washington Coll., Govtl. Research Inst.; hon. trustee George Washington U. Exec. sec. Nat. Security Council, 1947-50; spl. cons. (mil.-fgn.) to Pres. of U.S., 1950-53. Served to rear adm. USNR, 1940-46; first dir. of CIA. Decorated D.S.M. (Navy), Legion of Merit. Mem. Res. Officers Assn., Mil. Order World Wars, Navy League (bd. councilors St. Louis Council), World Affairs Council Greater St. Louis, U.S. Naval Acad. Found. (bd. govs.), Automobile Club Mo. (gov.), Ret. Officers Assn., Advt. Club Greater St. Louis, Mo. Acad. Squires, Delta Kappa Epsilon. Democrat. Presbyn. Clubs: La Coquille (West Palm Beach, Fla.); University; Boston (New Orleans, La.); Capital City Country (Atlanta); Armed Forces Officers, Mo. Athletic Assn., Noonday, Bogey Golf Roundtable, St. Louis, Media, Old Warson Country (St. Louis); Army and Navy, Metropolitan, Chevy Chase Country (Washington); Garden of Gods (Colorado Springs). Home: 625 S Skinker Blvd St Louis MO Died Jan. 14, 1973.

SOULE, EDWARD LEE, mfg. exec.; b. Little Shasta, Cal., Jan. 9, 1882; s. Stephen Hodgeboom and Lucinda Maria (Boyes) S.; B.S., U. Cal. at Berkeley, 1904; m. Addie McCurdy, Dec. 11, 1913; children—Lucile (Mrs. Daniel Arnon), Edward Lee, Stanley E., Howard S. Pres. Soule Steel Co., 1911-54, chmn. bd., 1954-71. Chmn. bd. trustees Edward L. and Addie M. Soule Found.; dir. Berkeley YMCA. Presbyn. Mason (Shriner). Club: Bohemian (San Francisco). Home: Berkeley CA Died Jan. 7, 1971; buried Sunset Cemetary, Berkeley CA

SOULE, ELIZABETH STERLING, nursing education; b. East Douglas, Mass., Oct. 13, 1884; d. Edwin (M.D.) and Adeline (Bates) Sterling; grad. Malden Hosp. Sch. of Nursing, 1907; A.B., U. of Wash., 1926, A.M., 1930; D.Sc., Mont. State Coll., 1944; m. Harry W. Soule, June 11, 1912. Engaged in public health nursing from 1909; mem. staff pub. health nursing, Mass., 1909-12; mem. Seattle, Walla Walla County, State Bd. of Health (Wash.), 1912-20; adminstrn. and teaching, Sch. of Nursing Education, U. of Wash., 1920-45, dean, 1945-50, dean, prof. emeritus, Traveling guest of the Rockefeller Foundation to study schs. of nursing in Europe, 1930. Fellow Am. Pub. Health Assn.; mem. Am. Nurses Association, American Sch. of Nursing, Nat. Orgn. for Public Health Nursing, National League Nursing Edn., American Assn. Univ. Professors, Assn. Collegiate Schs. Nursing (past pres.), Am. Legion Auxiliary, Pi Lambda Theta, Alpha Kappa Delta, Phi Mu. Author: Community Hygiene (with Christine MacKenzie), 1940. Alumnus summa laude dignatus, U. of Wash. Home: Alderwood Manor WA Died Feb. 19, 1972.

SOURDIS, EVARISTA, Colombian foreign min.; b. Sabanalarga, Atlantico, Colombia, Mar. 29, 1908; s. Aristides M. and Raquel Juliao S.; Baccalaureate studies Colegio de Barranquilla, Colombia; Dr. Law and Polit. and Social Scis., Law Faculty Externado de Colombia, Bogota, 1939; m. Adelaida Najera, July 11, 1936; children—Adelaida Maria, Maria Teresa, Evaristo de Jesus. Judge Barran-Quilla Dist., 1 yr.; sec. of state Dept. Atlantico, 2 mos.; mem. Ho. of Reps., 2 periods, 2 yrs. each; ex-senator of the Republic. Ambassador of Colombia to IX Pan Am. Conf., Bogota; minister of labour, minister of war, minister of justice, minister of fgn. affairs, 3 yrs.; ambassador and spl. envoy presiding the Mission to Rome in the Holy Year. Ambassador of Colombia to II Session of U.N. Gen. Assembly, chmn. Colombian delegation to VII session; later permanent del. to U.N. and prin. rep. of Colombia to Security Council, with rank of ambassador and envoy extraordinary and plenipotentiary; now minister fgn. affairs Colombia. Decorated Gran Cruz de Boyaca (Colombia), Orden Roben Dario. Mem. Colombian Acad. Jurisprudence. Author: La Teoria del Domicilio en el Derecho Internacional Privado. Home: Bogota Colombia Died Sept. 1970.

SOUSER, KENNETH, lawyer; b. Rockwell, Pa., Oct. 21, 1905; s. Russell R. and Grace (Critchfield) S. A.B., U. Pa., 1927, LL.B., 1930; m. Margaret Smith, Oct. 9, 1930. Admitted to Pa. bar, 1930; since practiced in Phila.; asso. firm Slocum & Ferguson, and successors, 1930-37; mem. firm Saylor Ferguson & Souser, and successors, 1938-59, Morgan, Lewis & Bockius, 1959-70. Chmn. bd. New Hope & Ivyland R.R. Co. Mem. Baker Street Irregulars, Phila. Bar Assn. Republican. Clubs: Lawyers Union League (Phila.). Home: Berwyn PA Died Sept. 4, 1970.

SOUTHWORTH, GEORGE CLARK, research engr., b. Little Cooley, Pa., Aug. 24, 1890; s. Freedom and Mary (Fleek) S.; B.S., Grove City Coll., 1914, M.S., 1916, Ph.D., Yale, 1923, D.Sc. (hon.), Grove City Coll., 1931; m. Lowene Smith, Aug. 14, 1913; children—Margaret Eleanor (Mrs. Arthur G. Pulis), George Howard. Asso. physicist, U.S. Bur. of Standards, 1917-18; instr., asst. prof. physics, Yale, 1918-23; radio research engineer, American Telephone & Telegraph Company, Bell Telephone Laboratory, 1923-55, radio consultant, from 1955. Recipient Medal of Honor, I.R.E., 1963. Fellow A.A.A.S., American Phys. Society, Inst. Radio Engrs.; member Sigma Xi. Awarded Morris Liebmann prize (I.R.E.) 1938, Levy medal (Franklin Inst.), 1946, Ballantine medal (Franklin Inst.) 1947. Republican. Presbyterian. Author: Principles and Applications of Wave-guide Transmission; Forty Years of Radio Research. Contributor of various articles relating to short electromagnetic waves and their application to problems in television and radar. Home: Chatham NJ Died July 6, 1972; buried Little Cooley PA

SOWELL, PAUL DIBRELL, business exec.; b. Little Rock, Ark., June 8, 1904; s. William J. and Dona (Smith) S.; student Ark. Law Sch., 1926, Northwestern U., 1944; m. Leota Ingram, Oct. 23, 1927;children—Jane Eloise (Mrs. Robert Smith Donoho), Paul David, Judith Ellen (Mrs. Walter Barroll Christmas). Clerk Southwestern Bell Tel. Co., 1921-22; clk. and salesman, Crane Co., 1922-26; asst. br. mgr. N. O. Nelson Mfg. Co., 1926-28; sales mgr., 555, Inc. (all at Little Rock), 1928-33; advt. mgr. Leonard Refrigerator Co., Detroit, 1933-36; buyer Montgomery Ward and Co., Chgo, 1936-42, asst. to operating v.p., 1942-44, gen. service mgr., 1944-47; pres. Brager Eisenberg, Inc., Balt., 1947-71; pres. Brager-Gutman, Inc., 1959-63, chmn. bd., 1963-68. Chmn. trustees Commn. govtl. efficiency and economy, Balt., 1963-66. Mem. Retail Mchts. Assn. (mem. bd.), Balt. Assn. Commerce (bd. mem.), Better Bus. Bur. of Balt. (pres. 1966-68; mem. bd. 1962-68), Balt. Retail Credit Bur.

(mem. bd. 1964-69), Md. Hist. Soc. Democrat. Clubs: L'Hirondell, Baltimore Country (Balt.). Home: Baltimore MD Died Dec. 11, 1971.

SOWERBY, LEO, composer, organist; born in Grand Rapids, Mich., May 1, 1895; s. John and Gertrude (Salkeld) S.; settled in Chicago, Ill., at 14; studied piano with Calvin Lampert and Percy Grainger, composition with Arthur Olaf Andersen; Master of Music, Am. Conservatory, Chicago, 1918; hon. Mus.D. from U. of Rochester, 1934; unmarried. Appeared as piano soloist at Norfolk (Conn.) Festival, 1917, and with various Am. and European orchestras since; instr. theory and composition, Am. Conservatory Music, Chgo., until 1962, organist, choirmaster, Cathedral of St. James (Episcopal), Chgo., until 1962; dir. Coll. of Church Musicians, Washington Cathedral, Washington, 1962-68. Enlisted as pvt. U.S. Army, Dec. 8, 1917; sergt., Apr. 1, 1918; bandmaster, Apr. 21, 1918; 2d lt., Aug. 21, 1918; hon. discharged, Feb. 28, 1919; service in U.S., Eng. and France with regimental band, 332d Field Arty. Recipient Pulitzer prize for musical composition, 1946; fellow Royal Sch. Ch. Music, Croydon, Eng., 1963; fellow Trinity Coll., London, 1957. Mem. A.S.C.A.P. Clubs: Cosmos (Washington, D.C.); Cliff Dwellers (Chicago). Compositions: (overture) Comes Autumn Time; Sonata for violin and piano; 2 concertos for piano-forte; Set of Four, for orchestra; Concerto for organ and orchestra; Sernade (string quartet); Quintet (wood wind instruments); Trio (flute, viola and piano); also choral works, organ pieces, piano pieces, songs, ballad for two solo pianofortes and orchestra; 5 symphonies for orchestra; Suite, From Northland"; symphonic poem, Prairie; Symphony in G for organ solo; etc. Apptd. as first Am. composer to the Rome Prize, established in music by the Am. Acad. in Rome, 1921; returned to America 1924. Home: Washington DC Died July 7, 1968; buried Washington Cathedral, Mt. St. Alban, Washington DC

SOWERS, JOSEPH CULLEN, coll. dean; b. Weldon, Tex., July 16, 1909; s. Jesse B. and Fannie (Matson) S.; B.S., Sam Houston State Tchrs. Coll., 1931; M.S., Tex. A. and M. Coll., 1936; Ph.D., U. Tex., 1949; m. Jeanette Cecile Venza, Sept. 5, 1934. High sch. tchr. Tex., 1931-33; supt. schs., Woodlake, Tex., 1934-37; asso. prof. sci. and agr. Sam Houston State Tchrs. Coll., 1937-42, registrar, 1946-51; dean Coll. East Tex. State U., Commerce, 1951-61, dean Faculties and Grad. Sch., 1961-64, provost Grad. Sch., 1964-67, dean, 1964-72. Mem. Commerce City Commn., 1956-72. Chmn. dirs. Commerce United Fund, 1958-72; bd. dirs. Hunt County chpt. A.R.C. Served with USAAF, 1942-46. Mem. N.E.A., Assn. Higher Edn., Tex. Tchrs. Assn., Phi Delta Kappa. Mason (32 deg., K.T.), Kiwanian (past lt. gov., dist. com. chmn.). Author: Some Phases of State Controls of Higher Education in Texas, 1950. Commerce TX Died Aug. 14, 1972; buried Beaumont TX

SPAAK, PAUL HENRI, Belgian govt. ofcl.; born Schaerbeck, January 25, 1899; m. Simonne Rikkers Hottlet Dear, April 1965. Socialist representative for the Arrondissement of Brussels, 1932-66; advocate (lawyer), Court of Appeals, Brussels; former communal counselor, Forest (Brussels), 1925-35; served as minister transport, minister post. telegraph and telphone, 1935; minister fgn. affairs and fgn. trade, 1936; prime minister, May 1938; retired (at own request) as minister fgn. affairs and fgn. trade, Jan. 1939; resigned as prime minister, Feb. 1939; named minister fgn. affairs and fgn. trade, Sept. 1939. Minister of labor, of social foresight and pub. health (London), 1940-44; resigned Sept. 1944, but continued as minister fgn. affairs and fgn. trade until 1957; secretary-general of NATO, 1957-61; vice premier of Belgium, minister of foreign affairs, 1961-66, also minister of African affairs. Pres., 1st Assembly Orgn. U.N.; prime minister and minister fgn. affairs, Mar. 12, 1946; resigned as prime minister, Mar. 21, but continued as minister fgn. affairs and fgn. trade; prime minister and minister fgn. affairs, Mar. 25, 1947; minister of state, 1949-66; chmn. council for European Recovery since 1948; pres. Consultative Assembly, Council of Europe, since 1949; chmn. Internat. Council, European Movement, 1950-66. Recipient 1959 Freedom Award, Freedom House, 1959. Home: Brussels Belgium Died July 1972.

SPAHR, BOYD LEE, lawyer; b. Mechanicsburg, Pa., Apr. 18, 1880; s. Murray Hurst and Clara (Koser) S.; Ph.B., Dickinson, 1900, A.M., 1903; LL.B., U. of Pa., 1904, LL.D., 1952; LL.D., Lafayette, 1933; D.C.L., Dickinson Coll., 1950; married Katharine Febiger, Oct. 8, 1908 (dec. June 1965); children—Boyd Lee, Christian C.F., John F. Admitted Pa. bar, 1904; in practice at Phila.; sr. mem. Ballard, Spahr, Andrews and Ingersoll. Served as major and member of the General Staff in United States Army, 1918. Trustee Dickinson Coll., 1908-70, pres. board, 1931-62, hon. pres., 1962-70. Mem. Hist. Soc. Pa. (past pres.), Society War 1812, Phi Kappa Sigma (nat. pres. 1920-23), Phi Beta Kappa. Episcopalian. Republican. Clubs: Rittenhouse, Union League, Merion Cricket; Century (N.Y.); Bar Harbor (Me.), The Pot and Kettle; Philadelphia. Home: Haverford PA Died Aug. 14, 1970.

SPAHR, WALTER EARL, economist; b. Centerville, Ind., June 27, 1891; s. Isaac Jenkins and Thursa LoRella (Kramer) S.; A.B., Earlham Coll., 1914; student U. Cal. at Berkeley, 1915; M.A., U.Wis., 1917; Ph.D., Columbia, 1925; m. Beulah Evelyn Lowry, Aug. 25, 1920 (dec. Oct. 1962); children—Carol Cecile (Mrs. Robert Bogdasarian) Kenneth Lowry, Jean Miriam (Mrs. Peter Segatto). Instr. history Pacific Coll., Newberg, Ore., 1914-15; instr. econ. history Manual Tng. High Sch., Indpls., 1915-16; asst. polit. sci. U. Wis., 1916-17; prof. polit. sci. Muskingum (O.) Coll., 1918-19; instr. econs. Dartmouth, 1919-20, Columbia, 1920-23; mem. faculty N.Y.U., 1923-56, prof. econs., 1928-56, chmn. dept., 1927-56, prof. emeritus, 1956-70; asso. prof. pub. finance Princeton, 1927; secretary, executive vice pres. Economists National Committee on Monetary Policy, 1933-70; trustee Tax Foundation, 1937-66. Ind. economist Republican Nat. convs., 1936, 40, 44. Recipient Alvin T. Simonds econ. prize Simonds Saw and Steel Co., 1929; Master Prophecy award Newsweek mag., 1939; Freedoms Found. award, 1949. Mem. Am. Econ. Assn. Author, editor books and articles in field; author Monetary Notes, monthly, numerous vols., 1940-70. Home: Bellerose LI NY Died Jan. 19, 1970; buried Greenfield Cemetery, Hempstead NY

SPAID, WILLIAM WESLEY, lawyer; b. Washington, Nov. 8, 1903; s. William Winfield and Ada (Bain) S.; B.S., Colgate U., 1926; J.D., U. Ariz., 1933; m. Estelle Abbott, Aug. 27, 1928; children—Estelle (Mrs. John U. Vincon), Salley (Mrs. Harold D. Adamson, Jr.). With Nat. Bank Commerce, N.Y.C., 1926-29; admitted to Ariz. bar, 1933, practiced in Tucson, 1933-72; partner firm Spaid, Fish, Briney & Duffield, 1963-72; Ariz. price atty. OPA, 1943. Mem. Ariz. Ho. of Reps., 1934-40, speaker spl. sessions of 14th Legislature, 1940. Mem. Am., Ariz. (gov. 1964-70), Pima County (pres. 1963-70) bar assns., Am. Bd. Trial Advocates (asso.), Am. Arbitration Assn. (arbitrator), Assn. ICC Practitioners, Phi Alpha Delta, Phi Gamma Delta. Presbyn. Mason (Shriner). Clubs: Tucson Country, Old Pueblo (Tucson). Home: Tucson AZ Died Apr. 1972.

SPALDING, ALFRED BAKER, M.D., obstetrics and gynecology; b. Atchison, Kan., July 19, 1874; s. Azel Wainwright and Olivia McConnell (Parker) S.; A.B., Stanford, 1896; M.D., Columbia, 1900; m. Mary Polhemus, of San Francisco, Calif., Oct. 29, 1902; children—Edward Polhemus, Alfred Baker. House surgeon Gen. Memorial Hosp., New York, 1900-01; asst. res. phys. Sloane Maternity Hosp., 1901-02; moved to San Francisco, 1902, and began practice as obstetrician and gynecologist; instr. in obstetrics, 1902-05, asst. prof., 1905-09, prof., 1909-12, U. of Calif.; prof obstetrics and gynecology, Stanford University Medical School, 1912-35, professor emeritus since 1935. Organized San Francisco Maternity, January 1, 1904. Member Pacific Coast Surg. Association, A.M.A., Calif. Med. Soc., Am. Gynecol. Soc. Am. Foundation for Musicians. Fellow Am. Academy of Arts and Sciences. Author: Tonal Counterpoint, 1904; (with Arthur Foot). Modern Harmony in Its Theory and Practice; Music—an Art and a Language, 1920; History of Music at Harvard, 1929; Music at Harvard-a Historical Review, 1935. Has had much to do with raising standard of music study in the public schools of New England; has often spoken in connection with N.E. Edn. League. Mem. Com. on Army and Navy Camp Music during war period. Lecturer on the appreciation of music in 9 French univs., 1920-21, under auspices of the James Hazen Hyde Foundation. Home: 985 Memorial Drive, Cambridge MA‡

SPALDING, ALICE HUNTINGTON, coll. prof.; b. Evanston, Ill., Feb. 3, 1875; d. John Joel and Cornelia Tracy (Pettis) S.; grad. Cumnock Sch. of Oratory (now Sch. of Speech), Northwestern U., 1897. Teacher of pub. speaking, since 1897, dean of women 1911-24, prof. pub. speaking since 1925, Allegheny Coll.; dramatic reader. Mem. Nat. Assn. Acad. Teachers of Pub. Speaking, Nat. Assn. Univ. Profs., Pub. Speaking Conf. of Middle and Eastern States. Home: Meadville PA‡

SPALDING, GEORGE R., army officer; b. Monroe, Mich., Jan. 25, 1877; s. Gen. George and Augusta (Lewis) S.; B.S., U.S. Mil. Acad., 1901; grad. Engr. Sch. of Application, 1905, Field Engring. Sch., 1911, Army War Coll., 1920; m. Alice Minnie Ruff, Sept. 17, 1904; children—George, Alice (Mrs. L. R. Wirak), Albert Ruff. Commd. 2d lt., Corps Engrs., 1901, and advanced through the grades to brig. gen., 1936; served in P.I., 1901-03; mapping and camp layout, Va. maneuvers, 1904; locks and dams, Ohio River, 1905-06; improvement Great Lakes and connecting channels, 1907; river and harbor works, Fla., 1908-11; instr. field engring., Command and Gen. Staff Sch., 1911-15; Ohio River Improvement, Cincinnati and Louisville, 1916-17; with A.E.F., as comdg. officer, 305th Engrs., div. engr., 80th Div., corps engr., 5th Corps.; chief engr., 1st Army and 3rd Army; deputy chief engr. A.E.F.; instr. Army War Coll., 1919-20; dir. course supply and transportation, 1920-23; charge, construction Wilson Dam, Tenn. River, 1923-25; Ohio River locks and dams, 1925-29; div. engr., improvement of Missouri, Upper Mississippi, Illinois and Ohio, 1929-33; comd. Engr. Sch. and Post, Ft. Belvoir, Va., 1933-34; div. engr. N.Y., 1935-36; asst. chief of staff, War Dept., 1936-38; retired for disability, 1938; recalled to Office of Chief of Staff in organization of Lend-Lease Adminstrn., 1941; army service forces in liaison with various civilian agencies; office of Chief of Staff, assisting in organization of Public Works Adminstrn., 1932. Awarded Officer Order of Leopold (Belgium), Legion of Honor (France); D.S.M., U.S. Life Saving medal. Awarded D.S.M., Oak Leaf Cluster. Returned to disability list, Jan. 7, 1945, and ordered home. Mem. Soc. Am. Military Engrs. Home: 202 N. 18th St., Bradenton FL‡

SPALDING, HUGHES, lawyer; b. Atlanta, Ga., Aug. 10, 1886; s. Jack Johnson and Elizabeth (Hughes) S.; A.B., Georgetown U., 1908, LL.D., 1956; LL.B., U. Ga., 1910; LL.D., Oglethorpe U., 1951; married Bolling Stovall Phinizy, February 7, 1912; children—Jack Johnson III, Eleanor (Mrs. George S. Craft), Hughes, Bolling (Mrs. J. Wallace Winborne, Jr.) Phinizy. Admitted to Georgia bar, 1910, and since in practice at Atlanta; sr. mem. King & Spalding; adv. dir. Trust Co. Ga.; mem. finance com. The Coca-Cola Co.; director of Coca-Cola International Corp., Whitehead Holding Co., Habersham Mills. Trustee of the Lettie Pate Evans Found., Emily and Ernest Woodruff Found. 1st lt. F.A., R.O.T.C., during World War. Chmn. bd. regents U. System Ga., 1933-34, 1949-51. Chmn. Fulton County Dem. Exec. Com., 1937-38. Privy Chamberlain Supernumerary of Sword and Cape to His Holiness, Pope Pius XXIII. Awarded Certificate of Merit by Alumni Soc. U. Ga., 1938; John Carroll award, Georgetown Univ., 1953. Mem. Am., Georgia State, Atlanta bar assns., U. Ga. Alumni Soc. (ex-pres.), Georgetown U. Alumni Assn. (mem. senate), Am. Law Inst., Am. Judicature Soc., Phi Beta Kappa, Chi Phi, Phi Delta Phi, Sphinx, Gridiron, Demosthenian Soc. (U. of Ga.). Mem. Am. Legion, Mil. Order of World Wars. Democrat. Catholic. Clubs: Lawyers', Capital City, Piedmont Driving (Atlanta). Home: Atlanta GA Died Mar. 30, 1969; buried Arlington Cemetery, Sandy Springs, nr. Atlanta GA

SPALDING, KEITH, rancher; b. Chicago, Ill., Oct. 7, 1877; s. Albert Goodwill and Sarah Josephine (Keith) S.; student Hill Sch., Pottstown, Pa., 1893-1896; B.A., Yale, 1902; m. Eudora Hull, Dec. 29, 1906 (dec. 1942); m. 2d Lois M. Fraser, July 2, 1947. President Durand Steel Locker Co., Chicago, 1906-28; adminstr. Rancho Sespe, Fillmore, Ventura Co., Calif., since 1908; dir. A. G. Spalding & Bros., Inc., 1917-44, Lyon Metal Products, Inc., 1928-44. Asso. dir., Div. Adminstrn., nat. hdqrs. Am. Red Cross, 1917-19. Trustee Am. Mus. of Natural History, New York, since 1943, Calif. Inst. of Tech., Pasadena, Calif. since 1942, Southwest Mus., Los Angeles, Calif. since 1945. Mem. Delta Kappa Epsilon. Republican. Clubs: Bohemian (San Francisco); California (Los Angeles); Twilight (Pasadena); Aiken (S.C.) Gun. Home: Huntington Hotel. Office: Huntington Hotel, Pasadena 15 CA‡

SPANG, JOSEPH PETER, JR., co. director; b. Boston, Feb. 1, 1893; s. Joseph Peter and Anna (Bosse) S.; Harvard, Class of 1915; L.H.D., Tufts Univ., 1954; LL.D., Northeastern Univ., 1948; married Gwendolen Green, Nov. 6, 1926 (dec.); children—Thomas Johnston Green, Joseph Peter, III. With Swift & Co., 1915-38, v.p. in charge of sales 1930-38; pres. Gillette Co., 1938-56, chmn. bd., 1956-58, past dir.; dir. N.Y. World's Fair 1964-65 Corporation; trustee of the Central Aguirre Sugar Company; director of Sheraton Corporation Am., U.S. Steel Corp., Internat. Packers, Ltd.; mem. corp. Northeastern U. Mem. Bus. Council; overseas econ. operations task force Hoover Commn.; chmn. sponsoring com. 1st Internat. Conf. Mfrs., N.Y., 1951, presided one session 2d conf., Paris, 1954; headed mission to France to evaluate Mut. Security Program, 1953; mem. group businessmen visiting Jugoslavia to study industry, make recommendations, 1954. Nat. chmn. Community Chests and Councils of Am., 1955-56; nat. chmn. United Community Campaigns of Am., 1955-56; pres. Greater Boston United Fund, 1957-59. Trustee, past chairman of finance committee Committee for Econ. Development; trustee of the Vincent Hosp., N.E. Deaconess, Mass. Meml. Hosps., U.S. Council Internat. C. of C.; director Boys' Club of Boston, Jr. Achievement. Served as lt. Balloon Service, U.S. Army. Decorated Chevalier Legion D'Honneur (France). Member of N.A.M., Legion of Honor. Clubs: Harvard, Union (Boston); The Links, Racquet and Tennis, The Brook (N.Y.C.); The Country (Brookline, Mass.). Home: Milton MA Died Dec. 19, 1969; buried Manchester-by-the-Sea MA

SPANGLER, JAMES WILLIAMS, banker; b. near Yankton, S.D., Aug. 5, 1874; s. Rev. James Wilson and Sarah Hannah (Richie) S.; ed. Ore. Agrl. Coll. (now Ore. State Coll.), Pacific U. and Willamette U. (non-grad.); m. Georgia Mabel MacLeod, Apr. 24, 1901 (dec.); m. 2d, Gertrude H. Tyrrell, Jan. 10, 1947. Supt. Bradstreet Co., Spokane, Wash., 1901, Seattle, 1902-05 (largely instrumental in credit orgn. and systematizing in Pacific Northwest); credit mgr. Dexter, Horton & Co., bankers, 1906-11; v.p. Seattle Nat. Bank, 1911, pres., 1920-29; v.p. Seattle-First Nat. Bank, 1929-46.

Sec. Clearing House Assn. of Seattle, 1906-43, pres. 1943-46; ex-pres. Seattle Credit Men's Assn.; ex-v.p. Nat. Credit Men's Assn.; mem. Am. council Inst. of Pacific Relations. Mem. Am. Bankers Assn., Wash. Bankers Assn. (exec. com.; president 1927-28), Sons of Veterans. Vice-president Seattle Chamber Commerce, World War, president, 1926-28 (now mem. bd. trustees, national affairs and fgn. trade coms.). Mem. exec. com., foreign commerce com., dir. and v.p. U.S. Chamber of Commerce until retirement 1946. Republican. Protestant. Elk, Eagle. Clubs: Rainier (past pres.), Seattle Golf, China Club (trustee), Washington Athletic; Washington State Press (life mem.); Tacoma Country and Golf (Tacoma). Home: 2724 Mt. St. Helens Place. Office: Seattle-First Nat. Bank, Seattle WA‡

SPANN, OTIS, pianist, singer; b. Jackson, Miss., Mar. 21, 1930; s. Frank H. and Josiephine (Evern) S.; studied with pianist Cose Davis; m. Lucille Wilson, May 2, 1969. With Muddy Waters Band, Chgo., 1947-70; recorded with Howling Wolf, Sonny Boy Williamson, Chuck Berry, Little Walter. Pres., Candid. Recorded Waters on Chess. Home: Chicago IL Died Apr. 24, 1970.

SPARKS, CHAUNCEY, former gov. of Ala.; b. Barbour County, Alabama, Oct. 8, 1884; s. George W. and Sarah (Castellow) S.; A.B., Mercer U., Macon, Ga., 1907, LL.B., (valedictorian), 1910; LL.D., Howard Coll., Birmingham, Ala., 1943, U. of Ala., 1947; unmarried. Admitted to Ala. bar and practiced in Eufaula, Ala., 1910-68; judge Inferior Court, Precinct 5, Barbour County, Ala., 1911-16. Secretary Barbour County Dem. Executive Committee, 1914-18; rep. Ala. State Legislature, 1919-23, 1931-39; governor of Alabama, Jan. 1943-47. Served as 2d lt. Co. G. 2d Inf., Ala. Nat. Guard, 1912-15. Trustee Ala. State Dept. Archives and History, 1920-47. Baptist. Mem. Ala. State Bar Assn. Club: Kiwanis. (Eufaula). Address: Eufaula AL Died Nov. 6, 1968.

SPARKS, N(ORMAN) R(OBERT), coll. prof.; born Alameda, Calif., May 22, 1900; s. Alfred Ethbert and Ellen Morrell (Lavell) S.; B.S., Clarkson Coll. of Tech., 1923, M.E., 1926; m. Ruth Ernestine Barbur, Sept. 2, 1923; 1 dau., Joan Louise. In motive power dept., N.Y.C.R.R., 1923-24; instr. mech. engring., Pa. State Univ., 1924-29, asst. prof., 1929-32, asso. prof., 1932-41, prof., 1941-72, head of dept. of mech. engring., from July 1946; various cons. and tech. adv. positions. Commd. lt., U.S.N.R., 1936; on active duty, advancing to grade of comdr., 1941-46, capt., 1951. Member Am. Soc. M.E., Am. Soc. Naval Engineers, Am. Society Engineering Education, Sigma Xi. Pi Tau Sigma (honorary M.E.). Theta Xi. Republican. Author: Theory of Mechanical Refrigeration, 1938. Contbr. articles to tech. jours. and mags. Home: State College PA Died Jan. 23, 1972.

SPATTA, GEORGE, mfr.; b. N.Y.C., Feb. 2, 1893. Hon. chmn. bd. Clark Equipment Co., Buchanan, Mich.; dir. Upper Ave. Nat. Bank,

SPAULDING, EUGENE RISTINE, magazine pub.; b. Galion, O., Oct. 30, 1889; s. Clement David and Jane (Ristine) S.; grad. Germantown Acad., 1906; B.S., Haverford Coll., 1911; m. Elizabeth Shaw, Apr. 22, 1913; children—Robert Eugene, Barbara Lee. Bus. mgr. The Churchman, N.Y.C., 1917-20, dir., from 1918, also chmn. bd.; bus. mgr., Town and Country, 1920-25; gen. mgr. New Yorker mag. from 1925, v.p. from 1926. Dir. Electronic Control Corp., 1947-48. Mem. bd. adjustment Village Ridgewood, N.J., 1938-47. Dir. Nat. Publicity Council 1945-49; mem. finance com. Nat. Orgn. Pub. Health Nursing, 1943-48; dir. Fed. Union, Inc.; mem. council Atlantic Union Com. Mem. Research Inst. of Am., Am. Forestry Assn., Triangle Soc., Newcomen Soc. Eng. (N.Y.). Clubs: The Players, Advertising (N.Y.). Home: Saddle River NJ Died Dec. 25, 1966; cremated.

SPAYD, MILFERD AARON, business exec.; b. Van Wert, O., Sept. 17, 1900; s. Noah P. and Bertha (Balyeat) S.; student Cornell; B.Sc., Ohio State U., 1922; Dr. Humanities U. Dayton, 1960; m. Mary Martha Vaughan, June 16, 1925 (dec. 1962); children—Robert, Jeralyn; m. 2d, Iola Ahlers Boyer. Sales exec. Gen. Motors Corp., 1925-33; exec. v.p., gen. mgr. Standard Register Co., Dayton, 1933, pres., 1944-64, chmn. bd., 1964-65; chmn. bd. Third Nat. Bank, Dayton, Metro Studies, Inc. Dir. Community Chest, Dayton Philharmonic, Dayton Art Inst.; past chmn. of the Salvation Army. Pres. bd. of trustees Univ. of Dayton. Member of Newcomen Society (former v.p.), Dayton C. of C. (pres. 1942-43), Delta Tau Delta, Alpha Kappa Psi. Republican. Presbyn. Clubs: Rotary, City, Moraine Country (Dayton); Queen City (Cin.); Metropolitan (N.Y.C.); Troy (O.) Country; Piqua (O.) Country. Home: East OH Died 1965.

SPEAKMAN, FRANK L., judge; b. Wilmington, Del., Aug. 11, 1874; s. Samuel and Anna M. (Ashbridge) S.; LL.B., Yale, 1897; unmarried. Admitted to Del. bar, 1897; engaged in independent practice at Wilmington, 1897-1935; dep. atty. gen. State of Del., 1919-21; now asso. justice Del. Supreme Court. Republican. Club: Wilmington. Home: Route 3. Address: Court House, Wilmington (33) DE‡

SPEAR, ELLWOOD BARKER, prof. chemistry; b. Aurora, Ont., Can., Feb. 22, 1875; s. James and Emma (Braund) S.; B.A., U. of Manitoba, 1899; studied univs. of Toronto and Leipzig; Ph.D., U. of Heidelberg, 1906; m. Edith W. Taylor, of Cambridge, Mass., Dec. 23, 1911. Asst. in chemistry, 1906, instr., 1907, asst. prof., 1910, asso. prof. since 1915, Mass. Inst. Tech. Mem. Am. Chem. Soc. Part Author and Translator: Chemistry of Colloids (Zsigmondy), 1917. Abstracter of Chemical Abstracts." Contbr. to Jour. Am. Chem. Soc. Home: 27 Walker St., Cambridge MA‡

SPEARE, FRANK PALMER, univ. pres.; b. Boston, Mass., 1869; s. Charles and Jeanette (Palmer) S.; grad. Bridgewater State Teachers Coll., 1889; studied at Harvard; M.H. (master of humanics), Springfield Coll., 1911; LL.D., Northeastern U., 1931, U. of N.H., 1934, Harvard U., 1941; m. May Cushing Whiting, Dec. 24, 1897 (dec.); m. 2d, Katharine May Vinton, July 6, 1914; 1 daughter, Marjorie Vinton (Mrs. John G. Carpenter). Was principal public grammar and high schools; established Northeastern University, 1896, Northeastern School of Law, 1898, School of Commerce and Finance, 1907, School of Engineering, 1909, Huntington (prep.) Sch., 1909, Sch. of Business Administration, 1922, Lincoln Prep. Sch., 1927 (formerly known as Northeastern Prep. Sch.), Lincoln Inst., 1927 (including what was formerly known as Northeastern Polytechnic Sch.), Lincoln Sch. of Liberal Arts, 1931; president emeritus Northeastern University; established divisions of the U. in Worcester, Springfield and Providence. Dir. Boston Y.M.C.A. Corporate mem. and trustee Northeastern U. Chmn. N.E. Regional Committee; chmn. bd., pres. and dir. Chandler Secretarial School, Boston; retired, 1947. Mem. Harvard Teachers' Assn. N.E.A., Mass. Schoolmaster's Club (pres. 1933, 34). Mason. Episcopalian. Clubs: University, Boston City, The Neighbors (Newton Center, Mass.). Home: 280 Beacon St., Boston MA (summer) Wolfeboro NH‡

SPEARE, WILLIAM MARTIN, librarian, educator; b. Las Cruces, N.M., March 8, 1908; s. Elias E. and Leona (Rudisill) S.; grad., Capitol Coll. of Pharmacy, 1930; B.S., N.M. Sch. Mines, 1931; m. Thelma May Blevins, Feb. 27, 1933; 1 d., Marian Louise. Practicing pharmacist, 1931-36; instr. of Spanish, N.M. Sch. Mines, (now N.M. Inst. Mining & Technology), 1936, and asst. librarian, 1937-41, librarian and asst. prof. of Spanish, 1941-68. Mem. A.L.A., Am. Assn. Tchrs. of Spanish and Portuguese, N.M. Library Assn., N.M. Sch. of Mines Alumni Assn. (sec.-treas.). Mason (past master). Contbr.: Geologic Literature of N.M. Through 1944, N.M. Bur. of Mines Bull. No. 22, 1945. Home: Socorro NM Died Oct. 28, 1968.

SPECTORSKY, AUGUSTE C., author, pub.; b. Paris, France, Aug. 13, 1910 (parents Am. citizens); s. Isaac and Frances (Herbert) S.; B.S., N.Y.U.; m. Lucille Hille, Aug. 6, 1937; 1 dau., Susan Ann; m. 2d, Elizabeth Bullock, Oct. 8, 1944; 1 dau., Katherine Michelle; m. 3d, Theo Feigenspan; children—Brooke Edwin, Lance Douglas. Senior v.p. Playboy Enterprises, Inc.; asso. pub., editorial dir. Playboy mag.; editorial supr. VIP magazine; director of Playboy Press. Bd. dirs. Urban Gateways. Mem. Shaw Society Chicago (v.p.), Soc. Midland Authors, International Soc. for General Semantics. Club: Chicago Press. Cliff Dwellers. Author: (with Fred Iselin) Invitation to Skiing, 1947; Man Into Beast, 1948; The Book of the Sea, 1954; The Exurbanites, 1955; The Book of the Mountains, 1955; The Book of the Sky, 1956; The Book of the Earth, 1957; The College Year's, 1958; (with Fred Iselin) The New Invitation to Skiing, 1958, Invitation to Modern Skiing, 1965. Life fellow Internat. Inst. Arts and Letters, Arts Club Chgo., Authors Guild, P.E.N., A.I.M., Urban Gateways, Phi Beta Kappa. Home: Chicago IL Died Jan. 17, 1972; buried at sea.

SPEED, JAMES BRECKINRIDGE, mcht.; b. Louisville, Ky.; s. William P. and Mary Ellen (Shallcross) S.; ed. public schools; bank clerk Louisville and Chicago until 1861; served in Union army, pvt. and later adj. 27th Ky. inf., 1861-5, serving in all the campaigns in the West; m. 1868, Cora, d. George W. Coffin, Cincinnati. In business in Louisville since war; pres. Louisville Cement Co., Louisville Street Ry. System, Ohio Valley Telephone Co.; head of J. B. Speed & Co., cement, etc., and Byrne & Speed, coal. Address: Louisville KY‡

SPEED, VIRGINIA PERRIN (MRS. W. S. SPEED), club woman; b. San Francisco, Mar. 1, 1881; d. Edward Burt and Ann Trewlett (Herndon) Perrin; LL.D., Transylvania Coll.; H.H.D., U. Louisville; m. William Shallcross Speed, Nov. 4, 1904; children—Alice (Mrs. B. V. Stoll), Virginia (Mrs. R. W. Condon). Pres. bd. dirs. Found. Louisville Collegiate Sch.; bd. curators. Transylvania Coll. Recipient Merit award D.A.R., 1954. Mem. Soc. Colonial Dames, Nat. Soc. Magna Charta Dames, Order of Garter. Episcopalian. Clubs: Garden of Am., Glenview Garden; Woman's Pendennis Country (Louisville). Home: Louisville KY Deceased.

SPEKKE, ARNOLDS, former diplomat; b. Vecmuiza, Courland, June 14, 1887; s. Andrejs and Doroteja (Zirul) S.; student pub. schs., Latvia; Faculty Letters, Imperial U., Moscow, 1915; m. Alexandra Sterste, Sept. 20, 1914; children—Andrejs Aleksandrs, Vija Violeta. Docent U. Riga, 1919, prof., 1929-31; dir. Classical High Sch. of Riga, 1920-22; Rockefeller Found. scholar. Poland, Vatican City, 1931-32; Latvian minister, Italy, 1933-40, emigrant in Italy, 1940-54; Latvian charge d'affaires, Washington, 1954-70. Author: History of Latvia, 1951; Latvia and the Baltic problem, 1954; The Ancient Amber Routes and the Geographical Discovery of the Eastern Baltic, 1956; The Baltic Sea in Ancient Maps, 1958; others. Died July 27, 1972.

SPELFOGEL, MORRIS RICHARD, lawyer; b. Malden, Mass., Oct. 14, 1907; s. Jacob and Mamie (Yessin) S.; A.B., Harvard, 1928, LL.B., 1931; m. Helen Steinberg, Oct. 7, 1934; children—Evan Jay, Bette-Ann. Admitted to Mass. bar, 1931; pvt. practice Boston, 1931-69; asst. atty. gen. Commonwealth of Mass., 1951-52; chief counsel Dept. Commerce and Devel., Mass. Pres. United Synagogues of America, New England region, 1947-60, honorary president, 1960-69; v.p. Asso. Synagogues of Greater Boston, 1950-69; chmn. Mass. Chaplaincy Commn. Trustee Boston Latin Sch.; founder, trustee Nantasket Youth Center, Hull, Mass.; rep. to Jewish Community Council, Boston. Mem. Am. Jewish Congress, Zionist of Am., Nat. Fedn. of Jewish Men's Clubs Am. and Can. (hon. nat. pres.), Boston Latin Sch. Alumni Assn. (pres.). Jewish religion (hon. life dir., v.p. temple). Mem. B'nai B'rith. Mason. Clubs: Brookline MA Died Mar. 7, 1969; interred Crawford St. Cemetery West Roxbury MA

SPELLACY, EDMUND FRANK, coll. dean; b. Lima, O., Feb. 28, 1906; s. Peter Edward and Floy Susan (Ticknor) S.; B.A., Stanford, 1927, M.A., 1931; Ph.D., Harvard, 1935; m. Frances Adele Phelps, Sept. 14, 1939; children—Floy Susan (Mrs. Fred Jones), and Nancy Adele (Mrs. Timothy Emmons). Lectr. government Univ. of Wash., 1935-36, asso. prof., 1936-46, vis. prof. polit. sci. summer 1962; vis. prof. govt. Stanford, 1948-49; mem. faculty U. Hawaii, 1946-68, prof. polit. sci., 1946-68, dean Coll. Gen. Studies, 1956-68. Mem. bd. selection Holloway Plan, 1947; subcom. exec. powers and functions Hawaii Statehood Comm., 1948-49; joint com. govt. health and welfare services Oahu Health Council-Council Social Agencies, 1953-59; subcom. community planning com. mental health Oahu Health Council, from 1954; Gov. Hawaii Adv. Com. Govt. Orgn., 1954-55; subcom. mental health services and orgn. Oahu Health Council, 1954-55; subcom. inservice edn. Tchr. Edn. Coordinating Com., 1957-58; adv. com. Small Bus. Mgmt. Inst., 1957-59; mem. Am. Micronesian Adv. Com., 1957-60; cons. Honolulu City and County Civil Service Commn., 1939-40. Served with USNR, 1942-46. Mem. Am. Polit. Sci. Assn., Am. Soc. Pub. Adminstrn., Nat. Univ. Extension Assn., Assn. Univ. Eve. Colls., Soc. Mental Hygiene, Friendly Sons. St. Patrick, Pi Sigma Alpha, Theta Xi, Hammer and Coffin. Clubs: Harvard; Stanford. Home: Honolulu HI Died Jan. 25, 1968; buried Nat. Meml. Cemetery of Pacific.

SPENCE, JOHN SELBY, clergyman, educator; b. Balt., May 1, 1909; s. John S. and Katherine G. (Hartman) S.; student Loyola Coll., Balt., 1927-29, St. Mary's Sem., 1929-30; S.T.B., Propanganda and Gregorian Univs., Rome (Italy), 1930, S.T.L., 1934. Ordained priest Roman Catholic Ch., 1933, papal chamberlain, 1948, domestic prelate, 1955; curate Sacred Heart Shrine, Washington, 1934-40, St. Anthony's Ch., 1940-42, St. Matthew's Cath., 1942-51; pastor St. John Baptist de La Salle Ch., Chillum, Md., 1951-58, Shrine of the Sacred Heart, Washington, 1958-73; named aux. to archbishop of Wash., 1964; judge matrimonial curia, 1936-73; dir. Women's Retreat League, Washington Archdiocese, 1934-44, dir. edn., 1948-64. Address: Washington DC Died Mar. 6, 1973; buried Mt. Olivet Cemetery.

SPENCER, ARTHUR COE, geologist; b. Carmel, N.Y., Sept. 27, 1871; s. Stephen Olin and Carrie (Adams) S.; B.S., Case Sch. Applied Science, Cleveland, 1892; Ph.D., Johns Hopkins, 1896; m. Betty Lublin, Mar. 19, 1902; children—Katharin, Oscar Lublin. Asst. geologist on geol. survey of Iowa in coal regions, 1893-94; geologist U.S. Geol. Survey, 1896-1939; retired, Oct. 1939. Worked upon geology of Rocky Mountains, San Juan Region, Colo., 1896-1900, geology of Copper River Region, Alaska, 1900-01; geol. studies in Cuba, under auspices U.S. Army, 1901-02; Pre-Cambrian and economic geology in Southern Wyo., 1902-03; Juneau gold belt, Alaska, 1903; Pre-Cambrian geology and ore deposits, N.J., 1904-07; Tex., 1908-09; copper deposits at Ely, Nev., 1909. Investigation of lands in Appalachian and White Mountains to determine if federal control of lands will promote navigability of dependent streams as prescribed under Weeks Act of 1911; studies relating to ore deposits of Wyo, Colo., N.M., Alaska and New Eng.; retired from Govt. service, 1939. Home: 3250 Highland Place, Washington 8 DC‡

SPENCER, GEORGE ALBERT, pub. utility co. exec.; b. Waterview, Va., Jan. 13, 1914; s. Albert Sidney and Louise (Powell) S.; student U. Richmond Evening Sch. Bus. Adminstrn., 1946-50, Ga. Inst. Tech., 1957; m. Laughlin Smith, Jan. 24, 1942; children—Bruce M.,

Jeffrey L., Judith A. With Va. Electric & Power Co., Richmond, 1936-73, asst. comptroller, 1961-63, comptroller, 1963-65, treas., 1965-73. Active Boy Scouts Am. Mem. town council, Town of Ashland, Va., 1948-50. Served to lt. USNR, 1941-45, 52-54. Mem. Am. Legion (past comdr.), Va., Richmond chambers commerce, Edison Electric Inst., Financial Execs. Inst., Ashland War Meml. Assn. (trustee 1948-73, treas. 1955-73). Methodist (trustee). Kiwanian. Clubs: Hanover, Hanover Country (Ashland). Home: Ashland VA Died Mar. 12, 1973.

SPENCER, HENRY RUSSELL, educator; b. Foxboro, Mass., Jan. 22, 1879; s. William Henry and Mary Eliza (Stevens) S.; B.A., Colby Coll., Waterville, Me., 1899, Litt.D., 1950; M.A., Columbia, 1901, Ph.D., 1905; LL.D., Ohio State U., 1950; m. Cornelia Powell, Oct. 15, 1912. Preceptor history and politics, Princeton, 1906-07; Ohio State U., 1903-06, since 1907, prof. polit. sci., 1909-49, emeritus, 1949-70. Mem. Am. Polit. Science Assn. (pres. 1948), Delta Kappa Epsilon. Leader of round-table on dictatorship, Williamstown Inst. of Politics, 1927. Conglist. Author: Government and Politics of Italy, 1932, Government and Politics Abroad, 1936. Co-author: The Mussolini Regime, 1935; Expanding Italy, 1939; The Corporative State, 1941. Home: Columbus OH Died Oct. 1970.

SPENCER, JAMES HARLAND, lawyer; b. Chgo., June 6, 1908; s. James Ezra and Dayse (Whitman) S.; A.B., U. Mich., 1929, J.D., 1931; m. Alliene Graham, May 22, 1934 (dec. 1956); children—Susan (Mrs. Donald Williams), Jean (Mrs. Donald Nichols), Donald E.; m. 2d, Alice Keane, June 7, 1958. Admitted to Mich. bar, 1931, practiced in Detroit; partner firm Dykema, Wheat, Spencer, Boodnow & Trigg, and predecessors, 1939-70. Vice pres., dir. Gross Telecasting, Inc.; asst. sec., dir. N.A. Woodworth Co.; dir. Air Products and Chems., Inc. Mem. Am. Bar Assn. (mem. com. partnerships and unincorporated bus. orgns.), Automotive Original Equipment Mfrs. Assn. (sec.), Am. Law Inst., Am. Judicature Soc., State Bar Mich. (chmn. com. corps. and securities 1953-55), Alpha Kappa Lambda (pres. 1933-34). Home: Birmingham MI Died Sept. 22, 1970.

SPENCER, LEE BOWEN, librarian; b. El Paso, Tex., Jan. 2, 1914; s. Lee Babers and Annabel (Bowen) S.; A.B., Okla. Baptist U., 1934; B.S. in L.S., U. Ill., 1940; M.A., U. Okla., 1946; m. Willa Belle Carter, Aug. 19, 1939; children—Lee Bowen, Mary Ann, Sarah Margaret. Asst. Carnegie Pub. Library, Shawnee, Okla., 1934-36; librarian Okla. Bapt. U., 1936-63, prof. library sci., 1946-63; librarian, prof. library science State College of Ark., Conway, 1963-70; chief acquisitions librarian Air Univ., 1947; vis. prof. Okla. State U., summers 1948, 49; dean men Okla. Bapt. U., 1951-54. Mem. hist. commn. So. Bapt. Conv., 1962-63. Bd. dirs., blood drive chmn. Pottawatomie County chpt. A.R.C., 1950-63; bd. dirs. Carnegie Pub. Library, 1961-63. Served to 1st lt. USAAF, 1942-46; lt. colonel Reserve. Member American, Southwestern, Arkansas (president 1969-70), Okla. (1950-51) library assns., S.A.R. (chaplain Oklahoma 1962-63), Res. Officers Assn. (pres. Shawnee 1961-62), Okla. (foundling mem., v.p. 1956-57), Ark. (pres. 1965-66) geneal. socs., Faulkner County Hist. Soc. (bd. dirs. 1[illegible]3—), Kappa Delta Pi, Phi Delta Kappa. Democrat. Baptist (deacon). Mason (K.T. Shriner), Rotarian (dist. gov. 1969-70; dir.). Contbr. profl. jours. Home: Conway AR Died June 12, 1970; buried Conway AR

SPENCER, LYLE MANLY, publisher; born Atlanta, Georgia, May 10, 1911; s. M. Lyle and Lois (Hill) S.; A.B., U. Wash., 1933, M.A., 1935; fellow sociology U. Chgo., 1936-37, Marshall Field fellow, 1937-38; Doctor of Laws degree, Syracuse U., 1967. Round-the-world debator, under auspices U. Wash. and U.S. Office Edn., 1933-34; instr. sociology U. Wash., 1934-35; pres. Sci. Research Assos., 1938-42, 45-68; dir. IBM. Mem. council advisers Nat. Scholarship Service and Fund for Negro Students, 1958; mem. adv. com. library research and tng. projects Dept. Health Edn. and Welfare Chmn. trustees Roosevelt U.; trustee Menninger Found., 1950-—, U. Chgo., Midwest Research Inst., Young Presidents' Found.; governing mem. Library Internat. Relations; trustee Center for Study Dem. Instns., Lawrence U., Center for Study Liberal Edn. Adults; bd. dirs. Adlai Stevenson Inst. Internat. Affairs, 1968. Served as lt. col. information, edn. div., AUS, 1943-45. Decorated Legion of Merit, Bronze Star; named one of 10 outstanding young men. U.S. Jr. C. of C., 1940. Fellow Am. Sociol. Soc.; mem. Young Pres.'s Orgn. (chmn. Chgo. chpt. 1952, nat. v.p. 1953), Am. Psychol. Assn., Am. Statis. Assn., Am. Textbook Pubs. Inst. (gen. com. testing), Phi Beta Kappa. Office: Chicago IL Died Aug. 21, 1968; buried Appleton WI

SPENCER, M(ATTHEW) LYLE, univ. dean; b. Batesville, Miss., July 7, 1881; s. Rev. Flournoy Poindexter and Alice Eleanor (Manes) S.; A.B., Kentucky Wesleyan Coll., 1903, A.M., 1904, Litt.D., 1942; A.M., Northwestern University, 1905, LL.D., 1928; Ph.D., University of Chicago, 1910; Litt.D., College of Puget Sound, Tacoma, Washington, 1932; LL.D. and Litt.D., Syracuse Univ., 1951; married Helen McNaughton, Sept. 8, 1920. Physical dir. Ky. Wesleyan College, 1901, instructor English, 1902, professor, 1903-04; fellow in English, U. of Chicago, 1905-07, 1910-11; asst. prof. English, Wofford Coll., S.C., 1907-10; prof. English, Woman's Coll., of Ala., Montgomery, 1910-11; prof. English, Lawrence Coll., Appleton, Wis., 1911-17; reporter, copy reader, editorial writer, Milwaukee Journal, 1913, 1917-19; capt. U.S. Army, 1918; lectr. in journalism U. of Wis., summer, 1919; dir. Sch. of Journalism, U. of Wash., 1919-26; pres. U. of Wash., 1927-33, dean Sch. of Journalism, Syracuse U., 1934-51, emeritus dean, 1951-69 awarded D.S.M., sch. journalism, 1951. Vis. prof. Am. U., Cairo, Egypt, 1937, 1945-46; lecturer, Oriental Culture Coll., Tokyo, Japan, 1940. Dir. Seattle Trust Co., 1924-31, Univ. Nat. Bank, 1925-27. Dir. Seattle Chamber of Commerce, 1925-33. Mem. S.A.R., Kappa Alpha. Phi Beta Kappa, Tau Kappa Alpha, Sigma Delta Chi, Alpha Delta Sigma; hon. mem. Washington Pub. Association, New York Press Association. Editor: Simms's Yemassee, 1911; N.Y. Laws Relating to Publications, 1943. Author: Corpus Christi Pageants in England, 1911; Practical English Punctuation, 1913; News Writing, 1917; Editorial Writing, 1924. Home: Fayetteville NY Died Feb. 1969.

SPENCER, PERCY CRAIG, business exec., lawyer; b. Jasper, N.Y., Sept. 8, 1893; s. Ward and Kathleen (Talmadge) S.; LL.B., U. of Neb., 1916, LL.D., 1964; LL.D., U. of Wyoming, 1949; L.H.D. (honorary), Clarkson College of Tech., 1958; m. Joan M. Maloney, April 5, 1926; 1 dau., Barbara Lee (Mrs. Rixon). Sec. to U.S. Senator Francis E. Warren, 1919, 1920; chmn. Republican State Central Com., Wyoming, 1922-28; gen. practice of law, Cheyenne, Wyo., 1922-27; gen. counsel, Producers and Refiners Corp. and subsidiaries, 1927-34; mem. legal dept., Sinclair Oil Corp., 1934-46, gen. counsel, 1946-47; pres. Sinclair Refining Co. (principal subsidiary of Sinclair Oil Corp.), 1947-54; pres., chief exec. officer Sinclair Oil Corp., 1949-58, chmn. bd. dirs., chmn. exec. com., chief exec. officer, 1958-61, chairman of the board, chairman executive committee, 1961-64, dir., chmn. finance com., from 1964; dir., chmn. finance com. Richfield Oil Corporation. Dir. Boys' Clubs of Am. Mem. Am. Bar Assn. Council on Foreign Relations. Am. Petroleum Institute (dir.), Chi Phi, Phi Delta Phi, Delta Sigma Chi. Clubs: River, Blind Brook, University, Links, Economic; National Press; Bath and Tennis; Everglades; Augusta National Golf. Home: New York City NY Died Nov. 12, 1969; buried Ch. of St. James The Less Scarsdale NY

SPENCER, PERCY LEBARON, inventor, radio engr.; b. Howland, Me., July 9, 1894; s. Jasper G. and Myrtle B. (Keene) S.; student Naval Wireless and Elec. Sch., Bklyn.; D.Sc., U. Mass., 1950; D.Sc., Nasson College, 1959, Univ. Me., 1961, Calvin Coolidge Coll. Liberal Arts, 1962; m. Louise Larsen, June 6, 1921 (died Feb. 10, 1956); children—John L., James H., Goerge R.; m. 2d, Lillian Ottenheimer, Nov. 18, 1960. Supt. operations Am. Radio and Research Corp., supt. Wireless Specialty Co., 1915-18; mgr. field engring. Submarine Signal Co., 1920-25; dir. development and engring. Raytheon Mgr. Co., Waltham, Mass., 1925-40, mgr., chief engr. microwave and power tube div., 1940-55, sr. v.p., director, 1955-65, director, consultant, until 1970; assisted in development photocell and gaseous rectifier tubes, mercury pool type tubes for welding, also subminiature tubes. Trustee Coburn Classical Inst., Waterville, Me. Served as radio electrician USN, 1912-15, radio aide Charlestown Navy Yard, 1918-20. Recipient Naval Ordnance award for exceptional service Bur. Ordnance, U.S. Navy, 1942, certificate commendation for outstanding service, 1947, distinguished pub. service medal, 1949. Fellow Am. Acad. Arts and Scis., Inst. Radio Engrs.; asso. mem. U.S. Naval Inst. Holder 100 patents on electronic tube processes. Home: Waban MA Died Sept. 7, 1970; buried Newton Cemetery Newton MA

SPENCER, ROBERT CLOSSON, architect, inventor; b. Milwaukee, Wis., Apr. 13, 1864; s. Robert C. and Ellen W. (Whiton) S.; B.M.E., U. of Wis., 1886; Rotch traveling scholarship in architecture (of Boston), 1891-93; m. Ernestine Elliott, Nov. 28, 1889 (died Nov. 1942); children—Marian L. (Mrs. John W. Smith), Ernestine M., Charles E. Entered archtl. work in Boston; came to Chicago, 1893; mem. Spencer & Powers, 1905-23; practiced alone in Chicago, 1923-28; associate professor architecture, Okla. A. and M. Coll., 1928-30; member faculty Sch. of Architecture and Allied Arts, U. of Fla., 1930-34. Designer of Oak Park (Ill.) High Sch. and many country houses; painted murals of 8 Fla. colonial houses for Federal Govt. and U. of Fla., 1935-38. Fellow Am. Inst. Architects; mem. Sigma Chi. Wrote article on Fla. architecture for Am. Guide, 1934-35. Inventor of widely used building appliances. Address: R.R. 4, Box 502, Tucson AZ*‡

SPENCER, ROBERT NELSON, clergyman; b. Tunnel, N.Y., Feb. 18, 1877; s. Nelson and Hannah (Pratt) S.; student Dickinson Coll., 1896-99, D.D., 1931, grad. Kan. Theol. Sch., 1904; m. Amy Frances Moffatt, Sept. 15, 1904; 1 dau., Kathleen, Deacon, 1904, priest, 1905, P.E. Ch.; rector Ch. of the Covenant, Junction City, and special preacher Ft. Riley, Kan., 1904-07; rector St. John's Ch., Springfield, Mo., 1907-09, Grace and Holy Trinity Ch., Kansas City, Mo., 1909-30; consecrated bishop of West Mo., 1930. Chaplain St. Luke's Hosp., Kansas City, 1923-30, now pres.; dep. to Gen. Conv. seven times. Lambeth Conf., Eng., 1920. Pres. Province of the Southwest, P.E. Ch., 1935-41; acting bishop of Salina, Kan., 1939-41. Dep. police commr., Kansas City, 1924-25; mem. Com. of 100 of Chamber Commerce, Kansas City. Mem. Missouri State Council of Defense, 1941. Trustee Drury College; member The Order of the Flag. Frequent lecturer summer school, P.E. Ch.; visiting lecturer on N.T., University of Kansas City, 1943. Beta Theta Pi, Pi Gamma Mu. Republican. Clubs: University, City, Country, Kansas City; Ludington (Michigan) Country. Associate editor Episcopal Quarterly. Author: Pere Marquette, a Pageant, 1936; collaborator, Presiding Bishop's Book, 1937. Delivered Centennial Sermon, Beta Theta Pi, 1939; The Seer's House, 1940. Home: 3725 Locust St., Kansas City 3, MO Office: 415 West 13th St., Kansas City 6 MO*‡

SPENCER, WILLIAM LORING, author, educator; b. St. Augustine, Fla.; d. Albert A. and Eliza M. (Loring) Nunez; (named in honor of her uncle, W. W. Loring, maj.-gen. C. S. A.); ed. partly in convent in U.S. and partly by tutors in Europe; m. 1877, Gen. George E. Spencer, U.S. senator from Ala. (died, Feb. 19, 1893). Since husband's death taught at Portland, Ore., a school of philosophy of thought, concentration of mind, public speaking, singing, oratory," etc.; about to establish similar school in New York. Author: Salt Lake Fruit, 1883; Story of Mary, 1884 D1; A Plucky One, 1887 C1; Calamity Jane, 1887 C1 (last 3 first published as serials in New York Tribune). Contributor to Pall Mall, Bachelors' and other mags. Christian Socialist; actively interested in civic reforms. Address: The Newport, Broadway and 52d St., New York NY‡

SPENCER, WILLING, b. Phila., Pa., Dec. 29, 1877; s. John T. and Rebecca B.W. (Wallace) S.; grad. Ecole Libre des Sciences Politiques, Paris, 1900; A.B., Harvard, 1899; LL.B., U. of Pa., 1903; m. Marion Parsons, of N.Y. City, Dec. 23, 1925. Practiced law in Phila., 1903-10; apptd. 3d sec. Embassy, Petrograd, Mar. 31, 1910; 2d sec. Embassy, Berlin, 1911-14; sec. of Legation, Caracas, Venezuela, 1914-15, Panama, 1915-16; charge d'affaires, Tegucigalpa, Honduras, 1916-17; assigned to Tokyo, Japan, Mar. 6, 1917; sec. Legation, Peking, China, 1918-19; charge d'affaires, Tegucigalpa, 1920-21; counselor Embassy, Madrid, Spain, 1922, Buenos Aires, resigned, 1924; now executor, trustee, lawyer. Empire Trust Co., 580 5th Av., New York NY‡

SPEWACK, SAMUEL, playwright, scenarist, author; b. Russia, 1899; s. Noel and Sema (Nightingale) S.; ed. N.Y. pub. schs. and Columbia U. (class of 1919); m. Bella (Loebel) Cohen, March 18, 1922. Reporter, N.Y. World, at age of 18; covered Genoa Conf., 1922; foreign corr., N.Y. World, Russia, Germany, 1922-26; returned to U.S. and devoted time to writing. Author: (under pseudonym of A.A. Abbott), Mon Paul, 1928; The Skyscraper Murder, 1928; The Murder in the Gilded Cage, 1929; in collaboration with wife, Bella, author of plays and screenplays (see above); screenplay Week-End At The Waldorf, 1945; play, Woman Bites Dog (with wife) produced 1946, published 1947); (novel) The Busy Busy People, 1948; author and director (play) Two Blind Mice, 1949; director of London production Kiss Me Kate, 1951; author Under the Sycamore Tree, 1952; author (with wife) My Three Angels, 1953; writer, dir. This is Russia, documentary film for USAF; debut with wife Bella in Mr. Broadway (musical teleplay NBC Showcase Productions, May 1957. Contributor of short stories and articles to Saturday Evening Post, Colliers. Red Book, Sec. In 1941, went to England for Look and N.Y. Evening Post; 1942 headed Domestic Film Unit of Office of War Information; 1943 press attache to U.S. Embassy in Moscow for Moscow Conf.; headed Russian division for Overseas Office of War Information. Address: New York City NY Died Oct. 1971.

SPICER, CLINTON ELBERT, physician; b. at Pardeeville, Wis., July 4, 1869; s. William H. and Emma J. (Morris) S.; ed. U. of Wis.; Valparaiso U., Ind.; M.D., Med. Dept., U. of Chicago, 1903; post-grad. work, Post-Grad. Med. Sch., New York; m. Eva M. Peterson, of Rio, Wis., June 21, 1893. Teacher, common, graded and high schs., 1889-99; in practice, N.D., 1903-—; asst. surgeon N.P.R.R. Mem. Ill. N.G., 1900-3. Pres. Litchville Bd. of Edn. Republican. Presbyn. Mem. A.M.A., N.D. State Med. Assn. (pres. 1911-12), Barnes Co. Med. Soc. Mason, K.T. Address: Litchville ND‡

SPICER, HENRY RUSSELL, air force officer; b. Colorado Springs, Colo., Feb. 16, 1909; s. Carroll Atchison and Bertha Agnes (Watson) S.; B.S., U. Ariz., 1931; student AC Flying Sch., 1934-35; m. Louise Frances Leonard, June 11, 1938; children—Henry A., Leonard R., Susan, James R. Commd. 2d lt. AC, 1935, advanced through grades to maj. gen. USAF, 1953; comdr. 357th Fighter Group, Eng., 1944; prisoner of war, Germany, 1944-45; comdr. 36th Fighter Group, Panama and Germany, 1946-48; instr. Armed Forces Staff Coll., 1949-50; comdr. Williams AFB, Ariz., 1950-51; comdr. Wichita AFB, Kan., 1951-53, Nellis

AFB, Nev., 1953; dep. comdr. Crew Tng. Air Force, 1954; insp. gen. Air Tng. Command, 1954-56, chief of staff, 1956-57, vice commander, 1957; commander of Flying Training Air Force, 1957-58; commander 17th Air Force, 1958-62, 25th Air Division (SAGE), McChord Air Force Base, Washington, 1962-64, ret., 1964. Decorated Distinguished Flying Cross, Bronze Star, Air Medal with clusters, Purple Heart, Legion of Merit with Cluster (U.S.); Croix de Guerre (France). Mem. Assn. Am. Rod and Gun Clubs (pres. Europe), Sigma Chi. Rotarian. Home: Tucson AZ Died Dec. 4, 1968; buried Nat. Cemetery, Ft. Sam Houston TX

SPICER, ROBERT BARCLAY, educator; b. Pleasantville, Harford Co., Md., Mar. 4, 1869; s. Simeon and Addie (Guyton) S.; grad. Swarthmore Coll., 1890; post-grad. studies Johns Hopkins, 1892-3, Breslau Univ., Germany, 1894, Leipzig, 1894-5, Meadville Theol. Sch., 1902, Univ. of Pa., 1903-4; m. Granby, Conn., May 1, 1900, Margaret Jones. Instr. Latin, Univ. of Cincinnati, 1895-8; resident worker in Cincinnati Social Settlement, 1896-8; pres. Franklin Coll., New Athens, O., 1900-2; student and instr. New Testament Greek, Meadville Theol. Sch., 1902. Editor Friends' Intelligence since 1902. Residence: Darby PA Office: 140 N. 15th St., Philadelphia PA‡

SPICER, WILLIAM AMBROSE, clergyman; b. Freeborn, Minn., Dec. 19, 1865; s. Ambrose Coats and Susan M. (Coon) S.; student Battle Creek (Mich.) Coll.; m. Georgia Harper, Apr. 17, 1890. Writer for religious press, London, Eng., 1887-90; sec. in U.S. of Foreign Mission Bd. of Seventh Day Adventist Ch., 1891-92; again writer religious press, in London, 1893-97, in Calcutta, India, 1898-1900; secretary General Conference, Seventh Day Adventists, 1901-22, president, 1922-30, field secretary, 1931-41, now retired. Author: The Hand of God in History, 1913; Our Day in the Light of Prophecy, 1917; The Hand That Intervenes, 1918; Youthful Witnesses, 1921; Providences of the Great War, 1923; Miracles of Missions, 1925; The Gospel in All the World, 1926; Certainties of the Advent Movement, 1929; Beacon Lights of Prophecy, 1934; Stories of Providential Deliverances, 1935; The Spirit of Prophecy," 1937; What Next?, 1939; Signs of Christ's Coming, 1941; Pioneer Days of the Advent Movement, 1941; Above the Din God Speaks, 1942. Home: 606 Carroll Av., Takoma Park MD*‡

SPICER-SIMSON, MARGARET, artist; b. at Washington, Mar. 6, 1874; d. E. L. and C. (Gutenrath) Schmidt; pupil of Knaus, Berlin, and of Boutet de Monvel and Carriere, Paris; m. Washington, Theodore Spicer-Simson, July 1, 1896. Miniature painter since 1896. Exhibited at Paris Salon, 1899, 1900, 1, 5, 6, 7; Royal Acad., London, 1900, 1901; Paris Expn., 1900. Address: 3 Rue Campagne lere, Paris‡

SPILMAN, BERNARD WASHINGTON, Sunday School worker; b. Weldon, N.C., Jan. 22, 1871; s. Bushrod Washington and Helvia Roxanna (Barham) S.; B.S., Wake Forest (N.C.) Coll., 1891, D.D., 1921; student Southern Bapt. Theol. Sem., Louisville, Ky., 1892-94; D.D., Stetson U., De Land, Fla., 1911, Baylor U., Tex., 1920; m. Mozelle Pollock, Jan. 24, 1900 (now dec.); children—Raymond Pollock (dec.), Agnes Mozelle (dec.); m. 2d, Esther Ward, August 12, 1939. Ordained to ministry of Bapt. Ch., 1891; pastor Kinston, 1895-96; elected Sunday School sec. Bapt. State Conv. of N.C., Apr. 1896 (inaugurating the modern era of Sunday School work among Baptists in the South); 1st field sec. Sunday School Bd. Southern Bapt. Conv., June , 1901-Jan. 1, 1941 (retired); founder 1907, gen. secretary, 1907-20, pres. 1921-33, The Ridgecrest Assembly, Ridgecrest, N.C.; lesson writer for Bapt. periodicals of Bapt. Sunday School Bd., 1907-14 and 1920-38. Mem. Board of Missions and Sunday Schs., Bapt. State Conv. of N.C., 1895-1919; pres. Bapt. State Conv. of N.C., 1918-24. Trustee Chowan Coll., N.C., 1924-27; pres. bd. Bapt. Orphanage of N.C., Thomasville, 1928-41; trustee Baptist Bible Inst., New Orleans. Democrat. Mason (K.T., Shriner). Author: Normal Studies for Sunday School Workers, 1902; Convention Normal Manual, 1909; The New Normal Manual, 1913; The New Convention Normal Manual, 1918; A Study in Religious Pedagogy, 1920; The Sunday School Manual, 1924; History of Ridgecrest, 1928; One Hundred Years of Baptist Sunday School Work in North Carolina, 1930; Sixty Years Old Today, 1931; The Mills Home-A History of the Baptist Orphan Work in North Carolina, 1932; also numerous articles in mags. and newspapers. Lecturer. Address: 604 N. Queen St., Kinston NC‡

SPILMAN, ROBERT SCOTT, JR., lawyer; b. Charleston, W.Va., Jan. 6, 1908; s. Robert Scott and Eliza (Dillon) S.; B.A., Va. Mil. Inst., 1928; LL.B., Harvard, 1932; m. Ann Hatfield, Apr. 18, 1941; 1 son, Robert Scott III (dec.). Instr. Am. history Va. Mil. Inst., 1928; admitted to W.Va. bar, 1932, since practiced in Charleston; partner firm Spilman, Thomas, Battle & Klostermeyer, 1937-69. Dir. Kanawha Banking & Trust Co., Charleston, Peerless Eagle Coal Co., Summersville, W.Va., James River Hydrate & Supply Co., Buchanan, Va. Mem. city council, Charleston, 1935-39, 47-51; mem. Charleston Municipal Planning Commn., from 1956, chmn., 1958-66. Bd. dirs. Charleston Community Chest, 1958-62; trustee Greater Kanawha Valley Found., 1960. Served to lt. col. USAAF, 1942-46. Mem. Am., W.Va. (exec. council 1966-69) bar assns., Am. Law Inst., Am. Judicature Soc., Kappa Alpha. Democrat. Episcopalian (vestryman). Clubs: Edgewood Country, Army and Navy, Press (Charleston); Farmington Hunt (Charlotteville, Va.); Springdale Hall (Camden, S.C.). Home: Charleston WV Died Nov. 3, 1969.

SPINGARN, ARTHUR B., lawyer; b. N.Y. City, March 28, 1878; s. Elias and Sarah (Barnett) S.; A.B., Columbia, 1897, A.M., 1899, LL.B., 1900; LL.D., Howard University, 1941; L.H.D., Long Island University, 1966; m. Marion Mayer, Jan. 27, 1918 (dec.). Admitted N.Y. bar, 1900, practiced N.Y. City since 1900. Served as capt. San. corps. U.S. Army, 1917-19; with A.E.F. Mem. Amer., N.Y. State, City N.Y., N.Y. Co. bar assns. Pres. Nat. Assn. for Advancement Colored People, 1940-66 (chmn. nat. legal com. and v. pres., 1911-40, pres. N.A.A.C.P. Legal and Ednl. Fund, Inc. 1940-57), chmn. legal com. Social Hygiene Div. N.Y. Tb and Health Assn.; mem. Manhattan Council State Commn. of Human Rights; past mem. legal com. N.Y. Probation Assn. Mem. Bibliog. Soc. (London). Oxford, Cambridge, Va. bibliog. socs., Society of Peintres Graveurs (France), Legion Fgn. Wars, Am. Legion (past post commdr.). Clubs: City, New York. Author: Laws Relating to Sex Morality in N.Y., 1915, rev. 1926; Legal and Protective Measures (with J. Goldberg), 1950. Contbr. articles and pamphlets on the Negro to nat. mags. Founder Springarn Collection of Negro Lit. at Howard U. Home: New York City NY Died Dec. 1, 1971.

SPINKA, MATTHEW, educator; b. Stitary, Czechoslovakia, Jan. 30, 1890; s. Joseph and Marie (Kratochvil) S.; A.B., Coe College, 1918, D.D., 1949; B.D., Chicago Theol. Sem., 1916; A.M., U. of Chicago, 1919, Ph.D., 1923; Th.D., Hus Protestant Theol. Faculty, Prague, Czechoslovakia; m. Zdenka Marie Dvorak, June 25, 1919. Came to United States, 1905, naturalized, 1911. Prof. church history, Central Theol. Sem., Dayton, O., 1919-26; librarian Chicago Theological Seminary, 1926-38, also assistant professor history of Eastern Christianity, asso. professor of church history 1938-43; also same at Div. Sch., U. Chgo.; prof. ch. history Hartford Theol. Sem. 1943-55; part-time prof. Claremont (Cal.) Sch. Theology and Grad. Sch., 1955-58, ret., 1958. Corr. mem. School of Slavonic Studies. King's College, Univ. of London, England; president Am. Soc. Church History, 1946. Congregationalist. Author, editor or contbr. numerous books relating to field; latest publs.: Nicolas Berdyaev: Captive of Freedom, 1950; Advocates of Reform: From Wyclif to Erasmus, 1953; the Church in Soviet Russia, 1956; John Hus at the Council of Constance, 1965; John Hus and the Czech Reform, 1966; John Hus Concept of the Church, 1966; John Amos Cominius, that Imcomparable Moravian, 1967; John Hus a Biography, 1968; Letters of John Hus, 1972. Home. Claremont CA Died Oct. 1972.

SPITZ, ARMAND N(EUSTADTER), author, inventor, astronomer; b. Phila., July 7, 1904; s. Louis and Rose (Neustadter) S.; student U. Pa., 1922-24, U. Cin., 1924-25; D.Sc., Otterbein Coll., 1956; m. Grace C. Scholz, Sept. 27, 1958; children by previous marriage Verne Carlin, Armand Lawrence. Editor, pub. Haverford Twp. News, 1928-36; pres. Spitz Pub. Co., 1928-35; asst. astronomer Haverford Coll. Obs., 1935-42; radio, TV lectr., 1935-71; staff Franklin Inst., 1936-55, editor The Inst. News, 1936-43, head dept. meteorology, 1940-47, asst. dir. pub. relations, 1941-43, lectr. Fels Planetarium, 1942-54, dir. edn., 1943-51; instr. astronomy Friends Central Sch., 1937-41; vis. cons. Dept. Edn., P.R., 1945; pres. Spitz Labs., 1949-53, dir., 1953-61, coordinator visual satellite observations Smithsonian Astro-physical Obs., 1956-61; spl. cons. Nat. Sci. Found., 1956-60; president Astro Murals, Incorporated, 1962-71. Asso. editor Review Popular Astronomy, 1958-71. Founder, former pres. Haverford Twp. Free Library; mem. intercultural com. World Affairs Council Phila.; mem. Phila. Sci. Council pres. 1948-52. Recipient silver medal Astron. Soc. Mexico, 1954; gold medal LaSalle Coll., Havana, Cuba, 1955. Fellow A.A.A.S. (council); mem. Am. Astron. Soc., Astron. League (award 1954), Am. Assn. Mus. Mem. Soc. Friends (trustee). Club: Cosmos (Washington). Author: The Pinpoint Planetarium, 1940; A Start in Meteorology, 1941; Dictionary of Astronomy and Astronautics, 1958; Weather, 1967; also mag. articles. Home: Fairfax VA Died Apr. 14, 1971.

SPIVACK ROBERT GERALD, newspaper columnist, editor; b. Dayton. O., Apr. 28, 1915; s. Mose K. and Leah C. (Tahl) S.; A.B., U. Cin., 1936; m. Adrienne Rauchwerger, Apr. 18, 1940; children—Lorna Ellen, Miranda Sheila. U.S. sec. Internat. Student Service, also free-lance writer, 1937-38; editor SOS, pub. Student Defenders Democracy, 1939; editorial dir. Fight For Freedom Com., 1940-41; free-lance writer, 1941-43; mem. staff N.Y. Post, 1943, polit. writer, reporter, Albany (N.Y.) corr., 1944-52, Washington corr., 1952-61; editor Contemporary Affairs, 1960-70; nat. and internat. affairs columnist N.Y. Herald Tribune Syndicate, also Pubs. Newspaper Syndicate, 1961-70; pres. chmn. Contemporary Affairs Soc., book club, 1960-70; preseident Potomac News Assos., syndication and distbn. news and feature columns, 1956-70; editor, pub. The Spivak Report, 1966-70; president Reporters' News Syndicate, 1968-70, consulting editor Basic Books, Incorporated, 1959-61. Mem. Legislative Corr. Assn. (pres. Albany 1949), White House Corr. Assn., Overseas Writers, Omicron Delta Kappa. Democrat. Jewish religion. Clubs: Washington Athletic, Nat. Press (Washington); Albany Soc., Inner Circle (N.Y.C.). Contbr.: The American Century, 1940; Our Sovereign State, 1949. Editor: (with Eric Sevareid) Candidates, 1960. Home: Alexandria VA Died June 25, 1970; buried Abel's Hill Cemememtery, Chilmark, Martha's Vineyard MA

SPRACHER, DWIGHT L., theatre co. exec.; b. Sibley, Ia., Nov. 15, 1903; s. Louis B. and Anna (Guttman) S.; student Yankton Coll., 1922-24; m. Lillian Lindstrom, June 25, 1933. Salesman real estate in Fla., 1924-25; salesman Paramount Pictures, Inc., 1927-46; sec.-treas. Kenmore Drive-In Theatre, Inc., Seattle, 1949-70; partner Aurora Drive-In, Seattle, 1946-70; officer Sno King Drive-In, Everett, 1960-70; sec.-treas. Harbor Drive-In, Aberdeen, 1949-70; partner Kitsap Lake & Rodeo Drive-In, Bremerton, 1949-70; organizer, dir. Bank of Kent (Wash.). State treas. Democratic State Central Com. Mem. Theatre Owners Am. (bd. dirs.), Theatre Owners Washington, No. Ida. and Alaska (pres.). Clubs: Washington, Athletic, Variety (chief barker), One Hundred and One, Rainier Golf (Seattle). Home: Seattle WA Died Jan. 14, 1970; interred Acacia Mausoleum Seattle WA

SPRAGUE, ALBERT TILDEN, JR., naval officer, educator; b. Revere, Mass., Mar. 13, 1898; s. Albert Tilden and Ella Worcester (Baker) S.; B.S., U.S. Naval Acad., 1918; M.S., Harvard, 1925; m. Ebba Briand, Sept. 15, 1920 (dec. Nov. 1938); children—June Elizabeth, Albert Tilden, Evageline Joy; m. 2d, Marie Ancona Robertson, June 6, 1940; children—Katharine Ancona, Caroline Robertson. Commd. ensign U.S. Navy, 1918, and advanced through grades to commodore Nov., 1945, ret. as rear adm., 1949; comd. U.S.S. Beaver (AS-5) and U.S.S. Raleigh (CL7) 1940-44; served as chief of staff comdr. amphibious group 8, 1944-45; comdr. 5th amphibious force, 1945; dep. commandant, Armed Forces Staff Coll., until 1949; asso. prof. elec. engring. Auburn (Ala.) U., 1949-67, prof. emeritus, 1967-68. Awarded Legion of Merit medal, 1944, Gold Star in lieu 2d medal, for services Auburn AL Died Apr. 8, 1968; buried Arlington Nat. Cemetery, Arlington VA

SPRAGUE, CHARLES ARTHUR, publisher, newspaper editor; b. Lawrence, Kan., Nov. 12, 1887; s. Charles Allen and Alice Caroline (Glasgow) S.; A.B., Monmouth (Ill.) Coll., 1910, LL.D., 1940; LL.D., Willamette University, 1939, Colby College, 1955; Litt.D., Albany (Ga.) College, 1939; married Blanche Chamberlain, Aug. 8, 1912; children—Martha (Mrs. Melvin T. Hurley), Wallace Arthur. Prin. schs. Ainsworth, Ia., 1906-08; supt. schs., Waitsburg, Wash., 1910-13; asst. supt. of public instrn., State of Wash., 1913-15; editor and pub. Journal-Times, Ritzville, Wash., 1915-24; business mgr. Corvallis (Ore.) Gazette Times, 1925-37; editor and mgr. Oregon Statesman, Salem, Ore., 1929-39, publisher since 1939; editor and pub., 1943-69. Pres. Ore. War Chest, 1943-46, 1951-52; chmn. Capitol Planning Commn., 1961-65, Regional Loyalty Bd.; pres. Colls. Ore's Future, 1963-69. Gov. of Ore., 1939-43. Pres. Ore. Council of Chs., 1943-47; bd. Carnegie Endowment Internat. Peace, 1954-58. Mem. board trustees Willamette University, Fellow Sigma Delta Chi. Republican. Presbyn. Rotarian. Home: Salem OR Died Mar. 13, 1969; interred Salem Mausoleum, Salem OR

SPRAGUE, HOWARD B., physician; b. Swampscott, Mass., Nov. 3, 1895; s. Henry Breed and Laura Loring (Brown) S.; A.B., Harvard, 1918, M.D., 1922; m. Lucy Sprague, June 14, 1919 (dec. Mar. 7, 1958); children—Priscilla Bulfinch Goldthwait, Elizabeth Howard Manson (M.D.), Howard B., Jr.; m. 2d, Marian B. Norton, Sept. 19, 1958. Intern Mass. Gen. Hosp., Boston, Mass., 1922-24, cardiac residency, 1924-25, asso. physician, 1931-53, physician, 1953-56, bd. consultants, 1956-67, hon. physician, 1967-71; physician specializing in diseases of heart, Boston, from 1925; former chief of staff House Good Samaritan; lectr. medicine Harvard Med. Sch., 1956-59; mem. nat. adv. heart council USPHS, 1954-59; sr. cons. in internal med. to U.S. Naval Hosp., Chelsea, Mass.; area chief in cardiology, New England area, Vets. Adminstrn., 1946-58. Served with Medical Corps, United States Naval Reserve, on active duty, 1941-45; promoted comdr., 1942, capt., 1943; on overseas service in Pacific, 17 mos. Decorated Asiatic-Pacific Theater Medal, Naval Reserve Medal (10 yrs. Service), Am. Theatre World War II Victory medal; gold-heart award of American Heart Assn., 1954; gold medal Am. Coll. Cardiology, 1965; Theodore and Susan Cummings humanitarian award, 1967. Trustee, treasurer Boston Med. Library, 1946-58, president, from 1958; mem. bd. directors Inter-Am. Soc. Cardiology, from 1946 (v.p. 1952); treas. Internat. Cardiology Found., from 1964.

Diplomate Am. Bd. Internal Medicine (Cardiology). Fellow Am. College of Physicians, American College of Cardiology; honorary mem. Mex., Chilean socs. of cardiology, Med. Soc. Santiago, Chile, med. faculty U. Chile; mem. Assn. Am. Physicians, Beacon Soc. Boston vice president 1952; president 1953-55), S.A.R., Soc. Colonial Wars, Harvard Alumni Assn. (dir. 1962-64), Bostonian Society, Am. Heart Assn. (sec. 1937-47, pres. 1950-51), Mass., N.E. Heart Assn. (pres. 1941-48), Mass. Med. Society, Am. Med. Assn., Am. Clin. and Climatol. Assn., Internat. Acad. Pathology, N.E. Cardiovascular Soc. (exec. com.), Internat. Soc. Cardiology, Phi Beta Kappa, Alpha Omega Alpha. Clubs: Harvard (Boston and N.Y.); Country (Brookline); Anglers (N.Y.C.); Cruising of Am. Contbr. numerous papers on diseases of circulation to med. publs. Home: Duxbury MA Died Nov. 4, 1971; buried Pine Grove Cemetery Lynn MA

SPRAGUE, KENNETH BURDETTE, corp. exec.; born Addison, N.Y., Apr. 18, 1908; s. Guy and Minnie (Swan) S.; B.S., Syracuse U., 1930, LL.B., Brooklyn Law Sch., 1941; m. Elizabeth Horton, Aug. 24, 1931; children—Richard Joan, Robert. Accountant Electric Bond & Share Co., N.Y. City, 1930-35; head tax dept. Am. & Foreign Power Co., Inc., 1935-43, asst. sec. Am. & Foreign Power Co., Inc., and Ebasco Internat. Corp., 1943-44, asst. sec. and asst. treas., 1944-45, sec. and asst. treas., 1945-46, asst. comptroller, 1946-52, v.p. in charge accounting and treasury, director; comptroller, treas., now financial v.p. Am. & Fgn. Power Co., Inc.; dir., v.p. Ebasco Internat. Corp. Mem. N.Y. State Bar, Phi Delta Phi. Home: Westfield NJ Died Aug. 10, 1967; buried Westfield NJ

SPRAGUE, THOMAS LAMISON, naval officer ret.; b. Lima, O., Oct. 2, 1894; s. Grant M. and Livia (Lamison) S.; B.S., U.S. Naval Acad., 1917; m. Evelyn Curry, Feb. 23, 1920; children—Isabel Curry (wife of Lt. Comdr. Louis Piollet Spear, U.S. Navy), Thomas Lamison (died Sept. 1, 1933), Martin Curry. Commd. ensign, U.S. Navy, advancing through the grades to vice adm., 1949; naval aviator (heavier than air) on staff of comdr. air force Pacific Fleet, 1921-22; sr. aviator U.S.S. Maryland, 1926-28; comd. Scouting Squadron 6, 1931, Scouting Squadron 10, 1932; asst. air officer, later air officer, U.S.S. Saratoga, 1935; navigator U.S.S. Langley, 1936; supt. aviation training, Naval Air Sta., Pensacola, Fla., 1937-40; exec. officer U.S.S. Ranger, 1940; comd. U.S.S. Pocomoke, 1941, U.S.S. Charger, 1942; chief of staff to comdr. fleet air, Quonset Point, R.I., Jan.-Feb. 1943, to comdr. air force Atlantic Fleet, Feb.-June 1943; comd. U.S.S. Intrepid, June 1943-Mar. 1944; comdr. fleet air, Alameda, Calif., 1944; comd. Carrier Div. 22, July 1944; comd. escort carrier group composed of 18 carriers with accompanying destroyers and escort vessels during battle for Leyte Gulf, 1944; comdr. carrier training squadron U.S. Pacific Fleet, Jan. 1945-46; comd. Task Group 38-I May-Dec. 1945; chief of naval personnel Feb. 1947; vice adm. serving under Presidential designation as comdr. Air Force, United States Pacific Fleet, 1949-52, retired with rank of admiral, April 1952. Decorated World War I Victory medal, Defense medal, Am. Area, Pacific Area, World War II Victory, Philippine Liberation, Navy Occupation, Navy Unit Citation, Presidential Unit Citation, Bronze Star, Legion of Merit with Gold Star, Distinguished Service medal, Navy Cross. Home: Oakland CA Died 1972.

SPRINGER, GEORGE PETER, univ. dean and adminstr.; b. Brno, Czechoslovakia, May 21, 1919; A.B., Harvard, 1942, M.A.T., 1943, Ph.D., 1954; fellow Georgetown U., 1953-54; div.; 3 children. Tchr. pub. schs. Mass., 1943-44; teaching fellow German, Harvard, 1952-53; research asso. Soviet studies, Human relations area files, New Haven, Conn., 1954-57; dir. admissions Grad. Sch., Yale, 1957-61, asst. dean Grad. Sch., 1961-65; prof. anthropology, dean Grad Sch., U. N.M., Albuquerque, 1965-72, v.p. research, 1968-72. Mem. bd. Grad. Record Exam. Mem. Linguistics Soc. Am., Soc. for Ethnomusicalogy, Council Grad. Schs. in U.S. (exec. com., pres.-elect 1972), Western Assn. Grad. (pres. 1969-70). Address: Albuquerque NM Died July 29, 1972.

SPRINGER, JOHN MCKENDREE, missionary bishop; b. Cataract, Wis., Sept. 7, 1873; s. Henry Martyn and Mary Ann (Durant) S.; Ph.B., Northwestern Univ., 1899; B.D., Garrett Biblical Institute, 1901, D.D., 1921; LL.D., Taylor Univ., 1939; m. Helen Emily (Chapman) Rasmussen (missionary Southern Rhodesia), Jan. 2, 1905. Ordained ministry M.E. Ch., 1901; supt. Old Umtali Industrial Mission, Southern Rhodesia, 1901-06; in 1907 accompanied by wife, crossed Central Africa from Umtali, Southern Rhodesia, to Malange, Angola, on west coast, traveling 1500 miles by foot paths, resulting in his founding Congo mission, M.E. Ch., 1910; supt. Congo Mission, 1910-21, 1923-36; in charge survey Central Africa missions for M.E. Ch., 1919, and all missions Central Africa for Inter-Church Movement, 1920; in charge Mutumbara Sta. and supt. dist. Southern Rhodesia, 1921-23; elected missionary bishop for Africa by Gen. Conf. M.E. Ch., 1936, in charge Umtali Area, 5 conferences (Angola Mission, Congo Mission, Liberia Annual, Rhodesia Annual, and South East Africa Mission); in charge Elisabethville Area, comprising within Africa Provisional Central Conf. 6 conferences, 1939-44; ret. from episcopal responsibilities, 1944, continuing as vol. in active missionary work with hdqrs. at Springer Inst. Mulungwishi, Belgian Congo, Africa. President Congo Protestant Council, 1934-36; represented council at International Missionary Council, Northfield, Mass., 1935. Mem. Delta Tau Delta. Decorated Chevalier Royal Order of the Lion (Belgium). Mason. Club: Overseas League (London). Author: Heart of Central Africa, 1908; Pioneering in the Congo, 1916; Christian Conquests in the Congo, 1926. Contbr. to religious jours. Home: Mulungwishi, via Elisabethville, Belgian Congo. Address: 150 5th Av., New York 11 NY‡

SPRINGER, THOMAS GRANT, writer; b. Sacramento, Calif., Dec. 26, 1873; s. Grant Horatio and Frances (Hamilton) S.; ed. pub. schs.; m. Edna Marione, of N.Y. City, Apr. 9, 1922. Author: The Red Cord (a Chinese Romance), 1925; Coffee and Conspiracy (romance of Central America), 1926; The Sword Peddler (satirical romance); The Sagebrush Buckaroo, 1932; Rodeo, 1935; The Californian, 1936. Contributor of over 175 stories to magazines, 200 play revs., over 250 poems, various articles, sketches and lyrics; has had 4 plays produced, several vaudeville sketches, including Reno and Return." Mem. Soc. Arts and Sciences.*‡

SPRINGHORN, CARL, artist; b. Broby, Sweden, May 13, 1887; s. Claes and Johanna (Edmundson) S.; came to U.S., 1904; ed. New York Sch. of Art and Henri Sch. of Art, New York; Colarossi Acad., Paris, etc.; unmarried. Exhibited in London, Kensington Mus., Stockholm, Gothenburg, Internat. Armory Show, New York, 1912, San Francisco Expn., 1915; one man shows in galleries of N.Y. City and Chicago; Worcester Art Mus., 1922; etc. Mgr. Henri Sch. of Art; dir. New Gallery; instr., Art Students' League, Los Angeles. Mem. Modern Artists America, New Gallery Art Club. Represented in permanent collection of Brooklyn Mus. Studio New York City NY Died Sept. 1971.

SPRINGWEILER, ERWIN FREDERICK, sculptor; b. Pforzheim, Germany, Jan. 10, 1896; s. Frederick and Emma (Kircher) S.; student Art Craft Sch. (Pforzheim), Fine Arts Acad. (Munich, Germany), Beaux Arts (N.Y.C.); m. Clara Kaeser, Oct. 27, 1921. Came to U.S., 1924, naturalized, 1939. Metal craftsman, sculptor, Germany, until 1922, Havana, Cuba, 1922-24, N.Y.C., 1924-68; works represented Nat. Zoo, Washington, Chester (Pa.) Post Office, Detroit-Highland Park Post Office, Manchester (Ga.) Post Office, Am. Swedish Museum, Phila., Broockgreen (S.C.) Gardens. Recipient Lindsay M. Sterling prize Nat. Sculpture Soc., 1937, Elin Speyer meml. prize NAD, 1938, 59; honorable mention New York World's Fair, 1939, Henry Avery prize Archtl. League N.Y., 1949, Hyatt-Huntington prize Nat. Acad. Design, 1949; Medal of Honor, National Arts Club N.Y., 1956; Sculpture prize National Art Club, 1965, 66. Mem. Nat. Sculpture Soc., Coun. Acad. Fine Arts, McDowell Colony (asso.), Soc. Animal Artists, N.A.D. Designer congressional medals. Home and studio: Wyandanch LI NY Died Mar. 18, 1968.

SPROSS, CHARLES GILBERT, musician, composer; b. Poughkeepsie, N.Y., Jan. 6, 1874; s. Michael and Alouisa (Rauch) S.; prep. edn., Poughkeepsie High Sch.; studied piano with Adolph Kuehn and Helen Andrus, later with Xaver Scharwenka, composition with Helen J. Andrus, of Poughkeepsie, and Emil Gramm, and Carl V. Lachmund, of New York; Mus.Doc., Capital Univ., Columbus, O., 1936; unmarried. Organist 2d Presbyn. Ch., Paterson, N.J., 7 yrs., Rutgers Presbyn. Ch., New York, 4 yrs., St. Paul's P.E. Ch., Poughkeepsie, 6 yrs., 1st Presbyn. Ch., Poughkeepsie, 17 yrs.; now organist First Congl. Ch., Poughkeepsie. Has served as accompanist to Melba, Amato, Schumann-Heink, Gluck, Destinn, Gadski, etc.; piano soloist with New York Philharmonic Orchestra, 1914. Presbyterian. Clubs: Musicians (New York); Amrita (Poughkeepsie, N.Y.). Composer of over 450 compositions, songs, sacred contatas, numerous piano and violin pieces, quartets, choruses, etc. Home: 4 Allen Pl., Poughkeepsie NY‡

SPROWLS, JOSEPH BARNETT, JR., educator; b. La Junta, Colo., Jan. 26, 1912; s. Joseph and Hilda Regina Theresa (Peterson) S.; Ph.C. and B.S., U. Colo., 1936, M.S., 1939, Ph.D., 1941; m. Rosalee Pearl Davy, Nov. 7, 1936; children—Joseph B., Marjorie Diane, Carol Lee, Rosalie Jean. Mem. faculty U. Colo., 1936-45, asst. prof. material medica, 1943-45; prof. and head dept. pharmacy U. Buffalo, 1945-48; prof. pharmacy Temple U. Sch. Pharmacy, 1948-50, dean, 1959-67; dean Coll. Pharmacy, U. Tex., Austin, 1967-71; consultant pharmacologist Meyer Memorial Hosp., Buffalo, 1945-48; mem. faculty of Pharmacy Seminar, Madison, Wis., 1949; mem. pharmacy seminar faculty Butler U., 1955. Mem. Pa. Drug, Device and Cosmetic Bd., 1962-67; mem. nat. adv. council, div. health manpower NIH. Chief pharmacist (Res.) USPHS. Registered pharmacist, Colo., N.Y. and Pa. Mem. Am. Public Health Association, A.A.A.S., American Pharm. Assn. (2d v.p., 1954), Am. Assn. Colls. Pharmacy (chmn. conf. pharmacy tchrs. 1950, chmn. exec. com. 1963-68), Am. Coll. Apothecaries, Am Foundation for Pharmaceutical Education (bd. of dirs.), Pa. Pharm. Assn. (exec. committee), Am. Pub Health Assn. Sigma Xi, Phi Delta Chi, Rho Chi Presbyn. (elder). Editor: Am. Pharm., 5th edit., 1960 6th edit., 1966; Prescription Pharm., 1964. Asso. editor Pharmaceutical Compounding and Dispensing, 2d edit 1955. Home: Austin TX Died Jan. 9, 1971; buried Austin TX

SPRUANCE, RAYMOND AMES, admiral; b Baltimore, Md., July 3, 1886; s. Alexander Peterson and Annie Ames (Hiss) S.; prep. edn. Stevens Prep. Sch. Hoboken, N.J.; grad. (with class of 1907), U.S. Naval Acad., 1906; m. Margaret Vance Dean, Dec. 30, 1914 children—Edward Dean (U.S.N.), Margaret (Mrs Bogart). Commd. ensign, U.S. Navy, 1908, and advanced through the grades to admiral, 1944; comd U.S.S. Mississippi, 1938-40; comdt. 10th Naval Dist. San Juan, P.R., 1940-41, with additional duty as comdr Caribbean Sea Frontier, July-Aug. 1941; became comdr Cruiser Div. 5, 1941; 2d in command operations in Marshall Islands, Wake Island and Marcus Island, 1942 jr. task force comdr. Battle of Midway, this force being built around carriers Enterprise and Hornet, 1942; chief of staff and aide to comdr. in chief Pacific Fleet June-Sept. 1942; dep. comdr. in chief Pacific Fleet Sept. 1942-Aug. 1943; comdr. Central Pacific Force later known as Fifth Fleet, 1944-45, in overall command of occupation of Gilbert Islands, invasion of Marshal Islands, in strikes against Truk, Palau, Yap and Woleai also in operations for capture of Saipan, Guam and Tinian (including Battle of Philippine Sea), and of Iwo Jima and Okinawa; comdr. in chief Pacific Fleet and Pacific Ocean Areas, Nov. 1945-Feb. 1946; pres. Naval War Coll., Newport, 1946; retired July 1, 1948 ambassador to the Philippines, 1952-55. Decorated D.S.M. with 2 gold stars (Navy), D.S.M. (Army) Presdnl. Unit Citation (Enterprise), Navy Cross Victory, Am. Defense, Fleet Clasp, Asiatic-Pacific Area Campaign and World War II Victory medals (U.S.) Gold Cross of Chevalier of Order of Savior (Greece) Hon. Companion Order of Bath (Gt. Britain); Grand Officer de l'Ordre de Leopold with palm, Croix de Guerre with palm, 1940 (Belgium). Address: Pebble Beach CA Died Dec. 13, 1969.

SPRUNT, ALEXANDER, JR., ornithologist; b. Rock Hill, S.C., Jan. 16, 1898; s. Alexander and Nell Richardson (Peck) S.; student Porter Mil. Acad. Charleston, S.C., 1910-11, Smith Sch., Charleston, S.C. 1912-13, Davidson (N.C.) Coll., 1914-18, Charleston Coll., 1954; D.Sc., Davidson Coll.; m. Margaret Malcolmson Vardell, Oct. 27, 1920 children—Alexander IV, Jean Vardell. Curator ornithology Charleston (S.C.) Mus., 1924-30, hon curator, 1930-73; supr. So. sanctuaries, Nat. Audubon Soc., 1935-40, So. rep. Nat. Audubon Soc., N.Y. 1940-73, also lectr. Served with USN 1918. Fellow Am Ornithologists Union. Author: Dwellers of the Silences 1935; Birds of South Carolina, 1949; Album Southern Birds, 1953; Florida Birdlife, 1954; North American Birds of Prey, 1955; Carolina Low Country; (with others) Warblers of America, 1957. Contbr. nature articles and stories to popular mags., also sci. articles on ornithology to tech. jours. Address: Charleston SC Died Jan. 3, 1973; buried Magnolia Cemetery, Charleston SC

SQUIRES, WALTER ALBION, clergyman; b. Cloud County, Kan., Dec. 26, 1874; s. Albion Caleb and Sarah-Isabel (McDonald) S.; Kan. State Normal Sch. 1898-1901; Northwestern U., 1903-04; grad. San Francisco Theol. Sem., 1910; A.B., Albany (Ore.) Coll. 1909; post-grad. work San Francisco Theol. Sem. Hartford Sch. Religious Pedagogy, Boston U.; D.D. Buena Vista Coll., Storm Lake, Ia., 1928; m. Elizabeth Thomson, Jan. 11, 1912; 1 son, Leslie Albion. Teacher country schs. and prin. high schs. until 1907; ordained Presbyn. ministry, 1912; pastor Stockton, Calif 1912-14, Lebanon Ch., San Francisco, 1914-17; exec sec. Calumet Fed. of Chs., Gary, Ind., 1918-20; dir. city surveys, Ind., 1920; became dir. Weekday Religious Inst. of Presbyn. Ch., 1920; pastor Community Presbyn Ch., Pismo Beach, Calif., 1937-39; minister of edn. First Presbyn. Ch., Stockton, Calif., 1939-42; First Church San Jose, Calif., since 1942. Member California Academy Sciences. Republican. Author: The Weekday Church School, 1921; God Revealing His Truth Through Patriarch and Prophet, 1921; Stories Jesus Told (with Elizabeth Squires), 1922; God Revealing His Truth Through His Son, 1922; New Testament Followers of Jesus, 1923; A Parish Program of Religious Education, 1923; Paul the Traveller and Missionary 1923; Christian Ideals for Young Disciples; World Tasks for Young Disciples; Psychological Foundations of Religious Education; The Pedagogy of Jesus in The Twilight of Today, 1927; Educational Movements of To-day, 1931. Home: 101 Glen Eyrie Av. Office: 60 N Third St., San Jose CA*‡

STACE, WALTER TERENCE, educator, author; b London, Eng., Nov. 17, 1886; s. Edward V. and Amy M (Watson) S.; B.A., Trinity Coll., Dublin (Ireland) U 1908, Litt.D., 1929; m. Blanche B. Beven, July 26, 1927 children—Noel J. (dec.), Jennifer J. (Mrs. Le Underwood). Came to U.S., 1933. Served Ceylon Govt 1910-33, judge, 1919-20; mayor of Colombo, Ceylon 1932-33; mem. faculty Princeton, 1933-55, pro hilosophy, 1944-55; retired, 1955. Mem. Am. Philos. Assn. (pres. 1949), Brit. Inst. Philosophy. Author: Critical History of Greek Philosophy, 1920; The Philosophy of Hegel, 1924; The Meaning of Beauty, 1929; The Theory of knowledge and Existence, 1932; The Concept of Morals, 1937; The Nature of the World, 1940; The Destiny of Western Man, 1942; The Gate of Silence, 1952; Religion and the Modern Mind, 1952; Time and Eternity, 1952; The Teachings of the Mystics, 1960; Mysticism and Philosophy, 1960; Man against Darkness, 1968. Home: Laguna Beach CA Died Aug. 3, 1967.

STACK, EDMUND JOHN, congressman; b. Chicago, Jan. 31, 1874; ed. high school, Chicago; LL.B., Lake Forest U. Law Sch., 1895; m. Mary A. R. Brazzell, of Chicago, Apr. 12, 1911. In practice at Chicago, 1895—. Served as asst. corpn. counsel, Chicago, and chief trial atty.; Dem. nominee for 60th Congress, 1906; elected 62d Congress (1911-13), 6th Ill. Dist.; Democrat. Home: 338 N. 40th Av. Office: Ashland Blk., Chicago IL‡

STACK, FREDERIC WILLIAM, naturalist; b. Poughkeepsie, N.Y., Nov. 21, 1871; s. George N. and Serena Martin (Macneil) S.; ed. pub. schs. and under pvt. tutelage of Prof. William B. Dwight, of Vassar Coll.; m. Cornelia Mollison Rockfellow, of Plainfield, N.J., Dec. 29, 1898. Mgr. dept. of publication mfr., Doubleday, Page & Co., since 1904. Served for 5 yrs. as pvt., 2d sergt. and sec. 15th Separate Co., N.G.S.N.Y.; formerly field collector for Mus. Natural History of Vassar Coll., and for mus. of the scientific sect. of Vassar Bros. Inst. Corr. mem. Delaware Valley Ornithol. Club; asso. mem. Am. Ornithologists' Union. Republican. Presbyn. K.T. Mason. Author: Wild Flowers Every Child Should Know, 1909. Extensive contbr. to mags. on nat. history and hort. subjects. Home: New Rochelle NY Office: 133 E. 16th St., New York NY‡

STACK, JOHN, engineer; b. Lowell, Mass., Sept. 13, 1906; s. Michael and Margaret (Connors) S.; B.S., Mass. Inst. Tech., 1928; m. Helen Sturtevant, Dec. 8, 1928; children—Martha (Mrs. John E. Sim), John Peter. Research, development, high-speed aerodynamics, 1928—; with Langley Aero Lab., NACA, beginning as research engr., successively sect. head, div. chief, then asst. dir.; mem. research adv. com. high speed aerodynamics, fluid mechanics, propellers, compressors; v.p. and dir. engring. Republic Aviation Corp., 1962-65; v.p. engring. Fairchild Hiller Co., from 1965; Wright Bros. lectr. Inst. Aero. Scis., 1944; Sci. Adv. Com. Tech. Adv. Panel Aero., Dept. Def.; vis. com. dept. mathematics Mass. Inst. Tech., 1954-56. Director Citizens & Marine Bank, Newport News, Va., Antilles Air Boats, Inc., St. Croix, V.I., Mac Aviation Corp., Ronkonkoma, L.I., United Virginia Bank/Citizens & Marine (Hampton, Va.). Recipient Science and Research award Air Forces Assn., 1948; awarded Collier trophy (with L. D. Bell, C. E. Yeager) for pioneer supersonic flight manned aircraft, 1948, for transonic wind tunnel development, 1952; awarded medal Soc. Engrs. Sweden, 1951, Wright Bros. Meml. Trophy, 1962. Fellow Royal Aero. Soc. Great Britian, Am. Inst. Aeros. and Astronautics (hon. mem.; recipient Sylvanus Albert Reid award 1953); hon. fellow Inst. Aerospace Scis.; mem. Air Force Assn. U.S. (hon.), Nat. Rifle Assn. Author sci. articles. Mem. editorial com. Jour. Aero. Scis. Home: Yorktown VA Died June 18, 1972; buried Grace Episcopal Churchyard, Yorktown VA

STACKPOLE, ALBERT HUMMEL, editor; b. Harrisburg, Pa., June 28, 1897; s. Edward James and Kate (Hummel) S.; grad. Harrisburg Acad., 1915; student Yale U., 1915-17, 1919; Doctor of Laws, Dickinson Law School, 1969; m. Mary Creighton, Oct. 9, 1920; children—Mary, Creighton. Reporter, city editor, publisher and columnist since 1919, vice pres., Telegraph Press, Inc.; pres. WHP, Incorporated, 1963-69, chairman of the board of directors, 1969-71. Del. Rep. National Conv., Phila., June 1948. Served with U.S. Army in A.E.F., 1917-19; commn. 1st lt. to col., 104th Cavalry, Fed. service, 1921-46; 2 yrs. in China with Chinese Combat Command, 1944-45; now ret. maj. gen. Reserve. Awarded Legion of Merit, Bronze Star; Yaun-Hui (Chinese). Mem. Reserve Officer's Assn., Alpha Delta Phi. Republican. Harrisburg PA Died July 31, 1971; buried Arlington Nat. Cemetery, Arlington VA

STADLER, WILLIAM LEWIS, business exec.; b. Lima, O., Aug. 27, 1897; s. Dr. Charles E. and Oma J. (Abbott) S.; A.B., B.S., U. Mich., 1922; m. Ruth R. Randall, Apr. 23, 1925; children—William Randall, Charles Edward, James Ralph. Vice pres. Backus-Fordon & Co., W.E. Reilly & Co., W. E. Moss & Co.; dir. Federal-Mongul-Bower Bearings, Inc., Dura Corp., Selected Securities Corp., Citizens Nat. Bank. Served with Tank Corps, U.S. Army, 1918-19. Mem. Newcomen Soc. Eng. Episcopalian. Mason. Clubs: Detroit, Detroit Athletic; Bloomfield Hills (Mich.) Country; Grose Ile Golf and Country, West Shore Golf, Round Island (Grosse Ile, Mich.); Bayou (La.); Surf (Miami Beach, Fla.); Urbana (O.) Country; Royal Palm Yacht and Country (Boca Raton, Fla.). Home: Urbana OH Died Jan. 14, 1972; cremated.

STAFFORD, JOHN RICHARD, author; b. Atchison County, Mo., Dec. 6, 1874; s. Richard and Phoebe Ann (Wilson) S.; State Normal Sch., Kirksville, Mo., 1887; B.A., Amity Coll., College Springs, Ia., 1896; m. Ethel M. McKillop, June 26, 1907; children—Mary Lee (Mrs. Harry J. Frichtel), Marjorie (Mrs. Edwin A. Pinkham, John Richard, Jean (Mrs. R.T.S. Lowell). Engaged in cattle ranching with father in Gray and Donley counties, Tex., 1896-98; newspaper writer, 1898-1900; in telephone business in Mo., 1900-05; mining in Ariz., 1905; went to Pacific coast, 1906; since engaged in writing fiction. Author: When Cattle Kingdom Fell, 1910. Contbr. to Century and other mags. Home: Oswego OR‡

STAFFORD, WENDELL PHILLIPS, judge; b. Barre, Vt., May 1, 1861; s. Frank and Sarah (Noyes) S.; grad. Barre Acad., 1878, St. Johnsbury Acad., 1880; LL.B. cum laude, Boston U., 1883; hon. A.M., Dartmouth Coll., 1901; LL.D., U. of Vt., 1905, Georgetown U., 1907; Litt.D., Middlebury Coll., 1910, George Washington U., 1916, U. of Vt., 1929; admitted to Vt. bar and began practice at St. Johnsbury, Vt.; m. Florence S. Goss, Feb. 24, 1886; children—Edward, Robert Sinclair (dec.). Mem. Vt. Ho. of Rep., 1892; reporter decisions of Supreme Court of Vt., 1896-1900; judge Supreme Court of Vt., 1900-04; asso. justice Supreme Court of D.C., 1904-31 (retired); prof. equity jurisprudence, George Washington U., since Sept. 1, 1908. Pres. Vt. Bar Assn., 1898-99. Lectured frequently in Vt. and occasionally in Boston, New York and Washington. Republican. Club: Cosmos. Author: North Flowers (poems), 1902; Dorian Days, 1909; Speeches, 1913; Voices, a Dramatic Ode, 1915; The Land We Love (poems), 1916; War Poems, 1917; A Handbook of Equity, 1934. Edited 69th, 70th and 71st vols. Vt. Reports. Contbr. poems and articles to mags. Washington DC‡

STAFSETH, H(ENRIK) J(OAKIM), coll. prof.; born Aalesund, Norway, Nov. 8, 1890; s. Knut Elias and Marie (Langset) S.; came to U.S., 1911, naturalized, 1918; student high sch. and gymnasium in Norway, 1904-11; B.S., N.D. State Agrl. Coll., 1915; D.V.M., Mich. State Coll., 1917, M.S., 1930, Ph.D., 1935; m. Inger Nordhem, Apr. 4, 1917; 1 son, Henrik Ekroll. Instr. and research asst. in bacteriology, Mich. State Coll., 1917-20, asst. prof. and research asst. in bacteriol., 1921-25, asso. prof. and research asso., 1926-30, prof. bacteriol. since 1930, head dept. bacteriol., bacteriologist, Mich. Agrl. Expt. Sta., dir. med. technol. and dir. div. biol. scis. Sch. Sci. and Arts, from 1948; cons. vet. edn. So. Regional Edn. Bd., 1949-52, U. Pa., 1956-57; dir. W. K. Kellogg Gull Lake biol. sta.; dist. veterinarian, Midtre Sondmor, Norway, Feb. 1910-July 1921; exchange prof. Royal Hungarian Vet. College, 1925-26; visited veterinary and other colls. and research labs., England, Norway, Sweden, Denmark, Germany, Austria, Switzerland, 1925-26; tech. adviser on poultry diseases to Dept. Agr. of Mexico, Nov. 1-Dec. 20, 1933. Chief veterinarian for U.N.R.R.A., China, Sept. 1945-Sept. 1946 (instrumental in establishing 1st modern vet. coll. in China at Lanchow, Kansu Province, summer 1946. Served in U.S. Army, 1917-19; discharged rank of 1st lt. Recipient Mich. State U. distinguished service award, 1955. Fellow Poultry Sci. Assn., Am. Pub. Health Assn., A.A.A.S.; mem. Royal Soc. Promotion Health, Am. Acad. Microbiologists, Am. and Michigan State Vet. Med. Assns., U.S. Live Stock San. Assn., Conf. Research Workers in Animal Diseases of N. Am., Soc. Am. Bacteriol., Am. Scandinavian Found., Mich. Acad. Science, American Legion, Military Order, Veterans of Foreign Wars, Sigma Xi, Sigma Chi, Alpha Psi, Phi Sigma, Phi Kappa Phi. Mem. People's Ch. (chmn. bd. trustees; chmn. Christian Student Foundation). Mason (K.T.), Kiwanian. Club: Walnut Hills Golf. Author: Laboratory Guide in Immunology and Lab. Guide in Pathogenic Bacteriology, 1942; Microbiology (with Ward Giltner), 1916; Diseases of Poultry (with Biester & Schwarte), 1948. Contbr. articles in profl. jours. Home: East Lansing MI Died Dec. 1, 1968.

STAHL, WILLIAM HARRIS, educator; b. N.Y.C., Dec. 20, 1908; s. John K. and Pauline (Pape) S.; B.A., N.Y.U., 1929, M.A. (A. Ogden Butler fellow 1930), 1930, Ph.D., 1934; m. Mattie L. Wallace, Sept. 18, 1934; children—Janice Ellen (Mrs. Daniel F. Mahoney, Jr.), Sara Judith (Mrs. David M. Logan). Instr. classics N.Y.U., 1930-43, asst. prof., 1945-51, asso. prof., chmn. classics dept. Univ. Coll., 1951-56; research analyst Engr. Research Office, Washington, 1943-45; Fulbright lectr. classics U. Melbourne (Australia), 1956; prof. classics, chmn. dept. classic and comparative lit. Bklyn. Coll., 1956-67; univ. seminar asso. classical civilization Columbia, 1959-69. Chmn. Ancient Civilization Group N.Y., 1954-69; member Com. on Internat. Exchange of Persons. Guggenheim fellow, 1962-63; hon. research asso. Greek, U. London (Eng.), 1962-63; Fulbright research fellow, fellow Univ. House, Australian Nat. U., 1963. Fellow A.A.A.S.; mem. History Sci. Soc. (council 1957-60, 65-68), Am. Philol. Assn. (chmn. com. textbooks 1950-55, 60-62), Medieval Club N.Y., Mediaeval Acad. Am., Renaissance Soc., N.Y. Classical Club, Classical Assn. Atlantic States, Classical Assn. Empire State, Am. Assn. U. Profs., Phi Beta Kappa. Author: Roman Science: Origins, Development and Influence to the Later Middle Ages, 1962; Macrobius' Commentary on the Dream of Scipio, 1952; Ptolemy's Geography: a Select Bibliography, 1953; The Odyssey of Homer, revision, 1955; Martianus Capella and the Seven Liberal Arts: Vol. I, The Quadrivium of Martianus Capella, 1971; also numerous articles. Home: Baldwin NY Died Apr. 20, 1969; buried Port Washington NY

STAIR, EDWARD DOUGLAS, general investments; b. Morenci, Michigan, Mar. 29, 1859; s. Jacob and Maryette (Beckwith) S.; public school education; m. Grace Crookson, July 2, 1888. Country newspaper pub. at Morenci, Midland, and Howell, Mich., and Cooperstown, N.D., 1876-88; entered theatrical management in New York, 1888, by producing a play he had written; reentered newspaper work by purchase of interest in Detroit Journal, 1901, and Detroit Free Press, 1906; chmn. bd. dirs. Detroit Free Press; also mem. board dirs. Detroit Creamery Realty Co., Buhl Stamping Co., Ann Arbor Ry., Wabash Ry. Co., Detroit Fire & Marine Ins. Co.; dir. Detroit Trust Co. Mem. Nat. Inst. Social Sciences. Republican. Mason (32 deg.). Clubs: Detroit, Old Club, Grosse Pointe, Nat. Press (Washington); Everglades (Palm Beach, Fla.). Home: 8330 Jefferson Av. Office: Free Press Bldg., Detroit 26 MI‡

STAKELY, CHARLES A., lawyer; b. Montgomery, Ala., Apr. 30, 1903; A.B., LL.B., U. Ala. Admitted to Ala. bar, 1926, since practiced in Montgomery; mem. firm Rushton, Stakely & Johnson. Mem. Ala. Senate, 1938-42, 42-46. Served to comdr. USNR, 1943-46. Mem. Am., Ala., Montgomery County bar assns., Phi Beta Kappa, Phi Delta Phi. Office: Montgomery AL Died June 2, 1965.

STALDER, JACKSON R., mech. engr.; b. Oakland, Cal., Dec. 12, 1915; s. John Reed and Maude (Wells) S.; B.S., U. Cal. at Berkeley, 1941; m. Virginia Hall, July 22, 1950; children—Suellen, Barbara Lynn, Kenneth Reed. Aero. research scientist NACA, 1941-58; exec. with Vidya, Inc., 1958-65; chief scientist USAF Flight Dynamics Lab., 1965-67; tech. asst. to dir. NASA, Ames Lab., 1967-68; pres. KOWL, Inc., Bijou, Cal., 1963-68, Beavercreek Farms (Ore.), 1964-68. Fellow Am. Inst. Aeros. and Astronautics (asso.); mem. Sigma Xi. Home: Palo Alto CA Died Sept. 10, 1968.

STALEY, A. ROLLIN, mfg. exec.; b. Baltimore, May 16, 1907; s. Augustus Eugene and Emma L. (Tressler) S.; student Staunton (Va.) Mil. Acad., 1923-24, Culver (Ind.) Mil. Acad., 1924-25, 1925-26; U. of Ill., 1926-29; married Nettie Lou Salisbury, July 24, 1949. Sales promotion mgr., A.E. Staley Mfg. Co., Decatur, Ill., then v.p. charge customer relations, resigned 1956; pres. Skylark Charter Lines. Dir. Decatur and Macon County Hosp.; trustee Naples Community Hospital; member U. Ill. Found. Served as 1st lt. USAF, 1942-44. Mem. Assn. of Commerce (recipient Civic Service award, 1940), Airplane Owners and Pilots Assn. (charter mem.), Alpha Tau Omega. Presbyn. Mason (K.T., Shriner). Clubs: Metropolitan (N.Y.C.); Jonathan (Los Angeles); Country, Decatur (dir.), Shrine, City (Decatur); Hole-in-the-Wall-Golf, Port Royal Beach (Naples, Fla.). Holder pilots license. Home: FL Died Oct. 11, 1968; buried Fair Lawn Cemetery, Decatur IL

STAM, JACOB, lawyer, orgn. ofcl.; b. Hawthorne, N.J., Sept. 18, 1899; s. Peter and Amelia E.A. (Willems& S.; LL.B., N.Y. Law Sch., 1922; m. Deana Bowman, Apr. 6, 1923 (dec. Nov. 1965); children—Paul B., Ruth M., John E., Mary E., David H., James H., Robert P. Amateur shorthand champion N.Y. Met. Dist., 1915, law office, 1915-22; admitted to N.J. bar, 1922, as counselor, 1928, U.S. Supreme Ct., 1950; gen. practice, Paterson, from 1922. Pres., trustee Latin Am. Mission, Star of Hope Mission of Paterson, D.M. Stearns Missionary Fund of Phila.; gen. counsel Gideons Internat.; charter mem., dir. Christian Legal Soc., Men in Action, Denver: trustee, past vice chmn. bd. Moody Bible Inst., Chgo.; life trustee Pocket Testament League. Served with U.S. Army, World War I. Mem. Am., N.J., Passaic County bar assns., Am. Judicature Soc. Republican. Home: Paterson NJ

STAMM, VINCIL R., welding supply mcht.; b. Dixon, Mo., June 19, 1901; s. Joseph and Anna S. (Houk) S.; student Benton Coll., St. Louis U.; m. Ruthanna Garnier, July 20, 1946. Bldg. contractor, St. Louis, 1928-44; operator, owner theater bus., Kansas City, Mo., 1944-50; owner, welding supply, Oxygen Service Co., Jayhawk Welding Supply, Topeka, Kan., Jay-Ox, Inc., Oxygen Service Co., Kansas City, Kan., Oxygen Service, Kansas City, Mo., now ret. Trustee Goodwill Industries. Mason (32 deg., Shriner). Home: Overland Park KS Died Nov. 1, 1968.

STANDEVEN, JAMES WYLIE, hosp. supt.; b. Hancock, Ia., Jan. 25, 1916; s. John Frank and Elsie (Wylie) S.; B.S., State U. Ia., 1940, M.D., 1940; m. Jean E. Beckwith, Apr. 30, 1960; children—John, Steven. Intern Neb. Meth. Hosp., Omaha; gen. practice medicine, Oakland, Ia., 1946-57; with VA, 1957-70, dir. VA Hosp., Montgomery, Ala., 1968-70. Mem. Gov. Ala. Com. Employment Handicapped. Councilman,

Oakland, Ia., 1950-54. Bd. dirs. local A.R.C. Served to capt. USAAF, 1941-45. Mem. Am. Coll. Hosp. Adminstrs., A.M.A., Aerospace Med. Assn., Fed. Execs. Assn., Alpha Omega Alpha, Alpha Kappa Kappa. Rotarian. Home: Tucson AZ Died May 20, 1972.

STANFIELD, THEODORE, peace advocate; b. Paris, France, Apr. 1, 1874; s. Adolph S. and Charlotte (Leviseur) S.; brought to U.S., 1874; Coll. City of New York, 1888-91, Harvard, summer 1921; m. Cora Rose Leopold, of N.Y. City, Oct. 11, 1905; 1 dau., Charlotte Leviseur; m. 2d, Susette M. Brunnschweiler, July 5, 1922. Began as office boy, Am. Metal Co., Ltd., 1891, and advanced to exec. mgr., treas. and dir.; retired 1917. Mem. Am. Peace Soc. (life), A.A.A.S., Inst. of Politics (Williamstown, Mass.), Acad. Polit. Science, Am. Acad. Polit. and Social Science, Am. Soc. Internat. Law. Republican. Unitarian. Clubs: Lotos, Nat. Arts, Bankers, Nat. Press, Harmonie. Wrote: Some Questions About Enduring Peace, 1920; A Coercive League Contrary to Teachings of American History, 1920; The Divided States of Europe and the United States of America, 1921; Europe's Road to Peace, 1923; An International Fact-Finding Body, 1926. Home: 151 Central Park W., New York NY*‡

STANGELAND, KATHARINA MARIE (MRS. CHARLES E. STANGELAND), author; b. Randers, Denmark, Mar. 20, 1877; d. Jacob and Sine (Bech) Brondum; ed. pvt. schs. and under tutors; m. Charles E. Stangeland, of Washington, D.C., Feb. 22, 1912. Author: Andrea, 1904; The Dangerous Age, 1910; Elsie Lindtner, 1912; The Governor, 1913; also various books pub. in Europe. Contbr. to Am. and European mags. Address: Thuro pr. Svendborg Denmark‡

STANISLAUS, I(GNATIUS) V(ALERIUS) STANLEY, chemist; b. at South Bend, Ind., 1870; s. M. Sylvester and Rosalie (Strans) S.; ed. Gynasium of Gnesen, Germany, 5 yrs.; Ph.C., U. of Ill., 1895; studied organic chemistry, Polytechnicum of Zurich, Switzerland, 1905-6; B.Sc., Univ. of Notre Dame, Ind., 1901; Dr. of Pharmacy, Brooklyn Coll. of Pharmacy, 1903; student, Brooklyn Poly. Inst., 1904; Ph.D., U. of Providence, O., 1907; studied at Harvard, 1907; M.A., Ursinus Coll., 1910; m. Lillian B. Smith, of Brooklyn, Oct. 17, 1903. Asso. chemist for Vanderhoof & Co., South Bend, Ind., 1888-93; dean dept. pharmacy and prof. industrial chemistry, U. of Notre Dame, 1896-1901; chemist for Osborn-Colwell Co., later De Ronde & Osborn Paint Co., New York, 1901-3; chief chemist for Hegeman & Co. Corpn., 1903-5; teacher pharmacy, Brooklyn College of Pharmacy, 1904; dean Medico-Chirurg. Coll. of Pharmacy, Phila., since July 1, 1906. Has done original work and investigation in chemistry of odorous principles and volatile oils and resins. Asso. editor, The Apothecary, Boston, since 1903. Mem. Am. Chem. Soc., Am., Pharm. Assn., Ind. Acad. Science, Phi Chi, Kappa Psi. Mason. Author: Systematic Qualitative Analyses, Inorganic and Organic, 1905; Text-Book on Pharmacy, 1907; Pharmaceutic Chemistry, 1908; Laboratory Guide Applied Pharmacy, 1909. Home: Landsdowne PA Office: 1715 Cherry St., Philadelphia PA‡

STANLEY, CARLETON WELLESLEY, pres. Dalhousie U.; b. (Canadian parents) Providence, R.I., July 6, 1886; B.A., U. of Toronto (highest place in Classics and gen. proficiency, two gold medals), 1911; B.A., New Coll. Oxford, Eng. (1st class honors, Literae Humaniores), 1913, M.A., 1916; LL.D., U. of Toronto, 1933, Litt.D., U. of Colo., 1935, LL.D., U. of Maine, 1935; m. Isabel Buchen Alexander, 1918; children—Carleton Alexander, Laura. Lecturer, English literature, Victoria Coll., U. of Toronto, 1913-16; engaged in business, 1916-25; prof. Greek, McGill U., 1925-31, asst. to prin., 1930-31; pres. Dalhousie U., 1931-71. Fellow Royal Soc. of Can. Author: Roots of the Tree, 1936; Matthew Arnold, 1938. Home: Halifax NS Canada. Died Nov. 30, 1971.

STANLEY, CLARANCE, corporation exec.; b. Pittsfield, Mass., Jan. 14, 1897; s. William and Lila C. (Wetmore) S.; student Berkshire Sch., 1909-14, Yale, 1915-17; m. Augusta G. Leovy, Jan. 9, 1929; children—William, Frank L., Lila C. Associated with Nat. Commercial Bank and Trust Co., Albany, N.Y., 1919-24; with Union Trust Co. of Pittsburgh, 1924-47, beginning in bond dept., pres. and dir., Jan. 1937-Sept. 1946, when company merged with Mellon Nat. Bank, becoming Mellon Nat. Bank & Trust Co., chmn. exec. com. and dir., 1946-47; gen. partner Morgan Stanley & Co., 1946-50; v.p. Gen. Motors Corp., N.Y.C., from 1950; dir. Brazilian Traction, Light & Power Co., Ltd., Can. Served with United States Naval Aviation Corps, 1917-18. Pres. and trustee Berkshire Sch. Republican. Episcopalian. Clubs: Yale, Links (New York); Pittsburgh Golf (Pittsburgh); Round Hill (Greenwich, Conn.). Home: Greenwich CT Died Feb. 1972.

STANLEY, EDWIN M(ONROE), dist. judge; b. Forsyth County, N.C., Mar. 9, 1909; s. John Brantson and Nettie Louise (Atkins) S.; LL.B., Wake Forest College, 1931, also received Doctor of Laws, 1964; m. Lottie Belle Myers, June 30, 1933; children—Susanne and Robert Myers (twins). Admitted to N.C. bar, 1930. practiced in Greensboro, 1931-54; judge Greensboro Juvenile Ct., 1951-54; U.S. atty. Middle Dist. N.C., 1954-57, U.S. dist. judge, 1957-71. Mem. com. trial practice and technique Jud. Conf. U.S., 1960-71; mem. Fed. Jud. Center Adv. Com. Innovation and Devel. Trustee Wake Forest Coll., 1953-57. Mem. Am., N.C., Greensboro bar assns., Greensboro Jr. C. of C. (past pres.), Gen. Alumni Assn. Wake Forest Coll. (pres. 1953). Baptist (deacon). Club: Greensboro Civitan (past pres.). Home: Greensboro NC Died Dec. 23, 1971.

STANLEY, THOMAS BAHNSON, gov.; b. Spencer, Va., July 16, 1890; s. Crockett and Susan Matildah (Walker) S.; ed. pub. schs. in Henry County, Va., and Eastman Bus. Coll., Poughkeepsie, N.Y.; hon. doctorate Coll. William and Mary; m. Anne Pocahontas Bassett, Oct. 24, 1918; children—Anne (Mrs. Hugh H. Chatham), Thomas Bahnson, John David. Mem. Va. House of Delegates, 1930-46, speaker, 1942, 44, 46; gov's adv. bd. on budget, 1930-46; mem. 79th to 83d Congresses, 5th Va. Dist.; resigned, 1953; elected gov. of Va., 1954. Chmn. bd. Stanley Furniture Co., Stanleytown, Va., Ferrum (Va.) Veneer Corp.; dir. Stanley Land & Lumber Corp., 1st Nat. Bank (Bassett, Va.). Former chmn. bd. trustees Ferrum Coll.; mem. bd. visitors Coll. William and Mary. Mem. Va. C. of C., Va. Mfg. Assn., Southern Furniture Mfrs. Assn. (High Point, N.C.), Omicron Delta Kappa. Democrat. Methodist. Mason (33 Stanleytown VA Died July 10, 1970; interred Roselawn Abbey Martinsville VA

STANLEY, WENDELL M(EREDITH), bio-chemist; b. Ridgeville, Ind., Aug. 16, 1904; s. James G. and Claire (Plessinger) S.; B.S., Earlham Coll., Richmond, Ind., 1926, hon. Sc.D., 1938; M.S., U. of Ill., 1927, Ph.D., 1929; Sc.D., 1959; Sc.D., Harvard, Yale, 1938, Princeton, 1947, U. Pitts., 1962, U. Penn., 1964, Gustavaus Adolphus College, 1963, University of Toledo, 1968, Butler U., 1968; LL.D., U. Cal., 1946, Indiana U., 1951, Jewish Theol. Sem., 1953, Mills Coll., 1960; Dr. honoris causa, U. Paris, 1947; m. Marian Staples Jay, June 15, 1929; children—Wendell, Marjorie (Mrs. Robert J. Albo), Dorothy (Mrs. Roger Erickson), Janet E. Research asso. and instr. in chemistry, U. of Ill., 1929; Nat. Research fellow, Munich, Germany, 1930-31; with Rockefeller Inst. for Med. Research since 1931, mem., 1940-48; Hitchcock prof. U. Cal., 1940, chmn. dept. biochemistry, 1948-53; prof. biochemistry, dir. virus lab. Univ. Cal. at Berkeley, 1948-69, professor, chmn. dept. viorology, 1958-64, professor of molecular biology, 1964-71. Vanuxem lectr. Princeton, 1942; Messenger lectr. Cornell, 1942; Silliman lectr. Yale, 1947. Trustee Mills Coll., 1951-58. Mem. expert adv. panel on virus diseases WHO, 1951-71; nat. adv. cancer council USPHS, 1952-56; chairman section biochemistry National Academy Sciences, 1955-58; dir.-at-large Am. Cancer Soc., 1955-61; mem. bd. scientific counselors National Cancer Inst., 1957-61, chmn. 1957-58; adv. com. to dir. Nat. Insts. Health, 1966-71; spl. adv. com. to sec. Dept. Health, Edn. and Welfare; pres. 10th Internat. Cancer Congress, Houston, 1970. Fellow N.Y. Acad. Scis.; mem. Japan Acad. (hon.), Am. Assn. Immunologists. Am. Philos. Soc., Am. Chem. Soc., Am. Phytopathological Society, Harvey Soc. (hon.), Am. Soc. Biol. Chemists (mem. council 1951-54), A.A.A.S., Sigma Xi, Alpha Omega Alpha, Gamma Alpha, Phi Lambda Upsilon (hon.), Alpha Chi Sigma, Phi Kappa Phi. Awarded A.A.A.S. prize, 1936; Isaac Idler prize by Med. Sch. of Harvard, 1938; Rosenberger medal by U. of Chicago, 1938; John Scott medal, certificate, and premium by the City of Phila., 1938; gold medal of Am. Inst. of the City of New York, 1941; Copernican Citation by the Copernican Quadricentennial Nat. Com., 1943; Nichols Medal of the N.Y. Sect. of American Chem. Society, 1946; Nobel Prize in Chemistry, 1946; Gibbs Medal of Chicago Sect. of Am. Chem. Soc., 1947; Franklin Medal of Franklin Inst., 1948; Presdl. Certificate of Merit, 1948; Modern Medicine award, 1958; Am. Cancer Soc. award, 1959; nat. award Am. Cancer Soc. 1963; Sci. Achievement award A.M.A., 1966; Wendell M. Stanley Hall named in his honor by U. Cal. decorated 2d class Order Rising Sun (Japan), Contbr. to sci. jours. Home: Berkeley CA Died June 15, 1971; buried Berkeley CA

STANSELL, ROBERT BASIL, clergyman; b. Groveoak, Ala., Nov. 2, 1875; s. Thomas Jefferson and Nancy (Gilbert) S.; grad. Walnut Grove (Ala.) Collegiate Inst., 1898; A.B., Grant U. (now U. of Chattanooga), 1901, D.D., 1913; B.D., Drew Theol. Sem., Madison, N.J., 1904; grad. study Harvard and Columbia; m. Frances Ryan, Jan. 24, 1897; children—Dorothy (dec.), Lucius Grant, Robert Basil; m. 2d, Mrs. Elizabeth Stewart Ganser, Aug. 18, 1925. Entered ministry M.E. Ch., 1897; Ala. rural pastorates, 1897-1900; pastor Alton Park, Tenn., 1901-02, East Moriches, L.I., N.Y., 1903-04, St. James Ch., Chattanooga, Tenn., 1905-07; dist. supt. Chattanooga Dist., 1908-09; prof. N.T. Greek, U. of Chattanooga, 1910, prof. English lit., 1911; dean of Athens Sch. (now Tenn. Wesleyan Coll.), 1912; v.p. U. of Chattanooga, 1913-14; financial agt. Asbury Hosp., Minneapolis, Minn., 1915; pastor Trinity Ch., St. Paul, 1916-20, Grand Av. (now 1st) M.E. Ch., Milwaukee, 1921-33; dist. supt. Milwaukee Dist. of M.E. Ch., 1933-40; pastor Summerfield Meth. Ch., Milwaukee, 1940-48; mem. bd. trustees Milwaukee Goodwill Industries, Wis. Annual Conf. Pres. bd. trustees Milwaukee Deaconess Girls' Home and Old People's Home. Mem. Interdenominational Relations Commn., 1928-32 and since 1936; mem. Gen. Conf. M.E. Ch., 1912, 20, 28 36; mem. Uniting Conf. Meth. Epis. Churches, Kansas City, Mo., 1939; mem. General Conf. Meth. Ch. Atlantic City, N.J., 1940, North Central Jurisdictional Conf. of Meth. Ch., Chicago, 1940; mem. Wisconsin Council Chs.; chmn. Wisconsin Conf. Commn. on World Service and Finance; mem. Entertainment Commn. North Central Jurisdiction, 1940-44; pres. Milwaukee Union of Meth. Ch. Pres. Milwaukee Meth. Ministerial Assn., 1944-45. Traveled extensively in Europe and Near East including Palestine and Egypt, 1930. Republican. Mason (32 deg.). Kiwanian. Home: 4916 N. Larkin St., Milwaukee 11 WI‡

STANTON, A. GLENN, architect; b. Humboldt, Ia. May 17, 1895; s. John Wellington and Carrie (Hupp) S. A.B., U. Ore., 1918; B.S., 1919; A.M., Mass. Inst. Tech. 1921; Am. Students Mission to Europe, 1921. Mem. firm Whitehouse, Stanton & Church, Portland, Ore., 1925-35; pvt. practice, Portland, 1935-55; sr. partner Stanton, Boles, Maguire & Church, architects, 1955-69. Mem. Met. Bd. YMCA, 1939-69; mem. Portland City Planning Commn., 1941-49, 55-69, pres. 1945-49. Fellow A.I.A. (national pres. 1951-53), Royal Archtl. Inst. Can. (hon.), Royal Society Arts Eng., Royal Society Encouragement Arts, Mfg. and Commerce; mem. Am. Arbitration Assn. (nat. panel), Royal Inst. Brit. Architects (hon. corr.), Philippine Institute Architects (corr. member), Portland Apprenticeship Council (chmn. 1944-1950), State Bd. Archt. Examiners (pres. 1941, 44, 52), Mass. Inst. Tech. Alumni Assn. (hon. sec. scholarship chmn.) Scarab. Conglist. Scottish Rite. Mason (Shriner). Clubs: University, Arlington, Architectural League of New York; Century Assn. (N.Y.); Cosmos (Washington); Tavern (Chgo.). Contbr. weekly column on city planning Sun. Ore. Jour., 1943-48. Home: Portland OR Died Oct. 16, 1969.

STANTON, HARRY LEAVENWORTH, banker; b. Sheridan, Mich., Aug. 28, 1875; s. Charles Hamilton and Cornelia Henrietta (Leavenworth) S.; ed. Lansing (Mich.) High Sch.; m. Grace Darrin Alsdorf, Nov. 22, 1899; children—Charles Frederick, Harry Leavenworth, Edward Hamilton. With E. Bements Sons, mfrs. agrl. implements and stoves, Lansing, 1894-1904, advancing to traffic mgr.; sales mgr. and gen. mgr. same co. and Central Implement Co., and The Lansing Co., 1904-07; gen. mgr. Glaziers Stove Co., Chelsea, Mich., 1907-09, Chelsea Stove Co., 1909-11; treas. Grant & Wood Mfg. Co., Chelsea Ball Co. and others, 1911-13; comptroller Abbott Detroit Motor Car Co., 1913; mgr. Michigan Buggy Co., 1914; with Detroit Trust Co. 1915-45, asst. sec. until 1917, vice pres. until 1945, now retired. Chmn. bd. Calaveras Land & Timber Co.; dir. W.H. Edgar & Co., Edgar Sugar House. Mem. Detroit Bd. of Commerce. Republican. Episcopalian. Club: Detroit. Contbr. on trust company adminstrn. Home: 13 Poplar Park, Pleasant Ridge, Detroit. Office: Detroit Trust Co., Detroit MI‡

STANTON, STEPHEN BERRIEN, author; b. Detroit, Mich., Mar. 12, 1864; s. Stephen Keyes and Mary Berrien (McCoskry) S.; A.B., Harvard, 1887; A.M., 1888, LL.B., 1889, Ph.D., Columbia, 1890; m. Hedwig Jeanne Quintard, Oct. 6, 1902. Practiced law in New York (Sherman & Stanton) to 1903; residing chiefly in New York or Washington, and engaged in writing. Member Assn. Bar City of New York, Phi Beta Kappa. Author: The Behring Sea Dispute, 1891; The Essential Life, 1908; Soul and Circumstance, 1910; Foam Flowers, 1911; The Hidden Happiness, 1917; The Fourth in the Furnace, 1927; Collected Poems, 1930. Contbr. to legal and other periodicals; also Just a Moment" column in Washington Post. Home: (summer) Bethel, Vt. Address: University Club, New York NY‡

STAREK, FRED, ex-dir. War Finance Corpn.; b. Cleveland, O., July 3, 1873; s. James and Gabrielle (Mondall) S.; grad. Cleveland Central High Sch.; student Western Reserve U., 1890. Began newspaper work, 1894; became staff corr. Cleveland Leader, at Washington, D.C., 1897, and later took charge of bureaus of Cincinnati Enquirer, Ohio State Journal (Columbus) and other newspapers; specialized in polit. and fiscal subjects, articles being made part of curriculum of U. of Cincinnati. Declined asst. secretaryship of the Treasury during the administration of President Roosevelt; appointed nat. bank examiner of N.Y. City by President Taft, 1912, resigning same yr. to assist in renomination of Taft. Offered option to purchase Washington Post and was about to close same when owner of the Post died, 1916, throwing estate into protracted litigation; at request of Senator Warren G. Harding of Ohio, made a wide survey in 1919, which led to announcement of Harding's candidacy for Rep. nomination for the Presidency, and later organized alliances resulting in his nomination, after deadlock between Wood and Lowden, at Chicago, June 20, 1920; associated with Harding in confidential capacity during fall campaign, and after his election was offered ambassadorship to Germany and other important posts abroad and in Washington, including membership Federal Reserve Bd. and Federal Trade Commn. and on European War Dept. Commn., but declined, finally accepting at President's insistence, directorship of War Finance Corpn. and served June 1922-June 1926; collaborated with Ex-Gov. Lowden of Ill. in promoting his second Presidential candidacy, 1927-28, but opposition of Coolidge administration to Lowden-Dawes theory of farm relief led to Lowden's withdrawal; conducted patent litigation against General Motors, 1930-31, involving potential awards of approximately $50,000,000, but rules of U.S. Supreme Court blocked final review, after U.S. District Court had rendered favorable decision; planned and engaged, 1934, in project to construct new Union Ry. Station (passenger and freight) in htart of N.Y. City, enabling all rys. lacking terminal facilities to enter the city through series of tunnels under Hudson River. Made official tour through South and Southwest in 1923 in Army and Navy airplanes, while dir. of war finance, covering 5,000 miles, entailing many risks and narrow escapes from disaster. Apptd. col. staffs of Govs. Glasscock and Hatfield of W.Va., 1908, 12. Presbyn. Clubs: Nat. Press (charter mem.), Congressional Country (Washington); Metropolitan, Calumet (New York). Address: 3211 19th St. N.W., Washington DC‡

STARK, ABE, city ofcl., civic leader; b. Manhattan, N.Y., Sept. 28, 1894; s. Hyman and Sarah (Becker) S.; student pub. schs.; m. Lilyan Goldman, Nov. 26, 1919; 1 son, Stanley. Founder retail clothing firm Abe Stark, Inc., 1915. Chmn. Retail Apparel Industry, N.Y.C., 1930; mem. adv. bd. N.R.A., 1934; mem. adv. council N.Y. City Dept. Hosps., 1948; commr. commerce N.Y.C., 1948-49; impartial labor-management arbitrator Retail Gasoline Industry, 1950-52; pres. N.Y.C. Council, 1953. Pres. Brownsville Boys Club, 1946-53; chmn. fedn. day Fedn. Jewish Philanthropies, 1952; mem. bd. Jewish Sanitarium and Hosp. Chronic Diseases, 1937; dir. Beth-El Hosp., 1938, Bklyn. Jewish Center, 1939; chmn. citizens com. Middlesex Med. Sch., 1940-48; dir. Brownsville and East N.Y. Y.M.H.A., 1943, Pride of Judea Children's Home, 1945. Awarded hon. key State of Israel, Am. Fund Israeli Instns., 1949, hon. professorship anatomy Chgo. Med. Sch., 1950, hon. professorship drama, Habima Chamber, Ohel Mate Theater of Israel, 1952; named man of year Children of Israel, 1951, man of year in child welfare Child Guidance League, 1951; outstanding citizen's award Good Neighbor League, 1952; man of year for promotion intergroup understanding Bapt. Pastors and Ch. Union, 1953. Mem. Nat. Conf. Christians and Jews (Bklyn. chmn. Brotherhood Week 1951), Pitkin Av. Mchts. Assn. (chmn. bd. 1935), Grand Street Boys, Anti-Defamation League, Hebrew Edn. Soc. (mem. bd.), Brooklyn C. of C., Americans Dem. Action. K.P., B'nai B'rith. Clubs: Dodger Knot Hole (dir. 1945), Brook Boro (pres. 1946), Forty-Six (chmn. bd.), Nonpareil, Elite. Home: Brooklyn NY Died July 1972.

STARK, CLARENCE OSCAR, oil co. exec.; b. Elk City, Kan., Feb. 9, 1898; s. Joel O. and Clara E. (Stark) S.; student pub. schs., Kan.; m. Julia Marie Glaze, 1924; children—Betty Jeanne (Mrs. Conrad S. Preston), Shirley Ann (Mrs. John E. Chouteau). Clk. oil accounting dept. Empire Oil & Gas Co. (now Cities Service Co.), 1918-19; with Phillips Petroleum Co., 1919-67; beginning in prodn dept., various positions land and geol. dept., 1919-38, v.p. charge land and geol. dept., 1938-67. Methodist. Home: Bartlesville OK Died Jan. 11, 1967.

STARK, DUDLEY SCOTT, bishop; b. Waverly, N.Y. Nov. 19, 1894; s. Rodney Jewett and Lelia May (Scott) S.; B.A., Trinity Coll., 1917, D.D., 1948; D.D., Episcopal Theol. Seminary, Cambridge, Mass., 1920; LL.D., Chicago Med. Sch., 1939; D.D., Kenyon Coll., 1940; Doctor of Sacred Theology, Hobart College, 1950; L.H.D., Alfred University, 1959; married to Mary Addie Leith, June 24, 1920; children—Mary Bliss and Rosalind (twins), Gregory Leith (killed in action, January 1945), and Dudley Scott. Deacon and priest in the P.E. Church, 1920, curate St. Mark's Church, Mauch Chunk, Pennsylvania, 1920-21, rector, 1921-26; vicar Ch. of the Holy Trinity, St. James Parish, N.Y. City, 1926-32; rector St. Chrysostom's Ch. Chicago, 1932-50; bishop Episcopal Diocese of Rochester, 1950-62; pastor Trinity Ch., York Harbor, 1963-71; chaplain of various civic orgns., York Harbor, Me. Trustee Chgo. Med. Sch.; chancellor, trustee Hobart Coll., 1950-62. Ensign U.S.N.R.F., 1918. Mem. Phi Beta Kappa, Alpha Delta Phi. Home: York Harbor ME Died Nov. 23, 1971; buried First Parish Cemetery York Village ME

STARK, FRANCIS RAYMOND, lawyer; b. N.Y. City, Aug. 15, 1877; s. William F. and Georgette A. (Flash) S.; A.B., Coll. of St. Francis Xavier, N.Y. City, 1893, A.M., 1894; LL.B., Columbia, 1896, Ph.D., 1897; univ. fellow in internat. law, same, 1897; m. Louise Tauber, 1924 (died 1931). With law dept. Western Union Telegraph Co. since 1899, asst. gen. atty., 1916-19, gen. attorney, 1919-26, general solicitor, 1926-41, v.p. and gen. solicitor 1941-46, v.p. and gen. counsel 1946, hon. gen. counsel 1947; director Am. District Telegraph Co. (N.J.); prof. law, Fordham U., 1908; attache U.S. and Spanish Peace Commn., Paris, France, 1898. Mem. Assn. Bar City of New York. Catholic. Clubs: Lawyers, Whist, New York Athletic. Author: The Abolition of Privateering and the Declaration of Paris (Columbia U.), 1897; also 200 page article on Telegraphs and Telephones" in Ency. of Law and Procedure, 1911. Home: 514 West End Av. Office: 60 Hudson St., New York, NY‡

STARK, HAROLD RAYNSFORD, naval officer; b. Wilkes-Barre, Pa., Nov. 12, 1880; s. Benjamin Franklin and Mary Frances (Warner) S.; grad. U.S. Naval Acad., 1903; m. Katharine Adele Rhoads, July 24, 1907; children—Mary (Mrs. Edwin Walker Semans). Katharine Rhoads (Mrs. Harold Perot Gillespie). Commd. ensign, U.S. Navy, Feb. 2, 1905; promoted through grades to admiral, August 1, 1939. Served on various ships and stations, 1903-17; aide on staff of Adm. Sims, comdg. U.S. Naval Forces operating in European waters, 1917-19; inspector in charge of ordnance, Naval Proving Ground, Dahlgren, Va., and Naval Powder Factory, Indian Head, Md., 1925-28; aide on staff and chief of staff, Destroyer Squadrons, Battle Fleet, 1928-30; aide to Sec. of Navy, Washington, D.C., 1930-33; comdg. U.S.S. West Virginia, 1933-34; chief of Bur. of Ordnance, Navy Dept., Washington, D.C., 1934-37; comdg. cruiser div. U.S. Fleet, 1937-38; comdg. cruisers, Battle Force, 1938-39; chief of naval operations, rank of admiral, August 1, 1939; comdg. U.S. Naval Forces in Europe, March 1942-August 1945; retired from active duty April 1, 1946. Decorated Mexican Campaign, and Dominican Campaign medals, World War Medal (U.S.); Expeditionary medal, D.S.M. (United States Navy) with three citations; Order of Crown of Italy; National Order of Southern Cross (degree of Grande Official) (Brazil); Distinguished Service Medal (U.S. Army); Hon. Knight of the Grand Cross, Military Division, Order of the British Empire; Comdr., Legion of Honor, Croix de Guerre with Palm (French); Grand Gross, Order of St. Olav (Norwegian). Episcopalian. Clubs: Army and Navy, Army and Navy Country, U. (Washington); Chevy Chase, Manor Country (Md.); Army and Navy (San Franciso); N.Y. Yacht, Westmoreland (Wilkes-Barre, Pa.). Home: Washington DC Died Aug. 20, 1972; buried Arlington Nat. Cemetery, Arlington VA

STARK, LLOYD CROW, ex-gov. of Mo.; b. Louisiana, Mo., Nov. 23, 1886; s. Clarence McDowell and Lilly (Crow) S.; B.S., U. S. Naval Acad., 1908; LL.D., Westminster Coll., U. of Mo., 1937, Central Coll., Fayette, Mo., 1939, Beloit (Wis.) Coll., 1941, Washington U., St. Louis, 1941; m. Margaret Pearson Stickney, Nov. 11, 1908 (died Oct. 12, 1930); children—Lloyd Stickney (Lt. Comdr., Killed on duty, 1946), John Wingate (major in Air Corps Reserve); m. 2d, Katherine Lemoine Perkins, Nov. 23, 1931; children—Mary (Mrs. Richard Strassner), Katherine (Mrs. Richard Clark Bull). Naval officer, 1904-12, serving in Turkey, 1909; South Am. waters, 1910; Submarines 1911; v.p., gen. mgr. Stark Brothers Nurseries, 1912-17, 1919-35, chmn. bd., 1935-37, 41-71, emeritus chmn. bd., 1971-72, also chief executive officer, nat. sales div. Discovered Stark Golden Delicious apple, 1913. Gov., State of Missouri, 1937-41. Chairman Governor's Conf. of United States, 1939; pres. Council of State Govts., 1939; member bd. of mgrs., 1941-47. Served as maj., batt. comdr. and (acting) asst. divisional chief of staff, 80th Div. and commanded 315th F.A., A.E.F., in Argonne, 1917-19. Decorated Victory medal and two battle clasps. Recipient Hall of Fame award, Am. Assn. Nurseymen, 1967; Patriots award S.R., 1969. Vice pres. and dir. Mo. State Chamber of Commerce, 1935-39; mem. exec. bd. Mo. Council Boy Scouts of Am., 1941, mem. at large Nat. Council; mem. nat. adv. council Arboretum, Washington, 1946-70; hon. life mem. Am. Assn. Nurserymen (pres. 1917, 1920), Fed. Garden Clubs of Mo., Mo. Soc. (Wash., D.C.); mem. Naval Inst., Mo. Hist. Soc. (past dir.), State Hist. Soc. of Mo., Garden Clubs of America, S.R., Am. Saddle Horse Breeders Assn. (past dir.), Naval Acad. Grads. Assn., Navy Athletic Assn., Navy League of the U.S. (v.p. and dir. 1941-46), Pan Am. Soc. (St. Louis com., 1941), Mo. Acad. Squires. Democrat. Episcopalian. Clubs: St. Louis Country, University (St. Louis); Army and Navy (Washington); Rotary. Home: Eolia MO Died Sept. 17, 1972; buried Riverview Cemetery, Louisiana MO

STARK, ORTON K(IRKWOOD), bacteriologist, educator; b. Cromwell, Ind., Sept. 21, 1898; s. Samuel Byron and Mary Elizabeth (Hart) S.; A.B., DePauw U., 1922; Ph.D., U. Ill., 1926; m. Mary Virginia Milligan, Sept. 10, 1926; children—Virginia Ruth (Mrs. Richard E. Sherrell), Edward William. Asso. prof. biology La. State Normal, Natchitoches, 1926-27; asst. prof. botany U. Wyo., 1927-29; asst. prof., then asso. prof. botany Miami U., 1929-44, prof., from 1944, chmn. dept., 1956-62. Served as pvt. U.S. Army, World War I. Mem. Soc. Am. Bacteriologists (pres. Ohio br. 1948), A.A.A.S., Am. Acad. Microbiology, N.Y. Acad. Scis., Am. Pub. Health Assn., Royal Soc. Health (Eng.), Sigma Xi, Phi Sigma. Contbr. research articles profl. jours. Home: Oxford OH Died Sept. 5, 1968; buried Oxford OH

STARKLOFF, MAX C(ARL), physician; b. Quincy, Ill., Dec. 30, 1859; s. Hugo Maximillian and Hermina von S.; prep. edn., Pa. Mil. Acad., Chester; studied medicine under Dr. John T. Hodgen, St. Louis Med. Coll.; m. Mary E. Flynn, 1879 (dec.); m. 2d, Genevieve Baldwin, 1903. In gen. practice, St. Louis, since 1882; surgeon Vulcan Steel Works, St. Louis, 1883-90; local surgeon Mo. Pacific R.R. since 1886; pres. U.S. Bd. of Pension Examining Surgeons, St. Louis, 1892-95; health commr., St. Louis, 1895-1903, and 1911-33. Mem. Vol. Med. Service Corps, Council of Nat. Defense, 1918. Mem. Internat. Assn. Med. Health Officers (pres. 1932 and 1933), A.M.A., St. Louis Med. Soc.; fellow Am. Pub. Health Assn. Home: 512 Dover Pl., St Louis MO*‡

STARKWEATHER, JOHN K., investment banker; b. Denver, Colo., June 16, 1891; s. James C. and Alice L. (Kent) S.; B.A., Brown U., 1913; m. Blanche L. Mason, Sept. 1, 1921; children—James O., Janet Kent (Mrs. Richard W. Besse). With Wm. E. Sweet & Co., Denver, 1913-15; with Harris, Forbes & Co., 1915-31, v.p., 1930-31; v.p. Chase, Harris, Forbes Corp., 1931-33; pres. Starkweather & Co., Inc., 1933-37, partner, from 1937; mem. N.Y. Stock Exchange, 1937-58, gov., 1940-44. Mayor, Scarsdale, 1943-45. Clubs: American Yacht, University, Scarsdale Golf, City Midday. Address: Scarsdale NY Died Mar. 29, 1972; buried Churchyard, Church of St. James the Less, Scarsdale NY

STARKWEATHER, WILLIAM EDWARD BLOOMFIELD, artist; b. Edinburgh, Scotland, May 16, 1879; s. John Henry and Hannah Elizabeth (Winchester) S.; brought to U.S., 1883; ed. Hillhouse High Sch., New Haven, Conn.; art edn., Art Students League (New York), Colarossi Acad., Paris; pupil of Sorolla, Madrid, Spain; independent study in Italy 3 yrs.; unmarried. Art teacher; formerly lecturer on art, Cooper Union and Traphagen School, N.Y. City, Pratt Institute, Brooklyn; prof. in art dept., Hunter Coll. of the City of New York, 1936-46. Represented in Metropolitan Museum, Brooklyn Museum, San Diego (Calif.) Museum, U. of Pa., Randolph-Macon Coll., Instituto le Valencia de Don Juan, Madrid, Spain. Popular vote for oils, New Haven, 1924; Mrs. William K. Vanderbilt prize, joint water color exhbn., N.Y. City, 1925; Dana gold medal for water color, Pa. Acad. Fine Arts, 1925; Jones prize, water color, Baltimore, 1926; Phila. prize, water color, Pa. Acad. Fine Arts, 1929. Mem. Am. Water Color Soc., Allied Artists America, Hispanic Soc. America (corr. mem.), New York Water Color Club. Republican. Episcopalian. Club: Salmagundi. Author: Drawings and Paintings by Francisco Goya in the Collection of the Hispanic Society of America. Home: Brooklyn NY Died May 14, 1969; buried Winchester CT

STARR, CORNELIUS V., ins. exec.; b. Ft. Bragg, Cal., Oct. 15, 1892; s. Cornelius Vander and Frances Arabella (Hart) S.; student U. Cal., 1910-11; m. Mary Helen Malcolm, Jan. 6, 1937. Admitted to Cal. State and U.S. Fed. bars, 1915. Organized Am. Asiatic Underwriters, Shanghai, China, 1919; formed Asia Life Ins. Co., Wilmington, Del. (now Am. Life Ins. Co.), 1921, dir., from 1921; organized Am. Internat. Underwriters Corp., N.Y., 1926, conducting home-fgn. ins. operations of group of Am. fire, marine and casualty ins. cos., and asso. co. Am. Internat. Underwriters Overseas, Inc., Bermuda, which supervises their worldwide operations abroad; chmn. C. V. Starr & Co., Inc. (N.Y.C.), 1951-68, sr. dir., 1968; chmn. bd. Am. Internat. Assurance Co. Ltd. (Hongkong), 1949-56, sr. dir., 1968; dir. Am. Internat. Marine Agency, Am. Life Ins. Co. (Wilmington, Del.), Ins. Co. State of Pennsylvania (Phila.), Philippine Am. Life Ins. Co. (Manila), American Home Assurance Co. (N.Y.), also United Service to China (N.Y.). Served with 24th Machine Gun Bn., World War I, 1917-18. Clubs: India House, Racquet and Tennis, River. Home: New York City NY Died Dec. 20, 1968.

STARR, HENRY FRANK, life ins. exec., physician; b. Greensboro, N.C., Feb. 1, 1894; s. Henry Francis and Annie Caroline (Young) S.; student U. N.C., 1911-14; M.D., Jefferson Med. Coll., 1916; m. Virginia Morton Goode, May 5, 1920; children—Elizabeth Frances (Mrs. James M. Jackson) (dec.); Henry Frank. Intern N.Y.C. Hosp., 1916; med. dir. Pilot Life Ins. Co., Greensboro, 1917-45, mem. bd. dirs., 1926-45, v.p., 1933-45; med. dir. Jefferson Standard Life Ins. Co., Greensboro, 1945-69, dir., 1947-51, v.p., 1951-69. Served as capt., 78th Div., U.S. Army, World War I. Mem. Assn. Life Ins. Med. Dirs. Am., Am. Life Conv., A.M.A., N.C. Med. Soc, Tri-State, So. med. assns. Presbyn. Kiwanian. Author articles on life ins. medicine. Home: Greensboro NC Died Sept. 24, 1969; buried Forest Lawn Cemetery Greensboro NC

STARR, LEE ANNA, minister, author; b. Point Pleasant, W.Va.; d. David Lee and Sarah Jane (Harper) S.; ed. high sch., Athens, O.; Sch. of Sacred Lit., Chautauqua, N.Y.; Yale U. and Kansas City U.; grad. Pittsburgh Theol. Sem., 1893; D.D., Kansas City U., 1911; LL.D., Adrian (Mich.) Coll., 1924. Began at 19 as lecturer for Pa. W.C.T.U.; later lecturer for Pa. Constl. Assn. and for Nat. Alliance, New York, and Nat. W.C.T.U. Bur. Ordained ministry M.P. Ch., 1895;

pastor successively Canton, Paris and Chicago, Ill., to 1922; pastor Adrian Coll. Ch., 1907-09. Rep. to Gen. Conf. M.P. Ch., Atlantic City, 1900, Baltimore, 1928. Has traveled in 22 countries. Author: The Ministry of Woman, 1900; The Bible Status of Woman, 1926. Home: 691 Lincoln Av., Bellevue PA‡

STARR, RAYMOND WESLEY, judge; b. Harbor Springs, Mich., Aug. 24, 1888; s. John Travis and Jeanette Amanda (Blackman) S.; grad. Ferris Inst., 1907; LL.B., University of Michigan, 1910; hon. J.D., Detroit Coll. of Law, 1938; honorary LL.D., Ferris Inst., 1945; m. Minnie Esseline Johnson, 1912; children—John Gerritt, Barbara. Admitted to Michigan bar, 1910, practiced Grand Rapids; mem. firm Starr & Starr; atty. gen. of Mich., 1937-38; apptd. justice of the Supreme Court of Mich., June, 1941; elected justice Supreme Court, 1942, reelected, 1945; appointed fed. judge, Western Dist. Mich. 1946, ret., 1961, sr. dist. judge. Chmn. bd. control Ferris Inst. Mem. Am., Mich., Grand Rapids bar assns. Democrat. Mason. Clubs: Peninsular, Torch. Home: East Grand Rapids MI Died Nov. 2, 1968.

STASON, E(DWIN) BLYTHE, lawyer, educator; b. Siouy City, Ia., Sept. 6, 1891; s. Edwin J. and Anna (Blythe) S.; A.B., U. of Wis., 1913, B.S., Mass. Inst. of Tech., 1916, J.D., U. of Mich., 1922, LL.D., 1970; m. Adeline Boaz, Sept. 14, 1921; children—Edwin Blythe, William Boaz. Instr. elec. engring., U. of Pa., 1916-17; asst. prof. elec. engring. U. of Mich., 1919-22; practiced law Sioux City, Ia., as mem. firm Stason & Stason, 1922-24; prof. of law, U. of Mich., from 1924, provost of the Univ. 1938-44, dean of the Law Sch., 1939-60; adminstr. American Bar Found., Chgo., 1960-64; prof. law Vanderbilt U., Nashville, 1964-67, Frank C. Rand professor of law, 1967-70. Michigan commissioner in Nat. Conf. of Commrs. on Uniform State Laws; member Michigan Constitution Revision Study Com., 1941; Mich. tax study commn., 1945; chmn. Michigan anti-subversive study com., 1950. Mem. United States Attorney Genls. Com. on Administrative Procedure 1939-41; cons. Pres.' Conf. on Adminstrv. Procedure, 1953-54, Hoover Commn. Task Force on Legal Services and Practices of Exec. Br. U.S. Govt., 1953-54; mng. dir. Fund for Peaceful Atomic Development, from 1955; trustee Power Reactor Development Co., from 1955; dir. Inst. for Tng. in Citizenship, N.Y. U., 1956-59; chmn. Mich. Commn. on Tax Administration, 1957-58; mem. of Council on Foreign Relations, from 1958. Served as capt. C.E., AUS, 1917-19. Recipient of award for outstanding research in law and government American Bar Found., 1965. Fellow Am. Bar Found.; mem. Am. Law Inst., Am. Judicature Soc. (dir. 1940-52), Univ. of Michigan Musical Society (dir. from 1938), Inter-Am. (council 1950), Am., Mich. (sec., editor Jour. 1929-35; com.-at-large 1946-61) bar assns., S.A.R., American Enterprise Inst. (adv. bd.), Order of the Coif, Gamma Eta Gamma. Republican. Presbyn. Clubs: University (Ann Arbor, Mich.); Detroit (Detroit); University (Nashville). Author: Cases and Materials on Municipal Corporations, 1935, rev. edit. 1959; Cases and Materials on Administrative Tribunals, 1937, revised 1956: (with S. D. Estep and W. J. Pierce) Atoms and the Ann Arbor MI Died Apr. 10, 1972; buried Ann Arbor MI

STATHAS, PERICLES PETER, elec. engr.; financial and mgmt. cons.; b. Tropaia, Greece, Apr. 7, 1898; s. Peter and Crissa (Constan) S.; student Milw. Sch. Engring., 1917-20; B.S., Marquette U., 1923, E.E., 1929; m. Mary Pegis, June 26, 1927; children—Diane, Thalia, Charles. Came to U.S., 1912, naturalized, 1920. Field engr, system engr. Wis. Electric Power Co., 1923-29, sr. engr. management staff, 1929-35; joined Duff & Phelps, pub. utility analysts and cons., 1936, partner, 1938, sr. partner, 1946-57; pres., dir. Duff & Phelps, Inc., 1958-60, chmn., chief exec. officer, dir., 1961-73; chmn., chief exec. Pa. & So. Gas Co.; chmn. bd. Southwest Gas Corp., Duff, Anderson & Clark, Inc., 1966-73; v.p. dir. Southeastern Mich. Gas Co.; dir., exec. com. Central La. Electric Co., Inc.; dir. Middle South Utilities, Inc., Selected Am. Shares, Inc., Piedmont Natural Gas Co., Inc., Pub. Service Co. N.M., Pubco Petroleum Corp.; also financial analyst. Trustee Northwestern Mil. and Naval Acad. Recipient McGraw Engring. award and Henry L. Doherty medal Edison Electric Inst., 1932; Distinguished Engring. Alumnus, Marquette U., 1967. Registered profl. engr., Wis., Ill. Mem. Am. Finance Assn., I.E.E.E., Am. Water Works Assn., So. Gas Assn., Pub. Utility Securities Club Chgo., Investment Analysts Soc., Western Soc. Engrs., Newcomen Soc., Eta Kappa Nu, Tau Beta Pi. Mason. Clubs: Union League, Attic, Executives, Exmoor, Chicago (Chgo.); Wall Street (N.Y.C.); Family (San Francisco); Harbor View, Author, lectr. pub. utilities papers. Expert witness pub. utility regulatory matters. Home: Lake Forest IL Died Feb. 22, 1973.

STATLER, ALICE SEIDLER (MRS. ELLSWORTH MILTON STATLER), hotel exec.; b. Hoboken, N.J., Aug. 25, 1882; d. Henry and Ellen Seidler; m. Ellsworth M. Statler, 1927; 1 stepson, Ellsworth M. Successively sec., chief asst. mgmt. Statler Hotel chain, from 1918; chmn. bd. Hotels Statler Co., 1928-45, hon. chmn., 1945-48. Trustee, later hon. life trustee Community Services Soc. N.Y.; chmn. Statler Found., 1934-69. Recipient plaque Hotel Sales Mgmt. Assn., 1960; Named Hotel man of Year, Sch. Hotel, Restaurant and Instl. Mgmt., Mich. State U., 1961. Found. Address: New York City NY Died Oct. 1969.*

STATTER, ARTHUR FREDERICK, government official; b. Carlisle, Eng., Sept. 9, 1870; s. George Frederick and Isabella (Joynson) S.; came to America, 1883; acad. edn.; m. Marie L. McCall, of Sioux City, Ia., June, 1898. Successively reporter and city editor Sioux City Journal, editor and mgr. Walla Walla (Wash.) Daily Union; sec. to Senator Levi Ankeny, of Wash.; sec. to Sec. of the Treasury L. M. Shaw; asst. sec. of the treasury, Jan. 22-June, 1907; personal representative of Sec. of the Treasury for Pacific Coast states since June, 1909; Republican. Episcopalian. Club: Army and Navy. Home: Walla Walla WA Address: Custom House, Portland OR‡

STAUBER, LESLIE ALFRED, educator; b. Newark, June 6, 1907; s. Ernest Gideon and Laura (Newton) S.; B.S., Rutgers U., 1929, M.S., 1930; Ph.D. (Logan fellow 1932-34), U. Chgo., 1937; m. Mabel Genevieve Fisher, July 27, 1930; children—Amy Ann Law, William T., T. Nelson. Asst. biologist, oyster investigations N.J. Agrl. Expt. Sta., 1935-43; asso. pharmacol. Squibb Inst. Med. Research, 1943-44; Squibb Inst. fellow 1945-46; asst. prof. zoology Rutgers U., 1944-47, assoc. prof., 1947-53, prof., 1953-72, chmn., dept., 1950-64, 65-68. Chmn. parasitology and tropical medicine study sect., div. research grants NIH, 1957-60, mem. microbiology tng. grant com., 1961-65, mem. allergy and infectious diseases tng. grant com., 1969-73; mem. commns. of parasitic diseases and malaria Armed Forces Epidemiological Bd. Active Boy Scouts Am. Fellow A.A.A.S., Am. Soc. Tropical Medicine and Hygiene (council 1962-65); mem. Am. Soc. Parasitologists (council 1955, 58, pres., 1962), Am. Soc. Protozoologists, N.Y. Soc. Tropical Medicine (pres. 1956), Theobold Smith Soc. (pres. 1954). Author articles on marine biology, parasitology. Home: Piscataway NJ Died Mar. 27, 1973.

STAUBLE, WILBUR CARL, mfr. computing instruments; b. New Haven, June 22, 1899; s. Arnold J. and Sophie (Shenkel) S.; m. Alice E. Thelin, July 1, 1922 (dec.); m. 2d, Mildred I. White, 1969. Vice pres. Holo-Krome Screw Corp., Hartford, 1929-45, exec. v.p., 1945-52, pres., 1952-72, also dir.; pres. dir. Veeder-Root, Inc., Hartford, 1958-66; chmn. Veeder Industries, 1966-70, chief exec., 1966-69; dir. Hartford Nat. Bank & Trust Co. Home: Bloomfield CT Died Sept. 27, 1972.

STAUFFER, CHARLES ALBERT, publisher; b. Sedgwick, Kan., Mar. 23, 1880; s. John Wesley and Mary Jane Richardson) S.; grad. Ariz. State Normal Sch. (now Ariz. State Tchrs. Coll.), Tempe, 1901; m. Edith Louise Bennett, Apr. 10, 1909; children—Dorothy, Eleanor, Sylvia, Charles Bennett. With Ariz. Republic (formerly Ariz. Republican), Phoenix, 1899-1946, circulation mgr., 1901-15, asst. bus. mgr., 1905-09, bus. mgr., 1912-20, dir., sec., 1915-29, gen. mgr., 1920-29, pres., gen. mgr., 1929-38, pub., 1929-46; chmn. bd., v.p. Ariz. Pub. Co., owners and operators Ariz. Republic, Phoenix Gazette, Republic and Gazette Engraving Co. Chmn. Ariz. circuit A.P. Vice pres. Heard Mus. Former mem. Phoenix City Council. Bd. dirs. Roosevelt council Boy Scouts Am. Mem. Phoenix C. of C. (dir.), Ariz. Hist. Soc. (v.p.), Ariz. Newspaper Assn. (past pres.), Ariz. State Tchrs. Coll. Alumni Assn. Clubs: Phoenix Country (dir., past pres.); Arizona. Home: Phoenix AZ Died Dec. 1970.

STAUFFER, HERBERT MILTON, physician; educator; b. Phila., Apr. 26, 1914; s. Milton F. and Anna (Hood) S.; M.D., Temple U., 1939, M.Sc., 1945; m. Joan Dunbar; 1 son, Scott. Intern, Temple U. Hosp., Phila., 1939-41, fellow in radiology, 1941-43; roentgenologist Univ. Hosp., Mpls., 1946-49; asst. prof. radiology U. Minn., Mpls., 1946-49; asso. prof. radiology Temple U., 1949-52, prof., 1952-70, head dept. radiology, 1957-70. Mem. radiation study sect. NIH, 1959-62, mem. internat. fellowship rev. panel, 1964-67, mem. diagnostic radiology tng. com., 1967-68; program USPHS. Bd. govs., mem. profl. edn. com. Heart Assn. Southeastern Pa., 1968-70. Served to lt., M.C., USNR, 1943-46. Diplomate Am. Bd. Radiology. Fellow Am. Coll. Radiology; mem. Assn. Univ. Radiologists (pres. 1963-64), Radiol. Soc. N.Am. (program com. 1964-66, dir. 1967-69, chmn. bd. dirs. 1970, pres.-elect. 1970), Am. (chmn. exec. council 1966, 2d v.p. 1969), Phila. (pres. 1969) roentgen ray socs., Phila. Tb and Respiratory Disease Assn. (dir. case detection com. Tb control adv. com. 1968-70). Contbr. numerous articles to med. jours., also chpts. to books. Home: Philadelphia PA Died Dec. 18, 1970.

STEALEY, SYDNOR LORENZO, seminary pres.; b. Martinsburg, W.Va., Mar. 7, 1897; s. Clarence Perry and Anna (Jamieson) S.; A.B., Okla. Baptist U., 1920, D.D., 1943; Th.M., So. Bapt. Theol. Sem., 1927, Ph.D., 1932; D.D., Wake Forest Coll., 1953; D.D., Furman U., 1954; LL.D., William Jewell Coll., 1959; m. Jessie Wheeler, Oct. 16, 1920; children—Jessie Louise (Mrs. Frank K. Vance), Sydnor Lorenzo. Tchr. high sch., 1920-22, coll., 1922-24; ordained to ministry Bapt. Ch., 1922; pastor in Mo., Ky., Ind., Va., N.C., 1925-42; tchr. ch. history So. Bapt. Sem., 1942-51; pres. Southeastern Bapt. Sem., Wake Forest, N.C., 1951-63, pres. emeritus, 1963-69; tchr. Bapt. Sem., Zurich, Switzerland, 1950, 55. Mem. exec. com. So. Bapt. Conv., 1938-44. Served to 2d lt. U.S. Army, World War I. Mem. Am. Soc. Ch. History. Lion. Club: Watauga (Raleigh). Editor: A Baptist Treasury, 1958. Home: NC Died July 24, 1969; buried Wake Forest NC

STEARLEY RALPH F., ret. air force officer; b. Brazil, Indiana, July 25, 1898; son William F. and Ella Lena (Kaelber) S.; B.S., U.S. Mil. Acad., 1918; student Yale U., 1920-21; m. Mildred S. Volandt, Sept. 19, 1931. Commd. 2d lt., U.S. army, 1918, and advanced through the grades to major general (temp.), Sept. 1949; Mil. Cav. School, 1920, Air Service Primary Flying Sch., 1925; Air Service Advanced Flying Sch., 1926; Air Corps Tactical Sch., 1935, Command and Gen. Staff Sch., 1936; Chemical Warfare Sch., 1938; asst. exec. officer, Office of Chief of Air Corps, Wash., D.C., 1940; mil. intelligence officer Flying Training Command, 1942; dir. of Air Support, Hdqrs. Army Air Forces, 1942; A-3 with 9th Air Force, E.T.O., May-Aug. 1944; G-3, 1st Allied Airborne Army, E.T.O., Aug. 1944-Mar. 1945; comdg. gen. 9th Tactical Air Command, E.T.O., Mar.-Sept. 1945; comdr. Air Sect., 15th Army Theater Gen. Bd., E.T.O., Sept. 1945-Jan. 1946; dep. chief War Dept. Spl. Staff Legislative and Liaison Div. 1946-48, chief, Air Force, 1948; comdg. general 14th Air Force, 1948-50; commanding gen. 20th Air Force, 1950-53, ret. as maj. gen. USAF, 1953; mil. advisor Twigg Industries, Martinsville, Ind. Chmn. Indiana Aeros. Commission. Rated command pilot and command observer. Decorations: D.S.M., second D.S.M. (with cluster), 1953, Legion of Merit, Air Medal, Bronze Star, L'Ordre de la Legion d' Honneur, degree de Chevalier, Croix de Guerre avec Palm (France); L'Ordre de Leopold II, Grede de Commandeur avec Palme, Croix de Guerre avec Palme (Belgium); Comdr. of Order of Orange-Nassau (Netherlands); Commander of Order British Empire. Mem. V.F.W., Am. Legion, C. of C. (pres.). Methodist. Mason, Elk. Clubs: Rotary; Terre Haute (Ind.) Country; Army and Navy (Washington). Home: Brazil IN Died Feb. 3, 1973.

STEARNS, CARL LEO, astronomer; b. Westbrook, Me., Sept. 14, 1892; s. Albert Joseph and Cora May (Weymouth) S.; A.B., Wesleyan U., Middletown, Conn., 1917; Ph.D., Yale, 1923; m. Mildred Parkhurst Booth, Aug. 9, 1923 (dec. 1966); children—Robert Leo, Elva Parkhurst (Mrs. Creeger), Doris Elizabeth (Mrs. Swain); m. 2d, Eddie McCormick. Asst. Dudley Observatory, Albany, N.Y., 1917-18; instr. in mathematics, Wesleyan U., 1918-19, instr. in astronomy, 1919-20; research asst., Yale Observatory, 1920-25; research asso. in astronomy, Van Vleck Obs., Wesleyan U., 1925-42, later dir. obs. asso. prof. astronomy 1942-44, prof. from 1944, instr. in nav. Naval Flight Prep. Sch., Wesleyan U., 1943; visiting instructor Trinity College, Hartford, Conn., 1940-41. Awarded Donohoe Comet medal by Astron. Soc. of the Pacific, 1927; Stearns comet named in his honor. Fellow Royal Astron. Soc., A.A.A.S.; mem. Am. Astron. Soc., Internat. Astron. Union, Middletown Sci. Assn. (past pres.), Phi Beta Kappa, Sigma Xi. Author: Stellar Parallaxes from Photographs Made with the 20-inch Refractor of the Van Vleck Observatory (with F. Slocum and B. W. Sitterly), 1938. Contbr. articles on stellar distances, solar eclipses, solar parallax, etc. to Astron. Jour. Home: Middletown CT Died Nov. 28, 1972; buried Indian Hill Cemetery.

STEARNS, LUTIE EUGENIA, lecturer; b. Stoughton, Mass.; d. Isaac Holden and Catharine (Guild) S.; grad. Milwaukee State Normal Sch., 1887. Taught pub. schs. 2 yrs.; in charge circulating dept. Milwaukee Pub. Library, 1890-97; connected with Wis. Free Library Commn., 1897-1914. Lecturer. Columnist Milwaukee Journal, 1932-—. Mem. Bd. of Regents Wis. Normal Schools, 1922-27. Mem. Woman's Internat. Soc. for Peace and Freedom. Club: Milwaukee Business and Professional Women's. Home: 2543 N. Prospect Av., Milwaukee WI‡

STEBBINS, G(EORGE) WARING, organist, vocal teacher; b. Albion, N.Y., June 16, 1869. s. George Coles (q.v.) and Elma (Miller) S.; ed. Brooklyn Poly. and Collegiate Inst.; studied piano under Robert Thallon; organ under Henry Eyre Browne, Brooklyn, and Guilmant, Paris; voice under Sbriglia, Paris, and Henschel, London; m. Caroline Tichenor Worth, of Brooklyn, June 1, 1898. Organist Westminster Presbyn. Ch., Brooklyn, 1892-3, Plymouth Ch., 1899-1902, Emmanuel Bapt. Ch., 1893-9, and 1902—; conductor The Singers Club, New York. Charter mem. Am. Guild Organists. Composer: When Love Is Gone; Thy Presence; also many songs, anthems and organ pieces. Address: 1171 Dean St., Brooklyn NY‡

STECHER, ROBERT MORGAN, physician; b. Cleve., Dec. 1, 1896; s. Frederick William and Lue (Morgan) S.; B.S., Dartmouth, 1919; M.D., Harvard, 1923; L.H.D., Fenn Coll., 1962; m. Florence McCarthy, Apr. 7, 1926; children—Mary (Mrs. Harold K. Douthit,

Jr.), Robert M., Sally J. (Mrs. Richard R. Hollington, Jr.). Intern Peter Bent Brigham Hosp., Boston, 1924-25; asso. clin. prof. internal medicine, Western Res. Med. Sch., Cleve., 1954-60, clin. prof. internal medicine, 1960-72; chief arthritis clinic Cleve. Met. Gen. Hosp., 1935-67. Pres. Ligue Internationale contre is Rhumatisme, 1953-57. Chmn. bd. Cleve. Health Museum; trustee Cleve. Mus. Natural History, C. F. Kettering Found., Sloan Kettering Inst. Cancer Research, Cuyahoga County Hosp. Found Cleve. Zool. Soc.; dir. Arthritis Found. Recipient Heberden award, London, 1954. Fellow A.C.P.; mem. Am. Rhêumatism Assn. (pres. 1947-48), Cleve. Acad. Medicine, A.M.A., Ohio Med. Assn., Central Soc. Clin. Research, Am. Genetic Soc., Am. Soc. Human Genetics, A.A.A.S., Cleve. Med. Library Assn. (pres. 1952-55), N.Y. Acad. Medicine, N.Y. Acad. Scis., Zool. Soc. London, Newcomen Soc., Sigma Xi, Beta Theta Pi, Nu Sigma Nu; hon. mem. numerous fgn. assns. for control of rheumatism. Republican. Episcopalian. Clubs: University (Cleve. and N.Y.C.); Grolier, Union, Clifton and Westwood Country. The Fifty, Rowfant, Contbr. articles to med. jours. Home: Lakewood OH Died Mar. 13, 1972; buried Riverside Cemetery, Cleveland OH

STECK, CHARLES CALVIN, mfg. exec.; b. Wheaton, Ill., Mar. 24, 1884; s. Calvin and Louisa Maria (Finch) S.; B.S., Wheaton Coll., 1906; M.S., U. Chgo., 1911; m. Jennie Ward Kinsman, Sept. 8, 1909; children—Helen Shirley (Mrs. Paul R. Swanson), Kenneth Kinsman, Richard Lamont; m. 2d, Etelka Holt Vincent. Instr. mathematics dept. U. N.H., 1911-19, head dept., 1917-19; with Spaulding Fibre Co., N. Rochester, N.H. from 1919, pres., gen. manager and dir., 1942-60, director and consultant, from 1960. Executive of Food Administration of N.H., 1917-18. Clubs: Park Country (Buffalo); Orchard Park (N.Y.) Country. Home: Orchard Park NY Deceased.

STEDDOM, RICE PRICE, sanitarian; b. Lebanon, O., Dec. 23, 1864; s. Isaac Kelley and Narcissa (Price) S.; ed. dist. schs.; V.S., Ont. Vet. Coll., 1886. Was in the employ of Springer & Willard, horse importers, Okaloosa, Ia., 1886-89; on ranch in Colo. 2 yrs., then in gen. practice, in employ of Springer & Willard, at Galesburg, Ill., 1891-97; with Bur. of Animal Industry, U.S. Dept. of Agr., since 1897; federal meat inspn. duty, at Kansas City, Mo., 1897-98; quarantine work in Tex. and Calif., 1898-99 spl. investigation of live stock diseases in Porto Rico 1899; organizer, and in charge of quarantine and transportation of southern cattle, east of Miss. River 1900-02; on duty in connection with eradication of foot and mouth disease in New Eng., 1902-03, and in charge at Boston, 1903-04; transferred to Washington, D.C., May 1904; apptd. asst. chief of Inspn. Div., Bur. of Animal Industry, 1905; chief of div., 1906; chief of Federal Meat Inspection Service, 1912-35, retired, Jan. 1, 1935. Mem. Friends Ch. Home: Summit Farm, R.D. 3, Lebanon OH‡

STEDMAN, LOUISE ADELLA, educator; b. Savanna, Ill., Oct. 17, 1907; d. Ira Marvin and Beulah Benton (Shepard) Stedman; A.B. with honors, U. Ia., 1930, A.M., 1937; student U. Wash., summer 1940; Ph.D., Purdue U., 1947. Tchr., Dawson (Ia.) Consol. High Sch., 1927-29; home econs. tchr. West Jr. High Sch., Des Moines, 1930-34, Roosevelt High Sch., 1934-37; instr. home econs. U. Ida., 1937-42; grad. asst. Purdue U., 1942-43, asst. dir. women's residence halls, 1943-44; asst. state supr. and itinerant tchr. trainer in home econs., Maine, 1944-47; asso. prof. home economics U. Me., 1947-48, prof., head dept. home econs., 1948-51; dir. Sch. Home Econs., U. Minn., 1951-70, prof. home econs. edn., 1970-72; cons. USDSEA Workshop, Karlsrhue, Germany, summer 1970. Mem. Am. Home Econ. Assn. (del. from Ida., 1941, Me., 1946-48, Minn., 1959, 60, 64, 65, v.p. 1967-69), Nat., Minn. councils family relations, N.E.A., Am. Vocational Assn., Internat. Fedn. Home Econs. (permanent council), A.A.A.S., Am. Assn. U. Women, Minn. Home Econs. Assn. (pres. 1959-60), Home Econs. Adminstrs. (chmn. North central region 1957-60), Phi Beta Kappa, Sigma Xi, Phi Kappa Phi, Omicron Nu (nat. sec. 1954-56), Pi Lambda Theta, Kappa Alpha Theta, Phi Upsilon Omicron (hon.), Gamma Sigma Delta. Club: Zonta. Author: (with H.H. Remmers) Bringing up Children; also articles in profl. jours., chpt. of book. Home: St Paul MN

STEEL, ROWE SUMMERVILLE, financial exec.; b. Bement, Ill., Aug. 20, 1899; s. William Anderson and Mary Jane (Coleberd) S.; m. Marion Louise Smith, Dec. 25, 1922; 1 son, Rowe Summerville. Comptroller, Greater New York Fund, Inc., 1938-43; budget comptroller Nat. War Fund, Inc., 1943-48; comptroller U.S.O., Inc., 1948-50, United Defense Fund, Inc., 1950-56; asst. comptroller Rockefeller Found., 1956, comptroller, 1957-65; comptroller Gen. Edn. Bd., N.Y.C. Mason. Home: Bronxville NY Died Jan. 12, 1970; buried Bement IL

STEEL, WESTBROOK, educator; b. Tuxedo Park, N.Y., Feb. 1, 1889; s. Henry T. and Louise (Bennett) S.; LL.D., Centenary Coll., La., 1938; LL.D., Lawrence College, 1956; m. Luverne Weismiller, June 15, 1931 (dec. Sept. 1958); m. 2d, Dorothea Hinman, 1959. Supr. Nat. System Co., 1910-17, 1919-21, gen. mgr., 1922-24; v.p. Western Theol. Sem., Ill., 1921-22, v.p. Centenary Coll., 1924-25, Westmoreland Coll., San Antonio Tex., 1925-26; cons. Coll. of Puget Sound, 1925; asst. to pres., Bradley Poly. Inst., Peoria, Ill., 1926-27; cons. ednl. instrns. on orgn. and finance, 1927-28; exec. sec. Lawrence Coll., Appleton, Wis. from 1929; exec. dir. Inst. of Paper Chemistry, Lawrence Coll. 1920-35, pres., trustee to 1955, emeritus pres., 1955. Served with U.S. Army, A.S., 38th Air Squadron, 1918-19. Exec. officer, Combined Prodn. and Resources Bd., WPB, 1943-44; mem. adv. bd. research and devel. br. Mil. Planning Div., Office Q.M. Gen., Army Service Forces. Fellow A.I.M. (president's council 1954); mem. A.A.A.S., Phi Delta Theta. Episcopalian. Club: Oceanside Country (Ormond Beach). Author pamphlets. Home: Daytona FL

STEELE, FRANK B., sec. gen. Sons Am. Revolution; b. Buffalo, N.Y., Mar. 28, 1864; s. Charles G. and Harriet V. (Snyder) S.; graduate State Normal Sch. (now State Teachers Coll.), Buffalo, N.Y., 1883; m. Helen Varian, Feb. 4, 1896; children—Helen Dorothy (Mrs. Hans W. Walter), Varian. Admitted to N.Y. State bar, 1890; law practice and dep. clerk Superior Court of Buffalo, 1892-94; dep. clk. Erie County, N.Y., 1894-97; clk. bd. supervisors, 1909-11; law practice, 1911-27; sec. gen. and registrar, Sons of Am. Revolution, 1921-50, now emeritus, Rep. committeeman, Buffalo, 10 yrs. Past gov. and dep. gov. gen. nat. society Mayflower Descendants in the Dist. of Columbia; mem. N.Y. State and Buffalo Hist. societies, Soc. of Founders and Patriots (gov. Dist. Columbia Soc.), Soc. of War of 1812 (past pres. and v.p. nat. soc.), Soc. Colonial Wars in D.C. (historian); former mem. bar assn. of Erie and sec. of Lawyers Club of Buffalo. Mem. Arts Club (past pres.), National Press Club (Washington, D.C.); Buffalo Club (Buffalo, N.Y.); N.Y. Advertising Club. Author of series of stories of Old Times in Buffalo for Buffalo Express. Unitarian. Editor, Sons of the Am. Revolution magazine. Made many addresses on hist. and patriotic subjects. Home: 1819 G St., N.W., Washington DC‡

STEELE, JOHN DUTTON, thoracic surgeon; b. Phila., Jan. 28, 1905; s. John Dutton and Edith (Williamson) S.; B.A., Williams Coll., 1926; M.D., U. Pa., 1932; M.S. in Surgery, U. Mich., 1937; m. Betsy Owen, July 2, 1936; children—Christopher, Polly (Mrs. W. Albert Munson), Wendy (Mrs. Harold Teasdale), Jenny (Mrs. Robert Allen). Intern Bryn Mawr (Pa.) Hosp., 1932-33; resident Internat. Grenfell Assn., St. Anthony, Newfoundland, 1933-35; resident thoracic surgery Univ. Hosp., Ann Arbor, Mich., 1935-37; pvt. practice thoracic surgery, Milw., 1938-55; chief surg. service Muirlale Sanatorium, Milw., 1938-55; asst. clin. prof. surgery Marquette U. Sch. Medicine, 1938-55; mem. faculty U. Cal. at Los Angeles Med. Sch., from 1957, clin. prof. surgery, from 1961; chief surg. service VA Hosp., San Fernando, Cal., 1955-67, cons. thoracic surgeon, from 1967; consulting thoracic surgeon Wadsworth VA Hosp., Los Angeles, Olive View Hospital, (Los Angeles). Diplomate Am. Bd. Thoracic Surgery (founder mem.). Fellow A.C.S.; mem. Am. Assn. Thoracic Surgery (sr.), A.M.A., Am. Thoracic Soc. (v.p. 1946-47, sec. 1950-53, pres. 1954-55, councilor 1962-65), Nat. Tb Assn. (dir. 1950-55, v.p. 1953-54; Trudeau medal 1962), Wis. Anti-Tb Assn. (dir. 1944-55) Cal. Thoracic Soc., Soc. Thoracic Surgeons (founder mem.). Author: The Solitary Pulmonary Nodule, 1964. Editor: (with others) The Surgical Management of Pulmonary Tuberculosis, Parasitic Diseases of the Chest, 1964; (with others) The Treatment of Mycotic and Alexander Monograph Series, 1957-65; The Annals of Thoracic Surgery, from 1965, Contbr. articles to med. jours. Home: Northridge CA

STEELE, JOHN MURRAY, cardio-vascular specialist; b. Newport, R.I., June 7, 1900; s. John Murray and Gertrude (Brooks) S.; student Marstons U. Sch. for Boys, Balt., 1910-17; A.B., Harvard, 1921; M.D., Johns Hopkins, 1925; m. Sylvia Moulton Ward, July 1, 1932; children—John Murray, Charles Nevett, Lucy Ann. Resident Billings Hosp., also instr. U. Chgo., 1928-29; asst. in medicine Rockefeller Inst. Hosp., 1929-35; asso., 1935-39; prof. N.Y.U., 1939-69; dir. N.Y.U. research service Goldwater Meml. Hosp. Welfare Assn., N.Y.C., from 1948. Cons. to Montreal Hosps. for chronic disease care. Mem. Welfare Council, N.Y.C., from 1938. Served as pvt. U.S.M.C., 1918; comdr. M.C., U.S.N.R., 1942-46; Research Inst. Nat. Naval Med. Center, Bethesda, Md. Mem. Am. Soc. Clin. Investigation, Am. Heart Assn., Am. Physiol. Soc., Harvey Soc., Century Assn., A.A.A.S., Democrat. Editor: Vol. VI: Methods in Medical Research, 1942. Research in chronic diseases. Home: New York City NY Died Oct. 13, 1969.

STEELE, JOSEPH M., building constrn.; b. Phila., Pa., Feb. 5, 1865; s. William and Ellen A. (Blair) S.; ed. pub. schs. and business coll., Phila.; m. Mary J. Stewart, Jan. 15, 1889; children—William III, May C. (widow of Dr. Leon Clemmer), Donald M., John S. Began in bldg., constrn. business, 1886; pres. Wm. Steele & Sons Co. since 1908; dir. Tradesman's Nat. Bank & Trust Co., Warner Co. Trustee Drexel Inst., Phila., Beaver Coll., Jenkintown, Pa., Geneva Coll., Beaver Falls, Pa., Am. Univ. at Cairo. Republican. Ref. Presbyn. Club: Union League. Home: Cambridge Apt., Germantown. Office: 661 Drexel Bldg., Philadelphia 8 PA‡

STEELE, ROBERT BENSON, prof. Latin; b. Lodi, Wis.; s. Robert and Rhoda Ann (Bower) S.; A.B., U. of Wis., 1883, A.M., 1888; Ph.D., Johns Hopkins, 1890; m. Elizabeth Jane Reed, of Monmouth, Ill., Sept. 6, 1894; 1dau., Mary Eleanor (dec.). Teacher of Latin, Antioch Coll., Yellow Springs, O., 1886-88, St. Olaf Coll., Northfield, Minn., 1890-91, Ill. Wesleyan U., Bloomington, Ill., 1891-1901, Vanderbilt since 1901. Mem. Am. Philol. Assn., Classical Assn. Middle West and South, Tenn. Philol. Assn., Brit. Classical Assn. Methodist. Writer of numerous philol. monographs. Home: 101 24th Av. S., Nashville TN‡

STEELE, ROBERT DENHAM, coll. pres.; b. Chicago, Ill., Jan. 26, 1901; s. John and Mary Maude (Barnes) S.; B.S., Coll. of Wooster, 1922, L.H.D., 1966; B.Th., Princeton Theol. Sem., 1926; student Grad. Coll., U. of Edinburgh, Scotland, 1928-29; D.D., Coll. of Ida., 1939; LL.D. (hon.), Westminster College, 1952, Ripon College, 1966; m. Elizabeth Louise Reherd, Sept. 20, 1928; children—Robert David, James Reherd. Coach and teacher of science, high sch., California, Pa., 1922-23; ordained to ministry Presbyn. Ch., May 1926; pastor Presbyn. Chs., Ridgebury, Centerville, Denton, N.Y., 1926; acting pastor Webb Horton Memorial Presbyn. Ch., Middleton, N.Y., 1927-28; dir. Christian edn. and asst. pastor Shadyside Presbyn. Ch., Pittsburg, Pa., 1929-34; v.p. Westminster Coll., Salt Lake City, 1934-36, asso. pres., 1936-39, pres., trustee, 1939-52; pres. Carroll Coll., Waukesha, Wis., 1952-67. President U. Council Chs., 1936-52; sec. Wis. Found. Independent Colls. Mem. regional exec. com. Boy Scouts Am. Mem. Wis. Assn. Pres. and Deans Liberal Arts Colls. (pres., 1956-59), Assn. Presidents and Deans Wis. Instns. Higher Learning (past pres.), C. of C. (past pres.). Clubs: University (Milw.), Kiwanis (pres.). Contbr. to ednl. and religious jours. Home: Waukesha WI Died Oct. 1972.

STEELE, ROBERT WILBUR, lawyer, judge; b. Denver, Apr. 8, 1891; s. Robert Wilbur and Anna (Truax) S.; A.B., Princeton, 1913; LL.B., U. of Denver, 1916, LL.D., 1958; m. Blanche Matteson, Oct. 10, 1946 (died July 1964); children—Robert Wilbur, Walter Arundel. Admitted to Colo. bar, 1916, pvt. practice, Denver, 1916-27; judge Juvenile Ct., Denver, 1927-30, Colo. Dist. Ct., 1930-69. Mem. Colo., Denver bar assns., Law Club of Denver. Home: Denver CO Died Apr. 8, 1969.

STEELE, SIDNEY JOHN, business executive; b. River Forest, Ill., Jan. 11, 1877; s. Ashbel J. and Julia (Rutherford) S.; ed. U. of Mich.; m. Florence De Lap, June 1909. In mfg. dept. Norton Brothers, 1898-1901; mfg. and sales depts. Am. Can Co., 1901-05; with Continental Can Co. since 1905, becoming exec. vice pres. and dir., 1923, vice chmn. of bd., ret. Clubs: Union League, Chicago Athletic (Chicago); Oak Park (Ill.) Country. Home: 1139 Lathrop Av., River Forest, Ill. Office: 135 S. La Salle St., Chicago 3‡

STEELE, WILBUR DANIEL, author; b. Greensboro, N.C., Mar. 17, 1886; s. Wilbur Fletcher (D.D.) and Rose (Wood) S.; A.B., U. of Denver, 1907, Litt.D., 1932; studied Museum of Fine Arts, Boston, 1907-08; Academie Julian, Paris, France, 1908-09; Art Students League, New York, 1909-10; m. Margaret Thurston, Feb. 17, 1913 (dec.); children—Thurston (dec.), Peter; m. 2d, Mrs. Norma Mitchell Talbot, Jan. 14, 1932. Mem. of Sigma Alpha Epsilon. Co-author of two plays; author several books from 1914; latest publs.; Diamond Wedding, 1951; Their Town, 1952; The Way to the Gold, 1955; also short stories in national magazines. Recipient second prize, 1919, from O. Henry Award Committee for story For They Know Not What They Do"; spl. award, same com., 1921, for maintaining highest level of merit for 3 yrs. among Am. short story writers; tied with Julian Street, same Com., for 1st honor, 1925; with story, The Man Who Saw Through Heaven"; first award, 1925, in Harper short story contest, for story, When Hell Froze"; first prize, O. Henry Award Com., 1926, for story, Bubbles"; first prize, same com., 1931, for story, Can't Cross Jordan." Home: Lyme CT Died May 26, 1970; buried Pleasantview Cemetery Hanbury CT

STEENROD, NORMAN EARL, educator; b. Dayton, O., Apr. 22, 1910; s. Earl Lindsay and Sarah (Rutledge) S.; B.A., U. Mich., 1932; M.A., Harvard, 1934; Ph.D., Princeton, 1936; m. Carolyn Witter, Aug. 20, 1938; children—Katherine, Charles. Instr. mathematics Princeton, 1936-39; asst. prof. mathematics U. Chgo., 1939-42; asst. prof. mathematics U. Mich., 1942-45, asso. prof., 1945-47; asso. prof. mathematics Princeton, 1947-51, prof., from 1951. Staff operations research group Navy Dept., Washington, 1944-45. Guggenheim fellow, 1950-51. Mem. Nat. Acad. Sci., Am. Math. Soc., Am. Assn. U. Profs., Math. Assn. Am., Sigma Xi. Author: The Topology of Fibre Bundles, 1951; (with S. Ellenberg) The Foundations of Algebraic Topology, 1952. Editor Annals of Mathematics, 1950-62. Home: Princeton NJ Died Oct. 14, 1971.

STEICHEN, EDWARD, photographer, artist, plant breeder; b. Luxembourg, Mar. 27, 1879; s. Jean Pierre and Marie (Kemp) S.; came to U.S., 1880; hon. M.A., Wesleyan U., Conn., 1942; A.F.D., U. Wis., 1957, U.

Hartford, 1960, Lincoln Coll., 1962; L.H.D., Bard Coll.; 1966; hon. degree Fairfield (Conn.) U., 1967; m. Clara Smith, 1903; children—Mary (Mrs. F. Calderone), Kate Rodina; m. 2d, Dana Glover, 1923 (dec. 1957); m. 3d, Joanna Taub, March 1960. One of the first to realize the possibilities of the new photography" and has produced many notable plates; has exhibited photographs and paintings at the great art centres of America and Europe; retrospective exhbn. photographs Mus. Modern Art, N.Y.C., 1961; paintings in Luxembourg (Paris), Met. Mus. (N.Y.C.), Whitney Mus. Am. Art, Portland Mus. Art, Toledo Mus. Art, numerous pvt. collections; chief photographer Conde Nast Publs., 1923-38; dir. dept. photography Mus. Modern Art, N.Y.C., 1947-62, dir. dept. emeritus, 1962-73. Made photographic mural decoration, subject aviation, in New Roxy Theatre, Radio City, N.Y.C., Commd. Photographic Div., Air Service, U.S. Army, World War I, with A.E.F., rank lt. col. Decorated Chevalier Legion d'Honneur (France). Served as capt., USNR, World War II; commd. U.S. Navy combat photography, dir. Navy Photographic Inst. Decorated D.S.M., Presdl. Medal of Freedom; grand officer de l'Ordre de Merit (Luxembourg). Directed making Road to Victory exhbn. for Museum of Modern Art, 1942; Power in the Pacific, 1944; supervised the photography of film, Fighting Lady. Recipient Ann. Advt. award, 1937; Fine Arts medal A.I.A., 1950; achievement award U.S. Camera Mag., 1949, Photography Mag., 1952; Internat. award Photog. Soc. Am., 1957; Silver Progress medal Royal Photog. Soc. (Eng.), 1960; spl. award Am. Soc. Mag. Photographers, 1961; Presdl. medal of freedom, 1963; Internat. Photog. Exposition award, 1965; award of merit medal Lotos Club, N.Y.C., 1965. Began cross-breeding of flowers, specializing in delphinium, 1910; one-man flower exhibit. Mus. Modern Art, 1936. Hon. pres. Am. Delphinium Soc.; hon. fellow Royal Photog. Soc. Great Britain, Photo. Soc. America. Created for Mus. Modern Art the Family of Man exhibition, 1955; recipient awards from Newspaper Guild, Am. Soc. Mag. Photographers, Phila. Mus. Art Urban League. Author: A Life in Photography, 1963. Editor: Sandburg Photographers View Carl Sandburg, 1966. Home: West Redding CT Died Mar. 25, 1973.

STEIL, WILLIAM NICHOLAS, univ. prof.; b. Highland, Wis., Sept. 4, 1876; s. Henry and Catherine (Steinhardt) S.; student Platteville State Teacher's Coll., 1895-97; Ph.B., U. of Wis., 1911; Ph.D., U. of Wis., 1916; m. Florence Vaughan, Aug. 19, 1902; children—Gerald William, Florence Madeline (Mrs. Bernard A. Wirth), Mary Katharine (Mrs. Frank Milton Bruce, Jr.). Taught sch., 1897-1903; teacher in secondary schools, 1904-10; instr., University of Wisconsin, 1910-22; with Marquette University since 1922, now professor botany. Fellow A.A.A.S.; mem. Bot. Soc., Am. Fern Soc. (life mem.), Wis. Acad. Arts, Science and Letters (v.p. 1942, 43), Torrey Bot. Club Stain Com., Sigma Xi. Contbr. over 40 papers to bot. jours. on apogamy, incomplete division, and antherozoids, etc. Home: 1926 N. 53d St. Office: 1217 W. Wisconsin Av., Milwaukee WI‡

STEIN, ALBERT HARVEY, govt. ofcl., lawyer; b. Omaha, May 23, 1917; s. Julius Allen and Dora (Green) S.; student U. Neb., 1933-35; A.B., U. Mich., 1937; LL.B., Harvard, 1940; m. Jay Foster, Sept. 30, 1939; children—Judith, Linda, John. Admitted to Neb. bar, 1940; counsel Bur. of Ships, USN, 1947-54; asst. gen. counsel Dept. Navy, 1954-57, dep. gen. counsel, 1957-72. Recipient Navy Distinguished Civilian Service award, 1961. Home: Bethesda MD Died Dec. 12, 1972.

STEIN, FRED W., SR., editor, publisher; b. Olean, N.Y., June 20, 1905; s. Frank E. and Margaret (Gaynor) S.; ed. Olean (N.Y.) High Sch. and U. of Pittsburgh; m. Amelia Wood, Aug. 5, 1929; children—Frederic William, Barbara Wood, Peter Kinne. Reporter, Olean (N.Y.) Herald, 1923-25; state editor, Buffalo (N.Y.) Express, 1925-26; copy editor, Pittsburgh (Pa.) Press, 1926, Pittsburgh Post, 1926, Buffalo News, 1927; telegraph editor, Orange (N.J.) Courier, 1927; feature writer, New York Telegram, 1927; with Binghamton (N.Y.) Press since 1928, telegraph editor, 1928-31, news editor, 1931-41, editor, 1941-70, gen. mgr., 1959-61; pub., 1961-70, also pres.; v.p.; sec. Binghamton Press Co., Inc.; dir. Gannett Co., Inc. Dir. Am. Press Inst., Valley Devel. Found.; mem. bd. dirs. Frank E. Garnett Newspaper Found., Inc.; adv. council St. Bonaventure Sch. Journalism, adv. bd. Journalism Sch. Syracuse U. Mem. Inter-Am. Press Inst., A.P., N.Y. Soc. Newspapers Editors (past pres.), Am., N.Y. State (past president) pubs. assns., Internat. Press Inst., Am. Soc. Newspaper Editors, Sigma Delta Chi. Clubs: Binghamton, Binghamton Country; Torch, Nat. Press (Washington). Home: Binghamton NY Died June 7, 1970; buried Oak Hill Cemetery, Towanda PA

STEIN, JAMES RAUCH, clergyman, church official; b. Schuylkill Haven, Pa., Apr. 18, 1868; s. George W. and Caroline Henry (Rauch) S.; A.B., Franklin and Marshall Coll., 1893, A.M., 1896, D.D., 1921; grad. Theol. Sem. Ref. Ch. in U.S., Lancaster, Pa., 1897; m. Blanche Marie Harnish (Bryn Mawr), June 14, 1898; children—Rev. Joseph Henry, Mrs. Caroline Rauch Gibson, Eleanor Robb, M.D., Rev. James Rauch and

George Harnish, M.D. Began career as teacher in public schools for 6 yrs.; teacher Mercersberg Acad., 1893; ordained Ref. Ch. ministry, 1897; asst. pastor First Ch., Lebanon, Pa., 1897; pastor St. Stephen's Ch., Perkasie, 1898-1900, St. John's Ch., Harrisburg, 1900-11, Christ Ch., Bethlehem, 1911-17, First Ch., Wilkes-Barre, 1917-23, Christ Church, Philadelphia, 1923-26. Stated clerk General Synod Ref. Ch. in U.S., 1909-34; stated clerk Gen. Synod Evang. and Ref. Ch., 1934-38; retired June 25, 1938, Continues as stated clerk Eastern Synod, 1909-42; president Phila. Classis of Reformed Church, 1933 (stated clerk, 1944), Phila. Ministerial Assn. since 1941; supply pastor Calvary Reformed Ch., Philadelphia, 1942, Heidelberg Ch., Hatfield, Pa., 1943, St. Mark's Ch., Phila., 1944-45, St. Matthews Ch., Phila., 1946; St. Luke's Ch., Philadelphia, 1947. Representative to Pennsylvania Council of Chs.; mem. Phila. Council Chs. Mem. Pennsylvania German Soc., American Academy Political and Social Science (Phila.), Lebanon County Hist. Soc., Pa. Anti-Saloon League. Phi Beta Kappa. Republican. Editor Minutes of Eastern Synod of Ref. Ch. in U.S. (annual); Minutes of General Synod of Evang. and Ref. Ch. (biennial), 1909-38; Minutes of Philadelphia Classes, 1943-46. Co-editor Statistical Tables Evang. and Ref. Church (Annual), 1935-39. Home: 804 N. 2d St., Harrisburg PA‡

STEINBACH, EVERETT MARK, coll. dean; b. L'Anse, Mich., Aug. 21, 1905; s. Herman Peter and Marie Ann (Pambrun) S.; A.B., No Mich. Coll. Edn., 1935; M.A., U. Detroit, 1951; m. Della M. Kinnucan, Feb. 2, 1946; 1 dau., Marie Louise. Dean freshman studies program U. Detroit, 1964-69. Home: Detroit MI Died Aug. 3, 1968; buried Evergreen Cemetery, L'Anse MI

STEINBACH, MILTON, business exec.; b. New Haven, 1902; s. Abdul D. and Ray (Hoffman) S.; grad. Phillips Andover Acad., 1920; grad. Yale, 1924; m. Ruth Adler, Dec. 8, 1925. Partner Wertheim & Co., N.Y.C., 1933-70; dir. Armour & Co., Baldwin-Lima-Hamilton Corp., Barber Oil Corp., Greyhound Corp. Gov. N.Y. Stock Exchange, 1964-69. Asso. treas Fedn. Jewish Philanthropies N.Y. Trustee Mt. Sinai Hosp.; pres. Mt. Sinai Sch. Medicine; charter trustee Phillips Acad., Andover, Mass. Served as maj. AUS, 1942-45. Clubs: Harmonie (N.Y.C.); Century Country. Home: Rye NY Died Dec. 1970.

STEINBECK, JOHN ERNST, writer; b. Salinas, Calif., Feb. 27, 1902; s. John Ernst and Olive (Hamilton) S.; grad. Salinas High School, 1918; student Stanford U., 1919; m. Carol Henning, 1930, (divorced Mar. 1943); m. 2d, Gwyn Conger, Mar. 29, 1943; 2 sons, Tom, John; m. 3d Elaine Scott, Dec. 28, 1950. Author: Cup of Gold, 1929; Pastures of Heaven, 1932; To a God Unknown, 1933; Tortilla Flat, 1935; In Dubious Battle, 1936; Of Mice and Men, 1937; Red Pony, 1937; dramatization of Of Mice and Men, 1937; Grapes of Wrath, 1939; The Moon is Down, 1942; Cannery Row, 1945; The Wayward Bus, 1947; Russian Journal, 1948; The Log from the Sea of Cortez, 1951; East of Eden, 1952; Sweet Thursday, 1954; Pipe Dream (musical), 1955; Reign of Pippin IV, 1957; Once There Was a War, 1957; The Winter of our Discontent, 1961; Travels with Charley, pub. 1962; America and the American, pub. in 1966. Recipient of Pulitzer prize, 1940, Nobel Prize for lit., 1962; Presdl. Medal of Freedom, 1964. War columnist overseas. Address: New York City NY Died Dec. 20, 1968.

STEINDEL, BRUNO, violoncello virtuoso; b. Zwickau, Saxony, Aug. 29, 1869; s. Albin S.; musical edn. under his father, a musical dir., and other teachers in Germany; m. Mathilde Stumpp, pianist, of Chicago, 1896 (dec.); 1 child. Soloist, Philharmonic Orchestra, Berlin, 1889-92; soloist with Thomas Orchestra, 1892, and Chicago Symphony Orchestra; later solo cellist Chicago Civic Opera Co. Address: Auditorium Bldg., Chicago IL*‡

STEINER, CELESTIN JOHN, association exec.; b. Detroit, Mich., Feb. 7, 1898; s. Edward P. and Mary Vandere (Brouker) S.; student U. of Detroit, 1916-18, St. Stanislaus Sem., Florissant, Mo., 1918-22; A.B., St. Louis U., 1923, M.A., 1925; Ph.D., Gregorian University, Rome, Italy, 1953; H.H.D. (honorary), Tampa University, 1953; studied Ignatiuskolleg, Valkenburg, Holland; Coll. Rue de Franklin, Paris, France; Maison de la Colombiere, Paray-le-Monial, France; St. Michael's Coll., Brussels, Belgium; Maison St. Louis, Jersey, Eng.; Marquette U., Milwaukee; Ohio State U.; joined Soc. of Jesus, 1918; instr., St. Louis U. High Sch., 1925-28; instr. French and German, Xavier U., Cincinnati, 1933-37; pres. St. Xavier High Sch., Cin., 1937-40, Xavier U., 1940-49; pres. U. Detroit, 1949-60, chancellor, 1960-67; dir. N. Am. commn. mass media Soc. Jesus, 1967-71; cons. to internat. sec. communications, 1967-71; extra-curricular lectr. in religion and philosophy. Dir. Detroit Symphony Orchestra, United Found.; mem. Detroit Round Table of Nat. Conf. of Christian and Jews. Mich. del. White House Conf. Edn. Mem. Cath. Coll. Pres. Assn. (pres. 1956), Ohio Coll. Assn., Assn. Cath. Colls. Mich., Assn. Am. Colls. (vice chmn. commn. Christian Higher Edn.), Nat. Cath. Broadcasters Assn. (pres.), Detroit Ednl. TV

Found. (chmn. finance com.), Fgn. Policy Assn. Detroit, Am. Soc. Engring. Edn., Am. Cath. Philos. Assn., Am. Cath. Sociol. Assn. Clubs: Detroit Athletic, Economic. Address: Detroit MI Died Oct. 25, 1971; interred Colombiere Coll., Clarkston MI

STEINER, MAX, composer, arranger; b. Vienna, Austria, May 10, 1888; student Vienna Conservatory, also pupil of Gustav Mahler. Went to Eng., 1904, to Paris, 1911; settled in U.S., 1914; wrote operetta at age fourteen; condr. musicals in N.Y.C.; film composer, conductor, Hollywood, Cal., 1929-71; filmscores include The Informer, Life With Father, Gone With the Wind. Address: Beverly Hills CA Died Dec. 28, 1971.

STEINERT, ALAN, business exec.; b. New Haven, Jan. 28, 1901; s. Rudolph and Hilda (Friedman) S.; A.B., Yale, 1923; m. Claire Hyman, Dec. 18, 1928; children—Susan (Mrs. Leo Poverman), Audrey (Mrs. William Barnett), Alan. Pres. Eastern Co., Cambridge, Massachusetts, 1933-66, chairman of board, 1966-69; director of Harvard Trust Co., United Research, Inc. Pres. James Jackson Putnam Children's Center, 1960-62, Eastern Charitable Found., from 1950; trustee Boston Mus. Sci., 1953-63, New Eng. Aquarium Corp., from 1963; trustee, pres. Peter Bent Brigham Hosp. Bd. overseers Shady Hill Sch., 1945-51; trustee Cambridge Sch. 1949-53; mem. Corp. Mass. Gen. Hosp.; pres. Cambridge Civic Assn., 1953-54. Mem. Am. Academy of Arts and Scis. Clubs: Yale, Harvard (Boston); St. Botolph, Belmont Country. Home: Cambridge MA Died July 1, 1969; buried Mt. Auburn Cemetery.

STEINGRUBER-WILDGANS, ILONA, soprano; d. Heinrich Steingruber and Rosa Kovacs; m. Friedr. Wildgans. State examiner piano, singing, stage performances; first appearance, Tilsit, 1943; on tour Holland, Belgium, France, Greece, to 1948, Hungary, Czechoslovakia, Germany, Italy, France, 1951-57; mem. State Opera, Vienna, 1948-51, from 1957; lectr. Holiday Music Courses, Darmstadt, also Jeunesses Musicales, Bayreuth, 1953; guest performance Mozart Festival, South Africa. Recipient Mozart medal, Wiener Konzerthaus, 1948. Schonberg medale, 1953. Address: Vienna Austria

STEINHAUS, ARTHUR H., physiologist; b. Chicago, Ill., Oct. 4, 1897; s. Henry D. and Rosa (Daehler) S.; B.P.E., George Williams Coll., 1921, M.P.E., 1926; S.B., U. of Chicago, 1920, M.S., 1925, Ph.D., 1928; m. Eva Kunzmann, June 23, 1921; 1 son, Robert Arthur. Instructor biological sciences, George Williams Coll., 1920-28, prof. physiology, 1928-63, Oscar G. Mayer Distinguished Service prof., 1963-65, dir. div health and phys. edn., 1953-62, dean coll., 1954-62, dean emeritus; Distinguished Service prof. physiology Chgo. Coll. Osteopathy, 1965-66; vis. professor Michigan State University, East Lansing, Michigan, 1966-70; chief Dir. Phys. Edn. and Health Activities, United States Office of Education, F.S.A., 1944; on leave as spl. adviser, The Robinson Foundation, Inc., Section on Health Edn., New York, 1945-46; lecturer biology Baptist Missionary Training School, 1935-45; visiting prof. U. of Calif. summers 1937, 39, 41, U. of Colo., 1942, Univ. Wis., 1943, Univ. Sask., 1946, U. Ore., 1950, 60 U. So. Cal., 1965; lectr. Internat. Congress Physical Edn., Internat. Sport Students' Congress in connection with XI Olympic Games, Berlin, 1936, 3d World Congress Phys. Edn., Istanbul, 1953, 1st Internat. Congress Phys. Edn. U.S., 1954; guest lectr. South African Assn. for Phys. Edn. and Recreation, 1965; cons. South African Fedn. for Youth and Sport, 1968. Consultant to Secretary of Navy on physical fitness and physical rehabilitation, during World War II. Fellow John Simon Guggenheim Memorial Foundation for study in Europe, 1931-32, Fulbright lectr. Germany, 1955, Japan, 1962-63. Recipient of Roberts-Gulick award, 1940, William G. Anderson Merit award, 1951; Honor award Am. College Sports Medicine, 1965; citation U. Toledo Div. Health, Phys. Edn. and Recreation, 1969. Fellow Am. Academy Physical Education (sec.-treas. 1936-41; v.p. 1941-42, pres. 1943-45), Am. Association Health, Physical Education and Recreation (pres. Midwest dist. 1955, Luther Halsey Gulick award 1969), Am. Pub. Health Assn., Am. School Health Assn., Am. Coll. Sports Medicine; membre appeles Fedn. Internat. Medico Sportive; mem. Fedn. Internat. Edn. Physique (v.p.), Ill. Assn. Health, Phys. Edn., Recreation (pres. 1948-49), Am. Physiol. Soc., Phys. Edn. Soc. New Zealand (v.p. 1963), South African Assn. for Phys. Edn. and Recreation (hon. v.p. 1967), Delta Psi Kappa (patron), Phi Epsilon Kappa (hon.), Kappa Delta Pi, Sigma Xi, Pi Gamma Mu. Baptist. Author: Tobacco and Health, 1939; The Romance of Service, 1940; How to Keep Fit and Like It, 1957; More Firepower for Health Education, 1945; Lectures on the Physiology of Exercise, 1948; Toward an Understanding of Health and Physical Education, 1963. Co-author Methods of Research in Health, Physical Education, and Recreation, 1959. Contbr. to Am. Journal Physiology, Jornal of Health and Phys. Edn., numerous other health jours. Home: East Lansing MI Died Feb. 8, 1970; buried Graceland Cemetery Chicago IL

STEINHAUS, EDWARD A(RTHUR), scientist, educator; b. Max, N.D., Nov. 7, 1914; s. Arthur Alfred and Alice (Rhinehart) S.; B.S., N.D. State Univ., 1936, Sc.D., 1962; Ph.D., Ohio State U., 1939; m. Mabry Clark, June 14, 1940; children—Margaret, Timothy Clark, Cynthia Alice. Asst. bacteriology Ohio State U., 1936-39; Muellhaupt scholar, 1939-40; asst. bacteriologist Rocky Mountain Lab., USPHS, 1940-41, asso. bacteriologist, 1942-44; asst. prof. bacteriology and insect pathology U. Cal., Berkeley 1944-49, insect pathologist Expt. Sta., 1945-63, organizer, dir. Lab. Insect Pathology, 1945-60, asso. prof. insect pathology, 1949-54, prof., 1954-63, vice chmn. dept. biological control, 1957-58, chairman of department insect pathol., 1960-63, prof., dean biol. scis., U. Calif. Irvine, Cal., 1963-68, dir. Center Pathobiology, 1968-69. Member United States Army Bullis Fever Commn., 1943-44; cons. NRC, 1951, Pacific Sci. Bd., 1951-69, USPHS, 1955-64; v.p. bacteriological sect. Internat. Congress Microbiology, 1950; mem. Internat. Com. Comparative Pathology, 1965-69; invertebrate cons. com. NRC, 1962-69; member NAS-NRC Com. Comparative Pathology, 1963-69; exec. com. Internat. Congress Insect Pathology, 1962-69. Guggenheim fellow, 1960-61. Fellow Entomol. Society America (president 1962-63, A.A.A.S., Am. Acad. of Microbiology; mem. Nat. Acad. Scis., Soc. Invertebrate Pathology (pres. 1967-68), Soc. Exptl. Pathology, Council of Biol. Editors, Soc. Am. Bacteriologists, Soc. Gen. Microbiology, Am. Soc. Protozoologists, Am. Inst. Biol. Scis. (governing bd.), Soc. Sci. and Tech., India, Entomol. Soc. USSR, Sigma Xi. Conglist. Author: Insect Microbiology, 1946; Principles of Insect Pathology, 1949. Editor Ann. Rev. Entomology, 1955-62, Jour. Invertebrate Pathology, 1959-69, Insect Pathology, an Advanced Treatise, 1962; mem. editorial bd. Jour. Econ. Entomology, Virology, U.C. Entomology Series; asso. editor Bergey's Manual of Determinative Bacteriology; editorial bd. Life Sciences. Author sci. papers. Home: Newport Beach CA Died Oct. 20, 1969; buried Corona del Mar CA

STEININGER, FRED H., social worker; b. Chgo. Nov. 8, 1915; s. Joseph and Rose (Moser) S.; B.A., St. Joseph's Coll. Rensselear, Ind., 1939; M.A., U. Chgo., 1945; m. Margaret Stalman, Sept. 1, 1941;children—Fred J., David A. Psychiat. social work supr. Lake County (Ind.) Mental Health Clinic, 1945-47; asst. prof. social work, and sociology Valparaiso U., 1947; field work instr. and adminstr. U. Chgo., Sch. Social Service Adminstrn, 1948; dir. Lake County Dept. Pub. Welfare, Gary, 1948-64; dir. bur. of family service welfare adminstrn. U.S. Dept. Health, Education and Welfare, 1964-73, asst. adminstr. Fed.-State Relations, Social and Rehab. Service, 1967, asst. commr. region IV social and rehab. service, Atlanta, 1969-73. Recipient Good Govt. award Gary Jr. C. of C., 1955; Page One Civic award Gary Newspaper Guild, 1956; Human Relations award Gary chpt. B'nai B'rith, 1959. Mem. Am. Pub. Welfare Assn. (pres. 1961-63, Howard E. Russell Meml. Merit award 1960), Council Social Work Edn. (v.p. 1957-62), Nat. Assn. Social Workers, K.C., Optimist. Home: Decatur GA Died Feb. 15, 1973.

STEINLE, ROLAND JOSEPH, lawyer; born Milw., Mar. 21, 1896; s. Joseph L. and Elizabeth (Baldauf) S.; student Marquette Coll. Law, 1920; m. Helen Sharpe, May 3, 1923; (dec. Dec. 1953); children—Roland Joseph, Betty (Mrs. David Labissoniere), Rosemary (Mrs. Joseph McCarthy); m. 2d, Nancy Sharpe, Decmeber 28, 1963. Admitted to Wis., bar, 1920; practice, Milw., 1920-40, 58-66; spl. asst. dist. atty. Milw. County, 1923-24, Forest County, 1925-26, County, Waukesha 1938-39, Dodge County, 1937; ct. commnr. Milw. County, 1937-40; circuit judge 2d Judicial Circuit Wis., 1940-54; asso. justice Wis. Supreme Ct. 1954-58; conciliator Circuit Ct. Milw. County, from 1958; instr. jurisprudence Marquette U., 1928-53; chmn. Bd. Circuit Judges Wis., 1946. Wis. chmn. Nat. Conf. Christians and Jews, 1956-57; twice mem. awards jury Freedom's Found. Chmn. Milw. County Republican Com., 1934-35; Rep. candiate lt. gov. Wis., 1936; Rep. candidate U.S. Senator from Wisconsin, 1958. Served from 2d lt. to 1st lt., inf., U.S. Army, 1917-18. Recipient Distinguished Service medal Vets. Fgn. Wars, 1928, citation Nat. Conf. Christians and Jews, 1956. Mem. Wis., Milw. (past pres.) bar assns., Am. Legion (1st judge adv. Wis.). K.C. (past dist. dep.), Cath. Knights Wis. (past v.p., dir.), Elk, Eagle, Moose. Home: Milwaukee WI Died Dec. 22, 1966.

STEINMETZ, MAURICE, Luxembourg ambassador; b. 1904; ed. Commercial Inst., Antwerp, Belgium; m. Mildred R. Laevens, 1947. With Luxembourg legation, Brussels, 1945-61; permanent rep. to UN, 1961-64; ambassador of Luxembourg to U.S., 1964-69, to Mexico, 1965, to Can., 1965. Recipient numerous Luxembourg and fgn. awards. Home: Luxembourg Died Dec. 15, 1969; buried Luxembourg.

STEINSAPIR, SAUL P., mfg. exec.; b. Pitts., Oct. 3, 1904; s. Julius L. and Libbie B. (Sherr) S.; LL.D. (hon.), U. Szczuzvn, Poland. Chmn., treas. Standard Die Tool & Forging Co., Pitts., then pres., gen. mgr. chief exec. officer. Home: Pittsburgh PA Died 1973.

STENGEL, FREDERICK WILLIAM, clergyman, educator; b. Watertown, Wis., Oct. 18, 1874; s. Charles William and Christina (Schumacher) S.; A.B., Moravian Coll., Bethlehem, Pa., 1896, D.D., 1921; B.D., Moravian Theol. Sem., 1898 (honor man); m. Elizabeth McLean High, Nov. 20, 1898; children—George Douglas, Charles William, James Frederick, Lowell Otis. Ordained ministry Moravian Ch., 1898; pastor Carver County, Minn., 1898-1901, Bethlehem, Pa., 1901-11, Dover, O., 1911-15; pres. Linden Hall Jr. Coll. and Sch. for Girls, Lititz, Pa., since 1915. Organizer, 1907, and mgr. Moravian Illustrated Lecture Bur., for production of missionary lectures; sec. Dept. of Missionary Edn., and chmn. Bd. Religious Edn. Moravian Ch. Home: Lititz PA*‡

STENZEL, LULA VINETTE, author; b. at Washington, Jan. 1, 1872; d. Jacob N. (inventor) and Elizabeth A. Kerper; ed. Washington pub. schs.; m. Washington, Aug. 9, 1900, Charles F. A. Stenzel. Author: Breta's Double (under pen-name of Helen V. Greyson), 1894 B26; The Darkwood Tragedy, 1902 N3. Address: 414 S. Capitol St., Washington DC‡

STEPELTON, NORMAN ALLEN, retail chain store exec.; b. Lima, O., Nov. 15, 1912; s. Aubrey Forest and Anna Florence (Hobbs) S.; student course exec. retail mgmt., Mich. State U., 1959; m. LaRee Marion Cross, May 9, 1934; children—Donald Douglas, David. With National Tea Co., Chgo., 1934-70, pres., 1961-70, vice chmn., 1970; dir. Am. Nat. Bank & Trust Co., Chgo., Ill. Member of Chicago Crime Commission. Chairman business division Chicago Heart Association, drive, 1957-62, Chgo. chpt. drive Am. Cancer Soc., 1958-62; chmn. food div. Combined Appeal-Community Fund Red Cross drive, Chgo., 1959-60; chmn. food industry Aiding Leukemia Stricken Am. Children drive, 1960-61; gen. chmn. Chicago Federation of Settlement and Neighborhood Centers, 1963-64. Mem. bd. dirs. Nat. Conf. Christians and Jews, Protestant Found. Greater Chgo.; mem. bd. trustees Chgo. Wesley Hosp., Nat. Jewish Hospital at Denver. Named Retailer of Year, Brand Names Found., 1961; named Man of Year, Aiding Leukemia Stricken Am. Children, 1961. Mem. Ill. Retail Merchants Assn. (dir.), Nat. Assn. Food Chains (dir.), Club: 100 of Cook County. Home: Winnetka IL Died Aug. 7, 1970.

STEPHAN, FREDERICK FRANKLIN, statistician; b. Chicago, May 17, 1903; s. Frederick William and Eirene Mary (Ford) S.; B.A., U. of Ill.; M.A., U. of Chicago; m. Eda Mildred Atwood, Sept. 10, 1925; children—Frederick Paul, Walter Franklin, Louise Elizabeth (Mrs. James P. Mergler), Janet Lucia (Mrs. Richard D. Greene). Instr., then asst. prof. U. of Pittsburgh, 1927-34; dir. Bureau Social Research. 1931-34; sec.-treas. and editor, Am. Statis. Assn., 1935-40; mem. Central Statis. Bd., 1935-40; lecturer, Columbia U., 1937; attended Internat. Population Congress, Paris, 1937; mem. Statis. Sec., Eighth Pan-Am. Sci. Congress, 1939; prof. of sociology and statistics, Cornell U., 1940-47; research cons., Office of Prodn. Management, 1941-42; dir. statis. service, War Manpower Commn., 1942-43; chief gen. statis. staff and asst. dir. research branch, WPB, 1944; European rep. for social sciences, Rockefeller Foundn., 1945-46; dir. studies of sampling. Social Science Research Council and Nat. Research Council, 1946-52; prof. social statistics and director office survey research and statis. studies Princeton, until 1971; sr. demographic cons. Population Council. Del., Assembly Inter-Am. Statis. Inst., 1947; cons. to various govt. research agencies. Civilian research analyst A.A.F. Evaluation Bd., ETO, 1944-45. Fellow Am. Statis. Assn. (pres. 1966), Inst. Math. Statistics, A.A.A.S. (v.p. econ. and social scis. 1947-61); member Operations Research Society, Social Science Research Council, Am. Sociol. Soc., Econometric Soc., Internat. Statis. Inst., Population Association of Am., Internat. Union for Sci. Study of Population, Am. Assn. Puplic Opinion Research (pres. 1957-58). Chilean Statistical Society (honorary member), Phi Beta Kappa, Sigma Xi. Club: Cosmos (Washington). Author: (with Philip J. McCarthy) Sampling Opinions: (with R. A. Gordon and others) Measuring Employment and Unemployment. Editor-Public Opinion Quarterly, 1958-64. Contbr. various articles to statis. and sci. jours. Home: Princeton NJ Died Aug. 2, 1971.

STEPHENS, BENJAMIN HUGHL, banker; b. Boonshill, Tenn., Dec. 30, 1869; s. Joseph M. and Julia Ann (Mouldin) S.; ed. college; m. Bessie M. Colbreath; two children. With St.L.S.W. Ry. as clerk to gen. agent; clerk Magnolia Petroleum Co., later v.p. and gen. mgr.; now chmn. bd. Mercantile Nat. Bank, dir. Southwestern Drug Corp., Dallas Federal Savings & Loan Assn. Mason. Club: Lakewood Country. Home: 4646 Shadywood Lane, Dallas 9*‡

STEPHENS, FERRIS J., assn. exec.; b. Fayette Co., Ind., Dec. 26, 1893; s. Alva Clayton and Mary W. (Ferris) S.; A.B., Butler Univ., 1915; B.D., Yale, 1923, Ph.D., 1925; m. Beulah B. Burkhardt, June 21, 1916; children—James Clayton, Mary Elizabeth (Mrs. Jorn Berg-Johnsen, Jr.). Prof. Old Testament and Ancient History, Culver-Stockton College, Canton, Mo., 1925-28; asst. prof. assyriology, Yale U., 1928-40, asso. prof., 1940-62, curator Babylonian Collection, 1933-62, emeritus, 1962-69; sec.-treas. Am. Oriental Soc., from 1939. Mem. Am. Oriental Soc., Soc. Biblical Lit. and Exegesis. Author: Personal Names from Cuneiform Inscriptions of Cappadocia, 1927; Votive and Historical Texts from Babylonia and Assyria, 1937; Old Assyrian Letters and Business Documents, 1944; numerous articles on assyriol. Subjects. Home: Hamden CT Died Oct. 31, 1969; buried Montowese North Haven CT

STEPHENS, HARLEY CLIFFORD, merchandising exec.; b. Linn County, Mo., July 21, 1900; s. Thaddeus Denzil and Anna Margaret (Hardinger) S.; ed. high sch., Kansas City; m. Cecelia Helen Bentz, Sept. 1, 1923 (dec. 1951); 1 dau., Janice Stephens Hagen; m. 2d, Dorothy Martha Louise Peterson, Apr. 7, 1952; step-children—Peter F. Pierce, Robert L. Pierce, Jacqueline Pierce Haugland. With J. C. Penney Co., 1924-60, dist. mgr., St. Louis, 1936-39, Mpls., 1940-55; v.p., dir., mem. exec. com., Gamble-Skogmo, Inc., Mpls., 1961-71; dir. Elsen Merc. Inc., Kansas City, Mode O'Day Corp., Mpls. Gas Co., retailers Growth Fund, Inc., Stedmans, Toronto, Macleods, Winnipeg. Pres. Minn. Retail Fedn., 1957-58. Episcopalian. Mason, Rotarian (past dir. Mpls.). Home: Excelsior MN Died Dec. 26, 1971; buried Minneapolis MN

STEPHENS, JAMES C(OLLINS), lawyer; b. Nashville, Jan. 13, 1894; s. Clay Greer and Mary (Collins) S.; B.S., Vanderbilt U., 1915; LL.B., Columbia, 1917; m. Dorothea Hall, Apr. 29, 1924; 1 son, Clay Greer. Admitted to N.Y. bar, 1917, practiced in N.Y.C., 1919-59; mem. Beekman, Bogue, Stephens & Black, 1925-44; partner Satterlee, Warfield & Stephens, 1944-59; counsel numerous corp. re-orgns. and recapitalizations; director Am. Home Mag. Corp. Served on fgn. econ. adv. matters Dept. State, Washington, 1942-43. Trustee Am. Coll., Sofia, Bulgaria, Near E. Coll. Assn., Seamans Ho., N.Y.C. Served as seaman to ensign USNR, 1917-18. Mem. Am., N.Y. State bar assns., Assn. Bar City of N.Y., S.R. Episcopalian. Clubs: University (N.Y.C.); Racquet & Tennis. Home: New York City NY Died Nov. 1969.

STEPHENS, OREN MELSON, govt. ofcl.; b. Blevins, Ark., June 7, 1914; s. Phillip Herbert and Lottie (Melson) S.; student Henderson State Tchrs. Coll., 1932-33; B.A., U. Ark., 1936; Nieman fellow journalism, Harvard, 1942-43; diploma Nat. War Coll., 1953; m. Naomi Lorene Vinson, Aug. 8, 1936; 1 son, Stephen Vinson. Sunday editor, columnist Ark. Democrat, Little Rock, 1937-42; psychol. war rep. O.W.I., Africa and Asia, 1943-45; dir. information Stanford, 1945-46; West Coast editor Newsweek mag., 1946-48; editor Santa Rosa (Cal.) Evening Press, 1948-49; information exec. Dept. State. U.S. Information Agy., Washington, 1949-69, dep. asst. dir. policy and programs, 1954-56, planning dir., rep. planning bd. Nat. Security Council, 1956-58, dir. research and analysis, 1959-64, dir. research and reference service, 1964-65; asst. dir. U.S. Information Agy. (research), 1965-66; sr. research officer European Research Center U.S. Information Agy., Geneva, Switzerland, 1966-69, attache U.S. Mission Internat. Orgns., Geneva, 1966-69; faculty Nat. War Coll., 1953-54; alternate member President's Spl. Com. Disarmament, 1956. Mem. Am. and World Assns. Pub. Opinion Research, Soc. Nieman Fellows, Sigma Delta Chi. Meth. Clubs: American of Geneva (Switzerland); Internat. (Washington). Author: Facts to a Candid World; America's Overseas Information Program, 1955. Contbr. articles nat. mags., Home: Geneva Switzerland Died July 7, 1969.

STEPHENS, PHILIP B(LANTON), newspaper exec.; b. Columbia, Mo., Oct. 20, 1900; s. James L. and Martha Bell (Blanton) S.; student U. Mo., 1918-20; m. Margaret Louise Wassmer, Sept. 30, 1925; children—Cynthia, Susan. Various plant jobs E.W. Stephens Pub. Co., Columbia, 1915-20; reporter Cleveland Press, 1923; linotype operator, Govt. Printing Office, Washington, 1924-25; advt. mgr. Magnus Chem. Co., Garwood, N.J., 1927-28; advt. copywriter Vacuum Oil Co., N.Y. City, 1929; with N.Y. News, 1930-72, bus. mgr. 1946-54, gen. mgr., 1954-72; asst. sec., dir. News Syndicate Co., Inc., 1951-72; dir. Met. Sunday Group. Industry mem. newspaper panel War Labor Bd., 1944-45. Mem. Phi Delta Theta. Clubs: Union League, Cloud (N.Y. City); National Golf Links of America (Southampton, L.I.); Westhampton Beach (L.I.) Country. Home: New York City NY Died Apr. 1972.

STEPHENS, W(ILLIAM) BARCLAY, ophthalmologist, otologist; b. Paris, Ky., Jan. 4, 1869; s. Charles and Mary (Miller) S.; A.M., Georgetown College, 1890; LL.D., 1926; M.D., Coll. Physicians and Surgeons (Columbia), 1893; m. Louise Bruce, 1903; children—Bruce Miller, Elizabeth Woodford, Stuart Barclay. Began practice at San Francisco, 1893; pres. Alameda Sanatorium; now retired. Mem. A.M.A., State and County Med. Societies, Am. Bd. Otolaryngology, Am. Bd. Ophthalmology, Pacific Coast Oto-Opthal. Society, Am. Forestry Assn., Calif. Bot. Soc., Calif. Acad. Sciences (hon. curator horology), Boy Scouts Am. Republican. Baptist. Clubs: Encinal Yacht, Rotary, Commonwealth, Sierra. Address: 1250 Bay St., Alameda CA‡

STEPHENSON, GILBERT THOMAS, born in Pendleton, N.C., Dec. 17, 1884; s. James Henry and Susan Anna (Fleetwood) S.; grad. Severn (N.C.) High Sch., 1899; A.B., Wake Forest (N.C.) Coll., 1902, A.M., 1904; A.M., Harvard, 1906, LL.B., 1910; m. Grace Morris White, Dec. 19, 1912; children—Thomas Wilson, James Henry. Admitted to N.C. bar, 1910 and practiced at Winston-Salem, N.C., 1910-19; mem. firm Hastings, Stephenson and Whicker, Winston-Salem, N.C., 1916-19; successively sec., asst. trust officer, asso. trust officer, v.p. Wachovia Bank & Trust Company of North Carolina, 1919-29; vice pres. in charge trust dept., Equitable Trust Co., Wilmington, Del., 1929-36, dir., 1929-51; mem. faculty Grad. Sch. of Banking, Am. Bankers Assn., N.Y., 1935-72, dir. trust research dept., 1937-51; mem. firm T.B. Stephenson & Sons, farmers, Pendleton, N.C., 1914-72; dir. Planters Nat. Bank & Trust Co., Rocky Mount, N.C.; lectr. law sch. Wake Forest Coll., 1951-72. Pres. trust div. Am. Bankers Assn., 1930-31; Dem. Baptist. Clubs: Quill and Grill; Ruritan (Pendleton-Severn, N.C.). Author of numerous books relating to field: latest publs.: Estates and Trusts, 1949; Studies in Trust Business (4th series), 1950; Your Estate and Your Family, 1951; Drafting Wills and Trust Agreements, Adminstrative Provisions, 1952. Address: Pendleton NC Died June 1972; interred Warren Place, Pendleton CA

STEPHENSON, HENRY THEW, univ. prof.; b. Cincinnati, April 22, 1870; s. Reuben Henry and Louisa (Wright) S.; B.S., Ohio State U., 1894; A.B., Harvard, 1898; M.A., Ind. U., 1911; m. Agnes Reynolds, Nov. 28, 1900 (died Feb. 24, 1931); 1 dau., Margaret Louise. Instructor, 1895-1900, asst. prof. English, 1900-08, asso. prof., 1908, prof. and head of department of English, 1919-—, Ind. Univ. Author: Patroon Van Volkenberg, 1901; The Fickle Wheel, 1901; Shakespeare's London, 1905; The Elizabethan People, 1909; A Handbook of Shakespeare, 1914; The Goldenrod (novel), 1918; The Ettrick Shepherd, a biography, 1923; Narrative Writing, 1929; The Mystery of the Murdered Bridegroom, 1931; also various mag. articles. Home: Bloomington IN‡

STEPHENSON, WENDELL HOLMES, educator; born at Cartersburg, Ind., Mar. 13, 1899; s. Robert Wans and Virginia (Rupe) S.; student Earlham Coll., 1916-17; A.B., Indiana U., 1923, A.M., 1924; Ph.D., U. Mich., 1928; Litt.D. (hon.), Duke U., 1950; LL.D., U.N.C., 1953; m. Hilda Huff Voyles, Aug. 31, 1924; 1 son, Lamar. Teacher in grade school, Plainfield, Ind., 1917-18; prin. Fairwood (Ind.) Grade Sch., 1918-19; prin. Clayton (Ind.) High Sch., 1919-21; instr. in history and polit. science, U. of Ky., 1924-25, asst. prof., 1925-26, professor of history, 1945-46; editor University of Kentucky Press, 1945-1946; asso. prof. of Am. History, Louisiana State University, 1927-32, prof., 1932-45, Walter Lynwood Fleming lectr. So. history, 1955, dean College of Arts and Sciences, 1941-44 (leave of absence with research grant from General Education Bd., 1944-45); prof. Southern history, chairman Division of Social Sciences, Tulane University, 1946-53; professor of history University Oregon, from 1953, special assistant to the president, from 1965; Fulbright professor of Am. history U. Southampton, 1959-60; tchr. summer scis., Ind. U., 1931, Duke, 1939-40; visiting prof. of Am. History, U. of Birmingham (Eng.), fall 1950; vis. prof. American history and instrns. Indian School Internat. Studies. New Delhi, India, 1962; lectr. Am. Studies Workshop, Mussorie, India, 1963. Carl Braun fellow in hist., U. of Mich., 1926-27. Member committee on grants of Hayes Foundation, 1939-42. Member Southern Historical Association (vice president, 1943, president 1944; member exec. council 1935-41 and 1943-47), Agrl. History Soc. (mem. exec. com., 1937-43, pres. 1940-41), Am. Hist. Assn., Miss. Valley Hist. Assn. (exec. com. 1941-44, 46-53, pres. 1957-58), La. Hist. Soc., Kan. State Historical Soc. (hon.), Am. Assn. Univ. Profs., Phi Beta Kappa, Phi Gamma Mu, Phi Delta Kappa, Omicron Delta Kappa, Phi Kappa Phi. Soc. Friends. Author: The Political Career of General James H. Lane, 1930; Alexander Porter, Whig Planter of Old Louisiana, 1934; Isaac Franklin, Slave Trade and Planter of the Old South, 1938; A Basic History of the Old South, published 1959. Editor of Journal of Southern History, 1935-41; editorial asso., 1942; member bd. editors, 1943-46; mng. editor Miss. Valley Hist. Review, 1946-53; (with C. W. Ramsdell and E. M. Coulter), A History of the South (10 volumnes), since 1938; (with Fred C. Cole) Southern Biography Series, 1939-46; The South Lives in History 1955; Southern History in the Making, pub., 1964. Contbr.: Dictionary Am. Biography, Dictionary Am. History, also hist. jours. Home: Eugene OR Died Apr. 14, 1970; buried Rest Haven Park, Eugene OR

STEPHENSON, WILLIAM PRETTYMAN, lawyer; b. Bentonville, O., July 31, 1868; s. Robert Amasa and Arcada (Hopkins) S.; student North Liberty (O.) Acad., 1890-91; LL.D., Cincinnati Law Sch., 1895; m. Stella M. Shriver, Mar. 14, 1893; 1 son, Sherwood Cummings. Admitted to Ohio bar, 1895; in practice, 1895-1906; pros. atty. Adams County, 1906-10; common pleas judge, 1915-32; judge (by apptd.) Supreme Court of Ohio Feb. 9 to Nov. election, 1932, when elected to fill unexpired term (ending Jan. 1, 1937) of Judge Robinson. Special counsel in office of Herbert S. Duffy, atty. general of Ohio, since Jan. 11, 1938. Mem. Am. and Ohio State bar assns., Delta Theta Phi. Democrat. Presbyterian. Mason. K.P., Elk, Odd Fellow, Eagle, Red Man. Clubs: Duckworth (Cincinnati); Izaak Walton (West Union); Athletic (Columbus). Author: Let's Go to Court, 1934. Home: 125 Clinton Heights, Columbus OH*‡

STERLING, BRUCE F., congressman; b. Masontown, Fayette Co., Pa., Sept. 28, 1870; ed. California (Pa.) State Normal Sch., Waynesburg (Pa.) Coll., and U. of W.Va.; m. May Conner, Dec. 14, 1899. Admitted to Pa. bar, 1895; now mem. firm Sterling, Higbee & Matthews, Uniontown, Pa.; mem. Pa. Ho. of Rep., 1907, 08; del. Dem. Nat. Conv., Baltimore, 1912; mem. 65th Congress (1917-19), 23d Pa. Dist. Home: Uniontown PA‡

STERLING, GEORGE MATHLESON, lawyer, judge; b. Xenia, O., May 7, 1910; s. James R. and Isobella (Mathieson) S.; pvt. study; m. Ruby Belle Trotter, Nov. 24, 1938; children—Karen, Ann, George Mathieson. Admitted to Ariz. bar, 1932; practiced in Phoenix, 1932-42, 45-61; judge Superior Ct., Maricopa County, Ariz., 1961-67. Served with USAAF, 1942-44. Mem. Am. Judicature Soc., Am. Legion, Am-vets. Mason (Shriner), Moose. Club: Arizona. Home: Phoenix AZPresbyn. Died Oct. 22, 1967; buried Greenwood Meml. Park Phoenix AZ

STERLING, GRAHAM LEE, lawyer; b. Poughkeepsie, N.Y., Apr. 30, 1904; s. Graham Lee and Mary Florence (Tousey) S.; student Phillips-Exeter Acad.; A.B., Williams Coll., 1925; LL.B., Harvard, 1928; m. Helen Robinson Davis, 1926 (div. 1938); children—Sally Lee (Mrs. Craig R. Norton), Graham Lee III; m. 2d, Margaret Lucy Burrall, Nov. 2, 1945. Admitted to Cal. bar, 1929; asso. O'Melveny & Myers, and predecessor firms, Los Angeles, 1928-42, 44-72, partner, 1932-52. Vice pres., gen. counsel, dir. indsl. relations Northrop Aircraft, Inc., 1942-44; dir. Hunt Foods & Industries, Inc., Jeffries Banknote Co., Nat. Theatres, Inc., Packard-Bell Electronics Corp., Suburban Gas Service, Inc. Mem. Cal. Com. Bar Examiners, 1948-53. Trustee Occidental Coll., Los Angeles. Mem. State Bar of Cal. (bd. govs. 1956-59, pres. 1958-59), Am., Los Angeles bar assns., Delta Kappa Epsilon. Club: California (Los Angeles). Author: (with Ballantine) California Corporation Laws, 1949. Home: Los Angeles CA Died Aug. 28, 1972.

STERN, BILL, sports dir.; b. Rochester, N.Y., July 1, 1907; s. Isaac and Lena (Reis) S.; student Hackley Preparatory Sch., Tarrytown, N.Y., 1925; B.S., Pa. Mil. Coll., Chester, Pa., 1930; m. Harriet May, Apr. 29, 1937; children—Peter, Mary, Patricia. Stage mgr. Roxy Theatre, N.Y.C., 1930-31; stage mgr. Music Hall, N.Y. City, 1932-35; sports announcer N.B.C., 1935-39, sports dir. MBS, 1940-71. Recipient Citation of Merit by Nat. Exchange Club for efforts toward curbing juvenile delinquency and youth crime, 1958. Mem. Sports Broadcasters Assn. (past pres.), Clubs: Century Country (White Plains, N.Y.). Selected by Nation's Radio Editors as Most Popular Sports Announcer in U.S., annually, 1939-71. Home: Port Chester NY Died Nov. 19, 1971.

STERN, HORACE, judge; b. Phila., Pa., Aug. 7, 1878; s. Morris and Matilda (Bamberger) S.; A.B., Central High Sch., Phila., 1895; B.S., U. of Pa., 1899, LL.B., summa cum laude, 1902, LL.D., 1933; Hahnemann Med. Coll., 1937 D.H.L., Dropsie Coll. Hebrew and Cognate Langs., 1948, Jewish Theological Seminary of America, 1956; LL.D., Pa. Mil. Coll., 1953, Temple University, 1954, Lafayette College, 1955, Villanova University, 1956; married Henrietta Pfaelzer, Feb. 12, 1906; 1 dau., Sophie S. (Mrs. Henry J. Friendly). Admitted to Pa. bar, 1902, practicing in Phila.; mem. Stern & Wolf, 1903-20; apptd. judge Court of Common Pleas, by Gov. Sproul, 1920, and elected to same office, 1922, term of 10 yrs.; pres. judge, 1924, reelected, 1932, term of 10 yrs.; elected justice Pa. Supreme Court, term 21 yrs., 1935; chief justice Supreme Court of Pa., 1952-56; lecturer University of Pennsylvania Law School, 1902-17; Trustee Dropsie College (vice president), University of Pennsylvania, Jewish Pub. Soc. Am. (v.p.); dir. Federation Jewish Charities of Phila. (honorary president). Maj. Ordnance Dept., U.S. Army, 1918-19. Mem. Am. Bar Assn., Pa. Bar Assn., Bar Assn. of Phila., Am. Judicature Soc., Am. Law Inst., Am. Acad. Polit. and Social Science, Hist. Soc. of Pa., Acad. Natural Sciences of Phila., Pennsylvania Society, Am. Jewish Hist. Soc., Am. Legion, Phi Beta Kappa, Beta Gamma Sigma, Order of the Coif. Republican. Mason. Clubs: Lawyers, Contemporary, Midday, Philobiblon, Univ. Home: Philadelphia PA Died Apr. 14, 1969.

STERN, JOSEPH SMITH, shoe mfg. exec.; b. Cin., Sept. 10, 1891; s. David Ralph and Fannie (Smith) S.; A.B., Cornell U., 1913; m. Miriam Haas, June 5, 1916; children—Joseph Smith, Robert D., Mary Ann (Mrs. David Simon). With Stern-Auer Co., 1913-35, dir., 1916-35, pres., 1921-35; partner mail order companies Fashion Wear Shirts, Crane Kent Clothes, Style Arch Shoes, 1921-28; joined U.S. Shoe Corp., Cin., 1931, became dir., 1931, pres., 1931-39, chairman of board, 1949-65 chairman executive committee, from 1965; bd. of dirs. Joyce Shoe Company, Wm. Hahn Sons Company. Member of the shoe adv. com., World War II; adv. com. Community Chest, nat. A.R.C., Sister Kenney Found. Trustee University Sch., Cin., Jewish Hosp. Assn. (also vice chmn.); chmn. May Inst. Med. Research. Mem. Nat. Shoe Mfrs. Assn. (pres.), Nat. Shoe Inst. (chmn.), Mid-West Shoe Fair Assn. (vice chmn.), Cin. C. of C. Jewish. Mason (32 deg.). Clubs: Rotary, Losantiville Cincinnati OH Died May 1971.

STERN, JULIUS DAVID, editor, pub.; Phila., Pa., Apr. 1, 1886; s. David and Sophie (Muhr) S.; grad. William Penn Charter School, Philadelphia, 1902; A.B., University of Pennsylvania, 1906, LL.B., 1909; m. Juliet Lit, Nov. 22, 1908; children—David III, Jill, Meredith, Jonathan. Reporter Phila. Public Ledger, 1908; gen. mgr. Providence (R.I.) News, 1911; purchased New Brunswick (N.J.) Times, 1912, Springfield (Ill.) News, 1914, Springfield Record, 1915, Camden (N.J.) Evening Courier, 1919, Camden Morning Post, 1926, and the Philadelphia Record, 1928; pub. New York Post, 1933-39; suspended publn. of all newspapers, Feb. 1, 1947. Clubs: Manhattan Chess, Lotos, Overseas Press (N.Y.C.). Author: Ediolon (philos. novel), 1952; Memoirs of A Maverick Publisher (autobiography), 1962. Home: Palm Beach FL Died Oct. 10, 1971.

STERN, LOUIS, stock broker; b. Newark, Feb. 29, 1904; s. Joseph and Fannie (Tenzer) S.; B.S. in Econs., U. Pa., 1924; Ph.D. in Chemistry; m. Francis Baum, Mar. 7, 1929; 1 son, Robert L. Partner Stern Bros., N.Y.C.; dean Oakland U., Rochester, Mich.; mem. N.Y. Stock Exchange. Pres. Jewish Community Council Essex County, N.J., 1952-55, Council Jewish Fedns. and Welfare Funds, N.Y.C., 1962-64; pres. Nat. Jewish Welfare Bd., N.Y.C., 1965-69. Home: South Orange NJ Died Nov. 11, 1972.

STERN, WILLIAM BERNHARD, librarian; b. Wurzburg, Germany, Mar. 10, 1912; Dr. Jur., Julius Maximilian U., 1933; m. Ruth H. Yarnell. Cataloger U. Chgo. Law Sch., 1937-39; fgn. law librarian, head cataloger Los Angeles County Law Library, 1939-45, fgn. law librarian, from 1945. Mem. Internat. Assn. Law Libraries (pres. 1962-65), Am. Assn. Law Libraries (chmn. com. fgn. law indexing from 1960, pres. 1969-70), Internat. Law Assn., Sierra Club, Am. Fgn. Law Assn. Editor Law Library Jour., 1953-54. Office: Los Angeles CA

STERNBERGER, MRS. ESTELLE MILLER, b. Cincinnati, O.; d. Abraham and Hannah (Greeble) Miller; student U. of Cincinnati, 1907-11, Community Sch. of Jewish Philanthropy, Cincinnati, 1907-14; married; 1 dau., Minnette Cathryn (wife of Dr. Jacob Easton Holzman). Engaged in vol. assn. work, Cincinnati, 1905-19; spl. lecturer for business women, Cincinnati, under auspices Federal Edn. Com., 1916-18; executive secretary National Council of Jewish Women, 1920-32; first vice-pres. National Council of Women of U.S.; mem. exec. com. Progressive City Com., 1937; internat. sec. World Orgn. of Jewish Women (1923-32); sec. Conf. Com. of Nat. Jewish Women's Orgns., 1923-33; mem. exec. com. Nat. Conf. of Jews and Christians; chmn. Good Neighbor League, 1936-37; founder Children for Israel, Incorporated. Mem. board of directors World Peaceways since 1931. Editor of The Jewish Woman, 1921-32, The Woman's Review, 1932-40. Trustee Bethune-Cookman Coll., Daytona Beach, Fla.; mem. com. A Living Mus. of Cities in Evolution. Received first award of Albert Einstein Foundation, for Goodwill and Internat. Peace, 1936. Mem. League of Am. Penwomen, Am. Women's Assn. of N.Y. City. Jewish religion. Club: Women's City. Author: The Supreme Cause, 1936. Contbr. to publications. Radio commentator. Home: New York City NY Died Dec. 23, 1971.

STERNE, THEODORE EUGENE, physicist; b. N.Y.C., Nov. 23, 1907; s. Eugene Washington and Dora (Kohn) S.; B.Sc., Princeton, 1928; Ph.D., Trinity Coll., Cambridge U., 1931; NRC fellow physics, Harvard and Mass. Inst. of Tech., 1931-33; M.A., Harvard, 1956; m. Grace Isabel DeRoo, Aug. 5, 1932; children—Theodore Drummond, John Robert; m. 2d Lois Cremins Isenberg, on Nov. 28, 1964. Research asso. Harvard Obs., 1933-34, astronomer, 1934-41, lecturer astrophysics, tutor Harvard, 1934-41, Simon Newcomb professor astrophysics, 1956-59; chief ballistician Ballistic Research Labs., Aberdeen Proving Ground, Md., 1946-56, chief spl. prob. br., 1941-45, comptng. lab., 1945-47, 52-53, term. ballistic lab., 1946-52, sci. adviser to dir., 1953-56; cons. operations research office Johns Hopkins, 1954-59; staff mem. Research Analysis Corp., 1961-65, Inst. Def. Analyses, Arlington, Va., 1965-70. Asso. director Astrophys. Obs., Smithsonian Instn., 1956-59; staff member of Johns Hopkins University Operations Research Office, Bethesda, Maryland, 1959-61, acting chief Air Def. division, 1960-61. Served from first lieut. to lieut. col., F.A., Ordnance Corps, AUS, 1941-46; col. Res. Fellow Am. Acad. Arts and Scis., A.A.A.S., Am. Physics Soc., Royal Astron. Soc.; mem. Am. Astron. Soc., Astron. Society of Pacific Operations Research Society of America, Cat Fanciers of Washington (pres. 1966-67), also Phi Beta Kappa, Sigma Xi. Club: Cosmos (Washington). Author: Introduction to Celestial Mechanics, 1960. Contbr.

articles sci. jours., govt. publs. Home: Chevy Chase MD Died Feb. 6, 1970; buried Arlington Nat. Cemetery, Arlington VA

STERNHELL, CHARLES MAX, life ins. co. exec.; b. Bklyn., Dec. 6, 1915; s. Maurice Louis and Freda (Haas) S.; B.Sc. cum laude, City Coll. N.Y., 1936; m. Mabel Lyons, Oct. 11, 1941; children—Susan Gale, Richard Michael, Amy Marcia. Actuarial research Met. Life Ins. Co., 1936-51; with N.Y. Life Ins. Company, 1951-71, 2d v.p., actuary, 1957-60, v.p., actuary, 1960-67, sr. v.p. planning and development, 1967-69, executive vice president of co., 1969-71; pres. N.Y. Life Fund, 1970-71; developed actuarial principles for variable life ins. Sec. indsl. actuarial adv. com. that devel. 1958 commnrs. standard ordinary mortality table. Civilian scientist operations research group, U.S. Navy, 1943-45. Fellow Society Actuaries (bd. govs. 1963-66, 69-71); mem. Internat. Congress Actuaries, Am. Acad. Actuaries, Operations Research Soc. Am., Am. Statis. Assn., Actuaries Club N.Y. (chmn. 1959-60), Sr. Actuaries Club, Phi Beta Kappa. Author articles profl. jours. Home: Lynbrook NY Died Aug. 31, 1971.

STEVENOT, FRED GABRIEL;, b. Oakland, Calif., Aug. 15, 1877; s. Emile K. and Sara (Stephens) S.; ed. pub. sch., high sch. and private instruction in engring.; m. Adeline J. DeLuca, June 5, 1907; children—Eileen M., Edward W., Helen M. Mining and engring. work, 1898; engr. Bay Counties Power Co., 1899-1902; dir. natural resources State of Calif., 1927-31; state R.R. commr. State of Calif., 1931-33; v.p. Bank of America, 1934-42; pres. Bank America Co. 1937-40, Puget Sound Pulp and Timber Co. since 1942. Home: 162 Alhambra St. Office: 300 Montgomery St., San Francisco CA‡

STEVENS, ALDEN, writer, assn. exec.; b. Chgo., July 1, 1907; s. Thomas Wood and Helen (Bradshaw) S.; B.S., U. Chgo., 1931; m. Marion Groezinger, Dec. 16, 1935; 1 dau., Dinah Elizabeth. Ednl. mus. exhibits designer Nat. Park Service, 1935-38; writer TV shows for Omnibus, Adventure, Wide Wide World, other series; designed exhibits for Am. Mus. of Immigration to be located at Statue of Liberty; sec. Assn. Am. Indian Affairs, N.Y.C., 1943-63, pres., 1964-68; pres. Alden Stevens Assos., Inc. Dir. Mobil Travel Guide, 1957-68. Club: Players (N.Y.C.). Author: Dove Creek Rodeo, 1936; Arms and the People, 1942; (with Roger Burlingame) Victory Without Peace, 1944; (with Marion Stevens) The Stevens America, 1950. Contbr. articles nat. mags. Home: Montclair NJ Died Apr. 28, 1968; cremated.

STEVENS, ALEXANDER RAYMOND, physician; b. Baltimore, May 9, 1876; s. George O. and Rebecca R. (Tibbetts) S.; A.B., Johns Hopkins, 1896, M.D., 1903; m. Mary Lane Davis, Oct. 25, 1919; 1 son, Alexander Raymond. Intern Johns Hopkins Hosp. (Baltimore) and Presbyn. Hosp. (N.Y. City), in practice in N.Y. City from 1909; mem. vis. staff Bellevue Hosp., 1909-37, attending surgeon in charge urol. dept., 1923-37; attending surgeon New York Hosp., also prof. urology Cornell U. Med. Sch., 1935-46; cons. urologist Bellevue, St. Vincent's, Beckman, St. Mary Immaculate (Jamaica), Tarrytown, Englewood, Stamford and Sharon hosps. Served as capt. to maj., Med. Corps, U.S. Army, France, 1917-19. Fellow A.C.S.; mem. A.M.A., Am. Urol. Assn., N.Y. Acad. Medicine. Club: Century (N.Y. City). Contbr. articles and chpts. on urologic surgery to med. publs. Home: Alstead NH Died June 1968.*

STEVENS, ANNA C. MANN (MRS. FRANK JAY STEVENS), club woman; b. Troy, N.Y., Jan. 7, 1889; d. Herbert Roome and Adelaide (Spicer) Mann; grad. pvt. sch.; m. Frank Jay Stevens, Dec. 13, 1913. Treas. Isolantite Manufacturing Corp. Pres. Missionary Ridge Garden Club, Chattanooga, 1941-43, treas., 1945-47, founder A.R.C. chpt. club, 1941; treas. Council Garden Clubs, Chattanooga, 1944. Mem. Am. Rose Soc., Hort. Soc. N.Y. Clubs: Towne, Fortnightly. Home: Summit NJ Died May 6, 1969.

STEVENS, DON ALBERT, grain exec.; b. Crary, N.D., July 15, 1903; s. Fred Ray and Rose (Southam) S.; student San Diego Army and Navy Acad., 1919-21, U. N.D., 1921-24; m. Dorothy Cutler, Oct. 23, 1926; children—Donna Marie, Joan Maxene, Kathryn Alayne. Crop reporter, grain buyer Washburn Crosby Co., 1924-28; with Gen. Mills, Inc., Minneapolis, from 1938, v.p., dir. grain operations, 1949-52, v.p., dir., from 1952, also gen. mgr. flour div.; dir. First National Bank of Minneapolis. Mem. National Agrl. Adv. Commn. Mem. Sigma Nu. Club: Minneapolis. Home: Minneapolis MN

STEVENS, ELLEN YALE, educator; b. Saratoga Springs, N.Y.; d. Edward Robbins and Catherine (Yale) S.; diploma. Teachers Coll. (Columbia), 1893; Ph.B., U. of Chicago, 1900; unmarried. Prin. Brooklyn Heights Sem., 1903-18. Presbyn. Mem. Assn. Collegiate Alumnae. Clubs: Head Mistresses, Women's University. Author: A Guide to the Montessori Method, 1913. Editor Montessori dept. McClure's Mag., Feb.-Aug. 1913. Contbr. to mags. on ednl. subjects. Home: Bellport, L.I. Office: 24 Columbia Heights, Brooklyn NY‡

STEVENS, ELMER T., merchant; b. Avon, Ill.; s. Charles A. and Fannie Stevens; m. Harriet Straight, May 3, 1930; children—Katherine Fannie, Carol Alta, Gail Thompkins. Chmn., dir. Charles A. Stevens & Co.; dir. Wilson & Co. Trustee Northwestern U. Home: Chicago IL Died Dec. 14, 1968; buried Delavan WI

STEVENS, ERNEST JAMES, hotel mgr.; b. Colchester, Ill., Feb. 13, 1884; s. James William and Jessie Louise (Smith) S.; Ph.B., U. of Chicago, 1904; LL.B., Northwestern U., 1907; m. Elizabeth Street, of Michigan City, Ind., Apr. 17, 1907; children—Ernest, Richard James, Wm. K., John Paul. With Ill. Life Ins. Co., 1904-07; admitted to Ill. bar, 1907; pres. and mgr. Hotel La Salle Co.; pres. Stevens Hotel Co.; dir. Ill. Life Ins. Co., Charles A. Stevens & Bros., Stevens Brothers Corp., Congress Trust & Savings Bank. Mem. Chicago Bar Assn., Psi Upsilon, Phi Delta Phi. Republican. Presbyn. Mason. Clubs: Union League, Quadrangle, Chicago Athletic, South Shore Country, Chikaming Country. Home: Chicago IL Died Feb. 1972.

STEVENS, EVERETT DUNCAN, elec. engr.; b. Goldsboro, N.C., Feb. 13, 1920; s. David Edgar and Stella (Benton) S.; student Wake Forest Coll., 1936-37, Mercer U., 1946; B.S., N.C. State U., 1950; m. Alma Ruth Jones, Nov. 28, 1940; children—Terell Everett, Nancy Lee. Equipment technician Western Electric Co., Raleigh, Charlotte N.C. and Charleston, S.C., 1938-43; indsl. sales mgr. Carolina Power & Light Co., Raleigh. Engring cons. to pvt. cons. firms. Vice chmn. Indsl. Sales Com., Southeastern Elec. Exchange, Indsl. Group, Edison Electric Inst. Mayor, Vetville, N.C., 1948-50. Mem. Rex. Hosp. Found. Served with USNR, 1944-45; ETO. Registered profl. engr., N.C. Mem. N.C. Soc. Engrs. (past pres., dir.), Profl. Engrs., N.C., Nat. Soc. Profl. Engrs., Raleigh C. of C., N.C. State U. Alumni Assn. (dir. 1966-69, pres. Wake County chpt. 1959). Democrat. Methodist (edn. commn.). Kiwanian. Club: Raleigh Engineers, Raleigh City, MacGregor Downs County. Research elec. power applications in industry. Home: Raleigh NC Died Jan. 17, 1969; buried Raleigh Meml. Park Raleigh NC

STEVENS, FRANCIS BOWDEN, writer, columnist; b. Norwich, N.Y., Apr. 6, 1905; A.B., Union Coll., 1926; student U. of Berlin, 1926-27, U. of Geneva, 1927, University of Besancon, summer 1927; LL.D. (honorary), Union College, 1951; 1 son, Nicholas B. Clerk, Am. consulate gen., later vice consul, Prague, 1931-32; vice consul. Warsaw, 1933; vice consul and language officer, Paris, 1934; 3d sec., Riga, 1935, Pretoria, 1936; Dept. of State, 1939; 2d sec. and vice consul Moscow, 1942; asst. chief Division of Eastern European Affair, Dept. of State, 1945-47, chief 1947-48; chief Spl. Research Div., Office of U.S. High Commr. for Germany, Frankfurt-on-Main, 1949-52; spl. asst. to dir. Office Eastern European Affairs, Dept. State, 1952-55, dir., 1955-56; dep. chief Mission, Tehran, 1956-57; ret., 1957; staff mem. Pres.' Com. on Internat. Information Activities, 1953; sr. editor U.S. Joint Pubs. Research Service, 1957-58; tour div. for Soviet delegations visiting U.S., 1958-59; mem. nat. staff U.S. News & World Report, 1959-71. Home: Washington DC Died Nov. 1971.

STEVENS, FRANK JAY, ceramic co. exec.; b. South Easton, N.Y., Apr. 27, 1890; s. Daniel B. and Eliza (Eddy) S.; E.E., Rennsselaer Poly. Inst., 1913; m. Anna C. Mann, Dec. 13, 1913. Jr. engr. Pub. Service Commn., N.Y.C., 1913-16; prodn. mgr., supt. Locke Insulator Co., Balt., 1916-27; asst. gen. mgr. Isolantite Co. of Am., Belleville, N.J., 1927-31; dir., v.p. engring. Am. Lava Corp., Chattanooga, 1931-45; v.p. D.M. Stewart Co., Chattanooga, 1945-47; pres., dir. Isolantite Mfg. Corp., Stirling, N.J., 1948-70. Registered profl. engr., N.J. Fellow I.E.E.E. (chmn. East Tenn. sect. 1943-44), A.A.A.S.; mem. Am. Ceramic Soc., Inst. Ceramic Engrs., Ceramic Association of New Jersey. Episcopalian. Mason. Research on antenna insulation for broadcasting transmitters. Originator high speed automatic pressing of steatite insulators. Home: Summit NJ Died June 29, 1970.

STEVENS, HENRY LEONIDAS, JR., judge; b. Warsaw, N.C., Jan. 27, 1896; s. Henry Leonidas and Fannie (Walker) S.; grad. Porter Mil. Acad., Charleston, S.C., 1913; student U. of N.C., 1913-17, Harvard Law Sch., 1919-20; m. Mildred Anderson Beasley, June 21, 1922; 1 son, Henry Leonidas III. Admitted to N.C. bar, 1921; jr. mem. Stevens, Beasley & Stevens, 1921-27; mem. Beasley & Stevens since 1927. Judge county ct., 1929-31; nat. comdr. Am. Legion, 1931-32; pres. Am. Legion Pub. Co., 1931-32, now dir.; judge of Superior Court of N.C. (resident judge 4th Jud. Dist.), 1938-62, emergency judge N.C. for life, 1963-71. Served as lt. World War; in action St. Die sector and Meuse-Argonne; now lieut. colonel of Specialist Reserve. Mem. Golden Fleece, Phi Delta Phi, Kappa Sigma, La Societe des Quarante Hommes et Huit Chevaux, Society of the Cincinnati. Comdr. Legion of Honor (France); N.C. Mil. D.S.M., 1971; brevet col. N.C. N.G., 1971; hon. chief Blackfeet Indians. Democrat Presbyn. (elder). Mason, Jr. Order United Am. Mechanics. Clubs: Army and Navy (Washington, D.C.); Indianapolis Athletic; Harvard of N.C. Home: Warsaw NC Died Aug. 5, 1971; buried Devotional Gardens, Warsaw NC

STEVENS, HOWARD EVELETH, civil engr.; b. Bluehill, Me., Mar. 8, 1874; B.C.E., U. of Me., 1897. With N.P. Ry. since 1904, successively inspr., draftsman, asst. engr., bridge engr., and chief engr., now v.p. in charge of operation and maintenance. Home: 725 Linwood Place. Office: Fifth and Jackson Sts., St Paul MN*‡

STEVENS, INGER, actress; b. Stockholm, Sweden; student drama, N.Y.C., divorced. Fist performances in little theatres and summer stock, also TV, motion pictures include Man on Fire, Cry Terror, The Buccaneer, Five Branded Women, The New Interns, The Long Ride Home, The Borgia Stick, A Guide For the Married Man, Firecreek; TV appearances in Route 66, Adventures in Paradise, Playhouse 90, Studio One, Philco Playhouse, Kraft Theatre, others; formerly feature actress in TV series Farmer's Daughter; starred on Broadway in Debut, Roman Candle, Mary Mary. Chmn. Cal. Council Retarded Children. Recipient Fgn. Press TV award, Emmy award. Address: Beverly Hills CA Died May 1970.

STEVENS, JAMES FLOYD, author; b. Albia, Ia., Nov. 15, 1892; s. Hague Augustus and Octavia (Turner) S.; ed. pub. schs.; Litt.D. (hon.), Pacific University, 1958; m. Theresa Seitz Fitzgerald, July 11, 1929. Began writing for publication, 1924. Member Cultural Arts directors Century 21 Exposition for the Seattle 1962-63 World's Fair. Public relations counsel, West Coast Lumbermen's Assn., ret.; member board of trustees Keep Washington Green Assn., Washington Foresty Conference; pub. relations chmn. Wash.-No. Ida., Seattle-King County Council Chs. Pvt. corpl. and sergt., Co. D., 162d Infantry, United States Army, 1917-19; in France 14 months. Mem. Am. Soc. Foresters, Am. Legion, American Forestry Association, and U. Wash. Foresters Alumni Association (honorary life mem.). Democrat. Congregationalist. Club: Seattle Free Lancers. Author: Paul Bunyan, 1925; Brawnyman, 1926; Mattock, 1927; Homer in the Sagebrush, 1928; Saginaw Paul Bunyan, 1932; Timber Seattle WA Died Dec. 31, 1971; buried Lakeview Cemetery Seattle WA

STEVENS, LAWRENCE M., business exec. Partner, Hornblower and Weeks-Hamphill, Noyes, Phila. Dir. Moore Products, Inc., Capitol Products Corp. Died Dec. 31, 1969.

STEVENS, LEITH, composer, conductor; b. Mt. Moriah, Mo., Sept. 13, 1909; s. Andrew and Elizabeth (Wooderson) S.; grad. Horner Inst. Music, Kansas City, Mo., 1927; student Juilliard Mus. Found., 1928-30; m. Mary McCoy, Oct. 3, 1930 (div. 1944); m. 2d, Peggy Joan McCartney, Dec. 15, 1945 (div. 1954); m. 3d, Elizabeth Struan Hughes, Dec. 17, 1955 (dec. 1970). Concert pianist, accompanist, 1923-29; composer, condr. arranger CBS, N.Y.C., 1930-40, Hollywood, 1939—; with OWI, 1942; dir. Radio Sydney, Australia, 1942-45; composer, condr. Alice in Wonderland, John Brown's Body, No Help Wanted, story of FBI (for BBC), Edward G. Robinson series, 1939-41, Ford Sunday Evening Hour, 1940, Free Company, 1941, Lionel Barrymore series, 1942, Abbott and Costello series, 1942, Dr. Fights series, Request Performance series, 1945, Acad. Award radio series and Dick Powell series, 1946; prod. Rise Stevens series, 1945; composed and conducted numerous motion picture scores, including Syncopation, All My Sons, Night Song, Destination Moon, The Wild One, Five Pennies, The Interns, New Kind of Love; composed and conducted television series including Ann Southern, 1958, Michael Shane, 1960, Dante in 1960, Mr. Novak, 1963, 1964, also numerous individual programs in TV series, among them Hotel de Paree, Cheyenne, Twilight Zone, Climax, Shower of Stars, Gunsmoke, Have Gun Will Travel, Dick Powell Theatre, Empire, Untouchables, Rawhide, Daniel Boone, Lost in Space, Voyage to the Bottom of the Sea, Long Hot Summer, Jesse James, Lancer, Custer, Land of the Giants, Judd for the Defense. Tchr. film scoring and film scoring workshop U. Cal. extension dept., Los Angeles, from 1960; mus. dir. Paramount TV, 1969. Mem. nat. adv. council Inst. Studies Am. Music, U. Mo. Nominated for Acad. Award for song, Julie, 1956, for scoring of musical picture, Five Pennies, 1959, scoring of musical picture New King of Love, 1963. Mem. Composers and Lyricists Guild Am. (pres. 1954-62). Club: Racquet (Palm Springs, Cal.) Author: Film Scoring, 1963. Home: Mountain Center CA Died July 23, 1970.

STEVENS, MILTON J., mfg. co. exec.; b. Chgo., 1913; ed. Northwestern U.; m. Marylyn Stevens; children—Joyce (Mrs. Rimer), Gayle (Mrs. Gorman), April, Nick Barbaro (step-son). Chmn. bd., chief exec. officer Republican-Transcon Industries, Inc.; chmn. pres., chief exec. officer Briggs Mfg. Co., Detroit; chmn. exec. com., dir. Chevron Water Heater Corp.; chmn. bd. Texlite, Inc., Fowler Mfg. Co., Republic Air-Conditioning Co., Republic-Odin Appliance Corp., Mathes Air Conditioning Co; dir. Western Auto Stores. Home: Dallas TX Died Nov. 1969; buried Rosemont Park, Chicago IL*

STEVENS, ROBERT SPROULE, educator; b. Attica, N.Y., May 29, 1888; s. Frederick C. and Isabel C. (Sproule) S.; A.B., Harvard, 1910, LL.B., 1913; m.

Pauline Croll, Aug. 16, 1922 (dec.); 1 son, Robert Croll; m. 2d, Eva Howe, March 30, 1940. Admitted to N.Y. bar, 1913, and practiced at Buffalo; with Rogers, Locke, & Bancock, 1913-16; mem. Stevens & Reynolds, 1916-17; lecturer Cornell Law Sch., 1919-21, prof. law, 1921-54, emeritus, 1954-68, acting dean, 1930, 34, dean 1937-54. N.Y. commr. Nat. Conference on Uniform State Laws, 1926-48; spl. asst. to U.S. atty. gen., 1935; spl. consultant to N.Y. State Law Revision Com., 1936; asst. gen. counsel Office of Lend Lease Adminstrn., 1942-43, Fgn. Econ. Adminstrn., 1943-45; chmn. Appeal Bd., Office of Contract Settlement, 1945; chief consultant to the joint legislative committee appointed to revise corp. laws of N.Y., from 1957. Served as 2d lt., F.A. and A.S., U.S. Army, 1917-19. Trustee Hackley Sch., Tarrytown, N.Y., 1937-41; faculty rep. to bd. trustees, Cornell U., 1934-39. Mem. Am., N.Y. State and Tompkins County bar assns., Am. Law Inst., Am. Judicature Soc., Order of Coif, Delta Theta Phi, Phi Kappa Phi. Republican. Mason. Author: Stevens on Corporations, 1936; Stevens and Larson Cases and Materials on the Law of Corporations, 1947. Contbr. to law revs. Home: Ithaca NY Died Nov. 1968.

STEVENS, S(TANLEY) SMITH, psychophysicist; educator; b. Ogden, Utah, Nov. 4, 1906; s. Stanley S. and Adeline (Smith) S.; Student U. Utah, 1927-29; A.B., Stanford, 1931; Ph.D., Harvard, 1933; m. Maxine Leonard, Mar. 28, 1930 (dec.); 1 son, Peter Smith; m. 2d, Geraldine Stone, Apr. 11, 1963. Asst. in psychology Harvard, 1932-34, nat. research fellow Med. Sch., 1934-35, research fellow in physics, 1935-36, faculty, 1936-73, prof., 1946-62, prof. psychophysics, 1962-73, dir. psychoacoustic lab., 1944-62, lab. psychophysics, 1962-73, psychol. labs., 1949-62. Sect. mem. NDRC, 1942-45; expert cons. Research and Devel. Bd., 1946-52; chmn. NRC Div. Anthropology and Psychology, 1949-52; mem. sensory diseases study sect. NIH, 1956-58; mem. Nat. Acad. Scis. NRC Physiol. Psychology Fellowship Bd., 1954-58; mem. space sci. bd. Nat. Acad. Sci., 1958-60. Recipient Beltone Inst. award for distinguished accomplishment, 1966; Rayleigh gold medal Brit. Acoustical Soc., 1972. Fellow Acoustical Soc. Am. (exec. council 1946-49), Am. Psychol. Assn. (Sci. award 1960); mem. Am. Philos. Soc., Nat. Acad. Sci., Soc. Exptl. Psychologists (Howard Crosby Warren medal 1943), Am. Physiol. Soc., Eastern Psychol. Assn. (past pres.), Psychonomic Soc. (governing bd. 1960-61), A.A.A.S. (v.p. sect. I 1955), Am. Acad. Arts and Scis., Philosophy Sci. Assn. (governing bd. 1957-59), Optical Soc. Am., Soc. for Neurosci., Am. Inst. Physics, Phi Beta Kappa, Sigma Xi, Pi Kappa Alpha. Mem. Ch. of Jesus Christ of Latter-day Saints. Author: (with Hallowell Davis) Hearing, Its Psychology and Physiology, 1938; (with W.H. Sheldon, W.B. Tucker) The Varieties of Human Physique, 1940; (with W.H. Sheldon) Varieties of Temperament, 1942; (with F. Warshofsky) Sound and Hearing, 1965; The Story of Psychophysics, 1974. Editor: Handbook of Experimental Psychology, 1951. Contbr. articles to various publs. Home: Cambridge MA Died Jan. 18, 1973.

STEVENS, WILLIAM HARRISON SPRING, economist; b. Eau Claire, Wis., Apr. 15, 1885; s. Wallace D. and Marcia E. (Spring) S.; A.B., Colby Coll., 1906; A.M., George Washington Univ., 1909; studied Univ. of Chicago, Cornell Univ., Univ. of Pa., Ph.D., Univ. of Pa., 1912, Dr. Soc. Sci. (honorary), Colby College, 1947; m. Mary Elizabeth Laird, June 16, 1923 (died 1940); m. 2d, Rachel I. Bretherton, 1944. Asst. in economics, Univ. of Pa., 1911-12; instructor same, Columbia, 1912-15; prof. business orgn. and management, Tulane University Coll. Commerce and Bus. Adminstration, 1915-16; temporary examiner Federal Trade Commn., summer 1916, spl. expert same, 1916-17, asst. chief economist same, 1918-36; asst. dir. Bur. Transport Economics and Statistics, Interstate Commerce Commission, 1936-44, dir., 1944-55; consultant Office of Production Management, 1941. Directed Federal Trade Commission inquiries into cotton, grain, bread, stock dividends, chain stores, textiles, milk and agrl. income. Prof. business finance and orgn., Am. U., 1921-23; lecturer in marketing and finance, Grad. Sch. same univ., 1928-32, adj. prof., 1932-44; lecturer on corp. finance, U. of Md., 1921-27, prof. marketing and finance, 1924-25; extension lecturer in marketing and corp. finance, Johns Hopkins, 1925-32 and 1939-45; mem. N.R.A. Policy Com., 1934; mem. Central Statis. Bd. 1933-36. Mem. Am. Econ. Assn., Am. Marketing Assn., Am. Statis. Association, Am. Finance Association, Delta Upsilon. Conglist. Clubs: University, Nat. Press. Author: Unfair Competition, 1917; also editor, author or co-author books relating to field; and numerous articles on finance, marketing and monopoly. Home: Alexandria VA Died Sept. 14, 1972.

STEVENS, WILLIAM LESTER, artist; b. Rockport, Mass., June 16, 1888; s. George Forrest and Annie Grover (Marshall) S.; ed. pub. schs., Rockport; art edn., Museum of Fine Arts, Boston; m. Angelina Vannini, Aug. 7, 1926; 1 son, Milton Howe. Represented in collections in Eng., Switzerland, France and Italy, also in public schs., art galleries and museums in the United States. Awarded fourth William A. Clark prize, Corcoran Art Gallery, Washington, D.C., 1921; Gedney Bunce prize, Conn. Acad. Fine Arts, Hartford, 1924; landscape prize, Springfield, Mass., 1925; 2d Altman prize, Nat. Acad. Design, 1927; William A. Delano purchase prize, Am. Water Color Soc., New York, 1927; Mr. and Mrs. Burton Mansfield prize, New Haven, Conn., 1929; medal of honor, Springville, Utah, 1931; patrons' prize, Springfield, Mass., 1931; medal Quincy (Mass.) Art League, 1932; New Haven Paint and Clay Club prize, 1933; 1st prize Meriden, Conn., 1938; Tonsburg prize, 1940; Springville purchase prize, 1941; purchase prizes, Mass. State Fedn. of Women's Clubs, 1930, 31, 33 and 37. Downes prize New Haven Paint and Clay Club, 1942; 2d prize Washington Water Color Club, 1942; 2d prize Washington Landscape Club, 1940. Eaton prize best oil, 1954, Epstein prize N. Shore Art Assn. 1954; best water color, Jackson, Miss., 1955; first prize Academic Artists Assn., 1955; first prize, mems. show, Academic Artists Association, 1955, popular prize, Worthington Grange, 1955, portrait prize Rockport, Massachusetts, 1956, landscape prize Ogunquit, Maine, 1956. Served with C.A.C. 11 months, World War. Member Guild of Boston Artists, New Haven Paint and Clay Club, Springfield Art League, North Shore Art Assn., Rockport Art Assn., Philadelphia Water Color Soc., New York Water Color Club, Boston Soc. Water Color Painters, Washington Water Color Club, Baltimore Water Color Club, Conn. Acad. of Art; hon. mem. Washington Landscape Club. Asso. Nat. Acad., 1935; N.A., 1943. Home: Conway MA Died June 10, 1969; buried Cricket Hill Cemetery, Conway MA

STEVENSON, ALEC BROCK, investment banker; b. Toronto, Ont., Dec. 29, 1895; s. James Henry and Evelyn (Sutherland) S.; brought to U.S., 1896, naturalized, 1920; B.A., Vanderbilt U., 1916; m. Florence Elise Maney, Nov. 10, 1920; children—Alec Brock, Florence Elise. Newspaper reporter, 1916-17, 19; asst. sec. Am. Nat. Co., investment bankers, Nashville, 1920-33; v.p. Gray, Shillinglaw & Co., investment bankers, 1933-40; v.p., trust officer Am. Nat. Bank of Nashville, 1940-51, dir., 1944-51; with Vance, Sanders and Co., sponsors mut. investment funds, Boston, 1951-59, partner, 1953-59; vice president Vance Sanders & Co., Inc., 1959-69. Commr., vice mayor, Belle-Meade, Tenn., 1938-40. Pres. Community Chest of Nashville and Davidson Co., 1950-51. Trustee Vanderbilt U., Joint U. Libraries Sgt. to lt. F.A., A.E.F., 1917-19. Mem. Phi Beta Kappa, Sigma Chi, Omicron Delta Kappa. Methodist. Club: Bellemeade Country, Cumberland (Nashville). Author: Shares in Mutual Investment Funds, 1946; Investment Company Shares, 1947. Mem. group. editing and pub. The Fugitive, a mag. of verse, Nashville, 1922-25. Home: Nashville TN Died May 27, 1969; buried Mt. Olivet Cemetery Nashville TN

STEVENSON, C. ALBERT, oil exec.; b. Adalmana, Ariz., June 8; the son of Carl Albert and Lula (Jones) S.; high sch. grad.; m. Artie F. Hair, July 25, 1925; children—Ethel Severson. In oil fields in all capacities, Cal., 1923-29; ind. oil operator, Cal., Alaska, Wyo., Libya, Algeria, Italy, Angola, 1929-68; pres. Orbit Petroleum Co., Los Angeles, 1963-68. Specialist in negotiating for acquisition fgn. holdings for maj. oil cos. U.S. Active Boy Scouts Am., YMCA; mem. adv. bd. Goldwater campaign, Long Beach. Mem. Wine & Food Soc., Western Oil and Gas Assn., Ind. Petroleum Assn., Nat. Petroleum Landman Assn., Anchorage, Alaska, Los Angeles petroleum clubs. Rep. Baptist. Clubs: Eldorado Country (Palm Desert, Cal.); Pacific Coast, Virginia Country (Long Beach, Cal.); Balboa Bay (Newport Beach, Cal.); Tennis (Palm Springs, Cal.). Home: Long Beach CA Died June 26, 1968.

STEVENSON, ELDON, JR., ins. exec.; b. Nashville; s. Eldon Boisseau and Minnie (Gleaves) S.; B.S., Vanderbilt U., 1914; m. Sarah Shannon, June 2, 1920. With Nat. Life and Accident Ins. Co., 1913-72, beginning as agent successively branch office cashier, inspector, supervisor and dist. mgr., later transferred to home office and made asst. mgr. of ordinary dept., later mgr. and then v.p. in charge of ordinary, dir. of co., 1925-72, exec. v.p., 1938, pres., 1953-72, vice chmn. corp., 1963-65, hon. vice chmn., 1965-72, cons. to co., 1970-72; vice chmn. bd. Radio WSM and WSM-TV; also past chmn. Combination Cos. Past chmn. bd. Life Ins. Sales Research Bur., Hartford, Conn.; mem. bd. Life Insurers Conf., Richmond, Va., 1948-72, pres., 1954-55. Trustees, hon. v.p. bd. trust Vanderbilt U. Enlisted USN, World War I; commd. ensign; instr. U.S. Naval Acad.; officer in U.S.S. George Washington. Mem. Vanderbilt Alumni Assn. (past mem. bd., exec. com. and nat. pres.), Phi Delta Theta. Mason. Clubs: Links, Brook, (N.Y.C.); Cumberland, Belle Meade Golf and Country (Nashville); Linville (N.C.) Golf; Augusta (Ga.) National Golf; Everglades and Mountain Lake Colony (Fla.). Home: Nashville TN Died Nov. 23, 1972.

STEVENSON, MARCIA JACOBS, lecturer; b. at Galena, Ill., Mar. 25, 1875; d. Henry Hayes and Elizabeth (Stephens) Jacobs; Platteville (Wis.) State Normal Sch.; B.A., State U. of Ia., 1898; m. Samuel Kirkwood Stevenson, of Iowa City, Ia., Aug. 2, 1898. Lecturer on Bible Study." The Lumbermen and Miners of Western Canada," Woman's Work," etc., before many leading colls. in middle west, also before state S.S. convs., women's clubs, and chautauquas. Presbyterian. Mem. King's Daughters. Clubs: Philosophical, Cosmopolitan, Hindusthan, Art; Dickens' Fellowship (London); Nat. Arts (New York); Arts (Washington); Drama League. Women's University. Home: Iowa City IA‡

STEVENSON, MARION, clergyman, editor; b. West Jersey, Ill., Dec. 26, 1861; s. Andrew and Martha Ann (Johnson) S.; A.B., Eureka (Ill.) Coll., 1883; diploma Coll. of the Bible, Lexington, Ky., 1885; D.D., Spokane U., 1926; m. Lucy A. Huston, May 18, 1886; children—Marian Coleman, Paul Huston, Ermine June, Lucy Margaret. Ordained ministry Ch. of Christ (Disciples), 1885; various pastorates until 1905; state supt. Sunday Schs. for Ch. of Christ, Ill., 1906-07; sec. Nat. Bible Sch. Assn., Disciples of Christ, 1908-09; editor in chief church sch. lit., Christian Bd. of Publication, St. Louis, 1910-35; now retired; mem. Internat. Sunday Sch. Lesson Com. since 1917. Author: Studies of the Books of the Bible, 1908; Teacher Training Handbook, 1908; Outline of the Gospel of Matthew, 1930; Guide to Study of the Old Testament, 1932. Home: 5844A Enright Av., St Louis 12 MO*‡

STEVENSON, WADE, mfg. exec.; b. Bradford, Pa., Aug. 31, 1885; s. Charles Porter and Louise (Wade) S.; student pvt. schs.; m. Josephine Gibson, Dec. 31, 1911. Shipping dept. Eastman Machine Co., 1908, pres., 1909-72; trustee Western Savs. Bank. Past pres. Erie County Soc. Prevention to Cruelty to Animals. Mem. Buffalo C. of C. (past pres.), N.Y. Automobile Assn. (past pres.). Clubs: Saturn (dem 1937), Buffalo (pres. 1955-56), Automobile (pres. 1936), Tennis and Squash (Buffalo): Racquet (N.Y.C.). Home: Buffalo NY Died May 9, 1972.

STEWARD, JULIAN H., anthropologist; b. Washington, Jan. 31, 1902; s. Thomas G. and Grace (Garriott) S.; A.B., Cornell U., 1925; A.M., U. Cal., 1926, Ph.D., 1929; m. Jane Cannon, June 21, 1934; children—Gary Cannon, Michael. Instructor anthropology U. Mich., 1928-30; asso. prof. U. Utah, 1930-33; lectr. U. Cal., 1934; anthropologist Bur. Am. Ethnology, 1935-38, sr. anthropologist, 1938-43; dir. Inst. Social Anthropology, Smithsonian Instn., 1943-46; prof. Columbia, 1946-52; research prof. anthropology U. Ill., from 1952, acting head dept., 1959-60, mem. Center Advanced Studies, from 1959, dir. Studies Cross-Cultural Regularities; fellow Center Advanced Study Behavorial Scis., Stanford, 1960-61; dir. Kyoto (Japan) Am. Studies Seminar, 1956. Mem. Ethnohistorical Soc., Am. Assn. U. Profs., Andean Inst., Franciscan Hist. Soc. (hon. mem.), Nat. Acad. Sci., Am. Anthrop. Assn. (Viking medalist 1952.) Society Am. Archaeology, A.A.A.S., Association Asian Studies, Soc. Asiatic Studies, Academy de la Cultura Guarani Paraguay (hon.), Soc. Applied Anthropology, Am. Ethnol. Soc. Author: Theory of Culture Charge, 1955, also papers and monographs. Co-author: People of Puerto Rico, 1956: Native People of South America, 1959. Editor: Handbook of South American Indians, vols. 1, 2, 1946, vols. 3, 4, 1948, vols. 5, 6, 1949; Contemporary Change in Traditional Societies, 3 vols., 1967. Home: Fithian IL Died Feb. 6, 1972.

STEWART, CHARLES ALLAN, former ambassador; b. Florence, Ariz, Jan. 27, 1907; s. Dugald and Franc May (Bailey) S., A.B., U. Ariz., 1929; m. Marion Selby, July 16, 1938. Newspaper reporter, editor, Tucson, 1927-31, Nogales, Ariz., 1931, Salinas, Cal., 1932-35, Burlingame, Cal., 1935-36; with A.P., San Francisco, N.Y.C., 1936-42, Latin Am. Desk, N.Y.C., 1941-42, chief bur., Bogota, Colombia, 1942-43, Caracas, Venezuela, 1943-46; pub. affairs officer Am. embassy, Havana, Cuba, 1947-49; 1st sec., consul Am. embassy, Santiago, Chile, 1949-53; counselor Am. embassy, San Jose, Costa Rica, 1953-56; assigned Dept. State, 1956-60; counselor embassy, dep. chief mission Am. embassy, Caracas, 1960-61; U.S. ambassador to Venezuela, 1961-64; spl. asst. Bur. Inter-Am. Affairs, 1965; dir. Office Caribbean Affairs, 1965-66, ret., 1967. Detailed to 4th meeting Consultation Ministers Fgn. Affairs, Washington, 1951, 5th meeting, Santiago, Chile, 1959. Recipient Honor award, 1964. Mem. Phi Delta Theta, Pi Delta Epsilon. Club: Congressional Country. Address: Caracus Venezuela Died Feb. 1973.

STEWART, CHARLES D., author; b. Zanesville, O., Mar. 18, 1868; s. Andrew Hugh and Sarah J. (Emery) S.; ed. pub. schs. of Milwaukee, Wis.; m. Emily Thompson, Aug. 18, 1898. Author: The Fugitive Blacksmith, 1905; Partners of Providence, 1907; Essays on the Spot, 1910; The Wrong Woman, 1912; Finerty of the Sand-house, 1913; Some Textual Difficulties in Shakespeare (pub. under auspices Elizabethan Club, by Yale Univ. Press), 1914; Prussianizing Wisconsin, 1919; Buck (novel), 1919; Valley Waters, 1922; Fellow Creatures (collected essays), 1935; also prize essay, Atlantic, May 1940. Also short stories, poems, etc., in mags. Exec. sec. to gov. of Wis., 1915-16. Vice-pres. Soc. of Midland Authors. Rotarian. Address: Hartford WI‡

STEWART, DUNCAN, educator; b. Detroit, Oct. 2, 1905; s. Duncan and Stella (Woodbridge) S.; B.S., U.

Mich., 1928, Ph.D., 1933; Sc.M., Brown U., 1930; m. Graziella Furkart, Dec. 28, 1937; children—Duncan VIII, Arzelie, Stella. Instr. geology Carleton Coll., 1933-35, asst. prof., 1939-41, prof., 1945-62, chmn. dept., 1945-69, Charles L. Denison prof. geology, 1962-69; instr. Michigan State Coll., 1935-39, asst. prof., 1939; asst. prof. Lehigh U., 1941-43, asso. prof., 1943-45; cons. Lehigh Portland Cement Co., Penn-Dixie Cement Corp., Mo. Portland Cement Co., 1944-59, Ash Gorve Lime and Portland Cement Co., 1961, Wilson Nuttall Raimond Engrs., Inc., Costa Rica, 1964-69. Cons. U.S. Army in Alaska, 1960. Researcher, IGY under Hill Foundation, Scott Polar Research Inst., Cambridge U., Eng., 1956. Recipient grants for Antarctic petrography Sigma Xi, 1935-36, Geol. Soc. Am., 1935-36, Mich. State Grant Patent Fund, 1937-38, Geol. Soc. Am., 1952-53, Louis W. and Maud Hill Family Found., 1956; recipient Congressional medal, 1968; Stewart Hills in West Antarctica named in his honor. Fellow Geol. Soc. Am., Mineral. Soc. Am., American Association for Advancement of Sci.; mem. Soc. Econ. Paleontologists and Mineralogists (asso.), Minn., Pa. Acads. sci., Mich. Acads. Sci., Mich. Acad. Sci. Arts and Letters, Arctic Inst. Am. (charter asso.), Sci. Research Soc. Am., Rochester Earth Sci. Soc. (hon.), Am. Geophys. Union, Yorkshire Geol. Soc. (Eng.). Home: Northfield MN Died Nov. 5, 1969; buried Detroit MI

STEWART, ELLA SEASS, lecturer; b. Arthur, Ill., Feb. 22, 1871; d. Levi and Elizabeth (Powell) Seass; A.B., Eureka (Ill.) Coll., 1890, A.M., 1893; A.B., U. of Mich., 1892; m. Oliver Wayne Stewart, Aug. 20, 1890. Lecturer for franchise dept. Nat. W.C.T.U., Chicago, 1898-1908. Pres. Ill. Equal Suffrage Assn., 1905-11 (v.p. 1902-05); rec. sec. Nat. Am. Woman Suffrage Assn., 1908-11. Trustee Eureka Coll. Mem. Disciples of Christ. Mem. Chicago Woman's Club, Woman's City Club, College Club, Am. Assn. Univ. Women; pres. dept. of school patrons N.E.A., 1918-19; v.-chmn. dept. social and industrial conditions of Gen. Federation of Woman's Clubs, 1918-20. Mem. bd. Disciples' Foundation at U. of Ill. Mgr. women's dept. University State Bank, Chicago. Dir. Assn. of Chicago Bank Women. Home: 1157 E. 56th St., Chicago IL‡

STEWART, FORD, pub.; b. Oak Park, Ill., May 3, 1909; s. Graham and Maude (Ford) S.; student Grinnell (Ia.) Coll., 1926-1929; B.A., U. Mo., 1930; m. Mercedes Jeisma, Oct. 4, 1930; children—Nancy, James, Susan, Constance, Steven. Pres. Christian Herald Assn., pub. Christian Herald Mag., ret., 1967. Vice pres., dir. Christian Herald Children's Home; dir. Bowery Mission and Young Men's Home, Meml. Home Community, Penney Farms, Fla., Nat. Council Alcoholism, Layman's Nat. Committee, Inc. Christian Children's Fund, Richmond, Va. Vice pres. Christian Herald's Family Bookshelf (book club). Mem. Mag. Pub. Assn. (dir.), Phi Delta Theta, Sigma Delta Chi. Presbyn. Club: Union League (N.Y.C.). Office: New York City NY Died May 30, 1971; buried Lighthouse Point FL

STEWART, FRANCIS ROBERT, consular service; b. Evansville, Ind., Aug. 7, 1874; s. Ross Forward; ed. high sch.; m. Gertrud Bosche, 1923. Apptd. dep. consul gen., Hamburg, 1912, also consular agent at Cuxhaven, 1913; v. and dep. consul gen., Hamburg, 1914, and v. consul, 1915; consul, Vera Cruz, Mexico, 1917; detailed to Dept. of State, 1919, and successively to Berne, Switzerland, Coblenz and Hamburg; mem. Am. Commission to Germany, 1920-21; consul at Bremen, 1921-23, Santiago de Cuba, 1923-28, Niagara Falls, Can., 1928-31, Vienna, Austria, 1931; Venice, Italy, 1936. Sec. in Diplomatic Service, 1936; became first sec. Am. Legation, Vienna, 1936; retired Mar. 1, 1939. Mem. S.A.R., Nat. Geog. Soc., Penn Hist. Soc., Spanish War Vets. Episcopalian. Home: 14 Burbury Lane, Great Neck, N.Y. Address: care Department of State, Washington DC‡

STEWART, FRED, actor; b. Atlanta, Dec. 7, 1906; s. Fred IV and Sarah (Dugger) S.; B.A., Oglethorpe U., 1927; summer student, Columbia, 1925. Operator, The Playcrafters, little theatre, Atlanta, 1924-27; profl. actor with Stuart Walker Co. in W. Va., Ind. and Ohio, 1927-31; Broadway in Ladies of Creation, 1931; other Broadway prodns. include Robin Landing, 1936, Excursion, 1937, 200 Were Chosen, 1936, Murder in the Cathedral, 1935, The Devil and Daniel Webster, 1939, Night Music, 1940, Retreat to Pleasure, 1940, The Whole World Over, 1947, Brigadoon, 1950, Arms and the Man, 1950, An Enemy of the People, 1951, The Crucible, 1953, Cat on a Hot Tin Roof, 1955, The Girls in 509, 1957, The Gang's All Here, 1960, Romulus, 1962, Strange Interlude, 1963, The Deputy, 1964; summer theatre appearances in Mass., Va., Conn., N.Y. 1929-56; dir. plays for Barter Theatre, Abingdon, Va., 1938-46, Actors Studio, N.Y.C., 1954-64, Theatre Delys, N.Y.C., 1960, Nat. Arts Club, N.Y.C., 1960-62, Library of Congress, 1960, also in New Milford, Conn. and Fishkill, N.Y.; film appearance in Splendour in the Grass, 1961; numerous TV appearances from 1939; mem. Actors Studio, from 1947, mem. members com., 1956-57, 62-63, mem. prodn. bd., from 1962; appeared in Galileo, 1967, More Stately Mansions, 1967. Served with AUS, 1941-45. Died Dec. 5, 1970.

STEWART, FREDERICK WILLIAM, mfg. co. exec.; b. St. Louis, Apr. 9, 1894; s. Eugene Van Arsdale and Julia Agnes (Ward) S.; student St. Louis U., 1917, student Washington U., St. Louis, 1918, Alexander Hamilton Inst., 1919; m. 2d, Jeanne Lau, Apr. 17, 1937; children—Frederick N., Mary S. (Mrs. Jules Bush). With Century Electric Co., St. Louis, 1917-20; partner Indsl. Mgmt. Corp., St. Louis, 1920-23; with Huttig Sash & Door Co., St. Louis, from 1923, v.p., treas., 1942-65, v.p. finance, 1965-68, consultant, member board of directors, 1969; dir. Missoula White Pine Sash Co., Gen. Sash & Door Co., Park PM Corp., Pro-tech Service, Inc., Belt and Ricker Co., A. B. Chance Co.; dir., mem. exec. com. Protection Mut. Ins. Co. Dir., mem. exec. com. Asso. Industries Mo., St. Louis. Mem. St. Louis Met. C. of C., St. Louis Country Police Assn., St. Louis County Grand Jury Assn. Presbyn. Clubs: St. Louis (Clayton, Mo.); University, Rotary Manchester MO

STEWART, GEORGE, author, minister, soldier; b. Webb City, Mo., Feb. 11, 1892; s. George and Fanny (Meade) S.; A.B., Linfield Coll., McMinnville, Ore., 1914, Litt.D., 1928; A.B., Yale, 1915, LL.B., 1917, Ph.D., 1921, D.D., 1939; Dr. Theol., Faculte Libre de Theologie Protestante de Paris, 1927; L.H.D. (honorary), Temple U., 1955; LL.D., Norwich U., 1963; m. Sarah Malcolm Klebs, May 20, 1925 (dec. July 1957); children—Mary (Mrs. James Meath), Anne, Jane (Mrs. William McDermott), Sarah (Mrs. Kendall Preston); m. 2d, Leni Loosli, Sept. 16, 1958. Gen. sec. YMCA, 1919-21; asso. pastor, Madison Av. Presbyn. Ch., N.Y. City, 1921-28; minister of First Presbyn. Ch., Stamford, Conn., 1928-44; Turnbull Trust preacher Scots Church, Melbourne, Australia, 1941; lecturer Yale Divinity School, 1930-36. Private, non-commd. officer and capt., World War; vol. student relief work, Europe part time, 1918-25. Mem. com. on worship Federal Council of the Chs. of Christ in America; mem. bd. trustees Community Chest, Stamford; mem. bd. trustees Ferguson Library, Stamford; mem. Am. Com. on Religious Rights and Minorities; mem. Am. Com. of the Paris Theol. Sem.; past mem. numerous govtl. and orgn. coms. in social field; mem. subcom. on hist. records, Nat. Research Council, 1942-44; mem. bd. dirs. Am. Waldensian Aid Soc.; mem. Oecumenism Commn. World Student Christian Feln.; mem. Am. sect. World Council of Churches. Commander, Legion of Honor; medaille Militaire (France); Orders of St. George and St. Vladamir (Russia); Golden Cross of Merit with Crossed Swords, Officer Order Polonia Restituta (Poland) Grand Officer Order of the Crown, Military Cross; Criox d' Honneur, Union Franco-Belge Devouement, Croix de laFrance Leberee, Croix d'Honneur Le Ligue Entriaide Francaise de Merite, Cuique, Croix de Commander Societe d' Encouragement on De-voncment (France), Soldat premiere Classe Honor dise de la Legion Entrangere, Croix de Commandeur Ligne Universelle du Bien Public (France), Grand Cross, Order of The Holy Sepulchre. Fellow fo the Royal Geographical Society; member several profl. and geneol. socs. Clubs: Century Association (N.Y.C.); Dublin Lake (New Hampshire). Author: Soldiers' Spirit, 1917; (with Professor Henry B. Wright of Yale) The Practice of Friendship, 1918; (with same) Personal Evangelism Among Students, 1919; A History of Religious Education in Connecticut to the Middle of the Nineteenth Century (winner John Addison Porter prize at Yale University), 1921; Life of Henry B. Wright, 1925, also God and Pain; The Incarnation in Our Street; The Crucifixion in Our Street; The Resurrection in Our Street; Redemption—An Anthology of the Cross; Protestant Europe—Its Crisis and Outlook (with Adolh Keller), 1927; Ask Me a Bible Question, 1927; The Sanctuary, 1928; The Letters of Maxwell Chaplin, 1928; Can I Teach My Child Religion?, 1929; Jesus as a Friend, 1931. Compiler and editor of Dedication—An Anthology of the Will of God, 1931; The White Armies of Russia, 1933; Jesus Said I Am," 1934; Reluctant Soil, 1936; The Church, 1938; God in Our Street, 1939; I Met Them Once, 1940; A Face to the Sky, 1940; The Story of a Carillon, 1944. Contbr. to mags.; mem. editorial bd. Presbyterian Tribune. War missions in 37 countries, rank of col. Hon. chaplain to British armies; Col., USAF (Reserve) Dublin NH Died Feb. 19, 1972.

STEWART, GRACE BLISS, author, painter; b. Atchison, Kan. Apr. 18, 1885; d. Joseph Lyman and Caroline M. (Pierce) Bliss; ed. Lasell Sem., Auburndale, Mass. Extensive traveler; artist; exhibited Nat. Arts Club, North Shore Arts Assn., Gloucester, Mass., National Assn. Women Artists exhibitions, Pen and Brush Club, N.Y. City, Ogunquit Art Center, Art Inst., Dayton, O., Palm Beach Art Center, Delphic Studios, New York City, 1933, 34, Studio Guild, 1937, Argent Galleries (for War Relief), 1942. Solo exhbn. Norlyst Gallery, New York, 1946; showed in water color exhbn., Paris, France, 1949. Awarded 1st prize in oil Pen and Brush, N.Y. City, 1951. Episcopalian. Mem. Nat. Assn. Women Artists, Pen and Brush Club (N.Y.), American Artists Professional League, N.H. Art Assn. Author: In and Out of the Jungle, 1922; Jumping Into the Jungle, 1923; The Good Fairy, 1930. Home: New York City NY Died Apr. 1969.

STEWART, JOHN ALEXANDER, banker; b. Bay City, Mich., May 23, 1900; s. John A. and Margaret (MacDonald) S.; A.B., U. Mich., 1921; m. Mary K. Martin, Oct. 11, 1928; children—Albert W., John A., Dennis M., Robert M. With Second Nat. Bank of Saginaw, 1921-68, beginning as clk., successively asst. cashier, v.p., v.p. and cashier, exec. v.p., cashier, 1921-57, pres., 1957-65, chmn. bd., 1965-68, also director; director Morley Brothers, Michigan Sugar Company. Treas., v.p., dir. Saginaw Community Chest, 1956; dir. Children's Home Family Soc.; bd. dirs. Saginaw YMCA, 1958-68, pres., 1963-65; trustee Delta College. Served as pvt., infantry, United States Army, 1918, later lt. U.S. Coast Arty. Mem. Mich. Bankers Assn. (exec. com. 1937-40), Saginaw C. of C. (treas., dir. 1947-58), Newcomen Soc., Navy League. Republican. Conglist. Mason (Shriner). Clubs: Saginaw, Saginaw Country, Saginaw MI Died May 20, 1968.

STEWART, JOHN LESLIE, lawyer; b. Toronto, Ont., Can., Sept. 24, 1911; s. John Leslie and Mary Frances (Nicholson) S.; B.A., U. Toronto, 1932; B.C.L., U. Oxofrd, 1934, diploma politics and economics, 1935; m. Winifred Muriel Gibson, Dec. 6, 1941; children—Margaret Ann, John Leslie, Gordon Fraser, Robert David Roy, Janet Elizabeth Mary. Called to bar, London, Eng., 1935, Ont., 1936, apptd. Queen's Counsel, 1950; with Fraser & Beatty, and successor firms, Toronto, 1936-71, partner, 1936-71; dir. various Canadian corps. Exec. com. corp. Trinity Coll., Toronto; sec. Can. Rhodes Scholarship Trust. Legal adviser Royal Commn. on Taxation. Served as lt. col. Canadian Army, World War II. Decorated Order Brit. Empire; Officer Order Orange Nassau (Netherlands). Mem. Alpha Delta Phi. Clubs: University, Badminton and Racquet, Granite, Toronto, Lambton Golf, Toronto Golf. Editor: Fraser and Stewart Handbook on Canadian Company Law, 5th edit., 1960; Company Law of Canada, 5th edit., 1962. Home: Toronto Ontario Canada Died 1971.

STEWART, JOHN QUINCY, physicist, generalist; born at Harrisburg, Pennsylvania, on September 10, 1894; s. John Quincy and Mary Caroline (Liebendorfer) S.; B.S., Princeton U., 1915, Ph.D., 1919; m. Lillian V., d. John Howell Westcott, June 17, 1925; 1 son, John Westcott. Engineer dept. of development and research, Am. Telephone & Telegraph Co., New York, investigating speech and hearing, 1919-21; designed the first electrical voice"; with dept. of astronomy, Princeton University, 1921-63, asso. prof. astron. physics, 1927-63; prof. metaphysics of sci. Prescott Coll., 1966-72. Organized small party which successfully observed longest modern total solar eclipse, from S.S. Steelmaker in the Pacific, June 8, 1937; duration was more than seven minutes. Served with 29th Engrs., A.E.F. (sound ranging), 1918-19. Fellow American Physical Society, Am. Geog. Soc. (hon.); member Am. Astron. Soc., American Assn. Univ. Profs. (nat. 1st v.p., 1940-41), Phi Beta Kappa, Sigma Xi. Clubs: Princeton (New York); Nassau (Princeton); Randolph Mountain. Presbyterian. Author: Astronomy (with H. N. Russell and R. S. Dugan), 1927, 1938; Navigation (with N. L. Pierce), 1944; Coasts, Waves, and Weather, 1945. Contributor research results in physics, astronomy, nav., meteorol., demography; organized studies in social physics, metaphysics. Home: Sedona AZ Died Mar. 19, 1972; buried Sedone AZ

STEWART, MALCOLM CHILSON, lawyer; b. Brookline, Mass., Jan. 10, 1913; s. Ralph Aldace and Mary Wallace(Guilford) S.; student St. Mark's Sch., Southborough, Mass., 1924-30; A.B., Harvard, 1934, LL.B., 1937; m. Marian deForest Clark, Dec. 14, 1941. Admitted to Mass. bar, 1937, asso. mem. Choate, Hall & Stewart, Boston, 1937-41, 46-49; legal dept. Gillette Co. (formerly Gillette Safety Razor Co.), 1949-70, gen. counsel 1951-56, dir., 1956-70, treas., 1955-66, v.p., 1959-65, sr. v.p., 1965-66, vice chairman of the board, 1968-70; mem. bd. directors Mchts. Nat. Bank Boston. Dir., exec. com. Boston Municipal Research Bur.; director National Foreign Trade Council. Director Mutual Security, special mission to France, 1953; mem. Nat. Indsl. Conf. Bd. Trustee Peter Bent Brigham Hosp., Affiliated Hosps. Center, Inc., Boston. Served as lieut. col. F.A., AUS, 1941-45. Decorated Bronze Star, Air Medal. Mem. Am., Mass. State, Boston bar assns., Boston C. C. (dir.), Nat. Assn. Mfrs. Clubs: Myopia Hunt (Hamilton, Mass.); Somerset (Boston); Racquet (Chgo.). Home: Prides Crossing MA Died Apr. 3, 1970; buried Westport, Essex County NY

STEWART, OLINE JOHNSON, ex-Rep. Nat. Com. woman; b. Virginia City, Nev.; d. Eli Walter and Mary Jane (Black) Johnson; student Whitaker Hall; Aydelotte's Bus. Coll.; m. James Wesley Stewart, Mar. 16, 1898 (deceased); 1 son, Eli Reed (adopted). Teacher pub. schs.; court reporter, confidential clerk; county clerk and recorder, county recorder and auditor, Tonopah, Nye County, Nev. Rep. Nat. committeewoman, 1936-52. Mem. polit. sci. dept. Columbia Univ. Episcopalian. Mem. Rebekahs (past pres.), Eastern Star (past grand matron), Dau. of Nile, Am. Women's Voluntary Services, Inc., Nat. Fedn. Bus. and Prof. Women's Clubs, Inc. Home: Tonopah Nye County NV‡

STEWART, PHILIP BATTELL, b. Middlebury, Vt., Jan. 27, 1865; s. John Wolcott and Emma (Battell) S.; grad. Phillips Acad., Andover, Mass., 1882; B.A., Yale Univ., 1886, M.A., 1888; LL.D., Middlebury (Vt.) College, 1939, Colorado Coll., 1941; m. Frances Cowles, Sept. 13, 1893. Engaged in mining and pub. utility enterprises in Colo. many yrs.; prominently identified with Rep. and Progressive Party movements in Rocky Mountain region; Rep. nominee for gov. of Colo., 1896 (declined); also declined appmts. as U.S. civil service commr. and U.S. land commr.; mem. Colo. Ho. of Rep., 1914-15 (speaker of House); chmn. com. which formulated plans for reorganization of state depts., Colo., 1914-16; del. Congress of Nat. Service, Chicago, 1918. Trustee Colorado Coll. 20 yrs. Elk. Clubs: El Paso, Country (Colorado Springs); Denver, University, Elks (Denver); University, Century (New York). Home: 1228 Wood Av., Colorado Springs CO*‡

STEWART, TOM, former U.S. senator; b. Dunlap, Tenn., Jan. 11, 1892; ed. Emory Coll., Cumberland U.; m. Helen Turner, Dec. 19, 1914; children—Tom, Mrs. J. W. Dunn, Mrs. Charles S. Coffey, Lawrence F., Paul Turner. In practice of law; mem. U.S. Senate, 1939-49; practicing atty., Nashville, 1949-72. Democrat. Methodist. Mason (Shriner). Home: Nashville TN Died 1972.

STEWART, WALTER ALLAN, ret. optical mfr.; b. Toronto, Can., Oct. 19, 1889; s. Charles Edward and Hannah (Hyland) S.; came to U.S., 1900, naturalized, 1918; student Canadaigua (N.Y.) Acad., 1905-10, Georgetown U., 1912-14; m. Helen Hamilton, Aug. 9, 1926; 1 s., Robert H. Pres., trustee Am. Optical Co., 1949-61, ret.; dir. Am. Optical Co., Can., Ltd., Fleming & Brit. Am. Optical Industries, Ltd., London, Eng. Dir. Nat. Indsl. Conf. Bd.; chmn. Nat. Safety Council. Served as cpl., Signal Corps, U.S. Army, 1918-19. Home: Bristol RI Died July 15, 1970.

STICKLE, JOHN WESLEY, newspaper pub.; b. Livingston Manor, N.Y., Jan. 1, 1876; s. Andrew and Mary Elizabeth (Schoonmaker) S.; ed. pub. schs.; m. Clara Nobles, of Wellsville, N.Y., July 14, 1901 (dec.);children—Floyd Archibald, Stanley Schoonmaker, John Herbert; m. 2d, Carrie Nobles, of Wellsville, Aug. 12, 1927. Began as printer's apprentice, Wellsville Daily Reporter, 1895; pub. successively Cuba (N.Y.) Patriot, Poughkeepsie Enterprise, Virginia (Minn.) Enterprise; later gen. mgr. Morning Astorian, Astoria, Ore.; pres., pub. and gen. mgr. Allentown (Pa.) Chronicle and News, 1922-35, retired. Trustee Children's Aid Soc. Republican. Episcopalian. Mason (32 deg.). Clubs: Rotary, Livingston, Lehigh Country. Home: R.D. 2, Quakertown PA‡

STICKLES, ARNDT MATHIS, educator; b. Patricksburg, Ind., Jan. 4, 1872; s. Mathis and Elizabeth (Kefaber) S.; A.B., Ind. U., 1897; grad. student U. of Ill., 1897-98; A.M., Ind. U., 1904, Ph.D., 1923; student summers, U. of Chicago and Harvard; A.M., Harvard, 1910; m. Laura Gordon Chambers, of Louisville, Ky., July 26, 1911; children—Elizabeth Hume, Harriet Henry, James Channing. Prin. pub. schs., Yorktown, Ind., 1899-1901; head dept. of history, high schs., Elkhart, Ind., 1901-03, high sch., Evansville, 1903-08; head dept. of history, Western Ky. State Teachers Coll., since 1908. Lecturer before teachers' institutes, etc. Mem. N.E.A., Miss. Valley Historical Association, Phi Beta Kappa. Democrat. Presbyn. Mason. Kiwanian. Author: Elements of Government (text book), 1914; The Critical Court Struggle in Kentucky. Home: Bowling Green KY‡

STIEG, MAX, banker; b. Clintonville, Wis., Oct. 20, 1889; s. Bernhard G. and Mary (Dittberner) S.; grad. Sch. Banking, Rutgers U., 1951; m. Merle E. Overton, Nov. 27, 1915; children—Bernard O., Robert W., William D., Marjorie J., John C., Richard F. Messenger, teller Clintonville (Wis.) State Bank, 1906-10, asst. cashier, 1910-17; cashier 1st Nat. Bank, Clintonville, Wis., 1917-19; cashier Dairyman's State Bank, Clintonville, Wis., 1920-55, pres., 1955-64, chmn. bd., dir.; pres. Clintonville Elevator Co., also dir.; v.p., dir. Clintonville Mercantile Co. Past pres. Valley council, Boy Scouts of Am.; past v.p. Banking Review Bd. Wis.; past mem. Judicial Council for State of Wis.; treas., mem. Bd. of Edn., 1915-52. Chmn. Waupaca County Republican Com., 1945-53. Treas. Four Wheel Drive Found.; dir., treas. Clintonville Community Hosp. Assn. Appointed Waupaca County Chmn., U.S. War and Savings Bond Program. Recipient 25 year award, U.S. Treasury Dept., Alumnus Honorus award, Clintonville (Wis.) High Sch. Mem. Am. (past v.p., past mem. exec. council), Wis. (past pres.) bankers assns., Clintonville Assn. of Commerce (past pres.), Am. Inst. Banking, Wis. State Hist. Soc., Milw. Rose Soc. Conglist. Rotarian. (gov. dist. 622, 1958-59). Home: Clintonville WI Died Jan. 3, 1969.

STILES, FRED BAILEY, banker; b. Cherokee, Ia., Mar. 4, 1887; s. Charles A. and Frances Leah (Bailey) S.; student U. of Ia., 1906-07, U. of Wis., 1907-09; m. Frances Kenney, Feb. 15, 1911; 1 dau., Frances Bailey (Mrs. William M. Lamont). Cashier Owanka (S.D.) State Bank, 1910-16; cashier First Nat. Bank, Watertown, S.D., 1916-20, v.p., 1920-27, pres. 1927-32; pres. First Nat. Bank, Aberdeen, 1932-52, chmn. bd. dirs., 1952-57; pres. McCook County Nat. Bank, Salem, S.D., 1925-60, chmn. bd., from 1960. Admitted to S.D. bar, 1923; mem. War Finance Corp., Washington, 1921-23; v.p. Agrl. Credit Corp., Minneapolis, 1923-28; state senator, 1915; U.S. commr., 1926-30. Pres. S. D. Hist. Assn., 1955-57; mem. adv. bd. Northwest Bancorporation, Mpls., 1950-52. Presdient Aberdeen Civic Association, 1943. Honored by U.S. Treasury Dept. for 25 year service as regional coordinator U.S. Savs. Bond program. Mem. State Bankers Assn. (pres. 1924), State and Am. Bar Assn., Kappa Sigma, Newcomen Soc., Rotary. Republican. Episcopalian. Mason, Elk, Odd Fellow, Woodman. Club: Morse. Author articles in field. Home: Aberdeen SD Died Oct. 21, 1970; buried Oak Hill Cemetery, Cherokee IA

STILES, GEORGE K(EAN), consul; b. Baltimore, Nov. 14, 1873; s. William Lee and Elisabeth M. (White) S.; ed. Baltimore City Coll.; Johns Hopkins, 1891-4; m. Beatrice S. Clarke, of Baltimore, Feb. 18, 1899. Asso. editor, Baltimore Herald, 1901-3; trade editor Merchants and Manufacturers Journal, 1904-6; on editorial staff of Baltimore Evening News, 1906-8, 1912-15; spl. newspaper work in Europe, 1908-12; Am. consul at Teneriffe, Mar. 2, 1915-18, at Patras, Greece, 1919-23, at Stavanger, Norway, Apr. 15, 1923—. Author: The Dragonman, 1913; Zuleik, the Magnificent, 1914. Contbr. numerous short stories to newspapers and mags. Fellow Am. Geog. Soc. Club: National Press (Washington). Home: Baltimore MD Address: Am. Consulate, Stavanger Norway‡

STILES, HINSON, editor; b. Albert, N.B., Can., June 28, 1893; s. John Albion and Barbara (Downing) S.; brought to U.S., 1896, naturalized, 1924 student Brown U., 1914-15, Boston U., 1915-16, Harvard U., 1917-19, married to Claire Leonore Birnbaum. Reporter for the Providence (Rhode Island) News, 1913; copy editor Boston American, 1914-16, exchange editor, 1916-17, picture editor, 1918-23; picture editor Boston Record (Advertiser), 1923-28, asst. managing editor, 1928-33; assistant managing editor New York Daily and Sunday Mirror, 1933-35, mng. editor, 1935-61; asso. editor, administr. Mirror Youth Welfare Fund, from 1961. Mem. N.Y. Acad. Pub. Edn. Served as 2d lt. Brit. Royal Air Force, 1917-18. Hon. comdr. of Sea Cadets. Episcopalian. Mem. Airedale Terrier Clubs of America (past vice president), New York, Middlesex Kennel Club of N.J. Club: Palm Beach (Fla.) Athletic. Author: (plays) Room with the Black Door, 1927; Song O' The Sea, 1928. Home: New York CityNY also Palm Beach FL Died Jan. 1970.

STILL, ALFRED, elec. engr.; b. Gloucestershire, Eng., Jan. 28, 1869; s. Edmund Alexander and Julie Emma (Ott) S.; student College de Dieppe, France, 1879-85; grad. Finsbury Tech. Coll., London, 1889; m. Melita F.L. Gilbert, Sept. 17, 1902; children—Edmund Neville, Reginald Gilbert, Arthur John, Richard Waller. Designer of elec. machinery Edison & Swan Co., Manchester, Eng., 1890-99; chief engr. and mng. dir. Cowans, Ltd., Manchester, 1899-1911; chief elec. engr. Lake Superior Corp., Ont., Can., 1911-13; prof. elec. engring., Purdue Univ., 1913-34, retired. Fellow Am. Inst. Elec. Engrs.; mem. Institn. of Elec. Engineers (British), Eta Kappa Nu, Sigma Xi, Tau Beta Pi. Author: Polyphase Currents, 1906; Overhead Electric Power Transmission, 1913; Principles of Electrical Design, 1916; Electric Power Transmission, 1927; Principles of Transformer Design, 1919; Elements of Electrical Design, 1932; Soul of Amber, 1944; Soul of Lodestone, 1946; Communication Through the Ages, 1946. Contbr. on tech. and engring. subjects. Home: 6038 34th Av. N.E., Seattle 5 WA‡

STILSON, OSCAR REEVES, clergyman, coll. dean; b. Unadilla, Mich., June 1, 1876; s. Henry Noble and Frances (Reeves) S.; student Adrian (Mich.) Coll. Acad., 1897-99; A.B., Adrian Coll., 1903; A.M., U. of Mich., 1925; student, Oberlin Coll., summer 1910; m. Addie A. Hague, Sept. 15, 1898. Ordained to ministry Meth. Protestant Ch., 1903; pastor Jeddo, Mich., 1903-05, Capac, Mich., 1905-10; prof. history and economics, Adrian Coll., 1910-12, prof. philosophy and psychology, 1912-15, prof. psychology and edn., 1915-35, registar, 1916-35; dean and prof. of philosophy and Bible, Huntington (Ind.) College, 1935-46, dean emeritus, prof. philosophy and Bible since 1946. Sec. Mich. Annual Conf. Meth. Protestant Ch., 1906-10; pres. Mich. Assn. Collegiate Registrars, 1934-35. Charter mem. Pi Gamma Mu. Home: 1836 College Av., Huntington IN‡

STIMPSON, HERBERT BAIRD, author; b. at Font Hill, nr. Ilchester, Howard Co., Md., Jan. 31, 1869; s. William and Annie L. (Gordon) S.; ed. common schs.; aid Smithsonian Instn., 1882-92; LL.B., LL.M., Columbian (now George Washington) U., 1891; unmarried. In law practice at Baltimore since 1891. Democrat. Asso. editor Conservative Review, 1899. Author: The Regeneration, 1896; The Tory Maid, 1899. Home: 2100 14th St., Walbrook, Baltimore MD Office: 207 N. Calvert St., Baltimore MD‡

STIMSON, ARTHUR MARSTON, public health officer; b. Rome, N.Y., Nov. 30, 1876; s. William Hamilton and Anna Braddock (Gallup) S.; M.D., Long Island Coll. Hosp., 1898; m. Sarah Boyd, Dec. 9, 1903;children—Elspeth (dec.), Jean, William Hamilton, Allan Braddock. Commd. asst. surgeon Pub. Health Service of U.S., July 1902; passed asst. surgeon, Aug. 1907; surgeon, Aug. 1914; asst. dir. Hygienic Lab., Washington, D.C.; detail sanitation officer U.S. Navy, 1917-19; asst. surg. gen., Pub. Health Service, 1922, med. dir., 1930; directing studies of heart disease at Nat. Inst. of Health, Washington, D.C., 1931-42; retired. Mem. Am. Public Health Assn., A.M.A. Author: Facts and Problems of Rabies; also brief history of bacteriological investigations in Public Health Service, Communicable Diseases, and other public health writings. Home: 414 Raymond St., Chevy Chase 15 MD‡

STIMSON, PHILIP MOEN, pediatrician; b. St. Louis, Mo., Nov. 1, 1888; s. Henry Albert and Alice Wheaton (Bartlett) S.; ed. The Hill Sch.; A.B., Yale, 1910; M.D., Cornell, 1914; m. Elizabeth Baldwin, June 5, 1920. Interne N.Y. Hosp., 1914-16; asst. resident in pediatrics, St. Louis Childrens Hosp., 1916-17; dir. Poliomyelities Service, Knickerbocker Hosp., 1945-49; med. dir. Floating Hosp. of St. John's Guild at N.Y. City, from 1927; attending physician Willard Parker Hosp., N.Y.C., 1924-55; consulting pediatrician Meadowbrook, Bergen Pines, Norwegian, New York, Roosevelt, Horton Memorial and the St. Francis hosps.; prof. emeritus clin. pediatrics Cornell University Medical College. Served lieutenant to captain, United States Army, 1917-19. Awarded Purple Heart with oak leaf. Diplomate American Bd. Pediatrics; fellow Am. Acad. Pediatrics, A.M.A. life fellow in pediatrics, N.Y. Acad. Med. (chmn. Pediatrics Sect., 1938-39); founder mem. Clin. Research Soc., Pediatric Travel Club. Trustee The Hill Sch.; pres. of bd. of trustees St. John's Guild since 1951; member of the advisory committee of the Intercollegiate br., Y.M.C.A. Mem. The Century Assn. Author: (with Hodes) Common Contagious Diseases, 5th edit., 1956. Contbr. articles to various jours. Home: Hightstown NJ Died Sept. 13, 1971; inurned Columbarium, Riverside Ch., New York City NY

STINCHFIELD, ROGER ADAMS, govt. ofcl.; b. Clinton, Me., July 23, 1904; s. Roger F. and Rovena (Adams) S.; grad. Coburn Classical Inst., 1922; B.S., Colby Coll., 1926; LL.B., Suffolk Law Sch., 1930, LL.M., 1937; m. Pauline J. Sinclair, Aug. 6, 1926; 1 son, Carleton P. Admitted to Mass., Me. bars, 1930; chief dep. clk. U.S. Ct. Appeals, First Circuit, Boston, 1928-47, clk., 1947-70; lectr. in admiralty Boston U. Law Sch., 1957-70. Dir. Woburn Community Chest, 1942-56, pres., 1952-53; active Boy Scouts Am., sponsoring chmn., treas. Woburn area Cub Scouts, 1939-45; mem. Citizens Com. surveying Woburn schs., 1941-42; trustee Choate Meml. Hosp., Woburn, Mass., 1950-70, pres., 1958-59. Life trustee Woburn Pub. Library, pres. 1961-63. Mem. Woburn Bar Assn., Fed. Ct. Clks. Assn. (committeeman), New Eng. Historic Geneal. Soc., Phi Beta Kappa. Baptist. Mason. Author: The Woburn MA Died Jan. 4, 1970.

STINSON, JOHN TURNER, agriculturist; b. Pierceton, Ind., Sept. 5, 1865; s. Archibald D. and Elizabeth (Doke) S.; B.S., Ia. State Coll. Agr. and Mech. Arts, 1890; m. Roberta Trott, Aug. 15, 1894; children—Rebecca (wife of Dr. Ben M. Bull), Benjamin A., Ruth Elizabeth (Mrs. G.W. Billmyer, Jr.), John T. Horticulturist, Ark. Agrl. Expt. Sta., Fayetteville, 1891-1900; prof. horticulture, U. of Ark., 1895-1900; dir. Mo. State Fruit Expt. Sta., Mountain Grove, 1900-03; supt. pomology, in charge fruit exhibits, La. Purchase Expn., St. Louis, Mo., 1903-04; agrl. agt., Mo.P. R.R. Co., 1906-07; sec. Mo. State Fair, 1908-16; with extension forces, U. of Mo., 1917; sec. Am. Swine Growers Assn., 1918; sec. Southeast Mo. Agrl. Bur., 1919-21; dir. agrl. development, Mo. P.R.R. Co., St. Louis, 1921-45. Member Kappa Alpha. Democrat. Mem. Christian (Disciples) Ch. Mason. Home: 6820 Delmar Blvd. Office: Missouri Pacific Bldg., St Louis MO‡

STIRLING, J. BOWMAN, lawyer, banker; b. Pointe Coupee Parish, La., Jan. 15, 1870; s. Jacob Bowman and Penelope Jones (Stewart) S.; student U. of South, Sewanee, Tenn.; LL.B., cum laude, U. of Mo., 1891; m. Hallie Carter, of Jackson, Miss., June 9, 1897; children—Samuel Carter, Hallie. Began practice at Jackson, Miss., 1898; referee in bankruptcy, Jackson Div., Southern Dist., Miss., 1901-07 (resigned); atty.-gen., Miss., Nov. 16, 1908-Apr. 1910 (resigned); became pres. First Nat. Bank, Jackson, 1910; former pres. Union Savings & Deposit Bank, Plaza Investment Co. (both of Jackson, Miss.); pres. Standard Life Insurance Co. (Jackson); former v.p. Commercial Bank (Woodville, Miss.). Mem. and sec. Dem. State Exec. Com., Miss., 1907-11. Press. Miss. Bankers Assn., 1925-26. Commd. capt. of Cadets, U. of Mo., by Gov. David R. Francis; commd. capt. Capital Light Guards, Jackson, Miss., by Gov. A. J. McLaurin, 1898. Home: Jackson MS‡

STITT, WILLIAM BRITTON, lawyer; b. N.Y.C., Mar. 3, 1898; s. Edward W. and Jennie A. (Britton) S.; A.B., Amherst Coll., 1918; LL.B., Columbia, 1922; m.

'osephene Lloyd White, Feb. 8, 1923; children—Joan 3. (Mrs. Edward B. McMenamin), Barbara (Mrs. Clifford O. Greene), William Britton. Admitted to N.Y. ar, 1922; legal sec. Judge C. B. McLaughlin, N.Y. Ct. of Appeals, 1922-23; practice of law, N.Y.C., 1923-69, partner Havens, Wandless, Stitt & Tighe and predecessor firms, 1930-69. Director of the Chapman Machine Company, Information Systems, Incorporated, Watson-Flagg Machine Co., Tri-Con. Constrn. Co., Inc., Business Supplies Corp. Am., others; v.p. Kaiser Metal Products Co., Inc., Kaiser Fleetwings, Inc.; sec., dir. Island Flying Service, Ltd. Trustee Village of Scarsdale, 1938-42, acting mayor, 1941-42, mem. bd. appeals, 1956-61, chmn., 1959-61, Dir., secretary Speech Rehab. Inst. Served as naval aviator, World War . Member of the Assn. Bar City of N.Y., Am. N.Y. State, Westchester County bar assns., Royal Philatelic Soc. (London), Kipling Soc., Theta Delta Chi. Democrat. Presbyn. Mason (K.T.). Clubs: Century Collectors, Union League (N.Y.C.); Bohemian (San Francisco); University (Washington); Royal and Ancient (St. Andrews, Scotland); Lyford Cay (Bahamas) Tequesta Country (Jupiter, Fla.). Author: Corporate Practice of Engring. Home: Jupiter FL also Bridgehampton LI NY Died May 17, 1969; buried Edgewood Cemetery, Bridgehampton NY

STIX, SYLVAN L., business exec.; b. New York, N.Y., May 28, 1871; s. Louis and Henrietta (Hackes) S.; student Sach's School of New York; Mass. Inst. Tech.; m. Florence Deitsch, Mar. 16, 1898; children—Charlotte, Louis, Hugh, Susan (Mrs. Donald Weisman). Entire career with Seeman Bros., New York, N.Y., beginning 1891; partner, 1896; vice pres. Seeman Bros., Inc. when incorp., Dec. 1920, pres. since 1941. Dir. Duffy-Mott Co. Past commr. New York State Indsl. Council. Hon. life trustee New York and Brooklyn Federation. Mem. Nat.-Am. Wholesale Grocers' Assn. (past treas. and v.p.), N.Y. State Wholesale Grocers' Asso. (past pres.) Jewish Child Care Assn. of New York (vice pres.). Clubs: City, Town Hall, Wool, Fairview Country (past pres.). Home: Elmsford NY Office: 121 Hudson St., New York City 13 NY‡

STOCKDALE, ALLEN ARTHUR, clergyman; b. Zanesville, O., Sept. 15, 1875; s. Stephen Edward and Susan (Lawson) S.; A.B., Taylor U., Upland, Ind., 1896; grad. Boston U. Sch. of Theology, 1902; spl. work in philosophy and sociology, Boston U., resident student Oxford University, England, 1922-23; S.T.B., Boston U., 1923; D.D., Berea, 1924; LL.D., Marietta (Ohio) College, 1942; m. Ella Mae Reppard, Apr. 1, 1897. Ordained Congl. ministry, 1904; pastor Berkeley Temple, Boston, 1903-07; leader in combination of Berkeley Temple and Union Ch. and pastor of combined ch. (Union Ch.), Boston, 1907-14, 1st Congl. Ch., Toledo, O., 1914-28, Rogers Park Ch., Chicago, 1928-31, First Congl. Ch., Washington, D.C., 1931-36. Trustee Boston Univ.; served as dir. City Missionary Soc., Berkeley Infirmary, Toledo Art Museum and as chaplain Emerson Coll. of Oratory. Past grand prelate, Domain of Mass., K. of P. Mason. Clubs: Chicago Rotary, Congregational. Lectured among soldiers on Mexican border and in cantonments; in France 6 mos. as Red Cross field dir. with commn. of capt.; with 2d Div. near Soissons, July 1918. Author of booklet "Soldiers' Smiles." Editorial contbr. People's Home Jour., 1925; regular contbr. to Congregationalist. Editor Reveille, 1937-39. Well known as lecturer; dean speakers bur. of Nat. Assn. Mfrs. Home: 600 W. 115th St. Apt. 124 New York NY‡

STOCKING, CHARLES FRANCIS, author; b. Freeport, Ill., Sept. 4, 1873; s. Charles Henry and Matilda (Breed) S.; student Cornell U., 1894-95; S.B., U. of Chicago, 1898; grad. U. of Colo.; M.E., Colo. State Sch. of Mines, 1901; m. Jeannette Everett Porter, Feb. 27, 1915. Began as mining engr., 1901; engr. with Colo. Fuel & Iron Co., 1903-04, Colombia Remolino Mining & Development Co., 1904-05; mgr. Freeport Mining Co., Calif., 1905-08; mgr. in S. America, Andes Mining & Development Co., 1908-09; pres. The Maestro Pub. Co., Chicago, since 1915; pres. Maestro Productions, Inc., 1933. Became head of department of science The Forman Schools, Litchfield, Conn., 1941; president Craft House, Inc., 1951. Member of executive council Grant Area of Boy Scouts of America; member of executive council Stephenson County (Ill.) Civic League; pres. Freeport Student Loan Fund. Mem. Internat. Mark Twain Soc. (hon.), Eugene Field Soc. of St. Louis, Mo., Soc. Midland Authors, Phi Delta Theta. Christian Scientist. Mason. Clubs: Rotary (ex-pres.), Freeport Club. Author several books since 1912. Lectr. Redpath Bureau. Home: 1238 W. Freeport IL‡

STOCKTON, J(AMES) ROY, sports editor and commentator; b. St. Louis, Mo., Dec. 16, 1892; s. James R. and Hephzibah (Cook) S.; student, Washington Univ., 1910-13; m. Charlotte M. Burton, July 12, 1921 (deceased January 17, 1953); 1 son, Richard Burton; married second, Josephine K. Rassieur, July 31, 1954. Reporter, St. Louis Republic, St. Louis Globe-Democrat, St. Louis Post-Dispatch, 1917-48; sports editor, St. Louis Post-Dispatch, since 1946; sports commentator, radio sta. KSD, 1934-50. Protestant. Author: The Gashouse Gang, 1945. Contbr. to nat. mags. Home: Ladue MO Died Aug. 14, 1972.

STOCKTON, LOUISE, author; b. at Phila.; d. William S. and Emily H. S.; sister of late Frank R. Stockton. Has been connected with leading jours. as editorial writer, book editor and music critic. Contbr. to mags. of short stories, novelettes, and hist. essays; formerly pres. W. Phila. Centre Univ. Extension. Pres. The Round Robin Reading Clubs, a corr. system for individuals and classes designed for promotion of systematic study of lit. Mem. Browning Soc. Clubs: Contemporary (a founder), New Century (a founder). Author: Dorothea, 1882; Apple Seeds and Briar Thorn, 1887; A Sylvan City, 1883, republished as Quaint Corners, 1900. Address: 1408 31st St., Washington DC‡

STOCKWELL, EUGENE LAFAYETTE, lawyer, bus exec.; b. Moscow, Ida., Nov. 7, 1884; s. Frank Howard and Madora Ann (Hawley) S.; student Univ. of Ore., 1903-06; A.B., Stanford, 1908, J.D., 1909; m. Elizabeth Anne Wilder, Dec. 27, 1911; children—Marjorie Anne (Mrs. Frank A. Rhodes, Jr.), Eugene L., Mary Elizabeth (Mrs. William L. Hoyt, Jr.). With Garret McEnerney, atty., San Francisco, 1909-10; atty. in charge claim dept. Aetna Life Ins. Co. and affiliated cos., San Francisco, 1910-27; atty. in charge claim department Pacific Indemnity Company, Los Angeles, 1927-34, vice president and general counsel, 1934-46, exec. v.p., 1946-49, pres., 1949-51, ret. as pres. dir., mem. exec. com. Mem. Theta Delta Chi, Phi Delta Phi, Phi Beta Kappa. Republican. Clubs: Los Angeles Country, Los Angeles Breakfast. Home: Los Angeles CA Died June 23, 1971.

STOCKWELL, JOHN WESLEY, JR., clergyman; b. Portland, Me., Mar. 24, 1873; s. John Wesley and Eliza Jane (Mathias) S.; grad. New Ch. Theol. Sch., Cambridge, Mass., 1903; Ph.B., U. of Chicago, 1908; B.D., U. of Chicago Div. Sch., 1911; post-grad. study, U. of Chicago and Harvard; unmarried. Began as newspaperman; ordained ministry Ch. of the New Jerusalem (Swedenborgian), 1903; pastorates in Chicago and Phila.; specialized in social service. Special Minister to Portland, Ore., New Jerusalem Christian Ch., April-Sept., 1945. Missionary pastor of Maryland Assn. of New Church. Building secretary and acting chaplain, Camp Beauregard, Louisiana, World War I. Director Nat. New Ch. Group Study Bureau; mem. Nat. New Ch. Methods and Results Bur.; mem. exec. com. Nat. New Ch. Bd. of Missions; mem. New Ch. Pub. Relations Bur.; mem. U. of Chicago Div. Sch. Alumni Assn., Pa. Assn. Ch. of New Jerusalem. Founder, 1923, First Undenominational Radio Ch. America, Phila; radio speaker on special occasions, New York, Chicago, Philadelphia, Paterson, N.J., Portland, Me., Cincinnati, O.; founder Neo-Behaviorism and Knowledge Exten. Soc.; mem. com. Nat. New Ch. for Cent. of Prog. Expn., Chicago, 1933; chmn. radio com. Sesquicen. Expn., Phila.; chmn. Gen. Conv. of New Jerusalem 250th Swedenborg Birthday Commemoration, 1938; chmn. New Ch., N.Y. World's Fair Committee, 1939-40. Republican. Mason. Mem. Pennsylvania Soc. of Sons of the Revolution. Clubs: Union League, Army and Navy, Union. Author: Health from the Spiritual Sun, 1928; Introduction and Appendix to Kentucky Americans; Riding the Question Mark Through Life Situations and Progress, 1937; The Lord's Own Bible, 1930; Swedenborg: Noetic Mystic and Other Poems, 1940. Co-author of research volume, Johnny Appleseed, A Voice in The Wilderness. Writer of brochures, poems, etc. Awarded 1st prize in The Year Book of Modern Poetry, 1939. Home: 2025 Cherry St., Philadelphia PA Office: 15120 Detroit Av., Lakewood 7 OH‡

STODDARD, A(RTHUR) E(LSWORTH), railway exec.; b. Auburn, Neb., July 28, 1895; s. James P. and Maryvilla (Johnson) S.; student Springfield (Mo.) Bus. Coll.; Harvard U., 1917-18; m. Oceain L. Johnson, Jan. 24, 1920; children—Robert E. (killed in action on Iwo Jima, Mar. 5, 1945), Patricia D. (Mrs. John H. Caton), Richard J. Shop apprentice Frisco Lines, Springfield (Mo.) shops, 1915-16; student helper U.P.R.R., Gothenburg, Neb., 1916-17, operator, 1917-28, dispatcher, 1926-28, chief dispatcher, 1928-34, trainmaster, 1934-37, asst. supt., 1937-41, supt., 1941-46, asst. gen. mgr. Omaha, 1946-47, gen. mgr., 1947-48, v.p., 1948-49, pres. Omaha, 1949-65; dir. U.P.R.R., Omaha Nat. Bank, 1st Security Corp. USN operator and chief operator on transports, rank of C.P.O., 1917-18; duty in S. Am., 1918-19; called to active service, rank of col., Transporation Corps., U.S. Army, Sept. 1942; served in Iran, England, and E.T.O.; dep. dir. gen. of mil. rys. br., G-4 div. SHAEF, England, 1943-45, Europe gen. mgr. of 1st mil. ry. service, 1945-46; relieved active duty, 1946; dep. dir. gen. G.H.Q., Mil. Ry. Service Organized Res., 1949, dir. gen., from 1951; brig. gen. U.S. Army (Res.), 1949, maj. gen., 1954, ret. 1958. Mem. C. of C., Res. Officers Assn., Nat. Aero. Assn., Mil. Order World Wars, Vets. Fgn. Wars, Air Force Assn., Assn. Am. Railroads, Am. Legion, Mil. Railway Vets. Presbyterian. Mason (Shrine). Clubs: Country, The Omaha (Omaha). Home: Omaha NB Died Mar. 1969.

STODDARD, CHARLES COLEMAN, editor, author; b. Cedar Rapids, Ia., Jan. 25, 1876; s. Joseph C. and Mary (Weeks) S.; grad. Cedar Rapids High Sch., June, 1892; sp'l student 1 yr. Coe Coll.; grad. Lafayette Coll., 1897, A.M., 1900; sp'l work in geology, Lafayette, June, 1897, to Jan., 1898; m. Elizabeth, N. J., June 21, 1905, Anna Low Glen. In editorial dept. D. Appleton & Co., 1898-1904, advertising mgr., 1903-4; with F. A. Stokes Co., 1905-6. Regular contbr. to Appleton's Annual Cyclo., and has contributed verse and prose to many periodicals. Residence: 311 W. 94th St. Office: Astor Theater Bldg., New York NY‡

STODDARD, FLORENCE JACKSON, editor; b. nr. New Orleans, La.; d. Thomas J. and Fannie (Wright) Jackson; ed. by mother (a noted educator), and at Rutgers Coll.; later studied in Paris, France; m. Edward Learned Stoddard, of Pittsfield, Mass., Oct., 1885. Began as corr. from Buenos Aires for New York Evening Post, 1881; joined staff of Review of River Platte, 1891, Arrow, 1892; lived next in Europe and Cuba, corresponding for Am. jours.; returned to New York and became connected with staff on New York Tribune, 1897; editor Overland Monthly, San Francisco, 1902, 1903, McCall's Magazine, New York, 1904, Pictorial Review, 1906-7. Lecturer New York Bd. of Edn. Mem. Rutgers Alumnae Assn. (New York), Anna Shaw League (Brooklyn). Author: As Old as the Moon, Cuban legends, 1909. Contbr. to mags. and revs. Home: 1048A Sterling Pl., Brooklyn NY‡

STODDARD, HARRY G., business executive; Doctor of Engineering (honorary), Worcester (Mass.) Polytech. Inst.; Dr. Civil Leadership (hon.) Clark U., Worcester; LL.D., Coll. of Holy Cross, Worcester, Mass.; married; children—Robert W., Lincoln W. (dec.) Marion S. (Fletcher). Chmn. bd. Worcester Telegram & Gazette, Inc., until 1965; chmn. bd. Wyman-Gordon Co., until 1964; dir. at various times Boston & Me. R.R., Graton & Knight Mfg. Co., Worcester, Worcester County Nat. Bank, State Mutual Life Assurance Co. Am., Worcester, United Aircraft Corp., East Hartford, Conn., Liberty Mutual Ins. Co., Boston; former trustee Worcester Five Cents Savs. Bank. Served as dir. Worcester YMCA, Worcester Boys Club; bd. dirs., pres. Worcester Community Chest. Home: Worcester MA Died May 21, 1969.

STODDARD, HOWARD J., banker; b. Baker, Ore., Nov. 1, 1901; s. George Eckersley and Ellen (Izatt) S.; student Ore. State Coll., 1919-20; B.S., Columbia U., 1925; m. Jennie Creer, Sept. 4, 1924; children—Howard Preston, Virginia Clare, Stanford Creer, Charles Creer. Chmn. Mich. Nat. Bank, Lansing, from 1940; chairman of board Michigan Bank, Detroit; director Auto Owners Insurance Co., Mich. Millers Mut. Fire Insurance Company, Wolverine Ins. Company, Fed. Life & Casualty Ins. Co., Radio N.Y. Worldwide, Wickes Corp., Channing Corp. Home: East Lansing MI Died June 1971.

STODDARD, JAMES ALEXANDER, univ. prof.; b. Owings, S.C., Oct. 12, 1876; s. Robert James and Frances Deree (DuPree) S.; A.B., U. of South Carolina, 1902; A.M., George Peabody Coll. for Teachers, Nashville, Tenn., 1924; LL.D., Presbyterian Coll. of South Carolina, Clinton, S.C., 1930; m. Effie Linda Toland, Jan. 5, 1905; children—Mary Floride, Robert James, Hugh Toland, David Lowry, Effie Linda (Mrs. Edward Arthur Harter, Jr.). Teacher in rural schools, 1898-1900; prin. rural sch., 1902-03, village sch., 1903-05; prin. high sch., Darlington, S.C., 1905-07; supt. city schs., Heath Springs, S.C., 1907-11; asst. supt. edn., South Carolina 1911-18; prof. secondary edn., U. of South Carolina, also state high sch. inspector, 1918-20; prof. secondary edn. and dir. summer sch., 1920-45, prof. secondary education, 1945-46, prof. of education emeritus since 1946, U. of S.C. Mem. board trustee Queens College, Charlotte, N.C., 1932-44; hon. trustee since 1944. Mem. N.E.A., South Carolina Edn. Assn., Am. Assn. Sch. Adminstr., Phi Beta Kappa, Phi Delta Kappa, Kappa Phi Kappa, Kappa Sigma Kappa, Blue Key. Democrat. Modern Woodman. Club: Wardlaw Schoolmasters (Columbia, S.C.). Author: Geography of South Carolina, 1922; Backgrounds of Secondary Education in South Carolina, 1924. Home: 3323 Devereaux Rd., Columbia 55 SC‡

STODDARD, ROBERT CURTIS, lawyer; b. Milford, Conn., Jan. 31, 1875; s. William Buddington and Sarah (French) S.; Ph.B., Yale, 1894, LL.B., 1896; M. Dorothea Burt, Jan. 12, 1916. Admitted to Conn. bar, 1896; partner Stoddard, Persky, Eagan & Cobey, New Haven; judge Town Ct. of Milford, 1912-41; v.p., dir. Milford Savs. Bank; pres. and dir. Milford Cemetery Assn. Mem. Bd. Edn., Milford, 1908-33, chmn. Sewer Commn., 1934-37; v.p., dir. Taylor Library; dir. Milford Hosp. Chmn. Fowler Meml. Bldg., 1930-40. Mem. draft bd., World War I. Mem. Am., Conn. State and New Haven Co. bar assns. Home: 417 Gulf St., Milford, Conn. Office: 205 Church St., New Haven‡

STODDART, CHARLES WILLIAM, educator; b. Boscobel, Wis., Oct. 14, 1877; s. William and Emma (Sylvester) S.; B.A., Columbia, 1900, M.A., 1901; Ph.D. U. of Wis., 1909; m. Clara Coburn Cook, June 12, 1902; children—Charles William, Harold Coburn, Robert Cook. Mining business, in Colo., 1902-04; instr. and asst. prof. of soils, U. of Wis., 1904-10; prof. agrl. chemistry, 1910-20, dean Sch. Liberal Arts, 1920-45, dean emeritus, 1945-71, acting dean Sch. Natural Sciences, 1920-24, Pa. State Coll. Mem. Beta Theta Pi,

Phi Beta Kappa, Sigma Xi, Phi Kappa Phi, Alpha Zeta. Conglist. Author: Chemistry of Agriculture, 1915. Home: State College PA Died Aug. 2, 1971; buried Pine Hall Cemetery State College PA

STODDART, L(AURENCE) A., coll. prof., research ecologist; b. Trinidad, Colo., July 17, 1909; s. Laurence D. and Hilda (Green) S.; B.S., Colo. Agrl. Coll., 1931, M.S., 1932; Ph.D., U. of Neb., 1934; m. Ruth Young, May 28, 1932; children—Hilda Ruth, Elizabeth Ann, Laurence Charles. Teaching fellow Colo. Agrl. Coll., 1931-32; range agent U.S. Soil Conservation Serv., 1934-35; with Utah State University and Utah Expt. Sta., 1935-45, prof. and head dept. of range management, acting dean of forestry, 1942-43, 46-68; prof. and head of range mgt. dept. Tex. Agrl. and Mechanical Coll., 1945-46; chairman of the range and pasture com. Nat. Research Council 1949-62. Mem. Am. Soc. Range Mgmt. (nat. pres. 1952), Alpha Zeta, Sigma Xi, Xi Sigma Pi, Phi Kappa Phi. Republican. Episcopalian. Author: Range Management, 1943, rev. 1954; Technical Writing, 1938; rev., 1948. Contbr. articles to prof. jours.; author bulls. on range management, plant ecology, drought resistance, livestock mgt., soil conservation, animal nutrition, big game mgt. Mem. editorial staff Ecology, 1938-42; asso. editor Jour. of Forestry, 1946-50; mem. editorial bd. Jour. of Range Mgmt., 1948-50. Home: Logan UT Died July 17, interred Logan City Cemetery Logan UT

STOEPLER, AMBROSE M., govt. ofcl. Dist. dir. U.S. Internal Revenue Service, Detroit. Died Sept. 23, 1969.

STOKES, HAROLD PHELPS, newspaper man; b. N.Y.C., Jan. 10, 1887; s. Anson Phelps and Helen Louisa (Phelps) S.; grad. Groton (Mass.) Sch., 1904; B.A., Yale, 1909 (Phi Beta Kappa); traveled and studied in Europe, 1904-05, and in Far East, 1909-10; m. Elizabeth Miner King, Sept. 17, 1920; children—Helen Elizabeth, Lydia King, Anne Cornelia. Reporter N.Y. Evening Post, 1911-13; Albany corr., 1913-17; corr. for Evening Post at Peace Conf., Paris, France, 1919; Washington corr. Evening Post, 1919-23; sec. to Herbert Hoover, 1924-26; editorial staff N.Y. Times, 1926-37. Student 1st Plattsburg O.T.C., 1917; commd. 2d lt., Aug. 15, 1917; 1st lt., Sept. 2, 1918; served with 306th F.A., 77th Div., A.E.F., Sept. 1917-Apr. 1919; participated in Oise-Aisne and Meuse-Argonne campaigns. Trustee Trudeau (N.Y.) Sanatorium, 1913-38. Sec. Class of 1909, Yale, 1909-21. Episcopalian. Washington DC Died June 3, 1970.

STOKES, HENRY NEWLIN, social worker; b. Moorestown, N.J., Oct. 24, 1859; s. Dr. John H. and Tabitha (Jenkins) S.; B.S., Haverford Coll., 1878; Ph.D., Johns Hopkins, 1884; U. of Munich and Federal Polytechnic, Zurich, Switzerland, 1884-89; m. Wilhelmina van den Berg, 1884. Chemist U.S. Geol. Survey, 1889-92 and 1894-1903; asst. prof. inorganic chemistry, Univ. of Chicago, 1892-93; asso. chemist, Bureau of Standards, 1903-09. Retired from chemical work, 1909; founded The O.E. Library League and edits its organ, The O.E. Library Critic, in behalf of prison reform and aid to prisoners. Club: Cosmos. Address: 1207 Q St. N.W., Washington DC‡

STOKES, JOHN HARRISON, JR., army officer; b. Freehold, N.J., Oct. 27, 1895; s. John Harrison and Elizabeth (Ayres) S.; B.S., U.S. Mil. Acad., 1918; m. Marion Elizabeth Mitchell, July 25, 1934; 1 son, John Harrison, III. Commd. 2d lt., U.S. Army, 1918, advanced through grades to maj. gen., 1953; served as chief of staff and asst. div. comdr. 2d Inf. Div., 1941-45, chief of staff XV Corps, 1945-46; dep. comdr. Allied Control Commn., Hungary, 1946-47; mil. attache. Hungary, 1947-49; chief of staff 6th Army, 1950-51; asst. chief of staff plans and operations Allied Forces So. Europe, Naples, Italy, 1951-53; mem. Sec. of Army's Review Bd. Council, 1953-54; comdg. gen. Mil. Dist. of Washington, 1954-56. Decorated Silver Star with oak leaf cluster, Legion of Merit with oak leaf cluster, B.S.M.; Legion of Honor, Croix de Guerre with palms (France); Russian Order of the Fatherland; War Cross (Czechoslovakia). Mem. Delta Tau Delta. Home: Menlo Park CA Died Nov. 1968; buried Presidio Nat. Cemetery CA

STOKES, JOSEPH, JR., physician; b. Moorestown, N.J., Feb. 22, 1896; s. Joseph and Mary (Emlen) S.; student Haverford Coll., 1912-16, Sc.D. (honorary), 1952; M.D., U. Pa., 1920; Med. Sc.D. (honorary), 1963; m. to Frances D. Eikitnon, Mar. 24, 1921; children—Jean Frances, Joseph, III, Donald E., Eleanor. Instr. U. of Pa. Med. Sch., 1923-24, instr. pediatrics, 1924-28, asso. pediatrics, 1928-31, Wm. H. Bennett asst. prof., 1931-33, asst. prof. pediatrics, 1933-36, asso. prof., 1936-38, William H. Bennett prof. pediatrics, 1939-62, emeritus professor; asso. physician in chief, Children's Hospital, 1936-38, physician in chief, 1939-63; dir. pediatric service, Abington Hospital, 1930-39; chief pediatric service, Hosp. of U. of Pa., 1939-62; director medical education Burlington County Meml. Hosp.; consultant Merck & Company. Hon. consul gen. Phila. for Govt. of Japan, 1967-72. Dir. Commd. Measles and Mumps Bd. for the Investigation and Control of Epidemic Diseases; cons. to surgeon gen., U.S. Army; consultant to secretary of war; mem. subcom. on maternity care and child health Office Fgn. Relief and Rehabilitation, U.S. State Dept.; mem. U.S. com. U.N. International Children's Emergency Fund; mem. bd. dirs. Phila. World Affairs Council; mem. commission on liver diseases, Armed Forces Epidemiological Bd.; mem. com. on blood and blood derivatives, NRC, mem. subcom. on plasma; nat. com. 1960 White House Conf. Children and Youth. Mem. expert adv. panel of the WHO; chmn. commn. on plasma fractionation Protein Foundation, Recipient Medal of Freedom; James E. Bruce medal, A.C.P., 1962; John Howland medal, Am. Pediatric Soc., 1962; Gordon Wilson medal Am. Clin. and Climatol Association. Made nutrition survey of unoccupied France for Am. Friends Service Committee, 1940. Director Pocono Lake Preserve; co-chairman joint committee on public health and preventive medicine, Coll. of Physicians and Philadelphia County Medical Society; mem. medical advisory bd., Visiting Nurse Soc.; mem. Sydeham Coterie, Interurban Clinical Club. Mem. bd. dirs., Philadelphia Child Guidance Clinic, Phila. Child Health Soc. Was co-chmn. for Pa. Am. Acad. Pediatrics. Trustee Woods Schs., Haverford Coll., Children's Seashore House. Fellow Philadelphia Coll. Physicians (council); mem. Wistar Association, A.M.A. (mem. council Pharmary and Chemistry), Am. Philos. Soc., Am. Pediatric Soc. (pres. 1958-59), Assn. Am. Physicians, Soc. Am. Microbiologists, Phila. County Med. Soc., Soc. Pediatric Research (one of founders), John Morgan Soc., Triangle Soc. of Haverford Coll., Sigma Xi, Phi Beta Kappa, Alpha Omega Alpha, Alpha Mu Pi Omega, Phi Kappa Sigma. Republican. Mem. Society of Friends. Contbr. articles to med. jours. Home: Chestnut Hill PA Died Mar. 9, 1972; buried nr. Moorestown NJ

STOLTZ, CHARLES EDWARD, finance co. exec.; b. Evansville, Ind. Feb. 13, 1920; s. Edward M. and Neda (Buchenberger) S.; student exec. devel. program Ind. U., 1960-61; m. Rosemary Couch, Apr. 12, 1947; children—Joseph C., Sue Ellen, Diane Elizabeth, Gary E., Alan M. Mgmt. trainee CREDITHRIFT Financial Corp., Evansville, 1939-42, advt. mgr., 1946-65, mgr. pub. and stockholder relations, 1966-68, corp. sec., 1969-71. Served with AUS, 1942-45; ETO. Home: Evansville IN Died Dec. 30, 1971; buried Park Lawn Cemetery, Evansville IN

STOLZ, LEON, newspaperman; b. Chicago, Ill., Sept. 12, 1893; s. Joseph and Blanche Amelia (Rauh) S.; Ph.B., U. of Chicago, 1914; m. Marcia Preble, April 25, 1927; 1 son, Preble. Reporter Chicago Tribune, 1914-18, mem. staff Paris edition, 1919-21; telegraph editor Chicago Herald & Examiner, 1923-24; editorial writer Chicago Tribune 1925-42, chief editorial writer, 1942-63, editorial consultant, 1963-68. Served as private, United States Army, 1918-19. Member Am. Soc. Newspaper Editors. Republican. Jewish religion. Home: Chicago IL Died Oct. 14, 1968.

STONE, CHARLES FREDERIC, indsl. exec.; b. Chattanooga, Feb. 28, 1883; s. Francis Irwin and Emma A. (Kirkpatrick) S.; student pvt. schs., Chattanooga, also Ga. Inst. Tech., 1903; m. Virginia Butler, Jan. 17, 1906 (dec.); children—Lucile (Mrs. James C. Dunlap), Charles Frederic (M.D.). Office staff, traveling sales rep. F. I. Stone & Co., Atlanta, 1903-10; with Atlantic Steel Co. (formerly Atlanta Steel Co.), 1910-70, beginning as sales rep., successively mgr. sales, v.p. charge sales, pres., 1910-47, chmn., 1947-63, chmn. exec. com., 1956-70; dir. Trust Co. of Ga. Trustee Agnes Scott College, Lewis H. Beck Scholarship Fund, Atlanta. Mem. Sigma Alpha Epsilon (past nat. treas.; mem. Supreme Council). Presbyn. (elder). Club: Capital City (hon. life) (Atlanta). Home: Atlanta GA Died Jan. 25, 1970.

STONE, CLIFF WINFIELD, prof. edn.; b. Fisk, Wis., Oct. 19, 1874; s. Edmund George and Lena Victoria (Miller) S.; grad. State Normal Sch., Oshkosh, Wis., 1899; B.S., Columbia, 1904, Ph.D., 1908; m. Kate M. King, Aug. 8, 1906; children—Stillman Sanford (dec.), Vesta Virginia, Edmund Jefferson, Charles Irving. Prin. Jr. High Sch., Indianapolis, Ind., 1899-1903; prin. Ethical Culture Sch., N.Y. City, 1904-06; head of dept. of edn. and dir. teaching, State Normal Coll., Farmville, Va., 1908-14; dir. teaching, State Teachers' Coll., Cedar Falls, Ia., 1914-18; mem. faculty A.E.F. Univ., Beaune, France, 1919; prof. education, 1920-46, prof. emeritus of education, State College of Washington, since 1946. Mem. trade test division, Committee on Classification of Personnel in U.S.A., Newark N.J., 1918. Mem. N.E.A., Nat. Conf. on Ednl. Methods, Nat. Soc. for Study of Edn., Am. Assn. Univ. Profs., Pi Gamma Mu, Phi Kappa Phi, Phi Delta Kappa, Sigma Phi Epsilon. Author: Arithmetical Abilities, 1908; Reasoning Tests, 1914; Reasoning Tests in Arithmetic and How to Use Them, 1921; New Stone Reasoning Tests in Arithmetic, 1927 (all four pub. by Teachers' Coll.). Contbr. to ednl. mags. Collaborator: Teaching Elementary School Subjects, 1916. Home: Pullman WA‡

STONE, DAVID LAMME, army officer; b. Stoneville, Miss., Aug. 15, 1876; s. David Lamme and Katie (Hunt) S.; grad. U.S. Mil. Acad., 1898; m. Helen Hoagland, Oct. 3, 1903; children—David Lamme, Mrs. Mark A. Devine, Mrs. John Theimer; m. 2d, Ruth B. Warfield, Dec. 20, 1931; m. 3d, Anita Thorne Corse, Jan. 1, 1936 Commd. 2d lt. inf., U.S. Army, Apr. 26, 1898; advance through grades to major general, Oct. 1, 1936. Served in Cuba, 1898, Philippines, 1899-1903, with A.E.F. France, 1918-19. In charge mil. constrn. H.I.; buil Camp Lewis, Wash., at beginning of World War; with 3d Div. in France in Marne, Chauteau Thierry, St. Mihiel Argonne campaigns; staff Army of Occupation Germany, 1919; Am. rep. on Inter-Allied Rhineland High Commn., Coblenz, 1919-23; Gen. Staff, 1923-25 comd. 6th Inf., Jefferson Barracks, Mo., 1925-26; exec officer for asst. sec. of War in charge organized reserve affairs, 1926-30; comdg. 3d Inf., Ft. Snelling, 1931-32 prof. mil. science and tactics, U. of Ill., 1932-33; comdg Ft. Snelling, 88th Div. Organized Res. and Civilian Conservation Corps, Northern Minn., 1933-35; comdg gen. 3d Div., Ft. Lewis, Wash., 1935-36; dept. comdr Panama Canal Dept., 1936-40; retired. Awarde D.S.M.; Silver Star Medal for gallantry agains Philippine Insurgents (woulded in action); Maple Hear Decoration (U.S.); Comdr. Legion of Honor (France) Officer of Order of Leopold I (Belgium); Croix d Guerre (France). Episcopalian. Clubs: Chevy Chase Army and Navy (Washington); Minnesota, University Somerset (St. Paul); Minneapolis Club. Home Thornewood, Tacoma WA*‡

STONE, FREDERICK E., business executive; b Wilmington, Del., Feb. 9, 1871; s. George W. an Catherine C. (Graupner) S.; student Friends Sch., 1886 Swarthmore Coll., 1888; m. Bertha Linton Smith, Jun 1, 1896; children—George, Linton, Roger, Mrs Margaret S. Crawford. Pres. Wilmington Savings Fun Soc., Woodlawn Trustees, Inc.; dir. Farmers Mut. Fir Ins. Co., Del. Elec. Supply Co. (past pres.), Holding Co of Del. (past pres.), Crescent Foundry Co. (past treas.) Perpetual Savings & Loan Assn. (past v.p.). Mem. fed legislation and pub. utilities coms. Nat. Assn. of Mutua Savings Banks; formerly Del. chmn. Defense Saving Bond Com. for Mutual Savings Banks; dir. Security Research Bureau. Pres. Peoples Settlement Assn. Minquadale Home, Wilmington Fountain Society, Del Indsl. Sch. for Girls. Republican. Unitarian. Home 2501 Willard St. Office: 838 Market St., Wilmingto DE‡

STONE, H(ENRY) CHARLES, clergyman; b Monmouth, Eng., Sept. 13, 1873; s. George and Juli (Newbolt) S.; ed. in England; m. Irene Pope, o Roxborough, Pa., Jan. 29, 1914. Came to U.S., 1893 deacon, 1901, priest, 1902, P.E. Ch.; formerly asst. St Luke's Ch., and Ch. of the Epiphany, Phila.; asst. Ch. o Holy Trinity, and minister in charge Holy Trinity Memorial Chapel, 1910-14; founder, 1914, Stonemen' Fellowship (over 150,000 members, 1917). Democrat Mason. Home: St. Davids PA Office: 138 S. 22d St Philadelphia PA‡

STONE, H. CHASE, chmn. El Pomar Found. Address Colorado Springs CO Died Oct. 9, 1966.

STONE, HERBERT STUART, publisher (H. S. Stone & Co.); b. Chicago, May 29, 1871; son Melville E Stone, q. v.; grad. Harvard, 1894; founded and edite The Chap Book (discontinued). Not married. Autho First Editions of American Authors. Residence: 40 Erie St. Office: Eldridge Ct., Chicago IL‡

STONE, ISABELLE, educator; b. Chicago, Ill.; d Leander and Harriet H. (Leonard) S.; B.A., Wellesley 1893; M.S., U. of Chicago, 1897, Ph.D., 1898. Instr. in physics, Vassar, 1899-1908; prin. Sch. for Am. Girls in Rome, 1908-14; head of physics dept., Sweet Briar (Va. Coll., 1916-23; head of Misses Stone's Sch. for Girls Washington, D.C., since 1923. Mem. A.A.A.S., Am Fed. Arts, Am. Assn. Univ. Women, Nat. Assn Principals Schs. for Girls, English-Speaking Union o U.S., Inst. Francais de Washington, League Rep Women. Methodist. Home: 1626 Rhode Island Av N.W., Washington DC‡

STONE, IVAN MCKINLEY, edn. cons.; b. Jewel County, Kan., Oct. 3, 1899; s. Charles Edward an Minnie Gertrude (Hutchens) S.; A.B., U. Neb., 1923 A.M., U. Ill., 1926; Ph.D., 1930; m. Janice Shrimpton Sept. 12, 1926. Instr. polit. sci. U. Neb., 1923-24 teaching fellow polit. sci. U. Cal., 1924-25; asst. polit sci. U. Ill., 1926-29; asst. prof. dept. govt. Beloit (Wis. Coll., 1930-33; asso. prof., 1933-37, prof., head dept 1937-57, dean coll., 1951-64, dir. World Affairs Center 1964-68, cons., 1970-71, chmn. internat. relation concentration, 1968-70. Chmn., Nat. Summer Conf Acad. Deans, 1963; mem. staff Am. Com. in Geneva Switzerland, 1936, 37, chmn., 1939; co-dir. Geneva Inst. Internat. Relations, 1939; mem. div. internat. orgn affairs Dept. State, Washington, 1944-45; asst information officer U.N., Conf. on Internat. Orgn., San Francisco, 1945; vis. expert U.S. Dept. Army Germany, 1949, USIS, Germany, 1951, 52; lectr. Bri UN Assn., 1951; leader chmn. Quaker Europea Internat. Seminars, 1949, 50, 52, 64; dir. Semina Internat. Orgn., Geneva, 1962, 64, 66, 67, 69; vic chmn. Wis. Gov.'s Com. on UN, 1968-71. Mem. Am Soc. Internat. Law (exec. council 1956-59), N. Centra Assn. Acad. Deans (pres. 1957-58), Am. (exec. counci 1951-53), Midwest (exec. council 1956-58, v.p 1958-59) polit. sci. assn., Phi Beta Kappa, Phi Delt

Kappa, Omicron Delta Kappa, Phi Eta Sigma, Tau Kappa Epsilon. Rotarian. Club: Faculty and Alumni (Beloit College). Home: Beloit WI Died Aug. 25, 1971; buried Beloit WI

STONE, J(OHN) MCWILLIAMS, mfr.; b. Chgo., Sept. 11, 1896; s. James Dickey and Helen (Sweet) S.; B.S., Armour Inst. Tech., Chgo., 1920; m. Marion Tilley Jones, Dec. 11, 1926; children—J. McWilliams Jr., William Thomas. Comml. wireless operator, marine engr., 1913-15; trial trip engr. Bethlehem Shipbuilding Co., 1917-19; v.p. Van Dorn Coupler Co., 1920-22; founder, pres. Operadio Corp., from 1922, became DuKane Corporation, 1951, chairman, 1956-70. Trustee Illinois Institute of Technology, Lake Forest Acad. Member N.A.M. (past dir.), Nat. Security Indsl. Assn. (trustee), Electronic Industries Assn. (founder, mem. bd. 1924). Home: St Charles IL Died June 8, 1970.

STONE, JAMES LAURISTON, banker; b. St. Albans, Vt., July 8, 1873; s. James Palmer and Ruby Ann (Church) S.; student Ripon Coll., 1888-90; m. Louise Sherman, Nov. 27, 1914. Clerk in postoffice, advancing to asst. postmaster, Ripon, 1890-99; bookkeeper German Nat. Bank, Ripon, 1899-1901, asst. cashier, 1901-02, cashier, 1902-15; cashier Am. Nat. Bank, 1915-22, pres., 1922-30; pres. First Nat. Bank (consolidation of First and American nat. banks) since Mar. 19, 1930; dir. Universal Motor Co., Oshkosh, Wis., Oshkosh Overall Co., Ripon Knitting Works; city comptroller, Ripon, 1904-16. Pres. Wis. Bankers Assn., 1945-46. Trustee Ripon Coll. since 1908, sec. of bd., 1922-38, treas. since 1938. Republican. Conglist. Mason (32 deg., K.T., Shriner). Address: Ripon WI*‡

STONE, JOHN PAUL, librarian, prof. library sci.; b. Martinsville, Mo., Jan. 4, 1902; s. John Alexander and Sarah Elizabeth (Van Hoozer) S.; S.B., Northwest Mo. State Teacher's Coll., 1926; S.B. with honors, U. of Ill., 1929, S.M., 1930; Ph.D., U. of Chicago, 1945; m. Mary Katherine Jones, June 11, 1931; 1 son, John Edward. Teacher rural elementary sch. Bethany, Mo., 1922-23; teacher English and pub. speaking, high sch., Moberly, Mo., 1926-27, Joplin, Mo., 1927-28; asst. order dept. U. of Ill. library, 1928-29; organizer library curriculum and prof. library sci., La. State Coll., 1930; librarian and asso. prof. library sci., San Diego (Cal.) State Coll., 1930-47, librarian and prof. 1947-60, prof. and coordinator library science, 1960-66, study of library revenue for Am. Library Assn., 1939-40, surveyed services of regional union catalogues and bibliog. centers in U.S. for A.L.A., 1941; surveyed Radio, Sound and Electronics Library, U.S. Navy, 1946; chmn. com. on library standards for Cal. state colls., 1949-50. Treas. San Diego (Cal.) Sci. Library Bd., 1947-50; chmn. San Diego State Coll. Wesley Found. Bd., 1956-60; mem. Inter-Faith Found. Bd.; leader Great Books Study Group, 1948-49. Mem. Am. Library Assn., Cal. Library Assn. (pres. So. dist., 1939-40), Assn. Cal. State Coll. Librarians (exec. com. 1947-48, vice pres. 1948-49), American Association of University Professors, Beta Phi Mu. Republican. Methodist (mem. bd.). Author: Factors Influencing Reading Choices, 1930; Regional Union Catalogues (Am. Library Assn.), 1942. Co-author and editor: Standards for Cal. State College Libraries, 1949. Editor: Library Program San Diego State College, 1957-58. Contbr. to profl. jours. Home: San Diego CA Died June 6, 1966.

STONE, JOHN PITTMAN, lawyer; b. Carroll County, Miss., Oct. 9, 1890; s. Isaac Burgess and Katherine (Farmer) S.; B.S., U. Miss., 1913, LL.B., 1916; M. Ruth Sisler, Nov. 7, 1933; children—Nancy Ruth (Mrs. John E. Kimbrough), John Burgess. Admitted to Miss. bar, 1916; local atty. I.C. R.R., 1920-69; organized Tallahatchie Valley Electric Power Assn., 1936, gen. counsel, 1936-61; atty. Bank of Water Valley, Miss., municipality atty., Coffeeville, Miss.; assisted orgn. Oxford Prodn. Credit Assn., 1934, v.p., dir., 1934-44; organized Yalobusha County Soil Conservation Dist., 1938, now dir.; mem. stockholders com. of nine Nat. Farm Loan Assns., 1950-59; nat. adv. committeeman Fed. Loan Bank Assns., 5th Farm Credit Dist., 1950-59, chmn. nat. adv. com., 1955-56; mem. Fed. Farm Credit Bd., 1959. Mem. Miss. Legislature, 1920-28; sec. County Democratic Exec. Com., 1943-69. Served as lt., Air Corps, U.S. Army, 1917-19. Named col. staff gov. Miss. Mem. Miss. Bar Assn., Coffeeville C. of C., Am. Legion, Miss. Farm Bur., Phi Kappa Psi. Mason. Home: Coffeeville MS Died Aug. 22, 1969.

STONE, PHILIP CARLTON, educator, entomologist; b. Athol, Mass., Dec. 24, 1911; s. Harry Sylvester and Bernice May (Piedalue) S.; B.S., U. Mass., 1935, M.S., 1936; Ph.D., U. Ill., 1942; m. Ruth Evelyn Slabaugh, June 15, 1940; children—John Wyman, Helen Virginia, Paul Richardson, Charlotte Ruth. Lab. asst. entomology U. Ill., 1937-40; mem. faculty U. Mo., 1940-42, 46-68, prof. entomology, 1954-68, chmn. dept., 1954-68; cons. in field, 1950-68. Served to capt. AUS, 1943-46. Recipient citation research vacuum fumigation of lice U.S. Army, 1945. Fellow A.A.A.S.; mem. Entomol. Soc. Am. (pres. N.C. br. 1968), Kan. Entomol. Soc. (pres. 1967), Columbia Audubon Soc. (pres. 1968), Mo. Beekeepers Assn., Bee Research Assn., Mo. Pest Control Assn. (hon.), Sigma Xi, Phi Simga Kappa, Gamma Sigma Delta (Superior Teaching Achievement award 1965). Unitarian. Kiwanian. Author Columbia MO Died Nov. 7, 1968.

STONE, RALEIGH WEBSTER, economist; b. Portland, Ind., Dec. 18, 1889; s. Ezekiel and Emily (Brinkerhoff) S.; S.M., Valparaiso (Ind.) U., 1914; Ph.D., U. of Chicago, 1919; m. Ursula Chase Batchelder, Sept. 1, 1928; children—Mary Alzina, George Batchelder. Public sch. teacher, Portland, Ind., 1906-07, Union City, Ind., 1910, Bryant, Ind., 1913; asst. prof. social science Goucher Coll., Baltimore, 1920; asst. prof. economics, U. of Ia., 1920-23; dir. of research Nat. Industrial Conf. Bd., 1923-24; prof. indsl. relations U. of Chicago from 1924. Econ. counselor, Div. of Review, N.R.A., 1935-36. Cons. to bus. and union orgns. Served as capt., inf., U.S. Army, 1917-19. Mem. Am. Econ. Assn., Indsl. Relations Assn. of Chicago (mem. exec. com.). Club: Quadrangle (Chicago). Author: Financing Education (with William F. Russell and others), 1925; The Baking Industry under N.R.A. (with U. B. Stone), 1936. Editor: Problems in Collective Bargaining, 1938. Home: Chicago IL Died Apr. 29 1969.

STONE, ROBERT ELWIN, lawyer; born Oakland, Cal., Aug. 24, 1891; s. Elwin Lucius and Katie Lorena (Horton) S.; A.B., U. Cal., 1916, J.D., 1924; m. Alice Beckwith, June 28, 1918; children—Robert Beckwith, Albert Ward. Tchr., Honolulu, Hawaii, 1916-21; admitted to Cal., N.Y. bars; with Fitzgerald, Abbott & Beardsley, Oakland, 1924-27; tchr. law, sch. jurisprudence and coll. commerce U. Cal. at Berkeley, 1927-41; dir. survey project on establishment bur. govtl. and legal research, Ohio State U., summer 1946; prof. bus. law U. Syracuse, 1946, coll. dean, 1950-54; prof. bus. adminstrn., Harvard U. Grad. Sch. Bus. Adminstrn., 1954-59; Am. co-dir. Inst. Bus. Adminstrn., Istanbul U., Turkey, 1954-59; vis. prof. Istanbul U., 1953-54; asso. project dir. two Cal. state commns., Insanity and Criminal Offenders, 1959-62. Asso. chief automobile rationing br. OPA, Washington, 1942-43, historian hist. records br., 1943-46; three appointments to presdl. bds. under Sect. 10 Ry. Labor Act, 1946, 48. Mem. Am., Alameda County bar assns. State Bar of California (member committee personal injury claims 1962-67), UN Assn. U.S.A., Inc. (pres. local county chpt. 1964-66, bd.), Order of Coif. Republican. Conglist. Clubs: Cosmos (Washington) Outlook (Oakland). Author: Manual of Practice, 1937; Business and Property Law, 1941; co-author: Fundamentals of Business Law, 1950. Contbr. articles profl. publs. Address: Oakland CA Died Feb. 25, 1971; buried Alamo CA

STONE, ROBERT FRANKLIN, banker; b. Warsaw, Ill., Dec. 2, 1895; s. Jerry Robert and Mary M. (Hatchitt) S.; student pub. schs., Okla.; m. Ethel Belle Comer, Aug. 15, 1937; children—Sharon (Mrs. John F. Goar), Beverly (Mrs. Stanley J. Haynes), Barbara (Mrs. Jon Pressley). Principal owner, and manager Stone Grain & Elevator Co., Clovis, N.M., 1937-43; partner, mgr. Stockmens Feed Mfg. Co., 1939-45; dir. Clovis Nat. Bank, 1927-68, v.p., 1932-46, pres., 1947-56, chmn. bd. dirs., 1957-68. Served with U.S. Army, 1918-19. Mem. C. of C. Baptist (deacon). Home: Clovis NM Died Nov. 28, 1968.

STONE, ROBERT SPENCER, consultant radiologist; b. Chatham, Ont., Can., June 5, 1895; s. Spencer and Flora Maude (Campbell) S.; B.A., University of Toronto, 1919, M.A., 1922, M.B., 1924, M.D., 1928, LL.D. (hon.), Univ. of California, 1966; m. Willena Rose Crawford, June 24, 1924; children—Robert Spencer, Margaret Ishbol (Mrs. Richard Hager). Intern Grace Hosp., Detroit, 1924-25, asst. radiologist, 1925-28; asst. anatomy Peking (China) Med. Sch., 1919-21; asso. Rollin H. Stevens, Detroit, 1925-28; instr. radiology U. Cal., 1928-29, asst. prof., 1929-32, asso. prof., 1932-38, prof., 1938-62, now emeritus, chmn. dept. radiology, 1940-43, 46-62, dir. radiol. lab., 1951-64, now emeritus; asso. project dir. for health Metall. Project (atom bomb), U. Chgo., 1942-46, also vis. prof. roentgenology. Mem. Nat. Adv. Cancer Council, 1946-48; cons. U.S.P.H.S., 1949; mem. Nat. Com. Radiation Protection from 1946, Internat. Commn. Radiol. Protection 1953-65; mem. com. growth Nat. Research Council, 1952-56; past mem. radiol. safety adv. com. Cal. State Diaster Council. Recipient Medal for Merit for wartime activities, 1946, Gold Medal, Radiol. Soc. of N.A., 1946, Carman lectr., 1952, Janeway Medal, Am. Radium Soc., 1947, Medal for cancer control, Am. Cancer Soc., 1953, Gold Medal, Am. College of Radiology, 1959; citation and medallion United States AEC, 1964. Diplomate Am. Board of Radiology. Fellow Am. Coll. Radiology; mem. A.M.A., Radiol. Soc. N.A. (past pres.), Am. Roentgen Ray Soc., Cal. Acad. Medicine; hon. mem. Soc. de Cancerologica de Guadalajara, Coll. Physicians of Phila., Phila. Roentgen Ray Soc., Royal Soc. Medicine (London, Eng.). Author articles profl. jours. Editor: Industrial Medicine on the Plutonium Project, Vol. 20, Series 4, National Nuclear Energy Series. Home: San Francisco CA Died Dec. 16, 1966.

STONE, WALKER, newspaperman; b. Okemah, Okla., Mar. 8, 1904; s. John Seborn and Stella (Bynum) S.; B.S., Okla. State U., 1926; postgrad. George Washington U., 1927-29; m. Donna Mae Smith, July 17, 1930; children—Sharon (Mrs. Michael Sean Kilpatrick), Sabra (Mrs. David Allen Smith). Writer, exec. Scripps-Howard Newspapers in Washington, 1927-73, editor Scripps-Howard Newspaper Alliance, 1943-52; editor in chief Scripps-Howard Newspapers, 1953-69; pres., chmn. Scripps-Howard Found., 1969-73. Mem. Kappa Sigma. Clubs: National Press, Metropolitan. Home: Woodville VA Died Mar. 1973.

STONE, WILLIAM S(EBASTIAN), air force officer; b. Cape Girardeau, Mo., Jan. 6, 1910; s. William M. and Emma (Albert) S.; B.S. in Engring., U.S. Mil. Acad., 1934; M.S. in Meteorology, Cal. Inst. Tech., 1938; M.A. in Econs., Columbia, 1949; m. Myra McCarthy, Sept. 15, 1937; children—Susan, William McCarthy. Commd. 2d lt. U.S. Army, 1934, advanced through grades to gen., 1966; with meteorol. service USAAF, 1937-40, 42-47; instr. econs. and govt. U.S. Mil. Acad., 1940-42, asso. prof. social scis., 1947-50; assigned Nat. War Coll., 1950-51; with plans div. Hdqrs USAF, Europe, 1951-53; directorate personnel plans, asst. dep. chief staff, personnel Hdqrs. USAF, Washington, 1953-57; comdr. Eastern Air Force Transport, Mil. Air Transport Service, McGuire AFB, N.J., 1957-59; supt. USAF Acad., Colo., 1959-62; dep. chief staff, personnel Hdqrs. USAF, Washington, 1962-66; air dep. to supreme allied comdr. Europe, Paris, France, 1966-68. Mem. Order Daedalians. Clubs: Belle Haven (Va.) Country; Army and Navy (Washington); Rotary (hon.) (Colorado Springs). Author: Meteorology for Pilots, 1938; Strategic and Critical Raw Materials, 1950. Co-author: Economics of National Security, 1950; Contemporary Foreign Governments, 1940. Died Dec. 1968.

STONE, WILSON S(TUART), univ. prof.; b. Junction, Tex., Oct. 6, 1907; s. Donald Stuart and Grace (Finney) S.; Ph.D., Univ. Tex., 1935; m. Julia Jean Lampman, Jan. 28, 1930; children—Charles Stuart, Laurie Jean, Micael (dec.). Instr. dept. zoology, U. of Tex., 1932-36, asso. prof., 1936-42, prof., 1942-68, chairman of the department zoology, 1959-63, adviser to chancellor grad. and research affairs, 1963-64, vice chancellor, 1964-66. Served to capt. with U.S. Army Air Force, 1942-45. Mem. Am. Soc. Naturalists (sec. 1947-49), Am. Soc. Zoologists, Genetics Soc. Am., A.A.A.S., Radiation Research Soc., Nat. Acad. Sci., Soc. Study of Evolution, Am. Soc. Human Genetics, Sigma Xi. Author: (with J. T. Patterson) Evolution in the Genus Drosophila, 1952. Co-editor: Genetics (with C. P. Oliver), 1957-62. Contbr. articles in genetics and evolution to 70 publs. Home: Austin TX Died Feb. 28, 1968.

STONER, GEORGE HIRAM, engring. exec.; b. Mt. Pleasant, Pa., Oct. 22, 1917; s. Howard M. and Bernice (Grimm) S.; B.S. in Chemistry, Westminster Coll., New Wilmington, Pa., 1938, D.Sc., 1969; postgrad. Mass. Inst. Tech., Columbia; m. Yvonne Bebie, Sept. 26, 1942; children—Renee, Peter, Michael, David. With Standard Oil Co. Ind., 1940-41; with Boeing Co. 1941-69, asst. v.p., gen. mgr. divisional planning pilotless aircraft div., 1955-58, mgr. advance projects proposal team, 1958-62, mgr. Dyna-Soar program, 1956-61, Saturn program, 1961-63, became v.p., 1962, assignment manager of aerospace division, 1964-66, vice pres., general mgr. space division, 1966-67, group v.p. aerospace, from 1967, sr. v.p. until 1971, also dir. Leader survey to review guided missiles in Europe, 1951; spl. work B-29 design, ground to air missile, B-47 bomber, Bonarc missile. Recipient Distinguished Service medal NASA, 1971. Fellow Am. Inst. Aero. and Astronautics; Am. Inst. Chemists; mem. New York Acad. Scis. (life), New Orleans C. of C. Clubs: Nat. Rocket (bd. govs.) (Washington); Internat. House, Round Table (New Orleans). Home: Mercer Island WA Died Feb. 18, 1971.

STONOROV, OSKAR, architect; b. Frankfurt-am-Main, Germany, Dec. 2, 1905; s. Gregor and Helen S.; student U. Florence (Italy), 1924-25, Ecole Polytechnique Federale, Zurich, Switzerland, 1925-28; m. Elizabeth Foster, Sept. 17, 1938; children—Katrina, Barbara, Derek, Andrea. Came to U.S., 1929, naturalized, 1937. Gen. practice of architecture, 1928-70; engaged in gen., pub. housing and city planning practice, Phila. Dir. Phila. Housing Assn., Citizens Council on City Planning; mem. City Policy Com., Phila. Fellow A.I.A.; mem. Pa. Assn. Architects, N.J. Soc. Architects, Am. Inst. Planners. Clubs: Cosmos (Washington); Contemporary (Philadelphia). Author: Le Corbusier, His Work, 1929; You and Your Neighborhood, (with L.I. Kahn), 1945. Contbr. to mags. Breeder of Guernsey Cattle; mem. Am. Guernsey Cattle Club. Home: Phoenixville PA Died May 9, 1970.

STOOTHOFF, EVERETT O., former natural gas. co. exec.; b. Bklyn., June 9, 1905; s. Elliott and Edythe (Ohlrogge) S.; B.S., Colgate U., 1927; certificate Am. Inst. Banking, 1931; student N.Y.U. Law Sch., 1931-33; m. Marcella Hutchinson, Mar. 27, 1931; children—Judy, Robert H., Martha. Corp. adminstr. Chase Manhattan Bank N.Y.C., 1928-42; asst. sec. Chem. Bank N.Y. Trust Co., N.Y.C., 1942-52; sec. Tex.

Gas Transmission Corp., Owensboro, Ky., 1952-70, ret. 1970. Mem. Am. Soc. Corp. Secs., Am. Gas Assn., Phi Kappa Psi. Home: Owensboro KY Died Jan. 28, 1973.

STORCKMAN, CLEM FRANKLIN, judge; b. nr. Mt. Carmel, Ill., Mar. 8, 1899; s. Frank and Sarah Amelia (Schwartz) S.; J.D., U. Mich., 1922; m. Adeline Bob, May 17, 1938. Admitted to Mo. bar, 1923, practiced in St. Louis; associate Abbott, Fauntleroy, Cullen & Edwards, then Cullen, Fauntleroy & Edwards, 1923-36, partner Cullen, Storckman & Coil, 1936-40, Coburn, Storckman & Croft, 1949-55; judge Supreme Court of Missouri, 1955-70, chief justice, 1965-67. Delegate to the Mo. State Constl. Conv., 1943-44; mem. bd. freeholders to draft new charter for City St. Louis, 1949-50. Mem. St. Louis Board of Education. Life mem. bd. dirs. Tb and Health Assn. St. Louis, also past pres. Served with armed forces World War I; govt. appeal agt. for Selective Service Bds., 1940-52. Recipient Distinguished Non-Grad. award U. Mo. Law Sch. Alumni Assn., 1964; Sesquicentennial award U. Mich., 1967. Fellow of Am. Bar Foundation; member American, Mo. (past gov.) bar assns., Bar Assn. St. Louis (past pres.), Am. Judicature Soc. (dir. 1968-70), U. Mich. Alumni Assn. (dir. 7th dist.), Mo. Acad. Squires, Mo. (life), Cole County hist. socs., Delta Theta Phi. Presbyn. Mason (32 deg., Shriner). Clubs: Missouri Athletic; Jefferson City Country. Home: Jefferson City MO Died Mar. 16, 1970; buried Riverview Cemetery Jefferson City MO

STORKE, THOMAS MORE, newspaper pub.; b. Santa Barbara, Calif., Nov. 23, 1876; s. Charles Albert and Martha (More) S.; A.B., Stanford, 1898; LL.D., Univ. of Cal., 1960, Colby Coll., 1963; m. Elsie Smith, Santa Barbara, 1904 (dec.); children—Mrs. Jean Isabel Menzies, Mrs. Elsie Margaret Cox, Charles Albert; m. 2d, Marion Day, 1920; 1 son, Thomas More. Editor, pub., owner News-Press, Santa Barbara, Cal., 1901-64, emeritus, 1964-71. Postmaster, Santa Barbara, 1914-21; mem. U.S. Senate from Cal., 1938-39, mem. Cal. Crime Commn., 1951-52. Founder, pres. Thomas More Storke Found.; bd. regents U. Cal., 1955-60. Recipient Lauterbach award, 1961; Pulitzer prize editorial writing, 1962; Lovejoy award, 1962. Clubs: Santa Barbara City, University, Valley of Montecito (Los Angeles). Author: California Editor, 1959; I Write for Freedom, 1962. Home: Santa Barbara CA Died Oct. 12, 1971; buried Santa Barbara Cemetery, Santa Barbara CA

STORM, MILDRED RAUM (MRS. EDWARD D. STORM), civic worker; b. Camden, N.J., May 12, 1911; d. Archibald F. T. and Anna (Milman) Raum; A.B. summa cum laude, Western Md. Coll, 1931; m. Edward D. Storm, June 19, 1936; children—Mary Elizabeth, Penelope Annabelle. Tchr. math and sci. high sch. Frederick, Md., 1931-39. Mem. region III com. Girl Scouts, 1958-65, pres. Frederick council, 1955-57, troop leaders, 1948-55. Bd. dirs. Frederick Community Action Com., Mem. Federated Women's Clubs (sec. Md. fedn. 1959-61, pres. 1st dist. 1957-59, 1st v.p. Md. Fedn. 1964-66, pres. Md. Fedn.), Frederick Civic Club (pres. 1961-63), Frederick City Homemakers (pres. 1948-50), Western Md. Alumni Assn. (dir. 1952-58, alumni rep. to bd. trustees Western Md. Coll. 1956-58), Internat. Platform Assn. Presbyn. Club: Nat. Democratic. Author mag. articles. Home: Frederick MD

STORRS, HARRY ASAHEL, electrical engr.; b. Boston, Jan. 13, 1861; s. Asahel S. and Mahala (Parsons) S.; C.E., U. of Vermont, 1882; post-grad. Columbia, 1893-94; m. Alice E. Stillman, June 14, 1888;children—Nellie Stillman (Mrs. Rea W. Smith), Katherine Fay (Mrs. Wallace Henrich); m. 2d, Grace L. Cockle, June 11, 1914. In ry. work in Ohio and W.Va., 1882-83; supt. water works, Burlington, Vt., 1883-84; on topographic work in Va., 1884-85; with Western Electric Co., New York and Chicago, 1885-87, and laid cables from Nantucket to mainland and from Cape Charles to Cape Henry for signal corps, etc.; chief engr. for Pomona Land & Water Co., Calif., 1887; laid govt. cable across mouth of Columbia River for Western Electric Co., 1888; asst. prof. civ. engring., 1890-92, prof. elec. engring., 1892-99, U. of Vt.; also acting as cons. elec. and hydraulic engr. on elec. plants in Vt.; in summer of 1893 did instrumental work on survey of St. Lawrence River under U.S. Engr. Corps; in 1897 on constrn. work on sea coast fortifications, including elec. installations, and during summer of 1898 on same and was also chief electrician of harbor mines during Spanish-Am. War; elec. engr. under War Dept., designing and installing elec. plants, and also on river and harbor improvements, 1899-1903; elec. engr. U.S. Reclamation Service, 1903-09; cons. engr., chiefly hydro-electric power and pumping plants for irrigation, Denver, 1909-11, and reclamation of La. marsh lands by drainage, 1911-14, office, Chicago; constructing and operating irrigation systems and deep well pumping plants, Ariz., 1915-16; mgr. Yolo Water & Power Co., Woodland, Calif., 1917; hydrographic studies, Sacramento River basin, 1918-19; consulting engr., irrigation and hydro-electric projects, San Francisco, 1920-23; chief engr., Modesto (Calif.) Irrigation Dist., 1923-25; sr. insp. East Bay Municipal Utility Dist., 1925-39; elec. and mech. inspr. Possum Kingdom Dam and Power House, Brazos River Conservation and Reclamation Dist., 1939-40; cons. engr., Berkeley, Calif., since 1940. Address: 2115 Cedar St., Berkeley 7 CA‡

STORRS, LUCIUS SEYMOUR, ry. official; b. Buffalo, N.Y., Jan. 4, 1869; s. Origen Symour and Janet (Rankin) S.; B.Sc., U. of Neb., 1890, M.A., 1904, hon. Dr.Engring., 1927; m. Mary L. Cooper, June 26, 1894. Asst. geologist Colo. Fuel Co., 1890-94; geologist N.P. Ry. and special writer U.S. Geol. Survey, 1896-1906; tech. expert N.Y., N.H. & H. R.R., 1906; pres. New Eng. Investment & Security Co., 1907-11; v.p. N.Y., N.H. & H. R.R., 1912-14; pres. Conn. Co., New Haven, 1914-25; mag. dir. Am. Elec. Ry. Assn., 1925-29; chmn. and pres. United Rys. and Electric Co., Baltimore, 1929-36, receiver during reorganization; pres. Los Angeles Ry. Corp., 1936-39; retired. Mem. A.A.A.S., Sigma Xi. Pres. Am. Electric Ry. Assn., 1917; chmn. com. on nat. defense of Am. Electric Ry. Assn. in charge of transportation cooperation of electric rys. through Nat. Council of Defense. Home: Northampton MA Died July 4, 1945.

STORRS, ROBERT WILLIAMSON III, banker; b. Nashville, Aug. 30, 1912; s. Robert Williamson and Addie Sue (Payne) S.; student Va. Mechanics Inst., 1935-39, Rutgers U., 1949-51; m. Mary Joe Wynne, Sept. 21, 1946;children—Robert Williamson IV, Mary Lee. Various positions 1st & Mchts. Nat. Bank, Richmond, Va., 1934-41, and from 1946, sr. v.p., from 1962; clk. Va.-Carolina Chem. Co., 1941-42. Sect. leader several Richmond United Givers campaigns. Served to capt. AUS, 1942-46. Mem. Am. Inst. Banking (dir. 1940), Central Richmond Assn. (dir.). Episcopalian. Clubs: Country of Va.; Kiwanis (past dir.; pres. 1968); Downtown. Home: Richmond VA Deceased.

STORY, DOUGLAS, war corr., author; b. at Edinburgh, Scotland, Dec. 31, 1872; s. Daniel F. (J. P.) and Jane (Skirving) S.; ed. George Watson's Coll., Edinburgh; studied medicine Edinburgh Univ., 1890-4; m. Sept. 29, 1902, Idah Margaret, d. C. L. Canfield, San Francisco. Gave up study of medicine on eve of degree; went to S. Africa, 1895; became editor Standard and Diggers' News, Johannesburg, on night of Reformers' trial, Apr. 27, 1896. Wounded in second Matabele war, 1896; expelled from Transvaal by Boer gov't for political reasons, 1897. In Soudan was only civilian permitted to accompany Egyptian force that captured Osman Digna. In S. African war represented London Daily Mail with Boer forces—only British subject permitted to enter Transvaal after outbreak of hostilities; only British subject allowed to accompany Boer forces in the field; first war corr. ever openly to accompany his nation's enemy in war time; was arrested and imprisoned several times by Boers on suspicion. Came to U.S. Jan., 1901, by invitation of James Gordon Bennett to write impressions of country for New York Herald. Clubs: Players (New York); Edinburgh University, Playgoers, National Liberal (London). Author: Ten Miles from Anywhere, 1895; Arbitration or War?, 1899. Extensive contb'r to European mags. on S. African situation in English reviews; on general topics in Am. mags. Address: 987 Madison Av., New York NY‡

STOUT, CHARLES BANKS, flour mill exec.; b. Paoli, Ind., Oct. 11, 1882; s. John Thomas and Adeline (McCarrell) S.; B.S., Earlham Coll., 1904; m. Warda Stevens, Nov. 1, 1906; children—Alice (Mrs. Edwards), Charlotte (Mrs. Hooker). Flour milling bus., Paoli, 1906-09, at Baker, Ore., 1909-13, at Astoria, Ore., 1913-16, with Dixie Portland Flour Co., Memphis, Tenn., from 1916, ret. as pres.; dir. G.M. & A.R.R. Trustee Earlham Coll. Foundn. Mem. Nat. Assn. Mfrs., Nat. Millers Assn., Nat. and Memphis chambers commerce. Clubs: Memphis Country, country of Virginia: The Virginias Seniors; Wapenoca Hunting. Home: Memphis TN Died Nov. 9, 1965.

STOUT, CHARLES FREDERICK CLOUA, mfr.; b. Philadelphia, Pa., Apr. 2, 1869; s. Albert Gallatin and Mary (Robinson) S.; ed. pub. schs. and Barker Acad., Germantown; m. Mary Ridgeway Deacon, Nov. 16, 1898; children—Frederick Sturgis, Robert Gwynne, Mary Ridgeway (Mrs. Alan Lowther Day). Junior Clerk Thomas T. Lee & Co., 1885-86; sr. partner John R. Evans & Co., 1896-1938, pres. since 1938; director Federal Reserve Bank of Philadelphia, Jan. 1, 1928-Dec. 31, 1943 (resigned). Served as mem. Council of Nat. Defense; registered col. in Q.M. Dept. and dir. Hide, Leather and Leather Goods Div., U.S. War Industries Bd., World War I. Trustee U. of Pa., Evans Dental Sch. (U. of Pa.); Former pres. bd. Graduate Hosp., Phila. Pres. Pa. Hort. Soc. Republican. Episcopalian. Clubs: Union League, Rittenhouse, Midday, Gulph Mills Golf, Merion Cricket. Home: 214 Glenn Rd., Ardmore, Pa. Office: 2d and Erie Sts., Camden NJ*‡

STOUT, GEORGE ABEEL, director; b. Fairview, Fulton Co., Ill., Apr. 7, 1876; s. Lyman Vroom and Sarah Margaret (Joralemon) S.; grad. Knox Coll. Conservatory of Music, 1899; pupil of Scharwenka and Max Gruenberg, Berlin, 1905-6; m. Anna Ruby Redmon, of Fargo, N.D., June 28, 1905. Dir. music, Geneseo (Ill.) Collegiate Inst., 1899-1900; head of piano dept., Fargo (N.D.) Coll. Conservatory of Music 1900-5; dir. Wesley Coll. Conservatory of Music, Grand Forks, N.D., 1906-10; dir. music, U. of N.D., 1906-10 dir. violin dept. and prof. piano and conducting, Knox Coll. Conservatory of Music, Galesburg, Ill., Sept. 1910-June, 1913; dir. music, 1st M.E. Ch., Spokane Wash., 1913-17, 1st Presbyn. Ch., Spokane, 1917-— also dir. music, Lewis and Clark High Sch., Spokane Mus. B., Knox Coll., 1908. Mem. University Club Spokane Ad Club, Musical Art Soc., Knox Chapter of Phi Kappa Lambda. Address: 1228 W. 11th Av Spokane WA‡

STOUT, HENRY ELBERT, college pres.; b. Carroll Co., Mo., Nov. 12, 1873; s. William Patterson and Mary Elizabeth (Brakey) S.; Ph.B., Central Coll., Fayette Mo., 1901, A.B., 1909; m. Genelle Cunningham, of Hamburg, Ia., Nov. 5, 1902; children—Sidney Elbert Henry Lee. Ordained M.E. ministry, 1901; pastor Clark, Mo., 1901-02, Centrallia, 1902-06; pres. Howard-Payne Coll., 1906-19; pres. Tex. Woman's Coll., Ft. Worth, Tex., since Feb. 1, 1919. Club Kiwanis. Mem. commn. on family life, Federal Council Chs. of Christ in America. Home: Ft Worth TX‡

STOUT, HIRAM MILLER, educator, polit. scientist b. Indpls., Apr. 30, 1905; s. Joseph L. and Estelle (Miller) S.; B.A., DePauw U., 1926; diploma Oxford (Eng.) U., 1928; M.A., Harvard, 1931, Ph.D., 1934; m. Caroline Plugge, June 28, 1934. From instr. to asso. prof. polit. sci. DePauw U., 1928-37; sr. research staff mem. Civil Service Assembly, Chgo., 1937-39; asso. prof. Am. U., 1939-41; fgn. affairs specialist U.S. Govt. 1946-61; vis. prof. Duke, 1962; prof. internat. affairs George Washington U., 1962-72, dir. Univ. Center at Naval War Coll., 1962-64, chmn. dept. internat. affairs asst. dean Sch. Govt., 1964-66, acting dean Sch. Pub. and Internat. Affairs, 1966-67, dean Sch. Pub. and Internat. Afairs, 1967-69; Adm. King prof. Naval War Coll., 1955-56. Served with AUS, 1941-45. Mem. Am. Polit. Sci. Assn., Am. Acad. Polit. and Social Sci., Inst. Strategic Studies, Internat. Studies Assn., English Speaking Union, Sigma Nu. Club: Cosmos (Washington). Author: Public Service in Great Britain 1938; British Government, 1953. Home: Washington DC Died Nov. 11, 1972; buried Juniper Hill Cemetery Bristol RI

STOUT, LAWRENCE EDWARD, educator; b. Seymour, Ind., Mar. 30, 1898; s. Edward Wagner and Rosalie (Lewis) S.; A.B., DePauw U., 1919; M.S., Ohio State U., 1921, Ph.D., 1923, Chem. E., 1934; m. Catherine Mary Frasch, Sept. 8, 1925 children—Lawrence E., Catherine (Mrs. R. H. Vanderpearl). Asst. prof. chemistry Miami U., Oxford O., 1923-27; asso. prof. chemistry Washington U., St. Louis, 1927-34, asso. prof. chem. engring., 1934-38 prof., from 1938, head dept. chem. engring., 1940-63 dean sch. engring., 1948-55; dir. Sever Inst. Tech. 1948-55; cons. chemical engineer, 1923-66. Alderman Clayton, Mo., 1950-57. Mem. Am. Chem. Soc., Am. Inst. Chem. Engrs., Am. Soc. Engring. Edn., Mo. Soc. Profl. Engrs., Sigma Xi, Tau Beta Pi, Phi Lambda Upsilon. Presbyn. Mason. Clubs: Rotary, University (St. Louis). Author articles profl. jours. Home: Clayton MO Died Dec. 30, 1966.

STOUT, SELATIE EDGAR, prof. Latin; b. Jamesport Mo., Dec. 27, 1871; s. Theophilus Thompson and Sarah Elizabeth (Wilcoxon) S.; B.S., Grand River Coll. Edinburg, Mo., 1891; A.B., William Jewell College, Liberty, Mo., 1901, LL.D., honorary, 1942; graduate student in classics, University of Chicago, 12 terms; Ph.D., Princeton Univ., 1910; married Frances Mabel Blodgett, Dec. 30, 1905; children—Richard Edgar, Paul Blodgett, William Jewell. Instr. in Latin, 1906-08, prof., 1908-14, William Jewell Coll.; prof. Latin Indiana U. from 1914, asst. dean. Coll. of Arts and Sciences, 1918-20, dean, 1920-42, dean emeritus and emeritus prof. of Latin, 1942-69. Mem. Am. Philol. Association, Classical Assn. of Middle West and South, Am. Assn. University Profs. Republican. Baptist. Club: Faculty. Wrote: The Governors of Moesia, 1911; Latin in the Latin Class—A List of Convenient Latin Words and Expressions, 1917; also numerous articles in Bloomington IN Died Dec. 1969.

STOUT, WESLEY WINANS, editor; b. Junction City Kan., Jan. 26, 1890; s. Francis Wellington and Dora (Dougherty) S.; m. Mary Lee Starr, Sept. 15, 1923. Reporter and editor various newspapers in Kan., Mo., Tex., Calif., Wash., City of Mexico, New York and Okla., 1907-17 and 1921-22; asso. editor and writer Saturday Evening Post, 1922-36, editor in chief, 1937-42. Enlisted man U.S. Naval Air Force, World War, 1917-18; at sea for U.S. Shipping Bd., 1919-21. Died 1971.

STOWELL, KENNETH KINGSLEY, architect; b. N.Y., N.Y., Apr. 30, 1894; s. William Leland and Louise (Epenschied) S.; B.S., Dartmouth Coll., 1916; M. Arch., Harvard, 1921; m. Barbara Tompkins, June 27, 1942; children—Barbara, Margaret Elizabeth. Archtl. designer, 1921-24; asso. prof. architecture Ga. Sch. Tech., 1924-27; practicing architect firm Skinner, Bush-Brown & Stowell, Atlanta, 1924-27; editor Archtl. Forum, 1927-35; editor American Architect and

Architecture, 1935; House Beautiful, 1936-42; editor-in-chief Archtl. Record, 1942-49; v.p. Giffels & Vallet, Inc., and L. Rosetti, Asso. Engrs. and Architects, Detroit, from 1950; ret., 1958. Mem. A.I.A. (president Westchester chapter 1936-37), Architectural League N.Y. (pres. 1946), Soc. of Beaux Arts of Architects, Westchester Soc. of Architects (pres. 1940), Phi Delta Theta. Congregationalist. Clubs: Harvard, Salmagundi (N.Y.C.), Bronxville Field, Coffee House, (N.Y.C.). Author: Modernizing Buildings for Profit, 1935. Home: San Francisco CA Died Jan. 1969.

STRACHAN, PAUL AMBROSE, orgn. exec.; b. Perry, Mich., Feb. 26, 1894; s. James Alexander and Lula May (Calkins) S.; student pub. schs. Atlanta, pvt. study 1908-12; m. Avery Pearl Beall, Jan. 4, 1919 (dec. 1969); children—William, Robert Wallace, Frank LeRoy, Burce Carroll. With various theatrical enterprises, 1914-16, 22-23; advt., 1919; orgn., promotional exec., 1919-32; legislative representative, 1919-32; chief founder Am. Fedn. Govt. Employees, 1942; founder, pres. Am. Fedn. Physically Handicapped, Inc., 1940, exec. dir. Ednl. Fund, Inc.; in 1945, conceived, organized, and wrote adminstrv. policies for what is now Pres.'s Com. on Employment of Handicapped; cons. handicapped affairs; former spl. asst. to U.S. Sec. Labor. Author of the resolution 79th Congress, establishing the first week in Oct. of each year as Nat. Employ the Physically Handicapped Week; pres. founder Am. Fedn. of Physically Handicapped Inst. for Human Engring. 1952; pres. Am. Inst. Human Engring., 1963-72. Recipient distinguished award Pres.'s Com. Employment of Handicapped. Dem. Meth. Clubs Nat. Press. Author: Rehab. Rebel, 1965; also fed. and state laws benefitting handicapped. Home: Brooksville FL Died Sept. 17, 1972; buried Cedar Hill Cemetery, Washington DC

STRAFER, HARRIETTE R., artist; b. Covington, Ky., 1873; studied at Acad. of Fine Arts, Cincinnati, O.; also in Paris under Mme. Macmonnies, Gustave Courtois, and Collin. Exhibited at Paris Salon of 1896, and the Exp'n, 1900. Address: 13 E. 59th St., New York NY‡

STRAGNELL, GREGORY, neuropsychiatrist, editor; b. Boulder, Colo., Dec. 26, 1888; s. Canon and Marie (La Fevre) S.; student U. of Denver, 1906-07, Clumbia, 1907-09; M.D., Coll. Phys. and Surgeons (Columbia Univ.), 1913; married 2d, Louise Ebert; children—Barbara, Robert. Military surgeon with French Army, 1914-17; surgeon in chief mil. hosps. No. 2 and No. 81, Paris, 1916-17; editor Medical Record, N.Y. City, since 1917; asso. editor Journal of Nervous and Mental Diseases; former exec. v.p., dir. med. research, Schering Corp. Mem. Washington Psychoanalytic Assn., Am. Med. Editors Assn., Internat. Congress Med. Hygiene, Am. Assn. for Study of Epilepsy, Am. Psychopathol. Assn., Assn. for Study Internal Secretions, Am. Psychoanalytic Assn., Am. Chem. Soc., Soc. Chem. Industry, A.A.A.S., N.Y. Endoctrinol. Soc., Am. Inst, Med. Directors' Assn., Physicians' Equity Assn. Clubs: Advertising, Chemists (New York). Home: Los Angeles CA Died Dec. 10, 1963.

STRAKE, GEORGE WILLIAM, business exec.; b. St. Louis, Nov. 9, 1894; s. William and Anna (Casper) S.; B.S., St. Louis U., 1917, D.Sc., 1948; LL.D., U. Notre Dame, 1949; H.H.D., St. Michael's Coll., 1954, Our Lady of Pena-francia Sem. Coll., Philippines, 1968; m. Susan E. Kehoe, Sept. 10, 1924; children—Elizabeth Susan (Mrs. Robert Dilworth), Georganna Alice (Mrs. Robert H. Parsley), George William. Oil business, Mexico, 1919-25, Havana, Cuba, 1925-27, Houston, 1927-69; dir. Mercantile-Trust Co., Nat. Assn., St. Louis, Eversharp, Inc.; discoverer Conroe Oil Field, Montgomery County, Tex., 1931, also others. Official rep. of gov. and state of Tex., inauguration pres. of U.S., 1937. Mem. president's council St. Louis U.; mem. nat. com. U.S.O.; mem. Houston Crime Commn. Bd. bd. govs., Am. Nat. Red Cross, finance com., Red Cross; mem. dirs. nat. bd. exec. com., Nat. Conf. Christians and Jews; past pres., life mem. and mem. exec. bd., Sam Houston Area Council, mem. nat. exec. bd., and nat. council, regional exec. com. and nat. lay com. on Catholic service, Boy Scouts of Am.; trustee Variety Boys' Club, Houston, Am.'s Future, Inc.; life trustee St. Joseph Hosp., Houston; bd. govs., Southwest Research Inst.; adminstrv. bd., Boys Harbor, La Porte, Tex.; adv. bd. Grad. Sch. Social Service, Our Lady of Lake Coll., San Antonio; citizens com. Houston-Harris Co. civilian defense, World War II; Tex. rep. Belgian war relief; mem. adv. council, Coll. of Commerce, U. of Notre Dame; past mem. bd. lay trustees U. Notre Dam, U. St. Thomas, Houston; trustee Nat. Foundn. for Infantile Paralysis, Houston Optimist Club. Served Army Air Corps, World War I. Decorated Knight Grand Cross of Holy Sepulchre, Knight Sovereign Mil. Order of Malta, Knight Grand Cross of Order of St. Sylvester, by Pope Pius XII; recipient Citation Our Lady of Lake Coll., San Antonio, 1948, George Washington Honor medal Freedom's Found., 1953, Humanitarian award Sisters Charity Incarnate Word, 1966; named Man of Year, Charity Guild Catholic Women, 1966. Mem. Petroleum Assn. Am. (dir.), Mid-Continent Oil and Gas Assn. (dir.), Am. Petroleum Inst. (dir.), Navy League U.S.A. (life), Tex. Ind. Producers and Royalty Owners (dir.), A.I.M. (Pres.'s Council), Houston C. of C. (indsl. steering com.), Sons. Rep. Tex. (hon.), Tex. Soc. for Prevention Blindness, Catholic War Vets. Roman Catholic. Home: Houston TX Died Aug. 6, 1969; buried Garden of Gethsemani, Houston TX

STRANDJORD, NELS MAGNE, radiologist, educator; b. Grenora, N.D., Aug. 18, 1920; s. Selmer J. and Eunice (Langeland) S.; B.A., Luther Coll., 1942; M.D., U. Chgo., 1946; m. Margaret E. Fry, Sept. 10, 1944; children—David Christian, Sarah Eunice, Mark Charles, Daniel Theodore. Intern, Ancker Hosp., St. Paul, 1946-47; gen. practice medicine, Virginia, Minn., 1948-51; resident U. Chgo., 1955-57, instr. radiology, 1958-59, asst. prof., 1959-61, asso. prof., 1961-65; prof., chmn. dept. radiology U. Kan., Kansas City, 1965-67; asso. prof. radiology U. Chgo., 1967-68. Vis. prof. Nat. Def. Med Center, Taipei, Taiwan, 1960-61; mem. physicians team Care-Medico and Department of State, Algiers, 1962; Project Vietnam, 1966. Served to captain in Medical corps, AUS, 1951-54. Recipient James A. McClintock award for outstanding teaching U. Chgo., 1960. Picker scholar in radiol. research, 1959-62. Diplomate Am. Bd. Radiology. Mem. Am. Coll. Radiology, Assn. U. Radiologists, Chgo. Roentgen Soc., Sigma Xi. Contbr. profl. jours. Home: Chicago IL Died Sept. 11, 1968; buried Belview MN

STRATEMEYER, GEORGE E., air officer; b. Nov. 24, 1890; B.S., U.S. Mil. Acad., 1915; grad. Air Corps Tactical Sch., 1930; Command and Gen. Staff Sch., 1932, Army War Coll., 1939. Commd. 2d lt., June 12, 1915; promoted through grades to lieutenant general, 1945; chief of staff for the Army Air Forces, 1942; commander Army Air Forces, India-Burma sector, 1943; air comdr. Eastern Air Comd., 1944; comdg. gen., Army Air Forces China Theater, 1945; comdg. gen., Air Defense Comd., 1946-48; comdg. gen. Continental Air Comd., 1948; comdr. Far East Air Force in Korea, 1950-51, ret., 1952. Recipient Republic of Korea Order Mil. Merit with Gold Star. Address: Winter Park FL Died Aug. 1969.*

STRATHALMOND, LORD, British industrialist; b. Glasgow, Scotland, Nov. 3, 1888; s. William and Janet (Loch) F.; ed. Glasgow Acad. and Royal Tech. Coll., Glasgow; LL.D., Birmingham University, 1951; married Mary McLintock, October 7, 1913; children—William, Mary Joan (Mrs. Neil Gowanioch Westbrook). Served in works and tech. depts. Pumpherston Oil Co., Ltd., dir., 1913, mng. dir., 1915; established joint selling orgn. for products Scottish Shale Oil Cos., 1918, followed by formation Scottish Oils, Ltd., 1919; dir. The British Petroleum Co. (formerly Anglo-Iranian Oil Co.), 1923, dep. chmn., 1928, chmn., 1941-56; dir. Burmah Oil Co., Ltd., Nat. Provincial Bank, Limited. Honorary petroleum adviser to British War Office since 1935. Awarded Comdr. Order Brit. Empire, 1918. Knighted in 1939. Visited U.S. as mem. Henley-on-Thames Oxon England. Died Apr. 1, 1970.

STRATTON, CLIF (CLIFTON JARIUS), newspaperman; b. Reading, Kan., May 20, 1886; s. Jairus Litchfield and Martha J. (Hultz) S.; B.S., Kan. State Agrl. Coll., 1911; m. Lenore Monroe, Aug. 20, 1917; children—Clifton Jairus, Lee Monroe. In circulation dept. Topeka (Kan.) Daily Capital, 1911-12, reporter, 1912-13, state house reporter, 1913-17, 1919-20; sec. Kan. State Agrl. Coll. Alumni Assn., 1920-22; mng. editor Topeka Daily Capital, 1926-58, Clif Stratton Writes; ret. Oct. for Capper Publs. Trade Union Courier, Ohio Farmer, Kansas Farmer, Mo. Ruralist; editorial page column Capital, 1926-58, Clif Stratton Writes; ret. Oct. 1958. Served in 1st O.T.C., 1917; 1st lt., Inf., U.S. Army, 1917-19; successively 2d lt., capt., maj., Kan. Nat. Guard, 1920-30. Mem. Delta Tau Delta, Sigma Delta Chi. Republican. Conglist. Mason (Shriner). Clubs: National Press (Washington); Topeka KS Died Dec. 22, 1970; buried Mount Hope Cemetery Topeka KS

STRATTON, MELVILLE NORCROSS, educator; b. Denver, Apr. 22, 1884; s. Melville O. and Clara A. (Norcross) S.; student Garrick Dramatic Sch.; grad. Fitchburg Teachers Coll., 1913; M.A. (hon.), Holy Cross Coll., 1927; m. Helen E. Hickey, June 24, 1908; children—Eleanor Norcross (Mrs. John A. Geary), Elizabeth Gertrude (Mrs. Gerald Kemp), Geraldine Francis (Mrs. Lawrence Robillard), Helen Rosamond (Mrs. Douglas Martell), Melville Norcross. Head practicai arts sch., Springfield, Mass., 1912-16; instr. Fitchburg Tchrs. Coll., 1916-17; supr. Mass. State Dept. Edn., 1917-20, chief supr., 1920-37, asst. dir. div. vocational edn., 1927-42, dir. div., 1942-55; ret. cons. in vocational edn.; asst. dir. War Prodn. Tng., 1938-48, adv. cons. U.S. sec. of labor, 1950-52; adv. bd. U.S. Commr. Edn.; dir. Vet. Tng., Mass. Mem. Arlington Sch. Bd., 1924-57, chmn. 9 yrs., mem. bldg. com.; chmn. Personnel Bd., 1949-53, chmn. com. salaries and wages, 1948-68, chmn. com. investigate jr. high schs., 1929-30; justice peace, 1917-60; Town Meeting mem., 1924-68. Lt. (j.g.), U.S.N.R., 1931-37. Mem. Mass. Safety Council (dir.), Internat., N.E. fire chiefs' assns. (hon. life), Nat. Assn. State Dirs. Vocational Edn. (pres. 1949-50), Am. Vocational Assn. (life), Adult Edn. Council Boston (treas. 1946-62), Soc. Advancement Mgmt. (pres. 1948), Supts. Round Table, Mass. Supts. Assn., Mass. Vocational Assn. (life mem.) Sigma Delta Pi, Pi Epsilon Tau. Club: City (Boston). Author pamphlets, mans. and bulls. Contbr. articles in profl. and ednl. jours. M. Norcross Stratton elementary sch. named for him. Home: Arlington MA Died 1968.

STRATTON, SAMUEL SOMMERVILLE, coll. pres.; b. Lynn, Mass., Feb. 23, 1898; s. Samuel and Emma Mary (Bluston) S.; B.S., Dartmouth Coll., 1920; Ph.D., Harvard Univ., 1930; LL.D., U. Vermont, 1943, Dartmouth, 1950, St. Michael's Coll., 1955; L.H.D. (hon.), Bowling Green State U., O., 1964; m. Marjorie Austin, Mar. 14, 1925; 1 dau., Nancy Austin (Mrs. Malcolm L. Hall); m. Janet M. Howard, Oct. 31, 1946. Engaged as an instr. Harvard, 1927-30; asst. prof. econ., Harvard Bus. Sch., 1930-36; asso. prof., 1936-41; chmn. com. on price research, iron and steel. Nat. Bur. Econ. Research, 1938-40; fellow Internat. Bur. Econ. Research, 1939; dir. Priorities Review, WBP, Washington, D.C., 1941-43; pres. Middlebury College (Middlebury, Vt.), 1943-64, emeritus, 1963-69; v.p. edn. Prentice-Hall, Inc., from 1963; dir. Technical Cooperation Administration for Saudi Arabia and Yemen, 1952-53. Chmn. bd. trustees Am. Inst. Econ. Research. Public member of the Regional War Labor Board, 1944-1945. Elector Hall of Fame, New York Univ., from 1953. Served as ensign, flying corps, U.S.N.R., 1918-19. Mem. Am. Econ. Assn. N.E. Council; Newcomen Soc. in N. Am., Phi Beta Kappa, Delta Sigma Rho, Lambda Chi Alpha. Co-author: Problems in Corp. Finance, 1936; Economics of the Iron and Steel Industry, 1937; Financial Instruments and Instns., 1938; Price Research in the Steel and Petroleum Industry, 1940. Clubs: University (New York); University (Boston); Cosmos (Washington). Home: Rutland VT New York City NY Died Mar. 1, 1969; buried Middlebury VT

STRAUGHN, JAMES HENRY, bishop; b. Centreville, Md., June 1, 1877; s. James Henry and Laura (Simmons) S.; A.B., Western Md. Coll., 1899, A.M., 1901, D.D., 1921; B.D., Westminster Theol. Sem., 1901; LL.D., Adrian Coll., 1937, W.Va. Wesleyan Coll., 1941, Allegheny Coll., 1941; m. Clara Bellamy Morgan, June 1, 1904; 1 dau., Laurlene. Ordained Methodist Protestant ministry, 1903; pastor various chs., Washington, D.C., Lynchburg, Va., Laurel, Del., and Baltimore; pres. denominational Christian Endeavor Union, 1904-08; pres. West Lafayette Coll., 1906-10; treas. and promotional sec. Meth. Protestant Ch., 1928-32; pres. Gen. Conf., same, 1936-39; bishop Methodist Ch., Pittsburgh Area, 1940-48, ret. 1948; del. Ecumenical Meth. Conf., London, 1921; Universal Christian Council on Life and Work, Oxford, Eng., 1937. Pres. bd. trustees Western Md. Coll. Mason. K.P. Lecturer; writer of religious articles. Home: 3370 Gunston Rd., Alexandria VA‡

STRAUS, MICHAEL W(OLF), govt. official; b. Chicago, Ill., Mar. 20, 1897; s. Michael and Mary (Howe) S.; student U. of Wis., 1914-17; m. Nancy F. Porter, May 24, 1924; children—Lucy (deceased), Margaret, Michael, James. Reporter, later city editor, mng. editor, Chicago Evening Post, 1920-32; instr. journalism, Northwestern U., 1922-24; nat. corr. N.Y. Evening Post and Washington corr. Universal News Service, 1932-33; dir. information, Fed. Pub. Works Adminstrn., 1933-38; dir. information, Dept. Interior, 1938-41; dir. prodn. drive W.P.B., 1941-42; 1st asst. sec., Dept. Interior, 1942-45; U.S. Commn. of Reclamation, 1945-53. Served in U.S. Navy, 1918-19. Democrat. Unitarian. Author: Housing Comes of Age, 1939; numerous govt. publs. Clubs: Tavern (Chicago); Nat. Press (Washington, D.C.). Home: Washington DC Died Aug. 1970.*

STRAUS, SAMUEL J. TILDEN, investment banker; b. Ligonier, Ind., July 12, 1876; s. Frederick William and Madlon (Goldsmith) S.; ed. pub. schs., Harvard Sch. and Met. Business Coll., Chicago; m. Lillie Wolf, June 6, 1900; children—Frederick William 2d, Samuel J.T. (dec.), Mary Adelaide. With S. W. Straus & Co., real estate loans and investment securities, becoming mem. firm, 1899 (firm inc. 1905), chmn. bd. since 1931; pres. Straus Nat. Bank & Trust Co. of Chicago; dir. Straus Nat. Bank & Trust Co. of New York. Republican. Clubs: (Standard, Lake Shore Country. Office: 306 S. Michigan Av., Chicago IL‡

STRAUSS, HERBERT DONALD, advt. exec.; b. Rochester, N.Y., Apr. 21, 1909; s. Herman D. and Clare (Baum) S.; B.S. in Econs., U. Pa., 1931; m. Sarann Eisner, Apr. 22, 1949; children—Richard, Barbara. Dir. advt. Riggs Optical Co., Chgo., 1931-39; v.p. Grey Advt. Agy., Inc., N.Y.C., 1939-56, exec. v.p., supr. client contact and creative service, 1956-61, pres., 1961-68, chief exec., chmn. mgmt. com., 1968-73, sr. exec. officer, 1969-73. Past vice chmn. Region 2, Boy Scouts Am. Bd. dirs. Better Bus. Bur. of N.Y. Served with USNR, 1942-46; lt. comdr. Res. Recipient Silver Buffalo and Silver Antelope awards Boy Scouts Am. Mem. Am. Assn. Advt. Agys. (past chmn. N.Y. council), Nat. Outdoor Advt. Bur. (dir.). Home: New York City NY Died Mar. 17, 1973.

STRAVINSKY, IGOR FEDOROVICH, composer; b. near St. Petersburg (Leningrad), Russia, June 5, 1882;

studied law, St. Petersburg U.; studied music under Rimski-Korsakov; married 2d, Vera de Bossett, April 1904; four children by first marriage. Composer: Symphony, 1907; Fireworks; L'Oiseau de Feu," Fire Bird Suite, 1910; Petrouchka, 1911; LeSacre du Printemps, 1917; Chant du Rossignol, 1917; Renard; Concerto for Piano and Orchestra: Oedipus Rex; Capriccio; Symphony of Psalms, Persephone; also many others. Author: Poetics of Music, 1947. Naturalized 1946. Mem. Am. Acad. Arts and Letters. Recipient Internat. Sibelius prize, 1963. Address: New York City NY Died Apr. 1971; buried Cemetery of San Michele, Venice Italy

STRAWBRIDGE, FREDERIC H(EAP), retired merchant; b. Phila., Pa., Aug. 24, 1866; s. Justus Clayton and Mary (Lukens) S.; ed. Friends' Preparative Meeting Sch., Germantown, Phila., 1872-83; A.B., Haverford Coll., 1887; m. Bertha Gordon Walter, June 5, 1894; children—J. Clayton, Frederic H., Anna Walter (Mrs. John Winthrop Claghorn), Gordon Weld, Edward Ritchie II. Began as clk. with Strawbridge & Clothier, dept. store, Phila., 1887, continued through various depts. and admitted to firm, 1900, director. Member Troop A, Home Defense Reserve, World War; dir. S.E. Div. Am. Red Cross Warehouse. Mem. bd. dirs. Bryn Mawr Coll., Haverford Coll. Republican. Mem. Soc. of Friends. Clubs: University, Phila. Cricket. Home: 500 W. Moreland Av., Chestnut Hill, Phila. Office: 801 Market St., Philadelphia PA‡

STREETER, EDWARD CLARK, M.D.; b. Chicago, Ill., Nov. 10, 1874; s. John Williams and Mary (Clark) S.; A.B., Yale, 1898; M.D., Northwestern U., 1901; studied Harvard, Paris, Vienna and Berlin; m. Alice Martha Chase, of Waterbury, Conn., 1906; children—Helen Chase, John Williams, Gordon Chase, Edward Clark. Began practice at Chicago, 1901; settled in Boston, 1907; lecturer on med. history, Harvard, since 1921. Capt. Q.M.C., U.S.A., 1917-19; with A.E.F., Aug. 23, 1917-Jan. 22, 1919. Trustee Congl. Foundation for Edn. Republican. Clubs: Yale (Boston, New Haven, New York); St. Botolph, Odd Volumes (Boston). Asst. editor History of Anatomic Illustration, 1920, Osler's Evolution of Modern Medicine, 1921. Asso. editor Annals of Medical History. Contbr. numerous med.-hist. studies revs. Home: 280 Beacon St., Boston MA‡

STREETT, ST. CLAIR, army officer; b. Washington, D.C., Oct. 6, 1893; s. Shadrack Watkins and Lydia Ann (Coggins) S.; m. Mary Lois Williams, Jan. 18, 1922; 1 son, St. Clair. Military airplane pilot, 1916; commd. 1st lt. Aviation Sect., Signal Corps Reserve, 1917; advanced through the grades to maj. gen., Dec. 1942; grad. Command and General Staff Sch., Army War Coll., Naval War Coll.; comdr. of Army Alaskan flight, New York to Nome, Alaska, and return, 1920; became comdg. gen. 3d Air Force, Dec. 1942, 2d Air Force, Sept. 1943, 13th Air Force, S.W. Pacific, Apr. 1944; became dep. comdg. gen. Continental Air Force, Feb. 1945, Strategic Air Command, Mar. 1946; assigned chief, Mil. Personnel Procurement Service, AGO, Jan. 1947; assigned dep. inspector gen. U.S.A.F., Jan. 1948; assigned dep. comdg. gen. Air Materiel Comd., 1949; ret., 1952. Awarded Distinguished Flying Cross, Purple Heart, Air Medal, Mackay Trophy, D.S.M. with 2 oak leaf clusters, Legion of Merit; Italian Order of the Court in the Grade of Officer (Italy). Died Sept. 1970.

STRETCH, DAVID ALBERT, corporation executive; b. Trenton, N.J., Oct. 12, 1908; s. Albert T. and Ada M. (Rogers) S.; B.S., U.S. Naval Acad., 1930; LL.B., Harvard, 1933; m. Mary Schnitzius Osborn, Dec. 28, 1937. Admitted to Mass. bar, 1934, N.Y. bar, 1935; asso. Gaston, Snow, Saltonstall & Hunt, Boston, 1933-34; asso. Simpson, Thacher & Bartlett, N.Y.C., 1934-47, mem. firm, 1947-55; exec. v.p. Atlas Corp., 1956-58, pres., dir., 1958-59, pres., chief exec. officer, 1960-65; dir. Northeast Airlines, Inc.; dir., chmn. exec. com. Texas Industries, Inc., from 1965; hon. dir. Ritter Pfaudler Corp. Chmn. Validation Bd. for German Dollar Bonds in U.S., U.S. Dept. State-Fed. Republic Germany, 1953-65. Pres., Dallas Symphony Assn. Trustee Naval Acad. Found. Served with USNR, 1940-45, comdr. ret. Mem. Am., Tex., Dallas bar assns., Assn. Bar City N.Y., S.R., Naval Order U.S., Navy League. Clubs: Lotos, Recess (N.Y.C.); Storm King Golf (Cornwall, N.Y.); Brook Hollow Golf (Dallas); Nat. Aviation (Washington); LaQuinta (Cal.) Country. Home: Dallas TX Died Mar. 23, 1972; buried Hillcrest Meml. Park, Dallas TX

STRICKER, FREDERICK DAVID, health officer; b. Detroit, Mich., Mar. 24, 1875; s. Frederick D. and Loida (Wegener) S.; M.D., Detroit Coll. of Medicine, 1900; m. Bertha Stewart, Jan. 15, 1904; 1 dau., Rosamond. Resident Physician Grace Hosp., Detroit, 1900-02; practicing physician and county health officer, Josephine County, Ore., 1903-17; in practice at Tucson, Ariz., 1919-21; state health officer and exec. sec. State Bd. of Health, Ore., 1921-45; now retired. Served as capt. Med. Corps, U.S. Army, 1917-19; now lt. col. Med. Res. Corps, U.S. Army. Fellow Am. Pub. Health Assn. (pres. Western Branch 1939-40), Am. Med. Assn., Portland Acad. of Medicine. Republican. Mason. Clubs: City, University. Home: Route 1, Box 601, San Rafael CA‡

STRICKLAND, FREDERICK GUY, clergyman; b. Mishawaka, Ind., Dec. 14, 1869; s. Curtis Valentine and Mary A. (Pembroke) S.; ed. Antioch, Union Christian, Hillsdale, and Hiram, colls., A.B., Hiram, 1896; spl. studies Cleveland Coll. Phys. and Surg.; Cleveland Coll. of Oratory; m. A. May McDonald, of New Lexington, O., Mar. 14, 1891. Ordained Christian (Disciples) ministry, 1890; began agitation for Hiram House (1st social settlement of Cleveland), 1895, and was 1st head resident; 1st pastor People's Christian Ch., Chicago, 1899; 1st organizer of Federation for Social Justice, Chicago, 1900; sec. Nat. Conv. Social Dem. party, Indianapolis, Mar. 6-10, 1900; coll. sec. Nat. Christian Citizenship League, 1900; sec. Socialist Party of Ind.; corr. sec. Union Missionary Assn. Asso. editor The Social Forum, 1899-1900; editor of Social Justice, 1901-2; field editor The Iowa Socialist, 1903; pastor Central Christian Ch., Columbus, Ind., 1905; lecturer for Sunday Afternoon Lecture Club, Douglass Hall, Cincinnati, 1906; pastor First Christian Ch., Portland, Ind., 1907; nat. lecturer, Socialist Party, 1908-10; lecturer for The Workers' Ethical Platform, The Auditorium, Dayton, O., 1911-15; pastor Christian Ch., Roseville, O., and lecturer on peace, 1915; pastor Franklin, O., 1916; prof. economics, Defiance (O.) Coll., 1917—. Extensive writer on socialism and applied Christianity. Address: 2 College Pl., Defiance OH‡

STRICKLAND, SILAS A., business exec. Pres. Bower Roller Bearing Co. when merged into Fed.-Mogul Corp., 1955, dir. Fed.-Mogul, 1955-69, dir. emeritus, 1969-70. Address: Detroit MI Died May 29, 1970.

STRICKLER, CYRUS WARREN, SR., physician; b. near Fisherville, Augusta County, Va., Nov. 1, 1873; s. Rev. Givens Brown and Mary Frances (Moore) S.; student Washington and Lee U., 1891-94; M.D., with first honor, Atlanta Med. Coll. (now Emory U. Sch. of Med.), 1897; m. Anne Virginia Williams, Feb. 24, 1903; children—Givens Brown, II, Cyrus Warren. Served as intern and resident Grady Hosp., Atlanta, Ga., 1897-99; resident Elkin-Cooper Sanatorium, 1899-1901; out-patient dept., Atlanta Med. Coll., 1901-11, lecturer minor surgery, 1903-05, quiz master in surgery, 1903-05; asso. prof. of medicine, Atlanta Coll. Physicians and Surgeons, 1911-16; prof. of medicine, Emory U. Sch. of Med., 1916-30. Now emeritus prof. of clin. med., Emory Univ. Sch. of Medicine. On the visiting staff Emory Univ. Hosp. and Grady Memorial Hosp. and consultant on staff of St. Joseph's Infirmary. Consultant Grady Memorial Hospital. Served as chief Medical Service, with Base Hospital No. 43; later lieutenant colonel, executive officer of hospitals at Blois, France, 1918-19. Decorated Officer d'Academie. Fellow American Coll. Physicians; diplomate Am. Bd. of Internal Med.; mem. Fulton County and Fifth Dist. med. socs., Ga. State Med. Assn., Southern Med. Assn., A.M.A., Mil. Surgeons U.S., Assn. Study Internal Secretions, Am. Legion, Phi Chi. Phi Beta Kappa, Alpha Omega Alpha. Democrat. Presbyterian. Clubs: Atlanta Athletic, Druid Hills Golf, Capital City, Kiwanis (Atlanta). Contbr. to med. jours. Home: 871 Oakdale Road N.E., Atlanta GA Office: 123 Forrest Av. N.E., Atlanta 3 GA‡

STRINGHAM, WARDE BARLOW, elec. mfr.; b. Bountiful, Utah, June 16, 1898; s. Richard and Elizabeth (Barlow) S.; B.A., U. Utah, 1921; m. Golda Smedley, Feb. 21, 1920; children—Nadine (Mrs. S. A. Blake), Gale S. Sales mgr. Woods Cross Canning Co., Utah, 1921-28; pres. Warde B. Stringham Co., Des Moines, Ia., 1928-32; sales mgr. W. D. Alexander Co., Atlanta, 1932-34; pres. Southern Appliances (subsidiary Gen. Electric Co.), 1934-36; dist. mgr. Gen. Electric Supply Corp., New Orleans, 1936, Washington, Balt., Wilmington, Del., 1937-51, comml. v.p., Washington, 1951; asst. to v.p. Govt. Bus. Services, Gen. Electric Co., Washington, 1951, comml. v.p., mgr., 1952-55, comml. v.p. Atlantic region, Washington and Phila., govt. bus. services, 1955. Member industry adv. committee Dept. Def. Mem. Elec. Assn. Phila. (gov.), Electric Inst. Washington (gov.), U.S. C. of C. (nat. def. com.), N.A.M., Am. Ordnance Assn., Am. Soc. Naval Engrs., Washington Bd. Trade, Newcomen Soc. Clubs: Army and Navy, Carlton, Metropolitan, Rotary (Washington); Columbia Country (Chevy Chase, Md.); University, Engineers (Phila.). Home: Rockville MD Died Oct. 1968.

STROHM, ADAM JULIUS, librarian; b. Venersborg, Sweden, Feb. 16, 1870; s. John and Ida (Wettervik) S.; A.B., U. of Upsala, Sweden, 1888; came to America, 1892; B.L.S., U. of Ill., 1900; hon. D.Litt., Wayne Univ., 1941; m. Cecilia B. McConnel, Oct. 30, 1902; children—Harriet, John. Library asst., U. of Ill., 1899-1900; librarian, Armour Inst. Tech., Chicago, 1900-01, Pub. Library, Trenton, N.J., 1901-11; asst. to librarian, Detroit Public Library, 1911-12, actg. librarian, 1912-13, librarian, 1913-41, retired July 1, 1941. Secretary Wayne County Library Board, 1921-43; consultant Wayne County Library Board, 1943-45. Mem. A.L.A. (pres. 1930-31), Mich. Library Assn. (pres. 1918-19). Clubs: Acanthus. Home: 698 Burlingame Av., Detroit 2 MI‡

STROM, CARL WALTHER, fgn. service officer; b. Albert Lea, Minn., Dec. 22, 1899; s. Eimar Ingvald and Helen Marie (Nedrud) S.; A.B., Luther Coll., Decorah, Ia., 1919, LL.D., 1950; A.M., State U. Ia., 1924; B.A., U. of Oxford (Rhodes scholar, Queens Coll., 1924-27), 1927, M.A., 1950; Ph.D., U. of Ill., 1931; m. E. Camille Sperati, 1931; children—Sonja, Karen. Instr. math. and Greek Luther Coll., 1919-23; prof. math., registrar, dir. placements, 1927-29, and 1930-35; asst. instr. math. State U. of Ia., 1923-24, U. of Ill., 1929-30; apptd. fgn. service officer, Dept. of State, 1935, vice consul Vancouver, B.C., 1935-36, Zurich, Switzerland, 1937-39; with Dept. of State, Wash., 1941-43 and 1945-48 (asst. chief fgn. service planning); adminstrv. officer Am. Embassy Mexico City, 1943-45, counselor of embassy, consul gen., 1948-51; fgn. service inspector Dept. State, 1951-54; counselor of embassy, Seoul, Korea, 1954-56; ambassador Cambodia, 1956-59, Bolivia, 1959-61; dir. Fgn. Service Inst., Dept. State, 1961-62; prof. math. Luther Coll., 1962-64. Served as 2d lt., U.S. Army, 1918. Lutheran. Club: Cosmos. Home: Decorah IA Died Jan. 27, 1969.

STROMBERG, HUNT, motion picture producer; b. Louisville, Ky., July 12, 1894; s. Benjamin and Fannie (Laub) S.; ed. pub. schs. of St. Louis; m. Katherine Kerwin, Nov. 9, 1919; 1 son, Hunt. Reporter St. Louis Times, 1911-12; sports staff specializing in baseball and column by-line, 1913; rode circuits with St. Louis Browns and Cardinals as spl. corr., 1914; baseball writer Sporting News, St. Louis, 1915-16; idea man and copywriter Keeshen Advt. Agency, Oklahoma City, Okla., 1917; dir. publicity Goldwyn Co., N.Y. City 1918-19; dir. publicity Thomas H. Ince, Hollywood Calif., 1920-22; personal asst. to Mr. Ince, 1923 producer M.G.M., 1923-42; with Co., 1942-48 organized own independent prodn. orgn. for United Artists release under name of Hunt Stromberg Prodns. Inc.; prodns. include: The Strange Woman, Guest in the House, Lady of Burlesque, Dishonored Lady, Personal Column; Too Late for Tears. M-G-M prodns.: The Great Ziegfeld (Acad. Award winner, 1936); Maytime Rose Marie, Northwest Passage, Night Must Fall, The Thin Man, Treasure Island, Naughty Marietta, The Women, Pride and Prejudice, Ah, Widerness, Red Dust, Blonde Bombshell, Marie Antoinette, Idiot's Delight, Chained, Our Dancing Daughters, White Shadows of the South Seas, They Met in Bombay, The Firefly Sweethearts, many others. Recipient: Motion Picture Herald (in asso. with Fame mag.). Special Award of Achievement for being selected by exhibitors of U.S. and Canada as the Champion of Champion Producers for All Time, Jan. 1, 1947. Home: Los Angeles CA Died Aug. 1968; buried Whittier CA

STRONG, ANNA LOUISE, writer; b. Friend, Neb., Nov. 24, 1885; d. Sydney and Ruth Maria (Tracy) Strong; studied in Germany, 1902; Bryn Mawr, 1903; A.B., Oberlin, 1905; Ph.D., U. of Chicago, 1908; m. Joel Shubin, 1932. Organized Know Your City," institutes in Seattle, Portland, Walla Walla, Spokane, 1909-10; employed in child welfare exhibits, New York and Chicago, 1911; dir. child welfare exhibits in Kansas City, St. Louis, Rochester, Louisville, Providence, Montreal, Northampton, Dublin (Ireland), Panama P.I. Expn., etc.; exhibit expert, U.S. Children's Bureau, Washington, D.C., 1914-16; mem. Seattle Sch. Bd., 1916-18; feature editor Seattle Union Record, 1918-21; corr. Am. Friends Relief Mission in Russia, 1921-22; apptd. corr. Hearst's Internat. Magazine for Central and Eastern Europe, 1922; corr. North Am. Newspaper Alliance in Russia, 1925. Lecturer at Wellesley, Smith, Vassar, Columbia and Stanford, 1926; wrote newsletter Letter from China, Peking, China, 1958-70. Conglist. Author: Songs of the City, 1906; The King's Palace, 1908; Psychology of Prayer, 1909; On the Eve of Home Rule, 1914; Ragged Verse by Anise, 1918; History of the Seattle General Strike, 1919; The First Time in History, 1924; Children of Revolution, 1925; Chin'a Millions, 1928; Red Star in Samarkand, 1929; The Road to the Grey Pamir, 1930; The Soviets Conquer Wheat, 1931; I Change Worlds, 1935; This Soviet World, 1936; The Soviet Constitution, 1937; Spain in Arms, 1937; One Fifth of Mankind, 1938; My Native Land, 1940; Wild River, 1941. Organized Moscow Daily News, first English newspaper in Russia, 1930. Home: China Died Mar. 1970.*

STRONG, FREDERICK FINCH, M.D., inventor; b. Aurora, N.Y., June 6, 1872; s. Thomas Campbell (D.D.) and Mary Arabella (Finch) S.; grad. high sch., Ithaca, N.Y.; student Cornell U., 1889-93, Univ. of Berlin, 1893-94. Boston U. Med. Sch., 1895-97; M.D., Tufts Coll. Medical School, 1898; 1st Am. pupil of Dr. Paul Ehrlich, Berlin; m. Ethel Ellen Haley, Sept. 27, 1916. Instr. in clin. hematology, Tufts Coll. Med. Sch., 1898, lecturer in electrotherapeutics, 1898-1908; in gen. practice of medicine, Boston, 1898-1908; research in paper-pulp, St. Petersburg, Fla. (granted 4 patents on pulp process), 1910-13; in practice of medicine, St. Petersburg, 1913-15; lecture tour of U.S., 1917-18; began practice at Hollywood, 1919; becoming dir. Strong Therapeutic Inst., 1928; dean research dept. Arcanum Corp., Los Angeles; regent Life Research Foundation. Mem. Am. Medical Editors and Authors Assn., Pacific Physiotheraphy Assn. Mason. Republican. Theosophist. Author: Modern Electrotherapeutics, 1906; High-Frequency Currents, 1908; Science of a Living Universe, Vital

Normalization, Dance of the Octaves (scenario), 1939; (fiction) The Life Condenser, 1938; Prisoners of Space, 1940; (poetry) Book of Villanelles; Book of Sonnets; Echoes. Composer: Valse Petite," Minuet in C," Barcarole," Sanscrit Chant," Love in the Waves." Contbr. to N.E. Masonic Jour., Med. Herald, Archives of Medicine and Surgery and Archives of Radiology. Inventor of 1st Tesla-Thompson therapeutic high-frequency apparatus, cold quartz mercury ultra violet apparatus, cold ray monochromatic system, ultra-short wave for cure of high bood pressure, Photosonic Synchronizer, Photosonic Harmony System, Silent Music Therapy, Life Condenser for food preservation. Home: and Office: 6129 Fountain Av., Hollywood 28 CA‡

STRONG, SELAH BREWSTER, judge; b. N.Y. City, Jan. 18, 1873; s. Thomas Shepard and Emily (Boorman) S.; Columbia, 1891-92; LL.B., New York Law Sch., 1894; m. May Waring Lefferts, of New York, Feb. 14, 1897. Atty. to State Forest, Fish and Game Commn., N.Y., 1905, 06; asst. U.S. dist. atty., 1906-10; referee in bankruptcy, 1910-15; surrogate, Suffolk Co., N.Y., 1915-20; justice Supreme Court of N.Y., 2d Dist., term 1921-34. Republican. Clubs: Crescent Athletic, Brooklyn Univ., Zeta Psi. Address: Court House, Brooklyn NY‡

STROTHER, DAN J(AMES) F(RENCH), lawyer; b. Washington, Va., June 29, 1872; s. James French and Mary (Botts) S.; ed. pub. and pvt. schs.; studied law with father and short course in U. of Va.; m. Elizabeth Garnett Grant, Nov. 25, 1902. Admitted to Va. bar, 1893, and began practice at Washington, Va.; admitted to W.Va. bar, 1896; mem. Strother & Christie, attorneys for various public utility and coal corps.; pres. Bankers Pocahontas Coal Co.; dir. and officer bank and various corps. Mem. W.Va. State Bd. Law Examiners, W.Va. Constitutional Commn., 1930 (chmn.). Mem. W.Va. State Bar Assn. (pres. 1928-29), Am. Bar Assn. (ex-chmn. sect. mineral law; mem. com. on professional ethics and grievances 5 yrs.). Farmer. Republican. Home: Welch WV*‡

STROZIER, FRED LEWIS, newspaperman; b. McRae, Ga., Nov. 4, 1908; s. Reuben James and Mattie (Stokes) S.; student pub. schs.; m. Nancy Dickinson Boss, Jan. 11, 1941; children—Jay Howard, Susan Hart. Reporter Tarpon Springs (Fla.) Leader, 1925-33, St. Petersburg (Fla.) Times, 1933-36; reporter Asso. Press, Jacksonville, Fla., 1936-37, Tallahassee, 1937-39, corr., Miami, Fla., 1939-42, chief Havana bur., 1943-46, Buenos Aires, 1947-55, South Am. manager, Rio de Janeiro, Brazil, 1955-60, adminstrv. asst., membership dept., 1961-64, broadcast membership exec., 1964-69. Member of Press Collegium of Havana, Brazilian Press Assn., Sigma Delta Chi. Methodist. Club: Overseas Press (N.Y.C.). Home: New York City NY Died July 1969.

STRUB, PAUL, univ. dean; b. St. Louis, Sept. 5, 1917; s. Reuben David and Elva (Glenn) S.; B.S., N.E. Mo. State Coll., 1939, M.A., 1948; postgrad. U. Ind., 1951; Ed.D., U. Kan., 1957; m. Masel E. Burlingame, Apr. 6, 1946 (dec. Feb. 1972); 1 dau., Edith Ann (Mrs. William Mante, Jr.). Supt. music, Lincoln County, Mo., 1937-38; dir. bands and choirs Fulton (Mo.) pub. schs., 1939-42; dir. bands McBride High Sch., St. Louis, 1946-47; prof. music N.E. Mo. State Coll., 1947-62; dean Sch. Music, Eastern N.M. U., Portales, 1962-72. Served to 1st lt., C.E., AUS, 1943-46. Mem. Music Educators Nat. Conf., N.E.A., Portales, Roosevelt County (pres. 1972) chambers commerce, Phi Mu Alpha. Pi Kappa Lambda, Phi Delta Kappa, Sigma Tau Gamma. Democrat. Roman Catholic. Kiwanian (H. gov. div. 1972). Contbr. profl. jours. Home: Portales NM Died Nov. 3, 1972; buried Portales Cemetery, Portales NM

STRUBE, GUSTAV, conductor, composer; b. Ballenstedt, Germany, Mar. 3, 1867; s. Friedrich and Henriette (Meergarten) S.; ed. Leipzig Conservatory; studied violin with Brodsky, composition with Jadassohn and Reinicke and piano with Reckendorf; m. Martha Grosse, Jan. 29, 1893; children—Claire (Mrs. Henry Schradieck), Elfriede (Mrs. Frederick Lee). Came to U.S., 1890, naturalized, 1896. First violin, Boston Symphony Orch., 1890-1912, also condr. of pops" 10 yrs.; former mem. faculty Peabody Conservatory, Baltimore, Md., since 1913; organizer and condr. Baltimore Symphony Orchestra, 1915-30. Composer: 3 symphonies, 4 overtures, 3 violin concertos; Poeme Antique, for violin and orchestra; 1 cello concerto; 2 symphonic poems for viola and orchestra; Hymn to Eros, for male chorus and orchestra; American Rhapsody, for orchestra; Symphonic Sketch Ariequinade; Symphonic Fantasie; The Captive (grand opera); 4 preludes for orchestra; Americana for orchestra; Sonata, for violin and piano; Sonata, for viola and piano; Sonata, for cello and piano; string quintet (2violas); quintet for woodwind and horn; trio for piano, violin and cello; 2 string quartettes; trio for clarinet, horn and piano; Sinfonietta for orchestra; Sonatina for viola and piano; Der Harz (symphonic poem for orchestra); Concerto (A minor) for violin and orchestra; also many smaller pieces for violin and piano. Home: 2845 N. Calvert St., Baltimore MD‡

STUART, ALBERT RHETT, bishop; b. Washington, Jan. 20, 1906; s. Garden Clarkson and Florence (Beale) S.; student Episcopal High Sch., Alexandria, Va., 1920-24; A.B., U. Va., 1928; B.D., Va. Theol. Sem., 1931; D.D., Oglethorpe U., 1938, U. of South, 1955, Va. Theol. Sem., 1955; m. Isabelle Alston, Sept. 25, 1945 (dec. 1964); children—Garden C., Isabella A. Ordained deacon Episcopal Ch., 1931, ordained priest, 1931; rector, Ch. of Resurrection, Greenwood, S.C., 1931-36, St. Michael's Ch., Charleston, S.C., 1936-47, dean Christ Ch. Cathedral, New Orleans, 1947-54; consecrated bishop of Ga., 1954-72, ret. 1972. Mem. Nat. Council Episcopal Ch., 1939-43, 67-70; dep. Gen. Conv., 1934, 40, 46, 49, 52. Served with Chaplain Corps, U.S. Navy, 1943; served N.O.B., Norfolk, Va.; E.T.O.; U.S.N.T.C., Great Lakes; disch. rank of lt., 1946. Mem. St. Andrews Soc. Savannah (chaplain), Ravan Soc., Soc. Colonial Wars, Phi Beta Kappa, Omicron Delta Kappa, Phi Delta Theta. Democrat. Episcopalian. Club: Ogethrope. Home: Savannah GA Died Jan. 19, 1973.

STUART, DELLA TOVREA (MRS. WILLIAM P. STUART), company director; b. Blanco, Texas, October 8, 1888; d. James Steele and Irene (Anderson) Gillespie; grad. Austin (Tex.) High Sch., 1905; student U. of Texas, 1905-06; m. Edward A. Tovrea, Dec. 18, 1906 (died 1932); m. 2d, William P. Stuart, Nov. 16, 1936. Clerk, Tovrea Meat Co., Bisbee, Ariz., 1906-08, auditor, 1908-19; vice pres. Tovrea Packing Co., Phoenix, Ariz., 1919-46, dir., 1919-46; pres. Central Ariz. Broadcasting Co., Jerome, Ariz., 1937-44; sec.-treas. Prescott (Ariz.) Courier, Inc.; dir. Anvil Rock Cattle Co., Seligman, Ariz. Mem. exec. com. Dem. State Central Com. since 1940; Dem. nat. committeewoman for Ariz., 1940-56; delegate to Democratic National Convention, 1936. Mem. D.A.R. Mem. Elks Auxiliary (Prescott). Mem. Society of Friends. Clubs: Business and Professional Women's, Hassayampa Country (Prescott); Phoenix Phoenix AZ Died Jan. 17, 1969.

STUART, ELBRIDGE HADLEY, milk products exec., b. El Paso, Tex., Nov. 9. 1887; s. Elbridge Amos and Mary (Horner) S.; grad. Phillips Acad., Andover, Mass., 1908; B.S., Sheffield Sci. Sch. of Yale U., 1911; L.D., Whitman Coll., Walla Walla, Wash., 1964; m. Nan Fullerton, June 22, 1916 (dec. Aug. 1937); children—Elbridge Hadley, Reginald Fullerton, Dwight Lyman; m. 2d, Mrs. Evelyn Clark Ruble, Feb. 24, 1945; children—Elizabeth (Mrs. Clarke A. Nelson), Ann (Mrs. Herbert L. Lucas, Jr.). With the Carnation Co., processors of evaporated milk, 1911-72, supt. factory, 1912, asst. gen. supt. operations, 1914, v.p., 1916, exec. v.p., 1926, pres., 1932-57, chmn. bd., 1957-71, hon. chmn. bd., 1971-72. Trustee emeritus Cal. Inst. Tech. Republican. Clubs: Los Angeles Country; Washington Athletic; Eldorado Country. Home: Los Angeles CA Died Sept. 16, 1972.

STUART, HENRY WALDGRAVE, univ. prof.; b. Oakland, Calif., Dec. 1, 1870; s. Daniel and Victoria (Barlow) S.; Ph.B., U. of Calif., 1893; Ph.D., U. of Chicago, 1900; m. Terese Waters, Sept. 12, 1905; children—Arthur Waters, Margaret Moore. Instr. philosophy, State U. of Ia., 1901-04; asst. prof., same Lake Forest (Ill.) Coll., 1904-07; asst. prof. philosophy, 1907-08, asso. prof., 1908-09, prof., 1909-36, Stanford Univ., retired, 1936. Mem. Pacific br., Am. Philos-Assn., etc. Author: Liberal and Vocational Studies in the College, 1918. Contbr. to Studies in Logical Theory, Chicago, 1903, to Creative Intelligence, N.Y., 1917, etc. Home: P.O. Box 1943, Carmel CA‡

STUART, IAN, educator, savs. and loan exec.; b. Dublin, Ireland, Sept. 18, 1902; s. William Henry and Florence Ann (Bowen) S.; student Malvern Coll., 1917-20; B.A., Trinity Coll., Dublin U., 1924, M.A., 1929; m. Barbara Millar, Apr. 14, 1931; children—Mary Ann, Barbara Jean, David Bruce. Came to U.S., 1947, naturalized, 1951. Master St. Paul's Sch., London, 1925-27, Harrow Sch., 1927-31; joint prin. Marcy's London, 1931-33; heamaster Beaminster Grammar Sch., Eng., 1933-35, Portora Royal Sch., No. Ireland, 1935-47; licensed Lay reader Ch. of Eng. 1935-69; mem. senate Belfast U., 1935-47; dir. guidance Mercersburg Acad., Mercers; Pa.; dir. Ala. Ednl. Found., 1949-52; dir. pub. relations and edn. So. States Indsl. Council, 1953-57; dir. community relations Florist's Telegraph Delivery Assn., 1957-69; asst. to pres. Jefferson Fed. Savs. & Loan Assn., 1965-69. Recipient Royal Humane Soc. award for saving life at sea; Freedoms Found. award at Valley Forge, 1960; D.A.R. medal, 1964; Douglas MacArthur medal, 1964. Mem. Royal Soc. Tchrs., Headmaster's Conf. Ireland Protestant Schs. (hon. sec., founder), Old Malvernian Soc. (U.S. rep.). Author: Matriculation History of England; Simplified Shakespeare Series (8 vols.); Modern Rugby Football; Reminiscences of a Public Schoolboy; Scenes Selected from Shakespeare; Thoughts for Johnny; (also radio program). Address: Birmingham AL Died Aug. 10, 1969.

STUART, JAMES EDWIN, asso. exec.; b. Hemlock, N.C., Jan. 22, 1897; s. John W. and Nancy (Weaver) S.; A.B., Emory and Henry Coll., 1921; L.H.D.; Emory and Henry College, Emory, Va., 1961; LL.B., George Washington U., 1924, LL.M., 1926; student Am. U., 1926-27; m. Bethel Beery, Mar. 31, 1923; children—Betty Ruth (Mrs. David M. Sander), John DeWitt. Chief, div. child welfare Bd. Pub. Welfare D.C., 1923-27; supt. Westchester Co. (N.Y.) Soc. for Prevention Cruelty to Children, 1927-29; exec. sec. Ohio Humane Soc., Cincinnati, 1929-33; dir. Dept. Pub. Welfare, Hamilton Co., 1933-35; asst. dir. Community Chest, Cincinnati, 1935-38; exec. sec. Hamilton Co. Child Welfare Bd., 1938-41; exec. v.p. and dir. Hosp. Care Corp. (Blue Cross Plan for S.W. Ohio), 1942-57; exec. v.p., Blue Cross Assn., 1957-60, pres., 1960-61, chairman board, 1961-62, consultant, 1963-68; chmn. bd., chmn. executive com. Health Service, Inc., 1951-52; v. chmn. Blue Cross Commn., Am. Hosp. Assn., 1952, chmn. 1952-1954, chmn. government relations committee, 1956-57; mem. bd. govs., exec. com. Blue Cross Assn., 1956-57; cons. Health Edn. and Welfare Dept., 1954, Dept. Defense, from 1963. Recipient Justin Ford Kimball award Am. Hospital Assn., 1961. Mem. of the alien enemy hearing board So. Ohio Jud. Dist., 1942. Served with U.S. Army, 1917-19; disch. as 2d lt. Decorated Silver Star. Mem. Cincinnatus Assn., Ohio Hist. and Philos. Soc., Sigma Chi, Phi Alpha Delta. Methodist. Clubs: Literary (Cin.); Canadian (N.Y.C.); Lake Shore (Chgo.). Home: Scottsdale AZ Died Dec. 23, 1968.

STUART, JOHN, corp. official; b. Cedar Rapids, Ia., May 23, 1877; s. Robert and Margaret (Sharrar) S.; prep. edn., U. Sch. Chgo.; C.E., Princeton, 1900; H.H.D., 1949; Doctor of Humanities (hon.), Coe College, 1949; m. Ellen B. Shumway, Feb. 14, 1903; children—Joan S., Ellen P., John. Began as factory hand in mill of Quaker Oats Co., Cedar Rapids, 1900; moved to Chgo., 1903, and was employed in one of the plants of same co., later successively asst. supt., asst. operating mgr., 2d v.p., 1910, pres., 1922-42, chmn. bd., 1942-56, dir. and mem. exec. com. until 1964. Dir. Tax Fedn. of Illinois. Member of the National Industrial Conf. Board Trustee-emeritus, Princeton, hon. trustee, U. Chgo. Com. econ. devel. Mem. Cap and Gown (Princeton). Republican. Presbyn. Clubs: Chicago, University, Commercial, Indian Hill, Onwentsia Country. Home: Lake Forest IL Died Dec. 26, 1969; buried Lake Forest Cemetery, Lake Forest IL

STUART, WILLIAM HERVEY, newspaper man; b. Paris, Ill., Oct. 4, 1874; s. William and Helen C. (Henry) S.; grad. high sch., Grand Rapids, Mich., 1893; m. 2d, Ethel M. Sullivan, of Chicago, Mar. 5, 1921; 1 son, Donald H. (by previous marriage). Began as reporter Grand Rapids Herald, 1895; with Chicago Journal, 1896-1904; city editor Detroit Tribune, 1905; mng. editor Grand Rapids Herald, 1905-06; became polit. editor Chicago American, 1906, now retired; chief clk, Chicago Bd. Election Commrs., 1910-14. Made race around the world in 1909, and established record of 40 days, 17 hours and 23 minutes. Dem. mem. Bd. Election Commrs. Chicago, 1920-22; chmn. publicity com. mayoralty campaign Wm. Hale Thompson, 1927. Mem. Bd. Fish and Game Conservation Advisors. Mem. Gamma Delta Psi. Protestant. Clubs: Lake Shore Athletic, Forty, Chiwaukee Country. Author: The 20 Incredible Years, 1936; Share the Profits Chicago IL‡

STUBBS, JOHN OSMON, investment banker; b. Portland, Ore., Jan. 19, 1898; s. Osmon B. and Edith (Williams) S.; grad. Phillips Andover Acad., 1917; S.B., Harvard, 1921; m. Vera Howell, June 20, 1945. With Lee Higginson & Co., 1921-32, Lee Higginson Corp., 1932-34; v.p. Whiting, Weeks & Knowles, 1934-38; Partner Whiting, Weeks & Stubbs, 1939-52; mng. partner F. S. Mosley & Co., Boston, 1953-69, ltd. partner, 1969-72; mem. corp. Dedham Instn. for Savs.; mem. corp. and mem. bd. mgrs. Greater Boston Charitable Trust, Inc.; mem. corp. Provident Instn. for Savs. in Town of Boston. Mem. corp. United Community Services, Mass. Gen. Hosp. Gov. Boston Stock Exchange, 1950-55, N.Y. Stock Exchange, 1954-57. Chmn. victory fund com. 1st Fed. Res. Dist., World War II. Mem. Investment Bankers Assn. (past v.p.), Nat. Assn. Securities Dealers (past gov.), Nat. Assn. Health, Edn. and Welfare (past v.p.), Mass. Hort. Soc. (v.p., mem. exec. com.), Mass. Soc. Promoting Agr. (treas., trustee), Mass. Audubon Soc. (dir.). Club: Somerset (Boston). Home: Westwood MA Died Oct. 23, 1972; buried Dover MA

STUBBS, MERRILL, banker; b. Dewey, Okla., July 14, 1905; s. Frederick A. and Katharyn (Tucker) S.; student U. of Colo., 1923-26; m. Gretchen Bryant, Apr. 20, 1946; children—Blayney, Jill, Michael. Chmn. Ivy Corp., Atlanta, 1961-72; dir., mem. exec. com. Dover Corp.; dir. Pratt-Read Corp. Clubs: Lyford Cay (Nassau); Essex Yacht, Old Lyme Country, Wall Street, Fifth Avenue; Key Largo Angler's. Home: Essex CT Died Oct. 10, 1972.

STUBBS, TRUETT TRISTIAN, telephone co. exec.; b. Raleigh, Miss., Jan. 29, 1907; s. Joseph J. and May Maud (Little) S.; A.B., Miss. Coll., 1928; student Jefferson Sch. Law, 1935-37; m. Beatrice Rita Thomas, Sept. 2, 1932; children—Truett T., Joseph G., Richmond L. High sch. tchr., 1928-29; accountant So. Bell Telephone Co., Atlanta, 1929-41, auditor Tenn. area, 1941-49, labor relations work, 1949-56, sec., 1956-68, sec.-treas., 1968. Mem. Telephone Pioneers

Am., Armed Forces Communications and Electronics Assn. Presbyn. (elder). Kiwanian (pres. 1961). Home: Atlanta GA Died June 28, 1968; buried Arlington Cemetery.

STUEMPFIG, WALTER, painter; b. Germantown, Phila., Jan. 26, 1914; s. Walter and Flora (Townsend) S.; grad. Germantown Acad., 1930; student U. Pa., 1930, Pa. Acad. Fine Arts, 1931-34; m. Lila Agnes Kennedy Hill, Oct. 22, 1935 (dec. Nov. 1, 1946); children—George Randolph Kennedy, Anthony Alexander Penn. Cresson fgn. traveling scholar Pa. Acad. Fine Arts, 1933, now prof. composition; landscape painter. Named Academician Nat. Acad. Design, 1951; recipient grant Am. Acad. Arts and Letters, 1952; award Corcoran Gallery, Washington, 1948, Nat. Acad., 1952, Nat. Acad. Design, 1956. Mem. Nat. Inst. Arts and Letters, Century Assn. Home: Clover Springs PA Died Dec. 1970.*

STULL, CHARLES HENRY, church official; b. Quincy, Pa., 1873; s. John F. and Mary S. (Long) S.; A.B., Ewing Coll., 1894, Ph.D., 1912; m. H. Jeanne Thorne, of Kearney, Neb., 1896 (now deceased); children—Paul, Chas. Henry. Began ministry at Leadville, Colo., 1895; pastor in Kan. and Ia., and at Newark and Marietta, O., until 1921; supt. evangelism Ohio Bapt. Conv. and Am. Bapt. Home Mission Soc. since 1921. Author: The Christian Sabbath, 1908; Greater Evangelism and the Leading Trails, 1933. Home: Granville OH‡

STULL, RAY THOMAS, ceramic engr.; b. Elkland, Pa., Mar. 12, 1875; s. David W. and Mary (Thomas) S.; E.M. in Ceramics, Ohio State U., 1902; m. Lena Taylor, of Mansfield, Pa., Apr. 15, 1903. Chemist Am. Terra Cotta & Ceramic Co., Terra Cotta, Ill., 1902-4; supt. Mt. Savage Enamel Brick Works, 1904-6; supt. Steiger Terra Cotta & Pottery Works, 1907; with department of ceramics engring., U. of Ill., 1907-15, becoming acting dir.; ceramic engr. Dunn Wire-Cut Lug Brick Co., at Conneaut, O., 1915-17; chief ceramist U.S. Bur. of Mines since Sept. 1, 1917, also supt. Ceramic Expt. Sta. of same. Mem. Am. Ceramic Soc. (ex-pres.), Sigma Xi, Alpha Chi Sigma, Acacia. Mason. Home: 114 W. 10th Av., Columbus OH‡

STUMM, ERWIN C(HARLES), educator, museum curator; b. Berkeley, Cal., Sept. 15, 1908; s. Ernest C. and Augusta (Eschle) S.; A.B., George Washington U., 1932, A.M., 1933; Ph.D., Princeton, 1936; m. Elizabeth Coon, Aug. 29, 1936; children—Virginia, Diana, Ernest. Sci. aide U.S. Dept. Agr., Washington, 1926-30, U.S. Geol. Survey, 1930-34; instr. geology Oberlin Coll., 1937-45, asst. prof., 1945-47; asst. prof. geology U. Mich., also asso. curator Mus. Paleontology, 1947-52, asso. prof., 1952-57, curator, 1952-69, prof., 1957-69; cons. geologist. Fellow Geol. Soc. Am., Ohio Acad. Sci.; mem. Paleontol. Soc. (pres. 1966-67), Am. Assn. Petroleum Geeologists, Mich. Acad. Arts, Sci. and Letters, Mich. Geol. Soc., Sigma Xi. Editor and co-editor Jour. Paleontology, 1957-64. Contbr. articles profl. jours. Home: Ann Arbor MI Died Apr. 24, 1969.

STUMP, FELIX BUDWELL, ret. naval officer; b. Parkersburg, W.Va., Dec. 15, 1894; s. John Sutton and Lily (Budwell) S.; B.S., U.S. Naval Acad., 1917; M.S., Mass. Inst. Tech., 1924; m. Myra Morgan, Dec. 22, 1923; 1 son, John Morgan; m. 2d, Elizabeth Smith, Aug. 11, 1937; children—Frances, Felix. Commd. ensign USN, 1917, advanced through grades to adm., 1953; navigator U.S.S. Cincinnati, World War I; flight tng. Naval Air Sta., Pensacola, Fla., 1919-20; comdr. exptl. squadron Naval Air Sta., Norfolk, Va., 1921-22; staff comdr. Air Bat. For., 1924-25; with torpedo plane squadron U.S.S. Langley, 1925-27; staff Naval Air Sta., Norfolk, 1927-30; comdr. cruiser scouting squadrons, 1930-32; with bur. aero. Navy Dept., 1932-34; comdr. dive bombing squadron U.S.S. Saratoga, 1934-36; navigator U.S.S. Lexington, 1936-37; with bur. aero. Navy Dept., 1937-40; exec. U.S.S. Enterprise, 1940-41; comdr. U.S.S. Langley, 1941; dir. combined operations, intelligence center Am., Brit., Dutch, Aus. Com. Java, 1942; capt. new U.S.S. Lexington, 1943-44; comdr. Carrier Div. 24, 1944-45; chief naval air tech. tng., 1945-48; comdr. Air Force, Atlantic Fleet, 1948-51, 2d Fleet and NATO Striking Fleet, 1951-53; comdr.-in-chief Pacific and U.S. Pacific Fleet, 1953-58; chairman of the board of Air America, Incorporated, Air Asia Co., Ltd., from 1959. Decorated Navy Cross with gold star, D.S.M. War and Navy depts., Legion of Merit with gold stars, Silver Star medal, also fgn. decorations. Address: McLean VA Died June 13, 1972; buried Arlington Nat. Cemetery, Arlington VA

STURDIVANT, J(AMES) HOLMES, educator; born Greenville, Texas, June 22, 1906; s. Emmett C. and Gladys (Holmes) S.; B.A., U. of Texas, 1926, M.A., 1927; Ph.D., Calif. Inst. Tech., 1930. Prof. chemistry Cal. Inst. Tech., 1947-72. Address: Pasadena CA Died Apr. 21, 1972.

STURDY, HERBERT FRANCIS, lawyer; b. Chgo., Dec. 19, 1902; s. Harry and Mary J. (Leahy) S.; B.S., Yale, 1924, LL.B., 1927; M. Jane Adeline Kellogg, Aug. 18, 1933; children—Sally, Nancy. Admitted to Cal. bar, 1927, practiced in Los Angeles; mem. firm Gibson, Dunn & Crutcher. Dir. Menasco Mfg. Co., Rohr. Corp. Mem. Yale Corp., 1959-65; former chmn. Yale Alumni Bd. Mem. Internat., Am. (former chmn. corp., banking and bus. law), Los Angeles bar assns., Am. Judicature Soc., Am. Law Inst., Am. Acad. Polit. and Social Sci., Acad. Polit. Sci., Phi Beta Kappa, Zeta Psi, Phi Delta Phi, Order of Coif. Episcopalian. Clubs: Chancery, Bond, Stock Exchange, California (Los Angeles); Bel-Air Country. Home: Los Angeles CA Died Feb. 19, 1969.

STURGES, DONALD GEORGE, mfg. co. exec.; b. Altamont, N.Y., Oct. 18, 1911; s. Edward C. and Hila F. (Scott) S.; Chem. Engr., Rensselaer Poly. Inst., 1933; m. Barbara Lyon, Sept. 2, 1938 (dec.); children—Scott, Susan, David. Devel. engr., analytical chemist E. I. duPont de Nemours & Co., 1933-35; sales engr. E. D. Tierney & Co., 1935-36; shift supt. Skenandoa Rayon Co., 1936-37; analytical research chemist, tech. service engr. Fisher Sci. Co., 1937-39; advt. mgr. Mallinckrodt Chem. Works, 1939-42; asst. operations officer, then operations officers, Madison Sq. Area, Corps Engrs., Manhattan Project 1942-46; gen. mgr. Northwest Chemurgy Co., dir. operations Hanford office AEC, 1947-56; mgr. new products br., research and devel. div. Carborundum Co., Niagara Falls, N.Y., 1956-59, asso. dir. research and devel., 1959-60, dir. research and devel., 1960-62, v.p., dir. research and devel., 1962-67, sr. v.p. corporate planning, 1967-73. Mem. N.Y. State Adv. Council Advancement Research and Devel. Bd. dirs. N.Y. State Sci. and Tech. Found.; chmn. bd. trustees Rensselaer Poly. Inst. Recipient Legion of Merit, 1946, Silver medal AEC, 1956. Fellow Am. Inst. Chemists; mem. Am. Ceramic Soc., Am. Nuclear Soc., A.A.A.S., Indsl. Research Inst., Am. Mgmt. Assn., Buffalo, Niagara Falls chambers commerce, N.A.M., Newcomen Soc., Nat. Planning Assn. Home: Youngstown NY Died Jan. 23, 1973.

STURGIS, GUY HAYDEN, judge; b. New Gloucester, Me., Mar. 3, 1877; s. John I. and Mira (Hayden) S.; A.B., Bowdoin, 1898, LL.D., 1926. Student law dept. Columbia, 1898-99; m. Edna L. Bailey, June 5, 1903 (dec.); m. 2d, Adelaide V. Sweeney, Apr. 30, 1908 (dec.); m. 3d, Elizabeth F. Cram, Feb. 20, 1926. Began practice in Portland, 1900; alderman, 1912, 13; member exec. com. Rep. State Com., Me., 1912-23; atty. gen. of Me., 1917-20; was asso. counsel in Chandler Will Case, chief counsel Municipal Fuel Yard Case, and as atty. gen., was counsel for the people in the Me. Central R.R. Rate Case and Cumberland County Power & Light Case. Asso. justice Supreme Court of Me., Aug. 14, 1923-Aug. 8, 1940, chief justice Supreme and Superior Courts of Maine since August 8, 1940. Conglist. Mason, K.P. V.p. Nat. Assn. of Attys. Gen. of U.S., 1919-20. Home: 605 Brighton Av., Portland ME*‡

STURGIS, HENRY SPRAGUE, ret. banker; b. Cheyenne, Mar. 1, 1892; s. William and Anna Louisa (Sprague) S.; prep. edn., Phillips Acad., Andover, Mass.; A.B. cum laude, Harvard, 1915; m. Gertrude Lovett, June 19, 1916; children—Elizabeth Moorfield (Mrs. T. Suffern Tailer), Henry Sprague, Robert Lovett; m. 2d, Catharine Bartholomay Osborne, 1941. Began business career in association with father, 1915-17; with Spencer, Trask & Co., 1919-24; with First Nat. City Bank N.Y., 1925-56, v.p., 1928-56; asso. with Sanderson & Porter, bus. consultants, 1956-73; chmn. exec. com. Erie Railroad; bd. dirs. Gen. Mills, Inc. Asst. to Gov. of Ariz. for Indsl. Devel. Mem. bd. St. Joseph's Hosp., Phoenix. Sr. bd. mem. Nat. Indsl. Conf. Bd. Served from pvt. to capt., AS, U.S. Army, Sept. 1917-March 1919. Vice-pres. New York Hospital. Clubs: Harvard, Knickerbocker, Rockaway Hunting; Royal and Ancient Golf (St. Andrews, Scotland); Paradise Valley Country. Author: Investment—A New Profession, 1924; A New Chapter of Erie, 1948. Address: Scottsdale AZ Died Mar. 19, 1973.

STURGIS, LINDELL WYMORE, banker; b. Metropolis, Ill., Aug. 18, 1899; s. Isaac Aaron and Lyda (Wymore) S.; student accounting Internat. Corr. Schs., also Walton Sch. Commerce; m. Viola Jones, May 18, 1922; children—Dorothy Jean (Mrs. John Easley), Carolyn Sue (Mrs. Milton E. Wetherington). Pres., dir. City Nat. Bank, Metropolis, 1943-72; v.p. Good Luck Glove Co., Carbondale and Metropolis, 1938-72; dir. Peoples Nat. Bank, Paducah Ky., First Nat. Bank, Lacenter, Ky., Massal County Bldg. & Loan Assn. Trustee So. Ill. U., 1949-51, 53-71, chmn. bd., 1969-71, mem. Univ. Retirement Bd., Champaign and Urbana, Ill., 1961-72; pres. Sch. Dist. 35, Metropolis, 1925. Named Ky. col., 1957. Mem. Metropolis C. of C. Republican. Mason, Odd Fellow, Rotarian. Home: Metropolis IL Died Oct. 11, 1972; buried Metropolis Meml. Gardens, Metropolis IL

STURTEVANT, ALFRED HENRY, zoologist; b. Jacksonville, Ill., Nov. 21, 1891; s. Alfred H. and Harriet E. (Morse) S.; A.B., Columbia, 1912, Ph.D., 1914; Sc.D., Princeton, 1947, U. Pa., 1949, Yale, 1951; m. Phoebe Curtis Reed, Apr. 22, 1922; children—William C., Harriet M. (Mrs. Howard E. Shapiro), Alfred H. Employed as research assistant Carnegie Instn., Washington, 1915-28; prof. genetics, Cal. Inst. Tech., 1928-47, Thomas H. Morgan prof. biology, 1947-62, now emeritus; visiting professor Univ. Washington, 1960, University of Texas, 1962, Princeton University, 1963, University Wisconsin, 1964, U. Ore., 1966, U. Cal. at Santa Cruz, 1966; visiting Carnegie prof., Birmingham, 1932, Leeds and Durham, 1933; vis. lectr. Harvard, 1940. Recipient Kimber medal Nat. Academy Sci., 1957; John J. Carty medal Nat. Acad. Scis., 1965, National Medal of Science, 1968. Fellow Am. Assn. Advancement Sci. (pres. Pacific div. 1953-54); mem. Am. Soc. Zoologist (president 1934), Nat. Acad. Scis., Genetic Soc. Am. (pres. 1944), Am. Philos. Soc., British (hon.), Japanese genetical socs. Author: A History of Genetics, 1965. Address: Pasadena CA Died Apr. 6, 1970; buried Woods Hole MA

STURTEVANT, EDGAR HOWARD, prof. linguistics; b. Jacksonville, Ill., Mar. 7, 1875; s. Alfred Henry and Harriet (Morse) S.; prep. edn., Whipple Acad., 1890-93; student Ill. Coll., 1893-95 (both of Jacksonville); A.B., Indiana Univ., 1898; Ph.D., U. of Chicago, 1901; L.H.D., Illinois College, Jacksonville, 1929; honorary LL.D., Indiana University, 1940, University of Chicago, 1941; married Bessie Fitch Skinner, July 11, 1903; children—Grace, Cortland Asa, Julian Munson. Instructor in Latin, Indiana University, 1901-02; acting prof. Greek, Maryville (Tenn.) Coll., 1902-03; acting asst. prof. Latin, U. of Mo., 1903-05; same, Ind. U., 1905-07; instr. in classical philology, Columbia, 1907-13, asst. prof., 1913-20; clk. Irving Nat. Bank, N.Y. City, 1920-23; asst. prof. Greek and Latin, Yale, 1923-26, asso. prof. linguistics, 1926-27, professor, 1927-43, professor emeritus since 1943. Member New Jersey State Bd. of Education, 1914-18. Mem. Am. Oriental Soc. (pres. 1936-37), Am. Philological Association, Linguistic Society of America (president 1931), American Philosophical Soc., and Phi Beta Kappa. Author: Contraction in Case Forms of Latin io and ia Stems and of deus, is and idem, 1902; Studies in Greek Noun Formation (4 parts), 1910-13; Linguistic Change, 1917; The Pronunciation of Latin and Greek, 1920, 2d edit., 1940; Hittite Glossary, 1931; 2d edit., 1937; A Comparative Grammar of the Hittite Language, 1933; Hittite Chrestomathy, 1935; The Indo-Hittite Laryngeals, 1942; Introduction to Linguistic Science, 1947. Editor: P. Terneti Afri Andria, 1914; T. Macci Plauti Mostellaria, 1925; T. Macci Plauti Pseudolus, 1932. Home: 408 Whitney Av., New Haven CT

SUDJARWO, TJONDRONEGORO, Indonesian diplomat; b. Lawang (Malang), Java, Indonesia, Mar. 2, 1914; s. Raden Pandji Adi Tjondronegoro and Sumarmi S.; 2d Candidacy Law, Djakarta Law Faculty, 1934-36; Meester in de Rechten, U. Leiden, 1936-39; m. Laksmiharti Pawitro Hadinoto, Aug. 8, 1942; children—Estia Adiarti, Nehria Astriani, Adi Tresnoto. Chief personnel to gov. of Central Java, 1940-42, asst. to gov., 1942-45; sec. Provincial Republican Council, also sec. Rep. Govt., 1945-46; head Rep. Information Office, Central Java, 1946-47; head publicity dept. Rep. Ministry Information, 1947-49, United States of Indonesia fgn. and publicity depts., also chmn. Indonesian Film Censor Bd., 1949-50; counsellor Embassy, Gt. Britain, 1950-52; dep. permanent rep. of Indonesia with rank to E.E. & M.P. United Nations, 1952-53, acting permanent representative, May 1953-Feb. 1956, permanent representative, Feb. from 1956, with rank of A.E. and P., from 1954. Mem. bd. League for Indonesian Culture. Mem. Am. Soc. Internat. Law. Moslem. Club: Lotos. Editor: The Revolution Pictured: 1945-49, 1950. Home: Jakarta Indonesia Died Dec. 1972.

SUDLER, ARTHUR EMORY, advt. exec.; b. Balt., Apr. 1, 1905; s. Arthur Emory and Louise Stabler (Gilpin) S.; student Balt. City Coll., 1918-22, Md. Inst. Fine and Applied Art, 1922-26; student painting with John Sloan and Robert Henri; m. Janet Starr Whitson, June 27, 1927; 1 dau., Gail (Mrs. Thomas R. Rockwell). One man shows of paintings Feragil Gallery, N.Y.C., 1954, 56; rep. Whitney Collection at N.Y. Med. Center, also pvt. collections; art dir. E. R. Squibb & Sons, 1930-36; organizer, 1936, pres. Sudler & Hennessey, Inc., advertising agency, N.Y.C., 1936-66, chairman board, 1966-68, also head 2 divs. of company; v.p. Arranz & Sudler, Inc., export pharm. advt., 1950-68. Mem. N.Y. Acad. Scis., Pharm. Mfrs. Assn., Pharm. Advt. Club (mem. bd. Am. Watercolor Club, Dutchess County Hist. Soc. Club: Lotos (pres. 1967, dir.) (N.Y.C.). Home: Poughkeepsie NY also New York NY Died Apr. 5, 1968; buried Nine Partner's Cemetery, Millbrook NY

SUDLER, MERVIN TUBMAN, surgeon; b. Vestover, Md., Aug. 9, 1875; s. Albert and Alice (Musselman) S.; S.B., Md. Agrl. Coll., 1894; Ph.D., Johns Hopkins Univ., 1899; M.D., Coll. of Physicians and Surgeons (now U. of Md.), Baltimore, 1901; m. Mabel A. Britton, Sept. 4, 1909. Instr. anatomy, John Hopkins Med. Sch. 1899-1902, Cornell U., 1902-03; interne and resident surgeon, Gen. Memorial Hosp., New York, 1903-05; resident surgeon, St. Mary's Hosp. for Children, New York, 1905-06; dean scientific dept., Sch. of Medicine, U. of Kan., 1906-11, dean and prof. surgery, Sch. of Medicine, same univ., 1911-24, also in practice as surgeon. Fellow Am. Coll. Surgeons; mem. A.M.A., Phi Beta Kappa, Sigma Xi, Phi Gamma Delta, Nu Sigma

Nu. Republican. Episcopalian. Club: University (Kansas City). Developed Medical Sch., U. of Kan. Home: West Hills. Office: 800 Massachusetts St., Lawrence KS‡

SUHR, CHARLES LOUIS, oil exec.; b. Oil City, Pa., Mar. 30, 1877; s. Henry and Louise (Schormann) S.; student Philadelphia College of Pharmacy, 1896-98; married Kate A. Wilkins, October 16, 1901 (dec. Aug. 1959); children—Henry (dec.), Charles W. (dec.); m. 2d, Ada M. McCoy, Apr. 28, 1964. With S. Penn Oil Co. (formerly Pennzoil Co.), Oil City, 1892-62, successively office clk., refinery worker, refinery supt., dir., treas. mgr., pres., chmn., dir., 1935-62, ret.; dir. First Seneca Bank & Trust Co., Oil City, 1915-63, chmn. 1953-62. Mason. Home: Oil City PA Died Sept. 1970.

SUKARNO, pres. Republic of Indonesia; b. Surabaya, Java, 1901; degree in civil engring., Tech. Inst. of Bandung. Joined revolutionists, 1927; several times imprisoned or exiled by Dutch govt.; while in exile on Sumatra was released by Japanese following its capture, 1942; pres. of Indonseian Republic, 1945-67, also prime minister (republic proclaimed by Indonesians, 1945, recognized by Dutch govt., 1947). Address: Djakarta Republic of Indonesia Died June 1970.

SULLIVAN, DENNIS FRANCIS, religious orgn. exec.; b. Brookline, Mass., July 22, 1898; s. Dennis and Mary (Sullivan) S.; ed. pub. schs., Mass.; m. Anne D. Tansey, Oct. 11, 1941. Mem. K.C., from 1919, with welfare program for hospitalized and discharged service men, Boston, 1919-22, asst. supreme sec., 1948, supreme sec., from 1964, also dir., exec. and finance coms.; trustee K.C. Found. Preservation Hist. Documents at Vatican Library. Vice pres. employees Tb Relief Assn., New Haven. Chmn. Democratic Town Com., N.Haven, Conn., 1959-60. Served with USNRF, 1917-19. Decorated Knight of St. Gregory the Great (Pope Paul VI). Mem. V.F.W., Holy Name Soc. Home: North Haven CT Died Feb. 29, 1968; interred St. Mary's Cemetery Hamden CT

SULLIVAN, DONAL MARK, journalist; born Boston, Massachusetts, Oct. 25, 1910; s. John Andrew and Mary Elizabeth (Donovan) S.; A.B., cum laude, Harvard Coll., 1933, student Law Sch., 1933-35; LL.B., Boston U. Law Sch., 1937; m. Annette C. Bandler, Mar. 11, 1936;children—Gail, Marcia. Began as newspaperman, 1929; Harvard corr. Boston Globe, 1929-35, editorial writer, rewrite man, reporter, 1935-71; admitted to Mass. bar, 1937. Pres. Newspaper Guild of Boston, 1937; internat. v.p. Am. Newspaper Guild (Congress Indsl. Orgns.), 1938, 39, pres., 1940-41; pres. Greater Boston Indsl. Union Council, 1939-40; v.p. Mass. State Indsl. Union Council, 1940-42, New England dir., C.I.O. War Relief com., 1942; confidential sec., Mass. Commr. of Mental Health. Served as 2d lt., F.A., O.R.C., U.S. Army, 1933-38. 2d lt. and capt. C.A.C., U.S. Army, 1942-46. Permanent sec. Harvard Coll. Class of 1933. Democrat. Club: Harvard (Boston); Harvard (N.Y. City); Wellesley Country. Home: Wellesley Hills MA Died May 30, 1971.

SULLIVAN, ELIZABETH HIGGINS (ELIZABETH HIGGINS), author; b. Columbus, Neb., Dec. 14, 1874; d. John G. and Anna (O'Conor) Higgins; prep. ed'n Neb. pub. schs.; grad. St. Francis Xavier's Acad., Ottawa, Ill., 1892; m. Apr. 11, 1896, Florence E. Sullivan, Omaha. Author: Out of the West, 1902 H1. Address 544 S. 30th, Omaha NE‡

SULLIVAN, JEREMIAH FRANCIS, JR., banker; b. San Francisco, Mar. 31, 1891; s. Jeremiah F. and Helen (Bliss) S.; student Boon's Prep. Sch., 1907-08, U. Cal., 1908; m. Josephine Drown, May 24, 1924. Dir., mem. adv. com. Crocker-Citizens National Bank; hon. chairman of the board United States Leasing Corporation; director Schlage Lock Company, Pacific Lumber Co., Del Monte Properties Co., Interstate Co., Moore Dry Dock Co., Moore Securities Company. Foreman San Francisco Country Grand Jury, 1941; president of the San Francisco Police Commn., 1943-46. Served as lt. (j.g.) U.S.N., World War I. Received meritorious civilian award U.S.N., 1945. Mem. Cal. Bankers Assn. (pres. 1932-33), Chi Psi. Clubs: Pacific Union (San Francisco); Burlingame (Cal.) Country. Home: San Francisco CA also Saratoga CA Died Mar. 26, 1969.

SULLIVAN, LEO DENNIS, educator; b. Lapeer, Mich., Jan. 21, 1901; s. William D. and Margaret A. (Linehan) S.; A.B., Gonzaga U., 1925, M.A., 1926; S.T.L., St. Louis U., 1933; S.T.D., Gregorian U., Rome, Italy, 1936. Joined Soc. of Jesus, 1919, ordained priest Roman Cath. Ch., 1932; instr. philosophy W. Baden (Ind.) Coll., 1936-37, rector coll., 1942-43, 49-54; instr. theology St. Mary of Lake Sem., Mundelein, Ill., 1937-42; provincial Chgo. Province Soc. Jesus, 1943-49, Detroit Province, 1954-58; prof. theology U. Detroit, 1958-69. Member Catholic Theological Society of America, Soc. Cath. Coll. Tchrs. Sacred Doctrine, Religious Edn. Assn. Home: Detroit MI Died Aug. 24, 1969; buried Colombiere Coll., Clarkston MI

SULLIVAN, PATRICK J., ex-congressman; b. Pittsburgh, Pa., Oct. 12, 1877; s. Cumming and Catherine (O'Connor) S.; ed. pub. and parochial schs., Pittsburgh; m. Caroline Wallisch, of Pittsburgh, Nov. 1901; children—Margaret, Catherine, Loretta. Alderman, Pittsburgh, 1910-29; police magistrate, Pittsburgh, 1914-21; mem. bd. assessment and revision of taxes, Allegheny Co., Pa., 1921-28; mem. 71st and 72d Congresses (1929-33), 34th Pa. Dist. Republican. Knight of Columbus, Elk. Home: 176 1/2 Hallock St., Pittsburgh PA‡

SULLIVAN, RAYMOND F., advt. exec.; b. New London, Conn., Jan. 23, 1897; grad. Yale, 1920; m. Marion Reilly; children—Raymond F., Mrs. John Dezell, Mrs. Carl Teschemacher. Successively copywriter, contact exec., v.p., dir., chmn. plans bd. Ruthrauff & Ryan advt. agy., 1920-46; founder chmn., chmn. exec. com. Sullivan, Stauffer, Colwell & Bayles, Inc.; former chmn., dir. Noxell Corp., Balt., Scarsdale Nat. Bank and Trust Co. Mem. Am. Legion. Clubs: Yale of N.Y., Scarsdale Golf. Address: Scarsdale NY Died June 30, 1969.

SULLIVAN, TIMOTHY D., ex-congressman. Was mem. N.Y. Senate; mem. 58th, 59th Congresses (1903-7), 8th N.Y. Dist. (resigned); Democrat. Address: 38 E. 4th St., New York NY‡

SULZBERGER, ARTHUR HAYS, newspaper publisher; b. New York, N.Y., Sept. 12, 1891; s. Cyrus L. and Rachel Peixotto (Hays) S.; prep. edn. DeWitt Clinton and Horace Mann high schs., N.Y. City; B.S., Columbia, 1913; LL.D., Rollins Coll., 1939, Union Coll., 1940, Dartmouth, 1951, Harvard, 1955, Knox College, 1956, Colby College, 1956 Fairleigh Dickinson U., 1957, L.I.U., 1967; Litt.D., Brown U. and U. of Chattanooga, 1944, Jewish Theol. Sem., 1951, John Carroll U., 1953; L.C.D., Bishop's U., Can., 1951; Dr. Pub. Service, U. Denver, 1951; L.H.D., Hebrew Union College, 1953; H.H.D., University of Hawaii, 1954; LL.D., U. Pitts., 1958; Columbia University, 1959, Colgate Univ., 1959; m. Iphigene B. Ochs, November 17, 1917; children—Marian Effie (Mrs. Andrew Heiskell), Ruth Rachel (Mrs. A. William Holmberg, Jr.), Judith Peixotto (Mrs. Budd Levinson), Arthur Ochs. In newspaper business, 1919-68; publisher New York Times, 1935-61; president, director The New York Times Co., 1935-57, dir., 1935-68, chmn. bd., 1957-68; chmn. bd. Interstate Broadcasting Co., 1944-65, dir.; chmn. bd. Times Printing Co., Chattanooga, from 1957; chmn. Chattanooga Pub. Co. Trustee emeritus of N.Y. Found., Columbia U.; trustee Grant Monument Assn., Met. Mus. Art, 1945-64, Roger Williams Straus Meml. Found., Inc., 1957-66, dir. Soc. Friends Touro Synagogue (Nat. shrine, Newport, R.I.), A.R.C., Am.-Korean Found., Netherland-America Found.; governor of the Thomas Jefferson Memorial Foundation. Attended Bus. Mans Tng. Camp, Plattsburg, N.Y., 1916; commd. 2d lt. F.A., 1st Plattsburg camp, 1917. Fellow New York Academy of Sciences; mem. Council on Fgn. Relations, Mchts. Assn., Pilgrims of U.S., Acad. Polit. Sci. (dir.), Am. Arbitration Assn. (dir.), S.A.R., Sigma Delta Chi. Clubs: Economic, Advertising, Century Assn., Columbia, Grolier, Metropolitan (Washington); Mountain City (Chattanooga); Overseas Press of Am.; Athenaeum (London). Home: New York City NY also Stamford CT Died Dec. 11, 1968.

SUMMERFIELD, ARTHUR E(LLSWORTH), postmaster gen. U.S.; b. Pinconning, Mich., Mar. 17, 1899; s. William Henry and Cora Edith (Ellsworth) S.; Dr. Bus. Adminstrn. (hon.), Cleary Coll., 1956; LL.D., Defiance (O.) Coll., 1953, U. Mich., 1957, Miami U., Oxford, O., 1959, Theil Coll, 1961, Tusculum Coll.; m. Miriam W. Graim, July 22, 1918; children—Gertrude Miriam (Mrs. John E. MacArthur), Arthur E. Real estate broker, 1919-24; pres. Summerfield Oil Co., distributor for Pure Oil Co., Flint, Mich., 1924-37; pres. Summerfield Chevrolet Co., Flint, since 1929; pres. Bryant Properties Corp., from 1938, Sico Enterprises, Incorporated, Flint, Michigan; bd. dirs. Lumbermens Mut. Casualty Company, Chgo., American Motorists Insurance Company, Chgo., Kemper Life Ins. Co., Boston. Dir. Michigan Automobile Dealers Association from 1942; dir. Nat. Automobile Dealers Assn., from 1942, former regional vice pres., chmn. post war planning com., 1943-44, former chmn. automotive com.; mem. post war planning com., U.S. Chamber of Commerce, 1944; director Genesee County (Michigan) Real Estate Association; finance dir. Rep. State Central Com. of Mich., 1943-45; Rep. nat. committeeman for Mich. from 1944, appt. regional v. chmn. N. Central div., 1946; chmn. Rep. Nat. Com., 1952-53; postmaster gen. of U.S., 1953-61. Trustee Cleary Coll., Ypsilanti, Mich., Taft Inst. Mason (33 deg., K.T., Shriner), Elk. Clubs: Flint City (pres., dir.), Kiwanis (Flint); Detroit, Athletic (Detroit); Metropolitan, 1925 F Street, Capitol Hill (Washington). Author: U.S. Mail, The Story of United States Postal Service, 1969. Home: Flint MI Died Apr. 26, 1972.

SUMMERFORD, DEALVA CLINTON, govt. ofcl.; b. Bexar, Ala., Apr. 23, 1906; s. Howard and Della (Wigginton) S.; B.S., Auburn U., 1930; m. Dorothy Chancellor, July 22, 1933; children—Lynn (Mrs. Walter W. Hopkins), Ann Rogers. With Am. Tel. & Tel., 1930-32, WHAS radio, Louisville, 1932-48, WKLO-WKLO-TV, Louisville, 1948-55; with U.S. Govt., 1955-69, communications planner, Thomasville, Ga., 1962-69. Pres. Shawnee Broadcasting Co., Chillicothe, O., 1946-49; instr., U. Ky. Coll. Pharmacy, Louisville, 1949-52; Pres. dir. WCCW, Inc., Traverse City, Mich. Registered profl. engr., Ky., Ga. Mem. I.E.E.E., Phi Kappa Phi, Tau Beta Pi. Home: Tallahassee FL Died May 27, 1969.

SUMMERS, ANDREW ROWAN, lawyer, musicologist, singer; b. Abingdon, Va., Dec. 15, 1912; s. Lewis Preston and Ann Katharine (Barbee) S.; LL.B., U. Va., 1935. Admitted to Va. bar, 1935, practiced in Abingdon, 1934-40; editor Frank Shepard Co., N.Y.C., 1941-43; asso. Burroughs & Brown, 1943-45; propr. Andrew R. Summers Assos., N.Y.C., design specialists and mfr., 1947-68; owner-mgr. Abingdon House Antiques; singer of Am.-Scottish folk songs accompanied by dulcimer; albums include: Old World Ballads in America; Seeds of Love: The Unquiet Grave; The Ladye Gay; The Faulse Ladye; collector Appalachian folk songs; Mem. Am., Va. bar assns., Va. State Bar. Club: Rockefeller Luncheon (N.Y.C.). Home: New York City NY Died Mar. 14, 1968; buried Abingdon VA

SUMMERS, FESTUS PAUL, univ. prof.; b. on farm near Summerville, W.Va., Mar. 2, 1895; s. Paul Jones and Julia (Cutlip) S.; Diploma. Concord Normal School, 1917; A.B., W.Va. University, 1923; A.M., U. of Chicago, 1927; student Columbia U., 1927-28; Ph.D., W.Va. U., 1933; Litt.D., Marshall University, 1963, Morris Harvey Coll., 1965; L.H.D., Concord College, 1967; m. to Helen Page, Dec. 22, 1922; 1 dau., Jane (Mrs. Robert J. Wygal, Jr.). Teacher in the West Virginia public schools, 1911-15, prin. Spanishburg (W.Va.) High Sch., 1917-18; supt. Jane Lew (W.Va.) Ind. Dist. Schools, 1922-26; prof. history, Morris Harvey Coll., Barboursville, W.Va., 1928-31; archivist and lecturer, W.V.U., 1935-39; asso. prof. history, 1939-46, prof., 1946-65, professor emeritus, 1965-71, chmn. of the department, 1946-47, head, 1947-62; visiting prof. (summers) Concord Coll., 1930, Emory U., 1952. Lucy Webb-Rutherford B. Hayes Found. fellow Am. hist., 1940-42. Chmn. W.Va. War History Commn., 1943-53; past mem. W.Va. Commn. Historic and Scenic Markers. W.Va. Centennial Commn. In U.S. Army, World War I; capt. Inf. Res., 1929-39. Recipient Vandalia award W.Va. Univ., 1968. Mem. Authors League, Am. Hist. Assn., Miss. Valley Hist. Assn., Southern Hist. Assn., W.Va. Hist. Soc. (pres. 1943-44), Am. Mil. Inst., Am. Assn. U. Profs., Phi Beta Kappa. Phi Delta Theta. Mason (32 deg.). Rotarian. Author: Johnson Newson Camden: A Study in Individualism. 1937: The Baltimroe and Ohio in the Civil War, 1939; William L. Wilson and Tariff Reform, 1953; (with C. H. Ambler) West Virginia: The Mountain State, 1958. Editor: The Cabinet Diary of William L. Wilson, 1896-97, 1957; Borderland Confederate, 1962; (with Elizabeth Cometti) The Thirty-Fifth State, 1966. Contbr. to hist. jours., reference works. Home: Morgantown WV Died May 21, 1971.

SUMNER, CAROLINE LOUISE, educator; b. Holyoke, Mass., Oct. 7, 1867; d. William James and Eveline (Sturtevant) Sumner; A.B., Smith Coll., 1890; study Am. Sch. Classical Studies, Rome, Italy, 1908-09. Teacher of Greek and English, high sch., Titusville, Pa., 1890-95; teacher of Latin, Smith Coll., 1897-1902, 1905-08; teacher of Greek and Latin, Wheeler Sch., Providence, R.I., 1902-05; co-prin. Elmhurst Sch., Connersville, Ind., 1909-26; co-prin. Stoneleigh Sch. for Girls, Rye Beach, N.H., 1926-30; co-prin. Stoneleigh-Prospect Hill, Greenfield, Mass., 1930-41; retired, June 1941. Mem. Headmistresses Assn. of Middle West, Am. Assn. Univ. Women, New England Classical Assn., Smith Coll. Alumnae Assn., Nat. Travel Club, Woman's Club of Greenfield. Republican. Unitarian. Home: Greenfield MA‡

SUMNER, (BERTHA) CID RICKETTS, writer; b. Brookhaven, Miss., Sept. 27, 1890; d. Robert Scott and Bertha (Burnley) Ricketts; B.S., Millsaps College, Jackson, Miss., 1909; A.M., Columbia, 1910; grad. work Cornell Med. Sch., 1914-15; m. James Batcheller Sumner, July 20, 1915 (divorced 1930); children—Roberta Rand (Mrs. John Henry Cutler), Prudence Avery (Mrs. Edward Gamard), James Cosby, Frederick Burnley. Author novels: Ann Singleton, 1938; Quality, 1946 (movie Pinky, 1949); Tammy Out of Time, 1948; But The Morning Will Come, 1949; Sudden Glory, 1951; short stories in Woman's Home Companion. Address: Duxbury MA Died Oct. 16, 1970.

SUMNER, JOHN SAXTON, b. Washington, D.C., Sept. 22, 1876; s. George Watson (Rear Admiral, U.S. Navy) and Henrietta (Ruan) S.; LL.B., New York U., 1904; m. Eloise Peckham, Nov. 17, 1904; 1 dau., Eloise Elizabeth (Mrs. Harry Lee Powell, Jr.). Banking and brokerage business, 1895-1905; gen. law practice, 1905-13; asso. sec. N.Y. Soc. for Suppression of Vice, later Soc. to Maintain Public Decency, 1913-15, secretary, 1915-50; a leader in movements and legislation directed against demoralizing influences in publs., the screen, the stage, etc. Served as Y.M.C.A. sec. with 26th Div. and 82d Div., U.S. Army, St. Mihiel and Argonne offensives, 1918. Member Founders and Patriots America, S.A.R., Phi Delta Phi, Zeta Psi. Republican. Episcopalian. Home: Ft Pierce FL Died June 20, 1971; buried Union Cemetery, Stratford CT

SUMPTER, WILLIAM DAVID, surgeon; b. Pulaski, Tenn., June 28, 1872; s. James Asher (M.D.) and Mary Amanda (Rhea) S.; grad. Webb Sch., Bell Buckle, Tenn., 1891; M.D., U. of Va., 1894; post-grad. work New York Polyclinic; m. Tommie Florence Wrenne, Oct. 10, 1901; children—Clara Wrenne (Mrs. Thomas Wilson Clapham), Thomas Wrenne, Mary Rhea (Mrs. Thomas Edward Scheffer), William David. Served internship at Hosp. of Good Shepherd, Nashville, Tenn.; successively prof. microscopy, prof. anatomy and prof. surgery, med. dept. U. of Tenn., prof. anatomy, gen. and oral surgery, dental dept.; staff surgeon Protestant Hosp. Formerly lecturer on gynecology. Formerly director Thomas W. Wrenne & Co., bankers. Member Am. and Tenn. State med. assns., Middle Tenn. Med. Assn., Southern Med. Assn., Nashville Acad. Medicine, Davidson Med. Soc. Club: Executives. Democrat. Presbyterian. Mason (32 deg., K.T., Shriner), K.P. Home: 1108 19th Av. S. Office: 516-19 Bennie-Dillon Bldg Nashville TN‡

SUNDFOR, ZALIA HARBAUGH (MRS. GUTTORM SUNDFOR), educator; b. Lima, O., Sept. 13, 1905; d. William A. and Chloie (Bailar) Harbaugh; A.B., Bluffton Coll., 1938; B.S., Defiance Coll., 1941; M.A. in Edn., Bowling Green (O.) State U., 1951; m. Guttorm Sundfor, Nov. 22, 1950 (dec. July 1959); stepchildren—Annabel (Mrs. Don Stubb), Robert D. Tchr., Lincoln Sch., Lima, 1924-27; tchr. history South High Sch., Lima, 1927-39, dean of girls, 1939-55; dean of girls Lima Sr. High Sch., 1955-64; dir. Christian edn. West Elm United Ch. of Christ, Lima. Tchr., Y-M Adult Sch., 1948-49. Mem. Human Relations Commn., Lima, 1960-64; pres. Chautauqua Clubs, 1938-62. Bd. dirs. YWCA, Lima, pres. bd., 1952-56; bd. dirs. Bradfield Community Center, Allen County Community Welfare Council, 1962-63, Child and Family Society, Lima, Ohio; trustee Student Christian Union, Bowling Green State U. Named Woman of Yr., Lima Soroptimist Club, 1956. Mem. Nat. (citation for years of service 1965), Ohio assns. women deans and counselors, N.E.A., Ohio, Lima edn. assns., Am. Assn. U. Women, Lima Federated Women's Clubs. Mem. Congl. Christian Ch. (dir. jr. ch. 1926-40, dir. young people's work 1940-45). Club: Altrusa (pres. Lima 1959, 65-66, 66-67). Home: Lima OH Deceased.

SURKAMP, ARTHUR, business exec.; b. St. Louis, Feb. 23, 1893; s. Christopher Henry and Emma (Luedinghaus) S.; A.B., U. of Tex., 1913; LL.B., 1914; student Harvard Grad. Sch. Bus. Adminstrn., 1916-17; m. Mrs. Esther Moore, Oct. 12, 1935; children (by previous marriage)—Arthur T., Anne S. (Mrs. Henry Lee Hogan III), Patricia (Mrs. O. W. Gillenwater). Engaged in the practice of law, San Antonio, Tex., 1914-15; joined freight traffic dept. of Pa. R.R., 1917; with U.S. Rubber Co., 1919-56, dir. and chmn. finance com. mem. exec. com., v.p., dir. various subsidiaries and affiliates, until 1956; dir. Arkwright Mutual Fire Insurance Co. Served in 21st Engrs., World War I. Officer Order of Orange Nassau. Trustee Village of Roslyn Estates, 1949-51 Controllership Foundation; member advisory council Controllers Institute of America; trustee Phi Gamma Delta. East Moriches LI NY Died Nov. 3, 1971.

SURMANN, JOHN FRED, architect; b. Louisville, June 26, 1889; s. John Fred and Ida (Schwilke) S.; grad. U.S. Sch. Mil. Aero., 1918; student Armour Inst. Tech., 1913; m. Ruth Rice, Nov. 8, 1930; stepchildren—Leslie Foster, Bob, Gene J. Gen. practice John F. Surmann, architect, Dayton, O. Served with USAAF, 1917. Registered architect, Ohio, Ky., N.Y. Mem. A.I.A., Architects Soc. Ohio. Mason (32 deg., Shriner). Contbr. articles to profl. jours. Home: Dayton OH

SUTER, FRANCIS L., retired business executive; b. Pittsburgh, Pa., Jan. 9, 1877; s. John P. and Emma A. (Vickroy) S.; ed. Pittsburgh grammar and high schs., m. Mary M. Barr, Oct. 21, 1903; 1 dau., Elizabeth M. (Mrs. Lawrence H. Dunlap). Clerk Liberty Nat. Bank, Pittsburgh, 1893-1900; clerk Armstrong Cork Co., Pittsburgh, 1900-09; asst. gen. mgr. linoleum plant, Lancaster, Pa., 1909-29, gen. mgr., 1929-32; v.p. and treas. Armstrong Cork Co., 1932-38, 1st vice-pres. 1938-45; dir. since 1927; retired 1945. Dir. Farmers Bank & Trust Co. (Lancaster). Dir. Lancaster Gen. Hosp. Ex-pres. Lancaster Chamber of Commerce. Republican. Presbyterian. Clubs: Hamilton, Lancaster Country (Lancaster). Home: 1112 Wheatland Av. Office: Armstrong Cork Co., Lancaster PA‡

SUTHERLAND, ALLAN, banker; b. Edinburgh, Scotland, Oct. 30, 1871; s. David and Elizabeth (Brown) S.; ed. pub. schs.; LL.D., Beaver Coll., 1933; m. Loretto Mabel Hearst, June 7, 1899 (died 1935). Came to U.S., 1887, naturalized, 1892. Member of Presbyterian Board of Christian Education, U.S.A., 1901-38; asst. dir. Sunday School and Missionary Exposition, Rome, 1907. Now retired from business affairs. Author: Famous Hymns of the World, Their Origin and Romance, 1909. Home: The Lenox, Philadelphia PA‡

SUTHERLAND, ARTHUR EUGENE, educator; b. Rochester, N.Y., Feb. 9, 1902; s. Arthur E. and Eleanor (Reed) S.; ed. pub. and pvt. schs. U.S. and Switzerland; A.B., Wesleyan U., Middletown, Conn., 1922; LL.B., Harvard, 1925; J.S.D., Suffolk U., 1960; m. Margaret Adams, Sept. 10, 1927 (dec. Jan. 1958); children—David Adams, Peter Adams, Eleanor Reed, Prudence; m. 2d, Mary Genung Kirk, Feb. 21, 1959. Asso. with Am. Commn. Relief Near East, in Asia Minor and Thrace, 1919; admitted to N.Y. State bar, 1926, practiced in Rochester, 1926-41; sec. to justice O. W. Holmes, U.S. Supreme Ct., 1927-28; commr. Uniform State Laws of N.Y., 1948-50; prof. law Cornell U., 1945-50; prof. law Harvard 1950-55, Bussey prof. law. 1955-70, emeritus prof. 1970-73; Purington vis. prof. polit. sci. Mt. Holyoke Coll., 1958-59; Fulbright lectr. Oxford U., 1956. Del. N.Y. State Constl. Conv., 1938; mem. N.Y. State Commn. on Elementary and Secondary Edn. 1969-71. Trustee Mt. Holyoke Coll. Served to col. AUS, 1941-45; ETO; MTO Decorated Legion of Merit with oak leaf cluster, Bronze Star Medal (U.S.); Order Brit. Empire: Cross of War (2) (France); Czechoslovakian War Cross: Ouissam Alaouite (Morocco); Volontai della Liberta, Italy. Fellow Am. Acad. Arts and Scis; mem. Am. Law Inst., Am. N.Y. State bar assns. Republican. Episcopalian. Author: Cases and Materials on Commercial Transactions (with others), 1951; Constitutional Law Cases and Other Problems, 1952; The Law and One Man Among Many, 1956; Constitutionalism in America, 1965; Apology for Uncomfortable Change, 1965; The Law at Harvard, 1817-1967, 1967. Editor: The Path of the Law from 1967, 1968. Contbr. articles to various legal publs. Home: Cambridge MA Died Mar. 8, 1973.

SUTHERLAND, JOSEPH HOOKER, chaplain U.S.A.; b. Good Intent. Pa. Apptd. post chaplain, Apr. 4, 1898; Assigned to 23d Inf., Feb. 25, 1901; commd. maj. for exceptional efficiency," Dec. 29, 1908; transferred to 12th Inf., Aug. 15, 1911; retired on account of disability in line of duty, Mar. 21, 1912; restored to active duty at own request, 1917. Served in Spanish-Am. War, Philippine Insurrection and Moro campaigns; mentioned in orders for gallant conduct under fire. Known as writer, traveler and lecturer. Home: West Alexander PA‡

SUTLIFF, VINCENT E., publisher; b. N.Y.C., June 15, 1900; s. William Robert and Catherine Cecilia (Carley) S.; m. Katherine A. Kubler, Apr. 24, 1921 (dec. Jan. 1950); children—Vincent E., Katherine Ann (Mrs. Reaumur S. Donnally); m. 2d, Margaret M. Govern, Feb. 14, 1951. Asst. to gen. mgr. subscription dept. Dodd, Mead & Co., 1921-32; asst. to pres., gen. mgr. Ency. Brit., Inc., 1933-39; v.p. Americana Corp., 1939-47, bd. dirs., 1942-65, pres., 1947-62, chmn. bd., 1962-65, treasurer, 1947-65; founder, pres., dir., treas. of Americana Corp. of Can., Ltd., 1949-65; v.p. in charge Federal div. Grolier, Incorporated, from 1965; pioneered devel. of national subscription book cos., Nat. Better Bus. Bur. program, 1949. Director, trustee South Florida Education Center. Decorated Knight of Malta (Papal). Fellow Montgomery County Historical Society; mem. Grolier, Inc. (dir.; dir. Colo., and Washington), Elk. Clubs: N.Y. Athletic (N.Y.C.); Kenwood Country, Rotary (Bethesda, Maryland). Home: Gaithersburg MD Died Oct. 29, 1969.

SUTTON, CHARLES R(FUEL), landscape architect; b. Grand Ridge, Ill., Mar. 8, 1900; s. John Willis and Lillian C. (Bragg) S.; B.S. in Archtl. Engring., U. of Ill., 1921, in Landscape Architecture, 1926; Fellow in landscape architecture Am. Acad. in Rome, 1929-32; m. Theodora Stone, Nov. 22, 1941; children—Charles R., Jonathan. Landscape architect in office of Ferruccio Vitale, N.Y. City, 1926-29; asst. prof. landscape architecture Ohio State U., 1932-37, asso. prof., 1937-51, professor of landscape architecture since 1951; in private practice, Columbus, O., and Old Saybrook, Connecticut, 1932-63. Member board of managers Columbus Gallery of Fine Arts. Recipient prize in landscape architecture Am. Acad. in Rome, 1929. Fellow in landscape architecture, Am. Acad. in Rome. Fellow Am. Soc. Landscape Architects (sec. 1947-51), mem. Am. Soc. Planning Officials, Am. Planning and Civic Assn., Hwy. Research Bd., Alpha Rho Chi, Tau Sigma Delta, ULAS. Conglist. Clubs: Faculty, University Golf (Ohio State Univ.); University, Crichton (Columbus). Home: Columbus OH Died Sept. 13, 1963.

SUTTON, CHARLES WOOD, civil engr.; b. nr. Smyrna, Del., Jan. 26, 1877; s. Thomas Layton and Sara Edwards (Weaver) S.; B.S., U. of Washington, 1898; post-grad. work in engring. and economics, U. of Pa., 1902, and department of economics and public law, Columbia U., 1914. Civil and hydraulic engring, practice with Seattle & Internat. Ry., U.S. Geol. Survey, U.S. Reclamation Service, and Corps of Engrs. of Mines of Peru, 1898-1908; chief engr. Peruvian Irrigation Service and consulting engr. Peruvian Dept. of Agr., 1908-14; consulting engr. Bd. Water Supply City of Lima, Peru, 1913-14; consulting engr., New York and Lima, 1914-19; consulting and constructing engr., Dept. of Irrigation Works, Peruvian Govt., 1919-—. Mem. Am. Soc. C.E., Peruvian Soc. Engrs., Peruvian Geog. Soc. Clubs: Phoenix, National, Union (Lima). Address: Apartado 152, Lima Peru*‡

SUTTON, DALLAS GILCHRIST, med. naval officer; b. Washington, D.C., Sept. 1, 1883; s. Robert Gilchrist and Elizabeth (Fearson) S.; M.D.; George Washington Univ., 1906, Naval Med. Sch., 1907-08; m. Mabel Clara Pimper, Sept. 23, 1911 (dec. Dec. 1940); children—Margaret Virginia (Mrs. Raymond Ringness), Mabel Elizabeth; m. 2d Violet G. Posthoff, Jan. 16, 1946. Resident physician, Emergency Hospital, Washington, D.C., 1906-07; commd. lt. (j.g.) Med. Corps, U.S. Navy, 1907, and advanced through the grades to rear admiral, 1942; instr. psychiatry, Naval Med. Sch., 1916-20; exec. officer, Naval Hosp., Great Lakes, Ill., 1921-24; senior med. officer, U.S. Naval Acad., 1934-36; asst. surgeon gen., U.S. Navy, 1936-41; comdg. officer, Naval Hosp., Portsmouth, Va., 1941-46; retired from U.S. Navy Jan. 1947. Mem. staff, Am. Hosp. Assn. since Sept. 1946. Campaign ribbons, Nicaraguan, Mexican, World War I, and World War II. Mem. Delta Tau Delta. Club: Officers (Naval Acad., Annapolis, Md.). Home: Washington DC Died Sept. 16, 1970; buried Arlington Nat. Cemetery Arlington VA

SUTTON, FREDERICK I., lawyer; b. Kinston, N.C., Sept. 7, 1886; s. Levi Mewborn and Cora Elizabeth (Grimsley) S.; A.B., U. of N.C., 1908, law student, summer 1910; student Harvard, summer 1907, J.D., 1911; studied in Europe, 1911; m. Annie Gray Fry, Nov. 10, 1915; 1 son, Frederick Islen. Admitted to N.C. bar, 1910; began practice of law, Kinston, 1912; city atty., Kinston; mayor, Kinston, 1913-19; mem. Sutton & Greene, Kinston, N.C., 1922-73. Dir. A & NC R.R. Co., South Atlantic Bonded Warehouse Corp., exec. com. Carolina Tel. & Tel. Co., 1959, 61, 62, now dir., Life mem. Nat. Conf Commrs. Uniform State Laws. Mem. N.C. Gen. Assembly, 1924-33, state senator, 1939-40; presdl. elector, 1941; mem. Nat. Dem. Finance Com.; del. Dem. Nat. Conv., 1932. Sec.-treas. Carolina Municipal Assn.; v.p. N.C. Good Roads Assn.; mem. Bd. of Conservation of Devel. 1927-32; mem. Pan-Am. Congress; N.C. commr. on uniform laws, 1939-73. Trustee U. of N.C., 1927-59, N.C. State Coll., 1931-59, Woman's Coll., U.N.C., Greensboro, 1931-59; bd. govs. Harvard Law Sch.; chairman Lenoir County-City of Kinston Air Port Com., 1947-50. Served as chief Intelligence Bur. Kinston, mem. Home Guard, World War. Mem. Am. Bar Assn., N.C. Bar Assn. (pres, 1940-41), chmn. exec. com. 1938-39), 6th Dist. Bar Assn. (pres. 1931), Am. Judicature Soc. Am. Law Inst., 4th Circuit Fed. Jud. Conf. N.Y. C. of C., Acad. Polit. Sci, Newcomen Soc., Harvard Law Sch. Assn., Gen. Alumni Assn. of Univ. of N.C. (pres.), Harvard Southern Club, Beale Law Club, Alpha Tau Omega, Pi Sigma hon. mem. W.Va. and Va. bar assns., 11th and 5th Dist., bar assns., Alumni Assn. N.C. State Coll. Mason (K.T., 32, shriner, acting potentate and orator; Jester, noble dir. 1950-51). Clubs: Harvard (N.Y.); Monogram (U.N.C.); Doc Newton (N.C. State Coll.); Dunes (pres. 1939-40, govs., 1940-41), Country (dir.), Harvard of N.C. (exec. committee) Sphinx (Raleigh, N.C.); Coral Bay, King Neptune's Ct. and Order of Shellbacks; Order Golden Dragon; Around the World. Home: Kinston NC Died 1973.

SUTTON, JOSEPH LEE, univ. pres.; b. Oklahoma City, Mar. 22, 1924; s. Erville Clarence and Carolyn Elizabeth (Hatch) S.; A.B. in Oriental Langs., U. Mich., 1948, M.A. in Oriental Civilization, 1949, Ph.D. in Polit. Sci., 1954; m. Jean Elizabeth Harkness, Aug. 19, 1945; children—James Werner, Geoffrey Joseph, David Harkness, Abigail Jean; m. 2d, Elizabeth Hartke Josephson, Mar. 15, 1971. Instr., Western Res. U., 1952-53; mem. faculty Ind. U., 1953-72, prof. govt., 1962-72, chmn. Asian studies com., also Asian studies program, from 1959, asso. dean Coll. Arts and Scis., 1962-65, dean College of Arts and Scis., 1965-66, v.p., dean faculties 1966-68, pres., 1968-71; chief adviser of pub. adminstrn. Govt. Thailand, 1955-58; mem. fgn. area fellowship nat. com. of Ford Found., Social Sci. Research Council and Am. Council Learned Societies. Cons. to U.S. Ho. of Reps. Republican Policy Com., 1960-62. Served to 2d lt. AUS, 1934-46. Research asst. Center Japanese Studies, U. Mich., 1948-49; World Area fellow Social Sci. Research Council, 1951-52. Mem. Am. Polit. Sci. Assn., Assn. Asian Studies, Club Indiana Univ. Men's Faculty (pres. 1962-63). Contbr. articles profl. jours., chpts. in books. Editor, contbr.: Problems of Politics and Administration in Thailand, 1961. Home: Bloomington IN Died Apr. 28, 1972; buried Oklahoma City OK

SUTTON, LOUIS VALVELLE, utilities exec.; b. Richmond, Va., Aug. 6, 1889; s. Lee Edwards and Ella (Wagner) S.; student Petersburg (Va.) Acad., 1904-06; B.S. in elec. engring., Va. Poly. Inst., 1910; D.Eng. (hon.), N.C. State Coll., Raleigh, 1944; m. Cantey McDowell Venable, Apr. 30, 1912; children—Louis Valvelle, Sarah Tomlinson, Apprentice engr. test course, Gen. Electric Co., Lynn, Mass., 1910-12; successively statistician, asst. engr., div. mgr., commercial mgr., asst. to gen. mgr. Carolina Power & Light Co., Raleigh, N.C., 1912-24; asst. gen. mgr. Ark. Central Power Co., Little Rock, 1924-27; v.p., gen. mgr., dir. Miss. Power & Light Co., Jackson, 1927-33; pres., Carolina Power & Light Co., 1933-63, gen. mgr., 1933-49, dir., 1933-69, chmn. bd., chief exec. officer, 1949-69; v.p., dir. Carolinas Va. Nuclear Power Assos., Inc., Parr Shoals, S.C.; president and dir. of Capitan

Corp., Raleigh. Vice pres., dir., past pres. Bus. Found., U. N.C.; dir. Research Triangle Found. N.C. Recipient award for engrng. achievement, N.C. Soc. Engrs., 1953; Distinguished Alumnus award Va. Poly. Inst., 1961. Mem. Va. Poly. Inst. Alumni Assn. (past v.p., dir.), I.E.E.E., N.A.M. (past dir.), Southeastern Electric Exchange (dir., past pres.), Nat. Assn. Elec. Cos. (dir., past chmn.), Newcomen Soc., Soc. the Cincinnati (hon.), Edison Electric Inst. (past pres., director), National Electric Heating Association (director), Tau Beta Pi, Phi Kappa Phi, Omicron Delta Kappa. Episcopalian. Clubs: Rotary, Carolina Country, Sphinx, Milburnie (Raleigh); Cape Fear (Wilmington); Mountain City (Asheville); Coral Bay (Morehead City); Country of N.C. (Southern Pines). Home: Raleigh NC Died Jan. 1970.

SUTTON, MARY WOOSTER MUNSON, lawyer; b. Bridgeport, Fairfield County, Conn., Apr. 20, 1866; d. Thomas Hamilton and Mary Etta (Hill) Munson; ed. under parents (both professionally trained teachers), pvt. schs. high sch., and State Normal Sch., Willimantic, Conn. (full course and post-grad. course) to June 1902; student Newark (N.J.) Law Sch., 1909-10; LL.B., New York U., 1911, LL.M., 1912; studied piano under Alexander Lambert; diploma in harmony, New York Coll. of Music; m. William J. Sutton, Sept. 12, 1894 (died June 5, 1921). Began teaching in pub. schs. at 17; became prin. high sch., Watertown, Conn., prin. pub. schs., Red Bank, also spl. science teacher in high sch.; began study of law at age of 42, in office of Hon. John S. Applegate, Red Bank; admitted to N.J. bar as atty., 1913, counsellor, 1916; admitted to Fla. bar, 1922, to bar of Supreme Court of U.S., 1925, Conn. bar, 1930; has appeared in many suits in Court of Chancery, before Supreme Court of N.J., and in N.J. Court of Errors and Appeals; most notable case was Chancery suit of Reilly vs. Brown in which won alone against 6 lawyers; on opposite side, 1924; won case for construction of will for appellants, in Roberts et al. vs. Mosely, before Div. A and Div. B, Supreme Court of Fla., 1929-30. Mem. New York U. Alumni Assn., New London County Bar Assn., New London County Hist. Soc., Sarah Whitman Trumbull Chapter D.A.R. Democrat. Episcopalian. Founder, 1896, and first pres. Philomathian Coterie (now Woman's Club), Red Bank. Established first law class for women in Conn., at New London, 1932, followed by second sect. at Waterbury, 1933 (5th annual session 1937). Lecturer on law before Bunker Hill Lit. Club, Waterbury, 1935-36; spl. addresses on legal topics before various D.A.R. chapters in Conn., 1937. Home: 95 Starr Hill Road, Groton CT‡

SUYKER, HECTOR, merchant; b. Belgium, 1889. C.P.A., N.Y. State. Pres. The Fair, Chicago. Home: Winnetka IL Died Jan. 15, 1973.

SVEDBERG, THEODOR, Swedish scientist; b. 1884; Ph.D., M.D., D.Sc., Upsala U. Lectr. in chemistry, Upsala University, 1907, professor, 1912-49; director Gustaf Derner Institute, 1949-67. Nobel prize winner for chemistry, 1926; awarded the Franklin Medal, 1949. Mem. Swedish Acad. Sci., N.Y. Acad. of Sciences other fgn. acads. One of researchers on giant molecules such as proteins, cellulose and high polymers. Address: Upsala University Sweden Died Feb. 1971.

SVENDSEN, (JAMES) KESTER (OLAF), educator, writer; b. Charleston, S.C., May 25, 1912; s. Halvor Simon and Ethel Agnes Monica (Schachte) S.; A.B., Coll. of Charleston, 1934; M.A., U. N.C., 1935, Ph.D., 1940; m. Margaret Rae Webb, Dec. 9, 1933; 1 dau., Jenifer. Student asst. English. Coll. of Charleston, 1933-34, grad. asst., teaching fellow, instr. English, U. N.C., 1934-40; faculty U. Okla., 1940-59, David Ross Boyd distinguished prof. English, 1956-59; prof., head dept. English, U. Ore., 1959-68; vis. prof. U. N.C., 1949, 58, U. Tex., summer 1958. Faculty study fellow Am. Council Learned Societies, 1950-51; Guggenheim fellow, 1952-53; Huntington and Folger Library fellow, 1956, 57; recipient distinguished teaching award U. Willis Okla., Mem. Modern Lang. Assn., Milton Soc. Am. Author: Milton and Science, 1956; Milton's Pro Se Defensio, pub. 1966; also author of articles, monographs Milton and Renaissance lit. Contbg. editor Chess Life, 1948-61, Am. Chess Quar., 1962-64, English Lang. Notes, 1962-—; adv. editor College English, 1950-60. Home: Eugene OR Died Oct. 5, 1968.

SVOBODA, RALPH EDWARD, lawyer; b. Howells, Neb., Feb. 8, 1901; s. Joseph Louis and Mary M. (Misek) S.; A.B., Creighton U., 1921, LL.B. summa cum laude, 1923; m. Anna May Bonness, June 28, 1927; children—David A. B., James F. S., Joseph F. R., Susannah May (Mrs. Peter P. Trebtoske). Admitted to Neb. bar, 1923; law clk. firm Kennedy, Holland, DeLacy & McLaughlin, Omaha, 1920-23, asso. firm, 1923-30; partner firm Kennedy, Holland, DeLacy & Svoboda, Omaha, 1931-69; prof. corps. and damages U. Omaha Law Sch., 1947-53. Dir. Occidental Savs. & Loan Assn., 1935-69, Neb. Tractor & Equipment Co., 1940-65, Lyman-Richey Sand & Gravel Corp., 1959-69, C.G. Johnson Boiler Co., 1951-69, Boiler Services, Inc., 1963-69, Packers Nat. Bank, 1964-69; gen. counsel Catholic Mut. Relief Soc. Am., 1959-69. Co-chmn. Omaha chpt. Nat. Conf. Christians and Jews, 1939-61. Trustee Omaha Indsl. Found., 1952-69; bd. dirs. Omaha Jr. Achievement, 1962-69; bd. advisers Creighton Meml. St. Joseph's Hosp., 1940-69, mem. adv. council Sch. Nursing, 1955-69, chmn., 1960-62. Recipient citation Nat. Conf. Christians and Jews, 1962. Mem. Am., Neb. (pres. 1961-62), Omaha bar assns., Assn. ICC Practitioners, Am. Judicature Soc., Omaha C. of C. (pres. 1957-58), Advt.-Selling League Omaha (bd. dirs. 1964-69, chmn. fgn. relations com. 1960-61), Neb. Hist. Soc., Delta Theta Phi, Alpha Sigma Nu. Club: University (Lincoln). Librettist: MacArthur Redivivus, 1956. Composer: The Lord's Prayer, 1965. Home: Omaha NE Died 1969.

SWADOS, HARVEY, author; b. Buffalo, Oct. 28, 1920; s. Aaron Nyer and Rebecca (Bluestone) S.; B.A., U. Mich., 1940; m. Bette Beller, Sept. 12, 1946; children—Marco, Felice, Robin. Mem. faculty lit. div. Sarah Lawrence Coll., from 1958, later faculty U. Mass. Amherst. Hudson Rev. fellow in Fiction, 1957; Guggenheim fellow, 1961; award for novel Nat. Inst. Arts and Letters, 1965, also Arts and Letter grant for art, 1965; grant for fiction Nat. Endowment for Arts, 1968. Mem. Authors League, P.E.N. Club. Author: Out Went the Candle, 1955; On the Line, 1957; False Coin, 1960; Nights in the Gardens of Brooklyn, 1961; Years of Conscience: The Muckrakers, 1962; A Radical's America, 1962; The Will, 1963; A Story for Teddy And Others, 1965; The American Writer and the Great Depression, 1966, Standing Fast, 1970; Standing Up For the People, 1972. Home: MA Died Dec. 11, 1972.

SWAIN, JAMES RAMSAY, clergyman; b. Marlboro, N.J., Sept. 8, 1872; s. George and Ann Elizabeth (Beekman) S.; A.B., Princeton, 1894; student Princeton Theol. Sem., 1898-1901; D.D., Coe Coll., 1927, Park Coll., 1927; m. Fanny Mulford Jessup, June 11, 1902; children—Ann Jessup (wife of Rev. Edwin O. Kennedy), Mary Louise (wife of C. Andrew Herschel), Elisabeth Ramsay. Ordained ministry Presbyn. Ch., 1901; Y.M.C.A., sec. at Princeton U., 1894-95; instr. at Am. Univ., Beirut, Syria, 1895-98; pastor Dutch Reformed Ch., Flushing, L.I., 1901-05, Woodland Presbyn. Ch., Phila, 1905-43, pastor emeritus since 1943; summer preacher Llandudno, Wales, 1910; prof. of church history and Christian missions, Temple U., 1928-36, Hist. Geography of Holy Land, Bible manners and customs, and Bibl. archeology since 1937, professor of church history, since 1947. Director of Presbyterian Board of Publ. and Sunday Sch. Work, 1910-25, and 1939-43. Leader Young Peoples Summer Conferences. Trustee Washington College (Tennessee), 1932-36. Served as volunteer chaplain, Camp Upton, L.I., 1917-18. Moderator of Presbytery of Philadelphia, 1932-33; vice moderator, Synod of Pa., 1941-42. Mem. Phi Beta Kappa. Republican. Club: Adelphoi (Phila.). Contbr. to Sunday school lesson helps, church and Temple U. publications. Home: 826 S. 48th St., Philadelphia 43 PA‡

SWAIN, JOSEPH WARD, educator; b. Yankton, S.D., Dec. 16, 1891; s. Henry Huntington and Mira (Oimsted) S.; student Beloit (Wis.) Coll., 1908-10; A.B., Columbia, 1912, Ph.D., 1916; A.M., Harvard, 1913; student Ecole Pratique des Hautes Etudes, Paris, France, 1913-15; travels and researches in the Near E. and Italy, 1935; m. Margaret Hatfield, Aug. 15, 1921; children—Henry Huntington, Richard Hatfield (dec.), Martha, Theodore Merryman. Instr. modern langs. Wabash Coll., 1916-17; instr. history U. Mont., 1917-18; with U. Ill., 1919-71, successively instr. history, asst. prof., asso. prof., 1919-37, prof., 1937-60, prof. emeritus, 1960-71, chmn. history dept. 1956-60; prof. history Columbia summer 1945. Served with U.S. Army, 1918-19. Mem. Am. Hist. Assn., Am. Oriental Soc., Phi Beta Kappa. Episcopalian. Author books relating to field; latest publ: The Ancient World, 2vols., 1950; The Harper History of Civilization, 2 vols., 1958; vols., 1950; The Harper History of Civilization, 2 vols., 1958; The Peoples of the Ancient World, 1959; Edward Gibbon the Historian, 1966. Home: Urbana IL Died Sept. 4, 1971.

SWALWELL, JOSEPH ARTHUR, banker; b. Ottawa, Can., Oct. 5, 1873; s. George William and Elizabeth (Duff) S.; ed. high school; m. Mae Swartout, Apr. 15, 1897; children—William Howard, Gladys Maud, Joseph Frederick; m. 2d, Josephine Enright, May 17, 1940; children—Mary Josephine, Margaret I., Joseph Casey. Came to the United States, 1888; messenger First National Bank, Everett, Washington, 1891; elected cashier, 1900; cashier National Bank of Commerce, Seattle, 1908-12, v.p., 1912-17; elected pres. Union Nat. Bank. Seattle. 1917; consolidated Union Nat. Bank with Dexter-Horton Nat. Bank, 1924; chmn. bd. Dexter-Horton Nat. Bank, 1924; pres. Seattle-First Nat. Bank, now retired; pres. Farwest Timber Co.; dir. Superior Portland Cement Co., Seattle Brewing & Malting Co., Asso. Breweries of Can., Ltd. State chairman Liberty Loans. World War I; mem. State adv. com. for Wash. War Finance Com. Member American Bankers Association (executive board), Washington Bankers Association (president). Member board dirs. Seattle Chamber Commerce. Republican. Episcopalian. Mason. Clubs: Seattle Golf and Country. Woodinville WA‡

SWAN, LOWELL BENJAMIN, clergyman, educator; b. Chgo., July 7, 1910; s. Eric Phillip and Marie S. (Larson) S.; student De Pauw U., 1930-31, U. Neb., 1934-36; A.B., Drake U., 1934; Th.M., Iliff Sch. Theology, 1940, Th.D., 1951; m. Katherine M. Short, June 1, 1936; children—Mary K. (Mrs. Clifford A. Hodge), Martha A. (Mrs. Lee C. Dohm, Jr.), David Lowell, and Nancy J. Ordained to the ministry in the Methodist Ch., in 1934; also pastor in Harcourt, Ia., 1931-34, Lincoln, Neb., 1934-36, Savannah, Ill., 1941, Denver, 1936-62, pres. Iliff Sch. Theology, Denver, 1962-69. Served with Chaplains Corps., AUS, 1942-45; PTO. Decorated Bronze Star. Mem. Delta Tau Delta. Republican. Mason (K.T., Shriner), Kiwanian. Home: Denver CO Died Jan. 18, 1969.

SWAN, PAUL, dancer, painter, sculptor; b. Ashland, Ill.; s. John Randolph and Adah (Corson) S.; student Art Inst. of Chicago; m. Helen Gavit; children—Paula Swan Arnold, Flora. Began career as dancer in Greece; pioneer male dancer giving solo performances of classical dancing. Starred in motion picture in color, Diana. The Huntress; appeared in picture, The Ten Commandments. Appeared on legitimate stage as Romeo in Romeo and Juliet. As artist has had one-man shows in S.A. and executed commns. for portraits of notable persons; portraits and sculptured busts include those of famous persons. Exhibited in, and is represented in collections of, prin. museums and galleries of U.S. and abroad. Address: New York City NY Died 1972.

SWAN, THOMAS WALTER, jurist; b. Norwich, Conn., Dec. 20, 1877; s. Thomas Walter and Jane Adelaide (Maynard) S.; grad. Williston Acad., Easthampton, Mass., 1896; A.B., Yale, 1900, hon. M.A., 1916, LL.D., 1947; LL.B., Harvard, 1903; LL.D., Northeastern U., 1948, U. Chgo., 1953; m. Mabel Eleanor Dick, June 28, 1919. Began practice, Chicago, 1903; mem. Bentley, Burling & Swan, 1907-16; lecturer, Law Sch. U. of Chicago, 1903-04, 1908; dean and prof. law, Sch. of Law, Yale, 1916-27; judge U.S. Circuit Court, 2d Circuit, since February 1927. Trustee Williston Acad. Member Phi Beta Kappa, Phi Delta Phi, Alpha Delta Phi, Elihu Club (Yale). Republican. Conglist. Clubs: Graduate (New Haven); Century, Links, Yale (New York). Home: Guilford, Conn.; and 300 Livingston St., New Haven. Chamber: U.S. Court House, New Haven‡

SWAN, VERNE STURGES, architect; b. Sherburne, N.Y., Jan. 15, 1891; s. Edward Minor and Melissa (Sturges) S.; student Valaparaiso U., 1910-11, Ohio State U., 1911-15; Cornell U., 1919-21, bachelor of architecture; student Am. Art Training Center, 1919, Paris, France; m. Jane Carpenter, Aug. 3, 1922 (deceased April 14, 1957). Associated with the firm of I. V. Van Duzer, Architects, Cazenovia, N.Y., 1915-17, Bagg & Newkirk, Utica, N.Y., 1922-32; pvt. practice, 1932-40; architect Turner Constrn. Co. Bldg. Contractors, 1940-41; engrng. dept. General Cable Corp., Rome, N.Y., 1942-48; pvt. practice since 1948. Mem. Gargoyle Assn., (Cornell U.), A.I.A., N.Y. State Assn. Architects, Amateur Chamber Music Players, Sigma Nu, Alpha Rho Chi. Home: Utica NY Died Apr. 26, 1969.

SWANBERG, HAROLD, educator; b. Phila., July 13, 1891; s. William H. and Lillian (Goerz) S.; B.S., Loyola U, 1916, Md., 1916; Harvard, summer 1924; certificate, U. Vienna, 1931; ScD., Carthage (Ill.) Coll., 1963; m. Zoe Johnson, Dec. 10, 1919 (div. 1933); 1 son, William Harold; m. 2d Mildred Wilber Spiva, Feb. 10, 1934; 1 dau., Nancy Gail; step-children—JoAnn Spiva, Mary Spiva. Practice of medicine, 1916-61; resident St. Luke's Hosp., Chgo., also instr. anatomy sch. medicine Loyola U., 1917; radiologist, dir. Quincy X-Ray & Radium Labs., 1919-61, sec., mng. editor. Recipient Distinguished Service award, Miss. Valley Med. Soc., 1946, Am. Med. Writers Assn., 1952; Golden Deeds award, Quincy Exchange Club, 1962. Served as radiologist, lt. to maj. med. R.C., U.S. Army, 1917-19, 24-29. Fellow Am. Pub. Health Assn., A.C.P., A.A.A.S. Am. Geriatrics Soc., Soc. Academic Achievement; mem. A.M.A., Miss. Valley Med. Soc. (founder, sec. 1935-61), Am. Med. Writers' Assn. (founder, sec. 1940-60, hon. pres.), Radiol. Soc. N.A., Am. Roentgen Ray Soc., Society for Academic Achievement (founder, sec.-teeas. from 1959), Adams County (past sec., editor, pres., del.), Ill. (past chmn sect. radiology, secs. conf.) med. socs., Chgo. Am. Assn. Ret. Persons (past chpt. pres., v.p., del.), Quincy C. of C., Nat. Edn. Assn. U.S. Council Basic Edn., Med. Assn. Vienna, Hist. Soc. Quincy and Adams County, Am. Legion. Clubs: Art, Kiwanis (past president). Author: The Intervertebral Foramen, 1914; The Intervertebral Foramina in Man, 1915; Radiologic Maxims, 1932; History of American Medical Writer's Assn., 1965; also articles and editorials radiologic and ednl. subjects. Founder and editor Quincy Med. Bull., 1924-30, Miss. Valley Med. Jour., 1924-60; editor; Academic Achievement, from 1959; founder Swanberg Med. Found. 1943, Swanberg Kiwanis Found., 1948, Swanberg Collegiate Education Foundation, 1956. Member of the Golden Key Soc. (U. Vienna). Home: Quincy IL Died June 27, 1970; buried Quincy IL

SWANEBECK, CLARENCE W., insurance executive, agriculturist; b. Fenton, Michigan, September 14, 1896; s. Alfred and Jennie (Meyer) S.; student Mich. State Coll.; m. Ellen M. Berryman, Nov. 2, 1927;children—Donald Clarence, Barbara Ellen, Carol Ann. Chmn. Genessee Co. (Mich.) Agrl. programs, 1933-36; mem. Mich. State Grain Bd. East Lansing, 1935-36, State Agri. Conservation Com., 1936-45; sec.-treas., gen. mgr. Pioneer Mutual Ins. Company, Lansing, 1945-67, pres., 1936-45, dir., from 1923; v.p. cons. Pioneer State Mut. Ins. Co., Flint, 1968-70; mem. Mich. Bean Council, Saginaw, since 1946. Dir. and mem. of exec. committee State Assn. Mutual Insurance Cos., Lansing, 1945-55; Fed. Crop Ins. Corp., Washington, 1947-53. Member Fenton Grange, Izaak Walton chapter, Gleaner Life Ins. Soc., Mich. Bean Producers Assn. (pres. 1938-50). Mason (Shriner, K.T.); Odd Fellow. Pres. Fenton MI Died Oct. 8, 1970; buried St. John's Cemetery Fenton MI

SWANISH, PETER THEODORE, educator; b. Mpls., Apr. 21, 1895; s. Theodore and Pearl (Hosma) S.; B.S., U. Minn., 1921; M.B.A., Northwestern U., 1924; Ph.D., U. Chgo., 1930; m. Leela Hanson, Aug. 21, 1922. Head football, basketball coach Bismarck (N.D.) High Sch., 1921-22; prof. econs. Loyola U., 1922-30, head dept., 1931-34, prof. dept. indsl. mgmt., 1949-64; prof. mgmt. No. Ill. U., DeKalb, Ill., 1964-71; chief division of statistics and research Ill. Dept. Labor, 1934-37, commr. placement and unemployment compensation, 1937-42; dir. indsl. relations Quality Hardware & Machine Corp., Chgo., 1942-44; mem. staff spl. com. to investigate civil service (Ramspeck), U.S. Congress, 1944; asst. dir. vocational rehabilitation and edn. VA, 1946-49, now cons. Nat. bd. field advisors Small Bus. Adminstrn.; mem. Ill. State Small Bus. Adv. Council, 1964-65, Mem. Methods-Time Measurement Assn. Standards and Research, Indsl. Relations Research Assn. Soc. Advancement Mgmt., Society Indsl. Mgmt., Am. Econ. Assn., Nat. Council for Development of Small Business Management, Academy Management, American Legion, Sigma Iota Epsilon, also Delta Sigma Pi, Pi Gamma Mu, Alpha Sigma Phi. Club: Glencoe Golf. Author tech. studies, essays, reports. Home: Chicago IL Died Aug. 15, 1971; buried Oak Grove Cemetery, Fergus Falls MN

SWANK, FLETCHER B., ex-congressman; b. Davis County, Ia., Apr. 24, 1875; s. Wallace and Melinda (Wells) S.; student Noble (Okla.) Acad., U. of Okla., night law sch., Georgetown U.; LL.B., Cumberland U., Lebanon, Tenn., 1909; m. Ada Blake, Dec. 30, 1914; children—Fletcher B., James Wallace. County supt. schs., Cleveland County, Okla., 1903-07; pvt. sec. to Scott Ferris, congressman, 1907-08; county judge, Cleveland County, 1911-15; dist. judge 14th Jud. Dist., Okla., 1915-20; mem. 67th to 70th Congresses and 72d and 73d Congresses (1921-29 and 1931-35), 5th Okla. Dist.; now practicing law. Democrat. Mem. M.E. Ch., S. Mason, Odd Fellow, Elk, Woodman. Home: 700 Chautauqua Av. Office: 2071/2 E. Main St., Norman OK*‡

SWANLUND, LESTER HERMAN, accountant, corp. exec.; b. LaMoille, Ill., Jan. 27, 1908; s. Albert and Hannah (Isacson) S.; B.S., U. Ill., 1932; C.P.A., Ill., 1937; m. Maybelle Leland, July 11, 1936. Auditor, Ernst & Ernst, 1932-33; treas. The Found. Press, Inc., 1933-37; staff accountant The Brunswick Corporation (formerly Brunswick-Balke-Collender Company) Chicago, Ill., 1937-42, asst. comptroller, 1942-46, controller, 1946-51, treas., dir., 1951-54, v.p. and treas., 1954-56, financial v.p., 1956-61, now dir.; with subsidiary cos., in Can., Brazil, Mexico, Argentina, also dir.; pres. Brunswick-Murray Automatic Pinsetter Corp., 1956-58; pres., dir. Brunswick Credit Corp., 1960-71; adv. bd. Irving L. Straus Assos., Inc., N.Y.C. Mem. Controllers Inst. Am., Am. Inst. Accountants Meth. Clubs: Executive (Chgo.); Sharon Heights Golf and Country. Home: Atherton CA Died Nov. 9, 1971; interred Alta Mesa Cemetery, Palo Alto CA

SWANSON, ALBERT E., assn. exec.; b. Kingsburg, Cal., Aug. 4, 1896; s. Charles E. and Anna Marie (Hedberg) S.; B.S., U. So. Cal., 1922; m. Lola Alice Paulson, Dec. 10, 1924; children—Eunice Marian, Dean Albert. Mem. Sun-Maid Raisin Growers of Cal., 1927-65, advisor, 1928-35, dir., 1936-43, pres., 1944-65; dir. State Center Bank, Fresno, Cal. Treas. Consol. Irrigation Dist., 1934-44; pres. Agrl. Council Cal.; exec. bd. Central Valley Empire Assn., 1949-52. Mem. Cal. C. of C., Nat. Council Farmer Coops (dir.), Am. Inst. Cooperation, Am. Legion, Sigma Alpha Epsilon. Mason. Clubs: Kiwanis, Commonwealth of California. Home: Kingsburg CA Died Jan. 1965.

SWANSON, ALBERT GUSTAV, coll. ofcl.; b. Raritan, Ill., Oct. 12, 1906; s. Gustav A. and Emma (Johnson) S.; A.B., Augustana Coll., 1927; M.A., U. Neb., 1929; Ph.D., U. Mich., 1936; m. Martha M. Borg, June 16, 1934; children—Gustav A., Linda M., Herman B. Instr. mathematics and mechanics General Motors Inst., 1929-47; prof. mathematics Gustavus Adolphus Coll., 1947-55, academic dean, 1955-67, v.p. for academic adminstrn., 1967-71, acting pres., 1968-69. Mem. Am. Math. Assn., Inst. Math. Statistics, N.E.A. Home: St Peter MN Died Jan. 30, 1971; Clearwater FL

SWANSON, CHARLES EDWARD, ex-congressman; b. Galesburg, Ill., Jan. 3, 1879; s. Peter and Hannah Matilda (Johnson) S.; A.B., Knox Coll., Galesburg, 1902; LL.B., Northwestern U., 1907; m. Ione Westcott, June 29, 1910; 1 son, Charles Edward (killed in action, European area, December 24, 1944). Admitted to Ia. bar, 1907, and began practice at Council Bluffs; pros. atty. Pottawattomie County, Ia., 4 terms, 1915-23; mem. 71st and 72d Congresses (1929-33), 9th Ia. Dist.; pres. Park Building Corp., Council Bluffs. Trustee Christian Home Orphanage. Republican. Presbyterian. Mason. Elk. Home: Council Bluffs IA Died Aug. 22, 1970.

SWANSON, CLARENCE EMANUEL, retail co. exec., univ. regent; b. Wakefield, Neb., Mar. 15,1898; s. Nels and Christine (Erickson) S.; B.S., U. Neb., 1922; m. Helen Hovland, June 19, 1923; children—James H., Kathryn (Mrs. Jerome E. Druliner). Pres. Hovland Swanson Bldg. Corp., Lincoln, Neb., 1935-70; pres. Hovland-Swanson Co., Lincoln, 1935-60, chmn. bd., 1967-70. Member bd. regents U. Neb., 1956-68, pres. bd., 1959-61, mem. fund raising club for Kellogg Center at univ., from 1960; mem. Lincoln Sch. Bd., 1936-42, pres., 1938. Pres. Lincoln Better Bus. Bur., 1938; chmn. Downtown Lincoln Devel. Com., 1959-60. Bd. dirs. Lincoln Community Chest. Recipient Distinguished Service award U. Neb., 1944; recipient of the Nebraska Builder award, 1969. Life mem. Lincoln C. of C., Nat. Alumni Assn. U. Neb. (pres. 1942), Beta Gamma Sigma (hon.), Sigma Alpha Epsilon. Republican. Presbyn. (trustee). Mason (32 deg.), Shriner, Lion. Club: Univ. Country (dir.) (Lincoln). Home: Lincoln NB Died Dec. 3, 1970; buried Wyuka Cemetery Lincoln NB

SWANSON, EDGAR WALFRED, dentist, educator; b. Chgo., Feb. 18, 1899; s. Axel J. and Augusta (Carlson) S.; D.D.S., Northwestern U., 1921, M.S.D., 1936; m. Aldridge Ballard, Oct. 5, 1940; 1 son, Edgar Walfred. Engaged in pvt. practice, Chgo., from 1924; faculty Northwestern U. Dental Sch., from 1921, prof. operative dentistry, from 1926, sec. of faculty, from 1938. Bd. dirs. Tb Inst. Chgo. and Cook County; bd. dirs. Edward Sanatorium, Naperville, Ill., pres., 1948-52. Life mem. Art Inst. Chgo. Served to 1st lt., Dental Corps, U.S. Army, World War I. Recipient Service award Northwestern U., 1939, Merit award, 1960. Fellow Am. Coll. Dentists (pres. 1960-61); mem. Am. Ill., Chgo. dental assns., Fred. Dentaire Internationale, Am. Acad. Periodontology, Inst. Medicine Chgo., Northwestern U. Alumni Assn. (hon. life; pres. 1939), Northwestern U. Dental Alumni Assn. (pres. 1937), Omicron Kappa Upsilon, Xi Psi Phi. Presbyn. Mason (Shriner). Clubs: Lake Shore (Chgo.); Evanston (Ill.) Golf. Author articles. Home: Chicago IL Died Nov. 12, 1968; interred mausoleum Memorial Park Cemetery Skokie IL

SWANTEE, PAUL FREDERICK, communications exec.; b. Wakefield, Mass., Apr. 3, 1900; s. Fredrik John and Augusta Charlotte (Perry) S.; student Boston U., 1916-18, Northeastern U., 1920-22; grad. Bentley Sch. Accounting and Finance, 1920. Treas. Nat. Union Radio Corp., Newark, 1930-33; staff mem. Arthur Andersen & Co., accountants and auditors, 1925-30, resident mgr., K.C., Mo., 1933-39, Boston, 1939-43; asst. comptroller Internat. Telephone & Telegraph Corp., N.Y.C., 1943-52, comptroller, 1952-58, treas., 1958-61, asst. v.p., from 1961, ret.; chmn., mem. bd. directors Kellogg Credit Corp.; treas., dir. ITT Aetna Finance Co., ITT Credit Corp.; treas. ITT Communication Systems, Inc., ITT Farnsworth Research Corp., ITT Financial Services Inc. C.P.A., Mass. Mem. American Institute C.P.A.'s, Financial Execs. Inst., Mass., Mo. socs. C.P.A.'s, Am. Accounting Assn., Nat. Assn. Accountants. Am. Legion. Clubs: Downtown Assn., N.Y. Athletic New York City NY Died Nov. 1970.

SWANTON, WILLIAM T., lawyer; b. Birmingham, Alabama, October 8, 1893; L.B., Cornell University, 1919; m. Ethel Sibson, 1923 (dec. 1963); 1 daughter, Margaret (Mrs. Paxton Lane Jones). Admitted to Ohio bar, 1919; now partner firm Manchester, Bennett, Powers & Ullman, Youngstown. Mem. Am., Ohio, Mahoning County bar assns., Am. Judicature Soc., Ohio Hist. Soc., Com. Constl. Govt., Am. Inst. Econ. Research, C. of C., Am. Legion, Delta Theta Phi. Club: Youngstown. Home: Youngstown OH Died Oct. 7, 1970.

SWARTHOUT, GLADYS, mezzo-soprano; b. Deepwater, Mo., Dec. 25, 1904; d. Frank Leslie and Ruth (Wonser) Swarthout; grad. Central High Sch., Kansas City, Mo., 1920; student Bush Cons. of Music, Chicago, 1920-23; hon. Mus.D., Chicago Musical College; married Harry Richmond Kern, March 22, 1925 (died Oct. 20, 1931); m. 2d, Frank M. Chapman, Jr., 1932 (dec. July 1966). Ch. singer, then appeared in concerts; mem. Chgo. Civic Opera Co., 1924-25, Ravinia Co., Chicago, 1927-29, Metropolitan Opera Co. since 1929; creator role of Niejata in Sadko" Am. premiere, and role of Cathos in Lattuada's Le Preziose Ridicole" Am. premiere; leading mezzo-soprano in Norma," Peter Ibbetson," Gioconda," Forza del Destino," Lakme," Carmen," Mignon," etc.; has toured widely in concerts. Radio and recording artist; star of five motion pictures; title role first televised opera Carmen." Five successive years voted first female classical singer in radio by critics of U.S. and Canada. Author of novel Come Soon Tomorrow." Address: New York City NY also Florence Italy Died July 7, 1969; buried Engelwood Cemetery, Elgelwood NJ

SWARTWOUT, MARY COOKE, art museum dir.; b. Cleveland, O., Dec. 19, 1876; d. William Jay and Mary (Isom) Cooke; grad. Starret Sch., Oak Park, Ill., 1897; student Oberlin Coll. Conservatory, 1897-98; grad. in home economics, Lewis Inst., Chicago, Ill., 1899; m. Leslie George Swartwout, June 28, 1900 (now deceased). Staff mem. Toledo Museum of Art, 1920-24; dir. Grand Rapids (Mich.) Art Gallery, 1924-32; dir. Montclair (N.J.) Art Museum since 1932. Mem. Am. Assn. of Museums, Am. Fedn. Arts, Am. Artists Professional League. Republican. Episcopalian. Home: 28 Gates Av. Office: 1 S. Mountain Av., Montclair NJ‡

SWARTZ, HERMAN FRANK, educator; b. Carlisle, Pa., May 12, 1871; s. Rev. Joel (D.D.) and Adelia (Rosecrans) S.; Sc.B., with honors, Pa. Coll., Gettysburg, 1891, M.Sc., 1893; student Union Theol. Sem. and Columbia U., 1892-93; grad. Hartford Theol. Sem., 1895 (fellow in Social Sciences, 1895); spl. work in social sciences, univs. of Berlin, Paris, Rome; D.D., Fargo Coll., N.D., 1915; LL.D., Coll. of the Pacific, 1932, Gettysburg Coll., 1933; m. Omega Kinsell, Jan. 1, 1901; m. 2d, Edna M. Lindsay, June 27, 1917. Ordained Congl. ministry, 1898; pastor Mansfield, Mass., 1898-1901; supt. City Missionary Soc., Cleveland, 1901-07; pastor Webster Groves Ch., St. Louis, 1907-10; sec. of missions, Congl. Home Missionary Soc., 1911-18; exec. sec. Pilgrim Memorial Fund and corr. sec. Annuity Fund for Congl. Ministers, 1918-19; instr. in pastoral care, Hartford Theol. Sem., 1917-21; gen. sec. Congl. World Movement, 1920-22; pres. Pacific Sch. of Religion, Berkeley, Calif., 1922-38, pres. emeritus since 1938; pastor First Congregational Church, Santa Barbara, Calif., 1943-46, ret. Santa Barbara CA‡

SWARTZ, MIFFLIN WYATT, college pres.; b. at Winchester, Va., Oct. 12, 1874; s. Edward Pendleton and Laura Bertram (Clowe) S.; B.A., U. of Va., 1898, M.A., 1900, Ph.D., 1910; studied U. of Chicago, summer quarters, 1907, 8, 9; m. Gertrude Dora MacBrian, of Potsdam, N.Y., May 22, 1902. Began teaching, Ft. Worth, Tex., 1900; pres. Woman's Coll. of Ala. since June 1, 1915. Mem. Southern Assn. Schs. and Colls., Pi Kappa Alpha, Phi Beta Kappa. Democrat. Methodist. Club: Country. Author: Personal and Dramatic Characteristics of the Old in the Dramas of Euripides, 1910. Address: Montgomery AL‡

SWARTZ, OSMAN ELLIS, lawyer; b. Newark, O., Nov. 3, 1880; s. Samuel Ellis and Jane Harriet (Ellis) S.; Ph.B., Shurtleff Coll., Alton, Ill., 1899; LL.B., Washington and Lee U., 1902; m. Marion Stephenson Swartz, Feb. 21, 1929. Admitted to W.Va. bar, 1902, and began practice at Clarksburg; counsel Monongahela West Penn. Pub. Service Co., Fairmont, W.Va., 1918-23; counsel Consolidation Coal Co., Fairmont, 1918-23, gen. atty. at N.Y. City, 1923-28; gen. counsel United Carbon Co., Charleston, W.Va., 1928-56, ret.; president and dir. Thompson Land and Coal Co.; vice pres., dir. United Rubber & Chemical Co.; dir. Holley Land Co., United Carbon Co. Served as pvt., AUS, World War. Mem. Am. and W.Va. bar assns., N.Y. Law Inst., Phi Kappa Psi. Democrat. Baptist. Club: Edgewood Country. Home: Charleston WV Died May 17, 1971.

SWAVELY, ELI, educator; b. Spangsville, Pa., Jan. 7, 1876; s. George F. and Elmira (Clouser) S.; prep. edn., Arm's Acad., Pottstown, Pa.; E.E., Lafayette Coll., 1896, Litt.M., 1926; m. Sara Zerbe, Reading, Pa., Oct. 11, 1900. Founder, 1901, and pres. Army and Navy Prep. Sch., Washington, D.C. (now the Swavely School for Boys, Manassas, Va.). Episcopalian. Mason. Club: University (Washington, D.C.). Home: Manassas VA‡

SWEARINGEN, JOHN ELDRED, state supt. edn.; b. Trenton, Edgefield Co., S.C., Jan. 9, 1875; s. John C. and Anna (Tillman) S.; ed. dist. sch.; Trenton High Sch.; Ga. Acad. for the Blind; S.C. Sch. for the Deaf and the Blind; A.B., S.C. Coll., 1899; LL.D., U. of S.C., 1920, Erskine Coll., 1922; m. Mary Hough, June 29, 1916;children—John Eldred, George Van, Mary Douglas. Rendered totally blind by accidental discharge of gun while hunting, Jan. 13, 1888; farmer since 1893; taught sch., 1899-1908; state supt. edn., S.C., 1909-23. Democrat. Presbyn. Home: Columbia SC‡

SWEARINGEN, LLOYD EDWARD, educator; b. Rosendale, Mo., Aug. 30, 1897; s. William H. and Elizabeth (Trussel) S.; B.S., U. Okla., 1920, M.S., 1921; Ph.D., U. Minn., 1926; m. Lillian Weisenbach, June 12, 1925. Head dept. phys. sci. Southwestern State Coll., Weatherford, Okla., 1921-23; asst. prof. U. Okla., 1923-26, asso. prof., 1926-29, prof. chemistry, from 1929, research prof., 1948-53, v.p. for research and development, from 1953; dir. U. Okla. Research Inst., 1947-49, exec. director, 1953-58, dean of the Graduate College, 1958-59; director of basic sciences research Dept. of Army (on leave from U. Okla.) 1951-53, sci.

asst. dep. for research and development Asst. Chief of Staff G-4, Dept. Army, 1952-53. Served as col., U.S. Army, World War. I, also 1942-46; ETO. Decorated Bronze Star (U.S.); Croix de Guerre with palms (France). Recipient Outstanding Achievement award U. Minn., 1955; Lloyd Swearingen Research Park at U. Okla. named in his honor, 1968. Mem. Am. Chem. Soc. Okla. Acad. Sci., Phi Beta Kappa, Sigma Xi, Alpha Chi Sigma, Phi Lambda Upsilon, Alpha Epsilon Delta, Phi Delta Chi. Contbr. profl. jours. Address: Norman OK Died Mar. 9, 1972; interred I.O.O.F. Mausoleum Norman OK

SWEARINGEN, MACK BUCKLEY, educator; b. Jackson, Miss., Feb. 5, 1902; s. George Crawford and Anne (Buckley) S.; B.A., Millsaps Coll., 1922; M.A., U. Chgo., 1923, Ph.D., 1932; B.A., Oxford U., 1927; m. Mary Louise Foster, Sept. 2, 1933; children—George Lin., Frances Anne. Instr., Emory U., 1923-24; asst. prof. Millsaps Coll., 1927-28, Marshall Coll., 1928-29; asso. prof. Tulane U., 1931-38; prof., chmn. social sci. div. Ga. State Coll. for Women, 1938-42; prof., chmn. soc. sci. div. Elmira Coll., 1942-52, prof., 1952-66; prof. history Lake Erie Coll., 1966-68; prof. Ankara U., 1955-56; asst. prof. U. Tex. at Austin, summer 1929; prof. Duke, summer 1941, Cornell U., summer 1943, 44, 45, U. Vt. summer 1949-53. Rhodes scholar, 1924-27; recipient Rockefeller Found. grant, Turkey, 1957-58. Address: Painesville OH Died Oct. 10, 1969.

SWEARINGEN, VAN CICERO, lawyer; b. Nassau Co., Fla., Feb. 2, 1873; s. William and Mary (Blitch) S.; self-ed.; LL.B., Mercer U., Macon, Ga., 1900; m. Alice M. Padgett, of Fernandina, Fla., Jan. 1, 1900. Worked at blacksmith's trade until 1908; judge Municipal Court, Jacksonville, Fla., 1911-13; mayor of Jacksonville, 1913-15; atty. gen. of Fla., 1917-18. Democrat. Methodist. Mem. Fla. Bar Assn. Mason. Odd Fellow, K.P., etc. Home: Jacksonville FL‡

SWEARINGEN, VICTOR CLARENCE, govt. ofcl.; b. Science Hill, Ky., June 1, 1899; s. Charles Clark and Eva Lena (Hubble) S.; A.B., U. Ky., 1922; J.D., Detroit Coll. Law, 1925; post grad., U. Mich. Law Sch., 1928-29; LL.M., George Washington U. Law Sch., 1951; m. Beth Secord Elliott, Aug. 22, 1929; 1 dau., Janet. Admitted to Mich. bar, 1925; in practice of law, Detroit, 1925-36, instr. in internat. law U. Detroit, 1926-31; instr. in legislation Wayne State U., Detroit, 1932-38; asst. atty.-gen., State of Mich., Lansing, 1937-38; atty. Dept. of Agr., Washington, 1939-40; referee on wage rates Dept. of Labor, Washington, 1940-41; Mich. State labor mediator, Detroit, 1941-46; U.S. judge Internat. War Crimes Trials, Nurnberg, Germany, 1946-47; spl. asst. to atty. gen. of U.S., Washington, 1948-56; hearing examiner ICC, Washington, 1956-68. Served as enlisted man U.S. Army, World War I; AAF intelligence officer, 1942-44, comdg. officer 419th troop carrier group, A.A.F., 1944-45, chief of war crimes operations Gen. Staff, U.S. Army, Jan.-Oct. 1946, recalled to active mil. service as col. USAF Res., Mar. 1951, chief, investigations div. Office Insp. Gen., USAF, 1951-53, sec. UN Command-Mil. Armistice Commn., Panmunjom, Korea, 1954-55, colonel U.S. Air Force retired, 1960. Member of Fed., Mich., and Detroit bar assns., Am. Soc. Internat. Law, Am. Legion, S.A.R., Delta Phi Epsilon, Delta Theta Phi. Democrat. Methodist. Mason (K.T., Shriner). Club: Lions. Contbr. articles law and govtl. subjects to various legal pubs. Home: Washington DC Died Jan. 15, 1968.

SWEENEY, GEORGE CLINTON, judge; b. Gardner, Mass., July 23, 1895; s. John Francis and Sarah (Shields) S.; student Williston Sem., 1915-16; LL.B., Georgetown U., 1922; m. Winifred E. Johnson, Apr. 14, 1925; children—George C., Sheila Elizabeth, Judith Shields. Admitted to Mass. bar, 1924, practicing in Gardner; mayor of Gardner, Jan. 1, 1931-June 15, 1933, resigning to accept position as asst. atty. gen. of the U.S., 1933-35; U.S. dist. judge for Mass. from 1935, later chief. Former mem. Gardner City Council. Pvt. Co. A, 301st Mil. Police Batt., 1917, sergt. 1918; served with 76th Div. overseas. Mem. Am. Law Inst., Am. Judicature Soc., Am., Mass., Middlesex Co., Boston and Worcester Co. bar assns. Democrat. Catholic. Clubs: Ekwanok Country (Manchester, Vt.); Clover (Boston). Home: Boston MA Died Nov. 5, 1966; buried Wolfboro NH

SWEENEY, JAMES G., judge; b. Carson City, Nev., Jan. 22, 1877; s. Edward D. and Ellen (Cavanaugh) S.; B.A., St. Mary's Coll., Oakland, Cal., 1896, M.A., 1906; LL.B., Columbian (now George Washington) U., 1900; (LL.D., St. Mary's, 1909); m. Mabel Trembath, of Virginia City, Nev., Dec. 14, 1906. Mem. Nev. Ho. of Rep., 1901-2; atty.-gen. of Nev., 1902-7; asso. justice Supreme Ct. of Nev., 1907-11; chief justice, 1911-14. Chmn. Dem. State Central Com. Pres. Western Pacific Telephone & Telegraph Co.; treas. Nev. Consolidated Telephone & Telegraph Co. Address: Carson City NV‡

SWEENEY, JAMES J., bishop; b. San Francisco, June 19, 1898; s. John J. and Catherine (McCarrick) S.; A.B., St. Patrick's Sem., 1932. Ordained priest Roman Cath. Ch., 1925; asst. pastor St. Paul's Ch., San Francisco, 1925-31; dir. Soc. for Propagation of the Faith, Archdiocese of San Francisco, 1931-41; bishop of Honolulu from May 1941, consecrated, July 1941. Home: Honolulu HI Died June 19, 1968; buried Holy Cross Cemetery, San Francisco CA

SWEENEY, JOHN WILLIAM, judge; b. Westerly, R.I., Apr. 11, 1869; s. Martin and Mary (Feeley) S.; ed. pub. schools; read law in offices; LL.D., Manhattan, also Providence Coll., 1929; Master Business Science, Bryant College, 1937; m. Ellen C. Bennett, Sept. 26, 1898. Admitted to R.I. bar, 1893, and began practice at Westerly; clk. of judiciary com., R.I. Senate, 1895-1913; justice 3d Jud. Dist. of R.I., 1898-1905; asso. justice Superior Court, 1913-20; associate justice of the Supreme Court of R.I., 1920-35. Mem. bd. dirs. Providence Coll., St. Joseph's Hosp.; v.p., St. Vincent de Paul Infant Asylum. Mem. bd. of appeal, Selective Service System. Mem. Am. Bar Assn., R.I. Bar Assn., Am. Law Inst., Am. Irish Hist. Soc., Phi Kappa. K.C. Clubs: Catholic, Turks Head. Home: West Kingston RI‡

SWEENEY, MILDRED I. MCNEAL, author; b. Burnett, Wis., Aug. 30, 1871; d. William and Jane (Hall) McNeal; B.A., Lawrence U., Appleton, Wis., 1899; m. Peter M. Sweeney, of Mass., Nov., 1903. Author: (poems) When Yesterday Was Young, 1906; Men of No Land. Club: Boston Authors. Home: 151 Garden St., Lawrence MA‡

SWEENY, CHARLES AMOS, govt. ofcl.; b. Ida, Mich., Oct. 25, 1908; s. Alferd Wyre and Grace (Sellick) S.; student U. Toledo, 1926-30; LL.B., George Washington U., 1935; LL.M., M.P.L., Nat. U., 1939, m. Elizabeth Mary Klar, July 31, 1950; children—Sabelle (Mrs. Donald C. Schuessler), Nancy Jean (Mrs. Charles H. Marshall). With FBI, 1930-35; admitted to U.S. Ct. Appeals for D.C., 1939; also U.S. Supreme Ct.; with FTC, 1935-68, chief div. food and drug advt., 1961-65, dir. bur. deceptive practices, 1965-68, director Office of Program Review, 1968. Served with USCGR, 1941-45. Decorated Bronze Star. Mem. Fed. Bar Assn., Res. Officers Assn. (pres. Washington USCG chpt. 1955-60). Democrat. Mason (Shriner). Home: Arlington VA Died Dec. 12, 1968.

SWEENY, WILLIAM MONTGOMERY, writer; b. New York, Aug. 29, 1871; s. late Gen. Thomas W. (U.S.A.) and Eugenia Octavia (Reagan) S.; ed. New York pub. schs., Coll. City of New York (not. grad.), and Richmond Acad., Augusta, Ga.; unmarried. Has written for press and contributed biog. articles to National Cyclopaedia of American Biography, Lamb's Biographical Dictionary of United States Encyclopaedia Americana and other biog. publs. Mem New York Assn. Cal. Pioneers (ex-sec.), Mil. Order Foreign Wars, N.C. Soc. of the Cincinnati, Aztec Club of 1847 (secretary 1907-12), Society of Colonial Wars in Virginia. Club: Army and Navy (Washington, D.C.). Author: Memoir General Sweeny, United States Army, 1907. Editor: Military Occupation of California, 1849-53; Captain Thomas Cook (1752-1841), a Soldier of the Revolution; Some notices, geneal. and hist., of the Cook, Dandridge, Higginbotham, Morrison, Reagan, Refo. and Sweeny families. Address: Astoria, LI NY‡

SWEET, HAROLD EDWARD, manufacturing jeweler; b. West Mansfield, Mass., June 24, 1877; (desc. of John Sweet, who came from Wales and settled in Salem, Mass., 1630); s. Joseph Lyman and Florence May (Hayward) S.; grad. English and Classical Sch., Providence, R.I., 1894; A.B., Tufts Coll., 1898; m. Gertrude O. Hunton, Jan. 23, 1900; children—Hayward Hunton, Mrs. Marian Sweet Armstrong. Began with B.F. Simmons Co., mfg. jewelers, Attleboro, Mass. 1898, associated with father in ownership and management of firm until the latter's death, July, 1932; son, Hayward, admitted to partnership, 1935; pres. First Nat. Bank since 1926; dir. various cos. Served as 2d lt. Co. M, 14th Regt. Inf., Mass. State Guard, 1918-19. First mayor of Attleboro, 2 terms, 1915-19. Pres. bd. trustees Tufts Coll., since 1923; pres. Sturdy Memorial Hosp. since 1933. Mem. Delta Upsilon. Democrat. Universalist. Mason, Odd Fellow, Elk. Clubs: Universalist, Mayors' Club of Mass. (Boston); Lions (Attleboro). Home: 80 North Main St.; (summer) North Falmouth, Mass. Office: 191 North Main St., Attleboro MA‡

SWEET, MARION ATWOOD (MRS. HAMILTON HOWARD SWEET), club woman; b. Salem, Mass., Sept. 15, 1899; d. Frederick Monroe and Grace (Boomer) Atwood; student pub. schs.; m. Hamilton Howard Sweet, June 16, 1923; children—Elizabeth (Mrs. Charles E. Martin), Marilyn (Mrs. Robert C. McKnight), Deborah (Mrs. Dwight Summers). Mem. staff Childrens Hosp., Boston, 1921-22, Muhlenburg Hosp., Plainfield, N.J., 1943-44. Bd. dirs. Vis. Nurses, Falmouth, Mass., 1963-70. Mem. D.A.R. (state chmn. Am. Indians 1959-62, state historian 1962-65, state vice regent 1965-68), Nat. Soc. Women Descendants, Daus. of Founders and Patriots. Club: Garden (bd. dirs. 1962-70). Address: Falmouth MA Died May 13, 1970.

SWEITZER, CAESAR, physician; b. Chgo., May 8, 1911; s. Adolph and Katherine (Veron) S.; M.D., U. Ill., 1939; m. Rachel M. Fairbanks, July 1949; children—Caesar, Dean, Richard, David. Intern, Grant Hosp., Chgo., 1938-39, resident in gen. surgery, 1939-40, asso. surg. staff, until 1970; resident in gen. surgery Wesley Meml. Hosp., Chgo., 1946-48, chief resident in surgery, 1948, sr. attending surgeon, until 1970; asso. dept. surgery Northwestern U., Chgo., until 1971. Served to lt. col., M.C., AUS, 1945-46. Decorated Bronze Star. Diplomate Am. Bd. Surgery. Fellow A.C.S.; mem. A.M.A., Internat. Coll. Surgeons. Republican. Home: Wilmette IL Died May 31, 1970; buried Forest Home, Forest Park IL

SWETT, FRANK TRACY;, b. San Francisco, Calif., Nov. 22, 1869; s. John and Mary L. (Tracy) S.; prep. edn., pub. schs., San Francisco; student U. of Calif., 1887-90; m. Myrta Wallace More, June 15, 1897; children—Margaret, Elizabeth. Fruit grower and nurseryman, nr. Martinez, Contra Costa County, Calif., since 1890; hort. commr. Contra Costa Co., 1905-09, 1915-19; vice pres. Calif. State Viticultural Commn., 1913-19; pres. and gen. mgr. Calif. Pear Growers Assn., 1917-35. Editor Pacific Rural Press, 1923. Pres. Calif. Grape Growers Assn., 1916-20, Contra Costa Fruit Growers Assn., 1915-20, Contra Costa Farm Bur., 1917; dir. Calif. Canning Peach Assn., 1921-25 (reorganization mgr. 1935), Calif. Prune and Apricot Assn., 1922-25, Calif. Cherry Growers Assn., 1922-29, Nat. Hort. Council since 1929; chief of Farm Debt Adjustment Div., Resettlement Adminstrn., 5 southwestern states, 1935-36, resigned. Democrat. Unitarian. Clubs: Commonwealth, Hillside, Jawbone, Laymen's League, Foreign Trade. Home: Alhambra Valley, near Martinez CA‡

SWIFT, ERNEST FREMONT, conservation adminstr.; b. Tracy, Minn., Sept. 15, 1897; s. Henry Lee and Carrie May (Blanchard) S.; student U. Minn.; m. Rosalie Tarr, Oct. 6, 1926 (dec. Jan. 1943); children—Helen (Mrs. Fred Swanson), Thelma (Mrs. Anthony Stassi), Dennis; m. 2d, Goldie Pauline Flannum. Conservation warden, forest ranger Wis. Conservation Dept., 1926-35, supr. fur farms, 1935, dep. dir., 1935-47, dir., 1947-54; asst. dir. charge game mgmt. activities, adminstr. regional offices U.S. Fish and Wildlife Service, 1954-55; exec. dir. Nat. Wildlife Fedn., 1955-60, consultant and adviser, 1960-68. Vice chairman of natural resources com. Wis. State Agencies, 1951-54. Bd. mem. Trustees for Conservation, 1959-68. Recipient Haskell Noyes Conservation Warden award; Aldo Leopold medal, 1959. Member of Midwest Association of Fish and Game Commissioners (president 1938-39, 49-50), Internat. Assn. Game, Fish and Conservation Commrs. (chmn. exec. com. 1953-54), Am. Fisheries Soc., Soc. Am. Foresters, Nat. Waterfowl Council (chmn. 1953-54), Wis. Acad. Scis., Arts and Letters, Wildlife Soc., Wilderness Soc. Author: AHistory of Wisconsin Deer; Wildlife as a Forest Crop in the Lake States, 1948; Education the Sharpest Tool for Conservation of Resources, 1953; Business of Conservation 1953; By Which We Live; The Glory Trail; Count Down to Survival. Home: Rice Lake WI Died July 24, 1968; buried Hayward WI

SWIM, CHESTER LAWRENCE, oil co. exec.; b. Stillwater, Okla., June 15, 1894; s. Herbert Alton and Margaret Jane (Davidson) S.; student Central State Tchrs. Coll., Edmond, Okla., Baker U., Baldwin, Kan.; m. Inez Taylor, Apr. 28, 1918; 1 son, Richard Taylor. Admitted to Okla. bar; engaged in practice, from 1925; with Skelly Oil Co., Tulsa, from 1923; asst. sec.-treas., 1939-51, sec.-treas., 1951-56, v.p. charge legal dept., 1956-59, also dir. Treas., mem. bd. Tulsa area council Boy Scouts Am., 1952-53. Treas. Payne County (Okla.), 1916, 18. Served as pvt. U.S. Army, World War I. Home: Tulsa OK

SWIM, DUDLEY, corp. exec.; b. Bellingham, Wash., June 15, 1905; s. Arthur L. and Mary (Galbraith) S.; A.B. with great distinction, Stanford, 1926, M.B.A., 1928; m. Katherine Merrill, June 22, 1935; children—Marilyn L., Roger C., Gaylord K. Engaged in ranching; past sr. v.p. Nat. Investors Corp.; dir. Investors Diversified Service, Inc., Mpls., 1952-54; former director., member of exec. committee M.O. Pacific R.R.; now chmn. board National Air Lines, Inc.; now president Twin Falls Mortgage Loan Co., former dir., mem. finance com. Providence Washington Ins. Grp., Del Monte Corp; former chmn., dir. Baker Raulang Co. Former member of the California State Coordinating Council Higher Edn.; internat. advisory committee Information Council of Americas. Member policy bd. USNR, 1946; pres. Carmel Valley (Cal.) Assn., 1957, Monterey Bay Area council Boy Scouts Am., 1957; director of Stanford Research Inst. Trustee of Cordell Hull Found. Internat. Education; mem. national council Pomona Coll.; founder, managing trustee of Arthur L. Swim Found.; chmn. adv. council, nutrition dept. U. Cal. at Berkeley; pres. Monterey County Found. for Conservation; mem. adv. bd. Hoover Instn. on War, Revolution and Peace, Stanford trustee Cal. State Colls., Rockford Coll., Wabash Coll. Served to lt. comdr. USNR, 1942-45. Mem. Free Soc. Assn. (trustee), Am. Legion (nat. vice comdr. 1946), Stanford Alumni Assn. (pres. 1951-52), Phi Beta Kappa, Sigma Nu. Republican. Presbyn., Clubs: Bohemian, Commonwealth (San Francisco); Blue Lakes Country (Ida.); Hope (R.I.). Home: Carmel CA Died 1972.

SWING, RAYMOND, radio commentator; b. Cortland, N.Y., Mar. 25, 1887; s. Albert Temple and Alice Edwards (Mead) S.; ed. Oberlin Coll., Conservatory of Music; Litt.D., Oberlin Coll., 1940; LL.D., Olivet Coll., 1940; D.H.L., Williams, Muhlenberg and Lafayette colleges, 1941; Master of Art, at Harvard, 1942; married to Suzanne Morin, July 9, 1912; children—Albert George, Elizabeth Francoise; married 2d, Betty Gram, on Jan. 10, 1920; children—Peter Gram, Sally Gram, John Temple; m. 3d, Mary S. Hartshorne, Jan. 3, 1945; m. 4th Meisung Euyang Loh, 1957. Began newspaper work in Cleve., 1906, later at Orrville, O., Richmond, Ind., Indpls., Cin.; Berlin corr. Chgo. Daily News, 1913-17; examiner WLB, 1918; Berlin corr. N.Y. Herald, 1919-22; dir. fgn. service Wall Street Jour., 1922-24; with London bur. Phila. Public Ledger, N.Y. Evening Post, 1924-34; bd. editors The Nation, 1934-36; N.Y. corr. London News Chronicle, 1936-37; news commentator Am. affairs, BBC, 1935-45; commentator fgn. affairs Am. Sch. of the Air, CBS, 1935-36; commentator fgn. affairs MBS, 1936-45; commentator ABC, 1942-48; lectr., 1948-50; news commentator sta. WOR, 1950, Liberty network, 1950-51; polit. commentator Voice of Am., 1951-53, 59-64, asso. Edward R. Murrow, 1953-59. Trustee Oberlin Coll., 1946. Mem. Council for Democracy (chmn. bd. 1940-41), Ams. United for World Government (chmn., director 1946), Phi Beta Kappa. Author of: Forerunners of American Fascism, published in 1935; How War Came, 1940; Preview of History, 1943; In the Name of Sanity, 1946; Good Evening, A Professional Memoir, 1964. Contbr. Am. and English mags. Home: Washington DC Died Dec. 22, 1968.

SWINGLE, FRANK BELL, editor; b. Shopiere, Wis., Mar. 8, 1874; s. Warren Ward and Francelia (Bell) S.; student State Teachers Coll., 1894-97; m. Anna Bose Wensing, Nov. 15, 1899; children—Esther (Mrs. Ray Herman), Everett Bell. Teacher schs., 1897-1912; asso. editor Wis. Agriculturist, 1912-34; editor Wisconsin Agriculturist and Farmer since 1934. Methodist. Mason. Clubs: Kiwanis (Racine). Author: English for Evening Schools, 1912; Farmer Boy at College, 1917. Wrote The Story of the Twine Binder," for Wis. Hist. Society. Home: 255 Lafayette Av. Office: Wisconsin Agriculturist and Farmer, Racine WI‡

SWINGLER, WILLIAM S(HERMAN), govt. ofcl.; b. Columbia, Pa., July 29, 1901; s. Sherman E. and Elizabeth A. (Lutz) S.; B.S. in forestry, Pa. State Forest Sch., Mont Alte, Pa., 1921; m. Norma J. Menschel, June 7, 1924; children—Jean (Mrs. Tom Price), Ann (Mrs. James McLean), Sally (Mrs. Richard Burke), William Sherman. District forester Pennsylvania Department of Forests and Waters, 1921-34; forester U.S. Forest Service, 1934-37, 38-42; charge hurricane rehabilitation work, Vt., 1937; headed program to stimulate prodn. lumber in N.E., W.P.B., 1942-44; forestry advisor to Gen. MacArthur in Tokyo, 1946; asst. regional forester U.S. Forest Service, Cal. region, 1946-48, regional forester, N.E. region, 1948-52, asst. chief, Washington, 1952-63. Mem. Soc. Am. Foresters, Soil Conservation Soc. Am., A.A.A.S. Home: Bethesda MD Died Feb. 28, 1971; buried Holy Trinity Columbia PA

SWIREN, MAX, lawyer; b. Sioux City, Ia., Sept. 1, 1904; s. William and Cecilia (Katz) S.; grad. Francis Parker Sch., Chicago, 1920; student Northwestern, 1920-21, Ph.B., U. Chicago, 1925, J.D., 1927; m. Dorothy Y. Tepper, Feb. 5, 1957; children—Marcia Cecile, Paula Kay. Admitted to Ill. bar, 1927, practiced in Chicago; spl. counsel to dir. Economic Stabilization and Price Administrator, 1943-44; chmn. finance com., dir. MSL Industries, Inc.; dir. Glenshaw Glass Co., Inc. Mem. Am., Ill., Chgo. bar assns., Phi Beta Kappa, Order of Coif. Independent Democrat. Jewish religion. Club: Standard. Home: Honolulu HI Died Mar. 7, 1969; buried Chicago IL

SWITZ, THEODORE MACLEAN, ednl. adminstr.; b. Balt., Nov. 16, 1901; s. Theodore A. and Genevieve (MacLean) S.; Chem.E., Lehigh U., 1922; Ph.D., Royal Coll. Sci., U. London, 1926; m. Faye Pedersen, Aug. 12, 1923; children—Donald MacLean, Margaret Holland. Research Westinghouse, 1922-24; econ. surveys of chem. industries Investment Research Corp., also Lehman Corp., 1926-37, Hercules Powder Co., 1937; dir. export dept. Hercules Powder Co., 1941-45; v.p. Overseas Ency. Britannica Films, Inc., 1945-48; dir. Phys. Scis. Devel., U. Chgo., 1948-65; asso. dir. Inst. Advanced Pastoral Studies, Bloomfield Hills, Mich., from 1965; cons. adult edn. Nat. Council of Episcopal Ch., 1948-60. Mem. Chi Psi, Tau Beta Pi. Republican. Episcopalian. Editor of: The Prayerbook Speaks in Our Uncertain Age, 1949; Consider the Bible, 1950; Church History for Group Study, 1951; Communism and Christianity, 1951; Creative Choices in Life, 1953; Corporate Worship; The Call of Every Man, 1957. Author, editor: (with R. H. Johnstone) Great Christian Plays, 1956. Translator: Statistical Theory of Liquids by I. Z. Fisher from the Russian, Silver Spring MD Died Apr. 1971.

SWITZER, MARY ELIZABETH, government service; b. Newton (Upper Falls), Mass., Feb. 16, 1900; d. Julius F. and Margaret M. (Moore) Switzer; A.B., Radcliffe Coll., 1921. Asst. sec., Minimum Wage Board, Washington, D.C., 1921-22; exec. sec., Women's Internat. League for Peace and Freedom, 1922; junior economist (financial), sect. of statistics, Treasury Dept., 1922-23; chief clerk's office, Treasury Dept., 1924-28; in charge press intelligence for sec. of treasury, 1928-33; asst. chief, White House editorial reports service, 1929-33; asst. chief, corr. div., sec. of treasury, 1933-34; asst. to asst. sec. of treasury in charge of pub. health service, 1934-39; asst. to chmn. inter-departmental Commn. to Coordinate Health and Welfare Activities, 1935-38; asst. to administrator, Federal Security Agency, 1939-50; commr. Vocational Rehabilitation Administrn., Dept. Health, Edn. and Welfare, 1950-67, adminstr. social, and rehab. service, 1967-70, chairman of the dept. patent bd., 1950-60; v.p. World Rehab. Fund, Washington, 1970-71; asst. to chairman, Procurement and Assignment Service for Physicians, etc., War Manpower Commn., 1940-46. Mem. tech. com. on nat. relief policy of Nat. Resources Planning Bd., 1939-43; chmn. ednl. com., Nat. Women's Trade Union League, 1934-50. Mem. bd. of visitors of St. Elizabeth's Hosp., Washington, 1941-46; board of trustees Menninger Foundation; advisor mem. U.S. del. Internat. Health Conf., U.N., 1946; U.S. del., Internat. Cong. on Mental Health, 1948; mem. Council of Nat. Com. for Mental Hygiene; mem. U.S. Del. WHO, Rome, 1949; member advisory committee International Soc. for Rehab. Disabled; mem. council Assn. for Aid to Crippled Children; mem. bd. dirs. Georgetown University, 1969-71. Recipient Albert Lasker award in medicine, 1960. Mem. bd. overseers Florence Heller Grad. Sch. for Advanced Studies Social Welfare, Brandeis U. Hon. member Am. Congress Physical Medicine and Rehabilitation, Am. Psychiatric Assn.; mem. Nat. Conf. Social Welfare (1st vice pres.), National (president 1961), Va. (mem. bd.) rehabilitation assns., American Hearing Soc. (pres. 1961-63), American Association of Workers for the Blind, Phi Beta Kappa. President's Certificate of Merit. Home: Alexandria VA Died Oct. 16, 1971.

SWOPE, GUY J., state official; born Meckville, Pa., Dec. 26, 1892; s. Jeremiah Gerhart and Mary Jane (Smith) S.; student pub. schs. of Pennsylvania and Keystone State Teachers College, Kutztown, Pennsylvania, Columbia U.; married Mayme Catherine Gerberich, October 23, 1909 (died May 6, 1948); children—Marjorie Evelyn (Mrs. Leon Guyer), Harold Wesley, Lee Frederick; married Helen Y. Yoshimura, August 13, 1949. Public school teacher, 1909-13; U.S. internal revenue agt., 1913-18; private accountant, 1918-19; pub. accountant, banker, dept. store comptroller, 1919-35; mem. Swope and Nichols, pub. accountants, 1936-54; budget sec. State of Pennsylvania, 1935-37; mem. 75th Congress (1937-39), 19th Pa. Dist.; auditor of Puerto Rico, Jan. 29, 1940-Feb. 2, 1941; gov. of Puerto Rico, 1941; resigned to become dir. Div. of Territories, Dept. of Interior, July 1941. Dem. chmn. Dauphin County, Pa., 1934-37. Entered on active duty as naval officer July, 1943; Deputy Military Gov. of Saipan, 1944. Mem. General MacArthur's staff as Chief, Legislative Div., Aug., 1945 to Aug., 1946. Retired from active service as captain, November, 1946. Returned to Tokyo Feb., 1947 as Chief, Nat. Govern. Div., General MacArthur's Headquarters, in civilian status; spl. asst. to U.S. High Commr. in Germany, and Chief Displaced Populations div., 1949-54; comptroller Lake Asphalt & Petroleum Co. of Pa., Harrisburg, 1955-61; dep. state treas. Commonwealth of Pa., 1961-65; del. Pa. Constl. Conv., 1967-68. Decorated Legion of Merit; recipient Good Citizenship medal for distinguished pub. service S.A.R. C.P.A., Pa. Democrat. Lutheran. Mason (32 deg., Shriner). Home: Harrisburg PA Died July 25, 1969; interred Hamlin Cemetery Fredericksburg PA

SYDNESS, JOSEPH TRUMAN, food chain exec.; b. Randall, Ia., Feb. 22, 1912; s. John S. and Theressa (Handeland) S.; student Am. Sch. Bus., 1929, Am. Inst. Banking, 1929-32, U. Minn., 1935-38, Internat. Accountants Soc., 1938-39; m. Eileen W. Beier, Sept. 24, 1937; children—Joleen Karen, Marcia Lee. With Harriet State Bank, Mpls., 1929-33, Fed. Res. Bank, Mpls., 1933-35, Baker Properties, Inc., Mpls., 1936-40, H.C.J. Peisch, C.P.A., Mpls., 1940-47; with Red Owl Stores, Inc., Hopkins, Minn., 1947-70, corporate sec.; dir. Northwestern Nat. Bank Hopkins. Successively dir., vice chmn., chmn. United Fund, 1959-62; bd. dirs. Aquatenial Assn., Hopkins Music Assn. Pres. Gethsemone Meml. Fund. Mem. Minn. Soc. C.P.A.'s, Ins. Mgmt. Soc., Am. Soc. Corporate Secs., Am. Soc. Corporate Secs., Am. Mgmt. Assn., Hopkins C. of C. Lutheran. Mason (Shriner). Home: Hopkins MN Died 1970.

SYKES, EDWARD, banker and broker; b. New York, N.Y., June 13, 1874; s. Charles and Pauline (Payne) S.; ed. pub. schs.; m. Mary E. O'Brien, June 1903. Made hon. chief of police, City of New York, Nov. 10, 1924; apptd. dep. police commr., 1925; dep. police commr. of Nassau County, N.Y., since 1926; hon. police commr. of Long Beach, L.I., since 1926; trial judge, Nassau County, N.Y. Mem. Police Pension Fund (treas. until 1927); pres. Nassau County Police Relief Assn.; hon. mem. Police Conf. of Nassau County; treas. Long Beach Hosp. Dir. South Shore Trust Co., Rockville Center, N.Y. Trustee Met. Museum of Art. Mem. Municipal Com. for Relief Home Owners, N.Y. City. Mem. N.Y State Assn. Chiefs of Police, Vets. of Foreign Wars Served as pvt. Spanish-Am. War; capt. Vol. Coas Patrol, World War, 1917. Republican. Episcopalian Club: Bankers. Home: 173 N. Grand Av., Baldwin, L NY Office: 19 Rector St., New York NY‡

SYLVESTER, EMMA, author; b. Brooklyn, July 23 1874; d. Daniel and Elizabeth (Wilhelmi) S.; grad. New York Normal Coll., 1892; Pd.M., New York U. Sch. o Pedagogy, 1900; unmarried. Prin. Pub. Sch. No. 35 New York. Mem. N.E.A. Methodist. Club: Principals Author: The Language Readers, including Primer, First Reader, Second Reader, Third Reader, Fourth Reader Fifth Reader, 1905-8. Translator (from the German) Maennel's Auxiliary Education—The Care and Training of Backward Children, 1909. Home: 6 Queen's Av., Flushing, LI NY‡

SYME, JOHN P., business exec.; born Franklin, Mass. Sept. 1, 1904; s. James F. and Edith H. (Gates) S.; grad Moses Brown Sch., Providence, R.I.; M.E., Cornell 1926; m. Helen English, 1927; children—Lochlin Duncan. Engineer Johns-Manville Corp., 1926; gen engring. indsl. products, organizer and mgr. marke analysis dept., organizer indsl. and pub. relations dept. v.p. Johns-Manville Service Corp. (operator of Kan ordnance plant during war), asst. to pres., asst. to chmn bd., vice president executive department; organizer director, pres. and treas. Executive Book Club, 1945-49 Asso. Nat. Indsl. Conf. Bd. Ex.-dir. United Medica Service. Trustee Cornell U., chmn. council 1955-57 Mem. Cornell Soc. Engrs. (past pres.), Sons o Revolution, St. Andrew's Society. Republican. Clubs Cornell (bd. govs.), Union League, University (N.Y.C.) Old Lyme, Essex Essex CT Died Aug. 14, 1970; buried Essex CT

SYMONDS, GARDINER, corporation exec.; b. Pitts. Oct. 15, 1903; s. Nathaniel and Irene (Millberry) S. A.B., Stanford, 1924; M.B.A. with distinction, Harvard 1927; m. Margaret Clover, Aug. 11, 1928 children—Henry Gardiner, Williston Brandreth, Jonathan Taft, Samuel Millberry, Susan Clover. With Ill. Merchants Trust Co., Chgo., 1927-30; asst. treas. Chicago Corp., 1930-32, v.p., 1932-45, dir., 1938-45, with Tenn. Gas Transmission Co., Houston, from 1943 pres., 1943-58, chmn. bd., pres., 1958-60, chmn. bd., chief exec. officer, 1960-68, also dir.; chairman board Tenneco Inc., 1968-71; chairman bd. Houston Nat. Co.; dir. numerous affiliated cos., including Midwestern Gas Transmission Co., E. Tenn. Natural Gas Co., Tenneco Corp., Tenneco Oil Co., Houston Nat. Bank, Tenneco Chemicals, Inc., Newport News Shipbldg. & Dry Dock Co., Phila. Life Ins. Co., Packaging Corp. Am., Tenn. Gas Transmission Co., Kern County Land Co., J.I. Case Co., Walker Mfg. Co.; dir. So. Pacific Co., Gen. Telephone & Electronics Co. Grad. mem. Business Council, Washington; member industry advisory council U.S. Dept. Def. trustee Com. Economic Devel.; board of dirs. Stanford Research Inst.; councillor Nat. Indsl. Conf. Bd.; trustee Tax Found. Trustee Stanford U., Rice University; vis. com. Stanford Sch. Earth Scis. Mem. Assn. Res. City Bankers, Kappa Sigma (past worthy grand master, now chmn. endowment fund trustees). Episcopalian. Clubs: Recess, Links, Board Room (N.Y.C.); Metropolitan (Washington); Attic, University (Chgo.); Pacific-Union, Bohemian (San Francisco); Cypress Point (Monterey, Cal.); Eldorado Country (Palm Desert, Cal.), Bayou, Eagle Lake Rod and Gun, Internat., Ramada, River Oaks, Tejas (Houston); Cotton Bay (Eleuthra, B.W.I.). Home: Houston TX Died June 1, 1971; buried Hinsdale IL

SYMONDS, NATHANIEL MILLBERRY, banker; b. Chgo., Apr. 26, 1906; s. Nathaniel G. and Amy I. (Millberry) S.; student Ia. State Coll., 1923-25; A.B., Leland Stanford Jr. U., 1927; M.B.A., Harvard, 1929; m. Johnetta L. Marshall, Feb. 24, 1932; children—Nathaniel Marshall, Eleanor Margaret (Mrs. Roy F. Deng, Jr.). Joined Northern Trust Co., Chgo., 1929, vice president, 1946-62, senior vice president, 1962-67; director of Tenneco, Incorporated, Houston, Tex. Trustee West Suburban Council, Boy Scouts Am. President Village of Hinsdale, Ill., 1965-68. Mem. Stanford Associates, Kappa Sigma. Clubs: Hinsdale (Ill.) Golf; Chicago, Union League, California (Los Angeles); Bohemian (San Francisco). Home: Hinsdale IL Died Dec. 5, 1968; buried Bronswood Cemetery, Oak Brook IL

SYMONS, THOMAS BADDELEY, dean agr.; b. Easton, Md., Sept. 2, 1880; s. Robert and Susan (Baddeley) S.; B.S., Md. Agrl. Coll., 1902, M.S., 1905, D.Agr., 1918; m. Susie La Roche, Apr. 10, 1907; children—Helen (Mrs. Innis LaRoche Jenkins), Isabel (Mrs. Owen Godwin), Josephine (Mrs. James Robert Troth). Asst. entomologist, Md. Agrl. Coll., 1902-04, state entomologist, 1904-14, dean sch. of Horticulture, 1913-14; dir. of extension, U. of Md. from 1914, acting dean Coll. of Agr., 1937-39, dean, 1939-50, pres. pro tem U. Md., 1953-54; pub. relations dir. Suburban Trust Co., 1950-70, also dir.; dir. Prince Georges Bank & Trust Co. Mem. A.A.A.S., Md. State Hort. Soc., Md. Agrl. Soc., Kappa Alpha, Epsilon Sigma Phi. Democrat. Episcopalian. Club: Rotary. Home: College Park MD Died July 4, 1970; buried St. John's Cemetery Beltsville MD

SYPHERD, WILBUR OWEN, prof. English; b. Zion, Md., June 28, 1877; s. Jacob Owen and Josephine (Draper) S.; A.B., Del. Coll., Newark, 1896; B.S., U. of Pa., 1900; M.S., Harvard, 1901, Ph.D., 1906; LL.D., U. of Del., 1947; unmarried. Prin. schs. Port Penn, Del., 1896-98; instr. English, U. of Wis., 1901-03; prof. English, U. of Del., 1906-46; University professor, 1946-47; University professor emeritus, 1947; teacher summer session, N.Y. Univ., 1910, U. of Calif., 1922, Harvard, 1933. Acting pres. and pres. Univ. of Del., May 1944-June 1946. Sec. local bd. Newcastle County, World War. Mem. Modern Lang. Assn. America, Coll. Conf. on English in Central Atlantic States, Soc. for Promotion Engring. Edn., Nat. Council of Teachers of English, Shakespeare Assn. America, American Association Univ. Profs., Sigma Phi Epsilon, Phi Kappa Phi. Club: University (Philadelphia). Author: Studies in Chaucer's House of Fame, 1907; Handbook of English for Engineers, 1913; Manual of English for Engineers, 1933, revised edit., 1943; The Literature of the English Bible, 1938; The Book of Books, 1944. Editor: The English Bible—Selections, 1921; John Christopherson's Jephthah (with F.H. Forbes), 1928. Home: Newark DE‡

SZIGETI, JOSEPH, violinist; b. Budapest, Hungary, Sept. 5, 1892; s. Adolph and Dora (Faktor) S.; pupil of Jeno Hubay; hon. Mus.D., Acadia U.; m. Wanda Ostrowska, 1919; 1 dau., Mrs. Irene Magaloff. Debut at Royal Acad., Budapest, at age of 11; then played in Berlin and Dresden; lived in England 5 years giving concerts and appeared with Melba and others; toured Europe; tchr. violin master classes Geneva (Switzerland) Conservatory, 1917-24; debut in U.S. as soloist with Phila. Orch., 1925; annual concerts in U.S., 1926-73; made 2 world tours, giving 200 concerts; appearances with major orchs. throughout U.S.; frequent nationwide broadcasts; has also made recordings of an extensive list of standard works by Mercury Rec. Corp., Columbia Records, and Vanguard Rec. Corp.; concert tour, Japan, 1953, S.A., 1954; series 20th Century Master Sonatas in N.Y.C., Chgo., San Francisco, Phila., others, 1956-57. Decorated comdr. French Legion of Honor; officer Hungarian Order of Merit; comdr. Belgian Order of Leopold. Mem. Royal Acad. Music London (hon.). Contbr. articles to musical jours. Featured in Warner Bros. film Hollywood canteen; transcontinental tours. Author: With Strings Attached, 1947; A Violinist's Notebook; Beethoven's Violin Sonatas; Szigeti on the Violin, 1969. Address: Baugy sur Clarens (Vaud) Switzerland Died Feb. 20, 1973.

TAFT, KENDALL B(ENARD), educator; b. Hamilton, N.Y., Jan. 22, 1899; s. George Wheaton and Jessie (Humpstone) T.; A.B., State U. Ia., 1920; A.M., Washington U., St. Louis, 1927; Ph.D., U. of Chicago, 1936; m. Martha Kathryn Sulem, Sept. 5, 1936. Head English dept. Rio Grande (O.) Coll., 1919-21; teacher of English in secondary schs., Mo. and Tex., 1922-27; instr. Washington U., 1927-30, asst. prof. English, 1930-31; asso. prof. English, Central Y.M.C.A. Coll., Chicago, 1933-37, prof. Am. lit., 1937-45, chmn. English dept., 1942-45; prof. Am. lit. and chmn. dept. English and speech, Roosevelt University, 1945-66, professor Am. literature emeritus, 1966-72; lecturer, Northwestern U., 1949; vis. prof. English, N.Y.U., summer, 1950. Served with Central Machine Gun Officers Training Sch., Camp Hancock, Ga., 1918; 1st lt., O.R.C., 1923-33. Sec. bd. trustees Roosevelt U., 1950-53, trustee, 1962-66, marshal, 1945-66, research fellow, 1958. Mem. Am. Studies Association, American Association University Professors, Modern Lang. Assn., Nat. Council Tchrs. English, Coll. English Assn. (pres. Chgo. area 1951-53), N.Y. Hist. Soc. Text editor; J. B. Priestley's, The Good Companions, 1930. Editor: College Readings in Contemporary Thought (with J. F. McDermott and D. O. Jensen), 1929; Sex in the Arts (with J. F. McDermott), 1932; Contemporary Opinion (with J. F. McDermott and D. O. Jensen), 1933. Author: Technique of Composition (with J. F. McDermott and D. O. Jensen), 1931, rev. 1960; English Communication (with others), 1943; Minor Knickerbockers, 1947; History of John Wiley & Sons (with others), 1957. Contbr. articles and revs. to Am. Lit. Address: Winona Lake IN Died Jan. 25, 1972; buried Oakwood Cemetery, Warsaw IN

TAFT, KINGSLEY A., judge; b. Cleveland, O., July 19, 1903; s. Frederick L. Taft and Mary Alice (Arter) T.; A.B., Amherst Coll., 1925, LL.D., 1950; LL.B., Harvard, 1928, LL.D., Baldwin Wallace College, 1952, Kenyon Coll., 1969; married Louise Dakin, Sept. 14, 1927; children—Charles K., Kingsley Jr., Sheldon A., David D. In practice of law in Cleveland with McKeehan, Merrick, Arter and Stewart and predecessor firm, 1928-39, partner, 1940-48; dir. Land Title Guarantee and Trust Co. of Cleveland, 1938-63. Mem. Ohio House of Reps., 1933-34. Elected U.S. senator from Ohio, Nov. 1946 to fill unexpired term of Mr. Justice Burton; judge Supreme Court of Ohio, 1948-62, chief justice Supreme Court of Ohio, 1963-70. Trustee Baldwin-Wallace College. Served in Army of the United States, 1942-46, advanced through the grades to major, 1945. Awarded Army Commendation Medal with oak leaf cluster, 1946. Mem. Shaker Heights Bd. of Edn., 1940-42, pres., 1942. Member American Law Institute, Cleveland, Am., Ohio, Cuyahoga, Columbus bar assns., Am. Legion, Sons American Revolution, American Judicature Society, Phi Beta Kappa, Phi Kappa Psi, Phi Alpha Delta. Republican. Methodist. Mason. Clubs: University, Rocky Fork (Columbus); Union (Cleveland). Associate editor Harvard Law Review, 1927-28. Home: Columbus OH Died Mar. 28, 1970; buried Lake View Cemetery Cleveland OH

TAGGART, DAVID ALEXANDER, lawyer, banker; b. Wooster, O., Apr. 29, 1898; s. Frank and Elizabeth (Wallace) T.; A.B., Harvard, 1920, LL.B., 1923; m. Ruth Williams, May 4, 1929; children—James W., David W. Admitted to Ohio bar, 1924, practiced in Wooster, 1924-70; sr. partner firm Taggart, Cox, Moore & Hays, 1944-70; dir. Wayne County Nat. Bank, Wooster, 1932-70, pres., 1947-63; sec. Wooster Products, Ins., 1942-52, dir., 1942-70; sec., dir. D.C. Curry Lumber Co., 1949-70; dir. United Steel Fabricators, Inc., 1950-64, sec., 1957-64; dir., Magni Power Co., 1953-70, sec., 1953-68. Trustee Wooster Pub. Library and Museum, 1923-46, asst. curator, 1926-55; sec. Pee Wee Hollow Boy Scout Camp, 1950-70; hon. mem. Nat. council Boy Scouts Am., 1955-57. Trustee Wooster Cemetery Assn., 1935-64. Recipient Silver Beaver award Boy Scouts Am., 1953. Mem. Beta Theta Pi. Republican. Presbyn. (trustee 1942-45, 48-51). Mason. Clubs: Garden Study, Century (Wooster). Home: Wooster OH Sept. 24, 1970.

TAGGART, MARION AMES, author; b. Haverhill, Mass.; d. of Alfred Gilchrist and Sarah Porter (Ames) T.; ed. entirely at home, owing to delicate health. Contbr. since 1882 of verses, stories and articles to mags. Author: The Blissylvania Post Office, 1897; Three Girls and Especially One, 1897; By Branscome River, 1897; Aser, the Shepherd, 1899; Bezaleel, 1899; Loyal Blue and Royal Scarlet, 1899; The Wyndham Girls, 1902; Miss Lochinvar, 1902; At Aunt Anna's, 1903; The Little Grey House, 1904; Nut Brown Joan, 1905; Six Girls and Bob, 1906; Daddy's Daughters, 1906; Miss Lochinvar's Return, 1906; Pussy Cat Town, 1906; Six Girls and the Tea Room, 1907; The Daughters of the Little Grey House, 1907; The Doctor's Little Girl, 1907; Six Girls Growing Older, 1908; Six Girls and the Seventh One, 1909; Sweet Nancy (sequel to The Doctor's Little Girl), 1909; Betty Gaston, the Seventh Girl, 1910; Six Girls and Betty, 1911; Nancy, the Doctor's Little Partner, 1911; Six Girls Grown Up, 1912; Nancy Porter's Opportunity, 1912; The Little Aunt, 1913; Her Daughter Jean, 1913; Beth's Wonder Winter, 1914; Nancy and the Coggs Twins, 1914; Beth's Old Home, 1915; The Garden Girls, 1916; Captain Sylvia, 1917; A Pilgrim Maid—A Story of Plymouth Colony, 1920; The Annes, 1921; The Jack-in-the-Box Books, 4 vols., 1921; Who Is Sylvia? 1922; No Handicap, 1922; The Cable, 1923. Home: 901 N. Front St., Harrisburg PA‡

TALBERT, SAMUEL STUBBS, educator; b. Brinson, Ga., May 6, 1917; s. William Gary and Myra (Stubbs) T.; B.A. in Journalism, U. Fla., 1941, M.A., 1947; Ph.D., State U. Ia., 1952; m. Frances Selzer, Nov. 8, 1944; children—Michael John, Eugenia Adeline, Frances Susan, Elizabeth Joanne, Patricia Ann, Mary Jane, Virginia Fay. Editor, Warm Springs (Ga.) Mirror, 1936-38; corr. Sebring (Fla.) American, 1938-40; editor Univ. News, U. Fla., 1940-41; instr. journalism Lehigh U., 1947-48, U. Ia., 1949-50; asst. prof. journalist U. Miss., 1948-49, prof., chmn. dept., 1951-72; editor Ole Miss Rev., 1955-56; columnist Publisher's Auxiliary, 1956; author nat. syndicated column. Local Business, 1957-72; copy editor Comml. Appeal, 1960; corr. Clarion Ledger, 1962. Dir. Advt. Inst., Acad. Press. Served to lt. comdr. USNR, 1941-46. Mem. Miss. Journalism Assn. (exec. sec.), Miss. Scholastic Press Assn. (dir.), Assn. Edn. Journalism, Am. Soc. Journalism Sch. Adminstr., Radio and Television News Dirs. Assn., Phi Kappa Phi, Sigma Delta Chi, Alpha Delta Sigma, Kappa Tau Alpha. Author: (musical comedy) Enough Said, 1942; (book) Case Studies in Local Advertising, 1959; Reaching Alumni, 1962; The Amateur, 1963; also booklets. Home: Oxford MS Died Apr. 25, 1972; buried Oxford MS

TALBOT, EDITH ARMSTRONG, author; b. Stockbridge, Mass., Aug. 30, 1872; d. Samuel Chapman and Emma Dean (Walker) Armstrong; ed. Miss Mackie's Sch., Newburgh, N.Y., 1887-89, Wellesley Coll., mus. course, 1890-91, Mrs. Shaw's Sch., Boston, 1889-90, Teachers Coll., New York, 1894-96; m. Winthrop Tisdale Talbot, M.D., of Boston, Sept. 19, 1896 (divorced 1915). Episcopalian. Author: Samuel Chapman Armstrong, a Biographical Study, 1904; Lessons in Meditation, 1921. Contbr. articles and poems on religious topics to mags. Lecturer. Address: E.P. Dutton & Co., New York NY‡

TALBOT, GUY WEBSTER, pub. utility exec.; b. Centerville, Mich., Aug. 12, 1873; s. Charles R. and Sara Folsom (Webster) T.; ed. Coll. of Emporia, Kan.; m. Geraldine Wallace, Oct. 14, 1903; children—Sara Jane (Mrs. Charles Gravson Dimon), Prudence Gertrude (Mrs. H. G. Shaler), Guy Webster, Jr. With C.,B.&Q. Ry. Co., Des Moines, Ia., 1891-94, Des Moines Northern & Western Ry., 1894-98, Ia. Central Ry., Marshalltown, Ia., 1898-1901, Peoria & Pekin Terminal Ry. Co., Peoria, Ill., 1901-06, Astoria & Columbia River R.R. Co. and Corvallis & Eastern R.R. Co., Portland, Ore., 1906; v.p. and gen. mgr. Ore. Electric Ry. Co., 1907-10; chmn. Portland Gas & Coke Co., Elec. Products Corp. of Ore.; dir. Pacific Power & Light Co., Portland Gasoline Co. (A Tex. Co.). Former chmn. Portland Waterfront Development Com., finance com., Portland Symphony Orchestra; ex-pres. Portland Rose Soc. Mem. Portland Chamber Comfinance com., Portland Symphony Orchestra; ex-pres. Portland Rose Soc. Mem. Portland Chamber Commerce. Republican. Episcopalian. Clubs: Arlington, Press, Multnomah Amateur Athletic, Waverly Country. Home: 245 Portland OR‡

TALBOT, M(URRELL) W(ILLIAMS), forester, ecologist; b. Appleton City, Mo., Aug. 18, 1889; s. LeRoy Hitt and Lettie E. (Williams) T.; B.S., U. Mo., 1913; postgrad. U.S. Dept. Agr. Grad. Sch., 1931; m. Zenaida Merriam, Oct. 27, 1928; children—Lee Merriam, Zenaida (Mrs. William Penn Mott III). Various positions U.S. Forest Service and Bur. Plant Industry, 1913-31; sr. ecologist charge range research Pacific S.W. Forest & Range Expt. Sta., Berkeley, Cal., 1931-55, acting dir., 1941-45, also dir., 1946-55, cons., 1955-72; cons. Govt. Spain, Pack Found., Salt River Basin, Ariz., State Cal.; collaborator U.S. Department of Agriculture. Member Alameda County Grand Jury. Served to 2d lt. F.A., U.S. Army, 1918. Recipient Spl. Meritorious award U.S. Dept. Agr., 1945, Alumnus of year citation Merit U. Mo., 1959. Fellow A.A.A.S.; mem. Am. Soc. Range Mgmt. (pres. 1963), Soc. Am. Foresters, Ecol. Soc. Am., Wilderness Soc., Alpha Zeta, Xi Sigma Pi. Republican. Conglist. Mason (32 deg.). Clubs: Faculty University California, Outlook (Berkeley); Commonwealth (San Francisco); Hillside (Berkeley). Author articles in field. Home: Berkeley CA Died Jan. 12, 1972.

TALBOT, WINIFRED LUELLA WINTER (MRS. JOHN E. TALBOT), church worker, author; b. Wabasha, Minn., Jan. 4, 1894; d. Daniel and Emma T. (Quisel) Winter; student, U. Minn., 1919-22; m. John E. Talbot, June 29, 1923; children—Jeanne (Mrs. Albert Drobnick), Lincoln, Marilyn (Mrs. Dwight Hill). Elementary tchr., 1912-14, 16-18; ch. sec. Wesley Found., 1918-20; with Univ. Coop., 1919-23; pub. sch. tchr., 1920-23. Organizer women's prayer group Aldersgate Meth. Ch., Mpls., 1957, exec. bd., 1957-66, historian ch. prayer group, 1959-70; organizer ch. library, 1958, sec. library staff, 1958-70. Named Woman of Year, St. Cloud Times, 1950; recipient citation (with husband) in appreciation of exceptional service and leadership in advancing edn1. and community activities St. Cloud State Coll., 1968; award for vol. talks to children Mpls. parochial and pub. schs., 1967, 68. Mem. Nat. League Am. Pen Women (br. treas. 1965-67), Am. Assn. U. Pen Women. Author: Happy Hospital Surprises, 1961; Denny's Friend Rags, 1964. Home: Minneapolis MN Died Feb. 22, 1970.

TALIAFERRO, HARRY MONROE, corp. exec.; b. Boonville, Mo., 1882; s. James Edwin and Frances (Monroe) T.; student pub. schs., Boonville, Mo.; m. Mary Littlepage Williams, Nov. 17, 1909; children—Frances Monroe (Mrs. Edward J. Frey), William Muir, James Gardner, Mary Jane (Mrs. Neil Weathers, Jr.), Harry Monroe. With Am. Seating Co., 1911-61, pres. 1929-58, chairman of the bd., 1958-59. Member of the Grand Rapids Safety Council, pres. 1915-17; director of YMCA. Member advisory board Detroit Ordnance District, World War II; mem. local appeal bd., SSS, World War II; former mem. Fed. Adv. Council, Social Security Bd.; mem. Welfare and Relief Study Commn., Mich., Social Security Study Commn., Mich., Mich. Pub. Edn. Study Commn., United Health and Welfare Fund Mich. (state campaign chmn. 1949-50). Member of the board of trustees Michigan College Foundation. Mem. C. of C. (pres. 1939-41), Mich. Mfrs. Assn., N.A.M. (former dir.), U.S. C. of C., Soc. Mental Hygiene. Mason. Clubs: Rotary (past pres.), Peninsular, Kent Country, University (Grand Rapids); Indian. Home: East Grand Rapids MI Died Dec. 1968.

TALLE, HENRY O(SCAR), congressman; b. near Albert Lea, Minn., Jan. 12, 1892; s. John and Anna (Ovri) T.; A.B., Luther Coll., 1917; student U. Minn., summers 1916, 19, Boston Univ., Emerson Coll. of Oratory, 1921, Univ. of Chicago, 1925-27, 1931-32, summers, 1922, 24, 28, 30, 33; D.C.L., Luther College, 1950; married to Edith Margaret Huset, 1920 (died December 21, 1938); children—Helen Elaine (Mrs. Keith Allan Crown, Jr.), Marjorie (Mrs. Jack C. Merriman), Mary (Mrs. William Penn Tilton, Jr.); m. 2d, Gladyce B. Carey, 1950. tchr. and supt. of schs., Rugby and Rolette, N.D., 1917-20; teacher, Luther Acad., Albert Lea, Minn., 1920-21; prof. of economics, Luther Coll., Decorah, Ia., 1921-38, treas. of coll., 1932-38; mem. 76th and 77th Congresses (1939-43), 4th Iowa District, 78th to 85th Congresses, from 2d Iowa Dist.; asst. adminstr. for program policy Housing and Home Finance Agency, Washington, 1959-61. Del. to confs. Interparliamentary Union, Oslo, Norway, 1939, Cairo, Egypt, 1947, Rome, Italy, 1948, Stockholm, 1949, Dublin, 1950, Istanbul, Turkey, 1951,

Bern, Switzerland, 1952, Washington, 1953, Vienna, Austria, 1954; chmn. delegations to Helsinki, Finland, 1955, Bangkok, Thailand, 1956, London, Eng., 1957, Rio de Janeiro, Brazil, 1958; permanent sec. Am. group, 1949; chmn. delegation from U.S. Ho. of Reps., Conf. Commonwealth Parliamentary Assn., Bermuda, 1948. Served in U.S. Navy, 1917-19; commd. ensign, 1918. Mem. Am. Legion, Vets of Foreign Wars. Republican. Lutheran. Contbr. to ednl., polit. jours. Home: Washington DC also Decorah IA Died Mar. 14, 1969; buried Arlington Nat. Cemetery, Arlington VA

TALLEY, BASCOM DESTREHAN, JR., lawyer; b. Bogalusa, La., Jan. 18, 1916; s. Bascom Destrehan and Maude Hermine (Gentry) T.; B.A., Tulane U., 1937, LL.B., 1939; m. Imogene Wilson, July 29, 1943; children—Bascom Destrehan, Jean, Morris Wilson, James Edmund. Admitted to La. bar, 1939, since practiced in Bogalusa; mem. firm Talley, Anthony, Hughes & Knight, 1940-71. Pres. Columbia Road Land Co., 1947-71; sec. Bogalusa Daily News, Inc., 1954-71, Bogalusa Realty Co., Inc., 1950-71; chmn. bd. Parish Nat. Bank, 1968-71. Mem. Council Better La., Pub. Affairs Research Council; president La. Civil Service League. Commnr. edn., Bogalusa, 1942-46; chmn. planning commnr., Bogalusa, 1956-59. Mem. council La. Law Inst., 1954-71. Mem. bd. La. Assn. for Mental Health. Mem. Am. (mem. circuit com. on profl. greivance, standing com. on legal assistance for servicemen), La. (pres. sect. local bar orgns. 1951-55, bd. govs. 1953-55, chmn. com. pub. relations 1955-56, v.p. 1962-63, pres. 1963-64) bar assns., Am. Judicature Soc., Tulane Law Alumni Assn. (pres. 1958-59); Order Coif (hon.). Methodist (ofcl. bd., trustee). Home: Bogalusa LA Died July 27, 1971; buried Ponemah Cemetery Bogalusa LA

TALLMAN, CLAY, commissioner Gen. Land Office; b. Ionia Co., Mich., 1874; s. H. C. and Harriet T.; B.S., Mich. Agrl. Coll., 1895; studied U. of Colo.; LL.B., U. of Mich., 1904; m. Jean S. Robertson, of Wyoming, 1909. In pub. sch. work, 1895-02; began law practice, Rhyolite, Nev., 1905; mem. Nev. Senate, 1908-12; chmn. Dem. State Central Com., Nev., 1910-11; Dem. candidate for Congress from Nev., 1912 (defeated by 69 votes); apptd. chief law officer Reclamation Service, Apr. 1, 1913; commr. Gen. Land Office, June, 1913—. Home: Tonopah NV Address: Gen. Land Office, Washington DC‡

TAMIROFF, AKIM, actor; b. Russia; ed. Moscow Art Theatre; m. Tamara; came to U.S., 1923. Actor in motion pictures, 1934-72; movies include His Butler's Sister, Miracle of Morgan's Creek, Can't Help Singing, Pardon My Past, The Gangster, My Girl Tisa, For Whom the Bell Tolls, Desert Legion, You Know What Sailors Are, They Who Dare, Black Sheep, Lord Jim, Disputed Passage, Queen Christina, The Captain Hates the Sea, Anthony Adverse, King of the Gamblers, The Great Gambini, The Buccaneer, Spawn of the North, Ride a Crooked Mile, Tenth Avenue Angel, Union Pacific, Tortilla Flat, The Magnificient Fraud, The Way of All Flesh, The Corsican Brothers, The Bridge of San Luis Rey, Dragon Seed, Fiesta, Anastasia, Me and the Colonel, Ocean's Eleven, Romanoff and Juliet, The Trial, Topkapi, Tenderly, Funeral in Berlin, Outpost in Morocco, many others; guest star appearances on TV. Palm Springs CA Died Sept. 17, 1972.

TAMM, IGOR Y., physicist; b. Vladivistok, USSR, July 8, 1895; s. Eugen and Olga (Davydova) T.; grad. Moscow State U., 1918, Dr. Physics and Math. Scis., USSR, 1933; m. Natalie Shuiskaia, Sept. 16, 1917; children—Irene, Eugen. Tchr. physics, univs. and tech. instns., Simpheropal and Odessa, 1919-22; with U. Moscow, from 1924, prof., from 1927, chair theoretical physics, 1930-37; head theoretical dept. Lebedev's Physical Inst., Acad. Scis. of USSR, Moscow, from 1934; sr. physician virology and medicine Rockefeller U., from 1967; research in quantum theory, also controlled thermonuclear reactions. Recipient (with P. Cerenkov, I. Frank), Nobel prize in physics for discovery and interpretation of Cerenkov's radiation, 1958; Lomonssov Medal, Academy Scis. USSR, 1968. Mem. Am. Acad. Arts and Scis. (foreign member), Acad. Scis. USSR, Acad. Scis. of Poland. Address: Moscow USSR Died Apr. 1971.

TANNER, EUGENE SIMPSON, clergyman, educator; b. Union Star, Mo., Jan. 13, 1907; s. John Bradley and Harriet Louise (Simpson) T.; A.B., Midland Coll., Fremont, Neb., 1929; A.M., U. of Chicago, 1931, Ph.D., 1934; B.D., McCormick Theol. Sem., Chicago, 1932, New Testament fellow 1932-33; student Union Theol. Sem., summer 1940, Columbia, summer 1940; student University of Edinburgh, 1957-58; married to Ada Charlotte Thomas, June 20, 1935;children—Joan Elizabeth, Jane Ellen, John Edward, Julia Eleanor. Instructor in religion Wesley Coll., N.D., 1934-37; asst. prof. religion U. of Tulsa, 1937-39, asso. prof., 1939-43, prof., 1943-53; professor of religion and head of department of religion College of Wooster (Ohio) 1953-67, professor religion, 1967-70. Ordained to ministry of Presbyterian Church, 1932. Mem. Soc. Bibl. Lit. and Exegesis. Nat. Assn. Bibl. Instrs., Am. Assn. Univ. Profs., Am. Oriental Soc., Archaeological Institute of America, American Schools of Oriental Research. Author: Types of Religious Experience Reflected in the Christian Liturgy of the First Century, 1937; The Nazi Christ, 1942; Edinburgh Year, 1962; A Night in Ephesus. Contbr. to Jour. of Bible and Religion, Jour. of Bibl. Lit., Westminster Adult Bible Class, Social Progress, Books Abroad, Presbyn. Tribune, Presbyn. Outlook. Contbr. revs. of books to learned jours. in 6 langs., also to philos. abstracts. Home: Wooster OH Died June 15, 1970; inurned Chautauqua NY

TANNER, HAROLD BROOKS, lawyer; b. Pawtucket, R.I., Oct. 30, 1887; s. Willard Brooks and Annie Tingley (Dunlop) T.; Ph.B., Brown U., 1909, LL.D., 1949; LL.B., Harvard, 1912; m. Kate E. Cushman, Oct. 15, 1913; children—Ralph Cushman, Earl Chapin. Admitted to R.I. bar, 1911, practiced in Providence, corporate, banking, taxation and real estate; sr. partner Tillinghast, Collins & Tanner, from 1950; chancellor Brown U., 1952-64; dir. Mchts. Cold Storage & Warehouse Co., 1947-64. Member Commn. on Uniform Comml. Code, 1959-60. Member Rhode Island (president 1946-49) bar associations, Primaries and Corrupt Practices, 1939-40. Trustee Brown U., Greater Providence Y.M.C.A. Mem. Am., Rhode Island (president 1946-49) bar assns., Inst. Jud. Adminstrns., Soc. Colonial Wars (past gov. R.I.). Bapt. (moderator First Bapt. Ch. in Am., 1943-53). Clubs: Art, Hope, Agawam Hunt Providence RI Died Dec. 25, 1968; buried Swan Point Cemetery, Providence RI

TANNER, JACOB, religious educator; b. Molde, Norway, Oct. 15, 1865; s. Johannes Arnold and Anne Bergitte (Indholm) T.; student Molde Latin Sch., 1885-87; B.A., Christiania University, M.A., 1889, graduate of Theology (B.D.), 1892; S.T.D., Augustana Theology Seminary, 1921; married Ingeborg Sophie Aaroe, April 6, 1893 (died 1935); children—Olaf John (deceased), Arvid Biarne, Idar Jacob, Agnar Sverre, Bergliot Solveig (dec.). Ordained Luth. ministry, 1893; pastor various chs. in Ia., N.Y., Wis., Canada and N.D., 1893-1916; financial sec., Fairview Hosp., Minneapolis, 1907-09; teacher Concordia Coll., Moorhead, Minn., 1916-24; teacher dogmatics and Christian edn. Luther Theol. Sem., St. Paul, 1925-38; ret.; teacher of Bible, Waldorf Coll., Forest City, Ia., since 1944. Mem. Com. of Zion Soc. of Israel, 1900-08, pres. 1902-08; mem. Com. on Ordination, 1902-03; mem. Bd. Home Missions, 1915-17, Bd. Elementary Christian Edn., 1920-32. Editor Lutheraneren, 1924-25; editor-in-chief new graded Sunday Sch. lesson material prepared by The Norwegian Luth. Church of America, 1931-41. Author: Manual of Bible Teachings, 1929; Ten Studies in Biblical History; My Faith; The Senior Confirmation Book; The Junior Confirmation Book; Atonement and Forgiveness, 1948; also wrote many pamphlets on Bible teachings, catechism, etc. Co-editor Jour. of Am. Luth. Conf., 1936-39. Has collected translations of Luther's Small Catechism in 135 langs. Home: Forest City IA*‡

TANNER, ROLLIN HARVELLE, univ. prof.; b. Oberlin, O., Dec. 3, 1874; s. Henry Truman and Olive J. (Jason) T.; grad. Central High Sch., Cleveland, O., 1892; grad. Forest City Business Coll., 1892; A.B., Adelbert Coll. (Western Reserve U.), 1896; studied U. of Chicago, summers 1907, 08; Ph.D., Princeton, 1912; m. Mabel Elizabeth Phypers, May 8, 1901. Master, Kenyon Mil. Acad., Gambier, O., 1896-97; with Browning, King & Co., clothiers, Cleveland, 1897-1902; teacher and head dept. classics, Central High Sch., 1902-10; fellow in classics, Princeton U., 1910-11, instr., 1911-12; prof. Greek and Latin, Ill. Coll., Jacksonville, Ill., 1912-17; financial rep. of Gaston, Williams &Wigmore, New York, in S.A., 1917-18; prof. Greek, Denison U., Granville, O., 1918-23, also dean; asso. prof. classics, New York U., 1923-25, prof. classics, 1925-30, prof. edn. and classics and head department of foreign langs. of School of Edn., 1930-43, prof. emeritus since 1943; visiting prof. mathematics, Mary Washington Coll., 1943-44, professor of classics since 1945. Mem. Archeological Institute of America, American Philological Association, American Classical League, Classical Assn. Atlantic States, Classical Assn. Middle West and South, N.E.A., Am. Assn. Univ. Profs., Univ. Assn. for the Study of Calendar Reform, Nat. Travel Club, Phi Beta Kappa, Pi Gamma Mu, Phi Delta Kappa, Delta Tau Delta, etc.; pres. Ohio Classical Conf., 1922-23; sec. Classical Assn. Middle West and South, 1920-23. Baptist. Contbr. to Trans. and Procs. American Philol. Assn., Classical Philology, etc. Home: Fredericksburg VA‡

TAPLEY, WALTER MOORE, JR., justice; b. Rockland, Me., July 2, 1898; s. Walter Moore and Katie I. (Nixon) T.; ed. pub. schs., Me.; m. Olive W. Barker, Nov. 24, 1921; 1 dau., Gay. Admitted to Me. bar, 1921, since practiced in Portland; asst. county atty., 1928-30, county atty., 1930-36; reporter decisions, Me., 1937-41; justice Superior Ct. Me., 1954, Supreme Ct. Me., 1954-69; 1st pres. South Portland Bank & Trust Co. (Me.). Mem. Am. Judicature Soc., Me. Bar Assn. Republican. Home: Portland ME Died Nov. 23, 1971; buried Forest City Cemetery, Portland ME

TAPLINGER, RICHARD JACQUES, publisher; b. Phila., Apr. 14, 1911; s. Matthew and Eve (Brick) T.; m. Kate Serlin, Jan. 2, 1938 (div. 1968); children—Thomas Matthew, Lee Serlin; m. 2d, Cecily Theresse Lent, Aug. 28, 1970. Stock clk. J.B. Lippincott Pub. Co., 1929-32; salesman Emerson Books, Inc., 1932-37; advt. mgr. Little, Brown &Co., 1937-39; advt. and publicity mgr. William Morrow & Co., Co., 1937-39; advt. and publicity mgr. William Morrow & Co., Inc., 1939-42; dir. Dick Taplinger Pub. Relations, N.Y.C., 1946-64; pres. Asia Book Club, N.Y.C., 1955-57, Taplinger Pub. Co., Inc., N.Y.C., 1955-73. Publs. cons. Asia Found., 1953-70; mem. Nat. Book Awards Planning Com., 1951-63; mem. Writers Bd. for World Govt., 1953-63. Served with AUS, 1942-46. Mem. Pubs. Ad. Club. (pres. 1956-57), P.E.N. (exec. bd. Am. 1952-73). Clubs: Dutch Treat, Overseas Press (N.Y.C.). Author: (with J.Y. Henderson) Circus Doctor, 1951; (with Damco Dhotre) Wild Animal New York City NY Died Feb. 13, 1973.

TAPP, SIDNEY C., lawyer, author; b. on farm in N.C., Sept. 5, 1870; s. Ruffin R. and Mailisa (Dunagan) T.; Ph.B., Furman U., S.C., 1892; post-grad. course U. of Chicago; unmarried. Admitted to bar, 1893. Dem. presdl. elector Ga., 1905; Liberal party nominee for President of U.S., 1908. Baptist. Author: The Story of Anglo-Saxon Institutions, or the Development of Constitutional Government, 1904; The Struggle, 1905; The Story of the French Revolution; The Truth About the Bible; The Sexology of the Bible; The Bible—the Law of Spirit and the Law of Sex; The Secret of the Confessional; Why Jesus Was a Man and Not a Woman. Address: Box 710, Kansas City MO‡

TARR, LESLIE RILEY, lawyer; b. Santa Barbara, Cal., Nov. 1, 1897; s. Orrin W. and Donna (Talbott) T.; LL.B., U. So.Cal., 1923; m. Christine Langdon, Sept. 18, 1926; children—Patricia (Mrs. Leavitt), Barbara (Mrs. Kroninger). Admitted to Cal. bar; city pros. City of Glendale, 1923-26; dep. county counsel County of Los Angeles, 1926-28; pvt. practice of law, 1926-66; mem. firm Holbrook, Tarr & O'Neil, Los Angeles, now ret. Served with USNR, World War I. Mem. Bar of Cal., Los Angeles County Bar Assn., Am. Legion, Phi Alpha Delta. Order of Coif. Baptist. Mason (32 deg., Shriner). Elk. Home: Cameo Shores CA Died July 26, 1972.

TARRANT, WILLIAM THEODORE, naval officer (ret.); b. Black Hawk, Miss., July 28, 1878; s. Edward William and Anne Wilson (Spencer) T.; ed., U.S Naval Acad., 1898; m. Ruth Gibson, June 13, 1906. Commd. ensign U.S. Navy, 1900 and advanced through grades to vice adm., 1936; comdt. 11th Naval Dist., 1933-36; comdr. scouting force, U.S. Fleet, 1936-38; comdt. 1st Naval Dist., 1938-42; ret., 1942, recalled to active duty, 1943-46. Episcopalian. Club: Army Navy (Washington). Home: Washington DC Died Aug. 2, 1972.

TASHLIN, FRANK, writer, director; b. N.J., Feb. 19, 1913; Cartoonist for Walt Disney, Leon Schlesinger, Screen Gems; syndicated comic scrip Von Boring, 1934-37; motion pictures include Variety Girl, Fuller Brush Man, The Paleface, Miss Grant Takes Richmond, Woman of Distinction; screen play Kill the Umpire, Fuller Brush Girl; dir., collaborator screen play Son of Paleface, Artists and Models; dir. Hollywood or Bust; dir., collaborator, screen play Lieutenant Wore Skirts; producer, dir., collaborator screen play Girl Can't Help It; producer, dir., screen play Will Success Spoil Rock Hunter?; screen play, dir. Rock-a Bye Baby, The Geisha Boy; producer, dir. Save One for Me; dir., screen play Cinderella; collaborator screen play, dir. Bachelor Flat; dir., screen play Who's Minding the Store; dir. It's Only Money, The Man from the Diner's Club, The Alphabet Murders, Glass Bottom Boat; screen play, dir. The Disorderly Orderly. Address: Los Angeles CA Died May 1972.

TATE, H. THEODORE, treasurer of United States; b. Rutledge, Tenn., Dec. 28, 1875; s. Allen S. and Arianna (Peck) T.; ed. Madison Acad., Rutledge; m. Margaret L. Ritchie, Aug. 6, 1902. With gen. offices Southern Ry. Co., Washington, D.C., 1900-08; entered Govt. service, 1908; treas. of U.S. since Apr. 24, 1928. Republican. Presbyn. Mason (K.T.). Home: 1453 Belmont St. Address: U.S. Treasury Dept., Washington DC‡

TATE, JACK BERNARD, lawyer; b. Bolivar, Tenn., Aug. 14, 1902; s. Robert Wood and Louise (Sevestre) T.; A.B., University of Tennessee, 1924; LL.B., Yale, 1926, M.A. (honorary), 1954; LL.M., George Washington University Law School, 1927; married Elizabeth Thomas Nelson, June 16, 1928; children—Robert Wood, Thomas Nelson. Legal editor U.S. Daily, 1926-28; asst. legal adviser, Dept. of State, 1928-34; div. counsel Nat. Recovery Adminstrn., 1934-35, div. adminstr., 1935-36; asst. gen. counsel Social Security Bd., 1936-38, gen. counsel, 1938-39; gen. counsel, Fed. Security Agency, 1939-47, dep. legal adviser Dept. State, 1947-54; legal advisor to U.S. delegations to 4th-6th regular sessions Gen. Assembly U.N., 1949-51; alternate U.S. del. 9th Internat. Conf. Am States, Bogota, 1948; prof. of law, N.Y.U. Law Sch., 1954; asso. dean, prof. law at Yale Law School, 1954-68. Fellow of Silliman College, Yale. Member Am. branch Internat. Law Assn., Am. Bar Assn., Tenn. and D.C. bars, American Society of Internat. Law, Phi Beta Kappa, Phi Delta Phi, Corby Court. Contbr. to legal periodicals. Home: New Haven CT Died Mar. 21, 1968; buried Polk Cemetery Bolivar TN

TATE, JOHN MATTHEW, JR., mfr.; b. Pittsburgh, Pa., May 31, 1870; s. John M. and Sarah A. (Stouffer) T.; ed. Sewickley (Pa.) Acad.; m. Ernestine Payne, of Titusville, Pa., Mar. 16, 1899. Entered employ of Westinghouse Electric Co., Pittsburgh, 1888, and advanced to asst. gen. supt.; resigned, 1896, to become gen. mgr. Pleasant Valley Traction Co. and asst. to pres. United Traction Co., Pittsburgh; organizer, 1898, Tate-Jones & Co., engrs. and mfrs., of which has been pres. since incorporation, 1899. Republican. Presbyn. Clubs: Duquesne, Allegheny Country. Home: Pine Road, Sewickley PA Office: 545 William Penn Way, Pittsburgh PA‡

TAUB, EDWARD ALLEN, corrugated paper co. exec.; b. N.Y.C., Nov. 24, 1907; s. Max and Saddie (Diamond) T.; spl. courses in time and motion study, indsl. relations N.Y.U.; m. Rose Stoller, Nov. 27, 1927; children—Irwin M., Ronald H., Lynn M. Designer Interstate Corrugated Paper Co., 1924-25; designer to prodn. mgr. Gibraltar Corrugated Paper Co., 1925-32; prodn. mgr. Container Corp. Am., 1932-33; prodn. mgr. to v.p. charge prodn. Gibraltar Corrugated Paper Co., North Bergen, N.J., 1933-58, dir., 1946-59, v.p., charge prodn. display div., Jersey City, 1956-57; v.p. charge mfg. A & P Corrugated Box Corp., Inc., Lowell, Mass., 1958, Gardner, Mass., 1958-60; vice pres. in charge of prodn. and labor relations Interstate Container Corp., Glendale, N.Y., 1959-61; pres. Alpak Mfg. Co., Inc. Montgomery, N.Y., 1960-69. Mem. Packaging Inst., Material Ft Lee NJ Died Sept. 30, 1969; buried Clifton NJ

TAUSSIG, FRANCIS BREWSTER, publisher; b. Yonkers, N.Y., May 2, 1900; s. Walter Martin and Sophia Lewis (Brewster) T.; B.S., Harvard, 1922; m. Elizabeth Roff, June 10, 1930 (died Dec. 1969); m. 2d, Harriet Burket, Oct. 8, 1960. Pub., 1922-70; v.p. Americana Corp., 1948-70; exec. v.p. dir. Grolier Soc., Inc., 1949-70; chmn., director Richards Co., 1960-70; pres. Grolier Internat., 1966-70. Chmn. Nat. Postal Com. for Books, 1954. Chmn. joint foreign trade com. Am. Book Pub. Council-Am. Educational Pub. Council, 1968. Served with USNR, 1942-46; comdr. Res. ret. Clubs: Harvard (N.Y.C.); St. Andrew's Golf (Hastings, N.Y.); Onteora (Tannersville, N.Y.); Field (Sarasota, Fla.). Home: New York City NY Died May 25, 1970; buried Dorset VT

TAYLOR, AMOS ELIAS, economist; b. Glenville, Pa., July 4, 1893; s. William Franklin and Emeline (Albright) T.; A.B., Gettysburg Coll., 1915; M.A. U. Chgo., 1920; Ph.D., U. Pa. 1921; LL.D., Gettysburg Coll., 1966; m. Leah Tipton, Nov. 12, 1921; 1 son, Amos Elias (dec.). Tchr. sci., East Stroudsburg (Pa.) High Sch., 1915-16; prof. Latin and English, Pa. Mil. Coll., 1916-17; instr. econs. U. Pa., 1920-23, asst. prof. finance, 1923-29; asso. prof. finance, Northwestern U., 1929-30; with U.S. Dept. Commerce, 1931-47; asst. chief finance div., 1931-39, chief, 1939-42, chief div. research and statistics, 1942-43, dir. Bur. Fgn. and Domestic Commerce, 1943-47; exec. com. on Econ. Fgn. Policy, 1944-45; com. on Reciprocity Information, 1944-45; dir. Office Bus. Econ., 1946-47; dir. dept. econ. and social affairs OAS, 1947-58; exec. sec. Inter-Am. Econ. and Social Council 1947-58; adj. prof. econs. Grad. Sch., Am. U., 1932-59, prof. econs., 1959-64. Served as pvt. AEF, 1918-19; mem. Sorbonne Detachment, 1919. Asso. mem. com statis. experts League of Nations, 1938-46. Trustee Gettysburg Coll., 1932-59. Mem. Nat. Acad. Econs. and Polit. Sci. (chmn. bd.), Am. Econ. Assn. (v.p., 1945) A.A.A.S., Royal Econ. Soc., Acad. Polit. Sci., Phi Beta Kapp, Pi Gamma Mu, Chi Psi Omega, Alpha Tau Omega. Lutheran. Clubs: Cosmos (pres. 1948), Torch (pres. 1941) (Washington) Author: Balance of International Payments of the United States, 1931-40; Foreign Investments in the U.S., 1937; Economic and Social Problems of the Americas, 1960. Contbr. articles to econ. jours. Home: York PA Died Nov. 25, 1972; buried Stone Church Cemetery, Glenville PA

TAYLOR, CHARLES RALPH, editor, author; b. Arlington, Mass., Dec. 14, 1877; s. Myron and Elizabeth Pinkerton (Crosby) T.; A.B., Harvard, 1900; m. Irma Ethyl Wing, of Roxbury, Mass., June 30, 1906. Prin. pub. schs., Sheffield, Mass., Burrilville, R.I., Hyde Park, Mass., and Quincy, Mass., until 1910; jr. master Girls' High Sch., Boston, 1910-19; treas. and editor F.M. Ambrose & Co., pubs.; dir. The Ambrose Press. Mem. N.E. Assn. English Teachers, Harvard Teachers' Assn. Republican. Conglist. Clubs: Boston City; Highland. Unitarian (West Roxbury, Mass.). Author: Vital English, 1919. Editor: The Merchant of Venice (annotated), 1920; Macbeth (annotated). Trustee Appleton Acad., New Ipswich, N.Y. Home: 31 Pelton St., West Roxbury MA Office: 14 Beacon St., Boston MA‡

TAYLOR, DONALD STEPHEN, supreme ct. justice; b. Troy, N.Y., June 17, 1898; s. John Park and Jessie (Simmons) T.; A.B., Colgate U., 1919; LL.B., Albany Law Sch., 1922; m. Frances E. Mittenzwey, Aug. 19, 1925; children—John P., Carolyn (Mrs. Stanley B. Terhune), Dorothy S. (Mrs. Donald C. Howey). Admitted to N.Y. bar, 1922; partner firm Taylor and Taylor, Troy, 1924-48, Wager, Taylor, Howd & Le Forestier, 1948-70; justice Supreme Ct. State of N.Y., 1949-70; asso. justice then justice appellate division State Supreme Court, 3d judicial dept., 1961-70. Trustee Troy Savs. Bank. Trustee Samaritan Hospital (Troy), Albany Law School (Albany). Mem. Am., N.Y., Rensselaer Co. bar assns., S.R., Justinian Soc. Episcopalian. Clubs: Troy Country, Rotary; Fort Orange (Albany, N.Y.). Home: Troy NY Died June 23, 1970.

TAYLOR, EDWARD R., marketing exec.; b. Troy, N.Y., May 3, 1908; ed. pub. schs. Detroit; exec. course Mass. Inst. Tech., 1955; m. Bertha Lucele Palmer, Jan. 1, 1938; 1 dau., Pamela Anne. Advt. Agency work, 1924-42, copy writer specializing in automotive goods, account exec., 1942; dir. advtg. and sales promotion, Zenith Radio Corp., Chgo., 1942-47; with Hotpoint, Inc., 1947-52, v.p. charge marketing, 1951-52; v.p., asst. to pres. Motorola, Inc., 1952-56, exec. v.p., 1956-64; founder Ed Taylor Chevrolet, San Diego, Cal., 1965. Hon. life dir. Brand Names Found., Inc. Office: San Diego CA Died Apr. 11, 1972; buried Borrego Springs CA

TAYLOR, EMERSON GIFFORD, author; b. at Pittsfield, Mass., June 9, 1874; s. John Metcalf and Edith (Emerson) T.; B.A., Yale, 1895, Ph.D., 1899; m. Edith Pendleton Corwin, of Hartford, 1901. Author: A Daughter of Dale, 1904; The Upper Hand, 1906. Address: Hartford CT‡

TAYLOR, EMILY (HEYWARD) DRAYTON, miniature painter; b. Phila., Apr. 14, 1860; d. Henry Edward and Mary (Brady) Drayton; ed. by pvt. governess and abroad for several yrs.; studied painting in Paris under Cecile Ferrier, and at Acad. of Fine Arts, Phila.; m. J(ohn) Madison Taylor, M.D., Oct. 15, 1879 (died Oct. 3, 1931); children—Edith Moore (Mrs. Albert Mansfield Patterson), Percival Drayton, Mabel Heyward (Mrs. Taylor Cochran). Important miniatures those of President and Mrs. McKinley, Dr. S. Weir Mitchell, Mrs. Eugene Hale, Emmons Blaine, Mrs. Cyrus McCormick, George Hamilton, son of John McLure Hamilton, Mr. John A. Morris, Mr. Henry Howard Houston, Mr. Frank Thomson, and Cardinal Mercier, of Malines, Belgium (1924). In 1898 assisted Miss Anne Holingsworth Wharton with Heirlooms in Miniature and wrote part of the work. Mem. Fellowship Pa. Acad. Fine Arts; pres. Soc. Miniature Painters; mem. Colonial Dames, Geneal. Soc. of Pa., Hist. Soc. of Pa., Print Club of Pa., Water Color Club. Awarded gold medal, Earl's Court, London, 1900, Charleston Exposition, 1902; silver medal, San Francisco Expn., 1915; medal, Miniature Soc. of Pa.; Medal of Honor, 1919; Charles M. Lea money prize. Acad. Fine Arts, miniature exbn., 1920. Painted portrait of Cardinal Mercier, 1924, and awarded spl. money prize by Pa. Acad. Fine Arts for same. Home: 1504 Pine St., Philadelphia PA‡

TAYLOR, FRANK J., writer; b. Wessington, S.D., Oct. 8, 1894; s. John S. and Ellen (Stobbs) T.; student Stanford U., 1914-17; m. Katherine Elizabeth Ames, June 30, 1919; children—Franklin James (dec.), Paul Ames, Robert Wilson. Reporter for Los Angeles Examiner, 1913; corr. for San Francisco Examiner, 1916-17, for San Francisco Bur. of Asso. Press, 1915-17; war corr. for United Press, with A.E.F. in France, 1918; covered Germany, Austria, Hungary, Czechoslovakia and Soviet Russia during post-war revolutions, 1919; with U.P. in New York and Washington, 1919-20; asst. mng. editor New York Globe, later Albany and Washington corr., 1920-21; mgr. Washington bur. Scripps-Howard Newspapers, 1921-24; advertising writer, 1925-30; mag. and book writing since 1924; war corr., Pacific Area, for 1945. Mem. Sigma Chi. Clubs: San Francisco Press, Bohemian. Co-author: Oh, Ranger1931; Pop, Warner's Book for Boys, 1934; Our U.S.A.—A Gay Geography, 1935; Democracy's Air Arsenal, 1947; Black Bonanza, 1950; High Horizons, 1951; Southern Pacific, 1952. Pacific Coast reporter, Sat. Eve. Post, Readers Digest, and other nat. mags. Address: Los Altos CA Died Oct. 1972.

TAYLOR, GEORGE WILLIAM, educator, arbitrator; b. Phila., July 10, 1901; s. Harry D. and Anna C. (Lahnemann) T.; B.S. in Econs., Wharton Sch. U. Pa., 1923, Ph.D., Grad. Sch., 1928; m. Edith S. Ayling, June 18, 1924. Instr. industry U. Pa., 1923; head dept. bus. adminstrn. Albright Coll., Reading, Pa., 1924-29; research asso. indsl. research dept. U. Pa., 1930-49; asso. prof., then prof. labor relations, Wharton Sch., 1937-64, Harnwell prof., 1964-71, prof. emeritus, 1971-72. Impartial chmn. hosiery industry, 1931-41, men's clothing industry, Phila. 1935-60; impartial umpire Gen. Motors Corp. and U.A.W., 1941-42; acting chmn. Regional Labor Relations Bd. Phila., 1934-35; vice chmn. NWLB, 1942-45, chmn., 1945; pres. Indls. Relations Research Assn., 1949; impartial chmn. Gen. Bldg. Contractors Assn. and Bldg. and Constrn. Trades Council Phila., AFL, 1953-57. Sec., Pres.'s Labor-Mgmt. Conf., 1945; chmn. adv. com. Office War Mblzn. and Reconversion, 1946-47; cons. Hoover Commn., 1948-49; chmn. WSB, 1950; arbitrator C.I.O. Jurisdictional Disputes, 1952; chmn. Presl. Bd. Inquiry Steel Dispute, 1959-69; chmn. long range com. Kaiser Steel Corp., U.S. Steel Workers, 1960-72; mem. Pres.'s Com. on Labor-Mgmt. Policy, 1961-68; chmn. Pres.'s Aerospace Com., 1962; presdl. mediator R.R. Dispute, 1964; chmn. Gov. N.Y. Commn. Pub. Employee Relations, 1966. Bd. dirs. Am. Arbitration Assn. Recipient Pa. Medal Merit, 1956; Phila. award, 1963; Presdl. Medal of Freedom, 1963; Pa. award for excellence, 1966. Mem. Am. Philos Soc., Franklin Inn Soc., Phi Beta Kappa, Beta Gamma Sigma. Author: Government Regulations of Industrial Relations, 1948. Editor: Series on Labor Arbitration, 1953. Author (with others), editor: New Concepts in Wage

TAYLOR, HARRY GORDON, lawyer; b. Bartow, Fla., Apr. 10, 1891; s. Lewis T. and Catherine (Gandy) T.; student Stetson U. Coll. of Law, 1914-15; m. Jennie E. Weir, Nov. 25, 1919 (dec. 1970); 1 dau., Norma (Mrs. E. J. McGuire). Admitted to Fla. bar, 1915; practice of law, 1915-17, 19-23; state atty., 1923-27; circuit judge 10th Jud. Circuit of Fla., 1927-33; spl. asst. to chief counsel Internal Revenue Service, 1934-45; pvt. practice of law, specializing fed. tax law, Miami; mem. firm Culverhouse, Tomlinson, Taylor & DeCarion. Served with U.S. Army, 1917-19. Mem. S.A.R. Mason (past grand master). Club: Riviera Country (Coral Gables, Fla.). Home: Miami FL Died Jan. 28, 1970; buried Bartow FL

TAYLOR, JAMES H., univ. prof.; b. Sharon, Pa., Feb. 21, 1893; s. James and Cornelia (Jackson) T.; B.S., U. of Nebraska, 1916; A.M., Princeton, 1920; Ph.D., U. of Chicago, 1924; m. Ethel Victoria Graham, Dec. 24, 1919; children—Richard Jackson, Lawrence Martin. Instr. in mathematics, U. of Nebraska, 1920-22; Nat. Research fellow, Princeton, 1924-25; asst. prof. mathematics, Lehigh U., 1925-26, U. of Wis., 1926-29; prof. mathematics George Washington U., Washington, D.C., 1929-72. Served as 2d lt., 351st Inf., 88th Div., U.S. Army, 1917-18, 1st lt., 1918-19. Mem. Math. Assn. America, Am. Math. Society, Washington Academy of Sciences, Phi Beta Kappa, Sigma Xi. Mason. Club: Cosmos (Washington). Author: Vector Analysis, 1939. Home: Avlon Rockville MD Died Mar. 30, 1972.

TAYLOR, JAMES HENRY, management cons.; born Wooster, O., Sept. 4, 1908; s. Rob Curtis and Erma Jane (Rowe) T.; student Dartmouth, 1926-29; B.A., Ohio Wesleyan U., 1930, M.A., 1931; Ph.D., Ohio State U., 1933; m. Audra N. Zaugg, August 19, 1927 (dec. August 1965); children—Rob John, Jane (Mrs. J. Reed Coleman). Began his career as personnel manager Procter & Gamble Co., 1935-58; prof. indsl. relations U. Mich., 1958-59; exec. v.p. Indsl. Relations Counselors, N.Y.C., 1958-60; corp. v.p. Federated Dept. Stores, Cin., 1960-61; resident asso. Boyden Assos., Inc., Cin., 1961-66; dean Sch. Bus., Western Res. U., Cleve., 1966-67; management consultant, Leland, Mich., 1967-68. With WLB, 1942-45; asst. dir. ODM, 1954-55; cons. to White House, 1958-59. Mem. Am. Mgmt. Assn. (Service award 1958), Indsl. Relations Research Assn., Personnel Round Table, U.S. C. of C., Sigma Xi. Author: Personnel Adminstration, 1959. Address: Leland MI Died Jan. 31, 1968.

TAYLOR, JAMES MILBURN, clergyman, traveler, lecturer; b. Maryville, Tenn., July 27, 1873; s. Benjamin Cornelius and Sophia T.; ed. Friends Normal Sch. (Maryville, Tenn.), Maryville Coll., Grant U. (Chattanooga, Tenn.); m. Margaret Nannette Kaderly, of Knoxville, Tenn., Sept. 7, 1898. Evangelistic work in U.S., 1895-1906; visited foreign lands and lectured in U.S. between tours, 1906-14; spl. lecturer Bd. Foreign Missions M.E. Ch., 1914-21; returned to lecture platform. Writer on missionary, travel and hist. topics; conceived and organized the Church Chautauqua. Address: P.O. Box 1010, Washington DC‡

TAYLOR, JOHN BLYTH, investment banker; b. Chelsea, Que., Can., Feb. 20, 1904; s. James and Jean (Ramage) T.; B.A., Queen's U., Kingston, Ont., 1925, M.A., 1926; m. Mary Samson, Dec. 19, 1936;children—James C., Hugh R., Sarah B. Mem. Investment dept. Sun Life Assurance Co., 1929-35; research analyst Harriman, Ripley & Co., Inc., 1935-41; exec. asst. to minister of finance, Ottawa, Can., 1941-43; partner, pres. Taylor Deale & Co., N.Y.C., 1943-54; partner Osler & Hammond, Toronto, 1956-68; dir. Harris & Partners, Limited, investment bankers, Toronto, 1955-68, executive vice president, 1958-68. Presbyterian. Clubs: Metropolitan, Broad Street Lunch (N.Y.C.); Lake Placid (N.Y.). Home: Toronto ON Canada. Died Mar. 26, 1968; interred South Lincoln Farm Bristol VT

TAYLOR, JOSEPH ROBERT, newspaperman; b. Toronto, Ont., Can., Feb. 7, 1873; s. Alfred and Caroline (Hodgson) T.; ed. pub. schs., Can.; m. Lillie E. Green, of Grand Rapids, Mich., 1898; children—Robert W., Henry G., Joseph A. Came to U.S., 1891, naturalized citizen, 1896. Began as jr. bookkeeper, Grand Rapids Press, 1893, later cashier, adv. solicitor, circulation mgr. and asst. gen. mgr. until 1919; editor and gen. mgr. Flint (Mich.) Daily Journal since 1919. Mem. Mich. Authors' Assn. Republican. Mason, Elk. Home: 424 Crapo St. Address: Flint Daily Journal, Flint MI‡

TAYLOR, LILLIAN E., surgeon; b. San Francisco; d. Edward and Elizabeth (Wheatley) T.; Moulton Coll., Toronto, Ont.; B.A., U. of Toronto, 1899; M.D., C.M., 1906. Interne, Woman's Hosp., Phila., New England Hosp., Boston. Instr. U. of Ill. Med. Sch. 4 yrs.; specializes in surgery of ear, nose, and throat. Formerly of Chicago, Ill.

TAYLOR, LILY ROSS, educator; b. Auburn, Ala., Aug. 12, 1886; d. William Dana and Mary Forte (Ross) Taylor; A.B., U. Wis., 1906, Litt.D., 1950; student Am. Acad. in Rome (Italy), 1909-10, fellow archaeology, 1917, 19-20; Ph.D., Bryn Mawr Coll., 1912; Litt.D., Wilson Coll., 1944, Mills Coll., 1947, Columbia, 1954, Smith Coll., 1961. Reader archaeology Bryn Mawr Coll., 1910-12; from instr. to prof. Latin, Vassar Coll., 1912-27; prof. Latin, Bryn Mawr Coll., 1927-52, prof. emeritus, 1952-69, dean Grad. Sch., 1942-52; Sather prof. Classics, U. Cal., 1947; prof. charge Classics sect. Am. Acad. in Rome, 1934-35, 52-55; vis. prof. Harvard, 1959, U. Wis., 1962-63; Nat. Phi Beta Kappa lectr., 1956-57; Jerome lectr. U. Mich. and Am. Acad. in Rome, 1964-65, mem. Inst. Advanced Study, Princeton, 1959, Trustee Wellesley Coll., 1943-49. Served with A.R.C. in Italy and Balkans, 1918-19, with O.S.S., Washington, 1943-44. Recipient Achievement award Am. Assn. U. Women, 1952; Gold medal Cultori di Roma, City of Rome, 1962. Mem. Am. Philol. Assn. (pres. 1942; award of merit 1962), Archaeol. Inst. Am. (v.p. 1935-37, del. nat. commn. UNESCO 1956-58), Am. Philos. Soc., Am. Acad. Arts and Scis.; corr. mem. Pontifical Archaeology (Rome), British Acad., Bavarian Acad. Scis. Author: Local Cults in Etruria, 1923; The Divinity of the Roman Emperor, 1931; Party Politics in the Age of Caesar, 1949; The Voting Districts of the Roman Republic, 1960; Roman Voting Assemblies, 1966; also articles. Address: Bryn Mawr PA Died Nov. 18, 1969.

TAYLOR, NORMAN, botanist; b. Hereford, England, May 18, 1883; s. James Durham and Mary Ann (Preece) T.; student Cornell U., 1901-02; D.Sc. (honorary), Washington College, 1958. Came to U.S., 1889, naturalized, 1896. Asst. curator N.Y. Botanical Garden, Bronx Park, 1905-11; curator of plants Brooklyn Botanic Garden, 1911-29; botany, horticulture and forestry editor, Webster's New Internat. Dictionary, 2d edition; editor of The Garden Dictionary, Houghton, Mifflin Co., 1933-36; director of Cinchona Products Inst., Inc., 1937-50; advisor Cinchona Instituut, Amsterdam, 1951-53; plant exploring expdns. to Bahamas, Haiti, Cuba, Santo Domingo, Puerto Rico, Yucatan, Guatemala, Bolivia, Peru, Ecuador and Brazil. Awarded Massachusetts Horticultural Society gold medal, 1936, Distinguished Service Award, N.Y. Bot. Garden, 1961, Liberty Hyde Bailey gold medal Am. Hort. Soc., 1963. Fellow New York Academy of Sciences, A.A.A.S.; associate fellow N.Y. Acad. Medicine; mem. Massachusetts Horticultural Soc., Torrey Botanical Club. Episcopalian. Clubs: Century, Players, Explorers (N.Y.C.); Cosmos (Washington). Author: Botany, Science of Plant Life, 1924; Guide to the Wild Flowers, 1928; Cinchona in Java, 1945; Taylor's Encyclopedia of Gardening, 1948; Flight From Reality, 1949; The Permanent Garden, and Color in the Garden, 1953; Fragrance in the Garden, Herbs in the Garden, 1954; Fruits in the Garden, The Everblooming Garden, 1955; Wild Flower Gardening, 1956; Guide to Garden Flowers, 1957; Taylor's Garden Guide, 1957; The Ageless Relicts, 1962; 1001 Questions Answered About Flowers, 1963; Narcotics: Nature's Dangerous Gifts, 1963; Guide to Garden Shrubs and Trees, 1965; Plant Drugs that Changed the World, 1965. Contbr. mags., Ency. Brit. and Book of Knowledge. Home: Princess Anne MD Died Nov. 5, 1967; interred New Episcopal Cemetery Princess Anne MD

TAYLOR, ORVILLE, lawyer; born Sioux City, Iowa, the son of Orville J. and Eleanor Sarah (Harris) T.; U. of Chicago; LL.B., Northwestern University Law Sch., 1908; married Catherine E. Apperson, January 19, 1924. Admitted to Illinois bar, 1908; mem. Taylor, Miller, Magner, Sprowl & Hutchings, Chgo.; special asst. atty. gen. U.S., 1922; asst. sec. Army, Germany, 1948; commr. Ill. State Toll Highway Commn.; dir. N.Y. Central System, United Asbestos Co., Ltd. (Canada). Director LaFayette Fellowship Found., Inc.; pres. Am. Legion Founders Ltd., 1966-67; dir. U.S.O., Chgo., Ch. Fedn. Greater Chgo.; chmn. A. Montgomery Ward Found.; trustee Ill. Inst. of Tech.; trustee and founder Chicago World's Fair Centennial Celebration"; pres. Chicago Bd. of Edn., 1933; mem. Chicago Plan Commn.; mem. Northwestern U. Assos., Citizens Bd., U. of Chgo. Candidate for Republican nomination for United States senator, 1936. Maj. U.S. Army, overseas with 86th Div., World War I. Recipient Order of Lafayette. Trustee, Am. Legion Americanism Endowment Fund, Little League Foundation. Vice pres. and dir. Alliance Francaise; v.p. and dir. France-America Soc.; co-chmn. (Chicago) Treasury Dept. War Loan Drives, 3-8 inclusive; dir. and v.p., Bill of Rights Commemorative Soc.; mem. Am. Branch of Internat. Law Assn., Am., Ill. State and Chicago bar assns., Assn. Bar N.Y. City, English Speaking Union (v.p., dir.), S.A.R. (v.p., dir.), Chicago Law Inst., Am. Judicature Soc., Legion of Honor, Am. Legion, Society of American Legion Founders, Limited, Navy League U.S. (life), Army, Navy and Air Force Vets. in Can. (life), Comarade de Combat (France), Ill. St. Andrew Soc. (life), Beta Theta Pi, Phi Delta Phi. Republican. Episcopalian. Mason, Elk, Moose. Clubs: Chicago, Legal, Law, Saddle and Cycle, Tavern, Casino, Attic (Chgo.); Bohemian (San Francisco); Metropolitan (N.Y.C.). Home: Chicago IL Died Jan. 19, 1969.

TAYLOR, RICHARD (DENLSON), cartoonist, painter; b. Ft. William, Ont., Can., Sept. 18, 1902; s. Richard Lippincott Denison and Christine Elizabeth (Young) T.; studied under Harry Britton, Toronto, at age of 12; student Central Technical School, Ontario College of Art (Toronto), Los Angeles School of Art and Design; married Maxine MacTavish, July 6, 1936. Began career by coloring lantern slides for Sunday schs.; cartoonist, Goblin mag., Toronto, 1927; free lance commercial artist, 1932; cartoonist, The New Yorker mag., since 1935. Creator of imaginary world in paintings, called Frodokom. Has had one-man shows of unpublished water colors at Walker Galleries (New York City), Butler Art Institute (Youngstown, Ohio), Addison Gallery (Andover, Massachusetts), Roullier Galleries (Chicago), Hudson Gallery (Detroit), Valentine Gallery (N.Y. City), 1941. Also exhibited at Internat. Watercolor Exhibit, Chicago Art Inst., Internat. Watercolor Exhibit, Brooklyn Museum, The Modern Art Soc., Cincinnati, 1941; Metropolitan Museum of Art, 1942; M. H. deYoung Memorial Museum, San Francisco (self-portrait), 1943; Whitney Museum of Am. Art, 1943; Flint (Mich.) Inst. of Arts (with Steig), 1943; exhibited Am.-British Art Center, N.Y. City; Addison Gallery, Andover, Mass.; Whitney Museum, N.Y. City; Carnegie Inst., Pittsburgh. Represented in collections of Museum of Modern Art, Boston Museum of Fine Arts, The Albright Art Gallery (Buffalo), Wichita (Kan.) Museum, and several private collections. Author: The Better Taylors (book cartoons), 1944. Home: West Redding CT Died May 1970.

TAYLOR, ROBERT JOHN, dean; b. near Middlesex, Vt., Jan. 3, 1874; s. George William and Martha (Henry) T.; B.A., Hamline U., 1900, D.D., 1919; M.A., University of Southern California, 1910; m. Mary C. McNeil, Oct. 15, 1900; 1 son, Robert John. Meth. minister, Minn., 1898-1908, southern Calif., 1910-23; lecturer Missions and religious education, U. Southern Calif., 1911-17, prof. since 1929, dean Grad. Sch. Religion since 1940; acting prof. religious education and comparative religions, Pomona Coll., 1923-29. Dir. Nat. Religious Edn. Assn. Mem. Phi Chi Phi. Republican. Methodist. Mason. Home: 4323 S. Hobart Blvd., Los Angeles 37 CA*‡

TAYLOR, ROBERT LEE, dir. Federal Compress & Warehouse Co.; b. Providence, Miss., Nov. 10, 1871; s. George Washington and Icybell (Wiggins) E.; grad. T.M. and W. Sch., 1890; m. Sarah Lea, Aug. 22, 1905 (died 1936); 1 son, William Lea. Post Office clk., 1890-96; cotton seed oil mill fireman, 1896-97; ry. brakeman, later clk., 1897-99; plantation mgr., 1900-03; supt. Grenada Cotton Compress Co., 1903-08, gen. mgr., 1908-15, pres., 1915-25; consolidated 28 corps. into Federal Compress & Warehouse Co., and became pres. of same, 1925, now dir.; owner of 10,000 acre game preserve. Ind. Democrat. Episcopalian. Home: 2021 South Parkway E. Office: 81 Monroe Av., Memphis TN*‡

TAYLOR, S. EARL, b. New Hampton, Ia., Apr. 26, 1873; s. Charles H. and Elizabeth T.; B.A., Upper Ia. U., Fayette, Ia., 1893, M.A., 1895; B.D., Drew Theol. Sem., 1899; post-grad. work, New York U.; (LL.D., U. of Chattanooga, 1913); m. Amber Swem, of Epworth, Ia., Sept. 18, 1895. Connected with Bd. of Foreign Missions M.E. Ch. since 1902. Corr. sec., 1912-21; has been sec. Student Volunteer Movement, also of Internat. Y.M.C.A., Young People's Missionary Dept. M.E. Church, and Laymen's Missionary Movement M.E. Ch.; exec. sec. Centenary Movement of M.E. Ch., 1917-19; dir. gen. Centenary Celebration of Am. Methodism, Columbus, O., July 1919; gen. sec. Interch. World Movement of N.A., 1919-20. Author: Price of Africa, 1902. Joint Author: Studies in the Life of Christ; Studies in the Apostolic Church; Studies in Old Testament History. Lecturer on missionary topics. Republican. Home: Oakland NJ Address: 150 5th Av., New York NY‡

TAYLOR, S(AMUEL) N(EWTON), physicist; b. Farmingdale, N.Y., Apr. 24, 1858; s. Francis James and Ann (Newton) T.; Ph.B., Wesleyan U., Conn., 1887; fellow in physics, Clark U., Worcester, Mass., 1893-96, Ph.D., 1896; studied German univs., 1902-03; m. Mabel Wright Burr, Dec. 27, 1887; 1 dau., Mabel Burr. Expert electrician with Gen. Electric Co., 1887-93; instr. physics, Purdue U., 1896-99; asso. prof. physics, Syracuse U., 1899-1903; prof. physics and elec. engring., Univ. of Pittsburgh, 1903-08; in charge of astron. time service, Allegheny Obs., 1904-05; prof. elec. engring., U. of Cincinnati, 1908-11; became prof. physics, Goucher Coll., Baltimore, Sept. 18, 1911, now emeritus. Hon. fellow A.A.A.S., 1917; mem. Am. Inst. E.E., Soc. Promotion Engring. Edn., Alpha Delta Phi, Mystical Seven. Contbr. papers on elec. and tech. subjects. Methodist. Home: 2514 Maryland Av., Baltimore MD‡

TAYLOR, VERNON F., business exec.; b. Daguscahonda, Pa., May 14, 1888; s. Benson E. and Emma R. (Olmsted) T.; B.S., U. Pa., 1911; m. Ruth Hallock Campbell, June 16, 1915. Mine supt. McKnight Coal Co., Brockway, Pa., 1915-16, Cambria Smokeless Coal Co., Brockway, 1916-17; pres., dir. Peerless Oil & Gas Co., San Antonio, 1923-63; chmn. Wytana Cattle Co., 1947-72; dir. United Corp., U.S. Lines, Chem. Corp., Rexall Drug, Penick & Ford, Ltd., Internat. Minerals & Chem. Corp., Am. Zinc Lead & Smelting Co., Pan-Am. Airways. Bd. dirs. Trinity, U., Tulane U. Mem. Sigma Alpha Epsilon. Republican. Presbyn. Mason (32, Shriner). Clubs: San Antonio Country; Duquesne (Pitts.); Rolling Rock (Ligonier, Pa.); Bankers (N.Y.C.). Address: San Antonio TX Died Sept. 3, 1972; buried Clarion PA

TAYLOR, WILL SAMUEL, mural painter; b. Ansonia, Conn., Nov. 27, 1882; s. Henry Clarence and Emeline (White) T.; ed. Mass. State Art Sch., Boston, and Art Students League, N.Y. City; M.A., Brown U., 1930; m. Augusta Whipple, June 19, 1912; children—Virginia Augusta, Carol Ashby. Prin. works: 18 murals depicting North Pacific Coast Indians, Am. Museum Natural History, N.Y. City, 1911-21; 3 murals showing evolution of man, J. P. Morgan Hall of same museum; also mural at City Park Chapel, Brooklyn, N.Y.; 2murals Early Colonial History of Worcester, Mass., for Providence St. Jr. High Sch., Worcester, etc. Instr. in mural painting and composition, Pratt Inst., Brooklyn, 1915-26; became asst. prof. art and curator of art, Brown U., 1926, asso. prof. from 1930. Mem. Nat. Soc. Mural Painters, Art Fellowship, Archtl. League New York, Lyme Art Association, Allied Artists, Phi Beta Kappa; hon. asso., Am. Inst. Architects. Unitarian. Clubs: Providence Art; Salmagundi (New York). Home: Providence RI Died Dec. 1968.

TEARSE, HAROLD HORTON, business exec.; b. Winona, Minn., Nov. 5, 1894; s. Robert Emmett and Kate Warren (Horton) T.; student Harvard Sch., Chicago, 1909-11, Phillips Andover, 1911-12; Ph.D., Yale Sheffield Sci. Sch., 1916; m. Katherine Searle Apr. 22, 1922; children—Lucia Reynolds, Harold Horton, Helen Evelyn. Sec. Sterling Grain Co., 1919-29; became v.p., gen. mgr. Searle Grain Co., 1929, now pres., dir.; dir. Northwestern Nat. Bank, Mpls. Fire & Marine Ins. Co., Standard Lumber Co., Winona. Pres. Mpls. Grain Exchange, 1945-46 (mem.); sec. Mpls. Grain Clearing Corp.; mem. Chgo. Bd. Trade. Mem. Mpls. Terminal Elevator Grain Merchants Assn. (v.p.), bd. Park Commrs., bd. Council of Social Agencies, trustee Mpls. Inst. Arts, Mpls. Orchestral Assn., A.R.C. (chmn. Mpls. 1943-46), Community Fund (gen. chmn., 1940), Am. Legion, Knight of Malta. Republican. Episcopalian. Clubs: Woodhill, Minneapolis (past pres.). Home: Wayzata MN Died Jan. 14, 1972.

TEASDALE, KENNETH, lawyer; b. St. Louis, Feb. 10, 1895; s. George Willard and Mamie (Walsh) T.; LL.B., U. Mo., 1918; m. Anne Fulbright, June 25, 1921; children—Suzanne Zorn, Kenneth S. Admitted to practice law 1917; member Armstrong, Teasdale, Kramer & Vaughan and predecessor firms, from 1921; chairman Supreme Court Committee to Revise Mo. Civil Procedure, 1938. Appointed to St. Louis Public Library board, 1956-57; mem. of bd. of Police Commrs. of St. Louis, from 1957. Served as 1st lt., F.A., U.S. Army, World War I. Fellow American College of Trial Lawyers; member American, Mo. (pres. 1936-37) bar assns., Bar Assn. St. Louis (pres. 1935-36), Order of Coif. Clubs: Noonday, Racquet, Bellerive Country, Missouri Athletic, Jefferson (pres. 1926-27). Home: St Louis MO Died Aug. 22, 1970; buried Fayetteville AR

TEETERS, NEGLEY KING, educator; b. Steubenville, Ohio, Nov. 16, 1896; s. Harry Negley and Margaret (Wyeth) T.; A.B., Oberlin Coll., 1920; A.M., Ohio State U., 1925, Ph.D., 1931; m. Ruth Schendel, Sept. 1, 1927; children—Robert Duane, Ralph Negley. Field work, Playground Assn. of Am., N.Y. City, 1920-23; sec., C. of C., Stuebenville, 1923-24; grad. instr., Ohio State U., 1924-25; instr. Minn. State Teachers Coll., Moorhead, Minn., 1926-27; with Temple U., Phila., 1927-71, prof. sociology, 1946-64, prof. emeritus, 1964-71, chmn. dept., 1948-56; vis. prof. Hartwick Coll., 1964-71, H. Claude Hardy prof. sociology, 1971; cons. Prison Industries Sect., W.P.B., 1944; teacher U. of Chicago, summer 1946, University of Southern California, summer 1961. Member Pa. Joint State Govt. Commn. of Gen. Assembly to revise penal code, 1945-47; mem. Gov.'s Commn. on Correctional Matters, 1955-58. Recipient August Vollmer award Am. Soc. Criminol., 1962. Mem. Pa. Prison Soc. (p.p.), Am. Sociol. Soc., Am. Assn. U. Profs. Author: They Were in Prison, 1937 (work Pa. Prison Soc. founded Phila. Soc. for Alleviating the Miseries of Public Prisons, 1878); New Horizons in Criminology (with Harry E. Barnes), 1943, rev. 51, 59; World Penal Systems, 1944; Penology from Panama to Cape Horn, 1946; Deliberations of the International Penal and Penitentiary Congresses (sponsored by the International Penal and Penitentiary Commn., Berne, Switzerland), 1949; The Challenge of Delinquency (with John O. Reinemann), 1950; The Cradle of the Penitentiary, 1955; Cherry Hill; The Prison at Philadelphia (with J. D. Shearer), 1957. Public Executions in Pennsylvania, 1960; Scaffold and Chair,

1963; (with Jack Hedblom) Hang by the Neck, 1967. Contbr. Journal Criminal Law, Prison Jour. Awarded grant from Dept. of State to make study of prisons of several countries in S.A., 1944; condr. summer study groups, S.A., 1951, 60, European tours, 1952-59. Address: Oneonta NY Died Oct. 30, 1971; cremated.

TEETERS, WILBER JOHN, educator; b. Alliance, O., Oct. 10, 1866; s. Williamson and Dorcas E. (Johnson) T.; B.S., Mt. Union Coll., Alliance, 1893, M.S., 1897; Ph.C., U. of Mich., 1895; m. Anna Hollister, June 6, 1895 (died July 25, 1909); m. 2d, Sara Hayden Harrison, June 23, 1912 (died July 25, 1921); children—Wilber Otis, Wilber J.; m. 3d, Hazel R. Reynolds, Sept. 2, 1925 (died Nov. 1, 1930). Demonstrator of chemistry, Med. Coll., State U. of Iowa, 1895-1903; asso. prof. pharmacy, State U. of Ia., 1903-04, dean Coll. of Pharmacy, 1904-37; dean emeritus and prof. of pharmacy since 1937; mayor of Iowa City, 1943-47. Fellow A.A.A.S., American Pharm. Association; mem. Am. Conf. Pharm. Faculties (past sec., past pres.), Alpha Phi Omega, Gamma Alpha, Sigma Alpha Epsilon, Phi Delta Chi, Beta Phi Sigma, Rho Chi, Dolphin, Alpha Chi Sigma. Republican. Methodist. Mason (K.T., 32 deg.). Clubs: Country, Kiwanis. Home: Iowa City IA‡

TEICH, MAX LOUIS, hotel exec.; b. Greiz, Germany Feb. 21, 1873; s. Christian and Elise (Tamm T.); ed. jr. coll. in Germany; m. Sophie Roessler, Nov. 23, 1898; children—Frederick C., Elizabeth T. (Mrs. E.J. Lettie). Pres., mng. dir., Congress Hotel, Chicago, 1910-11; Hotel Jefferson, St. Louis, 1927-50; pres., dir., Internat. Hotel Co. operating Hotel Atlantic, Chgo., since 1903. Mem. Am., Chgo., So. Cal. hotel Assns., Chgo. Assn. Commerce. Club: Montecito Golf (Santa Barbara, Calif.). Mason. Address: Hotel Atlantic, Chicago IL‡

TELLER, HUGH HARLOW, ret. fgn. service officer; b. Montague, Mich., Dec. 25, 1896; s. Delmore Alton and Ina Maude (Grove) T.; C.F.S., Georgetown U., 1923; m. Erna Pistorius, Oct. 11, 1928. U.S. govt. service, 1917-24; fgn. service officer, Dept. State, 1924-61; vice consul, Stuttgart, Germany, 1924-41; assigned State Dept., Washington, 1941-45; consul, Zurich, Switzerland, 1945-50; consul, Naples, Italy, 1950-54; consul, attache, Copenhagen, Denmark, 1954-61, ret., 1961. Served as aerial photographer U.S. Army, 1918-19. Home: Heidelberg Germany Died Mar. 31, 1973.

TEMPLE, MARY BOYCE, welfare worker; b. Knoxville, Tenn.; d. Oliver Perry and Caledonia (Hume) T.; A.B., Vassar, 1877; LL.D., Lincoln Memorial U., 1921. Active in civic, patriotic and ednl. work, especially in carrying on work begun by father, who organized the first Farmers' Conv. in U.S., 1872; founded short course in agr., applied in various cos. of Tenn.; mem. Tenn. Farmers' Inst. and Conv. (v.p. for life 1919), Rural Credit Commn., which officially visited Europe to observe conditions there in behalf of U.S., 1913. Mem. Tenn. Commn., Atlanta Expn., 1895; 1st v.p. Woman's Bd. of Tenn. Centennial Expn., 1897; represented Tenn. at Paris Expn., 1900; only woman on Jury of Higher Edn., St. Louis Expn., 1904; commr. to Jamestown Expn., 1907; chmn. of Special Days National Conservation Expn., Knoxville, Tenn., 1913. Organizer, 1893, and regent various terms Bonny Kate Chapter D.A.R.; v.p. gen. Nat. Soc. D.A.R., 1898-1900, state regent for Tenn., 1906-08, state v.-regent, 1908-10; 1st corr. sec. Gen. Fed. Women's Clubs, 1890-94, and state chmn. correspondence various Southern states, 1894-96; organizer, 1885, and pres. 5 yrs., of Ossoli Circle; state chmn. Daniel Boone Trail for Tenn. and marked trail through Tenn., 1914; mem. council George Washington U., 1919; founder Oliver Perry Temple Plant Breeding Foundation of $25,000, U. of Tenn., 1919; a commr. to Brazilian Expn., Rio Janeiro, 1922-23; also to Sesquicentennial Expn., Philadelphia; dist. chmn. League of Women Voters, also of Good Roads Assn., 1922-28; pres. gen. of Women's Aux., Southern Commercial Congress, and made a study of ednl. system of Scandinavian countries, 1923; commr. to Sesquicentennial Expn., Phila., 1926. Charter mem. George Washington Memorial Assn., 1898; mem. woman's dept. Nat. Civic Federation. Mem. Archaeol. Inst. America, Tenn. Hist. Assn., Authors' League America, League of Am. Pen Women, English-Speaking Union; pres. Gov. William Blount Mansion Assn. Presbyn. Club: Am. Women's of London. Author: Sketch of Margaret Fuller Ossoli, 1886. Editor: Notable Men of Tennessee, 1912. Vice-chmn. woman's com. of council Nat. Defense of Knoxville; mem. War Library Commn.; financed the Hoover state food administrator's work, 1917-18; chmn. D.A.R. war relief work of Knoxville, again state regent Tenn. D.A.R., 1920-21, and began campaign resulting in raising $50,000 for a boys' dormitory for Lincoln Memorial U., dedicated Nov. 5, 1921. Home: 623 W. Hill Av., Knoxville TN‡

TEMPLE, WALTER PAUL, capitalist; b. Merced ranch, Old Mission, Calif., June 7, 1869; s. Francis Pliny Fisk and Antonia Margarita (Workman) T.; nephew of John T., founder of the family in Calif., 1826, and builder Temple Block, Los Angeles; ed. Temple Sch., St. Vincents Coll. and business coll.; m. Laura Gonzales, of Old Mission, Nov. 28, 1903. Propr. La Puente ranch; announced discovery of Montebello oil fields; lessor oil lands and producer of petroleum; pres. Temple Holding Co.; dir. Talbert Oil Co., San Gabriel Bank; prop. Temple Theatre, Alhambra, Calif. Elk. Club: San Gabriel Country. Active in erecting monuments to notable events in San Gabriel Valley, founding hist. collections, etc. Home: Alhambra CA Office: Title Ins. Bldg., Los Angeles CA‡

TEMPLETON, CHARLOTTE, librarian; b. Brinkley, Ark., Dec. 24, 1877; d. Robert and Jane (Coleman) Templeton; A.B., U. of Neb., 1902 (Phi Beta Kappa); studied Pratt Inst. Library Sch., 1905. Reference librarian, Omaha (Neb.) Pub. Library, 1902-04; librarian, Oshkosh (Wis.) Pub. Library, 1905-06; sec. Neb. Pub. Library Commn., 1906-19; sec. Ga. State Library Commn., 1919-22; librarian, Greenville (S.C.) Pub. Library, 1922-31; librarian, Atlanta University, 1931-42. Mem. A.L.A. Address: Sautee GA‡

TEMPLETON, RICHARD HARKNESS, lawyer; b. Buffalo, N.Y., Sept. 23, 1877; s. Thomas and Charlotte (Harkness) T.; prep. edn., Central High Sch., Buffalo; A.B., Syracuse U., 1899, studied law, same univ.; m. Mai Morgan, 1908; children—Richard Harkness, Mary Reese, Jean Morgan. Admitted to N.Y. bar, 1901, and began practice at Buffalo; lecturer on corps., U. of Buffalo, 1910-25; U.S. atty. Western Dist. of N.Y., by appointment of President Coolidge, 1925-35. Major of 74th Inf. of N.Y.N.G. Dir. Buffalo Assn. for the Blind, Legal Aid Bur., Buffalo Mus. of Science. Mem. Am., N.Y. State and Erie County bar assns., Phi Kappa Psi, Phi Delta Phi. Republican. Episcopalian. Mason (32 deg.). Home: 309 Porter Av. Office: White Bldg., Buffalo NY‡

TEMPLIN, LUCINDA DE LEFTWICH, educator; b. Nevada, Mo.; d. William Wayne and Ella (Rice) Templin; A.B., B.S., U. of Mo., 1914, A.M., 1915, Ph.D., 1926; post-grad. work, summers, Harvard, Columbia, 1922-23. Dean Lindenwood Coll. St. Charles, 1916-24, research scholar, 1924-25; prin. Radford Sch. for Girls since 1927, also chmn. bd. of dirs. Lectr. ednl. subjects. Trustee Radford Scholarship Fund. Mem. El Paso Co. Consumers Council. El Paso Opera Guild. Mem. Nat. Conf. Christians and Jews, El Paso, Womans, S.W. Tex. C.'s of C., Y.W.C.A., El Paso Archeology Assn. Edn., Nat. Assn. Prins. Schs. for Girls, Am. Assn. U. Women, Nat. Assn. Adminstrv. Women Edn., Nat. Vocational Guidance Assn., Pan-Am. Round Table, Texas Assn. Pvt. Schs. (v.p. 1953-54), Am. Assn. U. Profs., El Paso Hist. Soc., Am. Inst. Mgmt., Am. Geog. Soc., D.A.R., A.A.A.S., Am. Acad. Polit. Sci., N.E.A. Shakespeare Soc. Am., Mus. Modern Art, Am. Mus. Natural History, Am. Hist. Assn., Am. Social Assn., Phi Theta Kappa, Pi Lambda Theta, Alpha Pi Zeta. Democrat. Baptist. Clubs: Knife and Fork, College Women's, Woman's, City Government, Coronado Country (El El Paso TX

TENBROEK, JACOBUS, educator; b. Alberta, Can., July 6, 1911; s. Nicolaas and Gerte (Bogart) tenB.; came to U.S., 1919, naturalized, 1927; A.B., U. Cal. at Berkeley, 1934, M.A., 1935, LL.B., 1938, J.S.D., 1940; S.J.D., Harvard University 1947; D.Litt., Findlay College, 1956; LL.D., Parson's Coll. 1964; m. Hazel Feldheym, Apr. 10, 1937; children—Jacobus, Anna C., Nicolaas. Lectr., tutor Law Sch. U. Chgo., 1940-42; instr. U. Cal. at Berkeley, 1942-46, asst. prof., 1946-47, asso. prof., 1947-53, prof., 1953-68, chmn. dept. speech, 1955-68, professor department political science, 1963-68; vis. asst. prof. Law Sch. U. Colo., 1946. Pres. Nat. Fedn. of Blind, 1940-61, 66-68, Am. Brotherhood for Blind, 1945-68; mem. Cal. Welfare Bd., 1950-68, Pres.'s Com. Employ Physically Handicapped, 1950; mem. Cal. State Social Welfare Bd., 1950-63, chmn., 1960-63. Brandeis research fellow Harvard Law Sch., 1939-40; co-recipient Woodrow Wilson Found. award, 1955; fellow Center for Advanced Study in the Behavioral Sciences, 1959-60; Guggenheim fellow, 1954-55, 60-61. Mem. Speech Assn. Am., Am. Polit. Sci. Assn., Harvard, U. Cal. law sch. assns. Author: The Anti-Slavery Origins of the 14th Amendment, 1951; Prejudice, War and the Constitution, 1954; California's Adoption Law and Programs, 1955; Hope Deferred, 1959; Law of the Poor, 1966; California's Dual System of Family, 1964. Home: Berkeley CA Died Mar. 27, 1968; buried Rolling Hills Meml. Park CA

TENNEY, CHARLES WESLEY, educator; b. Vancouver, Wash., July 31, 1873; s. Horace Dewey and Ellen (Goddard) T.; Ph.B., Willamette U., Salem, Ore., 1898; student Ore. Law Sch., 1898-99; M.A., George Washington U., 1908; LL.D., Intermountain Union Coll., Helena, Mont., 1927; m. Alice Maude Huston, May 25, 1905; children—Charles Dewey, Helen Alice (dec.), Mary Elizabeth. Pres. and prof. Montana Wesleyan (now Intermountain Union) Coll., 1899-1913; rural sch. inspector of Mont. schs., 1913-17; supt. schs., Libby, Mont., 1917-18; pres. Gooding (Ida.) Coll., 1918-35; dir. and Bible instr. Inst. Christian Edn., U. of Ida., since 1935. Lecturer summer schs., and has engaged widely in extension work; ordained ministry M.E. Ch. Chmn. bd. trustees Ellison-White Chautauqua Assn. Mem. N.E.A., Ida. Teachers' Assn., Mont. State Teachers' Assn., Inland Empire Teachers' Assn., Phi Delta Phi. Del. Gen. Conf. M.E. Ch., 1924, 28, 32. Republican. Methodist. Home: Moscow ID‡

TENNEY, HENRY FAVILL, lawyer; b. Chicago, Ill., June 1, 1890; s. Horace Kent and Eleanor Baird (Favill) T.; Williams Coll., 1908-12; M.A. (hon.), 1946, Ph.B., U. of Chicago, 1913, J.D., 1915; m. Eleanor N. Elmer, Dec. 24, 1917. Admitted to Ill. bar, 1915, practiced in Chicago, mem. firm of Tenney, Sherman, Bentley & Guthrie, from 1916; dir. Inland Steel Company, Mid-West Forging &Mfg. Co., Bradner Smith & Company. President Village of Winnetka, Ill., 1927-29; chmn. Chicago chapter Am. Red Cross 1944-46; mem. bd. trustees, U. of Chicago and Wesley Memorial Hosp.; mem. bd. governors Am. Nat. Red Cross, 1948-54, and from 1960; mem. Ill. Civil Service Commn., from 1961; dir. Chicago Boys Club, club, Good Will Industries, Chgo. Community Trust; chmn. Public Aid Commission 1949-52. Capt. 332d F.A., 86th Div., U.S.A., Apr. 1917-Mar. 1919. Mem. Am., Ill. State and Chicago bar assns., Law Club, Legal Club, Chi Psi, Phi Delta Phi. Democrat. Clubs: Univ., Mid-Day, Indian Hill, Tavern, Commercial, Chicago. Home: Winnetka IL Died Sept. 1, 1971.

TENNY, LLOYD STANLEY, agricultural expert; b. Hilton, N.Y., Dec. 24, 1876; s. Delos P. and Fannie Elizabeth (Lee) T.; grad. State Normal Sch., Brockport, N.Y., 1896; A.B., U. of Rochester, 1902; scholarship for research, Marine Biol. Lab., Woods Hole, Mass., 1902; studied, Cornell, 1908; m. Abby Warn, June 1, 1907; children—Fannybelle Lee, Stanley Warn, Lloyd Stanley. With Cornell U., 1911-13, advancing to prof. of extension; 1st state leader of county agrl. agts. in N.Y. State and assisted in establishing the first country farm bureaus; in charge service and regulatory work and asst. chief Bur. Agrl. Economics, U.S. Dept. Agr., 1921-26; chief of Bur. Agrl. Economics, 1926-28; v.p. Calif. Vineyardists Assn., 1928-29; pres. Federal Fruit Stabilization Corp. of Calif., Apr.-Nov. 1929; gen. mgr. Chicago Mercantile Exchange since Nov. 1929. Mem. Advisory Com. War Finance Corp., 1921. Treas. 7th World Poultry Congress, Cleveland, O., 1939. Republican. Baptist. Clubs: Alpha Delta Phi (New York); Cosmos (Washington); Electric (Chicago). Author of articles in mags. and published addresses. Address: Chicago Chicago IL*‡

TEPOEL, LOUIS JOHN, lawyer, educator; b. Wahoo, Neb., Dec. 15, 1877; s. John A. and Hannah (Mahoney) T.; A.B., Fremont (Neb.) Coll., 1901; studied U. of Neb.; A.M., LL.B., Columbia, 1905; LL.D., Creighton U., Omaha, Neb., 1930; m. Harriett Service Barnett, Sept. 1927. Admitted to Neb. bar, 1905, and began practice at Omaha; part time prof. law, Creighton U., 1907-20; dean Coll. of Law, same Univ., 1920-47, emeritus; city atty. Omaha, 1921; corp. counsel of Omaha, 1933. Dir. Omaha Pub. Library, 1908-18; mem. Neb. State Constl. Conv., 1919-20; chmn. State Judicial Council, 1939-43; member bd. dir. since 1939. Omaha C. of C. since 1943; mem. Omaha City Planning Commission since 1938. Nat. chmn. Artists Veterans Hosp. Programs, 1947-50. Mem. Am. and Neb. State bar assns., Am. Law Inst. Democrat. Catholic. Elk. Club: Professional Men's. Home: 415 N. 38th St. Office: Omaha Nat. Bank Bldg., Omaha NE‡

TERMOHLEN, WILLIAM DEWEY, govt. official; b. Storm Lake, Ia., June 20, 1898; s. William and Susanna Charlotte (Lundgren) T.; B.S., Ia. State Coll., 1925, M.S., 1927; m. Marie Saloman, Sept. 17, 1923 (dec. 1954); children—Barbara, Mary; married second, Josephine Marsh, March 3, 1955. With feed and seed mfr., 1925; field specialist, poultry and egg marketing, Ia. State Coll., 1927-33; with U.S. Dept. Agr. since 1933, dir. poultry br., prodn. and marketing adminstrn., 1946-53, poultry div. agrl. marketing service, 1953-55; agrl. attache Fgn. Agrl. Service, Tokyo, Japan, from 1955. Served in U.S. Army World War I. Mem. Am., World's (pres. 1949-51) poultry sci. assns., Sigma Alpha Epsilon, Phi Kappa Phi, Gamma Sigma Delta, Alpha Zeta, Am. Legion. Lutheran. Co-author; Marketing Poultry Products, 1948. Address: Hendersonville TN Died Oct. 1970.

TERRELL, ROY, b. Houston, Tex., February 18, 1876; s. Edwin Ruthven and Kate (Scurry) T.; grad. S.C. Military Acad., Charleston, S.C., 1897; m. Anina Legendre, of New Orleans, La., Nov. 23, 1912. Clk. gen. freight office M.K. & T. Ry. Co., 1897-99; became connected with St.L.&S.F. R.R. Co., 1899, successively soliciting freight agt., at Dallas, Tex., until 1907, traveling freight agt., commercial agt., gen. freight and passenger agt. of one of subsidiary cos.; asst. gen. freight and passenger agt., Frisco System, at New Orleans, until 1916; continued with La. and S. Tex. properties of the rd. under receivership; asst. to pres. New Orleans, Tex. & Mexico Ry., 1916-17; v.p. same rd., 1917-27, sec., 1920-27; v.p., gen. mgr. New Orleans Pontchartrain Bridge Co. since Oct. 15, 1927. Mem. Am. Assn. Freight Traffic Officers (exec. com.). Democrat. Episcopalian. Mason. Clubs: Boston, Louisiana, Country, New Orleans Traffic, Southern Yacht (New Orleans); Traffic (Chicago). Home: Roosevelt Hotel. Office: Canal Bank Bldg., New Orleans LA‡

TERRELL, SCURRY LATIMER, oculist, aurist; b. Houston, Tex., Dec. 12, 1869; s. Edwin Ruthven and Kate (Scurry) T.; A.B., U. of Ala., 1889; M.D., Coll. Phys. & Surg., Baltimore, 1895; post-grad. work in New York, London, Paris, Vienna and Wurzburg; m. Joe C. Goode, of Fort Worth, Tex., Apr. 30, 1908 (died Apr. 9, 1910); 2d, Homer Collier Gaston, June 21, 1913. Practiced, Dallas, Tex., 1896; formerly surgeon Tex. & Pacific Coal Co.; prof. otology, med. dept., Southern Meth. U.; mem. staff St. Paul's Sanitarium; consulting oculist and aurist various rys.; served as specialist to Col. Theodore Roosevelt, campaign 1912. Maj. Med. Corps Tex. N.G., now U.S.A. Progressive. Episcopalian. Mem. A.M.A., Tex. State Med. Assn., Dallas Co. Med. Soc., Assn. Mil. Surgeons of U.S., Delta Tau Delta, etc. Clubs: Dallas, Dallas Press, Dallas Country. Aurist to Gen. Hosp. 23, British Expeditionary Force, France, summer, 1915. Home: 2807 Forest Av. Office: Wilson Bldg., Dallas TX‡

TERRELL, WILLIAM DANDRIDGE, govt. radio official; b. Golansville, Va., Aug. 10, 1871; s. Joseph Thomas and Susan Frances (Wood) T.; ed. pub. and pvt. schs. and business coll.; m. Estelle Wilkerson, Nov. 6, 1901; children—Charlotte, William Dandridge. Began with Postal Telegraph Co., Golansville, Va., 1889, mgr. office, Alexandria, Va., 1891-92, successively operator, traffic chief, wire chief, Washington, D.C., 1893-1900; in charge leased wire service, Am. Can Co., New York, 1900-01; wire chief, Postal Telegraph Co., Washington, 1901-03; telegraph service, customs service, U.S. Treasury Dept., 1903-11; radio insp., U.S. Dept. Commerce, N.Y. City, 1911-15; in charge radio div., same dept., Washington, D.C., 1915-32; chief of div. of field operations, Fed. Radio Commission, July-Dec. 1932; chief of field div., Fed. Communications Commn., 1934-43. Mem. national radio confs. called by sec. of Commerce, 1922, 23, 24, 25. Del. to internat. Radio-telegraph Conf., London, 1912, Washington, D.C., 1927; tech. adviser Internat. Telegraph Conf., Paris, 1925; del. to Am. Canadian Radio Conf., Ottawa, Can., 1929, Safety of Life at Sea Conf., London, 1929; chmn. Am. delegation European Broadcasting Conf., Prague, 1929; mem. Am. sect. Internat. Com. on Radio. Fellow, Inst. Radio Engrs.; hon. mem. Veteran Wireless Operators Assn.; mem. Sons of Confederate Veterans. Mason. Retired August 31, 1943. Home: Miami FL*‡

TERRIBERRY, WILLIAM S(TOUTENBOROUGH), U.S. Pub. Health Service; b. Paterson, N.J., July 3, 1871; s. George W. and Martha Griffith (Stoutenborough) T.; grad. St. Paul's Sch., Garden City, N.Y., 1889; A.B., Yale, 1893; M.D., Columbia, 1896; m. Emilie Varet Reinhart, of N.Y. City, Oct. 17, 1907. Asst. surgeon (1st lt.) N.J.V., 1898; contract surgeon U.S. Army, 1898-99; lt. col. Med. Corps, N.Y. Nat. Guard, 1916; lt. col. Med. Corps, U.S.A., 1918, assigned as comdg. officer Embarkation Hosp., Newport News, Va.; advanced to col., Aug. 1918, hon. discharged, Nov. 1919; commd. asst. surgeon U.S.P.H.S., Dec. 1919, sr. surgeon, Jan. 1920, asst. surgeon gen., July 1920, med. dir. 1930; retired, Nov. 1937. Awarded Conspicuous Service Cross, 1922. Mem. Zeta Psi. Clubs: Yale (N.Y. City); Army and Navy (Washington, D.C.). Home: Old Lyme CT‡

TERRIEN, PIERRE-ESDRAS, business exec.; b. St. Monique, Nicolet, Que., June 29, 1876; s. Herecules Hercules Louise (Provencher) T.; B.L., Seminaire de Nicolet, 1899; m. Eva Lemieux, June 29, 1909; children—Marguerite, Cecile, Jean, Therese (Mrs. Armand Filion), Marthe, Louis, Francois. Sec. to L. Joseph Tarte, gen. mgr. newspaper La Patrie, Montreal, Nov. 1899, to March, 1900; statis. clerk Customs Dept., Ottawa, 1903-21, prin. clerk, 1922-27; translator, 1928-35; chief translator 1936-42; gen. mgr. Le Droit, Ottawa, Ont., since 1942, pres. since 1916; pres. Le Syndicat d'Oeuvres Sociales Limitie (pub. Le Droit), since 1916. Treas. L'Association C. F. d'Education d'Ontario. Roman Catholic. Home: 256 Besserer St. Office: Le Droit, Ottawa ON Can‡

TERRILL, DEAN, lawyer; b. Colchester, Ill., Dec. 27, 1904; s. David Edward and Edith May (Webb) T.; student Western Ill. Normal Tng. Sch., 1916-17, Western Ill. Normal Acad., 1921; B.S., Knox Coll., 1925; LL.B., Harvard, 1929. Admitted to Ill. bar, 1929; began practice with Chapman & Cutler, Chgo., 1929; asso. Robert S. Kerr, Oklahoma City, 1935; v.p., dir., gen. counsel Kerr-McGee Corp. (formerly Kerr-McGee Oil Industries, Inc.), Oklahoma City, 1936-52, dir., spl. counsel, from 1952; pvt. practice, Chgo., 1952-72. Assisted drafting Ill. Bus. Corp. Act; practitioner Fed. Securities Act. Dir. Found. for Fgn. Affairs, Inc.; trustee, scholarship dir. Phi Sigma Kappa Foundation; past trustee of Oklahoma Symphony Soc. Mem. Okla. Jr. Symphony Soc. (1st Pres.), Am., Ill., Chgo. bar assns., Phi Beta Kappa Associates, mem. Phi Beta Kappa, Delta Sigma Rho, Phi Sigma Kappa. Mem. Christian Ch. Club: University (Chgo.). Past Chicago IL Died May 3, 1972; buried Mt. Auburn Cemetery Colchester IL

TERRY, CHARLES LAYMEN, JR., gov. Del.; b. Camden, Del., Sept. 17, 1900; s. Charles and Elizabeth (Maxson) T.; LL.B., Washington and Lee U., 1923; m. Jessica Irby, June 30, 1924; 1 son, Charles Laymen III.

Admitted to Del. bar, 1924; mem. firm Hughes, Terry & Terry, 1935-37; atty. Del. Legislature, 1933-34; sec. state, Del., 1937-38; became asso. judge Supreme Ct. of Del., 1938, later chief justice; gov. Del., 1964-68. Mem. electors Hall of Fame. Mem. Sons Colonial Wars, Phi Sigma Kappa. Democrat. Episcopalian. Clubs: Maple Dale Country (Dover); Indian River Beach (Rehoboth Beach, Del.); Wilmington (Del.). Home: Dover DE Died Feb. 6, 1970; buried Christ Church Yard.

TERRY, HOWARD LESLIE, poet, writer; b. St. Louis, Mo., Jan. 4, 1877; s. John Henry and Elizabeth Helen (Todd) T.; ed. Collinsville (Ill.) Pub. Sch., 1888-94, Rugby Acad., St. Louis, 1894-95, Gallaudet Coll., Washington, D.C., 1895-97 (hon. M.Litt. 1938); m. Alice Taylor, Mar. 5, 1901; children—Catherine Bassett (Mrs. Ellis Van Gorder), Howard Leslie, Victor Taylor. Deaf since 11 years of age. Civil service clerk St. Louis Post Office, 1899-1901 (resigned because of failing eyesight); farming, southwest Mo. and Ill. until 1908; began writing, in boyhood. Dir. Lit. Bureau, Nat. Assn. of Deaf, 1913-14. Pres. Guild of Am. Deaf Writers, 1941. Formerly member Poetry Club Southern California; member Eugene Field Society, Nat. Writers Club, Pi Gamma Mu. Episcopalian. Author: Waters from an Ozark Spring (poems), 1909; California and Other Poems, 1912; A Voice from the Silence (novel), 1914, pub. serially as Man of the Soil, 1946; Sung in Silence (poems), 1929. Contbr. verse, arts., stories to mags. and papers, and to papers and mags. pub. in the interest of the deaf. Reporter and correspondent St. Louis-Globe Hollywood CA‡

TERRY, WALLACE IRVING, surgeon; b. Sacramento, Calif., Nov. 26, 1868; s. Wallace Emmet and Laura Abigail (Morrill) T.; B.S., U. of Calif., 1890, M.D., 1892; univs. of Berlin and Paris, 1894-96; m. Mary Frances Dudley, Apr. 19, 1898; children—Elizabeth Dudley (Mrs. Robertson Ward), Wallace Irving. Interne, St. Luke's Hosp., San Francisco, 1892-93; city physician, Sacramento, 1893; asst. in surgery, U. of Calif., 1899-1903, instr., 1903-07, asst. prof., 1907-12, prof., 1912-32, clin. prof., 1932-39; clinical prof. emeritus since 1939. Fellow Am. Surgical Assn., Am. Coll. Surgeons, Pacific Coast Surg. Assn.; mem. Zeta Psi, Nu Sigma Nu, Alpha Omega Alpha, Sigma Xi; hon. mem. San Francisco County Med. Soc. Republican. Episcopalian. Mason. Club: Pacific Union. Home: 2712 Broadway, San Francisco 15 CA‡

TETLOW, PERCY, mem. Bituminous Coal-Commn.; b. Leetonia, O., Dec. 16, 1875; s. William and Ann (Hadfield) T.; ed. pub. schs.; m. Sadie M. Carrier, of Washingtonville, O., July 3, 1900; children—Harry Lester, Percy William, Jessie May. Began as coal miner and became union official; mem. 4th Constitutional Conv. of Ohio, 1912; mem. Ohio Ho. of Rep., 1913; dir. Industrial Relations of Ohio, 1921-22; mem. Bituminous Coal Commn., Washington, D.C., since Sept. 21, 1935, now chmn. Served as pvt. Co. B, 16th Vol. Inf., Spanish-Am. War, 1898; capt. 134th Machine Gun Batt., 37th Div., World War, 1917-19. Republican. Methodist. Home: Columbus OH Address: Investment Bldg., 15th and K Sts. N.W., Washington DC‡

TEWELL, HAROLD STRONG, foreign service officer; b. Drayton, N.D., Jan. 7, 1892; s. Harry A. and May Lodema (Strong) T.; student U. of N.D., 1910-12; m. Helen Katherine Stixrud, Aug. 21, 1917; children—Vivian Thora, Shirley May, Helen Louise Strong, Richard Harold. In pvt. business, 1912-13; U.S. Customs Service, 1913-18; U.S. Immigration Service, 1918-20; v.consul Winnipeg, Can., 1920-22, North Bay, Ont., 1922-24; consul Vancouver, B.C., 1924-33; consul Havana, Cuba, 1933-42, consul gen., Mar. 1942, first sec. of Embassy, July 1942; consul gen., Barcelona, Sept. 1942; first sec. of Embassy, Rio de Janeiro, Dec. 1942, also Consul gen. at Rio de Janeiro, Mar. 1944; assigned to Dept. of State, Mar. 1945; asst. Chief, Div. Foreign Service Personnel, Aug. 7, 1945; counselor of Embassy, Havana, Cuba, 1947-50, ret. Clubs: American, Country Club, Biltmore Yacht and Country Club (Havana). Methodist. Address: Coral Gables FL Died Apr. 1972.

TEXTOR, G(EORGE) C(LINTON), banker; b. Brooklyn, July 28, 1900; s. Emil and Georgina (Kirkpatrick) T.; ed. pub. schs. of N.Y. City; m. Janice Fleming, Mar. 17, 1939; children—(by former marriage)—Joan (Mrs. C. Mildrum), George, Donald. With Marine Midland Grace Trust Co., N.Y.C., 1916-68, became exec. v.p., 1950, pres. until 1966, chmn., chief exec. officer, 1966-67, chmn. bd. 1967-68; dir. Foremost-Mckesson, Inc., C F & I Steel Corp., Random House, Marine Midland Banks, Inc., PepsiCo, Inc., Ambac Industries, Inc., Houdaille Industries, Inc., Carrier Corp., Crum & Forster, Sperry Rand Corp. Chmn. bd. trustees Ithaca Coll.; trustee N.Y. Community Trust, Nat. Found.; dir. Salvation Army, Am.-Israel Cultural Found.; gov., treas. Arthritis and Rheumatism Found.; treas., dir. Fedn. Protestant Welfare Agencies. Mem. Am., N.Y. State bankers assns., Am. Inst. Banking, Res. City Bankers Assn., Federal Hall Meml. Assos. (gov.), N.Y. Clearing House Assn., National Association of Manufacturers (director), N.Y. C. of C. Republican. Episcopalian. Clubs: Bankers of America, Racquet and Tennis,

Downtown Assn., Economic, Pilgrims, Pinnacle, Newcomen Soc. (N.Y.C.); Garden City (N.Y.) Golf; Nat. Golf Links of America, Lawrence Beach; Deepdale Golf, Madison Square Garden, Metropolitan Opera, Links (N.Y.C.); Everglades (Palm Beach, Fla.). Home: Garden City NY Died Oct. 9, 1968.

THACKSTON, JOHN ANDY, educator; b. Cedar Grove, S.C., Apr. 16, 1876; s. Elijah Ray and Annie (Brown) T.; A.B., Furman U., 1899; Pd.M., New York U., 1907, Ph.D., 1908; m. Annie Gill, Dec. 24, 1903; children—James Fred, John Arla, Sara. Supt. schs. in S.C., 1899-1906; prof. mathematics, State Normal Sch., Winona, Minn., 1908-09; prof. edn. and philosophy, U. of Fla., 1909-10, dean Teachers Coll., 1910-16; state high sch. insp., Fla., 1910-16; prof. edn., Univ. of Tenn., 1916-49. Member State Textbook Commn., Tenn., 1919-24; dir. summer quarter, U. of Tenn., 1921-43, dean summer quarter, 1943-49; head Sch. of Education, same, 1923-26, dean College of Edn., 1926-43. Mem. Tenn. State Teachers Assn. (pres. 1931); chmn. Tenn. Edn. Assn., Code of Ethics Commn.; mem. Nat. Edn. Assn. adv. com. on professional ethics of N.E.A., sec.-treas. Tenn. Assn. of Pub. School Board Members, Am. Assn. of School Administrators, Am. Edn. Fellowship, Phi Kappa Phi, Phi Delta Kappa. Author: High School Manual, 1911; author-editor or co-author books relating to field. Home: 31 Highland Hills, Knoxville TN‡

THAETE, EDWARD H., banker; b. Phila., Nov. 3, 1876; s. Frederick and Paulina (Fleig) T.; ed. pub. sch.; student Temple Business Sch. (nights); m. Regina M. Frisby, June 27, 1900 (died Jan. 2, 1934); children—Edward H., John, Regina T. Clark, Geraldine K. Shipley; m. 2d, Evalina G. Keenan, May 12, 1943. With Land Title & Trust Co., Phila., 1892-1917; with F. P. Risline & Co. (mem. N.Y. Stock Exchange) since Mar. 1917; dir. Freeport Sulphur Co. since 1930. Mem. Catholic Philopatrian Literature Inst. Republican. Roman Catholic. Clubs: Racquet, Play and Players. Home: 1900 Rittenhouse Square, Philadelphia 3 PA Office: 123 S. Broad St., Philadelphia 9 PA‡

THATCHER, GEORGE WILSON, educator; b. Ogden, Utah, Aug. 1, 1913; s. Gilbert and Margret (Folkman) T.; B.S., U. Utah, 1936; Ph.M., U., Wis., 1939, Ph.D., 1951; m. Alberta Riegel Neiswonger, Aug. 17, 1941; children—Karen Margret, Jeffrey Kirk. Grad. asst. U. Wis., 1937-40; faculty Miami University, Oxford, Ohio, 1940-42, 45-71, professor of economics, 1957-71, chairman of the department, 1957-63. Served to lieutenant (s.g.) USNR, 1942; 45. Mem. Am. Econ. Assn., Nat. Tax Assn., Beta Gamma Sigma, Delta Sigma Pi, Omicron Delta Kappa. Home: Oxford OH Died May 9, 1971; buried Oxford Cemetery, Oxford OH

THATCHER, MAURICE HUDSON, govt. ofcl.; b. Chgo., Aug. 15, 1870; s. John Christopher and Mary Tyler (Graves) T.; student pvt., pub. schs.; LL.D., U. Ala., 1930; m. Anne Bell Chinn, May 4, 1910 (dec. 1960). Asst. atty. gen. Ky., 1898-90; asst. U.S. dist. atty. for western Ky., 1901-06; state ins. and examiner, Ky., 1908-10; mem. Isthmian Canal Commn., civil gov. C.Z., 1910-13; practice law, Louisville, 1913-23; mem. Bd. Pub. Safety, Louisville, 1917-19, counsel, 1919-23; mem. U.S. Ho. of Reps., 1923-33; gen. counsel Gorgas Meml. Inst. Tropical and Preventive Medicine, Inc., Panama City, Panama, 1939-69, v.p., 1948-69, hon. pres., gen. counsel, 1969-73. Named hon. gov. C.Z., 1970; recipient Panama Canal Hon. Pub. Service award, 1970; decorated Order al Merito and Eloy Alfaro, Found. Ecuador; Order del Libertador Venezuela, Order Vasco Nunez de Balboa, Comendador con Placa. Mem. Eastern Nat. Park-to-Park Hwy. Assn. (founder, pres.), Panama Canal Soc. Washington, S.A.R., Baronial Order Magna Charta, Mil. Order Crusades, Washington Soc. Mayflower Descs. (past gov., hon. life counselor gen.), Am. Bar Assn. (life). Republican. Editor, compiler Stories and Speeches of William O. Bradley, 1906. Contbr. poems to mags., newspapers. Home: Washington DC Died Jan. 16, 1973; buried Frankfort Cemetery, Frankfort KY

THATCHER, W. ROSS, premier Saskatchewan; b. Neville, Sask., Can., May 24, 1917; s. Wilbert and Marjorie Thatcher; B. Commerce, Queen's U., Kingston, Ont.; m. Adrah Leone McNaughton; 1 son, Wilbert Colin. Alderman, City of Moose Jaw, 1942-44; mem. Parliament 12 yrs.; mem. Legislature, constituency of Morse, 1960—; premier of Sask., 1964-71. Privy Councillor. Mason. Club: Lions. Home: Regina SK Canada. Died July 23, 1971; buried Rosedale Cemetery, Moose Jaw Sask Canada

THAYER, CHARLES W(HEELER), writer; born Villanova, Pa., Feb. 9, 1910; s. George Chapman and Gertrude May (Wheeler) T.; student St. Paul's Sch., Concord, N.H., 1923-28; B.S., U.S. Mil. Acad., West Point, 1933; m. Cynthia Dunn, Mar. 27, 1950; stepdaughter, Diana, 1 son, James Dunn. U.S. fgn. service officer 1933-53; in Moscow, 1933-37, Berlin, 1937-38, Hamburg, 1939-40, Moscow, 1940-42, Kabul, Afghanistan, 1942-43, London, 1943-44; served as lt. col., U.S. Army, chief of mil. mission to Yugoslavia, 1944-45; chief, O.S.S., Austria 1945-46; mem. U.S.-U.S.S.R. Commn. for Korea, 1946; at U.S. Nat.

War Coll., 1946; chief, div. internat. broadcasting, Voice of America, 1947-49; polit. liaison officer to German Govt., Bonn, Germany, 1950-51; U.S. consul gen., Munich, 1952-53. Clubs: Metropolitan (Washington). Author: Bears in the Caviar; Hands Across the Caviar; The Unquiet Germans, 1957; Diplomat, 1959; Russia (with others), 1960; Moscow Interlude, 1962; Checkpoint, 1963; Guerrilla, 1963; Muzzy, 1966. Home: Philadelphia PA Died Aug. 27, 1969; buried Bryn Mawr PA

THAYER, EMMA REDINGTON LEE (PEN NAME LEE THAYER"), designer, author; b. Troy, Pa., Apr. 5, 1874; d. Edgar James and Jane Eliza (Pomeroy) Lee; ed. pub. schs.; m. Henry W. Thayer, Jan. 9, 1909 (died 1941). Studied interior decoration under Mrs. Candace Wheeler, New York; associated with Dora Wheeler Keith in decorating Woman's Building, Chicago Expn., 1892-93; formerly director Decorative Designers, N.Y. Republican. Author numerous books since 1919; latest publs.: Within the Vault, 1950; Too Long Endured, 1950; Guilt Edged, 1951; Do Not Disturb (in prep.). Home: 2514 Cedar St., Berkeley CA‡

THAYER, LUCIUS ELLSWORTH, lawyer; b. Portsmouth, N.H., June 19, 1896; s. Rev. Lucius Harrison and Helen Chadwick (Rand) T.; grad. Phillips Exeter Acad., 1914; B.A., Amherst Coll., 1918; LL.B., Harvard, 1923; m. Virginia Speare, Sept. 13, 1924; children—Lucius Harrison II, Patricia V. Admitted to Mass. bar, 1923; asso. Hale & Dorr, Boston, 1923-68, sr. partner, 1932-68, pres., 1949-65. Chmn., Exolon Co., abrasives, Tonawanda, N.Y., 1961-68, also dir.; chmn. Sherwood Investors, Inc., Brookline, Mass. President Bd. of Ministerial Aid. Mass. Commissioner, sinking fund, City of Newton. Sec., trustee Robert Coll., Istanbul, Turkey; board of trustees (recipient layman's citation award) Andover Theological Sch. Served with Am. Field Service, French Army, 1917; with Nr. East Relief, Konia, Asia Minor, 1919. Mem. Newton Council Chs. (1st pres.), Boston Seaman's Friend Soc. (past. pres.), Am., Mass. bar assns., Newcomen Soc., Am. Soc. Internat. Law, UN League Lawyers (past v.p. Am. div.), Phi Beta Kappa, Psi Upsilon. Conglist. (trustee Mass. Conf., moderator 1947, auditor, past vice chmn. Am. bd. commrs. fgn. missions). Clubs: Union, Algonquin (Boston); Braeburn (Newton); Dublin (N.H.) Sake. Home: West Newton MA Died Apr. 8, 1968.

THAYER, WALTER, railway official; b. Wayne, Pa., Apr. 27, 1875; s. John B. and Mary R. T.; U. of Pa., 1892-5; unmarried. Began as receiving clk. in frt. sta., Pa. R.R. at Phila., 1895; clk. same rd., later frt. solicitor United Rys. of N.J.; spl. agt. frt. dept. Buffalo & Allegheny Valley div., Pa. R.R., at Pittsburgh, 1901-3; Eastern mgr. Erie & Western Transportation Co., at Phila., 1903-10; asst. gen. frt. agt. Pa. R.R. and gen. frt. agt. Erie & Western Transportation Co., 1910-12; gen. frt. agt. Pa. R.R., May 8, 1912-17; gen. coal frt. agt., same rd., Nov. 15, 1917. Home: Merion Station PA Address: Broad St. Station, Philadelphia PA‡

THEILER, MAX, research physician; b. Pretoria, South Africa, Jan. 30, 1899; s. Arnold and Emma (Jegge) T.; student U. Capetown 1917-18; L.R.C.P., Mem. Royal Coll. Surgeons, St. Thomas' Hosp., 1922; D.T.M. and H., London Sch. Tropical Medicine, 1922; m. Lillian Graham, Feb. 18, 1928; 1 dau., Elizabeth. Came to U.S. 1922. Asst., Instr. dept. tropical medicine, med. sch. Harvard, 1929-30; staff mem. Rockefeller Found., N.Y.C., 1930-72, dir. div. medicine and pub. health labs., 1951-64; prof. Yale Sch. Medicine, 1964-67, prof. emeritus epidemiology and microbiology, 1967-72, lectr.; extensive research on yellow fever, on mouse encephalomyelitis and viruses isolated in tropics, 1940-72. Recipient Chalmers' medal, 1939; Flattery medal, 1945; Lasker award, 1949; Nobel prize in physiology and medicine for devel. vacine against yellow fever, 1951. Mem. Am. Soc. Tropical Medicine, Harvey Soc., Royal Soc. Tropical Medicine and Hygiene. Author chpts. in med. books; also numerous. sci. articles. Home: New Haven CT Died Aug. 11, 1972.

THEIS, FRANK VICTOR, surgeon; b. Chgo., Feb. 25, 1899; s. Victor and Anna (Blonn) T.; B.S., U. Chicago, 1920, M.D., 1923; Francis Hardy fellow in surgery, Rush Med. Coll., 1926-28; post grad., U. Vienna, 1928-29; m. Hazel H. Ericsson, Dec. 9, 1931; children—Henry Ericsson. Peter Frank. Intern Cook Co. Hosp., Chgo., 1924-25. attending surgeon 1946—; prof surgery Cook County Grad. School Medicine; resident Presbyn.-St. Lukes Hosp., 1926-28, asso. attending surgeon, from 1943; surg. staff St. Joseph's Hosp., 1929-38; cons. surgeon Norweglan Am. Hosp.; pvt. practice surgery since 1929; asso. prof. surgery Rush Med. Coll., U. Ill. since 1941. Bd. dirs. Senior Centers Metropolitan Chgo. Served as comdr. M.C., U.S.N.R., since 1942. Diplomate Am. Bd. Surgery. Fellow A.C.S.; mem. Ill. State, Chgo. med. socs, Inst. medicine Chgo., Am. Heart Assn., Soc. Vascular surgeons, A.M.A., Chgo. Surg. Soc., Chgo. Inst. Medicine, Internat. Cardiovascular Soc., Central Surg. Soc., Am. Diabetic Assn., Pan Am. Med. Assn., Chgo. Council American Scandinavian Found., Internat. Surg. Soc., N.Y. Acad. Scis., Sigma Chi. Republican. Episcopalian. Clubs: Executives, University (Chgo.). Home: Chicago IL Died Mar. 12, 1972; buried Rosehill Cemetery, Chicago IL

THEISEN, WILLIAM W., educator; b. West Point, Neb., Jan. 16, 1886; s. Henry and Emma (Kerl) T.; B.S., U. of Neb., 1907; student U. of Wis. summers 1913, 14; A.M., Columbia, 1915, Ph.D., 1916; m. Blanche Shearer, Oct. 28, 1916. Teacher, high sch., West Point, 1907-08; prin. schs., Beemer, Neb., 1908-10; supt. schs., Pierce, 1910-14; statis. asst. Md. Edn. Survey, 1915; research fellow Teachers Coll. (Columbia), 1916; dir. ednl. measurements, Wis. State Dept. Pub. Instrn., 1916-20; dir. Bur. Reference and Research, pub. schs., Cleveland, O., 1920-22; asst. supt. schs., Milwaukee, Wis., 1922-49, elected superintendent pro tempore, April, 1949. Served as lecturer summers at various univs. and colls.; lecturer extension div. U. of Wis., 1922-26. Chmn. Milwaukee School Building Survey, 1923-69. Member of Milwaukee Technical Committee, 1944. Mem. Am. Ednl. Research Assn. (pres. 1923), Nat. Council on Schoolhouse Construction, Nat. Edn. Assn. mem. Yearbook Commn. of Dept of Superintendence, 1935, 1950), American Association of School Administrators, Phi Delta Kappa. Clubs: Inter-Professional, Civitan. Author, co-author or compiler books relating to field. Home: Milwaukee WI Died Apr. 27, 1969; interred Wis. Meml. Park Cemetery.

THELEEN, DAVID E., naval officer; b. Kenosha, Wis., Nov. 6, 1875; s. Charles G.T.; grad. U.S. Naval Acad., 1897; m. Mary C. Persons, of Auburn, Ala., June 2, 1903. Promoted ensign, July 1, 1899; lt. jr. grade, July 1, 1902; lt., Aug. 10, 1903; lt. comdr., July 1, 1909; comdr., Aug. 29, 1916; capt. (temporary), Feb. 1, 1918. Served on Massachusetts during Spanish-Am. War, 1898; on surveying cruises in West Indies 3 yrs. and with Atlantic Training Squadron 3 yrs.; duty at Naval Proving Gound, Indian Head, Md., and two times at Naval Gun Factory, Navy Yard, Washington, D.C.; comdr. U.S.S. Glacier in U.S. Pacific Fleet, at outbreak of World War; served in Brazil and off East Coast S. America; duty Navy Yard, Washington, D.C., Sept. 1917-19; assigned as comdr. U.S.S. St. Louis, Oct. 8, 1919. Has specialized in ordnance work and engring. Mem. Am. Soc. Naval Engrs., Naval Inst. Republican. Baptist. Mason. Clubs: Army and Navy (Washington, D.C., and Manila). Address: Navy Dept., Washington DC‡

THELEN, MAX, lawyer; b. Rising City, Neb., Oct. 2, 1880; s. Edmund and Fanny J. M. (Bayrhoffer) T.; B.L., U. Cal., 1904, LL.D., 1966; A.M. Harvard, 1906; m. Ora Emily Muir, May 1, 1913; children—Ora, Henry Muir, Max, Dorothy Elise. With firm Olney & Olney, San Francisco, 1906-07; asst. atty. and atty. Western Pacific Ry. Co., 1907-11; atty. Calif. R. R. Commn., 1911-15; mem., 1912-18, pres., 1915-18. Lectr. Internat. law U. Cal., 1907-13; pres. Nat. Assn. Ry. Commrs., 1916-17, chmn. spl. war com., 1917-18; chmn. com. on petroleum Cal. Council Def., 1917-18; surveyor of contracts Gen. Staff, War Dept., 1918-19, also chief purchase br., chmn. Superior Bd. of Contract Rev., Army rep. on Munitions Patent Bd., chmn. Adv. Bd. on Sales and Contract Termination, and asst. to dir. Purchase, Storage and Traffic div. Gen. Staff, U.S. Army, 1918-19; dir. pub. service, U.S. R.R. Adminstrn., 1919-20, dir. Liquidation Claims, 1920; practiced in San Francisco, 1920-72; sr. mem. firm Thelen, Marrin, Johnson & Bridges, Pres. Bd. of trustees S. H. Cowell Found. Decorated D.S.M. Mem. Am. Law Inst., Acad. Polit. Sci., Am. Econ. Assn., Am. Soc. Internat. Law, Am. Acad. Polit. and Social Sci., Am. Bar Assn., Phi Beta Kappa, Phi Delta Phi. Clubs: Commonwealth (gov., past pres.), Bohemian, Author of Public Utilities Act, enacted by Cal. Legislature, Dec. 1911, and other statutes; Leading Railroad and Public Service Commissions, 1912. Home: Berkeley CA Died Apr. 5, 1972.

THEODOROVICH, JOHN VOLODYMYR, clergyman; b. Ukraine, Oct. 6, 1887; s. Volodymyr A. and Agapie (Chervinska) T.; student schs., Zhitomyr, Volynia, Theol. Sem., 1915; m. Julia Kornievich, May 24, 1914 (dec. Aug. 15, 1915); 1 dau., Valentina (Mrs. E.M. Prosen). Came to U.S., 1924, naturalized, 1929. Ordained priest, 1915; served with Army Red Cross, Russia, 1915-17; chaplain Ukranian Army, 1918-19; ordained bishop, Diocese of Podolia, City of Vinnitza, 1921-23; archbishop Ukrainian Orthodox Ch. in U.S., 1924-71, archbishop Ukrainian Greek Orthodox Ch. in Can., 1924-47; metropolitan of the Church, 1950, in jurisdiction affiliated churches, Brazil and Argentina. Address: Bala Cynwyd PA Died May 1971.

THERREL, CATCHINGS, lawyer; b. Seattle, Nov. 25, 1890; s. Robert S. and Hattie (Catchings) T.; student Vanderbilt U., 1912; LL.B., Atlanta Law Sch., 1915; m. Bessie L. Huggins, Aug. 11, 1923 (dec.); m. 2d, Blanche Ash, 1955 (dec.); m. 3d, Ida M. Pelton, 1967. Admitted to Ga. bar, 1914; practiced in Atlanta, 1914-16, Miami Beach, Fla., 1927-71; mem. firm Copeland, Therrel, Baisden & Peterson. Dir. Miami Beach Abtract & Title Co., Chase Fed. Savs. & Loan Assn., Miami Beach First Nat. Bank; dir., v.p. Community Nat. Bank Bal Harbour. Entered N.G., 1916, served on Mexican Border; commd. capt. U.S. Army, 1917; served overseas with 328th Inf., 82d Div., disch. as maj., 1919. Mem. Am., Fla., Dade County bar assns., Am. Legion (past comdr.), Miami Beach C. of C. (dir.), Com. of 100 Miami Beach, Delta Theta Phi. Episcopalian. Clubs: LeGorce Country (sec.), Surf, Bal Harbour; Rivlera Country. Miami Beach FL Died Sept. 1, 1971; buried Woodlawn Park Cemetery, Miami FL

THIELE, WALTER G., judge; b. Washington, Kan., Sept. 10, 1885; s. George H. and Elizabeth B. (Baumberger) T.; LL.B., U. of Kan., 1910; m. Maude Baker, July 26, 1911; children—Walter G. (dec.), John Robert. Admitted to Kan. bar, 1910; in practice at Lawrence, 1910-13; mem. Norton & Thiele, 1913-17; in practice alone, 1927-33; city atty., Lawrence, 1918-24; justice Supreme Court of Kansas since 1933; chmn. Kan. Judicial Council, 1941-54. Mem. Am., Kan. State and Douglas Co. bar assns., Acacia, Phi Delta Phi; pres. U. of Kan. Alumni Assn., 1935-36. Republican. Methodist. Mason. Rotarian. Home: Topeka KS Died Mar. 14, 1968; interred Lawrence KS

THIESING, THEODORE H(ENRY), lawyer; b. Hildesheim, Germany, May 11, 1890; s. Theodore and Louise (Brannan) T.; came to U.S., 1910, naturalized, 1915; LL.B., Columbia, 1913; postgrad. U. Berlin, Germany, 1921-23; LL.D. (hon.), Heidelberg (Germany) U., 1952; m. Constance Russell Myles, Dec. 18, 1954; 1 dau., Lisa Allerton. Admitted to D.C. bar, 1918, U.S. Supreme Ct. bar, 1923, N.Y. bar, 1924; practice law specializing in internat. law Washington, N.Y.C., 1918—. Decorated Grand Cross Order of Merit, W. Germany. Mem. Internat., Am., N.Y. State, N.Y. County bar assns., Bar Assn. City N.Y., Fed. Bar Assn. N.Y., N.J. and Conn., Internat. Law Assn. (London), Columbia Law Alumni Assn., Consular Law Society (founder; trustee emeritus), Am. Council on Germany (dir.), German-Am. C. of C., German Soc. City N.Y., German Am. Sch. Assn. (hon. pres.), Cath. Lawyers Guild, Yale Inst. Medieval Canon Law (founder, chmn.), Nat. Carl Schurz Assn. Clubs: Capitol Hill (Washington), Downtown Athletic, German (hon. pres.), Met., University (N.Y.C.). Author: Dual Allegiance in the German Law of Nationality and American Citizenship, 1918; Investment Trust as a Channel for Investment Abroad, 1921; The Emergence of a New Economic World, 1936; Control of Foreign-Owned Property in the United States, 1941, others. Home: New York City NY Died Apr. 1970.

THOMAS, ALBERT SIDNEY, bishop; b. Columbia, S.C., Feb. 6, 1873; s. John Peyre and Mary Caroline (Gibbes) T.; B.S., State Mil. Coll., Charleston, S.C., 1892, LL.D., 1931; B.D., Gen. Theol. Sem., N.Y. City, 1900, S.T.D., 1930; grad. study S.C. Coll., U. of the South, Sewanee, Tenn.; D.D., U. of the South, 1929; m. Emily Jordan Carrison, Dec. 17, 1908; children—Henry Carrison, Albert Sidney, Emily Jordan. Teacher, pub. schs., Columbia, 1892-97; ordained deacon, 1900, priest, 1901, P.E. Ch.; rector St. Matthew's Ch., Darlington, S.C., 1900-08, St. David's Ch., Cheraw, 1908-21. Ch. of Good Shepherd, Columbia, 1918. St. Michael's Ch., Charleston, 1921-28; bishop of S.C., Nov. 30, 1928-Jan. 1, 1944. Sec. Conv. P.E. Ch., 1901-21; dep. to Gen. Conv. P.E. Ch., 1907-28; editor The Diocese," 1913-28; pres. standing com. of the Diocese, 1922-28, histroiographer since 1921. Trustee Porter Mil. Acad., Charleston. Member S.C. Society Colonial Wars (chaplain), Gen. Soc. Colonial Wars, Huguenot Soc. of S.C. (chaplain), S.C. Soc. Democrat. Mason. Address: 63 King Street, Charleston SC‡

THOMAS, CLEVELAND ANTHOINE, sch. adminstr.; b. Waltham, Mass., May 25, 1912; s. Harrison Cleveland and Doris (Anthoine) T.; A.B., Antioch Coll., 1936; postgrad. Harvard, 1947-48; M.A., Northwestern U., 1950, Ph.D., 1952; m. Rose Marie Ellis, Sept. 3, 1941;children—Anthony Cleveland, Joel Jordan, Katherine. Tchr. English New Canaan (Conn.) Country Sch., 1937-39; asst. dir. Yellow Springs (O.) Summer Theatre, 1936-42; tchr. English, Ethel Walker Sch., Simsbury, Conn., 1940-44; head English dept. North Shore Country Day Sch., Winnetka, Ill., 1944-56, dean of faculty, 1952-56; prin. Francis W. Parker Sch., Chgo., 1956-67; dir. Registration Office, 1956-61, mem. commn., 1965-67; summer session faculty Northwestern U., 1951-55, 61, 62, Johns Hopkins, 1959. Mem. com. exams. Coll. Entrance Exam. Bd., 1960-63. Mem. Cook County exec-.steering com., Ill. com. 1960 White House Conf. on Edn. Bd. dirs. Grant Hosp. Chgo. Mem. Nat. Council Tchrs. Eng., Ind. Schs. Assn. Central States (dir.), Ill. Assn. English Tchrs., Sch. and Coll. Conf. on English, Nat. Assn. Prins. Schs. for Girls, Assn. Coll. Admissions Counselors, Country Day Sch. Headmasters Assn. (exec. com. 1965-67, chmn. ednl. programs com.), Ind. Schs. Assn. Greater Chgo. (pres. 1963-64), Nat. Assn. Ind. Schs. (mem. bd.), Phi Delta Kappa. Clubs: University, Harvard (Chgo.). Author: Language Power for Youth, 1955. General editor: They Will Read Literature, 1955. Contbr. articles profl. jours. Home: Chicago IL Died Apr. 29, 1967.

THOMAS, COLUMBUS EUGENE, banker, mfr.; b. Goldhill, Lee Co., Ala., Feb. 11, 1869; s. William Crawford and Emma Jane (Avery) T.; prep. edn., high sch., Oakbowery, Ala.; A.B., U. of Ala., 1901; m. Augusta Pratt, of Prattville, Ala., Nov. 14, 1894; children—William Pratt, Emma Julia, Mary Augusta, Daniel Holcombe. Pres. Autauga Banking & Trust Co., Prattville; pres. Autauga Oil & Fertilizer Co., Prattville Mercantile Co.; v.p. Autauga Cotton Mill; dir. many corpns. and large land holder; was state supt. of banks; member board trustees Ala. State Dept. of Archives and History. Col. on staff of Gov. O'Neal, 1911. Trustee Tuskegee Inst.; treas. county and high sch. funds, etc; pres. Chamber of Commerce, Prattville. Del. Dem. Nat. Conv., 1924. Mem. Phi Delta Theta. Methodist. K.P., Woodmen, Maccabee. Home: Prattville AL‡

THOMAS, DAVID WINTON, educator; b. London, Eng., Jan. 26, 1901; s. David John and Sarah (Thomas) T.; M.A., St. John's Coll., Oxford, Eng., 1926; M.A., Cambridge, 1926; Hon. D.D., U. Durham, 1965, U. Wales, 1968; m. Edith Marion Higgins, Dec. 20, 1932; children—David John Winton, Arthur Barry Winton, Judith Mary Winton. Prof. Hebrew and Oriental langs. U. Durham, Eng., 1930-38; Regius prof. Hebrew, U. Cambridge (Eng.), 1938-68, emeritus Regius prof., 1968-72; fellow St. Catharine's Coll., Cambridge, 1943-68, pres., 1965-68, emeritus fellow, 1968-72. Fellow Brit. Acad. Burkitt medal for bibl. studies 1969; mem. Soc. for O.T. Study (pres. 1953). Editor (with Martin Noth) Waisdom in Israel and in the Ancient Near East, 1955; Documents from Old Testament Times, 1958; ((with W.D. McHardy) Hebrew and Semitic Studies, 1963; Archaeology and Old Testament Study, 1967; Liber Cambridge England Died June 18, 1972.

THOMAS, EDWIN STARK, judge; b. Woodstock, Ill., Nov. 11, 1872; s. Wilbur E. and Mary (Stark) T.; student Yale, 1 yr.; LL.B., Yale Univ., 1895; m. Louise L. Peck, of West Haven, Conn., Sept. 7, 1894 (dec.); 1 dau., Mrs. Lois T. Reiners; m. 2d, Lulu Gorton Morgan, Apr. 29, 1920 (dec.); m. 3d Jean Gordon, December 29, 1931. Began practice in New Haven, 1895; mem. Conn. House of Rep., 1899; sec., treas. Dem. State Central Com., 1902-12; exec. sec. to Gov. Simeon E. Baldwin, 1911-13; U.S. Dist. judge; Dist. of Conn., by appmt. of President Wilson, since Nov. 17, 1913. Episcopalian. Mason (32 deg.); Elk. Home: Overloch," Columbia CT Address: Hartford CT‡

THOMAS, ELWYN, judge; b. Ankona, Fla., July 5, 1894; s. Harry Samuel and Julia (Eldred) T.; ed. John B. Stetson U., Acad., 1908-12, Coll. Liberal Arts, 1912-13, LL.B., 1915, LL.D., 1951; M. Eva Banes, June 18, 1924; children—Patricia Ann (Mrs. W.M. Meginniss), Pamela Elyn (Mrs. Ralph B. Wilson Jr.). Admitted to the Florida bar, 1915; practiced at Deland, Fla., 1915-16, Ft. Pierce, 1916-25; city atty., Ft. Pierce, 1918-25, Vero Beach, 1919-23; prosecuting atty., St. Lucie County, Fla., 1917-19; judge 21st Judicial Circuit, 1925-35; sr. judge Ninth Judicial Circuit, 1935-38; justice Fla. Supreme Court, 1938-69, chief justice, 1947-49, 59-61. Chmn. Fla. Jud. Council, 1953-57. Fellow Am. Bar Found., Inst. Judicial Administration. Served with U.S. Coast Artillery, World War I, state director Victory Speakers Bureau, Florida Defense Council, during World War II. Mem. Am. (jud. council 1951-57, chairman of section on judicial administration 1956-57), Florida bar assns., Am. Legion, Phi Beta Kappa, Sigma Nu, Phi Alpha Delta (supreme justice 1956-58). Democrat. Episcopalian. Mason. Club: Capital City Country. Home: Tallahassee FL Died Feb. 28, 1971; buried Roselawn Cemetery, Tallahassee FL

THOMAS, EUGENE STUART, ednl. adminstr.; b. Fortville, Ind., Mar. 29, 1900; s. George H. and Anna Mary (Stuart) T.; A.B., Ind. U., 1923; M.A., U. Mich., 1939; M.A. (hon.), Western Mich. U.; LL.D., Kalamazoo Coll., 1962; m. Mary Gladys Burgan, Oct. 25, 1923; children—Richard S., Jane Burgan (Mrs. Donald Hagaman). Tchr. phys. edn., coach, Marion, Ind., 1923-28; tchr. social scis., coach Central High Sch., Kalamazoo, 1929-39, prin., 1945-65; ednl. dir. children's charter Juvenile Cts. Mich., 1965-70; prin. Vine Sch., Kalamazoo, 1939-45. Trustee Council Advancement Secondary Edn., Coll. Entrance Exam. Bd., 1963. Recipient various civic club service awards; honored posthumously by City of Kalamazoo, 1970, Mich. Senate, 1970. Mem. Nat. (pres.), Mich. (pres.) assns. secondary sch. prins., N.E.A., Headmasters Assn., Kalamazoo Tchrs. Assn. Methodist. Clubs: Kiwanis, Kalamazoo MI Died May 7, 1970.

THOMAS, FRANK EMMETT, judge; b. Deposit, N.Y., May 29, 1895; s. John E. and Emily (Lakin) T.; LL.B., Syracuse U., 1923; m. Marian Whitney Mastin, June 30, 1926; children—Frank Emmett, John M. Admitted to N.Y. bar, 1924, U.S. Fed. Ct. bar, 1926; practiced in Binghamton, N.Y., 1925-69; mem. firm Thomas & Ray, Binghamton, 1925-50; atty. Village of Port Dickinson (N.Y.), 1932-50, Town of Conklin N.Y.), 1935-50; judge Broome County Children's Ct., Binghamton, N.Y., 1946-62; spl. judge Broome County, 1951-62; judge Family Ct., Broome County, 1962-66; member exec. com. National Council Juvenile Court Judges, 1963-66. Secretary, treasurer Farm Loan Association, Binghamton. Vice president Broome County chpt. A.R.C.; pres. Broome County Council Chs., 1950; mem. Port Dickinson Bd. Edn., 1942-46, pres., 1945-46; pres. Port Dickinson Vol. Fire Assn.; charter mem. U.S.O., Binghamton, 1935. Bd. dirs. Binghamton Boys Club, Broome County chpt. Nat. Found., Broome County Spl. Agys., Pal. Mem. N.Y. State Assn. Children's Ct. Judges (pres. 1956-57). Presbyn. (elder). Mason, Rotarian. Home: Port Dickinson NY Died Sept. 12, 1969.

THOMAS, FREDERICK BRADLEY, banker; b. Evanston, Ill., Mar. 26, 1921; s. Frederick Bradley and Marian (Lindman) T.; student Northwestern U., also U. Ill.; m. Katherine K. Bingham, Oct. 3, 1944; children—Frederick Bradley III, Katherine C. Asst. cashier Harris Trust & Savings Bank, Chgo., 1953-61, asst. v.p., 1962-64, cashier, from 1964; v.p., dir. N.W. Harris Corp., Chgo., from 1960. Mem. Winnetka Caucus Com., 1963-65. Bd. dirs. treas. Chgo. Hearing Soc., 1955-60. Served with AUS, 1942-46. Mem. U. Ill. Exec. Devel. Alumni Assn. Republican. Conglist. Home: Winnetka IL Deceased.

THOMAS, FREDERICK LIONEL, lawyer; b. Lansing W.Va., June 14, 1892; s. Ullyses Grant and Cora Alice (Calloway) T.; J.D., W.Va. U., 1917; m. Leafy Woofter, Dec. 24, 1917; m. Virginia Alice (Mrs. Roy H. Jones, Jr.), Frederick Lionel, Robert S. Admitted to W.Va. bar, 1917; with legal dept. United Fuel Gas Co., 1917; partner firm Spilman, Thomas, Battle & Klostermeyer, and predecessors, Charleston, W.Va., from 1920. Pres., dir. Midwale Colliery Co.; dir. Crab Orchard Coal & Land Co., also dir. 8 comml. credit plan companies. Mem. Pub. Assistance Council, Kanawha County, W.Va., 1933-36; chmn. Kanawha Clay chpt. A.R.C., 1943. Served to 2d lt. U.S. Army, World War I. Mem. Am., W.Va., Kanawha County (pres. 1930) bar assns., Charleston Area and W.Va. C. of C. W.Va. State Bar, Order of Coif, Phi Delta Phi, Phi Sigma Kappa. Republican. Baptist. Clubs: Edgewood Country, Army-Navy Charleston WV Died Sept. 9, 1969.

THOMAS, GERALD BURISON, aircraft co. exec.; b. Greensboro, Ala., May 29, 1927; s. Parker B. and Cora L. (Talbott) T.; B.S. in Aero. Engring., Miss. State U., 1948; M.S. in Aero. Engring., Ga. Inst. Tech., 1949; m. Dorothy Ann Top, Jan. 7, 1951; children—Bryan T., Sherry, Todd. With Douglas Aircraft Co., 1949-72, supr. advanced design performance, 1959-60, rep. in N.Y.C., 1960-64, dir. sales devel., 1964, v.p. domestic comml. sales, 1964-71, v.p. comml. sales 1971-72. Served with USNR, 1945-46. Mem. Am. Inst. Aero. and Astronautics, Soc. Automotive Engrs., Newcomen Soc. N.Am. Clubs: Cloud, Wings (N.Y.C.); Long Beach Yacht. Home: Long Beach CA Died Aug. 26, 1972; buried Sunnyside Meml. Park, Long Beach CA

THOMAS, HOWARD DUDLEY, life ins.; b. Iowa County, Wis., May 2, 1870; s. James and Mary (Thomas) T.; student German-English Coll., 1887-91; m. Mary Annette Baker, Dec. 25, 1894; children—Foster Keith, Jean Elizabeth (Mrs. Jackson Burgess). Cashier Blanchardville Bank, 1891-1903; pres. Blanchardville State Bank, 1903-14; loan agent Northwestern Mutual Life Ins. Co. of Milwaukee, 1921-23; mgr. farm loans, 1923-32, vice pres. 1932-45; retired since 1945. Republican. Mason. Club: University (Milwaukee). Home: Route 4, Oconomowoc, Wis. Office: 925 East Wells St. Milwaukee 2 WI‡

THOMAS, JAMES JOHN, ex-mayor; b. Wrexham, Wales, Oct. 1, 1867; s. David J. and Jane (Jones) T.; brought to U.S. in infancy; ed. pub. schs., Columbus, O.; m. Maude Huston, Oct. 8, 1902; 1 son, William Huston. With U.S. Express, Co., Columbus, 1886-1914; a founder and mem. exec. com. Am. Insurance Union, 23 yrs.; mem. City Council, Columbus, 1898-1902 (pres. 1900-02); mayor of Columbus, 1920-32. Republican. Conglist. Mason (33 deg.). Home: 39 N. Ohio Av., Columbus OH‡

THOMAS, JOHN PARNELL, congressman; b. Jersey City, N.J., Jan. 16, 1895; s. J. Parnell and Georgianna (Thomas) Feeney; grad. high sch. Ridgewood, N.J., student Univ. of Pa., 1914-17; m. Amelia Stiles, Jan. 21, 1921; children—J. Parnell, Stiles. Bond salesman with Kountze Bros., N.Y. City, 1919-20; with Paine, Webber & Co., N.Y. City, as salesman, 1920-24, as mgr. N.Y. bond department, 1924-38; mem. Thomas & Godfrey, insurance brokers, N.Y. City. Mem. 75th to 81st Congresses (1937-49), 7th N.J. Dist.; mem. Com. on Armed Services House of Representatives, Chairman Committee on Un-American Activities. Mayor of Allendale, 1926-30; mem. N.J. Assembly, 1935-37. Served as 2d and 1st lt. and capt. inf., U.S. Army, with A.E.F., 1917-18. Mem. Psi Upsilon. Republican. Mason. Home: Allendale NJ Died Nov. 19, 1970.

THOMAS, JOSEPH LOREN, banker; b. Adams Co., Ill., Nov. 3, 1873; s. Eli R. and Mary A. (Beckett) T.; grad. Western Normal Coll., Bushnell, Ill., 1898; m. Mattie Ethel Gans, of Golden, Ill., Nov. 14, 1901; children—Harry Loren, Charles Clifford. Teacher, pub. schs., 1892-1902; asst. treas., Adams Co., Ill., 1902-06; reporter and editorial writer, Quincy (Ill.) Daily Herald, 1907-10; county treas., Adams Co., 1910-14; tax counsellor, Mississippi River Power Co., Keokuk, Ia., 1914-18; in administrative div. U.S. Income and Profits Tax Bur., Washington, D.C., 1919-20; v.p. Quincy Nat. Bank, 1920-22; cashier Quincy-Ricker Nat. Bank & Trust Co., 1925-28, pres. since 1928. Trustee Chaddock Boys Sch., Quincy. Democrat. Methodist. Mason (32 deg.). Home: 215 S. 16th St. Office: 413 Hampshire St., Quincy IL‡

THOMAS, NORMAN (MATTOON), b. Marion, O., Nov. 20, 1884; s. Welling Evan and Emma (Mattoon) T.; grad. high sch., Marion, 1901; A.B., Princeton, 1905; B.D., Union Theol. Sem., 1911; Litt.D., Princeton University, 1932; LL.D., Johnson C. Smith University; m. Frances Violet Stewart, Sept. 1, 1910 (dec.); five children. Ordained ministry Presbyn. Ch., 1911; asso. minister Brick Presbyn. Ch., N.Y. City, 1910-11; pastor East Harlem Ch. and chmn. Am. Parish, N.Y. City, 1911-18, demitted ministry, 1931; founder, editor, 1918-21, World To-Morrow, also sec. Fellowship of Reconciliation; asso. editor The Nation, 1921-22; dir. League for Industrial Democracy, 1922; chmn. Postwar World Council; columnist Denver Post. Candidate Socialist ticket gov. N.Y., 1924, twice for mayor N.Y.C., and for President United States, 1928, 32, 36, 40, 44, 48. Chmn. Inst. Internat. Labor Research. Decorated Order of the Condor of the Andes (Bolivia): Order of Solidarity (Italy). Author following books: The Conscientious Objector in America, 1923, later revised and reprinted under title: Is Concience a Crime?, 1927; America's Way Out—a Program for Democracy, 1930; As I See It, 1932; (with Paul Blanshard), What's the Matter with New York?, 1932; Human Exploitation, 1934; War—No Profit, No Glory, No Need, 1935; Socialism on the Defensive, 1938; We Have a Future, 1941; What is Our Destiny?, 1944; Appeal to the Nations, 1947; A Socialist's Faith, 1951; The Test of Freedom, 1954; Mr. Chairman, Ladies and Gentlemen, 1955; The Prerequisites for Peace, 1959; The Great Dissenter, 1961; Socialism Re-examined, 1963; also pamphlets. Home: Cold Spring Harbor LI NY Died Dec. 19, 1968.

THOMAS, P(URDOM) C(LARK), oil co. exec.; b. St. Louis, Dec. 4, 1906; s. Charles L. and Leona (Thomas) T.; student Westminister Coll., Fulton, Mo., 1924-25, St. Louis U., 1925-26; m. Lola D. Lundburg; stepson, H. George Lundburg; children—Patricia, Jacqueline, Purdom C. With Shell Oil Co., 1932-68, beginning as salesman, successively dist. mgr., div. sales mgr., division manager, general sales mgr., 1932-56, v.p., 1956-61, v.p. marketing 1961-68; dir. Buckley Bros., Bridgeport, Conn., Internat. Lubricant Corp., New Orleans, Shell Oil Co. (P.R.), Ltd. Clubs: Greenwich (Conn.) Country; Chicago Althletic Association (Chgo.); Hemisphere (N.Y.C.). Home: New York City NY Died July 28, 1968; buried Greenwich CT

THOMAS, PERCY CHAMPION, retired mfr.; b. St. Louis, Mo., Nov. 5, 1874; s. James Stringham and Jane Hunt (Dodge) T.; ed. Rome Free Acad.; m. Mary Minton Hoxsey, Sept. 2, 1902 (died July 1942); children—Louise Hoxsey (Mrs. Earl Martin), Jane Dodge (Mrs. Josiah N. Knowles); m. 2d, Jane Patten Waterbury, April 20, 1946. Began as clerk in railroad offices, Chicago, Ill., and St. Paul, Minn., 1887-91; with Rome Mfg. Company, manufacturers brass, copper, aluminum and steel products, since 1892, advancing through various offices, president, 1920-28, (retired). Major Ordnance Dept., U.S. Army, 1918; Republican presdl. elector, N.Y., 1920; commr. pub. works, Rome, 1921; ex-pres. Rome Community Chest; dir. Rome Chamber Commerce. Episcopalian. Clubs: Rome, Teugega Country (Rome); Tin Whistles (Pinehurst, N.C.); Burlingame (Calif.) Country; Everglades (Palm Beach, Fla.). Home: Delta Farms, Town of Lee, P.O. Box 266, Rome NY‡

THOMAS, ROBERT ELLIS, librarian; b. Racine, Wis., Nov. 9, 1920; s. David Robert and Eleanor (Williams) T.; B.A., U. Wis., 1950, M.L.S., 1951; m. Frances A. Heusdens, Sept. 3, 1948; children—Charles Richard, Gregory Ellis. Librarian Bismarck (N.D.) Pub. Library, 1951-56; dir. Hutchinson (Kan.) Pub. Library, 1956-60, Salt Lake City Pub. Library, 1960-69; dir. Ramopo Catskill Library System, Middletown, N.Y., 1969-72. Pres., N.D. Library Assn., 1954-55. Served with inf., AUS, 1942-45. Mem. A.L.A., Mountain-Plains (pres. 1958), N.Y. Library assns. Home: Middletown NY Died Jan. 17, 1972.

THOMAS, SAMUEL MORGAN, electrical engr.; b. Searcy, Ark., Dec. 12, 1903; s. George Crawford and Annie (Tapscott) T.; B.S., Ga. Sch. Tech., 1926; m. Bebe Wharton, June 21, 1930; 1 son, Samuel Morgan. Employed by Allis Chalmers Mfg. Co., Milw., 1926-31; elec. engr. Corps Engrs., U.S. Army, 1931-40; commd. capt. Signal Corps, Army U.S., 1940 and advanced through grades to brig. gen.; signal dir., Persian Gulf Comd., Teheran, Iran, U.S. Army, 1942-45, chief of staff, 1945; dir. communications and postal service, U.S. Control Group Council, Berlin, Germany, 1945; brig. gen., Signal Corps. Res., 1947; asst. chief engr., RCA Communications, Inc., 1947; v.p., 1947-51; spl. asst. to sec. of army, 1952; v.p. Hazeltine Electronics Corp. 1954-62, sr. v.p. Hazeltine Dir. Internat. div., 1962-73. Decorated Legion of Merit with oak leaf cluster, Bronze Star, Order of Kutuzov (Russia); Order British Empire. Mem. Phi Kappa Phi, Tau Beta Pi, Alpha Tau Omega.

Clubs: Greenwich Country; Army and Navy (Washington). Home: Greenwich CT Died Jan. 4, 1973; buried Arlington Nat. Cemetery, Washington DC

THOMAS, WILLIAM NATHANIEL, navy chaplain; b. Rankin County, Miss., Mar. 21, 1892; s. John C. and Annie Laura (Thompson) T.; A.B., Millsaps Coll., Jackson, Miss., 1912, diploma, Seashore Divinity Sch., Gulfport, Miss., 1913-15, Chicago Theological Seminary, 1925, D.D. (hon.) Millsaps Coll., 1935, Am. Univ., Washington, D.C., 1941; m. Martha Ellen Fondren, Feb. 18, 1913; children—William N., John Edward. Began career as Methodist clergymen, 1911; Milsaps Memorial Meth. Ch., Jackson, Miss., 1910-11, Daleville Meth., Ch., Miss., 1912-13; Meth. Ch., Summit, Miss., 1913-17. Apptd. to chaplaincy in 1918, first duty Receiving Ship, Boston, Mass., 1918; U.S.S. Madawaska, 1918-19, U.S.S. Imperator, 1919; Naval Hosp., Fort Lyon, Colo. 1919-22; U.S.S. Pennsylvania, 1922-24; Naval Acad. Annapolis, 1924-27; U.S.S. Raleigh, 1927-29; 14th Naval Dist., 1929-32; U.S.S. West Virginia, 1932-33; Naval Acad., Annapolis, 1933-45; apptd. chief of chaplains, U.S. Navy, with rank of rear adm., 1945, ret. Awarded Victory Medal with Bronze Star—Transport Service, 1918; American Area Campaign Service Ribbon, American Defense Campaign Service Ribbon, Victory Medal, World War II, Legion of Merit. Mem. Internat. Soc. of Theta Phi, Kappa Sigma Frat. Mason. American Legion. Home: Lake Junaluska NC Died Apr. 1971.

THOMPSON, C(LARENCE) BERTRAND, biochemist; b. Denver, Colorado, April 12, 1882; son of James Beauregard and Medora Gertrude (Reed) Thompson; LL.B., U. of So. Cal., 1900; A.B., Harvard, 1908, A.M., 1909; postgrad. U. Cal. at Berkeley, 1940-44; m. Maravene Kennedy, 1906 (divorced 1922); m. 2d, Lisbet Heimann, 1926. Mem. faculty, Grad. School of Business Administration, Harvard, 1911-16, also serving apprenticeship Taylor System of Business Management, 1912-15; counsel for Am., French, German and Italian concerns; research associate Instituto de Fisiologia, Facultad de Medicina. Montevideo. Decorated Legion d' Honneur (France). Member Am. Chemical Society, Sociedad de Biologia de Uruguay. Clubs: Rosburghe (San Francisco); Typophiles (New York City). Am. Association (Montevideo). Author: The Churches and the Wage Earners, 1909; How to Find Factory Costs, 1915; Theory and Practice of Scientific Management, 1917; Le Systeme Taylor (also in Polish) 1919; Methodes Americaines de Prix de Revient, 1920; (with others) La Reorganisation des Usines (2 vols.), 1926; articles in economic, engring. and chem. periodicals. Compiler and part author of Scientific Management, 1914, and editor of several vols. of translations of Am. business classics into French. Research on cancer. Home: Montevideo Uruguay Died Jan. 9, 1969; buried British Cemetery, Montevideo, Uruguay

THOMPSON, CHARLES H., b. Brattleboro, Vt., Feb. 4, 1870; s. Charles F. and Elizabeth C. (Eime) T.; grad. Brattleboro High Sch., 1892; m. Ruth Helen Noyes, of Brattleboro, June 9, 1896. Clk. and teller Vt. Nat. Bank, Brattleboro, 1885-1903; owner and operator ranch properties in the Southwest, 1903-13; now president and manager of independent water powers in Vermont. Served as bailiff, mem. Sch. Bd., mayor and chmn. Bd. of Auditors, Brattleboro. Trustee Boston Sunday Commons, and Colored Industrial Coll., Southern Pines, N.C. Mem. Prog. Nat. Exec. Com., 1912-16, also N.E. mgr. of party (without salary), and chmn. Progressive Party Exec. Com. of Vt. Advocate of minimum wage and abolishment of child labor. Mem. Vt. Fish and Game League, Lake Champlain Assn., Adirondack League, etc. Mason, K.T. Clubs: Vt. Wheel (Brattleboro); Art, City (Boston); Lotos (New York); Ethan Allen, Waubanakee (Burlington). Home: Burlington VT‡

THOMPSON, CHESTER CHARLES, trade assn. exec.; b. Rock Island, Ill., Sept. 19, 1893; s. Charles Lewis and Susan Isabella (Miller) T.; student pub. schs., Rock Island; m. Margaret Mary Flynn, Jan. 19, 1924. Contractor, 1910-32; co. treas. Rock Island Co., Ill., 1922-26; mayor City Rock Island, 1927-33; elected rep. 14th congl. dist. Ill., U.S. Ho. Reps, 1933-39; pres., chmn. bd. Inland Waterways Corp., 1939-44; pres. Warrior River Terminal Co., 1939-44, Am. Waterways Operators, Inc., 1944-57. Mem. Rock Island County Bd. Suprs., 1965-71. Served with U.S. Army, 1918. Mem. Def. Transportation Assn., Am. Soc. Traffic and Transportation, Soc. Naval Architects and Marine Engrs., Assn. I.C.C. Practitioners, Am. Legion. Elk. Home: Rock Island IL Died Jan. 1971.

THOMPSON, E.E., lawyer; b. Montgomery City, Mo., Nov. 4, 1898; s. James H. and Susan A. (Hudson) T.; student U. Mo., 1918-19; LL.B., U. Kansas City, 1925; m. Eleanor H. Schroer, Sept. 14, 1921; children—Forrest L., Eleanor Ann (Mrs. Donald W. Hinchman). Admitted to Mo. bar, 1925, Dist. Ct. bar, 1928, U.S. Supreme Ct. bar, 1966; practice in Kansas City, Mo., 1925-68; mem. firm Popham, Thompson, Popham, Trusty and Conway, Kansas City, 1948-68. Served with USN, World War I. Mem. Am., Kansas City bar assns., Mo. Bar, Fedn. Ins. Counsel, Liberty Meml. Assn. (life trustee, gov.), Am. Legion (adv. com. div. vets. affairs), Sigma Phi Epsilon. Mason (32 deg., Shriner). Home: Kansas City MO Died Feb. 9, 1968; buried Mount Moriah Cemetery, Kansas City MO

THOMPSON, FRED LAWRENCE, civil engr.; b. nr. Grendview, Edgar County, Ill., Feb. 1, 1872; s. Edward Taylor and Mima J. (McDonald) T.; B.S. in C.E., U. of Ill., 1896; m. Maude Nellie Martin, Nov. 21, 1900; children—Donna, Ruth. Entered engring. corps. I.C. R.R. as chainman, 1896; rodman, 1896-99, asst. engr., 1899-1903, roadmaster, 1903-07, asst. engr. of bridges, 1907-10, engr. of bridges and buildings, 1910-13, was engineer of construction, 1913-14, asst. chief engr., 1914-18, chief engr., 1918-25, v.p. since Feb. 1, 1925, all with I.C. R.R. Mem. Western Soc. Engrs., Am. Ry. Engring. Assn. Republican. Methodist. Clubs: Engineers, South Shore Country. Home: 6906 Constance Av. Office: Central Station, Chicago IL *

THOMPSON, FREDERICK GREGG, physician, assn. ofcl.; b. St. Joseph, Mo., Mar. 22, 1898; s. Frederick Gregg and Mary D. (McNeely) T.; grad. Phillips Acad., Andover, Mass., 1916; Ph.B., Yale, 1919; M.D., Harvard, 1923; m. Katherine C. Chesney, Sept. 14, 1927; children—Frederick Gregg III, John Chesney, Mary Katherine (Mrs. Richard Dahms). Resident surgeon N.Y. Hosp., N.Y.C., 1924-26; gen. practice surgery, St. Joseph, 1927-68; dir. Thompson-Brumm-Knepper Clinic, St. Joseph, 1947-68; chief staff Ellis Fischel Cancer Hosp., Columbia, Mo., 1955-56. Mem. Hill-Burton Com., 1955-58, mem. Mo. health div., 1955-58; bd. dirs. Blue Cross-Blue Shield Kan.-Mo., 1955-60. Served to comdr., M.C., USNR, 1942-46. Fellow A.C.S.; mem. Am. Assn. Med. Clinics (pres. 1964-65). Catholic. Contbr. profl. jours. Home: St Joseph MO Died June 1, 1968.

THOMPSON, GEORGE VICTOR, city ofcl.; b. Ekastown, Pa., May 3, 1918; s. James Victor and Ruth (Maizland) T.; student U. Tulsa, 1945-46, U. N.M., 1947-49; m. Opal Evelyn Karns, Dec. 26, 1945; children—Lynda Lee, Mary Lou, Gail, George. Schedule clk. in charge prodn. Allegheny Ludlum Steel Corp., Brackenridge, Pa., 1936-43; sales and service engr. Engring. Labs., Tulsa, 1945-46; jr. water engr. city Albuquerque, 1949-50, purchasing agt., 1951-56, mgr. service and stores, 1953-56, personnel mgr., 1952-56, safety dir., 1956-64, asst. dir. personnel, 1966-67, asso. dir. in charge safety and tng., 1964-68, N.M. chmn. health and safety Rio Grande dist. Kit Crason council Boy Scouts Am., 1962-68. Served with USMCR, 1943-45. Mem. Am. Soc. Safety Engrs. (pres. N.M. chpt.), Am. Soc. Personnel Adminstrn. Methodist (pres. men's club). Patentee smoke controlled incinerator. Home: NM Died May 12, 1968.

THOMPSON, GEORGE WILLISTON, business exec.; b. Phila., July 18, 1888; s. Geo. W. and Anna (Dooner) T.; ed. pub. schs. of N.Y. City; m. Florence Keet, 1914; 1 son. With Liggett & Myers Tobacco Company (original co.), 1911-54, vice pres. in charge of sales and dir. Clubs: Metropolitan, Athletic, Rockefeller Center Luncheon (bd. govs.). Home: New York City NY Died Oct. 1969.

THOMPSON, JAMES KIDD, clergyman; b. Tunnel Hill, Ga., Jan. 11, 1874; s. Gilbert Taylor and Josephine A. (King) T.; Drury Coll., Springfield, Mo.; A.B., Austin Coll., Sherman, Tex., 1892; M.A., Central U., Richmond, Ky., 1893; B.D., Presbyn. Theol. sem. of Ky., 1896; studied Free Church Coll., Edinburgh, Scotland, Edinburgh Univ.; D.D., Westminster Coll., Mo., 1911, also from Austin Coll., 1928; m. Innie Foster, Oct. 3, 1899; children—Joseph Gilbert, Mary Josephine. Ordained Presbyn. ministry 1896; supply 1st Ch., Texarkana, Tex., 1896-97; pastor 1st Ch., Calvert, Tex., 1897-1902, 1st Ch., Muskogee, 1902-19, 1st Ch., Fort Worth, Tex., since June 6, 1919. Engaged in war work, 1917-18. Mem. Jud. Commn. Presbyn. Ch. U.S.A., 1908-11; member 9th Council Alliance Ref. Chs. Holding Presbyn. System, N.Y., 1909, Aberdeen, Scotland, 1913; moderator Synod of Okla., 1909-10 (chmn. home mission com., 1911-19); stated clk. Presbytery of Muskogee, 1909-19; del. Okla. on Am. Commn. of Southern Commercial Congress to Europe, 1913. Trustee Henry Kendall Coll., Tulsa, Okla. Democrat. Mem. Assn. of Commerce (Ft. Worth), Sigma Nu. Mason. Clubs: University, River Crest Country, Rotary (pres. 1923-24). Author religious dramas The Inn-Keeper of Bethlehem and Saul of Tarsus. Contbr. to religious press. Columnist. Address: 1209 W. El Paso St., Fort Worth TX‡

THOMPSON, JAMES RALPH, dairy exec.; b. Cortland, Ind., Mar. 18, 1897; s. James B. and Mary H. (Holmes) T.; B.S., Purdue U., 1919; m. Helen L. Temple, Apr. 14, 1921; children—James T., Jane L. Vice pres. Bedford Dairy Co., 1928, Thompson Dairy, Inc., 1939, v.p. Thompson Glass Dairy Co., 1942; chmn. bd. Thompson Dairy Co., 1929; dir. Home Savs. & Loan Association. Member of Ind. Legislature, 1935-39. Pres. bd. trustees Purdue U.; trustee Hanover Coll. Mem. Ind. C. of C. (pres. 1961-62), Phi Delta Theta. Presbyn. Mason (32 deg., Shriner), Elk. Clubs: Rotary (past dist. gov. Ind.), Indianapolis Athletic. Home: Seymour IN Died July 29, 1968; buried Riverview Cemetery Seymour IN

THOMPSON, JEAN M., author; b. Guilford, Conn., Sept. 20, 1867; d. Alden LaFletcher and Caroline Dudley (Field) Fowler; ed. pub. schs.; m. Henry W. Thompson, of N.Y. City, July 1, 1895 (died Sept. 1912). Began writing for publication as a child; has specialized in nature work, and is known as The Jack Frost Lady." Mem. Authors' League America. Episcopalian. Author: Water Wonders Every Child Should Know, 1907; Three Bears of Porcupine Ridge, 1913; Wild Kindred of Fur, Feather and Fin, 1914; Over Indian and Animal Trails, 1917; Animal Adventures in the Deep Forest, 1920; also many poems, juvenile plays, etc. Wrote nationally known hymn Resurrection." Stories have appeared in nearly 100 mags. Home: 16 Windsor Terrace, Yonkers NY‡

THOMPSON, JOHN FAIRFIELD, industrialist; born at Portland, Me., Mar. 8, 1881; s. Frank E. and Mary J. (Clarke) T.; B.S., Sch. of Mines, Columbia, 1903, Ph.D., 1906; D.Sc. (honorary), Columbia University, 1950; LL.D., Queen's U., 1954, Bowdoin Coll., 1959; married Elizabeth Fisher Wheeler, October 10, 1911; children—John Fairfield, Barbara Warren (Mrs. Ralph R. Birdsall). Assistant in metallurgy, School of Mines, Columbia, 1903-06; associated with The International Nickel Company in a number of technical and executive positions from 1906, exec. v.p. and dir., 1935-49, pres., dir., 1949-52, chmn. bd., dir. since 1951. Exec. v.p. and dir., Internat. Nickel Co. of Can., Ltd., 1936-49, pres., dir., 1949-52, chmn. bd., dir., from 1951; mem. bd. dirs. Whitehead Metal Products Co., Inc., Texas Gulf Sulphur Company, Am. Bank Note Co., Am. Metal Climax, Inc., Bank of N.Y. Trustee Packer Collegiate Institute, Nat. Safety Council. Recipient Instn. Mining and Metallurgy Gold medal, London, 1957. Honorable mem. Inst. of Metals (Eng.). Mem. American Society for Metals, Am. Inst. Mining, Metall., and Petroleum Engrs. (Rand Meml. medal 1958), Mining and Metall. Soc. American (past pres.). Am. Soc. Testing Materials. Unitarian. Clubs; City Midday, Columbia University (New York), University, Down Town Assn., (New York); New Canaan (Conn.) Country. Thomas Egleston Medal from Columbia Engring Schs. Alumni Assn., 1944; Comdr. Order White Rose (Finland). Home: New Canaan CT Died July 1968.

THOMPSON, JOHN FAWDREY, JR., coast guard officer; b. Franklin, N.H., May 30, 1919; s. John Fawdrey and Anna (Hildrebrand) T.; student Syracuse U., 1937-38; B.S., U.S. Coast Guard Acad., 1941; m. Marjorie A. Dunton, July 8, 1956; children—Dan J., Sheri Ann, Mark Dale. Commd. ensign USCG, 1941, advanced through grades to rear adm., 1970; comdg. officer sub chaser, Greenland Patrol, 1942; staff officer antisubmarine warfare, 1943; exec. officer, comdg. officer U.S.S. Harveson, 1943-45; comdg. officer U.S.S. Joyce, Atlantic Fleet, 1945; adminstrv. aide to Chief Mcht. Marine Safety, 1945-48; Industry tng. Esso Co. N.Y., 1948-49; insp. Marine Insp. Office, N.Y.C., 1949-50, 52-53; exec. officer, comdg. officer cutter Mendota, 1950-52; insp., sr. investigating officer Marine Insp. Office, Jacksonville, Fla., 1953-58; comdg. officer cutter Cherokee, 1958-60; officer in charge Coast Guard Mcht. Marine Detail, Yokohama, Japan, 1960-63; exec. officer, officer in charge Marine Insp. Office, Phila., 1963-67; chief operations div., chief staff 7th Coast Guard Dist., 1967-70; supt. U.S. Coast Guard Acad., New London, Conn., 1970-72. Decorated Navy Commendation medal. Mem. Nat. Def. Transp. Assn., Propeller Club U.S., Newcomen Soc. N.Am., U.S. Power Squadrons (bd. govs.). Address: New London CT Died Jan. 19, 1972.

THOMPSON, JOSEPH H., business exec.; b. Oct. 29, 1900; s. Joseph H. T.; ed. Notre Dame U.; m. Elizabeth Lacey, Sept. 21, 1921; children—Mary D. (Mrs. William J. Clark), Elizabeth L. (Mrs. Philip R. Neuhaus). Asst. v.p. Union Trust Co., 1921-29; v.p. Midland Bank, 1929-31; v.p. Cleveland Trust Co., 1931-33; v.p. The National City Bank of Cleveland, 1933-37; vice president The M.A. Hanna Co., 1937-52, pres., 1952-60, vice chmn., 1960-61, chmn. exec. com., dir., 1961-64, vice chmn. bd., 1964-68; 1st pres. Hanna Mining Co., 1958, later chmn. bd., until 1966, chmn. exec. com., dir., 1966-68; pres. Iron Ore Co. Can., later chmn. bd.; dir. Pa. R.R. Co., Nat. Steel Corp. Served as pvt. USMC, 1918-19. Clubs: Kirtland, Tavern. Union (Cleve.): Links. Twenty-nine (N.Y.C.). Home: Willoughby OH Died Apr. 30, 1968; buried Mt. Olivet Cemetery, Nashville TN

THOMPSON, JOSEPH S(EXTON), mfg. exec.; b. San Francisco, June 16, 1878; s. James Alden and Josephine (Moroney) T.; student pub. schs., San Francisco; m. Marjorie Buffington, June 1906; children—Joseph Alden, Mary Kathleen; m. 2d, Germaine DeNarie Requet, June 21, 1931; 1 dau., Jacqueline DeNarie. Founder Pacific Electric Mfg. Corp., San Francisco, 1906, pres., 1906-54; pres. Federal Pacific Electric Co., from 1954. Fellow Am. Inst. E.E.; mem. San Francisco C. of C. (past dir.). Clubs: Bohemian, Press and Union League (San Francisco). Author: More Progress and Less Poverty, 1942. Home: San Francisco CA Died Sept. 1970.

THOMPSON, LAWRANCE ROGER, educator, author; b. Franklin, N.H., Apr. 3, 1906; s. Roger Everett and Lena (Keller) T.; B.A., Wesleyan U., Middletown, Conn., 1928; Ph.D., Columbia, 1939; m. Janet Arnold, Jan. 9, 1945; children—Nathaniel Arnold, Eleanor Ann, Joel, Thomas Neal. Instr. English, Wesleyan U., 1934-35; instr. English and comparative lit. Columbia Grad. Sch., 1935-36, research fellow, 1936-37; curator rare books Princeton U. Library, 1937-42, editor-in-chief Library Chronicle, 1938-42; Guggenheim fellow, 1946-47; asso. prof. English, Princeton, 1947-51, prof., 1951-73, Holmes prof. Belles-lettres, 1968-73. Ford Found. fellow, 1953-54; guest lectr. Salzburg (Austria) Seminar in Am. Studies univs. Ljubljana, Zagreb and Belgrade, Yugoslavia, U. Oslo, Norway, Hebrew Jerusalem, Israel. Trustee Princeton U. Press, 1955-60, chmn. editorial board, 1959-60. Served from lt. (j.g.) to lt. comdr., USNR, 1942-46. Decorated Legion of Merit; recipient Citation for Distinguished service as tchr., scholar, author, Wesleyan U., 1958. Author: Robert Frost: A Chronological Survey of His Work, 1933; Edwin Arlington Robinson: A Catalogue of An Exhibition (with H. Bacon Collamore), 1935; Young Longfellow, 1939; Fire and Ice: The Art and Thought of Robert Frost, 1942; The Navy Hunts the CGR 3070, 1944; Melville's Quarrel with God., 1952; A Comic Principle in Sterne, Meredith, Joyce, 1954; Robert Frost: A Critical Study, 1959; William Faulkner: An Introduction and Interpretation, 1963; Robert Frost; The Early Years (Melville Cane award 1967), 1966; Robert Frost: The Years of Triumph, 1970 (Pulitzer prize in biography 1971). Editor: Tilbury Town; Selected Poems of Edwin Arlington Robinson, 1954; Selected Letters of Robert Frost, 1964; (with Edward Connery Lathem) Robert Frost, Farm-Poultryman, 1963, Robert Frost and the Lawrence, Massachusetts, High School Bulletin, 1966; (with Benton Spruance) Moby Dick: The Passion of Ahab, 1968; (with Arnold Grade) New Hampshire's Child: The Derry Journals of Lesley Frost, 1969. Home: Princeton NJ Died Apr. 16, 1973.

THOMPSON, LEWIS, writer; b. Jersey City, New Jersey; s. Chester Arthur and Gertrude (Fauquier) T.; B.A., N.Y.U., 1943; B. Library Sci., Pratt Inst., 1943; m. Joan Wallace (div.); 1 son, Wallace. Reference librarian N.Y. Pub. Library, 1939-43; with publicity dept. Alfred A. Knopf, Inc., 1945-46; exec. asst. to pres. Henry Schuman, Inc., pubs., 1946-47; free-lance writer, 1947-72; guest lectr. on profl. write in U.S. today, also sociology of lit., Columbia Grad. Sch., 1955-72; mem. teaching panel on the mystery story, Columbia and N.Y.U., 1954-58; pub. relations Sidney J. Wain, Inc., 1961-63; pub. relations for the Pepsi-Cola Company, 1963-72. Served with U.S. Merchant Marine and U.S. Maritime Service, 1943-45. Mem. Mystery Writers Am. (regional v.p. N.Y. 1958, exec. v.p. 1955, 60, 61), Soc. Magazine Writers, Phi Beta Kappa. Club: Overseas Press, Players. Author (with Charles Boswell) The Girl in the Stateroom, 1951, The Girl in Lover's Lane, 1953, The Girl with the Scarlet Brand (Edgar award Mystery Writers Am. 1954), 1954, The Girls in Nightmare House, 1955, Surrender to Love, 1955, More Deadly Than the Male, 1951; co-editor Advocates of Murder, 1962, Practitioners of Murder, 1962, Curriculum of Murder, 1962, Business of Murder, 1963, Harvesters of Murder, 1963, Mistresses of Murder, 1963; also many articles. Home: New York City NY Died July 1972.

THOMPSON, LEWIS EUGENE, portrait painter, historian; b. Hillsdale, Mich., May 21, 1894; s. Eugene John and Julie Addie (Alfred) T.; student painting under pvt. instrs., 1913, 1915, 1924, 1927, 1937; Certificate, Hillsdale Coll., 1915; spl. work psychology U. Mich., 1936; m. Grace B. Rickard, Feb. 14, 1921; children—Ralph Eugene, Elouise Irene; m. Marion Sturm, Aug. 20, 1955. Art instr. pub. schs., So. Mich., 1922-36; also pvt. instr. designing, comml. and fine arts, Hillsdale; pvt. instr., art dir. comml. and fine arts, Chicago, 1936-42; chief dept. art br. Aircraft Lab., Wright-Patterson Field, Dayton, O., creating original paintings secret air craft for A.A.F. staff, Washington, 1942-47; portraits, commercial illustrations, Dayton, Ohio, 1947-59; professor of fine arts; works represented in numerous collections, national, internat., state, and pvt.; painted 100 portraits leading Am. flyers, aviation personalities; condr. program art instrn. TV sta. WHIO-TV, Dayton 1951-58; also lectr. portraiture and aviation history, N.Y.C., Cin.; sr. member Hoosier Salon Exhibition Jury, 1957; study and lecturer Europe, 1956; lecturer on television and radio Decatur, Ill., 1957; now portraiture and pvt. instructor, Santa Barbara, Cal. Mem. bd. Sabado and Domingo Art Assn. Co-founder Dayton Metropolitan Art Guild. Mem. North Shore Art Guild, Inst. Aeronautical Scis. (asso. mem. hist. sect.), Dayton Wright Air Mail Soc., Dayton Kennel, Inc., Am. Air Mail Society, International Institute Arts and Letters, C. of C. Mason. Clubs: Gem City Hobby, Air Corps Masonic (Dayton); Sphinx Society (honorary), Avignon (France). Author: American Aviation History, 1952. Editor: Who's Who in World Aviation, 1955. Home: Santa Barbara CA Died Mar. 24, 1968; buried Frontier MI

THOMPSON, LLEWELLYN E., JR., fgn. affairs cons.; b. Las Animas, Colo., Aug. 24, 1904; A.B., U. of Colo., 1928; married Mrs. Jane Monroe Goelet, Oct. 2, 1948; children—Jenny, Sherry. Accountant 1923-24, 1926, 1928; fgn. service ofcr. since 1929; vice consul, Colombo, 1929; vice consul, Geneva, 1933, consul, 1937; 2d sec. and consul, Moscow, 1941. Adviser, 20th, 21st, 23d and 24th Internat. Labor conferences, Geneva, 1936, 1937, 1938; adviser, governing body Int. Labor Office, Prague, 1937, Geneva, 1938, London, 1938, Geneva, 1939; adviser and sec. Am. delegation 2d Regional Conf. of Am. States Members of Int. Labor Orgn., Havana, 1939. Advisory mem. Am. com. Internat. Inst. of Agr., 1939-40; Army War Coll., Jan.-Nov. 1940; 2d Sec. and cons. at Moscow, Nov. 20, 1940, at London Sept. 20, 1944; polit. and liaison officer, U.S. del., U.N. Conf. on Internat. Orgn., San Francisco, 1945; polit. adv. Berlin conf. 1945, and meeting of Council of Fgn. Ministers, London, Sept. 1945; 1st sec. at London, July 23, 1945; polit. adv., U.S. del., 1st session of the Gen. Assembly, U.N., London, 1946; Dept. of State, Apr. 8, 1946; chief, Div. of Eastern European Affairs, June 12, 1946; dep. dir. for European Affairs, 1948; dep. asst. sec., 1949; minister-counselor Am. Embassy, Rome, Italy, 1950; A.E. and P., U.S. High Commr., Austria, 1952-55. A.E. and P., 1955-57; U.S. ambassador to Soviet Union, 1957-62, 67-69; ambassador-at-large Dept. State, 1962-67; fgn. affairs cons., 1969-72. Recipient Pres. award for Distinguished Fed. Civilian Service, 1962. Address: Washington DC Died Feb. 6, 1972; buried Las Animas CO

THOMPSON, MARSHALL PUTNAM, lawyer; b. Lawrence, Mass., Jan. 24, 1869; s. William Luther and Katherine Putnam (Marshall) T.; A.B., Dartmouth, 1892; LL.B., Harvard, 1897; m. Clara Collins Southworth, of Springfield, Mass., June 19, 1907. Practiced at Boston since 1897. Republican. Member Military Order Loyal Legion, Society of the War of 1812, S.R., S.A.R. Club: Harvard (Boston). Mem. Delta Kappa Epsilon. Author: The Lieutenant, The Girl and the Viceroy, 1907. Writer of short stories and lecturer on law subjects. Dir. Mass. com. of S.A.R., for relief of soldiers and sailors; mem. council of Mass. Mil. Efficiency Assn. Home: Brookline MA Office: 15 State St., Boston MA‡

THOMPSON, MERLE DOW, business executive; b. Candor, N.Y., Nov. 14, 1879; s. Norman J. and Lillian (Tyler) T.; B.A., Princeton, 1902; m. Louise Henry, Oct. 3, 1905; children—Tyler, Norma, Henry, Eunice. Dir. Marine Midland Trust Co. of So. N.Y. (formerly Elmira Bank & Trust Co.), 1915-70, vice pres., 1932-37, chmn. exec. com., 1938-70; director of and chmn. exec. com. Insular Lumber Co. (P.I.). Chmn. Philippine Com., Nat. Fgn. Trade Council, Inc.; pres. bd. of trustees Elmira College, 1950. U.S. alt. del. Econ. Conf. for Asia and Far East, Manila, P.I., 1953. Democrat. Conglist. Clubs: Princeton, India House (N.Y.C.); City, Country (Elmira, N.Y.). Home: Elmira NY Died Mar. 9, 1970

THOMPSON, MILTON JOHN, aeronautical engr.; b. Grand Rapids, Mich., July 28, 1904; s. Schuyler D and Jennie L. (Albertson) T.; B.S., U. of Mich., 1925, M.S., 1926; Sc.D., Warsaw Polytech. Inst. (Guggenheim fellow in aerodynamics, 1928-30) 1930; m. Helen B. Frank, Aug. 22, 1931; children—Richard D., Barbara J. Instr. engring. math., U. of Mich., 1926-28, asst. prof., aero. engring., 1930-37, asso. prof., 1937-41; prof. aeronautics dept. mech. engring. U. Tex., 1941-42, prof. dept. aero. engring., 1942-71, chmn., 1942-66; asso. dir. Def. Research Lab., from 1945; cons. aero engr., 1930-71; v.p. Haneman Assos., Inc., consultants, 1961-71. Recipient grants NSF, Ford. Found. and NATO for research at U. Gottingen, Imperial Coll. and Cambridge U., Liverpool U., 1967-68. Registered professional engineer, Texas. Fellow Am. Society M.E. (aviation sect., gen. com.); member American Institute of Aeronautics and Astronautics, A.A.A.S., Am. Astronautical Society, American Society of Engring. Edn., Phi Kappa Phi, Sigma Gamma Tau, Sigma Xi, Tau Beta Pi, Pi Tau Sigma. Mem. aerodynamics panel, Navy Bur. Ordnance Bumblebee Guided Missile project, 1945-65; mem. panel target drones Guided Missile Com. Research and Development Bd., 1950-52; mem. panel on boundary layers Navy Bur. Ordnance Com. on Aero-ballistics, 1949-52, chmn. panel on drag., 1953-55. Club: Exchange. Author: The Theory of Single Burbling (with C. Witoszynski), Vol. III, division F. of Aerodynamic Theory, ed. by W.F. Durand, 1943; Fluid Mechanics (with R.A. Dodge), 1935. Contbr. articles on aerodynamics and aero. engring; classified reports on aero. research for aircraft industry and mil. aero. agys. Home: Austin TX Died July 23, 1971; buried Austin Meml. Cemetery, Austin TX

THOMPSON, RALPH LEROY, pathologist; b. Lisbon, Me., Nov. 15, 1873; s. Haley P. and Mehitable (Smith) T.; A.B., Bates Coll., Lewiston, Me., 1896, A.M., 1901; M.D., Harvard, 1900; grad. student, U. of Berlin; fellow Rockefeller Inst., 1902-03; m. Elizabeth Scammell Schuyler, May 28, 1918. Pathol. house officer and 2d and 1st asst. in pathology, Boston City Hosp., 1901-05; asst. prof. pathology, St. Louis U., 1905-07, prof. since 1907, now prof. emeritus; dir. Nat. Pathol. Lab., St. Louis, also hosp. commr., 1933-41, 1st lt. U.S. Army Med. R. C., 1910-15; pathologist, 23d Gen. Hosp., B.E.F., Etaples, France, summer 1915. Editor Mo. State Med. Jour., 1942-47, editor emeritus, 1947. Mem. Am. Assn. Pathologists and Bacteriologists, Am. Assn. Cancer Research, A.M.A. Clubs: University, Artists Guild. Author: Glimpses of Medical Europe, 1908; Surgery and Pathology of the Thyroid and Parathyroid Glands (with Albert J. Ochsner), 1910; also papers and articles in med. jours., chiefly on immunity, infectious diseases and parathyroid glandules. Home: 4406 McPherson Av. 8. Office: 607 N. Grand, St Louis 3 MO‡

THOMPSON, ROBERT BRUCE, mfg. exec.; b. Balt., Feb. 2, 1906; s. Robert Bruce and Mary (Pattersen) T.; student Johns Hopkins, 1922-24; m. Helen A. French, Oct. 27, 1928; 1 dau., Janet F. (Mrs. John Knauth). With Am. Can Co., from 1922, successively serviceman, plant operations staff, plant mgr., Balt., mgr. Atlantic div., N.Y.C., gen. mgr., v.p. mfg., 1922-63, v.p. mfg., purchasing and engring, from 1963; civilian cons. to comdg. gen. Munitions Command, U.S. Army, 1966-70. Home: Stamford CT Died Jan. 1970.

THOMPSON, ROBERT FOSTER, judge; LL.B., U. of Mich., 1892, LL.M., 1893. Began practice at Canadaigua, N.Y., 1893; dist. atty., 1900-06; served as county judge, Ontario Co., N.Y.; justice Supreme Court of N.Y., 7th Dist., 1916-30. Republican. Home: Canadaigua NY‡

THOMPSON, ROBERT S., pres. Thompson Hayward Chem. Co. Address: Kansas City KS Died Feb. 17, 1969.

THOMPSON, RUPERT CAMPBELL, JR., bus. exec.; b. Newton, Mass., July 5, 1905; s. Rupert C. and Christine Rhoda (McLean) T.; ed. Browne & Nichols Sch., 1922-24; A.B., Dartmouth Coll., 1928; LL.B., Suffolk Law Sch., 1934; D.C.S., Suffolk U., 1960; Sc.D., Bryant Coll., 1966; m. Eleanor B. Ball, June 7, 1930; children—Peter Campbell, David Carlisle; m. 2d, Doris Colburn Billings, February 25, 1958. Began as bank clerk, Newton Trust Co., 1928, asst. treas., 1930; became asst. cashier Providence Nat. Bank, 1937, vice pres. and cashier, 1941, 1st v.p. and director, 1942, pres., 1943; exec. v.p. Providence Union Nat. Bank, 1951; exec. vice pres. Industrial Nat. Bank R.I., 1954; chmn. exec. committee Textron. Inc., 1956-57, pres. 1957-60, chmn. and chief executive officer, 1960-69, also dir.; partner Little, Casler & Thompson, 1970; dir. Gen. Telephone and Electronics Corporation, Indsl. Nat. Bank R.I., Indsl. Bancorp., Inc., Narragansett Capital Corporation, Sperry Rand Corp., MFB Mut. Ins. Co., Am. Research & Devel. Corp. Trustee R.I. Charities Trust, Nat. Indsl. Conf. Bd., Dartmouth College, General chairman R.I. United War Fund, 1943. Clubs: Agawam Hunt, Providence Art, Hope, Turk's Head (Providence); Vineyard Haven Yacht (Mass.); Edgartown (Mass.) Yacht; N.Y. Yacht, Union League (N.Y.C.); Lyford Cay (Nassau). Home: Providence RI Died June 23, 1970; buried Martha's Vineyard MA

THOMPSON, SAM(UEL) EVANS, physician; b. Claiborne Parish, La., May 24, 1871; s. Robert Evans and Maria Louise (Bush) T.; student Hendrix Coll., Conway, Ark., 1892-93; M.D., U. of Louisville, 1904; m. Annie Lee Pinson Melear, Aug. 13, 1914. Teacher and traveling salesman until 1900; began practice of medicine El Dorado, Ark., 1904; med. dir. Tex. State Tuberculosis Sanatorium, 1913-17; owner and manager Thompson Sanatorium, 1917-37; private practice since 1937; specializes in treatment of tuberculosis. Fellow Am. Coll. Physicians; mem. Am., Southern, Tri-State and Kerr County med. assns., Tex. State Med. Assn. (pres.), Am. Hosp. Assn., Nat. Tuberculosis Assn., Southwest Texas Med. Assn. (pres.), Asociacion Mexicana de Medicos Militares (hon.), Am. Medical Editors and Authors Assn., Am. Medical Assn. of Vienna. Democrat. Methodist. K.P., Elk. Clubs: Rotary, Kerrville Country; Tarpon Inn Club (Port Arkansas, Tex.); Aransas Pass (Tex.) Hunting. Address: Medical and Professional Bldg., Kerrville TX*‡

THOMPSON, THEOS JARDIN, scientist, nuclear engr.; b. Lincoln, Neb., Aug. 30, 1918; s. Theos Jefferson and Mabel E. (Dow) T.; A.B., U. Neb., 1941, M.A., 1942, Doctor of Science (honorary), 1964; Ph.D. in Nuclear Physics, University of Cal. at Berkeley, 1952; m. Dorothy Sibley, Feb. 14, 1947; children—Jeff, Edward, Robert, Elizabeth. Physicist U. Cal. Radiation Lab., 1948-52, lectr. physics, Berkeley, 1949-52; staff Los Alamos Sci. Lab., 1952-55, reactor design and constrn.; asso. prof. nuclear engring. Mass. Inst. Tech., 1955-58, prof., 1958-—, dir. nuclear reactor for design, constrn. and operation; cons. Mem. AEC adv. com. reactor safeguards, 1959-66, chmn., 1960; co-editor AEC project Safety Information for Technology of Reactors, 1962-70; commr. AEC, 1969-70. Served from 2d lt. to maj., C.W.S., AUS, 1942-46. Recipient E.O. Lawrence Meml. award, Atomic Energy Commn., 1964; Guggenheim Found. fellow, 1963-64. Fellow American Nuclear Soc. (director); mem. Am. Academy of Arts and Sciences, American Phys. Soc., Phi Beta Kappa, Sigma Xi. Home: Winchester MA Died Nov. 25, 1970; buried Lincoln NB

THOMPSON, W. STUART, architect; born at N.Y.C. Jan. 25, 1890; s. George and Mary (Stuart) T.; grad. Sch

Arch., Columbia, 1912; grad. study architecture, southeastern Europe, 1913-16; m. M. Gladys Slade, Aug. 22, 1913; children—William Stuart, George Clifford, Isabel F. (dec.). Critic archtl. design Cooper Union, 1917-20; practicing architect, N.Y.C., from 1918; architect: Gennadius Library and Loring Hall, Athens, Greece (J. Van Pelt partner); Pearce Coll.; Corinth Mus.; hosp., Manisa, Turkey (H.S. Churchill partner); Am. Hosp., Istanbul, Turkey; numerous bldgs. in Greece and Near East; pvt. houses, apts. and office bldgs. in U.S., including: State Tower Bldg., Syracuse, N.Y., Crucible Steel Bldg., Chgo.; Sterling Drug Plant, Gulfport, Miss.; Sterling-Winthrop Research Inst., Rensselaer, N.Y.; lab. for Sharp & Dohme, West Point, Pa.; master plan terminal bldgs. Conn. State Airport; sch. bldgs., Greenwich, Conn.; pharm. mfg. bldgs., Rio de Janeiro, Cali, Colombia, Durban, S. Africa; Byzantine chs. Church Holy Cross, Brookline, Mass., Greek Orthodox Ch. of Archangels, Stamford, Conn.; Med. Research Bldg. for Carter Products, Inc., Cranbury, N.J.; architect restoring Stoa Attalos (159 B.C.), Athens (Phelps Barnum, partner), and others; airport designer in def. program U.S. Govt. with Pan-Am. Airways, 1942-43. Archtl. fellow Am. Sch. Classical Studies, Athens, 1913-15. Mem. board Near East Found. Decorated Order of Saviour, 1926, Order of Phoenix, 1956 (Greece); named hon. citizen Athens, 1926, 56. Fellow N.Y. Acad. Sci.; mem. Am. Friends of Greece (sec.). A.I.A., Archaeol. Institute of Am., N.Y. Acad. Scis. (mem. bd.); hon. mem. Archaeological Society of Athens. Mem. various coms. for amelioration Greek people, 40 yrs. Clubs: Indian Harbor Yacht Columbia Univ. (N.Y.C.). Home: Greenwich CT Died Apr. 2, 1968.

THOMPSON, WILLIAM BLAINE, JR., railroad ofcl.; b. Falls Church, Va., Aug. 22, 1917; s. William Blaine and Catherine Elizabeth (Foley) T.; A.A., U. Fla., 1940; m. Margaret Louise Covey, Dec. 5, 1958; children—William Blaine III (dec.), Holland McTyeire, Gayle Tigert (Mrs. Carpenter). Asst. cashier Fla. Nat. Bank, Jacksonville, 1940-48; asst. to v.p. Fla. Power and Light Co., 1949; self-employed pub. relations cons., 1952-58, also v.p. Riddle Air Lines; asst. v.p. Assn. Am. Railroads, 1958-60, 64-70; pres. Fla. East Coast Ry. Co., 1961-64, dir., 1961-70; pres., dir. Florida East Coast Highway Dispatch Co., 1961-64; dir. Fla. Nat. Bank and Trust Co., Miami. Sec., asst. treas. Am. Taxpayers Assn., 1963-70. Served to lt. col. USMCR, World War II, Korea. Mem. Am. Legion. Club: Seminole (Jacksonville, Fla.). Home: Arlington VA Died Oct. 12, 1970; buried Falls Church VA

THOMPSON, WILLIAM W., accountant; b. Otsego, Mich., Apr. 4, 1870; s. John and Julia (Thompson) T.; student pub. schs. Chicago; spl. courses U. Chicago; m. Florence E. Ludwig, Apr. 4, children—William W., Charlotte Julia (Mrs. Art Barnard). Cashier, bookkeeper Fraser & Chalmers (now Allis Chalmers), Chicago; office mgr. Dodge Mfg. Co. of Mishawaukee, Ind.; accountant Chicago, since 1893; dir. Independent Grocers Alliance. Home: 1825 Castellana Rd., La Jolla CA Office: 176 W. Adams St., Chicago IL‡

THOMS, HERBERT, physician, teacher; b. Waterbury, Conn., Jan. 5, 1885; s. William Peter and Adeline Delia (Hart) T.; M.D., Yale Univ., 1910; post grad. student John Hopkins Univ., 1914-15; m. Edith May Comstock, Aug. 21, 1912; 1 dau., Margaret Alison. Intern, Backus Hosp., Norwich, Conn., Memorial Hospital, New London, Conn., 1910-11; asst. resident Sloane Hosp. For Women, 1912; became prof. obstetrics and gynecology, chmn. dept. Yale Univ. Sch. Medicine, 1947, prof. emeritus; curator Yale Medical School Library; member of the staff of Grace-New Haven Hosp., Meriden Hosp., New Britain Hosp., Hungerford Hosp., Norwalk Hosp., Stamford Hosp., Backus Hosp., Milford Hosp. Exhibited art work at Phila. Art Alliance, 1932, Am. Soc. Etchers, 1933, Old Lyme Art Assn, Salmagundi Club, others. Chmn. med. adv. com. Conn. Planned Parenthood League, 1961. Awarded Lasker Award, 1953, Yale medal, 1961. Mem. Am. Med. Assn., American Gynecological Society. Clubs: Acom. Beaumont Medical, Elizabethan. Author: The Estimation of Pelvic Capacity, 1940; The Obstetric Pelvis, 1935; Chapters in American Obstetrics, 1933; Classical Contributions to Obstetrics and Gynecology, 1935; Training for Childbirth, 1950; Understanding Natural Childbirth, 1950; Pelvimetry, 1956; The Doctors Jared of Connecticut, 1958; The Docters of Yale College, 1701-1815, 1960; Our Obstetric Heritage, 1960; Samuel Seabury, Priest and Physician, Bishop of Connecticut, 1963; Jared Eliot, Minister, Doctor, Scientist and His Connecticut, 1967; Yale Men and Landmarks in Old Connecticut, 1967. Home: Stony Creek CT Died Oct. 27, 1972; buried Stony Creek CT

THOMSON, JAMES SUTHERLAND, educator, former univ. dean; b. Stirling, Scotland, Apr. 30, 1892; s. John and Margaret (Sutherland) T.; student Craig's, Stirling, 1896-1903; Eastbank Acad., Glasgow, 1903-10; M.A., U. Glasgow, 1914, D.D., 1946; student Trinity Coll., Glasgow, 1919-21; D.D., U. Toronto, 1936; LL.D., State Coll. Wash., 1943, McGill U., 1946, Queen's U., 1946, Toronto University, 1947, Manitoba University, 1948, McMaster University, 1948, Alberta University, 1949, U. Sask., 1951; m. Margaret Stewart Troup, June 27, 1922; children—John, Margaret Stewart. Minister, Middle Ch., Coatbridge, Scotland, 1920-24; sec. of edn., Ch. of Scotland, 1924-30; prof. theology, Pine Hill Coll., Halifax, N.S., 1930-37; pres., U. of Saskatchewan, from 1937; prof. philosophy of religion, McGill U., 1949-61, lecturer philosophy of education, 1961-72. Moderator of United Church of Canada, 1956. Served with Queen's Own Cameron Highlanders, 1915-17; capt., Rifle Brigade, 1917-19; now hon. colonel C.O.T.C. Fellow Royal Society Can. Mem. United Ch. of Can. Author: Studies in the Life of Jesus, 1927; The Way of Revelation, 1928; The Hope of the Gospel, 1955; The Divine Mission, 1957; The Word of God, 1959. Contributor of articles to the Dalhousie Review, and other jours. Home: Montreal Quebec Canada Died Nov. 1972.

THOMSON, PHILIP LIVINGSTON, business exec.; b. Schenectady, N.Y., Nov. 28, 1879; s. Alexander and Mary Helen (Livingston) T.; A.B., Union College 1900, hon. A.M., 1925; A.B., Harvard U., 1902; m. Dorothy Eliot Tuthill, Apr. 21, 1909; children—Donald (dec.), Dorothy (Mrs. Robert Hayden), Philip Van Rensselaer. With Western Electric Co., 1903-44, dir. pub. relations, 1911-44. President Audit Bureau Circulation, 1927-50; director Glen Ridge (New Jersey) Trust Company, Howe Caverns, Incorporated, mem. Assn. of Nat. Advertisers (pres. 1923-24), Phi Beta Kappa, Chi Psi, Alpha Delta Sigma. Republican. Congregationalist. Clubs: Harvard, New York Advertising, Glen Ridge Country. Contributor to Nation's Business, Printers' Ink, Advertising and Selling. Trustee Union Coll. 1941-49. Frequent speaker on advt., public relations; delivered address at International Advertising Conv., London, 1924, Berlin, 1929; awarded gold medal for distinguished service to advertising, 1939 and gold medals for distinguished service to Union College, and to the Chi Psi fraternity, 1946. Home: Boynton Beach FL Died Feb. 2, 1969; buried Schenectady NY

THORBORG, KERSTIN, Swedish contralto; b. Venjan, Dalekarlia, Sweden, May 19, 1906; ed. privately and as 1 of 3 winners from 1000 candidates joined opera sch. of Stockholm Royal Opera, 1926-31; m. Gustav Bergmann, June 7, 1928. Debut in Aida, Stockholm Opera, 1931; sang in Prague opera houses, 1932, in Berlin, 1933, in Buenos Aires, 1934, at Vienna State Opera, 1935-37, in London, 1936; debut in U.S. at Met. Opera House, 1936, also appeared 1938, 39, mem. Met. Opera, 1940-50, made annual concert tours in U.S. and Can.; considered among greatest contraltos; generally ranked among first as interpreter of Wagner. Most distinguished role as Kundry" in Parsifal. Awarded Golden Medal of Art by King of Sweden. Home: Hedemora Sweden Died May 1970.*

THORGRIMSON, OLIVER BERNHARD, lawyer; b. Chicago, Ill., Nov. 5, 1874; s. Martin Ludwig and Emily Helen (Bell) T.; LL.B., U. of Neb., 1901; m. Myrtle Regina Gilkey, Dec. 26, 1906; 1 son, Richard Oliver (lt. col. U.S. Army). Admitted to Nebraska and Washington State bar, 1901; admitted to United States Supreme Court bar, 1919; in private practice of law, 1901-05 and since 1908; asst. corp. counsel of Seattle, 1905-07; counsel Port of Seattle, 1912-18; lecturer on municipal law, U. of Wash., since Jan. 1, 1938; dir., chmn. trust com. and chmn. exec. com. Seattle Trust & Savings Bank; dir., mem. finance com. and gen. counsel Northern Life Ins. Co.; dir. Equity Corp., vice-pres. and dir. Schwabacher Hardware Company; dir. Bon Marche Realty Company. Member Seattle School Board, 1923-29; president Seattle Municipal League, 1916; chairman Municipal League Advisory Council, 1946. Mem. Seattle Park Board, 1945-49. Director and president Seattle Gen. Hosp., Seattle Aboretum Foundation. Mem. Nat. Arboretum Advisory Council. Pres. Seattle Bar Assn., 1923, Wash. State Bar Assn., 1933-34; mem. Am. Bar Assn., Order of the Coif. Independent Republican. Clubs: College, Rainier (Seattle). Home: 7140 55th Av. S. Office: Northern Life Tower, Seattle WA‡

THORKELSON, HALSTEN JOSEPH, mechanical engr.; b. Racine, Wis., Jan. 18, 1875; s. Mathias and Mary (Eggen) T.; B.S., U. of Wis., 1898, M.E., 1901; m. Mary Schuyler Carver, June 14, 1900; children—Mary Elizabeth, Florence Carver, Martha Seymour, Halsten John. Laborer, clk. and draftsman in mfg. establishment 7 yrs.; asst. supt. J. I. Case Plow Works, Racine, Wis., 1901-02; instr. steam engring., asst. prof., asso. prof. and prof., Coll. of Engring., U. of Wis., 1902-14; acting business mgr. and business mgr., U. of Wis., 1914-21; with Gen. Edn. Bd., New York, 1921-28; with Kohler Co., Kohler, Wis., 1928-43, becoming vice pres. and dir.; dir. Security Nat. Bank, Sheboygan, Wis.; retired Dec. 1943. Mem. Wis. Acad. Arts, Letters and Science; fellow A.A.A.S. Mason. Presbyterian. Clubs: Madison, University. Author: Air Compression and Transmission, 1913. Address: University Club, 803 State St., Madison 5 WI‡

THORKELSON, JACOB, ex-congressman; b. Norway, Sept. 24, 1876; s. Thorkel and Maren (Petersen) Jacobsen; came to U.S., 1892, naturalized, 1900; M.D., Coll. of Physicians and Surgeons, U. of Md., 1911; m. Charlotte Sullivan, Oct. 1, 1934; children—Frances Clare, John Milton, Jacob Timothy. Navigator since 1896; capt. of ocean-going ships, 1900-07. Practice of medicine at Butte, Mont.; surgeon Mont. State Hosp., Warm Springs, Mont., since 1913; visiting surgeon to St. James Hosp., Butte, St. Ann's Hosp., Anaconda, Mont.; pres. Butte Neon Outdoor Advertising Co.; airplane pilot; mem. 76th Congress (1939-41), 1st Mont. Dist. Has served in U.S. Revenue Service, Va. Naval Reserves, U.S. Naval Reserves, 1936-39. Member American Association Anatomists, Association Military Surgeons, Aero Med. Assn., Phi Chi. Republican. Club: Exchange (Butte); Explorers (N.Y. City). Address: National Hotel Bldg., Butte MT*‡

THORNAL, BENJAMIN CAMPBELL, judge; b. Charleston, S.C., Oct. 15, 1908; s. Benjamin Campbell and Henrietta F. (Wagener) T.; LL.B. University Fla., 1930; m. Alyce Carolyn Letton, Nov. 7, 1936; children—Alyce (Mrs. Thomas H. Wyatt), Ben C. Admitted to Fla. bar, 1930, practiced in Orlando, 1930-55; city atty., Orlando, 1938-41. 46-48, 52-55; county atty. Orange County, Fla., 1941-43; justice Supreme Ct. of Fla., 1955-70, chief justice, 1965-67. Legislative aide to gov. of Fla., 1943, 53. Trustee U. Fla. Endowment Corp.; vice chmn. bd. trustees Fla. So. Coll. Served as lt., USNR, World War II. Mem. Am. Law Inst., Fla. Bar, U.S. (dir. 1939-41), Fla. (pres. 1939-40) Jr. C.'s of C., Order of the Coif, also frats. Phi Kappa Phi, Phi Delta Phi, Lambda Chi Alpha, Blue Key. Methodist. Author, compiler: Code City of Orlando, 1948. Home: Tallahassee FL Died Nov. 4, 1970; buried Orlando FL

THORNBER, JOHN JAMES, botanist; b. Rantoul, Ill., Feb. 8, 1872; s. James and Ann (Strickland) T.; B.S., S.D. Agrl. Coll., Brookings, 1895; B.S., U. of Neb., 1897, A.M., 1901; m. Harriet Ann Brown, June 26, 1897; 1 son, John Stickland; m. 2d, Miriam Rainier Harris, July 11, 1932. Prof. botany, U. of Ariz., and botanist Ariz. Agrl. Expt. Sta., 1901-43, also dir. Ariz. Agrl. Expt. Sta., 1921-28, and dean Ariz. Coll. of Agr., Tucson, 1922-28. Sabbatical leave to study in Smithsonian Instn. and Asa Gray Herbarium, 1911-12. Fellow A.A.A.S.; mem. Bot. Soc. America, Washington Acad. Sciences, Torrey Bot. Club, Sigma Xi, Phi Kappa Phi. Lambda Gamma Delta (hon. agrl. judging fraternity), Pi Gamma Mu. Mem. Presbyterian ch. Mason (32 deg., Shriner). Author: (with Margaret Armstrong) Field Book of Western Wild Flowers, 1915; (with Frances Bonker) Sage of the Desert and Other Cacti, 1930; (with same) The Fantastic Clan—The Cactus Family, 1931. Writer bulls. and articles on plants and plant life in Ariz. Built up herbarium of 100,000 sheets in the U. of Ariz.; has devoted much time to study of restoration of depleted grazing areas in Southwest, and to the introduction of trees and shrubs adapted to an arid, semitropical climate. Home: 2041 E. 2d St., Tucson AZ‡

THORNDIKE, WILLIS HALE, cartoonist; b. Stockton, Cal., Feb. 8, 1872; s. Albert and Mary F. (Page) T.; ed. pub. schs., Cal.; studied art San Francisco Art Sch., Art Students' League, New York, and Acad. Julien, Paris, under Jean Paul Laurens and Benjamin Constant, 2 1/2 yrs.; m. Anaconda, Mont., Irma R. Hunsicker, of Phila., Jan. 15, 1902. Artist on San Francisco Chronicle, 1890-2; on New York Herald, 1896-7; cartoonist, Boston Herald, 1897-8, Philadelphia Press, 1904-6, Baltimore American, 1906—. Awarded first prize for drawing from life, Paris, 1894. Home: Stockton CA Address: Baltimore MD‡

THORNE, ELISABETH GRIFFIN, librarian; b. Skaneateles, N.Y., Nov. 13, 1873; d. William Gifford and Adeline (Talcott) Thorne; A.B., Vassar, 1895; B.L.S., Univ. State of N.Y., 1897. Chief librarian Port Jervis (N.Y.) Free Library, 1898-1908, Kingston-on-Hudson Library, 1908-10; prof. Syracuse U. Library Sch., 1910-27; acting librarian, Syracuse U. Library, 1920-21, librarian, 1921-27, also dir. Syracuse U. Library Sch., 1921-27. Mem. A.L.A., N.Y. State Library Assn., Assn. Am. Univ. Women. Republican. Episcopalian. Home: Skaneateles NY‡

THORNE, JAMES REYNOLDS, r.r. exec.; b. Spearsville, La., Sept. 19, 1909; s. John William and May (Reynolds) T.; student pub. schs., Fla.; grad. Advanced Mgmt. Program at Harvard Univ.; m. Helen Connor, July 20, 1935. With S.A.L. Ry., 1926-43, successively sec., chief clk. to supt., yardmaster, terminal trainmaster, trainmaster, assistant supt., 1937-43; with Seaboard Air Line R.R. Company, 1946-67, successively asst. supt., supt., asst. gen. mgr., asst. v.p. operations, asst. to pres., 1952-58, exec. v.p., 1958-67; dir., 1960-67; v.p. operations, Seaboard Coast Line R.R. Co., 1967-70, v.p. exec. dept., Jan.-July 1970; exec. vice pres. and/or dir. subsidiaries; v.p. operations Athens Terminal Co., Gainsville Midland R.R. Co., Ga., Fla. & Ala. R.R. Co., Tavares & Gulf R.R. Co., Tampa & Gulf Coast R.R. Co.; exec. v.p., dir. Southeastern Investment Co.; mem. exec. com., dir. Fruit Growers Express Company; dir. Barnett National Bank of Jacksonville (Fla.), Seacoast Transportation Co., also Jacksonville Terminal Co., North Charleston Terminal Co., Duval Connecting R.R. Company, Richmond Terminal Railway Company, Trailer Train Company, Railway Express Agy., Inc., Norfolk &

Portsmouth Belt Line R.R. Co. Served as capt., maj. AUS, 1943-46. Mem. Am. Assn. R.R. Supts., Nat. Def. Transportation Assn. Baptist. Mason (Shriner). Clubs: River; Commonwealth (Richmond); Southern and Southwestern Railway. Home: Jacksonville FL Died July 9, 1970; buried Evergreen Cemetery, Jacksonville FL

THORNHILL, ARTHUR H., publisher; b. Hyde Park, Mass., Feb. 25, 1895; s. Joseph and Eliza (Jones) T.; ed. in pub. schs. of Hyde Park; m. Mary J. Petersen, Sept. 16, 1922; 1 son, Arthur H. With Little, Brown and Co., Boston, from 1913, mgr. N.Y. office, 1935-48, dir., 1938-41, vice pres., 1941-48, pres., 1948-62, chmn. bd., from 1948; dir. Atlantic Monthly Company; dir. Grosset & Dunlap, Inc., 1949-65, Bantam Books, Inc., 1949-65. Bd. dirs. Am. Book Pubs. Council, 1951-54. Mason. Clubs: Publishers' Lunch (N.Y.C.); Union (Boston, Mass.). Home: Duxbury MA Died Jan. 9, 1970; buried Mayflower Cemetery Duxbury MA

THORNLEY, FANT HILL, librarian; b. Pickens, S.C., June 1, 1909; s. John Lewis and Elizabeth (Hill) T.; A.B., Presbyn. Coll., 1930; B.L.S. (Carnegie fellow), U. N.C., 1936. Instr. schs. Va., S.C., 1930-33; head circulation, reference, cataloging depts., later asst. librarian Richland County Pub. Library, Columbia, S.C., 1934-49; pres. Bostick & Thornley, publishers, Columbia, 1938-70; head reference dept., asst. dir. Birmingham Pub. Library, 1949-53, dir. 1953-70. Chairman Southern Books Competition, 1959-62; del. Conf. Library Dirs. Asian-Pacific Area, Tokyo, 1958. Served staff sgt. USMC, 1943-45. Recipient Birmingham Festival Arts Lit. award, 1958. Mem. Caroliniana Soc., Am., Southeastern, Ala., S.C. (pres. 1936-38), library assns., Birmingham Art Assn., Ala. Hist. Assn., English Speaking Union (mem. bd. Birmingham chpt., pres. 1960-62), Bibliog. Society of America, Birmingham Hist. Soc. Club: Grolier (New York City, N.Y.). Editor: Mills' Atlas of S.C. Editor of Alabama Librarian, 1951-53. Contbr. various periodicals. Home: Birmingham AL Died Apr. 13, 1970.

THORNTON, HAMILTON, editor; b. St. Louis, Apr. 21, 1901; s. Francis A. and Stella (Ferris) T.; A.B., St. Louis U., 1922; m. Dorothy Elinore Whiteford, June 29, 1929; children—Mary Elinore, Ann Dorothy (Mrs. David J. O'Malley), Michael H. With St. Louis Star, 1925; editorial depts. St. Louis Globe-Democrat, 1925-72, asst. editor editorial page, 1941-59, editor editorial page, 1959-72. Lectr. journalism St. Louis U., 1936-51. Lt., Mo. State Guard, 1944. Mem. Am. Soc. Newspaper Editors. St. Louis Council Cath. Men (mem. bd. 1955-56), Sigma Delta Chi. Roman Catholic. Home: Ferguson MO Died Dec. 30, 1972.

THORP, CLARK ELWIN, chem. engr.; b. Cleve., Aug. 15, 1914; s. Ayers Clark and Ada (Mercy) T.; B.Sc., Fenn Coll., Cleve., 1935; m. Amelia Greenawalt, Aug. 14, 1937; 1 son, Clark Elwin. Research engr. Fullers Earth Co., Cleve., 1936-37; dir. research Ozo-Ray Process Corp., Chgo., 1937-41; suprv. chem. engring. Armour Research Found., Chgo., 1941-44, mgr. chemistry and chem. engring. research, 1950-58; president Fiber Products Research Center, Inc., Beaver Falls, New York, 1958-68. Mem. Am. Inst. Chem. Engrs., Tech. Assn. Paper and Pulp Industry, Am. Assn. Research Dirs., Am. Inst. of Chemists (chairman), Am. Ordnance Assn., Electrochem. Soc., Am. Soc. Testing Materials, Am. Mgmt. Assn., Ill. Acad. Sci., Paper Industry Mgmt. Assn., Sigma Xi, Sigma Chi Alpha. Contbr. profl. publs. Patentee in field. Address: Beaver Falls NY Died Aug. 15, 1968; buried Crown Hill Cemetery, Twinsburg OH

THORPE, BURTON LEE, dental surgeon; b. Wright Co., Ia., June 29, 1871; s. Charles O. and Emma (Ames) T.; D.D.S., Western Dental Coll., Kansas City, Mo., 1895; M.D., Barnes U., St. Louis, 1904; m. Berta Scott, of Gallatin, Mo., Dec. 4, 1895. Practiced in St. Louis, since 1899; dean of faculty, prof. operative dentistry and dental history, Barnes Dental Coll., 1903-5. Mem. Mo. State Bd. Dental Examiners, 1900-8 (pres. 1903); elected pres. Nat. Assn. Dental Examiners, 1903. Mem. Nat. Dental Assn. (pres. 1909-10; chmn. sect. on mouth hygiene, 1919-20), Mo. State Dental Assn. (pres. 1901; corr. sec. 1906, 7, 8), St. Louis Soc. Dental Science (pres. 1905), Delta Sigma Delta (Supreme Grand Master Supreme Chapter, 1914-15); hon. mem. Kan., Colo., Va., Ohio, Ia., Tenn. and Southern Ill. dental socs. Originator 4th Internat. Dental Congress, St. Louis, 1904; asst. sec. Internat. Dental Federation; originator of Jamestown (Va.) Dental Congress, 1907, and chmn. com. on orgn.; del. 5th Congress, Berlin, 1909, 6th Congress, London, 1914. Awarded diploma and gold medal St. Louis Expn., 1904. Asso. editor The Dental Brief, 1904-14. Devoted to dental history, and has served as chmn. or sec. various hist. committees of dental socs. Mem. S.A.R. Mason (32 deg., Shriner). Republican. Episcopalian. Clubs: University, Midland Valley Golf. Author: The History of Dental Surgery, 1910; The Founders of the Missouri State Dental Association, 1909. Home: 3703 Lindell Boul. Office: 415 Metropolitan Bldg., St Louis MO‡

THORSEN, DAVID S., physician; b. Minn., 1916; M.D., U. Minn., 1943. Intern, San Bernardino County Hosp., San Bernardino, Cal., 1943-44; tng. U. Minn., VA Hosp., Mpls., 1946-49; fellow in child psychiatry Wilder Child Guidance Clinic, 1952-53, staff, 1953-67, dir., 1968-69. Served to lt., M.C., USNR, 1944-46. Diplomate Am. Bd. Psychiatry and Neurology. Mem. A.M.A., Am. Psychiat. Assn., Am. Assn. on Mental Deficiency, Alpha Omega Alpha. Home: St Paul MN Died July 4, 1968.

THORSON, GUNNAR AXEL WRIGHT, marine biologist, educator; b. Copenhagen, Denmark, Dec. 31, 1906; s. Charles U. and Astrid (Gjertsen) T.; M.Sc., Copenhagen U., 1930, Ph.D., 1936; m. Ellen Johanne Gudrun Jorgensen, Dec. 23, 1940; children—Ole, Bodll (Mrs. Soren Larsen). Curator, Copenhagen Zool. Mus. 1934-57; lectr. marine biology Copenhagen U., 1946-57, prof., 1957-70; dir. Elsinore Marine Biol. Lab. (Denmark), 1958-70; pres. Nordic Council for Marine Biology, 1960. Mem. adv. bds., marine insts. Miami, Paris, Naples, Eilat. Decorated knight Order Dannebrog, officer Siamese White Elephant; recipient Danish Merit medal, 1935, Danish Sci. prize, 1947. Mem. Royal Danish Acad. Sci.; corr. or hon. mem. sci. socs. Finland, France, Italy, Norway, Spain, Sweden, U.K., U.S. Author: Reproduction and Larval Development of Danish Marine Bottom Invertebrates, 1946; Bottom Communities, 1957; Light as a Ecological Factor in Dispersal and Settlement of Marine Larvae 1964; Some Factors Influencing the Recruitment and Establishment of Marine Communities. Contbr. profl. jours. Home: Elsinore Denmark Died Jan. 25, 1971; buried Frederiksberg Old Cemetery, Copenhagen Denmark

THORVALDSON, GUNNAR S., lawyer; b. Riverton, Man., Can., Mar. 18, 1901; s. Sveinn and Margaret (Solmundson) T.; LL.B., U. Man., 1925; m. Edna Schwitzer, Oct. 9, 1926. Admitted to Man. bar, 1925; practiced in Winnipeg, Man., 1925-69; mem. firm Thorvaldson & Co.; apptd. King's counsel, 1941-69. Dir. Anthes Imperial Ltd., Gamble MacLeod Ltd., CAE Industries Ltd., Canadian Premier Life Ins. Co., Can. Security Assurance Co., Western Gypsum Products Ltd. Mem. Man. Legislature, 1941-49, Senate, Winnipeg, Man., 1958-69. Canadian del. Gen. Assembly, UN, 1958. Mem. Law Soc. Man. (pres. 1956-58), Winnipeg C. of C. (pres. 1952-53), Canadian C. of C. (pres. 1954-55), Zeta Psi. Progressive Conservative. Mem. United Ch. Mason. Clubs: Manitoba, St. Charles Country, Winnipeg Conservative, Optimist (Winnipeg); Rideau (Ottawa, Que.); Seigniory (Montebello, Que.). Address: Winnipeg NB Can. Died Aug. 2, 1969.

THREADGILL, FRANCES FALWELL (MRS. JOHN THREADGILL), b. Memphis, Tenn.; d. Samuel and Zarsko Zelo (Messick) Falwell; grad. Peabody Normal Coll. (now Peabody Coll. for Teachers), Nashville; m. John Threadgill, M.D., of Oklahoma City, Okla., Jan. 6, 1892; children—Mary Frances (Mrs. W. T. Allen), John Falwell. Active in promotion of ednl. work, and in obtaining legislation in Okla. for child labor, juvenile courts, etc.; established ednl. loan fund in Okla. State Federation of Women's Clubs, to enable girls to secure higher edn. Past treas. Gen. Federation of Women's Clubs; ex. pres. Okla. State Federation of Women's Clubs, Okla. City Federation of Women's Clubs; v.p. Okla. State Women's Suffrage Assn. (chmn. state campaign com.); mem. Okla. Woman's State War Savings Com. Was librarian Carnegie Library, El Reno, Okla.; later librarian, Free Pub. Library, Henryetta, Okla. Presbyn. Home: Henryetta OK*‡

THROCKMORTON, CHARLOTTE EDGERTON ALVORD (CHARLES EGERTON"), author; b. New York, Nov. 8, 1873; d. Alwyn A. and Frances D. (Edgerton) Alvord; m. New York, Oct. 28, 1896, C. Wickliffe Throckmorton. Author: The Coming Dawn, 1906 L22. Contb'r to mags. Address: Morristown NJ‡

THROPP, JOSEPH EARLSTON, ex-congressman; b. Valley Forge, Chester Co., Pa.; pub. sch. edn.; C.E., Poly. Coll. of Pa., 1868; m. d. of late Col. Thomas A. Scott, pres. Pa. R.R. Engr. in Minn., reaching rank div. engr. (youngest) on L.S. & M. R.R.; entered into iron business in 1870, partner, 1872; purchased iron, coal and ore properties Everett Iron Co., Bedford Co., Pa.; declined to be a candidate for Congress at 28; candidate for Congress, 1896, on nomination papers; mem. 56th Congress, 1899-1901, 20th Pa. Dist.; Republican. Mem. com. of legislation Eastern Pig Iron Assn.; organizer and v.-p. Am. Protective Tariff League; mem. com. on legislation Mfrs.' Club, Phila. In 1906 purchased all the property of the Blue Mountain Steel Co., Catoctin, Md., also all the central Pa. property of the Saxton Furnace Co.; is now the second largest individual pig iron manufacturer in U.S. Club: Chevy Chase. Winter Home: 1701 20th St., N. W., Washington DC Address: Everett PA‡

THURMOND, ERASMUS KHLEBER, banker, b. Tarrant County, Tex., May 29, 1875; s. Erasmus Gogin and Amanda (Harmon) T.; ed. pub. schs.; m. Pearl Moody, Mar. 27, 1907. Began in banking at Cheyenne, Okla., 1892; now vice-pres. First Nat. Bank, Sayre. Democrat. Baptist. Mason (32 deg.). Home: 315 W. 15th St. Office: Exchange Bldg., Stock Yards Oklahoma City OK‡

THURSTON, LLOYD, comdr.-in-chief United Spanish War Vets; b. Osceola, Ia., Mar. 27, 1880; s. S. and Margaret (Maloy) T.; LL.B., State U. Ia., 1902; m. Louella Bolibaugh, 1910. Admitted to Iowa bar, 1902, and began practice at Osceola; county atty. Clarke Co., Ia., 1906-10; mem. Ia. Senate, 1920-24; mem. 69th to 72d Congresses, 8th Ia. Dist.; and 73d to 75th Congresses, 5th Ia. Dist., successively mem. rules, appropriations and ways and means coms. Mem. nat. awards jury Freedoms Founds. at Valley Forge. Served in Spanish-Am. war, Philippine Insurrection and World War I. Mem. Library Bd., Farm Bureau, Am. Legion United Spanish War Vets. (comdr.-in-chief), Vets Fgn. Wars, Nat. Soc. Army of Philippines, Naval and Mil. Order Spanish War, Pioneer Lawnmakers Assn. Caribou Soc., Isaak Walton League of Am. Republican. Rotarian (past pres.). Home: Osceola IA Died May 7, 1970.

THYE, EDWARD JOHN, ex-U.S. senator; b Aberdeen, S.D., Apr. 26, 1896; s. Andrew and Bertha (Wangan) T.; ed. pub. schs. and bus. coll.; LL.D., Carroll Coll.; m. Hazel Ramage, 1921 (dec. 1936); 1 dau., Jean Robertha; m. 2d, Myrtle Oliver, Nov. 1942. Enlisted as pvt. USAAF, 1917; commd. 2d lt. in France, World War I. Slaes force Deere & Webber Co., Mpls., 1919-22 owner, operator farm, Northfield, Minn., 1922-69 appraiser Federal Land Bank, 1933-34; dairy and food commr. and dep. commr. of agr., State Minn., 1939-42 elected lt. gov., Minn., 1942; gov. Minn., 1943-46; U.S senator from Minn., 1946-59, congl. del. WHO conv. 1958. Pres. Sciota Town and Sch. bd., 1925-39. Pres Dakota County Farm Bur., 1929-40; dir. Twin City Milk Producers Assn., 1933-40. Mem. bd. dirs Gallaudet Coll.; mem. bd. vistors USAF Acad. supported establishment of Nat. Found. Ulcerative Colitis. Recipient citation Am. Cancer Soc., Cerebral Palsy Found., Nat. Epilepsy League; Silver Beaver award Boy Scouts Am.; hon. alumnus U. Minn., Class 1918. Lutheran. Mason. Elk. Club: Minnesota (St Paul). Home: Northfield MN Died Aug. 28, 1969.

TIBOLT, ROBERT P., business exec.; b. Gordon, Pa. Oct. 24, 1898; s. James and Elizabeth (Haas) T.; studen Bethlehem Prep. Sch., Harvard, Boston U., Suffolk Law Sch., m. Alexandra F. DuPuis, 1924; children—Rober A., Gilbert R., Olive M., Lawrence R. In accounting and taxation depts., Mass. Gas Co., 1920-25; asst. to pres. New England Fuel and Transportation Co., 1925-28 dir. New England Coke Co.; v.p. Eastern Gas and Fue Assn., 1947-55, exec. v.p., 1955-60, president, 1960-62 chmn. bd., from 1962; mem. corp. Home Savs. Bank dir. First Nat. Bank Boston, Charleston Savings Bank former dir., chmn. exec. com. Norfolk & Western Ry Co., trustee Eastern Gas and Fuel Assos. Membe American Coke, Coal Chemical Institute, Greate Boston C. of C. (pres.). Clubs: Laurel Valley Golf Rolling Rock, Union League, Algonquin, Commercial Pine Valley Golf, Cohasset Cohasset MA Died Aug. 6 971; buried Woodside Cemetery Cohasset MA

TICHENOR, ALFRED BENTON, business exec.; b Dunkirk, O., Mar. 13, 1903; s. Jacob Berry and Ila Om (McDowell) T.; student U. Akron, 1921-23; B.C.E. Ohio No. U., 1927; m. Evelyn Huston, June 7, 1930; son, Alfred Huston. Personnel, labor relations exec Goodyear Tire & Rubber Co., 1927-36; staff cons. Indsl Relations Counselors, Inc., 1936-40, 1942-46; dir. indsl relations Castle & Cooke, Ltd., Honolulu, T.H., 194 with Matson Nav. Co., 1946-60, v.p. indsl. relations 1949-55, dir. indsl. relations, 1955-60. Mem. U.S Regional Labor Management Com., 1947; chmn Pacific Coast Longshore Employers negotiation com. 1951. Vice chmn. bd. trustees Golden Gate Coll. trustee Pacific Maritime Assn.-Marine Engrs. Beneficial Association Pension Funds; mem. Citizen Adv. Com. to Atty. Gen. for Crime Prevention Cal 1953-58. Mem. San Francisco Employers Council (bd govs., 1947-52), Soc. Advancement Mgmt., Pacifi Maritime Assn. (dir.), Cal. Personnel Mgmt. Assn. (pas pres.), Fed. Employers San Francisco, N.A.M., Am Ordnance Assn., Phi Delta Theta. Clubs: Propeller c U.S., Commercial (San Francisco); Commonwealth c California. Home: San Rafael CA Died Feb. 25, 196 buried Mt. Tamalpais Cemetery San Rafael CA

TICHENOR, AUSTIN KENT, business exec.; b. Sa Francisco, Calif., Apr. 17, 1872; s. Stephen James an Eleanor Leonore (Brady) T.; ed. public schools an night school, San Francisco and San Mateo County California; married Matilda Ann Pringle (died April 2 1940); children—Austin Pringle, Stephen Wallace DeWitt Clinton, Helen (dec.). Began as office boy wit steamship company, 1887, and advanced to position a purser on vessels of various steamship companies; wit Alaska Packers Assn. since 1902, dock clerk, 1902-0 sec., 1909-14, sec.-treas., 1914-18, vice pres. and gen supt., 1918-22, dir. and mem. exec. com., 1922-41, pres since 1941; dir. Calif. Packing Corp., Shipowners an Merchants Tow Boat Co.; mem. bd. trustees Ass Pacific Fisheries. Vice chmn. bondholders com. We Sacramento Co. Mem. sub-com. of classificatio Lloyd's Register of Shipping. Served with Calif. Na uard; U.S. Transport Service, Spanish Am. War. Iason. Clubs: Commercial, Olympic, Propeller, Press San Francisco). Home: 1717 Dayton Av., Alameda, alif. Office: 111 California St., San Francisco 11 CA*‡

IERNEY, LEO FRANCIS, lawyer; b. Lead, S.D., ct. 23, 1894; s. John and Mary A. (Hilton) T.; student t. Marys Acad., 1910-12, St. Marys Coll., 1912-13, U. eorgetown, 1913-14, U. Ia., 1915-16; LL.B., U. S.D., 917; m. F. Genevieve Chase, Oct. 10, 1942; hildren—Dan L., Joan M. (Mrs. Colson), Thomas M., ohn B., Patrick J. (all by former marriage), Leo Francis . Admitted to S.D. bar, Ia. bar, 1917, Ill., D.C. bars, 941; pvt. practice, Manchester, Ia., 1917-24, Dubuque, a., 1924-33; spl. atty. U.S. Solicitor's Office, Dept. gr., 1933-35; spl. asst. to atty. gen. U.S., 1935-41; pvt. ractice, Chicago, 1941-42, partner Mayer, Meyer, ustrian & Platt, 1942-54, Mayer, Friedlich, Spiess, ierney, Brown & Platt, 1954-68; acted as special ssistant to United States attorney general in onnection with Cicero (Ill.) riots, 1952. Fellow merican College of Trial Lawyers; member of Am., ederal, Illinois State, Chicago bar assns., Bar Assn. ity of N.Y., Phi Kappa Theta, Phi Alpha Delta. emocrat. Clubs: South Shore Country, Mid-America, airymen's Country (Chgo.). Home: Scottsdale AZ ied Apr. 8, 1973.

IETJENS, PAUL, pianist, composer; b. St. Louis, Io., May 22, 1877; s. Henry and Mary R.; grad. high ch., St. Louis, 1895; studied under St. Louis musicians nd in Vienna with Leschetizky and Fuchs, later with arold Bauer; m. Eunice Strong Hammond, of vanston, Ill., 1904 (divorced 1914); 1 dau., Janet. ettled in New York, 1905; musical dir. for Maude dams, 1916-19; accompanist and teacher of piano and armony. Composer: Wizard of Oz"; incidental music or Barrie's A Kiss for Cinderella"; Carnival" orchestral composition); Rustic Sketches" (juvenile uite for orchestra); also songs, piano pieces, etc. ccompanist grand opera setting of Lord Dunsanv's he Tents of the Arabs." Home: 51 E. 59th St., New ork NY‡

IETSORT, FRANICS JUDSON, editor, author; b. etroit, Mich., Aug. 17, 1877; s. Ira and Mary (Banks) .; ed. high sch., pvtly. and by travel; m. Helena Anna lga S. Yunescu, of Russia, 1916. Sunday editor Buffalo vening Times, 1900-01; with Chicago Chronicle, 901-02, San Francisco Examiner, 1903-05; sporting ditor Denver Evening Times, 1905-06; with New York vening World, New York Times, Phila. Pub. Ledger, ntil 1909; contracting agt. United Wireless Telegraph o., New York and Rio de Janeiro, 1909-10; founder nd editor 1911-12, Revista de Automoveis, Rio de aneiro; with New York Herald, 1913-14; editor Realty Iag., 1916-17; asso. editor Nat. Marine Mag., 1917-18; ditor-in-chief Compressed Air Mag., 1919-21; science, ngring. and aviation editor, New York American, 922-27, asso. editor same, 1929—. Mem. advisory bd. lying Stories Mag. Mem. Inst. Arts and Sciences, oston Soc. for Psychic Research; hon. mem. First ursuit Group of U.S. Army Air Corps. Clubs: ewspaper, Explorers (New York); Pen and Pencil Phila.); Nat. Press (Washington, D.C.); Authors' London). Author: Temperance or New York NY‡

ILDEN, LOUIS EDWARD, advt. exec.; b. Chgo., ept. 12, 1900; s. Edward and Antje (Evenhuis) T.; B.S., rinceton, 1922; m. Hester Abbott, Sept. 12, 1923; hildren—Louis Edward, Rufus Abbott. Vice pres. verill Tilden & Co., 1922-32; partner Tilden Bros. & rannis, 1932-40; network sales dept. NBC, 1940-45; p. Sherman & Marquette, Inc., 1945-54, Wherry, aker & Tilden, Inc., 1954-59, Baker, Tilden, Bolgard & arger, Inc., 1959-60, Compton Advertising, Inc., hicago, 1960-70. Clubs: University Cottage Princeton, N.J.); University, Commonwealth (Chgo.); len View (Golf, Ill.). Home: Evanston IL Died July 24, 970; buried Delavan WI

ILESTON, WILDER, prof. medicine; b. Concord, Iass., Jan. 22, 1875; s. John Boies and Mary Wilder Foote) T.; A.B., Harvard, 1895, M.D., 1899; post-grad. ork, Vienna and Gratz, Austria; m. Clare Williams, ov. 18, 1903 (died 1905); m. 2d, Ethel Walker, d. of ev. Newman Smyth, June 20, 1912; children—Wilder lec.), Thomas Newman, Anne, David Edsall (dec.), eter Ayer. Intern, Mass. Gen. Hosp., Boston, 899-1900; practiced in Boston, 1902-09; asst. in clin. hemistry, Harvard Med. Sch., 1902-03, in clin. edicine, 1906-08; dir. Harvard Summer Sch. of Iedicine, 1909; asst. visiting physician, Long Island losp., Boston, 1902-09; consulting physician, Mass. haritable Eye and Ear Infirmary, 1905-09; asst. prof. edicine, Yale Med. Sch., 1909-19, and clin. prof. of ed. since Sept. 1919, emeritus, 1943; cons. phys. Ieriden Hosp., Griffin Hosp. (Derby), New Haven losp., Grace Hosp., Middlesex Hosp., Norwalk Hosp., hief of staff, Grace Hosp., 1926-29. Lecturer in edicine, Yale Med. Sch., 1943-46. Mem. Assn. merican Physicians, Am. Med. Assn. (sec. sect. on ractice of medicine, 1909-11, chmn. 1912), Am. Soc. lin. Investigation (sec. 1910-12), Conn. State Med. oc. (sec. 1912-13), Interurban Clinical Club. epublican. Unitarian. Club: Graduate. Home: 15 dgehill Road. Office: 442 Temple St., New Haven CT‡

TILFORD, HENRY JOHNSON, lawyer; b. Louisville, Ky., Apr. 11, 1880; s. Robert Johnson and Mary Elizabeth (Terry) T.; LL.B., U. of Louisville, 1901; m. Minnie F. Etly, Oct. 16, 1901 (dec.); 1 dau., Mary (Mrs. William Howard Clowes). Admitted to Ky. bar, 1901; jr. mem. firm Greene and Tilford, 1907-10; sr. mem. firm Tilford & Wetherby, 1935-39; special chancellor, Jefferson Circuit Court, 1938-39; asso. justice Court of Appeals of Ky., 1939 to Sept. 21, 1945; chief justice, Court of Appeals, 1945; later mem. Tilford & Dobbins; member of board of dirs. Lincoln-Income Life Insurance Company. Mem. Dem. State Central Com., 1920-32; chmn. Civil Service Bd., Louisville, 1936-37. Mem. Ky. State Bar Assn., Am. Bar Assn., Louisville Labor Mgmt. Com. Episcopalian. Mason (33 deg.). Home: Louisville KY Died 1968.

TILSON, ANN COE (MRS. DONALD HEATH TILSON), vol. educator; b. Mpls., Jan. 29, 1904; d. William T. and Annabel (Collins) Coe; B.S., U. Minn., 1924; m. Donald H. Tilson, Sept. 24, 1926; children—Donald Heath, William Coe, Hugh Hanna. An organizer Vol. Corps. Internat. Inst. for English to Fgn. Born, St. Louis, 1949, Vol. Corps for work with mental patients St. Louis State Hosp., 1952; vol. worker House Good Shepherd, Portland, Ore. 1956-61; scholarship chmn. Vancouver Meml. Hosp. 1960-61; Mem. Am. Assn. U. Women (status of women chmn.), D.A.R. (regent Ft. Vancouver chpt.). Republican. Episcopalian. Clubs: Town (Portland), Royal Oaks Country (Vancouver, Wash.). Home: Vancouver WA Died Nov. 6, 1968.

TILTON, ELIZABETH (MRS. WILLIAM TILTON), suffrage, prohibition worker; b. Salem, Mass., Mar. 13, 1869; d. James T. and Eleanor Fox (Jewett) Hewes; ed. Radcliffe Coll.; m. William Tilton, of Cambridge, Mass., Jan. 10, 1911. Active since 1912 in woman suffrage, prohibition and the peace movement; chmn. poster com., Boston Associated Charities, 1912; orgn. chmn. Mass. Woman's Suffrage Assn., 1918; nat. chmn. legislation, Nat. Congress of Parents and Teachers, 1921-31; dir. Women's Nat. Com. for Law Enforcement, Nat. Anti-Saloon League; chmn. Women's Nat. Com. for Education Against Alcohol; chmn. Radio Education Com., Washington, D.C.; pres. Unitarian Temperance Soc. of Am. Unitarian Assn. Author: Turning Off the Spigot, 1914; Save America, 1924. Contbr. to Woman's Journal, Current History, Survey. Asked by church and dry women to be candidate for U.S. Senate, 1930, but declined. Home: 11 Mason St., Cambridge MA‡

TIMM, JOHN A(RREND), prof. chemistry; b. New Haven, Conn., Oct. 31, 1898; s. Rev. John Arrend and Emma (Stein) T.; Ph.B., Sheffield Scientific Sch., Yale, 1919, Ph.D., Grad. Sch., Yale, 1922; m. Marguerite Benedict, June 9, 1923; 1 dau., Mrs. Jane Eagle. Instr. chemistry, Yale, 1922-27, asso. prof., 1927-41; prof. chemistry, chmn. dept., chmn. div. of science, director School of Science, Simmons Coll., 1941-66, prof. emeritus, 1966-69, dir. of summer inst. for high sch. tchrs. chemistry, 1959-69. Served as 2d lieutenant F.A., U.S. Army, 1918; 2d lt. O.R.C., 1918-23. Recipient Honor Scroll, American Institute of Chemists, 1958; James Flack Norris award, 1966. Member American Chemical Society (chairman of Northeast section 1951-52), N.E. Assn. Chemistry Tchrs. (hon. mem.; pres. 1954-55), Sigma Xi, Theta Xi, Alpha Chi Sigma, Gamma Alpha. Unitarian. Author: Charts of the Chemical Reactions of the Common Elements, 1924; An Introduction to Chemistry, 1930, 3d edit., 1938; General Chemistry, 1944, 4th edit., 1966, Spanish and French transl., 1968. Co-author: Laboratory Exercises in General Chemistry, 1930; Development of the Sciences, 1941. Co-editor: Marvels of Science, 1941. Contributor articles to Journal of American Chemical Soc. and Journal Chemical Edn. Co-author: Laboratory Exercises in General Chemistry, 1948. Home: Newton Centre MA Died Mar. 4, 1969; buried Congregational Cemetery Seymour CT

TIMMERMAN, ARTHUR HENRY, electrical engineer; b. New York, N.Y., May 1, 1871; s. John Henry and Celia (Lussen) T.; B.S., Coll. City of N.Y., 1891; M.E. in elec. engring., Cornell U., 1892. M.M.E., 1893; m. Mary E. Pearson, July 25, 1894; 1 son, Arthur Pearson; married 2d, Rooney G. Ousley, June 21, 1941. Instr. in physics, Washington University, St. Louis, 1893-94; prof. physics and elec. engring., Sch. of Mines and Metallurgy (U. of Mo.), Rolla, Mo., 1894-99; engr., 1899, chief engr., 1908-19, v.p. and chief engr., 1919-26, v.p. in charge engring. and mfg. since 1926, also dir., Wagner Electric Corp., St. Louis; dir. Wagner Brake Service Co., Ltd., Industry mem. St. Louis Regional Labor Bd., 1933-34. Mem. Liberty Truck Design Com. Second v.p., 1936-38, 1st v.p., 1938-40, pres., 1940-42, Nat. Metal Trades Assn. (mem. exec. com. 1936-44); pres., 1940-42, mem. exec. com. 1936-44); pres., 1940-42, mem. council, 1936-46, Acad. of Science of St. Louis; mem. exec. com., 1942-45, mem. council, 1937-45, Asso. Industries of Missouri. Mem. exec. com. St. Louis Safety Council, 1939-41; mem. indsl. com. Y.M.C.A., 1939-42. Fellow Am. Inst. E.E.; mem. Soc. Automotive Engrs., Nat. Electric Light Assn., Nat. Elec. Mgrs. Assn., St. Louis Acad. Science, Electric Power Club (pres. 1923-25), Phi Gamma Delta, Sigma Xi. Republican. Clubs: Engineers, Cornell, Bellerive Country (St. Louis). Home: 40 Ridgetop, Richmond Heights 17, Mo. Office: 6400 Plymouth Av., St Louis MO‡

TIMMERMAN, GEORGE BELL, judge; b. Edgefield County, S.C., Mar. 28, 1881; s. Washington Hodges and Henrietta Maria Wolfe (Bell) T.; grad. Patrick Military Inst., 1900, LL.B., S.C. Coll. (now Univ. South Carolina) 1902, LL.D., (honorary), 1952; m. Mary Vandiver Sullivan, Nov. 22, 1906, children—Margaret, George Bell. Gen. practice of law, 1902-42; appointed U.S. District judge for the Eastern and Western Districts of S.C., 1942. Captain, S.C. Militia, aide on Brigade Staff, 1905. Solicitor 5th Judicial Circuit, 1905-08, 11th Judicial Circuit, 1908-20; mem. House of Rep., Gen. Assembly of S.C., 1923-24; mem. State of S.C. Highway Commn., 1931-39, chmn., 1936-39; chmn. Lexington County, S.C., Dem. Com., 1914-16, Dem. State exec. committeeman, 1930-32, 1938-42; pres. Dem. State Convention, 1932. Chmn. Ridge Dist. Boy Scouts of Am., 1940-43, v.p. Central Council, 1942-44; chairman Batesburg-Leesville Park Commn., 1941-46. Trustee University of S.C., Columbia, S.C., 1941-47. Member S.C. and Am. bar assns., Phi Kappa Sigma, Omicron Delta Kappa. Clubs: Ridge Golf (Batesburg, S.C.), Internat. Assn. of Lions Clubs (dist. gov., dir.). Home: Batesburg SC Died Apr. 22, 1966; buried Batesburg SC

TIMMINS, JULES ROBERT, mining exec., stockbroker; b. Mattawa, Ont., Can., June 6, 1888; s. Louis Henry and Alphonsine (Pare) T.; grad. St. Michael's Coll., 1909; student McGill U., 1911-14, D.Sc., 1951; LL.D., Queen's U., 1950; m. Edna Nelson, Nov. 17, 1920; children—Pauline (Mrs. Paul Ouimet), Gloria (Mrs. Earl Ferguson), Julia, Joan (Mrs. J. G. Fitzpatrick, Jr.), Louis Henry, Robert, Jules Robert, Nelson Taschereau, William. With Axle Valve Co., N.Y.C., 1920-22, Fortier, Beauvais & Co., stockbrokers, 1922-27; sr. partner J. R. Timmons & Co., stockbrokers, Montreal, Toronto, and N.Y.C. from 1927; chmn. Hollinger Consol. Gold Mines, Ltd.; pres. Labrador Mining & Exploration Co., Ltd., Hollinger North Shore Exploration Co., Ltd., from 1942, Que. North Shore & Labrador Ry. Co., from 1947, Hollinger Ungava Transport, Ltd., from 1948, Hollinger-Hanna, Ltd., from 1950; v.p. Imperial Bank of Can., Windsor Hotel, Ltd.; dir. Mining Corp. of Can., Normetal Mines, Ltd., Noranda Mines, Ltd., Quemont Mining Corp., Ltd., Pamour Porcupine Mines, Ltd., Jerome Gold Mines, Ltd., Chromium Mining &Smelting Corp., Fire Ins. Co. of Can., Canadian Arena Co., Imperial Bank of Can., Royal Trust Co., Candaian Petrofina, Ltd., Combustion Engring., Inc. Served with Canadian Engrs., 1916-17. Decorated Officer Order British Empire. Roman Catholic. Clubs: Mt. Bruno Country, Mt. Royal, Toronto, York (Toronto); Montreal Nat.; River, Links (N.Y.C.); Rolling Rock (Ligonier, Pa.). Home: Westmount PQ Canada. Died Feb. 1971.*

TIMOSHENKO, STEPHEN, univ. prof., author; b. near Kiev, Russia, Dec. 23, 1878; s. Prokop and Jozefina (Sarnavskaja) T.; grad. Inst. of Engrs. of Ways of Communication, Russia, 1901; D.Sc., Lehigh U., 1936; D.Eng., Michigan University, 1938; D.Eng., l'Ecole Polytechnique, Zurich, 1948, Technische Hochschule, Munchen, 1948, University of Zagreb, 1956; LL.D., University of Glasgow, 1951; married Alexander Archangelskaja, March 3, 1902;children—Anna (Mrs. F. Hetzelt), Gregor, Marine (Mrs. J. N. Goodier). Came to United States, 1922, naturalized, 1927. Instructor Inst. of Engr. of Ways of Communication, 1902-03; asst. prof. Polytechnical Inst., St. Petersburg, Russia, 1903-06; prof. Polytechnical Inst., Kiev, 1906-11, Electrotechnical and Polytechnical Inst., St. Petersburg, 1912-17, Polytechnical Inst., Zagreb, Yugoslavia, 1920-22; research engr. Westinghouse Electric and Mfg. Co., Pittsburgh, 1923-27; prof. of engring. mechanics, U. of Mich., 1927-36; prof. of theoretical and applied mechanics Stanford, 1936-44, emeritus. Corr. mem. Acad. Sciences (Russia), Acad. Tech. Sciences (Poland). Corr. mem. French Acad. Sciences since 1939. Mem. American Philos. Soc., 1939; mem. Nat. Acad. Sciences, 1940. Foreign mem. Royal Soc. of London, since 1944, Accademia Nationale del Lincei, Rome, since 1948. Mem. Greek Orthodox Ch. Author or co-author books relating to field since 1925; also articles in profl. jours. Home: Wuppertal-Elbenfeld Germany Died May 30, 1972.

TIMS, JOHN FRANCIS, newspaper exec.; b. New Orleans, La., Aug. 15, 1892; s. John Francis and Anna Lee (Finnegan) T.; grad., Jesuits Coll., New Orleans, 1910; m. Mae Adele Laury, May 17, 1925. Advt. mgr., The Times-Picayune Pub. Co., New Orleans, 1919, bus. mgr., 1922, v.p. and gen. mgr., 1940-52; pres. 1952, dir. 1942, chmn. bd., 1967-69. Director, Nat. Conf. of Christians and Jews; treas., Greater New Orleans, Inc.; mem. bd. of dirs., New Orleans Assn. of Commerce. Democrat. Roman Catholic. Home: New Orleans LA Died Sept. 2, 1969.

TINDALL, GLENN MEANS, music dir., public relations cons.; b. Shelbyville, Ind., June 21, 1894; s. Urus E. and Maude (Means) T.; grad. Sch. Music, Northwestern U., Music, 1915, A.B., 1916, M.A., Sch.

Edn., 1936; grad. study Columbia, 1919; studied piano, pipe organ, oboe and composition under Arne Oldberg, others; m. Elizabeth Jane Caldwell, Dec. 23, 1935; children—Richard C., William L., James B. Supr. music, Kokomo, Ind., 1916-18, Glen Cove, N.Y., 1918; admitted to Ind. bar, 1918; asst. supr. music, St. Louis, 1919-20; dir. music New Utrecht High Sch., N.Y.C., 1921; mgr. dept. store, 1922-25; supr. municipal music, dept. playgrounds and recreation, Los Angeles, 1926-31; organist and choir dir. Rosewood M.E. Ch., Los Angeles, 1926-34; mgr. Hollywood Bowl Assn., 1929-34; dir. Los Angeles Civil Orch., 1928-31; minister of music Grace M.E. Ch., N.Y.C., 1934-35; mgr. Choralopera, N.Y.C., 1934-45; dir. pub. relations Glenwood (Ill.) Sch. for Boys, 1949-72, also cons. on music and pub. relations, 1936-72; v.p. Eureka Coll. (Ill.), 1940-46; organist and choir dir. First Universalist Ch., 1940-52; organist and choir-master St. Margaret's Episcopal Ch., Chgo., 1944-46, St. Clement's Episcopal Ch., Harvey, Ill., 1956-72; cons.; assn. exec. in numerous instances. Bd. edn. Bremen Community High Sch., Midlothian, Ill., 1958-64. Served in inf. U.S. Army, World War I. Chmn. Music in Motion Pictures Com. of N.E.A.; mem. adv. com. Nat. Bur. for Blind Artists; chmn. choir festivals and contests Nat. Fedn. Music Clubs. Mem. Am. Guild Organists, N.E.A., Nat. Assn. Composers and Conductors, Music Educators Nat. Conf., Am. Legion, Delta Tau Chi (hon.), Phi Kappa Sigma. Received Merit of Honor award Northwestern U., 1933. Republican. Mason (32, K.T., Shriner), Elk, Rotarian. Author: Indiana Course of Music Study for High Schools, 1918, also motion picture scenarios, numerous mag. articles. Editor: Phi Kappa Sigma Song Books, 1948, 1956. Home: Tinley Park IL Died June 12, 1972; buried Forest Hill Cememtery, Shelbyville IN

TINKER, EDWARD LAROCQUE, author; b. New York, N.Y., Sept. 12, 1881; s. Henry Champlin and Louise (Larocque) T.; prep. edn., Browning Sch., N.Y. City; A.B., Columbia University, 1902, Litt. D. (hon.), 1963; studied at Columbia University Law Sch., 2 yrs.; LL.B., New York Law Sch., 1905; Docteur de l'Universite de Paris (France), 1933; LL.D. (honorary), Middlebury Coll., 1949; Doctor, de la Universidad de Madrid, 1955; married Frances McKee, Jan. 16, 1916. Admitted to N.Y. bar, 1905; counsel Legal Aid Soc. 1 yr.; asst. dist. atty. 3 yrs.; pres. Tinker Realty Co.; installed, operated one of first safety first" systems in Southwest, El Paso & Southwestern R.R. Co. Excng. prof. Nat. Univ. of Uruguay and Argentina, 1945; prof. extraordinario Nat. U. Mex. Pres. Tinker Found.; adv. council Sch. Internat. Affairs Columbia Bd. dirs. Operation Amigo, The Americas Found. Formerly mem. Squadron A, N.Y.N.G.; lt. U.S. Navy, World War I. Decorated Officer d'Academie (France), 1933; Commendador de la Orden de Isabela Catolica; recipient gold medals by French Acad., 1934, 37, also 1962 award from the Americas Foundation; medal Fedn. French Alliances in the U.S., 1964. Trustee Marine Museum and Museum of City of N.Y. Decorated, Chevalier Legion of Honor, 1939; Order de Mayo al Merito by Argentina. Member of the Louisians Historical Society (honorary life mem.), Am. Antiquarian Society (chancillor), Council on Foreign Relations, Inst. Social Sciences, Soc. Am. Historians, Spanish Inst. (v.p.), Uruguayan-Am. Assn. (pres.), Pan-Am. Soc., Psi Upsilon; trustee Am. Bible Soc., France Am. Soc., Elysee Francaise, Hispanic Soc., Instituto Gonzalo Fernandez de Oviedo, Institute Geografico Historico del Uruguay. Republcan. Episcopalian. Clubs: University, Union, Dutch Treat, Coffee House (N.Y.); Pilgrims; Piping Rock. Author: Lafcadio Hearn's American Days, 1924; Toucoutou, 1928; (with Frances Tinker) Old New Orleans, 1930; Les Cenelles, 1930; Les Ecrites de Langue Francaise en Louisiane au XIXe, Siecle, Paris, 1932; The Palengenesis of Craps, 1933; Bibiliography of the French Newspapers and Periodicals of Louisiana, 1933. Gombo, the Creole Dialect of La., 1936; The Cult of The Gaucho and the Birth of a Literature, 1948; The Horsemen of the Americas and the Literatures They Inspired, 1953; Creole City, 1953; The Life and Literature of the Pampas, 1961; Corridos and Calaveros, 1961; Centaurs of Many Lands, 1963. Contbr. New Edits. Fine and Otherwise N.Y. Times, 1937-42. Vis. lectr. Mex. for Carnegie Endowment for Internat. Peace, 1943. Home: New York 6, July 1968.

TINKHAM, RICHARD PARSONS, lawyer; b. Valparaiso, Ind., July 28, 1902; s. Clare Bonar and Mabel (Parsons) T.; A.B., Wabash Coll., 1925; LL.B., Harvard, 1928; m. Marion McAleer, July 14, 1928; children—Charles B., Richard P. Admitted to Ind. bar, 1928; sr. partner Tinkham, Bechman, Kelly & Singleton, Hammond. Mem. Ind. Bd. Law Examiners, 1942-50, pres., 1945, 48; chmn. Nat. Conf. Bar Assn. Presidents, 1951-52. Fellow Am. Bar Found., Am. Coll. Trial Lawyers; mem. Am. Judicature Soc. (dir. 1959-62), Hammond (Pres. 1964-65), Chgo., Am. (mem. ho. of dels. 1950-52, gov. 1953-56, chmn. pub. relations com. 1954-63), Ind. (pres. 1950-51) bar assns., Am. Law Inst., Nat. Legal Aid and Defender Assn. (dir. 1958-61). Author articles legal subjects. Editor: Public Relations for Bar Association (manual). Home: Hammond IN Died Feb. 2, 1973.

TIPPETS, JOSEPH HENDERSON, govt. ofcl.; b. Arimo, Ida., Dec. 11, 1913; s. Joseph Alva and Josephine (Henderson) T.; D.Pub. Service (hon.), Brigham Young U., 1967; m. Alta Mahoney, Sept. 11, 1936; children—John, David, Robert, Marilyn. With U.S. Govt., 1932-68, with FAA, 1937-68, dir. Western region, 1961-67, asso. adminstr. for personnel, 1967-68. Chief U.S. delegate several internat. congs. aero.; chmn. Fed. Exec. Bd., 1965-67. Served with U.S. Navy, 1932-35. Recipient Gold medal Dept. Commerce, 1957; name hon. M Man, Ch. of Jesus Christ of Latter Day Saints, 1958. Home: Adelphi MD Died Oct. 18, 1968; buried Heber UT

TIPPETTS, CHARLES SANFORD, economist, educator; b. in Glens Falls, N.Y., Jan. 16, 1893; s. of William Henry and Emily Katharine (Bell) T.; student Mercersburg (Pa.), Acad., 1910-12; Litt. B., Princeton, 1916, A.M., 1922, Ph.D., 1924; studied law, Harvard, 1916-17; Litt. D. (hon.), Franklin and Marshall Coll., 1941; Sc.D., (hon.) Lafayette Coll., 1954; married Margaret Elizabeth Griffith, Apr. 4, 1920; children—Katherine Bell, Charles Sanford. Inst. economics, Princeton, 1919-21 and 1923-24; asst. prof. economics State U. of Ia., 1924-25, prof., 1925-28; prof. business adminstrn., U. of Wash., 1928-29; prof. economics, U. of Buffalo, 1929-35; dean Sch. of Business Adminstrn., U. of Pitts., 1935-41; headmaster, Mercersburg Acad., 1941-61, emeritus, 1961-67; vis. professor, summer sessions, U. of Wash., 1930, W.Va. U., 1931, Ohio State U., 1932; dir. Fed. Home Loan Bank of Pitts. Mem. State Hwy. Planning Commn., 1949-51, Pa. Citizens Committee for Welfare, 1946-67. Economist National Committee on Monetary Policy. Served as first lieutenant Infantry, 76th Division, A.E.F., 1917-19; captain inf., O.R.C., 1919-34, Decorated Sacred Order of St. Olaf (Norwegian). Mem. American Economic Association, Headmasters Association, Scabbard and Blade, Phi Beta Kappa, Beta Gamma Sigma, Delta Sigma Rho, Alpha Kappa Psi, Omicron Delta Kappa. Presbyn. Mason. Clubs: University, Harvard-Yale-Princeton (Pitts.); Franklin Inn (Phila.). Author: State Banks and Federal Reserve System, 1929; Business Organization and Control (with S. Livermore), 1932. Revisor (with L. A. Froman) of Horace White's Money and Banking, 1935. Contbr. econ. articles. Home: Mercersburg PA Died Aug. 27, 1967.

TIPPLE, BERTRAND MARTIN, writer, lecturer; b. Camden, N.Y., Dec. 1, 1868; s. Martin and Sarah Elizabeth (Squier) T.; A.B., Syracuse U., 1894, D.D., 1904; B.D., Drew Theol. Sem., 1897; m. Jane Baldwin Downs, June 2, 1897; children—Silva, Elizabeth, Bertrand Squier, Marion. Ordained ministry M.E. Ch., 1897; pastor Epworth Ch., New Haven, Conn., 1897-1900; Embury Memorial Ch., Brooklyn, N.Y., 1900-06; First Ch., Stamford, Conn., 1906-09; transferred to Rome, Italy, 1909, as pastor of Am. M.E. Ch.; pres. Reeder Theol. Sem., Rome, 1910-23; founder and pres. Collegio Internazionale di Monte Mario, 1911-24, Lecture trips, 1910-24, in the U.S., Great Britain, France, Germany. Del. to World Conv. of Y.M.C.A., Robert Coll., Constantinople, 1911; del. to Ecumenical Conf., Edinburgh, Scotland, 1913; maintained social service rooms in Methodist Building, Rome, for British and American soldiers and sailors during World War I. During coll. years was corr. for the New York Tribune and the Mail and Express, and for the Post-Standard of Sryacuse; corr.-at-large in Europe and North Africa for The Christian Science Monitor, 1912-24, archaeol. and misc. research work in Samaria, Jerusalem, Patmos and Mt. Athos, 1933; travel, lecturing and writing since 1934; asso. with Am. Archaeol. Expdn., Van, Turkey, 1938-40. Mem. Gen. Conf. M.E. Ch. 1916, 1920. Received at Italian Court in 1910, and knighted by Victor Emmanuel III, 1915. Comdr. Order of Crown of Italy, 1920. Mem. Delta Upsilon, Phi Beta Kappa. Mason (33 deg. of Italy). Author: Italy of the Italians; Europe's God; The People of the Great Sea; The Eighth Hill. Address: 1731 Monterey Rd., South Pasadena CA‡

TIPTON, ROYCE JAY, civil engr.; b. Litchfield, Ill., Mar. 23, 1893; s. Basil Foster and Sarah (Calvert) T.; student U. Colo., 1915-17, C.E. (hon.), 1940; m. Natalie Knight, Aug. 25, 1919 (dec. Oct. 1961); children—John Knight, Robert Royce, Natalie Jean (Mrs. Thomas Milaskey); m. 2d, Jincy Hunt, July 30, 1962. Pvt. practice civil engring., Monte Vista, Colo., 1922-28, Denver, 1933-67; pres. R.J. Tipton & Assos., Inc., 1945-54, Tipton and Kalmbach, Inc., Denver, Colo., 1954-67; designing engr. Rio Mante Project, Mexico, 1928; spl. engr. interstate water problems and water resources studies Colo. Engr.'s Office, 1929-33; assisted negotiation interstate compacts Upper Colo. River, Pecos River, Costilla Creek and Rio Grande, also negotiation Mexican Water Treaty, 1944, Indus Water Treaty, 1960; mem. bd. cons. Pecos River Joint Investigations, 1939-42, Nat. Resources Planning Bd., 1935-42, canal linings U.S. Bur. Reclamation, 1948; mem. task force water resources and power 2d Hoover Commn., 1953-55; cons. Colo. Water Conservation Bd., 1937-58, Colo. Planning Commn., 1933-37, Climax Molybdenum Co., 1935-52; tech. adviser Internat. Boundary and Water Commn., U.S. and Mexico, 1938-67; architect-engr. War Dept. projects, World War II. Served to 2d lt., C.E., U.S. Army, World War I; AE in France and Germany. Recipient Norlin medal U Colo., 1958. Mem. Am. geophys. Union Am. Inst. Cons Engrs., Soc. Am. Mil. Engrs., Colo. Engring. Counc (Gold Medal award 1963), Colo. Soc. Engrs., Am. So C.E. (v.p. 1965-67), Internat. Commn. Irregation an Drainage (pres. 1966-67), Internat. Commn. Larg Dams, Colo. Hist. Soc., Am. Legion, Alpha Sigma Ph Tau Beta Pi, Chi Epsilon. Mason. Clubs: Denve Athletic, Denver, University (Denver); Metropolita (Washington). Home: Denver CO Died Dec. 23, 196 buried Fairmount Cemetery, Denver CO

TIRRELL, HENRY ARCHELAUS, educator; b. S Chatham, Mass., Aug. 7, 1873; s. Eben and Julia Ann (Harding) T.; grad. Norwich Free Acad., 1890; A.B Wesleyan Univ., Conn., 1894; U. of Chicag 1899-1900; hon. M.A., Trinity Coll., Conn., 191 Wesleyan Univ., 1934; m. Agnes Helen Butler, Sept. 2 1899; children—Mary Agnes, Charles Henry, Hele Butler, William Harding. Teacher, Penningto Collegiate Inst., 1894-96; teacher, Norwich Free Acad 1896-99, 1900-03, prin., 1903-40; pres. Norwic Savings Soc.; dir. Thames Br., Hartford, Conn., Trus Co., Conn. Light & Power Co. Mem. Headmaster Assn., Alpha Delta Phi. Phi Beta Kappa. Clu Arcanum. Home: Norwich CT‡

TISCH, ALFRED FRANCIS, investment co. exec.; b N.Y.C., Nov. 12, 1908; s. Herman and Ella (Tisch) T B.A., St. John's U., 1930; m. Mildred Christin Schaffner, July 4, 1935; children—Alfred C., Susan Winters. Admitted to N.Y. bar; asso. Carl M. Loe Rhoades & Co., N.Y.C., 1964-68. Pres. Queens counc Boy Scouts Am., 1962-66. Mem. Nat. Security Trade Assn. (pres. 1963), Security Traders Assn. N.Y. (pre 1955), Nat. Assn. Security Dealers. Episcopalia (vestryman, lay reader). Editor Stany mag., Trader Ann., 1952-68. Home: Glendale LI NY Died Sept. 1968; interred St. Matthew's Ch. Woodhaven NY

TISDEL, FREDERICK MONROE, univ. dean; Belvidere, Ill., Jan. 7, 1869; s. James Monroe an Amanda (Clark) T.; ed. Northwest Acad., Evansto Ill., 1885-87; A.B., Northwestern U., 1891; A.M., U. Wis., 1893; A.M., Harvard, 1894, Ph.D., 1900; m Nellie Monroe, Sept. 8, 1898; 1 son, Nelson Clar Instr. elocution, U. of Wis., 1891-93; asso. prof. rhetor and oratory, Oberlin (O.) Coll., 1895-98; prof. Englis Armour Inst. of Tech., 1900-04; pres. U. of Wyo 1904-08; dean Coll. Arts and Sciences and pro English, Toledo U., 1909-10; lecturer and prof., U. Mo., 1910-39, dean, 1921-39, emeritus since 193 Mem. Modern Lang. Assn. America, Phi Beta Kapp Author: Studies in the English Classics, 1904; Studies Literature, 1913; Survey of English and America Literature, 1915; also articles in learned periodical Home: 1316 Wilson Av., Columbia MO‡

TISELIUS, ARNE (WILHELM KAURIN biochemist; b. Stockholm, Sweden, Aug. 10, 1902; Hans J. and Rosa (Kaurin) R.; Dr. phil., U. Upsal 1931; student Princeton, 1934-35; Dr. honoris caus univs. of Paris, Bologna, Glasgow, Madrid an Cambridge, Caroline Inst., Stockholm, U. Oxford, Os U., U. Lyon, U. Cal., Berkeley, Gustavus Adolph College; m. Ingrid Margareta Dalen, Nov. 26, 193 children—Eva, Per. Research asst. in phys. chemist U. Upsala, 1925, became asst. prof., 1930, pr biochemistry, 1938-68. Mem. nat. sci. research co Atomic Energy Research Com., Com. for Reformatio of the Univs., Med. Research Council of Swede 1944-47; president Swedish Natural Science Researc Council, 1946-50; vice president Nobel Foundatio 1947-60, pres., 1960-64, chmn. chemistry com.; hea Nobel Inst. of Swedish Royal Acad. Scis.; mem. sci. ad council Swedish Govt.; pres. Internat. Union Pure an Applied Chemistry, 1951-55. Awarded Nobel Prize chemistry, 1948. Hon. fellow Royal Inst. Chemist London; hon. member French Chem. Soc., Swedis Society Physicians, Harvey Soc. N.Y., N.Y. Acad. Scis N.Y. Acad. Medicine, Royal Inst. Great Britain, Che Soc. London, Internat. Assn. Allergists Zurich, Re Sociedad Espanola de Fisica y Quimica Madrid, So Sci. Helsingfors, Consejo Super. de Investigacion Scientificas Madrid, Am. Acad. Arts and Sci., Roy Dutch, Swiss chem. socs., National Acad. Scis. Indi fgn. mem. Royal Soc. and Soc. Chem. Industry Londo American Philosophical Society; correspondi member Society Philomat. Paris, Academie d Ciencias de Lisboa, Acad. des Sciences, Paris; me Pontificia Sci. Acad. of Vatican, Royal Swedish Aca Sci., Nobel Com. Chemistry, Royal Acad. Engrin Scis., Royal Soc. Sci. Upsala, Royal Soc. Scis. an Letters Gothenburg, Nat. Acad. Scis. Washingto Royal Danish Sci. Soc., Copenhagen and Accadem Nazionale De quaranta Roma, Polish Acad. Sc Warsaw, Rumanian Acad. Scis. (hon.); fgn. me Czeckoslovak Acad. Sci.; hon. mem. So Electropheresis, Tokyo, Indian Inst. Scis. Liberal. Lut Home: Upsala Sweden Died Oct. 29, 1971.

TISSERANT, H. E. CARDINAL EUGEN ecclesiastic; m. Nancy, France, March 24, 1884; Hippolyte and Octavia (Connard) T.; educated Gra Sem. de Nancy, Ecole du Louvre, Ecole Biblique d Jerusalem, Ecole des Hautes-Etudes de la Sorbonn

École des Langues Orientales Vivantes, Inst. Catholique de Paris; Dr. honoris causa, univs. Louvain, Princeton, Coimbre, Vienna. Ordained priest Roman Cath. Ch., 1907; curator Oriental manuscripts Vatican Library, 1908; prof. Assyrian, Apollinarium U., Rome, Italy, 1908-13; asst. prefect Vatican Library, 1919-30, pro-prefect, 1930; adviser Sacred Congregation for Eastern Ch. Affairs, 1926; prelate to The Pope, 1929; protonotary apostolic, 1936; sec. Sacred Congregation for Eastern Ch., 1936-59; cardinal-deacon, 1936; consecrated bishop, 1937; cardinal-priest, 1937; cardinal-bishop of Porto and Santa-Rufina, 1946-66, bishop of Ostia, 1951-66; sub-dean Sacred Coll., 1948, dean Sacred College, 1951-72. President Committee Bibl. Studies; mem. Com. Eastern Canon Law; librarian, archivist Holy Roman Ch.; mem. Sacred Coll. for Extraordinary Affairs. Decorated grand cross Legion of Honor. Mem. Inst. de France, Acad. Francaise. Author: Ascension d'Isaie, 1909; Codex Zuquinensis Rescriptus Veteris Testamenti, 1911; Specimina Codicum Orientalum, 1914; Codices Armeni Bibliothecae Vaticanae, 1927; Luigi Maria Grignion de Montfort; le Scuole di Carita e le Origini dei Fratelli de San Gabriele, 1943; Bybliothecae apostolicae vaticanae codices manuscripti recensiti. . Codices aethiopici vaticani et borgiani, barberinianus orientalis n, rossianus, 865, 2 vols., 1935-36. Address: Rome Italy Died Feb. 1972.

TITCHENER, JOHN BRADFORD, educator; b. Ithaca, N.Y., Jan. 2, 1898; s. Edward Bradford and Sophia Kellog (Bedlow) T.; A.B., Clark Coll., 1917; Ph.D., U. Ill., 1923; m. Frances Campbell Bonner, Aug. 20, 1925; children—Edward Bradford, Campbell Bonner, John McLellan. Instr. Greek, U. Mich., 1923-25; Instr. classical lang. Harvard, 1925-26, asst. prof., 1927-30, Ohio State U., 1930-33, asso. prof., 1933-39, prof. classical lang., 1939-68, prof. emeritus, 1968-72, chmn. dept. classical lang., lit., 1936-66. Fulbright lectr., Melbourne, Australia, 1960-61; vis. prof. U. Sydney, 1968-69. Served as ambulance driver, French, Am. armies, 1917-19. Mem. Am. Philol. Assn., Classical Assn. Middle West and South. Author: The Manuscript Tradition of Plutarch's Aetia Graeca et Aetia Romana, 1924; idem, Teubner text, 1934. Home: Columbus OH Died Mar. 9, 1972.

TITCOMB, HARVEY BURGESS, ry. pres.; b. Indianapolis, Ind., Dec. 10, 1871; s. Daniel and Emma (Brown) T.; prep. edn., high sch., Indianapolis; student Cogswell Poly. Coll., San Francisco, Calif.; m. Mabel Havens, of San Francisco, Aug. 25, 1900; 1 dau., Mildred Havens. Began with S.P. Co., 1889, successively telegraph operator, draftsman, asst. engr. and roadmaster Western div., to 1900, roadmaster and asst. engr., 1900-05, div. engr., 1905-08, dist. engr. Los Angeles and San Francisco, 1908-17, supt. Stockton div., 1917-18; v.p. and gen. mgr. Pacific Electric Ry. Co., Los Angeles, 1918-21; pres. S.P. R.R. Co. of Mexico, 1921-33, retired. Address: 600 N. June St., Los Angeles CA‡

TITCOMB, VIRGINIA CHANDLER, artist and writer; b. Otterville, Ill.; d. Hiram and Julania (Humiston) Chandler; ed. pub. and pvt. schs.; m. Brooklyn, John Abbot Titcomb (now deceased). Sculptor in bas relief; has exhibited at Nat. Acad. Design. Founder, 1884, and pres. Patriotic League of the Revolution. Memorialized 57th Congress for recognition of services rendered by Theodore R. Timby, the inventor of the revolving turrett as used on the Monitor and all battleships of U.S. since Civil War. Mem. Central Com. Christian Co-operative Business Assn., Sorosis, etc. Contbr. Harper's Bazaar, Demorest's Magazine, Brooklyn Eagle, etc. Address: 101 Lafayette Av., Brooklyn NY‡

TITSWORTH, CLARENCE E., fire insurance; b. Brooklyn, Pa., Apr. 4, 1872; ed. pub. and pvt. schs. Began as local agt. Newark Fire Ins. Co., spl. agt. for middle dept. until 1920, asst. sec., 1920-25, v.p. since 1925. Home: 250 Harrison St., East Orange NJ Office: 41 Clinton St., Newark NJ‡

TITTLE, ELMER ANTHONY, banker; b. Chgo., Apr. 4, 1903; s. Anton and Mary (Kerner) T.; student Am. Inst. Banking, 1924-26, Northwestern U., 1926-28; m. Marthe Christine Olsen, Nov. 29, 1933;1 dau., Marthe Christine (Mrs. Douglas F. Nelson). With First Nat. Bank Chgo., 1922-64, asst. v.p. loan div., 1949-59, v.p. loan div., 1959-64. Mem. Chgo. Mortgage Bankers Assn. (dir.). Clubs: Union League (Chgo.); Itasca Country; Brookwood Country. Home: Park Ridge IL Died June 24, 1972; buried Chicago IL

TITUS, ANDREW PHILLIPS, ry. official; b. near Princeton, N.J., Apr. 11, 1875; s. Andrew R. and Juliet (Phillips) T.; student Princeton Prep. Sch., 1888-92; m. Isabell Crowley, Nov. 3, 1903; children—Delphine (Mrs. W. B. King), Juliett (Mrs. Frank Weber), John, Andrew. Began as ry. clk., 1892; trainmaster, later supt., Wheeling & Lake Erie R.R., then gen. supt., later gen. mgr. and v.p. Alton R.R. Co.; v.p. Ill. Terminal R.R., 1929-32, pres. since 1932. Home: 641 Palo Drive. Office: 710 N. 12th Blvd., St Louis MO*‡

TITUS, EDWARD CODDINGTON, physician; b. New York, N.Y., Feb. 25, 1863; s. Delos Edwin and Isabel (Hunt) T.; lineal desc. of Capt. David Heusted of Revolutionary fame; ed. pub. schs., New York; M.D., Univ. Med. Coll. (New York U.), 1884; m. 2d, Helen Stark Gillis. Has been in practice of medicine in New York since 1884; clin. asst. dept. diseases of children, New York U. Med. Coll., 1884-88, Demilt Dispensary, 1884-88; lecturer diseases of children, New York Post-Grad. Med. Sch. and Hosp., 1889-96; consultant to Reconstruction Hosp. Awarded Gold Key for meritorious service by the Am. Coll. of Physical Therapy, 1940. Mem. A.M.A., Am. Electro-Therapeutic Assn. (pres. 1908-09), N.Y. State Med. Soc., N.Y. County Med. Soc. Author of articles on original research work. Address: 127 W. 11th St., New York NY*‡

TITUS, LOUIS, lawyer; b. Lodi, Calif., Mar. 6, 1872; s. Lyman and Adelia (Rattan) T.; Univ. of Calif., 1893; m. Alice Jane Rooney, of San Francisco, Oct. 10, 1911. Practiced law at San Francisco 18 yrs. and in Washington, D.C., 15 yrs.; pres. Conservative Oil Co. Mem. Phi Delta Theta. Republican. Clubs: Metropolitan, Chevy Chase, Burning Tree (Washington). Home: 1175 N St. Office: Investment Bldg., Washington DC‡

TITUS, PAUL, publishers rep.; b. N.Y.C., Mar. 29, 1905; s. William Samuel and Amy (Warren) T.; B.A., St. Stephens Coll., 1926; M.A., Columbia, 1927; m. Millicent A. Barwis, June 30, 1928 (dec. Oct. 1943); 1 dau., Barbara G. (Mrs. Lewis F. Cole); m. 2d, Catherine A. Sware, June 25, 1946; 1 dau., Cathleen deLacy. Field supr. marketing dept. N.Y. Evening Jour., N.Y.C., 1927, sales control supr., 1928-31; asst. mgr. plans dept. Rodney E. Boone Orgn., N.Y.C., 1931-36, mgr. plans dept., 1936-44; dir. plans, promotion, research Hearst Advt. Service, N.Y.C., 1944-51, Eastern regional sales mgr., 1951-55, v.p., 1960-66, sr. v.p., 1966-67; sr. v.p. Key Market Advt. Reps., Inc. Mem. Mayors Com. for Civilian Def., 1942, George Washington Bicentennial, 1932. Mem. Soc. Mayflower Descs., S.A.R., Sales Exec. Club N.Y. (dir. 1965), Mayflower Soc. (bd. assts. 1968), N.Y. Grand Jury Assn., Soc. Medalists, Am. Soc. for prevention Cruelty to Animals, Stoutenburg-Teller Family Assn., Nat. Guild Churchmen, Am. Marketing Assn., Sigma Alpha Epsilon (life). Mem. Anglican Catholic Ch. Club: Columbia University. Home: New York City NY

TOBIN, CHARLES MILTON, b. San Antonio, Tex., Mar. 30, 1871; s. William Girard and Josephine (Smith) T.; ed. U. of the South, Sewanee, Tenn.; m. Olivia Prescott, of San Antonio, June 13, 1893. Began as fire ins. agt., San Antonio, 1892; spl. agt., Commercial Union Ins. Co., Ltd., of London, Eng., for Western Dist. of N.Y. and Pa., 1906-14. Capt. Co. I, 3d Tex. Inf., 1886-8; capt. Troop H, 1st N.Y. Cav., 1914-16; service on Mexican border, June 1916-Mar. 1917; maj. 1st N.Y. Cav., Nov. 1916-Mar. 25, 1917; supervising officer for West Central Zone, Mil. Training Commn., State of N.Y., Mar. 1917. Grad. Sch. Musketry and Machine Gunnery, Fort Sill; comd. 102d Supply Train, 27th Div.; arrived in France, July 13, 1918; at Brest until Oct. 1918, when joined div. at front; after armistice on staff of comdg. gen. at Brest. Wrote official history of Am. occupancy of Brest for Gen. Staff U.S.A.; discharged as lt. col., Oct. 8, 1919. Pres. Underwriters' Assn. of N.Y. State, 1914; mem. Delta Tau Delta. Republican. Episcopalian. Mason. Club: Rochester. Author: (with Maj. James K. Parsons, U.S.A.) Complete Infantry Guide, 1917; Rochester NY‡

TOBIN, EDMUND PAUL, ins. exec.; b. Cambridge, Mass., Sept. 17, 1904; s. Daniel J. and Annie (Reagan) T.; grad. Cambridge Latin Sch., 1921; A.B., Harvard, 1925; m. Alice M. Brine, June 25, 1932;children—Edmund P., Elizabeth (Sister Maria Sarto), Constance. Agt. Travelers Ins. Co., also Conn. Mut. Life Ins. Co., 1925-27; with Union Labor Life Ins. Co., N.Y.C., 1927-69, successively agt., Chgo. br. office mgr., N.Y. br. office mgr., v.p. and agy. mgr., exec. v.p., 1927-55, dir., 1952-69, president, 1955-69, chief executive officer, 1956-69, also member of executive committee; member adv. bd. Chemical Bank New York Trust Co. Mem. sec. of labor's com. on pension costs in relation to employment of older persons, 1956-69; mem. N.Y. Gov.'s Conf. on the Problems of the aging, 1956-69. Dir. Sportsmanship Brotherhood. Active Cath. Interracial Council, Cath. Youth Organization. Board of trustees Xavier University, New Orleans, Louisiana, Salve Regina Coll., Newport, Rhode Island, Iona Coll., Lincoln Hall. Decorated Knight of the Order of the Most Holy Sepulchre; Knight of the Order of Malta. Mem. Life Ins. Association America, American Life Convention, Life Insurance Agy. Mgmt. Assn., Nat. Assn. Life Underwriters, Friendly Sons of St. Patrick, New Eng. Soc. (gov.). Clubs: Bldg. Trades Employers Assn. Harvard, Cornell (N.Y.C.); Westchester Country (Rye, N.Y.); Harvard Varsity. Home: Rye NY Died July 27, 1969.

TOBIN, JAMES EDWARD, educator; b. Fall River, Mass., Jan. 17, 1905; s. William J.J. and Mary L. (Kelleher) T.; B.A., Boston Coll., 1925; M.A., Fordham U., 1928. Ph.D., 1933; m. Lorraine Claire Walsh, Sept. 9, 1929; children—Jean, Robert, Richard, David, Philip. Staff Asso. Press. 1925-27; faculty Fordham U., 1927-46, asso. editor univ. press, 1928-53, prof., head dept. English grad. sch., 1936-46; editorial board Thought, 1939-46; vice pres., editor-in-chief Declan X. McMullen Co., Inc., 1946-48; assistant professor English Queens College, 1948-53, associate professor, 1954-58; prof., 1959-68, chmn. div. arts, 1958-61, dir. Sch. Gen. Studies, 1961-66, dean, 1966-68; editorial bd. Fathers of the Church, 1949-61, Catholic Book Club, 1949-62. Mem. adv. bd. Molloy Coll., 1955-67, trustee, 1967-68, library named in his honor at Molloy Coll., 1967; trustee Tuckahoe Pub. Library, 1949-68, pres., 1963-68; mem. Area II selection com. Woodrow Wilson Fellowship Found., 1960-68. Mem. Catholic Poetry Soc. Am. (chmn. bd. 1951), Cath. Renascence Soc. (bd. dirs. 1958-65), Modern Lang. Assn. (bibliography com. 1943-49, chmn. 1948-49), Bibliog. Soc., Modern Humanities Research Assn. Author: Eighteenth Century English Literature and Its Cultural Backgrounds, 1939; Alexander Pope: A Bibliography, 1945; Dictionary of Catholic Biography, 1961. Mng. editor Comparative Lit. News Letter, 1943-46; asso. editor Spirit, 1951-68. Office: Flushing NY Died Oct. 30, 1968; buried Holymount Cemetery, Eastchester NY

TOBIN, ROBERT JAMES, roofing co. exec.; b. Mpls., Aug. 18, 1897; s. Michael and Katherine (Donaghue) T.; B.S., Mass. Inst. Tech., 1920; m. Phyllis P. Lake, July 17, 1946. With Tilo Roofing Co., Inc., Stratford, Conn., 1920-62, successively salesman, v.p., exec. v.p., pres. and chmn. bd., 1920-36, pres., 1936-59, chmn. bd., 1959-62, ret. Clubs: Metropolitan (N.Y.C.); Brooklawn Country (Bridgeport, Conn.); Lake Placid (N.Y.) Home: Fairfield CT Deceased.

TOBOLSKY, ARTHUR VICTOR, educator; b. N.Y.C., May 16, 1919; s. William H. and Ruth (Lemanowitz) T.; B.A. (Albert Asher Green Meml. prize, John Dash Van Buren, Jr. prize math. 1940), Columbia, 1940; Ph.D. in Physics and Chemistry, Princeton, 1944; m. Dorothy Epstein, Jan. 18, 1943; children—Margo Linda, William Harris, Steven Bennett. Faculty Princeton, 1944-72, Eugene Higgins prof. chemistry, 1960-65, Russel Wellman Moore prof. chemistry, 1965-72; sci. cons. chem. companies; asso. editor Am. Scientist, 1958-72; research asso. Textile Research Inst., 1960-72; cons. editor John Wiley and Sons., 1960-72. Recipient Gold Medal award Soc. Plastics Engrs., 1970. Fellow Am. Phys. Soc. (Ford prize 1968); mem. Soc. Rheology (Bingham medal 1956), Am. Chem. Soc. (Witco award 1972), Sigma Xi. Author: Physical Chemistry of High Polymeric in Polymer chemistry Systems, 1950; Organic Peroxides, 1954; Properties and Structures of Polymers, 1960; Polymeric Sulfur and Related Polymers, 1965; Polymer Science and Materials, 1971; Synthetic Polymers, 1973; also numerous articles. Home: Princeton NJ Died Sept. 7, 1972.

TODD, CASEY, lawyer; b. Weakley Co., Tenn., Sept. 12, 1873; s. John C. and Martha (Younger) T.; ed. common sch. and normal sch., Dickson, Tenn.; studied law under Judge Joseph E. Jones, of Dresden, Tenn.; m. Brena E. Jackson, of Martin, Tenn., 1900. Began practice, in Dresden, Tenn., 1898; removed to Memphis; was asst. dist. atty., Western Dist. of Tenn., dist. atty., since June 8, 1910. Democrat. Address: 75 N. Cleveland St., Memphis TN‡

TODD, EDWARD HOWARD, coll. pres.; b. Council Bluffs, Ia., Apr. 2, 1863; s. John Wesley and Minerva (Payne) T.; B.S., Simpson Coll., Indianola, Ia., 1886, M.S., 1889, S.T.B., Boston U. Sch. of Theology, 1893; D.D., Simpson Coll., 1907; LL.D., 1925; L.H.D., Gooding College, 1936, and College of Puget Sound, 1948; D.Sc. in Education, Boston University, 1940; m. Florence Ann Moore, September 29, 1887; children—Edward Paul, Wesley Sanford, Junia Helen, Florence Ruth (dec.) Elizabeth Eileen (dec.). Pastor Valisca Circuit, Ia., 1886, Gravity, Ia., 1887-89; ordained deacon, 1888; student pastor W. Roxbury, Boston, 1890-93; ordained elder, 1893; pastor Oakesdale, Wash., 1893-94, Colfax, 1894-97, Montesano, 1897-99, Vancouver, 1899-1903, Epworth Ch., Tacoma, 1903-05; corr. sec. U. of Puget Sound, 1905-09; pastor Grace Ch., Seattle, 1909-10; v.p. Willamette U., June 14, 1910-13; pres. Coll. of Puget Sound 1913-42, pres. emeritus since Aug. 1, 1942. Appointed Official Historian of C.P.S. since 1944. Trustee Puget Sound University, 1897-1911; member Pacific Northwest Annual Conference Meth. Church; mem. Gen. Conf., 1916, 20, 24; del. Ecumenical Conf., London, 1921, Atlanta, Ga., 1931; member Univ. Senate Meth. Ch. since 1934-42; pres. Assn. Independent Colls. since 1934. Scottish Rite Mason (Shriner), Rotary, Tacoma. Lecturer. Author of A Practical Mystic" and History of College of Puget Sound." Home: 1604 N. Alder St., Tacoma 6 WA‡

TODD, ELMER KENNETH, investor; b. Elwood, Ind., June 10, 1894; s. Elmer LeRoy and May Rachel (Smith) T.; student pub. schs., Elwood; m. Dorothy Hoagland Pepple, June 12, 1915; 1 son, William Kenneth; m. 2d, Mary B. Lewis Thompson, Nov. 15, 1923. Newspaper reporter Anderson (Ind.) Herald 1912; with South Bend (Ind.) Tribune, 1913-15, South Bend News-Times, 1915-17; city editor Richmond (Va.) Times-Dispatch, 1918-19; sports writer Boston

Traveler, 1920-21; circulation mgr. Rockford Republic, 1922-30; mgmt. staff Rockford Consol. Newspapers, Inc.; 1930-33; gen. mgr., 1933-52; pres. Rockford Newspapers, Inc. (pub. Rockford Morning Star, Rockford Register-Republic), 1952-62, chmn. bd., 1962-69; pres. Rockford Broadcasters, Inc., 1952-63. Mem. Rockford Coll. Bd. Counselors; bd. trustees Rockford Meml. Hosp. Republican. Methodist. Mason (32 deg.). Elk. Clubs: Rockford Country, Forest Hills Country, Rockford University, Mid-day; Chicago Athletic; Thunderbird Country, Canyon Country, O'Dennel Country, Committee of Twenty Five (Palm Springs, Cal.). Home: Palm Springs CA Died Apr. 18, 1969.

TODD, EUGENE, JR., physician; b. Richmond, Ky., Jan. 29, 1916; s. Eugene and Sonora (Black) T.; M.D., U. Louisville, 1942; m. Laura Montgomery, Nov. 12, 1938; children—James Black, Jane M., Julia Gene. Intern, St. Elizabeth's Hosp., Covington, Ky., 1942-43; resident Lexington (Ky.) Clinic, 1944-49, pres., 1968-69; attending surgeon St. Joseph's Hosp., Lexington, until 1970, pres. staff, 1963; attending surgeon Good Samaritan Hosp., Lexington, until 1970. Diplomate Am. Bd. Surgery. Mem. A.M.A., So., Ky. med. assns., Fayette County Med. Soc., Southeastern Surg. Congress, Ky. Surg. Soc., Phi Chi. Home: Lexington KY Died Feb. 23, 1970; buried Richmond KY

TODD, FANNIE BURGESS (MRS. HAROLD ARTHUR TODD), civic worker; b. Baton Rouge; d. George Wesley and Anna (Willis) Burgess; B.A., La State U., 1913; m. Harold Arthur Todd, Dec. 18, 1916; children—Harold Arthur (Lt. j.g., USN, Dec. 1945), Wesley Scott. Tchr. English, algebra Terrebonne High Sch., Houma, La., 1913-16; pres. Wauwatosa Gold Star Mothers, 1947-50, co-chmn. City of Wauwatosa Meml. Album Com., 1955-57; mem. Mayor's Commn. Meml. Bd., City of Wauwatosa, Wis., 1957-64. Bd. dirs. Milw. chpt. D.A.R., 1961-68, state chmn. insignia Wis. D.A.R., 1959-65, state historian, 1965-68, trustee Wis. Soc., mem. Officers Club Wis. Soc.; bd. dirs. Wauwatosa Woman's Club, 1941-43, 53-55. Mem. Auxiliary of Harold A. Todd, Jr. post Am. Legion; mem. Woman's League. Conglist. (bd. deacons 1949-52). Clubs: Blue Mound Country, Wisconsin, University, Milw. Athletic (all Milw.); Oconomowoc Lake (Wis.); Book (Wauwatosa, Wis.); 20th Century Topic. Home: Wauwatosa WI Died Apr. 29, 1970.

TODD, FORDE ANDERSON, naval officer; b. Anderson, S.C., Feb. 20, 1881; s. Albert Whitner and Martha (Anderson) T.; student Richmond Acad., Augusta, Ga., 1896-98, Coll. of Charleston (S.C.), 1899-1900; B.S., U.S. Naval Acad., 1904; m. Sylvia Leland Barnes, June 21, 1917; children—Emily Harrison, Anderson, Dorothy Marilla, John Barnes. Commd. ensign, U.S. Navy, 1906, and advanced through the grades to rear adm., 1938; served as naval aid to Pres. Wilson; exec. officer U.S.S. Utah with Grand Fleet, during World War; naval attache, Rome, Italy, 1926-28; comdg. officer U.S.S. Idaho, 1933-34; comdt. of midshipmen, U.S. Naval Acad., 1935-37; comdr. Atlantic Squadron, 1938; comdg. Cruiser Div. 8, U.S. Fleet, 1938-40; retired for physical disability, May 1, 1941, and ordered Governor Naval Home, Philadelphia. Decorated Victory medal for World War, Mexican Campaign medal. Mem. Alpha Tau Omega. Democrat. Presbyn. Clubs: New York Yacht (New York); Rittenhouse, Racquet (Phila.); Army and Navy, Chevy Chase (Washington, D.C.). Home: Haverford PA Died Aug. 1971.

TODD, PAUL HAROLD, business exec.; b. Nottawa, Michigan, September 10, 1887; s. Albert May and Augusta (Allman) T.; B.S., U. Mich., 1909; m. Elizabeth Dewing, June 18, 1931; children—Paul Harold, Thomas A. Dir. Abacus Fund, Inc.; pres., mgr. Farmers' Chem. Co., Kalamazoo, Mich.; pres. Mentha Plantation, Inc. (Mich.); dir. Kalamazoo Spice Extraction Co., First Nat. Bank & Trust Co., Kalamazoo, Michigan. Mayor of City of Kalamazoo, 1937, 38, 49, 50; chairman of the Mich. Public Utilities Commn., 1937, 38; past mem. Mich. Econ. Development Commn. Trustee Kalamazoo Coll. Served as 2d lt., arty., U.S. Army, World War I. Mem. Am. Chem. Soc., A.A.A.S., Am. Pharm. Assn., Am. Pub. Power Assn., Am. Legion, Vets. Fgn. Wars Clubs: Torch, Kiwanis (Kalamazoo); Marshall Chess (N.Y.C.). Home: Kalamazoo MI Died Sept. 3, 1969; buried Mountain Home Cemetery, Kalamazoo MI

TODD, WALTER EDMOND CLYDE, ornithologist; b. Smithfield, O., Sept. 6, 1874; s. William and Isabella (Hunter) T.; ed. Beaver (Pa.) High Sch., 1887-91; m. Leila E. Eason, Dec. 9, 1907 (died 1927). Asst. in Div. of Econ. Ornithology and Mammalogy (later Bur. of Biol. Survey), U.S. Dept. of Agr., 1891-99; curator of ornithology, Carnegie Museum, Pittsburgh, 1899-1944; curator emeritus, 1945-67. Fellow American Ornithologists' Union; member of the Biological Society of Washington. Methodist. Conducted numerous scientific expdns. to the east coast of Hudson Bay and to the coast and interior of Labrador, 1901-45. Awarded Brewster medal (with M.A. Carriker), 1925, by Am. Ornithol. Union, for meritorious work on ornithology." Author: Birds of Western Pennsylvania, 1940. Contbr. numerous papers, mostly on neo-tropical birds. Home: Beaver PA Died June 1967.

TODD, WALTER LEDYARD, mfg. exec.; b. Gettysburg, S.D., May 6, 1886; s. George Walter and Grace (Ledyard) T.; A.B., Cornell, 1909. Asso. with The Todd Co., Inc., Rochester, N.Y., since 1909, successively sales mgr., gen. mgr., pres., chmn. board, from 1946, consultant Burroughs Corporation division; trustee Rochester Savs. Bank, Security Trust Co.; dir. Rochester Gas & Elec. Corp., Stromberg Carlson Telephone Mfg. Co., Widmer Wine Cellars, Inc., Naples, New York. Director Bur. of Municipal Research, Rochester Community Chest, Hillside Children's Centre (pres. 1951), Navy League of U.S. Trustee Cornell U., Rochester Inst. Tech., Rochester Y.W.C.A. (also mem. adv. bd. Y.M.C.A.), Conv. and Publicity Bur. Mem. exec. com. N.Y. State YMCA. Mem. Rochester C. of C. (pres., 1948). Clubs: University, Cornell (N.Y. City); University, Genesee Valley Country Club of Rochester (Rochester); R.C.Y.C. (Toronto). Home: Rochester NY

TOGNAZZINI, ROLAND, bus. exec.; b. San Francisco, July 2, 1903; s. Milo D. and Dora (Tognazzini) T.; A.B., Stanford, 1924, J.D., 1926; grad. study U. Lausanne, 1927-28; m. Page Pressley, Oct. 9, 1935; children—Terry, Roland, Bruce. Admitted to Calif. bar, 1927; practicing lawyer, San Francisco, 1928-37; gen. counsel Calif. State Bldg. & Loan Commr., 1931-33; pres., dir. Union Sugar Co., Union Sugar Div. Consol. Foods Corp.; pres. Rosenberg Bros., 1951-54, chmn. bd. 1954-59; v.p., dir. Consolidated Foods Corp.; dir. Bank of Am., Nat. Trust & Savs. Assn., Cal. Agrl. Dist. 1A. Dir. Stanford Research Inst.; v.p., director Salvation Army, 1945. Mem. San Francisco C. of C. (v.p., dir. 1943-46), San Francisco Y.M.C.A. (v.p., dir. 1945-46). Mem. Newcomen Soc., Delta Tau Delta. Clubs: Country (Burlingame, Calif.); Golf, Bohemian. Pacific Union (San Francisco). Home: San Francisco CA Died 1971.

TOLAND, CLARENCE G(AINES), prof. surgery; b. 1875; M.D., Univ. Med. Coll. of Kansas City, 1901; m. Nina Rowland; 1 dau., Madge. Formerly asso. prof. clin. surgery, now prof. surgery, U. of Southern Calif. Fellow A.M.A., Am. Coll. Surgeons; mem. Western Surg. Assn., Pacific Coast Surg. Assn. Club: California. Home: 501 S Lucerne Boul. Office: 1930 Wilshire Boul., Los Angeles CA*‡

TOLBERT, JOSEPH W(ARREN), Rep. Nat. committeeman; b. nr. Ninety Six, S.C., June 7, 1870; s John Robert and Betty Pope (Payne) T.; ed. common sch. of S.C. and Adger Coll., Walhalla, S.C.; m. Julia E. DeLoach, of Ninety Six, S.C., 1910; children—Julia Elizabeth, Joseph Lincoln. Planter Ninety Six, S.C., sbince 1890. Chmn. Rep. State Com., S.C., since 1900. mem. Rep. Nat. Com. since 1908. Baptist. Home: Ninety Six SC‡

TOLEDO-HERRARTE, LUIS, diplomat; b. Guatemala City, Guatemala, C.A., Mar. 28, 1871; s. Roderico and Jesus (Herrarte) Toledo-Mattei; B.A., Instituts Nacional Central, Guatemala City, 1887; M.D., Faculty of Paris, France, 1894; m. Eugenie Roquejoffre, of France, May 27, 1902. Began practice at Guatemala City, 1894; prof. Faculty of Medicine, Guatemala; dir. Nat. Inst.; twice representative in Guatemalan Congress; lt.-col. med. corps; del. of Guatemala to Med. Congress, Panama, 1905; sec. Guatemalan Legation, Rio de Janeiro, Brazil, 1906; E.E. and M.P. to U.S. and Cuba since 1907; mem. Permanent Ct. of Arbitration of The Hague. Mem. Am. Acad. Polit. and Social Science. Roman Catholic. Clubs: Metropolitan (hon.), Guatemala. Author: El papel de los mosquitos en la transmision de las enfermedades contagiosas. Address: The Highlands, Washington DC‡

TOLER, FRED W., mfg. co. exec.; b. St. Louis, Feb. 22, 1926; s. John W. and Roena (Butteiger) T.; grad. high sch.; m. Dolores H. Blake, May 15, 1946; children—Kathie L., Mark W. Salesman, Hill Behan Lumber Co., 1947, County Lumber Co., 1948, Wilhelm Lumber Co., 1949; founder So. Cross Lumber & Millwork Co., Hazelwood, Mo., 1950, pres., from 1950; v.p. O'Fallon Lumber Co. (Mo.) from 1970. Served with USNR, 1943-46. Home: Ladue MO

TOLLES, MARIAN DONAHUE (MRS. N. ARNOLD TOLLES), editor; b. Cleve., Nov. 13, 1902; d. Charles James and Mary (Crowell) Donahue; A.B., Smith Coll., 1925, M.A., 1932; m. N. Arnold Tolles, Sept. 4, 1929; children—Patricia (Mrs. Edward Eckert), Harriet (Mrs. Keith Clement). Instr., Mt. Holyoke Coll., 1929-31; instr. Smith Coll., 1931-35; economist WPA Research Project, 1936-37; economist NRC, 1937-38; economist Brookings Inst., 1938-40; economist Nat. Defense OPM, WPB, Civilian Prodn. Adminstrn., Washington, 1940-47; mng. editor Human Organ., Ithaca, N.Y., 1958-66; mng. editor Soc. Applied Anthropology Cornell U., 1958-66, managing editor Adminstrv. Sci. Quar., Bus. Sch., 1966-68. Sec. Women's Democratic Club, 1944-66. Mem. League Women Voters (voters service chmn. 1950-52), Soc. Applied Anthropology (sec.). Club: Women's Democratic. Author: A History of Subsidies to French Aviation, Ithaca NY Died Dec. 16, 1969.

TOLLES, NEWMAN ARNOLD, educato economist; b. N.Y.C., Sept. 21, 1903; s. Harry Newma and Elisabeth (Eurgens) T.; Ph.B., U. Chgo., 192 M.A., 1924, Ph.D., 1932; M.A., Harvard, 1926; r Marian Donahue, Sept. 4, 1929 (dec. Dec. 1969 children—Patricia (Mrs. Edward Eckert), Harriet (Mrs Keith Clement); m. 2d, Martha Morrow Tolles, Apr. 2 1971. U. Chgo. research fellow London Sch. Econs 1925-27; asst. prof. Mt. Holyoke Coll., 1929-35; lect Smith Coll., 1933-34, Am. U., 1935, 39, U. Cal 1936-39; economist U.S. Bur. Labor Statistics, 1935-38 asst. dir., dir. research, wage and hour div. U.S. Dep Labor, 1938-40; asst. to Commr. Sidney Hillman, U.S Def. Commn., 1940; br. chief, asst. commr. U.S. Bur Labor Statistics, 1940-45; prof., dir. teaching inst. econs Am. U., 1945-47; prof. labor market econs. Cornell U 1947-71; vis. prof. econs. N.Y. State U. Coll. a Geneseo, 1967-68, 70-73; guest prof. U. Munich, lect Chmn. N.Y. State Minimum Wage Bd. for Dyeing an Cleaning Industry, 1956; dir. N.Y. State Council o Econ. Edn., 1961. Alderman, City of Ithaca (N.Y. 1966-69. With USIS, Germany, 1953-54; organizer anr confs. teaching labor econs., 1945-50. Cons. U.S Conciliation Service, Nat. War Labor Bd., U.S. Civi Service Commn., 1935-45. Mem. Am. Econ. Assn Am. Statis. Assn., N.Y. State Econ. Assn. (pres 1961-62), Indsl. Relations Research Assn., Am. Assn U. Profs., Phi Beta Kappa, Delta Sigma Rho. Author (with Earl Brooks), Providing Facts and Figures fo Collective Bargaining, 1951; (with Robert L. Raimon) Sources of Wage Information: Employer Associations 1952; Labor Costs and International Trade, 1961 Origins of Modern Wage Theories, 1964. Contbr. articles to jours. Home: Ithaca NY Died Apr. 10, 1973

TOLLETT, RAYMOND LEE, lawyer, banker Petroleum Corp.; b. Temple, Okla., Dec. 9, 1907; s Franklin M. and Elizabeth Maude (Dodson) T.; LL.B Dixie Univ., 1932; m. Leta Marie Bennett, June 30 1929 (div. Sept. 17, 1943); 1 dau., Eugenia Kay; m. 2d Iris Evelyn Goodbrake, November 17, 1945 children—Raymond Lee, Jr., Jason Blake, Iris Anr Acct. independent oil cos. No. Tex., 1925-33; public practice of accounting and law, January-Sept. 1934; sp agt. and agent-in-charge, Federal Bur. Investigation 1934-37; sec-treas. Wrightsman Oil Co., Ft. Worth Tex., 1937-39; sec.-treas., exec. v.p. Cosden Oil & Chem. Co., 1939-40, pres., 1940-68. Regional exec com. Boy Scouts; regent N. Tex. State U. Mem. Tex Research League (dir.), Tex. Bar, Tex. Soc. C.P.A., Soc Former Spl. Agts FBI, C. of C., Am. Petroleum Inst (director), Newcomen Soc. N.Am., Nat. Petroleum Refiners Assn. (dir.), Army Ordnance Assn., Ind Petroleum Assn. of Am., American Inst. of C.P.A.s Republican. Episcopalian. Clubs: Ft. Worth (Tex.); Bi Spring Country. Home: Big Spring TX Died Oct. 26 1969; interred Big Spring TX

TOLLMIEN, WALTER GUSTAV, scientist; b. Berlin Germany, Oct. 13, 1900; s. Gustav and Amalia (Alschausky) T.; student U. Berlin, 1919-21; Dr. phil. U. Gottingen, 1924, Dr. phil. habil., 1935; Dr. rer. nat h.c. Tech. U., Clausthal Mining Acad. 1965; m. Sigric Kosch, Mar. 18, 1948; children—Uwe, Renate (Mrs Schultheis), Cordula, Franziska, Sibylle. Asst. Kaiser-Wilhelm-Institut for Stromungsforschung 1924-30, sect. leader, 1934-37; research fellow Cal. Inst Tech., 1930-33; privatdozent for applied mathematic and mechanics, Gottingen, 1936-37; prof. Technical U. Dresden, 1937-45; dir. Outside Institutes Gottingen 1945-46; sci. Royal Aircraft Establishment Farnborough, 1946-47; prof. U. Gottingen, 1947-68 dir. Max-Planck-Institut fur Stromungsforschung Permanent mem. organizing com. Internat. Congresses on Applied Mechanics. Mem. A.A.A.S., Gottinger Acad. Sci. Contbr. numerous articles on honorary layer theory, turbulence theory, gas-dynamics, dynamic meterology, other fields to profl. publs. Home Gottingen Germany Died Nov. 25, 1968.

TOLMAN, ALBERT WALTER, writer; b. Rockport Me., Nov. 29, 1866; s. Walter and Deborah Bourne (Eells) T.; A.B., Bowdoin, 1888, A.M., 1891; A.B. Harvard, 1889; m. Mary Gertrude Merrill, of Portland Me., June 23, 1903; children—Albert Walter, Edward Merrill. Tutor Greek and rhetoric, 1889-90, instr. elocution and rhetoric, 1890-93, asst. prof. English 1893-94, Bowdoin; admitted to Me. bar, 1899, and practiced at Portland, until 1912. Congregationalist Mem. Psi Upsilon, Phi Beta Kappa. Club: Bostor Authors. Author: Jim Spurling Series, 4 vols. Asst Editor of Vocations," 1911. Contbr. stories chiefly to young people's publs., etc. Home: 471 Cumberland Av. Portland ME‡

TOMAJAN, JOHN S., mfg. co. exec.; b. Worcester Mass., Apr. 11, 1892; s. Mardiros S.T. and Margaret (Garoian) Nahigian; A.B., Harvard, 1914, LL.B., 1918; m. Gladys Harlow, June 11, 1920 (dec. Aug. 1972) children—Gladys Harlow (dec.), Joan (Mrs. Arnost P Propper), Carol (dec.). With The Washburn Co. and its subsidiaries 1918-72, sec. to pres. and gen. mgr. 1918-19, Eastern sales mgr., 1919-23, Western sales mgr., 1924-25, gen. sales mgr., 1925, dir., v.p., 1926-39 gen. mgr., 1939-54, pres., 1941-61, chmn., 1958-60 pres. Mich. Wire Goods Co., 1941-61, dir., 1928-60 pres. Andrews Wire Works of Can. Ltd., 1941-46, chmn., 1946-67; trustee Worcester Mechanics Savs. Bank; dir. Worcester County Nat. Bank. Pres. Am. Hardware Mfrs. Assn., 1944-46; dir. Holden Dist. Hospital, 1939-49; mem. Harvard Fund Council, vice chmn., 1953-55; chmn., 1955-57; trustee Meml. Hosp., Worcester, pres. 1965-67; trustee First Unitarian Ch., Worcester Reginald Washburn Scholarship Fund; bd. dirs. Worcester Boys Club; former dir. Harvard Alumni Assn.; mem. exec. council Clark U.; mem. indsl. adv. council Worcester Poly. Inst.; mem. corp. Worcester Art Museum, 1956-72. Pres. N.E. Div. Asso. Harvard Clubs, 1938-40. Mem. Com. on Pub. Information. Mason (Quinsigamond). Clubs: University, Harvard, Worcester (Worcester, Mass.); Trowel (Holden). Contrbr. articles to Atlantic Monthly mag., Harvard Bus. Rev., and to trade publs. Home: Worcester MA Died Mar. 30, 1972.

TOMBER, MAX L., chain store exec.; b. Hungary, May 22, 1898; s. Sam and Lena T. Merchant, South Bend, 1920, Gary, Ind., 1920-31; pres. and dir. Miller-Whol Co., Inc., N.Y.C., from 1932; mem. adv. com. N.Y.C. Met. br. The Chase Manhattan Bank. Office: New York City NY Died July 10, 1968.

TOMEI, PETER ANDREW, lawyer; b. Chgo., July 12, 1934; s. Felix and Hortense (Schurman) T.; B.A. magna cum laude, Yale, 1956; J.D. cum laude, Harvard, 1959; m. Mary Cleopha Staciva, May 30, 1959; children—Peter Alexander, Jennifer Lee, John Adam, Joshua Ellsworth. Admitted to D.C., Ill. bar, 1959, since practiced in Chgo.; asso. firm Isham, Lincoln & Beale, 1959-67, partner, 1968-71. Del. Ill. Constl. Conv., 1969-70. Served to capt. AUS, 1959-62. Recipient Maurice Weigel award Chgo. Bar Found., 1968; named one of Chgo.'s ten outstanding young men Chgo. Jr. Assn. Commerce and Industry, 1969. Mem. Am., Ill., Chgo. (chmn. com. on constl. revision 1968-69) bar assns., Econ. Club Chgo. Am. Trial Lawyers Assn., Chgo. Hist. Soc., Adlai Stevenson Inst. Internat. Affairs, Phi Beta Kappa. Democrat. Roman Catholic. Contbr. articles on Ill. constl. reform. Home: Chicago IL Died May 16, 1971.

TOMLINSON, HOMER AUBREY, bishop; b. Westfield, Ind., Oct. 25, 1892; s. A.J. and Mary Jane (Taylor) T.; student U. Tenn., 1911-13; m. Marie Wunch, Nov. 22, 1919; children—Halcy, A. Jess, Homer E. Various positions Church of God Pub. House, Cleveland, Tenn., 1900-23; prin. high sch., Tenn., 1913-14; sec. Culver Mil. Acad. Summer Sch., 1914-17; various positions advt., schs., colls., publishers, N.Y., 1916-28; ordained to ministry Church of God, 1923; N.Y. State overseer, 1923-43, gen. overseer from 1943; pastor Jamaica Tabernacle, Church of God, 1923-43; with father, founded Lee Coll., Cleveland, Tenn. Candidate for U.S. pres., Theocratic Party, 1960, 64, 68. Served with USA, World War I. Mem. World Wars Tank Corps Assn. (former nat. chaplain), Am. Legion. Author numerous books, including: Home Study Bible Lessons, 20 vols., 1919; The Church of God, 1919; Diary of A.J. Tomlinson, 1901-43, 3 vols., 1949; Amazing Fulfillments of Prophecy, 1935; The Kingdom of God, 1960; Theocracy, 1962; The Shout of a King, 1968. Home: Queens Village NY Died Dec. 4, 1968; buried National Cemetery, Pine Lawn LI NY

TOMLINSON, ROY EVERETT, corporation executive; born Chicago, Dec. 4, 1877; s. Everett S. and Genevieve (Rush) T.; LL.B., U. of Wis., 1901; m. Eleanor Parsons, Dec. 25, 1905; children—Harriet, Everett. With Nat. Biscuit Co., 1902-68, in legal dept. until 1917, pres. 1917, then chmn. bd., later dir., then dir. emeritus, 1965-68; dir. Am. Sugar Refining Co., D.,L.&W. R.R. Co., Am. Can Co.; trustee Montclair Trust Co., Prudential Life Ins. Co. Republican. Conglist. Clubs: Union League (New York); Montclair Golf, Eastward Ho Golf. Home: Montclair NJ and I2Chatham MA Died Apr. 28, 1968.

TOMLINSON, WILLIAM GOSNELL, naval officer; b. Leavenworth, Kan., Dec. 17, 1897; s. John Cassett and Medora (Gosnell) T.; grad. U.S. Naval Acad., 1919; m. Katharine Estelle Dent, June 15, 1931. Qualified as naval aviator 1922; early test pilot; participated in development of dive bombing and carrier aircraft tactics; comd. patrol squadron which made early overseas flights; head Reserve Aviation, Bur. Aeronautics, Washington, D.C., 1932-35; in World War II served overseas or on sea duty, holding 4 comds., last—aircraft carrier U.S.S. Belleau Wood (ship received Presdl. Unit citation; chief air readiness, Navy Dept., Washington, D.C.; comdr. Pacific Division Mil. Air Transport Service. Awarded Navy Cross for heroism in action (Iwo Jima); Legion of Merit with gold star in lieu of 2d for action against enemy. Baptist. As racing pilot member Am. Schneider Cup Team, 1926; won Curtiss Marine Trophy, 1929. Home: Washington DC Died Oct. 13, 1972.

TOMPKINS, BOYLSTON ADAMS, banker; b. Harlingen, N.J., Jan. 13, 1891; s. L. Douglas and Emma (Slack) T.; grad. Phillips Acad., Andover, Mass., 1912; A.B., Yale, 1915; m. Eleanore Louise Marshall, May 1917; children—Boylston Adams, Eleanore Louise, Joan Daphne, Judith Lee. Began with Astor Trust Co., N.Y.C., 1917; sr. v.p. Bankers Trust Co., 1921-55, also member of executive committee, dir., mem. adv. bd.; mem. adv. bd. Internat. Paper Co.; dir. Gen. Am. Investors Co., Inc., Flintkote Co., Puralator Products, Inc., Nat. Aviation Corp., Babcock & Wilcox Co., Otis Elevator Co., Detroit Edison Co., Bowery Savings Bank. Mem. Psi Upsilon, Scroll and Key. Clubs: Yale, Links Golf; Links; Quisset Yacht. Home: New York City NY Died May 7, 1972.

TOMPKINS, LUCIUS DOUGLAS, business exec. (retired); b. Harlingen, N.J., May 13, 1889; s. Lucius Douglas and Emma (Slack) T.; B.A., Yale, 1913; m. Selma Moore, June 12, 1918 (died 1941); children—John Vinton, Elizabeth Thayer; m. 2d, Edith Duncan. With U.S. Rubber Co., 1916-44; retired; dir. U.S. Rubber Co., 1941-44. Asst. rubber dir.; also in charge of operations, Washington, D.C.; special asst. to Justice Byrnes; White House dir., WMAC. Mem. Squadron A, New York, 1917-19. Mem. Delta Phi, Theta Nu Epsilon. Republican. Episcopalian. Clubs: Yale, University, Wee Burn Country. Home: Wilton CT Died Feb. 23, 1971; inurned Columbarium of St. Philip's-in-the-Hills Tucson AZ

TONE, FRANCHOT, actor; b. Niagara Falls, N.Y., Feb. 27, 1905; s. Frank Jerome and Gertrude (Franchot) T.; A.B., Cornell University, 1927; married Joan Crawford, Oct. 11, 1935 (divorced 1939); married 2d, Jean Wallace, Oct. 1941 (div.); children—Pascal, Thomas; m. Barbara Payton; m. Zolorres Dorn-Heft. Began with Garry McGarry Stock Co., 1927; at New Playwrights Theatre, New York City, 1927-28; with Katherine Cornell's Age of Innocence, N.Y. City, 1928-29, Theatre Guild, 1929-31, Group Theatre, 1931-32; with Metro-Goldwyn-Mayer Studios, Culver City, Calif., since 1932; now heads own film co. Dir. Screen Actors' Guild. Mem. Phi Beta Kappa, Alpha Delta Phi. Nominated by Acad. Motion Pictures Arts and Sciences, as one of ten best performers in 1935. Address: New York City NY Died Sept. 1968.*

TONG, HOLLINGTON K., Chinese diplomat; b. Ningpo, Chekiang, China, Nov. 9, 1887; A.B., U. Mo., 1912; Ph.D. (hon.), Park Coll., Parkville, Mo.; postgrad. Columbia; m. Ying-Hsiang Chao; children—Mrs. Ben Chen, Mrs. Meili Tong Chen, Mrs. Yali Swigart, Yang-lung Tong, Tang-bu Tong, Sze-liang Tong. Served as the vice minister of information, China, 1938-45, dir. Govt. Information Office, 1947-48; minister without portfolio, Executive Yuan, 1948; gen. mgr. Broadcasting Corp. of China, 1950-52; chmn. bd. Central Daily News, 1950-52; ambassador to Japan, 1952-56, U.S., 1956-58. Author: Dateline: China, 1950; Biography of Chiang Kai-shek, 1953; Japanese Sense of Humor, 1955; What is Ahead for China, and Gems of Chinese Humor, 1957; American Sense of Humour, 1958. Address: San Jose CA Died Jan. 1971.

TOOKER, STERLING TWISS, ins. co. exec.; b. Hartford, Conn., May 23, 1913; s. Morris S. and Hazel (Twiss) T.; B.A., Wesleyan U., Middletown Conn., 1935; B. Ins., U. Conn., 1942; m. Alice Miller, Aug. 10, 1940; children—Adlin M., S. Christopher. With Travelers Ins. Companies, Hartford, 1935-68, v.p. exec. dept., 1959-62, exec. v.p., 1962-64, pres., 1964-68, also dir.; dir. Hartford National Bank and Trust Company (Conn.), Standard Screw Co., N.E. Utilities. Bd. dirs. Travelers Research Center, Inc., Am. Sch. Deaf; pres. bd. trustees Kingswood Sch., Hartford; bd. trustees Wesleyan U., Com., Econ. Devel.; mem. council Grad. Sch. Bus., U. Chgo.; dir. v.p. Greater Hartford YMCA; mem. bd. advisers Hartford Grad. Center, Rensselaer Poly Inst. Conn., Inc.; mem. bd. electors Ins. Hall Fame. Served as lt. (j.g.) USNR, 1943-46. Mem. Greater Hartford C. of C. (chmn. edn. com., West Simsbury CT Died June 6, 1969.

TOOKEY, CLARENCE H(ALL), ins. exec.; b. Sundridge, Ont., Can., May 30, 1896; s. Mark E. and Elizabeth H. (Hall) T.; A.B., U. Alberta, 1920; m. Minerva Anderson, July 15, 1922; children—William A., Robert C. Came to U.S., 1920, naturalized, 1926. Actuary and statistician Fraternal Brotherhood, Los Angeles, 1920-21; asst. actuary Occidental Life Ins. Co. of Calif., Los Angeles, 1921-36, asso. actuary, 1936-42, actuary, 1942-46, actuarial v.p. 1946-61, also dir.; cons. actuary, Pasadena, Cal., 1961-67; mem. bd. dirs. Am. Life Ins. Co. of New York. Fellow Society Actuaries (v.p.). Contbr. various written discussions to Rec. Am. Inst. Actuaries. Home: La Canada CA Died Dec. 29, 1967; interred Forest Lawn Meml. Park Glendale CA

TOOLE, S. WESTCOTT, ins. exec.; b. Winder, Ga., Sept. 30, 1900; s. Warren H. and Clifford (Westcott) T.; student Emory U., 1917-20; m. Dorothy Decker, Sept. 28, 1925; 1 dau., Patricia (Mrs. Barnes). With Fed. Res. Bank, Atlanta, 1919-23; asst. cashier Bank of Orange & Trust Co., Orlando, Fla., 1924-26; real estate broker, Orlando, Fla., also Tampa, 1926-31; with Prudential Ins. Co., from 1931, sr. v.p., ret. Trustee Newark Safety Council; commr. Newark Parking Authority; mem. State Capitol Redevel. Commn. General chmn. United Appeals Campaign, 1964. Mem. Greater Newark C. of C. (dir., past pres.), Nat. Assn. Bldg. Owners and Mgrs., Newark Econ. Development Commn., Sigma Alpha Epsilon. Clubs: Essex (Newark); Deal (N.J.) Golf and Country; Everglades (Palm Beach, Fla.). Home: Allenhurst NJ Died Feb. 26, 1969; buried Monmouth Meml. Park Asbury Park NJ

TOOLIN, JOHN MARTIN, grocery chain exec.; b. New London, Conn., July 27, 1891; s. Peter Frederick and Anne Maria (Kelly) T.; student bus. coll., 1905-07; m. Ellen Hayes, Oct. 7, 1914 (dec. Feb. 1952); children—Donald H., Barbara (Mrs. William O'Brien); m. 2d, Velma Cook, July 10, 1953. Pres. Central Western div. The Great Atlantic & Pacific Tea Co., Detroit, 1925-54, dir. Great Atlantic & Pacific Tea Co. N.J., Great Atlantic and Pacific Tea Co. Am. Mem. Econ. Club Detroit, Adcraft Club. Clubs: Detroit Country, Detroit, Detroit Athletic, Beavers (Detroit); Grosse Pointe (Mich.) Yacht. Home: Detroit MI Died Sept. 1971.

TOOMBS, HENRY JOHNSTON, architect; b. Cuthbert, Ga., Jan. 4, 1896; s. Robert Edwin and Rebecca Seymour (Johnston) T.; B.Arch., U. of Pa., 1921, M.Arch., 1922; m. Frances Bennett, Feb. 10, 1931 (divorced 1946); one son, Michael; married 2d, Adah Knight Hereford, August 11, 1948. Draftsman, Paul P. Cret, Phila., 1922-24, McKim, Mead and White, N.Y. City, 1924-27; practicing architect since 1928; architect for Ga. Warm Springs Foundation, Bridge building for Rich's, Inc., Atlanta, Rhone Cemetery for Am. Battle Monuments Commission, also other pub. and private bldgs. and residences N.Y. and Ga.; partnership with Wm. J. Creighton as Toombs and Creighton, Jan. 1946-49; partner Toombs & Co., 1949-53; Toombs, Amisano & Wells, 1955-67; architect Fed. Reserve Bank Atlanta. Ensign, U.S. Navy, 1917-19. Mem. Bd. of Zoning Appeals, Fulton County, Ga., 1940-44, mem. Co. Planning Commn., 1946-51; mem. Municipal Planning Bd. since 1952; mem. Fulton Co. Grand Jurors Assn. Capt., U.S. Army Air Corps, May 1, 1942, maj., Dec. 17, 1943; retired 1944. Fellow A.I.A. Clubs: St. Anthony, Army and Navy, Washington, D.C.; Century (N.Y.) Home: Atlanta GA Died June 15, 1967; buried Warm Springs GA

TOOTELL, ROBERT BALLARD, govt. ofcl.; b. Maiden Rock, Wis., Sept. 20. 1904; s. Albert Ballard and Stella (Denham) T.; Bachelor of Science, Montana State College, 1927, Doctor of Laws, 1956; M.S., U. Cal., 1931; M. Pub. Adminstrn., Harvard U., 1966; m. Helen Strong, Oct. 26, 1928; children—Robert Ballard, Donald B. Tchr. vocational agr., Deer Lodge, Mont., 1927; instr. agrl. economics Mont. State Coll., 1928-30, then head agrl. economics; land economist Mont. State Extension Service, 1931-34 1943-46, dir., 1946-53; with Fed. Land Bank of Spokane, Wash., 1934-43; gov. FCA, 1954-69; head spl. study groups on farm credit, Ethiopia and Kenya, 1969, Kenya, 1970; cons. Farmers Home Adminstrn.; dir. Wash. State Agrl. Extension Service, 1953-54; farm credit cons. to numerous countries, 1956-69; Am. adviser 4th Far East Farm Credit Workshop, Taipei, 1967; spl. cons. IV Congress Mondial Agrl. Credit, Zurich, 1967. Dir. Am. Institute of Cooperatives; trustee Farm Found., from 1953. Recipient Distinguished Service award Am. Agrl. Editors Assn., 1968; hon. Am. Farmer degree Future Farmers Am., also 4-H Spl. Recognition award, 1967. Member of Lambda Chi Alpha, Phi Kappa Phi, Alpha Zeta, Epsilon Sigma Phi, Mu Beta Beta. Presbyn. Author articles on agr. Home: Sumner MD Died Aug. 20, 1971; buried Bozeman MT

TOPPIN, HARRY PATTINSON, business exec.; b. Lazonby, England, Mar. 8, 1898; s. Isaac and Ruth (Pattinson) T.; m. Hazel M. Nowack, April, 1940. Came to U.S., 1914, naturalized, 1923. Past pres. Fasco Industries, Inc., Rochester, N.Y., now chmn. Clubs: Rochester, Oakhill Country (Rochester). Home: Rochester NY Died 1971.

TORBERT, WILLIAM SYDENHAM, lawyer; b. Laurel, Md., Dec. 21, 1872; s. John Peyton and Elizabeth (Bryant) T.; LL.B., Columbian (now George Washington) U., 1893; m. Janet Louise Whitcomb, Aug. 7, 1896; children—Janet Louise, Hugh Sydenham. Has practiced at Washington since 1894. Mem. Citizens Advisory Council of D.C., 1925-26. Mem. Bar Assn. of D.C., Columbia Hist. Soc., S.A.R. Episcopalian. Author: Legal References, D.C., 1899; Comprehensive Index to Code, 1903; Index Digest of District of Columbia Cases, 1908; Digest of Patent, Trademark and Copyright Cases, 1909; Supplemental Digests of District of Columbia Cases, 1914, 20, 31. Editor Code of Laws of D.C., and a number of legal works; contbr. to encyclos. Reviser. Com. on Revision of the Laws, U.S. Ho. of Rep., 1920. Address: 1920 Varnum St. N.E., Washington DC*‡

TORIAN, OSCAR NOEL, pediatrician; b. Evansville, Ind., Oct. 6, 1875; s. Augustine Garnett and Anna Shelby (Boswell) T.; A.B., U. of the South, 1896; M.D., U. of Pa., 1900; m. Sarah Hodgson, Sept. 19, 1907; children—Anna Garnett, Telfair Hodgson (dec.), John Potter (dec.). Interne King's County Brooklyn) Hosp., 1900-01; asst. in pediatrics, 1908, asso. and then clin. prof., 1915-20, prof. pediatrics, 1920-41, emeritus prof., 1941-71, Ind. U. Sch. Medicine; staff physician Riley, Meth. (mem. bd.) and St. Vincent's hosps.; mem. Ind. Com. Child Health and Maternal Welfare (chairman of pediatric section); pediatrician of Emerald-Hodgson Hospital, Sewanee, Tenn., since 1941, Licentiate American Bd. of Pediatrics. Former trustee U. of the South (mem. bd. regents). Mem. A.M.A., Central States

Pediatrics Soc., Am. Acad. Pediatrics (chmn. Ind. com.), Ind. Pediatric Soc. (pres. 1938), Tenn. State Med. Soc., Franklin County Med. Soc., Phi Rho Sigma, Omicron Delta Kappa, Sigma Xi, Phi Delta Theta. Democrat. Episcopalian. Clubs: E.Q.B., Sewanee Golf. Home: Sewanee TN Died Mar. 29, 1971; buried Sewanee TN

TORRANCE, HENRY, mfr.; b. Brooklyn, N.Y., Mar. 7, 1870; s. Henry and Sarah Creighton (Peet) T.; M.E., Stevens Inst. Tech., 1890; m. Mary Hedges Fisher, June 8, 1918. Mfg. ice and refrig. machinery since 1891; former pres. Carbondale (Pa.) Machine Co.; chmn. Norwalk Co., Inc., South Norwalk, Conn. Mem. Am. Soc. M.E., Am. Soc. Refrigerating Engrs. (pres. 1914), Delta Tau Delta, Tau Beta Pi. Clubs: Engineers', Economic, West Side Tennis (N.Y.); University Heights Tennis (New York); Heights Casino (Brooklyn). Contbr. numerous papers on refrigeration. Home: 112 E. 17th St. Office: 175 Christopher St., New York NY‡

TORRE, CARLOS DE LA, Cuban scientist; b. Matanzas, 1858; ed. Colegio Le Empresa"; degree of bachelor, Inst. of Havana; student Nat. U. of Havana; Licentiate in Medicine, Pharmacy, and Natural Science, Nat. U.; degree of Dr. of Natural Science, Central U. of Madrid. Taught in Los Normales" schools; San Carlos, Mantanzas; La Gran Antilla and El Progeso, Havana; one of founders of School of Arts and Crafts, Havana; appointed asst. in natural and physico-chemical sciences, Inst. of Havana, 1880; prof. natural history and physiology, Inst. of Porto Rico, 1883; prof. comparative anatomy and zoography, U. of Havana; prof. natural sciences in Mexico; prof. biology, zoology and zoography, 1919; del. to Paris Exposition, 1900; commr. pub. instr., Exposition of St. Louis, 1904; del. 10th Internat. Geological Congress, Mexico, 1906. Awarded: hon. Dr. of Science by Harvard; gold medal from native city, Matanzas. Mem. Societe Zoologique (France), Acad. of Science (Havana), Hispanic Society of Am., Anthropological Soc. (Cuba). Author: Libros de lectura y lenguaje; Le geografia de Cuba; La historia de Cuba; La instruccion moral y civica and several papers on malacology. Address: Havana Cuba*‡

TORRENCE, OLIVIA HOWARD DUNBAR, writer; b. West Bridgewater, Mass.; d. Nathaniel William and Olive (Howard) Dunbar; B.L., Smith Coll., 1894; m. Ridgely Torrence, of New York, Feb. 3, 1914. On staff New York World, 1895-1902; writer for mags. Address: Care Civic Club, 14 W. 12th St., New York NY‡

TORRENS, D.T., chmn. Kansas City Life Ins. Co.; b. Oakdale, Ill., Oct. 30, 1873; s. Francis and Mary Jane (Boyd) T.; student Southern Ill. State Normal U., Carbondale, 1893-95; m. Margaret Isabel Dague, Dec. 25, 1899. Engaged in mortgage loan bus., 1899-1920; with Kansas City Life Ins. Co. since 1920, pres. 1937-39, chmn. of bd. since 1939. Mem. Reformed Presbyterian Ch. Club: Kansas City Commercial. Home: 1111 Valentine Road. Office: 3520 Broadway, Kansas City MO ‡

TORREY, CHARLES CUTLER, univ. prof; b. East Hardwick, Vt., Dec. 20, 1863; s. Rev. Joseph and Maria (Noble) T.; A.B., Bowdoin Coll., 1884; grad. Andover Theol. Sem., 1889; Ph.D., Strassburg, 1892; hon. A.M., Yale, 1900; D.D., Bowdoin, 1900; Litt.D., Yale, Bowdoin, 1934; D.H.L., Jewish Inst. Religion, 1934, Jewish Theol. Sem. Am., 1935; m. Marian Edwards, d. of Charles B. Richards, June 16, 1911; 1 dau., Anne Noble. Teacher Auburn (Me.) High Sch., 1884-85; tutor Latin, Bowdoin Coll., 1885-86; instr. and prof. Semitic langs., Andover Theol. Sem., 1892-1900; dir. Am. Sch. Archaeology in Jerusalem (leave of absence from Yale), 1900-01; prof. of Semitic languages, Yale U., 1900-32, prof. emeritus since 1932. Chmn. mng. com., Am. Sch. Archaeology in Jerusalem, 1906-18; mem. Egypt Exploration Fund; mem. bd. overseers, Bowdoin Coll.; trustee Am. Schools of Oriental Research. Fellow Am. Acad. Arts and Sciences, Mediaeval Acad. America; mem. Conn. Acad. Arts and Sciences, Soc. Bibl. Lit. and Exegesis, Am. Oriental Soc., Am. Numis. Soc., Archaeol. Inst. America, Deutsche Morgenlandische Gesellschaft, Palestine Oriental Soc. (hon.). Author: The Commercial-Theological Terms in the Koran, 1892; Composition and Historical Value of Ezra-Nehemiah, 1896; The Mohammedan Conquest of Egypt and North Africa (from the Arabic of Ibn Abd al-Hakam), 1901; Ezra Studies, 1910; The Translations Made from the Original Aramaic Gospels, 1912; The Composition and Date of Acts, 1916; Mysticism in Islam (in Sneath's At One with the Invisible), 1921; The Futuh Misr of Ibn 'Abd al-Hakam (Arabic text, etc.), 1922; The Second Isaiah, 1928; Pseudo-Ezekiel and The Original Prophecy, 1930; The Jewish Foundation of Islam, 1933; The Four Gospels, a New Translation 1933; Our Translated Gospels, 1936; Documents of the Primitive Church, 1941; A Brief Introduction to the Apocryphal Literature, 1945; The Lives of the Prophets, 1946. Compiler: Selections from Bokhari, 1906. Co-editor Journal Am. Oriental Society, 1900-17. Contbr. to periodicals. Address: 191 Bishop St., New Haven CT‡

TORREY, MARIAN MARSH, educator; b. Malden, Mass., Dec. 9, 1893; d. Daniel Temple and Anna Louise (Marsh) Torrey; student Northfield Sem., 1909-12; A.B., Brown U., 1916, A.M., 1917; Ph.D., Cornell, 1924. Instr. math. W.Va. U., 1920-23, U. Ill., 1924-25, Goucher Coll., Towson, Md., 1925-27, asst. prof., 1927-32, asso. prof., 1932-42, prof. math., from 1942, asst. to dean, 1937-45. Mem. Am. Math. Soc., Math. Assn. Am., Inst. Math. Statistics, Am. Assn. U. Profs. Home: Towson MD Died Sept. 16, 1971.

TOULMIN, JOHN EDWIN, banker; b. Brookline, Mass., Nov. 1, 1902; s. John Edwin and Alice Munroe (Barbour) T.; ed. Country Day Sch., Choate Sch. and Harvard; m. Rose Cracroft Loveland, Sept. 25, 1926; children—Peter Noyes, Hugh Huidekoper, Paul Routledge; married 2d Virginia Belcher Campbell, Aug. 26, 1950 (div. 1963). With First Nat. Bank of Boston, 1925-67, v.p., 1932-47, sr. v.p., 1947-59, vice chmn. bd., 1959-67; dir. 1st Nat. Bank Boston, First Bank Boston Internat., Boston Overseas Financial Corp., Massanet Corp., Firstbank Financial Corp., MIF Industries, Inc., McGregor-Doniger, Inc., United Fruit Co., Arthur D. Little Co., 1st Small Bus. Investment Corporation of New England, Badger Company, Inc. Member board of trustees Free Hospital for Women. Col. A. U.S., 1942-45, overseas 1943-44. Member Association Reserve City Bankers, Unitarian. Clubs: Harvard (Boston and New York); Dedham (Mass.) Country and Polo, Harvard Varsity; The Country (Brookline, Mass.). Home: Westwood MA Died Apr. 9, 1968; buried Forest Hills Cemetery, Jamaica Plain MA

TOUPS, ROLAND LEON, sugar co. exec.; b. Thibodaux, La., July 25, 1911; s. Leonidas M. and Maude (Peltier) T.; B.S. in Mech. Engring., Ga. Inst. Tech., 1933; m. Gertrude Daigle, Sept. 27, 1935;children—Roland Michael and Leon Henry (twins), Henry Etta. With Godchaux Sugars, Inc., New Orleans, 1933-42; with South Coast Corp., New Orleans, 1945-69, v.p., gen. mgr., 1953-64, pres., 1964-69; dir. Raceland Bank & Trust Co. (La.), La. Agrl. Credit Corp., New Orleans, Gulf South Financial Advisers, Inc., Thibodaux. Past chmn. St. John and Terrebonne parishes Boy Scouts Am., past mem. exec. bd. New Orleans area; past pres. St. Francis Boys Sch. Fathers Club. Houma, La. Served to lt. col. AUS, 1942-45. Named King Sucrose XXVII for La. Sugar Cane Festival, 1968. Registered profl. engr., La. Mem. Sugar Industry Technicians, Am. Sugar Cane Tech. Assn. (past pres.), La. Engring. Soc., Nat. Soc. Profl. Engrs., Houma-Terrebonne C. of C. (bd. dirs.), Lambda Chi Alpha, Pi Tau Sigma, Scabbard and Blade. Home: Houma LA Died May 9, 1969; interred St. Francis de Sales Mausoleum Houma LA

TOUSANT, EMMA SANBORN, lawyer, civic worker; b. Bradford, Vt., Nov. 11, 1890; d. William C. and Abbie D. (Paine) Sanborn; student Bridgewater Normal Sch., 1918-19; LL.B., Boston U., 1924; LL.D (hon.), Albright Coll., 1959; m. John B. Tousant, Dec. 23, 1911 (dec. 1914). Tchr. pub. schs. St. Johnsbury, Vt., 1910-18, Melrose, Mass., 1919-21; admitted to Mass. bar, 1924, pvt. practice, Quincy, 1924-70; instr. Harvard Sch. Pub. Health, 1940-60; treas., dir. General Theol. Library, Boston, 1959-60, President Quincy YMCA, 1961-70. Mem. Mass. Indsl. Accident Bd., 1927-51, chmn., 1937-47, mem. Mass. council Nat. Council Crime and Delinquency. Trustee United Theological Seminary, Dayton, Ohio, Thayer Academy, Braintree, Mass. Mem. Am., Mass., Norfolk County, Quincy bar assns., Internat. Assn. Indsl. Accident Bds. and Comms. (pres. 1943-44), Mass. Women Lawyers Assn. (pres. 1929), Quincy Taxpayers Assn. (pres. 1952-56), Mass. Fedn. Taxpayers Assns. Inc. (dir. 1961-63), Quincy Hist. Soc. (v.p. 1960), Boston U. Alumni of Quincy (v.p. 1959). Mem. council adminstrn. and finance com. Evang. United Brethren Ch. Home: MA Died July 8, 1970.

TOVEN, JOSEPH RICHARD, educator; b. Reynoldsville, Pa., Oct. 1, 1901; s. Frank and Mary (Palaggo) T.; A.B., Pa. State U., 1924; M.A., N.Y.U., 1928; Ph.D., Fordham U., 1943; m. Mary Agnes Burke, June 25, 1929; children—Joseph Richard, Margaret Anne (Mrs. Joseph A. Coleman), Mary Alice (Mrs. John H. Allen). Mem. faculty N.Y.U., 1925-73, prof. Spanish and Portuguese, Washington Sq. Coll., 1960-70, emeritus, 1970-73, chmn. dept., 1960-66, dir. fgn. student center, 1947-61, chmn. adviser Fulbright com., 1949-70, dir. N.Y.U. in Spain, 1958-70; specialist U.S. Office Edn., 1948. Co-founder, past treas., past v.p., dir. Greater N.Y. Council Fgn. Students; mem., adviser Council Evaluation Fgn. Student Credentials. Decorated golden cross Royal Order Phoenix (Greece); commendador de numero Order de Isabel la Catolica (Spain); recipient Fulbright research award to Spain, 1965; Gt. Tchrs. award N.Y.U. Alumni, 1970. Mem. Modern Lang. Assn., Eastern Assn. Deans and Adv. Men (pres. 1956-57), Am. Assn. U. Profs., Nat. Assn. Fgn. Student Adv. (cofounder, past treas., past dir.), Am. Assn. Collegiate Registars and Admissions Officers, Phi Delta Kappa, Phi Mu Delta, Delta Phi Epsilon. Contbr. articles to jours., encys., yearbooks, also chpts. in books. Home: Mount Vernon NY Died Feb. 2, 1973; buried Gate of Heaven Cemetery, Hawthorne NY

TOWER, CARL VERNON, prof. philosophy; b. Dayton, O., Dec. 14, 1869; s. Charles Frederick and Ann Judson (Bisbee) T.; A.B., Brown U., 1893, A.M., 1895; Ph.D., Cornell, 1898; Gottingen U., 1908-9; m. Emma Worman Powell, of Dayton, O., June 10, 1896 (died Apr. 29, 1906); m. 2d, Elizabeth Burke, of Brockville, Ont., Sept. 8, 1908. Instr. philosophy, Brown U., 1895-6; fellow, Sage Sch. Philosophy (Cornell U.), 1896-7; instr. philosophy, U. of Mich., 1898-1900; asst. to president, Clark U., 1900-1; prof. philosophy, Knox Coll., Galesburg, Ill., 1901-2, U. of Vt., 1902-9; asso. prof. philosophy, U. of Mich., 1909-10; actg. prof. philosophy, Trinity Coll., Conn., 1912-13, Ursinus Coll. since 1913. Mem. Am. Philos. Assn., A.A.A.S., Delta Upsilon. Republican. Baptist. Contbr. to Philos. Rev., and Jour. of Philosophy, Psychology and Scientific Methods. Address: Collegeville PA‡

TOWER, WALTER SHELDON, b. West Bridgewater, Mass., July 26, 1881; s. Lorenzo A. and Mary S. (Thompson) T.; A.B., Harvard, 1903, A.M., 1904; Ph.D., U. of Pa., 1906; m. Lurena L. Wilson, Dec. 27, 1906 (dec. Aug. 1917); children—Walter Sheldon, James W.; m. 2d, Edith Florence Jones, Mar. 7, 1919; 1 son, Donald B. Taught econ. and comml. geography Wharton Sch., U. Pa., 1906-11; prof. econ. geography, U. of Chicago, 1911-17; trade expert U.S. Shipping Bd., 1918-19; trade adviser Consolidated Steel Corp., New York, 1919-21; commercial attache American Embassy, London, England, 1921-14; with Bethlehem Steel Corp., 1924-33; exec. sec. Am. Iron and Steel Inst., 1933-40; pres., 1940-52; retired 1952, Republican. Home: Carmel CA Died Feb. 5, 1969.

TOWER, WILLIAM LAWRENCE, zoologist; b. Halifax, Mass., Dec. 22, 1872; s. Lorenzo Augustus and Mary Sheldon (Thompson) T.; Lawrence Scientific Sch. (Harvard), 1893-96; Grad. Sch., Harvard, 1898-1900; S.B., U. of Chicago, 1902; m. Lucia Kieve, of Bloomington, Ill., Aug. 21, 1898. Prof. zoology, Antioch Coll., 1900-—; asst. in embryology, 1901-3, asso., 1903-4, instr., 1904-7, asst. prof., 1907-11, asso. prof., 1911-—, U. of Chicago. Fellow A.A.A.S.; mem. Am. Soc. Zoologists, Am. Soc. Naturalists, etc. Republican. Club: Quadrangle. Home: 5461 Lexington Av., Chicago IL‡

TOWERS, ALBERT GAREY, govt. official; b. Caroline Co., Md., Aug. 1, 1873; s. William Francis and Mary Ann (Garey) T.; student U. of Md., 1890-92; m. Mary Bernard, Jan. 31, 1900; children—Albert Garey, Henrietta Josephine (Mrs. William D. Williams), Mary Bernard (Mrs. Charles H. Symington), Priscilla Steele. Admitted to Md. bar, 1884; state's atty., Caroline Co., Md., 1899-1903; pres. Peoples Bank, Denton, Md., 1910-19; pres. Title Guarantee and Trust Co., Baltimore, 1919-32, Mortgage Guarantee Co., 1919-32; dir. and mem. exec. com., Fidelity and Deposit Co. of Md., 1926-33; dir. Fidelity Trust Co., 1927-33, Phila., Baltimore and Washington R.R. Co. since 1926; asst. to dir. Fed. Deposit Ins. Corp., since 1936. Engaged in civic and polit activities: elector at large for Md., Presdl. campaign, 1908; U.S. Naval Officer of Customs, Port of Baltimore, 1910-13; Md. del. Rep. nat. conv., 1912; chmn. speakers com. for Md., Liberty Loan drives, World War I; chmn. Pub. Service Commn. Md., 1914-19; chmn. bd. supervisor City Charities, Baltimore, 1923-34; president commissioners of finance, Baltimore, 1923-38. Republican. Protestant Episcopal (vestryman). Home: Cambridge Arms Apartments, Baltimore 18 MD Office: National Press Building, Washington 4 DC‡

TOWLER, THOMAS WILLARD, pub. rep.; b. Chgo., Aug. 20, 1891; s. Edward Thomas and Elizabeth Hadley (Davis) T.; A.B., Dartmouth, 1913; m. Lois Breckenridge, Apr. 27, 1918. Salesman The Knapp Co., N.Y.C., 1913-15; advt. mgr. Westinghouse, Church, Kerr & Co., 1915-17, 19-20, Dwight P. Robinson & Co., 1920-22; advt. rep. Cosmopolitan mag., Chgo., 1922-27; account exec. Ruthrauff & Ryan, N.Y.C., 1927-28; advt. mgr. United Engrs. & Constructors, 1927-33, Am. Architect mag., 1933-38; pub., v.p. Town and Country mag., N.Y.C., 1938-66; pub. rep. Men's Bazaar, also Am. rep. Brit. Bazaar, German Bazaarette, 1966-68; pres. Magazine Space Consultants, 1968-72. Served as 1st lt. C.W.S., U.S. Army, 1918. Mem. Beta Theta Pi. Presbyn. Clubs: University, Dartmouth (N.Y.C.); Baltusrol Golf (Springfield, N.J.). Home: Summit NJ Died June 22, 1972; buried Fairview Cemetery, Westfield NJ

TOWNE, WILLIAM ELMER, editor, author; b. Walpole, N.H., Nov. 20, 1874; s. Salem and E. J. (Carpenter) T.; ed. pub. schs.; m. Elizabeth Struble, May 26, 1900. Dir. The Elizabeth Towne Co., Inc.; joint editor Nautilus, magazine of New Thought, 1900-23, editor since 1923. Author: Hurry-Worry Cured, 1908; Health and Power from Within, 1910; The Way to Perfect Healing, 1911; Nature Notes at Netop, 1919. Hon. pres. Internat. New Thought Alliance. Home: Holyoke MA‡

TOWNSEND, OLIVER HENRY, govt. ofcl.; b. Elyria, O., Jan. 29, 1917; s. Henry and Agnes (Taylor) T.; A., Ohio Wesleyan U., 1939; M.A., U. Cin., 1941; m. Anna Jeanette Sheppard, Feb. 2, 1941. Pub. adminstrn.

›ecialist U.S. Govt. Agys., Washington, 1941-43, 7-51; asst. to chmn. U.S. AEC, Washington, 1951-53; ›c. Atomic Indsl. Forum, N.Y.C., 1953-59; dir. N.Y. ›tate Office of Atomic and Space Devel. N.Y.C., 959-68; mem. U.S. AEC com. of state ofcls., adv. com. n isotopes devel., adv. com. on tech. information. ›hmn., mem. N.Y. State Atomic and Space)evel-Authority, 1962-69. Served from ensign to lt., ›SNR, 1943-47, PTO. Mem. Council on Fgn. ›elations, Phi Delta Theta, Omicron Delta Kappa. ›resbyn. Club: Coveleigh. Author articles in field. ›ome: Scarsdale NY Died Dec. 2, 1969; interred Elyria)H

›OWNSEND, OSCAR, railroad official; b. Cleveland, ›., Apr. 15, 1874; s. Oscar and Elizabeth (Martin) T.; ›d. University Sch., Cleveland; m. Margaret Chandler, ›pr. 17, 1906; 1 dau., Mary Elizabeth. Successively ›affic freight agt., C.P. Ry., Pittsburgh; same, ›.,M.&St.P. Ry., Pittsburgh; then with C.G.W. Ry., as ›en. agt., Pittsburgh, asst. gen. freight agt., St. Paul, ›inn., gen. freight agt., Chicago, traffic mgr., and now ›.p. Republican. Conglist. Clubs: Union League, ›hicago Traffic, Westmoreland Country; Detroit ›raffic; Minneapolis Traffic. Home: 1337 Ashland Av., ›Vilmette IL Office: 309 W. Jackson Blvd., Chicago ›L*‡

›OWNSEND, WAYNE LASALLE, lawyer, ct. ofcl.; b. ›ook, Neb., Dec. 7, 1896; s. Adelbert and Anna (Cook) ›.; B.A., U. of Neb., 1918; LL.B., Yale, 1928, J.S.D., ›929; married to Dorothy Pierce, June 7, 1922; 1 ›aughter, Nancy (Mrs. Marvin E. Pyle). Assistant ›ashier Minatare (Nebraska) Bank, 1920-22; cashier ›tate Bank of Minatare, 1922-26; instr. law, Yale Sch. ›f Law, 1929-31; visiting prof. law, Tulane U., 1931-32; ›rof. law, Western Reserve U., 1932-45; asso. with firm ›hompson, Hine and Flory, Cleveland, 1943-45; dean ›ch. of law and prof. law, Washington U., 1945-51; ›istinguished service professor of law, 1951-65; Legion ›ex Distinguished visiting professor, University of ›outhern California, 1959-60. Labor arbitrator, Cleve. ›nd St. Louis since 1944; referee court of common pleas,)hio, 1942; judge, Magistrate Ct. of Jefferson County, ›o., 1963-65; commr. St. Louis Ct. of Appeals, St. ›ouis, 1965-69. Served as second lt., F.A., U.S.A., 1918. ›rustee and vice pres. bd., Cleveland Pub. Library, ›942-45; chmn. McBride Lecture Foundation, ›leveland, 1938-45; trustee Great Lakes Hist. Soc., ›leveland; pres. St. Louis Artists Guild, 1957-58, ›ustee, 1958-69. Compliance Commr., W.P.B., ›leveland, 1942-44. Fellow Am. Bar Foundation; ›ember Neb., Ohio, Mo. bars, International Society ›linical Laboratory Technologists (chairman ›ccrediting commission), Phi Beta Kappa, Phi Alpha ›elta, Alpha Theta Chi, Chi Phi, Sigma Delta Chi. ›uthor and editor: Townsend's Cases and Other Select ›aterials on the Law of Banking, 1938; Townsend's)hio Corporation Law, 1961. Home: Dittmer MO also ›ook NE Died Apr. 1969.

›OWNSLEY, LOUIS, Dem. nat. committeeman; b.)ttawa, Kan., Aug. 2, 1877; s. William and Martha Lilly ›Thurber) T.; m. Martha G. Loker, of St. Louis, Mo.,)ec. 20, 1905. Chief operator dredges, Panama Canal. ›em. Dem. Nat. Com. for Canal Zone since 1928. Sec. ›anama Canal Dredge Men (labor union); dist. ›rganizer; Canal Zone, for Am. Fed. Labor several yrs. ›resbyn. Home: Balboa CZ‡

›OZERE, FREDERIC, actor; b. Brookline, Mass., ›une 19, 1901; s. Frederick Richard and Florence ›meline Tozere; ed. Brookline, Mass., and N.Y.C.; ›tudent Alexis Kosloff, Beverly Sitgreaves, Yeatman ›riffiths; m. Mary Brady, January 9, 1927 (dec. May ›968). Made his New York debut with Russian Ballet in ›ole of Shah in Scheherazade and as Le Jeune Homme ›n Le Dieu Bleu, 1919; with Morgan Dancers, 1920, ›tepping Stones, 1924-26 Criss Cross, 1927; actor on ›egitimate stage, 1927-72; with stock cos. in various ›rge eastern cities of U.S., 1927-30; roles in N.Y. ›rodns.; Stepping Sisters, Journey's End, 1930; Betty Be ›areful, 1931; Blue Monday, 1932; Julius Caesar, 1933; ›urder' in the Cathedral, Road to Paradise, 1936; It ›an't Happen Here, The Sun and I, Red Harvest, A ›ero Is Born, As you Like It, 1937; Shoemaker's ›oliday, A Doll's House, Mme. Capet, Waltz in ›oosestep, Glorious Morning, 1938; Key Largo, 1939; ›ourney to Jerusalem, 1940; Garbielle, Trojan Women, ›uckoos on the Hearth, 1941; Solitaire, Watch on the ›hine 1942; Outrageous Fortune, 1943; Stovepipe Hat, ›he Letter (in Can.), Personal Appearance (in Chgo.), ›n Bed We Cry, 1944; Signature, The Rich Full Life,)edipus Rex, 1945; Salute to Murder 1946; Miracle in ›he Mountains, 1947; Tower Beyond Tragedy, 1950; ›he King of Friday's Men, First Lady, 1952; Josephine, ›953; Thieves' Paradise, 1956; St. Joan, 1956; appeared ›n Happy Town, 1959; Caliqula, 1960; Daughter of ›ilence, 1961; A Majority of One, 1961; The Advocate, ›n 1962; Hidden stranger, in 1963; A Perfect Frenzy and ›he Peacock Season, 1964; Teahouse of the August ›oon, 1964; Gigi, 1965; Man Who Came to Dinner, ›965; A Majority of One, 1965; A Case of Libel in 1966; ›he Sorrows of Frederick, in 1967; Little Boxes 1969; ›ostcards, 1970; Wars of the Roses, 1970; also appeared ›n numerous motion pictures, 1939-72, including, ›eturn of October, Live Today for Tomorrow, Iron Curtain, An Act of Murder, Madame Bovary, Father Was A Bachelor; on numerous TV programs, including Maugham Playhouse, Kraft Playhouse, Montgomery Presents, Studio One, Treasury Men, Broadway TV. Theatre, You Are There, Hallmark, Mem. Actors Equity Assn. (council 1944-49, 1952-57, 59-69), A.F.T.R.A. (mem. nat. and local bds.), Screen Actors Guild. Address: New York City NY Died Aug. 3, 1972.

TRABUE, MARION REX, b. near Kokomo, Ind., Apr. 30, 1890; s. Otto A. and Mary Emma (Long) T.; student DePauw U., 1907-08; A.B., Northwestern U., 1911; A.M., Columbia, 1914, Ph.D., 1915; m. Emma Wilkie Small, Apr. 20, 1913; children—Bruce McDougal, Douglas Small. Prin. high sch., Fairbury, Ill., 1911-12, Hinsdale, Ill., 1912-13; with Teacher's Coll. (Columbia), 1913-22, as research scholar, student asst., instr. and asst. prof. edn., 1917-22, dir. Bur. Ednl. Service, 1919-22; prof. ednl. administration, U. of N.C., 1922-37, dir. Bur. Ednl. Research, 1923-37, and dir. consolidated univ. div. of edn., 1935-37; dean Sch. of Edn. and dir. of summer sessions, Pa. State Univ., 1937-56; prof. higher edn. University of Kentucky, 1956-72; exec. sec. com. on diagnosis and training Employment Stabilization Research Inst., U. of Minn., 1931-33. Head of Diagnosis Div. of the Adjustment Service, N.Y. City, 1933; mem. Federal Council of U.S. Employment Service, 1934-39, tech. dir. occupational research, 1934-36; mem. staff Am. Youth Commn., Washington, 1936. Lt. and capt., psychol. examiner and psychologist, U.S. Army, 1917-18. Chmn. Emergency Subcom. on Learning and Training, Nat. Research Council, 1941-43. Mem. nat., state and local scientific and profl. orgns. and assns., has served as pres. or other exec. of several. Author or co-author of several books; latest publication: Language Arts for Boys and Girls series, 1941. Home: Lexington KY Died Jan. 1972.

TRACY, GEORGE ALLISON, association executive; b. Milw., May 21, 1907; s. Edward Lawrence and Georgia (Allison) T.; student Marquette U., 1925-26, U. Wis., 1926-27; m. Harriett Bock, Apr. 19, 1930; children—Suzanne (Mrs. W. J. Ryan), Peter. With The Milw. Sentinel, 1927-63, asst. city editor, 1932-36, city editor, 1936-52, mng. editor, 1952-62, asso. mng. editor, 1962-63; dir. publicity Daytona Beach Area C. of C., 1964-72. Mem. Sigma Delta Chi. Clubs: Daytona Beach (Fla.) Advertising: Milwaukee Press. Home: Daytona Beach FL Died Oct. 4, 1971; buried Bellevue Meml. Park, Daytona Beach FL

TRACY, (WILLIAM) LEE, actor; b. Atlanta, Apr. 14, 1898; s. William Lindsey and Ray (Griffith) T.; student Union Coll., Schenectady, N.Y., 1917-18; m. Helen Thomas, July 20, 1938. Began as actor, 1919; starred in play, Broadway, in N.Y.C., 1926-27, Front Page, 1928; entered motion pictures, 1928; returned to stage for plays Oh Promise Me, Louder Please, 1930; starred in various talking pictures under contract to Paramount Corp.; now under contract to RKO Radio Pictures; appeared in play The Gag Stays In, New York, 1938; Every Man for Himself, 1940; Idiots Delight, London, 1938; The Traitor, N.Y.C., 1948; Mr. Barry's Etchings, New York City, 1949; Caine Mutiny Court Martial, Sydney, Australia, 1955; The Best Man, New York City, 1960-61; Minor Miracle, 1965; starred in the TV series Martin Kane, N.B.C., 1952-53. Recent pictures: Betrayal from the East, 1945; High Tide, 1947; The Best Man, 1965. Served as 2d lt. inf., AUS, World War I; commd. 1st lt., U.S. Army, 1942; advanced to capt.; with Office of Provost Marshal Gen., War Dept., Washington. Presbyn. Clubs: Green Room (New York); Masquer's (Hollywood). Home: Pacific Palisades CA Died Oct. 18, 1968; buried Evergreen Cemetery, Shavertown PA

TRAEGER, CORNELIUS HORACE, physician; b. St. Louis, Aug. 14, 1896; s. Victor and Selma (Goetz) T.; B.A., Columbia, 1923, M.D., 1927; m. Janet Reisner, July 8, 1962; 1 son, Charles. Intern, Roosevelt Hosp., N.Y.C., 1927-29, clin. asst., 1929-31, cons. attending physician internal medicine and arthritis, chief arthritis clinic, 1940-64, cons., 1964-68; co-chief rheumatic diseases Hosp. Spl. Surgery, N.Y.C., 1930-64, chief emeritus, 1964-68; asst. prof. clin. medicine Cornell U., 1954-64; exec. med. dir. N.Y. Infirmary, 1962-64. Med. dir. Nat. Multiple Sclerosis Soc., 1948-55; mem. adv. council NIH Neurol. Diseases and Blindness, 1950-54, NIH Arthritis and Metabolic Diseases, 1962-66, regional med. programs for heart, cancer and stroke, 1965-68; spl. cons. to Surgeon Gen., USPHS, 1954-57, 62-68. Bd. govs. Arthritis Found., also N.Y. chpt. Recipient Floyd B. Odlum award, 1965. Fellow American College Physicians (life), N.Y. Acad. Medicine, N.Y. Acad. Sci., Am. Acad. Neurology; mem. WHO, Am. Rheumatism Assn., Arthritis and Rheumatism Foundation (all co-founder). Am. Geriatric Soc., Assn. Am. Med. Colls., A.M.A., N.Y. State, N.Y. County med. socs., A.A.A.S., Am. Pub. Health Assn., Assn. Mil. Surgeons, Assn. Am. Physicians and Surgeons, Assn. Research Nervous and Mental Diseases. Contbr. articles to med. jours. Home: New York City NY Died Sept. 24, 1968.

TRAIN, HAROLD CECIL, naval officer; b. Kansas City, Mo., Oct. 15, 1887; s. Harry D. and Dora (Langdon) T.; grad. U.S. Naval Acad., 1909; m. May Philipps, May 25, 1916; children—Marian Langdon (wife of Capt. Amos T. Hathaway, USN) (dec.), Harriett Cecil (widow of Lt. Comdr. David S. Wilson, USN, dec.), Harry D., II, Jane Bullen (Mrs. John R. Flynn). Commd. ensign, U.S.N., 1911, and advanced through the grades to rear adm., 1942; exec. officer, U.S.S. Siboney, in transport of troops to Europe, World War I; comd. U.S.S. Borie and U.S.S. Parrott, Asiatic Fleet, also fleet operations officer and aide on staff comdr. in chief Asiatic Fleet, 1924-26; fleet communications officer, staff comdr. in chief, Battle Fleet, 1930-31; tactical officer and aide on staff comdr. in chief U.S. Fleet 1931-32; exec. officer U.S.S. Mississippi, also comd. U.S.S. Vestal, 1935-37; asst. dir. officer personnel, 1937-38, dir., 1938-40; comd. U.S.S. Arizona, 1940-41; chief of staff to comdr. Battle Force, 1941-42, with additional duty as asst. chief of staff comdr. in chief Pacific Fleet, Jan.-Mar. 1942; dir. Naval Intelligence, 1942-43; comdt. 15th Naval Dist., comdr. Panama Sea Frontier, and comdr. Southeast Pacific Force, 1943-44; sr. naval mem. Joint Postwar Com., Joint Chiefs of Staff, Washington, 1944-46, retired. Member American delegations to 3d, 5th and 6th Preparatory Commissions for Reduction and Limitations of Armaments, Geneva; mem. Am. delegation Three Power Naval Conf., Geneva, 1927, London Naval Conf., 1930. One of U.S. reps. Dumbarton Oaks Conf., Washington, D.C., 1944; U.S. naval adviser Conf. Problems War and Peace, Mexico City, 1945; a U.S. naval adviser United Nations Conf. on Internat. Orgn., San Francisco, Calif., 1945. Naval aide to President-elect Herbert Hoover on trip through Central and So. America, 1928-29. Decorations: Legion of Merit with Oak Leaf Cluster, Commendation Ribbon, Nicaraguan Campaign, 1912, Mexican Service, Victory with transport clasp, Am. Defense with fleet clasp, Asiatic-Pacific Area and Am. Area medals (U.S.), World War II, Abdon Calderon (Ecuador), Mil. Order Boyaca (Colombia), Mil. Order Merit (Chile), Mil. Order Vasco Nunez de Balboa (Panama), Mil. Order Ayacucho (Peru), Polonia Restituta (Poland). Clubs: Army-Navy Country (Arlington, Va.); Army-Navy (Washington); Columbia Country (Chevy Chase). Home: Washington DC Died Sept. 7, 1968; buried Naval Acad. Cemetery, Annapolis MD

TRAINER, MAURICE NEWLIN, business exec.; born Trainer, Pa., Jan. 7, 1899; s. William E. and Eliza A. (Irving) T.; B.S. in E.E., U. of Pa., 1910; m. Roberta S. Knowles, Dec. 18, 1915; children—Robert S., Georgia L. Vice pres. Am. Malleables Co., 1926-27; v.p. Am. Brake Materials Co., 1927; asst. v.p. Am. Brake Shoe & Foundry Co., N.Y. City, 1928, v.p. 1933-43, 1st vice pres., 1943-50, dir. from 1944; pres. Brake Shoe and Castings Div. of Am. Brake Shoe &Foundry Co., 1938-50; pres. Am. Brake Shoe Co., 1950-54, vice chmn. bd., from 1954; chmn. bd. Dominion Brake Shoe Co., Ltd.; trustee East River Savings Bank; mem. adv. bd. 46th St. br. Chemical Corn Exchange Bank. Mem. Bd. Edn., East Orange, N.J. Clubs: Chicago (Chgo.); Cloud, University (N.Y.C.); Baltusrol Golf; Pine Valley Golf. Home: East Orange NJ Died Sept. 1969.

TRAMMELL, NILES, business cons.; b. Marietta, Ga., July 6, 1894; s. William and Bessie (Niles) T.; ed. Sewanee (Tenn.) Mil. Acad., 1912-15; Univ. of the South, 1915-17; LL.D., DePauw Univ., 1942; married Elizabeth Huff, Nov. 14, 1923 (divorced, 1945); married 2d, Cleo Murphy Black, April 7, 1945 (dec. 1971). Comml. rep. traffic dept. RCA, San Francisco, Mar. 1923, transferred to Seattle, May 1923; dist. mgr. Pacific Northwest, Radiomarine Corp., Seattle, 1924; asst. sales mgr. Pacific div. RCA, 1925; joined sales staff NBC, Chgo., 1928, mgr. then v.p. in charge Central div., Chicago, 1928-29, exec. v.p., NBC, 1939, pres., 1940-49, chmn. bd., 1949-53; pres., gen. mgr. Biscayne TV Corp., Miami, Fla., 1953-62; gen. bus. cons., Miami, 1962-73. Served as 2d lt. 36th Inf., 12th Div., U.S. Army, 1917; 1st lt., 1918; staff officer under Maj. Gen. Charles G. Morton, Presidio, San Francisco, until Mar. 1923. Mem. Kappa Alpha. Episcopalian. Clubs: University, Links Golf, Twenty-Nine, and River (New York City); Chicago (Chicago); Miami, LaGorce Country, and Indian Creek Country, Bath (Miami); National Golf; Links, South Hampton; Lake Placid; Key Largo Anglers. Home: Miami Beach FL Died Mar. 28, 1973; buried Woodlawn Mausoleum, Miami FL

TRANER, FREDRICK W., prof. edn.; b. Rockford, Ill., Mar. 20, 1886; s. Nels Per and Sophia (Samuelson) T.; A.B., Beloit (Wis.) Coll., 1908; A.M., U. of Calif., 1920, Ph.D., 1930; m. Carrie N. Anderson, Aug. 30, 1911 (died Oct. 26, 1938); children—Margaret Carolyn, Helen Elizabeth, Barbara Jean, Alice Martha, Patricia Marie. Teacher high sch., Lancaster, Wis., 1908-09, supt. schs., 1904-14; instr. elementary edn., U. of Nev., 1915-18, asst. prof. edn., 1918-20, asso. prof., 1920-24, prof., 1924-56, head of dept. secondary edn., 1931-56, dean Sch. of Edn., 1937-56, dir. summer session, 1925-39. Member N.E.A., Nev. State Edn. Assn. (pres. 1936-38), Dept. of Secondary Sch. Prins. of N.E.A., Nat. Soc. Study of Edn., Am. Assn. Univ. Profs. Am. Assn. School Adminstrs., Phi Beta Kappa, Phi Delta Kappa. Republican. Mason. Home: Reno NV Died Dec. 31, 1963; buried Mountain View Cemetery, Reno NV

TRANSEAU, EDGAR NELSON, botanist; b. Williamsport, Pa., October 21, 1875; s. Samuel and Martha Edith (Zimmerman) T.; A.B., Franklin and Marshall Coll., Lancaster, Pa., 1897; studied Marine Lab., Brooklyn Inst. Arts and Sciences, summer 1899; Univ. of Chicago, 1900-01; Ph.D., U. of Michigan, 1904; honorary Sc.D., Franklin and Marshall College, 1941, Ohio State University, 1949; married Gertrude Hastings (M.D.), August 23, 1906; 1 daughter, Elizabeth Hastings (Mrs. August Mahr). Prof. biology, Alma Coll., 1904-06; investigator Sta. for Experimental Evolution, at Cold Spring Harbor, L.I., N.Y., 1906-07; prof. botany, State Teachers Coll., Charleston, Ill., 1907-15; prof. plant physiology and ecology, Ohio State Univ., 1915-46, chairman of department, 1918-46, retired; plant ecologist in Europe, for U.S. Bur. Entomology, 1927; collaborator Central States Forestry Expt. Station, 1929-32. Fellow A.A.A.S.; mem. Botanical Soc. of America (pres. 1940), Assn. Am. Geographers, Ecol. Soc. America (pres. 1924), Phycological Society of America (president 1951), American Geographic Soc., Ohio Acad. Sciences (pres. 1924) Phi Beta Kappa, Sigma Xi, Phi Kappa Sigma. Author: Science of Plant Life, 1919; General Botany, 1923; (with H. C. Sampson) Laboratory Manual in General Botany, 1923; (with Sampson and Tiffany) Work Book in General Botany, 1934; Textbook of Botany (with Sampson and Tiffany), 1939; The Zygnemataceae, 1951. Contbr. to bot. jours. Home: 2079 W. 5th Av., Columbus OH‡

TRANT, JAMES BUCHANAN, coll. dean; b. Pitts., Fla., Oct. 15, 1890; s. Thomas Franklin and Mary Ann (Isler) T.; student Campbell Business Inst., Dothan, Ala., 1911-12; A.B., Howard Coll., Birmingham, Ala., 1920; A.M., Princeton U., 1921; Ph.D., U. of Ill., 1925; m. Pauline Willoughby, June 9, 1924; 1 dau., Jean. Acting prof. of econ. and history, Howard Coll., 1921-22; instr. in economics, U. of Ill., 1922-25; asst. prof. of economics, U. of Tex., 1925-26, asso. prof. of business adminstrn., 1926-28; prof. of banking and dean Coll. of Commerce, La. State U., 1928-56, dean emeritus, 1956-70. Vice pres. Guaranty Income Life Ins. Co., 1957-70. Chmn. compliance bd., President's Re-employment Agreement, Baton Rouge; mem. com. on study of business edn., Am. Assn. of Collegiate Schs. of Bus., 1933-39; also mem. exec. com., 1939-42; consultant Nat. Resources Planning Bd. for Southwestern Dist., La., Ark., Tex., and Okla.; mem. exec. com. in charge of program La. Coll. Conf., Mar. 1939 and 1940; chmn. Selective Service Board No. 2, East Baton Rouge, Parish, La.; mem. Econ. Development Com. of La. (chmn. subcom. on edn., mem. subcom. on unemployment, ins. and social security, 1943-44; vice chmn. and chmn. subcom. on research, 1944-46). Dir. American Legion High School Oratorical Contest for Louisiana, 1944-46; mem. Research Com., Gulf Southwest Indsl. and Agrl. Conf., 1945-47; vice chmn. bd., Dept. of Commerce and Industry, chmn. subcom. on Ednl. Research and Finance, 1946-48; bd. trustees So. Assn. Sci. and Industry, 1947-48; chmn. Baton Rouge chpt. A.R.C., 1948-49; bd. dirs. C. of C., 1949-51; exec. com. Economists Nat. Com. on Monatary Policy since 1951. Served as pvt., sergeant and lt., San. Corps, U.S. Army, 1917-18. Pres. Legionnaire-Schoolmasters Club, La. Dept. American Legion, 1942-43. Member Mil. Order World War (state commander 1947-48), American Econ. Assn., Royal Econ. Society, Southern Econ. Assn., Southwestern Social Science Assn. (chmn. business adminstrn. sec. 1930-31; v.p. 1936-37, pres. 1937-38), Southern Econ. Assn. (pres. 1932-33), Phi Kappa Phi, Pi Kappa, Tau, Beta Gamma Sigma (exec. com. 1939-42), Pi Gamma Mu (Nat. Adv. Council), Beta Nu Kappa. Democrat. Baptist. Mason (K.T.). Club: Rotary (Baton Rouge). Author: Bank Administration, 1931. Contbr. to jours. Mem. editorial advisory bd. Southwestern Social Science Quarterly, 1930-32. Home: Baton Rouge LA Died Feb. 3, 1970; buried Green Oaks Cemetery Baton Rouge LA

TRATMAN, EDWARD ERNEST RUSSELL, editor; b. Bristol, Eng.; ed. private schs., studied engring. as asst. under Edward Wilson, London, and in ry. and other practice; came to U.S., 1884; m. Florence R. Kirkwood, 1897. Was special agt. U.S. Govt. to report on metal and wooden ry. ties. For many years was editor Engineering News-Record. Mem. Am. Soc. C.E., Am. Inst. Mining Engrs., Am. Ry. Engring. Assn., Internat. Tramways Union, etc. Received Norman medal, Am. Soc. C.E., for paper on English Railway Track, 1888. Contbr. numerous papers on ry. engring., article, Railways," Johnson's Universal Cyclopaedia, etc. Author: Railway Track and Track Work, 1908-25; Specifications and Standards for Public Works Engineering, 1933; Railway Car-Ferries, 1936-40. Reports on Metal and Wooden Railway Ties and Preservation of Ties, 1890, 1894. Home: Wheaton IL‡

TRAUBEL, HELEN, opera and concert singer; b. St. Louis, Mo.; d. Otto and Clara (Stuhr) Traubel; educated at St. Louis High Sch.; hon. Mus.D. U. So. Cal., 1947, U. Mo.; m. William L. Bass. Orchestral debut with St. Louis Symphony; opera debut with Met. Opera Assn., N.Y.C., Dec. 28, 1939; first N.Y. recital and first N.Y. orch. engagement (with N.Y. Philharmonic under Barbirolli), 1939; prin. Wagnerian soprano Met. Opera Assn., 1939-53; and made first transcontinental concert tour, U.S. and Can., season 1940-41; followed by annual coast-to-coast tours; appeared at Teatro Colon in Buenos Aires, summer 1943; tour Japan, Manila, India, Korea, etc., 1952; has made RCA Victor and Columbia recordings; also coast-to-coast broadcasts for the Ford Motor Co., Bell Telephone Co., Metropolitan Opera, Met. Life. Ins. Co., and others; TV guest appearances; various night club appearances; starred in film Deep in My Heart, 1954; soloist with NBC Orch. under Toscanini, St. Louis Symphony, Phila. Orch., etc. Presented award for most outstanding performance of year by N.Y. Tau Alpha chapter of Mu Phi Epsilon, 1939, 42; citation of merit Nat. Assn. Am. Composers and Conductors; Key woman of year Federated Charities; three times Woman of Year in music A.P. First Am. born and entirely Am. trained singer to appear as Isolde and 3 Brunnhildes for Met. Opera (season 1942-43). Author: The Ptomaine Canary; the Metropolitan Opera Murders, 1951; St. Louis Woman (autobiography), 1958. Home: Santa Monica CA Died July 29, 1972.

TRAUDT, BERNARD G., clergyman; b. Milwaukee, Wis., Aug. 29, 1876; s. John and Mary Anne (Dienstberger) T.; ed. St. Francis (Wis.) Sem., 1890-99, B.A., M.A., 1922. Ordained priest R.C. Ch., 1899, asst. St. Michael's Ch., Milwaukee, 1899-1901; apptd. sec. to Archbishop Katzer, 1901, and continued as sec. to Archbishop Messmer; apptd. chancellor, 1908; given title of monsignor by Pope Benedict XV, 1921; vicar gen. to Archbishop Messmer, 1922-30, apostolic administrator of Diocese of Milwaukee, Aug. 1930-Nov. 1930, vicar gen. to Archbishop Stritch and chaplain Mount Mary Coll., 1931-34; pastor St. Ann Parish, Milwaukee, since Mar. 1934; apptd. apostolic administrator, Mar. 1940, vicar gen. to Archbishop Kiley, Mar. 1941. Home: 2474 N. 37th St., Milwaukee WI*‡

TRAUTMANN, WILLIAM EMIL, lawyer; b. at Caseyville, Ill., Aug. 16, 1872; s. Frederick and Dorothea (Deck) T.; ed. McKendree Coll., Lebanon, Ill., LL.B., Law Dept. 1893, B.S., Lit. Department, 1895, and M.S., 1898; m. Evelyn L. Kinne, of Bloomington, Ill., Nov. 25, 1910. Began practice, East St. Louis, Ill., 1897; mem. Ill. Ho. of Rep., 4 terms, 1898-06; apptd. U.S. atty. for Eastern Dist. of Ill., by Pres. Roosevelt, May 27, 1905, reapptd. by Pres. Taft, Feb. 22, 1910; judge Ill. Ct. of Claims, 1916-17; asst. atty. gen. of Ill. since Jan. 15, 1917; Republican and Laboratory Exercises in Physical Geography, 1905; Methods of Attracting Birds, 1906; Bird Friends, 1916; The Teaching of Science in the Elementary School, 1918; Science of Home and Community, 1919. Address: Mankato MN

TRAVEN, B., author; m. Rosa; children—Elena, Maria. Works include: The Death Ship: The Story of an American Soldier, 1934; The Treasure of the Sierra Madre, 1934; The Carreta, 1935; The Bridge in the Jungle, 1938; General from the Jungle; Rosa Blanca; The Rebellion of the Hanged, 1952; The Night Visitor and other stories, 1966. Home: Mexico City Mexico Died Mar. 1969.*

TRAVIS, IRA DUDLEY, mining exec.; b. Syracuse, N.Y., Oct. 20. 1858; s. John Lewis and Susan Ann (Spinning) T.; B.Sc., Albion Coll., 1889; A.M., U. of Mich., 1894, Ph.D., 1897; m. Harriet M. Doolittle, Sept. 27, 1893; teacher and high sch. prin. in Wis., 1890-93, and Utah, 1898-1917; entered mining industry, 1900; pioneered in development of Tintic Standard Mining Co., of which is now pres.; also pres. Eureka Standard Consol. Mining Co., Colo. Consol. Mines Co., Dividend Trading Co., Eureka Lily Consol., North Beck Mining Co., Sioux Mines Co., South Standard Mining Co., Pinyon Queen Mining Co., Copper Exploration Mining Co., Victoria Gold Mining Co. Republican. Mason. Contbr. to Yale Review and other mags.; author of The Clayton-Bulwer Treaty," in the Library of Congress. Home: 1326 3d Av. Office: Walker Bank Bldg., Salt Lake City UT‡

TRAVIS, WESLEY ELGIN, business exec.; b. Hamilton, Nev., July 22, 1870; s. E.J. and Hannah P. (Dahl) T.; student Riverview Mil. Acad., Harvard; m. Hazel McSherry Pettigrew, June 23, 1926. Pres., gen. mgr. Ida.-Nev.-Cal. State Co., 1894; pres. Cal. Taxicab Co., 1909, Cal. Transit Co., 1920; pres., chmn. exec. com. Pacific Greyhound Lines since 1933; dir. Greyhound Corp., Chgo.; pres., dir. Cal. Parlor Car Tours, Atlantic Greyhound Lines, Stockton Electric R.R., Fresno City Lines, San Jose & Santa Clara R.R., Pacific City Lines, San Jose City Lines, Inc. Clubs: Harvard (N.Y.C.); Chicago (Chgo.); Jonathan (L.A.); Family, Olympic, Golf (S.F.); Athens Athletic, Claremount Country (Oakland, Cal.). Home: 320 El Cerrito, Piedmont, Cal. Office: 201 Pine St., San Francisco 6‡

TRAWICK, ARCADIUS MCSWAIN, clergyman, educator; b. Henry County, Tenn., Nov. 21, 1869; s. Andrew Marcus and Martha (McSwain) T.; student Southwestern Presbyn. U., Clarksville, Tenn.; B.A., Vanderbilt, 1894, B.D., 1897; studied Columbia U. and Sch. of Philanthropy, New York; m. Emma Shapard, Sept. 7, 1897 (died Dec. 29, 1905); 1 dau., Martha; m 2d, Mary Maude Wilder, June 8, 1909;children—Mar Louisa, Sarah Catherine. Ordained ministry M.E. Ch S., 1892; pastor East End, Nashville, Tenn., 1892-96 Shelbyville, Tenn., 1897-99, Wifield Memorial, Littl Rock, Ark., 1899-1900, Magnolia, Ark., 1900-01 Hobson Chapel, Nashville, 1902-05, McMinnville Tenn., 1905-08; prof. sociology and psychology, Meth Training Sch., Nashville, 1908-11; student secretar Internat. Com. Y.M.C.A., 1911-19; prof. sociology an field work, Scarritt Bible and Training Sch., Kansa City, Mo., 1919-21; prof. religious edn., Wofford Coll. Spartanburg, S.C., since 1921; teacher of sociology summer school, Emory U., 1926; teacher of religiou education, same, 1927. Special lecturer Nat. War Work Council and Fosdick Commn. on Training Cam Activities, 1917-19, and on inter-racial cooperation i southern colls. Mem. Alpha Tau Omega, Pi Gamm Mu. Democrat. Author: City Church and Its Socia Mission, 1913; Studies for Intermediates and Seniors (vols), 1912-17; Social Investigations, (booklet), 1915 Service Visits to Institutions, 1916. Editor of New Voic in Race Relations, 1914. Home: Spartanburg SC*‡

TRAYNOR, PHILIP ANDREW, ex-congressman dentist; b. Wilmington, Delaware, May 31, 1874; s Andrew and Elizabeth (Durney) T.; student U. of Del. 1889-92; D.D.S., U. of Pa., 1895; m. Mary A. Doyle July 30, 1900 (dec.). Engaged in practice of dentistry since 1895. Mem. 77th to 79th Congresses (1941-47) Delegate-at-large, Delaware State Militia. V.p. bd trustees Ferris Industrial School. Pres. Del. State Denta Soc., 1914, treas., 1915-39. Fellow Am. Coll. Dentistry Democrat. Roman Catholic. K.C., Eagle, Elk. Address 807 Washington St., Wilmington DE*‡

TREADWELL, EDWARD FRANCIS, lawyer; b Woodland, Calif., May 19, 1875; s. William Brewste and Adelaide Augusta (Kirk) T.; LL.B., Hastings Coll of Law (U. of Calif.), 1897; m. Eulila May Ayres, Mar 31, 1900; children—Earl Francis, Willard Brewster Marshall Gain; m. 2d, Doris Skinner Birney, March 17 1944. Admitted to California bar, 1897, and begar practice at San Francisco; associated with Mastick, Var Fleet & Mastick, 1897-1907; gen. counsel Miller & Lux 1907-22; mem. Treadwell, Van Fleet & Laughlin since 1925. Asst., Calif. Code Commn., 1899-1901; mem Calif. Assembly, 1901-05 and spl. session 1906; mem Calif. State Commn. on Taxation, 1905-09; chmn. bd trustees Burlingame, Calif., 1908-11; mem. Calif Constl. Commn., 1930. Chmn. Greater San Francisco Assn., 1911. Mem. Am. and San Francisco bar assns. Phi Delta Phi. Republican. Mason. Author: Annotated Constitution of California, 1902, 6th edit., 1931; The Cattle King, 1931. Home: 2208 Oakdale Road Burlingame, Calif. Office: 505 Mills Bldg., San Francisco CA‡

TREADWELL, GEORGE A., metallurgist, miner; b Me.; ed. pub. schs., followed by courses in geology and metallurgy at Yale. Went to Calif. and Ariz.; became 1878, supt. of the Vulture mine, Ariz., and built an 80-stamp mill, then the largest in the world; went to Europe, 1884, lecturer Dexter Sch. of Mines, London 1884-7; in Ariz., 1887; discovered the copper deposits in the Verde country; now pres. George A. Treadwel Mining Co. Residence: The Waldord-Astoria. Office: 27 William St., New York NY‡

TREADWELL, NANCY CLAAR, obstetrician and gynecologist; born Chgo., March 27, 1924; d. Elmer A and Evelyn Janet (Smith) Claar; B.A., Smith Coll. 1944; B.S., U. Ill., 1948, M.D., 1950; m. Warren S Treadwell, Dec. 25, 1947; children—Susan Millard Jennifer Anne, Alan Clay. Intern Henrotin Hosp. 1950-51 resident, 1951-52, preceptorship Dr. Joseph B Teton, 1952-56, asso. attending obstetricia and gynecologist, 1953-58; attending obstetrician and gynecologist Louis A. Weiss Meml. Hosp., 1959-63 courtesy staff obstetrics and gynecology, Lutheran Gen Hospital 1962-63, associate attending cons. in obstetrics and gynecology, 1963-70; clin. asst. U. Ill. Coll Medicine, 1954-60, clin. instr., 1960-70; pvt. practice medicine specializing in obstetrics and gynecology 1956-70. Diplomate Am. Bd. Obstetrics and Gynecology, Nat. Board Med. Examiners. Fellow A.C.S., Am. Coll. Obstetricians and Gynecologists Chicago Gynecol. Soc., International Coll. Surgeons (asso. fellow); member of American Com. on Maternal Welfare, Am. Soc. Study Sterility, Am. Med. Women's Assn., Ill., Chgo. med. socs., A.M.A., Alpha Epsilon Iota, Alpha Omega Alpha. Conglist. Author articles in field. Home: Wilmette IL Died Dec. 15, 1970.

TREAT, PAYSON JACKSON, historian; b. New York, N.Y., Nov. 12, 1879; s. Erastus Buck and Rhoda Ann (Goslee) T.; A.B., Wesleyan U., Conn., 1900 L.H.D., 1931; A.M., Columbia Univ., 1903; Ph.D. Stanford Univ., 1910; m. Jessie D. McGilvray, June 23 1909; (deceased January 1961). Engaged as tchr Barnard Sch., New York City, N.Y., 1900-03; instr. in history, Stanford U., 1905-06, 1907-08; research travel in Far East and Australasia, 1906-07, 12, 21, 35; instr. govt., Harvard, 1908-09; asst. prof. history, Stanford Univ., 1909-11, asso. prof., 1911-15, professor, 1915-45, professor emeritus from 1945; executive head of department, 1922-29. Lecturer political science

University of California, 1916; Albert Shaw, lecturer, Johns Hopkins Univ., 1917; visiting prof. Columbia U., 1929, U. of Calif., 1929. Decorated Order of Sacred Treasure, 3d class. Fellow Royal Geog. Soc. (London); mem. Am. Hist. Assn. (exec. council, 1926-30, pres. Pacific Coast Br. 1922), Asiatic Soc. of Japan, Chinese Social and Polit. Sci. Assn. (Peking), Alpha Delta Phi, Phi Beta Kappa. Author: The National Land System, 1785-1820, 1910; Early Diplomatic Relations between U.S. and Japan, 1853-1865, 1917; Japan and the United States, 1853-1921, 1921, 2d edit., 1928; The Far East, 1928, 35; The Diplomatic Relations between U.S. and Japan, 1853-1895, 1932; The Diplomatic Relations between U.S. and Japan, 1895-1905, 1938. Contbg. editor Journal of International Relations, 1919-22; mem. editorial bd., Pacific Historical Review, 1932-34. Home: Stanford CA Died June 15, 1972; buried Palo Alto CA

TREMAIN, ALBERT WRIGHT, banker; born Rome, N.Y., May 5, 1872; s. Sylvester F. and Julia (Barnes) T.; grad. Rome Free Acad., 1899 (oratorical honor); m. Jennie Emma Harrington, Sept. 3, 1896; children—Albert B., S. Frank, Alice H. Clk. Central Nat. Bank, Rome, 1890-94, Oneida County Savings Bank, Rome, 1895-1911; with Douglas Fenwick & Co., bankers, New York, 1911-12; treas. Am. Bank & Trust Co., Bridgeport, Conn., 1912-20, pres., 1920-35; pres. Commercial Bank & Trust Co. from its orgn., 1919-35. Mem. Liberty Loan Com., Bridgeport, World War, handling in 5 campaigns upwards of $2,000,000. Acad. Polit. Science. Republican. Presbyterian. Mason. Home: 313 Post Rd., Fairfield CT‡

TREMAIN, GEORGE LEE, lawyer; b. Bartholomew County, Ind., Apr. 6, 1874; s. John W. and Eliza E. (Jones) T.; B.S., Central Normal Coll., Danville, Ind., 1899, A.B. and LL.B., 1900; m. Mary V. Littell, Sept. 27, 1910. Admitted to Ind. bar, 1900; practiced law in Greensburg, 1900-35; county atty., 1913-18; judge Ind. Supreme Court, 1935-41; returned to Greensburg and is sr. mem. Tremain, Woodfill and Goddard; dir. Union Trust Co.; pres. Times Pub. Co. Trustee Indiana World War Memorial, 1931-35. Mem. Am. Bar Assn., Ind. State Bar Assn. (former mem. bd. mgrs.), Phi Delta Phi. Democrat. Mason, K.P., Elk. Clubs: Ind. Athletic, Ind. Democratic. Address: Greensburg IN*‡

TREMAINE, CHARLES MILTON, musical dir.; b. Brooklyn, N.Y., June 28, 1870; s. Charles Milton and Marianna Downs (Newhall) T.; student Adelphi Acad. (now Adelphi Coll.), 1881-86, Gunnery Sch. (Washington, Conn.), 1886-88; m. Elizabeth Lyman Lord, June 7, 1900; children—Lyman Lord, Elizabeth Newhall (Mrs. William Niel Pierce). Advertising solicitor, 1897-98; advertising mgr. Aeolian Co., 1898-1903, v.p., 1903-09; pres. Bacon Piano Co., 1910-14; pres. Tremaine Piano Co., 1912-16; organizer and mng. dir. Nat. Bureau for Advancement of Music, 1916-43, pres. and chmn. Bd. of Directors 1936-42; member of Board since 1942; founder of National Music Week Com., 1924-48; organized National School Band Assn., 1926, Nat. Sch. Orchestra Assn., 1928, exec. sec. both assns. to 1932; organizer Inter-American Music Week, 1941. Originated school music memory contests in 1916, held in 1600 cities and towns; promoted outdoor Christmas caroling in 2000 cities and towns and group piano instruction in over 1000; organized Nat. Sch. Music Contests. Mem. Music Educators Nat. Conf., S.A.R. Episcopalian. Clubs: Town Hall (chmn.), Music Round Table (New York). Home: 560 Prospect St., Westfield NJ Office: care National Bureau for Advancement of Music, 315 Fourth Av., New York NY‡

TRENDLE, GEORGE WASHINGTON, TV producer; b. Norwalk, O., July 4, 1884; s. Peter and Pauline (Seufert) T.; LL.B., Detroit Coll. of Law, 1908, J.D., 1968; also student business coll. and Y.M.C.A. night school; m. 2d, Adelaide L. Huston, Dec. 9, 1933; children (by first marriage)—Mary Kathryn, George Washington Jr.; 1 stepdau., Mrs. George A. Beauchamp. Began as bookkeeper, 1899; chief accountant Ralston Purina Co., St. Louis, Mo., 1902-03; purchasing agent and office mgr. Caille Motor Co., Detroit, 1903-08; admitted to Mich. bar, 1908, and practiced in Detroit; pres. Kunsky Theatres Corp. and affiliates, 1920-30. Trendle Campbell Broadcasting Corp., 1946-54; president and gen. mgr. King-Trendle Broadcasting Corp (Station WXYZ), Detroit, 1930-46; pres., treas. Lone Ranger, Inc., 1946-54, Green Hornet, Inc., from 1957, Sgt. Preston of the Yukon, Inc., 1939-57; president and part owner Radio Station WTAC, Flint, 1947-54. Chairman of Huron Clinton Met. Authority to 1957. Fire commr. City of Detroit, 1925-45. Trustee Village of Grosse Pointe Shores, 1948-58. Mem. Delta Theta Phi. Mason (32 degree, Shriner). Clubs: Detroit Athletic; Grosse Pointe Yacht, Grosse Pointe Hunt. Creator The Lone Ranger, The Green Hornet, Sgt. Preston of the Yukon, radio and TV dramas. Home: Grosse Pointe Shores MI Died May 9, 1972; buried Woodlawn Cemetery Detroit MI

TRENERY, MATTHEW JOHN, clergyman; b. Mineral Point, Wis., Sept. 28, 1870; s. John Valentine and Emily (Roberts) T.; prep. edn., high sch., Elkhorn, Wis.; spl. courses New York U.; grad. Drew Theol. Sem., 1898; D.D., Ia. Christian Coll., Oskaloosa, 1908; m. Mabel Russell MacNichol, of Shawano, Wis., June 27, 1899; children—Marian Evelyn (Mrs. Ormal Leroy Miller), Eleanor Mabel, Gordon John, Robert Matthew. Gen. sec. Y.M.C.A., Orange, N.J., later Madison, N.J., 1891-98; ordained ministry M.E. Ch., 1898; pastor successively Mattoon, Milwaukee, Oshkosh and Green Bay, Wis.; apptd. field rep. Bd. of Sunday Schs. M.E. Ch. for Wis., 1910; supt. Extension Dept. Bd. of Sunday Schs. M.E. Ch., 1912; sec. Dept. of Ch. Schs., same bd. since 1924. Republican. Mason (K.T.). Home: Evanston IL Office: 740 Rush St., Chicago IL‡

TRESOLINI, ROCCO JOHN, educator, author; b. Dolgeville, N.Y., Mar. 17, 1920; s. Oronzo and Albina (Ruggierio) T.; A.B., Hartwick Coll., Oneonta, N.Y., 1942; M.A., Syracuse U., 1947, Ph.D., 1949; m. Virginia Krohn, Sept. 24, 1943; children—Roger Lawson, Carol Patricia, Kevin Karl, Justin Andrew. Instr. polit. sci. Syracuse U., 1948-49; mem. faculty Lehigh U., 1949-67, prof. polit. sci., 1958-67, chmn. dept. govt., 1962-67; lectr. advanced study program Brookings Instn., 1965-67; vis. lectr. Armed Forces Information Sch., A. and M. Coll. N.C. Served to 1st lt. USAAF, 1942-46; ETO. Recipient Hillman award Lehigh U., 1964. Mem. Am. Polit. Sci. Assn., Pa. Pub. Adminstrn. and Polit. Sci. Assn. (sec.-treas. 1956-57, v.p. 1966), Pi Gamma Mu, Phi Alpha Theta. Author: American Constitutional Law, 2d edit., 1965; Justice and the Supreme Court, 1963; These Liberties: Case Studies in Civil Rights, 1968. Sr. editor: Cases in American National Government and Politics, 1966. Home: Coopersburg PA Died June 27, 1967.

TRIMBLE, ERNEST GREENE, univ. prof.; b. Frenchburg, Ky., Sept. 13, 1897; s. Farmer Johnce and Alice (Hale) T.; A.B., Berea (Ky.) Coll., 1922; Ph.D., Yale, 1927; m. Lois Elizabeth Hirschy, June 10, 1928; children—Robert Greene, Ruth Elizabeth. Instr. in polit. sci. New York U., 1927-30; John W. Weeks prof. of citizenship, Lincoln Memorial U., Harrogate, Tenn., 1930-31; part-time instr. in polit. sci. U. of Ky., 1931-32, asst. prof., 1932-36, asso. prof., 1936-47, prof. 1947-72; head department political science, 1959-62. Admitted to Kentucky bar, 1935; member of Kentucky Personnel Board, 1960-69. Trial attorney and hearing commr. Com. on Fair Employment Practice, Washington, 1942-44; legal personnel officer, O.P.A., Washington, 1944-47. Served with S.A.T.C., Berea Coll., 1918. Rep. League Nations Assn., Am. Com. at League of Nations in Geneva, Switzerland, also traveled in Europe, summer 1932. Mem. Am. Polit. Sci. Assn., Am. Soc. Internat. Law, Ky. Bar Assn., Am. Assn. Univ. Professors. Expert on labor Com. for Kentucky, 1946, and author com.'s report on labor, 1947. Contbr. articles to Ency. of Social Scis., Am. Jour. Internat. Law, and other periodicals. Home: Lexington KY Died Feb. 9, 1972, buried Beren Cemetery, Beren KY

TRIMBLE, JAMES W., congressman; b. Osage, Ark., Feb. 3, 1894; s. Matthew Allen and Anna (McFarlane) T.; A.B., U. of Ark., 1917; m. Ruth Maples, February 14, 1922; children—Martha Carol (deceased), James Kerry. Teacher in Texarkana (Ark.) Junior High Sch. and pub. schs. in Carroll County, Ark, 1911-17; served as county clerk, tax collector, dist. atty. and circuit judge, Carroll County, Ark., 1920-44. Member 79th to 89th congresses, 3d Ark. Dist. Served in U.S. Army, World War I. Mem. Am. Legion. Democrat. Methodist. Mason. Rotarian. Home: Berryville AK Died Mar. 1972.

TRINE, RALPH WALDO, author, publicist; b. Mt. Morris, Ill., Sept. 9, 1866; s. Samuel G. and Ellen E. (Newcomer) T.; A.B., Knox Coll., 1891, A.M., 1893, Litt.D., 1938; grad. student in history, polit. and social science, Johns Hopkins, 1892; m. Grace Steele Hyde; 1 son, Robert. Engaged for a time in teaching, lecturing, as bank cashier and as spl. newspaper corr. Interested in social problems; dir. Am. Humane Education Soc. Author: The Life Books (including: What All The World's A-Seeking, 1896; In Tune with the Infinite, 1897; The New Alinement of Life, 1913; In the Hollow of His Hand, 1915); On the Open Road, 1908; The Winning of the Best, 1912; The Higher Powers of Mind and Spirit, 1917; My Philosophy and My Religion, 1921; The Power That Wins (an intimate talk with Henry Ford on the inner things of life), 1929; The Man Who Knew (an intimate interpretation of the life, purpose and message of the Master). Also author the Life Booklets: Every Living Creature; The Greatest Thing Ever Known; Character-Building Thought-Power. Books have been translated and published in over twenty different langs., also in Hollywood CA*‡

TRINKS, WILLIBALD, mech. engr.; b. Berlin, Germany, Dec. 10, 1874; s. Wilhelm and Bertha (Obst) T.; grad. with honors, Charlottenburg Poly., 1897; m. 2d, Edith Moore, Aug. 8, 1910 (dec.); 1 son, Harold Rodney (dec.); m. 3d, Ruth Eudora Bittner, June 13, 1938. Came to U.S., 1899; chief mech. engr. William Tod Co., Youngstown, O., 1902-05; prof. mech. engring., Carnegie Inst. Tech., Pittsburgh, 1905-43; consulting and research on ammunition, 1942-46; cons. engineer Jones & Laughlin Steel Co., 1920-49. Member Am. Soc. M.E., Engrs. Soc. of Western Pa., Assn. of Iron and Steel Engrs., Society for Metals, Am. Iron and Steel Inst. Author: Governors, and the Governing of Prime Movers, 1919; Industrial Furnaces, Vol. I, 1923, 3d edit., 1934, Vol. II, 1925, 2 edit., 1942; Roll Pass Design (3 vols), 1933. Home: R.D. 1, Ohiopyle PA‡

TRIPP, WILLIAM HENRY, JR., naval architect; b. N.Y.C., Sept. 22, 1919; s. William Henry and Ethel Mary (Moran) T.; grad. Dwight Prep. Sch., N.Y.C., 1939; m. Alice Shelly Williamson, Sept. 14, 1944; 1 son, William Henry III. Propr. W. H. Tripp & Co., Port Washington, N.Y., from 1954; designer specialized comml. craft, sail and power yachts, racing and cruising sail boats. Served to lt. (j.g.) USCGR, 1942-46; PTO. Mem. Soc. Yacht Brokers and Designers. Clubs: N.Y. Yacht; Manhasset Bay Yacht. Office: Port Washington LI NY Died Oct. 13, 1971; cremated.

TROCHE, ERNST GUNTER, art mus. dir.; b. Stettin, Germany, Sept. 26, 1909; s. Ernst Paul and Hedwig (Benner) T.; student U. Vienna, 1929; Ph.D., U. Munich, 1932; m. Elfriede Michaelis, Feb. 14, 1942. Came to U.S., 1951, naturalized, 1956. Asst. curator Prussian State Mus., Berlin, 1932-36; curator Municipal Mus., Breslau, 1936-38; curator Germanic Nat. Mus., Nuremberg, 1938-45, dir., 1945-51; dir. Achenbach Found. for Graphic Arts. Cal. Palace of Legion of Honor, San Francisco, 1956-71. Mem. Renaissance Soc. Am., Deutscher Verein fur Kunstwissenschaft. Democrat. Lutheran. Club: Roxburghe (San Francisco). Author: Italian Painting in the 14th and 15th Centuries, Berlin, 1935; Painting in the Netherlands, 15th and 16th Centuries, Berlin & London, 1936; also numerous articles in field. Home: San Francisco CA Died Oct. 30, 1971.

TROTT, CLEMENT AUGUSTUS, army officer; b. Milwaukee, Dec. 14, 1877; s. August Von and Anna (Paul) T.; grad. U.S. Mil. Acad., 1899; honor grad. Inf. and Cav. Sch., Ft. Leavenworth, 1904; grad. Staff Coll., Ft. Leavenworth, 1905, Army War Coll., Washington, 1920; m. Leah Wright, Nov. 28, 1899. Commd. 2d lt. 7th Inf., 1899; promoted through grades to major gen., 1941; 1st lt. inf. Philippine Insurrection, 1901-03, capt. inf. Punitive Expdn., Mexico, 1916, col., chief of staff, 5th Div. in World War, 1917-18, commanding 6th Division, 1939-40; commanding 5th Corps Area, 1940-41; retired, Dec. 31, 1941. Awarded Spanish War Service medal, Philippine Campaign. Mexican Campaign Victory with 4 battle clasps, Silver Star medals, and D.S.M. (all U.S.); Croix de Guerre with palm, and Officer Legion of Honor (France). Clubs: Army and Navy (Washington). University (Chicago). Home: Hawthorne Lane, Geneva IL‡

TROUYET, CARLOS, corp. exec.; b. 1904; student German Sch., Mexico City. Banker and adviser to Miguel Aleman, then chmn. with him in Continental Hilton Hotel, Mexico City; later Hilton's partner in bldg. Hotel Las Brisas, Acapulco; formerly chmn., now vice chmn. Telefonos de Mexico; officer Celulosa de Chihuahua, Viscosa de Chihuahua, Plywood Ponderosa de Mexico, Bosques de Chichuahua, Banco Comercial Mexicano, Compania Insl. de Orizaba. Catholic. Address: Mexico City Mexico Died Mar. 1971.*

TROWBRIDGE, ARTHUR CARLETON, geologist; b. Glasgow, Mo., March 4, 1885; s. Samuel Hoyt and Julia Almira (Goodhue) T.; B.S., U. of Chicago, 1907; Ph.D., 1911; m. Sue Estelle Bussey, Aug. 29, 1911; children—Charles Lambert, Carolyn Frances. Asst. in geology, U. of Chicago, 1907-09, instr., 1909-11; prof., U. of Ia., since 1911, head dept., since 1934; dir. and state geologist, Ia. Geol. Survey, 1934-47; field asst. Ill. Geol. Survey, 1907, geologist, 1910; asst. U.S. Geol. Survey, 1913-20, geologist, 1920-24, asso. geologist, 1924-32; geologist Turkish Petroleum Co., Ltd., in Iraq, 1925-26; cons. geologist Nine Foot Channel Bd. Miss. River, 1928-30. With Army Y.M.C.A., Camp Dodge, Ia., 1917-18, N.Y. City, 1918-19. Fellow Geol. Soc. America (v.p. 1943). Mem. A.A.A.S., Ia. Acad. Science (pres. 1937), Nat. Research Council (chmn. com. sedimentation, 1932-35), Sigma Xi, Phi Kappa Sigma. Republican. Methodist. Club: Triangle (Ia. City). Author books relating to field; editor other publs. Home: Iowa City IA Died Nov. 16, 1971.

TROWBRIDGE, CARL HOYT, coll. pres.; b. West Westminster, Vt., Oct. 24, 1874; s. Samuel Hoyt and Julia Almira (Goodhue) T.; A.B., Prichett Inst., Glasgow, Mo., 1893; studied U. of Chicago, summers 1896, 1903 and 1905; A.B., Harvard, 1901, A.M., 1902; grad. student U. of Ia., 1920-21; m. Emily Bond Lanius, of Palmyra, Mo., June 27, 1905; 1 dau., Eleanor Goodhue. Began as teacher rural sch., Howard Co., Mo., 1893, later teacher grade and high sch.; prof. science, Central Coll. for Women, Lexington, Mo., 1896-1900; instr. chemistry, St. Louis Manual Training Sch., of Washington U., 1902-07; prin. Brevard (N.C.) Inst., 1907-23; pres. Weaver Coll., Weaverville, N.C., 1923—. Developed a system of denom. vocational training for mountain boys and girls under direction of Woman's Missionary Council, M.E. Ch., S. Mem. N.E.A., Nat. Soc. for Study of Edn., Nat. Economic League (council), Phi Delta Kappa. Home: Weaver College, Weaverville NC‡

TROWBRIDGE, VAUGHAN, artist; b. New York, Dec. 3, 1869; s. Miner and Charlotte Fox (Tiffany) T.; gen. edn. Brooklyn Poly. Inst.; married. Left business life, 1897, and took up art studies in Paris with Jean Paul Laurens and Benj. Constant. Exhibited in painting and etching in Paris Salons, 1900-13, and in etching, printed in color, at St. Louis Expn., 1904. Illustrator: Paris and the Social Revolution (by Alvan F. Sanborn), 1905. Address: 21 Av. Libert, Draveil, Seine et Oise France‡

TROXELL, EDWARD LEFFINGWELL, geologist; b. Deshler, Neb., Apr. 15, 1884; s. Jacob and Evelyn Virginia (Leffingwell) T.; prep. edn., Collegiate Inst., Salt Lake City, Utah; A.B., Northwestern U., 1908, A.M., 1911; Ph.D., Yale, 1914; student Sorbonne, Paris, 1919; m. Jane Allen Campbell, Oct. 17, 1917. Research asst., Yale, 1919, research asso. in paleontology, 1920; asst. prof. geology, 1920-25, prof. since 1925, Trinity Coll., dean of Coll., 1925-28; dir. State Geol. and Natural History Survey since 1940; Red Cross first aid instr., 1941; member State Defense Minerals Resources Committee. Joined First O.T.C., Fort Sheridan, Ill., 1917; commd. capt. inf., Aug. 15, 1917; at Camp Custer, Aug. 1917-July 1918; overseas, July 1918-July 1919; with 82d and 86th Divs., Argonne Forest. Fellow Geol. Soc. America, Am. Geog. Soc., Am. Assn. for Advancement of Science, Paleontol. Soc.; mem. Assn. of Am. State Geologists (exec. com.; pres. 1947-48), Am. Soc. Mammalogists, Am. Assn. Univ. Profs., Phila. Acad. Natural Sciences, Sigma Xi, Pi Gamma Mu (vice chancellor), Alpha Delta Phi, Book and Bond of Yale. Congregationalist. Clubs: Hartford Engineers, Twentieth Century, Hartford Golf. Field trips and exploration in the West, specimens now in many museums; important discoveries in fossil reptiles, birds and mammals. Contbr. plans in flood control and engring.; Gildersleeve Canal, etc. Author of about 80 papers, mostly on paleontology, geology and education, in Am. Jour. Science, Scientific Monthly, Yale Alumni Weekly, etc. Inventor. Home: West Hartford CT Died Sept. 21, 1972.

TROXELL, THOMAS FRANKLIN, investment banker; b. Balt., Jan. 9, 1895; s. Frederick W. and Mary K. (Hopkins) T.; A.B., Johns Hopkins, 1915; m. Louise F. Chase, Sept. 22, 1923; children—Thomas Franklin, D. Chase. With Dillon, Read & Co., Inc., N.Y.C., 1925-57, v.p., 1946-57; pres. Nassau Assos., Inc., 1952-57; dir. New Amsterdam Casualty Co., U.S. Casualty Co. Served as capt. 4th Inf., U.S. Army, 1917-19: AEF in France. Decorated Purple Heart. Mem. Phi Beta Kappa. Home: Montclair NJ Died Jan. 8, 1971; buried Loudon Park Cemetery Baltimore MD

TROY, GEORGE FRANCIS, lawyer; b. Providence, R.I., May 8, 1876; s. Timothy and Isabella (Goodwin) T.; student Providence pub. schs., 1881-94; A.B., Brown U., 1898; student Harvard U. Law Sch., 1899-1901; m. Alice L. Wallace, July 20, 1908; children—George F., Jr., Martha A. (Mrs. Judson Hurd), Carolyn J. (Mrs. Benjamin A. Watts, Jr.). Admitted to R.I. bar, 1902, and since in gen. practice of law at Providence; mem. R.I. Ho. of Rep., 1907-08; became first asst. U.S. dist. atty., Dist. of R.I., 1935; now U.S. dist atty. Mem. R.I. Bar Assn. Democrat. Home: 40 Colonial Rd. Office: Federal Bldg., Providence RI‡

TRUBY, ALBERT ERNEST, army officer; b. Otto, N.Y., July 18, 1871; s. John and Minnie (Ackerman) T.; student Cornell, 1890-93; B.S., U. of Pa., 1894, M.D., 1897; m. Elizabeth Downing, Apr. 26, 1906; children—Elizabeth, Barbara, Albert Eliot (deceased), John Orrien. Surgeon Medical Corps, United States Army, 1898; captain, 1903; promoted through grades to brigadier general, Jan. 1, 1933; retired Aug. 1, 1935. Served in Spanish-Am. and World Wars. Fellow Am. Coll. Surgeons; mem. A.M.A. Mason. Author: Memoir of Walter Reed—The Yellow Fever Episode, 1943. Address: 145 Laurel St., San Francisco CA‡

TRUCCO, MANUEL, ambassador; b. Cauquenes, Chile, Mar. 18, 1875; s. Napoleon and Maria (Franzani) T.; B.C.E., U. of Chile, 1899; student Sch. of Bridges and Highways, Paris, 1902-04; m. Laura Gaete, of Santiago, 1902 (died 1934); children—Marta, Graciela, Rebeca, Manuel. Engr. Dept. of Pub. Works and Nat. State Rys., Chile, 1900-11, dir. of latter, 1918-26; dean faculty of mathematics and dir. schs. of architecture and engring., U. of Chile, 1912-18; senator of Chile, 1926-30; v.p. and pres. Radical Party, 1926 and 1931; minister of Interior, Chile, 1931, actg. president, 1931; A.E. and P. from Chile to U.S. since 1933. Mem. Chilean Inst. of Engring. (one of founders). Address: Chilean Embassy, 2154 Florida Av., Washington DC‡

TRUE, LILIAN (SARAH) CRAWFORD, illustrator; b. Boston; d. Charles Oscar and Dr. Sarah (Marcy) Crawford; studied art under Tommaso Juglaris and at Cowles Art Sch., Boston; m. John Preston True (q.v.), July 22, 1885. Began art career by illustrating for Wide Awake, Youth's Companion, etc.; now devotes her attention to book illustration for Little, Brown & Co., Lee & Shepard, etc. Address: Waban MA‡

TRUELL, ROHN, physicist; b. Washington, Apr. 6, 1913; s. Karl O. and Anna M. (Rohn) T.; B.S. in Engring. Physics, Lehigh U., 1935; postgrad. Columbia, 1936-38; Ph.D., Cornell U., 1941; m. Marjory Ann Schminck, Sept. 12, 1942; children—Ann Rohn, Marcia Lee. With RCA, 1935-38, RCA Labs., Princeton, 1941-44; staff Stromberg Carlson, 1944-46; asst. prof. Brown U., 1946-48, asso. prof., 1948-51, prof., 1951-68, chmn. div. applied mathematics, dir. metals research lab., chairman phys. science council. Member of the board of trustees Roger Williams Hosp. Guggenheim fellow, 1959-60. Fellow Am. Phys. Soc.; mem. I.E.E.E., (sr.), Am. Math. Soc. Author: Ultrasonic Methods in Solid State Physics, 1969. Home: Providence RI Died Jan. 10, 1968; buried Nashua NH

TRUEMAN, WALTER HARLEY, Justice Manitoba Court of Appeal; b. Saint John, New Brunswick, May 23, 1870; s. Thomas P. and Grace (Black) T.; LL.B., Dalhousie U., Halifax, N.S., 1892; m. Elizabeth Wade, Oct. 16, 1895; children—Dr. Kenneth R. Trueman, Dorothy Wade (wife of Major H. Rivers Rebitt). Began as barrister at law, 1893; lecturer, King's Coll. Law Sch., Saint John, N.B.; lecturer, Manitoba Law Sch.; apptd. King's Counsel, 1916; apptd. justice Court of Appeal, Fed. Govt., Apr. 13, 1923. Author: Trueman's Equity Reports, New Brunswick. Address: Court of Appeal, Winnipeg MB Can*‡

TRUEMAN, WILLIAM H., lawyer; b. Mobile, Apr. 16, 1904; A.B., U. Ala., 1925, LL.B., 1927; m. Caroline V. Rankin; 1 dau. (Mrs. John W. Sharp). Admitted to Ala. bar, 1927; sr. mem. firm Cabaniss, Johnston, Gardner & Clark. Mem. Am., Ala., Birmingham bar assns., Farrah Law Soc. (charter), Phi Alpha Delta. Home: Birmingham AL Died May 19, 1970; buried Elmwood, Birmingham AL

TRUITT, JAMES STEELE, atty. gen. of Alaska; b. Bentonville, Ark., Oct. 16, 1868; s. James Madison and Mary Elizabeth (Pyatt) T.; ed. pub. and pvt. schs. and Elmsprings (Ark.) Acad.; law clerk 1 yr.; studied law under Preceptor 3 yrs.; m. Susie A. Oldham, Oct. 10, 1895; children—G. James, Mrs. Vella Elizabeth Moehring. Admitted to Bar of U.S. Court, 1897, and practiced in U.S. courts at Vinita and Miami, Okla.; admitted to Supreme Court, Wash., 1905, Alaska courts, 1916; referee in bankruptcy and spl. master in chancery, Circuit Court of Appeals and 3d Div. U.S. Courts, Alaska, 1918-21; asst. U.S. atty. same div., 1932; atty. gen. Alaska since 1933. Served as appeal agt. for Bd. of Exemptions, 1917-18, World War. Mem. Am. Bar Assn. (mem. com. on uniform laws). Democrat. Presbyn. Mason (32 deg., Shriner); mem. O.E.S. Home: Juneau AK‡

TRUITT, RALPH PURNELL, physician; b. Snow Hill, Md., Aug. 4, 1885; s. George Worthington and Gertrude Duncan (Purnell) T.; grad. high sch., Snow Hill, student Washington Coll., Chestertown, Md.; M.D., U. of Maryland, 1910; m. Eleanor McConnell, Sept. 2, 1920 (died 1946); 1 son, James McConnell. Intern University Hospital, Baltimore, 1909-10; jr. assistant physician N.J. State Hospital, Trenton, 1910-12; psychiatrist in chief City Hosp. (insane department), Baltimore, Maryland, 1912; assistant resident Psychiatrist Johns Hopkins Hosp., 1913-14; clin. dir. La. State Hosp., Jackson, La., 1915; sr. physician N.J. State Hosp., 1916-17; lt., capt. and maj. Med. Corps, U.S. Army, 1917-19; med. dir. Ill. Soc. for Mental Hygiene and asst. prof. neurology and psychiatry, U. of Ill. Med. Dept., 1919-23; dir. Child Guidance Clinic Demonstration under auspices Nat. Com. for Mental Hygiene, Los Angeles, Calif., 1924; dir. Div. on Prevention of Delinquency, Commonwealth Fund Program, New York, 1925-27; asso. prof. psychiatry and dir. psychiatric clinic, U. of Md., 1927-46, prof. clin. psychiatry and chief of psychiatric service, 1946-50, chairman of the department of psychiatry, 1948-50. Mem. Am. Psychiat. Assn., Am. Orthopsychiatric Assn. (pres. 1935-36), Phi Sigma Kappa. Home: Stevensville MD Died June 20, 1966.

TRUMAN, HARRY S., 33d Pres. of U.S. (32d man to serve although officially designated 33d President); b. Lamar, Mo., May 8, 1884; s. John Anderson and Martha Ellen (Young) T.; educated in public schools, Independence, Mo.; student Kansas City Sch. of Law, 1923-25. Field Arty. Sch. (Fort Sill, Okla.) 1917-18; m. Bess Wallace, June 28, 1919; 1 dau., Mary Margaret (Mrs. Clifton Daniel). With Kansas City Star, 1901; timekeeper for r.r. contractor, 1902; with Nat. Bank of Commerce and Union Nat. Bank, Kansas City, 1903-05; operated family farm, 1906-17; judge Jackson County Court, 1922-24, presiding judge, 1926-34; elected to U.S. Senate from Mo., 1934, re-elected 1940; served as chmn. Special Com. to investigate Nat. Defense Program; elected v.p. of United States, Nov. 7, 1944; and took office, Jan. 20, 1945; succeeded to presidency on death of Franklin Delano Roosevelt, Apr. 12, 1945; elected Pres. of the U.S. 1949-53. Served as 1st lt. Battery F. and capt. Battery D. 129th Field Atty., 35th Div., U.S. Army, World War I; participated in Vosges operations, St. Mihiel and Meuse-Argonne offensives, A.E.F. discharged as major, May 1919; col. Field Atty., U.S. Res. Corps, since 1927. Baptist. Mason (past grand master, Mo.). Author: Years of Decisions, Vol. I, 1955; Years of Trial and Hope, Vol. II, 1956. Home: Independence MO Died Dec. 26, 1972; buried Garden of Truman Library, Independence MO

TRUSSELL, C(HARLES) P(RESCOTT), newspaper corr.; b. Chicago, Aug. 3, 1892; s. Homer Milton and Margaret (Shuck) T.; ed. pub. schs. of Md. and Ill.; m. Beatrice W. Tait, June 14, 1923; children—Charles Tait, Galen Douglas. Reporter Baltimore Sun, 1917-19, copyreader, 1919-22, asst. city editor, 1922-25, city editor, 1925-32, mem. Washington Bur., 1932-41; mem. Washington Bur. N.Y. Times, 1941-65. Served as 2d lt., Inf., U.S. Army, World War I. Mem. chmn. standing com. of corrs. U.S. Capitol, 1934-36. Awarded Pulitzer prize in journalism for distinguished reporting on nat. affairs, 1949. Mem. White House Corr. Assn., Sigma Delta Chi. Clubs: National Press (bd. govs. 1946-49), Gridiron. Occasional contbr. to current pubs. Home: Washington DC Died Oct. 2, 1968; buried Rock Creek Cemetery Washington DC

TRUSTY, S(AMUEL) DAVID, lawyer; b. Louisville, Dec. 12, 1913; s. Samuel L. and Dorothy (Lemmon) T.; A.B., U. Mo., 1935, LL.D., 1938; m. Jean Lois Murray, Dec. 22, 1938; children—David Michael, Jean Murray, Scott Townsend, Ann Wilson. Admitted to Mo. bar, 1938, also U.S. Treasury Dept., ICC; mem. firm Trusty, Pugh & Trusty, 1938-41; spl. asst. to dist. atty. for D.C., 1941; spl. atty. OPA, Washington, 1941; mem. firm Popham, Thompson, Popham, Trusty & Conway, and predecessor, Kansas City, 1946-68. Mem. Appellate Judicial Commn. State Mo., 1962-68. Mem. corporate bd. YMCA, Kansas City; bd. mgrs. S.W. br., bd. curators Lincoln U. Served to lt. comdr. USNR, 1942-45. Fellow Am. Coll. Trial Lawyers; mem. Am. Judicature Soc., Am., Fed., Mo., Kansas City (pres.) bar assns., Chancery, Lawyers Assn., Res. Officers Assn., Phi Delta Phi, Sigma Chi, Sigma Gamma Epsilon, Chi Chi Chi. Clubs: Kansas City, Mission Hills Country (Kansas City, Kansas City MO Died Dec. 12, 1968.

TRUXAL, ANDREW GEHR, coll. pres.; b. Greensburg, Pa., Feb. 2, 1900; s. Jacob Q. and Elizabeth (Gehr) T.; A.B., Franklin and Marshall Coll., 1920, A.M., 1923; B.D., Theol. Sem. Reformed Ch. in U.S.A., 1923; Ph.D., Columbia, 1928; LL.D., Franklin and Marshall Coll., 1948; LL.D., Western Maryland College, 1961; m. Leah Deldee Groff, May 26, 1923; children—John Groff, Nora Deldee. Instr. Dartmouth Coll., 1928-30, asst. prof. sociology, 1930-35, prof. sociology, 1935-48; pres. Hood Coll., Frederick, Md., 1948-61, pres. emeritus, 1961; dean Anne Arundel Jr. College, Annapolis, Md., 1961; pres. Anne Arundel Community College, Severna Park, Maryland, 1961-68, pres. emeritus, 1968-71. Mem. Am. Sociol. Society, Phi Kappa Psi, Phi Beta Kappa. Mem. Evangelical and Reformed Ch. Author: Outdoor Recreation Legislation and Its Effectiveness; co-author: The Severna Park MD Died Feb. 4, 1971; buried Mt. Olivet Cemetery, Frederick MD

TRYON, LILLIAN (WAINWRIGHT) HART (MRS. WINTHROP PITT TRYON), author; b. New Britain, Conn., June 3, 1870; d. Charles Edwin and Jane (Wainwright) Hart; A.B., Wesleyan U., Conn., 1892; m. Winthrop Pitt Tryon, Oct. 30, 1909; 1 dau., Agatha. Lecturer, reviewer, essayist. Author: Speaking of Home—Essays of a Contented Woman, 1916; The Story of New Britain, 1925; Life of William H. Hart, 1929. Home: 24 University Rd., Brookline MA‡

TRYON, WINTHROP PITT, musical critic; b. Cape Elizabeth, Me., June 10, 1869; s. Joseph and Ellen Bigelow (Cummings) T.; grad. high sch., Deering, Me., 1885, Boston Latin Sch., 1888; A.B., Harvard, 1892; studied musical theory with Henry J. Storer, of Boston; m. Lillian Wainwright Hart, Oct. 30, 1909; 1 dau., Agatha. Teacher Greek, high sch., Brookline, Mass., 1898-99, New Britain, Conn., 1900-04; musical critic Christian Science Monitor, Boston, 1908-18, and at N.Y. City for same paper, 1918-34, except for a short period, 1921, staff writer, Boston office, since 1934; retired 1947. Member Soc. of Biblical Literature and Exegesis. Democrat. Christian Scientist. Home: 24 University Rd., Brookline. Office: 1 Norway St., Boston MA‡

TSALDARIS, CONSTANTIN, premier of Greece, resigned Jan. 1947; formerly U.N. del. Chmn. delegation of Greece to United Nations. Address: Athens Greece Died Nov. 1970.*

TSCHAPPAT, WILLIAM H., army officer; b. Aug. 10, 1874; grad. U.S. Mil. Acad., 1896. Commd. add. 2d lt. arty., June 12, 1896; promoted through grades to col., Sept. 4, 1919; served as col. Ordnance Dept., N.A., Jan. 1918-Sept. 1919; apptd. asst. to chief of ordnance with rank of brig. gen. for 4 yrs., beginning June 3, 1930; apptd. maj. gen., chief of ordnance, Mar. 1934; retired Aug. 31, 1938. Mem. Nat. Inventors Council, 1942-45. Home: Box 264, Falls Church VA‡

TUBMAN, WILLIAM V(ACANARAT) S(HADRACH), pres. Liberia; b. Harper, Liberia, 1895; s. Alexander and Elizabeth (Barnes) T.; student Cape Palmas Sem., Cuttington Inst.; LL.D., Howard U., U. of Akron, Lincoln U., Atlanta U., Morgan State College, Lafayette College, Tuskegee Institute 1954; L.H.D. Morehouse College, Xavier University, 1954; married Antoinette Padmore, Sept. 17, 1948; children—Shadrack, John Hiliary Wilhemenia,

William. Called to bar, 1917; collector internal revenue Maryland County, Liberia, 1919-22; senator Liberia, 1923-31, 34-37, asso. justice Supreme Ct., 1937-44, pres. of Republic, 1944-71. Office: Monrovia Liberia Died July 1971.

TUCKER, B. FAIN, judge; b. Greencastle, Ind.; d. Dr. William W. and Bertha (Clark) Tucker; A.B., DePauw U.; J.D. cum laude, U. Chgo., LL.D., DePauw U. Admitted to Ill. bar, 1925, practiced in Chgo.; spl. lectr. U. Chgo., 1939-43; judge Circuit Court, Cook Co., Ill., 1953-70; chief justice, 1961-62. First woman to serve as judge Criminal Ct., Cook County. Dir. Infant Welfare Soc. Chgo., Randall House; mem. women's bd. Aux. House of Good Shepherd. Recipient various awards including Kappa Kappa Gamma alumnae achievement award, 1954; woman of distinction award Women's Advt. Club of Chicago, 1954; Woman of Year award Jewish War Vets. Ladies Aux., 1957; Distinguished Service award Phi Beta Kappa Assn., 1958; Zonta Club award, 1969; Achievement citation Women's Advt. Club Chgo., 1970. Mem. Daughters of Indiana, Am., Ill., Chgo. bar assns., National Assn. Women Lawyers, The Women's Bar Assn. Ill. (pres. 1941-42), Am. Judicature Soc., Met. Bus. and Profl. Club Chgo., 100 Club Cook County Inc., DePauw Alumnae Chgo. (past pres.), English Speaking Union, Council of Christians and Jews, The English Assn., Marquis Brog. Library Soc., Chgo. Hist. Soc., Chgo. Art Inst. (hon.), Phi Beta Kappa Assocs., Phi Beta Kappa, Kappa Kappa Gamma, Theta Sigma Phi, Kappa Beta Pi. Republican. Episcopalian. Contbr. various periodicals. Author: Guide to National Labor Relations Act, 1947. Home: Chicago IL Died Sept. 26, 1970; buried Forest Hill Cemetery Greencastle IN

TUCKER, BENJAMIN FERREE, retired banker; b. Macon County, Ill., Aug. 28, 1870; s. Joseph Clough and Emma (Ferree) T.; m. Dorothy May, May 28, 1908; 1 dau., Carolyn Gilman (Mrs. Curtis Ward Richards, dec.). Mem. Tucker & Mosiman, Morton, Ill., grain dealers, 1896-1904; organized City Nat. Bank, Long Beach, Calif., 1907, operating same until 1925 when merged with First Nat. Bank of Los Angeles; dir. Associated Telephone Co., Ltd. Pres. Community Hosp., Long Beach, Adelaide Tichenor Hosp. Sch. for Crippled Children. Republican. Conglist. Mason, Odd Fellow. Clubs: Rotary (life), Los Angeles Athletic (Los Angeles); Pacific Coast (Long Beach). Opened a bird sanctuary on Modjeska ranch, later given to Audubon Soc. Home: 850 E. Ocean Av., Long Beach 2 CA Office: 132 Pine Av., Long Beach CA CA Office: 132 Pine Av., Long Beach CA‡

TUCKER, BEVERLEY DANDRIDGE, bishop and educator; b. Warsaw, Va., Feb. 4, 1882; s. Rt. Rev. Beverley Dandridge and Anna Maria (Washington) T.; B.A., U. of Va., 1902; Va. Theol. Sem., 1902-05, B.D., 1915, D.D., 1920; Rhodes scholar, from Va. at Christ Church, Oxford U., 1905-08, B.A., 1908, M.A., 1912; D.D., Univ. of Richmond, 1932; LL.D., Univ. of Ala., 1932; Western Reserve Univ., 1939; S.T.D., Kenyon College, 1938; L.H.D., Baldwin-Wallace College, 1945; married Eleanor Carson Lile, April 20, 1915; children—Maud (Mrs. W. H. Drane), Beverley D., Eleanor S., Louisa Lile (Mrs. T. G. Bell), Maria Washington (Mrs. E. S. Bowerfind, Jr.). Ordained deacon, 1908, priest, 1909, P.E. Church; rector St. James and St. Luke's parishes, Mecklenburg County, Va., 1908-11; rector St. Paul's Memorial Ch., U. of Va., 1911-20; prof. practical theology, Va. Theol. Sem., 1920-23; rector St. Paul's Church, Richmond, Va., 1923-38; bishop Diocese of Ohio, 1938-52; deputy to Gen. Conv., P.E. Ch., 1928, 31, 34, 37. Pres. Cleveland Church Fedn., 1947-48. First lt., chaplain, U.S. Army, 1918-19; attached to 17th Engrs. (Ry.), Base Hosp. 41, A.E.F. Mem. bd. dirs. and overseers Sweet Briar (Va.) Coll.; mem. bd. trustees Kenyon Coll., Lake Erie Coll., Western Reserve U. Mem. Alpha Tau Omega, Phi Beta Kappa, Raven Soc. Episcopalian. Democrat. Clubs: Colonnade, Univ. of Virginia, Farmington (Charlottesville, Va.); Union, Kirtland Country (Cleveland). Home: Cleveland Heights OH Died July 4, 1969; buried University Cemetery Charlottesville VA

TUCKER, CHARLES COWLES, lawyer; b. Washington, Mar. 3, 1869; s. Charles C. and Mary (Cowles) T.; grad. Columbian Univ., 1890, LL. B., 1889, LL. M., 1890; m. Baltimore, Apr. 28, 1898, Helen Zimmerman. Admitted to bar, 1890; lecturer on common law practice, torts, and admiralty law, Nat. Univ. Law Sch., Washington; official reporter, Court of Appeals, D.C., since organization of that court, 1893. Mem. vestry All Saints Parish, Washington, Bar Assn., D.C. Club: Chevy Chase. Author: Reports Court of Appeals, D.C. (24 vols), 1983-1905 L28. Residence: Chevy Chase MD Office: Colorado Bldg., Washington DC‡

TUCKER, CLARENCE R., railroad ofcl.; b. Hallsville, Tex., Aug. 3, 1897; s. P.C. and Ella (Hays) T.; ed. high sch. and comml. coll.; m. Willie Ross George, Aug. 21, 1919; 1 dau., Emily Jane. Connected with railroad work, 1916-62; asst. gen. mgr. A. T. & S. F. R.R.,Amarillo, Tex., 1941-42, Los Angeles, 1943-45, acting gen. mgr., Los Angeles, 1945-46, asst. v.p., Chgo., 1946, v.p. operations div., also dir. Methodist. Mason (Shriner). Home: Chicago IL Deceased.

TUCKER, HUGH CLARENCE, clergyman; b. Williamson County, Tenn., Oct. 4, 1857; s. William Alexander and Susan Catherine (Crichlow) T.; ed. pvt. and pub. schs; student academic and theol. depts., Vanderbilt U., 1876-79; grad. in theology, 1879; D.D., Southwestern U., 1917; LL.D., Randolph-Macon Coll., Ashland, Va., 1929; m. Ella Winston, d. Bishop John C. Granbery, July 16, 1891; children—Elvira Granbery (Mrs. Lewis Alden Estes), Hugh Clarence (dec.). Ordained ministry M.E. Ch., S., 1879; various pastorates in Tenn. until 1886; went to Rio de Janeiro, and served as pastor English-speaking ch. 2 yrs.; agency sec. Am. Bible Soc. in Brazil since Sept. 1887; has traveled widely in Brazil, preaching in Portuguese language. A founder and trustee The Strangers' Hosp., Evangelical Hosp., and Y.M.C.A. and Peoples Central Inst.; pres. bd. trustees Granbery Coll., Juiz de Fora, since 1898; trustee Methodist Pub. House, Sao Paulo. Del. to world religious confs., Europe and America; active in assisting Dr. Oswaldo Cruz in fight against yellow fever; pioneer in securing playground for children, instruction for nurses, etc. Awarded Order of the Southern Cross (Brazil) for distinguished service, 1943. Author: The Bible in Brazil, 1902; Dr. Jose Carlos Rodrigues (biography), 1924. Address: 12 Av., Erasmo Braga, Rio de Janeiro Brazil‡

TUCKER, JOHN FRANCIS, lawyer, author; b. N.Y. City, Feb. 25, 1871; s. Francis J. and Mary O'Neill (Bateman) T.; grad. pub. schs., N.Y. City; LL.B., New York U. Law Sch., 1893, LL.M., 1894; post-grad. work U. of Pa.; traveled in Europe, Africa and U.S. Admitted to N.Y. bar, 1894; candidate for assembly on fusion ticket, 1903; was associated with late Austin Abbott in editorial work; editor University Law Review, 1895-8. Mem. Sons of St. Nicholas, Delta Upsilon, Delta Chi. Clubs: Twilight. Friars, Liberal. Author: Story of Washington Square, 1895; The Power Political, 1899; Collected Short Stories, 1905; also (play) Husbands by Purchase, prod. Citerion Theatre, London, 1899. Home: Scotch Plains NJ Office: 25 W. 42d St., NY City NY‡

TUCKER, RAYMOND R(OCHE), educator, city ofcl.; b. St. Louis, Dec. 4, 1896; s. William J. and Mary Ellen (Roche) T.; A.B., St. Louis Univ., 1917; B.S., Washington U., 1920; m. Mary Edythe Leiber, November 28, 1928; children—Joan Marie (Mrs. Leigh Doxsee), John Thomas. Instructor in mechanical engineering with Washington University, 1921-23, asst. professor,1923-24; asso. prof., 1927-34; secretary to mayor St. Louis, 1934-37; commr. smoke regulation and dir. pub. safety, St. Louis, 1937-42; head dept. mech. engring. Washington U., 1942-51; prof. urban affairs Washington Univ., from 1965. Dir. Civil Def., 1951-53; mayor of St. Louis, 1953-65. Mem. President's Adv. Commn. Intergovtl. Relations, 1962. Mem. Am. Municipal League (dir., past pres.), U.S. Conference of Mayors (past president), Sigma Xi, Tau Beta Pi. Club: University. Author numerous reports on smoke control. Home: St Louis MO Died Nov. 23, 1970; interred Calvary Mausoleum St Louis MO

TUDOR, CHARLES WILLIAM, artist; b. Akron, O., Apr. 24, 1903; s. Guy Adwill and Ethel (Sapp) T.; student Baldwin-Wallace Coll., 1919-21, Cleve. Art Sch., 1920-21; m. Anna Margaret Matthews, Dec. 24, 1933 (dec.); children—Guy Adwill, Charles William Matthews; m. 2d, Eti Primus, Mar. 11, 1967. Staff artist Cleve. Press, 1923-28, N.Y. Telegram, 1929, Parade Mag., Cleve., 1930-31; art dir. information Rural Resettlement Adminstrn., Greenbelt towns, Washington area, 1935-36; art dept. Life mag., 1936-39, asst. art dir., 1941-46, art dir., 1946-62; art editor PM, 1939-40; art dir. En Guardia mag., Office Co-ordinator Inter-Am. Affairs, 1940; art dir. Office Emergency Management, Washington, 1940-41; free lance artist New Yorker, Town and Country; designer picture books, Christmas Story by Margit Varga, 1946, American Past by Roger Butterfield, 1947, Life's Picture History of Western Man, 1951, World We Live in, 1955; World's Great Religions, 1957, Wonders of Life on Earth, 1960, Life Pictorial Atlas of the World, published 1961; now quality cons. corporate prodn. Time, Inc. Recipient medal Art Dirs. Club, 1951, 54, 56, spl. award, 1958. Designer of Picture Cook Book for Life Mag., 1959; Life Guide to Paris, 1962. Home: New York City NY Died Jan. 16, 1970; buried Truro MA

TUFTS, EDGAR, clergyman, educator; b. Kirkwood, Ga., Dec. 4, 1869; s. Joseph F. and Anna D. (Robinson) T.; A.B., Washington and Lee U., 1894; grad. Union Theol. Sem., Hampden-Sidney, Va., 1897; m. Bessie Hall, of Hampden-Sidney, Apr. 8, 1898. Ordained Presbyn. ministry, 1897; pastor Banner Elk, N.C., since 1897; founder, 1899, and pres. Lees-McRae Inst. Democrat. Home: Banner Elk NC‡

TUFTY, HERBERT IVER, automobile distbr., b. Nunda, S.D., Oct. 20, 1903; s. Iver P. and Tillie (Selland) T.; grad. high sch.; m. Margaret M. Bradfeldt, Apr. 23, 1943; children—Toni (Mrs. Mike Burleigh), Duke, Ted, Trudy. Various positions, 1923-39; part owner, pres. Duke Tufty Co., Sioux Falls, S.D., 1939-61; full owner, pres., 1961-73; pres. Motor Parts, North Sioux Falls, 1954-73; Motor Parts Central, Sioux City, Ia., 1954-73, Jobber Motor Parts, Omaha, Duke Tuffy Leasing, Sioux Falls, 1964-73; dir. So. Br. Nat. Bank, Sioux Falls, Sanders Pub. Co. Finance chmn. Sen. Mundt, 1948-73. Bd. dirs. Hills of Rest Cemetery, Sioux Falls, Children's Hosp. Sioux Falls. Mem. S.D. Auto Dealers Assn. (pres. 1943-45), Sioux Falls Dealers Dodge Adv., Dodge Advt. Assn., Chrysler Council, C. of C. Republican. Lutheran. Mason (Shriner), Elk, Rotarian. Home: Sioux Falls SD Died Jan. 7, 1973.

TUKEY, HAROLD BRADFORD, horticulturist; b. Berwyn, Ill., Sept. 30, 1896; s. James Bradford and Armenia (Mehrhof) T.; B.S., U. of Ill., 1918, M.S., 1920; Ph.D., U. of Chicago, 1932; D.H.C. (honorary), Hanover, Germany, 1957; m. Margaret Davenport. November 23, 1918 (deceased February 7, 1930); children—Loren Davenport, Lois (Mrs. W. D. Baker, Jr.), Ronald Bradford; married 2d, Ruth Ann Schweigert, Nov. 23, 1932; children—Harold Bradford, Ann. Asst. horticulturist N.Y. State Agrl. Expt. Station, 1920-23; horticulturist in charge Hudson Valley Fruit Investigations, 1923-27; chief in research (horticulture), N.Y. State Agricultural Experimental Station, professor pomology, Cornell University, 1927-45. Head dept. of horticulture, Mich. State U., 1945-62, now prof. emeritus; U.S. tech. adv. Internat. Conf. on Atomic Energy, 1955. Commd. 1st lt. F.A., U.S. Army, 1918, serving W.W. Awarded Jackson Dawson Medal, 1948, Marshall P. Wilder medal 1956, N. J. Colman award, 1956, citation Am. Hort. Council, 1957; Gold medal of Honor, 1967; Liberty Hyde Bailey medal, 1967. Fellow A.A.A.S., Royal Hort. Soc. (Eng.), Am. Inst. Biol. Scis. (organizing bd. 1946-47, v.p.); mem. Am. Pomol. Soc. (bd. mgrs. 1925-28; exec. bd., 1925-48; pres. 1950-52; chairman Wilder Medal Award 1942-56, 59-62), Internat. Soc. Horticultural Sci. (pres. 1962-66), Am. Soc. Hort. Sci. (sec.-treas. 1927-46; pres. 1946; editor proc., 1927-50), Bot. Soc. Am., Am. Society Plant Physiologists, American Society Naturalists, Society Growth and Development, Soc. Nationale d'Horticulture de France (hon.), Mass. Hort. Soc., Michigan Horticultural Soc. American Horticultural Society, Phi Kappa Phi, Pi Alpha Xi, Theta Chi, Sigma Xi, Alpha Zeta. Republican. Presbyterian. Rotarian. Author: (books) The Pears of New York (with others), 1921; The Pear and Its Culture, 1929; Plant Regulators in Agrl., 1954; Dwarfed Fruit Trees, 1964. Contbr. to jours., agrl. press, and bulls. expt. sta. Mem. editorial and exec. staff Rural New Yorker, 1923-64; asso. editor Am. Fruit Grower. Contbr. Fruit Year Book (Eng.). Delivered Amos Meml. Lectr. (Eng.), 1952. Del. Internat. Hort. Congress, London, 1952, Scheveningen, 1955, Brussels, 1962, U.S., 1966, pres. XVIIth, 1966. Home: Woodland MI Died Nov. 1971.

TULLER, EDWARD PRATT, clergyman; b. Hartford, Conn., Apr. 16, 1859; s. George Warren and Abby Loveland (James) T.; A.B., Brown U., 1884, A.M., 1887; grad. Newton Theol. Instn., 1887; D.D., Kalamazoo Coll., 1904; m. Ella E. Lawton, Sept. 2, 1884; children—Charles Lawton, Abbie Loveland. Ordained Bapt. ministry, 1886; pastor Providence, 1886-87, First Ch., Newport, R.I., 1887-92, Second Ch., Lawrence, Mass., 1892-1901, First Ch., Detroit, 1901-04, Memorial Bapt. Ch., Chicago, 1904-06, Brighton Avenue Ch., Boston, 1906-15, First Church, Hyannis, 1915-17, Glendale Bapt. Ch., Everett, Mass., 1917-30. Lecturer on psychology of religion, Newton Theol. Instn., 1909-10, 1918-19. Mem. bd. of mgrs., Am. Bapt. Foreign Mission Soc., 1888-1915, sec. bd., 1901-06. Trustee Kalamazoo Coll., 1902-05, Boston Sch. of Expression, 1904-24, Newton Theol. Instn., 1907-39 (exec. com. 1908-36, sec. of trustees 1910-36). Mem. Delta Upsilon, Phi Beta Kappa. Club: C.C." (Boston). Contbr. to religious press. Home: Barnstable MA‡

TULLIS, ROBERT LEE, lawyer; b. Tensas Parish, La., June 10, 1864; s. Eli and Caroline Juliet (Hadermann) T.; student La. State U., and Vanderbilt U.; LL.B., Tulane U., 1887; m. Maggie Josephine Texada, Oct. 3, 1891 (died Feb. 12, 1901); 1 son, Edward Hadermann; m. 2d, Octavia Gayden, Oct. 23, 1919. Practiced law at New Orleans, 1889-97; sec. to mayor of New Orleans, 1897-99; resumed practice, 1899; prof. La. jurisprudence, La. State U., 1907-33, and dean Law Sch., 1912-33, now dean emeritus. Mem. Am. and La. bar assns., Am. Law Inst., Nat. Conf. Commrs. on Uniform State Laws, Phi Kappa Phi. Order of the Coif. Address: 803 Lake Park Dr., P.O. Box 2334, Baton Rouge 2‡

TUMILTY, HOWARD T(INSLEY), lawyer, corp. exec.; b. Bowling Green, Mo., Sept. 19, 1898; s. John and Flora Louise (Krebs) T.; student pub. schs. of Mo.; m. Louise E. Edwards, Oct. 5, 1925; children—Jack E., Richard C. Admitted to Okla. bar, 1920, pvt. practice Oklahoma City, 1920-22, 26-34; asst. co. atty. Oklahoma Co., 1923-25; asso. Am.-First Title & Trust Co., 1934-59, gen. counsel, v.p., dir., 1937-59, pres., 1959-60; pres. Southwest Title & Trust Co., 1960-64, gen. counsel, 1964-65; mem. firm Hanson, Fisher, Tumilty, Peterson & Thompkins, attorneys, Oklahoma City, 1966-69. Private AUS, 1918. Mem. Am., Okla. (p. pres.) bar assns., Am. Law Inst., Am. Jud. Soc., Delta Theta Phi. Presbyn. Author: Title Guaranty Handbook, 1943; Attorney's Title Guaranty Manual, 1961. Home: Oklahoma City OK Died June 3, 1969; buried Memorial Park, Oklahoma City OK

TUNISON, ABRAM VORHIS, govt. ofcl.; b. Geneva, N.Y., Apr. 16, 1909; s. John Smalley and Kate (Quigley) T.; B.S., in Gen. Agr., Cornell U., 1930, M.S. in Animal Nutrition, 1932, student Grad. Sch., 1938-40; m. Frances Clementine Bishop, Aug. 9, 1930; children—June P. (Mrs. George M. Gans, Jr.), John B., Kay D. (Mrs. Lee M. Eidson). Technician. Gen. Seafoods Corp., 1930-31; aquatic biologist N.Y. State Conservation Dept., 1932-44; with Fish and Wildlife Service, Dept. Interior, 1944-71, dep. dir. Bur. Sport Fisheries and Wildlife, 1964-70, staff asst. to asst. sec. interior, 1970-71. Recipient Distinguished Service award Dept. Interior, 1967. Mem. Am. Fisheries Soc. (hon. lif), Wildlife Soc., Internat. Assn. Game and Fish Commrs., Am. Soc. Limnology and Oceanography, N.Y. Acad. Scis., Am. Chem. Soc., A.A.A.S. Home: Falls Church VA Died Jan. 3, 1971; buried Grove Cemetery, Trumansburg NY

TUPOLEV, ANDREI NIKOLAEVICH, aircraft designer; b. Pustomazovo, Tver, USSR Nov. 10, 1888; graduate Moscow Higher Technical Sch. in 1915. Began career as designer wind tunnels, glider; assisted establishment Aerodynamic Aircraft Design Bur., 1916, became Central Inst. Aerodynamics and Hydrodynamics, 1919, then head of designing bureau; dep. directors of the Main Adminstrn. of the Aircraft Industry, USSR People's Commissariat of Heavy Industry, 1932, also dir., chief designer Exptl. Aircraft Constrn. Plant to 1938; polit. prisoner, 1938-43; lt. gen. Air Force Engring. and Tech. Service; designed metal constrn. single-engine monoplane, eight-engine, forty ton aircraft, twin-engine, double-fin dive bomber, 1938, four-engine plane, 1944, super-heavy four-engine bomber, 1945-46; designed, produced jet passenger plane for 50 passengers, 1950; design and exptl. constrn. super-heavy jet aircraft for 170 passengers, 1955-56, deluxe improved design, 1957; designed double-deck airliner with four propjet engines, TU-144 Supersonic Transport. Deputy Supreme Soviet, USSR, 1950, 54. Decorated Order of Lenin; recipient Stalin prize, Lenin prize for aircraft design; Hero of Socialist Labor award (2), others. Mem. USSR Acad. Scis. Address: Moscow USSR Died Dec. 1972.

TUPPER, JAMES WADDELL, coll. prof.; b. Sheet Harbor, N.S., Mar. 31, 1870; s. John and Eliza Bedford (Waddell) T.; B.A., Dalhousie Coll., Halifax, N.S., 1891; Ph.D., Johns Hopkins, 1895; m. Mary Patterson Harmon, Dec. 30, 1903; 1 son, Harmon. Prof. of English and of history, Western U., London, Ont., 1897-1900; asso. in English, Bryn Mawr Coll., 1900-02; instr. in English, Harvard, 1902-04; asso. prof. English lit., Lafayette Coll., 1906-09, prof. 1909-47, prof. emeritus, 1947, lecturer, Johns Hopkins Unvi., Univ. of Tex., Rutgers, New York U., summers. Chmn. Conf. on English in the Cent. Atl. States, 1914, 1917-19, 1931. Mem. Modern Lang. Assn. America, Phi Beta Kappa. Editor: D'Avenant's Love and Honour, and The Siege of Rhodes, 1909; Representative English Dramas (with Frederick Tupper), 1914; Narrative and Lyric Poems, 1927; English Poems from Dryden to Blake, 1933. Address: 120 McCartney St., Easton PA‡

TURCK, FENTON BENEDICT, cons. engr.; b. Chgo., May 4, 1902; s. Fenton Benedict and Avis Loveland (Paine) T.; B.S., Sheffield Sci. Sch., Yale, 1923; m. Claire Schenck, 1925 (div. 1940); 1 dau., Lorraine; m. 2d, Eleanor Plenge, 1945; children—Fenton Benedict III, Nancy. With Am. Radiator & Standard Sanitary Corp., 1923-39, v.p., 1929-39; pres. F. B. Turck & Co., Inc., cons. engrs., from 1938. Am. del. to Internat. Congress, Paris, 1946; mem. Distbn. Hall Fame, Boston Conf. Distbn. Trustee Fla. Ocean Scis. Inst., Inc., Deerfield Beach. Decorated Officer Order of Orange Nassau (Netherlands); recipient citation for engring. contbn. to distbn. Am. Soc. M.E., 1953. Profl. engr., N.Y. Fellow Am. Soc. M.E.; mem. Am. Inst. Cons. Engrs., Holland Soc., Nat. Soc. Profl. Engineers, National Institute of Social Sciences, Newcomen Society, S.A.R., Soc. Colonial Wars. Clubs: University, Elizabethan, Metropolitan Opera (New York, City). Author: Applying Engineering Principles to Distribution; Scientific Methods of Distribution; The American Explosion; Changes in Distribution Economics; Distribution of Diversified New Products; Ideas, Inertia and Achievement; also papers on indsl. operations. Established Turck Lectures on Distbn., Yale, 1951. Home: New York City NY Died Sept. 19, 1970.

TURLEY, CLARENCE MILTON, realtor, appraiser; b. St. Louis, Sept. 16, 1893; s. Joseph Sylvester and Lorena (Vogel) T.; LL.B., Benton Coll., 1916; m. Clarice H. Koch, Sept. 14, 1968; children—Clarence M., Ruth Jeanne (Mrs. Herbert E. Hetzler). Vice pres. Isaac T. Cook Co., 1913-28; pres., dir. Clarence M. Turley, Inc., St. Louis, 1928-70, also Arcade Bldg. Co., Eighth & Locust Realty Co.; sec.-treas., dir. Ambassador-Missouri Bldg. Corp., Monogram Bldg. Corp.; dir. Title Ins. Co., Delmar Bank of University City, Hydraulic Press Brick Co., Roosevelt Fed. Savs. & Loan Assn. Dir., exec. bd. St. Louis council Boy Scouts Am.; treas., chmn. exec. com. St. Louis Redevel. Corp.; pres. Civic Progress, Inc., 1962-63. Dir. Govtl. Research Inst.; trustee Carthage Coll. Mem. C. of C., St. Louis Real Estate Bd., Nat. Assn. Real Estate Bds. (pres. 1956), Am. Inst. Real Estate Appraisers (pres. 1952), Inst. Real Estate Mgmt., Soc. Indsl. Realtors, Nat. Assn. Bldg. Owners and Mgrs. (pres. 1936), Am., St. Louis bar assns., Soc. Real Estate Councillors (trustee). Mason (Shriner). Club: Optimist (St. Louis). Home: St Louis MO Died June 6, 1970.

TURNAGE, ALLEN HAL, marine corps officer; b. Farmville, N.C., Jan. 3, 1891; s. William J. and Ora (Smith) T.; ed. Homer Mil. Sch., Oxford, N.C.; hon. LL.D., U. of N.C., 1946; m. Hannah Pyke Torrey, July 21, 1920. Commd. 2d lt., Marine Corps, 1913; promoted through grades to lt. gen.; comd. 3d Marine Div., July 1943-Sept. 1944; dir. personnel and asst. comdt. U.S.M.C., 1944-46. Decorated Navy Cross, Navy D.S.M., Navy Legion of Merit, Haitian D.S.M., Nicaraguan D.S.M., Medal of Merit, Santo Domingo. Mem. Sigma Nu. Home: Wide Water VA Died Oct. 22, 1971.

TURNBULL, ANDREW WINCHESTER, author, educator; b. Balt., Feb. 2, 1921; s. Bayard and Margaret Carroll (Jones) T.; A.B. with high honors, Princeton, 1942; M.A., Harvard, 1947, Ph.D. in European History, 1954; m. Joanne Tudhope Johnson, Dec. 18, 1954; children—Joanne Tudhope, Frances Litchfield. Clk., ECA, Paris, 1951-52; instr. humanities Mass. Inst. Tech., 1954-58; free-lance writer, 1958-67; Fulbright lectr. Am. lit. U. Bordeaux (France), 1967-68; vis. prof. Brandeis U., also Trinity Coll., Hartford, Conn., 1969, Brown U., 1969-70. Served to lt. USNR, 1942-46, Guggenheim fellow, 1964-65. Presbyn. Author: Scott Fitzgerald, 1962; Thomas Wolfe, 1968. Editor: Letters of F. Scott Fitzgerald, 1963. Address: Cambridge MA Died Jan. 10, 1970; buried Glencoe MD

TURNER, DANIEL LAWRENCE, civ. eng'r; b. Portsmouth, Va., Oct. 25, 1869; s. Daniel James and Mary Elizabeth (Lawrence) T.; early ed'n Norfolk (Va.) Acad.; grad. Rensselaer Poly. Inst., C.E., 1891; m. at Norfolk, Va., Feb. 3, 1896, Eva Barcine Denby. Asst. in mathematics, Rensselaer Poly. Inst., 1892-3; in active practice as civ. eng'r in Conn., N.Y. State and New York City since 1893; instr. in surveying and hydraulics, and in charge Harvard Eng'ring Camp, Harvard Univ., 1893-1903; asst. eng'r in charge of stations Rapid Transit R. R. Comm'n, New York. Mem. Am. Soc. Civ. Eng'rs. Author: Sketch and Note Book for Stadia Work, E15. Residence: 220 W. 107th St. Office: Rapid Transit R. R. Commission, 320 Broadway, New York NY‡

TURNER, DANIEL W(EBSTER), ex-gov.; b. Corning, Ia., Mar. 17, 1877; s. Austin Bates and Almira (Baker) T.; ed. Corning Acad.; m. Alice Sample, Sept. 27, 1900; children—Mrs. Marjorie Witt, Ned, Thomas. Engaged in farming near Corning since 1894. Mem. Ia. State Senate, 1904-08; gov. of Ia. for term 1931-33. Del. Rep. Nat. Conv., 1928, 32 and 36. Served with Iowa Vol. Inf., in P.I., Spanish Am. War, May 1898-Nov. 1899. Republican. Presbyterian. Home: Corning IA Died Apr. 15, 1969; buried Walnut Grove Cemetery, Corning IA

TURNER, GARDNER CLYDE, lawyer; b. Ludlow, Mass., Mar. 3, 1910; s. Clyde A. and G. (Estes) T.; A.B., Harvard, 1932, LL.B., 1935; hon. degree N.H. Sch. Accounting and Commerce; m. Virginia Wells, Aug. 16, 1941. Admitted to N.H. bar, 1937, U.S. Supreme Ct.; asso. pvt. law practice Philip H. Faulkner, Keen, N.H., 1937-43; pvt. practice, Keene, 1946-70; atty. gen. N.H., 1961, also newspaper columnist, polit. writer. Former gen. counsel U.S. Senate Appropriations Com. Investigations Staff; counsel to minority U.S. Senate Appropriations com., spl. asst. to Senator Styles Bridges; mem. N.H. Gen. Ct., 1947, 49-51 (chmn. judiciary com.; mem. rules com.; majority floor leader Ho. Reps.); chairman of the board of selectman Town of Sullivan, 1964-70; mem. N.H. Legislative Council. Past treas., co-owner Brentwood Products, Inc. Member adv. bd. registrants SSS, 1942-70. N.H. atty. War Manpower Commn., 1945; mem. Gov.'s Commn. for Reorgn. State Govt.; chmn. Interim Com. to Study Tax Exempt Property; chmn. exec. com. Cheshire County Legislative Conv.; del. N.H. Constl. Conv., 1948, mem. Bill of Rights Com. Mem. exec. com. N.H. Republican Com.; treas., finance chmn. Cheshire County Republican Com. Chmn. bd. trustees N.H. State Indsl. Sch. 1950-61; chmn. N.H. Bd. of Hosps., Instns. and Corrections, 1956-61; chmn. Gov's. Mental Health Survey Com., 1957-59; bd. dirs. N.H. Citizens Council Gen. Welfare, 1950-52; adv. bd. Spaulding Youth Center, Tilton, N.H.; adv. bd. New Eng. Coll. Served to lt. (j.g.) USNR, 1943-45. Mem. Harvard Alumni Assn., Harvard Law Sch. Alumni Assn., Monadnock Region Assn., Soc. Protection N.H. Forests, S.A.R., Atlantic Union, Am., Fed. N.H., Cheshire County bar assns., Farm Bur. Fedn., N.H. Maple Products Assn., N.H. Council of Towns (past dir.), Keene Jr. C. of C. (past v.p.). Episcopalian. Clubs: Harvard (Lowell, Mass.); Harvard of N.H. (Concord); Boothbay Harbor (Me.) Yacht; Sullivan Golf. Contbr. legal articles to trade jours., polit. feature stories to newspapers. Home: East Sullivan NH also Lowell MA Died Jan. 23, 1970; buried Lowell MA

TURNER, GEORGE KIBBE, author; b. Quincy, Ill., Mar. 23, 1869; s. Rodolphus K. and Sarah Ella (Kibbe) T.; A.B., Williams Coll., 1890; m. Julia Hawks Patchen, Oct. 19, 1892. Began newspaper work, 1891. Editor and staff writer on McClure's Magazine, 1906-17. Author: The Taskmasters, 1902; Memories of a Doctor, 1913; The Last Christian, 1914; The Autobiography of a Million Dollars, 1918; Red Friday, 1919; Hagar's Hoard, 1920; White Shoulders, 1921; The Girl in the Glass Cage, 1927. Contbr. short stories, articles and poems to various mags.; also motion pictures, including Held in Trust; Those Who Dance; Street of Forgotten Men. Home: Coconut Grove FL‡

TURNER, HENRY CHANDLEE, JR., constrn. co. exec.; b. Bklyn., Apr. 24, 1902; s. Henry C. and Charlotte H. (Chapman) T.; A.B., Swarthmore Coll., 1923; m. Virginia Melick, Aug. 16, 1928; children—Virginia Ann, Mary Chandlee. Vice pres. Phila. office, Turner Constrn. Co., 1938-47, pres., N.Y.C., 1947-65, chmn., 1965-70, chmn. exec. com., 1971-73, also dir.; dir. Liberty Mut. Ins. Co., Boston, Provident Nat. Corp., Phila., Liberty Mut. Fire Ins. Co.; trustee Conn. Gen. Mortgage & Realty Investments. Trustee Com. Econ. Devel., Colonial Williamsburg, Inc., Phipps Houses; bd. dirs. Econ. Devel. Council, N.Y.C. Mem. Commerce and Industry Assn. N.Y. (dir.) Clubs: Indian Harbor Yacht (Greenwich); Blind Brook (Port Chester); Pinnacle (N.Y.C.); Round Hill (Greenwich); Economic (dir.), Links (N.Y.C.). Home: Greenwich CT Died Apr. 12, 1973.

TURNER, HENRY H., physician; b. Harrisburg, Ill., Aug. 28, 1892; s. John William and Alice (Rose) T.; student St. Louis U., 1914-15, Sch. of Medicine, 1915-18; M.D., U. of Louisville 1921; m. Frances Bulkley, June 28, 1923; children—Marian Frances, Alice Ann. Asst. in medicine U. Louisville, 1921-24; instr. U. Okla. Sch. Medicine, 1924-28, asst. prof. medicine, 1928-29, asso., clin. prof. 1939-69, clin. prof. medicine emeritus, 1969-70, asso. dean, 1948-49; pvt. practice internal med., 1925-70; resident in medicine Louisville Hosp., 1922-24; vis. physician Okla. State U. Hosp., State Crippled Children's Hosp., St. Anthony's Hosp., Okla., 1924-70; cons. endocrinologist University and Children's Hosp., 1924-70; chief metabolic clinic out-patient dept., Univ. Hosp., 1924-70; sec.-treas., Endocrine Soc., 1941 (v.p. 1937-38, council 1938-41). Seale Harris award So. Med. Assn., 1961. Schering Scholar, 1959. Diplomate Am. Bd. Internatl Medicine. Fellow A.C.P.; mem. Am., So. (v.p. 1938-39, trustee 1962-63) med. assns., Soc. Nuclear Medicine (pres. 1959-60), Am. Therapeutic Soc. (pres. 1939-40), Central Soc. Clin. Research, Okla. Med. Assn. (pres. 1940-41). Oklahoma County Med. Soc., Endocrine Soc. (sec.-treas. 1941-66, pres. 1967-68), Oklahoma City Acad. Medicine (sec. 1937, pres. 1938). Clubs: Doctor's Dinner, Lotus, Tower. Contbr. articles to med. jours. and books. Home: Oklahoma City OK Died Aug. 4, 1970.

TURNER, ROSCOE, aviator; b. Corinth, Miss., Sept. 29, 1895; s. Robert Lee and Aquilla (Derryberry) T.; ed. pub. schs., business coll.; m. Carline Stovall, Sept. 29, 1924; m. 2d, Margaret Madonna Miller, Dec. 1946. Chmn. bd. Roscoe Turner Aero Corp.; cons. House Com. Science and Astronautics, 1960, 63, Barnstorming flyer and stunt performer, 1919-27; operated pioneer comml. air field, Richmond, Va., 1927-28; operated world's pioneer high speed air line, 1929-30; holder cross country speed records Nat. Air Races, as winner Bendix Race, 11 hrs. 30 mins. N.Y. to Los Angeles, 1933 (record still standing in 1938); Nat. Air Races as winner Thompson Trophy Race, 1934, 38, 39; finished 2d. Speed Div., Internat. Air Race from London to Melbourne, 1934. Awarded Harmon Trophy by Ligue Internationale des Aviateurs as America's premier aviator for 1932. Served Air Service. World War; disch. 1st lt., 1919. Decorated Distinguished Flying Cross, 1952; recipient Paul Tissandier Diploma, Federation Aeronautique Internationale, (Austria), 1956; Beechcraft Man of Year award, 1960; Spl. Recognition award Ind. Aviation Trades Assn., 1960; Silver Wings award, 1964; Distinguished Citizen award Ind. dept. Am. Legion, 1969; Distinguished Nat. Vets. award Combined Vets. Orgns., 1969; honored with Col. Roscoe Turner Day in City of Indpls., 1969; Roscoe Turner Musuem established in his honor. Formerly col. gov.'s staff of Nev. Nat. Guard, Miss. Nat. Guard, on staff gov. of Cal.; now colonel in Civil Air Patrol. Honorary mem. Los Angeles Police Dept.; Sheriff's Staff, Los Angeles; capt. Aero Police, St. Joseph, Mo.; C. of C. Pitts.; Jr. C. of C., Dayton, O.; New York Detective Endowment Assn. Mem. Quiet Birdmen, Nat. Aeronautic Assn., Racing Pilots Assn. of Nat. Aeronautic Assn., Ind. Soc. of Chgo., Nat. Pilots Assns., Conquistadores Del. Celo. Am. Legion, Ligue Internationale des Aviateurs, Texas Rangers, Ind., Indpls. chambers commerce, Civil Air Patrol, Civil Air Patrol Nat. Aerospace Edn. Assn., Am. Inst. Aeros. and Astronautics, Air Force Assn., Nat. Aviation Traders Assn., Nat. Defense Transp. Assn., Inst. Aero. Scis., Soc. Automotive Engrs., Sigma Alpha Tau, other orgns. Mason (Shriner); mem. Order Eastern Star. Clubs: Flying (Columbus, O.), Kiwanis (Cleve.); Lions (Anderson, S.C.). Home: Indianapolis IN Died June 23, 1970; interred Crown Hill Cemetary Mausoleum, Indianapolis IN

TURNER, ROY JOSEPH, ex-gov. of Okla.; b. Lincoln County, Okla., Nov. 6, 1894; s. Reason and Etta Louise (Rogers) T.; student Hill's Business Univ., Oklahoma City; m. Jessica E. Grimm, Aug. 11, 1937; children—Betty, Bill (adopted twins). Bookkeeper, Morris & Co. Packing Co., Oklahoma City, 1911-15; salesman Goodyear Tire and Rubber Co., 1916; real estate business Okla., Fla., Tex., 1920-28; partner Harper-Turner Oil Co., independent oil producers, Oklahoma City, 1928-73; founder Turner ranch, Sulphur, Okla., 1933, established Turner purebred Hereford herd, 1935; mem. Oklahoma City Bd. of Edn., 1939-46; gov. of Okla., 1946-50. Served as pvt. U.S. Army, World War I. Mem. Am. Hereford Assn. (pres. 1939, 1945-60), Am. Legion. Democrat. Methodist. Mason. Home: Oklahoma City OK Died June 11, 1973.

TURNER, SCOTT, mining; b. Lansing, Mich., July 31, 1880; s. James Munroe and Sophie Porter (Scott) T.; A.B., U. of Mich., 1902, D.Eng., 1930; B.S. and E.M., Mich. Coll. Mines, 1904, D.Eng., 1932; Sc.D., Colorado School of Mines, 1930; D.Sc., Kenyon Coll., 1940; m. Amy Prudden, June 25, 1919. Mining engr., Ida. and Ore., 1902, Ariz., 1904, Calif., Panama, Nev. and Colo., 1905; examining engr., Nev., 1906; mining engr., Ida., 1906; asso. editor Mining Scientific Press, 1907; mining engr., Alaska, Wash., 1908; mine geologist, Calif. and Pacific Coast, 1909-10; mine examiner, Europe, 1911; mine mgr., Norway and Spitzbergen, 1912-16; mining engr., Peru, Chile, Bolivia, 1916-17; cons. engr., Can., 1919-25; dir. U.S. Bur. Mines, 1926-34; v.p. and dir. various mining cos., consultant in mining. Mem. Nat. Research Council, tech. com. and Div. Fed. Relations; mem. Nuclear, orgn. and geophys. coms. of Internat. Geol. Congress; mem. research com. Engring. Foundation; Holmes Safety Assn. (past pres.); mem. Geol. Soc. of Am.; mem. Council and Bd., World Power Conf.; mem. tech. adv. com. Fed. Oil Conservation Bd., 1926-34. Sole U.S. del. to Empire Mining Congress, Can., 1928. Apptd. by Dept. of Justice as mem. U.S. Anaconda Smelter Smoke Commn., 1926; apptd. by sec. of state as U.S. del. to World Engring. Congress, Tokyo, 1929; to World Power Conf., Berlin, 1930; to Internat. Congress of Mining, Liege, Belgium, 1930; Apptd. by secy. of treas. to U.S. Assay Commission and other important Fed. posts. Past chmn. Nat. Interfrat. Conf.; chmn. Hoover Medal Bd. of Award; dir. Belgian-Am. Ednl. Foundation; mem. Nat. Technol. Adv. Com. apptd. by sec. of war. Recipient Hoover medal (engring.), 1957. Served as lieutenant (s.g.) USNRF, 1917-19. Mem. Am. Inst. Mining, Metall. and Petroleum Engrs. (past pres.), Am. Inst. of Cunsulting Engrs. (pres.), Mining and Metall. Soc. Am., Canadian Inst. Mining and Metallurgy, Lake Superior Mining Inst., hon. mem. Am. Zinc Inst., Coal Mining Inst. of Am., Am. Rifle Assn., S.A.R., Tau Beta Pi, Psi Upsilon (nat. pres.). Republican. Mason. Clubs: Leash; Hammonasset Fishing; Burning Tree, Chevy Chase, Cosmos, Met. (Washington); Round Hill, Milbrook Gun (pres.), Engineers, River Hills Fishing (Conn.); Turtle Lake (Mich.); University, Century Assn., Mining, Explorers; Camp Fire of Am.; Boone and Crockett; Preston Mountain Club, Incorporated, Verbank Hunting and Fishing, Economic, A.R.A. Assn. (New York). Home: Greenwich CT Died July 30, 1972; buried Mt. Hope Cemetery, Lansing MI

TURNER, WILLIAM WOOD, ins. co. exec.; b. Hartwell, O., Sept. 22, 1891; s. William Mather and Jorinne (Harris) T.; M.E., Cornell U., 1915; m. Dorothy Wilsey, Jan. 10, 1923; children—Marcia (Mrs. Kurt W. Kreyling), Judith (Mrs. Richard C. Blackwell). Investment banker, 1923-38; rep. sr. security holders, dir. Republic Natural Gas Co., Dallas, 1934-61, Central Ohio Light & Power Co., Findlay, 1930-55, Colo. Central Power Co., Denver, 1934-61; chmn. exec. com., dir. Old Republic Life Ins. Co., Chgo., from 1934; pres., dir. Fiberesin Plastics Co., Fiberform, Inc.; dir. Old Republic Ins. Co. Mem. Newcomen Soc. N.A., Soc. Mayflower Descendents. Clubs: University, Mid-America, Skyline, Tavern (Chgo.). Home: Winnetka IL Died May 22, 1971.

TURQUETIL, ARSENE, bishop; b. Reviers, France, June 3, 1876; s. Felix and Maria (Ducellier) T.; grad., Minor Sem. of Villiers-le-Sec., 1886-94, Maj. Sem. of Sommervieu, 1894-96, Novitiate of Oblate Fathers, Angers, 1896-97, Maj. Sem. of Oblate Fathers, Liege, Belgium, 1897-1900. Ordained priest R.C. Ch., Dec. 23, 1899; missionary to Eskimos, Northern Canada, 1900-43, Reindeer Lake Indian Mission, Northern Saskatchewan, 1900, with Eskimos in N.W. territories, 1901; founded 1st Eskimo mission, Chesterfield Inlet, Hudson Bay, 1912; established 13 mission-posts, erected 1 hosp.; apptd. Prefect Apostolic for Hudson Bay, 1924, Vicar Apostolic, 1931; consecrated bishop, 1932; ret., 1943. Decorated Knight, French Legion of Honor. Address: care Scholasticate of Oblate Fathers of Mary Immaculate, 391 Michigan Av., N.E., Washington‡

TUTEN, J(AMES) RUSSELL, govt. ofcl., congressman; b. Appling County, Ga., July 23, 1911; s. Joseph Alexander and Ruth (Rogers) T.; student South Ga. College, Georgia Southern Coll.; m. Hazel Wicker, Aug. 20, 1939; children—James Russell, John Alec, Ernest, Mark. Mem. 88th U.S. Congress, 9th Dist. Georgia, mem. 89th U.S. Congress, 8th District Ga.; spl. asst. to adminstr. Gen. Services Adminstrn., 1966-67; co-chmn. Coastal Plains Regional Commn., 1967-68. Past city commr., also mayor, Brunswick, Ga. Chmn. bd. trustees Brewton Parker Coll. Mem. Brunswick-Glynn County C. of C. Democrat. Baptist (deacon, chmn. bd. deacons), Elk, Mason (Shriner; past grand marshal Ga.), Kiwanian; mem. Order Eastern Star. Home: Falls Church VA Died Aug. 1968.

TUTHILL, ALEXANDER MACKENZIE, surg.; b. S. Lebanon, N.Y., Sept. 22, 1871; s. William H. and Christina (Mackenzie) T.; grad. high sch., Los Angeles, Calif., 1890; M.D., U. of Southern Calif., 1895; m. May E. Heimann, Nov. 16, 1896; children—Dorothy Ila Lange, Christine Elizabeth Warbasse. Began practice at Los Angeles, 1895; chief surgeon Detroit Copper Co., Morenci, Ariz., 1903-16; state supt. pub. health of Ariz., 1921-22. Mem. Constl. Conv., Ariz., 1910. Enlisted as pvt. Troop D, N.G. Calif., 1896; capt. Troop A, N.G. Ariz., 1903-10; col. 1st Ariz. Inf., 1910-17; apptd. brig. gen. N.A., Aug. 5, 1917; served on Mexican border, 1916-17; assigned as commdr. 79th Inf. Brig., Camp Kearny; with A.E.F., Aug. 1918-Mar. 1919; later major gen. Nat. Guard Ariz., comdg. 45th Div. (Okla., Colo., N.M. and Ariz.); retired at age limit with rank maj. gen. Ariz. for life and detailed as sr. tactical comdr. and asst. adj. gen., now the adjutant gen. state dir. Selective Service. Mem. A.M.A.; fellow Am. Coll. Surgeons. Mason (32 deg., Shriner). Home: 2 Pasadena Av., Phoenix AZ

TUTTLE, CHARLES H(ENRY), lawyer; b. New York, N.Y., Apr. 21, 1879; s. Henry Croswell and Penelope (Cooke) T.; A.B., Columbia, 1899, LL.B., 1902; m. Helene L. Wheeler; children—Evelyn, Charlotte, Croswell, Jasmine. Admitted to N.Y. bar, 1902, and began practice at N.Y. City; mem. firm Davies, Auerbach & Cornell, 1907-27; later mem. Breed, Abbott & Morgan. Chmn. Selective Service Bd. No. 145, N.Y. City, World War I. Chmn. of Appeal Bd., No. 4 N.Y. City World War II, U.S. atty., 1927-30. Mem. spl. com. Nat. Crime Commn. since 1927; mem. exec. com.. N.Y. State Reorgn. Commn., 1926. Trustee Coll. City of New York; mem. bd. higher edn., City of New York. One of incorporators Religious Edn. Foundation; chmn. Christian edn. Protestant Council of New York; trustee International Council Religious Education. Delegate to Rep. Nat. Conv., 1928. Mem. Am. and N.Y. State bar assns., New York County Lawyers Assn., Assn. Bar City of New York, Trade and Commerce Bar Assn., Alumni Assn. Columbia College Alumni Assn. Columbia Law Sch., Lake George Assn. Episcopalian. Mason (33 degree, Shriner), Elk. Clubs: National Republican, Lawyers, Columbia University, Church. Home: New York City NY Died Jan. 26, 1971; buried Evergreen Cemetery, Lake George NY

TUTTLE, EDWIN FRANK, b. Dedham, Mass., May 16, 1875; s. David Levi and Mary R. (Gilbert) T.; grad. Uxbridge (Mass.) High Sch., 1894; m. Colletta Alice Parker, of Melrose, Mass., July 27, 1898. One of founders of Nat. Prog. Party, 1912; delegate Progressive National Convention, 1912, 1916; mem. Prog. Nat. Com. from R.I., 1912-16; chmn. R.I. Progressive Executive Com. and State Central Com., 1912; Prog. candidate for Congress, 3d R.I. Dist., 1912, 1914. Stumped Mass., R.I. and N.Y., campaign of 1912, for Roosevelt; stumped Me., N.Y. and Pa. for Wilson, 1916; stumped N.H., Mass. and R.I. for Cox, 1920, also Mass. and R.I. for League of Nations; Democratic nominee for gen. treas. of R.I., 1916, declined. Civilian rep. Salvation Army since 1921. Baptist. Mason. Author: The Bee in Ancient History; The Mission of the Salvation Army. Home: Cloverlawn, South Milford MA Office: 39 Howard St., Boston MA‡

TUTTLE, THOMAS DYER, physician; b. Fulton, Mo., Feb. 17, 1869; s. Warren W. and Susan C. (Dyer) T.; B.S., Westminster Coll., Fulton, Mo., 1889; M.D., Coll. Phys. & Surg. (Columbia), New York, 1892; m. Lucile Wiseman, of Centralia, Mo., Sept. 23, 1896. Began practice New York, 1892; removed to Mont., 1898; exec. officer State Bd. of Health, Mont., 1903-12; pres. Mont. State Tuberculosis Sanatorium, Dec. 17, 1912-—. Mem. A.M.A., Am. Pub. Health Assn., Assn. State and Provincial Bds. of Health, Nat. Assn. Study and Prevention of Tuberculosis, etc. Democrat. Presbyn. Mason. Author: Principles of Public Health, 1910. Address: Uarmspring MT‡

TUTTLE, W(ILLIAM) B(UCKHOUT), pub. service exec.; b. Austinburg, O., July 3, 1874; s. Albert H. and Kate (Seeley) T.; student U. of Va.; m. Leila House, 1898. Was student-instr. U. of Va.; asst. to supt. Consol. Gas Co. of N.J., 1896-97, supt., 1898-1902, gen. mgr., 1902-06; asst. to engr. Am. Light & Traction Co., N.Y. City, 1897-98; v.p. and gen. mgr. San Antonio (Tex.) Gas & Electric Co. and San Antonio Traction Co., 1906-16; v.p., gen. mgr. San Antonio Pub. Service Co., 1916-18, v.p., 1918-22, pres.; 1922-35; chmn. bd., 1935-42; chmn. City Pub. Service Bd., 1942-48; cons. engr. since 1948. Chmn., Alamo Soil Conservation Dist. No. 330, San Antonio River Canal and Conservancy Dist. Asso. mem. Naval Consulting Bd., Feb.-Sept. 1916; col. 2d Tex. Cav., Apr.-July 1918; maj. Constrn. Div., Q.M.C., U.S.A., July 1918-Mar. 1919; maj. Engr. O.R.C., 1921-23, lt. col., 1923-26, col. since 1926. Pres. emeritus Alamo Council Boy Scouts of Am. Mem. Am. Soc. M.E., Am. Inst. E.E., Soc. Am. Mil. Engrs., Res. Officers Assn. of U.S., Izaak Walton League America. Mason (Shriner). Clubs: Rotary, San Antonio Country; Army Navy Country, Army and Navy (Washington, D.C.). Home: 185 Terrell Rd. Office: 201 N. St. Mary's St., San Antonio TX

TVARDOVSKY, ALEXANDR TRIFONOVICH, Russian poet; born in 1910; educated Moscow Inst. History, Philosophy and Lit. Editor: Novy Mir. Mem. Presidium, Union Soviet Writers. Decorated Order of Lenin; State prize winner, 1941, 45, 47, Lenin prize for Beyond the Beyond, 1961. Author: (anthologies) The Road, 1934; Village Chronicles, 1939; Zagorye, 1941; Muravia, 1936; Vasil Tyorkin, 1941-45; House by the Roadside, 1943-46; Beyond the Beyond, 1953-57; Articles and Notes on Literature; Home and Abroad (prose), 1960; Selected Poems, 1964; Tyorkin in the Other World, 1964; Complete Works in 5 Vols., 1966-71. Address: Moscow USSR Died Dec. 18, 1971; buried Novo-Devichie Cemetery, Moscow USSR

TWEED, HARRISON, lawyer; b. New York, N.Y., Oct. 18, 1885; s. Charles Harrison and Helen Minerva (Evarts) T.; prep. edn., St. Mark's Sch., 1899-1903; A.B., Harvard, 1907, LL.B., 1910, LL.D., 1958; LL.D. (hon.), Syracuse U. 1954; m. Barbara Banning, Nov. 21, 1942; 1 d., Sandra Barbette; children by previous marriages—Eleanor (Mrs. Herbert von Metzier), Katharine Winthrop. Admitted to the New York bar and began with Byrne & Cutcheon, New York, 1910, became member of law firm of Byrne, Cutcheon & Taylor, 1916; now mem. firm Milbank, Tweed, Hadley & McCloy. Pres., Legal Aid Soc. N.Y., 1936-45, dir., 1946-69; chmn. com. on continuing legal edn. Am. Law Inst.-Am. Bar Assn., 1947-66, mem., 1967-69; pres. Nat. Legal Aid and Defender Assn., 1949-55, dir., 1956-69; chmn. N.Y. Temporary Com. on Courts, 1953-58; co-chmn. Lawyers' Com. for Civil Rights Under Law, 1963-65, dir., 1966-69. Trustee Sarah Lawrence Coll., 1940-59, 60-65, chmn. bd., 1946-54, pres. coll., 1959-60, hon. trustee, 1965-69; trustee Cooper Union, 1951-67, emeritus, 1968-69; trustee Practising Law Inst., 1957-69; overseer Harvard Coll., 1950-56. Served with U.S. Army, 1918. Fellow Am. Acad. Arts and Scis.; mem. American Law Institute (president 1947-61, chairman council 1962-69), Inter-Am., Internat., Am., N.Y. State, N.Y. County bar assns., N.Y. Law Inst., Assn. Bar City N.Y. (pres. 1945-48), Harvard Alumni Assn. (chmn. 1948-49). Clubs: Harvard, Century, Down Town (New York); Porcellian (Cambridge, Mass.). Author: Legal Aid Society-New York City 1876-1951, 1954; Life time and Testamentary Estate Planning (with W. Parsons) 1949, rev. 1961; and various mag. articles. Home: New York City NY Died June 16, 1969.

TWITCHELL, HANNAH (MRS. MILTON C. TWITCHELL), author; b. Manchester, Ill.; d. James and Elizabeth (Chamberlin) Stackpole; A.B., Prairie du Chien Coll. (now R.C. instn. for men); spl. student of French lang. for many yrs.; m. Milton C. Twitchell, of Madison, Wis., Dec. 29, 1886. Formerly teacher high school, Prairie du Chien, and 1 yr. in acad. at Madison, Wis. Episcopalian. Author: Famous Children, 1903. Translator: (from the French) Beautiful Women in Art, 1902; Chinese Life in Town and Country, 1905; The Little Florentine, 1914. Contbr. numerous serials, short stories and essays (mostly transl.) to mags. and newspapers. Home: Madison WI‡

TWOHY, DANIEL W., retired banker; b. Copper Harbor, Mich., Apr. 4, 1864; s. John and Lucy (Casey) T.; ed. pub. schs; m. Sue Bell, 1904; children—Daniel W., Henry, Frank, John. Began in banking business at Superior, Wis., 1895; moved to Spokane, Wash., 1902; pres. Old Nat. Bank, 1902-20, chmn. bd., 1921-40. Democrat. Catholic. Home: Spokane WA‡

TWOMBLY, EDWARD BANCROFT, lawyer; b. Summit, N.J., Feb. 25, 1891; s. Henry Bancroft and Frances (Doane) T.; B.A., Yale, 1912; LL.B., Columbia Law, 1914; LL.D. (honorary), Temple University, 1958; married Mildred Hadra, Apr. 14, 1917; children—Doane, Gilmer and Edward B. Asso. with Putney, Twombly, Hall & Skidmore, 1914-69, partner 1919-66, senior partner, 1966-69. Troop C. 1st N.J. Cav., 1914-17; Mexican border service, 1916; commissioned first lieutenant cav. res., 1917; commd. capt., 1917; overseas with Co. B-304th Machine Gun Bn., 77th Div., 1918-19; received Silver Star; maj., inf. res., 1919; lieut. col., inf. res., 1922-37. Mayor, City of Summit, N.J., 1930-32; Common Council, 1922-30, pres., 1926-30; pres. Summit Rep. Club, 1932-38; pres., Organization Rep. Club of Union Co., N.J., 1935-38; chmn., Summit Defense Council, 1940-45; chmn., United Campaign, 1938; Chairman adv. com. National State Bank, Elizabeth, New Jersey, Summit, N.J. branch; director general counsel Distributors Group, Inc., Promenade Mags., v.p. general counsel member board and exec. com. Chemetals Corp., counsel Group Securities, Incoporated; gen. counsel, director Lobsitz Mills Company. Trustee Temple University; now honorary chmn. Berkshire Farm for Boys. Member of Assn. Bar N.Y.C., Am., New York State bar assns.,

S.A.R., Newcomen Soc. N.Am., English Speaking Union, Skull and Bones, Alpha Delta Phi. Presbyn. (elder). Clubs: Royal Bermuda Yacht; Short Hills, Balustrol Golf; Coral Beach (Bermuda), Down Town Assn. (N.Y.). Home: Short Hills NJ Died June 7, 1969; buried Fairmount Cemetery Chatham NJ

TYLER, ALICE SARAH, librarian; b. Decatur, Ill.; d. John William and Sarah (Roney) T.; ed. high sch., Decatur; certificate, Library Sch., Armour Inst. Tech., Chicago (now U. of Ill. Library Sch.), 1894. Asst. in Pub. Library, Decatur, 1887-93; catalog librarian, Cleveland Pub. Library, 1895-1900; sec. Ia. State Library Commn., 1900-13; dir. Ia. Summer Library Sch., State U. of Ia., 1901-12; dean Sch. of Library Science, Western Reserve U., 1913-29 (emeritus). Pres. League of Library Commns., 1906, Ohio Library Assn., 1916-17, Assn. Am. Library Sch., 1918-19, A.L.A., 1920-21, Cleveland Library Club, 1922-23; mem. D.A.R. Club: Women's City. Editor Iowa Library Quarterly, 1901-13; contbr. to library periodicals. Home: 2104 Lennox Rd., Cleveland OH‡

TYLER, ANSEL AUGUSTUS, prof. science Bellevue Coll. since 1900; b. East Bridgewater, Susquehanna Co., Pa., March 7, 1869; s. Leander Ansel and Mary J. (Dowlin) T.; grad. Lafayette Coll., Pa., 1892, A.M., 1895; post-graduate studies same, 1892-4; School of Pure Science, Columbia, 1894-7, Ph. D., 1897; m. Grove City, Pa., Aug. 16, 1900, Ada Welch. Asst. biology, Lafayette Coll., 1892-4; instr. biology, Union Coll., 1897-8; instr. botany, Syracuse Univ., 1898-9; asst. prof. biology, Univ. of Ariz., 1899-1900. Mem. Am. Soc. Naturalists, A. A. A. S., Neb. Acad. Science. Wrote: Nature and Origin of Stipules, Annals New York Acad. Science, Vol. X, 1897. Address: Bellevue NE‡

TYNAN, THOMAS J., ex-penitentiary warden; b. Niles, Mich., Jan. 15, 1874; s. Patrick and Margaret (Crawford) T.; ed. in pub. schs.; m. Florence E. Scott, July 9, 1908; children—Margaret Helen (Mrs. Oliver H. Snyder), Florence Patricia. Associated with A.F. Sheldon of the Sheldon Sch., Chicago, in the book pub. business, 1902; later house manager for Armour & Co., Pueblo, and traveling salesman for Morey Mercantile Co., Denver; warden Colo. State Penitentiary, Apr. 7, 1909-27. Democrat. Made first successful application of convict labor to road building in U.S., in inaugurating a system which has been adopted in whole or in part by about 40 states. Over 5,000 miles of highways constructed by convict labor in Colo. in 18 yrs.; this plan allows each prisoner to reduce his sentence by working on prison farms and in prison road camps under the honor system, the cost of construction being reduced to 20% of contractor's cost. Has lectured widely in U.S. on convict life and the prison parole system; a leader in representing advanced ideas as to possibilities of reform of convicts. Home: 312 S. High Denver CO‡

TYNDELL, CHARLES NOYES, clergyman; b. Fall River, Mass., May 2, 1876; s. Rev. Charles Henri and Martha Willson (Noyes) T.; prep. edn. St. John's Mil. Sch. (Manlius, N.Y.) and Browne and Nichol's Classical School (Cambridge, Mass); student Colgate U., Class of 1894; grad. Theol. Sem. in Va., 1900; S.T.D., Dickinson Coll., 1921; m. Rebecca Holmes Lewis, Oct. 3, 1900; children—Cary Noyes (Mrs. Peyton Jacquelin Marshall), Rebecca Holmes (Mrs. Francis Ryland Washington). Deacon, 1900, priest, 1901, P.E. Ch.; rector Christ Ch., Williamsport, Pa., 1914-23, Grace-St. Luke's Ch., Memphis, Tenn., 1923-30, St. Stephen's Ch., Terre Haute, Ind., 1930-31, Trinity Ch., Ft. Wayne, Ind., 1931-32 St. Peter's Ch., Niagara Falls, N.Y., 1932-42; Calvary Ch. (The Little Cathedral of the Shenandoah"), Front Royal, Va., 1942-47, emeritus 1947. Mem. bd. dirs., exec. com. and on faculty (chair of comparative religions), Williamsport Sch. of Religious Edn. Dep. Gen. Conv., P.E. Ch., from Diocese of Harrisburg 3 times to 1922, from Diocese of Tenn., 1925, from Diocese of Northern Ind., 1931; mem. and sec. Joint Commn. on Home and Family Life; mem. exec. com. Diocese of Tenn. and chmn. Dept. of Christian Social Service; served as trustee Yeates Episcopal Sch. for Boys (Lancaster, Pa.), James V. Brown Public Library, Williamsport, and mem. Pub. Safety Com., Pa., etc., World War I; mem. Commn. on Crime Prevention of Memphis (exec. com. and treas.); mem. Social Service Commn., Council of Social Agencies (of Memphis, and also of State of Tenn.); mem. Council of Social Agencies (Niagara Falls, N.Y.); chmn. Niagara County Ch. Mission of Help; ex-trustee Manlius Sch.; chmn. field dept. Diocese of Northern Ind., Was chmn. War Service Commn. Diocese of Harrisburg; spl. preacher at camps Mills, Hancock and Gordon under Nat. War Work Council Y.M.C.A., guest preacher United States Naval Academy, Spring of 1937. Chmn. Warren County War Finance Com., 1943-46; chmn. Nat. Affairs Com., Chamber of Com. Mem. Pi Gamma Mu. Democrat. Mason (33 deg., Sovereign Grand Insp. Gen., Knight Templar, Shriner, Grotto; past grand prelate Grand Commandery, Knights Templar of Tennessee; council of Thirty Third Degree, Williamsport, Pa.). Elk. Clubs: University, Egyptians (Memphis); Rotary (Front Royal, Va.); The Shrine (chaplain), Niagara Club (Niagara Falls); Thirty Third Degree Club (Buffalo). Wrote: Our Altar Guild, 1915; A Communicant's Companion, 1915. Also sermons, addresses and essays. Nominated for bishop-coadjutor of Los Angeles. Home: 103 S. Stewart St., Winchester VA‡

TYNER, GEORGE PARKER, army officer; b. Davenport, Ia., Apr. 26, 1876; s. Henry Richard and Katherine Ellen (Parker) T.; distinguished grad. Army Sch. of the Line, 1915, Army Staff Coll., 1916, Army War Coll., 1922, Field Arty. Sch. (advanced course), 1923; m. Louise Judson, Aug. 7, 1909. Served as capt. 1st Ill. Cav., Spanish-Am. War; 1st lt. 45th Inf. (Vols.), 1899; commd. 2d lt. Cav., U.S. Army, 1901, and promoted through grades to brig. gen., 1936; asst. chief of staff, 1937-40; served in Philippine Insurrection, 1899-1901. Cuban Occupation, 1901-02, on Mexican border, 1916; active duty in France, World War, 1918-19; retired, 1940. Awarded D.S.M.; Officer French Legion of Honor. Episcopalian. Address: 1718 Hoban Rd N.W., Washington

TYSEN, JOHN COLQUHOUN, real estate exec.; b. Paris, France, Jan. 6, 1913 (parents Am. citizens); s. Rowe and Rosalie (Tone) T.; student Downside Sch., Eng., Trinity Coll., Cambridge, 1932-34; m. Constance Lazo Manny, June 28, 1947; children—Anne Colquhoun, Elizabeth Lorenza. Salesman Horlick's Malted Milk Co., Ltd., London, 1935; with Previews, Inc., Nat. Real Estate Clearing House, N.Y.C., br. offices Boston, Washington, Palm Beach, Los Angeles, San Francisco, Denver, Chgo., Paris, France, 1936-72, chmn., 1950-72, also dir. Author syndicated real estate column Buying or Selling Your Home. Mem. Nat. Inst. Real Estate Brokers (gov.), Internat. Real Estate Fedn. (past pres., dir. Am. chpt.), Nat. Assn. Real Estate Bds. (dir., past gov.), Internat. Real Estate Fedn. (past pres., dir. exec. com.), Valuers, Surveyors and Estate Agts. Assn. Gt. Britain, Young President's Assn., Nat. Inst. Farm and Land Brokers (past gov.), Nat., N.Y., N.Y.C. real estate assns. Clubs: Racquet and Tennis, Brook (N.Y.C.); Travellers (Paris); White's (London); Lyford Cay (Nassau). Home: New York City NY Died Oct. 17, 1972; buried Woodlawn Cemetery, New York City NY

TYSON, JOHN AMBROSE, judge; b. Denmark, Tenn., Dec. 12, 1873; s. John A. and Elizabeth (Ewing) T.; B.S., Union U., Jackson, Tenn.; B.L., Cumberland U., Lebanon, Tenn., 1898; m. Annabel Broadley, Dec. 29, 1908; 1 dau., Elizabeth Nell. Practiced law, Jackson, Tenn., 1898-1904, Greenwood, Miss., 1904-35 (with exception of 3 1/2 yrs.). Commd. maj., Judge Advocate General's Dept., Washington, D.C., 1918; lt. col., 1919, hon. discharge, 1919; served as chief counsel, Bd. Contract Adjustment, War Dept., 1919-21. Mem. Tenn. Legislature, 1903-05; chmn. Ways and Means Com. House of Reps. 1903-05; mem. Miss. Legislature, 1908-10; atty. Yazoo-Miss. Delta Levee Bd., 1923-35; mem. U.S. Bd. of Tax Appeals Dec. 1935-Oct. 1942; judge, Tax Court of U.S. since 1942. Mem. Nat. Press Club (asso.), Sigma Alpha Epsilon. Democrat. Episcopalian. Home: Washington DC Died Nov. 14, 1971; buried Arlington Nat. Cemetery, Arlington VA

UIHLEIN, ERWIN C(HARLES), brewery exec.; b. Milwaukee; graduate Wahl Henius Brewers' Institute. Joergensen's Labs., Copenhagen, Denmark; LL.B., Cornell, 1914; m. Marie Zarwell, Feb. 5, 1944; three children. With Jos. Schlitz Brewing Co., Milw., 1906-68, pres., 1933-61, chmn., 1961-67; director First Wisconsin Nat. Bank, First. Wis. Trust Co., Wis. Bankshares Corp. Mem. Chi Psi, Phi Delta Phi. Clubs: Milwaukee University, Town, Milwaukee Country, Wisconsin, Milwaukee Yacht, Milwaukee Athletic (Milwaukee). Home: Grafton WI Died Oct. 20, 1968; buried Forest Home Cemetery, Milwaukee WI

ULBRICHT, WALTER, chmn. Council of State, former 1st sec. central com. Socialist Unity Party Germany; b. Leipzig, Germany, June 30, 1893; s. Ernst and Pauline Ulbricht; woodworker apprentice, 1907-11; m. Frau Kuhn. Mem. Socialist Worker Youth, 1908-12; joined German Woodworker's League, 1910; mem. Social Democratic Party, 1912-18; mem. Liebknecht-Gruppe, Leipzig, 1914-18; co-founder, mem. German Communist Party, 1918-46; mil. service, imprisoned because of anti-war propaganda, 1915-18; sec. dist. adminstr. of Communist Party, Greater Thueringia, 1921-23; mem. central com., 1923; mem. State Parliament, Saxony, 1926-29, German Parliament, 1928-33; elected to exec. com. Communist Internat., 1928-43; party work outside Germany, 1933-45; propaganda work on front and in prisoner-of-war camps in USSR, World War II; co-founder Nat. Com. for Free Germany, 1943; one of leaders in setting-up anti-fascist-democratic order in Soviet Zone of Germany and in creating of Unity of working class and Socialist Unity Party Germany (SED), 1945-46; dep. chmn. Socialist Unity Party Germany, 1946; gen. sec. central com., 1950-53, 1st sec., 1953-71, mem. People's Chamber, 1949-73, dep. chmn. Council of Ministers, 1949-60, chmn. Council of State of German Democratic Republic, 1960-73. Decorated Karl Marx Order, Patriotic Order Merit in gold, Order Lenin, named Hero of Soviet Union, Georgi Dimitrov Order (Bulgaria), other fgn. distinctions. Address: Berlin German Democratic Republic Died Aug. 1, 1973.

ULE, GUY MAXWELL, entrepreneur; b. Lorain, O. Feb. 17, 1907; s. Anton and Mary (Cekada) U.; A.B., U Chgo., 1936, M.B.A., 1937, grad. student, 1939-40; m Margaret Karahuta, Sept. 22, 1934;children—Gu Maxwell, Carol. With Ule, Ule & Ule, constrn., Lorain O., 1925-33; credit analyst Brunswick, Balke, Collende Co., Chgo., 1937-38; economist Oren Pub. Co., Chgo 1938-39; dir. research McCann Erickson, Inc., Chgo 1940-49; v.p. charge research Kenyon & Eckhardt, Inc advt., N.Y.C., 1949-55, dir., 1955-61, sr. v.p., 1956-61 mem. exec. com.; engaged in research in marketing an investments; cons. Milw. Advt. Lab.; lectr. confs. adv and marketing groups. Mem. direct mail advisory com Dept. of Agr., 1954; lectr. bus. U. Chgo., 1947-49 Trustee of the Episcopal Mission Society. Member o tech. com., Advt. Research Found. Member Academy of Television Arts and Sciences, Am. Marketing Assn (dir. Chgo. chpt. 1946-48), Am. Assn. Advt. Agys. (vic chmn. research com.), Radio TV Research Counci (pres. 1955-56), Market Research Council, Am. Econ Assn., Am. Statis. Assn., Phi Beta Kappa, Delta Sigma Pi. Club: Westchester Country. Home: Port Chester NY Died Sept. 23, 1971.

ULLMAN, JAMES RAMSEY, author; b. New York N.Y., Nov. 24, 1907; s. Alexander F. and Eunice (Ramsey) U.; student Phillips Acad., Andover, Mass. 1922-25; B.A., Princeton U., 1929; m. Ruth Fishman June 27, 1930; children—James Ramsey, William A. married 2d, Elaine Luria, January 25, 1946; marriec third, Marian McCown, March 18, 1961. Newspape reporter, and feature writer, 1929-33; playwright 1930-35; theatrical producer, 1933-37 (produced 10 Plays on Broadway); co-producer; Mem in White (Pulitzer prize play), 1934; exec. Fed. Theater Project N.Y. and Calif., 1937-39; free lance writer, 1939-71 partner, editor-at-large Caribbean Beachcomber; 1st lt Am. Field Service, with Brit. 8th Army, 1942-43 awarded Africa Star. Mem. Am. Mt. Everest Expedition, 1963. Bd. dirs. MacDowell Colony Peterborough, N.H. Author: Mad Shelley, 1930; Is Nothing Sacred, 1934; The Other Side of the Mountain, 1938; High Conquest, 1941; The White Tower, 1945; River of the Sun, 1951; Windom's Way, 1952; The Island of the Blue Macaws, 1953; The Sands of Karakorum, 1953; Banner in the Sky, 1954; The Age of Mountaineering, 1954; Tiger of the Snows (with Tenzing Norgay), 1955; The Day on Fire, 1958; Down the Colorado with Major Powell; Fia Fia, 1962; Where The Bong Tree Grows, 1963; Americans on Everest, 1964; Straight Up, 1967; (with Al Dinhofer) Caribbean Here and Now, 1968, rev. biannually; And Not to Yield 1970. Editor: Kingdom of Adventure; Everest 1947 Clubs: Explorers; Nassau (Princeton), Princeton, American Alpine, P.E.N., Overseas Press. Contbr. stories and articles to various mags. Home: Boston MA Died June 20, 1971.

ULLMANN, HARRY MAAS, coll. prof.; b. Springfield, Mo., Apr. 14, 1868; s. Ludwig and Sarah (Maas) U.; A.B., Johns Hopkins U., 1889, Ph.D., 1892; student Ecole des Mines, Paris, 1893-94; m. Rachel Barnett Mifflin, Aug. 21, 1919; children—Harriet Mifflin, Thomas Mifflin. Instr. in quantitative and industrial analysis, 1894-1904; asst. prof. in chemistry, Lehigh U., 1904-10, asso. prof., 1910-14, prof. of chemistry and chem. engring. and head of dept., 1914-38, prof. emeritus since 1938. Fellow London Chem. Soc.; mem. A.A.A.S., Am. Inst. Chem. Engrs., Am. Chem. Soc., Societe Chimique de Paris, Deutsche Chemische Gesellschaft. Theta Delta Chi, Sigma Xi, Tau Beta Pi. Research on drying oils and castor oils; holder several patents. Democrat. Episcopalian. Clubs: Bethlehem, Sancon Valley Country. Address: 20 W Church St., Bethlehem PA*‡

UMBECK, SHARVY GREINER, coll. pres.; b. Kankakee, Ill., Oct. 17, 1912; s. Frederick Paul and Myrtle Louise (Nelson) U.; A.B., Elmhurst (Ill.) Coll., 1933; A.M., U. Chgo., 1938, Ph.D., 1940; LL.D., Bradley U., 1959, Lincoln Coll., 1965, Elmhurst Coll., 1967; L.H.D., Monmouth Coll., 1968, Westminster Coll., 1968; m. Elsie Hoyle, Oct. 30, 1936; children—Frederick James, John, Gretchen, Jane. Asst. prof. sociology Coll. of William and Mary, 1938-42, asso. prof., 1942-45, prof. sociology, chmn. dept., 1945-49, dean of coll., 1946-49; pres. Knox Coll., Galesburg, Ill., 1949. Pres. Fedn. Ill. Colls., 1962-64; chmn. Ill. Com. on Selection Rhodes Scholars, 1965-66, AID, 1967-68; mem. adv. com. for instnl. relations NSF, 1971-73; mem. adv. bd. Arthur Vining Davis Found., 1971. Bd. dirs. Asso. Colls. of Midwest, 1959-73, chmn. bd., 1959-62; Bd. dirs. Tchrs. Ins. and Annuity Assn., 1966-73, Inst. for Ednl. Mgmt., 1969-73. Mem. Asso. Coll. Ill. (v.p. 1964-66), Assn. Am. Colls. (chmn. commn. coll. adminstrn., dir. 1966-73), Lincoln Acad. Ill., Presidents' Profl. Assn., Am. Council Edn. (dir. 1964-69, nat. chmn. 1967-68, chmn. commn. adminstrv. affairs 1962-64), Am. Assn. Colls. for Tchr. Edn., North Central Assns. Colls. and Secondary Schs. (exec. bd. 1965-71), Phi Beta Kappa, Mem. United Ch. Christ. Rotarian. Clubs: Galesburg, Scangetaha Country; University (Chgo.). Home: Galesburg IL Died May 5, 1973.

UMBREIT, SAMUEL JOHN, bishop; b. Manchester, Green Lake Co., Wis., Feb. 22, 1871; s. Henry E. and

Sophia (Forsy) U.; Ph.B., North Central Coll., Naperville, Ill., 1898, Ph.M., 1907; D.D., Theol. Sem. of North Central Coll., 1916; student U. of Chicago; m. Amanda Bauernfeind, of Nerstrand, Minn., June 29, 1899; children—Kenneth Bernard, Lucile Burdella. Entered ministry Evangelical Ch., 1897; pastor Berlin (Wis.) Circuit and Menominee Falls Circuit until 1905; sent to Japan as missionary, 1905; supt. Japan mission Evang. Ch., 1913-26; elected bishop, Oct. 13, 1926; in charge work of Evang. Ch. in Europe. Author: From Darkness to Light (in the Japanese), 1921; Twenty Years Missionary in Japan, 1929. Editor Christian Movement (Tokio), 1922. Home: Kaiser-Friedrich Str. 87, Berlin-Charlottenburg Germany‡

UNDERWOOD, MELL G., U.S. judge; b. Rose Farm, O., Jan. 30, 1892; ed. public schs.; student law dept. Ohio State U.; m. Flora E. Lewis; children—Mell G., Max Lewis, Linda Lou, Ned. Taught sch.; pros. atty. Perry County, 2 terms, 1917-20; Dem. candidate for Congress, 1920; mem. 68th to 74th Congresses (1923-37), 11th Ohio Dist.; resigned to become U.S. judge, Southern Dist. of Ohio, Feb. 1936. Home: New Lexington OH Died Mar. 1972.

UNGAR, ARTHUR ARNOLD, banker, investor, univ. trustee; b. St. Louis, May 3, 1884; s. Adolf and Henrietta (Lenz) U.; ed. pub. schs.; Doctor of Laws, University of Miami, 1965; m. Marcella Marshall, Oct. 19, 1913; children—Bertha (Mrs. Leonard L. Abess), Marcella (Mrs. Charles S. Werblow). Incorporator, Advanced Refrigeration Co., Atlanta, 1914, pres., 1914-58; incorporator, 1919, since pres. Ungar Buick Co., Miami, Fla.; pres. Ungar-Marshall Co., Miami 1958-69; dir. Miami Laundry Co., City Nat. Bank Miami, City Nat. Bank, Miami Beach, Mary MacIntosh Services, Incorporated.Organizer, director, past president Orange Bowl. Com.; mem., past pres. Orange Bowl Stadium; mem. Opera Guild Miami, Fla. Sheriffs Assn., Greater Miami Traffic Assn.; Miami Mus. Modern Art., Pres. Ungar-Abess Found., 1956-69; trustee, exec. com. U. Miami, 1934-69; trustee, founder mem. Mt. Sinai Hosp., Miami Beach; past bd. dirs. Dade County Community Chest, Dade County chpt. A.R.C., Recipient Gold medal award of merit U. Miami, 1957; named hon. citizen Fla., 1961; hon. mem. Miami Police Benevolent Assn. Mem. Dade County C. of C. (past dir.), Phi Epsilon Pi (life). Jewish religion (founder mem. life trusteetemple), Mason (Shriner). Clubs: Gridiron (charter, 1st pres.), Miami, Rotary, Westview Country (past pres.) (Miami). Home: Miami Beach FL Died Apr. 17, 1969.

UNGER, FREDERIC WILLIAM, journalist, author; b. Phila., Jan. 25, 1875; s. John Frederick and Lydia Louise (Miller) U.; Eastburn Acad., Phila., 1884-92; matric lated law dept., Univ. of Pa., 1893; unmarried. Went to Klondike, traversing 3,000 miles of interior Alaska, 1898; corr. London Times and London Express in S. Africa during Boer War; visited Japan, Korea, China and Machuria during Russo-Japanese War; active in Phila. and Pa. polit. reform movement, 1905; chmn. City Party Vigilance Com., Phila. Mem. Phila. Browning Soc. Club: Franklin Inn (Phila.) Author: With Bobs" and Kruger, 1901 C4; Russia and Japan and the War in the Far East, W24; Epitaphs, P5; also stories, character sketches and econ. articles in mags. and newspapers. Residence: Leesport PA Office: Land Title Bldg., Philadelphia PA‡

UNGERLEIDER, SAMUEL, JR., pulp and paper co. exec.; b. Columbus, O., Apr. 28, 1917; s. Samuel and Selma (Dallet) U.; A.B., Brown U., 1939; m. Joy Gottesman, Dec. 2, 1945; children—Peter, Steven, Jeane, Andrew. With Central Nat. Corp., 1956, v.p., dir., 1957-73; with Gottesman & Co., N.Y.C., 1956-73, v.p., dir., 1958-73; dir. Ungerleider Motors Co. Pres., trustee 92d St. YM-YWHA. Served from pvt. to capt., AUS, AUS, World War II. Clubs: Nat. Press (Washington); Brown University (N.Y.C.); Beach Point Yacht (Mamaroneck, N.Y.). Home: Larchmont NY Died 1973.

UNTERMEYER, JEAN STARR, author, b. Zanesville, O., May 13, 1886; d. Abram E. and Johanna (Shonfield) Starr; ed. Putnam's Sem. (Zanesville). Kohut Sch. for Girls (New York), and Columbia Extension Course; m. Louis Untermeyer, January 23, 1907 (div.). Made debut as singer in Vienna and London 1924, specializing in German songs. Club: P.E.N. Author: (poems) Growing Pains, 1918; Dreams Out of Darkness, 1921; Steep Ascent, 1927; Winged Child, 1936; Love and Need, 1940. Was one of the original group to publish the biennials, A Miscellany of American Poetry, 1920 and 1922. Translator Oscar Bie's Schubert, the Man, 1928 (chosen by Schubert Centennial Com. as the official (biography). Lecturer and teacher, Olivet Writer's Conf., Olivet Coll., Mich.; summers 1936, 37; teacher Writers Sch. League of Am. Writers, 1938-39; teacher, lectr. New Sch. Social Research since 1948. Translator of Hermann Broch's masterpiece The Death of Virgil, 1945. Recipient of Ford Madox Ford Chair of Creative Literature, Olivet Coll., Mich., 1940. Contbr. verse and criticism to mags. Author: Private Collection, a Memoir, 1965; New York City NY Died July 27, 1970.

UNWIN, SIR STANLEY, book publisher; b. London, Eng., Dec. 19, 1884; s. Edward and Elizabeth (Spicer) U.; student Abbotsholme Sch., Derbyshire, also Haubinda; LL.D. (hon.), Aberdeen U.; m. Mary Storr, Dec. 19, 1914; children—David Storr, Ruth S. (Mrs. Norman J. L. Brodrick), Rayner Stephens. Shipping and ins. broker, 1900-03; with T. Fisher Unwin, Ltd., book publs. 1903-12; founder George Allen & Unwin, Limited, 1914, then chairman; mem. of the board of directors Equitable Life Assurance Soc. Exec. Brit. Council Chmn. Sir Halley Stewart Trust. Decorated Order of Crown of Belgium, Officier d'Academie (France), Order of White Lion (Czechoslovakia), Order of Orange Nassau (Holland), Knight Commander Order of Falcon (Iceland); Knight Commander Order St. Michael and St. George; Fellow Royal Geographic Soc., Royal Economic Soc., Royal Soc. Literature; member of Publishers Assn. Gt. Brit. (past pres.), Internat. Pubs. Assn. (past pres.), Am. Acad. Arts, Scis., Royal Inst. Internat. Affairs. Club: Reform (London). Home: London England Died Oct. 14, 1968.

UPHAM, JOHN HOWELL JANEWAY, physician; b. Trenton, N.J., Aug. 12, 1871; s. Nathaniel Lord and Anna Howell (Janeway) U.; certificate in biology, U. of Pa., 1891, M.D., 1894; intern Johns Hopkins Hosp., Baltimore, 1894-96; studied Prague, Leipzig and Berlin, 1899-1900; m. Alice Lee, June 1897. Began practice, Columbus, 1896; instr. in medicine, 1897-1902, asso. prof. medicine, 1902-08, Starling Med. Coll.; prof. medicine and clin. medicine, Starling-Ohio Med. Coll., 1908-14; prof. medicine, Ohio State U. Coll. Medicine, since 1914, dean Coll. of Medicine, 1927-41, dean emeritus, same, since 1941. Member Ohio State Medical Board since 1913; advisory committee A.R.C., 1922. Member A.M.A. (jud. council since 1922, trustee, 1923-35, chmn. bd., 1933-35, pres. 1937-38), Ohio State Med. Assn. (sec. and editor Ohio State Med. Jour., 1907-13; pres. 1914-15; legislative com. since 1915), Columbus Acad. Medicine (pres. 1919; pres. elect Ohio Hospital Assn., 1941. Home: 244 N. Parkview, Bexley, Columbus OH‡

UPLEGER, ARTHUR C(HRISTAN), accountant; b. Mt. Clemens, Mich., Feb. 20, 1883; s. Joseph F. and Elizabeth (Ullrich) U.; B.C.S., N.Y.U., 1910; m. Leona Walthall, Dec. 7, 1915 (dec. 1965); m. 2d, Mrs. Naida Barnes Patton, Accountant 1907-69, in Tex., 1911-69. Chmn. Tex. Bd. Accountancy, 1924. Treas. St. Paul's House Bd., 1930-59, Waco Pub. Library Assn., 1955. C.P.A., Tex. Mem. Am. (pres. 1929), Tex. (pres. 1924) socs. C.P.A.'s, Am. Inst. C.P.A.'s (permanent council mem.), Civic Music Assn. Waco (treas.), So. States Accountants Conf. (exec. com.), Phi Delta Phi, Alpha Kappa Psi, Beta Alpha Psi. Republican. Episcopalian. Mason (Shriner, 33 deg.; imperial auditor 1949-69. Clubs: Waco Philosophers, Rotary (Hall of Fame, Dist. 587 Conf. 1964). Home: Waco TX Died Dec. 11, 1969; buried Oakwood Cemetery, Waco TX

UPSON, ARTHUR (WHEELOCK), author; b. Camden, N.Y., Jan. 10, 1877; s. Spencer Johnson and Julia Maria (Claflin) U.; ed. Camden (N.Y.) Acad. and Univ. of Minn., A.B.; unmarried. Lived abroad, 1900, and wrote Octaves in an Oxford Garden at Oxford; at present residing in Weimar, Germany. Mem. hon. soc. of Phi Beta Kappa. Author: The Sign of the Harp, 1900; Peoms, 1902 B53; Octaves in an Oxford Garden, 1902 B53; Westwind Songs, 1902 B53; The City (a poem-drama), 1904 S9; The City, and Other Poems, 1905 M1; The Tides of Spring, and Other Poems, 1907 S9, E18. Address: Am Market 2, Weimar Germany‡

UPSON, CHARLES AYRAULT, mfr.; b. Tonawanda, N.Y., Mar. 27, 1875; s. William Henry and Nella M. (Ayrault) U.; B.S. in Economics, Wharton Sch. of Finance and Commerce (U. of Pa.), 1900; m. Ella J. Morgan, Nov. 9, 1910; children—Marjorie Morgan, Jeanne Ayrault (Mrs. Henry Wilkins Schmidt). Asst. to pres. investment co., Phila., 1900-01; bldg. contractor, 1902; salesman Niagra Paper Mills, 1903-04, sales and advt. mgr. 1904, gen. mgr., 1905-06; asst. to pres. Tonawanda Board and Paper Co., 1907-08; gen. mgr. Beaver Board Co. (Buffalo), 1908-10; organizer, founder The Upson Co., mfrs. wallboard and fibre specialties, 1910, pres. 1910-47, chmn. bd., 1947-69, dir.; dir. Lockport br. Mfrs. and Traders Trust Co., (Buffalo), 1935-69, various other corporations. Originator City Manager Plan at Lockport, 1910; president Lockport Public Library Board, 1919-48, honorary counselor 1948-69; mem. Lockport Bd. Edn., 1919-55; mem. Western N.Y. Port Authority Commn., 1927-28; dir. Niagara Frontier Planning Commn., 1930-41; trustee N.Y. State Coll. Forestry, 1931-69; mem. N.Y. State Commn. on Sch. Bldgs., 1950-52, Western N.Y. Sch. Bd. Inst., 1954-55; del. to N.Y. State com. White House Conf. on Edn. and White House Conf., Washington, 1955; dir. Goodwill Industries (Buffalo), 1954-69. Recipient Distinguished Service award, 1952, citation for services rendered to pub. schs. of N.Y. during yrs., 1919-52, merit award and citation for services U. Pa., 1962, Am. Paper Institute Merit award, 1967. Mem. Am. Chem. Soc., Soc. Mech. Engrs., A.A.A.S., Delta Kappa Epsilon (founder U. Pa. chpt. 1899). Organized Western N.Y. U. Pa. Club, 1900; charter mem. Nat. Asso. U. Pa. Clubs, 1913; organizer Lockport Rotary, 1919, pres., 1919-20. Republican. Presbyn. Mason (32 deg.). Clubs: Town and Country (Lockport); University, Masonic, Rotary, Tuscarora. Holder patents. Home: Lockport NY Died Sept. 25, 1969.

UPSON, MAXWELL MAYHEW, engr.; b. Milwaukee, Wis., Apr. 22, 1876; s. Edwin M. and Kittie (Parsons) U.; A.B., U. of N. Dakota, 1896, Dr. Engring., 1931; M.E. Cornell U., 1899; m. Mary Shepard Barrett, Apr. 28, 1915; (died Dec. 14, 1963); 1 dau., Jeanette. With Westinghouse, Church, Kerr & Co., N.Y. City, advancing to mng. engr., 1899-1905; asst. to pres. and chief engr. Hockanum Mills Co., Conn., 1905-07; gen. mgr., chief engr., v.p. Raymond Internat., Inc., 1907-31, pres. 1931-46; chmn. bd., 1946-60, hon. chmn. bd., 1960-69. Mem. Com. Econ. Devel. Holds many patents on methods of bldg. and placing concrete piles and bldg. of retaining walls, seawalls and off-shore oil derrick founds. Vice pres. Boys Clubs Am.; trustee emeritus Cornell U., Awarded Edward Longstreth medal by Franklin Inst., 1940 also; pres.dl. councilor. recipient Nat. Golden Keystone award Boys Clubs Am., 1964. Member of the American Concrete Inst. (pres. 1926-28), Am. Soc. C.E., A.S. M.E., Am. Soc. for Testing Materials, Pan Am. Soc. Republican Presbyn. Clubs: University, Bankers, Cornell University of New York, Knickerbocker Country; Yeamans Hall (Charleston, S.C.). Co-author; American Individual Enterprise System. Home: Englewood NJ Died May 1, 1969.

UPSON, RALPH HAZLETT, aeronautical engr.; b. New York, N.Y., June 21, 1888; s. William F. and Grace (Hazlett) U.; M.E., Stevens Inst. Tech., 1910, hon. Aeronaut. Engr.; m. Frances Talbot Allen, May 19, 1915; children—Frank Allen, Julia Ann, Nancy, Brent Talbot. Research in aerodynamics and airship engring., 1908-12; won Internat. Balloon Race, 1913; won Am. nat. balloon race, 1913, 19, 21; chief engr. aeronautical dept. Goodyear Tire & Rubber Co., 1914-20, producing most of the Am. balloons and airships used during World War I. Flew first U.S. Navy coast patrol airship, Chicago to Akron, in demonstration flight, 1917; rep. U.S. Navy design mission in Europe, 1918-19. Chmn. lighter-than-air div. Aeronautical Safety Code Commn. of Bur. of Standards, 1922-24; chief engr. Aircraft Development Corp., 1922-27; designer ZMC-2, first successful metal-clad airship, 1929; engaged in airplane development with Aeromarine-Klemm Corporation, and other companies, 1928-42; chief aeronautical engineer with H. J. Heinz Co., 1942-44; applied aircraft design methods to other vehicles, including pioneer streamlined train of Union Pacific R.R., 1933; research specialist and lecturer, N.Y.U., 1944-46; prof. aero. engring. Univ. Minn., 1946-56, prof. emeritus, 1956-68; research specialist Aerospace div. Boeing Co., 1956-64. Fellow Am. Institute of Aeronautics and Astronautics, Royal Aeronautical Society (Gt. Britain); member of Soc. Automotive Engrs. Co-Author: Free and Captive Balloons. Contbr. papers on airplane and airship design. Holder of pilot certificates for balloon, airship and airplane. Recipient of award for outstanding service rendered aeronautics," by Am. Soc. Mech. Engrs., 1929; awarded Wright Brothers medal, Soc. of Automotive Engrs., for contribution to wing design, 1930. Home: Seattle WA Died Aug. 13, 1968.

UPSON, WALTER LYMAN, prof. elec. engring.; b. Cleveland, O., July 3, 1877; s. Joseph Edwin and Cornelia Maria (Lyman) U.; B.S., Princeton, 1899, E.E., 1902, M.S., 1903; University Coll., London, Eng., 1906-07; M.E.E., Harvard, 1908; m. Anna Leigh Richardson, Aug. 20, 1906; children—Joseph Edwin II, David Richardson. Began teaching at Princeton U., 1904; asst. prof. elec. engring., Ohio State U., 1908-10; prof. elec. engring., U. of Vt., 1910-12; asst. prof. elec. engring., 1912-14, asso. prof., 1914-20, Union U.; prof. elec. engring., Washington U., 1920-42; consulting engineer, Torrington Manufacturing Company, Torrington, Conn. Vice pres. Litchfield Water Co.; v.p. Progress, Inc. Founder St. Louis Museum Science and Industry; v.p. Wolcott and Litchfield Lending Library. Fellow A.A.A.S.; mem. Am. Inst. E.E., Sigma Xi, Tau Beta Pi. Repub. Conglist. Clubs: Sanctum, Princeton (New York). Author: (with E. J. Berg) Electrical Engineering, 1916; Electrical Engineering Studies, 1931. Contbr. numerous scientific and ednl. papers. Inventor of air impellers. Home: Litchfield CT‡

UPTON, ROBERT W., ex-senator; b. Feb. 3, 1884; s. Mark and Clara (Kendall) U.; LL.B., Boston University, 1907, Doctor of Laws (honorary), 1950; married Martha G. Burroughs, September 18, 1912;children—Richard F., Elise Wright, Frederic K., Allan E., George T., John G. Admitted to Massachusetts, N.H. bars, 1907; practicing lawyer, Concord, N.H., 1907-72; mem. Upton, Sanders & Upton, 1949-72; U.S. senator from N.H. to complete term of late Senator Tobey, 1953-54. Chairman committee on law New Hampshire State Council Def., 1941-45; mem. Interstate Commn. for Flood Control Compacts in Conn. and Merrimack River valleys, 1936. Mem. N.H. State Ho. Reps., 1911; del. N.H. State Constl. Conv., 1918, 1930, 1938, pres., 1948; chmn. delegation Rep. National Convention, 1960. State chmn. March of Dimes, 1952-54. Mem. N.H. Judicial Council (chmn. since 1945), Am. (mem. bd. govs.,

1948-51), N.H. (pres. 1940-41) bar assns. Republican (del. nat. conv., 1940, 44, 48, 56). Home: Concord NH Died Apr. 29, 1972.

UPTON, WILLIAM TREAT, prof. piano; b. Tallmadge, O., Dec. 17, 1870; s. Jonathan Sprague and Amoret Hutchins (Treat) U.; B.A., Oberlin (O.) Coll., 1896, Mus.B., 1906, M.A., 1924, Mus.D., 1946; grad. study, Vienna, 1896-98, Berlin, 1913-14; m. Lelia Elmore, Aug. 9, 1899; 1 dau., Elizabeth. Instr. in piano., Oberlin Conserv. Music, 1898-1906, prof., 1906-36, emeritus, 1936; organist Woodland Avenue Presbyn. Ch., Cleveland, O., 1891-1903; organist and choirmaster Calvary Presbyn. Ch., Cleveland, 1903-18; research in Library of Congress, Washington since 1936, and British Museum, 1927. Member Music Library Association. Member American Musicol. Soc., Bibliog. Soc. of America, Friends of Music in Library of Congress, Am. Guild Organists, Pi Kappa Lambda (ex-pres. Theta Chapter). Received 1st award, Sonneck Memorial Fund, for unpub. biography, A.P. Heinrich, 1932. Conglist. Author: Art-Song in America—A Study in the Development of American Music, 1930; Supplement, 1938; Anthony Philip Heinrich—A Nineteenth Century Composer in America, 1939; revision and enlargement of O.G. Sonneck's Bibliography of Early Secular American Music (18th Century), 1945. The Musical Works of William Henry Fry in the Library Company of Philadelphia, 1946. Music critic Oberlin Review, 1918-36. Contbr. to Musical Quarterly, Chesterian, Notes, and other musical mags.; also sketches in Dictionary of American Biography, Ency. Americana. Home: 221 Forest St., Oberlin OH‡

URBAN, WILBUR MARSHALL, coll. prof.; b. Mount Joy, Pa., Mar. 27, 1873; s. Abraham Linwood and Emma Louisa (Trexler) U.; A.B., Princeton, 1895; Chancellor Green fellow in univs. of Jena and Leipzig, 1895-97; Ph.D., Leipzig, 1897; hon. M.A., Yale, 1931; L.H.D., Trinity Coll., 1937; m. Elizabeth Newell Wakelin, July 27, 1896. Reader in philosophy, Princeton, 1897-98; prof. philosophy and psychology, Ursinus Coll., Pa., 1898-1902; prof. philosophy, Trinity Coll., Conn., 1902-20; Stone prof. philosophy, Dartmouth, 1920-30; became prof. philosophy, Yale, 1931, also chairman dept. philosophy and dir. grad. studies, prof. philosophy emeritus since July 1941. Member Am. Philos. Soc., Am. Psychol. Assn. Author: Valuation—Its Nature and Laws, 1909; The Intelligible World—Metaphysics and Value, 1929; Fundamentals of Ethics, 1930; Language and Reality, 1939; also articles in mags. Home: Hall of Graduate Studies, Yale University, New Haven CT*‡

URETZ, LESTER ROBERT, govt. ofcl.; b. Chgo., Jan. 10, 1922; s. Louis A. and Bertha (Simon) U.; A.A., Wilson Jr. Coll., Chgo., 1941; J.D., U. Chgo., 1948; m. Miriam Herman Schuman, June 9, 1966; children by previous marriage—Leslie, Laurie, Richard, Andrew. Admitted to Ill. bar, 1948, D.C. bar, 1951, also U.S. Supreme Ct.; trial atty. Fed. Security Agy., 1948-51, Dept. Health, Edn. and Welfare, 1952-53; with Internal Revenue Service, 1953-69, dir. refund litigation div., 1963-64, asst. to chief counsel, 1964-65, dep. chief counsel, 1965-66, chief counsel, 1966-69; partner firm of Cohen & Uretz, Washington, 1969-72; speaker in field, 1955-72. Exec. v.p. Galesburg Soy Products Co. (Ill.), 1951-52. Served with USAAF, 1942-45; China. Decorated Legion of Merit, Presdl. citation. Mem. Am., Fed., D.C. bar assns. Author articles in field. Home: Washington DC Died Apr. 23, 1972; buried Rockville MD

URIELL, FRANK (FRANCIS) HAROLD, lawyer, corp. exec.; b. Elkader, Ia., Mar. 28, 1899; s. Francis J. and Mary (Ryan) U.; student St. Thomas Coll., St. Paul, Minn., 1916-18; A.B., State U. Ia., 1920, LL.B., 1922; m. Georgia Niemeyer, Nov. 27, 1924; 1 son, Francis George. Admitted to Ia. bar, 1922, Ill. bar, 1923, since practiced Chgo., partner Pope and Ballard, now named Pope, Ballard, Uriell, Kennedy, Shepard & Fowle. Special assistant, member of the general counsel's committee, Bureau of Internal Rev., 1933-37; dir. Clayton Mark & Co., Nat. Bank N. Evanston, Cherry-Burrell Corp. Mem. Assn. Gen. Counsel Am. Judicature Soc., Law Club, American, Ill. and Chicago (board of managers, 1957-59) bar associations, Order of the Coif, Sigma Phi Epsilon, Phi Delta Phi. Clubs: Law, Union League, Midday; Evanston, (Ill.) Golf. Roman Catholic. Home: Evanston IL

URIS, PERCY, builder; b. N.Y.C., Aug. 19, 1899; s. Harris H. and Sadie (Copeland) U.; student Townsend Harris Hall, 1913-16, Columbia Coll., Columbia U. Sch. Bus., 1916-20, B.S., 1920; m. Joanne Diotte, Mar. 20, 1935; children—Julia Krulenwitch, Linda Leavitt. Chmn. bd. Uris Bldg. Corp., investment builders, N.Y.C., 1960, design, finance, rent and mgmt. co. properties, including office bldgs., apt. houses, hotels, also def. housing under govt. contract. Trustee, chmn. bldg. com. Lenox Hill Hosp. Trustee Columbia U. Clubs: City Athletic (N.Y.C.); Hollywood Golf (Deal, N.J.), Sands Point (L.I., N.Y.) Golf, Palm Beach (Fla.) Country. Home: Jericho NY Died Nov. 21, 1971.

URQUHART, NORMAN CURRIE, mining co. exec.; b. Toronto, Can., Oct. 7, 1893; s. Donald and Jennie (McGolpin) U.; student Collegiate Inst.; m. Lucy Fair; 1 son, Norman Allan. Dir. Royal Bank of Can., Simpson's Ltd., Simpsons-Sears, Ltd.; v.p., dir. Noranda Mines, Ltd. Chmn. Toronto General Hosp.; gov. U. Toronto. Decorated comdr. Order Brit. Empire; officer Legion of Honor (France). Home: Toronto ON Canada Died Sept. 3, 1966.

URY, RALPH JAY, lawyer; b. Middletown, N.Y., Oct. 3, 1890; s. Herman and Josephine (Brodek) U.; Ph.B., Union Coll., Schenectady, N.Y., 1909; LL.B., Albany Law Sch., 1911, J.D., 1968; married to Mary Baehner, June 25, 1916 (deceased February 1945); married 2d, Jane Masterson, Aug. 31, 1950. Admitted to N.Y. bar, 1911; pvt. practice in Schenectady, 1911-71. Dir., Gloversville Abraiding Co. (N.Y.). Pres., Adirondack Assn. Amateur Athletic Union, 1930-61-62, nat. bd. mgrs., 1932-71. Mem. Am., N.Y. State, Schenectady bar assns., Zeta Beta Tau (nat. pres., 1913-15). K.P. (chancellor, comdr.), Kiwanian. Address: Schenectady NY Died Sept. 27, 1971.

USINGER, ROBERT L(ESLIE), educator, entomologist; b. Ft. Bragg, Cal., Oct. 24, 1912 s. Henry Clay and Edith (Johnson) U.; B.S., U. Cal. at Berkeley, 1935, Ph.D., 1939; m. Martha Boone Putnam, June 24, 1938; children—Roberta Christine (Mrs. Ronald Manuto), Richard Putnam. With Bishop Museum, Honolulu, 1935-36, Cal. Acad. Scis., 1936-39; faculty U. Cal. at Berkeley, 1939-68, entomologist in expt. sta., 1953-68, prof. entomology, 1953-68, chmn. div. entomology and acarology, 1963-68. NIH spl. research fellow Brit. Mus. National History, 1948-49; chmn. Pacific sci. bd. NRC-Nat. Acad. Sci., 1961-63, participant bd.'s Coral Atoll study, Marshall Islands, 1950, Laysan expdn. 1961; chmn. biology div. Pacific Sci. Congress, Honolulu, 1961; mem. comite permanent Internat. Congresses Entomology and Internat. Union Biol. Scis., 1953-68; dir. Galapagos Internat. Sci. project, 1964; participant Congo expdn. Institut pour la Recherche Scientifique en Afrique centrale, 1959. Served to maj. sanitarian, USPHS, 1943-46. Decorated Gold medal King Frederick of Denmark, 1956; medal and award of merit Govt. of Ecuador, 1964; named hon. citizen Guayaquil, Ecuador, 1964. Fellow Royal Entomol. Soc. London, Linnean Soc. London; mem. Entomol. Soc. Am. (pres. 1966), Pacific Coast Entomol. Soc. (pres. 1952), Soc. Systematic Zoology (pres. 1967). Author: Elements of Zoology, 2d edit., 1961; General Zoology, 4th edit. 1965; Methods and Principles of Systematic Zoology, 1953; Classification of Aradidae, 1959; Aquatic Insects of California, 1956; Sierra Nevada Natural History, 1964; Life in Rivers and Streams, 1967; Autobiography of an Entomologist, 1972. Editor Pan-Pacific Entomologist, 1939-49. Home: Berkeley CA Died Oct. 1, 1968; buried Mountain View Cemetery, Oakland CA

UTNE, JOHN ARNDT, corp. exec.; b. Dalton, Minn., Mar. 1, 1890; s. Oliver Martinus and Ellen Thorine (Ryen) U.; student Sch. Agr., U. Minn., 1914; m. Dagny Thyse, June 22, 1920; children—June (Mrs. Lloyd Swan), Joycelyn (Mrs. Linwood Beck), John Richard. Sales and serviceman James Mfg. Co., Ft. Atkinson, Wis., 1923-33; owner, mgr. Fergus Hatchery, Fergus Falls, Minn., 1933-56; pres., dir. West Central Airways, 1948-60; v.p., dir. Security State Bank, Fergus Falls, 1957-70. Pres., dir. Minn. Hatchery Assn., 1955, Norbest Turkey Growers Assn., Salt Lake City, 1963-64; treas., dir. West Central Turkey Growers Assn., 1957-66. Mem. city council, Fergus Falls, 1949-57, acting mayor, 1955. Lutheran (chmn. trustees, past financial sec., treas.). Rotarian (treas. Fergus Falls). Home: Fergus Falls MN Died May 1, 1970.

UTT, JAMES BOYD, congressman; b. Tustin Cal., Mar. 11, 1899; s. Charles Edward and Mary M. (Sheldon) U., student Santa Ana (Cal.) Jr. Coll., 1942-43; LL.B., U. So. Cal., 1946; LL.D., Bob Jones Univ., Greenville, S.C., 1965; m. Charlena Elizabeth Dripps, May 7, 1921; 1 son, James Sheldon. Mem. Cal. State Legislature, 1933-37; state inheritance tax appraiser, Cal., 1937-52; admitted to Cal. bar 1947; practice of law, Utt & Hubbard, Santa Ana, 1947-70; mem. 83d to 87th Congresses, 28th Dist. Cal.; mem. 88th-90th Congresses from 35th Dist. Cal. Mem. Santa Ana C. of C., (dir.). Presbyn. K.P., Elk, Mason (Shriner). Home: Santa Ana CA Died Mar. 1, 1970, buried Fairhaven Cemetery.

UTTERBACK, JOHN GREGG, congressman; b. Franklin, Ind., July 12, 1872; s. James and Hannah Deliah (Maddock) U.; ed. pub. schs., Franklin; m. Helen Louise Porter, of Caribou, Me., Sept. 1, 1900; children—Elaine Collins, James Gregg, Alma Jean, John Dudley, Lucy Anna; m. 2d, Anna Esther Peek, of Franklin, Ind., Aug. 1, 1910; m. 3d, Florence Evelyn Clukey, of Bangor, Me., May 19, 1924. Traveling salesman, 1892-1922; in carriage-automobile business, Bangor, Me., 1904-34. Councilman and alderman, Bangor, 1912-13, mayor, 1914-15; mem. 73d Congress (1933-35), 3d Me. Dist. Democrat. Conglist. Clubs: Rotary, Tarratine, Penobscot Valley Country. Home: 201 Broadway. Office: 44 Summer St., Bangor ME‡

VACHON, LOUIS A., JR., mutual fund co. exec.; b. Newton, Mass., Aug. 21, 1905; s. Louis A. and Katharine (Cavanaugh) V.; student Holy Cross College 1925-28; LL.B., Boston College, 1940; married Virginia White, Oct. 26, 1935; children—Sandra Jeanne (Mrs. Boyd Van Ness), Henry W. With Merrill, Lynch, Pierce, Fenner & Smith, Boston, 1931-44; with Keystone Custodian Funds Co., 1944-68, Los Angeles, 1951-68; v.p., dir. Keystone Co., Boston, 1957-68. Mem. Mayors community adv. committee of Los Angeles. Member of the Greater Los Angeles Zoo Assn., Los Angeles, Beverly Hills stock exchange clubs, Los Angeles Bond Club, Navy League. Club: Los Angeles Country; Beverly Hills (Cal.) Club. Home: Los Angeles CA Died July 26, 1968.

VAGIS, POLYGNOTOS G(EORGE), sculptor; b. Thasos, Greece, Jan. 14, 1894; s. George and Angeliki (Hydreu) V.; came to U.S., 1910, naturalized 1919; student art, Copper Union Inst. and Beaux Arts Inst.; m. Sylvia Bender, Aug. 20, 1954. One man shows include Painters and Sculptors Gallery, 1932, Kraushaar Art Gallery 1934, Valentine Art Gallery, 1938, Hugo Art Gallery, 1946, Alexander Iolas Gallery, 1955, 56, 60; rep. permanent collections Whitney Mus. Art, Bklyn. Mus. Art, Toledo Mus. Art, Tel Aviv Mus., Art Student's League, Metropolitan Museum Art, Museum of Modern Art, also pvt. collections; group shows include Chgo. World's Fair, 1934, N.Y. World's Fair, 1938, 39, Corcoran Art Gallery, 1936, Phila. Mus. Art, 1940, Bklyn. Mus. Art 1932, 38, Met. Mus. Art, 1942, 52, Whitney Mus. Art, 1936, 45, 50, 52, 54, 60, 61, Museum of Modern Art, 1951, 52, Carnegie Institute, 1941, 58, Houston Museum of the Fine Arts, 1947; created monument for World War II veterans, entitled U.S. Forces, Bethpage, L.I., N.Y. Served with U.S. Navy, World War I. Recipient grant Whitney Mus. Am. Art, 1923-33, Shilling purchase prize, 1945, 1st sculpture prize Levittown (L.I.) Art Festival, 1951, Audubon Gold Medal of Honor for sculpture, 1955, grant for sculpture Nat. Inst. Arts and Letters, 1957; decorated medal Royal Order Phoenix (Greece). Fellow Internat. Inst. Arts; mem. Fedn. Modern Painters and Sculptors, Sculptors Guild, Audobon Artists. Home: Bethpage NY

VAIL, DERRICK TILTON, ophthalmologist; b. Cincinnati, O., May 15, 1898; s. Derrick Tilton and Della (Harriss) V.; A.B., Yale, 1919; M.D., Harvard, 1923; grad. study Oxford U., Eng., 1927; m; Elizabeth Yeiser, Aug. 30, 1921; children—Derrick Tilton, III (Royal Can; Air Force; killed in action, Feb. 22, 1942), David Jameson, Ann Elizabeth, Peter. Ophthalmic interne Mass. Eye and Ear Infirmary, Boston, 1923-24; instr. in ophthalmology, Coll. of Medicine, U. of Cincinnati, 1926-37, prof. of ophthalmology, 1937-45; dir. eye dept. Children's Hosp. and Cincinnati Gen. Hosp., 1937-45; prof. ophthalmology, head dept. Northwestern U. Med. Sch., 1945-66, prof. of ophthalmology emeritus, 1966-73. DeSchweinitz lecturer, 1945, Francis Proctor lecturer, 1947, Montgomery lecturer R.C.S. (Dublin, Ireland) 1952. Served in S.A.T.C., 1918; served as lt. col. to col., U.S. Army, 1942-45. Decorated Bronze Star, Legion of Merit (U.S.); Medaille de Reconnaisance (France); Officer Order Crown of Belgium. Mem. various civic health groups, former mem. council Nat. Institute Neurology & Blindness USPHS; vice president Ill. Soc. Prevention Blindness. Recipient Outstanding Contribution medal A.M.A. (sect. ophthalmology), 1956; Doyne lecture and medal Oxford Ophthalmological Congress (England), 1957; Leslie Dana gold medal, Nat. Soc. Prevention of Blind, 1959; Lucien Howe gold medal Am. Ophthal. Soc., 1960. Decorated Comdr. Knights St. John Jerusalem. Diplomate Am. Bd. Ophthalmology (dir. 1946-54, pres. 1954). Fellow A.C.S.; (2d v.p.); hon. mem. several fgn. profl. socs.; mem. Am. Ophthal. Soc. (pres. 1958-59), Internat. Council Ophthalmology (pres. 1962-66); member other nat., state and local profl. med. socs., past officer of several. Republican. Presbyn. Clubs: Literary, Commonwealth (Cincinnati); University, Commercial, Casino (Chgo.). Author: Truth About Your Eyes, 1950. Editor-in-chief, gen. mgr. emeritus American Jour. of Opthalmology; asso. editor Experta Medica, Ophthalmology; asso. editor Graduate Medicine. Editorial com. L'Annee Therapeutique en Ophthalmologie, Paris. Lake Bluff IL Died Apr. 24, 1973.

VAILLANCOURT, CYRILLE, Canadian senator; b. St. Anselme, Dorchester, Eng., July 17, 1892; s. Cyrille and Marie-Louise (Dorchester) V.; D.S.A., Laval U.; m. Blanche Lejole, June 1, 1920; three sons, five daus. Mem. Canadian Senate; mng. Coop. People's Savs. Banks, Desjardins Bldg., Levis, Que.; mgr. L'Union regionale des Caisses Populaires DesJardins de Que., La Caisse Centrale Desjardins de Levis; dir. La Caisse Populaire de Levis; mgr. Les Producteurs de Sucre d'Erable de Que.; v.p. La Societie D'assurances des Chaisses Populaires; dir. Les Prevoyants du Can.; pres. L'Assurance Vie Desiardins, Journalism clk. L'Etoile du Nord, Joliette, 1914; head agrl. service Dept. Agr. Que., 1915, head agrl. service and maple sugar service, Que., 1918; mgr. la Fedn. de Caisses Popularies Desjardins, 1932, dir., mgr., now mng. dir.; prof. coop. Laval U. Decorated comdr. St. Gregorie-le-Grand. Roman Cath.

Clubs: Garrison: Club Journalist (Que.); Un'versity (Laval); Saint-Denis (Montreal). Home: Levis Que Canada. Died Oct. 30, 1969; buried Levis Que Canada

VAJNA, GEORGE, book pub.; b. Budapest, Hungary, Apr. 18, 1889; s. Odon V. and Isabella (Hatsek) V.; student, sch. law and social sci., univs. of Budapest and Kolozsvar, 1907-11, Dr. Polit. Sci. (from these schs.), 1912; m. Veronika Reinitz, Mar. 4, 1914. Came to U.S., 1939. Ofcl. of tariff policy div. Royal Hungarain Ry. Adminstrn., 1912-19; propr. book pub. firm and book store, Dr. George Vajna & Co., Budapest, 1920-46; founder and pres. Transatlantic Arts Inc., book pub. co., Forest Hills, N.Y., 1939-68, also editor. Mem. A.L.A., English Speaking Union, Coll. Art Assn. Am. Home: Hollywood FL Died May 12, 1968.

VALENCIA, GUILLERMO LEON, president of Colombia; b. 1909; ed. U. Popayan. Formerly permanent rep. of Columbia to UN, also ambassador to Spain; pres. of Colombia, 1962-66. Mem. Conseative Party. Address: Bogota Columbia Died Nov. 1971.

VALENTINE, EDWARD ABRAM UFFINGTON, author; b. Bellefonte, Pa., January 29, 1870; s. Abram Sharpless and Elizabeth Uffington (Natt) V.; Haverford Coll., 1887-9; LL.B., U. of Md., 1894; m. Eleanor Elkins, 1912. Practiced law New York and Baltimore; was lit. editor Baltimore Evening News; spl. foreign corr. New York World. Author: The Ship of Silence (poems), 1902; Hecla Sandwith (novel), 1905; The Red Sphinx (with S. E. Harper), 1907; The Labyrinth of Life (novel), 1912. Address: Author's Club, 2 Whitehall Ct., London SW England‡

VALENTINE, EDWARD ROBINSON, bldg. co. exec.; b. Los Angeles, Jan. 23, 1908; s. William L. and Louise C. (Robinson) V.; A.B. Stanford, 1930; m. Mary C. Urmston, May 9, 1936 (dec.); married 2d. Carol Lapham Ophuls, Aug. 5, 1958. Vice pres., treas. Fullerton Oil Co. (Cal.), 1930-54; chmn., pres. J. W. Robinson Co., 1949-54; pres. dir. Robinson Bldg. Co., Los Angeles; dir., mem. exec. com. Security-First Nat. Bank Los Angeles; dir. Cal. Portland Cement Company, Associated Dry Goods Corp.; adv. bd. Am. Mutual Fund. Past chairman and campaign director of Los Angeles area Community Chest; past dir. Community Chest and Councils Am.; trustee Cal. Inst. Tech., chmn. bd., trustees Huntington Meml. Hosp. Served as comdr. USNR, 1942-45. Mem. Cal. C. of C. (past pres., past dir.), Automobile Club of Southern Cal. (dir. and past pres.). Republican. Club: Lincoln (past pres., dir.) (Los Santa Barbara CA Died July 21, 1968.

VALENTINE, JOHN W(ADSWORTH), business exec.; b. Boston, 1906; s. Joseph Loring and Albertine Whitney (Flershem) V.; grad. Harvard, 1929; m. Jean Purcell, July 10, 1930; children—Ann (Mrs. John W. Cobb), Jean (Mrs. Jean V. Chace), John. With Harris Trust & Savings Bank, Chgo., 1929-36; vice president, director Harris Hall & Co., N.Y.C., 1937-42, 45-51; gen. partner White, Weld & Company, Boston, 1951-62, limited partner, 1962-69. Served with U.S. Naval Reserves, 1942-45. Mem. Greater Boston C. of C., Investment Bankers Association (gov.). Republican. Clubs: Bond (Boston); The Country (Brookline, Mass.); Bond, Harvard (N.Y.C.); Owl (Cambridge, Mass.). Home: Boston MA Died Feb. 19, 1969.

VALEUR, ROBERT, economist; b. Lons Ie Saunier, France, Feb. 10, 1903; s. Eugene and Elise (Rudler) V.; Docteur en Droit, U. Lyon, France, 1922-28; research on Rockefeller fellowship, U. Chgo., Columbia, Harvard, Oxford and London, 1926-29; m. Lois Anne Perkins, July 27, 1936; 1 son, Michel. Lectr. comparative law U. Lyon, 1929-30; instr. econs. Columbia, 1930-35, lectr., 1935-43, asso. in internat. adminstrn., 1943-45; dir. French Information Center, N.Y., 1935-39; French Govt. News Service, 1939-40; Reference Div., Interallied Information Center, 1940-42; Fench Govt. Press and Information Service in U.S., 1942-45; asso. sec. gen. UN Information Office, 1942-45; prof. econs., Ecole Libre des Hautes Etudes, N.Y.C.; consul gen. of France in Sao Paulo, Brazil, 1946-52; chief Cultural Exchanges Div., French Ministry of Fgn. Affairs, also French permanent del. to UNESCO, 1952-55; 1st counselor of Embassy of France to U.S., Washington, 1955-57, minister plenipotentiary, 1957-60, ambassador of France to Ecuador, 1960-65, to Columbia, Bogota, 1965-67; ret., 1967. Chairman of the European Council for Nuclear Research, Geneva, also chairman com. cultural experts Council of Europe, Strasbourg, 1954-55. Decorated Office Legion of Honor, 1953. Clubs: Paris-America (N.Y.C.); Hamilton Street (Balt.); Metropolitan (Washington). Author: French texts, Lyon, France, 1928-30; Teaching of Law in France and the United States; French Government in Politics, 1935. Address: Cartagena Colombia Died Mar. 9, 1973.

VALK, JOSEPH ELIHU, lawyer, banker; b. N.Y.C., Mar. 13, 1915; s. Jacob Mandel and Miriam (Gottlieb) V.; A.B., Yale, 1935; LL.B., Columbia, 1938; m. Els Amanda Wyngaard, July 6, 1950; children—James Emil, Alec and Guy (twins). Admitted to N.Y. bar, 1938, Cal. bar, 1959; practiced in Mt. Vernon, N.Y., 1939-41, 46, N.Y.C., 1945-46; U.S. investigator, War Assets Adminstrn., 1946-48; partner Orange Belt Refrigeration Co., San Bernardino, Cal., 1949-50; sales mgr. Coronet Constrn. Co., North Hollywood Cal., 1950-52; asst. to prins. Diller-Kalsman Constrn. Co., Beverly Hills, 1953-57; sec., house counsel Fidelity Bank, Beverly Hills, Cal., 1957-67; Mr. Genius quiz show expert KTTV, KTLA television, Los Angeles, 1955-59. Served with CIC, AUS, 1941-45. Mem. Am., Cal., Los Angeles County, Beverly Hills bar assns. Jewish religion. Club: Yale of Southern California (Los Burbank CA Died Oct. 3, 1967.

VAN ALLEN, WILLIAM HARMAN, priest; b. Cameron, N.Y., Feb. 16, 1870; s. Daniel D. and Frances Jane (Holland) V.; Ph.B., Syracuse U., 1890, Ph.M., 1897; M.A., Hobart Coll., 1899; S.T.D., Syracuse, 1904; L.H.D., St. Stephen's Coll., 1910; D.C.L., Univ. of Bishop's Coll., Quebec, 1911; LL.D., Alfred U., 1912; read for orders while head master St. John's Sch., New York, and with Bishop Huntington; unmarried. English tutor, Rutgers Coll., 1890-91; head master St. John's Sch., New York, 1891-94; gen. sec. Ch. Assn. for Advancement Interests of Labor, 1892-94; ordained, 1894; pvt. sec. to Bishop Huntington, with charge of St. Luke's and St. Anna's chapels, Syracuse, 1894-95; acting prin. Camden (N.Y.) High Sch., 1895-96; rector Ch. of the Epiphany, Trumansburg, N.Y., 1896-97, Grace Parish, Elmira, N.Y., 1897-1902, Parish of the Advent, Boston, 1902-29. Mem. Phi Beta Kappa, Delta Kappa Epsilon, Holland Soc. of New York (v.p. for New England, 1913—); alumni trustee Syracuse U., 1915-21; pres. Actors' Ch. Alliance, Boston Chapter, 1904-06, Boston Browning Soc., 1908-10. Served with A.E.F. in France and Germany, 1919. Dep. to Gen. Conf., P.E. Ch., 1922. Memorial of Merit, St. Charles the Martyr, 1926. Traveled much abroad, and lectures extensively. Author many works, in prose and verse; on editorial staff Living Church," Pen name, Presbyter Ignotus." Clubs: Boston Authors', Boston City (Boston); Players, Clergy (New York); Authors' (London). Chevalier Order of Leopold II (Belgium), 1921.*‡

VAN ALSTYNE HENRY ARTHUR, engineer; b. N. Chatham, Columbia Co., N.Y., Oct. 9, 1869; s. Charles G. and Rachel Landon (Huyck) V.; ed. Nassau (N.Y.) Acad., Marshall Sem., Easton, N.Y.; C.E., Union U., 1893; m. Bertha Stone Neher of Rochester, N.Y., Oct. 11, 1899. Engr. in charge constrn. pub. works, 1893-4; asst. engr. in state engr.'s dept., N.Y., 1894-7; supt. constrn. and engr. for Furnaceville Iron Co. in connection with improvement of state canals, Western div., 1897, and on completion of work, with Union Bridge Co. at Athens, Pa., until 1899, when re-entered state engr.'s dept., N.Y., as asst. engr. Eastern div.; later promoted 1st asst., then to resident engr., and in 1901 to div. engr. Eastern div.; state engr., N.Y., 1904-7; v.-p. Acme Engring. & Contracting Co.; pres. Sterling Iron & Ry. Co. Republican. Clubs: Unconditional Republican, Ft. Orange. Home: 149 Echo Av., New Rochelle NY Office: 475 5th Av., New York NY‡

VAN ATTA, ROBERT S., Christian Science lecturer; b. Nelsonville, O.; s. Frank Andrew and Lucy (Smith) Van A.; M.E. in E.E., Ohio State U., 1911; m. Mildred Daniel, Oct. 25, 1913, (dec. Dec. 1959); 1 daughter, Mrs. Jane V. Brownell; m. 2d, Helen Freeman, Nov. 25, 1960. Served in engring. corps, Panama Canal, during constrn.; railroad surveys and constrn. in Bolivia and U.S.; jr. topographer with U.S. Geol. Survey; asst. master mechanic, N.Y. State Rys., Rochester, N.Y., later asso. aeronaut. engr., engring. div., U.S. Army Air Corps, McCook Field, Dayton, O.; registered Christian Science practitioner, Rochester, N.Y., from 1925; mem. Christian Science Bd. of Lectureship, The Mother Church, The First Ch. of Christ, Scientist in Boston, 1946-66. Mem. Alpha Tau Omega, Eta Kappa Nu. Home: Rochester NY Died Nov. 23, 1966.

VAN ATTEN, WILLIAM TEUNIS, business exec.; b. Kingston, N.Y., July 5, 1892 s. William Albert and Anna May (Dann) Van A; ed. pub. schs. of Albany, N.Y.; m. Elinor E. Munger, Oct. 9, 1912 (died May 1, 1943); children—Cynthia R. (wife of Dr. M. F. Stein), William T; m. 2d, Dorothy May Zell, Oct. 5, 1944. Reporter The Bradstreet Co., Albany, N.Y., 1913-16; officer in charge of credits N.Y. State Nat. Bank, Albany, 1916-20; mgr. The Bradstreet Co., Newark (N.J.) br, 1920-28, asst. sec. The Bradstreet Co., N.Y. City, 1928-29. sec., 1929-30, vice pres. and dir., 1930-33 (merged, became Dun & Bradstreet, Inc.). spl. rep. Dun & Bradstreet, Inc., 1933-49, v.p., 1949-54, cons. 1954-68, coordinated co. with war interests, World War II. Vice chmn. Munitions Bd., spl. asst. on NATO affairs Dept. of Defense, Washington, 1951, chmn. Armed Forces Regional Council, N.Y.C., 1952-53. Trustee N.Y. Coll. of Podiatry, L.I. U. Chmn. Boys Camp div. N.Y. YMCA. 1938-43; trustee Citizens Traffic Safety Bd., 1953-54; dir. Downtown Manhattan Assn., Mexico Pilgrims, N.Y. Bd. of Trade, Inc. (pres. 1950, chmn. bd. 1951), Albany Soc. of N.Y. (pres. 1949-50), Am. Arbitration Assn.; trustee Holland Soc. of N.Y. (pres. 1952-53); mem. Trade Assn. Execs., Navy League U.S. Mason (32 deg., Shriner). Presbyn. Clubs: Circus Saints and Sinners (ex-gov.), Lambs, Merchants. Home: South Londerry VT Died Nov. 23, 1968; buried Feura Bush NY

VANAUKEN, CHARLES S., banker, lawyer; b. Blairstown, N.J., April 7, 1888; s. Reuben H. and Elmira Jane (Hill) VanA.; Ph.B., Dickinson Coll., 1912, A.M., 1913; m. Bessie C. Kelley, June 24, 1914; children—Jean C., Marion E., Ruth E. Trust officer Citizens Co., Paterson, N.J., 1932-1968 (now New Jersey Bank and Trust Company), vice president, 1942-68; Paterson Mortgage & Realty Co., 1936-40; dir. Alexander Hamilton Garage, Inc. Treas. bd. trustees Paterson YMCA; pres. bd. trustees Centenary Coll. for Women; chmn. bd. trustees George Washington Meml. Park Cemetery Assn. Mem. Passaic Co. Welfare Bd., 1936-49. Selective Service Bd. 37, Passaic Co. Mem. Am., N.J. State, Passaic Co. Bar assns., Am., N.J. bankers assns., Am. Judicature Soc., Soc. Polit. Sci., Paterson C. of C., Phi Beta Kappa. Republican. Methodist. Clubs: Rotary, New York Economic, Republican. Home: Paterson NJ Died Nov. 27, 1968.

VAN BUSKIRK, ARTHUR B., business exec.; b. Pottstown, Pa., Mar. 27, 1896; s. Charles C. and Florence (McKinley) Van B.; A.B., Yale, 1918; LL.B., University of Pennsylvania, 1922; LL.D., Thiel College, 1956; LL.D., U. Pittsburgh, Marietta College, 1957; LL.D., Carnegie Institute of Technology, 1959; married Katharine Jones, October 17, 1925; children—George, Joseph, David. Law sec. to Chief Justice of Pa., 1922-24; asso. of Reed, Smith, Shaw & McClay, 1924-34, partner, 1934-41; deputy adminstr. Lend Lease adminstrn., 1942-43; vice-pres. Mellon Securities Corp., 1944-45; vice-pres. and gov. T. Mellon and Sons, from 1945; chmn. and dir. Fed. Reserve Bank Cleve., 1957-61; mem. bd. directors North Star Reinsurance Company, Consolidation Coal Co., Gen. Reinsurance Corp., Koppers Co., Inc., Equitable Life Assurance Soc. U.S.; mem. adv. com. Export-Import Bank of Washington, 1958-60. Trustee Richard King Mellon Found., Com. Econ. Devel., Eisenhower Exchange Fellowship; vice chairman Urban Redevelopment Authority Pittsburgh, 1947-51; chairman Allegheny Conference on Community Development, 1952-56; formerly dir. United Fund of Allegheny County, Pittsburgh, Symphony Society; bd. of mgrs. Children's Hospital of Pitts. Served as 2d lieutenant, with 312th F.A., 79th Div., Aug. 17, 1917 to July 25, 1919. Awarded Presdl. Certificate of Merit, 1947. Member American, Pa. and Allegheny County bar assns., Am. Judicature Soc., Am. Legion. Republican. Episcopalian. Clubs: Duquesne, Fox Chapel Golf (Pitts.); Rolling Rock, Laurel Valley (Ligonier, Pa.); Links (N.Y.C.); Union (Cleve.). Home: Ligonier PA Died Apr. 6, 1972.

VANCE, HENRY T(HOMAS), investment banker; b. Norwood, O., Oct. 20, 1906; s. Louis T. and Lillie (Stratton) V.; B.S., University of Pennsylvania, 1927; m. Laurie Burnaby, Apr. 10, 1933 (dec. Oct. 1954)children—Laurie (Mrs. Robert Adams), Sally Jean (Mrs. James W. S. Allen), Henry Thomas. With W. A. Harriman, Inc., 1927-31, Am. Trustee Shares Corp., 1931-34, Ryan & McManus, 1934-36; v.p. Mass. Distbrs., Inc., 1936-42, pres., 1942-44; partner Vance, Sanders & Co., 1944-59; pres. Vance, Sanders & Co. Inc., 1959-64, chmn. bd., dir., 1964-72; chmn. bd. Vance, Sanders & Co. Canada, Ltd.; chairman board, director of Diversification Fund, Boston Mgmt. & Research Co., Inc., Boston Fund, Inc., Exchange Fund of Boston, Inc., Boston Common Stock Fund, Inc.; dir. Vance, Sanders Spl. Fund, Inc.; chmn. Depositors Fund of Boston, Capital Exchange Fund, Inc. trustee Century Shares Trust. Chmn. banking div. Greater Boston Community Fund, 1944, chairman financial div., 1947; trustee Boys and Girls Camps, Inc.; trustee, bd. bus. edn., investment com. U. Pa.; bd. dirs. Beverly Hosp. Research Foud., Allergy Found. Am. Inc. Clubs: Union, Tennis and Racquet (Boston); Essex Country, Singing Beach, Manchester Yacht (Manchester, Mass.); Myopia Hunt (Hamilton, Mass.); Eastern Yacht (Marblehead, Mass.); San Diego (Cal.) Yacht; St. Francis Yacht (San Francisco); Capitol Hill (Washington). Home: Boston MA Died Apr. 24, 1972.

VAN DE GRAAFF, ROBERT JEMISON, physicist; born Tuscaloosa, Ala., Dec. 20. 1901; s. Adrian Sebastian and Minnie Cherokee (Hargrove) Van de G; B.S., U. of Ala., 1922, M.S., 1923, hon. D.Sc., 1941; student Sorbonne, 1924-25; B.Sc., Oxford, 1926; Ph.D., 1928; hon. degree Fla. State U., U. Utrecht; m. Catherine Boyden, April 12, 1936 (dec. Dec. 1972); children—John Hargrove, William Boyden. Rhodes scholar, 1925-28; Internat. Edn. Bd. fellow, Oxford, 1928-29; Nat. Research fellow, Princeton, 1929-31; Research associate, Mass. Inst. Tech., 1931-34; asso. prof., 1934-60; dir. OSRD radiographic project, 1941-46; dir. High Voltage Engring. Corporation 1946-67, mem. exec. com. 1957-67; chief scientist. Awarded Elliott Cresson medal, Duddell medal, Dudley medal; Naval Ordnance Devel. award, 1946. Fellow Am. Phys. Soc. (Bonnerprize 1966); mem. Am. Acad. Arts and Scis., Sigma XI, Lexington MA Died Jan. 16, 1967; buried Beverly MA

VAN DEMAN, RALPH HENRY, army officer; b. Delaware, O., Sept. 3, 1865; s. John Dodridge and Lydia Sieg (Runkle) Van D.; student Ohio Wesleyan U., 1883-86; A.B., Harvard, 1888; M.D., Miami Med. Sch., Cincinnati, 1893; grad. Inf. and Cav. Sch., Fort Leavenworth, Kan., 1895, Army War Coll.,

Washington, D.C., 1905; m. Irene Kingcombe, Mar. 3, 1917. Commd. 2d lt. inf., U.S. Army, Aug. 1, 1891; advanced through grades to brig. gen., Sept. 28, 1927; maj. gen., May 27, 1929; retired Sept. 3, 1929. Member Harbor Commission, San Diego, Calif. Participated in Spanish-American War, Philippine Insurrection and World War. Awarded D.S.M. (U.S.); Companion of the Bath (British); Officer Legion of Honor (French); Comdr. Crown of Italy. Mem. Phi Kappa Psi. Republican. Episcopalian. Mason (32 deg.). Club: Army and Navy (Washington, D.C.). Home: 3141 Curlew St., San Diego 3 CA‡

VANDERBILT, HAROLD STIRLING, capitalist; b. Oakdale, N.Y., July 6, 1884; s. William Kissan and Alvia E. (Smith) V.; A.B., Harvard, 1907; Harvard U. Law Sch., 1907-10. Began active career with N.Y.C. R.R.; for many years dir. various ry. and other corps. Pres. bd. trust Vanderbilt U. Served from lt. (j.g.) to lt. USNRF, 1917-18; comdg. officer Scout Patrol 56, later comdr. Block Island and New London sects., served with submarine chaser detachment 3, Queenstown, Ireland, 1918. Inventor contract bridge, 1925. Home: New York City NY Died July 4, 1970.

VANDERBILT, MERRITT DAVID, mfg. exec.; b. N.Y.C., July 17, 1893; s. David Bissett and Ann Elizabeth (Campbell) V.; student pub. schs.; m. Florence Birdseye Lewis, Aug. 29, 1919; children—Esther V., Clarissa V. Teller V. Teller Tradesmen's Nat. Bank, New Haven, 1911-16; dept. head Locomobile Co. of Am., Bridgeport, Conn., 1916-17; accountant Walk-Over Shoe Co., New Haven, 1919-24; internal revenue agt. U.S. Treasury Dept., 1924-25; pub. accountant, mgmt. cons., 1925-42; pres., treas., gen. mgr. Griest Mfg. Co., 1942-60, chmn. bd., 1960-61; chmn. bd., chief exec. officer High Standard Manufacturing Corp., Hamden, Conn., from 1961; president Central Services Building, Inc.; New Haven; chmn. bd. Westhaven Buckle Co.; dir. So. Conn. Gas Co. Past pres. Air Marine Motors, Inc., Amityville, Long Island, Los Angeles. Pres. United Fund Greater New Haven, 1958-59; chairman of the Stratford Board Education, 1925-27; member bd. Stratford Library. Served as sgt. U.S. Army, A.E.F. in France, 1917-19. C.P.A., Conn., 1929. Mem. Am. Legion. Club: Quinnipack (New Haven). Home: Trumbull CT Died June 8, 1971.

VANDERBILT, NEWELL FITZGERALD;, b. Tomales, Marin Co., Calif., June 4, 1874; s. William and Mary (Fitzgerald) V.; grad. Mt. Tamalpais Mil. Acad., San Rafael, Calif., 1894; B.S., U. of Calif., 1902; spl. studies summer sessions, same; m. Effie Pauline Murray, of San Rafael, Oct. 22, 1910; 1 son, William Murray. Began teaching at Mt. Tamalpais Mil. Acad. upon graduation, 1894; mgr. and headmaster same, 1916-25; mgr. Luther Burbank Experimental Farms, 1929-32; now with Jackson, Perkins Co.; editor Better Delphiniums (mag.). Mem. Calif. N.G. since 1894, now maj.; served as 1st sergt. U.S. Vol. Inf., Spanish-Am. War. Mem. United Spanish War Veterans, Alpha Delta Phi. Republican. Presbyn. Home: San Rafael CA‡

VAN DER GRACHT, W. A. J. M. VAN WATERSCHOOT, geologist; b. Amsterdam, Holland, May 15, 1873; s. W. S. J. van Waterschoot and M. C. A. J. van der Does de Willebois V.; prep. edn., Katwyk Coll., Holland; student Stonyhurst Coll., Eng., 1892; LL.D., Amsterdam U., 1899; M.E., Sch. of Mines, Freiberg, 1904; hon. Sc.D., Colo. Sch. of Mines, 1924; m. Baroness J. F. R. G. M. Hammer-Purgstall, of Styria, Austria, May 22, 1901; children—Idesbald W. P. J. M., Arthur B. T. J. M. Walter J. J. M. (dec.), Marie-Gisele M. J. Began practice at The Hague, 1904; dir. Netherlands Geol. Survey, 1905-17; explored mineral resources of Holland for the Govt. and discovered extensive deposits of coal and rock salt; drafted safety regulations for coal mines in Holland, and acted as adviser and explorer in various countries for mining and petroleum corpns.; came to U.S., 1915; pres. Roxana Petroleum Co. (Royal Dutch-Shell), 1917-21; v.p. Md. Oil Co. Mem. Am. Assn. Petroleum Geologist, Am. Inst. Mining Engrs., Geol. Soc. Belgium, Geol. Soc. Holland (ex-pres.), Internat. Geol. Congress; fellow Geol. Soc. London. Decorated Knight Order of the Lion of the Netherlands; Comariere Segreto by Popes Leo XIII, Pius X and Pius XI. Catholic. Author: The Deeper Geology of the Netherlands and Adjacent Regions, 1910; also numerous Netherland Govt. repts. and papers in periodicals of Netherlands, Germany and America. Home: Ponca City OK‡

VANDERHOOF, ALBERT WHITTIER, office equipment mfr.; b. Everett, Mass., May 9, 1902; s. Fred and Frances (Grinnell) V.; B.S., Tufts U., 1924, M.A., 1950; m. Helen Steere, Dec. 27, 1926 (div. 1944); 1 dau., Joyce (Mrs. Louis Trilsch). With Standard Duplicating Machines Corp., Everett, Mass., 1924—, beginning as jr. salesman, successively sales corr., field supr., asst. sales mgr. gen. sales mgr., v.p. and Gen. mgr., 1924-47, pres. chmn. bd., 1947—; dir. Columbia Ribbon & Carbon Mfg. Co., Inc., Glen Cove, N.Y., Middlesex County Nat. Bank, Everett. Mass. Lectr., Harvard Coll., Boston Coll., Boston U. Permanent chmn. Mass. Assembly on State Govt.; mem. governor's adv. council on Mass. self-survey; mem. Mass. Civil Rights Com.; chmn. Gov.'s Adv. Council Mass. Manpower Com.; adv. council WPB. Trustee Civic Edn. Found., Inc.; life trustee, mem. exec. committee Tufts U., also mem. Alumni Council, chmn. Tufts Trustee Development Com.; chmn. founds. com., steering com. New Eng. Med. Center. Mem. Office Equipment Mfrs. Inst. (past pres.), Newcomen Soc., Beacon Soc., Everett C. of C., Asso. Industries of Mass., Alpha Tau Omega (past dir.). Club: University (pres.) (Boston). State sr. champion Squash Racquet. Home: Boston MA Died Sept. 15, 1968.

VANDER LUGT, GERRIT T., coll. pres.; b. Rotterdam, Holland, Jan. 28, 1879; s. Teunis and Cornelia Adriana (Vander Meer) Vander L.; came to U.S., 1905; naturalized, 1914; B.A., Calvin Coll., Grand Rapids, Mich., 1922; M.A., U. of Mich., 1923, Ph.D., 1928; LL.D., Lawrence Coll., 1944; D.D., Central Coll., 1957; H.H.D., Buena Vista Coll., 1959; Litt.D., Hope Coll., Holland, Michigan, 1960; m. Anna Haga, Sept. 20, 1923; 1 dau., Jacoba Ann. Instr. rhetoric, U. of Mich., 1924-28; associate professor philosophy, Carroll Coll., Waukesha, Wisconsin, 1928-30, prof., 1930-39, dean of adminstrn., 1939-40, pres., 1940-46; president, Central Coll., Pella, Iowa, 1946-60; prof. systematic theology New Brunswick Theol. Sem., 1960-67. Ordained to ministry Presbyn. Ch., 1937; moderator Milwaukee Presbytery, 1941-42; moderator of the Synod of Wis. of the Presbyn. Ch.; minister Reformed Ch. of Am. (mem. bd. edn. and chmn. curriculum com.); past pres. Gen. Synod Reformed Ch., Am.; past pres. Ia. Coll. Found. Mem. Am. Philos. Assn., Mich. Acad. Sci. Republican. Author ednl. and religious articles. Home: Grand Rapids MI Died May 1, 1968; buried Chapel Hill Cemetery, Grand Rapids MI

VANDERWARKER, RICHARD DEAN, hosp. adminstr.; b. Boston, May 15, 1911; s. James Roy and Christina (Leithead) V.; B.S., Cornell U., 1933; M.H.A., Northwestern U., 1950; m. Josephine Prigmore, Dec. 30, 1934; children—Christine, Richard D. Exec. asst. mgr., Hotel Sherman, Chgo., 1933-42; mgr. Hotel Bellerive, Kansas City, Mo., 1946-47; dir. Passavant Meml. Hosp., Chgo., 1947-52; v.p., gen. mgr. Meml. Center Cancer and Allied Diseases, N.Y.C., 1952-62; pres. Meml. Sloan-Kettering Cancer Center, 1964-71. President of the Greater N.Y. Hosp. Assn., 1962, Hosp. Assn. N.Y. State, 1963-65. Served from lt. (j.g.) to lt. comdr., USNR, 1942-46. Fellow Am. Coll. Hosp. Adminstrs. (gov. 1965-69); mem. Cornell U. Alumni Assn. (pres. 1962-64), Pan Am. Hosp. Assn. (life), Assn. Am. Med. Colls., Am. Hosp. Assn., Cornell U. Council, Internat. Hosp. Fedn. Clubs: Cornell University (N.Y.C.); Quaker Hill Country (Pawling, N.Y.). Home: New York City NY Died May 2, 1971; buried Pawling NY

VAN DEUSEN, HENRY REED, lawyer; b. Laurens, N.Y., June 2, 1872; s. Henry Newton and Mary Jane (Porter) Van D.; A.B., Wesleyan U., Middletown, Conn., 1894; LL.B., U. of Pa. Law School, 1899; LL.D., Mt. Union College, 1946; m. Jessie Lawrence Dimmick, September 16, 1903; children—William Connell (dec.), Lawrence Reed, Henry Reed, Jr. Admitted to bar, 1899; since in gen. practice at Scranton; officer of dir. various corps. Sec. Judicial Council of Meth. Ch. Mem. Delta Kappa Epsilon, Phi Beta Kappa. Republican. Methodist. Home: 420 Quincy Av. Office: Scranton Life Bldg., Scranton PA‡

VAN DEUSEN, ROBERT HICKS, chmn. Stone & Webster Securities Corp.; b. Phila., Pa., July 10, 1891; s. Edwin H. and Adelaide Parmalee (Smith) van D.; ed. public and private schs.; m. Maidza Wakem, Dec. 11, 1920; children—Frederick, Robert H., Maidza. Chmn. and dir. Stone & Webster Securities Corporation (formerly Stone & Webster and Blodget, Inc.), 1932-51, dir., 1926-51. First lt. with 12th F.A., 2d Div., A.E.F. Episcopalian. Clubs: Recess, Knickerbocker (New York). Home: Roxbury CT Died May 1971.

VAN DE WATER, FREDERIC F(RANKLYN), author; b. Pompton, New Jersey, Sept. 30, 1890; s. Frederic Franklyn and Virginia Belle (Terhune) Van de W.; student New York U., 1910-12; B.Litt., Columbia, 1914; L.H.D. (honorary), Middlebury College, 1952; married Eleanor Gay, Oct. 4, 1916; 1 son, Frederic Franklyn. Reporter N.Y. American, 1914; reporter, spl. writer, night city editor N.Y. Tribune, 1915-22; book critic N.Y. Tribune, 1922-24; staff of Ladies' Home Journal, 1922-28; book critic, N.Y. Evening Post, 1928-32; corporator Vt. Savings Bank, 1936-68; dir. Vt. Children's Aid Soc., 1936-54; mem. Ft. Ticonderoga Bi-centennial Com., 1954-55; trustee Leland Gay Seminary 1938-58. Member Windham County Peace Officers' Association, 1939-68; president 1941. Recipient Honors Medallion, Columbia U., 1963. Fellow International Inst. of Arts and Letters; mem. S.A.R., Soc. Colonial Wars, P.E.N., Psi Upsilon. Mason. Clubs: Authors, Adventurers (hon. life). Author: Grey Riders, 1921; The Social Ladder (with May King Van Rensselaer), 1924; Horsemen of the Law, 1926; The Eye of Lucifer, 1927; The Family Flivvers to 'Frisco, 1927; Elmer 'n' Edwina, 1928; Hurrying Feet, 1928; Still Waters, 1929; Alibi, 1930; Havoc, 1931; The Real McCoy, 1931; Plunder, 1933; Thunder Shield, 1933; Glory Hunter, A Life of General Custer, 1934; Hidden Ways, 1935; Death in the Dark, 1937; A Home in the Country, 1937; Rudyard Kipling's Vermont Feud, 1938 We're Still in the Country, 1938; Fathers Are Funny 1939; The Circling Year, 1940; The Reluctant Republic Vermont, 1724-1791, 1941; Members of the Family 1942; Mrs. Applegate's Affair, 1944; Fool's Errand 1945; The Sooner to Sleep, 1946; Lake Champlain and Lake George (Lakes of America Series), 1946 Reluctant Rebel, 1948; Catch a Falling Star, 1949; In Defense of Worms, 1950; The Captain Called It Mutiny 1954; Wings of the Morning, 1956; This Day's Madness, 1957; Day of Battle, 1958; Tempest, 1959 Home: West Dummerston VT Died Sept. 16, 1968 buried Dummerston Center VT

VANDIVER, HARRY SHULTZ, educator; b. Phila. Oct. 21, 1882; s. John L. and Ida F. (Everett) V.; studen U. Pa., 1904-05, Sc.D. (hon.), 1945; m. Maude F Everson, July 25, 1923; 1 son, Frank Everson. Asso with John L. Vandiver as customs house broker, Phila. 1900-19; instr. math. Cornell U., 1919-24; asso. prof pure math. U. Tex., 1925-35, prof., 1935-66 distinguished prof. applied math., 1947, research prof. 1934-35, research fellow, 1939-40, 46-47, researcl grantee, 1928, 31, 35, 44-50, 52-65, fellow Researcl Inst., 1946, 48, prof. emeritus, 1966-73; vis. prof. math U. Chgo., summer 1922, Princeton, spring 1934, U Ind., spring 1947, Notre Dame U., summer 1947 Chmn. com. algebraic numbers NRC, 1923-28. Servec with USNRF, 1917-19. Guggenheim fellow, 1927, 30 grantee Am. Philos. Soc., 1934-40, Heckscher Researcl Found., Cornell U., 1920-23; basic research grante Nat. Sci. Found., 1955, 57-59, 59-65, sr. postdoctora fellow, 1956. Mem. A.A.A.S., Texas Acad. Sci., N.Y Acad. Scis., Am. Math. Society (v.p. 1935-37 colloquium lectr. 1935; Cole prize 1931), Math. Assn Am., Am. Assn. U. Profs., Nat. Academy of Sciences Artisans Order of Mutual Protection, Sigma Xi, Ph Kappa Phi. Author: (with others) Report on Theory o Algebraic Numbers (NRC), part I, 1923, part II, 1928 Associate editor Scripta Mathematica, 1958, Jour Mathematical Analysis and Application, 1959. Contbr articles to profl. jours. Home: Austin TX Died Jan. 4 1973.

VAN DOREN, MARK, author; b. Hope, Ill., June 13 1894; s. Charles Lucius and Dora Anne (Butz) Van D. A.B., U. Ill., 1914, A.M., 1915, Litt. D., 1958; Ph.D. Columbia, 1920, Litt.D., 1960, Bowdoin, 1944; L.H.D. Adelphi, 1957; L.H.D., Mt. Mary Coll., 1965; Litt.D. Knox Coll., 1966, Harvard, 1966, Jewish Theol. Sem Am., 1970; M.D. (hon.), Conn. Med. Soc., 1966; m Dorothy Graffe, 1922; children—Charles, John. Instr English, Columbia, 1920-24, asst. prof., 1924-35, assc prof., 1935-42, prof., 1942-59; lectr. St. John's Coll Md., 1937-57; lit. editor The Nation, 1924-28, motio picture critic, 1935-38. Participant in radio talk Invitation to Learning, 1940-42 (CBS); The Eterna Light, 1952 (NBC). Recipient Pulitzer prize for poetry 1939; Ann. Creativity award Huntington Hartfor Found., 1962; Emerson-Thoreau award Am. Acad. Ar and Scis., 1963; Brotherhood award Nat. Con Christians and Jews, 1960; Sarah Josepha Hale award 1960; Alexander Hamilton medal Columbia, 1959 Mem. Am. Acad. Arts and Letters. Author many work 1916-72, latest being: The Autobiography of Mark Va Doren, 1958; The Last Days of Lincoln (play), 1959 Morning Worship and Other Poems, 1960; The Happ Critic, 1961; Collected Stories, 1962, Vol. II, 1965, Vo III, 1968; Collected and New Poems, 1963; Th Narrative Poems of Mark Van Doren, 1964; Thre Plays, 1966; Somebody Came, 1966; 100 Poem Selected by The Author, 1967; Introduction to Poetry Commentaries on Thirty Poems, 1968; That Shinin Place, 1969. Home: Falls Village CT Died Dec. 10 1972; buried Cornwall Hollow CT

VAN DUYN, EDWARD SEGUIN, surgeon; b. a Syracuse, N.Y., Aug. 20, 1872; s. John and Sara (Faulks) Van D.; M.D., Syracuse U., 1897; m. Luc Leavenworth Ballard, Feb. 4, 1903; children—Mary L John, Constance. Practiced at Syracuse since 1897 prof. Syracuse U. Coll. of Medicine, 1917-37, emerit since 1937; surgeon University Hosp.; cons. surgeo Syracuse Free Dispensary. Pres. bd. visitors Syracus State Sch., State Dept. Mental Hygiene. Served as l col., M.C., U.S. Army, in World War I. Fellow Am. Co Surgeons; mem. A.M.A., Med. Soc. State of N.Y Republican. Presbyterian. Club: Century. Home: 60 James St. Office: Medical Arts Bldg., Syracuse NY‡

VAN DYKE, EDWIN COOPER, prof. entomology; b Oakland, Calif., Apr. 7, 1869; s. Walter and Rowen (Cooper) Van D.; B.S., U. of Calif., 1893; M.D., Coope Med. Coll. (now Stanford U.), 1895; m. Mary Ame June 7, 1915. In practice of medicine, San Francisc 1895-1913; instr. in entomology, U. of Calif., 1913-1 asst. prof. entomology, 1915-21, asso. prof., 1921-2 prof., 1927-39, prof. emeritus since 1939; hon. curat entomology Calif. Academy Science. Fellow A.A.A.S Entomol. Soc. Am. Mem. Pacific Const. Entomol. So (ex-pres.), Calif. Acad. Science (hon. curator). Bet Theta Pi, Phi Rho Sigma, Sigma Xi; corr. mem. An Entomol. Soc. Republican. Address: Calif. Acad. Science, San Francisco CA‡

VAN DYKE, HARRY BENJAMIN, university prof.; b. Des Moines, Ia., Jan. 31, 1895; s. Benjamin and Louise V. (Boody) van D.; B.S., Univ. of Chicago, 1918, Ph.D., 1921; M.D., Rush Medical College, 1923; m. Elizabeth E. Allan, Apr. 14, 1920; children—Jane Elizabeth (Mrs. John H. Felber), Arthur Cushny (dec.). National Research Council fellow, Edinburgh, 1924-25, Brussels, 1925, Freiburg in Breisgau, 1925-26; associate professor of pharmacology, University of Chicago, 1926-30, prof., 1930-32; prof. Peiping Union Med. Coll., 1932-38; head div. pharmacology, The Squibb Inst. for Med. Research, 1938-44; David Hosack prof. pharmacology, Coll. Physicians and Surgeons, Columbia University, 1944-63, professor emeritus, 1963-71; vis. prof. pharmacology, Taiwan, 1963-64, U. Malaya, Kuala Lumpur, 1965-67. Recipient Sir Henry Dale medal Brit. Soc. Endocrinology, 1970. Fellow N.Y. Acad. Med.; mem. Am. Soc. Pharmacol. and Experimental Therapeutics (president 1962), A.A.A.S., A.M.A., Am. Physiol. Soc., Am. Soc. Pharmacology and Exptl. Therapeutics, Assn. Am. Physicians, Assn. Study Internal Secretions, Biochem. Soc. (Gt. Britain), Harvey Soc., Soc. Exptl. Biology and Medicine, Sigma Xi, Alpha Omega Alpha, Alpha Kappa Kappa. Editor, Journal Pharmacology and Experimental Therapeutics, 1950-53. Author of two books on the pituitary body; also contributor sci. articles to various publications. Home: Englewood NJ Died Feb. 14, 1971.

VAN EPPS, CLARENCE, physician; b. Aug. 29, 1875; s. Charles H. and Elizabeth Van E.; B.S., Ia. State Coll., 1894; M.D., State U. of Iowa, 1897, Univ. of Pa., 1898; m. Ella P. Parsons, July 6, 1904. Professor and head department of neurology, State University of Iowa, to 1945 (now prof. emeritus). Lieutenant colonel Med. O.R.C., serving General Hosp. No. 54, U.S. Army. Mem. Am. Med. Assn., Iowa State Medical Society, Central Neuropsychiatric Association, Delta Tau Delta, Phi Rho Sigma, Sigma Xi, Alpha Omega Alpha. Home: 128 E. Fairchild, Iowa City IA‡

VAN EPPS, EUGENE FRANCIS, physician, educator; b. DeWitt, Ia., Jan. 31, 1912; s. Homer Eugene and Anna (Foley) Van E.; M.D., U. Ia., 1935; m. Yola Margaret Came, Sept. 2, 1937; children—Robert Francis, Marcia Ann, William Michael. Intern State U. Ia. Hosps., 1935-36, resident medicine and pediatrics, 1936-39, radiology resident, 1946-49, radiologist, 1949-70, asst. prof., then asso. prof. radiology, 1949-55, prof., head dept., 1955-67, Ia. prof., 1967-68, prof. Duke U. 1968-70. Mem. sch. bd., Iowa City, 1961-64, pres., 1961-62. Served as capt., M.C., AUS, 1942-46. Diplomate Am. Bd. Radiology (vice president 1966-67, treasurer, trustee, pres. 1969-70). Fellow Am. Coll. Radiology; mem. Radiology Society N.A., Ia. Radiol. Soc. (pres. 1957-58), Ia. Med. Soc. (sec., chmn. jud. council 1953-57, pres. 1960-61), Society for Pediatric Radiology, American Roentgen Ray Soc. (exec. council), N.Y. Acad. Scis., Sigma Xi, Alpha Omega Alpha. Home: Albuquerque NM Mar. 11, 1970.

VAN EVERA, BENJAMIN DOUGLASS, educator; b. Davenport, Ia., May 28, 1901; s. Charles and Henrietta (Kepler) Van E.; B.S., Coe Coll., 1923, Sc.D. (hon.), 1952; M.S., Ia. State Coll., 1925; Ph.D., State U. Ia., 1937; m. Margaret Lorimer, Sept. 12, 1925. With George Washington U., 1925-70, successively instr. chemistry, asst. prof., exec. officer chemistry dept., asst. prof., prof., 1938-70; adminstrv. dir. Allegany Ballistics Lab., 1942-46, coordinator sci. activities, 1946-57, dean for sponsored research, 1957-66. Survey for India Government of fertilizer plants with Nat. Research Council and Tech. Cooperation Adminstrn., 1952. Mem. Am. Chem. Soc., Chem. Soc. Washington (pres. 1949), Am. Assn. U. Profs., A.A.A.S., Am. Soc. Engring. Edn., Washington Acad. Scis. (pres. 1962-63), Am. Inst. Chemists (honor award 1956), Sigma Xi, Alpha Chi Sigma (profl. service award 1965), Phi Lambda Upsilon, Omicron Delta Kappa. Club: Cosmos (Washington). Asso. editor Jour. Chem. Edn., 1949-55. Home: Falls Church VA Died Apr. 9, 1970; buried Summit Cemetery, Davenport IA

VANHANSWYK, LOUIS JOHN, printing co. exec.; b. Ridgewood, N.J., May 14, 1905; s. Nicholas and Victoria (Horn) Van H.; B.A., N.Y. U.; m. Mary S. Duhig, June 6, 1926; children—Robert Louis, Jeanne M. Owner, Lou Van Typographers, Inc., N.Y.C. Pres. Internat. Assn. Printing House Craftsmen; past pres. N.Y. Club Printing House Craftsmen; cons. N.Y. Sch. Printing; chmn. graphic arts ednl. adv. commn. N.Y.C. and N.Y. State. Mason. Author articles in field. Home: Great Neck Estates NY Died Dec. 15, 1971.

VAN HORN, ROBERT BOWMAN, engring., educator; b. Nova, O., July 1, 1893; s. Francis J. (D.D.) and Amy Bell (Richards) Van H.; B.S. in Civil Engring., Univ. of Washington, 1916, C.E., 1926; m. Sydnia Caldan, Feb. 20, 1926. Sanitary inspector, U.S. Pub. Health Service 1916; acting instr. in civil engring., U. of Washington, 1920; designing and maintenance engr., U.S. Reclamation Service, Yakima, Wash., 1920-25; instr., Coll. of Engring., U. of Washington, 1925-28, asst. prof., 1928-34, asso. prof., 1934-38, prof. hydraulic engring. and head dept. civil engring. 1938-62, prof. emeritus, 1962-72; cons. hydraulic and sanitary engr.; with state highway dept. summer 1926; in irrigating engring. U.S. Bureau Reclamation (Wash.) summers 1927-29; asst. engr. designs and constrn. U.S. Nat. Park Service, Mount Rainier Nat. Park, summers 1930-33. Served as 1st lt., 20th Engrs., U.S. Army, 1917-19; with A.E.F., France, 1918-19. Mem. Am. Soc. C.E., Soc. Am. Mil. Engrs., Soc. Promotion Engring. Edn., Tau Beta Pi, Sigma Xi, Phi Kappa Sigma. Editor: Hydraulic Tables, 1933. Author: Cost Estimation of Irrigation Works, 1926; Sanitary Engineering Laboratory Manual, 1931; A Short Course in Plane Surveying, 1934; Discharge of Commercial Cippoletti Weirs, 1936. Home: Seattle WA Died May 5, 1972; buried Fox Island WA

VAN KLEECK, MARY, indsl. sociologist; b. Glenham, N.Y., June 26, 1883; d. Rev. Robert Boyd and Eliza (Mayer) Van Kleeck; A.B., Smith Coll., 1904; LL.D., St. Lawrence Univ., 1938. Investigations of women in industry, 1905-09; dir. indls. studies, Russell Sage Found., 1909-48; ret.; dir. women's br. indsl. service sect. Ordnance Dept., Washington, 1918; dir. Woman in Industry Service, U.S. Dept. Labor, also mem. of War Labor Policies Bd., 1918-19. Trustee Smith Coll., 1922-30. Asso. dir. Internat. Indsl. Relations Inst., 1928-48, chmn. program com. World Social Econ. Congress, 1931; pres. 2d Internat. Conf. of Social Work, Frankfurt-am-Main, Germany, 1932; mem. bd. dirs. Ency. of Social Scis. Fellow A.A.A.S., Am. Statis. Assn. (v.p. 1932, 35); mem. Fedn. Am. Scientists, Nat. Assn. Social Workers, Am. Econ. Assn., Am. Sociol. Assn. Acad. Credited Social Workers. Episcopalian. Club: Cosmopolitan (N.Y.C.) Author books on women in industry published by Russell Sage Found., also Miners and Management, 1934; Creative America, 1936. Joint Author: Employes' Representation in Coal Mines, 1924; Technology and Livelihood, 1944; Technological Basis for National Development, 1948; studies of social adjustment of atomic energy, efforts to abolish nuclear weapons, 1943-56; International Trade and Peace, 1961, 64, Joint Editor on Economic Planning, 1935. Home: Woodstock NY Died June 8, 1972.

VAN LARE, STANLEY EVERETT, ednl. adminstr.; b. Marion, N.Y., Nov. 2, 1908; s. J. D. and Sarah (Manhave) VanL.; A.B., Hope Coll., 1930; M.S., Syracuse U., 1937; m. Charlotte Forman, June 21, 1937; 1 dau., Mary Ann (Mrs. Ronald Kenne). Tchr. Fremont (Mich.) Pub. Schs., 1930-32; ins. agt. The White Agy., 1932-34; dir. adult edn. Guidance and Placement Vets. Inst., Alpena (Mich.) Pub. Schs., 1934-52; dean Alpena Community Coll., 1952-68, pres., 1968-69. Cons. program with developing instns. Am. Assn. Jr. Colls., 1968-69. Mem. Mich. Higher Edn. Assistance Authority; mem. exec. com. Mich. Council of Community Coll. Adminstrs., joint exec. com. Mich. Assn. Community Coll. Bds.; pres. Mich. Council of Community Coll. Adminstrs., 1967-68. Chmn. civil service commn. City of Alpena, 1957-69. Mem. Phi Delta Kappa. Home: Alpena MI Died May 14, 1969; buried Evergreen Cemetery Alpena MI

VAN LEER, CARLOS CLARK, b. Nashville, Tenn., Oct. 15, 1865; s. Samuel and Alice McCorry (Clark) Van L.; LL.B., Vanderbilt, 1895; m. Harriet Draper, Aug. 23, 1905; children—Carlos C., Jr., Anthony Wayne, Leila D. Clerk in post office, Nashville, 1887-97; paymaster's clk., U.S. Navy, 1897; same in office of auditor U.S. Treasury, 1900-15, chief clk., 1915-21; chief of treasury dept. div., gen. accounting office, 1921; investigator, Bur. of the Budget, 1922-27; asst. to dir. of Budget and chmn. Personnel Classification Bd., 1927-32. Served as 1st lt. and capt. Tenn. Vol. Inf., 1898-99. Mem. S.A.R., Sigma Alpha Epsilon. Christian Scientist. K.P. Club: Columbia Country. Home: 1858 Ontario Pl., Washington DC‡

VAN NAME, ELMER GARFIELD, lawyer; b. Camden, N.J., Mar. 29, 1888; s. Clarence Barrett and Xenia (Smith) Van N.; LL.B., Temple U., 1912, J.D., 1968, grad. student, 1915-16; LL.D., Grove City Coll., 1934; m. Emily O. Paul, Mar. 29, 1916; children—David E., Xenia E., Emily P. (dec.). Admitted to N.J. bar, 1912; counsellor at law, 1915; in practice till 1953; master in chancery, 1915, U.S. Supreme Court, 1932, spl. master, 1933; apptd. commr. N.J. Supreme Ct., 1935; partner N.J. Rivet Co.; gen. counsel for Radio Condenser Co. and affiliates, 1923-53; formerly N.J. counsel for Fire Assn. of Phila. and affiliates. Admitted to practice, U.S. Ct. Claims, U.S. Tax Ct. Mem. YMCA 53 yrs.; del. to triennial meetings. General Soc. S.R. Co-founder the Coll. of South Jersey and South Jersey Law Sch., now div. Rutgers U., president 1926-40. Mem. Baronial Order of Magna Carta, Pa. Academy of Fine Arts, Hist. Soc. Pa., Franklin Inst. Pa., Camden County Historical Society (trustee), Acad. Natural Sciences (Phila.), Staten Island Hist. Soc., Met. Opera Guild, General Alumni Assn. Temple U. (life mem.), The Netherland-America Foundation. Member Zoological Soc. Phila., Geneal. Soc. N.J., N.Y. Geneal. and Biog. Soc., Am.-Swedish Historical Foundation, N.J. Bar Assn., Huguenot Socs. of Wash., Pa., N.J. (chancellor), Netherlands Society of Phila., S.R. (pres. N.J. 1956-58), S.A.R., N.J. Historical Society Order Crown Charlemagne United States, Soc. Colonial Wars State N.J. (gov. 1968-—), Holland Soc. N.Y., Salem County (hon. life), Gloucester County, Haddonfield hist. socs., Geneal. Soc. Pa., Swedish Colonial Soc., Netherland Benevolent Soc. N.Y., Inc. Com. for Constl. Govt., Nat. Geneal. Soc., Sigma Pi (life). Mason. Author geneal. publs. Home: Haddonfield NJ

VAN NICE, ERRETT, banker; b. Chgo., Apr. 5, 1908; s. Errett I. and Lillian (Blaker) Van N.; A.B., U. Chgo., 1931; m. Ruth Swift, Nov. 22, 1935; children—Ruth, Peter, Paul. With Harris Trust & Savs. Bank, Chgo., 1932-70, v.p., from 1949, later senior vice president; director of the Fred Harvey Company. Active in YMCA, Nat. Found. Infantile Paralysis, Community Fund; bd. dirs., past pres. Tb Inst. Chgo. and Cook County, Children's Meml. Hosp.; asso. mem. United Charities Chgo.; trustee, treas. Adler Planetarium; bd. dirs., treas. Chgo. Crime Commn.; dir.-at-large Nat. Tb and Respiratory Disease Assn.; mem. citizens bd. U. Chgo. Served to comdr. USNR, 1942-45. Fellow Inst. Medicine Chgo.; mem. Am. Enterprise Assn., Chgo. Assn. Commerce and Industry (dir.), Assn. Res. City Bankers, Delta Kappa Epsilon. Clubs: Bankers, Casino, Chicago, Chicago Sunday Evening (v.p., trustee), Chicago Commonwealth (dir., treas.), Economic, Executives, Mid-America, Attic, Commercial, Old Elm, Onwentsia. Home: Chicago IL Died Dec. 9, 1970.

VAN NORDEN, RUDOLPH WARNER, cons. engr.; b. St. Albans, Vt.; s. Charles and Anna Hubbell (Mygatt) Van Norden; student Cornell University, 1892-94; A.B. in Mech. Engring., Stanford, 1896; m. Rowena Fay Jackson, Oct. 12, 1904 (died Jan. 11, 1929). Began as asst. engr. with Central Calif. Electric Co. (merged into Pacific Gas & Electric Co. 1905), Sacramento, 1896, div. supt., 1905-06; cons. engr., San Francisco, Calif., since 1906; tech. adviser to U.S. Sec. of Interior on Boulder Dam questions, 1929-30; cons. engr., U.S. Bur. of Reclamation. Chief statistician San Francisco Traffic Survey, 1937; asso. engr. Federal Power Commn., 1938; tech. engr. Fed. Pub. Works Adminstrn., 1938-39; cons. electrical engr., 9th Corps Area, Zone Construction, Quartermaster Corps, U.S. Army, 1941. Has been cons. engr. State of Calif., Dept. of Pub. Works of San Francisco, Oakland, Stockton Modesto, Susanville, Sacramento, Santa Cruz, various cos., irrigation dists. and individuals; supervising engr.; locomotive fueling plant (oil), So. Pacific relocation, Shasta Dam Central Valleys project, Calif., 1942. Tech. engr. on design and constrn. of low-head hydro-elec. powerplant for Truckee-Carson Irrigation Dist., Nev., 1946-47. Designed 30 hydro-elec. power plants and supervised constrn. of 8 of these; designed over 50 high dams; owner of patent on multicone type of dams, also on electric-magnetic reduction gear for ship propulsion; has frequently appeared as expert witness. Rated Head Engr. by U.S. Civil Service, 1942. Mem. of Court of Honor, San Francisco area, Boy Scouts of America. Fellow and life mem., Am. Inst. E.E.; life mem., Am. Soc. C.E.; mem. Kappa Alpha (Southern). Democrat. Mason. Club: Engineers. Address: 1500 Sutter St., San Francisco CA‡

VAN NORMAN, FREDERICK DEWEY, mfg. exec.; b. Hamilton, Ont., Can., Dec. 13, 1862; s. Caleb H. and Elizabeth S. (Dewey) Van N.; student Collegiate Inst., 1879, Mechanics Inst., 1881; m. Beatrice Ethel Robson, July 12, 1921; 1 dau., Barbara Elizabeth (Mrs. Gerald Whitman, Jr.). Came to U.S., 1883, naturalized, 1919. Co-founder Waltham (Mass.) Watch Tool Co., 1885, name later changed to Van Norman Co. and moved to Springfield, Mass., chmn. bd. dirs. since 1946; designer self-contained motorized and full ball-bearing equipped bore grinder, 1916. Trustee Wesson Meml. Hosp. Mem. Am. Soc. M.E., Travelers' Aid Soc. (corporator), Community Concert Assn., Springfield C. of C., Springfield Art League. Methodist (trustee). Republican. Clubs: Rotary, Colony, Longmeadow (Springfield). Home: 120 Clarenden St., Springfield MA‡

VAN PETTEN, EDWARD CYRUS, lumberman; b. Cropsey, Ill., Sept. 14, 1873; s. Nicholas Veeder and Clarissa Elenor Van P.; grad. high sch., Kingman, Kan.; m. Bertha G. Bowles, June 1, 1896; children—Paul Edward, Frank Nicholas. Engaged in lumbering since 1899; now pres. Van Petten Lumber Co.; pres. City Lumber & Coal Yards, Garren Lumber Co., Eder Hardware Co. Mem. President Hoover's Commn. for Conservation and Administration of Pub. Domain, 1930-31. Republican. Mason (Shriner). Club: Boise (Ida.) Country. Home: Ontario OR*‡

VAN RIPER, WALTER D., lawyer; b. Montville, N.J., May 18, 1895; s. John H. and Josephine M. (Peirine) Van R.; LL.B., N.J. Law School, 1912-15; m. Verna M. Williams, Nov. 22, 1921. Began as lawyer in 1920; served as mayor of West Orange, N.J., 1921-22; asst. U.S. dist. atty. for N.J., 1922-24; common pleas judge of Essex County, N.J., 1926-44; atty. gen. of New Jersey, 1944-49. Trustee Rutgers U. Entered the army as a private in 1917, served in France, discharged as sgt.-major, 1919. Clubs: Essex and Down Town (Newark, N.J.); Rock Spring Golf (West Orange, N.J.); Trenton (Newark, N.J.). Home: West Orange NJ Died Mar. 3, 1973.

VAN SANT, WILBUR, advt. exec.; b. Balt., Oct. 19, 1890; s. Wilbur C. and Caroline S. (Nelson) Van S.; student Balt. Polytech. Inst., Lehigh U., 1912; m. Freeman Garrett, Apr. 6, 1917; children—Mary Caroline Garrett (Mrs. P.J. Gebelein, Jr.), Nicholas. Various positions advt. agencies, Phila.; founder Van Sant, Dugdale & Co., Inc., Balt., 1914, pres., 1914-59, chairman board, 1959-70. Member of board and executive committee of Balt. Criminal Justice Commn. Trustee Randolph-Macon Women's College. Mem. Balt. Chamber of Commerce (dir., past president), Baltimore Better Bus. Bur. (dir.), Md. Hist. Society, Maryland Acad. Sci. (trustee) S.A.R., and Phi Gamma Delta. Republican. Methodist. Mason (Shriner). Clubs: Kiwanis, Merchants (past pres., director), Baltimore Country, Center. Chmn., Balt. mag. Contbr. articles advt. trade publs. Home: Baltimore MD Died Jan. 9, 1970.

VAN SCHAICK, CLARENCE LLEWELLYN, mfg. exec.; b. Rossie, N.Y., Aug. 28, 1904; s. Frank Willis and Isabelle (Evans) Van S.; B.S., Syracuse U., 1928; m. Loretta Horle, Oct 5, 1929; children—Pieter Horle, David Llewellyn. With Dixie Cup div. Am. Can Co., 1928-71, exec. v.p., dir., 1948-55, pres., dir., 1955-57, gen. mgr., 1957-71, v.p. of Co., 1957-63, exec. v.p. charge Dixie Cup, Marathon, milk container and internat. divisions. 1963-71, dir., 1959-71; chmn. bd. dir. Dixie Cup Co. (Can.) Ltd., 1957-71, Distribuidora De Vasos Dixie, C.A.; v.p., dir. Dixie Cup de Venezuela, C.A., 1959-71; director Hotel Easton; director AB Dixie, Lund, Sweden. Member board trustee Blair Academy. Recipient George Arents award Syracuse U., 1956. Clubs: Pomfret, Country of Northampton County; Canadian (N.Y.C.). Home: Easton PA Died May 8, 1971; buried Northampton Meml. Shrine, Easton PA

VAN SCOYOC, LELAND STANFORD, economist, educator; b. Luray, Kan., Oct. 5, 1900; s. John M. and Lenna M. (Butler) Van S.; B.S., Kan. State U., 1926, M.S., 1935; D. Bus. Administrn., Ind. U., 1953; m. Marthellen Ratcliff, 1947; 1 dau., Jeanette. Tchr., adminstr. pub. schs., Kan. and N.M., 1926-37; instr. Highland (Kan.) Pub. Jr. Coll., 1937-42; asst. prof. econs. U. Dubuque, 1945-46; asst. prof. dept. econs. Bowling Green (O.) State U., 1946-50, asso. prof., 1950-56, prof., 1956-71, prof. emeritus, 1971-72, chmn. dept., 1955-66. Served to maj., Transp. Corps, AUS, 1942-44; faculty Chem. Warfare Sch., 1944-45. Mem. Am. Econ. Assn., Transp. Assn., Am. Phi Delta Kappa, Beta Gamma Sigma. Delta Nu Alpha. Mason. Home: San Diego CA Died Jan. 6, 1972; buried Crown Hill Cemetery, Indianapolis IN

VAN SLYKE, DONALD D., biol. chemist; b. Pike, N.Y., Mar. 29, 1883; s. Lucius L. and Lucy (Dexter) Van S.; A.B., U. of Michigan, 1905; Ph.D., 1907, Sc.D., 1935; studied U. of Berlin, 1911; Sc.D., Yale, 1925; M.D., U. of Oslo, 1938; Sc.D., Northwestern University, 1940, University Chicago, 1941, University of London, 1951; M.D. (honorary), University of Amsterdam, 1962; m. Rena Mosher, June 24, 1907 (dec.); children—Elsa, Karl Keller; m. 2d, Else von Bardenfleth Brock Aug. 1948. Research chemist, Rockefeller Inst., since 1907; chief chemist at hosp. for same, 1914-48, emeritus; asst. dir. in chge. research in biology and medicine, Brookhaven Nat. Lab., 1948-51, research chemist, 1951-71; counselor Eli Lilly Research Grants, 1951-56; visiting professor at Peking Medical Sch., China, 1922. Pres. Am. Bureau for Med. Aid to China, John Phillips Meml. Award Am. Coll. Physicians, 1954, 57, Donald D. Van Slyke award Am. Soc. Clin. Chemistry, 1957; Franklin medal 1965. Mem. of American Chem. Soc., Biol. Chemists (pres. 1921-22), Harvey Soc. (pres. 1927-28), N.Y. Acad. Medicine, Assn. Am. Physicians, Nat. Acad. Science, Acad. Science of India (honorary), Royal Danish Academy of Science and Letters, Brit. Physiol. Soc. (hon.), Swedish Royal Acad. Science, Accademia Medica Lombarda (hon.), Societa Italiana di Biologia Sperimentale (hon.), Societe de Biologie Chimique (France), Societe de Pathologie Renale, Sigma Xi, Beta Theta Pi; hon. member Renal Association (London), Physiological Society (Britain), Am. Philos. Soc. Contbr. articles American and foreign jours., chiefly concerning chemistry of proteins and protein derivatives and their role in physiology and pathology, enzyme action, blood chemistry, and the metabolic conditions of diabetes and nephritis. Author: Factors affecting distribution of electrolytes, water, and gases in the animal body; Micromanometric Analyses. published in 1961; co-author (with J. P. Peters) Quantitative Clinical Chemistry; (with C. Lundsgaard) Cyanosis; (with E. Stillman and others) The Course of Bright's Disease. Awarded Conne medal, Assn. Am. Physicians, 1937; Willard Gibbs medal, 1939; Kober medal, 1942; Mickle fellowship for contbns. to medicine, 1936; Order of Jade (China); Am. Chem. Soc. award, 1953; Scientific Achievement award, A.M.A., 1962; Cresson medal Franklin Inst., 1965; Nat. Medal of Sci., 1965. Home: Port Jefferson NY Died May 4, 1971; buried Glenwood Cemetery, Geneva NY

VAN STEENDEREN, FREDERICK CORNELIUS LEONARD, coll. prof.; b. Arnhem, Netherlands, Mar. 13, 1864; s. Cornelius and Aleida (Volkers) Van S.; came to America, 1881; traveled and studied in Europe, 1884-90; M.A., Penn. Coll., Ia., 1893; Ph.D., State U. of Ia., 1905; m. Jessie E. S. Meachem, Dec. 31, 1891 (died Sept. 21, 1913); children—Mrs. Aleida Jessie Peterson, Mrs. Florence Elizabeth James, Harold Fdk., Dorothy Evelyn (Mrs. James McCarthy Hadley). Was teacher Vianen Inst., 1888-90, then at Racine Coll. Grammar Sch., 1890-91; prof. modern langs., Penn. Coll., 1891-94; prof. Romance langs., State U. of Ia., 1894-1905; master modern langs. and history, Lake Forest (Ill.) Acad., 1905-06; prof. Romance langs; Lake Forest Coll., 1906-36, now prof. emeritus. Author: French Exercises, 1897; Quatre Contes de Merime, 1903; Descriptive Catalogue of Carlo Goldoni's Dramatic Works and Other Appendices, in Chatfield-Taylor's Goldoni, a Biography, 1913; Goldoni on Playwriting, 1919; Cleopatra's Nose and Modern Externality. Far Whispering Tongues. Home: Evanston IL‡

VAN STONE, NATHAN EDWARD, business exec.; b. Bridgeport, Conn., May 18, 1890; s. James Sage and Susan (Sanford) V.; B.S., U. of Mich., 1916, Ph.D., 1916; m. Estella Wilde Brown, Nov. 4, 1916; children—James Williard and Suzanne (twins). Became superintendent of chemical departments, dir. chemical operations, vice pres. Sherwin Williams Co., Cleve., 1928, later v.p., gen. mgr., also dir. Republican. Congregationalist. Mem. Sigma Xi, Gamma Alpha, Phi Lambda Upsilon, Alpha Sigma Phi. Died Sept. 15, 1971.

VAN VALKENBURG, HERMON LEACH, business exec.; b. Wellsboro, Pa., Aug. 13, 1874; s. James William and Harriot Abbey (Truman) Van V.; ed. Wellsboro High Sch., spl. work, Western U. of Pa., Allegheny, Pa. started work with Westinghouse Electric & Mfg. Co., student's course, 1893, engr. dept., 1895-1904; engring. dept. Bullock Works of Allis-Chalmers Mfg. Co., Cincinnati, 1904-06; chief engr. Walker Electric Co., Phila., 1906-12; elec. engr. U.S. Pipe Co., Burlington, N.J., 1912-14; chief engr. Indsl. Controller Co., Milwaukee, 1914-29; chief engr. Indsl. Controller Div., Square D Co., Milwaukee, since 1929, vice pres. since 1933. Fellow Am. Inst. E.E.; mem. Milwaukee Engrs. Soc. Home: 7831 Warren Av., Wauwatosa WI Office: 4041 N. Richards St., Milwaukee WI‡

VAN WART, WALTER BRIGHT, steel co. exec.; b. Dallas, Aug. 25, 1900; s. Walter Henry and Eliza Bell (Bright) Van W.; student U. Tex., 1916-18; m. Charlotte Kramolis, Nov. 1, 1923; children—Walter Bright, Charles Donald. With Wyatt Industries, Incorporated, Dallas, 1919-67, v.p., 1938-55, pres., 1955-62, chmn. bd., 1962-67, dir.; dir. Tex. Nat. Bank, Steel Tank Constrn. Co., Austin Bros. Steel Co., Big Three Welding Equipment Co., Spring Branch State Bank. Dir. Mus. Natural Sci., Jr. Achievement, Houston, Cath. Charities Houston, Houston Fat Stock Show, Houston Horse Show, United Fund. Served as 2d lt. U.S. Army, 1918-19. Mem. C. of C. (past dir.), N.A.M. (dir.), Tex. Mfrs. Assn., Steel Plate Fabricators Assn., Beta Theta Pi. Roman Catholic. Home: Houston TX Died Mar. 17, 1967; buried Forest Park Cemetery.

VAN WINKLE, MARSHALL, congressman, lawyer; b. Jersey City, N.J., 1869; s. Adolphus W. Jr. and Elizabeth (Browne) Van W.; ed. pub. and high sch.; m. Jersey City, 1896, Florence Mills. Counsellor at law since 1890, in continuous practice; law firm of Vredenburgh, Wall & Van Winkle. At one time counsel to Co. Tax Bd.; asst. prosecutor of pleas of Hudson Co., N.J., several yrs.; resigned. Mem. Congress, 9th N.J. dist., 1905-7. Republican. Mem. Holland Soc. of New York. Contb'r to legal periodicals. Address: Jersey City NJ‡

VARELA, JACOBO, diplomat; b. Montevideo, Uruguay, Dec. 25, 1876; s. Jose Pedro and Adela (Acevedo) V.; B.Sc. and Litt., U. of Montevideo, 1897, D.C.L. and Social Sciences, 1905; LL.D., honoris causa, Boston University, 1929; m. Olga Capurro, of Montevideo, Aug. 3, 1908; children—Adela, Jacobo Adrian, Olga Mireya. Served as asst. prof. philosophy and internat. law, U. of Montevideo; sec. to President of the Republic, 1905-07; minister foreign affairs, 1907; mem. Ho. of Rep., 1910-12, Senate, 1915 (v.p.); E.E. and M.P. from Uruguay to United States, October 4, 1919-34 (resigned). Chmn. Internat. High Commn. Uruguayan Sect. 1918-20; plenipotentiary of Peace Conference, Paris, 1919; v.p. Pan-Am. Union, 1924-25; 1st del. plenipotentiary from Uruguay to sixth Pan-Am. Conf.; chmn. Permanent Commn. of Washington to prevent conflicts between Am. Republics. Clubs: Metropolitan, Racquet, Chess, Congressional Country (Washington); Chevy Chase (Chevy Chase, Md.); Lawyers' (New York). Office: American Bldg., 1317 F St., Washington DC‡

VARIAN, BERTRAM STETSON, judge; b. Unionville, Humboldt County, Nev., May 12, 1872; s. Charles Stetson and Florence L. (Guthrie) V.; grad. Mich. Mil. Acad., Orchard Lake, 1891; University of Michigan, 1894; married Inez Vaughan Trent, December 3, 1904; children—Charles Lamartine, Florence (Mrs. Arnold Brunkow), Nina Louise (Mrs. Lemoyne A. Jones), Bertram Stetson. Began practice at Salt Lake City, Utah, 1895; moved to Weister, Ida., 1899; apptd. judge 7th Jud. Dist. of Ida., 1919, elected to same office, 1922 and 1926; apptd. justice Supreme Court of Ida., 1929 for term expiring Jan. 1933; asso. with Richards & Haga at Boise; served as Supreme Court commr., 1923-29. Mem. Ida. Bar Assn., S.A.R., Phi Kappa Psi. Republican. Mason (K.T., Shriner). Club: Lawyers of Ann Arbor (hon.). Home: 1102 N. 9th St. Office: 517 Idaho Bldg., Boise ID*‡

VARIAN, DONALD CORD, naval officer; b. Washington County Md., Mar. 7, 1902; s. Walter and Alice Blake (Cord) V.; B.S., U.S. Naval Acad., 1925; m. Lydia Hill, Nov. 6, 1926; 1 dau., Alice Jean (wife of H. L. Blanton, USMC). Commd. ensign, USN, 1925, advanced through grades to rear adm., 1953; various sea and shore assignments, primarily destroyers; staff Office Sec. Def. 1956-61, dir. personnel policy, 1956-61; pres. Varian Internat. Corp., 1961-69. Home: Coronado CA Died Sept. 1969.

VASILIEFF, NICHOLAS LOANOVICH, artist; b. Moscow, Russia, Nov. 3, 1892; s. Loan and Natalie (Chekulaeva) V.; student Moscow Acad. Fine Arts; m. Eugenia Engles, 1915; children—Yuri Nicholaevich, Tamara Nicholaeova; m. 2d, Magda Tranberg. Came to U.S., 1921. Prof. at Moscow Acad.; one man show Amel Gallery, 1963; exhibited Pitts. Internat., Buffalo Fine Arts Acad., Am. Mus., U. Ill. Biennial of Contemporary Painting, 3d exhbn. Am. painting Bordighera, Italy, 1955; paintings rep. permanent collections Whitney Mus., Bklyn. Mus., Butler Inst., Pa. Acad. Fine Arts, Phila Mus., Corcoran Gallery, Del Gado Mus., Tweed Gallery Art, Tel Aviv Mus., others. Served with Russian Army, World War I. Recipient 1st prize 3d ann. La Tausca exhbn. Riverside Mus., N.Y.C., 1948. Home: Lanesboro MA Died Oct. 13, 1970.

VASILIEV, ALEXANDER ALEXANDROVICH, prof. ancient history; b. St. Petersburg, Russia, Sept. 22, 1867; s. Alexander Stepanovich and Olga (Alexandrovna) V.; student First Classical Gymnasium, St. Petersburg, 1880-87; grad. U. of St. Petersburg, 1892, Dr. of History, 1902; unmarried. Came to America, 1925, naturalized, 1931. Teacher of Gymnasium, 1892-1904; prof., U. of Dorpat, 1904-12, Pedagogic Inst. (St. Petersburg), 1912-22, U. of St. Petersburg, 1917-25; prof. ancient history U. of Wis., 1925-39, now emeritus; vis. prof. Columbia Univ., 1935-36; Haskell lecturer, Graduate School Theology, Oberlin, O., March 1942. Resident scholar of Dumbarton Oaks, research library and collection for 1944-48. Mem. Am. Medieval Acad., Academy of Sciences (Belgrade, Jugoslavia); dir. Kondakov Inst. (Belgrad, Jugoslavia), Hon. Dr. of the Univ. of Athens, 1938. Mem. Greek Orthodox Ch. Club: University. Author: Byzantium and the Arabs (2 vols.), 1900, 02; A History of the Middle Ages, 1915; Medieval Civilization, 1915; History of the Byzantine Empire (2 vols.; tr. into French 1932, Spanish 1946), 1928, 29; Byzance et les Arabes Tome I, 1935; The Goths in the Crimea, 1936; The Russian Attack on Constantinople in 860, 1946. Home: 3101 R St., Washington 7 DC‡

VAUGHAN, DAVID DAVIES, educator, sociologist; b. Titusville, Pa., Aug. 11, 1876; s. John and Margaret Ann (Potts) V.; B.S., Northwestern U., 1900; M.A., U. of Chicago; D.D., Kan. Wesleyan U., 1936; m. Elzie Gertrude Wiley, Jan. 6, 1902; children—Marion (Mrs. Thomas Jefferson Glover), Herbert Wiley. Organizer, and pastor Thoburn Church, Chicago, 1900-02; ordained Meth. ministry, 1902; pastor Wyanet, Ill., 1902-03, 47th St. Ch., Chicago, 1903-05, Halsted Street Institutional Ch., Chicago, 1905-10, Harvey, Ill., 1910-13, Galena Blvd. Ch., Aurora, Ill., 1913-18 River Forest, Ill., 1918-19; prof. social ethics Boston U. Grad. Sch. and Sch. of Theology, 1919-43, prof. geography, U.S. Army Specialized Training Program, Boston U., July 1943; Nat. War Labor Bd., Chicago, 1943-44; regional dir. New Eng. area, Inst. for Am. Democracy, 1944-47; lectr. Mass. State U. Extension, Bangor Theol. Sch., Garland Sch. of Homemaking, Stoneleigh Coll., Harvard-Boston Univ. Extension Courses; prof. sociology, Am. Internal Coll., 1947-52; pastor Enfield (Conn.) Congl. Ch., 1953. Mem. Rock River (Ill.) Conf. Meth. Ch., Am. Assn. Univ. Profs., A.A.A.S., Am. Sociol. Soc., Am. Acad. Polit. and Social Science. Mason. Author: Lessons for Methodists, 1910; The High Road of Marriage, 1940. Contbr. to newspapers and mags. Radio lectr., and widely known as lyceum and forum lectr., having appeared throughout the U.S., in Can., Australia, Europe, etc. Home: 16 Kent Sq., Brookline MA‡

VAUGHAN, HAROLD STEARNS, surgeon; b. Burlington, N.S., Can., Oct. 7, 1876; s. William Stearns and Clara Jane (McCulloch) S.; came to U.S., 1889; D.D.S., U. of Pa., 1899; M.D., College Physicians and surgeons, Columbia, 1904; Doctor of Scienc, Acadia Univ., 1948; married Sara M. Campbell, May 24, 1905; 1 son, Harold Campbell (dec.). Practiced N.Y.C. since 1905; specializes in plastic maxillo-facial surgery; attending surgeon N.Y. Post Grad. Hosp. 1919-47, ret.; cons. surgeon of Southampton, Manhattan Eye, Ear and Throat, N.Y. U. Bellevue Med. Center hosps.; former prof. clin. surgery, New York Post-Grad Medical School (Columbia). Formerly trustee Joseph Purcell Research Memorial. Fellow American College

Surgeons; mem. Am. Society of Plastic and Reconstructive Surgery, Am. Bd. Plastic Surgery (founder group), A.M.A., American Association Plastic Surgeons, N.Y. Acad. Medicine, New York Laryngological Society. Republican. Presbyterian. Clubs: Century; also Ardsley Country. Author: An Abstract of Literature on Mouth Infections, 1924; Mouth Infections and Their Relation to Systemic Diseases, Vol. I, 1930, Vol. II, 1933; The Surgery of Cleft Lip, Cleft Palate and Associated Nasal Deformities, 1939. Contbr. on maxillo-facial plastic surgery, including the surgical correction of harelip and cleft palate. Providing Harold Campbell Vaughan Meml. Library at Arcadia U. in N.S. Home: Irvington-on-Hudson NY

VAUGHAN, WILLIAM HUTCHINSON, coll. registrar; b. Madge, Ky., Feb. 22, 1899; s. William Jamison and Margaret (Hutchinson) V.; A.B., Georgetown Coll., 1923; A.M., Peabody Coll., 1927, Ph.D., 1937; student U. of Chicago, 1934; m. Ruth Woods, Nov. 27, 1924; children—William Hutchinson, Robert Woods. Began as instr. Louisa (Ky.) High Sch., 1924; prin., dean, Morehead (Ky.) State Teachers Coll., 1928-40, pres., 1940-46; registrar, George Peabody Coll. for Tchrs., 1946-72; on leave. Served in U.S. Army, 1918. Mem. Am. Assn. Sch. Adminstrs., N.E.A., Phi Delta Kappa, Pi Kappa Delta. Democrat. Methodist. Mason. Club: Morehead Men's. Author: Robert Jefferson Breckinridge as an Administrator, 1938. Home: Nashville TN Died Oct. 30, 1972.

VAUGHN, EARNEST VAN COURT, prof. history; b. Shelbyville, Mo., Sept. 30. 1877; s. Samuel Van Court and Mary Emma (Penn) V.; B.L., U. of Mo., 1900, M.A., 1904; Ph.D., U. of Pa., 1910; m. Edna Frances Scrutchfield, Nov. 9, 1901 (died Sept. 2, 1922); m. 2d, Lottie Milam, July 15, 1924. Instr. history, U. of Mo., 1905-11; Harrison fellow in history, U. of Pa., 1908-10; prof. history, U. of Del., 1911-22; Modesto Junior College, 1923-24; asso. prof. history, Oregon Agrl. Coll. 1924-37, prof. 1937-44, prof. emeritus since 1944. Mem. Phi Kappa Phi. Democrat. Methodist. Author: The Origin and Early Development of the English Universities, 1908; Early Trading Expeditions into Asia under Authority of the Muscovy Company, 1912. Home: Corvallis OR‡

VAUGHN, SAMUEL JESSE, educator; b. Elkton, Mo., Feb. 12, 1877; s. Alexander Shelton and Mary Elizabeth (Boone) V.; grad. Weaubleau (Mo.) Christian Coll., 1897; A.B., Drury Coll., Mo., 1908; U. of Chicago, summers, 1905-10; m. Florence Rose Perry, of Springfield, Dec. 31, 1900; children—Jesse Wendell, Rebecca Merle. Prin. Dadeville (Mo.) Acad., 1899-1902; supt. schs. in Mo., 1902-05; dir. industrial edn., Springfield, Mo., 1905-08; dir. industrial teacher training, Northern Ill. Teachers Coll., De Kalb, Ill., 1908-20; head dept. industrial edn., U. of Ill., 1920-21; pres. Hardin Coll., Mexico, Mo., 1921-26; pres. Colo. Woman's Coll. since 1926. Editor Industrial Arts Magazine since 1914. Served as 1st lt. Sanitary Corps, reeducation service, Ft. McHenry, Baltimore, World War; asst. editor of Carry On" for Surgeon General's Office, Washington, D.C. Pres. Western Arts Assn., 1915, Vocational Edn. Assn. of Middle West, 1916; mem. Phi Delta Kappa. Republican. Missionary Bapt. Club: Rotary. Author: Printing and Bookbinding for Schools, 1912; Content and Methods of the Industrial Arts, 1922. Lecturer on ednl., social and economic problems. Address: 2001 Josephine St., Denver CO*‡

VEACH, ROBERT WELLS, clergyman; b. New Castle, Pa., Oct. 5, 1871; s. George W. and Laura C. (Burnett) V.; B.A., Westminister Coll., New Wilmington, Pa., 1896, M.A., 1909; D.D., 1911; Auburn Theol. Sem., 1897-98, 1899-1900; Union Theol. Sem., 1898-99; Columbia, 1898-99; U. of Pa., 1911; m. Harriett Rebecca McLaughry, Sept. 13, 1900 (died Oct. 30, 1924); children—Elizabeth C., Harriett. Ordained Presbyn. ministry, 1900; pastor Mt. Hor Ch., Rochester, 1900-08; prof. religious pedagogy, 1908-12, dean, 1910-12, Bible Teachers' Training Sch., New York; pastor North Ch., Rochester, N.Y., 1912-15; ednl. sec. Presbyn. Bd. Publ. and Sabbath-School Work, Phila., Dec. 1915-20; pastor First Presbyn. Ch., Ridgewood, N.J., Jan. 1921-30; lecture tour in Orient and Near East, 1931; now chaplain Overlook Sanitarium and pastor First Presbyterian Church, New Bedford, Pennsylvania; pastor Presbyn. Ch., Crystal River, Fla., Winters; acting pastor Presbyterian Ch., Weirsdale, Fla. Member Kappa Phi Lambda, Pi Gamma Mu fraternities. With War Time Service Commission, Fort Bragg, 1943, Southern army camps, 1944. Democrat. Mason. Author: The King and His Kingdom, 1908; The Friendship of Jesus, 1911; Principles of Teaching; The Sunday School, Its Organization and Management; The Meaning of the War for Religious Education, 1919. Editor, Christian Educator. On leave of absence to direct Army Y.M.C.A. religious work at Camp Dix, in France with A.E.F., Apr. 22-Nov. 18, 1918. Club: New York Clergy. Lecture tour around world, 1930-31. Contbr. on religious subjects. Lecturer. Home: Weirsdale FL‡

VEAL, FRANK RICHARD, univ. pres.; b. Milledgeville, Ga., Sept. 13, 1913; s. Joseph and Minnie Frances (Dillard) V.; ed. Allen U., U. Chgo., Howard U., Boston U.; holder degrees A.B., M.A., B.D., S.T.M., D.D., LL.D.; m. Maude Carroll Thomas, June 22, 1940. Ordained to ministry of A.M.E. Ch., 1939; served as pastor St. Andrews Meth. Ch., Worcester, Mass.; Park Place A.M.E. Ch., Pitts.; Trinity A.M.E. Ch., Newark, O.; Brown Chapel A.M.E. Ch., Cin.; Emanuel A.M.E. Ch., Charleston, S.C. Mem. faculty, also football coach, Allen U., Columbia, S.C., 1932-39, also dean of men; asst. football coach Howard U., 1936-37; mem. faculaty Payne Theol. Sem., 1942-53; pres. Paul Quin Coll., Waco, Tex., 1953-57; pres. Allen U., from 1957. Pres. Palmetto Printing Co. Sec. Gen. Conf. Commn. of A.M.E. Ch.; mem. Gen. Bd. of A.M.E. Ch.; mem. Nat. Council of Chs; del. World Council of Methodism, Oxford, Eng., 1951; del. constitution conv. Nat. Council Chs., Cleve. Formerly: mem. bd. mgmt. Walnut Hill YMCA, Cin.; chmn. bd. mgmt. Cannon St. YMCA, Charleston, S.C.; mem. racial adjustment com. Cin. Bd. Edn.; chmn. March of Dimes, Waco; pres. bd. Reid House, Charleston, S.C. Mem. Gov.'s Com. on Integration, Tex., 1955. Home: Columbia CS Died Oct. 1969.

VEENEMAN, WILLIAM H., chmn. bd. Churchill Downs. Home: Louisville KY Died Dec. 3, 1968.

VERDI WILLIAM FRANCIS, surgeon; b. Vico Equeuse, Italy, Nov. 27, 1873; s. Domenico and Rosa (Ruggiero) V.; brought to U.S. in boyhood; high sch., New Haven; M.D., Yale, 1894, hon. A.M., 1914. Practiced in New Haven since 1895; clin. prof. surgery Yale Med. Sch.; chief surgeon St. Raphael's Hosp.; attending surgeon New Haven Hosp.; consulting surgeon St. Vincent's Hosp. (Bridgeport), St. Mary's Hosp. (Waterbury), Middlesex Hosp. (Middletown). Fellow Am. Surg. Assn., Am. Coll. Surgeons; mem. A.M.A., Conn. State Med. Soc., Am. Urol. Assn., N.E. Surg. Assn. Awarded D S M., World War I. Home: 703 Whitney Av. Office: 27 Elm St., New Haven CT‡

VERHOEFF, FREDERICK HERMAN, ophthalmologist; b. Louisville, Ky., July 9, 1874; s. Herman and Mary Jane (Parker) V.; Ph.B., Yale, 1895; M.D., Johns Hopkins, 1899; LL.D., 1953; A.M., Harvard, 1902; study ophthalmology, in Europe, 1902-03; Margaret F. Lougee, Sept. 17, 1902; children—Mary Josephine (dec.), Margaret. Externe Johns Hopkins Hospital, 1899-1900; asst. surgeon Baltimore Eye, Ear and Throat Charity Hosp., 1899-1900; asst. in pathology, Harvard Med. Sch., 1900-02; asst. ophthalmic surgeon Carney Hosp., Boston, 1902-06; pathologist, Mass. Charitable Eye and Ear Infirmary, 1900-31, asst. ophthalmic surgeon, 1905-13, ophthalmic surgeon, 1913-32, chief of research, 1925-32, cons. chief of ophthalmology since 1932; instr. in ophthalmic pathology, Harvard Med. School, 1907-16, asst. prof. of ophthalmic research 1916-21, asst. prof. ophthalmology, 1921-24, prof. ophthalmic research, 1924-40, emeritus since 1940; scientific dir. Howe Lab. of Ophthalmology, 1931-32, dir. 1932-40. Maj. Med. Corps, U.S. Army, 1918-19. Fellow Am. Acad. Arts and Sciences, A.A.A.S., Am. Coll. Surgeons; mem. Am. Ophthal. Soc. (awarded Howe medal 1932; pres. 1937). A.M.A. (chmn. sect. on ophthalmology, 1932; awarded Knapp medal 1922, ophthalmic research medal, 1930). Awarded Leslie Dana Medal, 1947. Clubs: Harvard, Yale, Longwood Cricket, Algonquin, Eastern Yacht. Home: 61 Monmouth St., Brookline 16 MA Office: 395 Commonwealth Av., Boston 15 MA‡

VERKUYL, GERRIT, field rep. Presbyterian Bd. Christian Edn.; b. near Haarlem, Holland, Sept. 18, 1872; s. Mathys and Janetje (Streefkerk) V.; B.A., Park Coll., Mo., 1901, D.D., 1921; M.A., Princeton, 1903, B.D., 1904; New Testament fellowship abroad, 1904-05; Ph.D., U. of Leipzig, 1906; studied U. of Berlin, 1906; m. Minnie Irene Roberts, Sept. 9, 1902; children—Dorothy, Janet. Came to U.S. Mar. 1894, naturalized citizen, 1902. Sec. local Y.M.C.A., 1892-94; was Presbyterian pastor in Philadelphia, 1906-08; began work with Bd. of Christian Edn. in Wis., 1908; field rep. with hdqrs. in Chicago, serving the Middle West, 1916-29, leadership training, from coast to coast, 1929-40; since then writing, lecturing and teaching; church correspondent for Northern California. Presbyterian. Author: Children's Devotions, 1917; Scripture Memory Work (graded), 1918; Devotional Leadership, 1925; Things Most Surely Believed, 1926; Qualifying Men for Church Work, 1927; Adolescent Worship, 1929; Christ in the Home, 1932; Christ in American Education, 1934; Reclaim Those Unitarian Wastes, 1935; Berkeley Version of the New Testament, 1945; Young People's Worship, 1950. Home: 2617 Dana St., Berkeley CA‡

VERMILYA, CHARLES E., clergyman; b. Savannah, O., 1872; s. Sidney S. and Amanda (Fluke) V.; student Ada Normal Sch. (now Ohio Northern U.); A.B., Ohio Wesleyan U., 1899, A.M., 1902; S.T.B., Boston University School of Theology, 1901; D.D. Wesley College, Grand Forks, N.D., 1932; m. Goldie Fausey, of Bowling Green, O., 1899; children—Harold Fay, Marjorie May, Mildred Glenn. Entered ministry M.E. Ch., 1902; successively pastor Fargo, Park River and Valley City, N.Dak.; sec. Frontier Dept. Bd. of Home Missions and Ch. Extension, M.E. Ch., 1920-23; exec. sec. The Home Missions Council, 1923-27; exec. sec. N.Y. State Council of Chs., 1927-30; now pastor (temp.) Morris, N.Y. Mem. Bd. of Regents, N.Dak., 1917-19; trustee Wesley Coll., Grand Forks, N.D. Del. to Gen. Conf. M.E. Ch., 1912-20. Mem. Pi Gamma Mu. Republican. Mason, K.P.; mem. Am. Order United Workmen. Home: Morris NY‡

VERNER, SAMUEL PHILLIPS, explorer; b. in S.C., 1873; grad. Univ. of S.C.; hon. fellow, Yale. Was supt. Stillman Inst., Tuskaloosa, Ala.; took 3 expd'ns to Central Africa; as comm'r La. Purchase Exposition brought the first group of Pygmies for anthrop. exhibit; discovered new mountains, lakes and territory in the Southern Congo. Dir. Am. Congo Concessions which he persuaded the King of Belgium to grant; collected ethnol. specimens for Smithsonian Inst'n. and bot. specimens for Mo. Bot. Garden. Contb'r to mags. Author: Pioneering in Africa; The Cape to Cairo Railway; The Baluba Language; The Pygmies; etc. Address: Kasai River, Congo Free State, and 358 W. 57th St., New York NY‡

VERNON, AMBROSE WHITE, prof. biography; b. New York, N.Y., Oct. 13, 1870; s. William and Rebecca Peace (White) V.; A.B., Princeton, 1891; grad. Union Theol. Sem., 1894; univs. of Berlin, Halle, and Gottingen, 1894-96; A.M., Yale, 1907; D.D., Dartmouth, 1907; LL.D., Colorado Coll.; Litt.D., Carleton, Northfield, Minn., 1933; m. Katharine Tappe, May 22, 1896 (died May 18, 1932). Ordained Congregational ministry, 1896; pastor First Church, Hiawatha, Kansas, 1896-99, First Church East Orange New Jersey, 1899-1904, Church of Christ, Dartmouth College, and prof. Bibl. lit., Dartmouth, 1904-07; prof. practical theology, Yale Div. Sch., 1907-09; minister of Harvard Ch., Brookline, Mass., 1909-18; prof. biography, Carleton Coll., Northfield, Minn., 1919-24; prof. biography, Dartmouth Coll., 1924-31; Dudleian lecturer, Harvard, 1913; Southworth lecturer, Andover Theol. Seminary, 1915; visiting lecturer in Christian biography, Union Theol. Sem., 1925-26; lecturer on Samuel Harris Foundation for Lit. and Life, Bangor Theol. Sem., 1926. Author: The Religious Value of the Old Testament, 1907; Turning Points in Church History, 1917; Ten Pivotal Figures of History, 1925. Co-author: Cambridge History of American Literature. Editor: Modern Religious Problems, 1909. Club: University (Winter Park). Home: Hanover, N.H.; (winter) 699 Osceola Av., Winter Park FL‡

VERNON, WILLIAM TECUMSEH, register of the treasury; b. Lebanon, Mo., July 11, 1871; s. Adam and Margaret (Hooker) V.; Bachelor of Diatactics and A.M., Lincoln U., Jefferson City, Mo.; (D.D., LL.D., Wilberforce U.); m. Emily Jane Emory, of Leavenworth, Kan., August 18, 1901. Pres. Western U. Quindaro, Kan., since 1896; register of the treasury, U.S., since June 12, 1906 (on leave of absence from univ.); Republican. Mem. A.M.E. Ch. Mason Address: 420 T St., Washington DC‡

VERRILL, HARRY MIGHELS, lawyer; b. Wiscasset, Me., Jan. 4, 1868; s. Byron De Creny and Harriet Augusta (Robinson) V.; Ph.B., Yale, 1889, LL.B., 1891; m. Louise Shurtleff Brown, Oct. 30, 1895; children—Robinson, Richard, Louise, John. Began practice at Portland, 1891; mem. firm Verrill, Dana, Walker, Philbrick & Whitehouse; dir. Central Me. Power Co.; conservator Casco Mercantile Trust Co. Mem. Am., Me., N.Y. and Cumberland County bar assns. Republican. Clubs: Graduate (New Haven); Yale (New York). Home: Standish, Me. Office: 57 Exchange St., Portland ME*‡

VERRILL, ROBINSON, lawyer; b. Portland, Me., Aug. 22, 1896; s. Harry Mighels and Louise Shurtleff (Brown) V.; A.B., Yale, 1918; LL.B., Harvard Law Sch., 1922; m. Agnes Walton Thompson, Apr. 27, 1925; children—Robinson, Eric. Admitted to Mass. and Me. bars 1922; partner Verrill, Dana, Philbrick, Whitehouse & Putnam, Portland; dir. Coca-Cola Bottling plants, Inc.; chmn. exec. com. Bates Manufacturing Co., Served as Volunteer with Am. Field Service and as 2d lieut. U.S. Army, with A.E.F., World War I; served as maj. and lt. col. with I Troop Carrier Command, 1st Allied Airborne Army, Office of Strategic Services, Air Corps in U.S. and European Theatre, World War II col. USAFR, ret. Decorated Bronze Star. Fellow American Bar Foundation; member American, Maine, Cumberland bar assns., Zeta Psi. Republican. Conglist. Home: Portland ME Died Aug. 13, 1970.

VERSON, DAVID C., mfg. exec.; b. Russia, May 24, 1894; s. Morris and Doris (Kaufman) V.; student pub. schs., Russia; m. Pauline Loraine Duxler, Nov. 15, 1925; children—Melvin David, Donald, Sidney, Deborah (dec.), Judy. With Vernon Allsteel Press Co., Inc. Chgo., from 1931, beginning as machinist, became chmn., 1967; chmn. bd. Verson Mfg. Co., Dallas, from 1945; former chmn. bd. Gateway Nat. Bank Chgo. Mem. Art Inst. Chgo., Chgo. Hist. Soc., Chgo. Natural Hist. Mus., Cleve. Engrs. Soc., Engrs. Soc. West Pa. Mason (Shriner). Clubs: Nat. Republican, Standard, Dallas Athletic. Home: Chicago IL Died Mar. 20, 1969.

VESSELLA, ORESTE, musician; b. Alife (Casterta), Italy, Mar. 18, 1877; s. Crescenzo V.; nephew of Allesandro V., dir. of the famous Rome Municipal Band; ed. Naples Conservatory, San Pietro a Maiella. Toured U.S., 1901, with Royal Italian Band; dir. Vessella's Band, at the Steel Pier, Atlantic City, N.J., since 1902. Composer: The Road to Mandalay (comic opera); also of dance music, compositions for the band and popular songs. Address: Atlantic City NJ‡

VEST, H. GRANT, coll. official; b. Salt Lake City, May 6, 1908; s. Hyrum and Eliza Ann (Kay) V.; B.S., Brigham Young U., 1933, M.S., 1938; student U. Chgo., 1943, Ed.D., Stanford, 1950; m. Gwendolyn Lund, Oct. 20, 1933; children—Grant, Margaret Ann, Jolyne. Tchr. Vernal Latter Day Saints Sem., Utah, 1934-41; supt. Uintah Sch. Dist. Vernal, 1942-47; supt. Logan City Sch., 1948-53; commr. edn. State Colo., 1953-59; dir. Utah Coordinating Council Higher Edn., 1959-61; dir. planning So. Colo. State Coll., 1961-62; sec. Trustees of State Colls. Colo., 1962-72; dir. planning Met. State Coll., 1963; sec. Utah State Bank, 1942-48, State senator Utah, 1944-49; research analyst Utah Legislative Council, 1949-51; sec. Utah Pub. Sch. Survey Commn., 1952-53; mem. White House Conf. on Edn., 1955. Mem. Phi Delta Kappa, Colo. Schoolmasters Club. Democrat. Mem. Denver CO Died Jan 17, 1972; buried Fairmount Cemetery, Denver CO

VESTINE, ERNEST HARRY, physicist; b. Mpls., May 9, 1906; s. Olaf Algot and Frida Christina (Lund) V.; B.S., U. Alberta, 1931; grad. study U. Toronto, 1933; Ph.D., Diploma Imperial Coll., Imperial Coll. Sci. and Tech., U. London, 1937; m. Lois Ann Reid, May 20, 1943; 1 son Henry Charles. Leader expdn. Internat. Polar Year, to Meanook, Can., 1932-33; staff mem., dept. terrestrial magnetism Carnegie Instn. of Washington, 1938-57; phys. scientist Rand Corp., Santa Monica, Cal., 1957-68; expert cons. Office Sec. of Def. to 1954, also to applied physics lab. John Hopkins. Chmn. internat. com. on world magnetic survey of International Union Geodesy and Geophysics; cons. Dept. Commerce, National Aeronautics Space Administration, 1959-68; professor meterology, U. California at Los Angeles director data coordination office. International Geophysical Year, National Acad. Scis., 1956; member Com. on Polar Research; member com. on aurora and airglow IGY; mem. committee on particles and fields Space Science Bd. Recipient John A. Fleming Gold Medal award, 1967. Member American Physical Society, Am. Geophysical Union, (chmn. com. Cosmic and Terrestrial Relationships, 1957, pres. sect. geomagnetism and aeronomy 1965-68), International Union Geodesy and Geophysics (secretary-general world magnetic survey bd.), Nat. (chmn. panel on world magnetic survey), Washington acads. scis. Author: Description of the Earth's Main Magnetic Field, 1947; Description and Analysis of the Geomagnetic Field, 1948; The Earth and its Atmosphere, 1957. Home: Pacific Palisades CA Died July 18, 1968.

VETH, MARTIN, clergyman, educator; b. Dettelbach, Bavaria, Germany, Sept. 25, 1874; s. John and Ottilia (Fick) V.; came to U.S., 1884; ed. St. Benedict's Coll., Atchison, Kan., and Collegio St. Anselmo, Rome, Italy. Joined Order of St. Benedict, 1894; ordained priest R.C. Ch., 1899; abbot St. Benedict's Abbey and pres. St. Benedict's Coll., Atchison, Kan., 1921-43; visitator American Cassinese Congregation, Order of St. Benedict, 1929-41, resigned July 6, 1943. Address: St. Benedict's College, Atchison KS‡

VEYRA, JAIME CARLOS DE, Philippine commissioner; b. Tanauan, Leyte, P.I., Nov. 4, 1873; s. Felix and Ildefonsa (Diaz) Veyra; A.B., San Juan de Letran Coll., Manila, 1893; post-grad. work, U. of St. Thomas, Manila, 1895-7; m. Sofia Reyes, of Arevalo, Iloilo, June 28, 1907. Sec. Mil. Revolutionary Govt. of Leyte, 1898-9; editor newspapers, 1903-5; gov. of Leyte, 1906; mem. P.I. Assembly, 1907, 1909; mem. Philippine Commn., 1913-16; exec. sec. P.I., Apr., 1916-Jan., 1917; resident commr. of P.I. to U.S. since 1917. Acting secretary Commerce and Police, Philippine Islands, Dec. 1, 1913-Feb. 23, 1914, and since April 5, 1915; chmn. Philippine Expn. Bd., 1914; chmn. Philippine Gen. Hosp. Advisory Bd. since 1914; mem. Sales Agency Bd., Welfare Bd., of P.E. State Bd. Am. Red Cross, Philippine Carnival Assn. (pres. for 1916), etc. Hon. pres. Sanghiran san Binisaya; hon. mem. Associacion Historico-Geografica de Filipinas. Catholic. Clubs: Nacionalista (dir.), El Ideal (Manila). Home: Leyte, P.I. Address: 2616 Connecticut Av. N.W., Washington DC‡

VEYRA, MRS. JAIME C. DE, b. Arevalo, Iloilo, P.I., Sept. 30, 1876; d. Santiago J. and Eulalia (Tiaozon) Reyes; pvtly. educated; m. June 28, 1907, Jaime C. de Veyra, then gov. of Leyte, now resident commr. at Washington, D.C., from the Philippines. For many yrs. a leader among women in the Philippines and officer or dir. various socs. and clubs; has lectured extensively in U.S., since 1919, on topics relating to P.I. Address: 2616 Connecticut Av., Washington DC‡

VIA, LEMUEL R., lawyer; b. Free Union, Va., Aug. 25, 1873; s. BeZael L. and Lucy Ellen (Maupin) V.; A.B., William and Mary Coll., 1896; LL.B., Georgetown U., 1898; LL.M., Columbian U., 1899; D.C.L., 1900; m. Garnet Ann Ashworth, Dec. 19, 1922; children—Lemuel Richard, Martha Lucy. Admitted to West Va., bar, 1898; pros. atty., Cabell County, W.Va., 1925-28; asst. U.S. atty., 1934-37; dir. trial examiners Nat. Bituminous Coal Commn., 1937-38; apptd. U.S. atty., Southern Dist. of W.Va., 1938 (recess appmt.); re-apptd. for full term, 1939-43, Ret., 1943. Dem. cand. for Congress, 4th W.Va. Dist., 1930. Mem. W.Va. State Bar Assn., Fed. Bar Assn., Am. Bar Assn. Elk, Odd Fellow, K. of P., K. of G.E., I.O. of R.M., J.O.U.A.M. Clubs: Guyandotte, Huntington Country. Home: 213 Oakland Av. Office: Post Office Bldg., Huntington WV*‡

VICK, ROBERT ELLSWORTH, engr.; b. Caroleen, N.C., June 16, 1914; s. Robert Willard and Elizabeth (Brown) V.; B.S., N.C. State U., 1937; m. Catherine Lasater Rollins, Sept. 3, 1938; children—Mary Catherine (Mrs. Thomas Marvin Vick III), Barbara Lois (Mrs. George Larry Ketchum, Jr.), Robert Ellsworth, Jr. Jr. engring. draftsman N.C. Budget Bur., 1937-57; cons. engr. div. property control and constrn. N.C. Dept. Adminstrn., Raleigh, 1957-59, chief standards engr., engring. and standards sect. Div. Purchase and Contract, 1959-69. Served with USAAF, 1942-46. Registered profl. engr., N.C. Mem. Profl. Engrs. of N.C. (past pres.). Presbyn. Home: Raleigh NC Died Sept. 3, 1967.

VICKERS, ENOCH HOWARD, prof. economics; b. Washington County, Md., Mar. 14, 1869; s. William and Jerusha (Mullen) V.; A.B., W.Va. U., 1890; A.B., Harvard, 1893, A.M., 1894; studied U. of Berlin, 1895-96, Paris, 1896-98; m. Kiyo Nellie Nishigawa, Dec. 20, 1899;children—Fanny Clay, Alethea Kate, Walter William Howard. Teacher English and Mathematics, Prep. Sch. W.Va. U., 1890-92; asst. in constl. law and govt., Harvard, 1894-95; Robert Treat Paine fellow, Harvard, and non-resident student, 1895-97; professor economics, Keiogijuku Univ., Tokyo, Japan, 1899-1910; professor economics, W. Virginia University, 1911-38, professor emeritus since 1938, state supervisor of inventory of publicly owned land in W.Va., 1939-41. Liberty Loan speaker and four minute man, World War I. Pres. State Conf. Charities and Correction, W.Va., 1916, 17. Mem. Am. Economic Assn., Am. Assn. for Labor Legislation, Am. Assn. Univ. Profs., Am. Acad. Polit. and Social Science, Asiatic Soc. of Japan (life), Phi Kappa Psi, Phi Beta Kappa. Decorated Order of Rising Sun (Japan). Republican. Episcopalian. Home: Morgantown WV‡

VICKERS, JAMES CATOR, lawyer; b. Taylors Island, Md., Aug. 5, 1877; s. Stewart and Annie (Robinson) V.; student Randolph-Macon Acad., Bedford City, Va., 1893-96; A.M., Randolph-Macon Coll., Ashland, Va., 1900; LL.B., U. of the Philippines, 1913; m. Daisy Usher, Apr. 20, 1904. Taught sch. in Va., 1900-02; in Philippine civil service, 1902-13; admitted to P.I. bar, 1913; mem. firm McVean & Vickers, 1914-26; judge Court of First Instance, Cebu, P.I., 1927-30, Manila, P.I., 1931-32; asso. justice Supreme Court of P.I., 1932-36, resigned; now mem. firm Vickers, Velilla & Balonkita, Manila. Mem. Kappa Alpha. Republican. Clubs: Army and Navy (Manila); Baguio (P.I.) Country; Wack Wack Golf and Country (Mandaluyong, Rizal). Home: 1944 Donada. Office: Perez Samanillo Bldg., Manila Philippines*‡

VIDAL, EUGENE LUTHER, aviation official; b. at Madison, S.D., Apr. 13, 1895; s. Felix Louis and Margaret (Rewalt) V.; C.E., U. of S.D., 1916; grad. U.S. Mil. Acad., 1918, U.S. Army Engring., Air Corps Pilot and Observation Schs., 1918-21; Sc.D., (hon.), Lawrence Coll. 1943; m. Nina Gore, Jan. 11, 1921 (div. 1935); 1 son, Gore; m. 2d, Katharine Roberts, 1939; children—Vance, Valerie. Served in U.S. Army, 1918-26, football coach University of Oregon, 1926-27; assistant general manager Transcontinental Air Transport, 1929-30; organizer and general manager Ludington Air Lines, 1930-32; dir. of air commerce, U.S. Dept. of Commerce, Washington, and mem. Nat. Advisory Committee for Aeronautics, 1933-37; aviation consultant Bendix Aviation, 1937-38; pres. Aircraft Research Corp. and Vidal Research Corp. (developing Vidal Process), and dir. and asso. Northeast Airlines since 1937; pres. Vidal Corp., 1943-45. Dir. Metropolitan Aviation Corp., 1946, Northeast Airlines; pres. Vidal Co., 1949-69, aviation adviser to chief of staff U.S. Army, 1955-65; cons. Phillips Petroleum Co., 1962-69, U.S. Army, 1963-69. Mem. U.S. Army Sci. Adv. Panel, also Transportation Corps adv. com., 1957-69, Gov. Flight Safety Found. Mem. Nat. Aero. Assn., Inst. Aero. Sci. Phi Delta Theta. Democrat. Club: Wings (N.Y.). Home: Avon CT Died Feb. 20, 1969.

VIDAVER, SIDNEY JOSEPH, educator, college adminstr.; b. N.Y.C., May 22, 1910; s. Samuel and Sarah (Fischer) V.; student N.Y.U., 1932-37; M. Elaine Fleckman, Sept. 14, 1941; children—Judith (Mrs. Robert S. Heuman), Lawrence. Pres. Vidaver Assos., Lakewood, N.J., 1946-69, Vidaver & Co., Inc., 1961-68; mng. dir. Inst. of Commerce and Industry; v.p., mem. faculty Ner Israel Yeshiva Coll., Willowdale, Ont., Can., 1969. Commr. Lakewood Indsl. Commn., 1961-65. Served with AUS, 1942-45. Recipient Gold award Internat. Assn. Health Underwriters, 1959, 62 Mem. Internat. Council on Social Disorders (v.p.) Internat. Assn. Health Underwriters, Am. Acad. Polit and Social Sci., Am. Jewish Hist. Soc., Inst. Jewish Edn (dir.), Am. Hist. Assn., Am. Legion, Jewish War Vets Jewish Religion (trustee congregation). Home Willowdale ON Canada. Died Oct. 26, 1969.

VIDMER, GEORGE, army officer; born Mobile, Ala. Aug. 16, 1871; s. John and Ella (Redwood) V.; student U. of Ala., 1888-89; grad. U.S. Mil. Acad., 1894, War Coll., 1920; m. Carol Richards, Sept. 5, 1894 children—Eleanor Redwood (wife of Col. Joseph P Aleshire), Julian Richards. Promoted through grades to brig. gen., Aug. 21, 1933; comd. troops in battle Santiago, Cuba, Spanish-Am. War, 1898; Army of Cuban Occupation, 1899-1902; in P.I., 1902-04; Army of Cuban Pacification, 1906-09; adjutant U.S. Mil Acad., 1912-14; on Mexican border, 1914-17; served in France, 1918-19; asst. chief of cavalry, U.S. Army 1920-24; chief of staff 61st Cav. Div., 1924-29; on staff 7th Corps Area, 1929-31; comdg. 2d Cav. Brig. 1933-35; retired from the active service, Aug. 31, 1935 Twice wounded in action. Awarded D.S.C., D.S.M. Silver Star Citation with oak leaf cluster, Order of Purple Heart (U.S.); Officer Legion of Honor and Croix de Guerre with Palms (France). Mem. Internat Equestrian Team, 1909-13. Mem. Sigma Nu. Democrat Methodist. Home: Spring Hill, Mobile AL‡

VIEHOEVER, ARNO, coll. prof.; b. Wiesbaden Germany, Nov. 3, 1885; s. Joseph and Franciska (Maldaner) V.; Pharmaceutical Chemistry degree University of Marburg, 1908, Food Chemistry degree 1912; Ph.D., 1913; Pharmaceutical D. (honorary) 1938; m. Mabel E. Johnson, Nov. 21, 1915 children—Arnold Joseph, Ellen Margaret, Kent. Asst and instructor, Bot. Pharmacognostical Inst., Marburg 1909-13; pharmacognosist and chemist in charge Pharmacognosy Lab., Bur. of Chemistry, U.S. Dept Agr., Washington, 1913-23; prof. in charge dept biology and pharmacognosy, Phila. Coll. Pharmacy and Science, 1923-34, research prof. and dir. biol. and biochemical research laboratory 1934-38, also curator, dir. micros. labs. and expt. gardens; research director Hyper Humus Co., Newton, N.J., Lincoln Labs., Ill. Phenolphthalein Research Inst., N.Y.C.; scientific adviser to Ministry of Economic Affairs. Dept. of Science, Bangkok, Thailand, also prof. Chulalongkorn U., 1939-42; assistant Chief, U.S. Economic Mission to Siam, 1945-46; editor Bulletin Thailand Research Society, 1940-42; advisor to Office of Coordinator of Inter-Am. Affairs, Div. of Food Supplies to office Food Programs, Fgn. Econ. Adminstrn., 1942-45; chief European Med. and Food investigations, O.T.S. Comm., 1946-48; chief research br., vet. div. Army Med. Dept. Research, 1948-50; chief pharmacol. biochem. and nutritional br., med. div. Office Sci. Information, CIA, 1950-57; mng. dir. Viehoever & Campbell, waste cons., 1965-68; owner Abbey Real Estate, 1963-69. Composer of songs and marches. Naturalized citizen of U.S., 1919. Recipient Ebert prize Am. Pharm. Assn., 1917; Local Outstanding Citizen award, 1964, Civic Congress Spl. Citation, 1966; meml. in Children's Hosp., Washington, 1969. Pres., Broad Creek Citizens Assn., 1920-23. Chmn., U.S. Pharmcopoeia Com., Bur. Chemistry, 1914-23. First registered profl. engr. in biochem. engring., Md. Fellow A.A.A.S.; mem. American Chemical Society, American Pharmacy Association (chmn. sci. sect.), Philadelphia Academy of Science, Franklin Inst. Bot. Society, Brazil Society of Nutrition (hon.); French Soc. Chemical Industry (honorary), Thailand Pharm. Soc., Thailand Research Soc.; honorary member Kappa Psi; mem. Sigma Xi. Referee Daphnia Methods of Assn. of Agrl. Chemists. Rotarian. Author: (petry) Jublance, 1969. Contbr. numerous articles to profl. jours. Home: Oxon Hill MD Died Dec. 11, 1969.

VIERECK, LOUIS C., aluminum co. exec.; b. 1911; B.S., U. So. Cal., 1932, J.D., 1934; married. Engaged in law practice, 1934-69; sec. Harvey Aluminum, Inc., 1942-69, also dir. Home: Torrance CA Died Dec. 1969.*

VIETH, HENRY ALVIN, lawyer; b. Horicon, Wis., Oct. 10, 1870; s. August and Louisa Maria (Rilling) V.; ed. Northwestern and Wis. univs.; holds life certificate as teacher, Wis.; LL.B., Columbian (now George Washington) U., 1899, LL.M., 1900, D.C.L., 1901; m. Lavinia Katherine Pieh, of Madison, Wis., Aug. 12, 1896; children—Dorothy, Kenneth. Prin. high sch., Middleton, Wis., 1893-96; admitted to bar, 1900, to practice in Supreme Court of U.S., 1905; expert statistician, U.S. Dept. Agr., 1896-1902; law clerk and asst. U.S. atty., Dept. of Justice, 1902-08; spl. counsel U.S. Dept. Commerce and Labor, 1908-09. Operator in suburban real estate, D. of C., 1902—. Mem. Washington Bd. of Trade. Mem. Phi Sigma Kappa. Mason (32 deg.). Club: City. Home: 1932 Jackson St. N.E., Washington DC‡

VIGRAN, NATHAN, investment co. exec.; b. Cin., Mar. 16, 1893; s. Alex and Agnus (Salaway) Vigransky; J.D., Chase Coll., 1920; certificate in Real Estate, U. Cin., 1947; m. Bertha Cohn, June 24, 1923 (dec. July 1952); m. 2d Blanche Miller Rosenstein, Aug. 23, 1959.

Admitted to Ohio bar, 1918; pvt. practice law, Cin., 1919-33; owner Vigran's Ladies Shop, Rushville, Ind., 1935-39; v.p. Eliokum Investment Corp., Cin., 1942-72. Active League Hamilton County Property and Home Owners Assn., Cin. Mem. Ohio House Reps., 1927-29. Civilian asst. adminstr. Air Service Command, Patterson Field, O., 1944-45. Served with U.S. Army, 1917-19; AEF. Mem. Soc. Residential Appraisers (sr.), Cin. Real Estate Bd., Am. Soc. Appraisers (sr.), Am. Right-of-Way Assn., V.F.W. (past dept. sr. vice comdr. Ind.), Jewish War Vets, U.S. (past dept. sr. vice comdr. Ohio), Am. Legion (organizer, 1st comdr. Wittstein post 1933). Jewish religion (past pres., congregation). Mason (Shriner). Club: Lawyers (Cin.). Home: Cincinnati OH Died Mar. 2, 1972.

VIGUERS, RICHARD THOMSON, hosp. adminstr.; b. Phila., Aug. 25, 1911; s. Frank Rutherford and Mary (Thomson) V.; B.S. in Econs., U. Pa., 1933; LL.B., 1938; student New Sch. for Social Research, 1939-40; H. H. D., Portia Law Sch., 1965, Dr. Humanities, 1965, Calvin Coolidge Coll., 1965; m. Ruth Alfarata Hill, June 2, 1937; children—Deborah Hill (Mrs. Dennis Hughes), Susan Thomson (Mrs. Barnard L. Berman), Doris Kimball. Engaged as a lectr. in economics Central China Coll., Wuchang, China, 1935-37; adminstrator Bound Brook (New Jersey) Hospital; 1939; asso. div. rural hosps. The Commonwealth Fund, N.Y., 1940-46; administrator of the Pratt Diagnostic Clinic, N.E. Center Hosp., Boston, 1947-65, New England Medical Center Hospitals, 1965-69; cons. in hospital adminstrn. Pres. Greater Boston Hospital Council, 1962; chmn. adv. com. Center of Continuing Edn. in Hosp. Adminstrn., Columbia U. Bd. dirs. Chinese br. YMCA, Boston; pres. Human Relations Service, Inc., Wellesley, Mass., 1956-59; lectr. Tufts Sch. Dental Medicine, 1968. Trustee Wellesley Free Library, 1963-69. Served from lt. to lt. col., Med. Adminstrv. Corps, AUS, 1942-46; China-Burma-India Theatre. Fellow Am. Pub. Health Assn., Royal Soc. Health Gt. Britain, Am. Coll. Hosp. Adminstrs.; mem. Am. (mem. council on adminstrv. practice 1955-58), Mass. (pres. 1965) hospital associations, Assn. Am. Med. Colls., New England Hosp. Assembly (pres. 1955), Hosp. Supts. Club (pres. 1959-61), Mass. Health Council (pres. 1961), Hosp. Adminstrs. Study Soc. (pres. 1964-65); asso. mem. Am. Assn. Hospital Cons. Democrat. Episcopalian. Author articles on hosps. adminstrn. Home: Wellesley Hills MA Died Oct. 31, 1969.

VIGUERS, RUTH HILL, educator, mag. editor; b. Oakland, Cal., July 24, 1903; d. Everett Merrill and Alfarata (Kimball) Hill; A.B., Willamette U., 1924; B.S. in L.S., U. Wash., 1926; Ed.D. (honorary), Portia Law School, 1965; married Richard Thomson Viguers, June 2, 1937; children—Deborah Hill (Mrs. Dennis Hughes), Susan Thomson (Mrs. Bernard Berman), Doris Kimball (twins). Children's librarian Seattle Pub. Library, 1926-27, N.Y. Pub. Library, 1927-29, 32-36, Am. Library in Paris, 1931-32; librarian Internat. Inst. for Girls in Spain, 1929-31; instr. library sci. Boone Library Sch., Wuchang, China, 1936-37; asst. supt. work with children N.Y. Pub. Library, 1937-43; instr. childrens lit. Simmons Coll., Boston, 1949-71; editor The Horn Book mag., Boston, 1958-67; freelance writer, lectr., 1967-71; Caroline M. Hewins lectr. Boston, 1955; Anne C. Moore lecturer, New York Public Library, 1962, Miriam A. Wessel lectr., Detroit, 1965; lectr. U. Hawaii, 1968. Delegate golden anniversary White House Conf. Children and Youth, 1960; judge N.Y. Herald Tribune Spring Book Festival, 1958, Book World Spring Festival, 1968, Boston Globe Childrens Book award, 1967-68. Bd. dirs. Internat. Inst. for Girls in Spain; bd. firends Wellesley (Mass.) Free Library. Recipient Distinguished Alumna awards Willamette U., 1967, U. Wash., 1969. Mem. Quota Internat., Nat. League Am. Pen Women, Women Nat. Book Assn. (Constance Lindsay Skinner award 1968) A.L.A. (mem. council). Democrat. Methodist. Co-author: Children's Books Form Foreign Languages 1936; A Critical History of Children's Literature 1953; rev. edit., 1969; Illustrators of Children's Books, 1946-56 1958. Author: Margin for Surprise, 1964. Mem. editorial adv. bd. Open Court Pub. Co., 1968-71. Home: Wellesley MA Died Feb. 3, 1971.

VIJITAVONGS, PHYA, diplomatic service; b. Bangkok, Siam, Jan. 31, 1877; ed. in England at Sandhurst Mil. Acad., Sch. of Musketry (Hythe), Sch. of Arty. (Okehampton) and Christ Ch. Coll., Oxford; m. Yubha Singhara, of Bangkok, 1903. Served as lt. gen. Siamese Army; E.E. and M.P. from Siam to U.S. since Sept. 1926. Address: Siamese Legation, 2300 Kalorama Rd., Washington DC‡

VILAS, GEORGE BYRON, ry. official; b. Ogdensburg, N.Y., Apr. 18, 1868; s. Erastus and Emeline (Lake) Vilas; ed. pub. schs., Ogdensburg, and Phillips Exeter Acad.; m. Emma Phebe Curtis, Mar. 23, 1893; children—Curtis N., George C., Joseph W. With C.&N.W. Ry. Co. since 1887, beginning at Eagle Grove, Ia., successively, ticket agt., Madison, Wis., 1888-90, agt., Kenosha, Wisconsin, 1890-96, freight agent, Milwaukee, 1896-1908, division superintendent, Baraboo, Wis., 1908-12, gen. supt., at Chicago, 1912-24, gen. mgr. since 1924, v.p. and gen. mgr. since Dec. 1, 1934. Retired July 1, 1937. Republican. Presbyterian. Mason (32 deg., Shriner). Club: Union League. Home: Ogdensburg NY‡

VILLEDA-MORALES, RAMON, Honduran govt. ofcl.; b. 1909. Formerly ambassador to U.S.; pres. of Honduras, 1957-63. Died Oct. 8, 1971.

VINCENT, HAROLD S(ELLEW), educator; b. Knox, Ind., Nov. 9, 1900; s. Burton Jones and Carrie (Black) V.; A.B., Greenville (Ill.) Coll., 1923; A.M., Ohio State U., 1932; student Western Reserve University, 1938-46; LL.D., Marquette University, 1954; Litt.D., (honorary), Greenville College, 1955; married Frances Willard Hill, August 22, 1924; children—Burton Judson, Dwight Harold. Jr. high sch. prin., Wessington Springs, S.D., 1923-24, sr. high sch. prin., 1924-26; elementary sch. teacher, Akron, O., 1926-27, high sch. teacher and asst. prin., 1927-34, asst. supt. schs., 1934-47; supt. of schs., Canton, O., 1947-50, Milwaukee, 1950-68. Member of National Education Association, Ohio (pres. 1948-49), Am. (vice pres. 1962-63), Wis. assns. sch. adminstrs., Horace Mann League, Phi Delta Kappa. Methodist. Mason (32 deg., Shriner). Club: City; Rotary Milwaukee WI Died July 10, 1968; buried Wisconsin Meml. Park.

VINCENT, JOHN CARTER, foreign service officer; b. Seneca, Kan., Aug. 19, 1900; s. Frank Tabor and Beulah Vincent; A.B., Mercer U., Macon, Ga., 1923; grad. work Peking (China) Lang. Sch., 1928-30, Georgetown U., 1937-38; m. Elizabeth Thayer Slagle; children—Sheila, Elizabeth, John Carter. Diplomatic and consular officer at Changsha, Hankew Peking, Tsinan, Mukden Dairen and Nanking, China, 1925-35; with div. far eastern affairs, Dept. of State, Washington, 1935-39; consul at Geneva, Switzerland, 1939-40; advisor Internat. Labor Conf. and governing body of Internat. Labor Office, 1939-40; consul at Shanghai, China, 1941; counselor of embassy, Chungking, China, 1942-43; asst. to chief div. far eastern affairs, Dept. of State, Washington, 1943; special asst. to administrator, Office of Fgn. Econ. Adminstrn., 1943-44; mem. delegation U.N.R.R.A. Conf., Atlantic City, N.J., 1943; chief div. Chinese affairs, Dept. of State, Washington, 1944; delegate to I. P. R. Conf., Hot Springs, Va., 1945; mem. Am. delegation, United Nations Conf., San Francisco, 1945; 3 power conf., Potsdam, 1945; 3 Foreign Secs. Conf., Moscow, 1945; Director, Office Far Eastern Affairs, Dept. State, Washington, 1945; minister, Switzerland, 1947; now chief resident U.S. Delegations to Internat. Orgns., Geneva. Served with United States Army, 1918. Mem. Sigma Alpha Epsilon. Club: Cosmos (Washington). Home: Cambridge MA Died Dec. 3, 1972.

VINCENT, WILBER DDWAIN, educator; b. Haddam, Kan., Feb. 22, 1876; s. Reubin and Alice (Larabee) V.; A.B., U. of Kan., 1903; grad. study (summers), Columbia; corr. course, U. of Chicago; M.S. from U. of Idaho, 1933; m. Nelle Alspaugh, June 16, 1909; 1 son, W. Ddwain. Teacher country and village schs., also prin. to 1900; instr. in science and athletics and asst. prin. high sch., Lawrence, Kan., 1903-04; instr. in edn. and sociology, U. of Kan., 1902-03; supt. schs., Washington, Kan., 1904-09; also condr. Washington County Teachers' Normal Sch., 1904-09; supt. schs., Blackfoot, Ida., 1909-19; supt. State Industrial Training Sch., St. Anthony, Ida. (converted sch. into juvenile vocational instn.), 1919-26; commr. edn., Ida., 1927-33; supt. schs., Boise, 1933-40. Dep. county treas. Washington County, 1897-98. State Representative 1943-49. Mem. Phi Beta Kappa. Republican. Conglist. Author: The Causes of Delinquency; Five Lessons in Narcotic Education. Contbr. articles on corrective edn. Home: 1009 Harrison Blvd., Boise ID‡

VINCI, HENRY, food chain exec. Chmn. Certified Grocers of Ill., Inc. Home: Chicago IL Died 1971.*

VINER, JACOB, economics; b. Montreal, Can., May 3, 1892; s. Samuuel Pinchus and Rachel (Smilovici) V.; B.A., McGill U., 1914; M.A., Harvard, 1915, Ph.D., 1922; LL.D., Lawrence College 1941, U. of Cal., 1945, Brown U., 1950, Queen's U., Can., 1951, McGill U., 1954, U. Chgo., 1955; L.H.D., Columbia, 1954; LL.D., Oberlin Coll., 1959; D.Sc., Univ. of Pa., 1960; LL.D., University of Toronto, 1961; D.Sc., Harvard, 1963; D.Litt., Univ. Glasgow, 1963; Doctor of Letters, Princeton University, 1967; m. to Frances Klein, September 15, 1919; children—Arthur, Ellen (Mrs. Frederick Seiler). Came to U.S., 1914, naturalized, 1924. Instr. in economics, U. of Chicago, 1916-17; spl. expert U.S. Tariff Commn. 1917-19, and U.S. Shipping Bd. part of 1918; with U. of Chicago from 1919 as asst. prof. economics until 1923, asso. prof., 1923-25, prof., 1925, Morton Hull distinguished service prof., 1940-46; prof. of economics, Princeton Univ., 1946-60, professor emeritus, 1960-70, member of the Inst. Advanced Studies, 1946-70. Walker prof. econs. and internat. finance, 1950; Taussig vis. research prof. Harvard, 1961-62; vis. prof. Institut Universitaire de Hautes Etudes Internationales, Geneva, Switzerland, 1930-31, 33-34; vis. prof., Stanford U., 1937; vis. prof., Yale U., 1942-43, fellow Davenport coll., 1942-70; Hitchcock prof., U. Cal., 1945, vis. prof. London Sch. Econs., 1946. National Univ., Brazil 1950; Marshall Lecturer, Cambridge University, 1946; special assistant to sec. of Treasury, Mar.-Dec. 1934. Cons. expert, United States Treasury, 1935-39; spl. asst. to Sec. of Treasury, parts of 1939, 1942; consultant, U.S. Dept. of State, 1943-52. Del. International Studies Conf., League for Intellectual Cooperation, London, May, 1933, Bergen, Norway, Sept. 1939; American representative (alternate), Economic Com. League Nations, Geneva, 1933. Recipient spl. award Am. Council Learned Socs., 1958; semicentennial medallist Rice Univ., 1962. Fellow Am. Acad. Arts and Sci., London School of Economics (honorary), American Philos. Soc. (Jayne lectr. 1966), Brit. Acad.; mem. Swedish Royal Acad., Am. Econ. Assn. (Richard T. Ely lectr. 1962; president in 1939; Francis A. Walker medallist 1962), Accademia dei Lincei, Manchester Statis. Soc. (corr.). Author: Dumping A Problem in International Trade, 1923; Canada's Balance of International Indebtedness, 1924; Studies in the Theory of International Trade, 1937; Trade Relations Between Freemarket and Controlled Economics, 1943; The Customs Union Issue, 1950; International Economics, 1951; International Trade and Economic Development, 1952; The Long View and the Short, 1958. Home: Princeton NJ Died Sept. 12, 1970.

VINES, JOHN FINLEY, clergyman; b. near Jonesboro, Tenn., Oct. 6, 1873; s. William L. and Nancy (Carr) V.; Carson and Newman Coll., Jefferson City, Tenn., 1894-98; grad. Southern Bapt. Theol. Sem., Louisville, Ky., 1902; D.D., Carson and Newman, 1909; m. Mabel V. Lawrence, June 17, 1902. Ordained Bapt. ministry, 1899; pastor Central Bapt. Ch., Chattanooga, Tenn., 1902-05, 1st Ch., Elizabeth City, N.C., 1905-08, 1st Ch., Anderson, S.C., 1908-15; was also pres. Anderson Coll. of Women; pastor 1st Ch., Roanoke, Va., 1915-26, Calvary Bapt. Ch., Kansas City, Mo., 1926-33; supt. Evangelism of Bapt. Gen. Assn. of Mo. 1933-44. Now supply Pastor and Evangelistic work. Mason (32 deg. Shriner). Home: 4113 Sunnybrook Drive, Nashville 5 TN‡

VINES, WILLIAM MADISON, clergyman; b. Jonesboro, Tenn., Dec. 18, 1867; s. William Lafayette and Nancy (Carr) V.; B.S., Central Normal Coll., Danville, Ind., 1893; Louisville Theol. Sem., 1894-95; U. of Chicago, 1898-99; (D.D., Carson-Newman Coll., Tenn., 1906); m. Ivy Henderson, Apr. 30, 1902. Ordained Baptist ministry, 1893; pastor Johnson City, Tenn., 1896-98, 1st Ch., Asheville, N.C., 1899-1905, Freemason St. Ch., Norfolk, Va., 1905-09, Hanson Pl. Ch., Brooklyn, 1909-10, 1st Ch., St. Joseph, Mo., 1911-13, 1st Ch., Charlotte, N.C., 1913-17, 1st Ch., Augusta, Ga., 1917-18, 1st Ch., Norfolk, Va., 1919-23, 1st Ch., Greenwood, S.C., 1923-27; gen. evangelist Southern Bapt. Conv., 1927-29; pastor First Bapt. Ch., Quincy, Fla., 1929-39; now instr. in Dept. of Religion, Howard Coll., Birmingham, Ala.; also supply minister. Author: Home Mission Task; also pub. addresses. Home: Birmingham AL‡

VINSON, ALBERT EARL, chemist; b. Dayton, O., Oct. 30, 1873; s. Samuel H. and Mary (Mull) V.; B.S., Ohio State U., 1901; Ph.D., Gottingen U., 1904; studied univs. of Chicago and Wis., also at Sorbonne, Paris, 1910; m. Louisa M. Albert, June 10, 1897 (dec.); m. 2d, Blanche Morrison, Apr. 20, 1940. Asst. in agrl. chemistry, Ohio State U., 1896-1901, instr., 1901-02; asso. chemist, Ariz. Expt. Sta., 1905-07, later chemist, also prof. agrl. chemistry, U. of Ariz., till 1924; chemist Service Technique du Departement de l'Agriculture, Port-au-Prince, Haiti, 1924-31. Fellow A.A.A.S.; mem. Western Soc. for Soil Management and Plant Nutrition (pres. 1923-24). Sigma Xi, Phi Kappa Phi. Methodist. Mason (32 deg.). Author of numerous bulletins on agrl. topics and articles in tech. mags.; has made extensive physiol. studies on ripening of the date; also studies on alkali soils and on the behavior of dry soils when wetted. Home: 811 E. Prince Rd., Tucson AZ‡

VINTON, WARREN JAY, govt. official; b. Detroit, Mich., Dec. 30, 1889; s. George Jay and Rosa Bemrose (King) V.; A.B., Univ. of Mich., 1911; grad. work in economics, Columbia, 1932-34; m. Mary Emerson Perkins, Dec. 19, 1940; children—Jay Emerson, Mary Warren. Sec. and dir., Vinton Co. (gen. contractors), Detroit, 1911-17; asst. science attache, U.S. Embassy, Paris, France, 1918; asst. to dir. of med. relief, A.R.C. mission to Balkans, 1919; asso. editor, Psyche (Jour. of Psychology), London, 1925-27; dir. of research, Am. Assn. for Social Security, New York City, 1931-34; research supervisor, Fed. Housing Adminstrn., Washington, 1934-35; chief of research, Div. of Suburban Resettlement (directing econ. and social planning of 3 Greenbelt towns), Resettlement Adminstrn., Washington, 1935-37; chief economist, U.S. Housing Authority (and successor bodies, Fed. Pub. Housing Authority and Public Housing Administration), 1937-49, first asst. commr., 1949-57; consultant and writer on housing and planning. Assisted Senator Wagner in drafting U.S. Housing Act, 1937. Mayor, Town of Somerset, Md., 1958-69; pres. Montgomery County Citizens Planning Assn., 1958-61. Secretary and treas. Hawthorne Sch., Washington. Mem. Nat. Housing Conf. (dir.), Nat. Assn. Housing and Redevelopment Ofcls., American Institute of Planners, Am. Soc. Planning Ofcls. (member of the board of dirs. 1962-64), Phi Beta Kappa, Sigma Xi, Phi Sigma Kappa. Co-author: Economic Consequences of the New Deal, 1935. Contbr. to other publs., also articles and reviews in profl. jours. Home: Chevy Chase MD Died Nov. 19, 1969.

VIRGIN, EDWARD HARMON, librarian; b. Boston, July 13, 1876; s. Edward Warren and Mary E. (Harmon) V.; A.B., Harvard, 1899; N.Y. State Library School, 1899-1900; unmarried. Asst. in Harvard U. Library, 1900-4; librarian General Theol. Sem. Library, 1904-16; research work, Montague Press, 1916-17; ordnance Bur., War Dept., Washington, 1917—. Pres. Dyke Mill Corpn., 1909-10. Mem. A.L.A., Ch. Hist. Soc., New York Library Club (treas., 1906-7, pres., 1911-12), Sigma Alpha Epsilon Fraternity (eminent supreme recorder, 1900-4). Club: Harvard (New York). Editor: The Intellectual Torch (by Jesse Torrey), 1913. Mng. editor Bulletin Gen. Theol. Sem., 1914-16. Address: Ordnance Bureau, War Dept., Washington DC‡

VIRGIN, HERBERT WHITING, clergyman; b. Mandeville, La., May 29, 1872; s. Edwin Forrest and Helen (Caruthers) V.; A.B., Georgetown (Ky.) Coll., 1896, D.D., 1909; studied Southern Baptist Theol. Sem., Louisville, Ky.; D.D., Union U., Jackson, Tenn., 1909; LL.D., 1926; m. Isabelle Josephine Goff, of New Orleans, La., Dec. 31, 1896; children—Ruth, Mary Helen (wife of Guy Owens, M.D.), Isabelle Herbert, Herbert Whiting. Ordained Baptist ministry, 1894; pastor successively Kansas City, Mo., Jackson, Tenn., Roanoke, Va., Amarillo, Tex., until 1924, North Shore Ch., Chicago, Ill., since 1924. served as regional dir. Y.M.C.A. overseas, 1918-19. Mem. Ill. Bapt. State Bd.; formerly mem. Bapt. State Bd., Mo., Tenn. and Tex., also pres. Ministers' Aid Soc., Tenn. Democrat. Mason. Address: 1311 Berwyn Av., Chicago IL*‡

VIRTUE, CHARLES FRANKLIN, educator; b. Iberia, O., Mar. 3, 1901; s. Delphus Brown and Leila Gertrude (Sawhill) V.; B.A., U. Cin., 1925; Ph.D., Yale, 1933; m. Mildred Ruth Brooks, June 10, 1930; 1 son, Robert Brooks. Tutor, Robert Coll., Istamboul, Turkey, 1925-26; master Holderness Sch. Boys, Plymouth, Vt., 1927-28; instr. philosophy U. Ida., 1935-38; asst. prof., then asso. prof. and head dept. philosophy and psychology U. Louisville, 1938-46; asso. prof. philosophy U. Me., 1946-56, prof., 1956-71, chmn. dept., 1962-71. Mem. Am. Philos. Assn., Metaphys. Soc. Am., Assn. Realistic Philosophy, Am. Assn. U. Profs. Episcopalian. Author articles, contbr. books. Home: Orono ME Died Nov. 9, 1971.

VIRTUE, GEORGE OLIEN, prof. of economics; b. Abingdon, Ill., Nov. 4, 1861; s. John Freeborn and Cynthia (Jackson) V.; A.B., U. of Kan., and Harvard U., 1892; A.M., Harvard, 1893, Ph.D., 1897; m. Meta Vogel, Sept. 14, 1897; children—John Bernard, Ruth Vogel (wife of Dr. Gerald M. Almy). Instr. in polit. economy, Harvard, 1894-95 and 1896-97; instr. U. of Chicago (extension), 1895-96; teacher State Normal Sch., Winona, Minn., 1897-1909; prof. of economics and pub. finance, U. of Neb., from 1909, chmn. Dept. of Econs., 1925-37, ret. Research spl. agt. U.S. Census Bur., 1912, U.S. Shipping Bd., 1918; research and editorial work Federal Trade Commission, 1919. Mem. bd. dirs. Social Welfare Soc., 1912-27; mem. Bd. of Municipal Works, Winona, Minn., 1906-09. Mem. Am. Econ. Assn., Tax Research Foundation, Alpha Kappa Psi, Beta Gamma Sigma, Phi Beta Kappa. Democrat. Unitarian. Mason. Clubs: Layman's, Economica (Lincoln). Author: Government of Minnesota, 1910; also pamphlets and tech. articles. Co-author and editor of The Nebraska Tax Primer, 1932. Home: 1415 C St., Lincoln NE‡

VISHER, STEPHEN SARGENT, geographer; b. Chicago, Ill., Dec. 15, 1887; s. Rev. John and Julia (Sargent) V.; B.S., U. of Chicago, 1909, M.S., 1910, Ph.D., 1914; M.A. U. of S.D., 1912; fellow U. of Chicago and Yale; m. Martha Bolks, June 20, 1914 (deceased 1949); children—Ruth (Mrs. D. A. Smalley), John Edwin, Paul Sargent, Mary (Mrs. R. L. Mayer); m. 2d, Halene Hatcher, Mar. 21, 1951; 1 dau. Peggy Mildred. Instructor geology, Univ. of S.D., 1910-13; prof. geography, State Coll. Moorhead, Minn., 1915-18; land classifier U.S. Geol. Survey, 1918-19; prof. geography Ind. U. since 1919; prof. summers, U. Colo., 1925, Cornell U., 1926, 27, 30, U. of Pa., 1928, U. of Brit. Columbia, 1937, 40; research professor U. of Indiana, 1957-58; acting associate geographer, U.S. Dept. of State, 1931-32. Mem. U. of Chicago ecological expdn. to Alaska, 1907; sci. asst. Carnegie Instn., Desert Lab., Ariz., 1909; geographer and asst. state geologist S.D. Geol. Survey, 1909, 1910-14; scientist in soil survey, U.S. Bur. Soils; with U.S. Soil Conservation Service, summer, 1936; geographer Ind. Geol. Survey, 1919-46. Investigations in West Indies, 1915; in Spain, Italy, Britain, 1920; mem. Yale Indiana Expdn. South Seas, Australia, Far East, 1921-22. Awarded Distinguished Alumnus citation, U. Chicago, 1943; Distinguished Service to Geography award, Nat. Council Geography Teachers, 1948; Outstanding Achievement award Association of American Geographers, 1959. Honorary life member National Geographic Society, 1945. Fellow Geol. Soc. Am., A.A.A.S., Am. Meteorol. Soc., Royal Meteorol. Soc., Ind. Acad. Sci. (pres. 1950), Assn. Am. Geographers (vice pres. 1933), Geographic Assn. (British), Phi Beta Kappa, Sigma Xi. Author: Geography of South Dakota, 1918; Climatic Changes, Their Nature and Causes (with E. Huntington), 1922; Economic Geography of Indiana, 1923; Laws of Climate, 1924; Tropical Cyclones of the Pacific and Their Effects, 1925; Geographic Supplement to New Century Dictionary, 1927; Geography of American Notables, 1928; Climate of Kentucky, 1930; Economic Geography of Europe (with W. O. Blanchard), 1931; Our Natural Resources and Their Conservation (co-author), 1936, 39, 65; Aids to Students of Conservation, 1937; Principles of Economic Geography (with E. Huntington), 1940; Climate of Indiana, 1944; Introduction to Global Geography (with G. T. Renner and others), 1944; Scientists Starred 1903-43 in American Men of Science, 1947; Indiana Scientists, 1951; Climatic Atlas of the U.S., 1954, 66; also reports, articles. Co-author: Conservation of Natural Resources, 1950, rev. edit., 1965; Geography in the Twentieth Century, 1951; Regional Geography of the Midwest (with Garland and others), 1955. Home: Bloomington IN Died Oct. 25, 1967.

VOEHRINGER, JOHN KASPER, JR., hosiery mfg. exec.; b. Phila., May 27, 1897; s. John K. and Henricke (Guhl) V.; student evening sch., Temple U., 1917, Wharton Evening Sch., U. of Pa., 1921; m. Alice Boyd, Nov. 18, 1918 (dec.); 1 son, John Lester (dec.); m. 2d. Mary King Tillman, Oct. 1954. Office boy (Harry Lehmuth Co., Phila., 1912-19; sec., treas. Oscar Nebel Co., 1919-25; pres., dir. Mojud Hosiery Co., Inc., N.Y.C., 1925-55, retired; pres., dir. Mock, Judson, Voehringer Co. of N.C., Inc., Greensboro, 1926-55, Ala. Hosiery Mills, Inc., Decatur, 1932-55, Port City Hosiery Mills, Inc., Wilmington, N.C., 1945-55, Woodland Realty Co., 1950-67, Elm Realty Corp., Greensboro, 1936-67, Wilmington Warp Knitting Co., 1950-55, Atlantic Throwing Co., 1952-55; real estate and investments, 1955-67. Dir. of Children's Home Society of N.C. Dir. Med. Found. of N.C., Miami Heart Inst. Mem. Greensboro C. of C. (past pres.), Delta Sigma Pi. Clubs: LaGorce Country, Greensboro Country. Home: Miami Beach FL Died Aug. 2, 1967; buried Forest Lawn Cemetery, Greensboro NC

VOELKER, PAUL FREDERICK, educator; b. Evart, Mich., Sept. 30, 1875; s. Henry and Catharine (Hey) V.; M.Di., Ia. State Normal Coll., Cedar Falls, Iowa, 1901; B.Ph., Drake U., 1906, A.M., 1907; Ph.D., Columbia, 1920; m. Jessie Ray, Aug. 24, 1898 (died Feb. 13, 1929); m. 2d, Margaret McCormick, Feb. 14, 1930; children—Robert F., Catharine Margaret. Became supt. of schs., Ackley, Ia., 1901, Ida Grove, Ia., 1903; editor Midland Schools, Des Moines, 1905; prof. modern langs., Drake U. 1907; sec. extension div., U. of Wis., 1913; pres. Olivet (Mich.) Coll., 1920-25; pres. Battle Creek College, 1925-33; superintendent public instruction, Michigan, 1933-35. Ordained Congregational ministry, Feb. 18, 1943; pastor Presbyn. Church, Centerville, Mich., since 1946. President Michigan Sunday School Council Religious Education, 1923-24. Mem. Phi Beta Kappa, Pi Delta Kappa. Democrat. Conglist. Author: Function of Ideals in Social Education, 1921; Moral Education, 1924; Character in the Making, 1934. Chautauqua and lyceum lecturer. Address: Hale MI*‡

VOETTER, THOMAS WILSON, consular service; b. Salem, O., July 10, 1869; s. Julius and Margaret E. (Humphreys) V.; M.E. in E.E., Cornell U., 1892; m. Margaret E. Laird, of Waverly, Ia., July 24, 1905. Elec. work, 1892-94; with iron foundry, 1894-95, with Pa. R.R., 1895; in Indian service, 1901-07; apptd. consul at Saltillo, Mexico, Aug. 15, 1907; consul at La Guaira, 1911-15, at Antonfagasta, Chile, 1915-21, at Caracas, Venezuela, Dec. 1922-24, at Curacao, W.I., since Aug. 1924. Republican. Episcopalian. Clubs: Curacao, Sports, Gazellígheid (Curacao). Home: Ft. Wayne IN Address: Am. Consulate, Curacao West Indies‡

VOGEL, JOSEPH RICHARD, business exec.; born N.Y. City, Sept. 7, 1895; married Lina Lloyd, October 15, 1942; 1 son, Richard Lloyd. Pres., dir. Metro-Goldwyn-Mayer, Inc., 1956-63, Loew's Theatre and Realty Corp.; dir. Will Rogers Meml. Hosp.; mem. lay adv. bd. Met. Hosp. Dir. Motion Picture Assn. Am. Recipient Star of Sodilarity Comdr. Order of Merit (Italy). Home: Palm Beach FL Died Mar. 1, 1969.

VOGEL, JOSHUA HOLMES, planning and pub. works cons.; lb. White Lake, S.D., Jan. 25, 1889; s. John Peter and Genevieve (Anderson) V.; B.Arch., Ohio State U., 1912, M.Arch., 1917, postgrad., 1918; m. Helen Hollister, June 2, 1915 (dec.); children—Peter, Barbara (Mrs. Edwin H. Pope Jr.), Timothy, Ruth (Mrs. Don Knoke), Caroline (Mrs. Vernon Tyler, Jr.), Marianne (Mrs. Merle Gordon). Practice architecture, Japan, China, 1912-17, 21-27, northwestern U.S., 1918-21, 27-34; engr. in charge land use, zoning, san. and bus. survey, Seattle, 1934-35; planning engr., exec. officer King County Planning Commn., Seattle, 1936-41; cons. Nat. Resources Planning Bd., N.W. Pacific area, 1941-42, FSA, Seattle, 1944; cons. engr., exec. officer Puget Sound Regional Planning Commn., 1941-45; cons. Wash. State Planning Council, 1941-45; individual practice planning cons. Wash. cities and counties, 1941-45; cons. Bur. Reclamation, Columbia River Dist., 1948-53, also architect cons.-planner Coulee Dam City; planning pub. works cons. Bur. Govtl. Research and Services, U. Wash., Seattle, 1945-59, emeritus, 1960-70. Registered profl. engr., Wash. Fellow Am. Soc. C.E. (life); mem. A.I.A. (emeritus); hon. mem. Am. Soc. Planning Ofcls., Am. Inst. Planners. Prin. archtl. works include recreational centers in Far East. Contbr. articles to profl. jours. Home: Bellevue WA Died June 28, 1970.

VOGEL, ROBERT WILLIS, mfr. spark plugs; b. Toledo, Mar. 15, 1914; s. Willis Anderson and Florence Elizabeth (Haag) V.; B.B.A., U. Toledo, 1938; m. Dorothy Lucille Woolford, Sept. 10, 1938; children—Jill Barbara, Carolyn Eileen, Marilyn Christine. Accountant purchasing agt. M.V.C. Labs., Inc., Toledo, 1939-41; accountant Konopak, Hurst and Dalton, C.P.A.'s, Toledo, 1941-43; with Buckeye Traction Ditcher Co., Findlay, O., 1943-46, asst. sec.-asst. treas., 1944-46; accountant R. A. Hurst, C.P.A., Toledo, 1947-48; with Champion Spark Plug Co., Toledo, from 1948, controller, asst. treas., 1954-64, treas., 1965-68, also dir., chmn. exec. com.; v.p., treas. Champion Spark Plug Co. Can. Ltd., Toledo, Hellertown Mfg. Co. (Pa.), Iowa Industries, Inc., Iowa, from 1968; bd. dirs. Magnaflux Corp., Chgo.; dir., mem. exec. com. Devilbiss Co., Toledo, from 1967; dir. Baron Drawn Steel Corp. Mem. Financial Execs. Institute (pres. Toledo 1957-58, nat. dir. 1962-65, N. Central area v.p. 1964, v.p., trustee research found.). Mason (Shriner). Clubs: Toledo, Toledo Country, Exchange. Home: Toledo OH Died Nov. 14, 1971.

VOGEL, RUDOLPH EMERSON, investment broker; b. Milwaukee, Apr. 30, 1900; s. Augustus H. and Anita (Hansen) V.; A.B. Princeton, 1922; m. Marjorie Niedringhaus, Jan. 7, 1929; 1 dau., Helen Johnson. Vice pres., Rich Shoe Co., Milwaukee, 1922-24; 2d v.p., Ill. Merchants Trust Co. (later Continental Ill. Nat. Bank), Chicago, 1924-37; mem. underwriting dept., Glore, Forgan & Co., 1937-44, partner, 1944-67, vice president, 1967-68; director American Potash & Chemical Corporation, Glenmore Distilleries Co., Cory Corp., N.Am. div. Car Corp. Co., Knape & Vogt Mfg. Co. Mem. Community Fund of Chicago. Club: Saddle and Cycle, The Attic. Home: Delray Beach FL Died Jan. 1971.

VOGELGESANG, SHEPARD, architect; born San Francisco, California Feb. 9, 1901; s. Carl Theodore (rear adm. U.S. Navy) and Zenaide Stevens (Shepard) V.; diploma Phillips Acad., Andover, Mass., 1920; student Mass. Inst. Tech., 1920-26; traveling fellowship in architecture; studied in Vienna, Austria, 1927-28; grad. Mass. Inst. Tech., 1942; m. Camilla Herbert Boone, Aug. 6, 1942 (divorced 1949); 1 dau., Carlyle V. Archtl. draftsman in offices in Boston and New York until 1931; in charge interior color design, Century of Progress, Chicago, 1933, director of color, Century of Progress, 1934; assistant director decorative arts and dir. design Fine Arts Com., Golden Gate Internat. Expn., San Francisco, 1938-39; asso. dir. and designer of America at Home," N.Y. World's Fair, 1940; color consultant for Fed. Defense Housing, 1941; architectural practice Whitefield, N.H., 1941-69. Registered architect in N.H. and Vt. Lieutenant U.S.N.R., August 1942, comdr. October 1944. Member Beaux Arts Inst. Design (N.Y.C.), A.I.A. (also mem. N.H. chpt.), Dalton Grange, Phi Gamma Delta. Mem. Ch. of England. Rotarian. Contbr. to archtl. mags. Writer, lecturer, designer. Home: Whitefield NH Died Feb. 18, 1969; buried Cushman Cemetery, Dalton NH

VOGELTANZ, EDWARD LOUIS, lawyer; b. Wahoo, Neb., Oct. 12, 1895; s. Joseph and Mary (Jisa) V.; student Grand Island Bus. Coll., 1911-12, Peru State Normal Sch., 1914-16, U. Cal., Berkeley, summer 1918; A.B., LL.B., U. Nev., 1919; m. Amelia Polak, Jan. 4, 1921; children—Bette (Mrs. James Cornwell), Roselien (Mrs. James Staats), Raymond (dec.). Sec. for atty., David City, Neb., 1913-14; asso. atty. Norval Bros., Landis, Coleman & Mastin, Seward, Neb., 1919; gen. practice Ord, Neb., 1920-68; asso. Davis & Vogeltanz, 1928-58; Ord city atty., 1949-52; partner Vogeltanz & Kubitschek, Ord, 1965-68; pres. Arcadia State Bank (Neb.), State Bank of Scotia, Neb.; dir. sec. North Loup Valley Bank; v.p., dir. Protective Savs. & Loan Assn. Served with USAF, 1918. Named Boss of Year, Ord Jr. C. of C., 1967. Mem. C. of C. K.C., Elk. Home: Ord NE Died Apr. 9, 1968.

VOGLER, WILLIAM L., ins. exec.; b. Lodgepole, Neb., Nov. 27, 1898; ed. Northwestern U. Agt., asst. mgr. Metropolitan Life Ins. Co., Denver, 1923-29; mgr. Continental Life Ins. Co., Salt Lake City, 1929-32; mgr. Am. Nat. Ins. Co., Salt Lake City, 1932-44, exec. vice president, 1944-61, chairman, pres., 1961-69, also chief exec. officer; director FIF Mgmt. Corp., Braniff Airways, Inc. Home: Galveston TX Died Sept. 15, 1969.

VOGT, WILLIAM, ecologist; born Mineola, N.Y., May 15, 1902; s. William and Frances Bell, (Doughty) V.; A.B., St. Stephens (now Bard) Coll., New York, 1925; Sc.D., Bard College, 1953; m. Johanna von Goeckingk, Dec. 26, 1959. Assistant editor N.Y. Acad. Sciences, 1930-32; curator Jones Beach State Bird Sanctuary, 1932-35; editor Bird-Lore Magazine, and field naturalist and lecturer for Nat. Assn. Audubon Socs., 1935-39; cons. ornithologist, Compania Administradora del Guano, Lima, Peru, 1939-42;

udied in Chile on fellowship of Com. for ter-American Artistic and Cultural Relations, 1942; pert consultant, War Dept., 1942; asso. director, Div. Science and Education. Office Coordinator ter-Am. Affairs, 1942-43; chief Conservation Sect., an.-American Union, 1943-49; national director anned Parenthood Federation of America, 1951-61; c. Conservation Foundation, N.Y.C., 1964-68; del. to e International Planned Parenthood Conf., Bombay, dia, 1952, Stockholm, 1953, Tokyo, 1955; Delhi, 959. Recipient field research prize Linnaean Soc. .Y., 1938, Mary Soper Pope medal, 1949. Lasker oundation award 1951. Member A.A.A.S. American rnithologists Union, N.Y. Zoological Soc. (Fellow), m. Pub. Health Assn., Linnaean Society of New York ormer pres. and sec.), Ecological Soc. Am., Soc. Gen. emantics, Am. Geog. Society, Sociedad Geografica de ima, Sociedad Mexicana de Historia Natural also opulation Association U.S. Clubs: Century Assn.; osmos (Washington). Author: Audubon's Birds of merica, 1937; El Hombre y la Tierra, 1944; Road to urvival, 1948; People New York City NY Died July 2, 1968; cremated.

OLKOV, VLADISLAV N., Russian cosmonaut; b. ov. 23, 1935. Flight engr. on space craft Soyuz 7, 969. Address: Moscow USSR Died June 30, 1971.

OLLAND, ROSCOE HENRY, dental educator; b. unlap, Ia., Sept. 19, 1877; s. Henry Volland and Mary (Van Scoy) V.; B.Di., Ia. State Teachers Coll., 1898, .Di., 1899; D.D.S., State U. of Ia., 1902, M.D., 1905; .Sc., Northwestern U., 1927; m. Mabel Montgomery, ne 23, 1903; m. 2d, Marguerite Moore White, Oct. 19, 936. Served as demonstrator in operative and osthetic dentistry, State U. of Iowa, 1902-08, prof. d head of dept. of operative technic and dental athology, 1908-23; spl. lecturer in operative dentistry, orthwestern U., 1923-25, clin. prof. of operative entistry, 1925-44. Conductor of short term graduate hools for practitioners of dentistry at Baltimore, Md., ewark, N.J., Chicago, Ill., Washington, D.C., etc. em. Med. Advisory Bd., World War. Fellow Am. oll. of Dentists (regent 1920-26; pres. 1929-30); mem. m. Dental Assn. (pres. 1927-28; treas. 1928-48); c.-treas. Scientific Foundation and Research ommn., 1919-27, Internat. Dental Federation, ternat. Assn. for Dental Research, Ia. State Dental c. (ex-pres.). Mem. Am. Dental Congress, San ancisco, Calif., 1915; mem. bd. Internat. Dental ongress, Phila., Pa., 1926. Republican. Episcopalian. o-editor American Textbook of Operative Dentistry, '20, 26; (revision) Black's Operative Dentistry, 1924. ontbr. to dental jours. Home: 4 Bella Vista Pl. Office: rst Capital Nat. Bank Bldg., Iowa City IA‡

OLPE, PAUL ANTHONY, educator; b. Vancouver, C., Can., Oct. 7, 1915; s. Vincent and Ester (Volpe) ; A.B., U. British Columbia, 1939; A.M., Catholic niversity of America, 1942, Ph.D., 1943; m. Marie eresa Schrei, July 3, 1943; children—Paul Vincent, arie, Virginia, Mark, Peter, Marian, Ester. Came to .S., 1939, naturalized, 1944. Instr. dept. econ. Seattle ; asst. prof. econ. Carroll Coll., Helena, Mont.; asso. of. commerce and finance Seattle U., becoming prof., so dean Sch. Commerce and Finance; chmn. bd. acific Gen. Constrn. Co., Seattle; financial cons. rious firms. Mem. wage stblzn. panel Regional Office, age Stblzn. Bd., 1944-45; price adminstr. 13th egion, Price Stblzn. Agy., 1951-53; mem. Wash. Tax dv. Council, 1945-56, Wash. Gov.'s Bus. Adv. ouncil, 1950-65, Wash. Atty. Gen.'s Consumer Adv. ouncil, 1959-61; chmn. council of economists adv. to ash. Dept. Commerce and Econ. Devel., 1959-68; em. Wash. Trade Mission to Alaska, 1959, Hawaii, 960. Ford Motor Co. fellow, 1956. Mem. Nat. Assn. ost Accountants, Am. Econ. Assn. Roman Catholic. .C. Author: The International Financial Crisis of 1931; undamentals of Economics. Home: Edmonds WA ied Jan. 22, 1968.

ON BEKESY, GEORG, physicist; b. Budapest, ungary, June 3, 1899; s. Alexander and Paula Mazaly) von B.; student U. Berne, 1916-20; Ph.D., U. udapest, 1923; M.D. (hon.), Wilhelm U., Munster, ermany, 1955; M.D. (hon.), Univ. Berne, Switzerland, 959; M.D. (hon.) U. Padua, Italy, 1962; D.Sc., ustavus Adolphus Coll., 1963; D.Sc., U. Pa., 1965, at. U. Cordoba, 1968, U. Buenos Aires, 1968, U. awaii, 1969. With research lab. Hungarian Tel. ystem, 1923-46, Central Lab., Siemens & Halske A.G., erlin, Germany, 1926-27; privatdozent U. Budapest, 932-39, ausserordentlicher prof., 1939-40, dentlicher prof., 1940-46; Karolinski Inst., ockholm, Sweden, 1946-47; research lectr. ycho-Acoustic Lab., Harvard, 1947-49, sr. research llow psycho-physics, 1949-66; prof. of sensory sci. U. Hawaii, 1966-72. Recipient Denker prize in otology, 931, Guyot Prize for speech and otology, Groningen , 1939, Leibnitz Medal, Akademic der issenchaften, Berlin, 1937, Acad. Award, Academy of i., Budapest, 1946, Shambaugh prize in otology, 1950, oward Crosby Warren medal, Soc. Exptl. ychologists, 1955, gold medal Am. Otol. Soc., 1957; hievement award Deafness Research Found., 1961; obel prize for medicine for research on how the man ear hears, 1961. Fellow of the Acoustical Society of America; mem. American Acad. Arts and Scis.; hon. mem. Am. Otol. Soc., Nat. Acad. Scis., several fgn. sci. socs. Contbr. sci. publs. Address: Honolulu HI Died June 13, 1972.

VON BERTALANFFY, LUDWIG, educator; b. Atzgersdorf, Austria, Sept. 19, 1901 (Canadian citizen); s. Gustav and Charlotte (Vogl) von B.; student U. Innsbruck; Ph.D., U. Vienna, 1926; m. Maria M. Bauer, 1925; 1 son, Felix D. Lectr., then prof. U. Vienna, 1934-48; prof., dir. biol. research U. Ottawa, Can., 1949-54; vis. prof. U. So. Cal., 1955-58, dir. biol. research Mt. Sinai Hosp., Los Angeles, 1955-58; Sloan vis. prof. Menninger Found., 1958-59; prof. theoretical biology U. Alberta (Can.), 1961-69; faculty professor State U. N.Y., Buffalo, 1969-72. Fellow Notgemeinschaft der Deutschen Wissenschaft, 1930-32, Rockefeller Found., 1937-38, Lady Davis Found., 1949, Center for Advanced Study Behavioral Sciences, 1954-55, others. Fellow of A.A.A.S., American Psychiatric Assn. (hon.), International Academy Cytology; founder, life mem. Soc. Gen. Systems Research (vice president, 1956-60); mem. Deutsche Akademie der Naturforscher. Awarded gold medal Postal History Society of the Americas, 1963. Author: Modern Theories of Development, 1933, 62, Theoretische Biologie (2 vols.), 1932, 42, 51; Problems of Life, 1952, 1960, Robots, Mem and Minds, 1967, General System Theory, 1968; others in English, German, French, Spanish, Japanese, Dutch langs. Editor Handbuch der Biologie, from 1942, Yearbooks Soc. Gen. Systems Research, from 1956. Contbr. papers sol. jours. Home: Williamsville NY Died June 12, 1972.

VON BONNEWITZ, ORLANDO R., rectal surgeon; b. Van Wert, O., July 16, 1868; s. Franklin James and Elizabeth (Orr) von B.; Ph.C., Phila. Coll. Pharmacy, 1886; M.D., Hahnemann Med. Coll., Chicago, 1897; spl. course in rectal surgery, Post Grad. Sch. of Medicine, 1902; spl. course in proctology, Polyclinic Coll. and Hosp., N.Y. City, 1904; spl. study, London, Berlin, Vienna, 1929; m. Anne C. Bonham, Aug. 20, 1906. Began practice at N.Y. City, 1897; now prof. emeritus proctology and head dept., New York Med. Coll.; founder of rectal clinic, Flower Hosp., 1910; cons. proctologist to same and to Community, Flower and Jamaica hosps., New York Ophthalmic Coll. and Hosp. Mem. Acad. Path. Science (pres.), Am. Inst. Homoeopathy, N.Y. State Med. Soc., N.Y. County Med. Soc., Flower Hosp. Surg. and Gynecol. Soc., Alpha Kappa Kappa (pres.). Hon. alumnus N.Y. Homoe. Med. Coll., 1928. Lutheran. Clubs: Amsterdam Democratic, Columbia Yacht, Mahopac Golf, Dunwoodie Golf and Country. Contbr. papers on rectal diseases. Home and Office: 30 E. 76th St., New York NY (summer) Bonnie Bend," Erskine Lakes NJ*‡

VONDERLEHR, RAYMOND ALOYSIUS, ret. public health ofcl.; b. Richmond, Va., April 25, 1897; s. August Leonard and Marguerite (Hulcher) V.; M.D., U. of Va., 1920; m. Mary Truitt, Oct. 11, 1921; 1 dau., Mary Truitt. Asst. in pharmacology and materia medica, U. of Va., 1919-20; instr. dermatology and syphilology, Med. Coll. of Va., 1922-24; commd. asst. surgeon U.S.P.H.S., 1925, passed asst. surgeon, 1929, surgeon, 1937, asst. surgeon gen., 1935-43; med. adviser from U.S. to Anglo-American Caribbean Commn., 1943-47; med. dir. in charge of communicable disease center, U.S.P.H.S., 1947-51; regional medical director Region IV, Dept. Health, Edn. and Welfare, 1952-55; asst. surgeon gen. (ret.), 1955. Mem. Am. Pub. Health Assn. Club: Cosmos (Washington). Home: Atlanta GA Died Jan. 28, 1973.

VON ELM, HENRY C., banker; b. Brooklyn, N.Y., Nov. 10, 1887; s. Christian and Katharine (Gerken) Von E.; ed. pub. schs., L.I. Business Coll., Brooklyn, and Am. Inst. Banking, N.Y. City; m. Margaret D. Meyer, Apr. 20, 1910; children—Mrs. Dorothy Putnam, Henry Walter, Charles Arthur. Began, 1903, with Mfrs. Nat. Bank, merged with Mfrs. Trust Co., 1914, of which was asst. sec., 1915-18, v.p., 1919-27, director, 1925, chmn. exec. com., 1928, pres., 1929, vice-chmn. bd., 1931-47, chmn. bd., 1947-50, pres., 1950-51, hon. chmn. bd. 1951; dir. George W. Rogers Construction Co., Geo. A. Fuller Co., Home Insurance Co. (ex-mem. finance committee), Sperry & Hutchinson Co., Mem. Am. Inst. Banking. Robert Morris Assos. Lutheran. Clubs: National Golf Links of America, Maidstone, Bankers, Metropolitan, Everglades, Devon Yacht, Wyandanch. Home: Forest Hills NY Died July 17, 1969; buried Kensico Cemetery, Westchester County NY

VON GRAVE-JONAS, ELSA (BARONESS), concert pianiste; b. Cologne, Germany, June 4, 1875; d. Mortimer Baron von Grave and Rosalie von G.; ed. Munich; grad. Royal Acad. Music, Munich (was protege Hans von Bulow), receiving 1st prizes and pub. hon. mention; frequently asked to play before Royal family of Bavaria; m. Ann Arbor, Mich., Dec. 20, 1899, Alberto Jonas, pianist. Came to U.S. 1894; has toured with Boston Festival Orchestra; soloist on tour with Victor Herbert, Pittsburgh Orchestra, spring 1903. Asso. dir. Mich. Conservatory of Music. Address: 68 W. Alexandrine Av., Detroit MI‡

VON GRUNEBAUM, GUSTAVE E(DMUND), orientalist, educator; b. Vienna, Austria, Sept. 1, 1909; s. Egon and Edith Lucy Amalia Hedwig (Weissel) von G.; Ph.D., U. Vienna, 1931; fellow Notgemeinschaft der Deutschen Wissenschaft, U. Berlin, 1932-33; Dr. h.c., U. Frankfurt, 1964, Hebrew Union Coll., 1969; m. Giselle Eugenie Steuerman, Sept. 9, 1941; children—Tessa Jennifer, Claudia Constance. Came to U.S., 1938, naturalized, 1944. Leader of the extension institute, Oriental Inst., U. Vienna, 1936-38; asst. prof. Arabic and Islamic studies Asia Inst., N.Y.C., 1938-42, chmn. dept. Arabic, 1942-43; asst. prof. Arabic, U. Chgo., 1943-46, asso. prof., 1946-49, prof. Arabic, 1949; prof. history, dir. Near Eastern Center, U. Cal. at Los Angeles. Pres. Am. Research Center in Eqypt, Inc., 1966-72, bd. govs. Am. Research Inst., Turkey, Center for Arabic Studies Abroad; chmn. internat. com. Biennial Levi Della Vida Confs. Fellow Am. Acad. Arts, Scis., Middle East Inst.; mem. Am. Oriental Soc., Bombay (India) Islamic Research Assn. (hon.), Am. Philos. Soc., Accademia Nazionale dei Lincei, Institut d'Egypte. Author: Palestine, A Study of Jewish, Arab and British Policies (with others), 1947; Az-Zarnuji, Instruction of the Student—The Method of Learning (with T. M. Abel), 1947; Die Wirklichkeitweite der fruharabischen Dichtung, 1937; Medieval Islam, A Study in Cultural Orientation, 1946; A Tenth-Century Document of Arabic Literary Theory and Criticism, 1951; Muhammadan Festivals, 1951; Islam: Essays in the Nature and Growth of a Cultural Tradition, 1955; Modern Islam: The Search for Cultural Identity, 1962; French African Literature: Some Cultural Implications, 1964; Islam: Experience of the Holy and Concept of Man, 1965; Stadium zum Kulturbild und Selbstverstandnis des Islams, 1969; Classical Islam, 1970. Co-editor, contbr. The Dream and Human Societies, 1966, Muslim Self-Statement in India and Pakistan, 1970, Studia Islamica, 1971-72; editor Logic in Classical Islamic Culture, 1970; Theology and Law in Islam, 1971; Der Islam II. Fischer Weltgeschichte, 1971; Arabic Poetry; Theory and Development, 1973; editor-in-chief Bibliothek des Morgenlandes (Switzerland), Eng. series The Islamic World. Contbr. Am. and European periodicals. Cons. editor Jour. Nr. Eastern Studies, U. Chgo. Address: Los Angeles CA Died Feb. 27, 1972; buried Westwood Los Angeles CA

VON GUTTENBERG, KARL THEODORE, German govt. ofcl.; b. Weisendorf, Germany, May 23, 1921; s. George and Elisabeth (von der Tann) Von G.; m. Rose Sophie, Princess Arenberg, July 6, 1943; children—Elisabeth, Enoch, Michaela, Praxedis. One of founders of Christian Social Party; mem. Bundestag (Parliament), mem. fgn. relations com.; family participated Resistance Movement, World War II; Parliamentarian state-sec. to fed. chancellor, 1967-69. Decorated Knight of Holy Sepulchre. Home: Guttenberg Died Oct. 4, 1972; buried Guttenberg Germany

VON KAHLER, ERICH GABRIEL, author, educator; b. Prague, Oct. 14, 1885; s. Rudolph and Antoinette (Schwarz) von K.; Ph.D., U. Vienna, 1912; D.h.c., Princeton, 1969; m. Josephine Sobotka, 1913 (dec.); m. 2d, Alice Loewy, 1969. Came to U.S., 1938, naturalized, 1944. Author and lectr. in Munich and Heidelberg, Germany, 1913-33; lectr. New Sch. Social Research, 1941-42, Black Mountain Coll., 1946; tchr. Cornell U., 1947-55; Lord Simon fellow U. Manchester (Eng.), 1955-56; Mershon vis. prof. Ohio State U., 1959-60; tchr. Princeton, 1960-63, Faber lectr. Princeton, 1967; mem. Inst. Advanced Study, Princeton, 1949. Mem. Com. to Frame World Constitution, U. Chgo., 1945-48. Fellow Bollingen Found., 1947-50, 60-61; fellow Leo Baeck Inst., 1965-70. Mem. Deutsche Akademie fur Sprache and Dichthung. Author: Man the Measure, A New Approach to History, 1943; The Tower and the Abyss, An Inquiry into the Transformation of the Individual, 1957; The Meaning of History, 1964; Out of the Labyrinth, Essay in Clarification, 1967; The Disintegration of Form in the Arts, 1968: The Orbit of Thomas Mann, 1969: The Jews Among the Nations, 1968 (Wolff-Anisfeld award 1968); The Inward Turn of Narrative, 1973; Letters in Exile, Thomas Mann-Erich Kahler, 1973. Address: Princeton NJ Died June 28, 1970.

VON KLEINWAECHTER, LUDWIG PAUL VIKTOR, Austrian govt. official; b. Czernowitz, Austria, Oct. 9, 1882; s. Dr. Friedrich K.; ed. Univ. of Czernowitz, Austria; LL.D., U. of Berlin, 1908; LL.D. (hon.) U. of Southern Calif., 1946; m. Anna Neschuetz, Dec. 14, 1921; children—Gunda, Ebbe. Entered Austro-Hungarian foreign service, 1911; vice consul at New York, 1912; with Austro-Hungarian Embassy, 1915, Austro-Hungarian Ministry Fgn. Affairs, Vienna, 1917; sec. legation, Rome, 1920; consul gen. Republic of Austria, 1921-25 (Chicago); counsellor of legation, Austrian Legation, Washington, 1925-27; fgn. office, Vienna, 1927-29; Austrian consul gen., Ottawa, 1929-31; Fed. Press Bur. of Austrian Fgn. Office, Vienna, 1932-38; sent to Dachau, later Buchenwald concentration camps for anti-Nazi activities in 1938, released, 1939; reentered Fgn. Office, Vienna, 1945; acted as liaison officer between the Austrian govt. and U.S; Austrian political rep. to U.S. with rank of envoy extraordinary and minister plenipotentiary, Jan. 1946 to Dec. 1946, Austrian minister to U.S. 1946-52; ret., 1952. Home: Vienna Austria Died Mar. 5, 1973.

VON SCHLIEDER, ALBERT, clergyman; b. West Leyden, N.Y., Jan. 13, 1869; s. Frederick Ernest and Mary Constantine (Lohr) V.; A.B., Rutgers, 1893, A.M., 1896; B.D., New Brunswick Theol Sem., 1896; D.D., Central Coll., Pella, Ia., 1913; m. Harriet Schenck, of Canarise, N.Y., 1896 (died 1902); 1 dau., Evanita Schenck; m. 2d, Minnie Newkirk, of Hurley, N.Y., 1907; children—Elizabeth Newkirk, Karl Lohr. Ordained ministry Ref. Ch. America, 1896; pastor Hurley, N.Y., 1896-1902, Montclair, N.J., 1902-10, First Ch., Hackensack, N.J., since 1910. Chaplain, title of capt., State Defense Regt., Hackensack, World War; four minute man; mem. Americanization Com. Supt. New Brunswick Theol. Sem., 1916, pres., 1920; chmn. Ref. Ch. Synod Com. of Domestic Missions, 1921; now chmn. com. corr. and program, Synod Ref. Ch. in America. Pres. Hackensack Bd. of Health, Bergen Co. Health Centre. Mem. Am. Legion (hon.), D.K.E., Theta Nu Epsilon. Pres. Alumni Assn. New Brunswick Theol. Sem., 1923-24. Republican. Mason. Clubs: Rotary, Hackensack Golf, Kiwanis (hon.). Home: 128 Overlook Av., Hackensack NJ*‡

VON TRESCKOW, EGMONT CHARLES, b. Mamaroneck, N.Y., June 18, 1872; s. Egmont and Jane Augusta (Eldredge) von T.; ed. private instrn. and schs. in Austria; LL.B., Univ. of S.C., 1900; student U. of Va., summer, 1900; m. Sadie Belton Kennedy, July 22, 1907. Admitted to S.C. bar, 1900, in practice, 1900-16 and 1919-21; consul at Arica, Chile, 1921-26, Berlin, Germany, 1926-29, Rotterdam, Netherlands, 1929-32, Zagreb, Jugoslavia, 1932-35, St. John, N.B., 1935-37. Retired. Major S.C. Nat. Guard, Mexican border service; served with A.E.F., World War; was lt. col. S.C. Nat. Guard; now lt. col. O.R.C., Inactive List Mem. S.A.R. Associate member of Carlton Branch Canadian Legion of the British Empire Service League. Episcopalian. Home: Camden SC‡

VON WENING, ANTHONY, bus. exec.; b. Brooklyn, May 24, 1897; s. Adolph and Paula (Kriegel) von W.; student Cornell, 1914-17; m. Anne Sachse, Sept. 7, 1921; 1 son, Anthony F. With Continental Ill. Nat. Bank & Trust Co., Chicago, 1919-40, v.p., 1929-40; asst. to pres. A. O. Smith Corp., Milwaukee, 1940-45, v.p. 1945-53, chmn. finance com., 1953-55; dir. 1945-55; pres. Basic Products Corp. (formerly The Froedtert Corp), Milw., 1958-60, chmn. bd., chief exec. officer, 1953-62, mem. exec. com.; past chmn. board, chmn. exec. com. Cherry-Burrell Corp. Cedar Rapids, Ia.; chmn. Froedtert Malt Corp. Clubs: Milw., Milwaukee Country, University (Milw.); Chicago. Home: Milwaukee WI Died May 18, 1971.

VON WICHT, JOHN, artist; b. Malente, Germany, Feb. 3, 1888; s. Alfred and Adele (Strohmeyer) von W.; student pvt. art sch. of Grand Duke of Hesse, Darmstadt, 1909-10; B.A., Acad. Sch., Berlin, 1912; m. Kunigunde Petz, Dec. 31, 1912. Came to U.S., 1924, naturalized, 1936. One man shows include Artists Gallery, N.Y.C., 1944, Kleemann Gallery, N.Y.C., 1946, 47, Passedoit Gallery, N.Y. C., 1950, 51, 52, 54, 56, 57, 58, John Herron Inst., Indpls., 1953, Carl Schurz Meml. Found., Phila., 1954, Robles Gallery, Los Angeles, 1959, Santa Barbara (Cal.) Mus. Art, 1959, Pasadena (Cal.) Mus., 1959, Bertha Schaefer Gallery, N.Y.C., 1960, also in Paris, Belgium, Madrid; exhbns. include Met. Mus. Art, Mus. Modern Art, Whitney Mus. Am. Art, Corcoran Bienniel, Pa. Acad., Bklyn. Mus., Phila. Mus., Guggenheim Mus., Carnegie Inst., Nat. Acad., Art Inst. Chgo., Boston Mus. Fine Arts, numerous others U.S. and Europe; rep. permanent collections Musee D'Art Moderne, Paris, Museum of Fine Arts, Boston, Met. Mus., Whitney Mus., Bklyn. Mus., Library of Congress, Balt. Mus., Mus. Modern Art, Phila. Mus., Yale Art Gallery, Riverside Mus., N.Y.C., Cin. Mus., W. F. Chrysler Mus., Provincetown, Mass., Jewish Mus., N.Y.C., also in Madrid, Stockholm and Liege, Belgium, univ. and pvt. collections; executed mural commns. and mosiacs in N.Y.C., Miami, Fla., Trenton, N.J., St. Louis, Montreal, Can., Bklyn., Brewton, Ala., Helsingfors, Finland, Knoxville, Tenn., N.Y. World's Fair; tchr. Art Student's League, N.Y.C., summers 1951-52; vis. artist John Heron Art Sch., 1953. Recipient 1st prize for watercolor Bklyn. Mus., 1948, 1st prize for oil, 1949, purchase prize, 1951, prize for oil, 1958, purchase prize 12th nat. print exhbn., 1960; hon. mention for oil Audubon Artists, 1952, 53, prize for oil, 1954. Medal of Honor, 1958; 1st prize color lithograph Bklyn. Soc. Artists, 1953, 1st prize for oil, 1957, 1st prize for print, 1960; Mary Collins purchase prize for color lithograph Phila. Print Club, 1953, William H. Walker Meml. prize for lithograph, 1957; Mrs. A.W. Erickson prize for lithograph Soc. Am. Graphic Artists, 1954; prize for oil Riverside Mus., 1958; prize Boston Arts Festival, 1958; grand prize for color lithograph Art in Am. exhbn., N.Y.C., 1959; purchase prize H. Ford Found., 1960. Mem. Am. Abstract Artists, Audubon Artists (dir.), Am. Soc. Contemporary Artists (medal of merit 1966), Fedn. Modern Painters and Sculptors, Internat. Inst. Arts and Letters. Home: Brooklyn NY Died Jan. 20, 1970.

VON WILLER, HARRY WALTER, railroad exec.; b. Greensburg, Ind., Aug. 11, 1896; s. William H. and Estella (Lawson) Von W.; ed. pub. schs., manual training high sch., Indianapolis, Ind.; student Purdue University, 1913-15, University of Minnesota, 1930-31; LL.D., Alfred U., 1958; m. Roberta L. Terrell, Jan. 28, 1922; 1 daughter, Roberta Linda (Mrs. J. Morris Taylor, Jr.). Clk. local freight house, C., C., C. & St. L. Ry., 1915-17, in various positions, 1919-23; with Erie R.R., 1923-71, chief clerk and commercial agent, Indianapolis, Ind., 1923-27, gen. agent, Springfield, O., 1927-30, Minneapolis, Minn., 1930-31, div. freight agent, Youngstown, O., 1931-35, asst. gen. freight agent, Pittsburgh, Pa., 1935-38, asst. freight traffic mgr., Cleveland, O., 1938-39, freight traffic mgr., Chicago, Ill., 1939-40, asst. to vice pres., Cleveland, 1941, asst. vice pres., 1941-42, v.p. charge traffic, 1942-56, pres. 1956-60; chairman, chief exec. officer, Erie-Lackawanna R.R., 1960-62. Served with 113th Field Signal Bn., U.S. Army, 1917-19; disch. with rank sergt. 1st class, acting sergt. major. Mem. Assn. Interstate Commerce Commn. Practitioners. Clubs: Union (Cleveland); Union League (Chicago). Home: Shaker Heights OH Died May, 1971.

VOORHEES, JAMES D., physician; b. at Morristown, N.J., May 21, 1869; s. of George E. and Mary G. V.; grad. Princeton, 1890; A.M., 1893; Coll. Phys. and Surg., Columbia University, 1893. Resident physician Prby'n Hospital, 1894-6; New York Foundling Hosp., 1896-7; Sloane Maternity Hosp., 1897-1900; instr. in obstetrics from 1897, Coll. Physicians and Surgeons; secretary faculty Coll. Phys. and Surg., 1901-1905. Republican. Presby'n. Contb'r to med. jours. Address: 106 E. 60th St., New York NY‡

VOORHIES, FRANK COREY, author; b. at Woodbury, N.J., June 1, 1877; s. Cornelius Clark and Carolyn (Mann) V.; grad. Penn Charter Sch., Phila., 1895, Princeton Univ., 1899; m. 2d, Lyda May Pickett, of Omaha, Nebraska, Sept. 23, 1912. Became reporter on Omaha Daily News; later editor of The Spatula, Boston; left that to join advertising writers of W.C. Lewis Co. Success of first book led to devoting entire time to writing. Episcopalian. Republican. Clubs: Tiger Inn (Princeton, N.J.), Princeton (Boston). Author: Love Letters of an Irishwoman, 1901; Story of Lizzie McGuire, 1902; Mrs. McPiggs of the Very Old Scratch, 1903; Reflections of Bridget McNulty, 1902; The Knocker, 1903; Twisted History, 1904; That Settles the Nolans, 1904; Twisted Biographies. Contbr. squibs, jokes and short sketches to leading comic jours. Address: 1104 S. 35th Av., Omaha NE‡

VOORHIS, CHARLES BROWN, b. Olathe, Kan., Mar. 13, 1870; s. Aurelius Lyman and Levisa Ann (Brown) V.; prep. edn., Racine (Wis.) Coll. Grammar Sch.; student U. of Kan., 1887-91; m. Ella Ward Smith, Dec. 26, 1895; children—Horace Jeremiah, Virginia Jean. Became cashier Waddell Investment Co., Kansas City, Mo., 1895; in retail hardware and implement business, Ottawa, Kan., 1899-1908; mgr. Kingman Plow Co., Oklahoma City, Okla., and Kansas City, 1908-13; v.p. and sales mgr. Oakland Motor Car Co., Pontiac, Mich., 1913-16; v.p. and sales dir. Nash Motors Co., Kenosha, Wis., 1916-23; mem. bd. dirs. Los Angeles Branch Federal Reserve Bank, 1930-36, chmn. board, 1935-36. Builder and endower with wife of Voorhis Sch. for Homeless Boys, nr. San Dimas, Calif.; made gift of school, including 150 acres, buildings and equipment, to State of Calif., for Calif. Polytechnic School, Voorhis Unit," 1938. Asso. Calif. Inst. of Tech. since 1928. Mem. Sigma Chi. Democrat. Episcopalian. Clubs: University, Valley Hunt, Twilight, Annandale Golf. Home: 60 Los Altos Drive, Pasadena CA‡

VOROSHILOV, MAZSHAL KLIMENT YEFREMOVICH, mem. presidium USSR; b. Verkhneye, Drepzopetrovsk region, Feb. 4, 1881. Worker, Lugansk Engine-Building Works; joined Russian Social Democratic Labour Party, 1903; sent to Donbass with plenipotentiary powers by Communist Party Central Com., October Revolution of 1917; participated in rout of white-guard generals and fgn. interventionists during Civil War; mem. Central Com., Russian Communist Party, 1921-61; mem. Polit. Bur., 1926-52; comdr. North Caucasian Mil. area, 1921-24, Moscow Mil. area, 1924-25, people's commissar for mil. and naval affairs, 1925-34, people's commissar of def., USSR, 1934-40. Vice chmn. people's commissars of USSR, chmn. def. com., 1940-46; chmn. Allied Control Commn., Hungary, 1945-47; vice chmn. USSR Council Ministers, 1946-53; pres. Presidium of USSR Supreme Soviet, 1953-60, mem. Presidium, 1960-69. Decorated orders of Lenin, orders of Red Banner, Order of Suvorov 1st class other orders and medals; named marshal of Soviet Union, 1935, Hero of the Soviet Union, 1956, Hero of Socialist Labour, 1960. Author books on mil. sci. and history. Moscow USSR Died Dec. 2, 1969.

VORYS, JOHN MARTIN, congressman; b. Lancaster, O., June 16, 1896; s. Arthur Isaiah and Jeanny (McNeil) V.; A.B., Yale, 1918; J.D., Ohio State U., 1923; LL.D., Ohio Wesleyan University, 1949; married Lois West, February 5, 1927; children—Martin West, Jeanny Esther, Mary. Teacher, Coll. of Yale in China, 1919-20; admitted to Ohio bar, 1923, and began practice in Columbus; partner firm Vorys, Sater, Seymour & Pease, 1926-38; vice pres., dir. Vorys Bros.; member of 76th to 85th Congresses from the 12th Ohio District (member fgn. affairs com.); mem. Commission on Foreign Eco Policy, 1953-54; asst. sec. Am. delegation Conference on Limitation of Armaments, Washingto D.C., 1921-22; mem. Ohio Gen. Assembly, 1923-2 Ohio Senate, 1925-26; 1st dir. of aeronautics, Ohi 1929-30; dir. Columbus Y.M.C.A. Served as pilot, U. Naval Air Service, overseas, World War I; Civil A Patrol Pilot, 1942. Mem. U.S. Del. 6th Gen. Assembl UN, Paris, 1951. Mem. Columbus Bar Assn. (presiden 1938), Ohio Bar Assn., Psi Upsilon, Phi Beta Kappa, P Delta Phi, Delta Sigma Rho, Pi Sigma Alpha, Order Coif. Republican. Methodist. Clubs: Rocky Fork Hu and Country (Gahanna, Ohio). Home: Columbus O Died Aug. 25, 1968.

VORYS, WEBB ISAIAH, lawyer; b. Lancaster, O July 23, 1892; s. Arthur I. and Jeanny (McNeil) V A.B., Williams Coll., 1914; J.D., Ohio State U., 1917; r Adeline Werner, Apr. 27, 1918 (dec. May 1952 children—John W., Arthur Isaiah II, Margo. Admitte to Ohio bar, 1917, engaged in practice of la Columbus; now mem. firm Vorys, Sater, Seymour Pease; dir. Western & Souther Life Ins. Co., Credit Li Ins. Co., Marble Cliff Quarries Co., Kauffman Lattim Co.; gen. counsel Ohio Mfrs. Assn. Mem. Chi Psi, P Delta Phi, Order of Coif. Home: Gahanna OH Di Aug. 30, 1972.

VOTIPKA, THELMA, opera singer; b. Cleve., Dec. 2 1898; d. Emil and Jessie Votipka; student Oberl Conservatory; studied with Anna Schoen Rene N.Y. Lila Robeson, Cleve.; m. John C. Groth, Dec. 24, 194 Operatic debut as singing countess Marriage of Figar Am. Opera Co., 1927; soprano Chicago Opera, 1929-3 Stadium Opera, 1930, Phila., 1932, San Francisc 1938, 48, 52, Hartford, Conn., 1942, Cinn., 194 Puerto Rico, 1954; mem. Metropolitan Opera C 1935-63; ret., 1963. Mem. A.G.M.A. (v.p., mem. bd. Home: New York City NY Died Oct. 24, 1972.

VOX, HERMAN H(AROLD), univ. prof.; bo Norwood, Minn., Jan. 10, 1911; s. Herman a Margaret Elisa (Kloempken) V.; A.B. summa cu laude, Hamline U., St. Paul, 1932; A.M., U. of Minn 1933, Ph.D., 1939; m. Anita Corinne Lilie, Aug. 2 1941; children—Vicki, Margaret (Mrs. Robe Graham), Juli, Steven, Carla. High sch. prin. Claremon Minn., 1933-34; instr. German and modern Europe history, Rochester Sr. High Sch., 1934-36; teaching as in German, U. of Minn., 1936-39; prof. German Drak U., 1939-40, head dept. of German, 1940-57, pr German, from 1957, chmn. dept. fgn. langs., 1957-6 Served as U.S. Govt. translator, summer 1942. Award first prize for essay, George Washington's Contributio to Education, 1932. Member Am. Assn. Teachers German (president Ia. chapter, 1948-49), Modern Lan Assn., Am. Assn. Univ. Profs. (past pres. Dra chapter), Ia. Fgn. Lang. Assn., Kappa Phi Sigma, Kap Phi Kappa, Pi Gamma Mu, Alpha Lambda P Lutheran. Club: Faculty Men's (past pres.). Author: T Historical Element in the Dramas of Heinrich v Kleist, 1949. Home: Des Moines IA Died Dec. 3 1971; buried Glendale Cemetery, Des Moines IA

VREELAND, HAMILTON, JR., educator, lawyer; Jersey City, Jan. 19, 1892; s. Hamilton and Ella (Coward) V.; grad. Hasbrouck Inst., Jersey City, 190 Litt.B., Princeton, 1913; A.M., Columbia, 1915; LL. 1916, Ph.D., 1917; m. Marion Jefferson, 193 children—Hamilton, Marion. Admitted to N.Y. b 1916; mem. D.C. and U.S. Supreme Ct. bars; beg practice N.Y.C.; member firm Stockton & Stockto 1921-25, Stockton, Kerfoot & Vreeland, 1925-27; me Boyd, Adams, Chapman & Vreeland, 1927-30; White Case, 1943-45. Special counsel to agent of the Unit States, Mixed Claims Commns., United States a Mexico, 1930-31; professor law, Catholic University America, 1931-38; head of Grad. Dept. of Law Sc 1932-38; visiting lecturer internat. relations, Yale Gr Sch., 1937; prof. law, Washington Coll. Am. 1939-42; spl. lecturer Fordham Univ. Law Sc 1943-45; visiting prof. law New York Univ. Sch. of La 1945-47; adjunct professor Government N.Y. 1958-69; special asst. to atty. gen. of U.S., 1943. Serv in United States Navy, 1917; on legal staff U.S. De of State, 1917-19. Mem. Am. and Federal bar assn Am. Soc. Internat. Law, Internat. Law Assn., Am. L Inst., Inst. Juridique Internat. (The Hague), Am. Aca of Polit. and Social Science, S.A.R., Holland Soc. N. Mem. Dutch Reformed Ch. Clubs: Cosm (Washington); Campus (Princeton); Lotos, Columb U., N.Y. University Faculty (N.Y.C.). Author: Hu Grotius, 1917 (translated into Japanese, 1925); Validi of Foreign Divorces, 1938; Twilight of Individu Liberty, 1944; Russian Communism and Wo Domination, 1956; The Supreme Court, State Righ and Liberty, 1964; also contbr. articles on pub. and p law. Cons. Counsel. Pub. lectr. on current problems nat. and internat. affairs. Home: Bantam CT Died N 18, 1969; buried Kensico Cemetery, Valhalla NY

VULTEE, HOWARD FLEMING, financial a investment consultant; b. Rutherford, New Jersey, J 2, 1905; son of Edwin L. and Sarah (Fleming) student N.Y.U., also Grad. Sch. Bus. Adminstr 1933-35; m. Carrie I. Maynard, Sept. 14, 19 children—Lynn (dec.), Howard F. Financial sec. Co

Mut. Life Ins. Co., Hartford, 1944-46; adminstrv. v.p. the Marine Midland Trust Co. N.Y., also v.p., chmn. adminstrv. com. Marine Midland Corp., 1946-55, 5-58; financial and investment cons., 1958-73; dir. ffice Econ. Affairs, U.S. Mission to NATO, 1955-56; nancial adviser Eastman Dillon, Union Securities & o., 1958-70; dir. Papercraft Corp. Mem. N.Y. Society ecurity Analysts. Clubs: Recess (N.Y.C.); Everglades, ailfish (Palm Beach, Fla.). Address: Palm Beach FL Died Feb. 24, 1973.

WACHENFELD, WILLIAM A., judge; b. Orange, N.J., Feb. 24, 1889; s. Thomas and Elisa (Baumann) W.; L.B., N.Y.U., 1910; LL.D., N.Y.U., 1951, Upsala ollege, 1951; married Anne Gilmour Weir, Feb. 26, 1925; children—William T., Donand Weir (deceased), Howard G., David R., Elise (Mrs. Zsolt G. de Papp). Admitted to N.J. bar 1911; associate firm Lum, Fairlie and Wachenfeld, Newark, N.J., 1910-46; prosecutor of Pleas Essex County, N.J., 1932-46; asso. justice N.J. Supreme Ct., 1946-59; cons. Lum, Fairlie & Foster, 1959-69. Pres. Law Center Found.; trustee N.Y.U. Dir. Civil Def. N.J., World War II. Mem. Am. and Essex County bar assns., Kappa Sigma. Democrat. Episcopalian. Club: Baltusrol Golf. Home: Orange NJ Died Apr. 22, 1969.

WADDELL, CHARLES WILKIN, prof. edn.; b. near Taylorsville, Ill., Mar. 6, 1875; s. James and Adaline (Wilkin) W.; student Monmouth (Ill.) Coll. 3 yrs. to 1896, Colo. State Teachers Coll., Greeley, 1 semester; A.A., Colorado Coll., Colorado Springs, 1901, M.A., 1903; Ph.D., Clark Univ., 1905; m. Viola B. McCloskey, Aug. 27, 1902; 1son, James Eliot; m. 2d, Mrs. Lillias Jaquins Franklin, June 2, 1924 (died Mar. 1947); stepson, Philip Jaquins Franklin. Teacher rural sch. near Greeley, Colo., 1896-97; training teacher Colo. State Teachers Coll., 1905-06, asst. supt. Training School of same, 1906-09; prof. of psychology, Colo. State Teachers Coll., 1909-10, head dept. of psychology and edn., Los Angeles State Normal Sch., 1910-17, head of training dept., 1917-19; director training dept. and asso. prof. of edn., U. of Calif. at Los Angeles, 1919-21, prof. edn. and dir. training dept., July 1921-June 1940; prof. edn. 1940-45, prof. emeritus since 1945; prof. edn. and coordinator for student teaching Immaculate Heart Coll. since 1945. Fellow A.A.A.S.; member N.E.A. asso. for student teaching, dept. of supervision and curriculum development), Nat. Soc. for Study of Edn., Nat. Ednl. Fellowship, Am. Assn. Univ. Professors; member of Phi Delta Kappa fraternity. Republican. Conglist. Clubs: Educational Book Review Club. Author: Syllabus and Bibliog. of Child Study (with W. F. Root), 1915; An Introduction to Child Psychology, 1918; A Six-Year Experiment with a Nursery School with Barbara Greenwood and others), 1931; Major Units in the Social Studies (with Corinne A. Seeds, Natalie White and others), 1932; A Handbook for Student Teachers, 1935. Contbr. to ednl. mags. Home: 367 Midvale Av., Los Angeles 24 CA‡

WADDINGTON, RALPH HENRY, metal co. exec.; b. Leicester, Eng., Aug. 30, 1900; s. Frank Gladstone and Elizabeth (Hings) W.; became Canadian citizen, 1918; B.Sc. in Metallurgy, Queen's U., Kingston, Can., 1923; m. Jane Bates Freeman, Aug. 27, 1924. With Internat. Nickel Co. of Can., Ltd., 1923-67, v.p., 1960-64, senior vice president, 1964-67, v.p. Internat. Nickel, Inc., 1962-67. Mem. Am. Inst. Mining, Metall. and Petroleum Engrs., Canadian Inst. Mining and Metallurgy. Clubs: Canadian, Mining, City Midday (N.Y.C.); Toronto; (Toronto). Author papers metallurgy nickel and copper; spl. work electrothermal metallurgy of copper. Home: Died June 10, 1967.

WADE, JASON LLOYD, rubber co. exec.; b. Paris, Ill., Apr. 10, 1901; s. Luther E. and Marietta (jones) W.; A.B., U. Mich., 1924; m. Jean Palmer, May 14, 1955; children—Jean Kathleen, Julie Anne, Thomas Jason; 1 step-son, Rory O'Neil. Office mgr. D. M. Woodruff Co., Detroit, 1924-36; tax dept. mgr. Gen. Motors Corp., Detroit, 1936-43; asst. sec. Gen. Tire & Rubber Co., Akron, O. 1943-68. Chmn., Ohio Republican Finance Com., Summit County, 1966-68. Vice pres. M. G. O'Neil Found., Inc. Trustee Goodwill Industries, Akron, Summit County Tb and Health Assn., Akron, Mem. Chi Phi. Roman Catholic. Clubs: Portage Country, University; Rockwell Springs Trout (Castalia, O.). Home: Akron OH Died Apr. 1, 1968.

WADE, JOHN E., educator; born August 13, 1877; B.S., College City, New York, 1897; M.A., Columbia Univ., 1902; married; children—Mrs. Theodore Riehl, Mrs. Laurence Dantzler. Began as teacher Pub. Sch. 54, Manhattan, N.Y. City, 1898; became asst. to bd. of examiners in trade subjects in vocational and trade schools, 1919; associate city supt., 1927-34, dept. supt., 1934-42; supt., 1942-47. Lecturer on school adminstrn., Coll. City, N.Y. for 10 years. Home: 2267 Andrews Av., The Bronx, New York NY Office: Board of Education, 110 Livingston, Brooklyn NY*‡

WADE, WILLIAM LIGON, educator; b. Whitesboro, Tex., Nov. 11, 1906; s. George Henry and Jennie (Ligon) W.; A.B., St. Louis U., 1930, A.M., 1931; Ph.D., 1935, S.T.L., 1938. Joined Soc. of Jesus; instr. St. Louis U. High Sch., 1933-34; prof. St. Louis U., 1939-68, dir. dept. philosophy, 1942-65. Mem. Am., Am. Catholic philos. socs. Home: St Louis MO Died Jan. 1, 1968.

WADHAMS, WILLIAM HENDERSON, lawyer; b. Annapolis, Md., Dec. 7, 1873; s. Admiral A. V. (U.S.N.) and Caroline E. (Henderson) W.; grad. Phillips Acad., Andover, Mass., 1892; A.B., Yale, 1896; LL.B., Harvard Law Sch., 1899; m. Caroline D. Reed, of Andover, Mass., Apr. 26, 1900. Admitted to bar, N.Y. City, 1898; law sec. to Justice John Proctor Clarke, of Supreme Ct. of N.Y., 4 yrs.; apptd. to vacancy on bench of City Court by Gov. Hughes, 1907; apptd. by U.S. Court spl. master to determine claims against receivers of N.Y. City Ry. Co.; apptd. commr. by Gov. Hughes to investigate office of state supt. of elections; judge Court of Gen. Sessions, N.Y., term 1914-28. Resigned Jan. 1, 1921; engaged in practice of internat. law with offices in Paris. Legal adviser to the Chamber of Princess, India, since 1936. Mem. Am. and N.Y. State bar assns., Assn. Bar City of New York. Clubs: Union Interalliee, Univers of Paris. Address: 39 Av. George V, Paris France‡

WADSWORTH, ARTHUR LITTLEFORD, banker; b. Ft. Thomas, Ky;, July 30, 1910; s. Arthur W. and Bernice (Littleford) W.; Ph. B., U. Wis., 1933; M.B.A., Harvard, 1935; m. Betty Nevin, Feb. 3, 1940; children—Anne, Nancy, Arthur William. With Dillon, Read & Co., N.Y.C., 1935-70, v.p., 1949-63, exec. v.p., 1963-70; chairman executive com., dir. Copperweld Steel Co. (Pitts.); dir. The Jeffrey Co., Columbus, O., Dillon Read & Co., Inc., Grumman Aircraft Corp. Staff, of the WPB, 1942-43. Trustee of Wis. Alumni Research Foundation. Served from lt. (j.g.) to comdr., USNR, 1943-46. Decorated Legion of Merit, Order of Rising Sun 3d class (Japan). Mem. Investment Bankers Assn. Am. (v.p. 1959), Chi Psi. Episcopalian (vestryman 1954-60). Clubs: Creek, Manhasset Bay Yacht (L.I., N.Y.); Harvard, Wall Street, Links (N.Y.C.); Duquesne (Pitts.). Home: Roslyn NY Died June 2, 1970; buried Evergreen Cemetery, Ft Thomas KY

WADSWORTH, CRAIG WHARTON, foreign service officer; b. Philadelphia, Jan. 12, 1872; s. Craig Wharton and Evelyn Willing (Peters) W.; graduate of Hill School, Pottstown, Pa., 1892; student Harvard, 1892-93; unmarried. Mem. 1st U.S. Cav. (Rough Riders"), Spanish-Am. War, 1898; mem. governor's staff, N.Y., 1899-1900; apptd. 3d sec. Am. Embassy at London, May 14, 1902, 2d sec. May 10, 1905, resigned, 1909; sec. of legation and counsel-gen. at Teheran, Persia, 1912-15; sec. Legation, Bucharest, Roumania, 1915-16; sec. Legation, Montevideo, Uruguay, 1916-17; charge d'affaires, Buenos Aires, Aug.-Sept. 1916, Montevideo, 1917-18; assigned to Rio de Janeiro, May 25, 1918; apptd. counsellor of embassy, Rio de Janeiro, June 28, 1920; assigned temporarily to Buenos Aires as charge d'affaires, July 24-Nov. 4, 1920; as counsellor of embassy, a mem. of Sec. of State Colby's party visiting Brazil, Uruguay and Argentina, Nov. 19, 1920-Jan. 2, 1921; assigned to Dept. of State, Washington, Jan. 12, 1921; assigned to Brussels, as counsellor of embassy, May 23, 1921. Placed upon the list of unassigned secretaries, Sept. 27, 1923; apptd. foreign service officer, class 2, July 1, 1924; assigned to Lima, Peru, as counsellor of legation, Dec. 23, 1924; retired Nov. 6, 1927. Decorated Order of the Sun (Peru). Republican. Episcopalian. Clubs: Metropolitan, University (Washington, D.C.); Knickerbocker (New York); Roehampton (London). Home: Geneseo NY‡

WAGENAAR, BERNARD, composer; b. Arnhem, The Netherlands, July 18, 1894; s. Hendrikus Wijnandus and Charlotta Jacoba M. M. (van Rooijen) W.; ed. in private sch., The Netherlands; studied violin with Gerard Veerman, piano with Mme. Veerman-Bekker, composition with Dr. Johan Wagenaar; m. Irene Chadwick, Sept. 11, 1921; children—Theodore van Rooijen, Anneke (Mrs. Alexander Bacon Brook). Came to the United States, 1920, naturalized, 1927. Teacher and conductor, Holland, 1914-20; mem. of violin sec. New York Philharmonic Orchestra, 1921-23; teacher Inst. of Musical Art, 1925-37; teacher of fugue, orchestration and composition, Julliard Sch. Music, 1927-71. Compositions: (songs) Three Songs from the Chinese (voice, flute, harp, piano), 1921; From a Very Little Sphinx, 1921; (chamber music) Sonata for Piano, 1925; Sonata for Violin and Piano, 1926; Sonatina for Violoncello and Piano (Columbia recording) 1934; Second String Quartet, 1932; Third String Quartet, 1936; (orchestra) Sinfonietta for small orchestra, 1929; Violin Concerto, 1940; Three Symphonies: Triple Concerto for Flute, Harp, Cello and Orchestra; Divertimento for Orchestra, 1927; Fanfare for Airmen (for brass instruments); Concertino for 8 instruments; Feuilleton for orchestra; Fourth String Quartet (commissioned by the Kindler Foundation); Four Vignettes for harp; also various other compositions in manuscript. Awards: 1st place for Sonata for Violin and Piano by Soc. for Publ. of Am. Music, 1928. Sinfonietta was only Am. work chosen for festival of Internat. Soc. for Contemporary Music, Liege, Belgium, 1930; Triple Concerto, N.Y., 1941; Two Arrangements of Spanish Folk Songs, 1942; Chamber opera, commissioned by Alice M. Ditson Fund, Columbia U. Chamber opera, Pieces of Eight," 1944. Song of Mourning," (memoriam (for orchestra), for fallen Dutch patriots), 1944, Washington-New York radio, and others; Symphony, Number 4, 1949; Five Tableaux for Cello and Orch., 1952; Divertimento for Small Orch., 1952; Concert Overture for small orchestra, commd. by Louisville orchestra, 1952; Five Tableaux for cello and orchestra, 1955; Preamble for Orchestra, commendation by Juilliard Sch., Music, 1956; and several others; decorated Officer of Orange-Nassau (Netherlands). Works have been played by the leading orchestras both United States and foreign, including New York Philharmonic Orchestra, London Symphony, Detroit, National and Minneapolis Symphony orchestras, Chicago, Phila., Los Angeles, Cincinnati, St. Louis, Colorado Springs, C.B.S. symphony orchestras. Mem. Internat. Soc. Contemporary Music (mem. bd. dirs. Am. sect.), Am. Soc. Composers, Authors and Pubs., Composers Com. of League of Composers, Netherlands Soc. for Contemporary Music, Soc. for Netherlands History of Music. Home: 450 Riverside Dr. Address: care Juilliard School of Music, Home: New York City NY Died May 1971.

WAGENER, ANTHONY PELZER, coll. prof.; b. Charleston, S.C., May 27, 1887; s. Emil Aristide and Lillie Eva (Pelzer) W.; A.B., Coll. of Charleston, 1906; Ph.D., Johns Hopkins, 1910; grad. study Am. Sch. of Classical Studies, Rome, Italy, 1910-11; m. Frances Rebecca Keister, Aug. 16, 1916; children—Anthony Pelzer, Frances Keister. Instr. in Latin and Greek, Williams Coll., 1912-13; acting professor Latin and Greek, Coll. of Charleston, 1913-14; prof. of Latin, Roanoke Coll., 1914-19, prof. of Latin and Greek, 1919-26, also dir. of summer and extension courses, 1922-26; prof. of Latin, W.Va. U., 1926-28, prof. Latin and Greek, 1928-29; prof. ancient langs. and head of dept., Coll. of William and Mary, 1929-58, chancellor professor of ancient languages, 1955-58; John Hay Whitney Found. scholar, vis. prof. Austin Coll., Sherman, Tex., 1958-59; prof. of Latin, U. of Va., summers, 1926, 27, 29, Univ. of N.C., summer, 1935. Commissioned 2d lt. infantry, 1918; captain, Infantry Reserve, 1930-40. Mem. American Philological Assn., Archeol. Inst. America, Classical Assn. of Middle West and South (president, 1948 to 1949); chmn. com. on present status of classical edn., 1935-45), Scabbard and Blade, Am. Legion (past comdr. 3d Dist., Dept. of Va.), Pi Kappa Phi (past nat. pres.), Eta Sigma Phi, Omicron Delta Kappa, Phi Beta Kappa. Club: Cosmos (Washington). Democrat. Lutheran. Mason. Editor. Course of Study in Latin for High Schools of Virginia, 1945. Author: Latin and The Romans (with Thornton Jenkins), Book I, 1941, 1951, Book II, 1942, 1952; Learning Through Latin, 1944; The Heritage of European Literature (with Weatherly, Zeydel, and Yarmolinsky), 1948. Home: Williamsburg VA Died Jan. 31, 1972; buried Bethany Cemetery, Charleston SC

WAGENHEIM, MICHAEL BENJAMIN, lawyer; b. Norfolk, Va., Jan. 6, 1900; s. Herman and Sophie (Sheffield) W.; B.L., U. Va., 1922. Admitted to Va. bar, 1921, practiced in Norfolk, 1922-72. Mem. Norfolk Sch. Bd., 1931-46, chmn., 1943-46; mem. bd. Hampton Roads Sanitation Commn., 1947-54. Dir. Norfolk Community Fund, Child and Family Service (v.p. 1949-50), Travelers Aid Soc. (v.p. 1938-41), Goodwill Industries (v.p. 1936-37), Norfolk Community Concert Assn. (v.p. 1950-51), Norfolk Forum (charter mem., v.p. 1936-37), Boy Scouts Am. (awarded Silver Beaver 1940, v.p. 1948-49). Mem. bd. De Paul Hosp. Mem. commn. to revise charter of Norfolk. Recipient Arthur V. Briesen award Nat. Legal Aid and Defender Assn., 1967. Charter mem. Norfolk Jr. C. of C., pres., 1924-26, hon. life mem. Fellow Am. Bar Found.; mem. C. of C. (chmn. com. edn., 1953-54, dir. 1952-57), Am., Va. (chmn. exec. com. 1950-51, pres. 1954-55), Norfolk (pres. 1950-51) bar assns., Am. Judicature Soc., Gen. Alumni Assn. U. Va. (bd. mgrs. 1934-37, 43-46), U. Val. Law Sch. Assn. (exec. council 1953-70, pres. 1963-64), Am. Law Inst., Am. Soc. Internat. Law, Maritime Law Assn., Navy League (judge advocate Hampton council 1963-70), Raven Honorary Soc., Phi Beta Kappa, Phi Delta Phi (hon.), Omicron Delta Kappa (hon.), Zeta Beta Tau (supreme council 1926). Mason, Elk (hon. life mem., dist. dept. E. Va. 1933, pres. Va. assn. 1940-41), Lion. Clubs: Norfolk Boat, Hague; Lawyers (N.Y.C.); Harbor. Home: Norfolk VA Died Aug. 8, 1972.

WAGNER, JAMES ELVIN, clergyman; b. Savannah, Tenn., Oct. 6, 1873; s. William Mathias and Annie Josephine (Walker) W.; A.B., Parsons Coll., Veal's Station, Tex., 1893; A.B., Upper Ia. U., 1904, D.D., 1910; grad. study, Ill. Wesleyan U.; m. Mary Catherine Britt, Dec. 17, 1893; children—Alta Anne (Mrs. John Carmichael Clark), William Lowel, Eugene Palmer, Harry Hughes. Prin. pub. sch., Norman, Okla., 1893-94; pastor Cumberland Presbyn. Church, Henrietta, Tex., 1894-96; joined M.E. Ch., 1898; pastor various charges until 1908; pastor Enid, Okla., 1908-13, Mason City, Ia., 1913-17, Newton Center, Mass., 1917-21, Wesley M.E. Ch., Worcester, Mass., 1921-23, Omaha, Neb., 1923-26, Wheeling, W.Va., 1926-29, Mt. Lebanon Ch., Pittsburgh, Pa., 1929-33, First Church, Greensburg, Pa., 1933-37; St. Luke's Church, Long Branch, N.J., 1937-40, Baker Memorial Ch., Corcord, N.H., 1940-43; retired. Lecturer on evangelism, edn. and homiletics, in college and univs. for M.E. Board of Home Missions, 1919-22. Worked as carpenter, Fore River Ship Yard, building submarines, World War I; worked as custodian of records for U.S. Engrs. Redistribution center, Newton Upper Falls, Mass., through 1945. Republican.

Mason (K.T.). Clubs: Fort Henry (Wheeling); Kiwanis (Concord); Itinerant (Boston). Author: Rural Evangelism, 1921. Contbr. to Zion's Herald, Christian Advocate, Northwestern Christian Advocate. Home: 52 Westminster Rd., Newton Centre MA‡

WAGNER, JONATHAN HOWARD, educator; b. Columbia City, Ind., Jan. 7, 1873; s. Simon Peter and Angeline (Thomas) W.; A.B., Manchester Coll., 1895; grad. Ind. State Normal Sch., 1897; studied U. of Mich., U. of Chicago, U. of Wash.; m. Pearl Blickenstaff, Aug. 27, 1901; children—Frederick T., Robert H., Clyde L., Charles B., Martha A. Admitted to bar, Auburn, Ind., 1902; cashier Savings & Loan Trust Co., Auburn, 5 yrs.; high sch. prin., Ind., 8 yrs.; supt. schs., Las Cruces, N.M., 2 yrs., Santa Fe, 5 yrs.; state supt. pub. instrn., N.M., 1917-21; supt. city schs., Pueblo, Colo., 1921; pres. N.M. Normal U., 1922-23; chief, Alaska div., U.S. Office of Edn., 1923-30; prin. John Hay Sch. and in charge Children's Orthopedic Hosp. Sch. and Convalescent Home Sch., Seattle, 1930-1940; also dir. Pacific School of Research and Genealogy. State dir. U.S. Pub. Service Res. and Boys' Workers Res., N.M., World War I; Investigator for U.S. Army, 1941-47. Regional director White House Conference and Child Health and Protection. Former pres. and sec. N.M. Ednl. Assn.; pres. Seattle Principals' Assn., 1941-42. Mem. Nat. Council Edn., N.E.A., Am. Sch. Archeology, Knights of the Round Table. Republican. Mem. United Brethren in Christ. Mason (32 deg.). Author of a study entitled The Amount of Time Expected by the Teachers and the Amount of Time Actually Given to Their Studies by Pupils in the High Schools"; A Course of Study for United States Schools for Natives of Alaska; also numerous articles for magazines and papers on the natives of Alaska. Awarded Hudson's Bay Co. medal for services in rescuing crew of twenty-three from ship, Lady Kindersley, crushed in ice of Western Arctic, Aug. 31, 1924. Home: 6825 12th Av., N.E., Seattle WA‡

WAGNER, OSCAR, pianist; b. Corydon, Ia., Oct. 8, 1893; s. Joseph Benjamin and Mary Elizabeth (Goudy) W.; grad. Cosmopolitan Sch. of Music, Chicago, Ill., 1917; later studied with Ernest Hutcheson, New York; Dr. of Music, Muskingum Coll., New Concord, O., 1943; Dr. of Music, Philadelphia Conservatory, 1945; unmarried. Concert tours through U.S., Can., Hawaii, Australia; mem. faculty, Cosmopolitan Sch. of Music, Chicago, 1917-19; mem. faculty Eureka Coll., 1918-24, dir., 1922-24; mem. faculty, Juilliard Sch. Music, New York, 1925-46, asst. dean, 1928-37, in charge Inst. of Musical Art of same, 1934-37; dean Juillard School of Music, 1937-39; dean, Juilliard Grad. Sch., 1939-46; member faculty Los Angeles Conservatory of Music and Arts, 1946-54; member of faculty Univ. Utah, Salt Lake City, 1954-65; pres. Soc. Publ. Am. Music, 1940-46. Mem. Lambda Chi Alpha. Clubs: Bohemians, Century, Sinfonia New York. Home: Salt Lake City UT Died 1971.

WAGSTAFF, HENRY MCGILBERT, prof. history; b. Roxboro, N.C., Jan. 27, 1876; s. Clement McGilbert and Sara Elizabeth (Paylor) W.; Ph.B., U. of N.C., 1899; Ph.D., Johns Hopkins, 1906; m. Mary Jefferson Stephens of Roxboro, N.C., June 28, 1907; children—Mary Frances, Henry McGilbert. Prof. mathematics, Rutherford (N.C.) Coll., 1900-02; actg. prof. history and economics, Allegheny Coll., Meadville, Pa., 1906-07; asso. prof. history, 1907-09, prof. since 1909, U. of N.C. Mem. Am. Assn. Univ. Profs., N.C. Hist. Soc., Phi Beta Kappa. Methodist. Odd Fellow. Author: State Rights and Political Parties in North Carolina, 1776-1861, 1906; The Harrington Letters, 1914; The Harris Letters, 1916; The John Steele Papers; Publs. N.C. Hist. Commn. (2 vols.), 1924. Editor: The James Sprunt Historical Publications (N.C. Hist. Soc.). Home: Chapel Hill NC‡

WAHRHAFTIG, FELIX SOLOMON, lawyer, b. Sacramento, Oct. 14, 1909; s. M. S. and Irma R. (Levy) W.; A.B., U. Cal. at Berkeley, 1930, LL.B., 1933. Admitted to Cal. bar, 1933; legal staff Cal. Bd. Equalization, Sacramento, 1933-52, cons. tax counsel, 1942-52; pvt. practice of law, specializing taxation, 1952-69; mem. McDonough Holland, Schwartz, Allen & Wahrhaftig, spl. cons. atty. gen., Cal., 1953-62. Cons. expert Treasury Dept., Washington, 1942-44; cons. Cal. Legislature Com. on Revenue and Taxation, 1959-66, dept. finance State of Cal., 1959-66. Home: Sacramento CA Died Feb. 18, 1969.

WAILES, EDWARD THOMPSON, ex-ambassador; b. in Brooklyn, N.Y., Feb. 16, 1903; son of Montgomery Blair and Johanna (Thompson) W.; grad. Lawrenceville Sch., 1921; B.S., Princeton, 1925; m. Cornelia Lyon Wailes, Dec. 30, 1933. Vice counsul, Shanghai, China, 1930, Nanking, 1931-33; assigned State Dept., Far Eastern Div., 1933-34; in sec. of state's office, 1935-36; 2d sec. of embassy, Brussels, Belgium, 1937-39, Ottawa, Can., Mar.-July 1939; assigned Dept. of State, European Div., 1939-42; sec. of embassy, Algiers, Algeria, 1943-44; asst. polit. adviser to supreme comdr. A.E.F., London, Eng., 1944; sec. of embassy, The Hague, The Netherlands, Dec. 1944-Feb. 1945; chief, division of British Commonwealth Affairs, Dept. of State, 1945; fgn. service inspector, 1948-52, chief inspector, 1952; Asst. Sec. of State for Adminstrn., 1953-54; ambassador to Union of S. Africa, 1954; minister to Hungary, 1956-57; dep. commandant Nat. War Coll., 1957-58; ambassador to Iran, 1958-61; ambassador to Czechoslovakia, 1961-62. Trustee of Sweet Briar College. Clubs: Chevy Chase, Metropolitan (Washington); Quadrangle (Princeton). Home: Washington DC Died June 25, 1969; buried Rock Creek Cemetery, Washington DC

WAILES, GEORGE HANDY, clergyman, educator; b. Salisbury, Md., Aug. 22, 1866; s. Ebenezer Leonard and Annie (Todd) W.; A.B., magna cum laude, Princeton, 1894, A.M., 1896; grad. Princeton Theol. Sem., 1897; D.D., Ursinus Coll., 1913; m. Lucretia Mott Franklin, Oct. 8, 1902 (died Aug. 8, 1918). Ordained Presbyn. ministry, 1897; pastor Scots Ch., Phila., 1897-1908; Prof. English Bible and Greek lang., Ursinus Coll., 1908-19; prof. exegetical theology, Reformed Episcopal Theol. Sem., since 1919; prof. biblical langs. and English Bible, Temple U., 1926-49; visiting prof. of Hebrew, Princeton Theol. Sem., 1928-37. Mem. Phi Beta Kappa. Home: 517 S. 48th St., Philadelphia PA‡

WAINDLE, ROGER F(RANCIS), engr.; b. Madison, Wis., May 6, 1909; s. Francis J. and Mary (Riordan) W.; B.S. in mech. engring., Ill. Inst. Tech., 1932; m. Helen Irene Keane, June 15, 1940; children—Mary Kathryn, Roger John, Frank K. Successively marine engr., sales engr., sales mgr., chief engr., ordnance engr;, mgr., gen. mgr. Cannon-Muskegon (Mich.) Corp., v.p., gen. mgr., dir., 1951-63; general mgr. indsl. products div. Elgin Nat. Watch Co. since 1944; gen. mgr. Alloy Casting Co., Champaign, Ill., 1944-63; pres. Wai Met Engineering Co., 1953-63; chmn. bd., pres. Ziebart Process Co., 1963-73; vice pres., dir. Blake-Waindle Corp., West Newton, Mass.; research dir. Nugent Sand Co.; dir. Standard Sand Co. Chief tank-automotive prodn. War Dept., Chgo. Ordnance Dist., A.S.F., 1942-44; adv. non-metallic minerals Munitions Bd. Registered profl. engr., Mich., Ill. Mem. Am. Soc. Tool Engrs. (nat. dir., v.p.), Am. Ordnance Assn. (dir., past chmn. instrument bearings nat. com., member nat. coms. gage industry), Indsl. Diamond Assn. Am. (past nat. chmn. diamond abrasives), Am. Soc. for Metals, Engring. Soc. Det., Newcomen Soc. Am., Triangle, Tau Beta Pi, Pi Tau Sigma. Clubs: Columbia Yacht (Chgo.); Muskegon (Mich.) Country. Author articles tech. jours. Home: Chicago IL Died Apr. 15, 1973.

WAITE, HARVEY RICE, insurance exec.; b. Jefferson County, N.Y., May 30, 1876; s. Harlow Benjamin and Nettie (Oatman) W.; ed. Watertown (N.Y.) High Sch.; m. Lillian Herrick, 1898 (died 1909); 1 son, Harlow Oatman; m. 2d, Irene M. Allen, 1928. Asso. with Agrl. Ins. Co. (fire ins.) since July 5, 1894, beginning as office boy, cashier, 1915-20, treas., 1920-24, sec. and treas., 1924-28, pres. since 1928; pres. Empire State Insurance Co.; chmn. bd., 1945-47, hon. chmn. since 1947; trustee Watertown Savings Bank; pres. Watertown Foundn. Republican. Conglist. Mason (Shriner). Clubs: Black River Valley, Jefferson County Golf (Watertown). Home: 324 Winslow St. Office: 215 Washington St., Watertown NY‡

WAITT, ERNEST LINDEN, author; b. Lynn, Mass., June 29, 1872; s. Charles Hood and Laura Anna (Ward) W.; descendant of Revolutionary patriots on both sides; ed. pub. schs.; studied law and dramatic history, technique and construction, under tutors; m. Marian M. P. Webber, of Lynn, Apr. 17, 1892. Began newspaper work on Lynn Bee, 1886; assisted in establishing the Brockton Times; spl. writer on Associated Press, 7 yrs.; news editor Boston Herald, 1901; published Grand Army Record, 1901, 02, 03; dramatic critic and feature writer Boston American, 1905-8; editor Boston Courier, 1909-10; sec. Fitchburg (Mass.) Bd. of Trade, 1911-13; literary editor, Boston Journal, 1914; pub. Boston Courier since Sept. 1, 1914. Compiled History of 19th Massachusetts Vols., 1861-5; lecturer on newspaper and dramatic subjects. Republican. Universalist. Author: (plays) The Puppet, 1908; In the Enemy's House; The German Politician, 1909; (vaudeville sketches) Publicity; Fireworks; The Wrong House; A Dressing Room Romance, etc. Home: Somerville MA Office: 31 Milk St., Boston MA‡

WAKEFIELD, EVA INGERSOLL, author; b. Dobbs, Ferry, N.Y., Aug. 27, 1891; d. Walston Hill and Eva Robert (Ingersoll) Brown; student Masters Sch., 1910-13; extension student New Sch. Social Research, Columbia, 1926-31; m. Sherman Day Wakefield, July 8, 1932. Radio chmn. Manhattan br. Women's Internat. League for Peace and Freedom, 1933-38; mem. Citizen's Com. on Hoover Report, 1947-49; exec. sec. Robert G. Ingersoll Meml. Assn., 1946-55. Editor: The Letters of Robert G. Ingersoll, 1951. Contbr. articles, poetry, essays to newspapers, mags. Mem. Nat. Soc. Colonial Dames in State of N.Y., United World Federalists, Assn. on Am. Indian Affairs, Euthanasia Soc. Am., Vivisection Investigation League, Am. Civil Liberties Union, Am. Humanist Assn. (mem. ch.-state com. 1961-63, pres. N.Y. chpt. 1956-57), Ams. for Pub. Schs. (bd. dirs. 1965-67). Home: New York City NY Died Apr. 1, 1970.

WAKEFIELD, PAUL M., county ofcl.; b. nr. St. Joh Mich., Mar. 31, 1905; s. Elmer and Katherine (Dy W.; grad. high sch.; m. Cressie Matthews, June 16, 19 children—Dean M., David L. With Office of Clint County Clk., St. Johns, Mich., 1931-67, county c 1945-67. Mem. Mich. Assn. County Clks. (past pres Republican. Methodist. Home: St Johns MI Died D 26, 1967.

WAKEFIELD, RALPH, clergyman; b. Pittsburgh, P July 14, 1876; s. William Henry Harrison and Ma Jane (Edgar) W.; A.B., Baker U., Baldwin, Kan., 18 A.M., 1899; B.D., Drew Theol. Sem., 1902; gr student Columbia, 1901-02; m. Mary Catherine Bla Oct. 12, 1903; children—William Edgar, Mary Lou (wife of Rev. Harry C. Spencer). Ordained to minis of Meth. Ch., 1902; successively pastor Wago Memorial Ch., St. Louis, Trinity Ch., St. Louis, Clint Mo., Litchfield, Ill., First Ch., East St. Louis, First C Galesburg, Ill., First Ch., Aurora, Ill., First Ch. Englewood, Chicago, First Ch. of Irving Park, n pastor River Forest, Ill. Mem. exec. com. Anti-Saloon League; president Chicago Church Fed 1939-41. Club: Loch Vista (Geneva Lake, Wis.). Mas (K.T.). Home: 187 Conference Point Rd., Williams B WI‡

WAKEFIELD, SHERMAN DAY, editor, a bibliographer, writer; b. Bloomington, Ill., July 12, 18 s. Homer and Julia Pearson (Sherman) W.; gra Suffield Acad., Suffield, Conn., 1915, Meadville The Sch., Chicago, 1923; Ph.B., U. of Chicago, 192 post-grad. student Pacific Unitarian Sch. for t Ministry, Berkeley, 1925; B.S., Sch. of Library Ser Columbia U., 1928; hon. Litt.D., De Landas U., L Angeles, 1940; m. Eva Ingersoll (Brown) Swasey, Ju 8, 1932. Research asst. to minister, West Side Unitari Ch., New York, 1925-26; asst. New York Pub. Librar 1928-29; bibliographer Encyclopaedia of the Soc Sciences, New York, 1929-34; geneal., researcher a writer Am. Hist. Co., New York, 1937-39; asso. edit The Arbitrator, New York, 1939-43; genealogist f Wakefield family. Editor Research Inst. America, Ne York, 1941-42; indexer, Encyclopedia America 1942-43; staff editor and bibliographer, The Groli Encyclopedia, 1943-47; Collier's Encyclopedi 1947-49, World Wide Ency., 1949-50, Home Universi Ency., 1950-51, 55-63, New Human Interest Librar 1955-63. Served from pvt. to sgt. U.S. Engrs., 1918-1 Sec. Lincoln Fellowship of N.Y., 1936-40; mem. ad bd. First Humanist Soc. N.Y. Mem. A.A.A.S., Il McLean Co. hist. socs., Am. Humanist Assn. (memb church and State Committee 1955-63), Rationali Press Association (London), American Civil Liberti Union. Author: How Lincoln Became President, 193 Abraham Lincoln and the Widow Bixby, 194 Abraham Lincoln and the Bixby Letter, 1948, revis edit., 1955; Theodore Roosevelt and Robert Ingersoll As Revealed in Their Letters, 1969. Editori asst., The Humanist, 1944-55, consulting a contributing editor, 1955-59; co-editor Progressi World, 1948-51, cons. editor, 1951-71; contbr. to mag Home: New York City NY Died May 22, 1971.

WAKEHURST, LORD (JOHN DEVERE LODER b. London, Eng., Feb. 5, 1895; s. Gerald and La Louise DeVere (Beauclerk) L.; student Eton Col 1908-14; LL.D. (honorary), Queen's Univ., Belfa 1957; m. Margaret Tennant, June 3, 192 children—Henrietta (Mrs. John Reader-Harris Christopher, David, Robert. Fgn. service, 1919-2 mem. Parliament (Conservative) for East Leicest 1924-29, and for Lewes, Sussex, 1931-36; gov. Ne South Wales, Australia, 1937-46; gov. No. Irelan 1952-64. Bd. govs. Royal Ballet. Me English-Speaking Union (chmn. 1946-51). Served a capt. Royal Sussex Regt. and Intelligence Corps, Roy Army. Lord Prior of the Order of St. John of Jerusale since 1947; created Knight Order of Garter, 196 Home: London England Died Nov. 1970.

WAKELAND, CHARLES RICHARD, pres. Clinto Female Coll.; b. Carroll Co., Ind., Nov. 4, 1870; s. C. and Rebecca W.; grad. Northern Ind. Normal Schoo 1893; sp'l courses in pedagogy, State Normal Univ Normal, Ill.; m., 1895, Annette, d. S. H. Graves, Vil Ridge, Ill. Prin. Lostant Pub. schs., 1898-1900; pre Pike Coll., Mo., 1900; thence to present position. Wrot and published several articles on science in the grade 1897-1900; Republican. Address: Clinton MO‡

WAKELEY, THOMPSON MORRIS, investme exec.; b. St. Louis, Aug. 18, 1897; s. Lucius Wincheste and Helen Louise (Weeks) W.; A.B., Cornell U., 192 m. Natalie Noyes Nickerson, July 6, 1929; 1 dau Natalie Allyn. With A. C. Allyn & Co., Chgo., 1927— now partner; v.p. Nat. Shareholders Corp., 1926-3 Pres. bd. trustees Village of Kenilworth, 1949-5 Served as quartermaster 1st class, USN, 1918-1 Member of the Sons of Am. Revolution, Phi Be Kappa, Alpha Delta Phi. Republican. Conglist. Club Midday, Bondmen's, Cornell, Bond Traders, Uni (Chgo.); Indian Hill Country (Winnetka, Ill.) Kenilworth. Home: Winnetka IL Died March 1972.

WAKEMAN, SETH, med. cons., b. Batavia, N.Y., Ma 18, 1893; s. Wm. Sprague and Jennie (DeBow) W.; A.B

Hobart Coll., 1916, A.M., 1917; Ph.D., Cornell, 1922; m. Marion Delamater Freeman, May 29, 1926, 1 son, Seth Freeman; m. 2d, Mary Perley Storer, Nov. 18, 1961. Instr. edn. Cornell, 1919-22, asst. prof., 1922-25; prof. education Smith Coll., Northampton, Mass., 1925-57, dir. exptl. schs., 1945-46; asso. Robert Boggs, Assos., cons. med. affairs, 1956-61; in charge medicine and med. edn. Samuel H. Kress Found., N.Y.C., 1949-51. Asst. adminstr. Services to Armed Forces A.R.C., 1943-45, cons., 1946-47. Bd. trustees Martha's Vineyard Hosp.; bd. dirs. Martha's Vineyard Community Services, Edgartown Boys Club; chmn. Martha's Vineyard chpt. A.R.C. Served with psychology div., U.S. Army, 1918-19, A.R.C., 1919. Fellow A.A.A.S.; mem. Phi Delta Kappa, Phi Kappa Phi. Clubs: Edgartown Yacht, Edgartown Golf, Reading Room (Edgartown). Contbr. sci. jours. Home: Martha's Vineyard MA Died Feb. 8, 1968; buried Chilmark MA

WALBRIDGE, NELSON LEE, educator; b. Montpelier, Vt., June 27, 1902; s. Karl Howe and Lena (Colby) W.; B.S. in Chemistry, U. Vt., 1924, M.S. in Physics, 1926; Ph.D. in Physics, U. Chgo., 1941; m. Ethel V. Nealy, Aug. 25, 1927; children—Karl Deane, Eric Lee. Faculty U. Vt., 1924-73, prof. physics, 1948-73, chmn. dept., 1952-61, regional dir., 1961-64. Dir. summer physics Insts. Nat. Sci. Found., 1958, 60-68. Home: Cambridge VT Died Jan. 19, 1973.

WALDEN, WALTER, author; b. Milan, Ill., June 1, 1870; s. Lars P. Bergstrom and Dorothea Amelia (Axelson) W.; student Augustana Coll., Rock Island, Ill., 1888-90, Northwestern U., 1890-1892; M.D., Northwestern U. Med. Sch., 1896; m. Henri Albertine Wilhelm, of Chicago, Dec. 3, 1902; children—Viola, Walford. Began practice at Chicago, 1896. Commd. capt. M.C., U.S.A., Jan. 7, 1918; apptd. comdg. officer med. detachment 1st Div., Field Arty., Oct. 15, 1919; hon. discharged Sept. 14, 1920; passed asst. surgeon, U.S.P.H.S. Reserve, Nov. 1920; capt. O.R.C., U.S.A., Feb. 1921; hon. discharged U.S.P.H.S., Aug. 17, 1923; maj. Auxiliary Res. since June 1, 1934. Mem. Soc. Midland Authors, Am. Legion. Episcopalian. Author: Boy Scouts Afloat, 1918; The Hidden Islands, 1920; The Voodoo Gold Trail, 1922. Contbr. serials and short stories to Boy's Life Mag., Boy Scouts' Year Book, etc. Home: Campbell's Island, P.O. East Moline IL‡

WALDO, FULLERTON LEONARD, editor; b. Cambridge, Mass., Apr. 5, 1877; s. Leonard and Dora (Fullerton) W.; A.B., Harvard, 1888; Litt.D., Ursinus, 1920; unmarried. Teacher, chiefly at Pomfret (Conn.) Sch., 1898-1907; was mem. editorial staff Public Ledger, Phila. War corr. in Balkans, 1915, on British front, 1917, American front, 1918; Am. corr. London Observer, 1917-18; commr. Near East Relief, Southern Russia and Asia Minor, 1920. Decorated Order Cross of Mercy and Officer Order of St. Sava (Serbian). Fellow Royal Geog. Soc.; mem. Soc. Mayflower Descendants, Shakespeare Soc., Phi Beta Kappa, Delta Upsilon; hon. corr.-sec. English-Speaking Union. Republican. Presbyn. Clubs: Harvard, Franklin Inn. Author: Good Housing That Pays, 1917; America at the Front, 1918; With Grenfell on the Labrador, 1920; The Seashell (play), 1921; Down the Mackenzie, 1923; Philadelphia Music Pageant, 1924; Grenfell, Knight Errant, 1924; Rex, 1925; The Saga of a Super-Cargo, 1926; Early Italian and French Opera, 1927; German and Russian Opera, 1927; Modern French and Italian Opera, 1927.*‡

WALDO, LILLIAN MCLEAN, author; b. Rochester, N.Y., July 16, 1873; d. Alexander E. and Emma A. (Crouch) McLean; grad. Normal Sch., Rochester, 1892; univ. extension work 3 yrs.; m. Charles S. Waldo, of New York, Aug. 16, 1905. Teacher pub. schs. and supervising critic, Normal Sch., Rochester, 1892-1906; instr. psychology and pedagogy, Chautauqua, N.Y., summers 1904-07. Presbyn. Author: Around the World, Book V. (with Clarence F. Carroll); First Journeys in Numberland, 1911; Toy Shop Book (with Ada Van Stone Harris), 1915; Little Folks in Busy Land, 1916; Arithmetic Games for Primary Grades, 1917; Safety First for Little Folks, 1918; Civic Reader, 1933. Collaborated in preparing Stories of Luther Burbank and His Plant School, 1920. Contbr. to mags. Address: 32-32 159th St., Flushing LI NY‡

WALDRIP, MARION NELSON, clergyman; b. Caulksville, Ark., Nov. 23, 1873; s. Samuel Monroe and Martha Jane (Walters) W.; ed. Old Field Sch. and Elm Springs Acad., Ark.; Vanderbilt Univ., 1904; D.D., Henderson-Brown Coll., Ark.; m. Nancy Caroline Herron, Apr. 30, 1895; children—Paul Bascom (dec. World War), Sergeant Marion Fitzhugh, Seaman Lovick Pierce, Martha, Gladstone (U.S. Army Signal Corps), Mary Susan. Ordained ministry Methodist Episcopal Church, South, 1893; pastor Dyer Circuit, Arkansas, 1896-97, Huntington and Jenny Lind, 1896-97, Huntington, 1897-1901, Bentonville, 1900-03, Fort Smith, 1904-08, Morrillton, 1908-10, Fayetteville, 1910-14, Pine Bluff, 1915-16, Hot Springs, 1916-19, McKendree Ch., Nashville, Tenn., 1919-22, Central Ch., Kansas City, Mo., 1922-27, Missouri Meth. Ch. of Mo. Meth. Foundation at U. of Mo., Columbia, 1927-30, Lafayette Park Ch., St. Louis, 1930-31, Centenary Ch., Cape Girardeau, Mo., 1931-33, First Ch., South, Lexington, Ky., 1933-35, First Ch., Covington, Ky., 1935-37, Court Street Ch., Fulton, Mo., 1937-38, Marvin-McMurry Meth. Ch., Saint Joseph, Mo., 1938-40, Troost Av. Ch., Kansas City, Mo., 1940-47, Institutional Meth. Ch., Kansas City, since 1947. Mem. Free Art League America. Mason (K.T.). Orator for universities and colls., lyceum lecturer, after-dinner speaker. Home: 3638 Flora Av. Office: 702 Admiral Blvd., Kansas City MO‡

WALDRON, JOHN J., business exec.; b. New Bedford, Mass.; m. Janet Waldron; 1 son, 2 daus. Formerly pres. Ruppert Knickerbocker Brewery, P. Ballantine & Sons; pres. Robbin-Dale Uniform Co., Balt., 1970-71. Past pres. Boston Celtics basketball club. Died July 1971.

WALES, JAMES ALBERT, advertising; b. New York, N.Y., Oct. 6, 1879; s. James Albert and Claudia Marshall (Cooper) W.; A.B., Trinity Coll., Hartford, Conn., 1901; m. Ethel Holbrook Beach, Sept. 30, 1909 (now dec.); children—James Albert, Richard Beach, Nancy H. (Swaffield); married 2d Greta Marketa Zukar, June 9, 1951. Advertising writer with Charles Austin Bates, New York, 1902-03; partner Morris & Wales, Phila., 1903-08, Bartlett-Wales Co., New York, 1908-12; pres. and treas. Wales Advertising Co., Inc., 1912-42; dir. travel publicity Charles W. Hoyt Co., Inc., advertising, New York City, 1951-65. Mem. bd. trustees Trinity Coll., Hartford, Conn., 1932-35; senior fellow, 1917-32. Mem. S.R., Phi Beta Kappa, Alpha Chi Rho (nat. president, 1920-21). Episcopalian. Mason. Clubs: University, Church (N.Y. City); Housatonic Boat Stratford, Conn. (commodore 1924-34). Author: Residence in Bermuda, 1936; The Tourist Dollar, 1938; The Story of Alpha Chi Rho, 1963. Contbr. articles on travel, sports, humor, and advt. to periodicals. Home: New York City NY Died Jan. 12, 1970.

WALET, EUGENE HENRY, JR., lawyer; b. New Orleans, Sept. 24, 1901; s. Eugene Henry and Mary (Gauche) W.; A.B., Springhill Coll., 1922; student Georgetown U., 1923-24; LL.B., Loyola U., New Orleans, 1927; m. Celia Redman, Feb. 19, 1944; 1 son, Eugene Henry III. Admitted to La. bar, 1927, practiced in New Orleans, 1927-45; spl. asst. atty. gen. La., 1933; counsel Jefferson Lake Sulphur Co., Inc., New Orleans, 1936, v.p., 1936-46, pres., 1946-68, also dir.; chmn. bd. chief exec. officer, dir. Jefferson Lake Petra chem. of Can. Ltd.; exec. v.p., dir. Occidental Petroleum Corp.; dir. Sulphur Export Corp. Member Am., La. bar assns., Am. Law Inst., New Orleans Assn. Commerce, Phi Alpha Delta. Clubs: The Houston, Petroleum, Cork (Houston); Metairie Country, Southern Yacht, International House, New Orleans Athletic, Petroleum New Orleans LA Died Apr. 2, 1968.

WALK, CHARLES EDMONDS, author; b. Memphis, Tenn., Mar. 18, 1875; s. Rev. David and Joanna Marshall (Blinn) W.; ed. high schs., under pvt. tutors and at U. of Pacific; m. May Hamilton, of Kokomo, Ind., May 3, 1893. News editor Daily Tribune, Kokomo, since 1920. Democrat. Mem. Christian (Disciples) Ch. Elk. Club: Kiwanis. Author: The Silver Blade, 1908; The Yellow Circle, 1909; The Paternoster Ruby, 1910; The Time Lock, 1912; The Green Seal, 1914; The Crimson Cross (with Millard Lynch), 1913; also numerous short stories in mags. Home: Galveston IN Address: Daily Tribune, Kokomo IN‡

WALKER, ALICE JOHNSTONE, author; b. New Haven, Conn., Aug. 13, 1871; d. James and Martha Hall (Johnstone) Walker; ed. Miss Johnstone's Sch. for Girls (New Haven), history and art, at Yale, Alliance Francaise Summer Sch. (Paris, France), Summer Sch. of Langs. (Amherst, Mass.). Teacher history, French and elementary studies, Miss Johnstone's Sch., 1890-1918; associated with sister, Edith C., 1918-35, as one of principals of the Misses Walkers' School, New Haven. Conglist. Author: Little Plays-from American History for Young Folks, 1914; La Fayette, Columbus, The Long Knives (brief plays), 1919; Dolly Peckham's Clothes Line (play), 1928; Mary Muldoon's Morning (play), 1929; Abe's First Fish (play), 1929; The Sanctuary Knocker (play), 1930; Caesar Rodney's Ride (pageant), 1930; The Thursday (play), 1931; Episodes from Colonial Connecticut—Tercentenary Commission of the State of Connecticut (with Elisabeth Woodridge Morris), 1935. Home: 162 Bishop St., New Haven CT‡

WALKER, ANNIE KENDRICK, editor of woman's dept., Birmingham Age-Herald, since 1898; b. Bullock Co., Ala., Nov. 19, 1876; d. John A. W.; ed. private tutors; grad. L. Crozier French's School for Girls, Knoxville, Tenn. Contributor of many sp'l articles to leading Am. journals. Residence: South Highlands. Office: Age-Herald, Birmingham AL‡

WALKER, CHARLES BERTRAM, artist, educator; b. Warren, N.Y., Oct. 18, 1875; s. Charles Wm. and Rachel (Hotaling) W.; student Richfield Spa. Union Free School and Acad., 1890-94; B.P., Syracuse Univ., 1899; student Academie Julian, Acad. Colarossi, Paris, France, 1900-09; m. Ruth W. Weller, June 10, 1910; children—Ann Elizabeth (Mrs. Charles Hartwell Maltby). Mem. faculty, coll. fine arts, Syracuse Univ., 1900-46, instr., 1910-20, asso. prof., 1920-45, full prof. painting, 1946, dir. sch. of art, 1930-46; ret. 1946; Rep. permanent collections: Oswego County Court House (mural), Syracuse Mus. Fine Arts, numerous pvt. collections. Exhibitor: Paris Salon, Pa. Acad. Fine Arts, Buffalo Acad. Fine Arts, Springfield Art League, High Mus. Fine Arts, Atlanta, Rochester, N.Y. Awarded Hiram Gee fellowship for fgn. study, Syracuse Univ., 1900. Recipient Silver medal, work in art edn., Sesquicentennial Exposition, Phila., 1926; first prize oils, Assn. Artists of Syracuse, 1936. Mem. Paris-Am. Art Assn., Associated Artists of Syracuse, Iroquois Art Assn.; (hon.) Phi Kappa Phi, Alpha Delta Sigma, Tau Sigma Delta, Phi Syracuse 10 NY‡

WALKER, CHARLES CLEMENT, engr.; b. Highgate, London, Eng., Aug. 25, 1877; s. William Thomas and Claudia Ann (Smith) W.; student London U. Coll., 1892-95; m. Eileen Kenneth Hood, Sept. 2, 1916. Apprenticeship John Abbot & Co., Newcastle-on-Tyne, 1895-98; articled to J. J. Taylor, 1899-1904; various civil engring. positions rys., water supply, drainage, 1915; chief technician Aircraft Mfg. Co., 1915-20; chief engr., dir. De Havilland Aircraft Co., Ltd. since 1920. Asso. mem. Inst. C.E. Home: Foresters, Stanmore Common, Middlesex. Office: Hatfield Aerodrome, Hatfield Hertfordshire England‡

WALKER, CHARLES WELLINGTON, architect; b. Strang, Neb., June 30, 1889; s. Charles Wellington and Elmira Jane (Campbell) W.; student U. Pa., 1910-11; m. Louise Porter, June 18, 1912; children—Florence (Mrs. John R. Turner), Charles Wellington. Fellow A.I.A.; mem. Nat. Acad. Design, Archtl. League N.Y. Mason. Rotarian. Home: Stratford CT Died Mar. 12, 1967.

WALKER, FRED LIVINGOOD, army officer; b. Fairfield County, O., June 11, 1887; s. William Henry and Belle (Mason) W.; E.M., Ohio State U., 1911; grad. Infantry Sch., 1923, hon. grad. Command and Gen. Staff Sch., 1927; grad. Army War Coll., 1933; m. Frances M. Messmore, Aug. 19, 1911; children—Mary Elizabeth (dec.), Fred Livingood, Charles. Commd. 2d lt. Inf., 1911; promoted through grades to major gen., Jan. 1942; Comdt. The Inf. Sch., July 1944-45; retired from active service Apr. 30, 1946. Served in P.I., Mexico, China and with A.E.F. in France, Italy and Germany; instr. Army War Coll., 1933-37. Decorated D.S.C. with oak leaf cluster, D.S.M., Purple Heart with oak leaf cluster. Author: From Texas to Rome, 1969. Home: Charleston OH Died Oct. 1969.

WALKER, GEORGE HENRY, army officer; b. Muskogee, Okla., Apr. 2, 1914; s. George H. and Estelle (McRae) W.; B.S., U.S. Mil. Acad., 1937; M.S. in Civil Engring., U. Cal. at Berkeley, 1941; grad. Army War Coll., 1955; grad. Advanced Mgmt. Program, Harvard, 1961; m. Jo Dorsey Ballantine, Apr. 9, 1938; children—Joan VanNess (Mrs. Thomas H. O'Connor), George Henry III. Commd. 2d lt. U.S. Army, 1937, advanced through grades to maj. gen., 1964; served in PTO, also comdr. 1103d Engr. Combat Group, ETO, World War II; staff and command assignments Dept. Army, also U.S. Army Europe, 1945-52; dist. engr. U.S. Army, Engrs., San Francisco, 1952-54; corps engr. I U.S. Army Corps, Korea, 1957-58; asst. comdr. Army Engr. Sch., 1961-63; div. engr. Mo. River div. U.S. Army Engrs., 1963-65, S. Atlantic div., 1965-69. Mem. Miss. River Commn., Bd. Engrs. for Rivers and Harbors, Coastal Engring. Research Bd. Decorated Legion of Merit, Bronze Star for valor with oak leaf cluster; Croix de Guerre (France). Registered profl. engr., Neb. Mem. Soc. Am. Mil. Engrs. Home: Atlanta GA Died Sept. 1969.

WALKER, GUY MORRISON, lawyer, financial expert; b. Ft. Wayne, Ind., Jan. 24, 1870; s. Rev. Wilbur F. and Mary Florence (Morrison) W.; A.B., DePauw, U., 1890, LL.B., 1891, A.M., 1893; m. Minnie L. Royse, of Terre Haute, Ind., Dec. 15, 1891; children—Merle R., Ray M. Admitted to Ind. bar, 1891, and since in N.Y., Mich., Calif., Tenn., Ark.; resided in China 10 yrs.; expert on Chinese matters; edited all matter relating to China in Leslie's Weekly during the period following the Boxer outbreaks, and was called in consultation by President McKinley during the complications between the powers in the Chinese Empire; was offered commn. in U.S.A. for service in China, on Gen. Chaffee's staff, but declined. Organized Terre Haute Trust Co., 1894, Security Trust Co., of Toledo, O., 1898; located in New York, 1898. Expert on reorganization; spl. counsel for Everett-Moore ry. syndicate, 1901; reorganized Detroit & Toledo Shore Line Ry. Co., Columbus, Delaware & Marion Ry. Co., Pittsburgh Ry. & Light Co., etc.; chmn. Knickerbocker Trust Co. reorgn. com., 1907; reorganized U.S. Light & Heating Company, 1915. Founded, 1909, and endowed the Horizon" lecturers at DePauw U. Author: Measure of Civilization; Railroad Rates and Rebates; The Things That Are Caesar's; A Defense of Wealth, 1919; Can We Escape War With Japan? also many articles in financial and transportation jours., and of pamphlets on financial and econ. questions, Chinese matters, etc. Unofficial adviser to the Chinese delegation at the Conf. on Limitation of Armanents, Washington, 1921. Home: 924 West Edn Av. Office: 370 Lexington Av., New York NY‡

WALKER, HARRY, physician; b. LaCrosse, Va., Dec. 10, 1900; s. Benjamin Watkins Leigh and Ina Elizabeth (Puryear) W.; student Randolph-Macon Coll., 1921-22, LL.D., 1960; M.D., Med. Coll. Va., 1926; m. Pamelia Anne Gary, Dec. 8, 1928; children—Harry, Anne Gary. Interne, Med. Coll. of Va. Hosp., Richmond, Va., 1926-30; res. in med. Med. Coll. of Va., 1930-32; pvt. practice med., Richmond, 1932, specialist in internal med.; vis. physician, Med. Coll. of Va. Hosps., 1932-65; mem. faculty Medical Coll. of Va., 1932-65, prof. clin. medicine 1940-57, prof. of medicine, 1957-65, chmn. dept. of medicine, Medical Coll. Va., 1957-58; cons. internal medicine U.S. Veterans Hospital, McGuire, 1956-65. Served as pvt., Inf., U.S. Army, 1917-19; overseas; wounded in action, Oct. 23, 1918. Fellow A.C.P., Am. Coll. Cardiology; mem. Am. Clin. and Climatol. Assn., Alpha Omega Alpha, Omicron Delta Kappa. Club: Country of Va. Author: Physical Diagnosis (textbook). Home: Richmond VA Died May 2, 1968.

WALKER, HARVEY, prof. polit. sciences; b. Des Moines, Ia., Feb. 24, 1900; s. Marion McCreary and Lillie May (Harvey) W.; A.B., U. of Kan., 1923; M.A., University of Minnesota, 1927, Ph.D., 1928; LL.B., Ohio State University, 1948; m. Myra Lois Lingenfelter, May 18, 1924; children—Harvey, John Vaughan, Jeanne Carolyn. Instr. polit. science, U. of Kan., 1924-25, prof., 1969-70; instr. U. of Minn., 1927-28; asst. prof. polit. science, Ohio State U.; 1928-30, asso. prof., 1930-33, professor, 1933-67, prof. emeritus, 1967-71; also engaged in practice of law; superintendent of budget of State of Ohio, 1928-31; lt. col. Finance Reserve, U.S. Army; deputy finance officer and finance officer, Columbus, O., 1941-42; asst. Corps Area finance officer, 5th Corps Area, Fort Hayes, O., 1942; finance officer South Atlantic Ferrying Wing, Air Transport Command, 1942-43; finance officer, Services of Supply, U.S. Army Forces South Atlantic, 1943-44, chief Administrative Management Section, Office of Fiscal Dir. War Dept., 1944. Chief, Employee Relations Section, Indusl. Personnel Div., Army Service Forces, 1944; relieved from active duty, Aug. 1944; with UN Tech. Assistance Adminstrn., Rio de Janeiro, Brazil, 1951-52, C.Am., 1956-57. Fellow Social Sciences Research Council, 1932-33. Fellow Inst. Public Adminstrn. (London); mem. Internat. City Mgrs. Assn. (affiliate), Am. Polit. Science Assn. (secretary-treas.), Am. Acad. Polit. and Social Science, Am. Soc. for Public Adminstrn., Am. Assn. University Profs., Columbus, Ohio State and Am. Bar Assos., Order Coif, Phi Beta Kappa, Delta Sigma Pi, Pi Sigma Alpha, Acacia, Republican. Unitarian. Mason, K.T. Club: Faculty. Author, co-author, translator of books relating to field, also tech. articles. Home: Worthington OH Died May 22, 1971; cremated.

WALKER, HOBART ALEXANDER, architect; b. Brooklyn, N.Y., Nov. 1, 1869; s. Dr. Jerome and Helen (Oakley) W.; ed. Brooklyn Polytechnic, Pratt Inst.; m. Jessie M. Olcott, Apr. 12, 1898; children—Hobart Alexander Jr., Barbara (Mrs. Edmund A. Staub). Practiced architecture, 1889-1941. F.A.I.A.; mem. N.J. Soc. Architects. Republican. Club: Sketch (pres., New York, 1906). Home: 4327 Marble Hall Road, Baltimore 18 MD‡

WALKER, IRVING MILLER, lawyer; b. Louisville, Mar. 9, 1885; s. Walter and Mary Sydnor (Perkins) W.; B.A., University of Virginia, 1905; LL.D., Claremont College; m. Evangeline E. Duque, Oct. 6, 1914; 1 dau., Elita (Mrs. Fritz Caspari). Admitted to Cal. bar, 1906, since practiced in Los Angeles; mem. firm Loeb, Walker & Loeb, 1914-38, Walker, Adams, Duque & Smith, 1938-42, Walker, Adams & Duque, 1942-45, Walker, Wright, Tyler & Ward, 1956-69. Hon. dir. United Cal. Bank; dir. Farmer Bros. Co., other corps. Adviser com. on adminstrv. justice State Bar of Cal. Active Community Chest, Welfare Planning Council, Legal Aid Found. Los Angeles; pres. U.S.O., World War II; dir., hon. chmn. Travelers Aid Soc. Los Angeles, pres., 42 years; director National Travelers Aid Society, Director and trustee of Claremont Coll., Good Samaritan Hosp., Scripps Coll., (pres. 32 years); hon. life bd. dirs. of Claremont U. Coll. Fellow Am. Bar Found.; mem. Am., Cal. (v.p.), Los Angeles County (pres., recipient first Shattuck-Price award) bar assns., Am. Judicature Soc., Am. Coll. Trial Lawyers, Phi Beta Kappa. Democrat. Episcopalian. Home: Los Angeles CA Died June 9, 1969; buried Los Angeles CA

WALKER, J(OSEPH) FREDERIC, chemist; b. Perth Amboy, N.J., Dec. 7, 1903; s. Joseph F. and Mary (Hall) W.; B.S., Mass. Inst. Tech., 1925, M.S. (du Pont fellow 1926-27), 1928, Ph.D., 1929; m. Lois E. Lefler, Aug. 22, 1929; children—Lois M. (Mrs. John W. Wagner), Frederic R., Alan H. Research chemist Roessler & Hasslacher Chem. Co., Perth Amboy, 1927-30; with E. I. du Pont de Nemours & Co., Inc., 1930-64, research supr. electrochems. dept., Perth Amboy, 1945-50, Niagara Falls, N.Y., 1950-55, patent agt. patent sect., Niagara Falls, 1955-60, spl. assignment Exptl. Sta. Wilmington, Del., 1961-64; cons., Haddam, Conn., 1964-69; editorial asst. Choice, A.L.A., Middleton, Conn., 1965-69. Amateur artist, exhibiting at Studio Group Niagara Falls, 1950-69, Essex Art Assos., 1958-69. Recipient James E. Reid award for oil painting Western N.Y. Exhibit, Buffalo, 1959; Jacob F. Schoellkopf medal award Am. Chem. Soc., 1957. Licensed U.S. patent agt. Mem. Am. Chem. Soc. (chmn. Western N.Y. 1943-44), Am. Inst. Chemists (chmn. Niagara chpt. 1960-61, chmn. Del. chpt. 1962-63, chmn. com. ethics and status 1964-67), Conn. Patent Law Assn. Episcopalian (lay reader). Author Am. Chem. Soc. monograph, also articles in encys. World authority on formaldehyde chemistry. Address: Haddam CT Died Jan. 8, 1969.

WALKER, J(OHN) RANDALL, congressman; b. nr. Blackshear, Pierce Co., Ga., Feb. 23, 1874; grad. Jasper (Fla.) Normal Coll., 1895; LL.B., Dept. of Law, U. of Ga., 1898. Began practice of law, Valdosta, Ga., 1900; mem. Ga. Ho. of Rep., 1907-8; mem. 63d to 65th Congresses (1913-19), 11th Dist., Ga. Democrat. Home: Valdosta GA‡

WALKER, JOHN LEONARD, banker; b. Kenora, Ont., Can., Sept. 30, 1909; s. James and Marjorie (Morrison) W.; ed. Collegiate Inst., Sault Ste. Marie, Ont.; m. Helen Emily Simpson, Sept. 5, 1936; children—Judith, Nancy. With Bank of Montreal, from 1927, mgr. main Montreal br., 1957-59, asst. gen. mgr., dep. gen. mgr. B.C. div., 1959-64, gen. mgr. head office, 1964-66, sr. exec. v.p., gen. mgr., 1967, pres., chief operating officer, dir., from 1968; dir. Bank of Montreal Nassau, Kaiser Resources Ltd., Consol. Pipelines Co., Canadian Canners Ltd., Patagonia Corp., Tucson, Bank of Montreal (Cal.), Australian Internat. Finance Corp. Mem. adv. bd. Salvation Army, YMCA; bd. govs. Royal Victoria Hosp., Douglas Hosp., Montreal Gen. Hosp.; bd. dirs. Canadian Red Cross, Jr. Achievement Can., Boys Clubs Can.; exec. com. of adv. bd. Sch. Bus. Adminstrn., U. Western Ont. Mem. Canadian Forestry Assn. (nat. adv. council), Canadian Am. Com. Clubs: Mount Royal, St. James's, Forest and Stream, Royal St. Lawrence Yacht, Mt. Bruno Country (Montreal); Royal Vancouver Yacht, Vancouver. Home: Westmount Quebec Canada Deceased.

WALKER, LEWIS, 3D, bus. exec.; b. Pittsburgh, 1913; grad. Lehigh U., 1936. Pres. Talon div. Textron; dir. N.W. Pa. Bank & Trust Co., Oil City, Pa., Lightning Fastener Co., Ltd., (St. Catherines, Can.). Trustee Allegheny Coll. Meadville City Hosp. Address: Meadville PA Died Jan. 27, 1973.

WALKER, NELLIE VERNE, sculptor; b. Red Oak, Ia., Dec. 8, 1874; d. Everett A. and Rebecca J. (Lindsey) W.; pupil Lorado Taft, and Art Inst. of Chicago, unmarried. Executed monuments, W. S. Stratton, Colorado Springs, Colo.; Senator Harlan. Washington, D.C.; Decker Family, Battle Creek, Mich., D.F. Diggins, Cadillac, Mich.; statue of Chief Keokuk at Keokuk, Ia., 1913; monument to Senator Isaac Stephenson, Marinette, Wis., 1922; sculptural decorations, exterior of Library, State Coll., Amos, Ia., 1924; Polish-Am. war memorial, Chicago; also portrait busts and several large ideal groups. Mem. Painters and Sculptors of Chicago, Nat. Scultpure Soc., D.A.R., Daughters of 1912. Clubs: Little Room, The Cordon (pres. 1919-21). Home-Studio:6016 Ingleside Av., Chicago IL‡

WALKER, RALPH THOMAS, architect; b. Waterbury, Conn., Nov. 28, 1889; s. Thomas I. and Marion A. (Shipley) W.; prep. edn., Classical High Sch., Providence; Mass. Inst. Tech., 1911; Rotch Traveling scholarship, 1916; Litt.D., Syracuse U., 1965; m. Stella Forbes, Aug. 30, 1913 (dec.); m. 2d, Christine Foulds, Mar. 25, 1972. Began practice at N.Y.; cons. Haines, Lundberg & Waehler, firm architects for N.Y.C. Telephone Bldg., Irving Trust Co. Bldg., Western Union Telegraph Bldg.; Bklyn. Edison Office Bldg., telephone bldgs., N.Y., N.J., Washington, D.C., and vicinity, Travelers Ins. Bldg. (Hartford), several bldgs. N.Y. World's Fair, Bell Telephone Lab. (Murray Hill, N.J.), Roger Williams Meml. (Providence, R.I.), George Eastman Meml. (Rochester, N.Y.), Prudential Bldg., Newark, N.J., govt. project for Army Def. bases in Caribbean at Trinidad, St. Lucia, Antigua, British Guiana, town of Nicaro Nickel Co., Cuba; Belgian Chancellery, Washington, Argonne Nat. Lab., Chgo., IBM Research Center, Poughkeepsie, N.Y., Gen. Foods Office Bldg., White Plains, N.Y., Am. Fedn. Labor Bldg., Washington. Mem. adv. bd. of design of fgn. bldgs. State Dept., 1954-56, Commn. of Fine Arts, Washington, 1959; chmn. Benjamin Franklin Stiftung, Berlin, 1955-58. Mem. Archtl. Commn. Chgo. World's Fair Expn., 1933. Fellow Pierpont Morgan Library; trustee New Sch. Social Research, Lavanburg Found. Served as 2d lt., Engrs., camouflage sect., U.S., Army, World War I. Recipient Medal of Honor of N.Y., Phila. chapters of A.I.A.; gold medal Archtl. League of N.Y., 1927; on Honor Roll, The Nation, 1927; Honor Roll citation Am. Artists Profl. League, 1947, spl. Centennial medal A.I.A., 1957; Founders medal New Sch. Social Research, 1962; decorated chevalier Legion of Honor (France); officer Order of Crown (Belgium). Fellow A.I.A. (1st chancellor, past pres.); mem. Regional Plan Assn. (dir. 1956), Union Internationale Des Architects (v.p. 1948-57), Nat. Inst. Arts and Letters, Nat. Acad. Design (academician), Archtl. League N.Y. (past pres.), Beaux Arts Inst. of Design (trustee 1933-41), Municipal Art Soc. (past pres.), Am. Inst. Planners, Nat. Sculpture Soc., Citizens Housing Council of N.Y.; hon. corres. mem. Royal Inst. Brit. Architects, Philippine Inst. Architects, Bund Deutscher Architekten, Colegio Nacional de Arquitectos (Cuba), El Institute de Urbanism del Peru. Clubs: Technology, Union League (N.Y.C.); Cosmos (Washington). Author: London, 1943; Humans-Materials-Architecturs, 1948; Vidi, 1951; Ralph Walker, Architect, 1957; The Fly in the Amber, 1957. Home: Chappaqua NY Died Jan. 17, 1973; buried Fairlawn Cemetery, Ridgefield CT

WALKER, ROBERT BARNEY, tobacco co. exec.; b. Cape Vincent, N.Y., Oct. 27, 1913; s. John E. and Dolly A. (McMillan) W.; grad. high sch.; m. Helen G. Tingley, Apr. 17, 1938 (dec.); children—Patricia (Mrs. Stephen John Schulte), John Jeffrey, Michael David; m. 2d, Muriel E. Plate, 1956. With Am. Tobacco Co. (name changed to Am. Brands, Inc. 1969), N.Y.C., 1937-73, asst. to v.p. charge sales, 1951-53, exec. sales mgr., 1953-55, dir. of co. and dir. sales, 1955-57, v.p. charge sales, 1957-61, v.p. advt. and sales, 1961, exec. v.p., 1962, pres., chief exec. officer, 1963-65, pres., chmn. bd., 1965-69, chairman of board, chief exec. officer, 1969-73, dir., 1955-73. Episcopalian. Clubs: Pinnacle, Sky (N.Y.C.); Wee Burn Country, Ox Ridge Hunt (Darien, Conn.). Home: Darien CT Died Jan. 17, 1973.

WALKER, ROSS H., stockbroker; b. Currituck, N.C., 1894. Stockbroker Paine, Webber, Jackson & Curtis Inc. Home: Mechanicsville VA Died Oct. 25, 1972.

WALKER, STANTON, engr.; b. Vevay, Ind., Mar. 18, 1894; s. Harvey Edwin and Emma Deane (Williamson) W.; B.S., Univ. of Ill., 1917; m. Amelia Bertha Ramseyer, Aug. 12, 1916; children—John Stanton Robert, Richard David. Asso. research and research engr. for Portland Cement Assn., Structural Materials Research Lab., Lewis Inst., Chicago, 1917-26; dir. of engring. Nat. Sand and Gravel Assn., Washington 1926-62, emeritus, 1962-71, also dir. assn.'s Research Found., U. Md.; dir. engring. Nat. Ready Mixed Concrete Assn., 1930-62; emeritus 1962-71, also dir. Assn.'s Research Found. U. Md.; lectr. materials dept. civil engring. U. Md.; cons. or concrete and mineral aggregates; cons. engr. Nat. Indsl. Sand Assn., 1935-62. Recipient Roy W. Crum award, Highway Research Bd., 1956. Mem. Am. Soc. C.E. (hon.), Am. Soc. Testing Materials (mem exec. com. 1952-53, dir. 1951-54; recipient Award of Merit 1951, and Frank E. Richart award 1957 Sanford E. Thompson award 1960, Turner medal 1961; hon. mem.), Am. Concrete Inst. (mem. bd. 1940-50, pres. 1947, hon. mem.), Hwy. Research Bd. (exec. com. 1941-49, chmn. 1944-45), Am. Inst. Mining and Metall. Engrs. Contbr. articles dealing with research in concrete and mineral aggregates in tech. pubs. and in transactions and proc. profl. socs. Home: Blacksburg VA Died July 1971.

WALL, HUBERT STANLEY, mathematician, educator,; b. nr. Rockwell City, Ia., Dec. 2, 1902; s. Samuel H. and Gratia (Wright) W.; B.A., Cornell Coll., 1924, M.A., 1924, D.Sc. (hon.), 1970; Ph.D., U. Wis., 1927, postgrad. Inst. Advanced Study, 1937-38; m. Mary Kate Parker, Oct. 18, 1947. Fellow U. Wis., Madison, 1924-26, asst., 1926-27; instr. math. Northwestern U., 1927-30, asst. prof., 1930-36, asso. prof., 1936-43, prof., 1943-44; lectr. Ill. Inst. Tech., Chgo., 1944-45, prof., 1945-46; prof. U. Tex., Austin, 1946-70, prof. emeritus, 1970-73. Mem. Am. Math. Soc. Author: Analytic Theory of Continued Fractions, 1948; Creative Mathematics, 1963. Contbr. articles to profl. jours. Home: Austin TX Died Sept. 12, 1971; buried Rockwell City IA

WALLACE, DAVID A., automobile exec.; b. Castleton, Kan., Mar. 1, 1888; student Highland Park Coll. Engring.; E.D. (hon.), Mich. Coll. Mining and Tech., 1951. Employee A.T. & S.F. R.R. Shop, Dodge City, Kan., 1906; machinist, tool designer, service and sales rep. Buick Automobile Co., Flint, Mich. and Tex.; mech. supt. Concheno Mining Co., Mexico; tool room foreman, master mechanic, supt. Hart-Parr Tractor Co., Charles City, Ia.; master mechanic, supt., woris mgr. John Deere Tractor Co., Waterloo, Ia.; staff master mechanic Chrysler Corp., Detroit, 1929, v.p. in charge mfg. Chrysler div., 1930, pres. Chrysler Marine and Indsl. Engine Div., 1936-48, Chrysler div., 1937-53, Pekin Wood Products Co., Helena, Ark., 1932-48, Walco, Inc.; dir. Chrysler Sales Corp., Chrysler Export, Pekin Wood Products Indsl. Engine Div., Detroit Trust Co. Served as pvt. to capt., with Motor Transport, U.S. Army, World War I. Clubs: Detroit Athletic (pres.), Grosse Pointe Yacht, Country, Detroit, Yondotega (Detroit); Gulfstream Bath and Tennis, Gulfstream Golf, Little (Delray Beach, Fla.). Address: Grosse Pointe Farms MI Died Jan. 21, 1970; buried Nat. Chapel Cemetery, Lontana FL

WALLACE, DAVID M., lawyer; b. Middletown, Pa., July 6, 1892; A.B., Dickinson Coll., 1915, LL.B., 1917, M.A., 1920. Admitted to Pa. bar, 1920; now partner firm McNees, Wallace & Nurick, Harrisburg. Trustee Dickinson Coll., 1950-67. Mem. Pa., Dauphin County (pres. 1944) bar assns. Address: Harrisburg PA Died Aug. 26, 1967.

WALLACE, LURLEEN BURNS, gov. of Ala.; b. Tuscaloosa, Ala., Sept. 19, 1926; d. Henry Morgan and Estelle (Burroughs) Burns; grad. Tuscaloosa Bus. Coll., 1942; m. George Corley Wallace, May 22, 1943; children—Bobbi Jo (Mrs. James A. Parsons), Peggy Sue, George Corley, Janie Lee. Gov. of Ala., 1967-68. Mem. Women for Constl. Govt., Disabled Am. Vets. Aux. (life), Am. Legion Aux., Ninety-Nines, Nat. Rehab. Assn. Odd Fellow; mem. Order Amaranth, Order Eastern Star. Democrat. Home: Montgomery AL Died May 7, 1968; buried Greenwood Cemetery, Montgomery AL

WALLACE, MARGARET ADAIR, phys. therapist; b. St. Paul, July 24, 1900; d. Albert James and Mabel (McKinstry) Wallace; student Hamline U., 1918-20; grad. Chgo. Normal Sch. Phys. Edn., 1922; student phys. therapy Harvard, 1924; m. Wallace E. Krueger, Mar. 25, 1933 (dec.). Phys. therapist Elyria (O.) Meml. Hosp., 1922-24; pvt. practice, Chgo., 1925-29, Evanston, Ill., 1929-69; head posture clinic Evanston Meml. Hosp., 1930-53; phys. therapist Pope Found., Kankakee, 1931-42. Mem. bd. Evanston Northwestern Community Clubs, 1953-61, pres. 1955-61. Mem. Am. Phys. Therapy Assn. (past pres. Ill.). Club: Zonta (Evanston). Home: Des Plaines IL Died Mar. 5, 1969.

WALLACE, SCHUYLER CRAWFORD, author, univ. prof.; b. N.Y. City, Nov. 29, 1898; s. Homer Hugh and Ruth (Egbert) W.; A.B., Columbia Coll., 1919; A.M., Columbia U., 1920, Ph.D., 1928; m. Esther Clara Griffin, July 6, 1931. Instr. in govt. and history, Columbia, 1920-22, Gottsberger fellow in polit. science, 1922-23, instr. in govt., 1923-28, asst. prof., 1928-37, asso. prof., 1937-39, prof., 1939-50, Ruggles professor of public law and government, 1950-64, Ruggles professor emeritus, 1964-69; director of program of training for internat. adminstrn. and of Naval Sch. of Mil. Govt. and Adminstrn., 1942-45, exec. officer dept. pub. law and govt., 1945-60, dir. Sch. Internat. Affairs, 1946-60, dean School Internat. Affairs, Columbia 1960-62; dir. European Inst., 1950-61, Centers of Iranian, Pakistan and Turkish Studies, 1949-54; dir. Columbia U. Press, 1955-62, dir. fgn. area fellowship program of Social Sci. Research Council and Am. Council Learned Socs., 1962-68; lectr. polit. sci. various univ. summer sessions. Cons. Pres's. Com. on Adminstrv. Mgmt., 1937, Navy Dept., 1943-45, Ford Foundation, 1952-60. Trustee Free University Europe, 1953-58, dire. Near and Middle East Inst., 1954-62, Russian Inst., 1955-56. Mem. Social Science Research Council (director 1952-58), Turkish-American Society (director 1954-62), American Political Science Association, Academy Political Science. Clubs: Century Association (New York City). Author: Our Governmental Machine, 1925; State Administrative Supervision over Cities in the United States, 1928; The New Deal in Action, 1934; Federal Departmentalization: A Critique of Theories of Organization, 1941. Contbr. to periodicals and quarterlies. Contbg. editor Today, 1933-34, lit. editor, 1934-35. Home: New Preston CT Died July 9, 1969; buried Kensico Cemetery, Kensico NY

WALLACE, THOMAS F., banker; b. of Am. parents, Bogota, Colombia, S.A., Nov. 7, 1871; s. Thomas F. and Martha (Torrance) W.; A.B., U. of Minn., 1893, LL.B., 1895; unmarried. Admitted to Minn. bar, 1896, and practiced at Minneapolis until 1918; treas. Farmers & Mechanics Savings Bank of Minneapolis, 1918-29, pres., 1929-39, chmn. bd. since 1939, dir. Minneapolis Art Institute; dir. Northwestern Nat. Life Ins. Co. Mem. Phi Beta Kappa, Chi Psi, Phi Delta Phi. Presbyterian. Clubs: Minneapolis Minikahda. Home: 124 Groveland Av. Office: 90 S. 6th St., Minneapolis MN‡

WALLACE, WILLIAM CHARLES, clergyman, educator; b. Jamestown, Pa., Apr. 20, 1875; s. Rev. Joseph R. and Isabella (Robinson) W.; A.B., Geneva Coll., Beaver Falls, Pa., 1899; grad. Pittsburgh Theol. Sem., 1904 (D.D., Cooper Memorial Geneva and Muskingum colls., 1916); m. Sadie L. Morrow, of New Sheffield, Beaver Co., Pa., Feb. 16, 1905; children—Charles Alfred, Mary Graham (dec.), Rebecca Robinson and Wilhelmina Jane (twins). Ordained ministry U.I. Church, 1904; pastor Colorado Springs, Colo., 1904-07, Sheridan, Pa., 1907-12, 1st Ch., Braddock, 1912-16; pres. Westminister Coll. since Sept. 1916. Chmn. gen. com. Young People's Christian Union, 1916. Clubs: The Hungry (Pittsburgh), Community, Rotary, New Castle. Home: New Wilmington PA‡

WALLACE, WILLIAM MCLEAN, physician; b. Montclair, N.J., Jan. 12, 1912; s. Albert Howard and Ethel (McLean) W.; A.B., U. Pa., 1934, M.D., 1938; m. Patricia Raymond, July 2, 1949; children—William, Andrew, Jane, Harriet, Patricia. Intern Robert Packer Hosp., Sayre, Pennsylvania, 1938-39; NRC fellow Harvard, 1939-41, Rockefeller Found. fellow, 1946-48, asst. prof. pediatrics, med. sch., 1948-51; intern, resident Children's Hosp., Boston, 1941-42; prof. pediatrics Western Res. U. Sch. Medicine, 1951-68; dir. pediatrics Univ. Hosp., Cleve., 1951-68. Mem. human embryology and devel. study sect. NIH. Served from 1st lt. to maj. M.C., AUS, 1941-45. Decorated Silver Star, Bronze Star, Purple Heart. Diplomate Am. Bd. Pediatrics. Mem. A.M.A., Am. Soc. Clin. Investigation, Soc. Pediatric Research, Am. Pediatric Soc., American Institute Nutrition, Am. Assn. Advancement Sci., Am. Cleveland Heights OH Died Nov. 9, 1968; cremated.

WALLAU, HERMAN L., elec. engr.; born Brooklyn, N.Y., Jan. 26, 1877; s. George Jacques and Marie Lucile (Neuville) W.; B.S., Brooklyn Poly. Institute, 1896 (valedictorian), E.E. from same inst., 1897; m. Irene Louise Owers, Dec. 3, 1902; children—Irene Owers, Lucille Marian. With elec. engring. div. Brooklyn Rapid Transit Co., 1897-98, line constrn. same, 1898-99; draftsman Goodson Graphotype Co., Apr.-Aug. 1899; multiple unit equipment insp., Brooklyn Rapid Transit Co., Sept.-Dec. 1899; with Elec. Launch Co., Jan.-Oct. 1900, Westinghouse Electic & Mfg. Co., 1900-01; with Cleveland Electrical Illuminating Co., Oct. 1901-Jan. 1942; became chief electrical engr., 1907, designing elec. features of its Lake Shore, Avon and Ashtabula stations; dir. installation first 66,000 volt underground transmission circuits in U.S.; retired Jan. 1942. Fellow Am. Inst. E.E.; mem. Edison Electric Inst., Assn. Edison Illuminating Cos. Episcopalian. Home: 3051 E. Derbyshire Rd., Cleveland Heights 18 OH‡

WALLEN, SAUL, labor abritrator; b. N.Y.C., June 29, 1910; s. Samuel and Sarah (Zevin) W.; B.S. in Econs., N.Y.U., 1933; m. Mary Kirschner, May 27, 1934; children—Joan, James, Barbara. Labor disputes adjuster United Dress Mfrs. Assn., 1933-36; indsl. relations researcher N.Y. State Dept. Labor, 1936-40, U.S. Dept. of Labor, 1940-42; chmn. New Eng. Regional War Labor Bd., 1942-45; adviser President's Labor-Mgmt. Conf., 1945; chmn. Western Union Fact-Finding Bd., 1946; apptd. to nat. emergency boards, 1947-—; umpire Gen. Motors Corp.-UAW, 1948-49, Ford Motor Co.-UAW, 1955-69, Trans World Airlines-Internat. Assn. Machinists, 1959-69, B.F. Goodrich-United Rubber Workers, 1960-69; dir. Mass. Blue Cross Spl. lectr. Harvard, 1946-63; director New York Coalition, 1968-69. Mem. N.Y.C. Office Collective Bargaining, 1966-69. Chmn. Emergency Bd. 100 Railroads and Nonoperating Employees, 1962. Trustee Beth Israel Hospital. Mem. Nat. Acad. Arbitrators (pres. 1954), Indsl. Relations Research Assn. (exec. bd. 1955-57). Home: Brookline MA Died Aug. 5, 1969; buried Chilmark MA

WALLENBERG, AXEL FINGAL, diplomat; b. Stockholm, Sweden, Sept. 13, 1874; s. Andre Oscar (banker) and Anna W.; ed. at Stockholm; m. Elsa Lilliehook, May 17, 1900. In mii. service 10 yrs.; then mng. dir., forestry and lumber business; E.E. and M.P. from Sweden to U.S. since Mar. 1921. Clubs: Metropolitan (Washington, D.C., and New York). Address: Swedish Legation, 2249 R St., Washington DC‡

WALLENBERG, MARC JR., banker; b. London, Eng., June 28, 1924; s. Marcus and Dorothy (Mackay) W.; M.B.A., Harvard Bus. Sch., 1949; m. Olga Wehtje, Nov. 26, 1955; children—Marcus, Axel, Mariana; Caroline. Asst. v.p. Stockholms Enskilda Bank (Sweden), 1953-55, v.p., 1955-56; dir., 1955, vice mng. dir., 1956-58, mng. dir., 1958-71; chmn. svenska Dataregister AB; dir. Atlas Copco AB, Stockholm, Orkla Grube AB, AB Papyrus, G.K.N. Stenman AB, AB Svenska Jarnvagsverkstaderna. Goodyear Gummifabriks AB. Saab-Scania, AB Svenska Ostasiatiska Kompaniet, Forsakrings AB Skandia Treas., Stockholm Sch. Econs. Bd. dirs. Knut and Alice Wallenberg Found. Decorated Comdr. Order Vasa (Sweden); officer de l'ordre de la Republique Tunisienne Comdr. of Most Excellent Order of Brit. Empire. Mem. Swedish Banks' Assn., Brit.-Swedish C. of C. (chmn. 1964-66, hon. v.p. 1966-71), Internat. C. of C. (treas. Swedish nat. com., dep. treas). Club: Royal Swedish Yacht (treas.). Home: Stockholm Sweden Died Nov. 19, 1971.

WALLENSTEIN, MERRILL BERNARD, govt. ofcl., chemist; b. Idaho Falls, Ida., Feb. 8, 1920; s. George and Stella (Daniels) W.; B.S., U. Utah, 1948, Ph.D., 1951; m. Mary M. Weight, June 14, 1953; children—Helen Ann, Merrill Bernard, Mary Ann. Vice pres. research Operations Research Inc., Silver Springs, Md., 1956-58, William H. Johnston Labs., Inc., W. Lafayette, Ind., 1958-59; with Nat. Bur. Standards, 1959-68, dept. dir. Inst. Basic Standards, 1965-68, also chmn. ednl. com. Served with USAAF, 1941-45. Mem. Am. Chem. Soc., Sigma Xi, Phi Kappa Phi, Sigma Pi Sigma. Home: Washington DC Died July 2, 1968.

WALLER, WILMER JOYCE, banker; b. Sabetha, Kan., May 25, 1889; s. Charles Carter Page and Annie C. (Joyce) W.; student pub. schs.; m. Courtenay Towne Greenough, Nov. 9, 1910 (dec. 1947); children—Courtenay Page, Anne Carter, Wilmer Joyce, Robert Nelson; m. 2d, Anne Lee Gaines Surles, Feb. 3, 1951 (dec. 1967). Runner Am. Nat. Bank, Washington, 1906, asst. cashier, 1917, cashier, 1918; v.p. Fed. Am. Nat. Bank, 1922-33; v.p., cashier Hamilton Nat. Bank, 1933-43, pres, 1943-54, chmn. bd., dir., 1954; chmn. bd. Nat. Bank of Washington, 1954-67; dir. Potomac Electric Power Co. Treas. The Harry S. Truman Library, Inc. Member Washington Clearing House Association (v. chmn.), Washington Bd. Trade, Am. Inst. Banking (pres. Washington chpt. 1920), D.C. (pres. 1929), Am. (v.p. D.C. chpt. 1930, exec. council D.C. chpt. 1938-41; exec. com. nat. bank div. 1936, treas. 1944-45) bankers assns., Assn. Res. City Bankers. Mason. Clubs: Chevy Chase, Burning Tree (Chevy Chase, Maryland); Metropolitan (Washington). Home: Washington DC Died May 7, 1969.

WALLERSTEIN, EDWARD, business cons.; b. Kansas City, Mo., Dec. 9, 1891; s. David and Helen (Coons) W.; ed. Germantown Acad., Phila.; A.B., Haverford Coll.; m. Helen Perry Ault, Sept. 2, 1927; children—E. Perry, Jane Hastings, David V. Eastern mgr. music div. Brunswick-Balke-Collender Co., 1925-30; sales mgr. Brunswick Record Corp., 1930-32; mgr. record div. R.C.A. Victor, 1933-38; pres. Columbia Records, Inc., and all its subsidiaries, 1939-48, 49-59, chmn. bd., 1948-59; head Belock Recording Co. div. Belock Instrument Corp., also v.p. of corp., 1959-60; business cons., 1961-70. Served as 1st lt., inf., World War I. Club: Brodheads Forest and Stream (Stroudsberg). Home: Pomono Beach FL Died Sept. 1, 1970.

WALLICHS, GLENN EVERETT, record co. exec.; b. Grand Island, Neb., Aug. 9, 1910; s. Oscar and Mayme (Hoober) W.; m. Dorothy Kueker, Sept. 27, 1933; children—Linda Ann, Susan. Co-founder, v.p., sec.-treas., gen. mgr. Capitol Records, Inc., Hollywood, Cal., 1942-44, exec. v.p., 1944-47, pres., 1947-62, chmn. bd., 1962-68; dir. Electric & Musical Industries, Ltd. (Eng.), Am. Mut. Fund; chmn. bd. Capitol Industries, Inc., from 1968; founder Music City Stores. Trustee U. Redlands. Mem. Record Industry Assn. Am. (dir., past pres.). Hollywood Jr. C. of C., Television Acad. Arts and Scis. Club: Friars (Beverly Hills, Cal.). Home: Beverly Hills CA Died Dec. 23, 1971.

WALLIN, J(OHN) E(DWARD) WALLACE, psychologist; b. Page County, Ia., Jan. 21, 1876; s. C. Henry and Emma M. (Johnson) W.; A.B., Augustana Coll., Ill., 1897; M.A., Yale, 1899, Ph.D., 1901; m. Frances Geraldine Tinsley, June 21, 1913; children—Virginia Stanton, Mrs. Geraldine Tinsley Sickler. Research assistant in psychology, Clark University, 1901-02; assistant in experimental psychology, University of Mighigan, 1902-03; demonstrator in experimental psychology, Princeton University, 1903-06; vice prin. and head dept. psychology and edn., State Teachers College E. Stroudsburg, Pa., 1906-09; head dept. of psychology and edn., Normal Training Sch., Cleveland, 1909-10; dir. psychol. research to oral hygiene com., National Dental Association, 1910-11; dir. lab. of clin. psychology, N.J. State Village for Epileptics, 1910-11; prof. clin. psychology and dir. psycho-ednl. clinic, U. of Pittsburgh, 1912-14; psychologist on smoke investigation to the Mellon Inst., 1912-13; dir. psycho-ednl. clinic and spl. schs., and instr. in Harris Teachers Coll., dept. instrn., St. Louis, 1914-21; dir. bur. spl. edn. and psycho-ednl. clinic, and prof. clin. psychology, Miami U., 1921-29; dir. spl. edn. Baltimore Dept. of Edn., and lecturer Johns Hopkins, 1929-30; prof. psychology and dir. mental hygiene clinic, Atlantic U., Virginia Beach, Va., 1930-32; dir. div. spl. edn. and mental hygiene, Dela. State Dept. Pub. Instrn. 1932-47 and Wilmington Pub. Schs., 1932-45; vis. prof. numerous colls. and univs. Has served as chmn., leader, adv., or mem. numerous profl. orgnl. and govtl. coms. and commns., in fields of edn. and psychology, 1915-69; hon. life mem. or life mem. ten national orgns.; mem. nat. confs. Mem. nat., state, local profl. and scientific assns. and orgns. Former coop. editor Jour. of Applied Psychology, Journal of Delinquency; member advisory bd. Jour. Exceptional Children. Author books relating to field; latest: Children with Mental and Physical Handicaps, 1949; The Education of Mentally Handicapped Children, 1955; The Odyssey of a Psychologist, Wilmington DE Died Aug. 5, 1969.

WALLING, WILLIAM HENRY, printer; b. Potsdam, N.Y., Mar. 17, 1895; s. William W. and Ada (Coats) W.; student Hamilton Coll., 1913-14; grad. U. Ill. Sch. Mil. Aeros., 1917; m. Peggy Wood, Oct. 1, 1946; children—Janet Barclay, Ann Jermain. Asst. to advt. mgr. Packard Motor Car Co., 1919-20; v.p. Mortimer & Walling, printers, N.Y.C., 1920-73, dir. Dirs. Co., 1931-58, pres., 1958-73; chmn. Rogers Kellogg-Stillson, Inc., 1946-55, Hawley-Lord, Inc., Somerset Pub. Co., Shelter Industries; chmn. bd. dirs. Graphic Arts Mut. Ins. Co., 1957-73; pres. Boreal, Inc., 1964-73, Kewal Paper Co., 1957-73, Graphic Arts Mgmt. Corp., 1964-73, Overseas Devel. Services, Inc., 1966-73; dir. Utica Mut. Ins. Co. Served to lt. col. USAF. Decorated Bronze Star medal, Air medal. Mem. N.Y. Employing Printers Assn., Printing Industry Am. (pres., dir.), Printers League N.Y., Mayflower Descs., Colonial Wars, Air Force Assn., Soc. Am. Wars, Quiet Birdmen. Clubs: Metropolitan, Players, Saint Nicholas of New York, Turf and Field, Dutch Treat (N.Y.C.). Author: Backgammon Standards, 1930. Home: Stamford CT Died Feb. 5, 1973.

WALLIS, GEORGE EDWARD, business exec.; b. Beverly, Mass., July 20, 1886; s. Ed. F. and Mary E. (Wilson) W.; B.S., Mass. Inst. of Tech., 1909; m. Marcia K. Perkins, July 12, 1911; children—Elizabeth (Mrs. A.

W. Dodge), Frances Perkins (Mrs. A. L. Sandford). Pres. and gen. mgr. The Creamery Pkg. Mfg. Co., Chgo., 1933-52, chairman of the board, 1952-63; past pres. Creamery Pkg. Mfg. Co. Ltd. of Can. Formerly pres., dir. Dairy Industries Supply Assn.; former treas., dir. Nat. Dairy Council. Mem. Am. Soc. Refrigerating Engineers. Clubs: Union League (Chgo.); Salem (Mass.) Country Club. Home: Wenham MA Died Sept. 12, 1971; interred North Beverly MA

WALLIS, WILLIAM FISHER, magnetician; b. Baltimore, Md., June 5, 1874; s. William Hawkins and Maria Isabella (Griffith) W.; grad. Baltimore City Coll., 1893; A.B., Johns Hopkins, 1896; B.S., Mass. Inst. Tech., 1913; m. Mary Alberta Sigelen, Dec. 25, 1920; 1 son, Richard Fisher. Magnetic observer, U.S. Coast and Geodetic Survey, 1900-10; magnetician, Dept. Terrestrial Magnetism, Carnegie Instn., Washington, D.C., 1913-39; retired. Recalled to active duty by the Dept. Terrestrial Magnetism to assist in the Department's war service. Retired again Dec. 1946. Magnetic survey work in U.S., Europe, Africa, Hawaii, Australia and S. America. Mem. Philos. Soc. Washington, etc. Home: 5219 42d St. N.W., Washington 15 DC‡

WALLS, FRANK XAVIER, physician; b. Toronto, Can., Dec. 3, 1869; s. Thomas and Catherine (Ahern) W.; South Division High Sch., Chicago; M.D., Northwestern U. Med. Sch., 1891; m. Cecelia Cunningham, of Chicago, June, 1896; m. 2d, Mrs. Elizabeth G. Dickason, Sept. 1917. Attending phys. Cook Co., St. Luke's and Wesley hosps.; prof. pediatrics, Northwestern Univ. Med. Sch., since Feb. 1911. Mem. Chicago Med. Soc.; apptd. 1st lt. Med. R.C., U.S.A., 1911. Home: 999 Lake Shore Drive. Office: 30 N. Michigan Av., Chicago IL‡

WALMSLEY, WALTER NEWBOLD, JR., govt. ofcl.; b. Philadelphia, Pennsylvania, April 4, 1904; s. Walter Newbold and Harriet Hoskins (Preston) W.; grad. Gilman Country Sch., Baltimore, Md., 1922; student Rensselaer Poly. Inst., 1922-24; m. Maria Teresa Sanchez Domenech, Jan. 14, 1936. Clk., Am. consulate, Sao Paulo, Brazil, 1927, vice consul, 1928-31; vice consul, Aden, 1931-33, Prague, 1933; vice consul, Havana, 1934, consul, 1935-37; consul Pernambuco, 1937; asst. chief, div. of the Am. Republics, Dept. of State, 1941-42; 2d sec. and consul, Rio de Janeiro, 1943; chief, div. Brazilian affairs, Dept. of State, 1944, also acting chief, div. River Plate affairs, Mar.-May 1944; 2d sec. and consul, Lisbon, June 1944-45; 1st secretary, Paris, June 1945. Mem. secretariat, U.N. Conf. on Internat. Orgn., San Francisco, 1945; polit. adv., U.S. del., Preparatory Commn., UN, London, 1945; Nat. War Coll., 1946-47; Councelor Econ. Affairs, Rome, March 1947. Alternate del. Inter-Am. Coffee Bd., 1944; polit. adviser U.S. delegation, Paris Peace Conf., 1946; adviser U.S. delegation to 2d Assembly of Economic Com. for Europe, Geneva, 1947, Multilateral Civil Aviation Conf., Geneva, 1947; spl. asst. to Ambassador-at-large, Dept. State, 1950, to the counselor, 1951; minister Am. Embassy, Rio de Janeiro, 1952; minister Am. Embassy, Moscow 1954; deputy assistant Sec. of State, 1956-59; ambassador to Tunisia, 1959-62. Member of the Foreign Service Association, Delta Phi. Clubs: Metropolitan, Chevy Chase (Washington). Home: Washington DC Died Apr. 1, 1973.

WALSH, ALLAN B., congressman; b. Trenton, N.J., Aug. 29, 1874; ed. parochial, pub. schools. Formerly supt. elec. testing dept. John A. Roebling's Sons Co., Trenton; mem. N.J. Ho. of Rep., 2 terms; sec. Mercer County Bd. of Taxation, 1912-13; mem. 63d Congress (1913-15), 4th Dist. N.J.; Democrat. Catholic. Home: Trenton NJ‡

WALSH, SISTER FRANCES MARIE, educator; b. Kansas City, Mo., Feb. 13, 1893; d. Frank P. and Katherine M. (O'Flaherty) Walsh; student Mahattanville Coll. of the Sacred Heart, N.Y. City, 1911-12; A.B., Webster Coll., Webster Groves, Mo., 1923; A.M., Creighton U., Omaha, 1926. Joined Order of Sisters of Loretto, 1915, took vows, 1917; prin. Nerinx Hall, Webster Groves, Mo., 1925-28; prof. edn., Webster Coll., 1928-31, dean of women, 1931-39; pres. Loretto Heights Coll., Denver, 1946-64. Mem. Assn. Am. Colls., Am. Council on Edn., Catholic Endl. Assn. of Colls., North Central Assn. of Colls. (commr.), Asso. Colls. Colo. Home: Denver CO Died Sept. 3, 1968; buried Loretto Heights Coll., Denver CO

WALSH, JOHN EDWARD, educator; b. Grand Junction, Colo., May 28, 1919; s. Henry Edward and Lulu (Boren) W.; B.S. in Math., U. Notre Dame, 1941; M.A. in Math., U. Cal. at Los Angeles, 1944; Ph.D., Princeton, 1947; children—Luanne (Mrs. Glen Frisby), John Edward; m. 2d, Grace Kelleher, Sept. 1969. Research specialist Lockhead Aircraft Corp., 1941-45, 54-58; mathematician RAND Corp., 1947-51, U.S. Naval Ordnance Test Sta., 1951-54; sr. scientist System Devel. Corp., Santa Monica, Cal., 1958-67; v.p., treas. OR-Stat, Inc., Glendale, Cal., 1960-68; v.p. Computer Aid Companies, Inc., 1967-72; Mobil prof. statistics So. Meth. U., 1967; vis. prof. Stanford, 1962, U. Hawaii, 1964, U. So. Cal., 1965-66, So. Meth. U., 1966, U. Colo., 1957; cons. to industry, 1960. Fellow Am. Statis Assn.; mem. Operations Research Soc. (treas. 1962-65; pres. 1967-68), Internat. Fedn. Operational Research Socs. (mem. council 1963, 66), Inst. Math. Statistics, Biometric Soc., Inst. Mgmt. Scis., Internat. Assn. Statistics Phys. Scis., Soc. Actuaries, Research Assn. Am., Soc. Tech. Writers and Pubs. Author handbooks, articles. Home: Dallas TX Died Aug. 24, 1972.

WALSH, JOSEPH PATRICK, lawyer; b. Bklyn., Oct. 12, 1902; s. Patrick and Mary (Ryan) W.; A.B., St. Francis Coll., 1922; LL.B. Fordham U.; 1925; Doctor Jurisprudence, St. Lawrence University, 1926; m. Mary Bergin, June 1926 (deceased May 1964). With Sinclair Oil Corp., 1928-68, gen. counsel, 1947-68. Dir. Hosp. Rev. and Planning Council So. N.Y., Inc.; trustee Automotive Safety Found. Decorated knight St. Gregory, knight grand cross Order Holy Sepulchre Jerusalem. Home: Jamaica Estates NY Died June 21, 1971.

WALSH, LAWRENCE ALOYSIUS, emeritus provost; b. N.Y.C., N.Y., Aug. 23, 1896; s. Michael J. and Nano (Walsh) W.; diploma, Fordham Prep. Sch. (New York), 1913; student St. Andrew-on-Hudson, Poughkeepsie, N.Y., 1913-17; A.B., A.M., Woodstock Coll., Woodstock, Md., 1920; Ph.D., Gregorian U., Rome, Italy, 1938. Mem. Society of Jesus (Jesuit); ordained priest Roman Cath. Church. Treas. Woodstock Coll., 1930-32; dean grad. Sch. Fordham U., 1932-38; Dean Fordham Coll., Fordham U., 1938-49, provost Fordham U., 1949-66, emeritus, 1966-68. Mem. Nat. Cath. Edn. Asso., Middle Atlantic States Asso. of Coll. and Secondary Schs. Home: Bronx NY Died June 3, 1968.

WALSH, ROY EDWARD, real estate broker; b. N.Y.C., May 29, 1920; s. Roy and Elizabeth (Rodier) W.; B.A., Yale, 1947; m. Lenore Todd, June 21, 1947; 1 dau., Elizabeth Todd. Pres., R. E. Walsh & Co., real estate, 1965-68. Mem. Bd. Natural Resourses State of Md., 1963-64, chmn., 1964-68; mem. Seafood adv. com. Wye Inst., 1965-68. Trustee Benedictine Sch. for Retarded Children, Ridgely, Md. Served with AUS, 1942-43. Episcopalian. Clubs: Ocean City Marlin, Talbot Country, Chesapeake Bay Yacht (bd. mem.); Tred Avon Yacht. Author: Gunning the Chesapeake, 1963; Sanctuary Pond, 1967. Home: Easton MD Died Aug. 1968.

WALSH, THEODORE EDWIN, univ. prof.; b. Calcutta, India, Sept. 1, 1900; s. Theodore Newton and Edith May (Hillier) W.; A.B., Kings Coll., Cambridge U., Eng., 1921; med. tng. St. Thomas' Hosp., London, Eng., 1921-25; m. Octavia McNamara, June 14, 1930; 1 son, Peter Newton; came to U.S., 1929, naturalized citizen, 1937. Asst. med. officer, Sarawak, Borneo, 1926-29; instr. oto-laryngology, U. of Chicago, 1931-33, asst. prof., 1933-35, asso. prof., 1935-40; prof. oto-laryngology, Washington U., St. Louis 1940-68, prof. emeritus, 1968-71, chmn. dept. otolaryngology, 1940-66. Med. service cons. USAF, VA, NIH, Dept. Health, Edn. and Welfare. Licentiate, Royal Coll. Physicians, Royal Coll. Surgeons. Fellow American College of Surgeons, American Laryngological Association; member A.M.A., American Otol. Soc. (pres. 1963-64), Acad. Ophthalmology and Oto-laryngology, Am. Laryngol., Rhinol. and Otol. Soc. (pres. 1960; editor Transactions 1946-67), Alpha Omega Alpha. Editor of Laryngoscope, 1942-71. Home: St Louis MO Died Apr. 29, 1971.

WALTER, ELLIOT VINCENT, merchandiser; born New York City; s. Charles Frederick and Katherine (Cleary) W.; student N.Y.U.; m. Paula Senner, June 1925; children—Elliot Paul, Paula Katherine. With R. H. Macy & Co., Inc., 1924-59, beginning as asst. controller, successively asst. buyer housewares dept., dept. mgr. maj. basement housewares, mdse. counsel houseware and silverware depts., v.p., sr. vice pres. in charge home furnishing, 1924-56, president Macy's New York, 1956-58, chmn. bd., 1958-59, ret.; dir. Am. Surety Co. Active in civic work including Boy Scouts, A.R.C., Greater New York Fund, Cath. Charities. Home: Manhasset NY Died May 30, 1971.

WALTER, WILLIAM EMLEY, editorial director; b. Green Tree, Chester Co., Pa., Dec. 3, 1870; s. John Hannum and Henrietta Deacon (Emley) W.; grad. Friends' Central Sch., Phila., 1889; B.S., Swarthmore Coll., 1892; m. Caroline Packer Sargent, of St. Paul, Minn., Dec. 28, 1897. Began with Curtis Pub. Co., Phila., 1894, and asst. sec.; editorial dir. same, 1911-14. Dir. Curtis Inst. of Music Phila. Home: Swarthmore PA*‡

WALTERS RAYMOND, educator, author; b. Bethlehem, Pa., Aug. 25, 1885; s. L. F. and Ida (Keller) W.; B.A., Lehigh U., 1907, M.A., 1913, LL.D., 1932; Litt.D., Washington Coll., 1933; LL.D., Coll. of Charleston, 1935, U. of Toledo, 1935, Swarthmore Coll., 1937, Northwestern U., 1942, Northeastern U., 1947, U. Chattanooga, 1951, U. Akron, Xavier U., 1954, Miami U., U. Cin., 1955; D.H.L., Hebrew Union Coll., 1945; A.F.D. (hon.), Cin. Conservatory of Music, 1955; m. Elsie Rosenberg, Oct. 26, 1909 (dec.); children—Raymond, Everett, Philip Garrison. Newspaper work, 1907-11; instr. English, Lehigh U., 1911-17, asst. prof., 1917-21, registrar, 1912-21; dean, also tchr. in English Dept., Swartmore Coll., 1921-32; pres. U. Cin., 1932-55, pres. emeritus; lectr. Tokyo, Kyoto and other Japanese Universities, 1949. Served as registrar, capt., A.G.D., Central O.T.S., Camp Zachary Taylor, Ky., June 1918-Feb. 1919. Coll. inspector, Assn. Am. Univs., 1930-48. Mem. com. on fed. relations Am. Council on Edn., 1942-55. Mem. Senate United Chpts. Phi Beta Kappa, 1942-55; pres. Ohio Coll. Assn., 1935-36; trustee Cin. Inst. Fine Arts, Soc, for Advancement of Edn.; mem. Archeol. Inst. America, Cincinnati Chapter Alliance Francaise, Cin. Hist. Soc. (hon.), English Speaking Union (trustee Cin. branch), Modern Language Assn. American, Society Engineering Education, American Legion, S.A.R., Hon. Order Ky. Colls., Beta Gamma Sigma, Phi Beta Kappa, Kappa Delta Pi, Omicron Delta Kappa, Scabbard and Blade; Va. Soc. of the Cincinnati (medal); fellow A.A.A.S. Author: The Bethlehem Bach Choir, 1918; (with others) The Story of the Field Artillery Central Officers. Tng. Sch., 1919; Bethlehem Long Ago and To-Day, 1923; Silver Anniversary edit. The Bethlehem Bach Choir, 1923; Educational Jottings Abroad, 1924; Stephen Foster: Youth's Golden Gleam, 1936; Historical Sketch of the University of Cincinnati, 1941; One Branch of the Walters Family (history), 1956); Gifts and Bequests to Higher Education, 1959. Contbr. about 450 articles on ednl. and literary subjects in magazines, revs. Asso. editor School and Society, 1921-27, staff mem. since 1929. Statistician of Am. univ. and coll. enrollment since 1919. Episcopalian. Clubs: Commercial (hon.), Literary, University (Cincinnati); Franklin Inn (Phila.). Home: Cincinnati OH Died Oct. 25, 1970; buried Spring Grove Cemetery, Cincinnati OH

WALTERS, WILLIAM H., business exec.; m. Mary Constance Savage, Jan. 31, 1925; children—William C. (dec.), Richard J., Bernard F. Chmn. bd., chief exec. officer, dir. Diamond Internat. Corp.; dir. U.S. Playing Card Card Co., Security Nat. Bank of L.I.; trustee Emigrant Indsl. Savs. Bank. Clubs: Athletic, Union League, Canadian, Sky, Manhasset Bay Yacht (all N.Y.). Home: Manhasset LI NY Died Sept. 3, 1970.

WALTON, ALFRED GRANT, clergyman; b. Kalamazoo, Mich., Oct. 17, 1887; s. David and Margaret (Thomson) W.; A.B., Oberlin Coll., 1911, D.D., 1927; B.D., Oberlin Theol. Sem., 1914; A.M., Columbia, 1913; LL.D., Am. Internat. Coll., Springfield, Mass., 1935; L.H.D., Kalamazoo Coll., 1941; m. Mary I. Ingell, Jan. 1, 1916; children—Carolyn Margaret (Mrs. John Thayer Taintor), Gloria Louise (Mrs. Burton Knust), Alfred Grant. Ordained to ministry Congl. Ch., 1914; asst. pastor Pilgrim Ch., St. Louis, 1914-17; pastor first congl. ch. Stamford, Conn., 1917-31, Hope Congl. Ch., Springfield, Mass., 1931-34, Tompkins Av. Congl. Ch., Bklyn., 1934-42, Flatbush-Tompkins Congl. Ch., Bklyn., 1942-70. Served as capt. A.R.C. Bur. Personnel, Paris, 1918-19; dir. Bklyn. chpt. A.R.C., 1953-70. Trustee Bklyn. Pub. Library, 1951-70, Le Moyne Coll., Memphis, 1934-37; mem. Bd. Pub. Welfare, Springfield, Mass., 1934; pres. Fairfield County. (Conn.) Council Religious Edn., 1927-29; moderator Fairfield County Assn. Congl. Chs. and Ministers, 1929-30; dir. Boston Seaman's Friend Soc., 1929-31; mem. exec. com. Brooklyn Fedn. Chs., 1935-70; sec. adminstrv. com. Am. Missionary Assn. N.Y., 1925-35; dir. Bklyn. Home for Blind, 1936-70; pres. Bklyn. Brotherhood of Congl. Ministers, 1938-39; v.p. Home Bds. Congl. Chs. in U.S., 1940, pres. 1942-48; moderator N.Y.C. Congl. Ch. Assn., 1940; dir. Corp. for Gen. Council Congl. Christian Chs. in U.S. 1954-70; dir. Bklyn. div. Protestant Council, 1963. Dir Bklyn. chpt. A.R.C., 1959-70; mem. N.Y. State Com Cemeteries, 1960-63; dir. Congl. Hist. Soc., 1960-70 Trustee Berkeley Institute, 1943-70, Trustee Bklyn Pub. Library; director Brooklyn Eye and Ear Hosp. 1945-54. Republican nominee for U.S. Congress Bklyn., 1966. Mason (grand chaplain Grand Lodg N.Y. 1965-70. Clubs: Rotary, Brooklyn, Clerical, Quil Apollo (director). Author: Stamford Historic Sketches, 1922; This I Can Believe, 1935; For Mind an Heart, 1937; Highways to Happiness, 1939; Life I What You Make It, 1942; Living Waters, 1946; Song for the Seasons, 1947; The Radiant Way, 1948; Walkin with God, 1948; Lyrics for Living, 1963, also brochure and religious articles. Radio preacher: Fed. Council Chs Christ in Am. Syndicated prayers Nat. Council Chs U.S., 1958-70. Home: Brooklyn NY Died July 9, 197(

WALTON, ARTHUR CALVIN, educator; Meadville, Pa., Oct. 16, 1892; s. Calvin Levi and Minn Belle (Stevens) W.; B.A., Northwestern U., 1914, M.A 1915; student Harvard, 1915-17; Ph.D., U. of Ill., 192 student U. of Colo., summer, 1926; m. Isyl Spiker, Ju 30, 1919; children—James Calvin, Robert Lesli Richard Earl. Instr. biology, North Central Col Naperville, Ill., 1917-18, asst. prof., 1919-21, pro 1921-22 and 1923-24; prof. biology, Knox Col Galesburg, 1924-25, chmn. dept. biology, 1925-54, pro geology and geography, chmn. dept., 1954-67, Walla C. Abbott, prof., 1940-67; civilian instr. med. arts a geography, Army Air Forces Tech. Training Com Knox Coll., 1943-46; mem. summer faculty U. of I 1924, 25, 27; mem. summer faculty U. of Col

1928-33; visiting asso., Brit. Museum Natural History, London, Eng., 1932; mem. zoology staff U.S.P.H.S., Washington, D.C., 1939-40, summer 1941. Served with San. Service, A.E.F., 1918-19. Mem. Corp. of Bermuda (B.W.I.) Biol. Sta. Fellow A.A.A.S.; mem. Am. Soc. Zoology, Am. Soc. Parasitologists (pres.), Am. Soc. Systematic Zoology, Am. Micros. Soc., Ill. Acad. Sci., Phi Beta Kappa, Sigma Xi. Republican. Presbyn. Co-author: Introduction to Nematology, 1940. Contbr. numerous articles on parasitology and cytology to scientific jours. Home: Galesburg IL Died Apr. 23, 1967.

WALTON, ARTHUR KEITH, mdsg. co. exec.; b. Kalamazoo, May 25, 1909; s. Arthur and Rena (Moore) W.; B.S. in Elec. Engring., Mich. State U., 1930; m. Hazel Elizabeth Chapman, Nov. 24, 1932; children—Stephen K., Pamela (Mrs. Pat Byers), Donald K. Mdse. devel. technician Sears, Roebuck & Co., Chgo., 1931-42; mdse. mgr.-chief engr. Newark Stove Co. (O.), 1942-45, v.p., 1945-48; sr. buyer tire and tube dept. Sears, Roebuck & Co., 1948-51, nat. supr. dept., 1951-58, v.p. charge factories, 1958-66, gen. mgmt. cons., corp. dir., from 1966; former chmn. bd., dirs. Copolymer Rubber and Chem. Corp., Baton Rouge; past pres., dir. Calcasieu Chem. Corp., New Orleans; dir. Hazeltine Corp., Little Neck, N.Y., Du-Wel Metal Products, Inc., Bangor, Mich. Bd. dirs. Chgo. YMCA. Mem. president's council of bus. assos. Elmhurst Coll. Member of American Management Association, Ill. C. of C., Chgo. Assn. Commerce and Industry, Midwest Research Inst., Coll. Engring, Alumni Assn. Mich. State U., Newcomen Soc. N.Am. Conglist. Club: Chicago. Home: Elmhurst IL Died Jan. 13, 1972.

WALTON, CHARLES M(ILTON), JR., lawyer; b. Stamford, Conn., June 15, 1891; s. Charles M. and Mary A. (Lippoth) W.; A.B., Yale, 1914; LL.B., Harvard, 1917; m. Lorna Folsom Davenport, Dec. 29, 1917; children—Allison Davenport (Mrs. J. Conrad Breiby, Jr.), and Mary Folsom (Mrs. Norman A. Perry, Jr.). Assistant counsel for the Emergency Fleet Corp., Washington, 1917-19; admitted to N.Y. State bar, 1920, and since practiced in N.Y. City; asso. Rushmore, Bisbee & Stern, 1919-21, with Hornblower, Miller and Garrison and successor firms since 1922, mem. firm, 1926-68; now Wilkie Farr & Gallagher. Mem. Am., N.Y. State, N.Y. City bar assns., Am. Judicature Soc., Zeta Psi. Republican. Episcopalian. Clubs: Yale, Down Town Assn. (N.Y.C.); Orienta Beach (Mamaroneck, N.Y.). Home: Larchmont NY Died June 6, 1968; buried Woodlawn Cemetery, Stamford CT

WALTON, ELEANOR GOING, author; b. in Wilmington, Del.; classical ed'n at Madame Reed's Sem., New York. Made success on amateur stage, but now devotes herself to literature. Contb'r to mags. and newspaper syndicates. Author: She Will Not When She May, 1898 A9. Home: Wilmington DE Studio: 13 W. 26th St., New York NY‡

WALTON, HOWARD CHARLES, clergyman; b. Bethany, Ill., Jan. 18, 1897; s. John Azor and Anna Camilla (Bone) W.; B.A., Bethel Coll., McKenzie, Tenn., 1918; B.D., Cumberland Presbyn. Theological Seminary, McKenzie, 1920; M.A., Birmingham Southern College, 1924; D.D., Bethel College, 1942; married Ruby Louise Parham, Feb. 3, 1918; children—Maurine (Mrs. William J. Lanier, Jr.), Rev. Howard Charles, Jr. Began preaching 1914 and served as supply pastor during college and seminary periods; ordained Cumberland Presbyn. ministry, 1917; pastor First Ch., Birmingham, Ala., 1929-30, First Ch., Jackson, Tenn., 1932-43; pastor Central Cumberland Presbyterian Ch., Memphis, Tennessee, 1943-53; organized Calvary Cumberland Presbyn. Ch., 1959; services broadcast over Station WTJS, 1932-43; now engaged in evangelistic work. First president Young Peoples General Assembly, Austin Texas, 1924; mem. and campaign mgr. Educational Endowment Commission, Chattanooga since 1929, member executive committee since 1931, v.p. since 1941; denominatl. supt. Ala. Christian Endeavor Union, 1920-30, also represented the ch. in Internat. Council Religious Edn. (Chicago), 1926-30, Ala. Council Christian Edn., 1920-30, Birmingham Sunday Sch. Council, 1920-30; supervisor budget and tithing, Ala.-Miss. Synod of Cumberland Presbyn. Ch., 1922-30, same for Synod of W. Tenn., 1934-41; elected moderator Centennial Gen. Assembly Cumberland Presbyn. Ch., 1929, Synod of West Tenn., 1943; pres. Cumberland Presbyn. Ministers Association, Memphis, 1944, 1950; president Pan-Presbyterian Association, 1950. Trustee Y.M.C.A.; president City Pastors Association, 1934, 41; mem. bd. Internat. Daily Vacation Bible Schs. (New York), 1922-30; chmn. com. on lit. and theol., mem. com. on missions and pastoral supplies, Madison Presbytery. Mem. Southern Advisory Bd. of Internat. Soc. Christian Endeavor (Boston), 1923-30. Pres. Bd. of Missions and mem. com. on Literature and Theology, Memphis Presbytery. Mason. Contbr. to Book of Sermons, The Cumberland Presbyterian Pulpit, 1929, religious mags.; daily newspaper columnist; author gospel tracts. Compiler of Bethel College Centennial Book of Sermons, 1943. Home: Jackson TN Deceased.

WALTON, NORTON HALL, chem. engr.; b. Phila., Nov. 26, 1910; s. William Berkheimer and Emma Jane (Hall) W.; B.S. U. Pa., 1932; m. Ruth Anne Bowen, Oct. 12, 1934 (div.); 1 son, William Alfred; m. 2d, Margarete Wilson, Nov. 1967. Asst. supt. chemicals Atlantic Refining Co., Phila., 1933-60; operating supt., asst. to plant mgr. Sun Olin Chem. Co., Claymont, Del., 1960-66, marketing tech. asst., 1966-67, manager commercial development, 1967-69. Registered profl. engr., Pa., Del. Mem. Nat. Soc. Profl. Engrs., Am. Inst. Chem. Engrs., Am. Chem. Soc. Engring. and Tech. Socs. Council Delaware Valley (chmn. 1960-61), Phila. Sci. Council (pres. 1960-63), Phila. Engrs. Club, Alpha Chi Sigma, Sigma Zeta. Republican. Episcopalian. Home: Springfield PA Died Sept. 12, 1969; buried Boehm's Cemetery Blue Bell PA

WANDLESS, EDGAR GRIFFIN, lawyer; b. Bklyn., Oct. 29, 1892; s. William Richard and Charlotte Frances (Griffin) W.; m. Florence E. Keenan, Oct. 12, 1918. Admitted to N.Y. bar, 1914, practiced in N.Y.C., 1914-66; sr. mem. Havens, Wandless, Stitt & Tighe; spl. asst. U.S. atty., also spl. asst. U.S. atty. gen., 1926-29. Dir. North Jersey Trust Co. Dist. counsel N.Y.-U.S. Shipping Bd., World War I. Clubs: Arcola Country (N.J.); Black Meadow, Anglers (N.Y.C.); Tabusintac (New Brunswick, Can.); Union League. Home: Ridgewood NJ Died Dec. 10, 1966.

WANGCHUK, MAHARAJA JIGME DORJI, ruler of Bhutan. Address: Paro Thimbu Bhutan Died July 1972.

WANK, ROLAND ANTHONY, architect; b. Budapest, Hungary, Oct. 2, 1898; attended Royal Polytechnicum, Budapest, 1917-19, Tech. U., Brunn, Czechoslovakia, 1919-21; also studied Coll. of Beaux-Arts and Sch. of Applied Arts, Budapest; LL.D., Fairleigh Dickinson University, 1959; m. Piroska Szabo, Dec. 2, 1922; children—Peter John, Andrew George. Came to U.S., 1924, naturalized, 1930. Chief architect, European engring. and constrn. orgns., 1921-24; asso. with George Springsten, Fellheimer and Wagner firms, 1924-33; chief designer, Grand St. Apts., N.Y. City (A.I.A. gold medal), Cincinnati Union Terminal (A.I.A. gold medal); head architect, Tenn. Valley Authority, 1933-44; chief architect, Greenhills (Ohio) Resettlement Adminstrn.; chief cons. architect, Rural Electrification Adminstrn.; designer engring. structures, towns, pub., semi-pub. and comp. bldgs. Chief designer, Albert Kahn Asso. Architects & Engr., Inc. 1944-45; mem. firm Wank, Adams & Slavin, architects and engrs., 1945-70, sr. partner, 1958-70; archtl. cons. UN Hdqrs. Commn., 1946. Past mem. Planning Bd., City of New Rochelle, N.Y. Fellow A.I.A.; member American Inst. Planners, Nat. Association Planning Officials, Nat. Planning Assn., Nat. Assn. of Housing Officials. Contbr. articles to mags; spl. lectures at Harvard and M.I.T.; critic at Princeton. Home: New Rochelle NY Died Apr. 22, 1970.

WANLASS, RALPH PAGE, lawyer; b. at Provo, Utah, Sept. 17, 1912; s. William L. and Eva (Page) W.; A.B., Utah State U., 1936; LL.B. with distinction, George Washington U., 1936; m. Kathryn Caine, June 15, 1939; children—George R., Kathryn Ellen, Elizabeth Caine. Admitted to D.C. bar, 1935, Ohio bar, 1965; practice in Washington, 1935-52; mem. firm Mayle & Wanlass, 1940-52; with Champion Papers, Inc., Hamilton, O., 1952-65, sec., 1960-65, legal counsel, 1960-65; partner firm Frost & Jacobs, Cin., 1965-68. Mem. bd. edn. Wyoming, O., 1958-65, pres., 1960. Served to capt. AUS, 1943-46. Mem. Am. Bar Assn., Order of Coif, Phi Kappa Phi, Phi Delta Phi. Club: Maketewah Country (Cin.). Home: Cincinnati OH Died Apr. 7, 1968.

WANNAMAKER, OLIN DANTZLER, educator; b. Bamberg, S.C., July 16, 1875; s. Francis Marion and Eleanor Margaret (Bellinger) W.; A.B., Wofford Coll., Spartanburg, S.C., 1896; A.M., Vanderbilt U., Nashville, Tenn., 1900; A.M., Harvard, 1902; m. Katharine Hume, of New Haven, Conn., Feb. 7, 1907; 1 dau., Margaret Bushnell. Actg. head dept. English, Wofford Coll., 1900-01; prof. English, Canton (China) Christian Coll., 1902-08; actg. head dept. English, U. of Ark., 1909-11; head dept. English, Ala. Poly. Inst., 1911-15, Southern Methodist U., Dallas, Tex., 1915-19; adminstr. Am. ednl. instns. in China since 1921. American director trustees Lingnan U., Canton, China; trustee. Asso. Bds. Christian Colls. in China; director Anthrop. Soc. America; mem. Chi Phi, Phi Beta Kappa. Author: A Practical Grammar of English (Shanghai), 1915; With Italy in Her Final War of Liberation, 1922; Rudolf Steiner—An Introduction to His Life and Thought, 1928. Translator of several works by Rudolf Steiner and other books from the German. Home: 54 Morningside Drive. Office: 150 5th Av., New York NY‡

WANNAMAKER, WILLIAM HANE, university administrator; born at Bamberg, South Carolina, September 28, 1873; son of Francis Marion and Eleanor Margaret (Bellinger) W.; A.B., Wofford Coll., Spartanburg, S.C., 1895; A.M., Trinity Coll., Durham, N.C., 1901; studied Harvard Grad. Sch., 1901-03, univs. of Berlin, Tubingen, Leipzig and Bonn, 1903-05; A.M., Harvard, 1902; Litt.D., Wofford, 1917; m. Isabel Stringfellow, June 30, 1903; children—Margaret Elizabeth, William Hane, Isabel, Harriet Foote. Prof. of German lang. and lit., Trinity Coll. (now Duke University), 1902-42, dean, 1917-42, dean of Duke Univ. and vice president educational division, 1926-48, vice chancellor since 1948. Trustee Watts Hosp. Mem. Phi Beta Kappa, Chi Phi. Dem. Methodist. Commd. 2d lt. inf., U.S. Army, 1918. Home: Durham NC‡

WANTLAND, WAYNE W(ARDE), univ. prof.; born Sheridan, Ill., Sept. 5, 1905; s. Hosmer Vorhees and Elma Maude (Burgess) W.; student North Central Coll., Naperville, Ill., 1923-24, Northern Ill. State Teachers Coll., DeKalb, 1924-25 and summers of 1925, 1926 and 1927; B.S., Northwestern U., Evanston, Ill., 1930, M.A., 1932, Ph.D. 1935; m. Edna Marie Lohmeyer, Aug. 19, 1928 (deceased September 11, 1963); 1 son, William Stanley; m. second, Evelyn Kendrick Kinney, Apr. 29, 1964. Principal of Newark (Ill.) High Sch., 1925-27, supt., 1927-29; asst. in zoology, Northwestern U., 1930-34, instr., 1934-37; prof. biology, DePaul U., Chicago, 1935-37; instructor zoology, Eastern Ill. State Teachers Coll., Charleston, Ill., 1937-38; dir. biol. sci., Stephens Coll., Columbia, Mo., 1938-42; fellow Am. Council on Edn., U. of Chicago, 1940-41; prof. and head dept. of biology, Ill. Wesleyan U., Bloomington, 1944-45, dean of men, 1944-45, chmn. div. natural sciences, 1945-71, and George C. and Ella Beach Lewis prof. of biology, 1947-71, dir. Cancer Research Program, 1948-51, dir. Biol. Research Lab., 1951-71, dir. U.S. Pub. Health Research on mouth protozoa, 1956-64, also bd. dirs. Ill. Wesleyan U. Served as lt. administration and malariology, USN, 1942-44. Fellow A.A.A.S.; mem. Internat. Assn. Dental Research, Am. Soc. Zoologists, Am. Inst. Biol. Scis., Am. Soc. Parasitologists, Am. Cancer Soc., Ill. Acad. Sci., N.E.A., Research Soc. Am., Soc. Protozoologists, Am. Legion, Sigma Xi, Phi Kappa Phi. Republican. Methodist. Mason. Club: College Alumni (Bloomington). Contbr. profl. jours. Home: Bloomington IL Died Mar. 4, 1971; buried Bloomington IL

WARBASSE, JAMES PETER, surgeon, economist; born Newton, New Jersey, November 22, 1866; son Joseph and Harriet (Northrup) Warbasse; M.D., Columbia University, post-graduate universities of Gottingen and Vienna; m. Agnes Dyer, Apr. 15, 1903; children—Henry D., Agnes, James P., Richard N., Eric, Vera. Intern, 1889-91, attending surgeon, until 1909, M.E. Hosp., Brooklyn, N.Y.; attending surgeon, 1903-06, chief surgeon, 1906-19, German Hosp., Brooklyn. Editor N.Y. State Jour. Medicine, 1906-09; spl. editor Am. Jour. Surgery, 1909-19. Fellow Am. Coll. Surg. A.M.A., N.Y. Acad. Med. Retired from surgery, 1919, to devote time to social and economic study. Lecturer on med. sociology, L.I. Coll. of Medicine, since 1932. Mem. Consumers Bd. of NRA. Pres. Coop. League of U.S.A., 1916-41; organizer and pres. Rochdale Inst. since 1937; mem. Central Com. Internat. Coop. Alliance; Am. del. to all Internat. Coop. Congresses since 1913. Author: Doctors of Samuel Johnson, 1908; Medical Sociology, 1909; The Conquest of Disease, 1910; Surgical Treatment, 3 vols., 1919; Cooperative Democracy, 1923, 27, 36, 42, 47; What Is Cooperation?, 1927; The Doctor and the Public, 1935; Cooperation, a Way of Peace, 1939, 47; Problems of Cooperation, 1941; The Cooperative Way: A Method of World Reconstruction, 1945; Peace Through Cooperation, 1949. Contributor to International Text Book of Surgery, Keen's Surgery, Encyclopedia of Soc., and other works; also many surg. monographs and a continuous series of articles on cooperation since 1919. Has lectured and given courses on cooperation in more than 100 colleges and universities in the United States, Canada, England, Switzerland, Germany, Czechoslovakia, Russia and France. Home: Woods Hole MA‡

WARBURG, GERALD FELIX, musician; b. N.Y.C., May 12, 1901; s. Felix Moritz and Frieda (Schiff) W.; grad. Middlesex Sch., 1919; student Harvard, 1923, Inst. Musical Art, 1920-21; m. Marion Bab, June 5, 1923; children—Felix Max, Geraldine (Mrs. Louis Zetzel); m. 2d, Natica Nast, Dec. 23, 1933; children—Jeremy (Mrs. William Russo), Jonathan Frederick. Debut cello soloist N.Y. Philharmonic Symphony, 1925; mem. Stradivarius Quartet, 1930-36; founder Stradivarius Soc., 1940-41; cons. sec. of war on V disc. program, 1943-44; condr. Bklyn. Symphony Orch., 1939-41. Chmn. Music adv. com. High Sch. Performing Arts, N.Y.C.; v.p. Carnegie Hall Corporation; v.p., incorporator City Center N.Y., 1942-53; dir. Musicians Found. Mem. N.Y.N.G., 1920-21. Clubs: Harvard, Lotos, Century Assn., Coffee House, Bohemians (N.Y.C.); Harvard Faculty (Cambridge, Mass.). Home: New York City NY Died Feb. 14, 1971; buried Salem Fields, Queens NY

WARBURG, JAMES PAUL, author; born Hamburg, Germany, Aug. 18, 1896; s. Paul M. and Nina J. (Loeb) W.; brought to U.S. in infancy; grad. Middlesex Sch., Concord, Mass., 1913; A.B., Harvard U., 1917; m. Jean Melber, Aug. 28, 1948; children—James Paul, Jennifer Joan, Philip Neff, Sarah Neff; April, Andrea, Kay (by previous marriage). With B.&O. Railroad Company, 1916, National Metropolitan Bank, Washington, D.C.,

1919, First Nat. Bank of Boston, 1919-21; v.p. Internat. Acceptance Bank, N.Y. City, 1921-29, pres., 1931-32; pres. Internat. Manhattan Co., 1929-31; vice chmn. of bd. Bank of the Manhattan Co., 1932-35; director of The Bydale Co., Fontenay Corp.; dir. Polaroid Corporation. Special assistant to coordinator of information, 1941-42; deputy director, Overseas Branch, Office of War Information, July, 1942-Feb. 1944; stationed London and Washington. Seaman 2d class, later lt. j.g. Navy Flying Corps, 1917-18. Financial advisor World Econ. Conf., London, 1933. Chmn. bd. Julliard School of Music. Member Am. Acad. Polit. and Social Sci. (dir.), Phi Beta Kappa. Democrat. Hebrew religion. Clubs: Econ., Harvard (N.Y.); Cosmos (Washington); Authors' (London). Author: Wool & Wool Manufacture, 1920; Cotton & Cotton Manufacture, 1921; Hides and Leather Manufacture, 1921; Acceptance Financing, 1922; Three Textile Raw Materials, 1923; And Then What (verse), 1931; Shoes, Ships and Sealing Wax (verse), 1932; The Money Muddle, 1934; It's Up to Us, 1934; Hell Bent for Election, 1935; Still Hell Bent, 1936; Peace in Our Time?, 1940; Our War and Our Peace, 1941; Man's Enemy and Man (verse) 1942; Foreign Policy Begins at Home, 1944; Unwritten Treaty, 1945; Germany, Bridge or Battleground, 1947; Put Yourself in Marshall's Place, 1948; Last Call for Common Sense, 1949; Faith, Purpose and Power, 1950; Victory Without War, 1951; How to Co-exist, 1952; Germany-Key to Peace, 1953; The United States in a Changing World, 1954; Turning Point Toward Peace, 1955; Danger and Opportunity, 1956; Agenda for Action—Peace Through Disengagement, 1957; The West in Crisis, 1959; Reville for Rebels, 1960; Disarmament-the Challenge of the 1960s, 1961; The Liberal Papers, 1962; Toward a Strategy of Peace, 1964; The Long Road Home (autobiography), 1964; Time for Statesmanship, 1965; The U.S. in the Postwar World, 1966; Western Intruders, 1967; Crosscurrents in the Middle East, 1968. Home: Greenwich CT Died June 3, 1969.

WARBURG, OTTO HEINRICH, scientist, biology; b. Freiburg, Baden, Oct. 8, 1883; s. Emil Warburg and Elizabeth Gertner; Dr. der Chemie, Berlin, 1906; Dr. der Medizin, Heidelberg U., 1911. Dir. Max Planck Inst. Zellphysiologie, Berlin-Dahlem, 1933-70. Served with Prussian Horse Guards, 1914-18. Decorated Ordre pour le Merite, Great Cross Star and Shoulder Ribbon, Bunderrepublik; recipient Nobel prize for medicine, 1931. Fgn. mem. Royal Soc. Author: Freedom of West Berlin, 1963. Address: Berlin-Dahlem Germany Died Aug. 1970.

WARD, ALGER LUMAN, chemical cons.; b. Easthampton, Mass., May 4, 1890; s. Oscar and Ella Jeanette (Alexander) W.; grad. Williston Acad., Easthampton, 1910; B.S. in chemistry, Syracuse U., 1914, M.S., 1915, Sc.D., 1941; m. Emma Undritz, June 5, 1915. Research chemist for E. I. du Pont de Nemours & Co., 1915-20, discovering processes for synthesis of acetic acid, acetone, alky anilines, ethylene glycol and glycerine, covered by basic Am. and foreign patents; research chemist for United Gas Improvement Co., Phila., 1920-34; mgr. chem. labs. United Gas Improvement Co., 1934-35; principal work in physical properties, separation and polymerization of hydrocarbons; cause and prevention of formation of liquid-phase and vapor-phase gums in gas distribtuion systems (basic Am., fgn. patents); metal corrosion; dir. Research Laboratory, Pa. Industrial Chemical Corporation, 1946-55; principal work in synthetic resins, plasticizers for synthetic rubber, binders for asphaltic floor tile. Discovered and exponent (with S. S. Kurtz, Jr.) the Refractivity Intercept. Awarded Louis E. Levy medal Franklin Inst. 1938. Mem. Franklin Inst., Am. Chem. Soc., Soc. of Chem. Industry, Sigma Beta, Alpha Chi Sigma. Republican. Episcopalian (vestryman St. Clement's Ch., Phila.). Co-author: Styrene, 1951; Styrene Monomer, Ency. Chemical Technology, 1954. Contbr. to and honorary associate editor of The Science of Petroleum, 1938. Contributor numerous articles to profl. jours. Home: Bala-Cynwyd PA Died Jan. 19, 1969; buried West Laurel Hill Cemetery, Bala-Cynwyd PA

WARD, ARCHIBALD ROBINSON, bacteriologist; b. Ithaca, N.Y., Sept. 12, 1875; s. Albert Riley and Henrietta (Robinson) W.; B.S.A., Cornell U. Coll. of Agr., 1898; D.V.M., N.Y. State Vet. Coll. (Cornell), 1901; m. Flora Lillian Pinkham, May 21, 1914 (died 1915); m. 2d, Augusta Wolfe Russell, July 25, 1917 (died 1945); 1 daughter, Alice Russell. Assistant in dairy bacteriology, Cornell University College of Agriculture, 1898-1901; with University of Calif., 1901-10 (except 1 yr.), in many capacities, including instr. and asst. prof. vet. science, dir. State Hygienic Lab., asst. prof. bacteriology, research in infectious diseases of animals, of man, etc.; leave of absence, 1909-10, at Hygienic Lab. of U.S. Pub. Health and Marine Hosp. Service; in P.I., 1910-14, serving as chief veterinarian Bur. of Agr., dean Coll. Vet. Science and prof. preventive vet. medicine of U. of Philippines, also pres. Vet. Examining Bd. of P.I.; sr. pathologist and acting chief Pathol. Div. Bur. of Animal Industry, U.S. Dept. Agr., June 15, 1914, title sr. pathologist, 1918; prof. bacteriology and pathology in charge of Biol. Lab., Md. State Coll. Agr., 1918; asst. chief dairy research

bur. of The Mathews Co., Detroit, Mich., 1923-32; operating dairy testing laboratory and milk quality control service since 1932; consultant, dairy research bur., The Mathews Co., Detroit, 1940-45. Pres. P.I. Vet. Med. Assn., 1913-14; mem. Soc. Am. Bacteriologists (charter mem., pres. Mich. br. 1936-38), Am. Vet. Med. Assn., Am. Pub. Health Assn., Kappa Sigma, Sigma Xi; hon. member Alpha Zeta (California Chapter). Club: Faculty (Berkeley). Author: Pure Milk and the Public Health, 1909; Diseases of Domesticated Birds (with B. J. Gallagher), 1919. Contbr. articles on bacteriology of milk, city milk supply, diseases of fowls, diseases of cattle (more particularly rinderpest), etc. Home: 1986 Waverly Av., Detroit 6 MI*‡

WARD, ARTHUR SPRAGUE, writer; b. Grenada, Miss., July 28, 1869; s. Henry Clay (brig. gen. U.S.A) and Susie M. (Denny) W.; ed. Worcester (Mass.) Acad., Chauncy Hall Sch., Boston; unmarried. Far Eastern corr., respectively, United Press, Boston Herald, New York Herald, New York Times, 1904-14; with Am. Ambulance Corps in France, 1914-15; sec. Am. Red Cross Sanitary Commn. to Serbia, 1915; assigned Intelligence Corps, U.S.A., 1918; mem. Com. on Pub. Information, Paris, 1919; lay writer med. information dept., League Red Cross Socs., Geneva, Switzerland, 1920-21; historian, Am. Graves Regist. Service, France, 1922. Mem. Loyal Legion. Republican. Episcopalian. Clubs: Nat. Press (Washington, D.C.); Explorers (New York); Authors', Connaught (London); Touring Club of France. Awarded medal by Govt. of France; Order of St. Sava by King Alexander of Serbia. Home: 367 Worcester St., Wellesley Hills MA‡

WARD, CLARENCE RICHARD, architect; b. Niles, Mich., Dec. 19, 1870; s. James and Helen Maria (Everts) W.; ed. high sch.; spl. tech. course in architecture and engring., Calif. Mil. Acad., 1887-90; married. In professional practice, Calif., 1892——; architect of 100 bldgs. built in San Francisco after the fire of 1906; also of a large number in San Francisco and elsewhere before the fire. Mem. exec. council of archtl. commn. of Panama-Pacific Internat. Expn., and designer, with J. H. Blohme, of Palace of Machinery. Ex-pres. Calif. State Bd. Architecture. Mem. A.I.A. and Northern Calif. Chapter same; hon. mem. San Francisco Architectural Club. Clubs: Family, Bohemian. Home: 150 Lake St., Oakland CA Office: 24 California St., San Francisco CA‡

WARD, GEORGE EHINGER, lawyer; b. Roswell, N.M., Mar. 3, 1932; s. Charles Francis and Emily (Stephens) W.; B.S., N.M. Mil. Inst., 1954; LL.B., Washington and Lee U., 1959; m. Mary Lane Reed, Jan. 2, 1960; one son, George Ehinger. Admitted to N.M. bar, 1959; practiced in Roswell, N.M., 1959-67. Mem. Chaves County Safety Council. Dep. sheriff, Chaves County, 1967-67; mem. N.M. Republican Central Com. Chmn. bd. dirs. Chaves County Heart Assn.; bd. regents N.M. Mil. Inst., 1967. Served to 1st lt. AUS, 1954-56. Mem. N.M. Mil. Inst. Polo Assn. (v.p.), American, Chaves County bar assns., State Bar N.M., S.C.V., S.A.R. (pres. Southeastern N.M.), N.M. Mil. Inst. Alumni Assn. (pres. Roswell), Aqualantes, Sojourners (sec.), Delta Kappa Epsilon, Phi Alpha Delta. Mason, Rotarian. Home: Roswell NM Died Apr. 7, 1967.

WARD, HALLETT SYDNEY, ex-congressman; b. Gates Co., N.C., Aug. 31, 1870; s. Nathan O. and Martha (Matthews) W.; ed. pub. schs. and under tutorship of Capt. Julien Henri Picot; studied law summer session U. of N.C.; m. Aileen Latham, of Plymouth, N.C., Sept. 23, 1896. Admitted to N.C. bar, 1894, and practiced at Plymouth; moved to Washington, N.C., 1904; mem. firm Ward & Grimes. Mem. N.C. Senate, 1899, 1901; solicitor 1st Jud. Dist. of N.C., 1906-10; mem. 67th and 68th Congresses (1921-25), 1st N.C. Dist.; mem. N.C. Senate, 1931. Democrat. Episcopalian. Mason (32 deg., Shriner). Home: Washington DC*‡

WARD, HENRY HEBER, b. W. Haven, Conn., July 20, 1871; s. Israel Kimberly and Katharine Louise (Hannah) W.; apptd. U.S. Naval Acad. from N.J., and grad. 1893; m. Mary Minturn Hartshorne, of Highlands, N.J., Nov. 9, 1898; children—Katharine L., Julia, Mary Minturn, Henrietta, Henry H. Commd. ensign U.S.N., 1895; lt. jr. grade, 1899; advanced 10 numbers and commd. lt., 1901. On U.S.S. Baltimore, Asiatic Sta., 1893-95; U.S.S. Maine, 1895-97; Navy Dept., Washington, 1897; served as spy in Spanish-Am. War, 1898, and awarded medal for extraordinary heroism" during the war; asst. to judge advocate on Schley Court of Inquiry, 1901; sec. Gen. Bd. of the Navy, and flag lt. European Sta.; resigned from Navy, 1903. Sec. Navy League of U.S., 1907-12, v.p., 1912-16. Officer and dir. various corpns. Clubs: Union, Brook, New York Yacht, University (New York); Metropolitan (Washington); Graduate (New Haven). Author: Naval Operations of the War with Spain, 1898. Address: 1 E. 51st St., New York NY‡

WARD, JOSHUA, lawyer; b. Georgetown, S.C., Jan. 22, 1894; s. S. Mortimer and Katherine (LaBruce) W.; B.S. in Elec. and Mech. Engring., Clemson U., 1915; LL.B., Fordham U., 1927, J.D., 1968; m. Marie Greves, Oct. 20, 1928; children—Joshua John, Penelope

Bentley. Admitted to N.Y. bar, 1928; practiced in N.Y.C., 1928-70, specializing in patents and trademarks; sr. partner firm Ward, McElhannon, Brooke and Fitzpatrick. Mem. Am. Bar Assn., Am. N.Y. patent law assns., Bar Assn. City N.Y., N.Y. County Lawyers Assn., N.Y. Southern Soc., Soc. Cincinnati. Republican. Episcopalian. Mason. Home: Summit NJ Died Mar. 21, 1970.

WARD, KENNETH WILLIAM, food co. exec.; b. Eureka, Cal., Mar. 5, 1909; s. William H. and Stella (Cureton) W.; ed. pub. schs., Eureka; m. Barbara Phares Laird, Mar. 5, 1954; children—Stephen, Susan (Mrs. Alvin J. Steffens), Timothy, John Laird. With Western Condensing Co., 1926-55, pres., dir., 1954-55, co. merged with Foremost Dairies, Inc., 1955, v.p. 1955-67, merged with McKesson & Robbins, Inc. becoming Foremost-McKesson, Inc., 1967, v.p. 1967-72; v.p. Foremost Foods Co., 1967-70, pres. 1970-72; pres. dir., Peebles Products Ltd., Can. 1954-72; chief exec. officer, dir. Montreal Casein Co. Ltd., Can., 1964-72. Vice-chmn. bd. dirs. Am. Dry Milk Inst., Inc. Mason (Shriner). Elk. Home: Woodside CA Died Aug. 12, 1972.

WARD, ORLANDO, army officer; b. Macon, Mo. Nov. 4, 1891; s. Ethelbert and Ada (Smith) W.; B.S. U.S. Mil. Acad., West Point, N.Y., 1914; attended Field Arty. Sch., 1923-24; distinguished grad. Command and Gen. Staff Sch., 1925-26; attended Army War Coll. 1936, Army Gen. Staff Coll., Langres, France, 1919 D.Sc. (honorary), University of Denver, 1946; married Edith Hanington, June 16, 1915; children—Katherine Hanington (dec.), Edith Hanington, Ada Smith Commd. 2d lt., Cav., U.S. Army, advanced through ranks to major general, 1942; served on Mexican border and with Punitive Expdn. in Mexico, 1916-17 transferred F.A., 1917, in 10th F.A., 3d Div., France Army of Occupation, Germany, 1917-19; on R.O.T.C. duty, U. of Wis., 1919-23; Ft. F.E. Warren, Wyo. 1926-29; gen. staff, Philippines, 1929-31; instr. and dir. gunnery dept., Ft. Sill, Okla., 1931-35; comdg. 1s Batln., 83d F.A., Ft. Benning, Ga., 1936-38; on Gen Staff, War Dept., 1938-41; sec. Gen. Staff, 1939-41 brig. and comdg. gen. 1st Armored Div., Ft. Knox, Ky. 1941-42; comdg. gen. 1st Armored Div., 1942-43 comdg. gen. Tank Destroyer Center, Camp Hood, Tex. June 1943-Jan. 1944; comdt. Field Arty. Sch., Ft. Sill Okla., Jan.-Oct., 1944; comdg. gen. 20th Armored Div. Germany, Oct. 1944-July 1945; comdg. Inf. Advanced Replacement Tng. Center, Camp Gordon, Ga., 1945 with War Dependency Bd., Washington, 1945; mem then pres. Confidential Personnel Bd., 1946; comdg. V Corps, Ft. Jackson, S.C., 1946, Replacement Sch Command, Ft. Bragg, N.C., 1946; In command of 6t Div., Korea, 1946-49; chief historical div., Dept. of the Army 1949-53. Awarded D.S.C., Legion of Merit wit oak leaf cluster, Silver Star with oak leaf cluster, Purpl Heart, D.S.M., Bronze Star Medal. Home: Denver CO Died Feb. 4, 1972; buried Fairmount Cemetery Denver CO

WARD, OSSIAN PEAY, architect; b. Louisville, Oc 21, 1875; s. John Hardin and Eliza C. (Peay) W.; E.E Cornell U., 1896, M.E.E., 1897; m. Isabel Hogan, Apr 27, 1922; children—Gertrude (dec.), Margaret (Mrs Dean C. Lauffer). Draftsman, Snead Archtl. Iro Works, Louisville, 1897-1901, D. H. Burnham & C Chgo., 1903-05; structural engr., Louisville, 1905-13 pvt. practice as architect and engr., Louisville, 1913-6 Fellow A.I.A.; mem. Phi Delta Theta. Unitarian. Home Louisville KY Died Feb. 2, 1966; buried Cave Hi Cemetery Louisville KY

WARD PEIRCE COLTON, company dir., farmer; b Lafayette, Ind., Nov. 3, 1885; s. Frederic William an Elizabeth (Peirce) W.; student Purdue U., 1906; m Edith Aishton, Sept. 23, 1911; children—Jean (Mr Ward Woollett), Peirce Colton, Edith. Engaged i farming, Rochester, Ind., 1936-70; dir. Public Servic Co. of Indiana, Inc., Plainfield, Ind., Indiana Gas Water Co., Indpls., Western Power & Gas Co., Lincoln Neb., Central Telephone Co., La Crosse Telephone Corp. (Wis.), Morris Telephone Co. (Ill.), Southeaster Telephone Co., Tallahassee, Worthington Telephor Co. (Minn.). Address: Rochester IN Died Jan. 1970

WARD, ROBERT W., business exec., cons.; b Washington, July 4, 1891; s. James M. and Lyda M (Brewer) W.; student Davidson's Bus. Coll., 1906-07; r Mayme H. Wellman, Nov. 28, 1912; children—Nanc (Mrs. R. C. Shutts), Bettie (Mrs. J. T. Callaham), W to dist. mgr., Am. Car & Foundry Co., Huntington, W Va., 1909-20, supt. stores and yards, 1920-21, supt. ca dept., 1921-25, gen. supt., 1925-32, asst. dist. mgr 1932-37, dist. mgr., 1937-46, vice pres. in charge mfg New York office, 1946-47, v.p. in charge of productio 1947-69; chairman of the board of the Huntingto Federal Savings & Loan Assn.; dir. Ohio Valley Bus. C Dir. St. Mary's Hosp. Mem. Am. Ordnance Assn. In Democrat. Roman Catholic. Clubs: New York Railroa Machinery, New York Railroad. Home: Huntingto WV Died Dec. 9, 1969.

WARD, WILLIAM EDGAR, banker; b. Cleveland, May 9, 1874; s. William E. and Annie E. W.; ed. pu schs., Cleveland; unmarried. In employ Euclid Av. Na

Bank, Cleveland, 1892-8; with Colonial Nat. Bank, 1898-04; became connected with Union Nat. Bank, 1904, 1st v.p. 1914; dir. Cuyahoga Lumber Co., Williamson Securities Co., Crawford Land Co., H. C. Christy Co. Home: 2020 Cornell Rd. Office: 308 Euclid Av., Cleveland OH‡

WARD, WILLIAM EVANS, mfg. exec.; b. Port Chester, N.Y., Nov. 14, 1912; s. Evans and Edna R. (Freeman) W.; student Taft Sch., Watertown, Conn., 1926-31; m. Mary Scott Piel, May 29, 1937. With Russell, Burdsall & Ward Bolt and Nut Co., Port Chester, 1931-73, beginning as apprentice machinist, successively asst. plant supt., plant supt., gen. mgr., v.p., then gen. mgr., pres., dir. Home: Greenwich CT Died Apr. 5, 1973.

WARDALL, WILLIAM JED, business executive; born at Tuscola, Ill., Feb. 22, 1885; son of Xenophon Leonidas and Emma A. (Sawyer) W.; A.B., University of Illinois, 1908; married Mary Sherrill Burry, April 20, 1912 (died January 17, 1942); married 2d, Suzette F. Beavers, November 18, 1947. Bond salesman, 1909-16; western mgr. Bonbright & Co., Inc., 1916-32; pres. and dir. of Asso. Telephone Utilities Co. and various subsidiaries, New York, 1932-33; co-receiver Asso. Telephone Utilities Co., 1933-34, trustee in reorganization, 1934-35; pres. General Telephone Corp., successor, 1935-36; corporate reorganization work for various other corps., 1937-38; trustee in reorganization of Broad St. Hosp., New York, 1938-39; sole trustee in reorganization of McKesson & Robbins, Inc., 1938-41; chmn. bd. The Best Foods, Inc., 1942-50. Mem. Phi Gamma Delta, Beta Gamma Sigma. Republican. Presbyterian. Clubs: University (N.Y.C. and Chgo.). Home: Syossett NY Died July 19, 1972; buried Cold Spring Harbor NY

WARDLE, ROBERT, JR., power co. exec.; b. Bklyn., Oct. 14, 1911; s. Robert and Margaret (Lang) W.; B.S. in Civil Engring., Ga. Inst. Tech., 1934; m. Elizabeth Collier, July 3, 1935; children—Margaret Elizabeth, Charles Collier, Robert III. With Ga. Power Co., 1934-41, 45-58, asst. to v.p. and gen. mgr., 1951-53, asst. to v.p. charge finance, 1953-58; v.p. Southern Co., Atlanta, 1958-62, Southern Services, Incorporated, 1963-69. Consultant Office Energy and Utilities, Exec. Office of President, Nat. Security Resources Bd., 1948-50; cons. to adminstr. Def. Prodn. Adminstrn., 1951. Served to lt. col., C.E., AUS, 1941-46; col. Res. Decorated Bronze Star. Mem. Soc. Am. Mil. Engrs., Ga. Engring. Soc., Illuminating Engring. Soc., Am. Legion, Ga. Inst. Tech., Alumni Assn., Phi Gamma Delta. Clubs: Cherokee Town and Country (Atlanta); Civitan. Home: Atlanta GA Died June 27, 1969; buried Westview Cemetery, Atlanta GA

WARDLEY, RUSSELL GEORGE, investment banker; b. Akron, O., Dec. 12, 1909; s. John George and Isabelle (Kelley) W.; student Cleve. Coll., Fenn Coll.; m. Helen L. Dawson, Aug. 22, 1946; children—Christine A., Russell Paul. With Fulton, Reid & Co., Cleve., 1947-68, v.p., 1951-68, also dir. Bd. govs. Midwest Stock Exchange. Served with AUS, World War II. Mem. Cleve. C. of C. Methodist. Kiwanian. Club: Cleve. Athletic. Home: Bedford OH Died Aug. 5, 1968; buried Crown Hill Cemetery, Twinsburg OH

WARDWELL, FRANK CARLTON, civil engr.; b. Conneaut, O., Aug. 30, 1887; s. Jonn B. and Anna J. (Wilcox) W.; B.S., Ohio State U., 1911, C.E., 1920; m. Nettie E. Peirsol, Aug. 23, 1912 (dec. Mar. 1952); 1 son, Frank P.; m. 2d, Grace Andress Grant, Nov. 18, 1958. Draftsman to asst. chief engr. various R.R.'s, 1912-24; engr. hydroelec. project Stone & Webster, 1925-35, chief engr., project mgr., 1941-50, cons. devel. Canadian iron ore fields, 1951-54; cost engr., sr. accountant, asst. project mgr. power projects TVA, 1936-40; cons. 1200 mile r.r. rebldg. Govt. of Mexico, 1955-59; exec. v.p., dir. Wardwell, Inc., Retail Mdse., Ft. Meade, Fla., 1960-68. Mem. panel Nat. Safety Council, 1947-50. Registered profl. engr., Ind. Fellow Am. Soc. C.E. Contbr. articles in field to profl. jours. Address: Winter Haven FL Died Jan. 22, 1968.

WARE, HARRY HUDNALL, JR., physician; b. Baltimore, Md., Mary 24, 1898; s. Harry Hudnall and Lucile (Reynolds) W.; student Coll. of William and Mary; M.D., Med. Coll. of Va., 1924; m. Mary Warren Williams, Feb. 1929; children—Harry Hudnall, III, James Latane, Marshall Taylor, Isabel Williams. Prof. obstetrics and gynecology Med. Coll. Va., chmn. dept. obstetrics and gynecology Med. Coll. of Va. Hosps. Mem. board visitors, College of William and Mary; mem. bd. trustees, endowment assn., Coll. of William and Mary. Diplomate Am. Bd. Obstetrics and Gynecology; fellow Am. Gynecol. Soc. (vice president 1961), American Association of Obstetricians and Gynecologists (vice pres. 1962), A.C.S., South Atlantic Assn. Obstetricians, Gynecologists (pres. 1953), Southeastern Surg. Congress, A.M.A., So. Med. Soc., So. Gynec. and Obstet. Soc. (pres. 1947-48); mem. Med. Soc. Va., Richmond Acad. Medicine (pres. 1948), Va. Obstet. and Gynecol. Soc. (pres. 1940), Alumni Assn. Medical College Virginia (pres. 1952), Am. Coll. Obstetricians and Gynecologist (bd. govs.), American Fertility Society (president-elect 1968-69), Phi Beta Kappa, Alpha Omega Alpha, Omicron Delta Kappa. Clubs: Commonwealth of Virginia; Country of Virginia; Rappahannock River Yacht, Tappahannock Yacht. Contbr. numerous papers in med. jours. Home: Richmond VA Died Feb. 6, 1973.

WARE, PAUL, lawyer; b. Chgo., Dec. 29, 1904; s. Charles Homer and Bertha (Chamberlain) W.; B.S., Northwestern, 1926, J.D., 1929; m. Betty Fulton, Nov. 29, 1935; children—Dale Chamberlain, Linda. Admitted to Ill. bar, 1930; atty. Wilson & Co., Inc., Chgo., 1930-69, sec., 1949-69; guest lectr. law sch. Northwestern. Dir. Chgo. Area Project (member of advisory committee 1958-69). Member American Society Corporate Secs. (Chgo. adv. com. 1955-58), Am., Chgo. bar assns., Phi Delta Phi, Phi Kappa Psi. Clubs: Executives, Economic. Contbr. law revs. Home: Glencoe IL Died Jan. 7, 1969.

WARE, SEDLEY LYNCH, prof. history; b. Jackson, Miss., Nov. 15, 1868; s. William Lynch and Mary Smith (Dabney) W.; Bachelier-es-Lettres, Ecole Libre Sainte Barbe, Paris, 1891; B.A., Oxford U., Eng., 1895; LL.B., Columbia, 1900; Ph.D., Johns Hopkins, 1908; m. Alice Turner Porter, Sept. 17, 1901; children—William Lynch, John Davis Dabney, William Porter, Mary Dabney (Mrs. Robert Daniel), Elizabeth Osborne (Mrs. Harry Ford), Alice Marye (Mrs. Alice Pember). Admitted to Va. bar, 1901; instr. Porter Mil. Acad., Charleston, S.C., 1903-04; instr. in history, Stanford, 1908-10; lecturer in English history, U. of Wis., 1910-11; Francis Houghteling prof. history, U. of the South, 1913-44. Mem. Phi Beta Kappa, Sigma Nu. Home: Univ. of the South, Sewanee TN‡

WARFIELD, HARRY RIDGELY, JR., engineer, research dir.; b. Morgantown, W.Va., Aug. 17, 1904; s. Harry Ridgely and Susan Elizabeth (Sadtler) W.; B.Engring., Johns Hopkins, 1928; m. Juliet Linn Reaney, June 17, 1932 (dec. Apr. 1968); children—Harry Ridgely III, Susan Linn; m. 2d, Helen Gardner Howard, Oct. 31, 1968. With works mgmt. course Westinghouse Electric Co., 1928; application engr. Silica Gel Corp., 1930; dist. engr. Frigidaire div. Gen. Motors Corp., 1932; partner Fonda and Warfield, cons. engrs., 1938-41; mem. Inst. Coop. Research, Johns Hopkins, 1947-69, research engr., 1948-50, asst. dir., 1950-53, dir., 1953-69. Mem. Md. N.G., 1931-53; served from 2d lt. to col. F.A., AUS, 1941-45, ETO. Decorated ETO Service Medal with Assault Arrowhead, Normandy, No. France, Rhineland and Central Germany battle stars, Legion of Merit, B.S.M. (U.S.); Legion of Honor, Croix de Guerre with palm (France); Order of Leopold, Croix de Guerre with palm (Belgium). Mem. Soc. Colonial Wars, Alpha Delta Phi. Tau Beta Pi, Omicron Delta Kappa. Episcopalian (exec. council Diocese Md. 1951-57). Home: Baltimore MD Died Oct. 3, 1969.

WARHEIT, ISAREL ALBERT, computer co. exec.; b. Toronto, Ont., Can., Dec. 12, 1912; s. Nathan and Anna (Gutzin) W.; came to U.S., 1928, naturalized, 1936; A.B., Eastern Mich. U., 1933; M.A., U. Mich., 1934, Ph.D., 1940; postgrad. U. Zurich (Switzerland), 1935-36; m. Elizabeth Grace Limberg, June 30, 1939; children—David Charles, Ruth Leah. Librarian, Allison div. Gen. Motors Co., Indpls., 1941-46; chief library br. U.S. AEC, Oak Ridge, 1946-52, head library dept. Argonne, Ill., 1952-56, chief library br., Washington, 1956-59; systems analyst IBM, Washington, 1959-60, program adminstr., San Jose, Cal., 1960-73. Instr. Purdue U. Extension, Indpls., 1945. Mem. Assn. for Computing Machinery, Am. Soc. for Information Sci., A.L.A., Inst. for Information Scientists, Spl. Libraries Assn. Home: San Jose CA Died Feb. 2, 1973.

WARK, HOMER ETHAN, clergyman, educator; b. Spencer, Ind., Aug. 1, 1875; s. George B. and Elizabeth Rachel (Miller) W.; B.A., Campbell Coll., Holton, Kan., 1900; M.A., Washburn Coll., Topeka, Kan., 1904; S.T.B., Boston U. Sch. of Theology, 1906; Ph.D., Boston U., 1908; m. Gertrude Eliza Beecher, Sept. 5, 1900. Entered M. E. ministry, in Kan., 1900; pastor at Topeka Leavenworth and Kansas City, Kan., until 1912, Calcutta, India, 1912-15; prof. Bible, Southwestern Coll., Winfield, Kan., 1915-18; prof. history of religion, etc., Boston U., 1921-26; became pres. W.Va. Wesleyan Coll., 1926; now pastor First Meth. Ch., Clarksburg. Chaplain U.S. Army, May 1917-Feb. 22, 1919; with 137th Inf. in France 1 yr. Mem. Acad. Polit. Science. Republican. Mason. Club: Rotary (Clarksburg). Author of volumes on The Religion of a Soldier" and New Era in Missions." Home: Parkersburg WV*‡

WARNER, ALBERT LYMAN, radio news corr., editor; b. Bklyn., Mar. 1, 1903; s. Edwin G. and Euphemia Jane Gray (Lawson) W.; Bachelor of Arts, Amherst College, 1924, Master of Arts (honorary), 1954; student Columbia, 1925-26; m. Harriet West Rowe, Apr. 27, 1929;children—Edwin Gaylord II, Albert Lyman, Jr.; reporter Daily Eagle, 1924; legislative corr., N.Y. Times, Albany, 1926-29; asst. chief Washington Bur., N.Y. Herald-Tribune, 1930-36, chief of bur., 1936-39; covered Presdl. campaigns, 1928-56, World Econ. Conf., London, 1933, Inter Am. Conf., Havana, 1940. Washington Corr. and Commentator, C.B.S., March 1939-42; chief Washington news bur. Mutual Broadcasting Co., 1945-49, Am. Broadcasting Company, 1949-50, 54-56, NBC Three Star Extra, 1950-53; asso. editor U.S. News and World Report, 1956-71. Mem. White House Com. on Employment Physically Handicapped, 1946-56. Commd. major in Army the U.S., July 2, 1942, col., chief War Intelligence Div., Bur. Public Relations; temporary duty, ETO; broadcast Army Hour review of military operations; pioneered boradcasting of Congressional hearings. Received the first annual award for radio newswriting, Sigma Delta Chi, 1940; Legion of Merit, 1945; Headliners Radio News award, 1948. Mem. Amherst Alumni Council, 1925. Mem. White House Corr. Assn. (v.p. 1933-34, pres. 1935-36), Radio Corr. Assns. (v.p. 1939-40; pres. 1940-41 and 1948-49), Delta Kappa Epsilon, Phi Beta Kappa. Conglist. Clubs: Nat. Press, Gridirion, Cosmos, Overseas Writers (Washington). Contbr. mags. Home: McLean VA Died Jan. 11, 1971; buried Burdett NY

WARNER, C(HARLES) A(LBERT), cons. (petroleum); b. Jefferson, New York, April 27, 1894; son of Michael Silas and Anna B. (Dyckman) W.; A.B., Cornell University, Ithaca, New York, 1920; m. Jean R. Davis, Oct. 28, 1942. Field geologist, Empire Gas & Fuel Co., Okla. and Kan., 1917-19; dist. geologist, Emerald Oil Co., Lawton, Okla., 1919-20, Empire Gas & Fuel Co., Okmulgee, Okla., 1920-21; midcontinent dist. mgr. Houston Oil Co. of Tex., Okmulgee and Tulsa, Okla., 1921-32; mid-continent dist. mgr. and petroleum engr., Houston, 1932-34, mgr. land and lease department, Houston, 1932-50, director, 1941-44, v.p., director, 1944-51, v.p., secretary, dir., 1951-56; secretary Houston Pipe Line Company, Southwestern Settlement and Development Co., 1951-56; cons. (petroleum), 1956-68. Member Independent Petroleum Association, Texas Midcontinent Oil and Gas Association, American Association Petroleum Geol., Am. Inst. Mining and Metall. Engrs. (chmn. petroleum div. 1943), Am. Petroleum Inst., Houston Geol. Soc., Nat. Oil Scouts and Landmens Assn., Houston Landmens Assn., Tex. Gulf Coast Historical Association (trustee), also member Texas Surveyors Association. Clubs: Austin (Austin); Houston (Houston, Texas); Beeville (Tex.) Country. Author: Field Mapping for the Oil Geologist, 1921; Texas Oil and Gas since 1543, 1939; contbr. articles on oil industry to various publs. Home: Houston TX Died Nov. 6, 1968.

WARNER, HENRY BYRON, actor; b. London, Eng., Oct. 26, 1877; s. Charles and Fanchette (Hardes) W.; father a noted actor; ed. University Coll., London; m. Rita Stanwood, May 4, 1915. First appeared in company with father in Streets of London," 1883; professional debut as Rev. Mr. Eden, in Never Too Late to Mend," 1897; came to U.S. as leading man with Eleanor Robson, 1905, making appearance as John Danbury M.P., in Nurse Marjorie"; toured U.S. in Alias Jimmy Valentine," The Ghost Breaker," etc.; played in You and I," 1922; now playing in and directing motion pictures; pictures include— Let Freedom Ring," Nurse Edith Cavell," The Rains Came," Mr. Smith Goes to Washington," Torpedoed"; New Moon," 1940; Topper Returns," City of Missing Girls," 1941. Address: Care of United Artists, Hollywood CA*‡

WARNER, RAWLEIGH, corporation exec.; b. Chgo., Ill., May 14, 1891; s. Samuel Rohrer and Mary Belle (Rawleigh) W.; student Lawrenceville (N.J.) School; Litt.B., Princeton University, 1913; LL.D., Marietta Coll., 1955; m. Dorothy Haskins, October 14, 1914; children—Mary (Clifford), Dorothy (Ryburn), Rawleigh, Suzanne (Kenly). Treas. Central Sugar Co., 1915-17; with Dawes Bros. Inc., 1919-39, as v.p., dir.; v.p., treas., dir. Pure Oil Co., 1926-47, chmn. bd., 1947-63, dir., chmn. exec. com., 1963-65. Spl. adviser to sec. of Navy, World War II; mem. Hoover Commn. Life trustee Northwestern U., Crerar Library, Chgo.; bd. dirs. Soc. Prevention Blindness; trustee Lawrenceville Sch., 1938-52. Served as 1st lt. U.S. Army, 1917-18. Recipient Distinguished Service award Dept. Navy. Mem. 25 Year Club Am. Petroleum Industry (pres. 1952-53). Conglist. Clubs: Commercial, Chicago, Winnetka IL Died Jan. 8, 1971; buried Winnetka Congl. Ch. Churchyard, Winnetka IL

WARNER, WILLIAM EVERETT, educator; b. Roanoke, Ill., Aug. 22, 1897; s. Issac and Eva (Redmon) W.; diploma Wis. State U., Platteville, 1917; B.S., U. Wis., 1923, M.S., 1924; Ph.D. in Ednl. Research, Columbia, 1928; m. Ellen A. Todd, Aug. 14, 1920. Tchr. and prin. pub. and vocational schs., Wis. and N.Y., 1917-24; from asst. prof. to grad. prof. edn. Ohio State U., 1925-67, prof. emeritus, 1967-71; exec. dir. Civil Def. Ohio, 1950-53; cons. U.S. Office edn., 1934, Tuskegee Inst., 1936-37, 68, U.S. Office Civil Def., 1943, Am. Legion, 1946, Nat. Safety Council, 1948-51, Indonesia In-Service Indsl. Tng. Program, 1957-59, Philippine Indsl. Arts Assn., 1962, Canadian Indsl. Arts Assn., 1964-71, So. Assn. Colls. and Schs., 1965-71; pres. Adv. Com. Indsl. Safety, 1948. Served as pvt. F.A.C.O.T.S., World War I; as lt. col. World War II at SHAEF. Member International Executive Service Corps. Decorated Bronze Star, Purple Heart; Order Leopold II, Mil. Cross, Premier medal Nat. Red Cross (Belgium); named Colonel in Kentucky and Oklahoma; recipient Distinguished Alumnus award Wis. State U.

and Inst. Tech., Platteville, 1963; Distinguished Service citation Ohio State U. Seminar, 1966; citation eminence Kent State U., 1967; registered Coll. of Arms, London, Eng., 1944. Fellow Internat. Inst. Arts and Letters: mem. Newcomen Soc. Eng., Am. Legion, Am. Vocational Assn., Am. Indsl. Arts Assn. (founder 1939, pres. 1939-41), Res. Officers Assn. (pres. Ohio 1948-49, security officer 1947-56), Am. Council Indsl. Arts Tchrs. Edn. (hon.), Mil. Order Purple Heart, Phi Delta Kappa, Kappa Delta Pi, Omicron Delta Kappa, Epsilon Pi Tau (hon.; founder 1929, exec. sec. 1929-71). Republican. Rotarian. Clubs: Faculty (Columbus); Army and Navy (Washington). Author 2 books, other writings. Editor Epsilon Pi Tau brochure series, 1929-71), Western Arts Assn. publs., 1932-37; cons. editor Arts and Industries series. A pioneer indsl. arts edn., speaker, lectr. before numerous groups in field. Address: Columbus OH Died July 12, 1971; buried Forest Cemetery, Stevens Point WI

WARNICK, SPENCER K(ELLOGG), banker; b. Amsterdam, N.Y., Sept. 14, 1874; s. Middleton and Marion (Kellogg) W.; A.B. cum laude, Yale, 1895; m. Jane M. Greene, June 1, 1898; children—Spencer K., Henry G. Admitted to N.Y. State bar, Nov. 1897; in pvt. practice, Amsterdam, N.Y., 1897-1925; asst. dist. atty., Montgomery County, N.Y., 1900-02; exec. vice pres. Montgomery County, N.Y., 1900-02; exec. vice pres. Montgomery County Trust Co., 1925-36, pres. since 1936, dir. since 1912. Dir. Mohawk Carpet Mills. Served as mem. N.Y. State Senate, 1902-06, chmn. com. on public instrn., 1902-06; appointed mem. commn. authorized by legislature of State of N.Y. to investigate and revise tax laws of state, June 7, 1906. Post master Amsterdam, N.Y., 1921-25. Commd. major, J.A.G.D., N.G. N.Y., July 31, 1917; disch. rank of maj., U.S. Army, 1919. Dir. and enrollment officer N.Y. State Mil. census, 1916. Trustee: Amsterdam Free Library Assn., Green Hill Cemetery Assn. Trustee Montgomery County Hist. Soc., Mem. Zeta Psi. Republican. Presbyterian (trustee). Elk. Mason (Shriner). Club: Antlers Country. Home: 21 Grant Av. Office: Six Market St., NY‡

WARREN, ARTHUR FISKE, educator; b. Woburn, Mass., Jan. 21, 1875; s. Edson Parker and Helen Amelia (Fiske) W.; grad. Lawrence Acad., 1890; Monson (Mass.) Acad., 1892; B.A., Amherst Coll., 1897, honorary M.A., 1922; L.H.D., honoris causa, Rutgers Univ., 1928; m. Aline Glass, of Bangor, Me., July 15, 1914. Master of English and pub. speaking, Riverview Mil. Acad., Poughkeepsie, N.Y., 1897-1901; same, William Penn Charter Sch., Phila., 1901-02; master of English, Lawrenceville (N.J.) Sch., 1902-11 (sr. master Upper House, 1904-11); headmaster Collegiate Sch. (founded 1638), N.Y. City, 1911-30; headmaster Western Reserve Acad., Hudson, O., since 1930. Mem. Coll. Entrance Examining Bd. Mem. School Masters' Assn. of New York and Vicinity (pres. 1914-15), Head Masters' Assn. (sec. 1917-20; exec-com. 1921-23; pres. 1924), Assn. of Colls and Secondary Schools of Middle States and Md. (pres. 1928), Soc. Colonial Wars, S.R., N.E. Soc., Chi Phi. Republican. Conglist. Trustee Monson Academy. Clubs: University, Amherst, Chi Phi. Home: Hudson OH‡

WARREN, CONSTANCE, coll. pres.; b. Plymouth, N.H., Nov. 5, 1880; d. Henry Pitt and Annie Laurie (Lyman) Warren; A.B., Vassar, 1904; A.M., Columbia, 1905; D.Ped., N.Y. State Coll. for Teachers, Albany, 1932; Ed.D., Russell Sage Coll., 1934; Litt.D., Keuka Coll., Keuka Park, N.Y., 1942; LL.D., Allegheny College, 1945; L.H.D., U. Me., 1962. Teacher of history, successively New Haven High School, St. Timothy's School, Catonsville, Maryland, Brearley School, N.Y. City, Louisville (Ky.) Collegiate School, 1905-17; head of history department, Dana Hall and Pine Manor, Wellesley, Mass., 1917-20; asst. prin. University Sch. for Girls, Chicago, 1920-21; head of history dept. Dana Hall and Pine Manor, 1921-28; pres. Pine Manor Jr. Coll., 1928-29; pres. and trustee Sarah Lawrence Coll., Bronxville, Nov. 1929-July 1945; retired. Pres. Assn. of Colls. and Univs., State of N.Y., 1941, Mental Hygiene Assn., Westchester Co., 1945. Dir., chmn. Ednl. Com., American Association of Univ. Women. U. Me. TV sta. named in her honor. Mem. N.E.A., Vassar Alumnae Assn., Foreign Policy Assn., Am. Assn. United Nations, Am. Edn. Fellowship, Nat. Inst. Social Sciences. Democrat. Presbyterian. Clubs: Cosmopolitan, Vassar (New York). Author: A New Design for Women's Education. Contbr. articles to jours. and mags. Home: Hastings-on-Hudson NY Died June 15, 1971; buried Exeter NH

WARREN, CORNELIA, author; b. Waltham, Mass.; d. late Samuel D. Warren, paper mfr.; on local com. for Denison House Coll. Settlement. Author: Miss Wilton, 1892 H5. Address: Cedar Hill Waltham MA‡

WARREN, FRANK EDWARD, newspaper exec.; b. Navasota, Tex., Dec. 29, 1919; s. William S. and Myra (Otts) W.; B.B.A., S. Tex. Coll. Commerce, 1948; m. Mildred Ellen Guinn, Nov. 14, 1941; children—Cynthia Lea, Richard Alan. Staff mem. Houston Chronicle Pub. Co., 1937-50, chief accountant, 1950-52, asst. sec.-treas., controller, 1952-58, sec.-treas., 1958-65, exec. v.p., gen. mgr., 1965-71, pres., 1971-72; also dir.; dir. Belfort State Bank, Rusk Corp. Served with USAAF, 1942-45. Mem. Tex. Soc. C.P.A.'s. Presbyn. Home: Houston TX Died Aug. 18, 1972.

WARREN, FRANK LINCOLN, lawyer; b. Van Buren, Ark., Nov. 29, 1875; s. John Jay and Charlotte Olive (Hayford) W.; father and grandfather soldiers in Union Army; grad. high sch., Van Buren, 1889; B.S., Nat. Normal U., Lebanon, O., 1895; m. Annie G. Leaming, June 25, 1903; children—John Leaming, William Hayford. Settled in Ind. Ty. (now Okla.), 1902, and practiced law at Holdenville more than 40 yrs.; successively mem. firms Kistler & Warren, Pitman & Warren, Warren & Miller, and Warren, Miller & Crutcher, Warren & Warren; pres. Atlas Abstract Co.; v.p. First Nat. Bank, Holdenville. Mem. State Senate, Okla., 1909-12 inclusive; apptd. by gov. asso. justice Supreme Court of Okla., Mar. 1924, to fill vacancy from 8th Dist., Okla., ret. Del. at large to Rep. Nat. Conv., Chicago, 1932, and vice-chmn. of delegation. Episcopalian. Mason. Club: Holdenville. Home: 308 Country Club Drive, Holdenville OK‡

WARREN, IRENE, librarian; b. Rochelle, Ill., 1875; d. Solon Francis and Anna Francis (Dunning) W.; grad. Armour Inst. Tech. Library Sch., Chicago, 1896; Ph.B., U. of Chicago, 1910. Began as organizer of libraries, Armour Inst. Tech., 1895; librarian, Sch. of Edn., U. of Chicago, since 1900; lecturer on sch. libraries and allied subjects. Life mem. A.L.A.; mem. Ill. Library Assn., Drama League America, N.E.A. (chmn. library sect. 1915-16). Clubs: Chicago Library. Cordon. Francis W. Parker Club (pres. 1915). Home: 6056 Stony Island Av., Chicago‡

WARREN, SPEED, corp. exec.; b. Rushville, Ill., July 14, 1870; s. Augustus and Mary (Speed) W.; student pub. schs. of Rushville; m. Hettie B. Clemmer, Feb. 15, 1893; children—Ruth W., Herbert, Dorothy M. (Mrs. R. A. Parker). Asso., Lake Superior Corp., Saulte Ste. Marie, Ont., 1896-1911; Lake Superior Paper Co., Spanish River Pulp & Paper Mills, Ltd., Saulte Ste. Marie, 1911-17; employed G. H. Mead Co., Dayton, O., 1917-19; with Mead Pulp & Paper Co. (now The Mead Corp.) since 1919, v.p., 1942-51, now advisor and mem. finance com.; dir., chmn. bd. The Midwest Fulton Machine Co., Dayton, since 1925; Dir. Ohio C. of C. Republican. Presbyn. Home: 25 Harmon Terrace, Dayton 9. Office: 118 W. First St., Dayton 2 OH‡

WARREN, THOMAS DAVIS, lawyer; b. nr. Edenton, Chowan Co., N.C., Jan. 21, 1872; s. William Young and Fannie Roulac (Badham) W.; student Horner Mil. Sch., Oxford, N.C., 1888-90 inclusive, U. of N.C., 1891-93, 1896-98, LL.B., 1898; m. Mary Stevenson, of Kinston, N.C., June 4, 1904. Teacher langs. in Horner Mil. Sch., 1895; instr. U. of N.C. Law Sch., 1897-98; practiced at Trenton, N.C., 1898-1909; moved to Newbern, 1909; pres. Trenton Land & Lumber Co.; sec. Jones-Onslow Land Co., Southern Realty Co. Mem. N.C. Senate, 1901-03, Ho. of Rep., 1905; mem. Dem. State Exec. Com. since 1910, chmn., 1914-22; U.S. dist atty., Eastern Dist. of N.C., by apptmt. of President Wilson, 1919-20. Trustee U. of N.C.; trustee Newbern Graded Sch.; ex-chmn. Bd. Edn. Craven Co., N.C.; mem. N.C. State Tax Commn. Episcopalian. Elk. Home: 22 Pollock St. Office: Elks Bldg., Newbern NC‡

WARRINER, REUEL EDWARD, metal co. exec.; b. Johannesburg, South Africa, Apr. 19, 1910; s. Ruel Chaffee and Suzanne (Gutherz) W.; grad. Hill Sch., 1929; B.A., Yale, 1933; m. Doris Stanley, June 6, 1936 (dec. Feb. 1967); children—Reuel Edward, Alma Timolat, Robert Stanley; m. 2d, Ellen H. Saltus, Feb. 24, 1968. Came to U.S., 1918. With Western Mining Corp., 1933-34, Lake View & Star, Kalgoorie, West Australia, 1934-35, Internat. Nickel Co., Huntington, W.Va., 1935-42; with civilian ordnance dept. U.S. Army, 1942-43; charge steel and iron section nickel sales dept. Internat. Nickel Co., N.Y.C., 1943-54; v.p. sales Am. Metal Climax, Inc., 1954-68, v.p. nickel project, 1968-72. Mem. Am. Iron and Steel Inst., Am. Inst. Mining and Metall. Engring., Am. Soc. Testing Materials, Am. Ordnance Assn. Episcopalian. Clubs: Yale, Mining, Farm (N.Y.C.); Duquesne (Pitts.); American Cattle (N.H.); Field (Morristown, N.J.). Home: Montrose PA Died Nov. 8, 1972; buried Montrose PA

WARWICK, HERBERT SHERWOOD, JR., educator, historian; b. Columbus, O., Mar. 4, 1910; s. Herbert Sherwood and Hazel (Hain) W.; A.B., Princeton, 1930, M.A., Ohio State U., 1931, Ph.D., 1934; student Louisville Presbyn. Sem., 1950-55; m. Bertella Mae Lee, Aug. 30, 1941; 1 dau., Judith Lee (Mrs. Derek Thompson). Successively univ. scholar, fellow, asst. history Ohio State U., 1930-33; mem. faculty U. Louisville, 1934-70, prof. history 1951-70, head dept., 1964-70. Sec. Atlantic Union Com., 1949-62. Served to capt. USAAF, 1942-45. Mem. Am. Hist. Assn., Orgn. Am. Historians, English Speaking Union. Democrat. Episcopalian. Mason. Home: Louisville KY Died 1970.

WASHBURN, ALFRED HAMLIN, physician; b. Boston, Mar. 14, 1895; s. George H. and Anna M. (Hoyt) W.; A.B., Amherst Coll., 1916, D.Sc., 1956 M.D., Harvard, 1921; D.Sc., Denver U., 1958; m. Laura A. Orbison, Feb. 15, 1923; children—Alfred D., Arthur O., Thomas C. Interne, Presbyn. Hosp., N.Y.C. 1921-23, Infants and Children's Hosp. and Boston City Hosp., Boston, 1923-25; in pvt. practice pediatrics Portland, Ore., 1925-26, San Francisco, 1926-30; instr in pediatrics U. Ore., 1925-26; instr. U. Cal. Med. Sch. 1926-27, asst. prof., 1927-28, asso. prof., acting chief dept. pediatrics, 1928-30; asso. prof. pediatrics U. Colo Med. Sch., 1930-36, research prof., 1936-60, prof emeritus, 1960-72; dir. child research council, 1930-60 active mem. research staff, 1960-70; pediatric cons Children's Bur., Dept. Health, Edn. and Welfare 1946-62. Mem. various nat., state and municipal coms on child health, welfare and research. Recipient Borden award Am. Acad. Pediatrics, 1949, C. Anderson Aldrich award, 1965; Lord & Taylor award, 1952 Florence R. Sabin award Colo. Pub. Health Assn., 1967. Mem. Am. Pediatric Soc. (pres. 1954-55); Soc Research in Child Devel., Soc. Pediatric Research, Soc. Exptl. Biology and Medicine, A.A.A.S., Sigma Xi, Alpha Omega Alpha. Contbr. to several vols. on pediatrics, also articles in med. and sci. jours. Home: Denver CO Died Mar. 1972.

WASHBURN, EDWARD ROGER, educator chemist; b. Big Rapids, Mich., Sept. 22, 1899; s. Edward Rush and Myrtilla (Rogers) W.; B.S., U. Mich., 1922, M.S., 1923, Ph.D., 1926; m. Dorothy May Adams, Aug. 23, 1926; children—Dorothy Elaine (wife of Dr. Robert Dudley Olney), Edward Roger, Robert Henry, Carolyn May. With dept. chemistry U. Neb., 1926-67, successively instr., asst. prof., asso. prof., 1926-41, prof., 1941-67, chmn. dept. chemistry, 1955-64. Served with USNRF, 1918; with Chem. Warfare Res., U.S. Army, 1927-37. Mem. Am. Chem. Soc., A.A.A.S., Am. Assn. U. Profs., Neb. Acad. Sci., Sigma Xi, Phi Lambda Upsilon, Alpha Chi Sigma. Author sci. articles on solubility, surface tension, monomolecular films. Home: Lincoln NE Died Aug. 31, 1967; buried Wyuka Cemetery Lincoln NB

WASHBURNE, HELUIZ CHANDLER (MRS. CARLETON W. WASHBURNE), writer; b. Cin., Jan. 25, 1892; d. Charles Colby and Julia Georgianna (Davis) Chandler; student Sch. Indsl. Arts, 1908-09, and Women's Sch. Design, 1909-10 (both Phila.); m. Carleton Wolsey Washburne, Sept. 15, 1912; children—Margaret Joan (Mrs. Donald Kainer Marshall), Beatrice (Mrs. John Visher), Chandler. Comml. artist, 1910-12; fashion adviser Carson Pirie Scott & Co., Chgo., 1928-30; traveled extensively in Europe, Asia, Mexico, S.A., Australia, Africa; lectr. travel, 1933-49; travel column Chgo. Daily News, 1943-44. Author: Land of the Good Shadows (with Anauta), also numerous books for children; lates: (with Anauta) Children of the Blizzard, 1952, Japanese edit., abridged, 1957, Brit. edit., 1960; Tomas Goes Trading, 1959. Home: Falls Church VA

WASHINGTON, GEORGE THOMAS, judge; b. Cuyahoga Falls, O., June 24, 1908; s. William Morrow and Janet Margaret (Thomas) W.; Ph.B., Yale Coll., 1928; Litt.B., (Law), Oxford U., 1931; LL.B., Yale Law Sch., 1932; m. Helen Goodner, 1953. Practiced law, New York City, 1932-38; mem. faculty Cornell U. Law Sch., 1938-42, prof. law, 1942; atty. Office Emergency Mgmt. 1942; U.S. econ. rep., Baghdad, Iraq, 1942-43; chief U.S. Lend-Lease Mission, Teheran, Iran, 1943-44; spl. asst. to U.S. Atty. Gen. Nov. 1944-46; asst. solicitor gen. of U.S., 1946-49; acting solicitor gen. of U.S., 1946-47, charge govt. cases U.S. Supreme Ct.; legal adviser U.S. delegation to UN Conf. on Freedom of the Press, Geneva, 1948; apptd. judge U.S. Court of Appeals for D.C. Circuit, Oct. 1949, then sr. U.S. circuit judge. Mem. Assn. Am. Rhodes Scholars, Soc. of the Cincinnati (as rep. of Pres. Washington by descent from Col. Samuel Washington), U.S. Supreme Ct. Bar, D.C., San Francisco bar assns., Assn. Bar City of New York, Order of Coif, Phi Beta Kappa. Club: Elizabethan (New Haven). Editor Atty. General's Manual on Administrative Procedure Act, 1947. Author: Corporate Executives Compensation, 1942; Compensating the Corporate Executive (with V. Henry Rothschild, 2d), 1951, 3d edit., 1962; (with Joseph W. Bishop, Jr.) Indemnifying the Corporate Executive, 1963; contbr. articles. Home: Santa Barbara CA Died Aug. 21, 1971.

WASINGER, GORDON BERNARD, educator; b. Menasha, Wis., May 25, 1922; s. Alexander A. and Cora (Dahms) W.; B.S. with high distinction, Stout State U., 1950, M.S., 1951; Ph.D., U. Ia., 1961; m. Magna Marian Jorgensen, Sept. 5, 1945; children—Carl F., Kaaren M. Tchr. high sch., Kingsport Tenn., 1950-53; dir. adult edn. Davenport (Ia.) pub. schs., 1953-56; supr. adult edn. Ia. Dept. Pub. Instrn., 1958-61; asso. dir. instructional services, asst. prof. U. Ia. 1961-70; dean div. continuing edn., asso. prof. U. N.D., Grand Forks, 1970-72; cons. examiner Commn. Higher Edn., N. Central Assn. Colls. and Secondary Schs., 1969-72; cons. Army Mgmt. Engring. Tng. Agy., A. Assn. Jr. Colls. Served with USAAF, 1942-45; ETO. Mem. Nat. (dir.), Ia. (Achievement award 1969) assns. pub. continuing and adult edn., Mo. Valley Adult Edn. Assn. (Achievement award 1965), N.D. Adult Edn. Assn., ıat. Univ. Extension Assn., Nat. Assn. State Univs. and ınd Grant Colls. Home: Grand Forks ND Died Oct.), 1972.

'ASKEY, FRANK HINMAN, miner; b. at Lake City, Ɩinn., Apr. 20, 1875; s. George Washington and Julia melia (Hurd) W.; ed. grammar and high schs., ıinneapolis, 1883-7; m. Ballard, Wash., Aug. 10, 1904, dna Norma Blodgett. Went to Alaska and mined at ook's Iniet, 1898-9, at Nome, since 1900; pres. Nome old Quartz Mining Co.; dir. Nome Bank & Trust Co., ome Nugget Pub. Co. First del. in Congress from laska, 1906-7; Democrat. Residence: Nome, Alaska. ffice: Ballard WA‡

'ASLEY, RUTH ELLEN, educator; b. Shenandoah, ı., Feb. 20, 1914; d. Harry Malcolm and Ellen Aorgan) Wasley; A.B., Goucher Coll., 1935; M.A., olumbia, 1936; Ph.D., N.Y.U., 1953; diplome La orbonne, Paris, France, 1956. Tchr. sr. high sch., Ɩillville, Pa., 1937-39, Doylestown, Pa., 1939-46; asst. rof., supr. student teaching N.Y. State Coll. for Tchrs., he Milne Sch., Albany, N.Y., 1946-49; asso. prof. ıpr., 1949-58; on leave, supr. dept. student teaching, ıstr. modern fgn. langs. N.Y.U., 1950-51; Fulbright cholar Seminar in France, 1956; prof. and supr. modern ın. langs. Milne Sch., State U. of N.Y. at Albany, 958-69. Mem. N.E.A., Assn. Supervision and urriculum Development, Am. Assn. U. Profs., N.Y. ate Tchrs. Assn., Faculty Assn. State U. of New York, m. Assn. Tchrs. French, Am. Assn. Tchrs. Spanish ıd Portuguese, Nat. Fedn. Modern Lang. Tchrs. ıssns., N.Y. State Fedn. Fgn. Lang. Tchrs., French ugenot Soc., Am. Assn. U. Women, Assn. Student eaching, Delta Kappa Gamma. Contbr. Modern Lang. our., Hispania, Clearing House. Home: Albany NY ied May 29, 1969.

'ASSERMAN, EARL REEVES, educator; b. Vashington, Nov. 11, 1913; s. Samuel and Jennie Applestein) W.; Ph.D., Johns Hopkins, 1937; m. leanor B. Franklin, Oct. 15, 1937. Instr., asst. prof., sso. prof. U. Ill., 1938-48; asso. prof. Johns Hopkins, 948-53, prof., 1953-69, Caroline Donovan prof., 969-73. Vis. prof. U. Wis., summer 1951, Columbia, 959, 61, U. Wash., 1962, U. Colo., 1963, Harvard, 966. Guggenheim fellow, 1967-68. Served as lt. (j.g.) JSNR, 1944-46. Mem. Modern Lang. Assn., Am. ıcad. Arts and Scis., Phi Beta Kappa. Clubs: Johns Iopkins, Tudor and Stuart (Balt.). Author: Elizabethan oetry in the Eighteenth Century, 1947; The Finer one, Keats' Major Poems, 1953; The Subtler anguage; Critical Reading of Neo-classic and omantic Poems, 1959; Pope's Epistle to Bathurst, 960; Shelley's Prometheus Unbound; A Critical eading, 1965. Senior editor ELH WASSERMANJour. English Literary History; ditorial board Studies in English Literature. Contbr. rof. jours. Home: Towson MD Died Mar. 3, 1973.

'ASSERMANN, FRIEDRICH, anatomist; b. Aunich, Germany, Aug. 13, 1884; s. Franz and Amalie Fechheimer) W.; M.D., U. Munich, 1910; Ph.D. honorary), University of Frankfurt, 1958; M.D. honorary). University of Giessen, 1959; m. Margaret chmidgall, M.D., Feb. 3, 1917; children—Gertrude Mrs. Fetcher) Franz Walter. Came to U.S., 1937, aturalized, 1943. Privatdozent anatomy U. Munich, 914, teaching and research work in anatomy, histology nd cytology, 1919-30, prof. anatomy and head dept. istology and embryology, 1931-36; prof. of anatomy U. hicago, 1937-49; sr. biologist Argonne Nat. Lab., hicago, 1949-69; visiting prof. anatomy Western eserve University, 1942, U. Heidelberg, Germany, 952, University of Frankfurt, Germany, 1954, Albert instein College of Medicine, N.Y., 1955, 57. Mem. ıed. mission Unitarian Serv. Com. to Germany, 1948. erved as med. officer, German Army, 1914-18. Decorated Comdr. Cross of Order of Merit (Germany). Aem. Am. Soc. Zoologists, Internat. Soc. for Cell iology, Internat. Soc. Dental Research, Am. ssociation Anatomists, Anatomische Gesellschaft hon.), Soc. Exptl. Biology and Medicine, Society of rowth, A.A.A.S., Chicago Ethical Soc., Deutsche kademie der Naturforscher Leopoldina, Sigma Xi. lubs: Quadrangel (Chgo.). Author: Growth and eproduction of the living matter, 1929. Home: Downers Grove IL Died June 16, 1969; buried Valdfriedhof, Stuttgart Germany

VASSON, THERON, geologist; b. nr. Springville, V.Y., Apr. 23, 1887; s. George Fuller and Hattie Bevins Smith) W.; student Griffith Inst., Springville, N.Y., 905; B.S., Carnegie Inst. Tech., 1910; student Columbia, 1919-20; m. Isabel D. Bassett, June 11, 1920 div. May 1953); children—Elizabeth (Mrs. E.A. Bergstrom), Edward B., Anne (Mrs. Gregory Harney); ı. 2d, Ann M. Hand, June 3, 1959. Assistant surveys oal mines, railroads, oil and gas fields, pipe lines, New 'ork, Pa., N.J., Cal., 1903-15; designer hydraulic fill ake Almanor Dam. Gt. Western Power Co., San rancisco, 1913; water engr. Geol Survey State of N.J., renton, 1916; field geologist Twin State Oil Co., Tulsa, lso topographer U.S. Geol. Survey, 1917; chief eologist Am. Oil Engring. Corp., Ft. Worth, 1920; with eonard Exploration Co., N.Y., explorations east of the Andes in Ecuador, 1921; chief geologist The Pure Oil Co., Chgo., 1922-52, sr. geologist, advisor exec. com., 1952-54, consulting geologist. 1954-70. Advisory committee constrn. geol. exhibits Chgo. Century Progress, 1932-33; credited with discovery new oil fields of So. Ill., 1937; adv. council department geological engring. Princeton, 1941-55; radio program Adventures in Ecuador. Adventurers Club, Chgo., 1947; exec. com. oil exhibits Chgo. Mus. Sci. and Industry, 1947-58; del, UN Sci. Conf. on Conservation and Utilization of Resources, Lake Success, 1949; vis. geol. advisor Naval Petroleum Res. No. 4, Point Barrow, Alaska, 1950. Served as 2d lt. 117th and 1st Engrs., U.S. Army, 1917-19; city engr. Sinzig on Rhine, Germany, 1919. Recipient Award of Merit Carnegie Inst. Tech., 1951, certificate appreciation, Am. Petroleum Inst., 1955. Registered engr., Ill. Fellow Geol. Soc. Am.; mem. Am. Petroleum Inst. (adv. com. research occurrence and recovery of petroleum 1940-50), A.A.A.S., Western Soc. Engineers, American Geog. Society, American Association of Petroleum Geologists (honorary), Society of Econ. Geologists (vice pres. 1954), Am. Geophys. Union. Am. Inst. Mining and Metall. Engrs., Rainbow Div. Vets., Am. Geol Inst. (founder), Ill. Soc. Mayflower Descs., Tau Beta Pi. Unitarian. Mem. Order of the Top of the World. Clubs: Adventurers (Chgo.); Sierra (San Francisco); Petroleum (Denver). Author: Explorations in Eastern Ecuador, 1923; Geological Explorations East of the Andes in Ecuador, 1927; Geology of Cabin Creek Field, West Virginia, 1927; The First Geological Studies in the Eastern Region of Ecuador in a zone between Baeza-Coca and Canelos-Macas, 1937; Los Primeros Estudios Geologicos del Oriente, 1937; Geology of the Creole Oil Field, Gulf of Mexico, 1948; also ann. reports, oil and gas devel., various states, 1932-47. Editor of Mineral Map of Europe, 1940. Home: North Riverside IL Died Aug. 6, 1970; buried Maplewood Cemetery, Springville NY

WASSON, WILLIAM WALTER, physician, radiologist; b. Chrisman, Ill., Aug. 19, 1884; s. William Alexander and Matilda Ann (Layne) W.; diploma Northwestern U. Acad., 1904; student U. Ill., Urbana, 1904-06; A.B., U. Colo., 1908, M.D., 1910; m. Katharine L. Crouch, Sept. 24, 1908; children—Richard Van Cleave and Madolin Layne (Mrs. Richard Des Jardins) (twins). Asso. electrotherapeutics, Dr. E.H. Robertston, Boulder, Colo., 1910-13; practice of radiology, Boulder, 1910-16, Denver, 1916-68; asso. Dr. John Samuel Bouslog, 1918-68; established x-ray depts. St. Anthony's Hosp., Children's Hosp., Denver; co-founder, mem. bd. control Solmene Winter Found., 1922-68, dir., 1922-27; adv. com. Radiol. Research Inst.; radiology cons. Presbyn., Children's, St. Luke's hosps., Denver. Mem. com. on growth and development White House Conf. Child Health and Protection, 1929-32; radiologist to med. adv. bd. Rocky Mountain Region, World War II. recipient gold medal for studies in chest disease, Radiol. Soc. N.A., 1926, for distinguished service Am. Coll. Radiology, 1958; recipient Norlin award, University Colorado, 1960. Fellow A.M.A. (chairman sect. on radiology 1947-48), Am. Coll. Radiology (charter 1923; v.p. 1932-33, chancellor 1923-30, 42-47), Clin. and Pathological Soc. of Denver; mem. Western Roentgen Ray Soc. (dist. counsellor 1919), Radiol. Soc. N.A. (exec. com. 1920, past counselor, pres. 1941-42), Am. Roentgen Ray Soc. (v.p. 1947), Am. Radiol. Soc., Child Research Council (co-founder, mem. bd. control 1927-34, dir. 1927-30), Colo., Denver County med. socs., Colo., Rocky Mountain radiol. socs., Sigma Xi, Delta Upsilon, Pi Beta Phi. Clubs: Denver Country. Author: The Auxiliary Heart, 1954. Contbr. articles med. jours. Former profl. pitcher Western Baseball League. Home: Golden CO Died Apr. 14, 1968; buried Fair Mount Cemetery.

WATERHOUSE, GEORGE SHADFORD, banker; born Honolulu, T.H., July 10, 1875; s. John Thomas and Elizabeth (Pinder) W.; A.B., Princeton, 1898; m. Bess Burwell, July 17, 1901 (dec.); m. 2d Gertrude Gordon, Apr. 26, 1927; children—George Shadford, Wayne Gordon, Samuel Douglas. Began bus. career with Pacific Foundry; later with H. May & Co., Guardian Trust Co.; new pres. Bishop Nat. Bank of Hawaii; pres. Waterhouse Investment Co., Ltd., The Bishop Co., Ltd.; dir. The von Hamm-Young Co., Ltd., Territorial Bldg. & Loan Assn., Hawaiian Securities, Ltd., Hawaiian Pineapple Co. Apptd. commr. Hawaii Housing Authority, 1938 (resigned). Trustee Territory of Hawaii Employees' Retirement System, Chmn. for Hawaii. U.S. Savings Bonds Div.; chmn. for Hawaii, ABA Treasury Savings Bonds Com. Conglist. Clubs: Oahu Country, Waialas Country, Pacific (Honolulu). Home: 110 Coelho Way, Honolulu 10 HI Office: Bishop Nat. Bank of Hawaii, Honolulu 1 HI‡

WATERMAN, FRANK ALLAN, physicist; b. Oswego, N.Y., July 9, 1865; s. David Allen and Eliza Dunning (Van Vorst) W.; A.B., Princeton U., 1888, Ph.D., 1896; m. Florence Tower, Aug. 19, 1891; children—Alan Tower, Lesley (Mrs. Edward Kramer Funkhouser), Ransom. Instr. physics, 1891-92, prof., 1892-93, Purdue U., Lafayette, Ind.; instr. physics, Princeton U., 1893-97; prof. physics, Smith Coll., Northampton, Mass., 1897-1933, prof. emeritus since 1933. Fellow A.A.A.S., Am. Phys. Soc.; member Societe Francaise de Physique, Sigma Xi. Author: Laboratory Experiments in Physics, 1892. Contbr. to scientific jours. and revs. Address: Northampton MA‡

WATERMAN, LEROY, prof. Semitics; b. Pierpont, O., July 4, 1875; s. Hadley and Louesa (Lombard) W.; A.B., Hillsdale (Mich.) Coll., 1898, B.D., 1900; studied Oxford U., 1900-02, U. of Berlin, 1906-07; Ph.D., U. of Chicago, 1912; Litt.D., Hillsdale Coll., 1925; m. Mabelle A. Walrath, July 25, 1906; children—Dorothea Lydia, Donald Leroy (dec.). Prof. Hebrew, Hillsdale Coll., 1902-10; fellow U. of Chicago, 1910-12; prof. O.T. and history of religions, Meadville Theol. Sch., 1913-15; prof. Semitics and chmn. dept. Oriental langs. and lits., U. of Mich., 1915-45. Mem. Am. Oriental Soc., Soc. Bibl. Lit. and Exegesis, Nat. Assn. Biblical Inst., Royal Asiatic Soc. Research Club of Univ. of Mich., Palestinian Oriental Society, A.A.A.S. Progressive Baptist. Club: The University (Ann Arbor, Michigan). Annual president of American Oriental Society, 1936-37; annual pres. Soc. Biblical Lit. and Exegesis, 1946. Books: Some Koujunjik Letters and Related Texts, 1912; Business Documents of the Hammurabi Period, 1916. Translator: (with others) The Bible—An American Translation, 1927; mem. transl. com., revised standard version of Bible since 1937. Editor Vol. XIV R.F. Harper's Assyrian and Babylonian Letters; Royal Correspondence of the Assyrian Empire (Michigan Humanistic Series, volumes 17-20); First Preliminary Report upon the Excavations at Tel Umar, Iraq, 1931, Second Preliminary Report, 1933; Preliminary Report of the University of Michigan Excavations at Sepphoris, Palestine, 1937; Religion Faces the World Crisis, 1943; Song of Songs, 1948; The Religion of Jesus, 1952; The Historical Jesus, Hope of Mankind, 1955; Forerunners of Jesus, 1959; The Role of Religion in Tomorrow's World, 1963; The Christian Objective, 1970. Home: Ann Arbor MI Died May 9, 1972; buried Ann Arbor MI

WATERS, CAMPBELL EASTER, chemist, botanist; b. Baltimore County, Md., Sept. 14, 1872; s. Charles E. and Anne M. (Easter) W.; A.B., Johns Hopkins, 1895, Ph.D., 1899; m. Mary Snedeker, Apr. 16, 1907; children—Charles Emory, Elizabeth (Mrs. Allan H. Graeff). Professor of chemistry and physics, Connecticut Agricultural College, 1900-01; assistant in chemistry, Johns Hopkins, 1901-04; asst. chemist, Nat. Bureau Standards, 1904, asso. chemist, May 1, 1909, chemist, 1919-42, asst. chief chem. Aug. 1937-Sept. 1942; retired. Fellow A.A.A.S.; mem. Am. Chem. Soc., Md. Hist. Soc., Va. Hist. Soc., Chem. Soc. of Washington, Washington Academy Sciences, Wild Flower Preservation Society; hon. and charter mem. Am. Fern Soc. Democrat. Author: Ferns, 1903. Contbr. to Am. Chem. Jour., Jour. Am. Chem. Soc., Industrial Engring. Chemistry, Nat. Bur. of Standards publs.; also on bot. topics, especially ferns, to the Fern Bulletin, Rhodora, and the Plant World. Home: 5812 Chevy Chase Parkway, Washington 15 DC‡

WATKEYS, CHARLES W., prof. mathematics; b. Syracuse, N.Y., Sept. 30, 1877; s. Henry and Zerviah Temple (Colman) W.; A.B., U. of Rochester, 1901; grad. study, U. of Chicago; A.M., Harvard, 1908; m. Ollie Braggins, June 21, 1910; children—Jean de Garmo, Charlotte Allen. Instr. in mathematics, Kings Sch., Stamford, Conn., 1901-03, U. of Rochester, 1903-06, Harvard, 1906-08, U. of Chicago, summer 1908; instr. in mathematics, U. of Rochester, 1908-10, asst. prof., 1910-18, prof. since 1918, dir. Univ. Survey since 1925, pres. Bd. of Control of Student Activities, 1925-31. Mem. Phi Beta Kappa, Theta Delta Chi. Unitarian. Clubs: Mathematics (pres. since 1915), Torch (dir.; pres. 1930). Joint Author: Elementary Functions, 1920. Composer of coll. and fraternity songs. Home: 287 Dartmouth St., Rochester NY‡

WATKINS, DALE BAXTER, physician, teratologist; b. Chinook, Mont., June 9, 1914; s. Dale Baxter and Elsie (Laughton) W.; M.D., U. Minn., 1943; m. Celia Justina Cross, Oct. 15, 1944; children—Wendy Ann, Dale Baxter III, Diane Grace. Commd. ensign M.C. USNR, 1943, advanced through grades to capt. M.C. USN, 1957; grad. tng. in medicine USN Hosp., Bethesda, Md., 1946, San Diego, 1947-49, Oakland, 1950-51; tng. in dermatology USN Hosp., Phila. U., 1955-58; research Walter Reed Army Med. Center, Washington, 1951-52; head medicine USN Hosp., Pensacola, Fla., 1952-53; chief, outpatient clinics, allergy Tripler Army Hosp., Honolulu, 1953-55; chief dermatology USN Hosp., Key West, Fla., 1958-63; ret., 1964; dir. Cross Inst. Teratology, Honolulu, 1964-71. Teaching fellow Hahnemann Med. Sch., Phila., 1955-57. Active Key West Players, 1958-63, Community Concert Assn., Key West, 1958-63. Fellow Am. Acad. Dermatology; mem. A.C.P., A.A.A.S., A.M.A., Am. Geriatric Soc., Am. Soc. Tropical Medicine and Hygiene Am. Genetic Assn., Soc. for Study Evolution, Soc. Investigative Dermatologists, Am. Inst. Biol. Sci., Am. Fedn. for Clin. Research, Internat. Soc. Tropical Dermatologists, Internat. Leprosy Assn., U.S. Naval Inst., Assn. Mil. Surgeons, Assn. Mil. Dermatologists, Ret. Officers Assn. Researcher in field, 1964-71. Address: Honolulu HI Died Feb. 7, 1971; buried Arlington Nat. Cemetery.

WATKINS, FRANKLIN CHENAULT, artist; b. N.Y.C., Dec. 30, 1894; s. Benjamin Franklin and Shirley (Chanault) W.; student Groton Sch., 1908-10, U. Va., 1911-12, U. Pa., 1912-13, Pa. Acad. Fine Arts, 1914-20; A.F.D., Franklin and Marshall Coll., 1954; m. Ida

Quigley, 1942. One-man show Mus. Modern Art N.Y., 1950; one man Retrospective Exhibit Phila. Mus. Art, 1964. Instr. painting Pa. Acad. Fine Arts. Mem. bd. dirs. Pa. Acad. Fine Arts. Recipient Phila. Art Festival award, 1955; medal for achievement Phila. Art Allaince, 1958; Temple Gold medal, Pa. Acad. Fine Arts, Gold medal of honor, 1949; 1st prize, Carnegie Internat., Pitts.; gold medal Coreoran Biennial, Washington, A.N.A., Book award, 1972. Hon. life fellow Am. Acad. in Rome; mem. Nat. Inst., Arts and Letters, Pa. Acad. Fine Arts (bd. dirs.), Am. Philos. Soc. Home: Naples FL Died Dec. 4, 1972; buried Christ Ch., Philadelphia PA

WATKINS, FREDERICK MUNDELL, educator; b. Providence, Mar. 26, 1910; s. David Mundell and Velena Worth (Babcock) W.; A.B. summa cum laude, Harvard, 1930, Ph.D., 1937; LL.D., McGill U., 1971. Instr. Harvard, 1937-39, vis. lectr. Sch. Overseas Adminstrn., 1943-45; asst. prof. govt. Cornell U., 1939-42; research analyst OSS, 1945; Bronfman prof. polit. sci. McGill U., 1946-51, Angus prof. polit. sci., 1951-52, warden Douglas Hall, 1949-52, chmn. dept. polit. sci., economics, 1950-51; prof. polit. sci. Yale, 1952-71, chmn. dept., 1955-56. Pres. D. M. Watkins Co., Providence, 1935-58. Bd. overseers, mem. museum vis. com. Harvard. Mem. Am., Canadian polit. sci. assns., Am. Soc. for Legal and Polit. Philosophy (pres. 1962-64), Am. Numismatic Soc. (council), Providence Athenaeum. Clubs: Yale Faculty, New Haven Lawn (New Haven). Author: Constitutional Emergency Powers Under the German Republic, 1939; The Political Tradition of the West, 1948. Editor: Hume's Theory of Politics, 1951; Rousseau's Political Writings, 1953; The Age of Ideology, 1964. Home: North Scituate RI Died Mar. 29, 1972; buried Woodlawn Cemetery Attleboro MA

WATKINS, G. ROBERT, congressman; b. Hampton, Va., May 21, 1902; m. Hilda Jane Smerbeck; children—Robert G., Dwain Joseph. Organizer, pres. Chester Stevedoring Co. (Pa.), 1920-31; co-partner, organizer Blue Line Transfer Co., 1932; breeder thoroughbred horses, Delaware County, Pa., 1937-70; sheriff Delaware County, 4 years; mem. Pa. Senate, 12 years, commnr. Delaware County, 4 years; mem. 89th-91st congresses from 7th dist. Pa. Republican. Home: Delaware County PA Died Aug. 7, 1970.

WATKINS, HENRY HITT, judge; b. Laurens County, S.C., June 24, 1866; s. Henry Hitt and Hannah Elizabeth (Culbertson) W.; M.A., Furman U., 1883, LL.D., 1922; LL.D., Erskine College, Due West, S.C., 1932; read law under Wells & Orr, of Greenville, and Murray & Murray, Anderson, S.C.; summer course of law lectures U. of Va., under John B. Minor, 1890; m. Maude Wakefield, Dec. 27, 1892. Taught sch. 4 yrs. and prin. Prep. Sch., Furman U., 4 yrs.; admitted to S.C. bar, 1892, and practiced, Anderson, S.C. Q-m.-gen. on staff of Gov. Heyward, 1903-07; capt. Co. C, 1st S.C. Regt., U.S. Volunteers, 1898. Chmn. Dem. County Com., 1902-06; mem. Dem. State Exec. Com., 1906-10; Dem. presdl. elector, 1904; del.-at-large Dem. Nat. Conv., 1908. Became U.S. dist. judge, Western Dist. of S.C., 1919, now retired. Pres. bd. trustees Anderson Coll., 1911-27; trustee Anderson Hosp. Assn., Anderson Library Assn. Baptist. Mem. Am. Bar Assn. (v.p. for S.C., 1911, 12), S.C. Bar Assn., Sigma Alpha Epsilon. Mason (K.T.). Home: Anderson SC‡

WATKINS, J(AMES) STEPHEN, engr.; b. London, Ky., Nov. 14, 1892; s. Nathaniel and Dorcas (Chestnut) W.; student Sue Bennett Coll., London, Ky., 1907-12; B.S. in Civil Engring., U. Ky., 1930, C.E., 1938, LL.D., 1964; m. Martha Willis, June 21, 1923; 1 dau., Martha L. (Mrs. Barrett McVey Morris), County highway engr. Laurel County, Ky., 1916-17; engr. Briar Hill Steel Works, also Goodyear Tire & Rubber Co., 1919; hwy. engr. Ky. State Hwy. Dept., 1919-29. chief engr., 1927-29; chief engr., constrn. supt. Codell Co., 1930-32; pres. Watkins & Assos., Inc., 1962-66, chmn. bd., 1966-67; partner Wilson, Bell & Watkins, architects, engrs., 1941-45, Gillig, Watkins & Wilson, 1950-55, Balke & Watkins, Cons. engrs., 1952-55; sr. partner Watkins, Burrows & Assos., architects and engrs.; pres. East High Corp. of Lexington (Ky.); commr. hwys. Commonwealth Ky., 1943-48; dir. Security Trust Co. (Lexington). Vice pres. Ky. Mountain Laurel Festival, 1954-55; hwy. study com. Commn. on Intergovtl. Relations, 1954-55; mem. Ky. Adv. Commn. Div. Library Extension; bd. Fayette County chpt. Am. Cancer Soc. Pres. Ky. Med. Found.; trustee U. Ky., Coll. of Bible, Lexington; sponsor's com. Bellarmine Coll.; mem. Ky. State Fair Bd., 1956; chmn. exec. com. Ky. Sesquicentennial Commn.; dir. Ky. Constl. Edn. Found.; mem., bd. dirs. Ky. Spindletop Research Center; pres. Ky. Better Rds. Council. Served as 2d lieut. U.S. Army, 1918. Named Ky. Engr. of Year by Ky. Soc. Profl. Engrs., 1955. Member Kentucky C. of C. (director, past pres.), Am. Society C.E., American Road Builders Association (director), American Inst., Cons. Engrs., Am. Soc. Testing Materials, Am. Water Works Assn., Internat. Soc. Soils Mechanics and Foundation Engring., Newcomen Soc. Eng. in N.A., Ky. Soc. Profl. Engrs. (past pres.), Civil War Round Table, Sigma Nu. Member of the Christian Church. Clubs: Filson (Louisville); Lexington, Idle Hour Country, Lexington Country, Rotary, Kentucky Mountain (Lexington). Conbtr. tech. profl. jours. Home: Lexington KY Died Nov. 2, 1967.

WATKINS, JAMES (KEIR), lawyer; b. Normal, Ill., May 24, 1887; s. Amos and Agnes (Harvey) W.; A.B., U. Mich., 1909; LL.B., Detroit Coll. Law, 1911; B.C.L., Oxford U., 1914; m. Margaret B. Hosmer, Aug. 18, 1917; children—James K., George H., John B., Margaret Harvey. Admitted to Mich. bar, 1911; asso. Trowbridge & Lewis Detroit, 1914-19, mem. Trowbridge, Lewis & Watkins, later Lewis & Watkins, 1934-70; member bd. of directors of Michigan-Dynamics, Incorporated, Woodmere Cemetery Assn. Commr. police, Detroit, 1931-33; chmn. Mayor's Interracial Com., 1945-48. Republican. Episcopalian. Clubs: Detroit, Country of Detroit, Yondotega, University. Home: Grosse Pointe Farms MI Died Feb. 26, 1970.

WATKINS, JOSEPH CONRAD, dentist; b. Yadkin County, N.C., Nov. 27, 1873; s. Charles Jones and Flora Olivia (Conrad) W.; grad. Salem Boys Sch., Winston-Salem, N.C., 1891; LL.B. and A.B., Wake Forest (N.C.) Coll., 1897, Sc.D., 1922; D.D.S., U. of Md., 1900; F.A.C.D., 1925; m. Irene Montague, June 24, 1902; children—Joseph Conrad, Jr. (A.B., M.D., dec.), Richard Montague, Mary Elizabeth (dec.), William Henry, Eleanor (Mrs. W. A. Starbuck). Admitted to N.C. bar, 1897; began practice of dentistry at Winston-Salem, 1900; chief of dental staff City Memorial Hosp., 1937-42, Kate Bitting Memorial Hosp., 1937-42, Winston-Salem Health Center since 1938; dental dir. N.C. Bapt. Hosp. since 1940; visiting dental surgeon Forsyth County Hosp., also Forsyth County Tubercular Hosp., since 1942; member Forsyth County Board of Health, 1941-45; prof. periodontia and clin. dental surgery, Bowman Gray Med. Coll. of Wake Forest, Winston-Salem, N.C., since 1941. Awarded certificate of efficiency Am. Bd. Periodontology, 1941. Dir. Forsyth County Dentists, doing free dentistry to equip mem for mil. service, World War I. Trustee Wake Forest College since 1928. Mem. Internat. Dental Congress 6 times to 1939, Jamestown (Va.) Dental Congress, 1907. Life mem. Am. Dental Soc., Am. Acad. Periodontology, Southern Acad. Periodontology (pres. 1927), N.C. Dental Soc. (sec. 1905; pres. 1910; chmn. oral hygiene com. 1910-20), 2d Dist. Dental Soc. (chmn. orgn. com. 1921; pres. 1942), N.C. State Lit. and Hist. Assn., Delta Sigma Delta, Omicron Kappa Upsilon; asso. mem. for N.C. of Am. Dental Assn. Relief Fund Com. Has given series of lectures to nurses of City Memorial Hosp., 1927-38. Democrat. Baptist. Mason (K.T.), K.P. Rotarian. Contbr. many reports, papers and lectures on oral hegiene. Home: 417 Forsyth St. Winston-Salem NC Office: R. J. Reynolds Tobacco Co. Office: 1508-11 Reynolds Bldg., Winston-Salem, N.C.‡

WATKINS, VERNON PHILLIPS, poet; b. Maesteg, S. Wales, June 27, 1906; s. William and Sarah (Phillips) W.; student Magadalene Coll., Cambridge, 1924-25; D.Litt., U. Wales, 1966; m. Gwendoline Mary Davies, Oct. 2, 1944; children—Rhiannon Mary, Gareth Vernon, William Tristan David, Dylan Valentine, Conrad Merdith. With Lloyds Bank, 1925-66; vis. prof. poetry U. Wash., Seattle, 1964, 67; Gulbenkian fellow Swansea U., 1966-67. Served with R.A.F., 1941-46. Fellow Royal Soc. Lit.; mem. Societe Europeenne de Culture. Author: Ballad of the Mari Lwyd and Other Poems, 1941; The Lady With the Unicorn, 1948; The North Sea, 1951; The Death Bell, 1954; Cypress and Acacia, 1960; Affinities, 1963; Selected Poems, 1930-1960, 1967; Fidelities, 1968. Editor: Dylan Thomas's Letters to Vernon Watkins, 1957. Address: Pennard nr Swansea South Wales Died Oct. 8, 1967; buried St. Mary's, Pennard, nr. Swansea South Wales

WATSON, CHARLES G., steel co. exec.; b. Penfield, N.Y., Jan. 16, 1891; s. Abram Merrill and Martha (Gamble) W.; student Columbia; D. Engring., Youngstown U.; m. Sally Leedy, June 3, 1920. Tchr. schs. in N.Y. and Ohio, 1912-16; field engr. Youngstown Sheet & Tube Co., 1916-17; asst. chief engr. W.B. Pollock Co., Youngstown, 1919-21; with Youngstown Welding & Engring. Co., from 1921, pres., 1937-58, chmn. bd., from 1958, also dir.; dir. Powell Pressed Steel Co., Youngstown. Bd. dirs. Mahoning Valley Indsl. Council, Youngstown Better Bus. Bur. Trustee Youngstown U., from 1939, chmn. bd., from 1962; bd. dirs. Youngstown Community Fund. Served with U.S. Army, World War I. Decorated letter of commendation, World War I, World War II; Charles G. Watson Elementary Sch., Youngstown, named for him. Mem. Am. Soc. Naval Engrs., Soc. Naval Architects and Marine Engrs., Youngstown C. of C. (bd. 1940-58, pres. 1950-51), V.F.W. (life), Am. Legion (life), Youngstown Symphony Soc. Republican. Mason (Shriner), Kiwanian. Home: Canfield OH

WATSON, DAVID ROBERT, publisher; b. Chester, Pa., Feb. 13, 1902; s. James Henry and Elizabeth Emerick (Bradbury) W.; A.B. in Econs., Swarthmore Coll., 1924; m. Irene Duncan, July 5, 1952; children—Robert, Gregory, Deborah, Jill, Thomas. Pres. Watson Publs., Inc., Chgo., pubs. Modern Railroads, Appliance Mfrs., Traffic Mgmt., 1945-68. Bd. dirs. Bus. Publs. Audit of Circulation, 1962-68; chmn. Nat. Bus. Publs., 1962-68. Mem. Western Ry. Club, Assn. Indsl. Advertisers. Clubs: Union League (Chgo.); Biltmore Country (Barrington, Ill.); Royal Yacht and Country (Boca Raton). Home: Boca Raton FL Died Nov. 1968.

WATSON, DUDLEY CRAFTS, artist; b. Lal Geneva, Wis., Apr. 28, 1885; s. William Weldon ar Augusta Crafts (Tolman) W.; grad. high sch., Chicag 1904; studied Armour Inst. Tech., Art Inst. Chicag studied in Madrid and Valencia, Spain, Paris, ar London; pupil of Sorolla and Sir Alfred East; A.F.D Beloit Coll., 1935; m. Laura Josephine Hale, May 2 1908; children—Augusta Crafts, Emily Hale, Marjo Ann, Kathleen Laura. Mem. faculty, and tchr. wat color painting Art Inst. Chicago, 1908-13, membersh lectr. 1926-60, also extension lectr. to pub. sch 1934-60, Art through Travel lectr., 1950-60; dir. Mil Art Inst., 1913-26; U. Wis. externion lectr. 1926-60; a editor Milw. Jour., 1917-20; dramatic editor Milw. Fr Press, 1915-16. Dir. art edn., Minn. State Fair, 1915-2 conducted ann. art pilgramages to Europe, Russia, Asi Latin Am., 1956; ofcl. fine arts lecturer Century Progress Expn., Chicago, 1933, 1934, Texas Centennia 1935, Great Lakes Exposition, 1936, New York World Fair, 1939-40. Annual lecturer Carnegie Interna Exhbn., Pittsburgh, 1928-60. Originator and produc of music picture symphonies; author and produc pageants. Author: Nineteenth and Twentieth Centur Painting; Taste Through the Ages; Occupation Opportunities in the Fine and Industrial Arts; als numerous magazine and trade journal articles. Radi commentator, Station WGN, 1934-35 and 1939-4 Recorded color-film lectures in nat. distribution Mast Paintings of Art Inst. Chicago, and National Galler Washington, First prize, water color painting, A League, Chicago, 1907; exhibitor water colors, variou exhbns.; one-man show, 1944, Grand Central Gallerie New York, 1944-45; art assns., Terre Haute, Ind Atlanta, Ga., Charlotte, N.C.; Galesburg, Ill. Decorate Al Merito, en el Grado de Oficial (Ecuador); Knight Crown (Belgium). Clubs: Arts, Cliff Dweller University. Home: Lake Bluff IL Died Dec. 24, 197

WATSON, EARNEST CHARLES, physicist; bor Sullivan, Ill., June 18, 1892; s. Charles Grant and Alic Bell (Smith) W.; Ph.B., Lafayette Coll., Easton, Pa 1914; postgrad. U. Chgo., 1914-17; Sc.D., Lafayet Coll., 1958; m. Elsa Jane Werner, October 6, 1954. Ass in physics Univ. of Chicago, 1914-17; asst. prof. physics, Calif. Inst. Tech., 1919-20, associate professo 1920-30, professor, 1930-62, emeritus, 1962-70, dea faculty, 1945-60 chairman faculty board, chmn. di Physics, Mathematics and Astronomy, 1946-49, actin pres., 1956-57; cons. Ford Found. S. and S.E. As Program, 1964-70. Sci. attache to Am. Embassy Ne Delhi, India, 1960-62; del. to various confs. Served i U.S.N.R.F., 1917-1919; member Division 3, Nation Defense Research Committee, 1941-44. Offici Investigator, OSRD Contract OEMsr-418 (researc and development work on artillery rockets, torpedoe atomic bomb and other ordnance devices), 1941-4 Chmn. library adv. bd. City Pasadena, 1956-60. Fello Am. Phys. Soc., A.A.A.S.; mem. Am. Assn. Physic Teachers, History of Science Soc., Am. Assn. Univ Profs., Fgn. Policy Assn., Indian Internat. Centre, Ph Beta Kappa, Sigma Xi, Tau Beta Pi, Gamma Alpha Clubs: Athenaeum. Author: Mechanics, Molecula Physics, Heat and Sound, 1937. Contbr. sci. jours Home: Santa Barbara CA Died Dec. 5, 1970.

WATSON, ERNEST W(ILLIAM), artist, autho pub.; b. Conway, Mass., Jan. 14, 1884; s. Daniel an Lucinda (Moody) W.; grad. Monson (Mass.) Acad 1901, Mass. Normal Art Sch., Boston, Mass., 1906 Pratt Inst. Art Sch., 1907; travel and study in Eng. an Europe, 1926, Mexico, 1936; m. Eva M. Auld, June 2 1911 (dec. 1948); children—Lyn A. Aldren A.; m. 2d Eve Brian, April 9, 1949. Tchr. of drawing and desig at the Pratt Institute Art Sch., 1908-29, supervisor da and evening classes, 1919-29; co-founder (wit Raymond P. Ensign), The Berkshire Summer Sch. c Art, Monterey, Mass., 1915, withdrew from sch., 1927 art editor Scholastic mag., New York, N.Y., 1931-37 founder (with Ralph Reinhold, pres., and Arthur L Guptill, vice pres.), Watson-Guptill Pubs., Inc., Ne York, N.Y., 1937, v.p., 1937-55; editor-in-chief Am Artist, 1937-55, emeritus, 1955-69; artist adv illustrations in pencil since 1913, color woodcuts sinc 1920. Rep. in collections Smithsonian Inst., Library c Congress, N.Y. Pub. Lib., Bklyn. Mus., Balt. Mus. Ar Albert H. Wiggin Print Collection, Boston Publi Library, Nat. Collection Fine Arts, Washington. Mem Soc. Illustrators, Nat. Sculptors Soc. Republica Author: Lineolum Printing, 1925; Pencil Drawing 1937; Color and Method in Painting, 1942; Outdoo Sketching; Forty Illustrators, 1946; Twenty Painter and How They Work, 1950; How to Use Creativ Perspective, 1955; Course in Pencil Sketching, Book 1 Streets and Buildings, 1956, Book 2, Trees an Landscapes, 1957, Book 3, Boats and Harbors, 1957 Gallery of Pencil Techniques, 1958; Pictoria Composition in Landscape and Still Life, 1959; (wit Aldren Watson) The Watson Drawing Book, 1962 Perspective for Sketchers, 1964; Ernest W. Watson' Sketch Diary, 1965; The Art of Pencil Drawing, 1968 Recipient Alumni award Monson Acad., 1951, Ga Melchers Gold medal Artists Fellowship, 1959; Prat Inst. Alumni gold medal, 1965. Contbr. over 30 articles to Am. Artist mag. Home: New Rochelle NY Died Jan. 23, 1969; ashes interred at Hillside Cemetery Monson MA

WATSON, FLOYD ROWE, physicist; b. Lawrence, Kan., Apr. 23, 1872; s. Norman Allen and Helen Altana (Hitchcock) W.; grad. State Normal Sch., Los Angeles, Calif., 1893; B.S., U. of Calif., 1899; Ph.D., Cornell U., 1902; m. Estelle Jane Barden, Aug. 14, 1902; children—Norman Allen, Robert Barden. Asst. in physics, U. of Calif., 1897-99; fellow in physics, U. of Calif. and Cornell U., 1899-1902; instr. in physics, U. of Ill., 1902-04, asst. prof., 1904-15, asso. prof., 1915-17, prof. experimental physics, 1917-40, prof. of physics, emeritus since 1940. Fellow A.A.A.S., Am. Physical Soc., Acoustical Society of America, Sigma Xi. Methodist. Expert in acoustics. Home: 1504 Milan Av., South Pasadena CA‡

WATSON, JOHN FRANKLIN, church official; b. Clintonville, Ala., Oct. 7, 1871; s. John H. and Anna (Bell) W.; A.B., Howard Coll., Birmingham, Ala., 1896, D.D., 1914; Th.G., Southern Bapt. Theol. Sem., Louisville, Ky., 1898; m. Willenor Heloise Abbott, Oct. 11, 1898; children—William Harris, John Franklin (dec.). Ordained Bapt. ministry, 1894; pastor successively Orrville, Ala., Midway, Ky., Holdenville, Okla., Pomona, Calif.; exec. sec. Southern Calif. Bapt. Conv., 1912-18; exec. sec. and supt. missions Western Wash. Bapt. Conv., 1918-31; exec. sec. Wash. Bapt. Conv., 1931-34. Mem. Bd. of Missionary Cooperation of Northern Bapt. Conv. Trustee, mem. exec. com., Linfield Coll., McMinnville, Ore.; trustee Berkeley (Calif.) Bapt. Divinity Sch. Home: Woodinville, Wash. Office: Ranke Bldg., Seattle WA‡

WATSON, KENNETH NICOLL, investment banker, lawyer; b. Washington, Mar. 27, 1907; s. Walter Scott and Maude (Arthur) W.; A.B., George Washington U., 1928, LL.B., 1930; grad. student Harvard U. Bus. Sch., 1937; m. Diane G. Maitland (dec. Mar. 1949); m. 2d, Virginia Evans Carey, Dec. 1951; children—Nicole Carey, Diane Nicoll. Admitted to D.C. bar, 1930; atty. NRA, 1933-35, FTC, 1935-41; exec. WPB, 1941-43; mem. U.S. Tech. Mission to Brazil, 1942; pvt. practice law, Washington, also Europe, 1947-53; partner of Jones, Kreeger & Co., Washington, mem. N.Y. Stock Exchange, from 1953; dir. Allied Capital Corp., Peoples Bank, Buena Vista, Va. Vice chmn. President's Com. on Employment Handicapped; dir. U.S. Expn. Sci. and Industry, Washington. Trustee Washington chpt. Am. Cancer Soc. Served from lt. (j.g.) to lt. comdr., USNR, 1943-47; asst. naval and air attache Am. embassies, Colombia and Panama, 1945-47. Mem. Assn. Customers Brokers, Am., D.C. bar assns., Washington Bd. Trade, Soc. Cin., Washington Inst. Fgn. Affairs. Episcopalian. Clubs: Metropolitan (Washington and N.Y.C.); Burning Tree (Md.); City Tavern, Army Navy, 1925 F Street (Washington). Home: Washington DC Died June 4, 1970; buried Arlington Nat. Cemetery, Arlington VA

WATSON, RUSSELL ELLSWORTH, lawyer; b. New Brunswick, N.J., Oct. 8, 1885; s. Frank Ellsworth and Elizabeth (Painter) W.; student Rutgers Coll., 1902-05, LL.D., Rutgers U., 1949; LL.B., N.Y. Law Sch., 1907; m. Beulah Fraleigh Fingar, Mar. 24, 1909; children—Russell Ellsworth, Malcolm (dec.), Jean (Mrs. William B. Moses, Jr.), Sarah Elizabeth (Mrs. Kendall B. DeBevoise). Admitted to N.J. bar, 1909, counsellor at law, 1912-70; gen. practice of law, New Brunswick, 1909-70; with firm R.E. & A.D. Watson, 1920-70; asst. pros. of pleas. Middlesex County, N.J., 1909-12; asso. counsel in N.J., Port of N.Y. Authority, 1930-70; dep. atty. gen., N.J., 1931-48. Counsel N.J. Legislative Com., 1928-30, 45; counsel to gov. N.J., 1947-50; counsel Rutgers U., 1944-70, vice chmn. trustee, 1944-56. Fellow Am. Bar Found.; mem. Am. Bar Assn., Chi Psi. Republican. Mem. Reformed Ch. Home: Belle NJ Died Dec. 11, 1970.

WATSON, WILLARD OLIPHINT, ins. exec.; b. Orange, Tex., Apr. 8, 1902; s. Martin A. and Jennie (Oliphint) W.; student So. Methodist U., 1919; LL.B., U. Tex., 1928. With Am. Nat. Ins. Co., Galveston, Tex., from 1929, asst. treas., from 1931, then sr. v.p., dir.; dir. Commonwealth Life & Accident Ins. Co. Mem. Delta Kappa Epsilon. Clubs: Delta Kappa Epsilon (N.Y.C.); Artillery, Galveston, Galvez (Galveston). Home: Galveston TX

WATT, BARBARA HALL, instn. adminstr.; b. Lake Orion, Mich., Oct. 16, 1912; d. John Thomas and Nettie (Rodenbo) Hall; A.B., U. Mich., 1934; M.A., U. Chgo., 1940; part-time student, U. Toledo Coll. Law, 1961-64; m. Wallace F. Watt, Mar. 9, 1946; 1 adopted dau., Dorothy Marie (Mrs. Raymon C. Lewis). Caseworker, supr. social service Oakland and Bay counties (Mich.) emergency relief adminstrns., 1934-39; child welfare worker and cons. children's div. Mich. Dept. Social Welfare, 1941-46, 48-50; exec. sec. Upper Peninsula br. Mich. Children's Aid Soc., Marquette, 1947-48; casework supr. Bapt. Children's Home, Detroit, 1950-51, Meth. Children's Soc., Detroit, 1951-53; supt. Mich. State Girls' Tng. Sch., Adrian, 1953-67; asso. dir. Michigan Department Social Services Bureau Group Care Services, 1967-70. Named Mich. Child Welfare Worker of Year, 1961. Mem. Am. Assn. U. Women, Nat. Assn. Social Workers, Nat. Assn. Supts. Correctional Institutions for Girls and Women (president 1963-64), Bus. and Profl. Women, Am. Pub. Welfare Assn., Nat. Assn. Welfare Tng. Schs. and Juvenile Agys., Mich. Welfare League (dir. 1947-53), Mich. Assn. Children's Agys. (treas. 1960-61), Alpha Kappa Delta, Delta Kappa Gamma, Kappa Phi. Home: Lansing MI Died Apr. 1, 1970.

WATTERS, REV. PHILIP SIDNEY, clergyman; b. Dobbs Ferry, N.Y., Feb. 4, 1890; s. Philip M. and Hyla Ada (Stowell) W.; ed. Kingston (N.Y.) Acad.; A.B., Princeton, 1910; B.D., Drew Theol. Sem., 1913; M.A., N.Y.U., 1918; D.D., MacMurray Coll., 1950; m. Grace Catharine Briggs, Sept. 3, 1914; children—Catharine (Mrs. Davison), Philip S., Dorothy B. (Mrs. John Brand). Ordained to the ministry Methodist Church; asst. minister Centenary Ch., Newark, N.J., 1913; became minister churches, Tenafly, Demarest, Port Jervis, and Madison, N.J.; lectr. in hymnology Crew Theol. Sem., 1921; minister First Ch., Plainfield, N.J., 1927, Meml. Ch., White Plains, N.Y., 1930-43; pres. Drew Sem. for Young Women, Carmel, N.Y., 1943-50; minister Washington Sq. Meth. Ch., N.Y.C., 1950-61, Meth. Ch., Grand Gorge, N.Y., 1961-69, United Meth. Ch., Broadway, N.J., 1970-72. Trustee Drew U. Mem. Phi Beta Hackettstown NJ Died Sept. 21, 1972; buried Sleepy Hollow Cemetery, Tarrytown NY

WATTS, ALBERT EDWARD, petroleum producer; b. Washington, D.C., June 5, 1881; s. Sidney Smith and Mary Jane (Wichelow) W.; grad. Business High Sch., Washington, D.C.; m. Laura Bell Joseph, Oct. 27, 1911; children—Albert Edward, Robert Hoober, Mary Louise, Laura Bell. In oil business since 1900; v.p., dir. Sinclair Oil Corp. and Sinclair subsidiaries and affiliated corporations, retired, then retained as a counsultant. Umpire Cushing Field, 1914, by suggestions of pipe line cos. and crude oil producers jointly. Apptd. receiver Naval Reserve No. 3 (Teapot Dome), by Fed. Court, Cheyenne, Mar. 1924; apptd. mem. of planning and coordinating com. Administrating Petroleum Code under NRA, Washington, D.C. Democrat. Episcopalian. Mason (32 deg.). Club: Lotos. Home: Great Neck LI NY Died Jan. 1969.

WATTS, ARTHUR S., ceramic engr.; b. Zanesville, O., Mar. 27, 1876; s. Arthur H. and Reliance M. (Holton) W.; B.S., Ohio State U., 1901; Ceramic Engr. (professional), Ohio State U., 1928; studied Technische Hochschule, Charlottenburg, Germany, 1909-10; m. Olive May Graham, July 26, 1917; children—Arthur Graham, Richard Lee. With Locke Insulator Co., Victor N.Y., 1901, Bell Pottery Co., Findlay, O., 1902-03, New Lexington (O.) Insulator Co., 1904, Locke Insulator Co., Victor, 1905-08; quarry technologist, U.S. Bur. of Mines, 1911-13; prof. ceramic engineering, Ohio State University, 1914-46, prof. emeritus, 1946. Member American Ceramic Society, American Society for Testing Materials, Sigma Xi, Tau Beta Pi. Mason (K.T., Shriner). Baptist. Author: Feldspars and Kaolins of the South Appalachians (U.S. Bureau Mines), 1913; Feldspars of the New England and North Appalachian States (U.S. Bur. Mines), 1916; The Selection of Dinnerware for the Home, 1930. Home: 172 16th Av., Columbus OH*‡

WATTS, HERBERT CHARLES, physician; b. San Francisco, Calif., Mar. 1, 1874; s. Charles and Eliza Mills (Newman) W.; M.D., U. of Calif., 1900; m. Emily Cornelia Veirs, Apr. 26, 1905 (died June 30, 1908); 1 dau., Jessie (Mrs. Alan Scott); m. 2d, Silvia Josefa Varela, Oct. 10, 1914; children—Herbert Charles, George Joseph. House physician and surgeon City and County Hosp., San Francisco, 1900-01; surgeon Pacific Mail S.S. Co., 1902-04; resident surgeon Calif. Powder Works, Pinole, Calif., 1904-06; private practice, Modesto, Calif., 1906-08; physician and quarantine officer Panama Canal Service, 1909-20; commd. passed asst. surgeon U.S. Pub. Health Reserve, 1920, surgeon, 1921, sr. surgeon, 1923; transferred to Vets. Adminstrn. as chief med. officer, 1924; mgr. combined facility, Ft. Harrison, Mont., since 1929, retired Jan. 1, 1947. Served in Calif. Nat. Guard, 1893-1901, hosp. steward, 1898-1901; 1st lt. Med. Corps, U.S. Army, 1918-19; capt. Med. Sec., O.R.C., 1920. Mason (32 deg., Shriner). Home: 115 El Camino Real, Menlo Pk CA‡

WATTS, JOHN CLARENCE, congressman; b. Nicholasville, Ky., July 9, 1902; s. William Montague and Frances Elizabeth (Wilson) W.; A.B., U. Ky., 1926, LL.B., 1927; m. Nora Mae Wilburn, Mar. 27, 1945; 1 dau., Lillian Frances. Admitted to Ky. bar, 1927, since practiced in Nicholasville; police judge, Nicholasville, 1929-33; farmer Jessamine Co. since 1934; co. atty., 1933-45; maj. floor leader ho. of reps., Ky. State Leg., 1947; commr. motor transportation, State of Ky., 1948-51; member 82d to 89th Congresses, 6th Ky. Dist. Mem. Phi Delta Phi. Democrat. K.P. Club: Lions. Home: Nicholasville KY Died Oct. 1971.

WATTS, STANLEY SAUL, life ins. co. exec.; b. Richmond, Va., Sept. 29, 1922; s. Robert C. and Celia (Goodman) W.; B.S., U. Richmond, 1943; C.L.U., 1961; m. Velma L. Phillips, Dec. 27, 1947; children—Thomas Henry, Dorothy Phillips, Peggy Ann. Vice pres. G & W Constrn. Co., Asheville, N.C., 1946-49; with Equitable Life Assurance Soc. U.S., 1949-72, agy. mgr., South and Central Fla., then divisional agy. v.p., Norfolk, Va., 1963-72; v.p., dir. Ocean Electric Corp., Norfolk, Va., Rosanne Corp., Washington; United Va./Seaboard Nat. Bank. Past dir. Norfolk (Va.) Life Underwriters Assn., Norfolk C.L.U. Assn.; past pres. Norfolk Gen. Agts. and Mgrs. Assn. Div. Chmn., Norfolk United Fund, 1959-62, Norfolk United Jewish Appeal, 1959-62, Miami (Fla.) United Fund, 1964-65, Miami United Jewish Appeal, 1965; pres. Norfolk chpt. Am. Jewish Com., 1960-61, bd. dirs. Miami chpt., 1964-67. Bd. dirs. Norfolk United Fund. Served with USNR, 1943-46. Named Norfolk-Portsmouth Sales Exec. of Year, 1960. Mem. Million Dollar Round Table (exec. com. 1965-72, pres. 1969—), Miami Estate Planning Council. Jewish religion (bd. dirs. temple 1967). Home: Norfolk VA Died Dec. 3, 1972.

WAUGH, KARL TINSLEY, psychologist; b. of Am. parents, Cawnpore, India, Nov. 30, 1879; s. James Walter (D.D.) and Jennie Mary (Tinsley) W.; B.A., Ohio Wesleyan U., 1900, M.A., 1901, LL.D., 1927; studied Columbia; M.A., Harvard, 1906, Ph.D., 1907; m. Emily L. Sprightley, Sept. 4, 1912; children—Eleanor Tinsley (Mrs. J.A. Hanley; now dec.), Charles MacCarthy. Professor of philosophy and mathematics, Claflin University, S.C., 1900-04; Weld fellow and asst. in philosophy to prof. William James, Harvard, 1906-07; associate in psychology, U. of Chicago, 1907-09; head dept. philosophy and psychology, Beloit Coll., 1909-18; dean and prof. psychology and philosophy, Berea (Ky.) Coll., Sept. 1919-23; dean Coll. Arts and Sciences, and prof. psychology, U. of Southern Calif., 1923-31; prof. psychology, chmn. div. psychology and edn., Long Island U., Brooklyn, N.Y. 1930-31; pres. Dickinson Coll., Carlisle, Pa., 1931-34; dean Charles Morris Price Sch., Phila., 1934-39; state dir. of student aid, Nat. Youth Adminstrn. for Pa., 1935-37; exec. dir. Fed. Cooperative Health Service during 1937; personnel officer, Dept. of Public Assistance of Pa., 1939-42; field rep., student war loans fund, U.S. Office of Edn., 1942-43. Supervisor, Vocational Advisement, U.S. Vets. Adminstrn. from 1944; conducted educational and psychological investigation in China and India, 1916-17; lecturer in psychology, Univ. of Colorado, 1909, 14, Northwestern Univ. 1921. Served as 1st lt., capt. and maj. U.S. Army, psychol. div., World War, Aug. 1917-Feb. 5, 1919; in Surgeon General's Office, Washington, D.C.; chief psychol. examiner at Camp Gordon, Ga., Camp McClellan, Ala., trans. to Ft. McPherson, Ga.; supervisor Fed. Bd. for Vocational Edn., 5th Dist., Feb.-Sept. 1919. Treated successfully, by suggestion, nervous disorder, hysterical blindness, stammering, shell shock, etc.; organized first university courses leading to motion picture careers, Los Angeles. Fellow A.A.A.S.; mem. Am. Psychol. Assn., Am. Acad. Polit. and Social Science, Ky. Acad. Science, Soc. Psychical Research, Engenics Research Assn., Western Psychol. Assn., Psychol. Corp. (pres. Calif. br.), N.Y. Acad. of Sciences, Society for Adv. of Education, Sigma Xi, Phi Beta Kappa, Phi Delta Theta, Phi Kappa Phi, Pi Gamma Mu, Acacia, Omicron Delta Kappa. Methodist. Mason. Clubs; Poor Richard, Schoolmen's, Mendelssohn, Blackstonian, Executive Advancement. Author of articles: Vision in Animals, 1910; Mental Diagnosis of College Students, 1915; Comparative Mentality of Oriental and American Students, 1920; Rational Empiricism Views Teleology, 1927; The Liberal Arts College Faces the Present Age, 1932; Psychology in Modern Industry, 1934; Personal Hurdles (with J.W. Irwin), 1936; The Humanizing of Psychology; Saturday Night Thoughts," contributed to newspaper columns. Specialist in the writings of Rudyard Kipling; editor poetry sect. Artland Mag. and California Southland, 1925-30. Home: Washington DC Died May 9, 1971.

WAUGH, SAMUEL CLARK, banker, former government official; born Plattsmouth, Nebraska, on April 28, 1890; s. Sam and Flora (Rawlins) W.; student U. Neb., 1911-12, LL.B., 1964; LL.D., Doane Coll., 1955; LL.D., Rensselaer Polytech. Inst., 1959; D.S.M., U. Nuevo Leon, 1958; m. Ruby Barns, May 1, 1913 (dec. July 1934); m. 2d, Della Ladd Romans, Apr. 11, 1942. With First Trust Co., Lincoln, Neb., 1913-61, pres., 1946-53, dir., 1948-61; asst. sec. of state, 1953-55, dep. under sec. of state, 1955; pres., chmn. bd. Export-import Bank, 1955-61; dir. Gen. Reins. Corp., Citizens State Bank; cons. Bank of N.Y., Blaw-Knox Co. of Pitts. Trustee U. Neb. Found. Decorated Order So. Cross (Brazil); Order Golden Horse (Taiwan); Order Aztec Eagle (Mex.); commdr. Order of Merit (Chile); Grand Cross of Queen Isabella (Spain); Order of Rising Sun (Japan); Grand officer Order of Merit (Italy; Meritorious Service Medal (Philippines). Mem. Am. Bankers Assn. (past pres. trust div.), C. of C. (past pres.), Delta Upsilon. Republican. Clubs: Chevy Chase, Metropolitan (Washington); Links (N.Y.C.). Home: Washington DC Died July 30, 1970; buried Lincoln NB

WAUGH, WILLIAM HAMMOND, ex-army officer, civil engineer; b. Greenville, Pennsylvania, April 13, 1875; son John Harold and Ella Louise (Hammond) W.; educated Shattuck School, 1892-93; married Queen Scott Lawson, January 23, 1909; children—William Hammond (lieutenant colonel, C.A.C.), Dorothy Scott (Mrs. G. M. Watson). Began with Pecos Irrigation and Improvement Co., N.M., 1893; with Bessemer & Lake Erie Railroad, Greenville, Pa., 1895-98, locating engineer, same, 1903-04; contracting in Cuba, 1899-1902; chief engineer Shenango Traction Company, Greenville, Pennsylvania, 1904-07, Little Rock & Pine Bluff Traction Co., 1907-09; div. engr. Bur. Pub. Works, Manila, P.I., 1909-15; consulting practice, Riverside, Calif., 1915-17; pres. Alaska Road Commn., 1917-20, also acting district engr. Bur. Pub. Rds. and cons. engr., Ty. of Alaska, 1917-20. Corpl. Pa. Nat. Guard, 1897-98; corpl. 15th Pa. Vol. Inf., May-July 1898; 1st sergt. 3d Regt., U.S. Vol. Engrs., July 1898-April 1899; constructing engr. Q.-M. Dept. U.S. Army, Apr.-Oct. 1899; capt. Engr. Corps, Calif., 1916-June 1917; capt. engrs. U.S. Reserve, June 1917-June 1918; maj. engrs. U.S. Army, 1918-20; capt. Corps of Engrs., 1920-36, maj., 1936-39, retired; real estate dealer since 1940. Mem. Am. Soc. C.E., S.A.R. Republican. Episcopalian. Mason. Home: 345 Elmhurst Av., San Antonio TX‡

WAUGH, WILLIAM JASPER, news agy. exec.; b. Visalia, Cal., Oct. 10, 1913; s. Harry V. and Catherine E. (O'Shea) W.; student pub. schs., Cal.; m. Jane Inez Schafer, July 8, 1936 (dec.); children—Stephen Schafer, Susan Catherine; m. 2d, Renee Rochester; stepchildren Medlinda, Rhea, Deborah, Jamie. Reporter, Visalia (Cal.) Times-Delta, 1934-41; sports writer Fresno (Cal.) Bee, 1941-42; with A.P., 1942-72, corr. Korean War, 1950-51, chief bur., Honolulu, 1952-56, Louisville, 1956-59, Atlanta, 1959-63, San Francisco, 1963-67, Los Angeles, 1967-71, ednl. writer, Washington, 1971-72. Served with USNR, World War II. Mem. Sigma Delta Chi. Home: Vienna VA Died Nov. 25, 1972; buried Vienna VA

WAY, WILLIAM, clergyman; b. Asheville, N.C., Dec. 18, 1877; s. Charles Burr and Martha Julia (Howell) W.; Asheville High Sch. and Ravenscroft High Sch., Asheville; Gen. Theol. Seminary, 1901; Harvard Summer School of Theology, 1907, 09, 10; D.D., U. of S.C., 1922; m. Marie Wagener, Jan. 12, 1904. Deacon, 1901, priest, 1901, Episcopal Ch.; asst. Grace Ch., New York, 1901-02; rector Grace Ch., Charleston, S.C., 1902-46, emeritus. Preacher Clemson College, 1907-09, U. of S.C., 1913, Converse Coll., 1914, U. of N.C., and S.C. Mil. Coll., 1921; preacher Duke U., 1937. Trustee and mem. standing com. Diocese of S.C.; dep. to Gen. Conv. Trustee Gen. Theol. Sem. (N.Y. City), St. Mary's Coll. Pres. N.E. Soc. of Charleston (author of its history), S.C. Hist. Soc. Mem. Am. Peace Soc. (dir.), St. George's Soc. of S.C., S.C. Hist. Soc. (pres.), Mason (32 deg., K.T., Shriner). Club: Rotary International (dist. gov.). Author: The Old Exchange and Custom House, 1921; History of Grace Church, Charleston, S.C.; The Story of Two Portraits; History of the New England Society of Charleston, S.C. Home: SC‡

WEAKLEY, CHARLES ENRIGHT, naval officer; b. St. Joseph, Mo., June 11, 1906; s. Lawrence O'Niel and Jeanette (Landis) W.; student U. Mo., 1924; B.S., U.S. Naval Acad., 1929; student U. Cambridge (Eng.), 1937-39; grad. Nat. War Coll., 1951; m. Geraldine Cullen, Mar. 31, 1934; children—Geraldine Louise, Linda Enright. Commd. ensign U.S. Navy, 1929, advanced through grades to vice adm., 1963, served at sea in cruisers, destroyers, anti-submarine ships, U.S.S. Omaha, 1929-33, U.S.S. Talbot, 1933-36, U.S.S. New Mexico, 1939-40, U.S.S. Sampson, 1940-41; comdr. U.S.S. Goff, 1941-42, Convoy Escort, 1941-44, anti-submarine warfare unit, Naval Operating Base, Norfolk, Va., 1944-45; assigned Office Chief Naval Operations, Washington, 1945-48; comdg. officer surface anti-submarine devel. detachment Atlantic, Key West, Fla., 1948-50; naval adviser NSC staff, internat. affairs div. Office Chief Naval Operations, 1951-53; comdr. U.S.S. Cambria, 1953-54, U.S.S. Northampton, 1954-55; asst. chief naval personnel for naval res., Navy Dept., 1955-56; with Office Chief Naval Operations, 1956-57, dir. undersea warfare div., 1957-58, anti-submarine warfare readiness exec., 1958-59; comdr. Destroyer Flotilla 2, 1959-60, Destroyer Force, U.S. Atlantic Fleet, 1960-61; asst. chief naval operations (devel.), 1961-63, dep. chief, 1963; comdr. Anti-submarine Warefare Force, U.S. Atlantic Fleet, 1963-67; asst. adminstr. mgmt. devel. NASA, Washington, 1967-72. Decorated Legion of Merit with combat V, Bronze Star, D.S.M., numerous campaign medals; U.S. Navy Destroyer Sch. at Newport, R.I. named Weakley Hall. Home: Chevy Chase MD Died Dec. 23, 1972; buried Arlington Nat. Cemetery.

WEAR, FRANK LUCIAN, clergyman, coll. pres.; b. Verona, Miss., Mar. 16, 1873; s. Archibald Smiley and Elizabeth (Ratliff) W.; A.B., Trinity U., San Antonio, Tex., 1899, LL.D., 1942; B.D., Cumberland U., Lebanon, Tenn., 1902, D.D., 1908; grad. Union Sem., New York, 1905; grad. work Columbia, 1904-05; m. Maude Ware Denson, Feb. 11, 1903; 1 son, Frank Denson. Organized Presbyn. Ch., Ensley, Ala., 1901; ordained to ministry Presbyn. Ch., 1902; pastor Ensley, Ala., 1902-04, Bronx Mission, New York, 1904-05, Central Ch., Denton, Tex., 1905-08, Central Ch., Huntsville, Ala., 1908-19; field sec. and dir. Million Dollar Endowment Campaign for Trinity U., 1919-21; pastor Central Ch., Paris, Tex., 1921-37; president Trinity Univ., San Antonio, Tex., 1937-42. Moderator Synod of Ala., Presbyn. Ch., U.S.A.; chmn. com. on nat. missions, Synod of Ala., 1908-19, Presbytery of Huntsville, Ala., 1908-19, Presbytery of Paris, Tex., 1922-37; chmn. Am. Red Cross Roll, 1921; chmn. com. to establish junior coll., Paris, Tex.; sec. com. on nat. missions, Synod of Tex., 1922-37. Trustee Trinity U., 1921-42, Reynolds Presbyterian Home since 1933; moderator Synod of Texas Presbyn. Ch., U.S.A., 1939-40. Sect. mem. Tex. Acad. of Science; mem. Poetry Soc. of Tex., Nat. Poetry Soc. of Am., Pi Kappa Alpha. Mason. Club: Rotary of Paris, Tex. (hon.). Home: 164 6th S.E., Paris TX‡

WEATHERFORD, WILLIS DUKE, coll. prof.; b. Weatherford, Tex., Dec. 1, 1875; s. Samuel L. and Margaret (Turner) W.; B.S., Weatherford Coll., 1895; B.A., Vanderbilt U.; 1899, M.A., 1900, Ph.D., 1907; m. Julia McCrory Weatherford, May 27, 1915. Internat. student sec. of Y.M.C.A., 1901-19; pres. Y.M.C.A. Grad. Sch., Nashville, 1919-36; head Dept. of Religion and Humanities, Fisk Univ., 1936-46. Trustee Berea Coll.; pres. Blue Ridge Coll., Inc., 1906-44. Dir. Am. Cast Iron Pipe Co. Mem. A.A.A.S., Am. Acad. of Polit. and Social Science, Tenn. Acad. of Science, Alpha Tau Omega. Methodist. Author: Fundamental Religious Principles in Browning's Poetry, 1907; Negro Life in the South, 1910; Introducing Men to Christ, 1911; Present Forces in Negro Progress, 1912; Christian Life a Normal Experience, 1916; Personal Elements in Religious Life, 1916; The Negro from Africa to America, 1924; Race Relations (with Charles S. Johnson), 1934; Life Sketch of James Brownson Dunwoody De Bow, 1935; The American Churches and the Negro; Analytical Index of De Bows Review, 1946; Pioneers of Destiny, 1955; American Churches and the Negro, 1957; Studies in Christian Experience, 1962. Editor of Report on Law and Order Conf., 1917. Editor of Interracial Cooperation, 1920; Survey of Negro Boy Life in Nashville, Tenn., 1934. Mem. Phi Beta Kappa, Pi Gamma Mu. Home: Blue Ridge NC Died Feb. 21, 1970; buried Blue Ridge Assembly Grounds, Black Mountain NC

WEATHERLY, W(ILLIAM) H., banker; b. Munford, Ala., Apr. 22, 1864; s. John J. and Margaret (Smyth) W.; ed. pub. schs. and Moores Bus. Coll., Atlanta, Ga.; m. Alice Stone, Nov. 13, 1888; children—Mary (Mrs. Walker Reynold), Alice (Mrs. James C. Inzer), Robert S., James C., William S. Organizer, 1887, gen. mgr. until 1899, Anniston (Ala.) Mercantile Co., wholesale grocers; organizer, 1899, mgr., 1899-1907, owner, 1907-27, Bell & Weatherly, wholesale grocers; pres. Talladega Grocery Co., 1910-22, First Nat. Bank, Anniston, 1914-29, since chmn. bd.; dir. Ala. Power Company, M. & H. Valve & Fittings Company, Birmingham (Ala.) Fire Insurance Co.; dir. Community Chest. Chmn. 5th zone, 6th federal dist., Liberty Loan drive, World War. Democrat. Presbyterian. Mason (Shriner). Club: Anniston Country. Home: 1200 Leighton Av. Office: First Nat. Bank, Anniston AL‡

WEATHERRED, PRESTON ALONZO, lawyer; b. Oceola, Tex., Aug. 11, 1884; s. Thomas Preston and Elizabeth (King) W.; student Carlisle Mil. Acad., Arlington, Tex., 1901-03; LL.B., U. Tex., 1908; grad. Army War Coll., 1922, Inf. Sch., 1941; m. Irene Desole Warren, Oct. 14, 1907; children—Mary Elizabeth, Julia Augusta, Preston Alonzo. Practiced law, 1912-67, except for military service, 1916-25, 1940-42; specializes in indsl., administrative ins. and corporation practice; counsel Blanchette, Smith & Shelton, Dallas; gen. counsel Code Authority Ice Industry, Washington. 1934-35. Senior vice president, gen. counsel Internat. Fidelity Ins. Co.; dir. widespread coop. effort behalf conservation state govt.; dir. seminars labor relations, Arlington State Coll., oil industry, others. Served as maj. comd. 1st Battn. 2d Tex. Inf. Mexican Border, 1916-17; comd. 132d Machine Gun Battn., 36th Div., in France, 1918; lt. col., 1923, col., 1926, Tex. Nat. Guard; chief of staff, 36th Div., 1926-39; brig. gen. in command of 72d Inf. Brigade, 36th Div., 1939-42; transferred to inactive status, Sept. 26, 1942; recalled to active status as maj. gen. and assigned command 36th inf. div., Tex. Nat. Guard, April 29, 1946; made lt. gen., Tex. Nat. Guard, placed in commd. all Tex. N.G. Forces, 1948; ret. 1948. Mem. Bar Assn. of Dallas, Texas Bar Assn., Am. Bar Assn., Delta Chi. Clubs: Country, Executives' Dinner (1st pres.), Athletic, Rotary, Dallas, City, Imperial; Austin (Tex.). Contbg. editor: Ice and Refrigeration. Co-author: Pointers for Infantry Troop Leaders, 1940, 43, 50, 64. Author: Brochures on Labor-Management Relations and Fed. Wage and Hour Law; other publs. Home: Dallas TX Died Dec. 2, 1967; buried Tex. State Cemetery, Austin TX

WEATHERWAX, HAZELETT PAUL, retired naval officer, business executive; born at Honolulu, Hawaii, October 25, 1907; s. Charles Washington and Agnes May (Bookstaver) W.; student St. Louis Coll., Honolulu, 1923-27; B.S., U.S. Naval Acad., 1931; grad. U.S. Naval Postgrad. Sch., 1939, U.S. Naval War Coll., 1950; m. Alyce E. Hofmann, Apr. 15, 1933; children—Alyce Jean (Mrs. Robert A. Cornell), Susan Ann (Mrs. Clyde M. Walter). Commd. edsign U.S. Navy, 1931, advanced through grades to rear adm., 1959; assigned U.S.S. Childs, U.S.S. Leary U.S.S. Mississippi, U.S.S. Alexander J. Dallas, U.S.S. Massachusetts, 1941-43; ordance control officer staff comdr. Western Sea Frontier, 1943-46; comdr. U.S.S. Hanson, 1946-47; staff comdr. Second Task Fleet, 1947-49; asst. to dir. material div. Bur. Ordnance, Navy Dept., 1950-52. Comdr. U.S.S. Delta, 1952-53; asst. dir. research and devel. div., 1953-54, assigned Office Chief Naval Operations, 1954-56; comdr. Destroyer Sqdn. 5, 1956-57; asst. dir. surface type warfare div. Office Chief Naval Operations, Navy Dept., 1957-58; comdr. Destroyer Flotilla 1, 1958-59; insp. gen., asst. chief Bur. Naval Weapons for Adminstrn., Navy Dept., 1959-61; chief U.S. Naval Mission to Brazil, 1961-65; dir. Pan-Am. affairs Navy Dept., 1965-66, ret., 1966. Pres. Apito Assos. S.A., 1966-67. Decorated Commendation ribbon, numerous others. Home: Alexandria VA Died May 26, 1967; buried Arlington Nat. Cemetery, Arlington VA

WEAVER, BENNETT, educator; b. Sussex, Wis., Aug. 11, 1892; s. John Franklin and Ann (Bennett) W.; student Carroll Acad., 1907-10; A.B., Carroll Coll., Waukesha Wis., 1914, Litt.D., 1938; A.M., U. Chgo., 1915; Ph.D. U. Mich., 1930; m. Clarice A. Colby, Dec. 28, 1916; m. 2d Georgiana Colby Brown, Dec. 19, 1959. Professor speech Coll. Emporia, Kan., 1915-16; instr. English, Mich. State Coll., 1916-18, asst. prof., 1918-28; instr. English, U. Mich., 1928-30, asst. prof., 1930-34, asso. prof., 1935-49, prof. English, 1950-61, emeritus, 1961-70; professor of English literature University of California, Irvine, 1966-70; dir. Hopwood awards, 1930-31; lectr. English lit. U. Ia., summers 1932, Ohio State U., summer 1940, U. N.C., 1948; research scholar Huntington Library, 1930, 48. Mem. Modern Lang. Assn., Nat. Council Tchrs. English, Nat. Poetry Soc., Mich. Acad. Arts and Scis., Delta Sigma Rho, Phi Kappa Delta, Phi Gamma Delta. Author: The Garden of Seven Trees (poems), 1921; Sussex Poems, 1926; New Michigan Verse (with others), 1940; Braithwaite's Anthology, 1926, 1927, 1928, and others; Toward the Understanding of Shelly, 1932; Poetry and Criticism of the Romantic Movement (editor with O.J. Campbell, J.F.A. Pyre), 1932; The English Romantic Poets (with Ernest Bernbaum, Samuel C. Chew, Thomas M. Raysor, Clarence D. Thorpe, Rene Wellek), 1950, rev. 1956; The Major English Romantic Poets (editor with C.D. Thorpe and Carlos Baker), 1957; Prometheus Unbound, 1957; Wordsworth Poet of The Unconquerable Mind, 1965. Reviewer and contbr. articles profl., scholarly jour. Home: South Laguna CA Died Mar. 1, 1970; buried Sussex WI

WEAVER, FRED(ERICK H(ENRY), found. ofcl.; b. Aberdeen, N.C., Dec. 13, 1915; s. Frederick Henry and Ada Kelly (Stewart) W.; A.B., U. of N.C., 1937; A.M., in history, Harvard, 1950; Ph.D. in History, Duke University, 1968; m. Frances Louise Angas, Nov. 10, 1951; children—Elizabeth Gale, Margaret Dunn, Stewart Angas, Robert Moore. Teaching fellow in economics University of N.C., 1937-38, asst. dean of students, 1938-41, dean of men and instr. econs., 1946-48, became dean of students, 1948, dean student affairs, 1954-61, secretary U. N.C., 1961-74, v.p. adminstrn., 1964-65, v.p. for univ. relations, 1965-68; project adviser ednl. adminstrn. Ford Found., New Delhi, 1968-72. Am. vice consul, Rio de Janeiro, Brazil, 1941-42. Mem. North Carolina Seashore Commission, 1963-66, Gov.'s Commn. Reorgn. State Govt. N.C., 1959-63. Mem. bd. dirs. Institute for Services to Edn.; trustee of St. Augustine's Coll. Served in USN, 1942-46. Recipient Carnegie Travel Grant for Young Adminstrs., 1952, Rockefeller Found. study grant, 1956-57. Mem. Nat. Assn. Student Personnel Adminstrs. (pres. 1961-62). Democrat. Episcopalian. Home: Chapel Hill NC Died Jan. 8, 1972.

WEAVER, GILBERT GRIMES, educator; b. Highspire, Pa., June 14, 1889; s. Samuel Ringold and Elmira (Whorley) W.; student Pa. State Coll., 1911-13, U. Chgo., summers 1913-15; B.S., U. Pitts., 1922, M.A., 1924; m. Beulah Catherine Long, Dec. 27, 1917; children—Louise (Mrs. Harry Reiss), Janet (Mrs. Ralph Porter), Nancy (Mrs. John Kelso). Engaged in indsl. employment, 1910-13; tchr. Rankin Sch., St. Louis, 1913-15; dir. Coop Sch., York, Pa., 1915-17, Dayton (O.) Indsl. Inst., 1917-19; employment mgr. subsidiary Gen. Motors Co., 1919-20; supt. Patton Sch., Elizabethtown, Pa., 1924-26; service mgr. Frederick Loeser Co., Bklyn., 1926-29; prof. indsl. edn. U. Pitts., 1920-24; dir. indsl. tchr. tng. N.Y. State Dept. Edn., 1929-59; sec.-treas. Am. Rehab. Center Disabled, N.Y.C., 1959-68. Cons. Inter-Am. Affairs Com., 1950-54; chmn. vocational education committee Iran Foundation, 1956-68, pres., 1966-68; mem. of the reference board of Hadassah, 1956-59; chmn. publs. com. American Vocational Assn., 1949-68. Trustee N.Y. Trade Sch. Recipient medal Order Tai (Iran), 1963, Merit award N.Y. State Vocational High Sch. Tchrs. Assn., 1959. Mem. Nat. Assn. Indsl. Tchrs. Edn. (past pres.), Phi Delta Kappa, Iota Lambda Sigma, Epsilon Pi Tau. Republican. Conglist. Author: Trade Analysis and Course organization, 1945; Practical Hints on the Use of Motion Pictures, 1946; Visual Aids—Their Construction and Use, 1949; Shop Organization and Management, 1955; Applied Techniques of Teaching, 1960; (with Cenci) Teaching Occupational Skills, 1968. Address: Manhasset NY Died Dec. 20, 1968; buried Greenmount Cemetery, York PA

WEAVER, JAMES HARVEY, coll. athletic commr.; b. Rutherford, N.C., Mar. 29, 1903; s. Charles Clinton and Florence (Stacy) W.; student Emory and Henry Coll., 1919-21; B.S., Centenary Coll., Shreveport, 1925; m. Kate Speed Dunn, Aug. 16, 1938; 1 dau., Florence. Football coach Nacogdoches (Tex.) High Sch., 1926-27, Oak Ridge (N.C.) Acad., 1928-33; football coach Wake Forest (N.C.) Coll., 1933-36, athletic dir., 1937-54; commnr. Atlantic Coast Conf., 1954-70. Served to lt. comdr. USNR, 1942-45. Home: Greensboro NC Died July 11, 1970; buried Greensboro NC

WEAVER, PHILIP JOHNSON, supt. schs.; b. Emory, Va., Apr. 18, 1913; s. Charles Clinton and Florence (Stacy) W.; A.B., Duke U., 1934; A.M., U. N.C., 1937; postgrad. U. N.C., U. Chgo.; m. Elizabeth Winston Cobb, June 18, 1943; children—Philip Johnson, Lyn. Tchr. pub. schs., Kannapolis, N.C., 1934-35, Southern Pines, N.C., 1935-36; tchr. Darlington Sch. for Boys, Rome, Ga., 1937-39; supt. schs., Southern Pines 1939-51; asst. supt. pub. schs., Greensboro, N.C., 1951-58, supt., 1958-69; mem. summer sch. staff Woman's Coll. U. N.C., 1951-57. Mem. naturalization com. U.S. Dist. Ct., 1962-65, chmn., 1965; chmn. N.C. Textbook Commn., 1962-65. Mem. bd. higher edn. W. N.C. Conf. Meth. Ch., 1960-69. Bd. dirs. Greensboro A.R.C. div. chmn. United Fund Greater Greensboro, 1961; mem. exec. com. Gen. Greene council Boy Scouts Am., 1952-69, chmn. Eagle bd. rev., 1961-69; mem. City Greenboro's Youth of Month Program, 1959-69. Recipient Silver Beaver award Boy Scouts Am., 1960. Mem. N.E.A., N.C. Edn. Assn., Am. Assn. Sch. Adminstrs., Horace Mann League Am. (dir., pres. 1967-68), N.C. Congress Parents and Tchrs., N.C. Supts. (pres. 1968-69), Northwestern Schoolmasters Club (pres.). Democrat. Methodist (chmn. ofcl. bd. 1963-65). Rotarian (pres. 1960-61). Home: Greensboro NC Died Mar. 15, 1969.

WEAVER, R.C., v.p., sec. Am. Nat. Ins. Co. Home: Galveston TX Died Jan. 6, 1968; buried Meml. Park Cemetery, Hitchcock TX

WEBB, ATTICUS, state supt. Anti-Saloon League; b. Moscow, Ky., Feb. 6, 1869; s. Watkins and Mary Bennett (Barnes) W.; M.A., Southwestern U., Georgetown, Tex., 1896; studied U. of Chicago, 1906-07; m. Mattie Elma Fugitt, Dec. 25, 1896; children—Charles Galloway, Mattie Dell. Ordained ministry M.E. Ch. S., 1896; pastor Holliday, Archer City, Montague, Sanger, Bailey, Kemp and Detroit, Tex., until 1906; pres. University Training Sch., Blooming Grove, Tex., 1907-08; pres. Granbury (Tex.) Coll., 1908-11; dist. supt. Anti-Saloon League, Fort Worth, Tex., 1911-18; state supt. Anti-Saloon League, Tex., since 1918; mem. bd. dirs. Anti-Saloon League of America; dir. Wesley Foundation at Panhandle A. & M. Coll., 1935; pastor Aspermont, Tex., 1936. Member American Academy Political and Social Science, Kappa Sigma Fraternity. Democrat. Member Woodmen of the World. Club: Civitan; del. Civitan Internat., Nashville, Tenn., 1926. Author: Crime, Our National Shame, 1924; Face the Facts, 1927; Dry America (textbook for study of temperance from standpoint of the church), 1931; (drama) Who's to Blame, 1934 (used in Tex. by Anti-Saloon League as part of its ednl. program). Contbr. to newspapers and mags. Editor Home and State (mag.). Home: 3412 Univ. Boul., Dallas TX‡

WEBB, CHARLES M., judge circuit court 7th circuit Wis.; ed. U.S. Mil. Acad., West Point; served in Co. G, 12th Wis. regt., in Civil war; engaged in practice as lawyer until elected judge; voted for in Wis. legislature, 1899, as a Republican candidate for U.S. senator. Address: Grand Rapids Wood Co WI‡

WEBB, EDWIN DOUGLAS, prof. law; b. LaFayette Onondaga County, N.Y., Feb. 8, 1873; s. Emory L. and Ella A. (Peters) W.; LL.B., New York U., 1901, LL.M., 1902, J.D., 1910, also B.S. in Pedagogy, 1909; m. Lucy A. Weeks, Aug. 25, 1903. Admitted to N.Y. bar, 1901; mem. Van Zandt & Webb, N.Y. City, 1910-21; prof. law, New York U., 1905-37, prof. emeritus since 1937; also sec. Law Sch., 1922-33. Mem. Phi Delta Phi. Republican. Mason. Author: Elements of Practice Under the New York Practice Act, 1926. Joint Author: Commercial Law, 1924. Editor: Select Cases on New York Code of Civil Procedure, 1912; Cases on Equity, Pleading and Practice, 1934. Home: 390 Yarmouth Rd., Rochester 10 NY‡

WEBB, STUART WESTON, b. Worcester, Mass., Nov. 27, 1883; s. Stephen W. and Martha (Boyden) W.; A.B., Harvard, 1906; m. Marcia Sewall, July 9, 1910; children—Marcia S., Barbara, Elinor. Formerly pres. Eastern Mfg. Co., Boston; now pres. and dir. Pathe Exchange, Inc., New York; pres. and dir. Brightwater Paper Co., Adams, Mass.; dir. Dupont Film Mfg. Corp., New York. Regional adviser for N.E. of War Industries Bd., World War. Republican. Episcopalian. Clubs: Racquet and Tennis, Harvard (New York); Country Club (Boston). Home: Stonington CT Died Aug. 7, 1968.

WEBB, T(HOMAS) DWIGHT., mem. Federal Home Loan Bank Bd.; b. Memphis Tenn., Jan. 16, 1867; s. William H. and Margaret (Kerr) W.; grad. East Nashville Acad., 1886; m. Cora A. Crockett, Sept. 3, 1902; children—Edward C., Dwight, George C., Corinne (Mrs. William D. Spears). Became clerk Cumberland Telephone & Telegraph Co., Nashville, 1887, treas., 1890-1912; v.p. Fourth & First Nat. Bank and Nashville Trust Co., 1912-31; retired, Jan. 1, 1931. Mem. Fed. Home Loan Bank Bd. since 1933 (vice chmn.). Consultant in business operations to Alien Property Custodian, Washington, D.C., 1942. Life mem. Telephone Pioneers of America. Democrat. Presbyterian. Clubs: Belle Meade Country; Press (Washington). Home: 2400 16th St. N.W. Address: Press Bldg., Washington DC‡

WEBB, VIVIAN HOWELL (MRS. THOMPSON WEBB), educator; b. Marion, Ill., Aug. 14, 1894; d. Robert Paine and Louise (Nance) Howell; A.B., N. Tex. Coll., 1912; postgrad. So. Meth. U., U. Cal. at Los Angeles, U. N.M.; m. Thompson Webb, June 22, 1915; children—Thompson, Robert Howell, William Robert, John Lambeth. With English dept. Webb Sch. Cal., Claremont, 1922-23, asst. to headmaster, 1922-71; founder, dir. Mrs. Webb's Country Day Sch., 1926-34. Pres., Campus Club of Scripps Coll., 1935. Recipient Gold Cross pin Woman's Soc. Christian Service, 1961. Mem. Am. Assn. U. Women (chpt. dir.), League Women Voters. Club: Shakespeare of Pomona Valley (dir.). Home: Claremont CA Died Oct. 24, 1971.

WEBB, WILLARD ISAAC, JR., banker; b. Toledo, July 26, 1902; s. Willard Isaac and Belle N. (Dew) W.; B.A., Williams Coll., 1924; student law U. Mich., 1924-26; m. Mary Catherine Millard, July 12, 1924; children—Willard Isaac III, Thomas Irwin, John Millard. With Ohio Citizens Trust Co., Toledo, 1933-72, pres., 1940-64, chmn. bd., 1964-72; v.p., dir., sec. Commodore Perry Co.; dir. Cambria Land Co., Sheller-Globe Corp., Ohio Plate Glass Co., Monroe Equipment Co., Standard Am. Life Ins. Co. Mem. bd. Toledo Area Devel. Council, 1961. Past pres. Ottawa Hills Village Bd. Edn. Bd. dirs. Toledo Safety Council, 1960-72, Toledo Girl Scouts Am., 1935-72, Toledo chpt. A.R.C., 1958, Defiance (O.) Coll., 1961-72, Flower Hosp., Toledo, 1934-72, Hosp. Service Assn. Toledo, 1946-72; treas., dir. Cancer Cytology Research Fund Toledo, 1956-72; chmn. Nat. Found., 1950-54; adv. bd. St. Vincent Hosp., Toledo, 1946. Mem. Williams Alumni Assn. (past pres. Toledo), Chi Psi, Phi Delta Phi. Rotarian. Mason (Shriner). Clubs: Toledo Country, Toledo, Toledo Tennis (past pres.), Inverness, Ottawa Skeet (Toledo); Williams (N.Y.C.). Home: Toledo OH Died Mar. 4, 1972.

WEBBINK, PAUL, economist; b. Detroit, Sept. 12, 1903; s. George William and Sophie (Lindenmeyer) W.; A.B., U. Mich., 1925, grad. work, 1925-26; grad. work Robert Brookings Grad. Sch., 1926-28; m. Gladys R. Friedman, Apr. 14, 1934; children—Jane Barbara, Douglas William. Sec. Bur. of Govt. U. of Mich., 1924-26; research asst. U.S. Senator LaFollette, 1927-33; also on staff Editorial Research Reports Inc., Washington, 1928-32; asst. statistician to asst. dir. research, statistics, finance Fed. Emergency Relief Adminstrn., 1933-36, dir. research Com. Social Security, 1936-43; head Washington office Social Sci. Research Council, 1943-48, v.p., 1948-70; cons. govt. war manpower agencies, 1941-45. Fellow A.A.A.S.; mem. Am. Statis. Assn., Am. Econ. Assn., Indsl. Relations Research Assn., Phi Beta Kappa. Unitarian. Club: Cosmos (Washington). Home: Scarsdale NY Died Jan. 7, 1973.

WEBER, ADNA FERRIN, economist; b. Springville, Erie County, N.Y., July 14, 1870; s. Blanchard B. and Philena (Ferrin) W.; Ph.B., Cornell, 1894; post-grad. study Cornell, U. of Berlin, Columbia U.; Ph.D., Columbia, 1899; m. Mabel Norris, May 3, 1899; children—Harold Norris, Lawrence Adna. Studied social science in Europe as traveling fellow Cornell; later fellow in Columbia; sec. Cornell Summer Sch., 1898; deputy commr. labor statistics, N.Y., 1899-1901; chief statistician N.Y. State Dept. Labor, 1901-07; chief statistician (in charge of statistics and accounts), Pub. Serv. Commn. N.Y., 1st Dist., 1907-21; chief accounting div., Public Service Commn., 1921-23. Spl. agt. U.S. Census, 1902. Corr. Internat. Assn. for Labor Legislation, 1st sec. Am. Assn. for Labor Legislation, 1906-07; director Cities Census Committee, Inc., 1924-32. Fellow American Statis. Assn.; mem. Am. Econ. Assn., Acad. Polit. Science, Phi Beta Kappa. Author: The Growth of Cities in the Nineteenth Century, 1899 (awarded Grant Squires prize, Columbia); state statis. reports, occasional contbr. to periodicals. Home: 8521 114th St., NY‡

WEBER, ARTHUR WILLIAM, engr., mfg. exec.; b. Bklyn., May 17, 1910; s. William A. and Alice E. (Fisher) W.; B.S. in M.E., Yale, 1933; M.S. in Bus. Adminstrn., Mass. Inst. Tech., 1941; m. Margaret Jensen, Sept. 4, 1937; children—William A., Roger A., James S., John M. Lab. engring. asst. Nat. Sugar Refining Co., 1933-34; tech. trainlee Am. Thread Co., 1934-35; with Corning Glass Works (N.Y.), 1935-68, beginning as mech. engr. research lab., successively mech. engr., Charleroi, Pa. and Central Falls, R.I., asst. plant mgr., Wellsboro, Pa., asst. to gen. mgr., Charleroi, gen. mgr., Charleroi, mgr. mfg. consumer products div., asst. to dir. mfg. and engring., chief mech. engr., dir. engring., 1935-57, dir. engring. and mfg. staffs, 1957-68, v.p., 1957-61, vice pres. and dir. mfg. services, 1961-66, v.p., dir. facilities div., 1966-68. President, dir. Three Rivers Development Foundation, 1966. Adv. com. engring. Bucknell, also Carnegie Tech. Alfred P. Sloan fellow, 1941. Registered profl. engr. N.Y., N.J. Fellow Am. Soc. M.E. (v.p. 1957-59); chmn. bd. edn.); mem. Engrs. Council Professional Development (pres. 1967-68, dir.), Am. Soc. Engring. Education, Am. Ceramic Soc., Nat., N.Y. State socs. profl. engrs., New York State Bd. of Examiners Professional Engineers (chairman 1967-68), Newcomen Society of North Am., Yale Engring. Assn. (v.p.), Sigma Xi, Tau Beta Pi, Phi Gamma Delta. Episcopalian (vestry, warden). Clubs: Engineers, Yale (N.Y.C.); Rotary (Corning). Home: Corning NY Died Sept. 14, 1968.

WEBER, EDOUARD, ex-ofcl. Universal Postal Union; b. Biel, Switzerland, Oct. 2, 1901; s. Edouard and Marie Weber-Kapp; student univs. Lausanne. Berne and Paris; m. Margrit Kapp, Apr. 18, 1933; children—Marianne Strahm-Weber, Elisabeth Weber. Practice of law 1 yr., then sec. Ct. of Adminstrn. of Canton Berne, 8 yrs.; gen. sec. Fed. Dept. Posts and Railroads., 1941-49; dir. gen. Swiss Posts, Telegraphs and Telephones, 1950-60; founder, pres. Conf. European Postal and Telecommunications Adminstrns.; former dir. internat. bur. Universal Postal Union; past mem. bd. dirs. Swiss Broadcasting Corp. and Swissair; pres. Radio Switzerland, Ltd. Served as officer Swiss Army Gen. Staff. Home: Berne Switzerland Died Jan. 6, 1970.

WEBER, JOE NICHOLAS, labor leader; b. Ner Beschenowa, Hungary, June 21, 1866; s. Joseph and Katharine (Wasmer) W.; ed. normal sch. and gymnasium, Hungary; m. Gisela Liebholdt, Sept. 22, 1891. Came to U.S., 1879, naturalized, 1887. For many years active in theater and symphony orchestras; pres. Am. Fed. of Musicians; v.p. Am. Fed. of Labor. Mason. Office: 1450 Broadway, New York NY*‡

WEBER, SAMUEL EDWIN, supt. of schs.; b. Ellis, Vernon County, Mo., July 23, 1875; s. George Jacob and Elizabeth (Zilliox) W.; grad. Lock Haven Normal Sch., Pa., 1895; Ph.B., Lafayette Coll., 1901, Litt.D., 1941; Ph.D., U. of Pa., 1905; m. Mary Louise Knarr, Aug. 7, 1901; 1 son, Orville Ethelbert. Teacher in elementary schs., 1894-97; fellow in pedagogy, U. of Pa., 1903-05; prin. North Wales (Pa.) High Sch., 1901-03; supt. Cortland Normal Training Sch., N.Y., 1905-07; state high sch. insp. of La., 1908-10; dean Sch. of Liberal Arts and prof. edn., Pa. State Coll., 1910-14, and dir. summer session for teachers, same; supt. schs., Scranton, Pa., 1914-22; supt. of schs., Charleston, W.Va., 1922-29; asso. supt. schs., Pittsburgh, Pa., in charge personnel, 1929-41, retired Sept. 1, 1941. Professor educational administration and supervision, University of Pennsylvania, summer session, 1922-23. Presbyterian. Mem. N.E.A., Pa. Ednl. Assn. Clubs: Literary, University (Pa. State Coll.). Author: Charity School Movement in Colonial Pennsylvania, 1905; A Course of Study for High Schools, 1909; Cooperative Administration and Supervision of the Teaching Personnel, 1937. Joint Author of Weber, Koch, and Moran Series of Arithmetics. Joint translator of Brumbaugh's Christopher Dock," 1905. Home: 165 Longuevue Drive, Mt Lebanon PA‡

WEBSTER, CLYDE IRVIN, lawyer; b. Eaton Rapids, Mich., Aug. 10, 1877; s. Hiram P. and Sarah J. (Pickard) W.; Ph.B., U. of Mich., 1899, LL.B., 1901; m. Edith May Hughes, of Eaton Rapids, Mich., Sept. 4, 1901. In law office, Detroit, of Don M. Dickinson, ex-Postmaster-Gen. of U.S., 1901-4; mem. firm of Choate & Webster, 1904-8, Choate, Webster, Robertson & Lehmann, 1908-Nov., 1912; U.S. dist. atty., Eastern Dist. of Mich., by appmt. of President Taft, Aug. 6, 1912-—. Republican. Mem. Jackson Prison Bd., by appmt. of Gov. Osborn, Jan.-Aug., 1912. Congregationalist. Mem. Mich. State Bar Assn., Bar Assn. City of Detroit. Mason (32 deg.). Club: Fellowcraft (Detroit). Home: 31 King Av. Office: 311 P.O. Bldg., Detroit MI‡

WEBSTER, EDWIN HARRISON, dairy expert; b. Yates Center, Kan., Feb. 25, 1871; s. Rufus Durkee and Harriett (Edwards) W.; B.S., Kan. State Agrl. Coll., Manhattan, 1896, M.S., 1901; B.S. Agr., Ia. State Coll., Ames, 1901; m. Eleanor Florence Fryhofer, of Randolph, Kan., Apr. 10, 1900. Asst. in dairying, Ia. State Coll., 1900-1; asst. prof. dairying, 1901-2, prof., 1902-3, Kan. State Agrl. Coll.; scientific expert in dairying, Dept. Agr., 1903-4; chief, dairy div., Bur. Animal Industry, Dept. Agr., 1905-8; dean agr. and dir. Expt. Sta., Kan. State Agrl. Coll., 1908-12; asso. editor Hoard's Dairyman, Ft. Atkinson, Wis., 1912-13; asst. gen. mgr. Cal. Central Creameries, 1915-19; dairy engr., 1920-—. Mem. Nat. Dairy Instrs'. Assn., A.A.A.S. Republican. Methodist. Mason. Office: Wholesale Terminal Bldg., Los Angeles CA‡

WEBSTER, MARGARET, actress, director; b. N.Y.C., Mar. 15, 1905; d. Ben Webster and Dame May Whitty (both distinguished in the theater); ed. Queen Anne Sch., Reading, Eng., 1918-23; studied for stage at Etlinger Dramatic Sch.; D.Litt., Lawrence Coll., 1942,

Russell Sage Coll., 1944; D.H.L., Smith Coll., 1945, Beloit Coll., 1966; D.Litt., Rutgers U., 1947, Fairfield U., 1964; LL.D., Boston U., 1965. Actress, 1917-72; first profl. appearance in chorus of The Trojan Women, 1924; played with John Barrymore in Hamlet, 1925; subsequently with Dame Sybil Thorndike in Henry VIII, Macbeth, and several of the Greek tragedies; appeared in leading roles in great plays with many famous actors and companies, 1926-72. Dir. successful prodns., 1935-72; latest prodns. include: The Devil's Disciple (with Maurice Evans), 1950; (revivals) Richard II, St. Joan (with Uta Hagen), 1951; Richard III (with Jose Ferrer), 1953; Merchant of Venice (Stratford-on-Avon), 1956; Measure for Measure (Old Vic), 1957; Back to Methuselah (with Tyrone Power), 1958; Waiting in the Wings, 1960; The Aspern Papers, 1962; Anthony and Cleopatra, Berkeley, Cal., 1963; 12 Angry Men, London, Eng., 1964. Appeared one-woman program The Brontes, U.S. and London, Eng., tours, 1963-65; toured U.S. with The Seven Ages of Bernard Shaw, 1966, Toured South Africa, Dept. State, 1961. Dir., producer Am. Repertory Theater, 1946-47, Marweb Shakespeare Co., 1948-51. Pioneer woman dir. Met. Opera House, with Don Carlo, 1950, Aida, 1951, Simon Boccanegra, 1960. Staged the following operas for N.Y.C. Opera Co.; Troilus and Cressida, Macbeth; Taming of the Shrew; The Silent Woman. Mem. Equity (founder), ANTA (dir.). Author: Shakespeare Without Tears, 1942; Royal Highness, 1949. Address: New York City NY Died Nov. 13, 1972.

WEBSTER, ROBERT MORRIS, air officer; b. Boston, Mass., Oct. 10, 1892; s. William Roland and Jennie Webster (Gorrie) W.; m. Flora Dorothy Bitzer, Mar. 19, 1921; children—Robert Morris, Roland Carl. Commd. 2d lt., Air Service, U.S. Army, 1918; promoted through the grades to major, Air Corps, U.S. Army, 1940; maj. gen., 1944; successively apptd. comdg. gen. 1st Air Support Command, Aug. 1942; 1st Tactical Air Force in France, Mar. 1945; Air Transport Command, Sept. 1946; 1st Air Force, 1947; East Air Defense Force, 1949; mem. Brazil-U.S. Mil. Com. 1950; Can.-U.S. Defense Bd., Mexico-U.S. Defense Com., Brazil-U.S. Defense Com.; Inter-Am. Defense Bd., 1953. Rated command pilot, combat observer. Awarded Victory Medal, Distinguished Flying Cross, Distinguished Service Medal, Silver Star, Legion of Merit, Comdr. Legion of Honor; Croix de Guerre with 3 palms; chief comdr. Order Aero Merit (Brazil). Mem. Order of Daedalians. Clubs: Wings, (N.Y.C.); Army and Navy (Washington). Address: Washington DC Died Mar. 6, 1972; buried Arlington Nat. Cemetery, Arlington VA

WEBSTER, WILLIAM, business exec.; b. Bel Air, Md., Dec. 6, 1900; s. Richard Henry and Harriet Archer (Williams) W.; grad. U.S. Naval Acad., 1920; B.S. and M.S., Mass. Inst. of Tech., 1923; D.Sc., Tufts Coll., 1950, Lowell Technol. Institute, 1961; LL.D., Bates College, 1950; D.S. in B.A., Bryant Coll., 1965; D. in C.S., Suffolk U., 1970; m. Eleanore Blodgett, April 21, 1924 (dec. April 1961); 1 son, Richard; m. 2d, Vollie Sanderson, November 29, 1963. Asst. to gen. mgr. New Eng. Power Assn., Boston, 1928-33, asst. to pres., 1933-35, asst. dist. mgr., 1935-42; pres. Narragansett Electric Co., Providence, past pres. United Electric Rys. Co.; vice pres. New Eng. Power Assn. and pres. Mass. Utilities Assos., 1942; exec. v.p., dir. N.E. Electric System, 1950-59, pres., 1959-63, chmn., chief executive, 1963-70; chmn., dir. Yankee Atomic Electric Company; v.p., dir. Vt. Yankee Nuclear Power Company, Maihe Yankee Atomic Co.; dir. Conn. Yankee Atomic Power Co., Huyck Corp., Arthur D. Little, Inc., State St. Bank & Trust, Mitre Corp., Fed. Res. Bank Boston; trustee Band Corp.; mgmt. cons. OPA, 1942-45; with Nat. Defense Research Com., 1943-46; appointed chairman Research and Development Board of U.S. Dept. of Defense, 1950; deputy sec. defense for atomic energy, chmn. mil. liaison com. Dir., v.p. Am. Inst. Counselling and Personnel Research; mem. gen. adv. com. AEC; dir. chmn. New Eng. Council; mem. NACA, 1950-51; mem. Sci. Adv. Bd., 1951-52, Army Sci. Adv. Panel, 1951-58; v.p., dir. Atomic Indsl. Forum; trustee Fund Peacetime Atomic Development; dir. Edison Electric Inst., Am. Transit Assn.; mem. Hudson Inst. Trustee Moses Brown Sch., 1940. Bates Coll., 1945, Sci. Engring. Inst., Woods Hole Oceanographic Institute, Baystate Sci. Found.; chairman advisory committee of Woodrow Wilson School, Princeton, 1959-66; life mem. corp. Mass. Inst. Tech. Served USN, 1917-28, naval constructor, 1922-28. Patriotic Civilian Service award; Exceptional Civilian Service award; New Eng. award Outstanding Engr., 1964, citation Atomic Energy Commission, 1967; John Fritz medal Am. Soc. M.E., 1971. Fellow Am. Academy of Arts and Scis.; mem. Am. Nuclear Soc. (charter mem.), Soc. Naval Architects and Marine Engrs., U.S.N. Acad. Grads. Assn., Delta Psi. Clubs: The Algonquin (Boston); Army and Navy, Cosmos (Washington). Home: Boston MA Died May 17, 1972; interred Bel Air MD

WEBSTER, WILLIAM CLARENCE, university dean; b. Lake Tp., Mich., May 14, 1866; s. Rev. James and Eliza A. (Whitten) W.; grad. Albion Coll., Mich., 1887; Johns Hopkins, 1889-90; fellow in history, U. of Chicago, 1893-5, in administrative law, Columbia, 1896-7, Ph.D., 1897; m. Mary Rippey, of Mt. Pleasant, Mich., Dec. 27, 1898. Prof. history, Cornell Coll., Ia., 1890-3; mgr. New York City gen. agency Etna Life Ins. Co., 1902-6; lecturer, New York U. Sch. of Commerce, Accounts and Finance, 1901-6; prof. commerce, U. of Neb., 1906-9; asst. prof., U. of Chicago, 1909-10; dean, Coll. of Economics, Marquette U., Milwaukee, June 1, 1910—. Contbr. to econ. publs. Author: General History of Commerce, 1903. Home: 136 20th St., Milwaukee WI‡

WECKLER, HERMAN L., corporation executive; b. Pittsburgh, Pa., Aug. 31, 1888; s. August L. and Elizabeth (Hornung) W.; student Carnegie Inst. Tech., 1905-10; children—Harold A., James L., Inez E., Judy Lee. In engring. div. Jones & Laughlin Steel Co., Pittsburgh, Pa., to 1908; shop engr. Am. Locomotive Works, Pittsburgh, 1908-11; later with Buick Motor Corp., Flint, Mich., works mgr., to 1932; with Chrysler Corp., Detroit, 1932, v.p., gen. mgr. DeSoto div., 1935-37, v.p. indsl. relations, 1937-38, v.p. operations, 1938-40, dir., v.p., gen. mgr., 1940-53; pres. Dodge Bros. Corp. 1943-46; dir., v.p., gen. mgr. Chrysler Corp., 1940-53; v.p., gen. mgr. Clevite Corp., Cleve., 1953. Mem. Soc. Automotive Engrs. Mason. Clubs: Grosse Pointe Yacht, Grosse Pointe, Detroit Country, Detroit Athletic. Home: Grosse Pointe MI Died Jan. 26, 1970; buried White Chapel, Troy MI

WEDEL, PAUL JOHN, accountant; b. Jersey City, Aug. 17, 1896; s. Fred Henry and Anna (Hunken) W.; student N.Y.U., 1914-16; m. Helen Agnes Cleary, Mar. 14, 1926; children—Paul George, Diana Clare (Mrs. John Joseph Riley, Jr.), Peter John. Sr. accountant J. H. Cohn Co., Newark, 1919-23; cons. accountant, Newark, 1923-34; sr. accountant Patterson, Teele & Dennis, C.P.A.'s, N.Y.C., 1934-38; utilities accountant SEC, 1939-40; accounting cons. Trustees Associates Gas & Electric Corp., 1940-43; chief accountant, bd. mem. Navy Price Adjustment Bd., 1943-47; mem. appeal bd. Office Contract Settlement, 1947-48; mem. Excess Tax Council, Internal Revenue Service, 1948-52; dir. office of accounting U.S. Renegotiation, Bd., 1952-57; became controller Craig Systems, Inc., 1957, retired. Served as 1st lt. USAAF, World War I; capt. USNR, World War II. Mem. Am. Inst. Ft Lauderdale FL Died Nov. 13, 1971.

WEDEL, THEODORE OTTO, clergyman; b. Halstead, Kan., Feb. 19, 1892; s. Cornelius and Susannah (Richert) W.; B.A., Oberlin College, 1914, Doctor of Divinity (honorary), 1957; M.A., Harvard, 1915; Ph.D., Yale, 1918; S.T.D., Seabury-Western Sem., 1940; D.D. (hon.), Brown U., 1953, Trinity Coll., 1956; LL.D., Carleton Coll., 1959; Dr. Canon Law, Kenyon Coll., 1960; m. Elizabeth Ewert, June 26, 1917 (died Mar. 24, 1932); children—Theodore Carl, Gertrude Elizabeth; m. 2d, Cynthia Clark, May 4, 1939. Began career as instructor of English, Yale Univ., 1919-22; prof. English, Carleton Coll., 1922-30, prof. biography, 1930-34; ordained ministry Episcopal Ch., 1929; sec. for coll. work, Nat. Council of Episcopal Ch., 1934-39; dir. of studies, Coll. of Preachers, Washington Cathedral, 1939-42, warden, 1942-60, warden emeritus, 1960-70, canon, 1939-70; pres. house deps. Gen. Conv. Episcopal Ch., 1952-61. Danforth Found. Research Scholar, Ecumenical Inst., Evanston, Ill., 1960-61; Harry Emerson Fosdick visiting professor Union Theol. Seminary, 1962-63, lectr., 1963-69. Chmn. dept. ministry Nat. Council Chs., 1964-70. Served with Coast Arty., AUS, 1918-19; commd. as 2d lt. Mem. Phi Beta Kappa, Delta Sigma Rho. Club: Cosmos (Washington, D.C.). Author: The Medieval Attitude toward Astrology, 1920; The Coming Great Church, 1945; The Christianity of Main Street, 1950; Expositor of Ephesians in Interpreter's Bible, 1953; The Pulpit Rediscovers Theology, 1956; The Gospel in a Strange New World, 1963. Editor: Addison's Essays, 1929. Contbr. to mags. Home: Alexandria VA Died July 20, 1970; buried Washington Cathedral, Washington DC

WEED, J. SPENCER, b. Middletown,N.Y., Dec. 24, 1879; s. John Hollister and Mary Ann (Sharp) W.; student Williams Coll., 1900-03; m. Hannah Broadley Bowman, Oct. 14, 1908 (dec.); children—Douglas Bowman, Janet Mary, J. Spencer; m. 2d, Ethel Randall Eddy, Dec. 1, 1934. Pres. Grand Union Co., 1924-27, chmn. bd. 1947-49; v.p. Great A & P Tea Co., 1918-24; chmn. bd. Food Mart, Inc.; dir. Stone & Webster. Dir. Manhattan Eye, Ear and Throat Hosp. Hon. dir. Am. Horse Shows Assn.; hon. pres., dir. Nat. Horse Show of America; dir. Monmouth Park Jockey Club. Team, Inc. Mem. adv. bd. Liberty Mutual Ins. Co. Served on U.S. Food Adminstrn., 1918-19. Republican. Clubs: Union, India House (N.Y.C.). Home: Morristown NJ Died Nov. 1969.

WEED, THEODORE LINUS, director Postal Savings System; b. Norwalk, Conn., Mar. 4, 1876; s. L. Walter and Julia Thomas (Ketcham) W.; ed. pub. and high schs., D.C., George Washington U.; m. Elizabeth Maud Newman, of Washington, Feb. 1, 1899. Stenographer, War Dept., 1898; official stenographer, U.S. Evacuation Commn. to Cuba, 1898-9; chief, civ. div. Mil. Govt. of Cuba, 1899-1902; pvt. sec. to Secretary of Commerce and Labor Oscar S. Straus (q.v.), 1906-8, to Hon. Frank H. Hitchcock (q.v.), chmn. Rep. Nat. Com. during campaign of 1908; chief clerk, Dept. of Commerce and Labor, 1909-10; chief clerk, Post Office Dept., Mar. 1910-Jan., 1912; sec. bd. trustees Postal Savings System, July, 1910-Jan., 1912; dir. Postal Savings System, Jan. 1, 1912—. Asst. Sec. Foundation for Promotion of Industrial Peace; mem. Sigma Alpha Epsilon. Club: National Press. Address: 1628 Riggs Pl. Washington DC‡

WEEKS, JOHN A., judge; b. Chgo., June 28, 1899; s John A. and Francenia (Collier) W.; LL.B., U. Minn., 1924; m. Gertrude F. Wisneiwska, Apr. 28, 1926; 1 dau., Sonia Nancy (Mrs. Godfrey V. Larson). Asst. atty. gen., 1939-42; Municipal Ct., 1942-45; judge Dist. Ct., 4th Jud. Dist., Mpls., 1945-68, chief judge, 1965-68. Served with USNR, 1917-19. Mem. Hennepin County, Minn. bar assns., Minn. Dist. Judges (past pres.), Alpha Sigma Phi. Mason (33 deg.). Club: Minneapolis Athletic. Home: Minneapolis MN Died Sept. 6, 1968.

WEEKS, SINCLAIR, former sec. of commerce; born at West Newton, Massachusetts, June 15, 1893; son of John Wingate and Martha A. (Sinclair) W.; student Newton (Massachusetts) High School, 1906-10; A.B., Harvard, 1914; m. Beatrice Dowse, Dec. 4, 1915 (Dec.);children—Frances Lee, John W., 2d, Martha S., Sinclair, William D., Beatrice; married 2d, Jane Tompkins Rankin, January 3, 1948; m. 3d, Alice Requa Low, August 22, 1968. In employ First Nat. Bank of Boston, Mass., as clerk to asst. cashier, 1914-23; hon. dir. United-Carr, Inc., 1 st Nat. Bank of Boston; chmn. Reed and Barton Corp.; dir. N.H. Ins. Co., Lancaster Nat. Bank; limited partner Hornblower & Weeks. United States Secretary of Commerce, 1953-58; appointed U.S. senator from Mass. to serve in place Henry Cabot Lodge, Jr., Feb.-Dec. 1944. Treas. Republican Nat. Com., 1941-44, chmn. finance com., 1949-52. Trustee U. of N.H., Fessenden Sch., Newton, Mass.; chmn. bd. trustees Wentworth Inst. Served as capt. F.A., U.S. Army, 1917-19, with A.E.F. in France. Unitarian. Home: Concord MA Died Jan. 27, 1972.

WEET, HERBERT SEELEY, educator; b. Shelby, Orleans County, N.Y., Feb. 23, 1871; s. Elroy Sabin and Jane (Smith) W.; B.A., U. of Rochester, 1899, M.A., 1901; Pd.D., N.Y. State Coll. for Teachers, Albany, N.Y., 1918; Litt.D., U. State of New York, 1933; m. Ada Eleanor Smith, June 20, 1894; 1 dau., Winifred Eleanor (Mrs. Duncan Rae MacKenzie). Began as teacher in the rural schools of Orleans County, N.Y., 1889-95; prin. high sch., North Tonawanda, N.Y., 1901-03; prin. Monroe Grammar Sch., Rochester, N.Y., 1903-05, West High Sch., 1905-10; asst. supt. schs., Rochester, 1910-11, supt., 1911-34; retired; now engaged in occasional school surveys; also armed services rep. and Administrative Officer U. of Rochester, 1942-45. Trustee of U. of Rochester, Colgate-Rochester Divinity Sch., Rochester, Y.M.C.A. Mem. Rochester Hist. Soc., Memorial Art Gallery, Phi Beta Kappa, Alpha Delta Phi, Kappa Phi Kappa. Republican. Baptist. Clubs: University, Rotary, Fortnightly, Oak Hill Country. Home: Medina NY‡

WEGLEIN, DAVID EMRICH, supt. schs.; b. Baltimore, Md., June 10, 1876; s. Morris and Rosa (Emrich) W.; grad. Baltimore City Coll., 1894; A.B., Johns Hopkins, 1897, Ph.D., 1916; A.M., Columbia, 1912; unmarried. Asst. prin. elementary sch., Baltimore, 1897-1900; 1st asst., Teachers' Training Sch., Baltimore, 1900-02; teacher and head of pedagogical dept., Baltimore City Coll., 1902-06; prin. Western High Sch., Baltimore, 1906-20; instr. in edn., Johns Hopkins, 1917-21, asso. in edn., 1921-28, asso. prof. edn., 1928-46; asst. supt. schs., Baltimore, 1921-24, 1st asst., 1924-25, supt. 1925-46. Mem. problems and plans com. of Am. Council of Education, 1930-35; mem. Middle States Assn. of Colls. and Secondary Schs. (pres. 1938; mem. exec. com.); mem. Nat. Advisory Com. of Nat. Youth Adminstrn., 1935. Fellow A.A.A.S.; mem. N.E.A. and Dept. Superintendence (2d v.p. of latter, also mem. joint emergency commission), Md. State Teachers Assn. (ex-pres.), Ednl. Soc. Baltimore (ex-pres.), Phi Beta Kappa, Phi Delta Kappa. Jewish religion; mem. bd. trustees Eutaw Pl. Temple. Mason. Rotarian. Clubs: Civitan, University, Johns Hopkins. Author: Correlation of Abilities of High School Pupils, 1916. Home: 2400 Linden Av., Baltimore 17 MD‡

WEHMEYER, LEWIS E(DGAR), educator; b. Quincy, Ill., Jan. 1, 1897; s. August H. and Emma (Grimm) W.; B.S., U. Mich., 1921, Ph.D., 1925; m. F. Elaine Prince, Sept. 1, 1927. NRC fellow, Harvard, 1925-28; mem. faculty, U. Mich., 1928-71; prof. botany, 1948-71. Served as sgt., C.E., U.S. Army, 1918. Fellow A.A.A.S.; mem. Mycol. Soc. Am., Mich. Acad. Sci., Arts and Letters, Sigma Xi, Gamma Alpha, Phi Sigma. Club: Research (U. Mich.). Contbr. articles on sci. publs. Home: Ann Arbor MI Died Sept. 11, 1971; interred Terrace Hill Cemetery Truro Nova Scotia Canada

WEHRMANN, HENRY, composer, violinist; b. New Orleans, Dec. 27, 1871; s. Henry H. and Clementine (Bohne) W.; pub. sch. edn.; began study of violin and piano under Oweczka and Hasse, New Orleans; studied in Paris under Kieszen, Berton and Lefort of the Conservatory. On return from Paris to New Orleans engaged as teacher of music; also organist and choir dir. of First Presbyn. Ch.; supervisor Music, Newman Manual Training Sch. Wrote music of comic operas, The Swimming Girl (prod. New Orleans, 1902), and King Capital (prod. 1903). Home: 4021 Carondelet St., New Orleans LA‡

WEIBLE, RILLMOND FERNANDO, supt. schs.; b. Paulding County, O., Aug. 12, 1912; s. Arthur John and Allie (Kleinhen), W.; B.S., Bowling Green State U., 1940; M.S., Ind. U., 1948; m. Ilo Beatrice Lighthill, Aug. 22, 1934; children—Suzanne Rilla, Kristine Allie, Sara Lee. Tchr. Auglaize Twp., 1934-37; prin. Melrose Village Sch., 1937-41; prin. elementary sch. Bellevue City, 1941-45; exec. head Ayersville Sch., 1945-56; county supt. schs. Paulding County, 1956-70. Active A.R.C., Tb Assn., Heart Fund, other civic orgns. Mem. Ohio, N.W. Ohio (past pres.) edn. assns., Am., Ohio assns. sch. adminstrs., Northwestern Ohio County Supts. (pres. 1961-62), Ohio County Supts. Assn. Methodist. Mason. Clubs: Lions (dir. past pres.), Kiwanis. Home: Paulding OH Died Dec. 14, 1970.

WEICHER, JOHN, violinist, orch. condr.; b. Chgo., Mar. 29, 1904; s. John and Marie (Fuchs) W.; student Prague Conservatory, 1912-16, Am. Conservatory, 1918-21; m. Ruth Agnes Watts, 1936; 1 son, John Charles; m. 2d, Geraldine Caroline Vito, 1947; children—Joseph John, Richard Edward. Charter mem. Civic Orch., 1919; with Cleve. Symphony, 1921-23; with Chgo. Symphony, 1923-28, 29-69, asst. concertmaster, 1929-36, concertmaster, 1936-58, condr. Civic Orch., 1957-67, personnel mgr., 1961-68, prin. 2d violin sect., 1963-69; concertmaster Seattle Symphony, 1928-29. Home: Chicago IL Died July 25, 1969; buried Bohemian Nat. Cemetery, Chicago IL

WEICHSEL, CHRISTIAN C(ARL), banker; b. Cleveland, O., Sept. 27, 1870; s. Francis and Ella (Schaper) W.; ed. high sch., La Porte, Ind.; m. Elma Lammers, Mar. 16, 1897 (dec. 1929); children—Elma, Carl, Robert, Amy, Elizabeth; m. 2d, Annie May Ely, Apr., 1935. Stenographer, mortgage loan office, 1888-92; in mercantile business, Dallas, Tex., 1892-1920; with Dallas Bank & Trust Co. since 1922, now chmn. bd. Dallas Nat. Bank, successor; also chmn. bd. Dallas Title & Guaranty Co. Served with Texas Nat. Guard, 1889-92. Club: Dallas Country. Home: 5009 Swiss Av. Office: Dallas Nat. Bank, Dallas TX*‡

WEICKER, THEODORE, business exec.; b. Stamford, Conn., Jan. 15, 1902; s. Theodore and Florence Edith (Palmer) W.; grad., Culver Mil. Acad., 1919, Lawrenceville Sch., 1921, Yale, 1925; m. Schatz Adams, June 15, 1927; children—Theodore, Cherie (Mrs. John Bennett), Etienne, Juliet (Mrs. Riccardo Cerro); m. second, Dorothy Reaves, Mar. 24, 1939; m. 3d, Elizabeth Robertson Miller, May 22, 1958. With E.R. Squibb & Sons since 1925, sec., dir., 1926, officer and dir. overseas subsidaires, 1942-52, adminstrv. v.p., N.Y.C., 1945, pres. 1952; partner Weicker & Co., mem. N.Y. Stock Exchange, 1931-38; partner E.F. Hutton & Co., mem. N.Y. Stock Exchange, 1939-42, 55-62; partner of Reynolds & Company, 1962-68; president Squibb-Mathieson overseas div., 1953; v.p. overseas operations and dir. Olin Mathieson Chem. Corp., 1952-54. Mem. Delta Psi. Presbyn. Clubs: University (N.Y.C.); River, Maidstone, The Recess, India House. Home: New York City NY Died Mar. 19, 1968; buried Ferncliff Cemetery, Hartsdale NY

WEIGEL, GEORGE KIBLER, railroad ofcl.; b. New Rochelle, N.Y., Oct. 29, 1915; s. George Alexander and Ellen (Bourke) W.; B.A., Cornell U., 1936; M.B.A., N.Y.U., 1941; m. Marion Katherine Lyons, Aug. 17, 1946; children—George A., Paul H., Peter B. With investment dept. Met. Life Ins. Co., N.Y.C., 1947-56; controller N. Am. Car Corp., Chgo., 1957-62, v.p. finanace, controller, 1959-62, dir., 1960-62; joined M.P.R.R., 1963, became controller, 1964, v.p., 1965; later v.p. finance Ill. Central Industries, Chgo., until 1972. Served to capt. AUS, 1941-46; ETO. Mem. Assn. ICC Practitioners, Financial Execs. Inst., Financial Analysts Soc. (bd. govs. St. Louis from 1964), Delta Tau Delta. Clubs: Cornell (N.Y.C.); Union League (Chgo.); Press (st. Louis). Home: Olympia Fields IL Died Mar. 21, 1972; buried St. Catherine's Cemetery Sea Girt NJ

WEIKEL, ANNA HAMLIN, author; b. Clinton Co., Pa.; d. Benjamin Baird (D.D.) and Rebecca Blake (Manley) Hamlin; ed. Irving Coll.; m. at Harrisburg, Pa., Henry Hummel Weikel, of Chicago, May 28, 1895. Author: Betty Baird, 1906; Betty Baird's Ventures, 1907; Betty Baird's Golden Year, 1909. Contbr. to mags. Address: 175 Hicks St., Brooklyn NY‡

WEIKEL, CHARLES HENRY HARRISON, steel co. exec.; b. Steelton, Pa., Dec. 13, 1894; s. John Jacob and Harriet Peyton (Surghnor) W.; D.Eng., Lehigh U., 1961; m. Dorothy Chubbuck, Sept. 20, 1919; children—Harriet (Mrs. W.P. Hitchcock), John Hart (dec. World War II). With Bethlehem Steel Corp. (Pa.), 1912-68, mgr. comml. research, 1933-57, asst. to pres., 1957-60, former v.p. research, dir., 1961-68. Exec. com., chmn. music com. Bach Choir of Bethlehem. Recipient certificate of merit U.S. C of C. Mem. Am. Iron and Steel Inst. (chmn. com. onf bldg. research and tech., past chmn. com. on comml. research), Am. Marketing Assn., Newcomen Soc. of Eng., Sons of Signers of Declaration of Independence. Clubs: Bethlehem, Saucon Valley Country (Bethlehem); Racquet (Phila.); Pinnacle (N.Y.C.). Home: Bethlehem PA Died Sept. 14, 1968; buried Niskey Hill Cemetery, Bethlehem PA

WEIL, ANN YEZNER, author; b. Harrisburg, Ill., Aug. 31, 1908; d. David and Rose (Shedorsky) Yezner; student, U. Ill., 1925-26; B.E., Evansville Coll., 1928; m. Sam Weil, Aug. 17, 1930 (dec. May 1959); children—Jon, Robert. Tchr. elementary schs., Eldorado, Ill., Evansville, Ind., 1928-30; mem. staff U. Ind. Writer's Workshop, Bloomington, 1947; tchr. creative writing, Evansville (Ind.) Coll., 1950-51. Dir. Children's Theatre Assn., Evansville, Ind., 1940-45, League Women Voters, Evansville, 1940-47. Bd. dirs. Planned Parenthood. Named Runnerup for John Newbery medal, 1953. Club: Musician's (Evansville, v.p. 1960-62). Author: The Silver Fawn, 1939, My Dear Patsy, 1941, Pussycat's Breakfast, 1944, John Quincy Adams, 1945, The Very First Day, 1946, Animal Families, 1946, Franklin Roosevelt, 1947, Red Sails to Capri, 1952, Betsy Ross, 1954, John Philip Sousa, 1959, Eleanor Roosevelt, 1965. Home: Evansville IN Died July 31, 1969.

WEIL, LEE HERMAN, lawyer; b. Huntsville, Ala., May 23, 1875; s. Isaiah and Emma (Wertheimer) W.; ed. pvt. schs., Huntsville, and pub. schs., Cincinnati; student Harvard Law Sch., 1892-94; m. Esther Roman, of Montgomery, Ala., Dec. 6, 1905; children—Emma Lee, Roman. Admitted to Ala. bar, 1894, and since practiced at Montgomery; sr. mem. firm of Weil, Stakely & Cater partner Bakewell & Weihe, architects, San Francisco, since 1928. Award: Paris prize in architecture (national competition) by Beaux Arts Inst. of Design, 1919. Served in O.T.C., 1916. Mem. Am. Inst. of Architects. Clubs: San Francisco Architectural (hon. mem.), Bohemian (San Francisco). Home: 970 Chestnut St. Office: 251 Kearney St., San Francisco CA‡

WEIMER, BERNAL ROBINSON, retired educator; b. Port Royal, Pa., Dec. 4, 1894; s. George McCullough and Ada Ruth (Robinson) W.; A.B., A.M., W. Va. U.; Ph.D., U. Chgo., 1927; m. Margaret Grace Robinson, Aug. 31, 1918; children—John Robinson, Margaret Brown, George Alexander. Supervising prin. schs., Mifflintown, Pa., 1918-21; prof. biology Bethany Coll., 1921-70, distinguished prof. biology, 1966-70, chmn. sci. and math. group, 1931-70, dean faculty, 1936-70, acting pres., 1952-57; instr. zoology W.Va. U., summers 1924, 32, U. Chgo., summer 1927. Served with inf., M.C., U.S. Army, World War I. Fellow A.A.A.S.; mem. Am. Soc. Zoologists, Am. Assn. Biology Tchrs., W.Va. Acad. Sci., W.Va. Biol. Survey, Phi Beta Kappa, Sigma Xi, Beta Beta Beta (nat. pres.). Democrat. Mem. Disciples of Christ Ch. Mason. Author: (with P. D. Strausbaugh) General Biology, 1938; A Manual for Biology Laboratory, 1938; Elements of Biology, 1944; (verse) Nature Smiles, 1940; (with E. M. Core) A New Manual for Biology Laboratory, 1944; Man and the Animal World, 1951; Of Things Bi-iilogical, 1957. Contbr. articles sci. and gen. mags. and jours. Address: Bethany WV Died July 20, 1970.

WEINBERG, BENJAMIN FRANKLIN, hotel exec.; b. Kansas City, Mo., Nov. 10, 1892; s. Michael and Fannie (Stern) W.; student Kan. Comml. Coll., 1910-12; m. Kathryn Maier, June 9, 1945. Early bus. career in merchandising and oil, Tex.; v.p. Steeldraulic Brake Corp., Det., 1923-32 (firm pioneered with mech. four-wheel brakes for automobiles); hotel operator, Colorado, Texas, Missouri, California, 1933-70; formerly exec. director, later pres. Park Lane Hotel, Denver; became exec. director Lankershim Hotel, Los Angeles, 1950, then pres.; became exec. dir. Hotel Kansas Citian (formerly Commonwealth Hotel), Kansas City, 1952, later pres.; exec. dir. Capitol Hotel, Amarillo, Tex., 1947-70, later pres. Active in various charity organizations including Shrine's Crippled Children's Home of Kansas City. Served as sgt. 26th Division AUS, AEF, World War I; overseas, France. Mem. Nat. Hotel Men's Assn., K.C. Philharmonic Assn., K.C., L.A., Denver C.'s of C., Am. Legion, Vets. Fgn. Wars. Mason (Shriner). Pioneer sponsor (1928) starting-gate since used in horse-racing. Home: Prairie Village KS Died Feb. 28, 1970; buried Mt. Moriah Cemetery, Kansas City MO

WEINBERG, BERNARD, educator; b. Chgo., Aug. 23, 1909; s. William and Anna (Goldstein) W.; Ph.B., U. Chgo., 1930, Ph.D., 1936; diploma U. Paris, 1931; study and research, Paris, London, Florence, Rome, 1930-31, 34-35, 38, 47-48, 50, 51-52, 57, 61, 63-64, 67-68. Asst. Romance langs. U. Chgo., 1932-37; instr. Washington U., St. Louis, 1937-39, asst. prof., 1939-46, asso. prof., 1946-49, prof., 1949; asso. prof. Northwestern U., 1949-51, prof., 1951-55; vis. prof. U. Chgo., summer 1947, prof., 1955, chmn. dept. Romance langs. and lit., 1958-67, William H. Colvin research prof., 1967-68, Robert Maynard Hutchins Distinguished Service prof., 1969-73; visiting prof. U. Ia., 1965, U. Minn., 1966; vis. Accademica dei Lincei prof. Scuola Normale Superiore di Pise, 1970. Chmn. Newberry Library Conf. Renaissance Studies, 1953, 62; mem. adv. council Renaissance Soc. Am., 1953, 63. Served to capt. USAAF, 1942-45. Am. Field Service fellow for France, 1934-35; Guggenheim fellow, 1947-48, 56-57, fellow Inst. Advanced Study, 1956-57; Fulbright sr. research award for Italy, 1951-52, for France, 1962-63. Fellow Am. Acad. Arts and Scis.; mem. Modern Lang. Assn. (1st v.p. 1963, exec. council), Accademia Toscana La Colombaria, Assn. Internationale des Etudes Francaises, Am. Assn. Tchrs. French, Am. Assn. U. Profs., Phi Beta Kappa. Author: French Realism: The Critical Reaction, 1830-1870, 1937; Critical Prefaces of the French Renaissance, 1950; Critics and Criticism, Ancient and Modern (with others), 1952; A History of Literary Criticism in the Italian Renaissance, 2 vols., 1961; The Art of Jean Racine, 1963; The Limits of Symbolism, 1966; Trattati di poetica e retorica del Cinquecento, vols. I and II, 1970. Editor: (with E. P. Dargan) The Evolution of Balzac's Comedie Humaine, 1942; French Poetry of the Renaissance, 1954. Editorial bd. Comparative Lit., 1964-66, Modern Philology, 1968-73; internat. editorial com. Rivista de leterature moderne, Florence, Italy. Author numerous articles and revs. to scholarly jours. in U.S., France, Italy, Switzerland. Home: Chicago IL Died Feb. 13, 1973.

WEINBERG, SIDNEY JAMES, investment banking; b. N.Y. City, Oct. 12, 1891; grad. pub. sch. No. 13, Bklyn., 1906, Browne's Business Coll., Bklyn., 1907; LL.D. (hon.), Trinity Coll., 1946, U. Kansas City, 1957, Harvard, 1959, Poly. Tech. Inst. Bklyn., 1960; m. Helen Livingston, Sept. 2, 1920; children—Sidney James, John; m. 2d, Regina Pierce, Dec. 24, 1968. With Goldman, Sachs & Co., 1907, partner, 1927-69; dir. Ford Motor Co., Corinthian Broadcasting Corporation. Seaman U.S. Navy, 1917, spl. agt. Navy Intelligence Dept.; spl. agt. War Trade Bd., dep. collector of customs Norfolk, Va.; demobilized Dec. 1918; hon. disch., 1921. Bus. Adv. Council U.S. Department of Commerce, 1933-69, later the Business Council; member of the industrial adv. bd. NRA, 1934; gov. N.Y. Stock Exchange, 1938-40; gov. Investment Bankers Assn. Am., 1934-37, v.p. 1937-38; asst. dir. purchases O.P.M., May 1941, chief, Bureau Industry adv. coms., June 1941; asst. to chmn. W.P.B., 1942-43, vice chmn., June-Aug. 1944; deputy adminstr. Office Def. Mobizn., 1950-51. Awarded Medal for Merit by President Truman, 1946. Member bd. trustees Presbyn. Hosp., N.Y.; chmn. Comptroller's Investment Adv. Council State N.Y.; com. corporate support Am. Univs.; trustee Com. Econ. Devel.; vis. com. Grad. Sch. Bus., Harvard; trustee Eisenhower Exchange Fellowships. Fellow Inst. Jud. Adminstrn.; mem. Am. Legion. Mason. Clubs: Bond, Century Country, Recess, Madison Square Garden, Fifth Avenue (N.Y.C.). Home: New York City NY Died July 23, 1969.

WEINBERG, TOBIAS, physician; b. Balt., Mar. 3, 1910; s. David and Yetta (Goodman) W.; B.A., Johns Hopkins, 1930, M.D., 1933; m. Rhoda Perlo, July 14, 1940; 1 son, David Jonathan. Intern, asst. resident in medicine Balt. City Hosps., 1933-36; fellow, asst. in pathology Mt. Sinai Hosp., N.Y.C., 1936-40; pathologist-in-chief, dir. labs. Sinai Hosp., Balt., 1940-69; asso. prof. pathology Dental Sch. U. Md., 1952-59, Med. Sch., 1954-69, Johns Hopkins Med. Sch., 1961-69; pathologist Johns Hopkins Hosp.; cons. pathologist Springfield State Hosp., Lutheran Hosp., Kernan's Hosp. Diplomate Am. Bd. Pathology. Fellow A.C.P., Am. Soc. Clin. Pathologists, Coll. Am. Pathologists; mem. A.M.A., Internat. Acad. Pathology, Md. Soc. Pathologists, Med. and Chir. Faculty of Md., Am. Assn. for Neoplastic Diseases, Am. Assn. Pathologists and Bacteriologists, Sigma Xi. Home: Pikesville MD Died Nov. 21, 1969.

WEINERMAN, EDWIN RICHARD, physician, educator; b. Hartford, Conn., July 17, 1917; s. David Tolner and Anna (Schwartz) W.; A.B., Yale, 1938; M.D., Georgetown U., 1942; M.P.H., Harvard, 1948; m. Shirley Basch, Dec. 23, 1940; children—Jeffrey Alan, Diane Lee. Med. house officer Beth Israel Hosp., Harvard and Tufts Services, Boston, 1942-43; resident communicable diseases Charles V. Chapin Hosp., Providence, 1942; resident internal medicine Drew Field Regional Hosp., Fla., 1943-44; spl. resident internal medicine San Francisco VA Hosp. U. Cal. Service, 1952-53; practice medicine, specializing in internal medicine, Berkeley, Cal. 1953-62; asst. chief med. officer health services div. FSA, Washington, 1946-47; asso. in med. care adminstrn. div. pub. health methods USPHS, 1947; asso. prof. med. econs., head div. med. care adminstrn. Sch. Pub. Health, U. Cal., 1948-50; med. dir. Permanente Health Plan, Oakland, Cal., 1950-51; med. dir. Herrick Meml. Hosp. Clinics, Berkeley, 1952-62; physician-in-charge Rheumatic Fever Clinic, Richmond, Contra Costa County Health Dept., 1953-62; dir. ambulatory services Yale-New Haven Hosp., Yale-New Haven Med. Center, 1962-66; prof. medicine and pub. health (med. care) Yale Sch. Medicine, 1962-70; cons., Group Health Corp. Puget Sound, Seattle, 1949; Am. fellow WHO, summer 1950; med. cons. San Francisco Labor Council, 1952; cons. med. group practice President's Commn. on Health Needs of Nation, 1952; med. plan adviser Sheet Metal Industry Welfare Fund, Oakland, 1956-62; med. cons Community Health Assn., Santa Rosa, Cal., 1961-62;

cons. United Automobile Workers and Am. Motors Co., Milw., 1961, Office Econ. Opportunity, 1964-65; mem. adv. bd., cons. dept. univ. health Yale, 1964-70; cons. med. adv. com. Commn. on Delivery Personal Health Services, N.Y.C., 1966-70; mem. adv. com. on Medicaid, Conn. Dept. Welfare, 1967-70. Served to capt., M.C., AUS, 1943-46. Sr. faculty award Commonwealth Fund, 1967. Diplomate Nat. Bd. Med. Examiners, Am. Bd. Preventive Medicine. Fellow A.M.A., Am. Pub. Health Assn. (com. chmn.); mem. Conn., New Haven med. assns., Conn. Pub. Health Assn., Assn. Tchrs. Preventive Medicine, Am. Heart Assn., Internat. Acad. Legal Medicine and Social Medicine, Group Health Assn. Am., Am., Conn. hosp. assns., Assn. Am. Med. Colls., Royal Soc. Health (Gt. Britain), Nat. Rehab. Assn., Delta Omega (past nat. pres.). Contbr. articles profl. jours. Home: Hamden CT Died Feb. 20, 1970.

WEINSTOCK, HERBERT, author, editor; b. Milw., Nov. 16, 1905; s. Henry Michael and Edna Browning (Oherndorfer) W.; student U. Chgo., 1925-26. Exec. editor Alfred A. Knopf, Incorporated, N.Y.C., 1943-59; consulting editor, 1963-71; editor, Doubleday & Company, 1959-63, The Macmillan Company, 1963; program annotator Little Orchestra Soc., 1950-71, Concert Opera Assn. and Friends of French Opera, 1962-71; record reviewer Sat. Review. Author: Tchaikovsky, 1943; Handel, 1946, rev. edit., 1959; Chopin: The Man and His Music, 1949; Music as an Art, 1953; Donizetti, 1963; (with Wallace Brockway) Men of Music, 1939, rev. ed. 1950; The Opera, 1941, rev. as The World of Opera, 1962; (with Irene Cass) Through an Opera Glass, 1958; Rossini: A Biography, published in 1968. Translator: Toward a New Music (Carlos Chavez), 1937; Jusep Torres Campalans (Max Aub), 1962; My Voyage around the World (Carletti), 1964. Contbr. articles periodicals and Ency. Americana. Home: New York City NY Died Oct. 1971.

WEINTAL, EDWARD, govt. ofcl.; b. Warsaw, Poland, Mar. 21, 1901; s. David and Leonie (Graff) W.; B.A. with honours, St. Catherine's Coll., Oxford (Eng.) U., 1924. Came to U.S., 1928, naturalized, 1941. With Polish Fgn. Service, 1928-35; dir. Polish Information Bur., 1935-39; co-editor Fgn. Corr., Washington, 1939-43; diplomatic corr., chief European Corr., contbg. editor Newsweek mag., 1944-69; spl. cons. to dir. USIA, 1969-73. Decorated Legion of Honor (France); Polish Gold Cross of Merit; Olva medal (Norway); St. Sava medal (Yugoslavia). Mem. State Dept. Corr. Assn. (pres. 1951), Assn. Internat. des Corr. Diplomatiques (hon.). Clubs: Metropolitan, Federal City (Washington). Author (with Charles Bartlett) Facing the Brink, 1967. Home: Washington DC Died Jan. 24, 1973.

WEIR, PAUL, mining engr.; b. Punxsatawney, Pa., Dec. 3, 1894; s. Charles Steele and Carrie M. (Bell) W.; student Indiana (Pa.) State U., 1913-14; B.S., Pa. State U., 1919, E.M., 1949; m. Lura Hickox, Sept. 28, 1921 (dec. 1963); children—Charles Richard, John Paul, Mary Frances; m. 2d, Venetta Lewis, Oct. 5, 1963. Instr. mining Case Inst. Tech., 1919-20; chief engr., later gen. supt., v.p. Bell and Zoller Coal Co., Chgo., 1920-37; cons. mining engr., 1937-72; founder Paul Weir Co., mining engrs., 1937, successively pres., chmn. bd., now cons. Mem. U.S. Coal Mission to U.K., Trustee Sch. Ozarks. Recipient Erskine Ramsay Gold medal award Am. Inst. M.E., 1950; medal, Distinguished Alumni award Pa. State U., 1954. Hon. mem. Inst. Mining Engrs. (U.K.); mem. Am. Inst. Mining, Metall. and Petroleum Engrs. (life), Am. Mining Congress, Ill. Mining Inst. (life), Coal Mining Inst. Am., Rocky Mountain Mining Inst., Alpha Tau Omega, Tau Beta Pi. Republican. Presbyn. Mason. Clubs: Tower (Chgo.); Missouri Athletic (St. Louis); Duquesne (Pitts.). Address: Lookout MO Died Oct. 26, 1972.

WEIR, WILLIAM CLARENCE, univ. pres.; b. Ind., Aug. 1, 1874; s. Benjamin Franklin and Barbara Ann (Hartley) W.; B.S., Borden (Ind.) Coll., 1895, M.S., 1896; studied Louisville U.; LL.D., Fairmont Coll., Kan.; m. Nettie L. Biery, of Scottsburg, Ind., Mar. 19, 1896;children—Vera Ann, Gladys, Vivian, Benjamin F., William C. Began teaching as instr. in rural and urban schools of Ind., 1896; prin. high sch., Bellingham, Wash., 1904; mem. Training Camps Activities Commn., 1917; community organizer and lecturer for State Normal Sch., Bellingham, 1920; pres. Pacific U., July 1, 1922-25. Has written and lectured largely throughout the country on community, recreational, inspirational and patriotic subjects. Republican. Conglist. Mason. Woodman. Club: University (Portland, Ore.). Home: 609 E. Jackson St., Orlando FL‡

WEISBERG, HAROLD CHARLES, educator; b. Bklyn., June 2, 1925; s. Samuel and Rose (Seligman) W.; B.A., Bklyn. Coll., 1946; M.H.L., Jewish Theol. Sem., 1950, Ph.D., Columbia, 1962; m. Edzia Frydman, June 24, 1950; children—Elizabeth, Emily. Asst. leader Soc. Advancement Judaism, 1950-52; dir. Jewish Reconstrn. Found., 1952-54, B'nai B'rith dept. adult Jewish edn., 1954-56; mem. faculty Brandeis U., 1956-70, prof. philosophy, 1967-70, chmn. philosophy dept., 1968-70, chmn. faculty senate, 1968-70, dean Grad. Sch. Arts and Scis., 1963-67, editor Bobbs-Merrill History Philosophy Series, 1965-70, Bobbs-Merrill Test and Commentary Philosophy Series, 1965-70, Dial Press Religion in the 20th Century Series, 1967-70. Nat. chmn. B'nai B'rith Commn. Adult Jewish Edn., 1966-70, Trustee Park Sch., Brookline, Mass., 1966-70. Mem. Am. Profs. for Peace in Middle East (chmn. New Eng. Sect. Newton MA Died July 17, 1970; buried Sharon Memorial Park, Sharon MA

WEISL, EDWIN LOUIS, lawyer; b. Chgo., Dec. 31, 1897; s. Carl and Regina (Herrmann) W.; Ph.A., Univ. of Chicago, 1914, Ph.B., 1917, J.D., 1919; m. Alice Todriff, Oct. 17, 1928; 1 s. Edwin L. Admitted to Bar of Ill., Oct. 1919, N.Y. Bar, Oct., 1933; partner law firm of Simpson, Thacher and Bartlett, New York, N.Y., 1935-72; asst. U.S. atty., Chicago, 1920-24; spl. asst. atty.-gen. of U.S., Washington, D.C., 1924-25; director and mem. exec. com. Paramount Pictures Corp., 1938-61, now chmn. exec. com.; director Cenco Instruments Corp., Gulf & Western Industries, Page Airways, One William St. Fund. Chief counsel U.S. Senate preparedness com., counsel to com. on space and astronautics, 1957-60. Nat. Democratic Committeeman, N.Y., 1964-68. Trustee John F. Kennedy Culture Center Performing Arts. Served as co. comdr. U.S. Navy, World War I; asst. dir. contract distrbn., W.P.B., counsel war savings loan div., Treasury Dept., World War II. Trustee Am. Heritage Foundation, Presbyn. Hospital; mem. council Columbia University School of General Studies. Member charitable and civic coms. Mem. Am., New York and Chicago bar assns., Wig and Robe, Delta Sigma Rho, Beta Epsilon. Clubs: Wall St., Madison Sq. Garden (N.Y.C.) Home: New York City NY Died Jan. 1972; buried New York City NY

WEISMANN, WALTER W., corp. exec.; b. N.Y.C., Aug. 11, 1891; s. Abraham and Minnie (Kirsconer) W.; grad. N.Y.U.; M. Dorothy Alterman, Jan. 1, 1920; children—Helen, Florence, Marjorie. Pres. Champlain Spinners, Inc., Whitehall, N.Y., Oscar Heineman Corp., Chgo., Trimont Mfg. Co., Boston, Utility Construction Co., New Brunswick, N.J., J. Breckwoldt & Son, N.Y.C., Graton and Knight Co., Inc., Worcester, Mass.; chmn. bd. F.H. Hill Company, Cleveland, Ohio, also the Modern Globe, Inc., Grand Rapids, Mich., Trans-Lux Corp.; pres., chmn. Aetna Indsl. Corp., N.Y. Dir., trustee Union Am. Hebrew Congregations, also Beth Israel Hosp., N.Y.C.; trustee, v.p. Congregation Rodeph Sholom, N.Y.C. Clubs: Harmonie (N.Y.C); Bayshore (N.Y.) Yacht. Home: New York City NY Died Oct. 13, 1969.

WEISS, ADOLPH A., composer, musician; b. Balt., Sept. 12, 1891; s. George E. and Sophia (Soennicksen) W.; student extension courses Columbia, also U. Cal. at Los Angeles; student Akademie der Kunste, Berlin, Germany, 1925-27; m. Agnes Henrietta Erpenbach, Oct. 27, 1926 (dec.). Bassoonist, N.Y. Philharmonic, N.Y. Symphony, Chgo. Symphony, Rochester Philharmonic, San Francisco Symphony, Los Angeles Symphony; founder New Music Wind Quintet; tour of S.Am., 1941; conductor Pan Soc., New Sch. Soc. Research, 1927-28, Conductorless Orch., Carnegie Hall, 1930; instr. Los Angeles Conservatory; lectr. Univ. of California, Santa Barbara; former solo bassoonist with Santa Barbara Symphony Orch.; bassoonist Ventura (Cal.) Symphony Orch.; also private tchr. Guggenheim fellow, 1931-32; grantee Inst. Arts and Letters, 1955. Mem. of Anton Weburn Society, American Federation of Musicians. Composer: L Segreti for Large Orchestra, 1923; String Quartet 1, 1925, 2, 1926; Chamber Symphony for 10 instruments, 1927; Libation-Bearers, choreographic Cantata, 1930; Quintet for Flute, Oboe, Clarinet, Horn, Bassoon, 1951, Seven Songs for Soprano and String Quartet, 1955; Concerto for Trumpet and Orchestra, 1954; Trio for Clarinet, Cello, Viola, 1967, others. Address: Woodland Hills CA Died Feb. 1971.

WEISS, GEORGE, profl. baseball exec.; b. New Haven, June 23, 1895; s. Conrad and Anna (Kapitzke) W.; student Yale, 1914-16; 1 foster son, Allen Wood III. Pres. New Haven Baseball Club, 1919-28; gen. mgr. Balt. Baseball Club, 1929-31; sec., v.p. Am. League Baseball Club, N.Y.C., 1932-47; gen. mgr. N.Y. Yankees, 1947-60; pres. N.Y. Nat. League Baseball Club, 1961-66, N.Y. Nat. League, 1967-72. Lutheran. Clubs: Greenwich (Conn.) Golf. Home: Greenwich CT Died Aug. 13, 1972; buried Evergreen Cemetery, New Haven CT

WEISS, SEYMOUR, hotel exec.; b. Bunkie, La., Sept. 13, 1896; s. Samuel and Gisella (Elias) W.; student pub. schs., La.; m. Notie Turner, Apr. 19, 1925; m. second, Elva L. Kimball, June 12, 1963. Manager of Roosevelt Hotel, New Orleans, 1924-31, headed corp. purchasing hotel, 1931, pres., mng. dir. Hotel New Orleans Corp., since 1931; dir. Internat. House; president American Hotel Credit Corporation; dir., mem. exec. com. Universal Drilling Co.; dir. Standard Fruit and S.S. Co., Nat. Am. Bank, Bankers Union Life Ins. Co., Terra Firma Trust. Pres. Lovely La. Tourist Assn. Treas. Nat. Rivers and Harbors Congress, 1936-39; pres. bd. commrs. Port New Orleans, 1932-39; chmn. 250th Anniversary of founding of New Orleans, Bd. dirs., mem. finance com. WYES Ednl. TV: mem. bd., exec. com. Meth. Hosp.; bd. dirs. Nat. Conf. Christians and Jews, Fairgrounds Corp.; chmn. adv. com. Dome Stadium; member of the bd., vice chairman of Salvation Army La.; pres. bd. mgrs. Delado Coll.; pres. Am. Hotel Motel Ednl. Found.; regent Loyola U. Mem. advisory com. U. Denver, Brandeis Univ. Served as pvt., U.S. Army, World War I. Named La's Hotel Man of Distinction, 1952, Hotel Man of the Year, 1957. Member of the Metropolitan Safety Council New Orleans (v.p., mem. bd. dirs. 1952), New Orleans C. of C. (mem. exec. com.), Internat. Trade Mart (mem. exec. com.). Mem. Am. (v.p. 1951, dir. 1952-53, 61-69, pres. 1957), La. (p. 1952, chmn. bd. dir.), La. (pres. 1952), New Orleans (pres. 1951, chmn. bd. dirs. 1952) hotel assns., La. Bd. Commerce and Industry (vice chmn., dir.), La. Historical Society (hon.), American Guild of Variety Artists (honorary life member). Democrat (nat. com. man 1936). Clubs: Tavern; Lotus, Marco Polo (N.Y.C.); Lakewood Country; Audubon Golf; New Orleans Athletic; International House, (chmn. house com.), Press (New Orleans). Address: New Orleans LA Died Sept. 17, 1969.

WEITZMAN, ELLIS, psychologist, educator; b. Atlanta, Nov. 26, 1910; s. Nathan and Rachel (Stieffel) W.; A.B., Emory U., 1932; M.A., Creighton U., 1935; Ph.D., U. Neb., 1940; m. Ann Goldenberg, Aug. 23, 1934; children—Sandra Rae, Warren Ray. Social case investigator Douglas County Relief Adminstrn., Omaha, 1934-36; ednl. dir. Bellevue (Neb.) Vocational Sch., 1936-37; grad. asst. U. Neb., 1938-40; supr. spl. problems, occupational analysis sect. USES, 1940-42; dir. student personnel, univ. examiner Am. U., 1946-53, asso. prof. psychology, 1946-50, prof. psychology, 1950-67, chmn. dept., 1960-67, chmn. div. social scis., 1960-67; vis. prof. Mt. Vernon Jr. Coll., 1956-58; pres. Ellis Weitzman Assos., Inc., 1960-67. Psychol. stress research USPHS, 1961-62, cons. psychometrics heart dis. control program, 1962-63; cons. D.C. Dept. of Vocational Rehab., 1963-67. Served to lt. comdr. USNR, 1942-46. Diplomate Am. Bd. Examiners in Profl. Psychology. Fellow A.A A.S., American Psychological Association, Royal Geographical Society; member Am. Personnel and Guidance Assn., Am. Assn. U. Profs. (chpt. pres.), D.C. Psychol. Assn., N.Y. Acad. Scis., Interam. Soc. Psychology, Phi Delta Kappa, Psi Chi. Author: Growing Up Socially, 1949; (with W.J. McNamara) Constructing Classroom Examinations, 1949; Guiding Children's Social Growth, 1951. Contbr. articles to psychol., ednl. jours. Home: Washington DC Died Aug. 17, 1967.

WELBORN, CURTIS R., fire prevention engr.; b. Ellisville, Miss., Jan. 10, 1894; s. Jefferson Lee and Lurline (Watson) W.; B.S. in Elec. Engring., Miss. State Coll., 1920; m. Ethel Len Privett, Aug. 17, 1920; 2 children. With Underwriters' Labs., Inc., Chicago, 1920-59, pres., 1948-59. Served as capt., A Co., 346th Regt., 87th Div., World War I. Mem. University Club, Tau Beta Pi. Home: Winnetka IL Died Apr. 1973.

WELBORN, IRA CLINTON, army officer; b. Laurel, Miss., Feb. 13, 1874; s. James L. and Tobitha (Welch) W.; grad. U.S. Mil. Acad., 1898; honor grad. Army Sch. of the Line, 1916; grad. Gen. Staff Sch., 1920; grad. Army War Coll., 1921; m. Margaret Sayles Kilbourne, of N.Y. City, Aug. 3, 1901; children—James Lawrence, John Clinton. Commd. 2d lt. 9th Inf., Apr. 26, 1898; promoted through grades to col., July 1, 1920. With expdn. to Cuba, Spanish-Am. War, 1898; participated in Battle of San Juan Hill, and engagements before Santiago; campaigned in Philippines, 1899-1900, and China Relief expdn., 1900; served on Mexican border, 1916; dir. Tank Corps, hdqrs. Washington, D.C., World War; mem. Gen. Staff, 1921-23. Awarded Congressional Medal of Honor for distinguished bravery" at Battle of Santiago; D.S.M. for especially meritorious and conspicuous service" in the organization and administration of the Tank Corps. Democrat. Clubs: Army and Navy (Washington, D.C.); New York Athletic. Address: War Dept., Washington DC‡

WELBORN, JESSE FLOYD, b. on farm in eastern Neb., Mar. 9, 1870; s. John Wesley and Rebecca Jane (Roberts) W.; ed. pub. schs., Indianola, Neb.; m. Ada Elizabeth Baker, of Milwaukee, Wis., June 2, 1903. Clk. and cashier, banks, Indianola and McCook, Neb., 1887-90; became connected with Colo. Fuel & Iron Co., Denver, Colo., Aug. 1890; clk. and asst. gen. sales agt., 1890-99; gen. agt., asst. sec. and asst. treas., N.Y. City, Feb.-Oct. 1899; gen. sales agt., Denver, 1899-1903; v.p., 1903-07; pres. C.F.&I. Co. and its subsidiary cos., 1907-29, became chmn. bd., 1929, now mem. bd. dirs. Clubs: Denver, Denver Country; Rocky Mountain (New York). Office: Chamber of Commerce Bldg., Denver CO‡

WELCH, DOUGLAS, columnist Seattle Post-Intelligencer. Address: Seattle WA

WELCH, HERBERT, bishop; b. N.Y.C., Nov. 7, 1862; s. Peter A. and Mary L. (Loveland) W.; A.B., Wesleyan U., 1887, A.M., 1890, D.D., 1902, LL.D., 1906; B.D., Drew Theol. Sem., 1890; student Oxford U., 1902-03; LL.D., Northwestern U., 1910, Western Res. U., and U. Vt., 1911, Ohio Wesleyan U., 1924, Allegheny Coll.,

1932; Litt.D., W.Va. Wesleyan Coll., 1928; D.D., Boston U., 1938; LL.D., Brooklyn Poly. Inst., 1958; L.H.D., Drew University, 1966; m. Adelaide Frances McGee, June 3, 1890 (dec. 1958); children—Dorothy McGee (Mrs. Anthony F. Blanks), Eleanor Loveland. Entered M.E. ministry, 1890; pastor Bedford Sta., N.Y., 1890-92, St. Luke's Ch., N.Y., 1892-93, Summerfield Ch., Bklyn., 1893-98, First Ch., Middletown, Conn., 1898-1902, Chester Hill Ch., Mt. Vernon, N.Y., 1903-05; pres. Ohio Wesleyan U., 1905-16; elected bishop M.E. Ch., 1916; resident bishop, Japan and Korea, 1916-28, Pitts. area, 1928-32, Shanghai area, 1932-36, ret., 1936,; resident bishop of Boston area, 1938-39; chmn. Meth. Com. for Overseas Relief, 1940-48; Carol Gardner Found. lectr. Coll. of Physicians and Surgeons, Columbia University, 1962. Member board mgrs. Missionary Soc., 1896-1905; trustee Wesleyan U., 1901-06, 1937-59; trustee Ohio Wesleyan U., Drew U.; pres. Assn. Ohio Coll. Presidents and Deans, 1907-08; pres. Meth. Fed. Social Service, 1907-12; mem. Univ. Senate, 1908-16; mem. Commn. Ch. and Social Service of Fed. Council, 1908-17; mem. state com. YMCA (Ohio), 1913-16; pres. Ohio Conf. Charities and Correction, 1913-14; frat. del. M.E. Ch. to Meth. Ch. of Can., 1914; pres. Meth. Edn. Assn., 1914-15; del. Gen. Conf. M.E. Ch., 1916; v.p. Nat. Christian Council, China, 1935-36; chmn. trustees John Street Ch., N.Y., 1936-44; mem. exec. com. Fed. Council, 1936-44; mem. Com. Internat. Relations; bd. govs. West China Union U., 1936-44, chmn., 1941-43; chmn. Nanking Theol. Sem., 1937-43; bd. mgrs. Am. Bible Soc., 1936-48, also chmn. com. fgn. agencies; bd. dirs. United China Relief, 1941-48; mem. Church Com. on China Relief, 1941-46; mem. Church Com. Overseas Relief and Reconstrn. until 1946; v.p., dir. Church World Service, Inc., 1946-48. Decorated Order of Sacred Treasure (Japan), 1928; recipient medal Republic of Korea, 1952; Hon. Citizen, Korea, 1956; honor citation Republic of China, 1952; citation for pub. service O. Wesleyan U., 1954, citation Alumni Assn., also Poe medal, Ohio Wesleyan U., 1957; named Methodist man year World Outlook, 1958; Alumni citation Golden Jubilee award, Bklyn. Poly. Inst., 1960, citation Alumnus of Century, Bd. Edn. Meth. Ch. and Nat. Assn. Schs. and Colls. Meth. Ch., 1964. Mem. Phi Beta Kappa, Psi Upsilon. Rep. Mason (33 deg.). Author: (with others) The Christian College, 1916; That One Face, 1935; College Lectures (in Korean), 1935; Men of the Outposts, 1937. Editor (with intro.): Selections from the Writings of John Wesley, 1901; As I Recall My Past Century, 1962. Contributor Methodist Review, Zion's Herald, Christian Advocate, Religion in Life, Together Mag., others. Home: New York City NY Died Apr. 4, 1969; buried Woodlawn Cemetery, New York City NY

WELCH, JOHN EDGAR, otolaryngologist; b. near Bloomington, Ill., Sept. 26, 1872; s. Lawson Downs and Arabel Jane (Lemen) W.; B.S., Ill. Wesleyan U., 1896; M.D., Columbia, 1900; m. Lucy Ragsdale Bates, Jan. 1, 1900; 1 dau., Lucy Bates. Interne Lincoln and N.Y. City hosps.; 1900-03; instr. in pathology, N.Y. and Bellevue Hosp. Med. Sch.; pathologist to N.Y. Lying-In Hosp., Knickerbocker Hosp., Fordham Hosp.; visiting physician to Knickerbocker and Fordham hosps.; prof. of medicine, Fordham U. Med. Sch.; dir. of otolaryngology, Knickerbocker Hosp.; otolaryngologist to St. Elizabeth and Queens Gen. hosps.; jr. surgeon, Manhattan Eye, Ear and Throat Hosp. Originated the human blood serum treatment for hemophilia neonatorum. Served as 1st lt. Med. Reserve Corps, U.S. Army, during World War. Fellow N.Y. Acad. Medicine; mem. Am. Bd. of Otolaryngology; mem. Med. Jurisprudence Soc. (chmn. bd. trustees), A.M.A., New York County Med. Soc. Riverside Practitioners Soc., N.Y. Otol. Soc. (pres.), Phi Gamma Delta. Methodist. Mason. Home: 138 W. 70th St., New York NY‡

WELCH, PAUL M., banker; b. 1905; with Comml. Credit Co. until 1945; with Citizens & Southern Nat. Bank, Atlanta, 1945-71, sr. v.p. installment lending, 1968-71. Address: Atlanta GA Died Oct. 12, 1971.

WELCH, WILLIAM MCNAIR, petroleum engr. and executive; b. Oil City, Pa., Aug. 23, 1874; s. John Collins and Eliza Jane (McNair) W.; M.E., Stevens Inst. Tech., 1898; m. Nina Oliver Thompson, of N.Y. City, Apr. 24, 1901; children—Marjorie Thompson, Elizabeth Hunter, Helen Collins, Wm. McN. Engring. work connected with natural gas industry until 1912; chief engr. Mexican Eagle Oil Co. (S. Pearson & Sons), Tampico, Mex., 1912-14; petroleum and natural gas engr., U.S. Bur. Mines, Washington, D.C., 1914-16; v.p. and gen. mgr. Tidal Refining Co., Okla., and Tidal-Western Oil Corpn., Texas, 1916-24; pres. White Oak Refining Company, Beaver Refining Co., Ltd.; retired from petroleum industry, 1928; engaged in grapefruit and orange growing, etc., since 1928; with Texas Railroad Commission, oil and natural gas department, engring. div., since 1935; preparing a statis. and hist. review of the natural gas industry in Texas. Pres. Assn. Natural Gasoline Mfrs., 1921-23; dir. Am. Petroleum Inst., Western Petroleum Refiners' Assn., Internat. Petroleum Expn. and Congress, 1924. Episcopalian. Mason (32 deg.). Home: TX‡

WELDIN, JOHN CHILCOTE, coll. dean; b. Washington, Ia., Aug. 4, 1891; s. Charles D. and M.

Christine (Chilcote) W.; B.S., Ia. State Coll., 1916, M.S., 1922, Ph.D., 1926; m. Mable F. Gallaher, July 15, 1919. Instr. bacteriology Ia. State Coll., 1919-25, asst. prof., 1925-27; prof., head dept. animal breeding and pathology, expt. sta., U. R.I., 1927-31, prof. bacteriology, dean freshmen, 1931-46, dean adminstrn., registrar, 1946-70. Served with M.C., U.S. Army, 1917-19. Mem. Am. Assn. Collegiate Registrars and Admissions Officers, Sigma Xi, Phi Kappa Phi, Sigma Alpha Epsilon. Home: Kingston RI Died Oct. 15, 1970.

WELDON, R. LAURENCE, paper co. exec.; b. Winnipeg, Can., Nov. 27, 1894; s. Alfred E. and Estelle B. (Trueman) W.; B.Sc., McGill U., 1917, M.Sc., 1920; m. Helen Isabel Reid, June 12, 1920 (dec.); 1 dau., Elspeth Anne; m. to Sylvia Thoresen Bethune, Dec. 23, 1954. Mech. engr., Laurentide Co., Ltd., Grand Mere, Que., 1919-20; engr. in charge design for paper mills, St. Lawrence Paper Mills, Montreal, and Three Rivers, 1920-23; designing engr., Newfoundland Power & Paper Co., 1923-25, asst. mill mgr. company's plant, Corner Brook, Newfoundland, 1925-28, mgr., 1928-32, dir., 1929-36; chief engr., Internat. Paper Co. and subsidiaries, N.Y., 1930-36; pres., mng. dir., Bathurst Power and Paper Co., Ltd. (now Bathurst Paper Ltd.), 1936-59, chmn., 1959—; dir. Baje Holdings, Ltd., Abitibi Bathurst (U.K.), Ltd., Can. Power & Paper Securities, Ltd., Chemcell (1963), Ltd., Power Corp. Can.; newsprint adminstr. for Can., 1942-43; dep. coordinator pulp and paper adminstrn., Can., 1943-45; chmn. exec. bd. Can. Pulp & Paper Assn., 1945. Decorated Officer of British Empire. Gov. Sir George Williams U., Montreal. Mem. Engring. Inst. Can. (life member), Corp. of Profl. Engrs. P.Q., American Society M.E. (life mem.; mem. tech. and woodlands sections), Can. Pulp and Paper Assn., Tech. Association of Pulp and Paper Industry. Clubs: St. James, University, Forest and Stream, Mount Royal, Seigniory, Bathurst Golf; gov. Canadian Club of N.Y. (1934-36). Contbr. to trade and tech. publs. Home: Montreal Can Died Mar. 11, 1968.

WELFORD, WALTER, ex-gov.; b. in Eng., May 21, 1869; s. Thomas and Jane (Murry) W.; brought to U.S. 1879; ed. pub. schs. of N.D.; m. Edith Bachmann, of Toledo, O., June 27, 1900 (died Aug. 18, 1937). Twp. clk. Pembina, N.D., 1900-1920; mem. Ho. of Rep. of N.D., 2 terms, 1906-08 and 1908-10; state senator, N.D., 1916-1920, lt. gov., 1934, gov., 1935-37. Pres. Pembina Co. Farmers Press since 1920. Mem. Nonpartisan League Polit. Party. Episcopalian. Mason. Home: Pembina ND Address: Bismarck ND*‡

WELLER, LEROY, educator, clergyman; b. Fort Plain, N.Y., July 31, 1873; s. Edwin and Mary J. (Copley) W.; A.B., Wesleyan U., Conn., 1899; studied Drew Theol. Sem., 1900, Union Theological Sem., 1901; A.M., Columbia, 1906; Litt.D., Waynesburg, Pa., Coll., 1916; m. Gertrude L. Hough, of Middletown, Conn., June 20, 1901. Ordained M.E. ministry, 1901; pastor Blue Mountain Lake, N.Y., 1901-02, Ft. Ann, 1903-04, Willsboro and Essex, 1905; prof. philosophy and psychology, 1906-10, pres., 1910-17, Beaver Coll.; research work, Columbia U., 1917-18; organizer, ednl. war worker for E.I. du Pont de Nemours Co., 1918; pres. City Normal Sch., Bridgeport, Conn., 1919-22; supt. schs., Oil City, Pa., 1922-26; research and sch. surveys, Teachers Coll. (Columbia), 1926-27; prof. Summer Sch., Rutgers U., 1927. Mem. Com. Coll. Entrance Bd., N.E.A. Rotarian. Home: 168 W. 96th St., New York NY‡

WELLES, EDWARD KENNETH, business exec.; b. Chgo., Nov. 7, 1898; s. Edward Phelps and Emelyn (Munch) W.; prep. edn. St. Paul's Sch., 1913-17; Ph.B., Yale, 1920; grad. study Cambridge U. (Eng.), 1920-21; m. Elizabeth Cluett Scott, Sept. 22, 1923; children—Edward Kenneth, John Scott, David Keith, Emilie Scott Hofmann. With Chgo. Trust Co., 1921, co. merged, 1929, with Nat. Bank of the Republic; asst. v.p. Nat. Republic Co., which later merged with Central Republic Co., resigned 1932; joined Brown Bros., Harriman & Co., 1932; pres. 1942-58, chmn. bd. Besly-Welles Corp., Chgo., 1958-65, dir.; cons. Bendix Corporation, Chicago, 1965-71. Mem. bd. of directors Carson, Pirie, Scott & Company, also dir. S.G. Taylor Chain Company, Union Spcl. Machine Co. Trustee Children's Meml. Hosp., Chgo. Sunday Evening Club; mem. exec. com. Chicago Community Trust; trustee Beloit Coll. Mayor. City of Lake Forest, Ill., 1946-48. Commd. 2d lt., F.A., U.S. Army, Sept. 1918. Mem. Delta Psi. Republican. Episcopalian. Clubs: Chicago, Attic, University (Chgo.); Onwentsia (Lake Forest, Ill.); Old Elm (Ft. Sheridan, Ill.). Home: Lake Forest IL Died Aug. 17, 1971; buried Lake Forest IL

WELLING, MILTON HOLMES, ex-congressman; b. Farmington, Utah, Jan. 25, 1876; s. Job and Emma L. (Holmes) W.; student Latter Day Saints U., 1892-93; U. of Utah, 1894-95; m. Bracie Richards, Fielding, Utah, Dec. 26, 1900 (died Mar. 14, 1905); children—Emma Irene, Virginia; m. 2d, Alice S. Ward, of Riverside, Utah, May 17, 1906;children—Ward Holmes, Lila, John Voss. Farmer; dir. Farmers Cash Union (Tremonton, Utah), Tremonton Furniture Co., Garland Milling Co. Mem. Utah Ho. of Rep. 2 terms, 1911-15; mem. 65th and 66th Congresses (1917-21), 1st Utah

Dist.; dir. of registration for Utah, 1927-29; sec. of state, Utah, term 1929-36; field rep. Dept. of the Interior, Washington, D.C., 1937. Democrat. Mem. Ch. of Jesus Christ of Latter Day Saints (Mormon). Home: Fielding UT Office: 268 N. State St., Salt Lake City UT‡

WELLMAN, CHARLES AARON, savs. and loan exec.; b. Chgo., June 29, 1915; s. Charles A. and Elizabeth (Barker) W.; student U. Cal. at Los Angeles, 1933-36, Columbia, 1936-38; LL.B., U. So. Cal., 1940; m. Lela J. Buckley, Feb. 18, 1939; children—Leslie, Deborah. Admitted to Cal. bar, 1940; practice in Los Angeles, 1940; v.p. Coast Fed. Savs. and Loan Assn., Low Angeles, 1940-48; with Glendale Fed. Savs. and Loan Assn. (Cal.), 1948-62, exec. v.p. and mng. officer, 1952-61, president, and mng. officer; pres. 1st Charter Financial Corp., Los Angeles, Cal., 1962-66; president of Equitable Savs. & Loan, Los Angeles, 1966-70. Served AUS, 1934-46. Mem. Am. Bar Assn., Nat. U.S., Cal. savs. and loan leagues, Lambda Alpha. Home: Los Angeles CA Died Mar. 19, 1970; buried Forest Lawn Memorial Park, Glendale CA

WELLMAN, CREIGHTON, physician; b. near Kansas City, Mo., Jan. 3, 1873; s. Wheeler Montgomery and Nellie Jane (Blake) W.; Central High Sch., Kansas City; M.D., Med. Dept., U. of Kan., Kansas City, 1894; clin. study Rush and Cook County hosps., Chicago; natural science and social science, Chicago; clin. pathology, London (Eng.) hosps.; tropical medicine and hygiene, London Sch. of Tropical Medicine, diploma, 1904; Charite and Nat. Mus., Berlin; British Mus.; Smithsonian Instn.; m. Kathryn Edna Willis, of Buffalo, N.Y., July 20, 1908. Interne City Hosp., Kansas City, 1894-5; practiced Bihe Dist., later Bailundo Dist., Portuguese West Africa, with several periods of study in Europe, 1898-1907; scientific exploration line of Lobito-Katanga Ry., 1907; prof. tropical medicine Oakland (Cal.) Coll. of Medicine, 1909-11; instr. summer sch. U. of Cal., 1911; prof. tropical medicine, hygiene and preventive medicine, head of dept. and dir. labs., 1911-12, dean Sch. of Hygiene and Tropical Medicine, 1913-15, Tulane U. Editor Am. Jouranl of Tropical Diseases and Preventive Medicine, 1913-15. Democrat. Fellow and Am. sec. Soc. Tropical Medicine and Hygiene, London; fellow Entomol. Soc., London; mem. Societe de Medicine and d'Hygiene Tropicales de Paris, Am. Soc. Tropical Medicine (v.-p.), Am. Climatol. Assn., Am. Micros. Soc. (pres.), Washington Helminthological Soc., Societe Entomologique de France, Societe Entomologique de Belgique, Deutsches Entomologisches Gesellschaft, Schweizes Entomologisches Gesellschaft, Societas Entomologica Zurich, Pacific Coast Entomol. Soc., Acad. Natural Sciences, Phila., New Orleans Acad. Sciences (curator), etc.; mem. permanent com. for Internat. Entomol. Congresses. Mem. Nu Sigma Nu and Stars and Bars Senior Med. Scholarship Soc., Tulane (pres.). Club: Boston. Wrote one vol. on insects, in series, Fauna of British India," 1912; contbr. to Forcheimer's Therapeusis of Internal Diseases, 1913. Has published over 150 papers in English, Latin, German, French and Portuguese on scientific and med. subjects. Home: 2231 Prytania St., New Orleans LA‡

WELLMAN, MABEL THACHER, coll. prof.; b. Boston, Mass., Aug. 23, 1872; d. Joseph Hiller and Ellen Maria (Crowell) W.; B.A., Wellesley, 1895; Ph.D., U. of Chicago, 1925. Teacher science and mathematics, pub. schs., Brookline, Mass., 1895-1900; instr. chemistry and home economics, Rockford (Ill.) Coll., 1902-06; instr. home economics, Lewis Inst., Chicago, 1906-08, asst. prof., 1908-13; asso. prof. and head of home economics dept, Ind. U., 1913-23, prof. since 1923. Mem. Am. Assn. Home Economics, Am. Assn. Univ. Profs., Ind. State Home Economics Assn., Omicron Nu. Sweden-borgian. Author: Food Study, 1917; Economy in Food, 1918; Food Planning and Preparation, 1923; Food Study for High Schools, 1925; Food—Its Planning and Preparation, 1928; also articles on home economics in various publs. Home: Bloomington IN‡

WELLS, CHANNING MCGREGORY, trustee Am. Optical Co.; b. Southbridge, Mass., Aug. 13, 1870; s. George W. and Mary Eliza (McGregory) W.; grad. Phillips Andover Acad., 1889, Mass. Inst. Tech., 1892; m. Irene Kelley, Nov. 9, 1898; children—Channing McGregory, Alfred Turner, Henry Cady, Mason Bacheller, Elizabeth (Mrs. Heywood Fox); m. 2d, Lucile Hannan, Feb. 12, 1941. With Am. Optical Co., Southbridge, Mass., since 1891, pres., 1913-36, trustee 1936-51. Mem. Sigma Chi. Republican. Episcopalian. Mason. Clubs: Union (Boston); Country (Brookline); Worcester; Southbridge, Cohasse Country (Southbridge, Mass.); Wianno (Wianno, Mass.). Home: Fiske Hill, Sturbridge MA‡

WELLS, DONALD A., advt. exec.; b. Chgo., Apr. 21, 1920; s. Harvey T. and Jessie (Alexander) W.; student Northwestern U.; m. Nancy Jane Keck, Feb. 3, 1940; 1 dau., Donna. Mem. sales dept. Armour and Co., Chgo., 1939-47; v.p., account supr. Leo Burnett Co., Inc., Chgo., 1947-57; marketing dir. Colgate-Palmolive Co., 1958-59; v.p., dir. marketing Batten, Barton, Durstine & Osborn, Inc., N.Y.C., 1959-64, exec. v.p., 1964-71, also mem. exec. com., gen. mgr., dir. Mem. Assn. Nat. Advertisers. Home: New York City NY Died May 19, 1971.

WELLS, EVERETT F., oil exec.; b. Aledo, Ill., Jan. 18, 1905; s. James A. and Rowena (Everett) W.; A.B., U. Ill., 1926; m. Mary Louise Cole, Apr. 21, 1937; children—Gayle Jackson, Sara Jane. With Ashland Oil & Refining Co., 1926-72, dir., 1937-72, v.p. charge of sales, 1940-50, exec. v.p., 1950-57, pres. 1957-72, chmn. exec. com., 1965-72; pres. Freedom-Valvoline Oil Co., 1951-72; dir. Second Nat. Bank, Ashland, 1942-72. Club: Bellefonte Country (Ashland). Home: Ashland KY Died Feb. 1972.

WELLS, JOEL REAVES, lawyer; b. Vernon, Fla., Feb. 26, 1903; s. Joel R. and Ruth (Warnock) W.; A.B. in Edn., U. Fla., 1922; m. Julia Talley, July 14, 1927; children—Joel Reaves, Charles Talley. Admitted to Fla. bar, 1923; asso. firm Maguire & Voorhis, Orlando, 1923-25; partner firm Dillon, Ferguson & Wells, Miami, 1925-29, Maguire, Voorhis & Wells, Orlando, 1929-69. Fellow Am. Bar Found.; mem. Am. Bar Assn., Am. Counsel Assn. (pres. 1965-66). Home: Orlando FL Died June 13, 1969; buried Orlando FL

WELLS, JOHN MASON, coll. prof.; b. Cheshire, Mass., Mar. 11, 1877; s. Oscar Darius and Millie (Smith) M.; B.A., Amherst, 1902; B.D., Yale, 1905, M.A., 1906; D.D., Hillsdale Coll., 1925; m. Mary Ada Billard, Sept. 1, 1904; children—Pearl Beatrice (Mrs. J. R. Alden), Mason Billard. Pastor Union Baptist Church, Montowese, Conn., 1904-06; ordained Bapt. ministry, 1906; pastor 1st Ch., Kennett Sq., Pa., 1906-15, 1st Ch., Ann Arbor, Mich., 1915-21; pres. Grand Island (Neb.) Coll., 1921-29; prof. religion and philosophy, Hillsdale (Mich.) Coll., 1929-47, and professor speech 1938-46; superintendent Swarthmore Chautauqua Assn., 1915-19 and 1921; taught on Univ. of Tours, summer 1936. Chaplain, 1st lt., Camp Grant, Ill., World War I; director Victory Speakers Bureau of Hillsdale County. Chmn. United Service Orgns., Hillsdale County, Mich. Mem. Nat. Assn. Bibl. Instrs., Mich. Bapt. Conv. (com. on higher edn.), Internat. Council of Religious Edn. (professional advisory sect.), Mich. Acad. Science, Arts and Letters (mem. philos. sect.), School Masters Club, Mich. Intercollegiate Speech League; Am. Legion (post chmn. Americanism com.), Mich. Assn. Teachers of Speech, Nat. Assn. Teachers of Speech, N.W. Ohio Philos. Assn., Am. Philos. Assn. (Western div.), N.E.A., Phi Kappa Delta; mem. exec. com. Mich. div. Religious Edn. Assn. Candidate for Mayor of Hillsdale 1942; candidate for Sec. of State in Michigan on Prohibition ticket in 1944 and 1946. Platform lecturer and commencement speaker. Author religious monographs and magazine articles. Joint author of 4 books. Home: Peconic, Long Island NY‡

WELLS, MARGUERITE JO VAN DALSEM (MRS. THADDEUS R. WELLS), writer; b. Perryville, Ark., Oct. 18, 1904; dau. of Mark Anthony and Mary Josephine (Rankin) Van Dalsem; grad. high sch.; m. Thaddeus R. Wells, Jr., Feb. 11, 1923; children—Robert Leslie (dec.), Thaddeus Mark, Vanna Carolyn (Mrs. Robert W. Smith). Free lance writer, Little Rock, 1940-70. Pres., Band Mothers, Russellville, Ark. 1934-36; pres. Lee Sch. P.T.A., 1946-47. Recipient KTHS Radio Poetry award, 1944, Poets Roundtable Ark. certificate of merit, 1958, C. C. Allard cup for poet of year, 1965, Kenneth Boudoin Gem Stone award for poetry, 1967. Mem. Poets Roundtable Ark. (past pres., anthology editor), Nat. League Am. Pen Women (br. sec.), Ark. Writers Conf. (sec.), Perry County (councilor), Searcy, Helena poetry study clubs (co-founder). Mem. Order Eastern Star. Writer working script for variety show, 1949. Home: Little Rock AR Died Mar. 9, 1970; buried Elmwood Cemetery Morrilton AR

WELLS, STUART WILDER, banker; b. St. Paul, Minn., Feb. 10, 1876; s. Edward Payson, and Nellie March (Johnson) W.; A.B., Amherst, 1900; m. Beatrice Goodrich Ireys, Feb. 8, 1905; children—Edward Payson, Stuart Wilder, Beatrice (Crosby). Identified with banking business since 1903; pres. Wells-Dickey Co.; former director Russell-Miller Milling Co., Minneapolis Foundation, First Bank Corp., First Nat. Bank, Minneapolis Trust Co., Equitable Loan Assn., Scandinavian Am. Nat. Bank. Republican. Conglist. Mem. Psi Upsilon. Clubs: Minneapolis, Woodhill. Home: 11 Dell Pl. Office: Northwestern Bank Bldg., Mpls‡

WELLS, THEODORE D(ONALD), naval architect; b. Hudson Falls, N.Y., Oct. 22, 1875; s. Thomas E. and Charlotte A. (Cornell) W.; B.S., Middlebury (Vt.) Coll., 1898; post-grad. work, U. of Glasgow (Scotland), 1902; m. Anna Miner Fletcher, Oct. 9, 1901; children—Fletcher, Theodora Fletcher. Began as mem. firm Herreshoff & Wells, N.Y. City, 1902; mem. firm Wintringham & Wells, 1903-07, alone, 1907-17 and since 1919; mgr. Tebo Yacht Basin Co., 1913-16. Mem. Constrn. Corps, U.S.A., 1917-19. Mem. Soc. Naval Architects and Marine Engrs., Inst. Naval Architects (London), Am. Legion, Delta Kappa Epsilon. Republican. Episcopalian. Mason. Club: Whitehall. Designer of many pvt. yachts, etc. Home: 33 St. Austin's Pl., W. New Brighton, SI NY*‡

WELLS, WILLIAM WIDNEY, landscape architect; born in Traverse City, Michigan, October 19, 1910; the son of Dr. Robert Elsworth and Alice Mary (Widney) W.; student at Denison University, 1928-29; B.F.A., Ohio State U., 1933; m. Mary Hazel Durio, Mar. 2, 1935 (dec.); children—William Durio, Diana Widney and Margaret Widney (twins); m. 2d, Gladys Lucile Campbell, April 21, 1962. Landscape architect Nat. Park Service, 1933-37; landscape architect La. State Parks Commn., Fontainebleau State Park, Mandeville, La., 1937-41, exec. officer, Baton Rouge, 1941-61, asst. dir., till 1961; supervisory landscape architect Bur. Outdoor Recreation, Div. State Planning and Tech. Assistance, 1961-67. Fellow Am. Soc. Landscape Architects; mem. Nat. Conf. State Parks (dir. 1948-67, pres. 1959-60), Nat. Recreation and Park Assn. Address: Rockville MD Died Dec. 3, 1967; buried Roselawn Cemetery, Baton Rouge LA

WELSH, GEORGE A., judge; b. Bay View, Cecil County, Md., Aug. 9, 1878; s. George and Sarah (Pickering) W.; student Temple U., 1892-94, LL.B., 1906, LL.D., 1939; m. Nellie Ross Wolff, June 27, 1906 (died Feb. 18, 1920); children—William, Conwell; m. 2d, Helen Reed Kirk, Oct. 31, 1921; children—Margaret, Patrick, Deborah. Sec. to mayor of Phila., 1904-06; asst. city solicitor of Phila., 1906-07; asst. dist. atty. of Phila., 1907-22; mem. law firm Welsh & Bluett; mem. 68th to 72d Congresses (1923-33), 6th Pa. Dist.; resigned May 31, 1932; U.S. dist. judge, Eastern Dist. of Pa., later sr. judge, 1932-70. Dir. and sec. Temple U. many yrs., v.p., 1939-70, mem. exec. bd., board trustees. Mem. Bd. of Edn., Phila. County, 11 yrs. Republican. Mason (K.T.). Club: Mid-Day. Home: Media PA Died Oct. 22, 1970.

WELSH, ROBERT JAMES, oil jobber exec.; b. Kouts, Ind., Aug. 16, 1903; s. John and Alice (Lamping) W.; degree Internat. Corr. Schs., 1923; m. Catherine Volk, Sept. 15, 1930; children—Marlene (Mrs. John H. Phillips), Robert James, Shirley (Mrs. Patrick G. Ryan), and Alice. Secretary-treasurer, director Welsh Bros. Motor Service, Inc., Hammond, Indiana, 1928-68; pres. Welsh Oil, Inc., Gary, Ind., 1925-68; sec.-treas. Seaburg-Welsh Auto Supply, Inc., Gary, 1949-68; dir. Gary Nat. Bank. Active Boy Scouts Am. Mem. Am. Petroleum Inst., Independent Oil Marketers Assn. of Indiana Inc., Indiana Automotive Wholesalers Assn., Nat. Oil Jobbers, Ill. Petroleum Marketers, Am. Trucking Assn., Gary C. of C. (past pres.). Roman Catholic. K.C. Home: Portage IN Died Oct. 9, 1968.

WELSH, VERNON M., lawyer; b. Galesburg, Ill., Aug. 15, 1891; A.B., Knox Coll., 1913; LL.B., Harvard 1916. Admitted to Ill. bar, 1916; mem. firm Kirkland, Ellis, Hodson, Chaffetz & Masters, Chgo. Mem. village council, Winnetka, Ill., 1956-69, pres., 1960-64. Chmn. bd. trustees Knox Coll., 1950-69. Mem. Am., Ill., Chgo. bar assns. Address: Chicago IL Died Sept. 10, 1969.

WELTY, BENJAMIN FRANKLIN, congressman; b. nr. Bluffton, O., Aug. 9, 1870; s. Frederick and Katherine (Steiner) W.; student Tri-State Normal Sch., Angola, Ind.; B.S., Ohio Northern U., Ada, O., 1894; LL.B., U. of Mich., 1896; m. Cora B. Gottschalk, of Berne, Ind., Sept. 28, 1903. Admitted to Ohio bar, 1896; city solicitor, Bluffton, O., 1898-1913; mem. Welty & Downing, Lima, since 1900; pros. atty., Allen Co., O., 1905-10; spl. asst. to atty. gen. of Ohio, 1910-12; spl. asst., Dept. of Justice, in charge of prosecutions under Sherman Anti-Trust Law, 1913-15; mem. 65th and 66th Congresses (1917-21), 4th Ohio Dist. Pvt. Co. C, 2d Regt. Ohio N.G., 1896, and served in 2d Regt. Ohio Vol. Inf., 1898, Spanish-Am. War; returned to Ohio N.G., 1898, and continued until 1913; retired as lt. col., commissary dept.; volunteered for World War but services refused because he was member of Congress. Democrat. Presbyn. Mem. Ohio State Bar Assn. Mason, Odd Fellow, K.P., Elk. Clubs: Lima, Shawnee Country. Home: 810 W. Spring St., Lima OH‡

WEMPLE, WILLIAM LESTER, lawyer; b. Waverly, Ill., May 22, 1877; s. Francis Holland and Mary Ann (Carter) W.; B.S., Ill. Coll., Jacksonville, 1898; LL.B., Harvard, 1903; m. Dorothy Gunnels, of Toledo, O., July 20, 1910. Admitted to bar, 1904; practiced at New York, 1904-9; asst. U.S. atty., Southern Dist., N.Y., 1909-11; asst. atty.-gen. U.S., at New York, Aug. 1, 1911-14. Mem. law firm Crim & Wemple. Republican. Mem. Assn. Bar City of New York, Am. Bar Assn. Club: Harvard. Home: Somerville NJ Office: 30 Broad St., New York NY‡

WEMYSS, WILLIAM HATCH, shoe mfr.; b. Gallatin, Tenn., June 1, 1879; s. James A. and Annie (Hatch) W.; ed. pub. schs. of Gallatin Hartsville Military Instn.; m. Helen Peters, Jan. 1, 1919 (dec. Apr. 1, 1934); children—William Hatch, Helen Margaret; m. 2d, Ellen Stokes More, June 20, 1939; 1 stepson, Livingfield More. With Witherspoon Bros., shoe mfrs., Louisville, Ky., 1896-1902; supt. J. W. Carter, Nashville, Tenn., 1904-24; co-founder (with J. F. Jarman), Jarman Shoe Co. Nashville, 1924, now Genesco Corp., exec. v.p., 1935-67, now dir.; dir. 3d Nat. Bank; livestock farmer, 1944—. Republican. Episcopalian. Clubs: Rotary, Belle Meade Country. Home: Gallatin TN Died Mar. 1973.

WENDEROTH, OSCAR, architect; b. at Phila., Apr. 10, 1871; s. Frederick Augustus and Mary (Blascheck) W.; pub. sch. edn.; m. Sara Robinson Keyser, of Phila., June 15, 1898. Entered office of local architect, Phila., at 15; became draftsman in office of supervising architect, Washington, 1897; was made asst. supt. of constrn. in charge erection Mint bldg., Phila.; head draftsman to supt. of U.S. Capitol in charge of work on House and Senate Office bldgs., 1904; advanced to position of architect; resigned, 1909, to become head draftsman to Carrere & Hastings, architects, New York; supervising architect to Treasury Dept., July 16, 1913—. Club: Cosmos. Home: 2036 O St. N.W. Address: Treasury Dept., Washington DC‡

WENGER, JOSEPH NUMA, naval officer; b. Patterson, La., June 7, 1901; s. Aloysius Bercthold and Frances Adele (Roussel) W.; B.S., U.S. Naval Acad., 1923; m. Mary Crippen, May 16, 1932; 1 son, Jeffrey Joseph. Commd. ensign U.S.N., 1923; promoted through grades to rear adm., 1951; various ship, shore and staff assignments, U.S. and abroad; specialist communications; dir. various naval communications research and operational activities; chmn. joint communications electronics com. Joint Chiefs of Staff; chmn. NATO communications-electronics bd., 1957. Decorated; D.S.M. (Navy); Comdr. Order of Brit. Empire; National Security Medal, 1953. Mem. Armed Forces Communications and Electronics Assn. (hon.), U.S. Naval Inst. Roman Catholic. Clubs: Chevy Chase; Army-Navy Town; Army-Navy Country (Arlington, Va.). Home: Washington DC Died Sept. 21, 1970; buried Arlington Cemetery, Arlington VA

WENNER, HOWARD THEODORE, paper mfr.; b. Catasauqua, Pa., Mar. 5, 1909; s. Clinton G. and Eliza Ann (Hoffman) W.; A.B., Harvard, 1930; m. Grace Evelyn Walker, July 25, 1931; children—Howard T., John S., Jerry W. With Price Waterhouse & Co., C.P.A.'s, 1930-52, mgr., 1940-52; asst. controller Scott Paper Company, Philadelphia, Pa., 1952-56, controller, 1957-65, vice pres., 1963-68. C.P.A., Pa. Mem. Am. Inst. Pub. Accountants, Pa. Inst. C.P.A.'s. Home: Media PA Died Feb. 15, 1968; buried Whitemarsh Memorial Cemetery Whitemarsh PA

WENRICH, CALVIN NAFTZINGER, physicist; b. Bernville, Pa., Nov. 21, 1873; s. Isaac S. and Emalina (Naftzinger) W.; B.E., Keystone State Normal Sch., Kutztown, Pa., 1896, M.E., 1898; A.B., Franklin and Marshall Coll., 1902, A.M., 1904; Ph.D., U. of Pa., 1910; m. Ivah Patterson, Dec. 21, 1910. Teacher pub. schs., Pa., 3 yrs.; teacher physics and mathematics, Franklin and Marshall Acad., 1900-04, 1906-07; prof. physics, Carthage (Ill.) Coll., 1904-06; instr. physics, U. of Pa., 1907-08, fellow in physics, 1908-10; instr. physics, U. of Pittsburgh, 1910, asst. prof., 1912, prof. and head of dept., 1914-20, research physicist, Armstrong Cork Co., 1920-42; now retired. Trustee Franklin and Marshall Coll. Mem. Am. Phys. Soc., A.A.A.S., Sigma Xi. Republican. Home: Country Club Drive, Battle Creek MI‡

WENTE, CARL FREDERICK, banker; b. Livermore, Calif., Mar. 27, 1889; s.Carl Heinrich and Barbara (Trautwein) W.; ed. grammar sch. and high sch., Livermore, Calif.; m. Jessie Huldah Orelup, Jan. 16, 1915. Began as runner, Central Bank, Oakland, Calif., Apr. 1907; with First Nat. Bank, Livermore, Sept. 1907-18, became asst. cashier; various positions, Madera Branch, later supervisor of credits for the system, Bank of America, 1918-34; pres. first Nat. Bank of Nevada, 1934-37; pres. Central Bank of Oakland, 1937-43; sr. v.p., and chairman managing com., member executive com. and bd. dirs., Bank of America Nat. Trust and Savings Assn., San Francisco, Calif., 1943-49, vice chmn. gen. exec. com. and dir., 1949-52, pres., 1952-54, chmn. exec. com., 1954-71, honorary chmn. bd., 1963-71; dir. Pacific Gas & Electric Co., Foremost-McKesson Incorporated. Member California State C. of C. Clubs: Commercial, Bohemian, Rotary, Stock Exchange; St. Francis Yacht. Mason (Shriner). Home: San Francisco CA Died Feb. 1, 1971.

WENTE, EDWARD CHRISTOPHER, physicist; b. Denver, Ia., Jan. 2, 1889; s. Christian William and Sophia (Biesterfeld) W.; B.A., U. of Mich., 1911; M.A., Lake Forest (Ill.) U., 1912; B.S. in E.E., Mass. Inst. Tech., 1914; Ph.D., Yale, 1918; m. Sophia Mary Brockman, Sept. 17, 1924; children—Edward Frank, Henry Christian. Asst. in physics and mathematics, Lake Forest (Ill.) Coll., 1911-12; with engring. dept. Western Electric Co., New York, 1914-16 and 1918-25; mem. tech. staff, Bell Telephone Labs., 1925-54, ret., acoustical research engr., 1927-33, research physicist 1933-48, research cons., 1949-54. Research optics, acoustics, telephony, recording. Recipient Biennial Gold Medal award, Acoustical Soc. Am., 1959. Fellow Am. Phys. Soc., A.A.A.S., Acoustical Soc. (pres. 1942-43); mem. Soc. of Motion Picture Engrs., Sigma Xi, Gamma Alpha. Awarded Wetherill medal, by Franklin Inst., 1931; 1st recipient of Progress medal, 1935, of Soc. of Motion Picture Engrs., for outstanding achievement in motion picture technology"; Award of Merit plaque, Acad. Motion Picture Arts and Scis., 1936; Modern Pioneer award, Am. Mfrs. Association, 1940. Lutheran. Inventions: Condenser and moving coil icrophones; loud speakers; light valves used in picture ransmission and in sound recording for motion ictures; acoustical instruments. Contbr. to scientific urs. Home: Summit NJ Died June 9, 1972; buried airview Cemetery Westfield NJ

VENTWORTH, MARION CRAIG, author; b. at St. aul, Minn., Jan. 25, 1872; d. Robert and Maggie (Bell) raig; B.S., U. of Minn., 1894; student Curry Sch. of xpression, Boston; m. Franklin H. Wentworth, of hicago, Mar. 31, 1900 (divorced, 1912). Engaged in ettlement work, Chicago, later teacher of expression in ormal Sch., Milwaukee, Wis.; readings and lecture latform, with headquarters in Boston, for 10 yrs., ppearing before many women's clubs and ednl. instns. 1em. Kappa Kappa Gamma. Socialist. Author: The lower Shop, 1911; War Brides, 1915; The Bonfire of)ld Empires, 1917. Home: Santa Barbara CA‡

VENTWORTH, WALTER ALLERTON, assn. ofcl.; . Dover, N.H., Sept. 6, 1888; s. Elmer Marston and arah Elizabeth (Towne) W.; B.S.A., Ia. State Coll., 910; m. Flora Beatrice Cochrane, Aug. 1, 1912 (dec. 1ay 1939); children—Elizabeth (Mrs. William H. hillips), Francis Marston, Charles Edward; m. 2d, ubyn Chinn Watson, Aug. 31, 1940. Engaged in dairy ndustry, Ia., 1911-23, Ohio, 1923-35; dir. industry elations Borden Co., N.Y.C., 1935-56; pres. Internat.)airy Show, Chgo., 1953-71. Pres. Dairy Products mprovement Inst., N.Y.C.; chmn. Dairy Industry om., Washington, Nat. Dairy Council, Chgo., 952-54, Sec. Borden Co. Found., Inc., N.Y.C., 945-56. Dep. zone comdr. Civil Def., N.Y.C., World Var II. Mem. Municipal Housing Commn., Frankfort, 960-68. Named Ky. col., 1957. Mem. Am. Dairy Sci. ssn., S.A.R. (pres. Empire State Soc. 1950, nat. ec.-gen., 1954-55, nat. exec. com. 1956-57, pres.-gen. 958), Ky. Hist. Soc. (1st v.p. 1960, exec. com. 1958-60, hmn. historical markers program 1962-71), Sigma lpha Epsilon. Presbyn. (ofcl. bd., exec. com.). Clubs:)airy Shrine (pres.) (waterloo, Ia.); Kiwanis (pres.) Columbus, O.). Home: Frankfort KY Died May 11, 971.

VERDEN, ROBERT M., lawyer; b. Mattoon, Ill., 1ar. 16, 1908; B.S., U. Ill., 1931, LL.B., 1933. Admitted o Ill. bar, 1933; mem. firm Craig & Craig. Mem. Am., l., Coles County bar assns. Author: Levy and Craig. 1em. Am., Ill., Coles County bar assns. Author: Levy nd Collection of Drainage Assessments, 1960. ddress: Matoon IL Died July 14, 1969; buried lumboldt IL

VERNAER, ROBERT MAXIMILIAN, author; b. ena, Germany, May 13, 1865; s. Anton Ottomar and lvine (Peisker) W.; prep. schs. and gymnasia in iermany; came to U.S., 1884; LL.B., Albany Law Sch. Union U.), 1887; A.B., Harvard, 1899, A.M., 1900, h.D., 1903; univs. of Leipzig, Heidelberg, Geneva, erlin; m. Esther Upham Farr, Mar. 31, 1891; m. 2d, 1aud May Parker, June 7, 1930. Admitted to bar, 1889; racticed at Brooklyn and New York, 1889-96; instr. ierman, Harvard, 1901-03, U. of Wis., 1904-05, larvard, 1905-06; lecturer German lit. Harvard, 1908; sst. prof. German, Simmons Coll., 1920-21. Mem. 1odern Lang. Assn. America; Am. Acad. Polit. and ocial Science. Club: Boston Authors. Author: Das sthetische Symbol, 1906; Romanticism and the omantic School in Germany, 1910; New Constructive riticism, 1911; The Soul of America, 1917; The cholar In our Universities, 1926; The Proposal For a ociety of Scholars, 1932. Editor and translator. Contbr. mags. and scientific jours. Address: 20A Prescott St., ambridge 38 MA‡

VERNER, VICTOR DAVIS, lawyer; b. Shawano, Vis., Jan. 6, 1901; s. Edgar Victor and Jessie Mabel Davis) W.; A.B., Lawrence Coll., 1922; LL.B., U. Wis., 924; J.D., 1966; m. June Dorothy Coddington, Oct. 9, 1927. Admitted to Wis. bar, 1924, N.Y., 1936; asso.)uarles, Spence & Quarles, Milw., 1925-30, jr. partner, 930-35; v.p., gen. counsel Reynolds Corp., also eynolds Fiscal Corp., affiliates of Reynolds Metals o., 1935-37; asso. counsel Reynolds Metals Co., 936-37; pvt. practice law, own firm, 1937-54; now sr. artner firm Werner, Kennedy, French, Relyea & 1olloy and predecessor firms, 1971-72. Incorporator, ounsel, dir. Community Chest, president Community hest of Douglaston, 1956-72; pres. Civic Assn., 943-46, dir. 1943-54; dir. North Shore chpt. A.R.C.; rustee of the North Shore Hospital. Member of the)ueen's County Republican Com., 1941-70, mem. 8th ssembly Dist., 1941-70, finance chmn. 1952, chmn. peaker's bur., 1947; treas. Queen's Rep. Com. of 200, 953, pres., 1960; Douglaston chmn., United Rep. inance Com., 1940, 44, 48, Queens Co. chmn. 1952; d v.p., life mem. Nat. Republican Club; del. N.Y. state onv. 1946, 50, 54; del. 10th Jud. Dist. Conv., 1946-60; .Y. State Presidential Elector, 1948, 52. Fellow Am. oll. Trial Lawyers; mem. Nat. Assn. R.R. Trial ounsel, Am. Judicature Soc., Am. (council labor elations, 1947-48; chmn. com. participation Lawyers as itizens Pub. Affairs, 1948-49, vice chmn. publs. com. ect. ins., negligence, compensation law), Internat., ed., N.Y. State, Wis., Milw., Queen's Co. bar assns., Vis., Lawrence Coll. alumni assns., Internat. Assn. Ins. ounsel, Federation Insurance Counsel (state chmn.; v.p. 1959-60, 62-63, gov. 1960-62), Ancient and Honorable Artillery Co. Mass., S.R., Soc. Colonial Wars, St. Nicholas Soc., N.Y. State C. of C., Phi Delta Phi, Phi Delta Phi Assn. of N.Y., Sigma Phi Epsilon, Tau Kappa Alpha. Clubs: Nassau Country; Douglaston, North Hills Golf (Manhasset); Republican (Shorewood, Richmond Hill; National Lawyers (Washington); Nat. (2d v.p., life mem.); University (Milw.); Lawycrs (N.Y.C.); Douglaston NY Died Oct. 14, 1972; buried Zion Episcopal Cemetery, Douglaston NY

WERTH, ALEXANDER, author, journalist; b. St. Petersburg, Russia, Feb. 4, 1901; M.A., U. Glasgow (Scotland), 1922; m. Freda H. Lendrum, 1931; 1dau., Nancy (Mrs. Leonard Gabrysh); m. 2d Aline B. Dawson, 1947; 1 son, Nicholas. Research asst. Columbia Research Council, Paris, 1927-28; Paris corr. Glasgow Herald, 1929-32, Manchester Guardian, 1932-40; Moscow corr. Sunday Times, BBC, London, 1941-48; European corr. The Nation, N.Y.C., 1949-69; Simon fellow Manchester U., 1953-55; vis. prof. Ohio State U., 1957. Author; France in Ferment, 1934; Which Way France, 1937; France and Munich, 1939; The Year of Stalingrad, 1947; France 1940-1955, 1956; Russia at War 1941-45, 1964; De Gaulle, 1965. Home: Paris France Died Mar. 5, 1969; buried Pere Lachaise, Paris France

WESCOAT, L. S., oil exec., b. Bridgeton, N.J. President mem. exec. com. and dir. Pure Oil Co., until 1954, chmn. exec. com., dir., 1954-56, dir. 1956-60; dir. mem. exec. com. U.S. Gypsum Co. Home: Chicago IL Died Mar. 27, 1973.

WESCOTT, ORVILLE DE WITT, physician; b. Gladbrook, Ia., July 21, 1871; s. Delos Gary and Mary Ruana (Dibble) W.; B.S., Cornell Coll., Ia., 1900; M.D., Rush Med. Coll., Chicago, 1904; m. Sue May Gailey, Alexandria, La., Oct. 8, 1910. Interne Muskoka Cottage Sanatorium for Consumptives, Gravenhurst, Ont., 1904-5; asst. phys., Agnes Memorial Sanatorium, Denver, 1905-9; in pvt. practice, specializing in diseases of chest, throat and nose, 1909—. Sec. Colo. State Assn. for Prevention and Control of Tuberculosis, 1908, dir., 1908-9-10; awarded gold medal for ednl. leaflet at Internat. Congress on Tuberculosis, Washington, D.C., 1908; mem. Nat. Assn. for Study and Prevention of Tuberculosis, A.M.A., Denver Med. Science Club, etc. Mem. Ia. Vol. Inf., Apr.-Nov., 1898, Spanish-Am. War; mem. Colo. N.G., 1910; commd. maj. and regtl. surgeon to 157th Inf., 40th Div., N.G., Camp Kearny, Cal., 1917. Republican. Mason (32 deg., Shriner). Clubs: University, Denver Athletic, Lakewood Country. Home: 2219 Ivy St., Denver CO‡

WESLEY, CLARENCE NEWTON, business exec.; b. North Branch, Mich., May 19, 1887; s. Frederick Newton and Elizabeth Louise (Melvin) W.; student Y.M.C.A. Bus. Coll., Detroit, 1903-07; M.A. (hon.), Trinity Coll., Hartford, Conn., 1952; m. Lulu B. Belknap, June 2, 1910; children—Beatrice Eva, Marian Louise (Mrs. Joseph R. Milmoe). Accountant Standard Ry. Equipment Co., 1905-15, asst. treas., treas., 1915-25, exec. v.p., treas., dir. from 1926; v.p. charge finance, dir. Standard Ry. Equipment Mfg. Co. (Can.), Ltd. Spl. rep. Walter P. Murphy, 1925-42, later exec. v.p., trustee Walter P. Murphy Found.; trustee Ill. Health Found., Inc., Lake Bluff Orphanage, Lake Bluff, Ill.; director cago Boys Clubs, Portal House, Chgo. Asso. mem. Nat. Coll. Edn., Evanston, also Northwestern. Mem. Newcomen Soc. Eng. Methodist. Mason. Clubs: Chicago, Union League (Chgo.) Home: Evanston IL Died Apr. 23, 1969.

WESSELINK, JOHN, clergyman, educator; b. Sioux Center, Ia., July 28, 1875; s. Gerrit Willem and Grada Cornelia (Rensink) W.; grad. Northwestern Classical Acad., Orange City, Ia., 1897; A.B., Hope Coll., Holland, Mich., 1901; student U. of Chicago, 1902-03; grad. Western Theol. Sem., Holland, Mich., 1905; D.D., Central Coll., Pella, Ia., 1923; m. Anna G. Van den Tak, of Holland, Mich., June 27, 1905; children—Elizabeth Grace, William David. Ordained ministry Ref. Ch. in America, 1905; pastor North Holland, Mich., 1905-10, Maurice, Ia., 1910-13, Pella, 1913-25; pres. Central Coll. since 1925. Mem. Board of Edn. Ref. Ch. of America; mem. Ia. State Council of Religious Edn.; exec. com. Alliance of Ref. Chs. throughout the World holding the Presbyn. System; mem. Library Board, Pella. Democrat. Home: Pella IA‡

WEST, ARTHUR, mechanical engr.; b. Milwaukee, Wis., Mar. 25, 1867; s. Hubbell and Helen (Roberts) W.; M.E., U. of Wis., 1887; m. Alice Florence Tourtellot, Dec. 22, 1900. Engr. Edward P. Allis Co., Milwaukee, 1887-98, asst. to chief engr., 1898-1900; asst. chief engr. Allis-Chalmers Co., Milwaukee, 1900-04, also mgr. pumping engine dept., 1901-04; chief engr. Westinghouse Machine Co., Pittsburgh, 1904-08, v.p., 1906-08; mgr. power dept., Bethlehem Steel Co., 1908-27. Consulting mechanical engineer New York, Board of Water Supply, 1903-08; lecturer Johns Hopkins, Lehigh Univ. and U.S. Naval Academy, 1909-27. Mem. Am. Soc. Mech. Engrs. (v.p. 1905-07), Inventor's Guild (New York), Chi Psi. Republican. Club: Lake Placid (mem. council). Home: Lake Placid Club, Essex County, N.Y. Address: First Nat. Bank and Trust Co., Bethelehem PA‡

WEST, ARTHUR BENJAMIN, retired pub. utility exec.; b. Rochelle, Ill., Apr. 18, 1875; s. Benjamin and Catherine (Rhodes) W.; A.B., Leland Stanford Jr. U., 1899; grad. work in law, Denver U., 1900; m. Grace Campbell, Feb. 12, 1905; children—Catherine Campbell, Elizabeth Dearing, Dorothy, Arthur Benjamin, Helen. Admitted to Colo. bar, 1901, and practiced at Denver until 1913; mem. Potter, West & Potter, 1910-12; v.p. and asst. to pres. Nev.-Calif. Power Co. and Southern Sierras Power Co., 1913-16, gen. mgr. Southern Sierras Co., 1916-23, pres. same and associated cos. since 1923; pres. Nev.-Calif. Electric Corp. and subsidiaries from 1929 to 1941. Pres. & director, California Electric Power Co. and Interstate Telegraph Co., 1941-46; mem. executive committee, board of dirs., and consultant, California Electric Power Co. General chairman or campaign manager American Red Cross, Liberty Bond and Community Chest drives, World War. Member Colorado State bar Assn., Phi Delta Phi, Sigma Alpha Epsilon. Republican. Clubs: Victoria, Newport Harbor Yacht; California (Los Angeles), and Denver Club (Denver, Colo.). Home: 6116 Hawarden Drive. Office: 3771 8th St., Riverside CA‡

WEST, CHARLES, lawyer; b. Savannah, Ga., Mar. 16, 1872; s. Charles Nephew and Mary (Cheves) W.; A.B., Johns Hopkins, 1891; post-grad. work, U. of Leipzig, 1892-93, Johns Hopkins, 1893-94; m. Sophia Lovell Haskell, of Abbeville, S.C., Mar. 27, 1900. Admitted to bar Okla. Ty., 1894, and practiced at Pond Creek and Enid; atty.-gen. of Okla., 1907-15; practiced in Oklahoma City, 1915-17; mem. West, Hall & Hagan, then West & Petry, now alone. Democrat. Pres. Atty. Gen. Assn. 1911-12; member Nat. Tax Assn. Active in Territorial and State N.G., 1898-1910 (retired as lt. col.). Lecturer on law, Oklahoma U. Episcopalian. Mason (32 deg.), Elk, Redman. Commd. 1st lt., N.A., 1917; capt. inf., June 1918; with A.E.F. in France till Aug. 1919; col. inf. R.C. Home: 1635 S. Cheyenne St., Tulsa OK‡

WEST, ERNEST HOLLEY, b. Dorset, Vt., May 21, 1874; s. Spafford H. and Augusta M. (Holley) W.; B.S. in C.E., U. of Vt., 1896; m. Bessie Chambers, Sept. 20, 1906; children—Elisabeth, Helen, George. Topographer, dept. docks, N.Y. City, 1896-1900; sec. Norcross-West Marble Co., Dorset, 1900-03, v.p., 1903-10; pres. Bennington (Vt.) Marble Co., 1905-10; owner and mgr. The West Orchards, Dorset; public service commr., Vermont, 1923-35; marble consultant Tenn. Valley Authority; dir. Factory Point (Vt.) Nat. Bank. Trustee Burr and Burton Sem., Manchester, Vt. Mem. Vt. Engrs., Vt. State Hort. Soc. (pres. 1915), Dorset Soc. Natural Science, Southern Vt. Artists (pres.), Lambda Iota. Republican. Mason. Clubs: Dorset Players, Dorset Field. Home: Dorset VT*‡

WEST, HENRY SKINNER, educator; b. Baltimore, Md., Dec. 23, 1870; s. Henry Montgomery and Mary Anna (Skinner) W.; diploma, Baltimore City Coll., 1890 (first Peabody prize); A.B., Johns Hopkins, 1893, Ph.D., 1899 (scholarship every yr. of residence, and fellowship, 1898-99); diploma, Md. Inst. of Art and Design, 1890 (2d Peabody prize); m. Anne Brown Downman, Nov. 17, 1900; children—Henry Downman, Harriot Lee, Julian Montgomery. Teacher elementary sch., Baltimore, 1890-91, Baltimore City Coll., 1894-97; instr. in English, Johns Hopkins, 1899-1900; prof. English and Latin, Baltimore City Coll., 1900; prin. Western High Sch., Baltimore, 1900-06; asst. supt. schs., supervising teacher training and high schs., Baltimore, 1906-11; dir. statis. dept. U.S. Fidelity & Guaranty Co., New York, 1911-12; prof. edn., U. of Cincinnati, 1912-17; prin. Md. State Normal Sch., Towson, 1917-20; supt. pub. instrn., Baltimore, 1920-25; became prof. education and dean Coll. of Liberal Arts, University of Miami, Miami. Fla., 1926, now dean emeritus. Mem. Phi Beta Kappa, Kappa Alpha (Southern) and Phi Delta Kappa fraternities. Democrat. Episcopalian. Mason. Author of various published reports, addresses, lectures, and articles. Home: The Plains VA‡

WEST, HOWARD H(IRAM), business exec.; b. Elizabeth, W.Va., Sept. 9, 1903; s. Roy O. and Amanda (Swisher) W.; student LaSalle Extension University student Harvard Business School; married to Helen Louise Fiscus, Apr. 12, 1926; children—David Eugene, Margaret Louise, Barbara Ann. With Marthon Oil Co. (formerly the Ohio Oil Co.), Findlay, from 1922, secretary to treasurer, 1926-27, sec. to pres., 1927-41, asst. to pres., 1941-51, asst. sec., 1948-51, sec., 1951-56, v.p. from 1954; dir., also v.p., dir. subsidiaries; president Marathon Oil Foundation, Inc.; vice pres. Mountain Fuel Supply Co., Salt Lake City, 1940-53; dir. Rock River Petroleum Co., from 1942; dir. 1st Nat. Bank of Findlay. Served as pres. local council Boy Scouts, 1935-46, commr., 1946-56, mem. nat. council, from 1947, member regional exec. com., from 1964. Recipient Silver Beaver award from Boy Scouts of America. Mem. 25 Yr. Club Petroleum Industry, Am. Petroleum Inst., Mid-Continent Oil and Gas Assn., Findlay Hosp. Assn. (past pres.) Republican. Presbyn. Elk. Clubs: Union (Cleve.); Athletic (Columbus); Country; Capitol Hill (Washington). Home: Findlay OH Died Oct. 21, 1971.

WEST, JAMES SAMUEL, clergyman; b. High Peak, Va., Mar. 17, 1875; s. Rev. William Wallace and Margaret Emeline (Underwood) W.; A.B., Denison U., 1904; grad. Rochester Theol. Sem., 1908; D.D., Denison U., 1926, Berkeley Div. School, 1926; m. Helen Elizabeth Tufts, of Canandaigua, N.Y., May 15, 1908; 1 dau., Virginia Aileen; m. 2d, Nancy Barbara West, of San Francisco, Jan. 31, 1933; step-children—Bruce, Ross, Betty. State dept. field sec., Ohio State Y.M.C.A., 1904-05; organized Bapt. ministry, 1908; pastor West Union, W.Va., 1908-09, 1st Ch., Bucyrus, O., 1909-11, 1st Ch., Bakersfield, Calif., 1911-15, 1st Ch., Tacoma, Wash., 1915-19, 1st Ch., Middletown, O., 1919-20, Beulah Ch., Detroit, Mich., 1920-22, 1st Ch., San Francisco, 1922-34. Conductor funeral service of President Warren G. Harding, Palace Hotel, San Francisco, Aug. 3, 1923. Pres. Calif. br., White Cross Anti-Narcotic Soc. of America, 1927-—; internat. pres. Anti-Narcotic League since July 1933. Mem. Kappa Sigma. Mason (K.T.), Odd Fellow, Moose. Clubs: Commonwealth, East Bay Country. Home: 2019 Lake St., San CA‡

WEST, LEVON, etcher, photographer; b. Centerville, S.D., Feb. 3, 1900; s. Avedis Martin and Henrietta West; student U. of Minn., 1920-24; Art Students League, 1925; pupil of Joseph Pennell, 1925-26; m. Louise Remington, June 11, 1943; 1 son, Peter. Mem. U.S.N.R., 1918; tchr., rural sch., Wells Co., N.D., 1919. Made 32 etchings in Spain, 1926; official artist, World Press Congress, Geneva, Switzerland, 1926; recorded Col. Lindbergh's Transatlantic Flight (3 etchings); 40 watercolors, American game and Western Ranch Life, 1934-35; watercolors, Bermuda, 1935. Awarded Charles M. Lea prize, Phila., 1928; gold medal for etching at Exposition Internationale des Art et des Techniques, 1937; award, Freedoms Found. at Valley Forge, 1955; Univ. Minnesota outstanding achievement award, 1959. Represented in Phila. Museum of Art, Boston Museum Fine Arts, Met. Museum, N.Y. City, New York Public Library, Congressional Library, Hispanic Museum, N.Y. City, Inst. Geog. Exploration, Harvard Univ., Honolulu Acad. Fine Arts, Modern Masters of Etching Series (Vol. 24, 1930). Began photography, 1935; introduced first Americana series color photography Saturday Evening Post, 1937; also appearing Fortune, Vogue, House and Garden, Popular Photography, etc. War corr., Air Transport Command and Saturday Evening Post, 1943-44; founder Photography in Fine Arts Project, 1959, now dir. Mem. Inst. Graphic Arts, U. of Minn. Alumni Assn. of N.Y., Am. Fedn. of Arts, Brooklyn Soc. Etchers, Soc. of Am. Etchers, Kappa Sigma, Delta Phi Delta, Photographic Soc. Am. Clubs: Coffee House, Western Univs., Overseas Press, Nat. Press, Nat. Press Photographers Assn., Dutch Treat. Illus. Vivid Spain, 1926. Author: Making an Etching, 1932; A Catalogue of the Etchings of Levon West, 1929; How to Use Your Candid Camera, 1936; Color in Photography, 1939; Kodachrome and How to Use It, 1940; Flight to Everywhere, 1945. Address: New York City NY Died Apr. 26, 1968.

WEST, OSWALD, ex-governor; b. near Guelph, Ont., Can., May 20, 1873; s. John Gulliver and Sarah (McGregor) W.; ed. pub. schs.; m. Mabel Hutton, Sept. 22, 1897; children—Helen (Mrs. Ellery W. Stone), Gordon (dec.), Jean (Mrs. Frank J. McHugh). Clerk and paying teller, Ladd & Bush Bank, Salem, Oregon, 1889-1900; paying teller, First National Bank, Astoria, Oregon, 1900-03; state land agent, Oregon, 1903-07; member Oregon Railroad Commission, 1907-10; gov. of Ore., term 1911-15. Democrat. Resumed law practice at Portland. Home: 636 N.W. 20th Av., Portland OR‡

WEST, PRESTON C., lawyer; b. Rodney, Miss., Aug. 19, 1868; s. Preston C. and Winifred Todd (Wilcox) W.; A.B., Southwestern Presbyn. Univ., Clarksville, Tenn., 1888; studied law in pvt. offices, and in Law Dept., U. of Va., 1888-90; m. Bessie Douglas Shelby, Oct. 20, 1897; children—Gustavus Wilcox, Winifred. Practiced, Ft. Smith, Ark., 1890-97, Muskogee, Okla., 1897-1913; chmn. Bd. of Freeholders that prepared charter for commn. form of govt. for Muskogee; asst. atty.-gen. of U.S., 1913-14; solicitor Dept. of the Interior, 1914-16; resumed practice at Tulsa, Okla.; retired from active practice, 1940. Democrat. Episcopalian. Mason, Elk. Mem. Am. and Okla. State bar assns., Internat. Law Assn., Sigma Alpha Epsilon. Clubs: Tulsa; Colonnade (U. of Va.). Home: 238 McDowell Rd., Lexington KY*‡

WEST, SAMUEL WALLENS, broker; b. N.Y.C., Mar. 17, 1899; s. Charles and Pauline (Wallens) W.; A.B., Columbia, 1920; m. Babette Weil, Mar. 16, 1928; children—Jill (Mrs. John R. Adler), Douglas. Partner L. F. Rothschild & Co., 1930-40; partner Beauchamp, West & Stava, 1953-69. Gov. N.Y. Stock Exchange. Dir. Columbia University Club Found. Club: The Buttonwood (pres.). Home: New York City NY Died Oct. 22, 1969.

WESTCOTT, CHARLES DRAKE, consular service; b. Phila., Pa., Aug. 3, 1871; asst. engr. with Brooklyn Ry. Co., 1894-96; with Dept. of Justice, Washington, D.C., 1902-09; cons. practice, 1909-17; apptd. consul, 1920, and detailed to Paris, France. Address: Am. Consulate, Paris France‡

WESTERFIELD, SAMUEL ZAZA, JR., ambassador; b. Chgo., Nov. 15, 1919; s. Samuel Zaza and Rachael (Waddleton) W.; A.B. magna cum laude, Howard U., 1939; M.A., Harvard, 1949, Ph.D., 1950; m. Helene Bryant, Sept. 5, 1945; children—Samuel Zaza, Shelia Helene. Instr. econs. and statistics Howard U., summers 1940, 41, 45; asst. prof. econs. W.Va. State Coll., 1945-46; asst. prof. econs., chmn. dept. econs. and bus. adminstrn. Lincoln U., 1947-50; asso. prof. econs. Atlanta U., 1950-52, dean Sch. Bus. Adminstrn., prof. econs., 1952-61; asso. dir. debt analysis staff Treasury Dept., 1961, sr. adviser to dir. Office Internat. Affairs, 1961-63; dep. asst. sec. Bur. Econ. Affairs, State Dept., 1963-64, dep. asst. sec. econs. and planning Bur. African Affairs, 1964-69; ambassador to Liberia, Monrovia, 1969-72; vis. prof. Harvard Grad. Sch. Bus., 1959-60; guest lectr. Univ. Coll., Ibadan, Nigeria, 1960, Univ. Coll. Addis Ababa, Ethiopia, 1960. Rep. U.S. numerous internat. confs. Treas. All-Citizens Registration Com., Atlanta, 1957-58. Bd. dirs. Atlanta Urban League, 1956-59. Anson Phelps Stokes scholar, 1940-42; Rosenwald Found. fellow, 1940-42; grantee Social Sci. Research Council, 1944-45, Am. Univs. Program-Merrill Trust Fund, 1960. Mem. Am. Econ. Assn., Kappa Mu. Club: Internat. Home: Washington DC Died July 1972.

WESTERN, FORREST, govt. ofcl.; b. Purdin, Mo., Aug. 25, 1902; s. William Wardall and Leonora (Powell) W.; A.B., Central Coll., 1924; M.A., U. Mo., 1926; Ph.D., U. Pitts., 1933; m. Isabel Dorothy Asher, Jan. 3, 1930; children—William Alexander, Judith Christine. Asst. prof. physics Mo. Valley Coll., Marshall, 1931-33, prof. physics, 1933-35; prof. physics, head dept. phys. scis. Lincoln Meml. U., Harrogate, Tenn., 1935-42; lectr. dept. physics U. Minn., 1942-44; physicist Manhattan Project, Tenn. Eastman Corp., Oak Ridge, 1944; dir. lab. No. 1 Fercleve Corp., Oak Ridge, 1944-45; physicist health physics div. Oak Ridge Nat. Lab., 1945-47, asst. dir. div., 1947-49, asso. dir., 1949-51; health physicist biophysics br. div. biology and medicine AEC, Washington, 1951-57, asst. dir. radiation protection, 1957-59, dept. dir. Office Health and Safety, 1959-61, dir. div. radiation protection standards, 1961-64, dir. div. safety standards, 1964-67, dir. div. radiation protection standards, 1967-69, sci. adviser to dir. div. radiation protection standards, 1969-72. Recipient Distinguished Service award AEC, 1970. Mem. Am. Indsl. Hygiene Assn., Health Physics Soc., Sigma Xi. Home: McLean VA Died July 27, 1972; buried St. Louis MO

WESTFALL, BYRON LEE, univ. dean; b. Bolivar, Mo., Nov. 14, 1903; s. Laurence L. and Nora (Davison) W.; B.S., U. Mo., 1929, A.M., 1932, Ph.D., 1935; m. Lucille Elizabeth Hickman, Dec. 28, 1935; 1 son, Robert L. Tchr., Paris (Mo.) High Sch., 1929-30, Vandalia (Mo.) High Sch., 1930-31, Ferguson (Mo.) High Sch., 1931-34; asso. prof. edn. Central Mo. State College, Warrensburg, 1935-45, Butler U., 1945-46; dir. div. teaching Ind. State U., 1946-49, prin. Lab. Sch., 1946-55, asso. prof. edn., 1946-50, prof., 1950-70, acting chmn. dept. edn. and psychology, 1966-67, chmn. dept., 1967-68, asso. dean Sch. Edn., 1968-70, emeritus, 1970-72; vis. prof. U. Chgo., 1945, U. Mo., 1945; specialist secondary edn. U.S. Office Edn., 1964-65. Mem. commn. research and service N. Central Assn. Colls. and Secondary Schs., 1944-51, 54-60. Mem. N.E.A., Nat. Assn. Secondary Sch. Prins., Am. Assn. Sch. Adminstrs., Nat. Soc. Coll. Tchrs. Edn., Am. Assn. U. Profs., Phi Delta Kappa, Delta Upsilon. Contbr. articles to profl. jours. Home: Terre Haute IN Died June 25, 1972.

WESTHUES, HENRY J., ret. judge; b. Westphalen, Germany, June 5, 1888; s. William and Theresa (Peters) W.; brought to U.S., 1892, naturalized, 1896; LL.B., St. Louis U., 1912; m. Helen Roer, Aug. 22, 1916; children—Rosemary (Mrs. Otto Rieke), Marie (Mrs. Henry Staub), Rev. John H., Marjorie (Sister Mary Joan Cordis), Jane (Mrs. Paul Schmidt), Elaine (Sister Frances Cabrini), Marilyn. Admitted to Mo. bar, 1911, practiced in Jefferson City, 1912; partner D.F. Calfee, 1915-22; judge 14th Jud. Circuit Ct., 1922-30; commr. Supreme Ct. Mo., 1930-54, judge, 1954-63, ret., 1963. City atty., Jefferson City, 1913-18; pros. atty., Cole County, 1918-22. Recipient Alumni Merit award St. Louis U., 1955, Certificate of Merit, 1963. Mem. Am., Mo., Cole County bar assns., Order of Coif (hon.), Phi Alpha Delta (hon.). Roman Catholic. K.C., Kiwanian. Home: Jefferson City MO Died Apr. 17, 1969.

WESTON, EDWARD F., business exec.; b. Newark, N.J., Oct. 24, 1878; s. Edward and Wilhelmina (Seidel) W.; Columbia U. Sch. Engring., 1900; m. Edith R. Parker, May 9, 1906 (dec. 1954); children—Cornelia (Mrs. Philip H. Cummings), Frances Ross (Mrs. Malcolm B. Hoyt). With Weston Elec. Instrument Co. since 1900; sec., 2d v.p., v.p., president since 1925, chmn. bd. since 1944, dir. Fidelity Union Trust, Motor Finance Corp.; v.p., dir. Newark Dist. Telegraph Co.; regional dir. Am. Mutual Liability Ins. Co., Boston Mfrs. Mutual Liability Ins. Co. dir. Mt. Pleasant Cemetery Assn., Presbyterian Hosp., Newark. Pres. bd. govs. Newark Coll. of Engring. (v.p.). Mem. Montclair Soc. of Engrs., N.J. State Chamber Commerce (dir.), Newark Chamber Commerce, U.S. Chamber Commerce, Am. Soc. for Metals, Nat. Assn. Mfrs. Sigma Xi. Clubs: Downtown (Newark); Baltusrol Gol (Springfield); Essex (Newark); Montclair. Home Montclair NJ Died Sept. 27, 1971.

WESTON, EUGENE, JR., architect; b. Bloomington Cal., Jan. 12, 1896; s. Eugene and Margaret Hanna (Fegan) W.; student Los Angeles Poly. High Sch. 1911-14; m. Beatrice Stiles, May 17, 1921 children—Eugene, III, Russell Stiles, Jane Elizabeth Archtl. draftsman, 1915-21; with Bertram G. Goodhue N.Y.C., 1921-23; in practice Los Angeles, 1923-64 Served in California Field Artillery, United State Army, Mexican Border, 1916; capt., 20th F.A., 5th Div., A.E.F., 1917-19. Awarded A.I.A. honor award 1929, 46, 51, 54, Certificate of Merit, 1936; Ceramics 1940; bronze medal, Art Fiesta, 1931. Fellow A.I.A (member emeritus); member of the Society o Mayflower Descendants, Southwest Museum, Am Legion, Hist. Soc. of So. Cal., Los Angeles C. of C Republican. Episcopalian. Home: Pauma Valley CA Died Dec. 23, 1969; buried El Camino Memorial Park San Diego CA

WESTON, FRANK MOREY, church official; b Phelps, N.Y., Sept. 26, 1873; s. Alexander John an Harriott Swan (Peck) W.; B.A., Hamilton Coll., 1900 D.D., 1921; B.D., Auburn Theol. Sem., 1903; m. Len May Cooper, June 30, 1903; children—Carolyn Coope Harry Peck. Ordained Presbyn. ministry, 1903; pasto First Ch., Ellicottville, N.Y., 1903-07, Brighton Ch Rochester, 1907-24, First Ch., Geneva, N.Y., 1924-31 exec. sec.-treas. Rochester Presbytery 1931-47; nov area dir. of restoration fund campaign Presbyn. Ch U.S.A. 4-minute man, Rochester, 1915-17; spl. speake of Y.M.C.A. at 10 camps and forts, 1918, in France Jan.-June 1919. Trustee Okolona (Miss.) Industria Sch., 1914-47. Mem. Theta Delta Chi. Republican Clubs: University, Rotary, Ad, City, Rochester Midvale. Home: 61 Dorchester Rd., Rochester 10 NY

WESTON, HAROLD, artist; b. Merion, Pa., Feb. 14 1894; s. Samuel Burns and Mary (Hartshorne) W.; A.B magna cum laude, Harvard, 1916; m. Faith Borton, Ma 12, 1923; children—Barbara (Mrs. Esty Foster, Jr.) Bruce, Haroldine (Mrs. William H. Sudduth II). Wit YMCA attached to Brit. Army in India, Mesopotamia 1916-20; ofcl. artist London War Office, 1918 organizer, exec. sec. Reconstrn. Service Com., 1942-43 exec. dir. Food For Freedom, Inc., 1943-47. U.S. de Internat. Assn. Plastic Arts, Vienna, 1960, N.Y., 1963 Tokyo, 1966, exec. com., 1957-63, v.p., 1961-62, pres 1962-63, hon. pres., 1963-72, pres. U.S. com., 1961-67 hon. president, 1967-72; vice chmn. Nat. Council Ar and Govt., 1954-61, chmn., from 1961. Life fello World Academy Arts and Sci.; mem. Soc. Am. Graphi Artists (honorary), National Society of Mural Painter (hon.), Fedn. Modern Painters and Sculptors (pre. 1953-57), Phi Beta Kappa. Recipient 3d prize for Am painting Golden Gate Internat. Expn., 1939; Am. Soc Contemporary Artists award, 1964. Works represented War Mus. (London), Meml. Art Gallery (Rochester Pa. Academy Fine Arts, Phillips Gallery (Washington Yale Art Mus., San Francisco Mus. Art, Fogg Art Mu (Cambridge, Mass.), Mus. Modern Art, Corcora Gallery Art, Smithsonian Instn., Whitney Mus. of Am Art, N.Y.U. Collection, Butler Inst. Am. A (Youngstown, O.), Oakland Art Mus., Syracuse U. A Mus., Purdue U., Fordham U., Everson Mus., Syracus St. Lawrence U.; portrait of Dr. Felix Adler, Butl Library, Columbia; executed murals (22 panels) U.S General Services Bldg., Washington. Home: St Huber NY Died Apr. 10, 1972; buried Norton Cemete Keene NY

WESTON, HARRY ELISHA, mfrs. rep.; b. Hinckle N.Y., Dec. 17, 1897; s. James Walter and Fann (Pooler) W.; B.S., N.Y. State Coll. of Forestr Syracuse, 1921; m. Harriett M. Whitney, Jan. 27, 192 (dec. Apr. 3, 1952); m. 2d. Lucile White, Nov. 24, 195 Instr. forest chemistry N.Y. State Coll. Forestr 1920-23, asst. prof. pulp and paper manufactur 1923-26; sales engr. Thomas H. Savery, 1926-27; adv mgr. The Paper Industry, trade publ., 1927-32, edito 1932-38, editorial dir. The Paper Industry and Pap World, 1938-48; asso. sec. treas., Am. Pulp and Pap Mills Supts. Assn., 1948-50, sec., treas., 1950-59; sec treas. Paper Industry Mgmt. Assn. (formerly Am. Pu and Paper Mill Supts. Assn.), 1959-61, exec. sec., treas 1961-64; mfrs. rep., Lombard, Ill., from 1964. Mem Paper Industry Mgmt. Assn., Tech. Assn. Pulp ar Paper Industry, Acacia, Sigma Xi, Alpha Chi Sigm Republican. Methodist. Mason. Author: Lectures o Pulp and Paper Mill Machinery (privately published 1925; A Book on 1927, Compiler: Engineerin Handbook-Useful Information for Pulp and Pap Manufacturers. Contbr. of numerous articles on pu and paper making subjects to bus. press, and lecturer same field. Awarded George Arents Pioneer Meda 1949, Syracuse U., for advancement indsl. edn. Hom Lombard IL Deceased.

WESTON, SIDNEY ADAMS, editor; b. Sharo Mass., Dec. 9, 1877; s. Rev. Henry Crosby and Cla Amelia (Loring) W.; B.A., Yale, 1900, M.A., 190 Ph.D., 1903; m. Mille Louise West, July 12, 1905; dau., Betsey Gerry Rice. With Congregation

Publishing. Soc. since 1904, becoming asst. editor, 1904, mng. editor, 1909, editor-in-chief, 1915, business mgr., 1921, now general sec. Mem. Phi Beta Kappa, Theta Delta Chi. Congregationalist. Mason. Author: The World a Field for Christian Service; Problems of Youth in Social Life; Studies in the Books of Ruth and James; (brochures) Jesus and the Problems of Life; Jesus' Teachings for Young People; Problems and Principles of Social Living; The World and Its Problems; The Prophets and the Problems of Life; Social and Religious Problems; Discovering Jesus; To Drink or Not to Drink; Finding Your Way in Life. Home: Sharon, Mass. Address: 14 Beacon St., Boston MA‡

WESTON, WILLIAM, physician; b. Eastover, S.C., Aug. 6, 1874; s. William and Caroline Elizabeth (Woodard) W.; prep. edn., Patrick Mil. Inst., Anderson, S.C., 1888-90; student U. of S.C., 1890-93; M.D., Med. Coll. of S.C., 1896, hon. Dr. P.H., 1929; student, U. of the South, 1896, hon. D.Sc., 1931; m. Elizabeth Vander Horst, June 16, 1896; children—Caroline (Mrs. Benjamin F. Few), William, Adele Allston (Mrs. Horace A. Steven). Practiced in Columbia, S.C., since 1896; founder of first uncinariasis clinic in U.S., 1901; chief of staff Columbia Hosp., 1919-25; chmn. S.C. Food Research Commn. since 1927. Maj. Med. Corps, U.S. Army, 1918-19, World War. Mem. A.M.A. (chmn. pediatric sect. 1930-31; mem. Ho. of Dels. same sect. since 1936), Southern Med. Assn. (chmn. pediatric sect. 1917-18), S.C. Med. Assn. (pres. 1913-14), Columbia Med. Soc. (pres. 1908), Am. Acad. Pediatrics, Sigma Alpha Epsilon. Democrat. Episcopalian. Club: Forest Lake (Columbia). Author: (brochure) Studies in Nutrition, 1926; also articles in med. jours. Home: 1231 Bull St. Office: 1428 Lady St., Columbia SC*‡

WETHERALD, CHARLES E., motor mfg. exec.; b. Wilson, N.Y., Nov. 26, 1884; s. William and Ida M. (Bigalow) W.; ed. pub. schs. of Mich.; m. Estella M. Albro, June 27, 1906. Mechanic, Gen. Motors, 1904-45; in gen. mfg., 1930-45; mgr. Chevrolet Motor Co. since 1946; pres. and dir. U.S. Sugar Corp., 1945-69, vice chmn., until 1969; dir. Mich. Nat. Bank. Club: Detroit Athletic. Home: Clewiston FL Died Oct. 1969.

WETHERBEE, FRANK IRVING, artist; b. Hyde Park, Mass., Mar. 3, 1869; s. Henry Russell and Margaret (Welton) W.; ed. pub. schs., Boston; studied marine painting under Marshall Johnson, landscape under C. E. L. Green, water color under Melbourn Hardwick (all of Boston), and at Boston Art Club; unmarried. Worked at general lithography for several yrs. Club: Press (Chicago). Author and Illustrator: Fun in Painting and Drawing, 1905; Teddy Bears Painting and Drawing Book, 1907; Juvenile Painting Gallery, 1908; Pony Paint Book, 1909. Home: 3976 Vincennes Av., Chicago IL‡

WETTERAU, THEODORE CARL, JR., food co. exec.; b. St. Louis, Nov. 13, 1927; s. Theodore Conrad and Edna (Ehrlich) W.; student Westminister Coll., 1948-52; m. Helen Elizabeth Killion, Feb. 20, 1956; children—Theodore Conrad II, Mark Stephen, Elizabeth Killion. With Wetterau Foods, Inc., Hazelwood, Mo., 1959-71, v.p. marketing, dir., 1960-63, exec. v.p., 1963-71; guest speaker Duttweiler Inst., Zurich, Switzerland, 1965. Served with AUS, 1945-47. Named Man of Month, Progressive Grocer mag., 1966. Mem. Knights of Cauliflower Ear, Sigma Alpha Epsilon. Republican. Presbyn. (deacon). Pioneer Package store. Home: St Louis MO Died 1971.

WEYER, EDWARD MOFFAT, prof. philosophy; b. Portsmouth, O., Oct. 1, 1872; s. George W. and Mary Letitia (Marshall) W.; U. of Wis., 1891-93; B.A., Yale, 1895; Ph.D., U. of Leipzig, 1898; m. Julia Morris Ross, July 25, 1900 (died 1911); children—Elliott Ross, Edward Moffat; m. 2d, Mary Rodes Christie, Apr. 10, 1924 (died 1945). Professor of philosophy or of psychology, Washington and Jefferson Coll., Washington, Pa., 1899-48, ret., also dean of the college, director extension work, and prof. philosophy, 1922-30, dean and prof. of philosophy, 1930-35, dean of faculty and prof. philosophy, 1936-42, v.p. and prof. of philosophy, 1943. Mem. American Psychological Association, American Philos. Assn., Phi Delta Theta. Contbr. on philos. and psychol. topics to Internat. Journal of Ethics, Forum, Yale Review, Psychol. Review, etc. Republican. Presbyn. Home: 49 S. College St., Washington PA‡

WEYHE, ERHARD, art dealer, publisher; b. Salzwedel, Germany, Sept. 28, 1882; m. Hannah Weyhe, June 3, 1914; children—Gertrude (Mrs. Seth Dennis), Arthur. Came to U.S., 1914. Founder E. Weyhe, art bookstore, N.Y.C., 1914 and art gallery; publisher art books. Home: New York City NY Died July 11, 1972; buried Digby Nova Scotia Canada

WEYL, CHARLES, engr.; b. Phila., May 22, 1896; s. Maurice N. and Carrie (Stein) W.; student Germantown Acad.; B.S., U. Pa., 1917, M.S., 1927; m. Elinor Fittelson, Apr. 28, 1920; children—Elinor Jean, Doris Anne; m. 2d, Helen Roberts, Dec. 4, 1948; children—Charles Frederick, Mary Caroline. Engring. design, adminstrn. various firms; dir. Moore Sch. X-Ray Lab., 1925-45, prof. elec. engring. Moore Sch. Elec. Engring., U. Pa., 1937-50, asso. prof. radiol. physics Grad. School Medicine, 1942-50; director IRC, Inc., 1929-67, pres., 1953-59, chmn., 1959-67; former chmn. Edward Stern & Co., Inc. Served as ensign, USNR, World War I; Naval Expt. Sta., New London, Conn., also submarine detection duty, 1918-19. Recipient Centennial citation, Schools of Engineering, University of Pennsylvania, 1955. Member of the Franklin Institute (Longstreth medal 1930), I.E.E.E., also A.A.A.S., Sigma Xi. Author: Apparatus and Technique for Roentgenography of the Chest (with S. Reid Warren, Jr.), 1935. Co-author: Radiologic Physics, rev. edit., 1951. Contbr. articles profl. publs., fiction mags. Home: Rydal PA Died Aug. 23, 1967.

WEYLER, GEORGE LESTER, naval officer; b. Emporia, Kan., May 14, 1886; s. John William and Laura Amelia (Schmidt) W.; student Emporia (Kan.) Coll., 1904-05; B.S., U.S. Naval Academy, 1910; LL.B., George Washington Law Sch., Washington, D.C., 1922; grad. Naval War Coll., 1938; m. Laura Gertrude Pearks, Mar. 22, 1917; children—Mary Elizabeth (wife of Lt. Col. Harold Jones Mitchener, U.S.M.C. Ret.), Laura Therese Christian. Comd. ensign, U.S. Navy, 1912, advancing through the grades to rear admiral, 1942; retired with rank of vice admiral, 1946; sea duty, chiefly in Pacific area, includes service on all types of naval ships except submarines and carriers, totals 22 years; shore duty includes service in Navy yards, Navy Dept., Naval Acad., Naval War Coll., Naval Operating Base (Guantanamo, Cuba), and as naval attache, Peru and Ecuador. Decorated campaign badges, Mexican, World War I and World War II (with citation), Legion of Merit with gold star (U.S.), Orden El Sol del Peru, Knight Comdr., Navy Cross. Home: Coronado CA Died Aug. 6, 1971; buried San Francisco National Cemetery.

WEYSSE, ARTHUR WISSWALD, biologist; b. Machias, Me., Nov. 16, 1867; s. Jacob and Margaret (Larrabee) W.; A.B., Harvard, 1891, A.M., 1892, Ph.D., 1894; studied Leipzig, Berlin, Paris, Naples, Harvard U. Med. Sch. and London; registered physician, Mass., 1905; M.D., Basel, Switzerland, 1907; unmarried. Asst. in botany and zoology, Harvard, and Radcliffe Coll., 1892-94; instr. zoology, Mass. Inst. Tech., 1896-1907; prof. exptl. physiology, Boston U. Sch. of Medicine, 1899-1924, also prof. biology, Boston U. since 1904; lecturer on venereal disease, Boston U. Sch. of Medicine, 1915-24; acting dean Grad. Sch. of Boston U., 1917-22; and dean, 1922-33, prof. emeritus since 1939. Fellow Am. Academy Arts and Sciences, A.A.A.S.; mem. Am. Soc. Zoologists, Am. Soc. Naturalists, Am. Assn. Anatomists, Am. Genetic Assn., Am. Social Hygiene Assn., Mass. Soc. for Social Hygiene, Boston Soc. Med. Sciences, Boston Soc. Natural History, Boston Med. Library. Republican. Episcopalian. Mason (32 deg., K.T.). Clubs: Harvard, Boston. Author: Human Histology, 1898; Textbook of Zoology, 1904; Medico-Legal Moral Offenses, 1911; also numerous original papers on anatomy, embryology, physiology. Home: 291 Mishawum Road, Woburn MA‡

WHAM, BENJAMIN, judge; born on farm near Carter, Ill., June 11, 1891; s. Henderson Boyakin and Nancy Jane (Stonecipher) W.; student So. Ill. U., 1907-11; A.B., U. of Ill., 1915, J.D., 1917; m. Virginia Buffington, June 27, 1931; children—Barbara (Mrs. Charles M. Waite), David. Admitted to Ill. bar, 1917, and practiced in Chicago, 1920-69; partner of the firm of Wham, Welch and Metzdorf, and predecessor firms, Chgo., 1923-62; past officer several corps.; circuit judge Circuit Ct. Cook County, 1962-69. Past chmn. Ill. Statewide Pub. Health Com.; past ofcl. Chgo. Crime Commn.; various offices in Community Fund, Polio (campaign chmn. 1956-57), and American Red Cross organizations. Trustee C. & E. I.R.R. Co., 1939-41. Mem. bd. Ill., Inst. Tech. Served in inf., U.S. Army, A.E.F., World War I; member Alien Hearing Board, World War II. Awarded prize in Ross Bequest essay contest, Am. Bar Assn., 1935. Mem. Am. (chmn. corp. banking, bus. law sect., 1947-49, Ill. state del., 1951-60, chmn. com. commerce, 1946-47, bd. govs. 1959-62), Ill. (pres. 1941-42) Chgo. (chmn. coms., mem. bd. mgrs. 1949-51) bar assns., Order of the Coif, Am. Bar Assn. Fellows, Phi Delta Phi, Phi Beta Kappa Assos., Phi Beta Kappa, Delta Sigma Rho. Republican. Episcopalian. Clubs: Chicago, University, Indian Hill; Mawanda, Law, Legal, Literary (Chgo.). Contbr. to legal jours. Home: Northfield IL Died Nov. 27, 1969; buried Centralia IL

WHARTON, ARTHUR ORLANDO, ex-pres. Internat. Assn. Machinists, b. Wabaunsee Co., Kan., Nov. 9, 1873; s. Albert and Margaret Ellen (Collins) W.; ed. pub. schs., Topeka; m. Ella Louise Korschgen, Feb. 7, 1895; children—Margaret Ellen (Mrs. C. E. Morrison) and Arthur Orlando; m. 2d, Celeste Ayers, March 13, 1940. Machinist and foreman; elected general chmn. Internat. Assn. Machinists, 1903; pres. Ry. Employes Dept. of Am. Federation of Labor, 1912-18; apptd. by Sec. of Interior Lane as adviser to Ry. Wage Commn., Jan. 1918; apptd. by William G. McAdoo, dir. gen. of railroads, as mem. Bd. Railroad Wages and Working Conditions, and served as v.-chmn. and chmn. until dissolution of the bd., Mar. 1920; resumed position as pres. Ry. Employes Dept. A.F. of L.; mem. U.S. Ry. Labor Bd., by apptmt. of Pres. Wilson, Apr. 19, 1920, reapptd. by President Harding for term 1922-27, but bd. abolished, May 1926, by Congressional action; apptd. pres. Internat. Assn. Machinists, effective July 1, 1926, and elected pres. for term July 1, 1927-July 1, 1929, reelected for terms, 1929-41, retired Nov. 30, 1939; fifth vice president and mem. executive council American Federation Labor, 1930-39; appointed conservator Mt. Vernon Savings Bank, Washington, 1933; director Union Labor Life Insurance Company. Was chmn. com. that negotiated first standard form of agreement between Southeastern rys. and machinists, boiler makers, blacksmiths, 1917; apptd. mem. Nat. Labor Advisory Bd., NRA, 1934; apptd. chmn. Labor Policies Bd., Works Progress Adminstrn., 1935. Methodist. York and Scottish Rite Mason (Shriner). Address: Route 2, Box 676, Tucson AZ‡

WHARTON, CHARLES S., lawyer, congressman; b. Aledo, Ill., Apr. 22, 1875; s. Henry and Aurilla (Whitelaw) W.; grad. Graham (pub.) Sch., Chicago, 1890, Lake High Sch., Chicago, 1894, Univ. of Mich., law dept., LL.B., 1896; unmarried. Admitted to bar, 1896; active in politics; apptd., 1899, atty. for Town of Lake (one of the townships of which Chicago is composed); asst. city atty. of Chicago, 1903-4; mem. Congress, 4th Ill. dist., 1905-7. Methodist. Republican. Residence: 735 W. 43d Pl. Office: Reaper Blk., Chicago IL‡

WHEAT, RENVILLE, lawyer; b. Leavenworth, Kan., July 28, 1893; s. Samuel Edwin and Ida (Clements) W.; A.B., U. Mich., 1914, J.D., 1916; m. Elizabeth Shearer Russel, May 26, 1923; children—Anne Davenport (Mrs. William P. Hodgkins, Jr.), John R., Elizabeth Clements (Mrs. Paul H. Townsend, Jr.). Admitted to Mich. bar, 1916, since practiced in Detroit; partner firm Dykema, Wheat, Spencer, Goodnow & Trigg and predecessors, 1923-68. Trustee Edwin S. George Found., 1947-68; pres. Mich. Children's Aid Soc., 1951-56; sec., trustee McGregor Fund; bd. dirs. Detroit Symphony Orch. Assn.; trustee Skillman Foundation; mem. com. mgmt., vice chmn. bd. govs. Assos. Clements Library. Served to 2d lt., F.A., U.S. Army, 1917-19. Decorated Silver Star medal, Croix de Guerre. Fellow Am. Bar Found. Mem. Am., Mich., Detroit bar assns., Am. Judicature Soc., Lawyers Club (U. Mich.), Order of Coif, Phi Beta Kappa, Psi Upsilon. Presbyn. (elder). Clubs: Detroit, University, Detroit Country (all Detroit), Grosse Pointe; Groiler (N.Y.C.), Huron Mountain (pres. 1962-65) (Big Bay, Mich.). Bd. editors: Mich. Law Review, 1915-16. Home: Grosse Pointe Farms MI Died Oct. 8, 1968; buried Elmwood Cemetery, Detroit MI

WHEATLEY, WILLIAM ALONZO, educator; b. Verona, N.Y., Feb. 28, 1869; s. William and Lottie (Fry) W.; A.B., Syracuse U., 1894, A.M., 1897; grad. work Yale, 1904-05, 1911-12, U. of Pittsburgh, 1933-34; m. Mabel Ballantine of Andes, N.Y., Aug. 8, 1901 (dec.); children—William Ballantine (dec.), Esther Mabel, John Carol. Prin. Minoa (N.Y.) Grammar Sch., 1894; vice-prin., East Syracuse (N.Y.) High Sch., 1895; prin. Andes High Sch., 1896-97, Syracuse U. Prep. Sch., 1898-99, Chester (N.Y.) High Sch., 1900-04; supt. schs., Fairchild, Conn., 1905; towns of Fairfield and Branford, Conn., 1906-10; prin. City High Sch. and supt. schs., Middletown, Conn., 1910-17; rep. War Camp Community Service, 1917-20; teacher Hartford (Conn.) High School, 1921-23; head dept. of edn., State Teachers Coll., Edinboro, Pa., 1923-36, dean instruction, 1936-39. Dir. Sch. and Coll. Service and United Air Lines, 1940-47; regional supt. of schools and colleges since 1947. Organized community recreation for soldiers of Camp Greene, Charlotte, N.C. Mem. N.E.A. Commn. on the Reorgn. of Secondary Edn., Phi Kappa Psi, Phi Beta Kappa. Republican. Conglist. Author: German Declension Made Easy for Beginners, 1895; (with Enoch B. Gowin) Occupations, a Textbook in Vocational Guidance, 1916; The Good Citizen, Sticking to the Main Issue, 1920; Teaching Aptitude Tests, 1927; (with Royce R. Mallory) Building Character and Personality, a Textbook in Orientation, 1936; Teachers Manuel of Aviation, 1940, 42, 44, 45; also ednl. articles, 1930-47, Peering Into The Hereafter, 1949. Home: 670 Irolo St., Los Angeles 5. Office: United Air Lines, 501 W. 6th St., Los Angeles 14 CA‡

WHEDON, JOHN FIELDING, advt. exec.; b. Lake Co., Fla., Dec. 23, 1899; s. Daniel Denison and Harriet (Fielding) W.; A.B., U. Cal., 1922; m. Charlotte Hesser, Mar. 9, 1923 (div. 1951); children—John Fielding, Daniel Denison; m. 2d, Sonya Edgar, October 8, 1954. Advertising salesman for Hearst Mags., 1922-23, Pacific Coast mgr., 1923-24; v.p., mgr. Lord & Thomas, San Francisco, 1934-39, exec. v.p., dir., Chgo., 1939-42; v.p., mgr. Young & Rubicam, Inc., Chgo., 1948-56, mem. exec. com., N.Y.C., 1956—. Served with U.S. Army, 1918. Mem. Sigma Chi. Methodist. Mason. Clubs: Chicago, Tavern (Chgo.). Home: San Mateo CA Died Apr. 1969.

WHEELER, ALBERT HARRY, mathematician; b. Leominster, Mass., Jan. 18, 1873; s. Albert Alpheus and Ella Louise (Gibson) W., B.S., Worchester (Mass.) Poly. Inst., 1894; A.M., Clark U., 1921; m. Helen Marion Bonzey, Aug. 19, 1901; 1 dau., Helen Marjorie (Mrs. Paul E. Haney). Teacher of mathematics, English High

Sch., Worcester, 1896-1916, North High Sch., Worcester, Mass., since 1916; retired, 1943; lecturer in mathematics, Brown Univ., 1924-26, Wellesley Coll., 1926-28; lecturer on math. subjects at ednl. meetings since 1905; prof. affiliate in mathematics, Clark U., 1943-44. Mem. American Math. Soc., Math. Assn. America, Assn. Teachers of Mathematics of New England. Republican. Mason. Author: First Course in Algebra, 1907; Examples in Algebra, 1914. Engaged in research on theory and construction of polyhedra; has collection of math. models which have been exhibited to univs. and math. socs. Home: 44 Beverly Rd., Worcester 5 MA‡

WHEELER, JEAN HULEATT (MRS. JOSEPH COOLIDGE WHEELER), dir. research, educator, author; b. Boston, May 16, 1927; d. Joseph Alexander and Miriam Wesley (Shovelton) Huleatt; B.A. magna cum laude, Radcliffe Coll., 1948; license es sci. politique, Grad. Inst. Internat. Studies, Geneva, Switzerland, 1949; M.A., Radcliffe Coll., 1950, Ph.D., 1961; m. Joseph Coolidge Wheeler, Feb. 1, 1949; children—Juliet, Rachel, Deborah, Caleb, Daniel. Dir., originator The Founders Project, 1961-68; Scholar The Radcliffe Inst. for Ind. Study, 1962-64; tchr. courses in polit. theory, consitutional law, Am. thought, Am. U., 1963-65; lectr. various univs. and orgns.; president of Institute for Research in Social Scis. and Humanities, 1968-69. Mem. Fairfax County (Va.) Democratic com., 1954-61. Recipient Caroline Wilby prize Radcliffe Coll. Mem. Am. Studies Assn., Am. Hist. Soc. Orgn. Am. Historians, Am. Polit. Sci. Assn., Modern Humanities Research Assn., Phi Beta Kappa, Editor, author: An Index to the Thought of the Founders of American Republic and related works. Address: McLean VA Died Aug 1969.

WHEELER, JOHN DEBERRY, lawyer; b. Cisco, Tex., June 29, 1888; s. Thomas Benton and Ida (DeBerry) W.; B.S., Southwestern University, 1908, Doctor of Literature, 1963; Doctor of Laws, Trinity U., 1942; m. Georgie Fisher, June 7, 1911; children—John DeBerry (dec.), Sterling Fisher. Admitted to Tex. bar, 1910; partner firm Boyle, Wheeler, Gresham, Davis & Gregory, San Antonio, 1925. Dir. Am. Hosp. & Life Ins. Co. Chmn. trustees Southwestern U.; trustee Trinity U.; vice gen. chmn., trustee United Capitals Funds, Inc. Recipient Algernon Sidney Sullivan award Southwestern U., 1957. Methodist. Rotarian (pres. 1945-46). Home: San Antonio TX Died 1969.

WHEELER, JOHN SAMUEL, physician; b. Boston, Mass., Jan. 8, 1904; s. Rev. John Lewis and Tryphenia Halfyard (Garland) W.; student Univ. of N.H., 1923-26, Wesleyan Univ., Middletown Conn., 1924; M.D., Boston Univ., 1930; M.P.H., Johns Hopkins, 1938; m. Marion Ernestine Mitchell, June 22, 1929; children—John M. W., Harold H. C., Mark L. B., Michael L. L. Interne Bridgeport (Conn.) Hosp., 1930-31; gen. practice of medicine, Wolfeboro, N.H. 1931-37; dir. div. of epidemiology and local health N.H. State Dept. of Health, Concord, N.H., 1937-40; state health officer and sec. state bd. of health, N.H. State Dept. of Health, 1945-56, consultant in pub. health, staff Concord Gen. Hosp., 1947-56; staff physician and cons. pub. health Fairview Hosp. & Tng. Center, Salem, Ore., 1958-62, N.H. Hosp., Concord, 1962-67. Sec. state bd. funeral dirs. and embalmers, since Dec. 1945; sec. state bd. registration in medicine from Feb. 1946, in chiropody from 1946; chairman State Hospital Survey and Construction Commission. Mem. N.H. State water pollution commn., cancer commn., TB commn., commn. on alcholism. Trustee N.H. State Tb. Sanitarium, Glencliffe. Served in U.S. Army as N.H. state med. officer for Selective Service, Sept. 1940-Apr. 1945; med. insp. and hosp. insp. 31st gen. hosp., Lingayen Gulf, P.I., Sept. 1945, med. insp. Camp Wolters, Tex., May 1945; disch. as lt. col. Nov. 1945; served as state surg., staff N.H. Nat. Guard, Aug.-Oct. 1940; apptd. col., chief Selective Service Staff, 1951; col. m.c. ret. Fellow A.M.A., A.P.H.A. Mem. founders group Am. Bd. Preventive Med. and Pub. Health. Mem. State and Terr. Health Ofcrs. Assn., Assn. State and Provincial Health Authorities, N.H. Med. Soc. (chmn. pub. health commn.), Merrimack Co. Med. Soc., N.H. Tuberculosis Assn. (mem. exec. com.) N.H. Social Hygiene Soc. (mem. exec. com.), Alpha Chi Rho, Alpha Kappa Kappa. Rep. Episcopalian. Mason. Home: Contoocook NH Died Apr. 16, 1968; buried Blossom Hill Cemetery, Concord NH

WHEELER, JOSEPH C., fgn. service officer; b. Columbus, O., Mar. 8, 1912; s. Wayne and Ella Belle (Candy) W.; A.B., Oberlin Coll., 1933, M.A., U. Cin., 1935; m. Shirley Price, Oct. 31, 1936; children—Christopher Wayne, Linda Anne, Robin Virginia. Budget analyst, div. head, asst. to dir. Office of Budget and Finance, Dept. of Agr., 1939-47, asst. to chief in charge adminstrn. Bur. Agrl. Econs., 1947-49, dep. dir. finance Dept. of Agr., 1949-53, director finance and budget officer, 1953-57; exec. and program officer U.S. Information Service Am. Embassy, Rome Italy, 1957-62, dep. pub. affairs officer USIA, Belgrade, Yugoslavia, 1962-64, dep. asst. dir. adminstrn., 1964-66; consul gen., Florence, Italy, 1966-70. Home: Minisink Hills PA Died July 5, 1970.

WHEELER, LESLIE ALLEN, agrl. cons.; b. Ventura, Ia., Dec. 20, 1899; s. Frank and Lottie (Rankin) W.; A.B., Pomona Coll., Claremont, Calif., 1921; M.B.A., Harvard, 1923; m. Louise Price, Nov. 17, 1927. Spl. agt. U.S. Dept. of Commerce, 1923-26; asso., sr. and prin. agrl. economist and chief of the Foreign Agrl. Service, Bur. of Agrl. Econ., U.S. Dept. of Agr., 1926-39, dir. of the Office of Foreign Agrl. Relations 1939-48; apptd. fgn. service officer (class 1) and sec. in diplomatic service, 1948; assigned Dept. of State, 1948; minister-counselor of Embassy, Mexico City, 1948-50; vice chmn., exec. com., Food and Agriculture orgn. of U.N.; chmn. Internat. Wheat Council; chmn. International Cotton Advisory Com., 1942-48; director Interim office for technical collaboration, 1950; cons. Internat. Fedn. Agricultural Producers, 1951-68; chief econ. advisory mission, Iran; del. to numerous internat. confs. Member American Farm Economic Assn. Club: Cosmos (Washington, D.C.). Contbr. articles on internat. trade in agrl. products to jours. Home: Chevy Chase MD Died Apr. 26, 1968.

WHEELER, MARY CURTIS, author, graduate nurse; b. Brooklyn, N.Y., July 12, 1869; d. Norman Willis and Emma Sophia (VanAmringe) W.; graduate Ripon (Wis.) Coll., 1890; Teachers Coll. (Columbia), 1903-4; grad. Ill. Training Sch. for Nurses, 1893. Supt. Sherman Hosp., Elgin, Ill., 1893-9, Blessing Hosp., Quincy, Ill., 1899-1910, Ill. Training Sch. for Nurses since 1913. Mem. Nat. Com. Am. Red Cross Nursing Service. Mem. Am. Nurses' Assn., Nat. League of Nursing Education, Ill. Training Sch. Alumnae, Ill. State Assn. Graduate Nurses. Congregationalist. Club: Woman's City (Chicago). Author: Nursing Technic, 1918. Home: 509 S. Honore St., Chicago IL‡

WHEELER, RICHARD SMITH, govt. ofcl.; b. Chgo., Mar. 30, 1909; s. Herbert M. and Orra M. (Smith) W.; B.A., U. Mich., 1930; m. Dora L. Hughes, June 3, 1937; children—Douglas H., Richard M., David L. Exec. merc. establishments, N.Y.C., Washington, 1930-35; staff information statistics div., Nat. Emergency Council and successor agy. Office of Govt. Reports, Exec. Office of the President, 1936-38, chief information statistics div., 1938-40; fgn. affairs officer, div. internat. conferences Dept. State, 1946-49, asst. chief in charge program br., 1950-52, asso. chief div., 1953-54; dep. dir. Office Internat. Conferences, Bur. Internat. Orgn. Affairs, 1954-57, 59-60; exec. officer U.S. Mission to Internat. Atomic Energy Agency, Vienna, Austria, 1958-60; foreign service officer Department State, 1955-62; dir. advt. Arlington (Va.) Trust Co., 1964-70, asst. treas., asst. v.p. advt. and pub. relations, 1970-71. Mem. numerous U.S. delegations, ofcl. various internat. meetings. Served from 1st lt. to lt. col. Office Mgmt. Control, Hdqrs. USAAF, 1941-46. Decorated Military Legion of Merit; Commendation medal with 2 oak leaf clusters. Home: Arlington VA Died June 20, 1972; buried Ivy Hill Cemetery, Alexandria VA

WHEELER, SCOTT, organist; b. Plano, Ill., Sept. 2, 1870; grad. Plano High School, 1886; studied at Northwestern Univ., 1892-4; studied organ with Louis Falk, Clarence Eddy and R. H. Woodman; studied theory with Frederic Gleason and Dudley Buck. Began playing organ in Cong'l Ch., Plano, at 14; between ages of 16 and 20 played in People's Ch. and 1st Cong'l Ch., Aurora, Ill.; 5 yrs. organist 1st Cong'l Ch., Evanston, Ill.; since 1897 organist Clinton Av. Cong'l Ch., Brooklyn; also concert organist; composer of songs and anthems; unmarried. Address: 354 Adelphi St., Brooklyn NY*

WHEELER, WILLIAM ARCHIE, agronomist, marketing specialist; b. Stockton, Minn., June 28, 1876; s. Charles and Sylvia M. (Allen) W.; B.Agr., U. of Minn., 1900, M.S., 1901; m. Harriet Maria Alden, June 3, 1901; children—Harold Alden, Helen, Margaret, Catherine, Harriet. Instr. bot., U. of Minn., 1898-1903; prof. bot. and head of dept., S.D. State Coll., 1903-07; sec. and mgr. Dak. Improved Seed Co., Mitchell, 1907-16; specialist in charge seed marketing, Bur. of Markets, U.S. Dept. Agr., 1916-19; in charge marketing information, same bur., 1920-22; chief, hay, feed and seed div., Bur. of Agrl. Economics, 1922-39; became special consultant in seed and forage marketing; Agricultural Marketing Service, 1939; in charge of greatly expanded vegetable seed production program of U.S. and of supplying all United Nations and neutrals with seeds under Lend-Lease Adminstrn. during World War II, 1941-46; dir. agr. research, Field Seed Inst. of N.A., since 1946. Commd. by Sec. of Agr. Houston to investigate and report on seed conditions in Europe immediately following signing of Armistice, 1919-20; initiated and supervised the publ. by the U.S. Dept. Agr., The Seed Reporter, 1918-19, and The Market Reporter, 1920-21; initiated and developed the field of broadcasting of official federal and state crop and market reports to agrl. interests by radio, 1920-21; U.S. Dept. Agr. rep. on Nat. Radio Service Commn.; apptd. by Secretary Wallace and P.M. General Hays to investigate use of radio for broadcasting information, 1921-22; rep. of U.S. Dept. of Agr. on 1st, 2d, 3d and 4th Nat. Radio confs., 1922-25. V.p. Nat. Corn Assn., 1908-11; mem. Sigma Xi, Am. Soc. Agronomy. Republican. Unitarian. Author: Forage and Pasture Crops, 1950. Editor of Farm Clip Sheet for Nat. Farm & Garden Bur., Chicago. Home: 3041 Sedgwick St., Washington 8 DC‡

WHEELWRIGHT, PHILIP ELLIS, educator; b Elizabeth, N.J., July 6, 1901; s. Charles Edward and Jessamine (Meeker) W.; A.B., Princeton, 1921, Ph.D. 1924; student Union Theol. Sem.; LL.D., University o California, 1968; married Maude Chase McDuffee June 8, 1940; 1 dau., Linda Jean. Instr. Latin Hun Prep Sch., 1923-24; instr. philosophy Princeton, 1924-25 instr. philosophy Washington Sq. Coll., N.Y.U. 1925-27, asst. prof., 1927-28, asso. prof., 1928-31, prof. 1931-35, chmn. philosophy dept., 1927-32; prof philosophy Dartmouth, 1937-53, chmn. div humanities, 1944-47; lectr. philosophy Bread Loaf Sch English, summers 1930, 42; vis. prof. philosophy Pomona Coll., 1953; prof. philosophy University o California at Riverside, 1954-66, professor emeritus 1966-70; research prof. Smith Coll., 1957-58; Churchil prof. U. Bristol, 1959-60; lectr. Amherst Coll., Vassa Coll., Wellesley Coll., Mt. Holyoke Coll., U. Tex., U. o South, Haverford Coll., Princeton, Yale, Syracuse U., U Mexico, U. So. Cal. Mem. American Philosophica Association (president Pacific division 1966), Am Assn. Aesthetics, English Inst., Soc. Am. Folklore, Ph Beta Kappa. Author: A Critical Introduction to Ethics 3d edit., 1959; The Way of Philosophy, 1954, rev. edit 1960; The Burning Fountain, A Study in the Language of Symbolism, 1954, rev. edit., 1968; Heraclitus, 1959 Valid Thinking, 1962; Metaphor and Reality, 1962; The Presocraties, 1966; The Hidden Harmony Essays Author of chapters in Language of Poetry, 1942, T. S Eliot on his Sixtieth Birthday, 1946. Editor: (with James Burnham), The Symposium, 1930-33. Contbr. article profl. jours., U.S. and Mexico. Home: Santa Barbara CA Died Jan. 6, 1970.

WHELAN, EDWARD J., univ. pres.; b. San Francisco Calif., Sept. 20, 1887; s. James J. and Mary A. (Kelly W.; A.B., U. of Santa Clara (Calif.), 1910; A.M Gonzaga U., Spokane, Wash., 1913; S.T.D., Coll. o Burgos (Spain), 1923; LL.D., Fordham U., 1930 Ordained priest Roman Catholic Ch., 1921; pres Loyola U., Los Angeles, Calif., 1942-49; Superio Manresa Retreat House, Azusa, Calif., since 1949 Home: Azusa CA Died Oct. 9, 1971; buried Catholic Cemetery, Santa Clara CA

WHELESS, JOSEPH, author, lawyer; b. Nashville Tenn., Nov. 13, 1868; s. Joseph and Ellen Thoma (Malone) W.; ed. Webb's Sch., Bellbuckle, Tenn., and under pvt. instructors; m. Mamie Willard Teasdale June 17, 1904. Admitted to Tenn. bar, 1889, Mo. ba 1895, N.Y. bar, 1920; practiced at Nashville and St Louis; specialized, after 1910, in Latin-Am. law an represented Am. interests in Mexico; associated wit Aldao, Campos & Gil, Argentine internat. firm, in Nev York office, 1919-24; mem. law staff of Western Unio Telegraph Co., 1924-32; now in gen. practice, specialt of Mexican and foreign law. Sent to S. America b Carnegie Endowment for Internat. Peace, 1915, t report on the industrial and economic effects of the wa in Argentina, Brazil and Paraguay. Speaks 5 moder langs. and has knowledge of 3 ancient langs. Maj., judg advocate, U.S. Army, on duty Central Dept., a Chicago, July 1917-Dec. 1918; instr. mil. law R.O.T.C U. of Ark., 1918; Army Intelligence Service (Spanis and Italian), May 1942-Oct. 1943. Mem. Rep. Count Com., N.Y. County, N.Y. Chmn. for Manhattan o Mayor's Com. on Tax Exemption and Tax Inequalities author of its report, 1934-35. Mem. Am., N.Y. State an New York County bar assns., Am. Law Inst., Am Arbitration Soc., A.A.A.S., New York Southern Soc Mo. Hist. Soc., Science League America, Inc., Nev York County Am. Legion (legal com.), S.C.V.; mem organization conv. of Am. Legion. Humanist Freethinker. Mason. Club: Authors. Autho Compendium of the Laws of Mexico, 1910, revise edition, 1938; Is It God's Word? (an exposition of fable and mythology of the Bible"), 1926; Forgery o Christianity, 1930; The Forgery Founded Church, 193 Debunking the Laws of Moses. Translator: The Civ Code of Brazil, 1920. Asso. editor (sect. comparativ law) Am. Bar Assn. Jour. Dir. and atty. for Freethinker of America, Inc. Also lecturer. Home: 780 Riverside Drive, New York 32 NY‡

WHELPLEY, MEDLEY GORDON BRITTAIN, b Bristol, New Brunswick, Can., Jan. 16, 1893; s. Charle Brown and Harriet (Brittain) W.; brought to U.S. i infancy; student Coe Coll., 1913-14, LL.D., 194 student University of Pa., 1914-15; m. Katharine M Dietz, Mar. 8, 1918; children—Gordon Brittain, Harrie (Mrs. Bruce C. Conklin), Katharine (Mrs. Georg Atcheson). With Harris Forbes and Company, Nev York, 1915-17, Mechanics & Metals Nat. Ban 1919-22, v.p., 1922-26; vice president Chase Nat. Ban 1926-28, Chase Securities Corp., 1928-30; organize 1930, and pres., dir. Am. Express Bank & Trust Co 1930-31; partner Guggenheim Brothers, 1931-4 assisted in reorganization Chilean nitrogen industry chairman Lautaro Nitrate Company, Ltd. (London 1932-44; pres. and dir. Pacific Tin Consol. Corp 1938-44, pres. and dir. Anglo-Chilean Nitrate Corp 1932-44; dir. U.S. Rubber Co. Trustee Solomon Guggenheim Found. Chairman committee for Contro of Nitrogen in Germany, National Engr. Council, 194 President Bond Club of N.Y., 1926-27. Studer Officers' Tng. Camp, Plattsburg, May-Aug. 1917; capt 305th F.A., 77th Div., N.A., Aug. 1917-June 1919; wit

A.E.F., France, Apr. 1918-Mar. 1919; cited in gen. orders for gallantry in action. Certificate of Merit for activities, World War II. Republican. Episcopalian. Clubs: Links, Racquet and Tennis. Home: New York City NY Died Mar. 23, 1968; buried Kensico Cemetery, Valhalla NY

WHIDDEN, BRUCE, banker; b. Dayton, O., Mar. 29, 1909; s. Howard P. and Katherine L. (Ganong) W.; B.A., McMaster U., 1931; grad. Stonier Grad. Sch. Banking, 1952; m. Kathleen T. Firestone, Dec. 20, 1941; children—W. Graham, Joyce T. (Mrs. Arnold J. Katz), Blair M. With Goodyear Tire & Rubber, 1932-36; securities rep. Otis & Co., Cleve., 1936-42; mem. trust devel. dept. Central Nat. Bank Cleve., 1942-44, asst. trust officer, 1944-47, trust officer, 1947-52, v.p. trust devel., 1952-63, v.p., gen. mgr. trust dept., 1963-66, sr. v.p. trust dept., 1966-72. Trustee Childrens Aid Soc., 1954, pres., 1956-58; trustee Laurel Sch., 1954, mem. financial com., 1955, treas., 1957; trustee Health Hill Hosp. for Convalescent Children, 1958, mem. exec. com., 1960-67; trustee Welfare Fedn. Cleve., 1962-72, chmn. solicitations com., 1965, treas., 1967. Mem. Am. Inst. Banking, Estate Planning Council Cleve. Clubs: Raquet, Skating, Union, Chargrin Valley Hunt (Cleve.). Home: Shaker Heights OH Died Mar. 17, 1972.

WHIPPLE, WILLIAM G., lawyer; b. Warehouse Point, Conn.; s. William J. and Pamelia Cook (Woodward) W.; A.B., Wesleyan U., Conn., 1857; LL.B., Albany Law Sch., 1859; m. Dencie S. Loomis, of Warehouse Point, 1862; 2d, Mary S. Dodge, of Little Rock, Ark., Oct. 26, 1870. U.S. dist. atty. Eastern Dist. of Ark., 1868-71; mayor Little Rock, 1887-91; register U.S. Land Office, Little Rock, 1897-1900; U.S. dist. atty., Eastern Dist. of Ark., since 1900; Rep. candidate for gov. Ark., 1892. Chancellor Episcopal Diocese of Ark., 16 yrs. Address: 415 Scott St., Little Rock AR‡

WHISTON, FRANK MICHAEL, realtor; b. Escanaba, Mich., July 6, 1894; s. Michael and Mary (Siles) W.; m. Frances Becker, Dec. 16, 1919; children—Robert (dec.), Jerome. Pres., chmn. bd. Frank M. Whiston & Co., Chgo. Pres. Central Bus. Dist. Com., Chgo., 1952-70; chmn. bd. Wabash Av. Assn., Chgo., 1938-70. Mem. Chicago Board of Education, 1948-70, president, 1964-70. Chairman of the lay board of Barat Coll., Lake Forest, Ill., St. Anne's Hosp., Chgo.; citizens bd. Loyola U., Chgo.; bd. dirs. Catholic Charities Chgo. Mem. Nat. Assn. Bldg. Owners and Mgrs. (past pres.). Clubs: Edgewater Golf (past pres.), Chgo. Dist. Golf Assn. (past pres.). Home: Chicago IL Died Sept. 8, 1970.

WHITACRE, FRANK EDWARD, physician; b. Wausau, Wis., 1897; M.D., Ia. State U., 1926. Intern U. Ill., Chgo., 1926-27, resident in obstetrics and gynecology, 1927-28; intern Chgo. Lying-In Hosp. and Dispensary, 1929, resident, 1930-31; resident in gynecology U. Chgo., 1931-32; asst. Womens Hosp., Leipzig (Germany) U., 1932; asst. path. labs. Womens Hosp., Berlin (Germany) U., 1936; asso. Ochsner Clinic, New Orleans, 1944; instr. U. Chgo. Clinics, 1933-35; prof., head dept. obstetrics and gynecology Peiping (China) Union Med. Coll., 1939-41; civilian prisoner war, physician Santo Tomas Internment Camp, Manila Philippines, 1942-43; prof., head dept. obstetrics and gynecology U. Tenn., Memphis, 1945, Vanderbilt U., Nashville, 1953. Diplomate Am. Bd. Obstetrics and Gynecology. Fellow A.C.S.; mem. A.M.A., Am. Gynecol. Soc., Am., Central assns. obstetricians and Nashville TN Died June 2, 1971.

WHITAKER, ALBERT CONSER, economist; b. Venango County, Pa., July 5, 1877; s. John Henry and Maud Lowrie (Conser) W.; A.B., Stanford U., 1899; Ph.D., Columbia, 1904; studied U. of Berlin, 1901-02; m. Mary Elizabeth Merritt, Mar. 26, 1901. Began as teacher economics, Stanford U., 1902, prof., 1911-42, prof. emeritus since Sept. 1942; lecturer in economics, U. of Calif., summer session, 1906, 11, 24; lecturer in same, Columbia, 1906-07; temporary prof. polit. economy, U. of Chicago, 1912-13. Mem. Am. Economic Assn. Club: Bohemian (San Francisco). Author: History and Criticism of the Labor Theory of Value; Foreign Exchange, 1919; and articles on economic subjects. Address: Stanford Univ CA‡

WHITAKER, HARRIET CATHERINE REED (MRS. CHARLES RICHARD WHITAKER);, b. Biltmore, N.C., July 8, 1869; d. Joseph and Catherine Harrison (Miller) Reed; ed. Asheville (N.C.) Female College, Judson Coll., Hendersonville, N.C.; m. Charles Richard Whitaker, April 5, 1887; 1 dau.—Louise Reed (Mrs. Ernest V. Perkinson); Portege Irene D. Latham (Mrs. Clyde A. Justice). President North Carolina Rebekah Assembly, 1909-11; president International Association Rebekah Assemblies, I.O.O.F., 1920-22; trustee J.O.O.F. Home, Goldsboro, N.C. Past president N.C. Tuberculosis Assn., past chmn. health N.C. Fed. Women's Clubs. Mem. Colonial Dames of XVII Century, Daughters Am. Colonists, Daughters Am. Revolution (past regent Alfred Moore and Col. Ninian Beall chapters, State regent N.C. D.A.R., 1928-31; past regent Edward MacDowell chapter), Daughters of Am. Revolution; also past regent Princess Herngua Chates D.A.R., St. Petersburg, Fla. past State chmn. Edn., Fla. D.A.R.; past chairman Health and Welfare Assn. of Moore County, N.C.; past state register Daughters of Founders of Pariots of America; past chmn. Henderson County Fall Festival Assn. A founder Patton Memorial Hosp., Hendersonville, N.C.; past. chmn. N.C. Radio Broadcast Com. of U.D.C. Pres. U.D.C. Chapter, Hendersonville, N.C. Democrat. Baptist. Club: Woman's of Hendersonville (1st v.p.). Home: 319 N. Main St., Hendersonville NC‡

WHITAKER, ORVIL R(OBERT), mining engr.; b. Frazesburg, O., Oct. 21, 1875; s. Reuben Barker and Jennie (Magruder) W.; M.E., Colo. Sch. of Mines, 1898; m. Mina Killgore, June 14, 1905; children—Mary, Charles Killgore (dec.), Orvil Robert, George Barker. Assayer and chemist Silver Lake Mines, Colo., 1898-99; supt. of mines H. C. Harrison properties, Mexico, 1900; asst. mgr. and engr. Silver Lake Mines, 1901-02; engr. Anaconda Copper Mining Co., Butte, Mont., 1902; foreman War Eagle Mines, Rossland, B.C., Canada, 1903; supt. of mines New York and Honduras Rosario Mining Co., Honduras, C.A., 1903-04; examining engr. Guggenheim Exploration Co., 1905; gen. supt. mines Compania Minera de Penoles, Mapimi, Duranzo, Mexico, 1906-11; gen. cons. and operating practice since 1912; cons. engr. Molybdenum Corp. of America, Howe Sound Co., Molybdenum Gold Mining Co., Aspen Leases, Humphreys Gold Corp.; has made extensive examinations for various large companies; conducted investigation of ore smelting contracts for State of Colo., 1918, Province of British Columbia, Canada, 1919. Mem. Am. Inst. Mining and Mining Engrs., Mining and Metall. Soc. of America, Colo. Soc. Engrs. Club: University (Denver). Home: 1819 Gaylord St. Office: Equitable Bldg., Denver CO*‡

WHITCHURCH, IRL GOLDWIN, educator, clergyman; b. Marissa, Ill., Sept. 7, 1889; s. Joseph Clinton and Caroline Sophia (Hachmeister) W.; A.B., Northwestern U., 1916; A.M. (grad. scholar), 1917; B.D., (traveling fellow), Garrett Bibl. Inst., 1919; Ph.D. (fellow Sage Sch. Philosophy), Cornell U., 1921; m. Anna Dean Kellman, Aug. 2, 1917; 1 son, Charles Goldwin; m. 2d, Dorothy Emmons Kremser-Stoddard, May 14, 1947; m. 3d, Jane Penny Boreing, Nov. 24, 1965. Student pastor Okla., Ill., N.Y., 1912-21; ordained to ministry Methodist Ch., 1912; instr. Garrett Bibl. Inst., 1921-23, registrar, asst. prof. theology, 1923-27, asso. prof. ethics and philosophy of religion, 1927-32, prof., 1932-45; dean Grad. Sch. Religion, prof. of philos. theology U. So. Cal., 1945-47; interim pastorates, Decatur and Peoria, Ill., Iowa City, 1927-32; lectr. schs. for ministerial tng. Meth. Ch., also philos., theol., civic and cultural clubs, 1921-69; pastor Old South Congl. Ch., Farmington, Me., 1953-56; founder First Congl. Ch. of Rangeley Region, 1956; mem. Sherwood Eddy Seminar, Eng., France, Yugoslavia, Russia, 1957; lectr. philosophy Springfield Coll., 1959-61, Denver U., 1962, Colo. U. Denver Center, 1962-68; minister Hilltop Community Ch., Parker, Colo., 1963-68, minister emeritus, 1968-69. Mem. Gov.'s Safety Council; chmn. co. fund drive A.R.C., 1952. Mem. corp. Franklin House. Mem. Internat. Platform Assn., Am. Philos. Assn., Am. Theol. Soc. (past pres., sec.-treas. Midwest br. 1942-45), Pi Epsilon Theta, Phi Chi Phi, Internat. Soc. Theta Phi. Clubs: University, Twenty, Sugarloaf Ski (dir.). Author: An Enlightened Conscience, Asceticism in the Platonic Writings, Philosophy Fascinates Me. Home: Parker CO Died Mar. 16, 1969; buried Fairmount Cemetery, Denver CO

WHITE, MRS. ALEXANDER B. (RASSIE HOSKINS);, b. Lexington, Miss.; d. Capt. E. and Lou (Pinkston) Hoskins; coll. edn.; m. Alexander B. White, banker, of Tenn., 1890 (died 1912); 1 dau., Mildred (wife of Dr. J. R. Wells). Pres. gen. U.D.C. two terms, 1911-13; state pres. Tenn. U.D.C., 1905-07; dir. gen. Shiloh Monument Com., 1907-18 (monument dedicated 1917); mem. D.A.R. Was editor U.D.C. dept. of The Confederate Veteran, 5 yrs., also mem. com. on history U.D.C., 1926-30, writing on monuments and memorials; founder Jefferson Davis Ocean to Ocean Nat. Highway. Clubs: Fortnightly (ex-pres.), Woman's, Sans Souci. Home: Paris TN (winter) Daytona Beach FL‡

WHITE, ALEXANDER M., investment banker; born Brooklyn, Mar. 24, 1904; s. Alexander Moss and Elsie Helen (Ogden) W.; grad. Poly. Prep. Country Day Sch., 1921; A.B., Harvard, 1925, LL.D., 1958; m. Mary Evelyn Lanman, Apr. 26, 1930; children—Sheila Ludlow, Alexander Moss, Jr., Elinor. With White Weld & Co., 1930-68, and partner, 1936-68; dir. Am. Cyanamid Co. Pres. Am. Mus. Natural History, 1951; trustee Bklyn. Children's Aid Soc., 1929-41, pres., 1939-41; overseer Harvard U., 1958-68. Served in U.S.N., 1941-45, disch. as comdr. Home: Oyster Bay NY

WHITE, ANDREW JOHN, JR., Lawyer; b. East St. Louis, Ill., Aug. 3, 1901; s. Andrew John and Anna Margaret (Von Nida) W.; B.S., Ohio State U., 1923, LL.B., 1926; m. Dorothy Mildred Veach, Apr. 8, 1927; children—Dorothy Jean (Mrs. Raymond Barr Robinson), Andrew John III. Admitted to Ohio bar, 1926, and practiced in Columbus. Mem. council, Village of Marble Cliff, O. 1942-52, mayor, 1952-54. Mem. Am., Ohio and Columbus bar assns., Internat. Assn. Ins. Counsel, Columbus Law Library Assn. (pres.), Gamma Eta Gamma. Lutheran (member executive board Synod of Ohio, United Luth. Ch. Am.). Mason (K.T., Shriner, 33 deg.; hon. supreme council No. Jurisdiction; past grand master). Clubs: University, York Temple Country (dir.). Co-author: Successful Jury Trials, 1952. Home: Columbus OH Died Mar. 3, 1970; interred King Cemetery Middlepoint OH

WHITE, (JOHN) BEAVER, engineer; b. Milroy, Pa., June 10, 1874; s. Rev. John W. and Mary Miller (Beaver) W.; B.S. in M.E., Pa. State Coll., 1894; M.E. in E.E., Cornell, 1899; m. in Buckinghamshire, Eng., Harriet H. Stevens, of Lewiston, Idaho, June 9, 1904 (died Mar. 25, 1928); children—Harriet, Clarissa, Joan, Louise; m. 2d, Margery Thompson Sperry, of London, Eng., July 25, 1934. Began with J. G. White & Company, engineers and builders, Baltimore, Md., 1894; gen. mgr. and engr. Eastchester Electric Co., Mt. Vernon, N.Y., 1896-98; practiced at Salisbury and Winston-Salem, N.C., 1899-1900; constructing electric light and power and street ry., San Juan, P.R., 1900-01; in Mandalay, Burma, and Hyderabad and Bombay, India, 1901-02; in charge street ry. constrn. in many cities in England, for J. G. White & Co., Ltd., 1902-04; financial dir. same company, in London, Eng., 1904-09; established firm Beaver White & Co., London, 1909; dir. Internat. Light & Power Co., Home and Foreign Securities Company. Member of American Relief Committee, London, 1914-15; dir. Commn. for Relief in Belgium, in charge purchase and shipping, London, 1914-15, in America, 1915-16; was mem. Advisory Com. for Belgian Relief; assisted in preliminary work of U.S. Food Administration; representative of U.S. Food Administrator on Exports Administrative Bd.; mem. War Trade Bd., representing the food administrator, Oct. 1917-Feb. 1919. Chmn. Am. delegation to Internat. Communications Conf., Paris, 1925; apptd. by President Coolidge del. to Internat. Radio Conf., Washington, 1927; apptd. by President Hoover as mem. Annual Assay Commn., 1933. Officer Order of the Crown, Belgium, 1919. Studying economic conditions in Eng., France and Germany. Home: Villa Nova PA Office: Land Title Bldg., Philadelphia PA‡

WHITE, BESSIE BRUCE, social worker; b. Venice, Mich., Nov. 10, 1876; d. Almon Gardner and Permelia (Wood) Bruce; A.B., Albion Coll., 1898, Dr. Humanities, 1935; A.M., Boston U., 1901; m. James Orm White, June 21, 1899; 1 dau., Elizabeth Almyra (wife of Lt. John Rankin Powers). Social worker at Union Bethal since 1910, now supt. and mem. bd. dirs. Trustee Albion College. Mem. Archaeol. Soc. America, Foreign Policy Assn., Pan-Am. League, Sch. of Religious Edn. (faculty), Delta Gamma (pres. alumni assn.). Republican. Methodist. Clubs: College, Woman's Board Zonta, City. Home: Third and Lytle Sts., Office: 501 E. Third St., Cincinnati OH‡

WHITE, BOUCK, author; b. Middleburg, N.Y., Oct. 20, 1874; s. Charles Addison and Mary (Bouck) W.; A.B., Harvard, 1896; grad. Union Theol. Sem., 1902; unmarried. Ordained Congl. ministry, July 1, 1904; minister, Clayton, N.Y., 1904-7, Lewis Av. Ch., Brooklyn, 1907-8; head resident, Trinity House, Brooklyn, 1908-13 (dismissed by the church on account of his socialism); pastor Ch. of the Social Revolution, New York City. Sentenced to Blackwell's Island as an agitator and in prison May-Nov., 1914; upon release resumed pastorate of the Revolutionists. Traveled extensively in Europe as war corr., summer of 1915, to study the subject, War and the Workers." Mem. Psi Upsilon. Author: Quo Vaditis, 1913; The Book of Daniel Drew, 1910; The Call of the Carpenter, 1911; The Mixing, 1913; The Immorality of Being Rich, 1914; A Message to the World, 1914; Letters from Prison, 1915; The Carpenter and the Rich Man, 1914; The Free City, 1919. In 1916, sentenced to N.Y. prison for attacking the principle of nationalism and suggesting the need of a new political ordering; re-sentenced to prison for repeating the Marlboro-on-the Hudson NY‡

WHITE, CHARLES STANLEY, surgeon; b. Washington, D.C., July 1, 1877; s. George and Adelaide (Harris) W.; M.D., Geo. Wash. U., 1898; Sc.D., 1946; m. Blanche M. Strong, Sept. 5, 1914; children—Charles Stanley, Mary Alice. Practiced at Washington, D.C., since 1898; hosp. interne 8 yrs.; specialized in surgery since 1908; prof. surgery, George Washington U., 1930-46; pres. Washington Med. Bldg. Corp., Columbia Medical Building Corp., Doctors Hospital, Inc.; surgical consultant to St. Elizabeth's and Gallinger Municipal Hosps. Trustee Geo. Washington U. Served as lt. comdr. Medical Reserve, U.S. Navy, 1918-21. Member American Board of Surgery. Fellow Am. Coll. Surgeons; mem. A.M.A., Med. Soc. of D.C. (ex-pres.), Sigma Xi, Phi Chi. Republican. Episcopalian. Mason. Clubs: Metropolitan, Army and Navy, University, Chevy Chase, Cosmos, Rotary (Washington); Loudoun Golf and Country. Contbr. to med. jours. Co-author med. volume. Washington DC Died Aug. 13, 1969; buried Rock Creek Cemetery Washington DC

WHITE, E(DWARD) LAURENCE, investment banker; b. Lowell, Mass., Aug. 11, 1884; s. Edward L.

and Ida V. (Mosely) W.; grad. St. Paul's Sch., Concord, N.H., 1903; student Harvard, 1904-06; m. Harriet W. Lancashire, Apr. 29, 1911; children—E. Laurence, Sarah White (Mrs. William G. Robinson). Began as mining engr. and operator; entered banking business, 1919, and engaged in banking as founder and partner firm of Watson & White, New York, N.Y.; pres. and dir. Investors and Traders, Inc., Watite Corp.; past dir. Internat. Utilities Corp. Clubs: Racquet and Tennis, Bankers (New York); Harvard (Boston). Home: Beverly Farms MA Died May 12, 1968; buried Mt. Auburn Cemetery, Cambridge MA

WHITE, EMMA EATON (MRS. EDWARD FRANKLIN WHITE), b. Black River Falls, Wis., Mar. 14, 1868; d. Albridge and Almira (Adams) Eaton; ed. normal sch., River Falls, Wis., and business coll., Canton, O.; LL.B., U. of Mich., 1894; spl. studies in lit. and history, State U. of Ia.; m. Edward Franklin White, Sept. 17, 1900 (dec.); 1 dau., Mira (Mrs. Franklin P. Lemons). Began practice of law at Creston, Iowa, 1894; legal editor West Publishing Co., St. Paul, Minn., 1897-1900, and Bobbs-Merrill Co., Indianapolis, 1915-20; dep. atty. gen. of Ind., 1921-25; reporter Supreme and Appellate courts of Ind., term, 1925-29; resumed law practice; now editor digest dept., Bobbs-Merrill Co. Legislative chmn. Gen. Fedn. Women's Clubs, 1920-24; 1st v.p., and legal adviser same, 1924-28, chmn. revisions, 1928-32; hon. vice-pres., trustee Indiana Federation of Clubs, 1929-32; mem. D.A.R., W.C.T.U., Pi Beta Phi, Phi Delta Delta. Republican. Mem. Christian (Disciples) Ch. Clubs: Women's Press, Woman's Rotary, Woman's Department Club. Home: 5222 E. Michigan St., Indianapolis IN*‡

WHITE, FRANCIS JOHNSTONE, educator; b. Decatur, Ill., Sept. 24, 1870; s. Henry and Minerva (Saunders) W.; student William Jewell Coll., Liberty, Mo., 1892-93; B.A., Ottawa (Kan.) U., 1898, M.A., 1901, D.D., 1914; grad. Rochester Theol. Sem., 1901; m. Ivy Edith Thompson, Aug. 7, 1901; children—Frances, Roberta, Gilbert, Philip. Ordained Bapt. ministry, 1897; missionary Am. Bapt. Fgn. Missionary Soc. to China, 1901; prin. Boys' Boarding Sch., Ningpo, 1901-04; prof. N.T. in Theol. Sem., Shaohsing, 1904-06; afounder, prof. history of religion, 1906-35, pres., 1912-28, pres. emeritus since 1935, U. of Shanghai (plant valued at over $1,200,000, faculty of 85 and 1,000 students in college). President East China Baptist Conf. Member American Acad. Polit. and Social Science, Royal Asiatic Soc., Soc. of Oriental Studies, Pi Gamma Mu. Club: El Camino Real. Author: (in Chinese) An Outline of Christian Theology, 1919; Character Building, 1927; A Christian College in China; The Struggle in the Far East; A History of the University of Shanghai; A Pilgrim of Asia. Address: University of Shanghai, Shanghai, Whittier CA‡

WHITE, GEORGE LORING, clergyman; b. Lake County, Ill., Feb. 15, 1872; s. Andrew J. and Abbie Chase (Smith) W.; A.B., U. of Chicago, 1898, B.D. from same, 1903, A.M., 1904; D.D., Grand Island (Neb.) Coll., 1925; m. Edna C. Pollock, Mar. 1, 1900; 1 son, Loring Pollock; m. 2d, Josephine Upton, June 8, 1920; children—Grace Upton, Frank Gwinn, Kenneth Harry. Ordained Baptist ministry, 1900; pastor McCook, Neb., 1900-03, Harvey, Ill., 1903-04; supt. Bapt. missions in Utah and Wyo., 1907-11; supt. work for Am. Bapt. Pub. Soc. in western states, 1911-19; joint sec., states west of Miss. River for Am. Bapt. Publ. Soc. and Am. Bapt. Home Mission Soc., 1919-23; western rep. Am. Bapt. Publ. Soc.; dir. Northern Bapt. Corr. Sch., 1923-26, western sec. Bapt. Ministers and Missionaries Benefit Bd., 1926-28; asso. sec. Bapt. Ministers and Missionaries Benefit Bd., 1928-41, field sec. 1941-43. Sec. of promotion and student aid of The Spanish-American Baptist Seminary of Los Angeles, 1943-45. Mem. Delta Tau Delta. Republican. Mason. Home: 700 Irving St., Alhambra CA‡

WHITE, H. LEE, attorney; born Oswego, N.Y., Aug. 13, 1912; s. Walter A. and Frances (Baslow) W.; A.B., Hamilton Coll., 1934; LL.B., Cornell, 1937; Doctor of Laws, Syracuse University, 1954; married Betty F. Johnson, Apr. 1, 1939. Admitted to N.Y. bar, 1937; spl. asst. to gen. counsel U.S. Casualty Co., N.Y.C., 1937-38; staff Pearis & Resseguie, Binghamton, N.Y., 1938-39; asso. Mangan & Mangan, Binghamton, 1939-41, partner, 1941-43; asso. Cadwalader, Wickersham & Taft, N.Y.C., 1946-49, partner, 1949-53, 1954-71; dir. Day Assos., Inc.; assistant sec. air force, 1953-54; chairman of bd. Trinity Shipping Group, Oswego Shipping Group, Am. Steamship Company, Boland & Cornelius, Inc., Reiss S.S. Co., Gartland S.S. Company, chmn. bd., president Marine Transport Lines, Inc.; dir. Am. Inst. Mcht. Shipping, International Minerals & Chemical Corporation, American S.S. Owners Mutual Protection & Indemnity Assn., Inc. Member Def. Adv. Com. on Profl. and Tech. Compensation, 1956; mem. Pres.'s Maritime Adv. Com. Bd. mgrs. Am. Bur. Shipping. Comdr. USNR, 1943-46, Office Secretary of the Navy. Recipient of the Secretary of Navy's Commendation Ribbon, 1945, Air Force Exceptional Meritorious Civilian award, 1954. Mem. Council Fgn. Relations, Am. Law Inst., Assn. Bar City N.Y., Am., N.Y. State bar associations, New York Chamber of Commerce, also mem. Theta Delta Chi. Episcopalian. Clubs: Canoe Brook Country (Summit, N.J.); Army Navy Country (Washington); Down Town Assn., Recess. Home: Short Hills NJ Died 1971.

WHITE, HENRY DALE, prof. pastoral theology; b. Skilly-scolvan, Dromore, County Down, Ireland, Mar. 25, 1869; s. John and Mary Dale (Wilson) W.; prep. edn., Mount Ida Nat. Sch., Banbridge, Ireland; student Park Coll. Acad., Parkville, Mo., 1891-93, Lake Forest (Ill.) Acad., 1894-96; A.B., Lake Forest College, 1909, D.D., 1921; grad. McCormick Theol. Sem., 1902; m. Charlotte Dickson, June 30, 1902 (died July 18, 1938); 1 daughter, Elizabeth Edwards (Mrs. Herbert Vincent Pate). Came to U.S., 1887, naturalized citizen, 1897. Ordained ministry Presbyn. Ch., 1902; missionary, Siam, 1902-19; served as editor North Siam News, 1910-19; prof. and dean McGilvary Theol. Training Sch., Siam, 1912-19; prof. systematic theology, Presbyn. Theol. Sem., Omaha, Neb., 1927-39, prof. pastoral theology since 1937; mem. of staff of Dundee Presbyn. Ch., Omaha. Served in Hosp. Corps, U.S.A., 1898-99. Asso. mem. Am. Schs. Oriental Research. Mem. Pi Gamma Mu. Republican. Mason; dept. chaplain U.S.W.V. Home: 3303 N. 21st St., Omaha NE‡

WHITE, IKE D., lawyer; b. La Vaca County, Tex., Apr. 26, 1867; s. James and T. Paralee (Close) W.; student Liberty Hill Normal and Business Coll., 1883-87; LL.B., Vanderbilt U., 1891; m. Susie Taylor, July 5, 1893. Admitted to Tex. bar, 1891; in practice at Burnet, Tex., 1891-1909; partner Cochran & White, Austin, Tex., 1909-14; sr. mem. of firm White, Taylor & Chandler, Austin, since 1941; gen. atty. Austin Transit Co. since 1909; dir. Austin Nat. Bank, County judge, Burnet County, Tex., 1898-1904. Democrat. Methodist. Episcopalian. Mason (Scottish Rite, Shriner). Address: 4108 Av. H., Austin TX*‡

WHITE, JAMES CHARLES, business exec.; b. Solon, Mich., Aug. 29, 1889; s. Andrew James and Clara Nellie (Ferris) W.; ed. business coll., Traverse City, Mich., 1905-07; LL.D. (hon.) King Coll., 1947, Brown U., 1953; m. Vera J. Wynkoop, Oct. 23, 1912; children—Dorothy N. (Mrs. Val Edwards), R. James, (dec.), Andrew, Barbara (Mrs. George T. Schilling). Partner A. J. White and Son, 1908-17; mgr. Hope Falls Logging Co., Northville, N.Y., 1919-20; expert on wood and timber operations Tenn. Eastman Corp., Kingsport, Tenn., 1920, successively plant supt., 1923-25, gen. supt., 1925-33, treas. and gen. mgr., 1933-35, v.p. and gen. mgr., 1934-45, dir., 1941-50, pres. and gen. mgr., 1945-61, chmn., 1961-69; chmn. Tex. Eastman Co., 1961-69; chmn. bd. Eastman Chem. Products, Tenn. Eastman Co., 1961-69, Tex. Eastman Co., 1961-69; chmn. bd. First Nat. Bank of Sullivan County; mem. bd. dirs. Kingsport Fed. Savings and Loan Assn., Community Chest, Kingsport, Tennessee; adv. bd. Holston Valley Community Hospital, Kingsport, Tenn.; director, vice president for Tennessee, Southern States Indsl. Council; pres. bd. trustees King Coll., Bristol, Tenn.; panel mem. Atomic Energy Symposium, Nat. Assn. Mfrs. Congress of Am. Industry, 1945. Served with U.S.A. as master engr. (s.g.), Tenth Engrs., 1917-19. Received Manhattan dist. special award for individual contribution to Atomic Bomb Program, 1945, Nathan W. Dougherty award, 1959. Decorated Order of the Purple Heart, 1919. Fellow A.S.M.E.; mem. Am. Chem. Soc., Am. Legion, Manufacturing Chemists' Assn. (past director). Republican. Presbyterian. Mason. Clubs: Ridgefields Country (Tenn.), Glen Lake Yacht (Mich.). Home: Kingsport TN Died Mar. 17, 1973.

WHITE, JAMES HALLEY, physician; b. Salt Lake City, May 21, 1906; s. James Iasic and Emma (Halley) W.; B.S., Okla. U., 1932, M.D., 1934; m. Gertrude June Wyatt, Dec. 21, 1933; children—Sally June (Mrs. George W. Salzman), Stephen H., Betsy C. (Mrs. Michael R. Osborn). Pvt. practice medicine, Wewoka, Okla., 1936-38; med. dir. Lowndes County Health Dept., Columbus, Miss., 1939-51, Weld County Health Dept., Greeley, Colo., 1952-67; mem. staff Weld County Gen. Hosp.; cons. in communicable diseases. Trustee Weld County Community Found. Fellow Am. Pub. Health Assn.; mem. Am. Assn. Pub. Health Physicians (charter mem.), A.M.A., Colo. Med. Assn., Colo. Pub. Health Assn. Home: Greeley CO Died June 21, 1967; interred Sunset Meml. Gardens Greeley CO

WHITE, JESSE HAYES, educator; b. Alamo, Montgomery Co., Ind., Mar. 5, 1877; s. John Marshal and Irene B. (Wirt) W.; A.B., Ind. U., Bloomington, 1903, A.M., 1904; fellow in psychology and edn., Clark U., 1906-08, Ph.D., 1908; m. Estella May Odle, of Selma, Ind., Sept. 7, 1912; children—Winifred Sharlene, Muriel Alberta, Jean Irene. Teacher pub. schs. Ind., 1896-99, asst. in exptl. psychology, Ind. U., 1903-04; supt. schs., Waveland, Ind., 1904-06; prof. psychology and edn., and head of dept., 1908-11, prof. and head of dept. of psychology, 1911-29, prof. psychology and dir. div. of research in personality problems, 1929-30, U. of Pittsburgh; pres. James Millikin U., 1930-34. Fellow A.A.A.S.; mem. Am. Psychol. Assn., N.E.A., Ill. State Teachers Assn. Republican. Home: 508 N. Fess Av., Bloomington IN‡

WHITE, JOHN P., govt. ofcl.; b. Mass., Dec. 18, 1915; student Boston Coll., 1935-40; m. Elaine A. White. Atty., Mass. Ho. of Reps., 1935-40; sec. staff gov. of Mass., 1940, legislative sec., 1953-57; legislative counsel, 1946-53; Congl. liaison officer Dept. State, 1957-69, then dep. asst. sec. for Congl. relations. Served to capt. AUS, 1940-45. Home: Rockville MD Died Oct. 2, 1969; buried Gate of Heaven Cemetery, Rockville MD

WHITE, JOHN PHILLIP;, b. Coal Valley, Rock Island Co., Ill., Feb. 28, 1870; s. Joseph and Catherine (Byrnes) W.; ed. pub. schs.; m. Ida Berthold, of Burlington, Ia., Feb. 27, 1891. Began as trapper boy in coal mines, at 14; sec.-treas. Ia. Miners' Assn., 1899-1904, pres. 1904-7 and 1909-10; internat. v.p. United Mine Workers of America, 1908, internat. pres. since Apr. 1, 1911. Associated with Hoynes Powder Co., Cleveland, O. Adviser to U.S. fuel administrator, Sept. 1917-Jan. 1, 1919; apptd. mem. commn. to consider differences bet. bituminous coal operators and miners, Dec. 1919. Del. to World's Mining Congress, London, 1906. Democrat. Catholic. Mem. Elks, Eagles, Foresters of America. Home: Cleveland OH‡

WHITE, JOSEPH HILL, sanitarian; b. Milledgeville, Ga., May 4, 1859; s. Edward J. and M.A. (Hill) W.; pvt. and high schs.; M.D., Coll. Phys. and Surg., Baltimore, 1883; m. Emily H. Humber, Jan. 8, 1885; children—Emily H. (Mrs. R.A. Herring), Mary Roberta, Josephine H., Joseph H. Entered U.S. Marine Hosp. Service (since changed to U.S. Pub. Health Service), Oct. 2, 1884; passed asst. surgeon, Oct. 1887; surgeon, Aug. 1898; detailed to asst. surg.-gen., in charge of service quarantine div., 1899-1903; senior surgeon, 1915; asst. surgeon gen., 1920; first chmn. National Leprosy Commn. Lecturer on hygiene and tropical diseases, University of Alabama, 1903-05. Sanitary work as quarantine officer, 1885-91; in charge of smallpox epidemic in Southern Ga., 1891; sanitary rep. of U.S. at Hamburg during cholera epidemic, 1893; inspecting quarantine officer from Norfolk to Jacksonville, 1894; in charge smallpox epidemic, Key West, Fla., 1896, yellow fever epidemics in La. and Miss., 1897-98; inspected the troops returning from Cuba, 1898; eliminated the yellow fever out-break at Soldiers' Home, Hampton, 1899; disinfected San Francisco after plague, 1900; given full control by nat., state and city authorities to stamp out yellow fever epidemic, New Orleans, 1905 (epidemic fully started—wiped out before frost, for first time in history of yellow fever); dir. for Latin-America, Internat. Health Commn., 1914. On request of sec. of war was detailed to war service, July 1917, and served through the war as gen. insp. of anti-malarial work for army; commd. col., May 1918; eradicated epidemic of yellow fever in Guatemala, Sept. 1918; chief general inspector U.S.P.H.S., February 1919-23. Vice director International Sanitary Bureau, 1920-25, retired; member Yellow Fever Council since 1921. Lecturer on public health, U. of Tenn. Summer School, 1915-19, and Peabody Coll., Nashville, Tenn. Decorated Grand Officer of Order of Quetzai by Govt. of Guatemala for distinguished service with commendation by the president personally, Jan. 1943. Chmn. Section of Hygiene and Sanitary Science A.M.A., 1909; pres. Am. Soc. Tropical Medicine, 1911; hon. mem. Orleans Parish Med. Soc.; U.S. del. 6th Internat. Sanitary Conf., Montevideo, 1920. Pioneer proponent of total eradication yellow fever and director yellow fever campaigns for International Health Board in all Latin-America, 1921-27. Clubs: Mobile Round Table (hon. life); Egyptians (Memphis); Cosmos (Washington). Author of many papers on sanitary science. Contbr. to Nelson's System of Medicine, 1927-29. Home: 2955 Newark St., Washington DC‡

WHITE, JOSH, singer; b. Greenville, S.C. 1908; married; 1 son, Josh. Tambourine, guitar player, traveled as Singing Christian; recorded numerous spirituals, as Pinewood Tom recorded blues songs; singer clubs and cafes, N.Y.C.; appeared in Broadway show, John Henry; starred in series Back Where I Came From, CBS; numerous concert appearances, some with son, Josh. Nat. tambourine champion.

WHITE, KEMBLE, lawyer; b. Bellton, W.Va., Apr. 5, 1873; s. Henry Solomon and Loviah Fields (Kemble) W.; prep. edn., Trinity Hall, Washington, Pa., and Lindsley Inst., Wheeling, W.Va.; A.B., W.Va. U., 1894, LL.B., 1900; m. Jane Louise Ferguson, of Greenville, S.C., Oct. 4, 1904; children—Harriet Kemble, Kemble. Admitted to W.Va. bar, 1900, and began practice at Fairmont; counsel Standard Oil Co. interests in W.Va. since 1906. Served as capt., W.Va. Vol. Inf., Spanish-Am. War; chmn. Selective Draft Bd., Marion Co., W.Va. Mem. com. to cooperate with legislative commn. to codify laws of W.Va; mem. W.Va. State Constl. Commn. Mem. Am. Bar Assn., W.Va. State Bar Assn. (mem. exec. council 1920-28; pres. 1924-25), Am. Law Inst., Alumni Assn. W.Va. U. (pres. 1921-24), Phi Sigma Kappa. Republican. Methodist. Club: Clarksburg Country. Home: Stonewall Jackson Hotel. Office: Hope Natural Gas Co. Bldg., Clarksburg WV‡

WHITE, LEE A., journalist; b. Flint, Mich., Nov. 23, 1886; s. Elam Worden and Clara May (Johnson) W.;

A.B., U. Mich., 1910, A.M., 1911; LL.D., Wayne State U., 1936; m. Florence Elizabeth Baker, July 1, 1912 (dec. 1943); children—Walton Stoddard, Elizabeth; m. 2d, Hazel Reavis, Mar. 17, 1945. Served successively as reporter, feature writer, copyreader, and editor extra editions Detroit News, 1911-14; asst. prof. journalism U. Wash., 1914-17, head dept., 1916-17; mem. editorial staff Detroit News, 1917-52, dir. pub. relations, 1936-52, ret.; asso. prof. rhetoric U. Mich., summer 1916; lectr. journalism U. Mich., 1917-18, U. Detroit, 1928; lectr. advt. Wayne State U., 1929-50; pres. La Choy Food Products, Inc., 1922-41, chmn. bd., 1941-43 (co. merged with Beatrice Foods, Inc.). Mem. Birmingham Village Commn., 1928-31, City Charter Commn., 1932-33; mem. Mich. Commn. on Reform and Modernization of Govt., 1938-39; mem. State Com. on Allocation of Sch. Appropriations, 1947-48, Mich. Commn. on Displaced Persons and Refugees, 1948-71, Director Cranbrook Sch., 1926-46, Kingswood Sch., 1930-52; trustee Cranbrook Acad. Art, 1945-52, Student Aid Found. Mich., Detroit Inst. Cancer Research; dir. pub. relations Cranbrook Instns., 1952-55; mem. bd. Internat. Inst. Med. Detroit, Met. Detroit council Am. Youth Hostels; chmn. nationality com. United Community Services; mem. adv. com. Wayne State U. dept. journalism, Michigan Citizens' Community Health; charter member, also trustee Friends Detroit Pub. Library, Friends Baldwin Pub. Library of Birmingham. Mem. U. Press Club of Mich. (ex-pres), Mich. Press. Assn., Mich. Welfare League (dir. 1952-55), Mich., Detroit hist. socs., Am. Acad. Polit. and Social Sci., Cranbrook Inst. Sci., Gerontological Soc., Soc. Medalists, Sigma Delta Chi (nat. historian 1912-18; nat. pres. 1921-22; editor The Quill (1915-20). Clubs: Prismatic, Torch (internat. pres. 1938-39). Author: The Detroit News; 1873-1917—A Record of Progress, 1918; (with others) Cranbrook Institute of Science: Its Founding and First Twenty-Five Years, 1959. Editor: Poems of Harold Brian Steele, 1908; Ihan New's When I Was a Boy in Korea, 1928. Co-author: Journalism in Wartime (symposium), 1943. Contbr. encys. and periodicals. Home: Birmingham MI Died Sept. 29, 1971.

WHITE, MARIAN AINSWORTH, lecturer; b. in England; d. Dr. John and M. E. Ainsworth; ed. in London and Paris; grad. Normal Sch. and Kensington Mus. Art Sch.; studied music under Sir Jules Benedict; m. London, 1870, J. Harrison White. In 1876-8 organized and conducted in London and Toronto, Can., choral classes of over 1,000 voices. Mem. Tonic Solfa Singing Soc., London; appeared in their concerts 7 yrs.; mem. Handel Choral Soc., London, 3 yrs. Asso. editor, Nat. Pop. Rev., 3 yrs.; editor art mag. 6 yrs.; edited and published The Greater West, 1905-6. Author: Essays and Criticisms on Am. Art and Artists; American History of Music, 1907. Contb'r to music and art publ'ns. Address: 1115 Pratt Av., Chicago IL‡

WHITE, PERCIVAL, marketing counselor; b. Winchendon, Mass., Jan. 8, 1887; s. Percival Wayland and Edith Frazar (Wheeler) W.; grad. Oahu Coll., Honolulu, T.H., 1904; post-grad. study same coll. 1 yr.; A.B., Harvard, 1909, A.M., 1910; research work, Lawrence Scientific Sch. (Harvard) and Mass. Inst. Tech., 1910; m. Mary Cliff; children—Matilda (Mrs. John W. Riley), Persis (Mrs. Louis MacMillen, Nancy (Mrs Calvin P. Bartlett), Jessica (Mrs. Meade Batchelor); m. 2d, Pauline Arnold. Feature writer for Denver Post, later Boston Post, 1910-12; mng. dir. Percival White Engring. Works, mfrs. motor cars, Highbury, London, Eng., 1912-14; mgr. Percival White Engring. Works, East Milton, Mass., 1915-17; automobile expert to Ordnance Dept., U.S. Army, Rock Island Arsenal, Ill., 1917; master mechanic and mgr. mech. and maintenance depts., U.S. Gas Defense Plant, Long Island City, N.Y., 1918; dir. of development, and foreign rep. in Europe, Aluminum Mfrs., Inc. (Aluminum Co. of America), 1919-20; co-founder with Pauline Arnold, Market Research Co. Am., cons. to Crowell Pub. Co., Internat. Mag. Co., Macfadden Publs., Ford Motor Co., Gen. Motors Corp., others, 1919-52, head business specialist, War Production Board, 1942; general manager, White engineering Works, product developers, Stamford, Conn., 1942-51; partner White and Arnold, N.Y.C., from 1951; dir. Telautograph Corp. Mng. dir. Am. Econ. Found., 1935; dir. research Amputees Research Found. Am., Inc. Mem. President Hoover's Emergency Com. for Employment, 1930-31. Mem. Market Research Council, Am. Soc. Mech. Engrs., Soc. Automotive Engrs., Soc. Industrial Engrs., Am. Marketing Assn., Am. Statis. Assn., Mass. Soc. Mayflower Descendants, Inst. of Automobile Engrs. (London), Business Research Assn. of Great Britain (London, England). Clubs: Harvard (New York); Sunrise Flying (L.I.); Stamford (Conn.) Yacht. Author or co-author books relating to field, 1921-70, including Rate Yourself, 1958; Food, America's Biggest Business, 1959; Homes, The Building Business, 1960; Clothes and Cloth, America's Apparel Business, 1961; Money, Make It, Spend It, Save It, 1962; The Automation Age, 1963; How We Named Our States, 1965; Food Facts for Young People, 1968; Young Explorers of the Northwest, 1968. Home: Pound Ridge NY Died June 4, 1970.

WHITE, PHILIP (RODNEY), research physiologist; b. Chgo., July 25, 1901; s. Henry K. and Mary J. (Pattee) W.; A.B., University of Montana, 1922, D.Sc. (hon.), 1956; student University of Wash., 1922-23, Ecole Normale d'Instituteurs, Valence, France, 1923-24; Ph.D., Johns Hopkins, 1928; guest investigator, U. Berlin, Germany, 1930-31; m. Caroline D. M. Smith, Nov. 22, 1935; children—Christopher John, Jonathan Peter (dec.). Asst. botany U. Mont., 1920-21; grad. asst. U. Wash., 1922-23; lectr. d'Anglais, Ecole Normale d'Instituteurs, Valence, France, 1923-24; microscopic technician Bur. Plant Industry, Dept. of Agr., 1925-26; research asst. botany and U. Fellow Johns Hopkins, 1924-26; Johns Hopkins Tropical Expdn., Jamaica, B.W.I., 1926; spl. investigator United Fruit Co., Jamaica, Panama, Costa Rica, 1926-28; asst. prof. botany and plant physiology U. Mo., 1928-29; Nat. Research Council fellow, Boyce Thompson Inst. for Plant Research, 1929-30; Rockefeller Found. fellow Pflanzenphysiologisches Inst., U. Berlin, 1930-31; fellow dept. animal and plant pathology, Rockefeller Inst. for Med. Research, Princeton, N.J., 1932-34, asst., 1934-38, asso., 1938-45; sr. mem., dir. div. gen. physiology Inst. for Cancer Research, Phila., 1945-51; research asso. Roscoe B. Jackson Meml. Lab., Bar Harbor, Me., 1951-56, sr. staff scientist, 1957-66. Summer lectr. Ia. State Coll., 1942; guest prof. Yale, 1947-48; in charge summer tissue culture program Mt. Desert Island Biol. Lab., 1947-53; exchange prof. University of Paris, 1958-59; Distinguished visiting prof. Pa. State University, in 1963; lecturer University Me., 1965-66, univs. Delhi, Poona, Bombav, Baroda, Calcutta. 1967-68. Recipient Centenary medal; Societe Bot. de France, 1954, Medal of Honor, U. of Liege, 1959; Philip White lectureship founded in his honor Indian Acad. Scis. Fellow Am. Acad. Arts and Scis., A.A.A.S. (Cleveland medal 1965); mem. Am. Soc. Plant Physiologists (Stephan Hales award, 1940). Internat. Soc. Cell Biology, Soc. Study Growth and Devel., Am. Bot. Soc., Internat. Society Plant Morphology, Am. Soc. Naturalists, Tissue Culture Assn. (pres. 1958-59). Soc. Gen. Physiologists, Scandinavian Society Plant Physiology. Societe Francais de Physiology Veget Sigma Xi. Sigma Upsilon. Phi Sigma. Author: A Handbook of Plant Tissue Culture, 1943; Micrurgical and Germ-Free Methods (with others). 1943: Cultivation of Animal and Plant Cells, 1954, rev. edit. 1963. Home: Bar Harbor ME Died Mar. 25, 1968; buried West Parish Cemetery, Winchester NH

WHITE, WALTER W(ILLIAM), pub.; born Highland Park, Ill., Feb. 4, 1900; s. Charles Henry and Agnes (Jones) W.; LL.B., University of Nebraska, 1923; married Frances Whitmore, October 24, 1923; children—Sarah Whitmore (Mrs. Robert L. Grainger), Charles Whitmore. Advertising rep. Lincoln (Neb.) Star, 1920-24, classified advt. mgr., 1924-27, advt. dir., 1927-43, bus. mgr., 1943-44, pub., 1944-69; sec.-treas. and dir. Journal-Star Printing Co., 1950-69; chmn. Mail-O-Graph; v.p., dir. Lee Foundation; executive vice pres., and director Lee Enterprises, Inc., 1950-69; exec. v.p., director KFAB Broadcasting Company Omaha, Nebraska, 1943-69; dir. Woodmen Accident & Life Company. Chairman Tuberculosis Assn. Christmas Seal sales, 1945-46, vice pres., Lancaster County Tb Assn., 1949, pres., 1950; mem. Lincoln and Lancaster County Safety Council, also post-war planning com.; chmn. Lincoln scrap metal drive and mem. Lincoln war appeals review bd.; mem. defense publicity and pub. relations com. for civilian defense, War Aid Com. N.A.E.A. Adv. to Treasury Dept.; mem. Gov.'s Human Relations Committee, 1953-54. Trustee U. Neb., ANPA Found. Mem. Am. Bar Assn., Inland Daily Press Assn., Newcomen Soc. of North America, Better Bus. Bur. (pres. 1943, chmn. bus. expansion com., 1949), Lincoln C. of C. (pres. 1944), Neb. and Lincoln Real Estate Bds. (sec. 1925-26), Neb. Newspaper Advt. Mgrs. Assn. (pres. 1939), Neb. Reclamation Assn., Am. Newspaper Pubs. Assn., Inc. (mem. bd., dir.; mem. bd. Research Inst. Inc.), Newspaper Advt. Exec. Assn., Neb. State Bar Assn., Neb. Art Assn., Asso. Press. Phi Delta Theta, Phi Delta Phi, Sigma Delta Chi. Presbyn. Mason (Scottish Rite, Shriner), Elk. Clubs: Lincoln University, Lincoln Country. Home: Lincoln NE Died Aug. 7, 1969; buried Lincoln Meml. Cemetery, Lincoln NE

WHITE, WILLIAM ALFRED, musician; b. at Baltimore, Mar. 9, 1876; s. Peter Low and Anastasia (Smith) W.; ed. high school, Baltimore; mus. edn. Clavier Piano Sch., New York, Peabody Inst., Baltimore, Columbia U.; m. Eugenia Katherine Small, of Fayetteville, N.C., Aug. 19, 1896; 2d, LaDora Gertrude Wright, March 2, 1913. In charge of music, N.C. Agrl. and Mech. Coll., and State Sch. for Blind, 1893-1901; in charge dept. of theory, Clavier Piano Sch., New York, 1901-3; prof. music, Syracuse U., 1903-9; dean Sch. of Music, State Normal Sch., Bowling Green, Ky., 1909; dir. dept. sch. music, Northwestern U., 1910-13; head of theory dept., Lyceum Arts Conservatory, Chicago, 1913-14; dir. of music, independent school dist., Des Moines, Ia., 1914-—. Was in charge of theory dept., Am. Inst. of Normal Methods, Chicago and Boston, 1905-11; lecturer, College of Education, University of Chicago, 1911. Member National Assn. of Musicians, N.Y. State Music Teachers' Assn., Assn. Nat. Supervision, Internat. Musick Gesellschaft. Author: Harmony and Ear Training; Harmonic Part Writing, 1911; Beginner's Book of Songs, 1912. Educational editor of The Lyric Music Series, 1913; Lake High School Song Book, 1915; Songs Without Words, 1917. Contbr. ednl. journals. Address: Garfield School, Des Moines IA‡

WHITE, WILLIAM L(INDSAY), newspaperman; b. Emporia, Kan., June 17, 1900; s. William Allen and Sallie (Lindsay) W.; student Kan. State U., 1918-20; A.B., Harvard, 1924; m. Kathrine Klinkenberg, Apr. 29, 1931; 1 dau., Barbara. Reporter on Emporia Gazette, 1914, later circulation mgr., managing editor, editorial writer, asso. editor and pub.; staff Washington Post, 1935, Fortune Mag., 1937; war. corr. for 40 Am. daily newspapers, also rep. Columbia Broadcasting System, European corr., 1939-40; Christmas, 1939, broadcast from Mannerheim Line in Finland; awarded first prize by Nat. Headliners Club as year's best European broadcast; went to England on one of 50 former American destroyers to represent North American Newspaper Alliance and Reader's Digest in London winter of 1940-41; became roving editor The Readers Digest, 1942. Chairman Rep. County Com., Lyon County, 1933-34; mem. Kan. State Legislature, 1931-32. Served in S.A.T.C., 1918. Member bd. of overseers Harvard University, 1950-56. Fellow Am. Numis. Soc.; mem. Am. Civil Liberties Union (dir.), Theodore Roosevelt Meml. Assn. (dir.), Bill of Rights Commemorative Soc. (dir.). Conglist. Clubs: Players, Century, Harvard, Overseas Press (New York City); National Press (Washington, D.C.). Author: What People Said," (novel), 1938; co-author Zero Hour" (foreign affairs), 1940; author Journey for Margaret" (war-time travel), 1941; They Were Expendable, 1942; Queens Die Proudly, 1943; Report on The Russians, 1945; Report on the Germans, 1947; Lost Boundaries, 1948; Land of Milk and Honey, 1949; Bernard Baruch, 1951; Back Down The Ridge, 1953. Contbr. to Reader's Digest. Home: Emporia KS Died July 26, 1973.

WHITE, WILLIAM WURTS, banker; b. Providence, Aug. 12, 1909; s. William Wurts and Janet (Innis) W.; grad. St. Marks Sch., 1928; B.A., Yale, 1932; m. Lilla Carlton Sammis, June 25, 1932; children—William Wurts, Sarah Woodhull (Mrs. Anthony Coates), Lilla Carlton (Mrs. Brierly Woodhouse). Clk., R.I. Hosp. Trust Nat. Co., Providence, 1932-40, asst. sec., 1940-49, v.p., 1949-57, exec. v.p., 1957-69, dir., 1959-69, vice chmn., 1962; dir. Providence Lithograph Co. (Providence), Crompton Co. (N.Y.C.), Dieges & Clust, Hill Realty Co.; treas. Sycamore Cove Co., Ltd.; v.p., treasurer Eta Realty Company; trustee Bus. Devel. Co. R.I. Chmn. R.I. Recreational Bldg. Authority. Treas., trustee Hosp. Service Corp. R.I. (Blue Cross); former trustee Indsl. Found. R.I.; trustee, Providence Lying-In Hosp.; treas. University of R.I. Found. Served from 1st lt. to capt., Med. Adminstrv. Providence RI Died Nov. 7, 1969.

WHITEFORD, WILLIAM KEPLER, petroleum exec.; b. Los Angeles, Nov. 28, 1900; s. Gustavus A. and Grace (Kepler) W.; student Stanford U.; m. Asenath Louise Mitchell, June 22, 1927; children—William Kepler, Jr., Peter. Exec. v.p. British Am. Oil Producing Co., Toronto Pipe Line Co., 1935; exec. v.p. British Am. Oil Co., Ltd., Toronto, 1942-43, pres., 1943, chmn. bd. 1951; exec. v.p. Gulf Oil Corp., 1951, pres., 1952, chief exec. officer, 1957-65, dir., chmn. bd., 1960-65; dir., mem. advisory bd. Internat. Nickel Co. Can., Ltd., 1960-65; director of Gen. Motors Corp., Procter &Gamble, Stouffer Corp., Jones & Laughlin Steel Corp. Mem. Gamble, Stouffer Corp., Jones & Laughlin Steel Corp. Mem. American Institute Mining and Metall. Engineers, Alpha Tau Omega. Home: Ligonier PA Died Sept. 11, 1968; buried St. Michael's of the Valley, Ligonier PA

WHITEHEAD, HENRY C., army officer; b. Mar. 22, 1873; grad. U.S. Mil. Acad., 1896; distinguished grad. Army Sch. of the Line, 1911; grad. Army Staff Coll., 1912. Commd. add. 2d lt. cav., June 12, 1896; promoted through grades to col. Q.M.C., June 30, 1920; col. Signal Corps (temp.), Sept. 1917-Aug. 1919; apptd. asst. to q.m. gen. with rank of brig. gen. for 4 yrs. from Apr. 16, 1930; retired, Feb. 28, 1934. Home: Winchester KY*‡

WHITEHEAD, ROBERT FREDERICK, law Examiner Patent Office; born at Lovingston, Virginia, February 28, 1869; son of Robert and Margaret (Baldwin) D.; Ph.B., University of Virginia, 1892, A.B., A.M., 1893; graduated study, Johns Hopkins, 1895-96 and 1899-1900; studied law Natural University, Washington, D.C., 1902-04; m. Edmonia Ware Powers, Dec. 27, 1904; 1 dau., Roberta Macky. Began with U.S. Patent Office, as asst. examiner, 1902, successively apptd. law examiner, 1909, asst. commr., 1914, 1st asst. commr., 1916, commr., 1920 (resigned 1921, reinstated 1923), solicitor, 1934, retired June 30, 1939, reinstated May 13, 1942, as law Examiner, retired Mar. 31, 1946. Democrat. Episcopalian. Home: 1524 28th St. N.W., Washington DC‡

WHITEHEAD, T(HOMAS) NORTH, coll. prof.; born Cambridge, Eng., Dec. 31, 1891; s. Alfred North and Evelyn Willoughby (Wade) W.; student Bedales

Sch., Petersfield, Hampshire, England; B.A., subsequently M.A. (Economics Tripos), Trinity College, Cambridge U. 1913; studied engring., U. Coll., London U., 1913-14, 1919-20; m. Margaret Schuster, Nov. 3, 1920 (died 1947); step-children—Roy Arthur Dehn, Sheila Dehn (Mrs. Myron Piper Gilmore); 1 s., Eric Arthur North; m. 2d, Harriet James Eaton, July 20, 1948; one son, George Alfred North. Science officer British Admiralty, 1921-31; assistant, later associate professor Harvard Grad. Sch. Bus. Administrn., 1931-39, 43-58; dir. of Management Training Program, Radcliffe Coll., 1944-55; advisor on Am. Affairs, British Foreign Office, London, 1940-43. Commissioned officer British Army, 1914-19, in France and East Africa; private British Home Guard, 1940-42. F., A.A.A.S. Author: The Design and Use of Instruments and Accurate Mechanism, 1934; Leadership in a Free Society, 1936; The Industrial Worker, 1938; also many articles. Home: Cambridge MA Died Nov. 22, 1969.

WHITEHOUSE, BROOKS, lawyer; b. Portland, Me., Apr. 21, 1904; grad. Phillips Exeter Acad.; A.B., LL.B., Harvard. Admitted to Me. Bar, 1928; partner firm Verrill, Dana, Philbrick, Whitehouse & Putnam, Portland. Mem. Am., Me., Cumberland bar assns. Home: Portland ME Died 1969.

WHITEHOUSE, FLORENCE BROOKS, author; b. Augusta, Me.; d. Samuel Spencer and Mary Caroline (Wadsworth) Brooks; ed. St. Catherine's Hall, Augusta; music in Boston under pvt. tutors, also languages, drawing and painting; m. Robert Treat Whitehouse (q.v.), June 19, 1894. Vocalist in Rossini Club, of Portland, Me. Traveled in Europe, Syria and Egypt, 1891-2. Author: The God of Things, 1902; The Effendi, 1904; also several plays, all of which have been produced. Address: 42 Deering St., Portland ME‡

WHITEHOUSE, ROBERT TREAT, lawyer; b. Augusta, Me, March 27, 1870; s. William Penn (q.v.) and Evelyn M. (Treat) W.; A.B., Harvard U., 1891, LL.B., 1893; m. Florence Brooks, June 19, 1894. Admitted to bar, 1893; county atty. Cumberland Co., Me., 1900; U.S. district attorney, District of Maine, 1906-14; Republican. Author: Equity Jurisdiction, Pleading and Practice in Maine, 1900; Criminal Directions and Forms, 1913; Whitehouse's Equity Practice (3 vols.), 1914. Pres. State Bd. Charities and Corrections, 1913—. Home: 108 Vaughan St. Office: 85 Exchange St., Portland ME‡

WHITEHOUSE, VIRA BOARMAN (MRS. NORMAN DE R. WHITEHOUSE), suffragist; b. Va., Sept. 16, 1875; d. Robert and Cordelia (Terrell) Boarman; ed. Newcomb Coll., New Orleans, La.; m. Norman de R. Whitehouse, of N.Y. City, Apr. 30, 1898; 1 dau., Alice. Active worker and speaker in behalf of woman suffrage since 1913, when became chmn. publicity council of the Empire State Campaign Com.; made chmn. N.Y. State Woman Suffrage Party, Jan. 4, 1916; leading factor in securing woman suffrage for N.Y. State at state election, Nov. 6, 1917; sent to Europe by U.S. Govt., Jan. 10, 1918, on spl. mission to organize publicity to combat the German propaganda and make plain the aims of the Am. people. Pres. and majority stockholder Whitehouse Leather Products Co., 1920-30. Mem. Pi Beta Phi. Episcopalian. Clubs: Colony, City. Author: A Year as a Government Agent, 1920. Home: 791 Park Av., New York; (summer) Newport RI‡

WHITEIS, WILLIAM ROBERT, surgeon; b. Urbana, Ia., Aug. 10, 1869; s. Uriah Boyd and Emeline (Sprott) W.; B.S., State U. of Ia., 1892, M.S., 1895, M.D., 1895; studied U. of Leipzig, 1895, U. of Vienna, 1896-97, London, 1897; m. Alice Fernstrom, of Lone Tree, Ia., Aug. 10, 1892. Prof. histology and embryology, 1898, asst. to chair of otology, rhinology and laryngology, 1901, asst. prof. gynecology and obstetrics, 1903-14, prof. gynecology and obstetrics, and head of dept., 1914-21, U. of Iowa; was made dir. State U. of Ia. Hosp., 1904, pres. hosp. staff, 1907, acting surgeon, 1913; staff Mercy Hosp., 1924—. Mem. A.M.A., Ia. State Med. Soc., Johnson Co. Med. Soc., Sigma Nu. Rotarian. Home: 15 1/2 S. Dubuque St., Iowa City IA*‡

WHITELAW, JOHN BERTRAM, educator; b. N.Y. City, Oct. 3, 1905; s. Aubrey George and Norah Beatrix (Osborne) W.; Ph.B., Yale, 1929, Ph.D., 1935; m. Helen Chase Streeter, June 28, 1930; 1 son, John Streeter. Teacher Brooks Sch., North Andover, Mass., 1929-31; grad. fellow Yale, 1931-34; instr., asst. prof. Smith Coll., 1933-35; asst. prof. edn., acting dean School Edn. George Washington U., 1935-37; head, dept. edn. State Tchrs. Coll., Brockport, N.Y., 1937-41; gen. supervisor pub. schs., Newton, Mass., 1941-42; training adviser personnel div. War Manpower Commn., Washington, 1942-43; asst. dir. Fgn. Service Inst., Dept. State, 1946-47; prof. edn., chmn. dept. edn. Johns Hopkins, 1947-51; ednl. advisor CIA, Washington, 1951-55; specialist for tchr. edn. Office Edn., Dept. Health, Edn. and Welfare, 1955-66; consultant in education and mgmt., 1966-68; dir. instl. research and devel. Asheville-Biltmore Coll. (N.C.), 1967-68; regional training officer for Tropical Africa, Agy. Internat. Development, 1959-62; prof. U. Chgo. summers 1939-40; cons. Resettlement Adminstrn., summer 1935, Am. Council Edn., summer 1938; community study workshops Balt. Pub. Schs., 1948-50; member of U.S. Ednl. Mission to USSR, 1958. Served from lt. (j.g.) to lt. comdr. USNR, 1943-46. Mem. Am. Assn. School Adminstrs. (life), N.E.A. (life), Phi Delta Kappa. Clubs: Elihu, Elizabethan (New Haven); 14 W. Hamilton Street (Balt.); Mountain City (Asheville). Author: The School and Its Community, rev., 1951. Contbr. ednl. publ., jours. Home: Arden NC Died Aug. 5, 1968.

WHITELEY, ISABEL NIXON, author; b. New York; d. Rev. J. Howard and Flora H. (Jewell) Nixon; m. Nov. 6, 1879, Henry Whiteley. Mem. Contemporary Club, Am. Catholic Hist. Soc., Confraternity of St. Gabriel. Author: The Falcon of Langeac, 1897 H20; For the French Lilies, 1898 H20. Residence: Rome Italy‡

WHITELEY, JAMES GUSTAVUS, writer; b. nr. Baltimore, July 9, 1866; s. William Stevens and Elizabeth Emmeline (Holmes) W.; ed. at private schs. and under private tutors; m. Emily Baily Stone, December 16, 1896; 1 dau., Sophia Bainbridge (Mrs. S. Bainbridge Fonda); m. 2d, Bernadine Allen Miller. Unofficial representative of President of U.S. at The Hague, 1898, of Le Congres Internat. d'Histoire Diplomatique, of which was v.p. and a founder. Mem. Internat. Com. which organized Le Congres International d'Histoire Comparee, Paris, 1900; official del. of U.S. Govt. to same; apptd. consul of the Congo Free State by H.M. Leopold II, 1904, consol-gen., Sept. 1, 1905; apptd. consul of Belgium at Baltimore, Dec. 1916; attached to Belgian spl. mission to U.S. during its visit, June-Aug. 1917; hon. attache to Belgian Mil. Mission, 1918-19, Knighted by King Leopold, 1909, and created Chevalier de l'Ordre de la Couronne (Belgium); created Commander de l'Ordre de Leopold II, Nov. 1917, for service to Belgian mission, Chevalier de l'Ordre de Leopold, 1924; promoted Comdr. of Order of the Crown, 1931; Officer of Ordre de l'Etoile Africaine (Belgium). Fellow Royal Hist. Soc. (Eng.); mem. Inst. Internat. Colonial; v.p. Belgian League of Honor; mem. Am. Soc. Internat. Law; hereditary companion Mil. Order Foreign Wars; hon. mem. (with medal) Royal Zool. Soc. of Antwerp; pres. Consular Soc. of Baltimore. Sec. Nat. Com. of U.S. for the Restoration U. of Louvain; sec.-gen. of Central Com. of Belgian Relief Fund, which organized Belgian relief cons. in 33 states, 1914-18; consul gen. of Belgium, at Baltimore since 1928. Awarded Medaille Civique, for 25 yrs. service as Belgian consul general, 1945. Catholic. Extensive contbr. to principal American and foreign revs. on subjects of internat. law, diplomatic history and foreign affairs. Address: 223 W. Lanvale St., Baltimore 17 MD‡

WHITEMAN, SAMUEL DICKEY, natural gas co. exec.; b. Mercer, Pa., July 24, 1900; s. Joseph D. and Mellie (Dickey) W.; B.S. in Indsl. Engring., Pennsylvania State University, University Park, 1922; children—Sara Jane (Mrs. Joseph A. Sonneland), Samuel Dickey, Joseph David; m. 2d, Mabel Tucker, Nov. 24, 1963. Assistant general mgr. Lakeshore Gas Co., Astabula, O., 1923-28; gen. mgr. Owensboro Gas Co. (Ky.), 1929-30; v.p., gen. mgr. Sioux Falls Gas Co. (S.D.), 1930-40; v.p., treas., dir. Kokomo Gas & Fuel Co. (Ind.), 1940-41; with Kan.-Neb. Natural Gas Co., Inc., 1941-72, pres., 1946-61, chmn. bd., 1961-72, also dir.; pres. dir. Excelsior Oil Corp., 1955-72; dir. City Nat. Bank, Hastings. Pres. Overland Trails council Boy Scouts Am., 1954-57, mem. exec. com., 1957-mem. Nat. council, 1960-72. Trustee Mary Lanning Meml. Hosp., Hastings; bd. dirs. Big Brothers Hastings. Served with U.S. Navy, World War I. Mem. Am. (past dir.), Midwest (past pres.) gas assns., Ind. Natural Gas Assn. Am. (dir.) Asso. Industries Neb. (past dir.), Nat. Petroleum Council, N.A.M., Rocky Mountain Oil and Gas Assn. (dir.), Interstate Oil Compact Commn., Am. Legion, Phi Kappa Sigma. Episcopalian. Mason (Shriner), Rotarian, Elk. Home: Hastings NE Died July 6, 1972; buried Hastings NE

WHITFORD, ALFRED E(DWARD), dean; b. Milton, Rock County, Wis., Sept. 4, 1875; s. Albert and Chloe Eliza (Curtis) W.; B.A., Milton (Wis.) Coll., 1896; B.A., U. of Chicago, 1900; M.A., U. of Wis., 1911; hon. Sc.D., Alfred U., 1926; m. Mary Whitford, Aug. 15, 1900; children—Alfred Edward, Dorothy Euphemia (Mrs. Nelson C. Lerdahl); m. 2d, Ruth A. Rogers, Dec. 27, 1938. Teacher, Waupun (Wis.) High Sch., 1896-97; prin. public schools, Milton, 1897-99; prof. physics and asst. mathematics, Milton Coll., 1901-11, prof., mathematics and physics, 1911-23, prof. mathematics, 1923-30, registrar, 1903-21, acting pres., 1921-23, pres., 1923-30; lecturer mathematics, U. of Wis., 1930-32; prof. mathematics, Alfred (N.Y.) U. since 1932, dean Coll. Liberal Arts; 1934-46, dean emeritus since 1946. Mem. Math. Assn. America, Am. Assn. Univ. Profs. Seventh Day Baptist. Home: 60 W. University St., Alfred NY‡

WHITING, FRED, journalist, educator; b. Glenville, W.Va., June 21, 1915; s. Fred M. and Frankie (Craddock) W.; A.B. Glenville State Coll., 1935; B.J., U. Mo., 1939. M.S. in Journalism, 1947; m. Frederica Louise Schmitt, Oct. 17, 1943; children—Mary Susan, William Charles, Joseph Karl. Corr., Clarksburg (W.Va.) Telegram, 1932-35; tchr. high sch., Gilmer County, W.Va., 1936-41, 45-46; news writer, editor, reporter NBC Central div., Chgo. 1947-49, 55-57, summers 1949-55, 58-60; lab. instr. Northwestern U. Medill Sch. Journalism, Evanston, 1947-49, faculty, 1949-69, asso. prof., 1954-59, prof. 1959-69, asst. dean, 1957-64. Served to lt. USNR, 1942-45. Mem. Assn. for Edn. in Journalism, Radio-Television News Dirs., Assn., Ill. News Broadcasters Assn. Republican. Methodist. Club: Headline (dir., v.p. 1963) (Chgo.). Co-editor: TV News Handbook, 1954. Home: IL Died Jan. 1, 1969.

WHITING, FREDERIC ALLEN, art official; b. Oakdale, Tenn., Jan. 26, 1873; s. Frederic Augustus and Catherine Tracy (Allen) W.; ed. pub. schs., Wellesley Hills, Mass.; hon. M.A., Kenyon Coll., 1920; hon. D.F.A., Lawrence Coll, 1931; m. Olive Cook, June 4, 1903; 1 son, Frederic Allen. Active in arts and crafts movement; sec.-treas. Soc. of Arts and Crafts, Boston, 1900-12; dir. of museum, John Herron Art Inst., Indianapolis, 1912-13; dir. Cleveland Mus. of Art, 1913-30; pres. Am. Fedn. of Arts, 1930-36. Superintendent div. of applied arts, Dept. of Art, St. Louis Expn., 1904 (awarded diploma and gold medal for this service, arrangement of exhibits, etc.); mem. Internat. Jury of Awards for Group 14, Dept. Art, in same. Mem. Am. Assn. of Museums (pres. 1921-23; v.p. 1924-27). Unitarian. Home: 536 McDonald St., Mount Dora FL (summer) Ogunquit ME‡

WHITING, WALTER ROGERS, bank vault engr.; b. Ashburnham, Mass., Apr. 10, 1875; s. Charles G. and Sarah E. (Rogers) W.; grad. Cambridge, Mass., and Boston pub. schs.; m. Gertrude W. Clarke, Apr. 10, 1893; children—George Clarke, Samuel Weston. Automobile mfr., 1899-1904; founded with others Bankers Electric Protective Assn., Boston, Mass., 1907, became v.p., 1907; active in strengthening ties between Boston, Mass., and Boston, Lincolnshire, England; vice pres. Friends of St. Botolph's Ch., Boston, Lincolnshire, England. Trustee Boston U., Hingham (Mass.) Trust Co. and Savings Bank; trustee and chmn. coms., Mass. Memorial Hosp., Boston; chmn. Hingham (Mass.) Municipal Light Bd. Now retired. Home: 17 Miles Rd., Hingham MA‡

WHITLEY, JAMES LUCIUS, ex-congressman; b. Rochester, N.Y., May 24, 1872; s. Wm. and Elizabeth (Dorman) W.; grad. Law Dept. Union U., Albany, N.Y., 1898; m. Ora May Marker, Jan. 21, 1901; children—George Aldridge, James L. Admitted to N.Y. bar, 1899, and began practice at Rochester; asst. corp. counsel, Rochester, 1900-01; chief examiner, Civil Service, 1902-04; mem. Whitley & Whitley. Served as sergt. U.S. Vol. Battery, Spanish-Am. War. Mem. N.Y. Assembly, 1905-11, N.Y. State Senate, 1918-28; mem. 71st to 73d Congresses (1929-35), 38th N.Y. Dist. Mem. Am. and N.Y. State bar assns., Spanish War Vets., Sons of Vets. Republican. Episcopalian. Mason. Clubs: Rochester, Masonic. Author: Law of Arrest, 1901; Whitley on Bills. Notes. Checks, 1918. Home: 254 Culver Road. Office: 39 State St., Rochester NY‡

WHITLEY, JOHNSON DECOSTA, mdse. exec.; b. nr. Charlotte, N.C., Oct. 19, 1910; s. Ayer and Ester (Mangum) W.; student Mars Hill Coll., 1927-29; m. Miranda Medlin, Mar. 20, 1934; children—Carole Jean (Mrs. Jim Lee Parks), Jonnie Diane (Mrs. Edgar Lee Dalrymple). Salesman, Belk Bros. Co., Charlotte, 1929-41; asst. mgr. Belk's Dept. Store, Greensboro, 1941-43; asst. mgr. Belk Robinson Co., Charleston, S.C., 1945-47, Belk-Hudson Co., Orangeburg, 1947-49; co-owner, mgr. Belk's Dept. Store, Americus, Ga., 1949-51, Belt Whitley Co., Hattiesburg, Miss., 1951-68. Bd. dirs. Salvation Army. Served with USNR, 1943-45, Mem. Gen. Retail Mchts. Assn. Hattiesburg (chmn. 1952-60), Miss. Retail Mchts. Assn. (dir. 1955-58). Mason, Lion. Home: Hattiesburg MS Died Aug. 3, 1968.

WHITLOCK, ELLIOTT HOWLAND, mech. engr.; b. Brooklyn, N.Y., May 5, 1867; s. Elisha Schanck and Sarah Jane (Elliott) W.; student Agrl. and Mech. Coll. of Texas, 1886; M.E. Stevens Inst. of Tech., Hoboken, N.J., 1890, hon. M.Sc., 1933; m. Mrs. Charles H. Wellman, Oct. 24, 1907. With motive power dept. Pa. R.R. at Columbus, O., 1890-91; prof. mech. engring., Agrl. and Mech. Coll. of S.D., 1891-92; constrn. and operation of gas plants and in commercial business, 1892-96; with Nat. Carbon Co., Cleveland, 1896-1914; cons. practice, 1914-17; owner Whitlock Mfg. Co.; gen. mgr. Am. Fire Clay and Products Co.; mem. bd. dirs. Wellman-Seaver-Morgan Co.; commr. Division of Smoke Inspection, Cleveland, 1925-30; research prof. smoke abatement, Stevens Inst. Tech., 1930-32. Commd. maj. Engrs. R.C., U.S. Army, Feb. 23, 1917; called to active duty, May 7, 1917; assigned to 24th Engr. Regt. (Shop and Supply); sailed for France, Feb. 16, 1918; with Service of Supply, 2d and 3d armies; promoted lt. col. 24th Engrs., Dec. 31, 1918, and returned to U.S. in comd. of regt., June 1, 1919; commd. col. 112th Engr. Regt., 37th Div., Ohio Nat. Guard, June 1928. Mem. Am. Soc. Mech. Engrs. (v.p.), Soc. Am. Mil. Engrs., Cleveland Engring. Soc. (ex-pres.), S.A.R. Presbyterian. Club: University (Cleveland). Home: 3813 Euclid Av., Cleveland 15‡

WHITMAN, EDMUND ALLEN, lawyer; b. Lawrence, Kan., June 11, 1860; s. Edmund Burke and Lucretia (Clapp) W.; A.B., Harvard U., 1881, A.M., 1882, LL.B., 1885; m. Florence Josephine Lee, June 27, 1895;children—Allen L., Frederic B., Mrs. Eleanor L. Young (dec.). Admitted to Mass. bar, 1886, bar of U.S. Supreme Ct., 1902; engaged in gen. practice, but makes specialty of copyright cases. Mem. Cambridge Bd. Overseers of the Pub. Welfare, 1916-31. Tr. Gardner State Colony, 1902-19. Fellow Am. Acad. Arts and Sciences; member Mass. Bar Assn., Boston Bar Association, American Branch International Law Association (president 1930), Phi Beta Kappa. Liquidator of Austro-Hungarian Bank, 1920. Democrat. Unitarian. Clubs: Appalachian Mountain (v.p. 1903). Home: 23 Everett St., Cambridge MA Office: Pemberton Bldg., Boston MA‡

WHITMAN, LEROY, editor; born at Washington, Sept. 14, 1902; s. Winfield Scott and Sarah Jane (Price) W.; student George Washington Univ., 1921-22; m. Lucetta Sabin, June 25, 1923; children—Jane Laura (Mrs. H. C. Patterson, Jr.), Lucetta Fay (Mrs. Donald D. Schneider), LeRoy Winfield. Reporter, picture editor, asst. city editor. The Washington Post, 1922-29; mng. editor, general mgr. Army, Navy Air Force Jour., Washington, 1929-30, editor, 1930-62, pub., 1958-62; editor Army Navy Airforce Jour. and Register, 1962-64; editorial cons. Air Force Mag. and Space Digest, 1964-68; v.p. Army and Navy Jour., Inc. Mem. exec. com. control of Periodical Press Galleries U.S. Senate and House of Rep., 78th, 79th and 80th Congresses. Served as lt. (j.g.) and lt., U.S.N.R., 1927-40; editor Army and Navy Jour. for period World War II (Jour. awarded certificate of achievement, Navy Dept.; certificate of appreciation, U.S. Coast Guard); vice pres. Army and Navy Journal, Inc., 1949-68. Mem. Robert J. Collier Trophy Com., 1954. Wright Bros. Meml. Trophy Committee, 1955. Member Aviation Space Writers Association (First vice president 1952-53, president 1954-55), White House Corrs. Association. Unitarian. Clubs: Overseas Writers, Nat. Aviation, Aero (Washington); Nat. Press. Editor U.S. at War (4 vols.), pub. annually during World War II. Contbg. editor Funk & Wagnalls New Internat. Year Book, 1940-60. Home: Silver Spring MD Died Oct. 17, 1968; buried Martha's Vineyard MA

WHITMARSH, FRANCIS LEGGETT, corp. exec.; b. N.Y.C., Oct. 4, 1893; s. Theodore F. and Lillian (Smith) W.; student St. Paul's Sch., Concord, N.H., 1912; A.B., Harvard, 1916; m. Mildred Ingersoll, Dec. 12, 1917; children—Anne (Mrs. F. Alexander Close), Francis Leggett. With F. H. Leggett & Co., 1916-59, beginning as buyer, successively v.p., pres., dir., 1936-59; dir. Irving Trust Co. Trustee N.Y. U.; v.p., dir. Nat. Multiple Sclerosis Soc. Served as 1st lt. 306th Inf., 77th Div. U.S. Army, World War I. Mem. Nat. Am. Wholesale Grocers Assn. (gov.), Clubs: Union League, Harvard, University, Met. Opera (N.Y.C.). Home: New York City NY Died July 16, 1969.

WHITMORE, EUGENE R(ANDOLPH), pathologist, medical educator; b. Lancaster, Wis., June 18, 1874; s. Eugene and Rosena Catherine (Beers) W.; B.S., U. of Wis., 1896; M.D., Coll. Physicians and Surgeons, Chicago, 1899; intern Cook County Hosp., 1899-1901; post-grad. work, London School Tropical Medicine, 1905 (grad. with distinction), Vienna, 1906, Koch's Inst., Berlin, 1910-11; Dr.P.H., Johns Hopkins, 1921; Ph.D., Georgetown, 1929; m. Josephine W. Baker, Nov. 9, 1918. Apptd. asst. surgeon, rank of 1st t., U.S. Army, June 29, 1901; capt. asst. surgeon, June 29, 1906, and capt. Med. Corps same date; maj., Jan. 1, 1910; lt. col., May 15, 1917; col., Nov. 30, 1917. Prof. pathology, Army Med. Sch., Washington, D.C., Sept. 1913-19, also prof. tropical medicine; curator Army Med. Museum, 1913-15; retired, Jan. 8, 1920. Prof. bacteriology and preventive medicine, George Washington U. Med. School, 1920-24; prof. parasitology and pathology, Georgetown U., 1924-46, emeritus; head div. tropical diseases, Doctors Hospital; dir. pathology labs., Casualty Hospital, Washington, D.C. Pathologist, Bureau of Science, Manila, P.I., 1908-10; sec. Sect. VIII (med. sciences and hygiene), 2d Pan-Am. Scientific Congress, Washington, 1915; pathologist Yellow Fever Commn. Internat. Health Bd., Rockefeller Foundation, S. Am., summer 1916. Sec. Am. Assn. for Study of Neoplastic Diseases. Diplomate Am. Bd. of Pathology; fellow Am. Coll. Physicians, A.M.A., A.A.A.S., Am. Soc. of Clin. Pathologists; mem. Washington Soc. of Pathologists, George Washington U. Med. Soc., Pan-Am. Med. Assn., Am. Assn. Pathologists and Bacteriologists, Am. Soc. Parasitologists, Southern Med. Assn., Nu Sigma Nu. Episcopalian. Clubs: Army and Navy, Cosmos, Army and Navy Country. Home: 2139 Wyoming Av. N.W. Office: 2139 Wyoming Av. N.W., Washington 8 DC‡

WHITNEY, ALLEN BANKS, banking; b. Mt. Vernon, ., Dec. 2, 1877; s. Amza Alfred and Mary Virginia (Henderson) W.; B.S., Ohio Wesleyan U., 1899; m. Jane Rouns, of Washington C.H., Ohio, Feb. 25, 1903 (dec.); children—Alfred Whitney (dec.), Charles Richard, Ella Virginia (Mrs. Herman A. Harding); m. 2d, Florence Nicholson of Mt. Vernon, Iowa, Feb. 1, 1936. Supt. of Schs., Chesterville, O., 1900-02; traffic mgr. U.S. Telephone Co., Cleveland, 1902-04; asst. cashier Nat. Bank of Morrow Co., Mt. Gilead, 1904-05; sec. Ohio Mfg. Co., 1905-09, pres., 1909-19; v.p. Citizens Savings Bank, Upper Sandusky, Ohio, 1906-21, president 1921-31; asst. liquidator First-Central Trust Co., Akron, O. Pres. Upper Sandusky Village Council, 1911. Pres. Ohio Bankers Assn., 1929-30; mem. council Am. Bankers Assn., 1930-31; trustee Ohio Wesleyan U., 1918-38. Mem. Phi Delta Theta (pres. Sigma Province, pres. Alumni Club since 1926). Pres. Alumni Assn. O. Wesleyan U., 1917-18. Democrat. Methodist. Mason. Address: Akron OH‡

WHITNEY, CARRIE WESTLAKE, librarian; b. on plantation in Va.; d. Wellington Bracee and Helen (Van Waters) Westlake; pvt. edn.; m. James Steele Whitney, of Kansas City, Mo., Dec. 1, 1885 (died 1890). Librarian Kansas City Public Library, 1882-1910. Corr. sec. Kansas City Hist. Soc.; mem. Mo. branch Am. Folk-Lore Soc.; asso. mem. Mo. Hist. Soc., St. Louis. Author: Kansas City, Missouri—Its History and its People, 1800-1908, 1908. Contbr. poems to mags. and newspapers. Address: 1222 E. 10th St., Kansas City MO‡

WHITNEY, COURTNEY, brig. gen., U.S. Army; now assigned duty with govt. section, G.H.Q., Supreme Comdr. Allied Powers, Tokyo, Japan. Home: Washington DC Died 1969.*

WHITNEY, FRANK I., passenger traffic mgr. of the Great Northern Ry. since July 1, 1898; was clerk, chief clerk, etc., in ticket dept. Mich. Central R.R.; asst. gen. passenger and ticket agt. same, 1881-7; city passenger agt. Lake Shore & Mich. Southern Ry., Chicago, April to July, 1887; western passenger agt., 1887-8. Address: 826 Dayton Av., St Paul MN‡

WHITNEY, GUILFORD HARRISON, business exec.; b. Cedar Rapids, Ia., Apr. 21, 1888; s. Guilford and Mary (Harrison) W.; grad. Punahou Acad., Honolulu, T.H., 1905; m. Grace Davis, Mar. 19, 1913; children—Elnora (Mrs. Nicholas), Louise (Mrs. Fletcher), Ruth (Mrs. Robinson). With Theodore H. Davies & Co., Ltd., Honolulu, 1905-14; with Whitney & Co., San Diego, 1914-68, pres. 1930-68; dir. First Nat. Trust & Savs. Bank, 1928-68, chmn. bd., 1953-65, chairman exec. com. Dir. City Transit System; v.p. Met. Garages, Inc.; pres. San Diego Civic Facilities Corp. Republican. Conglist. Clubs: Rotary, Cuyamaca (San Diego, California). Home: San Diego CA Died July 12, 1968.

WHITSON, ANDREW ROBESON, b. Stanton, Minn., Oct. 9, 1870; s. Andrew and Abigail (Dack) W.; student U. of Wis., 1891-92; S.B., U. of Chicago, 1894, post-grad. work, U. of Chicago, 1900, Berlin, 1907; m. Josephine Fitch, of Evanston, Ill., Aug. 11, 1897; children—Kenneth Fitch, Ruth (dec.), Merritt Bragdon, Rosamond Louise. Prin. Beloit (Wis.) High Sch., 1895-99; asst. prof. soil physics, 1899-1901, prof. since 1901, U. of Wis. Mem. A.A.A.S., Am. Geog. Soc., Alpha Zeta, Sigma Xi, Science Club (U. of Wis.). Author: Soils and Soil Fertility (with H. L. Walster), 1914; Soils of Wisconsin, 1927. Organizer and 1st pres., 1920, Am. Assn. of Soil Survey Workers. Home: Longview Acres, R. 7, Madison WI‡

WHITTEMORE, ARTHUR EASTERBROOK, state judge; b. Reading, Mass., June 3, 1896; s. Frederick Ellsworth and Edith L. (Easterbrook) W.; B.S., Harvard, 1917, LL.B., 1922; m. Suvia Lanice Paton, Oct. 11, 1924; children—Suvia E. (Mrs. Richard M. Judd), Arthur Paton, Elizabeth Bayles (Mrs. Robert H. MacArthur). Admitted to Mass. bar, 1922, asso. Nutter, McClennen & Fish, Boston, 1922-25, partner, 1929-55; asso. justice Supreme Jud. Ct. of Mass., 1955-69; spl. asst. atty. gen., Mass., 1942-44; past mem. President's emergency bds. under Railway Labor Act, also arbitrator. Town moderator, Hingham, Mass., 1939-55, Trustee Marlboro Coll.; trustee Marlboro Music School and the World Peace Foundation. Served from 2d lieutenant to 1st lieut., inf., U.S. Army, 1917-19. Fellow Am. Acad. Arts and Scis.; member Am. Law Institute. Home: Hingham MA Died Oct. 1, 1969.

WHITTIER, CHARLES COMFORT, cons. engr.; b. Somerset County, Me., Dec. 10, 1876; s. Philander Coburn and Laura Ann (Taylor) W.; B.C.E., Univ. of Me., 1899; m. Leonore Arlie Leuckel, Sept. 2, 1908; children—Charles Taylor, John Coburn. Asst. engr. maintenance of way, B.&M. R.R., Boston, 1899-1900; asst. engr., Southwestern R.R. of Ariz., Bisbee, Ariz., 1900-01; mining engr. with Robert W. Hunt Co., engrs., Chicago, 1901-07; chief engr. and asst. gen. mgr. Zeigler Coal Co., Ziegler, Ill., 1904-07; inspecting and reporting engr. Robert W. Hunt Co., 1907-13; gen. mgr. Robert W. Hunt Co., Ltd., Montreal, 1913-15; chief engr. and mng. dir. Field Mining & Milling Co., 1915-19; v.p. and cons. engr. Hunt Mining Co., 1919-23; cons. engr. with Robert W. Hunt Co., 1923-32; partner Nutrition Research Laboratories; was sec. Illinois Mineral Industries Com.; inventor of mineral materials, vitamins and foods. Specialist in value and use of industrial plants and processes, quality of mineral deposits and development of new and improved mineral commodities. Mem. Engring. Inst. Can., Am. Inst. Mining and Metall. Engrs. (dir. 1932-35), Western Soc. Engrs. (pres. 1934-35), Inst. of Food Technologists. Clubs: Chicago Engineers (ex-pres.), Union League. Home: 6758 Muirlands Drive, La Jolla, Calif. Office: 4210 Peterson Av., Chicago IL‡

WHITTINGHILL, DEXTER GOOCH, b. Hopkins County, Ky., April 7, 1866; s. David and Margaret (Phillips) W.; B.S., Madisonville, Ky. Normal School, 1885; student Bethel College, Russellville, Ky., 2 yrs.; Th.D., Southern Bapt. Theol. Sem., Louisville, Ky., 1894; U. of Rome, Italy; m. Susy Braxton Taylor, July 27, 1905; children—Diana Grace, David George, Arnold Braxton (dec.), Robert Braxton. Ordained Bapt. ministry, 1894; pastor Coliseum Place Ch., New Orleans, 1894-1900; 1st Ch., Bonham, Tex., 1900-01; missionary, Bapt. Conv. of North America, and pres. Bapt. Theol. Sem., Rome, since 1901; supt. Bapt. Missions in Italy, 1904-10 and 1916-39. Del. congresses, Italian Baptists, London, 1905, Berlin, 1908, Stockholm, 1913; del. Congress for Promotion Internat. Peace Through the Churches, at the Hague, 1919, London, 1920, S. Beatenberg, 1921. Founder Bilychnis (religious review), Rome, 1912; founder and editor La Biblioteca di Studi Religiosi (library religious studies, 21 vols. issued). Baptist mem. revision com. Diodati's New Testament, 1907-15; and Psalms in Diodati's Bible, 1915-17. Co-Author: I. Battisti, 1912; La Chiesa e Nuovi Tempi, 1917. Founder Conscientia," weekly religious newspaper pub. at Rome. Mem. Phi Gamma Delta. Address: 434 W. 120th St., New York NY‡

WHITTLES, THOMAS DAVIS, author, clergyman; b. Bardsley, Lancashire, Eng., Dec. 27, 1873; s. Robert and Emma (Davis) W.; Ursinus Coll.; A.B., Waynesburg Coll., Pa., 1896, Litt.D., 1931; Princeton Theol. Sem., 1899; D.D., Waynesburg Coll., 1916; m. Sarah Canning, July 16, 1902; children—Leonard C., Miriam C.; m. 2d, Neonetta Iams, of Waynesburg, Pa., Mar. 4, 1925, Ordained Presbyn. ministry, 1899; pastor Grandin, N.D., and Hendrum, Minn., 1900-03, Fergus Falls, Minn., 1904-09, North East, Pa., 1910-16; supervisor of logging camp work, Board of Home Missions of Presbyn. Ch. U.S.A., 1916-18; pastor 2d Ch., Duluth, 1918-24, 1st Ch., Eau Claire, Wis., 1925-32, Paine Memorial Ch., Carlton, Minn., since 1933. Mason. Author: The Lumberjack's Sky Pilot, 1908; The Parish of the Pines, 1912; Frank Higgins, Trail Blazer, 1920; also short stories and mag. articles. Asso. editor Eastern Star mag. Home: The Manse, Carlton MN‡

WHITWORTH, PEGRAM, army officer; b. Mansfield, La., Aug. 5, 1871; s. William Thomas and Laura (Pegram) W.; student Thatcher Mil. Inst., 1886-89; grad. U.S. Mil. Acad., 1894, Army Sch. of the Line, 1915, Gen. Staff Sch., 1920, Army War Coll., 1921; m. Emeline Cole Smith, Apr. 18, 1899; 1 son, Pegram. Commd. 2d lt. Inf., June 12, 1894, and advanced through grades to temp. brig. gen., 1918, brig. gen. regular army, May 1933, retired, Aug. 31, 1935, Served in Philippine Insurrection, 1898-1900; again in Philippines, 1901-02 and 1906-08; construction q.m., Ft. Crockett, Galveston, Tex., 1909-12; in Panama Canal Zone, 1912-16; instr. and comdr. 1st Bn., 1st O.T.C., Presidio, San Francisco, 1917; col. 362d Inf., 91st Div., Aug. 1917; with A.E.F. in France, July 1918; brig. gen. comdg. 71st Brig., 36th Div., Aug. 1918-July 1919; chief of staff, 2d Div., 1932-33; comdr. 6th Inf. Brig., Ft. Douglas, Utah, 1933-35, also Civilian Conservation Corps of about 30 camps; apptd. member of the Bd. of Police Commrs. of the City of Los Angeles, Calif., June 1940. Awarded 3 silver stars for bravery against Spaniards in Manila, 2 citations for bravery against insurgents; cited by Marshal Petain, Apr. 1, 1919; Cross of Mil. Service (U.D.C. of La.). Republican. Christian Scientist. Mason (32 deg., Shriner). Home: 10950 Wellworth Av., W Los Angeles CA‡

WHYBURN, GORDON THOMAS, univ. prof.; b. Lewisville, Tex., Jan. 7, 1904; s. Thomas and Eugenia Elizabeth (McLeod) W.; B.A., U. of Tex., 1925, M.A., 1926, Ph.D., 1927; Guggenheim fellow. University of Vienna, Austria, 1929-30; Sc.D., Washington and Lee Univ., 1949; married Lucille Enid Smith, Sept. 9, 1925; 1 son, Kenneth Gordon. Instructor mathematics, University of Tex., 1926-27, adjunct professor, 1927-29; asso. in mathematics, Johns Hopkins U., 1929-34; prof. mathematics, U. of Virginia, 1934-57, Alumni professor, 1957-69, chairman mathematics faculty, 1935-66, member of the Center for Advanced Studies, 1966-69, also director of the premeteorol. training program for the Army Air Forces, 1943-44; visiting prof., Stanford U., summers 1929, 32, 38, 41, prof., U. of Calif. at Los Angeles, summer 1940, University of Calif. at Berkeley, summer 1947. University of Colorado, summer 1956. Member of the War Policy Com. for Mathematics, Nat. Research Council Fellowship Bd. Awarded Chauvenet prize, Math. Assn. Am., 1938. Mem. National Academy Sciences, American Mathematical Society (president 1953-54, colloquium speaker, 1940; councillor chmn. editorial bd., of Colloquium series, v.p. 1944-45, trustee 1948-64, mng. editor Transactions 1949-52), A.A.A.S. (vice pres., chmn. sect. A, 1941), Math. Assn. Am. (gov.), Va. Acad. of Sci., Sigma Xi, Phi Beta Kappa, Phi Lambda Upsilon. Club: Colonnade (U. of Va.). Author of book on Analytic Topology, 1942; Topological Analysis, 1958; and numerous research articles on mathematics. Home: Charlottesville VA Died Sept. 8, 1969.

WHYBURN, WILLIAM MARVIN, educator; born Lewisville, Texas, Nov. 12, 1901; s. Thomas and Eugenia Elizabeth (McLeod) W.; B.A., U. of Tex., 1922, M.A., 1923, Ph.D., 1927; honorary LL.D., Texas Technol. College, 1948; married Marie Barfield, Dec. 29, 1923; children—Willa Marie, Clifton Thomas. Teacher in pub. schs., Denton County, Tex., 1918-20; instr. mathematics, South Park Jr. Coll., Beaumont, Tex., 1923-24; asst. prof. mathematics, Tex. Agrl. and Mech. Coll., 1924-25; asso. prof. mathematics, Tex. Technological Coll., 1925-26; Nat. Research Fellow, mathematics, Harvard U., 1927-28; asst. prof. mathematics, U. of Calif., Los Angeles, 1928-30, asso. prof., 1930-38, prof. and chmn. dept. mathematics, 1938-44; pres. Tex. Tech. Coll., Lubboc, 1944-48, Kenan prof. math. U. N.C., 1948-67, Kenan prof. emeritus of math., 1967-72, chmn. dept., 1960-65, v.p. grad. studies and research, 1956-60; Charles F. Frensley prof. math. So. Methodist University, from 1967; NSF and OECD grant for research, U. London, Eng., 1964. Ednl. supr. U. of Cal., Los Angeles, for engring., sci., management war training program, 1941-44; chief Operations Analysis Sect., Hq. 3d Air Force, 1944. Corr. mem. La Academia Nacional de Ciencias Exactas, Fisicas y Naturales de Lima, 1943. Mem. Am. Math. Soc. (council 1939-43), Math. Assn. America (1st vice pres. 1944-45), A.A.A.S. (mem. sect. A com. 1939-41), Philos. Soc. of Texas, Phi Beta Kappa, Sigma Xi. Author: (with P. H. Daus and J.M. Gleason) Basic Mathematics for War and Industry, 1944; (with P. H. Daus) First Year College Mathematics with Applications, 1948, Algebra for College Students, 1955, Introduction to Mathematical Analysis, 1958, Algebra with Applications to Business and Economics, 1960. Contbr. articles to math. jours. Home: Chapel Hill NC Died May 5, 1972; buried Lewisville TX

WICK, SAMUEL, psychiatrist, hosp. adminstr.; b. Marinette, Wis., 1906; M.D., Rush Med. Sch., 1929. Intern Lutheran Meml. Hosp., Chgo., 1929-30; resident psychiatry, behavior clinic Criminal Ct. Cook County, Chgo., 1931-32; psychiatrist Elgin (Ill.) State Hosp., 1932-37; sr. psychiatrist Milw. County Hosp. Mental Diseases, 1937-42; chief acute intensive treatment VA Neuropsychiat. Hosp., Sawtelle, Cal., 1948-52; dir. edn. and research Ariz. State Hosp., Phoenix, 1952-53, supt., 1953-64; pvt. practice, Phoenix, from 1964. Served to capt., USAAF, 1942-46. Diplomate Am. Bd. Psychiatry and Neurology. Fellow Am. Psychiat. Assn.; mem. A.M.A. Home: Phoenix AZ

WIDENER, GEORGE D., trustee; b. Phila., Mar. 11, 1889; s. George D. and Eleanore (Elkins) W.; ed. privately, also deLancey Sch., Phila.; m. Jessie Sloane, Mar. 20, 1917. Engaged in mgmt. of family personal affairs, Phila.; dir. Electric Storage Battery Co., Provident Nat. Bank, Phila. breeder Hereford cattle, Chevoit sheep; breeder, racer thoroughbred horses; hon. chmn., Jockey Club, N.Y.C., N.Y. Racing Assn. Mem. bd. trustees Phila. Museum Art; past bd. dirs. Chestnut Hill Hosp., Abington Meml. Hosp., Acad. Natural Scis. of Phila., Phila. Zool. Garden. Served to 1st lt. U.S. Army, World War I. Mem. S.R., Soc. War of 1812, Soc. Colonial Wars. Republican. Episcopalian. Clubs: Racquet (Phila.); Knickerbocker, Brooke, Racquet & Tennis, Links (N.Y.C.). Home: Whitemarsh Township PA Died Dec. 8, 1971; interred Widener Mausoleum, Laurel Hill Cemetery.

WIDMANN, BERNARD PIERRE, radiologist; b. Johnstown, Pa., July 21, 1890; s. John and Magdalene (Graf) W.; student St. Francis Coll., Johnstown, Pa., 1909-11, St. Vincent's Coll., Latrobe, Pa., 1911-12; Medico Chirurgical Coll. of Medicine and Surgery, Phila., 1912-16; LL.D., St. Vincent's College; D.Sc., Hanahman Medical College, 1952, St. Joseph's College, 1958; married Mary Eileen Maher, Aug. 27, 1919 (died May 1937); children—Mary Eileen, Ann Stevens. Asst. prof. radiology, grad. sch. of medicine, U. of Pa., 1921-37, prof. since 1937, chairman in radiology in Graduate School since 1945; dir. X-ray dept., Philadelphia Gen. Hosp. since 1928, Fitzgerald-Mercy Hosp., Philadelphia, since 1928. Dir. Our Lady of Lourdes Hosp., Camden, N.J. Served as radiologist, Army X-ray Sch., Camp Greenleaf, 1918. Recip. Gold medal Am. Coll. Radiology, 1964. Gold medal, Strittmater award Philadelphia County Medical Society. Diplomate of the American Board of Radiology (pres. 1959-60, trustee). Mem. Phila. Radiol. Soc. (past president), American Radium Soc., American Roentgen Ray Society (president 1950), Radiologic Society N.A., American College Radiology (v.p. 1954), A.M.A., American Board of Radiology (president 1958, trustee since 1935), Sigma Xi, Phi Chi. Contributor over 150 papers on radiological subjects to professional publs. Home: Philadelphia PA Died Feb. 26, 1971; buried Holy Cross Cemetery, Yeadon PA

WIDTSOE, LEAH DUNFORD, home economist; b. Salt Lake City, Utah, Feb. 24, 1874; d. Dr. Alma B. Dunford and Susa Young (now Susa Young Gates); student Harvard, summer 1893; grad. normal dept. U. of Utah, 1896; student Pratt Inst., Brooklyn, N.Y., 1896-97; B.Pd., Brigham Young U., 1898; traveled and studied in Europe, 1898-1900; m. John A. Widtsoe, of Salt Lake City, June 1, 1898; children—Anna Gaarden, John A. (dec.), Karl M., Mark A. (dec.), Leah Eudora. Condr. pioneer household insts., auspices Utah Agrl. Coll., 1900-05; woman's adviser and lecturer on economics, Brigham Young U., 1905-07; lecturer home economics and investigator problems of household engring. and human nutrition, 1907-16; gen. ednl. work since 1916. During war period, state chmn. com. of edn. Utah Women's Council of Defense; state chmn. Americanization work of Federation of Women's Clubs, etc. Mem. Am. Home Economics Assn., Salt Lake City Federation Women's Clubs (pres. 1919, 20), Women of Univ. of Utah; state pres. Nat. League of Women Voters, 1921-23. Mormon. Author: Labor Saving Devices for the Farm Home, 1911. Co-Author: The Women of the Mormon Church; The Life-Story of Brigham Young, both 1930; The Word of Wisdom, A Guide to Health, 1937. Home: 1425 Sigsbee Av., Salt Lake City UT‡

WIEBOLDT, ELMER F., dept. store exec.; s. William A. and Anna Louise (Krueger) W.; m. Helen Bersbach; children—Elmer F., Richard A., Dorothy (Mrs. Urion), Helen (Mrs. Hoxie), Elizabeth (Mrs. Daggett). Pres. Wieboldt Stores, Inc.; dir. Wieboldt Foundation (Chicago charitable corp.). Home: Tucson AZ Died Jan. 1972.

WIEBOLDT, RAYMOND CARL, contractor; b. Chicago, Ill., Apr. 6, 1886; s. William Adolph and Anna Louise (Krueger) W.; grad. Lewis Inst., Chicago, 1905; A.B., U. of Wis., 1909; m. Nydia W. Huth, Dec. 15, 1915; children—Raymond Carl, Nydia Ann, James Calvin, Mary Louise. Pres. R.C. Wieboldt Co., gen. contractors, 1913-53; dir. Wieboldt Stores, Inc. Pres. Wieboldt Found., Chgo. Trustee Northwestern U. Mem. Western Soc. Engrs., Psi Upsilon, Methodist. Clubs: University, Glenview Golf. Home: Evanston IL Died Mar. 27, 1968; buried Memorial Park, Evanston IL

WIEGAND, CHARLES DUDLEY, ret. army ofer.; educator; b. Balt., Apr. 28, 1906; s. Charles List and Daisy Viola (George) W.; student St. Johns' Coll., 1924-25; B.S., U.S. Mil. Acad., 1929; grad. study Command and Gen. Staff Sch., 1942-43; Master of Arts, Colorado State University, 1957-59; m. Claire Elizabeth Baker, Mar. 14, 1931; children—Robert Dudley, Marguerite Claire. Commd. 2d lt., U.S. Army, 1929, advanced through grades to col., 1950; various army stas., U.S., Hawaii, Canal Zone, 1929-43; combat duty, Sicily and Italy, 1943-44; mil. missions, Guatemala, C.A., also founded Escuela de Aplicacion de Armas y Servicios, Escuela de Artilleria and Escuela de Caballeria, 1945-48; prof. mil. sci. and tactics Howe Mil. Sch., 1948-50, U. Mich., 1950-52, Colo. State U., 1957-59; asst. chief of staff, G4, U.S. Army, Alaska, 1952-54; chief of staff U.S. Army, Alaska, 1954; dep. post comdr. Ft. George G. Meade, Md., 1954-56, post comdr., 1956-57; ret.; with dept. of English, Colo. State U., 1961-72. Decorated Silver Star, Bronze Star (U.S.), Cruz de Merito Militar 2d class (Guatemala). Lion, Elk. Home: Fort Collins CO Died Mar. 7, 1972.

WIEHE, THEODORE CHARLES, business exec.; b. Flushing, L.I., N.Y., Dec. 10, 1880; s. William and Augusta (Wruck) W.; ed. pub. schs.; m. Gertrude E. Drinkwine, Aug. 20, 1946; children by previous marriage, Kathryn (Mrs. Vahan Sewny), Dr. Theodore B. Began business career with Bethlehem Steel Co., later engaged in business for self, then joined Schenley Distillers Corp. (now Schenley Industries, Inc.); president and dir. Schenley Internat. Corp., 1933-68. Clubs: Athletic (N.Y.); Everglades Country (Palm Beach, Fla.); Westchester Country (Rye, N.Y.). Home: New York City NY Died Feb. 24, 1973.

WIEMAN, ELTON EWART, dean, athletic dir.; b. Orosi, Calif., Oct. 4, 1896; s. William Henry and Alma Florence (Morgan) W.; A.B., U. of Mich., 1921, grad. student, 1929; m. Margaret Gates Vogel, Dec. 2, 1922; children—Robert Allan, Helen Elizabeth. Line coach, U. of Mich., 1921-26, head coach football, 1927-28, asst. dir. athletics, 1924-29, supervisor professional training phys. edn. and athletics, 1929-30; part time line coach, U. of Minn., 1930-31; part time line coach, Princeton U., 1932-37, head coach of football, 1938-42; with State Mutual Life Assurance Co. of Worcester, Mass., 1930-38; part time line coach, Columbia U., 1944-45; dean of men, dir. athletics and phys. edn., U. of Maine, 1946-51; dir. of athletics University of Denver from 1951. Served in Air Service, U.S. Army, 1918-19; commd. 2d lt., 1919. Apptd. chief of physical training sect. Army Specialized Training Div., Army Service Forces, War Dept., Washington, D.C., March 1943-45; athletic cons., Japan, January to March, 1946. Member American Football Coaches Assn., Phi Beta Kappa, Kappa Sigma. Republican. Presbyterian. Club: Princeton (New York). Author: Football Technique, 1929; Practical Football (with H. O. Crisler), 1934. Contbr. to profl. jours. Address: Denver CO Died Dec. 26, 1971.

WIENER, MEYER, ophthalmologist; b. St. Louis, Mo., Jan. 10, 1876; s. Isidor Marcus and Julia (Meyer) W.; M.D., Mo. Med. Coll., 1896; grad. student U. of Berlin, 1897-98, U. of Heidelberg, summer, 1898, U. of Paris, 1898-99; m. Marguerite Edith Lesser, Dec. 28, 1915; children—Julia, Thomas Rodgers, Edith. Prof. of clin. ophthalmology, Washington University School of Medicine, 1910-46; emeritus professor since 1946; ophthalmic surgeon Missouri Pacific Hospital; retired from active practice 1936; now engaged in teaching research and writing. Formerly dir. of prevention of blindness, Mo. Commn. for the Blind. Commd. maj. Med. Corps, U.S. Army, 1918; organized and dir. Sch. of Ophthalmology, Med. Officers Training Group, Ft. Oglethorpe, Ga.; chief of eye dept. Gen. Hosp. No. 14, later chief plastic surgery of the eye, Gen. Hosp. No. 11; lt. col. Med. Reserve Corps.; now hon. consultant to Med. Dept., U.S. Navy. Certified by Am. Bd. Ophthalmic Examiners. Fellow Am. Coll. Surgeons; mem. A.M.A., Mo. State Med. Soc., St. Louis Med. Soc., St. Louis Acad. Science, Am. Acad. Ophthalmology and Otolaryngology (past exec. v.p.), St. Louis Ophthal. Soc. (past pres.); honorary mem. many socs., honorary asso. pres. Service Club for the Blind (St. Louis). Democrat. Unitarian. Author: Surgery of the Eye, 1939. Formerly editor St. Louis Med. Review, Annals of Ophthalmology, asso. editor Am. Jour. Ophthalmology, editor-in-chief Ophthalmology in the War Years, editorial board, Quarterly Review of Ophth. Home: 321 Alameda Blvd., Coronado CA‡

WIENS, HENRY WARKENTIN, government official; b. India, Oct. 3, 1911; s. Frank J. and Marie H. (Warkentin) W.; B.A. Fresno State Coll., 1933; M.A., U. Cal. at Berkeley, 1936; Ph.D., Northwestern U., 1940; Far Eastern seminar Rockefeller Found., 1936; spl. student U. Lyon. France, 1940-41; m. Isabel Ferguson, Nov. 8, 1941; children—Josephine, Denise, Ruth Gay. Deborah Tchr. Cal. secondary schs., jr. coll., 1934-37; teaching fellow U. Cal. at Berkeley, 1937-39, instr., Santa Barbara, 1941-42; research fellow Northwestern U., 1939-40; war relief worker. Lyon. France, 1940-41; rep. A.R.C., Teheran, Iran, 1942-43; financial adviser Govt. of Iran. 1943-47; finance expert Am. Mission for Aid to Greece, 1947-48; program officer, dep. chief of mission, ECA Mission to Turkey, 1948-53; dir. U.S. Operations Mission to Iraq, 1954-56; chief Near East div. ICA, 1956-57; chief U.S. Tech. Survey Mission to Yemen, 1957; spl. adviser to regional dir. and regional economist Office Near East and South Asian Affairs, ICA, 1958, evaluation officer, 1958-59; dep. asst. sec. labor for internat. affairs, Dept. Labor. 1959-61; ICA rep. in the Congo, 1961-62; dep. chief Internat. div. Bur. of Budget, 1962-63; mgmt. cons. Klein & Saks, Inc., 1963; with World Bank, 1964-67; sr. adviser to Govt. Jamaica, 1964-66, Govt. Peru, 1966-67, AID, 1967. U.S. del. Middle Eastern Land Problems Conf., FAO, Iraq, 1956. Chmn. panel econ. devel. World Council Chs., 1963-68. Mem. Am. Polit. Sci. Assn., Middle East Inst. Presbyn. Contbr. articles to profl. jours. Home: Bethesda MD Died June 30, 1968; buried memorial garden Bradley Hills Presbyn. Church, Bethesda MD

WIER, ROBERT WITHROW, corp. official; b. Avoyelles Parish, La., July 4, 1873; s. Thomas Dabney and Margaret Flora (Campbell) W.; ed. pub. and pvt. schs.; m. Mary Randolph Norwood, July 14, 1925; children—Ann Randolph, Mary Withrow. Pres. and gen. mgr. Wier Long Leaf Lumber Co.; also officer or dir. various other cos. Ex-pres. Houston Recreation and Community Service Assn., Houston Chamber of Commerce. Trustee Hermann Hosp. Estate. Democrat. Episcopalian. Mason. Clubs: Kiwanis, Houston (Houston), Houston Country. Home: 1411 North Blvd. Office: Wier Long Leaf Lumber Co., Houston TX‡

WIESE, OTIS L., editor; b. Davenport, Ia., Jan. 14 1905; s. Christian and Thekla (Mueller) W.; Ph.B., U. of Wis., 1926; m. Josephine Anne Lasher, Sept. 30, 1929 children—Peter Christian, Jeffrey Lasher, Linda Lee Susan Otis. Associated with Publishers Syndicate Chicago, July-Dec. 1926; asso. editor McCall's Magazine, Jan.-Dec. 1927, editor-in-chief since Jan 1928, pub., 1949-58; dir. McCall Corp. Member Delta Chi, Sigma Delta Chi, Phi Kappa Phi. Home: Yorktown Heights NY Died Mar. 2, 1972.

WIESENBERGER, ARTHUR, investment banker; b New York City, Oct. 10, 1896; s. Isidor and Mar (Herman) W.; B.A., Columbia U., 1919; marrie Frances Glendenning Bayes, May ll, 1952; 1 son Arthur Francis. Research asst. National Retail Dr Goods Association, 1919-20, dir. of research, 1920-23 general merchandise manager Alfred Fantl Mercantil Company, 1923-26; foreign correspondent Syster Magazine 1926, associate editor, 1927; merchandisin expert, L. S. Goldsmith Advertising Agency, 1926-28 organizer and operating v.p. Hahn Dept. Store 1928-30; merchandising expert E. Naumburg & Co comml. bankers, 1930-32; mgr. foreign dep Distributors Group, Inc., investment bankers, 1932-3 partner Arthur Wiesenberger & Co., member N.Y Stock Exchange, 1938-67. Fellow Metropolita Museum of Art of N.Y.C. Served in United States Nav Reserve, 1917-19. Received the Horatio Alger Awar 1950, 51. Author: Merchandising Bargain Basement 1922; Radio Merchandising, 1922; Department Sto Operating Statistics, 1923; Fantl's Tariff Facts, 192 An Option on Inflation, 1941; Investment Compani and Their Securities, 1942, 1943; Investme Companies, annually 1944-67; Solving Yo Investment Problems, 1948; The Modern Way ıvest, 1949; Your Program for Security, 1950; You and 'our Dollars, 1952; Ninth Year of the Atomic Age, 954. Pub. of Wiesenberger Investment Report semi-monthly), 1945-67; Findings and Forecast semi-monthly), 1963-67; Wiesenberger Self-Tutor eaching machine for security salesman), 1962; 1066 in 966, London, 1963; The Last 200 Points, 1965. Patron hila. Museum of Art, Minneapolis Museum of Art; life nem. Am. Museum Natural History, Met. Mus. Art; nem. adv. council Dept. Art and Archaeology, 'olumbia U. Lecturer N.Y. Stock Exchange, 1944, N.Y. Inst. of Finance, 1949. Home: Pound Ridge NY Died Jan. 12, 1970.

WIGGANS, CLEO CLAUDE, prof. horticulture; b. Mercer County, Mo., Oct. 20, 1889; s. Joshua Sherman nd Lucy Ann (Barnes) W.; B.S., Mo. Coll. Agr., 1912; A.M., U. of Mo., 1913, Ph.D., 1918; m. Martha Chinn, ept. 29, 1918; children—Samuel Claude, Donald herman. Instr. horticulture, U. of Mo., 1913-18; esearch horticulturist, U. of Del., 1918-19; asso. prof. orticulture, U. of Neb., 1919-24, prof. and chmn. dept., 924-67. Mem. Gamma Sigma Delta, Gamma Alpha, arm House, Sigma Xi. Mem. Disciples of Christ. Mason. Author various research bulls. and articles. Home: Lincoln NE Died Feb. 28, 1967; buried Lincoln NB

WIGHT, CHARLES ALBERT, business exec.; b. Platteville, Wis., Mar. 8, 1899; s. Charles Albert and Charlotte Mathilda (Burgis) W.; A.B., Yale, 1922; m. lizabeth Boardman Mosle, Oct. 26, 1925; hildren—Charles Albert, David H., Cornelia E. vice res. Bankers Trust Co., London office, 1931-35, New ork, 1936-48; chmn. exec. com. and dir. Freeport ulphur Co., N.Y. City, 1948-58, pres., dir., 1958-61, ice chmn. bd., from 1961; dir. Nat. Potash Co., Sulphur xport Corp., Madison Fund, Inc., Grumman Aircraft ngring. Corp., McGraw-Hill Pub. Co. Trustee Lenox ill Hospital, New York City. Mem. Council Fgn. elations, Nat. Indsl. Conf. Bd. Presbyterian. Club: niversity, Century Assn. (New York). Home: Niantic T Died Mar. 29, 1972.

WIGHT, JOHN FITCH, hosp. adminstr.; b. Broadus, Mont., May 15, 1928; s. John F. and Susan (Goeres) W.; .S., U. Cal. at Berkeley, 1949; m. Jean Ivadell Maffly, May 22, 1948; children—John Fitch III, David A., teven M. Adminstrv. asst. Herrick Meml. Hosp., erkeley, 1949-50, asst. adminstr., 1951-57, adminstrv. r., 1957-66, adminstr., 1966-70. Instr., U. Cal., erkeley, 1957-70. Columbia, 1964-66. Active various ommunity charity drs. Served to ensign USNR, 942-46. Fellow Am. Coll. Hosp. Adminstrs.; mem. m. Pub. Health Assn., Hosp. Council No. Cal. res.-elect 1966-67, bd. dirs.), E. Bay Hosp. Conf. res. 1959, 60, 61), Cal. Hosp. Assn., Assn. Western osps., Hosp. Service of Cal. (rep. mem.), Berkeley C. C., Sigma Alpha Epsilon. Republican. Lion (pres. erkeley 1959-60). Club: Commonwealth (San rancisco). Home: Orinda CA Died Oct. 11, 1970.

WIGHT, THOMAS, architect; b. Halifax, N.S., Can., ept. 17, 1874; s. Robert Adam and Emmaline MacLean) W.; ed. pub. schs., Can.; archtl. study, Italy nd Greece; m. Grace L. Sheridan, Oct. 3, 1905; hildren—Helen MacLean (Mrs. Glen Edward Riley), orothy Mary (Mrs. Delmer M. Buckley), Marjorie heridan (dec.). Came to the United States, 1891, ecame naturalized citizen, 1913. With McKim, Mead White, architects. N.Y. City, 1892-1904; began actice at Kansas City, Mo., 1904; owner Wight & ight. Among important bldgs. designed and pervised by him are: William Rockhill Nelson Gallery Art, Atkins Museum of Fine Arts, Kansas City Life s. Co. Bldg., St. Joseph Hosp., Wyandotte County ourt House (winner of competition), First Nat. Bank dg., Jackson County Court House (exterior design), Kansas City. Chmn. Art Commn., Kansas City, 906-07. Mem. Am. Inst. Architects, Kansas City (Mo.) hamber of Commerce. Club: Kansas City. Home: 3863 olmes St. Office: 923 Baltimore Av., Kansas City O‡

WILBAR, CHARLES LUTHER JR., physician; b. hila., June 8, 1907; s. Charles Luther and Clara May chmidt) W.; A.B., U. Pa., 1928, M.D., 1932; D.Sc., hila. Coll. of Pharmacy and Sci., 1966; m. Mildred ene Robinson, Sept. 3, 1935; children—Irene May, harlotte Ellen, Frederick Hanson. Gen. rotating intern bington (Pa.) Meml. Hosp. 1932-33; resident diatrics Mary Drexel Children's Hosp., Phila., 1943; sident medicine Queen's Hosp., Honolulu, H.I., 1935; . Ewa (H.I.) Health Project, research pub. health, trition and pediatrics, 1936-39; dir. bur. maternal and ild health Bd. Health, Honolulu, 1939-41, pres. Bd. ealth, 1943-53; pediatric tng. Children's Hosp., Cin., 940-41; part-time faculty U. Hawaii, 1936-53; dep. sec. alth, Pa., 1953-57, sec. health, 1957-67; lectr. Grad. h. Pub. Health U. Pitts., 1953-67; vis. prof. pub. health d preventive medicine U. Pa., 1958-67; asso. pub. alth adminstrn. dept. Sch. Hygiene and Pub. Health, hns Hopkins 1964-69; clin. prof. medicine W.Va. U. h. Medicine, 1967-69; director West Virginia egional Medical Program for Heart, Cancer and roke, since 1967. Chairman of the Ohio River Valley ater Sanitary Commn., 1961-62, Interstate Commn. on the Potomac River Basin, 1963-65. Chairman of the Central Pennsylvania chapter of the National Multiple Sclerosis Soc., 1958-61; mem. board dirs. Nat. Multiple Sclerosis Soc., 1962-69; bd. dirs. Pa. Tb and Health Soc., 1958-67. Served from capt. to major Medical Corps, AUS, 1941-42. Recipient citation for distinguished service American Podiatry Association, 1966. Diplomate of American Board of Pediatrics, Am. Bd. Pub. Health and Preventive Medicine, Fellow Am. Pub. Health Assn.; mem. A.M.A., Assn. State and Provincial Health Authorities N.A. (pres. 1951-52), Assn. State and Territorial Health Officers (pres. 1962-63), National (dir. 1959-61), Pa. (v.p. 1959-61) health councils. Unitarian (pres. bd. trustees 1959-64). Club: Lions (pres. Honolulu 1952-53; dist. gov. Pa. 1957-58). Contbr. articles sci. jours. Home: Morgantown WV Died Jan. 22, 1969; inurned Arlington Cemetery Philadelphia PA

WILBUR, JOHN MILNOR, clergyman, educator; b. Charleston, S.C., Jan. 30, 1870; s. Theodore Augustus and Mary Bee (Cuttino) W.; prep. edn. University Sch., Charleston; Th.G., Southern Bapt. Theol. Sem., 1892; D.D., Richmond (Va.) Coll., 1912; m. Emma Comey Ellison, Sept. 2, 1924; children—John Milnor, Frances Comey. Ordained Bapt. ministry, 1891; asst. Eutaw Pl. Ch., Baltimore, 1892-93; pastor North Av. Ch., Baltimore, and later asso. pastor Eutaw Pl. Ch., until 1902; pastor Narberth, Pa., and Central Ch., Trenton, N.J., until 1909; prof. Bapt. Inst. for Christian Workers, Phila., 1909-11, pres. 1911-37, now pres. emeritus. Pres. Bd. of Edn. Northern Bapt. Conv., 1925-27; editor The Baptist Commonwealth, Phila., 5 yrs. Trustee Bapt. Inst. Mem. Beta Theta Pi. Home: 1308 Pleasure Av., Ocean City NJ‡

WILCOX, CLAIR, economist; b. Cuba, N.Y., Jan. 29, 1898; s. Frederick R. and Estelle (Wilcox) Lown; B.S., U. of Pa., 1919, Ph.D., 1927; M.A., Ohio State U., 1922; m. Florence Chapman, June 10, 1923 (dec.); children—Andrea, Carolyn; married 2d, Marcia Lincoln Wallace, 1955. Instr. economics, Lafayette Coll., 1919-20; asst. prof. economics, Ohio Wesleyan U., 1920-23; instr. econ., U. of Pa., 1923-27; asst. prof. econ., Swarthmore Coll., 1927-29, asso. prof., 1929-31, prof., from 1931; adviser on indsl. econs., Planning Bd., Govt. Pakistan, 1956-57; consultant plan orgn. Government of Iran, 1960; cons. Southeast Asia, Ford Found., 1961-62, program specialist, Malaysia field office, 1963-64; visiting professor, Princeton University, 1965. Sec. Pa. Parole Commn., 1926-27; dir. research Nat. Commn. Law Observance and Enforcement, 1930-31; mem. gen. code authority and adv. council. Nat. Recovery Adminstrn., 1934-35; cons. economist Social Security Bd., 1936; econ. expert Temporary Nat. Econ. Com. 1939-40; price exec. iron and steel branch, OPA, 1942, dir. indsl. materials div., 1942-43; chmn. Conf. Price Research, 1944-45; dir. Office Internat. Trade Policy, Dept. of State, 1945-48; vice chmn. or chmn. U.S. dels. to internat. confs. Mem. editorial staff, St. Louis Post-Dispatch, 1933-35, Fortune Mag., 1944. Mem. Am. Assn. Univ. Profs., Am. Econ. Assn. (v.p. 1950). Author books relating to field. Home: Swarthmore PA Died Dec. 31, 1970.

WILCOX, DEWITT GILBERT, surgeon; b. Akron, O., Jan. 15, 1858; s. David Gilbert and Hannah (Whitney) W.; student Buchtel Coll., Akron; M.D., Cleveland Hosp. Med. Coll., 1880; post-grad. work, St. Bartholomew Hosp., London, Eng., 1882-83; New York Post-Grad. Sch., 1887; m. Jennie Green, 1883; children—Margaret (Mrs. John M. Colony), Helen (Mrs. Jacob H. Randolph), John Maxson (M.D.), DeWitt Gifford (killed in World War, 1918). Began practice at Akron, O., 1880; moved to Buffalo, N.Y., 1887; attending surgeon, Buffalo Homoe. Hosp., 1890-1908, Erie County Hosp., 1892-98; surgeon-in-chief of Lexington Heights Hosp., 1890-1909; prof. gynecology, Boston U. Sch. of Medicine, 1909-32. Retired after 59 years of service, June 15, 1939. Apptd. surgeon Mass. State Guard with rank of capt., by Gov. McCall; attached to Mass. State Base Hosp., Commonwealth Armory. Attending surgeon Newton Hosp., 1918-32; attending gynecologist Westboro State Hosp., 1920-32. Was the first to operate on criminal's brain, 1909, for purpose of effecting change in character, F.A.C.S.; mem. A.M.A., Am. Inst. Homoeopathy (pres. 1914), Phi Delta Theta; ex-pres. N.Y. State Homeoe. Soc. Ex-pres. Boston Bapt. Sociol. Union. Author: Health Hygiene, Happiness, 1910; Physical Awakening of the Boy, 1911. Home: 118 Homer St., Newton Center MA‡

WILCOX, EDWARD BYERS, pub. accountant; b. La Porte, Ind., Dec. 17, 1893; s. Franklin Trumbull and Helen (Byers) W.; B.S., Northwestern U., 1916; m. Mary Gore, Mar. 11, 1919; children—Robert Byers, Ann Rogers (Mrs. Robert H. Jones), and Lee Davis (Mrs. Arthur Kneerim). C.P.A., State Ill., 1923. Partner Edward Gore & Co., 1927-55, Wilcox, Harbison & Co., 1955-59, Scovell, Wellington & Company, 1959-62. Member board of examiners accountancy in Ill., 1935-38. Mem. bd. dirs. Chgo. Crime Commn., 1941-54. Served as 2d lt. inf. A.E.F., 1916-19. Mem. Ill. Soc. C.P.A.'s (pres. 1953-54), Am. Inst. Certified Public Accountants (pres. 1946-47), Beta Alpha Psi, Phi Delta Theta. Clubs: Literary (pres. 1953-54), University, Indiana of Chgo. Home: Winnetka IL Died Feb. 1972.

WILCOX, ELIAS BUNN, soldier, lawyer; b. Nash Co., N.C., June 28, 1869; s. Edward Warren and Mary (Bunn) W.; ed. pub. schs. and under pvt. instrn.; engaged in ednl. work; grad. in law, U. of N.C., 1895; m. Vardaman Cockrell, of New York, Nov. 5, 1910; children—Mary Winifred, Adah Louise. Admitted to Supreme Court of N.C., 1895, Supreme Court of U.S., 1907; capt. U.S. Vol. Inf. (Immunes), 1898; served at Santiago, Cuba; in comd. mil. forces of Dist. of Holguin, later comd. mounted troops to fight bandits, his reg. holding record for longest vol. service in Cuba. After being mustered out of mil. service was apptd. spl. insp. Pub. Instrn. for Cuba; formulated plan for grading of schs. of Cuba. In P.R., since Aug. 1902; was dist. supt. schs. of Guayama; spl. del. Govt. for inspection of elections of 1902; spl. asst. atty.-gen.; capt. Insular Constabulary and acting cheif same for several mos.; lt.-col. on governor's mil. staff; judge of Dist. Court of Ponce, P.R., 1903-04; asst. sec. of state; gen. supervisor of elections, Aug. 1, 1904-Jan. 14, 1905; spl. counsel of govt., prosecuting election fraud cases; dist. atty. Jud. Dist. of Guayama, 1905-08; dist. atty., 1909, resigned to practice law at San Juan, P.R. Prominently connected with citrus fruit culture in P.R.; pres. Rio Hondo Planters' Assn., Bayamon Fruit Growers' Assn. First comdr. Camp Spanish-Am. War Vets. in P.R. Hon. mention in Army and Navy Journal for mil. service in Cuba; medal of honor conferred for same by Nat. Congress of S.A.R., Nov. 26, 1917. Grad. as capt. N.A., and ranking officer from O.T.C., Henry Barracks, P.R.; served in world war with Porto Rico Brigade as ins. officer, judge advocate; comd. Development Battn.; detailed to organize, instruct and command Porto Rico Home Guard of 3,000 men and officers; bvtd. maj. just before armistice. Resumed practice of law, Feb. 18, 1919. Lt. col. Judge Advocate Gen's. Dept. Res., U.S.A. Revised and recorded titles of Federal property in Porto Rico, valued at $13,000,000, without compensation, under appointment of sec. of war who officially referred to the work as patriotic service." Author of article Birth of English Civilization in America," dedicated to the lasting friendship of English Speaking Peoples as an important factor in the preservation and progress of world civilization, in the Town San Juan PR‡

WILD, JOHN DANIEL, retired educator; b. Chgo., Apr. 10, 1902; s. John Daniel and Fanny (Eggleston) W.; Ph.B., U. Chgo., 1923, Ph.D., 1926; A.M., Harvard, 1925; L.H.D. (hon.), Ripon Coll., 1950; m. Catherine Alsager, Dec. 16, 1929; children—Cynthia Margaret, Mary Ruth. Instr. U. Mich., 1926-27; instr. philosophy Harvard, 1927-34, asst. prof., 1934-40, asso. prof., 1940-46, prof., 1946-61, mem. staff Div. Sch., 1954-61; chmn. dept. philosophy Northwestern U., 1961-63; prof. philosophy Yale, 1963-69; emeritus, 1969-72; vis. prof. U. Chgo., 1940, Honolulu, 1949, U. Wash., 1950-51, U. Fla., 1969-70; Powell lectr. U. Ind. 1953. Guggenheim fellow, 1930-31, 57-58. Mem. Assn. Realistic Philosphy (pres. 1947-50), Am. Philos. Assn. (v.p. 1950-51, pres. Eastern div. 1960), Metaphys. Soc. Am. (pres. 1953), Am. Acad. Arts and Scis., Soc. Phenomenological and Existential Philosophy. Episcopalian. Author: George Berkeley, 1936; Plato's Theory of Man, 1946; Introduction to Realistic Philosophy, 1948; Plato's Modern Enemies and the Theory of Natural Law, 1953; Challenge of Existenialism, 1955. Mem. East-West Philosopher's Conf. Editor: Spinoza, 1929; The Return to Reason, 1953; Human Freedom and Social Order, 1959; The Radical Empiricism of William James, 1969; Existence and the World of Freedom, 1963; mem. editorial bd. Philosophy and Phenomenological Research, 1947-72, Philosophy East and West, 1951-72. Contbr. essays, chpts., prof. publs. Address: Jaffrey Center NH Died Oct. 23, 1972; buried Jaffrey Center NH

WILD, LAURA HULDA, coll. prof.; b. Greensboro, Vt., Dec. 22, 1870; d. Azel W. and Ellen (Douglas) Wild; student Mt. Holyoke Sem. (now Coll.), 1886, 1887; A.B., Smith Coll., 1892; B.D., Hartford Theol. Sem., 1896. Sec. Y.W.C.A., Lincoln, Neb., 1896-98; nat. sec. Y.W.C.A., 1898-1901; ordained ministry Congl. Church, 1901; pastor Lincoln, Neb., 1901-05; prof. Bibl. lit., Doane Coll., Crete, Neb., 1905-09; prof. same, Lake Erie Coll., Painesville, O., 1910-17; prof. same Mt. Holyoke Coll., 1917-37, emeritus since 1937; visiting prof. Ginling Coll., China, 1923-24. Author: Geographic Influences in Old Testament Masterpieces, 1915; The Evolution of the Hebrew People, 1917; A Present-Day Definition of Christianity, 1920; A Literary Guide to the Bible, 1922; The Romance of the English Bible, 1929; Courageous Adventures: Bible Stories, 1936. Meditations: Suggested by Biblical and Other Poetry, 1937; also chapter on Tyndale's Linguistic Genius in Macdonald Presentation Volume, 1933; also the article on English Versions of the Bible, in Standard Bible Dictionary, 3d edit., 1935, and chapter on Maude Royden in Creative Personalities, Vol. II, 1940, and on Ignatius Loyola, Vol. III, 1941. Compiler: Ethical Readings from the Bible (with Harriet Keeler), 1915. Contbr. articles to Jour. of Bible and Religion: The Basic Teachings of Jesus, 1944, Teaching the Fourth Gospel, 1947. Received first hon. mention in prize contest for best essay on Religious Education in Public Schools, offered by N.E.A., 1915. Home: 467 W. 8th St., Claremont CA‡

WILDER, CHARLES WESLEY, educator; b. Cliftondale, Mass., Feb. 16, 1877; s. Rev. Charles Wesley and Janette Howe (Davis) W.; Dedham (Mass.) High Sch. and Adams Acad.; A.B., Boston U., 1899; A.M., Harvard, 1905; studied Harvard, 1905-06; m. Maude Janette Case, of Putnam, Conn., June 22, 1912; children—Charles Wesley, Janette Case. Instructor in Latin and Greek, Norwalk (Connecticut) Univ. Sch., 1899-1901, Pennington (N.J.) Sem., 1901-02, Trinity Hall, Washington, D.C., 1902-04; asst. history dept., Harvard, 1904-06; head of history dept., Worcester (Mass.) Acad., 1906-15; headmaster Thurston Sch. for Boys, Pittsburgh, Pa., 1915-19; headmaster Arnold Sch., successor to Thurston Sch., since 1919. Mem. Phi Beta Kappa, Theta Delta Chi. Episcopalian. Club: University. Home: 7553 Graymore Rd., Pittsburgh PA‡

WILDER, SALMON WILLOUGHBY, mfr.; b. Lawrence, Mass., Feb. 10, 1870; s. Salmon Willoughby and Rose Eaton (True) W.; grad. Lowell High School, 1886; studied abroad, 1886-87; S.B. in Chem. Engring., Mass. Inst. Tech., 1891; m. Marcia Russell Sawyer, 1895; children—Philip Sawyer, Rachel. Connected with Russell Paper Co., Lawrence, 1891-93 inclusive; with Wm. Russell & Son, Boston, and Fall Mountain Paper Co., Bellows Falls, Vt., 1894-97 inclusive; with Merrimac Chemical Co., Boston, 1898-1931, pres., 1904-28, chmn. bd., 1928-31; trustee Newton Center Savings Bank. Former mem. sch. bd., City of Newton; mem. Advisory Board, U.S. Chem. Warfare Service, Boston Procurement District; mem. Corporation Massachusetts Institute Technology. Mem. Synthetic Organic Chem. Mfrs.' Assn. of U.S.; ex-chmn. exec. com. Mfg. Chemists' Assn. of U.S.; mem. Am. Chem. Soc., Soc. of Chemical Industry. Republican. Clerk First Congl. Ch., Newton Centre, Mass. Home: 21 Institution Av., Newton Center 59 MA‡

WILDMAN, MARIAN WARNER (MRS. JESSE A. FENNER), author; b. Norwalk, O., Oct. 14, 1876; d. Samuel Augustus and Ellen Elisabeth (Howe) W.; A.B., Western Reserve U., 1898; m. Jesse A. Fenner, Oct. 7, 1914. Began writing as a child; winner of $250 prize offered by Century Magazine, 1899, for best poem by coll. grad. of preceding yr., receiving degree of A.B. Mem. Phi Beta Kappa. Club: Ohio Woman's Press. Author: A Hill Prayer and Other Poems, 1903; Loyalty Island, 1904; Theodore and Theodora, 1905; What Robin Did Then, 1907; Betty's Beautiful Nights; A Help Meet for Him. Contbr. to mags. Address: 2112 E. 83d St., Cleveland OH‡

WILES, KIMBALL, coll. dean; author; b. Ripley, O., Oct. 17, 1913; s. M.K. and Ethel (Griffith) W.; B.S. in Edn., Miami (O.) U., 1934; M.A., Ohio State U., 1938, Ph.D., 1940; m. Hilda Long, June 6, 1936; children—David Kimball, Jon Whitney, Wendy Ann, Ann Kimball. Tchr., Liberty Twp. schs., Hamilton, O., 1934-35, Middletown (O.) schs., 1935-37; research asst. Ohio State U., 1937-39; asst. prof. edn. U. Ala., 1939-42; tng. coordinator Sperry Gyroscope Co., 1942-44; curriculum cons., dir. sch. and coll. div. Nat. Safety Council, 1944-46; asso. prof., then prof. edn. N.Y.U., 1946-50; prof. edn., chmn. div. curriculum and instrn. U. Fla., 1950-69, dean College of Education, 1964-69. Vice pres. bd. dirs. Southwestern Ednl. Lab., 1966-69. Member of Assn. for Supervision and Curriculum Devel. (exec. com. 1952-53, president Fla. 1960-61, nat. pres. 1963-64), Am. Edn. Research Assn., Nat., Fla. edn. assns., Phi Beta Kappa, Phi Delta Kappa, Kappa Delta Pi. Methodist. Author: The Changing Curriculum of the American High School, 1963; Teaching for Better Schools, 2d edit., 1959; Supervision for Better Schools, 3d edit., 1967. Co-author: Supervision in Physical Education, 1956 (with G. Hass) Readings in Curriculum, 1965. Co-editor: Toward Better Teaching 1949; Assn. Supervision and Curriculum and Devel. Yearbook, 1949. Bd. editors: Ednl. Adminstrn. and Supervision, 1954-58, The Clearing House, 1946-51. Cons. editor Charles E. Merrill Pub. Co., Mathers McCormick Editorial bd. Edn. Digest, Edn. Forum. Home: Gainesville FL Died Feb. 2, 1968; buried Evergreen Cemetery, Gainesville FL

WILEY, H(ENRY) ORTON, coll. pres.; b. Marquette, Neb., Nov. 15, 1877; s. John Thompson and Alice Chloe (Johnston) W.; grad. Ore. State Normal Sch., Ashland, Ore., 1898; A.B., U. of the Pacific, San Jose, Calif., 1910; B.D., Pacific Theol. Sem., Berkeley, Calif., 1910, S.T.M., 1916; D.D., Pasadena (Calif.) College, 1925; S.T.D. from Pacific Sch. of Religion, 1929; m. Alice May House, Nov. 8, 1902; children—Alma Pearl, Lester Vernon, Henry Ward, Alice Ruth. Ordained ministry Ch. of the Nazarene, 1909; pastor Berkeley (Calif.) Ch. of the Nazarene, 1905-09; pres. Pasadena Coll., 1910-16 and 1926-49, emeritus; pres. Northwest Nazarene Coll., Nampa, Ida., 1916-26. Sec. Gen. Bd. of Edn., Ch. of the Nazarene, since 1915; editor official church organ., 1928-36. Home: 1389 N. Sierra Bonita Av., Pasadena 7 CA‡

WILEY, HUGH, writer; b. Zanesville, O. Feb. 26, 1884; s. Eliphalet Case and Rose (McDonald) W.; ed. in public schs. Engr. and contractor for bridges, power plants, mines, railroads, in U.S., Canada and Mexico. Served as captain, B Company 18th Engrs., A.E.F., France, 1917-19. Author: The Wildcat, 1920; The Prowler, 1921; Jade, 1921; Lady Luck, 1922; Lily, 1923; Four Meals a Day, 1927; Manchu Blood, 1928; Here's Luck, 1928; The Copper Mask, 1930; also short stories for Saturday Evening Post, Colliers, Cosmopolitan, Red Book; also tech. reports on various engring. projects, and studies in early Chinese jade and bronze. Home: Berkeley CA Died 1969.

WILEY, SAMUEL ERNEST, educator; b. Kirkwood, Mo., Nov. 7, 1904; s. Samuel Ernest and Caroline Emily (Grau) W.; A.B., Athaeneum of Ohio, Cin., 1926; Ph.D., Acad. Romana, Rome, Italy, 1930; m. Mary Kupir, Apr. 11, 1946; children—Julie Caroline, Mary Patricia. Tchr. high sch., Nashville, 1930-42; editor Culver City (Cal.) Citizens, 1946-48; also Features mag.; prof. philosophy Long Beach (Cal.) State Coll., 1949-68, chmn. div. humanities, 1961-67, assistant dean School of Letters and Science, 1967-68. Chmn. Academic Senate of Cal. State Colls., 1963-64. Mem. Orange County Orchid Soc. (past pres.), Tau Kappa Epsilon. Editor: History of Long Beach State College, 1960. Home: Long Beach CA Died Oct. 2, 1968.

WILFORD, LORAN FREDERICK, artist; b. in Kansas Sept. 13, 1893; s. John and Martha (Sparks) W.; student Kansas City Art Inst., 1914-18, George Pearse Eniss Sch., 1929-32; m. Eunice E. Daggett, Feb. 16, 1918; children—Norman D., Gordon F., Janis M. Began as newspaper illustrator, 1914, and later mag. illustrator; painter specializing in landscape, figures and murals from 1922, instr. Ringling Sch. of Art from 1950. Executed 7 panel murals in midwestern (Wis.) High School. Works have been exhibited in large galleries; illustrator nat. mags. Represented in collections of museums, clubs, etc. Recipient of many prizes. Home: Sarasota FL Died Dec. 5, 1972.

WILGRESS, L. DANA, diplomat; b. Vancouver, B.C., Can., Oct. 20, 1892; s. Henry Trollope and Helene Maud (Empey) W.; student Queen's Sch., Victoria, B.C.; B.A. with honors, McGill U., 1914; LL.D., U. B.C., 1953, McGill University, 1954; m. Olga Buergin, June 4, 1919; children—Victor Jura, Edward Dana, Diana Sonia. Jr. trade commr. Dept. Trade and Commerce, Ottawa, Can., 1914-16; trade commr., Omsk 1916-18, Vladivostok, 1918-19; spl. trade commr. for South-East Europe, 1920, London, 1921-22; trade commr., Hamburg, 1922-32; dir. Comml. Intelligence Service, Ottawa, 1932-40; dep. minister of Trade and Commerce, 1940-42; minister, later ambassador at Moscow, 1942-47; minister at Berne, 1947-49; High Commr. for Can. at London, 1949-52; under-sec. of State for External Affairs, 1952-53; permanent rep. to North Atlantic Council, 1953-58; chairman of Canadian section Permanent Joint Board on Defense (Canada and U.S.), 1958-69. Chairman Canadian delegation to Prep. Commn. of UN, 1945, chmn. com. V. Gen. Assembly, 1948, chmn. contracting parties to gen. agreement on tariffs and trades, 1948-51, 53-56; chmn. Canadian Delegation To Geneva and Havana trade confs., 1947, 48. Clubs: Rideau, Country (Ottawa, Can.). Home: Ottawa ON Canada Died July 21, 1969.

WILHELM, RICHARD HERMAN, educator; b. N.Y. City, Jan. 10, 1909; s. Ernst Richard and Ida Emma (Krebs) W.; B.S., Columbia, 1931, Ch. E., 1932, Ph.D., 1935; m. Rachel Marjorie Hixson, June 19, 1937 (dec. Sept. 1964); children—Karen Elise, Joan Andrea, Richard David Washburn; m. 2d, Sarah Kollock Strayer, July 2, 1966. Faculty Princeton, 1934-68, prof. chem. engring., 1946-68, chmn. dept. engring., 1954-68, Henry Putnam Univ. prof., 1968; indsl. cons. Ofcl. investigator, Nat. Defense Research Com., 1941-43; cons. chem. warfare panel, Research and Development Bd., 1949-53. Recipient Profl. Progress award Am. Inst. Chem. Engrs., 1952, Warren K. Lewis award in chem. Engring. edn., 1966, William H. Walker award, 1951; Indsl. and Engring. Chem. award Am. Chem. Soc., 1966. Registered profl. engr., N.J. Fellow Am. Acad. Arts and Scis.; mem. Am. Inst. Chem. Engrs. (dir. 1956-59), Am. Chem. Soc., Am. Soc. Engring. Edn., Nat. Acad. Engring., Sigma Xi, Tau Beta Pi. Presbyn. Club: Nassau. Home: Princeton NJ Died Aug. 6, 1968.

WILKE, OTTO JOHN, clergyman; b. Charles City, Ia., May 7, 1874; s. Christian Friedrich and Adelheid (Haering) W.; A.B., Wartburg Coll., Waverly, Ia., 1892; student Wartburg Sem., Dubuque, Ia., 1892-95; B.D., English Lutheran Sem., Chicago, 1896; grad. work, U. of Wis., 1896-97; D.D., Capital U., Columbus, O., 1939; m. Klara Marie Beck, May 7, 1901; children—Adelaide Marie, Erna Helen. Ordained Lutheran ministry, 1897; pastor Superior, Wis., 1897-1904; succeeded father as pastor St. John Lutheran Congregation, Madison, Wis., 1904; pastor emeritus since 1946; vice pres. and dir. Luth. Mutual Fire Ins. Assn., v.p. and dir. Provident Loan & Bldg. Assn., 1932-47. Mem. exec. com. and 2d v.p. Am. Luth. Church, 1932-38; 3d v.p. Wisconsin District of Am. Luth. Church, 1932-40; member Fellowship Commission American Lutheran Ch., 1932-41; member bd. trustees Madison Lutheran Hosp. and Sanatorium Assn.; chmn. directing com. Luth. Student Service, U. of Wis.; president Madison Free Library Board. Mem. Steuben Soc. (Madison), Sportsman's League, Madison Cine 8 mm Club. Home: Lake Mendota Dr., R. 2, Madison WI‡

WILKES, JACK STAUFFER, coll. president; born Honey Grove, Tex., Aug. 5, 1917; s. Rex Bozarth and Fay (Stauffer) W.; B.A., Hendrix Coll., Conway, Ark., 1938; B.D., So. Meth. U., 1941; D.D., Oklahoma City U., 1956; LL.D., McMurry Coll., Abilene, Tex., 1958; m. Myra Annette Germany, Aug. 20, 1941; children—Sarah Elisabeth, Rex Benjamin, Judith Ann, Susanna Ruth. Admitted to ministry Meth. Ch., 1941; pastor Meth. Ch., Deer Creek, Okla., 1941-43, Goodwell, Okla., 1945-47, Perry, Okla., 1947-50, First Meth. Ch., Muskogee, Okla., 1950-54. Crown Heights Meth. Ch., Oklahoma City, 1954-57; instr., coach, Panhandle A. and M. Coll., 1945-47; pres. Oklahoma City U., 1957-63; pastor Wesley Meth. Ch., 1963-64; mayor Oklahoma City, 1963-64; pres. Centenary Coll. of La., 1964-69; v.p. for univ. relations So. Meth. U., 1969. State chmn. Brotherhood Week, Nat. Conf. Chrisitans and Jews, 1958; pres. Okla. Ind. Coll. Found. 1960-61. Served as lt. (j.g.), Chaplains Corps, USNR 1943-45. Mem. N.E.A., Alpha Chi, Sigma Alpha Epsilon, Blue Key. Mason, Rotarian. Home: Shreveport LA Died Nov. 1969; buried Dallas TX

WILKES, JAMES CLAIBORNE, SR., lawyer; b. Petersburg, Va., Mar. 6, 1899; s. William and Lizzie (Ferguson) W.; LL.B., Georgetown U., 1921; A.B., George Washington U., 1925; m. Edna G. Cross, June 7, 1926; children—James Claiborne, Charles Latimer Admitted to D.C. bar, 1921, practiced in Washington partner Wilkes & Artis, 1940-68; asst. corp. counsel D.C., 1922-26; gen. counsel Washington Hotel Assn. Fed. City Council, YMCA of Washington, and Doctors Hospital, also the Home Builders Assn. Met Washington. Dir. Am. Security & Trust Co., Columbia Fed. Savs. & Loan Assn., Barber & Ross, Inc. Chmn D.C. Republican Com., 1936-49. Fellow Am. Coll. Tria Lawyers; mem. Am., D.C. bar assns., Lambda Alpha Mason (Jester). Clubs: National Lawyers, Metropolitan Barristers. Nat. Press, Columbia Country. Capitol Hil Republican (Washington). Home: Washington DC Died Nov. 30, 1968; buried Columbia Gardens Cemetery Arlington VA

WILKINS, RAYMOND SANGER, judge; b. Salem Mass., May 24, 1891; s. Samuel Herbert and Mariett Burke (Rowell) W.; A.B., Harvard, 1912, LL.B., 1915 Doctor Juridicial Sci. (hon.), Suffolk U., 1951; LL.D. Northeastern U., 1952, Western N.E. Coll., 1956 Boston U., 1957, Tufts U., 1960, Am. Internat. College 1963, Harvard, 1964; J.D., Portia Law Sch., 1960; m Mary Louisa Aldrich, Sept. 22, 1923 (dec.) children—Raymond Sanger, David (dec.), Herber Putnam; m. 2d, Katharine S. Choate, Nov. 18, 195 (dec. Nov. 1959); m. 3d, Georgie E. Hebbard, Augus 7, 1965. Admitted to Mass. bar, 1915; and practiced i Boston, 1915-44, with Storey, Thorndike, Palmer & Dodge, later known as Palmer, Dodge, Wilkins & Davis apptd. associate justice Supreme Judicial Ct. Mass. 1944; chief justice, 1956-70. Selectman, Winchester Mass., 1935-37, moderator, 1940-43; mem. gov' council, Mass. 1941-43. Served as 2d lt., 1st lt., an capt., 301st F.A., A.E.F., 1917-19. Trustee Soldier Home in Mass., 1942-44, Boston Athenaeum; Bosto Symphony Orchestra, Peabody Mus. Former oversee Harvard; mem. corp. Northeastern University Massachusetts Institute of Technology. Mem. counc Am. Law Institute; member Harvard Law School Ass (former pres.), Am. Antiquarian Soc., Am., Mass Boston, Middlesex and Essex bar assns., Boston Lega Aid Soc. (hon. pres.), Colonial Soc. Mass., Mass. Hist Soc., Vets. Fgn. Wars, Am. Legion, Phi Beta Kappa Unitarian. Clubs: Harvard, Union, Odd Volumes Somerset, Tavern (Boston); Myopia Hunt (Hamilton) Home: Boston MA Died May 1971.

WILKINSON, ALFRED DICKINSON, paper mfr.; b Centerville, S.D., May 25, 1907; s. William A. and Olli (Dickinson) W.; B.A., Cornell Coll., 1928; m. France Chassell, May 29, 1931; children—Sally, Sue, Kay With Kimberly Clark Corp., Neenah, Wis., 1928-70 formerly corporate v.p., then gen. mgr. Shasta Di Home: Redding CA Died Aug. 7, 1970; burie Riverside Cemetery, Appleton WI

WILKINSON, WILLIAM ALBERT, prof. edn.; b Buffalo, Mo., Mar. 4, 1873; s. Joseph S. and Margar Anne (Stanley) W.; B.Pd., M.Pd., State Normal Sch Warrensburg, Mo., 1907; B.S. in Edn., U. of Mo., 191 A.M., 1911, A.M., Teachers Coll. (Columbia), 1918; m Grace Greenwood Speaker, Sept. 5, 1918. Teacher M rural schs., 4 yrs.; county commr. schs., Dallas County Mo., 1894-96; prin. schs., Buffalo, Mo., 1897-190 Alton, 1901-06; supt. schs., Holden, 1907-09; hea dept. edn. State Normal Sch., Mayville, N.D., 1911-1 prof. edn. and dir. Sch. of Edn., U. of Del., since 191 Mem. N.E.A., Nat. Assn. Coll. Teachers of Edn., Na Soc. for Study of Edn., Delaware State Ednl. Ass (pres. 1925-26), Phi Delta Kappa, Phi Kappa Ph Republican. Methodist. Author: Rural Scho Management, 1917. Home: Newark DE*‡

WILKINSON, WILLIAM DONALD, educato geologist; b. Minot, N.D., Sept. 23, 1901; s. William A and Ella (Walker) W.; B.A., U. Ore., 1923, Ph.D de 1932; student U. Cal. at Berkeley, 1923-24; m Marguerite F. Hill, Jan. 16, 1926; 1 dau., Janet L (Mrs. James R. Snook). Instr., U. Ore., 1929-31; mem faculty Ore. State U., 1931-69, prof. geology, 1945-69, chmn. dept., 1960-69. Served to capt. USAAF, 1942-45. Fellow A.A.A.S., Geol. Soc. Am.; mem. Am. Inst. Metall. and Mining Engrs., Am. Inst. Profl. Geologists (charter, 1st pres. Ore. chpt.), Ore. Acad. Sci., Sigma Xi, Phi Kappa Phi. Mason. Contbr. profl. jours. Home: Corvallis OR Died Jan. 3, 1969; buried Oaklawn Cemetery, Corvallis OR

WILLARD, LILLIAN WINIFRED, b. Jacksonville, Ill., Jan. 28, 1876; d. James Polk and Lydia (Larimore) W.; A.B., U. of Denver, 1899; grad. student U. of Chicago, 1905; D.Litt., Kan. Wesleyan U., 1922. Teacher Greek and Latin, 1901-05; prof. English lit., Ia. Wesleyan Coll., 1906-07; second officer and dir. publicity of Philanthropic Finance (The Hancher Organization) since 1920. Mem. Am. Assn. Univ. Women, Gamma Phi Beta Sorority, Colo. D.A.R. Republican. Office: 740 Rush St., Chicago IL‡

WILLARD, ROY H(OBSON), accountant; b. Dubach, La., Aug. 16, 1902; s. John W. and Amanda (Oliver) W.; student Tulane U., 1925-28, LaSalle Extension U., 1934-35; m. Robbie Alexander Willard, May 1, 1932; 1 dau., Robbie Ann (Mrs. Thomas Carroll Thomas III). Previous to 1929, asst. auditor Fenner & Beane, New Orleans; sr. accountant Haskins & Sells, Chas. E. Wermuth & Co., Emile Bienvenu & Asso., New Orleans, 1929-41; auditing div. RFC, Washington, 1942-44; pvt. practice accounting, Ruston, La., 1944-68, C.P.A., La., Tex. Mem. C. of C., La. Soc. C.P.A's, Am. Inst. C.P.A.'s, A.I.M., Pub. Affairs Research Council La. Baptist. Mason (K.T., Shriner), Rotarian. Home: Ruston LA Died Mar. 2, 1968.

WILLARD, WILLIAM A(LBERT), biologist; b. Grinnell, Ia., Apr. 24, 1873; s. William Origin and Emma Elizabeth (Shaw) W.; A.B., Grinnell Coll., 1895; A.M., Tufts Coll., 1898; A.M., Harvard, 1899, Ph.D., 1910; m. Blanche Ellis Snider, July 2, 1907; children—William Raymond, Ruth Eleanor. Instr. biology, Grinnell Coll., 1895-97, acting head dept., 1901-02; instr., asst. prof. zoology, U. of Neb., 1902-10, prof. and head dept. embryology and histology, 1910-14, prof. anatomy, Coll. of Medicine, 1914-46, prof. emeritus since 1946; also directed research students in neuroanatomy in Grad. Coll.; mem. summer faculties, U. of Ill. and Northwestern U. Mem. Am. Assn. Anatomists, Am. Soc. Zool., Sigma Xi (pres. Neb. chap. 1936), Phi Beta Kappa, Nu Sigma Nu. Conglist. Home: 1029 Park Av., Omaha 5 NB Office: University of Nebraska College of Medicine, Omaha NB‡

WILLCOX, WESTMORE, banker, financial consultant; b. Norfolk, Va., Oct. 23, 1894; s. J. Westmore and Louise Price (Collier) W.; grad. Croton Sch., 1913; A.B., Harvard, 1917; m. Esther L. Jenkins, Nov. 17, 1917; children—Westmore III (1st lt. dec. active duty, June 6, 1944), Esther McK. (Mrs. Carleton Putnam). With Dillon, Read & Company, New York, 1919-32, partner in Boston, 1925-28, partner in charge European business, 1928-32; financial v.p. Fed. Water Service Corp., N.Y., 1932-36; v.p. Blyth & Co., N.Y., 1936-38; partner Jackson & Curtis, 1938-41; financial cons., 1941-49; dir. British Raw Materials Mission, 1941-43; chmn. area cons. for Italy and Central Europe, Office of Fgn. Econ. Coordination, State Dept., Washington, Aug.-Nov., 1943; chief of Fgn. Econ. Adminstrn. Mission to India at New Delhi, 1945-46; cons. to Econ. Cooperation Adminstrn. spl. Mission to Great Britain in London, June-Aug. 1948; minister in charge Econ. Cooperation Adminstrn. Spl. Mission to Austria in Vienna, Aug.-Nov., 1948; cons. The Chase Bank, 1951-58; former member board directors Seaboard Airline Ry., Beneficial Indsl. Loan Corp., Fisk Rubber Co., Fed. Water Service Corp., N.Y. Water Service Corp., Cities Service Power & Light Co., Old Colony Trust Co. (Boston); mem. English Speaking Union, N.Y. City (former vice chmn.); dir. and mem. exec. com. Nat. Economy League; pres. Council for Democracy; treas. com. on Public Affairs. Democrat. Episcopalian. Clubs: Harvard, New York City (former mem. bd. of mgrs.), Associated Harvard (v.p. at large), Down Town Association. Home: New York City NY Died May 12, 1971; buried Norfolk VA

WILLEN, PEARL LARNER (MRS. JOSEPH WILLEN), orgn. exec.; b. Chgo., Jan. 2, 1904; d. Meyer and Sarah (Pastel) Larner; B.A., Washington U., 1925; student N.Y. Sch. Social Work, 1925-26; diploma Grad. Sch. Jewish Social Work, 1927; M.A. (fellow adult edn.), Columbia, 1935; m. Joseph Willen, Dec. 29, 1925; children—Paul, Deborah (Mrs. Fred Meier). Case worker Foster Home Bur., N.Y., 1927-29; exec. dir. Parent Edn. Council, Westchester, N.Y., 1933-34; dir. Parent Edn. Inst., Works Project Adminstrn., 1935; sec. Am. Labor Edn. Service, 1944-68; dir. League for Indsl. Democracy, 1948-68; dir. Workers Def. League, 1947-68, chmn. bd., 1962-68; mem. steering com. Women's Com. Civil Rights, 1963-68; bd. govs. Hebrew U., Jerusalem, 1963-68; also bd. Friends, member National bd. Ednl., Scholarship and Def. Committee Racial Equality; mem. fgn. relations com. Am. Jewish Com.; mem. Conference Presidents of Major Am. Jewish Orgns., 1963-68. Bd. govs. Am. Nat. Red Cross; mem. policy and program com. Crusade Against Poverty. Mem. President's Com. on Employment Handicapped. Vice chairman Liberal Party, 1944-48, chmn. women's div., 1946-52. Recipient award for outstanding service Nat. Council Negro Women, 1951. Mem. Nat. Social Welfare Assembly (chmn. com. on internat. social welfare 1958-62), Nat. Council Women in U.S.A. (mem. bd. 1960-68), Nat. Council Jewish Women (chmn. edn. and social action, 1947-53, chairman of the program com. 1953-54, v.p. 1955-63, pres. 1963-68; pres. internat. council 1954-57, hon. v.p. 1957-68, hon. bd. mem. N.Y. sect. 1960-68), Nat. Assn. Social Workers (commn. on internat. social work), Nat. Citizens Com. for Community Relations. Home: New York City NY

WILLETS, DAVID GIFFORD, medical zoologist; b. Scullville, N.J., Dec. 28, 1873; s. John Hope and Elizabeth Gifford (Scull) W.; Ph.B., Wesleyan U., Conn., 1902; M.D., Med. Sch., George Washington U., 1907; m. Mary Esther Kirpatrick, of Colorado Springs, Colo., Feb. 6, 1913. Asst. in Zool. Lab., Hygienic Lab., U.S. Pub. Health and Marine Hosp. Service, Washington, 1903-7; pathologist, Ga. State Sanitarium, Milledgeville, Ga., 1908, 1909; asst. Biol. Lab., Bur. of Science, Manila, 1910-13; asst. prof. med. zoology, Coll. of Medicine and Surgery, U. of Philippines, 1910-13; asst. epidemiologist, U.S. Pub. Health Service, 1914—. Methodist. Mem. A.M.A., Ga. State Med. Assn., Southern Med. Assn., Helminthol. Soc. of Washington, Alpha Delta Phi, Phi Chi. Mason. Author of bulls. and articles on pellagra, intestinal parasites, conditions affecting pub. health in P.I., etc. Address: U.S. Public Health Service, Washington DC‡

WILLETS, GILSON, author, editor, traveler; b. at Hempstead, L.I., N.Y., Aug. 10, 1869; s. Gilson and Almira W.; m. Daisy May, d. J. R. Vanderveer, of New York, 1896. Editor Current Literature, 1892-3; editor Romance Magazine, 1895-6-7; went to Cuba after Maine disaster for Leslie's Weekly and Collier's Weekly; spl. corr. in the Southern camps during Spanish-Am. War, and was 1st corr. to journey through Cuba from Havana to Santiago after the war; went to India and journeyed about 1,000 miles through the famine district, 1900; made sledge journey across the north of Russia, Finland and Sweden, 1902; made tour of capitals of Europe and West Indies, 1904, and crossed Mexico on horseback for Leslie's Weekly, 1905; made trans-continental tours for Frank A. Munsey's publs., 1906-7; made two trips to Pacific Coast covering every state in the Union for The Railroad Man's Mag., 1908-9-10. Republican. Author: His Neighbor's Wife, 1897; Anita, the Cuban Spy, 1898; The Triumph of Yankee Doodle, 1898; The Loves of Twenty and One, 1899; The Rulers of the World, 1900; Travels in India, 1901; The Workers of the Nation (2 vols.), 1903; Commercial Invasion of Europe, 1903; The Double Cross, 1910; The First Law, 1911; also numerous articles and short stories in Am. and English publs. Address: Calumet Hotel, 57th St., New York NY‡

WILLETT, GEORGE F., manufacturer; b. at Walpole, Mass., Aug. 7, 1870; s. A. D. and L.E. W.; ed. Boston U.; m. Edith M. Winslow, of Norwood, Mass., June 6, 1893. Pres. Boston Belting Corpn., Boston Belting Co.; chmn. bd. trustees Industrial Real Estate Trust. Mem. bd. dirs. Norwood Housing Assn.; dir. Boston Belting Sales Co. (Mass., also Ill.). Home: Norwood MA Office: 153 Nahatan St., Boston MA‡

WILLETT, WILLIAM, JR., congressman; b. Brooklyn, Nov. 27, 1869; s. William and Marion (White) W.; ed. Brooklyn public schs.; LL.B., New York Univ., 1896; m. Marie R. Van Tassel, of Brooklyn, August 7, 1895. Engaged in law practice since 1896; dir. in many land cos.; candidate for Congress, 1st N.Y. Dist., 1904; mem. 60th and 61st Congresses (1907-11), 14th Dist.; Democrat. Methodist. Home: Long Island City NY Office: 18 Wall St., New York NY‡

WILLETTS, HERBERT, oil exec.; b. Troy, N.Y., Nov. 26, 1899; s. Daniel and Rose Hannah (Humphreys) W.; Bachelor of Arts, Union College, 1923; married Edith Mae Iveson, August 30, 1923; children—Barbara Mae (Mrs. Donald C. Torey), Herbert I. Joined Standard Oil Co. of N.Y. (now Socony Mobil Oil Co., Inc.), Albany, N.Y., 1923, various positions marketing dept., 1923-51, mem. bd. dirs., 1951-68, v.p., 1953-59, exec. v.p., 1959-61, pres. Mobil Oil Co. div. Socony Mobil Oil Co., Inc., 1959-61. pres. parent co., 1961-64, also vice chairman of the executive committee. Served as pvt., 27th Div., A.E.F., 1918-19. Home: Larchmont NY Died July 5, 1968.

WILLEVER, JOHN CALVIN, telegraph official; b. Montana, N.J., Mar. 9, 1865; s. Jacob H. and Ellen F. (Rush) W.; ed. public schools; married Georgette E. Dauxon, June 28, 1941. Began as telegraph operator with Western Union Telegraph Co., 1882, and advanced to commercial gen. mgr., 1914, v.p. in charge commercial dept. since 1915, 1st v.p. since 1925; pres., Ocean Telegraph Co. of Mass.; v.p. Am. Dist. Telegraph Co. of N.J., Gold and Stock Tel. Co., Pacific & Atlantic Tel. Co., N.Y. Mut. Tel. Co., Southern & Atlantic Telegraph Co. and 21 other telegraph cos.; also dir. 33 telegraph cos. Republican. Home: Milburn, N.J. Office: 60 Hudson St., New York NY*‡

WILLEY, CHARLES HERBERT, educator; b. Kearny, N.J., Sept. 2, 1898; s. John Joseph and Jessie (Conklin) W.; A.B., N.Y.U., 1922, M.S., 1924, Ph.D., 1929; student Columbia, 1924-28; m. Margaret A. Klein, Apr. 15, 1922; children—John Charles, Thomas Edward. Faculty N.Y.U., 1922-69, beginning as teaching fellow, successively instr. biology, asst. prof., 1922-52, asso. prof., then prof., 1952-64, professor emeritus, 1964-69, chairman of the department, 1954-62. Served with U.S. Army, 1917-19. Decorated Order of Quetzal (Guatemala); Overseas fellow Churchill Coll., Cambridge, Eng., 1968-69. Mem. A.A.A.S., Am. Soc. Zoologists, Soc. for Am. Archeology (pres. 1967), American Society of Parasitologists, Am. Micros. Society, Genetic Soc., N.Y. Zool. Soc., N.Y. Acad. Sci., Phi Beta Kappa, Sigma Xi. Contbr. articles sci., biol. jours. Home: Bronx NY Died May 19, 1969; buried Moravian Cemetery, New Dorp, Staten Island NY

WILLI, ALBERT B(OND), business exec.; b. Williamsport, Pa., Apr. 10, 1895; s. Harry R. and Daisy P. (Smith) W.; student pub. schs.; m. Helen Lucile O'Brian, June 13, 1914; children—Albert Bond, Jr., Doris Louise, Thomas Arthur. Various positions engring. dept. Continental Motors Corp., 1917-26, exec. engr., 1926, asst. chief engr., 1927-32; chief engr. Fed.-Mogul Corp., 1933-42; v.p., asst. gen. mgr. Continental Aviation & Engring. Corp., 1942-51; exec. v.p. Continental Motors Corp., 1951-65. Profl. engr., Mich. Mem. Soc. Am. Mil. Engrs., Detroit Engring. Soc., Am. Soc. M.E. Home: Twin Lake MI Died Jan. 2, 1968.

WILLIAMS, ALFRED HICKS, metals co. exec.; b. Nashville, Nov. 28, 1912; s. Alfred H. and Elise (Lipscomb) W.; student U. Va.; m. Virginia Nunn Eady, Dec. 30, 1944; children—Lawrence L., Keith L., Elizabeth Eady. Sales exec. Brown Williamson Tobacco Co., 1932-39; gen. mgr. Canada Dry Bottling Co., Louisville, 1939-42; v.p., dir., gen. sales mgr. Consider H. Willett Co., Louisville, 1946-54; v.p. Reynolds Metals Co., Richmond, Va., 1954-72. Mgr. industry and commerce div. Louisville Community Chest, 1955-56; mem. Louisville Met. Sewer Commn., 1955-58. Served to capt., Tank Corps, AUS, 1942-46. Decorated D.S.C., Bronze Star, Purple Heart. Clubs: Louisville Country, Pendennis, Harmony Landing Country, River, Wynn-Stay, Valley (Louisville); Country of Virginia, Deep Run Hunt, Commonwealth (Richmond). Home: Richmond VA Died 1972.

WILLIAMS, ALFRED MELVIN, clergyman, educator; b. Lebanon, Ore., June 30, 1874; s. Alfred Evans and Keziah Adelia (Bentley) W.; A.B., Albany (Ore.) Coll., 1896; B.D., Cumberland U., Tenn., 1903, D.D., 1920; m. Winona Josephine Irwine, of Albany, Ore., Feb. 3, 1897. Ordained Presbyn. ministry, 1896; pastor McMinnville, Ore., 1906-11; supt. religious edn. in Ore., Wash. and Ida., 1911-14; pastor Seattle, Wash., 1914-17; pres. Albany (Ore.) Coll., 1919-22; pastor First Presbyn. Ch., Madera, Calif., 1923-29, St. Paul's Ch., San Francisco, since 1929. Commr. World's S.S. Assn. Philippines, China and Japan, 1913. Mason. Rotarian. Address: St. Paul's Presbyn. Church, San Francisco CA‡

WILLIAMS, ALPHEUS AMERICUS, educator; b. Banner, Fulton Co., Ill., May 19, 1870; s. Isaac Green Bury and Martha Ann (Davis) W.; B.S., Valparaiso U., 1892, A.B., 1894, Sc.D., 1920; studied U. of Ill.; m. Nettie Edna Dowdell, of Valparaiso, Ind., Aug. 17, 1897. Asst. prof. commercial brances, Valparaiso U., 1890-95; pres. Southern Ia. Normal and Scientific Inst., Bloomfield, Ia., 1895-1902; prof. higher mathematics, 1902-21; v.p. and treas., June, 1921—. Valparaiso U. Mem. Ind. Acad. Science. Democrat. Methodist. Actively interested in scientific methods of growing fruits. Home: Valparaiso IN‡

WILLIAMS, ANNA WESSELS, M.D.; b. Hackensack, N.J., Mar. 17, 1863; d. William and Jane Amelia (Van Saun) Williams; M.D., Women's Med. Coll. New York Infirmary, 1891; grad. study, Germany, Pasteur Inst., Paris, Marine Biol. Lab. and Columbia. Began practice at N.Y. City, 1895; asst. to chair of pathology and hygiene, New York Infirmary for Women and Children, 1891-96, pathologist, 1902-05; bacteriologist, N.Y. City Bur. of Labs., 1895-1905; asst. dir. labs., Health Dept. of N.Y. City, 1905-34; served as lecturer New York U. Med. Bd. and as scientific asst. U.S. Pub. Health Service. Mem. A.A.A.S., Am. Pub. Health Assn., Soc. Am. Bacteriologists, Am. Assn. Immunologists, Am. Social Hygiene Assn., Women's Med. Assn. (pres. 1914), N.Y. Acad. Medicine, N.Y. Pathol. Soc. Club: Pascack Women's (N.J.). Author: Pathogenic Microorganisms, 1905, 10th edit., 1933; Who's Who Among the Microbes (with Dr. William H. Park), 1929; Streptococci in Relation to Man, 1932. Contbr. many bulls. to publs. Health Dept. N.Y. City and papers to Jour. Exptl. Medicine, etc. Home: Woodcliff Lake NJ‡

WILLIAMS, CLAYTON EPES, prof. of law; b. Woodstock, Va., June 24, 1890; s. William Twyman and Sallie Madison (Bird) W.; grad. Massanutten (Va.) Acad., 1908; student Washington and Lee Univ.,

1908-10; LL.B., 1912; student Columbia Univ. Sch. of Law, summers 1922, 26; LL.D., Hampden Sydney College, 1951; married Billie Joe Tompkins, December 30, 1918; 1 son, Samuel Clayton. Admitted to Va. bar, 1912; pvt. practice of law, Woodstock, Va., 1912-18; Commonwealth's atty. of Shenandoah County, Va., 1916-19; asso. prof. of law, Washington and Lee Univ., Lexington, Va., 1919-20, prof., 1920-68, acting dean of the School of Law, 1944-46, dean, 1946-60, dean emeritus, 1963-68, distinguished lectr. law of property, 1960-68; vis. prof. of law Univ. of Va. summer 1944; mem. legislative commn. to study possible improvement of adminstrn. of justice in Va., 1944-46. Mem. zoning bd. Lexington. Mem. Am., Va. State bar assns., Am. Law Inst., Pi Kappa Alpha, Omicron Delta Kappa, Phi Delta Phi. Order of Coif. Democrat. Presbyn. Editor: (with Martin P. Burks 3d) 3d edit. Burks on Pleading and Practice, 1934. Home: Lexington VA Died Mar. 25, 1968; buried Woodstock VA

WILLIAMS, CLIFFORD LELAND, physician; b. Delaware County, Ind., Mar. 1, 1901; s. John Luther and Lucinda Jane (Clevenger) W.; B.S., Ind. U., 1924, M.D., 1926; m. Helen Aubrey, Oct. 12, 1928 (dec. Jan. 1962); m. 2d, Martha Mayer, May 2, 1964. Intern Phila. Gen. Hosp., 1926-28; resident psychiatry Ind. U. Sch. Medicine clinics, 1933-36; pvt. practice medicine, specializing psychiatry Indpls., 1928-33, instr., asst. dept. mental and nervous diseases Ind. U. Sch. Medicine, 1929-33, asst. prof. neurology, psychiatry, 1954-67; asst. physician Evansville (Ind.) State Hosp., 1933; supt. Logansport (Ind.) State Hosp., 1933-46; med. dir. Ind. Council Mental Health, 1946-47; chief acute intensive treatment service VA Hosp., Marion, Ind., 1947-51; chief profl. service VA Hosp., Lexington, Ky., 1951-52; supt. Central State Hosp., Indpls., 1952-66. Diplomate in psychiatry Am. Bd. Psychiatry and Neurology, 1936. Mem. A.M.A., Ind., Marion County med. socs., Am. Psychiat. Assn., Ind. Neuropsychiat. Assn. (past pres.). Kiwanian. Contbr. articles med. jours. Home: Indianapolis IN Died Oct. 1, 1967; buried Mt. Tabor Cemetery, Delaware County Muncie IN

WILLIAMS, CLIFTON CURTIS, JR., astronaut; b. Mobile, Sept. 26, 1932; s. Clifton Curtis and Gertrude (Medicus) W.; student Spring Hill Coll., 1949-51; B.M.E., Auburn U., 1954; m. Jane Elizabeth Lansche, July 1, 1964. Commd. 2d lt., USMC, 1954, advanced through grades to maj., 1963; naval aviator, 1956-60; test pilot Naval Air Test Center, Patuxent River, Md., 1960-63; astronaut Manned Space Flight Center, NASA, Houston, 1963-67. Home: Dickinson TX Died Oct. 5, 1967.

WILLIAMS, CYRIL, newspaper exec.; b. Barbados, B.W.I., Feb. 22, 1907; s. John Wellsley and Ethel Anne Williams; student various pvt. schs., Barbados, 1912-18, Lodge Sch., Barbados, 1918-24, Harrison Coll., Barbados, 1924-27, Pace Inst., N.Y.C., 1929-31; m. Bernice Joan Lesniak, Mar. 13, 1947; 1 dau., Linda Anne. With Bovell & Skeet, chartered accountants, Barbados, 1927-29, Perley Morse & Co., C.P.A.'s, N.Y.C., 1929-34, Barrow, Wade, Guthrie & Co., C.P.A.'s, N.Y.C., 1934-37; with Gannett Newspapers, Rochester, N.Y., 1937-70; v.p. Gannett Co., Inc.; sec., treas., dir. WAVY, Inc., WHEC, Inc.; treas., asst. sec., dir. Newburgh-Beacon News Co., Inc., Binghamton Press Co., Inc., Elmira Star Gazette, Inc., Hartford Times, Inc., Ithaca Jour. News, Inc., Niagara Falls Gazette Publishing Corp., Northwestern Pub. Co., Plainfield Courier News Company, The Saratogian, Inc.; president, director Samuel Sloan and Company, Incorporated; treasurer, director Utica Observer-Dispatch, Inc.; sec. treas., director So. N.J. Newspapers, Inc., Westchester Rockland Newspapers, Inc. Treas., dir., Frank E. Gannett Newspaper Found., Inc., Frank Gannett Newspaperboy Scholarships, Inc. Clubs: Oak Hill Country, Rochester. Home: Rochester NY Died Sept. 26, 1970; buried White Haven Meml. Park, Perinton NY

WILLIAMS, D.B., lawyer; b. Wells County, Ind., Mar. 1, 1910; A.B., Kalamazoo Coll., 1932; LL.B., Harvard, 1935. Admitted to Ill. bar, 1935; mem. firm Leibman, Williams, Bennett, Baird & Minow. Mem. Chgo. Law Inst., Am., Ill., Chgo. bar assns. Home: Wilmette IL Died Oct. 27, 1969; buried Meml. Park Cemetery, Skokie IL

WILLIAMS, DANIEL ALBERT, librarian; b. Wichita, Kan., Dec. 30, 1914; s. Roy Daniel and Frances (Elliott) W.; A.B., U. Chgo., 1944, B.L.S., 1945; m. Edna H. Goble, Mar. 15, 1941; 1 dau., Nancy Frances. With U. Chgo. Libraries, 1935-43; reference librarian Gary (Ind.) Pub. Library, 1944-45; chief librarian Muncie (Ind.) Pub. Library, 1945-51; asso. librarian Pub. Library of Des Moines (Ia.), 1951-52, dir., 1952-68. Mem. A.L.A., Ia. Library Assn. (pres. 1956-57), Des Moines Com. Fgn. Affairs, Ia. Adult Edn. Assn. (pres. 1964-65), Ia. Hist. Soc., Des Moines C. of C., Torch International (pres. Des Moines chapter 1956-57). Unitarian. Kiwanian. Contributor to professional jours. Home: Des Moines IA Died May 24, 1968.

WILLIAMS, DANIEL RODERICK, lawyer; b. at Dawn, Mo., May 13, 1871; s. John H. and Margaret E. (Lewis) W.; student Avalon (Mo.) Coll., and U. of Mich.; LL.B., U. of Mich., 1896; m. Margaret E. Dow, of National City, Cal., Oct., 1902 (died Nov., 1904); m. 2d, Esther May Marlatt, of Poynette, Wis., Feb., 1916. Mem. Bishop & Wheeler, San Francisco, 1896-1900; pvt. sec. to Bernard Moses, mem. Taft Philippine Commn., 1900-1; sec. of Commn., 1901-3; asso. judge Philippine Court of Land Registration, 1903-5 (resigned); practiced in Manila since Feb., 1905; now mem. Williams, Ferrier & Sycip. Delta Chi. Baptist. Clubs: University (San Francisco); Army and Navy, Polo (Manila). Author: Odyssey of the Philippine Commission, 1913. Address: 6 Escolta, Manila PI‡

WILLIAMS, DAVID P., JR., corp. exec.; b. Indpls., 1908; ed. Williams Coll., 1930. Pres., Ayrway Stores; vice chmn. dir. L. S. Ayres & Co.; dir. Murray Showrooms Inc. Home: Indianapolis IN Died Dec. 28, 1971.

WILLIAMS, DION, officer U.S.M.C., author; b. Williamsburg, O., Dec. 15, 1869; s. Byron and Katherine (Park) W.; grad. U.S. Naval Acad., 1891; U.S. Naval War Coll., 1905-06; m. Helen M. Ames, Feb. 20, 1895. Commd. 2d lt. U.S.M.C., July 1, 1893; promoted through grades to brig. gen., June 3, 1924. Served on U.S.S. Atlanta, Baltimore, Olympia, Ore., Kearsarge, Me., Conn.; shore duty various posts in U.S., Cuba, Panama, Philippines and China. Comd. 1st co. that landed on Spanish soil after Battle of Manila Bay, and hoisted first U.S. flag on Spanish soil, May 2, 1898; fleet marine officer Atlantic Fleet, 1903-04, 1907-09; comd. Am. Legation guard, Peking, China, 1913-15; duty Gen. Bd. of Navy, Washington, D.C., 1915-18; comdr. 10th Regt. U.S.M.C., Quantico, Va., 1919; comdr. Northern Dist., Santo Domingo, 1919-21; U.S. Army War Coll., 1921-22, grad. 1922; comdg. 4th Brig., U.S. Marines, 1922-24; comdg. gen. Marine Barracks, Quantico, 1924; dir. Operations and Training, 1924-25; asst. to maj. gen. comdt. U.S.M.C., 1925-28; comdg. gen. Marine Corps Base, San Diego, Calif., 1928-29; comdg. gen. 2d Brigade of Marines in Nicaragua, 1929-30; apptd. pres. Marine Examining Bd. and Marine Retiring Bd., 1931; retired on account of age limit, Jan. 1, 1934. Mem. U.S. Naval Inst., Society Manila Bay, Mil. Order Foreign Wars, Mil. Order Carabao, United Spanish War Vets., S.R., Am. Legion. Awarded Congressional medal for Battle of Manila Bay, also medals Philippine Insurrection, Army of Cuban Pacification, Spanish-Am. War, Marine Expeditionary medal, Victory medal, Nicaraguan Presidential medal, Nicaraguan medal of merit, Nicaraguan campaign medal; also awarded D.S.M. (U.S.). Clubs: Army and Navy, Chevy Chase (Washington, D.C.); New York Yacht. Author: Naval Reconnaissance, 1906, 2d edit., 1917; Port Directory of Foreign Ports of the World, 1911; Army and Navy Uniforms and Insignia, 1918. Home: 1746 Q St. N.W., Washington 9 DC‡

WILLIAMS, EGERTON RYERSON, JR., lawyer, author; b. Toledo, O., Feb. 1, 1873; s. Egerton Ryerson and Ella Louise (Hayden) W.; ed. St. Paul's Sch., Concord, N.H., Yale, 1894; LL.B., Albany Law Sch., 1896; m. Florence Augusta Johnson, of Boonville, N.Y., May 10, 1898. Admitted to bar, 1896, and practiced at Rochester, N.Y., until Nov., 1907; since living in Italy. Author: Hill Towns of Italy, 1903; Ridolfo, 1906. Address: Care W. J. Turner & Co., Naples Italy‡

WILLIAMS, EMMA ELIZABETH THOMAS, broadcasting exec.; b. Vincennes, Ind.; d. Prosper Joseph and Leocadia (Tougaw) Thomas; grad. Vincennes (Ind.) Bus. Coll., 1927; student Lamson Bus. Coll., 1949-50; m. Perry A. Williams, Dec. 1, 1933 (div. June 1949); 1 son, Robert Alan. Sec., bookkeeper Ft. Wayne Corrugated Paper Co., Vincennes, Ind., 1929-34, Central Fibre Products Co., Vincennes, 1936-42; bookkeeper KPHO Radio, Phoenix, 1946-48 KOOL Radio-TV, Phoenix, 1948-49, comptroller, 1949, sec. corp., 1956-69, v.p., sec., 1962-69, also dir. Mem. Nat. Assn. Accountants, Inst. Broadcasting Financial Mgmt. Home: Phoenix Az Died Sept. 7, 1969.

WILLIAMS, ERNEST BLAND, JR., lawyer; b. Longtown, Tenn., July 14, 1899; s. Ernest Bland and Elizabeth (Shelton) W.; A.B., Vanderbilt U., 1921; LL.B., Yale, 1924; m. Anne Williams, Nov. 22, 1926; children—Ernest Bland III, David G. Admitted to Tenn. bar, 1924, since practiced in Memphis; asso. firm Shepherd, Heiskell & Williams, 1943-46, Chandler, Shepherd, Heiskill & Williams, 1946-64; mem. firm Heiskell, Donelson, Adams, Williams, & Wall, from 1964. Mem. Am., Memphis, Shelby County bar assns., Bar Assn. Tenn. Presbyn. Mason. Home: Memphis TN

WILLIAMS, EUSTACE LEROY, author; b. Culpeper, Va., Sept. 29, 1874; s. L. Eustace and Flora (McDonald) W.; ed. Louisville, Ky., 1882-8, San Diego, Cal., 1889-90, Shenandoah Univ. Sch., 1891-3; m. Elizabeth St. C. Smith, of Berryville, Va., June 21, 1900. Apptd. master commr. Jefferson Circuit Ct., 30th Jud. Dist., Ky., Jan. 4, 1909. Author: The Substitute Quarterback, 1900; The Mutineers, 1903; (co-author) That Kentucky Campaign, 1900. Address: Anchorage KY‡

WILLIAMS, EVERARD MOTT, educator, cons engr.; b. New Haven, Feb. 2, 1915; s. Cecil H. an Phyllis H. (Mason) W.; B.S., Yale, 1936, Ph.D., 1939 m. Mary Stansel, Apr. 2, 1938; children—Thoma Granville, Nancy Reid, Susan Mott, Peter Biddle. Instr elec. engring. Pa. State Coll., 1939-42; chief engr. devel br. spl. projects lab. (USAAF) Wright Field, 1942-45 asso. prof. Carnegie-Mellon U., 1945-49, prof., 1949-72 head dept. elec. engring., 1952-69, Georg Westinghouse prof. engring., 1969-72, chmn. applie space scis. program, 1963-69; cons. engr., Pitts. 1945-72; expert cons. research and devel. bd. Dept Def., 1949-51; sci. cons. USAF, 1951-53; cons. U.S Army Signal Corps, 1953, U.S. Army Ordnance Corps 1953-54; dir. research Method X Co., 1952-55; cons Method X div. Firth Sterling, Inc., 1955-60; mem scientific adv. com. Regional Indsl. Devel. Corp. 1962-72; cons. Def. Dept., 1955-72; research adv. com on control, data processing and instrumentation NASA 1963-64; adv. com. Diamond Ordnance Fuse Labs. U.S. Army Ordnance Corps, 1955-64; pres., chmn. bd El-Gar Rehab, Inc., 1968-72; dir. Microwavel Systems Inc., Narda Microwave Corp.; adv. com. Harr Diamond Labs. Mem. Edgewood (Pa.) Sch. Bd. 1961-65. Trustee C. C. Mellor Meml. Library, 1961-63 Recipient Pres.'s certificate merit outstanding servic World War II; Eta Kappa Nu award as most outstandin young elec. engr. in U.S.A., 1946; Man of Yr. i Engring. award Pitts., 1957; Western Electric award fo excellent instrn., 1971. Fellow I.E.E.E.; mem. Am. Soc Engring. Edn. Club: Cosmos (Washington). Author Careers in Electronics, 1955; Transmission Circuits 1957; Electrical Engineering Problems, 1960; Solution of OLDECC, 1968. Contbr. to bulls. and profl. jours Home: Pittsburgh PA Died Oct. 24, 1972.

WILLIAMS, FREDERICK BALLARD, artist; b Brooklyn, N.Y., Oct. 21, 1871; s. John K. and Jennie C (Williams) W.; ed. pub. schs., Bloomfield and Montclair N.J., art edn. in Cooper Inst., New York Inst., Artist and Artisans, Nat. Acad. Design, etc., under John War Stimson, William Hamilton Gibson, C.Y. Turner, Edga M. Ward; m. Marion Gerry Duncan, Oct. 16, 1901 children—Duncan B., F. Ballard. Landscape and figur painter; exhibitor at important art exhbns. in U.S. an in London, Paris, Venice and Rome. Pictures in Met Museum of Art (New York), Nat. Art Galler (Washington), Brooklyn Inst. Arts and Science (purchased N.A.D. figure picture, 1909), Herron Inst (Muskegon, Mich.), St. Louis Museum, Albrigh Gallery (Buffalo), Arnot Gallery (Elmira, N.Y.), Lo Angeles Museum, Nat. Arts Club, Lotos Club Engineers' Club (New York), Art Inst. Chicago Montclair (N.J.) Art Museum, Milwaukee Art Inst Grand Rapids Art Assn., Ft. Worth Museum of Ar Nat. Gallery (Lima, Peru), etc. Bronze medal Pan-American Expn.; Inness prize, Salmagundi Club Isador gold medal, Nat. Acad. Design, 1909; Medal o Honor, Salmagundi Club, 1943. Nat. Academician 1909; mem. New York Water Color Club; mem Council Nat. Acad. Design, 1910-11, asst. treas 1930-38, treas. 1940-41; nat. chmn. Am. Artist Professional League; pres., Montclair (N.J.) Art Assn 1919-21. Mem. Mayors Municipal Art Com. of 100 fo New York City, Municipal Planning Committee, Gle Ridge, N.J. Clubs: Lotos, Salmagundi (pres. 4 terms) Nat. Arts, Glen Ridge Country. Studio: 31 Highlan Av., Glen Ridge NJ‡

WILLIAMS, GEORGE C., educator; b. Dryden, N.Y. July 23, 1874; s. Charles D. and Emma E. (Trapp) W. grad. high sch., Dryden, 1890; grad. New Eng Conservatory of Music, 1893; B.O., Boston U., 1894 studied Cornell U., 1897; m. Ruth Robertson, Dec. 29 1897 (dec.); children—Marguerite Carol, Harol Robertson; m. 2d, Mary H. Dean, Feb. 15, 1930 (dec.) m. 3d, Margaret C. Entrekin, Jan. 10, 1938. Teacher o expression, Neb. Conservatory of Music, Lincoln, 1894 founder Neb. Coll. Oratory, Lincoln, 1895; teache oratory, Cotner U., Lincoln, 1895; founder, 1897, an dean Williams School of Expression, Ithaca, N.Y.; pres Ithaca Coll., 1925-32; lecturer and public reader. Mem oral English div. N.Y. State Teachers Assn. (pres 1909-11); member National Speech Arts Assn. (pres 1913-16), Com. of 100, Century Club, Pan Am. League Acacia. Co-founder Phi Mu Alpha, 1901 (nat. pres 1903-04). Rep. Presbyn. Mason (K.T.). Rotarian Author: The Speaking Voice, 1919; Shakespearea Questionnaire, 1920; The Art of Expression, 1923 Ethics Questionnaire, 1924; Problems in Religion 1927; this is My Story (autobiography), 1969. Sinc 1935, teacher of Bryan Memorial Bible Class (said to b the largest Bible Class in the world), organized b William Jennings Bryan, 1918. Moderator, Southeas Fla. Presbytery, 1946. Supply pastor, North-Eas Presbyn. Ch., Miami, Fla., 1942; supply pastor, Cora Way Presbyn. Ch., Miami, Fla., 1947. Travele extensively in Europe and Near East, 1928, 30, 38 Home: Miami FL Died Dec. 28, 1971; buried Willo Glen Cemetery, Dryden NY

WILLIAMS, GEORGE HOWARD, lawye ex-senator; b. California, Mo., Dec. 1, 1871; s. Joh Morrow and Alice Gray (Howard) W.; grad. Drur Coll. Acad., 1890; A.B., Princeton, 1894; LL.B Washington U. Law Sch., 1897; LL.D., Mo. Valle Coll., 1923; m. Harriet Chase Stewart, June 12, 190

ildren—Stewart, Howard. Admitted to Mo. bar, 896; settled in St. Louis, 1897; judge Circuit Court, 907-11; del. at large Mo. Constl. Conv., 1922-23; mem. ryan, Williams, Cave & McPheeters; apptd. U.S. enator by Gov. Samuel Baker, May 25, 1925, for period nding Mar. 3, 1927, to succeed Selden P. Spencer, dec. Mem. Am., Mo. State and St. Louis bar assns. Mem. for 2 yrs., and chmn., St. Louis Bd. of Children's uardians. Republican. Conglist. Clubs: Noonday, niversity. Home: Clayton Road and Log Cabin Lane, t Louis County MO Office: Boatmen's Bank Bldg., St ouis MO*‡

WILLIAMS, GLADSTONE, newspaper corr.; b. wainsboro, Ga., Dec. 10, 1898; s. George Herschel and ntoinette (Moring) W.; student Mercer U., Harvard; . Helene Livingston Kravadze, Mar. 5, 1944. Mem. ditorial staff Atlanta Constitution, 1921, Washington orr., 1922; Washington staff Internat. News Service nd Cosmopolitan News Service, 1923-24; Washington orrespondent McClatchy papers of California. ecipient Newsweek magazine award in 1940 for most ccurate forecast on outcome of presdl. election; and in 944 for most accurate forecast on outcome of House ection. Mem. Soc. of Cin. Sigma Nu. Clubs: King and ueen Rod and Gun of Virginia; Nat. Press. Home: 'ashington DC Died Jan. 22, 1968; buried Dacha riendship Garden, King and Queen County, tevensville VA

WILLIAMS, HAROLD E., supply co. exec.; b. ewark, Apr. 24, 1877; grad. mech. engring. Stevens st. Tech., 1900. Founder, Williams & Co., Inc., Pitts., 907, hon. chmn. bd., dir. until 1972; dir. Union Nat. ank, Pitts., Youngstown (O.) Welding and Engring. o. Bd. dirs. Seabury House. Episcopalian (vestryman, ector's warden). Clubs: Duquesne, Pittsburgh Golf, niversity (Pitts.); Bay Head (N.J.) Yacht. Home: ittsburgh PA Died Jan. 24, 1972; buried Allegheny emetery.

WILLIAMS, HELEN BURTON (MRS. EDWARD . WILLIAMS), educator; b. LaCrosse, Wis., Jan. 16, 877; d. Frank Adams and Sarah Abigail (Moulton) urton; A.B., Wellesley Coll., 1899; student Columbia, 907, Sorbonne, Paris, 1924-25, Grenoble, France, 925; m. Edward J. Williams, of Panama, Dec. 7, 1907; hildren—Charlotte (Mrs. Robert H. Bayer), Barbara urton. Teacher High Sch., LaCrosse 1900-07, lorentine Sch. for Girls, Florence, Italy, 1923; prin. nd trustee Barstow Sch. for Girls, Kansas City, Mo., nce 1927. Mem. Am. Assn. Univ. Women, Delta amma. Republican. Conglist. Clubs: Country (Kansas ity and LaCrosse). Home: 1018 Cass St., LaCrosse WI ddress: Barstow School, Kansas City MO‡

WILLIAMS, HERBERT PELHAM, lit. adviser; b. 'ashington, Sept. 29, 1871; s. Pelham and Helen largaret (Gunnell) W.; ed. pvt. tutors and various schs. ntil 1885, St. Stephen's Coll., Annandale, N.Y., till 888, Harvard, 1889-92. grad. in 3 yrs., A.B.; Harvard aw Sch., 1892-3; m. Boston, July 18, 1894, Mary Olive 'ard. Asst. to lit. editor, 1893-5, lit. editor, 1895-1903, oston Herald; head of lit. dept., The Macmillan Co., ublishers, 1903-6. Clubs: Harvard, Nat. Arts. Address: 7 W. 44th St., New York NY‡

WILLIAMS, IRA JEWELL, lawyer; b. Pennsville, Pa., ov. 20, 1873; s. David and Magdalen (Herr) W.; eLand (now Stetson) U., DeLand, Fla., 1885-87; L.B., Law Sch., U. of Pa., 1897; m. Mary Harton Jones, eb. 17, 1898; children—Ira Jewell, David Alexander ec.). Practiced, Phila., 1896; mem. firm of Brown & illiams, 1899-1940; White & Williams since 1944; dir. idelity Mutual Life Insurance Co., Central-Penn. ational Bank, Proctor Electric Co. Writer on legal ubjects. Mem. Pa. Bar Assn. (formerly chmn. com. on onstitutional law and com. on judicial authority), Phila. ar Assn. (com. on professional guidance; formerly em. bd. of govs. and com. of censors), Am. Bar Assn., ssn. Bar City of N.Y., Lawyers' Club. Republican. lubs: University, Union League, Philadelphia Cricket, unnybrook, Pine Valley. Home: 707 Kenilworth Apts., hiladelphia 44 PA Office: 1900 Land Title Bldg., hiladelphia 10 PA‡

WILLIAMS, JAMES THOMAS, JR., editor; b. incolnton, N.C., Aug. 10, 1881; s. of James Thomas nd Sarah (McBee) W.; A.B., Columbia, 1901; D.C.L., . of the South, 1921; LL.D., Norwich U., 1928; nmarried. Washington corr. of The State, Columbia, C., 1901-02; mem. Washington staff Associated Press, 902-06, and one of its representatives at the Rep. and em. nat. convs., 1904, and at the Portsmouth Peace onf., summer of 1905; Washington corr., Boston vening Transcript, 1906-08; U.S. Civil Service ommr., 1909; editor Tucson (Ariz.) Citizen, 1910-12, ditor Boston Evening Transcript, 1912-25, editor oston Evening American, 1925-27; Washington ntbg. editor to Nat. Syndicates, 1925-37; Washington p. Chicago Daily News fgn. service, 1937-38. Member dvisory council Civil War Centennial Commission. ppointed by President Coolidge member bd. visitors S. Naval Acad., 1924, U.S. Naval Inst. Mem. lvanus Thayer Hall Fame Com. Mem. Anglican Soc. nem. exec. com.), Sigma Alpha Epsilon. Hereditary em. Soc. of the Cincinnati (S.C. Br.). Decorated Knight Order of Leopold (Belgium), 1920; Comdr. Order of Crown of Italy, 1920. Episcopalian. Clubs: Metropolitan, Cosmos, Army and Navy (Washington); University (N.Y. City). Lecturer on national affairs and foreign relations. Home: Lincolnton NC Died Dec. 26, 1969; buried Lincolnton NC

WILLIAMS, JOHN JOSEPH JR., lawyer; b. Memphis, Aug. 4, 1886; s. John Joseph and Martha Hicks (Cheatham) W.; A.B., U. Va., 1907, LL.B., 1909; m. Hattie Moody, Apr. 26, 1917; children—Margaret Morrison (Mrs. W. C. Fitch), Charlotte Cheatham (Mrs. W.D. Parker), Ridley Moody (Mrs. James McGregor), John Joseph. Admitted to Tenn. bar, 1909, Fla. bar, 1925; city atty. City of Sarasota, 1933-35, 38-40; mem. Williams, Parker, Harrison & Dietz, Sarasota. Dir. Sarasota Bank & Trust Co., 1st Fed. Savs. & Loan Assn., Sarasota. Mem. bd. trustees Fla. Presbyn. Coll. Charter mem. YMCA. Mem. Fla. Bar, Am., Sarasota County bar assns., C. of C., Delta Chi, Sigma Alpha Epsilon. Mason (32 deg., K.T., Shriner). Elk. Presbyn. (elder). Democrat. Clubs: Field, Kiwanis (past pres.). Home: Sarasota FL Died June 11, 1968.

WILLIAMS, JOHN PAUL, educator; b. New York City, N.Y., Jan. 17, 1900; s. Clarence Milton and Ellen (Pinson) W.; A.B., Baker U., 1922, LL.D., 1956; B.D., Garrett Bibl. Inst., Evanston, Ill., 1927; Ph.D., Columbia, 1937; m. Louise Ringer, 1926 (now dec.); children—Numan Arthur, Katherine Louise; m. 2d, Helen Elizabeth Hobart, 1932; 1 dau., Sarah Ellen. Asso. dir. Wesley Foundation, Urbana, Ill., 1926-27; dir. United Religious Council, Mass. State Coll., 1928-39; asso. prof. dept. of Religion, Mt. Holyoke Coll., 1940-45, prof., 1945-66, prof. emeritus dept. of religion, 1967-73, chmn. dept. 1943-46, 51-54, 59-64, acting dean of Coll. Chapel, 1965-66; vis. prof. Sch. Edn., Univ. Ore., summer, 1937, 38, Stout Inst., summer 1939, U. of Pa., summer, 1940, State Coll. of Wash., 1941, Garrett Biblical Inst., 1947, Union Theological Seminary, summer, 1948, U. of New Mexico, summer 1964; vis. prof. in sch. of Religious Edn., Hartford Sem. Found., 1943-46, 67; pastor St. Andrews Am. Ch., Athens. Greece, 1955. Pres. Assn. of Ch. Workers in Colls. and Univs. (Eastern region), 1936-37; dir. Survey of Working Conditions Among the Child Laborers of Conn. Valley, 1931; former mem. Commn. on Religious Orgns., Nat. Conf. of Christians and Jews; mem. div. of Christian edn., Congl. Christian Chs., 1947-56. Co-founder Soc. for the Sci. Study of Religion. Mem. Nat. Assn. Bibl. Instr. (v.p. 1938, pres. 1946), Kappa Sigma, Phi Delta Kappa, Pi Kappa Delta. Conglist. Author: Some Aspects of Social Adjustment in Methodism, 1938; The New Education and Religion, 1945; What Americans Believe and How They Worship, 1952, rev., 1962, 69. Research editor Jour. of Bible and Religion, 1946-56; mng. editor Jour. for Sci. Study of Religion, 1961-64. Home: Claremont CA Died Mar. 8, 1973.

WILLIAMS, JOHN TAYLOR, coll. pres.; b. Minden, La., Oct. 24, 1904; s. Charles Williams Sr. and Mary (Scott) W.; B.S., Langston U., 1928; M.A., U. Cin., 1932; Ed.D., Ind. U., 1936; m. Jennie V. Wendell, Nov. 5, 1929 (dec.); 1 dau., Lorelle. Dir. athletics, head football and basketball Coach Ky. State Coll., 1928-32, dir. ednl. extension,, 1932-37, dean, registrar, also dir. summer sch., 1937-47; vis. prof. edn. Prairie View State Coll., summer 1946; pres. Md. State Coll., 1947-71. Member Philadelphia Commissioners, 1950-71; mem. community council Wye Inst., Inc., 1965-71; mem. Gov.'s Com. on Chesapeake Bay Bridge; mem. Md. Social Welfare Man-power Com., Md. Commn. on World's Fair. Trus. Peninsula Gen. Hosp., Salisbury, Md. Spl. cons. Am. Coun. Edn., 1942-45; spl. lectr. War Dept. Bur. Pub. Rels., 1942; adv. com. U.S. Armed Forces Inst., 1942-46, editorial staff, 1942-45; expert cons. Joint Army and Navy Com. Welfare and Recreation, 1942-43. Rec. achievement and eminence awd. Langston U. Club, Los Angeles, 1951; Alumni awd. for Demonstrated Distinguished Service, Maryland State College, 1960. Maryland State A.F.R.O.T.C. award; Citizen of year award Omega Psi Phi, 1967; also numerous citations. Member Nat. Assn. Collegiate Deans and Registrars (v.p. 1941, pres. 1942, exec. com. 1943), Ky. Edn. Assn. (chmn. secondary sch. dept. 1938-42), Princess Anne C. of C., Kappa Alpha Psi, Sigma Pi Phi, Alpha Kappa Mu, Beta Kappa Xi. Methodist (dir. Wesley Found.) Club: Faculty Men's Professional (pres.). Home: Salisbury MD Died July 13, 1971; buried Lewes Cemetery, Muskogee OK

WILLIAMS, JOSEPH JUDSON, JR., lawyer; born at Hanover County, Va., July 20, 1905; s. Joseph Judson and Roberta (Richardson) W.; B.A., U. Richmond, 1927, LL.B., 1930; m. Nellie Ruth Hoover, June 30, 1928; 1 dau., Elizabeth Ann. Admitted to Va. bar, 1929, and practiced in Richmond until 1960; mem. Fed. Home Loan Bank Bd., 1960-63; an organizer, gen. counsel, dir. Franklin Fed. Savs. and Loan Assn., Richmond, 1934-60, 63-68; mem. Williams, McGehee & Willey, attorneys. Mem. Va. Adv. Legislative Council, 1950-60. Mem. Va. Legislature from Henrico County, 1937-60, chmn. com. cts. of justice chmn. Democratic Caucus, 1956-60; chmn. 3d Dist. Dem. Com., 1950-60. Presbyn. Mason (Shriner). Home: Richmond VA Died 1968

WILLIAMS, LEWIS KEMPER, hon. govt. ofcl., banker; b. Patterson, La., Sept. 23, 1887; s. Francis Bennett and Emily Williamson (Seyburn) W.; student U. of South, Sewanee, Tenn., 1906-08, D.C.L., 1935; m. Leila Moore, Oct. 2, 1920 (dec.). Sec.-treas. F. B. Williams Sypress Co., Ltd., 1912-32, pres., 1932-34; past chmn. bd. Williams, Inc.; past pres., dir. City Center Realty Co.; past dir. Nat. Bank of Commerce, Internat Trade Mart, Central Gulf S.S. Co.; now hon. consul gen. of Monaco. Past dir. Pub. Affairs Research Council La.; former chmn. New Orleans Housing Authority; pres. Nat. Assn. Housing Ofcls., 1939. Past chmn. bd. regents, former trustee Univ. of the South; mem. nat. council Boy Scouts Am.; pres. New Orleans Community Chest, 1933; pres. trustees Episcopal Diocese La. Served from 2d lt. to maj., U.S. Army, 1917-18; brig. gen. Res. ret. Decorated Legion of Merit (U.S.). Mem. N.E. Geneal. Soc., Res. Officers Assn. (pres. 1931-34), Va. Antiquities, New Orleans Assn. Commerce, New Orleans Philharmonic Symphony Soc. (past pres.), Newcomen Soc., Soc. Cincinnati, Mayflower Soc., S.A.R., Phi Delta Theta, Omicron Delta Kappa. Republican. Episcopalian (sr. warden 1958-60). Clubs: Boson, Louisiana, Country (New Orleans); Chevy Chase Country (Washington); University (N.Y.C.); Valley, Monticito (Santa Barbara). Home: New Orleans LA Died Nov. 17, 1971.

WILLIAMS, MARTHA MCCULLOCH, author; b. Montgomery Co., Tenn.; d. William B. and Fannie (Williams) Collins; ed. at home; m. Thomas McCulloch-Williams (now deceased). Began lit. work, upon moving to New York, 1887. Author: Field Farings, 1892; Two of a Trade, 1894; Milre, 1894-6; Next to the Ground, 1901. Has also written and had published since 1892 several serials, and over 200 short stories, notably The Pianner Mares; An Eyelash Finnish; A Black Settlement; Sarsaparilla; A Backslider; A Red Fox; and In Jackson's Purchase (prize story in McClure competition); also, A Rose Distilled, included in Fifty Best Stories of 1916. An authority on household topics; contbr. to Youth's Companion and other magazines. Address: Care McBride-Nast & Co., New York NY‡

WILLIAMS, NATHAN BOONE, lawyer; b. near Whitener, Ark., Aug. 26, 1873; s. Garrett and Belle (Wilson) W.; grad. Hindsville (Ark.) Acad., 1892; studied law privately; m. Lida Ware, April 6, 1898; children—Philip Tutle, Helen Harriet, Louise Elizabeth (Mrs. Elgin E. Groseclose). Admitted to Arkansas bar, 1894, bar of Supreme Court of the Dist. of Columbia and of the Supreme Court of U.S., 1914; practiced in Fayetteville, 1894-1911, in Washington, D.C., since 1911; U.S. commr., 1898-1910; spl. law asst. U.S. Ho. of Rep. Com. on Expenditures in Post Office Dept., 1911-12; counsel U.S. Senate com. investigating pneumatic mail tube contracts, 1912-13; councel U.S. Ho. of Rep. Com. on Judiciary, 1913-15; mem. Commn. on Uniform State Laws, 1915-16; advisor to U.S. Dept. Commerce, 1923; lecturer, Northwestern U., Chicago, 1929; spl. counsel to industry assns. since 1918. Mem. Am. Bar Assn. Democrat. Club: Monday Lunch (chmn.). Author: American Postoffice, 1911; Laws on Trusts and Monopolies, 1913; Administrative Agencies in Government, 1935; A Constitutional Catechism, 1936; The Lawyer and Corporate Clients, 1937; The Dust Bin, 1938; Rust of Virginia, 1940, An Arkansas Traveler, 1941; We the People, 1944; The Search for a Catalyst, 1945. Home: 3917 McKinley St., Washington 15 DC‡

WILLIAMS, ORA, journalist, historian; b. Dallas Co., Ia., Jan. 16, 1862; s. Ephraim and Elizabeth (Parker) W.; ed. pub. schs. of Ia.; m. Nettie Diddy, Oct. 13, 1886; children—Marguerite, Jeannette, Roger. City editor Ia. State Register, 1885-90; mng. editor Sioux City Jour., 1890-98; editorial writer Omaha (Neb.) Bee, 1898; editor Sioux Falls Press, 1899; syndicate writer, 1900-15; editor Nat. Daily Review, Chicago, 1905; Campbells Soil Culture, 1906; sec. Governor of Iowa, 1909; State Document Editor, 1915-21; div. chief U.S. Internal Revenue Bur., 1921-27; sec. Iowa Indsl. Commn., 1927-37; curator Ia. State Dept. History & Archives since 1939. Sec. Ia. Pioneer Lawmakers Assn., 1938, editor Annals of Ia. since 1938, historian Ia. dept. S.A.R., vice pres. Assn. State and Local Hist. Socs. since 1941. Republican. Club: Des Moines Pioneer. Home: 1303 E. Grand Av. Office: State Historical Bldg., Des Moines IA‡

WILLIAMS, PHILIP FRANCIS, gynecologist; b. Martin's Ferry, O., Oct. 20, 1884; s. Brady O'Neill and Mary Armistead (Grove) W.; Ph.B., Lafayette Coll., Easton, Pa., 1905; M.D., U. of Pa., 1909; m. Catherine Toland Stewart, June 2, 1923 (died Sept. 25, 1940); children—Cay Stewart, Jeremiah, Eleanor Shelby. Began as physician, 1912, and practiced in Philadelphia, specializing in obstetrics and gynecology; prof. clin. obstetrics and gynecology, School of Med., U. of Pa.; cons. gynecologist, obstetrician Phila. Gen. Hosp., Jewish Hosp.; obstetrician Presbyterian Hosp.; consulting obstetrician Preston Retreat and Nazareth Hospital. Served as maj. M.C., U.S. Army, A.E.F., 1917-19; World War I. Director Am. Com. on Maternal Welfare, Inc. Diplomate Am. Bd. Obstetrics and Gynecology. Fellow Am. Gynecol. Soc., Coll.

Physicians of Phila.; member A.M.A. (chmn. Sect. Obstetrics and Gynecology, 1946), Philadelphia Obstet. Soc. (ex-president), South Atlantic Assn. Obstetricians and Gynecologists (hon.), Nat. Fedn. Obstet. and Gynecol. Socs. (pres.), Central Assn. Obstetricians and Gynecologists (hon.), Welsh Soc. of Phila., Pa. Soc. S.R., Nu Sigma Nu, Sigma Xi. Received Strittmater award (research in maternal mortality), 1934. Republican. Presbyn. Mason. Clubs: Medical, Bala Golf, Doctors' Golf Assn. Contbr. numerous professional articles to encys., text books and journals. Mem. Adv. Editorial Bd. Am. Jour. of Obstetrics and Gynecology. Home: Lake Forest IL Died Jan. 1950.

WILLIAMS, RANSOME JUDSON, ex-gov.; b. Cope, S.C., Jan. 4, 1892; s. Theophilus D. and Ida (Williams); ed. Med. Coll. of S.C. at Charleston; m. Virginia Allen, Oct. 11, 1916; children—Virginia Allen (Mrs. William D. Anderson), Nancy. Pres. Delta Drug Co., Myrtle Beach, S.C.; part owner drug store at Mullins, S.C.; mgr. Jefferson Standard Life Ins. Co., Florence, S.C. Has served as mayor of Mullins, S.C., rep. of Marion County in State Legislature and lt. governor S.C., gov. of S.C., 1945-47. Mem. Bd. Edn. Marion County; trustee Coker Coll.; chmn. bd. trustees Med. Coll. of S.C.; Univ. of S.C.; Citadel. Member S.C. Pharm. Assn. (past pres.), Mem. Jr. Order United Am. Mechanics (mem. state council); Phi Delta Kappa, Democrat. Baptist. Mason (Shriner), K.P., W.O.W. Club: Rotary. Home: Mullins SC Died Jan. 1970.*

WILLIAMS, ROBERT PARVIN, army officer; b. Greencastle, Ind., Aug. 29, 1891; s. Robert C(larence) and Arta (Parvin) W.; M.D., U. of Cincinnati, 1913; student Army Med. Sch., 1915-16; honor grad. Med. Field Service Sch., 1927; student, Command and Gen. Staff Sch., 1928-30; Army War Coll., 1934-35, Chem. Warfare Sch., 1935; m. Barbara Murray, July 21, 1917; 1 son, Charles Murray. Interne Ancon Hosp., Panama Canal Zone, 1912-13; Cincinnati Gen. Hosp., 1913-15; commd. 1st lt., Med. Corps, U.S. Army, 1915, promoted through grades to brig. gen., 1949. Army service; Mexican border, adjutant Camp Hosp., Douglas, Ariz., 1916-17; asst. div. surg., 1917-18; organized and comd. Gen. Hosp. No. 34, East Norfolk, Mass., 1918; camp surg. Camp Upton, N.Y., 1918; adj. Tripler Gen. Hosp., post surg. Ft. Kamehameha, Hawaii, 1919-22; duty in Post Hosp., attending surg. Vancouver Barracks, Wash., 1922-26; comdg. officer 1st Med. Squadron, 1st Cavalry div., Ft. Bliss, Tex., 1930-34; surg. No. Ariz. Dist., Civilian Conservation Corps, 1933-34; instr. The Inf. Sch., Ft. Benning, Ga., 1935-39; dir. training, Med. Field Service Sch., Carlisle Barracks, Pa., 1939-40; comdg. officer 1st Med. Regiment, march from Pa. to Calif., 1940; div. surg. 7th Inf. Div., Camp Ord, Calif., 1940; corps surg. IX Corps, Ft. Lewis, Wash., 1941-42; mem. Gen. Stilwell's Mil. Mission to China and Burma, Feb. 5, 1942; 1st Burma Campaign, liaison with Chinese armies, Feb.-May, 1942; surg. Gen. Stilwell's Column, retreat from Burma to India, May, 1942; 2d Burma Campaign, chief surg. Gen. Stilwell's China-Burma-India Theater and adv. to Chinese surg. gen., June 1942-44; chief surg. Gen. Dan I. Sultan's India-Burma Theater, 1944-45; Army surg. Fourth Army, 1945-July 1949; spl. asst. to surgeon gen., Sept.-Nov. 1949; chief surgeon Army Field Forces, Ft. Monroe, Va., 1949-56. Decorations: Legion of Merit, Bronze Star Medal with Oak Leaf Cluster, Army Commendation Ribbon, Order of Yin Whei (1st grade) (China), Chinese War Memorial Badge. Mem. Alpha Kappa Kappa, Theta Nu Epsilon, Assn. of Mil. Surgeons, Am. Med. Assn. Home: Carmel-by-the-Sea CA Died Nov. 20, 1967.

WILLIAMS, ROSWELL CARTER, JR., entomologist; b. Brooklyn, N.Y., Aug. 21, 1869; s. Roswell Carter and Ellen Sophia (Woodford) W.; B.S., Adelphi Acad., Brooklyn, 1888; M.E., Cornell U., 1892; m. Margaret Hamilton, of Belfast, Ireland, Mar. 5, 1910; children—Roswell Carter III, Hamilton, Arthur Phelps, Charles Montgomery; m. 2d, Carrie Hamsher, of Barnesville, Pa., Feb. 28, 1929. Elec. engr. and contractor, at Phila., Pa., 1894-1918; research asso. Acad. Natural Sciences, Phila., since 1918, dir. R. C. Williams & Co., groceries, N.Y. City. Served as capt. Ordnance Dept., U.S.A., 1 yr., World War. Mem. Entomol. Soc. America (pres.), Kappa Alpha. Republican. Mason (32 deg.). Clubs: Manufacturers, Penn Athletic. Contbr. to Entomol. News, Trans. Am. Entomol. Soc. Home: 4537 Pine St. Office: Acad. Natural Sciences, Philadelphia PA‡

WILLIAMS, SAMUEL LEONARD, govt. ofcl.; b. Kinston, N.C., Jan. 27, 1905; s. Joseph and Katie (Waller) W.; LL.B., Wake Forest Coll., 1928; m. Kay Cloaninger, May 18, 1934; children—Joseph L., Patricia A. Admitted to N.C. bar, 1927; practice in Kinston, 1928-34; with FTC, 1934-68, chief project atty., 1958-61, dir. Bur. Field Operations, 1961-68. Pres. Herndon (Va.) High Sch., P.T.A., 1959. Served to lt. comdr. USNR, 1943-45. Episcopalian (sr. warden). Home: Fairfax VA Died July 24, 1968; buried National Cemetery, Winchester VA

WILLIAMS, SEWARD HENRY, congressman; b. Amsterdam, N.Y., Nov. 7, 1870; s. John J. and Maria Louise (Montonye) W.; student Williams Coll., 1889-90; prep. course in law under Woodrow Wilson at Princeton; B.L., Washington and Lee U., Lexington, Va., 1895; m. Sarah Jeannette Reynolds, of Lorain, O., Sept. 29, 1897. Admitted to Ohio bar, 1895, and practiced in Lorain. City solicitor, Lorain, 1900-2 and 1908-10; mem. 64th Congress (1915-17), 14th Ohio Dist.; Republican. Mem. Bd. of Edn., Lorain, 1906-8; sec.-treas. City Solicitors' Assn. of State of Ohio, 1908-10. Mem. Lorain Co. Bar Assn., Sons of Vets. Baptist. Mason. Address: Lorain OH‡

WILLIAMS, STEPHEN RIGGS, zoologist; b. Kalgan, N. China, Aug. 22, 1870; s. Mark and Isabella Burgess (Riggs) W.; A.B., Oberlin Coll., 1892, A.M., 1893; A.M., Harvard, 1898, Ph.D., 1900; m. Mary Covington, of Brooklyn, N.Y. and Oxford, O., Sept. 14, 1904. Teacher high sch., Lima, O., 1894-96; asst. in zoology, Harvard, 1898-1900; asst. and instr., Cold Spring Harbor, L.I., summer sessions, 1900-04; prof., biology and geology, 1900-05, zoology since 1905, Miami U.; mem. staff, Lake Lab., Ohio State U., summer sessions, 1913-34. Mem. A.A.A.S., Am. Soc. Zoologists. Conglist. Contbr. Anatomy of the Texas Fever Tick, Specific Gravity of Fresh Water Organisms, etc. Home: Oxford OH‡

WILLIAMS, TRAVIS, lawyer; b. Rara Avis, Miss., Sept. 18, 1876; s. Gilbert Henry and Malinda (Franklin) W.; B.S., Oakland Normal Inst., Miss., 1898; m. Nancy Kennedy, Dec. 24, 1903; children—Franklin (Mrs. H. G. Spencer), Travis, Mary, Kennedy. Began as a school teacher, 1899; read law in law office, Russellville, Ala., and admitted to Ala. bar, 1903; atty. U.S. Dept. of Justice, 1936-37; asst. gen. counsel Nat. Bituminous Coal Commn. since June 1937. Mem. Ala. Ho. of Rep., 1923-27, Senate, 1927-31. Democrat. Mem. M.E. Church South. Mason. Home: Methodist Bldg. Office: 734 15th St., N.W., Washington DC‡

WILLIAMS, WHEELER, sculptor; b. Chicago, Nov. 3, 1897; s. Lawrence and Adele Holbrook (Wheeler) W.; Ph.B., magna cum laude, Yale U., 1919 (as of 1918); M.Arch., Harvard Grad. Sch. of Architecture, 1922; student Beaux Arts, Paris, France, 1922-23; m. Sylvia Cawston Gough, Oct. 16, 1924 (div. 1928); m. 2d, Margaret P. McManua. May 29, 1933; children—Diana Wheeler, Katrina Wheeler (Mrs. Anthony Lester). Sculptor, 1921-72. Served as 2d lt. U.S. Army Balloon Corps, 1918-19; and lt. comdr. U.S.N.R., World War II. Awarded hon. mention, Prix de Rome, 1922; gold medal, Paris Expn., 1937; E.P. Speyer award, Nat. Acad., 1940; Gold medal Nat. Arts Club, 1954; Gold medal, Am. Artists Profl. League, 1957. Past pres. Fine Arts Fedn. of New York; pres. Nat. Sculpture, 1951-54; past v.p. Archtl. League of N.Y.; mem. Inst. Arch. Design, Nat. Arts Club, Am. Artists Professional League (pres.), Municipal Art Soc., Nat. Acad. Book and Snake. Rep. Club: Century Assn. (N.Y. City). Works: Tablets to Pioneers," Mich. Av. Bridge, Chicago; Pioneer Woman," Phillips Gallery; Rhythm of the Waves Fountain," Grosse Pointe, Mich.; Century of Progress, Chicago; west pediment, Interstate Commerce Bldg., Washington; fountain, Regents Park, London; Steeds of Imagination," Reader's Digest Tower, Chapaqua, N.Y.; Indian Bowman," Canal St. Post Office, N.Y. City; Childhood of the Gods" and The Muses," N.Y. World's Fair; Black Panthers," Brookgreen Gardens, S.C.; Settlers of the Seaboard," Fairmount Park, Philadelphia; Fountain of Youth," the Norton Gallery of Art, West Palm Beach, Fla.; Am. Eagle Lectern, West Point; Am. Spirit Honor Medal, U.S. Army; insignia Citizens Commn. for Army and Navy; meml. tablet on U.S. Destroyer Stephen Potter; over entrance sculpture Am. Bureau of Shipping, N.Y. City; Pegasus the Winged Colt,", U. of Utah, Heroic Angel", Hedrick Meml, Salisbury, N.C.; Praise and Prayer," Madison Av. Presbyn. Ch., N.Y. City; U.S. Naval Acad.; Venus of Manhattan," N.Y. City; Eagle of Victory," City Productial Bldg., Houston; Clifford Holland, entrance Holland Tunnel, N.Y.C.; Foutain of the Water Babies, Seattle, Army, Navy, Air Force and Coast Guard; Wall of the Missing, Am. Battle Monument, Cambridge, Eng.; statue Col. R.R. McCormick, Baie Comeau, Can.; Heroic Head Col. McCormick, Tribune Tower, Chgo.; Sculptured Relief, fascade Morrisania Health Center, N.Y.C.; Robert A. Taft Meml., Washington; also numerous portrait busts, garden pieces, medals, etc. Works represented in museums and pvt collections in numerous states and D.C., Eng., Can., Mex., Spain, Ireland, France, S. Africa. Lectr., writer on art. Home: Madison CT Died Aug. 12, 1972.

WILLIAMS, WILLIAM CROW, truck sales co. exec.; b. St. Petersburg, Fla., June 25, 1925; s. Gilbert N. and Geraldine (Crow) W.; grad. Valley Forge Mil. Acad., 1943; student Culver Mil. Acad., 1941-42, Denison U., 1945-47; m. Doris Smith, Jan. 22, 1949; children—Charles Gilbert, Cynthia Elaine. Office mgr. G. N. Williams Trucking Co., Niles, O., 1948-56, owner, chmn. bd.; dir. Dollar Savs. Bank, Niles. Served to 1st lt., pilot, USAFR World War II. Mem. Niles C. of C., Mahoning Valley Truck Assn. Republican. Presbyn. Mason. Clubs: Trumbell Country. Home: Warren OH Deceased.

WILLIAMS, WILLIAM R., congressman; Brookfield, N.Y.; m. Bertha M. Risley;children—M Stuart Pughe, William R., Mrs. Jane E. Hurn. Farme Mem. N.Y. State Legislature, 1935-43; sheriff Onei Co., N.Y., 1943-51; mem. 82d to 85th Congresses, 34 dist. N.Y. Chmn., Oneida County Republican Con 1951-61. Home: Cassville NY Died May 9, 1972; buri Sauquoit Valley Cemetery, Sauquoit NY

WILLIAMSON, CLIFTON P., lawyer; b. Rocheste N.Y., 1876; LL.B., N.Y. Law Sch., 1899. Admitted N.Y. bar, 1899; now sr. mem. firm Alexander & Gree N.Y.C. Mem. N.Y. Law Inst., Am., N.Y. State b assns. Assn. Bar City N.Y., N.Y. County Lawyers Ass Home: New York City NY Died Dec. 23, 1968.*

WILLIAMSON, GEORGE, educator; b. Galesbur Ill., Feb. 20, 1898; s. Joseph Henry and Natalie Emi (Byloff) W.; A.B., Stanford, 1920, Ph.D., 1928; A.M Harvard, 1925; m. Jehanne Bacher, June 10, 1929; son, Alan. Mem. faculty Wash. State Coll., 1920-2 Pomona Coll., 1925-27, Stanford, 1927-28, U. Or 1928-36; Guggenheim fellow, 1931-32; with U. Chg 1936-68, prof. English, 1940-68, Martin A. Ryers distinguished service professor, 1959-63, emeritu 1963; engaged as summer teacher University Washington, 1930, Cornell U., 1942, Harvard, 195 Served with U.S. Army, 1917-18. Mem. Modern Lan Assn., Phi Beta Kappa. Lutheran. Author: Talent of S. Eliot, 1929; Donne Tradition, 1930; The Senec Amble, 1951; A Reader's Guide to T. S. Eliot, 1953, edit., 1966; Seventeenth Century Contexts, 1960, re edit., 1969; The Proper Wit of Poetry, 1961; Milton ar Others, 1965; Six Metaphysical Poets, 1967; A Reader Guide to the Metaphysical Poets, 1968. Co-author: Garland for John Donne, 1931. Editor Mode Philology, 1952-59. Home: Chicago IL Died Sept. 1968; buried El Carmelo Cemetery, Pacific Grove C.

WILLIAMSON, MRS. MARY ROBINSON, b. Jackson, Miss.; d. John William and Mary Ja (Bradford) Robinson; descendant of Gov. Willia Bradford, of Mass.; grad. Fairmount Coll., Monteag Tenn.; m. Chalmers Meek Williamson, of Jackso Miss., Oct. 26, 1887. State chmn. Playground Ass America; ex-v.-p.-gen. Nat. Soc. D.A.R.; mem. So Colonial Dames America, Soc. Descendants of Coloni Governors, Soc. Mayflower Descendants, Daughters Founders and Patriots of America, U.S. Daughters 1812, U.D.C., etc. Episcopalian. Home: 714 N. Sta St., Jackson MS‡

WILLIAMSON, OLIVER ROBISON, ch. official; Covington, O., May 6, 1871; s. Oliver and Sara (Robison) W.; mainly self-educated; m. Nina Mar Bolt, June 26, 1895 (died Sept. 4, 1935); 1 dau., Ru (Mrs. E.E. Ackland); m. 2d, Sally Ferry. Printer, write country newspapers, Ohio, Alabama, Indiana; report and editorial writer daily papers; mng. editor T Continent, 1910, pub. same, and sec. and manag McCormick Pub. Co., 1912-26; gen. dir. of C Relations, Presbyn. Ch. in U.S.A., 1929-36; di production and purchases, 1936-41; acting gen. se John Milton Soc. for the Blind, 1941-44; sec. com. o church relations, Save the Children Fedn., 1944-4 Pres. Chicago Presbyn. Social Union, 1914; chm Inter-Church War Work Com. of Chicago during Wor War; organizer religious press for Federal Foo Adminstrn.; commr. to Gen. Assembly Presbyn. Ch 1910, 21, 23; chmn. advisory commn. Chicago C Federation, 1917-26; mem. Federal Council Chs. Christ in Am., 1915-40; chmn. publicity com. Worl Alliance Presbyn. Chs., 1920-46; one of the founde publicity dept. Presbyn. Ch. Mem. S.A.R. Republica Home: 734 New York 10 NY‡

WILLIAMSON, WILLIAM, congressman; bor Mahaska County, Ia., Oct. 7, 1875; s. Wm. and Mar (Erland) W.; student Wayne (Neb.) Normal Sch.; A.B U. of S.D., 1903, LL.B., 1905; m. Clara Victoria Dic Oct. 5, 1910; children (adopted)—Mary Lavern Cleola Catherine, Gertrude Lucile (all sisters). Joir founder with bro. Albert W., of the Coyote, and Prair Sun, weekly newspapers, 1903 and 1904, also Williamson Hardware Co., 1906; pres. Lyman Coun Abstract Co.; state's atty., Lyman County, 1905-1 circuit judge 11th Jud. Dist., S.D., 1911-21; del. Re Nat. Conv., 1912; mem. 67th to 72d Congresse (1921-33), 2d S.D. District; later asst. atty. gen. of S.D council Public Utilities Commn.; gen. couns Rushmore Mut. Life Insurance Co. Republica Conglist. Mason. Home: Rapid City SD Died July 1 1972; buried Pine Lawn Meml. Cemetery.

WILLINGHAM, EDWARD BACON, clergyman; Richmond, Va., Oct. 30, 1899; s. Robert Josiah an Sarah Corneille (Bacon) W.; studied Washington U., S Louis and Columbia U.; B.A., U. of Richmond, 192 D.D., 1933; Th.M., So. Bapt. Theol. Sem., 1924; D.D McMaster U., Hamilton, Ont., 1959; married Harriet Sharon, Aug. 15, 1929; children—Harriet (Mrs. W. Johnson, Jr.), Edward Bacon. Ordained ministry Bap Ch., 1922; student pastor Glencoe, Ky., 1922-24; ass prof. of Bible, U. of Richmond, Va., 1924-26; field se Va. Bapt. Bd. of Missions and Edn., Richmon 1926-28; pastor Rivermont Av. Bapt. Ch., Lynchbur Va., 1928-32, Delmar Bapt. Ch., St. Louis, 1932-4

Fifth Av. Bapt. Ch., Huntington, W.Va., 1940-June 1, 1945; pastor National Baptist Memorial Ch., Washington, D.C., 1945-55; general secretary to American Baptist Fgn. Mission Socs., 1956-65; interim pastor 1st Bapt. Ch., Kansas City, Mo., 1965-66, Cherry Hill Bapt. Ch., Dearborn, Mich., 1966, North Yonkers (N.Y.) Community Ch., 1967, 1st Bapt. Ch., Alliance, O., 1967-68, Madison Av. Bapt. Ch., N.Y.C., 1968, Delmar Bapt. Ch., St. Louis, 1969, Bethany Bapt. Ch., Pontiac, Mich., 1970, North Bapt. Ch., Port Chester, N.Y., 1970-71, 1st Bapt. Ch., White Plains, N.Y., 1971-72. Former mem. Fgn. Mission Bd., So. Bapt. Conv. Relief and Annuity Board; associate general secretary, and past mem. Gen. Council, Am. Baptist Cov.; pres. W.Va. Bapt. Conv., 1943-44 Washington Ministerial Union, 1950-51; v.p. W.Va. Council of Chs. and Christian Edn., 1944-45, Washington Federation Churches; past western treas. Baptist World Alliance; exec. com. Theol. Edn. Fund Com. Internat. Missionary Council, 1958-63; gen. bd. Nat. Council Chs. of Christ, 1960-65, mem. exec. bd. Div. Foreign Missions, and the Division of Overseas Ministries; del. Internat. Missionary Council and World Council Chs. Assembly, New Delhi, 1961. Trustee So. Bapt. Theol. Sem., 1946-55, Former chmn. Bapt. Joint Com. on Pub. Affairs. Served as 2d lieutenant U.S. Army, 1918. Former dir. Mo. Bapt. Hosp., St. Louis. Mem. Phi Gamma Delta, Omicron Delta Kappa, Tau Kappa Alpha, Theta Phi, Phi Beta Kappa. Mason (32 deg.). Home: New York City NY Died Nov. 16, 1972; buried Richmond VA

WILLIS, CHARLES FRANCIS, mining engr., editor; b. Boston, Mass., Aug. 18, 1885; s. Frank Eugene and Elizabeth Ann (King) W.; S.B. in Mining Engring., Mass. Inst. Tech., 1906; E.M., N.M. Coll. of Mines, 1916; m. Helen Isabel Heckman, Feb. 20, 1908; children—Barbara Lee (Mrs. B. F. C. Miller), Anne Harrison (Mrs. James H. Quint), Manager of the Enterprise Mining Co., Cooney, N.M., 1906, Pelican Mining Co., Lake City, Colo., 1909; first dir. Ariz. Bur. Mines, Tucson, 1912; cons. supervisior dept. indsl. relations, Phelps Dodge Corp., Bisbee, Ariz., 1918; editor and pub. The Mining Journal, 1920-46 (Mining Jour. then consol. with Mining World); editorial writer Mining World since 1946. Was active in war work as state dir. 1st and 2d Y.M.C.A. drives, United War Work Drive, Armenian and Jewish Relief drives, Near East Relief; was mem. Ariz. Council of Defense and in charge war mineral production, World War I; cons. Metals Reserve Co., mem. Ariz. War Manpower Commn., industry panel. Mem. 10th Regional Labor Bd., Ariz., dir. Com. on Econ. Development, World War II. Chmn. bd. of govs., Ariz. Dept. of Mineral Resources; consultant, Metals Reserve Co.; state sec. Arizona Small Mine Operators Assn.; mem. Nat. Minerals Adv. Council (chmn. pub. lands com.); mem. nat. adv. council Small Bus. Adminstrn. Recipient Medallian of Honor, U. Ariz., 1960. Mem. Am. Inst. Mining and Metall. Engrs. (dir. Ariz. Sect.); Am. Mining Congress, (gov. Western div.), Am. Assn. Engrs. (ex-pres. Phoenix chpt.), Soc. Promotion Engring. Edn. Ariz. Newspapers Assn. (past sec.). Republican. Episcopalian. Clubs: Arizona, Phoenix, Kiwanis (former dist. gov. S.W. Dist.), Advertising (ex-pres.). Home: Phoenix AZ Died Dec. 10, 1968; buried Greenwood Meml. Park, Phoenix AZ

WILLIS, EDWIN EDWARD, congressman; born Arnaudville, La., Oct. 2, 1904; s. Olanda and Julia (Hardy) W.; LL.B., Loyola U., 1926; m. Estelle Bulliard, Dec. 9, 1929. Admitted to La. bar, 1926; practiced law in St. Martinville, La.; mem. Louisiana state senate, 1947-48; mem. 81st to 90th Congresses, 3d La. Dist. Law lectr., nights, 1928-36. Mem. La. Bar Assn. Democrat. Roman Catholic. K.C., Rotarian. Home: St Martinville LA Died Oct. 24, 1972; buried St. Martin of Tours Catholic Cemetery.

WILLIS, HERMAN ALLEN, finance co. exec.; b. Hillsboro, Tex., Sept. 17, 1905; s. Alfred Wilkerson and Aaron Josephine (Hester) W.; student S.W. Tchrs. Coll., 1925-27, Tex. Tech., 1925; m. Johnnie Frances Tucker, Sept. 1, 1934; children—Kay (Mrs. Frank Ford Smith). Allen Tucker. Tchr., Mission, Sherryland, Tex., 1926-27; coach Abilene (Tex.) High Sch., 1928-29; tchr. Abilene Jr. High Sch., 1928-30; with Gen. Motors Acceptance Corp., 1930-70, mgr., Louisville, 1944-45, San Antonio, 1946-53, Houston, 1953-59, regional mgr., N.Y.C., 1959-62, v.p., 1962-64, v.p., mgr. operations, 1964, exec. v.p., 1964-70. Vice pres. Better Bus. Bur., Houston, 1956-59, Little Rock, 1960-63. Clubs: Pine Forest Country (pres. 1958-59) (Houston); Oak Hills County (v.p. 1950-53) (San Antonio). Home: Austin TX Died 1971.

WILLIS, HORACE HAROLD, textile consultant; b. Spartanburg, S.C., April 25, 1891; s. James Henry and Julia Ann (Finley) W.; B.S., Clemson Agrl. and Mech. Coll., 1917; m. Alice Moore, Dec. 23, 1922; 1 son, Ernest Moore. Employee Clifton Mfg. Co. intermittently 1903-17; Lt. World War I, 1917-19; instr. Clemson Coll., 1920; asst. state supervisor textile indsl. edn., State Dept. Edn., North Carolina, 1920-21; cotton specialist supervising tests in California, Ariz., and Tex., Bur. Plant Industry, U.S. Dept. Agr., 1921-24; in charge cotton spinning research, U.S. Dept. Agr., 1924-30; dir. Textile Sch., Clemson Coll., 1927-33; in charge flax spinning research, Textile Foundation, 1933; dean, Textile Sch., Clemson Coll., 1933-43; consultant cotton mfg. and labor relations, 1943-70. Mem. Southern Textile Assn., Arkwrights, Southeastern Econ. Council; S.C. Acad. Science, Am. Soc. Testing Materials, Blue Key, Phi Psi. Club: Kiwanis (Anderson, S.C.). Mason. Joint author series textile texts; contbr. to textile journals; writer of many spinning test reports and bulletins for U.S. Dept. Agr. Home: Clemson SC Died Aug. 11, 1970; buried Old Stone Cemetery Clemson SC

WILLIS, PARK WEED, physician, surgeon; b. Umatilla County, Ore., July 10, 1867; s. William McCellan and Mary Arabella (Keyes) W.; U. of Wash., 1883-84; B.S., Whitman College, Walla Walla, Washington, 1888, M.S., 1891, LL.D., 1945; M.D., University of Pennsylvania, 1891; married Georgia Clark, June 15, 1892;children—Park Weed, Cecil Durand. Practiced at Seattle, Wash. since 1892. Trustee Whitman Coll., 1909-49. Founder, fellow Am. College Surgeons; fellow A.M.A.; mem. North Pacific Surgical Association, Pacific Coast Surgical Association, Washington State Med. Assn. (ex-pres.), King County Med. Soc. (ex-pres.), Phi Beta Kappa. Republican. Episcopalian. Clubs: Army and Navy (Washington, D.C.); Rainier, Swinomish Gun, Monday, Washington Athletic. Home: 1316 Columbia St. Office: 914 Second Av., Seattle WA‡

WILLISON, GEORGE F(INDLAY), author, editor, pub. relations; b. Denver, July 24, 1896; s. Robert and Anna (Brunton) W.; grad. U. Colo., 1918, U. Oxford (Rhodes scholar), 1920-23, U. Paris, 1924; m. Florence Hauser, 1928; 1 son, Malcolm. Journalist Denver, N.Y. City, 1925-27; head classics dept. St. John's Coll., Annapolis, Md., 1928; tchr. Hessian Hills Sch., Croton-on-Hudson, N.Y., 1929-35, mem. bd. trustees, 1930-35, acting dir., 1934; writer, later nat. editor-in-chief Fed. Writers Program, Provincetown, Mass., Washington, 1936-41; writer, pub. relations cons. civil aeronautics adminstrn. Dept. Commerce, 1942-43; writer, asst. to publicity dir. Dem. Nat. Com., 1944-45; editor-writer Dept. Pub. Information, U.N., N.Y. City, 1950; Senator Estes Kefauver's presidential campaign staff, 1952, 55; mem. gov.'s exec. chamber staff state of N.Y., 1955-59; dir. pub. information City of New York Commission Intergroup Relations, N.Y.C., 1959-60; dir. pub. relations N.Y.C. Dept. Commerce and Pub. Events, 1961-62. Served as officer machine gun corps, U.S. Army, 1918. Author: Here They Dug the Gold, 1931 (rev., enlarged edit., 1946, paperback edit., 1972); Why Wars are Declared, 1936; Let's Make A Play, 1940; Saints and Strangers, 1945, rev. edit., 1965; Behold Virginia, 1951; The Pilgrim Reader, 1953; History of Pittsfield (Mass.), 1916-1955, 1957; I am An American: Patrick Henry and His World, 1967. Contbr. nat. mags., critical jours. Home: Ballston Spa, NY Died July 30, 1972; cremated.

WILLISTON, ARTHUR LYMAN, engr., educator; b. Cambridge, Mass., Oct. 11, 1868; s. Lyman Richards and Anne E. (Gale) W.; S.B., Mass. Inst. Tech., 1889, grad. course, 1889-90; m. Irene L. Simmons, June 21, 1893 (died May 1, 1924); m. 2d, Mary de F. Denny, Dec. 9, 1925. Asst. to chief engr. C.C.C.&St.L. Ry., 1890-91; instr. steam engring. Mass. Inst. Tech., 1891-92; mech. engr. Lockwood & Greene, Boston, 1892-93; dir. dept. industrial arts and prof. engring., Ohio State U., 1893-98; dir. Sch. of Science and Technology, Pratt Inst., Brooklyn, 1898-1910; prin. Wentworth Inst., Boston, 1910-24; dir. ednl. and industrial survey, Norwood, Mass., 1925-27; ednl. research and asst. to dir. Am. Council on Edn., Washington, D.C., 1927-32; mem. Hawkes Com. on Personnel Research, 1929-32. Internat. examiner in steam engring. and machine design, Y.M.C.A., 1902-14; mem. expert advisory com. Carnegie Tech. Schs., Pittsburgh, 1902-05; educational expert for Reed College, Boston School Committee, 1908, also for superintendent of schools, New York City, 1908-09, for Wentworth Inst., 1908-10, Ohio Mechanics Inst., Cincinnati, 1917-18. Ednl. dir. New England edn. and spl. training com. U.S. War Dept., 1918-19; organizer and dir. for U.S. War Dept. of Boston Sch. of Occupational Therapy, 1918-19. Am. del. World Federation of Edn., Edinburgh, 1925, World Conf. on Adult Edn., Copenhagen, 1926. Mem. Exec. Comm. (N.E. Br.) Com. to Defend America by Aid to Allies, 1940-41; mem. Council and sec. Citizens Com. for a Nat. War Service Act, 1942-46; treas. Mass. Br. Citizens Com. for Universal Mil. Training of Young Men since 1946. Initiated and planned program of Experimental Unit in U.M.T. at Ft. Knox, Ky. for U.S. War Dept., 1947. Mem. Am. Soc. Mech. Engrs. (pres. Boston sect. 1916-17), A.A.A.S., Fedn. of Arts, N.E.A. (pres. vocational edn. and practical arts dept., 1912-14; pres. science dept., 1918-19). Soc. for Promotion Engring. Edn. (mem. council 1900-03 and 1904-07; sec. 1907-09; vice-pres. 1909-10), Nat. Soc. for Promotion Indsl. Edn. (exec. comm.; sec.-treas. N.Y. State Br.) Writer of numerous published articles and reports on industrial, engineering, and gen. edn. subjects. Author: Beyond the Horizon of Science, 1944. Address: 986 High St., Dedham MA‡

WILLITS, OLIVER GASTON, food manufacturing executive; b. Brooklyn, February 20, 1892; s. George S. and Sylvia (Gaston) W.; student U. Pa., 1910-12; B.S. in Econs., Pa. State Univ. 1914; LL.D., Beaver Coll., Temple U.; m. Margaret Fitler, Apr. 8, 1915 (dec. 1968); children—Margot (Mrs. Harold E. Jahn), Nan (Mrs. Wm. J. Blake), Sylvia (Mrs. Richard Rittenhouse). Former chmn. bd. Campbell Soup Co., ret., 1962, also dir.; dir. Detroit, Toledo, and Ironton R.R. Co. Nat. chmn. United Community Campaigns Am., 1960; chmn. exec. com. United Community Funds and Councils Am., 1962. Mem. Sigma Nu. Republican. Presbyn. Clubs: Racquet, Gulph Mills (Phila.); Merion Cricket (Haverford); Pine Valley Golf (trustee), Santee (S.C.); Twenty Nine Inc. (N.Y.C.); Carlton (Washington). Home: Haverford PA Died May 26, 1971.

WILLMAN, LEON KURTZ, clergyman; b. Pottstown, Pa., July 26, 1873; s. Mabery Ebling and Esther Guldin (Dry) W.; A.B., Wesleyan U., Conn., 1897, D.D., 1914; student Drew Theol. Sem., Madison, N.J., 1897-98; m. Anne Lydia Judkins, of Bristol, N.H., Jan. 17, 1901. Ordained M.E. ministry, 1898; pastor Waterbury, Vt., 1898-1902, Montpeller, Vt., 1902-04; instructor Bible history, The Hill School, Pottstown, Pa., 1904-07; pastor Spring Garden St. Ch., Phila., 1907-14, 1st Ch., Asbury Park, N.J., 1914-18; asso. field dir. Am. Red Cross, Army Hospitals, 1918-19; pastor Broadway Ch., Camden, N.J., 1919-20, First Ch. of Wilkes-Barre, Pa., since 1920. Mem. Phila. Social Service Commn., 1911-14; chmn. social service commn. Pa. Council of Chs., 1927-1935; lecturer Bible courses N.J. S.S. Assn., 1915-19; del. Gen. Conf. M.E. Ch., 1932. Mem. Phi Beta Kappa, Psi Upsilon. Republican. Mason; Grand Chaplain Knight Templars of Pa., 1930. Rotarian. Author: Men of the Old Testament; Pastor's Vade Mecum. Contbr. to Christian Advocate, etc. Home: 63 N. Franklin St., Wilkes-Barre PA*‡

WILLNUS, HARRY G., business exec.; b. Brooklyn, Aug. 14, 1897; s. Christopher and Ida (Oswald) W.; ed. pub. schs., Brooklyn; m. May Meade Cartwright, Sept. 14, 1921; 1 dau., Marion Cartwright. Pres., dir. Intertype Corp., Bklyn., also chief executive officer, 1952-57; president Intertype Company div. Harris-Intertype Corp., 1957-62; dir. Home Title Guaranty Co.; trustee Brooklyn Savs. Bank; mem. adv. com. Chase Manhattan Bank. Trustee Polytech. Inst. Bklyn.; dir. Nat. Indsl. Conf. Bd. Mem. C. of C. (dir.); Arbitrator for Am. Arbitration Assn.; mem. industry panel War Labor Bd. 1943-45; mem. industry adv. com. O.P.A., 1945-46; industry adv. com. W.P.B., 1942-45; citizens panel, milk dispute, N.Y.C., 1947. Mem. panel investigating elementary and high sch. tchrs., N.Y.C. 1950. Clubs: Union League (N.Y.); Brooklyn, Rembrandt. Home: Brooklyn NY Died Feb. 20, 1969; buried Cypress Hills Abbey, Brooklyn NY

WILLOUGHBY, CHARLES A., army officer; b. Heidelberg, Germany, March 8, 1892 (naturalized U.S. citizen, 1910); s. Freiherr T. von Tscheppe-Weidenbach and Emma (Willoughby) von T.; B.A., Gettysburg (Pa.) Coll., 1914; grad. student U. of Kan., 1933; grad. Inf. Sch., 1929, Command and Gen. Staff Sch., 1931, Army War Coll., 1936; commd. 2d lt. Inf., 1915; advanced through the grades to major general, 1945, reverted to brigadier general, 1946; served on Mexican Border, 1916-17; served with 1st Division, of A.E.F., 1917-18; chief of intelligence, Gen. MacArthur's staff, Philippine campaign, 1941, S.W. Pacific, 1942-46; veteran of Bataan and Corregidor; represented Gen. MacArthur to receive Imperial Japanese delegation for surrender negotiations, Aug. 15, 1945, Manila, P.I. Awarded D.S.C., D.S.M., both with oak leaf cluster, Silver Star, Legion of Merit (U.S.); Commander Order British Empire (Gr. Brit.); Medaille d'Honneur (Aff. Etr.); Legion of Honor (France); S. Maurizio e Lazzaro (Italy); Order of Bolivar (Venezuela); Al Merito and Star of Calderon (Ecuador). Member Phi Gamma Delta. Club: Army and Navy (Washington, D.C.). Mason. Author: United States Economic Participation World War, 1917-18, 1931; Maneuver in War, 1939. Columnist for Army-Navy Jour. Editor: General Staff Quarterly, 1931-35; editor in chief Gen. Intelligence Series, SWPA, prepared for Dept. of the Army. Home: Bronxville NY Died 1972.

WILM, GRACE GRIDLEY (MRS. EMIL CARL WILM), pianist, author; b. Benzonia, Mich., Jan. 25, 1877; d. Albert Leveritt and Prudence (Wood) Gridley; Mus.B., Oberlin Conservatory of Music, 1900; also studied under W. H. Sherwood, Chicago, George Proctor, Boston, and Robert Teichmueller, Leipzig, Germany; m. Emil Carl Wilm, September 15, 1903 (died January 30, 1932); children—Clara, Harold, Margaret, Carl. Instructor in music, successively Southwestern U., Washburn Coll., Lasell Sem. and Wellesley Coll. Author: The Appreciation of Music, 1928; A History of Music, 1930. Home: 1317 N. Tejon St., Colorado Springs CO‡

WILSON, MRS. ALFRED GASTON (MATILDA RAUSH WILSON), coll. trustee, civic worker; b. Walkerton, Ont., Can., Oct. 19, 1883; d. George and Margaret (Glinz) Rausch; brought to U.S. 1884; student pvt. tutors; LL.D., Mich. State U., 1955; D.H. (hon.),

Oakland U., 1963; m. John Francis Dodge, Dec. 10, 1907 (dec. 1920); children—Frances Matilda (Mrs. Frederich L. VanLennep), Daniel George (dec.), Anna Margaret (dec.); m. 2d, Alfred Gaston Wilson, June 29, 1925 (dec. Apr. 1962); children—Richard, Barbara (Mrs. Thomas S. Eccles). Chmn. bd. dirs. Fidelity Bank & Trust Co., Detroit, 1930; mem. state bd. agr., Mich., 1932-38; treas. Mich. Synodical, 1921-41; lt. gov., State Mich., 1940. Pres. aux., Salvation Army, 1951; mem. Friends Detroit Pub. Library, 1946-67. Trustee Beloit Coll., 1952-67. Presbyn. Found., Phila., 1956-67. Recipient Distinguished Aux. Service Cross, Salvation Army, 1947. Mem. Women's Nat. Farm and Garden Assn. (local council 1956-67., pres. 1964-66), Fedn. Women's Clubs Met. Detroit (hon. pres.), Historic Memls. Soc. (past pres.), Women's Assn. First Presbyn. Ch. Detroit (pres. 1941-43, hon. pres. 1952-67), Soc. Arts and Crafts, Detroit Hist. Soc., Am. Fedn. Arts, Detroit Mus. Art Founders Soc., Nat. Council Women U.S., Presbyn. Hist. Soc. Presbyn. (elder). Clubs: Village Women's (pres. 1962-64) (Birmingham, Bloomfield Hills, Mich.); Women's City (Detroit bd. mem. 1944-47). Home: Rochester MI Died Sept. 19, 1967.

WILSON, BERT, coll. pres.; b. Wick, Tyler Co., W.Va., Mar. 31, 1877; s. Jasper and Elizabeth Ann (Shriver) W.; A.B., Cotner Coll., Bethany, Neb., 1909, LL.D., 1921; post-grad. work, U. of Neb., 1909-11; m. Edith Burchell, of Minden, Kearney Co., Neb., Aug. 27, 1902; children—Star, Roma, Lenore, Violet, Beth, Elaine, Arlene, Eunice. Teacher country schs., Kearney Co., Neb., 1896-98; prof. English lit. and head dept. English, Cotner Coll., 1911-12; sec. Men and Religion Forward Movement for Neb., 1912-13; sec. Fgn. Christian Missionary Soc., Cincinnati, 1913-20; chmn. promotional div. United Christian Missionary Soc., St. Louis, 1920-23; pres. Eureka (Ill.) Coll. since Dec. 1, 1923. Journey around the world, 1919-20. Author: Dad's Letters on a World Journey, 1921; In the Land of the Salaam, 1922; The Christian and His Money Problems, 1923. Home: Eureka IL‡

WILSON, CHARLES A., lawyer; b. Mexico, Me.; s. Philander and Janet Ayer (Fairbanks) W.; desc. Jonathan Fairbanks of Dedham, Mass.; ed. pub. and pvt. schs. of Me.; m. Cornelia Blake, of Providence, R.I., 1892. Admitted to bar, 1875, and since practiced in Providence; mem. Wilson, Lovejoy Budlong & Clough. Member Common Council, Providence, 1888-90; mem. R.I. Ho. of Rep., 1891; U.S. dist. atty., Dist. of R.I., 1898-1911. On staff of Gov. George Peabody Wetmore, 1885-87; judge advocate general of R.I., 1887-98; chmn. Rep. State Central Com. and Exec. Com., Aug. 1911-14. Mason. Mem. Fairbanks Family of America. Club: Turks Head. Home: 18 Medway St. Office: Turks Head Bldg., Providence RI*‡

WILSON, CHARLES EDWARD, business executive; b. New York, N.Y., Nov. 18, 1886; s. George H. and Hannah Rebecca (Stiles) W.; ed. public schools of N.Y. City; m. Elizabeth Maisch, Nov. 18, 1907; 1 dau., Mrs. Hugh Pierce. Began in shipping dept., Sprague Works, Gen. Electric Co., N.Y. City, Sept. 1899, and served successively in accounting, production, engring., mfg. and marketing depts.; mgr. merchandise dept. and v.p., 1930-37, exec. v.p., 1937-39, pres., 1940-42, 1944-50; exec. vice-chmn. WPB, Sept. 1944; dir. Office of Defense Mobilization 1950-52; dir., chmn. exec. com., chmn. bd. W. R. Grace & Co.; dir. Guaranty Trust Co. of N.Y. Pub. rep. on bd. govs. N.Y. Stock Exchange, 1955-72. Recipient Medal of Merit, Air Force Exceptional Award, Navy Distinguished Pub. Service award. Baptist. Clubs: Scarsdale Country; Mohawk (Schenectady); Links (N.Y. City). Home: Scarsdale NY Died Jan. 3, 1972; buried Kensico Cemetery, Nalhalla NY

WILSON, CHARLES HENRY, chmn. Raymond & Whitcomb Co.; b. St. Johnsbury, Vt.; s. Squires J. and Abigail C. (Smith) W.; grad. St. Johnsbury Acad., 1872; m. Jane Snow Swan, of Taunton, Mass., Nov. 27, 1886. Ry. service, including telegraph operator, engineer, conductor; with Raymond & Whitcomb, tourist mgrs., since 1884; conducted excursions to Mexico, Alaska, North Cape, and through Europe, etc.; in charge daily Pullman train service to World's Fair, Chicago, 1893; was mgr. San Francisco and New York offices of the company; served as pres., 1908-27, chmn. exec. com. since 1927, also mem. finance com. Republican. Conglist. Mason (K.T., Shriner). Clubs: Boston City; Lyndon (Vt.). Home: Brookline MA Office: 126 Newbury St., Boston MA‡

WILSON, CLARENCE HALL, clergyman; b. New Wilmington, Pa., Apr. 17, 1863; s. Hiram Hall and Mary Scott (Cotton) W.; B.A., Westminster Coll., Pa., 1884; grad. Union Theol. Sem., 1887; D.D., Wabash Coll., 1905; m. Mary Gordon, Sept. 21, 1887 (died 1928); children—Clarence Gordon, Paul, Mary Lena (Mrs. E.T. Booth), Norman Hall; m. 2d, Margaret Scott Hughes, Oct. 6, 1932. Ordained to Presbyn. ministry, 1887; pastor First Ch., Sag Harbor, N.Y., 1887-1902, Center Ch., Crawfordsville, Ind., 1902-09, Glen Ridge (N.J.) Congl. Ch., 1909-27. Commr. to Eng. to conduct Brit. pilgrimage to America, 1928. Mem. bd. dirs. Corp. Nat. Council Congl. Chs., 1919-25; mem. exec. com. Nat. Council, 1925-31, chmn. 1927-31; mem. exec. committee. Gen. Council, 1934-40, chmn. 1936-40; member Am. Institute of Archaeology; trustee College of Madura, India; trustee Annuity Fund for Congl. Ministers and Bd. of Ministerial Relief, 1919-25, also chmn. adminstrn. com. of the Bd., 1928-35; chmn. commn. on Near East Relief, 1921-25; dir. Home Missionary Socs., 1927-33. Mem. Nat. Civic Fedn. Com. of 100 on Internat. Relations, 1922; mem. adminstrn com. Am. branch Universal Conf. on Life and Work; pastor ad interim Central Union Ch., Honolulu, 1930-31; mem. exec. com. Internat. Council of Congl. Chs., 1940; mem. Commn. on Edn. for Ministry since 1940. Republican. Mason. Clubs: Congregational (pres. 1919-21), Clergy (New York); Winthrop (Boston); Friars (Hartford). Author: Talks to Young People on Ethics, 1917; Fellowship of Prayer, 1929, 31; also numerous published sermons and addresses. Address: 1954 Albany Av., West Hartford 5 CT‡

WILSON, EDMUND, writer; b. Red Bank, N.J., May 8, 1895; s. Edmund and Helen Mather (Kimball) W.; prep. edn., Hill Sch., Pottstown, Pa., 1909-12; A.B., Princeton, 1916; m. Mary Blair, 1923; 1 dau., Rosalind; m. 2d, Margaret Canby, 1930; m. 3d, Mary McCarthy, 1938; 1 son, Reuel; m. 4th, Elena Thornton, 1946; 1 d., Helen. Began as reporter on the New York Evening Sun, 1916-17; mng. editor Vanity Fair, 1920-21; associate editor New Republic, 1926-31; book reviewer for The New Yorker, 1944-48. Served as enlisted man with Base Hosp. 36, and Intelligence Corps, U.S. Army, August 1917-19. Recipient Aspen award Aspen Inst. Humanistic Studies, 1968. Author: The Undertaker's Garland (with John Peale Bishop), 1922; Discordant Encounters (dialogues and plays), 1926; I Thought of Daisy (novel), 1929; Poets, Farewell1931; The American Jitter—A Year of the Slump, 1932; Travels in Two Democracies, 1936; This Room and This Gin and These Sandwiches (plays), 1937; The Triple Thinkers, 1938; To the Finland Station, 1940; The Boys in the Back Room, 1941; The Wound and the Bow, 1941; Note-Books of Night, 1942; The Shock of Recognition (anthology), 1943; Memoirs of Hecate County, (fiction), 1946; Europe Without Baedeker, 1947; The Little Blue Light (play), Classics and Commercials (criticism), 1950; The Shores of Light, 1952; Five Plays, 1954; The Scrolls From the Dead Sea, 1955; Red, Black, Blond and Olive, 1956; A Piece of My Mind, 1956; The American Earthquake, 1958; Apologies to the Iroquois, 1959; Patriotic Gore, 1962; The Cold War and the Income Tax, 1963; Bit Between My Teeth; A literary chronicle of 1950-65, 1965; O Canada: An American's Notes on Canadian Culture, 1965; A Prelude, 1967; The Fruits of the MLA; The Duke of Palermo and other Plays; The Dead Sea Scrolls: 1955-69; Upstate, 1971; Window on Russia, 1972. Address: Wellfleet MA Died June 12, 1972; buried Wellfleet MA

WILSON, EDWARD ARTHUR, artist; b. Glasgow, Scotland, Mar. 4, 1886; s. Edward Joseph and Euphemia Evangeline (Murray) W.; came with parents to U.S., 1893; art edn., Art Inst. Chicago and under Howard Pyle, Wilmington, Del.; m. Dorothy Roe, Oct. 24, 1913;children—Jane, Mary Elizabeth. Painter and illustrator; prints are in Metropolitan Museum, New York Public Library, Library of Congress, and in private collection of H. H. Rogers and others. Awarded Art Director medal, 1926 and 1930; Isidor prize, 1927; Shaw prize, 1942; Soc. Illustrators Hall of Fame and medal, 1962. Fellow Royal Soc. Arts; mem. Guild of Free Lance Artists (pres. 1926), Am. Inst. Graphic Arts, Soc. Illustrators. Clubs: Dutch Treat, Players, Salmagundi, Century Assn. A.N.A., 1948. Illustrator and author numerous books; illustrator for mags. Home: Truro MA Died Oct. 2, 1970; buried Truro MA

WILSON, EDWARD LATIMER, trade assn. exec.; b. Chgo., Aug. 15, 1909; s Edward Fay and Nellie (Latimer) W.; B.S., U. Ill., 1932; m. Harriet Hoskins, Feb. 16, 1934; children—Ellen Fay (Mrs. Ronald F. Prater), Edward Hoskins. Reporter editorial dept. Chgo. Tribune, 1934-46; mng. dir. Mobile Homes Mfrs. Assn., Chgo., 1946-68; exec. v.p. Asso. Mgmt. Service, 1968-71; executive vice president Bostrom Corporation. Served from lt. (j.g.) to lt. comdr., USNR, 1942-45. Mem. U.S. C. of C. (mem. assn. committee), American Trade Assn. Execs. (grand award 1947), Trade Assn. Execs. Forum of Chgo., Assn. Econs. Council. Club: University (Chgo.). Home: Elgin IL Died Nov. 2, 1971.

WILSON, EDWARD WILLIAM, exec.; b. Chgo., Feb. 6, 1899; s. Edward and Mary (Anderson) W.; student U. Chgo., 1918; LL.B., John Marshall Law Sch., 1925; m. Lillian Margaret Boyd, June 15, 1929; children—Mary (Mrs. D.J. Keller), Jane (Mrs. D.M. Stone). Admitted to Ill. bar, 1925; with Armour & Co., Chgo., 1922-67, v.p., 1949-55, group v.p. charge non-food operations, exec. v.p., 1956-61, pres. 1961-65, vice chmn. bd., 1965-67, also dir. Chmn., Com. on Urban Area Govts., 1968-73. Bd. govs. Met. Housing and Planning Council of Chgo.; trustee Farm Found., West Suburban Hosp., Oak Park, Ill. Mem. W.P.B., 1942-43. Mem. Am. Legion. Mason. Presbyn. Clubs: Oak Park Country, River Forest Tennis, Executives, Chicago, Mid-America; Rio Mar Country, Rio Mar Yacht. Home: Vero Beach FL Died Feb. 17,, 1973.

WILSON, EDWIN CARLETON, diplomatic service; b. Palatka, Fla., Feb. 7, 1893; s. Henry Seth and Marion Dennison (Brown) W.; student University of Michigan, 1911-14, Harvard, 1914-15; m. Winifred Steckley, 1916; 1 son, Seth; m. 2d, Edith de Koranyi, June 19, 1936. Apptd. to U.S. Diplomatic Service, Apr. 7, 1920; assigned as 3d sec. to Santiago, Chile, 1920, Tegucigalpa, 1921, to Dept. of State, Washington, 1922; sec. Am. Delegation to Conf. on Central Am. Affairs, Washington, 1922; asst. sec. Am. Delegation, 5th Internat. Conf. of Am. States, Santiago, 1923; acting chief clk. Dept. of State, June-July, 1924; foreign service officer, 1924; 1st sec. at Paris, 1926; acting Am. observer Reparations Commn., 1927; observer Internat. Conf. on Reparations and Rhineland Evacuation, The Hague, 1929, 30; foreign service insp., 1930; chief Div. of Latin Am. Affairs, Dept. of State, 1931-35, counselor of Am. Embassy, Paris, 1935-39; Am. minister to Uruguay, 1939; ambassador to Panama, 1941; U.S. rep. to French Com. of Nat. Liberation, Nov. 1943, with rank of ambassador; dir. Office Special Polit. Affairs, Dept. of State, May, 1944; del. Dumbarton Oaks Conf. on Internat. Orgn.; ambassador to Turkey, March, 1945. Ambulance service in France, 1915, 1916-17; in U.S. Army, 1917-19; commd. 2d lt. Field Arty. Clubs: Metropolitan, Chevy Chase. Address: Washington DC Died Sept. 10, 1972; buried Rock Creek Cemetery, Washington DC

WILSON, EDWIN MOOD, educator; b. Lenoir, N.C., July 26, 1872; s. J. R. and Louisa (Round) W.; Wilson Acad. and Finley High Sch., Lenoir; A.B., Guilford Coll., N.C., 1892; A.B., U. of N.C., 1893; A.M., Haverford Coll., 1894, U. of Pa., 1927; Sc.D., Dickinson Coll., 1933; Litt.D., Rutgers U., New Brunswick, N.J., 1934; m. Alice Green, of Wilmington, N.C., June 16, 1904 (died June 21, 1921). Connected with Haverford Sch., since Sept. 1895, now head master emeritus. Chmn. bd. Christian Assn., U. of Pa. Hon. mem. Head Masters' Assn. Presbyterian. Home: Hotel Normandie, 36th and Chestnut Sts., Philadelphia PA‡

WILSON, FRANK JOHN, govt. security consultant; b. Buffalo, N.Y., May 19, 1887; s. John Frank and Mary Ann (MdGreevy) W.; m. Judith Barbaux, Oct. 27, 1926. Contractor and real estate, Buffalo, 1907-17; chief investigator N.Y. State, U.S. Food Adminstrn., Nov. 1917-July 1919; mgr. Surplus Army Food Sale, Buffalo, July-Dec. 1919; mem. Fair Price Commn., Dept. of Justice, Jan.-July 1920; agent and agent in charge Internal Revenue Bur., Intelligence Unit of Treasury Dept., 1920-36; chief U.S. Secret Service, Aug. 1936-Dec. 1946; cons. on security Atomic Energy Commission, 1947-48. Pres. Nat. Assn. Retired Civil Employees. Served with the U.S. Army Aug.-Oct. 1917. Mem. Internat. Assn. Chiefs of Police (exec. com.); hon. mem. Washington Numismatic Soc.; hon. life mem. Chief Constables' Assn. Can. Catholic. Mem. K.C., Am. Legion. Clubs: Buffalo Yacht (Buffalo); Nat. Press (Washington), Writer of various articles. Author: Special Agent, 1965. Home: Washington DC Died June 22, 1970; buried Rock Creek Cemetery, Washington DC

WILSON, GEORGE ARTHUR, lawyer; b. Richmond, Va., Jan. 14, 1895; s. George Briton and Cora (Boisseau) W.; B.A., U. Va., 1917, LL.B., 1920; m. Elisabeth Haralson Dent, Oct. 12, 1926. Admitted to Va. bar, 1917, N.Y. bar, 1921; practice in N.Y.C., 1920-67; mem. firm Breed, Abbott & Morgan, 1928-67. Dir. Ritter Pfaudler Corp., Rochester, Coca-Cola Bottling Plants, Inc., Portland, Me., Coca-Cola Bottling Co. of Hartford (Conn.). Sec., counsel United Hosp. Fund N.Y., 1932-41, trustee, 1931-41, member council, 1946-55, mem.-at-large, 1955-67; mem. counsel Goldwater Com., sponsored by fund for study and recommendation hosp. service plan in N.Y.C., 1932-34; organizer N.Y.C. Blue Cross. Served as 1st lt., C.A.C., A.A., U.S. Army, 1917-19; AEF in France. Mem. Assn. Bar City N.Y., N.Y. County Lawyers Assn., Am., N.Y. bar assns. Protestant Episcopalian (warden St. Thomas Ch., N.Y.C.). Clubs: Down Town Assn., Wall Street, (Unviersity, Union, Church (N.Y.C.); Mid-Ocean (Bermuda); Farmington Country (Charlottesville, Va.). Home: New York City NY Died Dec. 18, 1967; buried Richmond VA

WILSON, GEORGE P(ICKETT), univ. prof.; b. Clarksville, Va., Apr. 3, 1888; s. Thomas and Mary Elizabeth (Phillips) W.; student Buie's Creek (N.C.) Acad., 1906-09; A.B., Univ. of N.C., 1913; A.M., Columbia, 1919; Mary Adams fellow, Univ. of Wis., 1922-23, grad. work, 1920-23; m. Helen Rembert Leeson, July 1, 1915; children—George Pickett, Robert Leeson (pilot, killed in World War II), Alice Elizabeth (Mrs. E. N. Pearce, Jr.). Instr. of English, Tex. A. and M. Coll., 1913-17, Ind. Univ., 1917-19; head English dept. and dir. summer sch., Bessie Tift Coll., Forsyth, Ga., 1919-20; instr. English, Univ. of Wis., 1919-22; head English dept. and dir. summer sch., Guilford (N.C.) Coll., 1924-27; asso. prof. English, Woman's Coll., Univ. of N.C., 1927-38, prof. English, 1938-72 Mem. Modern Lang. Assn. of Am., South Atlantic Modern Lang. Assn. (mem. com. on dialectal studies 1935-42, chmn. 1942-43; mem. com. on orgn. and work in English lang., 1942-44; co-chmn. of folklore com. 1947, 1949), Am. Dialect Soc. (chmn. com. on regiona

›eech and localisms 1942-50; sec.-treas. 1944-52; riginator and editor Publication of the American)ialect Society, American Folklore Society, American ssn. U. Profs., Coll. Eng. Assn., Southeastern Folklore oc. (vice-pres. 1947, 1949), N.C. Folklore Soc. vice-pres. 1935-36, pres., 1937-43), N.C. English eachers (chmn. research com. 1945-47), Am. Name oc. (bd. mgrs. 1953-72), Ind. Democrat. Baptist. uthor books in field including: Down in the Holler: A iallery of Ozark Folk Speech (with Vance Randolph), 953. Asso. editor or cons. other publs. Home: ;reensboro NC Died Feb. 28, 1972; buried Forest awn Cemetery Greensboro NC

VILSON, GRAFTON LEE, lawyer; b. Providence, pr. 11, 1894; s. George Grafton and Elizabeth (Rose) V.; student Brown U., 1910-11, Sorbonne, Paris, 'rance, 1912, U. Lausanne (Switzerland), 1913; A.B. agna cum laude, Harvard, 1915, LL.B., 1919; m. orothy U. Wilson, July 3, 1918; children—Grafton ee, Roger Bliss, Douglas Usher, Leonard Usher. dmitted to Mass. bar, 1919, since practiced in Boston; artner firm Hale and Dorr, 1923-68. Life dir. Urban eague Greater Boston; trustee Avon Home, ambridge, Mass. Served as capt., inf., U.S. Army, 917-19; AEF in France. Mem. Am., Mass., Boston bar ssns., Delta Phi. Episcopalian. Home: Cambridge MA)ied Dec. 18, 1968.

VILSON, HARRY ROBERT, educator, composer, onductor; b. Salina, Kan., May 18, 1901; s. Frank obert and Sarah (Gatschet) W.; B.S., Manhattan Kan.) State Coll., 1926; M.A., Columbia, 1932, Ed.D., 937; fellowships composition, 1930-32, and onducting, 1934-37, Juilliard Grad. Sch. Music; m. adine Cox, June 2, 1932; 1 son, Robert Dean. Profl. nger, conductor, Wichita, Kan., 1921-26; dir. music ıb. schs., Eureka, Kan., 1926-29, Hastings-on-Hudson, .Y., 1932-34; in charge music activities New Coll., olumbia, 1934-39, prof. music edn., in charge vocal nd choral activities Tchrs. Coll., 1939-58, head of usic and music edn. dept., 1958-66; guest lectr. music dn.; guest condr. choral festivals. Mem. Music Tchrs. at. Assn., Music Educators Nat. Conf., Nat. Assn. chrs. Singing, Nat. Assn. Composers and Condrs., m. Soc. Composers. Authors, Pubs., Am. Musicol. oc., Am. Choral Dirs. Assn. (nat. exec. com.), Delta au Delta, Phi Mu Alpha (nat. president). Author: horal Arranging; Music in the High Sch.; Lead a Song; chool Music Conductor (with P. Von Bodegraven); uide for Choral Conductors; Choral Program Series; horal Musicianship Series, Prentice-Hall Choral eries, Sing a Song at Sight, Building a Church Choir; rtistic Choral Singing, 1958. Composer: Upon This ock (oratorio). Editor, arranger 25 song collections for ıoral groups; composer-arranger 250 compositions nd arrangements. Bd. editors Prentice-Hall basic song ries, Growing with Music. Home: New York City NY ied Sept. 24, 1968.

'ILSON, HIRAM ROY, prof. English; b. Hamden, ., Sept. 12, 1874; s. Horace Carter and Naomi atharine (Bishop) W.; A.B., Ohio U., 1896, A.M., 397; studied Cornell U., 1901, Litt.D., Franklin (Ind.) oll., 1911; m. Florence M. Craig, Oct. 31, 1901. With hio U., since 1897, prof. English, since 1905, sec. of culty, 1919-36, chmn. exec. com. English department,)39-41; professor emeritus of English, 1945. Member ante Society, Alumni Association Ohio University res. 1927-29), Phi Beta Kappa, Delta Tau Delta ıember Distinguished Service Chapter, 1945), Phi Mu lpha. Author: A Teacher's Manual of English rammar and Analysis, 1912. Joint author: Freshman hetoric. Editor of and edition of Silas Marner, 1906, v. edit., 1940. Contbr. to the Classical Journal. Home: Elmwood Pl., Athens OH‡

ILSON, J. FRANK, business exec., b. Lexington, y., Nov. 19, 1897; s. Samuel and Lou Amy AcGrahanagan) W.; student U. of Ky., 1919; m. delaide Pettit, Feb., 1921; 1 dau., Adelaide (Mrs. alcolm W. Sublett). Oil field worker, 1920; mgr. roducers Pipe Line Co., Owensboro, Ky., 1928-35; nployed in prodn., transportation and crude ırchasing divs. Standard Oil Co. of Ohio since 1935, rmer v.p., cons., 1961-72. Served with the U.S. Army, A., 5th Div., World War I. Mem. Am. Petroleum st., Mid-Continent Oil and Gas Assn., Ky., Ill. and d. oil and gas assn. Presbyterian. Home: Houston TX ied May 1972.

ILSON, JAMES WALTER, biologist; b. anchester, N.H., June 17, 1896; s. James Walter and enieve Beatrice (Knight) W.; Ph.B., Brown U., 1918. ı.D., 1921; Ed.D. (honorary), R.I. College of Edn., 60; Sc.D. (hon.), Providence Coll., Coll. Holy Cross, 63; m. Hope Burgess, June 22, 1922; 1 dau., Margaret Irs. R. Weed). Instr. in biology, Brown U., 1921-22; st. prof., 1922-29, asso. prof., 1929-44, prof., 1944-45. 'ank L. Day prof. of biology, 1945-69, professor ıeritus of biology, chairman of the 1944-60; instructor biol. lab., Cold Spring Harbor, N.Y., 1919-24; mem. ɔrp. R.I. Hosp., Corp. of Marine Biol. Lab., Woods ɔle, Mass. Member President's Conf. on Heart and ıncer, 1961. Chmn. morphology and genetics study ct., U.S.P.H.S., 1949-54, mem. screening panel ıncer Chemotherapy Nat. Service Center, 1955-69, nat. adv. council health research facilities, 1956-61, Radiation Study Sect., 1955-56; nat. adv. cancer council, 1960-64; bd. scientific cons. Sloan-Kettering Inst., 1956-69; corp. mem. Miriam Hosp., R.I. Hosp.; mem. vis. com. Brookhaven Nat. Lab., 1949-55, chmn., 1950-55; advisory com. instl. grants Am. Cancer Soc. Mem. Com. Cons. Med. Research to Senate Appropriations Com., 1959-60; sec.-gen. XI Internat. Congress for Cell Biology, 1964. Fellow A.A.A.S., N.Y. Acad. Sci., Am. Acad. Arts, Scis.; mem. Am. Soc. Zool. (pres. 1953-54). Gerontological Soc., Am. Acad. Neurologists, Biometric Soc., Soc. for Cell Biology, Am. Physiol. Soc., Am. Assn. Anatomists, Histochem. Soc. (pres. 1953-54), Soc. Exptl. Biol., Medicine, Soc. Study of Development and Growth. Am. Microscopical Soc., Am. Soc. Cancer Research. History of Science Soc., Biol. Stain Commn., Genetics Soc. Am., Am. Soc. Naturalists, Am. Cancer Soc. (adv. com. personnel research 1956-59, research adv. council 1959-64), Phi Beta Kappa, Sigma Xi. Author articles sci. and med. jours. Home: Providence RI Died May 10, 1969; buried Swan Point Cemetery, Providence RI

WILSON, JAMES WILBUR, agriculturist; b. Traer, Iowa, Feb. 12, 1871; s. James and Esther (Wilbur) W.; B.S.A., Ia. State Coll., 1896, M.S.A., 1898; attended lectures at Georgetown U. Law Sch. and Nat. U. Law Sch., Washington, and received private instruction in law in office at Cedar Rapids, Ia.; LL.D., Univ. of S.Dak., 1922; m. Elsie Chappell, of Brookings, S.D., Apr. 18, 1906; children—James Wilson, Robert C., Thomas V. Asst. prof. agr., Ia. State Coll., 1897; pvt sec. to sec. of agr. Washington, 1897-1900; became dir. S.D. Expt. Sta. and prof. animal husbandry, S.D. Agrl. Coll., 1902, now emeritus. Sec.-treas. S.D. Improved Live Stock and Poultry Breeders' Assn. Mem. Internat. Jury of Awards, St. Louis Expn. Fellow A.A.A.S.; mem. Gamma Sigma Delta, Phi Kappa Phi. Republican. Mason (K.T., Shriner); mem. Grange. Author of numerous bulls. along agrl. lines, and articles in agrl. press. Home: Brookings SD*‡

WILSON, JOHN DAVID, cement mfr.; b. Belle Fourche, S.D., July 30, 1912; s. George and Margaret (Donaldson) W.; student S.D. Sch. Mines, 1930-31; A.B., U. Neb., 1934, LL.B., 1936; m. Margaret Elizabeth Bump, Sept. 1, 1939; children—Barbara Gay, David George. Admitted to S.D., Neb. bars, 1936; with Whiting, Wilson &Lynn, Rapid City, S.D., 1937-53; sec.-treas. S.D. Cement Lynn, Rapid City, S.D., 1937-53; sec.-treas. S.D. Cement Commn., 1946-53; exec. v.p., dir. Giant Portland Cement Co., Phila., 1953-58, pres., 1958-70. Served as lt. (j.g.) USNR, 1943-46. Mem. Am. Legion, Phi Beta Kappa, Delta Theta Phi. Presbyn. Mason. Club: Union League (Phila.). Home: Gladwyne PA Died Jan. 12, 1970.

WILSON, JOHN HADEN, congressman; b. at Nashville, Tenn.; s. Andrew and Jennie Graham (Spears) W.; A.B., Grove City (Pa.) Coll., 1891; m. Catherine Elizabeth Levis, of Rochester, Pa., 1899. Admitted to Pa. bar, 1893, and practiced at Butler since 1896; city solicitor, Butler, 13 yrs.; mem. 66th and 67th Congresses (1919-23), 22d Pa. Dist. Democrat. Presbyn. Home: Butler PA‡

WILSON, JOHN MADISON, criminologist; b. Washington, May 7, 1931; s. Edgar Holtzman and Melrose (Lewis) W.; B.J., U. Mo., 1954; M.A., U. Md., 1958; Ph.D., 1964; m. Beatrice Harlen Miller, Aug. 14, 1953. Spl. research investigator D.C. Dept. Corrections, 1957, Am. Correctional Assn., D.C. area, 1958, Correctional Research Assos., Inc., D.C. area, 1962-63; gen. sec. Am. Correctional Assn., D.C., N.Y.C., 1963-65; asso. prof. U. Md., College Park, 1965-69. Served with AUS, 1955-56. Mem. Am. Sociol. Assn., Nat. Council on Crime and Delinquency, Am. Correctional Assn., Sigma Delta Chi, Alpha Kappa Delta, Psi Chi, Phi Kappa Phi, Phi Eta Sigma. Author:(with others) Delinquency Prevention, Theory and Practice, 1967. Contbr. articles to profl. jours. Home: College Park MD Died July 11, 1969.

WILSON, JOSEPH C(HAMBERLAIN), office equipment mfg. co. exec.; b. Rochester, N.Y., Dec. 13, 1909; s. Joseph R. and Katherine M. (Upton) W.; A.B., U. Rochester, 1931; M.B.A., Harvard University, 1933; L.H.D. (honorary), LeMoyne Coll., 1964, Boston U., 1967; LL.D. (hon.), St. John Fisher Coll., 1965, Harvard U., 1967; Doctor of Humanics, Springfield College, in 1967; m. Marie B. Curran, Oct. 12, 1935; children—Joan, Joseph R., Katherine M., and Judith, Deirdre, Janet C. Joined the Haloid Co., Rochester, 1933, pres., gen. mgr., chief exec. officer, 1946-66, chmn. bd., chmn. exec. com., 1966-71 (name changed to Xerox Corp. 1961), also dir.; co-chmn., dir. Rank-Xerox, Ltd., London; dir. Fuji-Xerox Co., Ltd., Japan (Tokyo), Rochester Gas & Electric Corp., McCurdy & Co. Mass. Mut. Life Ins. Co., Springfield, The Rank Orgn., Ltd., London, Eng., Lincoln Rochester Trust Co., Am. Can Co., Lincoln Rochester Trust Co., 1st Nat. City Bank; trustee Rochester Savs. Bank. Hon. chmn. U. Rochester. Member board of trustees Carnegie Endowment for the International Peace, Com. Econ. Devel., George Eastman House, Rochester, Sidney Hillman Health Center, Alfred P. Sloan Found.; dir., exec. com. Community Chest; bd. dirs. Council for Financial Aid to Edn., Urban Am., Inc. Un Assn. Fellow of American Academy of Arts and Sciences; member of the fraternities Phi Beta Kappa, Delta Kappa Epsilon. Clubs: Metropolitan (Washington); Lyford Cay (Nassau); Lake Placid (N.Y.); Genesee Valley, Country, Rochester (Rochester, N.Y.); University (N.Y.C.). Home: Rochester NY Died Nov. 22, 1971.

WILSON, JULIAN ALEXANDER, army officer; b. Lavonia, Ga., Nov. 11, 1909; s. Robert Marion and Nancy (Fleming) W.; B.S. in Commerce, Ga. Sch. Tech., 1933; postgrad. Clemson Coll., 1939, Mercer U., 1939; grad. Armed Forces Staff Coll., 1948, Air U., 1953, Air War Coll., 1953; m. Nancy West, June 26, 1935; children—Nancy L. (Mrs. James Barker), Julian Alexander, Valerie J., Robert M., John P. Commd. 2d lt. inf.-res., U.S. Army, 1933, called to active duty as 1st lt., 1940, advanced through grades to maj. gen., 1961; served in Hdqrs. ETOUSA, later with 12th Army Group, ETO, World War II; assigned War Dept. Gen. Staff, Washington, 1945-46, Office Adj. Gen., Washington, 1947-49; dep. adj. gen., later adj. gen., USARCARIB, Ft. Amador, C.Z., 1949-52; adj. gen. Armor Center, Ft. Knox, Ky., 1953-56; assigned officers assignment div. Dept. Army, 1956-61; adj. gen. Hdqrs. USAREUR, 1960-61; dep. adj. gen. Dept. Army, 1961-62, dep. chief personnel operations, then chief. Decorated Legion of Merit, Bronze Star, Commendation ribbon with metal pendant; Croix de Guerre with palm (Belgium); Croix de Guerre with palm, Legion of Honor (France); Order British Empire. Home: Falls Church VA Died Aug. 6, 1969; buried Arlington Nat. Cemetery, Arlington VA

WILSON, LEONARD, editor, genealogist; b. London, Eng., July 4, 1869; s. Charles and Emma (Goodchild) W.; ed. under pvt. tutors; m. Rose Mary Easby-Smith, of Tuscaloosa, Ala., Oct. 26, 1899. Traveled in Europe, Syria and Egypt; pvt. sec. to Henry M. Stanley, in Egypt and Europe, 1889-90; attache at court of King of Belgians, 1891-2; spl. translator for U.S. and Great Britain, at Brussels Internat. Money Conf., 1892; secretary New Caloric Syndicate, 1893-7; sent on special mission by U.S. Govt. to report on Spanish possessions in West Indies, 1898; sec. for U.S. of commn. which negotiated the surrender of Santiago, 1898; mil. sec. and vol. a.d.c. to Maj. Gen. Joseph Wheeler, in Cuba, 1898-9; with office Sec. of War, Washington, D.C., 1899-1903; pres. Cleveland (O.) Varnish Co., 1904-10; engaged in chem. research and lit. owrk, 1911-15; v.p., treas. and editor-in-chief, B. F. Johnson, Inc., pubs., 1916-18. With British and Canadian recruiting mission, 1917-18; sec.-treas. British and Canadian Soc. in U.S., 1918-19; spl. asst. to dir., Bur. of Exports, U.S. War Trade Bd., 1918-19. Hon. mention in Gen. Orders of the Army, Feb. 13, 1900, for especially meritorious service in the field," Spanish-Am. War. Fellow Soc. of Antiquaries of Scotland, Royal Soc. of Antiquaries of Ireland, Royal Soc. Arts; asso. Soc. Genealogists of London; mem. Nat. Geneal. Soc. America, N.E. Historic-Geneal. Soc., Am. Hist. Assn., English Monumental Inscriptions Soc. (v.-p.). Author: With Wheeler at Santiago, 1899; also biographies in Makers of America, 1915-18. Contbr. to mags. and newspapers. Home: 1718 Rhode Island Av., Washington DC‡

WILSON, LEONARD SELTZER, geophysicist, geographer; b. Detroit, July 10, 1909; s. Clyde E. and Esther S. (Seltzer) W.; A.B., U. Mich., 1932, M.S., 1933, Ph.D. (Earhart fellow 1934-35, U. fellow 1935-36), 1936; m. Mary W. Jarboe, Nov. 15, 1944; children—Leonard J., Susan M. Teaching fellow U. Mich., 1934-36; from instr. to prof. geography Carleton Coll., 1936-49; chief map intelligence br. Dept. State, 1945-46; map officer internat. sect. UN Conf. of Internat. Orgn., 1945; geog. adviser internat. sect. UN, 1945; chief geog. br. G-2, Far East Command, Supreme Comdr. Allied Powers, Tokyo, Japan, 1949-55; chief geophys. scis. br. Office Chief Research and Development, U.S. Army, 1955-60, chief Environmental Research Div., 1960-68; nat. leader sub-group T tech. cooperation Program United States Department of Defense, 1968-70, national leader ground mobility panel technical Coordination Program 1968-70. Head U.S. Army delegation to Quadripartite Ground Mobility Conf., 1959, 61, 63, 65; U.S. delegation NATO Long Range Study Group Naples, Italy, 1961; United States alternate mem. research coordination com. Am., Brit. Canadian, Australian Armies Weapons Standardization Orgn., 1956-63, U.S. mem. and chmn., from 1963; U.S. Army rep. Dept. Def. Forum Environmental Scis., 1964-65; sr. member environmental sciences The Army Research Council, 1964-65; chairman Army Committee Environment, from 1955, Army Com. for Internat. Geophys. Year, 1957-59, Army Coordinating Com.; del. U.S. Nat. Acad. Scis., 9th Pacific Sci. Congress, Bangkok, Thailand, 1958. Served lt. (j.g.) to lt. comdr. USNR, 1943-46; dep. chief map div. OSS, 1942-45 (as civilian 1942); chief map div. OSS, ETO, 1944. Decorated Bronze Star medal; recipient Army commendation medal, commendation certificate, meritorious civilian award, Army certificate meritorious achievement, also decoration for exceptional civilian service awarded posthumously. Fellow A.A.A.S., Sigma Xi.; mem. Menn. Council Geography Tchrs. (pres. 1946-47),

Assn. Am. Geographers (treas. 1963-65; mem. finance com., mem. mil. geography com.), Am. Geog. Soc., Royal Geog. Soc. London, Tokyo Geog. Soc., S.A.R., Nat. (Am. Soc. com. 1959), Mich. Minn. acads. scis., Chi Gamma Phi, Theta Chi. Episcopalian. Asso. editor: Oxford Am. Atlas, 1951; editor, compiler: Terrestrial Globe, 1957. Author articles profl. jours. Home: Alexandria VA Died Dec. 6, 1970; buried Culpepper Nat. Cemetery Culpepper VA

WILSON, LEWIS ALBERT, educator; b. Bergen, N.Y., Feb. 3, 1886; s. John T. and Ella (Chapman) W.; grad. State Normal Sch., Brockport, N.Y., 1907, Mechanics Inst., Rochester, N.Y., 1910; studied Stout Inst., Menominee, Wis., and Tchrs. Coll. (Columbia); D.Sc., Stout Inst., 1926, Rensselaer Polytechnic Institute, 1955; Doctor of Law, Alfred (N.Y.) U., 1934, Syracuse U., 1942; U. Rochester, St. John's U., Columbia U., 1955; Litt.D., L.I. U., Siena Coll., 1951; L.H.D., Yeshiva U., 1951, St. Bonaventure U., 1955; m. Luella Ellis, of Niagara Falls, Ont., December 25, 1911; children—Ruth Dana (Mrs. Harry A. Willis), Robert Ellis, John Lewis, Lois Ann (Mrs. Richard Decker). Teacher, Rochester Shop Sch., 1908-09, prin., 1909-11; dir. vocational edn., Albany, N.Y., 1911-12; specialist in industrial edn. and teacher tng., State Dept. Edn., N.Y., 1912-15; dir. Industrial Edn. Survey, N.Y. City, 1915-16; specialist in industrial edn. and teacher training, State Dept. Edn., Albany, 1916-17; dir. Div. of Vocation and Extension Edn., same, 1917-27; asst. commr. of edn., State of N.Y., 1927-41, dep. commr., 1941-50; pres. University State of N.Y., also commissioner of education State of New York, 1950-55. Member summer school faculty, tchrs. coll. Columbia, 1923-24, Penn State Coll., 1927; delegate International Exposition Decorative Arts, Paris, 1925. Member advisory board Manhattan Trade School, New York; trustee Dudley Obs.; dir. N.Y. Assn. Crippled Children, Associated Industries of N.Y.; mem. White House Conference on Youth, 1950, White House Conf. on Education, 1955; mem. bd. advisers Vocational Service for Juniors, N.Y.; mem. N.Y. State Commn. for Study Ednl. Problems of Penal Instns. for Youth; chmn. div. labor industry and agr. State War Council, 1942. Awards: Testimonial N.Y. State Maritime Coll. Alumni, 1951; N.Y. Acad. Pub. Edn., 1951; N.Y. Times Sq. Club, 1951; Medalion N.Y. State Vocational and Practical Arts Assn., 1934; Medalion N.Y. State Assn. Crippled Children, 1951; Star of Solidarity, Italy, 1951, Officer Legion of Honor (France), 1953, gold medal Distinguished Citizenship, S.A.R., 1953, fellowship Rochester Mus. Arts and Scis., 1955. Member of the board of trustees N.Y. State Town and Co. O.T.S. Mem. Am. Assn. Adult Edn. (v.p. 1934), N.Y. Adult Edn. Council (v.p. 1935), Nat. Rehabilitation Assn. (legislative com.), N.E. Assn. Commnrs. Edn. (pres. 1951-53), Nat. Assn. Chief State Sch. Officers (bd. dirs.), Nat. Soc. Vocational Edn. (pres. 1921-23), N.E.A., Am. Assn. Sch. Adminstrn., Phi Delta Kappa. Club: University. Home: Albany NY Died May 4, 1969.

WILSON, LOUIS ROUND, librarian; b. Lenoir, N.C., Dec. 27, 1876; s. Jethro Reuben and Louisa Jane (Round) W.; student Haverford (Pa.) Coll., 1895-98, LL.D., 1932; A.B., U. of N.C., 1899, A.M., 1902, Ph.D., 1905, LL.D., 1934 (Phi Beta Kappa); Litt.D., U. of Denver, 1932; L.H.D., Catawba Coll. Salisbury, N.C., 1949; student Columbia, summer, 1910; m. Penelope Bryan Wright, June 10, 1909 (dec.); children—Elizabeth Wright, Louis Round (dec.), Penelope, Mary Louise. Librarian, U. of N.C., 1901-32; asso. prof. library administration, same, 1907-12, prof. same, 1912-20, and Kenan prof. same, 1920-32; dean Grad. Library Sch., U. of Chicago, 1932-42, dean emeritus since 1942; dir. of U. of N.C., bur. of extension, 1912-21; dir. of U. of N.C. Press, 1922-32; dir. Sch. of Library Science, 1931-32, prof. library adminstrn., 1942-47, director Sesquicentennial Publications, 1943, Sesquicentennial Celebration, 1944-45. Chairman North Carolina Library Commission, 1909-16. Mem. American Library Assn. (mem. bd. edn. for librarianship, 1925-32, chmn. bd., 1931; v.p. 1930-31, 1933-34, pres. 1935-36); chmn. Library Extension Bd. A.L.A., 1936-40; del. to Brit. Library Assn. and Com. Internat. Fedn. Library Assns. 1931); mem. N.C. Library Assn. (sec. 1904-09, pres. 1910, 1921-23, 1930-31); pres. Southeastern Library Assn., 1924-26; mem. exec. com., American Council on Education, 1936-39; chmn. exec. com. of the Tennessee Valley Library Council, 1946-49. Democrat. Author: Chaucer's Relative Constructions, 1906; The Geography of Reading, 1938; Library Planning, 1944; (with E. A. Wight) County Library Service in the South, 1935; (with Branscomb, Dunbar, and Lyle) Survey of the University of Georgia Library, 1939; (with Kuhlman and Lyle) Survey of the University of Florida Library, 1940; (with M. F. Tauber) The University Library, Its Organization, Administration and Functions, 1945; Survey of Univ. of S.C. Library, 1946 (with M. F. Tauber); also co-author of surveys of the following libraries: Stanford U., 1947, Cornell U., 1948, Ala. Polytech. Inst., 1949; also co-author of a syllabus, The Library in College Instruction, 1951; editor of the Alumni Review, 1912-24. The Community Service Bulletin, 1914; Education and Citizenship, 1919. Asso. editor Studies in Philology, 1910-14, Journal of Social Forces, 1922-32; mem. editorial bd. The Library Quarterly since 1932, Jour. of Adult Education, 1931-41, College and Research Libraries, 1939-41. Editor with introduction, Library Trends, 1936, The Role of the Library in Adult Education, 1937, The Practice of Book Selection, 1939. Chmn. com. on yearbook The Library in General Education, National Society for the Study of Education, 1941-43. Contributor to library and other jours. Del. to Internat. Congress of Librarians and Bibliography, Madrid, 1935. Home: 607 E. Rosemary St. Address: University of North Carolina, Chapel Hill NC‡

WILSON, MILBURN LINCOLN, agrl. edn. and adminstrn.; b. Atlantic, Ia., Oct. 23, 1885; s. John Wesley and Mary E. (Magee) W.; B.S.A., Iowa State Col. Ames, Ia., 1907; M.S., U. of Wis., 1920; hon. D.Sc., Mont. State Col., 1935; hon. D.Agr., N.D. Agrl. Coll., 1940; m. Ida Elizabeth Morse, Dec. 18, 1913; children—Elizabeth, Virginia. Began as farmer, 1907; asst. agronomist, Mont. State Coll., 1910-12; county agent, Custer County, Mont., 1912-14; state extension agent leader, 1914-22; extension agrl. economist, Mont. State Coll., 1922-24, prof. and head dept. agrl. economics, 1926-33; in charge div. farm management and cost accounting, U.S. Dept. Agr., 1924-26; consultant on large-scale wheat farming, U.S.S.R., 1929. Chief Wheat Production Sect., Agrl. Adjustment Administrn., U.S. Dept. of Agr., May 16-Sept. 1, 1933; dir. Div. of Subsistence Homesteads, U.S. Dept. Interior, Sept. 1, 1933-June 30, 1934; asst. sec. of Agr., 1934-37; under sec. of agr., Jan. 1, 1937 to Feb. 1, 1940, director of extension work, U.S. Dept. of Agr., 1940-53. Chief Nutrition Programs, Production and Marketing Adminstrn. 1943-49. Mem. A.A.A.S., American Farm Economic Association (president 1925), Epsilon Sigma Phi, Phi Kappa Phi, Alpha Zeta. Unitarian. Club: Cosmos. Author: Farm Relief and the Domestic Allotment Plan, 1933; Democracy Has Roots, 1939; Agriculture in Modern Life (with others), 1939; etc. Home: Washington DC Died Oct. 1969; buried Rock Creek Cemetery, Washington DC

WILSON, MURRAY ALDERSON, cons. engr.; b. Parmyra, Ia., Aug. 15, 1894; s. Charles Herbert and Harriet (Alderson) W.; A.B., Baker U., 1916; student U. Wis., summer 1919; B.S. in Civil Engring., Kan. State U., 1922, C.E., 1926, awarded Doctor of Science (honorary), 1963; L.H.D., Kansas Wesleyan U., 1953; m. Edith May Coffman, June 21, 1919; children—Mary Helen (Mrs. Donald Hayman), Dorothy (Mrs. Merrill H. Werts). Prin. high sch., Oswego, Kan., 1916-17; head dept. math. Neodesha (Kan.) High Sch., 1919-20; city engr., Hays, Kan., 1922-24; research engr. Bur. Pub. Roads, 1924-26; chief engr. Kan. Forestry, Fish and Game Commn., 1926-32; cons. engr., 1932-69; partner firm Paulette & Wilson, Salina, Kan., 1932-41; owner Wilson & Co., Salina, 1942-59, cons. to company, 1959-69; dir. Nat. Bank Am., Sunflower Prestress, Inc. (both Salina). Mem. Kan. Bd. Engring. Examiners, 1947-58; mem. Gov. Kan. Adv. Com. Flood Control, 1942-56; adv. com. for pvt. enterprise AID, 1966. Trustee Kan. Wesleyan U., 1945-69, chmn., 1948-53; mem. Kan. State U. Research Found. Recipient Distinguished Service award Baker U., 1954, Kan. State U., 1957. Served with U.S. Army, 1917-19. Registered profl. engr., Kan., N.M., Colo., Neb., Ga. Fellow Am. Soc. C.E. (pres. Kan. 1941); mem. Nat. Soc. Profl. Engrs. (pres. 1961, award for outstanding service to profession 1967), Kan. Engring. Soc. (pres. 1936, chmn. cons. sect. 1957-59), Kan. Sewage Works Assn. (pres. 1947), Am. Inst. Cons. Engrs., Am. Water Works Assn., Am. Road Builders Assn., Am. Pub. Works Assn., Water Pollution Control Assn., Am. Legion, Alpha Delta Sigma, Phi Kappa Phi, Sigma Tau, Zeta Chi. Methodist (del. world conf. 1961). Mason (33 deg., Shriner), Lion. Home: Salina KS Died Apr. 17, 1969; interred Williamsburg Mausoleum, Salina KS

WILSON, ORLANDO WINFIELD, criminologist and educator; b. Veblen, S.D., May 15, 1900; s. Ole Knut and Olive (Stoutland) Vralson; A.B., U. of Cal., 1924; LL.D., Carthage Coll. (Ill.), 1962; awarded LL.D. by Northwestern U., 1965; m. Vernis Haddon, 1923; children—Henry, Sally Jo; married second Ruth Eleanor Evans, 1950; one daughter Patricia Anne. Engaged as patrolman Berkeley (Cal.) police force, 1921-25; chief of police, Fullerton, 1925-26, Wichita, Kan., 1928-39; prof. police adminstrn., Univ. of Cal., Berkeley, 1939-60, dean, sch. criminology, 1950-60, now emeritus; police cons., Pub. Adminstrn. Service, Chgo., 1939-43, Insular Government, Puerto Rico, 1951; superintendent police, Chicago, 1960-67; ret., 1967; lectr. Bureau Street Traffic Research, Harvard, 1937. Served as lt. col., later col., Corps of Mil. Police, A.U.S. in Italy and Germany, 1943-47. Pres. Soc. for Advancement of Criminology, 1941-49. Mem. Internat. Assn. Chiefs of Police, Mil. Govt. Assn. Mason. Author: Police Records, 1942; Police Administration, 1950, 2d edit., 1963, 3d edit., 1972 (translated into Arabic, Chinese, Spanish, Korean); Police Planning, 1951; also several pamphlets and articles. Editor: Parker on Police, 1956. Home: Poway CA Died Oct. 18, 1972.

WILSON, OTIS GUY, coll. dean; b. Ritchie County, W.Va., Sept. 11, 1877; s. William Martin and Mary Jane (Nay) W.; A.B., West Virginia U., 1907; A.M., 1911; student U. of Chicago, summer 1908, Columbia, summer 1909, U. of Pittsburgh, 1930-31; Pd.D. (hon.) Salem Coll. (W.Va.), 1936; m. Helen Vance, Dec. 2 1913; children—William Guy, Vance Nay. Rural schoc teacher, W.Va., 1897; supt. schools, Elkins, W.Va 1908-15, Fairmont, W.Va., 1915-30; head dept. of edn Glenville State Coll., Glenville, W.Va., 1931-35; dear Teachers Coll., Marshall Coll., Huntington, W.Va 1935-45; retired. Mem. Nat. and W.Va. State (pre 1914) edn. assns., Am. Assn. Coll. Teachers of Edn Supervisors Student Teaching, Higher Edn. Assn., Pl Beta Kappa, Kappa Delta Pi. Presbyterian. Masor Teacher Men's Bible Class Johnson Memori Methodist Episcopal Ch. Home: 619 South Terrac Huntington 3 WV‡

WILSON, PAUL ORAN, live stock exec.; b. Vig County, Ind., Apr. 1, 1894; s. Curtis B. and Mar (Bartlett) W.; student Ind. State Tchrs. Coll., summe 1913-15; B.S. in Agr., Purdue U., 1922; m. Mar Grogan, Sept. 5, 1923; children—James B., Catherin T., Nancy J. Tchr. country schs., 1914-17; county agr agt. Vandenburgh County, Ind., 1922-24; mg Producers Live Stock Marketing Assn., Cin., 1925-2 became gen. mgr. Nat. Live Stock Marketing Assn Chgo., 1930, then executive vice president; manag National Feeder & Finance Corp., Chgo., 1934-5 mng. editor publ. Nat. Live Stock Producer, Chgo 1936-59. Served to 1st lt., F.A., U.S. Army, 1917-1 Home: La Grange IL Died Oct. 19, 1969.

WILSON, PHILIP DUNCAN, orthopedic surgeon; Columbus, O., Apr. 5, 1886; s. Edward J. and Id (Tudor) W.; A.B., Harvard, 1909, M.D., 1912; Docteu honoris causa, U. Paris, 1966; m. Germaine Porel, 191 children—Paul E., Philip Duncan, Marianne Rejan Began practice of surgery, 1914; practice of orthoped surgery, Boston, 1919; asso. chief of fracture servic Mass. Gen. Hosp., 1919-34; instr. in orthopedic surger Harvard Med. Sch., 1919-34; dir. of surgery, Hosp. f Special Surgery, New York, 1934-35, surgeon in chie 1935-55, director of research, 1955-69; clin. pro surgery Cornell Med. Coll., emeritus 1955; organiz and medical director American Hospital in Britai 1940-41; cons. Surgeon Gen., U.S. Army, 1942-4 Chevalier Legion of Honor (Fr. 1947), Hon. Comd Order British Empire. Pres. 9th Congress Internat. So Orthopedics and Traumatology. Served with Harva Unit, Neuilly, France, 1915, Am. Ambulance Servic Neuilly, 1916; maj. Med. Corps, AUS, as orthoped consultant, with A.E.F., 1917-19. Decorated Chevali Legion of Honor (France); King's Medal (England Commander Order of British Empire (Eng.). Fello Am. Coll. of Surgeons; mem. A.M.A., Am. Orthoped Assn., Am. Acad. Orthopedic Surgeons (past pres. hon. mem. British Orthopedic Soc., Brit. Orthoped Assn. Royal Acad. Medicine, Scandinavian Orthoped Society. Italian, Spanish and the Portuguese orthoped associations. Episcopalian. Clubs: Harvard, Centu (New York). Author: Fractures and Dislocations (wi W. A. Cochrane), 1926. Editor: Experience in th Management of Fractures, 1938. Co-editor: Huma Limbs and Their Substitutes (with P. Klopstig), 195 Contbr. to med. jours. Home: New York City NY Di May 7, 1969.

WILSON, RICHARD HENRY (RICHAR FISGUILL), univ. prof., author; b. Christian Co., K Mar. 6, 1870; s. Richard Henry and Margaret Fie (Smith) W.; B.A., South Ky. Coll., 1889, M.A., 189 B.A., Johns Hopkins, 1892, Ph.D., 1898; student univ of Paris and Berlin, and in Italy and Spain; m. Par Marie-Louise Ronceret, of Dourdan, Seineet-Ois France, June 24, 1893. Prof. Romanic langs., U. of V since 1899. Author: The Preposition A; Mazel, 190 The Venus of Cadiz, 1905. Contbr. to periodica Address: P.O. Box 179, Charlottesville VA‡

WILSON, ROBERT NORTH, chemistry; b. Leno N.C., Mar. 3, 1875; s. Jethro Reuben and Louisa Ja (Round) W.; student Guilford (N.C.) Coll., 1893-9 A.B., Haverford (Pa.) Coll., 1898; grad. study, Harvar 1905-06, U. of Ill., 1922-23; M.S., U. of Fla., 1909; Saza Hendrick Peck, of Greensboro, N.C., Sept. 1 1910; children—Robert North, Jane Bliss. Teacher chemistry and physics, Guilford Coll., 1898-1908; s chemist, Fla. Agrl. Expt. Sta., 1908-10; asst. pr chemistry, Trinity Coll. (now Duke U.), 1910-16, pr since 1916. Commr. Durham Council Boy Scou America. Mem. Am. Chem. Soc., A.A.A.S., So Promotion Engring. Edn., N.C. Acad. Science, So Mayflower Descendants. Democrat. Methodi Kiwanian. Home: 822 3d St., Durham NC‡

WILSON, ROBERT PERRY, vending co. exec.; Shelburne Falls, Mass., June 1, 1912; s. Earl Joseph a Jessie (Manning) W.; m. Inez Viles, July 8, 1939. Wi Canteen Corporation, Chicago, 1935-69, v.p., 1961-6 Home: Elmhurst IL Died Dec. 4, 1969; buried M Emblem Cemetery.

WILSON, RUSSELL H., investment banker; b. S Francisco, 1908; ed. Cal., 1930; m. Barbara D. Wilso children—Lee, Sharon. Pres., dir. Birr, Wilson & C Inc.; dir. Yacu-dry Co., Cyclotron Corp., Chandler P Co. Home: Piedmont CA

WILSON, THOMAS A., banker; b. Wilkes-Barre, Pa., Sept. 19, 1888; s. Leslie MacLean and Nellie Priscilla (Orr) W.; student Maplewood Acad., 1899, Nazareth Hall Mil. Acad., 1900-03, Tome Sch., 1904-05, Exeter Acad., 1905-08, Lafayette Coll., 1908-09; Litt.B., Princeton, 1913; m. Gertrude Amy Page, Apr. 14, 1915; children—Thomas A., Bruce Page, Roger Terrill. Dist mgr. Mututal Benefit Life Ins. Co., 1914-23; v.p. Empire Grain & Elevator Co., 1920-27; gen. agt. Mass. Mut. Life Ins. Co., 1924-28; pres. Peoples Trust Co., 1928-31; pres. Marine Midland Trust Co. of Southern N.Y., 1951-55; hon. vice chmn. bd. Marine Midland Bank-So., 1955-72, also chmn. dirs. adv. Council; dir. Sheraton-Binghamton, Inc., chmn., dir. Raymond Corp., Inc.; trustee Link Found., Inc. Mayor, City of Binghamton, 1920-23; chmn. N.Y. state dist. III Savings Bonds div. U.S. Treasury Dept.; mem. Armed Forces Adv. Com., 1947-72. Treas., dir. Susquehanna Valley Home, 25 yrs.; dir. Humane Soc., Salvation Army; hon. dir. Roberson Meml. Centre; mem. football adv. com. Princeton, 1925-72, trustee, 1930-34. Served from pvt. to capt. Calvary U.S. Army, 1917-19. Mem. N.Y. State Bankers Assn. (pres. 1938), Am. Legion, V.F.W., Navy League of U.S., 78th Div. Vets. Assn., Princeton, Lafayette alumni assns., Internat. Assn. Chiefs of Police (hon.), Police and Sheriffs Assn. (hon.) Republican (del. various state convs.). Presbyn. Clubs: Binghamton Contry, Binghamton City; Princeton (N.Y.C.); Nassau, Tiger Inn (Princeton); Junior Carlton (London, Eng.). Home: Binghamton NY Died Sept. 3, 1972.

WILSON, THOMAS JAMES, book publisher; b. Chapel Hill, N.C., Oct. 25, 1902; s. Thomas James and Lorena Frank (Pickard) W.; A.B., University of N.C., 1921; A.M., 1924, Litt.D. (honorary), 1963; D.Phil., University of Oxford, England, (Rhodes scholar), 1928; L.H.D., Harvard University, 1965; m. to Dorothy Stearns on June 9, 1928; one son, Thomas James; married second Phoebe de Kay (Rous) Donald, March 17, 1950; children—Peyton, Chase. Instr. of French, University of North Carolina, 1921-24, assistant professor, 1927-30; foreign language editor Henry Holt & Co., N.Y. City, 1930-34, mgr. coll. dept., 1934-39, dir., 1934-39, v.p., 1937-39; dir., mgr. coll. dept. and v.p. Reynal & Hitchcock, Inc., 1940-42; dir. U. of N.C. Press, 1946-47; dir. Harvard U. Press, 1947-67; v.p., dir. sr. editor Atheneum Pubs., N.Y.C., 1967-69; chmn. bd. Franklin Book Programs, Inc., 1960-64; dir. Beacon Press, 1958-60, chmn., 1960. U.S. govt. adv. com. Internat. Book Programs, 1962-64. Sci. information council Nat. Sci. Found., 1964-66; adv. com. pub. Nat. Endowment for Humanities. Entered U.S. Navy as lt., 1942, advanced to comdr., 1945; U.S.S. Enterprise, P.T.O., 1942-43. Mem. Am. Book Pubs. Council (dir.), Assn. Am. U. Presses (president 1951-53), Am. Assn. Rhodes Scholar, Am. Acad. Arts and Scis., Massachusetts Hist. Soc. (trustee), Colonial Soc. Massachusetts, Phi Beta Kappa, Zeta Psi. Independent Democrat. Clubs: Saturday, Odd Volumes (Boston); Harvard, Century Association (N.Y.C.); Harvard Faculty (Cambridge). Translator The Correspondence of Romain Rolland and Malwida von Meysenburg, 1934. Contbr. scholarly articles on the 17th Century French heroic novel, particularly works of La Calprenede. Home: MA Died June 27, 1969.

WILSON, WILLIAM EARL, ednl. cons.; b. Scottsburg, Ind., Mar. 1, 1896; s. William L. and Edith (Tipps) W.; A.B., Hanover Coll., 1919, LL.D., 1961; A.M., Ind. State Tchrs. Coll., 1931; LL.D., Ball State U. 1967; m. Mytrle Z. Huffman, Aug. 31, 1924. Rural sch. tchr., Washington County, Ind., 1920-26; prin. Borden Schs., 1926-33; supt. schs., Clark County, 1933-59; supt. pub. instrn., Ind., 1959-—; part-time instr. history of edn., philosophy Southeastern Center, Ind. U., 1945-57. Mem. gov's. legislative commn. to revise Ind. code on sch. house planning and constrn.; mem. commn. to revise tchr. tng. curricula Ind. Colls. and Univs.; chmn. Ind. commn. on gen. edn.; chmn. Ind., 1959-67, dir. manuscript acquisition Ind. Hist. Soc., 1967-71; now ednl. cons. Lilly Endowment, Inc.; part-time instr. history of edn., textbook commn.; dir. Ind. div. vocational edn.; mem. Gov's Commn. on Arts. Mem. Ind. Civil Def. Com.; ofcl. civil def. observer Atomic Test Exercises, 1955-57; del. White House Conf. Children and Youth, 1960; mem. Ind. Lincoln Found. Mission Vis. Schs., Japan, 1960. State dir. Ind. Soc. for Crippled Children. Trustee, Ball State Tchrs. Coll., Ind. State Tchrs Coll.; alumni adv. com. Ind. U. Served with C.E. U.S. Army, World War I. Recipient U.S. Treasury award, 1954, Nat. Congress Parents and Tchs. award 1958, award of merit Am. State and Local History, Alumni Achievement award Hanover Coll., 1968. Mem. N.E.A. (del. for Ind.), Ind. Tchrs. Assn. (pres. 1947), Am. Assn. Sch. Adminstrs., Am. Acad. Polit. and Social Sci., Ind. Hist. Soc., Chief State Sch. Officers (mem. council), Ind. Schoolmen's Club, Kappa Delta Pi, Phi Delta Kappa. Democrat. Mem. Disciples of Christ Ch. Mason (32), Lion Author: History of Borden Inst., 1931. Contbr. articles profl. jours. Home: Jeffersonville IN Died Mar. 4, 1971.

WILSON, WILLIAM EDWARD, ex-congressman; b. Mt. Vernon, Ind., Mar. 9, 1870; s. Jay William and Mary Ann (Chaffin) W.; ed. pub. schs. and Evansville (Ind.) Commercial Coll.; Certified Public Accountant (C.P.A.) State of Ind.; m. Nettie Ora Cook, of Evansville, June 12, 1900; children—Isabelle, William E. Began with Evansville Commercial Coll., 1888, prin. and owner same until 1907; owner Columbian Business Coll. and Columbian Commercial Coll.; head of William E. Wilson Ins. Agency; president of Lincoln Savings Bank, Feb. 1927-29. Dep. county auditor, Vanderburg Co., Ind., 1910-12; clk. Circuit Court, 1912-20; mem. 68th Congress (1923-25), 1st Ind. Dist. Democrat. Presbyn. Mason (K.T., 32 deg., Shriner), K.P. Home: Evansville IN‡

WILSON, WILLIAM HUNTINGTON, lawyer; b. Washington, Aug. 21, 1870; s. William Lyne W.; ed. Charlestown Acad., 1879-80, prep. school, Columbia Univ., 1880-5, Columbian, 1885-90; grad. Columbian Law School, 1892; engaged in practice in W.Va.; unmarried. Author: Rafnaland (novel), 1900 H1. His stories, sketches, rhymings, etc., have appeared in many of the leading mags. Address: Charlestown WV‡

WILSON, WILLIAM JAMES, manufacturer, inventor; b. at Boston; s. James W. and Jane W.; moved to Chicago, 1854. Inventor and patentee of present process, and the can used therewith, for compressing and preserving meats and other foods in cans; was pres. Wilson Packing Co., packers of compressed meats, etc., under his own patents, until retired from active business, 1883. Pres. Bd. W. Park Commrs., 1897. Republican. Club: Illinois (pres. 1890, 1900, 1901). Address: 211 Ashland Boul., Chicago IL‡

WILSON, WILLIAM RILEY, b. Fair Haven, Preble County, O., Sept. 5, 1860; s. David Sturgous and Mary Jane (Orr) W.; A.B., Washington and Jefferson Coll., 1886; grad. Allegheny (now Pittsburgh-Xenia) Theol. Sem., 1889; D.D., Westminster and Grove City colls., 1906; LL.D., Muskingum Coll., 1934; m. Lily Jane Brownlee, July 31, 1890; children—John Brownlee, David Porter, Robert McWatty (dec.), Ross Stevenson, Martha Ashton (Mrs. Andrew C. Daft), Mary Orr (Mrs. Christian F. Kenneweg), Lu Ellen Sutton (Mrs. James O. Paisley). Ordained ministry United Presbyn. Ch., 1889; pastor North Shenango Ch., Espyville Sta., Pa., 1889-92, 2d Ch., Mercer, Pa., 1892-99, 10th Ch., Allegheny, Pittsburgh, Pa., June 1899-1902, 1st Ch., Carnegie, Pa., 1902-06; prof. pastoral theology and homiletics, Pittsburgh-Xenia Theol. Sem., 1906-40, emeritus prof. since May 1940. Mem. Phi Gamma Delta. Home: Ben Avon PA‡

WINANS, JAMES ALBERT, prof. pub. speaking; b. Sidney Center, Delaware County, N.Y., Feb. 8, 1872; s. James Addison and Mary (Sewell) W.; A.B., Hamilton Coll., 1897, A.M., 1900, L.H.D., 1941; LL.B., Cornell U., 1907; m. Elizabeth Sweet, June 28, 1899. Teacher of English, Middleton (N.Y.) High Sch., 1897-99; instr. in elocution and oratory, Cornell U., 1899-1901, acting asst. prof., 1901-02; instr., 1903-04, asst. prof. oratory and debate, 1904-14, prof. pub. speaking, 1914-20; asst. prof. pub. speaking, U. of Calif., 1902-03; prof. pub. speaking, Dartmouth Coll., 1920-42; emeritus prof., 1942; visiting prof. of speech, U. of Mo., 1942-45, special lecturer summer sch. La. State U., 1943; prof. pub. speaking U. of Calif. summer 1916. Trustee George Junior Republic, .Freeville, New York, 1919-21. Member National Association Teachers of Speech (president 1915-16), Eastern Public Speaking Conference, (president 1913-15), Delta Kappa Epsilon, Phi Beta Kappa. Author: Notes on Public Speaking, 1911; Public Speaking, 1915. Co-author: Argumentation (with William E. Utterbach), 1930; First Course in Public Speaking (with Hoyt H. Hudson), 1931; Speech-Making, 1938. Address: 218 Eddy St., Ithaca NY‡

WINBORNE, JOHN WALLACE, justice; b. Chowan County, N.C., July 12, 1884; s. Dr. Robert H. and Annie F. (Parker) W.; prep. edn. Horner School, Oxford, N.C., 1900-02; A.B., U. of North Carolina, 1906; LL.D., 1946; m. Charlie May Blanton, March 30, 1910 (died Nov. 4, 1940); children—Charlotte (Mrs. Charles Milton Shaffer), John Wallace; married 2d, Lalage O. Rorison, June 14, 1947. Teacher Bingham Military School, Asheville, N.C., 1906-07; admitted to N.C. bar, 1906, and practiced in Marion, 1907-37; mem. Pless & Winborne, 1907-19, Pless, Winborne & Pless, 1919-26, Pless, Winborne, Pless & Proctor, 1926-27, Winborne & Proctor, 1928-37; atty. Marion and McDowell counties, 1918-37; associate justice of the Supreme Court of North Carolina, 1937-56, chief justice, 1956-62. Member board of aldermen, Marion, N.C., 1913-21; chmn. Democratic Exec. Com., McDowell County, N.C., 1910-12; mem. State Dem. Exec. Com., 1916-37; chmn., 1932-37; mem. Local Govt. commn. of N.C., 1931-33. Served on Selective Bd. during World War. Mem. N.C. Bar Assn. (hon.) N.C. Jud. Council (chmn.), Soc. of the Cincinnati, Delta Kappa Epsilon. Democrat. Episcopalian. Mason. Home: Marion NC Died 1967.

WINCH, HORACE CARLTON, lawyer; b. Buffalo, May 4, 1901; s. Frank and Harriet (Fenton) W.; B.A., Amherst Coll., 1922; LL.B., Harvard, 1925; m. Ruth N. Laughlin, Jun. 1, 1929; children—Julia (Mrs. Roger D. Severance), Frank II. Admitted to N.Y. bar, 1925, practiced in Buffalo; partner firm Ohlin, Damon, Morey, Sawyer & Moot, and predecessor, from 1968; govt. appeal agt. SSS, World War II. Trustee Nichols Sch., 1949-51. Mem. Am., N.Y. State, Erie County bar assns., Alpha Chi, Beta Theta Pi. Clubs: Buffalo, Gyro (Buffalo). Home: Buffalo NY Died Sept. 9, 1971; buried Buffalo NY

WINCHELL, JOHN H., govt. ofcl.; b. Le Mars, Ia., Aug. 29, 1892; s. John H. and Emma K. (Alline) W.; E.M., Colo. Sch. Mines, 1917, Engr. Metallurgy; LL.B., Westminster Law Sch., 1946; m. Harriet M. Parmelee, Aug. 3, 1918 (dec. 1934); 1 dau., Meredith W. (Mrs. Meredith S. Pruett); m. 2d, Teresa J. Connolly, May 17, 1936. Geologist U.S. Geol. Survey, 1917-19; chief engr. Eagle Mines Zinc Co., (N.J.), 1920-22; practice law, Denver, 1947-51; asst. atty. gen. of Colo., 1951-—; commr. pub. utilities commn. State of Colo., 1951-54, chmn., 1953-54; commr. ICC, 1954-61, chmn., 1959-60; asst. agency mgr. Equitable Life Assurance Soc. (Colo.-Wyo.). Chmn. Denver Co. Rep. Central Com., 1945-51 mem. Rep. State Central Com., 1940-51. C.L.U., Am. Col. Life Underwriters, 1938. Mem. Am. Bakers Assn. (past gov.), Nat. Assn. R.R. and Utilities Commr., Sigma Nu, Theta Tau. Washington DC Died Dec. 3, 1970; buried Gate of Heaven Cemetery, Montgomery County MD

WINCHELL, WALTER, newspaperman; b. New York, N.Y., Apr. 7, 1897; m. Elizabeth June Magee; 2 children. Drama critic, columnist; syndicated 50 states, 11 fgn. papers; narrator-commentator radio-TV; columnist Morning Telegraph; reporter, narrator U.P.I. TV news film and documentaries; asso. editor Washington-N.Y. Examiner. Founder, treas. Damon Runyon Meml. Fund for Cancer Research. Enlisted, USNR, 1917, comdr. ret. Author: The Private Papers of WW. Contbr. mags. Died Feb. 20, 1972; buried AZ

WIND, EDGAR, historian; b. Berlin, Germany, May 14, 1900; s. Maurice Delmar and Laura (Szilard) W.; student univs. Berlin, Freiburg, Vienna, Hamburg, 1918-22; Ph.D., Hamburg, 1922; m. Margaret Kellner, May 14, 1942; naturalized, 1948. Instr. and asst. prof. philosophy U. N.C., 1925-27; research asst. Bibliothek Warburg, Hamburg, 1927-33; privatdozent U. Hamburg, 1930-33; dep. dir. Warburg Inst., London, also hon. lectr. Univ. Coll., London, 1934-42; prof. art U. Chgo., 1942-44; William Allan Neilson research prof. Smith Coll., 1944-48, prof. philosophy and art, 1948-55; prof. history of art U. Oxford, fellow Trinity Coll., 1955-67, prof. emeritus and hon. fellow, 1967-71. Vis. lectr. St. John's Coll., Annapolis, 1939, Pierpont Morgan Library and Inst. Fine Arts, N.Y.U., 1940-42; Trowbridge lectr. Yale, 1940, Ryerson lectr., 1941; Colver lectr. Brown U., 1948; Martin Classical lectr. Oberlin Coll., 1949; Guggenheim fellow, 1950; vis. scholar Am. Acad. in Rome, 1950-51; Chichele lectr. Oxford, 1954; Rede lectr. Cambridge, 1960. Decorated Order of Merit, West German Republic; recipient Serena medal British Acad. Fellow Am. Acad. Arts and Scis.; mem. Aristotelian Soc. (London). Author: Humanitaetsidee and heroisiertes Portrait in der englischen Kultur des 18. Jahrhunderts, 1932; Das Experiment und die Metaphysik, 1934; Bellini's Feast of the Gods, 1948; Pagan Mysteries in the Renaissance, 1958, rev. and enlarged edit., 1967; Art and Anarchy, 1963, 1969; Michelangelo's Prophets and Sibyls, 1967; Giorgione's Tempesta, 1969. Editor: K.B. McFarlane's Hans Memling, 1971; joint editor: A Bibliography of the Survival of the Classics, 1934, 1938; Journal of the Warburg Inst., 1937-42. Contbr. articles on iconographical and philos. subjects to various publs. Home: Oxford England Died Sept. 12, 1971.

WINDELS, PAUL, lawyer; b. Brooklyn, N.Y., Dec. 7, 1885; John Henry and Pauline (Klink) W.; A.B., Columbia, 1908; LL.B., Brooklyn Law Sch., 1909, J.D., 1910; hon. LL.D., St. Lawrence U., 1937; m. Louise E. Gross, Feb. 22, 1919; children—Louise Margaret, Paul, Richard, Barbara. Admitted to N.Y. bar, 1910; began practice at Brooklyn, N.Y.; official referee Kings Co. Court, 1917-19; counsel N.Y. State Bridge and Tunnel Commn., 1918-30; asso. counsel Port of N.Y. Authority, 1930-33; corp. counsel City N.Y., 1934-37; spl. master U.S. District Ct., L.I. R.R. Reorgn. Consul New York City Housing Authority, Triborough Bridge Authority, 1934-37; mem. Bd. of Statutory Consolidation, City of N.Y., 1936; chmn. N.Y. City Traffic Commn., 1937. Officer Legion of Honor, France; awarded Distinguished Pub. Service medal, Columbia U., 1937. Del. Rep. Nat. Convs., 1920, 24, 28, 40; mem. com. on program Rep. National Com., 1937-39; Republican candidate for del. at large N.Y. State Constl. Conv., 1937; chmn. Brooklyn Housing Council, 1931-32; chmn. Committee of Fifteen 1940-50; mem. Mayor's Business Advisory Com., 1940-43; chmn. Citizens Transit Com., 1943-49; counsel, Joint Legislative Committee to Investigate Public Educational System, 1940, 1941. Pres. Regional Plan Assn. of New York, 1943-52, dir., from 1943. Mem. bd. dirs. Nat. War Fund, 1943-48, Downtown Brooklyn Association, Inc., 1946-48. Trustee Brooklyn Daily Eagle, 1934-37, Bowery Savings Bank from 1943. Brooklyn Public Library, 1940-49; v.p. Brooklyn Law Sch., 1952-58, trustee, from 1952; president Museum of French Art, French Institute in U.S., from 1955, trustee from 1928; trustee Lycee Francais de New York, from 1945, chmn. bd., 1965. Member A.I.A. (honorary), Assn. of Bar of City of N.Y. (mem. exec. com. 1937-41;

v.p. 1943-44, 59-60; chmn. com. on municipal affairs 1960-62), Am., N.Y. bar assns., L.I. Hist. Soc., Bklyn. Heights Assn. (pres., gov. 1962-65, adv. com. 1965), Phi Delta Phi, New Eng. Soc. Republican. Presbyn. Mason. Club: Down Town Assn. (N.Y.C.). Home: Darien CT Died Dec. 15, 1967.

WINDSOR H. R. H., The Duke of (Edward Albert Christian George Andrew Patrick David); b. Richmond Park, England, June 23, 1894; s. H.M. King George V and H.M. Queen Mary; cadet R.N. Coll., Osborne, 1907-09, cadet, at Dartmouth, 1909-11, Oxford, 1912-14; m. Mrs. Wallis Warfield, June 3, 1937. Personal a.d.c. to King George V, 1919-36 served as a Counsellor of State; ascended the throne as King Edward VIII, Jan. 20, 1936, abdicated Dec. 1936 in favor of brother, Duke of York, as King George VI; lived on continent of Europe, 1937-39; gov. and comdr.-in-chief of the Bahama Islands, 1940-45. Apptd. midshipman, Royal Navy, 1911, and advanced through the grades to Admiral of the Fleet, 1936; apptd. 2d lt., 1st batn. Grenadier Guards, 1914; a.d.c. to comdr.-in-chief of British Expeditionary Forces and on active service, 1914; served in Italy, France and Egypt, 1916; decorated Knight of the Garter; Military Cross, (1916). Author: AKing's Story. Address: Paris France Died May 28, 1972; buried Frogmore, Windsor Eng.

WINDSOR, JAMES H(ARVEY), II, life ins. exec.; b. Des Moines, June 6, 1904; s. James Raymond and Helen Treat (Howell) W.; Ph.B., Yale, 1927; m. Mary Belle Hubbell, Apr. 27, 1932; children—James Harvey, Grover Hubbell, William Raymond. Asst. supt. bonds Equitable Life Ins. Co. of Ia., Des Moines, 1934, asst. treas., 1944, supt. bonds, 1947, financial v.p., 1948, trustee, 1955, v.p. and treas., 1957, pres., 1959-71; dir. Meredith Corp., Bankers Trust Co., Des Moines. Dir. Greater Des Moines (Ia.) Com. Member of the Greater Des Moines C. of C. (dir. 1959-71). Clubs: Des Moines, Wakonda, Embassy. Home: Des Moines IA Died Aug. 14, 1971; buried Woodland Cemetery, Des Moines IA

WINDSOR, PHINEAS LAWRENCE, librarian; b. Chenoa, Ill., Feb. 21, 1871; s. Rev. John Alexander and Amy (Arnold) W.; Ph.B., Northwestern U., 1895; N.Y. State Library Sch., Albany, N.Y., 1897-99; Albany Law Sch., 1899-1900; Litt.D., Columbia U., 1939; m. Margaret Fursman Boynton, Jan. 1, 1902; children—Margaret, Mary Frances, Elizabeth Arnold. Asst. N.Y. State Library, 1899; in copyright office, Library of Congress, 1900-03; librarian, U. of Tex., 1903-09; librarian and dir. Library Sch., U. of Ill., 1909-40, prof. library science, 1924-41, emeritus since 1940. Director Commercial Building & Loan Assn., 1924-49; dir. Free Pub. Library, 1936-49; treas. Wesley Foundation, 1940-49; member advisory com. of State Library, Springfield, Illinois, 1934-49. Assistant to director A.L.A. war service, 1917. Life mem. A.L.A. (council, 1909-13, 1918-23, 1936, v.p., 1923-24); fellow A.L.I. (pres. 1940-43); pres. Assn. College and Reference Libraries, 1939-40; pres. Assn. Am. Library Schs., 1921-22, 1934-35; mem. Ill. Library Assn. (pres. 1913 and 1935), Bibliog. Soc. America, Am. Hist. Assn., Phi Beta Kappa, Delta Tau Delta, Phi Kappa Phi. Methodist. Clubs: Rotary, University. Editor of Handbook of Texas Libraries, 1904. Contbr. to library publs. Address: 701 Michigan Av., Urbana IL‡

WING, FRANK (FRANCIS MARION), newspaper artist, writer; b. Elmwood, Ill., July 24, 1873; s. Clifton Leonard and Eliza Maria (Tucker) W.; ed. Elmwood High School; Grinnell Coll.; m. Mina J. Morton, Oct. 12, 1904; children—David Clifton, Frank M., Jr. Cartoonist Minneapolis Journal, 1900-14; sketching for Chicago Tribune syndicate, Washington, 1st session of 64th Congress and for Newspaper Enterprise Assn. at Conference on Limitation of Armament; with St. Paul Pioneer Press and Dispatch 5 yrs.; chief instr. cartoon dept., Art Education, Inc., Minneapolis, since 1932. Special sketching for Minneapolis Star, 1937. Author: Yesterdays, 1910; The Fotygraft Album, 1915; Old Forty Dollars, 1916; The Fambly Album, 1917; series of Yesterdays" for Des Moines Register and Tribune Syndicate (book of these, 1930); also several books of sketches of individuals under the titles, Amiable Libels. We Present, and Fore Minneapolis MN‡

WING, WILSON MUNFORD, physician; b. Washington, Nov. 15, 1908; s. David LaForest and Mary Blanche (Mumford) W.; M.D., Columbia, 1936; M.P.H., Johns Hopkins U., 1947; m. Elsa June Stockfisch, Nov. 2, 1940; children—David Lohr, Deborah Thom, Daniel Cushing. Intern, Babies Hosp., Presbyn. Med. Center, N.Y.C., 1936-37, asso. attending pediatrician Vanderbilt Clinic, 4 years; house physician in pediatrics Children's Hosp., Boston, 1938-39, asst. pediatrician, 1939-40; research fellow in allergy Roosevelt Hosp., N.Y.C., 1940-42; staff internat. health div. Rockefeller Found., Eng., 1947-48; asst. in pediatrics Harvard; asso. prof. pub. health adminstrn. Johns Hopkins U., Balt., 1948-56, 57; U.S. dir. High Inst. Pub. Health ICA, Alexandria, Egypt, 1956-58; cons. pub. health adminstrn. WHO, Rio de Janeiro, Brazil, 1958-59; health officer Western health dist. Balt. City Health Dept., 1960-64, Eastern health dist., 1964—. Served from capt. to lt. col., M.C., AUS, 1942-46. Diplomate Am. Bd. Preventive Medicine, Am. Bd. Pediatrics. Fellow A.A.A.S., Am. Pub. Health Assn. Home: Baltimore MD Died Jan. 31, 1971.

WINGER, ALBERT E., publisher; b. Syracuse, N.Y., July 15, 1883; s. John and Mary (Coyne) W.; m. Irene Ridgely, 1920. Comptroller Am. Lithographic Co., 1915-20, pres., 1920-1929; treas. dir. Crowell-Collier Pub. Co., 1917-35, exec. v.p., 1934-46, pres., 1946-51, chairman of the board, 1951-53, retired 1954; mem. adv. bd. Fifth Av. br. Chem. Bank; dir. Crowell-Collier Pub. Co., Publication Corp. Dir. Knapp Found., Asso. Industries N.Y. State. Mem. Mag. Publishers Assn. (dir.), Advt. Council (dir.). Club: Deepdale. Home: New York City NY Died Apr. 1971.

WINGERT, EMMERT LAURSON, lawyer; born Mt. Carroll, Ill., Apr. 2, 1899; s. Alva F. and Almedia (Laurson) W.; B.S., Beloit Coll., 1919; LL.B., Harvard, 1923; m. Helen Bridge, June 7, 1925. Admitted to Wis. bar, 1923; staff atty. gen., 1923-24; pvt. practice of law, 1924-56, 59-71; exec. counsel to Gov. of Wis., 1929-30; justice Wisconsin Supreme Ct., 1956-59; lectr. Wis. Law Sch., U. Wis. Mem., vice chmn. Gov.'s Commn. Study Retirement Systems, 1955-56; mem. Wis. Ins. Law Revision Com., 1966-71, State Retirement Research Committee, 1967-71. Mem. Am., Dane County bar assns., State Bar Wis., Bar Assn. 7th Fed. Circuit (past pres.), Phi Beta Kappa, Beta Theta Pi. Club: Rotary. Home: Madison WI Died Feb. 1, 1971.

WINGET, ARTHUR KNOX, textile mfr.; b. Mecklenberg County, N.C., Oct. 26, 1882; s. Benjamin Henry and Lydia Catherine (Fisher) W.; student pub. schs.; m. Minnie Gray, May 8, 1912; children—Mary Gray, Bennie Wallace, Arthur Knox, Elizabeth Fisher (Mrs. W. L. Mauney). Mercantile bus., Pineville, N.C.; clk., bookkeeper, merc. bus., Gastonia, N.C., 1900-09; with Armstrong group cotton mills, 1909-31, sec.-treas., 1912-31; pres., treas. Efird Mfg. Co., Albemarle, 1932-52, merged with Am. Yarn & Processing Co. to become Am. & Efird Mills, Inc., 1952, honorary chmn. bd.; vice president Roberta Mills, Inc.; director Textiles, Inc. Assisted establishment Cotton States Arbitration Bd., Atlanta, 1926; assisted writing So. Mill Rules, rules and regulations Cotton States Arbitration Bd.; mem. N.C. State Conservation and Development Commn., 1945-48; mem. sch. bd., city council, Gastonia, N.C.; rep. carded yarn, combed yarn mills OPS, W.P.B., World War II. Pres. Central N.C. council Boy Scouts Am., awarded Silver Beaver. Trustee Stanley County Hosp., Wiscassett Meml. YMCA. Mem. Am. Cotton Mfrs. Inst. (pres. 1955, dir.; chmn. cotton com.), N.C. Textile Mfrs. Assn. (pres. 1938-39), Carded Yarn Assn. (pres. 1952-53), So. Combed Yarn Spinners Assn. (pres. 1929-30), Nat. Cotton Council Am. (dir.), Cotton Textile Inst. Presbyn. Mason (Shriner), Rotarian (pres. Albemarle 1936-37). Home: Albemarle NC Died July 8, 1971; buried Hollywood Cemetery, Gastonia NC

WINKING, CYRIL H., state ofcl. Dir. Ill., Dept. Child and Family Service. Home: Springfield IL Died Mar. 21, 1968.

WINLOW, CLARA VOSTROVSKY (MRS. ALBERT E. WINLOW), author; b. West Point, Neb., Oct. 27, 1871; d. Jerome Jaroslav and Anna (Witousek) Vostrovsky; A.B., Stanford, 1895; traveled and studied abroad, 1910-12; studied U. of Calif., 1916-17; m. Albert E. Winlow, of London, Ont., Can., Nov. 13, 1901; 1 dau., Anna Constance. With Tenement House Dept., N.Y. City, 1902-03; foreign extension work, Los Angeles Pub. Library, 1920-22; lecturer, Summer Sch., U. of Calif., 1925; on staff U. of Calif. extension. Author: Our Little Bohemian Cousin, 1911; Our Little Serbian Cousin, 1913; Our Little Bulgarian Cousin, 1913; Our Little Carthagenian Cousin of Long Ago, 1915; Our Little Roumanian Cousin, 1917; Our Little Finnish Cousin, 1918; Our Little Czechoslovak Cousin, 1920; Our Little Jugoslav Cousin, 1923; Our Little Ukranian Cousin (with Anna C. Winlow), 1925; The Story of the Kitten Who Grew Too Fat, 1927; also short stories and serials and many articles pertaining to child study and magazine features. Translator Ostrovsky's The Forest (with Geo. Rapall Noyes), 1926; Kozisek's The Magic Flutes, 1929; Flick and Flock, 1929; Sacramento CA‡

WINN, WILLIAM ALMA, physician; born Butte, Mont., Sept. 22, 1903; s. William Francis and Caroline Christina (Vystrcil) W.; A.B., Stanford, 1926, M.D., Harvard, 1930; m. Astrid Kristine Martensen, Oct. 9, 1934; children—William Richard, Barbara Carolyn, Judith Jane. Began by serving residency in pathology at the Boston City Hospital, 1930-31; research associate Trudeau Sanatorium, 1931-32; house officer Mass. General Hospital, 1933-34; med. dir., superintendent Springville County Hosp., 1935-67; pvt. practice, 1967; med. cons. Fresno br. Cal. Dept. Vocational Rehab., Visalia; cons. pulmonary disease Porterville State Hospital. Member Springville Union School board; F.A.C.P., American Coll. of Chest Physicians; certified Am. Bd. of Internal Medicine; mem. Tulare Co. Med. Soc. (pres. 1947-48), Calif. Sanatorium Assn. (pres. 1940), Alpha Omega Alpha Contbr. of articles on coccidioidal infection, tuberculosis to med. jours. Address: Porterville CA Died Dec. 18, 1967.

WINSEY, A(LEXANDER) REID, educator; b. Appleton, Wis., June 6, 1905; s. William Frederick and Emma (Hill) W.; B.S., U. Wis., 1930, M.S., 1959; postgrad. Yale, Ind. U.; m. Hazel Schultz, Sept. 17, 1934; 1 son, Peter Reid. Head art dept. DePauw U. Greencastle, Ind., from 1935, also prof. art. Condr. art tours for coll. credit, Europe, summers. Served to lt. col AUS, 1944-45. Fulbright scholar, 1950; Ford Found. Kress Found. and Fulbright grantee, 1967; Nat Endowment for Humanities grantee. Fellow Royal Anthrop. Inst., African Studies Assn.; mem. Hoosier Salon Patrons Assn. (bd. dirs.), Hoosier Salon, Ind. Fedn. Artists Clubs, Chgo. Soc. Etchers, Gold Key, Iron Cross, White Spades, Kappa Pi, Pi Kappa Alpha. Republican. Episcopalian. Elk. Author: Freehand Drawing, 1950; Drawing Simplified, 1950. Home: Greencastle IN

WINSHIP, WALTER EDWIN, petroleum products; b. Providence, R.I., June 16, 1872; s. John Bruce and Carra Bryant (Mills) W.; B.A., Standford, 1895, M.A., 1896; Ph.D., U. of Berlin, 1899; m. Magdalene Agnes Slagter, of Titusville, Pa., Aug. 11, 1908. Instr. mathematics, 1895-96, instr. elec. engring., 1899-1900, Stanford U.; with Gould Coupler and Gould Storage Battery cos., New York, 1902-13; gen. mgr. Gen. Lead Batteries Co., 1913-15; southern sales mgr. Mexican Petroleum Corpn., 1915-20; independent marketer of petroleum, 1920-27; pres. Winship Fuel Oil Service, Inc. Mem. Am. Soc. M.E., Am. Inst. E.E., Am. Electro-chem. Soc., Sigma Chi, etc. Republican. Presbyterian. Club: New Orleans Country. Home: 1448 Jackson Av. Office: 344 Camp St., New Orleans LA‡

WINSLOW, REX (SHELTON), univ. prof.; b. Indianola, Ia., Mar. 28, 1901; s. Guy Jabez and Eunice (Goodman) W.; A.B., Simpson Coll., 1923; A.M., U. of Ill., 1929; Ph.D., U. of N.C., 1936; m. Lucille Evans July 26, 1924; children—Bruce, Patricia. Instr., U. of Ill., 1927-29; successively instr., asst. prof., asso. prof. and prof. U. of N.C., 1929-68, dir. bureau of bus. services and research, 1945-68; ednl. dir. Management Devel., Inc., 1955-68. Asso. econ. adviser Office of the Sec., U.S. Dept. of Agr., 1940; economist, W.P.B. 1944-45. Mem. Am. Econ. Assn., So. Econ. Assn., Asso. U. Bur. Bus. and Econ. Research, Am. Mgmt. Assn., U.S. C. of C., Alpha Tau Omega. Methodist Author: Some Problems of Conflict (Economic Problems in a Changing World), 1939. Home: Chapel Hill NC Died Dec. 21, 1968.

WINSLOW, ROBERT LANE, JR., ins. co. exec.; b Kansas City, Mo., Feb. 22, 1917; s. Robert Lane and Ethel (Meyer) W.; student Kansas City Jr. Coll. 1934-36; B.S., Kan. U., 1938; m. Constance Elaine Bolton, Feb. 12, 1943; children—Henry, Rhea, Staff accountant Lunsford, Barnes & Co., C.P.A.'s, 1938-48, v.p. Mastin Ins. Group, 1948-70; v.p. Cimco Inc., ins. marketing, Kansas City, Mo., from 1970; dir. Grand Av Bank & Trust Co., Kansas City, Mo. Chmn. Jackson County Republican Finance Com., 1952-60; mem. Rep Nat. Finance Com., 1954-60. Served with USN, 1942-45. Mem. Am. Inst. C.P.A.'s. Episcopalian (mem. vestry 1954-56, 61-63). Clubs: University, Indian Hill Country (Kansas City, Mo.). Home: Shawnee Mission KS

WINSTEIN, S(AUL), univ. prof.; b. Montreal, Canada, Oct. 8, 1912; s. Louis and Anne (Dick) W.; A.B., U. of Calif., 1934, A.M., 1935; Ph.D., Calif. Inst. Tech., 1938, post-doctorate fellow, 1938-39; Nat. Research fellow, Harvard, 1939-40; Docteur Honoris Causa, U. Montpellier, 1962; m. Sylvia V. Levin, Sept. 3, 1937; children—Bruce, Carolee. Came to U.S., 1923, naturalized, 1929. Instr., Ill. Inst. Tech., 1940-41; instr., U. of Cal., Los Angeles, 1941-42, asst. prof., 1942-46, asso. prof., 1946-47, prof., 1947-69. Max Tishler lectr., Harvard U., 1954, G. N. Lewis lectr., U. Cal., 1955, Baker Non-Resident lectr., Cornell U., Spring 1957. Received Am. Chem. Soc. award in pure chemistry, 1948; Richards medal American Chemical Societry 1962, James Flack Norris award in phys. organic chemistry, 1967; Cal. Scientist of Year award, 1962. Mem. Am. Acad. Arts and Scis., Bayerische Akademie der Wissenenschaften, National Academy of Sciences, America Chemical Society, Phi Beta Kappa, Sigma Xi, Phi Lambda Upsilon. Specializes in physical-organic chemistry and reaction mechanisms. Home: Los Angeles CA Died Nov. 23, 1969.

WINSTON, SANFORD RICHARD, educator, sociologist; b. Jamaica, N.Y., Nov. 27, 1897; s. Ian W. and Mary (Franklin); A.B., Western Res. U., 1925 Ph.D., U. Minn., 1929; grad. student U. Chgo., U. N.C. Columbia; m. Ellen Black, Aug. 30, 1928. Mem. faculty U. N.C. at Raleigh, 1926-65, prof. sociology, 1932-65, head dept. sociology and anthropology, 1933-63; tchr. U. Minn. 1925-26, Cornell U., summer 1944; lectr. Wake Forest Coll., 1949-50, Meredith Coll., 1941-45, Peace Coll., 1951-66; lectr. Ft. Bragg, 1956-66. Pres. Raleigh Community Council, 1944-46, Raleigh Chamber Music Guild, 1948-50. Research fellow Laura Spelman Rockefeller Found., 1925-26; grantee Gen. Edn. Bd., 1943-46, Purnell Fund. 1941-42; cons. N.C Council Housing Authorities, 1945-48. Fellow Am Sociol. Assn.; mem. N.C. Archeol. Soc. (past pres.). Author: Culture and Human Behavior, 1933; Illiteracy in the United States, 1930; Social Aspects of Public Housing 1947; Leadership in War and Peace, 1947; also articles. Home: Raleigh NC Died June 13, 1969; buried Bryson City NC

WINTER, ALICE BEACH, artist; b. Green Ridge, Mo., Mar. 22, 1877; d. Edgar Rice and Frances Emeline (White) Beach; ed. pub. schs., St. Louis; student St. Louis Sch. of Fine Arts, 1892-98, Art Students' League, New York, 1901; m. Charles Allan Winter, Jan. 1, 1904. Painter and illustrator of childhood; has illustrated child-life stories and originated many cover designs in color for mags.; commd. to paint numerous portraits of children. Exhibited at National Acad. Design, New York; Pa. Academy Fine Arts, Phila.; Carnegie Inst., Pittsburgh; St. Louis Museum Fine Arts; Museum of History, Science and Art, Los Angeles, Calif. Dir. Gloucester Art Class; member North Shore Arts Association. Charter member Gloucester Business and Professional Women's Club. Home-Studio: 134 Mt. Pleasant Av., Gloucester MA‡

WINTERBURN, FLORENCE (MAY) HULL, author; b. Chicago, Illinois; d. of Capt. Stephen Chester and Laura (Bell) Hull; ed. pvt. schs. and by pvt. tutors, Washington; student of theory and practice of edn.; m. Goerge William Winterburn, M.D. Asso. editor Childhood Mag., 1892; asst. editor Godey's, 1893, Home and Country, 1895; etc. Author: Nursery Ethics, 1896; From the Child's Standpoint, 1899; The Children's Health, 1901; Southern Hearts (short stories), 1901; Vacation Hints, 1911; Principles of Correct Dress, 1914; Novel Ways of Entertaining, 1914; The Mother in Education, 1915; Liberty Hall, 1916. Spl. work on New York Sun and New York Times, 1916-—; editor Americana; lit. editor Screen Stories Service. Address: Authors' League, New York NY‡

WINTERS, HARRY S(UNDERLAND), univ. prof.; b. Wellsboro, Pa., Nov. 13, 1871; s. Augustus C. and Hettie M. (Payne) W.; A.B., John B. Stetson U., 1896; student U. of Chicago, summer 1898, Colgate U., 1890-93, Vanderbilt U., summers 1930-32; M.A., George Peabody Coll., 1932; m. Mabel Winifred Allen, May 23, 1901; 1 son, Allen Charles (M.D.). Prin. Melbourne (Fla.) High Sch., 1896-99; clerk Fla. Paper Co., Jacksonville, Fla., 1906-10; partner, 1910-20; retired, 1920-27; instr. math., English, Stetson U., 1927-33, asst. prof. history and polit. science, 1933-37, asso. prof., 1937-43, prof. since 1943. Trustee De Land Pub. Library. Past vice pres. Fla. Library Assn.; past trustee and treas. Jacksonville Y.M.C.A. Mem. Fla. Hist. Soc., Phi Kappa Psi, Pi Gamma Mu, Phi Alpha Theta (sponsor), Scroll and Key, Sigma Delta Pi. Baptist. Mem. Stetson Alumni Assn. (pres. 1897-1908). Home: 520 N. Boulevard, DeLand FL‡

WINTERS, ROBERT (HENRY), mem. parliament Can.; b. Lunenburg, Nova Scotia, Can., August 18, 1910; s. Henry Collins and Sophia Elizabeth (Conrad) W.; ed. Lunenburg Acad.; A.B., Mt. Allison U., Sackville, N.B., 1931, LL.D., 1949; S.M., Mass. Inst. Tech., 1934; E.D. (hon.), N.S. Tech. Coll., 1953; D.Sc. (honorary), University of New Brunswick, 1954; LL.D., Queen's U., 1962, St. Dunstan's Univ., 1966, Mt. Allison U., Western New Eng. U., Dartmouth, St. Lawrence U.; m. Eleanor McRobie Dixon, July 11, 1936; children—Henry Collins, Richard Dixon (dec.), Marjorie Pauline, Engr. with Bell Telephone Labs., N.Y. City, N.Y. Telephone Co., and Northern Elec. Co., Ltd., Montreal; later became mgr. Industrial Shipping Co., Ltd., Mahone Bay, N.S.; mem. Parliament for Queens-Lunenburg, N.S., 1945-65; mem. Parliament for York South, Can., 1965-68. Became parliamentary assistant to minister of nat. revenue, 1947, to minister of transport, 1948; mem. Privy Council and minister of resources and development; minister of public works, 1953-57; minister of trade and commerce, Can., 1966-68; ret., 1968; chmn. bd. Brascan Ltd., 1968-69; pres. Brinco, 1963-65, Rio Tinto Can., 1957-65. Life mem. corp. Mass. Inst. Tech.; bd. govs. Can. Opera Company; chairman of the bd. govs. York Univ. Served with Royal Canadian Elec. and Mech. Engineers, World War II, returning to civilian life with rank of lt. col., 1946. Mem. Engring. Inst. of Can. Clubs: Badminton and Racquet, Toronto Tennis (Toronto). Home: Toronto ON Canada Died Oct. 10, 1969; buried Lunenburg, NS Canada

WINTERSTEINER, OSKAR PAUL, chemist; b. Bruck a/d Mur. Austria, Nov. 15, 1898; s. Carl and Eva (Torkar) W.; Ph.D., U. Graz (Austria), 1921; D.Sc. (hon.), Western Res. U., 1968; m. Margaret Ralston Prest, Sept. 21, 1934; children—Peter, Susanne. Instr. med. chemistry and organic microanalysis U. of Graz, Austria, 1921-26; fellow Internat. Edn. Bd., Johns Hopkins Med. Sch., Rockefeller Inst., 1926-27; instr. pharmacology Johns Hopkins Med. Sch., 1927-29; asst. prof. biochemistry Coll. Phys. and Surgs., Columbia U., 1929-39, asso. prof., 1939-41; dir. div. organic chemistry, Squibb Inst. Med. Research, 1941-59, director biological chemistry, 1959-63, sci. adviser, 1961-63, cons., 1964-67, sr. sci. adviser, 1967-71; hon. prof. biochemistry Rutgers U., 1942-71, emeritus prof., 1968-71; cons. and mem. antibiotic study sect. National Inst. Health, 1946-49; member board of scientific advisers National Inst. Arthritis and Metabolic Diseases, 1957-59. Awarded Presdl. Certificate of Merit, 1948; Nichols medal, 1950. Mem. Nat. Acad. Scis., Am. Chem. Soc. (chmn. North Jersey sect. 1957), A.A.A.S., Harvey Soc., Soc. Exptl. Biology and Medicine, Swiss Chem. Soc., Sigma Xi. Editor: Proceedings Soc. Exptl. Biology and Medicine, 1938-43, 1948-50; mem. editorial bd. Jour. Biol. Chemistry, 1952-62, Jour. Am. Chem. Soc., 1959-68. Home: Graz Austria Died Aug. 15, 1971.

WINTHER, OSCAR OSBURN, historian; b. Weeping Water, Neb., Dec. 22, 1903; s. Anton and Sena (Lund) W.; A.B., U. Ore., 1925; A.M., Harvard, 1928; student U. Cal., 1929; Ph.D., Stanford, 1934; m. Mary Merriam Galey, Aug. 21, 1937; children—Ingrid Ellen (Mrs. James R. Scobie), Eric Anton. Acting instr. history Stanford, 1931-35, instr., 1935-36; translator Danish, Hoover War Library, 1932-33; asst. curator Wells Fargo Bank & Union Trust Co., San Francisco, 1934-35; instr. Adult Edn. Center, San Jose, Cal., 1934-36; tchr. Portland Center, U. Ore., summers 1936, 37; instr. history Ind. U., 1937-43, asst. prof. history, 1943-47, associate prof., 1947-50, prof., 1950-65, University professor of history, 1965-70, asst. dean grad. sch., 1948-53, acting dean, 1950, asso. dean, 1953-58, acting chmn. dept. history, summer 1957; faculty U. N.M., summer 1945, Cal. Inst. Tech., spring 1946, Johns Hopkins, summer 1948; vis. professor Brigham Young U., summer 1959, University of Washington, summer 1966, Alaska Methodist U., summer 1967. Recipient grants-in-aid for research Social Sci. Research Council, Henry E. Huntington Library, Library Congress; research fellow Henry E. Huntington Library, 1945-46, Newberry Library, 1966-67; Fulbright research fellowship U. Coll., London U., 1952-53; John Simon Guggenheim Meml. fellow, 1959; Fulbright grantee U. Birmingham (Eng.), 1966. Sr. research associate Henry E. Huntington Library, 1960. Mem. com. internat. student exchange Assn. of Graduate Schools in Assn. Am. Universities, 1956-58. Fellow Royal Hist. Society, Soc. American Historians; mem. Am. Hist. Assn., Orgn. Am. Historians, Western History Association (president 1963-64), Agrl. History Soc., Scandinavian-American Society, Oral History Assn. (v.p. 1968-69, pres. 1969-70), Phi Alpha Theta. Author: The Story of San Jose, California's First Pueblo, 1935; Express and Stagecoach Days in California from the Gold Rush to the Civil War, 1938; Via Western Express and Stagecoach, 1945; The Great Northwest, 1947; Old Oregon Country, 1950; The Transportation Frontier: Trans-Mississippi West 1865-1890, 1964. Co-author: The Story of Our Heritage, 1962; The Book of the American West, 1963. Mng. editor: Mississippi Valley Hist. Rev., 1963-64, Journal of American History, 1964-66. Editor: A Friend of the Mormons: The Diaries and Letters of Thomas Leiper Kane, 1937; With Sherman to the Sea, 1943; Diary of a Dying Empire, 1955. Compiled: The Trans-Mississippi West, A Guide. 1942; A Classified Bibliography of Trans-Mississippi West Periodical Literature, 1811-1957, 1960, (with Richard A. Van Orman) A Supplement, 1957-67, 1970. Home: Bloomington IN Died May 22, 1970.

WINZLER, RICHARD JOHN, biochemist b. San Francisco, Sept. 29, 1914; s. Joseph and Esther (Hoppe) Brand; student San Mateo Jr. Coll., 1932-34; B.S., Stanford, 1936, Ph.D., 1938; m. Georgann E. Martin, June 17, 1939; children—Joan, Natalie, Lee. Sterling fellow physiology Yale, 1938-39; NRC fellow med. sci. Wenner-Grens Inst., Stockholm, Sweden, 1939-40, Cornell U. Med. Sch., 1940-41; research fellow Nat. Cancer Inst., Bethesda, Md., 1941-43; asst. prof. biochemistry U. So. Cal. Sch. Medicine, 1943-46, asso. prof., 1946-49, prof., 1949-52; vis research prof. physiol. chemistry U. Wis. Sch. Medicine, 1951; prof., head dept. biol. chemistry U. Ill. Coll. Medicine, 1952-65; prof., head dept. biochemistry State U. N.Y. at Buffalo, 1965-69; prof. chemistry Fla. State U., Tallahassee, 1969-72. Cons. in med. edn. Chiengmai U. Med. Sch., Thailand, 1962. Mem. Nat. Bd. Med. Examiners, 1954-64. Commonwealth Fund scholar U. Freiburg, 1959. Mem. Soc. Exptl. Biology and Medicine, Am. Chem. Soc., Am. Assn. Cancer Research, A.A.A.S., Am. Fedn. Clin. Research, Am. Soc. Cell Biology, Am. Assn. Clin. Chemists, Am. Soc. Biol. Chemists, Sigma Xi. Bd. editors Proc. Soc. Exptl. Biology and Medicine, 1953-58, Cancer Research, 1955-60. Home: Tallahassee FL Died Sept. 28, 1972.

WIREBAUGH, EVELYN BURBANK (MRS. HAROLD W. WIREBAUGH), banker; b. Warren, O., Aug. 22, 1907; d. Burt William and Stella (Chinnock) Burbank; student pub. schs.; m. Harold W. Wirebaugh, May 29, 1937 (dec. 1968). Auditor, Second Nat. Bank, Warren, O., 1925-46, The Miami Beach First Nat. Bank (Fla.), 1946-62, comptroller, 1963-66; asst. to pres., 1966-67, v.p., 1967-69; sec., asst. treas. United Bancshares of Fla., Inc., 1966-67, treas.. 1967-69. Recipient Woman of Achievement award Fla. Fedn. Business and Professional Women's Organizations, 1955. Mem. Nat. Assn. Bank Auditors and Comptrollers (dir. Fla., pres. S. Fla. conf., 1955-56), Nat. Assn. Bank Women (treas. 1957), Fla. Bankers Assn., Am. Inst. Banking. Republican. Episcopalian. Clubs: Coral Gables (Fla.) Country; Country (Miami). Home: Coral Gables FL Died Dec. 1, 1969; buried Warren OH

WIRT, LOYAL LINCOLN, clergyman, publicist; b. Lamont, Mich., May 3, 1863; s. David and Sarah Osborne (Potter) W.; student Jamestown (N.D.) Coll., 1886-87; B.D., Pacific Theol. Sem., Oakland, Calif., 1890; Sc.D., Armour Inst. Tech., Chicago, 1912; D.D., Pacific Sch. of Religion, 1925; m. Harriet Eliot Benton, Oct. 6, 1890; children—Joseph Benton, George Boynton (dec.), Williston, Monica Alexandra, Lincoln Brown, Sherwood Eliot. Ordained Congl. ministry, 1890; Calif. state supt. Congl. Sunday Sch. and Pub. Soc., 1890-98; territorial supt. Alaska Missions, 1898-1900; U.S. commr. of edn., Alaska, 1900; pastor Wharf St. Congl. Ch., Brisbane, Australia, 1901-07, Harrow, Eng., 1908; asso. pastor First Ch., Oakland, Calif., 1909-12; lecturing and writing, 1913-17; with Am. Red Cross, title of capt., 1917-18; with Near East Relief service, 1918-24; western secretary Nat. Council for Prevention of War, 1924-30; dir. Golden Rule Foundation, 1930-40. Established first hosp. at Nome, Alaska, 1899, and first pub. sch. north of the Yukon River; first white man to cross Alaska in winter—1200 miles, Cape Prince of Wales to Pacific Ocean—to secure doctors, nurses and food, 1899, to relieve starvation, first gold rush to Cape Nome; organized internat. movement for relief of war orphans and refugess in Near East, and established branches in Hawaii, Japan, China, Philippines, Australia and New Zealand, and had charge of first shipload of food and clothing from Australia to Constantinople; raised over $2,000,000 for post-war relief, Founder Casa Colina Home for Crippled Children. Fellow Royal Geog. Soc.; mem. Am. Acad. Polit. and Social Science; chancellor Pi Gamma Mu. Decorated Near East Relief Service medal. Republican. Mason. Author: As a Nation Thinketh; Alaskan Adventures; The World is My Parish. Clubs: Scrooby Club, Rotary. Home: 592 Mayflower Rd., Claremont CA‡

WIRTH, RUSSELL D. L., food mfg. exec.; b. Milw., Nov. 25, 1905; s. Adolph Lee and Edna (Double) W.; student Williams Coll., 1924-26; A.B., Harvard, 1928; m. Mary Elizabeth McMahon, Sept. 7, 1929; children—Russell D. L., Harry McMahon, Mary Rogers. Tng. program Universal Foods Corporation, Milw., 1929-33, mfg. and research depts., also dir. of co., 1933-38, exec. v.p., 1938-50, pres., 1950-66, chmn. bd., 1966-68; dir. Northwestern Nat. Ins. Co., Columbian Art Works, Marine Nat. Exchange Bank, Marine Corp. Dir. Greater Milw. Com., Columbia Hosp., Met. Milw. Assn. Commerce, Trustee Nutrition Found., Chas. A. Krause Found. Episcopalian. Rotarian. Home: Milwaukee WI Died Sept. 20, 1968.

WISCOTT, WILLIAM JOSEPH, editor; b. Balt., Aug. 3, 1898; s. Murray James and Anna Louise (Schindele) W.; spl. student Johns Hopkins, 1918-20; m. Luise M. Gaubatz, Jan. 16, 1966. Chemist, advt. and sales dir. Jewett & Sherman Co., Milw., 1921-26; circulation mgr. Modern Quar., Balt., 1931-35; mng. editor, editor Current Med. Digest, 1950-69; exec. sec. Md. Acad. Gen. Practice, 1950-69; pub. News Bull. of Md. and D.C. acads. gen. practice; mng. editor Bull. U. Md. Med. Sch., Quarterly Phi Lambda Kappa medical fraternity. Named to Hall of Fame, Balt. City Coll., 1961. Mem. Nat. Assn. Sci. Writers, Am. Med. Writers Assn., A.A.A.S., Med. Soc. Execs. Assn., Nat. Assn. Physically Handicapped, Md. Acad. Medicine and Surgery, German Soc. Md. Presbyn. Mason (32 deg., Shriner). Home: Baltimore MD Died June 16, 1969.

WISE, BOYD ASHBY, educator; b. Stephens City, Va., July 7, 1874; s. Henry A. and Minerva Elizabeth (Pifer) W.; grad. Randolph-Macon Acad., Front Royal, Va., 1894; A.B., Randolph-Macon Coll., Ashland, Va., 1897, A.M., 1898; Ph.D., Johns Hopkins, 1905; m. Rubie Clayton Mansfield, Dec. 27, 1912; children—Vermell, Elizabeth (dec.), Lillian, Boyd Ashby. Instr. Latin, Randolph-Macon Acad., 1898-1901; fellow Latin, Johns Hopkins, 1903-05; master in Latin and history, Belmont (Calif.) Sch., 1905-06; acting prof. English, Millsaps Coll., Jackson, Miss., 1906-07, Emory Coll., Oxford, Ga., 1907-08; prof. German and Latin, Okla. Agrl. and Mech. Coll., Stillwater, Okla., 1908-11; acting prof. Latin, Richmond (Va.) Coll., 1911-12; acting prof. English, W.Va. Wesleyan Coll., Buckhannon, W.Va., 1912-13; prof. Latin and English, Henderson-Brown Coll., Arkadelphia, Ark., 1913-16; dean and prof. English, Lincoln Memorial U., Harrogate, Tenn., 1916-21; prof. rhetoric and pub. speaking, Centre Coll., Danville, Ky., Sept. 1921-29, prof. journalism and public speaking, 1929-33; prof. English and journalism Cox Coll., College Park, Ga., 1933-34; prof. English Lincoln Memorial University, 1935-49, also dean of Univ. Dean Emeritus, 1945; now prof. English, Lambuth Coll., Jackson, Tenn. Secretary Association East Tennessee Colleges, 1918-21, Associations of Tenn. Coll., 1919-20. Mem. Am. Philol. Assn., Phi Beta Kappa (Alpha of Md.), Pi Kappa Delta, Tau Kappa Alpha, Alpha Kappa Pi. Democrat. Methodist. Mason. Club: Thirty. Author: (thesis) The Influence of Statius on Chaucer, 1911; Major George Washington—A Drama of American Youth, 1943. Editor of Mountain Herald, 1917-21; editor Centre College Magazine, 1928-33; asso. editor Lincoln Herald, 1937-49. Address: Jackson TN‡

WISE, BYRD DOUGLAS, lawyer; b. Richmond, Va., Dec. 21, 1886; s. John Sergeant and Eva (Douglas) W.; A.B., Columbia, 1907, LL.B., 1909; m. Edith Murray Grandin, May 20, 1914; children—Grandin, Byrd

Douglas (Mrs. Samuel L. Hays), Sergeant Woodhull, Edith Hamilton (Mrs. George A. Burpee). Admitted to N.Y. bar, 1909, practiced law, N.Y.C.; engaged in pvt. law practice. Dir. Hudson's Bay Co., Inc., Hudson's Bay Co. Fur Sales, Inc. Mem. Bouvier des Flandres Club Am., Beta Theta Pi. Mason. Club: Union League. Home: Cape Vincent NY Died Jan. 30, 1969; buried Greenwood Cemetery Brooklyn NY

WISE, RUSSELL VINCENT, pub. accountant; b. Sterling, Ill., Aug. 9, 1904; s. Edward J. and Cora (Modler) W.; student Wabash Coll., 1922-23, Northwestern U., 1924-25; m. 2d, Charlotte M. Hagemann, Aug. 23, 1942; children by previous marriage—Jean (Mrs. Dean E. Smith), Roger Day. Chief accountant Worthy Mfg. Co., Chgo., 1925-28, controller, 1928-29; financial mgr. Benjamin Moore & Co., 1929-42; mem. Renegotiation Bd., U.S. Signal Corps, Chgo., 1942-46; controller Aieron S.A., Mexico City, Mexico, 1946-49; auditor Price Waterhouse & Co., Chgo., 1950-54; individual practice C.P.A. and mgmt. cons., Chgo., 1954-72. Treas., mem. bd. St. Leonard's House, Chgo., 1955-56. Mem. Am. Inst. C.P.A.'s Ill. Soc. C.P.A.'s. Am. Accounting Assn., Tau Kappa Epsilon. Republican. Episcopalian (asst. ch. treas. 1957-58). Club: The 71. Home: Evanston IL Died July 27, 1972.

WISH, HARVEY, educator; b. Chgo., Sept. 4, 1909; s. Samuel and Reve (Stone) W.; B.S., Ill. Inst. Tech., 1931; M.A., U. Chgo., 1933; Ph.D., Northwestern U., 1936; fellow Harvard, 1943-44; m. Anne Kruger, May 16, 1932; 1 dau., Dorothy. Asst. prof. history DePaul U., 1936-42; asso. prof. Smith Coll., 1944-45; prof. history Western Res. U., 1945-63, Elbert Jay Benton distinguished professor, 1963-68; Fulbright prof. U. Munich, U. Aix-Marseilles, 1954, including lectures U. Copenhagen, Uppsala U., U. Stockholm, U. Lund, U. Vienna, Freiburg U.; summer lectr. U. So. Cal., 1948, San Diego State Coll., 1949, University of Michigan, 1951, Columbia University, 1958; Carnegie visiting professor University Hawaii, 1956; John G. Winant distinguished lectureship Brit.-Am. Assos., London, 1961. Mem. Am. Assn. U. Profs., Am., Miss. Valley hist. assns. Author: George Fitzhugh, Propagandist of the Old South, 1943; Contemporary America (last edit.), 1966; Society and Thought in America (2 vols.), 1950-52; The American Historian, 1960. Home: Cleveland Heights OH Died Mar. 8, 1968.

WISWALL, FRANK LAWRENCE, lawyer; b. Colonie, N.Y., July 8, 1895; s. Dr. Charles D. and Mary Elizabeth (Lawton) W.; LL.B., Albany Law Sch., Union U., 1916; m. Clara E. Chapman, Aug. 28, 1924; children—Elaine Joyce (wife of Rev. Darby W. Betts), Betty (Mrs. F. Beale Betts), Frank Lawrence. Admitted to N.Y. bar, 1917, practiced Albany until 1960; admitted Me. bar, 1959; town atty. Colonie, 1931-54; co. atty. Albany Co., 1921-22. Mem. N.Y. State Assembly, 1920; N.Y. State Senate, 1921-22. Trustee Albany Law School, 1921-72, Maine Maritime Academy, 1959-72 (v.p. 1964). Exec. v.p. U.S. Trotting Assn., 1938-41, counsel, dir., hon. sec. 1938-57, chmn. bd. 1956-57, hon. v.p. 1958-72; pres. Saratoga Harness Racing Assn., Inc., 1945-63, chmn. bd. 1963; sec. N.Y. State Harness Racing Commn., 1940-44. Served as regtl. sgt. maj. Judge Adv. Gen.'s Dept., hdqrs. 76th Div., 18 mos., World War I. Mem. Am., N.Y. State, Me., Hancock County bar assns., U.S. Coast Guard Aux. (flotilla comdr.), Delta Chi. Republican (chmn. county com. 1921-23). Episcopalian. Mason (32 deg.). Clubs: Fort Orange, Tarratine, Castine Men's (pres. 1966-67), Yachting of America, Castine Golf (gov.), Castine Yacht. Home: Castine ME Died Oct. 24, 1972; buried Castine ME

WITEBSKY, ERNEST, physician; b. Frankfurt, Germany, Sept. 3, 1901; s. Michael and Hermine (Neuberger) W.; student U. Frankfurt, 1920-25; M.D., U. Heidelberg, 1926; Dr. Med., h.c., University of Freiburg, 1958; married Ruth Mueller-Erkelenz, June 23, 1935; children—Frank G., Grace E. Came to U.S., 1934, naturalized, 1939. Asso. prof. bacteriology U. Buffalo, 1936-40, prof. bacteriology and immunology, 1940-54, distinguished prof., 1954-69, head dept. bacteriology and immunology, 1941-67, dir. Center for Immunology, 1967-69, acting dean Sch. Medicine, 1958-59, dean, 1959-60; bacteriologist, serologist Buffalo Gen. Hosp., 1936-68, dir. blood bank, 1941-67; cons. bacteriology VA Hosp., 1951-69. Diplomate clin. microbiology Am. Bd. Pathology. Fellow Am. Soc. Clin. Pathologists; mem. A.M.A., Am. Assn. Pathologists and Bacteriologists, Am. Assn. Immunologists, Soc. Am. Bacteriologists, Soc. Exptl. Biology and Medicine, Am. Assn. Blood Banks, International Society of Hematology, Royal Society of Medicine, Sigma Xi. Contributor of English, German, French, Am. med. jours. Home: Buffalo NY Died Dec. 7, 1969; buried Buffalo NY

WITHERS, JOHN THOMAS, landscape architect and forester; b. N. Wales, Mar. 22, 1872; s. William and Mary W.; ed. Sch. of Horticulture, Walthon-on-Thames; came to America, 1893; m. Jersey City, N.J., Emma North, of Aylesbury, England, Oct. 23, 1895; children—John William, Clarence Thomas. Employed on the estate of William Rockefeller, Tarrytown, 1893-96; asst. supt. Keney Park, Hartford, Conn., 1896-1901; with Manning Bros. (landscape architects), Boston, 1901-02; removed to Jersey City, N.J., 1902. Noted for successful application of tree surgery" in preservation of historic trees by use of concrete. Address: Teaneck NJ‡

WITHERSPOON, WILLIAM WALLACE, banker, lawyer; b. Spokane, Nov. 15, 1905; s. Archibald William and Eda (Mauseth) W.; B.S., Princeton, 1928; LL.B., U. Wash., 1931; m. Charlotte Semple, May 17, 1941; children—William Wallace, Grant Thomas, James Stuart, Tannis Eda, Peter Archibald. Admitted to Wash. bar, 1931, practiced in Spokane, 1931-72; sr. partner firm Witherspoon, Kelley, Davenport & Toole, and predecessors, 1958-72; chmn. bd. Old Nat. Bank Wash., Spokane, 1959-72; pres. dir. Washington Bancshares, Inc. (formerly called Old Nat. Corp.), 1959-72, Old Nat. Bank Bldg. Co., 1959-72, Investment Securities Co., 1959-72, Davenport Investment Co., 1964-72; v.p., dir. Greenough Investment Co., 1947-72, Pend Oreille Mines & Metals Co., 1959-72; sec.-treas., dir. Inland Empire Paper Co., 1950-72; dir. First Nat. Bank Spokane, Reeves McDonald Mines, Ltd., Securities-Intermountain, Inc. Trustee St. George's Sch., Spokane. Mem. Assn. Registered Bank Holding Cos. (dir.), Phi Delta Phi. Clubs: Spokane Country. Home: Spokane WA Died Oct. 20, 1972.

WITMER, FRANCIS POTTS, civil engr.; b. Phila., Pa., Apr. 2, 1873; s. Ambrose E. and Imogene B. (Potts) W.; A.B., Central High Sch., Phila., 1891; B.S., U. of Pa., 1893, C.E., 1894; m. Minnie Sears Barr, June 24, 1897; children—Dorothy Imogene (dec.), Francis Potts; instr. in civil engring., U. of Pa., 1894; draftsman and designer Phoenix Bridge Co., 1897-1900; engr. in charge bridge design, Am. Bridge Co., Phila. office, later New York office, 1901-13; structural engr. New York, Municipal Ry. Corp. (Brooklyn Rapid Transit System), 1913-20; cons. engr., associated with Howard C. Baird, New York, since 1920; dir. civil engring. dept.; prof. civil engring., U. of Pa., 1924-43; retired. Asso. with Mr. Baird in constrn. of Bear Mountain Bridge over Hudson River, 1922-24. Mem. Am. Soc. C.E., Am. Soc. for Testing Materials, Am. Concrete Inst., Soc. for Promotion Engring. Edn., Engineers Club (Phila.), Franklin Inst., Sigma Xi, Tau Beta Pi, Phi Beta Kappa. Republican. Episcopalian. Home: 738 Penna. Av., Prospect Park, Pa. Office: 95 Liberty St., New York NY‡

WITMER, R(OBERT) B(ONNER), educator; born at Bathgate, N.D., Jan. 30, 1900; s. Samuel T. and Charlotte (Fizette) W.; B.S., U. of N.D., 1922, M.S., 1926; Ph.D., U. of Mich., 1935; student U. of Wash., summer 1930, Columbia, 1940; m. Lillian Leith, Aug. 15, 1927; 1 dau., Jean Leith (Mrs. Charles W. Meline). Grad. asst. U. of N.D., 1922-24, instr. physics, 1924-27, asst. prof. physics, 1927-34, asso. prof. physics. 1934-42, freshman adviser, 1936-39, dean of freshmen, 1939-42, prof. physics from 1938, dean of jr. div., 1946-49, acting dean College of Sci., Lit. and Arts, and dean jr. div., 1948-49, dean Coll. of Sci., Lit. and Arts, 1949-65, dean emeritus, hon. University prof., 1965-70, dean emeritus, hon. univ. prof. emeritus, 1970-72. Served with U.S. Army, 1918; lt., U.S.N.R., 1942. Instr. and head mathematics-physics dept. U.S. Navy Pre-Flight Sch., Iowa City, Ia., 1942-43. Mem. Am. Assn. Univ. Profs., N.D. Academy Sci., Nat. Edn. Assn., Sigma Xi, Sigma Tau, Phi Beta Kappa, Blue Key, Phi Delta Kappa, Phi Eta Sigma, Sigma Nu. Episcopalian. Mason. Specialist in measurement of long Xrays by means of ruled grating; resistivity of N.D. clays. Home: Grand Forks ND Died Feb. 21, 1972; buried Memorial Park Cemetery Grand Forks ND

WITSCHI, EMIL, biologist; b. Bern, Switzerland, Feb. 18, 1890; s. Johann and Elisabeth (Blank) W.; student State Teachers Coll. and State U., Bern, Switzerland, 1905-11; Ph.D., U. of Munich, 1913; M.D. honoris causa, University Basel, 1960; Rockefeller Foundation fellow, Yale, 1926, U. of Chicago, 1926, U. of Calif., 1927; m. Ida Martha Muehlestein, July 10, 1914; children—Marianne, Hans Walter. Came to U.S., 1926, naturalized, 1933. Teacher zoology and comparative anatomy, U. of Basel, 1921-23, lecturer exptl. zoology, 1924-27; prof. zoology, embryology and endocrinology, State U. Ia., 1927-58, professor emeritus, 1958-71; guest prof. Univ. of Tubingen, Germany, 1948-49; vis. prof. U. Paris, 1959, Yale, 1961, Taiwan U., 1962, Basel University, 1963-67; program specialist for reproducation physiology Ford Foundation, 1962-67; sr. scientist, biomed. div. Population Council Rockefeller University, New York City, N.Y., 1967-71. Member permanent committee Internat. Congress of Zoologists, Jubile Scientifique Sorbonne, 1959. Fellow A.A.A.S., N.Y., Idaho academies sci., Internat. Inst. Embryology (Utrecht); mem. German Acad. Sci., Swiss Soc. Natural Scis., Am. Soc. Zoologists (pres. 1959, 60), Am. Assn. Anatomists, Endocrine Soc., Am. Genetics Soc., Soc. Exptl. Biology and Medicine, Am. Naturalists, Sigma Xi (tour lectr. 1960), Gamma Alpha; hon. mem. Societe Zoologique France, Societe d'Endocrinologie Paris others; corr. mem. Swiss Genetics Soc., others. Kiwanian. Author: Sex Deviations, Inversions and Parabiosis, 1932, 2d edit., 1939; Development of Vertebrates, 1956. Contbr. to Ency. Brit., 1957: also articles to scientific jours. Home: New York City NY Died June 9, 1971.

WITSELL, EDWARD FULLER, army officer; b. Charleston, S.C., Mar. 29, 1891; s. Edward Fuller and Rosa Ella (Oliveros) W.; B.S., The Citadel, Charleston, S.C., 1911, LL.D., 1947; grad. Chem. Warfare Sch., 1924, Army War Coll., 1929; m. Daphne Dow, Dec. 13, 1917; children—Edward F., Barbara D., Mary Ellen. Commd. 2d lieut., inf., U.S. Army, 1912, advancing through grades to maj. gen., 1945; served as officer of inf., Chem. Warfare Service, War Dept. Gen. Staff and Adj. Gen.'s Dept., Hawaii, Japan, Philippine Islands, Panama Canal Zone, and at various posts in U.S., also in War Dept.; chief of staff, Hawaiian Dept., U.S. Army, during World War I; dir. mil. personnel div. Adj. Gen.'s Office, War Dept., Washington, D.C., 1943-45, acting adj. gen., July 1945; apptd. adjutant gen., Feb., 1946, reapptd. 1950, ret. June 1951; dir., Army Emergency Relief, July 1951. Decorated Distinguished Service Medal, Army Commendation Ribbon, Victory, American Defense, American Theater and World War II medals. Japanese language student, and asst. mil. attache, Tokyo, Japan. Home: Washington DC Died Nov. 1969.

WITT, JOSHUA CHITWOOD, engr.; b. Connersville, Ind., Aug. 5, 1884; s. Isaac Snyder and Amanda (Chitwood) W.; A.B., Butler U., 1908; B.S., U. of Chicago, 1909; M.S., U. of Pittsburgh, 1912, Ph.D., 1915; M.E., Armour Institute Technology (now Illinois Institute Technology), Chicago, 1935; m. Florence Ruth Oldham, Dec. 5, 1918. Testing and research asst. Swift & Co., Chicago, 1908-10; mgr. testing dept. R. W. Hunt Co., Pittsburgh, 1910-15; chief of sect. Bur. of Science, Manila, P.I., 1915-17; tech. dir. Rizal Cement Co., Manila, 1917-19; asst. prof. U. of Pittsburgh, and cons. engr., 1919-20; dir. chem. research Portland Cement Assn., Chicago, 1920-23; dir. research Universal Atlas Cement Co., Chicago, 1924-39; tech. dir. Marquette Cement Mfg. Co., 1939-48; cons. engr., 1948-71. Cons. U.S. Bur. of Mines, 1922-23. Sect. editor Chemical Abstracts, 1924-71; cons. editor, Concrete, 1933-48. Fellow Am. Soc. M.E., A.A.A.S., Am. Soc. C.E., Am. Inst. Chem. Engrs.; mem. Am. Inst. of Consulting Engineers, American Chem. Soc., Am. Concrete Inst., Am. Soc. Testing Materials, Ill. Acad. Sci., Sigma Xi, Phi Delta Theta, Tau Beta Pi. Rep. Presbyn. Mason (32 deg., K.T., Shriner), Clubs: Adventures, Engineers (Chgo.). Author of Portland Cement Technology (also in Spanish), second edition in English, 1966; also numerous science and tech. papers. Patentee in cement. Home: Chicago IL Died Apr. 7, 1971; buried Liberty IN

WITTE, FRED(ERICK) C(HRISTOPHER), banker; b. Brooklyn, Oct. 30 1898; s. Fred J. and Dora (Osterheld) W.; ed. pub. schs. Bklyn.; m. Darthea E. Benson, Apr. 1920 (dec.); children—Virginie (Mrs. William C. Miller, Jr.), Barbara (Mrs. Robert Stieglitz). Fred C.; married 2d, Olga A. Wilson, Aug. 20, 1953, Clerk Columbia Trust Company, N.Y.C. 1916-18, Equitable Trust Co., 1918-25, asst. mgr. credit dept., 1925-26, mgr. credit dept., 1926-30, asst. vice pres., 1930, when co. merged with Chase Nat. Bank; 2d vice pres. Chase Nat. Bank, 1930-46, vice pres. in charge of 11 Broad St. Office, 1946-59, v.p. N.Y.C. dist., Met. Dept., head office, 1959-61, v.p. charge Plaza Banking Office, 1961-63. Officer candidate of U.S. Navy, 1918. Member bd. edn. Rockville Centre Public Schs., 1938-47. Mem. Nat. Credit Men's Assn., Robert Morris Assos. (pres. 1950-51), Am. Legion, Newcomen Soc. Rep. Conglist. Clubs: Kiwanis (pres. 1947-48), Hempstead Golf, Skytop. Home: Rockville Centre NY Died Apr. 3, 1972; buried St. John's Meml. Cemetery Cold Spring Harbor NY

WITTEN, HAROLD BRYAN, psychiatrist, hosp. administr.; m.; 3 children. Med. supt. Western State Hosp., Ft. Supply, Okla. Served with M.C. U.S. Army. Diplomate Am. Bd. Psychiatry and Neurology. Kiwanian. Home: Fort Supply OK Died Mar. 19, 1969.

WITTER, DEAN, partner Dean Witter & Co.; b. Wausau, Wis., Aug. 2, 1887; s. Willis Guy and Elizabeth Louise (Gooding) W.; B.S., U. Cal., 1909, LL.D., 1964; m. Helen Josephine Perkins, Feb. 20, 1918; children—William, Dean Jr., Ann (Mrs. Edmond Gillette). With Louis Sloss & Co., 1910-14, Blyth Witter & Co., 1914-24; partner Dean Witter & Co., 1924-69. Served as captain, inf., U.S. Army, 1917-19, 91st Div., A.E.F. 1918 and asst. chief of staff, operations sect. Gen. Staff Hdqrs., Chaumont, France, 1918. Col. Ordnance, U.S. Army, Nov. 1942-44; deputy chief San Francisco Ordnance Dist., 1942-44, served for short period, in charge of contract termination, Ordnance Department, Washington, D.C.; chief San Francisco Ordnance District, 1950-54. Awarded Ordnance Assn. Medal for outstanding service, 1945; Silver Star Meuse Argonne, 1918, also cited for gallantry in action; named to Helm's Hall of Fame for Rowing. Clubs: Pacific Union, Bohemian (San Francisco); Links (N.Y.C.). Home: San Francisco CA Died May 25, 1969.

WITTER, JEAN CARTER, investment banker; b. Humbird, Wis., Jan. 3 1892; s. George F. and Mary Ann (Carter) W.; B.S. U. Cal. 1916; m. Catharine Maurer, Dec. 25, 1917; children—Jean Carter (dec.), William Maurer, Nancy, Thomas Winship. Investment banker, 1916; jr. partner Blyth, Witter & Co., San Francisco, 1922-24; joined in formation Dean Witter & Co., 1924;

rtner, 1924-70; hon. chmn. bd. Dean Witter & Co., c. 1970; dir. I Magnin and Co., Yosemite Park and rry Co., Leslie Salt Co. Entered 1st O.T.C., 1917, sch. from U.S. Army as capt. FA. 1919. Dir. Piedmont al.) Bd. Edn. 1935-47; campaign chmn. San Francisco mmunity Chest, 1940; chmn. Red Cross War Fund mpaign, 1945-46. Mem. Investment Bankers Assn. res. 1938-39). Cal. Alumni Assn. (pres. 1945-46). gent. U. Cal., 1945-46; trustee Mills Coll., 1947-57. em. Zeta Psi. Republican. Mem. Piedmont (Cal.) mmunity Ch. Clubs: Pacific-Union. Bohemian. mmercial. San Francisco Golf. Commonwealth of l. Bond (San Francisco); Claremont Country akland, Cal.); Cypress Point (Pebble Beach); cCloud River. Died June 24, 1972.

ITTKE, CARL FREDERICK, coll. adminstr.; b. lumbus, O., Nov. 13, 1892; s. Carl William Oswald d Caroline (Kropp) W.; A.B., Ohio State U., 1913; M., Harvard, 1914, Ph.D., 1921, LL.D., Lawrence llege, 1946, Fenn Coll., 1955; Litt.D., Marietta llege, 1951, Denison U., 1959; L.H.D., Lake Erie llege, 1956, Ohio State University, Columbus, Ohio, 63; m. Lillian Boeshans, 1916 (died 1918); married , Lillian Nippert, 1921; 1 son, Carl Francis. Instructor history, Ohio State Univ., 1916-21, asst. prof., 21-25, prof., 1925-37, chmn. of dept., 1925-37; prof. story, dean, Oberlin Coll., 1937-48; prof. history, dean ad. sch., Western Res. U., 1948-63, v.p., 1961-63; ctr. history U. Ia., 1924-25; prof. history, summers, U. ngo., 1926, 27, U. W.Va., 1930, 31. Decorated comdr. rder Merit (Republic West Germany). Bd. editors iss Valley Hist. Review, 1927-32, 50-53, Canadian ist. Rev., 1932-35, Ohio Archeol. and Hist. Quarterly, 34-71. Mem. Social Sci. Research Council, 1931-35. em. Am. Hist. Assn., Miss. Valley Historical ssociation (pres. 1940-41), Am. Assn. University ofessors; chairman Ohio War Records Commission, 41-47; Phi Beta Kappa (senator, 1946-52); honorary ember Deutsche Akademie, 1932; fellow Royal Hist. c. Appointed by Deutsche Akademie of Munich to liver George Washington Lectures" before German ivs., to celebrate the 200th anniversary of ashington's Birth, 1932. Author: The History of nglish Parliamentary Privilege, 1921; A History of anada, 1928, rev. edits., 1933, 1941; Tambo and ones—A History of the American Minstrel Stage, 30; George Washington und Seine Zeit, 1933; erman-Americans and the World War, 1936; We Who uilt America: The Saga of the Immigrant, 1939; gainst the Current: The Life of Karl Heinzen, 1945; he Utopian Communist, A Biography of Wilhelm eitling, 1950; Refugees of Revolution, 1952; The Irish America, 1956; The German Language Press in merica, 1957; William Nast: Patriarch of German ethodism, 1960; The First Fifty Years, The Cleveland useum of Art, 1916-66, 1966. Contbr. to historical agazines Editor: Prentice-Hall history series 1931-46; istory of the State of Ohio (6 vols.). Home: Cleveland H Died May 24, 1971.

ITTKOWER, RUDOLF, educator; b. Berlin, ermany, June 22, 1901; s. Henry and Gertrude nsbach) W.; Ph.D., U. Berlin, 1923; student U. unich; Dr. Fine Arts (hon.) Duke University, 1969; n. degrees Columbia, 1969, Leeds U. (Eng.), 1971; m. argot Holzmann, Dec. 31, 1923; 1 son, Mario Max. ssistant, research fellow Bibliotheca Hertziana, Rome, aly, 1923-32; lectr. Cologne U., 1932-33; staff arburg Inst., U. London, 1934-56, reader U. London, 45, prof., 1949; prof., chmn. art history and chaeology, Columbia, 1956-69, Avalon Found. prof. neritus in humanities, 1969-71; Kress professor ational Gallery, Washington, 1969-71. Slade prof. fine ts Cambridge U. (Eng.), 1970-71; mem. Inst. dvanced Studies, 1971. Hon. trustee Met. Mus. Art. ecipient Serena medal, British Academy, 1957; anister Fletcher prize, 1960; Guggenheim fellow, 61-62. Fellow British Academy, Warburg Institute, merican Academy of Arts and Sciences, Am. Philos. c., Royal Institute of British Architects (hon.); ember Archaeol. Institute Great Britain and Ireland, enaissance Soc. Am., Society Archtl. Historians, ollege Art Assn., Accademia Olimpica, Vicenza, ccademia dei Lincei, Rome, Accademia di Belle Arti, enice, Accademia delle Scienze, Turin, Phi Beta appa. corresponding member of the Max Planck esellschaft (Gottingen). Author: British Art and the editerranean, 1948; Architectural Principles in the ge of Humanism, 1949; Gianlorenzo Bernini, 1955; rt and Architecture in Italy, 1600-1750, 1958; Born nder Saturn, 1963. Home: New York City NY Died ct. 11, 1971.

ITTNER, FRED, advt. and public relations exec.; b. klyn., Aug. 26, 1909; s. Frederick and Cecilia (Bakel) .; B.A., U. Wis., 1931; m. Miriam Halperin, Aug. 30, 934; children—Simon David, Judith Ann (dec.), eborah Ellen. Sports staff New York Herald Tribune, 931-35; asso. Amelia Earhart & George Palmer utnam, 1935-37; asso. editor Sports Illustrated and merican Golfer, 1938-39; pres. Fred Wittner Co., Inc., 939-72, chmn., 1968-72; pres. Fred Wittner Pub. elations, Inc., 1961-72. Mem. U.S. Dept. Commerce's rade Mission to Yugoslavia, 1958; dir. Audit Bur. of irculations. Vice pres., dir. Music for Westchester mphony Orch. Recipient Distinguished Service citation U. Wis. Sch. Journalism, 1964. Mem. Am. Assn. Advt. Agys. (chmn. bus. publs. com. 1958-61, sec.-treas., bd. govs. Eastern region), Indsl. Advertisers Assn., Pub. Relations Soc. Am., Silurians, Sigma Delta Chi, Alpha Delta Sigma. Jewish religion (trustee temple). Clubs: Lotos (N.Y.C.); Fairview Country (Greenwich, Conn.). Home: Scarsdale NY Died July 6, 1972.

WITTY, WILLIAM HENRY;, b. McCracken County, Ky., Feb. 3, 1872; s. Henry Hawkins and Minerva Elmus (McKinney) W.; A.B., Blandville (Ky.) Bapt. Coll., 1895; hon. LL.D., Lindfield Coll., McMinnville, Ore.; m. Annie Christian Terrell, June 9, 1895 (died 1937); children—Richmond (dec.), Mary Elizabeth (wife of Dr. Frederic P. Hoskyn, Ph.D.); m. 2d, Esther Olson, May 21, 1938. Elected president Blandville College, 1895, and taught there and at Clinton Coll. 8 yrs.; began practice of law at Wickliffe, Ky., 1896; moved to Pocatello, Ida., 1904; city atty. Pocatello during 3 administrations, 1906-15; county atty. Bannock County, 1911; mem. Ida. Senate 2 terms, 1919-22. Active worker in Bapt. Ch.; was vice pres. Ida. Bapt. State Conv.; mem. exec. com. Men's Church League of New York; mem. General Council of Northern Bapt. Conv.; also mem. Council of Finance and Promotion of same conv.; mem. advisory council of Nat. Conf. of Jews and Christians; mem. administrative com. Intermountain Evang. Conf.; mem. advisory council of Yenching Univ., Peiping, China. Trustee Berkeley (Calif.) Divinity Sch., Westminster Coll., Salt Lake City, Utah, also of Colorado Woman's Coll., Denver, Colo. Member American, Ida., Ky. and Calif. State bar assns. Republican. Mason (32 deg., K.T., Shriner). Clubs: University, Shrine, Pocatello Country. Home: 656 W. Lewis St. Office: Pioneer Bldg., Pocatello ID*‡

WOERTENDYKE, JAMES H., lecturer; b. Monmouth, Ill., Nov. 24, 1869; s. Frederick and Mary Elizabeth (Romans) W.; self-educated; Ph.D., LL.B. Admitted to bar, 1904; chmn. Prohibition Party of Calif., 1909-13; returned to Ill., 1918; Prohibition candidate for Gov. of Ill., 1920; lecturer with Flying Squadron, Aug. 1921-June 1923; pres. Nat. League to Enforce Laws; gen. mgr. World League of Christian Faith. Methodist. Good Templar. Address: 2825 Troost Av., Kansas City MO*‡

WOGAN, JOHN B., army officer; b. New Orleans, La., Jan. 1, 1890; s. John A. and Marguerite H. (Beugnot) W.; A.B., Coll. of Immaculate Conception (now Loyola U.), 1908; student Spring Hill Coll., Mobile, Ala., 1906-07; B.S. U.S. Mil. Acad., 1915; grad. Command and Gen. Staff Sch., 1930, Army War Coll., 1933; m. Grace MacLain, July 7, 1921; children—Mary Patricia, John B. Commd. 2d lt., Coast Arty., U.S. Army, 1915, and advanced through the grades to brig. gen., Feb. 1942, major gen., Sept. 1942; served on Mexican Border Campaign, 1916; served as capt., later major, Coast Arty. Corps, France, Sept. 1917-Oct. 1920, taking part in Battles of St. Mihiel and Meuse-Argonne; transferred to Field Arty., Sept. 1920; served at Fort Sill, 1920-24; R.O.T.C., Harvard, 1924-28; comdg. 2d F.A. Batn., Panama Canal, 1930-32; Gen. Staff, War Dept., public relations, 1933-37; instr. Field Arty. Sch., 1937-40; comd. 68th F.A. Regt., 1940-41; chief of staff, 5th Armored Div., Aug. 1941-Jan. 1942, comd. Combat Command B" 2d Armored Div., Fort Benning, Ga., Jan.-July 1942; Commanding 13th Armored Div., Camp Beale, Calif., 1942-44; served in European Theater, Dec. 1944-Apr. 1945; participated in battle of the Bulge and battle of the Ruhr; severely wounded in Ruhr battle, Apr. 15, 1945; retired as maj. gen. for combat wounds, Oct. 31, 1946. Mgr. Veterans' Hosp., Oteen, N.C. Feb. 15, 1947. Decorated D.S.M., Silver Star, Legion of Merit, Purple Heart; E.T.O. campaign ribbon with 2 battle stars; Legion of Honor, Croix de Guerre (French). Mem. Asheville Civitan Club, Mark Twain Soc., Soc. Promotion and Encouragement of Barber Shop Quartet Singing in Am., Inc., Am. Legion, Disabled Am. Vets. K.C. (4th deg.). Clubs: Biltmore Forest Country, Mens Garden, Executives. Home: Ashville NC Died Sept. 30, 1968; buried Arlington Nat. Cemetery, Arlington VA

WOHLSEN, RALPH J., archtl. exec., churchman; b. Lancaster, Pa., Mar. 20, 1897; s. Peter Nicholas and Anna Susan (Schwebel) W.; corr. grad. U. Chgo., 1924; m. Mabel Mae McComsey, Oct. 3, 1917; 1 dau., Jean Eloise (Mrs. Theodore V. Zaloudek). Owner bldg. firm, 1919-25; mgr. White Plains br. Mahlstedt Lumber & Coal Co., 1926-34; sales exec. Leon Co., Yonkers, N.Y., 1935-42; organizer White Wholesale Milwork, 1943, chmn. bd., 1943-52. Archtl. exec. Louis Jallade, N.Y.C., Cross & Cross, N.Y.C., Fletcher-Thompson, Inc., Bridgeport, Conn. & Clifton, N.J., William F. Griffin & Assos., 1952-63; owner, operator The Wohlsen Drafting Service, Lititz, Pa. Archtl. works include, Orthodox Cathedral, Clifton, N.J., Am. Legion Home, Lancaster, Pa. pres.'s house Hartwick Coll., Oneonta, N.Y., Ascension Luth. Ch., Lancaster, Pa. Internat. pres. United Luth. Ch. Men, 1948-52. Served as pvt., M.C., U.S. Army, 1917-18. Mem. Luth. Brotherhood (hon. life), Am. Legion, Vets. 1st World War. Mason (32 deg., Shriner). Rotarian. Home: Lititz PA Deceased.

WOJDYLA, HENRY EDWARD, college counselor; b. Lublin, Wis., Aug. 2, 1918; s. Stanley and Mary (Rampala) W.; B.A. with honors, Sacramento State Coll., 1951; M.A., Baylor U., 1953-55; student St. Louis U., 1959; m. Gloria Mohn, May 20, 1944; children—Henry Edward, Richard. Enlisted USAAF, 1941, commd. and advanced through grades to col. USAF; squadron comdr. Connally AFB, Tex., 1953-55; exec. officer 13th Air Force, Clarke AFB, Philippines, 1956-57; asso. prof. St. Louis U., 1957-59; prof. air sci. Washington U., St. Louis, 1959-61; mem. faculty USAF Acad., 1961-68, prof. behavioral scis., head dept., 1963-68, ret., 1968; counselor Am. River Coll., Sacramento, 1968-71; Distinguished vis. prof. U. So. Cal., summer 1967; vis. lectr. Decorated Legion of Merit, 1968, D.F.C. with 2 oak leaf clusters, Army Commendation ribbon Air medal with 3 oak leaf clusters. Mem. Am., Rocky Mountain, Colo. psychol. assn., Soc. Clin. and Extl. Hypnosis, Nat. Council Family Relations, Acad. Behavioral Scis. (pres.), Spl. Research ednl. methodology and use hypnosis in hypnotherapy and learning. Home: Citrus Heights CA Died Nov. 11, 1971; buried U.S. Air Force Academy CO

WOLBARST, ABRAHAM LEO, physician; b. New York City, Aug. 4, 1872; s. Bernard and Jane (Appel) W.; student Coll. of City of N.Y., 1887-91, Coll. of Phys. and Surgs., Columbia U., 1894-98; m. Bessie Bernstein, Oct. 14, 1909 (died Apr. 13, 1938); children—Bernard Paul, John; m. 2d, Miriam Newmark, June 6, 1942. Attending and cons. urol. various hosps., N.Y. City; studied with Ehrlich and Wassermann, 1910 (secured trial supply of 606); former asso. editor, Jour. Internat. Coll. of Surg.; invented several new instruments and procedures notably 5-glass catheter test for diagnosis in urinary disease. Ret. Dir., treas. Euthanasia Soc. of Am.; mem. of Founders Group of Am. Bd. Urology. Mem. A.M.A., Am. Urological Assn., Am. Neisserian Assn., Am. Professional Artists League. Mason. Clubs: New York Musicians (Bohemians), New Era (founder). Translated and edited: Treatise on Cystoscopy and Urethrascopy (from the French), 1918; Treatment of Syphilis with Salvarsan (from the German), 1911. Author: Healthy Sex Life, 1930; Gonococcal Infection in the Male, 1927. Contbr. some 200 articles and editorials to med. jours. First prize in sculpture, Am. Phys. Art Assn., 1940. Home: 140 W. 69th St., New York 23‡

WOLCOTT, JESSE PAINE, govt. ofcl.; b. Gardner, Mass., Mar. 3, 1893; s. William B. and Lillis B. (Paine) W.; ed. Detroit Tech. Inst.; LL.B., Detroit Coll. Law; m. Grace A. Sullivan, Feb. 26, 1927; 1 son, Jesse Paine. Practice of law, Detroit, 1915-19, Port Huron, Mich., 1919-61; asst. police judge, Port Huron, 1921; asst. pros. atty., St. Clair County, 1922-26, pros. atty., 1927-30; member of the board Federal Deposit Insurance Corporation, chairman board, 1957-61. Member 72d to 84th Congresses, 7th Dist. Mich. Served as 2d lt. U.S. Army, World War I; AEF in France. Recipient Collier award for distinguished Congl. services, 1946. Mem. Vets. Fgn. Wars (Mich. comdr. 1925-26), Am. Legion. Republican. Universalist. Mason, K.P. (past chancellor), Odd Fellow, Elk, Lion (dist. gov. 1926-27). Home: Chevy Chase MD Died Jan. 28, 1969; buried Arlington Nat. Cemetery, Arlington VA

WOLCOTT, L. W., paint co. exec.; b. Wauseon, O., Sept. 2, 1872; s. Miles L. and Mary Jane (Lathrop) W.; ed. high sch. and Coll. of Pharmacy; married, Feb. 29, 1892; children—Van K., Robert L.; m. 2d, Sept. 1, 1933. Pharmacist, 1890-1900; with The Sherwin-Williams Co., Cleveland, since 1900, now dir.; dir. Oliver United Filters Co., Oakland, Calif. Mason (Shriner). Clubs: Bohemian (San Francisco); Claremont Country (Oakland). Home: 275 Alvarado Rd., Berkeley CA Office: The Sherwin-Williams Co., 3423 Piedmont Av., Oakland CA*‡

WOLCOTT, ROGER, lawyer; b. Milton, Mass., July 25, 1877; s. Roger (Gov. of Mass.) and Edith (Prescott) W.; A.B., cum laude, Harvard, 1899, LL.B., 1902; m. Claire Morton Prince, June 7, 1904; children—Roger (dec.), Clarissa (dec.), John Endicott (dec.); m. 2d, Barbara Hinkley Welch, June 21, 1928; 1 dau., Susan. Admitted to Mass. bar, 1902, began practice in law dept. Boston Elevated Ry. Co.; alone since 1906; trustee Suffolk Savings Bank. Private, 1st Mass. Heavy Arty., U.S. Vols., Spanish-Am. War; maj. inf. U.S. Army, here in charge Selective Draft, Mass., World War I; also v.p. N.E. Italian War Relief; treas. Friends of Poland; mem. Mass. Com. Public Safety; lt. col., insp. gen. and col. Mass. Nat. Guard (ret. 1910). Former chmn. bd. of selectmen, Milton; former member Mass. State Bd. of Insanity; former repr. in gen. court; former mem. Selective Service Board No. 103, Mass.; former overseer Harvard; trustee Boston Athenaeum. Member Massachusetts State and Boston bar assns., Mass. Hist. Soc. (mem. council; corr. sec.), Am. Antiquarian Soc., Soc. Colonial Wars, Massachusetts Soc. of Cincinnati (past pres.), Loyal Legion, United Spanish War Veterans, Mil. Order of World Wars. Agent (class 1899), former chmn. council Harvard Fund; class sec., Harvard Coll., 1899. Republican. Unitarian. Clubs: Milton (ex-pres.), Somerset; Union (ex-pres.), Harvard (Boston). Editor: The Correspondence of William

Hickling Prescott (1833-1847), 1925. Author: Family Jottings, 1939. Home: Milton MA Office: 60 State St., Boston MA

WOLDMAN, ALBERT ALEXANDER, lawyer; b. Russia, Jan. 1 1897; s. Isaac and Gertrude (Kudysh) W.; brought to U.S., 1898; A.B., Western Reserve U. 1917; student Western Reserve Law Sch., 1918; LL.B., Ohio Northern University, 1919; LL.D., Monrovia University, 1956; married Lydia Levin July 3, 1921; children—Robert Morton, Phyllis Joy, Stuart. Editor South Brooklyn (O.) Herald, 1916; reporter Cleveland Press, 1917, Cleveland Plain Dealer, 1918; asst. state editor Cleveland Plain Dealer, 1918-19; admitted to Ohio bar, 1919, and since practiced in Cleveland, editor Every Boy's Mag., 1920, Real Estate Outlook, 1921; teacher legal history and constl. law, John Marshall Sch. Law, Cleveland, from 1936; dir. Dept. Indsl. Relations of State of O., 1949-53; judge Juvenile Ct. Cuyahoga County (Cleve.), 1953-71. Asst. law dir. of Cleveland, 1941-45; chmn. bd. review, Bur. Unemployment Compensation, State of O., 1945-49; mem. cabinet gov. Ohio, 1949-53. Bd. trustees Cultural Gardens Assn., Cleveland Community Religious Hour. Mem. Ohio, Cuyahoga County (sec.) and Cleveland bar assns., Miss. Valley Hist. Assn., Abraham Lincoln Assn. of Ohio (president), Abraham Lincoln Assn. (Springfield, Ill.). Chicago Civil War Round Table; honorary mem. Lincoln Fellowship of Southern Cal., Tau Epsilon Rho (hon.). Democrat. K.P., B'nai B'rith (pres. dist. 2, Grand Lodge). Club: City (Cleveland). Author: Lawyer Lincoln, 1936; Mightier Than the Sword, 1940; Lincoln and the Russians, 1952; The Governors of Ohio, 1954. Contbr. to newspapers and legal jours. Home: Cleveland OH Died Dec. 30, 1971; buried Cleveland OH

WOLF, AUGUST STEPHEN, chemist Equitable Assurance Soc. since April 1, 1900; b. New York, April 2, 1869; s. Stephen and Marguerita W.; ed'n at Middletown, N.Y.; grad. New York Coll. of Pharmacy, Ph. G., 1889; m. Aug. 2, 1894, Henrietta Taylor, of Woodstock, Vt. Passed exam. in med. chemistry and toxicology, Bellevue Hosp. Med. Coll.; expert in urinary analysis. Mem. A.A.A.S., Soc. Chem. Industry. Residence: 540 W. 112th St. Office: 120 Broadway, New York NY‡

WOLF, CHARLES GEORGE LEWIS, chemist; b. London, Eng., Nov. 6, 1872; s. Joseph and Isobel (Davis) W.; A.B., Manitoba College, Can., 1890; C.M., M.D., McGill Univ., Montreal, 1894; studied chemistry at Cambridge and Wirzburg univs. and King's Coll., London, 1896-9; unmarried. Asst. prof. chemistry, Cornell Univ. Med. Coll., New York, since 1900. Author: Elements of Stereo-Chemistry (translation Hantzch's Stereochemie), 1901; Physiological Chemistry, 1902. Contbr. papers on chemical and med. subjects to jours. and chemical soc. transactions. Home: 128 Lexington Av., New York NY‡

WOLF, LEONARD GEORGE, found. exec.; b. Mazomanie, Wis., 1925; s. Frank C. and Gertrude (Linley) W.; B.S. in Agrl. Econs., U. Wis., m. Marilyn Margaret Adams, July 2, 1949; children—Steven Michael, Ann Marilyn, Jennifer Elizabeth. Propr. retail feed bus., 1953-58; travel lectures on Europe, Iron Curtain countries; mem. 86th Congress, 2d Dist. Ia.; dir. Food for Peace, Brazil, 1961-65; coordinator Operation Ninos, AID, Dept. State, later with Bur. Inter-American Affairs, Bur. for Latin AID, Department of State, Washington, D.C.; exec. dir. Am. Freedom from Hunger Found., 1968-71. Active youth activities, rural and urban. Served with USNR, World War II. Mem. Am. Legion. Democrat, Eagle, Lion. Home: Washington DC Died Mar. 28, 1970; buried Mazomanie WI

WOLFE, ALBERT BENEDICT, teacher; b. Arlington, Ill., Aug. 23, 1876; s. William Henry and Jane Losee (Tompkins) W.; student Ill. State Normal Sch., 1895-98; A.B., Harvard, 1902, A.M., 1903, Ph.D., 1905; m. Clara May Snell, Sept. 6, 1906. Instr. in English, Ill. State Normal Sch., summers, 1900, 1902; instr. in history, McKinley High Sch., St. Louis, 1904-05; asso. prof. economics and sociology, 1905-07, prof., 1907-14, Oberlin Coll.; prof. economics and sociology, U. of Tex., 1914-23; statis. expert, War Trade License Bd., 1917; head investigation service Industrial Relations Div., Emergency Fleet Corp., Phila., 1918; prof. economics, Ohio State U., 1923-46, emeritus professor since 1946; visiting professor economics, University of California, 1931-32. Member American Economic Association (asso. editor 1931-34, v.p. 1936, pres. 1943), Am. Assn. of Univ. Profs., Population Assn. America. Democrat. Author: The Lodging House Problem in Boston, 1906; Readings in Social Problems, 1916; Works Committees and Industrial Councils, 1919; Conservatism, Radicalism and Scientific Method, 1923; (with Columbus 8 OH‡

WOLFE, JAMES EDWARD, r.r. exec.; b. Shelbina, Mo., June 11 1902; s. William and Mary Ann (Butler) W.; student St. Joseph's Acad., Hannibal, Mo.; m. Grace A. Kirn, Nov. 21, 1928; 1 son, James R. With C., B&Q R.R., from 1918 beginning as machinist helper, successively machinist, yard clk., chief yard clk., chief timekeeper, switchman, yardmaster, supr. wage schedules, staff officer to exec. v.p., asst. to v.p., asst. v.p., v.p. personnel, from 1957. Mem., vice chmn. Western Carriers' Conf. Com., in wage and other union demand cases, from 1950. Mem. Ill. C. of C., Chgo. Assn. Commerce and Industry, Nat. Planning Assn. (nat. council), Clubs: Executives, Boys, Western Railway. Traffic. Union League (Chgo.). Home: Clarendon Hills IL Died Oct. 1, 1971.

WOLFE, KENNETH B., retired army officer and business executive; born in Denver, Colorado, August 12, 1896; son of George Frank and Selma Wilhelmena (Franzen) W.; grad. San Diego High Sch., 1915; grad. U.S. Sch. Mil. Aeronautics, Berkeley, Calif., 1918, Air Service Flying Instrs. Sch., San Antonio, 1918; Air Corps Engr. Sch., Wright Field, 1931, Air Corps Tactical School, Maxwell Field, 1936, Command and Gen. Staff Sch., 1937; m. Edwina Ray, Jan. 14, 1922 (dec. Dec. 1964); 1 dau., Beverley Ray; m. 2d, Margaret Parker, Hall, August 7, 1965. Began as flying cadet, United States Army, January 14, 1918; commissioned 2d lieutenant July 1918, advanced through grades to lieutenant gen., Sept. 1949; comdg. gen. 20th Bomber Commd. (first B-29 orgn. to bomb Japan), June 5, 1943-July 8, 1944; comdg. gen. Materiel Command, July-Sept. 1944; comdg. gen. Fifth Air Force (occupational air force, Japan and Korea), 1945-48; dir. procurement indsl. planning, Air Material Command, U.S.A.F., Wright-Patterson Field, Dayton, 1948-49; became deputy chief of staff Materiel, Hdqrs. U.S. Air Force, Washington, 1949; retired from service; pres., Oerlikon Tool & Arms Corp., 1951-56; asst. to chem. Garrett Corp., 1956-57, sr. v.p., director, 1957-65; cons. Garrett Corp., Cohu Electronics, Inc.; dir. Automation Industries, Los Angeles, Cal. Mem. Nat. Security Indsl. Assn. (hon.), Order of Daedalians. Home: San Marcos CA Died Sept. 20, 1971; buried Arlington Nat. Cemetery, Arlington VA

WOLFE, RICHARD RUSSELL, lawyer; b. Parsons, Kan., Sept. 24, 1907; s. M. R. and Gertrude (Hart) W.; student U.S. Naval Acad., 1925-27; B.S. in Elec. Engring., Mass. Inst. Tech., 1929, M.S., 1930; LL.B., George Washington U., 1934; m. Elizabeth Eleanor Laughlin, June 17, 1930; 1 daughter, Elizabeth Gertrude (Mrs. John Twyeffort Hubbell). Admitted to Dist. Columbia bar, 1934, Ill. bar, 1937; practice in Chgo., 1956-70; with patent dept. Gen. Electric Co., 1930-35; asso. Parker, Carlson, Pitzner & Hubbard, 1936-43; partner Carlson, Pitzner, Hubbard & Wolfe, 1943-58; sr. partner Wolfe, Hubbard, Voit & Osann, 1959-70. Fellow Am. Coll. Trial Lawyers; mem. Am., Chgo. bar assns., Am., Chgo. patent law assns., Am. Judicature Soc. Clubs: Chicago University; Exmoor Country. Home: Deerfield IL Died Apr. 29, 1970; buried Chico Cemetery, Chico CA

WOLFE, THOMAS KENNERLY, agronomist; b. Elkton, Va., July 14, 1892; s. Joseph Henry and Elizabeth (Coffman) W.; B.S., Va. Poly. Inst., Blacksburg, 1914, M.S., 1915; Ph.D., Cornell U., 1921; m. Helen Hughes, June 27, 1923. Asst. in agronomy, Va. Poly. Inst., 1914-15, instr. in agronomy, 1915-17, asso. prof. agronomy, 1917-23, prof., 1923-27; also asst. agronomist Va. Agrl. Expt. Sta., 1915-17, asso. agronomist, 1917-23, agronomist, 1923-27; editor Southern Planter, 1927-33; mgr. fertilizer service, later distribution service, Southern States Coop., since 1934. Asst. comdt. Va. Poly. Inst., 1914-16. Mem. Phi Kappa Phi, Sigma Xi. Democrat. Author: (with T. B. Hutcheson) The Production of Field Crops, 1924, rev. 1937, 48, 53. Contbr. bulls. Va. Expt. Sta. Discoverer of superiority of unhulled sweet clover seed over scarified seed. Home: Richmond VA Died 1972.

WOLFERS, ARNOLD OSCAR, univ. prof.; b. St. Gallen, Switzerland, June 14, 1892; s. Otto Gustav and Clara Eugenie (Hirschfield) W.; J.U.D. summa cum laude, U. of Zurich, 1917; Ph.D., U. of Giessen, 1924; Litt.D. (hon.), Mt. Holyoke Coll., South Hadley, Mass., 1935; A.M. (hon.), Yale, 1935; LL.D. (hon.) University of Rochester, 1945; student of law, univs. of Lausanne, Munich and Berlin, 1912-17, of economics and political science, univs. of Zurich and Berlin, 1920-24; m. Doris Emmy Forrer, May 13, 1918. Came to U.S., 1933, naturalized, 1939. Admitted to bar, Switzerland, 1917; engaged in practice of law, St. Gallen, 1917-19; lecturer in polit. science, Hochschule fur Politik, Berlin, 1924-30, dir. of Hochschule, 1930-33; privatdozent in economics, U. of Berlin, 1929-33; visiting prof. internat. relations, Yale, 1933-35, prof. internat. relations, 1935-49, Sterling Professor internat. relations, 1949-57, emeritus, 1957-68, master Pierson Coll., 1935-50; director Johns Hopkins Washington Center of Fgn. Policy Research, 1957-65, spl. adv., research asso., 1965-68; mem. resident faculty of Nat. War College, Washington, D.C., 1947, mem. bd. cons., 1947-51; cons. E.C.A., 1951. President of the World Peace Foundation, 1953. Served as first lieutenant in the infantry, Swiss Army, 1917-19. Special advisor and lecturer, Sch. of Mil. Govt., Charlottesville, Va., 1942-44; expert consultant Office of Provost Marshal Gen., 1942-44; cons. OSS, 1944-45. Inst. for Defense Analyses, 1960-61; cons. to Dept. of State, 1960-68. General rapporteur Internat. Studies Conf., London, 1933; mem. internat. adv. council Inst. Strategic Studies. Mem. Am. Polit. Sci. Assn., Council Fgn. Relations (N.Y.). Clubs: Yale, Century Associati (New York City); Cosmos (Washington, D.C.). Auth Die Verwaltungsorgane der Aktiengesellschaft, 191 Amerikanische und Deutsche Loehne, 1930; D Kartellproblem, 1931; Britain and France between Tv Wars, 1940; also of Discord and Collaboration, 196 Editor: (with L. Martin) The Anglo American Traditi in Foreign Affairs, 1956. Editor, Alliance Policy in t Cold War, 1959; Developments in Military Technolo and Their Impact on United States Strategy and Forei Policy, 1959. Home: Washington DC Died July 1968; buried Sils Baseglia, Engadin Switzerland

WOLFF, FRANK ALFRED, physicist; b. Baltimo Md., Apr. 8, 1871; s. Frank Andrew and There (Haupt) W.; A.B., Johns Hopkins, 1890, Ph.D., 189 fellow in physics and chemistry, 1892-93; studied U. Leipzig, 1894; m. Lillian Marie Jones, Jan. 28, 189 children—Frances H., Lyman H. Expert physicist Bu of Soils, U.S. Dept. of Agr., 1894-96; prof. physics ar elec. engring., Columbia (now George Washington) U 1894-1908; in office Standard Weights and Measure 1897-1901; asso. physicist, Bur. of Standards, 1901-1 physicist, 1917-24, prin. physicist, 1928, now pri telephone engr.; detailed to Federal Communicatio Commn., 1935-37. Engaged since establishment bureau in development of improved apparatus ar methods of measurement, and in research on th internat. standards of resistance and electromotiv force, and on the development of standards of servic for telephone utilities. Especially active in economi and its relation to the stabilization of the purchasir power of the dollar; the analysis of government expenditures and revenues; the principles underlyir public utility regulation and valuation, standardizatio and municipal advancement; retired Apr. 1941. Chi dept. social economy, Panama P.I. Expn., 1913-1 Mem. Am. Inst. E.E. Home: 2957 Tilden, Washingto DC*‡

WOLFIT, DONALD, actor-manager; b. Newark, Eng Apr. 20, 1902; s. William Pearce and Emm (Tomlinson) W.; ed. Magnus Sch., Newark; m. Rosalin Iden Payne, Apr. 20, 1948; children—Margaret, Harri (Mrs. John Graham), Adam Pearce. Began acting caree 1920; presented own company in Shakespeare, 1936-5 New Century Theatre, N.Y.C., 1947; latest stag appearances in London include All in Good Time an The Strong Are Lonely, Robert and Elizabeth, Treasur Island, John Gabriel Borkman; recent motion pictur appearances include Room at the Top, Lawrence Arabia, Becket, Dr. Crippen, Life at the Top; als numerous television and radio broadcasts; di Advanced Player Assn. Ltd. Pres. Royal Ge Theatrical Fund. Created knight. 1957; comdr. Ord British Empire, 1949. Clubs: Garrick (London); Playe (N.Y.C.). Author: (autobiography) First Interval, 195 Home: Andover Hampshire England Died Feb. 1968

WOLFORD, LEO THORP, lawyer; b. Linton, Ind May 1, 1890; s. Edwin Lafayette and Anna Emil (Thorp) W.; A.B., Franklin Coll. of Ind., 1912, LL.D 1948; J.D., U. Chgo., 1915; m. Leah Jackson, Sept. 1916 (dec. 1918); 1 son, Thorp Lanier. Admitted to K bar, 1919; partner firm Bruce & Bullitt, Louisvill 1921-42, Bullitt & Middleton, 1942-48, Middleto Seelbach, Wolford, Willis & Cochran, 1948-71; v.p., di Louisville Title Ins. Co.; dir. Royal Crown Bottling C Louisville Title Co., Louisville Gas & Elec. Co. Pa pres. Estate Planning Council of Louisville. Pres. b trustees Louisville Free Pub. Library; bd. dirs. So. Bap Theol. Sem., Franklin Coll. Served with U.S. Arm World War I; mem. Alien Hearing Bd., World War I Mem. Am. Ky., Louisville bar assns., Nat. Titl Underwriters Assn. (p.p.), Kappa Delta Rho (past na pres.). Democrat. Baptist. Clubs: Filson (pres., dir. Lawyers, Pendennis. Conversation (Louisville). Home Louisville KY Died Dec. 6, 1971; buried Cave Hi Cemetery, Louisville KY

WOLFROM, MELVILLE L(AWRENCE), chemis born Bellevue, O., Apr. 2, 1900; s. Frederick and Mari Louisa (Sutter) W.; A.B., Ohio State U., 1924; M.Sc Northwestern, 1925, Ph.D., 1927; Guggenheim fellow U. of Zurich, 1939; m. Agnes Louise Thompson, Jun 1, 1926; children—Frederick L., (dec.), Eva M., (Mrs David Frank), Betty J. (Mrs. Chalmers G. Hixson, Jr. Anne M. (Mrs. Wilson Fleming, Jr.), Carl T. Engage as development chemist with National Carbo Company, Fremont, O., 1917-18; U.S. Gypsum Co Gypsum, O. and Chicago, summers 1921-24; asst. inst chemistry Northwestern, 1924-27; Nat. Researc Council fellow in chemistry Nat. Bur. Standard Rockefeller Inst. for Med. Research, Ohio State U 1927-29, instr. in chemistry, 1929-30, asst. prof 1930-36, asso prof., 1936-40, prof., 1940-69, head div organic chemistry, 1948-60, research prof., 1960-65 Regents' prof., 1965-69. An ofcl. investigator Nat. De Research Com., 1940-45; chmn. symposium Internat Union Biochemistry, Vienna, Austria, 1958. Serve S.A.T.C., 1918. Recipient citation Government o Austria, 1959; Austin M. Patterson award for chem documentation Dayton chpt. Am. Chem. Soc., 1967 Kenneth A. Spencer award Kansas City sect. Am Chem. Soc., 1967; Wolfrom meml. issue Jour Carbohydrate Research pub. in his honor, 1970. Mem A.A.A.S., Am. Chem. Soc. (chmn. cellulose div. 1940 sugar div. 1948, chmn. carbohydrate romenclature com. carbohydrate div.), Am. Assn. Cereal Chemists, Nat. Acad. Scis., Am. Acad. Arts and Scis., Am. Soc. Biol. Chemists, Chem. Soc. (London), N.Y. Acad. Science, Ohio Acad. Sci., Technical Association Pulp and Paper Industry, Phi Beta Kappa, Sigma Xi, Phi Lambda Upsilon, Pi Mu Epsilon, Alpha Chi Sigma. Co-editor: Advances in Carbohydrate Chemistry, 1945-49, 52-69; editor Methods in Carbohydrate Chemistry; editor carbohydrates sect. Chem. Abstracts 1959-69; adv. bd. Chem. Abstracts Service, 1964-69. Author articles on organic chemistry of carbohydrates and natural products in chem. jours. Home: Columbus OH Died June 20, 1969; buried Bellevue OH

WOLFSON, HOWARD E(DWARD), mfg. exec.; b. Chgo., Dec. 5, 1898; s. Simon and Dora (Maremont) W.; student Greer Coll, Northwestern U., 1930-32; m. Harriet Levitt, Mar. 4, 1948; children—Dorothy, James, Madeline. With Maremont Corporation (formerly Maremont Automotive Products, Incorporated), 1917-70, as warehouse worker, prodn. employee, inventory, order depts., prodn. control, sales dept., charge sales of spring div., organizer market procedures, sales mgr., sec., pres., 1942-70, chmn. 1953-70; bd. Internat. Furniture Co., 1948-50. Market research com. NPA, World War II; automotive indsl. adv. bd. Gen. Service Adminstrn. Vice chmn. automotive sect. Community Fund; chmn. automotive section United Jewish Appeal. President Chgo. chpt. Brandeis. Sec., mem. bd. Jewish Welfare Fund; mem. bd. Gastro-Intestinal Research Found. Founder Roosevelt Coll. Jewish religion (hon. mem. bd.). Clubs: Standard (mem. bd.), Executive (Chgo.). Home: Chicago IL Died Mar. 12, 1970.

WOLFSON, KURT, corp. exec.; b. Landeshut, Germany, June 29, 1898; s. Arno and Margaret (Eisenstaedt) W.; B.S., U. Munich, 1921; M.S., U. Koenigsberg, 1922; Ph.D., U. Berlin, 1924; m. Kate Lasch, May 15, 1925; children—Marion, Hesse. Came to U.S., 1935, naturalized, 1944. Research synthetic medicinal pharm. preparations Dr. Joachim Wiernik & Co., 1925-26; tech. dir. Rotophot, Berlin, Germany, 1926-33, Journal La Meuse, Liege, Belgium, 1933-34, De Spaarne Stad, Harlem, Holland, 1935, Brown &Bigelow, St. Paul, 1936-39; Bd. dirs. Anken Chem. & Film Corp., Newton, N.J., 1950-67, v.p., 1952-67; pres. Sigma Photo-Chem. Labs., Newton, N.J., 1967-69. Served with German Army, 1916-18. Mem. Am. Chem. Soc., A.A.A.S., Soc. Photog. Scientists and Engrs. Patentee in field. Address: Newton NJ Died July 11, 1969.

WOLPE, STEFAN, composer; b. Berlin, Germany, Aug. 25 1902; s. David and Hermine (Strasser) W.; student Staatliche Hochschule fur Music, Berlin, 1919-24; pvt. student Feruccio Busoni, Anton Webern, Herman Scherchen; Dr. Music (hon.) New Eng. Conservatory; m. Ola Ouniewska, July 1927; 1 dau. Katharina Petra; m. 2d, Irma Schoenberg, Apr. 1934; m. 3d, Hilda Morley, Dec. 1948. Came to U.S., 1938, naturalized, 1944, Prof. composition Palestine (Jerusalem) Conservatory, 1934-38; theory and composition Settlement Music Sch., Phila., 1939-42; mus. dir., prof. composition Contemporary Music Sch., N.Y.C., 1948-52; prof. theory and composition Phila. Acad. Music, 1949-52, Black Mountain Coll., 1952-56, Chatham Sq. Music Sch., N.Y.C., 1957-63; prof. music, head music dept. C.W. Post Coll., Long Island University 1957-68. Distinguished professor 1966-68, adjunct prof. C.W. Post Coll., from 1968; prof.composition Mannes College of Music, from 1968. Recipient Am. Inst. Arts and Letters award, 1949, Rogers and Hammerstein League Composers-Internat. Soc. Contemporary Music Award, 1953, Bethsabee de Rothchild Found. Arts and Sci. award 1953, Fromm Found. award, 1960, New York Music Critics citation, 1963. Thorne-Ketchum Foundation award, 65, 66, 67, 68; award for distinction in music Brandeis University, 1966; Fulbright fellow, 1956-57; Guggenheim, fellow, 1962-63, 70-71. Mem. Am. Music Center, Nat. Inst. Art and Letters. Composer: Zeus and Elida, opera, 1929; Strange Stories, theater piece, 1929; March and Variations for two pianos, 1931; 10 songs from the Hebrew, 1938; Sonata for Oboe and Piano, 1938; Sonata for Violin and Piano, 1949; Quartet for Trumpet and Tenor Saxophone, Percussion Piano, 1950; Enactments for Three, Pianos, 1950-53; Symphony for Orchestra, 1956; Piece in Two Parts for Flute and Piano, 1960; Piece for Piano and 16 Instruments, 1960; Piece for 2 Instrumental Units, Piece for Flute, Cello and Piano, 1963; Piece in 2 parts for Violin Alone, 1964; Chamber Piece No. 1 for 14 instruments, 1964-65; Piece in Two Parts for Six Players, 1961-62; Trio for Flute, Cello and Piano, 1963-64; Solo Piece for Trumpet, 1966; Second Piece for Violin Alone, 1966; Chamber Piece No. 2, 1968; String Quartet No. 1, 1969; Concerto for Bass, Clarinet, Violin and Piano, 1968-69; Quartet for Oboe, Violin, Percussion, and Piano, 1956; Quintet with Voice, 1957; Chamber Piece No. 2 for 14 Instruments, 1968; Form for Piano, 1969; Concerto for Trumpet and Chamber Ensemble, 1971. Home: New York City NY Died Apr. 4, 1972.

WOLTERS, LARRY (LORENZ GERHARD), editor, critic; b. Waukon, Ia., Oct. 17, 1899; s. Louis F. and Mary (Winter) W.; A.B., U. Ia., 1924; m. Flora Mae Martin, May 3, 1932; children—Winifred (Mrs. Truman Edward Boyd), Karen (Mrs. Hubert Eugene Dutil). Reporter, The Des Moines Register, 1924, Pittsburgh Gazette Times, 1925-26, Chicago Journal 1926-29; reporter Chgo. Tribune, 1929, radio editor, 1929-69, TV editor, 1946-65; author syndicated column Radio-TV Gag Bag, 1950-69; chief pub. information Ill. Sesquicentennial Commn. Com. judges George Foster Peabody Radio-TV Awards. Mem. Sigma Delta Chi. Sigma Alpha Epsilon. Episcopalian. Contbr. articles to popular mags., articles on electronics to World Book Ency. Home: Evanston IL Died Feb. 27, 1969.

WOLTMAN, FREDERICK ENOS, newspaper writer; b. York, Pa., Mar. 16, 1905; s. Enos Frederick and Ella (Strayer) W.; B.A. magna cum laude, U. of Pittsburgh, 1927, M.A., 1928; m. Virginia Russell, Oct. 26, 1940 (deceased, August 3, 1952); married 2d, Nancy Winslow Jackson, October 31, 1952. Graduate assistant department of philosophy, University of Pittsburgh, 1926-27; reporter, later staff writer, New York World-Telegram, 1927-70. Assisted World-Telegram to win Pulitzer Award for most disinterested and meritorious pub. service for the year with series of articles which exposed real estate mortgage bond racket, 1931. Received hon. mention Pultizer Prize for distinguished example of reporter's work in 1946, 1947. Home: Sarasota FL Died Mar. 5, 1970.

WOLVERTON, CHARLES A., ex-congressman; b. Camden, N.J., Oct. 24, 1880; s. Charles S. and Martha W.; LL.B., U. Pa., 1900; 1 son, Donnell Knox. Admitted to N.J. bar, 1901; began practice at Camden; asst. city solicitor, Camden, 1904-06; asst. prosecutor Camden County, 1906-13; spl. asst. atty. gen., N.J., 1913-14; mem. N.J. Ho. of Assembly, 1915-18 (speaker of House, 1918); Prosecutor of pleas, Camden County, 1918-23; alternate del. at large Rep. Nat. Conv., 1920; dir. and asso. counsel First Camden Nat. Bank & Trust Co.; mem. 70th-85th congresses, 1st N.J. Dist. Fed. food adminstr. Camden County, 1917-19. Mem. Am. Bar Assn. Methodist. Mason (32 deg., K.T., Shriner), Elk, Moose, Rotarian (Camden, N.J.). Club: Union League (Phila.). Home: Merchantville NJ Died May 16, 1969; buried Harleigh Cemetery, Camden NJ

WOLVERTON, JOHN MARSHALL, ex-congressman; b. Bigbend, W.Va., Jan. 31, 1872; s. James S. and Eliza Ann (Ferrell) W.; student Glenville (W.Va.) State Normal Sch. and Fairmount State Normal Sch.; LL.B., W.Va. U., 1901; m. Laura V. Herold, of Hookerville, W.Va., Dec. 20, 1907; children—Helen N., James H., Barbara Ruth. Admitted to W.Va. bar, 1901, and began practice at Richwood. Pros. atty. Nicholas Co., W.Va., 1913-17, 1921-25; mayor of Richwood, 1918-19; mem. 69th and 71st Congresses (1925-27, 1929-31), 3d W.Va. Dist. Republican. Methodist. Mason (Shriner), K.P., Moose. Rotarian. Home: Richwood WV‡

WOMACK, JOSEPH PITTS, college president; b. Centerton, Ark., July 25, 1871; s. James Wilson and Elizabeth Jane (Gamble) W.; grad. Rogers (Ark.) Acad., 1894; B.A., U. of Ark., 1903; M.A., George Peabody Coll., 1919; m. Lottie Lee, of Pea Ridge, Ark., May 21, 1891. Founder, 1903, and prin. high sch., Stephens, Ark., 1903-09; supt. schs., Magnolia, 1909-13, Conway, 1913-17, Jonesboro, 1917-26; state supt. pub. instrn., Ark., 1927-29; now pres. Henderson State Teachers Coll., Arkadelphia. Mem. N.E.A., Ark. Edn. Assn., Kappa Delta Pi. Democrat. Methodist. Mason. Rotarian. Home: Arkadelphia AR‡

WOOD, BARRY, producer Bell Telephone Hour. Home: New York City NY Died July 19, 1970.*

WOOD, CHARLES P., indsl. engr.; b. Warrenton, Va., Mar. 11, 1883; s. Daniel Pollard and Sallie (Parkinson) W.; M.E. in E.E., Cornell U., 1904; m. Frances Laura Fay, Jan. 8, 1923. Asst. supt., Buckeye Cotton Oil Co., Macon, Ga., 1904-08; Gibbs Gas Engring. Co., Atlanta, Ga., Standard Gas Power Co., N.Y., 1908-16; Empire Floor and Wall Tile Co., Metuchen, N.J.), 1916-17; trade commr., U.S. Dept. Commerce in France and Belgium, 1919-20; partner, Lockwood Greene Engrs., N.Y.C., from 1920; dir. in charge of party sent to Russia to advise textile industry, 1929; govt. rep., code authority Ry. Car Building, Industry Nat. Recovery Adminstrn., 1934; consultant, Div. Contract Distbn., O.P.M., 1941; National Resources Planning Bd., 1941-43. Founder of Levere Memorial Found. Unit chmn. Greater New York Fund, 1963. Served as 1st lieutenant, Engr., O.R.C., 1917, advanced to lt. colonel, C.W.S., 1918, World War I. Consultant Control Division, A.S.F. and Q.m. Gen. offices, 1942-45, World War II. Awarded Croix de Guerre, gold star. Licensed professional engineer, N.Y., Conn., Pa., Va. Mem. Am. Inst. Elec. Engrs. (life), American Institute of Consulting Engineers, Society of Colonial Wars, Vet. Corps Artillery (member council of administration), Am. Indsl. Development Council (hon. life) (chmn. 1935-36; mem. advisory bd.), Am. Soc. Military Engrs., Am. Ordnance Assn., Cornell Soc. Engrs., Nat. Bur. Engring. Registration, S.A.R., N.Y. Southern Soc., Virginians (governor 1951-52, honorary member 1963), Wilderness Society, Society American Wars, Society War of 1812, Mil Order Foreign Wars, World Wars, Am. Legion, Am. Defense Soc., Ypres League, Order of Lafayette, American Order of the French Croix de Guerre, Sigma Alpha Epsilon (mem. nat. bd. trustees). Clubs: University, Engineers, Cornell (N.Y.C.); Merion (Phila.); Army and Navy (Washington). Author: Industrial Machinery in France and Belgium; Factors Controlling Location of Various Types of Industry. Contbr. papers on indsl. and econ. subjects to profl. jours. Baptist. Past cons. editor Textile World. Contbr. article on Factory Construction and Planning Ency. Britannica, 1952. Made indsl. surveys of S.A.L. Ry., States of Okla., Me., Cities of Flint, Troy, Dallas, Okla. City, Okmulgee, Wilkes-barre, Decatur, Wilmington, Huntington, Gloucester, Hannibal (Mo.); report for Mo. State Dept. Resources and Development; report on cotton textile mfg. in Cal.; indsl. surveys Alexandria, Va., Wichita, Kan. Home: New York City NY

WOOD, EDMUND PALMER, lawyer; b. Cincinnati, Ohio, Feb. 21, 1899; s. William Ray and Alice (Palmer) W.; A.B. Yale, 1921; LL.B., U. of Cincinnati, 1923; m. Barbara Carter Hunt, April 26, 1926 (dec. 1952); children—Barbara (Mrs. Robert W. Elder), Alice Janet (Mrs. John D. Stuart), William Hunt; m. 2d, Inez M. Ferris, July 18, 1953. Admitted to Ohio Bar, 1923, Bar of the Supreme Court of U.S., 1932. Began practice with Wood and Wood, law firm, Cincinnati, 1923, became partner, 1929; senior partner of Wood, Herron & Evans. Engaged in patent and anti-trust cases in Federal courts and Fed. Trade Commn. Mem. coms. of patent sect., Am. Bar Assn. Mem. Cincinnati Patent Law Assn. (past pres.). Republican. Clubs: Cincinnati Country, The Literary. Home: Cincinnati OH Died May 15, 1968.

WOOD, ERNEST EDWARD, congressman, lawyer; b. Chico, Calif., Aug. 24, 1875; s. Rev. Jesse (D. D.) and Alice C. (Tyson) W.; ed. Stockton High Sch. and U.S. Mil. Acad. (2 yrs.); unmarried. Admitted to bar, 1897, and since then engaged in practice at St. Louis, Mem. Congress, 12th Mo. dist., 1905-7. Capt. Mo. Nat. Guard. Democrat. Methodist. Club: Jefferson. Residence: 811 Locust St. Office: 503 Chemical Bldg., St Louis MO‡

WOOD, ISABEL WARWICK, educator; b. Brooklyn, N.Y., Jan. 4, 1874; d. William Warwick and Abbie Maria (Richards) Bliss; grad. Packer Collegiate Inst., Brooklyn, 1892; A.B., Brown U., 1895, A.M., 1897; m. Nathan Robinson Wood, June 14, 1900; children—Nathan Warwick, William Bliss. Teacher high schs., Providence and Quincy Mansion Sch., Boston, 1895-99; prof. rhetoric and lit., Gordon Coll. of Theology and Missions, Boston, 1911, exec. sec., 1921-28, dean of faculty, 1928-44, lecturer on lit. and missionary subjects. Hon. foreign v.p. Woman's Am. Bapt. Foreign Mission Society. Mem. bd. and exec. com., Am. Bapt. Home Mission Society. Republican. Home: 26 Academy St., Arlington 74 MA‡

WOOD, JOHN C(LARK), retail exec.; b. Newark, June 18, 1901; s. Charles S. and Margaret A. (Maring) W.; B.A., Dartmouth, 1922; m. Frances Kelley Keresey, May 4, 1954. With McCann-Erickson, Inc., 1923-32; dir., v.p. B. Altman & Co., N.Y.C., 1932-45; president Brooks Brothers, Inc., New York City, 1946-67, chairman, 1967-69; president of Fifth Av. Assn.; dir. Julius Garfinkel & Co., Inc., Better Bus. Bur. N.Y.C. Served as maj. AUS, 1942-45. Clubs: Union League (N.Y.C.); The Creek (Locust Valley, N.Y.); Burning Tree. Home: New York City NY Died Dec. 15, 1969; buried Locust Valley, LI NY

WOOD, JOHN STEPHENS, congressman; ed. Mercer Univ. Former mem. gen. assembly of Ga.; solicitor gen. Blue Ridge Judicial Circuit of Ga. and Judge Blue Ridge Judicial Circuit; mem. 72d and 73d Congresses (1931-35), 79th to 82d Congresses (1945-53), 9th Dist. of Ga. Served in U.S. Army Air Corps, World War I. Home: Atlanta GA Died Sept. 12, 1968.

WOOD, LEDGER, educator; b. Pueblo, Colo., Sept. 4, 1901; s. Samuel R. and Elizabeth (Tyler) W.; student Los Angeles Jr. Coll., 1918-20; A.B., U. of Calif., 1922; Ph.D., Cornell, 1926; m. Frances Elinor Jennings, July 27, 1929; children—Ellen Elizabeth, Roger Jennings, and Suzanne Elinor (Mrs. Walter Kuehn, Jr.). Engaged as assistant in philosophy Cornell U., 1925-26; instr. philosophy Stanford, 1926-27; lectr. history of philosophy Calif. Inst. Tech., 1926-27; mem. faculty Princeton since 1927, prof. philosophy, 1949-70, chairman of dept. philosophy, 1952-60, McCosh prof. philosophy, 1956-70; Sterling research fellow Yale, 1940-41; vis. prof. U. Cal., summer 1931, grad. sch. Bklyn. Coll., 1948-49, N.Y.U. summer 1951. Mem. Am. Philos. Assn., Am. Assn. U. Profs., Phi Beta Kappa, Phi Kappa Phi. Author: The Analysis of Knowledge, 1940; A History of Philosophy (with Frank Thilly), 1951. Contbr. to books and jours. Home: Princeton NJ Died Dec. 8, 1970.

WOOD, NATHAN ROBINSON, clergyman, educator; b. Wyocena, Wis., Aug. 13, 1874; s. Nathan Eusebius and Alice Robinson (Boise) W.; prep. edn., high sch. and Brooklyn Polytechnic and Collegiate Inst.;

student Harvard, 1894-96; grad. Newton Theological Institution, 1900, B.D., 1906; D.D., Wheaton (Ill.) College, 1927; m. Isabel Warwick Bliss, June 14, 1900; children—Nathan Warwick, William Bliss. Ordained Bapt. ministry, 1901; pastor West Medford, Mass., 1901-11; prof. Gordon Coll. of Theology and Missions, Boston, 1908, dean 1910, pres., 1919-44. Mem. bd. mgrs., Am. Bapt. Foreign Mission Soc.; interim pastorates, conf. lecturer and preacher, since 1944. Author: The Secret of the Universe, 1932; Seven Lamps of Fire, 1942. Home: 26 Academy St., Arlington 74 MA‡

WOOD, ROBERT E., director Sears, Roebuck & Co.; b. Kansas City, Mo., June 13, 1879; s. Robert Whitney and Lillie (Collins) W.; grad. U.S. Mil. Acad., 1900; m. Mary Butler Hardwick, Apr. 30, 1908; children—Anne Hardwick, Frances Elkington, Sarah Stires, Robert Whitney, Mary Stovall. Served in the U.S. Army during Philippine Insurrection as 2d and 1st lt., 3d Cavalry, 1900-02; asst. chief quartermaster, chief quartermaster and dir. of Panama Railroad Co., on construction of Panama Canal, 1905-15; col. and brig. gen. N.A., World War I, acting quartermaster gen. U.S. Army, 1918-19. Entered business life, 1915; asst. to pres. Gen. Asphalt Co., 1915-17; v.p. Montgomery Ward & Co., Chicago, 1919-24; v.p. Sears, Roebuck and Co., 1924-28, pres., 1928-39, chmn. bd. 1939-54, chmn. finance com., 1954-57, also director. Awarded P.I. Insurrection medal, Panama Canal medal, D.S.M., Legion of Merit; Companion Order of St. Michael and St. George (Brit.); Knight Legion of Honor (French). Clubs: Univ., Chicago, Commercial (Chgo.); Army and Navy (Washington); Old Elm, Onwentsia. Home: Lake Forest IL Died Nov. 6, 1969; buried Lake Forest Cemetery, Lake Forest IL

WOOD, WALTER AARON, mfr.; b. Union Grove, Racine Co., Wis., June 5, 1877; s. Lyman and Savilla (Jarvis) W.; grad. high sch., Racine, Wis., 1898; student La Salle Extension U., Chicago, LL.B.; studied violin under Prof. Henry Schulte 4 yrs.; unmarried. Owner Lyman Wood Mfg. Co., mfrs. saddlery and hardware specialties. Mem. Soc. Mayflower Descendants, S.C.W., S.A.R. Republican. Prebyn. Office: 1433 Junction Av., Racine WI‡

WOOD, WILLIAM ALLEN, corporation lawyer; b. Covington, Ind., Sept. 25, 1874; s. Samuel Fletcher and Mary (Allen) W.; ed. Covington High Sch., Ind. Normal Coll. (Covington), and Indiana Univ. (B.S., M.S.); unmarried. Held chair of economics and English in a Southern univ., 1896-7; lecturer on corp'n law, finance and management, Indianapolis Coll. of Law. Pres. Ind. Soc. S.R.; 1st v.-p. S.A.R.; mem. Am. Econ. Assn. Editor The Phi Gamma Delta (nat. mag.). Editor: The Book of the Society of Sons of the Revolution in Indiana. Author: Modern Business Corporations, B6. Joint author: Indiana Bonds and Security for Loans in Indiana. Address: Indianapolis IN‡

WOOD, WILLIAM BARRY, JR., physician; b. Milton, Mass., May 4, 1910; s. William Barry and Emily Niles (Lockwood) W.; A.B., Harvard, 1932; M.D., Johns Hopkins, 1936; m. Mary Lee Hutchins, July 2, 1932; children—William Barry III, Margaret, Peter, Jonathan, Jean. Medical house officer, Johns Hopkins Hosp., 1936-39; Nat. Research Council fellow in bacteriology, Harvard Med. Sch., 1939-40; asst., dept. of medicine, Johns Hopkins Med. Sch.; 1937-39, associate, 1940-42; prof. medicine, Sch. of Medicine, Washington U., St. Louis, 1942-55; v.p Johns Hopkins U. and Hosp., 1955-59; prof. microbiology Johns Hopkins School of Medicine, 1955-71, also director of department of microbiology, 1959-71. Member bd. trustees Rockefeller Found. Fellow A.C.P.; mem. Am. Soc. Clin. Investigation (pres. 1952), Soc. Exptl. Biology and Med., Central Soc. Clin. Research (pres. 1952), Soc. Am. Bacteriologists, Assn. Am. Physicians (president 1962-63), National Academy of Sciences (member council 1962-65), Sigma Xi, Alpha Omega Alpha, Phi Beta Kappa. Home: Owings Mills MD Died Mar. 9, 1971.

WOOD, WILLIS DELANO, investment securities; born N.Y. City, Aug. 31, 1872; s. Cornelius Delano and Helen (Ogden) W.; student Amherst Coll., 1894, hon. M.A., 1910; m. Anna Matheson, Oct. 11, 1905;children—Robert Matheson, Jean (Mrs. William M. Preston). Employed in stock broker's office, N.Y. City, 1894-98; mem. Wood, Low & Co., investment securities, 1902, limited partner Wood, Walker & Co.; trustee Title Guarantee & Trust Co.; dir. Fidelity Phenix Fire Ins. Co., Fidelity and Casualty Co., Corn Products Refining Co., New York City Omnibus Corp., Western Pacific R.R. Corp. Trustee Union Theol. Sem., New York Y.M.C.A. Mem. New York Stock Exchange since 1902. Mem. Alpha Delta Phi. Republican. Clubs: New York Bond, Economics, Century, Down Town, Midday, Union (N.Y. City); Huntington Golf, Beaver Dam, Cold Spring Yacht, Seawanhaka Yacht, Wayandauch (Long Island); Ausable (Adirondacks). Home: 635 Park Av., NY City NY also Lloyds Neck, Huntington, LI NY Office: 63 Wall St., NY City

WOODARD, CHARLES AUGUSTUS, surgeon; b. Wilson County, N.C., May 11, 1876; s. Francis Joseph

and Virginia Carolina (Bynum) W.; A.B., Trinity Coll. Durham, N.C., 1900; M.D., U. of Va., 1904; studied U. of Vienna, 1911; m. Dorothy Whitehead, Nov. 18, 1926; 1 dau., Dorothy Whitehead. Began practice at Durham, N.C., 1907; mem. Board of Health, Durham, 1909-13; mem. staff Watts Hospital, Durham, 1910-19, trustee, 1916-17; moved to Wilson, N.C., 1919; chief surgeon and president Woodard-Herring Hosp.; mem. staff of visiting surgeons, State Hosp., Raleigh, N.C. Commd. 1st lt. Med. Corps, U.S. Army, Aug. 30, 1917; capt., Feb. 11, 1918; maj., Oct. 14, 1918; served on surg. staff Base Hosp. 41, St. Denis, France, July 25, 1918-Feb. 2, 1919; hon. disch., Mar. 28, 1919. Fellow Am. Coll. Surgeons; mem. A.M.A., N.C. Med. Soc., Wilson County Med. Soc., Kappa Sigma, Nu Sigma Nu. Democrat. Methodist. Mason. Home: 908 W. Nash St., Wilson NC‡

WOODBERRY, MIRIAM L., missionary sec.; b. Somerville, Mass., June 4, 1872; d. Nicholas J. and Alice M. (Crosby) W.; grad. Somerville High Sch., 1891; unmarried. Asst. treas. Woman's Home Missionary Assn., Congl. Ch., 1892-1902; asst. treas. Woman's Bd. Foreign Missions, 1902-05; editor Work at Home, 1906; field sec. Woman's Home Missionary Assn., 1905-07; nat. sec. Woman's Dept. Congl. Home Missionary Soc., 1907-32; asso. sec. missions, Congl. Ch. Extension Bds. 28 yrs.; retired Mar. 31, 1934. Mem. Internat. Council for‧ Patriotic Service, Council of Women for Home Missions. Trustee Country Life Acad. (Star, N.C.), Am. Internat. Coll., Springfield, Mass., Schauffler Coll. (Cleveland). Clubs: Congregational, Monday (New York); Dickens (Boston). Has traveled extensively in nearly all parts of U.S., studying and reporting on conditions among Indians, negroes, ranchmen, homesteaders, industrial workers, etc. Home: South Sudbury MA‡

WOODBRIDGE, DUDLEY WARNER, educator; b. Bellaire, O., Feb. 24, 1896; s. George Morgan and Julia Belle (Warner) W.; student U. Wash., 1914-17, U. Chgo., 1917; A.B., U. Ill., 1922, J.D., 1927; m. Ruby Belle Mendenhall, May 23, 1921 (dec. Apr. 1972); children—Hensley Charles, Julia Belle, William Luther, Robert Dudley (dec.). Admitted to Va. bar 1929; asst. prof. law Coll. William and Mary, 1927, asso. prof., 1928-32, professor, 1932-66, dean of law school, 1950-62, dean emeritus, Chancellor prof. law, 1962-66; vis. prof. U. Va., summers, 1943-44, U. Ill. summer 1946, U. Fla., summers, 1947-48. Mem. Am., Va. bar assns., Phi Beta Kappa, Omicron Delta Kappa, Order of Coif. Home: Williamsburg VA Died Oct. 20, 1969; buried Cedar Grove Cemetery, Williamsburg VA

WOODBRIDGE, JOHN ARVEN, vice pres., gen. counsel Union Elec. Co. of Mo.; b. N.Y. City, Nov. 19, 1903; s. Frederick James Eugene and Helena Belle (Adams) W.; student Phillips Exeter Acad.; B.A., Amherst, 1924; LL.B., Columbia Law Sch., 1927; m. Elizabeth Somerville, June 1925 (died 1931); children—James Ormond, Thomas Middleton; m. 2d, Frances Kittredge Long, May 1932; 1 dau., Cecil Arven. Admitted to N.Y. bar, 1929, Mo. bar, 1939; associated with law firm Sullivan & Cromwell, N.Y. City, 1927-39; v.p. Union Elec. Co., 1939-71; dir. 1940-71; dir. St. Louis, Union Colliery Co. Served with the 107th Inf., N.Y. Nat. Guard, 1928-32, lt. 306th Inf., 1932-39, 406th Inf., 1939-41; capt. Mo. State Guard, July 1942; lt. col., asst. chief of staff, May 1943. Mem. Am. Bar Assn., St. Louis Bar Assn., Mo. Bar Assn., St. Louis Chamber of Commerce, Phi Beta Kappa, Phi Delta Phi, Alpha Delta Phi. Episcopalian. Clubs: University (N.Y.C. and St. Louis); Clayton; Racquet, Old Warson (St. Louis). Home: St Louis MO Died June 5, 1971.

WOODBURY, ROBERT MORSE, economist; b. Worcester, Mass., July 15, 1889; s. John Charles and Jennie (Morse) W.; A.B., Clark U., Worcester, 1910, A.M., 1912; Pres. White traveling fellow Cornell U., 1913-14, Ph.D., 1915; grad. study U. Berlin, 1913, University Munich, 1914; LL.D., Clark University, 1955; married Helen L. Sumner, Nov. 25, 1918; m. 2d, Mildred Fairchild, July 24, 1947. Instr. econs. Cornell U., 1912-13, 1915-16; asst. prof. econs. U. Kan., 1916-17; dir. statis. research Children's Bureau, Dept. of Labor, 1918-24; mem. staff Inst. of Economics, Washington, 1924-28; asso. editor Social Science Abstracts, 1928-33; labor adviser NRA, 1933-35., economist, labor research sect., 1935-36; tech. expert Com. on Population, Nat. Resources Com., 1936; became mem. statis. sect. Internat. Labor Office, 1936, statis. adviser, 1941-46, chief statistician, 1946-53; sec.-gen. 7th Internat. Conf. Labor Statisticians, 1949; member International Statis. Institute 1949-53. Papers deposited in U. Ore. Library, Eugene. Fellow A.A.A.S., Am. Pub. Health Assn., Am. Sociol. Soc., Royal Econ. Soc., Royal Statis. Soc.; member Am. Economic Assn., Internat. Population Union, Population Association Am. Statistical Association. Congregationalist. Clubs: Philadelphia Art Alliance; Cosmos (Washington, D.C.). Author: Social Insurance, 1917; Industrial Instability of Child Workers, 1920; Statures and Weights of Children Under Six Years of Age, 1921; Infant Mortality and Preventive Work in New Zealand, 1922; Causal Factors in Infant Mortality, 1925; Maternal Mortality, 1926; Infant Mortality and Its Causes, 1926; Workers' Health and Safety, 1927; Methods of Family Living Studies,

1940; International Comparisons of Food Costs, 1941 Food Consumption and Dietary Surveys in the Americas, 1942. Contbr. to Jour. Am. Statistical Assr Home: Bryn Mawr PA Died Jan. 17, 1970; buried Roc Creek Cemetery, Washington DC

WOODHULL, DANIEL ELLIS, retired; b. Newark New Jersey, February 3, 1869; s. Addison Waddell an Emma Taylor (Ellis) W.; grad. high sch., Newark, 1886 m. Mabel, d. Sir Albert and Lady Altman, of London Eng., Jan. 12, 1907; children—Daniel E., John V. William T. Began as jr. clk. Am. Bank Note Co., N.Y City, 1887, advancing to asst. sec., 1902, sent to Eng. 1903-07, to act as chmn. and mng. dir. of subsidiary Bradbury, Wilkinson & Co., Ltd.; v.p. Am. Bank Note Co., 1907-10, dir. and 1st v.p., 1910-19, pres., 1919-35 chmn. bd., 1935-39; now retired. Mem. Soc. Founder and Patriots, S.R., Loyal Legion. Republican. Presbyn Clubs: Metropolitan, Pilgrims (New York); Nassau (Princeton). Home: 162 E. 80th St., New York NY‡

WOODHULL, ZULA MAUD, author; b. N.Y. City; d Dr. Canning (U.S.A.) and Victoria (Claflin) W.; (mothe late Mrs. John B. Martin); ed. New York, Paris and London. Life mem. Royal Instn. of Great Britain; life gov. Royal Agrl. Soc.; mem. Brit. Psychol. Soc., Institu Psychologique, Paris, Soc. for Psychical Research London, etc. Clubs: Ladies' Automobile, Ladies Athenaeum, Lyceum. Author: The Proposal, a Dialogue, 1880; Affinities, a Play, 1896. Writer or scientific and social questions. Was co-editor with he mother of the Humanitarian Magazine. Mem. Mano House Club, Ango-American Center. Address: Norton Park, Bredon's Norton, near Tewkesbury Worcestershire England‡

WOODMAN, ALPHEUS GRANT, chemist; b. a Kingston, Mass., Oct. 30, 1873; s. Dr. Aurin Payson and Emily (Grant) W.; B.S. in chemistry, Mass. Inst. Tech. 1897; m. Marion L. Cade, of Brighton, Mass., Aug. 4 1902. Instr. chemistry, 1897-1907, asst. prof. of food analysis since 1907, Mass. Inst. Tech. Mem. Am. Chem Soc., Soc. of Arts, Boston, A.A.A.S., Nat. Geog. Soc Author: Air, Water and Food from a Sanitary Standpoint, 1900. Contbr. to chem. and photog. jours Home: Watertown MA‡

WOODMAN, LAWRENCE EWALT, elec. engr.; b Manhattan, Kan., June 27, 1904; s. Louis Hall and Augusta (Ewalt) W.; B.S. in Elec. Engring. Kan. State U., 1927; m. Grace Walsh, Nov. 2, 1935 children—Judith (Mrs. Charles R. Coons), James Walsh. Student engr. S.W. Bell Telephone Co., 1927 heating salesman Kansas City Fuel Oil Co., 1927-29 heating engr. Mo. Power & Light Co., 1929-32; owner operator Woodman Engring Co., Jefferson City, Mo Mem. Smoke Abatement Bd., Jefferson City, Greater Jefferson City Planning Commn.; mem. Jefferson City Symphony Orch., from 1929, pres., 1960-61. Bd. dirs Jefferson City Community Concert Assn Mem. Nat. Mo. socs. profl. engrs., Refrigeration Service Engrs Soc., Engrs. Club, Am. Soc. Heating Refrigeration and Airconditioning Engrs., Am. Soc. Refrigeration Engrs Presbyn. Rotarian. Home: Jefferson City MC

WOODRUFF, EDWIN BLANCHARD, clergyman; b Delhi, N.Y., June 3, 1872; s. John Worth and Eunice (Blanchard) W.; prep. edn., Delaware Acad., Delhi N.Y.; student St. Stephen's Coll., Annandale, N.Y. A.B., Columbia, 1896; B.D., Berkeley Divinity Sch. Middletown, Conn., 1899; D.D., Seabury Divinity School, Faribault, Minn., 1925; Litt.D., Sioux Falls Coll., 1938; m. Ellen Hart Brent, Apr. 9, 1902 children—Eunice Brent (Mrs. Francis Dilworth Calley), Kelly Brent, John Blanchard. Deacon and priest, 1899, P.E. Ch.; rector St. George's Ch., Kansas City, Mo., 1899-1908; instnl. dir. Grace Ch., Kansas City, 1908-10; rector St. Clement's Ch., St. Paul, Minn. 1910-17; dean of Calvary Cathedral, Sioux Falls, S.D. 1917-40, dean emeritus since 1940. Mem. Nat. Commn on Ministry, P.E. Ch.; asso. sec. field dept., Nat Council, P.E. Ch.; pres. Standing Com. of S.D.; chmn Bd. of Examining Chaplains, S.D.; dean of Eastern Deanery, S.D. Mem. charter commission of Kansas City, 1910, of St. Paul, 1912. Pres. S.S. Inst. of Minn. 1914-17. Pres. bd. All Saints' Sch.; trustee Seabury Div Sch. Arbitrator of packing house strike, Sioux Falls 1921; pres. County and City Welfare Bd. Mem. Sigma Alpha Epsilon. Republican. Mason (33 deg., K.T. Shriner). Rotarian. Author: The Life of Bishop Berkeley, 1898. Editor S.D. Churchman. Home Huntington WV‡

WOODRUFF, JAMES ALBERT, army officer (ret.) b. Ft. Shaw, Mont., June 19, 1877; s. Charles Albert and Louise Virginia (Duff) W.; grad. U.S. Mil. Acad., 1899 U.S. Engr. Sch., 1901, Army Staff Coll., 1906, Army War Coll., 1917; m. Margarett Worth Hubbell, Oct. 8 1904; children—Margarett Stoddard, James Albert Commd. 2d lt. Engr. Corps, Feb. 15, 1899, and promoted through grades to maj. gen., Mar. 1, 1938 Dept. dir. constrn. and forestry, A.E.F., 1918-19, World War; chief of staff Panama Canal Dept., 1924-27; div engr. N. Atlantic Div., 1934-35; comdr. San Francisco Port of Embarkation, 1935-37, Hawaiian Coast Arty Brigade, 1937-38, Hawaiian Div., 1938-39, First Corps

Area, 1939-41; retired June 30, 1941, returned to active duty in Hawaii as pres. of mil. commn. under martial law, 1941-43; retired Aug. 1, 1943. Awarded D.S.M. (United States); Officer Legion of Honor (France); Officer Order of St. Michael and St. George (Eng.); Officer Order of Leopold (Belgium). Clubs: Army and Navy (Washington, D.C.), Army and Navy (San Francisco). Author: Applied Principles of Field Fortification, 1912. Home: CA Died Aug. 20, 1969.

WOODRUFF, WILLIAM WIGHT, coal mining; b. Hartford, Conn., Feb. 7, 1872; s. Samuel Vincent and Emma Coe (Coite) W.; ed. Germantown Acad., 1889; m. Frances A. Robb, of Pittsburgh, Pa., 1898. With Thomas Roberts & Co., wholesale grocers, Phila., 1889-94, W. W. Woodruff, Pittsburgh, 1895-1905; dist. mgr. Jeffrey Mfg. Co., 1905-14; now pres. Barbara Mining Co., Woodruff Coal & Iron Co., Fobewood Coal & Iron Co.; v.p. and gen. mgr. Fuel Service Co. Pvt. and lt. Pa. N.G., 6 yrs. Republican. Episcopalian. Clubs: Duquesne (Pittsburgh); Art (Phila.). Home: Muncy, Lycoming Co., Pa. Office: 1415 Park Bldg., Pittsburgh PA‡

WOODS, ALICE (MISS), writer, illustrator; b. Goshen, Ind., Nov. 22, 1871; d. William Allen and Mata (Newton) W.; ed. Girl's Classical Sch., Indianapolis; art ed'n New York Sch. of Art and Art schs. in Paris, France. Was mem. Ind. hon. com. at Paris Exp'n, 1900. Mem. Nat. Arts Club, Woman's Art Club of New York. Wrote and illustrated Edges." Address: Nat. Arts Club, 37 W. 34th St., New York NY‡

WOODS, ANDREW HENRY, neurologist; b. Hartwood, Va., Aug. 25, 1872; s. Francis Marion and Julia Miller (Junkin) W.; A.B., Washington and Lee U., 1893; M.D., U. of Pa., 1899; m. Fanny Soutter Sinclair, Apr. 29, 1902; children—Thomas Sinclair, Francis Marion, Janet McCleery, Margaret Soutter, Robert Pirrie. Med. dir. and v.p. Lingnan U., Canton, China; asst. neurologist, U. of Pa. and Phila. Gen. Hosp., 1908-12; prof. and head dept. of neurology, Peking (China) Union Med. Coll., 1920-28; prof. and head dept. of psychiatry, Univ. of Iowa, 1928-41; dir. Iowa State Psychopathic Hosp., 1928-41; retired 1941; now consultant in neurology and psychiatry. Dir. First National Bank; president Sinclair Realty Co. Served as major, Medical Corps, U.S. Army in U.S. and France, World War I. Fellow Am. Psychiatric Association; mem. Am. Neurol. Assn. (past v.p.), Sigma Nu. Democrat. Conglist. Contbr. scientific jours. Home: 1100 N. Dubuque St. Office: First Nat. Bank Bldg., Iowa City IA‡

WOODS, HARRY IRWIN, educator; b. near Greenville, Pa., July 6, 1870; s. William and Nacy Ann (White) W.; A.B., Lafayette Coll., 1895, A.M., 1898; studied astronomy and physics, Columbia, 1899-1900, U. of Pa., 1900-1901; m. Jennie M. Reznor, of Pa., June 24, 1897. Instr. Lafayette Coll., 1895-99, U. of Pa., 1901-2; prof. and dir. obs., 1902-16, prof. physics, 1916-17, Washburn Coll., Topeka, Kan.; service in France, 1918-20; prin. Teachers' Training Sch., Alpena, Ark., 1921—. Home: Alpena AR‡

WOODS, HENRY COCHRANE, corp. exec.; b. Lincoln, Neb., Oct. 24, 1895; s. Frank H. and Nelle (Cochrane) W.; B.S., Yale, 1918, Harvard, 1919; m. Elouise Bixby, June 19, 1919; 1 s., Henry Cochrane. Chairman board, directors Sahara Coal Co., Inc.; member bd. dirs. Automatic Electric Co., Internat., Lincoln Telephone and Telegraph Company, Saline Coal & Dock Co. Pres., trustee Woods Charitable Fund, Inc., Chgo.; chmn. adv. com. on coal mining engring. U. Ill.; hon. mem. adv. com. Ill. State Geol. Survey. Served with A.E.F., World War I. Mem. Bituminous Coal Research, Inc. (dir.), Chgo. Assn. of Commerce, Midwestern Air Pollution Prevention Association, Nat. Coal Association (dir.), Beta Theta Pi. Clubs: Republican, Chicago, Yale, Saddle and Cycle (Chicago); Bath (Miami Beach, Fla.). Home: Chicago IL Died Sept. 4, 1968.

WOODS, LOUIS EARNEST, Marine Corps officer; b. N.Y., Oct. 7, 1895; m. Evelyn Ninde; 1 dau., Marjorie (Williamson). Commd. 2d lt. Marine Corps, Apr. 1917, and advanced through the grades to brig. gen., 1942, major gen., 1944; asst. dir. Marine Corps Air Force; in command all Army, Navy and Marine Corps aviation units based on Guadalcanal, comdg. gen. Aircraft Fleet Marine Force, Atlantic, and 2d Marine Air Corps Wing, Cherry Point, N.C.; ret. 1951; v.p. First Nat. Bank Quantico (Va.), from 1951. Awarded D.S.M., Legion of Merit with a V, two Gold Stars and one Bronze Oak Leaf Cluster. Home: Washington DC Died Oct. 20, 1971; buried Arlington Nat. Cemetery.

WOODS, MARK WHITE, corp. official; b. Belvidere, Ill., Jan. 23, 1870; s. Frederick Moffatt and Eliza Olivia (Eddy) W.; student U. of Neb., 1889-90; m. Louise Clarke Pace, Sept. 10, 1892; children—Vashti Eugenia (Mrs. E. Lee Metcalfe), Frederick Pace. Established a loan, insurance and real estate agency in Lincoln, Neb., 1890; pres. since 1909, Woods Bros. Corp., river and harbor constrn., industrial development, real estate and gen. investments; also v.p. Woods Bros. Constrn. Co.; chmn. bd. Fairfax Airports, Woods Bros. Industrial Corp.; dir. and mem. exec. com. Standard Timber Co., Lincoln Telephone & Telegraph Co.; dir. Woods-Updike Land Co., O'Gara Coal Co. (Chicago). Mem. Lincoln Chamber Commerce. Republican. Mem. Elks, Woodmen, Royal Highlanders, T.P.A. of America. Clubs: University, Kiwanis, Country (Lincoln). Home: 2101 Sheridan Blvd. Office: 1303 Sharp Bldg., Lincoln NE‡

WOODS, WALTER LESLIE JAMES, radio mfg. exec.; b. London, Eng., June 4 1897; s. Albert J. and Susan (Hopekirk) W.; Shebbear Coll., N. Devon, Eng., 1911-15; E.D. (honorary), Drexel Institute of Technology; m. Jasmine Clarence, Sept. 17, 1927; children—Leslie, Diana. Asst. engr. wireless Iraq Telegraph Dept., 1921-24; with Philco Corp., 1926-60, chief engr. vacuum tube, export and auto radio div., 1932-39, gen. mgr. auto radio div., Detroit, 1941, asst. mgr. comml. div. in Washington, 1941-42, v.p. charge indsl. div., 1948-49, v.p., dir. research and engring. 1949, dir. internat. div., 1952, exec. v.p., dir. engring., 1957-60; vice president and general mgr. Nat. Union Radio Corp., 1942-48. Trustee Drexel U.; mem. bd. Franklin Inst.; mem. Univ. City Sci. Center. Served as lt. Royal Engrs., British Army, 1915-21. Decorated Order Brit. Emire, 1965, comdr. Order Brit. Empire, 1972. Mem. Inst. Radio Engrs., Armed Forces Communications Assn., English Speaking Union (pres. Phila. br.). Home: Philadelphia PA Died Apr. 28, 1971; buried St. Thomas' Church Whitemarsh PA

WOODS, WILLIAM GEORGE, coll. dean; b. Denton, Tex., Aug. 11, 1904; s. William M. and Ettie Alma (Briggs) W.; B.A., North Tex. State Coll., 1930; M.A., So. Meth. U., 1937; m. Lillian Sheppard, Aug. 21, 1926. Prin., coach Raymondville (Tex.) High Sch., 1925-29; prin. Denton (Tex.) Jr. High Sch., 1930-37; asst. dean men North Tex. State U., 1937-42, asso. dean men, asso. prof. edn., 1942-48, dean men, 1948-70; lectr. edn. U. Mich., U. Chgo., 1940-41; dir. Summer Workshop for Tchrs., Decatur, Mich., 1940, Grand Ledge, Mich., 1941. Served with USAAF, World War II; lt. col. Res. Mem. Tex. Tchrs. Assn., Tex. Assn. Student Personnel Adminstrn., Coll. Classroom Tchrs. Assn., Phi Delta Kappa, Alpha Chi, Kappa Delta Pi, Sigma Delta Pi. Presbyn. Home: Denton TX Died Jan. 11, 1970.

WOODS, WILLIAM SHARPLESS DERRICK, lawyer; b. Charlottesville, Va., Sept. 20, 1901; s. Samuel B. and Lucretia (Gilmore) W.; LL.B., U. Va. 1924; m. Page Bird, Apr. 17, 1929; children—William Sharpless Derrick, Montgomery Bird. Admitted to Va., N.Y. bars; practiced in Richmond, Va. 1924-28, N.Y.C., 1929-38; partner firm McGuire, Woods & Battle, and predecessor firm, Richmond, Va., from 1938. Mem. Am., Va., Richmond bar assns., N.Y. County Lawyers Assn., Soc. Colonial Wars, Nat. Audubon Soc., Raven Soc., Phi Delta Theta, Phi Delta Phi. Club: Commonwealth. Home: Richmond VA

WOODWARD, COMER MCDONALD, prof. sociology; b. Hickory Creek, Warren County, Tenn., Apr. 28, 1874; s. William Benjamin and Amelia Elizabeth (Lockhart) W.; A.B., Emory Coll., 1900; A.M., U. of Chicago, 1916, B.D., 1917, fellow, 1917-18; Dr. of Humane Letters, Birmingham-Southern, 1932; m. Mary Anne Woodruff, Oct. 25, 1900. Prin. pub. schs., New Hope, Ala., 1894-95, Guntersville, Ala., 1895-96 and 1897-98; prin. Warthen Inst., Wrightsville, Ga., 1900-02, Sparks (Ga.) Inst., 1902-07, Stamford (Tex.) Coll., 1907-09; ordained ministry M.E. Ch., S., 1903; pastor M.E. Ch., S., Rotan, Tex., 1909-10, Abilene, 1910-14; prof. history and dean of Tex. Woman's Coll., Fort Worth, 1914-15; prof. sociology, Southern Meth. U., Dallas, 1918-24; prof. sociology, Emory University, 1924-42, dean of men, 1924-34; on leave, 1929, as exec. sec. Ga. State Dept. Pub. Welfare. Mem. bd. Civic Fedn. of Dallas, 1918-24 (dir. social edn. 1918-22), Child Guidance Clinic, Dallas, 1922-24; chmn. family sect. Tex. State Conf. for Social Work, 1921-23; chmn. advisory bd. Study of Rural Chs. in Tex., 1923-24; mem. bd. Family Welfare Soc., Ga. Interracial Commn. (hon. chmn.), Ga. Conf. on Social Work (mem. exec. com.). Mem. Am. Sociol. Soc., Am. Assn. Social Workers, Southern Sociol. Soc., Ga. Acad. Social Sciences, Sigma Nu, Delta Theta Chi, Omicron Delta Kappa, Phi Beta Kappa (Emory U. 1930). Retired 1942. Home: Emory University, GA‡

WOODWARD, ELLEN SULLIVAN, govt. ofcl.; b. Oxford, Miss.; d. U.S. Senator William V. and Belle (Murray) Sullivan; ed. San Souci Woman's Coll.; LL.D., Woman's Coll., U. N.C.; m. Judge Albert Y. Woodward of Miss.; 1 son, Capt. Albert Y. Mem. State Legislature of Miss., 1926-28; dir. community development Miss. State Bd. of Dev., 1926-29, exec. dir., 1929-33; exec. sec. Research Commn. of Miss., 1930-33; conducted weekly radio programs on State dev., 1929-33; asst. adminstr. in charge women's div. Civil Works Adminstrn. and Fed. Emergency Relief Adminstrn., 1933-35; asst. adminstr. W.P.A., 1935-38; mem. Social Security Bd., 1938-46; dir. Office of Internat. Relations, Fed. Security Agy., since July 1946 (rep. of agy. on interdepartmental com. on internat. social policy, also rep. on interdepartmental adv. council on tech. coop., Dept. of State); mem. U.S. delegation to all six sessions of Council of U.N.R.R.A. (adviser on welfare services 1943-46); U.S. mem. standing tech. com. on welfare U.N.R.R.A., also tech. sub-com. on welfare for Far East, 1944-45; mem. U.S. delegation 3d, 4th and 5th sessions, U.N. ECOSOC (adviser on welfare services); mem. U.S. com. Internat. Conf. of Social Work; mem. President's nat. vol. participation com. Civil Defense, 1941-42; mem. White House confs.; on child health and protection, 1930, on housing and home ownership, 1931, on needs of unemployed women, 1933, on children in a Democracy, 1940, on how women may share in postwar policy making, 1944, on children and youth, 1950; chmn. nat. women's adv. com. U.S. Defense Bonds Div., Treasury Dept., 1940-51; trustee Miss. State Charity Hosp. (Matty Hersee), 1924-29; dir. Miss. Children's Home Soc., 1928-41; exec. sec. Miss. Conf. of Social Work, 1929-30, Miss. com. President's Orgn. on Unemployment Relief, 1931; mem. exec. com. Miss. State Bd. Pub. Welfare, 1932-33; mem. Internat. and Nat. confs. social work; Com. on Women in World Affairs; Instructive Vis. Nurse Soc. (dir.), 1941-45; nat. adv. com. post war planning A.W.V.S., 1944-47; continuing com. Nat. Conf. on Prevention and Control Juvenile Delinquency; Internat. and Nat. fedns. bus. and profl. women's clubs, inc.; nat. chmn. com. on pub. affairs Bus. and Profl. Women's Clubs, Inc., 1944-46; Polit. Study Club; Pilot Internat. (hon.); Am. Newspaper Women's Club; Miss. State Soc. of Washington (pres. 1937-40); Women's Nat. Dem. Club; Colonial Dames; D.A.R.; Chi Omega. Del. at large from Miss. to Dem. nat. convs., 1928, 36; Dem. nat. committeewoman for Miss., 1932-34. Methodist. Contbr. to mags. and newspapers. Home: Washington DC Died Sept. 23, 1971; buried Louisville MS

WOODWARD, ERNEST, lawyer; b. Hartford, Ky., Nov. 18, 1877; s. William T. and Lucy (Paul) W.; student Beaver Dam (Ky.) Sem., 1896, Hartford Coll., 1897-98; m. Alice Fielden, Jan. 4, 1910; children—Fielden, Alice, Elizabeth, Ernest. Admitted to Ky. bar, 1898, and began practice at Hartford; county atty. Ohio County, Ky., 1905-09; dist. atty. Louisville, Henderson & St. Louis Ry., 1915-20; gen. atty. L.. R.R. co., 1921-22; mem. Woodward, Hamilton & Hobson, 1922-35; sr. counsel Woodward, Hobson & Fulton. Dir. Henry Fisher Packing Co. Mem. Am., Ky., Louisville bar assns., Assn. Bar City of N.Y., Am. Law Inst., Am. Counsel Assn. (ex-president). Republican. Baptist. Mason (K.T.). Clubs: Pendennis, Filson. Home: Louisville KY Died Apr. 2, 1968.

WOODWARD, FLETCHER D(RUMMOND), physician; b. Saluda, Va., Jan. 30, 1895; s. William Wallace and Katharine Roberta (Drummond) W.; student Va. Mil. Inst., 1913-14; M.D., U. of Va., 1919; m. Mildred Bacon Hart, May 18, 1923; children—Anne Mutter (Mrs. James Hageman), Fletcher D., Malcolm P. Interne U. of Va. Hosp., 1919-20; resident in surgery, Manhattan Eye, Ear, Nose and Throat Hosp., N.Y. City, 1920-23; pvt. practice medicine, Newport News, Va., 1923-25; practice limited to otolaryngology since 1923; clinical professor otolaryngology University Va. Medical Sch. and Hospital, 1925-69. Diplomate Am. Bd. Otolaryngology, 1925. Fellow Am. Coll. Surgeons; mem. A.M.A. (past sec. and past pres.), Am. Broncho-Esoph. Assn., Am. L.R.O. Soc., Am. Laryngol. Assn., Am. Otolog. Soc., So. Med. Assn., Va. State and Albemarle County med. socs. Past sec. and chmn. sect. on eye, ear, nose and throat, So. Med. Assn. Home: Charlottesville VA Died July 2, 1969.

WOODWARD, HUGH BEISTLE, lawyer; b. Clearfield, Pa., Apr. 29, 1885; s. Americus Hodge and Ella Jane (Beistle) W.; student Pa. State U., 1904-06; Ph.B., Dickinson Coll., 1908, M.A., 1910, LL.B., 1910, LL.D., 1959; LL.D. (honorary), University New Mexico, 1963; m. Helen E. Kisner, June 14, 1911. Admitted to Pa. bar, 1911, Colo. bar, 1914, N.M. bar, 1915, U.S. Supreme Ct., 1923, also 8th Circuit, 10th Circuit cts. appeals; practiced law, Clearfield, Pa., 1911-13, Greeley, Colo., 1914, Clayton, N.M., 1915-29; gen. practice, Albuquerque, 1933-51, limited, 1951-68; dist. atty. 8th Jud. Dist. N.M., 1920-24; lt. gov. N.M., 1929; U.S. dist. atty. N.M., 1929-33; spl. asst. U.S. atty. gen., 1942-46; pres. Southwest Finance, Inc., 1931-57, N.M. Credit Corp., 1941-68, Southwest Loan Co., 1954-57, Southwestern Construction Company. Member National Advisory Committee on Multiple Use of Nat. Forests, 1960-64; mem. bd. edn., Clearfield, Pa., 1911-13, pres. bd. edn., Clayton, N.M., 1917-22; legal adv. bd. Selective Service, Union County, N.M., World War I; exec. com. N.M. Council Def., 1942-46, N.M. Council Civil Def., 1950-52; mem. N.M. Game Commn., 1937-43, Albuquerque Plan Commn., 1948-57; pres. N.M. State Game Protective Assn., 1946-48, 51-53, sec., 1949-50, also pres., sec. Albuquerque Game Protective Assn. Chmn. N.M. Republican Central Com., 1922-23, chmn. N.M. Rep. Conv., 1922, 28. Bd. regents U. N.M., 1935-37; pres. Nat. Wildlife Fedn. Endowment, Inc., 1957-61, member of the board of trustees, 1961-68, also v.p.; dir. Nat. Wildlife Fedn., 1952-62, chmn. permanent home bldg. com., 1955-61. Recipient Presdl. citation for pub. service, 1933, certificate of appreciation U.S. Atty. Gen., 1947, spl. award N.M. Assn. Finance Cos., 1955, Nash Conservation award, 1953, numerous others. Mem. Am., N.M. (bar commr. 8th Jud. Dist. 1928-31), Albuquerque bar assns., N.M. Wildlife and

Conservation Assn. (pres. emeritus), Audubon Soc., Wilderness Soc., Izaak Walton League, Am. Forestry Assn., Albuquerque Lawyers Club, Newcomen Soc. N.A., Phi Beta Kappa, Phi Beta Kappa Assos. Presbyn. Mason. Club: Ten Don (Albuquerque). Home: Albuquerque NM Died Aug. 18, 1968.

WOODWARD, LESTER ARMAND, oil co. exec.; b. Goodland, Kan., Jan. 31, 1908; s. William A. and Gertrude A. (McDole) W.; A.B., Coe Coll., 1930, Doctor of Laws (honorary), 1966; M.B.A., Northwestern University, 1932, C.P.A., 1932; m. Frances M. Danberg, Aug. 1, 1936; children—Douglas Earl, Russell Clark. Staff, Arthur Anderson & Co., C.P.A.'s Chgo., 1932-40, mgr., 1941-44; treas. Mid-West Refineries, Inc., 1944-45, v.p., 1946-50. pres. 1950-56; financial v.p. Kerr-McGee Oil Industries, Inc., Oklahoma City, 1956-67; senior vice president Kerr-McGee Corp., 1967-71; dir. Moss-American, Inc., American Potash & Chemical Corporation, also Penn Square National Bank, Kerr-McGee Chem. Corp. Mem. Am. Inst. C.P.A.'s. Unitarian. Clubs: Petroleum, Chandelle, Oklahoma City Country. Home: Oklahoma City OK Died July 8, 1971.

WOODWARD, (ERNEST) LLEWELLYN, SIR, educator; b. London, Eng., May 14, 1890; s. George Ernest and Helen (Thwaites) W.; ed. Merchant Taylors' Sch., London; M.A., Oxford U., 1914; Rhodes traveling fellow, 1931; Litt.D. (hon.), Princeton, 1946; m. Florence Marle O'Loughlin, Sept. 19, 1917 (deceased September 26, 1961). Fellow All Souls Coll., Oxford, 1919-44, 62-71, lectr., tutor New Coll., Oxford, 1922-39, sr. proctor, Oxford, 1928-29, prof. internat. relations, 1944-47, prof. modern history, 1947-51; prof. Inst. Advanced Study, Princeton, 1951-60, emeritus professor, 1961-71. Served with the B.E.F., World War One, France, 1915-16, Salonika, 1916-18; staff member Fgn. Office, London, World War II. Knighted, 1952; hon. fellow of Corpus Christi College and Worcester College, Oxford. Fellow of the British Academy; mem. Am. Philos. Soc. Club: Athenaeum (London). Author: Christianity and Nationalism in the Later Roman Empire, 1916; Three Studies in European Conservatism, 1929; War and Peace in Europe, 1815-70, 1931; French Revolutions, 1934; The Twelve-Winded Sky, 1933; Short Journey, 1942; British Foreign Policy in the Second World War, Vol. I, 1962, Vol. II, 1971, Vol. III, 1972; The Age of Reform, 1962; History of England, 1938, 2d edit., 1962. Editor: Documents on British Foreign Policy (with Rohan Butler), 1919-39; Great Britain and The War of 1914-18, 1967; Prelude to Modern Europe, 1972. Home: Oxford England Died Mar. 11, 1971.

WOODWORTH, G(EORGE) WALLACE, musical educator; b. Boston, Mass., Nov. 6, 1902; s. George Loomis and Ruth Smith (Beckford) W.; A.B., Harvard, 1924, A.M., 1926; Litt.D., (honorary), Miami U., 1955; Mus.D. (hon.), New England Conservatory Music, 1958; Mus.D. (honorary), Hartford University, 1963; m. Evelyn Barnes, Dec. 20, 1928; children—Ellery Beckford, Harriet Tilden (Mrs. Albin C. Koch). Tchr. Harvard, 1926, prof. music, formerly coll. organist, choir master, condr. Harvard Glee Club, Radcliffe Choral Soc.; vis. prof. Royal Coll. of Music, London, Eng., 1966-67. Trustee Fisk U., New Eng. Conservatory of Music. Recipient Founders award Radcliffe Coll., 1969. Fellow Am. Acad. Arts and Scis. Mem. Am. Musicol. Soc., Coll. Music Soc. (pres. 1958-60), Phi Beta Kappa (pres. Harvard chpt. 1969). Republican. Episcopalian. Author: The World of Music, 1964. Home: Cambridge MA Died July 18, 1969; buried Woodlawn Cemetery, Everett MA

WOODY, MCIVER, physician; b. Louisville, Ky., Mar. 16, 1886; s. Samuel Elisha and Emma Calmes (McIver) W.; A.B., University of Louisville, 1903, University of Richmond (Virginia), 1905, Harvard College, 1907 (cum laude); M.D., Harvard Medical School, 1912; married Regina Llewellyn Jones, May 1, 1918; children—McIver Wallace, Regina Llewellyn (Mrs. John Ben Butler, Jr.), Emma McIver (Mrs. J. M. Sowa). Asst. physician, Butler Hosp., Providence, 1912-13; surgical interne, Boston City Hospital, 1913-14; Austin teaching fellow, Harvard Med. Sch., 1914-19, James Jackson Cabot fellow, 1914-15, asst. in pathology, 1916-18, physician to students, 1917-18, sec. of the Faculty of Medicine, 1917-18; asst. out patient surgeon Boston City Hosp., 1917-20; dean and prof. of surgery Univ. of Tenn., 1920-21, Baylor U., 1921-22; physician Standard Oil Co. of N.J., 1922-44, medical director of the Esso Standard Oil Co., 1944-51; med. cons. Railroad Retirement Bd., 1951-65. Member medical advisory board American Petroleum Inst., 1945-51, chmn., 1945-46. Served as lieutenant, personnel and sanitation divisions Surg.-General's Office, United States Army, 1918-19; maj., Med. Res. Corps, 1924-34. Fellow N.Y. Acad. of Med. Mass. Med. Soc., Indsl. Medical Association (president 1939-40), A.A.A.S., A.M.A., A.C.P.; member Med. Soc. State of N.Y., N.Y. Soc. Tropical Medicine (president 1941-43), Descs. of Colonial Clergy, Sons of Am. Revolution, Phi Beta Kappa, Kappa Alpha. Republican. Presbyterian. Clubs: Harvard (N.Y.C.). Home: Elizabeth NJ Died May 3, 1970; buried Evergreen Cemetery, Boston MA

WOOLDRIDGE, EDMUND TYLER, naval officer; b. Lawrenceberg, Ky., Jan. 5, 1897; s. Dewell Henderson and Minnie Gray (Hawkins) W.; B.S., U.S. Naval Acad. 1919; m. Marion Lee Johnson, Nov. 18, 1921; children—Edmund Tyler, Marion Lee, Marshall Homer. Commd. ensign U.S. Navy, 1919, and advanced through grades to vice admiral, April 1954; assigned naval duties including commands of submarine, destroyer and battleship, 1916-41; chief of staff to task force comdr., North Atlantic, engaged in anti-submarine warfare, 1941-43; dir. naval officer personnel, hdqrs., Navy Dept., Washington, D.C., 1943-44; comd. U.S.S. New Jersey (flagship at various times for Admirals Halsey and Spruance), 1944-45; comd. naval forces, Northeastern Japan, 1945-46; comdg. cruiser div. Western Pacific, 1946-47; became asst. chief naval operations Mil.-Politico Affairs, Washington, 1947; now commander 2d Fleet and commander NATO Striking Fleet, 1954-55; comdt. The National War College, 1956-58. Decorated Distinguished Service medal, Legion of Merit, Bronze star, Commendation ribbon, Victory ribbon (World War I), Haitian Campaign ribbon, 1919, Am. Defense ribbon, European Theatre ribbon, Am. Theatre ribbon, Asiatic-Pacific Theatre ribbon, Victory (World War II); C.B.E.; Comdr. Order of Ayachucho, Peru, 1956. Presbyn. Club: Army-Navy-Marine Corps Country (Washington). Home: Annapolis MD Died Dec. 15, 1968; buried U.S. Naval Acad. Cemetery, Annapolis MD

WOOLLEY, CLARENCE MOTT, mfr.; b. Detroit, Mich., Sept. 15, 1863; s. Smith Rensselaer and Marie Richardson (Smith) W.; ed. pub. schs., Detroit; LL.D., Colgate U., 1928, St. Lawrence U., 1931; m. Isabelle Baker; children—Dorianne, Clarence Mott (dec.), J. Carrington. With Fiske & Co., Detroit, until 1887; assisted in organizing Mich. Radiator & Iron Co., Detroit, 1887, of which was dir. and sec.; moved to Chicago, 1892; an organizer of Am. Radiator Co., 1892, pres., 1902-24, chmn. bd. since 1924; chmn. bd. Am. Radiator & Standard Sanitary Corp. from formation in 1929, to Nov. 1938, retired but still dir.; former dir., A.T.&S.F. R.y., Atlantic Mut. Inc. Co., Mut. Life Ins. Co. N.Y., First Nat. Bank (Chicago), Gold Dust Corp., Hecker Milling Co. (now Best Foods, Inc.), Hotel Waldorf Astoria Corp., N.Y. Gen. Motors Co., Gen. Electric Co., Johns Manville Co., N.Y. Reserve Bk. World's Fair, 1939; pres. trus. John B. Pierce Foundn.; trustee St. Lawrence U. Vice-chmn. War Trade Bd., Washington, D.C., during World War I. Mem. Am. Soc. of French Legion of Honor, Pan-American Society, Pilgrims of U.S., American Chamber Commerce in France, British Chamber Commerce. Appointed vice chairman War Trade Board, Washington, 1917. Decorated Chevalier Legion of Honor (France); Order of the Crown of Italy; Order of Leopold (Belgium). Clubs: Blind Brook, Economic, Nat. Republican, The Links (New York); Chicago Club: El Paso (Colorado Springs, Colorado); Detroit, Yondotega (Detroit); American, Royal Automobile Club (London); Saint Cloud Country (Paris). Home: Greenwich, Conn.; Santa Fe, N.M.; also Palm Springs, Calif. Office: 40 W. 40th St., NY City*‡

WOOLLEY, MRS (ANNA) LAZELLE THAYER, author; b. Port Allegany, Pa., June 17, 1872; d. Edwin G. and Jane E. (Wilkin) Thayer; ed. high sch., Port Allegany, and pvt. schs.; m. Milwaukee, Wis., Edward Mott Woolley, Dec. 20, 1898; children—Catherine, Marion. Episcopalian. Author: The Just Alike Twins, 1912; Faith Palmer at the Oaks, 1912; Faith Palmer at Fordyce Hall, 1913; Faith Palmer in New York, 1914; Faith Palmer in Washington, 1915. Contbr. to women's mags. Pres. Woman's Club of Passaic, 1919—; chmn. resolutions com. N.J. State Federation of Women's Clubs, 1921-22. Home: 71 Park Av., Passaic NJ‡

WOOLSEY, GEORGE, surgeon; b. New Haven, Conn., May 2, 1861; s. Theodore Dwight (pres. Yale) and Sarah Sears (Prichard) W.; A.B., Yale, 1881; 1 yr. post-grad. Sheffield Scientific Sch., Yale; M.D., Coll. Phys. and Surg. (Columbia), 1885; post-grad. work, Roosevelt Hosp., 1885-86, Germany, and France, 1887-88; m. Jean Paul Ellinwood, May 12, 1892; children—Marjorie Ellinwood (Mrs. John C. Kittle), George Pierpont (dec.), Laura Hurd. Prof. anatomy and clin. surgery, New York U. Med. Sch., 1890-98, Cornell Univ. Med. Sch., New York, 1898-1909; prof. clin. surgery same, 1909-26, prof. emeritus since 1926; surgeon to Bellevue Hospital, 1890-1921, Presbyn. Hospital, 1900-14; now consulting surgeon Bellevue and Memorial hospitals, New York Infirmary for Women and Children (New York), St. John's Hospital (Yonkers), Peekskill Hosp. Maj. Med. Officers Reserve Corps, 1917. Fellow Am. Surg. Assn., Am. Coll. Surgeons, New York Acad. Medicine; mem. Soc. Clin. Surgery, New York Surg. Soc. and Clin. Soc., A.M.A., State and County med. socs. Club: Century (New York). Author: Applied Surgical Anatomy, 1902, 1908. Contbr. to System of Genito-Urinary Diseases, Syphilology and Dermatology (Morrow), 1893; Medical Jurisprudence, Forensic Medicine and Toxicology (Witthaus & Becker), 1894; Text Book of Anatomy by American Authors (Gerrish), 1899, 1902; Keen's Surgery, Vols. II and VI. Address: 117 E. 36th St., New York NY*‡

WOOLSON, HARRY THURBER, engring. consultant; b. Passaic, N.J., Sept. 20, 1876; s. George C. and Sarah Martin (Thurber) W.; ed. priv. sch., Stevens Prep. Sch.; M.E., Stevens Inst. of Tech., 1897; m. Bessie Van Iderstine, Aug. 19, 1903; children—L. Irving, George Thurber, Herbert C. Served as 2d class machinist, U.S. Navy, Spanish-Am. War. Draftsman with Nat. Meter Co. of Brooklyn, N.Y., 1903; later draftsman with Gas Engine & Power Co.; then draftsman advancing to chief engr. with Charles L. Seabury & Co., N.Y. City, 1899-1915; truck engr. Packard Motor Car Co., Detroit, 1915-16; engring. dept. Studebaker Corp., Detroit, 1916-20; with Willys Corp., Elizabeth, N.J., and Zeder-Skelton-Breer Engring. Co., Newark, N.J., 1921; with Chrysler Corp., Detroit, 1921-47, as chief engr. and later exec. engr., 1935-47, retired Jan. 1, 1947; pres. Chrysler Inst. of Engring., 1940-47. Mem. Com. on Internat. Screw Thread Unification. Has designed steam and gasoline marine machinery, developed automobile chassis, medium tanks and other war equipment. Awarded Stevens Inst. medal for accomplishments in engring., 1945; 2 citations from U.S. Army Ordnance Dept. Fellow Am. Soc. Mech. Engrs.; mem. Franklin Inst., Brit. Inst. Automotive Engrs., mem. (life) Soc. Automotive Engrs. v.p. 1928; councillor, 1932-36; pres., 1937; chmn. Detroit. Sect., 1934; mem. Ordnance adv. com.); mem. Engring. Soc. of Detroit, Tau Beta Pi. Clubs: Detroit Athletic, Detroit Golf, Ingleside Golf, (Detroit). Mason. Presbyterian. Home: 1780 Strathcona Drive, Detroit MI‡

WOOLSTON, HOWARD BROWN, sociologist; b. Harrisburg, Pa., Apr. 22, 1876; s. William John and Annie Elizabeth (Brown) W.; B.A., Yale, 1898; S.T.B., University of Chicago, 1901; M.A., Harvard Univ., 1902; studied in Paris and Berlin, 1903-04; Ph.D., Columbia University, 1909; m. Katharine Nichols Dally, Aug. 10, 1922; children—John, Marian. Fellow University of Chicago, 1901, Harvard University, 1902; lecturer Chicago Sch. of Civics, 1907; Western Reserve Univ., 1907-08; instr., asst. prof. and prof. sociology and statistics, Coll. City of New York, 1909-18; prof. sociology, Univ. of Washington, Oct. 1919-47, now emeritus and research counsel; exchange professor U. of Pa., 1923. Dir. sch. and neighborhood work, Roxbury, Boston, 1902-03, New York, 1904-06; headworker Goodrich House, Cleveland, O., 1906-08; dir. wage investigation, N.Y. Factory Commn., 1913-14; investigator Bur. of Hygiene, 1917; major American Red Cross and mgr. Serbian Relief in France, 1918; mem. Balkan Commn., 1919. Mem. Am. Sociol. Soc., Phi Beta Kappa, Zeta Psi. Decorated Officer Order of St. Sava (Serbian). Author: Study of the Population of Manhattanville, 1909; Prostitution in the United States, 1921; Metropolis, 1938. Home: 1307 E. Boston St., Seattle WA‡

WOOSTER, LORRAINE ELIZABETH, educator; b. Steubenville, O., July 24, 1874; d. Charles C. and Nannie (Cullom) W.; A.M., State Normal U. of Kan.; unmarried. Engaged in writing school books many years, and pub. of same as Wooster & Co.; admitted to Kan. bar, 1914, bar of Supreme Court of U.S., 1924, and to practice in Ill. and Okla. Elected v.p. Nat. Woman's Bar Assn., 1929. Kan. state supt. public instruction, 1919-23. Author of numerous school publs. since 1897; new edits.—Primer (American Life and Hand Work), Wooster Arithmetics (books 1 and 2), Wooster Combination Reading Chart, Wooster Sentence Builders, Wooster Number Builders, The Wooster Readers (American Life, 8 books), Wooster Patriotic Speaker—all brought down to 1928 or 1930. Home: Salina KS Office: 2510 Prairie Av., Chicago IL‡

WOOTAN, JAMES K., oil co. exec.; b. Los Angeles, May 19 1911; s. John T. and Margaret E. (Kirkpatrick) W.; student Occidental Coll., 1929-32; B.S. in Bus. Adminstrn., U. So. Cal., 1936; m. Doris L. Harvey, Sept. 11, 1937; children—Doris D., James H. Bookkeeper 1st Fed. Trust & Savs. Bank, Pasadena, Cal., 1932-33; asst. office engr. Tidewater Assos. Oil Co., 1933-36; mgr. land dept. Sunset Oil Co., 1936-44; mgr. lands Signal Oil and Gas Co., 1946-56, mgr. exploration, dir. co., 1956-60, v.p. from 1960, mgr. fgn. operations, from 1962, mgr. joint operations and real estate, from 1964; pres. dir. Sunbeam Oil Co.; v.p., dir. Am. Ind. Oil Co., from 1963; pres. dir. Long Beach Oil Devel. Co., from 1963. Served to lt. (s.g.) USNR, 1944-46. Mem. Am. Assn. Petroleum Landmen (charter). Home: Pasadena CA Died Apr. 7, 1971.

WOOTEN, BENJAMIN HARRISON, banker; b. Timpson, Tex., Dec. 21, 1894; s. Samuel Davis and Eula May (Downing) W.; grad. North Tex. State U., 1917, LL.D., 1968; LL.D., U. Ark., 1950, Baylor U., 1963; m. Margaret Kay, August 7, 1919. Asst. cashier Alba (Tex.) Nat. Bank, 1919-23; cashier, operating exec. officer Farmers and Merchants Nat. Bank, Farmersville, 1923-26; state bank examiner, 1926, deptl. state bank examiner, 1927-32; chief examiner Fed. Home Loan Banking System, Washington, 1932; pres. Fed. Home Loan Bank of Little Rock, 1932-44, chmn. bd., 1944-53; v.p., mem. exec. com. Republic Nat. Bank of Dallas, 1944-50; pres. First National Bank in Dallas, 1950-60, chmn. bd., 1960-63; chmn. bd. Dallas Fed. Savs. & Loan Assn., 1964-72; past chmn. bd. Oaklawn Nat. Bank, ìreenville Av. State Bank; dir. Dallas Fed. Savings & oan Assn., Gulf, Colorado & Santa Fe Ry. Co., Murray o. of Texas. Civilian aide at large to sec. of the army, ir. Cotton Bowl Athletic Assn. (mem. exec. ommittee). Served as private, World War I; machine un battalion, France and Army Occupation; disch. as d lt., 1919. Gen. chmn. Community Chest campaign r Dallas County, 1949; co-chmn. Dallas drive for ruett Meml. Hosp., 1947; treas. Texas Heart Assn., 953; trustee Baylor U.; chmn. bd. trustees Baylor U. ledical Center, Chmn. bd. regents North Tex. State U. rustee Tex. Found. Voluntarily Supported Colls. and nivs., Southwest Research Inst., Tex. Heart Research ound., Tex. Research Found. Trustee Tax Found., nc., N.Y.C. Former v.p. of the United Defense Fund, nc., N.Y.C., N.Y. Trustee Southwestern Legal Found. outhern Meth. U. Dir. Tex. Research League; mem. xecutive com., hon. chmn. bd. Tex. United Fund, Inc.; hmn. trustees Hillcrest Found.; bd. govs. Am. Found. eligion and Psychiatry; mem. exec. council Circle 10, oy Scouts America, member at large Nat. Council. hmn. Ark. state civil defense council, 1941-44. Chmn. th War Loan Dr., Dallas Co. Recipient Horatio Alger ward American Schs. and Colls. Assn., 1959; ertificate of appreciation for civilian service U.S. rmy, 1967; named Dallas' Headliner of yr., Dallas ress Club, 1952; outstanding salesman of Dallas, Sales xecs. Club, 1950; Linz Award, Dallas community ervice, 1953. Mem. Dallas C. of C., U.S. C. of C. Sales xecs. Club of New York, Delta Sigma Pi, Sigma Phi psilon, Beta Gamma Sigma (all hon.). Baptist (mem. elief and annuity bd., Southern conv., dir. Bapt. oundation of Texas). Clubs: Dallas Country, City, rook Hollow. Office: Dallas TX Died Nov. 22, 1971.

VOOTEN, RALPH H., army officer; b. Independence, Miss., Aug. 30, 1893; B.S., Agrl. and Mech. Coll. of ex., 1916; commd. 2d lt. Inf. Aug. 1917, and advanced hrough the grades to major general, 1944; apptd. mil. ttache, Santiago, Chile, Aug. 1938; on temp. duty in Mil. Intelligence Div., War Dept. Gen. Staff, July 941-Sept. 1941, then on staff duty with Gen. Hdqrs. of he Army; later assigned to Army Air Forces Tech. raining Command, Miami, Fla.; commd. Sixth Air orce, Nov. 1943-May 1944; commd. U.S. Army orces South Atlantic, Recife, Brazil, May 944-November 1945, Duty with Foreign Liquidation Commn., State Dept., Washington, D.C., 1946; comdg. en. Pacific Air Comd., Hawaii, 1947-48; ret. 1948; xec. v.p. Mid-South Chem. Co., Inc., Memphis, 949-69. Home: Memphis TN Died Nov. 19, 1969; uried Memphis Memorial Park.

VORCESTER, HENRY E., business exec.; b. Tewksbury, Mass., Sept. 30, 1875; s. Horatio E. and Annie (Jarvie) W.; ed. Mass. Inst. of Tech.; m. Alice Duncan, Apr. 10, 1905; children—Mary J., Henry E., r., John D. With the United Fruit Co., Boston, Mass., ince 1914, v.p. 1929-46; v.p. Revere Sugar Refinery, Boston, 1919-46; ret. Clubs: Union, Univ., Engineers, Algonquin (Boston); Union League (New York). Home: 11 Church St., Winchester MA Office: 60 State St., Boston MA‡

VORCESTER, P(HILIP) G(EORGE), geologist, niv. administr.; b. Thetford, Vt., May 5, 1884; s. George Steele and Ida Eldora (Kinney) W.; student, U. of Mich., 1904-06; A.B. U. of Colo., 1909, A.M., 1911; Ph.D., U. of Chicago, 1924; m. Mollie Brown, Aug. 29, 1911; children—Willis G., John B. (1st lieut., U.S.A.A.F., killed in service), Mary Ellen (Mrs. Geo. R. Lewis), Thomas K. Instr. geology U. of Colo., 1912-14, asst. prof., 1914-18, asso. prof. 1915-24, dean of men, 1920-30, prof., 1924-69, head dept., 1934-49, dean grad. sch., 1943-69; geologist Colo. Geol. Survey, 1912-27; geologist Canadian Exploration Co., summers, 1927-30; consulting geologist, since 1914. Moderator 1st Congl. Ch.; mem. Sch. Bd. Boulder Dist. No. 3, 1934-40; trustee Chicago Theol. Sem., 1922-24. Fellow Geol. Soc. Am., A.A.A.S.; mem. Sigma Xi, Phi Beta Kappa, Alpha Chi Sigma, Sigma Gamma Epsilon. Awarded Norlin Medal by U. of Colo. Alumni Assn., 1946. Republican. Conglist. Mason. Club: Internat. Rotary. Author: Textbook of Geomorphology (D. Van Nostrand Co.), 1939, revised edition, 1948; Molybdenum Deposits of Colo., 1918; Geology of Boulder CO Died 1969.

WORCESTER, WILLIS GEORGE, educator; b. Boulder, Colo., June 26, 1918; s. Philip George and Mollie (Brown) W.; B.S. in Elec. Engring., U. Colo., 1939, M.S. in Elec. Engring., Cal. Inst. Tech., 1940; Ph.D., Stanford; 1952; m. Mary Isobel Toy Greenway, June 7, 1940; children—Robert L., Willis George. Engr., Gen. Electric Co., 1941-46, mem. faculty U. Colo., 1946-63, prof. elec. engring., 1956-63, acting dean Grad. Sch., 1960-61; chmn. dept. elec. engring., 1961-63; dean engring, Va. Poly. Inst., 1963-70; engring. cons., 1948-70; specialist in planning research Inst. Kabul (Afghanistan) U., summer 1960. Dir. Hathaway Instruments, Inc., 1960-62. Mem. Citizens Com. Edn. Handicapped Children, Boulder, 1957, Citizens Com. Water Supply Devel., Boulder, 1961. Registered profl. engr., Colo., Va. Sr. mem. I.E.E.E.; member of Sigma Xi, Tau Beta Pi, Eta Kappa Nu, Sigma Pi Sigma, Blacksburg VA Died Feb. 10, 1970.

WORDEN, CHARLES BEATTY, occupational medical work; b. Steubenville, O., Apr. 26, 1874; s. James Avery (D.D.) and Mary Reeder (Hendrickson) W.; A.B., Princeton, 1894; M.D., Med. Sch., Univ. of Pa., 1898; univs. of Berlin and Vienna 1 yr.; m. Ora Otis Williams, Dec. 18, 1907; children—Ora Otis, James Avery II, Philip Monroe. Began practice at Phila., 1898; resident physician Presbyn. Hosp., 1899-1900; asst. surgeon orthopedic dept., Univ. Hosp., and asso. prof. diseases of stomach, Polyclinic Hosp., 1900-07; mem. staff Phipps Inst., 1905-07; specialized in occupational med. work; med. dir. John Wanamaker Stores, New York, Phila., 1906-48, ret. Capt. U.S. Med. Corps, 1918-19. Formerly fellow A.M.A., Coll. Physicians, Phila.; mem. Phila. County Med. Soc., Loyal Legion. Republican. Presbyterian. Clubs: Princeton (Phila.); Nassan (Princeton, N.J.). Home: Box 245 Princeton NJ‡

WORMAN, BEN JAMES, editor, publisher; b. Madison, N.J., Aug. 19, 1870; s. Dr. James H. W. (former editor Outing, now U.S. consul at Munich); ed. Adelphi Acad., Brooklyn, and grad. high school, Albany, N.Y., 1890; course of eng'ring, with sp'l attention to English, at Harvard, to junior yr.; left 1893 because of sickness; m. Albany, N.Y., Apr. 28, 1897, Ama M. Atkinson. Took partial charge of Outing magazine, 1895-6; complete editorial and business management Outing Publishing Co., 1896-1900, resigning upon change of ownership; treas. U.S. Appraisal Co., Boston, since 1903. Address: 141 Franklin St., Boston MA‡

WORMWOOD, KENNETH MENDUM, lawyer; b. Kennebunk, Me., Oct. 15, 1902; s. Raymond C. and Augusta (Mendum) W.; LL.B., Denver U., 1926; m. Rose B. Combs, Aug. 14, 1926 (dec.); 1 dau., Sally (Mrs. Blaine D'Arcey); m. 2d, Geneva Stonemets, Aug. 5, 1968. Admitted to Colo. bar, 1926; U.S. Supreme Ct.; practiced in Denver, 1926-70; sr. partner Wormwood, Wolvington, Renner & Dosh, 1964-70; lecturer law schools of Colorado University, Denver University. Vice pres., dir. Fedn. Ins. Council; vice chmn. com. jury instrns. Colo. Supreme Ct. Fellow Am. Bar Found., Am. Coll. Trial Attys.; mem. Am. (Ho. of Dels.), Colo. (founder, chmn. Lawyers Fidelity Fund), Denver (past pres.) bar assns., Phi Delta Phi, Lambda Chi Alpha. Republican. Methodist. Mason. Clubs: Denver Athletic, Lakewood Country. Contbr. articles to legal jours. Home: Evergreen CO

WORRALL, AMBROSE ALEXANDER, aerospace cons.; b. Barrow-in-Furness, Eng., Jan. 18, 1899; s. Alexander and Rebecca (Mattocks) W.; came to U.S., 1923, naturalized, 1930; certificate Barrow-in-Furness Sch., 1918; student St. Ignatius Coll., Cleve., 1923-24, Cleve. Coll., 1927-29; diploma Nat. Radio Inst., 1964; Ph.D. (hon.); m. Olga Nathalie Ripich, June 7, 1928; children—Ambrose Mattocks and Alexander Karanczay (twins) (Dec.). Aero. engr. Vickers Ltd., Barrow-in-Furness, 1920; dept. mgr. Martin Co., Balt., 1924-64; cons. Martin Marietta Corp., Balt., 1964-68, Westinghouse Electric Corp., Balt., 1968-69; v.p. K & W Enterprises, Inc., Balt., 1964-73, Markari Research Labs, Inc., Englewood, N.J., 1966-73; dir. Life Energies Research, Inc., N.Y.C., 1968-73. Mem. corp. bd. Springfield (Mass.) Coll., 1962-73. Served with Brit. Army, 1918-19. Mem. Wainwright Center Devel. Human Resources, Spiritual Frontiers Fellowship, Chs. Fellowship for Psychial and Spiritual Studies, Radionic-Magnetic Centre Orgn. Methodist (asso. dir. New Life Clinic 1950-73). Mason. Author: Essay on Prayer, 1952; Meditation and Contemplation, 1956; Silentium Altum, 1961; The Philosophy and Methodology of Spiritual Healing, 1961; Basic Principles of Spiritual Healing, 1963; The Gift of Healing, 1965; The Miracle Healers, 1968; Explore Your Psychic World, 1970; Your Power to Heal. Address: Baltimore MD Died Feb. 2, 1973; buried Dulaney Valley Meml. Gardens, Cockeysville MD

WORTH, JAMES HUNTTING, chem. mfg. exec.; b. N.Y.C., Nov. 30, 1918; s. Huntting C. and Gladys S. (Robbins) W.; grad. Deerfield Acad., 1936; B.S., Princeton, 1940, Ch.E., 1941; m. Fay Meggee, Dec. 30, 1947; children—James Huntting, Susan Rowland, Pamela Case, Mark Robbins. Research chemist Monsanto Chem. Co., 1941-42, project supt., 1943-50, devel. engr., 1951-53; dir. tech. and econ. evaluation Celanese Corp. Am., 1953-57, asst. gen. mgr. chem. div., 1957-59, v.p. Celanese Chem. Co., 1959-60, pres., 1960-63; group v.p. plastics and chemicals Celanese Corp. Am., 1963-65; v.p. FMC Corp., 1965-71; v.p. Lummus Co., Bloomfield, N.J., 1971-72; sr. v.p. Lummus Co., Bloomfield, N.J., 1972; dir. Erkins Studios. Served to lt. (j.g.), USNR, 1944-46. Mem. Am. Inst. Chem. Engrs., Am. Chem. Soc. Clubs: Field (Greenwich); Bridgehampton Golf; Round Hill (Greenwich, Conn.); Greenwich CT Died Oct. 22, 1972; buried Bridgehampton NY

WORTHY, EDMUND HENRY, lawyer; b. Carollton, Ga., July 1, 1909; s. Henry Judson and Martha Emily (Chambers) W.; student Emory U., 1927-30; LL.B., Washington Coll. Law, 1933; grad. student Cath. U. of Am. Law Sch., 1933-34; m. Helen Elizabeth Brown, June 17, 1932; 1son, Edmund Henry. Admitted to Ga. bar, 1932, D.C. bar, 1934; asst. to Congressman Wright of Ga., 1930-31; asst. to auditor Dist. Ct. D.C., 1931-35; with SEC, 1935-68, asst. dir. div. corp. finance, 1955-62, dir. div., 1962-68; partner law firm Morison, Murphy, Abrams & Haddock, Washington, D.C., 1969-70. Mem. U.S. Civil Service Examiners. Member Administrative Conf. U.S., 1961-62. Served with AUS, 1944-45. Mem. Am. Legion (past post comdr.), Pi Kappa Phi. Episcopalian. Home: Chevy Chase MD Died Jan. 18, 1970.

WRAITH, WILLIAM, mining engr.; b. in Eng., Nov. 23, 1872; s. Samuel and Mary Jane (Hardy) W.; brought to U.S., 1882, naturalized, 1900; student U. of Ill., 1890-91; E.M., Mich. Coll. Mines and Tech., Houghton, 1894, D. Eng., 1938; m. Erma M. Davis, Jan. 12, 1897; children—William, Erma M. (Mrs. C.E. Carstens). Mine surveyor for fuel dept. A.,T.&S.F. Ry., 1894-97; construction engineer Boston & Mont. Co., Butte & Boston Co., Anaconda Copper Mining Co., 1897-1906; asst. supt. Washoe smelter of Anaconda Copper Mining Co., 1906-13; mgr. Internat. Smelting Co., Salt Lake City, 1913-18; now exec. vice-president Andes Copper Mining Co., Chile Copper Co., Chile Exploration Co., president Chile Steamship Co.; vice-president Greene Cananea Copper Co., Inspiration Consolidated Copper Co.; dir. Internat. Smelting & Refining Co. Mem. Am. Inst. Mining and Metall. Engrs., Am. Soc. Mech. Engrs. Clubs: Engineers, India House; Plandome (N.Y.) Golf; Manhasset Bay Yacht (Port Washington, N.Y.). Retired. Home: Lafayette Hotel, Long Beach 2 CA‡

WRAPE, JAMES WYRE, lawyer; b. Paragould, Ark., Feb. 14, 1903; s. Frank Stephenson and Bertha Lon (William) W.; student St. Mary's (Kan.) Coll.; J.D., U. Notre Dame; m. Lila Hodge McGehee, Sept. 26, 1934; children—Lila McGehee (Mrs. J. T. Sanders), Posey Rhea (Mrs. William Witherspoon), Lucia Hodge (Mrs. Lucia W. Brown). With firm of Wrape & Hernly, Memphis and Washington, becoming sr. partner, Vice pres., dir. Dealers Transit, Inc., Chgo., C & J. Comml. Driveway Co., Inc., Lansing, Mich., Automobile Carriers Inc., Flint, Mich.; v.p. Gordons Transports, Inc., Memphis. Mem. American, Tennessee, Memphis and Shelly County. Fed. Communications bar assns., Practioners Bar ICC, Motor Carrier Lawyers Assn. Home: Collierville TN Died Mar. 17, 1970; buried Forest Hill Cemetery, Memphis TN

WRAY, JAMES GLENDENNING, elec. engr.; b. Janesville, Wis., May 19, 1872; s. James and Helen (Edgar) W.; B.S. in E.E., U. of Wis., 1893; m. Clara May Williams, Sept. 25, 1895; children—Florence Vivian (Mrs. A. H. Ward), Ernest Lee (dec.), Alice May (Mrs. J.A. Bailey), Ethel Lois (Mrs. Stanley D. Grace), Helen Norma (wife of J.D. Emrich, Jr.), James Glendenning, Jr., Clara Grace (Mrs. Alvin H. Mitchell). With Chicago Telephone Co., 1893, served as asst. chief engr., asst. supt. of maintenance, supt. of maintenance, electrician, supt. of equipment and chief engr., until 1916; chief engr. Wis. Telephone Co., Mich. State Telephone Co., Cleveland Telephone Co., and Central Union Telephone Co., 1911-16; chief engr. receivers of Central Union Telephone Co., 1914; pres. and dir. United Telephone Co., 1927-29, dir., 1930; v.p., dir. Standard Telephone Co., 1927-28; pres., dir. Southeastern Telephone Co., 1929-31; president Pa Wray Pickle Co., J.G. Wray & Co. Member Board of Education, Wilmette, Ill. (president 1917-19); member Bd. of Visitors, University of Wisconsin, 1909-12; former director Chicago Regional Plan Commn.; mem. Glencoe (Ill.) Plan Commn., 1929-30, Glencoe Park Bd. (v.p. since 1930). Fellow Am. Inst. E.E. (chmn. Chicago sect. 3 yrs.), A.A.A.S.; mem. Western Soc. Engrs., Ill. Acad. Sciences, Wis. Soc. of Chicago (secretary, treasurer and president), U. of Wisconsin Alumni Assn. (exec. com.). Formerly mem. Wis. Nat. Guard. Republican. Conglist.; former dir. Chicago City Missionary Soc. Mason (past master). Clubs: University, University of Wis. Club of Chicago (pres., sec. and treas.). Home: 625 Washington Av., Glencoe IL Office: Bankers Bldg., Chicago IL*‡

WRIGHT, ARNAULD LEONARD, aerospace co. exec.; b. St. Isadore, Que., Can., Jan. 27, 1908; s. Athol Choate and Olive (Johnson) W.; B.S., Queens U., 1932; postgrad. Mil. Coll. Sci., London, Eng., 1941-42, U. Cal. at Los Angeles, 1957; m. Charlotte Adeline Gibson, June 29, 1935; children—Carol Heather, Rosemary Ann, Robert Athol. Came to U.S., 1948, naturalized, 1961. Engr., No. Electric Co., 1932-39; sci. attache Canadian Diplomatic Service, London, 1947-48, Washington, 1948-54; long range bus. planner N. Am. Aviation, El Segundo, Cal., 1954-70. Served to col. Canadian Army, 1940-47. Decorated Order Brit. Empire, Mem. Nat. Planning Assn., Operations Research Soc. Am., Am. Statis. Assn., Writers Inst., Solar Energy Soc. Home: Santa Ana CA Died June 2, 1970; buried Newport Beach CA

WRIGHT, CECIL AUGUSTUS, univ. dean, lawyer; b. London, Ont., Can., July 2, 1904; s. Thomas Augustus and Emily (Whitehall) W.; B.A., U. Western Ont., 1923, LL.D., 1948; S.J.D., Harvard, 1927; LL.D., U. B.C., 1949, Queen's U., 1960; m. Marie Therese Loughlin, July 8, 1930; children—John Augustus, Caroline Cecil,

William Edward. Called to Ont. bar, 1926; lectr. Osgoode Hall Law Sch., Toronto, 1927-48, dean, 1948-49; dean faculty law U. Toronto, 1949-67; counsel Tory, Tory, DesLauriers & Binnington, Toronto, 1950-67. Created Queen's counsel, 1938. Mem. Canadian Bar Assn. Mem. Liberal Party. Mem. Anglican Ch. Author: Wright's Cases on Torts, 4th edit., 1967. Editor-in-chief Dominion Law Reports, 1942-67, Ont. Reports, 1961-67; Canadian Criminal Cases, 1942-67; editor Canadian Bar Rev., 1935-46. Home: Toronto ON Canada Died Apr. 24, 1967.

WRIGHT, COBINA, columnist, singer; b. Lakeview, Ore.; d. Benjamin and Delaphine (Holmes) Cobb; student Mills College; m. Owen Johnson; married second, to William May Wright, in December 1920; 1 dau., Cobina (Mrs. Palmer T. Beaudette). Singer leading roles, opera in Germany, Monte Carlo, France; concerts with orchestras throughout U.S. and Can.; now columnist Hearst Newspapers; TV, radio appearances, motion pictures. Active, City of Hope; chmn. entertainment French, Am., English soldiers, World War I. Republican. Author: (autobiography) I Never Grew Up, 1951. Home: Hollywood CA Died Apr. 1970.

WRIGHT, DAVID MCCORD, economist, educator, author; born Savannah, Georgia, August 1, 1909; son of Anton Pope and Hannah McCord (Smythe) W.; student at The Citadel, Charleston, S.C., 1926-27, U. of Pa. 1927-30; LL.B., U. of Va., 1935; M.A., Harvard U., 1939, Ph.D., 1940; m. Caroline Noble Jones, June 27, 1940; children—Antony Pope, Peter M., Anna H. Admitted to Ga. bar, 1935; atty. R.F.C., 1936-37; lecturer, U. of Va. Law Sch. 1940, and 1947-55; econ. consultant National Resources Planning Board, 1943; lecturer U.S. Army Sch. Mil. Govt., 1943, Columbia, summer 1946, 50, 52, 53, 55, U. Cal., summer 1947, Harvard, summer 1948, 51, 66, U.S. State Dept., France, Germany summer, 1956, also numerous programs, insts.; asst. prof. bus. adminstrn. U. Va., 1939-42, asso. prof. econs., 1943-46, prof., 1946-55; Fulbright lecturer Oxford University, 1953-54; Rockefeller fellow, also Earhart fellow, 1954-55; William Dow prof. econs. and polit. sci. McGill U., 1955-62; prof. econs. U. of Ga., Athens, 1962-68. Econ. adviser Fed. Res. Bank of Atlanta, 1963-66. Mem. editorial com. UNESCO Dictionary of the Social Scis., 1959-63. Mem. Royal Econ. Soc., Am. (exec. com. 1952-55), So. (pres. 1950) econ. assns., Soc. Colonial Wars, Soc. Cincinnati, Huguenot Society of South Carolina (life), Phi Delta Phi, Alpha Kappa Psi, Delta Psi, Beta Gamma Sigma. Republican. Episcopalian. Clubs: Oglethorpe, Savannah Yacht (Savannah, Ga.); Wianne (Wianne, Mass.). Colonade. Author: The Creation of Purchasing Power (David Wells prize Harvard), 1941; The Economics of Disturbance, 1947; Democracy and Progress, 1948; Capitalism, 1951; A Key to Modern Economics, 1954; The Kevnesian System, 1962; Economics and Economic Growth-Elementary Economics, 1964; The Trouble With Marx, 1967. Co-author econ. symposia and reports. Editor: The Impact of the Labor Union, 1951. Contbr. articles to econ., legal, other jours. Home: Athens GA Died Jan. 7, 1968; buried Bonaventure Cemetery, Savannah GA

WRIGHT, ELIZABETH WASHBURNE (MRS. HAMILTON WRIGHT), author; b. Minneapolis, Minn.; d. late Hon. William Drew (U.S. senator) and Elizabeth (Muzzy) Washburne; ed. Misses Masters' Sch., Dobbs Ferry, N.Y., pvt. schs. and in Europe; m. Hamilton Wright, Nov. 22, 1899 (died 1917); children—Rosalind, Hamilton, Washburne, Barbara, Leslie. Author: The Color of the East, 1913. Contbr. articles on One Way of Governing Malays, The Passing of the Opium Problem, to North Am. Rev. and The Outlook, also studies of the Far East to Atlantic, Scribner's, Harper's, etc. Apptd. assessor on Opium Advisory Com. by Council League of Nations, serving, 1921-25; del. to Internat. Opium Conf., Geneva, 1924-25; in Philippines, 1930-31, on mission for U.S. Govt., to report on opium situation. Mem. Inst. of Pacific Relations. Awarded medal by Chinese govt., 1930. Home: Massachusetts Pl., Waterside Drive, Washington DC and Norland," Livermore ME‡

WRIGHT, ERNEST HUNTER, educator; b. Lynchburg, Va., Mar. 20, 1882; s. John and Fannie Ellen (Knight) W.; A.B., Columbia, 1905, A.M., 1907, Ph.D., 1910; m. Mary Hill Heritage, Nov. 29, 1916. Instructor in English, Columbia University, 1910; asst. professor, 1914, asso. professor, 1919, professor, 1928-47, emeritus professor, 1947-68. Mem. Modern Language Assn. of America, Societe Jean-Jacques-Rousseau (Geneva), English Inst. (chmn. from 1942 to 1946). Clubs: Century, Faculty, Marshall Chess. Author: The Authorship of Timon of Athens, 1910; The Meaning of Rousseau, 1929. Editor: As You Like It, 1916, Timons of Athens, 1928. Translator: Clemenceau's La France devant l'Allemagne, 1918; Jean des Vignes Rouges' Bourru, Soldat de France, 1919. Editor-in-chief of The Richards Cyclopedia, 1933. Contbr. of articles to mags. Home: New York City NY Died Dec. 20, 1968; buried Fantinekill Cemetery, Ellenville NY

WRIGHT, GEORGE FRANCIS, business exec.; b. Worcester, Mass., June 1, 1892; s. George M. and Minnie E. (Searle) W.; student Bryant & Stratton Business Sch., 1911-13; m. Mattie L. Hickok, Nov. 15, 1916; 1 son, Merrill William; married 2d Veva Penick Miller, June 12, 1951. Established G. F. Wright Steel & Wire Co.; dir. Coes Knife Co., Springfield Gas Light Co., Fitchburg Gas & Electric Co., Indsl. City Bank, Coca-Cola Bottling Co. Trustee Worcester Investment Associates. Trustee Boston U. Conglist. Mason (32 deg, Shriner). Clubs: Rotary (past pres.), Worcester; Indian Harbor Yacht (Greenwich, Conn.); Bath and Tennis, Everglades (Palm Beach, Fla.). Home: Greenwich CT Died Apr. 20, 1967; buried Worcester MA

WRIGHT, HARRY NOBLE, coll. pres. emeritus; b. Shelbyville, Ind., Oct. 3, 1881; s. David Alexander and Dollie (Hankins) W.; B.S., Earlham Coll., Richmond, Ind., 1904, LL.D., 1953; M.S., U. Cal., 1911, Ph.D., 1913; LL.D. Whittier Coll., 1947; LL.D. (honorary), College City New York, 1953; m. Edna Alice White, August 24, 1904; 1 dau., Dorothy Evelyn. Prin. grammar sch., Vermilion Grove, Ill., 1903-04; prof. mathematics Pacific Coll., Newberg, Ore., 1904-05, Whittier Coll., 1908-10; fellow in mathematics U. Cal., 1910-13, instr., 1913-17; dean Whittier Coll., 1917-18, pres., 1918-23; lectr. mathematics U. Cal., 1923-24; dean Earlham Coll., 1924-30; asst. prof. mathematics Coll. City of N.Y., 1931-36, asso. prof. 1937-41, prof. from 1941, dir. evening and summer sessions, 1939-42, acting pres., 1941, pres. 1941-52, emeritus, 1952-69. Mem. bd. dirs. Protestant Council, 1953-62; chmn. bd. mgrs. Schools branch YMCA, N.Y.C., 1957-62. Chmn. N.Y. State Rhodes Scholarship Com., 1946-49. Fellow A.A.A.S.; mem. Council Fgn. Relations (N.Y.), Math. Assn. Am., Am. Math. Soc., Sigma Xi, Phi Delta Kappa, Kappa Delta Pi. Mem. Soc. of Friends. Author: First Course in the Theory of Numbers, 1939. Home: Portola Valley CA Died May 4, 1969.

WRIGHT, HELEN R., dean; b. Glenwood, Ia., 1891; d. Carlton Clark and Lucy (Russell) Wright; A.B., Smith Coll., 1912; student Chicago Sch. of Civics and Philanthropy, 1912-13; Ph.D., U. of Chicago, 1922. Research staff, Inst. of Economics, 1922-24; Brookings Grad. Sch., 1924-28; faculty member, Sch. of Social Service Adminstrn., U. Chgo., 1928-56, dean, 1942-56; chief group to work with Indian Schs. Social Work, 1956-58. Mem. Am. Assn. Schs. Social Work (pres. 1950-51), Council Social Work Edn. (pres. 1952-54), Am. Assn. of Social Workers. Writer of 2 studies for U.S. Childrens Bureau. Co-author: (with Walton Hamilton), The Case of Bituminous Coal; A Way of Order of Bituminous Coal. Editor: Social Service Review, 1953. Contbr. articles to Social Service Review. Home: Pasadena CA Died Aug. 1969.

WRIGHT, HELEN SMITH, author; b. Washington, Feb. 9, 1874; d. late Rear Admiral David and Sarah Saunders Smith; ed. Paris, France, pub. schs. and Corcoran Art Sch., Washington; m. Charles Hewitt Wright, Pittsfield, Mass., Oct. 20, 1898 (dec.); 1 son, Charles Ashley. Mem. Daughters Am. Revolution, Red Cross; fellow Royal Geog. Soc., London. Clubs: Country, Wednesday Morning, Arts (Washington, D.C.). Author: Old Time Recipes, 1909; The Great White North, 1910; New England Cook Book, 1912; Valley of Lebanon, 1916; Our United States Army, 1917; The Seventh Continent, 1917 Coal's Worst Year, 1923; Voices of the Wind (poems), 1930. Address: 148 Bartlett Av., Pittsfield MA‡

WRIGHT, IRENE ALOHA, author; b. Lake City, Colo., Dec. 19, 1879; d. Henry Edward and Letitia O. (Ballard) W.; grad. Va. Coll., Roanoke, Va., 1898; A.B., Stanford University, 1904; daughter, Flor Alma, adopted 1933. Special writer Havana (Cuba) Post, 1904-05; city editor Havana Telegraph, 1905-07; spl. agt. Cuban Dept. Agr., 1908; owner and editor Cuban Mag., 1908-14. Encomienda, Royal Order Alfonso XII (Spanish), Order Carlos Manuel Cespedes (Cuban); gold medal Women Geographers, 1950. Mem. Royal Hist. Soc. Eng., Royal Hist. Soc. Netherlands, U.S. govt. del. 3d Congress Spanish Am. Geography and History, Seville, 1930 26th Session of Internat. Congress of Americanists, Seville, 1935; rep. Library of Congress in Spain, 1932-36; asso. archivist of U.S., The Nat. Archives, 1936-38; adviser 4th gen. assembly, Pan Am. Inst. Geography and History, Caracas, 1946; expert 1st gen. conference, United Nations Ednl., Scientific and Cultural Orgn., Paris, 1946; fgn. affairs specialist Dept. of State. Author several books since 1910; latest English Voyages to the Caribbean, 1580-1592; 1949. Home: Washington DC Died Apr. 1972.

WRIGHT, JESSIE, physician; b. Eccleshall, Eng., Sept. 5, 1900; d. James and Mary (Keightley) Wright; came to U.S., 1907, naturalized, 1924; B.Sc., U. Pitts., 1932, M.D., 1934. Intern Allegheny Gen. Hosp., Pitts., 1934-35; med. dir. D.T. Watson Sch. Physiatrics U. Pitts., 1935-67; chief staff D. T. Watson Home, affiliated U. Pitts., 1948-67; instr. orthopedics U. Pitts., 1936-51, asso. prof. phys. medicine and rehab., 1952-67; cons. U. Pitts. Med. Center Hosps., 1952-67, surgeon gen. USAF, 1950-53. Mem. nat. adv. com. Nat. Found., 1947-70, cons. to found. for ICA in Argentina, 1956; nat. clin. adv. com. United Cerebral Palsy Assn., 1954-67; rep. Nat. Soc. Crippled Childrens and Adu at Internat. Soc. Welfare Crippled, Amsterda Holland, 1954; moderator panel rehab. 3d Intern Conf. Poliomyelitis, Rome, Italy, 1954, participant 4 Internat. Conf., Geneva, Switzerland, 1957. Trustee Pitts., 1961-67. Named Pitts. Woman of Year, 195 Distinguished Dau. Pa., 1952. Mem. Am. Aca Cerebral Palsy (pres. 1962), Am. Rheumatism Ass Am. Acad. Phys. Medicine and Rehab., Internat. Sc Rehabilitation Disabled, American Medical Write Assn. Presbyn. (elder). Clubs: U. Pitts. Century, Civi Zonta, 20th Century (Pitts.). Developed electrical controlled rocking bed for treatment respirato paralysis, 1945. Contbr. articles med. Jours. Hom Pittsburgh PA Died Sept. 9, 1970.

WRIGHT, JOHN CALVIN, vocational edn.; Elkhart County, Ind., June 24, 1876; s. John J. ar Hannah (Postma) W.; grad. Kan. State Normal Sch Emporia, Kan., 1900, Latin course, 1901; B.S. in Edn U. of Mo., 1918, A.M., 1919; Sc.D. in Edn., Stout Ins Menomonie, Wis., 1926; m. Cordelia D. Bennett, Jun 4, 1903; children—Nadia Virginia Zimmerma Genevieve Grace Smith, Dale Jokshan. Teacher in rur schs., 1895, teacher high sch. and supt. schs., Bellevill Kan., 1900-04; teacher high schs., Kansas City, Mc 1904-14; dir. vocational instrn., same city, 1913-1 with Fed. Bd. Vocational Edn. from 1917, dir., 1922-3 asst. commr. for vocational edn., U.S. Office of Edn 1933 to date of retirement, June 30, 1946. Architect ar builder in Kansas City, 6 yrs. Chmn. U.S. delegates 2d Inter-American Conference on Education, Santiag Chile, 1934; delegate 2d Inter-American Conf. on Agri Mexico City, 1942; made survey of tech. edn. in Mexic City, 1942; chmn. U.S. Commn. Apptd. by U.S. Con of Edn. to study vocational edn. in Mexico, 1945; men U.S. Commn. on Life Adjustment Edn. for Yout 1947-50. Corpl. Co. H, 22d Kan. Vols., Spanish-An War, 1898; spl. agt. for war training, 1918. Men N.E.A., Am. Vocational Assn.; charter mem. Boon Family Assn., Am. Order of Pioneers. Presbyteria Mason. Author: Automotive Repair (4 vols. Co-author: Automotive Construction and Operatio Supervision of Vocational Education; Administration c Vocational Education; Efficiency in Educatior Efficiency in Vocational Education; You and Your Job Editor Trade Series of John Wiley & Sons. Made surve of pulp and paper industry. Home: 5624 Western Av Chevy Chase 15 MD‡

WRIGHT, JOHN KIRTLAND, geographer; b. a Cambridge, Mass., Nov. 30, 1891; s. John Henry an Mary (Tappan) W.; grad. Browne and Nicholas Sch 1909; A.B., Harvard, 1913, A.M., 1914, Ph.D., 1922 LL.D., Clark U., 1967; m. Katharine Wolcot McGiffert, Jan. 12, 1921; children—Austin McGiffert Gertrude Huntington, Mary Wolcott. Instr. in history Harvard, 1916-17; librarian Am. Geographical Soc 1920-36, research editor, 1936-37, director, 1938-49 research asso., 1949-56, ret.; vis. prof. Dartmouth Coll 1957, La. State U., 1968. Served as cpl., inf., U.S. Army Sept. 1917-Feb. 1919, attached to hist. sect., G.H.Q. Chaumont, France, Aug.-Dec. 1918. Recipient Charle P. Daly Medal, Am. Geog. Soc., 1954. Patrons meda Royal Geog. Soc., 1955, Outstanding Achievemen award Assn. Am. Geographers, 1956. Membe Association of American Geographers (president 1946) History of Science Society, A.A.A.S. (v.p., 1943) Author: Aids to Geographical Research, 1923, rev edit., 1947; The Geographical Lore of the Time of the Crusades, 1925, rev. edit., 1965; The Leardo Map of the World (1452 or 1453), 1928; The Geographical Basis o European History, 1928; Geography in the Making: The American Geographical Society, 1851-1951, 1952 Human Nature in Geography, 1966. Editor: Orienta Explorations and Studies (by Alois Musil), 6 vols. 1926-28; Atlas of the Historical Geography of the United States (by C. O. Paullin), 1932; New England's Prospect (by 27 authors), 1933, and other publs. of Am Geog. Soc. Home: Lyne NH Died Mar. 24, 1969.

WRIGHT, JOHN LLOYD, architect; b. Oak Park, Ill. Dec. 12, 1892; s. Frank Lloyd and Catherine (Tobine) W.; student U. Wis., 1910-11, Art Inst. Chgo., 1914-15 pvt. structural engring. study, Chgo., 1914-16; m. Haze Ludin. Sept., 1921; children—John Lloyd II, (Mrs Gordon Ingraham); m. 2d, Frances Polachek Welsh Sept. 23, 1942; 1 stepson, Louis M. Welsh. Draftsman Harrison Albright, architect, San Diego, 1911-12; asst to Frank Lloyd Wright, architect, 1913-18; propr. John Lloyd Wright Inc., toy designer, Chgo., 1919-22; pvt. practice, Long Beach, Cal., 1923-39; archtl. designer fed. def. projects, 1940-44; pvt. practice, Long Beach, 1945-46, Del Mar, Cal., 1947-72; instr. factors of art in modern architecture U. Cal. at San Diego extension, 1948-49; exhbt. Art Inst. Chgo., John Herron Art Inst. Indpls., Met. Mus. N.Y., Cliff Dwellers, Chgo., Art Center, La Jolla, Cal. A.I.A. del. Internat. Congress Architects, Rome, Italy, 1935; chmn. planning commn. Del Mar. 1959-60. Recipient cash award Chgo. Builders Assn., 1928; gold certificate Indpls. Archtl Exhibit, 1928; citation award Soc. Am. Registered Architects, 1967, gold medal, 1959. Fellow Am. Registered Architects; mem. A.I.A., Soc. Archtl. Historians, Delta Kappa Epsilon. Club: Cliff Swellers (Chgo.). Inventor Lincoln logs, 1918, Wright blocks, 1932 (both toys). Author: My Father Who Is On Earth, 1946; also articles. Home: Del Mar CA Died Dec. 20, 1972; cremated.

WRIGHT, JOSEPH ALEXANDER, prof. journalism; b. Mechanicstown, O., Feb. 12, 1877; s. Rev. John Alexander and Martha Ellen (Wiley) W.; grad. school, 1895; student Northeastern Ohio Normal Sch., Canfield, O., 1 yr.; A.B., Ohio Wesleyan U., 1900; post-grad. work, New York U., 1 term; m. Mary Minetta Swank, Nov. 16, 1904 (died 1944); 1 dau., Martha Ellen (Mrs. E. Britt Myrick); m. 2d, Isabel Irene Woolf, Sept. 10, 1945. Reporter, copy reader, Indianapolis Sentinel, 1900-02; asst. city editor Indianapolis Star, 1902; exchange and feature editor Indianapolis News, 1902-13; asst. prof. journalism, Ind. U., 1913-17; prof. journalism, U. of S.D., 1919-27; director of Alumnus issue and prof. journalism, Indiana U., 1927-47, emeritus. Served as pvt. O. Nat. Guard, Spanish-Am. War; commd. capt. U.S. Army, Aug. 15, 1917; instr. Officers' Sch., and arty. engr., Ft. McKinley, Me. Instructor govt. work, 1942-44. Mem. Nat. Editorial Assn., Am. Assn. Teachers of Journalism, Delta Tau Delta. Democrat. Methodist. Mason (32 deg.). Home: Scottsdale AZ‡

WRIGHT, JOSEPH PURDON, lawyer; b. Colorado Springs, June 10, 1884; s. Richard William and Sarah Louise (Carter) W.; student Baltimore City Coll., 1905; A.B., John Hopkins, 1908; LL.B., U. Md., 1905; m. Lucy Agnes Wright, June 24, 1914 (dec. Mar. 1961); children—Margaret Louise (Mrs. J. A. Sader), Joseph Purdon, Richard Armstrong; m. second, Margaret Larrimore, August 24, 1963. Admitted to the Maryland bar, 1909, since practiced in Baltimore; assistant attorney general of Md., 1920-24; gen. counsel Pub. Service Commn. of Md., 1935-41; commr. Uniform Laws for Md., 1935-39; 1st supt. Md. State Police, 1935; dir., v.p., counsel Am. Nat. Bldg. & Loan Assn. Balt. City since 1920; dir. U.S. Fidelity & Guaranty Co. Trustee University of Baltimore, 1941—. Mem. Am., Maryland bar assns., American Law Institute, Commercial Law League Am. (past pres.), Hibernian Soc., Md. Hist. Soc., Phi Gamma Delta. Republican. Episcopalian. Mason (Shriner). Clubs: Terrapin (U. Md.); Merchants (Baltimore). Home: Baltimore MD Died Sept. 26, 1967; buried Corraine Cemetery, Baltimore MD

WRIGHT, MARY CLABAUGH (MRS. ARTHUR F. WRIGHT), educator; b. Tuscaloosa, Ala., Sept. 25, 1917; d. Samuel F. and Mary (Duncan) Clabaugh; student Vassar, 1938; M.A., Radcliffe, 1939, Ph.D., 1951; LL.D., Wheaton Coll., 1965, Western Coll. for Women, 1965; LL.D. (hon.), Smith Coll., 1968; m. Arthur F. Wright, on July 6, 1940; children—Charles Duncan, Jonathan Arthur. China rep. Hoover Instn., Stanford University, 1945-47, asst. prof., 1947-54, asso. prof., 1954-59, curator Chinese collection Hoover Instn., 1947-59; asso. prof. history Yale, 1959-64, prof., 1964-70, dir. Chinese studies, 1961-66. Trustee Wesleyan U., 1969-70. Mem. Am. Hist. Assn., Assn. for Asian Studies. Democrat. Episcopalian. Club: Sachems Head Yacht. Author: The Last Stand of Chinese Conservatism, 1957. Editor, contbr. China in Revolution, The First Phase 1900-1913, Guilford CT Died June 18, 1970; buried Grove St. Cemetery, New Haven CT

WRIGHT, QUINCY, educator; born Medford, Mass., December 28, 1890; s. Philip Green and Elizabeth Quincy (Sewall) W.; A.B., Lombard Coll., Galesburg, Ill., 1912, LL.D., 1923; A.M., U. of Ill., 1913, Doctor of Philosophy, 1915, Doctor of Laws, 1967; m. Louise Leonard, June 15, 1922; children—Rosalind, Christopher. Research fellow, U. of Pa., 1915-16; asst. and instr. internat. law, Harvard, 1916-19; asst. prof. polit. science, 1919-21, asso. prof., 1921-22, prof., 1922-23, U. of Minn.; prof. polit. science, U. of Chicago, 1923-31, prof. internat. law, 1931-56, now emeritus; vis. research scholar Carnegie Endowment for Internat. Peace, New York City, 1956-57; vis. prof. internat. law, Indian Sch. Internat. Studies, New Delhi, 1957-58, 62, internat. relations Columbia U., 1962-63; professor internat. law U. Va., 1958-61; vis. prof. Am. U., Cairo, Egypt, 1964, U. Ankara (Turkey), 1964, Makerere University, Kampala, Uganda, 1964, Cornell U., Ithaca, N.Y., Syracuse U., 1965; vis. professor of international relations Rice U., 1966-67, Spl. asst. internat. law U.S. Navy Dept., 1918, 21. Consultant to Fgn. Econ. Adminstrn. and Dept. of State, 1943-44; technical adviser to American member Internat. Military Tribunal, Nuremberg, 1945; consultant UNESCO, 1949, to U.S. High Commr., Germany, 1949-50. Pres. Am. Assn. Univ. Profs., 1944-46. Trustee Knox College; director Foreign Bondholders Protective Council. Recipient award Am. Council Learned Socs., 1961. Fellow Am. Acad. Arts and Sciences; mem. bd. editors, Am. Jour. Internat. Law. Mem. Am. Political Science Association (pres. 1949), Internat. Polit. Sci. Assn. (pres. 1950), Am. Philos. Society, Am. Soc. Internat. Law (pres. 1955-56), Am. Inst. Pacific Relations, Conf. on Sci., Philosophy and Religion, Internat. Law Assn., UN Assn. Greater Chgo. (pres. 1953), Commn. to Study the Organization of Peace, Institut de droit International. Unitarian. Club: Cosmos (Washington); Quadrangle (Chicago). Author: Enforcement of Internat. Law through Municipal Law in the U.S., 1916; Control of Am. Fgn. Relations, 1922; Mandates Under the League of Nations, 1930; The Causes of War and the Conditions of Peace, 1935; Legal Problems in the Far Eastern Conflict, 1941; A Study of War, published in 1942, revised edition, pub. in 1965; Problems of Stability and Progress in International Relations, 1954; The Study of International Relations, 1955; Contemporary International Law, A Balance Sheet, 1955; International Law and the United Nations, Balance Sheet, 1955; International Law and the United Nations, 1956; The Strengthening of Internat. Law, 1959; The Role of International Law in the Elimination of War, 1961. Home: Charlottesville VA Died Oct. 17, 1970; buried Medford MA

WRIGHT, STANLEY WILLARD, physician, educator; b. Chico, Cal., Mar. 27, 1921; s. Carol Willard and Dorothy (Cooper) W.; M.D., U. Rochester, 1944; m. Phyllis Mann, Nov. 16, 1946; children—Carol Lynn, Brian Cooper. Intern, Strong Meml. Hosp., Rochester, N.Y., 1944-45, a-st. resident, 1948-49, chief resident, 1949-50; asst. resident Children's Hosp., Boston, Atomic Bomb Casualty Commn., 1950-52; prof. dept. pediatrics U. Cal. Med. Sch. at Los Angeles, until 1971, grantee Mental Retardation Research Center. Served from 1st lt. to capt., M.C., AUS, 1946-48. Named Distinguished fellow Am. Psychiat. Soc., 1971. Diplomate Am. Bd. Pediatrics. Mem. Am. Pediatric Soc., Am. Assn. on Mental Deficiency, Am. Soc. Human Genetics, Am. Acad. Pediatrics, A.A.A.S., Western Soc. for Clin. Investigation, Western Soc. for Pediatric Research (pres. 1963), Soc. for Pediatric Research, Los Angeles County Med. Assn., Sigma Xi. Editor: Perspectives in Cytogenetics, 1972; mem. editorial bd. Jour. Pediatrics; cons. editor Jour. Mental Deficiency. Contbr. articles to sci. jours. Home: Los Angeles CA Died Sept. 26, 1971.

WRIGHT, SYDNEY LONGSTRETH, educator, chemist; b. Germantown, Phila., Oct. 9 1896; s. William Redwood and Letitia Ellicott (Carpenter) W.; student Episcopal Acad. Phila.; B.S. (Princeton, 1918, A.M. (Sayre fellow), 1920, Ph.D. (Proctor fellow), 1928; Nat. Research Council fellow medicine U. Pa., 1928-30, fellow, 1930-32, 32-33; m. Catharine Wharton Morris, Feb. 28, 1925; children—Anna Wharton, William Redwood, Ellicott, Harrison Morris. Research chemist Barrett Co., Phila., 1919-21; chemist Ayer Clinic Lab., Pa. Hosp., 1923-28; instr. dept. research medicine U. Pa., 1931-34, instr. dept. physiol. chemistry, 1932-36; asso. dir. Franklin Inst., 1943-40, dir. membership, 1936-40 asst. to sec. 1939-40; dir. Library Co. of Phila., 1937-43; pres. Meadowbrook Sch., 1938-42; dir. Pa. Acad. Fine Arts 1939-59. Chmn. Cheltenham Twp. Def. Council, 1941-45. Trustee Wagner Free Inst. Sci. 1931-58, sec.; 1935-40, treas., 1940, vice pres., 1948-58; trustee Pa. Sch. Horticulture for Women Ambler, 1945-46; dir. Nat. Farm Sch., Doylestown, Pa., 1943-46; trustee of the Rhode Island Oceanarium. Served as private U.S. Army 1917-19. Mem. Franklin Inst. (Phila.), Am. Soc. Biol. Chemistry; Newport (R.I.) Hist., Soc. (dir. 1950-51, pres. since 1951), Keats-Shelley Assn. Am. (dir. 1949—). Am. Soc. Biol. Chemists. Clubs: Mid Ocean (Bermuda); Franklin Inn Univ. Barge (Phila.); Tower (Princeton); Saunderstown Yacht (dir. 1941-47); Royal Bermuda Yacht. Author: The Story of Franklin Institute, 1938. Editor of Bull. Wagner Free Inst. Pa., 1931-58. Home: Jamestown RI Died Oct. 8, 1970.

WRIGHT, THEODORE PAUL, aircraft engr.; b. Galesburg, Ill., May 25, 1895; s. Philip Green and Elizabeth Quincy (Sewall) W.; B.S., Lombard Coll., Galesburg, 1915, Mass. Inst. Tech., 1918; D.Sc., Knox Coll., Galesburg, 1937; m. Margaret McCarl, Dec. 4, 1918; children—Douglas Lyman, Theodore Paul. Began as naval insp. aircraft (in charge inspection NC Flying Boats which made pioneer Transatlantic crossing by air), 1918; exec. engr. Curtiss Aeroplane & Motor Co., 1921, asst. factory mgt., 1922, asst. chief engr., 1923-25, chief engr. airplane div., 1925-30, in charge orgn. which designed and produced Curtiss Tanager" airplanes, winner Guggenheim Found. prize, Safe Aircraft Competition, 1929; gen. mgr., chief engr., airplane div. Curtiss Wright Corp., 1930-34, v.p., dir. the corp., 1930-41, dir. engring., chmn. engring., policy and planning com., 1934-41; vice president research Cornell University, 1948-60, acting president, 1951; pres. Cornell Aero. Lab., Inc., 1948-58, chmn. board, 1948-60, chmn. exec. com., 1960-70; pres. Asso. Univs., Inc., 1965-66; dir. Power Reactor Devel. Corp. Trustee Sloan Kettering Cancer Research Inst., 1948-60. Director of Fund for Peaceim Atomic Development, Cornell-Guggenheim Aviation Safety Center; chairman of bd. dirs. Cornell Research Found.; dir., governor Flight Safety Foundation. Served with the National Defense Advisory Council, Washington, 6 months, 1940; asst. chief, aircraft sect. OPM, 1940; dir. Aircraft Resources Control Office, also mem. Aircraft Prodn. Bd., 1942-44; tech. sec. Internat. Aviation Conv. (which established Internat. Civil Aviation Orgn.), Chgo., 1944; adminstr. Civil Aeronautics, 1944-48; dir. aircraft div. U.S. Strategic Bombing Survey, 1945; mem. NACA, 1941-53, chmn. aerodynamics sub com., 1941-53, vice chmn., 1953. Recipient medal, citation exceptional civilian service, 1944, Medal of Freedom, 1946 (both War Dept.), Daniel Guggenheim medal for aeronautics, 1945. Medal for Merit from the Pres., 1945. Hon. fellow Inst. Aerospace Sci. (founder council; pres. 1938), Royal Aero. Soc. London, Canadian Aero. and Space Institute; member of Soc. Automotive Engrs. (Wright Brothers medal 1930), Council Fgn. Relations, Sigma Xi, Sigma Nu, Tau Beta Pi. Democrat. Unitarian. Club: Cosmos (Washington). Author papers on aero. and ednl. subjects, presented in numerous speeches, also tech. contbns. to mags.; articles and speeches pub. in 3 vols., 1962. Delivered 33d Wilbur Wright lecture, Royal Aero. Soc., 1945. Home: Ithaca NY Died Aug. 21, 1970.

WRIGHT, THEW, surgeon; b. Boston, Mass., June 19, 1877; s. William Burnet and Lucretia (Johnson) W.; A.B., Yale, 1899; M.D., U. of Buffalo, 1903; m. Nathalie Clinton, Mar. 14, 1904; children—Gertrude Clinton (Mrs. Samuel Dorr Lunt), Thew. Practicing surgeon since 1903; cons. surgeon, Buffalo Children's Hosp., cons. surgeon, Buffalo Gen. Hosp., and J. N. Adam Hosp. (Perrysburg, N.Y.), emeritus prof. of surgery, U. of Buffalo Sch. of Medicine. Served as lt. col. Med. Corps, U.S. Army, comdg. officer Base Hosp. 110 in France. Mem. Council U. of Buffalo. Fellow Am. Coll. Surgeons, Internat. Coll. Surgeons (state regent), Am. Assn. Obstetricians, Gynecologists and Abdominal Surgeons; mem. Founders Group, Am. Bd. Surgery; mem. Am., N.Y. State and Erie County med. socs., Buffalo Surg. Soc. (ex-pres.), Buffalo Acad. Medicine (ex-pres.), Am. Legion, A.A.O.W.I., Alpha Omega Alpha, Nu Sigma Nu. Author: Appendicitis, 1928. Contbr. to med. jours. Home: Tucson AZ‡

WRIGHT, WILLIAM WOOD, corporation executive; b. Doswell, Va., Oct. 5, 1917; s. John Alexander and Ina (Smith) W.; A.B., Randolph-Macon Coll., 1937; certificate Am. Inst. Banking, 1938; student Va. Mechanics Inst., 1938-41, Rutgers U., 1951; m. Phyllis Vick Wright, May 19, 1939; children—Steven Terry, William Alexander. Transit clk. State-Planners Bank & Trust Co., Richmond, Va., 1937-38; sr. accountant audit div. Va. Dept. Hwys., 1938-40; with Johns-Manville Corp., 1941-58, budget dir., 1956-58; v.p. finance Beckman Instruments, Inc., Fullerton, Cal., 1958-61, exec. v.p. adminstrn., 1961-63, past dir.; exec. v.p., dir. Bestwall Gypsum Co., 1964-65; prin. W.W. Wright Mgmt. Consultants, 1965-71; chmn. bd. Caelus Memories, Inc., 1967-71; dir. Internat. Video Corp., Electrac, Inc., Barr Lumber Co., Inc., Carmel Steel Products, Inc. Chmn. Adams County (Miss.) chpt. A.R.C., 1949-50. Mem. Nat. Assn. Accountants (Lybrand certificate of merit 1957; pres. Raritan Valley chpt. 1955-56, nat. v.p. 1962-63), Stuart Cameron McLeod Soc. (bd. govs. 1965-67, v.p. 1968), Financial Execs. Inst. Presbyn. Club: Balboa Bay (Newport Beach, Cal.). Home: Newport Beach CA Died 1971.

WRIGLEY, THOMAS, publicity director, newspaperman; b. Elmira, N.Y., July 27, 1882; s. John and Mattie (de Graw) W.; ed. pub. schs. and Elmira Academy; m. Elsie M. Nagle, October 14, 1909 (deceased November 1961). Reporter for the Elmira Gazette, later Elmira Star-Gazette until 1909; mng. editor Elmira Herald, 1913-20; corr. Internat. News Service, 1920, chief of Kansas City Bur., 1921, Chicago Bur., 1922; mng. editor Elmira Advertiser and Elmira Sunday Telegram, 1923; city editor Boston Advertiser and Boston Sunday American, 1923-25; staff corr. Washington Bur. Universal Service, 1925-29, chief of Bur., 1929-32; news editor New York headquarters, Universal Service, 1933, Washington Bur., 1934-37; firs publicized March of Dimes" in 1938 as fund-raising plan for Nat. Foundation Infantile Paralysis campaigns, continuing as dir. publicity until 1943, resuming as publicity consultant, 1946-60; Washington columnist for Elk's Mag., 1950-70. Emcee, publicity dir. Am. Banjo Fraternity. City historian Elmira, 1963-70. Adv. bd. D.A.R., 1956-59. Mem. N.G.N.Y. 6 yrs. Democrat. Mason, Elk. Clubs: National Press; City (Elmira, N.Y.). Under auspices U.S. govt. conducted official tour, U.S. and Can., of five Turkish editors and journalists making study America's war effort by visiting munitions, armaments and other war plants, shipyards, airfields, and army and navy training camps, 1942. Home: Elmira NY Died Jan. 2, 1970.

WROBLEWSKI, WLADYSLAW, diplomat; b. Krakow, Poland, Mar. 21, 1875; s. Vincenty and Valerya (Bossowska) W.; ed. coll. and univ. in Krakow; m. Sophie Obtulowicz, of Lemberg, Poland, Apr. 19, 1911. Was asst. prof. pub. law; gen. dir. Agrl. Syndicate, Krakow; under sec. of state and under sec. of cabinet; chmn. commn. to negotiate with German Govt., 1919, in regard to provinces returned by Germany to Poland; dep. chmn. Polish delegation for peace negotiations with Soviet Russia, 1920; E.E. and M.P. from Poland to Great Britian 1921-22, to U.S. since Nov. 15, 1922. Clubs: Metropolitan, Chevy Chase. Address: 2640 16th St. N.W., Washington DC‡

WUERPEL, EDMUND HENRY, artist; b. St. Louis, May 13, 1866; s. Edmund M. and Minnie (Taussig) W.; pupil of the St. Louis Sch. of Fine Arts; W. A. Bouguereau, Tony Robert-Fleury, Gabriel Ferrier and Edmund Aman-Jean, Paris; Dr. Fine Arts, Washington U., 1935; m. Minnie Clay Johnson, June 25, 1895; children—Althea Adele (dec.), Lois (Mrs. E.L. Bowles), Margaret (Mrs. J. Wendell Macleod, dec.). Instr. 1894, later dir., St. Louis Sch. of Fine Arts, 1909-38; now dir. emeritus. Exhibited at Paris salons. Life mem. the St.

Louis Artists Guild (ex-pres.), Soc. Western Artists (ex-pres.); hon. mem. Am. Art Assn., Paris. Exhibited at Paris Expn., 1900; mem. Nat. Jury, Paris Expn., 1900; corr. sec. Am. Jury in Paris for Chicago Expn., 1893; mem. Jury of Selection and of Internat. Jury of Awards, St. Louis Expn., 1904. Represented by pictures in St. Louis Museum of Fine Arts, Clayton (Mo.) Pub. Library, Indianapolis Art Museum, Museum of Art (Buenos Aires, Argentina); mural decorations in Missouri Athletic Club, St. Louis Ch. of the Unity; mural decoration Mo. Capitol Bldg. Lecturer and writer on history of art. Awarded bronze medal, Internat. Expn., Buenos Aires; 1st prize, St. Louis Artists' Guild, 1914; silver medal, Seattle Expn.; mural prize, Artist Guild Exhbn., 1920; silver medal of merit, St. Louis Art League. Mem. jury of selection and Internat. Jury of Awards, Panama, P.I. Expn., 1915. Home: 7717 Walinca Terrace, Clayton, Mo. Address: Washington U., St Louis MO‡

WULSIN, LUCIEN, piano mfr.; b. Cincinnati, O., Mar. 17 1889; s. Lucien and Katharine E. (Roelker) W.; grad. St. George's Sch., Newport, R.I., 1906; A.B., Harvard, 1910, M.E.E., 1911; D. Litt. (hon.), Cincinnati Conservatory of Music 1952; D.Sc., University of Cincinnati, 1957; married Margaret M. Hager, June 6, 1914; children—Katharine R. Lucien, John H., Eugene, Thomas M., Margaret M., Adele. Elec. engr. Stone & Webster, Boston, 1911, in statis. dept., 1911-12; with engrng. dept. Baldwin Piano Co., Cincinnati, 1912-13, sec., 1913-19, treas., 1919-24, v.p., 1924-26, pres. The Baldwin Piano Company and subsidiaries, 1926-62, chairman of the board, 1962-64. Served as 2d lt., later 1st lt., Engr. Res. Corps, 1917-18; capt. Engr. Corps, U.S. Army, 1918-19, office of chief engr. line of communications and engr. purchasing office, Paris, Oct. 1917-May 1919. Trustee and sec. Cin. Inst. of Fine Arts; mem. overseers com. Harvard. Mem. Hist. and Philos. Soc. of Ohio (president, trustee). Republican. Clubs: Queen City, Camargo, Cincinnati Country (Cin.); Harvard (N.Y.C. and Boston); Chicago; Century Assn. (N.Y.C.). Home: Cincinnati OH Died Jan. 13, 1964; buried Spring Grove Cemetery Cincinnati OH

WUORINEN, JOHN H., coll. dean; b. Vaasa, Finland, May 10, 1897; s. John H. and Sanna Elizabeth (Hautamaki) W.; A.B., Clark Univ., 1921, A.M., 1922; Ph.D., Columbia U., 1931; Dr. Polit. Sci. (hon.), U. of Helsinki, 1956; married Alfhild Kalijarvi, July 7, 1923;children—John Henry, Charles Peter. Asst. in econs., Clark U., 1920-21, asst. history, 1921-22; instr. history, State Univ. of Iowa, 1922-24, Columbia Univ., 1924-35; asst. prof. history, Columbia, 1935-43, asso. prof. history 1943-47, prof., 1947-65, prof. emeritus, 1965-69, chmn. dept. history, 1949-58; dean of faculty Mount Wachusett Community Coll., Gardner, Mass., 1965-67; special lecturer Columbia University, 1965-68, sec. faculty polit. sci. Columbia 1943-48; William Bayard Cutting Traveling Fellow of Columbia Univ., 1927-28; fellowship of Columbia U. Social Science Research Council, 1934-35; research in Finland and Sweden, summers, 1929, 37; vis. Ohrbach prof. history City Coll. N.Y., 1952-53; Brittingham Distinguished vis. prof. U. Wis., 1967-68; cons. Coordinator Information Office, Washington, D.C., 1942; chief Scandinavian-Baltic Sect., rsrch. and analysis branch, Office Strategic Service, Jan.-June 1943, cons. 1943-45. Knight, First Class, Order of the White Rose, and Commander Order of the Finnish Lion, Republic of Finland; Knight 1st Class Royal Order Vasa (Sweden). Correspondent mem. Finnish Acad. of Letters (Suomalaisen Kirjallisuuden Seura); life mem. Am. Hist. Assn.; mem. American-Scandinavian Foundation (trustee 1961-69), Acad. Polit. Science. Author: Nationalism in Modern Finland, 1931; The Prohibition Experiment in Finland, 1931; Suomalaisuuden Historia, 1935; The Finns on the Delaware, 1938; Intructor's Course Outline, Modern European History; and Modern European History, College Course, 1945 Finland and World War II, 1948; A History of Finland, 1965; Scandinavia, 1965; also articles, chapters, book reviews on various Scandinavian topics in Current History, Polit. Science Quarterly, Annuals of Am. Polit. Science Acad., Am.-Swedish Monthly, N.Y. Times, etc. Gardner MA Died Apr. 10, 1969; buried Green Bower Cemetery, Gardner MA

WURLITZER, FARNY R., pres. The Rudolph Wurlitzer Co.; b. Cincinnati, O., Dec. 7, 1883; s. Rudolph and Leonie (Farny) W. Vice-pres. and dir. The Rudolph Wurlitzer Co. (now the Wurlitzer Co.), prior to 1933, then pres. and chmn. exec. com., later chmn. bd. Address: North Tonawanda NY Died May 6, 1972; buried Spring Grove Cemetery, Cincinnati OH

WYATT, LANDON R., bus. exec.; b. Callands, Va., Jan. 1, 1891; s. Eli J. and Sue (Gardner) W.; m. Beulah H., Apr. 4, 1923; children—Landon R., Catherine S., Dorothy H., Bernice B. Pres. Piedmont Hardward Co., Danville Parts and Body Corp., Dickerson Buick Corp., Lynchburg; v.p. Richardson-Wyatt Buick, Martinsville, Va., Daville Livestock Auction Market; pres. 1st Fed. Savs. & Loan Assn.; dir. Dan River Mills, Inc., Smith Seed & Feed, Inc., Danville Frozen Food Service, Danville Traction & Power Co., Piedmont Broadcasting Corp.; chmn. of board of dirs. Danville Knitting Mills. Member Virginia Ho. of Dels., 1944-53, Va. State Senate, 1953-68. President Danville Fair Assn. Pres. bd. trustees Averett Coll., Danville; mem. bd. trustees Hargrave Mil. Acad., Chatham, Va. Mem. bd. dirs., Hughes Meml. Sch. Mem. Danville City Council 8 yrs. Mem. Va. Automotive Trade Assn., Anti Tuberculosis Assn., C. of C. (dir.). Baptist (deacon). Mason (Shriner). Club: Kiwanis. Home: Danville VA Died Aug. 13, 1971; buried Mt. View Cemetery, Danville VA

WYCKOFF, ALBERT CLARKE, clergyman, teacher; b. Germantown, Columbia County, N.Y., Oct. 27, 1874; s. Rev. James and Katharine (Talmage) W.; grad. Seymour Smith Acad., Pine Plains, N.Y., 1893; A.B., Union Coll., Schenectady, N.Y., 1897, D.D., 1924; B.D., Union Theol. Sem., 1900; m. Mary Eno, May 11, 1903. Ordained ministry Presbyterian Church, U.S.A., 1900; pastor Presbyterian Church, Valatie, New York, 1900-06, Emanuel Reformation Ch., Castlelon-on-Hudson, 1906-09, Spring Valley, N.Y. since June, 1909; prof. psychology of religion, Bibl. Sem., New York, since 1923; interim Teacher of systematic theology at New Brunswick (N.J.) Theological Seminary; Y.M.C.A. sec., World War I as transport sec. then as secretary with Ambulance Sect., 42d (Rainbow") Div. Mem. Vets. of Foreign Wars, Delta Upsilon. Republican. Mason (K.T.); grand chaplain of Grand Lodge of Masons, State of N.Y. Author: The Science of Prayer, 1918; The Non-Sense of Christian Science, 1921; Acute and Chronic Unbelief, 1924. Writer on psychology of religion for 15 yrs.; asso. editor Bibl. Rev. Book reviewer for Saturday Review of Spring Valley NY‡

WYCKOFF, CECELIA G., publisher, b. Detroit, May 30, 1888; d. Jacob and Anna (Edelsohn) Shere; ed. pub. schs.; m. Richard DeMille Wyckoff, Aug. 26, 1913 (div.); children—Dorothy (Mrs. W. Dallas Baker), Gloria (Mrs. Alfred G. Dennison) (dec.). Treas. and dir. Ticker Pub. Co. (pubs. Magazine of Wall Street), 1912-66, pres., 1926-66; regular contbr. mag. under non de plume of Charles Benedict. Mem. Child Welfare Com., Am. (dir.), Acad. Polit. Sci. Club: Overseas Press. Home: New York City NY Died 1966.

WYCKOFF, RICHARD DEMILLE, editor, pub.; b. Brooklyn, N.Y., Nov. 2, 1873; s. Charles Benedict and Judith Anne (Stoothoff) W.; ed. pub. schs.; m. Cecelia Gertrude Shere, of Detroit, Mich., Aug. 26, 1913; children—Gloria, Dorothy. In Wall Street 37 yrs. as partner in various brokerage houses; founder, 1907, and editor and pub. Magazine of Wall Street. Republican. Clubs: Lawyers' (New York); Lakeville Golf and Country (Great Neck). Author: Studies in Tape Reading, 1909; How I Trade and Invest in Stocks and Bonds, 1920. Home: Great Neck LI NY Office: 42 Broadway, New York NY‡

WYLIE, PHILIP GORDON, author; b. Beverly, Mass., May 12, 1902; s. Edmund Melville and Edna (Edwards) W.; student Princeton U., 1920-23; Litt.D. (honorary), U. Miami, Fla. State U.; m. Johanna Ondeck, Apr. 17, 1928 (divorced 1937); 1 dau., Karen (now Mrs. Taylor A. Pryor); m. second, to Frederica Ballard, on April 27th, 1938. Mem. staff The New Yorker, 1925-27; adv. mgr. Cosmopolitan Book Corp., 1927-28; writer for Paramount Pictures Corp., 1931-33, Metro-Goldwyn-Mayer Corp., 1936-37; editor, newspaper columnist; fiction and articles appear in leading mags.; monographs in sci. and scholarly publications; many writings included in textbooks. Member of the Delense Council of Dade County; chmn. 1940, Dade County chapter Com. to Defend America; pres. Dade County Conservation Council, 1942; bd. mem. Office of Facts and Figures, 1942; Bur. Personnel Narr. U.S. Army Air Forces, 1945; expert cons. Fed. Civil Def. Adminstrn., 1949-71; consultant Oceanic Institute, Hawaii; mem. steering com. Lerner Marine Lab., B.W.I. Editor, Farrar & Rinehart, 1944. Recipient Freedom Found. gold medal, 1953; Henry H. Hyman Memorial trophy, 1959; medal Lotos Club, New York City, 1966. Member Internat. Game Fish Assn. (gov.), UN Assn., Authors' Guild (council 1945), Tropical Audubon Soc. (dir.), Acad. Polit. Sci. City of N.Y., Sigma Tau Delta, Sigma Delta Chi. Clubs: Outdoor Writers; Angler's, Inc. (past dir.). Author: Heavy Laden, 1928; Babes and Sucklings, 1929; Gladiator, 1930; Footprint of Cinderella, 1931; Murderer Invisible, 1931; The Savage Gentleman, 1932; Finnley Wren, 1934; As They Reveled, 1936; Too Much of Everything, 1936; An April Afternoon, 1938; The Big Ones Get Away, 1940; Salt Daffy, 1941; The Other Horseman, 1942; Generation of Vipers, 1942 (annotated 1955); Corpses at Indian Stones, 1943, Fish and Tin Fish—Crunch and Des Strike Back, 1944; Night Unto Night, 1944; An Essay on Morals, 1947; The Best of Crunch and Des, 1955; Treasure Cruise, 1956; The Answer, 1956; The Innocent Ambassadors, 1957. Collaborator (with Edwin Balmer); Five Fatal Words, 1932; When Worlds Collide, 1933; After Worlds Collide, 1934; The Golden Hoard, 1934; The Shield of Silence, 1936; The Army Way (with William W. Muir), 1940. Author: Opus 21, 1949; Crunch and Des Stories, 1948; The Disappearance, 1951; Three to be Read, 1952; TomorrowMagic Animal, 1968; The Spy Who Spoke Porpoise, 1969; Sons and Daughters of Mom, 1971; The End of the Dream, 1972. Permanent collection of works known as Wylie Papers in Firestone Meml. Library, Princeton U. Home: South Miami FL Hawaii. Died Oct. 26, 1971.

WYLLIE, JOHN COOK, librarian; b. Palatka, Fla., Oct. 26, 1908; s. William and Mabel (Cook) W.; B.A., U. Va., 1929; m. Evelyn Elizabeth Dollens, Aug. 24, 1949; 2 daus., Elizabeth, Jane. Curator rare books University Virginia, 1929-56, librarian, 1956-67, dir. libraries, 1967-68; book editor Richmond News Leader, 1952-62. Rosenbach fellow University of Pa., 1960-61. Served in AFS with Brit. Army, 1941-43, N. Africa, USAAF, 1943-46, C-B-I; capt. USAF, ret. Mem. bd. William Faulkner, Ellen Bayard Weedon founds. Recipient Algernon Sydney Sullivan award, 1948; Raven award Raven Soc. of U. Va., 1952. Mem. Am. Antiquarian Soc., Phi Beta Kappa, Omicron Delta Kappa, numerous other profl. socs. Author tech. articles and monographs on bibliog. subjects. Episcopalian. Clubs: Grolier, Century Assn., Farmington. Home: Charlottesville VA Died Apr. 18, 1968; buried University Cemetery, Charlottesville VA

WYLLIE, ROBERT (EDWARD) EVAN, army officer (ret.); b. Assam, India, Apr. 3, 1873; s. Henry Shaw and Emily (Cobb) W.; grad. arty. sch., sch. submarine defense, Army War Coll., Navy War Coll.; m. Marjorie Zoe Stuart, July 23, 1909; children—Zoe Roberta, Jean Louise (Mrs. O. Reeves Cross). Came to U.S., 1888, naturalized, 1896. Enlisted U.S. Army, 1895; 2d lt., arty., 1898; promoted through grades to col., ret. as brig. gen., 1930; established 1st coast defenses in Philippines; chief equipment br. War Dept., gen. staff, during World War I. Awarded Distinguished Service Medal. Author: Orders, Decorations and Insignia, 1920; contbr. to mags. Home: 59 Parkside Dr., Berkeley 5 CA‡

WYMAN, CHARLES ALFRED, mfg. co., exec.; b. Ustin/L, Czechosolovakia, June 7, 1914; s. Hans and Stella (Parnas) W.; LL.D., U. Prague, 1936; m. Olga Perger, Apr. 9, 1938; children—John Howard, Thomas Michael, Virginia Ann. Came to U.S., 1941, naturalized, 1946. Asst. v.p. Eversharp, Inc., Chgo., 1942-44; pres. Universal Plastics Co., New Brunswick, N.J., 1944-45. 94th & Fifth Av. Corp., 1951-69; pres. chmn. H. O. Canfield Co., Inc.; chmn. Pantasote Co., Passaic, N.J., Europaische H.O. Canfield GmbH, Gartenberg, Germany. Galvarplast, Malgesso, Varese, Italy. President Panwy Found. Mem. U.S. Austrian C. of C. (dir. mem. exec. com.), Rubber Mfrs. Assn. Clubs: Quaker Hill Country (Pawling, N.Y.); Innis Arden Golf, Burning Tree Country (Greenwich, Conn.); N.Y. Athletic. Home: New York City NY Died Dec. 24, 1971.

WYMAN, EUGENE LESTER, lawyer; b. Los Angeles, July 21. 1924; s. Abraham and Betty (Koplowitz) W.; B.S., Northwestern U., 1947; LL.B., Harvard, 1949; m. Rosalind Wiener, Aug. 29, 1954; children—Betty Lyn, Robert Alan, Brad Hibbs. Admitted to Cal. bar, 1950, U.S. Dist. for D.C., 1969, also U.S. Supreme Court; practice Beverly Hills, 1951-73; mem. Wyman, Bautzer, Rothman & Kuchel, 1952-73; Mem. arts and edn. com. Los Angeles Music Center; mem. legacy com. Brandeis U.; gen. chmn. Los Angeles com. State of Israel Bonds, 1971. Vice chmn. Cal. Dem. Central Com., 1961-62, chmn., 1962-64; mem. Dem. Nat. Com. for Cal., 1964-68; treas. Western States Dem. Conf. Bd. govs. Cedars Med. Center; trustee Reiss-David Clinic; bd. dirs. Reiss-David Child Study Center, Am. Friends Hebrew U., Fund for Higher Edn., Israel. Recipient Mr. Am. Citizen award Los Angeles B'nai B'rith, 1964, citation work for mentally retarded children Reiss-Davis Clinic, 1964. Mem. Am., Los Angeles, Beverly Hills bar assns., State Bar Cal. Jewish religion (trustee temple). Clubs: Beverly Hills: Big Ten (Northwestern U.). Home: Los Angeles CA Died Jan. 19, 1973.

WYMAN, WILLARD GORDON, retired army officer; b. Augusta, Me., Mar. 21, 1898; s. John Monroe and Minnie (Haynes) W.; student Lincoln Acad., Newcastle, Me., 1912-15; grad. Coburn Classical Inst., Waterville, Me., 1916; student Bowdoin Coll., 1917, M.A. (hon.), 1951; B.S., U.S. Mil. Acad., 1919; grad. Coast Arty. Sch., Ft. Monroe, Va., 1920, Cav. Sch., Ft. Riley Kan., 1921, Signal Sch., Ft. Monmouth, N.J., 1926; student Chinese language Mil. Attache's Office, Peiping, China, 1928-32 (mem. Central Asiatic Expdn. under Roy Chapman Andrews, 1930); Command and Gen. Staff Sch., Ft. Leavenworth, Kan., 1937; m. Ethel Mae Megginson, Sept. 27, 1921; children—Patricia Anne (Mrs. Eugene Pinney), Nancy Lee (Mrs. Earl F. Geiger), Williard Gordon. Commd. 2d lt. Cav., 1918 and advanced through the grades to general, 1956; assistant commanding general of 1st U.S. Inf. Div., 1943-44; comdg. general 71st Inf. Div., 1944-45, G-2 Army Ground Forces 1945-46; chief of staff 1st U.S. Army, 1947-50, adminstrv. Dept. of Army, 1950-51, Comdg. Gen. IX U.S. Corps, 1951-52 Allied Land Forces Southeastern Europe, 1952-54; comdg. gen. 6th U.S. Army, Presido of San Francisco, 1954-55; deputy commanding general Continental Army Command, August 1955-March 1956; commanding general United States Continental Army Command, Ft. Monroe, Virginia, 1956-58, ret. Awarded Victory Medal, German Occupation Medal, Yangtze Service Medal (Naval), Nat. Defense Medal, Asiatic Theater Medal with 2 campaign stars, European Theater Medal with 7 campaign stars and arrowhead, Occupation Medal, Victory Medal World War II, Distinguished Service

Cross, Silver Star, Legion of Merit, Bronze Star with oak leaf cluster (U.S.), Legion of Honor, Croix de Guerre with palm (France), Russian Order of Great War, 1st class, Distinguished Service Medal with 1st Oak Leaf Cluster. Mem. Assn. Grads. U.S. Mil. Acad., Lambda Chapter Zeta Psi, 1st Div. Soc., Sons of Cincinnati, Mayflower Soc., Explorers Club, Natural Resources Council, Nat. Rifle Soc. Club: Army-Navy (Washington). Contbr. to publication Am. Museum Natural History of Topography of Mongolia." Home: ME Died Mar. 29, 1969; buried Arlington Nat. Cemetery, Arlington VA

WYUM, OBED ALONZO, farm orgn. ofcl.; b. Hills, Minn., Mar. 14, 1897; s. Henry Edward and Tolena (Haatvedt) W.; acad. Lutheran Coll., Fergus Falls, Minn., 1913-15; m. Susie Anna Kulzer, June 4, 1923; children—Robert, Evelyn (Mrs. Maurice Anderson), Earl, Inez (Mrs. Frank Orthmeyer), Phyllis (Mrs. Karl Osmundson), Dorothy (Mrs. Lewis Dohman). Dir. R-S-R Rural Electric Coop., 1943-53. Farmers Union Grain Terminal Assn., 1944-59. Chmn. Sargent County exec. com. Nonpartisan League, 1920-34;, chmn. Sargent County Rep. Central Com., 1922-34; county commr. Sargent County, 1931-42, chmn. county welfare bd., 1934-42, mem. land-use planning com., 1937-40; mem. N.D. Agrl. Adv. Council, 1942-48; state committeeman FSA, 1943-46, Farmers Home Adminstrn., 1948. Mem. N.D. (chmn. policy and program com. 1946-52), Sargent County (chmn. 1938-51), farmers unions, Nat. (dir. 1951-56), N.D. (pres. 1946-53) assns. rural electric coops., Nat. Planning Assn., N.D. Health Council. Lutheran. Mem. bd. govs. Agrl. Hall of Fame, 1958-69. Home: Rutland ND Died Feb. 17, 1969.

YAGER, LOUIS, engineer; b. Germantown, Wis., July 2, 1877; s. Frederick R. and Mary (Eberlein) Y.; grad. high sch., Preston, Minn., 1895; C.E., U. of Minn., 1900; m. Hester Elizabeth Whiteley, of Brainerd, Minn., Aug. 14, 1902. Rodman and insp. N.P. Ry., 1900, asst. engr. on constrn., 1901-02, supervisor bridges and bldgs., at Minneapolis, 1902-07, asst. engr., St. Louis Bay Bridge reconstrn., Duluth, and constrn. Glendive (Mont.) East Line, 1907-10, div. engr., St. Paul, 1910-17, engr. maintenance of way, St. Paul, 1917-19; chief maintenance of way engr., U.S. R.R. Administration, Washington, D.C., 1919-20; engr., maintenance of way, N.P. Ry., St. Paul, 1920-22, asst. chief engr. since 1922. Mem. Am. Soc. C.E., Am. Ry. Engrs. Assn. (pres. 1929). Republican. Presbyn. Mason (32 deg.). Club: St. Paul Athletic. Home: 1156 Lincoln Av. Address: Northern Pacific Ry. Co., St Paul MN‡

YATES, STEPHEN, realtor; b. Albany, N.Y., Nov. 24, 1873; s. Edward and Catharine Anne (Bogart) Y.; art edn., Art Students League, N.Y. City, Slade's Sch., London, Julian Acad., Paris; m. Marion Combs, Feb. 14, 1900; 1 dau., Marion. Early career as artist; began as realtor, 1902. Mem. Nat. Assn. of Real Estate Bds., New York State Assn. Real Estate Bds. (pres. 1925), Long Island Real Estate Bd. (pres. 1920, 21). Democrat. Episcopalian. Mason. Home: The Narrows, Setauket, LI NY‡

YEASTING, WILLIAM HENRY, banker; b. Gibsonburg, O., Mar. 27, 1874; s. John F. and Margaret (Friar) Y.; ed. Northwestern Coll., Naperville, Ill.; m. Jessie Sarnes, of Elmore, O., Sept. 21, 1898. Began as messenger boy, Gibsonburg Banking Co., 1896; pres. Commercial Savings Bank & Trust Co., Toledo, O., until 1931. Pres. Bd. of Edn., Gibsonburg, 1898-1907. Mem. Ohio Bankers Assn. (pres. 1922-23), Toledo Chamber Commerce (pres. 1923-24). Republican. Methodist. Home: 3703 Brookside Rd., Ottawa Hills, Toledo OH‡

YELLOWLEY, EDWARD C., district supervisor of Alcohol Tax Unit, Bureau of Internal Revenue; b. near Ridgeland, Miss., Aug. 12, 1873; s. James Brownlow and Jessie (Perkins) Y.; ed. high sch. and mil. acad., N.C.; m. Callie H. Gibbons, Dec. 29, 1912 (died Mar. 2, 1927). Formerly mgr. father's plantation; with Internal Revenue Service since 1899; promoted internal revenue agent in charge, 1910, and served in that capacity in Phila., St. Paul, San Antonio, Nashville, Atlanta, and San Francisco; called to Washington to reorganized field force, Income and Estate Tax Units of Internal Rev. Bur., 1919; apptd. head of Field Audit. Div.; apptd. supervising agent for the Pacific region, 1920, hdqrs. San Francisco; transferred to Prohibition Unit, 1921, to reorganize Prohibition force, and made chief of general prohibition agents; supervisor of industrial alcohol for 7th Dist. of U.S., comprising states of Ill., Ind. and Wis., 1925-30, supervisor of permits, 1930-34; dist. supervisor alcohol tax unit, Bur. Internal Revenue, since 1934. Mem. Southern Soc., Miss. State Soc. of Washington. Mason (Shriner). Chicago IL‡

YEOMANS, EARL RAYMOND, univ. adminstr.; b. Phila., July 24, 1894; s. George Heath and Alice (Witcher) Y.; B.S. in Edn., Temple U., 1929, M.S. in Edn., 1933, Ed.D., 1945; LL.D. (hon.), Phila. Coll. Osteopathy, 1954; m. Irene S. Pearce, Nov. 29, 1917. Dir. athletic Frankford High Sch., Phila., 1917-19; asst. to dir. health and phys. edn. Phila. pub. schs., 1919-21; dir. phys. edn. Phila. YMCA, 1921-27; mem. staff Temple U., 1927-65, sec. corp., 1945-62, v.p., 1957-65, v.p. emeritus, hon. life mem. bd. trustees, 1966-73. Dir. Indsl. Valley Bank & Trust Co., Indsl. Valley Title and Ins. Co., Commonwealth Fed. Savs. and Loan Assn. Mem. Pa. Recreation Council, 1954-57, Pa. Citizens Council Better Schs., 1958; mem. Liberty Bowl Com., 1958-65, U.S. Olympic Com., 1950-52, Phila. Olympic Com., 1952, 64. Bd. dirs. Germantown Boys Club, Phila. Coll. Osteopathy, Phila. chpt. Football Found. and Hall of Fame. Recipient Tchrs. Coll. Merit award Temple U. Gen. Alumni Assn., 1942, Distinguished Service award, 1957; Annual Achievement award Phila. Post Office Square Club, 1961. Mem. Eastern Coll. Athletic Conf. (past pres., chmn. reorgn. com. 1946; James Lynah Meml. award 1963), Intercollegiate Assn. Amateur Athletics Am. (past pres., chmn. local 75th anniversary com. 1951), Intercollegiate Soccer Football Assn. Am., Eastern Intercollegiate Football Assn. (past pres.), Eastern Intercollegiate Basketball Conf. (past pres.), Phi Delta Kappa, Phi Epsilon Kappa, Kappa Kappa Psi, Sigma Pi, Blue Key. Republican. Baptist. Mason. Clubs: Skytop (Pa.); Union League (bd. dirs.) (Phila.). Home: Philadelphia PA Died Jan. 5, 1973.

YEOMANS, FRANK CLARK, surgeon; b. Stillwater, N.J., Nov. 6, 1871; s. Martin John William and Selina Eleanor (Fleming) Y.; grad. Phillips Exeter Acad., Exeter, N.H., 1893; A.B., Yale, 1897; M.D., Cornell U., 1900; grad. study, U. of Berlin, 1905; m. Estelle Louise Moreau, Nov. 6, 1906; 1 son, Moreau. Interne, New York Hosp., 1900-02; prof. intestinal and rectal surgery, New York Polyclinic Med. Sch. and Hosp., 1924-50; consulting surgeon New York City Cancer Inst.; consulting proctologist Richmond Memorial Hospital (Staten Island), Vassar Brothers Hospital, Poughkeepsie, N.Y. Hon. consulting surgeon N.Y. City Police Dept. Mem. med. bd. Doctor's Hosp., N.Y. City. Lt. col. Med. O.R.C. Diplomate, Am. Bd. Surgery. Fellow Nat. Gastroenterol. Assn. (hon.), Am. Coll. Surgeons, Am. Proctologic Soc. (ex-pres.), A.M.A. (chmn. Sect. on Gastroenterology and Proctology, 1940-41), New York Acad. Medicine; mem. N.Y. Gastroenterol. Assn., S.R., Gov. Soc. Mayflower Descendants in State of N.Y., 1944-46; hon. mem. Royal Soc. Medicine. Presbyn. Clubs: Univ. (Winter Park, Fla.), Yale. Author: A Treatise on Proctology, 1929; 2d edition, 1936; also section Diseases of the Colon and Rectum in Bedside Diagnosis. Mem. editorial bd. Rev. of Gastroenterology; mem. editorial council Am. Jour. Digestive Disease. Contbr. to med. jours. Editor: Sclerosing Therapy, 1939. Home: Orlando FL Died Jan. 23, 1969; buried Kensico Cemetery, Valhalla NY

YEOMANS, HENRY AARON, prof. government; b. Ashtabula, O., Feb. 5, 1877; s. William Andrew and Eva Mandane (Nettleton) Y.; A.B., Harvard, 1900, A.M., 1901, LL.B., 1904; m. Olive Livingston Gilbert, May 1, 1905. Practiced law, N.Y. City, 1904-09; lecturer on govt., Harvard U., 1910-11, instr., 1911-12, asst. professor, 1912-17, professor, 1917-43, professor emeritus since 1943; assistant dean, Harvard College, 1912-16, dean, 1916-21. Dir. Am. Univ. Union in Europe, 1919; exchange prof. to U. of Paris, 1919-20; Cercle Francais lecturer at the French univs. (Hyde Foundation), 1920; lecturer on French govt. and politics, Lowell Inst. Mem. Am. Polit. Science Assn.; fellow Am. Acad. Arts and Sciences. Contbr. Cyclo. of Am. Government and various periodicals. Editor: Facts and Visions, Baccalaureate Sermons by Abbott Lawrence Lowell. Author: Biography of Abbott Lawrence Lowell. Home: Harvard, Mass. Address: 215 Widener Library, Cambridge 38 MA‡

YEOMANS, ROBERT DEWITTE, utilities exec.; b. Chgo., June 9, 1912; s. Chester Bebe and Marguerite (Dunlop) Y.; A.B., U. Wash., 1936, LL.B., 1939; m. Virginia Cedar Burton, Dec. 22, 1951; children—Jill Dunlap, Leigh Stuart; m. 2d, Eleanor Jean Perkins, Aug. 18, 1962. Admitted to Wash. bar, 1939; practiced in Seattle, 1939-42, 45-53; mem. firm Vedova, Horswill & Yeomans, 1949-51; practiced in Spokane, 1951-73; mem. Wash. Pub. Service Commn., Olympia, 1953-56; sec. Wash. Water Power Co., Spokane, 1956-68, v.p., sec., 1968-73; sec., dir. Limestone Co., Wash. Irrigation Devel. Co.; sec. Spokane Indsl. Park, Inc., Pacific N.W. Power Co. (all Spokane). Instr. U. Ida. Pub. Utilities Exec. Course. Vice pres. Spokane City Plan Commn. Served to lt. comdr. USNR, 1942-45. Mem. Am., Wash., Spokane bar assns., Am. Soc. Corporate Secs. (dir.). Clubs: Spokane, Spokane Country. Home: Spokane WA Died 1973.

YODER, WORTH NICHOLAS, engr.; b. Wakarusa, Ind., Apr. 7, 1899; s. Nicholas B. and Clara (Longenecker) Y.; A.B., Asbury Coll., 1920; B.S. in Civil Engring., Purdue U., 1923; m. Eva May Merrill, June 4, 1921; children—Worth Nicholas, C. Merrill, Betty Lane (Mrs. Robert Fulwider). Engr., Indiana Service Corp., Ft. Wayne, 1923-27; constrn. engr. W.F. Schulz, Memphis, 1927-28; engr. Cin. Street Ry. Co., 1928-39; city mgr. City of Tipton (Ind.), 1939-48, City of Sturgis (Mich.), 1948-68, retired, 1968; spl. engr. City of Bloomington (Ind.), 1948; cons. engr., 1968-72. Served with U.S. Army, 1918; to maj. AUS, 1943-44; ETO. fellow Am. Soc. C.E.; mem. Internat. City Mgrs. Assn. (life), Mich. Community Health Assn. (dir.), Mich. Health Officers Assn., C. of C. Mason (Shriner). Home: Sturgis MI Died July 4, 1972.

YORK, EDWARD HOWARD, JR., investment banker; b. Portland, Me., Oct. 31, 1890; s. Edward Howard and Anna (Longley) Y.; grad. Phillips Andover Acad., '1908; B.A., Yale, 1912; m. Elizabeth C. McCawley, Apr. 29, 1916; children—Edward Howard, III, Pauline (Mrs. Sims McGrath), Elizabeth (Mrs. John S. Wyner) (dec.), John W. With E. W. Clark and Co., Phila., 1912-21; asso. bond dept. Drexel & Co., Phila., 1921-30, partner, 1931-35, v.p. and later partner Morgan Stanley & Co., N.Y.C., 1935-43; partner Drexel & Co., 1943-61, limited partner, 1961-66; dir. Markle Corporation, Wentz Corp. Captain A.E.F. 1917-19. Member finance committee United Fund of Phila. Area, 1959-66. Mem. bd. mgrs. Children's Hosp. Phila., 1947-66. Mem. Investment Bankers Assn. Am. (gov. 1947-50). Republican. Episcopalian. Clubs: Philadelphia, The Rabbit, Racquet (Phila.); Gulph Mills Golf (Pa.); Yale (N.Y.C.). Home: Villanova PA Died May 19, 1966.

YORK, HARLAN HARVEY, prof. botany; b. near Plainfield, Ind., Sept. 8, 1875; s. Pleasant McPherson and Elizabeth (Hornaday) Y.; Ph.B., DePauw U., Greencastle, Ind., 1903; A.M., Ohio State U., 1905; student Columbia, 1905-06; Ph.D., Johns Hopkins, 1911; m. Edith Thayer Cline, Aug. 26, 1908; 1 son, James Thayer; m. 2d, Minnie White Taylor, June 23, 1934. Fellow in botany, Ohio State U., 1903-04, asst. in botany, 1904-05; fellow in botany, Columbia, 1905-06; asst. in U.S. Nat. Herbarium, 1906; instr. botany, U. of Tex., 1906-09; asst. in botany, Johns Hopkins, 1909-10, fellow, 1910-11; asst. prof. of botany, Brown U., 1911-19; prof. of botany, W.Va. Univ., 1919-23; pathologist div. of forest pathology, U.S. Dept. Agr., 1923; forest pathologist N.Y. State conservation dept., 1923-30; prof. of botany, U. of Pa., since 1930; asst. in cryptogemic botany, Biol. Lab., Cold Spring Harbor, L.I., summers, 1906-11, instr. in charge, summers 1912-15; pathologist div. of forest pathology, U.S. Dept. Agr., summers 1916-22; special investigator and cons. pathologist N.Y. Conservation Dept., summers since 1930. Mem. A.A.A.S., Phytopathological Soc., Torrey Bot. Club, Am. Foresters, Phi Beta Kappa, Sigma Xi, Gamma Alpha, Sigma Nu. Mason, K. of P. Clubs: Lenape (U. of Pa.); McAlpine Street (Phila.). Contbr. to Jour. Phytopathology, Science. Home: 419 S. 45th St., Philadelphia PA*‡

YOST, BARTLEY FRANCIS, consular service; b. Switzerland, Sept. 20, 1877; s. George and Elizabeth (Fluetsch) Y.; came with parents to U.S. in infancy; ed. pub. sch., Kan., and at Washburn Coll., and Normal Inst., Osborne Co.; m. Irma Cleopha Blau, of Kirkland, Wash., Oct. 7, 1908; 1 son, Robert Lloyd. Farmer and teacher pub. schs. until 1905; clk. dist. court and part owner Osborne County (Kan.) News, 1906-08; apptd. consular asst., 1908; dep. consul gen., Paris, 1909-13, consular agt., Almeria, 1913-17; vice consul, Genoa, 1917-18; consul Santa Rosalia, Lower Calif., 1918, Guaymas, Mexico, 1918-24, Torreon, Mex., 1924-26, Sault Ste. Marie, Can., 1926-31, Nogales, Sonora, Mexico, 1931-32, Cologne, Germany, 1932-35, retired. Republican. Home: 1736 Asbury Drive, Pasadena CA‡

YOUNG, ARCHER EVERETT, mathematician; b. Haddam Neck, Conn., Mar. 12, 1873; s. Hezekiah Russell and Sarah E. (Andrews) Y.; A.B., Wesleyan U., Conn., 1898; Ph.D., Princeton, 1903; m. Grace Louise Wiard, of New Britain, Conn., Sept. 1, 1903; children—Everett W., Mary Louse, James Russell, Marjorie Evelyn. Instr. Shadyside Acad., Pittsburgh, 1898-1901; prof. mathematics, Purdue U., Layayette, Ind., 1903-08; same, Miami U., Oxford, O., 1908-21, also dean, 1913-21; with Standard Oil interests, 1921-—. Mem. Am. Math. Soc., Phi Beta Kappa, Alpha Delta Phi. Presbyn. Frequent contbr. to math. publs. Home: 1524 Asbury Pl., Pittsburgh PA‡

YOUNG, CHARLES HENRY, hospital supt.; b. Everett, Mass., Mar. 22, 1876; s. Reuben and Sarah Elizabeth (Renouf) Y.; prep. edn. high sch., Woburn, Mass.; M.D., Tufts Coll. Med. Sch., 1905; m. Anna Ethel Rand, M.D., of Boston, Mass., June 20, 1905. Asst. supt. Presbyn. Hosp., N.Y. City, 1906-14, supt., 1914-23; supt. Good Samaritan Hosp., Syracuse, N.Y., since 1923; asso. prof. administrative medicine and supt. Univ. Hosp., Syracuse U. Served as lt. col. M.C., U.S.A., World War; chief of hospitalization, Base Sect. No. 3, A.E.F.; now lt. col. O.R.C., attached to 98th Div., 2d Corps Area. Mem. New York Acad. Medicine, Harvey Soc., Mil. Order World War. Republican. Presbyn. Clubs: University, Rotary. Home: 812 University Av. Office: 110 Marshall St., Syracuse NY‡

YOUNG, CHARLES SOMMERS;, b. Camden, N.J., Mar. 28, 1873; s. Charles Elmer and Sarah (Smith) Y.; grad. Friends' Central High Sch., Phila., Pa.; student Cornell University, 1891-95; m. Gladys Meyer, of Berkeley, Calif., Jan. 27, 1923; children—Charles Sommers, John Reynolds. Began as reporter Omaha (Neb.) Bee, 1895; with adv. dept. C.,B.&Q.R.R., 1899-1903; adv. mgr. C., M.&St.P.R.R., 1903-10; adv. and business mgr. San Francisco Examiner, 1910-16; western mgr. N.W. Ayer & Son, adv. agency, at Chicago, 1916-20; v.p. and gen. mgr. Omaha Bee, 1920-21; asst. to pres. Omaha Daily News, 1921-22; pub. Oakland (Calif.) Post-Enquirer, 1922-26; pub. San

Francisco Call, 1926-30; with U.S. Beet Sugar Assn., since 1931. Mem. S.A.R., Sigma Chi, Sphinx Head. Episcopalian. Home: 3041 Baker St., San Francisco CA*‡

YOUNG, CHARLES VAN PATTEN, prof. emeritus ret.; b. Middletown, O., Nov. 30, 1876; s. John Mumaw and Caroline (Van Patten) Y.; A.B. and B.S., Dickinson Sem., Williamsport, Pa., 1895; A.B., Cornell, 1899; grad. Princeton Theol. Sem., 1902; m. Eleanor Mahaffey, June 3, 1902; 1 dau., Eleanor. With physical training dept., Cornell U., since 1904, prof. physical edn., since 1906. Served as dir. athletics Cornell S.A.T.C., World War I. Mem. Am. Assn. Univ. Profs., A.A.A.S., Alpha Delta Phi. Club: Rotary. Author: Courtney and Cornell Rowing, 1923; How Men Have Lived, 1932; Across The Borderline, 1946. Home: 112 Lake St., Ithaca NY*‡

YOUNG, CHIC (MURAT BERNARD YOUNG), cartoonist; b. Chgo., Jan. 9, 1901; s. James Luther and Martha (Techen) Y.; ed. pub. schs. of St. Louis and arts schs. in Chicago, New York and Cleveland, O.; m. Athel L. Lindorff, Oct. 4, 1927; children—Wayne Roy (dec.), Dean Wayme, Jeanne Athel. With Newspaper Enterprise Assn., 1920-21, Bell Syndicate, New York, 1921-23, King Features Syndicate, 1923-73; orginated comic strip Dumb Dora, 1924, and drew it 6 yrs.; originated comic strip Blondie 1930, and has been drawing this strip daily for 1600 Am. and fgn. newspapers. Address: Clearwater Beach FL Died Mar. 14, 1973.

YOUNG, CLAIBORNE ADDISON, Unitarian clergyman; b. in Indiana; grad. Wabash Coll.; m., May 8, 1890, Lucy Conant Farnham. Author: Way Songs and Wanderings; Nancy Gilbreth of the Cumberland Mountains Kums ter Harvard. Address: Canton MA‡

YOUNG, CLARENCE MARSHALL, aviation cons.; b. Colfax, Ia. s. Theodore G. and Ella (Foy) Y.; student Drake U.; LL.B., Yale, 1910; m. Lois Moran, Feb. 10, 1935; 1 son, Timothy Marshall. Admitted to Ia. bar, 1910, and began practice at Des Moines; served as exec. sec. Municipal Research Bureau, Des Moines, 1922-25; dir. aeros. U.S. Dept. Commerce, 1926-29, asst. sec. of commerce for aeros., 1929-33; mgr. Transpacific Div. Pan Am. Airways, 1934-45, v.p. Pan Am. World Airways, 1950-59; mem. CAB, Washington, 1946-50. Mem. Air Service, U.S. Army, 1917-19; overseas 18 mos., including 5 mos. as prisoner of war, Austria; col. U.S. Air Forces Res., ret. Decorated Comdr. Order Crown of Italy; named Elder Statesman of Aviation, Nat. Assn. Aeros; named to Aviation Hall of Fame Oxs Club Am. Asso. fellow Am. Inst. Aeros. and Astronautics, Royal Aero. Soc. London; mem. Acacia. Republican. Mason. Clubs: Yale (N.Y.C.); Family (San Francisco); Army and Navy (Washington). Home: Sedona AZ Died Apr. 10, 1973.

YOUNG, EDWARD JOSEPH, clergyman; b. San Francisco, Nov. 29, 1907; s. Edward Eyestone and Julia Rapier (Tharp) Y.; A.B., Leland Stanford Jr. U., 1929; student Centro de Estudios Historicos, Madrid, 1930; Th.B., Th.M., Westminster Theol. Sem., 1935; student U. Leipzig, 1935-36; Ph.D., Dropsie Coll., 1943; m. Lillian Riggs, July 25, 1935; children—Lillian Jean, Davis Alan. Ordained to ministry Presbyn. Ch., 1935; prof. O.T., Westminster Theol. Sem., Phila., 1936-68; prof. Winona Lake Summer Sch. Theology, 1950-68, Winona Lake Flying Seminar, 1952, 62. Member committee on Christian education Orthodox Presbyn. Church, 1937-68, moderator Gen. Assembly, 1956. Mem. of the Am. Oriental Soc., Soc. Bibl. Lit. and Exegesis, Evang. Theol. Sem. Soc., Phi Beta Kappa. Author: The Prophecy of Daniel, 1949; Introduction to the Old Testament, 1949; Arabic for Beginners, 1950; Isaiah Fifty-Three, 1952; My Servants the Prophets, 1953; The Messianic Prophecies of Daniel, 1954; Studies in Isaiah, 1954; Thy Word is Truth, 1957; Studies in Genesis One, 1964; Psalm 139, 1965; Genesis Three, 1966. Editor: The New International Old Testament Commentary, Commentary on The Book of Isaiah, Vol. 1, 1965, Vol. 2, 1970, Vol. 3, 1972. Home: Huntingdon Valley PA Died Feb. 14, 1968; buried George Washington Meml. Park, Plymouth Meeting PA

YOUNG, ELIZABETH GUION (BAB SEARS), author; b. St. Louis, 1876; d. Eben and Clementine (Guion) Y.; ed. in pvt. sch. and by governess and tutors; never attended sch. more than a yr.; unmarried. Writer short stories in many mags. and newspaper. Author: The Circle in the Square, 1903. Address: Cos Cob CT‡

YOUNG, ERNEST CHARLES, univ. dean; b. Grove City, Pa., Sept. 29, 1892; s. Seymour Rankin and Ella (Struthers) Y.; B.S., Grove City (Pa.) Coll., 1914; Ph.D., Cornell U., 1921; honorary LL.D., Grove City College, 1947; married Eva Crowe (div.); children—Margaret Ella (Mrs. John Petroskas), Marion Elizabeth; m. 2d, Marjorie M. Knott, August 6, 1953. Teacher of science, high school, Mercer, Pa., 1914-16, instr. in agrl. economics, Cornell U., 1916-21; asst. prof. agrl. econ., Purdue U., 1921-23, asso. prof., 1924-27, prof. since 1927, asst. dean of grad. sch., 1933-42, dean, 1942-63, also vice president of university, 1961-63; (on leave) director research N.Y. State Commn. on Agr., 1948-49. Served with Army Air Service, 1918. Asst. to gov. Farm Credit Adminstrn., 1933-34; mem. exec. com., vice chmn. agrl. bd. National Research Council since 1950; board cons. for agr. Rockefeller Foundation, 1952-60. Mem. Am. Assn. Farm Mgrs. and Rural Appraisers, Am. Farm Econ. Assn. (pres. 1938), Internat. Conf. Agrl. Economists (vice president, 1947-52), Sigma Xi, Alpha Zeta, Alpha Gamma Rho. Contributor of numerous technical articles in field of agricultural econs. to various publs. Home: Lafayette IN Died Apr. 23, 1968; buried Rest Haven Cemetery, Lafayette IN

YOUNG, GEORGE HENRY, clergyman, educator; b. York, Eng., Jan. 21, 1876; s. Daniel and Elizabeth (Arnold) Y.; B.A., Colgate, 1901, M.A., 1904; Colgate Theol. Sch., 1901-04; D.D., Albany Coll., 1919; m. Ethel Lena House of Mexico, New York, June 18, 1903; children—Elizabeth Ann, Genevieve Edith, Robert House. Ordained Bapt. ministry, 1904; asst. in pub. speaking, Colgate U., 1901-04; pastor First Ch., Beaver Dam, Wis., 1904-07, First Ch., Superior, 1907-10, First Ch., Oswego, N.Y., 1910-12; asst. prof. rhetoric and pub. speaking, Colgate, 1912-15; pastor First Ch., Albany, Ore., 1915-20; dir. religious education for Baptists of Ore., Ida., and Utah, 1920; pastor First Ch., Hamilton, O., 1922-24, First Ch. Kalamazoo, Mich., 1924-27; supt. Lord's Day Alliance of Indiana since 1927. Pres. Mich. Bapt. Ministers' Conf.; trustee Wayland Academy, Beaver Dam, Wisconsin, 1906-09; mem. bd. Wis. Bapt. State Conv., 1907-10; served as pres. Ore. Bapt. Ministers' Conf., and prof. Bible, Albany Coll. Chmn. Linn Co. Chapter Am. Red Cross, World War; chmn. Linn Co. Bd. Instruction for Registrants, 1918; ex-chaplain 2d Regt., Ore. Vol. Guard. Mem. Phi Beta Kappa, Beta Theta Pi. Odd Fellow. Author: Illustrative Teachings of Jesus, 1914. His Mother's Story, 1916; Fruitage of Baptist Faith, 1921; The Man of Eternal Glory. Home: Colosse NY‡

YOUNG, GEORGE JOSEPH, mining engr.; b. San Francisco, Oct. 3, 1876; s. Joseph and Mary (Wilburn) Y.; B.S., U. of Calif., 1899; m. Wayman A. Atterbury, June 24, 1912 (dec.); 1 child, Marion Wayman; m. 2d, Hulda Hanson, 1920. Asst. prof. metallurgy, U. of Nev., 1900-03, prof. mining and metallurgy, 1903-13; in charge of Mackay Sch. of Mines, U. of Nev., 1908-13; prof. mining, U. of Minn., 1913-16; prof. metallurgy, Colo. Sch. of Mines, 1916-17; cons. mining and metall. engineer, San Francisco, since 1917. Was dir. of Cooperative Lab., potash investigations of Bur. of Soils, Dept. of Agriculture and Mackay School of Mines. Mem. Am. Inst. Mining and Metall. Engrs. Clubs: Engineers', Sierra. Author: Elements of Mining; The Working of Unstratified Mineral Deposits. Asst. editor Engineering and Mining Journal, 1918-19, asso. editor same, 1919-32, consulting editor since 1933. Lecturer in mining U. of Calif., 1946-48. Home: 5928 Keith Av., Oakland 18 CA‡

YOUNG, GORDON ELMO, U.S. judge; b. Malvern, Ark., Apr. 26, 1907; s. John Elmo and Edna (Murry) Y.; LL.B., U. Ark., 1931; m. Ruth Elizabeth Gregg, Aug. 16, 1932; children—Elizabeth Edna (Mrs. David Harton Newbern), Martha Louise (Mrs. Cecil Duke Allison, Jr.), Catherine Blount (Mrs. Harry Howard Cockrill, Jr.), Virginia Anne (Mrs. Edward Powell Kenney). Admitted to Arkansas bar, 1931; pvt. practice, Malvern, 1931-39; mem. firm Bridges & Young, Pine Bluff, 1939-59; U.S. dist. judge Eastern Dist. of Ark., 1959-69. Mem. Am., Fed., Ark. bar assns. Home: Little Rock AR Died Aug. 20, 1969; buried Malvern AR

YOUNG, JAMES THOMAS, college prof.; b. Phila., Sept. 23, 1873; s. Andrew J. and Louisa A. Y.; Ph.B., U. of Pa., 1893; Ph.D., U. of Halle, 1895; Litt.D., 1940. Dir. Wharton Sch. Finance and Commerce, 1904-12; now prof. public adminstrn. (retired), University of Pa.; also consultant on government and indsl. policy. Mem. Am. Philos. Soc. Am. Assn. Univ. Profs., Phi Beta Kappa. Author: The New Am. Government and Its Work, 1915, 4th edit., 1940; also articles on government, pub. regulation of business in various jours. and procs. Address: Wharton School, Univ. of Pa., Philadelphia PA‡

YOUNG, JAMES WEBB, advt. cons.; b. at Covington Ky., Jan. 20, 1886; s. James Davidson and Susan Anna (Webb) Y.; ed. pub. schs., Covington; LL.D., U. N.M., 1957; m. Elizabeth Johnson, Sept. 18, 1907; children—James Philip, Richard Johnson, Webb. Successively office boy, stenographer, advt. bus. through depts. and becoming v.p. and pres. of J. Walter Thompson Co., of New York, also dir.; later prof. bus. history and advt. U. Chgo.; dir. U.S. Bureau of Foreign and Domestic Commerce, Sept. 1939-Feb. 1941. Dir. Santa Fe National Bank. Founder, director, also past chmn. Advt. Council; hon. trustee Com. Econ. Devel.; hon. mem. Business Council; Past pres. Am. Assn. Advtg. Agencies. Awarded Gold Medal for distinguished career in advertising, 1945. Clubs: Tavern, Chicago (Chgo.); Cosmos (Wash.). Author: Advertising Agy. Compensation, 1934; A Technique for Producing Ideas, 1940; The Diary of an Ad Man, 1944; A Footnote to History, 1950; A Story Still Untold, 1951; Pills for the Angels, 1952; The Compleat Angler, 1953; Mirror For a Lady, 1954; Ego-Biography, 1955; His Girl and His Dinner, 1956; The Itch for Orders, 1957; Hometow Boy Makes Good, 1958; Full Corn in the Ear, 1959 How to Become an Advertising Man, 1962. Address Santa Fe NM Died Mar. 1973.

YOUNG, KENNETH TODD, writer; b. Toronto, Can. June 22, 1916; s. Kenneth Todd and Marion (Hunt) Y. student Middlesex Sch., 1934, Lingnan U., China 1934-35, Sorbonne, Paris, 1937; A.B., Harvard, 1939 M.A., 1942; m. Patricia Morris, Oct. 30, 1943 children—Stephen, Edward, Katherine, Christina Teaching fellow Harvard, 1940-42; research asst. Nat Resources Planning Bd., 1942; economist WPB 1942-43; polit. intelligence officer Dept. State, 1946-49 Far Eastern specialist Office Sec. Def., 1949-52, dir Office Northeast Asian Affairs, 1952-54; acting dir Office Philippine and Southeast Asian Affairs, 1954 dir., 1955; dir. Office Southeast Asian Affairs, 1956-58 with Standard Vacuum Oil Co., 1958-61; ambassador to Thailand, 1961-63; pres. Asia Soc., N.Y.C., 1964-69 engaged in studies and writing on S.E. Asia, 1970-72; sr vis. fellow Council Fgn. Relations, 1970-72; cons. AID dir. Overseas Nat. Airways. Adviser U.S. del. to Japanese Peace Conf., also to 7th, 11th, 12th Session of UN General Assembly, and Geneva Conference 1954; mem. U.S. Mission to Japan for negotiation Adminstrv. Agreement; mem. Spl. U.S. Missions to Korea, 1953. Served as capt. air combat intelligence USAAF, 1943-46. Trustee Asia Soc., Lingnan U. Harvard-Yenching Inst. Mem. Council of Fgn Relations. Unitarian. Clubs: D.U., Harvard (Washington); Century Assn., Harvard (N.Y.C. Author: The Southeast Asia Crisis, 1966; The Foreign Policies of Thailand; Negotiating with the Chinese Communists: The United States Experience, 1953-67 1968. Co-editor The Prospects of Southeast Asia, 1966 Home: Larchmont NY Died Aug. 29, 1972.

YOUNG, LAURENCE W., ret. army officer; b Swannanoa, N.C., Aug. 18, 1877; s. Robert H. and Pamelia (Gudger) Y.; student Warren Wilson Coll 1896-97, Southern Bus. Coll., 1898; m. Hester Johnson Sept. 19, 1900; children—Julia (Mrs. A. A. McNamee) Helen (Mrs. David D. Hedekin), Louise (Mrs. M. R Kammerer). Commd. as 2d lt. Inf., N.C. Nat. Guard 1905, advanced through grades to brig. gen., 1918 commd. maj., U.S. Army, 1918, promoted through grades to brig. gen., 1941; ret. 1941, recalled to active duty, relieved 1944. Democrat. Presbyterian. Home 2085 E. Lake Rd. N.E., Atlanta 6 GA‡

YOUNG, LEONARD, supt. of schs.; b. Wabash Co Ind., Mar. 8, 1871; s. John Davis and Christiana (Stacy Y.; ed. State Normal Sch., Terre Haute, Ind., 1889-93 A.B., Ind. U., 1898; m. Lillian M. Butler, of Evansville Ind., Dec. 25, 1909. Teacher twp. high schs., 1888-96 teacher high schs., Wichita, Kan., 1898-99, Evansville Ind., 1899-1907, prin., 1907-10; prin. Central High Sch Duluth, Minn., 1910-23; supt. schs., Duluth, 1923-36 Dir. Duluth Teachers' Retirement Fund Assn. Presbyn Mason (33 deg.). Retired. Address: 922 Bellemade Av. Evansville IN‡

YOUNG, LESTER WILLIS, saxophone player Played tenor saxophone with Bostonians, King Oliver Walter Page's Blue Devils; with Fletcher Henderson 1934, Andy Kirk; with Count Basie, Kansas City summer 1936, with Basie Quintet, 1936-40, 43 pioneered transition from full-tone dotted eight-sixteenths phrasing to moody, legato phrases in eighths; leader own combo, 1941; leader sextet with brother Lee Young, 1942; with own quintet toured U.S and Europe; Jazz at the Philharmonic, 1950-59 numerous appearances with Billie Holiday, Tedd Wilson; appeared in motion picture Jammin' the Blues recordings include Taxi War Dance, Back in Your Own Backyard, Sailboat in the Moonlight. Served with AUS 1944-45. Recipient silver award Esquire, 1945, 47 winner Down Beat mag. poll, 1944. Home: Jamaica NY Died Mar. 15, 1959.

YOUNG, LEVI EDGAR, educator; b. Salt Lake City Utah, Feb. 2, 1874; s. Seymour Bicknell and Elizabeth (Riter) Y.; B.S., U. of Utah, 1895; student Harvard 1898-99; attended lectures, U. of Strassburg, 1904 M.A., Columbia U., 1910; m. Valeria Brinton Young, of Salt Lake City, June 12, 1907; children—Harriet Wollerton, Jane Seymour, Eleanor Brinton. Prof., and head dept. of western history, U. of Utah, since 1900 lectured widely at Am. univs. on history of Utah. De Internat. Ednl. Assn., Nuremberg, Germany, 1904 pres. Temple Block Mission at Salt Lake City; member Com. on Edn. of Aliens, Salt Lake City. Mem. Am Academy of Political and Social Science, Am. Ethno Soc., Am. Hist. Assn. (pres. Pacific Coast br., 1919-20) S.A.R. (ednl. com.), Utah Soc. S.A.R. (historian); fellow Am. Geog. Soc. Republican. Member of First Counc of 70 of Church of Jesus Christ of Latter Day Saints Clubs: Bonneville (Salt Lake City); Authors' (London) Author: (thesis) Economic and Social Development of Utah under Brigham Young's Leadership, 1910; History of the Mormon Tabernacle, 1918; The Founding of Utah, 1923. Address: Salt Lake City UT‡

YOUNG, RICHARD, ex-congressman; b. in Ireland came to America with parents at age of 5; ed. pub. schs and commercial coll., Phila.; m. Harriet M. Wells, o

Wellsville, Pa., 1873. Engaged in leather trade; pres. Richard Young Co.; organized Flatbush Trust Co., Atlantic Mut. Ins. Co. School commr. of Flatbush, L.I., 7 yrs.; organized, and chmn., Erasmus Hall High Sch.; ex-park commr. for boroughs of Brooklyn and Queens; Rep. nominee for comptroller of New York, 1905; mem. 61st Congress (1909-11), 5th N.Y. Dist. Mem. New York Chamber of Commerce, Mfrs.' Assn. of New York, Brooklyn League. Club: Drug and Chemical. Home: Flatbush (Brooklyn). Office: 36-38 Spruce St., New York NY‡

YOUNG, RICHARD HALE, physician, dean med. sch.; b. Chicago, Ill. Jan. 26, 1905; s. Alben and Fannie (Knight) Y.; student Dartmouth, 1923-24; B.S., Northwestern, 1929, M.D., 1930; m. Ellen Stearns Oct. 10, 1934; children—Irving Stearns, Howard Stearns. Interne St. Luke's Hosp., Chicago, 1929-31; pvt. practice of medicine, Evanston, Ill., 1934-46; asst. prof. of medicine, Northwestern, 1938-46, asst. to dean med. sch., 1938-42, dir. student health, 1945-46; dean and associate professor of medicine, University of Utah School of Medicine, 1946-49; dean and professor of medicine, Northwestern Univ. Medical School from 1949. Served as lieut. col., M.C. with 12th Gen. Hosp. U.S. Army 1942-45. Diplomate Am. Bd. Internal Medicine. Fellow A.M.A., A.C.P. Mem. Central Soc. Clin. Research, Chicago Soc. Internal Medicine, Sigma Xi, Alpha Omega Alpha, Pi Kappa Epsilon. Conglist. Home: Willmette IL Died Dec. 26, 1970.

YOUNG, ROBERT THOMPSON, zoologist; b. Phila., Pa., Feb. 14, 1874; s. James Thompson and Lucy Stoddard (Peet) Y.; B.S., U. of Pa., 1896; Ph.D., U. of Neb., 1906; m. Ellen Farrar Pierce, Mar. 22, 1907; 1 son, Robert Thompson. With U. of N.Dak., 1906-26, prof. zoology, 1914-26; prof. zoology, U. of Mont., 1927-34. Mem. Am. Soc. Zoologists, Sigma Xi. Spl. researches in cytology and cestodes, protective coloration of animals, biology of lakes. Author: Biology in America. Home: La Jolla CA‡

YOUNG, SANBORN, b. Evanston, Ill., Mar. 2, 1873; s. Aaron Nelson and Anna Maria (Corell) Y.; married Ruth Comfort Mitchell, October 3, 1914. Grain commission merchant, Chicago, 1898-1912; member Young & Nichols, 1899-1908, Young & Company, 1908-12; now engaged in ranching near Los Gatos, Calif. Member California State Senate, terms 1925-38. Chmn. California State Narcotic Com.; appointed by President Hoover del. Internat. Narcotic Conf., Geneva, 1931, for limitation of mfr. of narcotic drugs; the treaty was adopted by 55 countries. Trustee, The Boy Scouts Memorial Foundation. Member Sons of Revolution, Associated Sportsmen. Republican. Protestant. Clubs: Commonwealth, La Rinconada Country. Wrote: Drug Addiction in California, 1926; Report of the State Narcotic Committee, 1928; Survey of Narcotic Drug Addiction in California, 1932; Report on Drug Addiction in California, 1936. Chmn. Calif. State Narcotic Com., 1925-31. Home: Los Gatos CA‡

YOUNG, WHITNEY MOORE, JR., social work adminstr.; b. Lincoln Ridge, Ky., July 31, 1921; s. Whitney Moore and Laura (Ray) Y.; B.S., Ky State Coll., 1941; student Mass. Inst. Tech., 1942-43; M.A., U. Minn., 1947; student Harvard, 1960-61; LL.D., N.C. A. and T. Coll., 1961, Princeton, 1967, Harvard, 1968, U. San Francisco, 1968, Washington U., 1970; numerous other hon. degrees; m. Margaret Buchner, Jan. 2, 1944; children—Marcia Elaine, Lauren Lee. Indsl. relations and vocational guidance dir. St. Paul Urban League, 1947-50; exec. sec. Omaha Urban League, 1950-53; dean Sch. Social Work, Atlanta U., 1954-60; exec. dir. Nat. Urban League, N.Y.C., 1961-71; instr. Sch. Social Work, U. Neb., 1950-58; frequent lectr. Mem. President's Commn. on Law Enforcement and Adminstrn. Justice; adv. bd. N.Y. Sch. Social Work, Columbia; mem. national adv. council U.S. Office Econ. Opportunity; mem. adv. council on vocational education U.S. Office of Education. Dir. Fed. Res. Bank of N.Y. Member of board Eleanor Roosevelt Meml. Found., John F. Kennedy Meml. Library. Served with AUS, World War II. Recipient Florina Lasker award, 1959, Outstanding Alumni award U. Minn., 1960, Charles Spurgeon Johnson award Fisk U., 1967, Golden Key award N.E.A., 1968, Outstanding Service award U.S. Jaycees, 1969, Medal of Fredom, 1969, Four Freedom's award Four Freedoms Found., 1970, numerous others. Mem. Nat. Social Welfare Assembly (exec. com.), Nat. Assn. Social Workers, Nat. Conf. Social Welfare (past pres.), Alpha Phi Alpha. Mem. Community Ch. Author: Intergroup Relations as a Challenge to Social Work Practice, 1960; Integration-The Role of Labor Education, 1959; Status of the Negro Community: Problems-Proposals-Projections, 1959; To Be Equal, 1964; also author weekly newspaper column. Co-author: A Second Look-The Negro Citizen in Atlanta, 1958; Beyond Racism, 1969. Home: New Rochelle NY Died Mar. 11, 1971; buried Ferncliff Cemetery, Hartsdale NY

YOUNG, WILLIAM LESQUEREUX, educator; b. Pendleton, Co., W.Va., Mar. 4, 1889; s. Edwin and Ida (Earhart) Y.; A.B., Capital U., LL.D., 1950; A.M., Ohio State Univ. 1916, Ph.D. 1931; married Meta Buehring, 1914 (dec. Jan. 1957); children—William E. L., Robert P. T., John P. H.; m. 2d, Hildegarde Heinzelman, Feb. 22, 1958. Prof. Hebron (Neb.) Acad.; 1911-21, acting president, 1919-21; instructor English, Capital University, 1922, professor education and head department, 1923-45, v.p., 1936-45; acting president, 1941-42; executive secretary, Board of Christian Higher Education, The Am. Luth. Church, 1945-60; prof. English, asst. to pres., Capital U., Columbus, O., 1961-63; sec. of Joint Union Com. Merging Luth. Bodies, 1949-60. Mem. Phi Delta Kappa, N.E.A. (life). Author: The Junior College Movement in Relation to Higher Education in Ohio. Republican. Lutheran. Home: OH Died Mar. 20, 1972; buried Obetz Lutheran Cemetery Obetz OH 5DM

YOUNGBERG, GILBERT A(LBIN), army officer (retired); b. Belle Creek, Minn., Feb. 12, 1875; s. Par Nord and Kjerste (Branfelt) Y.; student Carleton Coll., 1893-95; grad. U.S. Mil. Acad., 1900, B.S., 1929; student Army Staff Coll., 1905-06, Army War Coll., 1909-10; m. Adele Harriett de Raismes, Apr. 22, 1903; children—Helen Biddle (Mrs. Charles E. Richheimer), Adele de Raismes (Mrs. Fleming W. Smith). Commd. 2d lt. arty. corps U.S. Army, 1900, transferred to C.E. as 2d lt., Feb. 2, 1901, and advanced through all grades to brig. gen., June 13, 1940; instr. engring., Army Service Schs., 1902-05; div. engr. Northern div., 1906-07; map making and highway constrn. in Cuba, 1907-09; prof. military engring., U.S. Mil. Acad., 1910-14; U.S. dist engr., Charleston, S.C., 1914-17; exec. officer for chief of engrs. A.E.F., 1917-18 and in charge engring. div. supply and constrn. sect., hdqrs. gen. staff, A.E.F., 1918-19; asst. to chief of engrs. U.S. Army, Washington, 1919-22; U.S. Dist. engr., Jacksonville, Fla., 1922-26; ret. 1926; cons. engr. on various river and harbor improvements, electric light and water plants, Jacksonville, Fla. since 1926; dir. Title & Trust Co. of Fla., since 1930. Awarded distinguished service medal U.S. Army; Companion of Distinguished Service Order of Great Britain; Officer of the Legion of Honor (France); Officer of the Order of Saints Mauricio and Lazaro (Italy). Fellow Fla. Engring. Soc.; mem. Am. Soc. Civil Engrs., Soc. Am. Mil. Engrs. (founder-mem. and past pres.), Am. Shore and Beach Preservation Assn. Episcopalian. Clubs: Engineering Professions, Jacksonville Rotary, Timuquana Country (Jacksonville). Author: Brief History of Engineer Troops, U.S. Army (1906); articles in engring. and mil. publs., also in 1920-21 edit. of Ency. Britannica. Home: 3519 Oak St., Jacksonville 5. Office: 712 Graham Bldg., Jacksonville FL‡

YOUNGDAHL, BENJAMIN EMANUEL, social worker; b. Minneapolis, Minn., July 12, 1897; s. John Carl and Elizabeth (Johnson) Y.; A.B., Gustavus Adolphus Coll., 1920, LL.D., 1954; A.M., Columbia, 1923; LL.D., Washington Univ., St. Louis, 1968; m. Livia Alexandra Bjorquist, Aug. 25, 1925; children—James Edward, Kent Benjamin, Mark Alexander. Prin. high sch. and supt. schs., Marietta, Minn., 1920-22; prof. econ. and sociology, Gustavus Adolphus Coll., 1922-33; dir. social service, Minn. State Emergency Relief Adminstrn., 1933-37; dir. pub. assistance, State of Minn., 1937-39; lecturer Univ. of Minn. and So. Calif. summers 1938, 39, 41; asso. prof. of social work, George Warren Brown Sch. of Social Work, Washington Univ., St. Louis, Missouri, 1939-43, professor of social work, 1943-44, 62-66, professor emeritus, 1966-70, dean Sch. Social Work, Washington Univ., 1945-62; visiting prof. U. of Calif., summer 1950. Mem. national com. Midcentury White House Conference on Children and Youth (chmn. fact finding commn.), 1950. Served with U.S. Army as lt. field arty. World War I; overseas service U.N.R.R.A. as liaison officer to S.H.A.E.F. 1944-45. Awarded certificate of merit by Gen. Eisenhower; recipient Florina Lasker award in Social Work, 1963. Mem. Nat. Conf. Social Work (pres. 1955-56). Am. Assn. Social Workers (pres. 1951-53), American Association Schs. Social Work (pres. 1949), Phi Beta Kappa. Conglist. Author: Social Action and Social Work, 1967. Contbr. profl. jours. Benjamin E. Youngdahl lectureship established at Washington U., 1965. Home: Webster Groves MO Died Sept. 18, 1970; buried St. Peter MN

YOUNGDAHL, REUBEN KENNETH NATHANIEL, clergyman; b. Minneapolis, May 17, 1911; s. John and Elizabeth (Johnson) Y.; A.B., Gustavus (Adolphus Coll., St. Peter, Minn., 1931, D.D. (hon.), 1948; B.D., Augustana Theol. Sem., Rock Island, Ill., 1934; m. Ruth Wilma Youngberg, June 14, 1934; children—Paul Matthew, Susan Elizabeth, Stephen Mark. Ordained to ministry Luth. Ch. (Augustana Synod), 1934, pastor, Marshalltown, Ia., 1934-37, (Mount Olivet Ch., Minneapolis since 1938. Pres. Cathedral of the Pines Corp. (operates summer camp) 1949-68. Dir. Midwest Fed. Savs. & Loan Assn. Chmn. mayor's council human relations Mpls., 1946-49. Pres. Mt. Olivet Homes, Caribou Lodge, Inc., Mt. Olivet Home for Sr. Citizens, Inc., Mt. Olivet Careview Nursing Home, Inc., Mt. Olivet-Rolling Acres Home for Mentally Retarded; bd. dirs. United Fund; bd. dirs. Minn. Synod. Recipient Distinguished Service award for outstanding young man City of Mpls., by Jr. Assn. Commerce, 1945; chosen one of 100 living great state of Minn., Minn. Terr. Centennial, 1949; one of 11 nationally selected for study tour State Israel, 1949. Clubs: Mpls. Athletic, Interlachen Golf, Rotary. Author: Going God's Way; House for Tomorrow; Living God's Way; The Secret of Greatness, 1955; This is God's Day, 1956; Pathway to Peace, 1957; A Turbulent World-A Tranquil God, 1958; Live Today, 1959; The Unconquerable Partnership, 1960; This is God's World, 1961; Trumpets in the Morning, 1962; To-day, 1965; Looking God's Way, 1966. Home: Minneapolis MN Died Mar. 2, 1968; buried Lakewood Cemetery, Minneapolis MN

YOUNGMAN, FRANK NOURSE, pulp and paper co. exec.; b. Wis., June 21, 1893; s. Charles F. and Anna B. (Trickey) Y.; B.A., U. Wis., 1913; m. Marie Leavens; children—Frank N., Mary (Mrs. James Holland). With Crown Zellerbach Can. (formerly Pacific Mills, Ltd.), 1927-68; v.p. Crown Zellerbach Corp. (U.S.), 1938-54, dir., 1947-54, chmn. bd., dir. Crown Zellerbach Can., 1954-68, chmn. exec. com., 1954-68, also v.p., pres. dir. St. Helen's Pulp and Paper Co., 1953-68; chmn. bd. Canadian Western Lumber Co., Ltd., 1954-68; Elk Falls Co., Ltd., 1954-68; dir. Transamerica Corp., Burrard Dry Dock Co., Ltd.; Vancouver adv. bd. Nat. Trust Co., Ltd., Toronto. Home: Vancouver BC Canada. Died Mar. 21, 1968.

YOUNGS, J(OHN) W(ILLIAM) T(HEODORE), educator, mathematician; b. Bilaspur, India, Aug. 21, 1910 (parents Am. citizens); s. Cornelius Herman and Lulu Gertrude (Johnson) Suckau; student Philander Smith Sch., Naini Tal, India, 1922-28; B.S., Wheaton Coll., 1930; M.A., Ohio State U., 1931, Ph.D., 1934; m. Marguerite Davenport Strong, Sept. 3, 1938; children—John William Theodore, Christopher Emory Strong. Came to U.S., 1928. Master, Stony Brook Sch., 1934-37; instr. Ohio State U., 1937-41; instr. Purdue U., 1941-42, asst. prof., 1942-46; asso. prof. Ind. U., 1946-48, prof., 1948-65, chmn. dept. mathematics, dir. Grad. Inst. Mathematics and Mechanics, 1956-65; prof. math. Univ. Cal., Santa Cruz, 1965-70. Supt. Sandia Corp., 1951-52. Cons. OSRD, 1944, 8th Air Force, 1944-45, U.S. Strategic Bombing Survey, 1945, RAND Corp., 1948-70, Ramo-Wooldridge Corp., 1953-56; cons. Naval Research Laboratory, 1960-70. Trustee George Washington Carver Institute also Carver Research Foundation. Guggenheim fellow, 1946-47. Mem. NRC (chairman liaison com. division mathematics), Am. Math. Soc. (asso. sec. 1948-63), Institute for Defense Analyses, Mathematical Assn. Am., Sigma Xi. Editor Jour. Combinatorial Theory. Author articles on math. subjects. Home: Santa Cruz CA Died July 20, 1970; buried Youngs Meml. Cemetery, Oyster Bay NY

YOUNGSON, WILLIAM WALLACE, clergyman; b. Pittsburgh, Pa., Dec. 27, 1869; s. James Burn and Martha Jane (Parker) Y.; A.B., Allegheny Coll., 1891, A.M., 1895; D.D., 1906; B.D., Drew Theol. Seminary, 1895; LL.D., Oregon State Coll., 1929; m. Ida Honor Farrell, Oct. 20, 1897 (died July 31, 1928); children—Honor Farrell (Mrs. Lawrence Lister), William Wallace, Jr.; m. 2d, Mrs. Ruby M. Blake, Jan. 19, 1935. Ordained Methodist ministry, 1895; pastor Redstone Circuit, Pa., 1895-97, Vandergrift, Pa., 1897-1901, Crafton, Pa., 1901-04, Elizabeth, N.J., 1905-08, East Orange, N.J., 1908-13, Rose City Park, Portland, Ore., 1913-16; dist. supt. M.E. Ch., Portland, 1916-24, Rose City Park, 1924-30; dist. supt. M.E. Ch., Portland, 2d term, 1930-32, Portland, 1932-35, Tillamook, Ore., 1935-39; area dir. world service and publicity, Portland Area Headquarters of Methodist Church, 1939-40; retired, 1940. Dir. Willamette Iron & Steel Corp. for past 18 yrs. Del. Gen. Conf. M.E. Ch., 1920, 24, 32; del. to Ecumenical Meth. Conf., Atlanta, Ga., 1931; del. First United Gen. Conf. Meth. Church, 1940, First Western Jurisdictional Conf., 1940. Mem. advisory board Salvation Army. Mem. Phi Beta Kappa, Phi Kappa Psi, Pi Gamma Mu. Mason (33 deg.); Grand Prelate Grand Encampment K.T., U.S., 1916-21; Grand Chaplain Supreme Council 33 deg. Scottish Rite Masons, Southern Jurisdiction, U.S.A.; Grand Prelate, Grand Comdr. Oregon, Grand High Prelate, Red Cross of Constantine; U.S.A.; Grand Prelate, Grand Comdr. Ore. K.T. Clubs: Rotary, Professional Business Men's; Lions; Altrurian, Kiwanis. Author: The Binnacle of Phi Kappa Psi; The Cross and the Rose; The Faith of Tennyson; The Builders of the American Republic; The Symbolism of the Rose Croix Degree; The Cross and the Crown; Unhand Me; Masonic and Radio Addresses. Commencement speaker. Civic, Fraternal and state leader. Made world tour with the University Afloat," 1926-27. Home: 6114 N.E. Alameda, Portland 13 OR‡

YOUNT, NORMAN FLEMING, steel co. exec.; b. Pitts., Apr. 18, 1917; s. George Fleming and Mary (Schaefer) Y.; B.S., U. Pitts., 1938; m. Ruth Elizabeth Johnston, July 1, 1950. With Haskins & Sells, C.P.A.'s, Pitts., 1939-40; with Aristology steel div. Copperweld Steel Co., Warren, O., 1940-64, chief accountant, 1946-50, div. controller, adminstrv. asst. to exec. v.p., 1950-64; adminstrv. v.p. Copperweld Steel Co., Pitts., 1964-68, v.p., gen. mgr. wire and cable div., 1968-72; pres., chief exec. officer Copperweld Steel Internat. Co., 1970-72; dir. Copperweld Steel Co., Japan Alumoweld Co., Tokyo. Served with USAAF, 1943-46. Named Man of Year, Warren (O.) Jr. C. of C., 1960. Mem. Am.

Iron and Steel Inst., Am. Inst. C.P.A.'s, Ohio Soc. C.P.A.'s, Nat. Assn. Accountants (Lybrand certificate merit 1951). Presbyn. Mason (Shriner). Clubs: Pittsburgh Pittsburgh PA Died Nov. 24, 1972.

YOUTZ, PHILIP NEWELL, architect; born at Quincy Massachusetts, April 27, 1895; son of Herbert Alden and Mary Palmer (Newell) Y.; B.A., Amherst College, 1918; M.A., Oberlin Coll., 1919; m. Frances May Leffler, Nov. 1, 1919. Architect of various schs., Canton, China, 1920-25; instr. architecture, Teachers Coll., Columbia, also instr. philosophy, Columbia, 1926-28; supervisor adult edn. and art courses, People's Inst. of New York, 1926-29; curator 69th St. br., Pa. Museum of Art, Phila., 1930-31, curator of exhbns., 1932; asst. dir. Brooklyn Museum, 1933, dir., 1934-38. Pres. Am. Federation of Arts, 1936-38; dir. Pacific Area, Golden Gate Internat. Expn., San Francisco, 1938-39; travel and exploration in South America, 1939-41; chief of consumer branch, Office Prodn. Research and Development, War Prodn. Bd., Washington, D.C., 1942-44; dir. tech. research, Smaller War Plants Corp., 1944-45. Inventor of skyhook for constructing monolithic concrete floor slabs without forms. Mem. A.I.A., Phi Beta Kappa, Delta Upsilon; fellow Royal Soc. of Arts. Club: Cosmos (Washington). Editor: Outline of Aesthetics (5 vols.), 1928; The New Arts (5 vols.), 1929. Author: Sounding Stones of Architecture, 1929; American Life in Architecture, 1932. Home: Yorktown Heights NY Died Jan. 1972.

YUDAIN, THEODORE, newspaper editor; born Dwinsk, Russia, Jan. 25, 1907; s. Morris and Bertha (Jaffe) Y.; brought to U.S., July, 1907; ed. in pub. schs. of Stamford, Conn., and Art Student's League, N.Y. City, 1927; m. Mae Shand, Sept. 5, 1936; 1 son, Ted; m. 2d, Carol Gewirtz Rosenthal; 1 stepson, Marc Rosenthal. Newspaperman, columnist Stamford (Conn.) Advocate, 1927-36; editor Greenwich (Conn.) News-Graphic, 1936-38; mng. editor Greenwich Time, 1938-39, 1940-45, editor, 1945-64; editor Stamford (Conn.) Advocate, 1964-70; legislative reporter, polit. and editorial cartoonist, pólit. editor Bridgeport (Conn.) Herald, 1939-40; dir. Greenwich Pub. Co.; mem. Stamford adv. bd. State Nat. Bank of Conn. President Connecticut Circuit of AP, 1965-67. Mem. State Civil Defense Advisory Commission. Mem. State GOP Platform Com.; vice chmn. Community Chest publicity drive com.; dir., mem. exec. bd., Boy Scouts of Am., Greenwich Council; bd. dirs. Greenwich Boys Club; exec. bd. Stamford United Fund; dir. Greenwich Library Bd.; adv. bd. Fairfield County Jewish Home for Aged; mem. Gen. Legislative Com. Mem. U.N. Site Com. (apptd. by Gov.), 1946. Recipient Liberty Bell award Stamford-Greenwich Bar Assn., 1967. Mem. Conn. Editorial Assn., Greenwich Chamber of Commerce, Internat. Police Chiefs Assn., Conn. Daily Newspaper Assn., Am., N.E. Socs. Newspaper Editors, Silurians, Alpha Delta Chi. Republican (state policy com. 1950; now state finance committee). Clubs: Connecticut Laurel (Hartford); All-Stamford; Harpoon (pres.); Deadline; Roasters (founder, roastmaster). Contbr. cartoons to newspapers and magazines. Home: Cos Cob CT Died Apr. 19, 1970; buried Riversville Cemetery, Greenwich CT

ZABRISKIE, ROBERT LANSING, b. Aurora, N.Y., Oct. 23, 1872; s. N. Lansing and Louise (Morgan) Z.; g.s. Edwin B. Morgan, a founder and benefactor of Wells Coll.; A.B., Princeton, 1895, E.E., 1897; m. Aubin Markham Wells, of Natchez, Miss., May 11, 1899 (died 1917); m. 2d, Hazel Everingham, of Chicago, Ill., Apr. 17, 1922. Trustee Wells Coll. since 1906, sec. and treas. since 1905, actg. pres., 1912-13. Pres. Village of Aurora, 1910. Presbyn. Home: Aurora NY‡

ZAENGLEIN, PAUL CARL, accountant; b. Pottsville, Pa., July 16, 1892; s. Conrad William and Dora Anna (Dasch) A.; grad. Rochester (N.Y.) Bus. Inst., 1911; m. Caroline Louise Strauchen, Sept. 28, 1918; children—Catherine (Mrs. Edward Weisenbeck), Roger W., Eric W., Paul Carl (dec.). Accountant, Livingston Niagara Power Co., Avon, N.Y., 1910-12; pub. accountant Jackson & Wilson Audit Co., Rochester, N.Y., 1913-14; pub. account Zaenglein & Provost, also Zaenglein & Wilson, Rochester, 1914-18; auditor, div. mil. aeros. War Dept., Riverside, Cal., also Washington, 1918-19; partner Jackson & Zaenglein, Rochester, 1919-57 (formerly Rochester Certified Audit Corp., then Jackson, Zaenglein & Ellis); partner Price Waterhouse & Co., C.P.A.'s, Rochester, 1957-60. Bd. dirs. Ebsary Charitable Found. C.P.A., N.Y., Ind. Mem. Am. Inst. C.P.A.'s, Ind., N.Y. socs. C.P.A.'s, Rochester C. of C., Am. Inst. Mgmt. (mem. investment council). Presbyn. Rotarian. Clubs: Monroe Golf, Genesee Valley (both Rochester). Home: Rochester NY Died Dec. 13, 1969.

ZAHNISER, CHARLES REED, b. Mercer County, Pa., May 30, 1873; s. William Arthur and Jane (Bromley) Z.; A.B., Grove City (Pa.) Coll., 1896, A.M., 1896, Ph.D., 1909, S.T.B., U. of Chicago, 1900; m. Pearl Stroud, 1896 (died 1946); children—Virgil Stroud, Pearl Charline (dec.), Chalmers Flath. Student pastor Presbyn. Ch. in U.S.A., Chicago, 1898-1900; pastor Sorrento, Ill., 1900-01, Pittsburgh, Pa., 1901-14; sec. Pittsburgh Council of Chs., 1914-29; survey dir. Pittsburgh Area, Interchurch World Movement, 1919-20, mem. editorial staff Presbyterian Advance, 1904-12; editor Pittsburgh Christian Outlook, 1914-29; extension lecturer Federal Council Chs., 1929-35; prof. social science and applied Christianity, Boston University, 1929-40; dir. Division of Social Work, Boston University, 1931-37; special consultant and lecturer on personal counseling for Army and Navy Dept. of National Y.M.C.A. 1941-42. Inst., Univ. of Pittsburgh, since 1944. Trustee Pa. Penitentiary, 1923-29. Mason. Author: The Zahnisers—A Family History, 1904; Social Christianity, 1911; Casework Evangelism, 1927; Interchurch Community Programs, 1932; The Soul Doctor, 1938; Techniques of Counseling in Christian Service, 1946. Home: Penn-Hall Hotel, Pittsburgh PA‡

ZANGERIE, JOHN A., tax expert; b. Cleveland, O., Apr. 12, 1866; s. Adam and Maria (Riffer) Z.; ed. law sch. and U. of Berlin; m. Blanche Norton, Nov. 10, 1912; children—Willis John, Hildegarde, Jane Elizabeth. Admitted to Ohio bar, 1890, and began practice in Cleveland; long active in civic affairs; mem. Cleveland Bd. of Edn., 1890-92; mem. Cleveland Quadrennial Bd. Assessors, 1910-12; auditor Cuyahoga County, since 1912; sec. and treas. Ontario Realty Co. Mem. Nat. Municipal League, Gen. Tax League, Am. Polit. Science Assn., Nat. Tax Assn. (model plan of taxation com.), Ohio Tax Assn. (hon. pres.), Cleveland Real Estate Bd., Nat. Assn. Assessing Officers (ex-president), Tax Institute. Democrat. Clubs: City, Westwood Country (Cleveland). Author: Principles of Real Estate Appraising, 1924, 2d edit., 1927; also numerous pamphlets on taxation and valuation of property. Home: 10404 Lake Av. Address: Court House, Cleveland OH‡

ZAPP, CARROLL FRANCIS, gen. constrn. exec.; b. Idaho City, Ida., Aug. 28, 1904; s. Mathias A. and Anna (Carrigan) Z.; student U. Santa Clara, 1922-24; LL.B., DePaul U., 1929; m. Helen Blackinger, Sept. 11, 1933 (dec. Sept. 1970); children—Carol Ann (Mrs. Peter Shawver) (dec.), John F., Robert F. Admitted to Ill. bar, 1929, Ida. bar, 1934; practice of law, Chgo., 1929-32, Boise, Ida., 1934-38; with Morrison-Knudsen Co., Inc., 1938-68, sec., 1941-60, v.p., 1952, gen. counsel, v.p., 1960-68, also dir. Mem. Am., Ida. bar assns. Home: Boise ID Died Mar. 6, 1968.

ZARTMANN, PARLEY EMMETT, clergyman; b. Glenford, O., Feb. 19, 1865; s. Solomon K. and Malinda (Vogt) Z.; A.B., Heidelberg U., Ohio, 1889, M.A., 1893; Heidelberg Theol. Sem., 1892; D.D., Muskingum Valley Coll., 1906; m. Effie Kathleen Stevenson, June 25, 1897; m. 2d, Mabel Houser, February 26, 1940. Ordained to Presbyterian ministry, 1892; pastor Sioux City, Ia., 1892-95; sec. Y.M.C.A., Sioux City, Ia., 1896-97; pastor Three Rivers, Mich., 1898-1900, Phila., 1900-02; asst. sec. Gen. Assembly's Com. on Evangelistic Work, 1902-11; sec. extension dept., Moody Bible Inst., Chicago, 1911-14; gen. sec. Interdenominational Assn. of Evangelists, 1914-23, Nat. Evangelistic Bureau, since 1923; pastor Presbyn. Ch., Winona Lake, Ind., Oct. 1939-44. Editorial writer Christian World, 1895-96; retired Nov. 1944. Home: 3630 Indiana Av., Fort Wayne IN

ZECHMEISTER, LASZLO KAROLY ERNO, prof. organic chemistry; b. Gyor, Hungary, May 14, 1889; s. Charles and Irene (Mocsary) Z.; student Polytech. Inst., Zurich, Switzerland, 1907-11 (diploma in chemistry, 1911; Dr. Engring., 1913); married. Began as asst., Kaiser Wilhelm-Inst. fur Chemie, Berlin, 1912; instr. Danish Royal Vet. Acad., Copenhagen, 1921-23; prof. of chemistry and dir. chem. lab., Med. Sch., U. of Pecs, Hungary, 1923-40; prof. organic chemistry, Calif. Inst. Tech., Pasadena, Calif., 1940-59; Guggenheim fellow, 1949; Sigma Xi lecturer, 1948. Awarded Pasteur medal, Paris, 1935; Claude Bernard medal, Paris, 1947. Member Hungarian Acad. Science (received the great prize of this Acad. 1937), Roy Danish Acad. Sci. (foreign mem.), Jr. Am. Chem. Soc. Author: Textbook of Organic Chemistry, 1930, 1932; Carotinoide, 1934; Principles and Practice of Chromatography (by L. Z. and L. Cholnoky), 1941, 43; and about 200 research papers. Editor: Progress in the Chemistry of Organic Natural Products, 1938. Address: Pasadena CA Died Feb. 28, 1972.

ZEITLER, EMERSON WALTER, investment counselor; b. Simsbury, Conn., Jan. 7, 1897; s. Walter and Nettie (Vincent) Z.; A.B., Bowdoin College, 1920; married to Sarah Wheeler, Apr. 19, 1924; children—Marilyn (Mrs. Joseph C. Birg), Emerson Gilbert, Elizabeth (Mrs. Robert Roche Strang). Investment banking, 1923-69; with National City Company, N.Y.C., 1923-26; Ireland Company, Portland, Me., 1926-30; Fidelity-Ireland Co., Portland, 1930-33; State Investment Co., Portland, 1933-69. Active A.R.C., 1944-69, local chpt. chmn., 1947-61, nat. vice chmn. fund raising, 1951, 56-61, nat. gov., 1953-56, chmn. Brunswick chpt., 1956-57; chairman of Governor Maine Adv. Council on Civil Def. and Pub. Safety, 1954-69; v.p., trustee, Brunswick Community Hosp.; trustee Regional Meml. Hosp.; dir. Fullfilment Appeal; mem. Me. Civil Def. Staff. Mem. Me. Investment Bankers Assn., Zeta Psi. Episcopalian. Republican. Home: Brunswick ME Died Mar. 21, 1969; cremated.

ZELLER, WALTER GEORGE, banker; b. Elgin, N.D., June 15, 1912; s. George D. and Elizabeth (Breitling) Z.; student Capitol Comml. Coll., 1937, U. Wash. Grad. Sch. Finance, 1959; m. Esther G. Gunsch, Feb. 1, 1941; 1 dau., Patricia. With C.I.T. Corp., 1941-49; asst. cashier First Nat. Bank of Ore., Portland, 1949-55, asst. v.p., 1955-65, v.p., 1965-68. Faculty, U. Wash. Pacific Coast Banking Sch., 1961-68. Active A.R.C. Served to capt. Mil. Intelligence Corps, AUS, 1942-46. Mem. Am. Inst. Banking (faculty 1965-68), Robert Morris Assos., Ore. Bankers Assn. (chmn. consumer credit com. 1961), Sales and Marketing Execs., Portland C. of C. Republican. Lutheran. Mason, Elk. Clubs: International Aero of Oregon (Portland). Home: Portland OR Died Nov. 30, 1968; buried Sunset Hills Meml. Cemetery Portland OR

ZENDER, AUSTIN R., business exec.; b. Bklyn. Chmn. bd. dir. Peter Paul, Inc., Naugatuck, Conn.; dir. Hayton Switch & Instrument Co., Heminway Corp., (both Waterbury, Conn.), Harvey Hubbell, Inc., Bridgeport, Conn., Eastern Co., Risdon Mfg. Co. (both Naugatuck, Conn.); chmn. bd., dir. Conn. Nat. Bank; trustee Peoples Savs. Bank (both Bridgeport, Conn.); past pres., dir. Nat. Distillers and Chem. Corp. Home: Milford CT Died Dec. 30, 1971.

ZENTMAYER, WILLIAM, physician; b. Phila., Pa., Oct. 28, 1864; s. Joseph and Catharine (Bluim) Z.; M.D., U. of Pa., 1886; unmarried. Professor diseases of the eye, Graduate School of Medicine, U. of Pa., now emeritus; cons. surgeon to Wills (Eye) Hospital, St. Mary's Hospital and Glen Mills School. Fellow A.M.A. (chmn. section ophthalmology, 1916-17), Coll. Physicians of Phila. (chmn. sect. on ophthalmology, 1909-10); mem. Am. Ophthal. Soc. (pres. 1926-27), Acad Ophthalmology and Oto-Laryngology, Acad. Nat. Sciences, Pa. Acad. Fine Arts, Ophthal. Soc. of United Kingdom (British), A.A.A.S.; pres. local Med. Alumni Soc. of U. of Pa., 1922-23; chmn. sect. on eye, ear, nose and throat, Med. Soc. of State of Pa., 1935-36. Asso. editor Archives of Ophthalmology. Dir. of Nat. Soc. for Prevention of Blindness. Guest of honor of section on ophthalmology Annual Meeting of A.M.A., 1941. Awarded the Leslie Dana Gold Medal, 1945, by the St. Louis Soc. for the Blind. Home: 265 Forrest Av., Merion, Pa. Office: 1930 Chestnut St., Philadelphia 3 PA‡

ZERBE, KARL, painter; b. Berlin, Germany, Sept. 16, 1903; s. Karl Henrich and Maria (Krammer) Z.; student elementary and high schs., France and Germany; student art school, Munich, Germany, 1921-24, Rome, Italy, 1924-26; A.F.D. honoris causis, Fla. State U., 1963; m. Marion S. Koegel, Sept. 2, 1936; 1 dau., Maria Carolina. Came to U.S., 1934, naturalized, 1939. Became dir. painting dept. Sch. Mus. of Find Arts, Boston, 1937; prof. art Fla. State U., Tallahassee, 1954-71, prof. emeritus, 1971-72. One-man shows, Berlin Gallery Gurlitt, 1922, Munich and Berlin, Germanic Mus. of Harvard, 1934, Grace Horne Galleries, Boston, 1938, Vos. Gallery Centennial show, Boston, 1941, Buchholz Gallery, N.Y.C., 1941, Downtown Gallery, N.Y.C., 1943, 1946, Art Inst., Chgo., 1946, Art Inst., Detroit, 1946, Museu de Arte Moderna, Rio de Janeiro, 1963; also retrospective show Inst. Contempory Art, Boston De Young Mus., San Francisco, 3d retrospective LeMoyne Art Found., Tallahassee, 1972; represented in about 70 museums and pub. orgns. Recipient John Barton Paine medal Va. Mus. Fine Arts, 1942; Watson F. Blair prize Art Inst. Chgo., 1944, Norman Wait Harris silver medal, 1946; 3d prize Carnegie Inst., 1948; Henry Schiedt Meml. prize Pa. Acad., 1949; Phila. Watercolor prize, 1950; Grand prize Boston Art Festival, 1953; Ford Found. Retrospective Exhbn. award, 1960. Mem. Artists Equity Assn. (pres. 1957-59, hon. pres. 1960-72), Coll. Art Assn. (dir.). Home: Tallahassee FL Died Nov. 28, 1972.

ZIEGET, JULIUS, exec. dir. Phila. Museum Art Samuel S. Fleisher Art Meml. Home: Philadelphia PA

ZIEGLER, CHARLES EDWARD, physician, surgeon; b. Carlisle, Pa., Mar. 23, 1871; s. Abraham John and Barbara (Rebert) Z.; B.E., State Normal Sch., Millersville, Pa., 1891; Ph.B., Dickinson Coll., 1896, A.M., 1898; M.D., U. of Pa. Med. Sch., 1900; post-grad. study, Berlin and Dresden, 1904, 1905; m. Annetta Culbertson Bucher, of Carlisle, Pa., Nov. 21, 1901. For details see Vol. X (1918-19). Home: 4716 Bayard St., Pittsburgh PA‡

ZIEGLER, MAXINE EVELYN HOGUE (MRS. JAMES R. ZIEGLER), clin. psychologist; b. Memphis; d. Abner Gill and Florence (Hutchins) Hogue; B.A., U. So. Cal., 1948, Ph.D., 1955; m. James R. Ziegler, Feb. 10, 1952; children—Evalinda Aurelia, Charlotte Elaine, Curtis Wayman, Bruce Allan. Practice clin. psychology, Los Angeles, 1955-68. Bd. dirs. Turn-Key Computer Applications, 1968. Mem. League Women Voters, Am. Assn. U. Women, Los Angeles World Affairs Council, Am. Psychol. Assn., Phi Beta Kappa, Sigma Xi. Home: Rolling Hills CA Died Nov. 22, 1968.

IEGLER, WINFRED HAMLIN, bishop; b. Detroit, ov. 23, 1885; s. Paul and Mary Frances (Bell) Z.; A.B., olumbia, 1911, S.T.D., 1937; S.T.B., Seabury Western heol. Sem., Evanston, Ill., 1929, D.D., 1936; m. Marie leanor Bartron, June 12, 1911; children—Paul, David arlton (dec.), George Hamlin, Frederick Howden, lary Frances. Hardware salesman, 1899-1907; rdained to ministry Episcopal Ch., 1912; missionary aldez, Prince William Sound Missions, Alaska, 911-14, Port Angeles, Olympic Peninsula Missions, /ash., 1914-15; viscar All Saints Ch., Lehighton, Pa., 915-18; cathedral dean and archdeacon of N.M., lbuquerque, 1918-23; rector Ch. of Redeemer, Elgin, l., 1923-31; archdeacon of Chgo., 1931-36; bishop of Vyo., 1936-49, ret. Served as chaplain 14th Div. U.S. rmy, 1918-19; capt. O.R.C. 1919. Pres., Sherwood all for Boys and Girls and Ivinson Meml. Sch. for irls, Laramie, Wyo., 1936-49. Recipient Univ. medal olumbia, 1935. Mem. Newcomen Soc. of Eng., Arctic ist. N.Am., Acad. Polit. Sci., Am. Legion, Soc. hilatelic Ams., Am. Philatelic Soc., Alpha Chi Rho. lason, Elk, Rotarian. Home: Pinedale WY Died July 6, 972.

IER, MERLIN WILLIAM, clergyman; b. Odessa, Vash., June 12, 1928; s. George and Katherine L. Horn) Z.; B.A., Pacific Lutheran U., 1950; B.D., Vartburg (O.) Theol. Sem., 1955; S.T.M., Andover Jewton Theol. Sem., 1959; m. Alice Louraine Slyler, eb. 8, 1957; children—Sandra Joan, Stephen Merlin, haron Ann, Sarah Beth. Ordained to ministry Luth. h., 1955; pastor in Ore., 1955-58; chaplain Rainier ch., Buckley, Wash., 1959-60, asst. supt., 1961-62; upt. State Home and Tng. Sch., Wheat Ridge, Colo., 962—. Vice pres. Jefferson County Community enter; chmn. Morrow County (Ore.) Heart Fund, 956-57; mem. Mayor's Com. of 100, Arvada, Colo., 966-67. Mem. Am. Assn. Mental Deficiency (nat. hmn. sub-sect. cottage and ward life), Council xceptional Children, Inst. Pastoral Care, Blue Key. Iome: Wheat Ridge CO Died Nov. 12, 1967; buried /alby Church Cemetery, Valby OR

IMBALIST, MARY LOUISE CURTIS, born Boston, Massachusetts, August 6, 1876; d. Cyrus Herman Kotzschmar and Louise (Knapp) Curtis; ed. ub. schs. and Ogontz Sch., L.H.D., University of ennsylvania. Temple U., Bowdoin Coll.; Mus. D., Villiams College; Litt.D., Colby Coll.; m. Edward William Bok, Oct. 22, 1896; children—William Curtis, ary Williams; m. 2d, Efrem Zimbalist, July 6, 1943. Sr. .p. Curtis Pub. Co.; pres. Settlement Music School of hiladelphia, 1912-26; founded and endowed The urtis Institute of Music, 1924, pres., 1924-70. Republican. Episcopalian. Club: Art Alliance Print Philadelphia, Pa.). Brought Burrell Collection of Wagner's letters from Eng. to U.S., presented to Curtis nst. Music 1944. Home: Philadelphia PA Died Jan. 4, 1970.

ZIMMER, BERNARD NICOLAS, vice-pres. Am. Metal Co.; b. Luxembourg, Oct. 24, 1888; s. John Joseph and Matilde (Makel) Z.; student Ecole Industrielle et Commerciale, Luxembourg, 1900-07; m. Nellie Kontz; children—Margot, John B. Came to U.S., 1913, naturalized, 1918. In metal business in Germany and Russia, 1908-11, in France, Belgium and Luxembourg, 1911-13; with Am. Metal Co. from 1913, then vice-pres.; dir. Climax Molybdenum Co.; pres. Am. Zinc and Chem. Co., Blackwell Zinc Co.; dir. Tsumeb Corp., Ltd., O'Okiep Copper Co., Ltd., U.S. Metals Refining Co. Apptd. hon. consul gen. for Grand Duchy of Luxembourg at N.Y. City, Dec. 1946. Decorated Officer Odre Couronne de Chene (Luxembourg). Mem. Am. Zinc Inst., Am. Inst. Mining Metall. Engrs., U.S. Copper Assn. (exec. com.). Republican. Catholic. Clubs: India House, Midday (N.Y. City); Duquesne (Pittsburgh). Home: Larchmont NY Died Sept. 14, 1970; buried Gate of Heaven, Valhalla NY

ZIMMER, WILLIAM HOMER, utilities exec.; b. Constance, Ky., Nov. 23, 1905; s. William F. and Margaet (Dress) Z.; student U. Cin., 1922-25, D.C.S. (hon.), 1964; LL.D., Xavier U.; m. Esther Krueger, Nov. 1, 1925 (dec.); children—Betty Jane (Mrs. James Maxwell), William H.; m. 2d Margaret Loth, Apr. 18, 1942. Various accounting positions Cin. Gas & Electric Co., 1920-30, asst. treas., 1939-43, asst. sec., 1942-57, treas., 1943-58, dir., 1945-73, v.p., 1946-57, mem. exec. com. 1950-73, exec. v.p., 1957-62, pres., chief exec. officer, 1962-70, chmn. finance com., 1957-70, chmn. bd., 1970-73; dir. Union Central Life Ins. Co., Cin. Bangals, Inc., Central Trust Co., Eagle-Picher Co., Cin., Cin. Reds, Inc. Mem. Am. Gas Ann., Edison Electric Inst., The Hist. and Philos. Soc. Ohio, A.I.M., Omicron Delta Epsilon, Sigma Iota Epsilon, Delta Sigma Pi, Delta Mu Delta, Beta Alpha Psi. Episcopalian. Mason (33 deg.), Rotarian. Clubs: Bankers, Queen City, Cincinnati Country, Western Hills Country, Optimists; Coldstream Country; Commonwealth, Commercial. Home: Lake City FL Died Apr. 1, 1973.

ZIMMERER, CHARLES JOHN, company exec.; b. St. Louis, Dec. 23, 1899; s. George L. and Emily C. (Regel) Z.; Cornell, class 1923; m. Dorothy Virginia Monroe, Feb. 3, 1926. With Liberty Central Trust Co., St. Louis, 1923-24, Gen. Motors Acceptance Corp., N.Y.C., 1924-30; v.p. Canal Bank & Trust Co., New Orleans, 1930-33; exec. v.p. dir. Comml. Credit Co., Balt., 1933-64; dir. Union Trust Co. Balt. Episcopalian. Mason (32 degree). Home: Baltimore MD Died Sept. 1970.

ZIMMERMAN, CHARLES BALLARD, judge; b. Springfield, O. June 22, 1891; s. John Luther and Helen (Ballard) Zimmerman; A.B., Wittenberg College, Springfield, Ohio, 1911, LL.D., 1946; student Harvard Law Sch., 1911-13; D.J.S., Bowling Green State U., 1947; D.C.L., Susquehanna U. 1950; LL.D., U. Cin., 1958; m. Dorothy Gayford, Apr. 24, 1930; children—Charles Ballard, Richard Gayford, Helen Cooke (Mrs. Richard E. Stevens). Admitted to the Ohio bar, 1913; in general, state and federal practice, first with father, and later with father and younger brother, Springfield, O., 1913-33; appointed justice Supreme Court Ohio, 1933; elected for terms of 6 years, 1934, 40, 46, 52, 58, 64. Dem. nominee Congress, 1922, for atty. gen. Ohio, 1926, Supreme Court of Ohio, 1932. Mem. nat. exec. board United Lutheran Ch. Am., 1942-50. Served U.S. Army (Ohio National Guard, 4th Div., 82d Division), 1917-19; participated in St. Mihiel and Meuse-Argonne offensives; dich. maj. Recipient Fellows award Ohio State Bar Assn. Found., 1966. Past pres. Springfield (O.) Kiwanis Club. Mem. American Legion, 40 and 8, Vets of Foreign Wars, Society of Colonial Wars in Ohio (past governor), S.A.R. (past state president), Mil. Order Fgn. Wars. Society War of 1812, Am., Ohio State and Clark County bar assns., Order Founders and Patriots of America. Society of Descendants of the Colonial Clergy, Blue Key, Beta Theta Pi, Delta Theta Phi, Tau Kappa Alpha, Pi Sigma Alpha. Democrat. Lutheran (mem. et. adjudication Luth. Ch. in America, 1962-68). Clubs: University (Columbus); Springfield Country (Springfield Ohio). Contbr. to legal and other periodicals. Home: Springfield OH Died June 5, 1969.

ZIMMERMAN, HARVEY J., statistician; b. Stoyestown, Somerset Co., Pa., Oct. 5, 1869; s. Joseph J. and Elizabeth (Specht) Z.; grad. Central Teachers College of Pa., 1891; LL.B., Georgetown U., 1905; m. Bessie Dear Wynkoop, of Loudon Co., Va., Jan. 12, 1910. Teacher pub. schs. of Pa. 6 yrs.; served with 5th Regt. Pa. Vol. Inf., Spanish-Am. War, 1898; apptd. clk. Census Office, May 24, 1900; advanced to chief administrative grade; chief statistician for cotton and oils div., in general charge of the several processes involved in the collection, compilation and publication of the periodical reports of cotton ginned, cotton consumed and on hand, activity in cotton spinning, cottonseed and cottonseed products, and animal and vegetable fats and oils. Mem. Am. Statis. Assn., S.A.R., Pa. German Soc. Republican. Mem. Ref. Ch. Mason (Shriner). Home: 1517 Varnum St. N.W., Washington DC‡

ZIMMERMAN, HERBERT JOHN, lawyer; b. Fort Collins, Colo., Aug. 10, 1906; s. Casper and Helen (Cutler) Z.; A.B., U. Denver, 1928, LL.B., 1930; m. Wilmette Z. Jones, Sept. 15, 1931; children—William John, Robert, Joanne. Admitted to Tex., Colo. bars, 1930; practiced in Fort Worth, 1930-44, Denver, 1950-70; mem. firm Gorsuch, Kirgis, Campbell, Walker & Grover; pres. Pioneer Biscuit Co., Denver, 1946-50. Served with USAAF, 1944-45. Mem. Am., Colo., Denver bar assns., State Bar of Tex., Am. Judicature Soc., Petroleum Club, Beta Theta Pi, Phi Delta Phi, Episcopalian. Home: Denver CO Died June 10, 1970; buried Fairmont Cemetery, Denver CO

ZIMMERMAN, HYMAN HAROLD, retail drug co. exec.; b. N.Y.C., May 4, 1921; s. Alter Benjamin and Lena (Esterson) Z.; student U. Ariz., 1941-43; B.A., U. So. Cal., 1944, M.B.A., 1949; m. Beatrice Margolis, Dec. 19, 1948; children—Sandra, Judith, Elliot. Staff accountant Arthur Young & Co., C.P.A.'s Los Angeles, 1950-55; chief accountant Revell, Inc., Venice, Cal., 1955-57; treas. Thrifty Drug Stores Co., Inc., from 1957; dir. E.S. Dairy Farms. Lectr. Sch. Bus., U. So. Cal., 1946-50. C.P.A. Cal. Mem. Am. Inst. C.P.A.'s, Cal. Soc. C.P.A.'s, Am. Accounting Assn. Address: Los Angeles CA

ZIMMERMAN, LEANDER M., clergyman; b. Manchester, Md., Aug. 29, 1860; s. Henry and Leah Z.; A.B., Pa. Coll., 1884, also A.M.; D.D., Susquehanna U.; LL.D., Gettysburg College, 1939; unmarried. Ordained Lutheran ministry, 1887, pastor Christ Lutheran Ch., Baltimore, Dec. 1, 1887-1925; now emeritus. Mem. Luth. Deaconess Bd., apptd. May 1897, pres. since 1920; mem. Home Mission Bd., Lutheran Ch., 1899; pres. Md. Synod, Oct. 19, 1900; del. to General Synod 6 times since 1898; dir. Lutheran Theol. Sem. since 1909. Mem. Soc. Science, Letters and Art, of London, Phi Beta Kappa. Author: How to Be Happy When Married, 1893; The Little Grave, 1895; Daily Bread for Daily Hunger, 1895; Sunshine, 1896; Pearls of Comfort from Tennyson's In Memoriam," 1896; Expository Thoughts on Pilgrim's Progress, 1897; Paths that Cross, 1897; A Wedding Token, 1898; The Family, 1898; Oil of Kindness, 1899; Yvonne, 1900; The Child and the Church; Treasures of Faith in the Lutheran Church; Dot," 1911; Sparks," 1912; Cordelia, 1914; Somebody Loves You, 1916; Reminiscences After Thirty Years in the Ministry, 1917; Echoes from the Distant Battlefield, 1917; Digging Wells, 1923; The Church of Our Faith, 1923; For Love's Sake, 1924; My Philosophy and Life, 1929; The Gospel Minister, 1930; The Shepherding of Souls, 1931; Leaves for Healing, 1933; When Days Are Dark, 1934; Mother's Christmas Story, 1935; Hymns of the Heart, 1935; God's Rainbow, 1936; Mellow Fruits of Experience, 1937; Thoughts for Happiness, 1939; Prayers, 1939; Love and Sunshine, 1940; A Bow Unfading, 1941; The Preacher's Door Knob, 1942; Helps, 1943; God's Living Truths, 1944; Daily Bread, 1945; Daily Bread for Daily Hunger, 1946; Thoughts, 1947. Pioneer broadcaster (sermon) from Baltimore, Md. Home: Lafayette Hotel, Washington DC‡

ZIMMERMAN, M(AX) M(ANDELL), editor, economist; b. Holyoke, Mass., Aug. 1, 1889; s. Isaac and Annie (Cooperman) Z.; LL.B., Yale, 1911; m. Hylda Grant, Aug. 1921; 1 son, Richard Grant. Mem. editorial staff Printer's Ink, 1913-14; free lance writer, 1914-18; merchandising counsel since 1918; pub. trade publs., 1925-72; president Super Market Merchandising; founder, dir., hon. life mem. Super Market Inst.; founder Internat. Assn. Food Distbn., 1950; president of the Super Market Publishing Co. Originator of Nationally Advertised Brands Week; mem. Nat. Food and Grocery Conf. Com.; mem. nat. advisory council Boston Conf. on Distribution. Elected to Hall of Fame in Distribution, 1953. Col., Aide-de Camp to Gov. of New Mexico. Awarded Chevalier du merite commercial, 1950 (France); received honorary citizenship of Paris, 1950; Chevalier de l'Ordre dela Couronne (Belgium), 1953; Cavaliere Ufficiale dell 'Ordine Al Merito (Italy), 1956. Club: Yale (N.Y.C.). Author: Challenge of Chain Store Distribution, 1931; Super Market—Spectacular Exponent of Mass Distribution, 1937; The Super Market Grows Up, 1939; Surveying Europe's Food Picture, 1949; Food Congress Meets in Paris, 1950; New Self-Service Adventures in Europe, 1952; The Super Market: A Revolution in Distribution, 1955. Contbr. to mags. Donor annual Super Market Merchandising Fellowship, Brandeis U. Home: New York City NY Died May 1972.

ZINN, CHARLES JAMES, lawyer; b. N.Y.C., July 12, 1905; s. Oscar and Margaret (Donnelly) Z.; A.B., Fordham U., 1927, LL.B., 1930; LL.M., Georgetown U., 1951, S.J.D., 1954; m. Ethel Doner Cahill, June 30, 1931; 1 dau., Ethel Marie (Mrs. Raymond J. Kern). Admitted to N.Y. bar, 1931, D.C. bar, 1939; law asso. firm Clark & Baldwin, N.Y.C. 1931-37; with firm Halpin, Keogh & St. John, N.Y.C., 1938-70; law revision counsel U.S. Ho. of Reps., 1939-70; professorial lectr. George Washington U., 1952-70; parliamentary adviser Govt. Pakistan, 1964; guest lectr. numerous European univs., 1955-56. Dir. Panama Canal Co., 1961-69. Asst. judge adv. N.Y.C. Patrol Corps, 1942-45; mem. U.S. adv. com. Internat. Rules Civil Procedure, 1958-65; mem. adv. com. Virgin Islands code Dept. Interior, 1955-56; mem. Gov. Adv. Com. C.Z. Code, 1959-70. Recipient Encaenia award Fordham Coll., 1957; grantee Asia Found., 1965. Mem. Am., Fed. (Justice Tom. C. Clark award 1966, also Distinguished Service award 1969), New York State, Brooklyn (trustee 1945-51) bar assns., Bklyn. Guild Catholic Lawyers (bd. govs. 1942-45), Am. Peace Soc. (pres. 1964-66), Cath. Assn. Internat. Peace, Nat. Legislative Conf., Assn. Secretaries Gen. Parliaments (pres.), D.C. Polit Sci. Assn. (pres. 1958), Sons Vets Civil War (comdr. Lafayette camp 1943-45), Royal Arcanum (regent W. S. Hancock council 1939-40), Phi Alpha Delta (justice D.C. chpt. 1953-54). Author: The Veto Power of the President, 1951; How Our Laws are Made, 1952; American Congressional Procedure, 1958; Control of the Executive by Congress, 1962. Home: Washington DC Died Mar. 5, 1970.

ZINN, JAMES ALEXANDER, banker; b. Oklahoma City, Jan. 7, 1913; s. Alpha A. and Charlotte (Shelton) Z.; A.B., U. Mo., 1933; M.B.A., Harvard, 1935; m. Joanne Dissette, Sept. 23, 1940; children—Alice Elizabeth, James A., Mary Charlotte, William Michael. With Nat. Bank of Detroit, 1935-71, v.p., 1950-64, sr. v.p., 1964-68, executive v.p., 1968-71; dir. Safe Deposit Co. Detroit, Formsprag Co., Internat. Bank Detroit. Trustee Alma Coll. Home: Grosse Pointe MI Died May 4, 1971; buried Crown Hill Cemetery, Indianapolis IN

ZIRATO, BRUNO, mgr. symphony orchestra; b. Calabria, Italy; s. John and Josephine L. Zirato; student pvt. tutors, also Tech. Coll., Rome, Italy; m. Nina Morgana, June 15, 1921; 1 son, Bruno, Jr. Came to U.S., 1912, naturalized, 1917. Tchr. Italian, N.Y.U., summer sessions; Am. corr. several Italian newspapers; pvt. sec. Enrico Caruso, 1915, other operatic and concert artists; bus. mgr. Musical Digest; organizer, dir. Lyric Bur., rep. concert artists; personal rep. Arturo Toscanini, 1930-31; asso. mgr. Philharmonic-Symphony Soc. N.Y., 1931-47, mgr. (with Arthur Judson), 1946-55, supervised tour to West Coast, also Brit. Isles and Continent, 1955, mng. dir., 1956-59, advisor to the board, 1959-72; v.p. Columbia Artists Management, 1938-56; columnist La Follia, Italian lit. and polit. paper, N.Y.C. Republican. Roman Catholic. Home: New York City NY Died Nov. 28, 1972; buried Fair Ridge Cemetery, Chappaqua NY

ZIRKLE, CONWAY, biologist; b. Richmond, Va., Oct. 28, 1895; s. Charles Milton and Mary Louise (Timberlake) Z.; B.S., U. of Va., 1921, M.S., 1921; Ph.D., Johns Hopkins, 1925; student U. of London, Eng., 1923, U. of Geneva, Switzerland, 1924; m. Helen Emily Kingsbury, Oct. 4, 1923. Instr. in biology, U. of Va., 1920-21; asst. in botony, Johns Hopkins U. 1921-24; Nat. Research Council fellow, Harvard, 1925-28, research associate, 1929-30; asso. prof. of botany, U. of Pa., 1930-37, prof., 1937-72. Served with U.S. Army Med. Corps. 1918-19. Fellow A.A.A.S. (v.p. sect. L 1951-52); mem. Bot. America, Am. Soc. Naturalists (mem. editorial board), History of Science Soc., Raven Soc. of Va., Phi Beta Kappa, Sigma Xi, Gamma Alpha. Author: The Beginnings of Plant Hybridization, 1935; Death of a Science in Russia, 1949; also numerous scientific papers and monographs. Member editorial board of Isis since 1934, of Bot. Reviews from 1944, Stain Technology from 1946. Secretary board of trustees Biol. Abstracts, 1939-44. Home: Secane PA Died Mar. 28, 1972.

ZIROLI, NICOLA VICTOR, painter, artist, educator; b. Italy, May 8, 1908 (parents U.S. citizens); s. Michael and Sofia (DeMarco) Z.; grad. Art Inst. Chgo., 1930; m. Lucille Johnson; 1 dau., Jane. Supr. of art and craft exhbns. State of Illinois, 1937-39; camoflage artist Chgo. Park Dist., 1941; topographical map draftsman, editor Army War Coll., 1942; mem. faculty U. Ill., 1944-70, prof. of art; sabbatical in Italy, 1957-58; juror art exhbns.; painter, works permanently exhibited Met. Mus. Art, Whitney Mus. Am. Art, I.B.M. Corp., Ill. State Mus., Butler Inst. Am. Art, Springfield (Mo.) Art Mus., Chgo. Pub. Library, John H. Vanderpoel Art Assn. (Chgo.), Fenster Collection (Tulsa), Parker Collection (St. Louis), others; exhibited Columbia (S.C.) Mus. Art 1st painting biennial; Ill. Profl. Art Exhbn., Ill. State Fair, Springfield. Recipient first prize for landscape, Washington Soc. Artists, 1934, William H. Bartels award for figure, 1938, Clyde M. Carr Award for landscape, 1939, Medal of 1st Award, San Francisco Art Assn., 1939, Mrs. Alma Lohmeyer Meml. Purchase Prize, 1945, 1st prize in oils and prints, Mint Mus. Art, Charlotte, N.C., 1946, Gold Medal of Honor, Audubon Artists, 1947, Kenneth Hayes Miller Meml. Prize, Audubon Artists, 1953, 1st prize, Old N.W. Ty. Art Exhbn., Springfield, Ill., 1954, Audubon Patron's Prize for watercolor, Audubon Artists, 1955, purchase prize, watercolor, Butler Inst. Am. Art, 1955, cash award Audubon Artists, 1956, 1st prize watercolor Seven States Profl. Art Exhbn., Springfield, 1956; 2d prize Am. Painters in Casein, N.Y.C., 1957; Minnie R. Stern medal for oil Audubon Artists, 1959; 1st prize for water color Union League Club, Chgo., 1959; 1st prize oils and purchase for Still Life, Evansville (Ind.) Mus. Fine Arts, 1960; 1st award for oil painting, also 1st award realistic oil painting 7th Ann. Nat. Exhbn. at El Paso Mus. Art, picture Grande Bouquet selected as Nat. Painting of Distinction at 9th Ann.; Mead Competition Watercolor prize; also others. Member of Audubon Artists, Am. Assn. U. Profs., Am. Watercolor Soc., Internat. Platform Assn., Alumni Assn. Art Inst. Chgo., Am. Fedn. Artists, Phila. Water Color Club. Home: Urbana IL Died July 1970.

ZOELLER, HENRY ADOLPH, stock and commodity broker; b. Bklyn., July 6, 1902; s. Adolph and Margaretha (Gack) Z.; ed. pub. and parochial schs.; m. Marion E. Brodie, Oct. 3, 1923; children—Henry A., Marion E. (Mrs. Hilery P. Hogendorn), Donald J., James P. With Mergenthaler Linotype Co., Bklyn., 1916-17; with H. Hentz & Co., 1917-68, gen. partner, 1950-68, mem. exec. com., 1961-68. Pres. N.Y. Hide Clearing Assn., 1963-68; N.Y. Produce Clearing Assn., 1963-68; bd. dirs. Commodity Exchange, 1964-68, chmn. arbitration com., 1966-68; pres. N.Y. Coffee and Sugar Clearing Assn., 1967-68; bd. mgrs. N.Y. Cotton Exchange, 1962-68; N.Y. Citrus Exchange, 1966-68; chmn. Assn. Commodity Exchange Firms, 1964-68, bd. dirs., 1953-68. Bd. govs. Home Rule Party, Rockville Centre, N.Y., 1953-68. Mem. Cardinal's Com. of Laity, N.Y.C., 1957-68. Mem. Holy Name Soc. Rotarian. Clubs: India Rockville Centre NY Died Aug. 9, 1968.

ZORN, PAUL MANTHEY, pub. utility exec.; b. Columbus, O., Oct. 25, 1902; s. Hans Manthey and Antoinette (Feldner) Z.; B.S., Yale, 1923; m. Ruth Stephan, 1926 (dec. 1943); children—Paul Manthey, Elizabeth M. (Mrs. R. W. Mettler Jr.), Susan M., (Mrs. B. E. Richardson); m. Varley Sims Davidson, 1945; stepchildren—Charles M. and Ruth S. Davidson. With So. New Eng. Telephone Co., New Haven, 1923-63; gen. traffic mgr., 1945-51; gen. plant mgr., 1951-53; v.p., 1953-55; v.p., gen. mgr. 1955-63; dir. First New Haven Nat. Bank, Conn. Savs. Bank, Conn. Blue Cross, Inc. Dir., exec. com. Grace-New Haven Community Hosp., 1953-71. Mem. Sigma Xi (asso.), Tau Beta Pi. Home: Hamden CT Died Oct. 2, 1971.

ZOVICKIAN, ANTHONY, plastic surgeon; b. Boston, Oct. 5, 1918; s. Hovhannes and Haiganoush (DerMargossian) Z.; B.A. cum laude, Harvard, 1940; M.D., Yale, 1943; m. Barbara Starr Hurlin, Oct. 28, 1944; children—William H., John A. Clin. instr. surgery Yale, 1950-51; resident plastic surgery Johns Hopkins Hosp., instr. surgery Johns Hopkins Med. Sch., trainee in cancer USPHS, 1951-53; asso. clin. prof. surgery Boston U. Sch. Med., 1966-69, asst. prof. surgery Boston U. Sch. Grad. Dentistry, 1965-69; gen. practice Boston, 1953-69; asso. vis. surgeon Univ. Hosp., Boston U. Med. Center, Mass. Eye and Ear Infirmary; vis. surgeon pediatric surgery Boston City Hosp.; lectr. plastic surgery Tufts U. Med. Sch.; cons. plastic surg. Chelsea Naval Hosp. and VA Hosp., Providence. Served to capt. M.C., AUS, 1944-46. Fellow A.C.S.; mem. A.M.A., Am. Soc. of Plastic and Reconstructive Surgery, Am. Assn. Plastic Surgeons, Soc. Head and Neck Surgeons (a founder), New Eng. Soc. Plastic Surgeons, Mass. Med. Soc., Alpha Omega Alpha. Republican. Unitarian. Home: Winchester MA Died May 21, 1969.

ZUCKER, PAUL, educator, author-critic; b. Berlin, Germany, Aug. 14, 1888; s. Dr. Julius and Anna (Samter) Z.; student univs. and insts. of tech. Berlin and Munich; Ph.D., U. of Berlin, 1913; m. Rose Walter, September 16, 1916 (dec. 1962). Came to the United States, 1937, naturalized, 1944. Lecturer in history of art and architecture at State Acad. Arts, Berlin, 1928-33, Lessing Hochschule, Berlin, 1917-35; practicing architect, constrn. country houses, office bldgs., workers settlements, banks, city planning projects, Berlin, 1920-37; lectr. history of art, architecture and theatre New Sch. for Social Research, N.Y. City, 1937-70, Cooper Union Art Sch., 1938-63, adj. prof.; 1948-63, vis. lectr. 1966-69. Awarded 1st and 2d prizes archtl. competitions, Germany, 1913-33. Recipient Brunner scholarship award, A.I.A., 1953; Order Merit 1st class German Bundes-republik, 1968. Member College Art Association America, American Society Architectural Historians (past pres. N.Y. chpt.), Am. Soc. Aesthetics (past president of the New York chapter). Author: Space and Architecture in Paintings of the Florentine Quattrocento, 1913; The Bridge-Typology and History of Its Artistic Form, 1921; Stage Setting at the Time of the Baroque, 1925; Stage Setting at the Time of the Classicism, 1925; Theatres and Motion Picture Houses, 1926; Architecture in Italy at the Time of the Renaissance (in Handbuch der Kunstwissenschaft), 1927; The Development of the City, 1929; American Bridges and Dams, 1941; Styles in Painting, 1950, 63; Town and Square—From the Agora to the Village Green, 1959, 1970; Fascination of Decay: Ruins, Relic, Symbol, Ornament, 1968. Editor: New Architecture and City Planning, A Symposium, 1944. Home: New York City NY Died Feb. 14, 1971.

ZUGGER, ALOYSIUS HENRY, hotel exec.; b. Buffalo, Dec. 3, 1905; s. Henry and Carrie (Boesl) Z.; student Bryant and Stratton Bus. Coll., 1921, U. Buffalo, 1932-33; m. Lorraine Elizabeth Kersten, Sept. 3, 1934; children—Robert Aloysius, Deanna Mae. Clk. Hotel Statler, Buffalo, 1923-28, asst. mgr., 1928-31, credit mgr., 1931-34, office mgr., 1934-38, exec. asst. mgr., 1938-48, resident mgr., N.Y.C., 1948-52, gen. mgr., St. Louis, 1952-56, gen. mgr., Buffalo, 1956-59; gen. mgr. Pittsburgh Hilton Hotel, Pitts., 1959-63; Statler Hilton, Boston, 1963-67, Washington Hilton, 1967-68; v.p., gen. mgr. Ambassador Hotel, Los Angeles from 1968. Mem. Cal. Hotel Assn. Address: Los Angeles CA Deceased.

ZURN, MELVIN ACKERMAN, mfg. co. exec.; b. Erie, Pa., Jan. 10, 1901; s. John Arthur and Clara (Ackerman) Z.; grad. Ky. Mil. Inst., 1920; m. Marian Ruth Schmid, June 25, 1924; children—Frank W., Sarah E. (Mrs. James M. Mead), David M., Roger W. With J. A. Zura Mfg. Co., Erie, 1923-56, chmn. bd., 1952-56; chmn. bd. Zurn Industries, Inc., Erie, 1956-65, chmn. exec. com., 1965-70; dir. Marine Nat. Bank, Erie, Zurn Industries Can. Ltd., Zurn Industries Philippines, Inc., Zurn de Mexico, S.A. de C.U., Erie City Iron Works. Mem. adv. bd. Small Bus. Adminstrn., 1960-70; chmn. fgn. trade adv. bd. Pa. Dept. Commerce, 1965-70; mem. U.S. Trade Mission to Mexico, 1963, to Peru, 1965. Chmn. Erie Housing Authority, 1936-66. Alternate del. Democrat Nat. Conv., 1960, 64; mem. Electoral Coll., 1960-64. Bd. dirs. Zurn Found., 1952-70; pres. Erie Philharmonic Soc., 1953; trustee Hamot Hosp., 1965-70; bd. incorporators St. Vincent Hosp., 1960-70; mem. lay adv. bd. Gannon Coll., 1960-70. Mem. Am. Soc. M.E., Am. Soc. Naval Engrs., Navy League U.S., Newcomen Soc. N. Am., N.A.M. (bd. dirs. 1965-70), Mfrs. Assn. Erie (pres. 1964-66), Pa. C. of C. (pres. 1965, dir. 1958-70). Presbyn. Clubs: Erie, Erie Yacht; Kahkwa, University (Erie). Home: Erie PA Died Jan. 7, 1970; buried Erie Cemetery.

ZWEIFEL, HENRY, lawyer; b. Granbury, Hood County, Tex., Oct. 12, 1883; s. Andrew and Sarah Elizabeth (Smith) Z.; educated at Granbury College; married Mrs. Johnnye J. Kelly, April 11, 1911 (deceased September 19, 1950); children—Norma Jane (Mrs. A. B. Crawford), Doris (Mrs. John S. Luton). Admitted to Tex. bar, 1912; practiced at Granbury, 1912-21; del. Rep. Nat. Conv., 1912, 20; U.S. dist. atty. for Northern Dist. of Tex., by apptmt. of Pres. Harding, May 1, 1921-26; reapptd. by President Coolidge, Jan. 25, 1926; resigned 1927, to enter private practice; pres. First Nat. Bank, Granbury. Mem. from Tex., Rep. Nat. Com. 1950-52. Baptist. Club: Ft. Worth. Home: Granbury TX Died Aug. 31, 1970.

A

AANDAHL, Fred George 4
AARON, Charles Dettie 5
AARON, Marcus 3
ABARBANELL, 1
  Jacob Ralph
ABBATT, Agnes Dean 1
ABBATT, William 1
ABBE, Charles Minott 4
ABBE, Cleveland 1
ABBE, Cleveland Jr. 1
ABBE, Robert 1
ABBE, Truman 4
ABBELL, Maxwell 3
ABBETT, Leon H
ABBETT, Merle J. 3
ABBEY, Edwin Austin 1
ABBEY, Glenn Allan 4
ABBEY, Henry 1
ABBEY, Henry Eugene H
ABBIATI, F. Alexander 3
ABBINK, John 3
ABBOT, Abiel H
ABBOT, Alice Balch 4
ABBOT, Benjamin H
ABBOT, Charles Wheaton 1
ABBOT, Edwin Hale 1
ABBOT, 2
  Everett Vergnies
ABBOT, Ezra H
ABBOT, 1
  Francis Ellingwood
ABBOT, 1
  Frederic Vaughan
ABBOT, Gorham Dummer H
ABBOT, Henry Larcom 1
ABBOT, Joel H
ABBOT, Willis John 1
ABBOTT, 1
  Alexander Crever
ABBOTT, Allan 3
ABBOTT, Amos H
ABBOTT, Arthur James 4
ABBOTT, Arthur Vaughan 1
ABBOTT, Augustus Levi 1
ABBOTT, Austin H
ABBOTT, Benjamin H
ABBOTT, H
  Benjamin Vaughan
ABBOTT, Byrdine Akers 1
ABBOTT, Charles Conrad 1
ABBOTT, Charles David 4
ABBOTT, 1
  Charles Frederick
ABBOTT, Christopher J. 3
ABBOTT, 2
  Clinton Gilbert
ABBOTT, Edith 3
ABBOTT, 1
  Edville Gerhardt
ABBOTT, Edward 1
ABBOTT, 3
  Edward Farrington
ABBOTT, Edward Prince 4
ABBOTT, Edwin Milton 1
ABBOTT, Emma H
ABBOTT, Ernest Hamlin 1
ABBOTT, 1
  Frances Matilda
ABBOTT, Frank H
ABBOTT, Frank Danford 2
ABBOTT, Frank Frost 1
ABBOTT, Fred Hull 4
ABBOTT, Frederick H. 1
ABBOTT, 1
  Frederick Wallace
ABBOTT, 5
  Freeland Knight
ABBOTT, George Alonzo 5
ABBOTT, George Birch 1
ABBOTT, Gordon 1
ABBOTT, Grace 1
ABBOTT, 2
  Henry Pryor Almon
ABBOTT, 1
  Herbert Vaughan
ABBOTT, Horace 1
ABBOTT, H
  Horatio Johnson
ABBOTT, 2
  Howard Strickland
ABBOTT, Ira Anson 1
ABBOTT, Jacob H
ABBOTT, James Francis 1
ABBOTT, Jo 1
ABBOTT, Joel H
ABBOTT, John Jay 2

ABBOTT, H
  John Stevens Cabot
ABBOTT, Joseph Carter H
ABBOTT, 4
  Joseph Florence
ABBOTT, Josiah Gardner H
ABBOTT, Keene 2
ABBOTT, L. Jewett 1
ABBOTT, 1
  Lawrence Fraser
ABBOTT, Leon Martin 1
ABBOTT, Leonard Dalton 3
ABBOTT, Lyman 1
ABBOTT, Mary Perkins 1
ABBOTT, Mather Almon 1
ABBOTT, Nathan 1
ABBOTT, Nehemiah H
ABBOTT, Paul 5
ABBOTT, 2
  Robert Sengstacke
ABBOTT, 4
  Russell Bigelow
ABBOTT, 1
  Samuel Appleton Browne
ABBOTT, Samuel Warren 1
ABBOTT, Theodore Jacob 3
ABBOTT, W. Herbert 1
ABBOTT, Wallace Calvin 1
ABBOTT, Wilbur Cortez 2
ABBOTT, William H
ABBOTT, H
  William Hawkins
ABBOTT, William Lamont 5
ABBOTT, William Lewis 2
ABBOTT, William Martin 1
ABBOTT, William Martin 2
ABBOTT, William Rufus 2
ABBOTT, William Tabor 1
ABDUL-HUDA, 3
  Tawfiq Pasha
ABDUL-ILAH, Hashimi 3
ABDULLAH, Achmed 2
ABDULLAH, 3
  Ibn 'al Hussein
ABDUL RAHMAN, 3
  Prince Tuanka
ABEEL, David H
ABEEL, Essie O. 4
ABEL, 4
  Frederic Laurence
ABEL, John A. 3
ABEL, John Jacob 1
ABELES, Edward S. 1
ABELES, 5
  Julian Theodore
ABELL, H
  Arunah Shepherdson
ABELL, Edwin Franklin 1
ABELL, Harry Clinton 1
ABELL, Harry Clinton 2
ABELL, Irvin 2
ABELL, Theodore Curtis 4
ABELLS, Harry Delmont 3
ABEND, Hallett Edward 3
ABENDROTH, 5
  William Henry
ABERCROMBIE, 2
  Daniel Webster
ABERCROMBIE, James H
ABERCROMBIE, 1
  John William
ABERCROMBY, James H
ABERLY, John 5
ABERN, Oscar G. 3
ABERNATHY, Alonzo 1
ABERNATHY, Chess, Jr. 5
ABERNATHY, 5
  Harry Thomas
ABERNATHY, 3
  Milton Aubrey
ABERNETHY, 5
  Arthur Talmage
ABERNETHY, 5
  Charles Laban
ABERNETHY, George H
ABERNETHY, 3
  Robert Swepston
ABERNETHY, 3
  William Ellis
ABERNETHY, 5
  William Shattuck
ABERT, James William H
ABERT, John James 1
ABERT, Silvanus Thayer 1
ABERT, William Stone 1
ABHEDANADA, Swami 4
ABORN, Milton 1
ABOTT, Bessie Pickens 1

ABRAHAM, Abraham 1
ABRAHAM, Herbert 4
ABRAHAMS, Henry 1
ABRAHAMSON, 2
  Laurentius G.
ABRAMS, Albert 1
ABRAMS, Benjamin 4
ABRAMS, Charles 5
ABRAMS, LeRoy 5
ABRAMS, Stanley L. 3
ABRUZZO, Matthew T. 5
ABT, Henry E. 4
ABT, Isaac Arthur 3
ACCAU, Michel H
ACER, Victor 4
ACHER, Howard 3
  Mossman
ACHESON, Albert Robert 1
ACHESON, 4
  Alexander Mahon
ACHESON, Alexander W. 1
ACHESON, Barclay 3
ACHESON, 5
  Dean Gooderham
ACHESON, 1
  Edward Campion
ACHESON, 4
  Edward Campion
ACHESON, 1
  Edward Goodrich
ACHESON, 1
  Ernest Francis
ACHESON, John Carey 1
ACHESON, Marcus W. 1
ACHESON, 1
  Marcus Wilson Jr.
ACHESON, 5
  Mary Virginia Berry (Mrs.
  John C. Acheson)
ACHESON, 1
  William McCarthy
ACHOR, Harold Edward 4
ACHORN, Edgar Oakes 1
ACHRON, Isidor 2
ACHRON, Joseph 2
ACIKALIN, Cevat 5
ACKEN, Henry S, Jr. 5
ACKER, Charles Ernest 1
ACKER, George Nicholas 1
ACKERMAN, 5
  Carl Frederick
ACKERMAN, Carl 5
ACKERMAN, 5
  William
ACKERMAN, 5
  Edward Augustus
ACKERMAN, Ernest R. 1
ACKERMAN, Fred W. 5
ACKERMAN, 2
  Frederick Lee
ACKERMAN, John Henry 1
ACKERMAN, 5
  Nathan Ward
ACKERMAN, R. B. 3
ACKERMAN, Ralph 3
  Henry
ACKERMANN, Carl 2
ACKERS, Deane Emmett 4
ACKERSON, James Lee 1
ACKERT, Charles H. 1
ACKLEY, Charles Breck 4
ACO, Michel H
ACOSTA GARCIA, Julio 3
ACQUAVELLA, 5
  A. Lawrence
ACREE, Solomon Farley 3
ACRELIUS, Israel H
ACRET, George Edward 3
ACUFF, Herbert 3
ADAIR, Fred Lyman 5
ADAIR, George William 4
ADAIR, 3
  Henry Porterfield
ADAIR, Hugh Rogers 5
ADAIR, Jackson Leroy 1
ADAIR, James H
ADAIR, John H
ADAIR, John A. M. 1
ADAM, Charles Darwin 2
ADAM, James Noble 1
ADAM, John Douglas 1
ADAM, Paul James 5
ADAMIC, Louis 3
ADAMOWSKI, Joseph 1
ADAMS, Abigail H
ADAMS, Abijah H
ADAMS, 2
  Adeline Valentine Pond
ADAMS, Alva 1

ADAMS, Alva Blanchard 1
ADAMS, Alva Blanchard 2
ADAMS, Alvin H
ADAMS, Andrew 1
ADAMS, Andrew Addison 1
ADAMS, Andy 1
ADAMS, Annette Abbott 3
ADAMS, Arthur 1
ADAMS, Arthur 4
ADAMS, Arthur Barto 3
ADAMS, Arthur Frank 3
ADAMS, Arthur Lincoln 1
ADAMS, Asael Edward 1
ADAMS, Avery C. 4
ADAMS, Benjamin H
ADAMS, Benjamin Cullen 3
ADAMS, Bristow 3
ADAMS, Brooks 1
ADAMS, Cedric M. 4
ADAMS, Charles H
ADAMS, Charles 1
ADAMS, 5
  Charles Albertus
ADAMS, Charles Baker H
ADAMS, Charles Bayley 4
ADAMS, 3
  Charles Christopher
ADAMS, 2
  Charles Clarence
ADAMS, Charles Closson 2
ADAMS, Charles Darwin 1
ADAMS, Charles E. 1
ADAMS, Charles Edward 3
ADAMS, Charles F. 2
ADAMS, Charles Fellen 1
ADAMS, Charles Francis H
ADAMS, Charles Francis 1
ADAMS, Charles Francis 2
ADAMS, Charles Francis 3
ADAMS, Charles Henry 4
ADAMS, Charles Josiah 1
ADAMS, Charles Kendall 1
ADAMS, 1
  Charles Partridge
ADAMS, Charles R. H
ADAMS, 1
  Charles Remington
ADAMS, Charles Ryan 2
ADAMS, Chauncey 5
  Corbin
ADAMS, Clair Stark 1
ADAMS, Clarence Henry 2
ADAMS, 4
  Clarence Raymond
ADAMS, Claris 4
ADAMS, Claude Mitchell 3
ADAMS, Comfort Avery 4
ADAMS, Cuyler 1
ADAMS, Cyrus Cornelius 1
ADAMS, Daniel H
ADAMS, H
  Daniel Weissiger
ADAMS, Dorothy 5
ADAMS, Dudley W. 1
ADAMS, Earl Frederick 3
ADAMS, Ebenezer 1
ADAMS, Edward Dean 1
ADAMS, Edward Francis 1
ADAMS, 1
  Edward Le Grand
ADAMS, 4
  Edward Le Grand
ADAMS, 5
  Edward Richmond
ADAMS, Edwin 1
ADAMS, Edwin Augustus 1
ADAMS, Edwin Plimpton 5
ADAMS, Eliphalet H
ADAMS, 3
  Elizabeth Kemper
ADAMS, Elmer Bragg 1
ADAMS, Elmer E. 3
ADAMS, 1
  Ephraim Douglass
ADAMS, Ernest Germain 5
ADAMS, Eugene Taylor 5
ADAMS, Frances Smith 5
ADAMS, 5
  Francis Alexandre
ADAMS, Frank 5
ADAMS, Frank Durward 1
ADAMS, Frank Hicks 3
ADAMS, Frank Ramsay 4
ADAMS, Frank Yale 1
ADAMS, Franklin George 1
ADAMS, Franklin Pierce 1
ADAMS, Franklin Pierce 3
ADAMS, Fred Winslow 2

ADAMS, Frederic 1
ADAMS, 4
  Frederick Baldwin
ADAMS, Frederick 1
  Upham
ADAMS, Frederick W. H
ADAMS, George Bethune 1
ADAMS, George Burton 1
ADAMS, George Edward 5
ADAMS, George Edward 4
ADAMS, George Everett 1
ADAMS, George Francis 1
ADAMS, George Herbert 1
ADAMS, George Heyl 2
ADAMS, George Irving 1
ADAMS, George Matthew 4
ADAMS, George Moulton 1
ADAMS, George Sheldon 5
ADAMS, George Wendell 4
ADAMS, Granger 1
ADAMS, Green H
ADAMS, Hampton 4
ADAMS, Hannah H
ADAMS, 1
  Harriet Chalmers
ADAMS, Harry M. 1
ADAMS, Henry H
ADAMS, Henry 1
ADAMS, Henry 4
ADAMS, Henry Austin 1
ADAMS, Henry Carter 1
ADAMS, Henry Cullen 1
ADAMS, Henry Foster 5
ADAMS, Henry Heberling 1
ADAMS, Henry Herschel 1
ADAMS, Henry Martyn 1
ADAMS, Herbert 2
ADAMS, Herbert Baxter 1
ADAMS, Herbert H. 5
ADAMS, Isaac H
ADAMS, J. Ottis 1
ADAMS, J. Wolcott 1
ADAMS, James Alonzo 1
ADAMS, James Barton 3
ADAMS, James Dexter 1
ADAMS, 4
  James Forster Alleyne
ADAMS, James Hopkins H
ADAMS, James M'ckee 1
ADAMS, James Meade 4
ADAMS, James Randolph 3
ADAMS, James Truslow 2
ADAMS, Jasper H
ADAMS, Jed Cobb 1
ADAMS, Jedidiah Howe 3
ADAMS, Jesse Earl 4
ADAMS, Jewett W. 1
ADAMS, John * H
ADAMS, John Coleman 1
ADAMS, John Davis 2
ADAMS, John Emery 1
ADAMS, 1
  John Gregory Bishop
ADAMS, John Hampton 1
ADAMS, John Haslup 1
ADAMS, John Jay 1
ADAMS, John Quincy H
ADAMS, John Quincy 1
ADAMS, John Snyder 4
ADAMS, John Stokes 1
ADAMS, John Taylor 1
ADAMS, John Taylor 3
ADAMS, John William 1
ADAMS, H
  Joseph Alexander
ADAMS, Joseph Quincy 2
ADAMS, Julius Walker 1
ADAMS, Karl Langdon 2
ADAMS, Kenneth Miller 4
ADAMS, L. Sherman 3
ADAMS, Leverett Allen 5
ADAMS, Lewis Mulford 5
ADAMS, Lewis Whitaker 5
ADAMS, 4
  Luther Bentley
ADAMS, M. Ray 5
ADAMS, Maldon 5
  Browning
ADAMS, Mary Mathews 1
ADAMS, Maude 3
ADAMS, Maxwell 1
ADAMS, Melvin Ohio 1
ADAMS, Milton Butler 4
ADAMS, Milward 1
ADAMS, Morgan 3
ADAMS, Myron Eugene 1
ADAMS, Myron Winslow 1
ADAMS, Nathan 5
ADAMS, Nehemiah 1

ADAMS, 5
Nicholson Barney
ADAMS, 2
Numa Pompilius Garfield
ADAMS, Oliver Stephen 1
ADAMS, Oscar Fay 1
ADAMS, Oscar Sherman 4
ADAMS, Otto Vincent 5
ADAMS, Parmenio 1
ADAMS, Porter Hartwell 2
ADAMS, R. R. 3
ADAMS, Ralph Snyder 1
ADAMS, 3
Randolph Greenfield
ADAMS, 3
Raymond Fletcher
ADAMS, Robert Jr. 1
ADAMS, Robert Brooks 1
ADAMS, H
Robert Huntington
ADAMS, Robert J. 4
ADAMS, Robert Morton 5
ADAMS, Robert Newton 4
ADAMS, Robert Simeon 3
ADAMS, Roger 1
ADAMS, Romanzo 2
ADAMS, Samuel H
ADAMS, Samuel * 1
ADAMS, Samuel Barnard 4
ADAMS, Samuel Hopkins 3
ADAMS, Samuel Shugert 5
ADAMS, Silas 1
ADAMS, Stephen H
ADAMS, Suzanne 5
ADAMS, Thomas 1
ADAMS, Thomas Sewall 1
ADAMS, 4
Thurston Madison
ADAMS, Walter Sydney 3
ADAMS, Warren Austin 1
ADAMS, 2
Washington Irving Lincoln
ADAMS, Wayman 3
ADAMS, Wilbur Louis 1
ADAMS, William H
ADAMS, William, II 5
ADAMS, William A. 1
ADAMS, William Edward 3
ADAMS, William Forbes 1
ADAMS, William Grant 1
ADAMS, William H. 4
ADAMS, William Henry 1
ADAMS, William Jackson 1
ADAMS, William Milton 3
ADAMS, 4
William Montgomery
ADAMS, William Taylor H
ADAMS, William Wirt H
ADAMS, Winston Davis 1
ADAMSON, Alfred 1
ADAMSON, Charles 1
ADAMSON, J. E. 4
ADAMSON, Robert 2
ADAMSON, 1
William Charles
ADANK, J. L. 5
ADCOCK, 4
Clarence Lionel
ADCOCK, Edmund David 3
ADDAMS, Clifford Isaac 1
ADDAMS, Jane 1
ADDAMS, William 1
ADDEMAN, 1
Joshua Melancthon
ADDICKS, Frank F. 3
ADDICKS, George B. 1
ADDICKS, John Edward 1
ADDICKS, 1
Walter Robarts
ADDINGTON, 1
Keene Harwood
ADDINGTON, Sarah 1
ADDIS, Thomas 2
ADDISON, Daniel Dulany 1
ADDISON, James Thayer 3
ADDISON, 4
Julia 'de Wolf
ADDISON, William H. F. 1
ADE, George 2
ADEE, Alvey Augustus 1
ADENAUER, Konrad 2
ADERHOLD, Omer Clyde 5
ADGATE, Andrew H
ADGATE, Asa H
ADGATE, 1
Frederick Whitney
ADIE, David Craig 2
ADKINS, Charles 1
ADKINS, Curtis D. 3
ADKINS, Galen Horatio 1
ADKINS, Homer 3
ADKINS, Homer Martin 4
ADKINS, Jesse Corcoran 3
ADKINS, John Scudder 1
ADKINS, Leonard 4
Dawson
ADKINS, William H. 4

ADLER, Alfred H
ADLER, Alfred 4
ADLER, Buddy M. 4
ADLER, Clarence 5
ADLER, Cyrus 1
ADLER, Dankmar 4
ADLER, David 3
ADLER, Elmer 4
ADLER, Emanuel Philip 4
ADLER, F. Charles 3
ADLER, Felix 1
ADLER, 4
Frederick Henry Herbert
ADLER, Freyda Nacque 5
ADLER, George J. H
ADLER, Herman Morris 1
ADLER, Isaac 4
ADLER, Julius Ochs 3
ADLER, Leopold 5
ADLER, Max 3
ADLER, Samuel H
ADLER, Simon Louis 1
ADLUM, John H
ADNEY, Edwin Tappan 3
ADOLPHE, Albert Jean 1
ADOUE, 3
Jean Baptiste Jr.
ADRAIN, H
Garnett Bowditch
ADRAIN, Robert H
ADRIAN, G. 3
ADRIAN, 5
William Lawrence
ADRIANCE, John Sabin 4
ADSON, 3
Alfred Washington
AEBERSOLD, Paul C. 4
AFFELDER, William L. 4
AFFLECK, 2
Benjamin Franklin
AFFLECK, James Gelston 5
AFRICA, John Simpson 3
AGA KHAN, 3
Aga Sultan Mohamad Shah
AGAR, John Giraud 1
AGAR, 5
William Macdonough
AGASSIZ, Alexander 1
AGASSIZ, 1
Elizabeth Cabot
AGASSIZ, 3
George Russell
AGASSIZ, H
Jean Louis Rodolphe
AGASSIZ, 1
Rodolphe Louis
AGATE, Alfred T. H
AGATE, H
Frederick Styles
AGEE, Alva 2
AGEE, James H
AGEE, James 4
AGER, Waldemar 4
AGERSBORG, H. P. K. 4
AGETON, Arthur Ainslie 5
AGG, Thomas Radford 2
AGGELER, William Tell 1
AGGER, Eugene Ewald 4
AGNELLI, Joseph B. 5
AGNEW, Andrew Davison 3
AGNEW, 4
Benjamin Lashells
AGNEW, Cornelius Rea H
AGNEW, Daniel 1
AGNEW, David Hayes H
AGNEW, Eliza H
AGNEW, George Harvey 1
AGNEW, Hugh Elmer 3
AGNEW, P. G. 3
AGNEW, Peter Lawrence 5
AGNEW, Walter D. 5
AGNEW, William Henry 4
AGNEW, 5
William John Clarke
AGNON, 5
Shmuel Yosef Halevi
AGNUS, Felix 1
AGOOS, Solomon 5
AGRAMONTE, Aristides 1
AGRY, Warren C. 3
AGUILAR, 3
Roberto Trigueros
AGUINALDO, Emilio H
AGUINALDO, Emilio 4
AHALT, Arthur M. 3
AHERN, Eugene Leslie 3
AHERN, Mary Eileen 1
AHERN, Michael Joseph 3
AHL, Henry Hammond 5
AHL, John Alexander H
AHL, Orville Walter 4
AHLPORT, Brodie E. 5
AHLQUIST, 4
Robert Wilhelm
AHMAD, King 'of Yemen 4
AHMANSON, 5
Howard Fieldstead

AHRENS, Edward 2
Hamblin
AHRENS, Mary A. 4
AHRENS, Theodore 1
AID, George Charles 1
AIGLER, Ralph William 4
AIKEN, Alfred Lawrence 2
AIKEN, H
Charles Augustus
AIKEN, Charles Avery 1
AIKEN, Charles Francis 1
AIKEN, 1
Charles Sedgwick
AIKEN, David Wyatt H
AIKEN, E. Clarence 1
AIKEN, 5
Ednah (Mrs. Charles Sedgwick Aiken)
AIKEN, Frank Eugene 1
AIKEN, Gayle 4
AIKEN, George L. H
AIKEN, Howard 5
Hathaway
AIKEN, John Adams 1
AIKEN, Robert Leon 5
AIKEN, William H
AIKEN, 1
William Appleton
AIKEN, William Martin 1
AIKEN, Wyatt 2
AIKENS, Andrew Jackson 1
AIKENS, Charles Thomas 1
AIKIN, Wilford Merton 4
AIKINS, Herbert Austin 1
AIKMAN, 2
Walter Monteith
AIKMAN, William 1
AILES, Milton Everett 1
AILSHIE, 2
James Franklin
AILSHIE, Margaret Cobb 3
AILSHIE, Robert 2
AIME, Valcour 5
AIMES, 5
Hubert Hilary Suffren
AINEY, 1
William David Blakeslee
AINSLIE, George 1
AINSLIE, George 2
AINSLIE, Hew H
AINSLIE, James Stuart 4
AINSLIE, Peter 1
AINSWORTH, 5
Edward Maddin
AINSWORTH, 2
Frank Kenley
AINSWORTH, 1
Fred Crayton
AINSWORTH, 2
John Churchill
AINSWORTH, Walden L. 4
AINSWORTH, 2
William Newman
AIRD, Alexander N. 3
AIREY, 1
Charles Theodore
AIREY, John 4
AIREY, Richard 4
AIRHART, John C. 5
AISHTON, Richard Henry 1
AITCHISON, Clyde Bruce 4
AITCHISON, John Young 1
AITCHISON, Robert J. 4
AITKEN, David D. 1
AITKEN, Peter 4
AITKEN, Robert H
AITKEN, Robert Grant 3
AITKEN, 2
Robert Ingersoll
AKE, Russell Everett 4
AKED, Charles Frederic 1
AKELEY, Carl Ethan 1
AKELEY, Healy Cady 4
AKELEY, 4
Lewis Ellsworth
AKELEY, Mary L. Jobe 4
AKERBERG, 4
Herbert Vestner
AKERMAN, Alexander 1
AKERMAN, Amos 3
Tappan
AKERMAN, John D. 5
AKERS, Benjamin Paul 1
AKERS, Elizabeth 1
AKERS, Milburn Peter 5
AKERS, Oscar Perry 5
AKERS, Thomas Peter H
AKERSON, George 1
Edward
AKHARAJ 1
VARADHARA, Phya
AKIN, John 1
AKIN, Theron 1
AKIN, Thomas Russell 2
AKINS, Zoe 3
ALA, Hussein 4

ALABASTER, 3
Francis Asbury
ALANSON, 3
Bertram Edward
ALARCON, Hernando H
ALBACH, George H. 4
ALBANI, Emma H
ALBANI, Emma 4
ALBANI, Madame 3
ALBARDA, Horatius 4
ALBAUGH, 5
George Sylvanus
ALBAUGH, John W. 1
ALBEE, Edward F. 1
ALBEE, Ernest 1
ALBEE, Fred Houdlett 2
ALBEE, John 1
ALBEE, Percy F. 3
ALBER, David O. 5
ALBER, Louis John 4
ALBERS, George 5
ALBERS, Henri 4
ALBERS, Homer 2
ALBERS, Joseph H. 4
ALBERS, William Henry 3
ALBERT, 5
A(braham) Adrian
ALBERT, Allen Diehl 5
ALBERT, 1
Allen Diehl, Jr.
ALBERT, 4
Aristides Elphonso Peter
ALBERT, 1
Brother Sylvester
ALBERT, Calvin Dodge 5
ALBERT, 4
Charles Stanley
ALBERT, Charles Sumner 1
ALBERT, 4
Clifford Edmund
ALBERT, Elma Gates 3
ALBERT, Ernest 2
ALBERT, Henry 1
ALBERT, William Julian H
ALBERTS, Joseph Ortan 4
ALBERTSON, 4
Abraham Horace
ALBERTSON, 3
Charles Carroll
ALBERTSON, 1
George Roger
ALBERTSON, J. Mark 4
ALBERTSON, 4
James Herbert
ALBERTSON, Nathaniel H
ALBERTSON, Ralph 3
ALBERTY, 5
Bernard) Harold
ALBERY, Bronson James 5
ALBERY, 4
Faxon Franklin Duane
ALBIG, John William 4
ALBING, Otto Frederick 1
ALBION, James Francis 4
ALBRIGHT, Adam Emory 3
ALBRIGHT, Charles 1
ALBRIGHT, 2
Charles Edgar
ALBRIGHT, H
Charles Jefferson
ALBRIGHT, Edward 1
ALBRIGHT, Edwin 1
ALBRIGHT, 1
Frank Herman
ALBRIGHT, Fuller 5
ALBRIGHT, Guy Harry 5
ALBRIGHT, Jacob 5
ALBRIGHT, 5
Jacob Dissinger
ALBRIGHT, John Joseph 1
ALBRIGHT, Percy R. 1
ALBRIGHT, Raymond 4
Wolf
ALBRIGHT, 5
William Foxwell
ALBRIZIO, Humbert 1
ALBRO, Addis 1
ALBRO, 3
Mrs. Curtis Sanford
ALCIATORE, Roy Louis 5
ALCOCK, 3
Nathaniel Graham
ALCORN, Douglas Earle 5
ALCORN, Hugh Mead 3
ALCORN, James Lusk H
ALCOTT, Amos Bronson 4
ALCOTT, Carroll Duard 4
ALCOTT, Louisa May H
ALCOTT, William Andrus H
ALDEN, Bertram F. 1
ALDEN, Carlos Coolidge 1
ALDEN, Carroll Storrs 5
ALDEN, Charles Henry 1
ALDEN, Charles Henry 3
ALDEN, Ebenezer 1
ALDEN, Edward S. 3
ALDEN, Ezra Hyde 2

ALDEN, George Henry 4
ALDEN, Henry Mills 1
ALDEN, Herbert Watson 1
ALDEN, Ichabod H
ALDEN, 1
Isabella Macdonald
ALDEN, James H
ALDEN, John H
ALDEN, John 1
ALDEN, John B. 1
ALDEN, Joseph H
ALDEN, 1
Mrs. Cynthia May Westover
ALDEN, 1
Raymond Macdonald
ALDEN, Timothy 1
ALDEN, William Clinton 4
ALDEN, 1
William Livingston
ALDEN, William Tracy 3
ALDER, Byron 3
ALDER, Kurt 3
ALDERMAN, 4
Edward Sinclair
ALDERMAN, 1
Edwin Anderson
ALDERMAN, Grover 1
Henry
ALDERMANN, Lewis R. 5
ALDERSON, 2
Victor Clifton
ALDERSON, Wroe 4
ALDINGTON, Richard 3
ALDIS, Arthur Taylor 1
ALDIS, Dorothy Keeley 4
ALDIS, Graham 4
ALDIS, Mary Reynolds 1
ALDIS, Owen Franklin 2
ALDRED, John Edward 2
ALDREY Y 5
MONTOLIO, Pedro 'de
ALDRICH, Anne Reeve H
ALDRICH, Auretta Roys 4
ALDRICH, Bess Streeter 3
ALDRICH, Charles 1
ALDRICH, 2
Charles Anderson
ALDRICH, Charles Henry 1
ALDRICH, Charles John 1
ALDRICH, Chester Hardy 1
ALDRICH, 4
Chester Holmes
ALDRICH, 2
Chilson Darragh
ALDRICH, Cyrus H
ALDRICH, Darragh 4
ALDRICH, 4
Donald Bradshaw
ALDRICH, Edgar 1
ALDRICH, 3
Edward Burgess
ALDRICH, George Ames 1
ALDRICH, Henry Clay 1
ALDRICH, 4
Herbert Lincoln
ALDRICH, James H
ALDRICH, John Gladding 5
ALDRICH, John Gladding 1
ALDRICH, John Merton 1
ALDRICH, 1
Kildroy Philip
ALDRICH, 1
Leander Jefferson
ALDRICH, Louis 1
ALDRICH, Loyal Blaine 4
ALDRICH, Mary Jane 1
ALDRICH, Mildred 1
ALDRICH, 1
Morton Arnold
ALDRICH, 1
Nelson Wilmarth
ALDRICH, Orlando W. 4
ALDRICH, Perley Dunn 1
ALDRICH, Richard 1
ALDRICH, Richard S. 1
ALDRICH, Richard S. 2
ALDRICH, Sherwood 1
ALDRICH, 1
Truman Heminway
ALDRICH, William H
ALDRICH, 1
William Farrington
ALDRICH, 4
William Sleeper
ALDRICH, 4
William Truman
ALDRIDGE, 2
Clayson Wheeler
ALDRIDGE, H
George Washington
ALDRIDGE, 1
Ira Frederick
ALDUNATE, Walter Hull 3
ALDUNATE, Don 1
Santiago
ALEMANY, Jose Sadoc

LENCASTRE, Stephen Peter — 2
LERDING, Herman Joseph — 1
LESHIRE, Arthur William — 1
LESHIRE, Edward — 4
LESHIRE, James Buchanan — 1
LESSANDRI-PALMA, Arturo — 5
LESSANDRONI, Walter Edwin — 4
LEXANDER, Abraham — H
LEXANDER, Adam — H
LEXANDER, Adam Rankin — H
LEXANDER, Albert Victor — 4
LEXANDER, Armstead Milton — H
LEXANDER, Barton Stone — H
LEXANDER, Ben — 2
LEXANDER, Carter — 4
LEXANDER, Charles — 5
LEXANDER, Charles Beatty — 1
LEXANDER, Charles McCallon — 1
LEXANDER, Charles Tripler — 1
LEXANDER, Charlton — H
LEXANDER, Clyde C. — 4
LEXANDER, Cosmo — H
LEXANDER, DeAlva Stanwood — 1
LEXANDER, Donald — 3
LEXANDER, Douglas — 2
LEXANDER, Edward Albert — 2
LEXANDER, Edward Porter — 1
LEXANDER, Evan Shelby — H
LEXANDER, Francesca — 1
LEXANDER, Francis — H
LEXANDER, Franz — 5
LEXANDER, Frederick — 4
LEXANDER, George — 1
LEXANDER, George F. — 2
LEXANDER, Grace — 5
LEXANDER, Gross — 5
LEXANDER, Harold David — 5
LEXANDER, Hartley Burr — 1
LEXANDER, Hattie Elizabeth — 5
LEXANDER, Henry Clay — 5
LEXANDER, Henry Martyn — 1
LEXANDER, Henry Martyn — 3
LEXANDER, Henry Porteous — H
LEXANDER, Herbert G. B. — 1
LEXANDER, Hooper — 1
LEXANDER, Hubbard Foster — 3
LEXANDER, James — H
LEXANDER, James Jr. — 1
LEXANDER, James F. — 1
LEXANDER, James Patterson — 2
LEXANDER, James Strange — 1
LEXANDER, James Waddel — H
LEXANDER, James Waddell — 1
LEXANDER, James Waddell, II — 5
LEXANDER, Jerome — 3
LEXANDER, John — H
LEXANDER, John — 3
LEXANDER, John Brevard — 4
LEXANDER, John E. — 4
LEXANDER, John Henry — H
LEXANDER, John L. — 1
LEXANDER, John Macmillan — 3
LEXANDER, John Romich — 3
LEXANDER, John White — 1
LEXANDER, Joseph Addison — H
LEXANDER, Joshua W. — 1
LEXANDER, Julian Power — 3
LEXANDER, Leigh — 2

ALEXANDER, Lester Fisher — 3
ALEXANDER, M. Moss — 3
ALEXANDER, Magnus Washington — 1
ALEXANDER, Maitland — 1
ALEXANDER, Mark — H
ALEXANDER, Minnie (Rebecca) — 1
ALEXANDER, Moses — 1
ALEXANDER, Nathaniel — H
ALEXANDER, Oakey Logan — 2
ALEXANDER, Paul W. — 4
ALEXANDER, Robert — H
ALEXANDER, Robert — 1
ALEXANDER, Robert C. — H
ALEXANDER, Samuel Davies — H
ALEXANDER, Samuel Nathan — 5
ALEXANDER, Sir William — 3
ALEXANDER, Stephen — H
ALEXANDER, Suydenham B. — 4
ALEXANDER, Taliaferro — 1
ALEXANDER, Richard) Thomas — 5
ALEXANDER, Truman Hudson — 5
ALEXANDER, Vance J. — 4
ALEXANDER, Wallace McKinney — 1
ALEXANDER, Walter R. — 3
ALEXANDER, Wilford S. — 3
ALEXANDER, Will Winton — 3
ALEXANDER, William — H
ALEXANDER, William — 1
ALEXANDER, William Albert — 2
ALEXANDER, William DeWitt — 1
ALEXANDER, William Henry — 5
ALEXANDER, William Leidy — 1
ALEXANDER, William McFaddin — 3
ALEXANDER, William Valentine — 5
ALEXIS, Algert Daniel — 4
ALEXY, Janko — 5
ALEY, Robert Judson — 1
ALFANO, Vincenzo — 1
ALFARO, Colon Eloy — 5
ALFARO, Ricardo Joaquin — 5
ALFONCE, Jean — H
ALFORD, Julius Caesar — H
ALFORD, Leon Pratt — 1
ALFORD, Leon Pratt — 2
ALFORD, Mrs. Nell — 3
ALFORD, Theodore Crandall — 2
ALFORD, William Hays — 4
ALFRED, Frank H. — 4
ALFREDSON, Bernard V(ictor) — 5
ALFRIEND, Edward Morrisson — 4
ALGER, Cyrus — H
ALGER, Frederick M. Jr. — 4
ALGER, George William — 1
ALGER, Horatio Jr. — 1
ALGER, John Lincoln — 4
ALGER, Philip Rounseville — 1
ALGER, Russell Alexander — 1
ALGER, William Rounseville — 1
ALI, Mohammed — 4
ALI KHAN, Liaquat — 3
ALINSKY, Saul David,* — 5
ALISON, Francis — H
ALLAIRE, James Peter — 1
ALLAIRE, William Herbert — 1
ALLAN, Chilton — H
ALLAN, John — H
ALLAN, John J. — 1
ALLARD, John S. — 4
ALLARDICE, Robert Edgar — 1
ALLDERDICE, Norman — 3
ALLDREDGE, Eugene Perry — 3
ALLDREDGE, J. Haden — 1
ALLEE, James Frank — 1
ALLEE, Marjorie Hill — 2
ALLEE, Warder Clyde — 3
ALLEFONSCE, Jean — H
ALLEMAN, Gellert — 2

ALLEMAN, Herbert Christian — 3
ALLEMANG, Herbert John — 4
ALLEN, Abel Leighton — 1
ALLEN, Addison — 1
ALLEN, Alexander John — 5
ALLEN, Alexander Viets Griswold — 1
ALLEN, Alfred — 2
ALLEN, Alfred Gaither — 1
ALLEN, Alfred Reginald — 1
ALLEN, Amos Lawrence — 1
ALLEN, Andrew — H
ALLEN, Andrew Aniel — 4
ALLEN, Andrew Hussey — 1
ALLEN, Andrew Jackson — H
ALLEN, Andrews — 1
ALLEN, Anthony Benezet — 1
ALLEN, Arch Turner — 1
ALLEN, Arthur Augustus — 4
ALLEN, Arthur Francis — 2
ALLEN, Arthur Moulton — 3
ALLEN, Arthur Watts — 4
ALLEN, Arthur Wilburn — 3
ALLEN, Austin Oscar — 5
ALLEN, Benjamin — 1
ALLEN, Benjamin — 3
ALLEN, Benjamin Franklin — 5
ALLEN, Benjamin Leach — 1
ALLEN, Bennet Mills — 4
ALLEN, Beverly Sprague — 1
ALLEN, Calvin Francis — 2
ALLEN, Carlos Eben — 3
ALLEN, Charles — H
ALLEN, Charles — 1
ALLEN, Charles Claffin — 1
ALLEN, Charles Curtis — 3
ALLEN, Charles Dexter — 1
ALLEN, Charles Edward — 1
ALLEN, Charles Elmer — 1
ALLEN, Charles Herbert — 1
ALLEN, Charles Julius — 1
ALLEN, Charles Lucius — 1
ALLEN, Charles Metcalf — 3
ALLEN, Charles Morse — 1
ALLEN, Charles Ricketson — 2
ALLEN, Charles Warrenne — 1
ALLEN, Chester Arthur — 4
ALLEN, Claxton Edmonds — 3
ALLEN, Clay — 5
ALLEN, Clinton L. — 4
ALLEN, Courtney — 5
ALLEN, Crombie — 2
ALLEN, David Oliver — H
ALLEN, Devere — 3
ALLEN, Don B. — 4
ALLEN, Don Cameron — 5
ALLEN, Dudley Peter — 1
ALLEN, Duff S. — 3
ALLEN, Edgar — 2
ALLEN, Edgar 'van Nuys — 4
ALLEN, Edmund Thompson — 1
ALLEN, Edward Archibald — 4
ALLEN, Edward Bartlett — 4
ALLEN, Edward Ellis — 3
ALLEN, Edward Mortimer — 1
ALLEN, Edward Normand — 5
ALLEN, Edward Patrick — 1
ALLEN, Edward Tyson — 3
ALLEN, Edwin Madison — 2
ALLEN, Edwin West — 1
ALLEN, Eliot Dinsmore — 5
ALLEN, Elisha Hunt — H
ALLEN, Eric William — 1
ALLEN, Ernest Bourner — 1
ALLEN, Ethan — 1
ALLEN, Ethan — 2
ALLEN, Eugene Thomas — 4
ALLEN, Ezra Griffen — 3
ALLEN, F. Sturges — 4
ALLEN, Florence Ellinwood — 4
ALLEN, Frances — 1
ALLEN, Francis Henry — 4
ALLEN, Francis Richmond — 1
ALLEN, Frank — 1
ALLEN, Frank Bigelow — 3
ALLEN, Frank G. — 3
ALLEN, Frank Philip Jr. — 2
ALLEN, Fred — 3
ALLEN, Fred Hovey — 1
ALLEN, Frederic De Forest — H
ALLEN, Frederic Winthrop — 1
ALLEN, Frederick Baylies — 1
ALLEN, Frederick Henry — 4

ALLEN, Frederick Hobbes — 1
ALLEN, Frederick Innes — 1
ALLEN, Frederick James — 1
ALLEN, Frederick Lewis — 3
ALLEN, Freeman Harlow — 2
ALLEN, Gardner Weld — 2
ALLEN, Geo A. Jr. — 1
ALLEN, George — H
ALLEN, George Edward — 5
ALLEN, George Garland — 4
ALLEN, George Henry — 3
ALLEN, George Venable — 5
ALLEN, George Washington — 1
ALLEN, George Whiting — 1
ALLEN, Glover Morrill — 5
ALLEN, Gordon — 5
ALLEN, Gracie — 4
ALLEN, Grant — 5
ALLEN, Grosvenor Noyes — 3
ALLEN, Guy Fletcher — 5
ALLEN, Hamilton Ford — 4
ALLEN, Hans — 3
ALLEN, Harris Campbell — 5
ALLEN, Harrison — H
ALLEN, Heman * — 5
ALLEN, Henry Jr. — 4
ALLEN, Henry Butler — 5
ALLEN, Henry Crosby — 5
ALLEN, Henry D. — 5
ALLEN, Henry Justin — 2
ALLEN, Henry Tureman — 1
ALLEN, Henry Watkins — H
ALLEN, Hope Emily — 4
ALLEN, Horace Eugene — 5
ALLEN, Horace Newton — 1
ALLEN, Horatio — 1
ALLEN, Howard Cameron — 4
ALLEN, Hubert A. — 2
ALLEN, Ira — 1
ALLEN, Ira Wilder — 1
ALLEN, J. Weston — 1
ALLEN, James — 1
ALLEN, James E. — 4
ALLEN, James Edward — 2
ALLEN, James Edward, Jr. — 5
ALLEN, James Henry — 3
ALLEN, James Lane — 1
ALLEN, James Turney — 2
ALLEN, Jeremiah Mervin — H
ALLEN, Joel Asaph — 1
ALLEN, John * — 1
ALLEN, John Beard — 1
ALLEN, John Clayton — 3
ALLEN, John Denby — 4
ALLEN, John Eliot — 2
ALLEN, John F. — 1
ALLEN, John James — H
ALLEN, John Johnson — 4
ALLEN, John Kermott — 1
ALLEN, John Mills — 1
ALLEN, John Rex — 5
ALLEN, John Robert — 1
ALLEN, John Stevenson — 4
ALLEN, John Wesley — 4
ALLEN, John Weston — 5
ALLEN, John William — H
ALLEN, Joseph — H
ALLEN, Joseph Dana — 1
ALLEN, Joseph Henry — H
ALLEN, Joseph Holmes — 5
ALLEN, Judson — 1
ALLEN, Julian — 4
ALLEN, Junius — 4
ALLEN, Kenneth — 1
ALLEN, Leo Elwood — 4
ALLEN, Leon Menard — 1
ALLEN, Leroy — 5
ALLEN, Lewis Falley — H
ALLEN, Lewis George — 2
ALLEN, Louis J. — 1
ALLEN, Lucy Ellis — 2
ALLEN, Lyman Whitney — 5
ALLEN, M. Marshall — 3
ALLEN, Mrs. Marion Boyd — 5
ALLEN, Martha Meir — 1
ALLEN, Maryland — 1
ALLEN, Milton Irving — 4
ALLEN, Nat Burtis — 5
ALLEN, Nathan — H
ALLEN, Nathaniel — 5
ALLEN, Nellie Burnham — 5
ALLEN, Paul — 4
ALLEN, Paul S. — 4
ALLEN, Perry S. — 1
ALLEN, Philip — 5
ALLEN, Philip Loring — 1
ALLEN, Philip Ray — 5
ALLEN, Philip Schuyler — 4
ALLEN, Ralph — 5
ALLEN, Ralph Clayton — 4
ALLEN, Ray — 5
ALLEN, Richard — H
ALLEN, Richard Day — 2

ALLEN, Richard Frazer — 3
ALLEN, Richard Lamb — H
ALLEN, Riley Harris — 4
ALLEN, Robert * — H
ALLEN, Robert E. Lee — 4
ALLEN, Robert Emmet — 3
ALLEN, Robert Gray — 4
ALLEN, Robert H. — 2
ALLEN, Robert I. — 4
ALLEN, Robert Porter — 4
ALLEN, Roderick Random — 5
ALLEN, Rolland Craten — 4
ALLEN, Russell Morton — 4
ALLEN, Samuel Clesson —
ALLEN, Samuel Edward — 1
ALLEN, Samuel G. — 1
ALLEN, Samuel James McIntosh — 5
ALLEN, Sherman — 2
ALLEN, Sidney J. — 3
ALLEN, Stephen Haley — 5
ALLEN, Sturges — 3
ALLEN, Thomas — H
ALLEN, Thomas — 1
ALLEN, Thomas Grant — 5
ALLEN, Thomas M. — H
ALLEN, Thomas Stinson — 2
ALLEN, Timothy Field — 1
ALLEN, Viola — 2
ALLEN, Walter — 4
ALLEN, Walter Barth — 3
ALLEN, Walter Cleveland — 2
ALLEN, William * — H
ALLEN, William Fitch — 5
ALLEN, William Francis — H
ALLEN, William Frederick — 1
ALLEN, William H. Jr. — 4
ALLEN, William Henry * — H
ALLEN, William Hervey — 2
ALLEN, William Joshua — 1
ALLEN, William Orville — 1
ALLEN, William Ray — 1
ALLEN, William Reynolds — 1
ALLEN, William Sims — 3
ALLEN, William Vincent — 1
ALLEN, Willis — H
ALLEN, Willis Boyd — 1
ALLEN, Wilmar Mason — 3
ALLEN, Wyeth — 5
ALLEN, Zachariah — H
ALLENDOERFER, Carl W. — 3
ALLER, Howard Lewis — 3
ALLERTON, Isaac — H
ALLERTON, Samuel Waters — 1
ALLEY, Calvin Lane — 5
ALLEY, Charles Edwin (C. Ed) — 5
ALLEY, James Pinckney — 1
ALLEY, John Bassett — H
ALLEY, Rayford W. — 4
ALLEZ, George Clare — 3
ALLGOOD, Dwight Maurice — 5
ALLIBOXE, — H
ALLIN, Arthur — 1
ALLIN, Bushrod Warren — 1
ALLIN, Cephas Daniel — 1
ALLIN, George Litchfield — 5
ALLIN, Roger — 3
ALLINE, Henry — H
ALLING, Arthur Nathaniel — 2
ALLING, Asa Alling — 1
ALLING, Harold Lattimore — 4
ALLING, John Wesley — 1
ALLING, Joseph Tilden — 1
ALLING, Paul Humiston — 2
ALLINGTON, Homer C. — 1
ALLINSON, Anne Crosby Emery — 1
ALLINSON, Francis Greenleaf — 1
ALLIOT, Hector — 1
ALLIS, Edward Phelps — H
ALLIS, Edward Phelps Jr. — 4
ALLIS, Louis — 3
ALLIS, Oscar Huntington — 1
ALLIS, Oswald Thompson — 5
ALLISON, James Jr. — H
ALLISON, James Boyd — 3
ALLISON, James Edward — 5
ALLISON, James Nicholls — 1
ALLISON, John — H
ALLISON, John Maudridge Snowden — 2

ALLISON, John P. 4
ALLISON, Nathaniel 1
ALLISON, Noah Dwight 5
ALLISON, Richard H
ALLISON, Robert H
ALLISON, Samuel King 4
ALLISON, William Boyd 1
ALLISON, William Henry 1
ALLISON, William Henry H
ALLMAN, 5
  David Bacharach
ALLMAN, Justin Paul 5
ALLMAN, Leslie Coover 4
ALLMOND, Marcus
  Blakey 4
ALLOUEZ, Claude Jean H
ALLPORT, Fayette Ward 3
ALLPORT, Frank 1
ALLPORT, 5
  Gordon Willard
ALLPORT, 4
  Gordon Willard
ALLRED, James V. 3
ALLSOPP, 1
  Clinton Bonfield
ALLSOPP, 2
  Frederick William
ALLSTON, H
  Robert Francis Withers
ALLSTON, Washington H
ALLWARDT, 1
  Henry Augustus
ALLWORK, 5
  Eleanor Bloom (Mrs. Ronald
  Allwork)
ALLYN, Arden Lacey 4
ALLYN, Arthur Cecil 4
ALLYN, Harriett May 3
ALLYN, Robert H
ALLYN, Stanley Charles 5
ALMACK, John C. 5
ALMAND, Claude Marion 3
ALMERT, Harold 5
ALMON, Edward Berton 1
ALMOND, James Edward 3
ALMOND, Nina 4
ALMSTEDT, 5
  Hermann Benjamin
ALMY, Frederic 1
ALMY, John Jay H
ALMY, Robert Forbes 5
ALONSO, Amado 3
ALPERS, 1
  William Charles
ALPHONSA, Mother H
ALPHONSA, Mother 4
ALRICH, Samuel Nelson 1
ALSBERG, C. Lucas 1
ALSCHULER, Alfred S. 1
ALSCHULER, 5
  Benjamin Philip;
ALSCHULER, Samuel 1
ALSOP, George H
ALSOP, John H
ALSOP, Joseph Wright 3
ALSOP, Reese Fell 4
ALSOP, Richard H
ALSTON, George L. 4
ALSTON, Joseph H
ALSTON, Lemuel James H
ALSTON, Robert Cotten 1
ALSTON, H
  William Jeffreys
ALSTON, Willis H
ALSTORK, John Wesley 5
ALT, Howard Lang 5
ALTE, Visconde 'de 3
ALTER, David H
ALTER, Dinsmore 5
ALTER, George Elias 1
ALTER, 4
  Lucien Weaver Scott
ALTER, Nicholas M(ark) 5
ALTGELD, John Peter 1
ALTGLASS, Max Mayer 3
ALTHAM, John H
ALTHAUS, Edward 4
ALTHAUSER, Norman
  Ray 4
ALTHERR, Alfred 5
ALTHOFF, Henry 2
ALTHOUSE, Harry
  Witman 1
ALTHOUSE, 5
  Howell Halberstadt
ALTHOUSE, Paul Marcks 5
ALTHOUSE, Paul Shearer 3
ALTMAIER, Clinton John 3
ALTMAN, Benjamin H
ALTMAN, Benjamin 4
ALTMAN, Oscar Louis 5
ALTMEYER, 5
  Arthur Joseph
ALTON, Alfred Edward 5
ALTON, 4
  Charles De Lancey
ALTROCCHI, Rudolph 3

ALTSCHULER, Modest 5
ALTSHELER, 1
  Joseph Alexander
ALTVATER, H. Hugh 3
ALVARADO, H
  Juan Bautista
ALVAREZ, Alejandro 5
ALVERSON, Claude B. 4
ALVES, Henry F(red) 5
ALVEY, Richard Henry 1
ALVORD, Benjamin 4
ALVORD, Benjamin 1
ALVORD, 1
  Clarence Walworth
ALVORD, Corydon Alexis H
ALVORD, 4
  Elisworth Chapman
ALVORD, Henry Elijah 1
ALVORD, 5
  Idress Head (Mrs. Clarence
  W. Alvord)
ALVORD, James Church 1
ALVORD, James Church 4
ALVORD, John Watson 2
ALVORD, 5
  Katharine Sprague
ALWAY, Frederick James 5
ALWOOD, Olin Good 3
ALWOOD, 2
  William Bradford
ALWORTH, Royal D. 4
ALY KHAN, Shah H
AMADAS, Phillip H
AMAT, Thaddeus H
AMATEIS, Louis H
AMATEIS, Louis 4
AMATO, Pasquale 2
AMBAUEN, Andrew
  Joseph 4
AMBERG, Emil 2
AMBERG, Harold Vincent 4
AMBERG, Julius H. 3
AMBERG, Richard Hiller 5
AMBERG, Samuel 5
AMBLER, Benjamin
  Mason 1
AMBLER, Charles Henry 3
AMBLER, Chase P. 4
AMBLER, Frank Rhoades 4
AMBLER, 5
  James Markham Marshall
AMBLER, James Murray 4
AMBLER, Mason Gaither 4
AMBLER, Sara Ellmaker 4
AMBROSE, Arthur H
AMBROSE, 4
  Warren
AMBROSE, Paul 5
AMBRUSTER, 1
  Howard Watson
AMBRUSTER, Watson 1
AMDUR, Isadore 5
AMELIA H
AMEN, Harlan Page 1
AMEN, John Harlan 3
AMEND, 3
  Bernhard Gottwald
AMEND, Edward Bernard 4
AMENT, James E. 1
AMERMAN, Lemuel H
AMERMAN, Ralph
  Alonzo 1
AMES, Adelbert Jr. H
AMES, Butler 3
AMES, Charles Bismark 1
AMES, Charles Gordon 1
AMES, 5
  Charles Wilberforce
AMES, Edgar 2
AMES, Edward Elbridge 3
AMES, Edward Raymond H
AMES, Edward Scribner 3
AMES, Eleanor Kirk 1
AMES, Ezra 1
AMES, Fisher H
AMES, Fisher 4
AMES, 1
  Frederick Lothrop
AMES, 4
  Herman Vandenburg
AMES, Hobart 2
AMES, James Barr H
AMES, James Barr 1
AMES, James Barr 4
AMES, James Tyler H
AMES, Jesse Hazer 3
AMES, John Griffith 1
AMES, John Griffith 3
AMES, John Lincoln 4
AMES, John Ormsbee 1
AMES, Joseph Alexander H
AMES, Joseph Bushnell 1
AMES, Joseph Sweetman 1
AMES, Knowlton Lyman 1
AMES, Lewis Darwin 5
AMES, Louis Annin 3
AMES, Mary Lesley 1
AMES, Nathan Peabody H

AMES, Nathaniel H
AMES, Norman Bruce 4
AMES, Oakes H
AMES, Oakes 3
AMES, Oliver * H
AMES, Oliver 1
AMES, 4
  Robert Parker Marr
AMES, Samuel H
AMES, Susie M(ay) 5
AMES, William 1
AMES, 3
  William Lafayette
AMES, Winthrop 1
AMEY, Harry Burton 3
AMEZAGA, Juan Jose 3
AMHERST, Jeffery H
AMICK, 5
  Erwin Hamer, Jr.
AMIDON, Beulah 3
AMIDON, 1
  Charles Fremont
AMIDON, Samuel Barker 1
AMIGER, William 1
  Thomas
AMMANN, Othmar
  Hermann 4
AMMEN, Daniel H
AMMEN, Jacob 4
AMMEN, Samuel Zenas 4
AMMIDOWN, 4
  Edward Holmes
AMMONS, Elias Milton 1
AMMONS, Teller 5
AMORY, Arthur 1
AMORY, Charles Walter 5
AMORY, Harcourt 5
AMORY, John James 1
AMORY, Robert 1
AMORY, Robert 5
AMORY, Thomas H
AMORY, William 3
AMOS, Frank R. 4
AMOS, 1
  Thyrsa Wealhtheow
AMOS, 5
  William Frederick
AMOSS, Harold L. 3
AMRINE, 5
  William Frederick
AMSBARY, Frank C. Jr. 4
AMSBARY, Wallace Bruce 3
AMSTER, Nathan
  Leonard 1
AMSTUZ, John O. 5
AMWEG, Frederick James 1
AMYOT, 5
  Louis Joseph Adjutor
ANAGNOS, H
  Julia Romana Howe
ANAGNOS, Michael H
ANAGNOS, Michael 4
ANAST, James Louis 4
ANASTASSY, 5
ANCENEY, Charles L. 1
ANDEREGG, Frederick 1
ANDERES, Robert L. 3
ANDERLEDY, H
  Anthony Maria
ANDERMAN, William 4
ANDERS, James Meschter 1
ANDERS, John Daniel H
ANDERS, Paul R. 1
ANDERS, 1
  Thomas Jefferson
ANDERSEN, Albert M. 3
ANDERSEN, 2
  Arthur Edward
ANDERSEN, Arthur Olaf 3
ANDERSEN, Bjorn 5
ANDERSEN, 3
  Christian Schmidt
ANDERSEN, 1
  Hendrik Christian
ANDERSEN, 2
  Hendrik Christian
ANDERSEN, James Roy 2
ANDERSEN, John Dlbos 4
ANDERSEN, 1
  Joyce Marilyn Off (Mrs.
  Chester W. Andersen)
ANDERSON, 1
  Abraham Archibald
ANDERSON, 2
  Abraham Archibald
ANDERSON, Ada
  Woodruff 4
ANDERSON, Albert 1
ANDERSON, Albert 2
ANDERSON, i
  Albert Barnes
ANDERSON, Alden 2
ANDERSON, Alexander H
ANDERSON, 2
  Alexander Outlaw
ANDERSON, 2
  Alexander Pierce

ANDERSON, Amabel A. 1
ANDERSON, Amos
  Carey 5
ANDERSON, 1
  Andrew Freeman
ANDERSON, Andrew
  Runni 3
ANDERSON, Andrew
  Work 2
ANDERSON, Arch W. 4
ANDERSON, 4
  Archibald Watson
ANDERSON, 4
  Arthur Julius
ANDERSON, 4
  Arthur Marvin
ANDERSON, Asher 1
ANDERSON, Axel Henry 4
ANDERSON, 2
  Benjamin McAlester
ANDERSON, Carl C. 1
ANDERSON, Carl
  Magnus 5
ANDERSON, Carl
  Thomas 1
ANDERSON, 2
  Carlotta Adele
ANDERSON, 1
  Chandler Parsons
ANDERSON, 4
  Charles Albert
ANDERSON, 5
  Charles Hardin
ANDERSON, 5
  Charles Loftus Grant
ANDERSON, 1
  Charles Palmerston
ANDERSON, 1
  Clifford Le Conte
ANDERSON, David Allen 5
ANDERSON, Dice Robins 2
ANDERSON, Donald
  Brown 3
ANDERSON, 3
  Douglas Smith
ANDERSON, Dwight 3
ANDERSON, Dwight 4
ANDERSON, Earl W. 5
ANDERSON, Edgar 5
ANDERSON, Edward 1
ANDERSON, 3
  Edward Delmar
ANDERSON, Edw...u Lee 1
ANDERSON, 1
  Edward Lowell
ANDERSON, 2
  Edward Wharton
ANDERSON, 1
  Edwin Alexander
ANDERSON, 2
  Edwin Hatfield
ANDERSON, 2
  Elam Jonathan
ANDERSON, 1
  Elbert Ellery
ANDERSON, Elbridge R. 2
ANDERSON, 4
  Elizabeth Preston
ANDERSON, Elsie Grace 5
ANDERSON, Ernest 3
ANDERSON, Esther L. 5
ANDERSON, F. Paul 1
ANDERSON, Frank 3
ANDERSON, Frank
  Bartow 1
ANDERSON, 1
  Frank Leonard
ANDERSON, 2
  Frederick Irving
ANDERSON, Frederick L. 5
ANDERSON, 4
  Frederick Lincoln
ANDERSON, Galusha 1
ANDERSON, George 5
ANDERSON, George A. 5
ANDERSON, George
  Alburtus H
ANDERSON, 5
  George Edward
ANDERSON, 1
  George Everett
ANDERSON, 1
  George Lucius
ANDERSON, George
  Minor 2
ANDERSON, George
  Smith 1
ANDERSON, George
  Thomas H
ANDERSON, 1
  George Weston
ANDERSON, George
  Wood 5
ANDERSON, Harold 5
ANDERSON, 3
  Harold Durbin

ANDERSON, 1
  Harold MacDonald
ANDERSON, Harold V. 4
ANDERSON,
  Harry Bennett
ANDERSON, Harry
  Reuben
ANDERSON,
  Harry William
ANDERSON,
  Helen Natalie Johnson
ANDERSON, Henry Clay
ANDERSON, Henry Hill H
ANDERSON, Henry
  James
ANDERSON, H
  Henry Tompkins
ANDERSON,
  Henry Watkins
ANDERSON,
  Henry William
ANDERSON, Howard B. H
ANDERSON,
  Hugh Johnston
ANDERSON, Isaac H
ANDERSON, Isabel
ANDERSON,
  J(efferson) Randolph
ANDERSON, Jacob
  Nelson
ANDERSON, James
  Arthur
ANDERSON, James
  Cuyler
ANDERSON, James
  Howard
ANDERSON,
  James Nesbitt
ANDERSON, James
  Patton H
ANDERSON, James R. H
ANDERSON, John
ANDERSON, John *
ANDERSON, John Albert
ANDERSON, H
  John Alexander
ANDERSON, John
  August
ANDERSON,
  John Benjamin
ANDERSON, 3
  John Crawford
ANDERSON, John
  Edward
ANDERSON, John
  Edward
ANDERSON, John F.
ANDERSON,
  Francis
ANDERSON, John
  George
ANDERSON, John Hargis
ANDERSON, John Jacob
ANDERSON, John
  Murray
ANDERSON, John Will
ANDERSON, John
  William
ANDERSON, Joseph
ANDERSON, Joseph
ANDERSON,
  Joseph Gaudentius
ANDERSON,
  Joseph Halstead
ANDERSON, Joseph Reid
ANDERSON, Joseph Starr
ANDERSON,
  Josiah McNair
ANDERSON, Karl
ANDERSON, Karl
  Leopold
ANDERSON, Larz
ANDERSON, Lee
ANDERSON, Leroy Dean
ANDERSON, Lewis Flint
ANDERSON,
  Louis Francis
ANDERSON, Martin
ANDERSON,
  Martin Brewer
ANDERSON, Mary
ANDERSON, Mary *
ANDERSON,
  Mary Mortlock (Mrs. Walter
  Anderson)
ANDERSON, Maxwell
ANDERSON,
  Melville Best
ANDERSON,
  Merle Hampton
ANDERSON, Neal Larkin
ANDERSON, Nelson Paul
ANDERSON,
  Newton Mitchell
ANDERSON, Nils
ANDERSON, Oscar V.

ANDERSON, Paul Lewis 3
ANDERSON, Paul N(athaniel) 5
ANDERSON, Paul Vernon 5
ANDERSON, Paul Y. 1
ANDERSON, Peirce 1
ANDERSON, R. T. 4
ANDERSON, Ralph J. 4
ANDERSON, Rasmus Bjorn 1
ANDERSON, Richard Clough H
ANDERSON, Richard Clough Jr. H
ANDERSON, Richard Heron H
ANDERSON, Richard James 5
ANDERSON, Robert H
ANDERSON, Robert Campbell 3
ANDERSON, Robert Earle 4
ANDERSON, Robert Edward, Jr. 5
ANDERSON, Robert Gordon 3
ANDERSON, Robert Hargis 4
ANDERSON, Robert 'van Vleck 2
ANDERSON, Rose 4
ANDERSON, Rudolph John 4
ANDERSON, Rudolph Martin 4
ANDERSON, Rufus 1
ANDERSON, Samuel H
ANDERSON, Samuel Wagner 4
ANDERSON, Sherwood 1
ANDERSON, Simeon H. H
ANDERSON, Sophie H
ANDERSON, Stonewall 1
ANDERSON, Sydney 2
ANDERSON, Thomas Davis H
ANDERSON, Thomas H. 1
ANDERSON, Thomas Joel Jr. 4
ANDERSON, Thomas Lilbourne H
ANDERSON, Thomas McArthur 1
ANDERSON, Troyer Steele 2
ANDERSON, Victor E. 4
ANDERSON, Victor Emanuel 2
ANDERSON, Victor Vance 4
ANDERSON, W. C. 1
ANDERSON, Walter H
ANDERSON, Walter Alexander
ANDERSON, Wells Foster 3
ANDERSON, Wendell W. 3
ANDERSON, William 1
ANDERSON, William A. 1
ANDERSON, William A. 3
ANDERSON, William Allison 2
ANDERSON, William Beverly 5
ANDERSON, William Brennan 1
ANDERSON, William Clayton H
ANDERSON, William D. 3
ANDERSON, William Downs 5
ANDERSON, William Dozier 5
ANDERSON, William Franklin 2
ANDERSON, William Gilbert 2
ANDERSON, William Hamilton 5
ANDERSON, William Harry 1
ANDERSON, William Henry 4
ANDERSON, William Joseph Jr. 2
ANDERSON, William Ketcham 1
ANDERSON, William Madison 4
ANDERSON, William Otto 2
ANDERSON, William Thomas 4
ANDERSON, William Thompson

ANDERSON, William Wallace H
ANDERSON, Winslow 1
ANDERSON, Winslow Samuel 2
ANDERSSON, Alfred Oscar 3
ANDERTON, Stephen Philbin 2
ANDRADE, Cipriano 1
ANDRE, Floyd 5
ANDRE, John H
ANDRE, Louis H
ANDREA, Frank A. D. 4
ANDREASEN, Milian Lauritz 5
ANDREEN, Gustav Albert 1
ANDRESEN, Albert Frederick Ruger 4
ANDRESEN, August Herman 3
ANDRESS, James Mace 1
ANDRESS, James Mace 2
ANDRESS, Robert Joseph 4
ANDRETTA, S. A. 4
ANDREW, A. Piatt 1
ANDREW, Hardage L. 3
ANDREW, Harriet White Fisher 1
ANDREW, Henry Hersey 1
ANDREW, James Osgood H
ANDREW, John Albion H
ANDREW, John Forrester H
ANDREW, Joseph Atkins H
ANDREW, Samuel H
ANDREWS, Addison Fletcher 1
ANDREWS, Adolphus 2
ANDREWS, Alexander Boyd 1
ANDREWS, Alexander Boyd 2
ANDREWS, Alexander Boyd 5
ANDREWS, Alexander Speer
ANDREWS, Ambrose H
ANDREWS, Annulet 2
ANDREWS, Arthur Leonard 1
ANDREWS, Avery DeLano 3
ANDREWS, Bert 3
ANDREWS, Charles H
ANDREWS, Charles Bartlett
ANDREWS, Charles Cecil 4
ANDREWS, Charles Edgar Jr. 3
ANDREWS, Charles Henry 2
ANDREWS, Charles McLean 2
ANDREWS, Charles Oscar 2
ANDREWS, Charles Oscar, Jr. 5
ANDREWS, Chauncey Hummason H
ANDREWS, Christopher Columbus 1
ANDREWS, Clarence Edward
ANDREWS, Clarence L. 5
ANDREWS, Clayton Farrington 4
ANDREWS, Clement Walker
ANDREWS, Daniel Marshall 1
ANDREWS, E. Benjamin 1
ANDREWS, E. Wyllys 1
ANDREWS, Edmund 1
ANDREWS, Edward Gayer 1
ANDREWS, Eliphalet Frazer 3
ANDREWS, Eliza Frances 1
ANDREWS, Elmer Frank 4
ANDREWS, Ethan Allen 4
ANDREWS, Eugene Plumb 4
ANDREWS, Evangeline Walker 4
ANDREWS, Fannie Fern 3
ANDREWS, Frank 1
ANDREWS, Frank L. 4
ANDREWS, Frank Maxwell 2
ANDREWS, Frank Mills 2
ANDREWS, Frank Taylor 1
ANDREWS, Garnett 1
ANDREWS, Garnett 2
ANDREWS, George 1
ANDREWS, George Leonard

ANDREWS, George Leonard 1
ANDREWS, George Lippitt 1
ANDREWS, George Pierce 1
ANDREWS, George Rex H
ANDREWS, George Whitfield 1
ANDREWS, George William 5
ANDREWS, Gwendolen Foulke 4
ANDREWS, Harry Eugene 1
ANDREWS, Herbert Marston 1
ANDREWS, Hiram Bertrand 4
ANDREWS, Horace Ellsworth 5
ANDREWS, Irene Osgood (Mrs. John B. Andrews)
ANDREWS, Israel DeWolf 1
ANDREWS, Israel Ward H
ANDREWS, J. Warren 1
ANDREWS, James DeWitt 1
ANDREWS, James Parkhill 2
ANDREWS, Jesse 4
ANDREWS, John H
ANDREWS, John 3
ANDREWS, John Bertram 2
ANDREWS, John Newman 1
ANDREWS, John Tuttle H
ANDREWS, Joseph H
ANDREWS, Julia Lincoln Ray 4
ANDREWS, Justin M. 4
ANDREWS, Landaff Watson 5
ANDREWS, Launcelot 1
ANDREWS, Leila Edna 5
ANDREWS, Leland Stanford 5
ANDREWS, Lewis Whiting 4
ANDREWS, Lincoln Clark 3
ANDREWS, Lorin H
ANDREWS, Lorrin H
ANDREWS, Marietta Minnigerode 1
ANDREWS, Martin Register 1
ANDREWS, Mary Raymond Shipman 1
ANDREWS, Matthew Page 2
ANDREWS, Matthew Thomas 1
ANDREWS, Newton Lloyd 1
ANDREWS, Paul Shipman 4
ANDREWS, Philip 2
ANDREWS, Robert Christie 4
ANDREWS, Robert Day 1
ANDREWS, Robert Macon 5
ANDREWS, Robert Robbins 1
ANDREWS, Roger Mercein 3
ANDREWS, Roland Franklyn 1
ANDREWS, Roy Chapman 3
ANDREWS, Samuel George H
ANDREWS, Samuel James 1
ANDREWS, Schofield 5
ANDREWS, Sherlock James H
ANDREWS, Sidney H
ANDREWS, Sidney Francis 1
ANDREWS, Steffan 3
ANDREWS, Stephen Pearl H
ANDREWS, T. Wingate 1
ANDREWS, Thomas G. 4
ANDREWS, Thomas Galphin 2
ANDREWS, Timothy Patrick H
ANDREWS, Vernon Daniel 1
ANDREWS, W. Earle 4
ANDREWS, Walter Gresham 1
ANDREWS, Walter Pemberton 1
ANDREWS, Wilfred Leslie 3

ANDREWS, William E. 5
ANDREWS, William Given 1
ANDREWS, William Loring 1
ANDREWS, William Noble 5
ANDREWS, William Page 1
ANDREWS, William Shankland 1
ANDREWS, William Symes 1
ANDREWS, William Watson H
ANDRIEU, Mathuren Arthur H
ANDROS, Sir Edmund H
ANDRUS, Clift 5
ANDRUS, John Emory 1
ANDRUSS, E. Van Arsdale 1
ANFUSO, Victor L. 4
ANGAS, W. Mack 4
ANGEL, Benjamin Franklin 5
ANGEL, John 4
ANGEL, William G. H
ANGELA, Mother 5
ANGELESCO, Constantin 2
ANGELI, Pier (Anna Marie Pierangeli) 5
ANGELL, Alexis Caswell 1
ANGELL, Ernest 5
ANGELL, Frank 1
ANGELL, George Thorndike 1
ANGELL, Henry Clay 1
ANGELL, Israel H
ANGELL, James Burrill 1
ANGELL, James Rowland 2
ANGELL, Joseph Kinnicutt H
ANGELL, L(isbeth) Gertrude 5
ANGELL, Martin Fuller 1
ANGELL, Montgomery B. 5
ANGELL, Norman (Ralph Norman Angell Lane) 5
ANGELL, Robert Henderson 1
ANGELL, Sir Norman 4
ANGELL, Walter Foster 1
ANGELL, William Gorham H
ANGELL, William Robert 2
ANGELLOTTI, Frank M. 1
ANGER, Sister Mary Alacoque 5
ANGERT, Eugene Henry 2
ANGEVINE, Jay B(ernard) 5
ANGIER, Roswell Parker 2
ANGIER, Walter Eugene 1
ANGLAND, Emmett Cyril 5
ANGLE, Edward Hartley 1
ANGLE, Edward John 1
ANGLE, George Keyser 1
ANGLE, Glenn D(ale) 5
ANGLE, Jay Warren 3
ANGLE, Wesley Motley 1
ANGLEMAN, Sydney Winfield 5
ANGLIN, Margaret (Mary) 1
ANGLY, Edward 3
ANGOOD, Sidney Bernard 3
ANHEUSER, Eberhard 4
ANJARIA, Jashwantrai Jayantilal 5
ANKCORN, Charles M. 3
ANKENEY, John Sites 2
ANKENY, John D'Art 2
ANKENY, Levi 1
ANNADOWN, Ruth Vivian 5
ANNAND, Percy Nicol 3
ANSBERRY, Timothy Thomas 1
ANSCHUTZ, Karl H
ANSEL, Martin Frederick 1
ANSELL, Samuel Tilden 5
ANSERMET, Ernest Alexandre 5
ANSHEN, S. Robert 4
ANSHUTZ, Edward Pollock 1
ANSHUTZ, Thomas Pollock 1
ANSLEY, Clarke Fisher 1
ANSLOW, Gladys Amelia 5
ANSLOW, W. Parker Jr. 4

ANSON, Adrian Constantine H
ANSON, Adrian Constantine 4
ANSORGE, Martin Charles 4
ANSPACH, Brooke Melancthon 5
ANSPACHER, Louis Kaufman 2
ANSTADT, Henry 1
ANSTED, Harry Bidwell 3
ANSTICE, Henry 1
ANTES, Henry H
ANTES, John H
ANTHEIL, George 3
ANTHON, Charles H
ANTHON, Charles Edward H
ANTHON, John H
ANTHONY, Alfred Williams 1
ANTHONY, Andrew Varick Stout 1
ANTHONY, Ann 1
ANTHONY, Arthur Cox 3
ANTHONY, Benjamin Harris 1
ANTHONY, Brayman William 4
ANTHONY, Daniel Read 1
ANTHONY, Daniel Read Jr. 1
ANTHONY, Earle C. 4
ANTHONY, Edward 5
ANTHONY, Ernest Lee 4
ANTHONY, Gardner Chace 1
ANTHONY, George Tobey H
ANTHONY, Henry Bowen H
ANTHONY, John Gould H
ANTHONY, Joseph Biles H
ANTHONY, Katharine Susan 5
ANTHONY, Katharine Susan 4
ANTHONY, Lovick Pierce 5
ANTHONY, Luther B. 3
ANTHONY, Norman (Hume) 5
ANTHONY, Sister H
ANTHONY, Susan Brownell 1
ANTHONY, William Arnold 1
ANTISDALE, Louis Marlin 2
ANTISDEL, Clarence Baumes 5
ANTOINE, Josephine Louise 5
ANTOINE, Pere H
ANTON, Mark 5
ANTONIA, Sister 2
ANTRIM, Doron Kemp 4
ANTRIM, Ernest Irving 3
ANTRIM, Eugene Marion 3
ANTRIM, Minna Thomas 4
ANTROBUS, John 4
ANTROBUS, John H
ANUNDSEN, Brynild H
ANZA, Juan Bautista 'de 4
AOKI, Viscount Siuzo 4
APES, William 5
APGAR, Austin Craig 1
APLIN, Henry Harrison 4
APP, Frank 1
APPEL, Daniel Frederick 5
APPEL, George F(rederick) Baer 5
APPEL, John Wilberforce Jr. 1
APPEL, Joseph Herbert 2
APPEL, Monte 5
APPEL, Theodore 1
APPEL, Theodore Burton 1
APPELT, Frank R. 1
APPENZELLAR, Paul 3
APPENZELLER, Alice Rebecca 3
APPENZELLER, Henry Gerhard H
APPLE, Andrew Thomas Geiger 1
APPLE, Henry Harbaugh 2
APPLE, Joseph Henry 2
APPLE, Thomas Gilmore H
APPLEBY, Frank 1
APPLEBY, Thomas Henry Montague Villiers 1
APPLEBY, Troy Wilson 2
APPLEBY, William Remsen 1

APPLEGATE, Frank G. 1
APPLEGATE, H. W. 1
APPLEGATE,
Irvamae Vincent 5
APPLEGATE, Jesse H
APPLEGATE,
John Stilwell 1
APPLEGATE, Paul Ray 4
APPLEMAN,
Charles Orville 4
APPLESEED, Johnny
APPLETON, Charles W. 2
APPLETON, Daniel H
APPLETON, Daniel 1
APPLETON,
Edward Victor 4
APPLETON, Floyd 3
APPLETON,
Francis Henry 1
APPLETON,
Francis Randall 1
APPLETON, James H
APPLETON, Jesse H
APPLETON, John * H
APPLETON, John Adams 4
APPLETON, John
Howard 1
APPLETON, L. Estelle H
APPLETON, Nathan H
APPLETON,
Nathaniel Walker H
APPLETON, Samuel H
APPLETON, Thomas
Gold H
APPLETON, William H
APPLETON,
William Channing 5
APPLETON,
William Henry H
APPLETON,
William Henry 1
APPLETON, William
Hyde 3
APPLETON,
William Sumner 2
APPLETON,
William Worthen 1
APTHORP,
William Foster 4
ARAKI, Eikichi 3
ARAMBURU,
Pedro Eugenio 5
ARANETA, Gregorio 1
ARANNA, Oswaldo 3
ARANT,
Herschel Whitfield 1
ARBEELY,
Abraham Joseph 4
ARBUCKLE,
Charles Nathaniel 3
ARBUCKLE, Howard Bell 2
ARBUCKLE, John 1
ARBUCKLE, John D. 4
ARBUCKLE, Maclyn 1
ARBUCKLE, Matthew H
ARBUCKLE,
Roscoe Conkling 1
ARBUS, Diane 5
ARBUTHNOT,
Charles Criswell 5
ARBUTHNOT,
Charles Criswell 4
ARBUTHNOT,
May Hill (Mrs. Charles C.
Arbuthnot) 5
ARBUTHNOT, Thomas
Shaw 5
ARBUTHNOT, Wilson S. 1
ARCAYA, Pedro Manuel 5
ARCE, Jose 5
ARCHAMBAULT,
A. Margaretta 3
ARCHBALD, James VI 1
ARCHBALD,
Robert Wodrow 1
ARCHBOLD, John Dustin 1
ARCHDALE, John H
ARCHER, Allen Thurman 4
ARCHER, Belle 1
ARCHER, Branch Tanner H
ARCHER, Clifford Paul 5
ARCHER, Franklin Morse 2
ARCHER, Frederic 1
ARCHER,
Gleason Leonard 4
ARCHER, James J. H
ARCHER, John H
ARCHER, John Clark 3
ARCHER,
Julian Lawrence 4
ARCHER, Peter 4
ARCHER, Ralph Curtis 3
ARCHER,
Shreve MacLaren 2
ARCHER, Stevenson * H
ARCHER, Thomas P. 2
ARCHER, William Segar H

ARCHIBALD,
Andrew Webster 1
ARCHIBALD, Frank C. 1
ARCHIBALD,
James Francis Jewell 5
ARCHIBALD,
Maynard Brown 3
ARCHIBALD, Mrs.
George 1
ARCHIBALD,
Raymond Clare 3
ARCHIPENKO,
Alexander 4
ARCTOWSKA, Adrian
Jane 5
ARCTOWSKI, Henryk 3
ARDEN,
Edwin Hunter Pendleton 4
ARDEN, Elizabeth 4
ARDERY,
William Breckenridge 4
ARDISON, Robert Joseph 5
AREF, Abdul Salam 5
ARENALES
CATALAN, Emilio 5
ARENBERG, Albert Lee 5
AREND, Harry O. 4
ARENDT, Morton 5
ARENS, Egmont 4
ARENS, Franz Xavier 1
ARENS, Henry 5
ARENS, Richard 5
ARENSBERG,
Walter Conrad 3
ARENTS, Albert 4
ARENTS, George 4
ARENTZ, Frederic C. H. 4
AREY, Hawthorne 5
AREY, Melvin Franklin 1
ARGALL, Philip 1
ARGALL, Samuel H
ARGETSINGER, J. C. 5
ARGUELLO, Jose Dario H
ARGUELLO, Leonardo 2
ARGUELLO, Luis
Antonio H
ARGYLE,
William Robertson 4
ARJONA, Jaime Homero 5
ARKELL, Bartlett 2
ARKELL, William Clark 4
ARKELL, William J. 1
ARKUSH,
Ralph Montgomery 4
ARKWRIGHT,
George Alfred 5
ARKWRIGHT,
Preston Stanley 2
ARLEN, Michael 3
ARLISS, George 2
ARMAS, Carlos Castillo 5
ARMBRECHT,
William Henry 2
ARMBRISTER,
Victor Stradley 4
ARMBRUSTER,
Adolph Henry 3
ARMES, William Dallam 4
ARMISTEAD, George H
ARMISTEAD,
Henry Beauford 3
ARMISTEAD,
Henry Marshall 3
ARMISTEAD,
Jesse Warren 3
ARMISTEAD,
Lewis Addison H
ARMITAGE, Albert T. 5
ARMITAGE, Paul 4
ARMOR,
Mrs. Mary Elizabeth Harris 3
ARMOUR, A. Watson 3
ARMOUR,
Allison Vincent 1
ARMOUR, Bernard R. 2
ARMOUR, Herman
Ossian 1
ARMOUR, J. Ogden 1
ARMOUR,
Laurance Hearne 5
ARMOUR, Lester 5
ARMOUR,
Philip Danforth 1
ARMOUR,
Philip Danforth 3
ARMS, Frank Thornton 2
ARMS, John Taylor 3
ARMS, Samuel Dwight 4
ARMS, Thomas Seelye 5
ARMSBY, George Newell 2
ARMSBY, Henry Prentiss 1
ARMSTEAD,
George Brooks 3
ARMSTEAD, Henry
Howell 1
ARMSTRONG, A. Joseph 3
ARMSTRONG, Alexander 1

ARMSTRONG,
Andrew Campbell 1
ARMSTRONG,
Anne Wetzell 3
ARMSTRONG,
Arthur Henry 1
ARMSTRONG, C. Dudley 3
ARMSTRONG, Charles 4
ARMSTRONG,
Charles Dickey 1
ARMSTRONG,
Charles Wallace 5
ARMSTRONG,
Charlotte (Mrs. Jack Lewi) 5
ARMSTRONG, Clare
Hibbs 5
ARMSTRONG, D.
Maitland 1
ARMSTRONG,
Dallas Warren; 5
ARMSTRONG,
David Hartley H
ARMSTRONG,
David William 4
ARMSTRONG,
DeWitt Clinton 5
ARMSTRONG, Donald
Budd 5
ARMSTRONG,
Edward Ambler 1
ARMSTRONG,
Edward Cooke 2
ARMSTRONG, Edwin H. 5
ARMSTRONG,
Frank Alton, Jr. 5
ARMSTRONG, Frank C. 1
ARMSTRONG, Gayle
Geard 3
ARMSTRONG,
George Buchanan H
ARMSTRONG, George
Dod H
ARMSTRONG, George
Dodd 1
ARMSTRONG,
George Simpson 4
ARMSTRONG,
George W. Jr. 4
ARMSTRONG,
George Washington H
ARMSTRONG,
George William Jr. 1
ARMSTRONG, H. C. 5
ARMSTRONG,
Hamilton Fish 5
ARMSTRONG,
Helen Maitland 2
ARMSTRONG,
Houston Churchwell 5
ARMSTRONG,
J. P. Taylor 4
ARMSTRONG, James H
ARMSTRONG, James 1
ARMSTRONG,
James Edward 5
ARMSTRONG,
James Reverdy 5
ARMSTRONG, Jesse
Evan 4
ARMSTRONG, John * H
ARMSTRONG, John
Irvine 1
ARMSTRONG, John
Nelson 2
ARMSTRONG,
Joseph Gillespie 3'rd 4
ARMSTRONG, Leroy 1
ARMSTRONG,
Lilian Harden 5
ARMSTRONG, Louis 5
ARMSTRONG, Lyndon
King 2
ARMSTRONG, Lyndon
King 4
ARMSTRONG,
Margaret Neilson 2
ARMSTRONG,
Maurice Whitman 5
ARMSTRONG,
Moses Kimball 3
ARMSTRONG, Paul 1
ARMSTRONG,
Paul Galloway 3
ARMSTRONG,
Philander Banister 4
ARMSTRONG, Richard
H. 3
ARMSTRONG, Robert H
ARMSTRONG,
Robert Allen 1
ARMSTRONG,
Robert Burns 2
ARMSTRONG,
Robert Hayden 5
ARMSTRONG,
Robert Helms 4

ARMSTRONG, Robert
John 3
ARMSTRONG,
Samuel Chapman H
ARMSTRONG,
Samuel Treat 2
ARMSTRONG,
Samuel Turell H
ARMSTRONG, Thomas
Jr. 1
ARMSTRONG,
Walter Preston 2
ARMSTRONG, William H
ARMSTRONG, William 2
ARMSTRONG, William
C. 1
ARMSTRONG,
William Gilbert 5
ARMSTRONG,
William Jackson 4
ARMSTRONG,
William Park 2
ARMSTRONG,
William Wright 1
ARMSTRONG-
HOPKINS, Geroge Franklin
ARMSTRONG-
HOPKINS, Saleni 4
ARN, Elmer Raymond 3
ARN, William Godfrey 5
ARNAL, Leon E. 4
ARNDT, C. O. 5
ARNDT,
Elmer Jacob Frederick
ARNDT, Karl M. 3
ARNDT,
Walter Tallmadge 1
ARNDT,
William Frederick 3
ARNEILL, James Rae 3
ARNESEN, Sigurd J. 4
ARNESON, Ben 3
ARNETT, Alex Mathews 2
ARNETT,
Benjamin William 1
ARNETT, Clare Newton 3
ARNETT, Trevor 3
ARNETTE, D. W. 4
ARNEY, C. E. Jr. 4
ARNN, Charles Edward 3
ARNO, Peter 4
ARNOLD, Abraham
Kerns H
ARNOLD, Alfred Colburn 4
ARNOLD, Alma Cusian 5
ARNOLD, Almon Al 5
ARNOLD, Arthur 4
ARNOLD, Arthur Z. 4
ARNOLD, Augusta Foote 1
ARNOLD, Aza H
ARNOLD, Ben 3
ARNOLD, Benedict * H
ARNOLD,
Benjamin William, Jr. 5
ARNOLD, Bion Joseph 1
ARNOLD, Bion Joseph 2
ARNOLD, Birch 5
ARNOLD, Carl Franklin 2
ARNOLD, Carl Raymond 4
ARNOLD,
Constantine Peter 5
ARNOLD, Conway
Hillyer 1
ARNOLD, Earl Caspar 3
ARNOLD,
Edmund Samuel Foster 1
ARNOLD, Edward 3
ARNOLD, Edwin Gustaf 4
ARNOLD,
Eliza Almy Peckham 4
ARNOLD, Ernst Hermann 1
ARNOLD, Felix 1
ARNOLD, Felix 5
ARNOLD,
Francis A(rthur, Jr. 5
ARNOLD, Francis Joseph 2
ARNOLD, Frank Atkinson 3
ARNOLD, Frank Russell 5
ARNOLD, George H
ARNOLD,
George Stanleigh 1
ARNOLD,
George Stanleigh 2
ARNOLD,
Harold DeForest 1
ARNOLD, Harry Wayne 4
ARNOLD, Hazen S. 2
ARNOLD, Henry H. 3
ARNOLD, Henry J. 3
ARNOLD, Horace David 2
ARNOLD, Howard
Payson H
ARNOLD, Isaac Newton H
ARNOLD, James E. 5
ARNOLD, James Loring 4
ARNOLD, James Newell 4
ARNOLD, John Jr. H

ARNOLD, John Anderson
ARNOLD, John Carlisle 3
ARNOLD, John Himes
ARNOLD, John Jacob
ARNOLD, Jonathan
ARNOLD, Joseph
Addison
ARNOLD,
Julean (Herbert)
ARNOLD,
Julian Biddulph
ARNOLD, Lauren Briggs
ARNOLD, Laurence F.
ARNOLD,
Lemuel Hastings
ARNOLD, Leslie Philip
ARNOLD, Lewis Golding
ARNOLD, Lloyd
ARNOLD, Lois J.
ARNOLD, Lynn John
ARNOLD, Maurice
ARNOLD, Morris Allen
ARNOLD, Newton
Darling
ARNOLD, Olney
ARNOLD, Oswald James
ARNOLD, Peleg
ARNOLD, Remmie Leroy
ARNOLD, Reuben Rose
ARNOLD, Richard
ARNOLD, Richard
ARNOLD, Richard Dennis
ARNOLD, Samuel
ARNOLD, Samuel Greene
ARNOLD,
Samuel Tomlinson
ARNOLD, Sarah Louise
ARNOLD, Thomas
Dickens
ARNOLD, Thomas
Jackson
ARNOLD, Thurman
Wesley
ARNOLD, W. F.
ARNOLD, Waldo Robert
ARNOLD, Walter P.
ARNOLD, William C.
ARNOLD,
William Hendrick
ARNOLD, William Joseph
ARNOLD,
William Richard
ARNOLD,
William Rosenzweig
ARNOLD, William Wright
ARNOLD, Winifred
ARNOLDSON,
Sigrid (Mme. Fischof)
ARNOTE, Walter James
ARNOUX, William Henry
ARNSTEIN, Albert
ARNSTEIN, Henry
ARNSTEIN, Margaret G.
ARNY, Henry Vinecome
ARON, Albert William
ARONOWITZ, Leon
ARONSON, Albert Y.
ARONSON, Jacob
ARONSON, Maurice
ARONSON, Robert Louis
ARONSON, Rudolph
ARONSTAM, Noah
Ephraim
AROSEMENA, Carlos C.
ARP, Jean
ARPS, George Frederick
ARRASMITH, John W.
ARREL, George F.
ARRICITIVA, Juan
ARRICK, Clifford
ARRIGHI,
Antonio Andrea
ARRINGTON, Alfred W.
ARRINGTON,
Archibald Hunter
ARRINGTON,
Kenneth Barton
ARRINGTON,
Richard Olney
ARROWOOD,
Charles Flinn
ARROWSMITH, Robert
ARROYO DEL RIO,
Carlos
ARSCOTT, A. E.
ARTER,
Charles Kingsley
ARTER, Frank Asbury
ARTERS, John Manley
ARTHUR, Alfred
ARTHUR,
Alfred Franklin
ARTHUR, Chester Alan
ARTHUR, Harold John
ARTHUR, James B.
Mckee
ARTHUR, Joseph Charles

814

ARTHUR, Julia 5
ARTHUR, Paul Harrison 4
ARTHUR, Peter M. 1
ARTHUR, Thomas 1
ARTHUR, Timothy Shay H
ARTHUR, W(illiam) C(athcart) 5
ARTHUR, William H
ARTHUR, William Evans H
ARTHUR, William Hemple 1
ARTHURS, Stanley M. 5
ARTIN, Emil 4
ARTOM, Camilio 5
ARTZYBASHEFF, Boris 4
ARUNDELL, Charles Rogers 5
ARVIN, Newton 4
ARVINE, Earlliss Porter 1
ARY, Henry H
ASAKAWA, Kwanlchi 2
ASBOTH, Alexander Sandor H
ASBURY, Francis H
ASBURY, Herbert H
ASCH, Morris Joseph H
ASCH, Nathan 4
ASCH, Sholem 3
ASCHAM, John Bayne 3
ASCHER, Hans Albert 4
ASCHWARZ, William Tefft 4
ASDALE, William James 5
ASELTINE, Walter Morley 5
ASH, Louis Russell 1
ASH, Nichael Woolston H
ASH, Percy 1
ASHBRIDGE, Samuel H. 3
ASHBROOK, Ernest Shepardson
ASHBROOK, M(ilan) Forest 5
ASHBROOK, William Albert 1
ASHBURN, Percy Moreau H
ASHBURN, Thomas Quinn 1
ASHBURNER, Charles Albert H
ASHBURTON, 1'st baron H
ASHBY, George Franklin 3
ASHBY, Samuel 1
ASHBY, Thomas Almond 4
ASHBY, Turner H
ASHCRAFT, Lee 3
ASHCRAFT, Leon Thomas 2
ASHE, Bowman Foster 3
ASHE, Edmund Marion 4
ASHE, Edward Joseph 5
ASHE, George B(amford) 5
ASHE, John H
ASHE, John Bapista * H
ASHE, Samuel H
ASHE, Samuel A'Court H
ASHE, Thomas Samuel H
ASHE, William Francis Jr. 4
ASHE, William Shepperd H
ASHFORD, Bailey Kelly 1
ASHFORD, Emma Louise 1
ASHFORD, Mahlon 3
ASHHURST, Astley Paston Cooper
ASHHURST, John 1
ASHHURST, John Jr. 1
ASHHURST, Richard Lewis
ASHLEY, Barnas Freeman 4
ASHLEY, Charles Sumner 1
ASHLEY, Chester H
ASHLEY, Clarence Degrand 1
ASHLEY, Clifford Warren 2
ASHLEY, Daniel W. 2
ASHLEY, Delos Rodeyn H
ASHLEY, Edward 3
ASHLEY, Frederick William
ASHLEY, George Hall 3
ASHLEY, Henry H
ASHLEY, James Mitchell 1
ASHLEY, John Pritchard 1
ASHLEY, Maurice C. 4
ASHLEY, Ossian D. 1
ASHLEY, Roscoe Lewis 4
ASHLEY, William Henry 1
ASHMEAD, Isaac H
ASHMEAD, William Harris 1
ASHMORE, John Durant H
ASHMORE, Otis 4
ASHMORE, Sidney Gillespie 1

ASHMORE, William H
ASHMORE, William 4
ASHMUN, Eli Porter H
ASHMUN, George 1
ASHMUN, George Coates 1
ASHMUN, Jehudi H
ASHMUN, Margaret Eliza 1
ASHTON, Eve 4
ASHTON, Henry Rusling 5
ASHTON, John H
ASHTON, John 4
ASHTON, John William 5
ASHTON, Joseph Hubley 1
ASHTON, William 1
ASHTON, William Easterly 1
ASHTON, Winifred 4
ASHURST, Henry Fountain 4
ASHWORTH, Hattie Tiller (Mrs. Eugene Marvin Ashworth)
ASHWORTH, John H. 2
ASHWORTH, Robert Archibald 3
ASHWORTH, Walter C. 4
ASKENSTEDT, Fritz Conrad 2
ASKEW, Sarah Byrd 2
ASKEW, Thyrza Simonton 3
ASKIN, Robert J. 1
ASKREN, William David 4
ASPEGREN, John 1
ASPER, Joel Funk H
ASPINALL, Joseph 1
ASPINALL, Clarence Aikin 4
ASPINWALL, Glenn William 5
ASPINWALL, J. Lawrence 4
ASPINWALL, Thomas 1
ASPINWALL, William Billings 3
ASPINWALL, William Henry H
ASPLUND, Rupert Franz 3
ASQUITH, Anthony 5
ASSMUTH, Joseph 2
ASTON, Anthony H
ASTON, James H
ASTON, Ralph 1
ASTON, Richard Douglas 1
ASTOR, John Jacob * H
ASTOR, John Jacob 1
ASTOR, Vincent 3
ASTOR, Viscountess 4
ASTOR, William Backhouse
ASTOR, William Waldorf 1
ASTOR OF HEVER, Baron (John Jacob Astor) 5
ASWELL, Edward C. 3
ASWELL, James Benjamin 1
ATCHESON, George Jr. 2
ATCHISON, David Rice H
ATCHISON, Thomas Cunningham 1
ATEN, Fred N. 3
ATHEARN, Fred Goodrich 3
ATHEARN, Walter Scott 1
ATHENAGORAS, His All Holiness 5
ATHERTON, Charles Gordon
ATHERTON, Charles Humphrey H
ATHERTON, Edwin Newton 2
ATHERTON, Frank Cooke 2
ATHERTON, George W. 1
ATHERTON, Gertrude Franklin 2
ATHERTON, Gibson H
ATHERTON, Henry Francis 2
ATHERTON, John C. 3
ATHERTON, Joseph Ballard 4
ATHERTON, Joshua H
ATHERTON, Louis M. 3
ATHERTON, Percy Lee 4
ATHERTON, Ray 3
ATKESON, Floyd Warnick 3
ATKESON, Thomas Clark 1
ATKESON, William Oscar 4
ATKIELSKI, Roman R. 5
ATKIN, Isaac Cubitt Raymond 3
ATKINS, Albert Henry 4
ATKINS, Arthur 4
ATKINS, Charles Duke 4
ATKINS, Edwin F. 1

ATKINS, George Tyng 2
ATKINS, George Washington Ely 4
ATKINS, Harry T. 1
ATKINS, Harry Thomas 5
ATKINS, Henry Hornby 5
ATKINS, James 1
ATKINS, Jearum H
ATKINS, John De Witt Clinton 1
ATKINS, Mrs. Louise Allen 3
ATKINS, Smith Dykins 1
ATKINS, Willard Earl 5
ATKINSON, Albert Algernon
ATKINSON, Archibald H
ATKINSON, Arthur Kimmins 4
ATKINSON, Benjamin Searcy 3
ATKINSON, Charles Edwin 4
ATKINSON, Charles R. 5
ATKINSON, Christoper Joseph 1
ATKINSON, Donald Taylor 3
ATKINSON, Edward 1
ATKINSON, Eleanor 2
ATKINSON, Fred Washington 4
ATKINSON, Geoffrey 4
ATKINSON, George Francis 1
ATKINSON, George Henry H
ATKINSON, George Wesley 1
ATKINSON, Guy F. 5
ATKINSON; Harry Hunt 5
ATKINSON, Henry H
ATKINSON, Henry Avery 3
ATKINSON, Henry Morrell 1
ATKINSON, Herbert Spencer 3
ATKINSON, Herschel C. 4
ATKINSON, Isaac Edmondson 1
ATKINSON, J. Robert 4
ATKINSON, John H
ATKINSON, John Bradshaw 4
ATKINSON, Joseph Story 5
ATKINSON, Louis Evans 1
ATKINSON, Ralph 2
ATKINSON, Ralph Waldo 4
ATKINSON, Samuel C. 2
ATKINSON, Thomas H
ATKINSON, Thomas Edgar 4
ATKINSON, Thomas Wilson 1
ATKINSON, William Biddle 4
ATKINSON, William Brockliss 4
ATKINSON, William E. 1
ATKINSON, William Elrie 1
ATKINSON, William Sackston 1
ATKINSON, William Walker 1
ATKINSON, William Yates H
ATKINSON, William Yates 1
ATKINSON, William Yates 3
ATKINSON, Wilmer 1
ATLASS, H. Leslie 4
ATLEE, John Light H
ATLEE, John Light 3
ATLEE, Samuel John H
ATLEE, Washington Lemuel H
ATTEBERY, Olin Moody 3
ATTERBURY, Anson Phelps 1
ATTERBURY, Grosvenor 3
ATTERBURY, William Wallace 1
ATTERIDGE, Harold Richard
ATTERIDGE, Harold Richard 2
ATTLEE, Earl 4
ATTRIDGE, Richard 1
ATTUCKS, Crispus H
ATTWILL, Henry Converse 1
ATTWOOD, Frederic 5
ATTWOOD, Stephen S. 4
ATWATER, Caleb H
ATWATER, David Hay 2

ATWATER, Edward Perrin 5
ATWATER, Francis 1
ATWATER, George Parkin 1
ATWATER, Helen Woodard 2
ATWATER, Henry G. 3
ATWATER, John Wilbur 5
ATWATER, Lyman Hotchkiss H
ATWATER, Mary Meigs 3
ATWATER, Reginald Myers 3
ATWATER, Richard Mead 1
ATWATER, Wilbur Olin 1
ATWATER, William Cutler 1
ATWELL, Charles Beach 1
ATWELL, William Hawley 4
ATWILL, Douglass Henry 4
ATWILL, Edward Robert 1
ATWILL, Lionel 2
ATWILL, William 1
ATWOOD, Arthur R. 3
ATWOOD, Charles B. H
ATWOOD, Charles Edwin 1
ATWOOD, David H
ATWOOD, Edward Leland 5
ATWOOD, Edwin Byron 5
ATWOOD, Elmer Bugg 3
ATWOOD, Frank Ely 2
ATWOOD, George Edward 4
ATWOOD, Harrison 3
ATWOOD, Harry 1
ATWOOD, Henry 3
ATWOOD, Hinckley Gardner 2
ATWOOD, Isaac Morgan 1
ATWOOD, James Arthur 2
ATWOOD, Jesse H
ATWOOD, John Harrison 1
ATWOOD, John Murray 3
ATWOOD, Julius Walter 1
ATWOOD, Lemuel True 1
ATWOOD, Millard V. 1
ATWOOD, Millard V. 2
ATWOOD, Oscar 1
ATWOOD, Roy Franklin 4
ATWOOD, Wallace Walter 2
AUBERT, Lloyd Lees 5
AUBREY, Edwin Ewart 3
AUBREY, Henry George 5
AUBREY, James Thomas 4
AUBREY, John Edmond 5
AUBREY, William 1
AUCH, John F. 4
AUCHINCLOSS, Charles C. 4
AUCHINCLOSS, Gordon 2
AUCHINCLOSS, John Winthrop 1
AUCHINCLOSS, William Stuart 1
AUCHMUTY, Richard Tylden H
AUCHMUTY, Robert * H
AUCHMUTY, Samuel H
AUCHTER, Eugene Curtis 3
AUCOCK, Arthur Morgan 5
AUD, Guy 4
AUDRIETH, Ludwig Frederick
AUDSLEY, George Ashdown 4
AUDUBON, John James H
AUDUBON, John Woodhouse H
AUDUBON, Victor Gifford H
AUER, John 2
AUER, Joseph Lawrence 1
AUER, Leopold 1
AUERBACH, Beatrice Fox 5
AUERBACH, Erich 3
AUERBACH, Frank Ludwig 4
AUERBACH, Herbert S. 2
AUERBACH, Joseph S. 2
AUERBACH-LEVY, William 4
AUF DER HEIDE, Oscar Louis 1
AUGENSTEIN, Leroy George
AUGER, Charles L. 1
AUGHINBAUGH, William Edmund
AUGSPURGER, Owen Beal 5
AUGUR, Christopher Columbus
AUGUR, Hezekiah H

AUGUR, Jacob Arnold 1
AUGUST, Harry Wirt 5
AUGUSTINE, Harry Hamill 4
AUGUSTINE, William Franklin 2
AUGUSTUS, Ellsworth Hunt 4
AUGUSTUS, John H
AUGUSTYN, Godfrey William 2
AULD, George P. 4
AULD, John Maxwell 4
AULT, Bromwell 5
AULT, James Percy 1
AULT, Nelson Allen 4
AULT, Otto Thurman 3
AULTMAN, Dwight Edward 1
AUMAN, Orrin W. 3
AUMAN, Russell Frank 5
AUMAN, William 1
AURAND, Samuel Herbert 4
AURELL, Alvin Karl 4
AURELL, George Emanuel 5
AURINGER, Obadiah Cyrus 1
AURIOL, Vincent 4
AUSTELL, Alfred H
AUSTEN, Benjamin H
AUSTEN, Peter Townsend 1
AUSTIN, Albert E. 1
AUSTIN, Albert E. 2
AUSTIN, Archibald H
AUSTIN, Benjamin Fish 4
AUSTIN, Calvin 1
AUSTIN, Clyde Bernard 4
AUSTIN, Cyrus Brooks 1
AUSTIN, David H
AUSTIN, Dwight Bertram 3
AUSTIN, Ennis Raymond 4
AUSTIN, Eugene Munger 4
AUSTIN, Francis Marion 1
AUSTIN, Fred Thaddeus 1
AUSTIN, Frederick Carleton 1
AUSTIN, George Curtis 4
AUSTIN, Henry H
AUSTIN, Henry 4
AUSTIN, Herbert Douglas 5
AUSTIN, Howard 4
AUSTIN, Howard Albert, Jr. 5
AUSTIN, Isabella McHugh 1
AUSTIN, James Harold 3
AUSTIN, James Trecothick H
AUSTIN, Jane Goodwin H
AUSTIN, John Corneby Wilson 5
AUSTIN, John Langshaw 4
AUSTIN, John Osborne 1
AUSTIN, John Turnell 5
AUSTIN, Jonathan Loring H
AUSTIN, Leonard S. 1
AUSTIN, Lloyd Lewis 5
AUSTIN, Louis Winslow 1
AUSTIN, Mary 1
AUSTIN, Moses H
AUSTIN, Oscar Phelps 1
AUSTIN, Richard Loper 2
AUSTIN, Richard Wilson 1
AUSTIN, Samuel H
AUSTIN, Samuel Yates 5
AUSTIN, Stephen Fuller H
AUSTIN, Warren Robinson 4
AUSTIN, Wilbert John 1
AUSTIN, William H
AUSTIN, William Lacy 3
AUSTIN, William Lane 2
AUSTIN, William Liseter 1
AUSTIN-BALL, Thomas 5
AUSTRIAN, Alfred S. 1
AUSTRIAN, Carl Joseph 5
AUSTRIAN, Charles Robert 3
AUTEN, James Ernest 2
AUTHIER, George Francis 5
AVANCENA, Ramon 5
AVELLANUS, Arcadius 3
AVENT, Joseph Emory 3
AVERELL, William Woods H
AVERETT, Thomas Hamlet H
AVERILL, George G. 3
AVERILL, Glenn Mark 5
AVERILL, John H. 5
AVERILL, John Thomas H

AVERITT, George Alfred 5
AVERS, Henry Godfrey 2
AVERY, 4
  Alphonso Calhoun
AVERY, Benjamin Parke
AVERY, 1
  Catherine Hitchcock Tilden
AVERY, 3
  Christopher Lester
AVERY, 2
  Clarence Willard
AVERY, Coleman 1
AVERY, Cyrus Stevens 5
AVERY, Daniel H
AVERY, Delos 4
AVERY, Elroy McKendree 1
AVERY, George C.
AVERY, George True 2
AVERY, Henry Ogden 1
AVERY, Isaac Wheeler H
AVERY, Isaac Wheeler 1
AVERY, John * H
AVERY, John 1
AVERY, John 4
AVERY, Johnston 5
AVERY, Milton 1
AVERY, Moses Nathan 2
AVERY, Nathan Prentice 1
AVERY, Oswald Theodore 3
AVERY, Rachel Foster 1
AVERY, Robert 1
AVERY, Samuel 1
AVERY, Samuel Putnam 1
AVERY, Sewell Lee 4
AVERY, Susan Look 1
AVERY, Thomas Burt 4
AVERY, H
  William Tecumsah
AVERY, H
  William Waightstill
AVES, Dreda 2
AVES, Henry Damerel 1
AVILDSEN, Clarence 4
AVINOFF, Andrew 2
AVIS, John Boyd 1
AVIS, Samuel Brashear 1
AVITABILE, Salvatore 3
AVNET, Lester Francis 5
AVNSOE, Thorkild 3
AWL, William Maclay H
AXE, Emerson Wirt 4
AXE, Ruth Houghton 4
AXEL, Hans H
AXELROD, Haim Izchak 5
AXELSON, 5
  Charles Frederic
AXLINE, George Andrew 1
AXSON, Stockton 1
AXTELL, Decatur 1
  Rodarmel
AXTELL, Edwin 1
AXTELL, 4
  Frances Cleveland
AXTELL, Harold Lucius 3
AXTELL, John Thomas 1
AXTELL, Samuel Beach H
AXTON, John Thomas 1
AYALA, Juan Manuel 'de 5
AYARS, 5
  George W(ashington)
AYCOCK, 1
  Charles Brantley
AYCRIGG, John Bancker H
AYDELOTT, James 4
  Howard
AYDELOTTE, Dora 5
AYDELOTTE, Frank 3
AYDLETT, Edwin
  Ferebee
AYER, Benjamin F. 1
AYER, Charles Fanning 3
AYER, 5
  Charles Frederick
AYER, Clarence Walter 1
AYER, Edward Everett 1
AYER, F. Wayland 1
AYER, Franklin Deming 1
AYER, Frederic Eugene 5
AYER, Frederick 1
AYER, 1
  Frederick Fanning
AYER, Harriet Hubbard 1
AYER, James Bourne 4
AYER, James Cook H
AYER, John 4
AYER, Joseph Cullen 2
AYER, Richard Small H
AYER, Winslow B. 4
AYERS, Allan Farrell 4
AYERS, Clarence Edwin 5
AYERS, Edward Everett 4
AYERS, Fred Wesley 4
AYERS, Harry Mell 4
AYERS, Howard 1
AYERS, Lemuel 3
AYERS, Roy E. 5
AYERS, Rufus Adolphus 4

AYETA, Francisco 'de H
AYLER, Albert 5
AYLESWORTH, 1
  Barton Orville
AYLESWORTH, 3
  Merlin Hall
AYLING, 5
  Charles Lincoln
AYLLON, H
  Lucas Vasquez De
AYLSWORTH, Leon 5
  Emmons
AYLSWORTH, 4
  Nicholas John
AYLSWORTH, 1
  William Prince
AYLWIN, John Cushing H
AYME, Louis Henri 1
AYME, Marcel 4
AYNESWORTH, 2
  Kenneth Hazen
AYRES, Albert Douglass 2
AYRES, Anne H
AYRES, Atlee Bernard 5
AYRES, Brown 1
AYRES, Burt Wilmot 1
AYRES, Edward 1
AYRES, Eugene Edmond 1
AYRES, Frank C. 3
AYRES, Franklin Herman 4
AYRES, George Frederic 1
AYRES, Harry Morgan 2
AYRES, Joseph Gerrish 1
AYRES, Leonard Porter 2
AYRES, Louis 1
AYRES, Milan Church 1
AYRES, Milan Valentine 5
AYRES, Philip Wheelock 5
AYRES, Quincy Claude 4
AYRES, Romeyn Beck H
AYRES, Samuel Gardiner 2
AYRES, 1
  Samuel Loring Percival
AYRES, Stephen Cooper 2
AYRES, Steven Beckwith 1
AYRES, Thomas A. H
AYRES, 3
  William Augustus
AZAD, 3
  Abul Kalam Maulana
AZARIAS, Brother H
AZCARATE Y 5
  FLOREZ, Pablo de
AZEVEDO, Philadelpho 3
AZUELA, Mariano 5
AZUOLA, Eduardo 3

B

BAAB, Otto J. 3
BAADE, Walter 4
BAAR, Arnold R. 3
BABASINIAN, V. S. 1
BABB, Clement Edwin 1
BABB, Cyrus Cates 1
BABB, James Elisha 1
BABB, James T(inkham) 5
BABB, Max Wellington 2
BABB, 1
  Washington Irving
BABBITT, H
  Benjamin Talbot
BABBITT, Charles James 4
BABBITT, Edwin Burr 4
BABBITT, Edwin Dwight 4
BABBITT, Elijah H
BABBITT, Eugene Howard 4
BABBITT, Frank Cole 4
BABBITT, 4
  George Franklin
BABBITT, Irving H
BABBITT, Isaac H
BABBITT, Juliette M. 3
BABBITT, Kurnal R. 1
BABBITT, 1
  Lawrence Sprague
BABBOTT, Frank Lusk 1
BABBS, Arthur Vergil 4
BABCOCK, Albert 4
BABCOCK, Alfred H
BABCOCK, Allen 5
BABCOCK, Bernie 5
BABCOCK, Birton E. 5
BABCOCK, Charles 1
BABCOCK, Charles Henry 5
BABCOCK, Charles Henry 1
BABCOCK, Charles Henry 4
BABCOCK, 1
  Earle Brownell
BABCOCK, Earle Jay 1
BABCOCK, Edward Vose 2
BABCOCK, Ernest Brown 3
BABCOCK, George H
  Herman
BABCOCK, Harold Delos 5
BABCOCK, Harriet 3
BABCOCK, Harry Allan 4

BABCOCK, Havilah 4
BABCOCK, Howard 1
  Edward 3
BABCOCK, Irving Brown 4
BABCOCK, James Francis H
BABCOCK, James Woods 1
BABCOCK, 1
  John Breckinridge
BABCOCK, John Pease 4
BABCOCK, Joseph Weeks 1
BABCOCK, 5
  Kendric Charles
BABCOCK, Leander H
BABCOCK, Louis Locke 5
BABCOCK, H
  Maltbie Davenport
BABCOCK, Orville Elias H
BABCOCK, Richard Earle 3
BABCOCK, Robert Hall 1
BABCOCK, Robert 4
  Weston
BABCOCK, 1
  Samuel Denison
BABCOCK, Samuel Gavitt 2
BABCOCK, 1
  Stephen Moulton
BABCOCK, 2
  Warren La Verne
BABCOCK, 1
  Washington Irving
BABCOCK, William H
BABCOCK, William 1
  Henry
BABCOCK, 4
  William Waterman
BABCOCK, William 5
  Wayne
BABER, George W. 5
BABER, Ray Erwin 4
BABIN, Hosea John 4
BABIN, Victor 5
BABLER, Jacob L. 2
BABSON, Herman 1
BABSON, Paul Talbot 5
BABSON, Roger Ward 4
BABST, Earl D. 1
BACCALONI, Salvatore 5
BACH, Oscar Bruno 5
BACH, Ralph Edward 5
BACH, Richard F. 4
BACH, Thomas Cumming 5
BACHARACH, 5
  Eric William
BACHARACH, Isaac 3
BACHE, H
  Alexander Dallas
BACHE, H
  Benjamin Franklin
BACHE, Dallas 1
BACHE, Franklin H
BACHE, Harold L. 5
BACHE, Jules Semon 2
BACHE, Leopold Semon 1
BACHE, Louise Franklin 2
BACHE, Rene 4
BACHE, Richard 1
BACHE, Theophylact 1
BACHE, William H
BACHELDER, John H
  Badger
BACHELDER, 1
  Nahum Josiah
BACHELLER, 2
  Irving Addison
BACHELLER, 1
  Joseph Henry
BACHEM, Albert 3
BACHER, Otto Henry 3
BACHKE, 3
  Halvard Huitfeldt
BACHMAN, 4
  Absalom Pierre
BACHMAN, 5
  Allan Earnshaw
BACHMAN, 5
  Frank Puterbaugh
BACHMAN, John H
BACHMAN, 1
  Jonathan Waverly
BACHMAN, Nathan 1
BACHMAN, Nathan Lynn 1
BACHMAN, Paul Stanton 3
BACHMAN, 5
  Robert Abraham
BACHMANN, Raphael 5
  Otto
BACHMANN, 3
  Werner Emmanuel
BACHMEYER, 3
  Arthur Charles
BACHRACH, Louis 4
  Fabian
BACHRACH, 4
  Walter Keyser
BACIGALUPI, 1
  James Augustus
BACIGALUPI, Tadini 4

BACK, George Irving 5
BACKES, John H. 1
BACKHAUS, Wilhelm 5
BACKMAN, Kenneth B. 4
BACKSTRAND, 5
  Clifford J.
BACKUS, August Charles 3
BACKUS, Azel H
BACKUS, 1
  Edward Wellington
BACKUS, Edwin Burdette 3
BACKUS, Isaac H
BACKUS, 1
  Manson Franklin
BACKUS, Samuel Woolsey 4
BACKUS, Standish 1
BACKUS, Truman Jay 1
BACKUS, Wilson Marvin 2
BACOATS, J. Alvin 4
BACON, 1
  Albert Williamson
BACON, 1
  Albion Fellows
BACON, 1
  Alexander Samuel
BACON, Alice Mabel 1
BACON, 1
  Augustus Octavius
BACON, Benjamin Wisner 1
BACON, Charles Sumner 1
BACON, Clara Latimer 2
BACON, David H
BACON, David William 4
BACON, Delia Salter H
BACON, Edgar Mayhew 1
BACON, Edward 1
  Payson
BACON, Edward 1
  Rathbone
BACON, Edwin Munroe 1
BACON, Edwin Munroe 1
BACON, Ezekiel H
BACON, Francis 1
BACON, Francis Leonard 3
BACON, Francis R. 4
BACON, Frank 1
BACON, Frank Rogers 2
BACON, Gaspar Griswold 1
BACON, George Andrew 1
BACON, George Morgan 1
BACON, George P. 1
BACON, George Wood 3
BACON, Henry 1
BACON, John H
BACON, John Harwood 5
BACON, John Mosby 1
BACON, John Watson 1
BACON, 5
  Josephine Dodge Daskam
BACON, Leonard H
BACON, Leonard 3
BACON, Leonard Woolsey 1
BACON, 5
  Mary Schell Hoke
  ("Dolores Marbourg")
BACON, Nathaniel H
BACON, Raymond Foss 4
BACON, Robert 1
BACON, Robert Low 1
BACON, 5
  Robert Stillwell
BACON, Selden 2
BACON, Thomas H
BACON, Walter W. 1
BACON, William Johnson H
BACON, William Stevens 3
BADAWI PASHA, 4
  Abdel Hamid
BADE, William Frederic 1
BADEAU, Adam H
BADENBERGER, Henry 2
BADER, Jesse Moren 4
BADER, Ralph Hedrick 1
BADGER, 1
  Charles Johnston
BADGER, Dewitt Clinton 1
BADGER, George H
  Edmund
BADGER, George Henry 4
BADGER, Joseph * H
BADGER, Luther H
BADGER, Oscar Charles 1
BADGER, Oscar Charles 3
BADGER, Philip Owen 5
BADGER, Walter Irving 1
BADGER, Walter Lucius 3
BADGLEY, 5
  Maxwell Forrest
BADGLEY, Sidney Rose 1
BADIN, H
  Stephen Theodore
BADING, Gerhard Adolph 2
BADLEY, 1
  Brenton Thoburn
BADT, Milton B. 4
BAEHR, Carl Adolph 4
BAEHR, Max Joseph 2
BAEHR, William Alfred 2

BAEHR, 5
  William Frederick Otto
BAEKELAND, Celine 4
BAEKELAND, George 4
BAEKELAND, Leo 2
  Hendrik
BAENSCH, Emil 3
BAENSCH, Willy E. 5
BAEPLER, Walter A. 3
BAER, George Jr.
BAER, George Frederick 1
BAER, John M(iller) 1
BAER, John Willis 1
BAER, Joseph Louis 3
BAER, Libbie C. 4
BAER, Sidney R. 3
BAER, William Bush 3
BAER, William Jacob 1
BAERWALD, Paul 4
BAETJER, Edwin G. 2
BAETJER, 1
  Frederick Henry
BAEZ, Cecilio 4
BAEZA, Marco A. 4
BAGAR, Robert 3
BAGBY, Albert Morris 2
BAGBY, H
  Arthur Pendleton
BAGBY, George Franklin 4
BAGBY, 1
  George Poindexter
BAGBY, George William H
BAGBY, John Courts 1
BAGBY, 1
  John Hampden
  Chamberlayne
BAGBY, William Buck 4
BAGDATOPOULOS, 5
  William Spencer
BAGG, Lyman Hotchkiss 1
BAGG, Rufus Mather 1
BAGGER, Henry
  Horneman
BAGGETT, Samuel
  Graves
BAGGS, Arthur Eugene 2
BAGGS, Mae Lacy 1
BAGGS, William Calhoun 5
BAGLEY, Charles Leland 5
BAGLEY, Clarence Booth 1
BAGLEY, David Worth 4
BAGLEY, 2
  William Chandler
BAGLEY,
  Willis Gaylord Clark
BAGNELL, Robert 3
BAGOT, Sir Charles H
BAGSTAD, Anna Emilia 5
BAGSTER- 5
  COLLINS, Elijah William
BAHL, William Edgar 3
BAHN, Chester Bert 4
BAHNSON, Agnew
  Hunter
BAHR, Emory J. 4
BAHRENBURG,
  Louis P. H.
BAIER, Victor
BAILEY, Albert Edward 1
BAILEY, H
  Alexander Hamilton
BAILEY, Alfred Halsey 3
BAILEY, Alice Ward 4
BAILEY, Ann
BAILEY, Anna Warner H
BAILEY, Arthur Low 1
BAILEY, Arthur Scott 5
BAILEY, 2
  Benjamin Franklin
BAILEY, Bert Heald 1
BAILEY, Bertha 1
BAILEY, Calvin Weston 5
BAILEY, Carl Edward 2
BAILEY, Cassius Mercer 1
BAILEY,
  Charles Franklin
BAILEY, Charles Justin 2
BAILEY, 5
  Charles Langdon
BAILEY, Charles Olin 1
BAILEY, Charles Reuben 1
BAILEY, 4
  Charles William
BAILEY,
  Clarence Mitchell
BAILEY, David Jackson H
BAILEY, E. Stillman 1
BAILEY, Ebenezer H
BAILEY,
  Edgar Henry Summerfield
BAILEY, Edward
BAILEY, Edward Monroe 2
BAILEY, 1
  Elijah Prentiss
BAILEY, 1
  Everett Hoskins

ILEY, 2
lorence Augusta Merriam
ILEY, Francis H
ILEY, Frank 3
ILEY, Frank Harvey 4
ILEY, Frank Moye 4
ILEY, Fred Oliver 1
ILEY, 1
Frederick Randolph
ILEY, Gamaliel H
ILEY, George Davis 4
ILEY, 1
George Washington
ILEY, George Wicks 1
ILEY, Gilbert Ellis H
ILEY, Goldsmith Fox 1
ILEY, Guy Winfred 4
ILEY, 1
Hannah Johnston
ILEY, Harry Louis 4
ILEY, Henry Turner 1
ILEY, Hollis Russell 1
ILEY, Irving Widmer 4
ILEY, Ivon Arthur 4
ILEY, Jacob H
ILEY, Jacob Whitman H
ILEY, James Anthony 1
ILEY, James Edmund 1
ILEY, James Garfield 1
ILEY, H
James Montgomery
ILEY, Jennings 4
ILEY, Jeremiah H
ILEY, John H
ILEY, John Hays 5
ILEY, John Mosher 1
ILEY, John Ora 3
ILEY, John Wendell 4
ILEY, Joseph * H
ILEY, Joseph T. H
ILEY, Joseph Weldon 1
ILEY, 2
Joseph Weldon Jr.
ILEY, Josiah William 2
ILEY, Leonard Henry 4
ILEY, Liberty Hyde 3
ILEY, Loring Woart 1
ILEY, Louis Jonathan 4
ILEY, Lydia R. 3
ILEY, 3
Margaret Emerson
ILEY, Mark Jr. 4
ILEY, Mercer Silas 1
ILEY, Mervyn J. 3
ILEY, Milus Kendrick 4
ILEY, Morton 3
ILEY, Morton Shelley 1
ILEY, Pearce 4
ILEY, Ralph Edward 4
ILEY, Ray W. 3
ILEY, Rufus William H
ILEY, Solon Irving 1
ILEY, Steele 4
ILEY, Temple 1
ILEY, Theodore Mead 3
ILEY, Theodorus * H
ILEY, Thomas L. 2
ILEY, Thomas Pearce 2
ILEY, Vernon 2
ILEY, Vernon Howe 1
ILEY, Warren Worth 1
ILEY, William Arthur 3
ILEY, William Bacon 3
ILEY, 1
William Whitman
ILEY, 4
William Whitman
ILEY, Willis J. 1
ILHACHE, H
Preston Heath
ILIE, Earle 1
ILIE, Virginia 1
ILIE, William 4
ILIE, William Lamdin 1
ILLARGEON, Cebert 4
ILLIE, Archie Fraser 3
ILLIE, Hugh 4
ILLIE, John 4
ILLOT, Edouard Paul 4
ILLY, Joseph Alexis H
ILLY- 1
BLANCHARD, Arthur
ILOR, Edwin Maurice 5
ILY, Alfred William 4
ILY, Elisha Ingram 1
ILY, Harold James 1
ILY, Joshua L. 1
IN, Charles Wesley 1
IN, Edgar Collins 5
IN, Ferdinand R. 2
IN, Fred B. 5
IN, George Grantham 4
IN, H
George Luke Scobie
IN, 1
George Washington
IN, Harry Foster 2

BAIN, 1
Robert Edward Mather
BAINBRIDGE, 1
Alexander Gilbert
BAINBRIDGE, 1
Lucy Seaman
BAINBRIDGE, William H
BAINBRIDGE, 2
William Seaman
BAINES, 5
Edward Richards
BAINES-MILLER, 5
Minnie Willis
BAINTER, Fay Okell 5
BAIRD, Absalom 1
BAIRD, Andrew D. 1
BAIRD, Andrew McClung 4
BAIRD, Bruce 1
BAIRD, Cameron 4
BAIRD, H
Charles Washington
BAIRD, Cora 5
BAIRD, David 1
BAIRD, David Jr. 3
BAIRD, Frank Burkett 1
BAIRD, 1
George Washington
BAIRD, George William 1
BAIRD, Henry Carey 1
BAIRD, Henry Martyn 1
BAIRD, Henry W. 4
BAIRD, James 1
BAIRD, Jean Katherine 1
BAIRD, John L. 4
BAIRD, John Wallace 1
BAIRD, Joseph Edward 2
BAIRD, Julian William 1
BAIRD, Louise 5
BAIRD, Lucius Olmsted 1
BAIRD, Matthew H
BAIRD, Phil C. 1
BAIRD, Raleigh William 1
BAIRD, Richard F. 3
BAIRD, Robert H
BAIRD, Robert W. 5
BAIRD, Samuel John 1
BAIRD, H
Spencer Fullerton
BAIRD, Thomas H. 1
BAIRD, William Jesse 3
BAIRD, William Raimond 1
BAITER, Richard Englis 5
BAITS, Vera Burridge 4
BAITY, George Perry 4
BAITY, James L. 5
BAJPAI, 1
Sir Girja Shankar
BAKENHUS, Reuben 4
Edwin
BAKER, A. George 4
BAKER, H
Abijah Richardson
BAKER, Albert 2
BAKER, Albert C. 1
BAKER, Albert Rufus 1
BAKER, Alfred Brittin 1
BAKER, Alfred Landon 1
BAKER, 5
Alfred Zantzinger
BAKER, Alton Fletcher 4
BAKER, 1
Archibald Eachern
BAKER, 3
Arthur Josiah Mountford
BAKER, Arthur Latham 1
BAKER, Arthur Mulford 1
BAKER, Asa George 1
BAKER, Asher Carter 1
BAKER, Benedict J. 2
BAKER, 1
Benjamin Franklin
BAKER, Benjamin Webb 1
BAKER, Bernard Nadal 4
BAKER, Bertha Kunz 5
BAKER, Bertha Kunz 2
BAKER, Bryant 1
BAKER, Caleb H
BAKER, Charles Fuller 1
BAKER, Charles Henry H
BAKER, 1
Charles Hinckley
BAKER, Charles Samuel 4
BAKER, Charles Whiting 1
BAKER, Charles William 4
BAKER, Chauncey Brooke 1
BAKER, Claude Milem 4
BAKER, Cora Warman 5
BAKER, Cornelia 1
BAKER, Crosby Fred 3
BAKER, Daniel 1
BAKER, Darius 1
BAKER, David 4
BAKER, David Dudrow 3
BAKER, David Floyd 1
BAKER, David Jewett H
BAKER, Dorothy 5
BAKER, Earl Dewey 5

BAKER, Earle A. 3
BAKER, Edgar Robey 5
BAKER, Edna Dean 3
BAKER, H
Edward Dickinson
BAKER, Edwin George 4
BAKER, Elbert H. 1
BAKER, 5
Elizabeth Bradford
Faulkner
BAKER, Elizabeth Gowdy 1
BAKER, Ellis Crain 2
BAKER, 5
Emilie (Addoms) Kip (Mrs.
Franklin Thomas Baker)
BAKER, Everett Moore 3
BAKER, Ezra H
BAKER, Ezra Flavius 5
BAKER, Ezra Henry 1
BAKER, Francis Asbury 1
BAKER, Francis Elisha 1
BAKER, Frank * 1
BAKER, Frank Collins 2
BAKER, Frank E. 5
BAKER, Frank Kline 1
BAKER, Frank S. 4
BAKER, Franklin, Jr. 5
BAKER, Franklin Thomas 1
BAKER, Frederick Cecil 1
BAKER, 4
Frederick Storrs
BAKER, 5
Frederick Van Vliet
BAKER, George Augustus H
BAKER, George Augustus 4
BAKER, George Barr 1
BAKER, George Bramwell 2
BAKER, 1
George Danielson
BAKER, George Fisher * 1
BAKER, George Hall 1
BAKER, George Holbrook H
BAKER, George Holbrook 4
BAKER, George L. 4
BAKER, George Pierce 1
BAKER, George Randolph 1
BAKER, George Randolph 2
BAKER, George Theodore 4
BAKER, George Titus 1
BAKER, 4
Gordon Harrington
BAKER, Harold Bruss 1
BAKER, Harold Griffith 3
BAKER, H
Harriette Newell Woods
BAKER, Harry B. 3
BAKER, Harvey Almy 3
BAKER, 1
Harvey Humphrey
BAKER, Henry Dunster 1
BAKER, Henry Moore 1
BAKER, Henry Moore 4
BAKER, Herbert 1
BAKER, Herbert Abram 1
BAKER, Hollis 4
BAKER, 3
Holmes Davenport
BAKER, Horace 5
BAKER, Horace Forbes 1
BAKER, Howard H. 4
BAKER, Hugh Benton 4
BAKER, Hugh Potter 3
BAKER, Ira Osborn 1
BAKER, Isaac Post 1
BAKER, J. Thompson 1
BAKER, James H
BAKER, James Addison 1
BAKER, James Barnes 1
BAKER, James Heaton 1
BAKER, James Hutchins 1
BAKER, James Marion 1
BAKER, James Norment 2
BAKER, Jehu 1
BAKER, John H
BAKER, John Daniel 1
BAKER, John Earl 3
BAKER, John Harris 1
BAKER, John Stewart 4
BAKER, Joseph Dill 1
BAKER, 1
Joseph Richardson
BAKER, Josephine Turck 2
BAKER, Julia Wetherill 1
BAKER, Karle Wilson 1
BAKER, H
La Fayette Curry
BAKER, Lawrence Simons 1
BAKER, 3
Leonard Theodore
BAKER, Lewis H
BAKER, Lucien 1
BAKER, Lucius K. 1
BAKER, Marcus 1
BAKER, 5
Marjorie Montgomery Ward
BAKER, Martha Susan 1
BAKER, Mary Francis 5

BAKER, Moses Nelson 4
BAKER, Murray M. 5
BAKER, Murray M. 4
BAKER, Naaman Rimmon 4
BAKER, Newman Freese 1
BAKER, Newton Diehl 1
BAKER, Oliver Edwin 2
BAKER, 1
Orlando Harrison
BAKER, Osmon Cleander H
BAKER, Osmyn H
BAKER, Page M. 1
BAKER, Peter Carpenter 1
BAKER, Phil 4
BAKER, Purley A. 1
BAKER, Ralph Jackson 4
BAKER, Ray Stannard 2
BAKER, Raymond T. 1
BAKER, Remember H
BAKER, Robert 1
BAKER, Robert Homes 1
BAKER, Roland Morris 1
BAKER, Roy Newsom 5
BAKER, S. Josephine 2
BAKER, Sam A. 1
BAKER, 1
Sarah Schoonmaker
BAKER, Simon Strousse 1
BAKER, Smith 1
BAKER, Stephen H
BAKER, Stephen 2
BAKER, Tarkington 1
BAKER, 1
Thomas Rakestraw
BAKER, Thomas
Stockham 1
BAKER, Virginia 1
BAKER, W. Browne 5
BAKER, Walter Cummings 1
BAKER, Walter Hudson 2
BAKER, 4
Walter Ransom Gail
BAKER, William B. 1
BAKER, 4
William Clyde Jr.
BAKER, William Edgar 1
BAKER, 2
William Gideon Jr.
BAKER, William Henry 1
BAKER, William Jesse 3
BAKER, William L. 1
BAKER, William Mumford H
BAKER, William Pimm 1
BAKER, William Taylor 1
BAKER, William W. 4
BAKETEL, H. Sheridan 1
BAKETEL, 1
Oliver Sherman
BAKEWELL, 3
Charles Montague
BAKEWELL, 3
Donald Campbell
BAKEWELL, Paul 4
BAKHMETEFF, 3
Boris Alexander
BAKHMETEFF, George 1
BAKHSHI, 5
Chulam Mohammad
BAKKE, E. Wight 5
BAKKEN, Clarence John 5
BAKKEN, Herman Ernst 4
BAKKUM, Glenn A(lmer) 4
BAKLANOFF, Georges 1
BAKST, Henry Jacob 5
BALABAN, 1
Abraham Joseph
BALABAN, Barney 5
BALABAN, Emanuel 5
BALABAN, John 3
BALATKA, Hans H
BALBACH, Edward 4
BALBOA, H
Vasco Nunez 'de
BALCH, 1
Allan Christopher
BALCH, Edwin Swift 1
BALCH, Emily Greene 4
BALCH, Ernest Berkeley 1
BALCH, Franklin Greene 3
BALCH, George Beall 1
BALCH, Thomas Willing 5
BALCH, William Monroe 2
BALCOM, Max Fenton 4
BALD, J. Dorsey H
BALD, Robert Cecil 4
BALDANZI, George 5
BALDENSPERGER, 1
Fernand
BALDERSTON, John
Lloyd 3
BALDERSTON, Lydia
Ray 5
BALDES, 5
Raymond Charles
BALDINGER, 5
Albert Henry

BALDINGER, Lawrence
H. 5
BALDOMIR, Alfredo 2
BALDRIDGE, H. 2
Clarence
BALDRIDGE, 1
Howard Hammond
BALDRIDGE, 5
Kenneth Ferguson
BALDRIDGE, 4
Thomas Jackson
BALDWIN, A. Stuart 1
BALDWIN, Abel Seymour 4
BALDWIN, Abraham H
BALDWIN, Abram Martin 1
BALDWIN, 4
Albertus Hutchinson
BALDWIN, 3
Alexander Richards
BALDWIN, Alice Mary 4
BALDWIN, 3
Arthur Charles
BALDWIN, 5
Arthur Douglas
BALDWIN, Arthur J. 1
BALDWIN, Asa Columbus 2
BALDWIN, Asa Fred 4
BALDWIN, 1
Benjamin James
BALDWIN, 2
Benjamin James
BALDWIN, Bird Thomas 1
BALDWIN, 4
Charles Jacobs
BALDWIN, Charles Sears 1
BALDWIN, Clarke
BALDWIN, Edward 3
BALDWIN, Daniel Pratt 1
BALDWIN, 5
Edward Chauncey
BALDWIN, Edward J. H
BALDWIN, 2
Edward Robinson
BALDWIN, 1
Elbert Francis
BALDWIN, H
Elihu Whittlesey
BALDWIN, Evelyn Briggs 1
BALDWIN, F. Spencer 1
BALDWIN, 3
Francis Everett
BALDWIN, Francis Marsh 1
BALDWIN, Frank A. 3
BALDWIN, Frank Conger 2
BALDWIN, Frank Dwight 1
BALDWIN, Frank F. 4
BALDWIN, Geoffrey P. 3
BALDWIN, George Colfax 1
BALDWIN, 1
George Johnson
BALDWIN, Hadley 3
BALDWIN, Harmon Allen 1
BALDWIN, Harry Streett 3
BALDWIN, Henry 1
BALDWIN, Henry 2
BALDWIN, 2
Henry Alexander
BALDWIN, 2
Henry 'de Forest
BALDWIN, Henry Perrine 4
BALDWIN, Henry Porter H
BALDWIN, Howard C. 4
BALDWIN, James 1
BALDWIN, 1
James Fairchild
BALDWIN, James Fosdick 1
BALDWIN, James Fowler H
BALDWIN, James H. 5
BALDWIN, James Hewitt; 5
BALDWIN, James Mark 1
BALDWIN, Jane North 5
BALDWIN, Jesse A. 1
BALDWIN, John * 5
BALDWIN, John Brown 2
BALDWIN, John Denison H
BALDWIN, 4
John Finley Jr.
BALDWIN, Joseph Clark 3
BALDWIN, 1
Joseph Clark Jr.
BALDWIN, Joseph Glover
BALDWIN, LaVerne
BALDWIN, Le Roy
Wilbur
BALDWIN, 2
Lewis Warrington
BALDWIN, Loammi H
BALDWIN, Loammi Jr. H
BALDWIN, Maitland 5
BALDWIN, 5
Lawrence Counsell) Martin
BALDWIN, 1
Martin Mortimer
BALDWIN, H
Matthias William
BALDWIN, Minor Coe 3
BALDWIN, Neilson Abeel 1

Name		Name		Name		Name		Name	
BALDWIN, Nellie Elizabeth	4	BALL, Willis Manville	2	BANCROFT, Charles Parker	1	BANNING, Kendall	2	BARBOUR, Oliver Lorenzo	
BALDWIN, Noyes	H	BALLAGH, James Curtis	2	BANCROFT, Edgar Addison	1	BANNING, Pierson Worrall	1	BARBOUR, Percy E.	
BALDWIN, Oliver Hazard Perry	5	BALLAINE, Francis Knight	4	BANCROFT, Edward	H	BANNISTER, Edward M.	4	BARBOUR, Philip Foster	
BALDWIN, Ralph Lyman	5	BALLANTINE, Arthur Atwood	4	BANCROFT, Francis Sydney	3	BANNISTER, Harry Ray	4	BARBOUR, Philip Pendleton	
BALDWIN, Raymond Peacock	5	BALLANTINE, Edward	5	BANCROFT, Frederic	2	BANNISTER, Henry Martyn	4	BARBOUR, Ralph Henry	
BALDWIN, Robert James	5	BALLANTINE, Henry Winthrop	3	BANCROFT, George	H	BANNISTER, Lucius Ward	3	BARBOUR, Thomas	
BALDWIN, Roger Sherman	H	BALLANTINE, Joseph William	5	BANCROFT, Howland	4	BANNISTER, Nathaniel Harrington	H	BARBOUR, Thomas Seymour	
BALDWIN, Roger Sherman	2	BALLANTINE, Stuart	2	BANCROFT, Hubert Howe	1	BANNON, Henry Towne	1	BARBOUR, W. Warren	
BALDWIN, Roland Dennis	3	BALLANTINE, William Gay	1	BANCROFT, Hugh	1	BANNOW, Rudolph F.	4	BARBOUR, William	
BALDWIN, Samuel Atkinson	4	BALLANTYNE, John	2	BANCROFT, J. Sellers	1	BANTA, Arthur Mangun	2	BARBOUR, William Rinehart	
BALDWIN, Samuel Prentiss	1	BALLARD, Aaron Edward	1	BANCROFT, Jessie Hubbell	4	BANTA, N. Moore	1	BARBOUR, William Tefft	
BALDWIN, Sherman	5	BALLARD, Addison	1	BANCROFT, Joseph	1	BANTA, Parke Monroe	5	BARCHFIELD, Andrew Jackson	
BALDWIN, Simeon	H	BALLARD, Bland Williams	H	BANCROFT, Levi Horace	3	BANTEL, Edward Christian Henry		BARCK, Carl	
BALDWIN, Simeon Eben	1	BALLARD, Charles William	4	BANCROFT, Milton H.	2	BANVARD, John	H	BARCLAY, Bertram Donald	
BALDWIN, Sylvanus	H	BALLARD, Edward Lathrop	1	BANCROFT, Thomas Moore	5	BANVARD, Joseph	H	BARCLAY, Charles Frederick	
BALDWIN, Theodore Anderson	1	BALLARD, Ellis Ames	1	BANCROFT, Wilder Dwight	3	BANZHAF, Henry Leo	3	BARCLAY, Charles James	
BALDWIN, Theron	H	BALLARD, Ernest Schwefel	3	BANCROFT, William Amos		BAPST, John	H	BARCLAY, David	
BALDWIN, Thomas Scott	1	BALLARD, Frederic Lyman	4	BANCROFT, William H.	1	BAPST, Robert Thomas	3	BARCLAY, George A.	
BALDWIN, Wilbur McIntosh	1	BALLARD, Harlan Hoge	1	BANCROFT, William Poole		BARA, Theda	3	BARCLAY, James Edward	
BALDWIN, William	H	BALLARD, James Franklin	1	BAND, Charles Shaw	5	BARACH, Frederica Pisek		BARCLAY, McClelland	
BALDWIN, William Alpheus	3	BALLARD, Nathaniel Harrison		BANDARANAIKE, Solomon West Ridgeway Dias		BARACH, Joseph H.	3	BARCLAY, McKee	
BALDWIN, William Ayer	2	BALLARD, Russell Henry	1	BANDELIER, Adolph Francis Alphonse		BARACK, Louis Barry	5	BARCLAY, Robert	
BALDWIN, William Delevan	1	BALLARD, S. Thruston	1	BANDHOLTZ, Harry Hill	1	BARAGWANATH, John Gordon	4	BARCLAY, Shepard	
BALDWIN, William Edward	5	BALLARD, Sam M.	4	BANDLER, Clarence G.	3	BARANOV, Alexander Andrevich	H	BARCLAY, Thomas	
BALDWIN, William Edward	4	BALLARD, Sumner	2	BANDMANN, Daniel Edward	1	BARAZA, Frederic	H	BARCLAY, Wade Crawford	
BALDWIN, William Henry	1	BALLARD, W. C. Jr.	3	BANE, Juliet Lita	3	BARBA, Charles Elmer	5	BARCLAY, William Franklin	
BALDWIN, William Henry Jr.	1	BALLENGER, Edgar Garrison	5	BANFIELD, Richard Wallace	4	BARBE, Waitman		BARCLAY, William Kennedy Jr.	
BALDWIN, William James	1	BALLENGER, George Walter	1	BANFIELD, Thomas Harry	3	BARBEE, David Rankin	3	BARCUS, James Samuel	
BALDWIN, William Lester	4	BALLENGER, Howard C.	4	BANGHAM, Ralph Vandervort	4	BARBEE, Hugh Arthur	5	BARCUS, John M.	H
BALDWIN, William Wright	2	BALLENGER, William Lincoln		BANGS, Francis Nehemiah	H	BARBEE, James Thomas	4	BARCUS, Norman	
BALDY, Christopher	4	BALLENGER, William Sylvester	3	BANGS, Francis Reginald	1	BARBEE, William Randolph	H	BARD, A. T.	
BALDY, Edward Vincent	1	BALLENTINE, George Andrew	5	BANGS, George Archer	3	BARBELIN, Felix Joseph	H	BARD, Albert Sprague	
BALDY, John Montgomery	2	BALLENTINE, John Jennings	5	BANGS, Isaac Sparrow	1	BARBER, Amzi Lorenzo	1	BARD, Cephas L.	
BALENCIAGA, Cristobal	5	BALLIET, Thomas M.		BANGS, J. Edward	1	BARBER, Charles Newell	3	BARD, David	
BALES, James Anthony	4	BALLIN, Hugo	3	BANGS, John Kendrick	1	BARBER, Charles Williams	2	BARD, Guy Kurtz	
BALESTIER, Charles Wolcott	H	BALLIN, Max	1	BANGS, L. Bolton	1	BARBER, Daniel	H	BARD, Harry Erwin	
BALEWA, Alhaji Abubaker Tafawa	4	BALLINGER, Richard Achilles		BANGS, Nathan	H	BARBER, Donn	5	BARD, John	
BALFOUR, Donald Church	4	BALLMANN, Martin	1	BANGS, Outram	1	BARBER, Edward John	3	BARD, Roy Emerson	
BALFOUR 'OF BURLEIGH, Lord	4	BALLOCH, Edward Arthur	2	BANGS, Tracy R.	1	BARBER, Edwin AtLee	1	BARD, Samuel	
BALK, Robert	3	BALLOU, Adin Augustus	H	BANGSBERG, Harry Frederick		BARBER, Francis	H	BARD, Sara Foresman	
BALKE, Clarence William	2	BALLOU, Charles Clarendon		BANISTER, John *	H	BARBER, George Garfield	2	BARD, Thomas Robert	
BALKEN, Edward Duff	4	BALLOU, Frank Washington	3	BANISTER, Marion Glass	3	BARBER, George Holcomb		BARD, William	
BALL, A. Brayton	1	BALLOU, Hosea	H	BANISTER, William Brodnax	4	BARBER, Gershom Morse	4	BARDEEN, Charles Russell	
BALL, Alice Worthington	1	BALLOU, Hosea II	H	BANISTER, Zilpah Grant	H	BARBER, H(oratio)	5	BARDEEN, Charles Valde	
BALL, Caroline Peddle	2	BALLOU, Hosea Starr	2	BANKER, Howard James	2	BARBER, Henry A. Jr.	3	BARDEEN, Charles William	
BALL, Charles Backus	1	BALLOU, Levi Herbert	3	BANKHEAD, Henry McAuley	5	BARBER, Henry Hervey	4	BARDEL, William	
BALL, Charles Thomas		BALLOU, Maturin Murray	H	BANKHEAD, John Hollis	1	BARBER, Herbert Goodell		BARDEN, Graham Arthur	
BALL, Edward	H	BALLOU, Sidney	1	BANKHEAD, John Hollis	2	BARBER, Joel Allen	H	BARDGETT, Edward Russell	
BALL, Elmer Darwin	2	BALLOU, William Hosea	2	BANKHEAD, Tallulah Brockman		BARBER, John Warner	H	BARDO, Clinton Lloyd	
BALL, Ephraim	H	BALLY, Louis Henry	5	BANKHEAD, William Brockman		BARBER, Levi	H	BARDON, Thomas	
BALL, Farlin Q.	1	BALMANNO, Charles Gorden	1	BANKS, A. A.	3	BARBER, Mary I.	1	BARDON, Thomas	
BALL, Francis Kingsley	2	BALMER, Edwin	3	BANKS, Alexander French	2	BARBER, Milton Augustus		BARDWELL, Rodney Jewett	
BALL, Frank Clayton	2	BALMER, Frank Everett	3	BANKS, Alexander Robinson		BARBER, Noyes	H	BARDWELL, Winfield William	
BALL, Frank Harvey	2	BALMER, Thomas	3	BANKS, Aloysius Burton		BARBER, Ohio Columbus	1	BARGER, Milton Sanford	
BALL, Fred Samuel	2	BALOUGH, Charles	4	BANKS, Charles Eugene	1	BARBER, Orion Metcalf	1	BARGER, Samuel F.	
BALL, Frederick Joseph	4	BALSAM, Aldo R.	4	BANKS, E. S.	3	BARBER, Raymond Jenness	3	BARGERON, Carlisle	
BALL, George Alexander	3	BALTES, Peter Joseph	H	BANKS, Edgar James	1	BARBER, Sidman I(ra)	5	BARHAM, Charles	
BALL, George Harvey		BALTIMORE, 3'd 'baron	H	BANKS, Elizabeth	1	BARBER, Virgil	H	BARHAM, Frank Forrest	
BALL, Gordon Reginald	3	BALTIMORE, 2'd 'lord	H	BANKS, Frank Arthur		BARBER, William A.	2	BARHAM, John A.	
BALL, Henry Price		BALTIMORE, 1'st 'baron	H	BANKS, George B.	4	BARBER, William Henry	4	BARING, Alexander	
BALL, Herman Frederick	5	BALTIMORE, 1'st 'lord	H	BANKS, Harry Pickands		BARBEY, Daniel Edward	5	BARING, Maurice	
BALL, James Moores	1	BALTZ, William N.	1	BANKS, James Jones		BARBEY, John Edward	3	BARJA, Cesar	
BALL, John Rice		BALTZELL, Maude Day	4	BANKS, John	H	BARBIROLLI, Sir John	5	BARK, John Daly	
BALL, L. Heisler	1	BALTZELL, Robert C.	3	BANKS, John Henry	1	BARBORKA, Clifford Joseph	3	BARKAN, Adolf	
BALL, Louise Charlotte		BALTZELL, Winton James	1	BANKS, John Wallace	3	BARBOT, Louis J.	H	BARKAN, Otto	
BALL, Max W.	3	BALTZLY, Oliver Daniel	5	BANKS, Linn	1	BARBOUR, Anna Maynard Mrs.	1	BARKDULL, Charles J.	
BALL, Michael Valentine	2	BALZ, Albert George Adam	3	BANKS, Louis Albert	1	BARBOUR, Clarence Augustus	1	BARKDULL, Howard L.	
BALL, Norman T(ower)	5	BALZAR, Frederick Bennett	1	BANKS, Nathan	3	BARBOUR, Erwin Hinckly	5	BARKER, Albert Smith	
BALL, Oscar Melville	2	BAMBERGER, Ernest	3	BANKS, Nathanial Prentiss	H	BARBOUR, Frank Alexander	3	BARKER, Albert Winslow	
BALL, Otho Fisher	3	BAMBERGER, Louis	2	BANKS, Theodore H.	1	BARBOUR, George Harrison	1	BARKER, Benjamin Fordyce	
BALL, Raymond Nathaniel	4	BAMBERGER, Ralph	5	BANKS, William Nathanial	4	BARBOUR, Henry Ellsworth	2	BARKER, Charles Whitney Tillinghast	3
BALL, Robert Lee	5	BAMBERGER, Simon	1	BANKSON, Virgil Lee	5	BARBOUR, Henry Gray	2	BARKER, Clare Wright	
BALL, Sydney Hobart	2	BAMBOROUGH, William	5	BANNARD, Otto Tremont		BARBOUR, Henry Merlin	4	BARKER, David	
BALL, Thomas	1	BAMBOSCHEK, Giuseppe	5	BANNEKER, Benjamin	H	BARBOUR, James	H	BARKER, David Jr.	
BALL, Thomas Henry	2	BAMFORD, Mary Ellen	5	BANNER, John	5	BARBOUR, James Joseph	5	BARKER, David R.	
BALL, Thomas Raymond	2	BANAY, Ralph Steven	5	BANNER, Peter	H	BARBOUR, John Carlyle	4	BARKER, Ellen Blackmar ("Ellen Blackmar Maxwell")	
BALL, William David		BANCROFT, Aaron	H	BANNING, Ephraim	1	BARBOUR, John Humphrey	1	BARKER, Elsa	
BALL, William Lee	H	BANCROFT, Cecil Franklin Patch	1	BANNING, Henry Blackstone		BARBOUR, John S.	3	BARKER, Ernest Franklin	
BALL, William Sherman	5	BANCROFT, Charles Grey	3			BARBOUR, John Strode	H	BARKER, Franklin Davis	
BALL, William Watts	5					BARBOUR, John Strode Jr.		BARKER, Frederick William	
						BARBOUR, Lola Diehl	4	BARKER, George	
						BARBOUR, Lucien	H	BARKER, George Frederick	
								BARKER, Harold Richard	
								BARKER, Helen Morton	

Name	
BARKER, Henry Ames	1
BARKER, Henry Stites	1
BARKER, Howard Hines	1
BARKER, Jacob	H
BARKER, James Madison	H
BARKER, James Nelson	H
BARKER, James William	1
BARKER, Jeremiah	H
BARKER, John, Jr.	5
BARKER, John Marshall	1
BARKER, John Tull	3
BARKER, Joseph	1
BARKER, Josiah	H
BARKER, Lewellys Franklin	2
BARKER, Lillian Marion	5
BARKER, M. Herbert	2
BARKER, Nelson W(aite)	5
BARKER, Prelate Demick	4
BARKER, Ralph Hollenback	5
BARKER, Ralph Malcolm	3
BARKER, Reginald Charles	1
BARKER, Reginald Charles	2
BARKER, Samuel Haydock	5
BARKER, Theodore Gaillard	4
BARKER, Walter R.	3
BARKER, Wendell Phillips	1
BARKER, Wharton	1
BARKER, William Morris	1
BARKHORN, Henry Charles	2
BARKLEY, Alben William	3
BARKLEY, Henry L.	1
BARKLEY, James Morrison	1
BARKLEY, Jane Rucker	4
BARKLEY, William Elliot	2
BARKSDALE, Alfred Dickinson	5
BARKSDALE, Ethelbert	H
BARKSDALE, John Woodson	5
BARKSDALE, Joseph Downs	2
BARKSDALE, William	H
BARLEY, Rex	5
BARLOW, Arthur J.	2
BARLOW, Bradley	H
BARLOW, Claude Heman	5
BARLOW, De Witt Dukes	2
BARLOW, Elmer Elbert	5
BARLOW, Francis Channing	H
BARLOW, Fred Jr.	3
BARLOW, Harry Elmore	1
BARLOW, Howard	5
BARLOW, Joel	1
BARLOW, John	2
BARLOW, John Quincy	4
BARLOW, John Whitney	1
BARLOW, Maximillan A. J.	4
BARLOW, Milton Theodore	1
BARLOW, Samuel Kimbrough	H
BARLOW, Samuel Latham Mitchill	H
BARLOW, Stephen	1
BARLOW, T. Noble	4
BARLOW, W. Jarvis	1
BARLOW, William Edward	1
BARLOW, William Harvey	4
BARNABAS, Brother	1
BARNABEE, Henry Clay	1
BARNARD, Charles	1
BARNARD, Charles Francis	H
BARNARD, Charles Inman	2
BARNARD, Chester Irving	4
BARNARD, Daniel Dewey	H
BARNARD, Edward Chester	1
BARNARD, Edward Emerson	1
BARNARD, Ernest Sargent	H
BARNARD, Frederick Augustus Porter	
BARNARD, George Grey	1
BARNARD, George M.	2
BARNARD, Harrison Bernard	3
BARNARD, Harry Everett	2
BARNARD, Henry	H
BARNARD, Isaac Dutton	H
BARNARD, James Lynn	2
BARNARD, Job	4
BARNARD, John	H
BARNARD, John Gross	1
BARNARD, Joseph Folger	1
BARNARD, William Nichols	2
BARNARD, William O.	3
BARNASON, Charles Frederick	2
BARNDS, William Paul	1
BARNDT, Milton A.	4
BARNES, Albert	H
BARNES, Alfred Edward	4
BARNES, Alfred Victor	2
BARNES, Amos	1
BARNES, Annie Maria	4
BARNES, Benjamin F.	5
BARNES, Cassius McDonald	4
BARNES, Charles Albert	3
BARNES, Charles Benjamin	5
BARNES, Charles P.	3
BARNES, Charles Reid	1
BARNES, Charlotte Mary Sanford	H
BARNES, Clarence Alfred	5
BARNES, Clifford Webster	2
BARNES, Demas	H
BARNES, Dewey Loyd	4
BARNES, Earl	1
BARNES, Earl Brandon *	4
BARNES, Eric Wollencott	4
BARNES, Floyd Morgan	3
BARNES, Frances Julia	4
BARNES, Francis George	1
BARNES, Frank Haslehurst	5
BARNES, Fred Asa	3
BARNES, Fuller Forbes	3
BARNES, George Anthony	5
BARNES, George Edward	5
BARNES, George Emerson	2
BARNES, George O.	2
BARNES, Gilbert Hobbs	2
BARNES, Gladeon Marcus	4
BARNES, Harlan Ward	5
BARNES, Harold Arthur	3
BARNES, Harry George	4
BARNES, Helen Florence	3
BARNES, Henry A.	5
BARNES, Henry Burr	1
BARNES, Henry Whitmer	4
BARNES, Hiram Putnam	1
BARNES, Howard	5
BARNES, Irving Franklin	3
BARNES, James	H
BARNES, James	1
BARNES, James Martin	3
BARNES, Jasper Converse	1
BARNES, John	1
BARNES, John Beaumont	1
BARNES, John Bryson	3
BARNES, John Hampton	3
BARNES, John Peter	5
BARNES, John Potts	5
BARNES, John Wilcox	4
BARNES, Joseph Fels	5
BARNES, Joseph K.	H
BARNES, Julius Howland	3
BARNES, Lemuel Call	1
BARNES, Margaret Ayer	4
BARNES, Margaret Campbell	4
BARNES, Mary Clark	2
BARNES, Mary Downing Sheldon	H
BARNES, Maynard Bertram	5
BARNES, Morgan	4
BARNES, Mortimer Grant	1
BARNES, Mrs. John	H
BARNES, Nathaniel Waring	3
BARNES, Oliver Weldon	1
BARNES, Parker Thayer;	5
BARNES, Parry	3
BARNES, Ralph W.	1
BARNES, Raymond Flatt	1
BARNES, Raymond Joseph	5
BARNES, Roswell Parkhurst	2
BARNES, Stephen Goodyear	1
BARNES, Stuart Knowlton	5
BARNES, Stuart Knowlton	4
BARNES, Thomas Robert	1
BARNES, Thurlow Weed	1
BARNES, Will Croft	1
BARNES, William *	1
BARNES, William H.	1
BARNES, William Henry	1
BARNES, William Preston	2
BARNET, Herbert L.	5
BARNETT, Augustus Edward	4
BARNETT, Bion Hall	3
BARNETT, Charles Eldridge	4
BARNETT, Claribel Ruth	3
BARNETT, Claude A.	5
BARNETT, Claude A.	4
BARNETT, Eugene Epperson	5
BARNETT, Evelyn Scott Snead	1
BARNETT, Frank Willis	3
BARNETT, George	1
BARNETT, George Ernest	5
BARNETT, Harry	3
BARNETT, Herbert Phillip	5
BARNETT, James	1
BARNETT, James Foote	5
BARNETT, John T.	2
BARNETT, Otto Raymond	2
BARNETT, R(obert) J(ohn)	5
BARNETT, Samuel Jackson	1
BARNETT, Stanley Pugh	5
BARNETT, Stephen Trent	5
BARNETT, Tom P.	1
BARNETT, William	H
BARNETTE, William Jay	5
BARNEY, Austin Dunham	3
BARNEY, Charles Neal	3
BARNEY, Charles Tracy	1
BARNEY, Edgar Starr	1
BARNEY, John	H
BARNEY, Joshua	1
BARNEY, Mrs. Alice Pike	1
BARNEY, Samuel Stebbins	1
BARNEY, William Joshua	3
BARNHARDT, George Columbus	1
BARNHARDT, Jesse Homer	2
BARNHART, Henry A.	1
BARNHART, John D(onald)	5
BARNHART, Thomas Frederick	3
BARNHART, William Gray	1
BARNHILL, John Finch	2
BARNHORN, Clement J.	1
BARNHOUSE, Donald Grey	4
BARNICKEL, William Sidney	1
BARNITZ, Albert	4
BARNITZ, Charles Augustus	H
BARNOUW, Adriaan Jacob	5
BARNOWE, Theodore Joseph	1
BARNS, William Eddy	1
BARNUM, Charlotte Cynthia	1
BARNUM, Dana Dwight	3
BARNUM, Gertrude	3
BARNUM, Hedrick Ware	5
BARNUM, Henry A.	H
BARNUM, Henry Samuel	5
BARNUM, Herman Norton	1
BARNUM, Jerome	4
BARNUM, Malvern-Hill	2
BARNUM, Phineas Taylor	5
BARNUM, Samuel Weed	H
BARNUM, William Henry	H
BARNUM, William Milo	1
BARNUM, Zenus	5
BARNWELL, Charles Heyward	4
BARNWELL, John	H
BARNWELL, John Blair	4
BARNWELL, Middleton Stuart	3
BARNWELL, Robert	H
BARNWELL, Robert Woodward	
BARNWELL, Robert Woodward	1
BARON, Herman	4
BARON, Joseph Louis	4
BARR, Albert J.	1
BARR, Alfred Hamilton	1
BARR, Alton Parker	4
BARR, Amelia Edith	1
BARR, Arvil S.	4
BARR, Charles	H
BARR, Charles	4
BARR, Charles Elisha	4
BARR, David Goodwin	1
BARR, Frank	1
BARR, G. Walter	2
BARR, George Andrew	1
BARR, James Adam	4
BARR, James M.	4
BARR, John Henry	1
BARR, John W.	1
BARR, Joseph Seaton	5
BARR, Lyman	5
BARR, Norman B.	3
BARR, Richard Alexander	2
BARR, Robert	2
BARR, Samuel Davis	3
BARR, Samuel Fleming	3
BARR, Thomas Francis	1
BARR, Thomas Jefferson	H
BARR, Thomas T.	4
BARR, William A.	1
BARR, William Alexander	1
BARR, William Francis	1
BARRADALL, Edward	1
BARRALET, John James	H
BARRAS, Harry Watson	1
BARRATT, Norris Stanley	1
BARRELL, Joseph	1
BARRERE, Claude	2
BARRERE, Georges	4
BARRERE, Granville	H
BARRERE, Nelson	H
BARRETT, Albert Moore	H
BARRETT, Benjamin Fiske	3
BARRETT, Channing Whitney	
BARRETT, Charles D.	2
BARRETT, Charles F.	4
BARRETT, Charles J.	4
BARRETT, Charles Raymond	5
BARRETT, Charles Simon	1
BARRETT, Clifford Leslie	5
BARRETT, Darwin Sherwood Jr.	2
BARRETT, Don Carlos	2
BARRETT, Edward F.	1
BARRETT, Edward Ware	1
BARRETT, Frank A.	4
BARRETT, Fred Dennett	1
BARRETT, George Carter	1
BARRETT, George Horton	H
BARRETT, Harrison D.	1
BARRETT, Harry McWhirter	1
BARRETT, Jay Amos	4
BARRETT, Jesse W.	3
BARRETT, John	1
BARRETT, John Ignatius	2
BARRETT, John Patrick	1
BARRETT, Joseph Hartwell	1
BARRETT, Kate Waller	1
BARRETT, Lawrence	H
BARRETT, Leonard Andrew	2
BARRETT, Lillian Foster	4
BARRETT, Linton Lomas	5
BARRETT, Michael Thomas	1
BARRETT, Oliver Rogers	2
BARRETT, Oscar Fitzallen	1
BARRETT, Otis Warren	3
BARRETT, Raymond F.	5
BARRETT, Reginald	4
BARRETT, Richard Cornelius	4
BARRETT, Richard Warren	2
BARRETT, Robert South	1
BARRETT, Samuel Alfred	4
BARRETT, Stephen Melvil	
BARRETT, W. Franklin	4
BARRETT, Wilbert Hamilton	3
BARRETT, William E.	1
BARRETT, William Felton	3
BARRETT, William Hale	1
BARRETT, William M.	1
BARRETT, Wilson	1
BARRETTE, Joseph Marie) Antonio	5
BARRETTE, John Davenport	1
BARRETTO, Laurence Brevoort (Larry)	5
BARRIENTOS, Rene Ortuno	5
BARRIER, Joseph Henry	5
BARRIERE, Hippolite	H
BARRIGER, John Walker	1
BARRINGER, Daniel Laurens	H
BARRINGER, Daniel Moreau	
BARRINGER, Daniel Moreau	1
BARRINGER, Edwin C.	4
BARRINGER, Paul Brandon	
BARRINGER, Paul Brandon, Jr.	5
BARRINGER, Rufus	1
BARRON, Carter Tate	3
BARRON, Clarence Walker	1
BARRON, E. S. Guzman	3
BARRON, Elbert Macby	5
BARRON, Elwyn Alfred	1
BARRON, Ernest R.	4
BARRON, George Davis	2
BARRON, James	H
BARRON, Joseph Day	1
BARRON, Leonard	1
BARRON, Mark	1
BARRON, Robert E.	1
BARRON, Samuel	H
BARRON, William Andros Jr.	4
BARROW, Alexander	H
BARROW, David	4
BARROW, David Crenshaw	1
BARROW, Elizabeth N.	5
BARROW, Frances Elizabeth Mease	1
BARROW, Pope	1
BARROW, Washington	H
BARROWS, Anna	5
BARROWS, Arthur Stanhope	4
BARROWS, Charles Clifford	1
BARROWS, Charles Henry	1
BARROWS, Chester Willard	1
BARROWS, David Prescott	5
BARROWS, Edwin Armington	2
BARROWS, Harlan H.	4
BARROWS, Harold Kilbrith	3
BARROWS, Isabel Chapin	1
BARROWS, John Chester	4
BARROWS, John Henry	1
BARROWS, John Otis	1
BARROWS, Lewis Orin	4
BARROWS, Morton	1
BARROWS, Nathaniel Albert	2
BARROWS, Nathaniel Haven	3
BARROWS, Raymond H.	3
BARROWS, Samuel June	1
BARROWS, Stanley Hill	1
BARROWS, Thomas Nichols	4
BARROWS, William Morton	2
BARROWS, William Stanley	1
BARRUS, Clara	1
BARRUS, George Hale	1
BARRY, David Sheldon	1
BARRY, Edward Buttevant	1
BARRY, Etheldred Breeze	5
BARRY, Frederick Lehrle	4
BARRY, Henry W.	H
BARRY, Herbert	2
BARRY, James Henry	1
BARRY, John *	H
BARRY, John Daniel	2
BARRY, John H.	3
BARRY, John Stewart	H
BARRY, Joseph Gayle Hurd	
BARRY, Leland Clifford	4
BARRY, Maggie W.	4
BARRY, Patrick	H
BARRY, Patrick	1
BARRY, Peter	5
BARRY, Philip	2

Indicates More Than One Such Name Listed

BATTIN, 3
 Charles Reginald
BATTIN, Charles Thomas 4
BATTLE, Archibald John 1
BATTLE, Burrill Bunn 1
BATTLE, Cullen Andrews 1
BATTLE, George Gordon 5
BATTLE, Henry Wilson 2
BATTLE, 1
 Herbert Bemerton
BATTLE, 5
 Hyman Llewellyn
BATTLE, John S(tewart) 5
BATTLE, 1
 John Thomas Johnson
BATTLE, Kemp Plummer
 * 1
BATTLE, Richard Henry 1
BATTLE, S. Westray 1
BATTLE, Thomas Hall 1
BATTLE, William Horn H
BATTLE, William James 3
BATTLEY, Joseph F. 5
BATTS, Arthur Alanson 5
BATTS, Robert Lynn 1
BAUCUM, A. W. 5
BAUDER, Reginald I. 4
BAUDOIN, Michael 1
BAUER, Augustus H
BAUER, Benjamin F. 1
BAUER, 2
 Charles Christian
BAUER, George Neander 5
BAUER, H(ans) G(ustav) 5
BAUER, Harold 4
BAUER, Johannes Henrik 4
BAUER, L. A. 1
BAUER, Leland Mason 5
BAUER, Louis Hopewell 4
BAUER, Marion Eugenie 3
BAUER, Ralph S. 1
BAUER, Ralph Stanley 5
BAUER, Walter 4
BAUER, William Charles 5
BAUER, William Hans 3
BAUER, William Waldo 4
BAUGHER, A. Charles 4
BAUGHER, Henry Louis H
BAUGHER, Norman J. 5
BAUGHMAN, L. Victor 1
BAUGHMAN, Lyle 4
 Lynden
BAUGHMAN, Roland 4
BAUM, Dwight James 1
BAUM, Ellis Conrad 1
BAUM, Frank George 1
BAUM, Harry 3
BAUM, Henry Mason 4
BAUM, Isidor 4
BAUM, L. Frank 1
BAUM, Morton J. 1
BAUM, Paull Franklin 4
BAUM, Vicki 4
BAUM, Walter Emerson 3
BAUM, 1
 William Miller Jr.
BAUMAN, Edward H
BAUMAN, Val Samuel 4
BAUMANN, Rudolf 5
BAUME, James Simpson 1
BAUMER, Bertha 3
BAUMES, Caleb Howard 1
BAUMGARDT, B. R. 1
BAUMGARTEN, Gustav 5
BAUMGARTNER,
 Apollinaris
BAUMGARTNER, 4
 Warren William
BAUMGARTNER, 5
 William Jacob
BAUR, Bertha
BAUR, Bertha E. 3
BAUR, Bertha E. 4
BAUR, Clara H
BAUSCH, Edward 2
BAUSCH, John Jacob H
BAUSCH, William 2
BAUSLIN, David Henry 1
BAUSMAN, Benjamin 1
BAUSMAN, Frederick 1
BAUSMAN, J. W. B. 1
BAWDEN, Samuel Day 2
BAWDEN, William
 Thomas 5
BAXENDALE, 4
 Esther Minerva
BAXLEY, Henry Willis H
BAXTER, Batsell H
BAXTER, Bruce Richard 2
BAXTER, 1
 Clarence Hughson
BAXTER, Dow Vawter
BAXTER, Earl Hayes 5
BAXTER,
 Edmund Dillabunty
BAXTER, Edmund Francis 4
BAXTER, Elisha H

BAXTER, George Edwin 4
BAXTER, 5
 George Edwin, M.D.
BAXTER, George Strong 1
BAXTER, Gregory Paul 5
BAXTER, H. R. 4
BAXTER, Henry 1
BAXTER,
 Irving Franklin
BAXTER, James Phinney 1
BAXTER, Jere 1
BAXTER, John H
BAXTER, 2
 John Babington Macaulay
BAXTER, 3
 Lionel David MacKenzie
BAXTER, 3
 Norman Washington
BAXTER, 5
 Percival Proctor
BAXTER, Portus H
BAXTER, Sylvester 1
BAXTER, Warner 3
BAXTER, William 1
BAXTER, William Joseph 1
BAY, Charles Ulrick 3
BAY, Jens Christian 4
BAY, William Van Ness 1
BAYARD, Edwin Stanton 3
BAYARD, Fairfax; 5
BAYARD,
 James Asheton *
BAYARD, John H
 Bubenheim
BAYARD, Nicholas 1
BAYARD, Richard Henry H
BAYARD, Samuel 1
BAYARD, Thomas Francis H
BAYARD, Thomas Francis 2
BAYARD, William 1
BAYDUR, Huseyin Ragip 3
BAYER, Lloyd Felch 3
BAYLES, Edwin Atkinson 5
BAYLES, George James 1
BAYLES, James Copper 4
BAYLES, Theodore Floyd 3
BAYLESS,
 William Silver
BAYLEY, 1
 Edward Bancroft
BAYLEY, Francis Reed 5
BAYLEY, Frank Tappan 1
BAYLEY, H
 James Roosevelt
BAYLEY, Richard 1
BAYLEY, Warner Baldwin 1
BAYLEY, 3
 William Shirley
BAYLIES, 1
 Edmund Lincoln
BAYLIES, Edwin 4
BAYLIES, Francis H
BAYLIES, Walter Cabot 1
BAYLIES, William H
BAYLIS, Charles T. 5
BAYLIS, Robert Nelson 2
BAYLISS, Alfred H
BAYLISS, Clara Kern 4
BAYLISS, Major William 1
BAYLOR,
 Adelaide Steele
BAYLOR, H
 Frances Courtenay
BAYLOR, 4
 Frances Courtenay
BAYLOR, George H
BAYLOR, James Bowen 1
BAYLOR, John Roy 3
BAYLOR, H
 Robert Emmett Bledsoe
BAYLOR, William Henry 5
BAYLY, Thomas 1
BAYLY, Thomas Henry 1
BAYLY, H
 Thomas Monteagle
BAYMA, Joseph 1
BAYNE, Howard 3
BAYNE, Howard
 Randolph 1
BAYNE, Hugh Aiken 1
BAYNE, Reed Taft 3
BAYNE, Samuel Gamble 1
BAYNE, Thomas McKee 1
BAYNE, William 3
BAYNE-JONES, Stanhope 4
BAYNES, Ernest Harold 1
BAYNES, John 1
BAYNHAM, William H
BAYOL, Edgar Sansom 5
BAYS, Alfred William 5
BAYUK, Samuel 3
BAZETT, Henry Cuthbert 3
BAZIN, John Stephen H
BAZIOTES, William 4
BEA, Augustin Cardinal 5
BEACH, Albert Isaac 1
BEACH, Alfred Ely H

BEACH, 2
 Amy Marcy Cheney
BEACH, 1
 Arthur Grandville
BEACH, Charles Fisk * 1
BEACH, Charles Lewis 1
BEACH, Chester 3
BEACH, Daniel 1
BEACH, Daniel Magee 2
BEACH, David Nelson 1
BEACH, Edward Latimer 4
BEACH, Francis Asbury 4
BEACH,
 Frederick Converse
BEACH, 2
 George Corwin Jr.
BEACH, Harlan Page 1
BEACH, Harrison L. 1
BEACH, Harry Prescott 4
BEACH, 1
 Henry Harris Aubrey
BEACH, John Kimberly 1
BEACH, John Newton 4
BEACH, Joseph Warren 3
BEACH, King D. 4
BEACH, Lansing Hoskins 2
BEACH, Lewis H
BEACH, Miles 1
BEACH, Moses Sperry H
BEACH, Moses Yale H
BEACH, R. Clyde 3
BEACH, Rex Ellingwood 2
BEACH, S. Judd 3
BEACH, Seth Curtis 4
BEACH, Spencer Ambrose 1
BEACH, Stanley Yale 5
BEACH, 1
 Sylvester Woodbridge
BEACH, 2
 Walter Greenwood
BEACH, H
 William Augustus
BEACH, 1
 William Dorrance
BEACH, 4
 William Harrison
BEACH, 1
 William Mulholland
BEACH, 2
 William Mulholland
BEACH, Wooster H
BEACHAM, Joseph Jr. 3
BEACHLEY, Charles E. 3
BEACHLEY, 5
 Ralph Gregory
BEACOM, Thomas H. 3
BEACOM, Thomas H. 4
BEADLE, Chauncey Delos 3
BEADLE, Erastus Flavel H
BEADLE, 1
 William Henry Harrison
BEAHAN, Willard 1
BEAHM, 4
 William Mc Kinley
BEAIRD, Pat 4
BEAKE, Harold Carnes 1
BEAKES, Crosby Jordan 1
BEAKES, Samuel Willard 1
BEAL, Alvin Casey 1
BEAL, Carl H. 2
BEAL, 1
 Foster Ellenborough
 Lascelles
BEAL, Francis Leavitt 4
BEAL, George Denton 5
BEAL, Gerald F. 5
BEAL, Gifford Reynolds 3
BEAL, Harry 4
BEAL, Henry C. 3
BEAL, James Hartley 1
BEAL, John M. 3
BEAL, Junius Emery 2
BEAL, Mary Barnes 1
BEAL, Reynolds 3
BEAL, Royal 5
BEAL, Thomas Andrew 2
BEAL, Thomas Prince 1
BEAL, Walter Henry 4
BEAL, William James 1
BEALE, Arthur Stanley 1
BEALE, Charles Hallock 2
BEALE, Charles Willing 1
BEALE, H
 Edward Fitzgerald
BEALE, Frank D. 5
BEALE, George William 2
BEALE, Howard Kennedy 4
BEALE,
 James Madison Hite
BEALE, Joseph G. 4
BEALE, Joseph Henry 2
BEALE, 4
 Leonard Tillinghast
BEALE, Maria Taylor 1
BEALE, H
 Richard Lee Turberville
BEALE, Stephen 3

BEALE, Truxtun 1
BEALE, William Gerrish 1
BEALER, 3
 Alexander Winkler
BEALES, C. William 1
BEALES, LeVerne 5
BEALL, Elias James 4
BEALL, Forest Wade 5
BEALL, Jack 1
BEALL, Jack 1
BEALL, James Glenn 5
BEALL, John Yates H
BEALL, Mary Stevens 1
BEALL, Reasin H
BEALL, Samuel Wootton 1
BEALS, Charles Edward 4
BEALS, David Thomas 1
BEALS, Edward Alden 1
BEALS, Frank Lee 5
BEALS, Ralph Albert 3
BEALS, Robert Diggs 5
BEALS, Walter Burges 4
BEAM, Francis H. 4
BEAM, Harry Peter 4
BEAM, Walter Irvin 3
BEAMAN, 2
 Alexander Gaylord Emmons
BEAMAN, Bartlett 2
BEAMAN,
 Charles Cotesworth
BEAMAN, H
 Fernando Cortez
BEAMAN, George
 William 1
BEAMAN, Robert Prentis 4
BEAMAN, William Major 4
BEAMER, Elmer A. 1
BEAMER, John V. 4
BEAMISH, 2
 Richard Joseph
BEAMSLEY, 3
 Foster Gilman
BEAN, Arthur John 1
BEAN, Barton A. 4
BEAN, Benning Moulton H
BEAN, Charles Homer 5
BEAN, Francis Atherton 3
BEAN, George W. 3
BEAN, Henry J. 4
BEAN, Holly Marshall 4
BEAN, L. L. 4
BEAN, Robert Bennett 2
BEAN, Robert Sharp 1
BEAN, Tarleton Hoffman 1
BEAN, William Smith 2
BEANBLOSSOM, 1
 Moody Lewis
BEANE, Fred Emery 4
BEANE, John G. 4
BEAR, Firman Edward 5
BEAR, Harry 1
BEAR, Joseph Ainslie 3
BEARCE, Henry Walter 4
BEARCE, Ralph King 5
BEARD, Adelia Belle 1
BEARD, Augustus Field 1
BEARD, Charles Austin 2
BEARD, Charles Heady 1
BEARD, Cyrus 1
BEARD, Daniel Carter 1
BEARD, Edward E. 1
BEARD, George Miller H
BEARD, Gerald Hamilton 4
BEARD, James Carter 1
BEARD, James Henry H
BEARD, James Randolph 3
BEARD, James Thom 2
BEARD, James Thom 2
BEARD, John Grover 2
BEARD, Joseph Howard 3
BEARD, Lina 1
BEARD, Mary 1
BEARD, Mary Ritter 3
BEARD, Oliver Thomas 1
BEARD, Reuben Alview 1
BEARD, Richard H
BEARD, Thomas Francis 1
BEARD, W. D. 1
BEARD,
 William Holbrook
BEARD, 4
 Wolcott Le Clear
BEARDALL, 4
 John Reginald
BEARDSHEAR, 1
 William Miller
BEARDSLEE, Clark Smith 1
BEARDSLEE,
 John Walter Jr.
BEARDSLEE,
 Lester Anthony
BEARDSLEY, 2
 Arthur Lehman
BEARDSLEY,
 Charles Alexander
BEARDSLEY, 4
 Charles Sumner

BEARDSLEY, H
 Eben Edwards
BEARDSLEY, 3
 Frank Grenville
BEARDSLEY, Glover 4
BEARDSLEY, Grenville 4
BEARDSLEY, Guy
 Erastus 5
BEARDSLEY, Harry M. 3
BEARDSLEY, Henry
 Mahan 1
BEARDSLEY, 2
 James Wallace
BEARDSLEY, Samuel 1
BEARDSLEY,
 Samuel Arthur
BEARDSLEY, 2
 William Agur
BEARDSLEY, William H. 1
BEARDSLEY, William S. 3
BEARDWOOD, 5
 Joseph Thomas, Jr.
BEARDWOOD, Matthew 1
BEARY, Donald Bradford
BEASLEY, Frederick H
BEASLEY, John 1
BEASLEY, Mercer H
BEASLEY, Rex Webb 4
BEASLEY, Ronald Storey 5
BEASLEY, 3
 Rowland Fowler
BEATES, Henry Jr. 1
BEATH, Robert Burns 1
BEATLEY, 1
 Clara Bancroft
BEATON, David 1
BEATON, Kenneth Carrol 5
BEATON, Lindsay Eugene 5
BEATON, Ralph Hastings 2
BEATTIE, Charlton Reid 1
BEATTIE, 1
 Francis Robert
BEATTIE, James A. 4
BEATTIE, John Walter 1
BEATTIE, R. Leslie 2
BEATTIE,
 Robert Brewster
BEATTY, Adam H
BEATTY, Alfred Chester 5
BEATTY, Alfred Chester 1
BEATTY, Arthur 2
BEATTY, Bessie 1
BEATTY, H
 Charles Clinton
BEATTY, 5
 Clara Smith (Mrs. Jesse O.
 Beatty)
BEATTY, Frank Edmund 1
BEATTY, Henry Russell 5
BEATTY, Hugh Gibson 5
BEATTY, James Helmick 5
BEATTY, James Laughead 5
BEATTY, Jerome 1
BEATTY, John H
BEATTY, John 1
BEATTY, John W. 1
BEATTY, Richard
 Croom 4
BEATTY, Sir Edward 2
BEATTY, Troy 1
BEATTY, 4
 Willard Walcott
BEATTY, William 1
BEATTY, William Henry 1
BEATTYS, George Davis 2
BEATY, Amos Leonidas 1
BEATY, John Owen 4
BEATY, John Yocum 5
BEATY, Martin H
BEATY, Richard A. D. 3
BEAU, Jonathan 1
BEAUCHAMP, Edwin 4
BEAUCHAMP, Emerson 5
BEAUCHAMP, James K. 4
BEAUCHAMP, Lou Jenks 1
BEAUCHAMP, William H
BEAUCHAMP,
 William Benjamin
BEAUCHAMP, 1
 William Martin
BEAUDETTE, F. R. 3
BEAUDOIN, L. Rene 5
BEAUJOLAIS, H
 Louis Charles D'Orleans
BEAUMONT, Andrew H
BEAUMONT, 5
 Campbell Eben
BEAUMONT,
 Edmond Eckhart
BEAUMONT, John Colt H
BEAUMONT, John Colt 2
BEAUMONT, Lilian
 Adele
BEAUMONT, William H
BEAUPRE, 1
 Arthur Matthias

BEAUREGARD, Augustin Toutant 3
BEAUREGARD, Elie 3
BEAUREGARD, Marie Antoinette 1
BEAUREGARD, Pierre Gustave Toutant H
BEAUX, Cecilia 1
BEAVEN, Albert William 2
BEAVEN, J. C. 3
BEAVEN, Thomas Daniel 4
BEAVER, Harry C. 5
BEAVER, James Addams 1
BEAVER, Sandy 5
BEAVERBROOK, Lord 4
BEAVERS, Thomas N. 4
BEAZELL, William Preston 2
BEBAN, George 1
BEBB, Charles Herbert 2
BEBERMAN, Max 5
BECH, Georg 3
BECHDOLT, Frederick Ritchie 3
BECHET, Sidney 3
BECHET, Sidney 4
BECHMAN, William George 4
BECHT, J. George 1
BECHTEL, Edward Ambrose 5
BECHTEL, Edwin De Turck 3
BECHTEL, George M. 3
BECK, Adam L. 1
BECK, Brooks 5
BECK, Carl 1
BECK, Carl 4
BECK, Carol H. 1
BECK, Charles H
BECK, Claude Schaeffer 5
BECK, D. Elden 4
BECK, Edward Adam 1
BECK, Edward Scott 2
BECK, George H
BECK, Herbert Wardle 3
BECK, James Burnie H
BECK, James Montgomery 1
BECK, Jean-Baptiste 1
BECK, Johann Heinrich 1
BECK, Joseph David H
BECK, Lewis Caleb H
BECK, Marcus Wayland 2
BECK, Martin H
BECK, Martin 4
BECK, Mary H
BECK, Robert McCandlass, Jr. 5
BECK, Theodric Romeyn H
BECK, Thomas Hambly 3
BECK, Victor Emanuel 4
BECK, Walter 1
BECK, William 1
BECK, William A. 4
BECK, William Henry 1
BECK, William Hopkins 3
BECKER, Alfred Le Roy 2
BECKER, Arthur Dow 1
BECKER, Benjamin V. 2
BECKER, Carl Lotus 2
BECKER, Charles E. 5
BECKER, Charles W(ashington) 5
BECKER, Elery Ronald 5
BECKER, Elizabeth H. (mrs. Richard F. Becker)
BECKER, Florence Hague (Mrs. William A. Becker) 5
BECKER, Frederic Harry 3
BECKER, George Ferdinand 1
BECKER, Gustave Louis 3
BECKER, Howard 4
BECKER, Isidor Schultz 4
BECKER, James Herman 5
BECKER, Joseph 4
BECKER, Lawrence 5
BECKER, May Lamberton 4
BECKER, Neal Dow 3
BECKER, Nils Folke 4
BECKER, Owen Chauncey 5
BECKER, P. L. 4
BECKER, Robert 5
BECKER, Sheburn Merrill
BECKER, Thomas A. 1
BECKER, Tracy Chatfield 4
BECKER, Washington 1
BECKER, William Dee 2
BECKERS, William Gerard
BECKET, Frederick Mark 2
BECKET, Welton David 5
BECKETT, Percy Gordon 5

BECKETT, Richard Creighton 3
BECKETT, Thomas Gervus Jr. 3
BECKETT, Wesley Wilbur 1
BECKETT, William Wesley 4
BECKHAM, Clifford Myron 5
BECKHAM, J. Crepps Wickliffe 1
BECKINGTON, Alice 1
BECKJORD, Walter Clarence 4
BECKLER, William Alexander 5
BECKLEY, Quitman F. 4
BECKLEY, Zoe 4
BECKMAN, Francis Joseph 2
BECKMAN, Frederick William 3
BECKMAN, Henry Frederick 5
BECKMAN, L. J. 5
BECKMAN, Nils Arvid Teodor 5
BECKMAN, P. E. 4
BECKMAN, Theodore N. 5
BECKMAN, Vincent Henry 3
BECKMANN, Max 4
BECKNELL, William H
BECKNER, Lucien 5
BECKWITH, Charles Minnigerode 1
BECKWITH, Clarence Augustine 1
BECKWITH, Isbon Thaddeus 2
BECKWITH, J. Carroll 1
BECKWITH, Paul Edmond 1
BECKWITH, Theodore Day 2
BECKWOURTH, James P. H
BECTON, Joseph D. 1
BEDARD, Pierre (Pierre-Armand Bedard de La Perriere) 5
BEDAUX, Charles E. 2
BEDDALL, Edward Fitch 4
BEDDOWS, Charles Roland
BEDE, J. Adam 2
BEDELL, Frederick 4
BEDELL, Gregory Thurston H
BEDELL, Gregory Townshend H
BEDFORD, Alfred Cotton 1
BEDFORD, Edward Thomas 1
BEDFORD, F. H. Jr. 3
BEDFORD, Frederick Thomas 4
BEDFORD, Gunning * H
BEDFORD, Gunning S. H
BEDFORD, Henry Clark 2
BEDFORD, Paul 5
BEDFORD, Scott Elias William 5
BEDFORD-JONES, Henry James O'Brien 2
BEDINGER, George Michael H
BEDINGER, Henry H
BEDLE, Joseph Dorsett H
BEE, Barnard Elliott H
BEE, Hamilton Prioleau H
BEE, Thomas H
BEEBE, Brooks Ford 1
BEEBE, James Albert 4
BEEBE, James Lyndon 4
BEEBE, Katherine 3
BEEBE, Kenneth John 4
BEEBE, Lewis C. 3
BEEBE, Lucius Morris 4
BEEBE, Murray Anthony 2
BEEBE, Philip S. 4
BEEBE, Raymond Nelson 5
BEEBE, Royden Eugene Jr. 3
BEEBE, William 1
BEEBE, William 4
BEEBE, FREDERICK SESSIONS
BEEBER, Dimner 1
BEECH, Walter Herschel 3
BEECHAM, Sir Thomas 4
BEECHE, Octavio H
BEECHER, Amariah Dwight
BEECHER, Catharine Esther
BEECHER, Charles 4

BEECHER, Charles Emerson 1
BEECHER, Edward H
BEECHER, Frederick William H
BEECHER, Eunice White Bullard
BEECHER, George Allen 5
BEECHER, Henry Ward H
BEECHER, Laban S. H
BEECHER, Lyman H
BEECHER, Philemon H
BEECHER, Thomas Kinnicut
BEECHER, Willis Judson 1
BEECHLER, Glenn Curtis 3
BEECKMAN, R. Livingston 1
BEECROFT, John William Richard 4
BEEDE, Frank Herbert 1
BEEDE, Herbert Gould 2
BEEDE, Joshua William 3
BEEDY, Carroll Linwood 2
BEEHLER, William Henry 1
BEEK, Alice D. Engley 3
BEEKMAN, Charles K. 5
BEEKMAN, Fenwick 4
BEEKMAN, Frederick Warren 5
BEEKMAN, Henry Rutgers 4
BEEKMAN, John K. H
BEEKMAN, Thomas H
BEELER, John Allen 2
BEELER, Roy Hood 3
BEER, George Louis 1
BEER, Thomas 1
BEER, William 1
BEERBOHM, Sir Max 3
BEERS, Alfred Bishop 4
BEERS, Barnet William 5
BEERS, Clifford Whittingham 2
BEERS, Cyrus H
BEERS, Edward M. H
BEERS, Ethel Lynn H
BEERS, Frederick 3
BEERS, George Emerson 2
BEERS, Henry Augustin 1
BEERS, Lucius Hart 2
BEERS, William Harmon 2
BEESE, Charles William 3
BEESON, Charles Henry 4
BEESON, Henry White 4
BEESON, Jasper Luther 2
BEEST, Albert Van H
BEETLE, David Harold 5
BEETS, Henry 2
BEEUWKES, Adelia Marie 4
BEGEMAN, Louis 4
BEGG, Alexander Swanson 3
BEGG, James Thomas 5
BEGGS, George Erle 1
BEGGS, Gertrude Harper 5
BEGICH, Nicholas Joseph
BEGIEN, Ralph Norman 2
BEGLEY, Ed 5
BEGOLE, George Davis 5
BEGOLE, Josiah Williams H
BEHAN, Brendan Francis 4
BEHAN, Joseph C. 3
BEHAN, Warren Palmer 2
BEHAN, William James 1
BEHARRELL, Sir George 3
BEHM, Walter Henry John
BEHN, Hernand 1
BEHN, Sosthenes 3
BEHNCKE, David L. 4
BEHNER, Albert Jacob 1
BEHREND, Bernard Arthur
BEHREND, Ernst Richard 1
BEHREND, Ernst Richard 2
BEHRENDS, Adolphus Julius Frederick 1
BEHRENDT, Walter Curt 2
BEHRENS, Charles August 3
BEHRENS, H. Frederick
BEHRENS, Henry H
BEHRENS, Herman Albert 2
BEHRENS, William Wohlsen 4
BEHRMAN, Martin 1
BEHYMER, Arthur Livingstone 5
BEHYMER, Francis Albert 3
BEHYMER, Lynden Ellsworth 2
BEIDERBECKE, Leon Bix H
BEIDERBECKE, Leon Bix 4

BEIDLER, Jacob Atlee 4
BEINECKE, Edwin John 5
BEINECKE, Frederick William 5
BEINECKE, Richard Sperry 4
BEINECKE, Walter 3
BEIRNE, Andrew H
BEISSEL, Johann Conrad H
BEKINS, Melvin 2
BEKKER, Leander J. 'de 1
BELANGER, John W. 5
BELASCO, David 1
BELAUNDE, Victor Andres 4
BELCHER, Edwin Newton, Jr. 5
BELCHER, Frank Garrettson 3
BELCHER, Frank J. Jr. 3
BELCHER, Hilda 4
BELCHER, Hiram 5
BELCHER, James Elmer 5
BELCHER, Jonathan H
BELCHER, Nathan H
BELCHER, Supply H
BELCOURT, George Antoine H
BELDEN, Charles Dwight 1
BELDEN, Charles Francis Dorr
BELDEN, Ellsworth Burnett 1
BELDEN, George Oglivie H
BELDEN, Henry Marvin 4
BELDEN, James Jerome 1
BELDEN, Jessie Van Zile
BELDEN, Josiah H
BELDEN, William Burlingame 5
BELDING, Alvah Norton 1
BELDING, David Lawrence 5
BELDING, Don 5
BELDING, Frederick Norton 2
BELDING, Milo Merrick Jr. 1
BELDING, Milo Merrick Sr. 1
BELDOCK, George J. 5
BELFIELD, Henry Holmes 1
BELFIELD, William Thomas 1
BELFORD, James B. H
BELFORD, John L. 3
BELFOUR, C(ampbell) Stanton 5
BELGRANO, Frank N. Jr. 3
BELIN, G. 'd'andelot 3
BELISLE, Hector Louis 3
BELK, Henry 5
BELK, William Henry 5
BELKNAP, Charles 3
BELKNAP, Daniel 5
BELKNAP, Edwin Star 1
BELKNAP, George Eugene 1
BELKNAP, Henry Wychoff 4
BELKNAP, Jeremy H
BELKNAP, Morris Burke 1
BELKNAP, Raymond H. 4
BELKNAP, Reginald Rowan 3
BELKNAP, William Richardson 1
BELKNAP, William Worth H
BELL, Agrippa Nelson 1
BELL, Alexander Graham 1
BELL, Alexander Melville 1
BELL, Alphonzo Edward 2
BELL, Archie 5
BELL, Bennett D. 4
BELL, Bernard Iddings 3
BELL, Bert 3
BELL, Brian 1
BELL, Charles Henry H
BELL, Charles James * 1
BELL, Charles S. 1
BELL, Charles S. 4
BELL, Charles Webster 2
BELL, Clark 1
BELL, Daniel Wafena 5
BELL, Digby 1
BELL, E. T. 4
BELL, Earl Hoyt 4
BELL, Edward 1
BELL, Edward August 2
BELL, Edward Price 1
BELL, Edward Theodore 1
BELL, Enoch Frye 2

BELL, Frank Breckenridge 2
BELL, Frank Somers 1
BELL, Frederic Somers 2
BELL, George 1
BELL, George Jr. 1
BELL, George Alfred 3
BELL, George Fisher 1
BELL, George Kennedy Allen 3
BELL, George L. 3
BELL, George Maxwell 5
BELL, Graham Bernat 5
BELL, Harmon 2
BELL, Helene S. 1
BELL, Henry Haywood 4
BELL, Herbert Clifford Francis
BELL, Hill McClelland 1
BELL, Hillary 1
BELL, Hiram 1
BELL, Hiram Parks 5
BELL, Howard James Jr. 1
BELL, (Harold) Idris 4
BELL, Hugh McKee
BELL, Isaac H
BELL, J. Franklin 1
BELL, J. Spencer 4
BELL, Jacob 1
BELL, James 5
BELL, James Carleton 4
BELL, James Ford H
BELL, James Madison H
BELL, James Martin 1
BELL, James Montgomery 1
BELL, James Munsie 5
BELL, James S. 1
BELL, James Warsaw 5
BELL, James Washington 4
BELL, John * H
BELL, John C. H
BELL, John Cromwell 1
BELL, John G. 1
BELL, John Lewis 5
BELL, John W. 5
BELL, Joseph A(sbury) 1
BELL, Joseph B. 1
BELL, Joseph Clark 2
BELL, Joseph Milligan 1
BELL, Joshua Fry H
BELL, Kenneth C. 1
BELL, Laird 4
BELL, Laura Joyce 1
BELL, Lawrence Dale 3
BELL, Lilian 1
BELL, Louis 1
BELL, Luther Vose H
BELL, Major Townsend 1
BELL, Marcus Lafayette H
BELL, Mary Adelaide Fuller
BELL, Miller Stephens 1
BELL, Neil 4
BELL, Nicholas Montgomery 1
BELL, Ovid 4
BELL, Peter Hansborough H
BELL, Rae Floyd 5
BELL, Raley Husted 5
BELL, Rex 4
BELL, Robert 5
BELL, Robert Cook 1
BELL, Roscoe Rutherford 4
BELL, Samuel H
BELL, Samuel Newell H
BELL, Samuel Paris H
BELL, Solomon H
BELL, Theodore Arlington 1
BELL, Thomas Montgomery 1
BELL, Ulric 5
BELL, Wilbur Cosby 1
BELL, William Allen 4
BELL, William Augustus 1
BELL, William Bonar 4
BELL, William Brown 3
BELL, William Constantine 1
BELL, William H. 5
BELL, William Hemphill 4
BELL, William Melvin 1
BELL, William Roe 4
BELL, William Yancy 5
BELLAIRE, Robert Thomas 4
BELLAMAH, Jeanne Lees (Mrs. Dale John Bellamah)
BELLAMANN, Henry 1
BELLAMANN, Katherine 3
BELLAMY, Blanche Wilder 1
BELLAMY, Charles Joseph 2

ELLAMY, Edward — H
ELLAMY, Elizabeth Whitfield — 1
ELLAMY, F. Wilder — 3
ELLAMY, Francis — H
ELLAMY, Francis — 4
ELLAMY, Francis Rufus — 5
ELLAMY, John Dillard — 2
ELLAMY, Joseph — H
ELLAMY, Leslie Burgess — 4
ELLAMY, Paul — 3
ELLAMY, Raymond (Flavius) — 5
ELLAMY, William — 4
ELLANCA, Guiseppe Mario — 4
ELLATTI, C. Robert — 3
ELLATTY, Charles E. — 5
ELLEW, Frank Henry Temple — H
ELLEW, Kyrle — 1
ELLEZZA, Russell G. — 3
ELLEZZA, Vincenzo — 4
ELLINGER, Charles Byron — 1
ELLINGER, John Bellinger — 1
ELLINGER, Joseph — H
ELLINGER, Martha Fletcher — 5
ELLINGER, Patrick Niesen Lynch — 4
ELLINGER, William Whaley — 2
ELLINGHAM, Richard — H
ELLIS, Leon Robert — 5
ELLMAN, Lawrence Stevens — 5
ELLOC, Hilaire — 3
ELLOMONT, 1'st 'earl — H
ELLOWS, Albert Fitch — H
ELLOWS, George Wesley — 1
ELLOWS, Henry Adams — 1
ELLOWS, Henry Whitney — H
ELLOWS, Howard Perry — H
ELLOWS, Johnson McClure — 2
ELLOWS, Robert Peabody — 3
ELMONT, Alva E. Smith — 4
ELMONT, August — H
ELMONT, August — 1
ELMONT, Morgan — 3
ELMONT, Mrs. O. H. P. — 1
ELMONT, Oliver Hazard Perry — 1
ELMONT, Perry — 2
ELO, Alfred H. — 1
ELO, Alfred Horatio — 1
ELSER, James Edwin — H
ELSTERLING, Charles Starne — 3
ELT, Benjamin Carleton — 4
ELT, Harry H. — 3
ELT, William Bradley Tyler — 5
ELVISO, Thomas Henry — 1
ELYAYEV, Pavel Ivanovich — 5
EMAN, Nathan Sidney Smith — H
EMAN, Solon Spencer — 1
EMAN, Wooster Woodruff — 1
EMELMANS, Ludwig — 4
EMENT, Alburto — 1
EMENT, Alon — 3
EMENT, Caleb N. — H
EMENT, Clarence Edwin — 1
EMENT, Howard — 1
EMIS, Albert Farwell — 1
EMIS, Edward Webster — 1
EMIS, George — 1
EMIS, Harold Medberry — 5
EMIS, Judson Stephen — 1
EMISS, Samuel Merrifield — 4
ENADE, James Arthur — 1
ENARD, Henri 'Jean Emile — 4
ENBRIDGE, Henry — H
ENBROOK, Edward Antony — 4
ENCHLEY, Robert Charles — 2
ENCHOFF, Howard Johnston — 3
ENCHOFF, Robert J(ohnston) — 5
ENCKENSTEIN, Leonard Julius — 4
ENDA, Harry Jindrich — 5

BENDA, Wladyslaw Theodor — 2
BENDELARI, George — 1
BENDER, Albert Maurice
BENDER, Eric J. — 4
BENDER, George H. — 4
BENDER, Harold H. — 3
BENDER, Jack I. — 4
BENDER, Melvin T. — 5
BENDER, Prosper — 4
BENDER, Walter — 5
BENDER, Wilbur H. — 1
BENDER, Wilbur Joseph — 5
BENDINER, Alfred — 4
BENDIRE, Charles E. — H
BENDIX, Ella Crosby (Mrs. Ella Crosby Bendix) — 5
BENDIX, Max — 2
BENDIX, Vincent — 4
BENDIX, William — 4
BENECKE, Adelbert Oswald — 4
BENEDICT, A. L. — 4
BENEDICT, Alfred Barnum — 1
BENEDICT, Andrew Bell — 3
BENEDICT, Anne — 4
BENEDICT, Asa Gardiner — 4
BENEDICT, C. Harry — 5
BENEDICT, Cleveland Keith — 4
BENEDICT, Cooper Procter — 5
BENEDICT, David — H
BENEDICT, Elias Cornelius — 4
BENEDICT, Erastus Cornelius — H
BENEDICT, Francis Gano — 3
BENEDICT, Frank Lee — 1
BENEDICT, George Grenville
BENEDICT, George Wyllys — 5
BENEDICT, Harris Miller — 1
BENEDICT, Harry Yandell
BENEDICT, Henry Harper — 1
BENEDICT, James Everard — 2
BENEDICT, Jay Leland — 3
BENEDICT, Lorenzo — 1
BENEDICT, Ralph C. — 4
BENEDICT, Robert Dewey — 1
BENEDICT, Russell
BENEDICT, Ruth Fulton — 2
BENEDICT, Samuel Durlin — 5
BENEDICT, Samuel Ravaud
BENEDICT, Stanley R. — 1
BENEDICT, Wayland Richardson
BENEDICT, Wayne LeClaire — 5
BENEDICT, William Leonard — 1
BENEDIKTSSON, Bjarnl — 5
BENEDUM, Michael Late — 3
BENEKER, Gerrit Albertus — 1
BENES, Eduard — 2
BENET, Christie — 3
BENET, Laurence Vincent — 2
BENET, Stephen Vincent — 1
BENET, Walker — 4
BENET, William Rose — 3
BENEZET, Anthony — H
BENEZET, Louis Paul — 4
BENGOUGH, Elisa Armstrong — 1
BENHAM, Andrew Ellicott Kennedy
BENHAM, Henry Washington — H
BENHAM, John Samuel — 1
BENINGTON, Arthur — 1
BENINGTON, George Arthur — 4
BENIOFF, Hugo — H
BENIOFF, Hugo — 5
BENITZ, William Logan — 4
BENJAMIN, A. Cornelius — 5
BENJAMIN, Anna Northend — 1
BENJAMIN, Asher — H
BENJAMIN, Charles Henry — 1
BENJAMIN, David Joel * — 4
BENJAMIN, Dowling — 4
BENJAMIN, Eugene S. — 1

BENJAMIN, George Hillard — 1
BENJAMIN, Gilbert Giddings — 2
BENJAMIN, John Forbes — H
BENJAMIN, Judah Philip — H
BENJAMIN, Louis — 1
BENJAMIN, Marcus — 1
BENJAMIN, Nathan — H
BENJAMIN, Park — H
BENJAMIN, Park — 1
BENJAMIN, Raphael — 1
BENJAMIN, Raymond — 3
BENJAMIN, Reuben Moore — 1
BENJAMIN, Robert M. — 4
BENJAMIN, Samuel Greene Wheeler — 1
BENMOSCHE, M. — 3
BENNARD, George — 5
BENNER, Philip — H
BENNER, Raymond Calvin — 5
BENNER, Walter Meredith — 5
BENNER, Winthrop Webster — 3
BENNERS, Augustus — 5
BENNESON, Cora Agnes — 1
BENNET, A. A. — H
BENNET, Benjamin — H
BENNET, Robert Ames — 3
BENNET, Sanford Fillmore — H
BENNET, Walter Mills — 1
BENNET, William Stiles — 4
BENNETT, Albert Arnold — 5
BENNETT, Albert Dwight — H
BENNETT, Alfred Allen — 4
BENNETT, Alfred S. — 1
BENNETT, Andrew Carl
BENNETT, Andrew Carl
BENNETT, Archibald Synica — 3
BENNETT, Arthur Ellsworth — 5
BENNETT, Arthur Ellsworth — 2
BENNETT, Belle H. — 1
BENNETT, Burton Ellsworth — 1
BENNETT, Caleb Prew — H
BENNETT, Charles Andrew Armstrong — 1
BENNETT, Charles Edwin — 1
BENNETT, Charles Goodwin
BENNETT, Charles Henry — 3
BENNETT, Charles Washington
BENNETT, Charles Wilbur — 5
BENNETT, Clarence F. — 5
BENNETT, Claude Nathaniel — 1
BENNETT, Constance — 4
BENNETT, David Smith — H
BENNETT, De Robigne Mortimer — H
BENNETT, Donald Menzies — 5
BENNETT, Edmund Hatch — H
BENNETT, Edward — 3
BENNETT, Edward Brown
BENNETT, Edward Herbert — 3
BENNETT, Elbert G. — 3
BENNETT, Emerson — 1
BENNETT, Eugene Dunlap — 5
BENNETT, Frank Marion — 3
BENNETT, Frank Woodrow — 4
BENNETT, George Allen — 3
BENNETT, Granville G. — 1
BENNETT, Harriet — 5
BENNETT, Hendley Stone — H
BENNETT, Henry — H
BENNETT, Henry Eastman — 2
BENNETT, Henry Garland — 3
BENNETT, Henry Holcomb — 1
BENNETT, Henry William — 1
BENNETT, Horace Wilson — 2
BENNETT, Hugh Hammond — 4
BENNETT, Ida Dandridge — 1
BENNETT, Ira Elbert — 5
BENNETT, Irving T. — 3
BENNETT, James Eugene — 4
BENNETT, James Gordon — H
BENNETT, James Gordon — 1

BENNETT, James O'Donnell — 1
BENNETT, James William, Jr. — 5
BENNETT, Jesse Lee — 5
BENNETT, John — 3
BENNETT, John Bonifas — 4
BENNETT, John Foster — 1
BENNETT, John George — 3
BENNETT, John James — 1
BENNETT, John Newton — 3
BENNETT, John William — 1
BENNETT, Johnstone — 1
BENNETT, Joseph Bentley — 3
BENNETT, Lawrence — 5
BENNETT, Louis — 1
BENNETT, Louis L. — 2
BENNETT, Louis Winston — 3
BENNETT, M. Katharine Jones — 3
BENNETT, May Friend — 4
BENNETT, Melba Berry (Mrs. Frank Henry Bennett)
BENNETT, Michael John — 2
BENNETT, Nathaniel — H
BENNETT, Philip Allen — 2
BENNETT, Ralph Culver — 5
BENNETT, Rawson — 5
BENNETT, Richard — 1
BENNETT, Richard Heber — 4
BENNETT, Robert Root — 1
BENNETT, Samuel Crocker
BENNETT, Thomas Gray — 1
BENNETT, Thomas Warren — H
BENNETT, Victor Wilson — 3
BENNETT, W(illiam) R(eece) — 5
BENNETT, Walter Harper — 4
BENNETT, Wendell C. — 1
BENNETT, William James — H
BENNETT, William Lyon — 1
BENNETT, William Rainey — 5
BENNETT, William Wirt — 1
BENNETT, William Zebina — 1
BENNETTS, James Mitchell — 1
BENNING, Henry A. — 4
BENNING, Henry Lewis — 1
BENNION, Adam Samuel — 3
BENNION, Milton — 5
BENNION, Samuel Otis — 1
BENNITT, George Stephen — 1
BENNITT, Rudolf — 3
BENNY, Allan — 2
BENOIT-LEVY, Jean — 1
BENOLIEL, Solomon D. — 1
BENRIMO, Joseph Henry McAlpin
BENSEL, James Berry — H
BENSEL, John A. — 1
BENSINGER, Benjamin Edward — 1
BENSINGER, C. G. — 3
BENSLEY, Robert Russell — 3
BENSON, Alfred Washburn — 1
BENSON, Allan L. — 1
BENSON, Blackwood Ketcham — 4
BENSON, Carl — H
BENSON, Carville Dickinson
BENSON, Charles Emile — 4
BENSON, Egbert — H
BENSON, Einar William — 4
BENSON, Emanuel Mervyn — 5
BENSON, Eugene — 1
BENSON, Frank Weston — 3
BENSON, Frank Williamson — 1
BENSON, Franklin Thomas
BENSON, George A. — 3
BENSON, George Edward — 5
BENSON, Henry Kreitzer — 1
BENSON, Henry Lamdin — 1
BENSON, Henry Perkins — 4
BENSON, John — 4
BENSON, John Joseph — 1
BENSON, Louis FitzGerald
BENSON, Oscar Herman — 3
BENSON, Philip Adolphus — 2
BENSON, R. Dale — 4
BENSON, Ramsey — 1
BENSON, Reuel A. — 3
BENSON, Robert Dix — 1

BENSON, Sally — 5
BENSON, Samuel Page — H
BENSON, Simon — 2
BENSON, Stuart — 2
BENSON, Wilbur Earle — 5
BENSON, William Shepherd — 1
BENSWANGER, William Edward; — 5
BENT, Charles — H
BENT, Erling Sundt — 3
BENT, Josiah — 1
BENT, Myron Hammond — 1
BENT, Quincy — 3
BENT, Samuel Arthur — 1
BENT, Silas — H
BENT, Silas — 2
BENT, William — H
BENTE, Frederick
BENTHIN, Howard Arthur — 5
BENTLEY, Alvin Morell — 5
BENTLEY, Arthur — 1
BENTLEY, Arthur F. — 3
BENTLEY, Charles Edwin — 1
BENTLEY, Charles Eugene
BENTLEY, Charles Harvey — 1
BENTLEY, Charles Staughton — 4
BENTLEY, Clavin Pardee — 4
BENTLEY, Cyril Edmund — 1
BENTLEY, Edwin — 4
BENTLEY, Gordon Mansir — 3
BENTLEY, Harry Clark — 5
BENTLEY, Henry — 1
BENTLEY, Irene
BENTLEY, Jerome Harold — 4
BENTLEY, John Edward — 4
BENTLEY, Julian
BENTLEY, Madison — 3
BENTLEY, Percy Jardine
BENTLEY, Richard — 5
BENTLEY, Robert Irving
BENTLEY, Walter E. — 4
BENTLEY, William — H
BENTLEY, William Burdelle — 3
BENTLEY, William Frederick
BENTLEY, Wilson Alwyn — 1
BENTON, Alva Hartley — 2
BENTON, Angelo Ames — 1
BENTON, Arthur B. — 1
BENTON, Charles Swan — H
BENTON, Charles William
BENTON, Elbert Jay — 2
BENTON, Elma Hixson — 2
BENTON, Frank — 4
BENTON, George Alden — 1
BENTON, Guy Potter — 1
BENTON, Jacob — H
BENTON, James Gilchrist
BENTON, James Webb — 2
BENTON, Jay Rogers — 3
BENTON, Joel — 1
BENTON, John Edwin — 2
BENTON, John Keith — 3
BENTON, John Robert — 1
BENTON, Josiah Henry — 1
BENTON, Lemuel — H
BENTON, Maecenas E. — 4
BENTON, Mary Lathrop
BENTON, Stephen Olin — 1
BENTON, Thomas Hart * — H
BENTON, William — 5
BENYAURD, William H. H. — 1
BENZ, Francis E. — 3
BENZ, Harry Edward — 5
BENZ, Margaret Gilbert (Mrs. Luke L. Benz)
BENZE, C. Theodore — 1
BENZEL, Charles Frederick, Sr. — 5
BENZENBERG, George Henry — 1
BENZIGER, August — 3
BENZINGER, Frederic — 4
BEN-ZVI, Izhak — 1
BERANGER, Clara — 3
BERCH, Samuel Harry — 3
BERCKMANS, Bruce — 4
BERCOVICI, Konrad — 4
BERDAN, John — 3
BERDANIER, Paul Frederick — 4
BERDYAEV, Nickolai Alexadrovich — 4
BERENGER, Victor Henry — 3
BERENS, Conrad — 4

BERENSON, Bernard 3
BERESFORD, Harry 2
BERESFORD, Richard H
BERETTA, John King 2
BEREZOWSKY, Nicolai 3
BERG, Alban 4
BERG, Albert Ashton 3
BERG, Charles I. 1
BERG, Douglas Spearman 5
BERG, Ernst Julius 1
BERG, George Olaf 1
BERG, Gertrude 4
BERG, Irving Husted 1
BERG, J. Frederic 3
BERG, John Daniel 2
BERG, Joseph Frederic H
BERG, Kaj 5
BERG, Louis 5
BERG, Royal Howard 5
BERG, Walter Gilman 1
BERG, William Henry 1
BERGAN, Gerald T. 5
BERGE, Edward 1
BERGE, Irenee 5
BERGE, Wendell 3
BERGEL, Egon Ernest 5
BERGEMANN, Gustav Ernst 5
BERGEN, Fanny Dickerson 4
BERGEN, James J. 5
BERGEN, John Tallmadge 2
BERGEN, John Teunis H
BERGEN, Joseph Young 4
BERGEN, Teunis Garret H
BERGEN, Tunis G. 5
BERGEN, Van Brunt 1
BERGENGREN, Roy Frederick 3
BERGER, Adolph 1
BERGER, Augustin 4
BERGER, C. A. 4
BERGER, Calvin Michael
BERGER, Charles L. 2
BERGER, George Bart
BERGER, Lowe 4
BERGER, Maurice Wibert 5
BERGER, Meyer 3
BERGER, Victor L. 1
BERGER, Vilheim 1
BERGEY, David Hendricks 1
BERGH, Albert Ellery 4
BERGH, Arthur 4
BERGH, Christian H
BERGH, Henry H
BERGH, Lillie d'Angelo 5
BERGH, Louis De Coppet 1
BERGH, Louis O. 3
BERGHERM, Charles Russell 4
BERGHOFF, Robert S. 4
BERGHOLZ, Leo Allen 4
BERGIN, Alfred 4
BERGIN, Charles Kniese 4
BERGIN, John William 2
BERGLER, Edmund 4
BERGLUND, Abraham 2
BERGMAN, Walter James 5
BERGMANN, Carl H
BERGMANN, Werner H
BERGQUIST, J. Victor 1
BERGQUIST, Stanard Gustaf 3
BERGSAKER, Anders Johannessen 3
BERGSON, Henri H
BERGSON, Henri 4
BERGSON, Henri Louis 2
BERGSTROM, George Edwin 5
BERGTOLD, William Harry 1
BERING, Frank West 4
BERING, Vitus Jonassen H
BERINGER, George M. 1
BERINGER, Milton S. 4
BERKELEY, John H
BERKELEY, Norborne H
BERKELEY, Norborne 4
BERKELEY, Randolph Carter 3
BERKELEY, Sir William H
BERKELEY, William Nathaniel 1
BERKENMEYER, Wilhelm Christoph
BERKEY, Charles Peter 3
BERKEY, Peter 3
BERKLEY, Claude Wellington 4
BERKLEY, Henry Johns
BERKMAN, Alexander H
BERKMAN, Alexander 4
BERKNER, Lloyd Viel
BERKOWITZ, Abram 5
BERKOWITZ, Henry 1

BERKOWITZ, Mortimer 4
BERKOWITZ, Walter J. 4
BERKSON, Seymour 3
BERL, Ernst
BERL, Eugene Ennalls 3
BERLACK, Harris 5
BERLAGE, Hendrik Petrus
BERLE, Adolf Augustus 5
BERLE, Adolf Augustus 4
BERLIN, Alfred Franklin 1
BERLIN, Harold Robert 4
BERLIN, Theodore H. 4
BERLINER, Emile 1
BERLINER, Henry Adler 5
BERMAN, Benjamin Frank 5
BERMAN, Eugene 4
BERMAN, Louis 5
BERMAN, Morris 2
BERMAN, Oscar 3
BERMAN, Philip Grossman 5
BERMANN, Isidor Samuel Leopold 4
BERMINGHAM, Arthur Thomas 5
BERMUDEZ, Edouard Edmund H
BERN, Paul 1
BERNADOTTE FOLKE, Count 2
BERNADOU, John Baptiste 1
BERNARD, Frances Fenton 3
BERNARD, Frank Basil 5
BERNARD, Hugh Robertson; 5
BERNARD, John H
BERNARD, Lawrence Joseph 5
BERNARD, Luther Lee 3
BERNARD, Merrill 3
BERNARD, Sam 1
BERNARD, Simon H
BERNARD, Sir Francis H
BERNARD, Victor Ferdinand 4
BERNARD, William Bayle H
BERNARDIN, Joseph Mariotte 4
BERNATOWICZ, Albert John 5
BERNAYS, Augustus Charles 1
BERNBAUM, Ernest 3
BERNE, Eric Lennard 5
BERNE-ALLEN, Allan 5
BERNECKER, Edward M. 3
BERNEKER, Louis Frederick 1
BERNER, Harry M. 3
BERNET, John J. 1
BERNHARD, Alva Douglas 5
BERNHARD, Dorothy Lehman 5
BERNHARD, Joseph 3
BERNHARD, Richard J. 4
BERNHARD, William 5
BERNHARDT, Sarah 1
BERNHARDT, Wilhelm H
BERNHEIM, Bertram Moses 3
BERNHEIM, Oscar Frederick 4
BERNHEIMER, Charles L.
BERNHEIMER, Charles Seligman
BERNHISEL, John Milton H
BERNIE, Ben 2
BERNIER, Paul 4
BERNINGHAUS, Oscar Edmund
BERNSTEIN, Allne 5
BERNSTEIN, Charles 2
BERNSTEIN, David 5
BERNSTEIN, Herman 1
BERNSTEIN, Jacob Lawrence 5
BERNSTEIN, Louis 1
BERNSTEIN, Louis 4
BERNSTORFF, Count Johann
BERNSTROM, Victor 1
BEROLZHEIMER, Edwin Michael 2
BEROUJON, Claude H
BERRES, Albert Julius 5
BERRESFORD, Arthur William
BERRI, Wililam 1
BERRIEN, Cornelius Roach 5

BERRIEN, Frank Dunn 3
BERRIEN, John Macpherson H
BERRIGAN, Thomas Joseph 5
BERRY, Albert Edgar 1
BERRY, Albert Gleaves 5
BERRY, Albert Seaton 1
BERRY, Cecil Ralph 5
BERRY, Charles Harold 4
BERRY, Charles White 3
BERRY, Edward Wilber 5
BERRY, Edward Willard 5
BERRY, Frank 1
BERRY, Frank Allen 5
BERRY, George Leonard 2
BERRY, George Ricker 2
BERRY, George Titus 3
BERRY, Gilbert Milo 5
BERRY, Gordon Lockwood 2
BERRY, Harold Haile 4
BERRY, Harold Lee 5
BERRY, Hiram Gregory H
BERRY, Howard 2
BERRY, James Edward 4
BERRY, James Henderson 1
BERRY, John H
BERRY, John Cutting 4
BERRY, Joseph Flintoft 1
BERRY, Kearie Lee 4
BERRY, Lillian Gay 5
BERRY, Martha McChesney 2
BERRY, Nathaniel Springer H
BERRY, Raymond Hirst 5
BERRY, Robert Mallory 1
BERRY, Robert W. 4
BERRY, Thomas 3
BERRY, Wallace 2
BERRY, Walter Van Rensselaer 1
BERRY, Ward Leonard 4
BERRY, Wilbur Fisk 4
BERRY, William Franklin 1
BERRY, William H. 5
BERRY, William H. 4
BERRYMAN, Clifford Kennedy 2
BERRYMAN, James Thomas 5
BERRYMAN, Jerome Woods 5
BERRYMAN, John 5
BERRYMAN, John Brondgeest 2
BERRYMAN, W. A. 3
BERSELL, Petrus Olof Immanuel 5
BERSTED, Alfred 5
BERTHOLF, Ellsworth Price 1
BERTOLET, William S(chaeffer) 5
BERTRAM, Helen (Lulu May Burt) 5
BERTRAM, James 1
BERTRAM, John H
BERTRAND, Ernest 3
BERTRANDIAS, Victor Emile 4
BERTRON, Samuel R. 3
BERTRON, Samuel Reading 1
BERTSCH, Howard 5
BERWALD, William 4
BERWIND, Edward Julius 1
BESEMER, Howard Burhans 1
BESHLIN, Earl Hanley 5
BESLER, William George 2
BESLEY, Fred Wilson 5
BESLEY, Frederic Atwood 2
BESS, Demaree Caughey 4
BESS, Elmer Allen 5
BESSE, Arthur 3
BESSEY, Charles Edwin 1
BESSEY, Ernst Athearn 3
BESSON, Harlan 5
BESSON, Waldemar Max 5
BEST, Alfred M. 2
BEST, Clarence L. 3
BEST, Ernest Maurice 4
BEST, George Newton 1
BEST, Gertrude Delprat 2
BEST, Harry 1
BEST, Henry Riley 1
BEST, Howard Richard 5
BEST, James Irvin 4
BEST, James MacLeod 5
BEST, John G(arvin) 5
BEST, Nolan Rice 1
BEST, William 3
BEST, William Hall 4

BEST, William Parker 1
BESTIC, John Brereton 5
BESTON, Henry 5
BESTOR, Arthur Eugene 2
BESTOR, Paul 4
BESTROM, Leonard L. 5
BETETA, Ramon 4
BETH, Hilary Raymond 4
BETHEA, Jack 1
BETHEA, Solomon Hicks 1
BETHEL, George Emmett 4
BETHEL, John P. 3
BETHEL, Lawrence L. 4
BETHELL, Frank Hartsuff
BETHELL, Frank Hopkins; 5
BETHELL, Union Noble 1
BETHKE, William 4
BETHUNE, George Washington H
BETHUNE, Lauchlin H
BETHUNE, Louise 1
BETHUNE, Marion H
BETHUNE, Mary McLeod 5
BETTELHEIM, Edwin Summer J. 3
BETTEN, Cornelius 5
BETTEN, Francis Salesius 2
BETTENDORF, Joseph William 1
BETTENDORF, William Peter H
BETTENDORF, William Peter 4
BETTERIDGE, Walter Robert 1
BETTERS, Paul V. 3
BETTI, Ugo 4
BETTMAN, Alfred 2
BETTMAN, Gilbert 2
BETTMANN, Bernhard 1
BETTON, Silas H
BETTS, Albert Deems 4
BETTS, B. Frank 1
BETTS, Charles Henry 1
BETTS, Craven Langstroth 1
BETTS, Edgar Hayes 3
BETTS, Edward C. 2
BETTS, Frederic H. 1
BETTS, Frederick A. 4
BETTS, Frederick William 1
BETTS, George Herbert 1
BETTS, George Whitefield Jr. 3
BETTS, James A. 1
BETTS, Louis 4
BETTS, Philander III 2
BETTS, Samuel Rossiter 5
BETTS, Thaddeus H
BETTS, William James 4
BETTS, Noble Lycester
BETZ, Robert Milton 5
BEUGLER, Edwin James 5
BEUKEMA, Herman 5
BEURY, Charles E. 3
BEUTEL, Albert Phillip 5
BEUTENMULLER, William
BEVAN, Arthur Dean 2
BEVAN, Charles Frederick 5
BEVAN, Laurence A. 4
BEVAN, Lynne J. 3
BEVAN, Thomas Horatio 4
BEVAN, W. Lloyd 2
BEVEN, John Lansing 2
BEVERIDGE, Albert Jeremiah 1
BEVERIDGE, Andrew Bennie 5
BEVERIDGE, Frank Stanley 3
BEVERIDGE, Hugh Raymond 4
BEVERIDGE, John Harrie 1
BEVERIDGE, John Lourie 1
BEVERIDGE, Kuhne 5
BEVERIDGE, Lord William Henry 4
BEVERLY, Robert H
BEVIER, Isabel 2
BEVIER, Louis 1
BEVIN, Ernest 3
BEVIS, Howard Landis 5
BEWER, Julius August 3
BEWLEY, Anthony H
BEWLEY, Edwin Elmore
BEWLEY, Luther Boone 5
BEXELL, John Andrew 2
BEYE, Howard Lombard 1
BEYE, William 5
BEYEA, Herbert Writer 5
BEYER, Frederick Charles 4

BEYER, George Eugene
BEYER, Gustav
BEYER, Henry Gustav
BEYER, Otto Sternhof
BEYER, Samuel Walker
BEYERS, Henry Wendell
BEYL, John Lewis
BEZANSON, Osborne
BEZIAT, Andre
BHABHA, Homi Jehangir
BIANCHI, Julio Domingo
BIANCHI, Martha Dickinson
BIARD, Pierre
BIAS, Randolph
BIBB, George Motier
BIBB, William Wyatt
BIBBY, James Harry
BIBERMAN, Herbert J.
BIBIGHAUS, Thomas Marshal
BIBLE, Frank William
BIBLE, George Albert
BICKEL, Karl August
BICKEL, Shlomo
BICKELHAUPT, Carroll Owen
BICKELHAUPT, George Bernard
BICKERDYKE, Mary Ann Ball
BICKET, James Pratt
BICKETT, Fanny Neal Yarborough
BICKETT, Thomas Walter
BICKFORD, Thomas
BICKFORD, Walter Mansur
BICKHAM, Warren Stone
BICKING, Ada Elizabeth
BICKLE, Edward William
BICKLEY, George Harvey
BICKLEY, Howard Lee
BICKMORE, Albert Smith
BICKNELL, Bennet
BICKNELL, Ernest Percy
BICKNELL, Frank Alfred
BICKNELL, Frank Martin
BICKNELL, George Augustus
BICKNELL, George Augustus
BICKNELL, Lewis Williams
BICKNELL, Thomas Williams
BICKNELL, Warren Moses
BICKNELL, William Harry Warren
BICKS, Alexander
BICKSLER, W. Scott
BIDDINGER, Noble Lycester
BIDDLE, A. J. Drexel
BIDDLE, Alexander
BIDDLE, Andrew Porter
BIDDLE, Anthony Joseph Drexel
BIDDLE, Arney Sylvenus
BIDDLE, Charles J.
BIDDLE, Charles John
BIDDLE, Clement
BIDDLE, Clement Miller, Sr.
BIDDLE, Edward
BIDDLE, Edward William
BIDDLE, Francis
BIDDLE, Henry Chalmers
BIDDLE, Horace P.
BIDDLE, James
BIDDLE, James Stokes
BIDDLE, John
BIDDLE, John
BIDDLE, Nicholas *
BIDDLE, Nicholas
BIDDLE, Richard
BIDDLE, Ward Gray
BIDDLE, William Baxter
BIDDLE, William Phillips
BIDLACK, Benjamin Alden
BIDWELL, Annie Ellicott Kennedy
BIDWELL, Barnabas
BIDWELL, Charles Clarence
BIDWELL, Daniel Doane
BIDWELL, Edwin Curtis
BIDWELL, George Rogers
BIDWELL, John
BIDWELL, Marshall Spring
BIDWELL, Marshall Spring

Name	Vol
BIDWELL, Percy Wells	5
BIDWELL, Walter Hilliard	H
BIEBEL, Franklin Matthews	4
BIEBER, Charles L.	4
BIEBER, Sidney	5
BIEDERBICK, Henry	1
BIEDERMANN, August Julius	
BIEDERWOLF, William Edward	
BIEFELD, Paul Alfred	4
BIEGLER, Philip Sheridan	2
BIELASKI, Alexander Bruce	4
BIEN, Julius	1
BIEN, Morris	1
BIENVILLE, 'sieur 'de	H
BIERBAUM, Christopher Henry	2
BIERBOWER, Austin	1
BIERCE, Ambrose	4
BIERCE, Ambrose Gwinett	
BIERD, William Grant	1
BIERER, Andrew Gordon Curtin Jr.	3
BIERER, Andrew Gregg Curtin	3
BIERI, Bernhard Henry	
BIERRING, Walter Lawrence	
BIERS, Howard	4
BIERSTADT, Albert	1
BIESECKER, Frederick Winters	1
BIESTERFELD, Chester H.	3
BIFFLE, Leslie L.	4
BIGELOW, Abijah	H
BIGELOW, Archibald Pierce	3
BIGELOW, Bruce Macmillan	3
BIGELOW, Charles C.	3
BIGELOW, Daniel Folger	H
BIGELOW, Daniel Folger	4
BIGELOW, Edith Evelyn	4
BIGELOW, Edward Fuller	1
BIGELOW, Erastus Brigham	H
BIGELOW, Florence	3
BIGELOW, Francis Hill	1
BIGELOW, Frank Hagar	1
BIGELOW, Frank Hoffnagel	1
BIGELOW, Frederic Russell	2
BIGELOW, Frederick Southgate	3
BIGELOW, George Hoyt	1
BIGELOW, Harriet Williams	1
BIGELOW, Harry Augustus	2
BIGELOW, Henry Bryant	4
BIGELOW, Henry Forbes	1
BIGELOW, Henry Jacob	H
BIGELOW, Herbert Seely	3
BIGELOW, Jacob	H
BIGELOW, John *	1
BIGELOW, John Milton	4
BIGELOW, Lewis	H
BIGELOW, Marshall Train	1
BIGELOW, Mason Huntington	5
BIGELOW, Maurice Alpheus	
BIGELOW, Melville Madison	
BIGELOW, Poultney	3
BIGELOW, Prescott	5
BIGELOW, Robert Mansfield	
BIGELOW, Robert Payne	3
BIGELOW, Samuel Lawrence	2
BIGELOW, Willard Dell	1
BIGELOW, William Frederick	
BIGELOW, William Sturgis	
BIGGAR, Hamilton Fisk	
BIGGAR, Oliver Mowat	1
BIGGER, Frederick	4
BIGGER, Isaac Alexander	
BIGGER, Robert Rush	1
BIGGERS, Earl Derr	1
BIGGERS, George Clinton	4
BIGGIN, Frederic Child	2
BIGGS, Albert Welburne	1
BIGGS, Asa	H
BIGGS, Benjamin T.	1
BIGGS, Benjamin Thomas	H
BIGGS, David Clifton	1
BIGGS, Hermann Michael	1
BIGGS, J. Crawford	3
BIGGS, Walter	1
BIGHAM, Madge Alford	5
BIGHAM, Truman C.	3
BIGLER, Henry William	
BIGLER, John	H
BIGLER, John Adolph	4
BIGLER, Regina Marie	4
BIGLER, William	4
BIGLER, William H.	1
BIGLOW, Lucius Horatio	4
BIGNELL, Effie Molt	1
BIJUR, Nathan	1
BIKLE, Henry Wolf	1
BIKLE, Philip Melanchthon	1
BIKRAM, Tribhubana Bir	3
BILBO, Theodore Gilmore	2
BILBY, George N.	1
BILDERSEE, Adele	5
BILES, George Phineas	1
BILGRAM, Hugo	1
BILL, Alfred Hoyt	4
BILL, Earl Gordon	2
BILL, Edward Lyman	1
BILL, John G.	3
BILL, Ledyard	1
BILL, Nathan D.	1
BILL, Raymond	3
BILLADO, Francis William	4
BILLANY, Harry Hilton	4
BILLER, George Jr.	1
BILLHARDT, Fred A.	5
BILLIKOPF, Jacob	3
BILLINGHURST, Benson Dillon	1
BILLINGHURST, Charles	H
BILLINGS, Charles Ethan	4
BILLINGS, Cornelius Kingsley Garrison	1
BILLINGS, Edmund	1
BILLINGS, Edward Everett	1
BILLINGS, Frank	1
BILLINGS, Frank Seaver	4
BILLINGS, Franklin Swift	1
BILLINGS, Frederic Church	5
BILLINGS, Frederick	H
BILLINGS, Frederic Horatio	5
BILLINGS, George Herrick	1
BILLINGS, J(ohn) Harland	5
BILLINGS, John Shaw	1
BILLINGS, Josh	1
BILLINGS, Luther Guiteau	1
BILLINGS, Stephen Ellsworth	5
BILLINGS, W. Chester	1
BILLINGS, William	H
BILLINGSLEY, Allen Loren	3
BILLINGSLEY, Paul	4
BILLINGSLEY, Sherman	4
BILLINGSLEY, William Newton	4
BILLNER, Karl Paul	4
BILLOW, Clayton Oscar	2
BILLS, Hubert Leo	1
BILLSON, William Weldon	1
BILLY 'THE KID	H
BILMANIS, Alfred	2
BILOTTI, Anton	4
BIMELER, Joseph Michael	H
BIMSON, Lloyd A.	4
BINCH, Wilfred Reese	5
BINDER, Carroll	3
BINDER, Rudolph Michael	1
BINDERUP, Charles Gustav	3
BINES, Thomas	H
BINFORD, Jessie Florence	4
BINFORD, Lloyd Tilghman	3
BINFORD, Raymond	5
BINGAY, Malcolm Wallace	3
BINGHAM, Amelia	1
BINGHAM, Anne Willing	1
BINGHAM, Caleb	H
BINGHAM, David Judson	1
BINGHAM, Edward Franklin	4
BINGHAM, Eugene Cook	2
BINGHAM, Florence Cornell	4
BINGHAM, George Caleb	H
BINGHAM, George Hutchins	5
BINGHAM, Gonzalez Sidney	4
BINGHAM, Guy Morse	5
BINGHAM, Harry	4
BINGHAM, Henry Harrison	1
BINGHAM, Herbert Mackay	4
BINGHAM, Hiram	1
BINGHAM, Hiram	1
BINGHAM, Hiram	3
BINGHAM, Joel Foote	1
BINGHAM, John Armor	H
BINGHAM, Kinsley Scott	H
BINGHAM, Millicent Todd (Mrs. Walter V. Bingham)	5
BINGHAM, Norman Williams	3
BINGHAM, Ralph	1
BINGHAM, Robert	1
BINGHAM, Robert Fry	2
BINGHAM, Robert Worth	1
BINGHAM, Stillman	1
BINGHAM, Theodore Alfred	1
BINGHAM, Walter Van Dyke	3
BINGHAM, Wheelock Hayward	5
BINGHAM, William *	H
BINGHAM, William II	3
BINGHAM, William J.	5
BINGHAM, William Theodore	1
BINING, Arthur Cecil	3
BIN ISHAK, Inche Yusoff	5
BINKLEY, Almond M(adison)	5
BINKLEY, Christian Kreider	5
BINKLEY, Robert Cedric	1
BINKLEY, Wilfred Ellsworth	4
BINKLEY, William Campbell	5
BINNEY, Amos	H
BINNEY, Arthur	1
BINNEY, Charles Chauncey	1
BINNEY, Edwin	1
BINNEY, Horace	H
BINNEY, John	1
BINNICKER, Richard Johnson	5
BINNIE, John Fairbairn	4
BINNION, Randolph	1
BINNS, Archie	5
BINNS, Charles Fergus	3
BINNS, Jack	3
BINNS, John	H
BINNS, John Alexander	H
BINNS, Walter Pope	4
BIN-NUN, Dov	5
BINSSE, Louis Francis 'de Paul	H
BINSTED, Norman Spencer	4
BINYON, Robert Laurence	2
BIOLETTI, Frederic Theodore	4
BIPPUS, Rupert Frederick	3
BIRCH, David Robert	5
BIRCH, Reginald Bathurst	2
BIRCH, Stephen	1
BIRCH, T. Bruce	1
BIRCH, Thomas	H
BIRCH, Thomas Howard	1
BIRCH, William Russell	H
BIRCHARD, Clarence C.	4
BIRCHARD, Glen Robbins	4
BIRCKHEAD, Hugh	1
BIRCKHEAD, Oliver W.	4
BIRD, Abraham Calvin	4
BIRD, Anna Child	4
BIRD, Anna Pennock	5
BIRD, Arthur	3
BIRD, Charles	1
BIRD, Charles	3
BIRD, Charles Sumner	1
BIRD, Eugene Hunt	4
BIRD, Frederic Mayer	1
BIRD, George Emerson	1
BIRD, Hobart Stanley	4
BIRD, James Pyper	3
BIRD, John	H
BIRD, John E.	1
BIRD, Paul Percy	5
BIRD, Philip Smead	2
BIRD, Reginald William	3
BIRD, Remsen du Bois	5
BIRD, Robert Montgomery	H
BIRD, Robert Montgomery	1
BIRD, Wallace Samuel	5
BIRD, Winfield Austin Scott	4
BIRDSALL, Benjamin P.	1
BIRDSALL, Carl A.	3
BIRDSALL, James	H
BIRDSALL, Samuel	1
BIRDSALL, William W.	1
BIRDSEYE, Clarence	3
BIRDSEYE, Claude Hale	1
BIRDSEYE, Victory	H
BIRDWELL, Alton William	3
BIRGE, Edward Asahel	3
BIRGE, Edward Bailey	3
BIRGE, Henry Warner	H
BIRGE, Julius	3
BIRK, Newman Peter	4
BIRKBECK, Morris	H
BIRKE, William D.	4
BIRKENMEYER, Carl Bruce	5
BIRKHEAD, Claude Vivian	3
BIRKHEAD, Leon Milton	3
BIRKHIMER, William Edward	3
BIRKHOFF, George David	2
BIRKINBINE, John	1
BIRKMIRE, William Harvey	1
BIRMINGHAM, Henry Patrick	1
BIRNBAUM, Martin	5
BIRNEY, Arthur Alexis	1
BIRNEY, David Bell	H
BIRNEY, Hoffman	3
BIRNEY, James	H
BIRNEY, James Gillespie	3
BIRNEY, Lauress J.	1
BIRNEY, William	1
BIRNEY, William Verplanck	1
BIRNIE, Rogers	2
BIRNIE, Upton Jr.	3
BIRNKRANT, Michael Charles	4
BIRREN, Joseph P.	1
BIRTLEY, Robert Lewis	3
BIRTWELL, Charles Wesley	1
BISBEE, Eldon	4
BISBEE, Frederick Adelbert	1
BISBEE, Horatio	4
BISBEE, Joseph Bartlett	1
BISBEE, Marvin Davis	1
BISBEE, Spaulding	3
BISBEE, William Henry	2
BISBING, Henry Singlewood	1
BISCH, Louis Edward	4
BISCHOFF, Henry Jr.	1
BISCOE, Alvin B.	4
BISCOE, Howard Morton	3
BISCOE, Thomas Dwight	3
BISEY, Sunker Abaji	1
BISHOP, Abraham	H
BISHOP, Arthur Giles	2
BISHOP, Arthur Vaughan	3
BISHOP, Avard Longley	5
BISHOP, Bruce Clay	5
BISHOP, Charles Alvord	1
BISHOP, Charles McTyeire	1
BISHOP, Charles Reed	H
BISHOP, Charles Reed	4
BISHOP, Curtis Vance	4
BISHOP, Daniel Sanborn	3
BISHOP, David Horace	5
BISHOP, Eben Faxon	4
BISHOP, Edwin Whitney	2
BISHOP, Elias B.	1
BISHOP, Emily Montague	1
BISHOP, Ernest Simons	1
BISHOP, Eugene Lindsay	3
BISHOP, Everett L.	4
BISHOP, Farnham	4
BISHOP, Frederic Lendall	2
BISHOP, Geo(rge) Lee	5
BISHOP, George Sayles	1
BISHOP, George Taylor	1
BISHOP, Harry Gore	1
BISHOP, Heber Reginald	1
BISHOP, Henry Alfred	1
BISHOP, Hubert Keeney	5
BISHOP, Irving Prescott	4
BISHOP, James	H
BISHOP, James	1
BISHOP, James Robert Thoburn	3
BISHOP, Joel Prentiss	H
BISHOP, John Peale	2
BISHOP, John Remsen	1
BISHOP, Joseph Bucklin	1
BISHOP, Judson Wade	4
BISHOP, Louis Faugeres	1
BISHOP, Mrs. L. Brackett	
BISHOP, Nathan	H
BISHOP, Percy Poe	4
BISHOP, Phanuel	H
BISHOP, Robert H.	4
BISHOP, Robert Hamilton	H
BISHOP, Roswell P.	4
BISHOP, Samuel A.	5
BISHOP, Samuel Henry	1
BISHOP, Sereno Edwards	1
BISHOP, Seth Scott	1
BISHOP, William Darius	1
BISHOP, William Henry	1
BISHOP, William Samuel	2
BISHOP, William Warner	3
BISHOPP, Fred Corry	5
BISPHAM, David Scull	1
BISPHAM, George Tucker	1
BISSELL, Arthur Douglas	
BISSELL, Charles Spencer	5
BISSELL, Clayton Lawrence	5
BISSELL, Dougal	1
BISSELL, E. Perot	2
BISSELL, Edwin Cone	H
BISSELL, French Rayburn	
BISSELL, George Edwin	1
BISSELL, George Henry	H
BISSELL, George Welton	4
BISSELL, Herbert Porter	
BISSELL, Hezekiah	1
BISSELL, Howard	1
BISSELL, John Henry	1
BISSELL, John William	4
BISSELL, Mary Taylor	5
BISSELL, Pelham St George	2
BISSELL, Richard Mervin	1
BISSELL, Walter Henry	1
BISSELL, William Grosvenor	
BISSELL, William Henry	H
BISSELL, Wilson Shannon	1
BISSELLE, Hulbert T.	4
BISSETT, Clark Prescott	1
BISSIER, Julius	4
BISSIKUMMER, Charles Hills	4
BISSONNETTE, T. Hume	3
BISSOT, Francois Marie	H
BISSOT, Jean Baptiste	H
BISTLINE, Francis M.	5
BITNER, Harry Murray	4
BITTER, Francis	4
BITTER, Karl Theodore Francis	1
BITTING, William Coleman	1
BITTINGER, John Lawrence	1
BITTINGER, Lucy Forney	4
BITTNER, John Joseph	4
BITTNER, Van Amburg	2
BIXBY, Ammi Leander	5
BIXBY, Anna Pierce Hobbs	H
BIXBY, Augustus Rufus	4
BIXBY, Edson Kingman	1
BIXBY, Harold McMillian	4
BIXBY, Horace Ezra	H
BIXBY, Horace Ezra	1
BIXBY, James Thompson	1
BIXBY, Kenneth Roberts	5
BIXBY, Tams	1
BIXBY, William Herbert	1
BIXBY, William Keeney	1
BIXER, Edmond P.	5
BIXLER, Edward Clinton	5
BIXLER, James Wilson	4
BIZE, Louis A.	5
BIZZELL, James Adrian	2

BIZZELL, William Bennett 2
BJERREGAARD, Carl Henry Andrew 1
BJOERLING, Jussi 4
BJORK, David Knuth 4
BJORKMAN, Edwin 3
BJORNSSON, Sveinn 3
BJORNSTAD, Altrea William 1
BLABON, Joseph Ward 1
BLACK, Albert Gain 4
BLACK, Alexander 1
BLACK, Alfred Lawrence 1
BLACK, Arthur Davenport 1
BLACK, Benjamin Warren 2
BLACK, Carl E. 4
BLACK, Charles Clarke 2
BLACK, Charles E. 3
BLACK, Chauncey Forward 1
BLACK, Clinton R. Jr. 4
BLACK, Dugald 4
BLACK, E. Charlton 1
BLACK, Edward Junius H
BLACK, Ernest Bateman 2
BLACK, Eugene Robert 1
BLACK, Forrest Revere 2
BLACK, Frank B. 1
BLACK, Frank Swett 1
BLACK, Garland C. 3
BLACK, George Harold 3
BLACK, George Robison H
BLACK, Greene Vardiman 1
BLACK, Harold Alfred 5
BLACK, Harry Alfred 1
BLACK, Harry S. 1
BLACK, Henry H
BLACK, Henry Campbell 1
BLACK, Howard 4
BLACK, Hugh 3
BLACK, Hugh S. 3
BLACK, Hugo La Fayette 5
BLACK, James * H
BLACK, James Augustus H
BLACK, James Byers 4
BLACK, James C. C. 1
BLACK, James Dixon 1
BLACK, James Harvey 3
BLACK, James William 1
BLACK, Jenny O. 3
BLACK, Jeremiah Sullivan H
BLACK, John H
BLACK, John Charles 1
BLACK, John Clarke 1
BLACK, John Donald 3
BLACK, John Donald 4
BLACK, John Janvier 1
BLACK, Lloyd Llewellyn 3
BLACK, Loring M. 3
BLACK, Mrs. Madeleine Elmer; 5
BLACK, Malcolm Stuart 4
BLACK, Melville 5
BLACK, Newton Henry 5
BLACK, Norman David 2
BLACK, Norman David, Jr. 5
BLACK, Robert Howell 4
BLACK, Robert Lounsbury 3
BLACK, Ruby Aurora 3
BLACK, Ryland Melville 4
BLACK, S(amuel) Bruce 5
BLACK, Samuel Charles 1
BLACK, Samuel Duncan 3
BLACK, Samuel Luccock 4
BLACK, Van-Lear 1
BLACK, Walter Joseph 3
BLACK, William 1
BLACK, William Harman 5
BLACK, William Henry 1
BLACK, William Joseph 4
BLACK, William Murray 1
BLACK, William Wesley 2
BLACK, Winifred 1
BLACK, Witherbee 3
BLACKALL, Christopher Rubey 1
BLACKALL, Clarence Howard 1
BLACKALL, Clarence Howard 2
BLACKALL, Frederick Steele 1
BLACKALL, Frederick Steele Jr. 4
BLACKARD, James Washington 1
BLACKBEARD H
BLACKBURN, Alexander 1
BLACKBURN, Armour Jennings 5
BLACKBURN, Edmund Spencer 4
BLACKBURN, Frederick George 5
BLACKBURN, George Andrew 1
BLACKBURN, George Stebbins 4
BLACKBURN, Gideon H
BLACKBURN, John Henry 3
BLACKBURN, John Simpson 4
BLACKBURN, Joseph H
BLACKBURN, Joseph Clay Styles 1
BLACKBURN, Joseph E. 4
BLACKBURN, K. Wilde 3
BLACKBURN, Luke Pryor H
BLACKBURN, Merrill Mason 3
BLACKBURN, Robert 1
BLACKBURN, William J. 2
BLACKBURN, William Jasper 1
BLACKBURN, William Maxwell 1
BLACKBURN, William Wallace 4
BLACKBURN, Willis Clifford 5
BLACKBURNE, Mary Frances 5
BLACKER, Daniel James 5
BLACKERBY, Philip Earle 2
BLACKFAN, Kenneth D. 1
BLACKFORD, Eugene Gilbert 1
BLACKFORD, Katherine M(elvina) H(untsinger) 5
BLACKFORD, Launcelot Minor 1
BLACKFORD, Staige Davis 2
BLACKHAM, George Edmund 1
BLACK HAWK H
BLACK KETTLE H
BLACKLEDGE, William H
BLACKLEDGE, William Salter H
BLACKMAN, Edward Bernard 5
BLACKMAN, William Fremont 1
BLACKMAN, William Waldo 2
BLACKMAR, Abel Edward 1
BLACKMAR, Charles Maxwell 4
BLACKMAR, Esbon H
BLACKMAR, Frank Wilson 1
BLACKMARR, Frank Hamlin 5
BLACKMER, Henry M. 5
BLACKMER, Samuel Howard 3
BLACKMON, Frederick Leonard 1
BLACKMORE, Emil A. 4
BLACKMORE, George Augustus 2
BLACKMORE, Henry Spencer 4
BLACKMORE, Simon Augustine 1
BLACKMUR, Richard Palmer 4
BLACKNEY, William Wallace 4
BLACKSTOCK, Ira Burton 1
BLACKSTONE, A. E. 3
BLACKSTONE, Richard 1
BLACKSTONE, Timothy B. 1
BLACKSTONE, William H
BLACKTON, J. Stuart 1
BLACKWELDER, Charles Davis 4
BLACKWELL, Alice Stone 2
BLACKWELL, Antoinette Louisa Brown 1
BLACKWELL, Elizabeth 1
BLACKWELL, Emily 1
BLACKWELL, George Lincoln 4
BLACKWELL, Hubert Charles Hansard 3
BLACKWELL, James Shannon 4
BLACKWELL, Julius W. H
BLACKWELL, Otto Bernard 5
BLACKWELL, Robert Emory 1
BLACKWELL, Thomas Joseph 4
BLACKWOOD, Alexander Leslie 1
BLACKWOOD, Andrew Watterson 4
BLACKWOOD, Ibra C. 1
BLACKWOOD, Norman Jerome 1
BLACKWOOD, Oswald 3
BLADEN, William H
BLAESS, August F. 5
BLAFFER, Robert Lee 2
BLAGDEN, Augustus Silliman 4
BLAHD, Mose Emmett 1
BLAIKIE, William 1
BLAIN, Alexander William 4
BLAIN, Hugh Mercer, Sr. 5
BLAINE, Helen Louise Townsend 5
BLAINE, James Gillespie 5
BLAINE, James Gillespie H
BLAINE, John J. 1
BLAINE, Mrs. Emmons 3
BLAIR, Albion Zelophehad 4
BLAIR, Algernon 3
BLAIR, Andrew Alexander 1
BLAIR, Apolline Madison 4
BLAIR, Austin H
BLAIR, Bernard H
BLAIR, C. Ledyard 4
BLAIR, Charles Austin 1
BLAIR, Chauncey J. 1
BLAIR, Cowgill 4
BLAIR, David Ellmore 3
BLAIR, David H. 2
BLAIR, Edwin Foster 5
BLAIR, Eliza Nelson 1
BLAIR, Emily Newell 3
BLAIR, Emma Helen 1
BLAIR, Eugenie (Mrs. Robert L. Downing) 5
BLAIR, Floyd Gilbert 4
BLAIR, Francis Grant 1
BLAIR, Francis Grant 2
BLAIR, Francis Preston H
BLAIR, Francis Preston Jr. H
BLAIR, Frank Warrenner 3
BLAIR, Frederic Howes 3
BLAIR, Harry Wallace 4
BLAIR, Henry Alexander 5
BLAIR, Henry Augustus 1
BLAIR, Henry Patterson 2
BLAIR, Henry William 1
BLAIR, Herbert Francis 5
BLAIR, Hugh McLeod 1
BLAIR, Jack F. 5
BLAIR, James * H
BLAIR, James A. Jr. 1
BLAIR, James Carroll 3
BLAIR, James Lawrence 1
BLAIR, James T. Jr. 4
BLAIR, James Thomas 2
BLAIR, John * H
BLAIR, John Halsey 1
BLAIR, John Insley 1
BLAIR, John Leo 4
BLAIR, Joseph Cullen 1
BLAIR, Joseph Paxton 2
BLAIR, Margaret Josephine 4
BLAIR, Montgomery H
BLAIR, Samuel H
BLAIR, Samuel Steel H
BLAIR, Vilray Papin 3
BLAIR, Walter Dabney 3
BLAIR, Watson Franklin 1
BLAIR, William Allen 2
BLAIR, William Reid 2
BLAIR, William Wightman 3
BLAIR-SMITH, Robert M. 5
BLAISDELL, Albert Franklin 1
BLAISDELL, Anthony Houghtaling 1
BLAISDELL, Daniel H
BLAISDELL, Gideon Moores 5
BLAISDELL, James Arnold 3
BLAISDELL, Thomas Charles 2
BLAISDELL, Warren Carl 5
BLAKE, A. Harold 3
BLAKE, Charles S. 1
BLAKE, Chauncey Etheridge 2
BLAKE, Clarence John 1
BLAKE, Clinton Hamlin 2
BLAKE, Edgar 2
BLAKE, Edgar Jr. 2
BLAKE, Edward Everett 2
BLAKE, Eli Whitney H
BLAKE, Emily Calvin 3
BLAKE, Francis 1
BLAKE, Francis Gilman 3
BLAKE, Frederic Columbus 5
BLAKE, George H. 5
BLAKE, Harold Hamilton 5
BLAKE, Harrison Gray Otis H
BLAKE, Henry Nichols 1
BLAKE, Henry Seavey 3
BLAKE, Henry William 1
BLAKE, Homer Crane H
BLAKE, James Henry 4
BLAKE, James Vila 1
BLAKE, John Jr. H
BLAKE, John Charles 5
BLAKE, John George 1
BLAKE, John Lauris H
BLAKE, John Walter 4
BLAKE, Joseph Augustus 1
BLAKE, Katherine Alexander Duer 1
BLAKE, Lillie Devereux 1
BLAKE, Lucien Ira 1
BLAKE, Luther Lee 3
BLAKE, Lyman Reed H
BLAKE, Lynn Stanford 4
BLAKE, Mary Elizabeth 1
BLAKE, Mary Katharine Evans 4
BLAKE, Maxwell 3
BLAKE, Monroe Williams 3
BLAKE, Ralph Mason 3
BLAKE, Robert Pierpont 3
BLAKE, Sidney Fay 4
BLAKE, Theodore Evernghim 2
BLAKE, Thomas Holdsworth H
BLAKE, Tiffany 2
BLAKE, Warren Everett 4
BLAKE, William Phipps 1
BLAKE, William Rufus H
BLAKELEY, George Henry 2
BLAKELOCK, Ralph Albert 1
BLAKELY, Bertha Eliza 5
BLAKELY, George 5
BLAKELY, John Russell Young 2
BLAKELY, Johnston H
BLAKEMORE, Arthur Hendley 5
BLAKENEY, Albert Alexander 1
BLAKESLEE, Albert Francis 3
BLAKESLEE, Arthur Lyman 4
BLAKESLEE, Clarence 4
BLAKESLEE, Dennis A. 1
BLAKESLEE, Edwin Mitchell 4
BLAKESLEE, Erastus 1
BLAKESLEE, Francis Durbin 2
BLAKESLEE, Fred Gilbert 2
BLAKESLEE, George Hubbard 3
BLAKESLEE, Howard Walter 3
BLAKESLEE, Raymond Ives 1
BLAKEY, Roy Gillispie 5
BLAKSLEE, James I. 5
BLALOCK, Alfred 4
BLALOCK, Jesse Marion 5
BLALOCK, Myron Geer 3
BLALOCK, U(riah) Benton 5
BLAMER, DeWitt 5
BLANC, Antoine H
BLANCH, Arnold 5
BLANCHARD, Amy Ella 1
BLANCHARD, Arthur Alphonzo 4
BLANCHARD, Arthur Horace 5
BLANCHARD, Charles Albert 1
BLANCHARD, Clarence John 4
BLANCHARD, Ferdinand Quincy 5
BLANCHARD, Frank LeRoy 1
BLANCHARD, Frederic Thomas 2
BLANCHARD, George Roberts 1
BLANCHARD, Grace 2
BLANCHARD, Harold Hooper 5
BLANCHARD, Harold M. 4
BLANCHARD, Henry 1
BLANCHARD, James Armstrong 1
BLANCHARD, John H
BLANCHARD, Jonathan * H
BLANCHARD, LaFayette Randall 5
BLANCHARD, Lucy Mansfield 1
BLANCHARD, Murray 5
BLANCHARD, Nathan Weston 1
BLANCHARD, Newton Crain 1
BLANCHARD, Ozro Seth 3
BLANCHARD, Ralph Harris 5
BLANCHARD, Raoul 5
BLANCHARD, Rufus 1
BLANCHARD, Thomas H
BLANCHARD, William H. 4
BLANCHARD, William Martin 2
BLANCHET, Clement Theophilus 4
BLANCHET, Francois Norbert H
BLANCHET, John Baptiste 3
BLANCKE, Leo Mulford 4
BLANCKE, William Henry 3
BLANCKE, Wilton Wendell 5
BLANCO-FOMBONA, Rufino 5
BLAND, Henry Meade 1
BLAND, John Randolph 1
BLAND, Oscar E. 3
BLAND, Pascal Brooke 1
BLAND, Richard H
BLAND, Richard Howard 3
BLAND, Richard Parks 1
BLAND, Schuyler Otis 2
BLAND, Theodorick H
BLAND, Thomas H
BLAND, William Thomas 1
BLANDEN, Charles Granger 1
BLANDFORD, John Bennett, Jr. 5
BLANDIN, Charles Kenneth 3
BLANDING, Albert Hazen 5
BLANDING, Don 3
BLANDY, William Henry Purnell 3
BLANEY, Dwight 2
BLANEY, Henry R. 4
BLANEY, Isabella Williams 1
BLANEY, William Osgood 1
BLANKENBUEHLER-, John H. 4
BLANKENBURG, Lucretia Longshore 2
BLANKENBURG, Rudolph 1
BLANKENHORN, Marion Arthur 3
BLANKS, Robert Franklin 3
BLANTON, Annie Webb 2
BLANTON, John Diell 1
BLANTON, Joseph Philip 4
BLANTON, Lindsay Hughes 1
BLANTON, Smiley 4
BLANTON, Thomas Lindsay 3
BLANTON, Wyndham Bolling 4
BLASDEL, Henry Goode H
BLASH, Rudolph F. 3
BLASHFIELD, Albert Dodd 1
BLASHFIELD, Edwin Howland 1
BLATCH, Harriet Stanton 1
BLATCHFORD, Charles Hammond 3
BLATCHFORD, Eliphalet Wickes 1

BLATCHFORD, Richard Milford — H
BLATCHFORD, Richard Milford — 1
BLATCHLEY, Samuel — H
BLATCHLEY, Willis Stanley — 1
BLATT, William M(osher) — 5
BLATTEIS, Simon Risefeld — 5
BLATTENBERGER, Raymond — 5
BLAU, Max Friedrich — 1
BLAUER, William E. — 3
BLAUSTEIN, Jacob — 5
BLAUSTEIN, Louis — 5
BLAUVELT, Bradford — 5
BLAUVELT, Charles F. — 1
BLAUVELT, Lillian Evans — 2
BLAUVELT, Martin Post — 1
BLAUVELT, Mary Taylor — 5
BLAVATSKY, Helena Petrovna Hahn
BLAXTER, Henry Vaughan — 2
BLAYLOCK, Louis — 1
BLAYNEY, John McClusky — 1
BLAYNEY, T(homas) Lindsey — 5
BLAZER, Paul Garrett
BLEAKLEY, William Francis — 5
BLEASE, Coleman Livingston — 1
BLEASE, Coleman Livingston — 2
BLECKLEY, Logan E. — 1
BLECKWENN, William Jefferson — 4
BLEDSOE, Albert Taylor — H
BLEDSOE, Benjamin Franklin — 1
BLEDSOE, Jesse — H
BLEDSOE, Samuel Thomas — 1
BLEECKER, Ann Eliza — H
BLEECKER, Harmanus — H
BLEECKER, John Van Benthuysen — 1
BLEGEN, Carl William — 5
BLEICH, Clements Harry — 5
BLEICHER, Clarence E. — 3
BLEININGER, Albert Victor — 2
BLENDER, Dorothea Klotz — 5
BLENDINGER, Fred L. — 1
BLENK, James Hubert — 1
BLENKINSOP, Peter — 1
BLENNER, Carle John — 3
BLENNERHASSETT, Harman — H
BLESH, Abraham Lincoln — 1
BLESSE, Frederick Arthur — 3
BLESSING, Edgar M. — 5
BLESSING, George Frederick
BLESSING, Lewis Greene — 4
BLESSING, Riley Andrew — 5
BLETHEN, Alden Joseph — 2
BLETHEN, Clarence Brettun
BLETHEN, Frank Alden — 5
BLETHEN, William Kingsley — 4
BLEWER, Clarence Frederick — 5
BLEWETT, Ben — 1
BLEWETT, William E. Jr. — 4
BLEYER, Herman — 3
BLEYER, J. Mount — 4
BLEYER, Willard Grosvenor — 1
BLICHFELDT, Emil Harry — 5
BLICHFELDT, Hans Frederik — 2
BLICKENSDERFER-, Joseph Patrick — 4
BLICKENSDERFER, Robert — 4
BLIEM, Milton Jacob — 4
BLIGHT, Reynold E. — 3
BLINN, Holbrook — 1
BLINN, Randolph — 2
BLISS, A. Richard Jr. — 1
BLISS, Aaron Thomas — 1
BLISS, Charles Bemis — 4
BLISS, Collins Pechin — 2
BLISS, Cornelius Newton — 1

BLISS, Cornelius Newton — 2
BLISS, D. Spencer — 3
BLISS, Daniel — 1
BLISS, Don Alfonso — 4
BLISS, Don C. — 4
BLISS, Edwin Elisha — 1
BLISS, Edwin Munsell — 1
BLISS, Eliakim Raymond — 1
BLISS, Eliphalet Williams — 1
BLISS, Elmer Jared — 2
BLISS, Eugene Frederick — 4
BLISS, Frederick Jones — 4
BLISS, George * — 5
BLISS, George Laurence — 5
BLISS, George Yemens — 1
BLISS, Gilbert Ames — 3
BLISS, Harding — 5
BLISS, Harry Hayner — 1
BLISS, Henry Evelyn — 5
BLISS, Howard Sweetser — 1
BLISS, James Harris — 3
BLISS, John Carlton — 3
BLISS, Jonathan — H
BLISS, Louis Denton — 5
BLISS, Louis G. — 5
BLISS, Malcolm Andrews — 1
BLISS, Paul Southworth — 1
BLISS, Philemon — H
BLISS, Philip Elijah — 1
BLISS, Phillip Paul — H
BLISS, Porter Cornelius — H
BLISS, Raymond Whitcomb — 4
BLISS, Robert Pratt — 4
BLISS, Robert Woods — 4
BLISS, Tasker Howard — 1
BLISS, Walter Phelps — 1
BLISS, William — 5
BLISS, William Carpenter — 1
BLISS, William Dwight Porter
BLISS, William Henry — 1
BLISS, William J. — 5
BLISS, William Julian Albert — 1
BLISS, William Root — 1
BLISS, Zenas Randall — 1
BLISS, Zenas Work — 3
BLITZ, Anne Dudley — H
BLITZ, Antonio — H
BLITZSTEIN, Marc — 4
BLIXEN-FINECKE, Karen Christentze
BLIZZARD, Reese — 4
BLIZZARD, Warren Lale — 4
BLOCH, Albert — 4
BLOCH, Alexander — 4
BLOCH, Bernard — 4
BLOCH, Claude Charles — 4
BLOCH, Ernest — 3
BLOCH, Herbert Aaron — 4
BLOCH, Jesse A. — 4
BLOCH, Julius — 4
BLOCH, Louis — 4
BLOCH, Monroe Percy — 5
BLOCK, Adriaen — H
BLOCK, Edward — 4
BLOCK, Karl Morgan — 3
BLOCK, Leopold E. — 3
BLOCK, Louis James — 1
BLOCK, Melvin A. — 4
BLOCK, Paul — 1
BLOCK, Philip Dee — 2
BLOCK, Rudolph — 1
BLOCK, Samuel Westheimer — 5
BLOCKER, Dan — 5
BLOCKER, Daniel James — 4
BLOCKER, William Preston — 2
BLOCKLINGER, Gottfried — 1
BLOCKSOM, Augustus Perry
BLODGET, Lorin — 1
BLODGETT, Benjamin Colman — 4
BLODGETT, Francis Branch — 5
BLODGETT, Frank Dickinson
BLODGETT, Henry Williams — 1
BLODGETT, Hugh Carlton — 5
BLODGETT, Isaac N. — 1
BLODGETT, John Taggard
BLODGETT, John Wood — 4
BLODGETT, Mabel Louise Fuller — 3

BLODGETT, Rufus — 1
BLODGETT, Samuel * — H
BLODGETT, Thomas Harper — 4
BLODGETT, Thurston P(ond) — 5
BLODGETT, Wells Howard — 1
BLOEDE, Gertrude — 1
BLOEDE, Victor Gustave — 1
BLOEDEL, Julius Harold — 4
BLOIS, Marsden Scott — 4
BLOM, Frans — 4
BLOMGREN, Carl August — 4
BLOMQUIST, Edwin Oscar — 4
BLOMQUIST, Hugo Leander — 4
BLONDEL, Jacob D. — H
BLOOD, Charles H. — 4
BLOOD, Henry Ames — 1
BLOOD, Henry Hooper — 2
BLOOD, Robert McCutchins — 3
BLOOD, William Henry Jr. — 1
BLOODGOOD, Clare Sutton
BLOODGOOD, Delavan — 1
BLOODGOOD, Joseph Colt — 1
BLOODGOOD, Wheeler Peckham — 1
BLOODWORTH, Andrew Dunn Franklin — 3
BLOODWORTH, Timothy — H
BLOOM, Charles James — 2
BLOOM, Edgar Selden — 3
BLOOM, Issac — 2
BLOOM, Sol — 2
BLOOM, W. Knighton — 1
BLOOMBERG, Maxwell Hillel — 5
BLOOMER, Amelia Jenks — H
BLOOMER, Edgar Nelson — 4
BLOOMER, Millard J. — 5
BLOOMFIELD, Arthur Collier — 5
BLOOMFIELD, Daniel — 4
BLOOMFIELD, Joseph — H
BLOOMFIELD, Leonard — 2
BLOOMFIELD, Maurice — 1
BLOOMFIELD, Meyer — 1
BLOOMINGDALE, Charles — 2
BLOOMINGDALE, Emanuel Watson
BLOOMINGDALE, Samuel Joseph — 5
BLOOMSTEIN, Max Jr. — 1
BLOOR, Alfred Janson — 1
BLOOR, Walter Ray — 4
BLOSS, James Ramsdell — 3
BLOSSOM, Francis — 5
BLOSSOM, George W. Jr. — 4
BLOSSOM, Harold Hill — 1
BLOSSOM, Henry Martyn Jr. — 1
BLOUGH, Earl — 4
BLOUGH, Sanford P. — 5
BLOUNT, Henry Fitch — 4
BLOUNT, James Henderson — 1
BLOUNT, Thomas — H
BLOUNT, William — H
BLOUNT, William Alexander — 1
BLOUNT, William Grainger — H
BLOUNT, Willie — H
BLOW, Allmand M. — 2
BLOW, Henry Taylor — H
BLOWERS, Sampson Salter — H
BLOXHAM, William D — 1
BLUCHER, Franz — 2
BLUE, Burdette — 2
BLUE, Frederick Omar — 5
BLUE, John Howard — 5
BLUE, Rupert — 2
BLUE, Victor — 1
BLUETT, John Joseph — 4
BLUFORD, Ferdinand Douglas — 3
BLUGERMAN, Lee N. (leonid) — 5
BLUM, Daniel — 1
BLUM, Edward Charles — 2
BLUM, Harry — 5
BLUM, Harry H. — 5
BLUM, Leon — 2
BLUM, Robert — 4
BLUM, Robert Frederick — 1
BLUM, Samuel J. — 5
BLUM, William — 3
BLUMBERG, Hyman — 5
BLUMBERG, Nathan J. — 4

BLUME, Fred H. — 5
BLUMENBERG, Marc A. — 4
BLUMENFELD, Ralph David — 4
BLUMENFIELD, Samuel M. — 5
BLUMENSCHEIN, Ernest L. — 4
BLUMENSCHEIN, Mary Shepard Greene — 3
BLUMENSCHEIN, William Leonard — 1
BLUMENSCHINE, Leonard G. — 5
BLUMENTHAL, George — 1
BLUMENTHAL, Gustave Adolph — 1
BLUMENTHAL, Sidney — 1
BLUMER, G. Alder — 1
BLUMER, George — 3
BLUMEYER, Arthur Adolphus
BLUN, Henry — 1
BLUNT, Edmund March — H
BLUNT, George William — H
BLUNT, Hugh Francis — 5
BLUNT, James Gillpatrick — H
BLUNT, John Ellsworth — 1
BLUNT, John S. — H
BLUNT, Katharine — 3
BLUNT, Matthew M. — 1
BLUNT, Stanhope English — 1
BLY, Eleanor Schooley — 5
BLY, John Marius — 2
BLY, Nelly — H
BLY, Nelly — 4
BLY, Robert Stewart — 3
BLYDE, Lewis J(ohn) N(ewbery) — 5
BLYDENBURGH, Charles Edward
BLYLEY, Katherine Gillette — 4
BLYNN, Lloyd Ross — 5
BLYTH, Charles R. — 3
BLYTHE, David Gilmour — H
BLYTHE, Joseph L. — 3
BLYTHE, Joseph William — 1
BLYTHE, Samuel George — 3
BLYTHIN, Edward — 3
BLYTHIN, Robert — 4
BOAK, Arthur Edward Romilly
BOAL, Pierre 'de Lagarde — 4
BOARDMAN, Albert Barnes — 1
BOARDMAN, Charles Willis — 3
BOARDMAN, Elijah — H
BOARDMAN, George Dana — 1
BOARDMAN, George Henry — 5
BOARDMAN, George Nye — 1
BOARDMAN, Harold Sherburne — 5
BOARDMAN, Harry Clow — 3
BOARDMAN, Harry L. — 4
BOARDMAN, Henry Augustus — H
BOARDMAN, Henry Bradford — 1
BOARDMAN, Mabel Thorp — 2
BOARDMAN, Samuel Lane — 1
BOARDMAN, Samuel Ward — H
BOARDMAN, Thomas Danforth — H
BOARDMAN, Waldo Elias — 1
BOARDMAN, William Bradford — 4
BOARDMAN, William Henry — 1
BOARDMAN, William Whiting — H
BOARMAN, Aleck — 3
BOARTS, Robert Marsh — 4
BOAS, Emil Leopold — 1
BOAS, Ernst Philip — 3
BOAS, Franz — 2
BOATNER, Victor Vincent — 2
BOATRIGHT, Byron B. — 3
BOATRIGHT, Mody Coggin — 5
BOATRIGHT, William Louis
BOATWRIGHT, Frederic William — 3

BOATWRIGHT, Gertrude Floyd Harris — 5
BOAZ, Hiram Abiff — 5
BOAZ, Hiram Abiff — 4
BOBB, Byron Arthur — 5
BOBB, Clyde S. — 3
BOBB, Earl Victor — 3
BOBBITT, Franklin — 3
BOBBS, William Conrad — 1
BOBER, Sam Henry — 5
BOCHER, Maxime — 1
BOCK, Harold Pattendon — 5
BOCK, Otto — 2
BOCKEE, Abraham — H
BOCKMAN, Marcus Olaus — 2
BOCKUS, Charles E. — 1
BOCOCK, Clarence Edgar — 1
BOCOCK, John Holmes — 3
BOCOCK, Thomas S. — H
BOCOCK, Willis Henry — 4
BODANSKY, Meyer — 1
BODANZKY, Artur — 1
BODDE, John R. — 5
BODDINGTON, Ernest Fearby
BODDIS, George — 4
BODDY, E. Manchester — 4
BODDY, William Henry
BODE, Boyd Henry — 3
BODE, Frederick — 1
BODECKER, Carl Friedrich Wilhelm — 4
BODELL, David Eugene — 5
BODELL, Joseph James — 3
BODEN, Andrew — H
BODEN, Reynold Blomerley
BODENHAMER, Osee — 1
BODENHEIM, Maxwell — 3
BODENWEIN, Theodore — 1
BODER, Bartlett — 5
BODER, David Pablo — 4
BODFISH, Morton — 4
BODINE, A(ldine) Aubrey — 5
BODINE, Alfred Van Sant — 4
BODINE, James Morrison — 1
BODINE, Joseph Hall — 1
BODINE, Joseph Lamb — 3
BODINE, Samuel Louis — 3
BODINE, Samuel Taylor — 1
BODINE, William Budd — 3
BODINE, William Warden — 3
BODLE, Charles — H
BODLEY, Temple — 1
BODMAN, Ernest James — 3
BODMAN, Henry Edward — 4
BODMER, Karl — H
BODY, Charles William Edmund — 1
BOE, Lars Wilhelm — 2
BOECKLIN, Roland — 5
BOEGNER, Marc — 5
BOEHLER, Peter — H
BOEHM, Edward Marshall — 5
BOEHM, Henry — H
BOEHM, John Philip — H
BOEHM, Martin — H
BOEHME, Ernest Adolph — 4
BOEHMER, Max — 1
BOEING, William Edward — 3
BOELEN, Jacob — H
BOELTER, Llewellyn Michael Kraus — 4
BOERICKE, Garth Wilkinson
BOERNSTEIN, Ralph A(ugustus) — 5
BOERUM, Simon — H
BOESCHENSTEIN, Charles — 3
BOESCHENSTEIN, Harold — 5
BOETTCHER, Charles — 2
BOETTCHER, Charles II — 4
BOETTCHER, Claude Kedzie — 3
BOETTIGER, John — 3
BOEYE, John Franklin — 4
BOEYNAEMS, Libert Hubert John Louis — 3
BOFINGER, D. T. — 2
BOGAN, Louise — 5
BOGAN, R. A. L. — 3
BOGAN, William Joseph — 1
BOGARDUS, Everardus — H
BOGARDUS, James — H
BOGART, Ernest Ludlow — 3
BOGART, Humphrey DeForest — 3
BOGART, John — 1
BOGART, Paul Nebeker — 4
BOGART, Walter Thompson

BOGART, William Henry H
BOGARTE, Martin
Eugene 1
BOGEN, Emil 4
BOGEN, Jules Irwin 4
BOGER, Glen Alvin 5
BOGER, 5
Robert Forrester
BOGERT, Edward Strong 1
BOGERT, George H. 4
BOGERT, Marston Taylor 3
BOGERT, 5
Walter Lawrence
BOGGESS, 5
Arthur Clinton
BOGGS, Carroll Curtis 1
BOGGS, Charles Stuart H
BOGGS, Earl Huffner 5
BOGGS, Frank Cranstoun 5
BOGGS, Frank M. 1
BOGGS, 1
Gilbert Hillhouse
BOGGS, Lillburn W. H
BOGGS, Robert 4
BOGGS, S. Whittemore 3
BOGGS, Sara E. 1
BOGGS, Thomas Hale 5
BOGGS, Thomas 1
Richmond
BOGGS, William Brenton H
BOGGS, William Ellison 1
BOGGS, 5
William Robertson
BOGIE, Mord M. 3
BOGLE, James H
BOGLE, Robert Boyd 1
BOGLE, 1
Sarah Comly Norris
BOGLE, Thomas Ashford 1
BOGLE, Walter Scott 4
BOGOSIAN, Ares George 5
BOGOSLOVSKY, 4
Boris Basil
BOGUE, Harold J. 4
BOGUE, Jesse Parker 3
BOGUE, Morton Griswold 4
BOGUE, Virgil Gay 5
BOGUSLAWSKI,
Moissaye 2
BOGY, Lewis Vital H
BOHACHEVSKY, 4
Constantine
BOHAN, Peter Thomas 5
BOHANNON, 3
Eugene William
BOHANNON, 1
William Everette
BOHART, Philip Harris 4
BOHEN, Frederick Owen 4
BOHLEN, Diedrich A. H
BOHLEN, 2
Francis Hermann
BOHLMAN, 5
Herbert William
BOHLMANN, 4
Henry Frederic Theodore
BOHM, Max 1
BOHN, Charles B. 4
BOHN, Donald George 5
BOHN, Frank Probasco 4
BOHN, 2
William Frederick
BOHR, Frank 5
BOHR, 4
Niels Henrik David
BOHUNE, Lawrence H
BOICE, James Young 4
BOIES, Henry Martyn 1
BOIES, Horace 1
BOIES, William Artemas 4
BOIES, William Dayton 1
BOIFEUILLET,
John Theodore
BOILEAU, Philip 4
BOISE, Otis Bardwell 1
BOISOT, Emile Kellogg 4
BOISOT, Louis 1
BOISSEVAIN, 2
Charles Hercules
BOISSEVAIN, 1
Inez Milholland
BOJER, Johan 3
BOK, Cary William 5
BOK, Curtis 4
BOK, Edward William 1
BOKEE, David Alexander H
BOKER, George Henry H
BOKHARI, Ahmed Shah 3
BOKOR, Margit 3
BOLAND, Francis Joseph 4
BOLAND, Frank Kells 3
BOLAND, John J. 3
BOLAND, John Peter 4
BOLAND, Mary 4
BOLAND, Patrick J. 1
BOLDEN, Charles H
BOLDEN, Charles 4

BOLDT, George C. 1
BOLDT, 2
Hermann Johannes
BOLDUAN, 3
Charles Frederick
BOLE, 1
Benjamin Patterson
BOLE, William McLure 1
BOLEND, Floyd Jackson
BOLES, Edgar Howard 2
BOLES, H(enry) Leo 5
BOLES, John 5
BOLGER, Henry Joseph 4
BOLIVAR, Simon H
BOLL, Jacob H
BOLLAN, William 1
BOLLER, 1
Alfred Pancoast
BOLLES, Albert Sidney 1
BOLLES, 1
Edwin Cortlandt
BOLLES, Frank H
BOLLES, Frank Crandall 1
BOLLES, Stephen 4
BOLLING,
Alexander Russell
BOLLING, 5
George Melville
BOLLING, 1
Raynal Cawthorne
BOLLINGER, James Wills 3
BOLLMAN, Justus Erich H
BOLOTOV, Ivan Il'ich
BOLSTER, 5
Stanley Marshall
BOLSTER, Wilfred 2
BOLSTER, 4
William Wheeler
BOLT, Richard Arthur 4
BOLTE, William John 4
BOLTON, Abby H
BOLTON, Benjamin
Meade 1
BOLTON, Charles Edward 3
BOLTON,
Charles Knowles
BOLTON, Chester Castle 1
BOLTON, Elmer Keiser 5
BOLTON, Ethel 3
BOLTON, 5
Frederick Elmer
BOLTON, 1
Henry Carrington
BOLTON, Herbert Eugene 5
BOLTON, J. Gray 1
BOLTON, John H
BOLTON, Margaret 3
BOLTON, Paul H. 4
BOLTON, 2
Reginald Pelham
BOLTON, Sarah Knowles 1
BOLTON, H
Sarah Tittle Barrett
BOLTON, 2
Thaddeus Lincoln
BOLTON, 5
John) Whitney (French)
BOLTON, William Jay H
BOLTON, William Jordan 1
BOLTWOOD, 1
Bertram Borden
BOLTWOOD, Edward H
BOLTZIUS,
Johann Martin
BOLZA, Oskar 4
BOMANN, George Atkins 5
BOMAR, Edward Earle 4
BOMAR, Paul Vernon 1
BOMBERGER, H
John Henry Augustus
BOMBERGER, Louden
Lane 4
BOMFORD, George H
BOMPIANI, 4
Sophia Van Matre
BONACUM, Thomas 1
BONAPARTE, 1
Charles Joseph
BONAPARTE,
Charles Lucien
BONAPARTE,
Charlotte Julie
BONAPARTE, H
Elizabeth Patterson
BONAPARTE, H
Jerome Napoleon
BONAPARTE, H
Louis Napoleon
BONAPARTE, Napoleon H
BONARD, Louis
BONASCHI, 3
Alberto Cinzio
BONBRIGHT, 4
William Prescott
BONCI, Alessandro 5
BOND, A. Russell 1
BOND, Ahva J. C. 5

BOND, Albert Richmond 2
BOND, Bernard Q. 1
BOND, Carrie Jacobs 2
BOND, Carroll Taney 2
BOND, 5
Charles Grosvenor
BOND, Charles Sumner 3
BOND, Frederic) Drew 1
BOND, Edward Austin 1
BOND, Edward Johnson 1
BOND, Edwin E. 4
BOND, Elizabeth Powell 1
BOND, Ford 4
BOND, Frank 1
BOND, Frank Stuart 1
BOND, George Hopkins 3
BOND, George Meade 1
BOND, George Phillips H
BOND, H. Wheeler 4
BOND, Henry 1
BOND, Henry Whitelaw 1
BOND, Horace Mann 5
BOND, Hugh Lennox Jr. 1
BOND, Hugh Lenox H
BOND, James Leslie 5
BOND, Lester L. 1
BOND, Oliver James 1
BOND, Reford H
BOND, Richard H
BOND, Shadrach 1
BOND, Sirus Orestes 3
BOND, Thomas H
BOND, Thomas Emerson 2
BOND, Willard Faroe 5
BOND, William Cranch H
BOND, William Key H
BOND, William Scott 3
BOND, Young Hance 4
BONDS, Archibald 5
BONDURANT, 1
Alexander Lee
BONDURANT, 5
Eugene DuBose
BONDURANT, 4
William Walton
BONDY, William 4
BONE, 5
Alfred Rufus, Jr.
BONE, Homer Truett 5
BONE, Scott Cardelle 1
BONE, Winstead Paine 2
BONEBRAKE, Peter Oren 4
BONEHILL, Ralph 1
BONELL, 5
Benjamin Walter
BONER, John Henry 1
BONESTEEL, 4
Charles Hartwell
BONESTEEL, Verne C. 4
BONFIELD, George R. H
BONFIG, Henry Carl 4
BONFILS, H
Frederick Gilmer
BONFILS, 4
Frederick Gilmer
BONFILS, Helen G. 5
BONGGREN, Olof Jakob 4
BONHAM, 5
Kenneth Arlington
BONHAM, 2
Milledge Lipscomb
BONHAM, 1
Milledge Louis Jr.
BONHAM, Milledge Luke H
BONIFACE, Mother Mary 4
BONIFIELD, 1
Charles Lybrand
BONILLAS, Ygnacio 2
BONNAR, John Duncan 1
BONNELL, Henry
Houston 1
BONNER, Albert Sydney 2
BONNER, Arthur 3
BONNER, Campbell 5
BONNER, Charles 5
BONNER, David Findley 3
BONNER, David Mahlon 5
BONNER, Francis A. 3
BONNER, Geraldine 1
BONNER, Griffith 5
BONNER, 4
Herbert Covington
BONNER, Hugh 1
BONNER, James Bernard 5
BONNER, John H
BONNER, John Joseph 2
BONNER, John Woodrow 5
BONNER, 4
Joseph Claybaugh
BONNER, Paul Hyde 5
BONNER, Robert 1
BONNER, Robert Johnson 2
BONNER, Sherwood H
BONNER, Tom Wilkerson 5
BONNER, Walter D. 3
BONNET, Frank Henry 4

BONNEVILLE, H
Benjamin Louis Eulalie 'de
BONNEY, 1
Charles Carroll
BONNEY, Sherman Grant 2
BONNEY, Wilbert Lowth 5
BONNEY, William H. H
BONNHEIM, Albert 1
BONNYMAN, Alexander 3
BONOMO, Alfred J. 4
BONRIGHT, Daniel 1
BONSAL, Stephen 3
BONSALL, Amos 1
BONSALL, Edward Horne 1
BONSALL, 1
Elizabeth Hubbard
BONSALL, 1
William Hartshorn
BONSER,
Frederick Gordon
BONSER, Thomas A. 4
BONTE, George Willard 2
BONTECOU, Daniel 1
BONTECOU, 1
Reed Brockway
BONTEMPS, Arna
Wendell 5
BONVIN, Ludwig 1
BONWILL,
William Gibson Arlington
BONYNGE, 1
Robert William
BONZANO, John 1
BOODELL, Thomas J. 5
BOODIN, John Elof 3
BOODY, Azariah H
BOODY, Bertha M. 3
BOODY, David Augustus 1
BOOG, Carle Michel 5
BOOHER, Charles F. 1
BOOK, Dorothy L. 3
BOOK, George Milton 1
BOOK,
William Frederick
BOOK, William Henry 2
BOOKER, George Edward 3
BOOKER, George William H
BOOKER, Joseph Albert 1
BOOKER, William David 1
BOOKSTAVER,
Henry Weller
BOOKWALTER, 1
Alfred Guitner
BOOKWALTER, Charles
A. 4
BOOKWALTER, John W. 4
BOOKWALTER, Lewis 4
BOOLE, Ella Alexander 3
BOOMER, 4
George Ellsworth
BOOMER, 2
Lucius Messenger
BOOMER,
Robert DeForest
BOOMHOUR, J. Gregory 4
BOON, Henry George 3
BOON, Ratliff H
BOONE, Andrew
Rechmond H
BOONE, Arthur Upshaw 5
BOONE, 1
Charles Theodore
BOONE, Daniel H
BOONE, Daniel 2
BOONE, Henry Burnham 5
BOONE, John Lee 1
BOONE, Joseph Prince 4
BOONE, Richard Gause 1
BOONE, Thomas H
BOONE, William Judson 4
BOORAEM,
John Van Vorst
BOORAEM, Robert Elmer 1
BOORD, Cecil Ernest 5
BOORMAN, James 1
BOOS, Ludwig Charles 3
BOOTE, Ward E. 4
BOOTH, Agnes 1
BOOTH, Ballington 1
BOOTH, Ballington 2
BOOTH, Bradford Allen 5
BOOTH, Charles Arthur 5
BOOTH, Charles Gordon 2
BOOTH, 1
Christopher Henry Hudson
BOOTH, Clarence Moore 5
BOOTH, Edwin Prince 5
BOOTH, Edwin Thomas H
BOOTH, Evangeline Cory 3
BOOTH, Ewing E. 2
BOOTH, Fenton Whitlock 2
BOOTH, Frank Walworth 4
BOOTH, Franklin 4
BOOTH, George Francis 3
BOOTH, George Gough 2
BOOTH, Harold Simmons 5
BOOTH, Henry Kendall 4

BOOTH, Henry Matthias 1
BOOTH, Hiram Evans 1
BOOTH, Isaac Walter 5
BOOTH, James Curtis H
BOOTH, John Henry 4
BOOTH, John Wilkes H
BOOTH, Junius Brutus H
BOOTH, Mary Ann Allard 1
BOOTH, Mary Louise H
BOOTH, Maud Ballington 4
BOOTH, Newell Snow 5
BOOTH, Newton H
BOOTH, Ralph Douglas 1
BOOTH, Ralph Harman 1
BOOTH, Robert Asbury 1
BOOTH, Robert Highman 5
BOOTH, Robert Plues 1
BOOTH, Robert Russell H
BOOTH, Samuel Babcock 4
BOOTH, Thomas Butler 1
BOOTH, Walter H
BOOTH, Wilbur Franklin 4
BOOTH, William Stone 1
BOOTH, Willis H. 3
BOOTHBY,
Walter Meredith
BOOTHE, Gardner Lloyd 1
BOOTHROYD, 1
Samuel Latimer
BOOTH TUCKER, 1
Emma Moss
BOOTH TUCKER, 3
Frederick St George 'de
Lautour
BOOTT, Kirk H
BOOZ, Edwin George 5
BOPE, Henry P. 4
BORAAS, Julius 4
BORAH, Leo Arthur 4
BORAH, Wayne G. 4
BORAH, William Edgar 1
BORBER, William 3
BORCH, Gaston
BORCHARD, Edwin 3
BORCHARDT, Albert
Hugo
BORCHARDT, 4
Selma Munter
BORCHERS,
Charles Martin
BORDEN, Bertram Harold 4
BORDEN, C. Seymour 1
BORDEN, Daniel Carey 4
BORDEN, Daniel LeRay 4
BORDEN, Gail H
BORDEN,
George Pennington
BORDEN, Howard
Seymour 5
BORDEN, John 4
BORDEN, Lizzie Andrew 4
BORDEN, Lizzie Andrew 4
BORDEN,
Mary (Mary Borden Spears)
BORDEN, H
Nathaniel Briggs
BORDEN, Richard H
BORDEN, Simeon 1
BORDEN, Spencer 1
BORDEN,
William Alanson
BORDEN, William Cline 2
BORDEN,
William Silvers
BORDERS, Joseph H. 4
BORDERS, M. W. 4
BORDET, Jules 4
BORDEWICH, Henry 1
BORDLEY, John Beale *
BORDNER, Harvey
Albert 5
BORDWELL, Walter 1
BORE, Jean Etienne H
BOREING, Vincent 1
BOREMAN, Arthur
Ingram H
BOREMAN, Jacob Smith 4
BORG, Carl Oscar 1
BORG, George William 3
BORGER, Edward M. 3
BORGER, Hugh Donald 5
BORGERHOFF,
Elbert Benton Op'tEynde
BORGERHOFF,
Joseph Leopold
BORGESE, G. A. 3
BORGESS, Caspar Henry H
BORGLUM, Gutzon 1
BORGLUM,
Solon Hannibal
BORGMAN, 3
Albert Stephens
BORHEGYI, 5
Stephan Francis de
BORI, Lucrezia
BORIE, Adolph Edward H
BORIE, Adolphe

BORIE, Charles Louis 2
BORING, 5
Edwin Garrigues
BORING, 1
William Alciphron
BORLAND, Charles Jr. H
BORLAND, 5
Chauncey Blair
BORLAND, Solon H
BORLAND, Wilfred P. 4
BORLAND, 1
William Patterson
BORN, Max 5
BORNE, John E. 1
BORNSTEIN, Sol 4
BORNSTEIN, 1
Yetta Libby Frieden (Mrs. Harry Bornstein)
BOROVSKY, 4
Maxwell Philip
BOROWSKI, Felix 3
BORST, Guernsey J. 3
BORST, Henry Vroman 1
BORST, Peter I. H
BORTHWICK, John David H
BORTMAN, Mark 4
BORTZ, Edward LeRoy 5
BORZAGE, Frank 4
BOSCH, Herbert Michael 4
BOSCHEN, 2
Frederick Wegener
BOSE, Emil 1
BOSETTI, Joseph 3
BOSHER, 1
Kate Lee Langley
BOSHER, Lewis Crenshaw
BOSKOWITZ, George W. 4
BOSLAUGH, Paul E. 2
BOSLEY,
Frederick Andrew
BOSLEY, 5
William Bradford
BOSMAN, David 1
BOSS, Andrew 2
BOSS, Benjamin 5
BOSS, Henry M.
BOSS, John Linscom Jr. H
BOSS, Lewis 1
BOSS, William 4
BOSSANGE, 2
Edward Raymond
BOSSARD, Guido 1
BOSSARD, 3
James Herbert Siward
BOSSIDY, John Collins
BOSSIER, H
Pierre Evariste John Baptiste
BOSSOM, Alfred Charles 4
BOST, Ralph Walton
BOSTOCK, Edward Crary 4
BOSTON, 1
Charles Anderson
BOSTON, Joseph H. 3
BOSTON, L. Napoleon
BOSTROM, Wollmar Filip 3
BOSTWICK, 2
Arthur Elmore
BOSTWICK, 1
Charles Dibble
BOSTWICK, 1
Charles Francis
BOSTWICK, 2
Frank Matteson
BOSTWICK, Harry Rice 1
BOSTWICK, Lucius Allyn
BOSTWICK, Roy Grier 2
BOSWELL, 1
Charles Martin
BOSWELL, 3
Grover Cleveland
BOSWELL, Ira Mathews 2
BOSWELL, Peyton Jr. 3
BOSWORTH, 3
Arthur Harding
BOSWORTH, 1
Benjamin Miller
BOSWORTH, 5
Charles Wilder
BOSWORTH, 1
Edward Increase
BOSWORTH, 5
Edwin Carpenter
BOSWORTH, 2
Francke Huntington Jr.
BOSWORTH, 2
Hobart Van Zandt
BOSWORTH, 3
Robert Graham
BOSWORTH, Welles 4
BOTELER, H
Alexander Robinson
BOTETOURT, 1'st 'baron H
BOTHE, Walther 3
BOTHNE, Gisle 1
BOTKIN, 1
Alexander Campbell

BOTKIN, 5
Harold Mitchell
BOTKIN, 1
Jeremiah Dunham
BOTSFORD,
Elmer Francis
BOTSFORD, 5
Florence Hudson;
BOTSFORD, 1
George Willis
BOTSFORD, 4
Stephen Blakeslee
BOTT, Herbert Joseph 4
BOTTA, Anne Lynch H
BOTTA, Vincenzo H
BOTTHOF, Walter E. 5
BOTTINEAU, Pierre H
BOTTOLFSEN, C. A. 3
BOTTOM,
Raymond Blanton
BOTTOME, Harry
Howard 4
BOTTOME, Margaret 1
BOTTOME, Phyllis 4
BOTTOMLEY, Allen W. T.
BOTTOMLEY, John
Taylor
BOTTOMLEY, 3
William Lawrence
BOTTOMLY, 4
Raymond Victor Sr.
BOTTS, Charles Tyler H
BOTTS, Hugh Pearce 4
BOTTS, John Minor H
BOUATTOURA, Tewfik 5
BOUCHER, 5
Anthony (pseudonym for William Anthony Parker
BOUCHER, 3
Chauncey Samuel
BOUCHER, 1
Chauncey Watson
BOUCHER, Horace
Edward H
BOUCHER, Horace
Edward 4
BOUCHER, Jonathan H
BOUCICAULT, Dion H
BOUCICAULT, Dion G. 1
BOUCICAULT, 5
Ruth Baldwin Holt (Mrs. Aubrey Boucicault)
BOUCK, Francis Eugene 2
BOUCK, Joseph H
BOUCK, William C. H
BOUCK, Zeh 2
BOUCKE, Ewald Augustus 5
BOUCKE, O. Fred 1
BOUDE, Thomas H
BOUDEMAN, Dallas 4
BOUDET, Dominic W. H
BOUDET,
Nicholas Vincent
BOUDIN, Louis B. 3
BOUDINOT, Elias * H
BOUDINOT, H
Elias Cornelius
BOUDINOT, Jane J. 5
BOUDINOT, 2
Truman Everett
BOUGHTON, George
Henry H
BOUGHTON, George
Henry 1
BOUGHTON,
Martha Arnold
BOUGHTON, Willis 2
BOUGUEREAU, 4
Elizabeth Gardner
BOUILLON, Lincoln 5
BOULDIN, James Wood 4
BOULDIN, Thomas Tyler
BOULDIN, Virgil 5
BOULIGNY, Dominique H
BOULIGNY, John Edward H
BOULT, William Thomas
BOULTER, 3
Howard Thornton
BOULTER, Thornton 3
BOULTON, 4
Payne Augustin
BOUNETHEAU, H
Henry Brintell
BOUQUET, Henry H
BOUQUILLON, Thomas 1
BOURGADE, Peter 1
BOURGEOIS,
Lionel John Sr.
BOURGMONT, 'sieur 'de H
BOURGOINE, Joseph
John 3
BOURKE, John Gregory H
BOURKE-WHITE,
Margaret 5
BOURLAND, Albert Pike 1

BOURLAND, 2
Benjamin Parsons
BOURLAND, 5
Caroline Brown
BOURN, Augustus Osborn 1
BOURNE, Benjamin H
BOURNE, Edward
Gaylord 1
BOURNE, Frank Augustus 1
BOURNE,
Frederick Gilbert
BOURNE, George H
BOURNE, Henry Eldridge 2
BOURNE, Jonathan Jr. 1
BOURNE, Nehemiah H
BOURNE, Randolph H
BOURNE, Shearjashub H
BOURQUIN, George M. 3
BOURSKAYA, Ina 3
BOUSCAREN, 1
Louis Frederic Gustave
BOUSCAREN, Louis H.
G. 4
BOUSFIELD, 2
Midian Othello
BOUSH, Clifford Joseph 1
BOUTELL, Henry
Sherman 1
BOUTELLE, 1
Charles Addison
BOUTELLE, H
De Witt Clinton
BOUTELLE, 4
Richard Schley
BOUTON, 2
Archibald Lewis
BOUTON, Burrett Beebe 4
BOUTON, 1
Charles Leonard
BOUTON, Edward Henry 4
BOUTON, Emily St. John 5
BOUTON, John Bell 1
BOUTON, Nathaniel H
BOUTON, Rosa 4
BOUTON, 5
S(tephen) Miles
BOUTWELL, 1
George Sewall
BOUTWELL, John
M(ason) 5
BOUTWELL, Paul
Winslow 5
BOUTWELL, William
Rowe 4
BOUVE, Clement Lincoln 2
BOUVE,
Pauline Carrington
BOUVET, Jeanne Marie 4
BOUVET, 1
Marie Marguerite
BOUVIER, John H
BOUVIER, Maurice 5
BOVARD,
Charles Lincoln
BOVARD, Freeman Daily 1
BOVARD, George Finley 1
BOVARD, Warren Bradley 1
BOVARD,
William Sherman
BOVEE, 1
Christian Nestell
BOVEE, J. Wesley 1
BOVEE, Matthias Jacob H
BOVENIZER, 4
George Wallace
BOVEY, Charles Cranton 3
BOVIE, William T. 3
BOVING, Adam Giede 5
BOVING,
Charles B(rasee)
BOW, Frank Townsend 5
BOW, Jonathan Gaines 4
BOW, Warren E. 2
BOWATER, 4
Sir Eric Vansittart
BOWDEN,
Aberdeen Orlando
BOWDEN, 2
Garfield Arthur
BOWDEN, George Edwin 4
BOWDEN, John H
BOWDEN, Laurens Reeve 2
BOWDEN, Lemuel
Jackson H
BOWDITCH, 1
Charles Pickering
BOWDITCH, H
Henry Ingersoll
BOWDITCH, 1
Henry Pickering
BOWDITCH, Nathaniel H
BOWDITCH, Richard
Lyon 3
BOWDITCH, 1
Vincent Yardley
BOWDLE, Stanley Eyre 4
BOWDOIN, George E. 3

BOWDOIN, 1
George Sullivan
BOWDOIN, James * H
BOWDOIN, 4
William Goodrich
BOWDON, Franklin
Welsh H
BOWE, Augustine J. 4
BOWEN, Abel H
BOWEN, Albert E. 3
BOWEN, Arthur John 5
BOWEN, Asa Bosworth 3
BOWEN, Benjamin Lester 4
BOWEN, H
Christopher Columbus
BOWEN, 1
Clarence Winthrop
BOWEN, Clayton
BOWEN, Raymond 1
BOWEN, Daniel H
BOWEN, Earl 4
BOWEN, Edwin Winfield 3
BOWEN, 5
Elizabeth Dorothea Cole
BOWEN, Ezra 2
BOWEN, Francis H
BOWEN, George H
BOWEN, Harold Gardiner 4
BOWEN, Harry 2
BOWEN, Henry Chandler 1
BOWEN, Herbert Wolcott 1
BOWEN, Ira Sprague 5
BOWEN, Ivan 3
BOWEN, John C. 4
BOWEN, John Campbell 5
BOWEN, John Henry 1
BOWEN, John Templeton 1
BOWEN, 4
John Wesley Edward
BOWEN, Joseph Henry 4
BOWEN, Lem Warner 1
BOWEN, 3
Louise 'de Koven
BOWEN, Marcellus 1
BOWEN, Norman Levi 3
BOWEN, Rees Tate
BOWEN, Reuben Dean 1
BOWEN, Thomas M. 1
BOWEN, Wilbur Pardon 1
BOWEN, William 1
BOWEN, William
Abraham 5
BOWEN, William Miller 1
BOWER, Alexander 3
BOWER, Bertha Muzzy 2
BOWER, George Hoyle 4
BOWER, Gustavus Miller H
BOWER, Lucy Scott
BOWER, Raymond G. 4
BOWERMAN,
George Franklin
BOWERMAN, Guy
Emerson 2
BOWERS, 1
Alphonzo Benjamin
BOWERS, Claude G. 3
BOWERS, Eaton Jackson 4
BOWERS, Edgar 4
BOWERS, Edison Louis 5
BOWERS,
Edward Augustus
BOWERS, H
Elizabeth Crocker
BOWERS, George Meade 1
BOWERS, Henry Francis 1
BOWERS, Herbert
Edmund 1
BOWERS, John Hugh 1
BOWERS, John Myer H
BOWERS,
LaMont Montgomery
BOWERS, Larkin Bruce 1
BOWERS, Lloyd Wheaton 1
BOWERS, Robert Graves 5
BOWERS, Robert Hood 1
BOWERS, H
Theodore Shelton
BOWERS, 2
Thomas Wilson 2
BOWERS, William Gray 2
BOWERSOCK,
Donald Curtis
BOWERSOCK,
Justin DeWitt
BOWES, Edward Major 1
BOWES, Frank B. 2
BOWES, Joseph 4
BOWES, Theodore F. 5
BOWES, Theodore F. 4
BOWIE,
Clifford Pinckney
BOWIE, Edward Hall 2
BOWIE, James H
BOWIE, Oden H
BOWIE, Richard Johns H
BOWIE, Robert H
BOWIE, Sydney Johnston 1
BOWIE, Thomas Fielder H

BOWIE, Walter H
BOWIE, Walter Russell 5
BOWIE, William 1
BOWKER, Horace 3
BOWKER, Richard Rogers 1
BOWLBY, Joel Morgan 3
BOWLEN, John James 4
BOWLER, Edmond
Wesley 4
BOWLER, James B. 3
BOWLER, John William 1
BOWLER, Metcalf H
BOWLER, William
Howard 3
BOWLES, Charles 3
BOWLES, 4
Charles Phillips
BOWLES,
Francis Tiffany
BOWLES, Gilbert 5
BOWLES, Henry Leland 1
BOWLES, Oliver 3
BOWLES, Phillip Ernest 1
BOWLES, 1
Pinckney Downie
BOWLES, Samuel H
BOWLES, Samuel 1
BOWLES, Samuel II H
BOWLES, Sherman Hoar 3
BOWLES, H
William Augustus
BOWLEY, Albert Jesse 2
BOWLEY, Arthur Lyon 5
BOWLIN, Jamer Butler H
BOWLING, Edgar Simeon 3
BOWLING, 2
William Bismarck
BOWMAN, Albert Chase 1
BOWMAN, Alpheus
Henry 1
BOWMAN, Charles Calvin 1
BOWMAN, Charles
Grimes 1
BOWMAN, Charles Henry 5
BOWMAN, Clellan
Asbury 1
BOWMAN, 5
Crete Dillon (Mrs. John W. Boman)
BOWMAN, Edward J. 1
BOWMAN, Edward
Morris 1
BOWMAN, 1
Frank Llewellyn
BOWMAN, Frank Otto 3
BOWMAN, George Ernest 1
BOWMAN, George Lynn 3
BOWMAN, George T. 3
BOWMAN, Harold
Leonard 4
BOWMAN, Harold Martin 4
BOWMAN, Harry Lake 4
BOWMAN, 5
Howard H(iestand) M(innich)
BOWMAN, Isaiah * 2
BOWMAN, James H
BOWMAN, James Clinton 5
BOWMAN, James Cloyd 4
BOWMAN, John Brady H
BOWMAN, John Bryan H
BOWMAN, John Calvin 1
BOWMAN, John Gabbert 4
BOWMAN, John McEntee 1
BOWMAN, John R. 5
BOWMAN,
Joseph Merrell, Jr.
BOWMAN, Karl Murdock 5
BOWMAN, Lloyd David 4
BOWMAN, Milo Jesse 3
BOWMAN, Robert A. 1
BOWMAN, Robert Jay 3
BOWMAN, Roland
Claude 1
BOWMAN, Rufus David 3
BOWMAN, 1
Samuel Henry Jr.
BOWMAN, Thomas * 1
BOWN, Ralph 5
BOWNE, Borden Parker 1
BOWNE, John H
BOWNE, Obadiah H
BOWNE, Samuel Smith H
BOWNOCKER, John
Adams 1
BOWRA, Cecil Maurice 5
BOWRON, 4
Arthur John Jr.
BOWRON, Fletcher 5
BOWRON, James 1
BOWSER, Edward Albert 1
BOWSFIELD, Colvin C. 1
BOWYER, John Marshall 1
BOWYER, John Wilson 5
BOX, John Calvin 5
BOXLEY, Calvin Peyton 5

BRAINE, Robert D. 4
BRAINERD, 4
Arthur Alanson
BRAINERD, Cephas 1
BRAINERD, 1
Chauncey Cory
BRAINERD, David H
BRAINERD, Eleanor
Hoyt 2
BRAINERD, Erastus 1
BRAINERD, Ezra 1
BRAINERD, Frank 1
BRAINERD, 5
Henry Dean, Sr.
BRAINERD, Henry Green 1
BRAINERD, John H
BRAINERD, Lawrence H
BRAINERD, Thomas H
BRAISLIN, Edward 1
BRAISLIN, William C. 2
BRAISTED, 1
William Clarence
BRAITHWAITE, 4
William Stanley Beaumont
BRAITMAYER, 1
Otto Ernest
BRAKELEY, 4
George Archibald
BRALEY, Berton 4
BRALEY, Henry King 1
BRALLEY, 1
Francis Marion
BRALLIAR, Floyd Burton 3
BRAMAN, Dwight 1
BRAMER, Samuel Eugene 2
BRAMHALL, 4
Edith Clementine
BRAMHALL, 4
Howard Wellington
BRAMHAM, 2
William Gibbons
BRAMKAMP, John
Milton 5
BRAMLETTE, Thomas E. H
BRAMMER, George
Edward 2
BRAMUGLIA, Juan Atilio 4
BRANCH, Anna
Hempstead
BRANCH, 1
Charles Henry Hardin
BRANCH, Ernest A. 3
BRANCH, Ernest William 1
BRANCH, Harllee 4
BRANCH, Harold Francis 4
BRANCH, Houston 5
BRANCH, Irving Lewis 4
BRANCH, James Ransom 4
BRANCH, John H
BRANCH, John B. 1
BRANCH, John Patteson 1
BRANCH, Joseph Gerald 4
BRANCH, H
Lawrence O'Bryan
BRANCH, 1
Mary Lydia Bolles
BRANCH, Oliver Ernesto 1
BRANCUSI, Constantin 3
BRAND, Charles 4
BRAND, Charles Hillyer 1
BRAND, Charles John 2
BRAND, Charles L. 3
BRAND, Edward Parish 1
BRAND, Harrison, Jr. 5
BRAND, James Tenney 4
BRAND, John W. B. 1
BRAND, Louis 5
BRAND, Robert Henry 4
BRAND, William Henry 3
BRANDE, 2
Dorothea Thompson
BRANDEBERRY, 3
John Benjamin
BRANDEGEE, 1
Frank Bosworth
BRANDEIS, Erich 3
BRANDEIS, Frederic H
BRANDEIS, Frederick 1
BRANDEIS, 1
Louis Dembitz
BRANDEL, S. W. 3
BRANDELLE, 1
Gustaf Albert
BRANDEN, Paul Maerker 2
BRANDENBURG, 4
Earnest Silas
BRANDENBURG, 1
Edwin Charles
BRANDENBURG, 1
Frederick Harmon
BRANDENBURG, 1
George Clinton
BRANDENBURG, 1
William A.
BRANDES, Elmer Walker 4
BRANDJORD, 3
Iver Martinson

BRANDON, Edgar Ewing 3
BRANDON, Edmund
John 2
BRANDON, H
Gerard Chittocque
BRANDON, Jesse DeWitt 3
BRANDON, Morris 1
BRANDON, 5
Samuel George Frederick
BRANDON, 1
William Woodward
BRANDT, Allen Demmy 5
BRANDT, Carl Gunard 5
BRANDT, Carl Ludwig H
BRANDT, Carl Ludwig 3
BRANDT, 4
Erdmann Neumiester
BRANDT, George Louis 5
BRANDT, Harry 5
BRANDT, 3
Herman Carl George
BRANDT, John 1
BRANDT, John Lincoln 2
BRANDT, Joseph Granger 1
BRANDT, Nils 1
BRANDT, Olaf Elias 1
BRANDT, William Earle 1
BRANGWYN, Sir Frank 3
BRANHAM, 4
Sara Elizabeth
BRANHAM, 1
William Charles
BRANIFF, Thomas E. 5
BRANN, Donald W. 2
BRANN, 1
Henry Athanasius
BRANN, Louis Jefferson 2
BRANN, William Cowper 1
BRANNAN, John Milton H
BRANNAN, John Winters 1
BRANNAN, 1
Joseph Doddridge
BRANNAN, Samuel H
BRANNAN, 3
William Forrest
BRANNEN, 4
Burton Alexander
BRANNER, John Casper 1
BRANNER, 5
Martin Michael
BRANNIGAN, Gladys 2
BRANNON, Henry 1
BRANNON, Melvin Amos 4
BRANNON, 4
Peter Alexander
BRANNON, William W. 4
BRANNT, 4
William Theodore
BRANOM, Mendel
Everett 4
BRANSBY, Carlos 1
BRANSCOMB, John W. 3
BRANSCOMB, 1
Lewis Capers
BRANSFORD, 1
Clifton Wood
BRANSHAW, Charles E. 2
BRANSON, Edwin Bayer 3
BRANSON, 1
Eugene Cunningham
BRANSON, John William 3
BRANSON, Taylor 5
BRANSON, William
Henry 4
BRANSTROM, 4
William Jeremiah
BRANT, Joseph H
BRANTINGHAM, 4
Charles Simonson
BRANTLEY, 1
William Gordon
BRANTLY, Theodore 1
BRANTLY, Theodore Lee 4
BRANTLY, 4
William Theophilus
BRANTON, James
Rodney 5
BRAQUE, Georges 4
BRAS, Harry Leonard 1
BRASE, Hagbard 3
BRASHEAR, John Alfred H
BRASHEAR, John Alfred 1
BRASHEAR, John Alfred 4
BRASHEAR, 2
Peter Cominges
BRASHER, Rex 3
BRASKAMP, Bernard 1
BRASLAU, Sophie 1
BRASOL, Boris 2
BRASSERT, 5
Herman Alexander
BRASTED, Alva Jennings 5
BRASTED, Fred 1
BRASTOW, Lewis
Orsmond 1
BRASWELL, James Craig 4

BRATENAHL, 1
George Carl Fitch
BRATTLE, Thomas H
BRATTLE, William H
BRATTON, John H
BRATTON, John Walter 4
BRATTON, Leslie Emmett 3
BRATTON, H
Robert Franklin
BRATTON, Sam Gilbert 4
BRATTON, Samuel Tilden 1
BRATTON, 2
Theodore DuBose
BRATTON, Walter
Andrew H
BRAUCHER, Frank 5
BRAUCHER, Howard S. 2
BRAUDE, Jacob Morton 5
BRAUER, Alfred 4
BRAUER, George R. 3
BRAUER, John Charles 5
BRAUFF, Herbert D. 3
BRAUN, Carl Franklin 3
BRAUN, John F. 1
BRAUN, Maurice 3
BRAUN, Robert 3
BRAUN, Werner 3
BRAUNE, 1
Gustave Maurice
BRAUNER, 2
Olaf Martinius
BRAUSE, Edward 4
BRAWLEY, Benjamin 1
BRAWLEY, Frank 1
BRAWLEY, William H. 3
BRAXTON, A. Caperton 1
BRAXTON, Carter H
BRAXTON, Elliott Muse H
BRAY, Charles I. 3
BRAY, Frank Chapin 2
BRAY, Harold Bryan 5
BRAY, Henry Truro 1
BRAY, John Leighton 3
BRAY, John P. 1
BRAY, Patrick Albert 4
BRAY, Thomas H
BRAY, Thomas Joseph 1
BRAY, William Crowell 2
BRAY, William L. 3
BRAYMAN, Mason H
BRAYMER, Daniel
Harvey 1
BRAYTON, Aaron Martin 2
BRAYTON, 1
Alembert Winthrop
BRAYTON, Charles Ray 1
BRAYTON, Israel H
BRAYTON, 1
William Daniel
BRAZEAU, 5
Theodore Walter
BRAZELTON, 1
William Buchanan
BRAZER, 3
Clarence Wilson
BRAZER, John H
BRAZIER, 1
Miss Marion Howard
BREADON, Sam 2
BREADY, Charles J. 5
BREARLEY, David H
BREARLEY, 1
William Henry
BREASTED, James Henry 1
BREATHITT, James 4
BREAUX, Joseph A. 1
BREAZEALE, Phanor 3
BREBNER, John Bartlet 3
BRECHT,
Bertoit Eugen Friedrich
BRECHT, H
Bertolt Eugen Friedrich
BRECHT, Robert Paul 5
BRECK, Daniel H
BRECK, Edward 1
BRECK, George William 1
BRECK, James Lloyd 4
BRECK, John H. 4
BRECK, Joseph 1
BRECK, Samuel 3
BRECK, Samuel 1
BRECKENRIDGE,
Clifton Rodes H
BRECKENRIDGE, 1
Hugh Henry
BRECKENRIDGE, James H
BRECKENRIDGE, 4
James Miller
BRECKENRIDGE, John H
BRECKENRIDGE, John
C. 4
BRECKENRIDGE, 3
Lester Paige
BRECKENRIDGE, Ralph
W. 1
BRECKINRIDGE, 4
Aida 'de Acosta

BRECKINRIDGE, Desha 1
BRECKINRIDGE, Henry 4
BRECKINRIDGE, 2
James Carson
BRECKINRIDGE, H
James Douglas
BRECKINRIDGE, H
Jefferson
BRECKINRIDGE, John H
BRECKINRIDGE, H
John Cabell
BRECKINRIDGE, 1
Joseph Cabell
BRECKINRIDGE, 1
Madeline McDowell
BRECKINRIDGE, Mary 4
BRECKINRIDGE, 2
Sophonisba Preston
BRECKINRIDGE, 1
William Campbell Preston
.BRECKINRIDGE, 1
William Lewis
BRECKONS, Robert W. 1
BREDIN, R. Sloan 1
BREED, Charles Blaney 3
BREED, Charles Henry 3
BREED, David Riddle 3
BREED, Dwight Payson 1
BREED, Ebenezer H
BREED, R. E. 1
BREED, Robert Stanley 3
BREED, 3
William Constable
BREEDEN, Harvey Oscar 4
BREEDING, Glenn
Edward 5
BREEN, Aloysius Andrew 3
BREEN, Joseph Ignatius 4
BREEN, Patrick H
BREEN, Robert A. 3
BREEN, 5
William John, Jr.
BREEN, William P. 1
BREENE, Frank Thomas 1
BREES, Herbert Jay 1
BREESE, Burtis Burr 1
BREESE, Edmund 1
BREESE, H
Randolph Kidder
BREESE, Sidney H
BREESE, 3
William Llywelyn
BREG, W. Roy 3
BREGY, Francis Amedee 1
BREGY, 4
Katherine Marie Cornelia
BREHAN, Marquise 'de H
BREHM, Cloide Everett 5
BREHM, John S. 1
BREHM, Marie Caroline 1
BREIDENBAUGH, 1
Edward Swoyer
BREIDENTHAL, John W. 5
BREIDENTHAL, John W. 1
BREIDENTHAL, 4
Maurice L.
BREIDENTHAL, 5
Maurice Lauren, Jr.
BREIDENTHAL, 4
Willard J.
BREIL, Joseph Carl 1
BREISACH, Paul 3
BREISACHER, Leo M. D. 4
BREITHAUPT,
Louis Orville 1
BREITUNG, 3
Charles Adelbert
BREITUNG, Edward H
BREITUNG, 1
Edward Nicklas
BREITWIESER, 3
Joseph Valentine
BRELSFORD, 4
Charles Henry
BRELSFORD, Millard 2
BREM, Walter Vernon 1
BREMER, Adolf 1
BREMER, George A. 3
BREMER, John Lewis 3
BREMER, Otto 3
BREMNER, 1
George Hampton
BREMNER, 1
William Hepburn
BRENDLER, Charles 4
BRENDLINGER, 5
Margaret Robinson
BRENEMAN, Abram
Adam 1
BRENGLE, Francis H
BRENGLE, Henry Gaw 2
BRENKE, 5
William Charles
BRENNAN, 4
Alfred Laurens
BRENNAN, Andrew
James 3

BRENNAN, Edward
James 3
BRENNAN, 4
Frederick Hazlitt
BRENNAN, George E. 1
BRENNAN, George M. 3
BRENNAN, Gerald Leo 4
BRENNAN, James Dowd 1
BRENNAN, John Francis 3
BRENNAN, Martin Adlai 1
BRENNAN, Martin S. 2
BRENNAN, 4
Thomas Francis
BRENNAN, William
Henry 4
BRENNECKE, 3
Cornelius G.
BRENNECKE, Ernest 5
BRENNECKE, Henry 4
BRENNEMANN, Joseph 2
BRENNER, John L. 4
BRENNER, Mortimer 5
BRENNER, Otto 5
BRENNER, Victor David 1
BRENON, Herbert 3
BRENT, Charles Henry 1
BRENT, Frank Pierce 4
BRENT, Henry Johnson H
BRENT, 1
Joseph Lancaster
BRENT, Margaret H
BRENT, Richard H
BRENT, Theodore 1
BRENT, William Leigh H
BRENTANO, Arthur 2
BRENTANO, Lorenz H
BRENTANO, Lowell 3
BRENTANO, Theodore 1
BRENTON, 1
Charles Richmond
BRENTON, Clyde Edward 1
BRENTON, Cranston 1
BRENTON, Samuel H
BRENTON, 5
Woodward Harold
BRERETON, Lewis Hyde 4
BRES, Edward Sedley 5
BRESCHARD H
BRESLICH, Arthur Louis 4
BRESLICH, 5
Ernst Rudolph
BRESLIN, James H. 1
BRESNAHAN, Thomas F. 5
BRESNAHAN, William H. 4
BRESSLER, 2
Raymond G. Jr.
BRESSLER, 2
Raymond George
BRESTELL, 5
Rudolph Emile
BRETHERTON, 1
Sidney Elliott
BRETON, Andre 4
BRETON, Ruth 4
BRETT, Agnes Baldwin 3
BRETT, Alden Chase 5
BRETT, Axel 3
BRETT, George Platt 1
BRETT, Homer 5
BRETT, Lloyd M. 1
BRETT, 4
Philip Milledoler
BRETT, Rutherford 3
BRETT, Sereno E. 3
BRETT, William Howard 1
BRETT, William Pierce 4
BRETZ, Julian Pleasant 3
BREUER, Henry Joseph 4
BREUER, Louis Henry 4
BREVARD, Joseph H
BREVOORT, James
Carson H
BREVOORT, 1
James Renwick
BREWBAKER, 5
Charles Warren
BREWER, Abraham T. 1
BREWER, Charles H
BREWER, Charles Edward 3
BREWER, Charles S. 1
BREWER, Clara Tagg 1
BREWER, D. Chauncey 1
BREWER, David Josiah 1
BREWER, Earl LeRoy 2
BREWER, H
Francis Beattie
BREWER, 1
Franklin Nourse
BREWER, George 1
BREWER, George
Emerson 1
BREWER, George St P. H
BREWER, Hugh Graham 4
BREWER, James Arthur 3
BREWER, John Bruce 4
BREWER, John Hyatt 1
BREWER, John Marks 3

BREWER, Leigh
Richmond 1
BREWER, Leo 4
BREWER, 1
Luther Albertus
BREWER, Mark Spencer 1
BREWER, 2
Nicholas Richard
BREWER, Oby T. 5
BREWER, Robert Du Bois 2
BREWER, Robert Paine 1
BREWER, Thomas Mayo H
BREWER, William A. Jr. 4
BREWER, William Henry 1
BREWER, Willis 5
BREWSTER, 3
Albert Vincent
BREWSTER, Andre
Walker 2
BREWSTER, Benjamin 1
BREWSTER, H
Benjamin Harris
BREWSTER, 4
Benjamin Harris
BREWSTER, 1
Benjamin Harris Jr.
BREWSTER, 1
Chauncey Bunce
BREWSTER, David
Lukens 2
BREWSTER, David P. H
BREWSTER, 1
Edward Lester
BREWSTER, Edwin
Tenney 3
BREWSTER, Elisha Hume 2
BREWSTER, 2
Ethel Hampson
BREWSTER, 1
Eugene Valentine
BREWSTER, Few 3
BREWSTER, 4
Frances Stanton
BREWSTER, H
Frederick Carroll
BREWSTER, 2
George Thomas
BREWSTER, 1
George Washington Wales
BREWSTER, Henry
Colvin 1
BREWSTER, James H
BREWSTER, James Henry 1
BREWSTER, 3
James Henry Jr.
BREWSTER, Osmyn H
BREWSTER, Owen 4
BREWSTER, Raymond 5
BREWSTER, Reginald R. 2
BREWSTER, 1
Sardius Mason
BREWSTER, 3
Walter Stanton
BREWSTER, William H
BREWSTER, William 1
BREWSTER, 1
William Nesbitt
BREWSTER, William Roe 4
BREWSTER, 4
William Tenney
BREYER, Henry W, Jr. 5
BREYFOGEL, 5
Sylvanus Charles
BREZING, Herman 2
BRIAN, Donald 2
BRICE, Calvin Stewart H
BRICE, Charles Rufus 4
BRICE, Fanny 3
BRICE, John A. 2
BRICHER, 3
Alfred Thompson
BRICK, Abraham Lincoln 1
BRICK, Alyea M. 4
BRICK, 1
Nicholas William
BRICKELL, 3
Henry Herschel
BRICKELL, Robert
Coman 1
BRICKELL, 4
William David
BRICKEN, Carl Ernest 5
BRICKER, Edwin Dyson 4
BRICKER, 2
Luther Otterbein
BRICKER, Mead L. 4
BRICKLEY, 3
Bartholomew A.
BRICKNER, 3
Barnett Robert
BRICKNER, Walter M. 1
BRIDE, 1
William Witthaft
BRIDGE, Gerard 5
BRIDGE, James Howard 1
BRIDGE, Norman 1
BRIDGER, James H

BRIDGERS, Robert Rufus H
BRIDGES, 1
Calvin Blackman
BRIDGES, 2
Charles Higbee
BRIDGES, Charles Scott 4
BRIDGES, Edson Lowell 1
BRIDGES, Fidelia 1
BRIDGES, H
William Harlowe
BRIDGES, 2
George Washington
BRIDGES, 2
Hedley Francis Gregory
BRIDGES, Horace James 3
BRIDGES, 1
James Robertson
BRIDGES, Jesse B. 1
BRIDGES,
Milton Arlanden
BRIDGES, Robert * H
BRIDGES, Robert 1
BRIDGES, Ronald 4
BRIDGES, S. Russell 1
BRIDGES, H
Samuel Augustus
BRIDGES, Styles 5
BRIDGES, Thomas Henry 4
BRIDGES, Thomas Reed 2
BRIDGES, Willson Orton 4
BRIDGMAN, H
Elijah Coleman
BRIDGMAN, 1
Frederic Arthur
BRIDGMAN, George
Henry 4
BRIDGMAN, 4
George Herbert
BRIDGMAN, 3
Grenville Temple
BRIDGMAN, 5
Helen Bartlett (Mrs. Herbert L. Bridgman)
BRIDGMAN,
Herbert Lawrence
BRIDGMAN, Howard
Allen 1
BRIDGMAN, Laura
Dewey H
BRIDGMAN, Lewis Jesse 1
BRIDGMAN, 4
Percy Williams
BRIDGMAN,
Raymond Landon
BRIDGWATER, William 4
BRIDPORT, Hugh H
BRIEN, William Given 4
BRIER, Ernest 3
BRIER, Warren Judson 5
BRIERLEY,
Wilfrid Gordon
BRIERTON, John H
BRIESEN, Arthur 'von
BRIGANCE, W. Norwood 3
BRIGGS, Arthur Hyslop 5
BRIGGS, Asa Gilbert 2
BRIGGS, Charles 1
BRIGGS,
Charles Augustus
BRIGGS, H
Charles Frederick
BRIGGS, Charles S. 4
BRIGGS, Clare A. 1
BRIGGS, Clay Stone 1
BRIGGS, Corona Hibbard 4
BRIGGS, 1
Edward Cornelius
BRIGGS, 3
Elizabeth Darling
BRIGGS, Frank Alonzo 3
BRIGGS, Frank Obadiah 5
BRIGGS, Frank Richmond 5
BRIGGS, 3
Frederic Melancthon
BRIGGS, George H
BRIGGS, George Ernest 5
BRIGGS, George Isaac 2
BRIGGS, 3
George Nathaniel
BRIGGS, George Nixon H
BRIGGS,
George Waverley
BRIGGS, George Weston 4
BRIGGS, Gordon Dobson 3
BRIGGS, 1
Gilbert Nicholas
BRIGGS, Henry Harrison 1
BRIGGS, J. Emmons 1
BRIGGS, 4
John De Quedville
BRIGGS, John Ely 3
BRIGGS, L. Vernon 1
BRIGGS, 1
Le Baron Russell
BRIGGS, Lucia Russell 3
BRIGGS, Lyman James 4
BRIGGS, Robert Aldrich 4
BRIGGS, Roswell
Emmons 4

BRIGGS, Stephen Albro 4
BRIGGS, Thomas Henry 5
BRIGGS, Thomas Roland 3
BRIGGS, Walter Owen 3
BRIGGS, 5
Walter Owen, Jr.
BRIGGS, Warren Richard 2
BRIGGS, 3
William Harlowe
BRIGHAM, Albert Perry 1
BRIGHAM, Amariah H
BRIGHAM, Arthur Amber H
BRIGHAM, Carl Campbell 2
BRIGHAM, 4
Clarence Saunders
BRIGHAM, Elbert Sidney 4
BRIGHAM, Elijah H
BRIGHAM, 5
Gertrude Richardson ("Viktor Flambeau,")
BRIGHAM, 5
Harold Frederick
BRIGHAM, 4
Henry Randolph
BRIGHAM, Johnson 1
BRIGHAM, Joseph Henry 5
BRIGHAM, L. Ward 4
BRIGHAM, H
Lewis Alexander
BRIGHAM, Mary Ann H
BRIGHAM, Nat Maynard 1
BRIGHAM, 3
Richard Douglas
BRIGHAM, 1
Sarah Jeannette
BRIGHAM, 1
William Erastus
BRIGHAM, William Tufts 5
BRIGHT, Alfred Harris 1
BRIGHT, David Edward 4
BRIGHT, Edward H
BRIGHT, James Wilson 1
BRIGHT, Jesse David H
BRIGHT, John 2
BRIGHT, Louis Victor 1
BRIGHT, 1
Marshal Huntington
BRIGHT EYES H
BRIGHTLY, 4
Frank Frederick
BRIGHTLY, H
Frederick Charles
BRIGHTMAN, 1
Alvin Collins
BRIGHTMAN, 3
Edgar Sheffield
BRIGHTMAN, 1
Horace Irving
BRIGHTMAN, 2
Horace Irving
BRIGMAN, 1
Bennett Mattingly
BRILES, Charles Walter 1
BRILL, Abraham Arden 2
BRILL, 5
George Mackenzie
BRILL, George Reiter 1
BRILL, Harvey Clayton 5
BRILL, Hascal Russel 3
BRILL, Nathan Edwin 1
BRILL, William Hascal 1
BRILLHART, David H. 3
BRIMHALL, George
Henry 1
BRIMSON, 1
William George
BRINCKE, H
William Draper
BRINCKERHOFF, 1
Arthur Freeman
BRINCKERHOFF, 2
Henry Morton
BRIND, Charles Albert 5
BRIND, Sir Patrick 4
BRINDLEY, Paul 3
BRINEY, Russell 4
BRINGHURST, 1
Robert Porter
BRININSTOOL, 3
Earl Alonzo
BRINK, Francis G. 3
BRINK, 1
Gilbert Nicholas
BRINKEN, Carl Ernest 5
BRINKER, Howard
Rasmus 4
BRINKER, Josiah Henry 1
BRINKERHOFF, H
Henry Roelif
BRINKERHOFF, Jacob 1
BRINKERHOFF, 3
Robert Moore
BRINKERHOFF, Roeliff 1
BRINKMAN, Oscar H. 5
BRINKMAN, 1
William Augustus
BRINLEY, Charles A. 4

BRINLEY, Daniel Putnam 4
BRINLEY, 4
Katherine Gordon Sanger
BRINSER, Harry Lerch 2
BRINSMADE, 1
John Chaplin
BRINSMADE, 1
Robert Bruce
BRINSMADE, 4
William Barrett
BRINSON, 1
Samuel Mitchell
BRINSTAD, 2
Charles William
BRINTON, Christian 2
BRINTON, 1
Daniel Garrison
BRINTON, Howard T. 4
BRINTON, John Hill 1
BRINTON, 4
Paul Henry Mallet-Prevost
BRINTON, Willard Cope 4
BRISBANE, Albert H
BRISBANE, Arthur 1
BRISBIN, 5
Clarence Franklin
BRISBIN, James S. H
BRISBIN, John H
BRISBINE, Annie M'Iver 4
BRISCO, Norris Arthur 2
BRISCOE, 5
Birdsall Parmenas
BRISCOE, Herman T. 4
BRISCOE, John Parran 1
BRISCOE, Robert Pearce 5
BRISKIN, Samuel Jacob 5
BRISTED, Charles Astor H
BRISTED, John 3
BRISTER, Charles James 3
BRISTER, John Willard 1
BRISTOL, Arthur E. 3
BRISTOL, Arthur LeRoy 2
BRISTOL, 1
Augusta Cooper
BRISTOL, 1
Charles Lawrence
BRISTOL, Edward Newell 2
BRISTOL, Frank Milton 1
BRISTOL, 1
George Prentiss
BRISTOL, Henry P. 3
BRISTOL, John Bunyan 1
BRISTOL, 1
John Isaac Devoe
BRISTOL, Lee Hastings 4
BRISTOL, Leverett Dale 3
BRISTOL, Mark Lambert 5
BRISTOL, 1
Theodore Louis
BRISTOL, William Henry 1
BRISTOW, 1
Algernon Thomas
BRISTOW, Benjamin
Helm H
BRISTOW, 1
Francis Marion
BRISTOW, George F. 4
BRISTOW, H
George Frederick
BRISTOW, 4
George Washington
BRISTOW, Joseph Little 2
BRISTOW, Louis Judson 5
BRITAN, Halbert Hains 3
BRITT, James J. 1
BRITT, Walter Stratton 1
BRITTAIN,
Carlo Bonaparte
BRITTAIN, 2
Charles Mercer
BRITTAIN, Frank Smith 1
BRITTAIN, Joseph I. 1
BRITTAIN, 3
Marion Luther
BRITTAN, Belle H
BRITTEN, 4
Edwin Franklin Jr.
BRITTEN, 4
Flora Phelps Harley
BRITTEN, Fred Albert 4
BRITTEN, Fred Ernest 4
BRITTIN, 5
Lewis Hotchkiss
BRITTINGHAM, 1
Thomas Evans
BRITTINGHAM,
Thomas Evans Jr.
BRITTON,
Alexander Thompson
BRITTON, Edgar C. 1
BRITTON, Edward Elms 1
BRITTON,
Elizabeth Gertrude
BRITTON, 1
Frank Hamilton
BRITTON, Frederick O. 1

BRITTON, 1
John Alexander
BRITTON, 1
Nathaniel Lord
BRITTON, 1
Wilton Everett
BRIZZOLARA, 5
Ralph Dominic
BROADBENT, 5
James Thomas
BROADDUS, Bower 3
BROADFOOT, Grover L. 4
BROADHEAD, 1
Garland Carr
BROADHEAD, H
James Overton
BROADHURST, Edward
T. 3
BROADHURST, 4
Edwin Borden
BROADHURST, George
H. 3
BROADHURST, Jean 3
BROADUS, John Albert H
BROADWATER, J. A. B. 3
BROCH, Hermann Joseph 5
BROCK, Charles Robert 1
BROCK, 1
Charles William Penn
BROCK, Clifford Edward 3
BROCK, Elmer Leslie 3
BROCK, George William 2
BROCK, Henry Irving 5
BROCK, James Ellison 4
BROCK, Larry 5
BROCK, Loring Stewart 5
BROCK, Robert Alonzo 1
BROCK, Sidney Gorham 4
BROCK, Thomas Sleeper 5
BROCK, William Emerson 4
BROCKENBROUGH, H
William Henry
BROCKETT, H
Linus Pierpont
BROCKHAGEN, Carl
Homer 2
BROCKIE, Arthur H. 2
BROCKLESBY, John H
BROCKMAN, 2
Fletcher Sims
BROCKSON, Franklin 4
BROCKWAY,
Albert Leverett
BROCKWAY, Fred John 1
BROCKWAY, George A. 5
BROCKWAY, Howard 3
BROCKWAY, John Hall H
BROCKWAY, Zebulon
Reed 1
BRODBECK, Andrew R. 1
BRODE, Charles Geiger 4
BRODE, Howard Stidham 4
BRODEK, Charles Adrian 2
BRODERICK, 2
Bonaventure Finnbarr
BRODERICK, 5
Carroll Joseph
BRODERICK, Case 1
BRODERICK, H
David Colbreth
BRODERICK, John T. 1
BRODERICK, Joseph A. 1
BRODERICK, 4
William Stephen
BRODERS, 4
Albert Compton
BRODESSER, 1
Roman Adolph
BRODEUR, 1
Clarence Arthur
BRODHEAD, Daniel H
BRODHEAD, 5
George Livingston
BRODHEAD,
George Milton
BRODHEAD, J. Davis 1
BRODHEAD, John H
BRODHEAD, John Curtis H
BRODHEAD, John
Romeyn H
BRODHEAD, Richard H
BRODIE, 1
Alexander Oswald
BRODIE, Andrew Melrose 1
BRODIE, Edward Everett 1
BRODIE, Israel B. 3
BRODRICK, 4
Lynn Rosegrant
BRODRICK, 1
Richard Godfrey
BRODSKY, Paul 4
BRODY, Clark Louis 4
BRODY, Joseph Isaac 4
BRODY, Samuel 3
BROEDEL, Max 1
BROEDEL, Max 2
BROEK, John Yonker 4

ROEKMAN, 3
David Hendrines
ROENING, 3
William Frederick
ROGAN, Francis Albert 5
ROGAN, James M. 5
ROGAN, Thomas J. 4
ROGDEN, Willis James 1
ROGLIE, Duc 'de 4
ROIDY, Edward William 3
ROKAMP, Frank
William 4
ROKAW, 1
Charles Livingston
ROKAW, Howard
Crosby 3
ROKENSHIRE, 3
Charles Digory
ROKENSHIRE, Norman 4
ROKENSHIRE, 4
William Samuel Jr.
ROKMEYER, Henry C. H
ROKMEYER, Henry C. H
ROMBERG, 1
Frederick George
ROMER, 3
Edward Sheppard
ROMER, Ralph
Shepherd 3
ROMFIELD, John H
ROMFIELD, Louis 3
ROMLEY, 5
Charles Dunham
ROMWELL, 1
Charles Summers
ROMWELL, Jacob
Henry 4
RONDEL, John B. 1
RONFENBRENNER- 3
, Jacques Jacob
RONFMAN, Samuel 5
RONK, Isabelle 2
RONK, Mitchell 3
RONLEM, Isaac Hill 1
RONNER, Edmond D. 1
RONNER, Harry 4
RONSON, Bennet 3
RONSON, Charles Eli 4
RONSON, David H
RONSON, Dillon 2
RONSON, 4
Francis Woolsey
RONSON, 2
Harrison Arthur
RONSON, Henry
RONSON, Isaac Hopkins H
RONSON, 1
Samuel Lathrop
RONSON, Solon Cary 1
RONSON, 3
Thomas Bertrand
RONSON, 1
Walter Cochrane
RONSON, 5
William Howard
RONSON, 4
William Sherlock
ROOK, Charles Henry 4
ROOKE, Ben C. 5
ROOKE, Flavius Lionel 1
ROOKE, Francis Key 1
ROOKE, H
Francis Taliaferro
ROOKE, 1
Franklin Ellsworth
ROOKE, John Mercer 1
ROOKE, John Rutter 1
ROOKE, Mary Myrtle 5
ROOKE, Richard Norris 1
ROOKE, 1
St George Tucker
ROOKE, Thomas Preston 4
ROOKE, Tucker 2
ROOKE, Walter H
ROOKE, 5
William Ellsworth
ROOKE, 4
William Ellsworth
ROOKER, 1
Charles Frederick
ROOKER, John William 3
ROOKE-RAWLE,
William 1
ROOKES, 4
John St Clair Jr.
ROOKES, H
Samuel Marsdon
ROOKHART, Smith W. 2
ROOKINGS, 1
Robert Somers
ROOKINGS, 3
Walter DuBois
ROOKINGS, 4
Walter DuBois
ROOKINS, 3
Homer De Wilton
ROOKS, Alfred Hulse 1

BROOKS, 5
Alfred Mansfield
BROOKS, Allerton Frank 3
BROOKS, Alonzo Beecher 4
BROOKS, Anson Strong 1
BROOKS, Arbie Leroy 3
BROOKS, Arthur H
BROOKS, Arthur Alford 2
BROOKS, Arthur Thomas 4
BROOKS, Arthur Wolfort 2
BROOKS, 4
Benjamin Talbott
BROOKS, Bryant Butler 2
BROOKS, C. Wayland 3
BROOKS, Charles H
BROOKS, Charles Alvin 5
BROOKS, Charles Edward 4
BROOKS, Charles F. 3
BROOKS, 5
Charles Hayward
BROOKS, 1
Charles Stephen
BROOKS, H
Charles Timothy
BROOKS, 5
Christopher Parkinson
BROOKS, 5
Clarence Richard
BROOKS, David H
BROOKS, Edward 1
BROOKS, 3
Edward Schroeder
BROOKS, Edwin B. 4
BROOKS, 1
Elbridge Streeter
BROOKS, Erastus H
BROOKS, Eugene Clyde 2
BROOKS, Florence 4
BROOKS, Frank Hilliard 1
BROOKS, Frank Wilks 1
BROOKS, Franklin Eli 1
BROOKS, Fred Emerson 5
BROOKS, Frederick A. 5
BROOKS, George Merrick 4
BROOKS, George Sprague 4
BROOKS, H
George Washington
BROOKS, Geraldine 5
BROOKS, Harlow 4
BROOKS, Harry Sayer 3
BROOKS, Henry Luesing 5
BROOKS, Henry S. 4
BROOKS, Henry Turner 4
BROOKS, J. Wilton 1
BROOKS, Jabez 1
BROOKS, James H
BROOKS, James Byron 1
BROOKS, James Gordon 5
BROOKS, Jesse Wendell 1
BROOKS, John H
BROOKS, John G(aunt) 5
BROOKS, John Graham 1
BROOKS, John Pascal 4
BROOKS, Joseph Hudson 3
BROOKS, Joshua Loring 2
BROOKS, 5
Laurance Waddill
BROOKS, LaVerne W. 5
BROOKS, Leon Richard 4
BROOKS, Maria Gowen H
BROOKS, Mary Willard 3
BROOKS, Micah H
BROOKS, Morgan 2
BROOKS, Ned 5
BROOKS, Neil 5
BROOKS, Noah 1
BROOKS, Olin L. 4
BROOKS, Overton 4
BROOKS, Paul David 3
BROOKS, Peter Anthony 2
BROOKS, Peter Chardon H
BROOKS, Phillips H
BROOKS, Phillips Moore 5
BROOKS, Preston Smith 4
BROOKS, Ralph Gilmour 4
BROOKS, 2
Raymond Cummings
BROOKS, Richard E. 1
BROOKS, Robert Blemker 4
BROOKS, 1
Robert Clarkson
BROOKS, Robert Mary 2
BROOKS, 3
Robert Nathaniel
BROOKS, Rodney Joseph 3
BROOKS, Samuel Palmer 1
BROOKS, Sarah Warner 1
BROOKS, Stewart 2
BROOKS, 2
Stratton Duluth
BROOKS, Summer
Cushing 3
BROOKS, Thomas Benton 4
BROOKS, Van Wyck 4
BROOKS, Victor Lee 1
BROOKS, Walter Rollin 3

BROOKS, 4
Wendell Stanton
BROOKS, 1
William Benthall
BROOKS, William E. 5
BROOKS, William Keith 1
BROOKS, William Myron 1
BROOKS, William Penn 1
BROOKS, William Robert 1
BROOKS, 4
William Thomas Harbaugh
BROOKS, Winfield Sears 4
BROOKSHIRE, 1
Elijah Voorhees
BROOM, Jacob H
BROOM, James Madison H
BROOMALL, John Martin H
BROOME, 3
Edwin Cornelius
BROOME, Harvey 4
BROOME, Harvey 5
BROOME, Isaac 1
BROOME, Robert Edwin 4
BROOMELL, I. Norman 1
BROOMFIELD, 4
John Calvin
BROONZY, 4
William Lee Conley
BROPHY, C. Gerald 3
BROPHY, Daniel Francis 4
BROPHY, Ellen Amelia 1
BROPHY, Thomas D'Arcy 4
BROPHY, Truman William 1
BROPHY, William Henry 1
BROREIN, William G. 1
BROSE, Louis D. 1
BROSIUS, Marriott 1
BROSMAN, Paul William 3
BROSMITH, William 1
BROSNAHAN, 5
Patrick Edward
BROSNAHAN, Timothy 1
BROSS, Ernest 1
BROSS, William H
BROSSART, Ferdinand 4
BROSSEAU, Alfred J. 1
BROTHER, Doran Palmer 4
BROTHERTON, 1
Alice Williams
BROUGH, John H
BROUGH, William 4
BROUGHAM, John 1
BROUGHER, J.
Whitcomb 4
BROUGHER, 5
J(ames) Whitcomb
BROUGHTON, 3
Charles Elmer
BROUGHTON, 2
Joseph Melville
BROUGHTON, 1
Leonard Gaston
BROUGHTON, 5
Leslie Nathan
BROUGHTON, 2
Levin Bowland
BROUGHTON, William
R. H
BROUGHTON, William S. 3
BROUILLETTE, 5
T. Gilbert
BROULLIRE, John Merlin 5
BROUN, Heywood 1
BROUN, William Le Roy 1
BROUNOFF, Platon 1
BROUSE, Edwin Walter 4
BROUSSARD, 1
Edwin Sidney
BROUSSARD, 2
James Francis
BROUSSARD, Robert F. 1
BROUSSEAU, Kate 1
BROUWER, Dirk 4
BROUWER, 4
Luitzen Egbertus Jan
BROWARD, 1
Napoleon Bonaparte
BROWDER, Basil David 3
BROWDER, Earl (Russel) 5
BROWER, Alfred Smith 5
BROWER, Daniel Roberts 1
BROWER, 1
Harriette Moore
BROWER, 1
Jacob Vradenberg
BROWER, Walter Scott 4
BROWER, 1
William Leverich
BROWERE, 1
Albertus D. O.
BROWERE, H
John Henri Isaac
BROWN, A. Curtis 2
BROWN, A. Luther 3
BROWN, A. Page H
BROWN, Aaron Switzer 1
BROWN, Aaron Venable H

BROWN, Abbie Farwell 1
BROWN, Abram English 1
BROWN, Addison 1
BROWN, Alanson David 1
BROWN, Albert Edmund 5
BROWN, Albert Frederic 4
BROWN, Albert Gallatin H
BROWN, Albert Oscar 1
BROWN, Albert Sidney 5
BROWN, Alexander H
BROWN, Alexander 1
BROWN, Alexander 2
BROWN, 4
Alexander Cushing
BROWN, 1
Alexander Ephraim
BROWN, Alfred Hodgdon 5
BROWN, Alfred Seely 5
BROWN, Alice 2
BROWN, 2
Allen Van Vechten
BROWN, 5
Alvin (McCreary)
BROWN, 1
Amanda Elizabeth
BROWN, Ames 2
BROWN, Ames Thorndike 4
BROWN, Amos Peaslee 1
BROWN, 5
Ann Mary Marothy (Mrs.
Ernest M. Brown)
BROWN, Anson H
BROWN, Archer 1
BROWN, 3
Archibald Manning
BROWN, Arlo Ayres 4
BROWN, Armstead 4
BROWN, Arthur 1
BROWN, Arthur Jr. 3
BROWN, 2
Arthur Charles Lewis
BROWN, Arthur Edward 1
BROWN, Arthur Erwin 4
BROWN, Arthur Judson * 4
BROWN, Arthur Lewis 2
BROWN, Arthur Morton 2
BROWN, Arthur Voorhees 2
BROWN, Arthur William 4
BROWN, Arthur Winton 2
BROWN, Ashmun Norris 2
BROWN, Barnum 1
BROWN, Baxter Lamont 3
BROWN, Bedford H
BROWN, Benjamin 2
BROWN, 1
Benjamin Beuhring
BROWN, 1
Benjamin Chambers
BROWN, Benjamin Gratz H
BROWN, 3
Benjamin Henry Inness
BROWN, Bernard 3
BROWN, Bolton 1
BROWN, Buford Mason 4
BROWN, 2
Burdette Boardman
BROWN, C. Foster Jr. 4
BROWN, C. Henry 1
BROWN, Calvin Luther 1
BROWN, Calvin Smith 1
BROWN, Carleton 1
BROWN, Caxton 1
BROWN, Cecil Kenneth 3
BROWN, Charles H
BROWN, Charles Allen 4
BROWN, H
Charles Brockden
BROWN, Charles Carroll 2
BROWN, Charles Edward 2
BROWN, Charles Francis 1
BROWN, Charles H. 1
BROWN, Charles Harvey 1
BROWN, Charles Ira 1
BROWN, Charles Irwin 1
BROWN, Charles Leonard 4
BROWN, 1
Charles Reynolds
BROWN, Charles Rufus 1
BROWN, Charles Sumner 1
BROWN, Charles Walter 1
BROWN, Charles William 1
BROWN, Charles Wilson 5
BROWN, 3
Charlotte Emerson
BROWN, 1
Charlotte Harding
BROWN, Clarence J. 4
BROWN, 1
Clarence Montgomery
BROWN, Clyde 3
BROWN, Colvin W. 3
BROWN, Cyrus Jay 5
BROWN, Cyrus Perrin 1
BROWN, D. J. 3
BROWN, Daniel Russell 1
BROWN, David Abraham 1
BROWN, David Chester 2

BROWN, David Paul H
BROWN, 1
Demarchus Clariton
BROWN, Demetra Vaka 2
BROWN, Donald C. 3
BROWN, Donald Lamont 1
BROWN, Donald Lee 5
BROWN, Donaldson 4
BROWN, Downing P. 4
BROWN, Earl Theodore 3
BROWN, Earle Godfrey 5
BROWN, Ebenezer H
BROWN, Edgar 5
BROWN, Edith 5
BROWN, Edna Adelaide 2
BROWN, Edward Eagle 3
BROWN, Edward Killoran 3
BROWN, Edward Lee 4
BROWN, Edward Miles 1
BROWN, Edward
Norphlet 3
BROWN, Edward Osgood 1
BROWN, Edward Scott 1
BROWN, 5
Edward Vail Lapham
BROWN, Edwin Hacker 1
BROWN, Edwin Perkins 1
BROWN, Edwin Pierce 5
BROWN, Edwin Putnam 1
BROWN, Edwy Rolfe 1
BROWN, Eli Huston Jr. 2
BROWN, Elias H
BROWN, H
Eliphalet M. Jr.
BROWN, Elliott Wilber 1
BROWN, Elmer 5
BROWN, Elmer Ellsworth 1
BROWN, Elon Rouse 4
BROWN, Elzear Joseph 5
BROWN, 4
Emma Elizabeth
BROWN, Enoch 4
BROWN, Eric Gore 4
BROWN, Ernest William 1
BROWN, Estelle Aubrey 4
BROWN, Ethan Allen H
BROWN, Everett Chase 1
BROWN, Everett J. 2
BROWN, F. E. 3
BROWN, F. E. 4
BROWN, Fayette 1
BROWN, Fayette 3
BROWN, Fletcher 3
BROWN, Foster Vincent 4
BROWN, Francis 1
BROWN, Francis 1
BROWN, Francis Cabell 4
BROWN, Francis Henry 1
BROWN, Francis James 4
BROWN, Francis Shunk 1
BROWN, Frank 1
BROWN, Frank Chilton 1
BROWN, Frank Chouteau 2
BROWN, Frank Clyde 2
BROWN, Frank Llewellyn 1
BROWN, Frank Xavier 5
BROWN, Franklin Q. 3
BROWN, 5
Franklin Stewart
BROWN, Fred Comings 3
BROWN, Fred Herbert 3
BROWN, Frederic Kenyon 1
BROWN, Frederick Anson 1
BROWN, 3
Frederick Harvey
BROWN, 4
Frederick Walworth
BROWN, 5
Frederick William
BROWN, 5
Frederick Winfield
BROWN, Fredric 5
BROWN, George * H
BROWN, George 1
BROWN, George Francis 1
BROWN, George Garvin 5
BROWN, George Granger 3
BROWN, George H. 5
BROWN, George Houston H
BROWN, George Lincoln 1
BROWN, George Loring H
BROWN, George M. 5
BROWN, George Marion 2
BROWN, George Newland 4
BROWN, George Pliny 1
BROWN, George Rothwell 4
BROWN, 5
George Rowland, III
BROWN, George Samson 2
BROWN, George Stewart 1
BROWN, George Stewart 2
BROWN, George Stewart 2
BROWN, George Tiden 4
BROWN, 2
George Van Ingen
BROWN, George W. 1
BROWN, George Warren

BROWN, 1
George Washington
BROWN, George William H
BROWN, George William 2
BROWN, George
Woodford 5
BROWN, Gertrude Foster 4
BROWN, Gilmor 3
BROWN, Glen David 3
BROWN, Glenn 1
BROWN, Goold H
BROWN, Grace Marn 4
BROWN, H. Martin 1
BROWN, Harold Haven 1
BROWN, Harry B. 4
BROWN, Harry Fletcher 2
BROWN, Harry Joe 5
BROWN, Harry Sanford 2
BROWN, Harry Winfield 1
BROWN, Harvey H. Jr. 3
BROWN, Helen Dawes 1
BROWN, Helen Gilman 2
BROWN, Henry B. 1
BROWN, Henry Bascom 1
BROWN, Henry Billings 1
BROWN, Henry Collins 1
BROWN, Henry Daniels 5
BROWN, Henry Harrison 1
BROWN, Henry Kirke H
BROWN, Henry Matthias 5
BROWN, Henry Seymour 1
BROWN, Herbert Daniel 5
BROWN, Herbert Daniel 1
BROWN, Herbert J. 2
BROWN, Herman 4
BROWN, Hilton Ultimus 4
BROWN, Hiram Chellis 4
BROWN, Hiram Staunton 1
BROWN, Holcombe James 3
BROWN, Homer Caffee 3
BROWN, 1
Horace Manchester
BROWN, Howard Benner 4
BROWN, 1
Howard Nicholson
BROWN, Hugh Elmer 3
BROWN, Hugh Henry 1
BROWN, Hugh S. 4
BROWN, Isaac Eddy 1
BROWN, H
Isaac Van Arsdale
BROWN, J. Appleton 1
BROWN, J. Hammond 3
BROWN, J. Hay 1
BROWN, J. Stanley 1
BROWN, J. Thompson 3
BROWN, J. Vallance 1
BROWN, Jacob Jennings H
BROWN, James * H
BROWN, James * 1
BROWN, James B. 3
BROWN, James Barrett 5
BROWN, 3
James Dorsey Jr.
BROWN, James Elwyn Jr. 4
BROWN, James F. 1
BROWN, James F. 3
BROWN, James Greenlief 3
BROWN, James Henry 4
BROWN, James R. 3
BROWN, James Salisbury H
BROWN, James Sproat H
BROWN, James Thomas 3
BROWN, James Wright 3
BROWN, 5
James Wright, Jr.
BROWN, Jeremiah H
BROWN, Joe Evan 5
BROWN, Joel Bascom 5
BROWN, John * H
BROWN, John A. H
BROWN, John Albert 2
BROWN, John Bernis 5
BROWN, John C. 1
BROWN, John Calvin H
BROWN, John Carter H
BROWN, John Crosby 1
BROWN, John Elward 3
BROWN, John Franklin 1
BROWN, John George 1
BROWN, John Griest 2
BROWN, John Hamilton 4
BROWN, John Henry H
BROWN, 4
John Herbert Jr.
BROWN, John Howard 1
BROWN, John Jacob 2
BROWN, John Mackenzie 1
BROWN, John Marshall 1
BROWN, John Mifflin H
BROWN, John Newton 1
BROWN, John Pinkney 1
BROWN, John Porter 1
BROWN, John Richard 1
BROWN, John W. H
BROWN, John Young * 1
BROWN, Joseph H

BROWN, Joseph Alleine 5
BROWN, Joseph Clifton 2
BROWN, Joseph Eckford 3
BROWN, Joseph Emerson H
BROWN, Joseph Gill 1
BROWN, Joseph M. 1
BROWN, Joseph Real 4
BROWN, Joseph Rogers H
BROWN, Julius L. 1
BROWN, Junius Calvin 5
BROWN, Justus Morris 1
BROWN, Kate Louise 1
BROWN, 1
Katharine Holland
BROWN, Kenneth 4
BROWN, Kenneth Rent 3
BROWN, Herman) LaRue 5
BROWN, Lathrop 3
BROWN, Lawrason 1
BROWN, Leigh A. 3
BROWN, 4
Levant Frederick
BROWN, Lew 3
BROWN, Lewis H. 3
BROWN, Lloyd Arnold 4
BROWN, Lloyd Davidson 3
BROWN, Louis M(yron) 5
BROWN, Louise Fargo 3
BROWN, Lucius 1
BROWN, Lucius Polk 1
BROWN, Lucy Hall 1
BROWN, Lyndon Osmond 4
BROWN, Lytle 3
BROWN, M. Mcclellan 1
BROWN, M(ary) Belle 5
BROWN, Manuel Nicholas 5
BROWN, Margaret Wise 3
BROWN, Mark A. 5
BROWN, Marshall 4
BROWN, 2
Marshall Stewart
BROWN, Mather H
BROWN, 5
Maxine McFadden (Mrs.
Jack
T. Brown)
BROWN, May Belleville 1
BROWN, Milton H
BROWN, Milton Wilbert 5
BROWN, Morris 1
BROWN, Moses * H
BROWN, Moses True 1
BROWN, Nathaniel Smith 2
BROWN, Neal 1
BROWN, Neill Smith H
BROWN, Nicholas * H
BROWN, Norriw 3
BROWN, Obadiah H
BROWN, Olympia 1
BROWN, Orville Harry 2
BROWN, Orvon Graff 4
BROWN, Oswald Eugene 1
BROWN, Owen Clarence 5
BROWN, Owsley 3
BROWN, Parke 2
BROWN, Paul 4
BROWN, Paul Goodwin 2
BROWN, Paul Winthrop 1
BROWN, Percy 3
BROWN, Percy A. 4
BROWN, Percy Edgar 1
BROWN, Percy W. 3
BROWN, Philip E. 1
BROWN, Philip Greely 1
BROWN, Philip King 1
BROWN, Philip King 2
BROWN, Philip Marshall 1
BROWN, Phoebe Hinsdale H
BROWN, Preston 2
BROWN, R. Lewis 2
BROWN, Ralph Hall 2
BROWN, Ray 2
BROWN, Ray Andrews 5
BROWN, Raymond
Dwight 3
BROWN, Rexwald 1
BROWN, Reynolds Driver 5
BROWN, 3
Rezeau Blanchard
BROWN, Robert H
BROWN, Robert Abner 1
BROWN, 1
Robert Alexander
BROWN, 5
Robert Arthur, Jr.
BROWN, Robert Burns 1
BROWN, Robert Elliott 1
BROWN, 5
Robert Frederick
BROWN, Robert K. 2
BROWN, Robert Rankins 1
BROWN, Robert Sater 1
BROWN, Robert Young 4
BROWN, Rollo Walter 1
BROWN, Rome G. 1
BROWN, 2
Roscoe Conkling Ensign

BROWN, Roy 3
BROWN, Rufus Everson 4
BROWN, Ruth Mowry 4
BROWN, Samuel H
BROWN, Samuel Alburtus 3
BROWN, Samuel Gilman H
BROWN, 1
Samuel Horton Jr.
BROWN, Samuel Robbins H
BROWN, Sanford Miller 1
BROWN, Sanger 1
BROWN, Selden Stanley 1
BROWN, Seth W. 4
BROWN, 3
Sevellon Ledyard
BROWN, Simon H
BROWN, Solyman H
BROWN, Stanley Doty 4
BROWN, Stanley L. 4
BROWN, Stimson Joseph 1
BROWN, Sydney Barlow 3
BROWN, 3
Sydney MacGillvary
BROWN, Sylvanus H
BROWN, Thaddeus
Harold 1
BROWN, Thatcher M. 3
BROWN, Theron 4
BROWN, Theron Adelbert 5
BROWN, Thomas Allston 1
BROWN, Thomas Cook 4
BROWN, Thomas Edwin 4
BROWN, Thomas F. 4
BROWN, 1
Thomas Jefferson
BROWN, 3
Thomas Richardson
BROWN, Titus 1
BROWN, Vandyke H
BROWN, W. Cabell 1
BROWN, W. Kennedy 1
BROWN, 5
W(illiam) L(ee) Lyons
BROWN, Wade Hampton 2
BROWN, Wade R. 4
BROWN, Waldron Post 1
BROWN, Wallace Elias 1
BROWN, 1
Wallace Winthrop
BROWN, Walter Folger 5
BROWN, Walter Folger 4
BROWN, Walter Franklin 3
BROWN, Walter Lewis 1
BROWN, Warwick
Thomas 4
BROWN, Webster Everett 4
BROWN, Wilbur Vincent 1
BROWN, Willard Dayton 5
BROWN, William * H
BROWN, William 1
BROWN, William Adams 2
BROWN, 3
William Adams Jr.
BROWN, 5
William Atwell, Jr.
BROWN, William Averell 3
BROWN, William C. 1
BROWN, William C. 4
BROWN, William Carey 5
BROWN,
William Channing
BROWN, William Edward 1
BROWN, William G. Jr. 1
BROWN, H
William Garl Jr.
BROWN, William Garrott 1
BROWN, William Gay H
BROWN, William George 1
BROWN, William Henry 2
BROWN, William Henry * 1
BROWN, William Hill 1
BROWN, William Horace 1
BROWN, William Hughey H
BROWN, William John H
BROWN, William Lee 1
BROWN, William Liston 1
BROWN, 1
William Montgomery
BROWN, William O. 3
BROWN, William Perry 2
BROWN, William Thayer 3
BROWN, 4
William Thurston
BROWN, William Wallace 5
BROWN, William Wells H
BROWN, Wilson 3
BROWN, Wrisley 3
BROWN, Wylie 4
BROWN, Zaidee 5
BROWNE, Aldis Birdsey 1
BROWNE, Arthur Wesley 2
BROWNE, Belmore H
BROWNE, 3
Benjamin Frederick
BROWNE, Bennet 1
BROWNE, 2
Bernard
BROWNE, Byron 4

BROWNE, Causten 1
BROWNE, Charles 2
BROWNE, Charles Albert 2
BROWNE, Charles Farrar H
BROWNE, 1
Charles Francis
BROWNE, Daniel Jay H
BROWNE, Duncan Hodge 3
BROWNE, Edward Everts 2
BROWNE, Edward
Tankard 3
BROWNE, Francis Fisher 1
BROWNE, 4
Frederick William
BROWNE, George Elmer 2
BROWNE, George Henry 3
BROWNE, H
George Huntington
BROWNE, George Israel 3
BROWNE, George Waldo 1
BROWNE, Harry C. 3
BROWNE, 1
Herbert Wheildon Cotton
BROWNE, Irving H
BROWNE, J. Lewis 1
BROWNE, 1
Jefferson Beale
BROWNE, John H
BROWNE, John Ross H
BROWNE, Junius Henri H
BROWNE, Lewis 2
BROWNE, Lewis Allen 1
BROWNE, Louis Edgar 3
BROWNE, 5
Margaret Fitzhugh
BROWNE, Maurice 3
BROWNE, Nina Eliza 1
BROWNE, Page 5
BROWNE, Porter
Emerson 1
BROWNE, Ralph Cowan 3
BROWNE, Rhodes 1
BROWNE, Robert Bell 3
BROWNE, Robert H. 1
BROWNE, Thomas H
BROWNE, H
Thomas Henry Bayly
BROWNE, 1
Thomas McLelland
BROWNE, Waldo Ralph 3
BROWNE, William 1
BROWNE, William Hand 1
BROWNE, 1
William Hardcastle
BROWNELL, Atherton 1
BROWNELL, Baker 4
BROWNELL, 1
Clarence Ludlow
BROWNELL, 5
Eleanor Olivia
BROWNELL, Emery
Albert 4
BROWNELL, 3
Francis Herbert
BROWNELL, 1
George Francis
BROWNELL, 1
George Griffin
BROWNELL, 1
Harry Franklin
BROWNELL, Harry Gault 4
BROWNELL, Henry
Howard H
BROWNELL, Jane Louise 1
BROWNELL, Kenneth C. 3
BROWNELL, Silas B. 4
BROWNELL, H
Thomas Church
BROWNELL, Walter A. 1
BROWNELL, 1
William Crary
BROWNING, 1
Charles Clifton
BROWNING, 1
Charles Henry
BROWNING, Eliza
Gordon 5
BROWNING, 2
George Landon
BROWNING, Grace 3
BROWNING, John Hull 1
BROWNING, John M. 1
BROWNING, 1
Matthew Sandefur
BROWNING, McPherson 3
BROWNING, Miles 3
BROWNING, H
Orville Hickman
BROWNING, 1
Philip Embury
BROWNING, 4
Ralph Rushton
BROWNING, 5
Robert Turner
BROWNING, Webster E. 2
BROWNING, William 1

BROWNING, William
Hull
BROWNING, William J.
BROWNLEE,
Frederick Leslie
BROWNLEE, James F.
BROWNLEE, James
Leaman
BROWNLEE,
William Craig
BROWNLOW, Louis
BROWNLOW,
Walter Preston
BROWNLOW,
William Gannaway
BROWNSCOMBE, Jennie
BROWNSON,
Carleton Lewis
BROWNSON,
Henry Francis
BROWNSON, James Irwin
BROWNSON,
Marcus Acheson
BROWNSON, Mary
Wilson
BROWNSON, Nathan
BROWNSON,
Orestes Augustus
BROWNSON,
Truman Gaylord
BROWNSON,
Willard Herbert
BROY, Charles Clinton
BROYDE, Isaac
BROYLES, Joseph Warren
BRUBACHER, Abram
Royer
BRUBACK, Theodore
BRUBAKER,
Albert Philson
BRUBAKER, Howard
BRUCE,
Alexander Campbell
BRUCE,
Andrew Alexander
BRUCE, Andrew Davis
BRUCE, Archibald
BRUCE, Blanche Kelso
BRUCE, Charles Arthur
BRUCE, Charles Morelle
BRUCE, Donald Cogley
BRUCE, Dwight Hall
BRUCE, Edward
BRUCE, Eugene Sewell
BRUCE, Frank M. Sr.
BRUCE, Frank M. Sr.
BRUCE, George
BRUCE, H. Duane
BRUCE,
H(enry) Addington (Bayley)
BRUCE, Harold Lawton
BRUCE, Helm
BRUCE, Henry William
BRUCE,
Horatio Washington
BRUCE, Howard
BRUCE, Jackson Martin
BRUCE, James Deacon
BRUCE, James Douglas
BRUCE, John
BRUCE, John Edgar
BRUCE, John Edward
BRUCE, John Eldridge
BRUCE, Lenny
BRUCE, Logan Lithgow
BRUCE, Matthew Linn
BRUCE,
Philip Alexander
BRUCE, Phineas
BRUCE, Robert
BRUCE, Robert Glenn
BRUCE, Saunders Dewees
BRUCE, Wallace
BRUCE, William Cabell
BRUCE, William George
BRUCE,
William Herschel
BRUCE, William Paterson
BRUCE OF
MELBOURNE, Viscount
BRUCKER, Joseph
BRUCKER,
Wilber M(arion)
BRUCKNER, Aloys L.
BRUCKNER, Henry
BRUCKNER,
Jacob Herbert
BRUECKMANN,
John George
BRUECKNER, Leo John
BRUEGGEMAN,
Bessie Parker
BRUEGGER, John
BRUENING, Heinrich
BRUENING,
William Ferdinand

BRUERE, Henry 3
BRUERE, Robert Walter 5
BRUES, Charles Thomas 3
BRUESTLE, 1
George Matthew
BRUFF, H
Joseph Goldsborough
BRUFF, 1
Lawrence Laurenson
BRUGGMANN, Charles 4
BRUHL, Gustav
BRUHN, Carl 5
BRUHN, Wilhelm L. 3
BRUHN, Wilhelm L. 3
BRUINS, John H. 3
BRULE, Etienne
BRUMBAUGH, Clement 1
BRUMBAUGH, 5
Gaius Marcus
BRUMBAUGH, I. Harvey 1
BRUMBAUGH, 1
Martin Grove
BRUMBAUGH, Roy 3
Talmage
BRUMBY, Frank 5
Hardeman
BRUMBY, H
Richard Trapier
BRUMBY, Thomas Mason 1
BRUMIDI, Constantino H
BRUMLEY, 5
Benjamin Basil
BRUMLEY, Daniel Joseph 4
BRUMLEY, Oscar Victor 2
BRUMM, 3
Charles Napoleon
BRUMM, George Franklin 1
BRUMM, John Lewis 3
BRUMMITT, Dan 1
Brearley
BRUMMITT, Dennis G. 1
BRUN, Constantin 2
BRUNAUER, 3
Esther Caukin
BRUNCKEN, Ernest 4
BRUNDAGE, 1
Albert Harrison
BRUNDAGE, 5
Charles Edwin
BRUNDAGE, 1
Edward Jackson
BRUNDAGE, 1
William Milton
BRUNDIDGE, Oscar 3
Dean
BRUNDIDGE, Stephen Jr. 4
BRUNE, Adolf Gerhard 1
BRUNE, Frederick W. 5
BRUNER, Henry Lane 2
BRUNER, James Dowden 4
BRUNER, Lawrence 1
BRUNER, 5
Raymond Alphonse
BRUNER, Weston 4
BRUNER, William Evans 5
BRUNIA, William Frans 3
BRUNKER,
Albert Ridgley
BRUNNER, 1
Arnold William
BRUNNER, David B. 1
BRUNNER, Henry George 4
BRUNNER, John 1
BRUNNER, John 4
Hamilton
BRUNNER, H
Nicholaus Joseph
BRUNNER, William F. 4
BRUNNOW, H
Rudolph Ernest
BRUNO, Frank J. 3
BRUNOT, Harney Felix 4
BRUNS, Henry Dickson 1
BRUNS, Henry Frederick 2
BRUNS, 4
Thomas Nelson Carter
BRUNSCHWIG,
Alexander 5
BRUNSCHWIG, Roger E. 5
BRUNSON, James Edwin 4
BRUNSON, May Augusta 5
BRUNSWICK, Mark 5
BRUNSWIG, 2
Lucien Napoleon
BRUNTON, David
William 1
BRUSH, Alvin G. 1
BRUSH, Charles Francis 1
BRUSH, Daniel Harmon 1
BRUSH, 1
Edward Nathaniel
BRUSH, Florence 4
BRUSH, Frank Spencer 1
BRUSH, 5
Frederic (Louis)
BRUSH, 1
George 'de Forest

BRUSH, George Jarvis 1
BRUSH, 1
George Washington
BRUSH, Henry H
BRUSH, Henry Raymond 1
BRUSH, Howard Grafton 5
BRUSH, Jacob Henry 1
BRUSH, Katharine 3
BRUSH, Louis Herbert 2
BRUSH, 1
Matthew Chauncey
BRUSH, Murray Peabody 5
BRUSH, 5
William Whitlock
BRUSHINGHAM, 1
John Patrick
BRUSIE, 4
Charles Frederick
BRUSKE, 4
Augustus Fredrich
BRUST, Peter 2
BRUTE 'DE H
REMUR, Simon William
Gabriel
BRUTON, John Fletcher 5
BRUYN, Andrew De Witt H
BRUYN, Charles DeWitt H
BRYAN, Adolphus Jerome 3
BRYAN, Beauregard 4
BRYAN, 1
Benjamin Chambers
BRYAN, Charles Page 3
BRYAN, Charles W. Jr. 4
BRYAN, Charles Wayland 1
BRYAN, Claude S. 3
BRYAN, Daniel Bunyan 4
BRYAN, Edward Payson 1
BRYAN, Elmer Burritt 1
BRYAN, Enoch Albert 1
BRYAN, Enoch Albert 2
BRYAN, Ernest Rowlett 3
BRYAN,
Frederick Carlos
BRYAN, George H
BRYAN, George 1
BRYAN, George Sands 2
BRYAN, Guy Morrison 1
BRYAN, Henry Francis 3
BRYAN, Henry H. 1
BRYAN, Henry Lewis 1
BRYAN, 4
Henry Ravenscroft
BRYAN, James Wesley 3
BRYAN, James William 3
BRYAN, John Heritage
BRYAN, John P. Kennedy 1
BRYAN, John Stewart
BRYAN, Joseph H
BRYAN, Joseph 4
Hammond
BRYAN, Joseph Hunter H
BRYAN, Joseph Roberts 1
BRYAN, Kirk 3
BRYAN, L. R. Jr. 3
BRYAN, Lewis Randolph 1
BRYAN, Louis Allen 4
BRYAN, Malcolm Honroe 1
BRYAN, Mary Edwards 1
BRYAN, 1
Mrs. William Jennings
BRYAN, Nathan 1
BRYAN, Nathan Philemon 1
BRYAN, Oscar Eugene 1
BRYAN, Ralph 4
BRYAN, Robert Coalter 1
BRYAN, Sheldon Martin 5
BRYAN, Thomas Barbour 1
BRYAN, W. S. Plumer 1
BRYAN, William Alanson 2
BRYAN, William James 1
BRYAN,
William Jennings
BRYAN, William Lowe 3
BRYAN, 1
William Shepard Jr.
BRYAN, Winfred Francis 5
BRYAN, Worcester Allen 5
BRYANS, Henry Bussell 5
BRYANS, 4
William Alexander III
BRYANT, Anna Burnham 5
BRYANT, Arthur Peyton 1
BRYANT, David E. 1
BRYANT, 4
De Witt Clinton
BRYANT, Edgar Reeve 1
BRYANT, Edwin Eustace 1
BRYANT, Eliot H. 3
BRYANT, Ernest Albert 1
BRYANT, Eugene 5
BRYANT, Floyd Sherman 1
BRYANT, Frank Augustus 4
BRYANT, 2
Frederick Howard
BRYANT, George Archie 4
BRYANT, Gridley H
BRYANT, Henry H

BRYANT, 5
Henry Edward Cowan
BRYANT, Henry Grier 1
BRYANT, John H. 1
BRYANT, John Howard 1
BRYANT, Joseph Decatur 1
BRYANT, Lorinda
Munson
BRYANT, Louise Stevens 3
BRYANT, Ralph Clement 1
BRYANT, Randolph 3
BRYANT, Samuel Wood 1
BRYANT, Sara Cone 5
BRYANT, Thomas
Wallace
BRYANT, Victor Silas 1
BRYANT, W. Sohier 3
BRYANT, Waldo Calvin
BRYANT, William Cullen H
BRYANT, William Cullen 1
BRYANT,
William McKendree
BRYCE, James 1
BRYCE, Lloyd 1
BRYCE, 4
Robert Alexander
BRYCE, Ronald 1
BRYDEN, William 5
BRYN, Helmer Halvorsen 3
BRYNE, Andrew H
BRYNE, Edward H
BRYNE, John H
BRYNE, Richard 1
BRYNE, William H
BRYSON, Charles Lee 2
BRYSON, 1
Charles William
BRYSON, Gladys 3
BRYSON, John Paul 1
BRYSON, 2
Joseph Montgomery
BRYSON, Joseph Raleigh 3
BRYSON, Lyman 5
BRYSON, Olive Flora 5
BRYSON, 4
Robert Hamilton
BRYSON, Robert Hassey 1
BUBB, Henry Clay 4
BUBB, John Wilson 1
BUBER, Martin 4
BUCH, Joseph Godfrey 2
BUCHANAN, Andrew H
BUCHANAN, Andrew
Hays
BUCHANAN, 1
Arthur Stillingfleet
BUCHANAN,
Benjamin Franklin
BUCHANAN, 3
Daniel Houston
BUCHANAN, David H. 5
BUCHANAN, Ella 1
BUCHANAN, Frank 1
BUCHANAN, Frank 3
BUCHANAN, Franklin H
BUCHANAN, 4
Geogre Sidney
BUCHANAN,
George Edward
BUCHANAN, Hugh H
BUCHANAN, James H
BUCHANAN, 1
James Anderson
BUCHANAN, James Isaac 1
BUCHANAN, James L. 3
BUCHANAN, James P 1
BUCHANAN, 1
James Shannon
BUCHANAN, 3
James William
BUCHANAN, John H
BUCHANAN, 1
John Alexander
BUCHANAN, John
Jenkins 1
BUCHANAN, John Lee 4
BUCHANAN, John P. 3
BUCHANAN, Joseph H
BUCHANAN, Joseph Ray 1
BUCHANAN, Joseph Ray 4
BUCHANAN, Joseph
Rodes
BUCHANAN, Kenneth 4
BUCHANAN, Kenneth B. 1
BUCHANAN, 3
Leonard Brown
BUCHANAN, 1
Malcolm Griswold
BUCHANAN, 3
Mrs. Vera Daerr
BUCHANAN, 3
Norman Sharpe
BUCHANAN, Oswald C. 4
BUCHANAN, Roberdeau 1
BUCHANAN, H
Robert Christie
BUCHANAN, Scott 5

BUCHANAN, T. Drysdale 1
BUCHANAN, Thomas H
BUCHANAN, Thomas C. 3
BUCHANAN, Thompson 1
BUCHANAN, W. C. 5
BUCHANAN, 1
Walter Duncan
BUCHANAN, 3
William Asbury
BUCHANAN,
William Insco
BUCHBINDER, 3
Jacob Richter
BUCHEN, Walther 4
BUCHER, 1
August Johannes
BUCHER, John Calvin 2
BUCHER, John Conrad * H
BUCHER, John Emery 5
BUCHER, Walter H. 1
BUCHER, William Henry
BUCHHOLZ, 3
Heinrich Ewald
BUCHHOLZ, 3
John Theodore
BUCHHOLZ,
Ludwig Wilhelm
BUCHHOLZ, William 1
BUCHMAN, Frank N. D. 4
BUCHNER,
Edward Franklin
BUCHSER, Frank H
BUCHTA, J. Williams 3
BUCHTEL, 1
Henry Augustus
BUCHTEL, John Richards H
BUCK, Albert Henry 1
BUCK, Alfred Eliab 1
BUCK, 3
Beaumont Bonaparte
BUCK, Benjamin F. 1
BUCK, C. Douglas 4
BUCK, Carl Darling 3
BUCK, Carl E. 3
BUCK, Cassius M. 4
BUCK, Charles William 1
BUCK, Clarence Frank 2
BUCK, Daniel H
BUCK, Daniel 1
BUCK, H
Daniel Azro Ashley
BUCK, Dudley 1
BUCK, Ellsworth Brewer 5
BUCK, Florence 1
BUCK, Foster 5
BUCK, Frank 2
BUCK, Frank Henry 1
BUCK, Frank Henry 1
BUCK, George Machan 1
BUCK, George Sturges 3
BUCK, Gertrude 3
BUCK, Gurdon H
BUCK, Harold Winthrop 3
BUCK, Harry Lambert 5
BUCK, Henry William 4
BUCK, Jirah Dewey 1
BUCK, John Ransom 4
BUCK, Leffert Lefferts 1
BUCK, Norman Sydney 4
BUCK, Oscar MacMillan 1
BUCK, 5
Pearl Sydenstricker (Mrs.
Richard J. Walsh)
BUCK, Peter Henry 3
BUCK, Phillip Earl 2
BUCK, Philo Melvin 1
BUCK, Philo Melvin Jr. 3
BUCK, Raymond Elliott 5
BUCK, Richard Sutton 3
BUCK, Samuel Jay 1
BUCK, Solon Justus 4
BUCK, Walter Albert 3
BUCK, Walter E. 5
BUCK, Walter Hooper
BUCKALEW, Charles H. 4
BUCKBEE, Anna 4
BUCKBEE, John T. H
BUCKELEY, Peter 1
BUCKENDALE, L. Ray 3
BUCKHAM, James 1
BUCKHAM, John Wright 2
BUCKHAM, Matthew
Henry
BUCKHOUT, Isaac Craig 5
BUCKINGHAM,
Burdette Ross
BUCKINGHAM, 1
Charles Luman
BUCKINGHAM,
David Eastburn
BUCKINGHAM, Edgar 3
BUCKINGHAM,
Edward Taylor
BUCKINGHAM,
George Tracy
BUCKINGHAM, H
Joseph Tinker

BUCKINGHAM, Norman
S. 1
BUCKINGHAM, Walter
Jr. 4
BUCKINGHAM, H
William Alfred
BUCKLAND, 3
Albert William James
BUCKLAND, 5
Charles Clark
BUCKLAND, Cyrus H
BUCKLAND, Edward
Grant 3
BUCKLAND, H
Ralph Pomeroy
BUCKLAND, William H
BUCKLE, John Franklin 5
BUCKLER, 3
Richard Thompson
BUCKLER, H
Thomas Hepburn
BUCKLER, 3
William Hepburn
BUCKLEY, 1
Albert Coulson
BUCKLEY, Charles A. 4
BUCKLEY, Edmund 4
BUCKLEY, Edwin M. 1
BUCKLEY, 1
Ernest Robertson
BUCKLEY, George Wright 4
BUCKLEY, Harry D. 3
BUCKLEY, James Monroe 1
BUCKLEY, James R. 5
BUCKLEY, James V. 4
BUCKLEY, Jere D. 4
BUCKLEY, John Peter 2
BUCKLEY, Leo Jerome 3
BUCKLEY, May 5
BUCKLEY, 3
Oliver Ellsworth
BUCKLEY, H
Samuel Botsford
BUCKLIN, Edward C. 1
BUCKLIN, 5
George Augustus
BUCKLIN, James C. H
BUCKLIN, James W. 1
BUCKLIN, 4
Walter Stanley
BUCKMAN, C. B. 3
BUCKMAN, Harry Oliver 4
BUCKMAN, 5
Henry Holland, II
BUCKMASTER, 4
Leland Stanford
BUCKMINSTER, H
Joseph Stevens
BUCKNAM, Ransford D. 1
BUCKNELL, Howard, Jr. 5
BUCKNELL, William H
BUCKNER, 4
Albert Gallatin
BUCKNER, Alexander H
BUCKNER, Aylett Hawes H
BUCKNER, Aylette H
BUCKNER, 3
Chester Arthur
BUCKNER, David Ernest 3
BUCKNER, E. C. 4
BUCKNER, Emory Roy 1
BUCKNER,
George Washington
BUCKNER, 2
Mortimer Norton
BUCKNER,
Richard Aylett
BUCKNER, Simon Bolivar 1
BUCKNER, 2
Simon Bolivar Jr.
BUCKNER,
Thomas Aylette
BUCKNER, Walker 1
BUCKNER, 3
Walter Coleman
BUCKS, William Henry 4
BUCKSTONE, John B. H
BUCKWALTER, Tracy V. 2
BUCKY, Gustav 4
BUCKY, Philip Barnett 3
BUDA, Joseph 5
BUDD, Britton Ihrie 3
BUDD, Charles Henry 3
BUDD, Charles Jay 1
BUDD, Edward G, Jr. 5
BUDD, Edward G. 2
BUDD, Henry 4
BUDD, James Herbert 1
BUDD, Nathan P. 4
BUDD, Ralph 4
BUDDY, Charles F. 4
BUDENZ, Louis Francis 5
BUDER, 3
Gustavus Adolphus
BUDGE, Alfred 3
BUDGE, David Clare 2
BUDGE, Ross A. 2

BURKE, Stevenson 1
BURKE, Thomas H
BURKE, Thomas 1
BURKE, Thomas A. 5
BURKE, Thomas Henry 3
BURKE, Thomas Joseph 4
BURKE,
  Thomas Martin Aloysius
BURKE, Timothy Farrar 4
BURKE, Victor 3
BURKE, Webster H. 3
BURKE, William J. 1
BURKET, 3
  Harlan Fessenden
BURKET, Jacob F. 1
BURKETT, 5
  Charles William
BURKETT, 4
  Charles William
BURKETT, Elmer Jacob 1
BURKHALTER,
  Edward Read 1
BURKHALTER, 5
  John Thomas
BURKHARDT, Samuel Jr. 1
BURKHARDT, Wilbur
  Neil 1
BURKHART, Harvey
  Jacob 2
BURKHART, Roy Abram 4
BURKHART, Summers 1
BURKHOLDER, 4
  Charles Harvey
BURKHOLDER,
  Charles Irvine
BURKHOLDER, Paul
  Rufus 5
BURKLIN, 4
  Robert Reyburn
BURKLUND, Carl Edwin 4
BURKS, Jesse Desmaux 4
BURKS, Martin Parks 1
BURLEIGH, H
  Charles Calistus
BURLEIGH, Clarence 1
BURLEIGH, 1
  Clarence Blendon
BURLEIGH, Edwin Chick 1
BURLEIGH, 1
  George Shepard
BURLEIGH, 1
  George William
BURLEIGH, Harry T. 1
BURLEIGH, John Holmes H
BURLEIGH, 4
  May Halsey Miller
BURLEIGH, 5
  Nathaniel George
BURLEIGH, 1
  Sydney Richmond
BURLEIGH, H
  Walter Atwood
BURLEIGH, William H
BURLEIGH, H
  William Henry
BURLESON, 1
  Albert Sidney
BURLESON, Edward H
BURLESON, Hugh
  Latimer 1
BURLESON, 1
  Rufus Columbus
BURLEW, Ebert Keiser 2
BURLEY, 1
  Clarence Augustus
BURLIN, Natalie Curtis
BURLIN, Paul 5
BURLING, Albert E. 1
BURLING, Edward H
BURLING, 5
  Edward Burnham
BURLINGAME, Anson H
BURLINGAME, C.
  Charles 3
BURLINGAME, 1
  Edward Livermore
BURLINGAME, 1
  Eugene Watson
BURLINGAME, 5
  Leonas Lancelot
BURLINGAME, Leroy J. 4
BURLINGAME, Luther
  D. 1
BURLINGAME, Roger 4
BURLINGHAM, Aaron
  Hale 5
BURLINGHAM, Charles
  C. 3
BURLINGHAM, 2
  Louis Herbert
BURLIUK, 4
  David Davidovich
BURMA, John Harmon 5
BURMEISTER, Richard 4
BURN, 5
  Belle Sumner Angier

BURNAM, 1
  Anthony Rollins
BURNAM, Curtis Field 2
BURNAM, John Miller 1
BURNAP, H
  George Washington
BURNELL, Barker H
BURNELL, Edward John 3
BURNELL, 4
  Edward John Jr.
BURNELL, Max Ronald 3
BURNES, Alonzo D. 4
BURNES, James Nelson 5
BURNES, Matthews James 4
BURNET, H
  David Gouverneur
BURNET, Duncan 5
BURNET, Jacob H
BURNET, W. Everit 3
BURNET, William * 1
BURNETT, Charles 1
BURNETT, Charles Henry H
BURNETT, Charles Hoyt 5
BURNETT, 5
  Charles Hugh, Jr.
BURNETT, 2
  Charles Theodore
BURNETT, Dana 4
BURNETT, Edgar Albert 4
BURNETT, Edmund Cody 1
BURNETT, Edwin Clark 1
BURNETT, 1
  Frances Hodgson
BURNETT, George Henry 1
BURNETT, 5
  George Jackson
BURNETT, H
  Henry Cornelius
BURNETT, 1
  Henry Lawrence
BURNETT, 5
  Jesse McGarrity
BURNETT, John Lawson 1
BURNETT, John Torrey 1
BURNETT, Joseph H
BURNETT, 4
  Joseph Herndon
BURNETT, Leo 5
BURNETT, Paul Moreton 2
BURNETT, H
  Peter Hardeman
BURNETT, Robert M. 1
BURNETT, 4
  Rogers Levering
BURNETT, Swan Moses 1
BURNETT, Whit 5
BURNHAM, Alfred Avery H
BURNHAM, Charles
  Edwin 4
BURNHAM, Clara Louise 1
BURNHAM, Claude
  George 1
BURNHAM, Daniel
  Hudson 1
BURNHAM, Daniel
  Hudson 4
BURNHAM, E(noch)
  Lewis 5
BURNHAM, 1
  Frederic Lynden
BURNHAM, 5
  Frederick E(dwin)
BURNHAM, 2
  Frederick Russell
BURNHAM, 5
  Frederick William
BURNHAM, George 1
BURNHAM, George Jr. 1
BURNHAM, Henry Eben 1
BURNHAM, Hubert 5
BURNHAM, John Bird 1
BURNHAM, Michael 1
BURNHAM, Ralph W. 1
BURNHAM, Roger Noble 4
BURNHAM, 1
  Sherburne Wesley
BURNHAM, Silas Henry 1
BURNHAM, Smith 2
BURNHAM, Sylvester 1
BURNHAM, Walter
  Henry 5
BURNHAM, William
  Henry 1
BURNHAM, William
  Power 1
BURNITE, Caroline 5
BURNQUIST, 1
  Joseph Alfred Arner
BURNS, Allen Tibbals 3
BURNS, Andrew J. 1
BURNS, Anna Letitia 1
BURNS, Anthony H
BURNS, Bob 3
BURNS, Charles Wesley 4
BURNS, Clyde Edwin 4
BURNS, Cornelius F. 1
BURNS, Daniel M. 4

BURNS, David 5
BURNS, Dennis Francis 3
BURNS, Edward H. 3
BURNS, Edward McNall 5
BURNS, Elmer Ellsworth 3
BURNS, 1
  Francis Highlands
BURNS, Frank 2
BURNS, George Plumer 3
BURNS, 5
  Hendry Stuart Mackenzie
BURNS, Henry B. 4
BURNS, 3
  Herbert Deschamps
BURNS, Howard Fletcher 5
BURNS, James Aloysius 1
BURNS, James Austin 1
BURNS, James J. 1
BURNS, John Horne 4
BURNS, John Joseph 3
BURNS, Joseph H
BURNS, Kevin 3
BURNS, Lee 3
BURNS, Louis Henry 1
BURNS, Matthew D. 4
BURNS, Melvin P. 1
BURNS, Michael Anthony 1
BURNS, Otway H
BURNS, Owen McIntosh 1
BURNS, P. P. 3
BURNS, Robert H
BURNS, Robert Edward 5
BURNS, Robert Emmett 5
BURNS, Robert Whitney 5
BURNS, Walter Noble 1
BURNS, William Henry 1
BURNS, William John 1
BURNSIDE, H
  Ambrose Everett
BURNSIDE, Thomas H
BURPEE, 4
  Charles Winslow
BURPEE, George William 4
BURPEE, Lucien Francis 1
BURPEE, W. Atlee 1
BURPEE, 4
  William Partridge
BURQUE, Henri Alphonse 2
BURR, Aaron * H
BURR, Albert George H
BURR, Alexander George 1
BURR, Alfred Edmund H
BURR, Allston 2
BURR, Anna Robeson 1
BURR, Borden 3
BURR, C. B. 1
BURR, Charles Walts 3
BURR, Edward 1
BURR, Enoch Fitch 1
BURR, Eugene Wyllis 5
BURR, Freeman F. 5
BURR, George Elbert 1
BURR, George Howard 1
BURR, George Hutchison 4
BURR, 5
  George L(indsley)
BURR, George Lincoln 1
BURR, 1
  George Washington
BURR, Hanford Montrose 4
BURR, Harold S(axton) 5
BURR, Henry Turner 5
BURR, Hudson C. 3
BURR, I. Tucker 4
BURR, Joseph Arthur 1
BURR, Karl Edward 2
BURR, Leslie L. 1
BURR, Nelson Beardsley 1
BURR, Theodosia 1
BURR, William Henry 1
BURR, William Hubert 1
BURR, William P. 1
BURR, William Wesley 4
BURRAGE, 1
  Albert Cameron
BURRAGE, Champlin 5
BURRAGE, Charles Dana 1
BURRAGE, 5
  Dwight Grafton
BURRAGE, Guy Hamilton 3
BURRAGE, 1
  Henry Sweetser
BURRAGE, 1
  Walter Lincoln
BURRALL, H
  William Porter
BURRELL, 5
  David de Forest
BURRELL, David James 1
BURRELL, Edward Parker 1
BURRELL, 1
  Frederick Augustus
  Muhlenberg
BURRELL, George Arthur 3
BURRELL, George W. 5
BURRELL, H. Cayford 3

BURRELL, 1
  Herbert Leslie
BURRELL, John Angus 3
BURRELL, Joseph Dunn 1
BURRETT, 1
  Claude Adelbert
BURRILL, H
  Alexander Mansfield
BURRILL, Harvey D. 1
BURRILL, James H
BURRILL, 3
  Stanley Stinton
BURRILL, 1
  Thomas Jonathan
BURRINGTON, George H
BURRINGTON, 4
  Howard Rice
BURRIS, Benjamin J. 1
BURRIS, Quincy Guy 5
BURRIS, William Paxton 2
BURRITT, Bailey Barton 3
BURRITT, Eldon Grant 1
BURRITT, Elihu H
BURRITT, Henry W. 4
BURROUGH, 4
  Edmund Weldmann
BURROUGHS, Bryson 1
BURROUGHS, 4
  Charles Franklin
BURROUGHS, Edgar Rice 2
BURROUGHS, 1
  Edith Woodman
BURROUGHS, 1
  George Stockton
BURROUGHS, George W. 3
BURROUGHS, 2
  Harry Ernest
BURROUGHS, John H
  Curtis
BURROUGHS, John 4
  Jonothan Edington
BURROUGHS, Marie 4
BURROUGHS, 2
  Prince Emmanuel
BURROUGHS, 1
  Sherman Everett
BURROUGHS, H
  Silas Mainville
BURROUGHS, 5
  W(illiam) Dwight
BURROUGHS, 1
  William Seward
BURROW, James Randall 1
BURROW, Joel Randall 1
BURROW, Trigant 3
BURROWES, Alexander J. 1
BURROWES, Alonzo
  Moore 3
BURROWES, 5
  Arthur Victor
BURROWES, 1
  Edward Thomas
BURROWES, Katharine 1
BURROWES, Peter
  Edward 1
BURROWES, Thomas
  Henry 1
BURROWS, 1
  Charles William
BURROWS, Daniel H
BURROWS, Daniel Chapel 5
BURROWS, 4
  Frederick Nelson
BURROWS, Julius C. 1
BURROWS, Lansing 1
BURROWS, Lorenzo H
BURROWS, Mark 4
BURROWS, 2
  Montrose Thomas
BURROWS, Robert Jay 2
BURROWS, Warren Booth 5
BURROWS, William H
BURROWS, 3
  William Russell
BURRUS, John Perry 1
BURRUS, John T. 1
BURRUSS, Julian Ashby 2
BURRY, George W. 1
BURRY, William 1
BURSE, Walter Morrill 4
BURSLEY, 4
  Herbert Sidney
BURSLEY, 3
  Joseph Aldrich
BURSUM, Holm O. 1
BURT, Alonzo 1
BURT, Andrew Sheridan 1
BURT, Armistead H
BURT, Austin 5
BURT, Charles Kennedy 1
BURT, Charles Morrison 4
BURT, Clayton Raymond 1
BURT, David Allan 2
BURT, Edward Angus 1
BURT, Frank 4
BURT, Frank Henry 2

BURT, Frederic Percy 4
BURT, George Haskell 4
BURT, Henry Jackson 1
BURT, Horace Greeley 1
BURT, John H
BURT, Joseph Bell 5
BURT, Mary Elizabeth 1
BURT, Silas Wright 1
BURT, Stephen Smith 1
BURT, Struthers 3
BURT, Thomas Gregory 1
BURT, William 1
BURT, William Austin H
BURTIN, Will 5
BURTIS, Arthur 1
BURTNESS, Olger B. 4
BURTON, Alfred Edgar 1
BURTON, Andrew Mizell 4
BURTON, Asa H
BURTON, 1
  Charles Emerson
BURTON, 1
  Charles Germman
BURTON, Charles Luther 4
BURTON, Charles Pierce 4
BURTON, 1
  Clarence Monroe
BURTON, Edgar Gordon 5
BURTON, Edward Francis 1
BURTON, Ernest DeWitt 1
BURTON, 1
  Frederick Russell
BURTON, George Dexter 1
BURTON, George Hall 1
BURTON, George William 1
BURTON, Harold Hitz 4
BURTON, Harry Edward 2
BURTON, Harry Edwin 2
BURTON, Hazen James 1
BURTON, 1
  Henry Fairfield
BURTON, Hiram Rodney 3
BURTON, H
  Hutchings Gordon
BURTON, James 3
BURTON, Jean 3
BURTON, Joseph Ralph 5
BURTON, 5
  Laurence V(reeland)
BURTON, Lewis William 1
BURTON, Marion LeRoy 1
BURTON, Myron Garfield 1
BURTON, H
  Nathaniel Judson
BURTON, Oliver Milton 3
BURTON, Richard 1
BURTON, Robert H
BURTON, Robert Allen 5
BURTON, 5
  Robert Mitchell
BURTON, 1
  Theodore Elijah
BURTON, Virgil Lee 5
BURTON, Warren 1
BURTON, William H
BURTON, William Evans H
BURTON, William Henry 4
BURTON-OPITZ, Russell 3
BURTS, Charles Elford 1
BURTT, Wilson Bryant 3
BURWELL, Armistead 1
BURWELL, Arthur
  Warner 2
BURWELL, 1
  Benjamin Franklin
BURWELL, 4
  Charles Sidney
BURWELL, 5
  John T(ownsend), Jr.
BURWELL, H
  William Armisted
BURWELL, 1
  William Russell
BURWELL, 1
  William Turnbull
BUSBEE, Charles Manly 5
BUSBEE, Charles Manly 1
BUSBEE, Fabius Haywood 1
BUSBEE, Jacques 5
BUSBEY, Fred E. 4
BUSBEY, Hamilton 1
BUSBEY, 5
  Katherine Graves
BUSBEY, L. White 1
BUSBY, George Henry H
BUSBY, Leonard Asbury 1
BUSBY, Orel 4
BUSCH, 3
  Adolf Georg Wilhelm
BUSCH, Adolphus 1
BUSCH, Adolphus III 5
BUSCH, Fritz 3
BUSCH, H. A. 4
BUSCH, Henry Miller 5
BUSCH, Joseph Francis 3
BUSCHEMEYER, 1
  John Henry

BUSCHMAN, S. L. 2
BUSEY, Paul Graham 3
BUSEY, Samuel Clagett 1
BUSEY, Samuel Thompson 3
BUSH, Albert Peyton 1
BUSH, Alvin Ray 3
BUSH, Archibald Granville 4
BUSH, Asahel 1
BUSH, Benjamin Franklin 1
BUSH, Benjamin Jay 3
BUSH, Charles G. 1
BUSH, Earl J. 4
BUSH, Florence Lilian 4
BUSH, George H
BUSH, Gordon Kenner 4
BUSH, Henry Tatnall 2
BUSH, Ira Benton 1
BUSH, Irving T. 2
BUSH, John A. 4
BUSH, Katharine Jeannette 1
BUSH, Leonard T. 3
BUSH, Lincoln 1
BUSH, Prescott Sheldon 5
BUSH, Robert R(ay) 5
BUSH, Royal Robert 4
BUSH, Thomas Greene 1
BUSH, Wendell T. 1
BUSH-BROWN, Henry Kirke 1
BUSHBY, Wilkie 5
BUSHEE, Frederick Alexander 5
BUSHFIELD, Harlan J. 2
BUSHMAN, Francis X. 4
BUSHNELL, Asa Smith 1
BUSHNELL, Charles Joseph 3
BUSHNELL, David H
BUSHNELL, David I, Jr. 5
BUSHNELL, Edward 2
BUSHNELL, George Edward 4
BUSHNELL, George Ensign 1
BUSHNELL, Henry Allen 4
BUSHNELL, Henry Davis 5
BUSHNELL, Herbert Martin 2
BUSHNELL, Horace H
BUSHNELL, John Edward 4
BUSHNELL, Madeline Vaughan (Abbott) 5
BUSHNELL, Robert T. 2
BUSHNELL, Winthrop Grant 1
BUSHONG, Robert Grey 3
BUSICK, Adrien Fowler 5
BUSIEL, Charles Albert 1
BUSSER, Ralph Cox 3
BUSSEWITZ, Maxillian Alfred 2
BUSSEY, Cyrus 1
BUSSEY, Gertrude Carman 4
BUSSOM, Thomas Wainwright 3
BUSTARD, William Walter 1
BUSWELL, Arthur Moses 4
BUSWELL, Henry Clark 4
BUSWELL, Henry Foster 1
BUTCHER, Thomas Campbell 4
BUTCHER, Thomas Walter 5
BUTCHER, William Lewis 1
BUTIN, Romain Francois 1
BUTLER, Alford Augustus 1
BUTLER, Amos William 1
BUTLER, Andrew Pickens H
BUTLER, Arthur Pierce 3
BUTLER, Benjamin Franklin * H
BUTLER, Bert S. 4
BUTLER, Burridge Davenal 2
BUTLER, Charles H
BUTLER, Charles 3
BUTLER, Charles C. 2
BUTLER, Charles Henry 1
BUTLER, Charles St John 2
BUTLER, Charles Thompson 3
BUTLER, Charles William 5
BUTLER, Chester Pierce H
BUTLER, Clement Moore H
BUTLER, Dan B. 3
BUTLER, Edmond Borgia 3
BUTLER, Edward Burgess 1
BUTLER, Edward H. 1
BUTLER, Edward Hubert 1
BUTLER, Edward Hubert 3
BUTLER, Ellis Parker 1
BUTLER, Elmer Grimshaw 5
BUTLER, Ethan Flagg 4
BUTLER, Ezra H
BUTLER, Frank Osgood 5
BUTLER, Fred Mason 1
BUTLER, George Bernard 1
BUTLER, George Frank 1
BUTLER, George Harrison Jr. 2
BUTLER, Glentworth Reeve 1
BUTLER, Harold Lancaster 5
BUTLER, Harold Lancaster 3
BUTLER, Henry Varnum 3
BUTLER, Howard Crosby 1
BUTLER, Howard Russell 1
BUTLER, Hugh 1
BUTLER, Hugh Alfred 3
BUTLER, J. Glentworth 4
BUTLER, J. Vernon 4
BUTLER, James Davie 1
BUTLER, James Gay 1
BUTLER, James Joseph 2
BUTLER, James Orval 5
BUTLER, Jerome Ambrose 3
BUTLER, Joe Beaty 3
BUTLER, John H
BUTLER, John Ammi 1
BUTLER, John Cornelius 3
BUTLER, John Gazzam 1
BUTLER, John George 1
BUTLER, John Jay H
BUTLER, John Wesley 1
BUTLER, John Winchel Spencer 3
BUTLER, Joseph Green Jr. 1
BUTLER, Josiah H
BUTLER, Louis Fatio 1
BUTLER, Marion 1
BUTLER, Mary 2
BUTLER, Matthew Calbraith 1
BUTLER, Nathaniel 1
BUTLER, Nicholas Murray 2
BUTLER, Paul M. 4
BUTLER, Peter Walton 4
BUTLER, Pierce H
BUTLER, Pierce 1
BUTLER, Pierce * 3
BUTLER, Pierce Mason H
BUTLER, Ralph 3
BUTLER, Richard H
BUTLER, Richard 1
BUTLER, Robert 3
BUTLER, Robert Gordon 1
BUTLER, Robert Paul 5
BUTLER, Robert Reyburn 1
BUTLER, Rush Clark 3
BUTLER, Sampson Hale H
BUTLER, Samuel R. 4
BUTLER, Scot 1
BUTLER, Simeon H
BUTLER, Smedley Darlington 1
BUTLER, Tait 1
BUTLER, Thomas H
BUTLER, Thomas Baldwin 5
BUTLER, Thomas Belden H
BUTLER, Thomas S. 1
BUTLER, Walter N. H
BUTLER, William * H
BUTLER, William 1
BUTLER, William Allen * 1
BUTLER, William Frederick 1
BUTLER, William John 2
BUTLER, William Mill 2
BUTLER, William Morgan 1
BUTLER, William Morris 1
BUTLER, William Orlando H
BUTLER, Willis Howard 1
BUTLER, Zebulon H
BUTMAN, Arthur Benjamin 3
BUTMAN, Samuel H
BUTNER, Henry W. 1
BUTT, Archibald Willingham 1
BUTT, John D. 4
BUTT, William 4
BUTTE, George Charles 1
BUTTENHEIM, Edgar J. 4
BUTTENHEIM, Harold S. 4
BUTTENWIESER, Moses 1
BUTTERFIELD, Consul Willshire 1
BUTTERFIELD, Daniel H
BUTTERFIELD, Daniel 1
BUTTERFIELD, Ernest Warren 5
BUTTERFIELD, John H
BUTTERFIELD, Kenyon Leech 1
BUTTERFIELD, Martin H
BUTTERFIELD, Ora Elmer 1
BUTTERICK, Ebenezer H
BUTTERWORTH, Benjamin H
BUTTERWORTH, Charles Fred 3
BUTTERWORTH, G. Forrest 3
BUTTERWORTH, George Forrest 1
BUTTERWORTH, Hezekiah 1
BUTTERWORTH, Julian Edward 4
BUTTERWORTH, William 1
BUTTFIELD, W. J. 2
BUTTLES, John S. 2
BUTTON, Frank Christopher 1
BUTTON, Stephen D. H
BUTTRAM, Frank 4
BUTTRE, John Chester H
BUTTRICK, James Tyler 4
BUTTRICK, Wallace 1
BUTTS, Alfred Benjamin 4
BUTTS, Annice Esther Bradford 1
BUTTS, Arthur Clarkson 4
BUTTS, Charles 3
BUTTS, Edmund Luther 3
BUTTS, Edward 4
BUTTS, Isaac H
BUTTZ, Henry Anson 1
BUTZ, Jesse Samuel Cooper 4
BUTZ, Reuben Jacob 3
BUTZEL, Fred M. 2
BUTZEL, Henry Magnus 4
BUTZEL, Leo Martin 4
BUTZER, Albert George 5
BUWALDA, John Peter 3
BUXTON, Albert 1
BUXTON, Charles Lee 5
BUXTON, Edwin Orlando 4
BUXTON, G. Edward 2
BUXTON, John A. 4
BUXTON, L. Haynes 1
BUXTON, Robert William 5
BUYS, John L. 3
BUZBEE, Thomas Stephen 2
BUZBY, George Carroll 5
BUZZI, Alfred Antoni 4
BUZZNELL, Reginald W. 3
BYARS, Louis Thomas 5
BYARS, William Vincent 1
BYAS, Hugh 2
BYE, Carl R. 4
BYE, Frank Paxson 1
BYER, Herman Bailey 4
BYERLY, William Elwood 1
BYERS, John Frederic 2
BYERS, John Winford 5
BYERS, Joseph Perkins 4
BYERS, Maxwell Cunningham 1
BYERS, Mortimer W. 4
BYERS, Samuel Hawkins Marshall 1
BYERS, Vincent Gerard 4
BYERS, Walter Louis 5
BYERS, William Newton 1
BYFIELD, Ernest Lessing 4
BYFIELD, Joseph 1
BYFORD, Henry Turman 1
BYFORD, William Heath H
BYINGTON, Cyrus H
BYINGTON, Edwin Hallock 2
BYINGTON, Ezra Hoyt 1
BYINGTON, Homer Morrison 4
BYINGTON, Spring 5
BYINGTON, Steven Tracy 4
BYLES, Axtell J. 1
BYLES, Mather H
BYLLESBY, Henry Marison 1
BYNE, Arthur 1
BYNNER, Edwin Lassetter H
BYNNER, Witter 5
BYNUM, Curtis 4
BYNUM, Jesse Atherton H
BYNUM, Marshall Francis 5
BYNUM, William Dallas 1
BYNUM, William Preston 1
BYOIR, Carl 3
BYRAM, George Logan 1
BYRAM, Harry E. 2
BYRD, Adam Monroe 1
BYRD, Anderson Floyd 4
BYRD, Harry Clifton 5
BYRD, Harry Flood 4
BYRD, Richard Evelyn 1
BYRD, Richard Evelyn 3
BYRD, Samuel Craig 4
BYRD, William * H
BYRER, Charles Emory 5
BYRER, Harry Hopkins 5
BYRNE, Alice Hill 5
BYRNE, Amanda Austin; 5
BYRNE, Austin Thomas 1
BYRNE, Barry 4
BYRNE, Bernard Albert 1
BYRNE, Charles Alfred 1
BYRNE, Charles Christopher 1
BYRNE, Christopher Edward 3
BYRNE, Edwin Vincent 4
BYRNE, Frank M. 1
BYRNE, James 5
BYRNE, John 1
BYRNE, John Baird 4
BYRNE, Joseph 2
BYRNE, Joseph M. Jr. 4
BYRNE, Sister Marie Jose 5
BYRNE, Sister Marie Jose 3
BYRNE, Thomas Sebastian 1
BYRNE, William 1
BYRNE, William Thomas 3
BYRNES, Allen William 5
BYRNES, Charles Metcalfe 1
BYRNES, Eugene Alexander 4
BYRNES, James Francis 5
BYRNES, Ralph Leonidas 3
BYRNES, Robert Dennison 5
BYRNES, Timothy Edward 2
BYRNES, William M. 4
BYRNS, Clarence Franklin 4
BYRNS, Joseph W. 1
BYRON, Arthur William 2
BYRON, Charles Loomis 4
BYRON, Joseph Wilson 3
BYRON, Robert Burns, Jr. 5
BYRON, William Devereux 1
BYRUM, Enoch Edwin 4

C

CABANA, Oliver Jr. 1
CABANISS, Edward Harman 1
CABANISS, Edward M. 4
CABANISS, Henry Harrison 1
CABANISS, Thomas Banks 4
CABEEN, Charles William 1
CABEEN, David Clark 4
CABELL, Benjamin Francis 1
CABELL, Charles Pearre 5
CABELL, De Rosey Carroll 1
CABELL, Edward Carrington H
CABELL, George Craghead 1
CABELL, Isa Carrington 4
CABELL, James Alston 1
CABELL, James Branch 3
CABELL, James Lawrence H
CABELL, Joseph Carrington H
CABELL, Nathaniel Francis H
CABELL, Robert Hervey 2
CABELL, Royal Eubank 3
CABELL, Samuel Jordan H
CABELL, William H
CABELL, William H. H
CABELL, William Lewis 1
CABELL, Wymond 3
CABET, Etienne H
CABLE, Benjamin Stickney 1
CABLE, Benjamin Taylor 1
CABLE, Emmett James 5
CABLE, Frank T. 2
CABLE, George Washington 1
CABLE, John L. 5
CABLE, John Ray 3
CABLE, Joseph H
CABLE, Ransom R. 1
CABOT, Arthur Tracy 1
CABOT, Carolyn Sturgis 1
CABOT, Edward 4
CABOT, Edward Clarke H
CABOT, Ella Lyman 1
CABOT, Francis Higginson 3
CABOT, Frederick Pickering 1
CABOT, George H
CABOT, George E. 2
CABOT, Godfrey Lowell 4
CABOT, Henry Bromfield 1
CABOT, Hugh 2
CABOT, John H
CABOT, Philip 1
CABOT, Richard Clarke 1
CABOT, Sebastian H
CABOT, Stephen Perkins 3
CABOT, Ted 5
CABOT, William Brooks 2
CABRILLO, Juan Rodriguez H
CABRINI, Saint Frances Xavier H
CABRINI, Sanit Frances Xavier 4
CADDELL, Albert D. 3
CADDY, Edmund Harrington Homer 5
CADE, Cassius Marcellus 3
CADE, George Newton 5
CADEK, Ottokar T. 3
CADILLAC, Sieur 'de H
CADISCH, Gordon Francis 1
CADMAN, Charles Wakefield 2
CADMAN, Paul Fletcher 2
CADMAN, S. Parkes 1
CADWALADER, Charles Evert 1
CADWALADER, John * H
CADWALADER, John 1
CADWALADER, John Lambert 1
CADWALADER, Lambert H
CADWALADER, Richard McCall 1
CADWALADER, Thomas H
CADWALADER, Thomas Francis 5
CADWALLADER, Isaac Henry 1
CADWALLADER, Starr 1
CADWELL, Charles Stewart 5
CADY, Calvin Brainerd 4
CADY, Daniel H
CADY, Daniel Leavens 1
CADY, Edward Hammond 1
CADY, Everett Ware 4
CADY, George Luther 1
CADY, Hamilton Perkins 2
CADY, J. Cleveland 1
CADY, John Hutchins 5
CADY, John Watts H
CADY, Jonathan Rider 4
CADY, Philander Kinney 1
CADY, Putnam 4
CADY, Samuel Howard 2
CADY, Walter Guyton 5
CAESAR, Doris 5
CAESAR, Kathleen 4
CAESAR, Orville Swan 4
CAETANI, Gelasio 1
CAFFEE, Robert Henderson 3
CAFFERTY, James H. H
CAFFERY, Donelson 1
CAFFEY, Eugene Mead 4
CAFFEY, Francis Gordon 3
CAFFIN, Charles Henry 1
CAFFREY, James Joseph 4
CAGE, Harry H
CAGLE, Alvah Penn 4
CAGLE, Fred Ray 5
CAHAN, Abraham 3
CAHEN, Alfred 4
CAHILL, Arthur James 5
CAHILL, Bernard J. S. 2
CAHILL, Edward 1
CAHILL, Edward A. 4
CAHILL, Edward Cornelius 4
CAHILL, George Francis 3
CAHILL, Holger 4
CAHILL, Isaac Jasper 2
CAHILL, James Christopher 2
CAHILL, John Thomas 4
CAHILL, Marie 1
CAHILL, Michael Harrison 1

CAHILL, Michael Henry	1
CAHILL, Thaddeus	1
CAHN, Bertram Joseph	3
CAHN, Edmond	4
CAHN, Gladys D. Freeman	4
CAHOON, Edward Augustus	1
CAHOON, William	H
CAILLE, Augustus	1
CAILLOUET, Adrian Joseph	2
CAIN, George R.	5
CAIN, James William	1
CAIN, Joseph E.	4
CAIN, Richard Harvey	H
CAIN, Rolly Morton	2
CAIN, Walter	1
CAIN, William	1
CAINE, John Thomas III	3
CAINE, Milton A.	3
CAINES, George	H
CAIRNS, Alexander	3
CAIRNS, Anna Sneed	1
CAIRNS, Charles Andrew	1
CAIRNS, Frederick Irvan	2
CAIRNS, W. D.	3
CAIRNS, William B.	1
CAJORI, Florian	1
CAKE, RALPH HARLAN	5
CALABRESE, Giuseppe	4
CALDER, Alexander	4
CALDER, Alexander Milne	1
CALDER, Alexander Stirling	2
CALDER, Curtis Ernest	3
CALDER, Helen Barnetson	5
CALDER, Hugh Gordon	5
CALDER, Louis	4
CALDER, Louis Jr.	4
CALDER, Robert Scott	5
CALDER, William M.	2
CALDERHEAD, William Alexander	4
CALDERON, Ignacio	4
CALDERON, Manuel Alvarez	4
CALDERON GUARDIA, Rafael Angel	5
CALDERWOOD, Alva John	2
CALDWELL, Alexander	1
CALDWELL, Ben Franklin	4
CALDWELL, Benjamin Palmer	3
CALDWELL, Bert Wilmer	3
CALDWELL, Burns Durbin	1
CALDWELL, Capt Billy	H
CALDWELL, Charles	H
CALDWELL, Charles Henry Bromedge	H
CALDWELL, Charles Pope	1
CALDWELL, Clarence B.	4
CALDWELL, Clifford Douglass	1
CALDWELL, Daniel Templeton	3
CALDWELL, David	H
CALDWELL, Edwin Valdivia	4
CALDWELL, Eugene Craighead	1
CALDWELL, Eugene Wilson	1
CALDWELL, Francis Cary	3
CALDWELL, Frank Congleton	4
CALDWELL, Frank Merrill	1
CALDWELL, Fred T.	3
CALDWELL, George Alfred	H
CALDWELL, George Brinton	1
CALDWELL, George Chapman	1
CALDWELL, Greene Washington	H
CALDWELL, Henry Clay	1
CALDWELL, Howard Walter	1
CALDWELL, Hugh Milton	3
CALDWELL, J. G.	5
CALDWELL, James *	H
CALDWELL, James E.	2
CALDWELL, James H.	H
CALDWELL, James Henry	1
CALDWELL, Jesse Cobb	1
CALDWELL, John Curtis	1
CALDWELL, John Handly	3
CALDWELL, John Lawrence	1
CALDWELL, John Livy	5
CALDWELL, John Williamson	1
CALDWELL, Joseph	H
CALDWELL, Joseph Pearson	H
CALDWELL, Joseph Pearson	1
CALDWELL, Joshua William	1
CALDWELL, Josiah S.	4
CALDWELL, Lisle Bones	4
CALDWELL, Louis Goldsborough	3
CALDWELL, Mary Letitia	5
CALDWELL, Morley Albert	1
CALDWELL, Orestes Hampton	5
CALDWELL, Orestes Hampton	4
CALDWELL, Otis William	2
CALDWELL, Patrick Calhoun	H
CALDWELL, Robert Breckenridge	3
CALDWELL, Robert J.	3
CALDWELL, Robert Porter	H
CALDWELL, Samuel Cushman	1
CALDWELL, Samuel Hawks	4
CALDWELL, Samuel Lunt	H
CALDWELL, Stephen Adolphus	3
CALDWELL, Thomas Jones	4
CALDWELL, Victor Bush	1
CALDWELL, Waller Cochran	4
CALDWELL, Walter Lindsay	4
CALDWELL, William	3
CALDWELL, William Edgar	2
CALE, Thomas	4
CALEF, Robert	H
CALEY, Katharine	1
CALEY, Llewelyn N.	1
CALFEE, John Edward	1
CALHANE, Daniel Francis	3
CALHERN, Louis	3
CALHOON, John	H
CALHOON, Solomon Saladin	4
CALHOUN, Abner Wellborn	1
CALHOUN, Alexander McConnell	1
CALHOUN, Byron E.	3
CALHOUN, David Randolph	1
CALHOUN, Fred Harvey Hall	3
CALHOUN, Galloway	4
CALHOUN, George Miller	2
CALHOUN, Hall Laurie	1
CALHOUN, John	H
CALHOUN, John	1
CALHOUN, John Caldwell	H
CALHOUN, John Calwell	1
CALHOUN, John Darr	4
CALHOUN, John William	2
CALHOUN, Joseph	H
CALHOUN, Joseph Painter	4
CALHOUN, Newell Meeker	4
CALHOUN, Patrick	2
CALHOUN, Philo Clarke	4
CALHOUN, Ralph Emerson	5
CALHOUN, William Barron	H
CALHOUN, William James	1
CALHOUN, William Lowndes	4
CALIFF, Joseph Mark	1
CALIFORNIA JOE	H
CALIGA, Issac Henry	4
CALISCH, Edward N.	2
CALIVER, Ambrose	4
CALKINS, Earnest Elmo	4
CALKINS, Franklin Welles	1
CALKINS, Gary Nathan	2
CALKINS, Harvey Reeves	1
CALKINS, James E.	5
CALKINS, L. A.	4
CALKINS, Lyman Darrow	1
CALKINS, Mary Whiton	1
CALKINS, Norman Allison	H
CALKINS, Ransom M.	1
CALKINS, Raymond	5
CALKINS, Truesdel Peck	2
CALKINS, William Henry	H
CALKINS, Wolcott	1
CALL, Arthur Deerin	2
CALL, Edward Payson	1
CALL, Jacob	H
CALL, Manfred	1
CALL, Rhydon Mays	1
CALL, Richard Ellsworth	4
CALL, Richard Keith	H
CALL, S. Leigh	3
CALL, Wilkinson	1
CALLAGHAN, Alfred	3
CALLAGHAN, Stephen	3
CALLAHAN, Donald A.	3
CALLAHAN, Ethelbert	1
CALLAHAN, Henry White	4
CALLAHAN, James Yancy	4
CALLAHAN, Jeremiah Joseph	5
CALLAHAN, John	3
CALLAHAN, Patrick Henry	1
CALLAHAN, William Paul, Jr.	5
CALLAN, Albert Stevens	4
CALLAN, Charles Jerome	4
CALLAN, John Gurney	1
CALLAN, Peter A.	1
CALLAN, Robert Emmet	1
CALLANAN, Carolyn Williams	4
CALLANAN, Edward A.	3
CALLANDER, Cyrus N.	1
CALLANDER, Cyrus N.	2
CALLANDER, William Forrest	5
CALLAWAY, Cason Jewell	4
CALLAWAY, Ely Reeves Sr.	3
CALLAWAY, Enoch Howard	1
CALLAWAY, Fuller Earle	1
CALLAWAY, Llewellyn Link	3
CALLAWAY, Merrel Price	3
CALLAWAY, Morgan Jr.	1
CALLAWAY, Samuel Rodger	1
CALLAWAY, Trowbridge	4
CALLBREATH, James Finch	1
CALLCOTT, Wilfrid Hardy	5
CALLEN, Alfred Copeland	3
CALLEN, J. Spencer	4
CALLENDER, Edward Belcher	1
CALLENDER, George Russell	5
CALLENDER, Guy Stevens	1
CALLENDER, Harold	3
CALLENDER, James Thomson	H
CALLENDER, John	H
CALLENDER, Romaine	1
CALLENDER, Sherman D.	3
CALLENDER, Walter Reid	1
CALLER, Mary Alice	5
CALLERY, Francis Anthony	5
CALLERY, James Dawson	1
CALLES, Plutarco Elias	2
CALLEY, Walter	1
CALLIERES BONNEVUE, Louis Hector 'de	H
CALLISON, Tolliver Cleveland	4
CALLISTER, Edward Henry	1
CALLOS, George John	4
CALLOW, John Michael	1
CALLOWAY, Alfred W.	1
CALLOWAY, Walter Bowles	5
CALLVERT, Ronald Glenn	3
CALTHROP, Samuel Robert	1
CALVE, Emma	1
CALVE, Emma	2
CALVER, George Wehnes	5
CALVER, Homer Northup	5
CALVERLEY, Charles	1
CALVERT, Cecil	H
CALVERT, Charles	H
CALVERT, Charles Benedict	H
CALVERT, George	H
CALVERT, George Henry	H
CALVERT, John Betts	1
CALVERT, John F.	4
CALVERT, Leonard	H
CALVERT, Philip Powell	5
CALVERT, Richard Creagh Mackubin	5
CALVERT, Robert	5
CALVERT, Thomas Elwood	1
CALVERT, William Jephtha	5
CALVERTON, Victor Francis	1
CALVERY, Herbert Orion	2
CALVIN, Edgar Eugene	1
CALVIN, Henrietta Willard (Mrs. John H. Calvin)	5
CALVIN, Samuel	H
CALVIN, Samuel	1
CALVIN, William Austin	4
CALVO, Joaquin Bernardo	1
CALWELL, Charles Sheridan	1
CALYO, Nicolino	H
CAM, Helen Maud	4
CAMAC, Charles Nicoll Bancker	1
CAMACHO, Manual Avila	3
CAMBRELENG, Churchill Caldom	H
CAMDEN, Harry Poole	2
CAMDEN, Johnson Newlon	1
CAMDEN, Johnson Newlon	2
CAMERON, Adam Kirk	5
CAMERON, Albert Barnes	5
CAMERON, Alexander	H
CAMERON, Andrew Carr	H
CAMERON, Angus	H
CAMERON, Archibald	H
CAMERON, Arnold Guyot	2
CAMERON, Benjamin Franklin	4
CAMERON, Charles Conrad	3
CAMERON, Charles Raymond	5
CAMERON, D(onald) Ewen	5
CAMERON, Edgar Spier	2
CAMERON, Edward Herbert	1
CAMERON, Edwin J.	3
CAMERON, Frank Kenneth	3
CAMERON, George Hamilton	2
CAMERON, George Toland	3
CAMERON, Gordon Wyatt	3
CAMERON, Harold William	5
CAMERON, Henry Clay	1
CAMERON, James Donald	1
CAMERON, John	H
CAMERON, John Andrew	4
CAMERON, John M.	1
CAMERON, Norman W.	2
CAMERON, Ossian	4
CAMERON, Ralph Henry	3
CAMERON, Robert Alexander	H
CAMERON, Roderick William	1
CAMERON, Shelton Thomas	2
CAMERON, Simon	H
CAMERON, Turner Christian, Jr.	5
CAMERON, William Donald	4
CAMERON, William Evelyn	1
CAMERON, William J.	4
CAMERON, William John	3
CAMERON, William McC	3
CAMILLO, Michael Francis	5
CAMINETTI, Anthony	1
CAMM, John	H
CAMMACK, Edmund Ernest	3
CAMMACK, Ira Insco	1
CAMMACK, James William	1
CAMMACK, James William	3
CAMMACK, John Walter	5
CAMMERHOFF, John Christopher Frederick	H
CAMP, Albert Sidney	3
CAMP, Charles Wadsworth	1
CAMP, David Nelson	1
CAMP, Edgar Whittlesey	4
CAMP, Frederic Edgar	4
CAMP, Hiram	H
CAMP, Irving Luzerne	1
CAMP, John Henry	H
CAMP, John Lafayette	H
CAMP, John Spencer	2
CAMP, Lawrence Sabyllia	2
CAMP, Mortimer Hart	4
CAMP, Thomas Ringgold	5
CAMP, Walter	1
CAMP, Walter John Richard	4
CAMP, Wendell H.	4
CAMP, William McCutcheon	4
CAMPANARI, Giuseppe	1
CAMPANINI, Cleofonte	1
CAMPANIUS, John	H
CAMPAU, Daniel J.	1
CAMPAU, Francis Denis	3
CAMPAU, Joseph	H
CAMPA 'Y CARAVEDA, Miguel Abgel	4
CAMPBELL, Albert H.	H
CAMPBELL, Albert James	1
CAMPBELL, Alexander *	H
CAMPBELL, Alexander Boyd	4
CAMPBELL, Alexander Morton	5
CAMPBELL, Alfred Hills	1
CAMPBELL, Allan	H
CAMPBELL, Allan B.	4
CAMPBELL, Andrew	H
CAMPBELL, Archibald Brush	4
CAMPBELL, Archibald Murray	4
CAMPBELL, Arthur Griffith	3
CAMPBELL, Bartley	H
CAMPBELL, Benjamin	4
CAMPBELL, Brookins	H
CAMPBELL, Bruce Alexander	3
CAMPBELL, Bruce Jones	5
CAMPBELL, Chandler	3
CAMPBELL, Charles	H
CAMPBELL, Charles Atwood	1
CAMPBELL, Charles Diven	1
CAMPBELL, Charles E.	4
CAMPBELL, Charles King	5
CAMPBELL, Charles L.	3
CAMPBELL, Charles Macfie	2
CAMPBELL, Charles S.	3
CAMPBELL, Charles Sherman	3
CAMPBELL, Chesser M.	4
CAMPBELL, Chester I.	1
CAMPBELL, D. Scott	4
CAMPBELL, Daisy Rhodes	4
CAMPBELL, Daniel A.	4
CAMPBELL, Delwin Morton	3
CAMPBELL, Doak Sheridan	5
CAMPBELL, Donald Francis	5
CAMPBELL, Donald J.	2
CAMPBELL, Donald Malcolm	2
CAMPBELL, Douglas Houghton	3
CAMPBELL, Dwight	4
CAMPBELL, E(rnest) Ray	5
CAMPBELL, Edmond Ernest	1
CAMPBELL, Edmund Schureman	3
CAMPBELL, Edward De Mille	1
CAMPBELL, Edward Hale	5
CAMPBELL, Edward Hastings	4
CAMPBELL, Edward K.	1

*** Indicates More Than One Such Name Listed**

CAMPBELL, Eldridge 3
CAMPBELL, Elizabeth 4
CAMPBELL, Elmer Grant 5
CAMPBELL, Felix 1
CAMPBELL, Floyd D. 4
CAMPBELL, Frank 4
CAMPBELL, Frank L. 1
CAMPBELL, Gabriel 3
CAMPBELL, George 2
CAMPBELL,
George Alexander
CAMPBELL, 3
George Ashley
CAMPBELL, 1
George Hollister
CAMPBELL, H
George Washington *
CAMPBELL, Gerald 1
Gilbert Whitney
CAMPBELL, Gordon
Peter 4
CAMPBELL, H. Wood 1
CAMPBELL, H. Donald 5
CAMPBELL, 4
Hardy Webster
CAMPBELL, Harold
Denny 3
CAMPBELL, 2
Harold George
CAMPBELL, Harry Huse 1
CAMPBELL, Helen Stuart 4
CAMPBELL, Henry Colin 1
CAMPBELL, Henry
Donald 1
CAMPBELL, Henry
Fraser H
CAMPBELL, Henry
Munroe 1
CAMPBELL, 1
Herbert Grant
CAMPBELL, 4
Ira Alexander
CAMPBELL, J. W. 3
CAMPBELL, Jacob Miller H
CAMPBELL, James 1
CAMPBELL, James A. 1
CAMPBELL, 2
James Alexander
CAMPBELL, 1
James Archibald
CAMPBELL, James C. 4
CAMPBELL, 1
James Daniels
CAMPBELL, James E. 1
CAMPBELL, H
James Hepburn
CAMPBELL, James
Hobart 5
CAMPBELL, James
LeRoy 2
CAMPBELL, James Mann 2
CAMPBELL, 2
James Philander
CAMPBELL, 1
James Romulus
CAMPBELL, James U. 1
CAMPBELL, H
James Valentine
CAMPBELL, James
Watson 5
CAMPBELL, John * H
CAMPBELL, John * 1
CAMPBELL, John A. H
CAMPBELL, John Allen H
CAMPBELL, H
John Archibald
CAMPBELL, 3
John Bayard Taylor
CAMPBELL, 4
John Bradford
CAMPBELL, John Bulow 1
CAMPBELL, John Charles 1
CAMPBELL, John Henry 1
CAMPBELL, John Hull H
CAMPBELL, John Logan 4
CAMPBELL, John Lorne 4
CAMPBELL, John Lyle 1
CAMPBELL, John Neal 4
CAMPBELL, 1
John Pendleton
CAMPBELL, H
John Pierce Jr.
CAMPBELL, John Preston 4
CAMPBELL, 1
John TenBrook
CAMPBELL, John
Thomas 5
CAMPBELL, John Wilson 1
CAMPBELL, Johnston B. 3
CAMPBELL, 1
Josiah A. Patterson
CAMPBELL, Killis 1
CAMPBELL, L. j. 5
CAMPBELL, Leon 3
CAMPBELL, 3
LeRoy Brotzman

CAMPBELL, LeRoy
Walter 5
CAMPBELL, Lewis Davis H
CAMPBELL, Lily Bess 4
CAMPBELL,
Lucien Quitman
CAMPBELL, Luther A. 2
CAMPBELL, Macy 1
CAMPBELL, Marcus B. 2
CAMPBELL, Marguerite 4
CAMPBELL, 1
Marius Robison
CAMPBELL, Mrs. Patrick 1
CAMPBELL, 5
Oscar James, Jr.
CAMPBELL, H
Patrick Thomas
CAMPBELL, Philip Pitt 4
CAMPBELL, Price 4
CAMPBELL, 1
Prince Lucian
CAMPBELL, R. Granville 1
CAMPBELL, 1
Ralph Emerson
CAMPBELL, Richard 1
CAMPBELL,
Richard Kenna
CAMPBELL, Robert H
CAMPBELL, Robert Blair H
CAMPBELL, 4
Robert Donald
CAMPBELL, 2
Robert Fishburne
CAMPBELL, 1
Robert Willis
CAMPBELL, Ronald Neil 4
CAMPBELL, Ross Turner 2
CAMPBELL, Rowland 2
CAMPBELL, Roy Davies 5
CAMPBELL, Sam 4
CAMPBELL, Samuel H
CAMPBELL, 1
Theodorick Pryor
CAMPBELL, Thomas H
CAMPBELL, Thomas A. 5
CAMPBELL, 4
Thomas Donald
CAMPBELL, 2
Thomas Edward
CAMPBELL, 2
Thomas Huffman
CAMPBELL, H
Thomas Jefferson
CAMPBELL, 1
Thomas Joseph
CAMPBELL, 1
Thomas Mitchell
CAMPBELL, Thomas W. 1
CAMPBELL, Thompson H
CAMPBELL, Wallace 3
CAMPBELL, 5
Wallace Edwin
CAMPBELL, 5
Walter Gilbert
CAMPBELL, 3
Walter Stanley
CAMPBELL, Wayne 5
CAMPBELL, William * H
CAMPBELL, William 1
CAMPBELL, 1
William Alexander
CAMPBELL, 1
William Bowen
CAMPBELL, 4
William Carey
CAMPBELL, 1
William Francis
CAMPBELL, H
William Henry
CAMPBELL, 2
William James
CAMPBELL, 4
William Lyman
CAMPBELL, William
Neal 2
CAMPBELL, 5
William Purnell
CAMPBELL, 1
William Rogers
CAMPBELL, 1
William Taggart
CAMPBELL, William W. H
CAMPBELL, William W. 4
CAMPBELL, 1
William Wallace
CAMPBELL, 5
William Wilson
CAMPBELL,
Willis Cohoon
CAMPBELL, Worthington 4
CAMPELLO, 5
Count Solone Di
CAMPHOR,
Alexander Priestly
CAMPNEY, 4
Ralph Osbiurne
CAMPOS, Maria E. 3

CAMROSE, 3
1'st Viscount of Hackwood
Park
CAMSELL, Charles 3
CAMUS, Albert 3
CANADA, John Walter 2
CANADA, John William 5
CANADA, John William 3
CANADA, 5
Robert Owen, Jr.
CANADA, William
Wesley 1
CANADAY, Paul O'neal 4
CANARUTTO, Angelo 2
CANARY, Martha Jane H
CANARY, Martha Jane 4
CANBY, H
Edward Richard Sprigg
CANBY, Henry Seidel 4
CANBY, Richard Sprigg H
CANBY, 1
William Marriott
CANDEE, Charles Lucius 2
CANDEE, 2
Helen Churchill
CANDEE, Leverett H
CANDEE, Lyman 2
CANDLER, Allen Daniel 1
CANDLER, Asa G. 1
CANDLER, 3
Charles Howard
CANDLER, 1
Charles Murphey
CANDLER, 2
Ezekiel Samuel Jr.
CANDLER, Henry E. 5
CANDLER, 2
John Slaughter
CANDLER, 5
Samuel Charles
CANDLER, 5
Thomas Slaughter
CANDLER, Warren A. 1
CANDLER, William 1
CANDY, Albert Luther 2
CANEVIN, J. F. Regis 1
CANFIELD, 2
Arthur Graves
CANFIELD, Edward 4
CANFIELD, 2
George Folger
CANFIELD, Harry C. 2
CANFIELD, James Hulme 1
CANFIELD, Roy Bishop 1
CANFIELD, 1
William Walker
CANHAM, 4
Charles Draper William
CANJAR, 5
Lawrence Nicholas
CANN, James Ferris 1
CANN, Norman D. 3
CANNAN, Robert Keith 5
CANNIFF, William Henry 1
CANNING, George H
CANNON, A. Benson H
CANNON, Annie Jump 1
CANNON, Austin Victor 1
CANNON, 4
Cavendish Welles
CANNON, Charles A. 5
CANNON, Charles James H
CANNON, Clarence 1
CANNON, 5
Cornelia James (Mrs.
Walter Bradford Cannon)
CANNON, Frank Jenne 1
CANNON, 4
George Lyman Jr.
CANNON, George Quayle H
CANNON, 5
Grant Groesbeck
CANNON, Harriet Starr H
CANNON, Henry White 1
CANNON, James Jr. 2
CANNON, James Graham 1
CANNON, James III 3
CANNON, John 1
CANNON, John Franklin 1
CANNON, John Kenneth 3
CANNON, Joseph Gurney 1
CANNON, 1
Le Grand Bouton
CANNON, Martin L. 3
CANNON, Newton 1
CANNON, Raymond J. 3
CANNON, 2
Sylvester Quayle
CANNON, 2
Walter Bradford
CANNON, William H
CANNON, 5
William Cornelius
CANONCHET H
CANONGE, Louis Placide 1
CANONICUS H
CANOVA, Leon Joseph 4

CANRIGHT, 1
Dudley Marvin
CANSE, John Martin 5
CANT, 1
William Alexander
CANTELLI, Guido 4
CANTER, Howard Vernon 5
CANTER, Joshua H
CANTEY, Morgan Sabb 4
CANTILLON, 1
William David
CANTILO, Jose Maria 5
CANTOR, Eddie 4
CANTOR, Jacob Aaron 1
CANTOR, Nathaniel 3
CANTRALL, Arch Martin 5
CANTRELL, Charles E. 1
CANTRELL, 5
Deaderick Harrell
CANTRIL, 5
(Albert) Hadley
CANTRILL, 1
James Campbell
CANTRILL, James E. 1
CANTWELL, Alfred W. 4
CANTWELL, 1
James William
CANTWELL, John Joseph 2
CANTWELL, 1
Robert Murray
CANTY, Thomas 4
CAPA, Robert 4
CAPARO, Jose Angel 3
CAPE, Emily Palmer 1
CAPEK, Thomas 3
CAPEN, Charles Laban 1
CAPEN, Edward Warren 5
CAPEN, Elmer Hewitt 1
CAPEN, Nahum H
CAPEN, Oliver Bronson 3
CAPEN, Samuel Billings 1
CAPEN, Samuel Paul 3
CAPERS, Ellison 1
CAPERS, John G. 1
CAPERS, Walter Branham 5
CAPERS, William H
CAPERS, 2
William Theodotus
CAPERTON, Allen Taylor H
CAPERTON, Hugh 1
CAPERTON, 1
William Banks
CAPES, William Parr 2
CAPLES, Martin Joseph 1
CAPLES, Russel B. 5
CAPPER, Arthur 3
CAPPS, Charles R. 1
CAPPS, Edward 1
CAPPS, Joseph Almarin 4
CAPPS, Stephen Reid 2
CAPPS, Washington Lee 1
CAPRON, Adin Ballou 1
CAPRON, 3
Charles Alexander
CAPRON, Horace 1
CAPSTAFF, Albert L. 4
CAPSTAFF, John George 3
CAPSTICK, John Henry 1
CAPT, James Clyde 2
CAPTAIN JACK H
CARAWAY, Hattie Wyatt 3
CARAWAY, Thaddeus H. 1
CARBEE, Scott Clifton 4
CARBO, Luis Felipe 4
CARBONARA, 5
E(mil) Vernon
CARBONE, Agostino 4
CARBONNIER, 4
Claes Cecil
CARD, Benjamin Cozzens 1
CARD, Ernest Mason 5
CARDELLI, Pietro 1
CARDEN, Cap R. 1
CARDEN, Edward Walter 4
CARDEN, 2
George Alexander
CARDEN, William
Thomas 1
CARDENAS, H
Garcia Lopez 'de
CARDENAS, Lazaro 1
CARDIFF, Ira D. 5
CARDOFF, Thomas H. 4
CARDON, Philip Vincent 4
CARDOZO, 1
Benjamin Nathan
CARDOZO, Jacob
Newton H
CARDWELL, James R. 3
CARDY, Samuel H
CARENS, Thomas Henry 4
CAREW, Harold David 2
CAREW, James 1
CAREW, John F. 3
CAREY, Archibald 1
CAREY, Archibald James 1
CAREY, Arthur Astor 1

CAREY, Asa Bacon 1
CAREY, Charles Emerson 3
CAREY, Charles Henry 1
CAREY, Charles Irving 5
CAREY, Eben James 2
CAREY, Eustace W. 2
CAREY, Francis King 2
CAREY, Hampson 1
CAREY, Henry Charles H
CAREY, Henry Westonrae 1
CAREY, James F. 4
CAREY, James William 5
CAREY, John Joseph 5
CAREY, Joseph 1
CAREY, Joseph Maull 1
CAREY, Liguori John 4
CAREY, Mathew H
CAREY, Miriam Eliza 1
CAREY, Peter Bernard 2
CAREY, Robert 1
CAREY, Robert Davis 1
CAREY, Robert Lincoln 1
CAREY, William Francis 3
CAREY, 2
William Gibson Jr.
CARGILL, 5
Frank Valentine
CARGILL, Oscar 1
CARHART, Daniel 1
CARHART, Frank Milton 4
CARHART, Henry Smith 1
CARHART, 4
Winfield Scott
CARHARTT, Hamilton 1
CARHARTT, John Ernest 2
CARIAS ANDINO, 5
Tiburcio
CARKIN, Seth Ballou 1
CARKNER, James W. 4
CARL, Francis Augustus 1
CARL, 1
Katharine Augusta
CARL, Melvin Latshaw 3
CARL, William Crane 1
CARLAND, John Emmett 1
CARLE, Frank Austin 1
CARLE, Nathaniel Allen 4
CARLE, Richard 1
CARLES, Arthur B. 3
CARLETON, Bukk G. 1
CARLETON, Clifford 4
CARLETON, Guy 3
CARLETON, Henry H
CARLETON, Henry Guy 1
CARLETON, Mark Alfred 1
CARLETON, Murray 4
CARLETON, Peter H
CARLETON, Will 1
CARLEY, Henry
Thompson 4
CARLEY, Patrick J. 1
CARLEY, W. F. 3
CARLILE, John Snyder H
CARLILE, 5
William Buford
CARLIN, Andrew B. H
CARLIN, 1
Charles Creighton
CARLIN, Charles L. H
CARLIN, George Andrew 4
CARLIN, Henry A. 4
CARLIN, James Joseph 1
CARLIN, John H
CARLIN, Thomas H
CARLIN, 1
Walter Jeffreys
CARLIN, 1
William Passmore
CARLIN, William Worth 1
CARLISLE, 1
Charles Arthur
CARLISLE, Chester Lee 3
CARLISLE, Clifton Hugh 3
CARLISLE, Floyd Leslie 3
CARLISLE, 3
G. Lister Jr.
CARLISLE, 4
Harold Walter
CARLISLE, Helen Grace 5
CARLISLE, Howard Bobo 5
CARLISLE, James Henry 1
CARLISLE, H
James Mandeville
CARLISLE, James McCoy 4
CARLISLE, John Griffin 1
CARLISLE, John Nelson 1
CARLISLE, Marcus Lee 1
CARLL, John Franklin 1
CARLOCK, John Bruce 4
CARLOUGH, 1
David Jacobus
CARLSEN, Carl Laurence 1
CARLSEN, Clarence J. 4
CARLSEN, Dines 1
CARLSEN, Emil 1
CARLSEN, 2
Niels Christian

CARLSON, Anders Johan 5
CARLSON, Anton Julius 3
CARLSON, Chester 5
CARLSON, 3
  Clarence Erick
CARLSON, 5
  E(rnest) Leslie
CARLSON, Evans
  Fordyce 2
CARLSON, George Alfred 1
CARLSON, Gunard Oscar 5
CARLSON, Harry Johan 5
CARLSON, James Alfred 4
CARLSON, John Fabian 2
CARLSON, Loren Daniel 5
CARLSON, 5
  T(horgny) C(edric)
CARLSON, Wally 4
CARLSTON, Kenneth S. 5
CARLSTROM, Oscar E. 2
CARLTON, A. C. 3
CARLTON, Albert E. 1
CARLTON, Caleb Henry 1
CARLTON, Caleb Sidney 5
CARLTON, Clarence Clay 3
CARLTON, Doyle Elam 5
CARLTON, Ernest W. 4
CARLTON, Frank Tracy 5
CARLTON, 1
  Leslie Gilbert
CARLTON, Newcomb 3
CARLTON, Richard Paul 3
CARLTON, 2
  William Newnham Chattin
CARLYLE, Irving Edward 5
CARLYLE, William Levi 5
CARMACK, Edward
  Ward 1
CARMALT, James Walton 1
CARMALT, William
  Henry 1
CARMAN, Albert Pruden 3
CARMAN, 5
  Augustine Spencer
CARMAN, Bliss 1
CARMAN, Ezra Ayers 1
CARMAN, George Noble 5
CARMAN, Harry James 4
CARMELIA, 2
  Francis Albion
CARMICHAEL, 3
  Archibald Hill
CARMICHAEL, 4
  George Edgar
CARMICHAEL, George
  T. 1
CARMICHAEL, Henry 1
CARMICHAEL, John
  Hugh 5
CARMICHAEL, 4
  Oliver Cromwell
CARMICHAEL, Omer 3
CARMICHAEL, H
  Richard Bennett
CARMICHAEL, 4
  Robert Daniel
CARMICHAEL, 2
  Thomas Harrison
CARMICHAEL, William H
CARMICHAEL, 4
  William Donald Jr.
CARMICHAEL, 2
  William Perrin
CARMODY, John 3
CARMODY, John Michael 4
CARMODY, Martin
  Henry 3
CARMODY, 2
  Terence Francis
CARMODY, Thomas 1
CARMODY, Thomas
  Edward 2
CARMONA, 3
  Antonio Oscar 'de Fragoso
CARNAHAN, A.Sj. 5
CARNAHAN, David
  Hobart 5
CARNAHAN, 1
  George Holmes
CARNAHAN, Herschel L. 1
CARNAHAN, James H
CARNAHAN, 1
  James Richards
CARNAHAN, Paul
  Harvey 4
CARNAHAN, Wendell 4
CARNAP, Rudolf 5
CARNEGIE, Andrew 1
CARNEGIE, Dale 3
CARNEGIE, Hattie 3
CARNEGIE, 2
  Louise Whitfield
CARNEGIE, 5
  T(homas) Morris(on)
CARNELL, Edward John 4
CARNELL, Laura Horner 1
CARNES, Cecil 3

CARNES, Thomas Petters H
CARNEY, Francis Joseph 1
CARNEY, Frank 1
CARNEY, James Lorring 4
CARNEY, Leonard T. 4
CARNEY, Thomas H
CARNEY, Thomas Joseph 2
CARNEY, William Roy 5
CARNOCHRAN, H
  John Murray
CARO, Marcus Rayner 4
CAROL, Kate H
CARONDELET, H
  Baron Francisco Luis
  Hector 'de
CAROTHERS, Wallace H. 1
CARPENDER, Arthur S. 3
CARPENTER, 5
  Aaron Everly
CARPENTER, 2
  Allen Fuller
CARPENTER, 5
  Allen Harmon
CARPENTER, Alva
  Edwin 1
CARPENTER, 3
  Arthur DeVere
CARPENTER, Arthur
  Howe 3
CARPENTER, B. Platt 1
CARPENTER, Benjamin 1
CARPENTER, 1
  Charles Carroll
CARPENTER, 5
  Charles Colcock Jones
CARPENTER, Charles E. 1
CARPENTER, 2
  Charles Ernest
CARPENTER, 1
  Charles Lincoln
CARPENTER, Clarence 1
CARPENTER, Clinton E. 2
CARPENTER, 5
  Coy Cornelius
CARPENTER, Cyrus Clay 1
CARPENTER, Davis H
CARPENTER, 1
  Decatur Merritt Hammond
CARPENTER, Delph E. 3
CARPENTER, 1
  Edmund Janes
CARPENTER, 5
  Edward Childs
CARPENTER, 2
  Elbert Lawrence
CARPENTER, Ellen
  Maria 4
CARPENTER, Eugene R. 5
CARPENTER, 1
  Fanny Hallock
CARPENTER, Ford
  Ashman 2
CARPENTER, 1
  Francis Bicknell
CARPENTER, 1
  Frank George
CARPENTER, 4
  Frank Oliver
CARPENTER, 1
  Frank Pierce
CARPENTER, 5
  Frank Watson
CARPENTER, 4
  Franklin Reuben
CARPENTER, Fred Green 4
CARPENTER, 5
  Fred Warner;
CARPENTER, 1
  Frederic Ives
CARPENTER, 1
  Frederic Walton
CARPENTER, 2
  George Albert
CARPENTER, 1
  George Oliver
CARPENTER, George
  Rice 1
CARPENTER, 1
  Gilbert Saltonstall
CARPENTER, H. Beach 3
CARPENTER, 1
  Horace Francis
CARPENTER, 2
  Hubert Vinton
CARPENTER, J. Henry 1
CARPENTER, James D. 5
CARPENTER, James W. * 4
CARPENTER, John Alden 3
CARPENTER, 1
  John Slaughter
CARPENTER, 1
  Julia Wiltberger
CARPENTER, Levi D. H
CARPENTER, 1
  Louis George
CARPENTER, Louis
  Henry 1

CARPENTER, H
  Matthew Hale
CARPENTER, Myron Jay 4
CARPENTER,
  Newton Henry
CARPENTER, 4
  Ralph Emerson
CARPENTER, Ray
  Wilford 4
CARPENTER, Reid 1
CARPENTER, 2
  Robert Ruliph Morgan
CARPENTER, 5
  Robert Wilfred
CARPENTER, 1
  Rolla Clinton
CARPENTER, Samuel H. H
CARPENTER, H
  Stephen Cullen
CARPENTER, H
  Stephen Haskins
CARPENTER, William E. 1
CARPENTER, William H. 4
CARPENTER, 1
  William Henry
CARPENTER, 1
  William Leland
CARPENTER, 3
  William Seal
CARPENTER, 5
  William Weston
CARPENTIER, 4
  Charles Francis
CARR, Albert Zolotkoff 5
CARR, Alexander 2
CARR, Arthur R. 1
CARR, Benjamin H
CARR, 1
  Camillo Casatti Cadmus
CARR, Ceylon Spencer 1
CARR, Charlotte 3
CARR, Clarence Alfred 4
CARR, Clark E. 1
CARR, Clyde Mitchell 1
CARR, Dabney H
CARR, Dabney Smith 1
CARR, Elias 1
CARR, Emma Perry 5
CARR, Eugene Asa 1
CARR, Floyd LeVerne 1
CARR, Francis H
CARR, Gene 3
CARR, George H. 1
CARR, George Wallace 3
CARR, Harry 1
CARR, Harry C. 3
CARR, Harvey 3
CARR, Henry James 1
CARR, Herbert Wildon 1
CARR, Irving J. 5
CARR, James H
CARR, James O. 3
CARR, James Ozborn 2
CARR, John Foster 1
CARR, John Wesley 3
CARR, Joseph Bradford 1
CARR, 1
  Julian Shakespeare
CARR, Lawrence 5
CARR, Leland Walker 5
CARR, Lewis E. 1
CARR, Lucien 1
CARR, Nathan Tracy H
CARR, Ossian Elmer 5
CARR, Ralph L. 3
CARR, Reid Langdon 2
CARR, Robert Franklin 2
CARR, Samuel 1
CARR, Sarah Pratt 4
CARR, Sterling Douglas 1
CARR, Thomas Matthew H
CARR, Walter Lester 4
CARR, Walter Scott 1
CARR, Wilbert Lester 5
CARR, Wilbur John 1
CARR, William John 1
CARR, William Kearny 1
CARR, William Phillips 4
CARR, Wooda Nichols 3
CARRE, Henry Beach 1
CARRE, Jean Marie 3
CARREL, Alexis 5
CARRELL, H
  George Aloysius
CARRELL, William Beall 2
CARRERE, John Merven 5
CARRICK, 5
  Alice Van Leer (Mrs.
  Prescott Orde Skinner);
CARRICK, Lynn 4
CARRICK, Manton
  Marble 1
CARRICK, Samuel H
CARRICO, 2
  Joseph Leonard

CARRIER, H
  Augustus Stiles
CARRIER, Wilbur Oscar 1
CARRIER, 3
  Willis Haviland
CARRIGAN, Clarence 1
CARRIGAN, Edward 2
CARRIGAN, William L. 1
CARRINGTON, Edward H
CARRINGTON, 1
  Edward Codrington
CARRINGTON, Elaine 3
CARRINGTON, FitzRoy 5
CARRINGTON, 1
  Frances Courtney
CARRINGTON, 2
  Gordon 'de L.
CARRINGTON, 1
  Henry Beebee
CARRINGTON, 1
  James Beebee
CARRINGTON, Paul H
CARRINGTON, 3
  Richard Adams Jr.
CARRINGTON, 2
  William John
CARRINGTON, 1
  William Thomas
CARRIS, Lewis Herbert 3
CARRITHERS, Howard 4
CARROLL, Anna Ella 5
CARROLL, Augustus John 5
CARROLL, B. Harvey 1
CARROLL, Ben 1
CARROLL,
  Benajah Harvey
CARROLL, Beryl F. 1
CARROLL, 5
  Caroline Moncure Benedict
  (Mrs. Mitchell Carroll)
CARROLL, Charles * H
CARROLL, Charles 1
CARROLL,
  Charles Chauncey
CARROLL, Charles Eden 2
CARROLL,
  Charles Hobart
CARROLL, Daniel H
CARROLL, Dudley
  DeWitt 5
CARROLL, Earl 2
CARROLL, 2
  Edward Ambrose
CARROLL, 4
  Francis Patrick
CARROLL, Francis X. 5
CARROLL, 2
  Frederick Aloysius
CARROLL, George W. 4
CARROLL, Henry 1
CARROLL, Henry King 1
CARROLL, Horace Bailey 4
CARROLL, Howard 1
CARROLL, Howard
  Joseph 3
CARROLL, James 1
CARROLL, James Bernard 1
CARROLL, James F. 3
CARROLL, James Jordan 1
CARROLL, James Milton 1
CARROLL, John H
CARROLL, John 1
CARROLL, John D. 1
CARROLL, John F. 1
CARROLL, John Francis 1
CARROLL, John Haydock 1
CARROLL, John Joseph 1
CARROLL, John Lee 1
CARROLL, John P. 1
CARROLL, 3
  Joseph Francis
CARROLL, Leo G. 5
CARROLL, Louis Francis 5
CARROLL, Mitchell 1
CARROLL, 5
  Monroe Spurgeon
CARROLL, Paul Thomas 3
CARROLL, Paul Vincent 5
CARROLL, Phil 5
CARROLL, Philip A. 5
CARROLL, Raymond G. 2
CARROLL, 3
  Richard Augustine
CARROLL, Robert Paris 3
CARROLL, Robert Sproul 1
CARROLL, Samuel Sprigg H
CARROLL, Thomas
  Claude 4
CARROLL, Thomas F. 1
CARROLL, 4
  Thomas Henry II
CARROLL, 1
  Thomas Patrick
CARROLL, William H

CARROLL, William
  Henry 1
CARROON, Frank 5
CARROTHERS, 4
  George Ezra
CARROW, Fleming 4
CARRUTH, 4
  Arthur Jay Jr.
CARRUTH, 1
  Charles Theodore
CARRUTH, Hayden 1
CARRUTH, Louis 1
CARRUTH, 1
  William Herbert
CARRUTHERS, 3
  John Franklin Bruce
CARRUTHERS, 4
  Thomas Neely
CARRY, Edward Francis 1
CARRYL, Charles Edward 2
CARRYL, Guy Wetmore 1
CARSE, Elizabeth 1
CARSE, Matilda Bradley 1
CARSON, Adam Clarke 1
CARSON, 3
  Charles Averette
CARSON, 2
  Charles Clifton
CARSON, Charles L. H
CARSON, Christopher H
CARSON, Clifford 5
CARSON, Frank L. 3
CARSON, 4
  George Prentice
CARSON, 1
  Hampton Lawrence
CARSON, Harry Roberts 2
CARSON, Howard Adams 1
CARSON, James Carlton 4
CARSON, James Oliver 1
CARSON, James S. 5
CARSON, Jessie M(ay) 1
CARSON, John Fleming 1
CARSON, John Hargadine 5
CARSON, John Miller 1
CARSON, John Miller 3
CARSON, John Renshaw 1
CARSON, Joseph H
CARSON, 3
  Joseph Kirtley Jr.
CARSON, Luella Clay 3
CARSON, 5
  Matthew Vaughan, Jr.
CARSON, Norman Bruce 1
CARSON, Rachel L. 4
CARSON, Robert 3
CARSON, Samuel Price H
CARSON, Walter Lapsley 4
CARSON, William E. 2
CARSON, William Henry 4
CARSON, William Pierce 5
CARSON, William Waller 1
CARSS, 1
  William Leighton
CARSTARPHEN, 3
  Frederick Charles
CARSTARPHEN, 2
  William Turner
CARSTENS, 1
  Christian Carl
CARSTENS, J. Henry 1
CARSTENSEN, 1
  Gustav Arnold
CARSTENSEN, John 1
CARTER, A. F. 4
CARTER, Albert Paine 5
CARTER, Amon Giles 3
CARTER, 4
  Arthur Hazelton
CARTER, Asher H
CARTER, Benjamin Estes 2
CARTER, Bernard 1
CARTER, 4
  Bernard Shirley
CARTER, Boake 2
CARTER, C. C. 4
CARTER, Charles David 1
CARTER, 1
  Charles Francis
CARTER, 1
  Charles Frederick
CARTER, Clarence Edwin 4
CARTER, 3
  Clifton Carroll
CARTER, DeWitt 3
CARTER, Edward Carlos 3
CARTER, Edward Clark 3
CARTER, Edwin A. 2
CARTER, Edwin Farnham 3
CARTER, Elias H
CARTER, Emma Smuller 1
CARTER, 4
  Emmet Thoroughman
CARTER, Ernest Trow 3
CARTER, 1
  Francis Beauregard
CARTER, Francis Graves 4

Name	
CARTER, Franklin	1
CARTER, Fred Afton	2
CARTER, Fred G.	3
CARTER, Fred Mason	3
CARTER, Gale H.	3
CARTER, Gardner Lloyd	4
CARTER, George	3
CARTER, George Calvin	5
CARTER, George Henry	2
CARTER, George Milton	3
CARTER, George Robert	2
CARTER, George William	1
CARTER, Harold Samuel	4
CARTER, Henry Alpheus Pierce	H
CARTER, Henry Holland	3
CARTER, Henry Rose	1
CARTER, Herbert DeWayne	1
CARTER, Herbert Swift	1
CARTER, Hodding	5
CARTER, Horace A.	3
CARTER, Hubert Lazell	3
CARTER, James	2
CARTER, James Coolidge	3
CARTER, James Francis	5
CARTER, James Gordon	3
CARTER, James Madison Gore	1
CARTER, James Richard	1
CARTER, Jesse Benedict	4
CARTER, Jesse Francis	2
CARTER, Jesse McIlvaine	1
CARTER, Jesse Washington	3
CARTER, John *	H
CARTER, John Franklin Jr.	4
CARTER, John H.	4
CARTER, John Ridgely	2
CARTER, John S.	4
CARTER, Joseph Newton	1
CARTER, Landon	H
CARTER, Leyton E.	3
CARTER, Luther Cullen	4
CARTER, Mary Elizabeth	4
CARTER, Mrs. Leslie	1
CARTER, Nathan A. Sr.	3
CARTER, Oberlin Montgomery	2
CARTER, Oliver Clinton	1
CARTER, Orrin Nelson	1
CARTER, Philips John	4
CARTER, Randall Albert	3
CARTER, Raymond Lanson	3
CARTER, Richard Burrage	2
CARTER, Robert *	H
CARTER, Robert Allen	4
CARTER, Robert Inglee	4
CARTER, Russell Gordon	3
CARTER, Samuel Fain	1
CARTER, Samuel Powhatan	H
CARTER, Seth May	4
CARTER, Steven V.	3
CARTER, Thomas Coke	1
CARTER, Thomas Henry	1
CARTER, Timothy Jarvis	4
CARTER, Walter Steuben	1
CARTER, Wilbert James	5
CARTER, William	1
CARTER, William Blount	H
CARTER, William Curtis	5
CARTER, William Francis	3
CARTER, William Harding	1
CARTER, William Henric	1
CARTER, William Henry	3
CARTER, William Samuel	1
CARTER, William Spencer	2
CARTER, William V.	5
CARTER, Winthrop Lakey	2
CARTERET, Philip	H
CARTERET, Sir George	H
CARTIER, Jacques	H
CARTLAND, Donald Lee	4
CARTON, Alfred Thomas	4
CARTON, John Jay	1
CARTOTTO, Ercole	2
CARTTER, David Kellogg	H
CARTWRIGHT, Alexander Joy	H
CARTWRIGHT, C. Hawley	4
CARTWRIGHT, Frank Thomas	4
CARTWRIGHT, James Henry	1
CARTWRIGHT, Peter	H
CARTY, Donald Joseph	3
CARTY, John J.	1
CARTY, Roland Kenneth	5
CARUANA, George J.	3
CARUS, Emma	1
CARUS, Paul	1
CARUSI, Charles Francis	1
CARUSO, Enrico	1
CARUTHERS, Robert Looney	H
CARUTHERS, Samuel	H
CARUTHERS, William Alexander	H
CARVALHO, David Nunes	1
CARVALHO, Solomon Nunes	H
CARVALHO, Solomon Solis	2
CARVER, Clifford Nickels	4
CARVER, George	3
CARVER, George Washington	H
CARVER, George Washington	2
CARVER, George Washington	4
CARVER, Jay Ward	2
CARVER, John	H
CARVER, John Stuart	3
CARVER, Jonathan	H
CARVER, Thomas Nixon	4
CARVER, Walter Buckingham	3
CARVER, Walter Lexor	4
CARVER, Williard	3
CARVETH, Hector Russell	2
CARVILLE, E. P.	3
CARY, Alice	H
CARY, Annie Louise	1
CARY, Archibald	H
CARY, Austin	1
CARY, Charles	1
CARY, Charles Preston	4
CARY, Edward	1
CARY, Edward Henry	3
CARY, Edward Richard	4
CARY, Elisabeth Luther	1
CARY, George	H
CARY, George	2
CARY, George Booth	H
CARY, George Foster	2
CARY, George Lovell	1
CARY, Glover H.	1
CARY, Guy	3
CARY, Harry Francis	5
CARY, Henry Nathaniel	1
CARY, Jeremiah Eaton	H
CARY, Joyce	3
CARY, Lott	H
CARY, Lucian	5
CARY, Melbert Brinckerhoff	2
CARY, Phoebe	H
CARY, Robert John	1
CARY, Robert Webster	4
CARY, Shepard	H
CARY, William Joseph	1
CASADAY, L(auren) W(ilde)	5
CASADESUS, Robert	5
CASADY, Thomas	3
CASAMAJOR, George Holberton	4
CASANOWICZ, Immanuel Moses	1
CASE, Albert Hermon	5
CASE, Arthur Ellicott	2
CASE, Carl Delos	1
CASE, Charles	H
CASE, Charles Clinton	4
CASE, Charles Orlando	4
CASE, Clarence Edwards	4
CASE, Clarence Marsh	2
CASE, Clifford Philip	4
CASE, Dwight Samuel	4
CASE, Eckstein	4
CASE, Ermine Cowles	5
CASE, Francis Higbee	4
CASE, Francis Owen	5
CASE, George Sessions	3
CASE, Harold Claude	5
CASE, Harold Clayton M.	4
CASE, Howard Gregory	5
CASE, J(ames) Herbert	5
CASE, James Herbert Jr.	4
CASE, James Thomas	4
CASE, Jerome Increase	H
CASE, John Francis	4
CASE, Leonard *	H
CASE, Lorenzo Dow	5
CASE, Mary Emily	4
CASE, Maurice	5
CASE, Nelson	4
CASE, Norman Stanley	1
CASE, Ralph E.	5
CASE, Rolland Webster	3
CASE, Shirley Jackson	2
CASE, Theodore Spencer	1
CASE, Walter	H
CASE, Walter Summerhayes	1
CASE, William Scoville	1
CASEMENT, Dan Dillon	3
CASER, Ettore	3
CASESA, Philip Robert	5
CASEY, Charles Clinton	5
CASEY, Daniel Vincent	5
CASEY, Douglas	4
CASEY, Edward Pearce	1
CASEY, Francis 'de Sales	1
CASEY, George J.	4
CASEY, John Francis	2
CASEY, John J.	1
CASEY, John Schuyler	2
CASEY, Joseph	H
CASEY, Lee	3
CASEY, Levi	H
CASEY, Lyman R.	1
CASEY, Robert Joseph	4
CASEY, Robert Pierce	3
CASEY, Samuel Brown	4
CASEY, Silas	H
CASEY, Silas	1
CASEY, Thomas Lincoln	1
CASEY, William Joseph	3
CASEY, Zadoc	1
CASH, Albert D.	3
CASH, Wilbur Joseph	5
CASH, William Thomas	3
CASHEN, Thomas Cecil	3
CASHIN, John Martin	5
CASHMAN, Earl William	3
CASHMAN, Edwin James	5
CASHMAN, Joseph Thomas	1
CASHMORE, John	4
CASILEAR, John William	H
CASKEY, John Fletcher	4
CASKIE, John Samuels	1
CASKIE, Marion Maxwell	4
CASKODEN, Edwin	1
CASON, Hulsey	3
CASPARI, Charles Jr.	1
CASPARI, Charles Edward	2
CASS, Alonzo Beecher	1
CASS, Charles Anderson	3
CASS, George Washington	H
CASS, Joseph Kerr	1
CASS, Lewis	1
CASS, Louis S.	4
CASSADY, John Howard	5
CASSADY, Morley Franklin	5
CASSADY, Thomas Gantz	5
CASSANDRA	4
CASSATT, Alexander Johnston	5
CASSATT, Mary	1
CASSEDY, George	H
CASSEDY, John Irvin	1
CASSEL, Henry Burd	5
CASSEL, John H.	5
CASSELBERRY, William Evans	4
CASSELL, Wallace Lewis	4
CASSELMAN, Arthur Vale	3
CASSELS, Edwin Henry	2
CASSERLY, Eugene	H
CASSIDY, George Livingston	4
CASSIDY, George Washington	1
CASSIDY, George Williams	H
CASSIDY, Gerald	1
CASSIDY, James E.	3
CASSIDY, James H.	5
CASSIDY, Leslie Martin	4
CASSIDY, Lewis Cochran	2
CASSIDY, M. Joseph	3
CASSIDY, Massilon Alexander	1
CASSIDY, William	H
CASSILL, Harold E.	3
CASSILLY, Francis	4
CASSIN, John	1
CASSINGHAM, John W.	4
CASSINGHAM, Roy B.	3
CASSINO, Samuel Edson	1
CASSIRER, Ernst	5
CASSODAY, John B.	1
CASSON, Herbert Newton	5
CASTANEDA, Carlos Eduardo	3
CASTEGNIER, Georges	1
CASTELLANI, Aldo (Count of Chisimaio)	5
CASTELLO, Eugene	1
CASTELLO BRANCO, Humberto 'de Alencar	4
CASTELLOW, Bryant Thomas	5
CASTELNUOVO-TEDESCO, Mario	5
CASTER, George Brown	5
CASTIGLIONI, Arturo	3
CASTILLO, Ramon S.	2
CASTILLO NAJERA, Francisco	3
CASTLE, Eugene Winston	3
CASTLE, Frederick Albert	1
CASTLE, Harold Kainalu Long	4
CASTLE, Henry Anson	1
CASTLE, Homer Levi	4
CASTLE, John H, Jr.	5
CASTLE, Kendall Brooks	5
CASTLE, Lewis Gould	1
CASTLE, Nicholas	4
CASTLE, Vernon	4
CASTLE, William	4
CASTLE, William Ernest	4
CASTLE, William Richards	H
CASTLE, William Richards	1
CASTLEBERRY, John Jackson	1
CASTLEMAN, Francis Lee Jr.	3
CASTLEMAN, John Breckinridge	1
CASTLEMAN, Virginia Carter	3
CASTLEMON, Harry	1
CASTLES, Alfred Guldo Rudolph	2
CASTNER, Joseph Compton	2
CASTO, C. Everett	3
CASTON, Saul	5
CASTRO, Americo	5
CASTRO, Hector David	5
CASTRO, Jose	H
CASWELL, Albert Edward	3
CASWELL, Alexis	1
CASWELL, Irving A.	5
CASWELL, Lucien B.	4
CASWELL, Mary S.	1
CASWELL, Richard	1
CASWELL, Thomas Hubbard	1
CASWELL, Thomas Thompson	1
CATCHINGS, Thomas Clendinen	4
CATCHINGS, Waddill	5
CATE, Horace Nelson	1
CATE, Roscoe Simmons Jr.	4
CATES, Charles Theodore Jr.	1
CATES, Clifton Bledsoe	5
CATES, Gordon Dell	5
CATES, Junius Sidney	4
CATES, Louis Shattuck	3
CATES, Walter Thruston	3
CATESBY, Mark	H
CATHCART, Arthur Martin	2
CATHCART, Charles Sanderson	H
CATHCART, Charles William	H
CATHCART, James Leander	H
CATHCART, Robert Spann	2
CATHCART, Stanley H.	5
CATHCART, Thomas Edward (Tom Cathcart)	5
CATHCART, Wallace Hugh	4
CATHCART, William	1
CATHCART, William Ledyard	1
CATHELL, Daniel Webster	4
CATHELL, William T.	4
CATHER, David Clark	2
CATHER, Willa Sibert	2
CATHERWOOD, Mary Hartwell	1
CATHLES, Lawrence Maclagan	5
CATLIN, Albertus Wright	1
CATLIN, Charles Albert	1
CATLIN, George	H
CATLIN, George Smith	H
CATLIN, Henry Guy	4
CATLIN, Isaac Swartwood	H
CATLIN, Louise Ensign	
CATLIN, Randolph	
CATLIN, Robert Mayo	
CATLIN, Roy George	
CATLIN, Theron Ephron	
CATLIN, Warren Benjamin	
CATON, Arthur J.	
CATON, John Dean	
CATOR, George	
CATRON, Charles Christopher	
CATRON, John	
CATRON, Thomas Benton	
CATT, Carrie Chapman	
CATT, George William	
CATTELL, Alexander Gilmore	
CATTELL, Edward James	
CATTELL, Henry Ware	
CATTELL, James McKeen	
CATTELL, Jaques	
CATTELL, Richard Bartley Channing	
CATTELL, William Ashburner	
CATTELL, William Cassaday	
CATTELLE, Wallis Richard	
CATTERALL, Ralph Charles Henry	
CATTON, Charles Jr.	
CATTS, Sidney Johnston	
CAUFFMAN, Frank Guernsey	
CAULDWELL, Frederic Wadsworth	
CAULDWELL, John Britton	
CAULDWELL, Leslie Giffen	
CAULDWELL, Oscar Ray	
CAULFIELD, Bernard Gregory	
CAULFIELD, Henry Stewart	
CAULK, John Roberts	
CAULLERY, Maurice Jules Gaston Corneille	
CAUSEY, William Bowdoin	
CAUSIN, John M. S.	
CAUTHORN, Joseph Lurton	
CAVADAS, Athenagoras	
CAVAGNARO, James Francis	
CAVAGNARO, Robert John	
CAVALIERI, Lina (Mrs. Lucien Muratore)	
CAVALLARO, Joseph B.	
CAVALLITO, Albino	
CAVAN, Marie (Mary Cawein)	
CAVANA, Martin	
CAVANAGH, C. J.	
CAVANAUGH, James Michael	
CAVANAUGH, John William	
CAVANAUGH, John William	
CAVANAUGH, Robert Joseph	
CAVE, Edward Powell	
CAVE, H. W.	
CAVE, Henry Wisdom	
CAVE, Reuben Lindsay	
CAVELIER, Robert	
CAVERNO, Charles	
CAVICCHIA, Peter Angelo	
CAVINS, Lorimer Victor	
CAWEIN, Madison Julius	
CAWL, Franklin Robert	
CAWLEY, Edgar Moore	
CAWTHORN, Joseph Bridger	
CAYCE, Edgar	
CAYLOR, John	
CAYTON, Horace Roscoe	
CAYVAN, Georgia	
CAYWOOD, Roland Blanchard	
CAZEDESSUS, Eugene Romain	
CAZENOVE, Theophile	
CAZIARC, Louis Vasmer	
CECIL, Charles Purcell	
CECIL, George W.	
CECIL, James McCosh	

CECIL, John Giles 1
CECIL, Lamar 3
CECIL, Russell 1
CECIL, Russell LaFayette 4
CECIL 'OF CHELWOOD, Viscount 3
CEDERBERG, William Emanuel 5
CEDERGREN, Hugo 5
CEDERSTROM, Albert Gustaf 4
CEHRS, Charles Harold 5
CELENTANO, William C. 5
CELERON 'DE BLAINVILLE, Pierre Joseph 'de H
CELINE, Louis Ferdinand 4
CELL, George C.
CELL, John W(esley) 5
CELLA, John G. 5
CELLINI, Renato 4
CERACCHI, Guiseppe H
CERF, Barry * 2
CERF, Bennett Alfred 5
CERF, Edward Owen 3
CERMAK, Anton Joseph 1
CERRE, Jean Gabriel H
CESNOLA, Louis Palma Di 1
CESPEDES Y ORTIZ, Carlos Miguel 3
CESSNA, John
CESSNA, Orange Howard 1
CHABRAT, Guy Ignatius H
CHACE, Arnold Buffum H
CHACE, Elizabeth Buffum
CHACE, George Hart 3
CHACE, Jonathan 1
CHACE, Malcolmn Greene 3
CHADBOURN, Erlon R. 4
CHADBOURN, William Hobbs Jr. 4
CHADBOURNE, George Storrs 1
CHADBOURNE, Paul Ansel H
CHADBOURNE, Thomas Lincoln 1
CHADBOURNE, William Merriam 4
CHADDOCK, Charles Gilbert 1
CHADDOCK, Robert Emmet 1
CHADSEY, Charles Ernest 5
CHADWICK, Charles 3
CHADWICK, Charles Wesley 1
CHADWICK, Clarence Wells 1
CHADWICK, E. Wallace 5
CHADWICK, French Ensor 1
CHADWICK, George Halcott 3
CHADWICK, George Whitefield 1
CHADWICK, Henry Dexter 5
CHADWICK, James Read 1
CHADWICK, John Raymond 4
CHADWICK, John White 1
CHADWICK, Lee Sherman 5
CHADWICK, Stephen James 1
CHAFEE, Adna Romanza 1
CHAFEE, Henry Sharpe 4
CHAFEE, Zechariah Jr. 3
CHAFER, Lewis Sperry 5
CHAFFE, Henry Hansell 5
CHAFFEE, Adna Romanza 1
CHAFFEE, Arthur Billings 4
CHAFFEE, Calvin Clifford H
CHAFFEE, Jerome Bunty H
CHAFFEE, Jerome Stuart 2
CHAFFEE, Roger B. 1
CHAFFEY, Andrew M. 1
CHAFFEY, George 1
CHAFFIN, Lucien Gates 1
CHAFIN, Eugene Wilder 1
CHAILLE, Stanford Emerson 1
CHAILLE-LONG, Charles 1
CHAINEY, George 4
CHAISSON, John Robert 5

CHALFANT, Alexander Steele 4
CHALFANT, Harry Malcolm 1
CHALIAPIN, Feodor 1
CHALIFOUR, Joseph Onesime 3
CHALKLEY, Lyman 1
CHALKLEY, Otway H. 3
CHALKLEY, Thomas H
CHALLENER, William Albert 4
CHALMERS, Allan Knight 5
CHALMERS, Gordon Keith
CHALMERS, Harvey, 2d 5
CHALMERS, Henry 3
CHALMERS, Hugh 1
CHALMERS, James 1
CHALMERS, James Ronald H
CHALMERS, Joseph Williams
CHALMERS, Louis Henry 1
CHALMERS, Robert Scott 1
CHALMERS, Stephen 1
CHALMERS, Thomas 1
CHALMERS, Thomas Clark 4
CHALMERS, Thomas Hardie
CHALMERS, Thomas Mitchell 2
CHALMERS, Thomas Stuart
CHALMERS, William Everett 1
CHALMERS, William James 1
CHALMERS, William Wallace 4
CHAMBELLAN, Rene Paul 3
CHAMBERLAIN, Abiram 1
CHAMBERLAIN, Alexander Francis
CHAMBERLAIN, Allen 3
CHAMBERLAIN, Arthur Henry 2
CHAMBERLAIN, Arthur Van Doorn 5
CHAMBERLAIN, Charles Joseph 1
CHAMBERLAIN, Clark Wells 2
CHAMBERLAIN, Clarke E. 5
CHAMBERLAIN, Daniel Henry 1
CHAMBERLAIN, Dwight Lincoln 3
CHAMBERLAIN, Ebenzer Mattoon H
CHAMBERLAIN, Eugene Tyler 1
CHAMBERLAIN, Francis Asbury 1
CHAMBERLAIN, Frank 1
CHAMBERLAIN, Frederick Stanley 1
CHAMBERLAIN, George Agnew 4
CHAMBERLAIN, George Earle 1
CHAMBERLAIN, Glenn R. 4
CHAMBERLAIN, Henry 1
CHAMBERLAIN, Henry Richardson
CHAMBERLAIN, Henry Thomas 4
CHAMBERLAIN, Herbert Marvin 3
CHAMBERLAIN, Hiram Sanborn 1
CHAMBERLAIN, Mrs. Hope Summerell; Isaac Dearborn 1
CHAMBERLAIN, Jacob 1
CHAMBERLAIN, Jacob Payson H
CHAMBERLAIN, James Franklin 2
CHAMBERLAIN, John Curtis H
CHAMBERLAIN, John Loomis 2
CHAMBERLAIN, John M. 3
CHAMBERLAIN, Joseph Perkins 3
CHAMBERLAIN, Joseph Scudder 5
CHAMBERLAIN, Joshua Lawrence 1

CHAMBERLAIN, Leander Trowbridge 1
CHAMBERLAIN, Lucy Jefferies 5
CHAMBERLAIN, Mary Crowninshield Endicott 1
CHAMBERLAIN, Mellen 1
CHAMBERLAIN, Montague 1
CHAMBERLAIN, Nathan Henry H
CHAMBERLAIN, Orville Tryon 4
CHAMBERLAIN, Oscar Pearl 1
CHAMBERLAIN, Paul Mellen 1
CHAMBERLAIN, Robert F. 4
CHAMBERLAIN, Samuel Selwyn 1
CHAMBERLAIN, W. Lawrence 4
CHAMBERLAIN, William Isaac 1
CHAMBERLAIN, William W. 2
CHAMBERLAIN, Winthrop Burr 4
CHAMBERLAINE, William 1
CHAMBERLAYNE, Catharine Jane 1
CHAMBERLAYNE, Churchill Gibson 1
CHAMBERLAYNE, Lewis Parke 1
CHAMBERLIN, Chester Harvey 1
CHAMBERLIN, Clayton Jenkins 1
CHAMBERLIN, Edson Joseph 1
CHAMBERLIN, F. Tolles 4
CHAMBERLIN, Frederick 2
CHAMBERLIN, George Ellsworth 5
CHAMBERLIN, Harry Dwight 2
CHAMBERLIN, Henry Barrett 1
CHAMBERLIN, Henry Harmon 3
CHAMBERLIN, Joseph Edgar 1
CHAMBERLIN, Joseph Hanson 3
CHAMBERLIN, McKendree Hypes 4
CHAMBERLIN, Rollin Thomas 2
CHAMBERLIN, Stephen J. 5
CHAMBERLIN, Thomas Chrowder 1
CHAMBERLIN, Walter Howard 4
CHAMBERLIN, William H(enry) 5
CHAMBERLIN, Willis Arden 4
CHAMBERS, Charles Augustus 5
CHAMBERS, Charles Carroll 3
CHAMBERS, Charles Edward 2
CHAMBERS, David H
CHAMBERS, David Laurence 4
CHAMBERS, Edward 1
CHAMBERS, Ezekiel Forman H
CHAMBERS, Francis T, Jr. 5
CHAMBERS, Francis T. 1
CHAMBERS, Frank Taylor 1
CHAMBERS, Frank White 4
CHAMBERS, George H
CHAMBERS, Henry Edward 1
CHAMBERS, Henry H. 1
CHAMBERS, I. Mench 3
CHAMBERS, James H
CHAMBERS, John 1
CHAMBERS, Julius 1
CHAMBERS, Lenoir 5
CHAMBERS, Mary Davoren 1
CHAMBERS, Myron Gossette 4
CHAMBERS, Othniel Robert 3

CHAMBERS, Porter Flewellen 4
CHAMBERS, Robert 1
CHAMBERS, Robert 3
CHAMBERS, Robert Augustus 3
CHAMBERS, Robert Craig 2
CHAMBERS, Robert Foster 2
CHAMBERS, Robert William
CHAMBERS, Stuart Munson 4
CHAMBERS, Talbot Wilson H
CHAMBERS, Victor John 5
CHAMBERS, W. Irving 4
CHAMBERS, Walter Boughton 2
CHAMBERS, Will Grant 2
CHAMBERS, William 3
CHAMBERS, William Earl 4
CHAMBERS, William Lee 4
CHAMBERS, William Nesbitt 2
CHAMBLESS, John Robert 5
CHAMBLIN, Walter Williams Jr. 1
CHAMBLISS, Alexander Wilds 2
CHAMBLISS, Charles Edward 5
CHAMBLISS, Hardee 2
CHAMBRE, A. St John 1
CHAMLEE, Aquila 4
CHAMLEE, Mario 4
CHAMLEE, Mario 5
CHAMOT, Emile Monnin 3
CHAMOVE, Arnold S. 2
CHAMPION, Charles Sumner 1
CHAMPION, Epaphroditus H
CHAMPION, Fritz Roy 1
CHAMPION, John B. 3
CHAMPLAIN, Samuel H
CHAMPLIN, Christopher Grant
CHAMPLIN, Edwin Ross 1
CHAMPLIN, John Denison 1
CHAMPLIN, John Wayne 1
CHAMPLIN, Stephen H
CHAMPNEY, Benjamin 1
CHAMPNEY, Elizabeth Williams 1
CHAMPNEY, James Wells 1
CHANCA, Diego Alvarez H
CHANCE, Edwin Mickley 3
CHANCE, Henry Martyn 1
CHANCE, Jesse Clifton 1
CHANCE, Julie Grinnell 1
CHANCEL, Ludovic 1
CHANCELLOR, Charles Williams 1
CHANCELLOR, Eustathius A. 1
CHANCELLOR, William Estabrook 4
CHANCEY, Robert Edward Lee 2
CHANCHE, John Mary Joseph H
CHANDLER, Albert Brown 1
CHANDLER, Albert Edward 3
CHANDLER, Alexander J. 4
CHANDLER, Alfred Dupont 1
CHANDLER, Alfred N(oblit) 5
CHANDLER, Algernon Bertrand Jr. 1
CHANDLER, Anna Curtis 5
CHANDLER, Asa Crawford 1
CHANDLER, Bert D. 2
CHANDLER, Charles 1
CHANDLER, Charles 'deForest 1
CHANDLER, Charles Frederick 1
CHANDLER, Charles Henry 1
CHANDLER, Charles Quarles 2
CHANDLER, Elbert Milam 5
CHANDLER, Elizabeth Margaret H
CHANDLER, Francis Ward 1

CHANDLER, Frank Wadleigh 2
CHANDLER, Fremont Augustus 3
CHANDLER, George Brinton 2
CHANDLER, George Garvin 5
CHANDLER, Harry 2
CHANDLER, Izora 1
CHANDLER, Jefferson Paul 2
CHANDLER, John H
CHANDLER, John Gorham 1
CHANDLER, John Greene H
CHANDLER, John Winthrop H
CHANDLER, Joseph Hayes
CHANDLER, Joseph Ripley H
CHANDLER, Julian Alvin Carroll 1
CHANDLER, Katherine 5
CHANDLER, Kent 5
CHANDLER, Lloyd Horwitz 2
CHANDLER, Peleg Whitman H
CHANDLER, Percy Milton 2
CHANDLER, Philip 5
CHANDLER, Ralph Bradford 5
CHANDLER, Raymond Thornton 3
CHANDLER, Seth Carlo 1
CHANDLER, Theodore Edson 2
CHANDLER, Thomas 3
CHANDLER, Thomas Alberter
CHANDLER, Thomas Bradbury H
CHANDLER, Walter 4
CHANDLER, Walter Marion 1
CHANDLER, William Eaton 1
CHANDLER, William George 4
CHANDLER, William Henry * 1
CHANDLER, William Jessup 4
CHANDLER, Zachariah H
CHANDOR, Douglas 3
CHANEL, Gabrielle (Bonheur) (Coco)
CHANEY, James Eugene 4
CHANEY, John H
CHANEY, John Crawford 3
CHANEY, Lon H
CHANEY, Lon 4
CHANEY, Lucian West 1
CHANEY, Morris J. 3
CHANEY, Newcomb Kinney 4
CHANEY, Novetus Holland 1
CHANEY, Ralph Hill 4
CHANEY, Stewart 5
CHANFRAU, Francis S. 5
CHANG, Hsin-Hai 5
CHANG, John Myun 4
CHANG 'AND ENG H
CHANIS, Daniel 2
CHANLER, Lewis Stuyvesant
CHANLER, Lewis Stuyvesant 4
CHANLER, Margaret 3
CHANLER, Theodore Ward 4
CHANLER, William Astor 1
CHANNING, Edward 1
CHANNING, Edward Tyrrell H
CHANNING, George 3
CHANNING, Grace Ellery 1
CHANNING, John Parke 2
CHANNING, Walter 1
CHANNING, Walter H
CHANNING, William Ellery 1
CHANNING, William Ellery H
CHANNING, William Francis 1
CHANNING, William Henry H
CHANNON, Frank Ernest 1
CHANUTE, Octave 1
CHAPEAU, Ellen 4

CHAPELLE, 1
Placide Louis
CHAPIN, Aaron Lucius H
CHAPIN, Alfred Clark 1
CHAPIN, Alfred H. 4
CHAPIN, Anna Alice 1
CHAPIN, Arthur Beebe 2
CHAPIN, Augusta J. 1
CHAPIN, 1
Benjamin Chester
CHAPIN, Calvin H
CHAPIN, 1
Charles Frederic
CHAPIN, Charles Sumner 1
CHAPIN, Charles Value 1
CHAPIN, H
Chester William
CHAPIN, 5
Cornelia Van Auken
CHAPIN, 5
E(dward) Barton
CHAPIN, Edward 3
Whitman
CHAPIN, Edward Young 3
CHAPIN, Edwin Hubbell H
CHAPIN, Francis 4
CHAPIN, Fred H. 3
CHAPIN, Graham Hurd H
CHAPIN, Henry Barton 1
CHAPIN, Henry Dwight 2
CHAPIN, Henry Edgerton 1
CHAPIN, Howard Millar 1
CHAPIN, James Paul 4
CHAPIN, John Bassett 1
CHAPIN, Lloyd Walter 4
CHAPIN, H
Mrs. Jane Catherine Louise Value
CHAPIN, Robert Colt 1
CHAPIN, Roy Dikeman 1
CHAPIN, Selden 4
CHAPIN, 3
William Wallace
CHAPIN, 4
Willis McDonald
CHAPLIN, 4
Henry Prescott
CHAPLIN, James Crossan 5
CHAPLIN, Jeremiah H
CHAPLIN, John Howard 3
CHAPLIN, 1
William Edwards
CHAPLIN, 1
Winfield Scott
CHAPLINE, Jesse Grant 1
CHAPLINE, Vance Duncan 5
CHAPMAN, Alvah H. Sr. 4
CHAPMAN, H
Alvan Wentworth
CHAPMAN, Andrew Grant H
CHAPMAN, Arthur 1
CHAPMAN, Arthur 3
CHAPMAN, H
Augustus Alexandria
CHAPMAN, Bird Beers H
CHAPMAN, 1
Carlton Theodore
CHAPMAN, Charles H
CHAPMAN, 2
Charles Clarke
CHAPMAN, 2
Charles Edward
CHAPMAN, Charles Hiram 3
CHAPMAN, 4
Charles Shepard
CHAPMAN, Clowry 3
CHAPMAN, 5
Daniel Knowlton
CHAPMAN, 3
David Carpenter
CHAPMAN, 5
Dwight Westley, Jr.
CHAPMAN, E. B. 3
CHAPMAN, 3
Edward Mortimer
CHAPMAN, Edwin Garner 4
CHAPMAN, 3
Elbridge Gerry
CHAPMAN, Elverton R. 1
CHAPMAN, Emmanuel 2
CHAPMAN, Ervin S. 1
CHAPMAN, Francis 1
CHAPMAN, Frank Elmo 1
CHAPMAN, Frank Michler 2
CHAPMAN, Frederic A. H
CHAPMAN, 4
Frederick Lewis
CHAPMAN, 5
George Herbert
CHAPMAN, Gerald 4
Howard
CHAPMAN, Harry Powell 3

CHAPMAN, Henry H
CHAPMAN, 1
Henry Cadwalader
CHAPMAN, Henry Leland 1
CHAPMAN, Horace L. 3
CHAPMAN, Howard Rufus 2
CHAPMAN, Ira T. 3
CHAPMAN, J. H. 1
CHAPMAN, J. Wilbur 1
CHAPMAN, James Alfred 4
CHAPMAN, James Blaine 2
CHAPMAN, James Crosby 1
CHAPMAN, James Russell 4
CHAPMAN, 2
James Wilkinson Jr.
CHAPMAN, John * H
CHAPMAN, John (Arthur) 5
CHAPMAN, John A. 3
CHAPMAN, John Gadsby H
CHAPMAN, John Grant H
CHAPMAN, John Jay 5
CHAPMAN, John Martin 1
CHAPMAN, John Wayne 4
CHAPMAN, Joseph 2
CHAPMAN, Judson W. 3
CHAPMAN, H
Katharine Hopkins
CHAPMAN, 4
Kenneth William
CHAPMAN, Levi S(nell) 5
CHAPMAN, Lila May 1
CHAPMAN, Maria Weston H
CHAPMAN, 1
Mrs. Woodallen
CHAPMAN, Nathaniel H
CHAPMAN, Paul Wilber 3
CHAPMAN, 4
Pleasant Thomas
CHAPMAN, Reuben H
CHAPMAN, 1
Robert Hollister
CHAPMAN, Ross McClure 2
CHAPMAN, Roy H. 3
CHAPMAN, Theodore S. 2
CHAPMAN, 4
Theron Taggert
CHAPMAN, 4
Thomas Garfield
CHAPMAN, Virgil Munday 3
CHAPMAN, 5
W(ilbert) M(cLeod)
CHAPMAN, William Edgar 4
CHAPMAN, 2
William Gerard
CHAPMAN, H
William Williams
CHAPPEL, Alonzo H
CHAPPEL, James Edward 3
CHAPPELL, H
Absalom Harris
CHAPPELL, Edward A. 3
CHAPPELL, Edwin B. 2
CHAPPELL, 3
George Shepard
CHAPPELL, John Joel H
CHAPPELL, Joseph John 4
CHAPPELL, 5
Matthew N(apoleon)
CHAPPELL, 1
Walter Franklin
CHAPPELL, Will H. 2
CHAPPELLE, 2
Benjamin Franklin
CHAPPELLE, William D. 1
CHAPPLE, Joe Mitchell 3
CHARBONNEAU, Joseph 3
CHARBONNEAU, 5
Louis Henry
CHARDON, Jean Baptiste H
CHARIPPER, Harry A. 5
CHARLES, 1
Benjamin Hynes
CHARLES, Dorothy 3
CHARLES, Frances 5
CHARLES, Joseph D. 4
CHARLES, William H
CHARLES, 3
William Barclay
CHARLESS, Joseph H
CHARLEVOIX,
Pierre Francois Xavier 'de
CHARLS, George Herbert 2
CHARLTON, 5
Charles Magnus
CHARLTON, Clyde B. 3
CHARLTON, Earle Perry 1
CHARLTON, George James 1

CHARLTON, James 1
CHARLTON, Joseph W. 3
CHARLTON, Loudon 1
CHARLTON, Paul 1
CHARLTON, H
Robert Milledge
CHARLTON, H
Thomas Usher Pulaski
CHARLTON, 1
Walter Glasco
CHARNAUX-GRILLET, Raymond Paul 5
CHARNOCK, 5
Donald Austin
CHARSKE, F. W. 3
CHARTERS, 3
Werrett Wallace
CHARTRAND, Joseph 1
CHASE, Adelaide Cole 4
CHASE, Agnes Mrs. 4
CHASE, Arthur Horace 1
CHASE, Arthur Minturn 2
CHASE, Benjamin E. 1
CHASE, 1
Benjamin Franklin
CHASE, Charles E. 1
CHASE, Charles Parker 1
CHASE, Civilian Louis 4
CHASE, Cleveland King 3
CHASE, Dudley 1
CHASE, Edna Woolman 3
CHASE, Ellen 4
CHASE, Emory Albert 1
CHASE, Ethan Allen 1
CHASE, Eugene Parker 5
CHASE, Frank David 1
CHASE, Frank Herbert 1
CHASE, 2
Frederic Hathaway
CHASE, 1
Frederick Augustus
CHASE, 1
Frederick Lincoln
CHASE, 2
Frederick Starkweather
CHASE, George 1
CHASE, George Colby 1
CHASE, George Davis 2
CHASE, George Francis 1
CHASE, George Henry 3
CHASE, George Lewis 1
CHASE, George William H
CHASE, H. Stephen 5
CHASE, Harold Stuart 1
CHASE, Harold Stuart 4
CHASE, Harold Taylor 5
CHASE, 5
Harrie Brigham Chase
CHASE, Harry Woodburn 3
CHASE, Harvey Stuart 4
CHASE, Henry Sabin 1
CHASE, Irah H
CHASE, Irving Hall 3
CHASE, Isaac McKim 1
CHASE, J. Franklin 1
CHASE, J. Smeaton 1
CHASE, James Mitchell 3
CHASE, Jehu Valentine H
CHASE, H
Jeremiah Townley
CHASE, Jessie Anderson 5
CHASE, John Calvin 1
CHASE, John Carroll 1
CHASE, John F. 4
CHASE, Joseph Cummings 2
CHASE, Joshua Coffin 2
CHASE, Lewis 1
CHASE, H
Lucien Bonaparte
CHASE, Mary Ellen 5
CHASE, Mrs. Lewis 3
CHASE, Paul Addison 4
CHASE, Philander H
CHASE, Pliny Earle H
CHASE, Ray P. 2
CHASE, Robert Howland H
CHASE, Salmon Portland H
CHASE, Samuel * H
CHASE, Solon 1
CHASE, Stanley Perkins 3
CHASE, Thomas 1
CHASE, William Martin 1
CHASE, William Merritt 1
CHASE, William Sheafe 1
CHASSAIGNAC, 2
Charles Louis
CHASTAIN, Elijah Webb H
CHATARD, 1
Francis Silas Marean
CHATARD, Thomas Marean 4
CHATBURN, 1
George Richard
CHATFIELD, Thomas Ives 1
CHATFIELD, 1
Walter Henry

CHATFIELD, 5
William Hayden
CHATFIELD-TAYLOR, Hobart C. 2
CHATHAM, 1'st 'earl H
CHATHAM, Thurmond 3
CHATTERS, Carl Hallack 4
CHATTERTON, Fenimore 3
CHATTERTON, Ruth 4
CHAUMONOT,
Pierre Joseph Marie
CHAUNCEY, Isaac H
CHAUNCY, Charles * H
CHAUTEMPS, Camille
CHAUVENET, Regis 1
CHAUVENET, William H
CHAUVENET, 4
William Marc
CHAVE, Ernest J. 4
CHAVEZ, Dennis 4
CHAVIS, John H
CHEADLE, John Begg 4
CHEATHAM, H
Benjamin Franklin
CHEATHAM, 5
Elliott Evans
CHEATHAM, John Henry 3
CHEATHAM, 5
Owen Robertson
CHEATHAM, Richard H
CHEATNAM, B. Frank 4
CHEATNAM, Joseph J. 2
CHEAVENS, 5
David Anderson
CHECKLEY, John H
CHEEK, F. J. Jr. 3
CHEER, Miss H
CHEESMAN, Forman H
CHEETHAM, James H
CHEEVER, David 3
CHEEVER, 1
David Williams
CHEEVER, Ezekiel H
CHEEVER, H
George Barrell
CHEEVER, Harriet A. 1
CHEEVER, H
Henry Theodore
CHEFFETZ, Asa 4
CHEFFEY, John Howard 5
CHEHAB, Fuad 5
CHEKIB, Bey 5
CHELDELIN, Vernon H. 4
CHELEY, Frank Howbert 3
CHEN, Yi 5
CHENERY, 5
Christopher Tompkins
CHENERY, 5
William Elisha
CHENERY, Winthrop Holt 3
CHENEY, Albert Nelson 1
CHENEY, 3
Archibald Myron
CHENEY, Azio E. 4
CHENEY, 5
Benjamin Austin
CHENEY, H
Benjamin Pierce
CHENEY, Charles 2
CHENEY, 3
Charles Baldwin
CHENEY, Charles Edward 1
CHENEY, Charles Henry 2
CHENEY, Clarence Orion 2
CHENEY, Clifford D. 1
CHENEY, Ednah Dow 1
CHENEY, Elmer Erwood 1
CHENEY, Frank, Jr. 5
CHENEY, 5
Frank Woodbridge
CHENEY, Harold Clark 3
CHENEY, Howell 1
CHENEY, James William 1
CHENEY, Jerome Lucius 1
CHENEY, John H
CHENEY, John Moses 1
CHENEY, John Richard 4
CHENEY, John Vance 1
CHENEY, Louis Richmond 2
CHENEY, Monroe George 1
CHENEY, Orion Howard 1
CHENEY, Person Colby 1
CHENEY, Russell 2
CHENEY, Seth Wells H
CHENEY, 2
Sherwood Alfred
CHENEY, Thomas Perkins 3
CHENEY, Ward H
CHENEY, Ward 1
CHENEY, Warren 1
CHENEY, William Atwell 1
CHENEY, William Fitch 1
CHENG, Chen 4
CHENNAULT, Claire Lee 3

CHENOWETH, 1
Alexander Crawford
CHENOWETH, 4
Caroline 'van Deusen
CHENOWETH, 1
Catherine Richardson
CHENOWETH, 5
David Macpherson
CHENTUNG, 5
Liang-Cheng, Sir
CHERINGTON, 4
Charles Richards
CHERINGTON, Paul Terry 2
CHERONIS, 4
Nicholas Dimitrius
CHERRIE, George Kruck 2
CHERRINGTON, 2
Ernest Hurst
CHERRY, C. Waldo 4
CHERRY, Charles 4
CHERRY, Francis A. 4
CHERRY, Henry Hardin 4
CHERRY, James William 1
CHERRY, Kathryn Evelyn 4
CHERRY, Robert Gregg 3
CHERRY, 4
Thomas Crittenden
CHERRY,
Ulysses Simpson Grant
CHERRY, Walter L. 2
CHERRY,
Wilbur Harkness
CHERRY, William Stamps 4
CHERWELL,
1'st Baron 'of Oxford
CHESEBROUGH, H
Caroline
CHESEBROUGH,
Robert Augustus
CHESHIRE,
Fleming Duncan
CHESHIRE, H
Joseph Blount
CHESLEY, Albert Justus 3
CHESNEY, Alan Mason 4
CHESNEY, Cummings C. 4
CHESNUT, James Jr. H
CHESNUT, James Lyons 2
CHESNUT, Victor King 1
CHESNUT, 1
William Calvin
CHESNUTT,
Charles Waddell
CHESNUTT,
Nelson Alexander
CHESSIN, Alexander 5
CHESTER,
Albert Huntington
CHESTER, Alden 1
CHESTER, Colby Mitchel 4
CHESTER,
Colby Mitchell
CHESTER,
Colby Mitchell
CHESTER, Eliza 4
CHESTER, Frank Dyer 4
CHESTER,
Frederick Dixon
CHESTER,
George Randolph
CHESTER, Hawley 4
Thomas
CHESTER, John Needels 1
CHESTER, Joseph Lemuel H
CHESTER,
K(enneth) Starr
CHESTER, Samuel Hall 1
CHESTER,
Wayland Morgan
CHESTER,
William Merrill
CHESTERMAN,
Francis John
CHESTERMAN,
William Dallas
CHESTON, J. Hamilton 4
CHESTON,
Radcliffe, Jr.
CHETLAIN, Arthur Henry 4
CHETLAIN,
Augustus Louis
CHETTA, Nicholas John 4
CHETWOOD,
Charles Howard
CHETWOOD, John 5
CHETWOOD, William H
CHEVALIER, John B. 4
CHEVALIER,
Maurice (Auguste)
CHEVALIER, Stuart 4
CHEVALIER,
Willard Townshend
CHEVEE,
Charles Humbert
CHEVER, James W.

CHEVERTON, Cecil Frank 3
CHEVERUS, Jean Louis Anne Magdelene Lefebvre 'de H
CHEVES, Langdon H
CHEVIGNY, Hector 4
CHEVRIER, Edgar Rodolphe Eugene 4
CHEW, Benjamin H
CHEW, Beverly 1
CHEW, Ng Poon 4
CHEW, Oswald 2
CHEW, Samuel Claggett 1
CHEW, Samuel Claggett 3
CHEWNING, Edmund Taylor 5
CHEYDLEUR, Frederic Daniel 2
CHEYNEY, Barton 4
CHEYNEY, Edward Gheen 2
CHEYNEY, Edward Potts 2
CHEZ, Joseph 5
CHICHESTER, Sir Francis 5
CHICHESTER, Richard Henry Lee 1
CHICKERING, Allen Lawrence 3
CHICKERING, Charles A. 1
CHICKERING, John White 1
CHICKERING, Jonas H
CHICKERING, William Elbridge
CHIDESTER, John Young 3
CHIDLEY, Howard James 4
CHIDSEY, Thomas McKeen 3
CHIDWICK, John Patrick Sylvester 1
CHIEF JOSEPH H
CHIERA, Edward 2
CHIFLEY, The Rt Hon Joseph Benedict 3
CHILBERG, John Edward 4
CHILCOTT, Ellery Channing 1
CHILCOTT, George Miles H
CHILD, Charles Manning 1
CHILD, Clarence Griffin 2
CHILD, Clement Dexter 1
CHILD, David Lee 1
CHILD, Edwin Burrage 1
CHILD, Eleanor Dodge 2
CHILD, Francis James H
CHILD, Frank Samuel 1
CHILD, Fred S. 4
CHILD, George Newport 1
CHILD, Katherine Blake 3
CHILD, Lydia Maria Francis H
CHILD, Richard Washburn 1
CHILD, Thomas Jr. H
CHILDE, John H
CHILDERS, James Saxon 4
CHILDERS, Marvin Alonzo
CHILDERS, Sylvester Earl 2
CHILDRESS, John Whitsitt 4
CHILDRESS, Levi Wade 2
CHILDS, Arthur Edward 1
CHILDS, C. Frederick 3
CHILDS, Cephas Grier 1
CHILDS, Donald Smythe 4
CHILDS, Edward Powell 5
CHILDS, Eleanor Stuart 1
CHILDS, Eversley 3
CHILDS, Frank Aiken 1
CHILDS, Frank Hall 3
CHILDS, Geoffrey Stafford 3
CHILDS, George Theodore 4
CHILDS, George William 1
CHILDS, Harwood Lawrence 5
CHILDS, Henry A. 1
CHILDS, John Lewis 4
CHILDS, Joseph William 1
CHILDS, Prescott 5
CHILDS, Ross Renfroe 4
CHILDS, Samuel Beresford 4
CHILDS, Thomas H
CHILDS, Thomas Spencer 1
CHILDS, Timothy 1
CHILDS, William Hamlin 1
CHILES, Harry Linden 1
CHILES, James Alburn 5
CHILES, Joseph B. H
CHILLMAN, James, Jr. 5

CHILTON, Arthur Bounds 1
CHILTON, Cecil Hamilton 5
CHILTON, Cleo Madison 4
CHILTON, Horace 1
CHILTON, Robert S. 2
CHILTON, Samuel H
CHILTON, Thomas H
CHILTON, Thomas Hamilton 5
CHILTON, William Edwin 4
CHILTON, William Edwin Jr. 3
CHILTON, William Paris H
CHINARD, Gilbert 5
CHINDBLOM, Carl Richard 3
CHING, Cyrus Stuart 3
CHING, Cyrus Stuart 4
CHINLUND, Edwin F. 3
CHINN, Armstrong 3
CHINN, C. B. 3
CHINN, Joseph William 2
CHINN, Joseph William 4
CHINN, Thomas Withers 5
CHIPERFIELD, Burnett Mitchell 1
CHIPERFIELD, Robert Bruce 5
CHIPMAN, Daniel H
CHIPMAN, John Logan H
CHIPMAN, John Smith 1
CHIPMAN, John Sniffen 1
CHIPMAN, Nathaniel 1
CHIPMAN, Norris Bowie 3
CHIPMAN, Norton Parker 1
CHIPMAN, Ward 1
CHIPMAN, William Pendleton 1
CHIRSMEN, James Stone H
CHIRSTIE, Gabriel H
CHIRUG, James Thomas 5
CHISHOLM, Hugh J. 1
CHISHOLM, Hugh J. 1
CHISHOLM, Julian J. 5
CHISHOLM, Sir Joseph Andrew 3
CHISHOLM, William 1
CHISHOLM, William Sr. 1
CHISLETT, Howard Roy 1
CHISOLM, Alexander Robert
CHISOLM, Alexander Robert 4
CHISOLM, John Julian 5
CHISUM, John Simpson H
CHITTENDEN, Frank Hurlbut 1
CHITTENDEN, Hiram Martin 1
CHITTENDEN, J. Brace 1
CHITTENDEN, Kate S. 2
CHITTENDEN, Martin H
CHITTENDEN, Russell Henry 2
CHITTENDEN, Simeon Baldwin H
CHITTENDEN, Thomas H
CHITTENDEN, Thomas Cotton H
CHITTENDEN, William Lawrence 1
CHITWOOD, Joseph Howard 2
CHITWOOD, Oliver Perry 5
CHIVERS, Elijah Eynon 1
CHIVERS, Thomas Holley H
CHIVINGTON, John Milton H
CHOATE, Augusta 5
CHOATE, Charles Francis 1
CHOATE, Charles Francis Jr.
CHOATE, Isaac Bassett 1
CHOATE, Isaac W. 1
CHOATE, Joseph Hodges 1
CHOATE, Joseph Hodges Jr. 4
CHOATE, Joseph Kittredge
CHOATE, Nathaniel 4
CHOATE, Robert Burnett 4
CHOATE, Rufus H
CHOATE, Washington 1
CHOATE, William Gardner 1
CHODORCOFF, William 4
CHODOROV, Frank 4
CHOLMELEY-JONES, R. G. 1
CHOPIN, Kate 1
CHOQUETTE, Charles Auguste 4
CHORIS, Ludovik H
CHORPENNING, George H
CHOTZINOFF, Samuel 4

CHOUINARD, Carroll 5
CHOUINARD, Mrs. Nelbert Murphy 5
CHOULES, John Overton H
CHOUTEAU, Jean Pierre H
CHOUTEAU, Pierre H
CHOUTEAU, Pierre 1
CHOUTEAU, Pierre Auguste H
CHOUTEAU, Rene H
CHOVET, Abraham H
CHREITZBERG, Augustus McKee 5
CHRESTMAN, Marion Nelson 2
CHRISMAN, Arthur Bowie 3
CHRISMAN, Edward Robert 1
CHRISMAN, Lewis Herbert 4
CHRISMAN, Oscar 1
CHRIST, Harding Simon 5
CHRISTENBERRY, Charles W. 4
CHRISTENBERRY, Robert Keaton 5
CHRISTENSEN, Asher Norman 3
CHRISTENSEN, Bernard Victor 3
CHRISTENSEN, George Francis 4
CHRISTENSEN, J. J. 4
CHRISTENSEN, John Cornelius 3
CHRISTENSEN, Niels 1
CHRISTENSEN, Niels Anton 3
CHRISTENSEN, Parley Parker 3
CHRISTENSON, John August 2
CHRISTENSON, Louis P. 4
CHRISTENSON, Walter E. 5
CHRISTIAN, Andrew Dunscomb 2
CHRISTIAN, Edmund Adolph 1
CHRISTIAN, Eugene 1
CHRISTIAN, Frank Lamar 4
CHRISTIAN, George Busby, Jr. 5
CHRISTIAN, George Eastland 2
CHRISTIAN, George Llewellyn 4
CHRISTIAN, Henry Asbury 3
CHRISTIAN, John L. 5
CHRISTIAN, John Tyler 1
CHRISTIAN, Palmer 2
CHRISTIAN, Robert J. 4
CHRISTIAN, Sanders Lewis 2
CHRISTIAN, William H
CHRISTIAN, William Peter 2
CHRISTIANCY, Isaac Peckham H
CHRISTIANS, William F. 3
CHRISTIANSEN, Arthur 4
CHRISTIANSEN, Edward S, IV 5
CHRISTIANSEN, F. Melius 3
CHRISTIANSEN, N. Woodruff 4
CHRISTIANSON, Adolph Marcus 3
CHRISTIANSON, John Oscar 4
CHRISTIANSON, Theodore 2
CHRISTIANSON, Theodore 3
CHRISTIE, Alexander 4
CHRISTIE, Alexander Graham
CHRISTIE, Arthur Carlisle 3
CHRISTIE, Charles Johnson 4
CHRISTIE, Francis Albert 4
CHRISTIE, James 1
CHRISTIE, Jane Johnstone 1
CHRISTIE, Lansdell Kisner
CHRISTIE, Luther Rice 1
CHRISTIE, R. E. 3
CHRISTIE, Robert 4
CHRISTIE, Robert James 4

CHRISTIE, Thomas Davidson 1
CHRISTIE, William Wallace 1
CHRISTISON, J. Sanderson 1
CHRISTMAN, Henry Jacob 2
CHRISTMAN, W. W. 1
CHRISTMAN, Warren Ursinus 1
CHRISTOL, Carl 5
CHRISTOPHER, Frederick 4
CHRISTOPHER, George H. 5
CHRISTOPHER, George T. 3
CHRISTOPHERSON-, Charles Andrew 3
CHRISTY, David H
CHRISTY, Earl 4
CHRISTY, Edwin P. H
CHRISTY, Howard Chandler 3
CHRISTY, Samuel Benedict 1
CHRISTY, William C. 3
CHRITTON, George Alvah 2
CHRYSLER, Jack Forker 3
CHRYSLER, Mintin Asbury 5
CHRYSLER, Walter Percy 1
CHRYST, Robert D. 3
CHRYSTIE, Thomas Ludlow 3
CHRYSTIE, Thomas Witter
CHUBB, Chester Niles 3
CHUBB, Edwin Watts 4
CHUBB, Hendon 4
CHUBB, Lewis Warrington 1
CHUBB, Percival 4
CHUBB, Thomas Caldecot 5
CHUBBUCK, Thomas H
CHUJOY, Anatole 4
CHUNDRIGAR, Ismail Ibrahim
CHUPP, Charles David 5
CHURCH, Alonzo H
CHURCH, Alonzo 1
CHURCH, Angelica Schuyler 3
CHURCH, Archibald 1
CHURCH, Arthur Latham 4
CHURCH, Augustus Byington
CHURCH, Benjamin * H
CHURCH, Benjamin Butler 3
CHURCH, Denver Samuel 3
CHURCH, Earl D. 4
CHURCH, Edward Bentley 1
CHURCH, Francis Pharcellus
CHURCH, Frank Henry 1
CHURCH, Frederick Edwin 1
CHURCH, Frederick Stuart 1
CHURCH, George Hervey 1
CHURCH, Henry Ward 1
CHURCH, Irving Porter 1
CHURCH, James Edward 4
CHURCH, John Adams 1
CHURCH, John Fertig 4
CHURCH, John Huston 3
CHURCH, Melville 1
CHURCH, Pharcellus H
CHURCH, Ralph Edwin 2
CHURCH, Randolph 5
CHURCH, Samuel Harden 1
CHURCH, William Conant 1
CHURCH, William E. 1
CHURCH, William Howell 1
CHURCHILL, Alfred Vance 1
CHURCHILL, Charles Samuel 1
CHURCHILL, Edward Delos 5
CHURCHILL, Everett Avery 3
CHURCHILL, Frank Edwin 2
CHURCHILL, Frank Spooner 4
CHURCHILL, George Bosworth 1
CHURCHILL, George Morton 5
CHURCHILL, Henry Stern 4

CHURCHILL, John Charles 1
CHURCHILL, John Wesley 1
CHURCHILL, Joseph Richmond 1
CHURCHILL, Julius Alonzo 4
CHURCHILL, Lady Randolph Spencer 1
CHURCHILL, Lida A. 5
CHURCHILL, Marlborough 2
CHURCHILL, Sir Winston 4
CHURCHILL, Thomas J. 1
CHURCHILL, Thomas William 1
CHURCHILL, William 3
CHURCHILL, Winston 2
CHURCHMAN, John Woolman 1
CHURCHMAN, Philip Hudson 5
CHURCHMAN, William Henry H
CHURCHWELL, William Montgomery H
CHUTE, A(aron) Hamilton 5
CHUTE, Arthur Hunt 1
CHUTE, Arthur Lambert 1
CHUTE, Charles Lionel 3
CHUTE, Horatio Nelson 1
CILLEY, Bradbury H
CILLEY, C. C. 5
CILLEY, Gordon Harper 1
CILLEY, Greenleaf 4
CILLEY, Jonathan Longfellow 1
CILLEY, Jonathan Prince 1
CILLEY, Joseph * H
CIMIOTTI, Gustave 5
CIOCCO, Antonio 5
CIST, Charles * 1
CIST, Henry Martyn 1
CIST, Jacob 1
CLAASSEN, Peter Walter 1
CLABAUGH, Harry M. 1
CLABAUGH, Hinton Graves 2
CLAFLIN, Arthur Whitman 1
CLAFLIN, Horace Brigham H
CLAFLIN, John 1
CLAFLIN, William 1
CLAGETT, Clifton H
CLAGETT, John Rozier 1
CLAGETT, Wyseman 1
CLAGHORN, George H
CLAGHORN, Kate Holladay
CLAGUE, Frank 3
CLAIBORNE, John H
CLAIBORNE, John Francis Hamtramck H
CLAIBORNE, John Herbert 1
CLAIBORNE, Nathaniel Herbert H
CLAIBORNE, Thomas * H
CLAIBORNE, William H
CLAIBORNE, William Charles Coles 1
CLAIBORNE, William Stirling
CLAIR, Edward L. 3
CLAIR, Matthew Wesley 2
CLAIRE, Richard Shaw 5
CLAMER, Guilliam Henry 4
CLANCY, Albert Worthington
CLANCY, Frank J. 3
CLANCY, Frank Willey 1
CLANCY, George Carpenter 4
CLANCY, John Richard 1
CLANCY, John W. 5
CLANCY, Robert H. 1
CLAP, Nathaniel H
CLAP, Thoms H
CLAPHAM, Thomas 4
CLAPP, Asa H
CLAPP, Asa William Henry H
CLAPP, Augustus Wilson 2
CLAPP, Charles Horace 1
CLAPP, Clift Rogers 1
CLAPP, Clyde Alvin 3
CLAPP, Cornelia Maria 1
CLAPP, Earle Hart 5
CLAPP, Edward Bull 1
CLAPP, Edwin Jones 1
CLAPP, Elmer Frederick 1
CLAPP, Frank Leslie 1

CLAPP, Franklin Halsted 2
CLAPP, Frederick Gardner 2
CLAPP, Gordon Rufus 4
CLAPP, Harold L. 4
CLAPP, Henry Austin 1
CLAPP, Herbert Codman 1
CLAPP, Jacob Crawford 4
CLAPP, John Mantle 5
CLAPP, Moses Edwin 1
CLAPP, Paul Spencer 3
CLAPP, Philip Greeley 3
CLAPP, Verner Warren 5
CLAPP, William Warland H
CLAPPER, Raymond 2
CLAPPER, Samuel Mott Duryea 1
CLARAHAN, Leo E. 4
CLARDY, John D. 4
CLARDY, Kit 4
CLARE, Arthur James 1
CLARE, Israel Smith 1
CLARITY, Frank Edmund 1
CLARK, A. Howard 1
CLARK, Abraham H
CLARK, Addison 4
CLARK, Albert Montgomery 3
CLARK, Albert Warren 1
CLARK, Alden Hyde 4
CLARK, Alfred Edward 3
CLARK, Allan 3
CLARK, Allan Jay 3
CLARK, Allen Culling 2
CLARK, Alson Skinner 2
CLARK, Alva Benson 3
CLARK, Alvan H
CLARK, Alvan Graham H
CLARK, Ambrose Williams H
CLARK, Anne Kinnier 5
CLARK, Annie Maria Lawrence 4
CLARK, Anson Luman 3
CLARK, Arthur Bridgman 2
CLARK, Arthur Bryan 2
CLARK, Arthur Elwood 3
CLARK, Arthur Henry 3
CLARK, Austin Hobart 3
CLARK, B. Preston 1
CLARK, Badger 3
CLARK, Barrett H. 3
CLARK, Barzilla Worth 2
CLARK, Bennett Champ 3
CLARK, Bert Boone 5
CLARK, Bobby 3
CLARK, Bonnell Wetmore 3
CLARK, C. P. 4
CLARK, Calvin Montague 2
CLARK, Cameron 3
CLARK, Caroline Richards 5
CLARK, Champ 1
CLARK, Charles H
CLARK, Charles Benjamin H
CLARK, Charles Cleveland 5
CLARK, Charles Dickson 1
CLARK, Charles Edgar 1
CLARK, Charles Edward 4
CLARK, Charles Finney 1
CLARK, Charles Heber 1
CLARK, Charles Hopkins 1
CLARK, Charles Martin 1
CLARK, Charles Upson 4
CLARK, Charles Walker 1
CLARK, Charles William 1
CLARK, Chase Addison 4
CLARK, Chester Frederic 3
CLARK, Christopher Henderson H
CLARK, Clarence Don 1
CLARK, Clarence Munroe 1
CLARK, Clarence Sewall 4
CLARK, Claude Lester 4
CLARK, Clifford Pease 3
CLARK, Cyrus J. 3
CLARK, D. Worth 3
CLARK, Dan Elbert 3
CLARK, Daniel * H
CLARK, David L. 1
CLARK, David Wasgate H
CLARK, Davis Wasgatt 1
CLARK, Derral LeRoy 5
CLARK, Donald Lemen 4
CLARK, Duncan Campbell 4
CLARK, Dwight Edwin 3
CLARK, Edgar Erastus 1
CLARK, Edson Lyman 1
CLARK, Edward 1
CLARK, Edward Brayton 5
CLARK, Edward Gay 2
CLARK, Edward Hardy 2
CLARK, Edward L. 3
CLARK, Edward Lee 4
CLARK, Edward Lord 1
CLARK, Edward P. 1
CLARK, Edward W. 2
CLARK, Elijah H
CLARK, Eliot Round 4
CLARK, Ellery Harding 2
CLARK, Elmer Talmage 4
CLARK, Elroy Newton 4
CLARK, Emily 3
CLARK, Emmons 1
CLARK, Emory W. 3
CLARK, Eugene Bradley 2
CLARK, Eugene Francis 1
CLARK, Ezra Jr. H
CLARK, Ezra Westcote 2
CLARK, F. Lewis 1
CLARK, Felicia Buttz 4
CLARK, Felton Grandison 5
CLARK, Fontaine Riker 4
CLARK, Francis Edward 1
CLARK, Frank 4
CLARK, Frank Hodges 3
CLARK, Frank Sylvester 3
CLARK, Frank William 2
CLARK, Franklin H
CLARK, Franklin Jones 4
CLARK, Fred 5
CLARK, Fred Emerson 2
CLARK, Fred George 5
CLARK, Fred Pope 1
CLARK, Frederic Simmons 1
CLARK, Frederick Huntington 5
CLARK, Frederick John 1
CLARK, Frederick M. 5
CLARK, Frederick Pareis 5
CLARK, Frederick Timothy 1
CLARK, Friend Ebenezer 5
CLARK, Gaylord Parsons 1
CLARK, George 4
CLARK, George Archibald 1
CLARK, George Campbell 4
CLARK, George Crawford 1
CLARK, George Halford 3
CLARK, George Hardy 4
CLARK, George Harlow 5
CLARK, George J. 3
CLARK, George Lindenberg 5
CLARK, George Luther 5
CLARK, George Ramsey 2
CLARK, George Rogers H
CLARK, George Thomas 1
CLARK, George Whitefield 1
CLARK, Geroge Larkin 4
CLARK, Grenville 4
CLARK, Grenville 5
CLARK, Grover 1
CLARK, Hamilton Burdick 5
CLARK, Hannah Belle 4
CLARK, Harold Benjamin 3
CLARK, Harold Johnson 3
CLARK, Harold Terry 4
CLARK, Harry Camp 3
CLARK, Harry Granville 1
CLARK, Harry Henderson 3
CLARK, Harry Willard 4
CLARK, Harvey Cyrus 1
CLARK, Henry A. 3
CLARK, Henry Benjamin 5
CLARK, Henry Hunt 5
CLARK, Henry James H
CLARK, Henry Selby H
CLARK, Henry W. 2
CLARK, Herbert W. 4
CLARK, Herma N. 3
CLARK, Horace Francis H
CLARK, Horace Spencer 1
CLARK, Horatio David 3
CLARK, Howard J. 1
CLARK, Howard V. 4
CLARK, Hubert Lyman 2
CLARK, Imogen 1
CLARK, Isaac 1
CLARK, Isaiah Raymond 1
CLARK, J. Reuben Jr. 4
CLARK, J. Ross 1
CLARK, J. Scott 1
CLARK, James H
CLARK, James Edward 5
CLARK, James Edwin 2
CLARK, James G. 5
CLARK, James Truman 1
CLARK, James Waddey 1
CLARK, James West H
CLARK, Janet Howell 5
CLARK, Jesse Redman 1
CLARK, John H
CLARK, John Arvine 3
CLARK, John Bates 1
CLARK, John Brittan 2
CLARK, John Bullock H
CLARK, John Bullock 1
CLARK, John Chamberlain H
CLARK, John Cheesman 2
CLARK, John Edward 1
CLARK, John Emory 1
CLARK, John Goodrich 1
CLARK, John Howe 1
CLARK, John Jesse 4
CLARK, John Lewis 5
CLARK, John Marshall 1
CLARK, John Maurice 4
CLARK, John Robert 3
CLARK, John Spencer 4
CLARK, Jonas H
CLARK, Jonas Gilman H
CLARK, Joseph Bourne 1
CLARK, Joseph James 5
CLARK, Joseph Leon 4
CLARK, Joseph Sylvester H
CLARK, Josephine Adelaide 4
CLARK, Julian Jerome 5
CLARK, Kate Upson 1
CLARK, Keith 3
CLARK, L. Pierce 1
CLARK, Lee Hinchman 4
CLARK, Lester Williams 1
CLARK, Lewis Gaylord H
CLARK, Lewis Whitehouse 1
CLARK, Lincoln H
CLARK, Lindley Daniel 4
CLARK, Linwood L. 5
CLARK, Lloyd Montgomery 5
CLARK, Lot H
CLARK, Lucius Charles 2
CLARK, Mallie Adkin 1
CLARK, Marguerite 1
CLARK, Melville 1
CLARK, Melville 3
CLARK, Melvin Green 1
CLARK, Meriweather Lewis H
CLARK, Myron H. 3
CLARK, Myron Holley H
CLARK, Nathaniel Walling 1
CLARK, Olynthus B. 1
CLARK, Paul Burroughes 4
CLARK, Paul Dennison 5
CLARK, Paul Foster 5
CLARK, Percy Hamilton 4
CLARK, Randolph 4
CLARK, Ray Henry 3
CLARK, Reed Paige 3
CLARK, Rensselaer Weston 4
CLARK, Robert H
CLARK, Robert Bruce 5
CLARK, Robert Cariton 1
CLARK, Robert Lanier 4
CLARK, Robert Thomas Jr. 3
CLARK, Roe Sidney 3
CLARK, Roland Eugene 3
CLARK, Rollin M. 3
CLARK, Roy Wallace 2
CLARK, Rufus Wheelwright H
CLARK, Rufus Wheelwright 1
CLARK, Rush H
CLARK, Sam L. 4
CLARK, Samuel H
CLARK, Samuel M. 1
CLARK, Samuel Wesley 3
CLARK, Sheldon H
CLARK, Sheldon 3
CLARK, Solomon Henry 1
CLARK, Stephen Carlton 4
CLARK, Stephen Cutter 3
CLARK, Taliaferro 2
CLARK, Theodore 3
CLARK, Theodore Minot 1
CLARK, Thomas Arkle 1
CLARK, Thomas Collier 1
CLARK, Thomas Curtis 3
CLARK, Thomas Frederic 4
CLARK, Thomas Harvey 1
CLARK, Thomas March 1
CLARK, Victor Selden 3
CLARK, Virginius E. 2
CLARK, W. A. Graham 3
CLARK, Wallace 2
CLARK, Walter * 1
CLARK, Walter Appleton 1
CLARK, Walter Eli 2
CLARK, Walter Ernest 3
CLARK, Walter Eugene 4
CLARK, Walter Loane 1
CLARK, Walter VanTilburg 5
CLARK, Walton 1
CLARK, Washington A. 2
CLARK, Wilbur 4
CLARK, Will L. 4
CLARK, William * H
CLARK, William 3
CLARK, William Andrews 1
CLARK, William Andrews Jr. 1
CLARK, William Anthony 4
CLARK, William Arthur 1
CLARK, William Braddock 1
CLARK, William Bullock 1
CLARK, William Clifford 3
CLARK, William E. 4
CLARK, William Francis 4
CLARK, William Heermans 1
CLARK, William Henry 5
CLARK, William Irving 3
CLARK, William Mansfield 4
CLARK, William R. 5
CLARK, William Smith H
CLARK, William Smith, II 5
CLARK, William Thomas 4
CLARK, William Timothy 4
CLARK, William Walker 3
CLARK, Willis Gaylord H
CLARK, Willis Winfield 4
CLARK, Winfred Newcomb 3
CLARKE, Albert 1
CLARKE, Alfred 1
CLARKE, Andrew Stuart Currie 1
CLARKE, Archibald Smith H
CLARKE, Arthur Edward 2
CLARKE, Augustus Peck 1
CLARKE, Bascom B. 1
CLARKE, Bayard H
CLARKE, Benjamin Franklin 1
CLARKE, Beverly Leonidas H
CLARKE, Caspar Purdon Kt 1
CLARKE, Caspar William 3
CLARKE, Charles Cameron 1
CLARKE, Charles Ezra H
CLARKE, Charles Lorenzo 1
CLARKE, Charles S. 3
CLARKE, Charles W. E. 4
CLARKE, Charles Walter 4
CLARKE, Clement George 1
CLARKE, Creston 1
CLARKE, David Roland 3
CLARKE, Donald Henderson 3
CLARKE, Dumont 1
CLARKE, Edith Emily 1
CLARKE, Edmund Arthur Stanley 1
CLARKE, Edwin Leavitt 2
CLARKE, Elijah H
CLARKE, Eliot Channing 1
CLARKE, Elizabeth Crocker Lawrence 4
CLARKE, Ernest Perley 1
CLARKE, Ernest Swope 2
CLARKE, Francis West 1
CLARKE, Frank G. 1
CLARKE, Frank Wigglesworth 1
CLARKE, Freeman H
CLARKE, George H
CLARKE, George Herbert 1
CLARKE, George W. 1
CLARKE, Hans Thacher 5
CLARKE, Harley Lyman 3
CLARKE, Helen Archibald 1
CLARKE, Herbert Lincoln 2
CLARKE, Hermann Frederick 2
CLARKE, Hopewell 1
CLARKE, Horace Donald 3
CLARKE, Hugh Archibald 4
CLARKE, Ida Clyde 3
CLARKE, J. Calvitt 5
CLARKE, James Augustine 5
CLARKE, James Everitt 4
CLARKE, James Franklin 1
CLARKE, James Frederic 2
CLARKE, James Freeman H
CLARKE, James I. 4
CLARKE, James P. 1
CLARKE, Joe Alexander
CLARKE, John
CLARKE, John Davenport
CLARKE, John Hessin
CLARKE, John Hopkins
CLARKE, John Mason
CLARKE, John Proctor
CLARKE, John Sleeper
CLARKE, John Vaughan
CLARKE, Joseph Ignatius Constantine
CLARKE, Lorenzo Mason
CLARKE, Mary Bayard Devereux
CLARKE, Mary Francis
CLARKE, McDonald
CLARKE, Philip Ream
CLARKE, R. Floyd
CLARKE, Reader Wright
CLARKE, Rebecca Sophia
CLARKE, Richard
CLARKE, Richard Henry
CLARKE, Richard Wilton
CLARKE, Robert
CLARKE, Samuel Fessenden
CLARKE, Sarah J.
CLARKE, Staley Nichols
CLARKE, Thomas Benedict
CLARKE, Thomas Shields
CLARKE, Thurmond
CLARKE, Walter
CLARKE, Walter Irving
CLARKE, Walter James
CLARKE, William A.
CLARKE, William Fayal
CLARKE, William Francis
CLARKE, William Hawes Crichton
CLARKE, William Horatio
CLARKE, William Newton
CLARKIN, Franklin
CLARKSON, Coker Fiffield
CLARKSON, Coker Fifield
CLARKSON, Edward Everett
CLARKSON, Edward Rycroft
CLARKSON, Grosvenor B.
CLARKSON, Henry Mazyck
CLARKSON, Heriot
CLARKSON, James A(ndrew)
CLARKSON, James C.
CLARKSON, Louise
CLARKSON, Matthew *
CLARKSON, Percy William
CLARKSON, Ralph
CLARKSON, Richard Perkinhon
CLARKSON, Robert Livingston
CLARKSON, Thaddeus Stevens
CLARKSON, W. Palmer
CLARKSON, Wright
CLARSON, James Willis Jr.
CLARY, Albert G.
CLARY, Harold Franklin
CLARY, Joseph Monroe
CLARY, William Webb
CLARY-SQUIRE, Mary Louise
CLAS, Angelo Robert
CLASSEN, Anton H.
CLASSON, David Guy
CLATWORTHY, Fred Payne
CLATWORTHY, Linda May
CLAUDEL, Paul
CLAUS, Henry Turner
CLAUSE, William Lewis
CLAUSEN, Claus Lauritz
CLAUSEN, Frederick Harold
CLAUSEN, Jens (Christian)
CLAUSEN, Leon R.
CLAUSEN, Roy Elwood
CLAUSEN, Samuel Wolcott
CLAUSON, Clinton Amos
CLAUSON, Ivy P. Stewart (mrs. Edwin Clauson)
CLAUSON, J. Earl

CLAUSSEN, George 2
CLAUSSEN, Julia 1
CLAWSON, 3
Clinton Dudley
CLAWSON, Isaih Dunn 1
CLAWSON, Marion Don 3
CLAWSON, Rudger 2
CLAXTON, Allen Enes 4
CLAXTON, Brooke 4
CLAXTON, C. Porter 4
CLAXTON, Kate 1
CLAXTON, 3
Mary Hannah Johnson
CLAXTON, 3
Philander Priestley
CLAY, Albert Tobias 1
CLAY, 1
Alexander Stephens
CLAY, Brutus Junius H
CLAY, Brutus Junius 1
CLAY, 1
Cassius Marcellus
CLAY, Cecil 1
CLAY, 1
Christopher Field
CLAY, H
Clement Claiborne
CLAY, Clement Comer H
CLAY, Edward Williams H
CLAY, Green H
CLAY, Henry H
CLAY, Henry Brevard 5
CLAY, James Brown H
CLAY, John 1
CLAY, John Cecil 5
CLAY, Joseph * H
CLAY, Laura 1
CLAY, Matthew H
CLAY, Ryburn Glover 3
CLAY, William Rogers 1
CLAYBERG,
John Bertrand
CLAYBORN, John Henry 3
CLAYBOURN, John G. 4
CLAYBOURN, 5
John Geronold
CLAY-CLOPTON, 4
Virginia Carolina
CLAYPOLE, Edith Jane 5
CLAYPOLE, 1
Edward Waller
CLAYPOOL, Harold K. 3
CLAYPOOL, Horatio C. 5
CLAYPOOL,
J(ohn) Gordon
CLAYPOOL, James
Vernon 4
CLAYTON, H
Augustin Smith
CLAYTON, Bertram
Tracy 1
CLAYTON, Charles H
CLAYTON, Ernest 3
CLAYTON, H. G. 4
CLAYTON, 1
Henry De Lamar
CLAYTON, Henry Helm 2
CLAYTON, 4
James Benjamin
CLAYTON, John H
CLAYTON, H
John Middleton
CLAYTON, Joshua H
CLAYTON, Lawrence 2
CLAYTON, 5
Philip Thomas Byard
CLAYTON, Powell 1
CLAYTON, Thomas H
CLAYTON,
Victoria Virginia
CLAYTON, 3
William Brasher
CLAYTON, 4
William Lockhart
CLAYTON, 1
Willis Sherman
CLAYTOR, Archer Adams 4
CLAYTOR, Thomas Ash 1
CLEARWATER,
Alphonso Trumpbour
CLEARY, Alfred John 1
CLEARY, Daniel Francis 3
CLEARY, George J. 3
CLEARY, James M. 4
CLEARY, 5
James Mansfield
CLEARY, Michael Joseph 2
CLEARY, Owen J. 4
CLEARY, 1
Peter Joseph Augustine
CLEARY, William E. 1
CLEASBY, Harold Loomis 5
CLEAVELAND, 5
Agnes Morley
CLEAVELAND, 1
Elizabeth Hannah Jocelyn

CLEAVELAND, 2
Harry Hayes
CLEAVELAND, 3
Harry Hayes Jr.
CLEAVELAND, 1
Livingston Warner
CLEAVELAND, Moses H
CLEAVELAND, Parker H
CLEAVES,
Arthur Wordsworth
CLEAVES, 1
Henry Bradstreet
CLEAVES, Nelson C. 4
CLEAVES, 4
Willis Everett
CLEAVINGER, 3
John Simeon
CLEBORNE, 1
Christopher James
CLEBURN, H
Patrick Ronayne
CLEE, 3
Frederick Raymond
CLEE, Gilbert Harrison 5
CLEEMANN,
Richard Alsop
CLEGG, Cecil Hunter 5
CLEGG, Lee Milton 3
CLEGG, Moses Tran 1
CLEGHORN, 3
Sarah Norcliffe
CLELAND, 4
Alexander McIntosh
CLELAND, Charles S. 4
CLELAND, 1
Herdman Fitzgerald
CLELAND, John Scott 3
CLELAND, McKenzie 1
CLELAND, Ralph Erskine 5
CLELAND, Robert Glass 3
CLELAND, 4
Robert Wickliffe
CLELAND, Thomas Hann 1
CLELAND, 4
Thomas Maitland
CLEM, John Lincoln 1
CLEMEN, 5
Rudolf Alexander
CLEMENS, Charles Edwin 1
CLEMENS, James Ross 3
CLEMENS, Jeremiah H
CLEMENS, 1
Samuel Langhorne
CLEMENS, Sherrard H
CLEMENS, Wilbur T. 4
CLEMENS, 1
William Marshall
CLEMENS, 1
William Montgomery
CLEMENT, 3
Allan Montgomery
CLEMENT, 1
Charles Maxwell
CLEMENT, Clay 1
CLEMENT, Edmond 1
CLEMENT, Edward 1
Henry
CLEMENT, Ernest Wilson 1
CLEMENT, Frank Goad 5
CLEMENT, 1
George Clinton
CLEMENT, John Addison 2
CLEMENT, 4
Martin Withington
CLEMENT, Percival 1
Wood
CLEMENT, Rugus Early M
CLEMENT, 1
Stephen Merrell
CLEMENT, William
Tardy 3
CLEMENTE, 5
Roberto Walker
CLEMENTS, 4
Andrew Vernon
CLEMENTS, Berthold A. 2
CLEMENTS, C. R. 4
CLEMENTS, 2
Colin Campbell
CLEMENTS, 1
Courtland Cushing
CLEMENTS, 5
Edith Schwartz
CLEMENTS, Edward
Bates 1
CLEMENTS, 4
Francis Washington
CLEMENTS,
Frederic Edward
CLEMENTS, George P. 3
CLEMENTS, Judson C. 1
CLEMENTS, Newton N. 1
CLEMENTS, Robert 1
CLEMENTS,
William Lawrence
CLEMMER, Mary H
CLEMMONS, Joe Rainey 2

CLEMONS, 1
Charles Frederic
CLEMONS, Thomas
Green H
CLEMSON, Walter John 4
CLENDENIN, David H
CLENDENIN, 1
Frank Montrose
CLENDENIN, 1
Henry Wilson
CLENDENIN, 4
William Wallace
CLENDENING, Logan 2
CLEOPHAS, Mother
Mary 2
CLEPHANE, 1
James Ogilvie
CLEPHANE, 3
Walter Collins
CLERC, Laurent H
CLERGUE, 4
Francis Hector
CLERK, Ira 2
CLEVA, Fausto 5
CLEVELAND, Aaron H
CLEVELAND, 1
Abner Coburn
CLEVELAND, 4
Alexander Sessums
CLEVELAND, 5
Austin C(arl)
CLEVELAND, Benjamin H
CLEVELAND, 1
Chauncey Fitch
CLEVELAND, 4
Chester Wilson
CLEVELAND, Clement 1
CLEVELAND, 4
Cynthia Eloise
CLEVELAND, 3
Frank Ernest
CLEVELAND, 2
Frederick Albert
CLEVELAND, 4
George Henry
CLEVELAND, Grover 1
CLEVELAND, Helen M. 1
CLEVELAND, H
Horace William Shaler
CLEVELAND, James
Wray 4
CLEVELAND, H
Jesse Franklin
CLEVELAND, John
Bomar 4
CLEVELAND, 5
Lemuel Roscoe
CLEVELAND, Orestes H
CLEVELAND, Paul W. 3
CLEVELAND, 1
Reginald McIntosh
CLEVELAND, H
Richard Jeffry
CLEVELAND, 1
Rose Elizabeth
CLEVELAND, 5
Treadwell, Jr.
CLEVELAND, 5
William Davis
CLEVEN, 5
Nels Andrew Nelson
CLEVENGER, Cliff 1
CLEVENGER, Shobal Vail H
CLEVENGER, Shobal Vail 4
CLEVER, Charles P. H
CLEVER, Conrad 1
CLEVERLEY, Frank T. 3
CLEWELL, John Henry 1
CLEWS, Alonzo Charles 2
CLEWS, Henry 1
CLEWS, James Blanchard 1
CLEXTON, 1
Edward William
CLIFFE, Adam C. 4
CLIFFORD, Chandler R. 5
CLIFFORD, Charles P. 1
CLIFFORD, 1
Charles Warren
CLIFFORD, Edward 5
CLIFFORD, 1
Elmer Laurence
CLIFFORD, 3
Harry Ellsworth
CLIFFORD, John David 3
CLIFFORD, John Henry H
CLIFFORD, 5
Leslie Forbes
CLIFFORD, Nathan 1
CLIFFORD, 5
Reese F(rancis)
CLIFFORD, Walter 4
CLIFFTON, William H
CLIFT, Albert Earl 4
CLIFT, Montgomery 1
CLIFTON, Albert Turner 2
CLIFTON, 1
Chalmers Dancy

CLIFTON, Charles 1
CLIFTON, John Leroy 3
CLIFTON, 4
Joseph Clinton
CLIFTON, Josephine 1
CLIFTON, Louis 3
CLINCH, Charles Powell H
CLINCH, Duncan Lamont 4
CLINCH, Edward Sears 1
CLINCH, R. Floyd 1
CLINE, Cyrus 4
CLINE, Howard Francis 5
CLINE, Isaac Monroe 3
CLINE, Lewis Manning 5
CLINE, Lyle Stanley 5
CLINE, Pierce 2
CLINE, 3
Robert Alexander
CLINE, Russell Walter 4
CLINE, Sheldon Scott 1
CLINE, Thomas Sparks 5
CLINE, Walter Branks 1
CLINEDINST, B. West 1
CLINGAN, William H
CLINGMAN, H
Thomas Lanier
CLINKSCALES, 1
John George
CLINNIN, John V. 3
CLINTON, DeWitt H
CLINTON, Fred S. 5
CLINTON, George * 1
CLINTON, George 1
CLINTON, 1
George Perkins
CLINTON, George Wylie 1
CLINTON, James H
CLINTON, James Graham 1
CLINTON, 1
Louis Adelbert
CLINTON, Marshall 2
CLINTON, Sir Henry H
CLIPPINGER, 5
Donald Roop
CLIPPINGER, 1
Erle Elsworth
CLIPPINGER, 2
Walter Gillan
CLISE, James William 4
CLOAK, 3
Frank Valentine Centennial
CLOCK, Ralph H. 4
CLOKE, Paul 4
CLONNEY, James
Goodwyn H
CLOPPER, 3
Edward Nicholas
CLOPTON, David H
CLOPTON, John 1
CLOPTON, Malvern
Bryan H
CLORAN, Timothy 1
CLORIVIERE, H
Joseph-Pierre Picot 'ed
Limoelan 'de
CLOSE, 5
Charles Mollison
CLOSE, Charles William 1
CLOSE, James William 5
CLOSE, Lewis Raymond 3
CLOSE, Lyman Withrow 1
CLOSE, Ralph William 2
CLOSE, Stuart 1
CLOSSON, Henry
Whitney 1
CLOSSON, William B. 1
CLOTHIER, 1
Isaac Hallowell
CLOTHIER, Morris Lewis 2
CLOTHIER, 5
Robert Clarkson
CLOUCHEK, Emma Olds 1
CLOUD, Arthur David 4
CLOUD, Charles H. 2
CLOUD, Henry Roe 2
CLOUD, James Henry 1
CLOUD, John Hofer 1
CLOUD, Marshall Morgan 1
CLOUD, Noah Bartlett 1
CLOUD, 3
William Woodward
CLOUES, William Jacob 4
CLOUGH, Charles A. 4
CLOUGH, Charles C. 1
CLOUGH, David Marston 1
CLOUGH, Francis Edgar 3
CLOUGH, Frank C. 3
CLOUGH, George Albert 1
CLOUGH, George Hatch 3
CLOUGH, Merrill H. 5
CLOUGH, Paul Wiswall 5
CLOUGH, Raphael Floyd 3
CLOUGH, S. Dewitt 5
CLOUGH, W. P. 1
CLOUGH-LEIGHTER,
Henry 3
CLOUS, John Walter 1

CLOUSE, Wynne F. 2
CLOVER, 1
George Frederick
CLOVER, Lewis P. Jr. H
CLOVER, Richardson 1
CLOVER, Samuel Travers 1
CLOW, Allan Bowman 5
CLOW, Harry Beach 1
CLOW, James Beach 3
CLOW, Kent Sarver 3
CLOW, 3
William Ellsworth Jr.
CLOWES, 3
George Henry Alexander
CLOWNEY, H
William Kennedy
CLOWRY, Robert Charles 1
CLUBB, Merrel Dare 5
CLUESMANN, Leo 4
CLUETT, E. Harold 3
CLUETT, Robert 1
CLUETT, 5
Sanford Lockwood
CLUETT, W. Scott 5
CLUFF, Harvey H. 5
CLUGSTON, 4
Herbert Andrews
CLUTE, 4
Walker Stillwell
CLUTE, Walter Marshall 1
CLUTE, Willard Nelson 4
CLUTTS, Oliver Perry 4
CLUTZ, Jacob Abraham 1
CLUVERIUS, Wat Tyler 3
CLUYTENS, Andre 4
CLYCE, Thomas Stone 2
CLYDE, George Dewey 5
CLYDE, John
Cunningham 1
CLYDE, Norman Asa 5
CLYDE, William Gray 1
CLYDE,
William Pancoast
CLYMAN, James H
CLYMER, George H
CLYMER, George E. H
CLYMER, Hiester 1
CLYMER, Meredith 1
CLYMER, 5
R(euben) Swinburne
CLYNE, Charles F. 5
CLYNE, Charles F. 4
CLYNE, 5
James Francis, Jr.
COADY, Charles Pearce 1
COAKLEY,
Cornelius Godfrey
COAKLEY, Daniel Henry 4
COALE, Griffith Baily 3
COALE, Issac Jr. 4
COALE, James Johnson 2
COALE, Robert Dorsey 1
COAN, Charles Florus 4
COAN, 4
Frederick Gaylord
COAN, Titus H
COAN, Titus Munson 1
COAPMAN, Eugene H. 1
COAR, John Firman 1
COASH, Louis E. 5
COATE, Alvin Teague 5
COATE, Roland Eli 3
COATES, Charles Edward 1
COATES, Charles F. 3
COATES, David C. 4
COATES, Edward Hornor 1
COATES, Edwin Morton 1
COATES, Eric 3
COATES, Florence Earle 1
COATES, Foster 1
COATES, Henry Troth 1
COATES, Joseph Hornor 1
COATES, Robert Myron 5
COATES, Samuel 1
COATES, Thomas Jackson 1
COATS, 4
Adelbert Sumpter
COATS, Albert B. 4
COBB, Albert Clifford 1
COBB, Amasa 1
COBB, Andrew Jackson 4
COBB, Beatrice 1
COBB, Bernard C. 3
COBB, Bertha Browning 1
COBB, Bruce Benson 3
COBB, Calvin 5
COBB, Candler 3
COBB, Carolus Melville 5
COBB, 5
Charles Wellington
COBB, Clinton Levering H
COBB, Collier 1
COBB, Cyrus 1
COBB, Darius 1
COBB, David H
COBB, 5
Dudley Manchester, Jr.

COBB, Ebenezer Baker 1
COBB, Elijah H
COBB, Ernest 4
COBB, 2
  Florence Etheridge
COBB, Frank Irving 1
COBB, George Thomas H
COBB, Henry Everton 2
COBB, Henry Ives 1
COBB, Henry Nitchie 1
COBB, Herbert Edgar 1
COBB, Howell * H
COBB, Irvin Shrewsbury 2
COBB, James A. 3
COBB, James Shepard 3
COBB, John Blackwell 1
COBB, John Candler 1
COBB, John Nathan 1
COBB, John Robert 5
COBB, Jonathan Holmes H
COBB, Joseph Pettee 1
COBB, Levi Henry 1
COBB, Lloyd Joseph 5
COBB, Lyman H
COBB, Nathan Augustus 1
COBB, Randell Smith 2
COBB, Robert 4
COBB, Rufus Wills 1
COBB, Samuel Ernest 1
COBB, Sanford Hoadley 1
COBB, Seth Wallace 1
COBB, Stanley 4
COBB, Stephen Alonzo 1
COBB, Sylvanus * H
COBB, Thomas Reed H
COBB, H
  Thomas Reed Rootes
COBB, Thomas Willis H
COBB, Tyrus Raymond H
COBB, Tyrus Raymond 4
COBB, William Henry 1
COBB, William Titcomb 1
COBB, H
  Williamson Robert Winfield
COBBETT, William H
COBBEY, 1
  Charles Elliott
COBBEY, Joseph Elliott 1
COBE, Ira Maurice 1
COBERN, 1
  Camden McCormack
COBERO, H
  Pedro Rodriguez
COBLEIGH, 1
  Nelson Simmons
COBLEIGH, 5
  William Merriam
COBLENTZ, Edmond 3
  David
COBLENTZ, 1
  Emory Lorenzo
COBLENTZ, Virgil 1
COBLENTZ, 4
  William Weber
COBO, Albert E. 3
COBURN, Abner H
COBURN, Charles 4
COBURN, Foster Dwight 1
COBURN, 3
  Frederick William
COBURN, John 1
COBURN, Nelson Francis 2
COBURN, Stephen H
COBURN, William 1
COBURN, William Gibson 4
COCHEL, Wilber Andrew 3
COCHEMS, 1
  Henry Frederick
COCHEU, Frank 2
  Sherwood
COCHISE H
COCHRAN, Alexander G. 1
COCHRAN, 1
  Andrew McConnell January
COCHRAN, Archelaus M. 3
COCHRAN, 5
  Archibald Prentice
COCHRAN, 1
  Carlos Bingham
COCHRAN, 1
  Charles Fremont
COCHRAN, Claude A. 4
COCHRAN, David Henry 1
COCHRAN, Ernest Ford 1
COCHRAN, George G. 1
COCHRAN, George Ira 2
COCHRAN, Harry King 1
COCHRAN, Henry Jessup 1
COCHRAN, Homer Pierce 5
COCHRAN, James * H
COCHRAN, James 4
  Chester
COCHRAN, James Harvey 4
COCHRAN, Jean Carter 5
COCHRAN, John H
COCHRAN, John Joseph 2

COCHRAN, Robert 4
  LeRoy
COCHRAN, Samuel 1
  Poyntz
COCHRAN, Thomas 1
COCHRAN, 4
  Thomas Baumgardner
COCHRAN, 3
  Thomas Cunningham
COCHRAN, 1
  William J. Hamilton
COCHRANE, 2
  Aaron Van Schaick
COCHRANE, 1
  Charles Henry
COCHRANE, Clark H
  Betton
COCHRANE, Edward 3
  Lull
COCHRANE, Edward W. 4
COCHRANE, 5
  F(rancis) Douglas;
COCHRANE, Henry Clay 1
COCHRANE, John H
COCHRANE, John C. H
COCHRANE, 1
  John McDowell
COCHRANE, John Taylor 1
COCHRUN, James Lee 1
COCKAYNE, 2
  Charles Alexander
COCKCROFT, James 3
COCKCROFT, 4
  Sir John Douglas
COCKE, 2
  Charles Hartwell
COCKE, John H
COCKE, John Hartwell H
COCKE, Lucian Howard 1
COCKE, Matty L. 3
COCKE, H
  Philip St George
COCKE, William 1
COCKE, William Horner 1
COCKE, William Michael H
COCKE, 5
  William Ruffin Coleman
COCKERELL, 2
  Theodore Dru Allson
COCKERILL, John Albert 1
COCKERILL, H
  Joseph Randolph
COCKING, Walter Dewey 4
COCKRAN, W. Bourke 1
COCKRELL, 1
  Egbert Railey
COCKRELL, Ewing 5
COCKRELL, 1
  Francis Marion
COCKRELL, 1
  Joseph Elmore
COCKRELL, 5
  Robert Spratt
COCKRILL, Ashley 1
COCKRUM, John Barrett 1
COCKS, Orrin Giddings 5
COCKS, William Willets 1
COCKSHUTT, C. Gordon 4
COCKSHUTT, Henry 1
COCO, Adolphe Valery 1
COCTEAU, Jean 4
CODD, George Pierre 1
CODD, Leo A. 5
CODDINGTON, 4
  Edwin Broughton
CODDINGTON, 5
  Herbert Guibord
CODDINGTON, 1
  Merrill Franklin
CODDINGTON, 1
  Wellesley Perry
CODDINGTON, William H
CODE, Charles Joseph 4
CODE, James A, Jr. 5
CODE, William Henry 4
CODEL, Martin 5
CODERE, 4
  Charles Francis
CODMAN, Charles H
CODMAN, 1
  Charles Russell
CODMAN, Edmund 5
  Dwight
CODMAN, Ernest Amory 1
CODMAN, John H
CODMAN, John Sturgis 4
CODMAN, Julian 1
CODMAN, Robert 1
CODMAN, 4
  Russell Sturgis
CODRINGTON, Frank T. 4
CODRINGTON, George 4
  W.
CODY, Claude Carr 4
CODY, Frank 2
CODY, Henry John 3
CODY, John Christopher 4

CODY, 2
  Rev. Hiram Alfred
CODY, Sherwin 3
CODY, 1
  William Frederick
CODY, 4
  Zeachariah Thornton
COE, Albert Buckner 5
COE, Charles Francis 3
COE, Edward Benton 1
COE, Frank Winston 2
COE, Frantz Hunt 1
COE, Fred Joiner 3
COE, George Albert 3
COE, George Simmons H
COE, Henry Clarke 1
COE, Henry Waldo 1
COE, Israel H
COE, John Allen 2
COE, John Parks 4
COE, Robert 4
COE, Robert Lewis 4
COE, Wesley Roswell 5
COE, William Robertson 3
COE, William Rogers 5
COEFIELD, John 1
COEN, John Ralph 4
COERNE, Louis Adolphe 1
COES, Harold Vinton 3
COES, Mary 1
COESTER, Alfred 5
COFER, John Daly 5
COFER, 2
  Leland Eggleston
COFER, Martin Hardin H
COFFEE, 5
  Harry Buffington
COFFEE, Rudolph Isaac 3
COFFEE, William J. H
COFFEN, T. Homer 5
COFFEY, 1
  Alexander Brainard
COFFEY, Charles Shelby 4
COFFEY, Edward Hope 1
COFFEY, George Nelson 5
COFFEY, Harry K. 3
COFFEY, James V. 1
COFFEY, James Vincent 1
COFFEY, John Will 3
COFFEY, Martin Vincent 4
COFFEY, Robert Calvin 1
COFFEY, 1
  Robert Lewis Jr.
COFFEY, Walter Bernard 2
COFFEY, 1
  Walter Castella
COFFIN, Charles Albert 1
COFFIN, Charles Dustin H
COFFIN, Charles E. 1
COFFIN, 1
  Charles Franklin
COFFIN, Frank G. 1
COFFIN, Freeman C. 4
COFFIN, Henry Sloane 3
COFFIN, 1
  Howard Aldridge
COFFIN, Howard Earle 1
COFFIN, James Henry H
COFFIN, John H
COFFIN, H
  John Huntington Crane
COFFIN, John Lambert 2
COFFIN, Levi H
COFFIN, 4
  Lewis Augustus Jr.
COFFIN, Lorenzo S. 1
COFFIN, Marie T. Brown 3
COFFIN, O. Vincent 1
COFFIN, Oscar Jackson 3
COFFIN, Peleg Jr. H
COFFIN, 3
  Robert Peter Tristram
COFFIN, 1
  Selden Jennings
COFFIN, Sir Isaac H
COFFIN, 1
  Thomas Chalkley
COFFIN, Victor 4
COFFIN, William 1
COFFIN, 1
  William Anderson
COFFIN, William Carey 2
COFFIN, William Sloane 1
COFFIN, 1
  William Tristram
COFFMAN, De Witt 1
COFFMAN, 3
  George Raleigh
COFFMAN, L. Dale 2
COFFMAN, Leroy Mallon 1
COFFMAN, Lotus Delta 1
COFFMAN, Noah Beery 1
COFFMAN, Ray Harold 4
COGDELL, John Stevens H
COGGESHALL, 3
  Arthur Sterry
COGGESHALL, Chester 5

COGGESHALL, 1
  Edwin Walter
COGGESHALL, George H
COGGESHALL, 2
  George Whiteley
COGGESHALL, 1
  Henry James
COGGESHALL, Murray 4
  H.
COGGESHALL, H
  William Turner
COGGINS, 1
  Paschal Heston
COGGS, 5
  Theodore Washington
COGHILL, George Ellett 1
COGHILL, William Hawes 5
COGHLAN, Charles F. 1
COGHLAN, John 3
  Maxwell
COGHLAN, Ralph 4
COGHLAN, Rose 1
COGSHALL, 3
  Wilbur Adelman
COGSWELL, 1
  Frederick Hull
COGSWELL, 1
  Hamlin Elisha
COGSWELL, James 1
  Kelsey
COGSWELL, Joseph H
  Green
COGSWELL, Ledyard Jr. 3
COGSWELL, William H
COGSWELL, 1
  William Brown
COGSWELL, William F. 1
COGSWELL, 1
  William Sterling
COHAN, George M. 1
COHEN, A. Broderick 3
COHEN, Abraham 5
COHEN, 4
  Abraham Benjamin
COHEN, Alfred Morton 3
COHEN, Andrew 1
  Benjamin 5
COHEN, Archie H. 3
COHEN, Barnett 1
COHEN, Benjamin A. 3
COHEN, Charles Joseph 1
COHEN, David Solis 4
COHEN, 1
  Dolly Lurie (Mrs. A. B. Cohen)
COHEN, Felix S. 3
COHEN, George Harry 2
COHEN, Harry 5
COHEN, Henry 3
COHEN, Herbert Spencer 4
COHEN, Irvin Joseph 3
COHEN, Jacob Solis 5
COHEN, John Sanford 1
COHEN, Julius Henry 3
COHEN, Katherine M. 1
COHEN, Lewis 5
COHEN, Lily Young 5
COHEN, Louis 2
COHEN, Mendes 1
COHEN, Merrill Morris 4
COHEN, Morris Raphael 4
COHEN, Murray 4
COHEN, Octavus Roy 3
COHEN, Paul 5
COHEN, Paul Pincus 5
COHEN, William Nathan 1
COHEN, William W. 2
COHILL, 3
  Edmund Pendleton
COHN, Adolphe 1
COHN, Alfred Einstein 3
COHN, Alfred I. 4
COHN, 2
  Charles Mittendorff
COHN, Edwin Joseph 3
COHN, Harry 3
COHN, Jack 3
COHN, Joseph Hoffman 3
COHN, Morris M. 3
COHN, Ralph Morris 3
COHN, Saul 3
COHON, Morris 3
COHON, Samuel Solomon 4
COHU, La Motte T. 5
COIL, Everett Johnston 5
COILE, Samuel Andrew 1
COINER, Beverly Waugh 4
COIT, Alfred 2
COIT, Arthur Clinton 1
COIT, Henry Augustus H
COIT, J. Milnor 1
COIT, John Clarke 5
COIT, John Knox 1
COIT, John McLean 1
COIT, Joseph Howland 1

COIT, Joshua
COIT, Joshua
COIT, Judson Boardman
COIT, Olin Burr
COIT, Ruth
COIT, Stanton
COIT, Thomas Winthrop
COKE, Henry Cornick
COKE, James L.
COKE, John Story
COKE, Richard
COKE, Richard Jr.
COKE, Thomas
COKENOWER, James W.
COKER, David Robert
COKER, Francis William
COKER, James Lide
COKER, James Lide
COKER, Robert E(rvin)
COKER,
  William Chambers
COLACCI, Mario
COLAHAN,
  John Barron Jr.
COLAW, John Marvin
COLBERN, William H.
COLBERT, Carl Cato
COLBERT,
  Charles Francis, Jr.
COLBERT, Leo Otis
COLBERT,
  Richard Victor
COLBRON, Grace Isabel
COLBURN, Albert E.
COLBURN, Allan Philip
COLBURN,
  Burnham Standish
COLBURN, Dana Pond
COLBURN, Warren
COLBURN, Zerah
COLBY, Albert Ladd
COLBY, Bainbridge
COLBY, Branch Harris
COLBY, Charles Carlyle
COLBY, Clara Bewick
COLBY, Everett
COLBY, Frank C.
COLBY, Frank Harvey
COLBY, Frank Moore
COLBY, Franklin Green
COLBY, Gardner
COLBY, Gardner
COLBY,
  Harrison Gray Otis
COLBY, Henry Francis
COLBY, Irving Harold
COLBY, J. Rose
COLBY, James Fairbanks
COLBY, Leonard Wright
COLBY, Luther
COLBY,
  Nathalie Sedgwick
COLBY, Walter Francis
COLBY, William Edward
COLBY, William Edward
COLBY, William Irving
COLBY, Willoughby Amos
COLCOCK, F. Horton
COLCOCK,
  William Ferguson
COLCORD, Bradford C.
COLCORD,
  Charles Francis
COLCORD, Frank Forest
COLCORD, Joanna Carver
COLCORD, Lincoln Ross
COLCORD, Roswell
  Keyes
COLDEN, Cadwallader
COLDEN,
  Cadwallader David
COLDEN, Charles J.
COLDEN, Charles S.
COLDEN, Jane
COLDREN, Philip
COLE, Aaron Hodgman
COLE, Alfred Dodge
COLE, Ashley Trimble
COLE, Betty Joy
COLE, Carlos Merton
COLE, Charles F.
COLE, Charles H.
COLE, Charles Knox
COLE, Charles Nelson
COLE, Chester Cicero
COLE, Clarence Alfred
COLE, Cornelius
COLE, Cyrenus
COLE, Cyrus W(illard)
COLE, David
COLE, Douglas Seaman
COLE, Edward Smith
COLE, Eli Kelley
COLE, Elmer E.
COLE, Ernest E.
COLE, Fay-Cooper

COLE, Felix 5
COLE, 4
Francis Watkinson
COLE, Frank Nelson 1
COLE, Franklin 5
COLE, George Clarence 5
COLE, 3
George Douglas Howard
COLE, George E. *
COLE, George Lamont 1
COLE, George W. 1
COLE, George Watson 1
COLE, Glen Walker 3
COLE, Harold Mercer 5
COLE, Harry Outen 3
COLE, Henry Tiffany 1
COLE, Howard Ellsworth 3
COLE, Howard I. 5
COLE, Howard Ware 5
COLE, Jean Dean 1
COLE, John Adams 4
COLE, John Nelson 1
COLE, Joseph Foxcroft H
COLE, Lawrence Thomas 5
COLE, Lawrence Wooster 2
COLE, Leon Jacob 2
COLE, Lewis Gregory 3
COLE, Louis Maurice 4
COLE, Nat King 4
COLE, Nathan Jr. 1
COLE, Nelson 1
COLE, Ralph Dayton 3
COLE, Ralph R. 3
COLE, Richard Beverly 1
COLE, 3
Rossetter Gleason
COLE, Rufus 4
COLE, Rufus 5
COLE, Russell D. 4
COLE, Samuel Valentine 1
COLE, Samuel Winkley 1
COLE, Theodore Lee 1
COLE, Thomas H
COLE, Thomas F. 1
COLE, Timothy 1
COLE, Walton Adamson 1
COLE, Whitefoord R. 1
COLE, William Carey 1
COLE, William H. 1
COLE, William Hinson H
COLE, William Isaac 1
COLE, William Morse 4
COLE, 3
William Purrington Jr.
COLE, Wilson Giffin 3
COLEBAUGH, 2
Charles Henry
COLEGROVE, 4
Chauncey Peter
COLEGROVE, 4
Frederick Welton
COLEMAN, Algernon 1
COLEMAN,
Alice Blanchard
COLEMAN, Arch 4
COLEMAN, Arch 5
COLEMAN, 1
Benjamin Wilson
COLEMAN, Chapman 1
COLEMAN, Charles Caryl 1
COLEMAN,
Charles Elliott
COLEMAN, 1
Charles Philip
COLEMAN, 4
Charles Washington
COLEMAN, 2
Christopher Bush
COLEMAN, Claude C. 3
COLEMAN, 5
Cornelius Cunningham
COLEMAN,
Cynthia Beverley Tucker
COLEMAN, Cyril 3
COLEMAN, D'Alton
Corry 3
COLEMAN, Frank Joseph 1
COLEMAN, 2
Frederick W. B.
COLEMAN, 2
Frederick William
COLEMAN, 2
George Preston
COLEMAN,
George Whitfield
COLEMAN, 3
George William
COLEMAN, 4
Gilbert Payson
COLEMAN, 4
James Melville
COLEMAN, John 4
COLEMAN, John Dawson 4
COLEMAN, John Francis 2
COLEMAN, John
Hamline 4
COLEMAN, John Shields 5

COLEMAN, John Strider 3
COLEMAN, 4
Kathleen Blake
COLEMAN, Leighton 1
COLEMAN, Lewis Minor 1
COLEMAN, Lyman 5
COLEMAN, H
Nicholas Daniel
COLEMAN, Philip Frantz 3
COLEMAN, Ralph Pallen 5
COLEMAN, Richard B. 4
COLEMAN, Satis Narrona 5
COLEMAN, Stewart P. 5
COLEMAN, Sydney
Haines 3
COLEMAN, Thomas
Davies 1
COLEMAN, Thomas
Emmet 4
COLEMAN, Thomas
Wilkes 1
COLEMAN, Walter
Moore 1
COLEMAN, Warren 2
COLEMAN, William H
COLEMAN, 4
William Caldwell
COLEMAN, 3
William Coffin
COLEMAN, 1
William Emmette
COLEMAN, 4
William Harold
COLEMAN, William
Henry 3
COLEMAN, William John 5
COLEMAN,
William Magruder
COLEMAN, William Tell H
COLEMAN, 4
William Wheeler
COLER, Bird Sim 1
COLES, Alfred Porter 2
COLES, David Smalley 1
COLES, Edward H
COLES, Isaac 1
COLES, J. Ackerman 1
COLES, Walter H
COLESTOCK, 4
Henry Thomas
COLETTE, 3
COLEY, 4
Bradley Lancaster
COLEY, 2
Edward Huntington
COLEY, Francis Chase 1
COLEY, William Bradley 1
COLFAX, Schuyler H
COLFELT, 4
Lawrence Maclay
COLFLESH, 4
Robert William
COLFORD, 5
William Edward
COLGATE, Gilbert 1
COLGATE, Henry A. 3
COLGATE, James
Boorman 1
COLGATE, James Colby 2
COLGATE, Russell 1
COLGATE, S. Bayard 4
COLGATE, Sidney Morse 1
COLGATE, William 1
COLGROVE, 1
Philip Taylor
COLHOUN, John Ewing H
COLIE, Edward Martin 1
COLIE, Rosalie Littell 5
COLKET, Edward Burton 4
COLL, Raymond S. 4
COLLADAY,
Edward Francis
COLLADAY, 2
Samuel Rakestraw
COLLAMER, Jacob H
COLLAR, William Coe 1
COLLBRAN, Henry 1
COLLEDGE, William A. 1
COLLENS, Charles 3
COLLENS, 5
Clarence Lyman
COLLENS, H
Thomas Wharton
COLLER, 4
Frederick Amasa
COLLER, Julius A. 4
COLLES, Christopher H
COLLET, John Caskie 3
COLLETT, 2
George Richard
COLLETT, John 1
COLLIE, George Lucius 3
COLLIER, Barron 1
COLLIER, Daniel Lewis 1
COLLIER, David Charles 1
COLLIER, 3
Edward Augustus

COLLIER, Frank Wilbur 2
COLLIER, 1
George Haskell
COLLIER, Harry D. 3
COLLIER, Henry Watkins H
COLLIER, James William H
COLLIER, John 5
COLLIER, John Allen H
COLLIER, John Howard H
COLLIER, 5
Marie Elizabeth
COLLIER, Peter H
COLLIER, Peter Fenelon 1
COLLIER, Price 1
COLLIER, Robert Joseph 1
COLLIER, Theodore 4
COLLIER, William 2
COLLIER, 4
William Armistead
COLLIER, 3
William Miller
COLLIN, Alonzo 1
COLLIN, Charles Avery 4
COLLIN, Frederick 1
COLLIN, Harry E. 5
COLLIN, John Francis H
COLLINGS, Clyde Wilson 5
COLLINGS, 1
Crittenden Taylor
COLLINGS, 4
Gilbert Hooper
COLLINGS, Harry
Thomas 1
COLLINGS, 3
Howard Paxton
COLLINGS, John Ayres 5
COLLINGS, 1
Kenneth Brown
COLLINGS, Samuel Posey 1
COLLINGWOOD, Francis 1
COLLINGWOOD, G.
Harris 3
COLLINGWOOD, 1
Herbert Winslow
COLLINS, 5
A(rchie) Frederick
COLLINS, Alan Copeland 4
COLLINS, 1
Albert Hamilton
COLLINS, Alfred Morris 5
COLLINS, 1
Alfred Quinton
COLLINS, Atwood 1
COLLINS, 4
Bertrand Robson Torsey
COLLINS, Charles E. 5
COLLINS, Charles Edwin 4
COLLINS, 1
Charles William
COLLINS, 2
Clifford Ulysses
COLLINS, 1
Clinton DeWitt
COLLINS, Conrad Green 5
COLLINS, 4
Cornelius Vallance
COLLINS, 1
Cornelius Van Santvoord
COLLINS, Edgar Thomas 1
COLLINS, Edward Day 1
COLLINS, Edward Knight 1
COLLINS, Edwin R. 1
COLLINS, Ela 1
COLLINS, 1
Everell Stanton
COLLINS, Foster K. 1
COLLINS, 3
Francis Arnold
COLLINS, Francis Dolan H
COLLINS, Frank Shipley 1
COLLINS, 2
Franklin Wallace
COLLINS, 3
Frederick Lewis
COLLINS, George Lewis 1
COLLINS, George Stuart 1
COLLINS, George W. 5
COLLINS, 4
George William
COLLINS, Gilbert 1
COLLINS, Guy N. 1
COLLINS, 1
Harold Moorman
COLLINS, Henry W. 5
COLLINS, Herman LeRoy 1
COLLINS, Howard Dennis 4
COLLINS, Hubert Edwin 1
COLLINS, J. Franklin 1
COLLINS, 1
James Franklin
COLLINS, James H(iram) 5
COLLINS, James Lawton 4
COLLINS, John H
COLLINS, John Anderson H
COLLINS, 1
John Bartholomew
COLLINS, John Joseph 1

COLLINS, John Martin 3
COLLINS, 4
John Mathewson
COLLINS, John Timothy 4
COLLINS, Joseph 5
COLLINS, Joseph Henry 4
COLLINS, 1
Joseph Howland
COLLINS, Joseph Martin 3
COLLINS, Joseph Victor 2
COLLINS, 1
Joseph William
COLLINS, Joshua H
COLLINS, Laura G. 4
COLLINS, Loren Warren 1
COLLINS, Lorin Cone 1
COLLINS, Mark 5
COLLINS, 1
Matthew Garrett
COLLINS, Mauney D. 3
COLLINS, 1
Michael Francis
COLLINS, Napoleon H
COLLINS, Patrick A. 1
COLLINS, Paul Fisk 5
COLLINS, Paul Valorous 1
COLLINS, 2
Philip Sheridan
COLLINS, Ralph L. 4
COLLINS, Robert Moore 4
COLLINS, 5
Ross Alexander
COLLINS, Roy Charles 5
COLLINS, Stewart G. 2
COLLINS, Truman W. 1
COLLINS, 1
Varnum Lansing
COLLINS, Virgil Dewey 4
COLLINS, Vivian 3
COLLINS, 3
Whitley Charles
COLLINS, William H
COLLINS, William 3
COLLINS, William 1
COLLINS, William Henry 3
COLLINS, Winifred 2
COLLIP, James Bertram 1
COLLIS, Charles H. T. 1
COLLISON, Wilson 1
COLLISSON, 4
Norman Harvey
COLLITZ, Hermann 1
COLLITZ, 2
Klara Hechtenberg
COLLYER, Robert 1
COLM, Gerhard 5
COLMAN, Benjamin H
COLMAN, Henry H
COLMAN, James Douglas 5
COLMAN, John H
COLMAN, Norman Jay 4
COLMAN, Ronald 3
COLMAN, Samuel 1
COLMORE, 3
Charles Blayney
COLNON, Aaron 3
COLONNA, Paul
Crenshaw 4
COLPITTS, Edwin Henry 2
COLPITTS, 3
Walter William
COLQUHOUN, 4
Walter Alexander
COLQUITT, Alfred Holt H
COLQUITT, Oscar Branch 1
COLQUITT, Walter T. 1
COLQUITT, Walter Terry H
COLSON, Clyde Lemuel 4
COLSON, David Grant 1
COLSTON, Edward H
COLSTON, Edward 1
COLSTON, H
Raleigh Edward
COLSTON, 1
William Ainslie
COLT, Harris Dunscomb 4
COLT, 1
Le Baron Bradford
COLT, Samuel H
COLT, Samuel Pomeroy 1
COLTER,
Frederick Tuttle
COLTER, John H
COLTMAN, Robert 4
COLTMAN, 4
William George
COLTON, A. M. F. 1
COLTON, Arthur Willis 1
COLTON, Calvin H
COLTON, Charles Adams 1
COLTON, Charles Henry 1
COLTON, Don Byron 5
COLTON, 1
Elizabeth Avery
COLTON, 3
Elizabeth Sweetser

COLTON, Ethan
Theodore 5
COLTON, Ferry Barrows 3
COLTON, Gardner
Quincy H
COLTON, George Henry 1
COLTON, 1
George Radcliffe
COLTON, Julia M. 5
COLTON, Walter H
COLTRANE, Eugene J. 4
COLTRANE, John
William 4
COLUM, Mary M. 3
COLUM, Padraic 5
COLUMBUS, Christopher H
COLUMBUS, Diego H
COLUMBUS,
Fernando Colon
COLVER, Benton Noble 1
COLVER, Nathaniel 1
COLVER, William Byron 1
COLVIN, 3
Addison Beecher
COLVIN, Allan DeWitt 3
COLVIN, D. Leigh 3
COLVIN, Fred Herbert 4
COLVIN, George 1
COLVIN, H. Milton 3
COLVIN, James G. 5
COLVIN, Mamie White 5
COLVIN, Oliver Dyer 4
COLVIN, 1
Stephen Sheldon
COLVIN, Verplanck 1
COLVIN, W. H, Jr. 5
COLVOCORESSES, H
George Musalas
COLVOCORESSES, 1
George Partridge
COLWELL, Nathan Porter 1
COLWELL, 4
Robert Talcott
COLWELL, Stephen H
COLYER, Douglas 3
COLYER, Vincent H
COMAN, Charlotte Buell 1
COMAN, Edwin Truman 5
COMAN, Henry Benjamin 1
COMAN, Katharine 1
COMAN, Mary Meriam 4
COMAN, Wilber Edmund 1
COMBA, Richard 1
COMBS, 5
Everett Randolph
COMBS, George W. 3
COMBS, 1
Gilbert Raynolds
COMBS, J. M. 3
COMBS, James Horton H
COMBS, Leslie H
COMBS, Leslie 1
COMBS, 3
Morgan Lafayette
COMBS, Moses Newell H
COMBS, Thomas Selby 4
COMEAUX, C. Stewart 3
COMEGYS, H
Joseph Parsons
COMER, Braxton Bragg 1
COMER, Edward Trippe 4
COMER, George Legare 4
COMER, Harry D. 4
COMER, Hugh Moss 4
COMER, James
McDonald 4
COMERFORD, Frank 1
COMERFORD, Frank
Dowd 2
COMEY, Arthur Coleman 3
COMEY,
Arthur Messinger
COMFORT, Anna
Manning 1
COMFORT, 5
Charlotte Walrath
COMFORT, Frank J. 3
COMFORT, George Fisk 1
COMFORT, 3
Mandred Whitset
COMFORT, Walter R. 4
COMFORT, 1
Will Levington
COMFORT, 3
William Wistar
COMINGO, Abram H
COMINS, Linus Bacon H
COMINSKY, 5
Jacob R(obert)
COMLY, Samuel Pancoast 1
COMMONS, John Rogers 2
COMPARETTE, T. Louis 1
COMPHER, Wilber G. 4
COMPTON, 2
Alfred Donaldson
COMPTON, Alfred
George 1

COMPTON, Arthur H. — H
COMPTON, Arthur H. — 4
COMPTON, Charles Elmer — 1
COMPTON, Elias — 1
COMPTON, George Brokaw — 1
COMPTON, Karl Taylor — 4
COMPTON, Lewis — 2
COMPTON, Loulie — 1
COMPTON, Richard J. — 3
COMPTON, Walter — 3
COMPTON, William Randolph — 3
COMPTON, Wilson Martindale — 4
COMPTON-BURNETT, Ivy — 5
COMSTOCK, A. Barr — 3
COMSTOCK, Albert H. — 4
COMSTOCK, Alzada — 3
COMSTOCK, Anna Botsford — 1
COMSTOCK, Anthony — 2
COMSTOCK, Clarence Elmer
COMSTOCK, Cyrus Ballou — 1
COMSTOCK, Daniel Frost — 4
COMSTOCK, Elizabeth L. — H
COMSTOCK, Elting Houghtaling — 5
COMSTOCK, F. Ray — 2
COMSTOCK, Frank Mason — 1
COMSTOCK, George Cary — 1
COMSTOCK, George Franklin — H
COMSTOCK, Harriet Theresa — 5
COMSTOCK, Henry Tompkins Paige — H
COMSTOCK, John Henry — 1
COMSTOCK, Louis Kossuth — 4
COMSTOCK, Oliver Cromwell — H
COMSTOCK, Ralph J. — 4
COMSTOCK, Sarah — 3
COMSTOCK, Solomon Gilman — 1
COMSTOCK, Theodore Bryant — 1
COMSTOCK, William Alfred — 2
COMTOIS, Paul — 4
CONANT, Alban Jasper — 1
CONANT, C. Everett — 1
CONANT, Charles Arthur — 1
CONANT, Charlotte Howard — 1
CONANT, Ernest Bancroft — 5
CONANT, Frederick Odell — 1
CONANT, Gordon Daniel — 4
CONANT, Hannah O'Brien Chaplin — H
CONANT, Harold Wright — 4
CONANT, Helen Peters Stevens — 1
CONANT, Henry Dunning — 4
CONANT, Hezekiah — H
CONANT, John Willis — 4
CONANT, Levi Leonard — 1
CONANT, Roger — H
CONANT, Thomas Jefferson — 1
CONANT, Thomas Oakes — 3
CONARD, Frederick Underwood — 3
CONARD, Henry Shoemaker — 5
CONARD, John — H
CONARRO, Harry Wiborg — 4
CONARROE, George W. — H
CONATY, Thomas James — 1
CONAWAY, Charles Herman — 3
CONBOY, Martin — 2
CONBOY, Sara Agnes — 3
CONCANNON, Charles Cuthbert — 3
CONCHESO, Aurelio Fernandez — 3
CONDE, Bertha — 5
CONDEE, Robert Asa — 1
CONDICT, George Herbert — 1
CONDICT, Lewis — H
CONDICT, Silas — H
CONDIT, Blackford — 1
CONDIT, John — H
CONDIT, Silas — H
CONDO, Gus S. — 1
CONDON, Edward J. — 4

CONDON, Francis Bernard — 4
CONDON, Herbert Thomas — 3
CONDON, John Thomas — 1
CONDON, Randall Judson — 4
CONDON, Richard William — 1
CONDON, Thomas Gerald — 4
CONDRON, Theodore Lincoln — 5
CONE, Burtis Octavius — 4
CONE, Frederick Preston — 2
CONE, Helen Gray — 2
CONE, Herman — 1
CONE, Hutchinson Ingham — 1
CONE, Martin — 4
CONE, Marvin Dorwart — 4
CONE, Orello — 1
CONE, Russell G. — 4
CONE, Spencer Houghton — H
CONEY, Aims Chamberlain — 4
CONEY, Jabez — H
CONEY, John — H
CONFREY, Edward Elzear (ZEZ) — 5
CONGDON, Charles Harris — 1
CONGDON, Charles Howard — 1
CONGDON, Charles Taber — H
CONGDON, Chester Adgate — 1
CONGDON, Clement Hilman — 4
CONGDON, Edward Chester — 1
CONGDON, Ernest Arnold — 4
CONGDON, Gilbert Maurice — 4
CONGDON, Harriet Rice — 5
CONGDON, Joseph William — 1
CONGER, Abraham Benjamin — 3
CONGER, Albert C. — 5
CONGER, Seymour) Beach, III — 5
CONGER, Edward A. — 1
CONGER, Edwin Hurd — 1
CONGER, Everett Lorentus — 1
CONGER, George Perrigo — 4
CONGER, Harmon Sweatland — H
CONGER, James Lockwood — H
CONGER, John Leonard — 5
CONGER, John William — 1
CONGER, John William — 4
CONGER, Robert Alan — 4
CONGER, Seymour Beach — 1
CONGLETON, Jerome Taylor — 1
CONICK, Harold C. — 4
CONKEY, Elizabeth A. — 4
CONKEY, Henry Phillips — 3
CONKLIN, Abram — 4
CONKLIN, Arthur Stewart — 4
CONKLIN, Charles — 1
CONKLIN, Clifford Tremaine — 3
CONKLIN, Edmund Smith — 2
CONKLIN, Edwin Grant — 3
CONKLIN, Franklin Jr. — 1
CONKLIN, Jennie Maria Drinkwater — 1
CONKLIN, John F. — 5
CONKLIN, Roland Ray — 1
CONKLIN, Viola A. — 1
CONKLIN, William Augustus — 1
CONKLIN, William Judkins — 1
CONKLING, Alfred — H
CONKLING, Alfred Ronald — 4
CONKLING, Frederick Augustus — H
CONKLING, Grace Hazard — 3
CONKLING, Mark Le Roy — 4
CONKLING, Roscoe — H
CONKLING, Roscoe Powers — 3
CONLAND, Henry H. — 2
CONLEN, William J. — 3

CONLEY, Alonzo Theodore — 4
CONLEY, Clyde — 5
CONLEY, Edgar Thomas — 3
CONLEY, Elmo Hansford — 3
CONLEY, George J. — 3
CONLEY, John Wesley — 1
CONLEY, William Gustavus — 1
CONLEY, William Maxwell — 3
CONN, Donald Deans — 3
CONN, George Chester — 4
CONN, Granville Priest — 1
CONN, Harry L. — 1
CONN, Herbert William — 1
CONN, Ulysses Sylvester — 1
CONNAH, Douglas John — 1
CONNALLY, Elijah L. — 4
CONNALLY, Tom — 4
CONNELL, Albert James — 2
CONNELL, Arthur J. — 4
CONNELL, Carl W. — 2
CONNELL, Charles R. — 1
CONNELL, Francis J. — 4
CONNELL, George Boyce — 3
CONNELL, Horatio — 1
CONNELL, James Mark — 4
CONNELL, Karl — 1
CONNELL, Richard — 1
CONNELL, Richard E. — 1
CONNELL, Wilfrid Thomas — 4
CONNELL, William — 1
CONNELL, William Henry — 2
CONNELL, William Lawrence — 1
CONNELL, William Phillips — 1
CONNELL, Wilson Edward — 1
CONNELLEY, Clifford Brown — 1
CONNELLEY, Earl John — 3
CONNELLEY, William Elsey — 1
CONNELLY, Celia Logan — H
CONNELLY, Cornelia — 2
CONNELLY, Edward Michael — 5
CONNELLY, Emma Mary — H
CONNELLY, Henry — 1
CONNELLY, James H. — 5
CONNELLY, John R. — H
CONNELLY, Pierce Francis — 3
CONNELY, Emmett Francis — 4
CONNELY, Willard — 1
CONNER, Benjamin Coulbourn — 5
CONNER, Bruce — H
CONNER, David — 1
CONNER, Eli Taylor — 5
CONNER, Fox — H
CONNER, James — 1
CONNER, James Keyes — 4
CONNER, James Moyer — 4
CONNER, James Perry — H
CONNER, John Coggswell — 3
CONNER, Lewis Atterbury — 4
CONNER, Martin Sennett — 1
CONNER, Phineas Sanborn — 1
CONNER, Samuel Shepard — 5
CONNER, Walter Thomas — 1
CONNERS, William James — 3
CONNERS, William James Jr. — 1
CONNERY, Lawrence J. — 4
CONNERY, Thomas Bernard Joseph — 1
CONNERY, William Patrick Jr. — 2
CONNESS, John — 2
CONNESS, Leland Stanford — 4
CONNICK, Arthur Elwell — 2
CONNICK, Charles Jay — 4
CONNICK, Harris De Haven — 5
CONNIFF, Frank — 5
CONNIFF, Paul R. — 1
CONNING, John Stuart — 1
CONNOLLY, Christopher Powell — 1
CONNOLLY, Daniel Ward — H
CONNOLLY, Francis X. — 4
CONNOLLY, James Austin — 1
CONNOLLY, James Brendan — 3

CONNOLLY, James J. — 3
CONNOLLY, John * — H
CONNOLLY, Joseph Peter — 2
CONNOLLY, Joseph Vincent — 2
CONNOLLY, Louise — 4
CONNOLLY, Maurice — 1
CONNOLLY, Michael William — 4
CONNOLLY, Mike — 3
CONNOLLY, Robert Emmet — 3
CONNOLLY,. Terence Leo — 4
CONNOLY, Theodore — 4
CONNOR, Aloysius J. — 5
CONNOR, Edward — 1
CONNOR, George L. — 1
CONNOR, George Whitfield — 2
CONNOR, Guy Leartus — 1
CONNOR, Henry Groves — H
CONNOR, Henry William — 4
CONNOR, Jacob Elon — 1
CONNOR, Leartus — 3
CONNOR, Louis George — H
CONNOR, Patrick Edward — 1
CONNOR, Ray — 2
CONNOR, Robert Digges Wimberly — 1
CONNOR, Seldon — 4
CONNOR, Washington Everett — 1
CONNOR, William Durward — 1
CONNOR, William Neil — 4
CONNOR, William Ott — 1
CONNORS, John P. — 4
CONNORS, Joseph Mathew — 1
CONOLLY, Richard L. — 1
CONOVER, Adams Jewett — 1
CONOVER, Charles H. — 3
CONOVER, Elbert Moore — 1
CONOVER, Harvey — 3
CONOVER, James) Milton — 5
CONOVER, Obediah Milton — H
CONOVER, Samuel Seymour — 4
CONQUEST, Ida — 1
CONRAD, Arcturus Z. — 1
CONRAD, Carl Nicholas — 3
CONRAD, Casper Hauzer Jr. — 3
CONRAD, Charles — H
CONRAD, Charles Magill — 3
CONRAD, Charles Wearne — 3
CONRAD, Cuthbert Powell — 1
CONRAD, Frank — 2
CONRAD, Frank L. — H
CONRAD, Frederick — 1
CONRAD, Frowenus — 4
CONRAD, G. Miles — 4
CONRAD, Henry Clay — 4
CONRAD, Marus Edward — 3
CONRAD, Nicholas John — 1
CONRAD, Paul C. — 4
CONRAD, Robert Taylor — 4
CONRAD, Stephen — 1
CONRAD, Timothy Abbot — 4
CONRAD, Victor Allen — 2
CONRADI, Edward — 1
CONRIED, Heinrich — 3
CONROW, Wilford Seymour — 1
CONROY, John Joseph — H
CONROY, Joseph H. — 1
CONROY, Peter Joseph — 3
CONROY, Thomas Francis — 3
CONROY, Thomas Michael — 5
CONRY, Michael Francis — 1
CONRY, Thomas — 2
CONS, Louis — 2
CONSIDERANT, Victor Prosper — H
CONSIDINE, James W(illiam) — 5
CONSTABLE, Albert — 1
CONSTANCY, Frank Alan — 2
CONSTANT, Frank Henry — 1
CONSTANT, Samuel Victor — 3
CONSTANTINE, Earl Gladstone — 4
CONSTANTINOPLE-, Panaglotes S. — 2
CONTEE, Benjamin — H
CONVERSE, Amasa R. — H

CONVERSE, C. Crozat — 1
CONVERSE, Costello C. — 1
CONVERSE, Edmund Cogswell — 1
CONVERSE, Francis Bartlett — 1
CONVERSE, Frederick Shepherd — 1
CONVERSE, George Albert — 1
CONVERSE, George Leroy — H
CONVERSE, George Peabody — 4
CONVERSE, Harriet Maxwell — 1
CONVERSE, Harry E. — 3
CONVERSE, Harry Pollard
CONVERSE, James Booth — 1
CONVERSE, John Heman — 1
CONVERSE, Marquis Mills — 3
CONVERSE, Myron Frederick
CONVERY, Neil Joseph — 5
CONWAY, Albert — 5
CONWAY, Barret — 2
CONWAY, Carle Cotter — 1
CONWAY, Edwin Stapleton — H
CONWAY, Elias Nelson — H
CONWAY, Frederick Bartlett
CONWAY, Henry Wharton — H
CONWAY, Herbert — 5
CONWAY, James Ignatius — 4
CONWAY, James Sevier — 1
CONWAY, John Edward — 2
CONWAY, John Severinus — 1
CONWAY, Joseph M. — 4
CONWAY, Joseph W. — 1
CONWAY, Katherine Eleanor — H
CONWAY, Martin Franklin
CONWAY, Moncure Daniel — 1
CONWAY, Patrick — 1
CONWAY, Thomas — H
CONWAY, Thomas Jr. — 4
CONWAY, Walter — 3
CONWELL, Russell Herman — 1
CONWELL, Walter Lewis — 2
CONYNGHAM, Gustavus — 2
CONYNGHAM, William Hillard — 2
COOGAN, Edward Francis — 1
COOK, Albert John — 1
COOK, Albert Samuel — 3
COOK, Albert Stanburrough — 1
COOK, Alfred A. — 2
COOK, Alfred Newton — 1
COOK, Alice Rice — 5
COOK, Allan Nehrands — 4
COOK, Alton — 5
COOK, Andrew Bruce — 5
COOK, Ansel Granville — 1
COOK, Burton Chauncey — H
COOK, Carroll Blaine — 4
COOK, Cary Wilson — 1
COOK, Charles Alston — 4
COOK, Charles Augustus — 1
COOK, Charles Emerson — 5
COOK, Charles R. — 3
COOK, Charles Sumner — 1
COOK, Charles T. — 1
COOK, Chauncey William — 2
COOK, Chester Aquila — 3
COOK, Clarence Chatham — H
COOK, Clinton Dana — 1
COOK, Daniel Pope — H
COOK, David C. — 1
COOK, Donald — 4
COOK, Ebenezer — 1
COOK, Edward Noble — 5
COOK, Elmer Jay — 4
COOK, Ermond Edson — 4
COOK, Ernest Fullerton — 4
COOK, Eugene — 2
COOK, Fannie — 1
COOK, Fayette Lamartine — 1
COOK, Francis Augustus — 1
COOK, Frank Gaylord — 4
COOK, Frederic White — 3
COOK, Frederick Albert — 4
COOK, George Cram — 1
COOK, George Crouse — 4
COOK, George Fox — 4
COOK, George Frederick — 4
COOK, George Hammell — H

COOK, George Roy 5
COOK, 4
  George Washington
COOK, George Wythe 4
COOK, Gilbert Richard 4
COOK, Grant L. 3
COOK, H. Earl 5
COOK, Harold James 4
COOK, Henry Clay 1
COOK, Henry Mudd
COOK, Henry Webster 4
COOK, Irving Winthrop 3
COOK, Isaac H
COOK, J. Clinton Jr. 4
COOK, James H
COOK, James Henry 2
COOK, James Merrill 1
COOK, Joe 4
COOK, Joel 1
COOK, John 1
COOK, John 3
COOK, John Henry 5
COOK, John Parsons
COOK, John Williston 1
COOK, Joseph
COOK, Joseph Platt H
COOK, Marc H
COOK, 4
  Martha Elizabeth Duncan Walker
COOK, 3
  Melville Thurston
COOK, 3
  Orator Fuller Jr.
COOK, Orchard H
COOK, Otis Seabury 1
COOK, Paul 1
COOK, Peter, Jr. 5
COOK, Philip 1
COOK, Philip 1
COOK, Raymond Mack 4
COOK, Richard Briscoe 1
COOK, Richard Yerkes 1
COOK, Robert George
COOK, Robert Harvey 2
COOK, Roy Bird 4
COOK, Roy H. 4
COOK, Russell S. H
COOK, Samuel A. 1
COOK, Samuel C. 1
COOK, Samuel E. 4
COOK, Samuel Richard 4
COOK, Sidney Albert
COOK, 4
  Theodore Augustus
COOK, Vernon 3
COOK, Virgil Y. 1
COOK, Waldo Lincoln 3
COOK, Walter 1
COOK, Walter W. 4
COOK, Walter Wheeler 2
COOK, 4
  Walter William Spencer
COOK, William Cassius 3
COOK, William Henry * 1
COOK, William Locke 2
COOK, William Wallace 1
COOK, William Wilson
COOK, Willis Clifford 1
COOK, Willis Clifford 2
COOK, Zadock H
COOK, Zebedee H
COOKE, A. Wayland 1
COOKE, 2
  Alexander Bennett
COOKE, Arthur Bledsoe 5
COOKE, Bates
COOKE, 5
  Charles Maynard, Jr.
COOKE, 2
  Charles Montague Jr.
COOKE, Clarence Hyde 2
COOKE, Douglas H. 2
COOKE, Ebenezer 1
COOKE, Edmund Vance 1
COOKE, Edward Dean H
COOKE, 4
  Elbridge Clinton
COOKE, Eleutheros H
COOKE, Elisha * 1
COOKE, Flora Juliette 3
COOKE, George H
COOKE, George Anderson 1
COOKE, George Henry 1
COOKE, George Willis 1
COOKE, Grace 4
  MacGowan
COOKE, Harold Groves 1
COOKE, Harrison Rice 5
COOKE, Helen Temple 1
COOKE, Henry D. 3
COOKE, Henry David 1
COOKE, Hereward Lester 2
COOKE, James Francis 3
COOKE, Jay 1
COOKE, Jay 4
COOKE, John Daniel 5

COOKE, John Esten * H
COOKE, John Rogers H
COOKE, Joseph Brown 4
COOKE, Joseph Platt 4
COOKE, Josiah Parsons H
COOKE, Juan Isaac 3
COOKE, Leslie Edward 4
COOKE, Lorenzo Wesley 1
COOKE, Lorrin Alanson 1
COOKE, Marjorie Benton 1
COOKE, 3
  Morris Llewellyn
COOKE, H
  Philip Pendleton
COOKE, H
  Philip St George
COOKE, Richard Dickson 3
COOKE, Richard Joseph 1
COOKE, Robert Anderson 4
COOKE, Robert Locke 3
COOKE, Rose Terry 4
COOKE, Samuel 4
COOKE, Thomas Burrage 1
COOKE, Thomas Turner 4
COOKE, Thornton 1
COOKE, Walter Platt 1
COOKE, William Parker 1
COOKMAN, Alfred H
COOKSEY, George
  Robert 2
COOKSON, Walter John 1
COOLBAUGH, 3
  Melville Fuller
COOLBRITH, Ina Donna 1
COOLE, Thomas Henry 1
COOLEY, 1
  Alford Warriner
COOLEY, Anna Maria 5
COOLEY, 5
  Arthur Henderson
COOLEY, Charles Horton 1
COOLEY, 5
  Charles Parsons
COOLEY, Edwin Gilbert 1
COOLEY, 5
  Ethel Halcrow (Mrs. John B. Cooley)
COOLEY, 2
  Frederick Boyden
COOLEY, Hollis Eli 1
COOLEY, LeRoy Clark 1
COOLEY, Lyman Edgar 1
COOLEY, Mortimer 2
  Elwyn
COOLEY, Robert Allen 5
COOLEY, 3
  Robert Lawrence
COOLEY, Roger William 1
COOLEY, Stoughton 1
COOLEY, Thomas Benton 1
COOLEY, H
  Thomas MacIntyre
COOLEY, Thomas Ross 3
COOLEY, William Forbes 4
COOLIDGE, Algernon 4
COOLIDGE, 3
  Archibald Cary
COOLIDGE, 3
  Arthur William
COOLIDGE, Calvin 1
COOLIDGE, 1
  Charles Allerton
COOLIDGE, 1
  Charles Austin
COOLIDGE, Cora Helen 1
COOLIDGE, Cornelius H
COOLIDGE, Dane 1
COOLIDGE, 3
  Elizabeth Sprague
COOLIDGE, 2
  Emelyn Lincoln
COOLIDGE, Emma 4
  Downing
COOLIDGE, George 3
  Greer
COOLIDGE, 3
  Grace Goodhue
COOLIDGE, 1
  Harold Jefferson
COOLIDGE, Herbert 5
COOLIDGE, J. Randolph 1
COOLIDGE, James Henry 4
COOLIDGE, John 1
  Gardner
COOLIDGE, 4
  Joseph Bradford
COOLIDGE, 3
  Julian Lowell
COOLIDGE, Lawrence 3
COOLIDGE, Louis Arthur 1
COOLIDGE, Marcus 2
  Allen
COOLIDGE, Mary 1
  Roberts
COOLIDGE, 4
  Richard Bradford

COOLIDGE, Sherman 1
COOLIDGE, Sidney 1
COOLIDGE, T. Jefferson 1
COOLIDGE, T. Jefferson 3
COOLIDGE, 1
  T. Jefferson Jr.
COOLIDGE, 1
  William Henry
COOM, Charles Sleeman 4
COOMARASWAMY, 2
  Ananda Kentish
COOMBE, 5
  Harry E. (james)
COOMBE, Thomas H
COOMBS, C. Whitney 1
COOMBS, Frank L. 1
COOMBS, George Holden 2
COOMBS, Harrison S. 1
COOMBS, William Jerome 1
COOMBS, Zelotes Wood 2
COON, Charles Lee 1
COON, J. R. 4
COON, Jesse Drake 3
COON, John Sayler 4
COON, Owen L. 2
COON, Stephen Mortimer 1
COONAN, Frederick Leo 4
COONE, Henry Herbert 4
COONEY, Charles Edwin 3
COONEY, Frank H. 1
COONEY, James 4
COONEY, James D. 5
COONEY, Michael 1
COONEY, Percival John 1
COONEY, 4
  Russell Conwell
COONLEY, Howard 4
COONLEY, Lydia Avery 1
COONLEY, 5
  Prentiss Loomis
COONRADT, Arthur C. 3
COONS, Albert 1
COONS, Arthur Gardiner 5
COONS, Henry N. 4
COONS, James Ephraim 5
COONS, Leroy Wilson 2
COONS, Samuel Warwick 4
COONTZ, Robert Edward 1
COOPER, Alfred Duff 4
COOPER, Allen Foster 4
COOPER, 5
  Armwell Lockwood
COOPER, Brainard 1
COOPER, Bryant Syms 3
COOPER, 4
  Charles Champlin
COOPER, 1
  Charles Hermance
COOPER, 1
  Charles Lawrence
COOPER, 3
  Charles Phillips
COOPER, 4
  Charles Proctor
COOPER, 1
  Clayton Sedgwick
COOPER, Colin Campbell 1
COOPER, Courtney Ryley 1
COOPER, Cyril Bernard 5
COOPER, Douglas Harold 4
COOPER, Drury W. 3
COOPER, Edward 1
COOPER, Edward 1
COOPER, Edward Nathan 5
COOPER, Elias Samuel H
COOPER, 2
  Elisha Hilliard
COOPER, 5
  Elizabeth (Mrs. Clayton Sedgwick Cooper)
COOPER, Ellwood 1
COOPER, Emma Lampert 1
COOPER, Ezekiel H
COOPER, Frank 2
COOPER, Frank B. 4
COOPER, Frank Edward* 3
COOPER, Frank Irving 1
COOPER, Frederic Taber 1
COOPER, Gary 4
COOPER, George 3
COOPER, George Bryan H
COOPER, 3
  George Franklin
COOPER, George Victor H
COOPER, Gladys 5
COOPER, Harold 5
COOPER, Henry H
COOPER, Henry Allen 1
COOPER, Henry Elliott 3
COOPER, Henry Ernest 1
COOPER, Herman Charles 5
COOPER, Homer Eber 5
COOPER, Homer H. 4
COOPER, Hugh Lincoln 1
COOPER, Irving Steiger 1
COOPER, 5
  Isabelle Mitchell

COOPER, Jacob 1
COOPER, James H
COOPER, James Fenimore 4
COOPER, James Graham H
COOPER, James Wesley 3
COOPER, Jere 3
COOPER, Job A. 1
COOPER, John 4
COOPER, John Cobb 4
COOPER, John Gordon 5
COOPER, 3
  John Montgomery
COOPER, Kent 4
COOPER, Lane 3
COOPER, Mark Anthony H
COOPER, Merian C. 5
COOPER, Myers Y. 1
COOPER, Myles H
COOPER, Oscar Henry 4
COOPER, Peter H
COOPER, Philip Henry 1
COOPER, Prentice 5
COOPER, H
  Richard Matlack
COOPER, Richard Watson 1
COOPER, Robert Archer 3
COOPER, 4
  Robert Franklin
COOPER, Robert 4
  Muldrow
COOPER, Sam Bronson 1
COOPER, Samuel * H
COOPER, 4
  Samuel Williams
COOPER, 4
  Sanson Milligan
COOPER, H
  Sarah Brown Ingersoll
COOPER, Susan Fenimore H
COOPER, Theodore 1
COOPER, Thomas * H
COOPER, H
  Thomas Abthorpe
COOPER, H
  Thomas Buchecker
COOPER, Wade Hampton 5
COOPER, Wade Hampton 4
COOPER, William * H
COOPER, William Albert 4
COOPER, William Alpha 1
COOPER, 5
  William Goodwin
COOPER, 1
  William Irenaeus
COOPER, William John 1
COOPER, 1
  William Knowles
COOPER, H
  William Raworth
COOPER, Wyllis 3
COOPER-
  POUCHER, Matilda S. 1
COOPERRIDER, George
  T. 5
COORS, D. Stanley 4
COOTE, Richard H
COOTER, James Thomas 4
COOVER, John Edgar 1
COOVER, Melanchthon 3
COPASS, 5
  Benjamin Andrew
COPE, Alexis 4
COPE, Arthur Clay 4
COPE, Caleb H
COPE, Edward Drinker 5
COPE, Gilbert 3
COPE, Henry Frederick 1
COPE, Millard 4
COPE, Quill Evan 5
COPE, Robert S. 3
COPE, Thomas Pym H
COPE, Walter H
COPELAN, Robert W. 4
COPELAND, 3
  Alfred Bryant
COPELAND, 2
  Arthur H(erbert, Sr.
COPELAND, Charles 2
COPELAND, 3
  Charles Townsend
COPELAND, Charles W. H
COPELAND, 3
  Edward Rivers
COPELAND, 5
  Edwin Bingham
COPELAND, Fayette 4
COPELAND, Foster 1
COPELAND, 1
  Frederick Kent
COPELAND, 1
  Guild Anderson
COPELAND, 3
  Lennie Phoebe
COPELAND, Oren S. 3
COPELAND, Paul L. 1
COPELAND, Royal 1
  Samuel

COPELAND, Theodore 1
COPELAND, Walter Scott 1
COPELAND, 4
  William Adams
COPELAND, 3
  William Franklin
COPLAND, Douglas Berry 5
COPLEY, Ira Clifton 2
COPLEY, John Singleton H
COPLEY, Lionel H
COPLIN, 1
  William Michael Late
COPP, Arthur Woodward 1
COPP, Owen 1
COPPEE, Henry H
COPPEE, Henry St Leger 1
COPPENS, Charles 1
COPPER, 5
  Joseph Benjamin
COPPERNOLL, William
  D. 4
COPPERS, George Henry 4
COPPIN, Levi J. 3
COPPINGER, John 1
  Joseph
COPPINI, Pompeo 3
COPPRIDGE, 3
  William Maurice
COPWAY, George H
COQUARD, Leon H
COQUELIN, H
  Benoit Constant
COQUELIN, 4
  Benoit Constant
COQUILLETT, 1
  Daniel William
COQUILLETTE, St. Elmo 5
CORAM, Joseph A. 5
CORAM, Thomas * H
CORBALEY, Gordon
  Cook 4
CORBE, Zenan M. 1
CORBETT, H
  Gail Sherman (Mrs. Harvey Wiley C.)
CORBETT, Harvey Wiley 3
CORBETT, Henry L. 2
CORBETT, Henry 1
  Winslow
CORBETT, Hunter 1
CORBETT, James John 4
CORBETT, James John 4
CORBETT, Jim 2
CORBETT, 2
  Lamert Seymour
CORBETT, Laurence Jay 3
CORBETT, Lee Cleveland 1
CORBETT, Robert James 5
CORBETT, Timothy 1
CORBIN, Alvin LeRoy 5
CORBIN, Arthur Linton 1
CORBIN, 5
  Arthur Linton, Jr.
CORBIN, Austin H
CORBIN, 4
  Caroline Fairfield
CORBIN, 2
  Charles Russell
CORBIN, Daniel C. 1
CORBIN, Henry Clark 1
CORBIN, Henry Pinkney 1
CORBIN, Horace Kellogg 3
CORBIN, John 3
CORBIN, Joseph Carter 4
CORBIN, Margaret 1
CORBIN, Philip 2
CORBIN, 1
  William Herbert
CORBIN, William Lee 3
CORBIND, Jon 4
CORBITT, 1
  Charles Linwood
CORBITT, James Howard 2
CORBLY, 4
  Lawrence Jugurtha
CORBUS, Budd Clarke 3
CORBY, William H
CORCORAN, Brewer 5
CORCORAN, 1
  Francis Vincent
CORCORAN, 4
  George Fancis
CORCORAN, John 1
  William
CORCORAN, Katherine H
CORCORAN, Michael H
CORCORAN, 2
  Sanford William
CORCORAN, Thomas J. 3
CORCORAN, 4
  William Warwick
CORCORAN, H
  William Wilson
CORDELL, 4
  Wayne Wellington
CORDES, Frank 3
CORDES, Frederick Carl 4

COWEN, Joshua Lionel 4
COWEN, Lawrence 5
COWEN, Myron Melvin 4
COWEN, William B. 4
COWGER, William Owen 5
COWHERD, 1
William Strother
COWIE, David Murray 1
COWIE, Jack Baron 1
COWIE, 1
Thomas Jefferson
COWIN, John Clay 1
COWING, Hugh Alvin 2
COWL, Jane 3
COWLES, Alfred 1
COWLES, 1
Alfred Hutchinson
COWLES, 1
Augustus Woodruff
COWLES, Cheney 2
COWLES, Edward 1
COWLES, Edward
Spencer
COWLES, Edwin H
COWLES, Emma Milton 4
COWLES, Eugene Chase 1
COWLES, 3
Frederic Albert
COWLES, Gardner 2
COWLES, Henry Booth 1
COWLES, Henry Chandler 1
COWLES, James Lewis 1
COWLES, 1
John Guiteau Welch
COWLES, John Henry 3
COWLES, Julia Darrow 1
COWLES, LeRoy Eugene 3
COWLES, Maude Alice 1
COWLES, 4
Mrs. Josiah Evans
COWLES, Torris Zalmon 1
COWLES, 1
Walter Cleveland
COWLES, 5
William Hutchinson
COWLES, 2
William Hutchinson
COWLES, William Lyman 1
COWLES, 1
William Sheffield
COWLEY, Charles 1
COWLEY, Matthew 3
COWLING, Donald J. 4
COWPER,
Harry Mattingly
COWPERTHWAITE, 4
Allen Corson
COX, Abraham Beekman 1
COX, Albert Lyman 4
COX, Albert Scott 4
COX, Alonzo Bettis 5
COX, Archibald 1
COX, Argus 4
COX, Attilla 1
COX, Benjamin 5
COX, C(larence) Brown 5
COX, Channing Harris 5
COX, Charles Elbridge 1
COX, Charles Finney 5
COX, Charles Raymond 4
COX, Creed Fulton 5
COX, Creed Fulton 2
COX, Daniel Hargate 3
COX, Douglas Farley 1
COX, Edward Eugene 3
COX, Edward Weston 1
COX, Eleanor Rogers 1
COX, Forrest Dale 3
COX, Frank P. 4
COX, Frederick Irving 4
COX, G. Howland 1
COX, Garfield V. 5
COX, George Clarke 4
COX, 2
George Howland Jr.
COX, George James 2
COX, Guy Henry 1
COX, Guy Wilbur 3
COX, Hannah Pierce H
COX, Harvey Warren 2
COX, Henry Hamilton H
COX, Henry Joseph 5
COX, 1
Charles) Hudson Baynham
COX, Isaac Joslin 5
COX, J. Elwood 1
COX, Jacob H
COX, Jacob Dolson 1
COX, Jacob Dolson 3
COX, James H
COX, James B. 4
COX, James C. 3
COX, James M. 3
COX, James Monroe 5
COX, 5
Jocelyn Meridith Nolting
(Mrs. Rowland Cox Iii)

COX, John Harrington 4
COX, Joseph Winston 1
COX, 1
Katherine Hamilton Cabell
COX, Kenyon 1
COX, Leander Martin H
COX, Leilyn Munns 5
COX, Lemuel H
COX, Leonard Martin 2
COX, Lester Edmund 5
COX, Linton A. 5
COX, Louis Sherburne 5
COX, 2
Louise Howland King
COX, Millard F. 4
COX, 5
Nellie I. Mcmaster (mrs. William Cox)
COX, Nicholas Nichols 4
COX, Oscar Larken 5
COX, Oscar Sydney 1
COX, Palmer 1
COX, Raymond Benjamin 3
COX, Rowland H
COX, Samuel Hanson 4
COX, Samuel Sullivan H
COX, Taylor H. 4
COX, Theodore Sullivan 2
COX, W(illiam) Rowland 5
COX, Wally 5
COX, Walter Smith 1
COX, William Elijah 4
COX, William Ruffin 1
COX, William Stakely 3
COX, William Van Zandt 1
COX, William Wesley 4
COX, Wilson Naylor 5
COXE, Alfred Conkling 1
COXE, Alfred Conkling 1
COXE, Arthur Cleveland H
COXE, Daniel H
COXE, Eckley Brinton 1
COXE, Frank Morrell 1
COXE, 1
James Clarke Watson
COXE, John Redman 1
COXE, Macgrane 1
COXE, Richard Smith H
COXE, Tench 1
COXE, William H
COXE, William Briscom 1
COXE,
William Ellery C.
COXETTER, H
Louis Mitchell
COXEY, Jacob S. 3
COY, Edward Gustin 1
COY, Eliah Washburn 1
COY, Wayne 3
COYE, William Henry 1
COYKENDALL,
Frederick 3
COYL, Horace Edward 4
COYLE, David Cushman 5
COYLE, Eugene 5
COYLE, Frank J. 5
COYLE, Henry 1
COYLE, James Edwin 1
COYLE, Marvin E. 4
COYLE, Robert Francis 1
COYLE, Robert McCurdy 1
COYLE, William Radford 4
COYNE, Frederick E. 4
COYNE, John Nicholas 1
COYNER, Charles Luther 4
COZENS, 3
Frederick Warren
COZIER, Robert V. 5
COZZENS, H
Frederick Swartwout
CRABB, H
George Whitfield
CRABB, Jeremiah H
CRABBE, George William 3
CRABBE, John Grant 1
CRABBS, George Dent 2
CRABITES, Pierre 2
CRABTREE, Charlotte 1
CRABTREE, 2
Ernest Granville
CRABTREE, Frederick 1
CRABTREE, Harold Roy 3
CRABTREE, 4
James Anderson
CRABTREE,
James William
CRABTREE, Nate L. 4
CRACCHI, Guiseppe H
CRADDOCK, 1
Charles Egbert
CRADLEBAUGH, John H
CRAFT, 1
Clarence Christian
CRAFT, E. A. 3
CRAFT, Edward Beech 1
CRAFT, Frost 1
CRAFTON, Allen 4

CRAFTS, 4
Annetta Stratford
CRAFTS, Clayton Edward 4
CRAFTS, James Mason 1
CRAFTS, Leland Whitney 5
CRAFTS, Leo Melville 1
CRAFTS, H
Samuel Chandler
CRAFTS, Sara Jane 5
CRAFTS, Walter 4
CRAFTS, Wilbur Fisk 5
CRAFTS, William H
CRAGHAN, George 1
CRAGIN, Edwin Bradford 1
CRAGIN, 4
Francis Whittemore
CRAGO, Thomas Spencer 1
CRAGUN, John Wiley 5
CRAIG, Alexander Kerr 1
CRAIG, 1
Alexander Righter
CRAIG, Alfred Edwin 1
CRAIG, Alfred M. 1
CRAIG, Asa Hollister 1
CRAIG, Austin H
CRAIG, Austin 3
CRAIG, Charles 4
CRAIG, Charles Curtis 4
CRAIG, 3
Charles Franklin
CRAIG, Charles Patton 1
CRAIG, Clarence Tucker 5
CRAIG, Daniel Frank 3
CRAIG, Daniel H. H
CRAIG,
Donald Alexander
CRAIG, Edward Chilton 3
CRAIG, Edwin Wilson 5
CRAIG, Frank 1
CRAIG, George M. 3
CRAIG, Hardin 5
CRAIG, Hector H
CRAIG, James 1
CRAIG, James Alexander 4
CRAIG, James Edward 5
CRAIG, John 1
CRAIG, Joseph Davis 1
CRAIG, Joseph Edgar 1
CRAIG, Katherine L. 1
CRAIG, Locke 1
CRAIG, Malin 2
CRAIG, Oscar John 3
CRAIG, Palmer Hunt 5
CRAIG, Robert H
CRAIG, 5
Robert S(pencer)
CRAIG, Samuel G. 4
CRAIG, Thomas H
CRAIG, Thomas Bigalow 1
CRAIG, Wallace 5
CRAIG, Walter 1
CRAIG, William Bayard 1
CRAIG, 1
William Benjamin
CRAIG, William Edward 1
CRAIG, Willis Green 1
CRAIG, 3
Winchell McKendree
CRAIGE, Francis Burton H
CRAIGE, Francis Burton 2
CRAIGHEAD, Edwin
Boone 3
CRAIGHEAD, Erwin 1
CRAIGHILL, 5
George Bowdoin, Sr.
CRAIGHILL,
William Price
CRAIGIE, Andrew H
CRAIGIE, 1
David Johnston
CRAIGIE, 1
Pearl Mary-Teresa
CRAIGIE,
William Alexander
CRAIK, James H
CRAIK, William H
CRAIL, Joe 1
CRAIN, John Hillier 4
CRAIN, William Henry H
CRAM, Franklin Webster 4
CRAM, George F. 1
CRAM, Harold Edgerly 2
CRAM, Ralph Adams H
CRAM, Ralph Adams 2
CRAM, Ralph Adams 4
CRAM, Ralph Warren 1
CRAM, Willard Gliden 5
CRAM, William Everett 3
CRAM, Wingate Franklin 1
CRAMBLET, Thomas E. 1
CRAMER, Frederic 5
CRAMER, Harriet Laura 4
CRAMER, John H
CRAMER, John Francis 5
CRAMER, John Luther 4
CRAMER, John Wesley 4
CRAMER, Kenneth Frank 3

CRAMER, Michael John H
CRAMER, Myron Cady 4
CRAMER, Sterling B. 3
CRAMER, Stuart Warren 1
CRAMER, 2
Stuart Warren Jr.
CRAMER, W. Stuart 1
CRAMER, William 2
CRAMP, Arthur Joseph; 5
CRAMP, Charles Henry 1
CRAMP, 1
Walter Concemore
CRAMP, William H
CRAMPTON, Albert M. 3
CRAMPTON, C. Ward 4
CRAMPTON, 1
Charles Albert
CRAMPTON, George S. 5
CRAMPTON, Guy 3
Chester
CRAMPTON, Henry 3
Edward
CRAMTON, Louis C. 5
CRANCH, H
Christopher Pearse
CRANCH, John H
CRANCH, William H
CRANDALL, 3
Albert Rogers
CRANDALL, 4
Andrew Wallace
CRANDALL, 3
Arthur Fitz James
CRANDALL, Bruce Verne 4
CRANDALL, 1
Charles Henry
CRANDALL, Charles Lee 1
CRANDALL, 1
Charles Spencer
CRANDALL, 5
Clifford Waldorf
CRANDALL, 1
Floyd Milford
CRANDALL, 1
Francis Asbury
CRANDALL, 4
George Strachen
CRANDALL, H. Burr 4
CRANDALL, 1
Lathan Augustus
CRANDALL, Lee 5
Saunders
CRANDALL, Prudence H
CRANDALL, Shannon 5
CRANDALL, Shannon Jr. 1
CRANDON, 1
Le Roi Goddard
CRANE, A. W. 1
CRANE, Aaron Martin 1
CRANE, Albert Sears 2
CRANE, Anne Moncure 1
CRANE, Arthur Griswold 5
CRANE, Arthur Henry 4
CRANE, Augustus 5
CRANE, Bruce 1
CRANE, 1
Caroline Bartlett
CRANE, Cephas Bennett 1
CRANE, Charles Alva 1
CRANE, Charles Howard 3
CRANE, 1
Charles Kittredge
CRANE, Charles P. 5
CRANE, Charles Richard 1
CRANE, 3
Charles Richard II
CRANE, Clinton Hoadley 3
CRANE, Cyrus 1
CRANE, Earl H(oward) 5
CRANE, Edward Andrew 4
CRANE, Edward 4
Matthews
CRANE, 4
Elvin Williamson
CRANE, Evan Jay 4
CRANE, Frank 1
CRANE, Frederick Evan 1
CRANE, Frederick Lea 2
CRANE, G. Stewart 1
CRANE, George Francis 1
CRANE, Hart 1
CRANE, Jason George 5
CRANE, Jasper Elliot 5
CRANE, Jay Everett 5
CRANE, Jefferson Davis 3
CRANE, John 3
CRANE, John Alden 3
CRANE, 1
Jonathan Townley
CRANE, Joseph Halsey 5
CRANE, Lawrence 5
Gordon
CRANE, Louis Burton 5
CRANE, Martin McNulty 1
CRANE, Michael Joseph 1

CRANE, Oscar W. 5
CRANE, R. B. 1
CRANE, R. Newton 1
CRANE, Ralph Thompson 1
CRANE, Raymond E. 3
CRANE, Richard 1
CRANE, Richard Teller 1
CRANE, 1
Richard Teller Jr.
CRANE, Robert Clark 4
CRANE, Robert Treat 4
CRANE, Ronald Salmon 5
CRANE, Ronald Salmon 4
CRANE, Ross 2
CRANE, Stephen H
CRANE, Stephen 4
CRANE, Theodore 1
CRANE, 1
Thomas Frederick
CRANE, W. Murray 1
CRANE, Walter Richard 5
CRANE, William G. 3
CRANE, William H. 1
CRANE, William Iler 1
CRANE, H
William Montgomery
CRANE, 5
Winthrop Murray, Jr.
CRANE, Zenas Marshall 1
CRANE-GARTZ, Kate 4
CRANFILL, 2
James Britton
CRANFORD, William
Ivey 4
CRANMER, Gibson L. 1
CRANMER, William H. 4
H.
CRANNELL, 5
Elizabeth Keller Shaule
(Mrs. Winslow Crannell)
CRANNELL, 1
Philip Wendell
CRANSTON, Claudia 2
CRANSTON, Earl 1
CRANSTON, Earl 5
CRANSTON, Henry
Young H
CRANSTON, John H
CRANSTON,
Robert Bennie
CRANSTON, Samuel H
CRANWELL, James
Logan 4
CRANWELL,
Thomas George
CRAPO, Philip M. 1
CRAPO, Stanford Tappan 1
CRAPO, William Wallace 1
CRAPSEY, 1
Algernon Sidney
CRARY, George Waldo 4
CRARY, Gordon B. 1
CRARY, Isaac Edwin H
CRASSWELLER, Frank 2
CRATHORNE, 2
Arthur Robert
CRATTY, Mabel 1
CRATTY, Robert Irvin 4
CRAVATH, Erastus Milo 1
CRAVATH, Paul Drennan 1
CRAVEN, Alex 4
CRAVEN, Alfred 1
CRAVEN, Braxton 4
CRAVEN,
Charles Edmiston
CRAVEN, 1
Elijah Richardson
CRAVEN, Frank 2
CRAVEN, George Warren 1
CRAVEN, Hermon Wilson 2
CRAVEN, James Braxton 2
CRAVEN, John Joseph H
CRAVEN, Leslie 3
CRAVEN, Thomas 5
CRAVEN, Thomas Tingey 3
CRAVEN, Thomas Tingey 3
CRAVEN,
Tunis Augustus Macdonough
CRAVEN, H
Tunus Augustus
Macdonough
CRAVEN, William Reno 4
CRAVENS, Ben 1
CRAVENS,
Du Val Garland
CRAVENS, James
Addison H
CRAVENS, H
James Harrison
CRAVENS, John William 1
CRAVENS, 5
Kenton Robinson
CRAVENS, Oscar Henry 5
CRAVER,
Harrison Warwick
CRAVER, Samuel Porch 1

Name	
CRAWFORD, Andrew Murray	1
CRAWFORD, Andrew Wright	1
CRAWFORD, Angus	4
CRAWFORD, Angus	5
CRAWFORD, Arch	1
CRAWFORD, Arthur	4
CRAWFORD, Charles	3
CRAWFORD, Charles Wallace	3
CRAWFORD, Clarence K.	4
CRAWFORD, Coe Isaac	4
CRAWFORD, David A.	3
CRAWFORD, David McLean	4
CRAWFORD, Earl Stetson	5
CRAWFORD, Eben G.	2
CRAWFORD, Edward Grant	1
CRAWFORD, Edwin Robert	1
CRAWFORD, Eugene Lowther	1
CRAWFORD, F. Stuart	1
CRAWFORD, Finia Goff	5
CRAWFORD, Francis Marion	1
CRAWFORD, Fred Lewis	3
CRAWFORD, George Gordon	1
CRAWFORD, George Washington	H
CRAWFORD, Harry J.	3
CRAWFORD, Harry Jennings	3
CRAWFORD, Isabel	4
CRAWFORD, Ivan Charles	4
CRAWFORD, Jack Randall	5
CRAWFORD, James Pyle Wickersham	1
CRAWFORD, James Stoner	4
CRAWFORD, Jerry Tinder	1
CRAWFORD, Joel	H
CRAWFORD, John	H
CRAWFORD, John Forsyth	1
CRAWFORD, John Jones	4
CRAWFORD, John M.	3
CRAWFORD, John Martin	1
CRAWFORD, John Raymond	1
CRAWFORD, John Wallace	1
CRAWFORD, Joseph E(manuel)	5
CRAWFORD, Leonard Jacob	1
CRAWFORD, Leonidas Wakefield	3
CRAWFORD, Martin Jenkins	H
CRAWFORD, Mary Caroline	1
CRAWFORD, Mary Sinclair	4
CRAWFORD, Medorem	4
CRAWFORD, Meriwether Lewis	1
CRAWFORD, Morris Barker	1
CRAWFORD, Morris Barker	2
CRAWFORD, Nelson Antrim	4
CRAWFORD, Porter James	2
CRAWFORD, Ralph Dixon	3
CRAWFORD, Robert A.	1
CRAWFORD, Russell Tracy	3
CRAWFORD, Samuel Johnson	1
CRAWFORD, Stanton Chapman	4
CRAWFORD, Thomas	H
CRAWFORD, Thomas Dwight	1
CRAWFORD, Thomas Hartley	H
CRAWFORD, Thomas Henry	1
CRAWFORD, Walter Joshua	1
CRAWFORD, William *	H
CRAWFORD, William Alfred	1
CRAWFORD, William Campbell	1
CRAWFORD, William Harris	H
CRAWFORD, William Henry	2
CRAWFORD, William Hopkins	4
CRAWFORD, William L.	1
CRAWFORD, William T.	4
CRAWFORD, William Thomas	1
CRAWFORD, William Webb	3
CRAWFORD-FROST, William Albert	1
CRAWLEY, Clyde B.	3
CRAWLEY, David Ephraim	1
CRAWLEY, Edwin Schoffield	2
CRAWSHAW, Fred Duane	5
CRAWSHAW, William Henry	1
CRAZY HORSE	H
CREAGER, Charles E.	5
CREAGER, John Oscar	2
CREAGER, Marvin H.	5
CREAGER, Rentfro Banton	3
CREAGER, William Pitcher	3
CREAL, Edward Wester	2
CREAMER, David	H
CREAMER, Thomas J.	2
CREASER, Charles W.	4
CREATH, Jacob *	H
CREBS, John Montgomery	H
CRECRAFT, Earl Willis	2
CREE, Archibald Cunningham	3
CREECH, Harris	2
CREECH, John W.	3
CREECH, Oscar, Jr.	5
CREECH, Oscar Jr.	4
CREED, Thomas Percival	1
CREED, Wigginton Ellis	1
CREEDE, Frank J.	4
CREEDEN, Daniel W.	3
CREEGAN, Charles Cole	1
CREEL, Enrique C.	3
CREEL, George	3
CREEL, Robert Calhoun	3
CREELMAN, Harlan	3
CREELMAN, James	1
CREESE, James	4
CREESE, Wadsworth	5
CREESY, Josiah Perkins	1
CREEVEY, Caroline Alathea Stickney	4
CREHORE, Albert Cushing	1
CREHORE, William Williams	1
CREIGHTON, Albert Morton	4
CREIGHTON, Edward	H
CREIGHTON, Elmer Ellsworth Farmer	1
CREIGHTON, Frank Whittington	2
CREIGHTON, James Edwin	1
CREIGHTON, John Thrale	1
CREIGHTON, Martha Gladys	4
CREIGHTON, William	H
CREIGHTON, William Henry	1
CREIGHTON, William J.	3
CREIM, Ben Wilton	3
CREITZ, Charles Erwin	4
CRELLIN, Edward Webster	2
CREMER, Jacob Theodoor	1
CRENIER, Henri	1
CRENSHAW, Bolling Hall	1
CRENSHAW, H. F.	1
CRENSHAW, James Llewellyn	3
CRENSHAW, Ollinger	5
CRENSHAW, Thomas C.	4
CRERAR, Henry Duncan Graham	4
CRERAR, John	H
CRESAP, Mark W. Jr.	4
CRESAP, Mark Winfield	2
CRESAP, Michael	H
CRESAP, Thomas	H
CRESON, Larry Barkley	5
CRESPI, Juan	4
CRESPO 'Y MARTINEZ, Gilberto	4
CRESS, George Clifford	3
CRESS, George Oscar	3
CRESSEY, George Babcock	4
CRESSEY, George Croswell	1
CRESSLER, Alfred Miller	1
CRESSLER, Isabel Bonbrake	3
CRESSON, Elliott	H
CRESSON, Ezra Townsend	4
CRESSON, W. Penn	1
CRESSWELL, Robert	2
CRESSY, Warren Francis	3
CRESSY, Wilfred Wesley	1
CRESSY, Will Martin	1
CRESWELL, Edward J.	3
CRESWELL, Harry I. T.	5
CRESWELL, John Angel James	H
CRET, Paul Philippe	2
CRETIN, Joseph	H
CREVECOEUR, Michel-Guillaume Jean De	H
CREW, Henry	3
CREW, William Binford	1
CREWS, Floyd Houston	4
CREWS, Leslie F.	5
CREWS, Ralph	3
CRICHTON, Alexander Fraser	1
CRICHTON, Kyle S.	4
CRIDER, John Henshaw	5
CRIDLAND, Charles	5
CRIDLER, Thomas Wilbur	4
CRILE, Austin Daniel	1
CRILE, Dennis Rider Wood	1
CRILE, George Washington	2
CRILLEY, A. Cyril	3
CRIM, John William Henry	1
CRIMMINS, Harry Benedict	4
CRIMMINS, John Daniel	1
CRIMONT, Joseph Raphael	2
CRINKLEY, Matthew S.	4
CRIPPA, Edward David	4
CRIPPEN, Henry Durrell	1
CRIPPEN, Lloyd Kenneth	5
CRIPPS, Sir Stafford	3
CRISCUOLO, Luigi	3
CRISFIELD, John Woodland	H
CRISP, Charles Frederick	1
CRISP, Charles R.	1
CRISPIN, M. Jackson	3
CRISS, Clair C.	3
CRISS, Neil Louis	5
CRISSEY, Forrest	2
CRISSINGER, Daniel Richard	2
CRIST, Bainbridge	5
CRIST, Harris McCabe	2
CRIST, Henry	H
CRIST, Raymond Fowler	4
CRISTY, Albert Barnes	4
CRISTY, Albert Moses	1
CRISWELL, George Stuart	1
CRITCHFIELD, Howard Emmett	4
CRITCHLOW, Francis B.	3
CRITTENBERGER, George Dale	4
CRITTENDEN, Christopher	5
CRITTENDEN, Eugene Casson	3
CRITTENDEN, George Bibb	H
CRITTENDEN, John Jordan	1
CRITTENDEN, Thomas Leonidas	H
CRITTENDEN, Thomas Theodore	1
CRITTENDEN, Walter Hayden	2
CRITZ, Hugh	5
CRITZ, Richard	5
CROASDALE, Jack Finch	4
CROASDALE, Stuart	1
CROCE, Benedette	1
CROCHERON, Henry	H
CROCHERON, Jacob	H
CROCKARD, Frank Hearne	1
CROCKER, Alvah	H
CROCKER, Arthur W.	4
CROCKER, Augustus Luther	4
CROCKER, Bosworth	1
CROCKER, Charles	H
CROCKER, Charles Henry	1
CROCKER, Edward Savage	5
CROCKER, Francis Bacon	1
CROCKER, Frank Longfellow	2
CROCKER, George	1
CROCKER, George Glover	1
CROCKER, Hannah Mather	H
CROCKER, Henry E.	1
CROCKER, Samuel Leonard	H
CROCKER, Sarah G.	1
CROCKER, Stuart Miller	3
CROCKER, Templeton	2
CROCKER, Theodore D.	2
CROCKER, Uriel	H
CROCKER, Uriel Haskell	1
CROCKER, Walter James	2
CROCKER, William	2
CROCKER, William Henry	1
CROCKER, William Willard	4
CROCKETT, Albert Stevens	5
CROCKETT, Arthur Jay	4
CROCKETT, Charles Winthrop	1
CROCKETT, David	H
CROCKETT, Eugene Anthony	1
CROCKETT, Horace Guy	4
CROCKETT, Ingram	4
CROCKETT, John Wesley	4
CROCKETT, Montgomery Adams	1
CROCKETT, Walter Hill	1
CROCKETT, William Day	1
CROCKETT, William Goggin	1
CROES, John James Robertson	1
CROFFUT, William Augustus	1
CROFT, Albert Jefferson	1
CROFT, Delmer Eugene	1
CROFT, Edward	1
CROFT, George William	1
CROFT, Harry William	1
CROFTAN, Alfred Careno	1
CROFTS, Frederick Sharer	3
CROGHAN, George	H
CROGHAN, Hubert McLeod	4
CROGMAN, William Henry Sr.	1
CROISSANT, De Witt Clinton	2
CROIX, Teodoro 'de	H
CROKER, Richard	1
CROLL, Morris William	2
CROLL, Philip C.	4
CROLL, William M.	1
CROLY, David Goodman	H
CROLY, Herbert	1
CROLY, Jane Cunningham	1
CROMELIN, Paul Bowen	3
CROMER, George Benedict	1
CROMER, George Washington	4
CROMER, S. S.	4
CROMIE, William James	5
CROMMELIN, Henry	5
CROMPTON, George	H
CROMPTON, George	1
CROMPTON, William	H
CROMWELL, Arthur Dayton	5
CROMWELL, Bartlett Jefferson	1
CROMWELL, Emma Guy	3
CROMWELL, Frederic	5
CROMWELL, Frederick	1
CROMWELL, George	1
CROMWELL, Lincoln	3
CROMWELL, Michael Jenkins	5
CROMWELL, William Nelson	2
CRONAU, Rudolf	1
CRONBACH, Abraham	4
CRONE, Frank Linden	5
CRONE, R. Bertram	5
CRONEIS, Carey	5
CRONIN, Con P.	1
CRONIN, David Edward	4
CRONIN, Edward Joseph	3
CRONIN, John J.	4
CRONIN, John William	1
CRONIN, Marcus Daniel	1
CRONIN, Timothy T.	3
CRONIN, William Francis	4
CRONKHITE, Adelbert	1
CRONYN, George William	5
CROOK, Alja Robinson	1
CROOK, George	H
CROOK, Isaac	1
CROOK, James King	1
CROOK, James Walter	1
CROOK, Jere Lawrence	3
CROOK, William McKissack	2
CROOKE, Philip Schuyler	1
CROOKER, Florence Kollock	1
CROOKER, Joseph Henry	1
CROOKS, Alexander Richard	5
CROOKS, Arthur	H
CROOKS, Ezra Breckenridge	1
CROOKS, Ezra Breckenridge	2
CROOKS, George Richard	H
CROOKS, Ramsay	H
CROOKS, Richard M.	5
CROOKSHANK, Angus James	4
CROPLEY, Charles Elmore	1
CROPPER, Walter V.	1
CROPSEY, James Church	1
CROPSEY, Jasper Francis	1
CROPSEY, Nebraska Miss	1
CROSAS, Andres Bernardino	1
CROSBY, Alpheus	1
CROSBY, Charles Noel	1
CROSBY, Dick J.	1
CROSBY, Edward Harold	1
CROSBY, Edwin L.	1
CROSBY, Edwin Stanislau	3
CROSBY, Ernest Howard	1
CROSBY, Evan	2
CROSBY, Everett Nathaniel	1
CROSBY, Everett Uberto	5
CROSBY, Fanny	1
CROSBY, Franklin Muzzy	5
CROSBY, Frederic Van Schoonhoven	1
CROSBY, George Harrington	1
CROSBY, George Heman	4
CROSBY, H. E.	3
CROSBY, Harley N.	3
CROSBY, Herbert Ball	1
CROSBY, Howard	1
CROSBY, James Ott	1
CROSBY, John	1
CROSBY, John Crawford	1
CROSBY, John Schuyler	1
CROSBY, Nathan	1
CROSBY, Oscar Terry	1
CROSBY, Peirce	1
CROSBY, Pierce	1
CROSBY, Raymond Moreau	1
CROSBY, Sheldon Leavitt	1
CROSBY, Stephen Moody	1
CROSBY, Walter Wilson	1
CROSBY, William Dorr	3
CROSBY, William Hugh	5
CROSBY, William Otis	1
CROSE, William Michael	5
CROSIER, Edwin Neil	1
CROSKEY, John Welsh	5
CROSLAND, John Everett	1
CROSLEY, Powel Jr.	1
CROSLEY, Walter Selwyn	4
CROSMAN, Charles Sumner	1
CROSMAN, Henrietta	2
CROSS, Anson Kent	2
CROSS, Arthur Chester	1
CROSS, Arthur Lyon	4
CROSS, Asa Beebe	1
CROSS, Cecil Frank	4
CROSS, Charles Robert	1
CROSS, Charles Whitman	1
CROSS, Clarence Eland	4
CROSS, E(than) A(llen)	1
CROSS, Earle Bennett	4
CROSS, Edward	1
CROSS, Edward Makin	5
CROSS, Edward Weeks	1
CROSS, George	1
CROSS, Hardy	1
CROSS, Harold L.	3
CROSS, Harry Parsons	1
CROSS, Henry H.	1
CROSS, Henry H.	1

CROSS, John W(alker) 5
CROSS, John Walter 3
CROSS, Joseph 1
CROSS, Judson Lewis 2
CROSS, Judson Newell 1
CROSS, Lewis Josephus 5
CROSS, Michael Hurley H
CROSS, Oliver Harlan 5
CROSS, Peter F. 1
CROSS, Richard James 1
CROSS, 4
  Roselle Theodore
CROSS, Roy 2
CROSS, Samuel Hazzard 2
CROSS, Thomas Joseph 4
CROSS, Walter Snell 5
CROSS, Wilbur Lucius 2
CROSS, 3
  William Campbell
CROSSE, 2
  Charles Washburn
CROSSE, Mentor 4
CROSSEN, George
  Edward 3
CROSSEN, 3
  Harry Sturgeon
CROSSER, John Roach 3
CROSSER, Robert 4
CROSSETT, Edward C. 4
CROSSETT, Lewis Abbott 4
CROSSFIELD, 3
  Richard Henry
CROSSKEY, 4
  William Winslow
CROSSLAND, Edward H
CROSSLAND, Paul
  Marion 5
CROSSLAND, 4
  Weldon Frank
CROSSLEY, 5
  Arthur Webster
CROSSLEY, 1
  Frederic Beers
CROSSLEY, James Judson 5
CROSSLEY, Robert J. 3
CROSSLEY, 5
  Robert Pierce
CROSSMAN, Edgar
  Gibson 4
CROSSMAN, Edgar O. 5
CROSSMAN, 5
  Jerome Kenneth
CROSSWELL, William H
CROSWELL, Edwin H
CROSWELL, Harry H
CROSWELL, 1
  James Greenleaf
CROTHERS, Austin L. 1
CROTHERS, Bronson 3
CROTHERS, 3
  George Edward
CROTHERS, 4
  Harold Marion
CROTHERS, Rachel 3
CROTHERS, 1
  Samuel McChord
CROTHERS, 1
  Thomas Davison
CROTT, Homer Daniel 5
CROTTI, Andre 3
CROUCH, Austin 3
CROUCH, Calvin Henry 1
CROUCH, Charles T. 5
CROUCH, Edward H
CROUCH, 3
  Leonard Callender
CROUCH, Richard Edwin 4
CROUCH, 5
  Sydney James Leonhardt
CROUSE, Lorenzo 3
CROUSE, George Nellis 2
CROUSE, Mary Elizabeth 5
CROUSE, Russel 4
CROUTER, 1
  A. L. Edgerton
CROW, Charles Augustus 3
CROW, Charles Langley 2
CROW, Herbert Carl 1
CROW, Herman Denton 1
CROW, Martha Foote 4
CROW, Orin Faison 3
CROW, Randolph Fairfax 1
CROW, William E. 1
CROWDER, Enoch
  Herbert 1
CROWDER, 1
  Frank Warfield
CROWDER, John Batte 3
CROWDER, 5
  Render Lewis, Jr.
CROWDER, Thomas Reid 5
ROWE, 2
  Francis Trenholm
CROWE, John A. 4
CROWE, R. L. 3
CROWE, Thomas Bennett 1
CROWE, William 4

CROWELL, 3
  Bowman Corning
CROWELL, 1
  Chester Theodore
CROWELL, Edward
  Payson 1
CROWELL, 5
  Grace Noll (Mrs. Norman
  H. Crowell)
CROWELL, Henry
  Coleman 4
CROWELL, Henry
  Parsons 2
CROWELL, James Foster 1
CROWELL, 1
  James McMullin
CROWELL, John * H
CROWELL, John 1
CROWELL, John Franklin 1
CROWELL, John Stephen 1
CROWELL, 1
  Katharine Roney
CROWELL, 3
  Lester Avant Sr.
CROWELL, Luther Childs 1
CROWELL, Merle 3
CROWELL, 4
  Thomas Irving Jr.
CROWLEY, 3
  Charles Francis
CROWLEY, Henry J. 1
CROWLEY, John Dennis 5
CROWLEY, Joseph Burns 4
CROWLEY, Karl Allen 2
CROWLEY, Leo T. 5
CROWLEY, 1
  Mary Catherine
CROWLEY, 3
  Patrick Edward
CROWLEY, Xavier 3
CROWN, James Evans 2
CROWNE, John H
CROWNE, William H
CROWNFIELD, Gertrude 2
CROWNHART, 1
  Charles Henry
CROWNHART, 2
  Jesse George
CROWNINSHIELD, 1
  Arent Schuyler
CROWNINSHIELD, H
  Benjamin Williams
CROWNINSHIELD, 1
  Bowdoin Bradlee
CROWNINSHIELD, 1
  Caspar Schuyler
CROWNINSHIELD, 2
  Frank
CROWNINSHIELD, 1
  Frederic
CROWNINSHIELD, H
  George
CROWNINSHIELD, H
  Jacob
CROWNINSHIELD, 1
  Mary Bradford
CROWNOVER, Arthur Jr. 4
CROWNOVER, Arthur Sr. 2
CROWSON, 1
  Benjamin Franklin
CROWTHER, Cyril Irwin 4
CROWTHER, Frank 3
CROWTHER, James
  Edwin 2
CROWTHER, Samuel 2
CROXTON, Fred C. 4
CROY, Homer 4
CROY, Homer 5
CROZER, John Price H
CROZER, Samuel Aldrich 1
CROZET, Claude H
CROZIER, 1
  Herbert William
CROZIER, John Hervey H
CROZIER, Norman
  Robert 1
CROZIER, Robert H
CROZIER, W. J. 3
CROZIER, William 2
CRUCE, Lee 5
CRUCHAGA-
  TOCORNAL, Miguel 5
CRUDUP, Josiah H
CRUGER, Daniel H
CRUGER, Henry H
CRUGER, John H
CRUGER, Mary 1
CRUICKSHANK, H. W. 4
CRUICKSHANK, Alfred B. 1
CRUIKSHANK, Margaret 1
CRUIKSHANK, R. J. 3
CRUIKSHANK, Russell V. 4
CRUIKSHANK, 2
  William Mackey
CRULL, Harry Edward 5

CRUM, 3
  Bartley Cavanaugh
CRUM, Roy W. 3
CRUM, William Demos 1
CRUM, William Leonard 4
CRUMB, Frederick Waite 4
CRUMBACKER,
  William Pollock 1
CRUMBINE, Samuel Jay 3
CRUMLEY, Thomas 3
CRUMLEY,
  Thomas Ralston 1
CRUMMER, Le Roy 1
CRUMP, Edward Hull 3
CRUMP, George William H
CRUMP, Rousseau O. 1
CRUMP, Walter Gray 2
CRUMP, William Wood H
CRUMPACKER, Edgar
  Dean 1
CRUMPACKER,
  Maurice Edgar 1
CRUMPTON,
  Washington Bryan 1
CRUNDEN,
  Frederick Morgan 1
CRUNELLE, Leonard 2
CRUSE, Thomas 2
CRUSINBERRY, 3
  William Alfred
CRUTCHFIELD, 3
  James Stapleton
CRUTCHFIELD, William H
CRUTCHFIELD, 5
  William Gayle
CRUTHCER, 5
  Lewis Pinkerton
CRUTTENDEN, 2
  Walter Barnes
CRUZ, Anibal 1
CRUZE, James 2
CRYDERMAN, 5
  Mackie Macintyre (Mrs.
  Clifford William
CRYER, George Edward 4
CRYER, Matthew Henry 1
CSATORDAY, Karoly 5
CUBBERLEY, 1
  Ellwood Patterson
CUBBERLY, Fred 1
CUBBINS, 3
  William Robert
CUCKSON, John 1
CUDAHY, Edward A. 1
CUDAHY, 1
  Edward Aloysius Sr.
CUDAHY, John 1
CUDAHY, John 2
CUDAHY, Joseph M. 1
CUDAHY, Michael 1
CUDAHY, 5
  Michael Francis
CUDAHY, Patrick H
CUDDEBACK, Allan W. 1
CUDDEBACK, 1
  William Herman
CUDDIHY, 3
  Herbert Lester
CUDDY, Warren N. 3
CUDLIP, Merlin A. 5
CUENY, Elizabeth 1
CUFFE, Paul H
CUFFE, Thomas E. 4
CULBERSON, Charles A. 1
CULBERSON,
  David Browning 1
CULBERTSON, Albert L. 1
CULBERTSON, Alexander H
CULBERTSON, 4
  Anne Virginia
CULBERTSON, Ely 3
CULBERTSON, 1
  Emma Valeria Bicknell
CULBERTSON, Henry
  Coe 1
CULBERTSON, James
  Coe 1
CULBERTSON, 5
  James Gordon
CULBERTSON, John J. 1
CULBERTSON, William 5
CULBERTSON, 4
  William Smith
CULBRETH, 4
  David Marvel Reynolds
CULBRETH, Thomas H
CULIG, Ivan Conrad 4
CULIN,
  Alice Mumford (Mrs.
  Stewart Culin) 1
CULIN, Frank Lewis 4
CULIN, Stewart 1
CULKIN, Francis D. 2
CULKINS, 1
  William Clement
CULLEN, Countee 2

CULLEN, 1
  Edgar Montgomery
CULLEN, H
  Elisha Dickerson
CULLEN, Frederick John 5
CULLEN, Glenn E. 1
CULLEN, Hugh Roy 3
CULLEN, Richard J. 2
CULLEN, Thomas Ernest 5
CULLEN, Thomas H. 2
CULLEN, 4
  Thomas Joseph Vincent
CULLEN, Thomas
  Stephen 3
CULLEN, Vincent 4
CULLER, Arthur Jerome 2
CULLER, Arthur Merl 4
CULLER, 1
  Joseph Albertus
CULLIMORE, 3
  Allan Reginald
CULLIMORE, Clarence 4
CULLINAN, 3
  Craig Francis
CULLINAN, 3
  Edith Phillips
CULLINAN, 1
  Joseph Stephen
CULLIS, Charles H
CULLISON, 1
  James Buchanan
CULLMAN, Howard
  S(tix) 5
CULLOM, Alvan H
CULLOM,
  Marvin McTyeire 1
CULLOM, Shelby Moore 1
CULLOM, William H
CULLOM, Willis Richard 5
CULLOP, William Allen 1
CULLUM, H
  George Washington
CULMER, Henry L. A. 1
CULP, Charles Cantrell 4
CULP, John M. 1
CULPEPER, John H
CULPEPER, Thomas 1
CULPEPPER, John H
CULTER, Mary McCrae 4
CULVER, Bernard Mott 3
CULVER, Bertram Beach 3
CULVER, Charles Beach 5
CULVER, 1
  Charles Mortimer
CULVER, Erastus Dean H
CULVER, Frank Pugh 1
CULVER, Harry Hazel 2
CULVER, Helen 1
CULVER, Henry S. 4
CULVER, John Yapp 3
CULVER, 5
  Montgomery Morton
CULVER, Raymond B. 1
CULVER, Romulus Estep 4
CUMBERLAND, 3
  William Wilson
CUMING, Fortescue 1
CUMING, Sir Alexander H
CUMINGS, Edgar Roscoe 5
CUMMER, 3
  Clyde Lottridge
CUMMING, Alfred H
CUMMING, 1
  Charles Atherton
CUMMING, Hugh S. 2
CUMMING, H
  Thomas William
CUMMING, William H
CUMMINGHAM, 2
  William Burgess
CUMMINGS, Amos 4
CUMMINGS,
  Bertrude Fields Mrs. 1
CUMMINGS, Charles
  Amos 1
CUMMINGS, Clara Eaton 1
CUMMINGS, D. Mark 1
CUMMINGS, Edward 1
CUMMINGS, 4
  Edward Estlin
CUMMINGS, 4
  George Donald
CUMMINGS, George W. 1
CUMMINGS, H
  Gordon Parker
CUMMINGS, Harold Neff 4
CUMMINGS,
  Henry Johnson Brodhead 4
CUMMINGS,
  Henry Johnson Brodhead 4
CUMMINGS, Homer
  Stille 3
CUMMINGS, James
  Howell 1
CUMMINGS, H
  Jeremiah Williams
CUMMINGS, Joe Brown 3

CUMMINGS, John H
CUMMINGS, John 1
CUMMINGS, Joseph H
CUMMINGS, 5
  Marshall Baxter
CUMMINGS, Marvin Earl 5
CUMMINGS, O. Sam 1
CUMMINGS, Thomas Seir H
CUMMINGS, Walter J. 4
CUMMINGS, Wilbur Love 1
CUMMINGS, Albert Baird 1
CUMMINGS, Albert Wilson 1
CUMMINS, Alexander H
CUMMINS, 2
  Alexander Griswold
CUMMINS, Claude 1
CUMMINS, Claude 5
CUMMINS, Clessie Lyle 5
CUMMINS, George David 1
CUMMINS, John 1
CUMMINS, John D. H
CUMMINS, 3
  Joseph Michael
CUMMINS, Maria
  Susanna H
CUMMINS, Ralph 4
CUMMINS, Robert
  Rankin 3
CUMMINS, 4
  William Fletcher
CUMMINS, William J. 1
CUMMINS, 3
  William Taylor
CUMNOCK, Robert
  McLean 1
CUNHA, Felix 4
CUNINGGIM, Jesse Lee 5
CUNLIFFE, John William 2
CUNLIFFE-OWEN, 1
  Frederick
CUNLIFFE-OWEN, 2
  Sir Hugo
CUNNIFF, Michael Glen 1
CUNNINGHAM, 4
  Albert Benjamin
CUNNINGHAM, 1
  Andrew Chase
CUNNINGHAM, 1
  Andrew Oswald
CUNNINGHAM, Ann
  Pamela H
CUNNINGHAM, 3
  Augustine Joseph
CUNNINGHAM, 2
  Benjamin B.
CUNNINGHAM, 5
  Benjamin Frazier
CUNNINGHAM, Bert 1
CUNNINGHAM, 5
  Burris Bell
CUNNINGHAM, 5
  C. Frederick
CUNNINGHAM, 2
  Charles Henry
CUNNINGHAM, 3
  Cornelius Carman
CUNNINGHAM, David
  West 1
CUNNINGHAM, 2
  Donnell LaFayette
CUNNINGHAM, 1
  Edward Henry
CUNNINGHAM, 3
  Edwin Sheddan
CUNNINGHAM, Edwin
  W. 4
CUNNINGHAM,
  Elijah William 4
CUNNINGHAM, Eugene 3
CUNNINGHAM, H
  Francis Alanson
CUNNINGHAM, Frank 4
CUNNINGHAM, 5
  Frank Harrison
CUNNINGHAM,
  Frank Simpson 4
CUNNINGHAM, George
  A. 4
CUNNINGHAM, 3
  George William
CUNNINGHAM, Harry
  A. 4
CUNNINGHAM, 1
  Henry Vincent
CUNNINGHAM, 5
  Holly Estil
CUNNINGHAM, 5
  Horace Herndon
CUNNINGHAM, I. A. 1
CUNNINGHAM, James
  A. 4
CUNNINGHAM, 4
  James Dalton
CUNNINGHAM, 5
  John Charles
CUNNINGHAM, 3
  John Ferguson

CUNNINGHAM, John Henry 5
CUNNINGHAM, John Lovell 4
CUNNINGHAM, Joseph Oscar 1
CUNNINGHAM, Julian W. 5
CUNNINGHAM, Louis Wyborn 1
CUNNINGHAM, Milton Joseph 1
CUNNINGHAM, Paul 4
CUNNINGHAM, Paul Davis 1
CUNNINGHAM, Richard Hoope 1
CUNNINGHAM, Robert Sydney 4
CUNNINGHAM, Ross MacDuffee 4
CUNNINGHAM, Russell McWhorter 1
CUNNINGHAM, Solomon M. 4
CUNNINGHAM, Sumner Archibald
CUNNINGHAM, Thomas F. 1
CUNNINGHAM, Thomas Mayhew 5
CUNNINGHAM, Warren W. 3
CUNNINGHAM, Wilfred Harris 5
CUNNINGHAM, William 4
CUNNINGHAM, William Francis 4
CUNNINGHAM, William James 5
CUNZ, Dieter 5
CUPPIA, Jerome Chester 4
CUPPLES, Samuel 1
CUPPY, Hazlitt Alva 1
CUPPY, William Jacob 2
CURETON, Calvin Maples 5
CURL, Robert Floyd 5
CURLEE, Francis M. 3
CURLEY, Daniel J. 1
CURLEY, Edward W. 1
CURLEY, Frank E. 1
CURLEY, James H
CURLEY, James Michael 1
CURLEY, Michael Joseph 2
CURLEY, Walter J. 5
CURLEY, William A. 5
CURME, George Oliver 2
CUROE, Philip R(aphael) V(incent) 5
CURRAN, Charles Courtney 2
CURRAN, Henry Hastings 4
CURRAN, Kenneth James 5
CURRAN, Thomas Jerome 3
CURRAN, William Reid 5
CURRELL, William Spenser 2
CURREY, Brownlee Own 3
CURREY, J. Seymour 1
CURREY, John 1
CURRICK, Max Cohen 2
CURRIE, Barton Wood 4
CURRIE, Brainerd 4
CURRIE, Donald Herbert 1
CURRIE, Edward James 1
CURRIE, George Graham 1
CURRIE, Gilbert Archibald 1
CURRIE, John S. 3
CURRIE, Thomas White 2
CURRIER, Albert Dean 4
CURRIER, Albert Henry 4
CURRIER, Amos Noyes 1
CURRIER, Charles Francis Adams 1
CURRIER, Charles Warren
CURRIER, Frank Dunklee 1
CURRIER, George Harvey 5
CURRIER, J. Frank 1
CURRIER, John C. 4
CURRIER, Moody H
CURRIER, Nathaniel H
CURRIER, Raymond Pillsbury 5
CURRIER, Richard Dudley 2
CURRIER, Thomas Franklin 2
CURRY, Albert Bruce 1
CURRY, Allen 5
CURRY, Arthur Mansfield 4
CURRY, Charles Forrest 1
CURRY, Charles Madison 2
CURRY, Edward Rufus 1
CURRY, George 2

CURRY, George Law H
CURRY, Jabez Lamar Monroe 1
CURRY, James Bernard 1
CURRY, James J. 4
CURRY, James Rowland 5
CURRY, John F. 3
CURRY, John Steuart 2
CURRY, Michael John 3
CURRY, Neil James 1
CURRY, Peter H. 3
CURRY, R. Granville 1
CURRY, Samuel Silas 1
CURRY, William Melville 1
CURTICE, Harlow Herbert 4
CURTIN, Andrew Gregg H
CURTIN, Austin 1
CURTIN, D. Thomas 4
CURTIN, Jeremiah 1
CURTIN, Roland Gideon 1
CURTIS, A. J. R. 3
CURTIS, Alfred Allen 1
CURTIS, Arthur Melvin 2
CURTIS, Asahel 5
CURTIS, Augustus Darwin 1
CURTIS, Benjamin Robbins H
CURTIS, C. Densmore 1
CURTIS, Carlton Brandaga H
CURTIS, Carlton Clarence 2
CURTIS, Charles 1
CURTIS, Charles Albert 1
CURTIS, Charles Boyd 1
CURTIS, Charles Clarence 4
CURTIS, Charles Gordon 3
CURTIS, Charles Minot 1
CURTIS, Charles Pelham 2
CURTIS, Charles Pelham 3
CURTIS, Constance 3
CURTIS, Cyrus Hermann Kotzschmar
CURTIS, David A. 1
CURTIS, Edward H
CURTIS, Edward 1
CURTIS, Edward Gilman 5
CURTIS, Edward Glion, Jr.
CURTIS, Edward Harvey 4
CURTIS, Edward Lewis 1
CURTIS, Edward S. 4
CURTIS, Edwin Upton 1
CURTIS, Eugene Judson 3
CURTIS, Eugene Newton 1
CURTIS, F. Kingsbury 1
CURTIS, Florence Rising 2
CURTIS, Francis 4
CURTIS, Francis Joseph 4
CURTIS, Frederic Colton 4
CURTIS, Frederick Smillie 1
CURTIS, George H
CURTIS, George Carroll 1
CURTIS, George Lenox 4
CURTIS, George Lewis 3
CURTIS, George Martin 1
CURTIS, George Martin, II 5
CURTIS, George Milton 1
CURTIS, George Morris 1
CURTIS, George Munson 1
CURTIS, George Ticknor H
CURTIS, George William 1
CURTIS, Georgina Pell 1
CURTIS, Gerald Beckwith 1
CURTIS, H. Holbrook 1
CURTIS, Harry Alfred 4
CURTIS, Harvey Lincoln 3
CURTIS, Heber Doust 1
CURTIS, Henry G. 1
CURTIS, Henry Stoddard 3
CURTIS, Howard James 5
CURTIS, Howard Junior 1
CURTIS, Isabel Gordon 1
CURTIS, James Freeman 3
CURTIS, Jesse William 1
CURTIS, John Green 1
CURTIS, John Jay 1
CURTIS, John Talbot 3
CURTIS, John Thomas 4
CURTIS, Mattoon Monroe 4
CURTIS, Melville Goss 3
CURTIS, Moses Ashley 4
CURTIS, Newton Martin 1
CURTIS, Oakley Chester 1
CURTIS, Olin Alfred 1
CURTIS, Otis Freeman 1
CURTIS, Richard Cary 3
CURTIS, Roy Emerson 4

CURTIS, Samuel Ryan H
CURTIS, Sumner 1
CURTIS, Vivian Critz 5
CURTIS, Wardon Allan 1
CURTIS, William Buckingham 1
CURTIS, William Edmond 1
CURTIS, William Eleroy 1
CURTIS, William Franklin 1
CURTIS, William Fuller 5
CURTIS, William John 1
CURTIS, William Samuel 1
CURTIS, Winterton Conway 5
CURTISS, Charles Chauncey 1
CURTISS, Charles Franklin 2
CURTISS, David Raymond 3
CURTISS, George Boughton 4
CURTISS, Glenn Hammond 1
CURTISS, Julian Wheeler 2
CURTISS, Lawrence Meredith 5
CURTISS, Philip 4
CURTISS, Ralph Hamilton 1
CURTISS, Richard Sydney 5
CURTISS, Samuel Ives 1
CURTISS, William Hanford 3
CURTISS, William John 3
CURTIZ, Michael 4
CURTS, Lewis 1
CURWEN, John 1
CURWEN, Samuel H
CURWEN, Samuel M. 1
CURWOOD, James Oliver 1
CURZON, Mary Victoria 1
CUSACK, Thomas Francis 1
CUSHING, Caleb H
CUSHING, Charles C. S. 1
CUSHING, Edward Harvey 5
CUSHING, Ernest Watson 1
CUSHING, Frank Hamilton H
CUSHING, George Holmes 5
CUSHING, Grafton Dulany 1
CUSHING, Harry Alonzo 3
CUSHING, Harry Cooke 4
CUSHING, Harvey 1
CUSHING, Henry Platt 1
CUSHING, Herbert Howard 5
CUSHING, Howard Gardiner 1
CUSHING, John E. 3
CUSHING, John Pearsons 1
CUSHING, John Perkins 1
CUSHING, John Thayer 1
CUSHING, Luther Stearns H
CUSHING, Oscar K. 2
CUSHING, Richard Cardinal 5
CUSHING, Samuel Tobey 1
CUSHING, Stephen S. 3
CUSHING, Thomas H
CUSHING, William H
CUSHING, William Barker H
CUSHING, William Erastus 1
CUSHING, William Lee 1
CUSHMAN, Allerton Seward 1
CUSHMAN, Arlon Vannevar 3
CUSHMAN, Austin Sprague 1
CUSHMAN, Beulah 4
CUSHMAN, Charlotte Saunders H
CUSHMAN, Edward Everett 4
CUSHMAN, Francis W. 1
CUSHMAN, Frank 3
CUSHMAN, George Hewitt
CUSHMAN, Henry W. 4
CUSHMAN, Herbert Ernest 4
CUSHMAN, Horace O. 5
CUSHMAN, John Paine H
CUSHMAN, Joseph Augustine 2
CUSHMAN, Joshua H
CUSHMAN, Lewis Arthur 4
CUSHMAN, Pauline H

CUSHMAN, Ralph Spaulding 4
CUSHMAN, Robert H
CUSHMAN, Robert Eugene 5
CUSHMAN, Samuel H
CUSHMAN, Susan Webb H
CUSHMAN, William Michael 4
CUSTER, Elizabeth Bacon 1
CUSTER, George Armstrong
CUSTER, Omer Nixon 2
CUSTIS, George Washington Parke H
CUSTIS, John Trevor 1
CUSTIS, Marvin A. 3
CUSTIS, Vanderveer 4
CUTBUSH, James H
CUTCHEON, Byron M. 1
CUTCHEON, Franklin W. M. 1
CUTHBERT, Alfred H
CUTHBERT, John Alfred H
CUTHBERT, Lucius Montrose 1
CUTHELL, Chester Welde 2
CUTHRELL, Hugh H. 3
CUTLER, Anna Alice 3
CUTLER, Arthur Hamilton 1
CUTLER, Augustus William H
CUTLER, Bertram 3
CUTLER, Carroll H
CUTLER, Charles Frederic 1
CUTLER, Condict Walker 1
CUTLER, Condict Walker Jr. 3
CUTLER, Elbridge Gerry 1
CUTLER, Elliott Carr 2
CUTLER, Everett Alonzo 1
CUTLER, Frederick Morse 2
CUTLER, Garnet Homer 4
CUTLER, George Chalmers
CUTLER, Harry Morton 1
CUTLER, Henry Edwin 1
CUTLER, Henry Franklin 4
CUTLER, Ira Eugene 1
CUTLER, James Elbert 3
CUTLER, James Goold 1
CUTLER, James Gould H
CUTLER, James Gould 4
CUTLER, John Christopher 1
CUTLER, John W. 3
CUTLER, Lizzie Petit H
CUTLER, Manasseh H
CUTLER, Otis Henderson 1
CUTLER, Ralph William 1
CUTLER, Timothy H
CUTLER, William Frye 3
CUTLER, William Parker 1
CUTRIGHT, Harold Glen 4
CUTSHALL, H. Walton Jr.
CUTTEN, Arthur W. 1
CUTTEN, George Barton 1
CUTTEN, Ruloff Edward 4
CUTTER, Benjamin 1
CUTTER, Charles Ammi 1
CUTTER, Ephraim 1
CUTTER, Mrs. George Albert (florence Maxim Cutter) 5
CUTTER, George Washington
CUTTER, Irving Samuel 2
CUTTER, John Ashburton 4
CUTTER, K. K.
CUTTER, Victor Macomber 3
CUTTER, Victor Macomber Jr. 4
CUTTER, William Dick 1
CUTTER, William Parker 1
CUTTING, Bronson 1
CUTTING, Charles Sidney 1
CUTTING, Charles Suydam 5
CUTTING, Churchill Hunter
CUTTING, Elisabeth Brown 2
CUTTING, Francis Brockholst
CUTTING, Hiram Adolphus H
CUTTING, James Ambrose H
CUTTING, Mary Stewart 1
CUTTING, R. Fulton 1

CUTTING, Starr Willard 1
CUTTING, W. Bayard 1
CUTTING, Windsor Cooper 5
CUTTLE, Francis 5
CUTTS, Charles H
CUTTS, Elmer Henry 4
CUTTS, Marsena Edgar 1
CUTTS, Richard H
CUYLER, Cornelius Cuyler
CUYLER, T. De Witt 1
CUYLER, Theodore H
CUYLER, Theodore Ledyard
CYR, Paul Narcisse 1
CZARNOMSKA, Marie Elizabeth Josephine
CZERWONKY, Richard Rudolph 2

D

DABLON, Claude H
DABNEY, Charles William
DABNEY, Edwin 1
DABNEY, Julia Parker 1
DABNEY, Lewis Stackpole 1
DABNEY, Richard H
DABNEY, Richard Heath 1
DABNEY, Robert Lewis H
DABNEY, Samuel Gordon 2
DABNEY, Thomas Smith Gregory
DABNEY, Virginius 1
DABNEY, William C. 4
DABO, Leon 1
DABO, Theodore Scott 1
DABOLL, Nathan H
DABROWSKI, Joseph 1
DACOSTA, Albert Lloyd 1
DA COSTA, Chalmers 1
DA COSTA, Jacob M. H
DA COSTA, John C. Jr. 1
DADANT, Camille Pierre 1
DADE, Alexander Lucien 1
DADMUN, Frances May 4
DAEGER, Albert Thomas 1
DAFOE, John Wesley 2
DAFT, Leo 1
DAFT, Leo 4
'DA GAMA, Vasco 1
DAGER, Forrest Eugene 1
DAGG, John Leadley 1
DAGGETT, Aaron Simon 1
DAGGETT, Athern Park 5
DAGGETT, David 1
DAGGETT, Ellsworth 1
DAGGETT, Harriet Spiller
DAGGETT, Leonard Mayhew 1
DAGGETT, Mabel Potter 1
DAGGETT, Mary Stewart 1
DAGGETT, Naphtali 1
DAGGETT, Parker Hayward 4
DAGGETT, Robert Frost 1
DAGGETT, Stuart 1
DAGGY, Maynard Lee 5
DAGWELL, Benjamin Dunlap
DAHL, Francis W. 5
DAHL, George 4
DAHL, Gerhard Melvin 1
DAHL, Myrtle Hooper 1
DAHL, Theodore H. 1
DAHLBERG, Arthur Chester
DAHLBERG, Bror Gustave 3
DAHLE, Herman B. 1
DAHLE, Herman Bjorn 1
DAHLE, Herman Bjorn 1
DAHLERUP, Ioost Baron 1
DAHLGREEN, Charles W. 3
DAHLGREN, B. E. 4
DAHLGREN, John Adolphus Bernard H
DAHLGREN, Sarah Madeleine Vinton
DAHLGREN, Ulric 1
DAHLMAN, James Charles 2
DAHLQUIST, Thomas Wilford
DAIGNEAU, Ralph H. 3
DAILEY, Morris Elmer 1
DAILY, Francis L. H
DAILY, Joseph Earl 1
DAILY, Samuel Gordon 1
DAINE, Robert 1
DAINES, Lyman Luther 1
DAINGERFIELD, Elliott 1

DAINGERFIELD, Foxhall Alexander — 1
DAINS, Frank Burnett — 2
DAISH, John Broughton — 1
DAISLEY, Robert Henry — 4
DAKE, Charles — 2
DAKE, Charles Laurence — 1
DAKIN, Henry Drysdale — 3
DAKINS, John Gordon — 4
DALAND, Judson — 1
DALAND, William Clifton — 1
DALBEY, Josiah T. — 4
DALBY, Zachary Lewis — 5
DALE, Alan — 1
DALE, Albert Ennis — 3
DALE, Chester — 4
DALE, Coudoashia Bernice Watts (Mrs. Luther W. Dale) — 5
DALE, Edward Everett — 5
DALE, Frank — 1
DALE, Harry Howard — 1
DALE, Sir Henry Hallett — 5
DALE, James Wilkinson — H
DALE, Porter Hinman — 1
DALE, Richard — H
DALE, Samuel — H
DALE, Thomas — H
DALE, Thomas Henry — 1
DALE, Thomas Nelson — 1
DALE, Warren Jefferson — 4
DALESIO, Carmine — 4
DALEY, John F. — 4
DALEY, John Phillips — 4
DALEY, Robert Morris — 3
DALEY, William Raymond — 5
DALGLEISH, Oakley Hedley — 4
DALL, Caroline Healey — 4
DALL, William Healey — 1
DALLAS, Alexander James — H
DALLAS, Charles Donald — 3
DALLAS, George Mifflin — H
DALLAS, George Mifflin — 4
DALLAS, Jacob A. — H
DALLAS, John Thomson — 4
DALLAS, Trevanion Barlow
DALLA VALLE, Joseph Maria — 3
DALLENBACH, Karl M. — 5
DALLIN, Cyrus Edwin — 4
DALLIN, David Julievich
DALLMAN, Vincent Y. — 4
DALLMANN, William — 3
DALLSTREAM, Andrew John — 4
DALMORES, Charles — 1
DALRYMPLE, Louis — 1
DALRYMPLE, William Haddock — 1
DALSIMER, Samuel — 5
DALSTROM, Oscar Frederick — 5
DALTON, Albert Clayton — 5
DALTON, Henry George — 1
DALTON, James L. — 2
DALTON, John Call — H
DALTON, John M(ontgomery) — 5
DALTON, Joseph N. — 4
DALTON, Mary Louise — 1
DALTON, Robert — H
DALTON, Sidna Poage — 4
DALTON, Test — 2
DALTON, Tristram — H
DALTON, W. R. Inge — 1
DALTON, William — 5
DALY, Arnold — 1
DALY, Augustin — 1
DALY, Brenton L. — 3
DALY, Carroll John — 3
DALY, Sister Cecilia — 5
DALY, Charles Frederick — 1
DALY, Charles Patrick — 4
DALY, Edward C. — 4
DALY, Edward James — 3
DALY, Edwin King — 3
DALY, Howard J. Sr. — 4
DALY, J. Burrwood — 1
DALY, J. J. — 2
DALY, John Fidlar — 5
DALY, John J. — 4
DALY, John Wallace — 4
DALY, Joseph Francis — 1
DALY, Marcus — 1
DALY, Reginald Aldworth — 3
DALY, Thomas Augustine — 2
DALY, William Barry — 2
DALY, William D. — 1

DALZELL, John — 1
DALZELL, Lloyd Howland — 4
DALZELL, Robert M. — H
DALZELL, William Sage — 4
DAM, Henry Jackson Wells — 1
DAMBACH, Charles Arthur — 5
DAME, Elizabeth L. — 5
DAME, Frank Libby — 1
DAME, Harriet Patience — 1
DAME, J. Frank — 5
DAMESHEK, William — 5
DAMIANO, Celestine Joseph — 4
DAMIANOV, Georgi — 3
DAMM, Henry Christian Augustus — 1
DAMM, Walter J. — 4
DAMMANN, John Francis — 4
DAMMANN, Milton — 4
DAMMANN, Theodore — 3
DAMON, Alexander Martin — 2
DAMON, Alonzo Willard — 1
DAMON, Frank Hardy — 5
DAMON, George Alfred — 1
DAMON, Howard Franklin — H
DAMON, Lindsay Todd — 1
DAMON, Norman Clare — 5
DAMON, Ralph Shepard — 3
DAMON, S(amuel) Foster — 5
DAMON, Samuel Mills — 3
DAMON, William Emerson — 1
D'AMOURS, Ernest R. — 4
DAMRELL, William Shapleigh — H
DAMROSCH, Frank Heino — H
DAMROSCH, Leopold — H
DAMROSCH, Walter Johannes — 3
DANA, Amasa — H
DANA, Charles Anderson — H
DANA, Charles Edmund — 1
DANA, Charles Loomis — 1
DANA, Edward Salisbury — 1
DANA, Floyd G. — 4
DANA, Francis — H
DANA, Francis E. — 1
DANA, Frank M. — 5
DANA, Harvey Eugene — 2
DANA, Henry Wadsworth Longfellow — 3
DANA, Israel Thorndike — 1
DANA, James — H
DANA, James Dwight — H
DANA, James Dwight — 3
DANA, James Freeman — H
DANA, John Cotton — 1
DANA, John Fessenden — 4
DANA, Judah — H
DANA, Lynn Boardman — 1
DANA, Marvin — 4
DANA, Myron T. — 4
DANA, Napoleon Jackson Tecumseh
DANA, Paul — 1
DANA, Richard — H
DANA, Richard Henry * — H
DANA, Richard Henry — 1
DANA, Richard Turner — 1
DANA, Samuel — H
DANA, Samuel Luther — H
DANA, Samuel Whittelsey
DANA, Stephen Winchester — 1
DANA, William Franklin — 1
DANA, William Henry — 1
DANA, William Parsons Winchester
DANCEL, Christian — H
DANCER, H. M. — 3
DANCKAERTS, Jasper — H
DANCY, Alexander Brown — 4
DANDRIDGE, Danske — 4
DANDRIDGE, Dorothy — 4
DANDRIDGE, N. Pendleton
DANDY, George Brown — 1
DANDY, Walter Edward — 2
DANE, Ernest Blaney — 2
DANE, Joseph — H
DANE, Nathan — H
DANE, Walter Alden — 5
DANELY, Alfred Marion — 4
DANENHOWER, John Wilson
DANEY, Eugene — 2

DANFORD, Lorenzo — 1
DANFORTH, Charles — H
DANFORTH, Charles H. — 5
DANFORTH, Elliott — 1
DANFORTH, George Jonathan — 3
DANFORTH, George Washington — 4
DANFORTH, Henry Gold — 1
DANFORTH, Isaac Newton — 1
DANFORTH, Joshua Noble — H
DANFORTH, Loomis Le Grand — 4
DANFORTH, Moseley Isaac — H
DANFORTH, Thomas — H
DANFORTH, William H. — 3
DANGAIX, William Joseph — 2
DANHOF, Ralph John — 5
DANIEL, Charles Ezra — 4
DANIEL, Charles William
DANIEL, David R. — 4
DANIEL, Ferdinand Eugene — 1
DANIEL, Henry — H
DANIEL, J. Mctyeire — 5
DANIEL, John — 2
DANIEL, John Franklin — 2
DANIEL, John Moncure — H
DANIEL, John Reeves Jones — H
DANIEL, John Warwick — 1
DANIEL, Lewis C. — 3
DANIEL, Peter Vivian — H
DANIEL, Richard Potts — 5
DANIEL, Robert Norman — H
DANIEL, Robert Prentiss — 4
DANIELL, Francis Raymond — 5
DANIELL, Moses Grant — 1
DANIELLS, Arthur Grosvenor — 2
DANIELLS, William Willard — 1
DANIEL-ROPS, Henry — 4
DANIELS, Arthur Hill — 1
DANIELS, Arthur Simpson — 4
DANIELS, Benjamin — 3
DANIELS, Charles — H
DANIELS, Charles Herbert — 1
DANIELS, Charles Nelson — 1
DANIELS, Cora Linn — 1
DANIELS, Farrington — 5
DANIELS, Francis Cummings — 3
DANIELS, Francis Potter — 2
DANIELS, Frank — 1
DANIELS, Fred Harris — 1
DANIELS, George Henry — 1
DANIELS, Harold Kennan — 4
DANIELS, Henry H. — 3
DANIELS, John — 3
DANIELS, John Karl — 3
DANIELS, Joseph J. — 5
DANIELS, Joseph Leonard — 1
DANIELS, Josephus — 2
DANIELS, Josephus Jr. — 4
DANIELS, Lilla Wood — 4
DANIELS, Milton J. — 2
DANIELS, William S. — 1
DANIELS, Winthrop More — 2
DANIELSON, Clarence Hagbart — 3
DANIELSON, Jacques — 3
DANIELSON, Reuben Gustaf — 3
DANIELSON, Richard Ely — 3
DANIELSON, Wilmot Alfred — 4
DANLEY, William L. — 4
DANN, Alexander William — 4
DANN, Hollis Ellsworth — 1
DANNAT, William T. — 1
DANNELLY, John Milton — 1
DANNENBAUM, Walter — 4
DANNER, Arthur Vincent — 5
DANNER, Harris Leslie — 5
DANNER, Joel Buchanan — H
DANNER, Peter C. — 5
DANNREUTHER, Gustav — H
DANNREUTHER, Gustav — 4
DANNREUTHER, Walter T. — 3
DANSINGBERG, Paul — 2

D'ANTONI, Salvador — 3
DANZIGER, Henry — 1
DA PONTE, Lorenzo — 3
'DA PONTE, Lorenzo Brooke
DAPPING, William Osborne — 5
DARBY, Ada Claire — 3
DARBY, Edwin Tyler — 1
DARBY, Ezra — 1
DARBY, John * — H
DARBY, John Eaton
DARBY, John Fletcher — H
DARBY, John Frederick — 3
DARBY, William
DARBY, William Johnson — 1
DARBY, William Lambert
DARBYSHIRE, Leonard — 4
D'ARCY, William Cheever — 2
DARDEN, Thomas
DARE, Virginia
DARGAN, Edmond Strother — H
DARGAN, Edwin Charles — 1
DARGAN, Edwin Preston — 1
DARGAN, Henry McCune — 5
DARGAN, Olive Tilford — 5
DARGAVEL, John William
DARGEON, Harold William — 5
DARGUE, Herbert Arthur — 2
DARKE, William — H
DARKENWALD, Gordon Gerald — 4
DARLEY, Felix Octavius Carr — H
DARLEY, Jane Cooper — H
DARLING, Arthur Beebe — 5
DARLING, Arthur Burr — 5
DARLING, C. Coburn — 4
DARLING, Charles Kimball — 1
DARLING, Charles William — 1
DARLING, Flora Adams — 1
DARLING, Henry — H
DARLING, Herbert Franklin — 5
DARLING, Jay Norwood — 4
DARLING, John Augustus — 1
DARLING, Joseph Robinson; — 5
DARLING, Louis, Jr. — 5
DARLING, Mary Greenleaf — 4
DARLING, Mason Cook — H
DARLING, Robert Ensign — 5
DARLING, Samuel Taylor — 1
DARLING, Sid L(ouis) — 5
DARLING, William Augustus — H
DARLING, William Lafayette — 1
DARLINGTON, Charles Francis — 1
DARLINGTON, Charles Goodliffe — 4
DARLINGTON, Charles Joseph — 4
DARLINGTON, Edward — H
DARLINGTON, Frederick — 3
DARLINGTON, Henry — 3
DARLINGTON, Isaac — H
DARLINGTON, James Henry — 1
DARLINGTON, Joseph James — 1
DARLINGTON, Thomas — 1
DARLINGTON, Thomas — 2
DARLINGTON, Urban Valentine W. — 3
DARLINGTON, William — H
DARLOW, Albert Edward — 4
DARMS, John Martin George — 2
DARNALL, Carl Rogers — 1
DARNALL, Marcy Bradshaw — 4
DARNALL, William Edgar — 1
DARNELL, Henry Faulkner — 1
DARNELL, Linda — 4
DARNTON, Eleanor Choate — 5
DARR, Earl A. — 4
DARR, Edward A. — 3
DARR, John Whittier — 5
DARR, Loren Robert — 5
DARRACH, William — 2
DARRAGH, Ann Sophia Towne — H

DARRAGH, Archibald Bard — 4
DARRAGH, Cornelius — H
DARRAH, Thomas W. — 3
DARRIN, Erwin N. — 4
DARROW, Chester William — 5
DARROW, Clarence — 1
DARROW, Daniel Cady — 4
DARROW, George Potter — 2
DARSIE, Darsie Lloyd — 4
DARSIE, Marvin Lloyd
DARST, Joseph Miltenberger — 3
DARST, Thomas Campbell — 2
DART, Carlton Rollin — 1
DART, Henry Plauche — 1
DARTON, Nelson Horatio — 2
D'ARVILLE, Camille — 1
DARWIN, Charles Carlyle
DARWIN, Charles Galton — 4
DARWIN, Gertrude Bascom — 1
DAS, Taraknath — 3
D'ASCENZO, Nicola — 3
DASCH, George — 3
DASHER, Benjamin Joseph — 5
DASHER, Charles Lanier, Jr. — 5
DASHIELL, Alfred Sheppard — 5
DASHIELL, Paul Joseph — 3
DASHIELL, William Robert — 1
DASKAM, Walter Duryee
DATER, Alfred Warner — 1
DATES, Henry Baldwin — 5
DATTNER, Bernhard — 3
DAU, William Herman Theodore — 2
DAUBIN, Freeland Allen — 3
DAUGETTE, Clarence William — 2
DAUGHERTY, Arthur Cornelius — 5
DAUGHERTY, Charles M. — 1
DAUGHERTY, Duncan W(ilmer) — 5
DAUGHERTY, Edgar Fay — 3
DAUGHERTY, Harry Kerr — 3
DAUGHERTY, Harry Micajah — 1
DAUGHERTY, James Alexander — 4
DAUGHERTY, Jerome — 4
DAUGHERTY, Lewis Sylvester
DAUGHTERS, Freeman — 3
DAULTON, Agnes McClelland — 2
DAULTON, George — 1
DAUMONT, Simon Francois — H
D'AUNOY, Rigney — 1
DAUZVARDIS, Petras Paulius — 5
DAVANT, Thomas S. — 5
DAVEE, Henry A. — 3
DAVEE, Thomas — H
DAVEIS, Charles Stewart
DAVEISS, Joseph Hamilton — H
DAVELER, Erle Victor — 3
DAVENPORT, Basil — 4
DAVENPORT, Bennett Franklin — 1
DAVENPORT, Charles Benedict — 2
DAVENPORT, Edward Loomis — H
DAVENPORT, Erwin R. — 4
DAVENPORT, Eugene — 1
DAVENPORT, Fanny Lily Gypsy — H
DAVENPORT, Frances Gardiner — 1
DAVENPORT, Franklin — H
DAVENPORT, Frederick M. — 3
DAVENPORT, Frederick Parker — 1
DAVENPORT, George — H
DAVENPORT, George Edward — 1
DAVENPORT, George William — 5
DAVENPORT, Gideon I. — 4
DAVENPORT, Henry Joralemon — 4
DAVENPORT, Herbert Joseph — 1
DAVENPORT, Holton — 4

DAVENPORT, Homer Calvin — 1
DAVENPORT, Ira — 1
DAVENPORT, Ira Erastus — H
DAVENPORT, Ira Erastus — 4
DAVENPORT, James * — H
DAVENPORT, James Henry — 1
DAVENPORT, James LeRoy — 1
DAVENPORT, James Sanford — 1
DAVENPORT, John * — H
DAVENPORT, John Gaylord — 1
DAVENPORT, Leroy Benjamin — 4
DAVENPORT, Louis M. — 5
DAVENPORT, R. Briggs — 1
DAVENPORT, Richard Graham — 1
DAVENPORT, Roy Leonard — 4
DAVENPORT, Russell — 3
DAVENPORT, Samuel Arza — 4
DAVENPORT, Stanley Woodward — 4
DAVENPORT, Thomas * — H
DAVENPORT, Walter — 5
DAVENPORT, Walter Rice — 2
DAVENPORT, William Henry Harrison — H
DAVEY, James Charles — 1
DAVEY, John — 1
DAVEY, Martin L. — 2
DAVEY, Randall — 4
DAVEY, Robert C. — 1
DAVEY, Wheeler P. — 3
D'AVEZAC, Auguste Genevieve Valentin — H
DAVID, Edward Wandell — 4
DAVID, John Baptist Mary — H
DAVID, Vernon Cyrenius — 4
DAVIDGE, John Beale — H
DAVIDGE, William Pleater — H
DAVIDOW, H. M. — 3
DAVIDS, James — H
DAVIDSON, Alexander Caldwell — H
DAVIDSON, Alfred James — 1
DAVIDSON, Anstruther — 4
DAVIDSON, Arnold — 4
DAVIDSON, Augustus Cleveland — H
DAVIDSON, Benjamin — 1
DAVIDSON, Carter — 4
DAVIDSON, Charles — 1
DAVIDSON, David J. — 2
DAVIDSON, Donald (Grady) — 5
DAVIDSON, Donald Miner — 4
DAVIDSON, Edwin Lee — 1
DAVIDSON, George — 1
DAVIDSON, George — 1
DAVIDSON, George A. — 4
DAVIDSON, Hannah Amelia
DAVIDSON, Harlan Page — 1
DAVIDSON, Irville Fay — 1
DAVIDSON, Israel — 1
DAVIDSON, J. Brownlee — 3
DAVIDSON, James Edward — 2
DAVIDSON, James Edward — 3
DAVIDSON, James Hamilton — 3
DAVIDSON, James Henry — 1
DAVIDSON, James O. — 1
DAVIDSON, James Wheeler — 1
DAVIDSON, James Wood — 3
DAVIDSON, Jo — 3
DAVIDSON, John Wynn — H
DAVIDSON, Joseph G. — 5
DAVIDSON, Joseph Quentin — 5
DAVIDSON, Laura Lee — 5
DAVIDSON, Levette Jay — 3
DAVIDSON, Loucretia Isobel — 5
DAVIDSON, Louis Rogers — 1
DAVIDSON, Lucretia Maria — H
DAVIDSON, Lyal Ament — 3
DAVIDSON, Margaret Miller
DAVIDSON, Mary Blossom, (Mrs. Charles S. Davidson) — 5
DAVIDSON, Maurice P. — 1
DAVIDSON, Robert * — H

DAVIDSON, Robert James — 1
DAVIDSON, Roy Elton — 4
DAVIDSON, Royal Page — 2
DAVIDSON, Samuel Presley
DAVIDSON, Theodore Fulton
DAVIDSON, Thomas — 1
DAVIDSON, Thomas Green — H
DAVIDSON, Thomas William — 4
DAVIDSON, Victor H. — 3
DAVIDSON, Ward Follett — 1
DAVIDSON, Wilbur Leroy — 1
DAVIDSON, William — H
DAVIDSON, William Andrew — 3
DAVIDSON, William Lee — 1
DAVIDSON, William Mehard
DAVIE, Maurice R. — 4
DAVIE, William Richardson — H
DAVIES, Acton — 1
DAVIES, Arthur B. — 1
DAVIES, Arthur Ernest — 4
DAVIES, Arthur Powell — 3
DAVIES, Caroline Stodder — 4
DAVIES, Charles — H
DAVIES, Charles Frederick — H
DAVIES, David Charles — 1
DAVIES, Edward — H
DAVIES, Ernest Coulter — 4
DAVIES, George Reginald — 5
DAVIES, Harry William — 3
DAVIES, Henry Eugene — H
DAVIES, Hywel — 1
DAVIES, James — 4
DAVIES, James William Frederick
DAVIES, John Rumsey — 1
DAVIES, John Vipond — 1
DAVIES, Joseph Edward — 3
DAVIES, Julian Tappan — 1
DAVIES, Marion — 4
DAVIES, Percy Albert — 4
DAVIES, Samuel — H
DAVIES, Thomas Frederick * — 1
DAVIES, Thomas Stephen — 5
DAVIES, Thurston Jynkins — 4
DAVIES, Valentine — 4
DAVIES, William Gilbert — 1
DAVIES, William Preston — 2
DAVIES, William Rupert — 4
DAVIES, William Walter — 1
DAVIESS, Maria Thompson
DAVILA, Carlos — 3
DAVILA, Charles Alexander — 4
DAVIN, John Wysor — 2
DAVIS, A. M. — 5
DAVIS, Abel — 1
DAVIS, Achilles Edward — 4
DAVIS, Addison D. — 4
DAVIS, Albert Gould — 1
DAVIS, Alexander Jackson — H
DAVIS, Alexander Macdonald — 4
DAVIS, Alexander Mathews — H
DAVIS, Alfred Cookman — 2
DAVIS, Alton Frank — 3
DAVIS, Alva Raymond — 4
DAVIS, Amos — H
DAVIS, Andrew Jay — 3
DAVIS, Andrew McFarland — 1
DAVIS, Arlene — 4
DAVIS, Arlene (Mrs. Max T. Davis)
DAVIS, Arnold Lyman — 1
DAVIS, Arthur Cayley — 4
DAVIS, Arthur Kyle — 3
DAVIS, Arthur Marshall — 4
DAVIS, Arthur Newton — 5
DAVIS, Arthur Powell — 1
DAVIS, Arthur Vining — 5
DAVIS, Arthur Vining — 4
DAVIS, Arthur William — 2
DAVIS, Asa Barnes — 1
DAVIS, Beale — 4
DAVIS, Benjamin Marshall
DAVIS, Benson Willis — 3
DAVIS, Bergen — 3

DAVIS, Bernard George — 5
DAVIS, Bert Byron — 2
DAVIS, Boothe Colwell — 1
DAVIS, Bradley Moore — 3
DAVIS, Brinton Beauregard — 5
DAVIS, Byron Bennett — 1
DAVIS, Calvin Olin — 3
DAVIS, Cameron Josiah — 3
DAVIS, Carl Braden — 1
DAVIS, Carlisle R. — 4
DAVIS, Carroll Melvin — 1
DAVIS, Cecil Clark — 3
DAVIS, Charles Albert — 1
DAVIS, Charles B. — 2
DAVIS, Charles Belmont — 1
DAVIS, Charles Edward Law Baldwin — 1
DAVIS, Charles Ernest, Jr. — 5
DAVIS, Charles Gilbert — 1
DAVIS, Charles Harold — 1
DAVIS, Charles Henry — H
DAVIS, Charles Henry — 1
DAVIS, Charles Henry Stanley — 1
DAVIS, Charles K. — 4
DAVIS, Charles Lukens — 1
DAVIS, Charles Moler — 5
DAVIS, Charles Palmer — 1
DAVIS, Charles Russell — 1
DAVIS, Charles Strout — 3
DAVIS, Charles Thornton — 4
DAVIS, Charles Wellington — H
DAVIS, Chester R. — 4
DAVIS, Claude Jefferson — 5
DAVIS, Clifford — 5
DAVIS, Clinton Wildes — 3
DAVIS, Clyde Brion — 4
DAVIS, Cushman Kellogg — 4
DAVIS, D. Dwight — 4
DAVIS, Daniel Franklin — H
DAVIS, Darrell Haug — 4
DAVIS, David — H
DAVIS, David Jackson — 1
DAVIS, David John — 3
DAVIS, David William — 5
DAVIS, Donald Derby — 3
DAVIS, Donald W. — 3
DAVIS, Dwight Filley — 2
DAVIS, E. Asbury — 3
DAVIS, E. Gorton — 1
DAVIS, E. Asbury — 5
DAVIS, Earl Fred — 4
DAVIS, Earl J. — 1
DAVIS, Edith Smith — 1
DAVIS, Edmund Jackson — H
DAVIS, Edward — 1
DAVIS, Edward C. P. — 3
DAVIS, Edward E. — 5
DAVIS, Edward Everett — 3
DAVIS, Edward Parker — 4
DAVIS, Edwin — 4
DAVIS, Edwin G. — 5
DAVIS, Edwin Hamilton — H
DAVIS, Edwin Weyerhaeuser — 4
DAVIS, Effa Vetina — 1
DAVIS, Ellery Williams — 1
DAVIS, Elmer — 3
DAVIS, Elmer Joseph — 5
DAVIS, Emerson — H
DAVIS, Ewin Lamar — 2
DAVIS, Fay — 2
DAVIS, Francis Breese Jr. — 4
DAVIS, Frank Jr. — 1
DAVIS, Frank De Montibirt — 4
DAVIS, Frank Garfield — 3
DAVIS, Frank Parker — 3
DAVIS, Fred Henry — 1
DAVIS, Frederick Henry — 1
DAVIS, Garret — H
DAVIS, Gaylord — 5
DAVIS, George — 1
DAVIS, George Breckenridge
DAVIS, George Burwell — 4
DAVIS, George Gilman — 4
DAVIS, George H. — 2
DAVIS, George Harvey — 3
DAVIS, George Royal — 1
DAVIS, George Russell — 4
DAVIS, George Samler — 1
DAVIS, George Thomas — H
DAVIS, George Thompson Brown — 5
DAVIS, George Washington — 4
DAVIS, George Whitefield — 1
DAVIS, George William — 4

DAVIS, Gladys Rockmore — 4
DAVIS, Graham Lee — 3
DAVIS, Gwilym George — 1
DAVIS, H. L. — 4
DAVIS, Hal Strange — 3
DAVIS, Hallie Flanagan — 5
DAVIS, Harry Ellerbe — 5
DAVIS, Harry Lyman — 1
DAVIS, Harry Orville — 4
DAVIS, Harry Phillips — 1
DAVIS, Harvey Henry — 5
DAVIS, Harvey Nathaniel — 3
DAVIS, Hassoldt — 3
DAVIS, Hayne — 1
DAVIS, Helen Clarkson Miller, (Mrs. Harvey Nathaniel Davis) — 5
DAVIS, Henry — H
DAVIS, Henry — 4
DAVIS, Henry Edgar — 1
DAVIS, Henry Gassaway — 1
DAVIS, Henry Gassett — 1
DAVIS, Henry Winter — H
DAVIS, Herbert Burnham — 1
DAVIS, Herbert John — 4
DAVIS, Herbert Spencer — 5
DAVIS, Herman S. — 1
DAVIS, Horace — 1
DAVIS, Howard — 4
DAVIS, Howland Shippen — 5
DAVIS, Hugh Orton — 5
DAVIS, Ira Cleveland — 4
DAVIS, Irving Gilman — 1
DAVIS, J. Dewitt — 1
DAVIS, J. Frank — 1
DAVIS, J. Mccan — 1
DAVIS, J. F. — 5
DAVIS, J(ohn) Lionberger — 5
DAVIS, Jackson — 1
DAVIS, Jacob Cunningham — H
DAVIS, James — 1
DAVIS, James Cox — 1
DAVIS, James Harvey — 1
DAVIS, James John — 2
DAVIS, James Sherman — 5
DAVIS, James Thomas — 3
DAVIS, Jeff — 1
DAVIS, Jefferson — H
DAVIS, Jefferson Columbus — H
DAVIS, Jess Harrison — 5
DAVIS, Jesse Buttrick — 3
DAVIS, Jesse Duke — 1
DAVIS, Joan — 4
DAVIS, Joe L. — 2
DAVIS, John * — H
DAVIS, John — 1
DAVIS, John A. G. — H
DAVIS, John Chandler Bancroft — 1
DAVIS, John Charles — 1
DAVIS, John D. — 1
DAVIS, John Francis — 1
DAVIS, John Givan — H
DAVIS, John Ker — 5
DAVIS, John Lee — 1
DAVIS, John Marcus — 2
DAVIS, John Merrill — 1
DAVIS, John Moore Kelso
DAVIS, John Patterson — 1
DAVIS, John Rose Wilson — 4
DAVIS, John Staige — 2
DAVIS, John Wesley — H
DAVIS, John William — 1
DAVIS, John William — 3
DAVIS, John Williams — 1
DAVIS, John Woodbridge — 1
DAVIS, Jonathan McMillan — 2
DAVIS, Joseph Baker — 1
DAVIS, Joseph Jonathan — 1
DAVIS, Joseph Phineas — 1
DAVIS, Joseph Robert — 5
DAVIS, Joseph Smith — 5
DAVIS, Joshua A. — 4
DAVIS, Kary Cadmus — 1
DAVIS, Katharine Bement
DAVIS, LeCompte — 3
DAVIS, Lemuel Clarke — 1
DAVIS, Leonard Moore — 1
DAVIS, Lyman Edwyn — 1
DAVIS, Malcolm McTear — 5
DAVIS, Malvin Edward — 4
DAVIS, Manton — 3
DAVIS, Manvel — 1
DAVIS, Mary Evelyn Moore
DAVIS, Mary Gould — 3
DAVIS, Matthew Livingston — H

DAVIS, Michael Marks — 5
DAVIS, Milton Fennimore — 1
DAVIS, Minnie S. — 4
DAVIS, Monnett Bain — 1
DAVIS, Nathan Smith * — 1
DAVIS, Nathan Smith — 3
DAVIS, Nathaniel French — 1
DAVIS, Neal Balbach — 5
DAVIS, Nelson Fithian — 1
DAVIS, Newton Eads — 1
DAVIS, Noah — 1
DAVIS, Noah Knowles — 1
DAVIS, Norman H. — 2
DAVIS, Olive Bell — 4
DAVIS, Oscar Franklyn — 5
DAVIS, Oscar King — 1
DAVIS, Owen — 3
DAVIS, Ozora Stearns — 1
DAVIS, Paul (Alexander) — 5
DAVIS, Paul A. — 2
DAVIS, Paul Arthur — 4
DAVIS, Paul Hazlitt — 5
DAVIS, Paulina Kellogg Wright — H
DAVIS, Philip — 1
DAVIS, Phineas — H
DAVIS, Pierpont — 3
DAVIS, Pierpont V. — 4
DAVIS, R. C. — 4
DAVIS, Ralph Waldo — 3
DAVIS, Raymond Cazallis — 1
DAVIS, Rebecca Harding — 1
DAVIS, Reuben — H
DAVIS, Reuben Nelson — 1
DAVIS, Richard Beale — 1
DAVIS, Richard Bingham — H
DAVIS, Richard David — H
DAVIS, Richard Hallock — 5
DAVIS, Richard Harding — 1
DAVIS, Richard J. — 3
DAVIS, Richmond Pearson — 1
DAVIS, Robert Courtney — 2
DAVIS, Robert Hobart — 1
DAVIS, Robert McNair — 3
DAVIS, Robert Stewart — 1
DAVIS, Robert W. — 4
DAVIS, Roblin Henry — 2
DAVIS, Roger — 1
DAVIS, Roger Wolcott — 3
DAVIS, Rowland Lucius — 3
DAVIS, Roy — 3
DAVIS, Royal Jenkins — 1
DAVIS, Royall Oscar Eugene — 2
DAVIS, Sam — H
DAVIS, Samuel — H
DAVIS, Samuel T. — 4
DAVIS, Sheldon Emmer — 4
DAVIS, Stephen Brooks — 1
DAVIS, Stuart — 4
DAVIS, Sturgiss Brown — 5
DAVIS, Susan Topliff — 1
DAVIS, T. Lawrence — 2
DAVIS, Tenney Lombard — 1
DAVIS, Theodore Russell — H
DAVIS, Thomas — H
DAVIS, Thomas Archibald — 1
DAVIS, Thomas Bealle — 4
DAVIS, Thomas Crawley — 4
DAVIS, Thomas Davis — 1
DAVIS, Thomas Edward — 1
DAVIS, Thomas Francis — 3
DAVIS, Thomas Jefferson
DAVIS, Thomas Latham — 3
DAVIS, Thomas Terry — H
DAVIS, Thomas Treadwell
DAVIS, Thomas Walker — 3
DAVIS, Timothy * — H
DAVIS, Titus Elwood — 4
DAVIS, Tobe Coller — 4
DAVIS, Tom J. — 3
DAVIS, Varina Anne Jefferson — 3
DAVIS, Varina Jefferson — 1
DAVIS, Vernon Mansfield — 1
DAVIS, Wallace McRae — 5
DAVIS, Walton — 4
DAVIS, Warren Bartlett — 1
DAVIS, Warren Blair — 4
DAVIS, Warren Johnson — 3
DAVIS, Warren Ransom — H
DAVIS, Watson — 5
DAVIS, Webster — 1
DAVIS, Westmoreland — 1
DAVIS, Will J.

DAVIS, William Augustine — H
DAVIS, William Church — 3
DAVIS, William Francis Jr. — 3
DAVIS, William Garland — 4
DAVIS, William H. — 5
DAVIS, William H. — 4
DAVIS, William Hammatt — 4
DAVIS, William Harper — 5
DAVIS, William Hersey — 3
DAVIS, William Holmes — 5
DAVIS, William Horace — 1
DAVIS, William Morris — H
DAVIS, William Morris — 1
DAVIS, William Philip — 3
DAVIS, William R. — 1
DAVIS, William Rees — 2
DAVIS, William Stearns — 1
DAVIS, William Thomas — 1
DAVIS, William Thornwall — 2
DAVIS, William Warren — 1
DAVIS, William Watts Hart — 1
DAVIS, William Whiting — 4
DAVIS, William Z. — 1
DAVIS, Wirt — H
DAVIS, Wirt — 2
DAVISON, Albert Watson — 4
DAVISON, Archibald Thompson — 4
DAVISON, Charles — 1
DAVISON, Charles Stewart — 2
DAVISON, Donald Angus — 2
DAVISON, Edward — 5
DAVISON, Frank Elon — 4
DAVISON, George Stewart — 2
DAVISON, George Willets — 3
DAVISON, Harry P. — 4
DAVISON, Mrs. Henry Pomeroy — 5
DAVISON, Henry Pomeroy — 1
DAVISON, Homer R(eese) — 5
DAVISON, John — 1
DAVISON, John A. — 2
DAVISON, Peter Weimer — 2
DAVISON, Thomas Callahan — 3
DAVISON, Wilburt Cornell — 5
DAVISON, William Anthony — 4
DAVISSON, Albert Eugene — 1
DAVISSON, Clinton Joseph — 3
DAVOL, Ralph — 5
DAVY, John M. — 1
DAWBARN, Charles — 4
DAWE, George Grosvenor — 2
DAWE, Helen Cleveland — 5
DAWES, Anna Laurens — 1
DAWES, Beman Gates — 3
DAWES, Charles Gates — 3
DAWES, Chester Mitchell — 1
DAWES, Henry Laurens — 1
DAWES, Henry May — 3
DAWES, Irving D. — 5
DAWES, James William — 3
DAWES, Norman James — 4
DAWES, Rufus Cutler — 1
DAWES, William — H
DAWES, William Ruggles — 3
DAWKINS, Henry — H
DAWLEY, Frank E. — 1
DAWLEY, Thomas Robinson Jr. — 1
DAWSON, Albert Foster — 5
DAWSON, Allan — 1
DAWSON, Allan — 2
DAWSON, Archie Owen — 4
DAWSON, Arthur — 1
DAWSON, Benjamin Elisha — 1
DAWSON, Cecil Forrest — 4
DAWSON, Charles I. — 5
DAWSON, Claude Ivan — 5
DAWSON, Clyde C. — 2
DAWSON, Edgar — 2
DAWSON, Edward — 2
DAWSON, Francis Warrington — H
DAWSON, Fred — 4
DAWSON, George — H
DAWSON, George Ellsworth — 1
DAWSON, George Louis — 4
DAWSON, George Walter — 3
DAWSON, Henry Barton — H
DAWSON, James Frederick — 5

DAWSON, John — H
DAWSON, John Bennett — H
DAWSON, John Littleton — H
DAWSON, John Shaw — 4
DAWSON, Lemuel Orah — 1
DAWSON, Marion Lindsay — 5
DAWSON, Mary — 5
DAWSON, Miles Menander — 2
DAWSON, Thomas Cleland — 1
DAWSON, Thomas S. — 4
DAWSON, William — 5
DAWSON, William Crosby — H
DAWSON, William James — 1
DAWSON, William Johnston — H
DAWSON, William L. — 5
DAWSON, William Leon — 1
DAWSON, William Mercer Owens — 1
DAWSON, William Warren — 2
DAWSON-WATSON, Dawson — 1
DAY, Addison Blanchard — 5
DAY, Arthur Louis — 4
DAY, Benjamin Franklin — 1
DAY, Benjamin Henry — H
DAY, Bernard Pope — 4
DAY, Charles — 1
DAY, Charles Ivan — 3
DAY, Charles Manley — 2
DAY, Charles Orrin — 1
DAY, Clarence — 1
DAY, Clifford Louis — 5
DAY, Clive — 5
DAY, Cyrus Lawrence — 5
DAY, David Alexander — H
DAY, David Sheldon — 4
DAY, David Talbot — 1
DAY, Edmund — 1
DAY, Edmund Ezra — 4
DAY, Edward — 4
DAY, Edward Cason — 1
DAY, Edward Charles — 1
DAY, Edward Marvin — 2
DAY, Erastus Sheldon — 1
DAY, Ewing Wilber — 2
DAY, Fisk Holbrook — 1
DAY, Florence Roberts — 3
DAY, Francis — 1
DAY, Frank Leighton — 4
DAY, Frank Leslie — 4
DAY, Frank Miles — 1
DAY, Frank Parker — 3
DAY, G. Z. — 2
DAY, George Armstrong — 1
DAY, George Calvin — 1
DAY, George Edward * — 1
DAY, George Parmly — 3
DAY, Harold Briggs — 4
DAY, Henry — H
DAY, Henry Noble — H
DAY, Herbert James — 3
DAY, Holman Francis — 1
DAY, Horace H. — H
DAY, James E. — 4
DAY, James Gamble — H
DAY, James Roscoe — 1
DAY, James W. — 1
DAY, Jeremiah B. — H
DAY, Jerome J. — 1
DAY, Jesse Erwin — 4
DAY, John Boynton Wilson — 1
DAY, John Boynton Wilson — 4
DAY, John Dabney — 1
DAY, John Francis — 1
DAY, John William — 1
DAY, Joseph Paul — 2
DAY, Karl S. — 5
DAY, Kenneth — 5
DAY, L. B. — 1
DAY, Leigh Gross — 4
DAY, Luther — H
DAY, Luther — 4
DAY, Mary Anna — 1
DAY, Oscar Fayette Gaines — 4
DAY, Ralph E. — 2
DAY, Richard Edwin — 1
DAY, Richard Ellsworth — 1
DAY, Robert Henry — 1
DAY, Rowland — H
DAY, Sarah J. — 1
DAY, Stephen — H
DAY, Stephen A. — 2
DAY, Thomas Fleming — 1
DAY, Thomas Franklin — 1
DAY, Timothy Crane — H
DAY, William A. — 1
DAY, William A. — 3
DAY, William Baker — 1

DAY, William Cathcart — 1
DAY, William Cyrus — 4
DAY, William Horace — 1
DAY, William Louis — 1
DAY, William Plummer — 1
DAY, William Rufus — 1
DAYAN, Charles — H
DAY-LEWIS, Cecil — 5
DAYTON, Alston Gordon — 1
DAYTON, Arthur Spencer — 1
DAYTON, Charles Willoughby — 1
DAYTON, Ellas — H
DAYTON, George Draper — 5
DAYTON, Hughes — 5
DAYTON, James Henry — 1
DAYTON, John Havens — 3
DAYTON, Jonathan — H
DAYTON, Lewis Seeley — 1
DAYTON, Roy — 3
DAYTON, William A. — 3
DAYTON, William Lewis — 1
DAYTON, William Lewis — 5
D'AZAMBUJA, Lucien Henri — 5
DAZEY, Charles Turner — 1
DEADERICK, William Heiskell — 2
DEADY, Matthew Paul — H
DEAK, Francis — 5
DEAKIN, Gerald — 4
DEAKYNE, Herbert — 2
DEAL, Edson H. — 4
DEAL, Erastus Charles — 5
DEAL, Herbert L. — 4
DEAL, Joseph T. — 2
DEAL, Roy Walter — 4
'DE ALARCON, Hernando — H
'DE ALBA, Pedro — 5
DEALEY, Edward Musgrove (Ted) — 5
DEALEY, George Bannerman — 2
DEALEY, James Quayle — 1
DEALY, Patrick Francis — 1
DEAN, Alexander — 1
DEAN, Amos — H
DEAN, Arthur Davis — 1
DEAN, Arthur Lyman — 3
DEAN, Bashford — 1
DEAN, Basil — 4
DEAN, Ben — 3
DEAN, Benjamin — H
DEAN, Charles — H
DEAN, Edwin Blanchard — 1
DEAN, Ezra — H
DEAN, Francis Winthrop — 1
DEAN, George Adam — 5
DEAN, George Reinald — 4
DEAN, Gilbert — 1
DEAN, Gordon Evans — 3
DEAN, H. Trendley — 3
DEAN, Howard B. — 3
DEAN, Hugh — 4
DEAN, James — 4
DEAN, James Renwick — 1
DEAN, James Theodore — 1
DEAN, John — 1
DEAN, John Candee — 1
DEAN, John Marvin — 1
DEAN, John Ward — H
DEAN, Josiah — H
DEAN, Julia — H
DEAN, Lee Wallace — 2
DEAN, Reginald Scott — 4
DEAN, Richard Crain — 1
DEAN, Richard Doggett — 3
DEAN, Richmond — 1
DEAN, Robert Augustus — 1
DEAN, Sara — 1
DEAN, Sidney — H
DEAN, Vera Micheles — 5
DEAN, Walter Carleton — 1
DEAN, Walter Lofthouse — 1
DEAN, William Blake — 1
DEAN, William John — 1
DEAN, William Laird — 1
DEAN, Willis Johnson — 2
DEAN, Willis Leonard — 2
DEANDRADE, Anthony J. — 5
'DE ANDREIS, Andrew James Felix Bartholomew — H
DEANE, Charles Bennett — 5
DEANE, Charles J. — 4
DEANE, Gardiner Andrus Armstrong — 4
DEANE, John Hall — 1
DEANE, Ruthven — 1
DEANE, Samuel — H
DEANE, Silas — H
DEANE, Walter — 1
DE ANGELIS, Jefferson — 1
DE ANGELIS, Pascal Charles Joseph — 1

'DE ANZA, Juan Bautista — H
DEAR, J. Albert — 3
DEAR, J. Albert — 4
DEAR, Joseph Albert — 2
DEAR, Walter Moore — 4
DEARBORN, Benjamin — H
DEARBORN, Donald Curtis — 4
DEARBORN, Earl Hamilton — 5
DEARBORN, George Van Ness — 1
DEARBORN, Henry — H
DEARBORN, Henry Alexander Scammell — H
DEARBORN, Henry M. — 1
DEARBORN, John — 1
DEARBORN, Nathaniel — H
DEARBORN, Ned — 4
DEARBORN, Ned Harland — 4
DEARBORN, Richard Harold — 2
DEARBORN, Walter Fenno — 3
DEARDORFF, Neva Ruth — 3
DEARHOLT, Hoyt E. — 5
DEARING, Charles Lee — 5
DEARING, John Lincoln — 1
DEARING, William Prentice — 3
DE ARMOND, David A. — 1
DEARMONT, Russell Lee — 4
DEARMONT, Washington Strother — 2
DEARTH, Henry Golden — 1
DEAS, Charles — H
DEAS, Zachariah Cantey — H
DEASY, John Francis — 3
DEASY, Luere B. — 1
DEAVER, Bascom S. — 2
DEAVER, John B. — 1
DEAVOURS, Stone — 1
DE AYALA, Juan Manuel — H
DE AYLLON, Lucas Vasquez — H
DEBARDELEBEN, Charles Fairchild — 2
DE BARDELEBEN, Henry Fairchild — H
DE BARDELEBEN, Henry Fairchild — 4
DEBARDELEBEN, Henry Ticknor — 3
DE BARR, Edwin — 4
DE BASTOS, Emil — 5
'DE BEAUMONT, Guerin Jean Michel 'du Bosco — 3
DE BECK, William — 2
DE BELLEVILLE, Frederic — 1
DE BENEVIDES, Alonzo — H
DE BERARD, Wilford Willis — 4
DE BERDT, Dennys — H
DEBERRY, Edmund — H
DEBERRY, William Nelson — 2
DEBEVOISE, P. Leroy — 4
DEBEVOISE, Thomas — 3
DEBEY, Cornelia Bernarda — 4
DEBISSCHOP, Frank J. — 3
DE BLOIS, Austen Kennedy — 2
DE BLOIS, George Lewis — 1
DEBOARD, Elmer H. — 3
DEBOE, William J. — 1
DE BOER, John J. — 5
DE BOER, Joseph Arend — 1
DEBOLT, John T. — 4
DE BOLT, Rezin A. — H
'DE BONNEVILLE, Benjamin Louis Eulalie — H
DE BOOY, Theodoor — 2
DE BOST, William Ludlam — 3
DEBOW, Charles Louis — 1
DE BOW, James Dunwoody Brownson — H
'DE BOWER, Herbert Francis — 1
DE BRA, Harvey Rufus — 4
DE BRAHM, William Girard — H
'DE BREHAN, Marquise — H
DEBS, Eugene Victor — 1
DEBUCHI, Katsuji — 2
DEBUSK, Burchard Woodson — 1
DEBUYS, Laurence Richard — 3

DEBYE, Peter Joseph William — 4
DE CALLIERES BONNEVUE, Louis Hector — H
DE CAMP, George — 5
DE CAMP, John A. — 3
DE CAMP, Joseph Rodefer — 1
DE CAMP, William Scott — 1
DE CAPRILES, Jose Rafael — 5
'DE CARDENAS, Garcia Lopez — H
'DE CARONDELET, Francisco Luis Hector — H
'DE CARTIER DE MARCHIENNE, Baron Emile — 2
DECASSERES, Benjamin — 2
DE CASTRO, Hector — 1
'DE CASTRO, Morris F. — 4
DECATUR, Emmett Daniel — 1
DECATUR, Stephen * — H
DE CELERON DE BLAINVILLE, Pierre Joseph — H
DECELL, John Lloyd — 2
'DE CHAMPLAIN, Samuel — H
'DE CHARLEVOIX, Pierre Francois Xavier — H
DE CHAVANNE, Countess Loveau — 4
DECHERD, H. Ben — 5
DECHERT, Henry Martyn — 1
DECHERT, Henry Taylor — 1
'DE CHEVERUS, Jean Louis Anne Magdelen Lefebre — H
DE CISNEROS, Eleonora — 1
DE CISNEROS, Eleonora — 2
DECKER, Alonzo Galloway — 3
DECKER, Benton Clark — 1
DECKER, Charles Elijah — 5
DECKER, Clarence Raymond — 5
DECKER, Edward William — 5
DECKER, Edward William — 3
DECKER, Floyd F. — 3
DECKER, Marion Emory — 5
DECKER, Martin Snyder — 1
DECKER, Orlady Paul — 4
DECKER, Perl D. — 5
DECKER, Sarah Platt — 1
'DE CLORIVIERE, Joseph-Pierre Picot 'de Limoelan — H
DECORMIS, Louis — 1
DECOSTA, Benjamin Franklin — 4
DE COU, Branson — 1
DE COU, Edgar Ezekiel — 2
DE COURCY, Charles A. — 1
'DE CREVECOEUR, Michel-Guillaume Jean — 1
DEDERICK, Peter Kells — 1
DEEDMEYER, Frank — 4
DEEDS, Edward Andrew — 4
DEEGAN, William Joseph — 2
DEEKS, William Edgar — 1
DEEMER, Elias — 3
DEEMER, Horace Emerson — 1
DEEMS, Charles Force — H
DEEMS, Edward Mark — 1
DEEMS, J. Harry — 1
DEEN, Joshua Lee — 3
DEEPING, Werwick — 3
DEER, George Harvison — 4
'DE ERDELY, Francis — 4
DEERE, Charles Henry — 1
DEERE, John — H
DEERFOOT — 1
DEERING, Charles — 1
DEERING, Frank Prentiss — 1
DEERING, James — 1
DEERING, Nathaniel — H
DEERING, Nathaniel Cobb — 1
DEERING, Robert Waller — 4
DEERING, William — 1
DEES, Randall Euesta — 5
DEESZ, Louis A. — 3
DEETER, Paxson — 1
DEETJEN, Rudolph Henry — 4
DEETZ, Charles Henry — 3
DEFAUW, Desire — 4

DEFEBAUGH, James Elliott 1
DEFENBACH, Byron; 5
DEFERRARI, Roy Joseph 5
DEFFENBAUGH, Walter Sylvanus 5
'DE FLOREZ, Luis 4
DEFOE, Harry Joseph 3
DE FOE, Louis Vincent 1
DE FONTIANE, Felix Gregory H
DE FOREST, Alfred Victor 2
DE FOREST, Charles Mills 2
DE FOREST, David Curtis H
DE FOREST, Erastus Lyman H
'DE FOREST, Henry Lockwood 3
'DE FOREST, Henry Pelouze 2
DE FOREST, Henry S. 1
DE FOREST, Henry Wheeler 1
DE FOREST, John William H
DE FOREST, John William 4
DE FOREST, John Williams 4
DEFOREST, Johnston 3
DE FOREST, Katharine 5
DE FOREST, Lee 4
DE FOREST, Lockwood 1
'DE FOREST, Marian 1
DE FOREST, Robert Weeks 1
DE FRANCA, Manuel Joachim H
'DE FRANCESCO, Italo Luther 4
'DE FRANCISCI, Anthony 4
DEFREES, Donald 5
DEFREES, Joseph Holton 1
DEFREES, Joseph Hutton H
DEFREES, Joseph Rollie 3
'DE FREYRE 'Y SANTANDER, Manuel 1
'DE GALVEZ, Bernardo H
DE GARMO, James M. 4
DE GARMO, William 1
DEGAS, Hilaire Germain Edgar H
DEGAS, Hillaire Germain Edgar 4
'DE GASPERI, Alcide 3
DE GAULLE, Charles Andre Joseph Marie 5
DE GELLEKE, Gerrit Jacob 5
DEGENER, Edward H
DEGERING, Edward Franklind 4
'DE GERSDORFF, Carl August 2
DEGETAU, Federico 4
'DE GHELDERODE, Michel 4
DEGLMAN, George Anthony 5
DE GOGORZA, Emilio Eduardo 5
DE GOGORZA, Emilio Eduardo
DE GOLYER, E. L. 3
DE GOLYER, Robert Seeley 3
DE GRAEFF, Dr. A. C. D. 3
DE GRAFF, John Isaac H
DE GRAFF, Lawrence 1
DE GRAFF, Mark H. 4
DE GRAFFENRIED, Christopher H
DE GRAFFENRIED, Edward 1
DE GRAFFENRIED, Mary Clare 4
DE GRAFFENRIED, Reese Calhoun 1
'DE GRASSE, Francois Joseph Paul H
DE GRAW, Peter Voorhees 1
DEGROAT, George Blewer
DEGROAT, Harry DeWitt 5
DE GROOT, William A. 1
DE HAAN, John Jr. 2
DE HAAS, Jacob Jaudah Aaron

DE HAAS, Jacob Judah Aaron H
DE HAAS, John Philip H
DE HART, John H
DE HART, William Henry 1
DE HART, William Mathias 4
'DE HASS, Mauritz Frederick Hendrick H
DE HAVEN, David William 2
DE HAVEN, Edwin Jesse H
DE HAVEN, Frank 4
DE HAVEN, Franklin 1
DEHAVEN, John B. H
DE HAVEN, John Jefferson 1
'DE HAVILLAND, Sir Geoffrey 4
'DE HEVESY, George Charles 4
DEHN, Adolf 5
DEHON, Theodore H
DEIBLER, Frederick Shipp 4
DEICHMAN, Carl F. 5
DEILER, John Hanno 1
DEIMEL, Henry L. 4
DEIMLER, Paul Ellas 5
DEINES, Ernest Hubert 5
DEININGER, William 1
DEISS, Charles F. 3
DEITRICH, Theodore C. 1
DEITRICK, Elizabeth Platt 5
DEITRICK, Frederick Simpson 3
DEITRICK, James 4
DEITZ, Archibald Edwin 5
DEITZLER, George Washington H
DE JARNETTE, Daniel Coleman H
DEJARNETTE, Joseph Spencer 5
DE JESOS, Angel Roman 3
DE JONG, David Cirnel 4
DE JURENEV, Nicholas 4
DE KALB, Courtenay 1
DEKALB, Frances Douglas (Mrs. Courtenay Dekalb) H
DE KAY, Charles 1
DE KAY, George Colman H
DE KAY, James Ellsworth H
DE KAY, John Wesley 5
DEKKER, Albert 5
DE KLEINE, William 3
DE KNIGHT, Clarence Woods 1
'DE KOVEN, Anna Farwell 3
DE KOVEN, James H
DE KOVEN, Reginald 1
DEKRAFFT, William 4
DE KROYFT, S. Helen A. 1
DE KRUIF, Paul 5
DE LA BARRA, Francisco Leon H
DE LA BARRE, Cecil Franzen 3
DELABARRE, Edmund Burke 2
DELABARRE, Frank Alexander H
DE LABOULAYE, Ander Lefebvre 4
DE LABOULAYE, Andre Lefebvre 5
DELACOUR, Reginald Beardsley 2
DE LACY, Walter Washington H
DELAFIELD, E. M. 2
DELAFIELD, Edward H
DELAFIELD, Francis 1
DELAFIELD, John * H
DELAFIELD, John Ross 4
DELAFIELD, Lewis Livingston 2
DELAFIELD, Lewis Livingston 3
DELAFIELD, Maturin Livingston 1
DELAFIELD, Richard H
DELAFIELD, Richard 1
DE LA HABA, Gabriel 4
DELAHANTY, William John 5
DELAHAY, Mark William H
DELAMANO, William H
DE LAMAR, Joseph Raphael 1
DE LAMAR, Joseph Raphael 4

DE LA MARE, Walter 3
DELAMARTER, Eric 3
DELAMATER, Cornelius Henry H
DELAMATER, Nicholas B. 1
DE LA MATYR, Gilbert H
'DE 'LA MOTHE, Antoine H
DELANCEY, Darragh 1
DE LANCEY, Edward Floyd 1
DE LANCEY, James * H
DE LANCEY, Oliver H
DE LANCEY, William Heathcote H
DE LAND, Charles Edmund 3
DE LAND, Charles Victor H
DE LAND, Clyde Osmer 2
DELAND, Ellen Douglas 1
DELAND, Margaretta Wade 2
DELAND, Paul Stanley 4
DELANDER, N. Paul H
DELANEY, George Philip 5
DELANEY, John J. 2
DELANEY, Matthew A. 5
DE LANEY, Paul 4
DELANEY, Peter A. 1
DELANEY, Sadie Peterson 3
DE LANGLADE, Charles Michel H
DELANO, Aline P. 4
DELANO, Amassa H
DELANO, Charles H
DELANO, Columbus H
DELANO, Edith Barnard 2
DELANO, Eugene 1
DELANO, Frances Jackson 4
DELANO, Francis Henry 1
DELANO, Frederic Adrian 3
DELANO, Jane Arminda 1
DELANO, Jane Arminda 4
DELANO, Lyman 2
DELANO, William Adams 3
DELANY, John Bernard 1
DELANY, John Joseph 1
DELANY, Joseph Francis 2
DELANY, Martin Robinson H
DELANY, Patrick Bernard 1
DELANY, Selden Peabody 1
'DE 'LA OSSA, Ernesto 4
DELAPLAINE, Isaac Clason H
'DE 'LA PUENTE, Don Juan Joseph Eligio H
DE LARGE, Robert Carlos H
DE LARGENTAYE, Jean 5
DE LA RICHARDIE, Armand H
DE LARME, Alonzo Alvin 1
'DE 'LA ROCHE, Mazo 4
'DE 'LA RONDE, Louis Denis H
DELATOUR, Henry Beeckman 1
'DE LAUBENFELS, Max W 3
'DE LAUDONNIERE, Rene Goulaine H
DELAUP, Sidney Philip 1
DELAVAN, David Bryson 2
DELAVAN, Edward Cornelius H
DE 'LA WARR, 'baron H
DELBOS, Julius 5
DE LEE, Joseph Bolivar 2
DE LE MONTANYA, James H
DE LEON, Daniel 1
DE LEON, Edwin H
DE LEON, Edwin Warren 1
DE LEON, Pablo Ocampo 4
DE LEON, Thomas Cooper H
'DE LEQUERICA 'Y ERQUIZA, Jose Felix 4
DELERY, Francois Charles H
'DE LERY, Joseph Gaspard Chaussegros H
DE LESTRY, Edmond Louis 1
DELEUW, Charles Edmund 5

DEL GAUDIO, Matthew William 4
'DE L'HALLE, Constantin H
'DE LIMA 'E SILVA, R. 1
DE LISSER, Horace 1
DELIUS, Frederick H
DELIUS, Frederick 1
DELK, Edward Buehler 3
DELK, Edwin Heyl 1
DELL, Floyd 5
DELL, Francis William 4
DELL, Roger LeRoy 5
DELL, Roger LeRoy 5
DELLA PIETRA, Alfonso 1
DELLA TORRE ALTA, Il Marchese (Albert-Felix Schmitt) H
DELLENBAUGH, Frederick Samuel 1
DELLENBAUGH, Harriet Rogers Otis 1
DELLET, James H
DELLINGER, John Howard 4
DELLPLAIN, Morse 5
DEL MAR, Alexander 1
DEL MAR, Algernon 5
DEL MAR, Eugene 2
DELMAS, Delphin Michael 1
DELMONICO, Lorenzo H
DELOACH, Robert John Henderson 5
DE LOM D'ARCE, Louis-Armand H
DE LONG, George Washington 1
DE LONG, Ira Mitchell H
DE LONG, Irwin Hoch 5
DE LONGPRE, Paul 1
'DE 'LOS RIOS, Fernando 2
'DE LOUTHERBOURG, Annibale Christian Henry H
DELSASSO, Leo Peter 1
DEL TUFO, Raymond, Jr. 5
DELUCA, Giuseppe 3
'DE LUNA 'Y ARELLANO, Tristan H
DELUREY, Laurence Augustine 4
DEL VALLE, Manuel Angel 5
DELWICHE, Edmond Joseph 2
DELZELL, James Ellis 4
DELZELL, Thomas White 5
DE MAR, John L. 3
DEMAREE, Albert Lowther 1
DEMAREST, George Stuart 5
DEMAREST, Henry Samuel 1
DEMAREST, William Henry Steele 3
DEMAREST, William Thomas 1
'DEMARTINO, Nobile Giacomo 3
'DE MARTINO, Nobile Giacomo H
DEMBITZ, Lewis Naphtali 1
DEMBY, V. E. Thomas 3
'DEMEISSNER, Sophie Radford 4
'DE MENASCE, Jacques 3
DE MENIL, Alexander Nicolas 1
DE MENT, Byron Hoover 4
DEMEREC, Milislav 4
DE MERITTE, Edwin 4
DEMERS, Albert Fox 2
DEMERS, Pierre Paul 5
DE MEZIERES 'Y CLUGNY, Athanase H
DEMIASHKEVICH, Michael John 1
DE MILHAU, Louis John de Grenon H
'DE MILLE, Cecil Blount 1
DE MILLE, Henry Churchill H
'DE MILLE, William Churchill 3
DE MILT, Aida Rodman 5
DEMING, Benjamin F. H
DEMING, Clarence 1
DEMING, Edwin Willard 1
DEMING, Harold S. 3
DEMING, Henry Champion 1

DEMING, Horace Edward 1
DEMING, Judson Keith 4
DEMING, Lucius Parmenias H
DEMING, Philander 1
DEMING, Therese O. 2
DEMING, Thomas Harlan 3
DEMING, William Chapin 1
DE MIRANDA, Francisco H
DEMME, Charles Rudolph 1
DEMMON, Isaac Newton 1
DE MOKCSA, Agoston Haraszthy H
DE MONCHY, W. H. 5
DEMOREST, Frederic Coe 4
DEMOREST, William Curtis 1
DEMOS, Raphael 5
'DE MOSCOSO 'DE ALVARADO, Luis H
DE MOTT, John H
DEMOTT, Richard Hopper 5
DE MOTTE, Harvey Clelland 1
DE MOTTE, Mark L. 1
DEMPSEY, Clarence Haines 1
DEMPSEY, Edward John 4
DEMPSEY, Edward Joseph 3
DEMPSEY, Elam Franklin 1
DEMPSEY, James Howard 4
DEMPSEY, John Bourne 4
DEMPSEY, John J. 3
DEMPSEY, John Stanley 3
DEMPSEY, Stephen Wallace 2
DEMPSIE, Ephraim 2
DEMPSTER, Arthur Jeffrey
DEMPSTER, John H
DEMPSTER, William John 1
DEMPWOLF, Reinhardt 2
DEMUTH, Charles H
DEMUTH, Charles 4
DEMUTH, Laurence Wheeler H
'DE NANCREDE, Paul Joseph Guerard H
DENARI, Andrew F. 3
'DE NARVAEZ, Panfilo H
DENBIGH, John Halliday 1
DENBY, Charles * 1
DENBY, Edwin 1
DENCH, Edward Bradford 1
DENDRAMIS, Vassill 3
DENE, Shafto Henry Monckton 3
DENECHAUD, Charles Isidore 3
DE NECKERE, Leo Raymond H
DENEEFE, Robert 3
DENEEN, Charles Samuel 1
DENEGRE, Walter Denis 1
DENFELD, Louis Emil 5
DENFELD, Robert Edward 1
DENHAM, Edward 1
DENHAM, Henry Henderson 1
DENHAM, Robert Newton 3
DENHAM, Thomas Palmer 4
DENHARD, Charles Edward 1
DENHARDT, Henry H. 1
DENIG, Robert Gracey 1
DENIG-MANOE, Rudolf Karl Robert 1
DENIO, Francis Brigham 1
DENIOUS, Jess C. 3
DENIOUS, Wilbur Franklin 3
DENISE, Larimore Conover 5
DENISON, A. Rodger 4
DENISON, Arthur Carter 2
DENISON, Charles H
DENISON, Charles H
DENISON, Charles Simeon 5
DENISON, Edward Everett 5
DENISON, Frederic H
DENISON, George H
DENISON, Henry Willard 1
DENISON, John Henry * 1
DENISON, John Hopkins 1
DENISON, John Ledyard 1
DENISON, Lindsay 1
DENISON, Mary Andrews 1

DENISON, Robert Charles — 1
DENISON, Robert Fuller — 5
DENISON, Thomas Stewart — 1
DENISON, William Cecil — 4
DENISON, Winfred Thaxter — 1
'DE NIZA, Marcos — H
DENMAN, Burt J. — 1
DENMAN, Ira O. — 1
DENMAN, Leroy Gilbert — 1
DENMAN, William — H
DENMAN, William — 3
DENNEN, Ernest Joseph — 1
DENNEN, Jeanne Whitney — 1
DENNETT, Carl Pullen — 3
DENNETT, Edward Power — 3
DENNETT, Fred — 2
DENNETT, John Richard — H
DENNETT, Raymond — 4
DENNETT, Roger Herbert — 1
DENNETT, Tyler — 3
DENNEY, James Arlando — 4
DENNEY, Joseph Villiers — 1
DENNEY, Lawrence Vincent — 5
DENNEY, Oswald Evans — 2
DENNEY, William 'du Hamel — 4
DENNIE, Charles Clayton — 5
DENNIE, Joseph — H
DENNING, Forrest Wayne — 4
DENNING, James Edwin — 5
DENNING, Joseph M. — 1
DENNING, Reynolds McConnell — 5
DENNING, William * — H
DENNIS, Alfred Lewis Pinneo — 1
DENNIS, Alfred Pearce — 1
DENNIS, Charles Henry — 2
DENNIS, David Worth — 1
DENNIS, E. Willard — 4
DENNIS, Fred L. — 1
DENNIS, Frederic Shepard — 3
DENNIS, Gabriel Lafayette — H
DENNIS, George Robertson — H
DENNIS, Graham Barclay — 4
DENNIS, James Shepard — 1
DENNIS, James Teackle — 1
DENNIS, John * — H
DENNIS, John Cobb — 4
DENNIS, John Hancock — 4
DENNIS, John M. — 1
DENNIS, Joseph Charles — 5
DENNIS, Lindley Hoag — 3
DENNIS, Littleton Purnell — H
DENNIS, Louis Munroe — 1
DENNIS, Ralph Brownell — 2
DENNIS, Samuel K. — 3
DENNIS, Samuel Shepard — 1
DENNIS, William B. — 1
DENNIS, William Cullen — 1
DENNIS, William Henry — 1
DENNIS, William Henry Jr. — 4
DENNISON, Aaron Lufkin — H
DENNISON, Clare — 3
DENNISON, E. Haldeman — 1
DENNISON, Ethan Allen — 3
DENNISON, Henry Strugis — 3
DENNISON, Henry Sturgis — 5
DENNISON, Jackson Belden — 3
DENNISON, Walter — 1
DENNISON, William — 1
DENNISTON, Henry Martyn — 1
DENNY, Charles Eugene — 4
DENNY, Collins — 2
DENNY, Collins Jr. — 1
DENNY, Ebenezer — H
DENNY, Frank Lee — 3
DENNY, George Hutcheson — H
DENNY, George Vernon Jr. — 3
DENNY, Harmar — H
DENNY, Harmar Denny — 4
DENNY, Harold Norman — 2
DENNY, James W. — 5
DENNY, Ludwell — 5
DENNY, Reginald Leigh — 1
DENNY, Robert H. — 3

DE NORMANDIE, James — 1
DE NORMANDIE, Robert L. — 3
'DE NOYAN, Pierre-Jacques Payen — H
DENOYELLES, Peter — H
DENOYER, L. Philip — 4
DENSLOW, Dorothea Henrietta — 5
DENSLOW, Herbert McKenzie — 2
DENSLOW, William Wallace — 1
DENSMORE, Emmet — 1
DENSMORE, Frances — 1
DENSMORE, Hiram D. — 1
DENSMORE, John B. — 3
DENSMORE, John Hopkins — 2
DENSON, Nimrod Davis — 1
DENSON, Samuel Crawford — 1
DENT, Frederick Rodgers, Jr. — 5
DENT, Frederick Tracy — H
DENT, George — 2
DENT, Hawthorne K. — 3
DENT, Louis Addison — 4
DENT, Marmaduke Herbert — 1
DENT, Stanley Hubert — 3
DENT, William Barton Wade — H
DENTON, George Kirkpatrick — 1
DENTON, J. Furman — 5
DENTON, James Clarence — 2
DENTON, James Edgar — 5
DENTON, Lyman Morse — 5
DENTON, Minna Caroline — 3
DENTON, Winfield K. — 5
DENVER, James William — H
DENVER, Matthew Rombach — 3
DENYES, John Russell — 1
'DE ONATE, Juan — H
DE ONIS, Federico — 4
'DE OTERMEN, Antonio — H
'DE PADILLA, Juan — H
DE PAOLIS, Alessio — 4
DE PARIS, Wilbur — 5
'DE PAUGHER, Adrien — H
DEPAUW, Washington Charles — H
DE PENA, Carlos Maria — 1
'DE PENALOSA, BRICENO, Diego Dionsio — H
'DE PERALTA, Pedro — H
DEPEW, Chauncey Mitchell — 1
DEPEW, Claude Ira — 3
DEPEW, Joseph William — 5
DE PEYSTER, Abraham — 1
DE PEYSTER, Frederic James — 1
DE PEYSTER, John Watts — 1
DEPONAI, John Martin — 1
'DE PORTOLA, Gaspar — H
'DE POUILLY, Jacques Nicholas Bussiere — H
'DE POURTALES, Louis Francois — H
DEPPERMANN, William Herman — 5
DE PRIEST, Oscar — 3
DEPUE, David A. — 1
DEPUTY, Manfred Wolfe — 2
DE PUY, William Harrison — 1
DE QUILLE, Dan — H
DERAMUS, William Neal — 4
DERBIGNY, Irving A. — 3
DERBIGNY, Pierre Auguste Charles Bourguignon — H
DERBY, Donald — 5
DERBY, Elias Hasket * — H
DERBY, George Horatio — H
DERBY, George McClellan — 3
DERBY, George Strong — 1
DERBY, Jeanette Barr — 1
DERBY, Orville Adelbert — 4
DERBY, Richard — H
DERBY, Richard — 4
DERBY, Samuel Carroll — 1
DERBY, Stephen Hasket — 2
DERCUM, Francis X. — 1
DE REMER, John A. — 1
DE RESZKE, Edouard — 1
DE RESZKE, Jean — 2
DERICKSON, Donald — 4
DERICKSON, Samuel Hoffman — 1
DERIEUX, Samuel Arthur — 1

DERLETH, August (William) — 5
DERLETH, Charles, Jr. — 5
DERN, Alfred L. — 2
DERN, George Henry — 1
DERN, John — 1
DERN, John — 3
DE ROALDES, Arthur Washington — 1
DE ROSE, Peter — 3
DE ROSSET, Frederick Ancrum — 1
DE ROSSET, Moses John — 4
DE ROSSET, William Lord — 3
DE ROUEN, Rene L. — 2
'DE ROUSSY 'DE SALES, Raoul — 2
DERR, Cyrus George — 1
DERR, Homer Munro — 5
DERR, Louis — 1
DERRICK, Samuel Melanchthon — 5
DERRICK, Sidney Jacob — 2
DERRY, George Hermann — 2
DERSE, Alexander Anthony — 4
DERSHEM, Franklin Lewis — 4
DERTHICK, Frank A. — 4
DERTHICK, Henry J. — 5
DERTINGER, Georg — 4
DE RUSSY, Isaac Denniston — H
DERWENT, Clarence — 3
DERY, D. Geofge — 3
'DE SAINT EXUPERY, Antoine — 2
DE SAINT-MEMIN, Charles Balthazar Jullen Fevret — H
DE SALVIO, Alfonso — 5
DESANCTIS, Adolph George — 4
DE SAULLES, Charles August Heckscher — 5
DE SAUSSURE, Henry William — H
'DE SAVITSCH, Eugene Constantine — 4
'DE SCHWEINITZ, Edmond Alexander — H
'DE SCHWEINITZ, Paul — 1
DESHA, Joseph — H
DESHA, Mary — 1
DESHA, Robert — 1
DESHON, George — 1
DESIDERIO, Anthony — 5
DESJARDINS, Arthur Ulderic — 4
DESLOGE, Joseph — 5
DE SMET, Pierre Jean — H
DESMOND, Daniel Francis — 2
DESMOND, Humphrey Joseph — 1
DESMOND, Thomas Charles — 5
DESMOND, Thomas Henry — 3
DE SOLLAR, Tenney Cook — 4
DE SOTO, Hernando — H
DE SOTO, Hernando — 1
DESPARD, Clement L. — 3
DES PLANCHES, Baron Ed Mayor — 4
DES PORTES, Fay Allen — 2
D'ESPOSITO, Joshua — 3
DESPRADELLE, Constant Desire — 1
DESPRES, Emile — 5
DESPRES, Maurice Samuel — 3
DESSAR, Leo Charles — 2
DESSAR, Louis Paul — 3
DESSES, Jean — 5
DESSION, George Hathaway — 3
DE ST. Aubin, Percival Ovide — 1
'DE ST. Denis, Louis Juchereau — H
'DE ST. Vrain, Ceran De Hault Delassus — H
'DE STEIGUER, Louis Rodolph — H
DESTINN, Emmy — 1
DESTREHAN, John Noel — H
DESVERNINE, Raoul Eugene — H
DE SYLVA, George Gard — 3
DETCHON, Adelaide — 1
DETELS, Martin Paul — 5
DETHMERS, John R. — 5
DETMER, Julian Francis — 3

DETMOLD, Christian Edward — H
'DE TOCQUEVILLE, Alexis Henri Maurice Clerel — H
'DE TONTY, Henry — H
'DE TORRENTE, Henry — 4
'DE TOUSARD, Anne Louis — 1
DE TREVILLE, Yvonne — 3
DETRICK, Jacob Stoll — 4
'DE TROBRIAND, Regis Denis 'de Kereden — H
DETT, Robert Nathaniel — 2
DETWEILER, A(lbert) Henry — 5
DETWEILER, Charles Samuel — 4
DETWEILER, Frederick German — 3
DETWEILER, George H. — 3
DETWILER, Frederick Knecht — 3
DETWILER, Samuel Randall — 3
DETWILER, W. Frank — 3
DEUEL, Alanson Chase — 4
DEUEL, Harry James Jr. — 1
'DE ULLOA, Antonio — H
DEUPREE, John Greer — 4
DEUSSEN, Alexander — 4
DEUTSCH, Albert — 4
DEUTSCH, Bernard Seymour — 1
DEUTSCH, Gotthard — 1
DEUTSCH, Henry — 5
DEUTSCH, Monroe Emanuel — 1
DEUTSCHER, Isaac — 5
DEVAN, Harriet Beecher Scoville — 5
DE VANE, William Clyde — 4
DEVANEY, John Patrick — 1
DEVANEY, Michael R. — 5
'DE VARGAS ZAPATA 'Y LUJAN PONCE DE, Leon Diego — H
'DE VEGH, Imrie — 4
DEVENDORF, Irving R. — 1
DEVENDORF, James Franklin — 2
DEVENS, Charles — H
DEVER, Paul Andrew — 3
DEVER, William Emmett — 1
DEVEREUX, F. Ramsey — 4
DEVEREUX, John C. — H
DEVEREUX, John Henry — 1
DEVEREUX, Mary — 1
DEVEREUX, Nicholas — 3
DEVILBISS, Howard P. — 5
DEVIN, Thomas Casimer — 1
DEVIN, William Augustus — 3
DEVINE, Edward Thomas — 2
DEVINE, James Gasper — 5
DE VINE, James Herbert — 1
DEVINE, John M. — 5
DEVINE, Joseph McMurray — 1
DEVINE, Thomas Hume — 1
DE VINNE, Theodore Low — 1
DEVINS, John Bancroft — 1
DEVINY, John Joseph — 3
DE VLIEG, Ray Albert — 3
DEVLIN, Robert Thomas — 1
DEVLIN, Thomas Francis — 1
DEVOE, Alan — 3
DE VOE, Emma Smith — 4
DEVOE, Frederick William — 1
DE VOE, John M. — 2
DEVOE, Ralph Godwin — 4
DEVOE, Robert W. — 5
DE VOE, Walter — 5
DEVOE, William Beck — 3
DEVOL, Carroll Augustine — 1
DE VOLL, F. Usher — 1
DEVOORE, Ann (Mrs. Reginald Prescott Walden) — 5
DEVOR, Donald Smith — 4
DEVORE, Daniel Bradford — 4
DEVORE, Harry S. — 2
DE VORE, Rebecca Jane — 5
DE VOS, Julius Emilius — 3
DEVOSS, James Clarence — 3
DE VOTO, Bernard Augustine — 3
DEVOY, John — 4
DEVOY, John — H
DEVREE, Howard — 4

DE VRIES, David Pieterson — H
DEVRIES, Herman — 2
DE VRIES, Marion — 1
DE VRIES, Tiemen — 4
DE VRIES, William Levering — 1
DEW, Louise E. — 4
DEW, Thomas Roderick — H
DEW, Thomas Roderick — 4
DE WAHA, Baron Raymond — 5
DEWALT, Arthur Granville — 1
DEWART, Frederick Wesley — 5
DEWART, Lewis — H
DEWART, Murray Wilder — 1
DEWART, William Herbert — 1
DEWART, William Lewis — H
DEWART, William Thompson — 2
DEWEERD, James A. — 5
DEWEES, William Potts — 4
DE WEESE, Truman Armstrong — H
DEWESSE, Arville Ottis — 5
DEWEY, Byrd Spilman — 5
DEWEY, Charles — 1
DEWEY, Charles Almon — 3
DEWEY, Charles Melville — H
DEWEY, Chester — H
DEWEY, Daniel — H
DEWEY, Davis Rich — 2
DEWEY, Francis Henshaw — 1
DEWEY, Frederic Perkins — 1
DEWEY, George — 1
DEWEY, Harry Pinneo — 1
DEWEY, Henry Bingham — 1
DEWEY, Henry Sweetser — 1
DEWEY, James F. * — 3
DEWEY, John — 4
DEWEY, Julian Hiland — 4
DEWEY, Lloyd Ellis — 4
DEWEY, Lyster Hoxie — 2
DEWEY, Mary Elizabeth — 1
DEWEY, Melvil — 1
DEWEY, Orville — H
DEWEY, Richard — 1
DEWEY, Stoddard — 1
DEWEY, Thomas Edmund — 5
DEWEY, W. A.
DEWHURST, Frederic Eli — 1
DEWHURST, J. Frederic — 4
DEWILDE, Brandon — 5
'DE WINDT, Delano — 3
DEWINDT, Harold Clifford — 5
DEWING, Arthur Stone — 5
DEWING, Francis — H
DEWING, Maria Oakey — 1
DEWING, Thomas Wilmer — 1
DE WITT, Alexander — H
DE WITT, Benjamin Parke — 4
DE WITT, Calvin — 1
DE WITT, Charles — H
DE WITT, Charles Gerrit — H
DE WITT, David Miller — 1
DE WITT, George Ashley — 5
DE WITT, George Gosman — 1
DE WITT, Jacob Hasbrouck — H
DE WITT, John — 1
DE WITT, John — 4
DEWITT, John Doyle — 1
DE WITT, John Hibbett — 1
DEWITT, John Lesesne — 4
DE WITT, Julia Woodhull — 1
DE WITT, Lydia Maria — 1
DEWITT, Norman Johnston — 4
DEWITT, Simeon — H
DE WITT, William Converse — 4
DE WITT, William Hedges — 1
DE WOLF, Frank Walbridge — 3
DE WOLF, James — H
DE WOLF, John — H
DEWOLF, Richard Crosby — 2
DE WOLF, Wallace Leroy — 1
DEWOLFE, Donald Joseph — 4
DE WOLFE, Elsie — 4
DE WOLFE, James Pernatte — 4
DEWOODY, Charles Frederick — 1

DONNELLY, Phil M. 4
DONNELLY, 5
  Richard Carter
DONNELLY, 2
  Samuel Bratton
DONNELLY, Simon Peter 4
DONNELLY, 1
  Thomas Frederick
DONNELLY, Thomas
  James 4
DONNELLY, 5
  Walter Joseph
DONNER, George H
DONNER, Tamsen H
DONNER, William Henry 3
DONOGHUE, Thomas J. 5
DONOHO, Ruger 1
DONOHOE, Denis 1
DONOHOE, James A. 5
DONOHOE, Michael 4
DONOHOE, Thomas
  Joseph 1
DONOHOE, William A. 4
DONOHUE, Charles 1
DONOHUE,
  Francis Michael
DONOHUGH, Thomas
  Smith 5
DONOVAN, 2
  Edward Francis
DONOVAN, 5
  George Francis
DONOVAN, Herman Lee 4
DONOVAN, James Britt 5
DONOVAN, James J. 5
DONOVAN, Jeremiah 1
DONOVAN, 2
  Jerome Francis
DONOVAN, John Joseph 1
DONOVAN, Richard 2
DONOVAN, 3
  William Joseph
DONOVAN, 4
  Winfred Nichols
DONWORTH, George 2
DONWORTH, Grace 2
D'OOGE, 3
  Benjamin Leonard
D'OOGE, Martin Luther 1
DOOLAN, John Calvin 2
DOOLAN, 2
  Leonard Weakley
DOOLEY, Channing Rice 3
DOOLEY, 1
  Henry Williamson
DOOLEY, Joseph Brannon 4
DOOLEY, Lucy 2
DOOLEY, M. S. 3
DOOLEY, Michael F. 1
DOOLEY, 4
  Thomas Anthony III
DOOLEY, 1
  William Francis
DOOLEY, William Henry 2
DOOLIN, John B. 1
DOOLING, Maurice T. 1
DOOLING, Peter J. 1
DOOLITTLE, Amos H
DOOLITTLE, 1
  Charles Camp
DOOLITTLE, 1
  Charles Leander
DOOLITTLE, Dudley 3
DOOLITTLE, Eric 1
DOOLITTLE, 3
  Frederick William
DOOLITTLE, Hilda 4
DOOLITTLE, 1
  Hooker Austin
DOOLITTLE, James Rood H
DOOLITTLE, 1
  Roscoe Edward
DOOLITTLE, 1
  Thomas Benjamin
DOOLY, Oscar Earle 5
DOORLY, Henry 4
DOPP, 5
  Katherine Elizabeth
DORAN, James M. 5
DORAN, 1
  Joseph Ingersoll
DORAN, Thomas Francis 1
DORAN, William Thomas 3
DORCHESTER, Daniel 1
DORCHESTER, Daniel 2
DORCHESTER, 3
  Liverus Hull
DORE, John F. 1
DOREMUS, Charles
  Avery 1
DOREMUS, 2
  Frank Ellsworth
DOREMUS, Henry M. 4
DOREMUS, Robert
  Ogden H
DOREMUS,
  Sarah Platt Haines

DOREN, Electra Collins 1
DORESAM, Charles
  Henry 2
DOREY, Halstead 2
DORGAN, H
  Thomas Aloysius
DORGAN, 4
  Thomas Aloysius
DORIA, Clara 1
DORIGAN, Harry William 5
DORIGAN, Harry William 4
DORION, 2
  Eustache Charles Edouard
DORION, Marie H
DORLAND, Ralph E. Sr. 2
DORLAND, 4
  William Alexander Newman
DORMAN, 4
  Edmund Lawrence
DORMAN, William Edwin 1
DORN, Harold F. 4
DORNE, Albert 4
DORNIN, Bernard H
DORNIN, H
  Thomas Aloysius
DOROSHAW, 4
  Jennis Milford
DORR, 4
  Dudley Huntington
DORR, Edward Monroe 4
DORR, George Bucknam 2
DORR, Harold M. 5
DORR, 4
  John Van Nostrand
DORR, 1
  Julia Caroline Ripley
DORR, Rheta Childe 3
DORR, 1
  Robert East Apthoep
DORR, Robert John 4
DORR, Thomas Wilson H
DORRANCE, 2
  Arthur Calbraith
DORRANCE, 2
  George Morris
DORRANCE, Gordon 3
DORRANCE, 1
  John Thompson
DORRANCE, Sturges
  Dick 5
DORRELL, William H
D'ORSAY, Lawrance 1
DORSCH, Eduard H
DORSET, Marion 1
DORSETT, P. H. 4
DORSETT, 1
  Walter Balckburn
DORSEY, 5
  Clarence Wilbur
DORSEY, 2
  Clayton Chauncey
DORSEY, Clement H
DORSEY, Ella Loraine 4
DORSEY, Francis Oswald 1
DORSEY, Frank J. G. 2
DORSEY, George Amos 1
DORSEY, Harry
  Woodward 5
DORSEY, Herbert Grove 5
DORSEY, Hugh Manson 2
DORSEY, James Emmet 3
DORSEY, James Owen 1
DORSEY, John Syng H
DORSEY, LeRoy Howard 3
DORSEY, Maxwell J. 4
DORSEY, H
  Sarah Ann Ellis
DORSEY, Stephen Palmer 4
DORSEY, Stephen W. 1
DORSEY, Susan M. 4
DORSEY, Thomas Francis 3
DORSEY, W. Roderick 4
DORSHEIMER, H
  William Edward
DORST, Joseph Haddox 1
DORT, J. Dallas 1
DORWARD, 4
  William Thompson
DOSDALL, 3
  Chester Arthur
DOSKER, Henry E. 1
DOS PASSOS, 5
  John (Roderigo)
DOS PASSOS, 1
  John Randolph
DOSS, Clay 3
DOSS, Roscoe James 2
DOSTER, Frank 4
DOSTER, James Jarvis 2
DOSTERT, Leon Emile 5
DOTEN, Carroll Warren 2
DOTEN, Samuel Bradford 3
DOTSON, Floyd D. 5
DOTTERWEICH, 5
  June (Mrs. Frank Henry
  Dotterweich)
DOTY, Alvah Hunt 4

DOTY, 1
  Douglas Zabriskie
DOTY, Elihu H
DOTY, James Duane H
DOTY, Paul 1
DOTY, William Furman 5
DOUBLEDAY, Abner H
DOUBLEDAY, 1
  Frank Nelson
DOUBLEDAY, George 3
DOUBLEDAY, Nelson 2
DOUBLEDAY, 1
  Netje De Graff
DOUBLEDAY, Russell 2
DOUBLEDAY, H
  Ulysses Freeman
DOUDNA, Edgar George 4
DOUGAL, William H. H
DOUGHERTY, 4
  Blanford Barnard
DOUGHERTY, Curtis 1
DOUGHERTY, Denis J. 3
DOUGHERTY, 5
  Edward Archer
DOUGHERTY, Edward E. 2
DOUGHERTY, George A. 4
DOUGHERTY, George S. 1
DOUGHERTY, Hugh 1
DOUGHERTY, J.
  Hampden 1
DOUGHERTY, John 1
DOUGHERTY, 5
  Joseph P(atrick)
DOUGHERTY, Paul 2
DOUGHERTY, 5
  Proctor Lambert;
DOUGHERTY, 1
  Raymond Philip
DOUGHERTY, 4
  Richard Erwin
DOUGHERTY, 2
  William Edgeworth
DOUGHTON, Robert L. 3
DOUGHTY, Howard
  Waters 2
DOUGHTY, Mrs. Alla 1
DOUGHTY, Thomas H
DOUGHTY, 1
  Walter Francis
DOUGHTY, 5
  William Ellison
DOUGHTY, William
  Henry 1
DOUGHTY, 1
  William Henry Jr.
DOUGLAS, Albert 4
DOUGLAS, Alexander 4
DOUGLAS, Alice May 2
DOUGLAS, Amanda
  Minnie 1
DOUGLAS, Archibald 2
DOUGLAS, Arthur F. 3
DOUGLAS, Benjamin H
DOUGLAS, 2
  Beverly Browne
DOUGLAS, 5
  Bruce Hutchinson
DOUGLAS, Charles A. 1
DOUGLAS, Charles
  Henry 3
DOUGLAS, 2
  Charles Winfred
DOUGLAS, 5
  Clarence Brown
DOUGLAS, David Dwight 3
DOUGLAS, 1
  Davison McDowell
DOUGLAS, Ernest 1
DOUGLAS, Fred James 2
DOUGLAS, 3
  Frederic Huntington
DOUGLAS, Frederick A. 4
DOUGLAS, George Bruce 1
DOUGLAS, 1
  George William
DOUGLAS, 2
  George William
DOUGLAS, Hamilton 3
DOUGLAS, Henry Kyd 1
DOUGLAS, 4
  Henry Trovert Jr.
DOUGLAS, James 1
DOUGLAS, James H. 4
DOUGLAS, James Stuart 2
DOUGLAS, John 1
DOUGLAS, John Francis 1
DOUGLAS, 4
  John Frederick Howard
DOUGLAS, Julia S. 1
DOUGLAS, Lee 3
DOUGLAS, Lloyd C. 4
DOUGLAS, 5
  of Kirtleside, Lord
  (William Sholto Douglas)
DOUGLAS, 1
  Orlando Benajah
DOUGLAS, Oscar Berry 4

DOUGLAS, 4
  Percy Liningston
DOUGLAS, Richard 4
DOUGLAS, Robert Martin 1
DOUGLAS, H
  Silas Hamilton
DOUGLAS, H
  Stephen Arnold
DOUGLAS, 1
  Stephen Arnold
DOUGLAS, Thaddeus 2
DOUGLAS, 4
  Theodore Wayland
DOUGLAS, 4
  Wallace Barton
DOUGLAS, Walter 2
DOUGLAS, Walter G. 5
DOUGLAS, William H
DOUGLAS, 3
  William Archer Sholte
DOUGLAS, 2
  William Harris
DOUGLAS, William Lewis 1
DOUGLAS, 1
  William Wilberforce
DOUGLASS, 1
  Andrew Ellicott
DOUGLASS, 4
  Andrew Ellicott
DOUGLASS, 3
  Aubrey Augustus
DOUGLASS, 1
  Benjamin Wallace
DOUGLASS, Dana Carroll 5
DOUGLASS, David Bates H
DOUGLASS, Earl 1
DOUGLASS, Earl Leroy 5
DOUGLASS, 1
  Edwin Herbert
DOUGLASS, Frank 1
DOUGLASS, 4
  Harvey
DOUGLASS, Frederick H
DOUGLASS, 3
  Frederick Melvin
DOUGLASS, 5
  Gaylord William
DOUGLASS, George C. 1
DOUGLASS, 3
  George Shearer
DOUGLASS, H. Paul 3
DOUGLASS, 5
  H(erbert) Ellwood
DOUGLASS, John Joseph 5
DOUGLASS, 1
  John Watkinson
DOUGLASS, 4
  Lucille Sinclair
DOUGLASS, Mabel Smith 5
DOUGLASS, Matthew
  Hale 2
DOUGLASS, Robert M. J. H
DOUGLASS, 4
  Rufus Collins
DOUGLASS, 4
  Thomas VanKirk
DOUGLASS, 5
  Truman Bartlett
DOUGLASS, 1
  Truman Orville
DOUGLASS, William H
DOULL, James Angus 4
DOUNCE, Harry Esty 3
DOUTHIRT, Walstein F. 5
DOUTHIT, Claude 3
DOUTHIT, Harold 4
DOUTHIT, Jasper L. 4
DOUTRICH, Isaac H. 1
DOUTY, Nicholas 5
DOVE, David James H
DOVE, 5
  W(illiam) Franklin
DOVELL, Ray C. 5
DOVENER, 4
  Blackburn Barrett
DOVER, Elmer 1
DOW, Alex 2
DOW, Allan Wade 3
DOW, Arthur Wesley 1
DOW, Caroline Bell 1
DOW, Charles Mason 2
DOW, Earle Wilbur 4
DOW, Edward Albert 2
DOW, Fayette Brown 4
DOW, Frederick Neal 4
DOW, George Francis 1
DOW, Henry H
DOW, Herbert Henry 4
DOW, Howard Malcolm 1
DOW, Lorenzo 5
DOW, Neal H
DOW, Roger 4
DOW, Willard Henry 2
DOWD, 1
  Charles Ferdinand
DOWD, Charles North 1
DOWD, David L(loyd) 5
DOWD, James Edward 4

DOWD, Jerome 4
DOWD, John Worthington 1
DOWD, W. Carey Jr. 4
DOWD, 4
  Wallace Rutherford
DOWD, William 1
DOWDALL, Edward 4
DOWDALL, Guy Grigsby 5
DOWDELL, H
  James Ferguson
DOWDELL, James
  Render 3
DOWDNEY, Abraham H
DOWE, 1
  Jennie Elizabeth Tupper
DOWELL, Alvis Yates 5
DOWELL, Benjamin B. 4
DOWELL, Cassius C. 1
DOWELL, Floyd Dee 4
DOWELL, Greensville H
DOWELL, Spright 4
DOWER, Walter H. 1
DOWLING, Alexander 1
DOWLING, Austin 1
DOWLING, 4
  Emmett Patrick
DOWLING, George
  Thomas 4
DOWLING, John Joseph 2
DOWLING, John William 1
DOWLING, Michael John 1
DOWLING, Noel Thomas 5
DOWLING, Oscar 1
DOWLING, Victor James 1
DOWLING, William E. 1
DOWMAN, Charles
  Edward 4
DOWNER, Alan Seymour 5
DOWNER, Charles Alfred 1
DOWNER, Eliphalet H
DOWNER, James Walker 1
DOWNER, Samuel 4
DOWNES, Anne Miller 4
DOWNES, Bruce 2
DOWNES, James R. 3
DOWNES, John H
DOWNES, John 3
DOWNES, Olin 3
DOWNES, 2
  William Augustus
DOWNES, William Howe 1
DOWNEY, David George 1
DOWNEY, Francis X. 4
DOWNEY, Francis Xavier 2
DOWNEY, George Eddy 1
DOWNEY, George Faber 1
DOWNEY, Hal 3
DOWNEY, Hermon
  Horatio 5
DOWNEY, John H
DOWNEY, John Florin 1
DOWNEY, June E. 1
DOWNEY, Mary
  Elizabeth 3
DOWNEY, Sheridan 4
DOWNEY, 1
  Stanley Wilson Crowell
DOWNEY, Walter Francis 4
DOWNEY, William H. 3
DOWNIE, Robert C. 4
DOWNING, H
  Andrew Jackson
DOWNING, Augustus 1
DOWNING, Charles * H
DOWNING, 2
  Elliot Rowland
DOWNING, H
  Frances Murdaugh
DOWNING, George 1
DOWNING, Harold Kemp 2
DOWNING, John
  Franklin 1
DOWNING, John Robert 1
DOWNING, Lewis King 5
DOWNING, Maj Jack 4
DOWNING, Paul M. 2
DOWNING, 3
  Robert Everard
DOWNING, Robert L. 2
DOWNING, 5
  Russell Vincent
DOWNING, 4
  Warwick Miller
DOWNS, Francis Shunk 4
DOWNS, 4
  George Sheldon Mrs.
DOWNS, John Ayman 4
DOWNS, 4
  John William Sr.
DOWNS, Joseph 3
DOWNS, 4
  Lawrence Aloysius
DOWNS, Le Roy
  Donnelly 5
DOWNS, 4
  Solomon Weathersbee
DOWNS, William Findlay 4

864

DOWNS, William Smith 3
DOWRIE, George William 4
DOWS, Sutherland 5
DOWSE, Edward H
DOWSE, Thomas H
DOWSE,
  William Bradford Homer 1
DOX, Charles E. 5
DOX, Peter Myndert H
DOXTATER, Lee Walter 1
DOYLE, 5
  Albert Pryor Edward
DOYLE, Alexander 1
DOYLE, Alexander P. 1
DOYLE, Bernard Wendell 3
DOYLE, C. W. 1
DOYLE, Clyde Gilman 4
DOYLE, Cornelius James 1
DOYLE, Edward H. 1
DOYLE, Edward John 4
DOYLE, Gregory 1
DOYLE, Henry Grattan 4
DOYLE, Howard L. 3
DOYLE, James Harold 5
DOYLE, John Hardy 1
DOYLE, John T. 1
DOYLE, 5
  Martha Claire MacGowan
  ("Martha James,")
DOYLE, 5
  Sister Mary Peter
DOYLE, Michael Francis 3
DOYLE, Price 5
DOYLE, 5
  Rhederick Elwood, Jr.
DOYLE, Richard Smith 5
DOYLE, Robert Morris 1
DOYLE, Sarah Elizabeth 1
DOYLE, Sherman Hoadley 5
DOYLE, Thomas Aloysius 1
DOYLE, Thomas
  Henchin 5
DOYNE, John James 3
DOZER, 4
  Russell Shinnick
DOZIER, Curtis Merry 4
DOZIER, Elizabeth Gist 4
DOZIER, Melville 4
DOZIER, Orion T. 4
DRABKIN, Israel Edward 4
DRACH, Edmund L. 5
DRACHMAN, Bernard 2
DRACHSLER, Julius 1
DRAEMEL, 5
  Milo Frederick
DRAFFAN, 4
  George Livingston
DRAGER, Walter Louis 3
DRAHMS, August 4
DRAIN, James Andrew 2
DRAKE, 1
  Alexander Wilson
DRAKE,
  Archie Augustus Jr.
DRAKE, Benjamin H
DRAKE, C. St Clair H
DRAKE, Charles Daniel H
DRAKE, Daniel 1
DRAKE, Durant 1
DRAKE,
  Edwin Laurentine
DRAKE, 4
  Emma Frances Angell
DRAKE, Emmet Addis 4
DRAKE, H
  Frances Ann Denny
DRAKE, Francis Marion 1
DRAKE, Francis Samuel H
DRAKE, 1
  Franklin Jeremiah
DRAKE, Fred Raymond 1
DRAKE, Frederic Nelson 4
DRAKE, Harry Trevor 4
DRAKE, James Calhoun 1
DRAKE, James Madison 1
DRAKE, Jeannette May 3
DRAKE, John Burroughs H
DRAKE, John Poad H
DRAKE, John Reuben H
DRAKE, John Walter 2
DRAKE, 2
  Joseph Horace Sr.
DRAKE, Joseph Rodman H
DRAKE, Lauren J. 3
DRAKE, Milton Jay 4
DRAKE, Nathan Lincoln 4
DRAKE, Noah Fields 2
DRAKE, Russell Payson 5
DRAKE, Samuel H
DRAKE, Samuel Adams H
DRAKE, Samuel Gardner H
DRAKE, Sir Francis H
DRAKE, Tracy Corey 1
DRAKE, William A. 4
DRAKE, William Henry 1
DRANE, Herbert Jackson 2
DRANSFIELD, Jane 1

DRANT, Patricia 3
DRAPER, Alfred Pearman 3
DRAPER, Andrew Sloan 1
DRAPER, 2
  Benjamin Helm Bristow
DRAPER, Daniel 1
DRAPER, 5
  Dorothy (Tuckerman)
DRAPER, Eben Sumner 1
DRAPER, Edward Bailey 1
DRAPER, 3
  Ernest Gallaudet
DRAPER, Frank Winthrop 1
DRAPER, George Otis 1
DRAPER, Henry H
DRAPER, Ira H
DRAPER, John H
DRAPER, John William H
DRAPER, Joseph H
DRAPER, Lyman
  Copeland 1
DRAPER, Margaret Green H
DRAPER, Norman 4
DRAPER, Richard H
DRAPER, Ruth 3
DRAPER, Warren Fales 5
DRAPER, 1
  William Franklin
DRAPER, William H. 1
DRAPER, William Henry 1
DRAPER, 1
  William Kinnicutt
DRAUGHON, Ralph
  Brown 5
DRAYTON, Charles O. 1
DRAYTON, Grace Gebbie 1
DRAYTON, Henry
  Shipman 1
DRAYTON, John H
DRAYTON, Percival H
DRAYTON, Samuel 2
DRAYTON, H
  Thomas Fenwick
DRAYTON, William * H
DRAYTON, William
  Henry H
DREES, Charles William 1
DREFS, Arthur George 3
DREHER, Julius Daniel 1
DREHER, LeRoy Herbert 4
DREHER, 5
  Monroe Franklin
DREHER, William Counts 1
DREIER, Mary Elisabeth 4
DREIKURS, Rudolph 5
DREISER, Theodore 2
DRELLER, Louis 5
DRENNAN, Michael C. 1
DRESBACH, Glenn Ward 5
DRESBACH, Melvin 3
DRESCHER,
  Theodore Bausch
DRESDEN, Arnold 3
DRESEL, Ellis Loring 1
DRESEL, Otto H
DRESEN, Oswald Mathew 4
DRESLER, Earl Louis 5
DRESSEL, Edwin Henry 4
DRESSEN,
  Charles Walter
DRESSER, Daniel Le Roy 1
DRESSER, 3
  Horatio Willis
DRESSER, Louise 1
DRESSER, Paul H
DRESSER, Paul 4
DRESSER, Raymond H. 1
DRESSER,
  Solomon Robert
DRESSLAR, 1
  Fletcher Bascom
DRESSLAR, Frank A, Sr. 1
DRESSLER,
  Louis Raphael
DRESSLER, Marie 1
DREVER, Thomas 4
DREVES, Walter Julius 5
DREW, 5
  Alfred Stanislaus
DREW, Charles Richard 3
DREW, Daniel 1
DREW, Frank Gifford 1
DREW, Franklin Mellen 1
DREW, George Alexander 5
DREW, Gerald Augustin 5
DREW, Gilman Arthur 4
DREW, Ira Walton 5
DREW, Irving Webster 5
DREW, James Byron 5
DREW, John H
DREW, John 4
DREW, John Graham 4
DREW, Louisa Lane 1
DREWES, 5
  Alfred H(erman)
DREWES, Alfred H. 4
DREWRY, Patrick Henry 2

DREWRY, 1
  William Francis
DREXEL, Anthony Joseph H
DREXEL, H
  Francis Anthony
DREXEL, Francis Martin H
DREXEL, 2
  George W. Childs
DREXEL, Joseph William H
DREYER, George Peter 1
DREYER, 2
  Jorgan Christian
DREYER, Leslie Hayes 4
DREYER, Walter 3
DREYFUS, 3
  Camille Edouard
DREYFUS, Carl 3
DREYFUSS, Henry 5
DREYFUSS, Leonard 5
DREYSPRING, Adolphe 1
DREYSTADT, Nicholas 5
DRIEMEYER, Henry 4
DRIGGS, Edmund Hope 2
DRIGGS, Frank Howard 5
DRIGGS, Frank Milton 5
DRIGGS, Howard Roscoe 5
DRIGGS, John Fletcher H
DRIGGS, 2
  Laurence La Tourette
DRILL, Lewis L. 5
DRINKER, Cecil Kent 1
DRINKER, Henry Sturgis 1
DRINKER, Philip 5
DRIPPS, Isaac L. H
DRIPPS, 4
  Joseph Frederick
DRISCOLL, 4
  Arthur Francis
DRISCOLL, 3
  Charles Benedict
DRISCOLL, Clara 2
DRISCOLL, 5
  Daniel Angelus
DRISCOLL, Denis J. 3
DRISCOLL, Frederick 4
DRISCOLL, 4
  George Walter
DRISCOLL, Joseph 3
DRISCOLL, Louise 5
DRISCOLL, 1
  Michael Edward
DRISCOLL, William H. 3
DRISLER, Henry H
DRIVER, James 1
DRIVER, John Merritte 1
DRIVER, 1
  Leeotis Lincoln
DRIVER, Samuel Marion 3
DRIVER, William J. 5
DRIVER, 4
  William Raymond
DROEGE, John Albert 5
DROKE, George Wesley 3
DROKE, Maxwell 5
DROMGOOLE, George
  Coke H
DROMGOOLE, Will
  Allen 1
DRONE, Eaton Sylvester 1
DROPPERS, Garrett 1
DROSSAERTS, Arthur 1
DROUET, Robert 1
DROUGHT, 5
  Arthur Bernard
DROUGHT, Henry
  Patrick 3
DROUIN, Mark Robert 4
DROWN, Edward Staples 1
DROWN, 1
  Thomas Messinger
DROZNIAK, Edward 4
DRUCKENMILLER, 4
  Barton W.
DRUCKER, Arthur Ellert 2
DRUECK, Charles 1
DRUFFEL, John Henry 4
DRUILLETTES, Gabriel 1
DRUKKER, Dow Henry 5
DRUKKER, Dow Henry 5
DRUKKER, Richard 5
DRUM, A. L. 1
DRUM, Augustus 1
DRUM, Hugh Aloysius 3
DRUM, John Sylvester 5
DRUM, Richard Coulter 1
DRUM, Walter 1
DRUMGOOLE, H
  John Christopher
DRUMHELLER, Joseph 5
DRUMHELLER, 2
  Roscoe Maxson
DRUMM, Thomas W. 1
DRUMMOND, Alexander
  M. 3
DRUMMOND, 5
  Harrison Irwin

DRUMMOND, 3
  Huntly Redpath
DRUMMOND, I. Wyman 1
DRUMMOND, 3
  James Herbert
DRUMMOND, 1
  Josiah Hayden
DRUMMOND, 5
  Sara King Wiley
DRUMMOND, 5
  Thomas Russell
DRUMMOND, 5
  Wilbert Ivanhoe
DRURY, Alexander Greer 1
DRURY, Augustus Waldo 3
DRURY, 3
  Francis Keese Wynkoop
DRURY, John 5
DRURY, John Benjamin 1
DRURY, Lacy H
DRURY, 1
  Marion Richardson
DRURY, Samuel Smith 1
DRURY, Victor Montague 4
DRURY, Walter Maynard 2
DRURY, Wells 1
DRUSHEL, J. Andrew 1
DRYDEN, 1
  Forrest Fairchild
DRYDEN, George
  Bascomb 3
DRYDEN, Hugh Latimer 4
DRYDEN, James 1
DRYDEN, John Fairfield 1
DRYDEN, John Lester 3
DRYDEN, John N. 3
DRYER, Charles Redway 1
DRYER, George William 3
DRYFOOS, Orvil Eugene 4
DRYSDALE, Matthew
  Watt 1
DRYSDALE, Robert A. 4
DRYSDALE, 1
  Thomas Murray
DRYSDALE, William 1
DUANE, Alexander 1
DUANE, James H
DUANE, James Chatham H
DUANE, James May H
DUANE, Russell 1
DUANE, William 1
DUANE, William J. 2
DUANE, William John H
DU BARRY, Beekman 1
DUBARRY, William H. 3
DUBBINK, 1
  Gerrit Hendrik
DUBBS, Henry A. 1
DUBBS, Joseph Henry 1
DUBILIER, William 5
DUBLE, Lu 4
DUBOC, Frank Windsor 5
DU BOIS, Augustus Jay 1
DUBOIS, 1
  Charles Gilbert
'DU BOIS, Coert 4
DU BOIS, Durwood Carl 5
DU BOIS, Edward Church 1
DUBOIS, Eugene Floyd 3
DUBOIS, Fred Thomas 1
DUBOIS, 3
  Gaston Frederic
'DUBOIS, Guy Pene 3
DU BOIS, James T. 1
DUBOIS, Jean Joseph 1
DUBOIS, John H
DU BOIS, John Ezekiel 1
DUBOIS, Jules 5
DU BOIS, Julian Arthur 3
DU BOIS, 3
  Mary Constance
DU BOIS, Patterson 1
DUBOIS, Samuel F. H
DU BOIS, 4
  William Edward Burghardt
DU BOIS, William Ewing H
DUBORD, Richard Joseph 5
DU BOSE, 4
  Catherine Anne
DU BOSE, Dudley McIver H
DUBOSE, 5
  Francis Goodwin
DU BOSE, Henry Wade 3
DU BOSE,
  Horace Mellard
DU BOSE, Joel Campbell 4
DU BOSE,
  John Witherspoon
DU BOSE,
  William Haskell
DU BOSE,
  William Porcher
DU BOSE, 4
  William Richards

DU BOSQUE, 1
  Francis LeBrun
DU BOURG, H
  Louis Guillaume Valentin
DUBOURJAL, H
  Savinien Edme
DUBRAY, Charles Albert 5
DUBUIS, Claude Mary H
DUBUQUE, Julien H
DUCASSE, Curt John 5
DUCE, Hugh Marlo 4
DUCE, James Terry 4
DUCEY, Thomas James 1
DU CHAILLU, 1
  Paul Belloni
DUCHE, Jacob H
DUCHESNE, H
  Rose Philippine
DUCKER, 2
  Edward Augustus
DUCKWORTH, 5
  George Eckel
DUCKWORTH,
  William Henry
DUCOMMUN,
  Edmond Frederick
DUCOMMUN,
  Jesse Clarence
DU COUDRAY,
  Philippe Charles Jean
  Tronson
DUCRUE, Francis Bennon H
DUDDY, Edward
  Augustin
DUDGEON, Matthew S. 3
DUDLEY, A. Dean 5
DUDLEY, Albert Henry 3
DUDLEY, Albertus True 3
DUDLEY, 1
  Augustus Palmer
DUDLEY, H
  Benjamin Winslow
DUDLEY, Bide 2
DUDLEY, Charles
  Ashman 4
DUDLEY, 1
  Charles Benjamin
DUDLEY, Charles Edward. H
DUDLEY, 1
  Charles Rowland
DUDLEY, 1
  Edgar Swartwout
DUDLEY,
  Edgar Swartwout
DUDLEY, Edward Bishop 4
DUDLEY, Emelius Clark 1
DUDLEY, Frank Alonzo 2
DUDLEY, Frank Virgil 3
DUDLEY, 4
  Frederick Merritt
DUDLEY, 4
  Guilford Swathel
DUDLEY, Helena Stuart 3
DUDLEY, Henry C. H
DUDLEY, Irving Bedell 1
DUDLEY, James Benson 1
DUDLEY, James G. 4
DUDLEY, John Benton 4
DUDLEY, John Gant 4
DUDLEY, Joseph H
DUDLEY, Joseph Grassie 5
DUDLEY, Lucy Bronson 1
DUDLEY, Mrs. Guilford 3
DUDLEY,
  Nathan Augustus Monroe
DUDLEY, Paul H
DUDLEY, Pemberton 1
DUDLEY, Pendleton 5
DUDLEY, Plimmon Henry 1
DUDLEY, Samuel
  Madison 2
DUDLEY, Samuel William 4
DUDLEY, Thomas H
DUDLEY, 1
  Thomas Underwood
DUDLEY, Wesley
  Coleman 4
DUDLEY,
  William Lofland
DUDLEY, William Russel 1
DUDLEY, William Wade 1
DUDLEY, Winfield Ware 1
DUDYCHA, George
  J(ohn) 5
DUEL, Arthur Baldwin 1
DUELL, 5
  Charles Halliwell
DUELL, Charles Holland 1
DUELL, Prentice 4
DUELL, Robert Holland 1
DUEMLING, Hermann 4
DUER, Caroline King 3
DUER, Edward Louis 4
DUER, John H
DUER, William * H
DUER, H
  William Alexander

DUERR, Alvan Emile 2
DUFF, Alexander Wilmer 3
DUFF, Edward Aloysius 1
DUFF, G. Lyman 3
DUFF, James H. 5
DUFF, Mary Ann Dyke H
DUFF, Philip Grandy 4
DUFF, Philip Sheridan 4
DUFF, Sir Lyman Poore 3
DUFF, William McGill 3
DUFFEE, 5
  Warren S(adler)
DUFFEY, Warren Joseph 1
DUFFIELD, 1
  Edward Dickinson
DUFFIELD, George * H
DUFFIELD, Henry 1
  Martyn
DUFFIELD, Howard 1
DUFFIELD, John Thomas 1
DUFFIELD, 5
  Marcus McCampbell
DUFFIELD, Pitts 2
DUFFIELD, 1
  Samuel Augustus Willoughby
DUFFIELD, 4
  Samuel Pearce
DUFFIELD, William Ward 1
DUFFUS, Robert Luther 5
DUFFY, 5
  Bernard Cornelius
DUFFY, Charles 5
DUFFY, Edmund 4
DUFFY, Francis Patrick 3
DUFFY, Francis Patrick 4
DUFFY, Frank H. 5
DUFFY, Herbert Smith 4
DUFFY, James Albert 5
DUFFY, James Albert 4
DUFFY, James O. G. 1
DUFFY, John A. 4
DUFFY, 5
  Joseph Alexander
DUFFY, Richard 2
DUFFY, Ward Everett 4
DUFNER, Edward 3
DUFOUR, Frank Oliver 5
DUFOUR, John James H
DUFOUR, 5
  William Cyprien
DUFOURCQ, 1
  Edward Leonce
DUFY, Raoul 3
DUGAN, Caro Atherton 5
DUGAN, Howard Francis 4
DUGAN, James 4
DUGAN, Larry Hull 5
DUGAN, Raymond Smith 1
DUGAN, Thomas
  Buchanan 1
DUGANNE, H
  Augustine Joseph Hickey
DUGARDIN, Herve 5
DUGDALE, Ralph E. 4
DUGDALE, Richard
  Louis H
DUGGAN, B. O. 3
DUGGAN, Charles F. 4
DUGGAN, John J. 3
DUGGAN, Laurence 2
DUGGAN, Mell L. 5
DUGGAN, Stephen 3
DUGGAN, Walter Teeling 1
DUGGAN, William H. 4
DUGGAR, Benjamin
  Minge 3
DUGGAR, John Frederick 2
DUGGAR, Reuben Henry 5
DUGMORE, 5
  Arthur Radclyffe
DUGRO, P. Henry 1
DUGUE, Charles Oscar 5
DU HAMEL, William 5
DUHRING, 1
  Louis Adolphus
DUJARDIN, 4
  Rosamond Neal
DUKE, Basil Wilson 1
DUKE, Benjamin Newton 1
DUKE, Charles Wesley 3
DUKE, Claude Walter 4
DUKE, James Buchanan 1
DUKE, James Thomas 5
DUKE, Nathaniel 1
DUKE, 1
  Richard Thomas Walker Jr.
DUKE, Samuel Page 3
DUKE, T. Seddon 4
DUKE, Vernon 5
DUKE, Victor LeRoy 1
DUKE, William Richard 4
DUKE, William Waddell 2
DUKELOW, 1
  Charles Thomas
DUKES, Charles Alfred 2
DUKES, 3
  Richard Gustavus

DULANEY, 1
  Benjamin Lewis
DULANEY, Henry Stier 1
DULANEY, William
  Leroy 4
DULANY, Daniel * H
DULANY, 3
  George William Jr.
DULANY, 2
  Henry Rozier Jr.
DULANY, William Henry 2
DULCAN, Charles B. 5
DULING, G. Harold 4
DULLES, Allen Macy 4
DULLES, Allen Welsh 5
DULLES, 1
  Charles Winslow
DULLES, John Foster 3
DULLES, Joseph Heatly 2
DULUTH, H
  Daniel Greysolon
DULZELL, Paul 4
DUMAINE, 3
  Frederic Christopher
DUMAS, Gustave 3
DUMAS, Walter A. 3
DUMAS, William Thomas 4
DUMBA, 1
  Constantin Theodor
DUMBAULD, 3
  Horatio Snyder
DUMBLE, Edwin
  Theodore 1
DUMETZ, Francisco H
DU MEZ, Andrew Grover 2
DUMLER, Martin George 1
DUMM, Benjamin Alfred 5
DUMMEIER, Edwin F. 2
DUMMER, Edwin Heyse 4
DUMMER, Jeremiah * 1
DUMOND, Frank Vincent 3
DU MONT, Allen Balcom 4
DUMONT, Ebenezer H
DUMONT, 1
  Frederick Theodore
  Frelinghuysen
DUMONT, Wayne 5
DU MOUCHEL, 5
  Leandre Arthur
DU MOULIN, Frank 2
DUN, Angus 5
DUN, Edwin 1
DUN, James 1
DUN, Robert Graham 1
DUNAWAY, John Allder 5
DUNAWAY, Thomas F. 4
DUNBAR, Arthur White 5
DUNBAR, 4
  Charles Edward Jr.
DUNBAR, 1
  Charles Franklin
DUNBAR, 5
  Duke Wellington
DUNBAR, Erroll 1
DUNBAR, Flanders 3
DUNBAR, James Robert 1
DUNBAR, James Whitson 2
DUNBAR, John H. 5
DUNBAR, Moses H
DUNBAR, Newell 1
DUNBAR, Paul Laurence 1
DUNBAR, Ralph O. 1
DUNBAR, Robert H
DUNBAR, 1
  Ulric Stonewall Jackson
DUNBAR, William * H
DUNBAR,
  William Harrison
DUNBAUGH, Harry Joy 5
DUNCA, Frederick S. 3
DUNCALF, Frederic 4
DUNCAN, Albert Greene 1
DUNCAN, Alexander 5
DUNCAN,
  Alexander Edward
DUNCAN, Carson Samuel 3
DUNCAN, Charles 1
DUNCAN, Charles Miguel 4
DUNCAN, Daniel H
DUNCAN, David Shaw 1
DUNCAN, Edward
  Carlton 1
DUNCAN, 5
  Frances (Mrs. John L. Manning)
DUNCAN, Garnett H
DUNCAN, George Brand 2
DUNCAN, George Martin 1
DUNCAN, Gerald 5
DUNCAN, Glenn A. 3
DUNCAN, Greer
  Assheton 4
DUNCAN, Herschel Mills H
DUNCAN, Isadora 1
DUNCAN, Isadora H
DUNCAN, James H
DUNCAN, James 1

DUNCAN, James
  Cameron 1
DUNCAN, James Floyd 5
DUNCAN, James Henry H
DUNCAN, James R. 4
DUNCAN, John Harris 1
DUNCAN, Joseph H
DUNCAN, Joseph Wilson 1
DUNCAN, Lewis
  Johnston 5
DUNCAN, Louis 1
DUNCAN, Luther Noble 2
DUNCAN, Norman 1
DUNCAN, Oscar Dibble 2
DUNCAN, Robert
  Kennedy 1
DUNCAN, 5
  Ruth Henley (Mrs. Isaac Greenwood Duncan)
DUNCAN, Samuel
  Edward 5
DUNCAN, Stuart 3
DUNCAN, Thomas
  Shearer 4
DUNCAN, W. Butler 1
DUNCAN, Walter Jack 5
DUNCAN, 2
  Walter Wofford Tucker
DUNCAN, Warren W. 1
DUNCAN, Watson Boone 1
DUNCAN, H
  William Addison
DUNCAN, William Cary 1
DUNCAN, 2
  William McKinley
DUNCAN, 1
  William Wallace
DUNCAN-CLARK, 1
  Samuel John
DUNCANSON, Robert S. H
DUNCANSON, 5
  Thomas Sherriff
DUNCKLEE, John Butler 1
DUNDEY, Charles L. 5
DUNFORD, 4
  Edward Bradstreet
DUNFORD, Ralph
  Emerson 5
DUNGAN, Albert Wallace 4
DUNGAN, David Roberts 4
DUNGAN, Paul Baxter 2
DUNGAY, Neil Stanley 3
DUNGLISON, 1
  Richard James
DUNGLISON, Robley H
DUNHAM, Arthur 1
DUNHAM, H
  Cyrus Livingston
DUNHAM, Daniel H. 1
DUNHAM, Edward
  Kellogg 1
DUNHAM, Franklin 4
DUNHAM, 1
  Frederic Gibbons
DUNHAM, George Earl 1
DUNHAM, Henry
  Goodrich 4
DUNHAM, Henry Kennon 1
DUNHAM, Henry Morton 1
DUNHAM, James Henry 3
DUNHAM, James Webb 4
DUNHAM, John Dudley 1
DUNHAM, 1
  Ransom Williams
DUNHAM, Robert James 3
DUNHAM, Russell H. 3
DUNHAM, Samuel Clarke 4
DUNHAM, Sturges Sigler 2
DUNHAM, 1
  Sylvester Clark
DUNHAM, 4
  William Russell
DUNIWAY, Abigail Scott 4
DUNIWAY, 5
  Clyde Augustus
DUNKEL, Joel Ambrose 5
DUNKIN, Damon
  Duffield 1
DUNKLEY, 3
  Ferdinand Luis
DUNLAP, Andrew 1
DUNLAP, Boutwell 1
DUNLAP, Charles Bates 1
DUNLAP, Charles Edward 4
DUNLAP, Charles
  Graham 1
DUNLAP, 2
  Charles Kephart
DUNLAP, 5
  David Richardson
DUNLAP, Elbert 5
DUNLAP, Frederick Levy 5
DUNLAP, 1
  George Washington
DUNLAP, Harry 4
DUNLAP, Hiram J. 1
DUNLAP, James Boliver H

DUNLAP, John H
DUNLAP, John Bettes 4
DUNLAP, John Robertson ·1
DUNLAP, Knight 2
DUNLAP, 4
  Millard Fillmore
DUNLAP, 5
  Orrin Elmer, Jr.
DUNLAP, Renick William 4
DUNLAP, Robert 1
DUNLAP, Robert Finley 1
DUNLAP, Robert Henry 5
DUNLAP,
  Robert Pinckney 1
DUNLAP, Roy J. 1
DUNLAP, Roy John, Jr. 1
DUNLAP, William H
DUNLAP,
  William Claiborne 1
DUNLAVY, Edwin
  Wesley 5
DUNLEVY, 3
  Robert Baldwin
DUNLOP, James H
DUNMORE, 4'th 'earl 1
DUNMORE, Walter
  Thomas 2
DUNN, Alexander Gordon H
DUNN, Arthur David 1
DUNN, Arthur Wallace 1
DUNN, Arthur William 1
DUNN, Ballard 5
DUNN, Beverly Charles 5
DUNN, Byron Archibald 4
DUNN, Charles H
DUNN, Charles Gwyllym 1
DUNN, Charles John 1
DUNN, Charles Putnam 1
DUNN, Charles Wesley 3
DUNN, Edward Gregory 2
DUNN, Elias Bound 1
DUNN, Emmett Reid 3
DUNN, Fannie Wyche 1
DUNN, Frank Harold 4
DUNN, Frank Kershner 4
DUNN, Frederick Julian 4
DUNN, 4
  Frederick Sherwood
DUNN, Gano 3
DUNN, George Grundy 1
DUNN, George Hedford H
DUNN, George M. 4
DUNN, Harris Ashton 1
DUNN, Harry Thatcher 5
DUNN, Harvey 3
DUNN, Henry Wesley 5
DUNN, Herbert Omar 1
DUNN, Ignatius J. 3
DUNN, Jacob Piatt 1
DUNN, James Phillip 1
DUNN, Jesse James 1
DUNN, John Joseph 2
DUNN, John Randall 1
DUNN, Joseph 1
DUNN, Joseph Allan 1
DUNN, Martha Baker 4
DUNN, Matthew A. 1
DUNN, Richard J. 2
DUNN, Robert 1
DUNN, Robert A. 2
DUNN, Samuel O. 1
DUNN, Sir James Hamet 5
DUNN, Thomas B. 1
DUNN, Waldo Hilary 1
DUNN, William Edward 4
DUNN, William Frank 1
DUNN, William Le Roy 1
DUNN, William McKee H
DUNN, William Warren 4
DUNN, Williamson 1
DUNNACK, Henry E. 1
DUNNE, Charles D. 4
DUNNE, Edmond M. 1
DUNNE, 1
  Edward Fitzsimons
DUNNE, Edward Joseph 1
DUNNE, Finley Peter 1
DUNNE, James Edward 2
DUNNE, 4
  James Edward Craven
DUNNE, Peter Francis 1
DUNNELL,
  Elbridge Gerry 1
DUNNELL, Mark
  Boothby 1
DUNNELL, Mark Hill 1
DUNNETT, Alexander 1
DUNNING, Albert Elijah 1
DUNNING, Alden W. 2
DUNNING, Charles A. 3
DUNNING, Edwin James 5
DUNNING, 1
  George Freeman
DUNNING, 5
  Harry Westbrook
DUNNING, 4
  Henry Armitt Brown

DUNNING, Henry Sage 3
DUNNING, James
  Edmund 5
DUNNING, James Edwin 3
DUNNING, John Sullivan 5
DUNNING, John Wirt 5
DUNNING, Lehman H. 1
DUNNING, Morton
  Dexter 5
DUNNING, N. Max 2
DUNNING, Philip 5
DUNNING, 5
  Robert M(ackenzie)
DUNNING, Stewart N. 3
DUNNING, 1
  William Archibald
DUNNINGTON, 4
  Francis Perry
DUNNINGTON, 5
  Walter Grey
DUNPHY, Charles 1
DUNPHY, William Henry 1
DUNSCOMB,
  Charles Ellsworth 1
DUNSCOMB, 1
  Samuel Whitney Jr.
DUNSHEE, Jay Dee 5
DUNSMORE, Andrew B. 1
DUNSMORE, John Ward 2
DUNSMORE, Philo
  Cordon 5
DUNSTAN,
  Arthur St. Charles 5
DUNSTAN, 5
  Edmund Fleetwood
DUNSTER, Henry H
DUNTLEY, John Wheeler 1
DUNTON, Edith Kellogg 3
DUNTON, Frank Holt 1
DUNTON, Larkin 1
DUNTON, Lewis Marion 1
DUNTON, 1
  William Herbert
DUNWELL, 1
  Charles Tappan
DUNWELL, James
  Winslow 1
DUNWODY, Thomas
  Edgar 4
DUNWODY, 3
  William Elliott
DUNWOODY, 3
  Henry Harrison Chase
DUNWOODY, William
  Hood 1
DUPALAIS, H
  Virginia Poullard
DUPEE, John 5
DUPLESSIS, Maurice L. 3
DUPONCEAU, H
  Pierre Etinne
DU PONT, A. Felix 5
DU PONT, Alfred I. 1
DU PONT, Alfred Rhett 5
DU PONT, 4
  Eleuthere Irenee
DUPONT, Francis V. 4
DU PONT, Henry H
DU PONT, 1
  Henry Algernon
DUPONT, Henry B. 5
DUPONT, Henry Francis 5
DUPONT, Irenee 4
DUPONT, Irenee 5
DUPONT, 1
  Jessie Ball (Mrs. Alfred Irenee Dupont)
DU PONT, Lammot 2
DU PONT, Pierre Samuel 3
DU PONT, H
  Samuel Francis
DU PONT, T. Coleman 1
DU PONT, Victor Marie 5
'DU PONT, William Jr. 4
DUPRATZ, H
  Antoine Simon Le Page
DU PRE, Arthur Mason 2
DU PRE, Daniel Allston 4
DUPRE, Henry Garland 1
DUPRE, Marcel 5
DUPUIS, Raymond 5
DUPUY, Eliza Ann H
DU PUY, Herbert 5
DUPUY, Pierre 5
DU PUY, Raymond 1
DU PUY, 1
  William Atherton
DUQUE, Henry
  O'Melveny 1
DUQUESNE DE
  MENNEVILLE, Marquis H
DURAN, F. Mutis 4
DURAN, Narcisco H
DURAND, Asher Brown H
DURAND, Cyrus H
DURAND, David 5

DURAND, E(dward)
  Dana 5
DURAND, Elias Judah 1
DURAND, Elle Magioire H
DURAND, 5
  G(eorge) Harrison
DURAND, Loyal, Jr. 5
DURAND, 2
  Sir Henry Mortimer
DURAND, 3
  William Frederick
DURANT, Charles Person H
DURANT, 4
  Frederick Clark Jr.
DURANT, Henry H
DURANT, Henry Fowle H
DURANT, Thomas Clark H
DURANT,
  Thomas Jefferson
DURANT, William Crapo H
DURANTE, Oscar 2
DURANTY, Walter 3
DURBIN, Elisha John H
DURBIN, John Price H
DURBIN, 1
  Winfield Taylor
DURELL, Daniel Meserve H
DURELL, Edward Henry H
DURELL, Edward Hovey 4
DURELL, George B. 4
DU RELLE, George 4
DURET, Miguel Lanz 3
DUREY, Cyrus 4
DUREY, John C. 5
DURFEE, Edgar Noble 3
DURFEE, 4
  Herbert Augustus
DURFEE, Job H
DURFEE, H
  Nathaniel Briggs
DURFEE, Thomas 1
DURFEE,
  William Franklin
DURFEE, William Pitt H
DURFEE, William Pitt 2
DURFEE, 1
  Winthrop Carver
DURFEE, Zoheth
  Sherman H
DURFREY, John Cooper 4
DURGIN,
  Calvin Thornton
DURGIN, Cyrus W. 4
DURGIN, George Francis 4
DURGIN, Samuel Holmes 4
DURHAM, Caleb Wheeler H
DURHAM, Calen Wheeler H
DURHAM, Charles Love 4
DURHAM, Donald B. 3
DURHAM, Edward 1
DURHAM, 3
  Edward Miall Jr.
DURHAM, Fred
  Stranahan 3
DURHAM, Henry Welles 5
DURHAM, Hobart Noble 5
DURHAM, Isreal W. 4
DURHAM, James Ware 5
DURHAM, John Stephens 1
DURHAM, Knowlton 4
DURHAM, Milton
  Jamison
DURHAM, Nelson Wayne 1
DURHAM, Plato Tracy 4
DURHAM, Robert Lee 2
DURIER, Antoine 1
DURIVAGE, H
  Francis Alexander
DURKEE, Charles
DURKEE, Frank Williams 1
DURKEE, 5
  J(ames) Stanley
DURKEE, John H
DURKIN, Martin 1
DURLAND, Kellogg 1
DURLING, Edgar Vincent 5
DURRELL, Joseph H. 4
DURRETT, Reuben
  Thomas 1
DURRIE, Daniel Steele H
DURRIE, George Henry H
DURST, William Arthur 1
DURSTINE, Roy Sarles 4
DURSTON, John Hurst 1
DURY, Charles 4
DURYEA, Charles Edgar H
DURYEA, Charles Edgar 4
DURYEA, 5
  Dan(iel) (Edwin)
DURYEA, Edwin 1
DURYEA, Hiram 1
DURYEA, Nina Larrey 3
DURYEA, Wright 4
DURYEE, Abram H
'DU SABLE,
  Jean Baptiste Point H

'DU SACRE 4
  COEUR, Mother Marie
DUSCHAK, Lionel
  Herman 2
DUSE, Eleonora H
DUSE, Eleonora H
DU SHANE, Donald 2
DUSHANE, Graham 4
DUSHMAN, Saul 3
DU SIMITIERE, H
  Pierre Eugene
DUSSER 'DE 1
  BARENNE, Joannes
  Gregorius
DUSTIN, Hannah H
DUTCHER, Charles
  Mason 1
DUTCHER,
  George Matthew
DUTCHER, Silas Belden 1
DUTCHER, William 1
DUTREMBLAY, 3
  Pamphile-Real
DUTTON, Benjamin F. 1
DUTTON, Charles Judson 1
DUTTON, 1
  Clarence Edward
DUTTON, Edward A. 3
DUTTON, Edward Payson 1
DUTTON, Emily Helen 2
DUTTON, George Burwell 1
DUTTON, George Elliott 3
DUTTON, Henry H
DUTTON, Joseph 1
DUTTON, Richard King 5
DUTTON, Samuel Train 1
DUTTON, Walter C. 4
DUTTON, William Jay 4
DUVAL, Charles Warren 4
DU VAL, Frederic Beale 4
DUVAL, H. Rieman 1
DUVAL, Isaac Harding 1
DUVAL, Laurel 3
DUVAL, William Pope 1
DUVALIER, Francois 5
DUVALL,
  Charles Raymond
DUVALL, 5
  Donald Chauncey
DUVALL, Gabriel H
DUVALL, James William 4
DUVALL,
  Trumbull Gillette
DUVALL, William Penn 1
DUVEL, 2
  Joseph William Tell
DUVENECK, Frank 1
DUVERNAY, Ludger 3
DUWE, George E. 5
DUXBURY, George H. 3
DUYCKINCK,
  Evert Augustus H
DUYCKINCK, George
  Long H
DUYCKINCK, Gerrit H
DVORAK, Antonin H
D'VYS, 1
  George Whitefield
DWAN, Ralph Hubert 4
DWENGER, Joseph H
DWIGGINS, Clare Victor 3
DWIGGINS,
  William Addison
DWIGHT, Arthur Smith 1
DWIGHT, H
  Benjamin Franklin
DWIGHT, H
  Benjamin Woodbridge
DWIGHT, Edmund H
DWIGHT, Edmund 1
DWIGHT, Edwin Welles 4
DWIGHT, Francis H
DWIGHT, 3
  Harrison Griswold
DWIGHT, Henry Otis 1
DWIGHT, Henry Williams 4
DWIGHT, H
  Jeremiah Wilbur
DWIGHT, John Sullivan H
DWIGHT, John Wilbur 1
DWIGHT, Jonathan 1
DWIGHT, Mabel 5
DWIGHT, Minnie Ryan 3
DWIGHT, Nathaniel H
DWIGHT, Ogden Graham 5
DWIGHT,
  Richard Everett
DWIGHT, Sereno
  Edwards H
DWIGHT, Theodore * H
DWIGHT, H
  Theodore William
DWIGHT, Thomas H
DWIGHT, Thomas 1
DWIGHT, Timothy H
DWIGHT, Timothy 1
DWIGHT, William H

DWIGHT, William Buck 1
DWINELL, Justin H
DWINNELL, 1
  Clifton Howard
DWIRE, Henry Rudolph 2
DWORKIS, Martin B. 4
DWORSHAK, 4
  Henry Clarence
DWYER, Charles 1
DWYER, Edward Martin 3
DWYER, James A. 1
DWYER, James Francis 3
DWYER, Jeremiah 4
DWYER, John B. 3
DWYER, John William 4
DWYER, Robert Arthur 4
DWYER, Robert E. 4
DWYER, William Joseph 3
DWYRE, Dudley G. 2
DYAR, Harrison Gray 1
DYAS, Ada H
DYAS, Ada 1
DYCHE, Howard Edward 3
DYCHE, Louis Lindsay 1
DYCHE, William Andrew 4
DYE, Alexander Vincent 3
DYE, Clair Albert 2
DYE, Eugene Allen 4
DYE, Eva Emery 3
DYE, John T. 1
DYE, William Holton 1
DYER, Alexander Brydie H
DYER, Alexander Brydie 1
DYER, 1
  Catherine Cornelia
DYER, Clifton G. 3
DYER, David Patterson 1
DYER, Eliphalet H
DYER, Elisha 1
DYER, Francis John 1
DYER, Frank 1
DYER, Frank Lewis 1
DYER, 4
  Franklin Benjamin
DYER, Frederick Rainey 1
DYER, George Leland 1
DYER, Gustavus Walker 4
DYER, Heman 1
DYER, Hezekiah Anthony 2
DYER, Isaac Watson 1
DYER, Isadore 1
DYER, James Ballard 1
DYER, James Edward 5
DYER, Jesse Farley 5
DYER, John H. 4
DYER, John LaFayette 1
DYER, John Lewis 1
DYER, John Napier 3
DYER, Joseph Henry 2
DYER, Leonard Huntress 3
DYER, 3
  Leonidas Carstarphen
DYER, Louis 1
DYER, Mary H
DYER, Nehemiah Mayo 1
DYER, Oliver 1
DYER, Walter Alden 2
DYETT, Herbert Thomas 5
DYKE, Charles Bartlett 1
DYKE, Herbert H. 4
DYKEMA, 5
  Karl W(ashburn)
DYKEMA, Peter William 3
DYKEMA, Raymond K. 5
DYKEMAN, King 1
DYKHUIZEN, 5
  Harold Daniel
DYKSTRA, 3
  Clarence Addison
DYKSTRA, Gerald Oscar 5
DYKSTRA, John 5
DYLANDER, John H
DYM, Aaron 4
DYMENT, Colin Victor 1
DYMOND, Florence 5
DYNES, Owen William 1
DYOTT, Thomas W. H
DYRENFORTH, 1
  Robert St George
DYSINGER, Holmes 4
DYSON, Charles Wilson 1
DYSON, James Lindsay 4

E

EACHES, Hector H
EACHES, Owen Philips 1
EADE, Charles 4
EADS, James Buchanan H
EAGAN, Charles Patrick 1
EAGAN, 5
  Edward Patrick Francis
EAGAN, John Joseph 1
EAGELS, Jeanne 1
EAGER, George
  Boardman H
EAGER, George Eugene 4

EAGER, Helen 3
EAGER, Henry Gossett 5
EAGER, John M. 3
EAGER, Samuel Watkins H
EAGLE, J. Frederick 4
EAGLE, James Phillip 1
EAGLE, Joe Henry 5
EAGLE, Mary Kavanaugh 1
EAGLE, The 1
EAGLES, 1
  Theophilus Randolph
EAGLESON, James Beaty 1
EAGLESON, Thomas R. H
EAGLETON, Clyde 5
EAGLETON, 2
  Wells Phillips
EAKIN, Robert 1
EAKINS, Thomas 1
EAKLE, Arthur Starr 1
EAMAN, Frank Dwight 4
EAMES, Alfred Warner 5
EAMES, Charles H
EAMES, Charles Holmes 2
EAMES, Emma 1
EAMES, Hayden 1
EAMES, Henry Purmort 3
EAMES, John Capen 4
EAMES, Wilberforce 1
EAMES, William S. 1
EARDLEY, Armand John 5
EARHART, Amelia 1
EARHART, Harry Boyd 3
EARHART, Lida Belle 4
EARHART, 5
  Robert Francis
EARHART, Will 5
EARL, Augustus H
EARL, Charles 2
EARL, Edward 1
EARL, Edwin T. 1
EARL, George Goodell 1
EARL, George H. 4
EARL, Guy Chaffee 1
EARL, Harley J. 5
EARL, John Arthur 1
EARL, 1
  Mrs. Elizabeth Claypool
EARL, N. Clark, Jr. 5
EARL, Ottis M. 2
EARL, H
  Ralph Eleaser Whiteside
EARL, Robert 1
EARL, Robert 2
EARLE, Alice Morse 1
EARLE, 3
  Clarence Edwards
EARLE, Edward Mead 3
EARLE, Elias H
EARLE, 1
  Frank Breckenridge
EARLE, Franklin Sumner 3
EARLE,
  Genevieve Beavers
EARLE, George Howard 1
EARLE, James H
EARLE, John Baylis H
EARLE, H
  Joseph Haynsworth
EARLE, 1
  Lawrence Carmichael
EARLE, Mortimer Lamson 1
EARLE, Pliny * H
EARLE, Ralph 1
EARLE, Ralph 1
EARLE, Robert L. 4
EARLE, Samuel H
EARLE, Samuel T. Jr. 1
EARLE, Thomas H
EARLE, Walter Frank 4
EARLE, Walter Keese 5
EARLE, William Hughes 4
EARLEY, John Joseph 3
EARLING, Albert J. 1
EARLING, Herman B. 5
EARLL, Jonas Jr. H
EARLL, H
  Nehemiah Hezekiah
EARLY, Eleanor 5
EARLY, 2
  Gilbert Garfield
EARLY, John H
EARLY, John Jacob 2
EARLY, John Jacob 3
EARLY, Jubal Anderson H
EARLY, Maurice 3
EARLY, Peter 1
EARLY, Robert Lee 4
EARLY, Stephen 3
EARLY, William Wallace 4
EARNEST, 5
  Herbert Ludwell
EARNHEART, Harold 3
EARNSHAW, Manuel 1
EARP, Edwin Lee 1
EARP, James William 3

EARP, John Rosslyn 1
EARP, H
  Wyatt Berry Stapp
EARP, 4
  Wyatt Berry Stapp
EASBY-SMITH, James S. 5
EASCH, Albertina 4
EASLEY, 2
  Claudius Miller
EASLEY, Gertrude Beeks 2
EASLEY, Katherine 5
EASLEY, 1
  Ralph Montgomery
EASON, George Millar 4
EAST, Edward Murray 1
EASTBURN, L. A. 3
EASTER, 5
  Charles Whittlesey
EASTER, 1
  De 'la Warr Benjamin
EASTERBROOK, Arthur
  E. 3
EASTERBROOK,
  Edmund Pepperell
EASTERBY, James Harold 4
EASTERWOOD, 1
  William Edward Jr.
EASTIN, Bertrand P 5
EASTLAND, 4
  Florence Martin
EASTMAN, Annis Ford 1
EASTMAN,
  Arthur MacArthur
EASTMAN, Barrett 1
EASTMAN, Ben C. H
EASTMAN, 4
  Charles Alexander Ohiyesa
EASTMAN,
  Charles Gamage
EASTMAN, 1
  Charles Rochester
EASTMAN, 3
  Clarence Willis
EASTMAN, Edwin
  Gamage 1
EASTMAN, Enoch
  Worthen H
EASTMAN, Fred 4
EASTMAN, George 1
EASTMAN, Hal Pond 3
EASTMAN, Harry L. 4
EASTMAN, H
  Harvey Gridley
EASTMAN, Helen 3
EASTMAN, Ira Allen H
EASTMAN, John Coates 1
EASTMAN, John Robie 1
EASTMAN, Joseph 1
EASTMAN, 2
  Joseph Bartlett
EASTMAN, Joseph Rilus 2
EASTMAN, 1
  Julia Arabella
EASTMAN, LeRoy
  Emerson 5
EASTMAN, Linda Anne 4
EASTMAN, Lucius Root 2
EASTMAN, M. Gale 3
EASTMAN, 5
  Max (Forrester)
EASTMAN, Nehemiah H
EASTMAN,
  Rebecca Lane Hooper (Mrs.
  William Franklin
EASTMAN, Samuel Coffin 1
EASTMAN, Samuel
  Palmer 1
EASTMAN, Seth H
EASTMAN, H
  Timothy Corser
EASTMAN, William Reed 4
EASTON, Burton Scott 2
EASTON, Edward
  Denison 1
EASTON, John H
EASTON, Morton William 1
EASTON, Nicholas H
EASTON, Rufus H
EASTON, 4
  Stanly Alexander
EASTVOLD, Carl Johan 1
EASTVOLD, 4
  Seth Clarence
EASTWOOD, A. J. 4
EASTWOOD, Alice 3
EASTWOOD, Everett
  Owen 5
EASTWOOD, 4
  George Anderson
EATON, Amasa Mason H
EATON, Amos H
EATON,
  Arthur Wentworth Hamilton
EATON, Barney Edward 2
EATON,
  Benjamin Harrison

EATON, C. Harry 1
EATON, Charles Aubrey 3
EATON, Charles Frederick 4
EATON, Charles H. H
EATON, Charles H. 1
EATON, Charles ·Warren 1
EATON, Cyrus H
EATON, D. Cady 1
EATON, Daniel Cady H
EATON, Dorman Bridgeman 1
EATON, Edward Dwight 2
EATON, Elon Howard 1
EATON, Emma Florence 4
EATON, Ephraim Llewellyn 4
EATON, Ernest Theophilus 3
EATON, Fred Laurine 1
EATON, Frederick Heber 1
EATON, George Daniel 1
EATON, George Francis 2
EATON, George Franklin 3
EATON, Harvey Doane 1
EATON, Henry William 1
EATON, Homer H
EATON, Horace Ainsworth 5
EATON, Hubert 4
EATON, James Briggs 4
EATON, James Murchie 3
EATON, James Shirley 3
EATON, James Tucker 1
EATON, James Webster 1
EATON, John H
EATON, John Henry H
EATON, John Wallace 2
EATON, Joseph Giles 1
EATON, Joseph Horace H
EATON, Joseph Oriel 1
EATON, Joseph Oriel 3
EATON, L. Mckendree 2
EATON, Lewis H
EATON, Lewis Tillson 1
EATON, Lucien 3
EATON, Marquis 1
EATON, Marquis G. 3
EATON, Melvin Carr 4
EATON, Nathaniel H
EATON, Paul B. 4
EATON, Philip Bentley 1
EATON, Russell 5
EATON, Samuel H
EATON, Seymour 1
EATON, Theodore Hildreth 4
EATON, Theophilus H
EATON, Thomas Treadwell 1
EATON, Walter Prichard 3
EATON, William H
EATON, William Colgate 1
EATON, William H. 4
EATON, William Hanmer 3
EATON, William Robb H
EATON, Wyatt H
EAVENSON, Howard Nicholas 3
EAVES, George 1
EAVES, Lucile 5
EBAUGH, Franklin Gessford 5
EBEL, William K. 5
EBELING, Philip Calvin 4
EBELING, Willi Henry 4
EBERBACH, Carl Walter 4
EBERHARD, Ernst 5
EBERHARDT, Charles Christopher 4
EBERHARDT, Charles Christopher 2
EBERHARDT, Frederick L. 2
EBERHART, Nelle Richmond 3
EBERHARTER, Herman Peter 2
EBERLE, Abastenia St Leger 4
EBERLE, E. G. 4
EBERLE, Edward Walter 4
EBERLE, Frederick J. 4
EBERLE, J. Louis H
EBERLE, John 4
EBERLEIN, Harold Donaldson 5
EBERLY, George Agler 5
EBERSOLE, Ezra Christian 5
EBERSOLE, J(acob) Scott 2
EBERSOLE, John Franklin 3
EBERSOLE, William Stahl

EBERSTADT, Ferdinand 5
EBERSTADT, Rudolph 4
EBERT, Edmund Francis 5
EBERT, Robert Edwin 5
EBERT, Rudolph Gustav 4
EBY, Frederick 4
EBY, Frederick 5
EBY, Ivan David 1
EBY, Kermit 4
EBY, Kerr 2
EBY, Robert Killian 4
ECCLES, James A. 3
ECCLES, Robert G. 1
ECCLESTON, Samuel H
ECHOLS, Angus B. 4
ECHOLS, Charles Patton 1
ECHOLS, John H
ECHOLS, John Warnock 4
ECHOLS, Leonard Sidney 5
ECHOLS, Oliver P. 3
ECHOLS, Robert 3
ECHOLS, William Holding Jr. 1
ECHOLS, William Joseph 1
ECIJA, Juan 'de 4
ECKARD, Elisabeth Ellen Gilliland 5
ECKARD, James Read H
ECKARD, Leighton Wilson 1
ECKARDT, Lisgar Russell 2
ECKART, E. Albert 5
ECKEL, Charles Lewis 1
ECKEL, Edwin Clarence 2
ECKELS, James Herron 1
ECKER, Enrique E. 4
ECKER, Frederic W. 4
ECKER, Frederick H. 4
ECKERSALL, Edwin Robert 4
ECKERSALL, Walter H. 1
ECKERT, Charles R. 4
ECKERT, George Nicholas H
ECKERT, Howard Haines 1
ECKERT, Thomas Thompson 1
ECKERT, Wallace J. 5
ECKERT, William D(ole) 5
ECKFELDT, Howard 2
ECKFELDT, Thomas Hooper 1
ECKFORD, Henry H
ECKHARD, George Frederick 2
ECKHART, Bernard Albert 1
ECKHART, Percy Bernard 5
ECKHOUSE, Joseph L. 4
ECKLES, Clarence Henry 1
ECKLES, Isabel Lancaster 5
ECKLEY, William Thomas 1
ECKMAN, Donald Preston 4
ECKMAN, George Peck 1
ECKOFF, William Julius 1
ECKSTEIN, Frederick H
ECKSTEIN, John H
ECKSTEIN, Louis 1
ECKSTEIN, Nathan 2
ECKSTORM, Fannie Hardy 4
ECKSTROM, Lawrence Joel 4
ECTON, Zales Nelson 3
ED, Carl Frank Ludwig 3
EDBROOKE, Willoughby J. H
EDDINGER, Wallace 1
EDDINS, Henry A. 4
EDDIS, William H
EDDY, Alfred Delavan 1
EDDY, Allen 4
EDDY, Arthur Jerome 1
EDDY, Brayton 3
EDDY, Charles Brown 3
EDDY, Clarence 1
EDDY, Condit Nelson 4
EDDY, Daniel Clarke H
EDDY, David Brewer 2
EDDY, Forrest Greenwood 1
EDDY, Frank Woodman 1
EDDY, Harrison Prescott 1
EDDY, Henry Brevoort 5
EDDY, Henry Stephens 1
EDDY, Henry Turner 1
EDDY, Isaac H
EDDY, Manton S. 4
EDDY, Mary Baker Glover 1
EDDY, Milton Walker 4
EDDY, Nathan Browne 5
EDDY, Nelson 4

EDDY, Norman H
EDDY, Oliver Tarbell H
EDDY, Richard 1
EDDY, Samuel H
EDDY, Sherwood 4
EDDY, Spencer 1
EDDY, Thomas H
EDDY, Thomas Mears H
EDDY, Walter Hollis 3
EDDY, William Abner 4
EDDY, William Alfred 4
EDDY, Zachary H
EDEBOHLS, George Michael 1
EDELHERTZ, Bernard 1
EDELMAN, John W. 5
EDELMAN, Nathan 5
EDELSTEIN, Ludwig 4
EDELSTEIN, M. Michael 2
EDEN, Charles 1
EDEN, Robert H
EDENBORN, William 1
EDENS, Arthur Hollis 5
EDENS, James Benjamin 5
EDENS, William Grant 3
EDER, Phanor James 5
EDES, Benjamin H
EDES, Henry Herbert 1
EDES, Robert Thaxter 1
EDES, William Cushing 1
EDESON, Robert 1
EDGAR, Charles Bloomfield 1
EDGAR, Charles Leavitt 1
EDGAR, Graham 3
EDGAR, J. Clifton 1
EDGAR, Randolph 1
EDGAR, Randolph 2
EDGAR, Robert Franklin 1
EDGAR, Thomas Delbert 3
EDGAR, William Crowell 1
EDGCOMB, Ernest Isaac 4
EDGE, Walter Evans 3
EDGECOMBE, Samuel 3
EDGELL, George Harold 3
EDGERLY, Winfield Scot 1
EDGERTON, Alfred Peck 1
EDGERTON, Alice Craig 2
EDGERTON, Alonzo Jay H
EDGERTON, Charles Eugene 1
EDGERTON, Franklin 4
EDGERTON, Halsey Charles 4
EDGERTON, Henry White 5
EDGERTON, Herbert Oliver 5
EDGERTON, Hiram H. 1
EDGERTON, James Arthur 1
EDGERTON, John Emmett 1
EDGERTON, John Warren 1
EDGERTON, Justin Lincoln 5
EDGERTON, William Franklin 5
EDGETT, Edwin Francis 2
EDGINGTON, Thomas Benton 1
EDGREN, John Alexis 1
EDHOLM-SIBLEY, Mary G. Charlton 4
EDIE, Guy Lewis 1
EDIE, John Rufus H
EDIE, Lionel Danforth 4
EDINGS, William Seabrook 1
EDINGTON, Arlo Channing 4
EDISON, Charles 5
EDISON, Charles B. 5
EDISON, Harry 4
EDISON, Mark Aaron 3
EDISON, Oskar E. 4
EDISON, Samuel Bernard 5
EDISON, Thomas A. 1
EDMAN, Irwin 3
EDMAN, V. Raymond 4
EDMANDS, John 1
EDMANDS, John Wiley H
EDMANDS, Samuel Sumner 1
EDMISTON, Andrew 4
EDMISTON, R. W. 4
EDMISTON, William Sherman 5
EDMOND, William H
EDMONDS, Dean Stockett 5
EDMONDS, Douglas Lyman 4
EDMONDS, Francis William

EDMONDS, Franklin Spencer 2
EDMONDS, George Washington 1
EDMONDS, Harry Marcus Weston 2
EDMONDS, Henry Morris 4
EDMONDS, John Worth H
EDMONDS, Richard Hathaway 1
EDMONDSON, Cathrine Elizabeth 5
EDMONDSON, Clarence Edmund 2
EDMONDSON, James Howard 5
EDMONDSON, Thomas William 1
EDMONDSON, William John 5
EDMUNDS, Albert Joseph 1
EDMUNDS, Albert Joseph 2
EDMUNDS, Charles Carroll 4
EDMUNDS, Charles Keyser 2
EDMUNDS, Charles Wallis 1
EDMUNDS, George Franklin 1
EDMUNDS, Harry Nicholas 1
EDMUNDS, James Richard Jr. 3
EDMUNDS, Samuel Henry 1
EDMUNDS, Sterling Edwin 2
EDMUNDS-HEMINGWAY Mme H
EDMUNDSON, Henry Alonzo H
EDMUNDSON, James Depew 1
EDOUART, Alexander H
EDOUART, Auguste H
EDRINGTON, William Reynolds 1
EDROP, Percy T. 5
EDSALL, David Linn 2
EDSALL, Joseph E. H
EDSALL, Preston William 5
EDSALL, Samuel Cook 1
EDSFORTH, Charles Dugdale 4
EDSON, Andrew Wheatley 1
EDSON, Carroll Everett 1
EDSON, Cyrus 1
EDSON, Franklin 1
EDSON, Gus 5
EDSON, Howard Austin 5
EDSON, Job Adolphus 1
EDSON, John Joy 1
EDSON, Katherine Philips 1
EDSON, Merritt Austin 3
EDSON, Robert Clay 5
EDSON, Stephen Reuben 5
EDSON, Tracy R. 5
EDSON, Winfield 3
EDSTROM, David 1
EDWARD, Harvey 2
EDWARDS, Alanson W. 1
EDWARDS, Alba M. 5
EDWARDS, Alfred Shenstone 4
EDWARDS, Arthur Robin 1
EDWARDS, Bela Bates 1
EDWARDS, Benjamin H
EDWARDS, Benjamin D. 1
EDWARDS, Benjamin Franklin 4
EDWARDS, Charles H
EDWARDS, Charles Gordon 1
EDWARDS, Charles Lincoln 1
EDWARDS, Charles Vernon 5
EDWARDS, Charles William 3
EDWARDS, Chauncey Theodore 5
EDWARDS, Clarence Ransom 1
EDWARDS, Clement Stanislaus 5
EDWARDS, David Frank 4
EDWARDS, David George 4
EDWARDS, David Morton 1
EDWARDS, Deltus Malin 5
EDWARDS, Don Calvin 1

EDWARDS, Edward B. 2
EDWARDS, Edward Irving 1
EDWARDS, Edward William 3
EDWARDS, Elisha Jay 4
EDWARDS, Everett Eugene 3
EDWARDS, F. Boyd 4
EDWARDS, Frank 4
EDWARDS, Frederick 5
EDWARDS, George Herbert 2
EDWARDS, George Lane 5
EDWARDS, George Porter 1
EDWARDS, George Thornton 1
EDWARDS, George Wharton 2
EDWARDS, George William 3
EDWARDS, Gordon L. 3
EDWARDS, Granville Dennis 3
EDWARDS, Gurney 5
EDWARDS, Harrison Griffith 1
EDWARDS, Harry Stillwell H
EDWARDS, Heber L. 4
EDWARDS, Henry Waggaman H
EDWARDS, Howard 1
EDWARDS, Howard Wesley 4
EDWARDS, Ira 2
EDWARDS, James Thomas 1
EDWARDS, John * 1
EDWARDS, John Cummins H
EDWARDS, John Harrington 4
EDWARDS, John Homer 2
EDWARDS, John Palmer 4
EDWARDS, John Richard 2
EDWARDS, John Rogers 1
EDWARDS, Jonathan * 5
EDWARDS, Joseph Lee 5
EDWARDS, Joseph Lee 1
EDWARDS, Julian 1
EDWARDS, Justin H
EDWARDS, Landon Brame 1
EDWARDS, Le Roy Mallory 4
EDWARDS, Leroy D. 3
EDWARDS, Linden Forest 5
EDWARDS, Loren McClain 2
EDWARDS, Louise Betts 4
EDWARDS, Margaret Messenger H
EDWARDS, Morgan French 4
EDWARDS, Murray 5
EDWARDS, Myrtle Sassman (Mrs. Harlan H. Edwards) 1
EDWARDS, Nathaniel Marsh H
EDWARDS, Ninian H
EDWARDS, Ninian Wirt 1
EDWARDS, Ogden Matthias 3
EDWARDS, Paul Kenneth 5
EDWARDS, Percy Noyes H
EDWARDS, Philip R. 1
EDWARDS, Pierpont H
EDWARDS, Ray Gwyther 1
EDWARDS, Richard 3
EDWARDS, Richard Henry 3
EDWARDS, Richard Stanislaus 5
EDWARDS, Robert Ernest 5
EDWARDS, Robert Wilkinson 1
EDWARDS, Samuel 1
EDWARDS, Samuel 1
EDWARDS, Stephen Ostrom H
EDWARDS, Talmadge H
EDWARDS, Thomas Allison 5
EDWARDS, Thomas Cynonfardd H
EDWARDS, Thomas McKey H
EDWARDS, Thomas Owen 5
EDWARDS, Velma Green (Mrs. Lowell Wayne Edwards)

EDWARDS, 2
  Vere Buckingham
EDWARDS, 1
  Victor Everett
EDWARDS, Walter Alison 4
EDWARDS, H
  Weldon Nathaniel
EDWARDS, William H
EDWARDS, William A. 3
EDWARDS,
  William Augustus
EDWARDS, 5
  William Hanford;
EDWARDS, William
  Henry 1
EDWARDS,
  William Seymour
EELLS, Dan Parmelee 1
EELLS, 4
  Elsie Eusebia Spicer
EELLS, Hastings 5
EELLS, Howard Parmelee 1
EELLS, Myron 1
EELLS, Stillman Witt 1
EELLS, Walter Crosby 4
EERDMANS,
  William Bernard
EFFINGER, John Robert 1
EFFLER, Erwin R. 3
EFNER, Valentine H
EFROYMSON, Abram B. 4
EFROYMSON, Gustave
  A. 2
EGAN, Hannah M. 2
EGAN, John M. 2
EGAN, Joseph L. 2
EGAN, Louis Henry 3
EGAN, Martin 1
EGAN, Maurice Francis 1
EGAN, Michael H
EGAN, Thomas Aloysius 3
EGAR, John Hodson 4
EGAS, Camilo 4
EGBERT, H
  Albert Gallatin
EGBERT, Donald Drew 5
EGBERT, 2
  James Chidester
EGBERT, Joseph H
EGBERT, Percy T. 5
EGBERT, Seneca 1
EGBERT, Sherwood Harry 5
EGBERT, W. Grant 1
EGE, George H
EGE, Hattie B. 5
EGELSON, Louis I. 3
EGERTON, Graham 1
EGGERS, George William 5
EGGERS, Harold Everett 4
EGGERS, Otto R. 5
EGGERSS, H. A.; 4
EGGERT, Carl Edgar 4
EGGERT, 1
  Charles Augustus
EGGERT, Harry T. 5
EGGIMANN, 2
  Edward Daniel
EGGLESTON, 4
  Allan Arthur
EGGLESTON, Benjamin H
EGGLESTON, Cary 5
EGGLESTON, David
  Quinn 4
EGGLESTON, Edward 1
EGGLESTON, George
  Cary 1
EGGLESTON, Joseph H
EGGLESTON, 3
  Joseph Dupuy
EGGLESTON,
  Sir Frederic William
EGGLETON, 5
  Frank E(gbert)
EGLE, William Henry 1
EGLESTON, Thomas 1
EGLIN,
  William Charles Lawson
EGLOF, Warren K. 4
EGLOFF, Gustav 3
EGLOFFSTEIN, H
  Frederick W. Von
EGLY, Henry Harris 3
EGNER,
  Arthur Frederick
EGNER, Frank 3
EHNES,
  Morris Wellington
EHRENFELD,
  Charles Hatch
EHRENFELD,
  Charles Lewis
EHRENFRIED, Albert 3
EHRENREICH, Joseph 5
EHRENSVARD,
  Johan Jacob Albert
EHRHARDT,
  Julius George

EHRHORN, 1
  Edward Macfarlane
EHRICH, Harold Louis 1
EHRICH, Louis R. 1
EHRICH, 5
  William E(rnst) (Hermann
  Heinrich)
EHRINGHAUS, 2
  John Christoph Blucher
EHRLICH, Harry 3
EHRLICH, Jacob W. 5
EHRLICHMAN, Ben B. 5
EHRMAN, 1
  Mary Bartholomew
EHRMAN, Sidney M(yer) 5
EHRMANN, Max 1
EICHBERG, Julius H
EICHELBERGER, 4
  Robert Lawrence
EICHELBERGER, 5
  William Snyder
EICHENAUER, 3
  Charles Frederick
EICHER, Edward Clayton 2
EICHER, Henry Martin 3
EICHHEIM, Henry 2
EICHHOLTZ, Jacob H
EICHHORN, William A. 3
EICKEMEYER, Rudolf H
EICKEMEYER, Rudolf 1
EIDEM, Olaf 5
EIDLITZ, Charles Leo 1
EIDLITZ, Otto Marc 1
EIDMANN, Frank Lewis 4
EIELSEN, Elling H
EIESLAND, John (Arndt) 5
EIFERT, 4
  Virginia Snider
EIGENMANN, Carl H. 1
EIKENBARY,
  Charles Franklin
EIKENBERRY, 4
  Dan Harrison
EIKENBERRY, 3
  William Lewis
EILENBERGER, 1
  Clinton B.
EILERS, Anton 1
EILERS, Karl 4
EILERT, 1
  Ernest Frederick
EILSHEMIUS, 1
  Louis Michel
EILSHEMIUS, 2
  Louis Michel
EIMBECK, William 4
EINAUDI, Luigi 5
EINHORN, David H
EINHORN, Max 4
EINSIDEL, D. 1
EINSTEIN, Albert 3
EINSTEIN, Alfred 3
EINSTEIN, Lewis 2
EIS, Frederick 4
EISELEN, 1
  Frederick Carl
EISEN, Gustavus A. 1
EISENBERG, 5
  Irwin Weinman
EISENBERG, Maurice 5
EISENDRATH, 1
  Daniel Nathan
EISENHARDT, Raymond 4
EISENHARDT, Raymond
  F. 5
EISENHART, 4
  Charles Marion
EISENHART, 4
  Luther Pfahler
EISENHOWER, Arthur B. 3
EISENHOWER, 5
  Dwight David
EISENHOWER, 5
  Edgar Nuton
EISENMAN, William
  Hunt 3
EISENSCHIML, Otto 4
EISFELD, Theodor H
EISNER, J. Lester 5
EISNER, Mark 1
EITEL, George Gotthilf 1
EKBLAW, Walter Elmer 2
EKBLOM, John Olof 1
EKELEY, John Bernard 3
EKENGREN,
  Wilhelm August Fredinand
EKERN, Herman Lewis 3
EKINS, H. R. 5
EKLUND, Fred Nils 3
EKSERGIAN, Rupen 3
EKWALL,
  William Alexander
ELA, David Hough 4
ELA, Jacob Hart H
ELA, John Whittier 5
ELAM, Emma Lee 1
ELAM, John Babb 1

ELAM, Joseph Barton H
ELAN, Meir 5
ELANDER, Albin Eskel 4
EL AZHARI, Ismail 5
ELBERT, John Aloysius 4
ELBERT, Samuel 1
ELDEN, John Aten 1
ELDER, Bowman 3
ELDER, Cyrus 1
ELDER, Frank Ray 4
ELDER, George H
ELDER, John Adams H
ELDER, Joseph Freeman 5
ELDER, Orr Jay 3
ELDER, Paul 2
ELDER, Robert Henry; 5
ELDER, Samuel James 1
ELDER, Susan Blanchard 4
ELDER, William H
ELDER, William Henry 1
ELDER, William Line 1
ELDERKIN, 4
  George Wicker
ELDERKIN, John 4
ELDERKIN, Karl Osler 4
ELDERKIN, Noble Strong 4
ELDRED, Byron E. 3
ELDRED, Lewis 4
ELDREDGE, Arch Bishop 1
ELDREDGE, H
  Charles Augustus
ELDREDGE, 1
  Charles Henry
ELDREDGE, 1
  Joseph U. Jr.
ELDREDGE, H
  Nathaniel Buel
ELDREDGE, 1
  Zoeth Skinner
ELDRERGE, 3
  Elliott Minton
ELDRIDGE, Edward
  Henry 5
ELDRIDGE, 2
  Francis Howard
ELDRIDGE, Frank
  Harold 1
ELDRIDGE, Frederick L. 4
ELDRIDGE, 1
  Frederick William
ELDRIDGE, 1
  George Homans
ELDRIDGE, Maurice
  Owen 5
ELDRIDGE, Seba 3
ELDRIDGE, H
  Shalor Winchell
ELDRIDGE, 3
  William Angevine
ELGHAMMER, H.
  William 5
ELIAS, Albert Barnes 5
ELIAS, Harold Lee 3
ELIASBERG, Wladimir G. 5
ELIASON, James Bayard 5
ELIOT, Amory 3
ELIOT, Charles H
ELIOT, Charles William 1
ELIOT, 2
  Christopher Rhodes
ELIOT, 5
  Douglas Fitch Guilford
ELIOT, Edward Cranch 1
ELIOT, Frederick May 3
ELIOT, George Fielding 5
ELIOT, Jared H
ELIOT, John H
ELIOT, Samuel H
ELIOT, Samuel Atkins H
ELIOT, Thomas Dawes H
ELIOT, Thomas Lamb 1
ELIOT, Thomas Stearns H
ELIOT, Walter Graeme 1
ELIOT, H
  William Greenleaf
ELIOT, 3
  William Greenleaf Jr.
ELIOTT, Van Courtlandt 5
ELISOFON, Eliot 5
ELIZALDE, 5
  Rafael Hector
EL-KHOURY, Bechara 4
ELKIN, Daniel Collier 3
ELKIN, John Pratt 1
ELKIN, William Lewis 1
ELKIN, William Simpson 1
ELKINS, Davis 3
ELKINS, George W. 1
ELKINS, James Anderson 5
ELKINS, Stephen Benton 1
ELKINS, William Lukens 1
ELKINS, 2
  William McIntire
ELKUS, Abram I. 2
ELKUS,
  Charles 'de Young

ELLABARGER, 3
  Daniel Rudolph
ELLARD, 4
  Roscoe Brabazon
ELLEFSON, 5
  Bennett Stanley
ELLEGOOD, 1
  Robert Grif.
ELLENDER, Allen Joseph 5
ELLENDER, 5
  Raphael Theodore
ELLENSTEIN, Meyer C. 4
ELLENWOOD, Frank
  Oakes 2
ELLENWOOD, Fred
  Alden 2
ELLER, Adolphus Hill 2
ELLERBE, Alma Martin 4
ELLERBE, James Edwin 4
ELLERBE, 1
  William Haselden
ELLERHUSEN, 3
  Florence Cooney
ELLERHUSEN, 3
  Ulrich Henry
ELLERMAN, Ferdinand 1
ELLERY, Christopher H
ELLERY, Edward 5
ELLERY, Eloise 5
ELLERY, Frank H
ELLERY, William H
ELLET, Charles H
ELLET, H
  Elizabeth Fries Lummis
ELLET, Henry Thomas H
ELLETT, Edward
  Coleman 2
ELLETT, Thomas Harlan 3
ELLETT, Walter Beal 2
ELLICK, Alfred George 2
ELLICOTT, Andrew H
ELLICOTT, Benjamin H
ELLICOTT, Eugene .4
ELLICOTT, John Morris 3
ELLICOTT, Joseph 1
ELLIFF, Joseph Alonzo 5
ELLIFF, Joseph Doliver 5
ELLIMAN, 3
  Douglas Ludlow
ELLIMAN, 3
  Lawrence Bogert
ELLING, Henry 1
ELLINGER, Moritz 4
ELLINGHAM, 1
  Lewis Glendale
ELLINGSON, Carl
  Herman 3
ELLINGTON, Buford 5
ELLINGTON, 5
  Jesse Thompson
ELLINGWOOD, 1
  Albert Russell
ELLINGWOOD, Finley 1
ELLINWOOD, Everett E. 2
ELLINWOOD, Frank
  Field 1
ELLINWOOD, 1
  Ralph Everett
ELLINWOOD, 1
  Truman Jeremiah
ELLIOT, Charles H
ELLIOT, Daniel Giraud 1
ELLIOT, George Thomson 1
ELLIOT, 1
  Henry Rutherford
ELLIOT, James H
ELLIOT, John Wheelock 1
ELLIOT, Jonathan H
ELLIOTT, A. Marshall 1
ELLIOTT, Alfred J. 5
ELLIOTT, 4
  Arthur Richard
ELLIOTT, Benjamin H
ELLIOTT, 1
  Byron Kosciusko
ELLIOTT, 1
  Charles Addison
ELLIOTT, Charles Burke 1
ELLIOTT, 1
  Charles Gleason
ELLIOTT, H
  Charles Loring
ELLIOTT, Claude 1
ELLIOTT, Curtis Miller 5
ELLIOTT, 2
  Daniel Stanley
ELLIOTT, Edward 2
ELLIOTT, 1
  Edward Charles
ELLIOTT, Edward Loomis 3
ELLIOTT, Ernest Eugene 1
ELLIOTT, Francis Perry 1
ELLIOTT, Frank Rumsey 4
ELLIOTT, George 1
ELLIOTT, George Blow 2
ELLIOTT, George Frank 1

ELLIOTT, 4
  George Frederick
ELLIOTT, Gertrude 3
ELLIOTT, 2
  Harriet Wiesman
ELLIOTT, 3
  Harrison Sacket
ELLIOTT, Henry Wood 4
ELLIOTT, Homer 3
ELLIOTT, Howard 1
ELLIOTT, Huger 2
ELLIOTT, J. M. 2
ELLIOTT, Jackson S. 2
ELLIOTT, James H
ELLIOTT, James Douglas 1
ELLIOTT, James Lewis 5
ELLIOTT, James Robert 4
ELLIOTT, James Thomas 5
ELLIOTT, Jesse Duncan H
ELLIOTT, John H
ELLIOTT, John 1
ELLIOTT, John Asbury 1
ELLIOTT, John B. 4
ELLIOTT, John Barnwell 5
ELLIOTT, John Henry * 4
ELLIOTT, John Lovejoy 2
ELLIOTT, John M. 1
ELLIOTT, John Mackay 1
ELLIOTT, John Milton H
ELLIOTT, John Stuart 4
ELLIOTT, John Wesley 5
ELLIOTT, John Wesley 4
ELLIOTT,
  Joseph Alexander
ELLIOTT, Lewis Grimes 2
ELLIOTT, Martin Kelso 2
ELLIOTT, Maud Howe 2
ELLIOTT, Maxine 1
ELLIOTT, 3
  Middleton Stuart
ELLIOTT,
  Milton Courtright
ELLIOTT, Oliver Morton 1
ELLIOTT, Orrin Leslie 1
ELLIOTT, Philip Lovin 5
ELLIOTT,
  Phillips Packer
ELLIOTT, 5
  Richard Hammond
ELLIOTT, Richard Nash 2
ELLIOTT, Robert Brown H
ELLIOTT, Robert Irving 2
ELLIOTT, 4
  Robert Michael
ELLIOTT, Roy Gordon 3
ELLIOTT, 1
  Sarah Barnwell
ELLIOTT, 5
  Shelden Douglass
ELLIOTT, Simon Bolivar 4
ELLIOTT, Stephen H
ELLIOTT, Stuart Rhett 5
ELLIOTT, Thompson Coit 2
ELLIOTT, Walter 1
ELLIOTT, H
  Washington Lafayette
ELLIOTT, William H
ELLIOTT, William 1
ELLIOTT, William 2
ELLIOTT, William 1
  William Arthur
ELLIOTT, William Henry 1
ELLIOTT, 3
  William Sanders
ELLIOTT, William Swan 1
ELLIS, 2
  Alexander Caswell
ELLIS, Alston
ELLIS, Anderson Nelson 2
ELLIS, Anna M. B. 1
ELLIS, Arthur McDonald 1
ELLIS, Caleb H
ELLIS, Calvin H
ELLIS, Carleton 1
ELLIS,
  Challen Blackburn
ELLIS, Charles Alton 2
ELLIS, Charles Calvert 3
ELLIS, Charles S. 4
ELLIS, Chesselden H
ELLIS, 4
  Crawford Hatcher
ELLIS, David Abram 1
ELLIS, Don Carlos 3
ELLIS, Edgar Clarence 1
ELLIS,
  Edward Sylvester
ELLIS, Edwin Erastus 1
ELLIS, Ezekiel John H
ELLIS, Frank Burton 5
ELLIS, G. Corson 4
ELLIS, George Adams 3
ELLIS, George David 4
ELLIS, George Edward H
ELLIS, George Edwin 4
ELLIS, 3
  George Price Sr.

ELLIS, George Washington 1
ELLIS, George William 5
ELLIS, Griffith Ogden 2
ELLIS, H. Bert 1
ELLIS, Harold Milton 2
ELLIS, Harvey 1
ELLIS, Hayne 5
ELLIS, Henry H
ELLIS, Horace 1
ELLIS, Howard 4
ELLIS, Howard 5
ELLIS, Ira Howell 4
ELLIS, J. Breckenridge 3
ELLIS, James Tandy 4
ELLIS, Job Bicknell 1
ELLIS, John Dayhuff 3
ELLIS, John Washington H
ELLIS, John Washington 4
ELLIS, John William 1
ELLIS, John Willis H
ELLIS, Leighton Arthur 4
ELLIS, Mary 1
ELLIS, Max Mapes 3
ELLIS, Milton Andrew 4
ELLIS, Overton Gentry 1
ELLIS, Perry Canby 1
ELLIS, Powhatan H
ELLIS, Ralph 3
ELLIS, Robert Walpole 1
ELLIS, Rudolph 1
ELLIS, Samuel Mervyl 2
ELLIS, Seth H. 1
ELLIS, Tharon J. 4
ELLIS, Theodore Thaddeus 1
ELLIS, Thomas Cargill Warner 4
ELLIS, Thomas David 3
ELLIS, W. R. 3
ELLIS, Wade H. 2
ELLIS, Willard Drake 2
ELLIS, William Cox H
ELLIS, William D. 4
ELLIS, William Hull 2
ELLIS, William John 2
ELLIS, William Russell 1
ELLIS, William Thomas 3
ELLISON, Andrew H
ELLISON, Everett Monroe 1
ELLISON, George Robb 3
ELLISON, Joseph Roy 5
ELLISON, Robert S(purrier) 5
ELLISON, Thomas Emmet 1
ELLISON, William Bruce 1
ELLISTON, George 2
ELLISTON, Grace 3
ELLISTON, Herbert Berridge 3
ELLITHORP, John Stafford Jr. 4
ELLMAKER, Amos H
ELLMAKER, Lee 3
ELLS, Arthur Fairbanks 4
ELLSBERRY, William Wallace H
ELLSLER, Effie 1
ELLSLER, Effie 2
ELLSWORTH, Albert LeRoy 3
ELLSWORTH, Elmer Ephriam H
ELLSWORTH, Franklin Fowler 3
ELLSWORTH, Fred Winthrop 3
ELLSWORTH, Henry Leavitt H
ELLSWORTH, James Drummond 1
ELLSWORTH, James William 1
ELLSWORTH, John Jay 5
ELLSWORTH, Lincoln 3
ELLSWORTH, Oliver H
ELLSWORTH, Oliver B. 5
ELLSWORTH, Samuel Stewart H
ELLSWORTH, Sidney Ernest 4
ELLSWORTH, William Webster 1
ELLSWORTH, William Wolcott H
ELLWANGER, George Herman 1
ELLWANGER, William De Lancey 1
ELLWOOD, Charles Abram 2
ELLWOOD, Isaac Leonard 1
ELLWOOD, John Kelley 4
ELLWOOD, Reuben H
ELLYSON, J. Taylor 1
ELMAN, Mischa 4
ELMAN, Robert 3
ELMEN, Gustaf Waldemar 3
ELMENDORF, Dwight Lathrop 1
ELMENDORF, Francis Littleton 5
ELMENDORF, Henry Livingston 1
ELMENDORF, Joachim 1
ELMENDORF, John E. Jr. 4
ELMENDORF, Lucas Conrad H
ELMENDORF, Theresa Hubbell 1
ELMER, Ebenezer H
ELMER, Henry Whiteley 1
ELMER, Herbert Charles 4
ELMER, Jonathan H
ELMER, Lucius Quintius Cincinnatus H
ELMER, S. Lewis 4
ELMER, S(amuel) Lewis 5
ELMER, William 1
ELMER, William 3
ELMER, William Price 3
ELMORE, Franklin Harper H
ELMORE, George Sutherland 3
ELMORE, Jefferson 1
ELMORE, Samuel Edward 1
ELMORE, Wilber Theodore 1
ELMQUIST, Axel Louis 2
ELMSLIE, George Grant 3
ELOFSON, Carl L. 3
ELROD, Morton John 4
ELROD, Ralph 3
ELROD, Samuel Harrison 1
ELSBERG, Charles Albert 2
ELSBERG, Louis H
ELSER, Frank B. 1
ELSER, Maximilian Jr. 4
ELSER, William James 5
ELSNER, Henry Leopold 1
ELSOM, James Claude 4
ELSON, Alfred Walter 2
ELSON, Arthur 1
ELSON, Henry William 3
ELSON, Louis Charles 1
ELSON, William Harris 1
ELSTAD, Rudolph T. 3
ELSTON, Dorothy Andrews (Mrs. Walter L. Kabis) 5
ELSTON, Isaac Compton 1
ELSTON, Isaac Compton Jr. 4
ELSTON, John Arthur 1
ELSWORTH, Edward 1
ELTHON, Leo 4
ELTING, Arthur Wells 2
ELTING, Howard 3
ELTING, Victor 3
ELTING, Winston 5
ELTINGE, Julian 1
ELTINGE, LeRoy 1
ELTON, J. O. 3
ELTON, James Samuel 1
ELTON, John Prince 2
ELTZHOLTZ, Carl Frederick 1
ELVEHJEM, Conrad Arnold 4
ELVERSON, James 1
ELVEY, Christian Thomas 5
ELVINS, Politte 2
ELWELL, Charles Clement 1
ELWELL, Francis Edwin 1
ELWELL, John Johnson H
ELWELL, Levi Henry 1
ELWOOD, John Worden 4
ELWOOD, Philip Homer Jr. 4
ELWOOD, Robert Arthur 3
ELWYN, Alfred Langdon H
ELY, Albert Heman 1
ELY, Alfred H
ELY, Charles Russell 1
ELY, Charles Wright 1
ELY, Elizabeth L. 5
ELY, Frederick David 1
ELY, Grosvenor 4
ELY, Hanson Edward 3
ELY, John H
ELY, John Hugh 1
ELY, John Slade 1
ELY, Joseph Buell 3
ELY, Lafayette G. 4
ELY, Leonard Wheeler 4
ELY, Richard R(oyal) 5
ELY, Richard Theodore 2
ELY, Robert Erskine 2
ELY, Roy J. W. 4
ELY, Sims 3
ELY, Smith 1
ELY, Sterling 4
ELY, Sumner Boyer 5
ELY, Theodore Newel 1
ELY, Wayne 3
ELY, William H
ELY, Wilson C. 3
ELZAS, Barnett Abraham 1
ELZEY, Arnold H
ELZNER, Alfred Oscar 1
EMANUEL, Victor 4
EMBER, Aaron 1
EMBLETON, Harry 3
EMBODY, George Charles 1
EMBREE, Charles Fleming 1
EMBREE, Edwin Rogers 2
EMBREE, Elihu H
EMBREE, Elisha H
EMBRIE, Jonas Reece H
EMBRY, John 4
EMBURY, Aymar II 4
EMBURY, David A. 4
EMBURY, Philip H
EMCH, Arnold 5
EMERICH, Martin 4
EMERICK, Charles Franklin 1
EMERICK, Edson James 3
EMERSON, Benjamin Kendall 1
EMERSON, Charles Franklin 1
EMERSON, Charles Phillips 1
EMERSON, Charles Wesley 1
EMERSON, Cherry Logan 4
EMERSON, Edward Randolph 1
EMERSON, Edward Waldo 1
EMERSON, Edwin 4
EMERSON, Edwin, Jr. 5
EMERSON, Ellen Russell 1
EMERSON, Evalyn (stage name, Evalyn Earle) 5
EMERSON, Frank Collins 1
EMERSON, Frank Nelson 5
EMERSON, George Barrell H
EMERSON, George H. 5
EMERSON, Gouverneur H
EMERSON, Guy 5
EMERSON, Harold Logan 4
EMERSON, Harrington 1
EMERSON, Haven 3
EMERSON, Henry Pendexter 1
EMERSON, Jabez Oscar 5
EMERSON, James Ezekiel 1
EMERSON, Jay Noble 2
EMERSON, John 3
EMERSON, Joseph H
EMERSON, Justin Edwards 4
EMERSON, Kendall 5
EMERSON, Linn 5
EMERSON, Lousis W. 4
EMERSON, Luther Orlando 1
EMERSON, Merton Leslie 2
EMERSON, Nathaniel Bright 1
EMERSON, Nathaniel Waldo 1
EMERSON, Oliver Farrar 1
EMERSON, Paul 1
EMERSON, Philip 4
EMERSON, Ralph H
EMERSON, Ralph 1
EMERSON, Ralph Waldo H
EMERSON, Robert 3
EMERSON, Robert Alton 4
EMERSON, Robert Stephen 1
EMERSON, Rollins Adams 2
EMERSON, Samuel Franklin 1
EMERSON, Summer Brooks 5
EMERSON, Susan Mabel 4
EMERSON, Willard I. 4
EMERSON, William H
EMERSON, William 3
EMERSON, Willis George 1
EMERTON, Ephraim 1
EMERTON, James H. 1
EMERY, Albert Hamilton 1
EMERY, Ambrose R. 2
EMERY, Charles Edward H
EMERY, DeWitt McKinley 3
EMERY, Edward Kellogg 1
EMERY, Fred Azro 4
EMERY, Fred Parker 1
EMERY, Grenville C. 1
EMERY, Henry Crosby 1
EMERY, Ina Capitola 1
EMERY, James Augustan 3
EMERY, John Runkle 1
EMERY, Lewis Jr. 1
EMERY, Lucilius Alonzo 1
EMERY, Matthew Gault 1
EMERY, Natt Morrill 1
EMERY, Richard Runkel 4
EMERY, Roe 3
EMERY, Sarah Anna 1
EMERY, Stephen Albert H
EMERY, Susan L. 1
EMERY, William Marshall * 4
EMERY, William Morrell 4
EMERY, William Orrin 3
EMERY, Z. Taylor 1
EMHARDT, William Chauncey 3
EMIG, Arthur S. 3
EMIG, Elmer Jacob 3
EMISON, John C. 5
EMISON, John C. 4
EMKEN, Cecil Wheeler 5
EMLAW, Harlan Stigand 3
EMMERICH, F.J. 5
EMMERICH, Herbert 5
EMMERSON, Henry Read 3
EMMERSON, Louis Lincoln 1
EMMERT, John Harley 2
EMMET, Grenville Temple 1
EMMET, John Patten H
EMMET, Lydia Field 3
EMMET, Thomas Addis H
EMMET, Thomas Addis 1
EMMET, William LeRoy 1
EMMET, William Temple 1
EMMETT, Daniel Decatur H
EMMETT, Daniel Decatur 2
EMMONS, Arthur Brewster III 4
EMMONS, Charles Demoss 1
EMMONS, Delos Carleton 4
EMMONS, Ebenezer H
EMMONS, George Foster H
EMMONS, George Thorton 2
EMMONS, Grover Carlton 2
EMMONS, Harold Hunter 4
EMMONS, Lloyd C. 3
EMMONS, Nathanael H
EMMONS, Samuel Franklin 1
EMMONS, William Harvey 2
EMORY, Frederic 1
EMORY, Frederick Lincoln 1
EMORY, John H
EMORY, Samuel T. 3
EMORY, William Hemsley H
EMORY, William Hermsley 1
EMOTT, James * H
EMPEY, Arthur Guy 4
EMPRINGHAM, James 5
EMRICH, Frederick Ernest 1
EMRICH, Jeannette Wallace 2
EMSWELLER, Samuel Leonar 5
ENANDER, John Alfred 1
ENCKELL, Carl J. A. 3
ENDALKATCHOU, Bitwoded Makonnen 4
ENDECOTT, John H
ENDELMAN, Julio 2
ENDERS, George Christian 4
ENDERS, Howard Edwin 5
ENDERS, John Ostrom 3
ENDICOTT, Charles Moses H
ENDICOTT, George H
ENDICOTT, H. Wendell 3
ENDICOTT, Henry 1
ENDICOTT, Mordecal Thomas 1
ENDICOTT, William H
ENDICOTT, William 1
ENDICOTT, William Crowninshield * 1
ENDLICH, Gustav Adolf 1
ENDORE, Samuel) Guy 5
ENELOW, Heman Gerson 1
ENESCO, Georges 3
ENFIELD, Gertrude Dixon (Mrs. John Enfield) 5
ENGBERG, Carl Christian 1
ENGEL, Albert Joseph 3
ENGEL, Carl 2
ENGEL, Carl Henry 5
ENGEL, Edward J. 2
ENGEL, K. August 4
ENGEL, Katharine Asher 3
ENGEL, Michael Martin 5
ENGEL, Peter 1
ENGELHARDT, Francis Ernest 4
ENGELHARDT, Fred 2
ENGELHARDT, Nickolaus Louis 3
ENGELHARDT, Zephyrin 1
ENGELKEMEIR, Donald William 5
ENGELMANN, George H
ENGELMANN, George Julius 1
ENGEN, Hans Kristian 4
ENGER, Melvin Lorenius 3
ENGERRAND, George C. 4
ENGERUD, Edward 1
ENGLAND, Edward Theodore 5
ENGLAND, George Allan 1
ENGLAND, John H
ENGLAND, William Henry 5
ENGLAR, D. Roger 3
ENGLE, Clair 4
ENGLE, Earl T. 3
ENGLE, Jesse A. 4
ENGLE, John Summerfield 5
ENGLE, Wilbur Dwight 5
ENGLEBRIGHT, Harry Lane 2
ENGLEBRIGHT, William F. 4
ENGLEHARD, Charles William 5
ENGLEHART, Robert William 4
ENGLEMAN, James Ozro 2
ENGLER, Edmund Arthur 1
ENGLIS, Charles Mortimer 1
ENGLIS, John H
ENGLISH, Charles Henry 2
ENGLISH, Conover 4
ENGLISH, David Combs 1
ENGLISH, Earle Walter 4
ENGLISH, Elbert Hartwell H
ENGLISH, Frank A. 3
ENGLISH, Frank Clare 5
ENGLISH, George Bethune H
ENGLISH, George Letchworth 2
ENGLISH, George Washington 4
ENGLISH, Harry David Williams 1
ENGLISH, Horace Bidwell 4
ENGLISH, James Edward H
ENGLISH, John Francis 5
ENGLISH, John Mahan 1
ENGLISH, Merle Neville 2
ENGLISH, Robert Byrns 3
ENGLISH, Robert Henry 2
ENGLISH, Sara John (Mrs. Henry W. English) 5
ENGLISH, Thomas Dunn 1
ENGLISH, Virgil P. 4
ENGLISH, William Eastin 1
ENGLISH, William Hayden H
ENGMAN, Martin Feeney 3
ENGSTROM, Howard Theodore 4
ENGSTROM, Sigfrid Emanuel 3
ENLOE, Benjamin Augustine 1
ENLOW, Robert Cooke 4
ENMAN, Horace Luttrell 4
ENNEKING, John Joseph 1
ENNIS, Alfred 4
ENNIS, George Pearse 1
ENNIS, H. Robert 2
ENNIS, Joseph 3
ENNIS, Luna May 1
ENNIS, Thomas Leland 3
ENNIS, William Duane 2
ENO, William Phelps 2

ENOCHS, 5
Herbert Alexander
ENOCHS, William Henry H
ENOS, George M. 3
ENRIGHT, Earl F.
ENRIGHT, Elizabeth 5
ENRIGHT, 3
Richard Edward
ENRIGHT, 5
Walter J(oseph)
ENSEY, Lot 5
ENSIGN, Forest Chester 5
ENSIGN, Josiah Davis 1
ENSIGN, Orville Hiram 1
ENSLEN, Eugene F. 2
ENSLEY, Enoch H
ENSLOW, Linn Harrison 3
ENSOR, James 4
ENSTROM, William N. 2
ENT, Uzal Girard
ENTRATTER, Jack 5
ENTRIKIN, John Bennett 4
ENTWISTLE, James
ENWALL, Hasse Octavius 2
EPES, Louis Spencer 1
EPES, Sydney P.
EPLER, Percy H(arold) 5
EPLEY, Lloyd L. 5
EPP, George Edward 5
EPPES, John Wayles H
EPPLEY, Eugene C. 2
EPSTEIN, Abraham 3
EPSTEIN, Henry 4
EPSTEIN, Jacob 2
EPSTEIN, Jacob 3
EPSTEIN, Joseph Hugo 4
EPSTEIN, Louis M. 2
EPSTEIN, Max 3
EPSTEIN, Paul Sophus 4
EPSTEIN, Ralph C. 3
EQUEN, Murdock 4
ERB, Carl Lee, Jr. 5
ERB, Donald Milton 2
ERB, Frank Otis 3
ERB, John Lawrence 2
ERB, John Warren 3
ERB, Newman 1
ERBEN, 3
Henry Vander Bogert
ERBES, Philip Henry 5
ERDLAND,
Bernard August
ERDMAN, 4
Charles Rosenbury
ERDMAN, 5
Frederick Seward
ERDMAN, Jacob H
ERDMAN, John Frederic 3
ERDMANN, 4
Charles Albert
ERDMANN, 4
William Lawrence
ERHARDT, Joel Benedict 5
ERHARDT, John George 3
ERICHSEN, Hugo 2
ERICKSON,
Alfred William
ERICKSON, Clifford E. 4
ERICKSON, Cyrus 5
ERICKSON, Frank
Morton 3
ERICKSON, 5
J(ulius) L(yman) E(dward)
ERICKSON, John E. 2
ERICKSON, Knut Eric 4
ERICKSON, Reinhart H
ERICSON, 1
Charles John Alfred
ERICSON, John Ernst 1
ERICSSON, Frans August 3
ERICSSON, John H
ERICSSON, Leif H
ERIC THE RED
ERIKSON, Carl Anthony 4
ERIKSON, David Junkin 4
ERIKSON, Henry Anton 3
ERIKSSON, 1
Erik McKinley
ERIKSSON, Herman 2
ERK, Edmund Frederick 3
ERLANGER,
Abraham Lincoln
ERLANGER, Joseph 4
ERLANGER, Milton S. 5
ERLANGER, 1
Mitchell Louis
ERMATINGER, Francis H
ERMENTROUT, Daniel 1
ERMINGER, 3
Howell B. Jr.
ERN, Henri 4
ERNEST, Albert 4
ERNSBERGER,
Millard Clayton
ERNST, Alwin Charles 2
ERNST, August Frederic 3

ERNST, 1
Bernard Morris Lee
ERNST, Carl Clark 4
ERNST, Carl Wilhelm 4
ERNST, Clayton Holt 2
ERNST, Edward Cranch 2
ERNST, Edwin Charles 1
ERNST, Fritz B. 3
ERNST, 1
George Alexander Otis
ERNST, Harold Clarence 1
ERNST, Henry 1
ERNST, Oswald Herbert 1
ERNST, Richard Pretlow 1
ERNSTENE, 5
Arthur Carlton
ERNY, Charles G. 4
ERPF, Armand Grover· 2
ERRETT, Edwin Reader 5
ERRETT, Isaac H
ERRETT, Russell 3
ERSKINE, Albert Russel 1
ERSKINE, Ebenezer 1
ERSKINE, Emma Payne 1
ERSKINE, Howard Major 1
ERSKINE, John H
ERSKINE, John 3
ERSKINE, Robert 1
ERTEGUN, Mehmet
Munir 2
ERTZ, R. B. A. Edward 4
ERVIN, Charles Edwin 2
ERVIN, James H
ERVIN, James S. 1
ERVIN, Jee W. 2
ERVIN, 3
Morris Donaldson
ERVIN, Robert Tait 4
ERVINE, St. John Greer 5
ERVING, George William H
ERVING, Henry Wood 4
ERVING, William Gage 1
ERWAY, Richard Eugene 5
ERWIN, Claude Mayo 5
ERWIN, Clyde Atkinson 3
ERWIN, George L. Jr. 3
ERWIN, Guy Burton 5
ERWIN, Henry Parsons 3
ERWIN, Howell Cobb 5
ERWIN, 1
James Brailsford
ERWIN, Marion Corbett 3
ERWIN, Richard Kenney 1
ERWIN, 3
Robert Gallaudet
ESAREY, Logan 5
ESBERG, Milton Herman 1
ESBJORN, Lars Paul 4
ESCALANTE, Diogenes 4
ESCALANTE, H
Silvestre Velez 'de
ESCH, John Jacob 1
ESCHER, Franklin 1
ESCHWEILER, 1
Franz Chadbourne
ESCOBAR, Adrian C. 3
ESCOBOSA, Hector 4
ESENWEIN, Joseph Berg 1
ESHBACH, Ovid Wallace 4
ESHELMAN, 5
Walter Witmer
ESHKOL, Shkolnik) Levi 5
ESHLEMAN, Fred
Koontz 4
ESHLEMAN, John
Morton 1
ESHNER, 3
Augustus Adolph
ESKEW, 5
Samuel W(illiams)
ESKILDSEN, 4
Clarence Raymond
ESKOLA, Pentti Eelis 4
ESKRIDGE, J. T. 5
ESKRIDGE,
James Burnette
ESLICK, Edward Everett 1
ESLING, 1
Charles Henry Augustine
ESMAY, Rhodolph Leslie 4
ESPEJO, Antonio 'de H
ESPENSHADE,
Abraham Howry
ESPIL, Felipe A. 5
ESPINA, Concha 3
ESPINOSA,
Aurelio Macedonio
ESPINOSA DE 3
LOS MONTEROS, Antonio
ESPINOSA Y SAN 5
MARTIN, Antonio
ESPOSITO, 5
Vincent Joseph
ESPOSITO, 4
Vincent Joseph
ESPY, James Pollard H
ESQUIROL, John Henry 4

ESS, Henry N. 4
ESSARY, 2
Jesse Frederick
ESSELEN, Gustavus John 1
ESSER, Sigurd Emanuel 5
ESSERY, Carl Vanstone 4
ESSEX, William Leopold 3
ESSIG, 5
Benjamin C(lark)
ESSIG, Edward Oliver 4
ESSINGTON, 4
Thurlow Gault
ESTABROOK, Arthur F. 1
ESTABROOK, Experience H
ESTABROOK, Fred
Watson 1
ESTABROOK, Henry
Dodge 1
ESTABROOK, John D. 5
ESTABROOK, Joseph H
ESTABROOK, Leon
Moyer 1
ESTABROOK, 3
Merrick Gay Jr.
ESTAING, H
Charles Hector
ESTAUGH, H
Elizabeth Haddon
ESTBERG, Edward Robert 2
ESTEE, James Borden 1
ESTEE, Morris M. 1
ESTENSON, Lyle Osbern 5
ESTEP, Preston 5
ESTERBROOK, Richard H
ESTERLINE, Blackburn 1
ESTERLY, Calvin Olin 2
ESTERLY, George H
ESTERLY, Henry Minor 5
ESTERQUEST, 5
Ralph Theodore
ESTERS, Bernard E. 4
ESTERS,
Charles Thompson
ESTES, Dana 1
ESTES, David Foster 1
ESTES, George Henson 5
ESTES, Ludwell H. 4
ESTES, 1
Webster Cummings
ESTES,
William Lawrence
ESTES, William Lee 1
ESTEY, Alexander R. 1
ESTEY, Jacob H
ESTEY, James Arthur 4
ESTEY, Stephen Sewall 1
ESTIGARRIBIA, 2
Jose Felix
ESTIL, Benjamin H
ESTILL, 3
George Castleman
ESTILL, 2
Harry Fishburne
ESTILL, John Holbrook 1
ESTOPINAL, Albert 1
ESTREM, Thomas Sabin 4
ESTY, Edward Tuckerman 2
ESTY, William 1
ESTY, William Cole 1
ESTY, William Cole III 3
ETCHEVERRY, 3
Bernard Alfred
ETCHISON, 3
Page McKendree
ETHEL, Agnes H
ETHEREDGE, 5
M(ahion) P(adgett)
ETHERIDGE, Emerson 1
ETHRIDGE, 1
Willam Nathaniel, Jr.
ETS-HOKIN, Louis 5
ETTER, William Kirby 2
ETTINGER, 2
George Taylor
ETTINGER,
Richard Prentice
ETTINGER, William L. 2
ETTWEIN, John H
ETZ, Roger Frederick 3
EUBANK, Earle Edward 2
EUBANK, Jessie Burrall 4
EUBANK, John Augustine 3
EUBANK, Victor 4
EUBANKS, Sam B. 4
EULER, William D. 3
EULER,
William Gilman Badger
EUMENES H
EUSDEN, Ray Anderson 5
EUSTACE,
Bartholomew Joseph
EUSTIS, Arthur Galen 3
EUSTIS, 5
Augustus Hemenway
EUSTIS, 5
Frederic Augustus
EUSTIS, George * H

EUSTIS, Henry Lawrence H
EUSTIS, James 1
EUSTIS, James Biddle H
EUSTIS, John Edward 1
EUSTIS, Percy Sprague 4
EUSTIS, William H
EUSTIS, William H. 1
EUWER, 5
Anthony Henderson
EVALD, Emmy 2
EVANS, Alexander H
EVANS, 3
Alexander William
EVANS, Allan 5
EVANS, Alvin 1
EVANS, Alvin Eleazer 3
EVANS, Andrew Wallace 4
EVANS, 2
Anthony Harrison
EVANS, H
Anthony Walton Whyte
EVANS, Arthur Grant 1
EVANS, Arthur Maybury 4
EVANS, Arthur Thompson 2
EVANS, 1
Aurelius Augustus
EVANS, 4
Austin Patterson
EVANS, Beverly Daniel 1
EVANS, Britton Duroc 1
EVANS, Cadwallader Jr. 4
EVANS, Charles 4
EVANS, Charles 4
EVANS, 4
Charles Napoleon
EVANS, Charles Robley 1
EVANS, 1
Charles Rountree
EVANS, Clement Anselm 1
EVANS, Clinton Buswell 1
EVANS, Curtis Alban 5
EVANS, Dafydd Joshua 1
EVANS, Daniel 1
EVANS, Daniel Henry 4
EVANS, David Ellicott H
EVANS, David Reid 1
EVANS, De Scott 4
EVANS, Donald 1
EVANS, Donald 3
EVANS, Dudley 1
EVANS, Earle Wood 1
EVANS, Edgar Hanks 3
EVANS, Edith Brazwell 1
EVANS, Edward 1
EVANS, Edward Andrew 4
EVANS, Edward Baker 4
EVANS, Edward Benjamin 5
EVANS, Edward Payson 2
EVANS, Edward Steptoe 2
EVANS, Elizabeth Edson 1
EVANS, 4
Elizabeth Gardiner
EVANS, Elwyn 2
EVANS, Ernestine 4
EVANS, Evan Alfred 2
EVANS, Everett Idris 3
EVANS, Frank 1
EVANS, Frank Edgar 2
EVANS, 5
Fred(eric) M(aurice)
EVANS, Frederic Dahl 1
EVANS, Frederick 4
EVANS, Frederick Noble 1
EVANS, H
Frederick William
EVANS, George 4
EVANS, George 1
EVANS,
George Ballentine
EVANS, George E. 2
EVANS, George Edward 1
EVANS, George Henry H
EVANS, George Watkin 3
EVANS, H. Clay 1
EVANS, H(enry) David 5
EVANS, Harold Sulser 3
EVANS, Harry Carroll 1
EVANS, Harry G. 1
EVANS, Henry 1
EVANS, Henry Clay 1
EVANS, Henry Ridgely 2
EVANS, Herbert Francis 4
EVANS, Herbert P. 3
EVANS, Hiram Kinsman 1
EVANS, Howard Rector 4
EVANS, Howell Gershom 4
EVANS, Hugh Ivan 4
EVANS, Ira Hobart 1
EVANS, Isaac Blair 3
EVANS, James 1
EVANS, Jervice Gaylord 1
EVANS, Jessie Benton 5
EVANS, John * H
EVANS, John 1
EVANS, John Brooke 3
EVANS, John C. 3
EVANS, John Fairhurst 5

EVANS, John Gary 2
EVANS, John Morgan 4
EVANS, John Morris 2
EVANS, John Norris 3
EVANS, John William 2
EVANS, Joseph E(arly) 5
EVANS, Joseph Spragg 2
EVANS, Joshua, Jr. 5
EVANS, Joshua Jr. H
EVANS, Josiah James H
EVANS, Lawrence Boyd 1
EVANS, Lawton Bryan 1
EVANS, Lemuel Dale H
EVANS, Letitia Pate 3
EVANS, Lewis Orvis 1
EVANS, Marcellus Hugh 3
EVANS, 5
Marshall Blakemore
EVANS, Mary 4
EVANS, Milton G. 1
EVANS, Montgomery 4
EVANS, Nathan H
EVANS, Nelson Wiley 1
EVANS, Newton Gurdon 2
EVANS, Oliver H
EVANS, Percy Henriques 5
EVANS, Peyton Randolph 5
EVANS, Ray O. 3
EVANS, Richard Bunton 4
EVANS, Richard Joseph 3
EVANS, Richard Louis 5
EVANS, Robert Emory 1
EVANS, Robert Kennon 1
EVANS, Robert T. 4
EVANS, 1
Robley Dunglison
EVANS, Rudolph Martin 3
EVANS, Rudulph 3
EVANS, Silas 3
EVANS, Silliman 3
EVANS, Silliman Jr. 4
EVANS, Thomas H
EVANS, Thomas 3
EVANS, Thomas Crain 1
EVANS, Walter 3
EVANS, Walter Chew 4
EVANS, Walter Harrison 5
EVANS, Walter Howard 3
EVANS, Ward Vinton 4
EVANS, William 3
EVANS, 2
William Augustus
EVANS, William D. 1
EVANS, 5
William Dent, Jr.
EVANS, William E. 3
EVANS, William Frank 1
EVANS, William Gray 3
EVANS, William John 1
EVANS, William Lloyd 3
EVANS,
William Prentice
EVANS, Wilmot Roby 1
EVARTS, Allen Wardner 1
EVARTS, Edward Mark 1
EVARTS, Hal G. 1
EVARTS, Maxwell 1
EVARTS, 5
Richard Conover
EVARTS, 1
William Maxwell
EVATT, Herbert V. 4
EVATT,
William Steinwedell
EVE, Duncan 4
EVE, Henry Prontaut 5
EVE, Joseph H
EVE, Paul Fitzsimons H
EVELAND, Samuel S. 1
EVELAND, William Perry 1
EVELEIGH, Nicholas H
EVELETH, 5
True Ballentine
EVELYN, Judith 4
EVELYN, Sister Mary 3
EVENDEN, Edward
Samuel 1
EVERARD, Lewis Charles 2
EVERENDON, Walter H
EVEREST, David Clark 3
EVEREST, Frank Fort 1
EVEREST, Harold Philip 4
EVERETT, H
Alexander Hill
EVERETT, Arthur Greene 1
EVERETT, 3
Charles Carroll
EVERETT,
Charles Horatio
EVERETT, Edward H
EVERETT, George Abram 3
EVERETT, Harry Harding 3
EVERETT, Henry A. 1
EVERETT, H
Herbert Edward
EVERETT, Horace H
EVERETT, Howard 4

EVERETT, 4
Louellea Dorothea
EVERETT, Robert Ashton 5
EVERETT, 2
Sidney Johnston
EVERETT, 1
Walter Goodnow
EVERETT, William
EVERETT, William Henry 1
EVERETT, William Wade
EVERETT, Willis Mead 2
EVERGOOD, 5
Philip (Howard Francis Dixon)
EVERHART,
Benjamin Matlack
EVERHART, James
Bowen H
EVERHART, 3
Mahlon Thatcher
EVERHART, William H
EVERILL, 5
Royal Burdette
EVERIT,
Edward Hotchkiss
EVERITT, 2
Charles Raymond
EVERITT, George Bain 1
EVERMANN,
Barton Warren
EVERSMAN, Walter A.
EVERSON, 3
William Graham
EVERSULL, 4
Frank Lissenden
EVERSULL, Harry Kelso 3
EVERSZ, Moritz Ernst 4
EVERTS, Orpheus 1
EVERWIJN, 5
Jan Charles August
EVINS, John Hamilton H
EVINS, Robert Benson 1
EVJEN, John Oluf 5
EVJUE, 5
William Theodore
EVVARD, John Marcus 2
EWALD, Henry Theodore 3
EWART, Frank Carman 2
EWART, Hamilton Glover 1
EWART, J. Kaye 3
EWBANK, Henry Lee 4
EWBANK, Louis B. 5
EWBANK, Thomas H
EWELL, Arthur Woolsey 5
EWELL, Elliott Gordon 4
EWELL, Ervin Edgar 1
EWELL, James H
EWELL, Marshall Davis 1
EWELL, H
Richard Stoddert
EWEN, Edward C. 1
EWEN, John Meigss 5
EWEN, Melvin M. 4
EWEN, W. C. 3
EWER, Bernard Capen 5
EWER, H
Ferdinand Cartwright
EWER, Warren Baxter
EWERS, Ezra Philetus 1
EWERS, John Ray 5
EWING, Alonzo B(yron) 5
EWING, Andrew H
EWING, Arthur Eugene 1
EWING, Arthur Henry 1
EWING, Charles * H
EWING, Charles H. 1
EWING, Cortez A. M. 4
EWING, David L. 1
EWING, Emma Pike 2
EWING, Fayette Clay 3
EWING, Finis H
EWING, Henry Ellsworth 3
EWING, Hugh Boyle 2
EWING, James H
EWING, James 2
EWING, 1
James Caruthers Rhea
EWING, James Dunlop 4
EWING, James Stevenson 1
EWING, John * H
EWING, John 1
EWING, John Dunbrack 3
EWING, John Gillespie 4
EWING, John Hoge H
EWING, John Thomas 1
EWING, Lynn Moore 3
EWING, Majl 4
EWING, Nathaniel 1
EWING, Philemon H
EWING,
Presley Kittredge
EWING,
Presley Underwood
EWING, Robert 1
EWING, Robert Legan 1
EWING, Russell Charles 5
EWING, Samuel Edgar 2

EWING, Thomas * H
EWING, Thomas 2
EWING, William 3
EWING, William 4
EWING, William F. C. 4
EWING, H
William Lee Davidson
EWOLDT, Harold Boaden 5
EXALL, Henry 1
EXCELL, Edwin Othello
EXLINE, Frank 4
EXNER, Max Joseph 1
EXTON, James Anderson 4
EXTON, William Gustav 2
EYANSON, Charles Louis 4
EYCLESHYMER, 1
Albert Chauncey
EYERLY, Elmer Kendall 4
EYERLY, James Bryan 4
EYERMAN, John 4
EYMAN, Frank P. 4
EYMAN, Henry C. 1
EYRE, Laurence 3
EYRE, Wilson 4
EYRING, Carl Ferdinand 3
EYSMANS, Julien L. 5
EYSTER, George Senseny 3
EYSTER, 4
Nellie Blessing
EYSTER, William Henry 5
EYTINGE, Rose 1
EZEKIEL, Moses 1
EZEKIEL,
Walter Naphtali
EZELL, B. F. 4

F

FABENS, Joseph Warren H
FABER, Eberhard 2
FABER, John Eberhard H
FABER, John Lewis 5
FABER, Lothar W. 1
FABER,
William Frederic
FABIAN, Simon H. 5
FABIANI, Aurelio 5
FABING, Howard Douglas 5
FABRICIAN, 4
Rev. Brother
FABYAN, George 1
FACCIOLI, Giuseppe 4
FACKENTHAL,
Benjamin Franklin Jr.
FACKENTHAL, 5
Frank Diehl
FACKLER, David Parks 1
FACKLER, 3
Edward Bathurst
FADDIS, Charles I. 5
FAELTEN, Carl 1
FAELTEN, Reinhold 1
FAESCH, John Jacob H
FAESI, Robert 5
FAGAN, 1
Charles Aloysius
FAGAN, James Fleming H
FAGAN, James J. 1
FAGAN, James Octavius 4
FAGAN, William Long H
FAGERBURG, Dewey 4
Frank
FAGERGREN, Fred C. 5
FAGES, Pedro H
FAGET, Guy Henry 2
FAGET, Jean Charles H
FAGG, John Gerardus 1
FAGGI, Alfeo 4
FAGIN, N. Bryllion 5
FAGLEY, 3
Frederick Louis
FAGNANI, 1
Charles Prospero
FAHEY, John H. 3
FAHNESTOCK, 1
Harris Charles
FAHNESTOCK,
James Frederick
FAHNESTOCK, 5
James Murray
FAHNESTOCK,
Karol James
FAHNESTOCK, William 1
FAHNESTOCK, 3
Zephine Huphrey
FAHS, David Wesley
FAIG, John Theodore 3
FAIGLE, Eric H. 4
FAILLA, Gioacchino 4
FAILOR, Isaac Newton 1
FAINSOD, Merle 5
FAIR, Eugene 4
FAIR, Gordon Maskew 5
FAIR, H. H. 4
FAIR, James Graham H
FAIRBAIRN, 1
Henry Arnold

FAIRBANK, Alfred 2
FAIRBANK, Arthur Boyce 1
FAIRBANK, Calvin H
FAIRBANK, 4
Herbert Sinclair
FAIRBANK, Janet Ayer 3
FAIRBANK, Kellogg 1
FAIRBANK, Leigh Cole 4
FAIRBANKS, Arthur 2
FAIRBANKS,
Charles Warren
FAIRBANKS, 1
Cornelia Cole
FAIRBANKS, Douglas 1
FAIRBANKS, 1
Edward Taylor
FAIRBANKS, Erastus H
FAIRBANKS, 1
Frank Perley
FAIRBANKS, 1
Frederick Cole
FAIRBANKS, 4
George Rainsford
FAIRBANKS, 4
Harold Wellman
FAIRBANKS, Henry 1
FAIRBANKS, John Leo 2
FAIRBANKS, Richard 2
FAIRBANKS, Thaddeus H
FAIRBANKS, 1
Warren Charles
FAIRBURN, 2
William Armstrong
FAIRCHILD, 3
Arthur Wilson
FAIRCHILD, 2
Benjamin Lewis
FAIRCHILD, 1
Charles Stebbins
FAIRCHILD, Clarence A. 5
FAIRCHILD, David 3
FAIRCHILD, 1
David Sturges
FAIRCHILD, 1
Edward Thomson
FAIRCHILD, Fred Rogers 4
FAIRCHILD, 1
George Thompson
FAIRCHILD, 1
George Winthrop
FAIRCHILD, Henry Pratt 3
FAIRCHILD, 4
Herman Le Roy
FAIRCHILD, 1
James Harris
FAIRCHILD, 4
Joseph Schmitz
FAIRCHILD, Julian D. 1
FAIRCHILD, Lucius H
FAIRCHILD, Milton 1
FAIRCHILD, 2
Muir Stephen
FAIRCHILD, 3
Raymond Wilber
FAIRCHILD, 1
Salome Cutler
FAIRCHILD, Sherman M. 5
FAIRCHILD, 1
Thomas Everett
FAIRCLOTH, James M. 4
FAIRCLOTH, 1
William Tyson
FAIRCLOUGH,
George Herbert
FAIRCLOUGH, 1
Henry Rushton
FAIRFAX, Albert Kirby 5
FAIRFAX, Thomas H
FAIRFAX, 2
Donald McNeill
FAIRFIELD,
Arthur Philip
FAIRFIELD, 1
Edward George
FAIRFIELD, John H
FAIRFIELD, Louis W. 1
FAIRFIELD, H
Sumner Lincoln
FAIRFIELD, Wynn
Cowan
FAIRHURST, William 3
FAIRLAMB, 1
James Remington
FAIRLEIGH,
David William
FAIRLESS, Benjamin F. 4
FAIRLEY, Edwin 1
FAIRLEY, William 1
FAIRLIE,
John Archibald
FAIRMAN, F. E. Jr. 3
FAIRMAN, Gideon H
FAIRMAN, James 4
FAIRMAN,
James Ferdinand
FAIRMAN, Seibert 4

FAIRWEATHER, 3
Clement Wilson
FAIRWEATHER, 2
Jack Hall Alliger Lee
FAISAL II, 3
King of Iraq
FAISON, John Miller 1
FAISON, Samson Lane 1
FAITHORN, 1
John Nicholson
FAKE, Guy Leverne 3
FALCK, Alexander Diven 3
FALCKNER, Daniel H
FALCKNER, Justus H
FALCONER, 5
Douglas Platt
FALCONER, 5
Jacob Alexander
FALCONER, 1
John Ironside
FALCONER, 4
John Ironside
FALCONER, John Mackie 1
FALCONER, 1
Robert Clemons
FALCONER, 1
William Armistead
FALCONIO, Diomede 1
FALES, De Coursey 4
FALES, 3
Frederick Sayward
FALES, Herbert Peck 5
FALES, Jonathan Cilley 3
FALES, 5
Winnifred (Shaw)
FALK, Harold Sands 3
FALK, K. George 3
FALK, Louis 1
FALK, Maurice 2
FALK, Myron Samuel 2
FALK, Otto Herbert 1
FALK, Ralph 4
FALK, Sawyer 4
FALKNER,
Jefferson Manly
FALKNER, Roland Post 1
FALL, Albert Bacon 2
FALL, Bernard B. 4
FALL, Charles Gershom 1
FALL, 1
Clifford Pervines
FALL, Delos 1
FALL, Frank Andrews 3
FALL, Gilbert Haven 3
FALL, Henry Clinton 1
FALLEY, 4
George Frederick
FALLIGANT, Robert 1
FALLIS, 3
Iva Campbell Doyle
FALLON, Bernard Joseph 3
FALLON, 5
Lester (Raymond)
FALLOWS, 1
Alice Katharine
FALLOWS, 1
Edward Huntington
FALLOWS, Samuel 1
FALLS, Charles Buckles 3
FALLS, Charles Buckles 4
FALLS, DeWitt Clinton 1
FALLS, Raymond Leonard 3
FALSEY, William J. 1
FALVEY, Daniel Patrick 4
FALVEY, Timothy J. 2
FALVEY, Wallace
FANCHER, Bertram Hull 1
FANCHER, Elvadore R. 1
FANCHER, 4
Frederick Bartlett
FANCIULLI, Francesco 1
FANE, Frances Gordon 4
FANER, Robert Dunn 5
FANEUIL, Peter H
FANNIN, James Walker H
FANNING, 1
Alexander Campbell Wilder
FANNING, Cecil 1
FANNING, David H
FANNING, Edmund * H
FANNING, John Thomas 1
FANNING, 5
Lawrence Stanley
FANNING, Nathaniel H
FANNING, Ralph 5
FANNING, Tolbert H
FANSLER, Michael Louis 4
FANT, John Clayton 1
FANT, Lester Glenn 2
FARABEE, Samuel
Howard 1
FARABEE, 1
William Curtis
FARAGHER, 5
Donald Qualtrough
FARAGHER, Warren
Fred 4

FARAN, James John H
FARBER, John Clarke 5
FARBER, Sidney 5
FARBER, William Sims 4
FARENHOLT, Ammen 5
FARENHOLT, 1
Oscar Walter
FARGO, Charles 1
FARGO, James Congdel 1
FARGO, William George H
FARIBAULT, H
Jean Baptist
FARIS, Barry 4
FARIS,
Charles Breckenridge
FARIS, Ellsworth 3
FARIS,
George Washington
FARIS, Herman Preston 1
FARIS, James Edge 2
FARIS, John Thomson 2
FARIS, Paul Patton 5
FARIS, Robert Lee 1
FARISH,
Frederick Garesche
FARISH,
Hunter Dickinson
FARISH, William Stamps 1
FARLEE, Isaac Gray H
FARLEY, Edward Philip 3
FARLEY, Eliot
FARLEY, Ephraim Wilder H
FARLEY, Frank Edgar 1
FARLEY, Franklin 5
FARLEY, 4
Frederic Henry Morton
Stanley
FARLEY, Hugh D. 5
FARLEY, J. W. 3
FARLEY, James I. 2
FARLEY, James
Thompson
FARLEY, John Murphy 1
FARLEY, Joseph Pearson 1
FARLEY, Michael F. 1
FARLEY,
Richard Blossom
FARLEY, Robert E. 1
FARLIN, Dudley H
FARLOW, Alfred
FARLOW, Arthur Clark 4
FARLOW, William Gilson 1
FARMAN, Elbert Ell H
FARMER,
Arthur Lafayette
FARMER, 3
Chester Jefferson
FARMER, Clyde F. 5
FARMER, Donald Francis 5
FARMER, Edward
FARMER, Edward
McNeil
FARMER, F. Malcolm 5
FARMER, Fannie Merritt 1
FARMER, Ferdinand
FARMER, Garland Sr. 5
FARMER, Gene 4
FARMER, Harry
FARMER, James Eugene 4
FARMER, John * 1
FARMER, Leslie P.
FARMER, Lydia Hoyt
FARMER, Moses Gerrish 1
FARMER, S. J.
FARMER, Sarah Jane 4
FARMER, Silas
FARMER, Thomas Harris H
FARMER, William Burton H
FARMER, William M.
FARNAM, Henry H
FARNAM, Henry Walcott 4
FARNAM, Ruth Stanley 1
FARNAM,
William Whitman
FARNDON, Walter 5
FARNELL,
Frederic James
FARNESS, 5
Orin Jocevious
FARNHAM,
Charles Chittenden
FARNHAM,
Charles Haight
FARNHAM, Charles
Wells
FARNHAM,
Dwight Thompson
FARNHAM, Edwin
Pickett
FARNHAM, 4
Eliza Woodson Burnhans
FARNHAM, Mateel Howe 1
FARNHAM, Robert
FARNHAM, Roswell 1

FARNHAM, Russel — H
FARNHAM, Sally James — 2
FARNHAM, Thomas Jefferson — H
FARNSWORTH, Charles Hubert — 2
FARNSWORTH, Charles Stewart — 3
FARNSWORTH, Elon John — H
FARNSWORTH, Frederick Eugene — 1
FARNSWORTH, George Low — 4
FARNSWORTH, Joseph Eastman — 4
FARNSWORTH, Louis Henderson — 1
FARNSWORTH, Philo Judson — 4
FARNSWORTH, Philo Taylor — 5
FARNSWORTH, Ray D. — 4
FARNSWORTH, Sidney Woods — 5
FARNSWORTH, Wilson Amos — 1
FARNUM, Dustin — 1
FARNUM, George Rossiter — 5
FARNUM, Loring Nelson — 1
FARNY, Henry F. — 1
FAROUK, I. — 4
FARQUHAR, Arthur B. — 1
FARQUHAR, Edward — 1
FARQUHAR, Henry — 1
FARQUHAR, John Hanson — H
FARQUHAR, John McCreath — 1
FARQUHAR, Norman 'von Heldreich — 1
FARQUHAR, Samuel Thaxter — 3
FARQUHAR, Silas Edgar — 2
FARQUHAR, Thomas Lippincott — 5
FARQUHARSON, James — 3
FARR, Albert George — 1
FARR, Clifford Bailey — 5
FARR, Evarts Worcester — H
FARR, Finis King — 1
FARR, Frederic William — 4
FARR, Harry Willson — 4
FARR, Henry Bartow — 5
FARR, Hilda Butler — 5
FARR, John Richard — 1
FARR, Marcus Stults — 5
FARR, Newton Camp — 4
FARR, T. J. — 4
FARRAGUT, David Glasgow — H
FARRAGUT, George — H
FARRAGUT, Loyall — 4
FARRAH, Albert John — 2
FARRAH, Clarence B. — 5
FARRAND, Beatrix
FARRAND, George E. — 3
FARRAND, Livingston — 1
FARRAND, Max — 1
FARRAND, Wilson — 1
FARRAND, Wilson
FARRAR, Clarence B. — 5
FARRAR, Edgar Howard
FARRAR, Fred — 5
FARRAR, Geraldine — 4
FARRAR, Gilbert Powderly — 3
FARRAR, James McNail — 1
FARRAR, John — H
FARRAR, Roy Montgomery — 2
FARRAR, Thomas James — 5
FARRAR, Timothy — H
FARRAR, William Edmund
FARRELL, Benjamin Peter — 2
FARRELL, Charles LeRoy — 1
FARRELL, Gabriel — 5
FARRELL, Glenda — 5
FARRELL, Henry Edward — 4
FARRELL, J. Fletcher — 1
FARRELL, James Augustine — 2
FARRELL, James Charles — 1
FARRELL, John D. — 4
FARRELL, John J. — 5
FARRELL, Joseph D. — 5
FARRELL, Patrick Joseph Hoshie — 5
FARRELL, Thomas Francis — 4
FARRELL, William Elliston — 2
FARRELLY, John P. — 1
FARRELLY, John Wilson — H

FARRELLY, Patrick — H
FARREN, George P. — H
FARREN, Marie Ann Russell — H
FARRER, Henry — 1
FARRINGTON, Carl Coleman — 5
FARRINGTON, Donald H. — 4
FARRINGTON, Edward Holyoke — 1
FARRINGTON, Edward Irving — 5
FARRINGTON, Edward Silsby — 1
FARRINGTON, Ernest Albert — 1
FARRINGTON, Frank — 4
FARRINGTON, Frank George — 1
FARRINGTON, Frederic Ernest — 1
FARRINGTON, Harold P. — 4
FARRINGTON, Harry Webb — 1
FARRINGTON, Isabelle Scudder (Mrs. F. E. Farrington) — 5
FARRINGTON, James — H
FARRINGTON, John D. — 4
FARRINGTON, Joseph Rider — 3
FARRINGTON, Oliver Cummings — 1
FARRINGTON, Robert I. — 3
FARRINGTON, Wallace Rider — 1
FARRINGTON, William George — 1
FARRINGTON, William Giddings — 4
FARRIS, Edmond J. — 4
FARRIS, Frank Mitchell — 3
FARRIS, John Wallace de Beque — 5
FARRIS, Ralph W. — 5
FARRIS, Robert Perry — 1
FARRISEE, William James — 4
FARRISS, Charles Sherwood — 1
FARROW, Edward Samuel — 1
FARROW, Edward Samuel — 4
FARROW, John Villiers — 4
FARROW, Miles — 5
FARROW, Samuel — H
FARSON, John — 1
FARWELL, Arthur — 3
FARWELL, Arthur Burrage — 1
FARWELL, Charles Benjamin — 4
FARWELL, Frederick Marcus * — 4
FARWELL, John Villiers — 1
FARWELL, John Villiers — 2
FARWELL, John W. — 1
FARWELL, Nathan Allen — H
FARWELL, Thomas Abbot — 1
FARYON, Reginald Richard — 4
FASSETT, Charles Marvin — 1
FASSETT, Cornelia Adele Strong — H
FASSETT, Helen Mary Revere — 2
FASSETT, Jacob Sloat — 1
FASSETT, James Hiram — 1
FASSETT, Norman C. — 5
FASSETT, William M. — 5
FASSIG, Oliver Lanard — 1
FAST, Gustave — 2
FASTEN, Nathan — 3
FATH, Jacques F. — 1
FAUBEL, Arthur Louis — 4
FAUCETTE, William Dollison — 2
FAULCONER, Albert — 1
FAULEY, Wilbur Finley — 2
FAULK, Andrew Jackson — H
FAULK, C. E. — 1
FAULKES, James Nelson — 3
FAULKES, William Fred — 1
FAULKNER, Barry — 4
FAULKNER, Charles James — H
FAULKNER, Charles James — 1
FAULKNER, Charles James — 3
FAULKNER, Georgene ("The Story Lady") — 5
FAULKNER, Harold Underwood — 5

FAULKNER, Harry Charles — 4
FAULKNER, Herbert Nelson — 4
FAULKNER, Herbert Waldron — 1
FAULKNER, John Alfred
FAULKNER, Leon Charles — 2
FAULKNER, Lester Bradner — 5
FAULKNER, Roy H. — 3
FAULKNER, William — 4
FAULKNER, William Harrison — 5
FAULKS, Theodosia — 1
FAULL, Joseph Horace — 4
FAUNCE, Daniel Worcester — 1
FAUNCE, William Herbert Perry — 1
FAUQUIER, Francis — H
FAUST, Albert Bernhardt — 3
FAUST, Allen Klein — 3
FAUST, Charles Lee — 3
FAUST, John Bernard — 3
FAUST, Paul E. — 1
FAUST, Samuel D. — 1
FAUST, Walter Livingston — 3
FAUSTMANN, Edmund C. — 2
FAUVER, Edgar — 2
FAUVER, Edwin — 1
FAVERSHAM, William — 1
FAVILL, Henry Baird — 1
FAVILLE, David Ernest — 5
FAVILLE, Frederick F. — 5
FAVILLE, Henry — 1
FAVILLE, John — 1
FAVILLE, William Baker — 5
FAVOUR, Alpheus Hoyt — 1
FAVREAU, Guy — 4
FAVROT, Charles Allen — 1
FAVROT, George Kent — 1
FAVROT, Laurence Harrison — 1
FAVROT, Leo Mortimer — 3
FAW, Walter Wagner — 1
FAWCETT, Angelo Vance — 1
FAWCETT, Edgar — 1
FAWCETT, George D. — 1
FAWCETT, Howard Samuel — 2
FAWCETT, Jacob — 4
FAWCETT, M. Edward — 1
FAWCETT, Owen — 1
FAWCETT, Wilford Hamilton, Jr. — 5
FAWCETT, William H. — 3
FAWCETT, William Vaughn Moody — 4
FAXON, Charles Edward — 1
FAXON, Frederick Winthrop — 1
FAXON, Henry Darlington — 1
FAXON, Walter — 1
FAXON, William Bailey — 1
FAXON, William Otis, II — 5
FAY, Albert Hill — 1
FAY, Amy — 3
FAY, Arthur Cecil — 4
FAY, Charles Ernest — 2
FAY, Charles Norman — 2
FAY, Charles Robert — 3
FAY, Charles W. — 5
FAY, Edward Allen — 1
FAY, Edwin Whitfield — 1
FAY, Francis Ball — H
FAY, Frederic Harold — 2
FAY, George Morris — 3
FAY, Henry — 4
FAY, Irving Wetherbee — 1
FAY, James H. — 2
FAY, John — H
FAY, Jonas — H
FAY, Lucy Ella — 2
FAY, Oliver James — 2
FAY, Sidney Bradshaw — 4
FAY, Sidney Bradshaw — 4
FAY, Temple — 4
FAY, Theodore Sedgwick — 4
FAY, Waldo Burnett — 4
FAY, William Patrick — 5
FAYANT, Frank H. — 4
FAYER, Margaret Wilson — 1
FAYERWEATHER, Daniel Burton — H
FAYSSOUX, Peter — H
FEAD, Louis H. — 2
FEAGIN, Noah Baxter — 5
FEAGIN, William Francis — 5
FEARING, Daniel Butler — 1

FEARING, Kenneth Flexner — 4
FEARING, Paul — H
FEARN, John Walker — H
FEARN, Richard Lee — 4
FEARON, Henry Dana — 2
FEATHERS, William C. — H
FEATHERSTON, Winfield Scott — 3
FEATHERSTONE, William B. — 3
FEBIGER, Christian — H
FECHET, James Edmond — 2
FECHNER, Robert — 1
FECHTELER, Augustus Francis — 4
FECHTELER, William Morrow — 4
FECHTER, Charles Albert — H
FECHTER, Oscar Augustus — 1
FEDERBUSH, Simon — 5
FEDERSPIEL, Matthew Nicholas — 3
FEDIGAN, John J. — 1
FEE, Charles S. — 1
FEE, Chester Anders — 3
FEE, James Alger — 3
FEE, Jerome John — 1
FEE, John Gregg — H
FEE, William Thomas — 1
FEEHAN, Daniel F. — 1
FEEHAN, Patrick A. — 1
FEELEY, James Patrick — 4
FEELEY, William P. — 5
FEELY, Edward Francis — 4
FEELY, John Joseph — 1
FEEMAN, Harlan Luther — 3
FEEMSTER, Robert M. — 4
FEENEY, Daniel J. — 5
FEENEY, Joseph Gerald — 1
FEGAN, Hugh J. — 3
FEGAN, Joseph Charles — 2
FEGTLY, Samuel Marks — 2
FEHLANDT, August Frederick — 1
FEHR, Arthur — 5
FEHR, Harrison Robert — 1
FEHR, Herman — 5
FEHRENBACH, John — 4
FEIBELMAN, Herbert U. — 5
FEIDELSON, Charles N. — 4
FEIERABEND, Raymond H. — 5
FEIGL, Hugo — 4
FEIKER, Frederick Morris — 5
FEILCHENFELD, Ernst H. — 3
FEININGER, Lyonel Charles Adrian — 3
FEIS, Herbert,* — 5
FEISAL II — 3
FEISS, Paul Louis — 3
FEJOS, Paul — 4
FEKE, Robert — H
FELAND, Faris Robison II — 3
FELAND, Logan — 1
FELCH, Alpheus — H
FELDBERG, Morris — 5
FELDBUSH, Harry A. — 4
FELDER, C. S. — 3
FELDER, John Myers — H
FELDMAN, Charles K. — 5
FELDMAN, Herman — 3
FELDMAN, Leonard G. — 5
FELDMANN, Markus — 3
FELDMANS, Jules — 3
FELGAR, James Huston — 3
FELIX, Anthony G. — 3
FELIX, Elizabeth Rachel — H
FELKEL, Herbert — 1
FELKER, Samuel Demeritt — 1
FELL, Alpheus Gilbert — 1
FELL, Charles Albert — 5
FELL, D. Newlin — 1
FELL, Frank J. Jr. — 1
FELL, George Edward — 5
FELL, Harold Bertels — 4
FELL, John — H
FELL, John R. — 4
FELL, Thomas — 2
FELLAND, Ole Gunderson — 3
FELLER, Abraham — 1
FELLER, Alto Edmund Howard — 4
FELLER, William — 5
FELLERS, Carl Raymond — 3
FELLHEIMER, Alfred — 3
FELLINGHAM, John Henry — 5
FELLOWS, C. Gurnee — 1

FELLOWS, Dorkas — 1
FELLOWS, Frank — 3
FELLOWS, George Emory — 1
FELLOWS, Grant — 1
FELLOWS, Harold E. — 3
FELLOWS, John Ernest — 4
FELLOWS, John R. — H
FELLOWS, Oscar F. — 1
FELLOWS, William Bainbridge — 1
FELLOWS, William Kinne — 2
FELMLEY, David — 1
FELS, Joseph — 1
FELS, Mary — 3
FELS, Samuel S. — 1
FELS, William Carl — 4
FELSING, William August — 3
FELT, Charles Frederick Wilson — 1
FELT, Dorr Eugene — 1
FELT, Edward Webster — 1
FELT, Ephraim Porter — 2
FELT, Joseph Barlow — H
FELT, Truman Thomas — 1
FELTER, Harvey Wickes — 1
FELTES, Nicholas Rudolph — 3
FELTON, Charles — H
FELTON, Cornelius Conway — H
FELTON, Edgar Conway — 1
FELTON, George Hurlburt — 4
FELTON, Lloyd Derr — 3
FELTON, Rebecca Latimer — 1
FELTON, Samuel Morse — 5
FELTON, Samuel Morse — 1
FELTON, William Hamilton
FENDALL, Josias — H
FENETRY, Clare Gerald — 3
FENGER, Christian — 1
FENHAGEN, George Corner — 3
FENHAGEN, James Corner — 3
FENKELL, George Harrison — 3
FENLEY, Oscar — 1
FENLON, John F. — 2
FENN, E. Hart — 1
FENN, George Karl — 1
FENN, Harry — 1
FENN, Stephen Southmyd — 5
FENN, Wallace Osgood — 1
FENN, William Wallace — 1
FENNELL, William George — 1
FENNEMAN, Nevin M. — 2
FENNER, Arthur — H
FENNER, Burt L. — 1
FENNER, Charles E. — 4
FENNER, Charles Erasmus — 1
FENNER, Charles Payne — 3
FENNER, Clarence Norman — 3
FENNER, Edward Blaine — 2
FENNER, Erasmus Darwin — 2
FENNER, Harlan K. — 4
FENNER, Hiram Walter — 1
FENNER, James — H
FENNER, Robert Coyner — 5
FENNING, Frederick Alexander — 3
FENNO, John — H
FENOLLOSA, Ernest Francisco — 1
FENOLLOSA, Mary McNeill — 3
FENSHAM, Florence — 1
FENSKE, Merrell Robert — 5
FENSKE, Theodore H. — 4
FENSTERMACHER, R. — 4
FENSTERWALD, Bernard — 3
FENSTON, Earl J. — 1
FENTON, Hector Tyndale — 1
FENTON, Howard Withrow — 3
FENTON, Jerome D. — 4
FENTON, Joseph Clifford — 5
FENTON, Lucien Jerome — H
FENTON, Ralph Albert — 4
FENTON, Reuben Eaton — H
FENTON, William David — 1
FENTRESS, Calvin — 3
FENWICK, Benedict Joseph — H
FENWICK, Charles G. — 5
FENWICK, Charles Philip — 3

FENWICK, Edward Dominic — H
FENWICK, Edward Taylor — 2
FENWICK, George — H
FENWICK, John — H
FERBER, Edna
FERBERT, Adolph Henry — 2
FERDON, John William — 5
FEREBEE, Enoch Emory — 4
FERGUSON, Alexander Hugh — 1
FERGUSON, Charles — 4
FERGUSON, Charles Eugene — 4
FERGUSON, DeLancey
FERGUSON, Edmund Sheppard — 1
FERGUSON, Edward — 5
FERGUSON, Elsie — 4
FERGUSON, Emma Henry — 1
FERGUSON, Everard D.
FERGUSON, Farquhar — 4
FERGUSON, Fenner — H
FERGUSON, Finlay Forbes — 1
FERGUSON, Frank Cardwell — 4
FERGUSON, Frank William — 1
FERGUSON, Franklin La Du — 4
FERGUSON, Fred Swearengin — 3
FERGUSON, Garland Sevier Jr. — 4
FERGUSON, George Albert — 1
FERGUSON, Georgia Ransom — 4
FERGUSON, Harley B(ascom) — 5
FERGUSON, Harriet R. — 4
FERGUSON, Harry George — 4
FERGUSON, Henry — 1
FERGUSON, Henry A. — 1
FERGUSON, Henry Gardiner — 4
FERGUSON, Hill — 5
FERGUSON, Homer Lenoir — 3
FERGUSON, Ira Alfred — 5
FERGUSON, James Edward — 2
FERGUSON, John Calvin — 2
FERGUSON, John Donald — 4
FERGUSON, John Lambuth — 3
FERGUSON, John William — 1
FERGUSON, Kenneth Reinhard — 3
FERGUSON, Louis Aloysius — 1
FERGUSON, Margaret Clay — 3
FERGUSON, Melville Foster — 5
FERGUSON, Milton James — 1
FERGUSON, Miriam A. — 3
FERGUSON, Olin Jerome — 4
FERGUSON, R. J. — 3
FERGUSON, Robert Gracey — 5
FERGUSON, Robert Gracey — 1
FERGUSON, Samuel — 2
FERGUSON, Samuel David — 1
FERGUSON, Smith Farley — 3
FERGUSON, Thomas Ewing — 4
FERGUSON, Thompson B. — 1
FERGUSON, Walter — 1
FERGUSON, William H. — 4
FERGUSON, William J. — 1
FERGUSON, William Law — 4
FERGUSON, William Porter Frisbee — 1
FERGUSON, William Scott — 3
FERGUSSON, Arthur Walsh — 1
FERGUSSON, E. Morris, — 1
FERGUSSON, Frank Kerby — 1
FERGUSSON, Harvey Butler — 1
FERLAINO, Frank Ralph — 3
FERMI, Enrico — 3
FERN, Fanny — H
FERNALD, Bert M. — 1
FERNALD, Charles Henry — 1

FERNALD, Chester Bailey — 1
FERNALD, Frank Lysander — 1
FERNALD, Gustavus Stockman
FERNALD, Henry Barker — 4
FERNALD, Henry Torsey — 3
FERNALD, James Champlin — 1
FERNALD, Merritt Caldwell — 1
FERNALD, Merritt Lyndon — 3
FERNALD, Robert Foss — 4
FERNALD, Robert Heywood — 1
FERNALD, Walter Elmore — 1
FERNANDEL, Ferdinand Joseph Desire Contandin) — 5
FERNANDEZ, Antonio M. — 3
FERNANDEZ, John D. — 5
FERNBACH, R(obert) Livingston — 3
FERNBERGER, Samuel Weiller — 5
FERNLEY, George Anderson — 1
FERNOW, Bernhard Eduard — 1
FERNOW, Berthold — 1
FERNSTROM, Henning — 5
FERON, Madame Hoffman — H / 1
FERRARA, Orestes — 5
FERRARI, Louis — 3
FERRARI-FONTANA, Edoardo — 1
FERRATA, Giuseppe — 1
FERRE, Nels Fredrik Solomon — 5
FERREE, Barr — 4
FERREE, Clarence Errol — 2
FERREL, William — H
FERRELL, Chiles Clifton — 1
FERRELL, John Appley — 1
FERRELL, John Atkinson — 4
FERREN, John (Millard) — 5
FERRERO, Edward — 4
FERRIER, Kathleen — H
FERRIER, Kathleen — 2
FERRIER, William Warren — 5
FERRIN, Augustin William — 4
FERRIN, Dana Holman — 4
FERRIN, William Nelson — 5
FERRIS, Albert Warren — 1
FERRIS, Charles Edward — 5
FERRIS, Charles Goadsby — H
FERRIS, Cornelius — 1
FERRIS, David — 1
FERRIS, David Lincoln — 2
FERRIS, Elmer Ellsworth — 1
FERRIS, Eugene B. Jr. — 3
FERRIS, George Floyd — 4
FERRIS, George Hooper — H
FERRIS, George Washington Gale — 1
FERRIS, Harry Burr
FERRIS, Helen (Josephine) — 5
FERRIS, Isaac — H
FERRIS, Jean Leon Gerome — 1
FERRIS, John Mason — 1
FERRIS, Mary Lanman Douw — 1
FERRIS, Morris Patterson
FERRIS, Ralph Hall — 3
FERRIS, Scott — 5
FERRIS, Theodore Parker — 5
FERRIS, Walter Rockwood
FERRIS, Walton C. — 3
FERRIS, Woodbridge Nathan
FERRISS, Franklin — 1
FERRISS, Hugh — 4
FERRISS, James Henry — H
FERRISS, Orange — H
FERRY, David William — 3
FERRY, Dexter Mason
FERRY, Dexter Mason Jr. — 1
FERRY, E. Hayward — H
FERRY, Elisha Peyre — 3
FERRY, Ervin Sidney — 5
FERRY, Frederick Carlos

FERRY, George Bowman — 1
FERRY, George Francis — 3
FERRY, Hugh J. — 5
FERRY, Orris Sanford — H
FERRY, Thomas White — H
FERRY, William Mont — 1
FERSON, Merton Leroy — 4
FERST, Monie Alan — 4
FESS, Simeon D. — 1
FESSENDEN, Edwin Allan — 5
FESSENDEN, Francis — 1
FESSENDEN, Franklin Goodridge — 1
FESSENDEN, Frederick J. — 4
FESSENDEN, James Deering — H
FESSENDEN, Laura Dayton — 3
FESSENDEN, Reginald Aubrey — 1
FESSENDEN, Russell Green — 2
FESSENDEN, Samuel — H
FESSENDEN, Samuel — 1
FESSENDEN, Samuel Clement — H
FESSENDEN, Thomas Amory Debiols — H
FESSENDEN, Thomas Green — 1
FESSENDEN, William Pitt — 1
FEST, Francis B. — 4
FETHERS, Ogden Hoffman — 1
FETHERSTON, John Turney — 4
FETTER, Frank Albert — 2
FETTER, Norman — 4
FETTERMAN, William Judd — H
FETTEROLF, Adam H. — 1
FETZER, Frank L. — 3
FETZER, Gottlob — 4
FETZER, Wade — 3
FETZER, Wade, Jr. — 5
FEUCHTWANGER, Lion — 3
FEUER, Mortimer — 5
FEUILLERAT, Albert Gabriel — 3
FEUSTEL, Robert M. — 1
FEW, Ignatius Alphonso — H
FEW, William — H
FEW, William Preston — 1
FEWKES, J. Walter — 1
FEWSMITH, Joseph — 3
FEZANDIE, Clement — 4
FFOULKE, Charles Mather — 1
FFRENCH, Charles Dominic — H
FIALA, Anthony — 3
FIALA, Sigmund Nicholas — 5
FICHTE, Harold O. — 5
FICK, George Henry — 1
FICK, Henry H. — 1
FICKE, Arthur Davison — 2
FICKEL, Jacob Earl — 4
FICKEN, George John — 4
FICKEN, H. Edwards — 3
FICKEN, Henry Horlbeck — 3
FICKES, Robert O. — 5
FICKLEN, John Rose — 1
FICKLIN, Orlando Bell — 5
FICSHER, Mario McCaughin — 5
FIDLER, Harry L. — 1
FIEANDT, Rainer von — 5
FIEBACH, Albert H. — 3
FIEBEGER, Gustav Joseph — 1
FIEKERS, Bernard Albert — 5
FIELD, Allan Bertram — 5
FIELD, Allen W. — 4
FIELD, Archelaus G. — 4
FIELD, B. Rush — 1
FIELD, Benjamin Hazard — 1
FIELD, Caroline Leslie — 1
FIELD, Carter — 4
FIELD, Charles Neale — 3
FIELD, Charles William — 1
FIELD, Cortlandt 'de Peyster — 1
FIELD, Crosby — 5
FIELD, Cyrus West — H
FIELD, Daniel F. — 1
FIELD, David Dudley — H
FIELD, David Mason — 4
FIELD, E. B. — 4
FIELD, Edward — 4
FIELD, Edward Pearsall Jr. — 4
FIELD, Elisha C. — 1

FIELD, Erastus Salisbury — H
FIELD, Eugene — H
FIELD, Frank Harvey — 4
FIELD, Fred Tarbell — 3
FIELD, George Wilton — 4
FIELD, Hamilton Easter — 1
FIELD, Harry Ashby — 5
FIELD, Harry Hubert — 2
FIELD, Heman M. — 4
FIELD, Henry — 2
FIELD, Henry Alonzo — 3
FIELD, Henry Martyn — 1
FIELD, Herbert H. — 3
FIELD, Herbert Haviland — H
FIELD, Hugh W. — 4
FIELD, Isaac S. — 1
FIELD, Jacob — 4
FIELD, James Alfred — 1
FIELD, James Gaven — 1
FIELD, Joseph M. — H
FIELD, Marshall — 1
FIELD, Marshall — 1
FIELD, Marshall IV — 4
FIELD, Mary Katherine Keemie — H
FIELD, Maunsell Bradhurst — H
FIELD, Moses Whelock — H
FIELD, Neill Brooks — 1
FIELD, Oliver Peter — 3
FIELD, Rachel — 2
FIELD, Richard Stockton — 1
FIELD, Richard Stockton — 3
FIELD, Robert — H
FIELD, Robert E. Lee — 4
FIELD, Robert Michael — 2
FIELD, Robert Patterson — H
FIELD, Roswell Martin — 1
FIELD, Scott — 5
FIELD, Stanley — 4
FIELD, Stephen Dudley — 1
FIELD, Stephen Johnson — H
FIELD, Theron Rockwell — 1
FIELD, Thomas Warren — H
FIELD, Walbridge Abner — 1
FIELD, Walter Taylor — 1
FIELD, Wells Laflin — 1
FIELD, William Henry — 1
FIELD, William Hildreth — 4
FIELD, William Jefferson — 4
FIELD, William Lusk Webster — 5
FIELD, William Perez — 5
FIELD, Winston Joseph — 5
FIELDE, Adele Marion — 1
FIELDER, Clarence Hunt — 4
FIELDER, James Fairman — 3
FIELDER, William — 1
FIELDING, Mantle — 1
FIELDING, Michael Farlow — 4
FIELDNER, Arno Carl — 4
FIELDS, Annie Adams — 2
FIELDS, Ernest Seymour — 4
FIELDS, Harold — 4
FIELDS, Herbert — 3
FIELDS, James Thomas — H
FIELDS, John — 4
FIELDS, Joseph E. — 3
FIELDS, Lew — 4
FIELDS, Louis Glenn — 3
FIELDS, Mitchell — 4
FIELDS, W. C. — 2
FIELDS, William Craig — H
FIELDS, William Henry — 4
FIELDS, William Jason — 3
FIENE, Ernest — 4
FIERO, J. Newton — 1
FIESER, James Louis — 4
FIFE, George Buchanan — 1
FIFE, Joseph Paul — 2
FIFE, Ray — 4
FIFE, Robert Herndon — 3
FIFER, Joseph Wilson — 1
FIFER, Orien Wesley — 2
FIFIELD, Albert Frank — 1
FIFIELD, Benjamin F. — 1
FIFIELD, Henry Allen — 4
FIFIELD, Lawrence Wendell
FIFIELD, Lawrence Wendell — 4
FIFIELD, Samuel Stillman — 1
FIGGINS, Jesse Dade — 4
FIGGIS, Dudley Weld — 4
FIGL, Leopold — 4
FIGUERAS-CHIQUES, Jose Maria — 4
FIKE, Charles Laird — 3

FIKE, Pierre Hicks — H
FILBERT, Ludwig S.
FILBERT, William J. — 4
FILBEY, Edward Joseph — 4
FILBEY, Edward Joseph — 1
FILENE, Edward A. — 1
FILENE, Lincoln — 2
FILER, Harry Lambert — 4
FILER, Herbert Augustus — 1
FILES, Howard W. — 1
FILIPOWICZ, Tytus — H
FILLEBROWN, Charles Bowdoin — 1
FILLER, Mervin Grant — 4
FILLEY, Chauncey Ives — 1
FILLEY, Everett R. — 1
FILLION, Francis — 1
FILLIS, Ben Earle — 5
FILLMORE, Charles — 5
FILLMORE, John Comfort — H
FILLMORE, Millard — 1
FILLMORE, Parker — 4
FILLMORE, Waldo Rickert — H
FILSINGER, Ernst B. — 1
FILSON, John — 1
FIMPLE, John H. — 5
FINAN, Joseph B. — 3
FINCH, Edward Ridley — 4
FINCH, Francis Miles — H
FINCH, Frederick L. — 1
FINCH, George Augustus — 4
FINCH, Henry LeRoy — 5
FINCH, Herbert Isaac — 1
FINCH, Isaac — 4
FINCH, James Kip — 4
FINCH, John Aylard — 4
FINCH, John Wellington — 4
FINCH, Morton Easley — 4
FINCH, Peyton Newell, Jr. — 3
FINCH, Royal George — 3
FINCH, Ruy Herbert — 4
FINCH, Stanley Wellington — 3
FINCH, Thomas Austin — 4
FINCH, Vernor Clifford — 4
FINCH, Volney Cecil — 4
FINCH, William Albert — 4
FINCH, William Rufus — 5
FINCHER, Edgar Franklin — 4
FINCK, Edward Bertrand (Bert Finck) — 4
FINCK, Henry Theophilus — H
FINCKE, Clarence Mann — 1
FINCKEL, Martin Luther — 2
FINDLAY, Hugh — 5
FINDLAY, James — 1
FINDLAY, John — H
FINDLAY, John Van Lear — H
FINDLAY, William — H
FINDLEY, Alvin Irwin — 1
FINDLEY, Earl Nelson — 1
FINDLEY, Palmer — 1
FINDLEY, Thomas Maskell — 4
FINDLEY, William — 1
FINE, Henry Burchard — H
FINE, Irving Gifford — 4
FINE, John — 3
FINEGAN, James Emmet — 1
FINEGAN, Thomas Edward — 4
FINER, Herman — 3
FINERTY, John Frederick — 1
FINESINGER, Jacob Ellis — 3
FINFROCK, Clarence Millard — 4
FINGER, Aaron — 4
FINGER, Charles Joseph — 1
FINGER, Henry James — 4
FINGERHOOD, Boris — 4
FINGOLD, George — 4
FINGOLD, Samuel — 4
FINK, A. J. — 4
FINK, Albert — 4
FINK, Bruce — H
FINK, Colin Garfield — 4
FINK, David N. — 4
FINK, Denman — 4
FINK, Emil C. — 1
FINK, Francis A. — 4
FINK, George R. — 4
FINK, Henry — 1
FINK, Joseph Lionel — 4
FINK, Louis Maria — H
FINK, Ollie Edgar — 4
FINK, Reuben — 4
FINK, William Green — 1
FINKE, George — 4

INKE, Walter William 5
INKE, William F. 4
INKEL,
　Benjamin Franklin 2
INKELNBURG, G. A. 1
INKLE,
　Frederick Cecil 3
INKLER,
　Rita V. Sapiro 5
INKS, Nettie Velier 4
INLAY, Charles John 5
INLAY, George Irving 5
INLAY, Hugh H
INLAY, James Ralph 5
INLAY, John Jerome 5
INLAY, Kirkman George 1
INLAY,
　Walter Stevenson Jr. 3
INLAYSON,
　Frank Graham 2
INLAYSON, John
　Duncan 3
INLEY, Charles 1
INLEY,
　Charles William 3
INLEY, David Edward 1
INLEY, Emmet 3
INLEY, Ernest Latimer 5
INLEY, James H
INLEY, James Bradley 5
INLEY, John Huston 1
INLEY, John Huston 2
INLEY, Joseph William 1
INLEY, Martha 5
INLEY, Robert 1
INLEY, Ruth Ebright 3
INLEY, Samuel 1
INLEY,
　Solomon Henderson 2
INLEY, William Henry 1
INLEY, William Lovell 3
INLEY, William Wilson 1
INN, Francis James H
INN,
　Henry James William
INN, Howard Joseph 4
INN, John F. X. 3
INN, William Joseph 4
INNEGAN, Edward
　Rowan 5
INNEGAN, James A. 3
INNEGAN, James
　Edward 4
INNEGAN,
　Joseph Francis 4
INNEGAN, Philip J. 3
INNEGAN,
　Richard James 3
INNEGAN, William A. 4
INNELL, Woolsey 4
INNEY,
　Benjamin Ficklin 2
INNEY,
　Charles Grandison H
INNEY, Darwin Abel H
INNEY, Edward Clingan 5
INNEY,
　Frederick Norton 1
INNEY, James Imboden 1
INNEY,
　John Miller Turpin 2
INNEY, Ross Lee 1
INNEY, William Parker 2
INNIGAN,
　George Joseph 1
INOTTI, Joseph Maria H
INTA, Alexander 3
INTY, Tom Jr. 1
IPPIN,
　Elmer Otterbein 3
IREMAN, Peter 4
IRESTEIN, Alfred 5
IRESTONE,
　Clark Barnaby 3
IRESTONE,
　Harvey Samuel 1
IRESTONE,
　Harvey Samuel, Jr. 5
IRESTONE, Ray Ernest 4
IRESTONE,
　Roger Stanley 1
IRING, Thoralf Otmann
IRKINS, Oscar W. 1
IRM, Joseph Lannison 4
IRMIN,
　Albert Bancroft Wilcox 4
ISCHEL, Victor Arnold 5
ISCHEL,
　Washington Emil 1
ISCHER, Anton Otto 4
ISCHER,
　Arthur Frederick
ISCHER, Earl Britzius 4
ISCHER, Earl W. 5
ISCHER, Edward Louis 5
ISCHER, Ernst Georg 1

FISCHER,
　George Alexander 1
FISCHER, George August 2
FISCHER, Henry W. 4
FISCHER,
　Hermann Otto Laurenz 4
FISCHER, Israel F. 4
FISCHER, Jacob 5
FISCHER, Karl 3
FISCHER, Kermit 5
FISCHER, Leo H. 5
FISCHER, Leo J. 2
FISCHER, Louis 2
FISCHER, Louis 5
FISCHER, Louis Albert 1
FISCHER, Martin Henry 5
FISCHER,
　Mary Ellen Sigsbee (Mary
　Sigsbee Fischer)
FISCHLER, Peter K. 3
FISET,
　Sir Eugene (Marie-Joseph)
FISH, Alfred Lawrence 3
FISH, Bert 2
FISH, C. W. 4
FISH, Carl Russell 1
FISH, Daniel 1
FISH, Edwards R. 1
FISH, Frank Leslie 1
FISH, Fred Alan 5
FISH, Frederick Perry 5
FISH, Frederick Samuel 1
FISH, Hamilton H
FISH, Herbert Henry 5
FISH, Horace 1
FISH, Irving Andrews 2
FISH,
　John Charles Lounsbury 5
FISH, Milton Ernest 5
FISH, Nicholas 1
FISH, Nicholas H
FISH, Pierre Augustine 1
FISH, Preserved H
FISH, Stuyvesant 1
FISH, Walter Clark 4
FISH, William Hansell 1
FISH, William Henry 1
FISH, Williston 4
FISHBACK,
　George Welton 1
FISHBACK,
　William Meade
FISHBERG, Maurice 1
FISHBURN, John Eugene 1
FISHBURN, Junius Blair 3
FISHBURN,
　Junius Parker 1
FISHBURN,
　Randolph Eugene
FISHBURNE, Edward Bell 5
FISHBURNE, John Wood 5
FISHER, Albert Kenrick 2
FISHER, Alphonse Louis 3
FISHER, Alvan 5
FISHER, Anna 3
FISHER, Anne B(enson) 5
FISHER, Anne B. 4
FISHER, Arthur 5
FISHER, Arthur William 5
FISHER, Ben S. 3
FISHER, Bud 5
FISHER, Cassius Asa 1
FISHER, Charles * H
FISHER, Charles A. 1
FISHER, Charles Asbury 2
FISHER, Charles E. 5
FISHER,
　Charles Thomas Jr.
FISHER, Clara H
FISHER,
　Clarence Stanley
FISHER, Daniel C. 4
FISHER, Daniel Webster 1
FISHER, David H
FISHER,
　Dorothy Canfield 3
FISHER,
　Dorsey Gassaway 5
FISHER, Ebenezer H
FISHER, Edgar Jacob 4
FISHER, Edmund Drew 4
FISHER, Edward Dix 5
FISHER, Edward F. 5
FISHER, Edwin 2
FISHER, Edwin Lyle 5
FISHER, Elam 1
FISHER,
　Elizabeth Florette 1
FISHER, Emory Devilla 5
FISHER, Frank Cyril 5
FISHER, Franklin L. 1
FISHER, Fred Douglas 3
FISHER, Frederic John 1
FISHER, Frederick Bohn 1
FISHER,
　Frederick Charles 5

FISHER, 4
　Frederick Vining
FISHER, Galen Merriam 3
FISHER, 5
　Geoffrey Francis
FISHER, George H
FISHER, George Clyde 2
FISHER, George Egbert 1
FISHER, George J. 4
FISHER, George Jackson H
FISHER, George Park 5
FISHER, George Purnell 4
FISHER, Gordon 3
FISHER, Haldane S. 3
FISHER, Hammond
　Edward 5
FISHER, Harrison 1
FISHER, Harry Linn 4
FISHER, Henry C. 4
FISHER, Henry Johnson 4
FISHER, Henry Wright 5
FISHER, Horace Newton 4
FISHER, Horatio Gates H
FISHER,
　Hubert Frederick 5
FISHER, Irving 2
FISHER, James Blaine 3
FISHER, 5
　James Maxwell McConnell
FISHER, John H
FISHER, John Dix H
FISHER, John Frederick 1
FISHER, John S. 1
FISHER, John Wesley 3
FISHER, Jonathan H
FISHER, Joseph Anton 5
FISHER, Joshua Francis H
FISHER, Lawrence Peter 4
FISHER, Lewis Beals 1
FISHER, Lucius George 1
FISHER, Mahlon Leonard 2
FISHER, William) Mark 5
FISHER, Martin Luther 5
FISHER, Mary 4
FISHER, Miles Bull 5
FISHER, Oliver David 4
FISHER, Oscar Louis 1
FISHER, Ralph Talcott 1
FISHER, 1
　Richard Thornton
FISHER, Robert 4
FISHER, Robert Farley 1
FISHER, Robert Jones 1
FISHER, Robert Joseph 1
FISHER, 4
　Robert Joseph Jr.
FISHER, Robert Welles 1
FISHER, Robert Welles 4
FISHER, Russell Todd 3
FISHER, 5
　Samuel Brownlee
FISHER, Samuel Herbert 5
FISHER, Samuel Jackson 1
FISHER, Samuel Ware 1
FISHER, Sidney George H
FISHER, Stokely S. 1
FISHER, Sydney George 1
FISHER, 4
　Theodore Willis
FISHER, Thomas Edward 5
FISHER, Thomas Kaufman 4
FISHER, Thomas Russell 4
FISHER, Vardis 5
FISHER, Waldo Emanuel 1
FISHER, Walter L. 1
FISHER, Willard Clark 5
FISHER, 5
　William A(ndrew)
FISHER, William Arms 2
FISHER, 1
　William Cummings
FISHER, William H. 4
FISHER, William Orris 5
FISHER, William Victor 5
FISHER, 1
　Willis Richardson
FISK, Bradley 4
FISK, Charles Henry 1
FISK, Charles Joseph 1
FISK, Clinton Bowen H
FISK, Daniel Moses 4
FISK, Eugene Lyman 1
FISK, Everett Olin 1
FISK, 4
　Frederick Mewborn
FISK, George Mygatt 4
FISK, Harlan Wilbur 4
FISK, Harold N. 4
FISK, Herbert Franklin 1
FISK, James * H
FISK, Jessie (Gladys) 5
FISK, Jonathan 1
FISK, Katharine 4
FISK, Kerby H. 5
FISK, 3
　Louisa Holman Richardson
FISK, Samuel Augustus 1

FISK, Wilbur H
FISKE, Adam Hastings 3
FISKE, Amos Kidder 1
FISKE, Arthur Irving 4
FISKE, Asa Severance 4
FISKE, Bradley Allen 2
FISKE, Charles 1
FISKE, Charles Parker 5
FISKE, Daniel Willard 1
FISKE, Edmund Walter 1
FISKE, Eugene Allen 1
FISKE, Fidelia H
FISKE, George Converse 5
FISKE, 4
　George McClellan
FISKE, George Walter 2
FISKE, Gertrude 4
FISKE, Haley 1
FISKE, Harold Benjamin 5
FISKE, Harrison Grey 2
FISKE, Horace Spencer 1
FISKE, James Porter 1
FISKE, John H
FISKE, John 1
FISKE, Lewis Ransom 1
FISKE, Minnie Maddern 1
FISKE, Stephen 1
FISKE, Thomas Scott 1
FISKE, William F. 5
FISKE, 1
　William Mead Lindsley
FISKE, 5
　Wyman P(arkhurst)
FISKEN, John Barclay 2
FISKER, Kay 4
FISTELL, Harry 5
FITCH, Albert Parker 2
FITCH, Asa * H
FITCH, Ashbel Parmelee 1
FITCH, Cecil 4
FITCH, Charles Elliott 1
FITCH, Charles Hall 4
FITCH, Clifford Penny 1
FITCH, Clyde 1
FITCH, Edward 2
FITCH, Ezra Charles 3
FITCH, Florence Mary 4
FITCH, Frank E. 1
FITCH, George 1
FITCH, George Hamlin 2
FITCH, Graham Newell H
FITCH, Grant 4
FITCH, James Burgess 4
FITCH, John H
FITCH, John Andrews 3
FITCH, John Hall 5
FITCH, Joseph Henry 4
FITCH, Rachel Louise 3
FITCH, Samuel H
FITCH, 5
　Tecumseh Sherman
FITCH, Thomas 1
FITCH, Thomas Davis 1
FITCH, Thomas F. 1
FITCH, Walter 1
FITCH, William Edward 1
FITCH, 1
　William Foresman
FITCH, William Kountz 5
FITE, Alexander Green 4
FITE, Emerson David 3
FITE, Warner 1
FITE, William Benjamin 4
FITE, William Conyers 4
FITHIAN, Edward 1
FITKIN, Abraham Edward 1
FITLER, Edwin Henry H
FITTERER, John Conrad 4
FITTON, James 2
FITTS, Alice Evelina H
FITTS, Charles Newton 5
FITTS, Dudley 5
FITTS, George Henry 3
FITTS, William Cochran 1
FITTZ, Austin Hervey 4
FITZ, Henry H
FITZ, Hugh Alexander 5
FITZ, Reginald 3
FITZ, Reginald Heber 1
FITZ-GERALD, 4
　Aaron Ogden
FITZGERALD, 4
　Adolphus Leigh
FITZGERALD, Barry 2
FITZGERALD,
　David Edward 1
FITZGERALD, Desmond 1
FITZGERALD, E. Roy 3
FITZGERALD, Edward 5
FITZGERALD, 1
　Edward Aloyslus
FITZGERALD, 1
　Francis Alexander James
FITZGERALD, 1
　Francis Scott Key
FITZGERALD, 1
　Frank Dwight

FISK, Wilbur H
FITZGERALD,
　Harrington 1
FITZ GERALD, James 1
FITZGERALD, James J. 2
FITZGERALD, 1
　James Merlin
FITZ GERALD, 1
　James Newbury
FITZGERALD, 4
　James Wilford
FITZ-GERALD, 2
　John Driscoll II
FITZGERALD, 3
　John Francis
FITZGERALD, 3
　John Joseph
FITZGERALD, 3
　John Morton
FITZGERALD, Joseph 1
FITZGERALD, Leo David 3
FITZ GERALD, 1
　Leslie Maurice
FITZGERALD, Louis 1
FITZGERALD, 4
　Matthew Joseph
FITZGERALD, Maurice
　A. 3
FITZGERALD, 1
　Michael Edward
FITZGERALD, Oscar
　Penn 1
FITZGERALD, 1
　Robert Mullins
FITZGERALD, Roy
　Gerald 4
FITZGERALD, 4
　Rufus Henry
FITZGERALD, Ruth 4
FITZ GERALD, 4
　Susan Walker
FITZGERALD, 5
　Theodore Clinton
FITZGERALD, Thomas * H
FITZGERALD, Thomas 2
FITZGERALD, 4
　Thomas Edward
FITZGERALD, W. 4
　Thomas
FITZGERALD, 2
　Walter James
FITZGERALD, William H
FITZGERALD, William
　A. 1
FITZGERALD, 2
　William Joseph
FITZGERALD, 3
　William Joseph
FITZ GERALD, 1
　William Sinton
FITZGIBBON, Catherine H
FITZGIBBON, 3
　John Harold
FITZGIBBON, 4
　Thomas O'Gorman
FITZ GIBBON, William 4
FITZGIBBONS, John 1
FITZGIBBONS, 4
　John Joseph
FITZHENRY, Louis 1
FITZHUGH, Edwin A. 5
FITZHUGH, George H
FITZHUGH, 1
　Guston Thomas
FITZHUGH, Millsaps 4
FITZHUGH, Percy Keese 3
FITZHUGH, Thomas 4
FITZHUGH, William * H
FITZHUGH, 5
　William Wyvill
FITZMAURICE, Edmond
　J. 4
FITZMAURICE, John E. 3
FITZPATRICK, Benjamin H
FITZPATRICK, 5
　Daniel Robert
FITZPATRICK, 5
　Edward Augustus
FITZ-PATRICK, Gilbert 1
FITZPATRICK, Herbert 4
FITZ-PATRICK, 4
　Hugh Louis
FITZPATRICK, H
　John Bernard
FITZPATRICK, 1
　John Clement
FITZPATRICK, 1
　John Francis
FITZPATRICK, 1
　John Tracy
FITZPATRICK, Morgan
　C. 3
FITZPATRICK, 1
　Paul Edward
FITZPATRICK, Thomas H
FITZPATRICK, 1
　Thomas Vanhook

FITZPATRICK, Thomas Y. — 4
FITZPATRICK, William Samuel — 5
FITZ-RANDOLPH, Corliss
FITZROY, Herbert William Keith — 5
FITZSIMMONS, Cortland — 2
FITZSIMMONS, Thomas — H
FITZSIMON, Laurence Julius — 3
FITZSIMONS, Charles — 1
FITZ SIMONS, Ellen French — 2
FITZWATER, Perry B. — 3
FITZWILLIAM, Fanny — H
FLACCUS, — H
FLACK, Joseph — 3
FLACK, Marjorie — 3
FLACK, William Henry — 1
FLAD, Edward — 5
FLAD, Henry — H
FLAGET, Benedict Joseph — H
FLAGG, Azariah Cutting — H
FLAGG, Charles Allcott — 1
FLAGG, Charles Noel — 1
FLAGG, Edmund — 1
FLAGG, Edward Octavus — 1
FLAGG, Ernest — 2
FLAGG, George Whiting — H
FLAGG, Isaac — 4
FLAGG, James Chester — 4
FLAGG, James Montgomery — 4
FLAGG, Jared Bradley — 1
FLAGG, Josiah — H
FLAGG, Josiah Foster — H
FLAGG, Josiah Foster — 1
FLAGG, Montague — 1
FLAGG, Paluel Joseph — 5
FLAGG, Rufus Cushman — 3
FLAGG, Thomas Wilson — 1
FLAGLER, Clement Alexander Finley — 5
FLAGLER, Harry Harkness
FLAGLER, Henry M. — 1
FLAGLER, Isaac Van Vleck
FLAGLER, John Haldane — 4
FLAGLER, Thomas Thorn — H
FLAGSTAD, Kirsten — 4
FLAHERTY, Frederick H. — 1
FLAHERTY, Lawrence J. — 1
FLAHERTY, Robert Joseph — 3
FLANAGAN, Dan Collins — 4
FLANAGAN, Edward Joseph — 4
FLANAGAN, Harold Francis — 4
FLANAGAN, Henry Clinton — 3
FLANAGAN, James Wainwright — H
FLANAGAN, James Winright
FLANAGAN, John — 3
FLANAGAN, Thomas Edmund — 4
FLANAGAN, Webster — 1
FLANAGIN, Harris — H
FLANDERS, Alvan — H
FLANDERS, Benjamin Franklin — H
FLANDERS, Fred C. — 3
FLANDERS, George Lovell — 4
FLANDERS, Henry — 1
FLANDERS, James Greeley — 1
FLANDERS, Ralph Edward — 5
FLANDERS, Ralph Lindsay
FLANDRAU, Charles Eugene — 1
FLANDRAU, Charles Macomb — 5
FLANDRAU, Grace Hodgson — 5
FLANIGAN, Edward Joseph — 1
FLANIGAN, Howard Adams — 4
FLANNAGAN, John William Jr. — 4
FLANNERY, John — 4
FLANNERY, John Rogers — 2
FLANNERY, John Spalding — 3
FLANNERY, Vaughn — 3
FLANNIGAN, Richard Charles
FLASCH, Kilian Casper — H

FLATH, Earl Hugo — 5
FLATHER, — 5
FLATHER, Frederick Arthur
FLATHER, John Joseph — 1
FLATTERY, M. Douglas — 1
FLAVIN, Martin — 4
FLEBBE, — 5
FLEBBE, Beulah Marie Dix (Mrs. George H. Flebbe)
FLECK, Alexander — 5
FLECK, Henry Thomas — 1
FLECK, Wilbur H. — 5
FLEEGER, — H
FLEEGER, George Washington
FLEEK, John Sherwood — 3
FLEESON, Doris — 5
FLEESON, Howard Tebbe — 3
FLEET, —
FLEET, Alexander Frederick
FLEET, Thomas — H
FLEETWOOD, — 1
FLEETWOOD, Benjamin Franklin
FLEETWOOD, Frederick Gleed
FLEGENHEIMER, Albert — 5
FLEISCHER, Charles — 2
FLEISCHMANN, — H
FLEISCHMANN, Charles Louis
FLEISCHMANN, Julius — 1
FLEISCHMANN, Max C. — 1
FLEISCHMANN, Raoul H. — 5
FLEISCHMANN, Simon — 2
FLEISHER, Benjamin Wilfrid
FLEISHER, Samuel S. — 2
FLEISHER, Walter Louis — 3
FLEISHHACKER, Herbert — 1
FLEISHHACKER, Mortimer — 5
FLEMER, John Adolph — 5
FLEMING, — 1
FLEMING, Adrian Sebastian
FLEMING, Aretas Brooks — 1
FLEMING, Arthur Henry — 2
FLEMING, Bryant — 1
FLEMING, Burton Percival
FLEMING, Charles A. — 1
FLEMING, — 5
FLEMING, Daniel Johnson
FLEMING, Dewey Lee — 3
FLEMING, Ernest Joseph — 5
FLEMING, Francis Philip — 1
FLEMING, — 2
FLEMING, Francis Philip
FLEMING, Fred W. — 1
FLEMING, — 3
FLEMING, Frederic Sydney
FLEMING, Harvey Brown — 1
FLEMING, Henry Stuart — 1
FLEMING, Ian Lancaster — 4
FLEMING, James Wheeler
FLEMING, John * — H
FLEMING, John Adam — 3
FLEMING, — 1
FLEMING, John Donaldson
FLEMING, — 5
FLEMING, Joseph Barclay
FLEMING, Lamar Jr. — 4
FLEMING, Matthew Corry — 2
FLEMING, — 3
FLEMING, Philip Bracken
FLEMING, Robert Vedder — 4
FLEMING, Rufus — 4
FLEMING, Samuel Wilson Jr.
FLEMING, Sir Alexander — 3
FLEMING, Victor — 2
FLEMING, Wallace B. — 3
FLEMING, — 1
FLEMING, Walter Lynwood
FLEMING, Willard C. — 5
FLEMING, William * — H
FLEMING, William Bennett
FLEMING, William Bowyer
FLEMING, William Hansell
FLEMING, William Maybury — H
FLEMING, — 1
FLEMING, Williamina Paton
FLEMINGTON, William Thomas Ross — 5
FLETCHER, Alice Cunningham — 1
FLETCHER, Andrew — 1
FLETCHER, Angus Somerville — 4
FLETCHER, Austin Barclay — 1

FLETCHER, Austin Bradstreet — 1
FLETCHER, Benjamin — H
FLETCHER, Calvin — H
FLETCHER, Daniel Howard — 5
FLETCHER, Duncan Upshaw — 1
FLETCHER, Emerson Armor — 2
FLETCHER, Frank Friday — H
FLETCHER, Frank Jack — 5
FLETCHER, Frank Morley
FLETCHER, Frank Ward — 3
FLETCHER, Fred Leland — 5
FLETCHER, Frederick Charles
FLETCHER, Henry — 3
FLETCHER, Henry Jesse — 4
FLETCHER, Henry Prather — 3
FLETCHER, Horace — 1
FLETCHER, Inglis (Mrs. John G. Fletcher)
FLETCHER, Isaac — H
FLETCHER, James Cooley — H
FLETCHER, James Donald — 5
FLETCHER, Jefferson Butler
FLETCHER, John — 5
FLETCHER, John Gould — 3
FLETCHER, John Madison
FLETCHER, John Storrs — 4
FLETCHER, Julia Constance — 4
FLETCHER, Loren — 1
FLETCHER, Mona — 4
FLETCHER, Montgomery — 1
FLETCHER, Mordecai Hiatt — 1
FLETCHER, Orlin Ottman — 4
FLETCHER, Paul Franklin
FLETCHER, Richard — H
FLETCHER, Robert — 1
FLETCHER, Robert Howe — 4
FLETCHER, Robert S. — 4
FLETCHER, Robert Stillman — 3
FLETCHER, Robert Virgil — 4
FLETCHER, Samuel Johnson — 3
FLETCHER, Stevenson Whitcomb — 5
FLETCHER, Thomas — H
FLETCHER, Thomas Clement — H
FLETCHER, Walter D. — 5
FLETCHER, William Asa — 5
FLETCHER, William Baldwin — 1
FLETCHER, William Bartlett — 3
FLETCHER, William Isaac — 1
FLETCHER, William Meade — 2
FLEWELLING, Ralph Carlin — 3
FLEWELLING, Ralph Tyler — 5
FLEXNER, Abraham — 3
FLEXNER, Anne Crawford — 3
FLEXNER, Bernard — 5
FLEXNER, Magdalen Glaser Hupfel
FLEXNER, Simon — 2
FLICK, Alexander Clarence — 2
FLICK, Lawrence F. — 1
FLICK, Walter A. — 3
FLICKINGER, Daniel Kumler — 1
FLICKINGER, Roy Caston — 2
FLICKINGER, Samuel Jacob — 1
FLICKINGER, Smith M. — 1
FLICKWIR, David Williamson — 1
FLIEGEL, Leslie — 5
FLING, Fred Morrow — 1
FLINN, Alfred Douglas — 1
FLINN, John Joseph — 1
FLINN, Richard Orme — 2
FLINNER, Ira Arthur — 3
FLINT, Albert Stowell — 1
FLINT, Austin — H
FLINT, Austin — 1
FLINT, Austin — 3

FLINT, Charles Louis — H
FLINT, Charles Ranlett — 1
FLINT, Charles Wesley — H
FLINT, Mrs. Edith Foster — 5
FLINT, Frank Putnam — 1
FLINT, James Milton — 1
FLINT, Joseph Marshall — 5
FLINT, Leon Nelson — 3
FLINT, Motley H. — 4
FLINT, Noel Leslie — 4
FLINT, Timothy — H
FLINT, Weston — 1
FLIPPEN, Edgar Lucas — 5
FLIPPER, Joseph Simeon — 2
FLIPPIN, James Carroll — 1
FLIPPIN, Percy Scott — 1
FLOERSH, John A. — 5
FLOM, George Tobias — 3
FLOOD, Francis Arthur — 3
FLOOD, Gerald F. — 4
FLOOD, Henry Jr. — 4
FLOOD, Henry Delaware — 1
FLOOD, Ned Arden — 1
FLOOD, Theodore L. — 1
FLOOD, Walter Vincent — 3
FLOODY, Robert John — 4
FLOOK, William M. — 4
FLORANCE, Ernest Touro
FLORANCE, Howard — 3
FLORE, Edward — 2
FLORENCE, Elias — H
FLORENCE, Fred Farrel — 1
FLORENCE, Mrs. William J.
FLORENCE, Thomas Birch — H
FLORENCE, William Jermyn — H
FLORER, Warren Washburn
FLOREY, Lord Howard Walter — 5
FLOREY, Lord Howard Walter — 4
FLORIDABLANCA, 'conde 'de — H
FLORIDIA, Pietro — 1
FLORIO, Caryl — 1
FLORSHEIM, Irving S. — 3
FLORSHEIM, Leonard S. — 4
FLORY, Arthur Louis — 5
FLORY, George Daniel — 1
FLORY, Ira S. — 4
FLORY, John Samuel — 4
FLORY, Joseph — 1
FLOTA, George W. — 3
FLOURNOY, Harry L. — 1
FLOURNOY, Parke Poindexter
FLOURNOY, Thomas Stanhope — H
FLOURNOY, William Walton
FLOWER, Anson Ranney — 1
FLOWER, Benjamin Orange
FLOWER, Elliott — 1
FLOWER, Frank Abial — 1
FLOWER, George — H
FLOWER, Henry Corwin — 2
FLOWER, J(oseph James) Roswell — 5
FLOWER, Richard — H
FLOWER, Rosewell Pettibone — H
FLOWER, Walter C. — 1
FLOWERS, Alan Estis — 2
FLOWERS, Allen Gilbert — 5
FLOWERS, Herbert Baker — 1
FLOWERS, James Nathaniel — 3
FLOWERS, John Garland — 4
FLOWERS, Montaville — 3
FLOWERS, Robert Lee — 3
FLOY, Henry — 1
FLOY, James — H
FLOYD, Charles Albert — H
FLOYD, Charles Miller — 1
FLOYD, David Bittle — 1
FLOYD, Frank Monroe — 4
FLOYD, Ivy Knox — 3
FLOYD, John * — H
FLOYD, John Buchanan — H
FLOYD, John C. — 4
FLOYD, John Charles — 1
FLOYD, John Gelston — H
FLOYD, Richard C. — 3
FLOYD, Robert Mitchell — 1
FLOYD, William — H
FLOYD-JONES, De Lancey — 1
FLUG, Samuel S. — 4
FLUGEL, Ewald — 1
FLY, James Lawrence — 4

FLYE, Edwin
FLYNN, Albert T.
FLYNN, Benedict Devine
FLYNN, Dennis Joseph
FLYNN, Dennis T.
FLYNN, Edmund W.
FLYNN, Edward
FLYNN, Edward Francis
FLYNN, Edward Joseph
FLYNN, Errol Leslie
FLYNN, Frank Earl
FLYNN, John Aloysius
FLYNN, John E.
FLYNN, John Thomas
FLYNN, Joseph Crane
FLYNN, Joseph Michael
FLYNN, P. J.
FLYNN, Thomas
FLYNN, Thomas E.
FLYNN, Thomas P.
FLYNN, Vincent Joseph
FLYNN, William James
FLYNN, William Smith
FLYNT, Charles Fremont
FLYNT, Henry Needham
FLYTHE, William P.
FOBES, Joseph Henry
FOCHT, Benjamin K.
FOCHT, John Brown
FOCKE, Theodore Moses
FOELKER, Otto Godfrey
FOELL, Charles Michael
FOELLINGER, Oscar G.
FOERDERER, Percival Edward
FOERSTE, August Frederick — 1
FOERSTER, Adolph Martin — H
FOERSTER, Otto Hottinger — H
FOERSTER, Robert Franz — 3
FOERSTER, Roland Constantine
FOGARTY, James Francis — 4
FOGARTY, John Edward — 4
FOGARTY, Thomas — 1
FOGDALL, Sorenus P.
FOGEL, Edwin Miller — 1
FOGG, George Gilman — H
FOGG, Isaac
FOGG, Lawrence Daniel — 1
FOGG, Lloyd Clarke — 1
FOGHT, Harold Waldstein — 3
FOGLESONG, John E.
FOGO, James Gordon — 3
FOHS, Ferdinand Julius — 2
FOIK, Paul Joseph — 1
FOKINE, Michel
FOKKER, Anthony H. G. — 1
FOKMA, Jan Jelle — 5
FOLDS, Charles Weston
FOLEY, Arthur Lee — 2
FOLEY, Francis B(enedict) — 5
FOLEY, Frederick Clement
FOLEY, George Cadwalader
FOLEY, James A. — 1
FOLEY, James Bradford — H
FOLEY, James Owen — 4
FOLEY, James William Jr. — 1
FOLEY, John Burton — H
FOLEY, Margaret F. — H
FOLEY, Margaret Mary — 5
FOLEY, Max Henry — 1
FOLEY, Thomas J. — 1
FOLEY, Thomas Patrick Roger — H
FOLGER, Alonzo Dillard
FOLGER, Charles James — H
FOLGER, Henry Clay — H
FOLGER, James A. — 1
FOLGER, Peter — H
FOLGER, Walter — H
FOLGER, William Mayhew — 1
FOLIN, Otto — 1
FOLINGSBY, George Frederick — H
FOLINSBEE, John Fulton — 5
FOLK, Carey Albert
FOLK, Edgar Estes — 1
FOLK, Joseph Wingate — 1
FOLK, Marion Hayne Jr. — 4
FOLKMAR, Daniel — 4
FOLKMAR, Elnora Cuddeback
FOLKS, Homer — 4
FOLLAND, William Henry — 2
FOLLANSBEE, George Alanson

FOLLANSBEE, George Edward — 5
FOLLANSBEE, John — 3
FOLLANSBEE, Mitchell Davis — 1
FOLLANSBEE, Robert — 4
FOLLEN, Charles F. C. — H
FOLLEN, Eliza Lee Cabot — H
FOLLETT, Charles Walcott — 3
FOLLETT, Martin Dewey — 1
FOLLETT, Mary Parker — 5
FOLLETT, William W. — 1
FOLLEY, Walter Clark — 4
FOLLMAN, Matthew A. — 4
FOLLMER, Harold Newton
FOLSOM, Alfred Iverson — 2
FOLSOM, Benjamin — 1
FOLSOM, Charles — H
FOLSOM, Charles Follen — 1
FOLSOM, George — 4
FOLSOM, Justus Watson — 1
FOLSOM, Nathaniel — H
FOLSOM, Sarah Blanton (Mrs. Douglas Lawrence Folsom, Jr.) — 5
FOLSTER, George Thomas — 4
FOLTS, Aubrey Fairfax — 4
FOLTZ, Clara Shortridge — 5
FOLTZ, Frederick Steinman — 3
FOLTZ, James A. Jr. — 5
FOLWELL, Amory Prescott — 5
FOLWELL, Arthur Hamilton — 4
FOLWELL, Samuel — H
FOLWELL, William Hazelton — 2
FOLWELL, William Watts — 1
FOLZ, Stanley — 3
FONDA, John H. — 5
FONDE, George Heustis — 2
FONDILLER, Richard — 4
FONG, Jacob — 4
FONT, Pedro — H
FONTAINE, Arthur Benjamin — 5
FONTAINE, Lamar — 3
FONTAINE, William Morris — 1
FONTANA, Lucio — 5
FONVILLE, Richard Henry — 3
FONVILLE, William Drakeford — 4
FOOKS, D(aniel) W(ebster) — 5
FOORD, Archibald Smith — 5
FOORD, James Alfred — 5
FOOT, Edwin Hawley — 3
FOOT, Nathan Chandler — 3
FOOT, Samuel — 5
FOOT, Solomon — H
FOOTE, Allen Ripley — 4
FOOTE, Andrew Hull — H
FOOTE, Arthur — 1
FOOTE, Charles Augustus — H
FOOTE, Dellizon Arthur — 1
FOOTE, Edward Bliss — 1
FOOTE, Edward Bond — 4
FOOTE, Elizabeth Louisa — 4
FOOTE, Harry Ward — 1
FOOTE, Harry Ward — 2
FOOTE, Henry Stuart — H
FOOTE, Henry Wilder — 4
FOOTE, John A. — 5
FOOTE, John Taintor — 2
FOOTE, Lucius Harwood — 1
FOOTE, Mark — 3
FOOTE, Mary Hallock — 1
FOOTE, Morris Cooper — 1
FOOTE, Nathaniel — 2
FOOTE, Paul D(arwin) — 5
FOOTE, Percy Wright — 4
FOOTE, Stephen Miller — 4
FOOTE, Will Howe — 5
FOOTE, William Henry — H
FOOTE, William Wirt — 4
FOOTNER, Hulbert — 2
FORAKER, Burch — 1
FORAKER, Forest Aimes — 2
FORAKER, Joseph Benson — 1
FORAND, Aime Joseph — 5
FORBES, Alexander — 1
FORBES, Allan — 3
FORBES, Allen Boyd — 1
FORBES, Allyn Bailey — 1
FORBES, B. C. — 3

FORBES, Bruce Charles — 4
FORBES, Charles Henry — 1
FORBES, Edgar Allen — 5
FORBES, Edward Waldo — 5
FORBES, Edwin — 1
FORBES, Elmer Severance — 4
FORBES, Ernest Browning — 4
FORBES, Esther — 4
FORBES, Francis Murray — 4
FORBES, Frederick Faber
FORBES, Frederick Levi — 1
FORBES, George Mather — 4
FORBES, Gerrit Angelo — 1
FORBES, Harriette Merrifield — 3
FORBES, Harrye Rebecca Piper Smith (Mrs. Armitage S.C.) — 5
FORBES, Henry Prentiss — 1
FORBES, James — H
FORBES, James — 1
FORBES, Jesse Franklin — 4
FORBES, John * — H
FORBES, John F. — 4
FORBES, John Franklin — 4
FORBES, John Murray * — H
FORBES, John Sims — 4
FORBES, Richard Tasker — 4
FORBES, Robert — 1
FORBES, Robert Bennet — H
FORBES, Robert Humphrey — 5
FORBES, Russell — 3
FORBES, Stephen Alfred — 4
FORBES, Theodore Frelinghuysen — 1
FORBES, W. Cameron — 3
FORBES, W. O. — 1
FORBES, William C. — H
FORBES, William Trowbridge — 1
FORBES-ROBERTSON, Johnston — 1
FORBUSH, Edward Howe — 1
FORBUSH, Gayle T. — 5
FORBUSH, William Byron — 1
FORCE, Juliana — 2
FORCE, Manning Ferguson — 1
FORCE, Peter — H
FORCE, Raymond Charles — 3
FORCHHEIMER, Frederick — 1
FORD, Alexander Hume — 2
FORD, Amelia Clewley — 1
FORD, Arthur Hillyer — 1
FORD, Arthur R. — H
FORD, Arthur Younger — 1
FORD, Charles F. — 5
FORD, Charles Halsey Lindsley — 1
FORD, Clyde Ellsworth — 5
FORD, Corey — 5
FORD, Cornelius — 4
FORD, Daniel — 5
FORD, Daniel Sharp — 1
FORD, David McKechnie — 3
FORD, Edsel — 5
FORD, Edsel Bryant — 2
FORD, Elias Allen — 4
FORD, Emory M. — 5
FORD, Ford Madox — H
FORD, Ford Madox — 2
FORD, Ford Madox — 4
FORD, Francis Chipman — 1
FORD, Frank Richards — 1
FORD, Frazer L. — 3
FORD, George Alfred — 4
FORD, George Burdett — 4
FORD, George Michael — 1
FORD, Gordon Lester — H
FORD, Guy Stanton — 4
FORD, H. Clark — 1
FORD, Harriet French — 3
FORD, Henry — 1
FORD, Henry Clinton — 1
FORD, Henry Clinton — 1
FORD, Henry Jones — 1
FORD, Henry P. — 1
FORD, Hiram Church — 5
FORD, Hugh — 5
FORD, Isaac Nelson — 1
FORD, Jacob — H
FORD, James — H
FORD, James — 2
FORD, James Buchanan — 2
FORD, James Lauren — 1
FORD, James W. — H
FORD, Jeremiah Denis Matthias — 3
FORD, John — 1
FORD, John Baptiste — H
FORD, John Battice — H
FORD, John Donaldson — 1

FORD, John Thompson — H
FORD, Joseph C. — 3
FORD, Julia Ellsworth (Mrs. Simeon Ford) — 5
FORD, Leland Merritt — 4
FORD, Leonard Augustine — 5
FORD, Mary Hanford — 4
FORD, Mason — 3
FORD, Melbourne Haddock — H
FORD, Nancy Keffer — 4
FORD, Nicholas — 1
FORD, Patrick — 1
FORD, Paul Charles — 5
FORD, Paul Leicester — 4
FORD, Peter J. — 4
FORD, Peyton — 5
FORD, Richard — 5
FORD, Richard Clyde — 3
FORD, Sallie Rochester — 4
FORD, Samuel Clarence — 4
FORD, Samuel Howard — 1
FORD, Sewell — 4
FORD, Shirley Samuel — 2
FORD, Simeon — 1
FORD, Smith Thomas — 1
FORD, Stanley Myron — 5
FORD, Sumner — 4
FORD, Thomas — H
FORD, Thomas Francis — 3
FORD, Tirey Lafayette — 4
FORD, Walter Burton — 5
FORD, Willard Stanley — 3
FORD, William D. — H
FORD, William Ebenezer — 1
FORD, William Henry — 4
FORD, William Miller — 1
FORD, William Webber — 1
FORD, Worthington Chauncey — 4
FORDHAM, Herbert — 3
FORDNEY, Joseph Warren — 1
FORDYCE, Charles — 1
FORDYCE, Claude Powell — 3
FORDYCE, John Addison — 1
FORDYCE, Samuel Wesley — 1
FORDYCE, Samuel Wesley — 2
FOREHAND, Brooks — 3
FOREMAN, Albert Watson — 3
FOREMAN, Alvan Herbert — 3
FOREMAN, Grant — 3
FOREMAN, Harold Edwin — 3
FOREMAN, Henry Gerhard — 1
FOREMAN, Lester B. — 5
FOREMAN, Milton J. — 1
FOREMAN, Oscar G. — 1
FOREPAUGH, Adam — H
FORESMAN, Hugh Austin — 3
FOREST, John Anthony — 1
FORESTER, Cecil Scott — 4
FORESTER, Frank — H
FORESTER, John B. — H
FORESTI, Eleutario Felice — 1
FORGAN, David Robertson — 1
FORGAN, James Berwick — 1
FORGASH, Morris — 4
FORIO, Edgar Joseph — 5
FORKER, John Norman — 3
FORMAN, Allan — 1
FORMAN, David — 4
FORMAN, Henry James — 4
FORMAN, Joshua — 1
FORMAN, Justus Miles — 1
FORMAN, Samuel Eagle — 4
FORMAN, William St John — 1
FORMENTO, Felix — 1
FORMES, Karl Johann — H
FORNANCE, Joseph — H
FORNELL, Earl Wesley — 5
FORNES, Charles Vincent — 1
FORNEY, Daniel Munroe — 4
FORNEY, James — 1
FORNEY, John H. — 1
FORNEY, John Wien — H
FORNEY, Peter — H
FORNEY, William — H
FORNEY, William R(ufus) — 5
FORNIA, Rita — 1
FORREST, Aubrey Leland — 3
FORREST, Edwin — H
FORREST, French — H
FORREST, Jacob Dorsey — 1

FORREST, Nathan Bedford — H
FORREST, Nathan Bedford — 2
FORREST, Thomas — H
FORREST, Uriah — H
FORREST, William Mentzel — 4
FORREST, William Sylvester — 4
FORRESTAL, Frank Vincent — 3
FORRESTAL, James — 2
FORRESTAL, James — 4
FORRESTER, D. Bruce — 3
FORRESTER, Elijah Lewis — 5
FORRESTER, Graham — 2
FORRESTER, Henry — 4
FORRESTER, James Joseph — 1
FORREY, George C. Jr. — 3
FORRY, John Harold — 4
FORSANDER, Nils — 1
FORSE, Charles Thomas — 4
FORSTALL, Armand William — 2
FORSTER, Alexius Mador — 4
FORSTER, E(dward) M(organ) — 5
FORSTER, Frank Joseph — 2
FORSTER, James Franklin — 5
FORSTER, Rudolph — 5
FORSTER, Weidman Wallace — 5
FORSTMANN, Curt — 1
FORSTMANN, Erwin — 3
FORSTMANN, Julius G. — 4
FORSYTH, David Dryden — 1
FORSYTH, George Alexander — 1
FORSYTH, Henry Hazlett — 1
FORSYTH, James McQueen — 1
FORSYTH, James W. — 1
FORSYTH, Jessie — 4
FORSYTH, John * — H
FORSYTH, Robert — 1
FORSYTH, Thomas — H
FORSYTH, William — 1
FORSYTHE, George Elmer — 5
FORSYTHE, Newton Melville — 4
FORSYTHE, Robert Stanley — 1
FORSYTHE, W. B. — 3
FORT, Franklin William — 1
FORT, George Franklin — H
FORT, Gerrit — 3
FORT, Greenbury Lafayette — H
FORT, J. Franklin — 1
FORT, Jardine Carter — 3
FORT, Joel B. Jr. — 4
FORT, Marion Kirkland Jr. — 2
FORT, Rufus Elijah — 2
FORT, Tomlinson — H
FORTEN, James — H
FORTENBAUGH, Abraham — 4
FORTENBAUGH, Robert — 3
FORTESCUE, Granville — 3
FORTH, Edward Walter — 4
FORTIER, Alcee — 1
FORTIER, Michel J. — 3
FORTIER, Samuel — 3
FORTUNE, Alonzo Willard — 1
FORTUNE, J(ohn) Robert — 5
FORTUNE, William — 4
FORWARD, Chauncey — H
FORWARD, John F, Jr. — 5
FORWARD, Walter — H
FORWOOD, William Henry — 1
FOSBROKE, Gerald Elton — 4
FOSBROKE, Hughell Edgar Woodall — 3
FOSCUE, Edwin Jay — 5
FOSDICK, Charles Austin — 1
FOSDICK, James William — 4
FOSDICK, Lucian John — 4
FOSDICK, Nicoll — H
FOSDICK, Raymond Blaine — 5
FOSDICK, William Whiteman — H
FOSHAG, William Frederick — 3
FOSHAY, James A. — 1
FOSKETT, James Hicks — 4
FOSS, Claude William — 1
FOSS, Cyrus David — H

FORREST, — H
FOSS, Feodore Feodorovich — 5
FOSS, George Edmund — 1
FOSS, George Ernest — 3
FOSS, Noble — 5
FOSS, Sam Walter — 1
FOSS, Wilson Jr. — 3
FOSSEEN, Carrie S. (mrs. Manley L. Fosseen)
FOSSLER, Laurence — 1
FOSTER, A. Lawrence — H
FOSTER, Abiel — H
FOSTER, Abigail Kelley — H
FOSTER, Addison Gardner — 1
FOSTER, Agnes Greene — 2
FOSTER, Albert Douglas — 5
FOSTER, Alexis Caldwell — 2
FOSTER, Alfred Dwight — 1
FOSTER, Allyn King — 1
FOSTER, Ardeen — 4
FOSTER, Arthur Borders — 1
FOSTER, Austin Theophilus — 4
FOSTER, Ben — 1
FOSTER, Bernard Augustus, Jr. — 5
FOSTER, Cassius G. — 1
FOSTER, Charles — 1
FOSTER, Charles Elwood — 1
FOSTER, Charles Henry Wheelwright — 3
FOSTER, Charles James — H
FOSTER, Charles Kendall — 2
FOSTER, Charles Richard — 1
FOSTER, David Johnson — 1
FOSTER, David Nathaniel — 1
FOSTER, David Skaats — 1
FOSTER, Dwight — H
FOSTER, Edna Abigail — 2
FOSTER, Edward K. — 4
FOSTER, Ellsworth D. — 1
FOSTER, Enoch — 1
FOSTER, Ephraim Hubbard — H
FOSTER, Ernest Le Neve — 4
FOSTER, Eugene Clifford — 1
FOSTER, Fay — 4
FOSTER, Finley M. K. — 3
FOSTER, Francis Apthorp — 5
FOSTER, Frank Hugh — 1
FOSTER, Frank Keyes — 1
FOSTER, Frank Pierce — 1
FOSTER, George Burgess Jr. — 3
FOSTER, George Burman — 1
FOSTER, George Nimmons — 3
FOSTER, George P. — 4
FOSTER, George Sanford — 4
FOSTER, Glen Edward — 4
FOSTER, Hannah Webster — H
FOSTER, Harry Ellsworth — 4
FOSTER, Harry LaTourette — 1
FOSTER, Henry Allen — H
FOSTER, Henry Bacon — 3
FOSTER, Henry Donnel — 1
FOSTER, Henry Hubbard — 2
FOSTER, Herbert Darling — 1
FOSTER, Herbert Hamilton — 2
FOSTER, Horatio Alvah — 1
FOSTER, Irving Lysander — 1
FOSTER, Israel Moore — 3
FOSTER, James Peers — 4
FOSTER, James William — 4
FOSTER, Jeanne Robert (Mrs. Matlack Foster) — 5
FOSTER, John — H
FOSTER, John Early — 1
FOSTER, John Gilman — 1
FOSTER, John Gray — H
FOSTER, John Hopkins — 1
FOSTER, John McGaw — 1
FOSTER, John Morrell — 1
FOSTER, John Morton — 5
FOSTER, John Pierrepont Codrington
FOSTER, John Shaw — 2
FOSTER, John Watson — 1
FOSTER, John Wells — H
FOSTER, Joseph — 1
FOSTER, Joshua Hill — 5

FOSTER, Judith Ellen Horton 1
FOSTER, Julian Barringer 2
FOSTER, LaFayette Sabine H
FOSTER, Laurence 5
FOSTER, Luther 4
FOSTER, Mabel Grace 5
FOSTER, Major Bronson 3
FOSTER, Marcellus Elliott 2
FOSTER, Martin D. 1
FOSTER, Matthias Lanckton H
FOSTER, Maximilian 5
FOSTER, Milton Hugh 5
FOSTER, Murphy James 1
FOSTER, Nathaniel Greene H
FOSTER, Nellis Barnes 1
FOSTER, Paul F. 5
FOSTER, Paul Hadley 4
FOSTER, Paul Pinkerton 5
FOSTER, Percy Semple 1
FOSTER, Randolph Sinks 1
FOSTER, Reginald 2
FOSTER, Richard Clarke 5
FOSTER, Robert Arnold 5
FOSTER, Robert Frederick 2
FOSTER, Robert Sandford 1
FOSTER, Robert Verrell 5
FOSTER, Roger 1
FOSTER, Rufus Edward 2
FOSTER, Rufus James 4
FOSTER, Samuel Monell 5
FOSTER, Sheppard Walter 2
FOSTER, Stephen Clark H
FOSTER, Stephen Collins H
FOSTER, Stephen Symonds H
FOSTER, T. Stewart 4
FOSTER, Theodore 1
FOSTER, Theodosia Toll 3
FOSTER, Theodosia Toll 4
FOSTER, Thomas Arnold 5
FOSTER, Thomas Flournoy H
FOSTER, Thomas Henry 3
FOSTER, Thomas Jefferson H
FOSTER, Thomas Jefferson 4
FOSTER, Virgll Elwood 5
FOSTER, Volney William 1
FOSTER, W(alter) Bert(ram) 5
FOSTER, Warren William 2
FOSTER, Wilder De Ayr H
FOSTER, William 1
FOSTER, William Davis 1
FOSTER, William Eaton 1
FOSTER, William Edward * 1
FOSTER, William Frederick 3
FOSTER, William Garnett 2
FOSTER, William Heber Thompson 2
FOSTER, William Henry 3
FOSTER, William James 3
FOSTER, William Trufant 3
FOSTER, William Wallace 3
FOSTER, William Wilson Jr. 1
FOSTER, William Z. 4
FOTHERGILL, John Vincent 3
FOTITCH, A. Constantin 3
FOUGNER, Ernest Hjalmar 5
FOUGNER, G. Selmer 1
FOUILHOUX, Jacques Andre 2
FOUKE, Philip Bond H
FOUKE, William Hargrave 1
FOULDS, Henry W. 3
FOULK, Charles William 3
FOULK, Claude Claude 5
FOULK, George Clayton H
FOULK, William Henry 1
FOULKE, Elizabeth E. 5
FOULKE, William Dudley 1
FOULKROD, Harry Ellsworth 5
FOULKROD, William W. 1
FOULOIS, Benjamin Delahauf 4

FOUNTAIN, Claude Russell 2
FOUNTAIN, Percy Coleman 3
FOUNTAIN, Reginald Morton 5
FOUNTAIN, Richard Tillman 2
FOUNTAIN, Samuel Warren 1
FOUNTAIN, William Alfred Sr. 3
FOURNIER, Alexis Jean 2
FOURNIER, Alphonse 4
FOURNIER, Leslie Thomas 4
FOUSE, Levi Garner 1
FOUSE, Winfred Eugene 3
FOUST, Julius Isaac 2
FOUT, Henry H. 2
FOWKE, Gerard 1
FOWLE, Daniel H
FOWLE, Frank Fuller 2
FOWLE, Luther Richardson H
FOWLE, William Bentley H
FOWLER, Alfred 3
FOWLER, Arthur Thomas 5
FOWLER, Benjamin Austin 1
FOWLER, Burton Philander 4
FOWLER, C. Lewis 5
FOWLER, Carl Hitchcock 2
FOWLER, Charles Evan 2
FOWLER, Charles Henry 1
FOWLER, Charles Newell 4
FOWLER, Charles Rollin 3
FOWLER, Charles Wesley 4
FOWLER, Chester Almeron 2
FOWLER, Clifton Lefevre 4
FOWLER, David 1
FOWLER, Edmund P. Jr. 5
FOWLER, Edmund Prince 4
FOWLER, Elbert Hazelton 1
FOWLER, Elbert Hazelton 2
FOWLER, Elting Alexander 1
FOWLER, Frank 5
FOWLER, Frederick Curtis, II 1
FOWLER, Frederick Hall 2
FOWLER, Gene 4
FOWLER, George Little 1
FOWLER, George Ryerson 1
FOWLER, George S. 4
FOWLER, H. Robert 1
FOWLER, Harold North 5
FOWLER, Harry Atwood 5
FOWLER, Helen Frances Wose (Mrs. Albert Vann Fowler) 1
FOWLER, Henry Thatcher 2
FOWLER, James Alexander 3
FOWLER, Jessie Allen 1
FOWLER, John H
FOWLER, John 2
FOWLER, Joseph Smith 1
FOWLER, Laurence Hall 5
FOWLER, Leonard Burke 2
FOWLER, Nathaniel Clark Jr. 1
FOWLER, Orin H
FOWLER, Orson Squire H
FOWLER, Raymond Foster 2
FOWLER, Rex H. 5
FOWLER, Richard Labbitt 5
FOWLER, Robert Lambert 3
FOWLER, Robert Ludlow 1
FOWLER, Russell Story 1
FOWLER, Samuel H
FOWLER, Thomas Powell 1
FOWLER, Trevor Thomas H
FOWLER, Walter William 3
FOWLER, William Charles 1
FOWLER, William Edward 5
FOX, Abraham Manuel 1
FOX, Albert Charles 1
FOX, Alex P. 4
FOX, Andrew Fuller 4
FOX, Austen George 1
FOX, Carl 1
FOX, Charles Eben 1
FOX, Charles Eli 4
FOX, Charles James 5
FOX, Charles Kemble H

FOX, Charles Shattuck 1
FOX, Daniel Frederick 2
FOX, Della 2
FOX, Dixon Ryan 2
FOX, Early Lee 2
FOX, Edward J. 1
FOX, Emma Augusta 1
FOX, Fayburn L. 4
FOX, Felix 1
FOX, Fontaine Talbot Jr. 4
FOX, Francis Morton 5
FOX, Fred C. 4
FOX, Fred Lee 5
FOX, Frederick S(hartle) 5
FOX, Genevieve 3
FOX, George Henry 1
FOX, George Levi 1
FOX, George Washington Lafayette H
FOX, Gilbert 1
FOX, Gustavus Vasa H
FOX, Harry H
FOX, Henry 5
FOX, Herbert 2
FOX, Herbert Henry Heywood 5
FOX, Howard 3
FOX, Jabez 4
FOX, James Butler 4
FOX, James D. 1
FOX, James Harold 5
FOX, Jared Copeland, III 5
FOX, Jesse William 1
FOX, John 1
FOX, John Jr. 2
FOX, John McDill 1
FOX, John Pierce 5
FOX, Joseph John 1
FOX, L. Webster 1
FOX, Luther Augustine 4
FOX, Margaret H
FOX, Matthew 4
FOX, Norman 1
FOX, Norman Arnold 3
FOX, Oscar Chapman 4
FOX, Philip 2
FOX, Sherwood Dean 5
FOX, Victor Samuel 3
FOX, Walter Dennis 1
FOX, Walter Gordon 4
FOX, William 3
FOX, William Freeman 1
FOX, William H. 3
FOX, William Henry 5
FOX, William Joseph 2
FOX, Williams Carlton 1
FOXALL, Henry H
FOXCROFT, Frank 1
FOY, Byron Cecil 1
FOY, Eddie 1
FOY, Mary Emily 5
FOY, Robert Cherry 2
FOYE, Andrew Jay Coleman 1
FOYE, Wilbur Garland 1
FRACHTENBERG, Leo Joachim
FRACKER, Stanley Black 5
FRACKLETON, Susan Stuart 4
FRADENBURGH, Adelbert Grant 1
FRADENBURGH, J. N. 4
FRAILEY, Carson Peter 3
FRAILEY, Leonard August 1
FRAIN, Andrew Thomas 4
FRAKER, George W. 3
FRALEIGH, Arnold 5
FRALEY, Frederick H
FRAME, Alice Browne 1
FRAME, Andrew Jay 1
FRAME, James Everett 3
FRAME, Nat Terry 2
FRANCA, Manuel Joachim 'de H
FRANCE, Beulah Sanford 5
FRANCE, Charles E. 3
FRANCE, Evalyn Smith 5
FRANCE, Harry Clinton 5
FRANCE, Jacob 4
FRANCE, Joseph Irwin 1
FRANCE, Lewis B. 4
FRANCE, Melville Jefferson 3
FRANCE, Mervin B. 5
FRANCE, Royal Wilbur 4
FRANCHERE, Gabriel 1
FRANCHOT, Charles Pascal 3
FRANCHOT, Richard H
FRANCINE, Albert Philip 1

FRANCIS, Arthur J. 5
FRANCIS, Brother Clement 4
FRANCIS, Charles Edward 1
FRANCIS, Charles Inge 5
FRANCIS, Charles Spencer 1
FRANCIS, Charles Stephen H
FRANCIS, Convers 1
FRANCIS, David Rowland 1
FRANCIS, Edward 5
FRANCIS, Emily A. 4
FRANCIS, G. Churchill 5
FRANCIS, George Blinn 1
FRANCIS, Herbert Cadogan 4
FRANCIS, James A. 1
FRANCIS, James Bicheno H
FRANCIS, James Draper 5
FRANCIS, John Jr. 3
FRANCIS, John Brown 1
FRANCIS, John F. H
FRANCIS, John Haywood 1
FRANCIS, John Miller 1
FRANCIS, John Morgan H
FRANCIS, John Morgan 1
FRANCIS, John Wakefield H
FRANCIS, Joseph H
FRANCIS, Joseph G. 1
FRANCIS, Joseph Marshall 1
FRANCIS, Kay 5
FRANCIS, Lee Masten 5
FRANCIS, Mark 1
FRANCIS, Parker B. 3
FRANCIS, Richard Clarence 1
FRANCIS, Richard J. 5
FRANCIS, Samuel Ward H
FRANCIS, Sarah Dimon Chapman 4
FRANCIS, Sir Josiah 4
FRANCIS, Tench H
FRANCIS, Thomas, Jr. 5
FRANCIS, W. A. 3
FRANCIS, William Bates 5
FRANCIS, William Howard 2
FRANCIS, William Howard Jr.
FRANCIS, William Mursell 3
FRANCISCO, John Bond 1
FRANCK, Charles 5
FRANCK, Harry Alverson 4
FRANCKE, Kuno
FRANCOIS, Samson 5
FRANCOIS, Victor Emmanuel 4
FRANCOLINI, Joseph Nocola 4
FRANDSEN, Julius Herman 4
FRANDSEN, Peter 5
FRANGES, Ivan 5
FRANK, Abraham 1
FRANK, Alfred 2
FRANK, Alfred Swift 1
FRANK, Arthur Albert 4
FRANK, Augustus H
FRANK, Eli 3
FRANK, Everett 1
FRANK, Fritz John 1
FRANK, Glenn 1
FRANK, Graham 5
FRANK, Henry 1
FRANK, Isaac William 1
FRANK, Jerome N. 3
FRANK, John Mayer 4
FRANK, Joseph Otto 5
FRANK, Lawrence Kelso 4
FRANK, Lawrence Louis 5
FRANK, Lewis Crown, Jr. 5
FRANK, Maude Morrison 5
FRANK, Nathan 1
FRANK, Pat Harry Hart 4
FRANK, Royal Thaxter 1
FRANK, Tenney 1
FRANK, Theodore 4
FRANK, Theodore McConnell 4
FRANK, Waldo 4
FRANK, Walter 5
FRANKAU, Pamela 5
FRANKE, Gustav Henry 5
FRANKE, Louis 4
FRANKEL, Bernard Louis 5
FRANKEL, Emil 1
FRANKEL, Lee Kaufer 1
FRANKEL, Max 5
FRANKEL, William Victor 5

FRANKENBERG, Theodore Thomas
FRANKENFIELD, Harry Crawford
FRANKENSTEIN, Godfrey N.
FRANKENSTEIN, John Peter
FRANKENTHAL, Adolph Levy
FRANKFORT, Henri
FRANKFORTER, George Bell
FRANKFURTER, Felix
FRANKL, Paul Theodore
FRANKLAND, Frederick Herston
FRANKLAND, Frederick William
FRANKLAND, Lady Agnes Surriage H
FRANKLIN, Alfred
FRANKLIN, Benjamin *
FRANKLIN, Benjamin A.
FRANKLIN, Chester Arthur
FRANKLIN, Edward Curtis
FRANKLIN, Fabian
FRANKLIN, Frank
FRANKLIN, George
FRANKLIN, James
FRANKLIN, James Henry
FRANKLIN, Jesse
FRANKLIN, John Eddy 5
FRANKLIN, John Rankin
FRANKLIN, Leo M. 2
FRANKLIN, Lewis Battelle
FRANKLIN, Lindley Murray
FRANKLIN, Lucy Jenkins
FRANKLIN, Lynn Winterdale
FRANKLIN, Marvin Augustus
FRANKLIN, Melvin M.
FRANKLIN, Meshack H
FRANKLIN, Philip
FRANKLIN, Philip Albright Small
FRANKLIN, Samuel Petty
FRANKLIN, Samuel Rhoads
FRANKLIN, Sidney Arnold
FRANKLIN, Thomas Levering
FRANKLIN, Wallace Collin
FRANKLIN, Walter Alexander
FRANKLIN, Walter Simonds
FRANKLIN, Walter Simonds
FRANKLIN, William H
FRANKLIN, William Buel 5
FRANKLIN, William Suddards
FRANKLIN, Wirt
FRANKS, E. T. 4
FRANKS, John B. 2
FRANKS, Robert A. 1
FRANT, Samuel 4
FRANTZ, Edward 4
FRANTZ, Frank 1
FRANTZ, Frank Flavius 1
FRANTZ, Joseph Henry 1
FRANTZ, Robert Benjamin
FRANTZ, Virginia Kneeland 4
FRANZ, Elmer Franklin
FRANZ, Shepherd Ivory
FRANZEN, August 1
FRANZEN, Carl G. F.
FRANZHEIM, Kenneth
FRANZONI, Charles William
FRAPRIE, Frank Roy 5
FRAPS, George Stronach 5
FRARY, Ihna Thayer 5
FRASCA, William Robert
FRASCH, Herman H
FRASCH, Herman
FRASER, Abel McIver
FRASER, Alexander David
FRASER, Arthur McNutt 5
FRASER, Blair 5
FRASER, Carlyle
FRASER, Cecil Eaton 2
FRASER, Charles H
FRASER, Chelsea Curtis 3
FRASER, Daniel 1
FRASER, Duncan William

FRASER, 1
Elisha Alexander
FRASER, Forrest L. 3
FRASER, Frank Edwin 5
FRASER, Harry Wilson 3
FRASER, Horace John 5
FRASER, Horatio Nelson 4
FRASER, Hugh John 3
FRASER, James Earle 5
FRASER, John Falconer 5
FRASER, Laura Gardin 3
FRASER, Leon 2
FRASER, Malcolm 3
FRASER, Melvin 1
FRASER, Peter 3
FRASER, Samuel 3
FRASER, Thomas Boone 1
FRASER, Wilber John 3
FRASER, 1
William Alexander
FRASER, William Lewis 1
FRASIER, 3
George Willard
FRATER, 4
George Ellsworth
FRAUENHEIM, 5
George Meyer
FRAUNCES, Samuel H
FRAWLEY, John Edward 3
FRAWLEY, John Milan 5
FRAWLEY, Michael P. 5
FRAWLEY, William 4
FRAYNE, Hugh 1
FRAZAR, Everett Welles 3
FRAZAR, Lether Edward 1
FRAZEE, Harry Herbert 1
FRAZEE, John H
FRAZER, David Ruddach 1
FRAZER, Elizabeth 4
FRAZER, George Enfield 5
FRAZER, John 4
FRAZER, John Fries H
FRAZER, John G. 2
FRAZER, John Stanley 1
FRAZER, 2
Joseph Christie Whitney
FRAZER, 5
Joseph Washington
FRAZER, Leslie 2
FRAZER, Oliver H
FRAZER, Persifor H
FRAZER, Persifor 1
FRAZER, Robert Sellers 1
FRAZER, William Henry 3
FRAZIER, Arthur Hugh 4
FRAZIER, Benjamin West 1
FRAZIER,
Charles Harrison
FRAZIER, Chester North 5
FRAZIER, 3
Clarence Mackay
FRAZIER, 4
Edward Franklin
FRAZIER, 1
George Harrison
FRAZIER, James B. 1
FRAZIER, John Robinson 4
FRAZIER, Kenneth 2
FRAZIER, Lynn Joseph 2
FRAZIER, 3
Raymond Robert
FRAZIER, Robert Thomas 1
FRAZIER, William Fiske 4
FREAR, James A. 1
FREAR, Walter 4
FREAR, Walter Francis 2
FREAR, William 1
FREAS, Howard George 5
FREAS, Thomas Bruce 1
FREAS, 1
William Streeper
FREASE, Donald William 5
FRECHETTE, 5
Annie Howells
FREDENTHAL, David 3
FREDERIC, Harold H
FREDERICK, 4
Daniel Alfred
FREDERICK, 1
George Aloysius
FREDERICK,
Karl Telford
FREDERICK, Pauline 5
FREDERICK, 5
Robert Tryon
FREDERICK, 4
Russell Adair
FREDERICKS, 2
John Donnan
FREDERICKS, R. N. 3
FREDERICKSON, 3
Charles Richard
FREDERICKSON, George 4
FREDERIK, 5
Christian Frederik Franz
Michael Carl Valdemar

FREDERIKSEN, 4
Ditlew Monrad
FREDRICK, John E. 2
FREDRICK, Leopold 1
FREE, Arthur Monroe 3
FREE, Edward Elway 1
FREE, Lincoln Forrest 3
FREE, Montague 4
FREE, Spencer Michael 1
FREE, Walter Henry 4
FREEBORN, Stanley B. 4
FREEBOURN, Harrison J. 3
FREEBURG, Victor Oscar 4
FREED, Arthur 5
FREED, Charles Abram 1
FREED, Emerich Burt 1
FREED, Isadore 5
FREEDLANDER, A.L. 5
FREEDLANDER, 2
Joseph Henry
FREEDLEY, 1
Angelo Tillinghast
FREEDLEY, 1
Edwin Troxell
FREEDLEY, George 4
FREEDLEY, John H
FREEDLEY, Vinton 5
FREEDMAN, Andrew 1
FREEDMAN, 5
Emanuel R(alph)
FREEDMAN, John Joseph 3
FREEDMAN,
William Horatio
FREEHILL, Joseph Hugh 4
FREELING, 5
Sargent Prentiss
FREEMAN, A. F. Patrick 4
FREEMAN, Abraham
Clark 1
FREEMAN, Albert
Howard 4
FREEMAN, Alden 4
FREEMAN, Alfred Bird 4
FREEMAN, Allen Weir 3
FREEMAN, Bernardus H
FREEMAN, 5
Charles Seymour
FREEMAN, Charles West 4
FREEMAN, Charles Yoe 4
FREEMAN, 1
Clarence Campbell
FREEMAN, Clayton E. 5
FREEMAN, 3
Douglas Southall
FREEMAN, Edmond
Wroe 2
FREEMAN, Edward
Monroe 4
FREEMAN, 5
Ernest Bigelow
FREEMAN, 3
Ernest Harrison
FREEMAN, 2
Francis Breakey
FREEMAN, Frank Nugent 4
FREEMAN, George H
FREEMAN, George
Fouche 1
FREEMAN, 3
Hadley Fairfield
FREEMAN,
Harrison Barber
FREEMAN,
Henry Blanchard
FREEMAN, Henry
Raymond 1
FREEMAN, Henry
Varnum 1
FREEMAN, James H
FREEMAN,
James Crawford
FREEMAN, James
Edward 1
FREEMAN, James
Edwards
FREEMAN, 1
James Midwinter
FREEMAN, John Charles 1
FREEMAN, John D. H
FREEMAN, John Dolliver 2
FREEMAN, John Ripley 1
FREEMAN, John William 4
FREEMAN, Jonathan H
FREEMAN, Joseph 4
FREEMAN, Joseph
Hewett
FREEMAN,
Julia S. Wheelock
FREEMAN, Leonard 1
FREEMAN, Leonard 4
FREEMAN, Luther 1
FREEMAN,
Mary E. Wilkins
FREEMAN, Miller 3
FREEMAN, Monroe
Edward 5
FREEMAN, Nathaniel H

FREEMAN, Nathaniel Jr. H
FREEMAN, Ralph Evans 5
FREEMAN, 2
Richard Austin
FREEMAN, Richard D. 5
FREEMAN, 2
Richard Patrick
FREEMAN, Robert 1
FREEMAN, 2
Rowland Godfrey
FREEMAN, Talbot Otis 3
FREEMAN, Thomas H
FREEMAN, Thomas J. A. 1
FREEMAN, Thomas Jones 1
FREEMAN, 5
W(eldon) Winans
FREEMAN, 1
Walker Burford
FREEMAN, Walter 5
FREEMAN, Will 4
FREEMAN, William Perry 3
FREEMAN, Winfield 1
FREEMAN, 5
Y(oung) F(rank)
FREER, Charles Lang 1
FREER, Eleanor Everest 2
FREER, 1
Frederick Warren
FREER, 5
Hamline Hurlburt
FREER, Otto 1
FREER, Paul Caspar 4
FREER, Robert Elliott 4
FREER, Romeo Hoyt 3
FREER, William Davis 1
FREESE, John Henry 5
FREESTON, 5
William D(enney)
FREESTONE, Fred James 4
FREIBERG, Albert Henry 1
FREIBERG, 3
Leonard Henry
FREIBERG, Maurice 1
FREIBERGER,
Isadore Fred
FREIDIN, Jesse 5
FREILER, Abraham J. 4
FREIMAN, Henry David 5
FREIMANN,
Frank Michael
FREIN, Pierre Joseph 3
FREITAG, 5
Joseph Kendall
FREITAG, Walter 3
FRELEY, Jasper Warren 4
FRELINGHUYSEN, H
Frederick
FRELINGHUYSEN, 4
Frederick
FRELINGHUYSEN, H
Frederick Theodore
FRELINGHUYSEN, 2
Joseph Sherman
FRELINGHUYSEN, 1
Theodore
FRELINGHUYSEN, H
Theodorus Jacobus
FREMMING, Morris A. 3
FREMONT, Jessie Benton H
FREMONT, John Charles H
FREMONT, John Charles 1
FREMSTAD, Olive 3
FRENCH, Aaron H
FRENCH, Alice 1
FRENCH, Allen 1
FRENCH, Amos Tuck 1
FRENCH, Amos Tuck 2
FRENCH, Anne Warner 1
FRENCH, Arthur Willard 4
FRENCH, Asa Palmer 1
FRENCH, Augustus C. H
FRENCH, Burton Lee 1
FRENCH, Calvin Hervey 1
FRENCH, 1
Charles Wallace
FRENCH, Daniel Chester 1
FRENCH, 5
Edward L(ivingstone)
FRENCH, Edward
Sanborn 5
FRENCH, Edward Vinton 3
FRENCH, Edwin Davis 1
FRENCH, Ezra Bartlett H
FRENCH,
Ferdinand Courtney
FRENCH, Frances
Graham 1
FRENCH, Francis Henry 1
FRENCH, Frank 1
FRENCH, Frank
Chauncey 3
FRENCH, George 1
FRENCH, Harlan Page 1
FRENCH, 5
Harley Ellsworth
FRENCH, Henry Willard 4
FRENCH, Herbert Greer 2

FRENCH, Hollis 1
FRENCH, Horace S. 4
FRENCH, Howard Barclay 1
FRENCH, J. Milton 4
FRENCH, Jacob H
FRENCH, James Adolphus 5
FRENCH, James J. 4
FRENCH, John Robert 5
FRENCH, John Shaw 5
FRENCH, John Stewart 5
FRENCH, Joseph Lewis 4
FRENCH, Leigh Hill 4
FRENCH, 4
Lillie Hamilton
FRENCH, H
Lucy Virginia Smith
FRENCH, Mary Adams 1
FRENCH, 3
Mary Montagu Billings
FRENCH, 1
Nathaniel Stowers
FRENCH, Owen Bert 4
FRENCH, Paul Comly 4
FRENCH, Pinckney 4
FRENCH, Ralph Lines 4
FRENCH, Richard H
FRENCH, Robert Dudley 5
FRENCH, Roy LaVerne 5
FRENCH, Samuel Gibbs 1
FRENCH, 3
Seward Haight Jr.
FRENCH, Thomas H
FRENCH, Thomas Ewing 2
FRENCH, Willard 1
FRENCH, Willard S. 3
FRENCH, William 4
FRENCH, William Henry 5
FRENCH, William Henry 4
FRENCH, William John 1
FRENCH, William John 2
FRENCH, 1
William Merchant
Richardson
FRENCH, William W, Jr. 5
FRENEAU, Philip Morin H
FRENZEL, 2
John Peter Jr.
FRENZENY, Paul H
FRERET, James H
FRERET, William Alfred 4
FRERI, Joseph 3
FRERICHS, 3
William Reinhard
FRESEMAN,
William Langfitt
FRESHWATER, 4
Robert Marquis
FRETTER, Frank B. 1
FRETWELL, 4
Elbert Kirtley
FRETZ, Franklin Kline 2
FREUCHEN, Peter 5
FREUD, Sigmund H
FREUD, Sigmund 4
FREUDENBERGER, 2
Clay Briscoe
FREULER, John Rudolph 3
FREUND, Ernst 1
FREUND, Erwin O. 3
FREUND, Hugo Abraham 3
FREUND, Jules 4
FREUND, Sanford H. E. 3
FREUTEL, Guy Scott 3
FREW, Walter Edwin 1
FREW, William 2
FREW, William Nimick 1
FREY, Adolf 4
FREY, Albert R. 1
FREY, Calvin Alexander 2
FREY, Charles Daniel 3
FREY, Erwin Mortimer 3
FREY, John Philip 3
FREY, John Walter 5
FREY, John Weaver 5
FREY, H
Joseph Samuel Christian
Frederick
FREY, Oliver W. 1
FREY, 4
Walter Guernsey Jr.
FREYBERG, Sir Bernard 4
FREYER, William
Norman 4
FREYVOGEL, 2
Charles Ernest Cecil
FRICK, Frank H
FRICK, Henry 1
FRICK, Henry Clay 1
FRICK, John Henry 3
FRICK, Joseph E. 1
FRICK, Philip Louis 5
FRICK, William Jacob 1
FRICK, William Keller 1
FRICKE, William A. 2
FRICKS,
Lunsford Dickson
FRIDAY H

FRIDAY, David 2
FRIDEN, John H. 4
FRIDENBERG, Percy 4
FRIDGE, 3
Benjamin Franklin
FRIED, George 5
FRIEDEL, 3
Francis Joseph
FRIEDEN, Alexander 3
FRIEDEN, John Pierre 1
FRIEDEN, Pierre 3
FRIEDENWALD, Aaron H
FRIEDENWALD, Harry 1
FRIEDENWALD, Herbert 2
FRIEDENWALD, 3
Jonas Stein
FRIEDENWALD, Julius 1
FRIEDLAENDER, Israel 1
FRIEDLAENDER, Walter 4
FRIEDLANDER, Alfred 1
FRIEDLANDER, Israel 2
FRIEDLANDER, Leo 4
FRIEDLANDER,
Theodore
FRIEDMAN, Bernard 4
FRIEDMAN,
Elisha Michael
FRIEDMAN, 3
Emanuel David
FRIEDMAN, Francis Lee 4
FRIEDMAN, Harry G.
FRIEDMAN, 3
Herbert Jacob
FRIEDMAN, Isaac Kahn 1
FRIEDMAN, Lee Max 3
FRIEDMAN, Moses 3
FRIEDMAN, Samuel 5
FRIEDMAN, Sol H. 3
FRIEDMAN, 4
Stanleigh Pohly
FRIEDMAN, 5
William Frederick
FRIEDMAN, 4
William Henry
FRIEDMAN, 2
William Sterne
FRIEDMANN, Max E. 3
FRIEDMANN, 5
Wolfgang Gaston
FRIEDSAM, Michael 1
FRIEL, Arthur Olney 3
FRIEL, 4
Francis 'de Sales
FRIEL, Henry Craig 5
FIELDS, Eva Christine 5
FRIEND, 3
Albert Mathias Jr.
FRIEND, Albert Wiley 5
FRIEND, Emil 1
FRIEND, Oscar Jerome 4
FRIEND, Robert Ellas 4
FRIENDLY, Edwin
Samson 5
FRIERSON, Horace 3
FRIERSON, James Nelson 4
FRIERSON, John Woods 3
FRIERSON, 3
William Little
FRIES, 2
Adelaide Lisetta
FRIES, Amos Alfred 5
FRIES, Archibald 1
FRIES, Elmer Plumas 3
FRIES, Francis H
FRIES, Francis Henry 1
FRIES, George H
FRIES, J. Elias 3
FRIES, John H
FRIES, John William 1
FRIES, 1
William Otterbein
FRIESEKE, 1
Frederick Carl
FRIESELL, H. Edmund 2
FRIESEN, 3
Abraham Penner
FRIESNER, Ray Clarence 3
FRIETCHIE, Barbara H
FRIEZE, Henry Simmons 1
FRILEY, Charles Edwin 3
FRIMI, Rudolf 5
FRINK, Fred Goodrich 1
FRINK, 1
John Samuel Hatch
FRIPP, William J. 4
FRISBIE, Alvan Lillie 1
FRISBIE, Guy Stoddard 5
FRISBIE, Henry Samuel 1
FRISBIE, Levi H
FRISBIE, Robert Dean 2
FRISBIE, 4
William Albert
FRISBY, Edgar 1
FRISCH, Hartvig 2
FRISCH, Martin 3
FRISCH, 3
Ragnar Anton Kittil

FRISCH, William 1
FRISON, Theodore Henry 2
FRISSELL,
Algernon Sydney
FRISSELL, Hollis Burke 1
FRITCH, Louis Charlton 5
FRITSCH, Homer Charles 3
FRITSCHEL, H
Conrad Sigmund
FRITSCHEL, George John 4
FRITSCHEL,
Gottfried Leonhard Wilhelm
FRITSCHEL, 5
Herman L(awrence)
FRITTS, Carl Emerson 5
FRITZ, Herbert Daniel 5
FRITZ, John 1
FRITZ, 3
John Henry Charles
FRITZ, 5
Lawrence G(eorge)
FRITZ, Oscar Marion 3
FRITZSCHE, 4
Carl Ferdinand
FRIZELL, Joseph Palmer 1
FRIZOL, Sylvester M. 5
FRIZZELL, 1
Albert Burnett
FRIZZELL, 5
Donald Leslie
FROBISHER, Sir Martin H
FROEDTERT, Kurtis R. 3
FROEHLICH, Jack E. 1
FROEHLINGER, 3
Richard Anthony
FROELICHER, 4
Francis Mitchell
FROELICHER, Hans 1
FROHLICH, 5
Ludwig William
FROHMAN, Charles 1
FROHMAN, Daniel 1
FROHMAN, Philip Hubert 5
FROHMAN, Sidney 1
FROHRING, William Otto 3
FROLICH, Finn Haakon 2
FROMENTIN, Eligius H
FROMKES, Maurice 1
FROMMELT, Henry
Julius 5
FROMUTH, Charles
Henry 4
FRONING, 4
Henry Bernhardt
FRONTENAC, H
Louis 'de Baude
FROST, Albert D. 2
FROST, Albert Ellis 1
FROST, Alfred Sidney 1
FROST, Arthur Burdett 1
FROST, Charles Sumner 1
FROST, Edward J. 2
FROST, Edward Wheeler 4
FROST, Edwin Brant 1
FROST, Eliott Park 1
FROST, Frances 3
FROST, 5
Frederick George
FROST, Fredric Worthen 1
FROST, George H
FROST, 4
George Frederick
FROST, George Henry 1
FROST, Harry Talfourd 2
FROST, Henry Atherton 3
FROST, Henry Weston 3
FROST, James Marion 1
FROST, Joel H
FROST, John 1
FROST, John Edward 1
FROST, Joseph H. 3
FROST, 5
Leslie Miscampbell
FROST, Norman 4
FROST, Robert 4
FROST, Rufus Smith H
FROST, Stanley 2
FROST, Thomas C. 5
FROST, Thomas Gold 2
FROST, 1
Timothy Prescott
FROST, Wade Hampton 1
FROST, Walter Archer 4
FROST, Wesley .4
FROST, William Dodge 3
FROST, William Goodell 1
FROST, William Henry 1
FROTHINGHAM, 1
Arthur Lincoln
FROTHINGHAM,
Channing
FROTHINGHAM, Ellen 1
FROTHINGHAM, 5
Eugenia Brooks
FROTHINGHAM, James H
FROTHINGHAM, James 1

FROTHINGHAM, 2
Jessie Peabody
FROTHINGHAM, 1
Louis Adams
FROTHINGHAM, H
Nathaniel Langdon
FROTHINGHAM, H
Octavius Brooks
FROTHINGHAM, 1
Paul Revere
FROTHINGHAM, H
Richard
FROTHINGHAM, Robert 1
FROTHINGHAM, 3
Theodore Longfellow
FROTHINGHAM, 3
Thomas Goddard
FRUEAUFF, Frank W. 1
FRUEAUFF, Harry Day 3
FRUEHAUF, 4
Harry Richard
FRUEHAUF, 5
Harvey Charles
FRUEHAUF, Roy A. 4
FRUIT, John Phelps 4
FRUITNIGHT, John
Henry 1
FRY, Alfred Brooks 1
FRY, Anson Clifton 5
FRY, Birkett Davenport H
FRY, C. Luther 1
FRY, Carl 4
FRY, Clements Collard 3
FRY, Francis Rhodes 4
FRY, Franklin Clark 5
FRY, Franklin Foster 1
FRY, Georgiana Timken 4
FRY, Harry Shipley 3
FRY, Henry Davidson 1
FRY, Jacob 1
FRY, Jacob Jr. H
FRY, James Barnet H
FRY, John A.B. 5
FRY, John Hemming 2
FRY, Joseph Jr. H
FRY, Joshua H
FRY, Lawford H. 2
FRY, Morton Harrison 5
FRY, Richard H
FRY, Samuel Roeder 5
FRY, 1
Wilfred Washington
FRY, William Henry H
FRY, William Wallace 3
FRYBERGER, Agnes
Moore 1
FRYE, Alexis Everett 1
FRYE, Benjamin Porter 5
FRYE, Frank Augustus 5
FRYE, Jack 3
FRYE, James Albert 1
FRYE, John H. 2
FRYE, Joseph H
FRYE, L. Arnold 4
FRYE, 5
Louise Alexander (Mrs.
Royal M. Frye)
FRYE, Newton Phillips 3
FRYE, Prosser Hall 1
FRYE, 5
Theodore Christian
FRYE, William 4
FRYE, William Clinton 3
FRYE, William Pierce 1
FRYER, Douglas 4
FRYER, Eli Thompson 5
FRYER, 5
Jane Eayre (Mrs. John
Gayton Fryer)
FRYER, John 4
FRYER, 1
Robert Livingston
FTELEY, Alphonse 1
FUCHS, Emil 1
FUERBRINGER, 2
Ludwig Ernest
FUERST, P. Placidus 3
FUERTES, 1
Estevan Antonio
FUERTES, 1
James Hillhouse
FUERTES, Louis Agassiz 1
FUESS, Claude Moore 4
FUESSLE, 1
Newton Augustus
FUGARD, John Reed 5
FUJKHOUSER, 4
Raymond Joseph
FULBRIGHT, James F. 2
FULCHER, Paul Milton 3
FULD, Leonhard Felix 4
FULEIHAN, Anis 5
FULKERSON,
Frank Ballard
FULKERSON, Monroe 4
FULLAM, James Edson 3

FULLAM, 1
William Freeland
FULLBROOK, Earl S. 4
FULLER, 4
Abraham Lincoln
FULLER, Alfred Howard 3
FULLER, Alvin Tufts 3
FULLER, Andrew S. H
FULLER, Anna 1
FULLER, 4
Arthur Davenport
FULLER, Ben Hebard 1
FULLER, 5
Caroline Macomber
FULLER, Charles E. 5
FULLER, Charles E. 1
FULLER, Charles Gordon 1
FULLER, 5
Claude A(lbert)
FULLER, Claude A. 4
FULLER, Clyde Dale 5
FULLER, Edward 1
FULLER, 1
Edward Hawley Laton
FULLER, Ellis Adams 3
FULLER, Emily Guillon 4
FULLER Eugene 1
FULLER, Frank Lanneau 3
FULLER, Frank Manly 3
FULLER, George H
FULLER, George Freeman 5
FULLER, George Gregg 5
FULLER, George 5
Newman
FULLER, George R. 1
FULLER, George Warren 1
FULLER, 1
George Washington
FULLER, H. Harrison 4
FULLER, Harold 'deWolf 3
FULLER, Hector 1
FULLER, Helen 5
FULLER, Henry Amzi 1
FULLER, Henry Blake 1
FULLER, Henry Brown 1
FULLER, Henry Jones 3
FULLER, Henry Mills H
FULLER, Henry Starkey 4
FULLER, Hiram H
FULLER, Homer Taylor 4
FULLER, Howard G. 1
FULLER, Hulbert 1
FULLER, J(ohn) Douglas 5
FULLER, John Wallace H
FULLER, Leo Charles 4
FULLER, Leslie Elmer 1
FULLER, Levi Knight 1
FULLER, Loie 1
FULLER, 1
Lucia Fairchild
FULLER, 1
Lucius Eckstein
FULLER, 1
Marcellus Bunyan
FULLER, Margaret 3
FULLER, 1
Melville Weston
FULLER, Myron Leslie 5
FULLER, 5
Olive Beatrice Muir
FULLER, Oliver Clyde 2
FULLER, Paul Jr. 1
FULLER, Philo Case H
FULLER, 1
Raymond Garfield
FULLER, Richard H
FULLER, 1
Robert Higginson
FULLER, Robert Stevens 5
FULLER, Samuel L. 4
FULLER, Sarah Margaret 1
FULLER, 1
Stuart Jamieson
FULLER, Teddy Ray 5
FULLER, Thomas 4
FULLER, Thomas Charles 4
FULLER, H
Thomas James Duncan
FULLER, Thomas Staples 1
FULLER, Timothy H
FULLER, Walter Deane 4
FULLER, Warner 3
FULLER, Wiley Madison 3
FULLER, William David 1
FULLER, William Eddy 1
FULLER, William Elijah 5
FULLER, William Hayes 5
FULLER, H
William Kendall
FULLER, William Oliver 1
FULLER, 5
William Parmer, Jr.
FULLER, 1
Williamson Whitehead
FULLERTON, Anna M. 5
FULLERTON, Baxter P. 1

FULLERTON, 3
Charles Alexander
FULLERTON, David H
FULLERTON, 1
Edith Loring
FULLERTON, 1
George Stuart
FULLERTON, Hugh
Stuart 5
FULLERTON, Kemper 1
FULLERTON, Mark A. 1
FULLERTON, 5
Samuel Clyde
FULLERTON, 4
William Morton
FULMER, Clark Adelbert 1
FULMER, Ellis Ingham 1
FULMER, Elton 1
FULMER, Hampton Pitts 2
FULMORE,
Zachary Taylor
FULP, James Douglas 5
FULTON, Albert Cooley 5
FULTON, Andrew Steele H
FULTON, Charles Herman 5
FULTON, 1
Charles William
FULTON, Chester Alan 3
FULTON, Elmer Lincoln 4
FULTON, Frank Taylor 4
FULTON, Hugh 1
FULTON, James A. 3
FULTON, James Grove 5
FULTON, John 1
FULTON, John Allen 1
FULTON, John Farquhar 1
FULTON, John Hall H
FULTON, John Hamilton 1
FULTON, John Samuel 1
FULTON, Joseph Samuel 4
FULTON, Justin Dewey 1
FULTON, Kerwin Holmes 3
FULTON,
Maurice Garland
FULTON, Robert H
FULTON, Robert Burwell 1
FULTON, Robert Irving 1
FULTON, 3
Samuel Alexander
FULTON, Walter Scott 3
FULTON, H
Weston Miller Sr.
FULTON, 4
Weston Miller Sr.
FULTON, William H
FULTON, William John 4
FULTON, 1
William Pomeroy
FULTON, William Savin H
FULTON, 4
William Shirley
FULTON, 1
William Stewart
FULTZ, Francis Marion 4
FULWOOD, Charles Allen 4
FUMASONI-BIONDI,
Peter 1
FUNCHESS, Marion Jacob 3
FUNK, Casimir 3
FUNK, Charles Earle 3
FUNK, Clarence Sidney 1
FUNK, Erwin Charles 5
FUNK, Eugene Duncan 1
FUNK, Frank Hamilton 1
FUNK, Henry Daniel 1
FUNK, Isaac Kaufman 1
FUNK, John Clarence 3
FUNK, Miles Conrad 5
FUNK, Wilfred 4
FUNK, Wilhelm Heinrich 1
FUNK, William R. 1
FUNKHOUSER, Abram
Paul 4
FUNKHOUSER, George
A. 1
FUNKHOUSER, 2
William Delbert
FUNSTEN, Benjamin
Reed 5
FUNSTON, James Bowen 1
FUNSTON, Edward
Hogue 1
FUNSTON, Frederick 1
FUQUA, Henry 1
FUQUA, James Henry 4
FUQUA, Stephen Ogden 1
FURAY, James Henry 3
FURAY, John Baptist 3
FURBER, Fred Nason 3
FURBER, Henry Jewett 1
FURBER, Pierce T. H
FURBRINGER, Max
Henry 3
FURBUSH, 1
Charles Lincoln
FURCHES, David Moffatt 1
FURER, Julius Augustus 4

FURER, William Charles
FUREY, Francis Thomas
FUREY, John Vincent
FURGUSON,
Elizabeth Graeme
FURLONG,
Atherton Bernard Sr.
FURLONG,
Charles Wellington
FURLONG, Thomas J.
FURLOW, Floyd Charles
FURMAN,
Bess (Mrs. Robert B.
Armstrong, Jr.)
FURMAN,
Franklin De Ronde
FURMAN, James Cement
FURMAN, John Myers
FURMAN, Lucy
FURMAN, N. Howell
FURMAN, Richard
FURNALD, Henry Natsch
FURNAS, Clifford Cook
FURNAS, Elwood
FURNAS,
Robert Wilkinson
FURNESS,
Caroline Ellen
FURNESS,
Clifton Joseph
FURNESS, Horace
Howard
FURNESS,
Horace Howard Jr.
FURNESS, William Henry
FURNESS,
William Henry III
FURNISS,
Edgar Stephenson
FURNISS,
Edgar Stephenson Jr.
FURNISS, Henry Dawson
FURRER, Rudolph
FURROW, Clarence Lee
FURRY, William Davis
FURST, Clyde
FURST, Joseph
FURST, Moritz
FURST, Sidney Dale
FURSTENBERG,
Albert Carl
FURTH, Albert Lavenson
FURTWANGLER,
Wilhelm
FURUSETH, Andrew
FUSON, Samuel Dillard
FUSSELL, Bartholomew
FUSSELL, Joseph Hall
FUSSELL, Lewis
FUSSELL, M. Howard
FUSTING,
Frederick Erwin
FUTCHER, Thomas
Barnes
FUTHEY, Bruce
FUTHEY, John Smith
FUTRALL, John Clinton
FUTRELL, Junius Marion
FUTRELLE, Jacques
FUTRELLE, May
FYAN,
Robert Washington
FYFE, John William
FYLES, Franklin

G

GAARDE, Fred William
GABA, Meyer Grupp
GABALDON, Isauro
GABB, William More
GABBARD, Elmer Everett
GABBERT,
Mont Robertson
GABBERT, William Henry
GABEL, Carl W.
GABLE, Clark
GABLE, George Daniel
GABLE, Morgan Edwards
GABLEMAN, Edwin
Wilson
GABRIEL, Charles L.
GABRIEL, Gilbert Wolf
GABRIEL, John Huston
GABRIEL,
Mgrditch Simbad
GABRIELS, Henry
GABRILOWITSCH, Ossip
GADDIS, Cyrus Jacob
GADE, John Allyne
GADLOW, David Berman
GADSBY, George M.
GADSBY, Robert Charles
GADSDEN, Philip Henry
GADSEN, Christopher
GADSEN, James

GADSKI, Madame
  Johanna 1
GAEBELEIN, 2
  Arno Clemens
GAEDE, William R. 4
GAEHR, Paul Frederick 3
GAENSLEN,
  Frederick Julius
GAERTNER, 3
  Carl Frederick
GAERTNER, Fred Jr. 4
GAERTNER,
  Herman Julius
GAERTNER, William 2
GAFFEY, Hugh J. 2
GAFFNEY, Dale V. 3
GAFFNEY, 4
  Emmett Lawrence
GAFFNEY, Hugh H. 4
GAFFNEY, John Jerome 4
GAFFNEY, John Marshall 5
GAFFNEY, Leo Vincent 5
GAFFNEY, Matthew Page 4
GAFFNEY, 2
  Thomas St John
GAG, Wanda 2
GAGARIN, 5
  Yuri (Alekseyevich)
GAGE, Alfred Payson 1
GAGE, Brownell 2
GAGE, Charles Amon 5
GAGE, Elbert Mauney 5
GAGE, H
  Frances Dana Barker
GAGE, George Williams 1
GAGE, Harry Morehouse 1
GAGE, Henry Tifft 1
GAGE, Homer 1
GAGE, John Bailey 5
GAGE, John H. 4
GAGE, Joshua H
GAGE, Lyman Judson 1
GAGE, Matilda Joslyn H
GAGE, Simon Henry 2
GAGE, Susanna Phelps H
GAGE, Thomas H
GAGE, Thomas Hovey 1
GAGE, Walter Boutwell 5
GAGE-DAY, Mary M. D. 1
GAGEL, Edward 1
GAGER, Charles Stuart 2
GAGER, Curtis H. 4
GAGER, Edwin Baker 1
GAGGIN, Edwin Hall 3
GAGLIARDI, Tommaso H
GAGNON, J-Romeo 5
GAGNON, Onesime 4
GAGNON, Wilfrid 4
GAHN, Harry C. 4
GAIGE, Crosby 2
GAIL, William Wallace 3
GAILLARD, 1
  David Du Bose
GAILLARD, Edwin
  Samuel H
GAILLARD, Edwin White 1
GAILLARD, Felix 5
GAILLARD, John H
GAILLARDET, H
  Theodore Frederick
GAILOR, Frank Hoyt 3
GAILOR, Thomas Frank 1
GAINE, Hugh H
GAINER, Joseph Henry 2
GAINES, Charles Kelsey 2
GAINES, 4
  Clement Carrington
GAINES, H
  Edmund Pendleton
GAINES, 2
  Edward Franklin
GAINES, 4
  Francis Pendleton
GAINES, Frank Henry 1
GAINES, H
  George Strother
GAINES, John Pollard H
GAINES, John Wesley 1
GAINES, John William 5
GAINES, Joseph Holt 4
GAINES, L. Ebersole 3
GAINES, 1
  Lewis McFarland
GAINES, Paschal Clay 4
GAINES, Reuben Reid 1
GAINES, Robert Edwin 1
GAINES, Wesley John 1
GAINEY, Percy Leigh 5
GAIR, George West 1
GAITHER, Frances 2
GAITHER, H. Rowan Jr. 4
GAITHER, Nathan H
GAITHER, 5
  P(erry) Stokes
GAITHER, 4
  William Cotter Jr.

GAITSKELL, 4
  Hugh Todd Naylor
GAITSKILL, Bennett S. 1
GALARNEAULT, John
  Toan 5
GALATTI, Stephen 4
GALBERRY, Thomas H
GALBRAITH, Anna Mary 1
GALBRAITH, 5
  Archibald Victor
GALBRAITH, 3
  Clinton Alexander
GALBRAITH, John H
GALBRAITH, Nettie May 2
GALBREATH, 1
  John Morrison
GALBREATH, 4
  Robert Ferguson
GALE, Arthur Sullivan 5
GALE, Benjamin H
GALE, Clement Rowland 4
GALE, Edward Chenery 2
GALE, Edward Justus 5
GALE, Esson McDowell 4
GALE, George H
GALE,
  George Washington
GALE, Henry Gordon 2
GALE, Hoyt Stoddard 3
GALE, Joseph Wasson 5
GALE, Laurence Edward 4
GALE, Levin 1
GALE, Minna K. 5
GALE, Noel 5
GALE, Oliver Marble 5
GALE, Philip Bartlett 2
GALE, Samuel Chester 1
GALE, Stephen Henry 1
GALE, William Holt 5
GALE, Willis Donald 4
GALE, Zona 1
GALEN, Albert John 4
GALER, Roger Sherman 3
GALES, George M. 1
GALES, Joseph * H
GALITZEN, Elizabeth H
GALL, H
GALL, John Christian 3
GALLAGHER,
  Charles Eugene
GALLAGHER, 1
  Charles Theodore
GALLAGHER, 1
  Charles Wesley
GALLAGHER, Daniel J. 3
GALLAGHER,
  Francis Edward
GALLAGHER, Henry M. 5
GALLAGHER,
  Howard William
GALLAGHER, Hugh 5
GALLAGHER, 1
  Hugh Clifford
GALLAGHER, H
  Hugh Patrick
GALLAGHER, John
  James 5
GALLAGHER, 5
  Louis Joseph
GALLAGHER, Michael 3
GALLAGHER, 1
  Michael James
GALLAGHER, 1
  Nicholas Aloysius
GALLAGHER, 4
  Ralph Aloysius
GALLAGHER, Ralph W. 3
GALLAGHER, Sears 3
GALLAGHER, Thomas 1
GALLAGHER, William 1
GALLAGHER,
  William Davis
GALLAGHER, William J. 2
GALLAHER, Ernest Yale 5
GALLAHUE, 5
  Dudley Richard
GALLAHUE, 5
  Edward Francis
GALLALEE, John Morin 1
GALLAND, 2
  Joseph Stanislaus
GALLANT, Albert Ernest 1
GALLATIN, Albert H
GALLATIN, 3
  Albert Eugene
GALLATIN,
  Francis Dawson
GALLAUDET, Bern Budd 1
GALLAUDET, 1
  Edward Miner
GALLAUDET, Thomas 1
GALLAUDET, H
  Thomas Hopkins
GALLAWAY, Robert
  Macy 1
GALLEGOS, Jose Manuel H
GALLICO, Poole 3

GALLI-CURCI, Amelita 4
GALLIE, William Edward 3
GALLIER, James H
GALLIGAN, 4
  Matthew James
GALLIHER, 1
  William Thompson
GALLINGER, Jacob H. 1
GALLISON, 1
  Henry Hammond
GALLITZIN, H
  Demetrius Augustine
GALLIVAN, 1
  James Ambrose
GALLIVER, 1
  George Alfred
GALLIZIER, Nathan 1
GALLO, Fortune 5
GALLOWAY, 1
  Beverly Thomas
GALLOWAY, 3
  Charles Anderson
GALLOWAY, 1
  Charles Betts
GALLOWAY, 5
  Charles Henry
GALLOWAY, 5
  Charles Mills
GALLOWAY, 1
  Charles William
GALLOWAY, David
  Henry 3
GALLOWAY, 3
  Floyd Emerson
GALLOWAY, 4
  Irene Oti'lia
GALLOWAY, J. J. 4
GALLOWAY, John Stuart 4
GALLOWAY, Joseph H
GALLOWAY, Lee 4
GALLOWAY, Robert E. 4
GALLOWAY, Samuel H
GALLOWAY, 1
  Thomas Walton
GALLOZZI, Tommaso 3
GALLUP, Albert H
GALLUP, Anna Billings 3
GALLUP, Clarence Mason 2
GALLUP, 5
  Edward Hatton, Jr.
GALLUP, Frank Amner 3
GALLUP, Joseph Adams H
GALLUP, William Arthur 5
GALPIN, Charles Josiah 4
GALPIN, Kate Tupper 1
GALPIN, Stanley Leman 1
GALPIN, 4
  William Freeman
GALSTON, Clarence G. 4
GALT, Alexander H
GALT, Herbert Randolph 1
GALT, Howard Spilman 1
GALT, John Randolph 1
GALUSHA, 5
  Hugh Duncan, Jr.
GALVEZ, Bernardo 'de H
GALVIN, John 1
GALVIN, John Francis 1
GALVIN, Joseph A. 1
GALVIN, Leroy Spahr 3
GALVIN, Michael Joseph 4
GALVIN, Paul Vincent 5
GAMA, Domicio 'da 1
GAMACHE, George Paul 5
GAMAGE, 3
  Frederick Luther
GAMBEL, William H
GAMBER, 3
  Branson Van Leer
GAMBLE, Cecil Huggins 3
GAMBLE, Donald Phelps 5
GAMBLE, E. Ross 4
GAMBLE,
  Eleanor Acheson McCulloch
GAMBLE, Hamilton
  Rowan H
GAMBLE, James H
GAMBLE, James Lawder 4
GAMBLE, James Norris 1
GAMBLE, John Rankin 1
GAMBLE, 3
  Ralph Abernethy
GAMBLE, Robert Bruce 1
GAMBLE, Robert Howard 3
GAMBLE, Robert Jackson 1
GAMBLE, Roger Lawson H
GAMBLE, Samuel Walter 5
GAMBLE, Sidney David 5
GAMBLE, 5
  Theodore Robert
GAMBLE, 4
  Theodore Roosevelt
GAMBLE, 4
  William Elliott
GAMBRELL, James
  Bruton 1
GAMBRELL, Joel Halbert 1

GAMBRILL, Charles D. H
GAMBRILL, 3
  J. Montgomery
GAMBRILL, 3
  James Henry Jr.
GAMBRILL, 1
  Stephen Warfield
GAME, Josiah Bethea 1
GAMEL, W. Warren 5
GAMER, Helena Margaret 4
GAMERTSFELDER,
  Solomon Jacob
GAMERTSFELDER, 4
  Walter Sylvester
GAMEWELL, 3
  Francis Dunlap
GAMMACK, Arthur
  James 5
GAMMACK, James 1
GAMMAGE, Grady 5
GAMMELL, Robert Ives 1
GAMMELL, William 2
GAMMON, Edgar
  Graham 4
GAMMON, Elijah
  Hedding H
GAMMON, Robert
  William 2
GAMMONS, 4
  Charles Clifford
GAMON, Wylena Clarissa 5
GAMORAN, Emanuel 4
GAMOW, George 5
GANDHI, 2
  Mohandas Karamchand
  Mahatma
GANDY, Charles Moore 1
GANDY, John Manuel 1
GANDY, Joseph Edward 5
GANEV, Dimiter 5
GANEY, J. Cullen 5
GANFIELD, 1
  William Arthur
GANIERE, 1
  George Etienne
GANIÓDAIIO H
GANLY, James Vincent 1
GANN, Edward Everett 1
GANNAM, John 4
GANNETT, Anne
  Macomber 3
GANNETT, Barzillai 1
GANNETT, Ezra Stiles H
GANNETT, Farley 3
GANNETT, Frank Ernest 3
GANNETT, Guy
  Patterson 3
GANNETT, Henry 1
GANNETT, 4
  Lewis Stiles *
GANNETT, 1
  Thomas Brattle
GANNETT, 1
  William Channing
GANNETT, 2
  William Howard
GANNON, Anna 5
GANNON, 1
  Frank Stanislaus
GANNON, John Mark 5
GANNON, Sinclair 2
GANNON, Thomas
  Joseph 1
GANO, John H
GANO, Roy A. 5
GANO, Seth Thomas 3
GANO, Stephen H
GANOE, 5
  William Addleman
GANONG, 1
  William Francis
GANS, Edgar Hilary 4
GANSEVOORT, Leonard H
GANSEVOORT, Peter H
GANSON, John 1
GANT, Samuel Goodwin 5
GANTENBEIN, 1
  Calvin Ursinus
GANTENBEIN, 4
  James Watson
GANTT, Ernest Sneed 2
GANTT, Henry Laurence 1
GANTT, James Britton 1
GANTVOORT, 1
  Arnold Johann
GANTZ, Hallie George 5
GANUS, Clifton L. 3
GANZ, Albert Frederick 1
GANZ, Rudolph 5
GARAKONTHIE, Daniel H
GARBER, Earl Augustus 4
GARBER, 3
  Frederick William
GARBER, Harvey C. 4
GARBER, J(ames) Otis 5
GARBER, John Palmer 1

GARBER, Milton Cline 2
GARBER, Paul Neff 5
GARCELON, Alonzo 1
GARCELON, William
  Frye 2
GARCES, H
  Francisco Tomas
  Hermenegildo
GARCIA, Carlos P. 5
GARCIA, Fabian 3
GARCIA LORCA,
  Federico
GARCIA-VELEZ, Carlos 4
GARD, Warren 1
GARD, Willis Lloyd 1
GARDEN, Alexander * H
GARDEN, 4
  Hugh Mackie Gordon
GARDEN, 1
  Hugh Richardson
GARDEN, Mary 4
GARDENER, Cornelius 1
GARDENER, 1
  Helen Hamilton
GARDENHIRE, 1
  Samuel Major
GARDENIER, Barent H
GARDINER, Asa Bird 1
GARDINER, 1
  Charles Alexander
GARDINER, Curtiss C. 2
GARDINER, Frederic 1
GARDINER, 1
  George Schuyler
GARDINER, Glenn L. 4
GARDINER, Harry
  Norman 1
GARDINER, 4
  James Garfield
GARDINER, James L. 3
GARDINER, James Terry 1
GARDINER, John * H
GARDINER, John Hays 4
GARDINER, H
  John Sylvester
GARDINER, Lion H
GARDINER,
  Robert Hallowell
GARDINER, 1
  Robert Hallowell
GARDINER, Silvester H
GARDINER, H
  Sir Christopher
GARDINER, Sylvester 1
GARDINER, T. Momolu 1
GARDINER, 3
  William Howard
GARDINER, 3
  William Tudor
GARDNER, Addison
  Leman 5
GARDNER, 4
  Albert TenEyck
GARDNER, Archibald K. 4
GARDNER, Arthur 4
GARDNER, 1
  Augustus Peabody
GARDNER, 5
  Bertie Charles
GARDNER, Caleb H
GARDNER,
  Celia Emmeline
GARDNER, Charles 1
GARDNER, 4
  Henry
GARDNER, H
  Charles Kitchel
GARDNER, Charles M. 3
GARDNER, 2
  Charles Spurgeon
GARDNER, Dillard Scott 5
GARDNER, 5
  Earl Wentworth
GARDNER, 4
  Edward Frederic
GARDNER, Edward
  Joseph 3
GARDNER, Edward
  Tytus 3
GARDNER, Eugene C. 1
GARDNER, Eugene
  Elmore 3
GARDNER, Francis H
GARDNER, Frank 2
GARDNER, Frank Duane 1
GARDNER, Frank Saltus 1
GARDNER, 1
  Frederick Dozier
GARDNER,
  George Peabody
GARDNER, George W. 1
GARDNER, Gideon H
GARDNER, Gilson 1
GARDNER, Grandison 4
GARDNER, Halbert Paine 4
GARDNER, Harold Ward 5
GARDNER, 5
  Harry Wentworth

---

* Indicates More Than One Such Name Listed

GAY, Robert Malcolm 4
GAY, Sydney Howard H
GAY, Taylor Scott 4
GAY, W. Allan 1
GAY, Walter H
GAYARRE,
  Charles Etienne Arthur H
GAYER, Arthur David 3
GAYLE, John H
GAYLE, R. Finley Jr. 1
GAYLER, Charles H
GAYLEY, Charles Mills 1
GAYLEY, James 1
GAYLORD, Charles Seely H
GAYLORD,
  Clifford Willard 3
GAYLORD,
  Franklin Augustus 2
GAYLORD,
  Harvey Russell 1
GAYLORD, James
  Madison H
GAYLORD, Joseph Searle 4
GAYLORD,
  Truman Penfield 1
GAYLORD, Willis H
GAYNOR, Frank R. 1
GAYNOR, Jessie Smith 1
GAYNOR, William Jay 1
GAYOSO 'DE
  LEMOS, Manuel H
GAZLAY, P. M. 4
GAZLEY, James William 1
GAZZAM, Joseph M. 1
GEAR, Harry Barnes 3
GEAR, Hiram Lewis 4
GEAR, John Henry 1
GEAR, Joseph 1
GEARE, Randolph Iltyd 1
GEARHART, 3
  Bertrand Wesley
GEARIN, John M. 1
GEARY, George Reginald 5
GEARY, John White H
GEARY, Joseph James 2
GEBELEIN,
  George Christian
GEBERT, Herbert George 4
GEBHARD, John H
GEBHARD, Willrich 4
GEBHARDT, Ernest A. 4
GEBHARDT, 5
  George Frederic
GEBHARDT, Raymond L. 3
GEDDES, Alice Spencer 5
GEDDES, 1
  Frederick Lyman
GEDDES, H
  George Washington
GEDDES, James H
GEDDES, James Jr. 2
GEDDES, James Loraine H
GEDDES, John Joseph 2
GEDDES, Norman Bel 3
GEDDES, 3
  Sir Auckland Campbell
GEDDES, 4
  William Findlay
GEDDES, 1
  Williamson Nevin
GEDDY, Vernon Meredith 3
GEDYE, 5
  George Eric Rowe
GEE, Edward 3
GEE, Nathaniel Gist 4
GEE, Wilson 4
GEER, Bennette Eugene 4
GEER, Curtis Manning 1
GEER, Danforth 4
GEER, E. Harold 3
GEER, Everett Kinne 3
GEER, George Jarvis 4
GEER, 4
  Theodore Thurston
GEER, Walter 1
GEER, William Chauncey 4
GEER, William Clarke 2
GEER, William Henry 1
GEER, William Montague 1
GEERY, 4
  William Beckwith
GEHAN, John Francis 4
GEHL, Edward J. 3
GEHLBACH,
  Herman Hunter
GEHLE, Frederick W. 4
GEHLKE, Charles Elmer 5
GEHRIG, Lou 4
GEHRING, Albert 1
GEHRING, John George 1
GEHRMANN, Adolph 1
GEHRMANN, Bernard
  John 3
GEHRMANN, 3
  George Howard
GEHRON, William 3
GEHRS, John Henry 1

GEIBEL, Adam 1
GEIBEL, Victor B. 4
GEIER, 1
  Frederick August
GEIER, Philip Otto 3
GEIER, Philip Otto 4
GEIFFERT, Alfred Jr. 1
GEIGER, Alfred B. 3
GEIGER, Ferdinand A. 1
GEIGER, Jacob 1
GEIGER, Marlin George 1
GEIGER, Roy Stanley 2
GEIGER, 5
  William Frederick
GEIJSBEEK, John Bart 5
GEIL, William Edgar 1
GEIS, George (Sherman) 5
GEISEL, Carolyn 1
GEISER, Karl Frederick 3
GEISSINGER, 1
  James Allen
GEISSLER, Arthur H. 2
GEISSLER, 1
  Ludwig Reinhold
GEIST, Clarence Henry 1
GEIST, Emil Sebastian 1
GEIST, Samuel Herbert 2
GEIST, Walter 3
GELBACH, Loring Lusk 4
GELEERD,
  Elisabeth Rozetta (Mrs.
  Rudolph M. Loewenstein) 1
GELERT,
  Johannes Sophus
GELLATLY, John Arthur 5
GELLER, David 4
GELLERMANN, William 4
GELLERT, N. Henry 4
GELLES, Paul P. 4
GELLHORN, Ernst 5
GELLHORN, George 1
GELMAN, Samuel Joseph 4
GELSTON, David H
GEMMELL, 1
  Robert Campbell
GEMMELL, William
  Henry 4
GEMMILL, 1
  Benjamin McKee
GEMMILL, 1
  Willard Beharrell
GEMMILL, 3
  William Headrick
GEMMILL, 1
  William Nelson
GEMUNDER, H
  August Martin Ludwig
GENET, Arthur Samuel 4
GENET, Edmond Charles H
GENGEMBRE, H
  Charles Antoine Colomb
GENIN, John Nicholas 1
GENIN, Sylvester H
GENNET, 2
  Charles Westcott Jr.
GENT, H
  Mrs. Sophia S. Daniell
GENTELE, C. Goran
  H.A. 5
GENTH, H
  Frederick Augustus
GENTH, 1
  Frederick Augustus Jr.
GENTH, Lillian 3
GENTHE, Arnold 4
GENTHE, Karl Wilhelm 5
GENTILE, Edward 3
GENTILE, Felix Michael 3
GENTLE, Alice True 3
GENTRY, Charles Burt 5
GENTRY, Cyrus S. 4
GENTRY, Martin Butler 3
GENTRY, H
  Meredith Poindexter
GENTRY, North Todd 2
GENTRY, Thomas George 4
GENTRY, William Lee 4
GENTRY, 4
  William Richard
GENUNG,
  George Frederick
GENUNG, John Franklin 1
GEOFFROY, W. J. 3
GEOGHAN, William F.
  X. 3
GEOGHEGAN,
  Anthony Vincent Barrett 4
GEOHEGAN,
  William Anthony
GEORG, 5
  Walter Ferdinand
GEORGE, Albert Eugene 4
GEORGE, Albert Joseph 4
GEORGE, Andrew
  Jackson 1
GEORGE, Andrew
  Jackson 4

GEORGE, Charles Albert 3
GEORGE,
  Charles Carlton
GEORGE, Charles P. 2
GEORGE, Edgar Jesse 1
GEORGE, Edwin Black 4
GEORGE, Harold Coulter 1
GEORGE, Henry H
GEORGE, Henry 1
GEORGE,
  James Zachariah H
GEORGE, 5
  Jennings Burton
GEORGE, John J. 4
GEORGE, Joseph Henry 1
GEORGE, Joseph Warren 4
GEORGE, Manfred 4
GEORGE, Robert James 1
GEORGE, Robert Mabry 4
GEORGE, Rufus Lambert 4
GEORGE, Russell D. 4
GEORGE, Vesper Lincoln 1
GEORGE, VI 3
GEORGE, W. Perry 3
GEORGE, 3
  Walter Franklin
GEORGE, William 2
GEORGE, William
  Reuben 1
GEORGE I H
GEORGE II H
GEORGE III H
GEORGESON, 1
  Charles Christian
GEOTHALS, 1
  George Washington
GEPPERT, Otto Emil 5
GERAGHTY, James M. 1
GERAGHTY, Martin John 1
GERALD, Mother Mary 4
GERAN, 3
  Elmer Hendrickson
GERARD, Felix Roy 2
GERARD, James Watson 1
GERARD, James Watson 1
GERARD, James Watson 3
GERARDI, Joseph A. 4
GERASIMOV, 5
  Mikhall Mikhaylovich
GERBER, Frank 3
GERBERDING, 1
  George Henry
GERBERDING, 5
  Richard Henry
GERBRANDY, P. S. 4
GERCKE, Daniel James H
GERDEMANN, 5
  Herbert Edmund
GERDES, John 3
GERDINE, 1
  Thomas Golding
GERE, Charles Henry 1
GERE, George Grant 3
GERE, 4
  George Washington
GEREN, Paul Francis 5
GERGEN, John Jay 4
GERHARD, 5
  Gerhard Russell
GERHARD, William Paul 1
GERHARD, William
  Wood H
GERHARDT, 2
  August Edward
GERHARDT, Karl 4
GERHARDT, Paul Jr. 4
GERHART, Emanuel
  Vogel 1
GERHAUSER, 3
  William Henry
GERICKE, Wilhelm 1
GERIG, John Lawrence 3
GERIG, William 2
GERKEN, Rudolph A. 2
GERKEN, 5
  Walter Diedrick
GERLACH, Arch C. 5
GERLACH, Charles L. 2
GERLACH, George W. 3
GERLACH, John Joseph 1
GERLAUGH, Paul 3
GERLING, Henry Joseph 3
GERMAIN, George H
GERMAN, John S. 2
GERMAN, Obadiah 1
GERMAN, William J. 4
GERMANE, Charles E. 2
GERMANOS 3
GERMANY, 5
  Eugene Benjamin
GERMER, Lester Halbert 5
GERMUTH, 4
  Frederick George
GERNERD, Fred
  Benjamin 2
GERNON, Frank E. 3
GERNSBACK, Hugo 4

GERONIMO H
GERONIMO 4
GEROULD, Gordon Hall 3
GEROULD, James Thayer 3
GEROULD, John Hiram 4
GEROULD, 2
  Katharine Fullerton
GEROULD, 3
  Winifred Gregory
GEROW, 5
  Leonard Townsend
GERRER, Gregory 3
GERRISH, 1
  Frederic Henry
GERRISH, Theodore 4
GERRISH, Thornton 3
GERRISH, 5
  Willard Peabody
GERRITY, 4
  Thomas Patrick
GERRY, Elbridge * H
GERRY, Elbridge Thomas 1
GERRY, James H
GERRY, Louis Cardell 4
GERRY, 5
  Margarita Spalding
GERRY, 2
  Martin Hughes Jr.
GERRY, Peter Goelet 3
GERSBACHER, 5
  Eva Nina Oxford (Mrs.
  W.M. Gersbacher)
GERSHON-COHEN, 5
  Jacob
GERSHOVITZ, Samuel D. 4
GERSHWIN, George 1
GERSON, Felix Napoleon 2
GERSON, Oscar 5
GERSON, 5
  Theodore Perceval
GERST, Francis Joseph 5
GERSTELL, 5
  Robert Sinclair
GERSTEN, E. Chester 5
GERSTENBERG, 2
  Charles William
GERSTENBERGER, 3
  Henry John
GERSTENFELD, Norman 5
GERSTER, Arpad Geyza 1
GERSTER, Jack Alan 5
GERSTLE, Lewis H
GERSTLE, Mark Lewis 5
GERVAIS, John Lewis H
GERWIG, George William 3
GESELL, Arnold 4
GESELL, Robert 3
GESNER, Anthon Temple 1
GESNER, Bertram Melvin 5
GESSLER, 1
  A(lbert) E(dward)
GESSLER,
  Theodore A. K.
GESSNER, 2
  Hermann Bertram
GESSNER, Robert 5
GEST, John Marshall 1
GEST, Joseph Henry 1
GEST, Morris 2
GEST, William Purves 1
GESTEFELD,
  Ursula Newell
GESTIDO, General Oscar 4
GETCHELL, 4
  Charles Munro
GETCHELL, J. Stirling 4
GETCHELL,
  Noble Hamilton
GETHOEFER, Louis
  Henry 2
GETHRO, Fred William 5
GETLER, Charles 2
GETMAN, 2
  Frederick Hutton
GETSCHOW, Roy Martin 5
GETSINGER, 4
  Edward Christopher
GETTELL, 3
  Raymond Garfield
GETTEMY, 1
  Charles Ferris
GETTY, H
  George Washington
GETTY, Robert 5
GETTY, Robert N. 1
GETZ, Forry Rohrer 4
GETZ, George Fulmer 1
GETZ, Hiram Landis 2
GETZ, James Lawrence H
GEYER, Bertram Birch 5
GEYER, Ellen M. 3
GEYER, Henry Sheffie H
GEYER, Lee Edward 3
GEYL, Pieter 4
GHALI, Paul 5
GHEEN, Edward Hickman 1

GHENT, William James 2
GHEORGHIU-DEJ, 4
  Gheorghe
GHERARDI, Bancroft * 1
GHERARDI, 1
  Walter Rockwell
GHOLSON, James
  Herbert H
GHOLSON, H
  Samuel Jameson
GHOLSON, Thomas Jr. H
GHOLSON,
  Thomas Saunders
GHOLSON, William Yates H
GHORMLEY, Alfred M. 4
GHORMLEY, John
  Wallace 5
GHORMLEY, Ralph K. 3
GHORMLEY, Robert Lee 3
GHULAM, Mohammed 3
GIACOMETTI, Alberto 4
GIANELLONI, 3
  Vivian Joseph
GIANNINI, Amadeo
  Peter 2
GIANNINI, Attilio H. 2
GIANNINI, 3
  Lawrence Mario
GIANNINI, Vittorio 4
GIAUQUE, Florien 1
GIAVER, Joachim G. 1
GIBAULT, Pierre H
GIBB, Arthur Norman 3
GIBB, 5
  Frederick William
GIBB, 5
  Hamilton Alexander
  Rosskeen
GIBBES, Heneage 1
GIBBES, Robert Wilson H
GIBBINS, Henry 2
GIBBON, John H
GIBBON, John Heysham 3
GIBBON, 5
  John Heysham, Jr.
GIBBON, Thomas Edward 1
GIBBONEY, 2
  Stuart Gatewood
GIBBONS, H
  Abigail Hopper
GIBBONS, Cedric 3
GIBBONS, Charles David 5
GIBBONS, Douglas 4
GIBBONS, Edmund F. 5
GIBBONS, Edmund F. 4
GIBBONS, Floyd 1
GIBBONS, George Rison 3
GIBBONS, Henry H
GIBBONS, Henry 1
GIBBONS, Henry Jr. 1
GIBBONS, Herbert Adams 1
GIBBONS, 1
  James Cardinal
GIBBONS, James Edmund 3
GIBBONS, James Sloan H
GIBBONS, John 1
GIBBONS, Stephen B. 3
GIBBONS, Thomas H
GIBBONS, 5
  Walter Bernard
GIBBONS, William * H
GIBBONS,
  William Cephus
GIBBONS, H
  William Futhey
GIBBS, A. Hamilton 4
GIBBS, Alfred Wolcott 1
GIBBS, Carey A. 5
GIBBS, Edwin C. 1
GIBBS,
  Frederick Seymour
GIBBS, George * H
GIBBS, George 1
GIBBS, George 2
GIBBS, George Couper 2
GIBBS, George Sabin 2
GIBBS, Harry Drake 1
GIBBS,
  James Ethan Allen
GIBBS, 5
  Jeannette Phillips
GIBBS, John Sears Jr. 3
GIBBS, Josiah Willard H
GIBBS, Josiah Willard 1
GIBBS, 2
  Lincoln Robinson
GIBBS, Ralph A. 4
GIBBS, Robert Adams 3
GIBBS, Sir Philip 1
GIBBS, William Francis 4
GIBBS, William Hasell H
GIBBS, Willis Benjamin 1
GIBBS, Winifred Stuart 4
GIBBS, Wolcott H
GIBBS, Wolcott 1
GIBIER, Paul 1
GIBLIN, Walter M. 1

GIBNEY, Virgil Pendleton 1
GIBSON, Anna Lemira 4
GIBSON, Axel Emil 1
GIBSON, Ben J. 2
GIBSON, Cable Morgan 5
GIBSON, Carleton Bartlett 1
GIBSON, Charles Brockway 4
GIBSON, Charles Dana 1
GIBSON, Charles Donnel 4
GIBSON, Charles Hammond 3
GIBSON, Charles Hopper 1
GIBSON, Charles Langdon 2
GIBSON, Edgar J. 1
GIBSON, Edwin T. 3
GIBSON, Ernest Willard 1
GIBSON, Ernest William 5
GIBSON, Eva Katherine Clapp 1
GIBSON, Finley F. 5
GIBSON, Frank Markey 1
GIBSON, George H
GIBSON, George Miles 1
GIBSON, Harvey Dow 3
GIBSON, Henry Richard 1
GIBSON, Horatio Gates 1
GIBSON, Hugh 3
GIBSON, J(ohn) J(oseph) 5
GIBSON, James Alexander 1
GIBSON, James Edgar 3
GIBSON, James King H
GIBSON, James Lambert 2
GIBSON, John H
GIBSON, John Bannister H
GIBSON, Joseph Thompson 1
GIBSON, Lorenzo P. 1
GIBSON, Louis Henry 1
GIBSON, Paris 1
GIBSON, Paul Emil 4
GIBSON, Preston 1
GIBSON, Randall Lee H
GIBSON, Robert Atkinson 1
GIBSON, Robert Edward Lee 4
GIBSON, Robert Murray 2
GIBSON, Robert Newcomb 4
GIBSON, Robert Williams 1
GIBSON, Samuel Carrol 4
GIBSON, Stanley 3
GIBSON, Truman Kella 5
GIBSON, Walter Murray H
GIBSON, William H
GIBSON, William Campbell 1
GIBSON, William Hamilton H
GIBSON, William Meredith 1
GIBSON, William Richie 1
GIBSON, William Wesley 4
GIDDINGS, Franklin Henry 1
GIDDINGS, Howard Andrus 2
GIDDINGS, Joshua Reed H
GIDDINGS, Napoleon Bonaparte H
GIDE, Andre Paul Guillaume 3
GIDEON, Abram 4
GIDEON, Dave 2
GIDEON, Peter Miller H
GIDEON, Valentine 3
GIDLEY, James Williams 1
GIDNEY, Herbert Alfred 4
GIE, Stefanus Francois Naude 2
GIEDION, Siegfried 5
GIEGERICH, Leonard Anthony 1
GIELNIAK, Jozef 5
GIELOW, Martha Sawyer 1
GIERING, Eugene Thomas 1
GIES, William John 3
GIESE, Augustus Albert 4
GIESE, Herman Robert 5
GIESE, Oscar W. 2
GIESE, William Frederic 4
GIESECKE, Frederick Ernest 5
GIESECKE, Friederich Ernst 5
GIESEKING, Walter Wilhelm 3
GIESEL, Frederick W. 4

GIESLER, Jerry 4
GIESLER-ANNEKE, Mathilde Franzisha H
GIESY, John Ulrich 2
GIFFEN, James Kelly 1
GIFFEN, John Kelly 1
GIFFIN, William M. 4
GIFFORD, Augusta Hale 1
GIFFORD, Charles L. 2
GIFFORD, Frances Eliot 4
GIFFORD, Franklin Kent 4
GIFFORD, George 1
GIFFORD, George 3
GIFFORD, Glen J. 3
GIFFORD, Harold 1
GIFFORD, James Meacham 1
GIFFORD, John Clayton 2
GIFFORD, Kenneth C. 4
GIFFORD, L. C. 5
GIFFORD, Livingston 4
GIFFORD, Miram Wentworth 1
GIFFORD, Orrin Philip 1
GIFFORD, Ralph Clayton 1
GIFFORD, Ralph Waldo 1
GIFFORD, Robert Ladd 4
GIFFORD, Robert Swain 1
GIFFORD, Roy Wellington 3
GIFFORD, Sanford Robinson H
GIFFORD, Sanford Robinson 2
GIFFORD, Seth Kelley 1
GIFFORD, Sidney Brooks 4
GIFFORD, Walter John 3
GIFFORD, Walter Sherman 4
GIFFORD, William Logan Rodman 5
GIGLI, Benjimino 3
GIGNILLIAT, Leigh R(obinson, Jr. 5
GIGNILLIAT, Leigh Robinson 5
GIGNOUX, Regis Francois H
GIGOT, Francis Ernest 1
GIHON, Albert Dakin 5
GIHON, Albert Leary 1
GILBER, James Henry 3
GILBERT, Abijah H
GILBERT, Albert Clark 3
GILBERT, Alfred Carlton 4
GILBERT, Alfred Carlton Jr. 4
GILBERT, Arthur Hill 5
GILBERT, Arthur Witter 1
GILBERT, Benjamin Davis 4
GILBERT, Cass 1
GILBERT, Charles Allan 1
GILBERT, Charles Benajah 1
GILBERT, Charles Calvin Sr. 3
GILBERT, Charles Henry 1
GILBERT, Charles Kendall 3
GILBERT, Charles Pierrepont H. 3
GILBERT, Clinton Wallace 1
GILBERT, Donald Wood 3
GILBERT, Earl C. 4
GILBERT, Edward H
GILBERT, Edward Martinius 5
GILBERT, Eliphalet Wheeler H
GILBERT, Ezekiel H
GILBERT, Frank Bixby 5
GILBERT, Frederick Spofford 5
GILBERT, George Blodgett 2
GILBERT, George Burton 3
GILBERT, George Gilmore 1
GILBERT, George Holley 1
GILBERT, Grove Karl 1
GILBERT, Harvey Wilbarger 3
GILBERT, Henderson 4
GILBERT, Henry Franklin Belknap 1
GILBERT, Hiram Thornton 1
GILBERT, Horace Mark 1
GILBERT, James Eleazer 1
GILBERT, John 1
GILBERT, John 4
GILBERT, John Gibbs H

GILBERT, John Ingersoll 1
GILBERT, Joseph Oscar 5
GILBERT, Joseph Walter 2
GILBERT, Katharine 1
GILBERT, L(ouis) Wolfe 5
GILBERT, Levi 1
GILBERT, Linda H
GILBERT, Lyman D. 1
GILBERT, Mahlon Norris 1
GILBERT, Marie Dolores Eliza Rosanna H
GILBERT, Marion L. 4
GILBERT, Matthew William 1
GILBERT, Mrs. George Henry 1
GILBERT, Nelson Rust 4
GILBERT, Newell Clark 3
GILBERT, Newton Whiting 1
GILBERT, Osceola Pinckney 2
GILBERT, Prentiss Bailey 1
GILBERT, Ralph 1
GILBERT, Robert Randle 1
GILBERT, Rufus Henry H
GILBERT, S. Price 3
GILBERT, Samuel T. 2
GILBERT, Seymour Parker 1
GILBERT, Sir Humphrey H
GILBERT, Sylvester 1
GILBERT, Vedder Morris 5
GILBERT, Virgil O. 1
GILBERT, Walter Bond 4
GILBERT, William Augustus H
GILBERT, William Ball 1
GILBERT, William Edward 2
GILBERT, William Lewis 1
GILBOY, Glennon 3
GILBREATH, James Richard 4
GILBREATH, Sidney Gordon 5
GILBREATH, W(illiam) Sydnor, Jr. 5
GILBRETH, Frank Bunker 1
GILBRETH, Lillian Moller 5
GILCHRIST, Albert Waller 1
GILCHRIST, Alexander 1
GILCHRIST, Beth Bradford 3
GILCHRIST, Donald Bean 1
GILCHRIST, Fred C. 3
GILCHRIST, Harry Lorenzo 2
GILCHRIST, Jack Cecil 5
GILCHRIST, John Foster 1
GILCHRIST, John Raymond 5
GILCHRIST, Robert H
GILCHRIST, T. Caspar 1
GILCHRIST, Thomas Byron 4
GILCHRIST, William Wallace 3
GILCREASE, Thomas 4
GILDER, Jeannette Leonard 1
GILDER, John Francis 1
GILDER, Joseph B. 1
GILDER, Richard Watson 1
GILDER, Robert Fletcher 1
GILDER, Rodman 3
GILDER, William Henry H
GILDERSLEEVE, Basil Lanneau 1
GILDERSLEEVE, Ferdinand 1
GILDERSLEEVE, Henry Alger 1
GILDERSLEEVE, Oliver 1
GILDERSLEEVE, Virginia Crocheron 4
GILE, John Fowler 3
GILE, John Martin 1
GILE, M. Clement 1
GILES, Chauncey H
GILES, Dorothy 4
GILES, Howard Everett 3
GILES, J. Edward 4
GILES, Malcolm R. 3
GILES, William Alexander 1
GILES, William Branch H
GILES, William Fell H
GILHAMS, Clarence C. 3
GILKEY, Charles Whitney 5

GILKEY, Geraldine Gunsaulus Brown 3
GILKINSON, Howard 4
GILKISON, Frank E. 3
GILKYSON, Thomas) Walter 5
GILL, Adam Capen 1
GILL, Augustus Herman 1
GILL, Benjamin 1
GILL, Bennett Lloyd 1
GILL, Charles Clifford 2
GILL, Corrington 2
GILL, Elbyrne Grady 4
GILL, Everett 1
GILL, George Carleton 4
GILL, Henry Z. 1
GILL, James Presley 4
GILL, Joe Henry 2
GILL, John H
GILL, John Jr. 1
GILL, John Edward 1
GILL, John Goodner 4
GILL, Joseph A. 1
GILL, Joseph J. 4
GILL, Joseph Kaye 1
GILL, Kermode Frederic 5
GILL, Laura Drake 1
GILL, Patrick Francis 1
GILL, Paul Ludwig 1
GILL, Richard C. 3
GILL, Theodore Nicholas 1
GILL, Thomas Augustus 1
GILL, Thomas Harvey 5
GILL, Waltus Hughes 1
GILL, William Andrew 1
GILL, William Fearing 1
GILL, William Francis 1
GILL, William Hugh 1
GILL, Wilson Lindsley 1
GILLAM, Bernhard H
GILLAM, Manly Marcus 1
GILLAN, Silas Lee 4
GILLANDERS, John Gordon 2
GILLEAUDEAU, Raymond
GILLEM, Alvan Cullem H
GILLEM, Alvan Cullom, Jr. 5
GILLEN, Charles P. 3
GILLEN, Courtland C. 3
GILLEN, Wilfred Donnell 5
GILLES, Verner Arthur 3
GILLESPIE, Alexander Garfield 3
GILLESPIE, Barnes 1
GILLESPIE, Charles Bowen 1
GILLESPIE, Dean Milton 2
GILLESPIE, George H
GILLESPIE, George Benjamin 3
GILLESPIE, George De Normandie 1
GILLESPIE, George Lewis 1
GILLESPIE, James H
GILLESPIE, James Edward 4
GILLESPIE, James Frank 3
GILLESPIE, Julian Edgeworth 1
GILLESPIE, Louis Frank 5
GILLESPIE, Mabel H
GILLESPIE, Mabel 4
GILLESPIE, Neal Henry H
GILLESPIE, Oscar William 4
GILLESPIE, Richard Thomas 1
GILLESPIE, Thomas A. 1
GILLESPIE, William 2
GILLESPIE, William Lane 3
GILLESPIE, William Mitchell H
GILLET, Charles 5
GILLET, Charles William 1
GILLET, Guy Mark 5
GILLET, Joseph Eugene 3
GILLET, Paul 5
GILLET, Ransom Hooker H
GILLETT, Arthur Dudley Samuel 2
GILLETT, Arthur Lincoln 1
GILLETT, Charles Ripley 4
GILLETT, Ezra Hall H
GILLETT, Frederick Huntington 1
GILLETT, James Norris 1
GILLETT, John Henry 1

GILLETT, Leonard Godfrey 3
GILLETT, Philip Goode 1
GILLETT, William Kendall 1
GILLETTE, Albert Cooley 3
GILLETTE, Clarence Preston 1
GILLETTE, Edward Hooker 1
GILLETTE, Fanny Lemira 4
GILLETTE, Francis H
GILLETTE, Frank Edward 4
GILLETTE, Halbert Powers 3
GILLETTE, John Morris 3
GILLETTE, King Camp 1
GILLETTE, Leon N. 1
GILLETTE, Lewis Singer 1
GILLETTE, Walter Robarts 1
GILLETTE, William 1
GILLETTE, Wilson D. 3
GILLHAM, Robert 1
GILLIAM, David Tod 4
GILLIAM, Donnell 1
GILLIARD, E. Thomas 4
GILLICK, James T. 5
GILLICK, Laurance Henry 5
GILLIES, Andrew 2
GILLIES, Donald B. 3
GILLIES, James Lewis 3
GILLIES, John A. 2
GILLIG, Edward M. 1
GILLILAN, Strickland 3
GILLILAND, Clarence Vosburgh 1
GILLILAND, John W. 4
GILLIN, John Lewis 3
GILLINGHAM, Clinton Hancock 5
GILLIS, James Henry 1
GILLIS, James Lisle H
GILLIS, James Louis 1
GILLIS, James Martin 1
GILLISPIE, Robert Wallace 4
GILLISS, James Melville H
GILLMAN, Henry 1
GILLMAN, Robert Winthrop 3
GILLMER, Gipson P. 1
GILLMOR, Horatio Gonzalo 5
GILLMOR, Horatio Gonzalo
GILLMOR, Reginald E. 3
GILLMORE, Frank 1
GILLMORE, James Clarkson
GILLMORE, Quincy Adams H
GILLMORE, Quincy Adams H
GILLMORE, Rufus 1
GILLMORE, William E. 2
GILLON, Alexander 1
GILLON, John William 4
GILLPATRICK, Wallace 4
GILLSON, Joseph Lincoln 1
GILMAN, Albert Franklin 3
GILMAN, Alfred Alonzo 1
GILMAN, Arthur 1
GILMAN, Arthur Delevan H
GILMAN, Benjamin Ives 1
GILMAN, Bradley 1
GILMAN, Caroline Howard H
GILMAN, Charlotte Perkins 1
GILMAN, Daniel Colt 1
GILMAN, Harry A. 1
GILMAN, James Henry 1
GILMAN, John E. 1
GILMAN, John Ellis 1
GILMAN, John R. 1
GILMAN, John Taylor H
GILMAN, Lawrence 1
GILMAN, Luthene Clairmont 2
GILMAN, Margaret 1
GILMAN, Mary Rebecca Foster
GILMAN, Max M. 4
GILMAN, Nicholas H
GILMAN, Nicholas Paine 1
GILMAN, Roger 1
GILMAN, Samuel H
GILMAN, Samuel P. 1
GILMAN, Stella Scott (Mrs. Marion Vaughn) 5

GILMAN, Stephen Warren 1
GILMAN, Theodore 1
GILMAN, W. Stewart 2
GILMARTIN, 4
  Eugene Richard
GILMER, Albert Hatton 3
GILMER, 5
  Elizabeth Meriwether
  (Dorothy Dix)
GILMER, 3
  Elizabeth Meriwether
GILMER, Francis Walker H
GILMER, H
  George Rockingham
GILMER, John Adams H
GILMER, Thomas H
GILMER, Thomas Lewis 1
GILMER, William Wirt H
GILMOR, Harry H
GILMORE, Albert Field 2
GILMORE, Alfred 5
GILMORE, 2
  Charles Whitney
GILMORE, 4
  Eddy Lanier King
GILMORE, Edward 4
GILMORE, Eugene Allen 3
GILMORE, 5
  Eugene Allen, Jr.
GILMORE, 1
  George William
GILMORE, James Roberts 1
GILMORE, John 1
GILMORE, John Curtis 1
GILMORE, 2
  John Washington
GILMORE, Joseph Albree H
GILMORE, Joseph Henry 1
GILMORE, Joseph Henry 1
GILMORE, Joseph Henry 4
GILMORE,
  Joseph Michael
GILMORE, Maurice E. 3
GILMORE, 1
  Melvin Randolph
GILMORE, Myron T. 4
GILMORE, Pascal Pearl 4
GILMORE, H
  Patrick Sarsfield
GILMORE, Robert 2
GILMORE, Samuel Louis 1
GILMORE, 3
  Thomas Francis
GILMORE, Thomas
  Mador 1
GILMOUR, 3
  Abram David Pollock
GILMOUR, George Peel 4
GILMOUR, Ray Bergantz 2
GILMOUR, Richard H
GILPATRIC, Guy 3
GILPATRICK, John Lord 4
GILPIN, C. Monteith 5
GILPIN, Charles Sidney H
GILPIN, H
  Edward Woodward
GILPIN, Henry Dilworth H
GILPIN, Joseph Elliott H
GILPIN, William H
GILROY, Thomas F. H
GILRUTH, Irwin Thoburn 3
GILSON, Roy Rolfe 1
GILTNER, Frank Carlton 1
GILTNER, Leigh Gordon 3
GILTNER, Ward 2
GIMBEL, Adam Long 5
GIMBEL, Benedict, Jr. 1
GIMBEL, Bernard F. 4
GIMBEL, Charles 1
GIMBEL, Ellis A. 3
GIMBEL, Jacob 2
GIMBREDE, Thomas H
GIMMESTAD, Lars
  Monson 2
GIMSLEY, George Perry 4
GINDER, Philip DeWitt 5
GINGRICH, Curvin
  Henry 3
GINGRICH, John Edward 4
GINN, Curtiss Jr. 4
GINN, Edwin 1
GINN, Frank Hadley 1
GINN, James Theda 4
GINSBURG, 4
  William Irving
GINSBURGH, A. Robert 1
GINTER, Lewis H
GINTER, Ribert McNiel 5
GINTHER, 3
  Mrs. Pemberton
GINZBERG, Louis 1
GIORDANO, Alfred S. 3
GIPPRICH, John L. 3
GIPSON, James Herrick 4
GIRARD, Alfred Conrad 1
GIRARD, Andre 5

GIRARD, H
  Charles Frederic
GIRARD, Joseph Basil 1
GIRARD, Stephen H
GIRARDEAU, H
  John Lafayette
GIRARDIN, Ray 5
GIRD, Richard 4
GIRDLER, Tom Mercer 4
GIRDLER, 4
  Walter Higgins Jr.
GIRDNER, John Harvey 2
GIRL, Christian 2
GIRSCH, Frederick H
GIRTY, George Herbert 1
GIRTY, Simon H
GIST, Arthur Stanley 3
GIST, Christopher H
GIST, Joseph H
GIST, Mordecai H
GIST, Nathan Howard 4
GIST, William Henry H
GITELSON, M. Leo 4
GITELSON, Maxwell 4
GITHENS, Alfred Morton 5
GITHENS, Perry 4
GITLIN, Irving Joseph 4
GITLOW, Benjamin 4
GITT, Charles Moul 5
GITTINGER, Roy 3
GITTINGS, J. Claxton 3
GITTINS, Robert Henry 1
GIVAGO- 1
  GRISHINA, Nadeshda
GIVEN, John LaPorte 3
GIVEN, Josiah 1
GIVEN, Leslie Emmett 4
GIVEN, 5
  William Barns, Jr.
GIVENS, Raymond L. 5
GIVENS, 5
  Spencer Hollingsworth
GIVENS, Willard Earl 5
GIVLER, J. P. 3
GJELSNESS, Rudolph H. 5
GJERSET, Knut 1
GLACKENS, William J. 1
GLADDEN, George 1
GLADDEN, Washington 1
GLADDING, Albert F. 1
GLADDING, 3
  Ernest Knight
GLADDING, Timothy H
GLADSON, Guy Allen 5
GLADSON, 4
  William Nathan
GLADSTONE, 3
  Robert William
GLADWIN, Henry H
GLADWIN, 1
  Mary Elizabeth
GLADWIN, 1
  Malcolm
GLADWIN, 1
  William Zachary
GLAENZER, 1
  Richard Butler
GLAESER, 4
  Martin Gustave
GLAMAN, Eugenie Fish 3
GLANCY, 3
  Alfred Robinson
GLARNER, Fritz 5
GLASCOCK, Hugh
  Grundy 1
GLASCOCK, Thomas H
GLASCOFF, Donald G. 4
GLASER, Lulu 3
GLASER, Otto 3
GLASGOW, Arthur
  Graham 3
GLASGOW, Ellen 2
GLASGOW, Frank
  Lawson 5
GLASGOW, Hugh H
GLASGOW, Hugh 2
GLASGOW, 1
  William Anderson Jr.
GLASGOW, 2
  William Hargadine
GLASGOW, 4
  William Jefferson
GLASIER, 5
  Gilson Gardner
GLASOE, Paul Maurice 5
GLASPELL, Susan 2
GLASS, Carter 2
GLASS, Carter Jr. 3
GLASS, Franklin Potts 1
GLASS, Gilbert 1
GLASS, Henry 1
GLASS, Hiram 1
GLASS, Hugh H
GLASS, James H. 1
GLASS, H
  James William Jr.
GLASS,
  Joseph Sarsfield
GLASS, Meta 4

GLASS, Montague 1
GLASS, Powell 2
GLASS, Robert Camillus 3
GLASSCOCK, 2
  Carl Burgess
GLASSCOCK, 4
  Samuel Sampson
GLASSCOCK,
  William Ellsworth
GLASSER, Otto 4
GLASSFORD, 3
  William Alexander II
GLASSIE, Henry
  Haywood
GLASSMAN, Oscar 5
GLASSON, William Henry 2
GLATFELTER, Samuel F 1
GLATFELTER,
  William Lincoln
GLAVIN, Charles C. 5
GLAVIS, Louis Russell 1
GLAZEBROOK, Otis
  Allan 1
GLAZEBROOK, 3
  Otis Allan Jr.
GLAZIER, Robert Cromer 3
GLAZIER, Willard 1
GLAZIER, William S. 1
GLEASON, 1
  Arthur Huntington
GLEASON, 1
  Carlisle Joyslin
GLEASON, 1
  Clarence Willard
GLEASON, Daniel Angell 1
GLEASON, 1
  Edward Baldwin
GLEASON, Elliott Perry 4
GLEASON, 1
  Frederic Grant
GLEASON, Gay 3
GLEASON, 4
  Herbert Wendell
GLEASON, James 3
GLEASON, James E. 1
GLEASON, Kate 1
GLEASON, Lafayette B. 1
GLEASON, 1
  William Palmer
GLEAVES, Albert 1
GLEED, Charles Sumner 1
GLEED, James Willis 1
GLEESON,
  Joseph Michael
GLEIS, Paul G. 3
GLEISS, Henry Crete 1
GLEISSNER, John M. 1
GLEN, Henry H
GLEN, Irving Mackey 1
GLEN, James Allison 2
GLENDINNING,
  Malcolm
GLENDINNING, Robert 1
GLENN, Charles Bowles 5
GLENN, Edgar Eugene 3
GLENN, Edwin Forbes 1
GLENN, Garrard 2
GLENN, 3
  Gustavus Richard
GLENN, J. Lyles 1
GLENN, James Dryden 3
GLENN, James W. 4
GLENN, John Brodnax 1
GLENN, John Mark 3
GLENN, John McGaw 1
GLENN,
  Leonidas Chalmers
GLENN, Mary Willcox 1
GLENN, Milton Willits 4
GLENN, Otis Ferguson 3
GLENN, Robert Brodnax 1
GLENN, Thomas Kearney 2
GLENN, Thomas L. 4
GLENN, 1
  William Schaeffer
GLENNAN, Arthur
  Henry 4
GLENNON, James Henry 1
GLENNON, John Joseph 2
GLESSING, Thomas B. H
GLESSNER, John Jacob 1
GLICK, Carl 5
GLICK, 1
  George Washington
GLICKMAN, Irving 5
GLICKMAN, Mendel 2
GLIDDEN, 1
  Charles Jasper
GLIDDEN, H
  Joseph Farwell
GLIDDEN, 4
  Joseph Farwell
GLIDDEN, Minnie Maud 1
GLINES, Earle Stanley 4
GLINTENKAMP,
  Hendrik 2
GLOCK, Carl

GLOGAUER, Fritz 1
GLONINGER, John H
GLORE, Charles Foster 3
GLORIEUX, 1
  Alphonsus Joseph
GLOSE, Adolf 4
GLOSSBRENNER, H
  Adam John
GLOTZBACH, 1
  William Edward
GLOVER, Arthur James 2
GLOVER, Charles 1
GLOVER, 1
  Charles Carroll
GLOVER, David D. 3
GLOVER, 3
  Frederic Samuel
GLOVER, George Henry 5
GLOVER, James
  Waterman 1
GLOVER, John George 5
GLOVER, 1
  John Montgomery ·
GLOVER, Lyman Beecher 1
GLOVER, Robert Hall 2
GLOVER, Roy Henry 3
GLOVER, Townend H
GLOVER, William
  Howard H
GLUCK, Alma 1
GLUECK, Bernard 5
GLUECK, 5
  Eleanor Touroff, (Mrs.
  Sheldon Glueck)
GLUECK, Nelson 1
GLUHAREFF, Michael E. 4
GLYNDON, Howard 4
GLYNN, James H
GLYNN, James P. 1
GLYNN, Martin H. 1
GMEINER, John 1
GOAN, Orrin S. 4
GOBBLE, Aaron Ezra 4
GOBEIL, Samuel 4
GOBEILLE, 3
  Harrold Le Fevre
GOBER, William Mathis 5
GOBIN, Hillary Asbury 1
GOBIN, 1
  John Peter Shindel
GOBLE, 4
  George Washington
GOBRECHT, Christian H
GOCK, A. J. 4
GODARD, George
  Seymour 1
GODBE, William Samuel H
GODBEER, George H. 4
GODBEY, Allen Howard 2
GODBEY, Earle 2
GODBEY, John Campbell 1
GODBEY, John Emory 1
GODBOLD, Edgar 3
GODBOLD, Norman
  Dosier 1
GODBOUT, 3
  Joseph Adelard
GODCHARLES, 1
  Frederic Antes
GODCHAUX, Charles 3
GODCHAUX, Frank A. 4
GODCHAUX, Jules 3
GODDARD, Calvin H
GODDARD, Calvin
  Hooker 3
GODDARD, Calvin
  Luther H
GODDARD, 3
  Charles William
GODDARD, 4
  Christopher Marsh
GODDARD, Edwin C. 2
GODDARD, Harold
  Clarke 1
GODDARD, 1
  Harry Williams
GODDARD, Henry
  Herbert 4
GODDARD, Henry
  Newell 1
GODDARD, Henry
  Warren 3
GODDARD, John H
GODDARD, John Calvin 2
GODDARD, Karl B. 3
GODDARD, Leroy Albert 3
GODDARD, 4
  Loring Hapgood
GODDARD, Luther M. 1
GODDARD, Morrill 1
GODDARD, O. Fletcher 4
GODDARD, Oscar Elmo H
GODDARD, Paul Beck 1
GODDARD, Pliny Earle 1
GODDARD,
  Ralph Bartlett
GODDARD, Ralph Willis 1

GODDARD, 2
  Robert Hale Ives
GODDARD, 1
  Robert Hales Ives
GODDARD, 2
  Robert Hutchings
GODDARD, William H
GODDARD, William 1
GODDING, 4
  Adelaide M. Smith
GODDING, 1
  John Granville
GODDING, 1
  William Whitney
GODEFROY, Maximilian H
GODEHN, Paul M. 3
GODEY, Louis Antoine H
GODFREY, 5
  Alfred Laurance
GODFREY, Benjamin H
GODFREY, Edward Settle 1
GODFREY, Fletcher 4
GODFREY, Hollis 1
GODFREY, Lincoln 1
GODFREY, Stuart C. 2
GODFREY, Thomas * H
GODING, 1
  Frederic Webster
GODKIN, Edwin
  Lawrence 1
GODLEY, 4
  Frederick Augustus
GODLOVE, Isaac Hahn 3
GODMAN, John
  Davidson 1
GODOWSKY, Leopold 1
GODOY, Jose Francisco 4
GODSHALK, William 5
GODSHALL,
  Lincoln Derstine
GODSHALL, Wilson Leon 3
GODWIN, Earl 3
GODWIN, Edward Allison 1
GODWIN, 5
  Hannibal La Fayette
GODWIN, Harold 1
GODWIN, Herbert 5
GODWIN, Parke 1
GOEBEL, Frank J. 4
GOEBEL, Herman Philip 1
GOEBEL, Julius 4
GOEBEL, Peter W. 1
GOEBEL, William H
GOEKE, John Henry 1
GOELET, 1
  Augustin Hardin
GOELET, Robert 4
GOELET, Robert Walton 1
GOEPP, Philip Henry 4
GOERTNER, Francis B. 4
GOERTZ, Raymond C. 5
GOESSMANN, 1
  Charles Anthony
GOESSMANN, 3
  Helena Theresa
GOETCHIUS, 1
  Henry Richard
GOETHE, 4
  Charles Matthias
GOETSCHIUS, John
  Henry H
GOETSCHIUS, Percy 4
GOETZ, Albert Gillies H
GOETZ,
  George Washington
GOETZ, Norman S. 5
GOETZ, Philip Becker 3
GOETZ, William 3
GOETZE, Albrecht 5
GOETZE, Arthur Burton 3
GOETZE, 3
  Frederick Arthur
GOETZMANN, 3
  Jule Lawrence
GOFF, Emmet Stull H
GOFF, Ernest Lucius 4
GOFF, Frederick Harris 1
GOFF, Guy Despard 1
GOFF, Harold 1
GOFF, John W. 1
GOFF, Nathan 1
GOFF, Thomas Theodore 2
GOFFE, J. Riddle 1
GOFFE, William 1
GOFORTH, William H
GOGARTY, 1
  Oliver St John
GOGGIN, Catharine 5
GOGGIN, 1
  William Leftwich
GOHDES, Conrad Bruno 3
GOHEN, Charles Marsh 5
GOIN, Sanford Williams 1
GOING, Charles Buxton 5
GOING, Jonathan H
GOING, Maud 1

Indicates More Than One Such Name Listed

GOLATKA, Walter Francis 4
GOLAY, John Ford 5
GOLD, Harry 5
GOLD, Howard R. 3
GOLD, Nathan Jules 5
GOLD, Pleasant Daniel, Jr. 5
GOLD, Thomas Ruggles
GOLD, William Henry 4
GOLD, William Jason 1
GOLDBECK, Albert Theodore 4
GOLDBECK, Edward 1
GOLDBECK, Robert 1
GOLDBERG, Isaac 5
GOLDBERG, Leo 5
GOLDBERGER, Isidore Harry 5
GOLDBERGER, Joseph 1
GOLDBLATT, Maurice Henry 4
GOLDBLATT, Nathan 2
GOLDEN, Ben Hale 5
GOLDEN, Clinton Strong 4
GOLDEN, Grace 5
GOLDEN, James S. 5
GOLDEN, John 3
GOLDEN, Michael Joseph 4
GOLDEN, Richard 1
GOLDEN, S. Herbert 1
GOLDEN, S. M. 3
GOLDENBERG, Morris 1
GOLDENWEISER, Alexander
GOLDENWEISER, Emanuel Alexander 3
GOLDER, Benjamin M. 2
GOLDER, Frank Alfred 1
GOLDESBERRY, John Milford 5
GOLDET, Antoine Gustave 4
GOLDFOGLE, Henry M. 1
GOLDING, Frank Henry 1
GOLDING, Jerrold R. 1
GOLDING, Louis 3
GOLDING, Louis Thorn 4
GOLDING, Samuel H. 5
GOLDMAN, Albert 4
GOLDMAN, Edward Alphonse 2
GOLDMAN, Edwin Franko 3
GOLDMAN, Emma H
GOLDMAN, Emma 4
GOLDMAN, Frank 4
GOLDMAN, Hetty 5
GOLDMAN, Maurice Harry
GOLDMAN, Mayer C. 1
GOLDMAN, Samuel P. 5
GOLDMAN, Solomon 5
GOLDMANN, Franz 5
GOLDMARK, Pauline Dorothea 5
GOLDMARK, Pauline Dorothea 4
GOLDMARK, Rubin 1
GOLDNER, Jacob Henry 5
GOLDSBERRY, Louise Dunham 5
GOLDSBOROUGH, Charles H
GOLDSBOROUGH, Laird S. 3
GOLDSBOROUGH, Laird Shields 2
GOLDSBOROUGH, Louis Malesherbes H
GOLDSBOROUGH, Phillips Lee 2
GOLDSBOROUGH, Richard Francis 1
GOLDSBOROUGH, Robert H
GOLDSBOROUGH, Robert Henry H
GOLDSBOROUGH, T. Alan 3
GOLDSBOROUGH, W. Elwell 3
GOLDSBOROUGH, Washington Laird 5
GOLDSBOROUGH, Worthington 1
GOLDSCHMIDT, Jakob 3
GOLDSCHMIDT, Richard Benedict 3
GOLDSCHMIDT, Samuel Anthony 1
GOLDSMITH, Alan Gustavus 4
GOLDSMITH, Brooks P. 5
GOLDSMITH, Clifford 5
GOLDSMITH, Deborah H
GOLDSMITH, Goldwin 5

GOLDSMITH, Jonothan H
GOLDSMITH, Middleton H
GOLDSMITH, Milton 3
GOLDSMITH, Philip H. 3
GOLDSMITH, Robert 1
GOLDSPOHN, Albert 1
GOLDSTEIN, Irving 5
GOLDSTEIN, Louis 4
GOLDSTEIN, Max Aaron 5
GOLDSTEIN, Molse Herbert
GOLDSTEIN, Sidney Emanuel 3
GOLDSTINE, Harry 3
GOLDTHWAIT, James Walter 2
GOLDTHWAIT, Joel Ernest 5
GOLDTHWAIT, Nathan Edward 3
GOLDTHWAIT, Sheldon Forrest 4
GOLDTHWAITE, Anne 2
GOLDTHWAITE, 'du Val R. 3
GOLDTHWAITE, George H
GOLDTHWAITE, George Edgar 4
GOLDTHWAITE, Henry Barnes H
GOLDTHWAITE, Nellie Esther 2
GOLDTHWAITE, Vere 5
GOLDWATER, Richard M. 5
GOLDWATER, Robert 5
GOLDWATER, Sigismund Schultz 2
GOLER, George W. 1
GOLER, William Harvey 4
GOLLADAY, Edward Isaac 4
GOLLADAY, Jacob Shall H
GOLLOMB, Joseph 3
GOLOVIN, Nicholas Erasmus 5
GOLSCHMANN, Vladimir 5
GOLTMAN, Maximilian 5
GOLTRA, Edward Field 1
GOLUB, Jacob Joshua 3
GOMBERG, Moses 2
GOMBROWICZ, Witold 5
GOMEZ, Laureano 4
GOMEZ-MORENO MARTINEZ, Manuel 5
GOMPERS, Samuel 1
GOMPERT, William Henry 2
GONCE, John Eugene Jr. 3
GONDELMAN, Sidney 5
GONGWER, Lillian May 5
GONS, James Walker H
GONZALES, Ambrose Elliott 1
GONZALES, William Elliott 3
GONZALEZ, Bienvenido M.
GONZALEZ, Rosa Mangual 4
GOOCH, D. Linn 4
GOOCH, Daniel Wheelwright H
GOOCH, Frank Austin 1
GOOCH, Sir William H
GOOCH, Tom Carbry 3
GOOD, Adolphus Clemens H
GOOD, Alice Campbell 3
GOOD, Charles Winfred 2
GOOD, Edward Ellsworth 1
GOOD, Edwin Stanton 5
GOOD, Fredrick Hopkins 5
GOOD, Howard Harrison 4
GOOD, Irby J. 2
GOOD, James Isaac 1
GOOD, James William 1
GOOD, Jeremiah Haak H
GOOD, Paul Francis 1
GOODALE, Charles Warren 4
GOODALE, Dora Read 4
GOODALE, George Lincoln 1
GOODALE, George Pomeroy 1
GOODALE, Greenleaf Austin 1
GOODALE, Joseph Lincoln 5
GOODALE, Joseph Lincoln
GOODALE, Stephen Lincoln H
GOODALE, Stephen Lincoln 3

GOODALL, Albert Gallatin H
GOODALL, Charles Edward 5
GOODALL, Harvey L. H
GOODALL, Louis Bertrand 1
GOODBAR, Joseph Ernest 3
GOODCHILD, Frank Marsden 1
GOODE, Clement Tyson 2
GOODE, George Brown H
GOODE, George William 5
GOODE, J. Paul 1
GOODE, John 1
GOODE, Patrick Gaines H
GOODE, Richard Livingston 5
GOODE, Richard Urquhart 1
GOODE, Samuel H
GOODE, William Athelstane Meredith 5
GOODE, William Osborne H
GOODELL, Charles Elmer 1
GOODELL, Charles Le Roy 1
GOODELL, David Harvey 1
GOODELL, Henry Hill 1
GOODELL, Raymond Batchelder 3
GOODELL, Reginald Rusden 2
GOODELL, Roswell Eaton 5
GOODELL, Thomas Dwight 1
GOODELL, William * H
GOODENOUGH, Erwin Ramsdell 4
GOODENOUGH, George Alfred 1
GOODENOUGH, Luman W. 3
GOODENOW, John Milton H
GOODENOW, Robert H
GOODENOW, Rufus King H
GOODERHAM, Melvill Ross 3
GOODFELLOW, Edward 1
GOODHEART, William Raymond Jr. 4
GOODHUE, Benjamin 1
GOODHUE, Bertram Grosvenor
GOODHUE, Edward Solon 4
GOODHUE, Francis Abbot 2
GOODHUE, James Madison H
GOODHUE, William Joseph 5
GOODIER, James Norman 5
GOODIN, John Randolph H
GOODING, Frank R. 1
GOODKIND, Gilbert E. 1
GOODKIND, Maurice Louis 1
GOODKNIGHT, James Lincoln 1
GOODLAND, Walter Samuel 2
GOODLOE, Daniel Reaves H
GOODLOE, William Cassius H
GOODMAN, Benedict Kay 4
GOODMAN, Charles H
GOODMAN, Charles 2
GOODMAN, Daniel Carson 3
GOODMAN, David 5
GOODMAN, Frank Bartlett 3
GOODMAN, Frank Croly 3
GOODMAN, George Hill 5
GOODMAN, Jack Arthur 3
GOODMAN, James E. 4
GOODMAN, Jess Dee 5
GOODMAN, John 4
GOODMAN, John Forest 4
GOODMAN, Jules Eckert 4
GOODMAN, Louis Earl 4
GOODMAN, Mary Ellen 5
GOODMAN, Mrs. Jean R. 1
GOODMAN, Nathan Gerson 3
GOODMAN, Paul 5
GOODMAN, William Edward
GOODMAN, William M. 3

GOODMAN, William Owen 1
GOODNIGHT, Charles H
GOODNIGHT, Charles 4
GOODNIGHT, Cloyd 1
GOODNIGHT, Isaac Herschel
GOODNIGHT, Scott Holland 5
GOODNO, William Colby 5
GOODNOW, Charles Allen
GOODNOW, Frank Johnson
GOODNOW, Isaac Tichenor H
GOODNOW, John 1
GOODNOW, Minnie 5
GOODPASTURE, Ernest William 4
GOODPASTURE, Wendell Williamson 5
GOODRELL, Mancil Clay
GOODRICH, Alfred John 3
GOODRICH, Annie Warburton
GOODRICH, Arthur 1
GOODRICH, Ben H
GOODRICH, Benjamin Franklin
GOODRICH, Caspar Frederick
GOODRICH, Charles Augustus
GOODRICH, Chauncey * H
GOODRICH, Chauncey 1
GOODRICH, Chauncey Allen H
GOODRICH, Chauncey William 3
GOODRICH, David Marvin 3
GOODRICH, Donald Reuben 2
GOODRICH, Edgar Jennings 5
GOODRICH, Elizur H
GOODRICH, Elizus
GOODRICH, Ernest Payson 3
GOODRICH, Foster Edward 5
GOODRICH, Francis Lee Dewey 5
GOODRICH, Frank 1
GOODRICH, Frank Boott H
GOODRICH, Frederick William 4
GOODRICH, Hale Caldwell
GOODRICH, Herbert F. 4
GOODRICH, Hubert Baker 4
GOODRICH, James Clarence 3
GOODRICH, James Edward 3
GOODRICH, James Putnam 1
GOODRICH, John Ellsworth
GOODRICH, John Zacheus H
GOODRICH, Joseph King 5
GOODRICH, L(awrence) Keith
GOODRICH, Levi H
GOODRICH, Lowell Pierce 2
GOODRICH, Milo H
GOODRICH, Nathaniel Lewis
GOODRICH, Ralph Leland 4
GOODRICH, Robert Eugene
GOODRICH, Samuel Griswold
GOODRICH, Wallace H
GOODRICH, William Marcellus
GOODRICH, William W. 4
GOODRIDGE, John 4
GOODRIDGE, Malcolm 5
GOODRIDGE, Sarah H
GOODSELL, Charles True 1
GOODSELL, Charles True 5
GOODSELL, Daniel Ayres 1
GOODSELL, Willystine 5
GOODSON, Edward Fletcher
GOODSPEED, Arthur Willis 4
GOODSPEED, Charles Barnett 2

GOODSPEED, Charles Ten Broeke
GOODSPEED, Edgar Johnson
GOODSPEED, Frank Lincoln
GOODSPEED, George Stephen
GOODSPEED, Thomas Harper
GOODSPEED, Thomas Wakefield
GOODSPEED, Walter Stuart
GOODWILLIE, David Herrick
GOODWILLIE, David Lincoln
GOODWIN, Arthur C.
GOODWIN, Cardinal Leonidas
GOODWIN, Charles Archibald
GOODWIN, Charles Jaques
GOODWIN, Clarence Norton
GOODWIN, Daniel
GOODWIN, Daniel Raynes
GOODWIN, E. Mckee
GOODWIN, Edward C.
GOODWIN, Edward Jasper
GOODWIN, Edward Jewett
GOODWIN, Elijah
GOODWIN, Elliot H.
GOODWYN, Ernest Vance
GOODWIN, Frank Judson
GOODWIN, Frederick C.
GOODWIN, Godfrey G.
GOODWIN, Grace Duffield (Mrs. Frank J. Goodwin)
GOODWIN, Hannibal Williston
GOODWIN, Harold
GOODWIN, Harry Manley
GOODWIN, Henry Charles
GOODWIN, Ichabod
GOODWIN, J. Cheever
GOODWIN, James Junius
GOODWIN, John Benjamin
GOODWIN, John Edward
GOODWIN, John Noble
GOODWIN, Kathryn Dickinson
GOODWIN, Lavinia Stella
GOODWIN, Leo, Sr.
GOODWIN, Mark London
GOODWIN, Maud Wilder
GOODWIN, Nat C.
GOODWIN, Philip Arnold
GOODWIN, Philip Lippincott
GOODWIN, Richard Vanderburgh
GOODWIN, Russell Parker
GOODWIN, Wilder
GOODWIN, Willard T.
GOODWIN, William Archer Rutherford
GOODWIN, William Hall
GOODWIN, William Watson
GOODWYN, Peterson
GOODYEAR, Anson Conger
GOODYEAR, Charles *
GOODYEAR, Charles Waterhouse
GOODYEAR, John
GOODYEAR, William Henry
GOODYKOONTZ, Colin Brummitt
GOODYKOONTZ, Wells
GOOKIN, Daniel
GOOLD, Marshall Newton
GOOLRICK, C. O'conor
GOOLSBY, Robert Edwin Moorman
GOOSSENS, Eugene Sir
GORBACH, Alfons
GORBY, Paul Ford
GORDIN, Harry Mann
GORDINIER, Charles H.
GORDINIER, Hermon Camp

GORDON, — H
Adoniram Judson
GORDON, Alfred — 5
GORDON, Andrew — H
GORDON, Anna Adams
GORDON, Archibald D. — H
GORDON, — 1
Armistead Churchill
GORDON, — 3
Armistead Churchill Jr.
GORDON, Arthur Horace
GORDON, Charles — 2
GORDON, Charles Henry — 1
GORDON, Clarence
GORDON, — 5
Clarence McCheyne
GORDON, David Stuart — 1
GORDON, Donald — 5
GORDON, Dorothy
GORDON, Douglas — 2
GORDON, — 1
Edward Clifford
GORDON, Edwin Seamer — 1
GORDON,
Eleanor Elizabeth
GORDON, Eleanor Kinzie
GORDON, Elizabeth — 1
GORDON, — 5
Ernest (Barron)
GORDON, Francis — 1
GORDON, Frank
Malcolm — 2
GORDON, — 4
Fred George Russ
GORDON, — 3
Frederic Sutterle
GORDON,
Frederick Charles
GORDON, — 3
George Anderson
GORDON, George Angier — 1
GORDON, George Breed — 1
GORDON, George Byron — 1
GORDON, George C. — 4
GORDON, George Henry — H
GORDON, George
Phineas — H
GORDON, — 1
George Washington
GORDON, Gurdon
Wright — 3
GORDON, Hirsch Loeb — 5
GORDON, Irwin Leslie — 3
GORDON, Jacques — 2
GORDON, James — H
GORDON, James — 1
GORDON, James
Herndon — 1
GORDON, James Logan — 1
GORDON, James Marcus — 3
GORDON, John — 1
GORDON, John — 3
GORDON, John Brown — 1
GORDON, — 1
Joseph Claybaugh
GORDON, Julien — 1
GORDON, Laura De
Force — H
GORDON, Laura De
Force — 4
GORDON, Leon — 2
GORDON, Louis — 4
GORDON, M. Lafayette — 1
GORDON, Margaret — 4
GORDON, Merritt J. — 4
GORDON, Neil Elbridge — 2
GORDON, Ney Kingsley — 4
GORDON, Peyton — 2
GORDON, Ray P(ercival) — 5
GORDON, — 5
Richard Sammons
GORDON, Robert — 3
GORDON, Robert Loudon — 2
GORDON, S. D. — 1
GORDON, Samuel — 1
GORDON, Seth Chase — 1
GORDON, Thomas Sylvy — 3
GORDON, Walter Henry — 1
GORDON, William * — H
GORDON, William — 1
GORDON, William — 2
GORDON, William
Duncan — 4
GORDON, — H
William Fitzhugh
GORDON, William Knox — 2
GORDON, — 5
William Lawrence Sanford
GORDON, William
Robert — H
GORDON, — 1
William St Clair
GORDON, William W. — 1
GORDON, — H
William Washington

GORDON-DAVIS, — 5
Alfred Burwell (Davis
Brinton)
GORDY, J. P.
GORDY, Wilbur Fisk — 1
GORE, Christopher — H
GORE, Claude — 3
GORE, Elbert Brutus — 4
GORE, Herbert Charles — 5
GORE, Howard Mason — 2
GORE, James Howard — 4
GORE, John Kinsey — 4
GORE, Joshua Walker — 1
GORE, Quentin Pryor — 1
GORE, Thomas Pryor — 2
GORE, W. A.
GORGAS, — 4
Ferdinand James Samuel
GORGAS, Josiah — H
GORGAS, — 1
William Crawford
GORGES, Sir Ferdinando — H
GORHAM, Frederic Poole — 1
GORHAM, George
Congdon — 1
GORHAM, Jabez — H
GORHAM, John — H
GORHAM, Nathaniel — H
GORHAM, Willis Arnold — H
GORIN, Orville B. — 1
GORKY, Arshile — 4
GORMAN, Arthur Pue — H
GORMAN, Arthur Pue Jr. — 1
GORMAN, Charles
Edmund — 1
GORMAN, Daniel M. — 1
GORMAN, George
Edmond — 1
GORMAN, — 3
Herbert Sherman
GORMAN, James Edward — 2
GORMAN, — 3
Lawrence Clifton
GORMAN, Michael
Arthur — 3
GORMAN, Robert Nestor — 5
GORMAN, Thomas J. — 4
GOROSTIZA, Jose — 5
GORRELL, Edgar Staley — 2
GORRIE, John — H
GORRINGE,
Henry Honeychurch
GORSKI, Martin — 4
GORTATOWSKY, — 4
Jacob Dewey
GORTHY, Willis Charles — 4
GORTNER, Ross Aiken — 2
GORTON, David Allyn — 1
GORTON, Eliot — 1
GORTON, Samuel — H
GOSE, Mack F. — 3
GOSE, Thomas Phelps — 5
GOSHEN, Elmer Isaac
GOSHORN, Alfred Traber — 1
GOSHORN, — 3
Clarence Baker
GOSHORN, Lenore
Rhyno — 3
GOSHORN, R. C. — 3
GOSLEE, Hart John — 1
GOSLINE, — 2
William A. Jr.
GOSLING, — 1
Thomas Warrington
GOSNELL, John Ansley — 5
GOSNEY, Ezra Seymour — 2
GOSNOLD, Bartholomew — H
GOSS, Albert S. — 3
GOSS, Arthur — 1
GOSS, Bert Crawford — 5
GOSS, Charles A. — 1
GOSS, Charles Frederic — 1
GOSS, Chauncey P. — 4
GOSS, Chauncey Porter — 1
GOSS, Edward Otis — 1
GOSS, Elbridge Henry — 1
GOSS, Evan Benson — 1
GOSS, Francis Webster — 1
GOSS, Harvey Theo — 3
GOSS, John Henry — 2
GOSS, — H
Nathaniel Stickney
GOSS, Robert Whitmore — 5
GOSS, Warren Lee — 1
GOSS,
William Freeman Myrick
GOSS, — 4
William Middlebrook
GOSSARD, George Daniel — 1
GOSSARD, Harry Clinton — 5
GOSSETT, Alfred Newton — 2
GOSSETT,
Benjamin Brown
GOSSETT, Earl J. — 4
GOSSETT, John Taylor

GOSSETT, — 5
Robert Kenneth
GOSSLER, Philip Green — 2
GOSTELOWE, Jonathan — H
GOTSCH, Arthur Edward — 5
GOTSHAL, Sylvan — 5
GOTSHALL, — 1
William Charles
GOTT, Charles
GOTT, Daniel — H
GOTT, Edgar Nathaniel — 2
GOTT, William Thomas — 2
GOTTESMAN, D. Samuel — 3
GOTTFRIED, Louis Elio — 5
GOTTHEIL, Gustave — H
GOTTHEIL, — 4
Richard James Horatio
GOTTHEIL, — 4
William Samuel
GOTTSCHALK, — 1
Alfred L. Moreau
GOTTSCHALK, — 4
Louis Ferdinand
GOTTSCHALK, — H
Louis Moreau
GOTTSCHALL, Morton — 5
GOTTSCHALL, Oscar M. — 4
GOTTWALD, Klement — 3
GOTWALD, — 4
Luther Alexander
GOTWALS, John C. — 3
GOUCHER, John Franklin — 1
GOUDY, Frank Burris — 2
GOUDY, Franklin Curtis — 1
GOUDY, — 2
Frederic William
GOUDY, William Charles — H
GOUGAR, Helen M. — 1
GOUGE, William M. — H
GOUGH, Emile Jefferson — 2
GOUGH, — H
John Bartholomew
GOUGH, Lewis Ketcham — 4
GOUGH, Robert E. — 5
GOULD, Anna Laura — 5
GOULD, Arthur Robinson — 2
GOULD, Ashley Mulgrave — 1
GOULD, — H
Augustus Addison
GOULD, — H
Benjamin Apthorp
GOULD, — 1
Carl Frelinghuysen
GOULD, Charles Newton — 2
GOULD,
Charles Winthrop
GOULD,
Clarence Pembroke
GOULD, Edward Sherman — 1
GOULD, Edward Shuman — H
GOULD, Edwin — 1
GOULD, — 3
Edwin Miner Lawrence
GOULD, Edwin Sprague — 1
GOULD,
Elgin Ralston Lovell
GOULD,
Elizabeth Lincoln
GOULD, Ezra Palmer — 1
GOULD, Frank — 4
GOULD, Frank Horace — 1
GOULD, Frank Jay — 3
GOULD, Frank Miller — 2
GOULD, George Jay — 1
GOULD, George Milbry — 1
GOULD, Hannah Flagg — H
GOULD, Harris Perley — 2
GOULD, Harry — 4
GOULD, Harry Edward — 5
GOULD, Herman Day — H
GOULD, Howard — 1
GOULD, James — H
GOULD, Jay — H
GOULD, Kenneth Miller — 5
GOULD, Kingdon — 1
GOULD, Laura Stedman — 1
GOULD, Moses Joseph — 4
GOULD, Nathaniel Duren — H
GOULD, Norman Judd — 5
GOULD, Norman Judd — 4
GOULD, — 1
Samuel Wadsworth
GOULD, — 4
Theodore Pennock
GOULD, Thomas
Ridgeway — H
GOULD, William Edward — 3
GOULDEN, — 1
Joseph Augustus
GOULDER, — 1
Harvey Danforth
GOULDER, — 4
Harvey Danforth
GOULDING, Edmund — 3
GOULDING, — H
Francis Robert
GOULETT, Paul R. — 4

GOULEY, — 4
John William Severin
GOUPIL, St Rene — H
GOURDIN, Theodore — H
GOURLEY, Joseph
Harvey — 2
GOURLEY, Louis Hill — 3
GOURLEY, William B. — 1
GOUVERNEUR, Marian
GOVAN, Andrew Robison — H
GOVE, Aaron — 1
GOVE, Charles Augustus — 1
GOVE, Frank Edward — 4
GOVE, George — 3
GOVE, Philip Babcock — 5
GOVIN, Rafael R.
GOW, Charles R(ice) — 5
GOW, George Coleman — 4
GOW, James Steele — 5
GOW, John Russell — 1
GOW, Robert Macgregor — 4
GOWANS, Ephraim
Gowan — 4
GOWANS, William — H
GOWDY, John Kennedy — 2
GOWDY, Robert Clyde — 5
GOWDY, Roy Cotsworth — 1
GOWEN, Francis Innes — 1
GOWEN, — H
Franklin Benjamin
GOWEN, Herbert Henry — 5
GOWEN, Isaac William — 1
GOWEN, — 3
James Bartholomew
GOWEN, James Emmet — 5
GOWEN, — 4
John Knowles Jr.
GOWEN, John Wittemore — 4
GOWEN, Robert Fellows — 1
GOWENLOCK, — 4
Thomas Russell
GOWER, John Henry — 4
GOWMAN, T. Harry — 4
GRABAU, — 5
Amadeus William
GRABAU, — H
Johannes Andreas August
GRABAU, Martin — 5
GRABER, Edward Darwin — 5
GRABFELDER, Samuel — 1
GRABILL, — 5
Ethelbert Vincent
GRABLE, — 5
Betty (Elizabeth Ruth)
GRABLE, E. F. — 4
GRABLE, Errett Marion — 4
GRACE, Atonzo G. — 5
GRACE, Carl Guy — 5
GRACE, Edward
Raymond — 4
GRACE, Eugene Gifford — 5
GRACE, — 1
Francis Mitchell
GRACE, Frank W. — 2
GRACE, Harry Holder — 4
GRACE, — 5
James Thomas, Jr.
GRACE, John Joseph — 5
GRACE, Joseph Peter — 3
GRACE, Louise Carol — 5
GRACE, Thomas — 1
GRACE, Thomas L. — 5
GRACE, Thomas Langdon — H
GRACE, William — 1
GRACE, William Joseph — 5
GRACE, William Russell — 1
GRACEY, Samuel Levis — 1
GRACEY, Wilbur Tirrell — 5
GRACEY, — 2
William Adolphe
GRACIE, Archibald — H
GRADLE, Harry Searls — 3
GRADLE, Henry — 1
GRADY, Daniel Henry — 3
GRADY, Eleanor
Hundson — 5
GRADY, Henry Francis — 3
GRADY, Henry W. — 5
GRADY, Henry Woodfin — H
GRAEBNER,
August Lawrence
GRAEBNER,
Martin Adolph Henry
GRAEBNER, Theodore — 3
GRAEFFE, Edwin O(tto) — 5
GRAESSER, Roy French — 5
GRAESSL, Lawrence — H
GRAF, Herbert — 5
GRAF, Homer William — 5
GRAF, Oskar Maria — 5
GRAF, Robert Joseph — 2
GRAFF, Ellis U. — 1
GRAFF, Everett D. — 4
GRAFF, Frederic
GRAFF, Frederick — H
GRAFF, Fritz William — 3

GRAFF, George E. — 1
GRAFF, Joseph Verdi — 1
GRAFFENRIED, — H
Christopher
GRAFFLIN, — 3
Douglas Gordon
GRAFLY, Charles — 1
GRAFTON, — 1
Charles Chapman
GRAFTON, — 1
Robert Wadsworth
GRAHAM, Albert D. — 3
GRAHAM, — 2
Alexander William
GRAHAM, Allen Jordan — 1
GRAHAM, B.A. — 5
GRAHAM, — 5
Balus Joseph Windsor
GRAHAM, Ben George — 2
GRAHAM, — H
Charles Kinnaird
GRAHAM, — 4
Charles Vanderveer
GRAHAM, Christopher — 3
GRAHAM, Clarence
Henry — 5
GRAHAM, Dale — 3
GRAHAM, David — H
GRAHAM, David Wilson — 1
GRAHAM, Donald
Goodnow — 5
GRAHAM, Dorothy — 3
GRAHAM, Edward
Kidder — 1
GRAHAM, Edwin Charles — 3
GRAHAM, Edwin Eldon — 1
GRAHAM, Edwin R. — 1
GRAHAM, Ernest Robert — 1
GRAHAM, Evarts
Ambrose — 3
GRAHAM, Frank
GRAHAM, Frank
Dunstone — 2
GRAHAM, Frank Porter — 5
GRAHAM, George
Edward — 4
GRAHAM, George Rex — H
GRAHAM, George Scott — 1
GRAHAM, Gwethalyn — 4
GRAHAM, Henry Tucker — 1
GRAHAM, Horace French — 1
GRAHAM, Horace French — 1
GRAHAM, — 3
Horace Reynolds
GRAHAM, Hoyt Conlin — 1
GRAHAM, Hugh — 3
GRAHAM, Inez — 4
GRAHAM, — H
Isabella Marshall
GRAHAM, James * — H
GRAHAM, James B. — 5
GRAHAM, James Duncan — H
GRAHAM, James Francis — 4
GRAHAM, James Harper — 4
GRAHAM, James Hiram — 4
GRAHAM, James M. — 2
GRAHAM, John * — H
GRAHAM, John Andrew — H
GRAHAM, John Howard — 3
GRAHAM, John Hugh — H
GRAHAM, John Meredith — 5
GRAHAM, — 1
Jonathan Thomas
GRAHAM, Joseph — H
GRAHAM, — 4
Joseph Alexander
GRAHAM, Kelley — 4
GRAHAM, Lawrence Pike — 1
GRAHAM, — 5
Lena Forney Reinhardt
(Mrs. Joseph Graham)
GRAHAM, Louis Edward — 4
GRAHAM, Malbone
Watson — 4
GRAHAM, — 1
Margaret Collier
GRAHAM, Mary Owen — 5
GRAHAM, Neil F. — 4
GRAHAM, Philip L. — 4
GRAHAM, Ray Austin — 1
GRAHAM, Robert Cabel — 4
GRAHAM, Robert Henry — 5
GRAHAM, Robert
Orlando
GRAHAM, Robert X. — 3
GRAHAM, Samuel Jordan — 3
GRAHAM, Stephen A. — 4
GRAHAM, Stephen Victor — 5
GRAHAM,
Sterling Edward
GRAHAM, Sylvester — H
GRAHAM, Thomas
Wesley — 5
GRAHAM, Walter James — 2
GRAHAM, Willard J. — 4
GRAHAM, William — H

GRAHAM, H
William Alexander
GRAHAM, 3
William Alexander
GRAHAM, 4
William Harrison
GRAHAM, 1
William Johnson
GRAHAM, William
Joseph 4
GRAHAM, 1
William Montrose
GRAHAM, William Pratt 4
GRAHAM, William Tate 5
GRAHAME, Laurance
Hill 4
GRAINGER, Percy 4
GRAMBLING, 5
Allen Rowell
GRAMMER, 5
Allen L(uther)
GRAMMER, Carl
Eckhardt 2
GRAMMER, 1
Elijah Sherman
GRAMMER, Jacob 1
GRANAHAN, 3
William Thomas
GRANBERRY, C. Read 4
GRANBERY, John
Cowper 1
GRANBERY, John
Cowper 3
GRAND, Gordon, Jr. 5
GRANDFIELD, 4
Charles Paxton
GRANDGENT, 4
Charles Hall
GRANDIN, Egbert Henry 4
GRANFIELD, 3
William Joseph
GRANGER, Alfred Hoyt 1
GRANGER, Amos Phelps H
GRANGER, 5
Armour Townsend
GRANGER, Arthur Otis 1
GRANGER, Barlow 1
GRANGER, H
Bradley Francis
GRANGER, 1
Charles Trumbull
GRANGER, 1
Daniel Larned Davis
GRANGER, Francis 1
GRANGER, Frank Butler 1
GRANGER, Gideon H
GRANGER, Gordon 1
GRANGER, Miles Tobey 1
GRANGER, 1
Moses Moorhead
GRANGER, 5
Sherman Moorhead
GRANGER, Walter 1
GRANGER, 1
William Alexander
GRANIK, Theodore 5
GRANJON, Henry Regis 4
GRANNAN, Charles P. 1
GRANNIS, 1
Elizabeth Bartlett
GRANNIS, 1
Robert Maitland
GRANNISS, Anna Jane 4
GRANNISS, 1
Robert Andrews
GRANT, Abraham 1
GRANT, Abraham Phineas H
GRANT, Albert Weston 1
GRANT, Alsie Raymond 4
GRANT, Arthur Rogers 2
GRANT, Asahel H
GRANT, 5
Bishop F(ranklin)
GRANT, Carroll Walter 1
GRANT, Charles Henry 1
GRANT, 1
Claudius Buchanan
GRANT, David Elias 5
GRANT, 4
David Norvell Walker
GRANT, DeForest 5
GRANT, Elihu 2
GRANT, 5
Elliott Mansfield
GRANT, Frederick Dent 1
GRANT, George Barnard 1
GRANT, George Barnard 4
GRANT, George Camron 1
GRANT, George Ernest 3
GRANT, Gordon 4
GRANT, Harry Johnston 4
GRANT, Heber J. 2
GRANT, Henry Horace 1
GRANT, Henry William 5
GRANT, Hugh John 4
GRANT, James Benton 1
GRANT, James Benton 2

GRANT, James Richard 3
GRANT, Jesse R. 4
GRANT, John Black 1
GRANT, John Cowles 1
GRANT, John Gaston 3
GRANT, John Henry 1
GRANT, John MacGregor 1
GRANT, John Prescott 2
GRANT, John Thomas H
GRANT, Joseph Donohoe 2
GRANT, Joseph Henry 1
GRANT, Julia Dent 1
GRANT, 5
Lester Strickland
GRANT, Lewis Addison 1
GRANT, Madison 1
GRANT, Margaret 4
GRANT, Percy Stickney 1
GRANT, Richard Frank 3
GRANT, 1
Richard Ralph Hallam
GRANT, Robert 1
GRANT, Robert John 2
GRANT, 4
Roderick McLellan
GRANT, Rollin P. 1
GRANT, Thomas
McMillan 3
GRANT, Ulysses S. Jr. 1
GRANT, Ulysses S, III 5
GRANT, Ulysses Sherman 3
GRANT, Ulysses Simpson H
GRANT, Walter Bruce 1
GRANT, Whit
McDonough 1
GRANT, William Thomas 3
GRANT, William Thomas 5
GRANT, William West 1
GRANT, William West 3
GRANTHAM, 1
Edwin Lincoln
GRANTLAND, Seaton H
GRANT-SMITH, U. 1
GRANVILLE, 4'th Earl 3
GRANVILLE, 2
William Anthony
GRANVILLE-SMITH, W. 1
GRASON, C. Gus H
GRASS, John 3
GRASS, John H
GRASSE, Edwin 3
GRASSE, 1
Francois Joseph Paul 'de
GRASSELLI, 1
Caesar Augustin
GRASSELLI, 5
Thomas Fries
GRASSELLI, 2
Thomas Saxton
GRASSHAM, Charles C. 2
GRASSHOFF, Frank O. 3
GRASTY, Charles Henry 1
GRASTY, John Sharshall 1
GRATACAP, Louis Pope 1
GRATIOT, Charles H
GRATKE, Charles Edward 2
GRATZ, Bernard 1
GRATZ, Michael H
GRATZ, Rebecca H
GRATZ, W. Edward J. 3
GRAU, Maurice 1
GRAUDAN, Nikolai 5
GRAUEL, George Edward 4
GRAUER, A. E. 4
GRAUER, Natalie Eynon 3
GRAUER, Theophil Paul 4
GRAUPNER, 2
Adolphus Earhart
GRAUPNER, H
Johann Christian Gottlieb
GRAU SAN MARTIN, 5
Ramon
GRAUSTEIN, 5
Archibald R(obertson)
GRAUSTEIN, 1
William Caspar
GRAVATT, 2
William Loyall
GRAVE, Caswell 1
GRAVE, Frederick David 4
GRAVELY, 1
Joseph Jackson
GRAVEN, Henry Norman 5
GRAVES, Abbott Fuller 1
GRAVES, Alvin C. 4
GRAVES, Anson Rogers 1
GRAVES, Bibb 2
GRAVES, Charles 4
GRAVES, Charles Alfred 1
GRAVES, 1
Charles Burleigh
GRAVES, Charles Hinman 1
GRAVES, 3
Charles Marshall
GRAVES, Eli Edwin 1
GRAVES, Eugene Silas 3

GRAVES, 3
Frank Pierrepont
GRAVES, 1
Frederick Rogers
GRAVES, George Keene 2
GRAVES, 5
Grant Ostrander
GRAVES, Harold Nathan 4
GRAVES, Henry Solon 1
GRAVES, 1
Herbert Cornelius
GRAVES, Ireland 5
GRAVES, 1
Jackson Alpheus
GRAVES, James Robinson H
GRAVES, James Wesley 1
GRAVES, Jay P. 2
GRAVES, John 3
GRAVES, John Temple 1
GRAVES, John Temple 4
GRAVES, Louis 1
GRAVES, Lulu Grace 2
GRAVES, Mark 1
GRAVES, Marvin Lee 4
GRAVES, 1
Mary Wheat (Mrs. Billy Z.
Graves)
GRAVES, Nelson Zuingle 1
GRAVES, Ralph A. 1
GRAVES, Ralph H. 1
GRAVES, Robert John 3
GRAVES, 1
Schuyler Colfax
GRAVES, Waller W. 1
GRAVES, William Blair 1
GRAVES, William Jordan H
GRAVES, William Lucius 2
GRAVES, 1
William Phillips
GRAVES, William Sidney 1
GRAVES, 3
William Washington
GRAVES, H
Zuinglius Calvin
GRAVETT, Joshua 5
GRAVIER, Charles H
GRAVIER, Jacques 1
GRAWE, Oliver Rudolph 4
GRAWN, 4
Charles Theodore
GRAY, 5
Albert F(rederick)
GRAY, Alexander 1
GRAY, Alfred Leftwich 1
GRAY, Alfred Walter 1
GRAY, Andrew Caldwell 1
GRAY, Arthur Irving 4
GRAY, Arthur Romeyn 1
GRAY, Asa H
GRAY, Baron De Kalb 2
GRAY, Bowman 1
GRAY, Bowman 5
GRAY, Campbell 1
GRAY, Carl Raymond 1
GRAY, Carl Raymond Jr. 3
GRAY, Charles Harold 4
GRAY, Charles Oliver 4
GRAY, Charlotte Elvira 1
GRAY, Chester Earl 2
GRAY, Chester H. 5
GRAY, Clarence Truman 5
GRAY, Clifton Daggett 2
GRAY, Clifton Merritt 5
GRAY, Cyrus S. 1
GRAY, David H
GRAY, David 5
GRAY, David L. 1
GRAY, Donald Joseph 4
GRAY, Dudley Guy 1
GRAY, 4
Duncan Montgomery
GRAY, E. Mcqueen 4
GRAY, Earle,* 5
GRAY, Edward Winthrop 1
GRAY, Edwin 2
GRAY, Elisha H
GRAY, Finly H. 3
GRAY, Francis Calley 1
GRAY, George 1
GRAY, George Edward 4
GRAY, George Herbert 2
GRAY, George William 4
GRAY, George Zabriskie H
GRAY, Giles Wilkeson 4
GRAY, Gordon 4
GRAY, Harold (Lincoln) 4
GRAY, Harold Edwin 5
GRAY, Harold Parker 5
GRAY, Henry David 5
GRAY, Henry G. 3
GRAY, Henry Peteers 1
GRAY, Hiram H
GRAY, Hob 5
GRAY, Horace 1
GRAY, Howard Adams 3
GRAY, Howard Kramer 5
GRAY, Isaac Pusey H

GRAY, J. P. 4
GRAY, J. S. 5
GRAY, James 1
GRAY, James Alexander 3
GRAY, James Burdis 4
GRAY, James M. 1
GRAY, James Richard 1
GRAY, Jessie 2
GRAY, John Chipman 1
GRAY, John Clinton 1
GRAY, John Cowper H
GRAY, John Henry 2
GRAY, John Pinkham 1
GRAY, John Purdue H
GRAY, Joseph M. M. 3
GRAY, Joseph Phelps 4
GRAY, Joseph Preston 1
GRAY, Joseph W. H
GRAY, Joslyn 5
GRAY, Leon Fowler 5
GRAY, Louis Herbert 1
GRAY, Maria Freeman 4
GRAY, Mat 5
GRAY, Morris 1
GRAY, Oscar Lee 1
GRAY, 1
Prentiss Nathaniel
GRAY, Richard J. 4
GRAY, Robert H
GRAY, Roland 5
GRAY, Thomas 1
GRAY, William H
GRAY, William C. 1
GRAY, William H. H
GRAY, William John 1
GRAY, 4
William Price Jr.
GRAY, 1
William Rensselaer
GRAY, William Scott 4
GRAY, William Steele 4
GRAYDON, Alexander H
GRAYDON, James Weir 4
GRAYDON, 5
Joseph Spencer
GRAYDON, William H
GRAYSON, Cary Travers 1
GRAYSON, 4
Charles Prevost
GRAYSON, 4
Clifford Prevost
GRAYSON, Theodore J. 1
GRAYSON, 4
Thomas Jackson
GRAYSON, Thomas Wray 1
GRAYSON, William H
GRAYSON, William
Bandy
GRAYSON, William John H
GREACEN, Edmund 2
GREATHOUSE, Charles
A. 1
GREATHOUSE, H
Clarence R.
GREATHOUSE,
Clarence Ridgeby
GREATON, John H
GREATON, Joseph H
GREATOREX, Eliza Pratt H
GREATOREX, 3
Kathleen Honora
GREAVES, Joseph Eames 1
GREBE, 5
Marguerite Luckett
GREBENSTCHIKOF- 4
F, George
GREBLE, Edwin St John 1
GREBLE, John T. H
GREEAR, Fred Bonham 4
GREEF, Robert Julius 4
GREELY, Edwin Seneca 1
GREELEY, Horace H
GREELEY, Louis May 1
GREELEY, Samuel
Arnold 5
GREELEY, William B. 3
GREELEY, William Roger 1
GREELY,
Adolphus Washington
GREELY, Edward H
GREELY, John Nesmith 4
GREEN, Addison Loomis 2
GREEN, 1
Adolphus Williamson
GREEN, Adwin Wigfall 5
GREEN, Adwin Wigfall 4
GREEN,
Alexander Little Page
GREEN, Allen Percival 3
GREEN, Andrew Haswell 1
GREEN, Arthur Laurence 4
GREEN, Asa H
GREEN, Ashbel H
GREEN, Bartholomew H
GREEN, Beriah 1
GREEN, 1
Bernard Richardson

GREEN, Berryman 1
GREEN, Bert 2
GREEN, Byram H
GREEN, Charles Boden 5
GREEN, Charles Carrol 4
GREEN, Charles Edward 4
GREEN, Charles Henry 1
GREEN, Charles Henry 1
GREEN, 1
Charles Montraville
GREEN, Conant Lewis 3
GREEN, Darrell Bennet 3
GREEN, David Edward 1
GREEN, David I. 1
GREEN, Duff H
GREEN, Dwight H. 3
GREEN, Edward
Brodhead 3
GREEN, 1
Edward Howland Robinson
GREEN, Edward Melvin 1
GREEN, Edwin Luther 1
GREEN, Fitzhugh 2
GREEN, Francis H
GREEN, 1
Francis Harriet Whipple
GREEN, Francis Harvey 1
GREEN, Francis Mathews 1
GREEN, Frank Russell 1
GREEN, Fred Warren 5
GREEN, Frederick 1
GREEN, Frederick Robin 1
GREEN, H
Frederick William
GREEN, George Rex 5
GREEN, George Walter 1
GREEN, Grafton 2
GREEN, H. T. S. 2
GREEN, Harold L. 3
GREEN, Harry Joseph 5
GREEN, Henry 1
GREEN, Henry Irvin 5
GREEN, Henry Woodhull 1
GREEN, Henry Woodhull H
GREEN,
Hetty Howland Robinson
GREEN, Horace H
GREEN, Horace 1
GREEN, Howard Whipple 3
GREEN, Innis 1
GREEN, Isaiah Lewis H
GREEN, Jacob * H
GREEN, James 4
GREEN, James Benjamin 1
GREEN, James F. 2
GREEN, James Gilchrist 1
GREEN, James Monroe 1
GREEN, James Stephen H
GREEN, James Woods 1
GREEN, Jerome Joseph 2
GREEN, Jesse Cope 1
GREEN, John * H
GREEN, John 2
GREEN, John 4
GREEN, John Cleve 1
GREEN, John Edgar Jr. 2
GREEN, John F. 1
GREEN, John Garside 4
GREEN, John Orne 1
GREEN, John Pugh 1
GREEN, John Webb 2
GREEN, Jonas 1
GREEN, Joseph 4
GREEN, Joseph Andrew 4
GREEN, Julia M. 1
GREEN, Lewis Warner 4
GREEN, Lot 4
GREEN, Marcellus 1
GREEN, Nathan 1
GREEN, Nathan 4
GREEN, Nathan Williams 1
GREEN, Norvin H
GREEN, Norvin Hewitt 1
GREEN, Percy Warren 1
GREEN, Perry Luther 1
GREEN, Robert Gladding 1
GREEN, Robert McCay H
GREEN, Robert N. 4
GREEN, Robert Stockton H
GREEN, Rolland Lester 1
GREEN, Roy Monroe 5
GREEN, Rufus Lot 1
GREEN, Samuel 1
GREEN, Samuel Abbott H
GREEN, Samuel Bowdlear 1
GREEN, Samuel Swett 1
GREEN, Seth H
GREEN,
Theodore Francis
GREEN, Theodore Meyer 5
GREEN, Thomas H
GREEN, Thomas Dunbar 1
GREEN, Thomas Edward 1
GREEN, Walter Lawrence 1
GREEN, Walton Atwater 4
GREEN, Warren Everett 1
GREEN, Wharton Jackson 1

GREEN, William — H
GREEN, William — 1
GREEN, William — 3
GREEN, William Charles — 3
GREEN, William Elza — 1
GREEN, William Henry — 1
GREEN, William Joseph Jr. — 4
GREEN, William Marvin — 2
GREEN, William Mercer — H
GREEN, William Mercer — 2
GREEN, William Raymond — 2
GREEN, Willis — H
GREENAWALD, Paul Benjamin — 3
GREENBAUM, Edward S. — 5
GREENBAUM, Leo — 1
GREENBAUM, Max — 1
GREENBAUM, Samuel — 1
GREENBAUM, Sigmund Samuel — 2
GREENBERG, Bernard Samuel — 4
GREENBERG, Noah — H
GREENBERRY, Nicholas — H
GREENBIE, Marjorie Barstow — 4
GREENBLATT, Louis — 5
GREENDLINGER, Leo — 1
GREENE, A. Crawford — 4
GREENE, Aella — 1
GREENE, Albert Collins — H
GREENE, Albert Gorton — H
GREENE, Arthur Maurice, Jr. — 5
GREENE, Benjamin Allen — 1
GREENE, Charles Arthur — 5
GREENE, Charles Ezra — 1
GREENE, Charles Jerome — 2
GREENE, Charles Lyman — 1
GREENE, Charles Samuel — 1
GREENE, Charles Warren — 4
GREENE, Charles Wilson — 4
GREENE, Chester W. — 4
GREENE, Christopher — H
GREENE, Clay Meredith — 1
GREENE, D. Crosby — 1
GREENE, Daniel Crosby — 1
GREENE, David Maxson — 1
GREENE, Edward Belden — 3
GREENE, Edward Lee — 1
GREENE, Edward Martin — 3
GREENE, Edwin Farnham — 3
GREENE, Evarts Boutell — 2
GREENE, Floyd L. — 3
GREENE, Francis Vinton — 1
GREENE, Frank Lester — 1
GREENE, Fred T. — 4
GREENE, Frederick Stuart — 5
GREENE, Gardiner — 1
GREENE, George C. — 1
GREENE, George Francis — 1
GREENE, George Louis — 5
GREENE, George Sears — H
GREENE, George Sears Jr. — 1
GREENE, George Washington — H
GREENE, George Wellington — 1
GREENE, George Woodward — H
GREENE, Harry Irving — 4
GREENE, Harry Sylvestre Nutting — 5
GREENE, Henry Alexander — 1
GREENE, Henry Copley — 3
GREENE, Henry Fay — 1
GREENE, Henry Vincent — 3
GREENE, Herbert Eveleth — 2
GREENE, Herbert Wilber — 1
GREENE, Homer — 1
GREENE, Howard — 3
GREENE, Isabel Catherine — 4
GREENE, Jacob L. — 1
GREENE, James E(dward) — 5
GREENE, James H. — 4
GREENE, James Leon — 1
GREENE, James Nicholas — 5
GREENE, James Sonnett — 3
GREENE, Jerome Davis — 3
GREENE, John — 4
GREENE, John Ernest — 1
GREENE, John Holden — H
GREENE, John Morton — 4
GREENE, John Priest — H
GREENE, Joseph Ingham — 3
GREENE, Joseph Nathaniel — 5
GREENE, Katherine Glass — 2

GREENE, Lionel Y. — 4
GREENE, M(aria) Louise — 5
GREENE, Marc Tiffany — 4
GREENE, Mary Anne — 4
GREENE, Myron Wesley — 4
GREENE, Nathanael — H
GREENE, Nathaniel — H
GREENE, Oliver D. — 1
GREENE, Patterson — 5
GREENE, Raleigh W. — 3
GREENE, Ray — H
GREENE, Richard Gleason — 1
GREENE, Richard Thurston — 3
GREENE, Robert Holmes — 1
GREENE, Roger Sherman — 1
GREENE, Roger Sherman — 2
GREENE, S. Harold — 1
GREENE, Sam — 4
GREENE, Samuel Dana — H
GREENE, Samuel Harrison — 4
GREENE, Samuel Stillman — H
GREENE, Samuel Webb — 5
GREENE, Sarah Pratt — 1
GREENE, Theodore Ainsworth — 3
GREENE, Thomas L. — 1
GREENE, Thomas Marston — H
GREENE, Ward — H
GREENE, Warwick — 1
GREENE, William * — H
GREENE, William Brenton — 4
GREENE, William Cornell — 1
GREENE, William Houston — 1
GREENE, William L. — 1
GREENE, William Milbury — 4
GREENE, William Stedman — 1
GREENE, Winfield Wardwell — 4
GREENEBAUM, Henry Everett — 1
GREENEBAUM, Leon Charles — 5
GREENEBAUM, Moses Ernest — 1
GREENEFIELD, Nathan R. — 1
GREENER, John Hunter — 5
GREENER, Richard Theodore — 4
GREENFIELD, Albert Monroe — 4
GREENFIELD, Kent Roberts — 4
GREENHALGE, Frederick Thomas — H
GREENHOW, Robert — H
GREENING, Harry Cornell — 5
GREENLAW, Edwin — 1
GREENLAW, Lowell M. — 5
GREENLEAF, Benjamin — H
GREENLEAF, Carl Dimond — 3
GREENLEAF, Charles Ravenscroft — 1
GREENLEAF, Edmund — 1
GREENLEAF, Georgie H. Franck — 1
GREENLEAF, James Leal — 1
GREENLEAF, Jonathan — H
GREENLEAF, Moses * — H
GREENLEAF, Simon — H
GREENLEAF, Thomas — 4
GREENLEE, Karl B. — 4
GREENLEY, Howard — 4
GREENMAN, A. V. — 4
GREENMAN, Frederick Francis — 4
GREENMAN, Jesse More — 3
GREENMAN, Milton J. — 1
GREENMAN, Walter Folger — 2
GREENOUGH, Chester Noyes — 4
GREENOUGH, George Gordon — 5
GREENOUGH, Henry — 4
GREENOUGH, Horatio — H
GREENOUGH, James Bradstreet — 1
GREENOUGH, James Carruthers — 1
GREENOUGH, Jeanie Ashley Bates — 4
GREENOUGH, John — 1
GREENOUGH, Robert Battey — 1

GREENOUGH, William — 2
GREENQUIST, Kenneth Lloyd — 5
GREENSFELDER, Albert Preston — 3
GREENSHIELDS, Donn D. — 4
GREENSLADE, John Wills — 1
GREENSLET, Ferris — 3
GREENSTEIN, Jesse P. — 3
GREENSTONE, Julius Hillel — 3
GREENUP, Christopher — H
GREENWALD, Emanuel — H
GREENWALD, Herbert S. — 3
GREENWALT, Elmer Ellsworth — 1
GREENWAY, Charles Moore — 1
GREENWAY, Isabella Selmes — 3
GREENWAY, James Cowan — H
GREENWAY, John Campbell — 5
GREENWAY, Walter Burton — 1
GREENWELL, Darrell J. — 4
GREENWELL, Hiliary Johnson — 4
GREENWOOD, Alfred Burton — H
GREENWOOD, Allen — 2
GREENWOOD, Arthur H. — 4
GREENWOOD, Elizabeth Ward — 4
GREENWOOD, Ernest — 3
GREENWOOD, Ethan Allen — 1
GREENWOOD, Grace — H
GREENWOOD, Isaac — 1
GREENWOOD, James M. — 4
GREENWOOD, John — H
GREENWOOD, John Joseph — 5
GREENWOOD, Marion — 1
GREENWOOD, Miles — H
GREENWOOD, Thomas Benton — 2
GREER, Benjamin Brinton — 1
GREER, David Hummell — 1
GREER, Frank U. — 2
GREER, Herbert Chester — 2
GREER, Hilton Ross — 3
GREER, James Agustin — 1
GREER, Lawrence — 1
GREER, Margaret R. — 3
GREER, Samuel Miller — 1
GREET, William Cabell — 5
GREEVER, Garland — 4
GREEVER, Walton Harlowe — 4
GREGERSEN, Magnus Ingstrup — 5
GREGG, Alan — 3
GREGG, Alexander — H
GREGG, Alexander White — 1
GREGG, Alexander White Jr. — 3
GREGG, Andrew — H
GREGG, Curtis Hussey — 4
GREGG, David — 1
GREGG, David McMurtrie — 1
GREGG, Francis Whitlock — 5
GREGG, Frank Moody — 4
GREGG, Fred Marion — 4
GREGG, J. A. — 3
GREGG, James Bartlett — 1
GREGG, James Edgar — 2
GREGG, James Madison — H
GREGG, John — H
GREGG, John Andrew — 1
GREGG, John B. — 3
GREGG, John Price — 3
GREGG, John Robert — 2
GREGG, Josiah — H
GREGG, Maxcy — H
GREGG, Paul L. * — 3
GREGG, William — H
GREGG, William C. — 2
GREGG, William Henry — 4
GREGG, Willis Ray — 1
GREGOR, Elmer Russell — 3
GREGORY, Carl C. — 1
GREGORY, Caspar Rene — 1
GREGORY, Charles Noble — 1
GREGORY, Chester Arthur — 1
GREGORY, Clifford V. — 2
GREGORY, Daniel Seelye — 1

GREGORY, David Thomas — 3
GREGORY, Dudley Sanford — H
GREGORY, Edmund Bristol — 4
GREGORY, Eliot — 1
GREGORY, Elisha Hall — 1
GREGORY, Herbert Bailey — 3
GREGORY, Herbert E. — 3
GREGORY, Jackson — 3
GREGORY, John — 3
GREGORY, John Goadby — 3
GREGORY, John Henry — 1
GREGORY, John Herbert — 1
GREGORY, John Milton — H
GREGORY, Laurence Wilcoxson — 2
GREGORY, Leslie Roscoe — 3
GREGORY, Louis Hoyt — 3
GREGORY, Luther Elwood — 4
GREGORY, Martin LeRoy — 5
GREGORY, Menas Sarkis — 5
GREGORY, Noble Jones — 5
GREGORY, Oliver Fuller — 3
GREGORY, Raymond William — 3
GREGORY, Samuel — H
GREGORY, Stephen Strong — 1
GREGORY, Tappan — 4
GREGORY, Thomas B. — 3
GREGORY, Thomas T. C. — 1
GREGORY, Thomas Watt — 1
GREGORY, Warren Fenno — 1
GREGORY, William — 1
GREGORY, William Benjamin — 2
GREGORY, William Edward — 3
GREGORY, William Hamilton Jr. — 4
GREGORY, William K(ing) — 5
GREGORY, William Logan — 3
GREGORY, William Mumford — 5
GREGORY, William Voris — 1
GREGORY, Willis George — 1
GREHAN, Bernard H. — 3
GREIG, Alexander Simpson — 4
GREIG, John — H
GREINER, John E. — 2
GREINER, Tuisco — 4
GREIS, Henry Nauert — 2
GRELL, Louis — 4
GRELLET, Stephen — H
GRENELL, Zelotes — 1
GRENFELL, Helen Loring — 1
GRENFELL, Sir Wilfred Thomason — 1
GRENIER, Arthur Sylvester — 1
GRENNELL, George Jr. — H
GRESHAM, James Wilmer — 3
GRESHAM, LeRoy — 3
GRESHAM, Walter Quintin — H
GRESS, Ernest Milton — 5
GREUSEL, John Hubert — 2
GREVE, Charles Theodore — 1
GREVILLE, Mr. — H
GREVSTAD, Nicolay Andrew — 1
GREW, Henry S. — 3
GREW, Joseph Clark — 4
GREW, Theophilus — H
GREY, Benjamin Edwards — H
GREY, Elmer — 4
GREY, Samuel Howell — 1
GREY, Zane — 1
GRIBBEL, John — 4
GRICE, David Stephen — 4
GRICE, Warren — 2
GRIDER, Henry — H
GRIDLEY, Charles O. — 4
GRIDLEY, Charles Vernon — H
GRIDLEY, Jeremiah — H
GRIDLEY, Richard — H
GRIER, Albert Oliver Herman — 3
GRIER, Alvan Ruckman — 1
GRIER, Francis Ebenezer — 3
GRIER, James Alexander — 4
GRIER, James Harper — 4

GRIER, Norman MacDowell — 3
GRIER, Robert Cooper — H
GRIER, William — 1
GRIER, William Moffatt — 1
GRIERSON, Benjamin H. — 4
GRIERSON, Benjamin Henry — 1
GRIERSON, John — 5
GRIES, John Matthew — 3
GRIESEDIECK, Alvin — 4
GRIEST, William Walton — 1
GRIEVE, Miller — H
GRIFFES, Charles Tomlinson — H
GRIFFES, Charles Tomlinson — 4
GRIFFIN, Angus MacIvor — 5
GRIFFIN, Anthony Jerome — 1
GRIFFIN, Appleton Prentiss Clark — 1
GRIFFIN, Bulkley Southworth — 5
GRIFFIN, Cardinal Bernard — 3
GRIFFIN, Carroll Wardlaw — 3
GRIFFIN, Charles — H
GRIFFIN, Cyrus — H
GRIFFIN, Daniel J. — 1
GRIFFIN, Delia Isabel — 4
GRIFFIN, Edward Dorr — 1
GRIFFIN, Edward Herrick — 1
GRIFFIN, Eugene — 1
GRIFFIN, Frank Loxley — 5
GRIFFIN, Frederick Robertson — 5
GRIFFIN, Henry Lyman — 1
GRIFFIN, Isaac — H
GRIFFIN, James Aloysius — 2
GRIFFIN, James Arthur — 3
GRIFFIN, James H. — 3
GRIFFIN, James Owen — 4
GRIFFIN, John — 1
GRIFFIN, John Howard — 3
GRIFFIN, John Joseph — 1
GRIFFIN, John King — H
GRIFFIN, John W. — 4
GRIFFIN, Lawrence Edmonds — 5
GRIFFIN, Lee Henry — 5
GRIFFIN, Levi Thomas — 1
GRIFFIN, Mark Alexander — 5
GRIFFIN, Martin Eugene — 4
GRIFFIN, Martin Ignatius — 1
GRIFFIN, Martin Luther — 2
GRIFFIN, Michael — 1
GRIFFIN, Nathaniel Edward — 1
GRIFFIN, Robert Stanislaus — 1
GRIFFIN, Samuel — H
GRIFFIN, Simon Goddell — 1
GRIFFIN, Solomon Bulkley — 1
GRIFFIN, Thomas — H
GRIFFIN, Walter — 1
GRIFFIN, William Aloysius — 2
GRIFFIN, William Richard — 2
GRIFFIN, William Vincent — 3
GRIFFING, Josephine Sophie White — H
GRIFFIS, Elliot — 4
GRIFFIS, Lawrence W. — 4
GRIFFIS, William Elliot — 1
GRIFFITH, Armond Harrold — 4
GRIFFITH, Benjamin — H
GRIFFITH, Benjamin Whitfield — 1
GRIFFITH, C. J. — 4
GRIFFITH, Chauncey H. — 3
GRIFFITH, Clark — 3
GRIFFITH, Coleman Roberts — 4
GRIFFITH, David Lewelyn Wark — 2
GRIFFITH, David Wark — H
GRIFFITH, David Wark — 4
GRIFFITH, Earl L. — 4
GRIFFITH, Elmer Cummings — 1
GRIFFITH, Francis Marion — 4
GRIFFITH, Frank Carlos — 1
GRIFFITH, Frank Leslie — 5
GRIFFITH, Franklin Thomas — 3

GRIFFITH, 5
Frederic Richardson
GRIFFITH, George 1
GRIFFITH, 1
Griffith Jenkins
GRIFFITH, 4
Griffith Pritchard
GRIFFITH, 3
Hall McAlister
GRIFFITH, Harry Elmer 4
GRIFFITH, Harry Melvin 5
GRIFFITH, Heber Emlyn 1
GRIFFITH, 4
Helen Sherman
GRIFFITH, 1
Herbert Eugene
GRIFFITH, Ivor 4
GRIFFITH, J. P. Crozer 1
GRIFFITH, 1
Jefferson Davis
GRIFFITH, John 5
GRIFFITH, John L. 2
GRIFFITH, P. Merrill 1
GRIFFITH, 3
Reginald Harvey
GRIFFITH, Richard
GRIFFITH, H
Robert Eglesfield
GRIFFITH, Samuel H
GRIFFITH, 5
Samuel Henderson
GRIFFITH, 4
Thomas Stuart
GRIFFITH, Virgil A. 5
GRIFFITH, W. M. 3
GRIFFITH, 5
Wendell Horace
GRIFFITH, William H
GRIFFITH, William 1
GRIFFITH, William G. 4
GRIFFITHS, 1
Arthur Floyd
GRIFFITHS, David 1
GRIFFITHS, 1
Edwin Stephen
GRIFFITHS, 3
Farnham Pond
GRIFFITHS,
Frederick J.
GRIFFITHS, James Henry 4
GRIFFITHS, John Lewis 1
GRIFFITHS, John Willis H
GRIFFITHS, 4
William John Jr.
GRIGEBY, Hugh Blair H
GRIGGS, 1
Chauncey Wright
GRIGGS, David Cullen 3
GRIGGS, Edward Howard 3
GRIGGS, Everett Gallup 1
GRIGGS, Frederick 3
GRIGGS, Herbert Lebau 1
GRIGGS, James M. 1
GRIGGS, John William 1
GRIGGS, Nathan Kirk 1
GRIGGS, Thomas Newell 5
GRIGGS, 4
William Cornelius
GRIGSBY, Bertram James 3
GRIGSBY, William Fred 3
GRIM, Allan K. 4
GRIM, David H
GRIM, Paul Ridgeway 3
GRIMBALL, 3
Elizabeth Berkeley
GRIME, Sarah Lois 4
GRIMES, 3
Charles Pennebaker
GRIMES, Donald Robert 5
GRIMES, Frances 4
GRIMES, Frank 4
GRIMES, George 4
GRIMES, George Simon 1
GRIMES, J. Bryan 1
GRIMES, James Stanley H
GRIMES, James Wilson H
GRIMES, John 1
GRIMES, Waldo Ernest 2
GRIMES, William Henry 5
GRIMES, 3
William Middleton
GRIMKE, Angelina Emily H
GRIMKE,
Archibald Henry
GRIMKE, Francis James 4
GRIMKE, Frederick H
GRIMKE, H
John Faucheraud
GRIMKE, Sarah Moore H
GRIMKE, Thomas Smith H
GRIMM, Carl William 4
GRIMM, Jacob Luther 5
GRIMM, 5
John Crawford Milton
GRIMM, John Hugo 3
GRIMM, John Murchison 5

GRIMMELSMAN, 5
Henry Joseph
GRIMMELSMAN, Joseph 1
GRIMMER, 2
Ward Chipman Hazen
GRIMSHAW, Austin 4
GRIMSHAW, Robert 4
GRINDAL, Herbert W. 3
GRINDALL, 1
Charles Sylvester
GRINDLEY, Harry Sands 4
GRINDON, Joseph Sr. 3
GRINNELL, 1
Charles Edward
GRINNELL, Elizabeth 1
GRINNELL, 4
Frank Washburn
GRINNELL, Frederick 1
GRINNELL, George Bird 1
GRINNELL, 3
George Morton
GRINNELL, Harold C. 1
GRINNELL, Henry H
GRINNELL, Joseph H
GRINNELL, Joseph 1
GRINNELL, H
Josiah Bushnell
GRINNELL, Morton 1
GRINNELL, Moses Hicks 1
GRINNELL, Russell 2
GRINNELL, 1
William Morton
GRINSFELDER, H. J. 4
GRISCOM, 1
Clement Acton *
GRISCOM, John H
GRISCOM, 5
Lloyd Carpenter
GRISCOM, Ludlow 3
GRISCOM, 3
Rodman Ellison
GRISER, John Millen 3
GRISMER, Joseph Rhode 1
GRISMORE, 3
Grover Cleveland
GRISSOM, 5
Irene Welch (Mrs. Charles Meigs Grissom)
GRISSOM, Virgil Ivan 4
GRISWOLD, A. Whitney 4
GRISWOLD, H
Alexander Viets
GRISWOLD, 4
Alphonso Miner
GRISWOLD, Augustus H. 1
GRISWOLD, 2
Benjamin Howell Jr.
GRISWOLD, 1
Casimir Clayton
GRISWOLD, 5
Clayton Tracy
GRISWOLD, 3
Dwight Palmer
GRISWOLD, Edith Julia 1
GRISWOLD, F. Gray 1
GRISWOLD, Gaylord H
GRISWOLD, Glenn 1
GRISWOLD, Glenn 1
GRISWOLD, Hattie Tyng 1
GRISWOLD, 3
Hervey DeWitt
GRISWOLD, James F. 3
GRISWOLD, 1
John Augustus
GRISWOLD, Latta 1
GRISWOLD, Leon Stacy 4
GRISWOLD, Matthew 1
GRISWOLD, Merrill 4
GRISWOLD, Morley 3
GRISWOLD, 3
Oscar Woolverton
GRISWOLD, 5
Rettig Arnold
GRISWOLD, Roger H
GRISWOLD, Rufus H
GRISWOLD, 1
Sheldon Munson
GRISWOLD, Stanley H
GRISWOLD, 1
Stephen Benham
GRISWOLD, Thomas, Jr. 5
GRISWOLD, H
Victor Moreau
GRISWOLD, 1
William Edward Schenck
GRISWOLD, H
William McCrillis
GRISWOLD, 1
William McCrillis
GROAT, Benjamin Feland 2
GROAT, Carl D. 3
GROAT, George Gorham 3
GROAT, William Avery 1
GROCHOWSKI, Leon M. 5
GRODZINS, Morton 4

GROEDEL, 3
Franz Maximillian
GROESBECK, 3
Alexander J.
GROESBECK, George 2
Clarence Edward
GROESBECK, 3
Herman V. S.
GROESBECK, 1
Stephen Walley
GROESBECK, H
William Slocum
GROFE, 5
Ferde (Ferdinand Rudolph von Grofe)
GROFF, George G. 1
GROFF, George Weidman 3
GROGAN, James J. 2
GROLL, Albert Lorey 3
GROMAIRE, Marcel 5
GROMER, Samuel David 1
GRONDAHL, 1
Jens Kristian
GRONER, 5
Duncan Lawrence
GRONER, Frank Shelby 2
GRONER, John Vaughan 5
GRONLUND, Laurence 4
GRONLUND, Lawrence H
GRONNA, A. J. 4
GRONNA, Asle J. 1
GRONWALL, Thomas 5
Hakon
GROOM, Thomas J. 4
GROOMBRIDGE, H
William
GROOME, James Black 4
GROOVER, Paul 3
GROPIUS, Walter Adolf 5
GROS, John Daniel 5
GROSE, Clyde Leclare 2
GROSE, George 5
Richmond
GROSE, George
Richmond
GROSE, Howard Benjamin 1
GROSE, William H
GROSEILLIERS, H
'sieur 'de
GROSS, A. Haller 1
GROSS, Alfred Otto 5
GROSS, Charles 1
GROSS, Charles Edward 1
GROSS, Charles Welles 3
GROSS, Christian 1
GROSS, Ezra Carter 1
GROSS, Fred Louis 2
GROSS, Harold Judson 1
GROSS, John E. 1
GROSS, Joseph Leonard 1
GROSS, Mervin E. 2
GROSS, Milt 5
GROSS, Nathan L. 4
GROSS, Oskar 4
GROSS, 4
Robert Ellsworth
GROSS, Samuel H
GROSS, Samuel David H
GROSS, Samuel Elbely H
GROSS, Samuel Weissell H
GROSS, Sidney 3
GROSS, Walter W. 3
GROSS, 2
William Jennings
GROSSCUP, 1
Benjamin Sidney
GROSSCUP,
Peter Stenger
GROSSCUP, Walter T. 3
GROSSET, Alexander 4
GROSSET, Alexander 4
GROSSINGER, Jennie 5
GROSSMAN, Georg H
Martin
GROSSMAN, Marc Justin 5
GROSSMAN, Moses 2
Henry
GROSSMANN, Louis 1
GROSSMANN, Rudolph 1
GROSVENOR, 4
Abbie Johnston
GROSVENOR, 1
Charles Henry
GROSVENOR, 1
Edwin Augustus
GROSVENOR, 1
Edwin Prescott
GROSVENOR, 4
Gilbert Hovey *
GROSVENOR, 2
Graham Bethune
GROSVENOR, 1
Lemuel Conant
GROSVENOR, H
Thomas Peabody
GROSVENOR, H
William Mason

GROSVENOR, 2
William Mason
GROSVENOR, 1
William Mercer
GROSZ, George 3
GROSZMANN, 1
Maximilian Paul Eugen
GROTE, August D. 3
GROTE, H
Augustus Radcliffe
GROTE, Irvine Walter 5
GROTEWOHL, Otto 4
GROTH, Arnold William 5
GROTON, 1
William Mansfield
GROUARD, Frank H
GROUITCH, Slavko Y. 5
GROUT, Abel Joel 2
GROUT, 4
Daniel Alexander
GROUT, Edward Marshall 1
GROUT, Frank F. 3
GROUT, John Henry 4
GROUT, Jonathan H
GROUT, Josiah 1
GROUT, Lewis 1
GROUT, William Wallace 1
GROVE, Asa Porter H
GROVE, Charles Gordon 3
GROVE, James Harvey 4
GROVE, Lon Woodfin 4
GROVE, William Barry H
GROVER, Cuvier H
GROVER, Delo Corydon 3
GROVER, Eulalie Osgood 1
GROVER, 4
Frederick Orville
GROVER, 5
Frederick Warren
GROVER, James Hamilton 5
GROVER, La Fayette 1
GROVER, Martin H
GROVER, 3
Nathan Clifford
GROVER, Oliver Dennett 1
GROVER, 5
Wayne C(layton)
GROVES, Charles Stuart 2
GROVES,
Ernest Rutherford
GROVES, Frank Malvon 5
GROVES, Leslie Richard 5
GROVES, Owen Griffith 5
GROVES, Robert Walker 5
GROW, Galusha Aaron 1
GROWER, Roy William 1
GROWOLL, Adolf 1
GROZA, Petre 4
GROZIER, Edwin Atkins 1
GROZIER, Richard 2
GRUBB, Edward Burd 4
GRUBB, Eugene Housel 4
GRUBB, George Albert 3
GRUBB, Ignatius Cooper 1
GRUBB, William Irwin 4
GRUBBE, Emil Herman 3
GRUBBS, Samuel Bates 2
GRUBE, Bernhard Adam H
GRUBER, John Lewis 3
GRUBER, L. Franklin 1
GRUBER, Leo Ray 4
GRUBER, Lewis 4
GRUEHR,
Anatole Rodolph
GRUEN, 2
Frederick Gustavus
GRUEN, George John 3
GRUENBERG, Benj C. 1
GRUENBERG, Louis 4
GRUENER, Gustav 1
GRUENER, Hippolyte 5
GRUENSTEIN, 3
Siegfried Emanuel
GRUENTHANER, 4
Michael J.
GRUGER, 5
Frederic Rodrigo
GRUHL, Edwin 1
GRUITCH, Jerry M. 5
GRULEE, 4
Clifford Grosselle G.
GRUMBINE, 2
Harvey Carson
GRUMM, Arnold Henry 4
GRUND, Francis Joseph H
GRUNDY, Felix 1
GRUNDY, Joseph R. 4
GRUNERT, 1
Francis Eugene
GRUNERT, Robert W. H
GRUNEWALD, Gustavus H
GRUNEWALD, Max 5
Eugene
GRUNITZKY, Nicholas 5
GRUNN, Homer 1
GRUNSKY, Carl Ewald 1
GRUNWALD, Kurt 4

GRUPPE, Charles Paul 1
GRUSKIN, Alan Daniel 5
GRUVER, Harvey Snyder 5
GRUWELL, Hugh Clifton 5
GRYLLS, 2
Humphry John Maxwell
GUARD, Samuel R. 5
GUARD, Samuel R. 5
GUARESCHI, Giovanni 5
GUBB, Larry E. 2
GUCK, Homer 2
GUCKER, Frank Thomson 5
GUDAKUNST, 1
Donald Welsh
GUDDE, Erwin Gustav, 5
GUDE, Ove 1
GUDEBROD, Louis 5
Albert
GUDEMAN, Alfred 4
GUDEMAN, Edward 4
GUDGER, Eugene Willis 3
GUDGER, Hezekiah A. 1
GUDGER, 4
James Cassius Lowry
GUDGER, 4
James Madison Jr.
GUE, Benjamin F. 1
GUEDALLA, Philip 2
GUENDLING, J. H. 5
GUENTHER,
August Ernest
GUENTHER,
Francis Luther
GUENTHER, Louis 3
GUENTHER, Richard 1
GUENTHER, Rudolph 1
GUEPIN,
Felix Alouis Caspar
GUERARD, Albert Leon *
GUERBER,
Helene Adeline
GUERIN, Anne-Therese 4
GUERIN, Jules 4
GUERIN, William Estil 4
GUERIN, William Eugene 4
GUERLAC, Othan Goepp 1
GUERNSEY, 1
Alice Margaret
GUERNSEY, Egbert 1
GUERNSEY, Frank
Edward
GUERNSEY, Henry
Newell
GUERNSEY, James
Seeley
GUERNSEY, Lucy Ellen 1
GUERNSEY,
Nathaniel Taylor
GUERNSEY, Peter Buel 4
GUERNSEY,
Rocellus Sheridan
GUERNSEY, Samuel
James
GUERNSEY,
Sarah Elizabeth
GUERRANT, 1
Edward Owings
GUERRERO, Jose
Custavo
GUERRIER, Edith 4
GUERRY, Alexander 2
GUERRY, Dupont 2
GUERRY, Le Grand 2
GUERRY,
William Alexander
GUERTIN, George Albert 2
GUESS, George H
GUESS, Harry Adelbert 2
GUEST, Edgar Albert 5
GUEST, Harold Walter 4
GUEST,
Richard Clarence
GUEVARA, Ernesto 5
GUFFEY, James McClurg 1
GUFFEY, Joseph F. 3
GUFFY,
Bayless Leander Durant
GUGGENHEIM, Daniel 1
GUGGENHEIM, 5
Edmond Alfred
GUGGENHEIM, Isaac 1
GUGGENHEIM, M. 1
Robert
GUGGENHEIM, Murry 1
GUGGENHEIM, 5
Olga H. (mrs. Simon Guggenheim)
GUGGENHEIM, Simon 1
GUGGENHEIM, Solomon
R. 4
GUGGENHEIM, William 1
GUGGENHEIMER,
Charles S.
GUGGENHEIMER,
Minnie
GUGGENHEIMER,
Randolph

GUGLER, Henry — H
GUGLIELMI, Louis O. — 3
GUIGNAS, Michel — H
GUIHER, James Morford — 4
GUILBERT, Frank Warburton — 1
GUILBERT, Yvette — 4
GUILD, Courtenay — 2
GUILD, Curtis * — 1
GUILD, George A. — 2
GUILD, Henry J. — 4
GUILD, Josephus Conn — 5
GUILD, LaFayette — H
GUILD, Lewis Thurber — 2
GUILD, Reuben Aldridge — H
GUILD, Reuben Aldridge — 4
GUILD, Roy Bergen — 2
GUILD, William Huntoon — 2
GUILDAY, Peter — 2
GUILER, Henry Anderson — 1
GUILFOILE, Francis Patrick — 5
GUILFORD, Nathan — H
GUILFORD, Simeon Hayden — 1
GUILL, John Hudson — 3
GUILLE, Andrew J. — 1
GUILLE, Peter — 5
GUILLEBEAU, Joseph Edwin — 3
GUINEE, William Fenton — 3
GUINEY, Louise Imogen — 1
GUINEY, Patrick Robert — H
GUINEY, Patrick William — 1
GUINTHER, Robert — 3
GUINZBURG, Harold K. — 4
GUINZBURG, Ralph K. — 3
GUINZBURG, Roland Hay — 4
GUION, Connie M. — 5
GUION, Lewis — 1
GUION, Walter — 1
GUIRAUD, Ernest — H
GUITEAU, Charles Julius — H
GUITERAS, Gregorio Maria — 1
GUITERAS, Juan — 1
GUITERAS, Ramon — 4
GUITERMAN, Arthur — 2
GUITTEAU, William Backus — 4
GUIZADO, Jose Ramon — 4
GULICK, Archibald A. — 4
GULICK, Charles Burton — 4
GULICK, Charles P. — 3
GULICK, Edward Leeds — 1
GULICK, John Thomas — 4
GULICK, John W. — 5
GULICK, Luther Halsey — H
GULICK, Luther Halsey — 4
GULICK, Sidney Lewis — 2
GULICK, Thomas Lafon — 1
GULLAGER, Christian — H
GULLETTE, George Albert — 5
GULLEY, Needham Yancey — 4
GULLION, Allen Wyant — 2
GULLIVER, Frederic Putnam — 4
GULLIVER, Julia Henrietta — 1
GUM, Walter Clarke — 5
GUMBEL, Irving — 4
GUMMERE, Amelia Mott — 4
GUMMERE, Francis Barton
GUMMERE, John — H
GUMMERE, Samuel James — H
GUMMERE, Samuel Rene — 1
GUMMERE, William Stryker
GUMMEY, Henry Riley, Jr. — 5
GUMP, Louis Franklin — 5
GUMPERT, Martin — 3
GUNBY, Andrew Augustus — 4
GUNCKEL, John Elstner — 4
GUNCKEL, Lewis B. — 1
GUND, George — 4
GUNDELL, Glenn — 4
GUNDER, Dwight Francis — 4
GUNDERSEN, Adolf — 1
GUNDERSEN, Henrik — 1
GUNDERSON, B. Harry — 5
GUNDERSON, Carl — 1
GUNDERSON, Clark Young — 4
GUNDRY, Richard Fitz Harris
GUNLOCK, V. E. — 4
GUNN, Alexander Hunter III

GUNN, Archibald — 4
GUNN, E. L. Jr. — 4
GUNN, Frederick William — H
GUNN, Herbert Smith — 4
GUNN, James — H
GUNN, James Newton — H
GUNN, James Newton — 4
GUNN, John Edward — 1
GUNN, John W. — 5
GUNN, John William — 1
GUNN, Ross — 4
GUNN, Selskar Michael — 2
GUNN, Walter Thomas — H
GUNNELL, Francis M. — 1
GUNNELL, George — 1
GUNNISON, Almon — 1
GUNNISON, Binney — 1
GUNNISON, Foster — 4
GUNNISON, Frederic Everest — 1
GUNNISON, Herbert Foster — 1
GUNNISON, John Williams — H
GUNNISON, Raymond M. — 5
GUNNISON, Royal Arch — 5
GUNNISON, Royal Arch — 2
GUNNISON, Walter Balfour — 1
GUNSAULUS, Edwin Norton — 1
GUNSAULUS, Frank Wakeley — 1
GUNSETT, Helen Tossey — 5
GUNTER, Archibald Clavering — 1
GUNTER, Clarence — 3
GUNTER, Felix Eugene — 5
GUNTER, Julius Caldeen — 1
GUNTHER, Charles Frederick
GUNTHER, Charles Otto — 3
GUNTHER, Ernest Ludolph
GUNTHER, Franklin Mott — 1
GUNTON, George — 1
GUNTON, Rebecca Douglas (Mrs. George Gunton) — 5
GUPTILL, Arthur Leighton — 3
GUPTON, William — 1
GURD, Fraser Baillie — 2
GURIAN, Waldemar — 3
GURKOFF, Eugene — 4
GURLER, Henry Benjamin — 1
GURLEY, Henry Hosford — H
GURLEY, John Addison — H
GURLEY, Ralph Randolph — H
GURLEY, William Fitzhugh — 1
GURLEY, William Wirt — 1
GURNEY, Augustus M. — 1
GURNEY, Charles Henry — 4
GURNEY, Deloss Butler (D. B.) — 5
GURNEY, Ephraim Whitman — 1
GURNEY, James Paul — 1
GUROWSKI, Adam — H
GURSEL, Cemal — 4
GUSHEE, Edward Manning — 1
GUSHEE, Edward T. — 3
GUSS, Uriah Cloyd — 3
GUST, John Lewis — 3
GUSTAFSON, Airik — 4
GUSTAFSON, Axel Carl Johan
GUSTAFSON, Carl Henry — 5
GUSTAFSON, Frank August — 5
GUSTAFSON, G(ustaf) Joseph — 5
GUSTAFSON, Gilbert Eugene — 3
GUSTAFSON, William — 1
GUSTAFSON, Zadel Barnes — 1
GUSTAVUS V — 3
GUSTE, William Joseph Sr. — 3
GUSTIN, Albert Lyman Jr.
GUSTINE, Amos — 1
GUTELIUS, Frederick Passmore — 1
GUTENBERG, Bene — 3
GUTERMAN, Carl Edward Frederick — 3
GUTH, William Westley — 1
GUTHE, Karl Eugen — 1
GUTHEIL, Emilian Arthur — 3

GUTHERZ, Carl — 1
GUTHNER, William Ernest — 3
GUTHRIE, Alfred — H
GUTHRIE, Anna Lorraine — 1
GUTHRIE, Charles Claude — 4
GUTHRIE, Charles Ellsworth — 1
GUTHRIE, David Vance — 4
GUTHRIE, Donald — 2
GUTHRIE, Edward Sewall — 4
GUTHRIE, Ernest Graham — 2
GUTHRIE, George Wilkins — 1
GUTHRIE, James — 1
GUTHRIE, James Alan — 5
GUTHRIE, James Alan — 4
GUTHRIE, Joseph Edward — 1
GUTHRIE, Kenneth Sylvan — 1
GUTHRIE, Lewis Van Gilder — 1
GUTHRIE, Robert R. — 5
GUTHRIE, S(eymour) Ashley — 5
GUTHRIE, Samuel — H
GUTHRIE, Stanley Walter — 3
GUTHRIE, Thomas Joseph — 5
GUTHRIE, Walter James — 1
GUTHRIE, William Anderson — 1
GUTHRIE, William Buck — 1
GUTHRIE, William Dameron — 1
GUTHRIE, William Norman — 2
GUTHRIE, William Tyrone — 5
GUTHRIE, Woody — 4
GUTHUNZ, Henry — 3
GUTMANN, Addis — 5
GUTSCH, Milton Rietow — 5
GUTSTADT, Richard E. — 3
GUTT, Camille — 4
GUTTERSON, George H. — 1
GUTTERSON, Henry H. — 3
GUTTERSON, Herbert Lindsley — 3
GUTTMACHER, Manfred S. — 4
GUTTRIDGE, G(eorge) H(erbert) — 5
GUY, Charles Lewis — 1
GUY, Francis — H
GUY, Harvey Hugo — 1
GUY, J. Sam — 3
GUY, Seymour Joseph — 1
GUY, William Evans — 1
GUY, William George — 5
GUYER, Michael Frederic — 5
GUYER, Ulysses Samuel — 2
GUYER, William Harris — 1
GUYON, James Jr. — H
GUYOT, Arnold Henry — H
GUYTON, David Edgar — 4
GUZE, Henry — 5
GWALTNEY, Leslie Lee — 3
GWATHMEY, Edward Moseley
GWATHMEY, James Tayloe — 1
GWIN, Earl Stimson — 1
GWIN, William McKendree — H
GWINN, Joseph Marr — 5
GWINN, Ralph W. — 4
GWINNETT, Button — H
GWYN, Herbert Britton — 5
GWYNN, J(ohn) Minor — 5
GWYNNE, Charles Thomas — 2
GWYNNE, Walker — 1
GYGER, Edgar Grant — 1

H

HAACKE, Henry — 1
HAAG, Harvey B. — 4
HAAG, Joseph Jr. — 3
HAAKE, Alfred Paul — 4
HAAKON VII — 3
HAAN, William George — 1
HAANEL, Charles Francis — 4
HAANSTRA, John Wilson — 5
HAAS, Francis Joseph — 3
HAAS, George Christian Frederick — H
HAAS, Gustav — H
HAAS, Jacob Judah Aaron 'de

HAAS, Jacob Judah Aaron 'de — 4
HAAS, John A. W. — 1
HAAS, Otto — 3
HAAS, Samuel — 5
HAAS, Sidney Valentine — 4
HAAS, William David — 4
HAAS, William H. — 5
HAAS, William H. — 4
HAASS, Julius Henry — 1
HABBERTON, John — 1
HABER, Ernest Straign — 5
HABERMAN, Phillip William, Jr.
HABERMAN, Sol — 5
HABERSHAM, Alexander Wylly — H
HABERSHAM, James — H
HABERSHAM, John — H
HABERSHAM, Joseph — H
HABERSHAM, Richard Wylly — H
HACK, Elizabeth Jane Miller — 4
HACK, George — H
HACK, Gwendolyn Dunlevy Kelley — 1
HACK, Roy Kenneth — 2
HACKEMANN, Louis Frederick — 4
HACKENBURG, William Bower — 4
HACKER, Fred A. — 3
HACKER, Newton — 3
HACKETT, Arthur — 5
HACKETT, Charles — 1
HACKETT, Charles Megginson — 5
HACKETT, Charles Wilson — 3
HACKETT, E. Byrne — 3
HACKETT, Francis — 4
HACKETT, Frank D. — 3
HACKETT, Frank S. — 3
HACKETT, Frank Warren — 1
HACKETT, Horatio Balch — 1
HACKETT, James Dominick — 5
HACKETT, James Henry — H
HACKETT, James Keteltas — 1
HACKETT, Karleton Spalding
HACKETT, Lewis Wendell — 5
HACKETT, Richard Nathaniel — 3
HACKETT, Robert Phillip — 4
HACKETT, Samuel Everett — 5
HACKETT, Thomas C. — H
HACKETT, Wallace — 4
HACKETT, William Stormont
HACKH, Ingo W. D. — 1
HACKLEY, Aaron Jr. — 4
HACKLEY, Charles Elihu — 4
HACKLEY, Charles H. — 1
HACKMAN, Abe — 3
HACKNEY, Ed T. — 3
HACKNEY, Leonard J. — 4
HACKNEY, Thomas — 2
HACKNEY, Walter S. — 1
HADAMARD, Jacques Salomon — 5
HADAS, Moses — 4
HADDEN, Alexander — 1
HADDEN, Archibald — 1
HADDEN, Charles — 3
HADDEN, Crowell — 1
HADDEN, Maude Miner — 4
HADDOCK, Charles Brickett — H
HADDOCK, Frank Channing — 1
HADDOCK, John Courtney — 4
HADEN, Annie Bates (Mrs. Charles J. Haden)
HADEN, Charles Jones — 5
HADEN, Russell Landram — 3
HADFIELD, Barnabas Burrows — 4
HADFIELD, George — H
HADING, Hane — 4
HADLEY, Arthur Twining — 1
HADLEY, Carleton Sturtevant — 2
HADLEY, Cassius Clay — 1
HADLEY, Chalmers — 3
HADLEY, Charles William
HADLEY, Edwin Marshall — 5
HADLEY, Ernest Elvin — 3
HADLEY, Everett Addison

HADLEY, Henry Harrison * — 1
HADLEY, Henry K. — 1
HADLEY, Herbert Spencer — 1
HADLEY, Hiram — 1
HADLEY, Hiram Elwood — 1
HADLEY, James — H
HADLEY, John Vestal — 1
HADLEY, Lindley Hoag — 5
HADSALL, Harry Hugh — 5
HADSELL, Irving W. — 4
HADZSITS, George Depue — 3
HAEBERLE, Arminius T. — 5
HAECKER, Theophilus Levi — 2
HAENSEL, Fitzhugh William — 2
HAENSEL, Paul — 2
HAERING, George John — 4
HAERTLEIN, Albert — 4
HAESCHE, William Edwin — 1
HAESHMAN, Walter Scott — 1
HAEUSSLER, Armin — 4
HAFEN, Ann Woodbury (Mrs. Leroy R. Hafen) — 5
HAFEY, William Joseph — 3
HAFF, Delbert James — 2
HAFFENREFFER, Rudolf Frederick — 3
HAFNER, John A. — 3
HAGA, Oliver Owen — 2
HAGAN, Edward James — 3
HAGAN, Horace Henry — 1
HAGAN, John Campbell Jr. — 3
HAGAN, William Arthur — 4
HAGAR, Edward McKim — 1
HAGAR, George Jotham — 1
HAGAR, Gerald Hanna — 4
HAGAR, Stansbury — 5
HAGEBOECK, Alfons Ludwig — 1
HAGEDORN, Hermann — 4
HAGEMAN, Harry Andrew — 5
HAGEMAN, Richard — 4
HAGEMANN, Harry H. — 5
HAGEN, Harold C. — 3
HAGEN, Hermann August — H
HAGEN, Jere — 5
HAGEN, John George — 4
HAGEN, Oskar Frank Leonard — 3
HAGEN, Sam — 3
HAGENBARTH, Francis Joseph — 4
HAGER, Albert Davis — H
HAGER, Albert Ralph; — 5
HAGER, Alice Rogers — 4
HAGER, Clint Wood — 2
HAGER, George Caldwell — 3
HAGER, John Sharpenstein — H
HAGER, Luther George — 2
HAGERMAN, Edward Thomson — 4
HAGERMAN, Frank — 1
HAGERMAN, Herbert James
HAGERMAN, James — 1
HAGERTY, Christian Dane
HAGERTY, Edward Daniel — 5
HAGERTY, George James — 4
HAGERTY, James Edward — 2
HAGERTY, Melvin Everett
HAGGARD, Alfred Martin — 1
HAGGARD, Fred Porter — 4
HAGGARD, Sir Godfrey Digsby Napier — 5
HAGGARD, Howard Wilcox — 3
HAGGARD, Sewell — 1
HAGGARD, William David — 1
HAGGE, Hans Jergen — 3
HAGGERSON, Fred H. — 3
HAGGERTY, Cornelius J. — 5
HAGGERTY, James E. — 5
HAGGERTY, Melvin Everett — 1
HAGGETT, Arthur Sewall — 1
HAGGIN, Ben Ali — 3
HAGGIN, James B. — 1
HAGGIN, Louis Terah — 1
HAGGOTT, Warren Armstrong — 4
HAGIN, Fred Eugene — 1
HAGNER, Alexander Burton

HAGNER, Francis Randall 1
HAGNER, Peter H
HAGOOD, Johnson
HAGOOD, Johnson 2
HAGSPIEL, Bruno Martin
HAGSTROM, G. Arvid 3
HAGUE, Arnold 1
HAGUE, Frank
HAGUE, James Duncan 1
HAGUE, Louis Marchand
HAGUE, Maurice Stewart 2
HAGUE, Parthenia Antoinette Vardaman 4
HAGUE, William H
HAGY, Henry B. 3
HAHN, Adolf
HAHN, Albert George 5
HAHN, Benjamin Daviese 1
HAHN, Conrad Velder
HAHN, E. Adelaide 4
HAHN, Frederic Halsted
HAHN, Frederick E. 2
HAHN, George Philip
HAHN, Herman F. 3
HAHN, J. Jerome
HAHN, John H
HAHN, Lew 3
HAHN, Michael Georg Decker H
HAHN, Otto 5
HAHN, Paul M. 4
HAHN, Willard E.
HAHNE, Ernest Herman 3
HAID, Leo 1
HAID, Paul L. H
HAIDT, John Valentine H
HAIG, Vernon Lester Hague) 5
HAIG, John T. 4
HAIG, Robert Murray 3
HAIGHT, Albert 1
HAIGHT, Cameron 5
HAIGHT, Charles H
HAIGHT, Charles Coolidge 1
HAIGHT, Charles S. 5
HAIGHT, Edward 4
HAIGHT, Elizabeth Hazelton H
HAIGHT, George Ives 3
HAIGHT, H. W. 5
HAIGHT, Henry Huntly H
HAIGHT, Raymond LeRoy 2
HAIGHT, Thomas Griffith 1
HAIGIS, John William 4
HAILE, Columbus 1
HAILE, William H
HAILEY, Orren Luico 1
HAILEY, Thomas Griffin 4
HAILMANN, William Nicholas H
HAILPERIN, Herman 5
HAILS, Raymond Richard 4
HAIN, Jacob L. 5
HAINER, Bayard Taylor 1
HAINES, Charles Glidden H
HAINES, Charles Grove 5
HAINES, Charles Henry 4
HAINES, Daniel H
HAINES, Elwood Lindsay 2
HAINES, Frank David 3
HAINES, Harry B. 5
HAINES, Harry L. 2
HAINES, Helen 5
HAINES, Helen Elizabeth 5
HAINES, Henry Cargill 1
HAINES, Jennie Day 4
HAINES, John Allen 1
HAINES, John Michener 1
HAINES, John Peter 1
HAINES, Matthias Loring
HAINES, Robert Terrel 5
HAINES, Thomas Harvey 3
HAINES, Walter Stanley 1
HAINES, William T. 1
HAINS, Peter Conover 1
HAINS, Thornton Jenkins
HAIRE, Andrew J. 3
HAISH, Jacob H
HAISH, Jacob 4
HAISLIP, Wade Hampton 5
HAJI ALI H
HAKANSSON, Erik Gosta 3
HAKE, Harry 3
HAKLUYT, Richard H
HALBERSTADT, Baird 1
HALBERT, Henry Sale 1
HALBERT, Homer Valmore 1

HALD, Henry Martin 4
HALDEMAN, Bruce 2
HALDEMAN, Frederick Dwight 4
HALDEMAN, Harry Marston 1
HALDEMAN, Isaac Massey 1
HALDEMAN, Richard Jacobs H
HALDEMAN, Samuel Steman H
HALDEMAN, Walter Newman
HALDEMAN, William Birch 1
HALDEMAN-JULIUS, E. 3
HALDEN, Alfred A. 3
HALDEN, Leon Gilbert 3
HALDERMAN, John A. 1
HALE, Albert 1
HALE, Albert Cable 1
HALE, Anne Gardner 1
HALE, Annie Riley 2
HALE, Artemas H
HALE, Benjamin 1
HALE, Chandler 3
HALE, Charles H
HALE, Charles Reuben 1
HALE, Clarence 1
HALE, David 5
HALE, David C. H
HALE, Earl Melvin 4
HALE, Edward Everett * 1
HALE, Edward Joseph 1
HALE, Edward Russell 1
HALE, Edwin Moses H
HALE, Edwin Moses 1
HALE, Ellen Day 2
HALE, Enoch H
HALE, Eugene 1
HALE, Fletcher 1
HALE, Florence 1
HALE, Floyd Orlin 1
HALE, Frank Judson 5
HALE, Franklin Darius 1
HALE, Fred Douglas 4
HALE, Frederick 1
HALE, Gardner 1
HALE, George Ellery 1
HALE, Harris Grafton 4
HALE, Harry Clay 2
HALE, Horatio Emmons H
HALE, Hugh Ellmaker 3
HALE, Irving 4
HALE, James Tracy H
HALE, John Howard 1
HALE, John Parker H
HALE, John Philetus 1
HALE, Ledyard Park 1
HALE, Lillian Westcott 4
HALE, Lincoln Bell 1
HALE, Louise Closser 1
HALE, Lucretia Peabody 1
HALE, Marshal 2
HALE, Matthew 1
HALE, Morris Smith 2
HALE, Nathan * H
HALE, Nathan Wesley 1
HALE, Oscar 3
HALE, Philip 1
HALE, Philip Leslie 1
HALE, Philip Thomas 1
HALE, Prentis Cobb 1
HALE, Ralph Tracy 3
HALE, Reuben Brooks 1
HALE, Richard Walden 2
HALE, Robert Lee 5
HALE, Robert Safford 1
HALE, Salma H
HALE, Sarah Josepha Buell
HALE, Susan 1
HALE, Walter 1
HALE, Will T. 4
HALE, William * 1
HALE, William Barton 1
HALE, William Bayard 1
HALE, William Benjamin 1
HALE, William Browne 2
HALE, William Gardner 1
HALE, William Green 3
HALE, William Henry 1
HALE, William J. 3
HALE, William Thomas 1
HALE, Willis H. 4
HALE, Wyatt Walker 2
HALEY, Andrew Gallagher
HALEY, Dennis C. 4
HALEY, Elisha H
HALEY, George Franklin 1
HALEY, James Frederick 5
HALEY, Jesse James 1
HALEY, Ora 1
HALEY, William J. 3
HALFHILL, James Wood 1

HALFORD, Albert James 1
HALFORD, Elijah Walker 1
HALFORD, John Henry 5
HALIFAX, Earl 'of 3
HALL, A. Cleveland 1
HALL, A. Neely 3
HALL, Abraham Oakey H
HALL, Alaistair Cameron 5
HALL, Alexander Wilford 1
HALL, Allen Garland 1
HALL, Alton Parker 3
HALL, Alvin William 5
HALL, Ansel Franklin 4
HALL, Arethusa H
HALL, Arnold Bennett 1
HALL, Arthur Crawshay Alliston
HALL, Arthur Fletcher 2
HALL, Arthur Graham 1
HALL, Arthur Jackson 2
HALL, Arthur Pinckney 1
HALL, Asaph H
HALL, Asaph Jr. 1
HALL, Augustus H
HALL, Baynard Rush H
HALL, Benjamin Mortimer 1
HALL, Benton Jay H
HALL, Bolling H
HALL, Bolton 1
HALL, C. Lester 1
HALL, Chaffee E(arl) 5
HALL, Chapin H
HALL, Charles Badger 1
HALL, Charles Cuthbert 1
HALL, Charles Edward 4
HALL, Charles Francis H
HALL, Charles Henry 1
HALL, Charles Hershall 1
HALL, Charles Martin 1
HALL, Charles Mercer 1
HALL, Charles Philip 3
HALL, Charles Winslow 1
HALL, Chester Wallace 4
HALL, Christopher Webber 1
HALL, Claude Caleb 5
HALL, Damon Everett 3
HALL, Daniel 1
HALL, David 1
HALL, David McKee Jr. 3
HALL, Dominick Augustin H
HALL, Edmond 4
HALL, Edward Bigelow 1
HALL, Edward Hagaman 1
HALL, Edward Henry 1
HALL, Edward Kimball 1
HALL, Edwin Herbert 1
HALL, Edwin S. 3
HALL, Elmer Edwards 1
HALL, Emery Stanford 1
HALL, Ernest 1
HALL, Everett Wesley 5
HALL, Fitzedward H
HALL, Fitzgerald 2
HALL, Florence Marion Howe 1
HALL, Ford Poulton 3
HALL, Francis Joseph 1
HALL, Frank A. 5
HALL, Frank Herbert 4
HALL, Frank Hillman 3
HALL, Frank Lucas 1
HALL, Frank M. 1
HALL, Frank Oliver 5
HALL, Franklin 1
HALL, Fred(erick) L. 5
HALL, Fred Smith 5
HALL, Frederic Aldin 5
HALL, Frederic Byron 1
HALL, G. Stanley 1
HALL, G(eorge) Edward 1
HALL, Gene W. 3
HALL, George H
HALL, George Edward 4
HALL, George Eli 1
HALL, George Elisha 2
HALL, George Gilman 4
HALL, George Henry 3
HALL, George Martin 1
HALL, George Washington 1
HALL, Gertrude 4
HALL, Grover Cleveland 4
HALL, Grover Cleveland, Jr. 5
HALL, Harold 4
HALL, Harry Alvan 1
HALL, Harry Hinckley 1
HALL, Harry Melville 1
HALL, Harvey Monroe 5
HALL, Henry * 1
HALL, Henry B. 4
HALL, Henry Bryan H

HALL, Henry Clay 1
HALL, Henry Harrington 1
HALL, Henry Noble 5
HALL, Herbert Edwin 4
HALL, Herbert James 1
HALL, Herman 4
HALL, Hilland H
HALL, Holworthy 5
HALL, Homer William 5
HALL, Howard 5
HALL, Howard Judson 2
HALL, Isaac Harry 4
HALL, Isaac Hollister 1
HALL, James * H
HALL, James 1
HALL, James Alexander 1
HALL, James Glenn 3
HALL, James Jabez 2
HALL, James King 1
HALL, James Knox Polk 4
HALL, James Morris Whiton 4
HALL, James Norman 3
HALL, James Parker 1
HALL, James Pierre 4
HALL, James Whitney 1
HALL, Jennie 1
HALL, John * H
HALL, John Dean 4
HALL, John Elihu 1
HALL, John Ellsworth 2
HALL, John H. H
HALL, John L. 1
HALL, John Lesslie 1
HALL, John Raymond 1
HALL, John William 5
HALL, Joseph 4
HALL, Joseph Kevin 1
HALL, Josephine 1
HALL, Josiah Newhall 1
HALL, Juanita H
HALL, Lawrence Washington H
HALL, Lee Davis 4
HALL, Leland 3
HALL, Lemuel C. 2
HALL, Lester W. 1
HALL, Lloyd Augustus 5
HALL, Louis Harrison 1
HALL, Louis Phillips 1
HALL, Louis Phillips 2
HALL, Louisa Jane Park H
HALL, Luther Egbert 1
HALL, Lyman 1
HALL, Lyman 1
HALL, Lyman Beecher 1
HALL, Matthew Alexander 2
HALL, Matthew Walton 4
HALL, Maurice Crowther 1
HALL, Nathan Kelsey H
HALL, Newton Marshall 1
HALL, Nichols 1
HALL, Norman Brierley 4
HALL, Obed 1
HALL, Oliver Leigh 2
HALL, Orson Loftin 5
HALL, Pauline 1
HALL, Percival 3
HALL, Philip Louis 1
HALL, Philo 3
HALL, Prescott Farnsworth 1
HALL, Randall Cooke 1
HALL, Ray Ovid 1
HALL, Reynold Thomas 1
HALL, Richard Cartwright 1
HALL, Robert Bernard H
HALL, Robert Henry 1
HALL, Robert Samuel 1
HALL, Robert William 5
HALL, Rufus Bartlett 1
HALL, Ruth 4
HALL, Samuel * H
HALL, Samuel Read H
HALL, Sarah Ewing 1
HALL, Sharlot Mabridth 3
HALL, Sherman 1
HALL, Sidney Bartlett 3
HALL, Thomas * 1
HALL, Thomas 3
HALL, Thomas Bartlett 1
HALL, Thomas Cuming 1
HALL, Thomas H. H
HALL, Thomas Seavey 1
HALL, Thomas Winthrop 1
HALL, Tomas Proctor 1
HALL, Walter Henry 1
HALL, Walter Perley 3
HALL, Wilbur Curtis 5
HALL, Willard H
HALL, Willard Merrill 3
HALL, Willard Preble 1
HALL, William H
HALL, William Augustus H

HALL, William Baldwin Fletcher 5
HALL, William Bonnell 4
HALL, William Dickson 5
HALL, William Edwin 4
HALL, William Leroy 4
HALL, William Phillips 1
HALL, William Preble 1
HALL, William Shafer 2
HALL, William Thomas 5
HALL, William Whitty H
HALL, Wilmer Lee 3
HALL, Winfield Scott 4
HALLAERT, Charles 1
HALLAM, Clement Benner 5
HALLAM, Julia Clark 1
HALLAM, Lewis H
HALLAM, Oscar 2
HALLAM, Robert Alexander H
HALLANAN, Walter Simms 4
HALLAUER, Carl S. 5
HALLBECK, Elroy Charles 5
HALLBERG, Carl Savante Nicanor 1
HALLDEN, Karl William 5
HALLE, Edward Gustav 1
HALLE, Samuel H. 2
HALLE, Stanley Jacques 5
HALLE, Walter Murphy 5
HALLECK, Fitz-Greene H
HALLECK, Henry Wager H
HALLECK, Reuben Post 1
HALLENBECK, Edwin Forrest 4
HALLER, Frank Louis 1
HALLER, H(erbert L(udwig Jacob) 5
HALLET, Etienne Sulpice H
HALLET, Richard Matthews 4
HALLETT, Benjamin H
HALLETT, Benjamin Franklin
HALLETT, George Hervey 2
HALLETT, Herbert K. 3
HALLETT, Moses 1
HALLETT, Robert Leroy 3
HALLEY, George 4
HALLEY, James 1
HALLEY, Rudolph 3
HALLEY, William J. 4
HALLGREN, Mauritz Alfred 3
HALLIBURTON, Erle Palmer 3
HALLIBURTON, Richard 1
HALLIDAY, Richard 5
HALLIDAY, Samuel Dumont
HALLIDIE, Andrew Smith H
HALLIGAN, Howard Ansel 1
HALLIGAN, John 1
HALLINAN, Paul John 5
HALLIWELL, Ashleigh C. 4
HALLOCK, Charles 1
HALLOCK, Frank Hudson 1
HALLOCK, Frank Kirkwood
HALLOCK, Gerard H
HALLOCK, Gerard 1
HALLOCK, Gerard Benjamin Fleet 5
HALLOCK, Henry Galloway Comingo 3
HALLOCK, John Jr. H
HALLOCK, Joseph Newton 1
HALLOCK, Julia Isabel 4
HALLOCK, Mary Elizabeth 3
HALLOCK, Robert Crawford
HALLOCK, William 1
HALLOCK, William Allen 5
HALLORAN, Edward Roosevelt
HALLORAN, Paul James 3
HALLOWAY, Ransom H
HALLOWELL, Anna Davis 4
HALLOWELL, Benjamin H
HALLOWELL, George Hawley 5
HALLOWELL, John White 1
HALLOWELL, Norwood Penrose 1
HALLOWELL, Richard Price 5
HALLOWELL, Robert

Name	
HALLOWELL, Sara Catherine Fraley	4
HALLSTEAD, William F.	4
HALLWORTH, Joseph Bryant	5
HALPER, Benzion	1
HALPERN, Jacob	5
HALPERN, Julius (Jules)	5
HALPERN, Michael	4
HALPERN, Philip	4
HALPERT, Edith Gregor	5
HALPIN, George H.	3
HALPIN, James G.	4
HALPINE, Charles Graham	H
HALSALL, William Formby	4
HALSEY, Abram Woodruff	1
HALSEY, Benjamin Schuyler	3
HALSEY, Francis Whiting	1
HALSEY, Frederick Arthur	1
HALSEY, George Armstrong	H
HALSEY, Jehiel Howell	H
HALSEY, Jesse	3
HALSEY, John	H
HALSEY, John Julius	5
HALSEY, John Taylor	5
HALSEY, Leroy Jones	H
HALSEY, N. Wetmore	H
HALSEY, Nicoll	H
HALSEY, Rena Isabelle	H
HALSEY, Richard T. Haines	1
HALSEY, Silas	H
HALSEY, Thomas J.	4
HALSEY, Thomas Lloyd	H
HALSEY, William Frederick	3
HALSTEAD, Albert	2
HALSTEAD, Albert Edward	1
HALSTEAD, Alexander Seaman	1
HALSTEAD, Alexander Seaman	2
HALSTEAD, Kenneth Burt	
HALSTEAD, Laurence	3
HALSTEAD, Murat	1
HALSTEAD, Ward Campbell	5
HALSTEAD, William	H
HALSTEAD, William Riley	1
HALSTED, Abel Stevens	1
HALSTED, Byron David	1
HALSTED, George Bruce	1
HALSTED, Thomas Henry	3
HALSTED, William Stewart	1
HALTOM, William Lorenz	5
HALVERSON, Wilton L.	4
HAM, Arthur Harold	3
HAM, Clifford Dudley	5
HAM, Edward Billings	4
HAM, Guy Andrews	1
HAM, Marion Franklin	3
HAM, Roscoe James	3
HAM, William Felton	1
HAMAKER, John Irvin	3
HAMAKER, Winters D.	4
HAMAN, B. Howard	1
HAMANN, Anna	5
HAMANN, Carl August	1
HAMANN, Carl Ferdinand	1
HAMBIDGE, Gove	5
HAMBIDGE, Jay	5
HAMBLEN, Archelaus L.	5
HAMBLEN, Edwin Crowell	4
HAMBLEN, Herbert Eliott	4
HAMBLETON, Samuel	H
HAMBLETON, Thomas Edward	1
HAMBLIN, Charles Henry	1
HAMBLIN, Joseph Eldridge	H
HAMBLIN, Thomas Sowerby	
HAMBRECHT, George Philip	2
HAMBRO, C. J.	4
HAMBRO, Sir Charles Jocelyn	5
HAMBROOK, Richard Edward	5
HAMBURGER, Louis Philip	5
HAMBURGER, Walter Wile	1
HAMBY, William Henry	1
HAMEL, Charles Dennis	5
HAMELE, Ottamar	4
HAMER, Edward Everett	5
HAMER, Francis Gregg	4
HAMER, James Henry	4
HAMER, Jesse Dewey	4
HAMER, Philip May	5
HAMER, Thomas Lyon	H
HAMER, Thomas Ray	4
HAMERSCHLAG, Arthur Arton	1
HAMERSCHLAG, Robert Joseph	5
HAMERSLAG, Victor	3
HAMERSLEY, James Hooker	1
HAMERSLEY, William	1
HAMET KARAMANLI	H
HAMFF, Christian F.	4
HAMID, George Abou	5
HAMILBURG, Ira M.	4
HAMILBURG, Joseph M.	5
HAMILL, Alfred Ernest	3
HAMILL, Charles Humphrey	1
HAMILL, Ernest Alfred	1
HAMILL, Howard M.	1
HAMILL, James A.	1
HAMILL, Patrick	H
HAMILL, Samuel McClintock	2
HAMILTON, A. J.	5
HAMILTON, Albert Hine	1
HAMILTON, Alexander *	H
HAMILTON, Alexander *	1
HAMILTON, Alexander	5
HAMILTON, Alice	5
HAMILTON, Allan McLane	1
HAMILTON, Alston	1
HAMILTON, Andrew *	H
HAMILTON, Andrew Holman	H
HAMILTON, Andrew Jackson	H
HAMILTON, Arthur Stephen	2
HAMILTON, Aymer Jay	4
HAMILTON, Bertis Frank	3
HAMILTON, Charles Elbert	1
HAMILTON, Charles Memorial	H
HAMILTON, Charles Robert	3
HAMILTON, Charles Smith	H
HAMILTON, Charles Sumner	1
HAMILTON, Charles Whiteley	5
HAMILTON, Clarence Grant	1
HAMILTON, Clayton Meeker	2
HAMILTON, Cornelius Springer	H
HAMILTON, Daniel Webster	4
HAMILTON, David Gilbert	1
HAMILTON, Donald Ross	5
HAMILTON, Edith	4
HAMILTON, Edward John	1
HAMILTON, Edward La Rue	1
HAMILTON, Edward Wilbur Dean	2
HAMILTON, Elwood	2
HAMILTON, F. F.	H
HAMILTON, Finley	1
HAMILTON, Francis Frazee	4
HAMILTON, Frank Hastings	H
HAMILTON, Frank Hastings	1
HAMILTON, Franklin Elmer Ellsworth	1
HAMILTON, Frederic Rutherford	3
HAMILTON, Frederick William	1
HAMILTON, Gail	H
HAMILTON, Garrison W.	4
HAMILTON, George Anson	
HAMILTON, George E.	2
HAMILTON, George Hall	1
HAMILTON, George Henry	2
HAMILTON, George Livingstone	1
HAMILTON, Gilbert Van Tassel	2
HAMILTON, Grant E.	4
HAMILTON, Hamilton	1
HAMILTON, Harold Lee	5
HAMILTON, Henry	H
HAMILTON, Hollister Adelbert	1
HAMILTON, Hugh Ralston	4
HAMILTON, Isaac Miller	3
HAMILTON, J. Kent	1
HAMILTON, J. Taylor	3
HAMILTON, James *	H
HAMILTON, James Jr.	5
HAMILTON, James Alexander	5
HAMILTON, James Alexander	H
HAMILTON, James E.	3
HAMILTON, James Edward	1
HAMILTON, James Henry	4
HAMILTON, James Lemmon Jr.	4
HAMILTON, James McLellan	1
HAMILTON, James Wallace	5
HAMILTON, Jamin Hannibal	4
HAMILTON, Jay Benson	1
HAMILTON, John *	H
HAMILTON, John	1
HAMILTON, John Alan	1
HAMILTON, John C.	5
HAMILTON, John Carroll	3
HAMILTON, John L.	1
HAMILTON, John Leonard	3
HAMILTON, John Marshall	1
HAMILTON, John McLure	1
HAMILTON, John Sherman	5
HAMILTON, John Taylor	1
HAMILTON, John William	5
HAMILTON, Kate Waterman	5
HAMILTON, Maxwell M.	3
HAMILTON, Morgan Calvin	H
HAMILTON, Norman Rond	4
HAMILTON, Paul	H
HAMILTON, Peter	H
HAMILTON, Peter Joseph	1
HAMILTON, Peter Myers	H
HAMILTON, Ralph Scott	4
HAMILTON, Robert	5
HAMILTON, Robert Patrick	4
HAMILTON, Rolland Jerome	2
HAMILTON, Roy William	3
HAMILTON, Samuel King	1
HAMILTON, Samuel L.	3
HAMILTON, Schuyler	1
HAMILTON, Stanislaus Murray	1
HAMILTON, Thomas Benton	5
HAMILTON, Thomas Jefferson	1
HAMILTON, Thompson A.	5
HAMILTON, Walton Hale	3
HAMILTON, William	4
HAMILTON, William Benjamin	2
HAMILTON, William F.	4
HAMILTON, William Henry	5
HAMILTON, William Peter	3
HAMILTON, William Pierson	1
HAMILTON, William Reeve	1
HAMILTON, William Thomas *	H
HAMILTON, William Thomas	3
HAMILTON, William Wistar	1
HAMILTON, Williard I.	3
HAMILTON, Wilson H.	3
HAMLEN, James C.	1
HAMLEN, Joseph Rochemont	1
HAMLET, Harry Gabriel	3
HAMLETT, Barksdale	1
HAMLIN, Alfred Dwight Foster	1
HAMLIN, Augustus Choate	1
HAMLIN, Charles	1
HAMLIN, Charles Sumner	1
HAMLIN, Chauncey J.	4
HAMLIN, Clarence Clark	1
HAMLIN, Conde	4
HAMLIN, Courtney Walker	4
HAMLIN, Cyrus	1
HAMLIN, Edward Stowe	H
HAMLIN, Elbert Bacon	1
HAMLIN, Emmons	H
HAMLIN, Fred	3
HAMLIN, George John	1
HAMLIN, Hannibal	1
HAMLIN, Hannibal Emery	1
HAMLIN, John	3
HAMLIN, John N(ellis)	5
HAMLIN, Simon Moulton	1
HAMLIN, Talbot Faulkner	3
HAMLIN, Teunis Slingerland	1
HAMLIN, William	H
HAMLINE, John Henry	1
HAMLINE, Leonidas Lent	H
HAMM, Beth Creevey	3
HAMM, Margherita Arlina	1
HAMM, William	1
HAMM, William, Jr.	5
HAMMAKER, Wilbur Emery	5
HAMMAN, Louis	2
HAMMARSKJOLD, Dag Hjalmar Agne Carl	4
HAMMEL, Wilbert C.	4
HAMMEL, William Charles Adam	3
HAMMELL, Alfred Lawson	4
HAMMELL, George M.	1
HAMMER, Edwin Wesley	3
HAMMER, John Schackelford	1
HAMMER, Kenneth S.	5
HAMMER, Trygve	2
HAMMER, William C.	1
HAMMER, William Joseph	1
HAMMERLING, Louis Nicholas	1
HAMMERSTEIN, Oscar	1
HAMMERSTEIN, Oscar 2'd	4
HAMMETT, Edward	5
HAMMETT, Henry Pinckney	H
HAMMETT, Samuel Adams	H
HAMMETT, Samuel Dashiell	4
HAMMETT, William H.	H
HAMMILL, Fred H.	1
HAMMILL, John	1
HAMMITT, Jackson Lewis	1
HAMMON, Jupiter	H
HAMMOND, Alonzo John	2
HAMMOND, Andrew B.	1
HAMMOND, Bray	5
HAMMOND, Charles	H
HAMMOND, Charles Herrick	5
HAMMOND, Charles Parker	3
HAMMOND, Creed Cheshire	1
HAMMOND, Edward	H
HAMMOND, Edward Payson	1
HAMMOND, Edward Sanford	5
HAMMOND, Edwin	H
HAMMOND, Edwin Pollock	1
HAMMOND, Eleanor Prescott	1
HAMMOND, Eli Shelby	1
HAMMOND, Frank Clinch	5
HAMMOND, George Francis	4
HAMMOND, George Henry	H
HAMMOND, George Young	4
HAMMOND, Godfrey	5
HAMMOND, Graeme Monroe	2
HAMMOND, Harold	1
HAMMOND, Harry Parker	3
HAMMOND, Jabez Dean	1
HAMMOND, Jabez Delano	H
HAMMOND, Jack	5
HAMMOND, James Jr.	1
HAMMOND, James Bartlett	H
HAMMOND, James Bartlett	4
HAMMOND, James Henry	H
HAMMOND, Jason E.	H
HAMMOND, John	H
HAMMOND, John Dennis	4
HAMMOND, John Hays	1
HAMMOND, John Hays Jr.	4
HAMMOND, John Henry	2
HAMMOND, John Wilkes	1
Winthrop	1
HAMMOND, Lily Hardy	1
HAMMOND, Lyman Pierce	3
HAMMOND, Matthew Brown	1
HAMMOND, Monroe Percy	1
HAMMOND, Nathaniel Job	H
HAMMOND, Norma Mae	4
HAMMOND, Ogden Haggerty	3
HAMMOND, Percy	1
HAMMOND, Robert Hanna	4
HAMMOND, Roland	4
HAMMOND, Samuel	H
HAMMOND, Stevens Hill	3
HAMMOND, Theodore Augustus	1
HAMMOND, Thomas Stevens	3
HAMMOND, William Alexander	1
HAMMOND, William Alexander	4
HAMMOND, William Churchill	2
HAMMOND, William Gardiner	1
HAMMOND, Winfield Scott	1
HAMMONS, David	H
HAMMONS, Earle Wooldridge	4
HAMMONS, Earle Woolridge	
HAMMONS, Joseph	1
HAMP, Sidford Frederick	H
HAMPDEN, Walter	3
HAMPSON, Alfred Aubert	2
HAMPTON, Aubrey Otis	3
HAMPTON, Benjamin Bowles	1
HAMPTON, Edgar Lloyd	3
HAMPTON, George	2
HAMPTON, Ireland	2
HAMPTON, James Giles	H
HAMPTON, Moses	H
HAMPTON, Wade	H
HAMPTON, Wade	1
HAMRIN, Shirley Austin	3
HAMSUN, Knut	3
HAMSUN, Knut	4
HAMTRAMCK, John Francis	
HAMUDA PASHA	H
HANAN, John H.	1
HANAU, Kenneth John	3
HANAUER, Jerome J.	1
HANAW, Henry	1
HANBACK, Lewis	1
HANBY, Benjamin Russel	H
HANCEY, Carlos	4
HANCH, Charles Connard	2
HANCHER, John William	4
HANCHER, Virgil Melvin	4
HANCHETT, Benton	1
HANCHETT, George Tilden	5
HANCHETT, Henry Granger	1
HANCHETT, Lafayette	3
HANCHETT, Luther	1
HANCOCK, Albert Elmer	1
HANCOCK, Arthur Boyd	5
HANCOCK, Clarence Eugene	2
HANCOCK, Elizabeth Hazlewood	1
HANCOCK, G. Allan	4
HANCOCK, George	H
HANCOCK, Glover Dunn	3
HANCOCK, H. Irving	1

HANCOCK, Harris 4
HANCOCK, James Cole 1
HANCOCK, John * H
HANCOCK, John M. 3
HANCOCK, La Toucha 1
HANCOCK, Theodore E. 1
HANCOCK, Thomas H
HANCOCK, · 2
  Thomas Hightower
HANCOCK, 5
  W(alter) Scott
HANCOCK, William
  Wayne 4
HANCOCK, H
  Winfield Scott
HAND, Alfred 1
HAND, H
  Augustus Cincinnatus
HAND, Augustus Noble 3
HAND, Chauncey Harris 4
HAND, Daniel 1
HAND, Edward H
HAND, 5
  George Trowbridge
HAND, Harold Curtis 5
HAND, John Pryor 1
HAND, Learned 4
HAND, Richard Lockhart 1
HAND, Thomas Millet 3
HAND, William Flowers 1
HANDBURY, John D. 5
HANDERSON, 4
  Henry Ebenezer
HANDFORTH, Thomas 2
HANDLEY, 4
  Carroll Alfred
HANDLEY, Harold Willis 5
HANDLEY, William
  White 1
HANDLIN, 3
  Frank Augustine
HANDMAN, Max Sylvius 2
HANDSCHIN, Charles H. 4
HANDWORK, Bentley S. 5
HANDY, H
  Alexander Hamilton
HANDY, Anson Burgess 2
HANDY, Burton 3
HANDY, 1
  Henry Hunter Smith
HANDY, James A. 5
HANDY, Parker Douglas 1
HANDY, Ray D. 5
HANDY, 3
  William Christopher
HANECY, Elbridge 1
HANEMAN, 4
  Frederick Theodore
HANES, Frederic Moir 2
HANES, James Gordon 5
HANES, Leigh (Buckner) 1
HANES, Robert March 3
HANES, S. B. Jr. 4
HANEY, Bart Emory 2
HANEY, Carol 4
HANEY, Dick 2
HANEY, James Parton 1
HANEY, John Louis 5
HANEY, Lewis Henry 5
HANFORD, Ben 1
HANFORD, 1
  Charles Barnum
HANFORD, 1
  Cornelius Holgate
HANFORD, Franklin 1
HANFORD, James Holly 5
HANGER, 5
  Franklin M(cCue)
HANGER, 1
  G. Wallace William
HANGER, Harry Baylor 1
HANGER, 5
  Robert Kittrell
HANGER, William A. 2
HANIFAN, Lyda Judson 1
HANISCH, Arthur Oscar 4
HANK, Frederick Borter 4
HANK, Oscar Charles 1
HANKINS, 5
  Frank Hamilton
HANKS, Abbott Atherton 1
HANKS, Bryan Cayce 5
HANKS, Charles Stedman 1
HANKS, Henry G. 1
HANKS, Lucien Mason 5
HANKS, 2
  Marshall Bernard
HANKS, Mrs. Bernard 4
HANKWITZ, 5
  Arthur Walter
HANLEY, Elijah Andrews 5
HANLEY, 5
  Herbert Russell
HANLEY, John Chaney 3
HANLEY, Joseph Rhodes 5
HANLEY, L. E. 3
HANLEY, Miles L. 3

HANLEY, Sarah Bond 3
HANLEY, Stewart 1
HANLEY, 5
  Thomas James, Jr.
HANLEY, William
  Andrew 4
HANLIN, Merton E. 3
HANLON, Edward I. 4
HANLON, Edward K. 5
HANLON, 5
  Lawrence Wilson
HANLON, Thomas J. Jr. 4
HANLY, J. Frank 1
HANMER, Lee Franklin 5
HANN, Charles 3
HANNA, 3
  Charles Augustus
HANNA, Dan R. 1
HANNA, 4
  Daniel Rhodes Jr.
HANNA, Edward J. 2
HANNA, Frank Willard 2
HANNA, Guy Carleton 4
HANNA, Howard Melville 2
HANNA, Hugh Henry 1
HANNA, Hugh Sisson 2
HANNA, James Robert 1
HANNA, John H
HANNA, John 4
HANNA, John Andre H
HANNA, John Hunter 2
HANNA, Kathryn Abbey 5
HANNA, 3
  Leonard Colton Jr.
HANNA, Louis Benjamin 2
HANNA, Marcus Alonzo 1
HANNA, Margaret M. 4
HANNA, Matthew Elting 1
HANNA, Mrs. John M. 3
HANNA, Philip C. 1
HANNA, Philip Sidney 3
HANNA, Richard Henry 2
HANNA, Robert H
HANNA, Septimus James 1
HANNA, William Brantly 1
HANNAFORD, 1
  Charles Edward
HANNAFORD, Jule
  Murat 1
HANNAGAN, 3
  Stephen Jerome
HANNAH, Harvey
  Horatio 2
HANNAN, 1
  Frederick Watson
HANNAN, Jerome Daniel 4
HANNAY, 4
  Neilson Campbell
HANNEGAN, Edward
  Allen H
HANNEGAN, Robert E. 2
HANNIGAN, 1
  Francis James
HANNIKAINEN, Tauno 5
HANNON, W. H. 4
HANOVER, 4
  Clinton DeWitt Jr.
HANRAHAN, 3
  Edward Mitchell
HANSBERRY, Lorraine 4
HANSBROUGH, Henry
  Clay 1
HANSCOM, 1
  Charles Ridgely
HANSCOM, 3
  Elizabeth Deering
HANSCOM, Frank
  Edward 1
HANSCOM, John Forsyth 1
HANSEL, Charles 1
HANSEL, 1
  John Washington
HANSEL, 3
  John Washington
HANSELL, Granger 5
HANSELL, Howard Forde 1
HANSELMAN, 1
  Joseph Francis
HANSEN, A. B. 2
HANSEN, Alice G. 3
HANSEN, Arild Edsten 3
HANSEN, Armin Carl 4
HANSEN, Augie Louis 4
HANSEN, Carl W. 4
HANSEN, Einar A. 5
HANSEN, Eric H. 5
HANSEN, Eric H. 4
HANSEN, 5
  Florence Froney
HANSEN, George 4
HANSEN, George 5
HANSEN, George Troup 4
HANSEN, 3
  Hans Christian Svane
HANSEN, 4
  Hans Christian Svane
HANSEN, Niels Ebbesen 3

HANSEN, Oskar J. W. 5
HANSEN, Paul 2
HANSEN, Walter William 4
HANSEN, William W. 3
HANSMANN, William H. 3
HANSON, Albert Hoit 4
HANSON, H
  Alexander Contee *
HANSON, Arthur Edwin 4
HANSON, Bert 1
HANSON, Burton 1
HANSON, Charles Lane 5
HANSON, Elisha 1
HANSON, Ephraim 5
HANSON, 3
  Felix Valentine
HANSON, Frank Blair 2
HANSON, George Charles 1
HANSON, George M. 1
HANSON, Henry W. A. 4
HANSON, 2
  James Christian Meinich
HANSON, John H
HANSON, John Fletcher 1
HANSON, Joseph Miles 5
HANSON, Karl P(eter) 5
HANSON, Leonard G. 4
HANSON, Martin Gustav 4
HANSON, Martin H. 1
HANSON, 5
  Michael Francis
HANSON, Miles 4
HANSON, Murray 5
HANSON, 4
  Norwood Russell
HANSON, O. B. 1
HANSON, Ole 1
HANSON, Richard Burpee 2
HANSON, Richard Locke 3
HANSON, H
  Roger Weightman
HANSON, Thomas
  Grafton 2
HANSON, Victor Henry 2
HANUS, Paul Henry 1
HANUS, Paul Henry 2
HANWAY, J. E. 2
HANZLIK, Paul John 3
HANZSCHE, 3
  William Thomson
HAPGOOD, Hutchins 2
HAPGOOD, 1
  Isabel Florence
HAPGOOD, Marshall Jay 1
HAPGOOD, Neith Boyce 3
HAPGOOD, Norman 1
HAPPER, Andrew Patton H
HARADA, Tasuku 4
HARADEN, Jonathan H
HARAHAN, 1
  James Theodore
HARAHAN, 1
  William Johnson
HARALSON, H
  Hugh Anderson
HARALSON, Jonathan 1
HARBACH, 1
  Abram Alexander
HARBACH, Otto Abels 4
HARBAUGH, 5
  Charles William
HARBAUGH, Henry H
HARBAUGH, 4
  James Fleming Linn
HARBAUGH, 1
  Thomas Chalmers
HARBEN, Will N. 1
HARBER, Giles Bates 1
HARBERT, 1
  Elizabeth Morrisson
  Boynton
HARBESON, William
  Page 5
HARBISON, E. Harris 4
HARBISON, Ralph
  Warner 3
HARBISON, 1
  Robert Cleland
HARBISON, 3
  William Albert
HARBO, Elias Peter 1
HARBOLD, Peter Monroe 5
HARBORD, James
  Guthrie 2
HARBOROUGH-
  SHERARD, Mrs. Robert 5
HARBOUR, Jefferson Lee 1
HARBY, Isaac H
HARBY, Lee Cohen 4
HARCOURT, Alfred 3
HARCUM, Edith Hatcher 5
HARD, Gideon H
HARD, William 4
HARDAWAY, 1
  William Augustus
HARDEE, Cary Augustus 3
HARDEE, Theodore 4

HARDEE, William Joseph H
HARDEMAN, 5
  Nicholas Brodie
HARDEMAN, Thomas Jr. H
HARDEN, Edward Walker 5
HARDEN, John Henry 4
HARDEN, Orville 3
HARDEN, William 2
HARDENBERGH, 1
  Henry Janeway
HARDENBERGH, H
  Jacob Rutsen
HARDENBERGH, 4
  John Gerard
HARDENBURGH, H
  Augustus Albert
HARDESTY, Frederick A. 3
HARDESTY, Irving 2
HARDESTY, Shortridge 3
HARDEY, H
  Mother Mary Aloysia
HARDGROVE, George P. 4
HARDGROVE, 5
  John Gilbert
HARDIE, George Robert 1
HARDIE, James Allen H
HARDIE, Robert Gordon 4
HARDIN, Benjamin H
HARDIN, Charles Henry 4
HARDIN, Charles Roe 3
HARDIN, Everitt C. 5
HARDIN, George A. 1
HARDIN, John H
HARDIN, John J. H
HARDIN, John Ralph 5
HARDIN, John Ralph 4
HARDIN, John Wesley H
HARDIN, Martin D. 5
HARDIN, Martin D. * 1
HARDIN, Robert Allen 5
HARDIN, Willett Lepley 4
HARDING, Aaron H
HARDING, Abner Clark 1
HARDING, Albert Austin 3
HARDING, Alfred 4
HARDING, Alfred 5
HARDING, 2
  Arthur McCracken
HARDING, Carroll Rede 4
HARDING, 1
  Charles Francis
HARDING, Charles L. 3
HARDING, Chester H
HARDING, Chester 1
HARDING, Edwin Forrest 5
HARDING, Garrick M. 4
HARDING, George 1
HARDING, 1
  George Franklin
HARDING, George M. 3
HARDING, Harry Alexis 1
HARDING, Harry Patrick 5
HARDING, Henry 1
HARDING, J. Horace 1
HARDING, J. M. 4
HARDING, Jesper H
HARDING, John Cowden 4
HARDING, John Eugene 2
HARDING, John Thomas 2
HARDING, John William 4
HARDING, Louis A. 3
HARDING, Nelson 2
HARDING, Robert H
HARDING, 3
  Robert Ellison
HARDING, Russell 1
HARDING, 1
  Samuel Bannister
HARDING, Seth H
HARDING, Warren G. 1
HARDING, 4
  William Barclay
HARDING, William Lloyd 1
HARDING, William P. G. 1
HARDING, William
  White H
HARDINGE, Hal 2
HARDISON, 3
  Osborne Bennett
HARDMAN, 1
  Lamartine Griffin
HARDT, Frank McCulley 2
HARDT, John William 5
HARDWICK, 5
  Charles Cheever, Jr.
HARDWICK, Charles Z. 4
HARDWICK, 5
  Clifford Emerson
HARDWICK, 4
  Thomas William
HARDWICKE, 1
  Cedric Webster Sir
HARDY, 1
  Arthur Sherburne
HARDY, Ashley Kingsley 1
HARDY, Caldwell 1

HARDY, Charles J. 3
HARDY, Charles Oscar 2
HARDY, David Phillip 3
HARDY, Edward Lawyer 5
HARDY, Edwin Noah 5
HARDY, Ewing Lloyd 5
HARDY, George Erastus 1
HARDY, George Fiske 2
HARDY, Guy U. 2
HARDY, Irene 4
HARDY, James Graham 3
HARDY, John Crumpton 1
HARDY, John Henry 1
HARDY, Joseph Johnston 1
HARDY, Josiah H
HARDY, Kenneth 5
  Burnham
HARDY, Lamar 3
HARDY, Le Grand Haven 1
HARDY, Marjorie 2
HARDY,
  Martha Eugenia Sidebottom
  (Mrs. Donald Hardy)
HARDY, Mary Earle 1
HARDY, Oscar J. 3
HARDY, Ralph W. 3
HARDY, Robert Marion 4
HARDY, Rufus 1
HARDY, Samuel H
HARDY, Summers 1
HARDY, Thomas Walter 4
HARDY, 1
  Warren Follansbee
HARDY, William Edwin 1
HARE,
  Arley Munson (Mrs. James
  A.)
HARE, Clifford LeRoy 2
HARE, Darius Dodge H
HARE, Emlen Spencer 4
HARE, George Andrew 1
HARE, George Emien H
HARE, Hobart Amory 1
HARE, Hugh F. 2
HARE, James H. 2
HARE, James Madison 4
HARE, John Innes Clark 1
HARE, Marmaduke 3
HARE, Robert H
HARE, S. Herbert 4
HARE, William Hobart 1
HARER, William Benson 5
HARGADON, I. Leo 3
HARGER, Charles 3
  Moreau
HARGEST, 2
  William Milton
HARGIS, Thomas Frazier 1
HARGITT, 1
  Charles Wesley
HARGRAVE, 4
  Homer Pearson
HARGRAVE, Thomas
  Jean 4
HARGREAVES, 3
  John Morris
HARGREAVES, 5
  Richard T(heodore)
HARGROVE, 3
  Reginald Henry
HARGROVE, 1
  Robert Kennon
HARING, Alexander 3
HARING, Clarence Henry 4
HARING, 1
  Clarence Melvin
HARING, 5
  Douglas Gilbert
HARING, John H
HARING, Philip Erwin 5
HARISON, Beverly Drake 1
HARK, J. Max 1
HARKER, Catherine 1
HARKER, Joseph Ralph 1
HARKER, Oliver Albert 1
HARKER, Ray Clarkson 1
HARKEY, Simeon 5
  Walcher
HARKINS, 5
  Edward Francis
HARKINS, Henry Nelson 4
HARKINS, Matthew 1
HARKINS, 1
  William Draper
HARKNESS, Albert 1
HARKNESS, 1
  Albert Granger
HARKNESS, 1
  Charles William
HARKNESS, 1
  Edward Stephen
HARKNESS, 1
  Gordon Follette
HARKNESS, Harvey W. 1
HARKNESS, 1
  James Stewart
HARKNESS, William 1

HARKNESS, William Hale 3
HARL, Maple Talbot 3
HARLAN, Aaron H
HARLAN, Byron Berry 3
HARLAN, Campbell Allen 5
HARLAN, Edgar Rubey 1
HARLAN, George Cuvier 1
HARLAN, Henry David 2
HARLAN, James * H
HARLAN, James 1
HARLAN, James Elliott 1
HARLAN, James S. 1
HARLAN, John Marshall 5
HARLAN, John Marshall 1
HARLAN, John Maynard 1
HARLAN, Josiah H
HARLAN, Otis 1
HARLAN, Richard H
HARLAN,
  Richard Davenport 1
HARLAN, Rolvix 5
HARLAND, Edward 1
HARLAND, Henry 1
HARLAND, James
  Penrose 5
HARLAND, Thomas H
HARLEY,
  Charles Richard 1
HARLEY,
  Lewis Reifsneider 4
HARLING, W. Franke 3
HARLLEE, William Curry 5
HARLOW, Alvin Fay 4
HARLOW, Jean H
HARLOW, Jean 4
HARLOW, John Brayton 4
HARLOW, Louis Kinney 4
HARLOW, Ralph Volney 3
HARLOW,
  Richard Cresson 4
HARLOW, S. Ralph 5
HARLOW,
  Victor Emmanuel 3
HARLOW, William Burt 4
HARLOW, William Elam 3
HARLOW, William Page 1
HARMAN, Arthur Fort 2
HARMAN, Harvey Jones 5
HARMAN, Henry Elliott 1
HARMAN, Jacob
  Anthony 5
HARMAN, James Lewie 5
HARMAN, Pinckney
  Jones 1
HARMAN, Pinckney
  Jones 4
HARMANSON, John
  Henry H
HARMAR, Josiah H
HARMATI, Sandor 1
HARMELING, Henry 4
HARMELING,
  Stephen John 3
HARMER, Alfred C. 1
HARMON,
  Andrew Davidson 3
HARMON, Arthur Loomis 3
HARMON, Austin Morris 3
HARMON, Benjamin
  Smith 1
HARMON, Cameron 5
HARMON, Claude Moore 3
HARMON,
  Daniel Williams H
HARMON, Frank Wilson 1
HARMON, Harold Elliott 4
HARMON, Henry Gadd 4
HARMON, Hubert Reilly 5
HARMON, John Francis 3
HARMON, Judson 1
HARMON, Leo Clinton 5
HARMON,
  Miliard Fillmore 2
HARMON, Paul M. 4
HARMON, William Elmer 1
HARMONY, David Buttz 1
HARMS, John Henry 2
HARN, Orlando Clinton 3
HARNDEN,
  William Frederick H
HARNED, Perry L. 4
HARNED,
  Robert Ellsworth 5
HARNED, Thomas Biggs 4
HARNED, Virginia 1
HARNER, Nevin Cowger 3
HARNETT, Cornelius 1
HARNEY, George Edward 1
HARNEY, John Milton H
HARNEY, William Selby H
HARNLY, Andrew
  Hoerner 4
HARNO, Albert James 4
HAROLD, Raymond
  Paget 5
HAROUTUNIAN, Joseph 5
HARPER, Alexander H

HARPER, Carrie Anna 1
HARPER,
  Cornelius Allen 3
HARPER, Donald 3
HARPER, Earl Enyeart 4
HARPER, Edward
  Thomson 1
HARPER, Fletcher H
HARPER, Floyd Arthur 5
HARPER, Fowler Vincent 4
HARPER, Francis Jacob H
HARPER, George Andrew 1
HARPER, George McLean 1
HARPER,
  George Washington Finley 3
HARPER, H. Mitchell 4
HARPER, Harold 5
HARPER, Harry F. 2
HARPER, Harvey W. 3
HARPER, Henry Winston 2
HARPER, Ida Husted 1
HARPER, Jacob Chandler 1
HARPER, James * H
HARPER,
  James Patterson Jr. 1
HARPER, James R. 5
HARPER, John Adams H
HARPER, John Erasmus 1
HARPER, John Lyell 1
HARPER, Joseph Morrill 4
HARPER, Mary McKibbin 5
HARPER, Merritt Wesley 4
HARPER, Paul Tompkins 1
HARPER, Paul Vincent 2
HARPER, Robert Almer 4
HARPER, Robert Francis 1
HARPER, Robert Goodloe H
HARPER, Robert N. 1
HARPER, Robert S. 4
HARPER, Roland M. 4
HARPER,
  Samuel Northrup 2
HARPER,
  Samuel Williams 3
HARPER,
  Theodore Acland 2
HARPER, Thomas Henry 4
HARPER, William H
HARPER, William Allen 2
HARPER,
  William Rainey 4
HARPER,
  William St John 1
HARPER, William Wade 1
HARPHAM,
  Gertrude Tressel Rider 5
HARPSTER,
  Charles Melvin 1
HARPSTER, John Henry 4
HARPUR, Robert H
HARR, Luther 3
HARR, William R. 3
HARRAH,
  Charles Jefferson H
HARRAH,
  Charles Jefferson 4
HARRAH,
  William Ferguson 3
HARRAL, Jared Alphonso 4
HARRAL, Stewart 4
HARRE, T. Everett 2
HARRELD, John William 5
HARRELL, Alfred 1
HARRELL, Joel Ellis 5
HARRELL, John H
HARRELL,
  Linwood Parker 5
HARRELL, Mack 4
HARRELSON,
  John William 3
HARRER,
  Gustave Adolphus 2
HARRIES,
  George Herbert 1
HARRIGAN, Edward 1
HARRIGAN, Nolan 4
HARRIMAN, H. Alice 1
HARRIMAN, Alonzo
  Jesse 5
HARRIMAN,
  Charles Conant 2
HARRIMAN, Edward
  Avery 5
HARRIMAN, Edward
  Henry 4
HARRIMAN,
  Florence Jaffray 4
HARRIMAN, Frank Black 4
HARRIMAN,
  Frederick William 3
HARRIMAN,
  Henry Ingraham 3
HARRIMAN, Job 1
HARRIMAN, John Walter 5
HARRIMAN,
  Joseph Wright 2
HARRIMAN, Karl Edwin 4

HARRIMAN,
  Lewis Gildersleeve 5
HARRIMAN, Mary W. 1
HARRIMAN, Oliver 1
HARRIMAN,
  Raymond Davis 5
HARRIMAN, Walter H
HARRINGTON,
  Arthur William 4
HARRINGTON, Charles 1
HARRINGTON, Charles
  A. 5
HARRINGTON,
  Charles Kendall 1
HARRINGTON,
  Charles Medbury
HARRINGTON, David L. 4
HARRINGTON,
  Emerson Columbus 4
HARRINGTON,
  Francis Bishop 1
HARRINGTON,
  Francis Clark
HARRINGTON,
  Frank Annibal 3
HARRINGTON,
  George Bates 4
HARRINGTON,
  Harry Franklin 1
HARRINGTON, Henry
  Hill 4
HARRINGTON,
  Henry William H
HARRINGTON, John
  Lyle 2
HARRINGTON, John T. 1
HARRINGTON,
  John Thomas 2
HARRINGTON,
  John Walker 3
HARRINGTON, Joseph 5
HARRINGTON,
  Karl Pomeroy 4
HARRINGTON, Leon W. 4
HARRINGTON,
  Louis Clare 3
HARRINGTON,
  Mark Raymond 5
HARRINGTON,
  Mark Walrod H
HARRINGTON,
  Mark Walrod 4
HARRINGTON, Philip 2
HARRINGTON,
  Purnell Frederick 1
HARRINGTON,
  Russell Chase 5
HARRINGTON,
  Samuel Maxwell H
HARRINGTON,
  Samuel Milby 2
HARRINGTON,
  Stuart William 5
HARRINGTON, Thomas
  F. 3
HARRINGTON,
  Thomas Francis
HARRINGTON,
  Vincent Francis 2
HARRINGTON,
  William Watson 5
HARRINGTON, Willis F. 4
HARRIOTT, Frank 4
HARRIS,
  Abram Lincoln 1
HARRIS,
  Abram Winegardner
HARRIS, Addison C. 1
HARRIS, Agnes Ellen 3
HARRIS, Albert Hall 1
HARRIS, Albert Mason 2
HARRIS,
  Albert Wadsworth 5
HARRIS, Alexander 5
HARRIS, Alfred F. 2
HARRIS, Alfred S. 1
HARRIS,
  Amanda Bartlett 1
HARRIS, Andrew Lintner 1
HARRIS, Arthur Emerson 3
HARRIS, Arthur I. 4
HARRIS, Arthur M. 1
HARRIS, Arvil Ernest 1
HARRIS, Basil 2
HARRIS, Benjamin H
HARRIS, Benjamin Bee 4
HARRIS,
  Benjamin Franklin 1
HARRIS, Benjamin Gwinn H
HARRIS, Beverly Dabney 2
HARRIS,
  Bravid Washington
HARRIS, Caleb Fiske H
HARRIS, Carlton Danner 1
HARRIS, Chapin Aaron 1
HARRIS, Charles 2
HARRIS, Charles Butler

HARRIS,
  Charles Cuthbert 4
HARRIS, Charles Joseph 2
HARRIS, Charles K. 1
HARRIS, Charles Murray H
HARRIS,
  Charles Tillman Jr. 4
HARRIS, Charles Willis 3
HARRIS, Christopher C. 4
HARRIS,
  Cicero Richardson 1
HARRIS, Corra May 1
HARRIS, Credo Fitch 3
HARRIS, Daniel Lester H
HARRIS, Dawson Bailey 3
HARRIS, Duncan G. 4
HARRIS, Edwin Ewell 2
HARRIS, Elijah Paddock 1
HARRIS, Elisha H
HARRIS, Ella Isabel 5
HARRIS, Emerson Pitt 1
HARRIS, Eugene Dennis 5
HARRIS, Everett Earl 3
HARRIS, Frank 1
HARRIS,
  Franklin Stewart 4
HARRIS,
  Frederic Robert 2
HARRIS,
  Frederick Brown 5
HARRIS, Garrard 1
HARRIS, George 1
HARRIS, George B. 1
HARRIS, George Barnes 5
HARRIS,
  George Ellsworth 4
HARRIS, George Simmons 2
HARRIS, George Stiles 3
HARRIS, George Upham 5
HARRIS, George Waldo 3
HARRIS,
  George Washington H
HARRIS, George William 1
HARRIS, George William 3
HARRIS,
  Gilbert Dennison
HARRIS, Guy W(alter) 5
HARRIS, Hamilton 1
HARRIS, Heaton W. 4
HARRIS,
  Henry Burkhardt 1
HARRIS,
  Henry Fauntleroy 4
HARRIS, Henry Hiter 3
HARRIS,
  Henry Tudor Brownell
HARRIS, Herbert Eugene 5
HARRIS, Hugh Henry 5
HARRIS, Ira H
HARRIS, Isham Green 1
HARRIS, J. Andrews Jr. 1
HARRIS, J. Arthur 2
HARRIS, James A. 2
HARRIS, James Coffee 1
HARRIS, Joel Chandler 1
HARRIS, John * H
HARRIS, John Andrews 3
HARRIS, John Augustus 3
HARRIS, John Burke 5
HARRIS, John Harper 5
HARRIS, John Howard 4
HARRIS, John Peter 5
HARRIS, John Royall 1
HARRIS, John Warton 3
HARRIS, John Woods H
HARRIS, Joseph 1
HARRIS, Joseph 1
HARRIS, Joseph B. 4
HARRIS,
  Joseph Hastings
HARRIS, Joseph Smith 1
HARRIS, Julia Collier 5
HARRIS, Julian LaRose 4
HARRIS, Lancelot Minor 4
HARRIS,
  Leslie Huntington 2
HARRIS, Loe A. 2
HARRIS, Louis Israel 1
HARRIS, Louis Marshall 3
HARRIS, M. Anstice 1
HARRIS,
  Malcolm LaSalle
HARRIS, Mark H
HARRIS, Mary Belle 3
HARRIS, Mattie Powell 5
HARRIS, Maurice Henry 1
HARRIS, May 1
HARRIS,
  Merriman Colbert
HARRIS, Miriam Coles 4
HARRIS, Montefiore M. 3
HARRIS, Morris Bedford 2
HARRIS, Moses H
HARRIS, Moses Henry 1
HARRIS, Mrs. Ralph A. 3
HARRIS,
  Nathaniel Edwin 1

HARRIS, Newton Megrue 5
HARRIS, Norman Dwight 5
HARRIS, Norman W. 4
HARRIS, Norman Wait 1
HARRIS, Overton 1
HARRIS, Paul Percy 2
HARRIS, Peter Charles 3
HARRIS, Philip H. 3
HARRIS, Pierce 5
HARRIS, Ralph Scott 4
HARRIS, Reese Harvey 3
HARRIS, Robert H
HARRIS, Robert Alfred 1
HARRIS, Robert Le Roy 2
HARRIS, Robert Orr 1
HARRIS, Rollin Arthur 1
HARRIS, Ruth Miriam 5
HARRIS, Sam H. 1
HARRIS, Sampson Willis H
HARRIS, Samuel H
HARRIS, Samuel 1
HARRIS, Samuel Henry 1
HARRIS, Samuel Smith H
HARRIS, Seale 3
HARRIS,
  Sherwin Bentley 5
HARRIS, Stanley G. 5
HARRIS, Thaddeus Mason H
HARRIS,
  Thaddeus William H
HARRIS, Thomas Green 4
HARRIS,
  Thomas Jefferson 2
HARRIS, Thomas K. H
HARRIS,
  Thomas Langrell H
HARRIS, Thomas
  LeGrand 1
HARRIS, Thomas Luther 4
HARRIS, Titus Holliday 5
HARRIS, Townsend H
HARRIS, Uriah Rose 1
HARRIS, Victor 5
HARRIS, W. Hall 1
HARRIS, W. John 3
HARRIS, Wade Hampton
HARRIS, Wade N. 5
HARRIS,
  Walter Alexander 3
HARRIS, Walter Butler 1
HARRIS, Walter Edward 1
HARRIS, Walter William 3
HARRIS, Wiley Pope
HARRIS, William H
HARRIS, William Jr. 2
HARRIS,
  William Alexander H
HARRIS,
  William Alexander 1
HARRIS,
  William Alexander
HARRIS,
  William Charles 1
HARRIS,
  William Fenwick 1
HARRIS, William Julius 1
HARRIS, William Laurel 1
HARRIS,
  William Littleton H
HARRIS, William Logan H
HARRIS, William Torrey 1
HARRIS, William Welton 1
HARRIS, Willis Overton 1
HARRIS, Winder Russell 5
HARRISON,
  Albert Galliton
HARRISON, Alexander 1
HARRISON,
  Alfred Craven, Jr. 5
HARRISON, B. George 3
HARRISON,
  Belle Richardson 4
HARRISON, Benjamin H
HARRISON, Benjamin 1
HARRISON, Benjamin 5
HARRISON,
  Benjamin Franklin 4
HARRISON,
  Benjamin Inabnit
HARRISON, Birge 1
HARRISON,
  Carter Bassett H
HARRISON, Carter Henry H
HARRISON, Carter Henry 3
HARRISON, Charles A. 3
HARRISON,
  Charles Custis
HARRISON, Charles Yale 3
HARRISON, Christopher H
HARRISON,
  Constance Cary 1
HARRISON, DeSales 5
HARRISON, Earl Grant 3
HARRISON, Edith Ogden 3
HARRISON, Edward
  Tyler 4
HARRISON, Edwin 1
HARRISON, Elizabeth 1
HARRISON, Fairfax 1

* Indicates More Than One Such Name Listed

HARRISON, Floyd Reed 4
HARRISON, 3
Francis Burton
HARRISON, Fred 1
HARRISON, Gabriel 1
HARRISON, 5
George Billingsley
HARRISON, George L. 3
HARRISON, 1
George McGregor
HARRISON, 1
George Moffett
HARRISON, George Paul 4
HARRISON, Gessner H
HARRISON, Hall 1
HARRISON, Hamlett 5
HARRISON, Harry P. 5
HARRISON, 2
Harvey Thomas
HARRISON, Henry
Sydnor
HARRISON, H
Horace Harrison
HARRISON, Ida Withers 4
HARRISON, Ike H(enry) 5
HARRISON, James H
HARRISON, James Albert 1
HARRISON, James D. 5
HARRISON, James Jabez 1
HARRISON, 4
Jamison Richard
HARRISON, John H
HARRISON, John B. 2
HARRISON, John Ellis 4
HARRISON, John Green 1
HARRISON, John Higgins 5
HARRISON, John Scott H
HARRISON, John Smith 5
HARRISON, 1
, Jonathan Baxter
HARRISON, Joseph H
HARRISON, 3
Joseph Le Roy
HARRISON, Leland 3
HARRISON, Leon 1
HARRISON, 4
Lester Stanley
HARRISON, Luther 3
HARRISON, Lynde 1
HARRISON, Mark Robert H
HARRISON, 1
Mary Scott Lord
HARRISON, 3
Maurice Edward
HARRISON, 2
Milton Whately
HARRISON, 1
Orla Ellsworth
HARRISON, Pat 5
HARRISON, Peleg Dennis 4
HARRISON, Perry G. 3
HARRISON, Peter H
HARRISON, 1
Ralph Chandler
HARRISON, Ray 3
HARRISON, 4
Raymond Leyden
HARRISON, 1
Richard Almgill
HARRISON, Richard B. 1
HARRISON, 1
Roland Rathbun
HARRISON, 4
Roland Wendell
HARRISON, 3
Ross Granville
HARRISON, 1
Russell Benjamin
HARRISON, Samuel
Smith H
HARRISON, 5
Shelby Millard
HARRISON, 4
Stephen Noble
HARRISON, 2
Thomas Perrin
HARRISON, 1
Thomas Skelton
HARRISON, 4
Thomas Walter
HARRISON, W. Vernon 1
HARRISON, 4
Walter Munford
HARRISON, Ward 5
HARRISON, William Jr. H
HARRISON, 2
William Benjamin
HARRISON, 5
William Groce
HARRISON, H
William Henry
HARRISON, 3
William Henry *
HARRISON, 4
William Mortimer
HARRISON, William Pope H

HARRISON, 1
William Preston
HARRISON, 1
William Robert
HARRISON, Zadok 4
Daniel
HARRITY, 1
William Francis
HARROD, 1
Benjamin Morgan
HARROD, James H
HARROFF, Fred F. 3
HARROLD, 2
Charles Cotton
HARROLD, Orville 1
HARRON, Marion Janet 5
HARROP, 1
George Argale Jr.
HARROP, 4
Leslie DeVottie
HARROW, Benjamin 5
HARRY, Joseph Edward 2
HARSH, David Newby 1
HARSH, James Birney 1
HARSH, Philip Whaley 4
HARSHA, 2
William McIntire
HARSHA, William
Thomas 3
HARSHAW, William
Jacob 4
HARSHBARGER, 4
William Asbury
HARSHBERGER, 1
John William
HARSHE, 1
Robert Bartholow
HARSON, M. Joseph 1
HARSTROM, Carl Axel 1
HART, Abraham H
HART, Albert Bushnell 2
HART, Alden Leonard 1
HART, 1
Archibald Chapman
HART, Boies Chittenden 2
HART, Burdett 1
HART, Charles A. 3
HART, Charles Arthur 3
HART, Charles Edward 1
HART, Charles Henry 1
HART, Edmund Hall 1
HART, Edward 1
HART, Edward J. 4
HART, Edward Payson 3
HART, Edwin Bret 3
HART, Elizur Kirke 1
HART, Emanuel Bernard H
HART, Ernest Eldred 1
HART, Frances Noyes 2
HART, Francis Russell 4
HART, 1
Franklin Augustus
HART, Freeman H. 4
HART, George H. 3
HART, George Overbury 1
HART, H. Martyn 1
HART, Harris 5
HART, Hastings Hornell 4
HART, Henry Clay 4
HART, Henry Hersch; 5
HART, 5
Henry Melvin, Jr.
HART, Hornell 4
HART, Howard Stanley 1
HART, Irving Harlow 3
HART, James A. 3
HART, James MacDougall 1
HART, James Morgan 1
HART, James Norris 1
HART, Jerome Alfred 1
HART, Jesse Cleveland 4
HART, Joel Tanner H
HART, John H
HART, John Francis 4
HART, John Marion 5
HART, John Nathaniel 1
HART, John Seely H
HART, John William 4
HART, Joseph Kinmont 2
HART, Lasher 1
HART, Lorenz 1
HART, Louis Bret 1
HART, Louis Folwell 4
HART, Luke Edward 4
HART, Marion Weddell 1
HART, Merwin Kimball 4
HART, Michael James 3
HART, Moss 4
HART, Oliver Philip 3
HART, 5
Percie (William Edward)
HART, Ringgold 5
HART, Roswell H
HART, Samuel 1
HART, Simeon Thompson 4
HART, Sophie Chantal 2
HART, Theodore Stuart 3

HART, Thomas Charles 5
HART, Thomas Norton 4
HART, Thomas Patrick 5
HART, Walter Morris 5
HART, William H
HART, William H. 1
HART, 4
William Henry Harrison
HART, William Lee 3
HART, William Lincoln 5
HART, William Michael 4
HART, William Octave 4
HART, William Richard 4
HART, William S. 2
HARTE, Bret 5
HARTE, Emmet Forrest 5
HARTE, Houston 5
HARTE, Richard 5
HARTE, Richard Hickman 4
HARTE, Thomas John 4
HARTENSTEIN, 4
Robert Franklin
HARTER, Dow W(atters) 5
HARTER, George Abram 5
HARTER, Isaac 3
HARTER, J. Francis 5
HARTER, Michael Daniel H
HARTFIELD, 4
John McCallum
HARTFIELD, 4
Joseph Manuel
HARTFORD, 1
Fernando Wood
HARTFORD, H
George Huntington
HARTFORD, 4
George Huntington
HARTFORD, George L. 3
HARTFORD, John A. 3
HARTHORN, 5
Drew Thompson
HARTIGAN, 2
Charles Conway
HARTIGAN, 5
Raymond Harvey
HARTINGER, 5
William Calvert
HARTLEY, 5
Charles Pinckney
HARTLEY, Ellis Taylor 1
HARTLEY, Eugene Fuller 4
HARTLEY, Frank 5
HARTLEY, 5
Fred Allan, Jr.
HARTLEY, Harold H. 4
HARTLEY, 4
Henry Alexander Saturnin
HARTLEY, 1
Isaac Smithson
HARTLEY, James Joseph 2
HARTLEY, 1
Jonathan Scott
HARTLEY, Leslie Poles 5
HARTLEY, Lowrie C. 5
HARTLEY, 5
Robert Willard
HARTLEY, Roland H. 3
HARTLEY, Thomas H
HARTMAN, Carl G. 4
HARTMAN, Charles S. 1
HARTMAN, 5
Charles William
HARTMAN, 1
Douglas William
HARTMAN, Edwin
Mitman 2
HARTMAN, Ernest
Herman 5
HARTMAN, 5
Frank Alexander
HARTMAN, Gertrude 3
HARTMAN, Harold
Hoover 4
HARTMAN, 4
Harvey Clarence
HARTMAN, Henry 4
HARTMAN, 3
Howard Russell
HARTMAN, Jesse L. 1
HARTMAN, John A. 5
HARTMAN, John Clark 1
HARTMAN, John Peter 2
HARTMAN, Lee Foster 1
HARTMAN, Leon Wilson 2
HARTMAN, Lewis Oliver 3
HARTMAN, Louis Francis 5
HARTMAN, Louis H. 5
HARTMAN, Sara 5
HARTMAN, 5
Siegfried Frisch
HARTMANN, Alexis 4
HARTMANN, F. M. 1
HARTMANN, George W. 3
HARTMANN, 2
Jacob Wittmer

HARTMANN, 5
Carl) Sadakichi
HARTMANN, William V. 5
HARTNESS, James 1
HARTNEY, Harold Evans 2
HARTRANFT, 1
Chester David
HARTRANFT, H
John Frederick
HARTRATH, Lucie 4
HARTREE, 3
Douglas Rayner
HARTRIDGE, 4
Clifford Wayne
HARTRIDGE, 2
Emelyn Battersby
HARTRIDGE, John Earle 1
HARTRIDGE, Julian 5
HARTS, William Wright 4
HARTSFIELD, 5
William Berry
HARTSHORN, 1
William Henry
HARTSHORN, 1
William Newton
HARTSHORNE, Charles 1
HARTSHORNE, 1
Charles Hopkins
HARTSHORNE, Henry H
HARTSHORNE, Hugh 4
HARTSUFF, Albert 1
HARTSUFF, George
Lucas H
HARTT, H
Charles Frederick
HARTT, 3
George Montgomery
HARTT, Mary Bronson 5
HARTT, Rollin Lynde 2
HARTUNG, 5
Albert Michael
HARTWELL, 4
Alfred Stedman
HARTWELL, Burt Laws 4
HARTWELL, 1
Edward Mussey
HARTWELL, Ernest Clark 4
HARTWELL, Henry
Walker 3
HARTWELL, 1
John Augustus
HARTWELL, 3
Shattuck Osgood
HARTWICH, Herman 2
HARTWIG, H
Johann Christoph
HARTY, Jeremiah J. 1
HARTZ, William Homer 5
HARTZELL, Charles 1
HARTZELL, J. Culver 1
HARTZELL, Joseph Crane 1
HARTZELL, 5
Milton Bixler
HARTZELL, Thomas B. 5
HARTZLER, Henry Burns 4
HARTZLER, 5
John Ellsworth
HARTZOG, Henry Simms 4
HARTZOG, Justin R. 5
HARVARD, John H
HARVEY, Alexander 2
HARVEY, Andrew Magee 3
HARVEY, 1
Basil Coleman Hyatt
HARVEY, Byron 5
HARVEY, 1
Byron Schermerhorn
HARVEY, Charles Henry 1
HARVEY, Charles Milton 5
HARVEY, 1
Charles Mitchell
HARVEY, Daniel Robert 4
HARVEY, Edmund
Newton 3
HARVEY, Eli 3
HARVEY, Ethel Browne 1
HARVEY, Ford 1
HARVEY, 1
Frederick Loviad
HARVEY, George H
HARVEY, George 5
HARVEY, 1
George Cockburn
HARVEY, George U. 2
HARVEY, Harold Brown 5
HARVEY, H
Haywood Augustus
HARVEY, Holman 5
HARVEY, Horace 3
HARVEY, I. J. Jr. 4
HARVEY, James Madison H
HARVEY, Jean Charles 5
HARVEY, John (Lacey) 5
HARVEY, Jonathan 1
HARVEY, Kenneth G. 5
HARVEY, Lawson Moreau 1
HARVEY, LeRoy 1

HARVEY, 5
Lillian A. (mrs. Raymond
F. Harvey)
HARVEY, Lorenzo Dow 1
HARVEY, Louis Powell H
HARVEY, Matthew 2
HARVEY, Paul 2
HARVEY, Philip Francis 5
HARVEY, Ralph Hicks 3
HARVEY, Ray Forrest 2
HARVEY, Rodney
Beecher 2
HARVEY, 2
Roland Bridendall
HARVEY, Rowland Hill 5
HARVEY, Samuel Clark 3
HARVEY, Sir John 5
HARVEY, 5
W(illiam) W(est)
HARVEY, William Edwin 5
HARVEY, William Hope 5
HARVEY, William Lemuel 4
HARVEY, 4
William Patrick
HARVEY, William Riggs 3
HARVIE, John H
HARVIE, John Bruce 1
HARVIE, Peter Lyons 2
HARWOOD, Andrew
Allen H
HARWOOD, Charles 3
HARWOOD, 4
Charles McHenry
HARWOOD, Cole Leslie 1
HARWOOD, Edwin 1
HARWOOD, Frank James 1
HARWOOD, 1
George Alexander
HARWOOD, John H
HARWOOD, John E. H
HARWOOD, Thomas A. 4
HARWOOD, 1
William Sumner
HARZA, Leroy Francis 3
HASBROUCK, H
Abraham Bruyn
HASBROUCK, H
Abraham Joseph
HASBROUCK, Alfred 1
HASBROUCK, 1
Charles Alfred
HASBROUCK, 1
Gilbert D. B.
HASBROUCK, H
Henry Cornelius
HASBROUCK, Josiah H
HASBROUCK, Lydia
Sayer H
HASBROUCK, Lydia
Sayer 4
HASCALL, H
Augustus Porter
HASCALL, Milo Smith 1
HASCALL, Wilbur 1
HASCHE, 3
Rudolph Leonard
HASE, 5
William Frederick
HASELDEN, Kyle
Emerson 5
HASELTINE, Burton 1
HASELTINE, George 4
HASELTINE, Herbert 5
HASELTINE, 4
Nathan Stone
HASELTON, Page Smith 5
HASELTON, Seneca 4
HASEMAN, Charles 2
HASENCLEVER, Peter H
HASKELL, 1
Charles Nathaniel
HASKELL, 1
Clinton Howard
HASKELL, Dudley Chase H
HASKELL, Earl Stanley 5
HASKELL, Edward
Howard 1
HASKELL, 4
Edwin Bradbury
HASKELL, H
Ella Louise Knowles
HASKELL, 1
Ella Louise Knowles
HASKELL, Eugene Elwin 1
HASKELL, 5
Freda Rew (Mrs. George S.
Haskell)
HASKELL, 1
Frederick Tudor
HASKELL, Glenn Leach 5
HASKELL, 1
Harold Clifford
HASKELL, 1
Harriet Newell
HASKELL, Harry Garner 3
HASKELL, Harry Leland 5

HAYCRAFT, 5
Julius Everette
HAYDEN, Amos Sutton H
HAYDEN, 4
Arthur Gunderson
HAYDEN, Austin Albert 1
HAYDEN, 5
Carl (Trumbull)
HAYDEN, Charles 1
HAYDEN, Charles H. 1
HAYDEN, Charles Sidney 1
HAYDEN, Edward 1
Everett
HAYDEN, H
Ferdinand Vandiveer
HAYDEN, Frank 1
HAYDEN, 4
Frederick Smith
HAYDEN, Horace Edwin 1
HAYDEN, Horace H. 1
HAYDEN, Jay G. 5
HAYDEN, Joel Babcock 2
HAYDEN, John Louis 1
HAYDEN, Joseph H
HAYDEN, Joseph Ralston 2
HAYDEN, Josiah Willard 3
HAYDEN, Moses H
HAYDEN, Philip Cady 1
HAYDEN, Velma Denison 4
HAYDEN, Warren 1
Sherman
HAYDEN, William 1
HAYDN, Hiram Collins 1
HAYDOCK, George
Sewell 5
HAYDON, Glen 4
HAYES, Alfred 4
HAYES, Anson 4
HAYES, Arthur Badley 2
HAYES, Augustus Allen H
HAYES, C. Willard 1
HAYES, 4
Carlton Joseph Huntley
HAYES, Charles Harris 1
HAYES, Clifford Barron 4
HAYES, Daniel Webster 1
HAYES, David J. A. 3
HAYES, Doremus Almy 1
HAYES, Edward Arthur 3
HAYES, Edward Cary 1
HAYES, Edward Mortimer 1
HAYES, Ellen 1
HAYES, Everis Anson 1
HAYES, Francis Little 1
HAYES, 4
Frederick Albert
HAYES, George Miller 3
HAYES, Hammond Vinton 4
HAYES, Harold M. 4
HAYES, 5
Harvey Cornelius
HAYES, Henry 4
HAYES, Henry Reed 3
HAYES, Isaac Israel 1
HAYES, James Edward 2
HAYES, James Leo 5
HAYES, Jay Orley 1
HAYES, John Herman 4
HAYES, John Lord 1
HAYES, John Russell 3
HAYES, John William 1
HAYES, Johnson Jay 5
HAYES, Joseph H
HAYES, Joseph P.; 5
HAYES, Lucy Webb H
HAYES, 5
Mary Sanders (Mrs. William Henry Hayes);
HAYES, Max S. 2
HAYES, Montrose W. 1
HAYES, Myron J. 1
HAYES, Patrick Joseph 1
HAYES, Philip 2
HAYES, 1
Philip Cornelius
HAYES, R.S. 5
HAYES, H
Rutherford Birchard
HAYES, Samuel Perkins 3
HAYES, Samuel Walter 1
HAYES, Simeon Mills 4
HAYES, Stephen Quentin 1
HAYES, Thomas Gordon 1
HAYES, Thomas Sumner 1
HAYES, Wade Hampton 3
HAYES, Warren Howard 1
HAYES, Watson McMillan 1
HAYES, 5
Wayland J(ackson)
HAYES, Webb Cook 1
HAYES, Webb Cook II 3
HAYFORD, John Fillmore 1
HAYGOOD, Atticus
Green H
HAYGOOD, Laura Askew H
HAYHOW, Edgar Charles 3
HAYHURST, Emery Roe 4

HAYKIN, David Judson 3
HAYLER, Guy Wilfrid 5
HAYLEY, John William 1
HAYMAKER, Jesse N. 1
HAYMAN, Al 1
HAYMOND, Frank Cruise 5
HAYMOND, Thomas S. 5
HAYMOND, H
Thomas Sherwood
HAYMOND, H
William Summerville
HAYNE, H
Arthur Peronneau
HAYNE, Coe 5
HAYNE, Isaac 1
HAYNE, James Adams 5
HAYNE, Paul Hamilton H
HAYNE, Robert Young 1
HAYNE, 1
William Hamilton
HAYNER, Rutherford 1
HAYNES, Arthur Edwin 1
HAYNES, 4
Benjamin Rudolph
HAYNES, 3
Carlyle Boynton
HAYNES, Charles Eaton 1
HAYNES, Daniel H. 3
HAYNES, David Oliphant 1
HAYNES, Eli Stuart 1
HAYNES, 3
Elizabeth A. Ross
HAYNES, Elwood 1
HAYNES, Emory James 1
HAYNES, Evan 3
HAYNES, Fred Emory 4
HAYNES, George
Edmund 1
HAYNES, George Henry 2
HAYNES, 5
Harley A(rmand)
HAYNES, 1
Henry Williamson
HAYNES, Ira Allen 3
HAYNES, Irving Samuel 2
HAYNES, John H
HAYNES, John Randolph 1
HAYNES, Joseph Walton 5
HAYNES, Justin O'Brien 5
HAYNES, Myron Wilbur 1
HAYNES, 1
Nathaniel Smith
HAYNES, Robert Blair 3
HAYNES, Rowland 4
HAYNES, Roy Asa 5
HAYNES, Thornwell 3
HAYNIE, Henry 1
HAYS, Alexander H
HAYS, Arthur Alexander 3
HAYS, Arthur Garfield 1
HAYS, Calvin Cornwell 1
HAYS, Charles H
HAYS, Charles Melville 1
HAYS, Charles Thomas 2
HAYS, Daniel Peixotto 1
HAYS, Edde K. 4
HAYS, Edward D. 1
HAYS, Edward Retilla H
HAYS, Elmer D. 1
HAYS, Frank Lazmer 3
HAYS, Frank W. 1
HAYS, 1
George Washington
HAYS, Harry Thompson H
HAYS, Howard H. 5
HAYS, I. Minis 5
HAYS, Isaac H
HAYS, Jack Newton 5
HAYS, John 1
HAYS, John Coffee 1
HAYS, Margaret Gebbie 1
HAYS, Mortimer 4
HAYS, Samuel H
HAYS, Samuel Lewis H
HAYS, Silas B. 4
HAYS, Walter Lee 4
HAYS, Will H. 4
HAYS, Willet Martin 4
HAYS, William Charles 4
HAYS, William Jacob H
HAYS, William Jacob 1
HAYS, 1
William Shakespeare
HAYT, Charles D. 1
HAYWARD, 1
Benjamin Dover
HAYWARD, 1
Edward Farwell
HAYWARD, Florence 1
HAYWARD, Fred Preston 5
HAYWARD, George H
HAYWARD, Harry 1
HAYWARD, Harry Taft 1
HAYWARD, Joseph H
HAYWARD, 1
Warren
HAYWARD, Monroe
Leland 1

HAYWARD, Nathan 2
HAYWARD, H
Nathaniel Manley
HAYWARD, Ralph A. 3
HAYWARD, 5
Walter Brownell
HAYWARD, William 2
HAYWARD, William Jr. H
HAYWARD, William
Leete 3
HAYWOOD, Allen S. 3
HAYWOOD, Harry
LeRoy H
HAYWOOD, John H
HAYWOOD, John Kerfoot 1
HAYWOOD, John Wilfred 5
HAYWOOD, Marshall, Jr. 5
HAYWOOD, 1
Marshall De Lancey
HAYWOOD, H
William Dudley
HAYWOOD, 4
William Dudley
HAYWOOD, H
William Henry Jr.
HAZARD, H
Augustus George
HAZARD, Caroline 2
HAZARD, Clifton T. 4
HAZARD, Daniel Lyman 3
HAZARD, Ebenezer H
HAZARD, 1
Frederick Rowland
HAZARD, Henry Bernard 3
HAZARD, Jonathan J. H
HAZARD, 1
Lauriston Hartwell
HAZARD, 1
Marshall Curtiss
HAZARD, Rowland
Gibson H
HAZARD, Rowland
Gibson 1
HAZARD, Samuel H
HAZARD, 3
Spencer Peabody
HAZARD, Thomas H
HAZARD, 5
Thomas Pierrepont
HAZARD, 1
Thomas Robinson
HAZARD, 3
Willis Hatfield
HAZEL, John Raymond 5
HAZELBAKER, 5
Norval Denver
HAZELIUS, Ernest Lewis 4
HAZELRIGG, 4
James Hervey
HAZELTINE, Abner H
HAZELTINE, Alan 4
HAZELTINE, 1
George Cochrane Jr.
HAZELTINE, 5
Harold Dexter
HAZELTINE, Horace 4
HAZELTINE, 2
Mary Emogene
HAZELTINE, 1
Mayo Williamson
HAZELTON, John H. 3
HAZELTON, John Wright H
HAZELWOOD, John H
HAZEN, Allen 1
HAZEN, Azel Washburn 1
HAZEN, Charles Downer 1
HAZEN, Henry Allen * 1
HAZEN, Henry
Honeyman 1
HAZEN, John Vose 1
HAZEN, Joseph Chalmers 4
HAZEN, 1
Marshman Williams
HAZEN, 4
Maynard Thompson
HAZEN, Moses H
HAZEN, William Babcock H
HAZEN, 2
William Livingston
HAZLETT, Harry Fouts 4
HAZLETT, Robert 1
HAZLETT, Samuel M. 3
HAZLEWOOD, Craig
Beebe 3
HAZZARD, Charles 1
HAZZARD, Jesse Charles 5
HAZZARD, John Edward 4
H'DOUBLER, 1
Francis Todd
HEACOCK, Frank Ahern 4
HEACOCK, Roger Lee 4
HEACOX, Arthur Edward 5
HEAD, Franklin Harvey 1
HEAD, Henry Oswald 1
HEAD, James Butler 1
HEAD, James Marshall 1
HEAD, James Milne 5

HEAD, John Benedict 1
HEAD, John Frazier 1
HEAD, Leon Oswald 4
HEAD, Mabel 5
HEAD, T. Grady 4
HEAD, Walter Dutton 4
HEAD, Walter William 3
HEAD, Walton O. 5
HEADDEN, 1
William Parker
HEADE, Martin Johnson H
HEADLAND, Isaac
Taylor 2
HEADLEE, Thomas J. 2
HEADLEY, Cleon 3
HEADLEY, Joel Tyler H
HEADLEY, John William 3
HEADLEY, Leal Aubrey 4
HEADLEY, Phineas Camp 1
HEADLEY, Roy 3
HEAFFORD, George
Henry 4
HEAL, Gilbert B. 3
HEALD, Daniel Addison 1
HEALD, 3
Frederick De Forest
HEALD, Kenneth Conrad 5
HEALD, William Henry 1
HEALE, Charles J. 2
HEALEY, Arthur Daniel 1
HEALEY, Charles C. 1
HEALEY, Michael J. 5
HEALY, A. Augustus 1
HEALY, Daniel Joseph 1
HEALY, 1
Daniel Ward, Jr.
HEALY, Ezra Anthony 1
HEALY, Fred Albert 2
HEALY, H
George Peter Alexander
HEALY, James Augustine 1
HEALY, Joseph H
HEALY, Patrick Joseph 1
HEALY, Robert E. 2
HEALY, Robert Wallace 1
HEALY, Thomas Henry 2
HEALY, William 3
HEANEY, John William 3
HEANEY, Noble Sproat 1
HEAP, David Porter 1
HEAP, Samuel Davies 1
HEAPS, William James 5
HEARD, Arthur Marston 1
HEARD, Augustine H
HEARD, Augustine 1
HEARD, Bill James 1
HEARD, Dwight Bancroft 1
HEARD, Franklin Fiske 1
HEARD, Gerald 5
HEARD, James Delavan 5
HEARD, Oscar Edwin 1
HEARD, William H. 1
HEARD, William Wright 1
HEARE, Clayton 5
HEARN, Clint Calvin 1
HEARN, David William 2
HEARN, Hardie B. 4
HEARN, Lafcadio H
HEARNE, Edward Dingle 1
HEARNE, John J(oseph) 5
HEARON, Charles Oscar 5
HEARST, Charles Ernest H
HEARST, George H
HEARST, 5
George Randolph, Sr.
HEARST, John Randolph 3
HEARST, 1
Phoebe Apperson
HEARST, 3
William Randolph
HEATH, Clyde J(ames) 5
HEATH, 1
Daniel Collamore
HEATH, Edwin Joseph 3
HEATH, Ferry Kimball 1
HEATH, Fred H. 1
HEATH, 1
Frederic Carroll
HEATH, Harold 3
HEATH, Hubert A. 4
HEATH, Hugh Austin 1
HEATH, James Ewell 1
HEATH, James P. H
HEATH, John H
HEATH, Perry Sanford 1
HEATH, S. Burton 2
HEATH, William H
HEATH, William Ames 4
HEATH, William Womack 5
HEATHCOTE, Caleb 1
HEATHCOTE, 4
Charles William
HEATLEY, Stuart Alden 4
HEATON, Arthur B. 3
HEATON,
Augustus Goodyear 1
HEATON, David H

HEATON, Harry Clifton 3
HEATON, Herbert 1
HEATON, John Langdon 1
HEATON, 3
Lucia Elizabeth
HEATON, Percy 5
HEATON, Robert Douglas 1
HEATWOLE, 1
Cornelius Jacob
HEATWOLE, 1
Joel Prescott
HEATWOLE, Lewis
James 1
HEATWOLE, 4
Timothy Oliver
HEAVEY, John William 2
HEBARD, Arthur Foster 2
HEBARD, Grace
Raymond 1
HEBDEN, John Calder 1
HEBEL, John William 1
HEBERT, Felix 1
HEBERT, Paul Octave H
HEBRARD, Jean 3
HECHT, Ben 3
HECHT, David Stanford 3
HECHT, Hans H. 5
HECHT, Julius Lawrence 3
HECHT, Moses S. 3
HECHT, Rudolf S. 3
HECHT, Selig 3
HECK, Barbara Ruckle H
HECK, Nicholas Hunter 3
HECK, 1
Robert Culbertson Hays
HECK, William Harry 1
HECKE, G. H. 4
HECKEL, 1
Edward Balthasar
HECKEL, George Baugh 1
HECKEL, Norris Julius 4
HECKER, Frank Joseph 1
HECKER, H
Friedrich Karl Franz
HECKER, Isaac Thomas H
HECKER, John Valentine 4
HECKERT, 1
Charles Girven
HECKERT, John Walter 3
HECKETT, Eric Harlow 1
HECKEWELDER, H
John Gottlieb Ernestus
HECKLER, Edwin Little 4
HECKMAN, James Robert 2
HECKMAN, Samuel B. 1
HECKMAN, Wallace 1
HECKSCHER, August 1
HECKSCHER, August 2
HECKSCHER, 1
Celeste Delongpre
HEDBACK, Axel Emanuel 3
HEDBLOM, Carl Arthur 1
HEDBROOKE, Andrew H
HEDENSTROM, Paul
Henry 5
HEDERMAN, T. M. 2
HEDGCOCK, George
Grant 1
HEDGE, Charles Gorham 1
HEDGE, Frederic Henry H
HEDGE, Frederic Henry 1
HEDGE, Henry Rogers 5
HEDGE, Levi 1
HEDGE, Thomas 4
HEDGE, William Russell 2
HEDGES, 5
Benjamin Van Doren
HEDGES, Frank Hinckley 1
HEDGES, J. Edward 4
HEDGES, James Blaine 3
HEDGES, Job Elmer 1
HEDGES, Joseph Harold 3
HEDGES, 3
Marion Hawthorne
HEDGES, 2
Samuel Hamilton
HEDLESTON, Winn
David 1
HEDLEY, Frank 3
HEDLY, Arthur Howard 1
HEDRICH, Kenneth 5
HEDRICK, Bayard
Murphy 4
HEDRICK, Charles Baker 3
HEDRICK, 3
Charles Embury
HEDRICK, E. H. 3
HEDRICK, Earle
Raymond 2
HEDRICK, Ira Grant 1
HEDRICK, Tubman Keene 5
HEDRICK, 3
Ulysses Prentiss
HEDRICK, Wyatt Cephas 4
HEDSTROM, Carl Oscar 5
HEDTOFT, Hans

HEEBNER, Charles 1
HEED, Thomas D. 3
HEEKIN, Albert Edward, Jr. 5
HEELAN, Edmond 2
HEELY, Allan Vanderhoef 3
HEENAN, John Carmel H
HEENEHAN, James T. 5
HEENEY, Arnold Danford Patrick 5
HEERMAN, Ritz Edwin 4
HEERMANCE, Edgar Laing 5
HEERMANN, Adolphus L. H
HEERMANS, Augustyn H
HEERMANS, Charles Abram 4
HEERMANS, Forbes 1
HEERMANS, Josephine Woodbury 4
HEES, William Rathbun 2
HEETER, Silvanus Laurabee 5
HEFELBOWER, Samuel Gring 3
HEFFELFINGER, Frank Totton 3
HEFFELFINGER, George W. P. 5
HEFFERAN, Thomas Hume 5
HEFFERAN, W. S. Jr. 4
HEFFERN, Andrew Duff 4
HEFFERNAN, James Joseph 4
HEFFRON, John Lorenzo 1
HEFFRON, Patrick Richard 1
HEFLIN, J. Thomas 3
HEFLIN, Van 5
HEFNER, Ralph A(ubrie) 5
HEFTY, Thomas R. 4
HEG, Elmer Ellsworth 4
HEGEMAN, John Rogers 1
HEGER, Anthony 1
HEGGEN, Thomas Orlo 2
HEGLAND, Martin 2
HEGNER, Bertha Hofer Mrs. 4
HEGNER, Robert William 2
HEHER, Harry 5
HEHIR, Martin A. 1
HEIDEL, William Arthur 4
HEIDER, Raphael 5
HEIDINGER, James Vandaveer 2
HEIDINGSFIELD, Myron S(amuel) 5
HEIKES, Victor Conrad 2
HEIL, Charles Emile 3
HEIL, Julius Peter 1
HEIL, William Franklin 1
HEILAND, Carl August 5
HEILBRONNER, Louis 5
HEILBRUNN, Lewis Victor 3
HEILEMAN, Frank A. 4
HEILIG, Sterling 4
HEILMAN, Fordyce R. 4
HEILMAN, Ralph Emerson 1
HEILMAN, Russell Howard 5
HEILMAN, William H
HEILMAN, William Clifford 2
HEILNER, Samuel 1
HEILNER, Van Campen 5
HEILPRIN, Angelo 1
HEILPRIN, Louis 1
HEILPRIN, Michael 1
HEIM, Herbert E. 5
HEIM, Jacques 4
HEIMANN, Henry Herman 3
HEIMBACH, Arthur E. 5
HEIMBACH, Howard Anders 5
HEIMERICH, John James 5
HEIMKE, William 1
HEIMROD, George 4
HEIN, Carl 2
HEIN, Carl Christian 1
HEIN, Otto Louis 4
HEIN, Walter Jacob 4
HEINBERG, John Gilbert 3
HEINDEL, Augusta Foss 4
HEINE, Peter Bernard William H
HEINEMAN, Walter Ben 1
HEINEMANN, E. 1
HEINER, Gordon Graham 2
HEINER, Moroni 5
HEINGARTNER, Robert Wayne 2

HEINICKE, Arthur John 5
HEINL, Robert D. 3
HEINLEIN, Mary Virginia 4
HEINMILLER, Louis Edward 1
HEINMULLER, John P. V. H
HEINO, Albert Frederic 3
HEINRICH, Antony Philip H
HEINRICH, Edward Oscar 3
HEINRICH, Wilhelm 1
HEINRICHS, Charles E. 4
HEINRICHS, Jacob 2
HEINROTH, Charles 5
HEINS, George Lewis 1
HEINSHEIMER, Edward Lewis 1
HEINSOHN, Alvin Frederick 5
HEINTZ, Philip Benjamin 2
HEINTZELMAN, Arthur William 4
HEINTZELMAN, Samuel Peter H
HEINTZELMAN, Stuart 1
HEINTZELMAN, Percival Stewart 1
HEINZ, Fred C. 4
HEINZ, Henry John 1
HEINZ, Howard 1
HEINZ, John Bernard 4
HEINZE, F. Augustus 1
HEINZE, Otto Charles 5
HEINZEN, Karl Peter H
HEISCHMANN, John J. 1
HEISE, Fred H. 2
HEISEL, Thomas Bayard 1
HEISEN, Aaron Jonah 5
HEISER, Victor George 3
HEISERMAN, Clarence Benjamin 3
HEISING, Raymond Alphonsus 4
HEISKELL, Frederick Hugh 1
HEISKELL, Henry Lee 1
HEISKELL, John Netherland 5
HEISKELL, Samuel G. 1
HEISLER, John Clement 1
HEISS, Austin Elmer 1
HEISS, Gerson Kirkland 5
HEISS, Marion Welch 1
HEISS, Michael H
HEISSENBUTTEL, John diedrich 4
HEISTAND, Henry Olcot Sheldon 1
HEITFELD, Henry 1
HEITMAN, Charles Easton 3
HEITMAN, Francis Bernard 4
HEITSCHMIDT, Earl T. 5
HEIZER, Oscar Stuart 4
HEIZMANN, Charles Lawrence 4
HEKKING, William Mathews 5
HEKMA, Jacob 2
HEKMAN, John 3
HEKTOEN, Ludvig 3
HELBRON, Peter H
HELBURN, Theresa 3
HELD, Anna 1
HELD, John Jr. 3
HELDER, H. A. 3
HELFEN, Mathias 3
HELFENSTEIN, Edward Trail 2
HELFENSTEIN, Ernest H
HELFFENSTEIN, John Albert Conrad H
HELGESEN, Henry T. 1
HELLAND, Andreas 5
HELLBAUM, Arthur Alfred 4
HELLEMS, Fred Burton Renney 1
HELLENTHAL, John Albertus 2
HELLER, A. Arthur 4
HELLER, Edmund 1
HELLER, Edward Hellman 4
HELLER, Florence Grunsfeld 5
HELLER, Frank Henry 5
HELLER, Frank Morley 5
HELLER, George 3
HELLER, Helen West 3
HELLER, James Gutheim 5
HELLER, Joseph Milton 2

HELLER, Maximilian 1
HELLER, Otto 1
HELLER, Victor H. 4
HELLER, Walter E. 5
HELLER, William 4
HELLIER, Charles Edward 1
HELLINGER, Ernst David 2
HELLINGER, Mark 2
HELLMAN, F. J. 4
HELLMAN, George Sidney 3
HELLMAN, Isias William 1
HELLMAN, Isias William Jr. 1
HELLMAN, Maurice S. 4
HELLMAN, Milo 2
HELLMUND, Rudolph Emil 2
HELLSTROM, Carl Reinhold 4
HELM, Harry Sherman 2
HELM, Harvey 1
HELM, James Meredith 1
HELM, John Charles H
HELM, John Larue H
HELM, Joseph Church 1
HELM, Nelson 4
HELM, Roy 3
HELM, Thaddeus Geary 4
HELM, Thomas Kennedy 1
HELM, Wilbur 5
HELM, William P. 3
HELMER, B. Bradwell 1
HELMER, Frank Ambrose 1
HELMHOLZ, Henry Frederic 3
HELMICK, Eli Alva 2
HELMICK, Milton John 3
HELMICK, William H
HELMING, Oscar Clemens 1
HELMLE, Frank J. 1
HELMPRAECHT, Joseph 1
HELMS, Edgar James 4
HELMS, Elmer Ellsworth 3
HELMS, Paul Hoy 3
HELMS, William H
HELMSLEY, William H
HELMUTH, Justus Henry Christian 1
HELMUTH, William Tod 1
* 1
HELPER, Hinton Rowan 1
HELPMAN, Dell A. 1
HELSER, Albert D. 5
HELSER, Maurice David 3
HELTMAN, Harry Joseph 4
HELVERING, Guy Tresillian 2
HELYAR, Frank G. 4
HEMANS, Lawton Thomas 1
HEMBDT, Phil Harold 1
HEMBORG, Carl August 4
HEMENWAY, Alfred 1
HEMENWAY, Augustus 1
HEMENWAY, Charles Clifton 5
HEMENWAY, Charles Reed 2
HEMENWAY, Henry Bixby 1
HEMENWAY, Herbert Daniel 2
HEMENWAY, James Alexander 1
HEMENWAY, Mary Porter Tileston H
HEMING, Arthur 1
HEMINGTON, Francis 2
HEMINGWAY, Allan 5
HEMINGWAY, Ernest 4
HEMINGWAY, Harold Edgar 1
HEMINGWAY, Harry J. 4
HEMINGWAY, James S. 4
HEMINGWAY, Samuel Burdett 3
HEMINGWAY, Walter Clarke 3
HEMINGWAY, Wilson Edwin 1
HEMINGWAY, Wilson Linn 3
HEMLEY, Cecil 4
HEMLEY, Cecil 5
HEMLEY, Samuel 5
HEMMETER, Henry Bernard 2
HEMMETER, John Conrad 1
HEMPEL, Charles Julius H
HEMPEL, Frieda 3
HEMPHILL, Alexander Julian 1

HEMPHILL, Charles Robert 1
HEMPHILL, Clifford 4
HEMPHILL, James Calvin 1
HEMPHILL, John H
HEMPHILL, John James 1
HEMPHILL, Joseph H
HEMPHILL, Joseph Newton 1
HEMPHILL, Victor Herman 3
HEMPHILL, William Arnold 1
HEMPHILL, William P. 4
HEMPL, George 1
HEMPSTEAD, Clark 3
HEMPSTEAD, Edward H
HEMPSTEAD, Fay 1
HEMRY, Charles W. 4
HEMSTREET, Charles 4
HENCH, Jay Lyman 4
HENCH, Philip Showalter 4
HENCHMAN, Daniel H
HENCK, John Benjamin 4
HENDEE, George Ellsworth 1
HENDEL, John William H
HENDERLITE, James Henry 3
HENDERSON, Alexander Iselin 4
HENDERSON, Alfred Edwin; 5
HENDERSON, Archibald 1
HENDERSON, Archibald 4
HENDERSON, Bennett H. H
HENDERSON, Byrd Everett 4
HENDERSON, C. Hanford 1
HENDERSON, Charles 1
HENDERSON, Charles Belknap 3
HENDERSON, Charles English 1
HENDERSON, Charles J. 4
HENDERSON, Charles Richmond 1
HENDERSON, Charles William 2
HENDERSON, Daniel 3
HENDERSON, David 1
HENDERSON, David Bremner 1
HENDERSON, David English H
HENDERSON, Earl C. 3
HENDERSON, Edward 5
HENDERSON, Eldon Hazelton 1
HENDERSON, Elmer Lee 3
HENDERSON, Ernest 4
HENDERSON, Ernest Flagg 1
HENDERSON, Ernest Norton 1
HENDERSON, George Bunsen 5
HENDERSON, George Logan 4
HENDERSON, Gerard C. 5
HENDERSON, Grace Mildred 5
HENDERSON, Helen Weston 5
HENDERSON, Howard Andrew Millet
HENDERSON, Isaac 4
HENDERSON, James Fletcher
HENDERSON, James Henry Dickey H
HENDERSON, James Monroe 4
HENDERSON, James Pinckney
HENDERSON, John H
HENDERSON, John Armstrong 1
HENDERSON, John Brooks *
HENDERSON, John H. 4
HENDERSON, John Joseph 1
HENDERSON, John Moreland 1
HENDERSON, John Steele 3
HENDERSON, John Thompson
HENDERSON, Joseph H
HENDERSON, Joseph Lindsey 4
HENDERSON, Joseph W. 3
HENDERSON, Junius 1

HENDERSON, Kenneth Manning 5
HENDERSON, Lawrence Joseph 1
HENDERSON, Leland John 1
HENDERSON, Leon N. 4
HENDERSON, Leonard H
HENDERSON, Lizzie George 4
HENDERSON, Mary N. Foote
HENDERSON, Melvin Starkey 3
HENDERSON, Peronneau Finley 5
HENDERSON, Peter H
HENDERSON, Philip Eldon 3
HENDERSON, Richard H
HENDERSON, Robert 2
HENDERSON, Robert 2
HENDERSON, Robert Burns 1
HENDERSON, Robert Miller 1
HENDERSON, Samuel H
HENDERSON, Theodore Sommers 1
HENDERSON, Thomas H
HENDERSON, Thomas Howard 5
HENDERSON, Thomas Jefferson
HENDERSON, Thomas Stalworth 1
HENDERSON, Walter Brooks Drayton 2
HENDERSON, Walter C. 3
HENDERSON, William D. 2
HENDERSON, William James 1
HENDERSON, William Olin
HENDERSON, William Penhallow 2
HENDERSON, William Price 2
HENDERSON, William Thomas 5
HENDERSON, William Williams
HENDERSON, Yandell 2
HENDLER, L. Manuel 4
HENDREN, Paul 3
HENDREN, William Mayhew 1
HENDRICK H
HENDRICK, Archer Wilmot 1
HENDRICK, Burton Jesse 4
HENDRICK, Calvin Wheeler
HENDRICK, Ellwood 1
HENDRICK, Frank 5
HENDRICK, Ives 5
HENDRICK, John Thilman 2
HENDRICK, Michael J. 1
HENDRICK, Peter Aloysius 1
HENDRICK, Thomas Augustine 4
HENDRICK, William Jackson 5
HENDRICKS, Allan Barringer, Jr. 5
HENDRICKS, Eldo Lewis 1
HENDRICKS, Francis 4
HENDRICKS, Ira King 5
HENDRICKS, Thomas Andrews H
HENDRICKS, Thomas Armstrong 2
HENDRICKS, William H
HENDRICKSON, Charles Elvin 1
HENDRICKSON, George Lincoln 4
HENDRICKSON, Homer O. 3
HENDRICKSON, Robert C. 4
HENDRICKSON, William Woodbury 1
HENDRIX, Eugene Russell 1
HENDRIX, Jimi 5
HENDRIX, Joseph Clifford 1
HENDRIX, William Samuel 2
HENDRIXSON, Walter Scott 1
HENDRYX, James Beardsley 4

899

HERVEY, Walter Lowrie 3
HERVEY, 1
  William Addison
HERVEY, William Rhodes 3
HERZBERG, Max J. 3
HERZIG, Charles Simon 1
HERZOG, Anna Edes 3
HERZOG, Felix Benedict 1
HERZOG, 1
  Maximilian Joseph
HERZSTEIN, Joseph 5
HESCHEL, 5
  Abraham Joshua
HESLIN, Thomas 1
HESS, Alfred Fabian
HESS, Elmer 4
HESS, Finley B. 5
HESS, Frank L. 5
HESS, Franklin 1
HESS, Harry Hammond 5
HESS, Henry 1
HESS, Herbert William 2
HESS, Jerome Sayles 5
HESS, Julius Hays 3
HESS, Leslie Elsworth 3
HESS, Max 5
HESS, Myra 5
HESS, Victor Francis 4
HESS, 5
  Wendell Frederick
HESSBERG, Albert 1
HESSBERG, Irving Kapp 2
HESSE, Bernard Conrad 1
HESSE, Frank McNeil 3
HESSE, Hermann 5
HESSE, Seymour David 4
HESSELBERG, 1
  Edouard Gregory
HESSELIUS, Gustavus H
HESSELIUS, John H
HESSELTINE, 4
  William Best
HESSER, 3
  Frederic William
HESSLER, John Charles 2
HESSLER, William Henry 4
HESTER, Clinton Monroe 5
HESTER, John Kenton 1
HESTER, St Clair 1
HESTER, William 1
HESTER, William John 3
HESTER, 1
  William Van Arden
HESTON, J(ohn) Edgar 5
HESTON, John William 1
HETERICK, 3
  Robert Hynton
HETERICK, 5
  Vincent Richard
HETH, Henry H
HETHERINGTON, 1
  John Edwin
HETLER, Donald McK 3
HETTINGER, 4
  Frederick C.
HETTRICK, 5
  Elwood Harrison
HETZEL, Ralph Dorn 2
HETZLER, Howard
  George 1
HETZLER, Theodore
HEUCHLING, Fred G. 5
HEUER, George J. 3
HEUER, John Harland 5
HEUER, William Henry 4
HEUSER, Emil 4
HEUSER,
  Frederick William Justus
HEUSER, Gustave A. 5
HEUSNER, 5
  William Samuel
HEUSS, John 4
HEUSS, Theodor 4
HEUSTIS, 4
  Charles Herbert
HEVESY, George 'de 4
HEWAT, Alexander H
HEWE, Laurence Ilsey 4
HEWES, Amy 5
HEWES, Clarence Bussey 4
HEWES, Fletcher Willis 1
HEWES, Joseph 3
HEWES, M. Lewin 1
HEWES, Robert H
HEWES, Thomas 4
HEWETSON, H. H. 5
HEWETT, Donnel Foster 5
HEWETT, Edgar Lee 2
HEWETT, Edwin
  Crawford 1
HEWETT, Hobart 4
HEWETT, 1
  Waterman Thomas
HEWETT, 4
  William Wallace
HEWETT-THAYER, 4
  Harvey Waterman

HEWINS, Caroline Maria 1
HEWIT, H
  Augustine Francis
HEWITT, A. 2
HEWITT, Abram Stevens 1
HEWITT, 1
  Charles Nathaniel
HEWITT, 3
  Clarence Horace
HEWITT, 3
  Edward Ringwood
HEWITT, Edward Shepard 4
HEWITT, Edwin Hawley 1
HEWITT, Emma
  Churchman 4
HEWITT, Erastus Henry 5
HEWITT, Erskine 1
HEWITT, Fayette 1
HEWITT, George Ayres 4
HEWITT, H
  Goldsmith Whitehouse
HEWITT, H. Kent 5
HEWITT, Harvey 3
HEWITT, Henry Jr. 1
HEWITT, Herbert
  Edmund 2
HEWITT, James H
HEWITT, John Haskell 5
HEWITT, John Hill H
HEWITT, 4
  John Napoleon Brinton
HEWITT, Joseph William 5
HEWITT, 4
  Leland Hazelton
HEWITT, Ogden Blackfan 4
HEWITT, Peter Cooper 1
HEWITT, Richard Miner 5
HEWITT, Theodore Brown 3
HEWITT, William 1
HEWITT, William Keesey H
HEWLETT, A. Walter 2
HEWLETT, James Howell 3
HEWLETT, James Monroe 1
HEWSON, Addinell 1
HEXAMER, Charles John 1
HEXNER, Ervin Paul 5
HEXTER, Irving Bernard 4
HEXTER, Joseph 3
HEYBURN, 1
  Weldon Brinton
HEYDECKER, 4
  Edward Le Moyne
HEYDLER, Charles 5
HEYDON, Henry Darling 1
HEYDRICK, 5
  Benjamin Alexander
HEYDT, Herman A. 1
HEYE, Carl T. 2
HEYE, George Gustav 3
HEYER, H
  John Christian Frederick
HEYL, Bernard Chapman 4
HEYL, Paul Renno 5
HEYMAN, Clarence
  Henry 4
HEYMANN, Edgar 5
HEYMANN, Hans 2
HEYMANS, 5
  Corneille (Jean)
  (Francois)
HEYMSFELD, Ralph Taft 5
HEYNE, Maurice 5
HEYNE, Roland 4
HEYNS, Garrett 5
HEYROVSKY, Jaroslav 4
HEYSHAM, Theodore 1
HEYSINGER, 4
  Isaac Winter
HEYWARD, Dorothy 4
HEYWARD, DuBose 1
HEYWARD, Duncan
  Clinch 2
HEYWARD, Thomas H
HEYWOOD, Abbot
  Rodney 4
HEYWOOD, Alba 1
HEYWOOD, Albert
  Samuel 1
HEYWOOD, Charles 1
HEYWOOD, Ezra Hervey 4
HEYWOOD, Gene Bryant 5
HEYWOOD, Levi H
HEYWORTH, James
  Omerod 1
HIACOOMES H
HIATT, Walter Sanders 3
HIBBARD, Addison 2
HIBBARD, 5
  Aldro Thompson
HIBBARD, Angus Smith 2
HIBBARD, 3
  Benjamin Horace
HIBBARD, Carlisle V. 3
HIBBARD, 4
  David Sutherland
HIBBARD, Ellery Albee 1
HIBBARD, Frank 3

HIBBARD, 3
  Frederick Cleveland
HIBBARD, H
  Freeborn Garrettson
HIBBARD, George 1
HIBBARD, George Albee 5
HIBBARD, H. Wade 4
HIBBARD, 5
  Rufus Percival
HIBBEN, John Grier 1
HIBBEN, Paxton 1
HIBBEN, 1
  Samuel Galloway
HIBBERD, 1
  James Farquhar
HIBBINS, Ann H
HIBBS, Harold Dickson 5
HIBBS, Henry C. 2
HIBSHMAN, Jacob H
HICHBORN, Franklin 5
HICHBORN, Philip 1
HICKAM, John Bamber 5
HICKENLOOPER, 1
  Andrew
HICKENLOOPER, 5
  Bourke Blakemore
HICKENLOOPER, Smith 1
HICKERNELL, 4
  Latimer Farrington
HICKEY, Andrew J. 2
HICKEY, James Burke 1
HICKEY, 3
  Jeremiah Griffin
HICKEY, John F. 4
HICKEY, John Joseph 5
HICKEY, 3
  Joseph Aloysious
HICKEY, Lee Cole 5
HICKEY, Leo J. 1
HICKEY, 5
  Matthew (Joseph, Jr.
HICKEY, Philip J. 4
HICKEY, 1
  Preston Manasseh
HICKEY, Turner Paul 5
HICKEY, 1
  William Augustine
HICKLING, D. Percy 4
HICKMAN, Adam Clark 1
HICKMAN, 3
  Cuthbert Wright
HICKMAN, Emily 2
HICKMAN, 1
  Eugene Christian
HICKMAN, 3
  Herman Michael
HICKMAN, John H
HICKMAN, John Edward 4
HICKMAN, Norman 3
HICKMAN, 4
  William Howard
HICKOK, Charles Thomas 3
HICKOK, James Butler H
HICKOK, H
  Laurens Perseus
HICKOK, Paul Robinson 2
HICKOK, Ralph Kiddoo 2
HICKOX, Ralph W. 1
HICKS, Ami Mali 5
HICKS, Clarence John 2
HICKS, 5
  Clifford E(rving)
HICKS, Douglas Mallory 4
HICKS, Edward H
HICKS, Elias H
HICKS, Francis Marion 4
HICKS, Frank M. 3
HICKS, 3
  Frederick Charles
HICKS, Frederick Cocks 1
HICKS, George 4
HICKS, Hanne John 5
HICKS, John 1
HICKS, John Donald 5
HICKS, Joseph Emerson 5
HICKS, Joseph Winstead 4
HICKS, Josiah Duane 4
HICKS, 3
  Lawrence Emerson
HICKS, Leonard 4
HICKS, Lewis Ezra 4
HICKS, Marshall 1
HICKS, Robert Emmet 5
HICKS, Thomas H
HICKS, Thomas E. 4
HICKS, Thomas Holliday H
HICKS, Thomas Holliday 3
HICKS, W. B. 5
HICKS, William Arthur 3
HICKS, William Minor 5
HICKS, Wilson 3
HICKS, Xenophon 3
HICKSON, William James 5
HIDDEN, William Earl 1
HIDER, Arthur 5
HIEBERT, Joelle C. 2

HIEBERT, 4
  Peter Cornelius
HIERONYMUS, 2
  Robert Enoch
HIERONYMUS, 3
  William Peter
HIESTAND, 5
  Edgar Willard
HIESTAND, Jean Carter 3
HIESTAND, John Andrew H
HIESTER, Anselm Vinet 1
HIESTER, Daniel * H
HIESTER, H
  Isaac Elimaker
HIESTER, John H
HIESTER, Joseph 1
HIESTER, William H
HIGBEE, Albert Enos 1
HIGBEE, Harry 1
HIGBEE, Irving Jackson 3
HIGBIE, Carlton M. 5
HIGBIE, 2
  Edgar Creighton
HIGBIE, 1
  Robert Winfield
HIGBY, Chester Penn 4
HIGBY, Gilbert C. 3
HIGBY, William H
HIGGINBOTHAM, 4
  Alfred Leslie
HIGGINBOTTOM, Sam 3
HIGGINS, A. Foster 1
HIGGINS, Aldus Chapin 1
HIGGINS, Alice Louise 1
HIGGINS, 1
  Allan Herbert Webster
HIGGINS, 1
  Alvin McCaslin
HIGGINS, 3
  Andrew Jackson
HIGGINS, Anthony 1
HIGGINS, 2
  Archibald Thomas
HIGGINS, Charles H. 4
HIGGINS, 4
  Charles Melbourne
HIGGINS, Daniel Paul 3
HIGGINS, Edward 1
HIGGINS, Edwin Werter 1
HIGGINS, 1
  Elmore Fitzpatrick
HIGGINS, Eugene 3
HIGGINS, Francis G. 4
HIGGINS, Frank James 1
HIGGINS, Frank Wayland 1
HIGGINS, 3
  George Frederick
HIGGINS, George
  Thomas 5
HIGGINS, Harry B. 4
HIGGINS, 4
  Herbert Newton
HIGGINS, James Bennett 5
HIGGINS, James Henry 1
HIGGINS, John Clark 3
HIGGINS, John Patrick 3
HIGGINS, John W. 4
HIGGINS, John Wilfred 5
HIGGINS, Joseph 2
HIGGINS, 1
  Katharine Elizabeth Chapin
HIGGINS, Marguerite 4
HIGGINS, Milton Prince 1
HIGGINS, 1
  Richard Thomas
HIGGINS, 1
  Robert Barnard
HIGGINS, 4
  Robert William
HIGGINS, 4
  Rodney Gonzales
HIGGINS, Samuel 4
HIGGINS, 5
  Stanley Carmen, Jr.
HIGGINS, Victor 2
HIGGINS, 1
  William Edward
HIGGINS, 3
  William Lincoln
HIGGINSON, Ella 1
HIGGINSON, Francis H
HIGGINSON,
  Francis John
HIGGINSON, Francis Lee 5
HIGGINSON, Francis Lee 1
HIGGINSON, Henry Lee 1
HIGGINSON, John H
HIGGINSON,
  Mary P. Thacher
HIGGINSON, Nathaniel H
HIGGINSON, Stephen H
HIGGINSON,
  Thomas Wentworth
HIGH, Robert King 4
HIGH, Stanley 5
HIGHFILL, Robert David 4
HIGHLAND, Cecil Blaine 3

HIGHLAND, Virgil Lee 1
HIGHSMITH, J. Henry 3
HIGHSMITH, 1
  Jacob Franklin
HIGHT, Clarence Albert 2
HIGHTOWER, Emmett 1
HIGHTOWER, 5
  Louis Victor
HIGHTOWER, Robert E. 4
HIGHTOWER, 2
  William Harrison
HIGINBOTHAM, 1
  Harlow Niles
HIGINBOTHAM, John U. 1
HIGLEY, 2
  Adelbert Pankey
HIGLEY, Albert Maltby 5
HIGLEY, Brodie Gilman 2
HIGLEY, Cyrus Martin 5
HIGLEY, Henry Grant 5
HIGLEY, Miles M. 3
HIGLEY, Walter Maydole 5
HIGLEY, Warren 1
HILAND, James H. 1
HILBERSEIMER, 4
  Ludwig Karl
HILBRANT, 5
  Robert Edward
HILBUN, Ben Frank 4
HILD, Frederick Henry 5
HILD, Oscar F. 3
HILDEBRAND, 2
  Daniel Munroe
HILDEBRAND, H.
  Edward 4
HILDEBRAND, Ira Polk 2
HILDEBRAND, 1
  Jesse Richardson
HILDEBRANDT, Fred H. 4
HILDEBRANDT, 4
  Harvey Thornton
HILDEBRANDT, Howard
  L. 3
HILDEBRANT,
  Charles Quinn
HILDEBURN, 1
  Charles Swift Riche
HILDER, Howard 1
HILDER, John Chapman 1
HILDINGER, 4
  Wade Wheeler
HILDRETH, 1
  David Merrill
HILDRETH, 4
  Harold Mowbray
HILDRETH, John Lewis 1
HILDRETH, Joseph S. 5
HILDRETH, 2
  Melvin Andrew
HILDRETH, Melvin Davis 3
HILDRETH, Richard H
HILDRETH, H
  Samuel Prescott
HILDRETH,
  William Sobieski
HILDT, John Coffey 1
HILDUM, Clayton
  Edward 3
HILGARD,
  Eugene Woldemar
HILGARD, H
  Ferdinand Heinrich Gustav
HILGARD,
  Julius Erasmus
HILGARTNER, 1
  Henry Louis
HILKEY, Charles Joseph 4
HILL, Adams Sherman 1
HILL, Agnes Leonard 1
HILL, Albert Hudgins 1
HILL, Albert Ross 2
HILL, Alferd J. 3
HILL, Alfred Gibson 5
HILL, Ambrose Powell H
HILL, Arthur Dehon 2
HILL, Arthur Edward 1
HILL, Arthur Joseph 4
HILL, Arthur Middleton 5
HILL, Arthur Turnbull 1
HILL, Bancroft 3
HILL, Benjamin Harvey H
HILL, Bert Hodge 3
HILL, Carlton 5
HILL, Carolyn Bailey 4
HILL, Charles 4
HILL, Charles Edward 1
HILL, Charles Leander 3
HILL, Charles Lewis 3
HILL, Charles Shattuck 1
HILL, 5
  Chester James, Jr.
HILL, Claiborne Milton 3
HILL, Claude Eugene 3
HILL, Clyde Milton 4
HILL, Crawford 1
HILL, Daniel Harvey H
HILL, Daniel Harvey

HILL, David Bennett 1
HILL, David Garrett 5
HILL, David Jayne 1
HILL, David Spende 3
HILL, Eben Clayton M. D.
HILL, Ebenezer J. 1
HILL, Edgar Preston 1
HILL, Edward Burlingame 4
HILL, Edward Curtis 4
HILL, Edward Gurney 1
HILL, Edward Llewellyn 3
HILL, Edward Yates 1
HILL, Edwin Conger 3
HILL, Emory 1
HILL, Ernest Rowland 2
HILL, Ernest W. 4
HILL, Ernie 3
HILL, Felix Robertson, Jr. 5
HILL, Charles) Francis 5
HILL, Frank Alpine 1
HILL, Frank Davis 1
HILL, Frank Ernest 1
HILL, Frank Pierce 4
HILL, Fred Burnett 1
HILL, Frederic Stanhope H
HILL, Frederic Stanhope 4
HILL, Frederick Sinclair 3
HILL, Frederick Thayer 5
HILL, Frederick Trevor 1
HILL, G. Albert 4
HILL, George Alfred Jr. 2
HILL, George Andrews 1
HILL, George Anthony 1
HILL, George Griswold 1
HILL, George Handel H
HILL, George Washington 1
HILL, George William * 1
HILL, Gershom Hyde 1
HILL, Grace Livingston 2
HILL, Grover Bennett 4
HILL, Harold O. 1
HILL, Harry Granison 3
HILL, Harry Harrison 4
HILL, Harry W. 5
HILL, Henry Albert 4
HILL, Henry Alexander 4
HILL, Henry Barker 1
HILL, Henry Clarke 3
HILL, Henry Wayland 4
HILL, Herbert Wynford 1
HILL, Hiram Warner 1
HILL, Horace Greeley 2
HILL, Howard Copeland 1
HILL, Hugh Lawson White H
HILL, Irving 5
HILL, Isaac H
HILL, Isaac William 4
HILL, J. B. P. Clayton 1
HILL, J. Gilbert 1
HILL, J. Murray 4
HILL, J. Stacy 1
HILL, James H
HILL, James 4
HILL, James Jr. 3
HILL, James Brents 3
HILL, James Ewing 1
HILL, James J. 1
HILL, James Langdon 1
HILL, James Michael 4
HILL, James Norman 1
HILL, James Perminter 3
HILL, James W. 1
HILL, Janet McKenzie 1
HILL, Joe H
HILL, Joe 4
HILL, John * H
HILL, John A. 3
HILL, John Alexander 1
HILL, John Edward 1
HILL, John Ethan 4
HILL, John Fremont 1
HILL, John Godfrey 5
HILL, John Henry H
HILL, John Lindsay 4
HILL, John Sprunt 1
HILL, John Wesley 1
HILL, John William H
HILL, Joseph Adna 1
HILL, Joseph Henry 1
HILL, Joseph Knoerle 5
HILL, Joseph Morrison 1
HILL, Joseph St Clair 1
HILL, Joshua H
HILL, Judson Sudborough 1
HILL, Julien Harrison 2
HILL, Knute 5
HILL, Lamar 1

HILL, Laurance Landreth 1
HILL, Leslie Pinckney 3
HILL, Louis A. 4
HILL, Louis Clarence 1
HILL, Louis Warren 2
HILL, Lysander 1
HILL, Mabel Jones 3
HILL, Marion 1
HILL, Mark Langdon H
HILL, Max 2
HILL, Mozell Clarence 5
HILL, Mrs. Caroline Miles 3
HILL, Nathaniel Peter 1
HILL, Nathaniel Peter 1
HILL, Noble 4
HILL, Norman Stewart 5
HILL, Owen Aloysius 1
HILL, Owen Duffy 1
HILL, Patty Smith 2
HILL, Percival Smith 1
HILL, Pierre Bernard 3
HILL, Ralph Waldo Snowden 3
HILL, Randolph William 3
HILL, Reese Franklin 5
HILL, Reuben L. 3
HILL, Richard H
HILL, Robert Andrews H
HILL, Robert Carmer 2
HILL, Robert E. Lee 1
HILL, Robert Potter 1
HILL, Robert Thomas 1
HILL, Robert William 4
HILL, Rolla Bennett 1
HILL, Roscoe R. 4
HILL, Samuel 1
HILL, Sherwin A. 4
HILL, Theophilus Hunter 1
HILL, Thomas H
HILL, Thomas 1
HILL, Thomas Edie 1
HILL, Thomas Guthrie Franklin 1
HILL, Tom Burbridge 3
HILL, Ureli Corelli H
HILL, Vassie James 3
HILL, Walker 1
HILL, Walter Barnard 1
HILL, Walter Clay 4
HILL, Walter Henry 1
HILL, Walter Newell 3
HILL, Warren E. 4
HILL, Whitmel H
HILL, William 1
HILL, William A. 1
HILL, William Austin 1
HILL, William Bancroft 2
HILL, William Edwin 1
HILL, William Free 1
HILL, William H. 5
HILL, William Henry 1
HILL, William Henry 1
HILL, William S. 1
HILL, William Silas 5
HILL, Wilson Shedric 1
HILLARD, Charles W. 1
HILLARD, George Stillman H
HILLARD, Mary Robbins 1
HILLAS, Robert M. 3
HILLBRAND, Earl K. 4
HILLE, Gustav 4
HILLE, Hermann 4
HILLEARY, Edgar D. 5
HILLEBRAND, Harold Newcomb 3
HILLEBRAND, William Francis 1
HILLEGAS, Howard Clemens 1
HILLEGAS, Michael H
HILLEN, Solomon Jr. H
HILLENMEYER, Louis Edward 4
HILLER, Alfred 3
HILLER, Hiram Milliken 1
HILLES, Charles Dewey 1
HILLES, Frederick Vantyne Holbrook 5
HILLES, William Samuel 1
HILLHOUSE, James H
HILLHOUSE, James Abraham H
HILLHOUSE, William 1
HILLIARD, Benjamin Clark 3
HILLIARD, Benjamin Clark, Jr. 5
HILLIARD, Curtis Morrison 5
HILLIARD, Francis H
HILLIARD, Henry Washington H
HILLIARD, Isaac 5

HILLIARD, John Northern 1
HILLIARD, Raymond Marcellus 4
HILLIARD, Robert Cochran 1
HILLIARD, Thomas C. 4
HILLINGER, Raymond Peter 5
HILLIS, David H
HILLIS, Mrs. Newell Dwight 1
HILLIS, Newell Dwight 3
HILLMAN, Alex L. 5
HILLMAN, James Frazer 5
HILLMAN, John Hartwell Jr. 3
HILLMAN, John William 5
HILLMAN, Lucy Rosaltha 4
HILLMAN, Sidney 2
HILLMAN, William 4
HILLQUIT, Morris 1
HILLS, Ada A. 4
HILLS, Elijah Clarence 1
HILLS, Franklin Grant 4
HILLS, Joseph Lawrence 5
HILLS, Laura Coombs 3
HILLS, Laurence 1
HILLS, Lewis Samuel 1
HILLS, Oscar Armstrong 3
HILLS, Richard Charles 1
HILLS, Victor Gardiner 1
HILLS, William Henry 1
HILLYER, H. Stanley 3
HILLYER, Homer Winthrop 2
HILLYER, Junius H
HILLYER, Robert Silliman 4
HILLYER, Thomas Arthur 4
HILLYER, Virgil Mores 1
HILLYER, William Hurd 4
HILMER, William Charles 5
HILPRECHT, Herman Volrath 1
HILSBERG, Alexander 4
HILSON, Edwin I. 3
HILTMAN, John Wolfe 1
HILTON, Alexander 1
HILTON, Clifford L. 2
HILTON, David Clark 2
HILTON, Henry Hoyt 2
HILTON, Hugh Gerald 5
HILTON, James 3
HILTON, Warren 3
HIMES, Charles Francis H
HIMES, Charles Francis 3
HIMES, John Andrew 1
HIMES, Joseph Hendrix 4
HIMES, Joshua Vaughan H
HIMES, Norman Edwin 2
HIMLER, Leonard E. 5
HIMMEL, Joseph 1
HIMMELBLAU, David 4
HIMMELWRIGHT, Abraham Lincoln Artman H
HIMSTEAD, Ralph E. 3
HIMSWORTH, Winston E. 5
HINCKLE, William 4
HINCKLEY, Allen Carter 3
HINCKLEY, Edwin Smith 2
HINCKLEY, Frank Erastus 3
HINCKLEY, Frank L. 3
HINCKLEY, Frederic Allen 1
HINCKLEY, Frederick Wheeler 1
HINCKLEY, George Lyman 1
HINCKLEY, George W. 4
HINCKLEY, Robert 1
HINCKLEY, Thomas 1
HINCKS, Carroll Clark 4
HINCKS, Clarence Meredith 4
HINCKS, Edward Young 1
HINDEMITH, Paul 4
HINDERLIDER, Michael Creed 1
HINDLE, Norman Frederick 4
HINDLEY, George 1
HINDLEY, Howard Lister 2
HINDMAN, Albert Clare 1
HINDMAN, Baker Michael 1
HINDMAN, James Edward 4
HINDMAN, Thomas Carmichael H
HINDMAN, William H
HINDMARSH, Harry Comfort 3
HINDS, Anthony Keith 4

HINDS, Asher Crosby 1
HINDS, Ernest 1
HINDS, Frederick Wesley 2
HINDS, Henry 4
HINDS, James H
HINDS, John Iredelle Dillard 1
HINDS, Thomas 1
HINDS, Warren Elmer 1
HINDS, William Alfred 1
HINDS, William Lawyer 1
HINDUS, Maurice Gerschon 5
HINE, Charles Daniel 1
HINE, Charles De Lane 1
HINE, Clint C. 1
HINE, Francis Lyman 1
HINEBAUGH, William Henry 1
HINERFELD, Benjamin 3
HINES, Charles 4
HINES, Duncan 1
HINES, Earle Garfield 4
HINES, Edgar Alphonso 1
HINES, Edward 1
HINES, Edward Norris 1
HINES, Edward Warren 1
HINES, Frank Thomas 3
HINES, Harry Matlock 1
HINES, James Kollock 1
HINES, John Fore 1
HINES, John Leonard 5
HINES, Laurence Edward 1
HINES, Linnaeus Neal 1
HINES, Murray Arnold 5
HINES, Ralph J. 3
HINES, Richard H
HINES, Walker Downer 1
HINGELEY, Joseph Beaumont 1
HINITT, Frederick William 1
HINKE, Frederick William 4
HINKE, William John 2
HINKLE, Beatrice M. 3
HINKLE, Elmer Forry 3
HINKLE, Frederick Wallis 3
HINKLE, James Fielding 4
HINKLE, Ross Oel 3
HINKLE, Thomas Clark 4
HINKLE, Thornton Mills 1
HINKLEY, Alonzo Gibbs 4
HINKLEY, H. Lawrence 1
HINKLEY, J. William Iii 4
HINKLEY, John 1
HINMAN, Alice Hamlin 1
HINMAN, Dale Durkee 3
HINMAN, E(dgar) Harold 5
HINMAN, Elisha 1
HINMAN, George Elijah 5
HINMAN, George Warren 1
HINMAN, George Wheeler 1
HINMAN, Harold J. 3
HINMAN, Harvey DeForest 3
HINMAN, Joel H
HINMAN, Russell 1
HINMAN, Thomas Philip 1
HINRICHS, Gustavus Detlef 1
HINRICHS, Gustavus Detlef 4
HINRICHSEN, Walter 5
HINRICHSEN, William H. 1
HINSCH, Charles Arthur 1
HINSDALE, Burke Aaron 1
HINSDALE, Ellen Clarinda 4
HINSDALE, Grace Webster 1
HINSDALE, Guy 2
HINSDALE, John Wetmore 1
HINSDALE, Wilbert B. 2
HINSHAW, Carl 3
HINSHAW, David 3
HINSHAW, Edmund Howard 4
HINSHAW, Joseph Howard 5
HINSHAW, Virgil Goodman 3
HINSHAW, William Wade 2
HINSHELWOOD, Sir Cyril (Norman) 5
HINSHELWOOD, Sir Cyril 4
HINSMAN, Carl B. 5
HINSON, M. R. 4
HINSON, Noel Bertram 3
HINSON, Walter Benwell 1

HINTON, Charles Louis 3
HINTON, Edward Wilcox 1
HINTON, H. D. 4
HINTON, Harold B. 3
HINTON, James William 5
HINTON, Raymond J. 3
HINTZ, Alfred Edward 4
HINTZ, Howard William 4
HIPPLE, Alpheus Hugh 1
HIPPLE, Frank K. 1
HIPSHER, Edward Ellsworth 2
HIPSLEY, Elmer R. 5
HIRE, Chas 1
HIRES, Charles Elmer H
HIRES, Charles Elmer 4
HIRES, Harrison Streeter 4
HIRONS, Frederic C. 1
HIRONS, Frederic Charles 2
HIRSCH, Alcan 1
HIRSCH, Edwin Frederick 5
HIRSCH, Emil Gustav 1
HIRSCH, Frank E. 1
HIRSCH, Gustav 3
HIRSCH, Harold 1
HIRSCH, Irene Dorothea 5
HIRSCH, Isaac E. 2
HIRSCH, John Frederick 1
HIRSCH, Julius 4
HIRSCH, Max 1
HIRSCHBERG, Michael Henry 1
HIRSCHBERG, Sanford Leon 4
HIRSCHFELD, Hans M. 1
HIRSCHFELDER, Arthur Douglass 2
HIRSCHFELDER, Joseph Oakland 1
HIRSCHHORN, Fred 2
HIRSCHLER, Frederic Salz 5
HIRSH, Herbert William 5
HIRSH, Hugo 1
HIRSHBERG, Herbert Simon 3
HIRSHBERG, Leonard Keene 5
HIRSHFELD, Clarence Floyd 1
HIRST, Barton Cooke 1
HIRST, Henry Beck H
HIRST, Robert Lincoln 4
HIRTH, Emma P. 1
HIRTH, Friedrich 1
HISAW, Frederick Lee 5
HISCOCK, Frank 1
HISCOCK, Frank Harris 2
HISE, Elijah H
HISGEN, Thomas Louis 1
HITCH, Arthur Martin 3
HITCH, Calvin Milton 5
HITCH, Robert Mark 1
HITCHCOCK, Abner Edward 4
HITCHCOCK, Albert Spear 1
HITCHCOCK, Alfred H
HITCHCOCK, Alfred Marshall 3
HITCHCOCK, Alvirus Nelson 4
HITCHCOCK, Caroline Hanks 4
HITCHCOCK, Charles A. 1
HITCHCOCK, Charles Baker 5
HITCHCOCK, Charles Henry 1
HITCHCOCK, Curtice 2
HITCHCOCK, Edward 1
HITCHCOCK, Edward Embury Asbury 2
HITCHCOCK, Enos H
HITCHCOCK, Ethan Allen H
HITCHCOCK, Ethan Allen 1
HITCHCOCK, Frank Harris 1
HITCHCOCK, Frank Lauren 3
HITCHCOCK, Frederick Collamore 1
HITCHCOCK, Frederick Hills 1
HITCHCOCK, George 1
HITCHCOCK, George Collier 5
HITCHCOCK, Gilbert Monell 1
HITCHCOCK, Henry

HITCHCOCK, Henry Booth 1
HITCHCOCK, Herbert E. 4
HITCHCOCK, 5
Lauren Blakely
HITCHCOCK, 2
Lucius Wolcott
HITCHCOCK, Peter H
HITCHCOCK, H
Phineas Warrener
HITCHCOCK, Ripley 1
HITCHCOCK, Romyn 4
HITCHCOCK, H
Roswell Dwight
HITCHENS, 2
Arthur Parker
HITCHLER, Theresa 3
HITCHLER, 3
Walter Harrison
HITE, Bert Holmes 1
HITE, George E. Jr. 3
HITE, Jost H
HITE, Lewis Field 2
HITER, Frank Ambrose 3
HITLER, Adolf
HITREC, Joseph George 5
HITT, R. S. Reynolds 1
HITT, 5
Robert Melvin, Jr.
HITT, Robert Roberts 1
HITTEL, Charles J. 4
HITTELL, John Sherzer 1
HITZ, John 1
HITZ, Ralph 1
HITZ, William 1
HIX, Asa Witt 4
HIX, Charles H. 1
HIXON, Ernest Howard 5
HIXSON, Fred White 1
HLAVATY, Vaclav 5
HO, Chi-Minh 5
HOAD, 4
William Christian
HOADLEY, David H
HOADLEY, George 1
Arthur
HOADLEY, John H
Chipman
HOADLY, George 1
HOAG, David Doughty 1
HOAG, Ernest Bryant 4
HOAG, Frank Stephen 4
HOAG, George Grant 5
HOAG, Gilbert Thomas 3
HOAG, Joseph 1
HOAG, Junius Clarkson 1
HOAG, Truman Harrison H
HOAG, 4
William Ricketson
HOAGE, Robert J. 5
HOAGLAND, Denis 4
Robert
HOAGLAND, John Hurle 4
HOAGLAND, Moses H
HOAGLAND, 5
Warren Eugene
HOAN, Daniel Webster 4
HOAR, H
Ebenezer Rockwood
HOAR, George Frisbie 1
HOAR, Leonard 1
HOAR, Rockwood 1
HOAR, Samuel H
HOARD, Charles Brooks 1
HOARD, 1
William Dempster
HOARE, Elmer Joseph 5
HOBAN, Edward Francis 4
HOBAN, James 1
HOBAN, Michael John 1
HOBART, Aaron 4
HOBART, Alice Tisdale 4
HOBART, Alvah Sabin 4
HOBART, 4
Franklin Gatfield
HOBART, 1
Garret Augustus
HOBART, George Vere 1
HOBART, Henry Metcalf 2
HOBART, 1
Horace Reynolds
HOBART, John Henry 4
HOBART, John Sloss H
HOBART, Lewis Parsons 3
HOBART, 5
Mrs. Lowell Fletcher
(edith Liela)
HOBART, 1
Marie Elizabeth Jefferys
HOBBIE, Henry Martin 3
HOBBIE, Selah Reeve H
HOBBINS, James R. 1
HOBBLE, Deborah Sharp 5
HOBBS, Alfred Charles 4
HOBBS, Allan Wilson 4
HOBBS, Charles Seright 5
HOBBS, Charles Wood 1

HOBBS, Edward H. 1
HOBBS, Franklin Warren 3
HOBBS, George Sayward 4
HOBBS, 3
Gustavus Warfield Jr.
HOBBS, Ichabod Goodwin 1
HOBBS, James Randolph 2
HOBBS, John Edward 1
HOBBS, John Weston 4
HOBBS, Leland Stanford 4
HOBBS, Lewis Lyndon 4
HOBBS, Morris Henry 4
HOBBS, Perry L. 4
HOBBS, Ralph Waller 1
HOBBS, Roe Raymond 1
HOBBS, Sam Francis 3
HOBBS, William Herbert 3
HOBBS, William J. 1
HOBBY, William Pettus 4
HOBDY, John Buford 5
HOBEN, Allan 1
HOBEN, Lindsay 1
HOBGOOD, Frank P. 5
HOBLITZELL, 4
John Dempsey Jr.
HOBLITZELLE, Harrison 2
HOBLITZELLE, Karl 5
HOBSON, 5
A(lphonzo) Augustus
HOBSON, Alfred Norman 1
HOBSON, Benjamin Lewis 1
HOBSON, Edward Henry 1
HOBSON, Jesse Edward 5
HOBSON, John Peyton 1
HOBSON, 4
Joseph Reid Anderson
HOBSON, 1
-Richmond Pearson
HOBSON, Robert Louis 5
HOBSON, Robert P. 4
HOBSON, Sarah Matilda 4
HOBSON, Stanley H. 4
HOBSON, T. Francis 4
HOBSON, Thayer 4
HOBSON, Wilder 4
HOBSON, William 5
Andrew
HOBSON, William Horace 1
HOCA, Myron Myroslaw 5
HOCH, August 1
HOCH, Daniel K. 5
HOCH, Edward Wallis 1
HOCH, Homer 2
HOCH, Paul H. 4
HOCHBAUM, Hans 3
Weller
HOCHDOERFER, 4
Richard
HOCHE, Herman Emanuel 4
HOCHMUTH, Bruno 4
Arthur
HOCHSTETTER, 5
Robert William
HOCHWALD, 5
Fritz G(abriel)
HOCHWALT, 1
Albert Frederick
HOCHWALT, Frederick 4
G.
HOCKADAY, Ela 5
HOCKEMA, Frank C. 3
HOCKENBEAMER, 4
August Frederick
HOCKENSMITH, 3
Wilbur Darwin
HOCKER, Lon O. 2
HOCKER, William Adam 4
HOCKETT, Homer Carey 5
HOCKING, 4
William Ernest
HOCKLEY, Chester Fox 4
HOCKSTADER, 4
Leonard Albert
HODDER, Alfred 1
HODDER, Frank 1
Heywood
HODDINOTT, 5
Mary Loretta
HODELL, Charles Wesley 1
HODES, Henry Irving 4
HODGDON, Charles 3
HODGDON, 1
Frank Wellington
HODGDON, Frank 4
Wilbert
HODGE, 4
Archibald Alexander
HODGE, H
Bachman Gladstone
HODGE, Caspar Wistar 1
HODGE, Charles H
HODGE, Clifton Fremont 4
HODGE, Edward B. 1
HODGE, 2
Edward Blanchard
HODGE, Edwin Rose Jr. 4
HODGE, Frederick Webb 3

HODGE, Henry Wilson 1
HODGE, Hugh Lenox H
HODGE, Hugh Lenox 1
HODGE, John Aspinwall 1
HODGE, John R. 4
HODGE, Kenneth LaVern 4
HODGE, Oliver 4
HODGE, Richard Morse 1
HODGE, Tobe 1
HODGE, Walter Roberts 1
HODGE, 4
Willard Wellington
HODGE, William 1
HODGE, William Irvine 5
HODGEN, John H
Thompson
HODGES, Arthur 4
HODGES, Brandon Patton 3
HODGES, 2
Campbell Blackshear
HODGES, Charles 4
HODGES, Charles Drury H
HODGES, Charles H. 1
HODGES, 1
Charles Libbens
HODGES, Courtney H. 4
HODGES, Frank 5
HODGES, George 1
HODGES, 2
George Hartshorn
HODGES, George Tisdale H
HODGES, Gilbert 5
HODGES, 3
Gilbert Tennent
HODGES, Harry Foote 4
HODGES, Harry Marsh 4
HODGES, Henry Clay 1
HODGES, James Leonard H
HODGES, John Cunyus 5
HODGES, John Cunyus 4
HODGES, 1
John Sebastian Bach
HODGES, Johnny 5
HODGES, Joseph Gilluly 5
HODGES, Leigh Mitchell 3
HODGES, LeRoy 2
HODGES, 5
Louise Threete;
HODGES, 1
Nathaniel Dana Carlile
HODGES, Richard 4
Edward
HODGES, Thomas 4
Edward
HODGES, Walter Edward 2
HODGES, 3
William Franklin
HODGES, William 2
Thomas
HODGES, William V. 4
HODGHEAD, Beverly 1
Lacy
HODGIN, 4
Charles Elkanah
HODGIN, Cyrus Wilburn 1
HODGINS, Eric 5
HODGKIN, 1
Henry Theodore
HODGKIN, 4
William Newton
HODGKINS, Alton Ross 3
HODGKINS, 1
Howard Lincoln
HODGKINS, 1
Louise Manning
HODGKINS, 1
William Candler
HODGKINSON, Francis 2
HODGKINSON, John H
HODGMAN, Burns P. 4
HODGMAN, T. Morey 4
HODGMAN, 1
William Lansing
HODGON, Anderson 2
Dana
HODGSDON, 1
Daniel Bascome
HODGSON, Albert James 2
HODGSON, 1
Carey Vandervort
HODGSON, Caspar 1
Wistar
HODGSON, Frank Corrin 5
HODGSON, Fred Grady 4
HODGSON, Harry 5
HODGSON, 5
Joseph Frederick
HODGSON, Joseph Park 5
HODGSON, 1
Laurence Curran
HODGSON, 5
Marshall Goodwin Simms
HODGSON, 3
Morton Strahan
HODGSON, Richard 1
HODGSON, 4
Robert Willard

HODGSON, Thekla Roese 5
HODGSON, William H
Brown
HODGSON, William Roy 3
HODNETTE, John K. 4
HODOUS, Lewis 2
HODSON, Clarence 1
HODSON, William 2
HODUR, Francis 5
HOE, Richard March H
HOE, Robert H
HOE, Robert 1
HOE, Robert 3
HOEBER, Arthur 1
HOECHST, Edward John 5
HOECK, Theodor Albert 4
HOECKEN, Christian H
HOEFELD, Norman 3
HOEFER, Charles Wenzel 3
HOEHLER, Fred Kenneth 5
HOEHLING, 2
Adolph August
HOEHLING, 2
Adolph August
HOEHN, Kenneth William 5
HOEING, Charles 1
HOEING, 4
Frederick Waldbridge
HOELSCHER, 5
Randolph Philip
HOELZEL, John P. 3
HOEN, August H
HOENSHEL, Eli J. 3
HOERR, Normand Louis 4
HOEY, Clyde Roark 3
HOEY, James J. 2
HOF, Samuel 1
HOFF, 4
Charles Worthington
HOFF, Emanuel Buechley 5
HOFF, John Edward 4
HOFF, 1
John Van Rensselaer
HOFF, Nelville Soule 1
HOFF, Olaf 1
HOFF, 1
William Bainbridge
HOFFECKER, John H. 1
HOFFENSTEIN, 2
Samuel Goodman
HOFFHERR, Frederic G. 3
HOFFLUND, John Leslie 4
HOFFMAN, Abram 3
HOFFMAN, Arnold 4
HOFFMAN, Arthur 1
Gilman
HOFFMAN, Burton C. 3
HOFFMAN, Carl 2
HOFFMAN, Charles 1
Fenno
HOFFMAN, 1
Charles Frederick
HOFFMAN, Charles W. 5
HOFFMAN, 1
Christian Balzac
HOFFMAN, Clare E. 4
HOFFMAN, David H
HOFFMAN, David 1
Murray
HOFFMAN, Dean Meck 5
HOFFMAN, Edward 1
George
HOFFMAN, 3
Edward Richard
HOFFMAN, 1
Eugene Augustus
HOFFMAN, Frank 1
Sargent
HOFFMAN, Fred William 4
HOFFMAN, 2
Frederick John
HOFFMAN, 1
Frederick Ludwig
HOFFMAN, 1
George Matthias
HOFFMAN, Harold Giles 3
HOFFMAN, Harry Leslie 1
HOFFMAN, Heman Leslie 5
HOFFMAN, Henry H
William
HOFFMAN, Herman S. 2
HOFFMAN, 3
Horace Addison
HOFFMAN, 3
Hugh French T.
HOFFMAN, James David 1
HOFFMAN, 5
James Franklin
HOFFMAN, James I. 4
HOFFMAN, John C. 1
HOFFMAN, John H
Thompson
HOFFMAN, 3
John Washington
HOFFMAN, John Wesley 5
HOFFMAN, Josiah Ogden H
HOFFMAN, Leroy E. 5

HOFFMAN, Malvina 4
HOFFMAN, Michael H
HOFFMAN, Ogden H
HOFFMAN, Ralph 4
HOFFMAN, Richard 1
HOFFMAN, 1
Richard Curzon
HOFFMAN, Roy 5
HOFFMAN, Samuel 3
David
HOFFMAN, W. D. 3
HOFFMAN, Wickham 3
HOFFMAN, 3
William George
HOFFMANN, Ernst 3
HOFFMANN, 1
Francis Arnold
HOFFMANN, Ralph 1
HOFFSTOT, Frank N. 1
HOFFY, Alfred M. 4
HOFFZIMMER, 5
Ernest K(aspar)
HOFMAN, Heinrich Oscar 1
HOFMANN, Hans 4
HOFMANN, 5
Herbert Andrew
HOFMANN, Hugo 5
HOFMANN, Josef 3
HOFMANN, Julius 5
HOFSTADTER, Richard 5
HOGAN, 2
Aluysius Gonzaga Joseph
HOGAN, Bernard Francis 3
HOGAN, Dana 2
HOGAN, Denis Patrick 4
HOGAN, Edgar Poe 5
HOGAN, Edward A. Jr. 1
HOGAN, Frank J. 2
HOGAN, Frank J. 1
HOGAN, 5
George Archibald
HOGAN, Henry Michael 5
HOGAN, John H
HOGAN, John Henry 1
HOGAN, John Joseph 1
HOGAN, John Philip 1
HOGAN, 4
John Vincent Lawiess
HOGAN, 1
Louise E. Shimer
HOGAN, Michael J. 1
HOGAN, O. T. 5
HOGAN, William H
HOGAN, William Ransom 5
HOGATE, Enoch George 1
HOGATE, Kenneth 2
Craven
HOGE, Arthur Kenworthy 1
HOGE, James Doster 1
HOGE, James Fulton 5
HOGE, John H
HOGE, John H
HOGE, John Blair H
HOGE, Joseph Pendleton H
HOGE, Moses H
HOGE, Moses Drury H
HOGE, Peyton Harrison 4
HOGE, Vane Morgan 5
HOGE, William H
HOGE, William James H
HOGEBOOM, H
James Lawrence
HOGELAND, 1
Albert Harrison
HOGG, Astor 5
HOGG, George H
HOGG, Herschel M. 1
HOGG, James Stephen 1
HOGG, Samuel H
HOGG, William Clifford 1
HOGG, William Stetson 1
HOGGATT, Wilford 1
Bacon
HOGGSON, William John 1
HOGLE, James A. 3
HOGSETT, William Sloan 4
HOGUE, Addison 4
HOGUE, S. Fred 1
HOGUE, Walter Jenkins 1
HOGUE, Wilson Thomas 1
HOGUET, Robert Louis 4
HOGUN, James H
HOH, Paul Jacob H
HOHENBERG, A. Elkan 4
HOHENTHAL, 4
Emil Louis George
HOHF, Silas Matthew 5
HOHFELD, Edward 4
HOHFELD, 4
Wesley Newcomb
HOHFELD, 4
Wesley Newcomb
HOHLFELD, 2
Alexander Rudolf
HOHLFELD, 3
Alexander Rudolf
HOHMAN, Leslie B. 5

HOIDALE, Einar 3
HOILES, Raymond Cyrus 5
HOISINGTON, Henry Richard H
HOIT, Henry Ford 5
HOITT, Charles William 5
HOKE, Elmer Rhodes 1
HOKE, Kremer J. 2
HOKE, Michael 2
HOKE, Robert Frederick 2
HOKE, Travis Henderson 3
HOKE, William Alexander 1
HOLABIRD, John Augur 2
HOLABIRD, Samuel Beckley 1
HOLABIRD, William 1
HOLADAY, Ross Edgar 1
HOLADAY, William P. 2
HOLAHAN, Maurice Fenelon 3
HOLAND, Hjalmar Rued 5
HOLAND, Hjalmar Rued 5
HOLBEN, Ralph Penrose 4
HOLBORN, Hajo 5
HOLBROOK, Alfred 1
HOLBROOK, Donald 5
HOLBROOK, Dwight 4
HOLBROOK, Edward Dexter H
HOLBROOK, Elmer Allen 3
HOLBROOK, Evans 1
HOLBROOK, Florence 1
HOLBROOK, Frederick * 1
HOLBROOK, Henry Crosby 4
HOLBROOK, John 5
HOLBROOK, John Edwards H
HOLBROOK, John Swift 1
HOLBROOK, Josiah 5
HOLBROOK, Lucius Roy 5
HOLBROOK, Martin Luther 1
HOLBROOK, Richard Thayer 1
HOLBROOK, Roland C. 3
HOLBROOK, Silas Pinckney H
HOLBROOK, Stewart Hall 4
HOLBROOK, Willard Ames 1
HOLCH, Arthur Everett 1
HOLCOMB, Amasa H
HOLCOMB, Horace Hale 3
HOLCOMB, Lynn Howe 2
HOLCOMB, Marcus Hensey 1
HOLCOMB, Oscar Raymond 1
HOLCOMB, Richard Roy 4
HOLCOMB, Silas Alexander 1
HOLCOMB, Thomas 4
HOLCOMBE, Amasa Maynard 5
HOLCOMBE, Armstead Richardson 1
HOLCOMBE, Chester H
HOLCOMBE, George H
HOLCOMBE, Henry H
HOLCOMBE, James Philemon H
HOLCOMBE, John Lavallee 4
HOLCOMBE, John Marshall 1
HOLCOMBE, Oscar Fitzallen 5
HOLCOMBE, William Frederic 1
HOLCOMBE, William Henry H
HOLDEN, Albert James 1
HOLDEN, Alice M. 3
HOLDEN, Carl Frederick 3
HOLDEN, Charles Arthur 4
HOLDEN, Charles Revell 1
HOLDEN, Edgar 2
HOLDEN, Edward Henry 1
HOLDEN, Edward Singleton 1
HOLDEN, Edwin Chapin 2
HOLDEN, Frederick Clark 2
HOLDEN, George Parker 1
HOLDEN, George Walter 1
HOLDEN, Gerry Rounds 2
HOLDEN, Hale 1
HOLDEN, Hale 3
HOLDEN, Horace Moore 1
HOLDEN, James 1
HOLDEN, James Austin 2
HOLDEN, James Franklin 1
HOLDEN, James Stansbury 5
HOLDEN, John Burt 1

HOLDEN, Liberty Emery 1
HOLDEN, Louis Edward 1
HOLDEN, Louis Edward 2
HOLDEN, Louis Halsey 5
HOLDEN, Oliver H
HOLDEN, Perry Greeley 4
HOLDEN, Roy Jay 2
HOLDEN, Thomas Steele 3
HOLDEN, Ward Andrews 1
HOLDEN, William Woods 1
HOLDER, Arthur Ernest 1
HOLDER, Charles Adams 3
HOLDER, Charles Frederick H
HOLDER, Edward Perry 3
HOLDER, Francis Jerome 1
HOLDER, Joseph Basset H
HOLDER, Oscar Curtis 4
HOLDERBY, Andrew Roberdeau 4
HOLDERBY, William Matthew 1
HOLDING, Archibald M. 1
HOLDING, Elisabeth Sanxay 3
HOLDING, Robert Powell 3
HOLDOM, Jesse H
HOLDREGE, George Ward H
HOLENSTEIN, Thomas 4
HOLGATE, Thomas Franklin 2
HOLIDAY, Eleanor 1
HOLIDAY, Herman Joe 4
HOLL, Carl Waldo 4
HOLL, Die Lewis 3
HOLLADAY, Alexander Quarles 3
HOLLADAY, Alexander Richmond H
HOLLADAY, Ben H
HOLLADAY, James 4
HOLLADAY, Waller 4
HOLLAMAN, Rich William 2
HOLLAND, Clifford Milburn 1
HOLLAND, Cornelius H
HOLLAND, Edmund Milton 1
HOLLAND, Edward Everett 1
HOLLAND, Edwin Clifford H
HOLLAND, Elmer Joseph 5
HOLLAND, Elmer Leonard Jr. 4
HOLLAND, Ernest O. 3
HOLLAND, Frank P. 1
HOLLAND, Frederic May 1
HOLLAND, George H
HOLLAND, Henry Finch 4
HOLLAND, James H
HOLLAND, James Buchanan 1
HOLLAND, James M. 4
HOLLAND, James William 1
HOLLAND, John Joseph 1
HOLLAND, John Philip H
HOLLAND, John Philip 4
HOLLAND, Joseph Jefferson 1
HOLLAND, Josiah Gilbert H
HOLLAND, Laurier Fox-strangways 3
HOLLAND, Leicester Bodine 3
HOLLAND, Louis Edward 4
HOLLAND, Madeline Oxford (Mrs. John N. Mcdonnell) H
HOLLAND, Peter Olai 1
HOLLAND, Philip 1
HOLLAND, Robert Afton 1
HOLLAND, Robert Allen 3
HOLLAND, Rupert Sargent 3
HOLLAND, Rush 1
HOLLAND, Sidney George 4
HOLLAND, Spessard Lindsey 5
HOLLAND, Thomas Leroy 2
HOLLAND, Travis 5
HOLLAND, Ubert Cecil 3
HOLLAND, W. Bob 1
HOLLAND, William J. 1
HOLLAND, William Merideth 1
HOLLANDER, Franklin 1
HOLLANDER, Jacob H. 1
HOLLANDER, Sidney 5
HOLLEMAN, Joel H

HOLLEMAN, Willard Roy 5
HOLLENBACK, George Matson H
HOLLENBACK, John Welles 4
HOLLENBACK, Matthias H
HOLLENBECK, Don 3
HOLLERITH, Herman H
HOLLERITH, Herman 2
HOLLERITH, Herman H
HOLLEY, Alexander Lyman H
HOLLEY, Francis 1
HOLLEY, George Malvin 4
HOLLEY, Horace H
HOLLEY, Horace 1
HOLLEY, John Milton H
HOLLEY, John Milton 1
HOLLEY, Marietta 1
HOLLEY, Myron 1
HOLLEY, William Welles 4
HOLLICK, Arthur 1
HOLLIDAY, Carl 1
HOLLIDAY, Cyrus Kurtz H
HOLLIDAY, Elias S. 4
HOLLIDAY, Houghton 5
HOLLIDAY, John Hampden 1
HOLLIDAY, Judy 4
HOLLIDAY, Robert Cortes 2
HOLLIDAY, Robert Paul 3
HOLLIDAY, Wallace Trevor 3
HOLLIDAY, William Harrison 4
HOLLIDAY, William Helmus H
HOLLIDAY, William Helmus 1
HOLLIDAY, William Helmus .
HOLLIDAY, William Helmus 4
HOLLING, Thomas Leslie 4
HOLLINGSHEAD, Stewart 4
HOLLINGSWORTH, Amor 3
HOLLINGSWORTH, David A. 4
HOLLINGSWORTH, Frank 4
HOLLINGSWORTH, William Franklin 4
HOLLINGTON, Richard Deming 2
HOLLINGWORTH, Harry Levi 3
HOLLINGWORTH, Leta S. 1
HOLLINS, George Nichols H
HOLLIS, Allen 3
HOLLIS, Ernest Victor 4
HOLLIS, Henry French 2
HOLLIS, Henry Leonard 3
HOLLIS, Ira Nelson 1
HOLLIS, W. Stanley 1
HOLLISTER, Buell 1
HOLLISTER, Clay Harvey 1
HOLLISTER, Fred H. 3
HOLLISTER, Gideon Hiram 1
HOLLISTER, Granger A. 1
HOLLISTER, Horace Adelbert 1
HOLLISTER, Howard Clark 1
HOLLISTER, John Hamilcar 1
HOLLISTER, Joseph 3
HOLLISTER, Ned 1
HOLLISTER, Orlando Knapp 1
HOLLISTER, William Henry Jr. 1
HOLLMANN, Harry Triebner 2
HOLLOMON, James Arthur 1
HOLLOPETER, William Clarence 1
HOLLOWAY, David Pierson H
HOLLOWAY, Edward Stratton 1
HOLLOWAY, Harry Vance 4
HOLLOWAY, Jacob James 1
HOLLOWAY, John H
HOLLOWAY, John Lindsay 4
HOLLOWAY, Joseph Flavius H
HOLLOWAY, Thomas Beaver 1

HOLLOWAY, William A. 4
HOLLOWAY, William Grace 3
HOLLOWAY, William James 5
HOLLOWAY, William Judson 5
HOLLOWAY, William Lawson 1
HOLLOWAY, William M. 4
HOLLOWAY, William Robeson 4
HOLLS, George Frederick William 1
HOLLUMS, Ellis Clyde 2
HOLLY, Charles Harden 1
HOLLY, Henry Hudson H
HOLLY, James Theodore 1
HOLLY, William H. 3
HOLLYDAY, Richard Carmichael 4
HOLLYER, Samuel 4
HOLLZER, Harry Aaron 2
HOLM, Frits Vilhelm 1
HOLM, George Elmer 3
HOLM, Henry Jesse 1
HOLM, Theodor 1
HOLM, Victor S. 1
HOLMAN, Alfred 1
HOLMAN, Charles Thomas 4
HOLMAN, Eugene 4
HOLMAN, Frank 4
HOLMAN, Frank E. 4
HOLMAN, Frederick Van Voorhies 1
HOLMAN, Howard Francis 3
HOLMAN, Jesse Lynch H
HOLMAN, Jud McCarty 4
HOLMAN, Louis Arthur 1
HOLMAN, Minard Lafever 1
HOLMAN, Rufus C. 4
HOLMAN, Russell Lowell 4
HOLMAN, William Henry 4
HOLMAN, William Kunkel 5
HOLMAN, William Steele H
HOLMBERG, Adrian Otis 5
HOLMBERG, Allan Richard 4
HOLMBERG, George C. 1
HOLMBERG, Gustaf Fredrik 2
HOLME, John Francis 1
HOLME, Thomas H
HOLMES, Abiel 4
HOLMES, Arthur 4
HOLMES, Bayard 1
HOLMES, Burton 3
HOLMES, Champneys Holt 3
HOLMES, Charles Elmer 1
HOLMES, Charles Horace H
HOLMES, Christian R. 1
HOLMES, Clarence Leroy 4
HOLMES, David 4
HOLMES, David Eugene 2
HOLMES, Donald Safford 5
HOLMES, Dwight Oliver Wendell H
HOLMES, Edward H
HOLMES, Edward Jackson 3
HOLMES, Edward Marion, Jr. 5
HOLMES, Edward Thomas 5
HOLMES, Edwin Francis 4
HOLMES, Edwin Sanford, Jr. 5
HOLMES, Elias Bellows H
HOLMES, Ernest Shurtliff 4
HOLMES, Ezekiel H
HOLMES, Frank G. 3
HOLMES, Frederick 2
HOLMES, Frederick Lionel 2
HOLMES, Frederick S. 4
HOLMES, Gabriel 1
HOLMES, George Frederick H
HOLMES, George Kirby 1
HOLMES, George Robert 1
HOLMES, George Sanford 3
HOLMES, George William 4
HOLMES, Gerald Anderson 2
HOLMES, Gustavus S. 4
HOLMES, Guy Earl 2
HOLMES, Harry Nicholls 4
HOLMES, Henry Alfred 4
HOLMES, Henry Wyman 4
HOLMES, Howard Carleton 1

HOLMES, Isaac Edward H
HOLMES, Israel 5
HOLMES, Jack Alroy 5
HOLMES, James Thomas 4
HOLMES, Jesse Herman 2
HOLMES, John H
HOLMES, John * 4
HOLMES, John Haynes 4
HOLMES, John McClellan 5
HOLMES, John P. 4
HOLMES, John Simcox 4
HOLMES, Joseph Addison 4
HOLMES, Joseph Austin 5
HOLMES, Joses B. S. 5
HOLMES, Julius Cecil 5
HOLMES, Ludvig 5
HOLMES, Major Edward 2
HOLMES, Malcolm Haughton 5
HOLMES, Mary Caroline 1
HOLMES, Mary Elisabeth 1
HOLMES, Mary Emilie 1
HOLMES, Mary Jane 4
HOLMES, Merrill Jacob 4
HOLMES, Morris Grant 5
HOLMES, Nathaniel H
HOLMES, Oliver Wendell H
HOLMES, Oliver Wendell 3
HOLMES, Pehr G. 3
HOLMES, Phillips 2
HOLMES, Ralph Clinton 4
HOLMES, Ralston Smith 5
HOLMES, Richard Sill 1
HOLMES, Robert 4
HOLMES, Robert Shailor 1
HOLMES, Rudolph Wieser 1
HOLMES, Samuel Jackson 4
HOLMES, Samuel Van Vranken H
HOLMES, Sidney Tracy H
HOLMES, Theophilus Hunter H
HOLMES, Thomas James 5
HOLMES, Urban Tigner 5
HOLMES, Uriel H
HOLMES, Walton H. 4
HOLMES, Wilbur Fisk 4
HOLMES, William Henry H
HOLMES, William Henry 2
HOLMGREN, John R. 4
HOLMQUIST, Claire Walfred 5
HOLMSTROM, Andrew Birger 5
HOLMSTROM, Gus Edgar 5
HOLSAPPLE, Cortell King 5
HOLSCHUH, Louis William 5
HOLSEY, Hopkins H
HOLSEY, Lucius Henry 4
HOLSMAN, Henry K. 5
HOLST, Edvard 4
HOLSTEIN, Henry Lincoln 4
HOLSTEIN, Otto 5
HOLT, Adoniram Judson 3
HOLT, Andrew 3
HOLT, Andrew Hall 2
HOLT, Arthur Erastus 3
HOLT, Byron Webber 1
HOLT, Charles Sumner 1
HOLT, Edwin Bissell 4
HOLT, Edwin Michael H
HOLT, Erastus Eugene Sr. 1
HOLT, Erwin Allen 4
HOLT, Frank O. 4
HOLT, Fred Park 3
HOLT, George Chandler 1
HOLT, George Hubbard 1
HOLT, Guy 2
HOLT, Hamilton 4
HOLT, Hamilton Tatum 4
HOLT, Harold Edward 5
HOLT, Harry Howard Jr. 4
HOLT, Henry H
HOLT, Henry Chandler 1
HOLT, Henry Winston 1
HOLT, Hines H
HOLT, Ivan Lee 4
HOLT, John H
HOLT, John Herrimon 1
HOLT, Joseph H
HOLT, L. Emmett Lawrence Shackleford 4
HOLT, Lee Cone 1
HOLT, Lucius Hudson 1
HOLT, Marshall Keyser (Mrs. Leland Wallace Holt) 4
HOLT, Orren Thaddeus 1
HOLT, Orrin H
HOLT, Rackham 4
HOLT, Roland H

HOLT, Rosa Belle 5
HOLT, Rush Dew 3
HOLT, Walter Vincent 4
HOLT, William Franklin 3
HOLT, William Henry 4
HOLT, William Joseph 3
HOLT, William Sylvester 1
HOLT, Winifred 5
HOLTEN, Samuel H
HOLTER, Norman B. 3
HOLTHUSEN, Henry Frank 5
HOLTMAN, Dudley Frank 4
HOLTMAN, Louis 4
HOLTON, Edwin Lee 3
HOLTON, Elizabeth Curran (Mrs. Winfred Byron Holton, Jr.) 5
HOLTON, George Van Syckel 5
HOLTON, Henry Dwight 1
HOLTON, Holland 2
HOLTON, Jessie Moon 3
HOLTON, M. Adelaide 3
HOLTON, Winfred B. Jr. 3
HOLTZCLAW, Jack Gilbert 3
HOLTZMAN, John W. 4
HOLTZMANN, Jacob L. 4
HOLTZOFF, Alexander 5
HOLTZWORTH, Bertram Arthur 5
HOLYOKE, Edward 1
HOLYOKE, Edward Augustus H
HOLYOKE, Samuel H
HOLZBERG, Jules Donald 5
HOLZER, Charles Elmer 3
HOLZHEIMER, William Andrew 2
HOLZINGER, Karl John 3
HOLZKNECHT, Karl J. 3
HOMAN, Fletcher 1
HOMAN, Paul Thomas 5
HOMANS, Amy Morris 4
HOMBERGER, Alfred William 3
HOMBERGER, Ludwig Maximillian 3
HOMER, Arthur Bartlett 5
HOMER, Francis Theodore; 5
HOMER, John L. 4
HOMER, Louise Dilworth Beatty 2
HOMER, Sidney 3
HOMER, Soloman Jones
HOMER, William J. 1
HOMER, Winslow 1
HOMES, Henry Augustus H
HONAN, James Henry 1
HONAN, William Francis 1
HONDA, Masujiro 4
HONDORP, Peter 1
HONE, Philip H
HONEGGER, Arthur 4
HONEY, Robertson 1
HONEY, Samuel Robertson 1
HONEYCUTT, Francis Webster 1
HONEYCUTT, Jesse Vernon 5
HONEYWELL, Mark C. 4
HONEYWELL, Miss M. A. H
HONLINE, Moses Alfred 1
HONNOLD, William Lincoln 3
HONORE, Paul 3
HOO, Victor Chi-Tsai 5
HOOBLER, Bert Raymond 2
HOOD, Arthur A. 4
HOOD, Charles Crook 1
HOOD, Charles Emerson 4
HOOD, E. Lyman 1
HOOD, Edwin Milton 1
HOOD, Frazer 2
HOOD, Frederic Clark 2
HOOD, George E. 3
HOOD, Horace 1
HOOD, J. Douglas 4
HOOD, James Walker 1
HOOD, John 1
HOOD, John Bell H
HOOD, Oliver Roland 1
HOOD, Ozni Porter 1
HOOD, Raymond Mathewson 1
HOOD, Solomon Porter 4
HOOD, Washington H
HOOD, William 1
HOOGEWERFF, John Adrian 1

HOOK, Charles Ruffin Jr. 4
HOOK, Enos H
HOOK, James William 3
HOOK, Walter Williams 4
HOOK, William Cather 1
HOOKER, Charles Edward 4
HOOKER, Donald Russell 2
HOOKER, Edward 1
HOOKER, Edward Beecher 1
HOOKER, Ellen Kelley 1
HOOKER, Elon Huntington 1
HOOKER, Forrestine Cooper 1
HOOKER, Frank Arthur 1
HOOKER, George Ellsworth 1
HOOKER, Harry Mix 2
HOOKER, Henry Stewart 4
HOOKER, Isabella Beecher 1
HOOKER, James Murray 5
HOOKER, John Daggett 4
HOOKER, John Jay 5
HOOKER, Joseph H
HOOKER, Margaret Huntington 5
HOOKER, Philip H
HOOKER, Richard 4
HOOKER, Thomas H
HOOKER, Thomas 1
HOOKER, Warren Brewster 1
HOOKER, William H
HOOKER, William Brian 2
HOOKER, William P. 4
HOOKS, Charles 1
HOOLEY, Arthur 5
HOOLEY, Edwin Strange 4
HOON, Clarence Earl 1
HOOPER, Ben W. 3
HOOPER, C. E. 3
HOOPER, Charles Edward 4
HOOPER, Everett 4
HOOPER, Frank Finley 3
HOOPER, Franklin Henry 4
HOOPER, Franklin William 1
HOOPER, Jessie Annette Jack 1
HOOPER, John William 3
HOOPER, Johnson Jones 1
HOOPER, Joseph Lawrence 1
HOOPER, Louis Leverett 4
HOOPER, Lucy Hamilton H
HOOPER, Osman Castle 1
HOOPER, Philo O. 1
HOOPER, Robert P. 3
HOOPER, Samuel H
HOOPER, Shadrach K. 4
HOOPER, Sir Federic Collins 4
HOOPER, Stanford Caldwell 3
HOOPER, William H
HOOPER, William Henry H
HOOPER, William Leslie 1
HOOPER, William Thomas 1
HOOPES, Josiah 1
HOOPINGARNER, Dwight Lowell 1
HOOPINGARNER, Newman Leander 3
HOOSE, James Harmon 1
HOOTON, Caradine Ray 4
HOOTON, Earnest Albert 3
HOOTON, Mott 1
HOOVER, Arthur McCall 4
HOOVER, Bessie Ray 5
HOOVER, Blaine 1
HOOVER, Charles Franklin 1
HOOVER, Charles Lewis 2
HOOVER, Charles Ruglas 2
HOOVER, Donald Douglas 5
HOOVER, Frank G. 3
HOOVER, George Pendelton 3
HOOVER, Harvey Daniel 3
HOOVER, Herbert 4
HOOVER, Herbert, Jr. 3
HOOVER, Herbert William 3
HOOVER, Hubert Don 5
HOOVER, J(ohn) Edgar 5
HOOVER, John Howard 4
HOOVER, Lou Henry 2
HOOVER, Ray 4
HOOVER, Samuel Earle 5
HOOVER, Simon Robert 1

HOOVER, Stuart 4
HOOVER, Theodore Jesse 3
HOOVER, William D. 2
HOOVER, William H. 4
HOPE, Chester Raines 4
HOPE, Clifford Ragsdale 5
HOPE, Francis Moffat; 5
HOPE, James H
HOPE, James Barron 4
HOPE, James Haskell 5
HOPE, James William 4
HOPE, John 1
HOPE, Minnie Gazelle Welborn (Mrs. Tom Hope) 5
HOPE, Richard 3
HOPE, Walter Ewing 2
HOPEKIRK, Helen 1
HOPEWELL, John 1
HOPEWELL-SMITH, Arthur 1
HOPF, Harry Arthur 2
HOPFENBECK, George M. 4
HOPKINS, Abner Crump 4
HOPKINS, Albert J. 1
HOPKINS, Alphonso Alva 1
HOPKINS, Altis Skiles 5
HOPKINS, Amos Lawrence 4
HOPKINS, Anderson Hoyt 4
HOPKINS, Andrew Delmar 4
HOPKINS, Archibald 1
HOPKINS, Arthur Francis H
HOPKINS, Arthur John 1
HOPKINS, Arthur Melancthon 2
HOPKINS, B. Smith 3
HOPKINS, Benjamin Franklin H
HOPKINS, Benjamin Franklin 3
HOPKINS, Charlotte Everett 1
HOPKINS, Cyril George 1
HOPKINS, E. Washburn 1
HOPKINS, Edna Boies 5
HOPKINS, Edward H
HOPKINS, Edward Augustus H
HOPKINS, Edward Jerome H
HOPKINS, Edwin Butcher 1
HOPKINS, Edwin Mortimer 2
HOPKINS, Erasmus Guy 1
HOPKINS, Erastus 1
HOPKINS, Ernest Martin 4
HOPKINS, Esek 1
HOPKINS, Evan Henry 1
HOPKINS, Frank A. 4
HOPKINS, Franklin Whetstone 4
HOPKINS, Fred Mead 3
HOPKINS, Frederick Eli 4
HOPKINS, George Washington H
HOPKINS, Grant Sherman 1
HOPKINS, Harry L. 2
HOPKINS, Henry 1
HOPKINS, Herbert Muller 1
HOPKINS, Isaac Stiles 1
HOPKINS, James Campbell H
HOPKINS, James Frederick 1
HOPKINS, James Love 1
HOPKINS, James R. 5
HOPKINS, Jay Paul 5
HOPKINS, John Appleton Haven; 5
HOPKINS, John Burroughs H
HOPKINS, John Henry H
HOPKINS, John Henry 2
HOPKINS, John Henry Jr. H
HOPKINS, John Jay 3
HOPKINS, Johns 3
HOPKINS, Joseph Gardner 3
HOPKINS, Juliet Ann Opie H
HOPKINS, Lemuel H
HOPKINS, Lindsey 1
HOPKINS, Louis Bertram 1
HOPKINS, Louise Virginia Martin 4
HOPKINS, Margaret Briscoe 4
HOPKINS, Mark H
HOPKINS, Miriam 5
HOPKINS, Nanette 1

HOPKINS, Nevil Monroe 2
HOPKINS, Percy Earl 4
HOPKINS, Richard J. 2
HOPKINS, Robert Emmet 1
HOPKINS, Robert Holbrook 5
HOPKINS, Robert Milton 3
HOPKINS, Samuel * H
HOPKINS, Samuel Augustus 1
HOPKINS, Samuel Miles 3
HOPKINS, Samuel Miles 1
HOPKINS, Scott 1
HOPKINS, Selden G. 4
HOPKINS, Sherburne Gillette 5
HOPKINS, Stephen H
HOPKINS, Stephen Tyng 5
HOPKINS, Theodore Weld 4
HOPKINS, Thomas Cramer 3
HOPKINS, Thomas Snell 1
HOPKINS, Walter Lee 3
HOPKINS, William Hersey 1
HOPKINS, William John 1
HOPKINS, William Rowland 4
HOPKINSON, Charles 4
HOPKINSON, Edward Jr. 1
HOPKINSON, Ernest 1
HOPKINSON, Francis H
HOPKINSON, Joseph H
HOPKIRK, Howard William 4
HOPLEY, Elizabeth Sheppard 1
HOPLEY, John Edward 1
HOPLEY, Russell James 2
HOPPE, Herman Henry 5
HOPPER, David Claude 5
HOPPER, DeWolf 1
HOPPER, Edna Wallace 3
HOPPER, Edward 4
HOPPER, Frances Peters (Mrs. Eugene D. Hopper) 5
HOPPER, Franklin Ferguson 3
HOPPER, Hedda 4
HOPPER, Isaac Tatem H
HOPPER, James Marie 3
HOPPER, Rex Devern 4
HOPPES, John J. 4
HOPPIN, Augustus H
HOPPIN, James Mason 1
HOPPIN, Joseph Clark 1
HOPPIN, William Warner H
HOPPIN, William Warner 1
HOPPIN, William Warner 2
HOPPING, Andrew Daniel 1
HOPSON, George Bailey 1
HOPSON, William Fowler 1
HOPWOOD, Avery 1
HOPWOOD, Erie Clark 1
HOPWOOD, Herbert Gladstone 4
HOPWOOD, Josephus H
HOPWOOD, Robert Freeman 4
HORACK, Frank Edward 3
HORACK, Frank Edward Jr. 3
HORAN, Hubert Joseph, Jr. 5
HORAN, Philip Edward 5
HORAN, Walter Franklin 5
HORBERG, Leland 3
HORD, Donal 4
HORDYK, Gerard 5
HORENSTEIN, Jascha 5
HORINE, John Winebrenner 5
HORLICK, Alexander James 5
HORLICK, William 1
HORLICK, William Jr. 1
HORMEL, George Albert 2
HORMEL, Jay Catherwood 3
HORMELL, William Garfield 1
HORN, Aaron Charles 5
HORN, Carlton William 5
HORN, Charles Edward H
HORN, Charles J. 5
HORN, Clinton Morris 5
HORN, Edward Traill 1
HORN, Frank Churchill 1
HORN, George Henry H
HORN, Henry H
HORN, Henry John 1
HORN, Henry John 5
HORN, Nelson Paxson 3
HORN, Paul Whitfield 1
HORN, Raymond Edwin 4

HORN, Robert Chisolm 4
HORN, Tiemann Newell 1
HORN, William C. 4
HORN, William Melchior 1
HORNADAY, James Parks 1
HORNADAY, William Temple 1
HORNADY, John Randolph 2
HORNBEAK, Samuel Lee 2
HORNBECK, Donald Warner 4
HORNBECK, John Wesley 3
HORNBECK, John Westbrook H
HORNBECK, Marquis D. 4
HORNBECK, Stanley K. 4
HORNBECK, Vivienne B. (mrs. Stanley K. Hornbeck) 5
HORNBLOW, Arthur 2
HORNBLOWER, Henry 1
HORNBLOWER, Joseph Coerten H
HORNBLOWER, Joseph Coerten 1
HORNBLOWER, Josiah H
HORNBLOWER, Ralph 4
HORNBLOWER, William Butler 1
HORNBOSTEL, Henry 4
HORNBROOK, Henry Hallam 5
HORNE, Charles Francis 2
HORNE, Edmund Campion 2
HORNE, Frank Alexander 1
HORNE, Frederick Joseph 3
HORNE, Herman Harrell 2
HORNE, Joseph A. 3
HORNE, Mary Tracy Earle 5
HORNE, Nellie Mathes 5
HORNE, Perley Leonard 1
HORNER, Bernard Justine 5
HORNER, Charles Francis 4
HORNER, Henry 1
HORNER, James Richey 2
HORNER, John B. 1
HORNER, Junius Moore 1
HORNER, Leonard Sherman 2
HORNER, Wesley Winans 3
HORNER, William Edmonds H
HORNEY, Karen 3
HORNEY, Odus Creamer 5
HORNIBROOK, William Harrison 2
HORNIBROOKE, Isabel (Isabel Hornibrook) 5
HORNICK, Charles W. 1
HORNING, William Allen 4
HORNOR, Lynn Sedwick 1
HORNSBY, John Allen 1
HORNSBY, Rogers H
HORNSBY, Rogers 4
HORNUNG, Christian 4
HOROWITZ, Louis Jay 3
HORR, Alfred Reuel 1
HORR, George Edwin 1
HORR, Ralph A. 3
HORR, Roswell Gilbert H
HORRAX, Gilbert 3
HORRELL, George Robert 5
HORROCKS, James H
HORRWORTH, Charles A. 4
HORSBURGH, Robert Homer 2
HORSEY, Outerbridge H
HORSFALL, Frank Lappin, Jr. 5
HORSFALL, I. Owen 5
HORSFALL, Robert Bruce 2
HORSFIELD, Thomas H
HORSFORD, Cornelia 3
HORSFORD, Eben Norton H
HORSFORD, Jeremiah H
HORSKY, Edward 2
HORSLEY, John Shelton 2
HORSMANDEN, Daniel H
HORST, Emil Clemens 1
HORST, George Philip 1
HORST, John Joseph 2
HORST, Louis 4
HORST, Miles 5
HORSTMAN, Albert Adam 4

HORSTMANN, Ignatius Frederick 1
HORSTMANN, William H. H
HORSWELL, Charles 4
HORTENSTINE, Raleigh 5
HORTON, Albert Howell 1
HORTON, Benjamin Jason 5
HORTON, Douglas 5
HORTON, Edward Augustus 1
HORTON, Edward Everett 5
HORTON, Elmer Grant 2
HORTON, Frank Ogilvie 2
HORTON, George 2
HORTON, George Terry 2
HORTON, Henry Hollis 1
HORTON, Herbert L. 3
HORTON, Herman DeWitt 3
HORTON, Horace Babcock 3
HORTON, J(oseph) Warren 5
HORTON, Jesse M. 4
HORTON, Katharine Loren Pratt 1
HORTON, Lydiard Honeage 2
HORTON, McDavid 1
HORTON, Oliver Harvey 1
HORTON, Robert Elmer 2
HORTON, Samuel Dana H
HORTON, Thomas Corwin 1
HORTON, Thomas Raymond H
HORTON, Valentine Baxter H
HORTON, Walter Marshall 4
HORTON, Walter Shurts 4
HORTON, Wilkins P. 2
HORTON, William Edward 1
HORTON, William S. 4
HORVATH, Imre 3
HORVITZ, Aaron 5
HORWITZ, Phineas Jonathan 1
HORWITZ, Solis 5
HORWOOD, Murray Philip 3
HOSACK, Alexander Eddy 1
HOSACK, David H
HOSFORD, Charles Franklin Jr. 3
HOSFORD, Harry Lindley 2
HOSFORD, Willard Deere 3
HOSFORD, William Fuller 3
HOSHOUR, Harvey Sheely 3
HOSHOUR, Samuel Klinefelter H
HOSIC, James Fleming 3
HOSKIER, Herman C. 1
HOSKIN, Arthur Joseph 1
HOSKIN, Robert 4
HOSKINS, Fermin Lincoln 1
HOSKINS, Franklin Evans 1
HOSKINS, Fred 4
HOSKINS, George Gilbert H
HOSKINS, Halford Lancaster 4
HOSKINS, J. Preston 1
HOSKINS, James Dickcason 3
HOSKINS, James Preston 2
HOSKINS, John Deane Charles 1
HOSKINS, John Hobart 3
HOSKINS, John K. 3
HOSKINS, John M. 4
HOSKINS, Leander Miller 1
HOSKINS, William 1
HOSKINS, William Horace 1
HOSMER, Charles Bridgham 2
HOSMER, Frank Alvin 3
HOSMER, Frederick Lucian 1
HOSMER, George Stedman 1
HOSMER, Harriet Goodhue 1
HOSMER, Hezekiah Lord * H
HOSMER, James Kendall 1
HOSMER, Ralph Sheldon 4

HOSMER, Samuel Monroe 1
HOSMER, Titus H
HOSMER, William Howe Cuyler
HOSS, Elijah Embree 1
HOSS, George Washington 1
HOSTER, Herman Albert 3
HOSTETLER, Erwin Case 5
HOSTETLER, Joseph C. 3
HOSTETLER, Lowell Coy 5
HOSTETLER, Theodore Allen 2
HOSTETTER, Jacob H
HOSTY, Thomas Edward 5
HOTCHENER, Marie Russak
HOTCHKIN, Samuel Fitch 1
HOTCHKISS, Benjamin Berkeley H
HOTCHKISS, Chauncey Crafts 1
HOTCHKISS, Clarence Roland 3
HOTCHKISS, George Burton 3
HOTCHKISS, George W. 1
HOTCHKISS, Giles Waldo H
HOTCHKISS, Henry Dedwitt 1
HOTCHKISS, Henry Greene 4
HOTCHKISS, Henry Stuart 2
HOTCHKISS, Horace Leslie 1
HOTCHKISS, J. Elizabeth 5
HOTCHKISS, Julius H
HOTCHKISS, Loyal Durand 1
HOTCHKISS, Lucius Wales 1
HOTCHKISS, Willard Eugene 3
HOTCHKISS, William Horace 3
HOTCHKISS, William Otis 3
HOTCHKISS, Willis R. 5
HOTTENROTH, Adolph Christian 5
HOTTES, Charles Frederick 5
HOTZ, Ferdinand Carl 1
HOTZ, H(enry) G(ustave) 5
HOTZ, Robert Schuttler 1
HOUCK, Irvin Elmer 5
HOUCK, Jacob Jr. H
HOUCK, Louis 1
HOUDE, Camillion 3
HOUDINI, Harry 1
HOUGH, Alfred Lacey 1
HOUGH, Charles Merrill 1
HOUGH, David H
HOUGH, Emerson 1
HOUGH, Franklin Benjamin H
HOUGH, George Anthony 5
HOUGH, George Washington 1
HOUGH, Henry Hughes 2
HOUGH, Romeyn Beck 1
HOUGH, Samuel Strickler 2
HOUGH, Theodore 1
HOUGH, Walter 1
HOUGH, Warwick 1
HOUGH, William Jervis H
HOUGH, Williston Samuel 1
HOUGHTELING, James Lawrence 1
HOUGHTELING, James Lawrence 4
HOUGHTON, Alanson Bigelow 1
HOUGHTON, Albert Balch 5
HOUGHTON, Dorothy Deemer (Mrs. Hiram Cole Houghton) 5
HOUGHTON, Douglass 2
HOUGHTON, Edward Lovell 4
HOUGHTON, Edward Rittenhouse 3
HOUGHTON, Frederick Boies 4
HOUGHTON, Frederick Lowell 3
HOUGHTON, Frederick Percival
HOUGHTON, George Clarke 1

HOUGHTON, George Heindric H
HOUGHTON, H. Seymour 4
HOUGHTON, Henry Clarke 1
HOUGHTON, Henry Oscar H
HOUGHTON, Herbert Pierrepont 4
HOUGHTON, James Warren 1
HOUGHTON, John Henry 1
HOUGHTON, Louise Phillips 5
HOUGHTON, Louise Seymour 1
HOUGHTON, Sherman Otis 4
HOUGHTON, Will H. 2
HOUGHTON, William Addison 1
HOUGHTON, William Morris 4
HOUK, Eliza Phillips Thruston 1
HOUK, George Washington H
HOUK, Leonidas Campbell H
HOUKOM, John Asbjorn 3
HOULIHAN, D. F. 4
HOURIGAN, John A. 1
HOURWICH, Isaac A. 1
HOUSE, A. G. 4
HOUSE, Boyce 4
HOUSE, Byron Orvil 5
HOUSE, Edward Howard 1
HOUSE, Edward Mandell 1
HOUSE, Elwin Lincoln 1
HOUSE, Francis Edwin 1
HOUSE, Garry Campbell 5
HOUSE, Henry Alonzo 1
HOUSE, Homer Clyde 1
HOUSE, Homer Doliver 2
HOUSE, James Alford 1
HOUSE, James Arthur 5
HOUSE, Jay Elmer 1
HOUSE, John Forde 1
HOUSE, John Henry 1
HOUSE, Joseph Warren 3
HOUSE, Ralph Emerson 1
HOUSE, Robert Ernest 1
HOUSE, Roy Temple 4
HOUSE, Royal Earl 1
HOUSE, Samuel Reynolds H
HOUSEMAN, Julius H
HOUSER, Daniel M. 1
HOUSER, Frederick Wilhelm 2
HOUSER, Gerald Fred Tillman 5
HOUSER, Gilbert L. 3
HOUSER, Karl Musser 4
HOUSER, Shaler Charles 2
HOUSER, Theodore V. 4
HOUSER, Walter L. 1
HOUSMAN, Laurence 3
HOUSSAY, Bernardo Alberto 5
HOUSTON, Charles Albert 3
HOUSTON, Charles Hamilton 3
HOUSTON, Clarence Preston 4
HOUSTON, David Franklin 1
HOUSTON, Edwin James 1
HOUSTON, Edwin Samuel 1
HOUSTON, Frances C. 1
HOUSTON, Francis A. 1
HOUSTON, George Harrison 2
HOUSTON, George Smith H
HOUSTON, Grant 3
HOUSTON, Henry A. 3
HOUSTON, Henry Howard H
HOUSTON, Herbert Sherman 3
HOUSTON, John Wallace H
HOUSTON, Margaret Bell 4
HOUSTON, Oscar R. 5
HOUSTON, Persis Daniel 1
HOUSTON, Robert Griffith 2
HOUSTON, Samuel H
HOUSTON, Samuel Frederic 3
HOUSTON, Victor Steuart Kaleoaloha 5
HOUSTON, William Cannon 3
HOUSTON, William Churchill H
HOUSTOUN, John H

HOUSTOUN, William H
HOUTS, Charles Alfred 4
HOUX, Frank L. 3
HOVANNES, John 5
HOVDE, Bryn J. 3
HOVELL, Albert Armand 3
HOVENDEN, Thomas H
HOVER, William Adgate 3
HOVEY, Alvah 1
HOVEY, Alvin Peterson 4
HOVEY, Chandler 5
HOVEY, Charles Edward H
HOVEY, Charles Mason H
HOVEY, Chester Ralph 5
HOVEY, Edmund Otis 1
HOVEY, George Rice 3
HOVEY, Henriette (Mrs. Richard Hovey, formerly Mrs. 5
HOVEY, Horace Carter 1
HOVEY, Otis Ellis 1
HOVEY, Rexford William 3
HOVEY, Richard 1
HOVEY, William Simmons 3
HOVGAARD, William 2
HOVING, Johannes 5
HOVIS, William Forney 4
HOVLAND, Carl I. 5
HOW, Louis 2
HOWARD, A. T. 4
HOWARD, Ada Lydia 1
HOWARD, Albert Andrew 3
HOWARD, Alfred Taylor 2
HOWARD, Alice Sturtevant 2
HOWARD, Alvin Hayward 5
HOWARD, Arthur Ethelbert, Jr. 5
HOWARD, Arthur Platt 5
HOWARD, Ben Odell 5
HOWARD, Benjamin H
HOWARD, Benjamin Chew 4
HOWARD, Blanche Willis H
HOWARD, Bronson 1
HOWARD, Burt Estes 1
HOWARD, Burton James 2
HOWARD, Alan) Campbell Palmer 5
HOWARD, Cecil 'de Blaquiere 3
HOWARD, Charles Benjamin 4
HOWARD, Charles Danforth 2
HOWARD, Charles Pagelsen 4
HOWARD, Charles S. 3
HOWARD, Clara Eliza 1
HOWARD, Clarence Henry 1
HOWARD, Claud 1
HOWARD, Clifford 2
HOWARD, Clinton Norman 3
HOWARD, Clinton Wilbur 3
HOWARD, Dowell J. 3
HOWARD, Earl Dean 5
HOWARD, Eddy 4
HOWARD, Edgar 3
HOWARD, Edgar Billings 2
HOWARD, Edward Orson 2
HOWARD, Emma Pease 4
HOWARD, Eric 3
HOWARD, Ernest E. 3
HOWARD, Everette B. 1
HOWARD, Ezra Lee 5
HOWARD, Francis W. 2
HOWARD, Frank Atherton 4
HOWARD, Frank Eugene 4
HOWARD, Fred Leslie 1
HOWARD, Frederic Hollis 2
HOWARD, George Bronson 1
HOWARD, George C. H
HOWARD, George Elliott 3
HOWARD, George H. 1
HOWARD, George H. 4
HOWARD, Graeme Keith 4
HOWARD, Guy Clemens 4
HOWARD, H. Clay 1
HOWARD, Harry Clay 1
HOWARD, Harvey James 3
HOWARD, Hector Holdbrook 4
HOWARD, Henry H
HOWARD, Henry * 1
HOWARD, Henry 3
HOWARD, Herbert Burr 1
HOWARD, Jacob Merritt H
HOWARD, James E. 1
HOWARD, James Quay 1
HOWARD, James Raley 3
HOWARD, John Eager H

HOWARD, John Galen 1
HOWARD, John Raymond 1
HOWARD, John Tasker 4
HOWARD, Joseph Jr. 1
HOWARD, Joseph Henry 3
HOWARD, Joseph Whitney 5
HOWARD, Julia Palmer 5
HOWARD, Kathleen 3
HOWARD, Leland Ossian 3
HOWARD, Leslie 5
HOWARD, Louis Orrin 3
HOWARD, Lowry Samuel 1
HOWARD, Marion Edith 3
HOWARD, Milford W. 2
HOWARD, Nathaniel Lamson 2
HOWARD, Oliver Otis 1
HOWARD, Perry W. 4
HOWARD, Perry Wilbon 5
HOWARD, Philip Eugene 2
HOWARD, Ralph Hills 1
HOWARD, Robert Mayburn 4
HOWARD, Rossiter 2
HOWARD, Roy Wilson 1
HOWARD, Seth Edwin 1
HOWARD, Sidney Coe 1
HOWARD, Sir Esme William 1
HOWARD, Thomas Benton 1
HOWARD, Tilgham Ashurst H
HOWARD, Timothy Edward 1
HOWARD, Velma Swanston 1
HOWARD, Volney Erskine 1
HOWARD, Walter 1
HOWARD, Walter Eugene 1
HOWARD, Walter Lafayette 1
HOWARD, Wendell Stanton 4
HOWARD, Wesley O. 1
HOWARD, Wilbert Harvard 5
HOWARD, William H
HOWARD, William Alanson 4
HOWARD, William Clyde 3
HOWARD, William Eager, Jr. 5
HOWARD, William Gibbs 1
HOWARD, William Lauriston 1
HOWARD, William Lee 1
HOWARD, William Marcellus 5
HOWARD, William Schley 5
HOWARD, William Travis 5
HOWARD, Willie 1
HOWARTH, Ellen Clementine 1
HOWAT, William Frederick 4
HOWBERT, Irving 3
HOWDEN, Frederick Bingham 2
HOWE, Albert Richards H
HOWE, Albion Parris H
HOWE, Andrew Jackson H
HOWE, Anna Belknap 1
HOWE, Archibald Murray 1
HOWE, Arthur 3
HOWE, Arthur Millidge 2
HOWE, Burton Alonzo 3
HOWE, Carl 4
HOWE, Carl Ellis 4
HOWE, Charles Sumner 1
HOWE, Church 1
HOWE, Clarence Decatur 4
HOWE, Daniel Wait 1
HOWE, Edgar F. H
HOWE, Edgar Watson 1
HOWE, Edmund Grant 3
HOWE, Edward Gardner 4
HOWE, Edward Leavitt 3
HOWE, Elias H
HOWE, Ernest 1
HOWE, Frank William 4
HOWE, Frederic Clemson 1
HOWE, Frederic William 1
HOWE, Frederic William, Jr. 4
HOWE, Frederick Stanley 1
HOWE, Frederick Webster 2
HOWE, Gene Alexander 3
HOWE, George 3
HOWE, George 3

HUFFMAN, Oscar Caperton 1
HUFNAGEL, Edward Henry 2
HUFTY, Jacob H
HUG, George Willard 1
HUGE, Wilbert Erwin 4
HUGER, Alfred 1
HUGER, Benjamin *
HUGER, Daniel H
HUGER, Daniel Eliott H
HUGER, Francis Kinloch H
HUGER, Isaac H
HUGER, John H
HUGER, William Harleston 1
HUGET, J. Percival 4
HUGGENVIK, Theodore 5
HUGGINS, Eli Lundy 1
HUGGINS, George Augustus 4
HUGGINS, Miller James H
HUGGINS, Miller James 4
HUGGINS, R. Paul 4
HUGGINS, Raleigh Russell 1
HUGGINS, Richard Emmett 5
HUGGINS, William Lloyd 1
HUGGINS, William Ogburn 1
HUGHAN, Jessie Wallace 5
HUGHES, Aaron Konkle 1
HUGHES, Adella Prentiss 3
HUGHES, Albert Raymond 4
HUGHES, Charles H
HUGHES, Charles Colfax 2
HUGHES, Charles Evans 2
HUGHES, Charles Evans Jr. 2
HUGHES, Charles Frank 3
HUGHES, Charles Frederick 1
HUGHES, Charles Hamilton 4
HUGHES, Charles Haynes 5
HUGHES, Charles James Jr. 1
HUGHES, Christopher H
HUGHES, David Edward H
HUGHES, Donald James 4
HUGHES, Dudley Mays 2
HUGHES, Edward Smallwood 1
HUGHES, Edwin 1
HUGHES, Edwin Holt 2
HUGHES, Ellwood Clarke 1
HUGHES, Eugene Melvin 4
HUGHES, Everett S. 3
HUGHES, Francis Massie 5
HUGHES, Fred C. 1
HUGHES, George E. 1
HUGHES, George Wurtz H
HUGHES, Gerald 3
HUGHES, Harold L. 3
HUGHES, Hatcher 2
HUGHES, Hector James 1
HUGHES, Helen Sard 3
HUGHES, Henry 1
HUGHES, Herman Yeary 1
HUGHES, Hermann James 3
HUGHES, James 1
HUGHES, James Anthony 1
HUGHES, James Fredric 5
HUGHES, James H. 3
HUGHES, James Madison 1
HUGHES, James Monroe 5
HUGHES, James P. 4
HUGHES, John Chambers 5
HUGHES, John H. 3
HUGHES, John Henry 5
HUGHES, John Joseph H
HUGHES, John Newton 4
HUGHES, John T. 5
HUGHES, Joseph E. 4
HUGHES, Langston 5
HUGHES, Levi Allen 1
HUGHES, Louis C. 1
HUGHES, Matt Simpson 1
HUGHES, Merritt Yerkes 5
HUGHES, Mildred B. 5
HUGHES, Oliver John Davis 1
HUGHES, Percy 3
HUGHES, Percy Meredith 5
HUGHES, Peter Davis 1
HUGHES, Phillip Samuel 1
HUGHES, Price H
HUGHES, Ray Osgood 3
HUGHES, Raymond Mollyneaux 3
HUGHES, Reynold King 1
HUGHES, Richard Cecil 1
HUGHES, Robert Ball H
HUGHES, Robert M. Jr. 3

HUGHES, Robert Morton 1
HUGHES, Robert Patterson 1
HUGHES, Robert William 1
HUGHES, Rowland Roberts 3
HUGHES, Royal Delaney 1
HUGHES, Rupert 3
HUGHES, Russell Houston 5
HUGHES, Simon P. 1
HUGHES, Talmage Coates 4
HUGHES, Thomas Aloysius 4
HUGHES, Thomas Hurst H
HUGHES, Thomas Patrick 1
HUGHES, Thomas Welburn 2
HUGHES, Wilburn Patrick 1
HUGHES, William 1
HUGHES, William Edgar 4
HUGHES, William F. 1
HUGHES, William Joseph 1
HUGHES, William Leonard 3
HUGHITT, Marvin 1
HUGHITT, Marvin Jr. 2
HUGHSTON, Jonas Abbott H
HUGO, Albert Carl 3
HUGO, Trevanion William 4
HUGUELET, Guy Alexander 3
HUGUNIN, Daniel Jr. H
HUGUS, Wright 4
HUHLEIN, Charles Frederick 1
HUHNER, Leon 3
HUHNER, Max 2
HUIDEKOPER, Arthur Clarke 1
HUIDEKOPER, Frederic H
HUIDEKOPER, Frederic Louis 1
HUIDEKOPER, Frederic Wolters 1
HUIDEKOPER, Harm Jan 1
HUIDEKOPER, Henry Shippen 1
HUIDEKOPER, Reginald Shippen 2
HUIDEKOPER, Rush Shippen 1
HUIZENGA, Lee Sjoerds 2
HUIZINGA, Arnold 'van C. P. 3
HUIZINGA, Henry 1
HUKILL, Edwin Martin 4
HUKILL, Ralph LeRoy 5
HULBERT, Archer Butler 1
HULBERT, Calvin Butler 1
HULBERT, Edmund Daniel 1
HULBERT, Eri Baker 1
HULBERT, Geroge Murray 3
HULBERT, Henry Carlton 1
HULBERT, Henry Woodward H
HULBERT, Homer B. 2
HULBERT, John Whitefield H
HULBERT, Milan Hulbert 1
HULBERT, William Davenport 1
HULBURD, Calvin Tilden H
HULBURD, Charles Henry 1
HULBURT, David Willey 1
HULBURT, Lorrain Sherman 1
HULBURT, Ray Garland 2
HULEN, John Augustus 3
HULEN, Rubey Mosley 3
HULETT, Edwin Lee 2
HULETT, George Augustus 3
HULICK, George Washington 1
HULICK, Peter Vaughn 5
HULING, Ray Greene 1
HULING, Sara Hawks 1
HULINGS, Garnet 1
HULINGS, Willis James 1
HULINGS, Willis James 4
HULL, Albert Wallace 4
HULL, Alexander 1
HULL, Charles Henry 1
HULL, Clark Leonard 3
HULL, Cordell 3
HULL, David Carlisle 1
HULL, David Denton 2
HULL, George Huntington 1
HULL, George Ross 3

HULL, Gordon Ferrie 3
HULL, Harry Edward 1
HULL, Isaac H
HULL, John H
HULL, John Adley 2
HULL, John Albert Tiffin 1
HULL, Josephine 3
HULL, Lawrence Cameron 4
HULL, Merlin 3
HULL, Morton Denison 1
HULL, Nathan P. 3
HULL, Robert Johnson 4
HULL, Robert William 1
HULL, James) Roger 5
HULL, Roger Benton 1
HULL, Theodore Young 1
HULL, Thomas Everett 4
HULL, William H
HULL, William Edgar 2
HULL, William Isaac 1
HULLEY, Lincoln 1
HULLFISH, H. Gordon 4
HULLIHEN, Simon P. H
HULLIHEN, Walter 2
HULLINGER, Edwin Ware 5
HULME, Edward Maslin 1
HULME, Thomas Wilkins 1
HULME, William Henry 1
HULSE, George Egbert 4
HULSE, Hiram Richard 1
HULSHIZER, Stanford 5
HULST, Nelson Powell 1
HULSWIT, Frank Theodore 1
HULT, Adolf 2
HULT, Gottfried Emanuel 3
HULTEN, Charles M. 4
HULTEN, Herman H. 5
HULTMAN, Ivar Ninus 4
HULTZ, Fred Samuel 4
HULVEY, Otey Crawford 5
HUMASON, Harry Byrd 5
HUMASON, M. L. 5
HUMBER, Robert Lee 5
HUMBERT, Jean Joseph Amable H
HUMBERT, Russell J. 4
HUMBIRD, John Alexander 2
HUME, Alfred 3
HUME, Cyril 4
HUME, David 5
HUME, Edgar Erskine 3
HUME, Edward Hicks 3
HUME, H. Harold 5
HUME, James Cleland 3
HUME, Leland 4
HUME, Nelson 2
HUME, Omer Forest 3
HUME, Robert Allen 1
HUME, Robert Ernest 2
HUME, Thomas 1
HUME, William H
HUME, William 2
HUMES, Augustine Leftwich 3
HUMES, Harold Louis 4
HUMES, Thomas William H
HUMMEL, George F. 2
HUMMEL, George Henry 2
HUMMEL, R. A. 3
HUMMEL, William Grandville 1
HUMPHREY, Alexander Pope 1
HUMPHREY, Arthur Luther 1
HUMPHREY, Caroline Louise 1
HUMPHREY, Charles H
HUMPHREY, Charles Frederic 1
HUMPHREY, Charles Frederick, Jr. 5
HUMPHREY, Doris 3
HUMPHREY, Edward Frank 3
HUMPHREY, Evan H. 3
HUMPHREY, George Colvin 2
HUMPHREY, George Magoffin 5
HUMPHREY, George Thomas 5
HUMPHREY, Harry Baker 3
HUMPHREY, Helen F. 4
HUMPHREY, Heman H
HUMPHREY, Henry H. 2
HUMPHREY, Herman Leon 1
HUMPHREY, Herman Loin 1
HUMPHREY, J. Otis 1

HUMPHREY, James H
HUMPHREY, Lewis Craig 1
HUMPHREY, Lyman Underwood 1
HUMPHREY, Marie E. Ives 1
HUMPHREY, Reuben 1
HUMPHREY, Richard Lewis 1
HUMPHREY, Seth King 1
HUMPHREY, Walter R. 5
HUMPHREY, William Armine 4
HUMPHREY, William Brewster 4
HUMPHREY, William E. 1
HUMPHREY, William Francis 3
HUMPHREYS, Abram Stephanus 4
HUMPHREYS, Albert Edmund 5
HUMPHREYS, Albert Edmund 5
HUMPHREYS, Alexander Crombie 1
HUMPHREYS, Andrew Atkinson H
HUMPHREYS, Benjamin Grubb H
HUMPHREYS, Benjamin Grubb H
HUMPHREYS, Charles 1
HUMPHREYS, David H
HUMPHREYS, David Carlisle 1
HUMPHREYS, Frank Landon 1
HUMPHREYS, H. E. Jr. 4
HUMPHREYS, Harrie Moreland 2
HUMPHREYS, James H
HUMPHREYS, John J. 1
HUMPHREYS, Joshua H
HUMPHREYS, Lester Warren 1
HUMPHREYS, Marie Champney 1
HUMPHREYS, Mary Gay 1
HUMPHREYS, Milton Wylie 1
HUMPHREYS, Parry Wayne H
HUMPHREYS, Richard F(ranklin) 5
HUMPHREYS, Robert 4
HUMPHREYS, Solon 1
HUMPHREYS, T(homas) Hadden 5
HUMPHREYS, Walter 5
HUMPHREYS, West Hughes H
HUMPHREYS, Willard 1
HUMPHREYS, William Jackson 2
HUMPHREYS, William Yerger 1
HUMPHRIES, John Edmund 1
HUMPHRIES, George) Rolfe 5
HUMPHRISS, Charles H. 4
HUMPSTONE, Henry Judson 3
HUMSTONE, Walter Coutant 1
HUN, Henry 1
HUN, John Gale 2
HUND, H. E. 3
HUNDLEY, Henry Rhodes 1
HUNDLEY, John Robinson, Jr. 5
HUNDLEY, John Trible Thomas 4
HUNDLEY, Oscar R. 1
HUNEKE, William August 2
HUNEKER, James Gibbons 1
HUNGERFORD, Charles William 5
HUNGERFORD, Clark 4
HUNGERFORD, Edward 2
HUNGERFORD, Frank Louis 1
HUNGERFORD, John Newton H
HUNGERFORD, John Pratt H
HUNGERFORD, Orville H
HUNGERFORD, Samuel James 3
HUNKELER, Edward J(oseph) 5
HUNKER, John Jacob 1
HUNN, John 4

HUNNEMAN, William Cooper Jr.
HUNNER, Guy LeRoy
HUNNEWELL, Horatio Hollis
HUNNEWELL, James
HUNNEWELL, James Frothingham
HUNNEWELL, Walter
HUNNICUTT, Warren Towers
HUNSAKER, Walter Jerome
HUNT, Albert Clarence
HUNT, Albert Henry
HUNT, Alfred Ephraim
HUNT, Andrew Murray
HUNT, Arthur Prince
HUNT, Benjamin Weeks
HUNT, Carleton
HUNT, Caroline Louisa
HUNT, Charles Wallace
HUNT, Charles Warren
HUNT, Clara Whitehill
HUNT, Clyde Du Vernet
HUNT, D. F.
HUNT, Duane Garrison
HUNT, Edward Eyre
HUNT, Emory William
HUNT, Ernest Leroi
HUNT, Evert Merle
HUNT, Frank W.
HUNT, Frazier
HUNT, Frederick Salisbury
HUNT, Frederick Vinton
HUNT, Freeman
HUNT, Gaillard
HUNT, George Edwin
HUNT, George Wylie Paul
HUNT, Graham Putnam
HUNT, Harriet Larned
HUNT, Harriot Kezia
HUNT, Harry Hampton
HUNT, Henry Jackson
HUNT, Henry Warren
HUNT, Hiram Paine
HUNT, Isaac
HUNT, Isaac Hamilton
HUNT, James Bennett
HUNT, James Gallaway
HUNT, James Ramsay
HUNT, James Stone
HUNT, James Winford
HUNT, John Thomas
HUNT, Jonathan
HUNT, Leigh
HUNT, Leigh S. J.
HUNT, LeRoy Philip
HUNT, Lester Callaway
HUNT, Levi Clarence
HUNT, Livingston
HUNT, Mabel Leigh
HUNT, Marion Palmer
HUNT, Mary Hannah
HUNT, Myron
HUNT, Nathan
HUNT, O(ra) E(lmer)
HUNT, Ormond Edson
HUNT, Ralph Hudson
HUNT, Ralph Waldo Emerson
HUNT, Reid
HUNT, Richard Carley
HUNT, Richard Howland
HUNT, Richard Morris
HUNT, Robert
HUNT, Robert Woolston
HUNT, Roy Arthur
HUNT, Samuel
HUNT, Samuel Furman
HUNT, Seth Bliss
HUNT, Sumner P.
HUNT, Theodore Gallard
HUNT, Theodore Whitefield
HUNT, Thomas Forsyth
HUNT, Thomas Sterry
HUNT, Walter Reid
HUNT, Ward
HUNT, Washington
HUNT, Westley Marshall
HUNT, William Chamberlin
HUNT, William Gibbes
HUNT, William Henry
HUNT, William Henry
HUNT, William Morris
HUNT, William Peter
HUNT, William Prescott
HUNT, William Southworth
HUNT, Wilson Price
HUNTER, Aaron Burtis
HUNTER, Adison I.

HUNTER, 1
Alexander Stuart
HUNTER, Alfred M. 1
HUNTER, Andrew H
HUNTER, Andrew
Jackson 4
HUNTER, Arthur 4
HUNTER, Charles O. 4
HUNTER, Croil 5
HUNTER, Dard 4
HUNTER, David H
HUNTER, Edward 4
HUNTER, Fred Heaton 5
HUNTER, 4
George Bowditch
HUNTER, George King 1
HUNTER, George Leland 1
HUNTER, 4
George McPherson
HUNTER, George William 2
HUNTER, 4
Guy Breckenridge
HUNTER, Hiram Tyram 2
HUNTER, Horace
Talmage 4
HUNTER, Howard Owen 4
HUNTER, Hubert Samuel 1
HUNTER, James Boyd 4
HUNTER, Jay Tyler 3
HUNTER, Jesse Coleman 4
HUNTER, Joel 5
HUNTER, John H
HUNTER, John 1
HUNTER, John F. 3
HUNTER, John Lathrop 1
HUNTER, Joseph Rufus 3
HUNTER, Kent A. 1
HUNTER, Louis James 5
HUNTER, Matthew Albert 4
HUNTER, Merlin Harold 1
HUNTER, Morton Craig H
HUNTER, Narsworthy H
HUNTER, Oscar Benwood 3
HUNTER, Paull Stuart 1
HUNTER, R. M. 3
HUNTER, Richard H
HUNTER, 4
Richard Stockton
HUNTER, Robert H
HUNTER,
Robert Mercer Taliaferro
HUNTER,
Rudolph Melville 4
HUNTER, Samuel John 1
HUNTER,
Stephen Alexander
HUNTER, Thomas H
HUNTER, Thomas 4
HUNTER, Thomas
HUNTER, W. Godfrey 4
HUNTER, Walter David
HUNTER, Walter Samuel 3
HUNTER, Warren Clair 5
HUNTER, Wiles Robert 2
HUNTER, William * H
HUNTER,
William Armstrong
HUNTER, William Boyd 5
HUNTER, H
William Forrest
HUNTER, 1
William Forrest
HUNTER, William H. H
HUNTING, Fred Stanley 3
HUNTING, Gardner 4
HUNTING, 1
George Coolidge
HUNTING, Walter Judson 5
HUNTINGTON, Abel H
HUNTINGTON,
Adoniram Judson
HUNTINGTON, 3
Archer Milton
HUNTINGTON, 4
Arria Sargent
HUNTINGTON, 5
Arthur Franklin
HUNTINGTON,
Baldwin Gwynne
HUNTINGTON, Benjamin H
HUNTINGTON, 4
Charles Clifford
HUNTINGTON,
Charles Pratt
HUNTINGTON,
Clarence William
HUNTINGTON,
Collis Potter
HUNTINGTON, Daniel 1
HUNTINGTON, 3
Daniel Trumbull
HUNTINGTON,
David Lynde
HUNTINGTON,
DeWitt Clinton
HUNTINGTON, 5
Dorothy Phillips

HUNTINGTON, Ebenezer H
HUNTINGTON, 3
Edward Vermilye
HUNTINGTON, Elisha H
HUNTINGTON,
Ellsworth 2
HUNTINGTON, Emily 1
HUNTINGTON, Faye 4
HUNTINGTON, Ford 2
HUNTINGTON, 5
Frances Carpenter (Mrs.
William Chapin
HUNTINGTON, Frank 1
HUNTINGTON, 1
Frederic Dan
HUNTINGTON, George 1
HUNTINGTON, 3
George Herbert
HUNTINGTON, 1
George Sumner
HUNTINGTON, Harwood 1
HUNTINGTON, 1
Henry Alonzo
HUNTINGTON, 4
Henry Barrett
HUNTINGTON, 1
Henry Edwards
HUNTINGTON, Jabez H
HUNTINGTON, H
Jabez Williams
HUNTINGTON, 1
James Otis Sargent
HUNTINGTON, Jedediah H
HUNTINGTON, Lloyd
Lee 4
HUNTINGTON, 1
Margaret Evans
HUNTINGTON, 1
Oliver Whipple
HUNTINGTON, 5
Richard Lee
HUNTINGTON, 2
Robert Watkinson
HUNTINGTON, Samuel * 1
HUNTINGTON, 1
Theodore Sollace
HUNTINGTON, 1
Thomas Waterman
HUNTINGTON, 1
Tuley Francis
HUNTINGTON, 1
Warner Dare
HUNTINGTON, 4
Whitney Clark
HUNTINGTON, 3
William Chapin
HUNTINGTON, 1
William Edwards
HUNTINGTON, 1
William Reed
HUNTLEY, Charles R. 1
HUNTLEY, Elias DeWitt 1
HUNTLEY, Florence 1
HUNTLEY, 2
Samantha Littlefield
HUNTLEY, 5
Victoria Hutson
HUNTON, Eppa 1
HUNTON, Eppa Jr. 1
HUNTON, William Lee 1
HUNTOON, 1
Benjamin Bussey
HUNTOON, Gardner A. 5
HUNTOON, Louis
Doremus 2
HUNTRESS, 3
Carroll Benton
HUNTRESS, Frank G. 3
HUNTSMAN, Adam H
HUNTSMAN, 1
Owen Benjamin
HUNTSMAN, Robert F.
R. 2
HUNZIKER, 3
Otto Frederick
HUPP, John Cox 4
HUPPER, 3
Roscoe Henderson
HUPPUCH, Winfield A. 4
HURBAN, Vladimir S. 2
HURD, Albert Arthur 1
HURD, Archer Willis 3
HURD, Arthur William 1
HURD, Charles Edwin 1
HURD, Charles W.B. 5
HURD, Edward Melville 1
HURD, Edward Payson * 1
HURD, Eugene 1
HURD, Frank Hunt H
HURD, George Arthur 1
HURD, George Edward 5
HURD, Guilford Lansing 5
HURD, Harry Boyd 1
HURD, Harvey Bostwick 1
HURD, Henry Mills 1
HURD, John Codman H
HURD, Lee Maidment 2

HURD, Louis Guthrie 1
HURD, Nathaniel H
HURD, 1
Richard Melancthon
HURD, William Daniel 1
HURDLE, James Ernest 5
HURDON, Elizabeth 4
HURFF, 5
Lindley Scarlett
HURIE, Wiley Lin 3
HURLBERT, H
William Henry
HURLBUT, 1
Byron Satterlee
HURLBUT, Edwin Wilcox 1
HURLBUT, Jesse Lyman 1
HURLBUT, H
Stephen Augustus
HURLBUT, William N. 3
HURLEY, 2
Charles Francis
HURLEY, Edward Nash 1
HURLEY, Edward
Timothy 3
HURLEY, George 3
HURLEY, James E. 1
HURLEY, James Franklin 1
HURLEY, John Patrick 2
HURLEY, John Richard 1
HURLEY, Joseph Patrick 3
HURLEY, 1
Lawrence Francis
HURLEY, Leonard B. 4
HURLEY, 4
Margaret Helene
HURLEY, Neil C. 2
HURLEY, Neil C. Jr. 1
HURLEY, Patrick Jay 4
HURLEY, 5
Robert Augustine
HURLEY, Roy T. 5
HURLEY, Stephen
Edward 3
HURLEY, William E. 1
HURLL, Estelle May 1
HURRELL, Alfred 5
HURREY, 1
Clarence Barzillai
HURSH, Ralph Kent 4
HURST, Albert S. 2
HURST, Carlton Bailey 2
HURST, Charles Warner 2
HURST, Clarence Thomas 4
HURST, Fannie 2
HURST, Harold Emerson 5
HURST, John 1
HURST, John Fletcher 1
HURST, 5
Peter F(rederick)
HURST, William Henry 1
HURSTON, Zora Neale 3
HURT, Huber William 4
HURT, John Jeter 5
HURT, John Smith 2
HURT, Rollin 1
HURTH, Peter Joseph 1
HURTY, John N. 4
HURWITZ, Henry 3
HURWITZ, 5
Wallle Abraham
HUSAIN, Zaklr 3
HUSBAND, 1
George Rosewall
HUSBAND, Joseph 1
HUSBAND, 2
Richard Wellington
HUSBAND, 3
William Walter
HUSBANDS, Hermon H
HUSBANDS, Sam Henry 3
HUSE, Charles Phillips 3
HUSE, Harry Pinckney 2
HUSE, Raymond Howard 3
HUSE, William 4
HU-SHIH
HUSIK, Isaac 4
HUSING, Edward B. 1
HUSKINS, C. Leonard 4
HUSKINS, James Preston 2
HUSS, George Morehouse 2
HUSS, Henry Holden 3
HUSSERL, Edmond H
HUSSERL, Edmond 1
HUSSEY,
Charles Lincoln 1
HUSSEY, Curtis Grubb H
HUSSEY, John Brennan 4
HUSSEY, Obed 1
HUSSEY, Raymond 3
HUSSEY, Roland Dennis 4
HUSSEY, Tacitus 1
HUSSEY, William Joseph 3
HUSSLEIN, Joseph 1
HUSSMAN, George 5
HUSSON, 1
Chesley Hayward
HUSTED, James Delno 1

HUSTED, James William 1
HUSTED, Ladley,* 5
HUSTING, 2
Berthold Juneau
HUSTING, Paul Oscar 1
HUSTIS, James H. 2
HUSTON, 1
Abraham Francis
HUSTON, Charles H
HUSTON, 1
Charles Andrews
HUSTON, Charles Lukens 3
HUSTON, Claudius Hart 1
HUSTON, Henry Augustus 5
HUSTON, Howard Riggins 3
HUSTON, Joseph Waldo 1
HUSTON, Ralph Chase 3
HUSTON, Ralph Ernest 5
HUSTON, 5
S(imeon) Arthur
HUSTON, Stewart 1
HUSTON, Thad 5
HUSTON, Walter 4
HUTCHENS, 1
Frank Townsend
HUTCHEON, Robert
James 1
HUTCHERSON, 4
Dudley Robert
HUTCHESON,
Allen Carrington Jr. 4
HUTCHESON, David 4
HUTCHESON, Grote 2
HUTCHESON, John Bell 1
HUTCHESON, John Redd 4
HUTCHESON, 5
Joseph C, Jr.
HUTCHESON, 4
Joseph Chappell
HUTCHESON, 5
Martha Brookes
HUTCHESON,
William Anderson 1
HUTCHESON, William L. 3
HUTCHINGS, Frank Day 1
HUTCHINGS, 3
John Richard Jr.
HUTCHINGS, 3
Leslie Morton
HUTCHINGS, 4
Leslie Morton
HUTCHINGS, Lester 3
HUTCHINGS, 2
Richard Henry
HUTCHINS, 2
Augustus Schell
HUTCHINS, 4
Charles Clifford
HUTCHINS, 1
Charles Henry
HUTCHINS, 4
Charles Lewis
HUTCHINS, 1
Charles Pelton
HUTCHINS, 1
Charles Thomas
HUTCHINS, 1
Edward Webster
HUTCHINS, Frank Avery 3
HUTCHINS, 2
Frank Frazier
HUTCHINS, Harry Burns 1
HUTCHINS, 1
James Calhoun
HUTCHINS, 3
Jere Chamberlain
HUTCHINS, John H
HUTCHINS, John Corbin 1
HUTCHINS, Lee Wilson 1
HUTCHINS, Stilson 1
HUTCHINS, Thomas H
HUTCHINS, Waldo H
HUTCHINS, H
Wells Andrews
HUTCHINS, Will 2
HUTCHINS, William J. 3
HUTCHINSON,
Adoniram Judson Joseph
HUTCHINSON, Anne 4
HUTCHINSON,
Aubry Vaughan
HUTCHINSON, B. Edwin 4
HUTCHINSON, H
Benjamin Peters
HUTCHINSON, 1
Cary Talcott
HUTCHINSON,
Charles Lawrence
HUTCHINSON, 5
Edith Stotesbury
HUTCHINSON,
Elijah Cubberley
HUTCHINSON, 3
Ely Champion
HUTCHINSON, Emlen 4
HUTCHINSON, Forney 5

HUTCHINSON, 1
Frederick Lane
HUTCHINSON, 3
George Alexander
HUTCHINSON, 4
J. Raymond B.
HUTCHINSON, James H
HUTCHINSON, John 1
HUTCHINSON, 4
John Corrin
HUTCHINSON, John
Irwin 1
HUTCHINSON, 1
John Wallace
HUTCHINSON, 1
Joseph Baldwin
HUTCHINSON, 3
Knox Thomas
HUTCHINSON, 5
Mark Eastwood
HUTCHINSON, 3
Myron Wells Jr.
HUTCHINSON, Norman 1
HUTCHINSON, Paul 3
HUTCHINSON, 3
Robert Orland
HUTCHINSON, 1
S. Pemberton
HUTCHINSON, Thomas H
HUTCHINSON, William
K. 3
HUTCHINSON, 2
William Spencer
HUTCHINSON, Woods 1
HUTCHISON,
Benjamin Franklin
HUTCHISON, 4
Frances Kinsley
HUTCHISON,
Frederick William
HUTCHISON, 2
George Wayland
HUTCHISON, 3
James Brewster
HUTCHISON, James
Edgar 1
HUTCHISON, Martin Bell 1
HUTCHISON, 2
Miller Reese
HUTCHISON, 4
Ralph Cooper
HUTCHISON, 1
Robert Alden
HUTCHISON, Stuart Nye 5
HUTCHISON, Stuart Nye 4
HUTCHISON, Thomas L. 4
HUTCHISON, 3
William Easton
HUTCHMAN, 5
J(ohnston) Harper
HUTSON, 1
Charles Woodward
HUTSON, 3
Frederick Leroy
HUTSON, John B. 4
HUTSON, Joshua Brown 4
HUTSON, Leander C. 5
HUTSON, Richard H
HUTT, Henry 2
HUTTER, Francis 4
HUTTIG, Charles Henry 1
HUTTON, Colin Osborne 5
HUTTON, Edward F. 1
HUTTON, Edward Hyatt 1
HUTTON, 1
Frederick Remsen
HUTTON, James
Buchanan 1
HUTTON, James Morgan 1
HUTTON, John Edward H
HUTTON, Josiah Lawson 5
HUTTON, Laurence 4
HUTTON, Leon 4
HUTTON, Levi W. 1
HUTTON, Mancius
Holmes 1
HUTTON, Norman 1
HUTTON, Samuel Reed 4
HUTTON, William
Edward 3
HUTTY, Alfred 3
HUTZLER, Albert David 4
HUXFORD, Walter Scott 3
HUXLEY, Aldous Leonard 4
HUXLEY, Henry Minor 3
HUXMAN, Walter A. 5
HUYCK, Edmund Niles 1
HUYLER, John H
HUYSMANS, Camille 4
HYAM, Leslie Abraham 4
HYAMSON, Moses 2
HYATT, Alpheus 1
HYATT, Carl Britt 5
HYATT, Charles Eliot 3
HYATT, Edward 1
HYATT, Frank Kelso 3
HYATT, John Wesley 1

HYDE, Albert Alexander 1
HYDE, Ammi Bradford 1
HYDE, Arthur Knox 5
HYDE, Arthur M. 2
HYDE, Charles Cheney 3
HYDE, Charles Leavitt 1
HYDE, Clarence Ludlam 2
HYDE, Clayton H. 4
HYDE, 4
  Cornelius Willet Gillam
HYDE, D. Clark 3
HYDE, Donald Frizell 4
HYDE, Edward * H
HYDE, Edward Warden 1
HYDE, Edward Wyllys 1
HYDE, Edwin Francis 1
HYDE, 5
  Elizabeth A(dshead)
HYDE, George Merriam 1
HYDE, Grant Milnor 5
HYDE, Helen 1
HYDE, Henry Baldwin H
HYDE, Henry Morrow 5
HYDE, Howard Elmer 5
HYDE, Howard Kemper 5
HYDE, Howard Linton 5
HYDE, Ida Henrietta 3
HYDE, 2
  James Francis Clark
HYDE, James Hazen 3
HYDE, James Macdonald 5
HYDE, James Nevins 1
HYDE, Jeannette Acord 5
HYDE, Jesse Earl 1
HYDE, Joel Wilbur 1
HYDE, John 1
HYDE, John Bachman 5
HYDE, John McEwen 5
HYDE, John Sedgwick 1
HYDE, Joseph H
HYDE, Louis Kepler 4
HYDE, Mary Backus 5
HYDE, Mary Caroline 1
HYDE, Mary Kendall 1
HYDE, Miles Goodyear 4
HYDE, 5
  Nelson Collingwood
HYDE, Roscoe Raymond 2
HYDE, William Dedwitt 1
HYDE, William Henry 2
HYDE, William Waldo H
HYDE DE H
  NEUVILLE,
  Anne-Marguerite-
  Henriette
HYDRICK, Daniel
  Edward 1
HYER, David Burns, Jr. 5
HYER, Frank Sidney 3
HYER, Robert Stewart 1
HYLAN, John F. 1
HYLAN, John Perham 5
HYLAND, Francis E. 5
HYLAND, Philip David 3
HYLAND, William A. 4
HYLE, Michael William 4
HYLLESTED, 4
  August Frederick Ferdinand
HYLTON, John Dunbar 1
HYLTON, Joseph Roy 2
HYLTON-FOSTER, Harry 4
HYMAN, 5
  Albert Salisbury
HYMAN, Irving 4
HYMAN, John Adams H
HYMAN, 5
  Libbie Henrietta
HYMAN, 5
  Marion LaRoche Strobel
  (Mrs. John Patrick Hyman)
HYMAN, Stanley Edgar 5
HYMANS, Max 4
HYNDMAN, James
  Gilmore 1
HYNDS, John Arthur 2
HYNEMAN, John M. H
HYNES, John B. 5
HYNES, John William 3
HYNES, William J. 1
HYNICKA, 1
  Rudolph Kelker
HYNNINEN, P. J. 4
HYPES, Benjamin Murray 1
HYPES, Oran Faville 5
HYPES, Samuel L. 4
HYPES, William Findley 1
HYRE, 1
  Sarah Emma Cadwallader
HYRNE, H
  Edmund Massingberd
HYSLOP, James Augustus 3
HYSLOP, James Hervey 1
HYVERNAT, Henry 1
HYZER, Edward M. 1
HYZER, W. Edward 5

I

IARDELLA, Francisco H
IBANEZ DEL 4
  CAMPO, Carlos
IBERT, Jacques 4
IBSEN, Heman Lauritz 3
ICE, Harry Lawrence 4
ICHAILOVITCH, 5
  Lioubomir
ICKELHEIMER, Henry R. 4
ICKES, Harold L. 3
IDDINGS, Edward John 3
IDDINGS, Joseph Paxson 1
IDDINGS, Lewis Morris 1
IDE, Alba M. 1
IDE, Charles Edward 3
IDE, Fannie Ogden 1
IDE, George Edward 1
IDE, George Elmore 1
IDE, Henry Clay 1
IDE, John Jay 4
IDE, William B. H
IDELL, Albert Edward 3
IDEMA, Henry 3
IDESON, Julia Bedford 2
IDLEMAN, 1
  Finis Schuyler
IDLEMAN, 1
  Silas Ellsworth
IFFT, George Nicolas 2
IGLAUER, Samuel 2
IGLEHART, 2
  David Stewart
IGLEHART, 4
  Fanny Chambers Gooch
IGLEHART, 1
  Ferdinand Cowle
IGLESIAS, Santiago 4
IGOE, James Thomas 5
IGOE, Michael Lambert 4
IGOE, William L. 3
IHLDER, John 3
IHLE, Leo 3
IHLSENG, Axel Olaf 1
IHLSENG, 4
  Magnus Colbjorn
IHMSEN, 1
  Maximilian Frederick
IHRIE, Peter Jr. H
IHRIG, Harry Karl 4
IIAMS, Thomas Marion 4
IJAMS, Frank Burch 4
IJAMS, George Edwin 4
IKEDA, Hayato 4
ILAK, Abdul 4
ILES, George 4
ILES, Malvern Wells 1
ILES, Orlando Buff 1
ILGENFRITZ, Carl A. 4
ILGENFRITZ, E. K. 3
ILIFF, Thomas Corwin 1
ILL, Edward Joseph 1
ILLGES, John P. 3
ILLINGTON, Margaret 3
ILLINGWORTH, 3
  Sir Cyril Gordon
ILLOWAY, Henry 1
ILSLEY, Daniel H
ILSLEY, James Keeler 1
ILSLEY, James Lorimer 4
ILSLEY, 4
  Samuel Marshall
IMAHORN, Albert Peter 4
IMBERT, Antoine H
IMBODEN, John Daniel H
IMES, Birney Sr. 2
IMLAY, Gilbert H
IMLAY, James Henderson 1
IMLAY, Lorin Everett 1
IMMEL, Ray Keeslar 2
IMPERATORI, 3
  Charles Johnstone
INCE, Charles R. 4
INCE, Thomas Harper 1
INCH, Richard 1
INCH, Robert Alexander 4
INCH, Sydney Richard 4
INFELD, Leopold 4
INGALLS, 1
  Charles Russell
INGALLS, Fay 3
INGALLS, George Hoadly 1
INGALLS, James Monroe 1
INGALLS, Jeremiah 1
INGALLS, John James 1
INGALLS, Marilla Baker 1
INGALLS, Melville Ezra 1
INGALLS, 3
  Robert Ingersoll
INGALLS, 5
  Roscoe Cunningham
INGALLS, Walter Renton 3
INGALS, E. Fletcher 1
INGALSBE, 1
  Grenville Mellen
INGE, Francis Harrison 3

INGE, Samuel Williams H
INGE, William 5
INGE, William Marshall H
INGE, 3
  Zebulon Montgomery Pike
INGERSOLL, A. C. Jr. 4
INGERSOLL, 1
  Charles Edward
INGERSOLL, 2
  Charles Henry
INGERSOLL, 1
  Charles Jared
INGERSOLL, 2
  Colin Macrae
INGERSOLL, Ebon Clark H
INGERSOLL, Edward H
INGERSOLL, 1
  Edward Payson
INGERSOLL, Ernest 2
INGERSOLL, 1
  George Pratt
INGERSOLL, 1
  Henry Hulbert
INGERSOLL, 2
  Henry Wallace
INGERSOLL, Jared H
INGERSOLL, Joseph H
  Reed
INGERSOLL, 3
  Leonard Rose
INGERSOLL, H
  Ralph Isaacs
INGERSOLL, 1
  Raymond Vail
INGERSOLL, 1
  Robert Green
INGERSOLL, 1
  Robert Hawley
INGERSOLL, Roy Claire 4
INGERSOLL, 1
  Royal Rodney
INGERSOLL, Simon H
INGERSOLL, 5
  Tyrrell Meyer
INGERSOLL, 2
  William Harrison
INGHAM, H
  Charles Cromwell
INGHAM, Charles Samuel 2
INGHAM, Harvey 2
INGHAM, John Albertson 3
INGHAM, Lucius Edwin 3
INGHAM, Samuel H
INGHAM, H
  Samuel Delucenna
INGHAM, 1
  William Armstrong
INGLE, Edward 1
INGLE, James Addison 1
INGLE, Richard 1
INGLE, William 4
INGLESON, Robert G. 4
INGLEY, Fred 3
INGLIS, 1
  Alexander James
INGLIS, Charles H
INGLIS, James 2
INGLIS, Richard 3
INGLIS, 5
  William Wallace
INGMANSON, 4
  William Leslie
INGRAHAM, 1
  Darius Holbrook
INGRAHAM, H
  Duncan Nathaniel
INGRAHAM, 5
  Edgar Shugert
INGRAHAM, H
  Edward Duffield
INGRAHAM, 4
  Franc Douglas
INGRAHAM, 1
  Frances Adelaide Leverich
INGRAHAM, 1
  George Landon
INGRAHAM, Henry A. 4
INGRAHAM, 1
  Henry Cruise Murphy
INGRAHAM, 1
  John Phillips Thurston
INGRAHAM, Joseph 1
INGRAHAM, Joseph Holt H
INGRAHAM, Prentiss 1
INGRAHAM, 1
  William Moulton
INGRAM, 1
  Augustus Eugenio
INGRAM, Dwight 5
INGRAM, 4
  Edward Lovering
INGRAM, Eleanor Marie 1
INGRAM, 1
  Frederick Fremont
INGRAM, Henry Atlee 4
INGRAM, Jonas Howard 3
INGRAM, Leon John 5

INGRAM, Orrin Henry 4
INGVOLDSTAD, Orlando 5
INGWERSEN, John
  Arthur 3
INLOW, 3
  Richard Morehead
INMAN, Arthur Charles 4
INMAN, Edward
  Hamilton 1
INMAN, George H
INMAN, Henry H
INMAN, Henry 1
INMAN, Henry Arthur 5
INMAN, John H
INMAN, John Hamilton H
INMAN, Samuel Guy 4
INMAN, 3
  Walker Patterson
INNES, Frederick Neil 1
INNES, George 3
INNES, Harry H
INNES, James H
INNES, Katherine 4
INNES, Thomas Christie 1
INNESS, George H
INNESS, George Jr. 1
INNIS, George Swan 4
INNIS, 1
  William Reynolds
INNOKENTII H
INSKEEP, Annie Dolman 3
INSKIP, John Swanel H
INSLEY, William Henry 4
INSULL, 1
  Frederick William
INSULL, Martin John 5
INSULL, Samuel 3
INVERCHAPEL,
  Lord Archibald John Kerr
  Clark Kerr
INVERFORTH, Lord 3
INVILLIERS, 4
  Edward Vincent 'd
IOASAF H
IOOR, William H
IPATIEFF, 5
  Vladimir Nikolaevich
IPSEN, Ernest Ludvig 3
IRBY, 1
  John Laurens Manning
IRBY, John St John 1
IRBY, Nolen Meaders 3
IREDELL, 5
  Francis Raymond
IREDELL, James * H
IRELAN, Singer B. 3
IRELAND, Alleyne 5
IRELAND, 5
  Charles Thomas, Jr.
IRELAND, Clifford 1
IRELAND, John H
IRELAND, John 1
IRELAND, John 4
IRELAND, Joseph Norton H
IRELAND, 4
  Josias Alexander
IRELAND, Lloyd Owen 5
IRELAND, Mary E. 4
IRELAND, 3
  Merritte Weber
IRELAND, Oscar Brown 1
IRELAND, R.W. 5
IRELAND, 1
  Robert Livingston
IRELAND, Thomas 5
  Saxton
IRELAND, William 1
IRENE, Sister H
IRETON, Peter L. 4
IREY, Elmer Lincoln 2
IREYS, 2
  Charles Goodrich
IRION, 3
  Theophil William Henry
IRISH, Edwin M. 4
IRISH, Fred Abbott 1
IRISH, John Powell 1
IRISH, Rolland E. 4
IRLAND, George Allison 5
IRONQUILL 1
IRONS, Ernest Edward 3
IRONS, Henry Clay 4
IRONS, James Anderson 1
IRONSIDE, Henry Allan 3
IRVIN, Alexander H
IRVIN, Donald F. 3
IRVIN, James H
IRVIN, Leslie LeRoy 4
IRVIN, Rea 5
IRVIN, William Adolf H
IRVIN, William W. H
IRVINE, 1
  Alexander Fitzgerald
IRVINE, Alonzo Blair 1
IRVINE, 1
  Benjamin Franklin
IRVINE, Fergus Albert 4

IRVINE, Frank
IRVINE, James
IRVINE, James
IRVINE,
  Julia Josephine
IRVINE, Leigh Hadley
IRVINE, Robert Tate
IRVINE, William *
IRVINE, William
IRVINE, William Bay
IRVINE,
  William Burriss
IRVINE, William Mann
IRVINE, Wilson Henry
IRVING,
  Frederick Carpenter
IRVING,
  George Henry Jr.
IRVING, George Milton
IRVING, Isabel
IRVING, John Beaufain
IRVING, John Duer
IRVING, John Treat
IRVING, Minna
IRVING, Paulus A.
IRVING, Peter
IRVING, Pierre Munro H
IRVING, Roland Duer H
IRVING,
  Sir Henry Brodribb
IRVING, Thomas Patrick
IRVING, Washington H
IRVING, William H
IRWIN, Agnes
IRWIN,
  Bernard John Dowling
IRWIN, Charles Walter 4
IRWIN,
  Clinton Fillmore
IRWIN, Edward M. 4
IRWIN,
  Elisabeth Antoinette
IRWIN, 5
  Frederick Charles
IRWIN, George Le Roy 1
IRWIN, Harry N. 3
IRWIN, Harvey S. 4
IRWIN, Inez Haynes 5
IRWIN, Jared H
IRWIN, John 1
IRWIN, John Arthur 1
IRWIN, John Nichol 1
IRWIN, John Scull 1
IRWIN, Kilshaw McHenry 4
IRWIN, May 1
IRWIN, Noble Edward 1
IRWIN, Richard William 1
IRWIN, Robert Benjamin 4
IRWIN, 4
  Robert Forsythe Jr.
IRWIN, Robert Winfred 5
IRWIN, Solden H
IRWIN, Staford LeRoy 4
IRWIN, Thomas H
IRWIN, W. Francis 1
IRWIN, Wallace 3
IRWIN, Walter McMaster 4
IRWIN, Warren W. 1
IRWIN, William Andrew 4
IRWIN, William Glanton 2
IRWIN, William Henry 4
IRWIN, William Wallace H
ISAACS, Abram Samuel 1
ISAACS, Asher 5
ISAACS,
  Charles Applewhite
ISAACS, Edith J. R. 3
ISAACS, Hart 4
ISAACS, Hart 5
ISAACS, Henry G. 1
ISAACS, John Dove 1
ISAACS,
  Lewis Montefiore
ISAACS, Moses Legis 3
ISAACS, Myer Samuel 1
ISAACS, Nathan 1
ISAACS, Raphael 5
ISAACS, Samuel Myer H
ISAACS, Stanley Myer 1
ISAACSON,
  Charles David
ISACKS, Jacob C. H
ISBELL, Egbert Raymond 5
ISBRANDTSEN, Hans J. 4
ISELIN, Adrian 1
ISELIN, Charles Oliver 1
ISELIN,
  Columbus O'Donnell
ISELIN, 1
  Columbus O'Donnell
ISELIN, Ernest 3
ISELIN, Oliver 1
ISELY, Frederick B. 4
ISERMAN, Michael 5
ISHAM, Asa Brainerd 1

SHAM, 1
Frederic Stewart
SHAM, Henry Porter 5
SHAM, Mary Keyt 2
SHAM, Norman Morrison 2
SHAM, Ralph Heyward 3
SHAM, Samuel 1
SHERWOOD, 1
Benjamin Franklin
SLE, Walter Whitfield 3
SMAY, Lord 1
SOM, Edward Whitten 4
SOM, Mary Frances 4
ISRAEL, Arthur Jr. 4
ISRAEL, Edward L. 1
ISRAEL, Harold Edward 4
ISRAEL, Rogers 1
ISRAELS, 5
Carlos Lindner
ISSEKS, Samuel Shepp 3
ISSERMAN, 5
Ferdinand Myron
ISTEL, Andre 4
ITTEL, George Alfred 4
ITTLESON, Henry 2
ITTNER, Martin Hill 1
ITTNER, William Butts 1
IVANOWSKI, 5
Sigismond de
IVEAGH, The Earl 'of 4
IVERSEN, Lorenz 4
IVERSON, Alfred 1
IVERSON, 1
Samuel Gilbert
IVES, Augustus Wright 4
IVES, Brayton 1
IVES, Charles E. 3
IVES, Charles John 4
IVES, Charles Taylor 4
IVES, Chauncey Bradley H
IVES, Clarence Albert 5
IVES, Eli H
IVES, Frederic Eugene 1
IVES, Frederick Manley 3
IVES, George Burnham 1
IVES, Halsey Cooley 5
IVES, Herbert Eugene 3
IVES, Howard Chapin 2
IVES, Irving McNeil 4
IVES, James Edmund 2
IVES, James Merritt H
IVES, Joel Stone 1
IVES, John Hiett 5
IVES, John Winsor 3
IVES, Joseph Christmas H
IVES, Joseph Moss 1
IVES, Levi Silliman H
IVES, Percy 1
IVES, Ralph Burkett 1
IVES, Sarah Noble 5
IVES, Sumner Albert 2
IVES, Willard H
IVEY, Alphonso Lynn 1
IVEY, George Melvin 5
IVEY, Herbert Dee 4
IVEY, Joseph Benjamin 1
IVEY, Thomas Neal 1
IVIE, Joseph Henry 2
IVIE, William Noah 5
IVINS, Anthony W. 1
IVINS, Antoine Ridgway 5
IVINS, 4
Benjamin Franklin Price
IVINS, James S. Y. 4
IVINS, Lester Sylvan 4
IVINS, William Mills 1
IVINSON, Edward 1
IVISON, 1
David Brinkerhoff
IVY, Hardy H
IYENAGA, Toyokichi 3
IZARD, George H
IZARD, Ralph H
IZARD, Thomas C. 4

J

JACCARD, Walter M. 5
JACCHIA, Agide 1
JACK, 3
Frederick Lafayette
JACK, George Whitfield 1
JACK, James Robertson 3
JACK, John George 3
JACK, Summers Melville 4
JACK, Theodore Henley 4
JACK, William H
JACK, William Blake 2
JACKLIN, Edward G. 5
JACKLING, Daniel 3
Cowan
JACKMAN, Charles 3
Lyman
JACKMAN, Howard Hill 4
JACKMAN, Wilbur 1
Samuel
JACKS, Leo Vincent 5

JACKSON, 1
A. V. Williams
JACKSON, H
Abraham Reeves
JACKSON, 1
Abraham Willard
JACKSON, Albert Atlee 1
JACKSON, 1
Albert Mathews
JACKSON, Allan 4
JACKSON, Amos Henry 3
JACKSON, Amos Wade 5
JACKSON, Andrew H
JACKSON, Arnold S. 4
JACKSON, Arthur C. 3
JACKSON, 4
Bennett Barron
JACKSON, Burris C. 4
JACKSON, Carl Newell 2
JACKSON, Charles H
JACKSON, 5
Charles (Reginald)
JACKSON, 4
Charles Akerman
JACKSON, Charles Cabot 1
JACKSON, 4
Charles Douglas
JACKSON, 4
Charles H. Spurgeon
JACKSON, 1
Charles Loring
JACKSON, 1
Charles Samuel
JACKSON, 5
Charles Tenney
JACKSON, H
Charles Thomas
JACKSON, 1
Charles Warren
JACKSON, Chevalier 3
JACKSON, Chevalier L. 4
JACKSON, Claiborne Fox H
JACKSON, 2
Clarence Martin
JACKSON, 1
Clifford Linden
JACKSON, Daniel Dana 1
JACKSON, David H
JACKSON, David E. H
JACKSON, H
David Sherwood
JACKSON, 1
Dorothy Branch
JACKSON, Dugald Caleb 3
JACKSON, Dunham 2
JACKSON, E. Hilton 3
JACKSON, Ebenezer Jr. 1
JACKSON, Ed 3
JACKSON, Edward 2
JACKSON, Edward Brake 5
JACKSON, Edward 1
Payson
JACKSON, Elihu Emory 1
JACKSON, Ernest Bryan 4
JACKSON, Francis 1
JACKSON, Frank Dar 1
JACKSON, Frank Lee 1
JACKSON, Fred Schuyler 1
JACKSON, 2
Frederic Ellis
JACKSON, 1
Frederick John Foakes
JACKSON, 3
Frederick Mitchell
JACKSON, 4
Gabrielle Snow
JACKSON, George H
JACKSON, George 1
JACKSON, George Anson 1
JACKSON, George B. 4
JACKSON, 1
George Edwards
JACKSON, George K. H
JACKSON, George Leroy 5
JACKSON, George Pullen 3
JACKSON, 1
George Somerville
JACKSON, George 1
Thomas
JACKSON, 1
George Washington
JACKSON, Hall H
JACKSON, H
Helen Maria Fiske Hunt
JACKSON, Henry 1
JACKSON, Henry Ezekiel 1
JACKSON, 3
Henry Hollister
JACKSON, 1
Henry Melville
JACKSON, Henry Rootes H
JACKSON, Henry S. 1
JACKSON, 3
Herbert Spencer
JACKSON, 4
Herbert W. Jr.
JACKSON, Herbert Worth 4

JACKSON, 4
Holland Taylor
JACKSON, 1
Holmes Condict
JACKSON, 4
Howard Campbell Sr.
JACKSON, H
Howell Edmunds
JACKSON, J. Hugh 4
JACKSON, Jabez North 1
JACKSON, Jabez Young 1
JACKSON, James * H
JACKSON, James A. 1
JACKSON, James Arthur 3
JACKSON, James Caleb 1
JACKSON, James F. 1
JACKSON, 2
James Frederick
JACKSON, 2
James Hathaway
JACKSON, James 4
Kirkman
JACKSON, H
James Streshly
JACKSON, 2
Jesse Benjamin
JACKSON, John Adams H
JACKSON, 1
John Brinckerhoff
JACKSON, John Davies H
JACKSON, John Day 4
JACKSON, John Edward,* 5
JACKSON, John Edwin 5
JACKSON, John George 3
JACKSON, 3
John Gillespie
JACKSON, John Henry 1
JACKSON, John J. 5
JACKSON, John Jay 1
JACKSON, John Long 2
JACKSON, Jonathan 2
JACKSON, Joseph 2
JACKSON, Joseph Cooke 1
JACKSON, Joseph Henry 3
JACKSON, Joseph Henry 3
JACKSON, 5
Joseph Raymond
JACKSON, Joseph Webber H
JACKSON, 2
Josephine Agnes
JACKSON, 3
Katharine Johnson
JACKSON, 3
Lambert Lincoln
JACKSON, Mahalia 5
JACKSON, 1
Margaret Doyle
JACKSON, Martha 1
JACKSON, Mary Anna 1
JACKSON, McStay 4
JACKSON, H
Mercy Ruggles Bisbe
JACKSON, H
Mortimer Melville
JACKSON, Patrick Tracy H
JACKSON, Paul Rainey 5
JACKSON, Percival E. 1
JACKSON, Percy 1
JACKSON, 3
Philip Ludwell
JACKSON, H
Rachel Donelson
JACKSON, Ralph LeRoy 3
JACKSON, 5
Raymond Thomas
JACKSON, 1
Reginald Henry
JACKSON, Richard Jr. H
JACKSON, 1
Richard Arbuthnot
JACKSON, 3
Richard Harrison
JACKSON, 3
Richard Webber
JACKSON, 3
Robert Houghwout
JACKSON, Robert Tracy 2
JACKSON, 1
Roscoe Bradbury
JACKSON, Russell 1
JACKSON, Samuel H
JACKSON, Samuel Dillon 3
JACKSON, 1
Samuel Macauley
JACKSON, Samuel 2
Morley
JACKSON, Samuel P. H
JACKSON, Schuyler 4
Wood
JACKSON, Sheldon 4
JACKSON, Shirley 4
JACKSON, 4
Theodore Fredlinghuysen
JACKSON, H
Thomas Birdsall
JACKSON, Thomas Broun 5

JACKSON, 1
Thomas Herbert
JACKSON, H
Thomas Jonathan
JACKSON, Thomas 5
Wright
JACKSON, V. T. 5
JACKSON, 4
Virgil Thomas Sr.
JACKSON, Wilfrid J. 3
JACKSON, William * H
JACKSON, William 1
JACKSON, 1
William Alexander
JACKSON, 1
William Benjamin
JACKSON, 2
William H(arding)
JACKSON, William Henry 2
JACKSON, William Hicks 1
JACKSON, 1
William Humphreys
JACKSON, William J. 1
JACKSON, 5
William Kenneth
JACKSON, 1
William Nichols
JACKSON, William Payne 1
JACKSON, 1
William Purnell
JACKSON, William Terry H
JACKSON, 1
William Trayton
JACKVONY, Louis V. 3
JACOB, Richard Taylor 1
JACOB, Robert Byron 5
JACOBBERGER, 4
Francis Benedict
JACOBI, Abraham 1
JACOBI, Frederick 3
JACOBI, Herbert P. 5
JACOBI, Mary Putnam 1
JACOBS, 1
Benjamin Franklin
JACOBS, Carl Marlon 4
JACOBS, Charles M. 1
JACOBS, 5
Charles Michael
JACOBS, Edwin Elmore 3
JACOBS, 5
Elbridge Churchill
JACOBS, 1
Fenton Stratton
JACOBS, Ferris Jr. H
JACOBS, Fred Clinton 4
JACOBS, Harold Duane 3
JACOBS, Henry Barton 1
JACOBS, Henry Eyster 1
JACOBS, Henry L. 4
JACOBS, Israel H
JACOBS, J. Arthur 1
JACOBS, Jay Wesley 5
JACOBS, John Hall 4
JACOBS, John Marshall 4
JACOBS, Joseph 1
JACOBS, Joseph Earle 5
JACOBS, Joshua W. 1
JACOBS, Melville 5
JACOBS, Michael H
JACOBS, 4
Michael William
JACOBS, Michel 3
JACOBS, Myrl Lamont 3
JACOBS, Nathan Bernd 3
JACOBS, 4
Nehemiah Pitman Mann
JACOBS, Pattie Ruffner 1
JACOBS, Randall 1
JACOBS, Thornwell 3
JACOBS, Walter Abraham 1
JACOBS, Walter Ballou 1
JACOBS, Whipple 3
JACOBS, 2
William Plummer
JACOBS, William States 3
JACOBSEN, Alfred 4
JACOBSEN, 1
Bernhard Martin
JACOBSEN, Einar A. 5
JACOBSEN, Elnar A. 5
JACOBSEN, 5
Jerome Vincent
JACOBSOHN, 1
Simon Eberhard
JACOBSON, 3
Arthur Clarence
JACOBSON, 5
Belle Elizabeth
JACOBSON, Carl Alfred 5
JACOBSON, 2
Carl Frederick
JACOBSON, Fritz 1
JACOBSON, Gabe 2
JACOBSON, H
John Christian
JACOBSON, 4
Morris Lazarev

JACOBSON, 5
Moses Abraham
JACOBSSON, Per 4
JACOBSTEIN, Meyer 4
JACOBUS, David Schenck 3
JACOBUS, 1
Melancthon Williams
JACOBY, George W. 1
JACOBY, Harold 1
JACOBY, 3
Henry Sylvester
JACOBY, Ludwig Sigmund H
JACOBY, Raymond W. 4
JACOBY, William Lawall 1
JACOWAY, 5
Henderson Madison
JACQUES, 4
Sidney Bennett
JACQUES, William White 1
JADWIN, Edgar 1
JAECKEL, Theodore 1
JAEGER, Alphons Otto 3
JAEGER, Gebhard 4
JAEGER, Werner Wilhelm 4
JAEGERS, Albert 1
JAEKEL, Frederic Blair 2
JAFFA, Myer Edward 1
JAFFE, Louis Isaac 1
JAFFRAY, Clive Talbot 3
JAGEMANN, 1
Hans Carl Gunther 'von
JAGGAR, 1
Thomas Augustus
JAGGAR, 1
Thomas Augustus
JAGGARD, Edwin Ames 1
JAHN, Gunnar 5
JAHN, Walter J. 1
JAHNCKE, Ernest Lee 4
JAHNCKE, P.F. Sr. 5
JAHR, 5
Torstein (Knutsson Torstensen)
JAKOSKY, John Jay 1
JALLADE, Louis Eugene 3
JAMERSON, G(eorge) H. 5
JAMES, Addison Davis 1
JAMES, Albert Calder 4
JAMES, Alexander 2
JAMES, 3
Alice Archer Sewall
JAMES, Amaziah Bailey H
JAMES, Aphie 5
JAMES, Arthur Curtiss 1
JAMES, Arthur Horace 1
JAMES, 3
Bartlett Burleigh
JAMES, Ben 4
JAMES, Benjamin F. 4
JAMES, 1
Bushrod Washington
JAMES, Charles 1
JAMES, Charles Fenton 1
JAMES, Charles P. H
JAMES, 1
Charles Tillinghast
JAMES, D. Bushrod 1
JAMES, D. Willis 1
JAMES, Darwin Rush * 1
JAMES, Donald Denny 5
JAMES, Edmund Janes 1
JAMES, H
Edward Christopher
JAMES, Edward David 5
JAMES, Edward Holton 3
JAMES, 5
Edward Washington
JAMES, Edwin H
JAMES, Edwin Leland 3
JAMES, Edwin Warley 5
JAMES, Eldon Revare 2
JAMES, Fleming 3
JAMES, Francis H
JAMES, Francis Bacon 1
JAMES, Frank Cyril 5
JAMES, Frank Lowber 5
JAMES, George 5
JAMES, George Francis 1
JAMES, George Oscar 1
JAMES, George Roosa 5
JAMES, George Wharton 1
JAMES, Henry * H
JAMES, Henry 1
JAMES, Henry 1
JAMES, Henry 5
JAMES, Herman Brooks 5
JAMES, James Alton 4
JAMES, James Charles 5
JAMES, Jesse Woodson H
JAMES, John Edwin 4
JAMES, Joseph Hidy 2
JAMES, Louis 1
JAMES, Marquis 3
JAMES, Mary E. 1

JAMES, 5
Minnie Kennedy (Mrs. Wm.
Carey James)
JAMES, Ollie M. 1
JAMES, Ollie Murray 5
JAMES, Reese D. 4
JAMES, Samuel Catlett 4
JAMES, 4
Samuel Humphreys
JAMES, Thomas H
JAMES, Thomas Chalkley H
JAMES, Thomas Lemuel 1
JAMES, Thomas Potts H
JAMES, W. Frank 2
JAMES, Walter Belknap 1
JAMES, Walter Gilbert 2
JAMES, Warren William 2
JAMES, William 1
JAMES, William 4
JAMES, William Carey 1
JAMES,
William Hartford
JAMES, William John 1
JAMES, William Knowles 1
JAMES, William M. 3
JAMES, William P. 1
JAMES, 2
William Roderick
JAMES, William Stubbs 4
JAMESON, Edwin Cornell 2
JAMESON, Henry
JAMESON, Horatio Gates H
JAMESON, John H
JAMESON, H
John Alexander
JAMESON, John Butler 4
JAMESON, John Franklin 1
JAMESON, P. Henry 4
JAMESON, Patrick Henry 4
JAMESON, Robert Willis 3
JAMESON, 3
Russell Parsons
JAMIESON, 1
Charles Clark
JAMIESON, 1
Edmund Scudder
JAMIESON, 3
Francis Anthony
JAMIESON, Guy Arthur 4
JAMIESON, Robert Cary 4
JAMIESON, Thomas N. 4
JAMIESON, William D. 4
JAMIESON, 4
William Edward
JAMISON, Alpha Pierce 5
JAMISON, Atha Thomas 4
JAMISON, Cecilia Viets 4
JAMISON, 4
Charles Laselle
JAMISON, David H
JAMISON, David Lee 2
JAMISON, Joseph Warren 4
JAMISON, Minnie Lou 4
JAMISON, 1
Monroe Franklin
JAMISON, Paul Bailey 5
JAMISON, Robert H. 4
JAMISON, 4
Thomas Worth Jr.
JAMISON, 1
William Arbuckle
JANAUSHEK, Francesca 4
JANE, Robert Stephen 3
JANES, George Milton 1
JANES, Henry Fisk H
JANES, John Valle 5
JANES, Lewis George H
JANES, Lewis George 1
JANEWAY,
Edward Gamaliel
JANEWAY, Frank 4
Latimer
JANEWAY, Phineas Allen 4
JANEWAY, H
Theodore Caldwell
JANIS, Elsie 3
JANISSE, Denis R. 4
JANNEY, O. Edward
JANNEY, Russell 4
JANNEY, H
Samuel McPherson
JANNEY, Thomas B. 1
JANNOTTA, 5
Alfred Vernon
JANSEN, Ernest George
JANSEN, Marie 1
JANSEN, Peter 4
JANSEN, Reinier H
JANSEN, William 4
JANSS, Peter W(illiam) 4
JANSSEN, E. C. 2
JANSSEN, Henry 1
JANSSEN, John 1
JANSSENS, Francis H
JANSSON,
Edward Fritiof
JANUARY, William Louis 4

JANVIER, 1
Caesar A. Rodney
JANVIER, Catharine Ann 1
JANVIER, Charles 1
JANVIER,
Margaret Thomson
JANVIER,
Thomas Allibone
JANVRIN, Joseph Edward
JANZEN, Assar Gotrik 5
JANZEN, Danile H(ugo) 5
JAQUA, Albert Roscoe 5
JAQUA, Ernest James 5
JAQUES, Alfred 1
JAQUES, Bertha E. 2
JAQUES, 3
Charles Everett
JAQUES, Francis Lee 5
JAQUES, Herbert 1
JAQUES, Willard W. 1
JAQUES, William Henry 1
JAQUESS, James Frazier H
JAQUESS, 4
William Thomas
JAQUITH, 2
Harold Clarence
JARBOE, Henry Lee 4
JARDINE, David H
JARDINE, James Tertius 3
JARDINE, John Earle 3
JARDINE, 5
John Earle, Jr.
JARDINE, William M. 3
JARECKY, Herman 4
JARMAN, Joseph Leonard 2
JARMAN, Lewis Wilson 3
JARMAN, Pete 3
JARMAN, Sanderford 3
JARNAGIN, Spencer H
JARRATT, Devereaux 5
JARRATT, Hill 5
JARRELL, Albert Polk 5
JARRELL, Albert Polk 4
JARRELL, 5
Charles Crawford
JARRELL, Randall 4
JARRETT, Benjamin 2
JARRETT, Cora Hardy 5
JARRETT, Edwin Seton 3
JARRETT, 3
William Ambrose
JARRETT, William Paul 1
JARRETT, William Paul 2
JARROLD, Ernest 4
JARVES, James Jackson H
JARVIE, James Newbegin 1
JARVIS, Charles H. H
JARVIS, Chester Deacon 2
JARVIS, David Henry 4
JARVIS, 4
De Forest Clinton
JARVIS, Deming 1
JARVIS, Edward H
JARVIS, George Tibbals 5
JARVIS, 1
Harry Aydelotte
JARVIS, John Wesley H
JARVIS, Leonard H
JARVIS, 5
Robert Edward Lee
JARVIS, Samuel M. 1
JARVIS, Thomas Jordan 1
JARVIS, Thomas Neilson 2
JARVIS, William H
JARVIS,
William Chapman
JASPER, William H
JASSPON, William Henry 3
JASTRAM, 3
Edward Perkins
JASTROW, Joseph 2
JASTROW, Marcus 1
JASTROW, Morris Jr. 1
JASZI, Oscar 3
JAUNCEY, 2
George Eric MacDonnell
JAUREGUI, 1
Guillermo Patterson 'y
JAVIS, Abraham H
JAY, 3
Clarence Hollingsworth
JAY, John * 1
JAY, John Clarkson 1
JAY, John Edwin 4
JAY, Lawrence Merton 1
JAY, Mary Rutherford 3
JAY, Milton 1
JAY, Nelson Dean 5
JAY, Peter Augustus 1
JAY, Peter Augustus 1
JAY, Pierre 2
JAY, Sir James H
JAY, William * 1
JAY, William H
JAYCOX, Walter Husted 1
JAYNE, Anselm Helm 4
JAYNE, Benaiah Gustin 4

JAYNE, 1
Caroline Furness
JAYNE, Henry LaBarre 1
JAYNE, Horace 1
JAYNE, Joseph Lee 1
JAYNE, Walter Addison 1
JAYNES, Allan Brown 1
JEAN, Sister Anne 5
JEAN, Sally Lucas 5
JEANMARD, 3
Jules Benjamin
JEANS, Philip Charles 3
JECK, George G. 5
JEFFERIS, Albert Webb 4
JEFFERIS, William W. 1
JEFFERS, 1
Eliakim Tupper
JEFFERS, Henry William 3
JEFFERS, Katharine R. 1
JEFFERS, LeRoy 1
JEFFERS, Robinson 4
JEFFERS, 1
William Hamilton
JEFFERS, 3
William Martin
JEFFERS, H
William Nicholson
JEFFERSON, 5
Benjamin Lafayette
JEFFERSON, 4
Bradley Carter
JEFFERSON, 1
Charles Edward
JEFFERSON, 4
Clarence Ernest
JEFFERSON, H
Cornelia Burke
JEFFERSON, 5
Floyd Wellman
JEFFERSON, 4
Floyd Wellman Jr.
JEFFERSON, 1
John Percival
JEFFERSON, Joseph H
JEFFERSON, Joseph * 1
JEFFERSON, Mark 4
JEFFERSON, H
Martha Wayles
JEFFERSON, Robert 4
JEFFERSON, 1
Samuel Mitchell
JEFFERSON, Thomas H
JEFFERY, Edward Turner 1
JEFFERY, Elmore Berry 1
JEFFERY, Robert Emmett 1
JEFFERY, H
Rosa Griffith Vertner
Johnson
JEFFERY, 3
William Prentiss
JEFFERYS, 3
Charles William
JEFFERYS, 2
Edward Miller
JEFFERYS, 2
William Hamilton
JEFFORDS, Elza H
JEFFORDS, Olin Merrill 4
JEFFREY,
Edward Charles
JEFFREY, Frank Rumer 2
JEFFREY, Walter Roland 5
JEFFRIES, Benjamin Joy 1
JEFFRIES, Edward J. 3
JEFFRIES, John H
JEFFRIES, Louis Eugene 1
JEFFRIES, 1
Millard Dudley
JEFFRIES, Walter Sooy 3
JEFFRIES, Zay 4
JEFFRIS, 1
Malcolm George
JEFFS, 3
Charles Richardson
JEIDELS, Otto 2
JELKE, 1
Ferdinand Frazier
JELKE, John Faris 4
JELKS, James Thomas 4
JELKS, John Lemuel 2
JELKS, William Dorsey 1
JELLIFF, Horatio F. 1
JELLIFFE, Smith Ely 2
JELLINEK, Elvin M. 4
JELLINGHAUS, C. L. 4
JELLISON, 4
Walter Fremont
JEMISON, David Vivian 3
JEMISON, Mary 1
JEMISON, Robert Sr. 1
JENCKES, Joseph * H
JENCKES, 5
Joseph Sherburne, Jr.
JENCKES, Marcien 1
JENCKES, Thomas Allen H
JENCKS, Millard Henry 2
JENIFER, Daniel * H

JENKINS, H
Albert Gallatin
JENKINS, 3
Alfred Alexander Jr.
JENKINS, Arthur 1
JENKINS, Burris Jr. 4
JENKINS, Burris Atkins 3
JENKINS, C. Bissell 3
JENKINS, 1
Charles Francis
JENKINS, 3
Charles Francis
JENKINS, Charles Jones H
JENKINS, Charles Rush 1
JENKINS, 1
Daniel Edwards
JENKINS, David Rhys 3
JENKINS, E. Fellows 1
JENKINS, Edward Corbin 1
JENKINS, Edward Elmer 5
JENKINS, 1
Edward Hopkins
JENKINS, 4
Florence Foster
JENKINS, Frances 5
JENKINS, Francis A. 4
JENKINS, Frank Edwin 4
JENKINS, 1
Frederick Warren
JENKINS, 1
George Franklin
JENKINS, 5
Herbert F(ranklin)
JENKINS, 5
Herbert Theodore
JENKINS, Hermon Dutilh 1
JENKINS, Herschel V. 4
JENKINS, Hilger Perry 5
JENKINS, 1
Howard Malcolm
JENKINS, J. Caldwell 4
JENKINS, 5
James Alexander
JENKINS, 4
James Alexander
JENKINS, James Graham 1
JENKINS, John H
JENKINS, John J. 1
JENKINS, John Murray 3
JENKINS, John S. Jr. 5
JENKINS, John Stilwell 1
JENKINS, Joseph J. 4
JENKINS, Lemuel 1
JENKINS, MacGregor 1
JENKINS, Micah 1
JENKINS, Michael 1
JENKINS, Nathaniel 1
JENKINS, 1
Oliver Peebles
JENKINS, Paul Burrill 1
JENKINS, Perry Wilson 3
JENKINS, Ralph Carlton 2
JENKINS, Robert 1
JENKINS, Robert Edwin 1
JENKINS, 5
Romilly James Heald
JENKINS, Stephen 1
JENKINS, Thomas 5
JENKINS, Thomas Albert 3
JENKINS, 1
Thomas Atkinson
JENKINS, H
Thornton Alexander
JENKINS, Timothy H
JENKINS, Vernon Henry 3
JENKINS, 1
William Dunbar
JENKINS, William J. 3
JENKINS, William Leroy 1
JENKINS, William M. 1
JENKINS, William Oscar 4
JENKINS, 5
William Robert
JENKINSON, Isaac 1
JENKINSON, Richard C. 1
JENKS, Albert Ernest 3
JENKS, Almet 4
JENKS, Almet Francis 1
JENKS, Arthur Byron 2
JENKS, Arthur Whipple 1
JENKS, Benjamin L. 4
JENKS, Edward Watrous 1
JENKS, Edwin Hart 1
JENKS, George Augustus 1
JENKS, George Charles 1
JENKS, Henry Fitch 4
JENKS, James Lawrence 1
JENKS, 1
Jeremiah Whipple
JENKS, John Edward 1
JENKS, John Story 2
JENKS, 5
John Whipple Potter
JENKS, Joseph H
JENKS, H
Michael Hutchinson
JENKS, Orrin Roe 1

JENKS, 1
Phoebe A. Pickering
JENKS, Tudor 1
JENKS, William H
JENKS, William Jackson 3
JENNE, James Nathaniel 1
JENNESS, H
Benning Wentworth
JENNESS, Leslie George 5
JENNESS, Lyndon Yates 4
JENNESS,
Theodora Robinson
JENNEY, Charles Albert 4
JENNEY, 1
Charles Francis
JENNEY, Ralph E.
JENNEY, 1
William Le Baron
JENNEY, 5
William Sherman
JENNINGS, 1
Andrew Jackson
JENNINGS, B. Brewster 5
JENNINGS, 1
Charles Godwin
JENNINGS, David H
JENNINGS, David 3
JENNINGS, 5
Dean Southern
JENNINGS, Edward
Henry
JENNINGS, Edwin B. 4
JENNINGS, Elzy Dee 1
JENNINGS, Frank E. 5
JENNINGS,
Frederic Beach
JENNINGS, Hennen 1
JENNINGS,
Henry Burritt
JENNINGS, Henry C. 1
JENNINGS,
Herbert Spencer
JENNINGS, Isaac, Jr. 5
JENNINGS, Joe Leslie 5
JENNINGS, John H
JENNINGS, John Jr. 3
JENNINGS, John Joseph 1
JENNINGS, Jonathan H
JENNINGS, Judson Toll 2
JENNINGS, 5
Leslie Nelson
JENNINGS, Louis John H
JENNINGS, Maria Croft 1
JENNINGS,
Martin Luther
JENNINGS, Newell 4
JENNINGS, O. E. 4
JENNINGS, Oliver Gould 1
JENNINGS,
Richard William
JENNINGS, 4
Robert William
JENNINGS, Roscoe G. 4
JENNINGS, Rudolph D. 1
JENNINGS, 3
Samuel Clemens
JENNINGS,
Sidney Johnston
JENNINGS, 5
Stephen Richard
JENNINGS, W. Beatty 1
JENNINGS, Walter 2
JENNINGS, Walter Louis 5
JENNINGS,
Wesley William
JENNINGS, 1
William Sherman
JENNNINGS, T. Albert
JENSEN, Ben Franklin 4
JENSEN, Elmer C. 1
JENSEN, Frank A. 2
JENSEN, Howard C. 4
JENSEN, Jens 3
JENSEN, Johannes V. 4
JENSEN, John Christian 3
JENSEN, Leslie 4
JENSEN, Ralph Adelbert 5
JENT, John William 1
JENTE, Richard 4
JEPPSON,
George Nathaniel
JEPSON, Harry B. 3
JEPSON, Ivar Per 4
JEPSON, Samuel L. 1
JEPSON, William 1
JERGENS, Andrew
JERMAIN, Louis Francis 1
JERMAN,
Mrs. Cornelia Petty
JERMANE,
William Wallace
JERNBERG,
Reinert August
JERNEGAN, 2
Marcus Wilson
JERNEGAN,
Prescott Ford

JERNIGAN, Charlton C. 3
JEROLOMAN, John 4
JEROME, Brother 3
JEROME, Chauncey H
JEROME, Harry 1
JEROME, 1
 William Travers
JERSILD, 5
 Marvin A(mble)
JERVEY, Henry 2
JERVEY, 2
 Huger Wilkinson
JERVEY, James Postell 2
JERVEY, 2
 James Wilkinson
JERVIS, H
 John Bloomfield
JESSE, Richard Henry 2
JESSE, Richard Henry 3
JESSE, 5
 William H(erman)
JESSEN, Karl Detlev 1
JESSOPP, 4
 Dudley Frederick
JESSUP, 4
 Charles Augustus
JESSUP, Edgar B. 4
JESSUP, 5
 Everett Colgate
JESSUP, Henry Harris 1
JESSUP, Henry Wynans 1
JESSUP, Joseph John 3
JESSUP, Samuel 1
JESSUP, Walter Albert 2
JESTER, 1
 Beauford Halbert
JESTER, John Roberts 1
JESUP, Henry Griswold 1
JESUP, Morris Ketchum 1
JESUP, Thomas Sidney H
JETER, Frank Hamilton 3
JETER, Jeremiah Bell 1
JETT, Ewell Kirk 4
JETT, Robert Carter 5
JETT, Thomas M. 4
JEWELL, Edward Alden 2
JEWELL, 1
 Frederick Swartz
JEWELL, Harvey H
JEWELL, John Franklin 1
JEWELL, Louise Pond 2
JEWELL, Marshall H
JEWELL, 1
 Theodore Frelinghuysen
JEWELL, William Henry 3
JEWETT, 3
 Arthur Crawford
JEWETT, Charles 1
JEWETT, Charles Coffin H
JEWETT, David 1
JEWETT, Edward Hurtt 1
JEWETT, Frances Gulick 4
JEWETT, Frank Baldwin 2
JEWETT, Frank Fanning 3
JEWETT, H
 Frederick Stiles
JEWETT, H
 Freeborn Garrettson
JEWETT, George Anson 1
JEWETT, 1
 George Franklin
JEWETT, 3
 George Frederick
JEWETT, Harry Mulford 1
JEWETT, Harvey C. 1
JEWETT, 3
 Harvey Chase Jr.
JEWETT, Hugh Judge H
JEWETT, James Richard 2
JEWETT, John Howard 1
JEWETT, John Howard 4
JEWETT, John Punchard H
JEWETT, Joshua Husband H
JEWETT, Luther H
JEWETT, Milo Parker H
JEWETT, Nelson J. 3
JEWETT, H
 Rutger Bleecker
JEWETT, Sarah Orne 1
JEWETT, Sophie 1
JEWETT, Stephen Perham 5
JEWETT, 1
 Stephen Shannon
JEWETT, William H
JEWETT, H
 William Cornell
JEWETT, H
 William Samuel Lyon
JEWETT, William Smith H
JIGGITTS, 2
 Louis Meredith
JIMENEZ, Juan Ramon 3
JIMENEZ 2
 OREAMUNO, Ricardo
JINNAH, Mahomed Ali 2
JOANNES, Francis Y. 3
JOAREZ, Benito H

JOB, Frederick William 4
JOB, Herbert Keightley 1
JOB, Robert 4
JOB, Thomas 2
JOBES, Harry C. 5
JOBLING, James Wesley 4
JOCELYN, Nathaniel H
JOCELYN, Simeon Smith 1
JOCELYN, Stephen Perry 1
JOCHEMS, 4
 William Dennis
JOEKEL, 3
 Samuel Levinson
JOEL, 3
 George William Freeman
JOERG, W. L. G. 3
JOESTING, 4
 Henry Rochambeau
JOGUES, Isaac H
JOHANN, Carl 1
JOHANNES, Francis 1
JOHANNSEN, 4
 Oskar Augustus
JOHANSEN, George P. 4
JOHANSEN, John C. 4
JOHL, Edwin Phillips 4
JOHN, Augustus E. 4
JOHN, 5
 Francis, Sister Mary
JOHN, 1
 John Price Durbin
JOHN, Samuel Will 4
JOHN, 4
 Waldemar Alfred Paul
JOHN, 4
 William Mestrezat
JOHN, William Scott 3
JOHNES, Edward 1
 Rodolph
JOHNS, Carl Oscar 2
JOHNS, Charles A. 1
JOHNS, Choate Webster 4
JOHNS, Clarence D. 3
JOHNS, Clayton 1
JOHNS, Cyrus N. 5
JOHNS, Frank Stoddert 5
JOHNS, George Sibley 1
JOHNS, John H
JOHNS, Joshua Leroy 1
JOHNS, Kensey H
JOHNS, Kensey Jr. H
JOHNS, Roy William 4
JOHNS, 2
 William Hingston
JOHNSEN, Erik Kristian 1
JOHNSON, Aben 4
JOHNSON, Adam Rankin 4
JOHNSON, 4
 Adelaide McFadyen
JOHNSON, Adna 4
 Romulus
JOHNSON, Alba 1
 Boardman
JOHNSON, Albert 3
JOHNSON, Albert Henry 5
JOHNSON, Albert Mussey 2
JOHNSON, 4
 Albert Richard
JOHNSON, 3
 Albert Rittenhouse
JOHNSON, 3
 Albert Williams
JOHNSON, 4
 Albinus Alonzo
JOHNSON, Alden Porter 5
JOHNSON, Alex Carlton 4
JOHNSON, Alexander 1
JOHNSON, H
 Alexander Bryan
JOHNSON, 1
 Alexander Smith
JOHNSON, Alfred Le Roy 4
JOHNSON, Alfred Sidney 1
JOHNSON, Allan Chester 3
JOHNSON, Allen 1
JOHNSON, 5
 Alvin Saunders
JOHNSON, Andrew H
JOHNSON, 1
 Andrew Gustavus
JOHNSON, Andrew W. 4
JOHNSON, Anna 3
JOHNSON, Arnold Milton 3
JOHNSON, 3
 Arthur Charles
JOHNSON, Arthur 1
 Monrad
JOHNSON, 1
 Arthur Newhall
JOHNSON, Ashley Sidney 1
JOHNSON, Axel Petrus 3
JOHNSON, Bascom 3
JOHNSON, Ben * 3
JOHNSON, 2
 Benjamin Alvin
JOHNSON, 1
 Benjamin Franklin

JOHNSON, 1
 Benjamin Newhall
JOHNSON, H
 Benjamin Pierce
JOHNSON, Bernard 2
 Lyman
JOHNSON, 1
 Bolling Arthur
JOHNSON, Bradley Tyler 1
JOHNSON, Burt W. 1
JOHNSON, Bushrod Rust H
JOHNSON, Byron H
JOHNSON, Byron 1
JOHNSON, Byron Arthur 4
JOHNSON, 1
 Byron Bancroft
JOHNSON, 5
 Campbell Carrington
JOHNSON, Carl Edward 5
JOHNSON, Carl Gunnard 4
JOHNSON, Carl W. 3
JOHNSON, Cave H
JOHNSON, Chapman H
JOHNSON, Charles 5
 Charles Ellicott
JOHNSON, 1
 Charles Eugene
JOHNSON, Charles F. H. 3
JOHNSON, 3
 Charles F. Jr.
JOHNSON, 1
 Charles Fletcher
JOHNSON, 1
 Charles Frederick
JOHNSON, Charles Henry 2
JOHNSON, 1
 Charles Nelson
JOHNSON, Charles Oscar 4
JOHNSON, 1
 Charles Philip
JOHNSON, Charles Price 5
JOHNSON, 3
 Charles Spurgeon
JOHNSON, 4
 Charles Sumner
JOHNSON, 4
 Charles Williamson
JOHNSON, 2
 Charles Willis
JOHNSON, 1
 Charles Willison
JOHNSON, 2
 Charles Willison
JOHNSON, Clarence S. 3
JOHNSON, Clarke 1
 Howard
JOHNSON, Claude M. 4
JOHNSON, Clifton 1
JOHNSON, Cone 1
JOHNSON, Crawford Toy 5
JOHNSON, Crawford Toy 4
JOHNSON, Curtis Boyd 3
JOHNSON, David 1
JOHNSON, 1
 David Bancroft
JOHNSON, David Clayton 2
JOHNSON, 2
 Douglas Wilson
JOHNSON, Duncan Starr 1
JOHNSON, E. Fred 5
JOHNSON, Earl A. 5
JOHNSON, 3
 Earle Frederick
JOHNSON, Earle George 4
JOHNSON, Eastman 1
JOHNSON, Eben Samuel 1
JOHNSON, 5
 Edgar Augustus Jerome
JOHNSON, 2
 Edgar Hutchinson
JOHNSON, 5
 Edgar N(athaniel)
JOHNSON, 3
 Edith Christina
JOHNSON, Edward * H
JOHNSON, Edward 1
 Bryant
JOHNSON, Edward 5
 Gilpin
JOHNSON, Edward 1
 Payson
JOHNSON, 4
 Edward Roberts
JOHNSON, Edwin Carl 5
JOHNSON, 4
 Edwin Clifford
JOHNSON, Edwin Ferry H
JOHNSON, Edwin S. 1
JOHNSON, Effie 1
JOHNSON, Elbert Leland 2
JOHNSON, 2
 Eldridge Reeves
JOHNSON, Elias Finley 1
JOHNSON, Elias Henry 1
JOHNSON, Elijah 1
JOHNSON, Elizabeth H

JOHNSON, 4
 Elizabeth Winthrop
JOHNSON, Ellen H
JOHNSON, Ellen Cheney H
JOHNSON, Emil Fritiof 4
JOHNSON, Emory 2
 Richard
JOHNSON, Emsley 3
 Wright
JOHNSON, Ernest Amos 3
JOHNSON, Evan Malbone 4
JOHNSON, Francis 1
JOHNSON, Francis Ellis 5
JOHNSON, Francis Howe 1
JOHNSON, Francis Kirk 4
JOHNSON, 4
 Francis Rarick
JOHNSON, 4
 Francis Raymond
JOHNSON, Frank Asbury 4
JOHNSON, Frank Fisk 1
JOHNSON, Frank Pearson 1
JOHNSON, Frank Seward 1
JOHNSON, Frank Tenney 1
JOHNSON, Franklin 1
JOHNSON, 3
 Franklin Paradise
JOHNSON, 3
 Franklin Winslow
JOHNSON, Fred G. 5
JOHNSON, Fred Page 1
JOHNSON, Frederick 5
JOHNSON, H
 Frederick Avery
JOHNSON, 5
 Frederick Ernest
JOHNSON, 2
 Frederick Foote
JOHNSON, 1
 Frederick Green
JOHNSON, 3
 Frederick William
JOHNSON, George 2
JOHNSON, George 4
JOHNSON, George C. 4
JOHNSON, George E. Q. 2
JOHNSON, 1
 George Ellsworth
JOHNSON, 2
 George Francis
JOHNSON, George H. 3
JOHNSON, George K. 1
JOHNSON, George W. 3
JOHNSON, 2
 George William
JOHNSON, Gove Griffith 2
JOHNSON, Grace Allen 1
JOHNSON, Gustavus 4
JOHNSON, Guy H
JOHNSON, Hale 1
JOHNSON, Hallett 5
JOHNSON, 4
 Hansford Duncan
JOHNSON, 2
 Harold Bowtell
JOHNSON, 1
 Harry McCrindell
JOHNSON, Harry Miles 2
JOHNSON, Harvey Hull H
JOHNSON, Hayden 1
JOHNSON, 1
 Helen Kendrick
JOHNSON, Henry H
JOHNSON, Henry 1
JOHNSON, Henry Clark 1
JOHNSON, Henry 1
 Herbert
JOHNSON, Henry Lincoln 1
JOHNSON, 1
 Henry Lowry Emilius
JOHNSON, 3
 Henry Mortimer
JOHNSON, Henry U. 4
JOHNSON, Henry Viley 1
JOHNSON, Herbert 1
JOHNSON, Herbert Fisk 1
JOHNSON, 1
 Herbert Morris
JOHNSON, 2
 Herbert Spencer
JOHNSON, Herman E. 5
JOHNSON, Herrick 1
JOHNSON, Herschel V. 4
JOHNSON, H
 Herschel Vespasian
JOHNSON, Hewlett 1
JOHNSON, Hiram Warren 2
JOHNSON, Homer Hosea 4
JOHNSON, Horace 4
JOHNSON, Howard 5
JOHNSON, Howard 3
 Cooper
JOHNSON, Hugh McCain 2
JOHNSON, Hugh S. 2
JOHNSON, Irving Peska 1
JOHNSON, Isaac Cureton 1
JOHNSON, J. Ford 4

JOHNSON, J. Lovell 1
JOHNSON, J. Sidney 5
JOHNSON, Jackson 1
JOHNSON, Jacob 3
JOHNSON, James * H
JOHNSON, H
 James Augustus
JOHNSON, James Buford 4
JOHNSON, 4
 James Clarence
JOHNSON, James Gibson 1
JOHNSON, 1
 James Granville
JOHNSON, H
 James Hutchins
JOHNSON, James Leeper H
JOHNSON, 3
 James McIntosh
JOHNSON, James Weldon 1
JOHNSON, Jed Joseph 4
JOHNSON, 4
 Jefferson Deems Jr.
JOHNSON, 1
 Jeremiah Augustus
JOHNSON, Jeromus H
JOHNSON, Jesse 3
JOHNSON, John H
JOHNSON, John A. 1
JOHNSON, John Albert 1
JOHNSON, John B. 1
JOHNSON, 5
 John Bockover, Jr.
JOHNSON, John Butler 1
JOHNSON, John Davis 4
JOHNSON, John Edward 5
JOHNSON, John Edward 1
JOHNSON, John Gilmore 1
JOHNSON, John Graver 1
JOHNSON, John 3
 Lipscomb
JOHNSON, John Mitchell 4
JOHNSON, John Monroe 4
JOHNSON, 1
 John Samuel Adolphus
JOHNSON, John T. 4
JOHNSON, H
 John Telemachus
JOHNSON, John 2
 Theodore
JOHNSON, John William 1
JOHNSON, H
 Jonathan Eastman
JOHNSON, 4
 Jonathan Eastman
JOHNSON, Joseph * 2
JOHNSON, Joseph French 1
JOHNSON, 1
 Joseph Horsfall
JOHNSON, Joseph 5
 Lowery
JOHNSON, Joseph Taber 1
JOHNSON, Joseph Travis 1
JOHNSON, Joseph Travis 4
JOHNSON, Jotham 4
JOHNSON, 1
 Julia Macfarlane
JOHNSON, Justin H
JOHNSON, Justin 4
JOHNSON, Keen 5
JOHNSON, Kenneth D. 3
JOHNSON, 3
 Lambert Dunning
JOHNSON, Lee Payne 4
JOHNSON, 3
 Leighton Foster
JOHNSON, Leon H. 5
JOHNSON, 5
 Lester Bicknell
JOHNSON, Levi H
JOHNSON, Lewis Edgar 2
JOHNSON, Lewis Jerome 3
JOHNSON, Ligon 3
JOHNSON, 1
 Lilian Wyckoff
JOHNSON, Lincoln 3
JOHNSON, Livingston 1
JOHNSON, 2
 Loren Bascom Tabor
JOHNSON, Lorenzo M. 1
JOHNSON, Louis Arthur 4
JOHNSON, Lucius E. 1
JOHNSON, Lucius Henry 1
JOHNSON, H
 Luther Alexander
JOHNSON, 1
 Luther Appeles
JOHNSON, Lyndon 5
 Baines
JOHNSON, Magnus 1
JOHNSON, Malcolm 3
JOHNSON, Margaret 4
JOHNSON, 2
 Marietta Louise
JOHNSON, Marion Alvin 4
JOHNSON, Marmaduke H
JOHNSON, Martin 1

JOHNSON, Martin Nelson 1
JOHNSON, Max Sherred 4
JOHNSON, 3
Melvin Maynard
JOHNSON, 4
Melvin Maynard Jr.
JOHNSON, Merle DeVore 1
JOHNSON, Milbank 2
JOHNSON, 1
Mortimer Lawrence
JOHNSON, Nathaniel H
JOHNSON, Nels G. 3
JOHNSON, 3
Nelson Trusler
JOHNSON, Noadiah H
JOHNSON, Oliver H
JOHNSON, 1
Oliver Francis
JOHNSON, Osa Helen 3
JOHNSON, Oscar John 2
JOHNSON, Otis Coe 1
JOHNSON, Otis R. 3
JOHNSON, Owen 3
JOHNSON, Palmer O. 3
JOHNSON, Paul Burney 3
JOHNSON, Paul Rodgers 2
JOHNSON, Perley Brown 3
JOHNSON, 1
Philander Chase
JOHNSON, Philip H
JOHNSON, Philip Gustav 3
JOHNSON, Ralph Blake 4
JOHNSON, Ray Prescott 4
JOHNSON, 3
Reginald Davis
JOHNSON, Reverdy H
JOHNSON, Richard H. 3
JOHNSON, 1
Richard Harvey
JOHNSON, H
Richard Mentor
JOHNSON, 5
Richard Newhall
JOHNSON, Richard W. H
JOHNSON, Richard Zina H
JOHNSON, Robert H
JOHNSON, 4
Robert Livingston
JOHNSON, 5
Robert Livingston, Jr.
JOHNSON, 1
Robert Underwood
JOHNSON, Robert W. 4
JOHNSON, Robert Ward H
JOHNSON, 1
Robert Wilkinson
JOHNSON, Robert Wood 5
JOHNSON, 5
Robert Wood, Jr.
JOHNSON, 3
Roger Bruce Cash
JOHNSON, Rosamond 3
JOHNSON, Rossiter 1
JOHNSON, Roy William 4
JOHNSON, Royal Cleaves 1
JOHNSON, S. Arthur 4
JOHNSON, Samuel * H
JOHNSON, 1
Samuel William
JOHNSON, Silas 3
JOHNSON, Simeon Moses 3
JOHNSON, Sir John H
JOHNSON, Sir William H
JOHNSON, Stanley 2
JOHNSON, Stanley H. 1
JOHNSON, Sveinbjorn 2
JOHNSON, 1
Sylvanus Elihu
JOHNSON, Talmage
Casey 4
JOHNSON, Theodore 3
JOHNSON, Thomas 1
JOHNSON, Thomas Cary 1
JOHNSON, 1
Thomas Humrickhouse
JOHNSON,
Thomas Joseph Allan
JOHNSON, Thomas
Moore
JOHNSON, Tillman Davis 3
JOHNSON, Tom Loftin 1
JOHNSON, Treat Baldwin 2
JOHNSON, Virgil Lamont 4
JOHNSON, 1
Virginia Wales
JOHNSON, W. Ogden 4
JOHNSON, Waldo Porter H
JOHNSON, Wallace 4
JOHNSON, Wallace Clyde 1
JOHNSON, Walter H. 4
JOHNSON, 4
Walter Lathrop
JOHNSON, Walter
Nathan 3
JOHNSON, Walter Perry H
JOHNSON, Walter Perry 4
JOHNSON, Wanda Mae 5

JOHNSON, Wayne 2
JOHNSON, Wendell A. L. 4
JOHNSON, William * H
JOHNSON, William Allen 1
JOHNSON, 3
William Arthur
JOHNSON, H
William Bullein
JOHNSON, 3
William Burdett
JOHNSON, William C. H
JOHNSON, 1
William Christie
JOHNSON, William Cost H
JOHNSON, 5
William Driscoll
JOHNSON, 2
William Eugene
JOHNSON, William F. 4
JOHNSON, 4
William Franklin
JOHNSON, William Geary 4
JOHNSON, 4
William Hallock
JOHNSON, 1
William Hannibal
JOHNSON, 5
William Harold
JOHNSON, William
Henry H
JOHNSON, 4
William Houston
JOHNSON, 1
William Howard
JOHNSON, 4
William Martin
JOHNSON, 1
William Mindred
JOHNSON, H
William Ransom
JOHNSON, H
William Samuel
JOHNSON, 1
William Samuel
JOHNSON, 3
Lawrence Albert
JOHNSON, 1
William Templeton
JOHNSON, 1
William Woolsey
JOHNSON, Willis Ernest 3
JOHNSON, 1
Willis Fletcher
JOHNSON, Willis Grant 1
JOHNSON, Wingate M. 1
JOHNSTON,
Adelia Antoinette Field
JOHNSTON, H
Albert Sidney
JOHNSTON, Alexander H
JOHNSTON, Alva 3
JOHNSTON, Alvanley 1
JOHNSTON,
Annie Fellows
JOHNSTON, Archibald 4
JOHNSTON, Augustus H
JOHNSTON, Charles 4
JOHNSTON, Charles 1
JOHNSTON,
Charles Clement
JOHNSTON, 3
Charles Eugene
JOHNSTON, Charles G. 2
JOHNSTON,
Charles Haven Ladd
JOHNSTON, 1
Charles Hughes
JOHNSTON,
Charles Worth
JOHNSTON, Christopher 1
JOHNSTON,
Clarence Howard
JOHNSTON, 5
Clarence Thomas
JOHNSTON, H
David Claypoole
JOHNSTON, David E. 4
JOHNSTON, David Ira 3
JOHNSTON, Douglas T. 4
JOHNSTON, 1
Elizabeth Bryant
JOHNSTON, Ella Bond 4
JOHNSTON, Eric A. 4
JOHNSTON, Forney 4
JOHNSTON, 3
Frances Benjamin
JOHNSTON, 4
Francis Wayland
JOHNSTON, 5
Franklin Davis
JOHNSTON, Gabriel 1
JOHNSTON, George Ben 1
JOHNSTON, 1
George Doherty
JOHNSTON, Gordon 1
JOHNSTON, Gordon 1
JOHNSTON,
Harold Whetstone
JOHNSTON, Harry Lang 2

JOHNSTON, 5
Harvey Pollard
JOHNSTON, Henrietta H
JOHNSTON, Henry Alan 3
JOHNSTON, 4
Henry Donaldson
JOHNSTON, Henry
Phelps 1
JOHNSTON, Herrick Lee 4
JOHNSTON, Howard
Agnew 1
JOHNSTON, Hugh 1
JOHNSTON, Ivan Murray 4
JOHNSTON, J. Stoddard 1
JOHNSTON, James 4
JOHNSTON, James A. 3
JOHNSTON, James
Martin 4
JOHNSTON,
James Steptoe
JOHNSTON, John H
JOHNSTON, John 1
JOHNSTON, John 1
JOHNSTON,
John Alexander
JOHNSTON, John Black 2
JOHNSTON, 3
John Lawrence
JOHNSTON, John T. M. 1
JOHNSTON, John Taylor H
JOHNSTON, H
John Warfield
JOHNSTON, H
Joseph Eggleston
JOHNSTON, 1
Joseph Forney
JOHNSTON, H
Josiah Stoddard
JOHNSTON, 1
Julia Harriette
JOHNSTON, Kilbourne 5
JOHNSTON, L. S. 3
JOHNSTON, 1
Lawrence Albert
JOHNSTON, Leon H. 4
JOHNSTON, 5
Leslie Morgan
JOHNSTON, Lucy
Browne 1
JOHNSTON, Marbury 1
JOHNSTON, 5
Maria Isabella
JOHNSTON, Mary 1
JOHNSTON, 4
Nathan Robinson
JOHNSTON, Olin Dewitt 4
JOHNSTON,
Oliver Martin
JOHNSTON, 3
Oscar Goodbar
JOHNSTON, 3
Percy Hampton
JOHNSTON, Peter H
JOHNSTON, Richard Hall 5
JOHNSTON, 3
Richard Holland
JOHNSTON, H
Richard Malcolm
JOHNSTON, 1
Rienzi Melville
JOHNSTON, Robert Born 5
JOHNSTON, 4
Robert Daniel
JOHNSTON, 1
Robert Matteson
JOHNSTON, Robert Story 2
JOHNSTON, Rowland L. 1
JOHNSTON, Rufus Perry 1
JOHNSTON, Russell M. 1
JOHNSTON, Samuel H
JOHNSTON, Samuel 4
JOHNSTON, Samuel M. 5
JOHNSTON, Stanley 4
JOHNSTON, Stewart 1
JOHNSTON, Thomas H
JOHNSTON, 1
Thomas Alexander
JOHNSTON, H
Thomas Murphy
JOHNSTON, 1
Thomas William
JOHNSTON, Victor A. 4
JOHNSTON, W. Dawson
* 1
JOHNSTON, W. Fenton 4
JOHNSTON, Walter Vail 4
JOHNSTON, Wayne
Andrew 4
JOHNSTON, William H
JOHNSTON, William 1
JOHNSTON, 1
William Agnew
JOHNSTON, 1
William Atkinson
JOHNSTON, 5
William Drumm, Jr.

JOHNSTON, 3
William Greer
JOHNSTON, William
Hugh 1
JOHNSTON, 1
William Milton
JOHNSTON, 1
William Pollock
JOHNSTON, 1
William Preston
JOHNSTON, 1
William Waring
JOHNSTON, Wirt 5
JOHNSTON,
W(illia)m Allen
JOHNSTON, Zachariah H
JOHNSTONE, 5
Arthur Edward
JOHNSTONE, Bruce 5
JOHNSTONE, 2
Edward Ransom
JOHNSTONE, 1
Edward Robert
JOHNSTONE, 2
Ernest Kinloch
JOHNSTONE, 4
Henry Fraser
JOHNSTONE, Henry
Webb 5
JOHNSTONE, Job H
JOHNSTONE, 4
John Humphreys
JOHNSTONE, 1
William Jackson
JOHN XXIII, 4
His Holiness
JOHONNOTT, 1
Edwin Sheldon
JOLIET, Louis H
JOLINE, Adrian Hoffman 1
JOLIOT-CURIE, Frederic 3
JOLIOT-CURIE, Irene 5
JOLLES, 5
Otto Jolle Matthijs
JOLLIFFE, 5
Charles Byron
JOLLIFFE, Norman H. 4
JOLLY, Austin Howell 1
JOLLY, Robert Garland 3
JOLSON, Al 3
JOME, Hiram L. 1
JONAH, Frank Gilbert 2
JONAS, 1
August Frederick
JONAS, 1
Benjamin Franklin
JONAS, Charles Andrew 5
JONAS, Edgar A. 4
JONAS, Jack Henry 5
JONAS, Maryla 3
JONAS, Nathan S. 4
JONAS, Ralph 3
JONAS, Russell E. 5
JONES, Aaron H
JONES, Abner H
JONES, Ada 4
JONES, Adam Leroy 1
JONES, Albert Marshall 2
JONES, Albert Monmouth 1
JONES, Albert R. 5
JONES, Alexander H
JONES, 4
Alexander Francis
JONES, Alfred 1
JONES, Alfred 2
JONES, Alfred B. 4
JONES, Alfred Miles 1
JONES, Allen H
JONES, Allen Northey 3
JONES, 1
Amanda Theodosia
JONES, 1
Andrieus Aristieus
JONES, Anson H
JONES, Archibald A. 4
JONES, Arthur Gray 1
JONES, Arthur Julius 5
JONES, Augustine 1
JONES, Barton Mills 3
JONES, Bassett 3
JONES, Benjamin H
JONES,
Benjamin Franklin *
JONES, 1
Benjamin Franklin Jr.
JONES, Bob 4
JONES, Breckinridge 1
JONES, Brian 5
JONES, Bruce Carr 3
JONES, Buell Fay 1
JONES, Burr W. 1
JONES,
Burton Rensselaer
JONES, C. Edward 1
JONES, C. Hampson 1
JONES, Calvin H
JONES, Carl H. 3

JONES, Carl Waring 3
JONES, Carlton Allen 3
JONES, Carter Helm 2
JONES, H
Catesby Ap Roger
JONES, Charles Alfred 2
JONES, Charles Alvin 1
JONES, Charles Andrews 3
JONES, Charles Colcock H
JONES, 5
Charles Colcock, III
JONES, Charles Davies 1
JONES, Charles F. 5
JONES, Charles Fremont 1
JONES, Charles Henry 1
JONES, Charles Reading 1
JONES, Charles S. 5
JONES, Charles Sumner 1
JONES, Cheney Church 1
JONES, Chester Lloyd 1
JONES, Chester Morse 2
JONES, Claud Ashton 1
JONES, Clement Ross 1
JONES, Cliff C. 1
JONES, Clyde E. 1
JONES, Cyril Hamlen 1
JONES, Daniel Fiske 1
JONES, Daniel Jonathan 1
JONES, Daniel Terryll H
JONES, Daniel Webster 1
JONES, David H
JONES, David Dallas 1
JONES, David Hugh 1
JONES, David Percy 1
JONES, David Rumph H
JONES, Donald Forsha 1
JONES, Dwight Bangs 3
JONES, E. Lester 1
JONES, E(mmett) Milton 5
JONES, Earl J. 5
JONES, Edgar DeWitt 1
JONES, Edgar Laroy 1
JONES, Edith Kathleen 1
JONES, Edmund Adams 1
JONES, Edward Campbell 5
JONES, Edward David 3
JONES, Edward E. 3
JONES, Edward Franc 1
JONES, Edward Groves 1
JONES, Edward Perry 1
JONES, Edwin Frank 1
JONES, Edwin Lee 1
JONES, Edwin Whiting 1
JONES, Eleanor Louise 1
JONES, Eli Stanley 5
JONES, Eliot 5
JONES, 4
Elizabeth Dickson
JONES, Ella Virginia 4
JONES, Elmer Ellsworth 5
JONES, Elmer Ray 5
JONES, Elton B. 4
JONES, Evan J. 5
JONES, Evelyn Tubb 5
JONES, Everett Starr 1
JONES, F. Robertson 4
JONES, Fernando 1
JONES, Floyd William 4
JONES, Forrest Robert 1
JONES, Francis H
JONES, Francis Coates 1
JONES, Francis Ilah 3
JONES, Frank H
JONES, Frank Cazenove 2
JONES, Frank Johnston 1
JONES, Frank Leonard 1
JONES, Franklin D. 4
JONES, Franklin Elmore 5
JONES, 2
Frederic Marshall
JONES, 2
Frederick Robertson
JONES, Gabriel H
JONES, Gaius J. 1
JONES, Gardner Maynard 1
JONES, George * 1
JONES, George H. 1
JONES, George Heber 1
JONES, George Herbert 1
JONES, George James 4
JONES, 5
George Lewis, Jr.
JONES, George Salley 1
JONES, George Wallace H
JONES, H
George Washington
JONES, 1
George Washington
JONES, George William 1
JONES, Grinnell 1
JONES, Guernsey 1
JONES, H. Bolton 1
JONES, Harold Ellis 4
JONES, 1
Harold Wellington
JONES, Harriot Hamblen 1
JONES, Harrison 1

JONES, Harry Burnell 5
JONES, Harry Clary 1
JONES, Harry Stewart 4
JONES, 1
  Harry Stuart Vedder
JONES, Harry Wild 1
JONES, Heber 1
JONES, Henrietta Ord 4
JONES, Henry Craig 1
JONES, Henry Lawrence 4
JONES, Herbert Vincent 2
JONES, Herschell V. 1
JONES, Hilary Pollard 1
JONES, Hilton Ira 3
JONES, Horace Conrad 1
JONES, Howard 4
JONES, Hugh H
JONES, Hugh McK 4
JONES, I. Howland 5
JONES, Idwal 4
JONES, Ilion Tingnal 5
JONES, Isaac Dashiell H
JONES, Isaac Thomas 1
JONES, Isham 4
JONES, J. Catron 1
JONES, J. Claude 1
JONES, J. Levering 1
JONES, J. Morris 4
JONES, J. S. William 2
JONES, J. Shirley 3
JONES, J. Sparhawk 1
JONES, J. William 1
JONES, Jacob H
JONES, James * H
JONES, James Archibald 4
JONES, H
  James Chamberlayne
JONES, James Coulter 2
JONES, James Emlyn 1
JONES, James Hazlitt 5
JONES, James Kimbrough 1
JONES, 1
  James Marion Jr.
JONES, James Mills 4
JONES, James Sumner 1
JONES, James Taylor 4
JONES, Jefferson 4
JONES, Jehu Glancy 4
JONES, Jenkin Lloyd 1
JONES, Jerome 1
JONES, Jesse Holman 3
JONES, Joe 4
JONES, Joel H
JONES, John H
JONES, John B. 1
JONES, John Beauchamp H
JONES, John Carleton 1
JONES, John Edward 1
JONES, John George 3
JONES, John Logan 4
JONES, John Paul H
JONES, John Paul 4
JONES, John Percival 1
JONES, John Price 1
JONES, John Sills 1
JONES, John Taylor H
JONES, John Wesley 4
JONES, John William H
JONES, John Winston H
JONES, Jonathan 4
JONES, Joseph * H
JONES, Joseph Addison 2
JONES, Joseph Merrick 4
JONES, Joseph Russell 1
JONES, Joseph Seawell H
JONES, Joseph Stevens H
JONES, Joshua H. 1
JONES, 4
  Kate Emery Sanborn
JONES, Lake 1
JONES, Lawrence Clark 5
JONES, Lawrence Donald 4
JONES, Lawrence E. 4
JONES, 1
  Leonard Augustus
JONES, Lester Martin 3
JONES, Lewis Barrett 4
JONES, Lewis Henry * 1
JONES, Lewis Howel 5
JONES, Lewis Ralph 1
JONES, 2
  Livingston Erringer
JONES, 1
  Livingston French
JONES, Llewellyn 1
JONES, Lloyd E. 3
JONES, Louis R. 5
JONES, Louise Tayler 2
JONES, Loyd Ancile 3
JONES, Lynds 3
JONES, Mabel Cronise 1
JONES, Marcus Eugene 4
JONES, Marvin Fisher 3
JONES, Mary Harris H
JONES, Mary Harris 4
JONES, Matt Bushnell 1
JONES, Mattison Boyd 1

JONES, Melvin 4
JONES, Meredith Ashby 2
JONES, 3
  Millard Franklin
JONES, Minetry Leigh 4
JONES, Montfort 3
JONES, Morgan H
JONES, Morton Tebbs 4
JONES, Nard 5
JONES, Nathaniel H
JONES, 3
  Nellie Sawyer Kedzie
JONES, Nelson Edwards 1
JONES, Newell N. 5
JONES, Noble Wymberley H
JONES, Norman Edward 5
JONES, Norman L. 1
JONES, O. Garfield 4
JONES, Olin McKendree 4
JONES, 5
  Olive M. (olivia Mary)
JONES, Owen H
JONES, Paul 4
JONES, Paul Fouts 3
JONES, Peter Smith 5
JONES, Philip Harold 5
JONES, Philip Lovering 1
JONES, Philip Mills 1
JONES, Phineas H
JONES, Quill 1
JONES, Ralph Beaumont 4
JONES, Ralph M. 1
JONES, Reginald Lamont 4
JONES, Richard 1
JONES, 1
  Richard Channing
JONES, Richard Hugh 4
JONES, Richard Lloyd 4
JONES, Richard Mott 1
JONES, Richard Saxe 1
JONES, Richard Uriah 4
JONES, Richard Walter 4
JONES, Richard Watson 3
JONES, Robert Edmond 3
JONES, Robert Ellis 1
JONES, Robert Franklin 5
JONES, Robert Lee 4
JONES, Robert Looney 4
JONES, Robert Otis 4
JONES, Robert Taylor 3
JONES, 5
  Robert Tyre, Jr. (bobby Jones)
JONES, Robert Vernon 5
JONES, 1
  Robinson Godfrey
JONES, Roland H
JONES, 3
  Roy Bergstresser
JONES, Roy Childs 4
JONES, Rufus Matthew 2
JONES, Samuel * H
JONES, Samuel Augustus 5
JONES, Samuel Fosdick 2
JONES, Samuel J. 4
JONES, Samuel Milton 1
JONES, Samuel Porter 1
JONES, Seaborn H
JONES, 1
  Sebastian Chatham
JONES, Seth Benjamin 1
JONES, Seward William 4
JONES, Stephen Alfred 1
JONES, Sullivan W. 3
JONES, Sybil H
JONES, T. Sambola 1
JONES, Thomas H
JONES, Thomas Alfred 1
JONES, H
  Thomas Ap Catesby
JONES, Thomas Clive 2
JONES, Thomas Davies 1
JONES, Thomas Dow H
JONES, Thomas Goode 1
JONES, Thomas Hoyt 5
JONES, Thomas Hudson 5
JONES, Thomas Jesse 2
JONES, Thomas Laurens H
JONES, Thomas P. H
JONES, 1
  Thomas Samuel Jr.
JONES, Victor Owen 5
JONES, Vincent Lloyd 4
JONES, Virginia Smith 1
JONES, W. A. Fleming 4
JONES, W. Paul 3
JONES, 1
  Mrs. W.J. (mollie Roberts Jones)
JONES, Walk Claridge 4
JONES, Wallace Thaxter 2
JONES, Walter * H
JONES, Walter 1
JONES, Walter Burgwyn 4
JONES, Walter Clinton 2
JONES, Walter Clyde 1
JONES, Warren Francis 5

JONES, Washington 1
JONES, Wesley Livsey 1
JONES, Wharton Stewart 1
JONES, Wiley Emmet 1
JONES, Wilie 4
JONES, Will Owen 1
JONES, William * H
JONES, William A. 4
JONES, William Albert 1
JONES, 1
  William Alexander
JONES, William Alfred 4
JONES, William Alton 4
JONES, William Ambrose 1
JONES, 1
  William Atkinson
JONES, William Carey * 1
JONES, 1
  William James Jr.
JONES, 3
  William Larimer Jr.
JONES, 1
  William Otterbein
JONES, William Palmer H
JONES, H
  William Patterson
JONES, William Richard H
JONES, William Russell 1
JONES, H
  William Theopilus
JONES, Willie H
JONGERS, Alphonse 3
JONSON, Jep C. 1
JONSSON, Axel 3
JOPP, Charles B. 5
JOPLIN, Janis 5
JOPSON, John Howard 1
JORDAN, Arthur 1
JORDAN, 2
  Charles Bernard
JORDAN, 1
  Chester Bradley
JORDAN, Clarence Lorin 5
JORDAN, Conrad N. 1
JORDAN, David Francis 2
JORDAN, David Starr 1
JORDAN, Eben Dyer 1
JORDAN, 3
  Edward Benedict
JORDAN, Edward 1
  Stanlaw
JORDAN, Edwin Oakes 1
JORDAN, Elizabeth 2
JORDAN, Floyd 1
JORDAN, Francis Jr. 1
JORDAN, Frank Craig 1
JORDAN, Frank Morrill 5
JORDAN, 1
  Frederick Freas
JORDAN, G. Gunby 1
JORDAN, G. Ray 4
JORDAN, Harvey Bryant 4
JORDAN, Harvey Herbert 5
JORDAN, Harvie 5
JORDAN, Howard 4
  William
JORDAN, Isaac M. H
JORDAN, James Henry 1
JORDAN, John H. 4
JORDAN, John Woolf 1
JORDAN, Jules 1
JORDAN, Kate 1
JORDAN, 1
  Lyman Granville
JORDAN, Mahlon Kline 4
JORDAN, Marian 4
JORDAN, Mary Augusta 1
JORDAN, Ralph Curtis 4
JORDAN, Richard Henry 5
JORDAN, 3
  Riverda Harding
JORDAN, Samuel Martin 1
JORDAN, Sara Murray 3
JORDAN, Thomas 1
JORDAN, Thomas Walden 1
JORDAN, Virgil 5
JORDAN, Weymouth 1
  Tyree
JORDAN, Whitman 5
  Howard
JORDAN, 1
  William Frederick
JORDAN, William George 4
JORDAN, William Mark 4
JORDEN, 1
  Edward Fletcher
JORGENSEN, Joseph H
JOSAPHARE, Lionel 1
JOSEPH, Don Rosco 1
JOSEPH, Lawrence Edgar 1
JOSEPH, Lazarus 4
JOSEPHI, Isaac A. 5
JOSEPHSON, 2
  Aksel Gustav Salomon
JOSEPHSON, 5
  Clarence Egbert
JOSHI, Samuel Lucas 1

JOSLIN, Cedric Freeman 1
JOSLIN, 4
  Elliott Proctor
JOSLIN, Falcon 1
JOSLIN, Harold Vincent 1
JOSLIN, 2
  Theodore Goldsmith
JOSLIN, William Cary 1
JOSLYN, 4
  Marcellus Lindsey
JOSS, John 3
JOSSELYN, Benage S. 1
JOSSELYN, Charles 4
JOSSELYN, 1
  Freeman Marshall
JOSSELYN, John H
JOSSET, Raoul Jean 3
JOST, Henry Lee 3
JOST, Hudson 1
JOSTEN, Werner Eric 4
JOSTES, 3
  Frederick Augustus
JOUBERT 'DE H
  'LA MURAILLE, James Hector
  Marie Nicholas
JOUETT, 5
  Edward Stockton
JOUETT, James Edward 1
JOUETT, John 4
JOUETT, John Hamilton 5
JOUETT, Matthew Harris 1
JOUHAUX, Leon 3
JOUIN, Louis 1
JOURDAN, James H. 1
JOURNET, Marcel 1
JOUTEL, Henri 1
JOUVENAL, Jacques H
JOWETT, John Henry 4
JOY, H
  Agnes Elisabeth Winona Leciercq
JOY, H
  Agnes Elisabeth Winona Leclercq
JOY, Charles Frederick 4
JOY, Charles Turner 3
JOY, Henry Bourne 1
JOY, James Frederick 1
JOY, James Richard 3
JOY, Richard Pickering 1
JOY, Thomas H
JOYCE, Adrian Dwight 1
JOYCE, Charles Herbert 4
JOYCE, Dwight P. 5
JOYCE, Isaac W. 1
JOYCE, J(ames) Wallace 5
JOYCE, James 1
JOYCE, John Alexander 1
JOYCE, John Michael 4
JOYCE, Kenyon Ashe 3
JOYCE, Matthew M. 1
JOYCE, Patrick H. 2
JOYCE, R. Edwin 3
JOYCE, Thomas Martin 1
JOYCE, Walter Eves 5
JOYCE, Walter Frank 1
JOYCE, William B. 4
JOYCE, William Henry 1
JOYES, John Warren 2
JOYNER, Fred Bunyan 4
JOYNER, James Yadkin 3
JOYNES, Edward Southey 1
JUBE, Albert Riordan 1
JUCH, 1
  Emma Antonia Joanna
JUCHHOFF, Frederick 3
JUDAH, Noble Brandon * 1
JUDAH, Samuel H
JUDAH, 1
  Samuel Benjamin Helbert
JUDAH, Theodore Dehone H
JUDAY, Chancey 2
JUDD, Bertha Grimmell 2
JUDD, Charles Hubbard 2
JUDD, Climena Lyman 5
JUDD, Deane Brewster 5
JUDD, Edward Starr 1
JUDD, Gerrit Parmele H
JUDD, 5
  Gerrit Parmele, IV
JUDD, James Robert 2
JUDD, John Waltus 1
JUDD, Lawrence McCully 5
JUDD, Norman Buel H
JUDD, Orange H
JUDD, Orrin Reynolds 1
JUDD, Sylvester H
JUDD, Zebulon 1
JUDGE, William John 5
JUDGE, William Quan H
JUDKINS, Charles Otis 1
JUDSON, Adoniram H
JUDSON, Adoniram 1
  Brown
JUDSON, H
  Andrew Thompson

JUDSON, Ann Hasseltine H
JUDSON, 5
  Charles Wingfield
JUDSON, Clara Ingram 4
JUDSON, Clay 4
JUDSON, Edward 1
JUDSON, H
  Edward Zane Carroll
JUDSON, Egbert Putnam H
JUDSON, Emily 1
  Chubbuck
JUDSON, 5
  Fletcher Wesley
JUDSON, 1
  Frederick Newton
JUDSON, Harry Pratt 1
JUDSON, H
  Sarah Hall Boardman
JUDSON, Wilber 3
JUDSON, William Lees 1
JUDSON, 1
  William Pierson
JUDSON, 1
  William Voorhees
JUDY, Arthur Markley 4
JUENGLING, Frederick H
JUERGENS, Alfred 1
JUETTNER, Otto 1
JUHAN, Frank Alexander 4
JUHRING, 1
  John Christopher
JUIN, Alphonse Henri 4
JULDOON, Peter J. 1
JULIA, Sister H
JULIAN, H
  George Washington
JULIAN, 1
  George Washington
JULIAN, Isaac Hoover 1
JULIAN, John Herndon 4
JULIAN, 2
  William Alexander
JULIEN, Alexis Anastay 1
JULIEN, Juliette Marie 5
JULL, Morley Allan 3
JULLIARD, Augustus D. 1
JULLIARD, Frederic A. 1
JUMEL, Stephen H
JUMP, 1
  Herbert Atchinson
JUMP, William Ashby 2
JUMPER, Royal Thiesen 4
JUNEAU, H
  Solomon Laurent
JUNELL, John 3
JUNG, Carl Gustav 3
JUNG, Carl Gustav 5
JUNG, 5
  Franz August Richard
JUNGE, Carl Stephen 5
JUNGMAN, John George H
JUNKERMAN, Gustavus 1
  S.
JUNKERMANN, 4
  Charles Franklin
JUNKERSFELD, Peter 1
JUNKIN, 1
  Francis Thomas Anderson
JUNKIN, George H
JURENEV, Serge B. 4
JURGATIS, John Paul 5
JURICA, 1
  Hilary Stanislaus
JUSSERAND, 1
  Jean Adrien Antoine Jules
JUST, Ernest Everett 1
JUST, Theodor Karl 4
JUSTICE, Edwin Judson 1
JUSTIN, Margaret M. 5
JUUL, Niels 1

K

KABLE, Harry G. 3
KABRICH, 2
  William Camillus
KADING, Charles August 3
KAEDING, 2
  Charles Deering
KAELBER, William G. 2
KAELIN, Charles Salis 1
KAEMMERLING, Gustav 1
KAEMPFFERT, 3
  Waldemar Bernhard
KAGAN, Henry Enoch 5
KAGEY, Charles L. 2
KAGY, Elbert Osborn 5
KAHANAMOKU, Duke 4
  Paoa
KAHANE, 4
  Benjamin Bertram
KAHIN, George 5
KAHLENBERG, Louis 1
KAHLER, Erich Gabriel 1
KAHLER, 1
  Frederick August
KAHLER, Harry Adams 3

KAHLER, Hugh MacNair 5
KAHLER, John Henry 1
KAHLKE, Charles Edwin 5
KAHN, Albert 2
KAHN, Ely Jacques 5
KAHN, Florence Prag 2
KAHN, Henry Kastor 4
KAHN, Howard 3
KAHN, Julius 1
KAHN, Julius Bahr, Jr. 5
KAHN, Lazard 1
KAHN, Maurice Guthman 3
KAHN, Otto Hermann 1
KAHN, Samuel 3
KAIN, George Hay 3
KAIN, John Joseph 1
KAINS, Archibald Chetwode 2
KAINS, Maurice Grenville 2
KAISER, Albert David 3
KAISER, Henry J. 4
KAISER, Lewis 4
KAISER, Louis Anthony 5
KAIV, Johannes 4
KAL, Norman Coleman 5
KALANIANAOLE, J. Kuhio 1
KALB, Johann H
KALB, Lewis Powell 3
KALBFLEISCH, Martin H
KALBFUS, Edward Clifford 3
KALDENBERG, Frederick Robert 1
KALER, James Otis 1
KALES, Albert Martin 1
KALISCH, Isidor H
KALISCH, Samuel 1
KALISH, Max 2
KALKSTEIN, Mennasch 5
KALLAY 'DE NAGY KALLO, Miklos 4
KALLENBACH, Walter Dustin 2
KALLET, Arthur 5
KALLGREN, Carl Alfred 5
KALLIO, Elmer William 5
KALLMANN, Franz J. 4
KALLOCH, Parker Cromwell 3
KALMAN, Charles Oscar 1
KALMAN, Charles Oscar 3
KALMAN, Paul Jerome 1
KALMUS, Herbert Thomas 4
KALTENBORN, Hans V. 4
KAMAIAKAN H
KAMBESTAD, Howard S. 3
KAMEHAMEHA I H
KAMEHAMEHA III H
KAMENSKY, Theodore 1
KAMINSKI, Stephan 4
KAMMAN, William F. 4
KAMMER, Adolph Gottlieb 4
KAMMER, Alfred Charles 5
KAMMER, Herbert Anthony 4
KAMMERER, Frederic 1
KAMMERER, Percy Gamble 3
KAMMERER, Webb Louis 5
KAMMERT, Donald Milton 5
KAMMEYER, Julius Ernest 1
KAMPER, Louis 3
KAMPHUISEN, Pieter Wilhelmus 4
KANALEY, Byron Vincent 4
KANAVEL, Allen Buckner 1
KANBENSHUE, Paul 2
KANDEL, Isaac Leon 4
KANDER, Allen 5
KANDINSKY, Vasily 4
KANE, Elias Kent H
KANE, Elisha Kent H
KANE, Elisha Kent 1
KANE, Francis Fisher 3
KANE, Grenville 2
KANE, Howard Francis 2
KANE, James Johnson 1
KANE, John Kintzing H
KANE, Leo Aloysius 4
KANE, Matthew John 1
KANE, Nicholas Thomas H
KANE, Paul V. 3
KANE, Theodore Porter 2
KANE, Thomas Franklin 5
KANE, Thomas Leiper H
KANE, Thomas Leo 4
KANE, William Patterson 1
KANE, William T. 2
KANNER, Samuel Jacob 5
KANOUSE, Theodore Dwight 4
KANSKI, Francis 5
KANTER, Aaron E. 5
KANTER, Arron E. 4
KANTER, Charles Andrew 3
KANTOROWICZ, Ernst H. 4
KANTZLER, George R. 3
KANZLER, Ernest Carlton 4
KAPELL, William 3
KAPENSTEIN, Ira 5
KAPLAN, Benjamin 5
KAPLAN, Bernard Michael 1
KAPLAN, Ellezer 3
KAPLAN, Frank R. S. 3
KAPLAN, Harry 5
KAPLAN, Jacob Joseph 4
KAPLAN, Milton Lewis 5
KAPLAN, Morris 4
KAPLAN, Samuel 5
KAPP, Friedrich H
KAPP, Jack 2
KAPPEL, Gertrude 5
KAPPEL, Samuel 3
KAPPER, Isaac M. 4
KARAPETOFF, Vladimir 2
KARAVONGSE, Phya Prabha 5
KARCH, Charles Adam 1
KARCHER, Walter Thompson 3
KAREL, John Connell 5
KARELITZ, George Boris 2
KARFIOL, Bernard 3
KARGER, Gustav J. 1
KARIG, Walter 3
KARKER, Maurice Harmon 3
KARL, Tom 4
KARLEN, Sven Bernhard 5
KARLOFF, Boris 5
KARN, Daniel Earl 5
KARN, Harry Wendell 5
KARNES, Joseph V. C. 1
KARNEY, Rex Lambert 4
KAROLIK, Maxim 4
KARPINSKI, Louis Charles 3
KARPOVICH, Michael 3
KARR, Edmund Joseph 5
KARR, Elizabeth 5
KARR, Frank 5
KARRER, Enoch 2
KARRER, Paul 5
KARRICK, David Brewer 4
KARSNER, Howard 5
KARSTEN, Gustaf E. 1
KARTAK, Franz August 3
KARWOSKI, Theodore F. 3
KASANIN, Jacob Sergi 2
KASAVUBU, Joseph 5
KASBERG, Karl Gary 5
KASEBIER, Gertrude 1
KASNER, Edward 3
KASSABIAN, Mihran Krikor 1
KASSEL, Charles 2
KASSLER, Edwin Stebbins 4
KASSLER, Kenneth Stone 4
KASSON, Frank H. 4
KASSON, John Adam 1
KAST, Ludwig 1
KAST, Miller I. 2
KASTEN, Harry Edward 5
KASTEN, Walter 3
KASTEN, William Henry 4
KASTER, John P. 1
KASTLE, Joseph Hoeing 1
KATCHEN, Julius 5
KATEK, Charles 5
KATHRENS, Richard Donland 4
KATO, Frederick 1
KATTE, Edwin Britton 1
KATTE, Walter 1
KATTERLE, Zeno Bernel 5
KATZ, Abner Roland 4
KATZ, Benjamin Samuel 5
KATZ, Frank J. 1
KATZ, Joseph 4
KATZ, Mark Jacob 1
KATZ, Michael H. 4
KATZENBACH, Edward Lawrence 1
KATZENBACH, Frank S. Jr. 1
KATZENBERGER, William E. 5
KATZENELLENBOGEN, Adolf 4
KATZENTINE, A. Frank 3
KATZER, Frederic Xavier 1
KATZIN, Eugene M. 4
KATZ-SUCHY, Juliusz 5
KAUFFMAN, Benjamin Franklin 2
KAUFFMAN, Calvin Henry 1
KAUFFMAN, James Lee 5
KAUFFMAN, Lawrence A. 4
KAUFFMAN, Ruth Wright 3
KAUFFMANN, Alfred Otto 3
KAUFFMANN, Rudolph 1
KAUFFMANN, Rudolph Max 3
KAUFFMANN, Samuel Hay 5
KAUFFMANN, Samuel Hay 1
KAUFFMANN, Victor 5
KAUFMAN, Abraham Charles 4
KAUFMAN, David E. 5
KAUFMAN, David E. 4
KAUFMAN, David Spangler H
KAUFMAN, George S. 4
KAUFMAN, Herbert 2
KAUFMAN, Kenneth Carlyle 2
KAUFMAN, Louis Graveraet 2
KAUFMAN, Paul D. 3
KAUFMAN, Ralph Odell 3
KAUFMAN, Samuel H. 4
KAUFMANN, Christopher Alphonso 4
KAUFMANN, Ed 4
KAUFMANN, Edgar Jonas 3
KAUFMANN, Edmund I. 3
KAUFMANN, Gordon Bernie 3
KAUFMANN, John Heiden 5
KAUFMANN, Paul 4
KAUFMANN, Wilford E. 3
KAUL, John Lanzel 1
KAULBACK, Frank S. 3
KAUTZ, Albert 1
KAUTZ, August Valentine H
KAUTZ, John Arthur 1
KAUTZKY, Theodore 3
KAUVAR, C(harles) E(liezer) Hillel 5
KAVANAGH, Edward H
KAVANAGH, Francis Bernard 3
KAVANAGH, James Edward 3
KAVANAGH, Leslie J. 1
KAVANAGH, Marcus A. 1
KAVANAGH, Robert Vincent 3
KAVANAUGH, John Michael 5
KAVANAUGH, William Harrison 1
KAVANAUGH, William Kerr 1
KAVANAUGH, Williams Marmaduke 1
KAVELER, Herman Henry 4
KAWABATA, Yasunari 5
KAWAKAMI, Jotaro 4
KAWAKAMI, K. K. 2
KAY, Edgar Boyd 1
KAY, George Frederick 2
KAY, Gertrude Alice 1
KAY, Joseph William 2
KAY, William Edward 1
KAYAN, Carl F(rederic) 5
KAYE, James Hamilton Barcroft 1
KAYE, John William 1
KAYE, Joseph 4
KAYE-SMITH, Sheila 3
KAYN, Hilde B. 3
KAYS, Donald Jackson 3
KAZANTZAKIS, Nikos 3
KAZANTZAKIS, Nikos 4
KEAGY, John Miller H
KEAGY, Walter R. 4
KEALING, Joseph B. 1
KEALY, Philip Joseph 2
KEAN, Charles H
KEAN, Charles Duell 4
KEAN, Edmund H
KEAN, Hamilton Fish 1
KEAN, Jefferson Randolph 3
KEAN, John H
KEAN, John 1
KEAN, Thomas H
KEANE, Doris 2
KEANE, James John 1
KEANE, John Joseph 1
KEANE, Lee 3
KEANE, Theodore John 3
KEANE, William Edward 3
KEARFUL, Francis Joseph 1
KEARNEY, Andrew Thomas 4
KEARNEY, Belle 3
KEARNEY, Denis H
KEARNEY, Denis 4
KEARNEY, Drye H
KEARNEY, Edward Francis 1
KEARNEY, Edward James 1
KEARNEY, Erick Wilson 5
KEARNEY, George Fairchild 4
KEARNEY, Lawrence Francis 4
KEARNEY, Raymond Augustine 3
KEARNEY, Thomas Henry 3
KEARNS, Charles Cyrus 1
KEARNS, Gurney Harriss 4
KEARNS, John W. 3
KEARNS, Thomas 1
KEARNS, Thomas F. 4
KEARNS, William Michael 5
KEARNY, Francis H
KEARNY, Lawrence H
KEARNY, Philip H
KEARNY, Stephen Watts H
KEARNY, Warren 2
KEARSLEY, John H
KEASBEY, Edward Quinton 1
KEASBEY, George Macculloch 1
KEASBEY, Henry Miller 4
KEASBEY, Lindley Miller 4
KEATING, Anne C. 3
KEATING, Arthur 4
KEATING, Cecil A. 1
KEATING, Cletus 4
KEATING, Edward 4
KEATING, F(rancis) Raymond, Jr. 5
KEATING, Frank Webster 1
KEATING, John 5
KEATING, John H. 4
KEATING, John Marie H
KEATING, John McLeod 4
KEATING, Laurence Freeman 5
KEATING, William Hypolitus H
KEATON, Buster 4
KEATON, James R. 2
KEATOR, Alfred Decker 4
KEATOR, Frederic William 1
KEAYS, Hersilia A. Mitchell 4
KEBBON, Eric 4
KEBE, Kenneth Albert 4
KEBLER, Leonard 4
KEBLER, Lyman Frederic 3
KECK, Charles 3
KECK, Harry 4
KEDNEY, John Steinfort 1
KEDZIE, Frank Stewart 1
KEDZIE, Robert Clark 1
KEDZIE, William Roscoe 1
KEE, John 3
KEEBLE, Glendinning 2
KEEBLE, John Bell 1
KEEDICK, Lee 4
KEEDY, Charles Cochran 1
KEEFE, Daniel C. 4
KEEFE, Daniel J. 1
KEEFE, David Andrew 5
KEEFE, Frank B. 3
KEEFE, John C. 4
KEEFE, John Hancock 3
KEEFE, John William 1
KEEFE, William J. 3
KEEFER, Chester Scott 5
KEEFER, Frank Royer 3
KEEFER, Joseph Isadore 4
KEEGAN, Gilbert Kearnie 4
KEEGAN, Harry Joseph 5
KEEGAN, John Joseph 5
KEEHN, Clarence (Heckman) 5
KEEHN, Roy Dee 2
KEEL, Elmo W. 5
KEELER, Charles 1
KEELER, Fred Lockwood 1
KEELER, Harriet Louise 1
KEELER, Harry Stephen 4
KEELER, James Edward 1
KEELER, John Everett 1
KEELER, Leonarde 2
KEELER, Ralph Olmstead H
KEELER, Ralph Welles 3
KEELER, Stephen Edwards 3
KEELEY, Edward S. 4
KEELEY, James 1
KEELEY, Leslie E. 1
KEELEY, Patrick C. H
KEELING, Hal Ray 4
KEELING, Walter Angus 2
KEELY, John Ernst Worrell H
KEELY, Robert Neff 4
KEEN, Edward Leggett 2
KEEN, Gregory Bernard 1
KEEN, James Velma 4
KEEN, Kennard Garton Jr. 4
KEEN, Morris Longstreth H
KEEN, Victor 3
KEEN, William Williams 1
KEENA, James Trafton 1
KEENA, Martin J. 4
KEENAN, Albert Joseph, Jr. 5
KEENAN, Alexander Stanislaus 5
KEENAN, Frank 1
KEENAN, Geo M. 4
KEENAN, Henry Francis 4
KEENAN, James R. 3
KEENAN, Joseph Berry 3
KEENAN, Thomas Johnston 1
KEENE, Amor Frederick 1
KEENE, Arthur Samuel 5
KEENE, Carter Brewster 1
KEENE, Edward Spencer 1
KEENE, Floyd Elwood 1
KEENE, James Robert 1
KEENE, Laura H
KEENE, Thomas Wallace H
KEENER, Gladys M. 4
KEENER, John Christian 1
KEENER, Walter Ney 1
KEENER, William Albert 1
KEENEY, Albert Lawrence 4
KEENEY, Francis B. 3
KEENEY, Frederick Thomas 3
KEENEY, Mrs. Ralph D. 3
KEENEY, Paul Aloysius 5
KEENEY, Russell Watson 3
KEENEY, Willard F. 2
KEEP, Albert 1
KEEP, Charles Hallam 1
KEEP, Chauncey 1
KEEP, Henry H
KEEP, John Joseph 2
KEEP, Oliver Davis 4
KEEP, Robert Porter 1
KEEP, William John 1
KEESE, Richard H
KEESE, William Linn 1
KEESECKER, Raymond P. 4
KEESING, Felix Maxwell 4
KEESING, Frans Arnold George 5
KEESLING, Francis Valentine 4
KEETON, Robert Wood 3
KEEVIL, Charles Samuel 5
KEFAUVER, Clarence Eugene 5
KEFAUVER, Estes 4
KEFAUVER, Grayson Neikirk 2
KEFAUVER, Harry Joshua 2
KEFFER, Charles Albert 1
KEGEL, Arnold Henry 5
KEHL, John Elwin 5
KEHLENBECK, Alfred Paul 5
KEHOE, Arthur Henry 5
KEHOE, James N. 2
KEHOE, Joseph W. 3
KEHOE, James) Walter 5
KEIDEL, George Charles 2
KEIFER, J. Warren 1
KEIGWIN, A. Edwin 3
KEILBERTH, Joseph 5
KEILEY, Benjamin J. 1
KEILLER, William 1
KEIM, Franklin David 3
KEIM, George 'de Benneville 2
KEIM, George May H

KEIM, William High — H
KEIR, John Sibbit — 4
KEIRN, Gideon Isaac — 4
KEISER, Albert — 4
KEISER, Edward Harrison — 4
KEISER, George Camp — 3
KEISER, Laurence Bollon — 5
KEISTER, Abraham L. — 1
KEITH, Adelphus Bartlett — 5
KEITH, Allen Phelps — 3
KEITH, Arthur — 2
KEITH, Arthur Leslie — 2
KEITH, Arthur Monroe — 1
KEITH, Benjamin Franklin — 1
KEITH, Charles Penrose — 1
KEITH, Charles S. — 2
KEITH, David — 1
KEITH, David — 2
KEITH, Dora Wheeler — 1
KEITH, Elbridge G. — 1
KEITH, George — H
KEITH, George Eldon — 1
KEITH, Harold Chessman — 4
KEITH, James — 1
KEITH, John Alexander Hull — H
KEITH, Lawrence Massillon — H
KEITH, Marie Morrisey — 4
KEITH, Minor Cooper — 1
KEITH, Nathaniel Shepard — 1
KEITH, Sir William — H
KEITH, William — 1
KEITH, William Hammond — 4
KEITHAHN, Edward Linnaeus — 5
KEITT, George Wannamaker — 5
KELBY, Charles Hendre — 2
KELBY, James Edward — 4
KELCE, L. Russell — 3
KELCE, Merl C. — 5
KELCEY, Herbert — 5
KELEHER, William Aloysius —
KELHAM, George William — 1
KELIHER, John — 4
KELIHER, John Austin — 4
KELIHER, Sylvester — 4
KELKER, Rudolph Frederick, Jr. — 5
KELLAND, Clarence Budington — 4
KELLAR, Chambers — 3
KELLAR, Harry — 3
KELLAR, Herbert Anthony —
KELLAS, Eliza — 2
KELLAWAY, Herbert John — 2
KELLEHER, Daniel — 1
KELLEHER, Louis Francis — 4
KELLEHER, Michael T. — 3
KELLEN, William Vail — 4
KELLER, Adolph — 5
KELLER, Albert Galloway — 3
KELLER, Amelia R. (mrs. Eugene Buehler) — 5
KELLER, Arnold B. — 4
KELLER, Arthur Ignatius —
KELLER, Benjamin Franklin — 1
KELLER, Carl Tilden — 3
KELLER, Emil Ernest — 4
KELLER, Frederick — 4
KELLER, Gert — 4
KELLER, Harry Frederick —
KELLER, Helen Adams — 5
KELLER, Henry — 2
KELLER, Henry Jr. — 5
KELLER, Herbert Paist — 5
KELLER, James Albert — 2
KELLER, John William — 4
KELLER, Kaufman Thuma — 4
KELLER, Kent Ellsworth — 3
KELLER, Lewis Henry — 4
KELLER, Mathias — H
KELLER, May Lansfield — 5
KELLER, Mollie V. Everett (mrs. Charles C. Keller) —
KELLER, Oliver James — 4
KELLER, Oscar Edward — 1
KELLER, Oscar H. — 4
KELLER, Ralph Edward — 4

KELLER, Walter — 1
KELLER, Will E. — 4
KELLER, William Huestis — 2
KELLER, William Simpson — 1
KELLERMAN, Karl Frederic — 1
KELLERMAN, William Ashbrook — 1
KELLERSBERGER, Eugene Roland — 4
KELLETER, Paul Delmar — 3
KELLEY, Albert Wesley — 1
KELLEY, Alfred — H
KELLEY, Alfred Kendall — 1
KELLEY, Augustine Bernard — 3
KELLEY, Camille McGee — 3
KELLEY, Clement Earl, Jr. — 5
KELLEY, Cornelius Francis — 3
KELLEY, David Campbell — 1
KELLEY, Edgar Stillman — 2
KELLEY, Eugene Robert — 1
KELLEY, Florence — 1
KELLEY, Francis Alphonsus — 1
KELLEY, Francis Clement — 2
KELLEY, Frank Harrison — 3
KELLEY, Hall Jackson — H
KELLEY, Harold Hitchcock — 4
KELLEY, Harrison — H
KELLEY, Hermon Alfred — 1
KELLEY, Howard G. — 1
KELLEY, J(ames) Herbert — 5
KELLEY, James Douglas Jerrold — 1
KELLEY, Jay George — 1
KELLEY, Jerome Telfair — 4
KELLEY, Jessie Stillman — 2
KELLEY, Jessie Stillman — 4
KELLEY, John S. — 4
KELLEY, John William — 1
KELLEY, Lilla Elizabeth — 5
KELLEY, Louise — 4
KELLEY, Nicholas — 4
KELLEY, Oliver Hudson — H
KELLEY, Oliver Hudson — 4
KELLEY, Patrick Henry — 1
KELLEY, Pearce Clement — 5
KELLEY, Phelps — 4
KELLEY, Robert Hamilton —
KELLEY, Robert Michael — 5
KELLEY, Robert Weeks — 1
KELLEY, Samuel Walter — 1
KELLEY, Selden Dee — 2
KELLEY, Truman L. — 4
KELLEY, Walter Pearson — 4
KELLEY, William Andrew Gresham — 5
KELLEY, William Darrah — H
KELLEY, William Valentine — 2
KELLEY, William Vallandigham — 1
KELLICOTT, William Erskine — 1
KELLNER, Elisabeth Willard Brooks — 1
KELLNER, Max — 1
KELLOGG, Abraham Lincoln — 2
KELLOGG, Albert — H
KELLOGG, Amos Markham — 1
KELLOGG, Arthur Piper — 5
KELLOGG, Arthur Remington —
KELLOGG, Brainerd — 5
KELLOGG, Charles — H
KELLOGG, Charles Collins — 1
KELLOGG, Charles Wetmore — 5
KELLOGG, Clara Louise — 1
KELLOGG, Daniel Fiske — 1
KELLOGG, David Sherwood — 4
KELLOGG, Edgar Romeyn — 1
KELLOGG, Edward — H
KELLOGG, Edward Brinley — 4
KELLOGG, Edward Leland — 2
KELLOGG, Elijah — H
KELLOGG, Elijah Chapman — H

KELLOGG, Eva Mary Crosby — 4
KELLOGG, Francis William — H
KELLOGG, Frank Billings — 1
KELLOGG, Frederic Rogers — 1
KELLOGG, Frederick Conway — 1
KELLOGG, Frederick William — 1
KELLOGG, George Dwight — 3
KELLOGG, Gordon Hill — 3
KELLOGG, Harold Field — 4
KELLOGG, Henry Theodore — 2
KELLOGG, Howard Jr. — 1
KELLOGG, James C. — 1
KELLOGG, James G. — 4
KELLOGG, James H. — 5
KELLOGG, James Lawrence — 1
KELLOGG, John Harvey — 2
KELLOGG, John Morris — 1
KELLOGG, John Prescott — 1
KELLOGG, Joseph Augustus — 1
KELLOGG, Laura Cornelius (Mrs. Orrin Joseph Kellogg) — 5
KELLOGG, Louise Phelps — 3
KELLOGG, Luther Laflin — 1
KELLOGG, Martin — 1
KELLOGG, Morris W. — 3
KELLOGG, Olin Clay — 2
KELLOGG, Oliver Dimon — 1
KELLOGG, Orlando — H
KELLOGG, Paul Underwood — 3
KELLOGG, Peter Comstock — 4
KELLOGG, Ralph Averill — 4
KELLOGG, Robert James — 3
KELLOGG, Samuel Henry — H
KELLOGG, Scott D(ouglas) — 5
KELLOGG, Spencer — 1
KELLOGG, Stephen Wright — 1
KELLOGG, Theodore H. — 5
KELLOGG, Thomas Moore — 1
KELLOGG, Vernon Lyman — 1
KELLOGG, W. K. — 3
KELLOGG, Walter Guest — 3
KELLOGG, Warren Franklin — 4
KELLOGG, Wilbur Ralph — 3
KELLOGG, William — H
KELLOGG, William Pitt — 1
KELLOR, Frances — 3
KELLS, Clarence Howard — 3
KELLWAY, Cedric Vernon — 4
KELLY, Aloysius Oliver Joseph — 1
KELLY, Bradley — 5
KELLY, Charles E. — 5
KELLY, David George — 4
KELLY, Dennis Francis — 1
KELLY, Edward A. — 1
KELLY, Edward Joseph * — 3
KELLY, Eleanor — 1
KELLY, Eric Philbrook — 3
KELLY, Eugene — H
KELLY, Eugene Hill — 2
KELLY, Florence Finch — 1
KELLY, Francis Martin — 3
KELLY, Frank A. — 2
KELLY, Frank V. — 2
KELLY, Fred C. — 3
KELLY, Frederick James — 4
KELLY, George Alexander —
KELLY, George Arthur — 4
KELLY, George Henderson —
KELLY, Sir Gerald — 5
KELLY, Geroge B(radshaw) —
KELLY, Guy Edward — 1
KELLY, Harry Eugene — 1
KELLY, Harry Francis — 5
KELLY, Harry Joseph — 1
KELLY, Harry McCormick —
KELLY, Howard Atwood — 2
KELLY, Howard Charles — 4
KELLY, J. Redding — 1
KELLY, James — H
KELLY, James Edward — 1
KELLY, James Kerr — 1
KELLY, John — H
KELLY, John C. — 1

KELLY, John Forrest — 1
KELLY, John Grant — 4
KELLY, John H. — 1
KELLY, John William — 5
KELLY, Joseph James — 1
KELLY, Joseph Luther — 1
KELLY, Judith — 3
KELLY, Lon Hamman — 2
KELLY, Luther Sage — H
KELLY, Luther Sage — 4
KELLY, M. Clyde — 1
KELLY, Mervin J. — 5
KELLY, Michael D. — 5
KELLY, Michael J. — H
KELLY, Monroe — 3
KELLY, Myra — 1
KELLY, Orie R. — 5
KELLY, Paul — 3
KELLY, Percy R. — 4
KELLY, Ralph — 4
KELLY, Raymond — 5
KELLY, Robert James — 5
KELLY, Robert Lincoln — 1
KELLY, Robert Morrow — 1
KELLY, Stephen — 5
KELLY, T(homas) Howard — 4
KELLY, William * — H
KELLY, William — 4
KELLY, William A. — 4
KELLY, William Albert — 4
KELLY, William Anthony — 4
KELLY, William Arthur — 4
KELLY, William F. — 1
KELLY, William J. — 3
KELLY, William Joseph — 1
KELLY, William Louis — 4
KELLY, William Powers — 3
KELMAN, John — 4
KELPIUS, Johann — H
KELSEN, Hans — 5
KELSER, Raymond Alexander — 3
KELSEY, Albert — 3
KELSEY, Carl — 3
KELSEY, Charles Boyd — 1
KELSEY, Charles Edward — 1
KELSEY, Clarence Hill — 1
KELSEY, Francis Willey — 1
KELSEY, Frederick Trowbridge — 3
KELSEY, Frederick Wallace — 1
KELSEY, Harlan Page — 5
KELSEY, Henry Hopkins — 1
KELSEY, Hugh Alexander — 3
KELSEY, Joseph A. — 1
KELSEY, Preston Telford — 3
KELSEY, Rayner Wickersham — 1
KELSEY, William Henry — H
KELSO, James Anderson — 3
KELSO, John Bolton — 5
KELSO, John Russell — H
KELTON, John Cunningham — H
KELTON, Stanton Colt — 3
KELTY, Paul Ray — 4
KEM, James Preston — 4
KEMBLE, Edward Windsor — 1
KEMBLE, Frances Anne — H
KEMBLE, Gouverneur — H
KEMERER, Benjamin Tibbits — 5
KEMEYS, Edward — 1
KEMLER, Walter James — 4
KEMMERER, Edwin Walter — 2
KEMMERER, John L. — 2
KEMMLER, Edward Albert — 3
KEMP, Agnes — 1
KEMP, Alexander Nesbitt — 3
KEMP, Bolivar Edwards — 1
KEMP, Ellwood Leitheiser — 4
KEMP, Clarence) Everett — 5
KEMP, Harold Augustus — 3
KEMP, Harold Francis — 3
KEMP, Harry Hibbard — 4
KEMP, James — H
KEMP, James Furman — 1
KEMP, John — H
KEMP, Louis Wiltz — 5
KEMP, Matthew Stanley — 5
KEMP, Philip Claris — 2
KEMP, Robert H. — H
KEMP, Theodore — 1
KEMP, W. Thomas — 1
KEMP, William Webb — 2
KEMP, Wyndham — 4
KEMP, Zachariah Willis — 4
KEMPER, Arthur Bernard — 5

KEMPER, — 4
KEMPER, Charles Pendleton —
KEMPER, — 1
KEMPER, General William Harrison —
KEMPER, Graham Hawes — 4
KEMPER, Jackson — H
KEMPER, James Lawson — H
KEMPER, James Madison — 5
KEMPER, John Mason — 5
KEMPER, Reuben — H
KEMPER, William Mauzy — 5
KEMPER, William Thornton — 1
KEMPFF, Clarence S. — 4
KEMPFF, Louis — 2
KEMPNER, Aubrey John — 5
KEMPNER, Isaac Herbert — 5
KEMPNER, Isaac Herbert Jr. — 3
KEMPSHALL, Thomas — H
KEMPSTER, James Aquila — 5
KEMPSTER, Walter — 1
KEMPTON, Charles Walter — 5
KEMSLEY, James Gomer Berry) — 5
KENAN, Thomas — 4
KENAN, William Rand Jr. — 4
KENDAL, Mrs. — 4
KENDAL, William Hunter — 1
KENDALL, Amos — H
KENDALL, Calvin Noyes — 1
KENDALL, Charles Harry — 5
KENDALL, Charles Howard —
KENDALL, Charles Pierce — 5
KENDALL, Charles Shilling —
KENDALL, Courts P. — 5
KENDALL, Edward Calvin — 5
KENDALL, Edward Hale — 1
KENDALL, Elizabeth Kimball — 3
KENDALL, Elva Roscoe — 5
KENDALL, Ezra Fremont — 1
KENDALL, George R. — 5
KENDALL, George Valentine —
KENDALL, George Wilkins — H
KENDALL, Harry R. — 3
KENDALL, Henry Hubbard — 2
KENDALL, Henry Madison — 3
KENDALL, Henry Plimpton — 4
KENDALL, Henry Wiseman — 4
KENDALL, James — 3
KENDALL, John C. — 5
KENDALL, John Chester — 5
KENDALL, John Smith — H
KENDALL, John Wilkerson —
KENDALL, Jonas — H
KENDALL, Joseph Gowing — H
KENDALL, Margaret — 2
KENDALL, Messmore — 3
KENDALL, Myron A. — 4
KENDALL, Nathan E. — 1
KENDALL, Ralph Charles — 4
KENDALL, Samuel Austin — 1
KENDALL, Sergeant — 1
KENDALL, Valerius Horatio — 4
KENDALL, William Converse — 1
KENDALL, William Mitchell — 4
KENDALL, William Morgan — 5
KENDELL, Robert Lothar — 5
KENDIG, Calvin Miles — 3
KENDIG, H. Evert — 2
KENDRICK, Asahel Clark — H
KENDRICK, Benjamin Burks —
KENDRICK, Charles; — 5
KENDRICK, E. S. — 4
KENDRICK, Eliza Hall — 1
KENDRICK, Georgia — 1
KENDRICK, John — H
KENDRICK, John Benjamin — 1
KENDRICK, John Mills — 1
KENDRICK, John William — 1
KENDRICK, Nathaniel Cooper — 5
KENDRICK, W. Freeland — 3

KENDRICKS, Edward James 3
KENE, Joseph Alphonse 4
KENEALY, Ahmed John 4
KENEALY, Alexander C. 4
KENEFICK, Daniel Joseph 2
KENGLA, Hannah M. Egan 3
KENIN, Herman David 5
KENISTON, Ralph) Hayward 5
KENISTON, James Mortimer 1
KENKEL, Frederick P. 3
KENLON, John 1
KENLY, John Reese 1
KENLY, Julie Woodbridge Terry 2
KENLY, Ritchie Graham 1
KENLY, William Lacy 1
KENNA, Edward Dudley 4
KENNA, Frank 2
KENNA, John Edward H
KENNA, Joseph Norris 1
KENNA, Roger 4
KENNAMER, Charles Brents 3
KENNAN, George 1
KENNARD, Frederic Hedge 1
KENNARD, Joseph Spencer 2
KENNARD, Samuel M. 1
KENNEBECK, George Robert 5
KENNEDY, Ambrose J. 3
KENNEDY, Andrew H
KENNEDY, Annie Richardson 3
KENNEDY, Anthony 1
KENNEDY, Archibald H
KENNEDY, Arthur Garfield 3
KENNEDY, Charles A. 5
KENNEDY, Charles Rann 2
KENNEDY, Charles William 5
KENNEDY, Chase Wilmot 1
KENNEDY, Clarence 5
KENNEDY, Clarence Hamilton 3
KENNEDY, Clyde Raymond 5
KENNEDY, Crammond 1
KENNEDY, Daniel Joseph 1
KENNEDY, David Scott 1
KENNEDY, Elijah Robinson 1
KENNEDY, Emma Baker 1
KENNEDY, F. Lowell 1
KENNEDY, Foster 3
KENNEDY, Francis Willard 1
KENNEDY, Fred J(ohnston) 5
KENNEDY, Gall 5
KENNEDY, George A. 4
KENNEDY, Gilbert Falconer 5
KENNEDY, Henry L. 3
KENNEDY, Howard Samuel 1
KENNEDY, Howard Samuel 4
KENNEDY, James 1
KENNEDY, James Arthur 4
KENNEDY, James Henry 1
KENNEDY, James Madison 1
KENNEDY, James Melvin 1
KENNEDY, John Bright 5
KENNEDY, John Bright 1
KENNEDY, John Doby H
KENNEDY, John Fitzgerald 4
KENNEDY, John Lauderdale 4
KENNEDY, John Louis 4
KENNEDY, John Pendleton 5
KENNEDY, John Pendleton H
KENNEDY, John Stewart 1
KENNEDY, John Thomas 1
KENNEDY, Joseph 1
KENNEDY, Joseph Camp Griffith H
KENNEDY, Joseph Patrick 5
KENNEDY, Joseph William 3
KENNEDY, Josiah Forrest 4
KENNEDY, Julian 1

KENNEDY, Lloyd Ellison 4
KENNEDY, Lorne Edward 4
KENNEDY, Margaret 4
KENNEDY, Martin J. 3
KENNEDY, Merton Grant 4
KENNEDY, Michael Joseph 2
KENNEDY, Miles Coverdale 4
KENNEDY, Moorhead Cowell 1
KENNEDY, Olin Wood 5
KENNEDY, Paca 4
KENNEDY, Philip Benjamin 4
KENNEDY, Ralph Dale 4
KENNEDY, Raymond 3
KENNEDY, Richard Oakley 3
KENNEDY, Robert Francis 5
KENNEDY, Robert MacMillan 5
KENNEDY, Robert Morris 2
KENNEDY, Robert Patterson 1
KENNEDY, Roger L. J. 4
KENNEDY, Ruby Jo Reeves 5
KENNEDY, Samuel Macaw 1
KENNEDY, Sara Beaumont 1
KENNEDY, Sidney Robinson 5
KENNEDY, Stanley Carmichael H
KENNEDY, Sylvester Michael 5
KENNEDY, T. Blake 3
KENNEDY, Thomas 4
KENNEDY, Thomas F. 1
KENNEDY, W. Mcneil 5
KENNEDY, Walker 1
KENNEDY, Willard John 2
KENNEDY, William H
KENNEDY, William 1
KENNEDY, William Henry Joseph 2
KENNEDY, William Parker 5
KENNEDY, William Pierce 5
KENNEDY, William Sloane 1
KENNEDY, Wray David 5
KENNELLY, Arthur Edwin 1
KENNELLY, Edward F. 4
KENNELLY, Martin H. 4
KENNER, Albert Walton 3
KENNER, Duncan Farrar H
KENNER, Frank Terry 4
KENNERLY, John Hanger 1
KENNERLY, Thomas Martin 4
KENNERLY, Wesley Travis 2
KENNESON, Taddeus Davis 1
KENNETT, Luther Martin H
KENNEY, Edward A. 1
KENNEY, John Andrew 2
KENNEY, Richard Rolland 1
KENNEY, William Francis 1
KENNEY, William P. 1
KENNGOTT, George Frederick 4
KENNICOTT, Cass (Langdon) 5
KENNICOTT, Donald 4
KENNICOTT, Robert H
KENNISH, John 4
KENNON, Jack Eccleston 4
KENNON, Lyman Walter Vere 1
KENNON, William Jr. H
KENNON, William Lee 3
KENNON, William Sr. H
KENNY, Albert Sewall 1
KENNY, Elizabeth 3
KENNY, Michael 1
KENNY, Thomas James 5
KENNY, William John 1
KENRICK, Francis Patrick H
KENRICK, Peter Richard H
KENRICK, William H
KENSETT, John Frederick
KENT, Alexander H

KENT, Arthur Atwater 2
KENT, Charles Artemas 1
KENT, Charles Foster 1
KENT, Charles Stanton 5
KENT, Charles William 1
KENT, Donald Peterson 5
KENT, Edward H
KENT, Edward 1
KENT, Edward Mather 5
KENT, Elizabeth Thacher 4
KENT, Frank Richardson 3
KENT, Fred I. 3
KENT, Harry Llewellyn 2
KENT, Harry Watson 1
KENT, Henry Oakes 1
KENT, Herbert A. 5
KENT, Ira Rich 2
KENT, Jacob Ford 1
KENT, James H
KENT, James Tyler 1
KENT, John Harvey 4
KENT, Joseph H
KENT, Louise Andrews 5
KENT, Moss H
KENT, Norman 4
KENT, Norton Adams 2
KENT, R. H. 4
KENT, Raymond Asa 2
KENT, Richard T. 2
KENT, Robert Homer 3
KENT, Robert Thurston 2
KENT, Rockwell 5
KENT, Roland Grubb 3
KENT, Russell 1
KENT, Russell Alger 1
KENT, Stephen G(irard) 1
KENT, Walter Henry 5
KENT, William * 1
KENT, William J, Jr. 5
KENTON, Edna 3
KENTON, Simon H
KENYON, Alfred Monroe 1
KENYON, Alpheus Burdick 1
KENYON, Dorothy 5
KENYON, Douglas Houston 4
KENYON, Frederick Courtland 4
KENYON, George Henry 4
KENYON, James Benjamin 5
KENYON, John Samuel 5
KENYON, Otis Allen 2
KENYON, William Houston 5
KENYON, William Scheuneman H
KENYON, William Squire 1
KEOGH, Andrew 3
KEOGH, Martin Jerome 1
KEOGH, Thomas Bernard 4
KEOKUK H
KEOUGH, Austin Campbell 3
KEOUGH, Francis Patrick 4
KEPHART, Calvin Ira 5
KEPHART, Cyrus Jeffries 1
KEPHART, Ezekial Boring 1
KEPHART, Horace 1
KEPHART, Isaiah Lafayette 1
KEPHART, John William 2
KEPLER, Charles Ober 1
KEPLER, Thomas Samuel 4
KEPNER, Harold R. 4
KEPNER, Harry V. 4
KEPPEL, Charles John 4
KEPPEL, Frederick 1
KEPPEL, Frederick Paul 2
KEPPLER, Joseph H
KEPPLER, Joseph 5
KER, Severn Parker 2
KERBEY, Eric A. 3
KERBY, William Joseph 1
KERCHEVILLE, F(rancis) M(onroe) 5
KEREKES, Frank 4
KEREKES, Tibor 5
KERENS, Richard C. 1
KERENSKY, Alexander Fedorovitch 5
KERESEY, Henry Donnelly 4
KERFOOT, John Barrett 1
KERFOOT, Samuel Fletcher 1
KERFOTT, John Barrett H
KERKAM, William Barron 4
KERKER, Gustave Adolph 1
KERLEY, Charles Gilmore 2
KERLIN, Isaac Newton H

KERLIN, Robert Thomas 3
KERN, Edith Kingman 5
KERN, Edward Meyer H
KERN, Frederick John 1
KERN, Herbert Arthur 4
KERN, Howard Lewis 2
KERN, Jerome David 2
KERN, John Adam 1
KERN, John Dwight 2
KERN, John Worth 1
KERN, John Worth 1
KERN, Josiah Quincy 1
KERN, Maximilan 4
KERN, Olly J. 4
KERN, Paul Bentley 3
KERN, Richard Hovenden H
KERN, Robert H. 1
KERN, Walter McCollough 2
KERN, William Albert 1
KERNAHAN, Arthur Earl 2
KERNAN, Francis H
KERNAN, Francis Joseph 2
KERNAN, John Devereux 1
KERNAN, Thomas Jones 4
KERNAN, Will Hubbard 4
KERNE, Leo J. 4
KERNER, Otto 1
KERNER, Robert Joseph 3
KERNEY, James 1
KERNEY, Sarah M. 1
KERNO, Ivan 4
KERNOCHAN, Joseph Frederick 5
KERNS, Shirley Kendrick 3
KEROUAC, Jack (Jean-Louis Kerouac) 5
KERR, Abram Tucker 1
KERR, Albert Boardman 1
KERR, Alexander 1
KERR, Alexander Taylor 5
KERR, Alexander Thomas Warwick 1
KERR, Alvah Milton 1
KERR, Charles 2
KERR, Charles Volney 1
KERR, Charles William 3
KERR, Clarence D. 3
KERR, David Ramsey 1
KERR, Duncan J. 1
KERR, Eugene Wycliff 5
KERR, Frank Marion 1
KERR, H(enry) Farquharson 5
KERR, Henry H. 3
KERR, Henry Hampton 1
KERR, Hugh T. 3
KERR, James 1
KERR, James Bremer 1
KERR, James Taggart 1
KERR, John H
KERR, John Jr. H
KERR, John Bozman H
KERR, John Brown * 1
KERR, John Daniel 1
KERR, John Davis 4
KERR, John Glasgow H
KERR, John Henry 1
KERR, John Hosea 1
KERR, John Leeds H
KERR, John N. 5
KERR, John Steele 1
KERR, John Walter 5
KERR, Joseph H
KERR, LeGrand 5
KERR, Mark Brickell 1
KERR, Michael Crawford H
KERR, Robert Floyd 1
KERR, Robert Pollok 1
KERR, Robert Samuel 4
KERR, Sophie 1
KERR, Walter Craig 1
KERR, Washington Caruthers H
KERR, William Jasper 2
KERR, William Melville 5
KERR, William Watt 5
KERR, Winfield S. 1
KERRICK, Harrison Summers 5
KERRIGAN, Frank Henry 1
KERRIGAN, James J. 3
KERRIGAN, Walter C. 3
KERRISON, Philip D. 4
KERSHAW, John H
KERSHAW, Joseph Brevard H
KERSHNER, Frederick Doyle 3
KERWIN, Hugh Leo 1
KERWIN, J. S. 4
KERWIN, James Charles 1
KESCHNER, Moses 3
KESLER, John Louis 4
KESLER, Martin Luther 1

KESSELRING, Joseph Otto 4
KESSING, Oliver Owen 4
KESSLER, Alfred August Jr. 5
KESSLER, Bernard 5
KESSLER, George Edward 5
KESSLER, Harry Clay 1
KESSLER, Louis Robert 4
KESTEN, Paul W. 3
KESTER, Frederick Edward
KESTER, Paul 1
KESTER, Reuben P. 5
KESTER, Roy Bernard 4
KESTER, Vaughan 1
KESTERSON, M. M. 4
KESTNBAUM, Meyer 4
KETCHAM, Charles Burgess 3
KETCHAM, Daniel Warren 1
KETCHAM, Earle Hoyt 5
KETCHAM, Frank Atherton
KETCHAM, Heber Dwight 2
KETCHAM, John Clark 1
KETCHAM, John Henry 1
KETCHAM, Rosemary 1
KETCHAM, Victor Alvin 2
KETCHAM, William Alexander
KETCHAM, William Ezra 1
KETCHAM, William Henry 1
KETCHUM, Alexander Phoenix 1
KETCHUM, Edgar 1
KETCHUM, John Buckhout 1
KETCHUM, Milo Smith 4
KETCHUM, Omar Bartlett 4
KETCHUM, Richard Bird 1
KETCHUM, Winthrop Welles H
KETHLEY, William Marion 4
KETLER, Isaac Conrad 1
KETMAN, Tony Louis 4
KETNER, Forrest Guy 4
KETTELL, Samuel H
KETTERING, Charles Franklin
KETTERING, Eugene Williams
KETTIG, William Henry 1
KETTLE, Edgar Ulf 1
KETTLER, Stanton Peter 5
KETTNER, William 1
KETTON-CREMER, Robert Wyndham 5
KEW, William S. W. 4
KEY, Albert Lenoir 4
KEY, David McKendree 1
KEY, Francis Scott H
KEY, James Biggers 5
KEY, James Lee 1
KEY, John A. 5
KEY, Joseph Staunton 1
KEY, Philip H
KEY, Philip Barton H
KEY, Pierre 'van Rensselaer 2
KEY, V. O. Jr. 5
KEY, William Mercer 4
KEY, William Shaffer 3
KEYES, Charles Henry 1
KEYES, Charles Reuben 2
KEYES, Charles Rollin 2
KEYES, Conrad Saxe 4
KEYES, Edward Lawrence 1
KEYES, Edward Loughborough 2
KEYES, Elias H
KEYES, Erasmus Darwin H
KEYES, Frances Parkinson (Mrs. Henry Wilder Keyes) 5
KEYES, Geoffrey 4
KEYES, Henry Wilder 1
KEYES, Homer Eaton 1
KEYES, Michael J. 1
KEYES, Rollin Arthur 1
KEYES, Thomas Bassett 4
KEYES, Victor Ernest 4
KEYES, Winfield Scott 4
KEYNES, John Maynard 5
KEYS, Clement Melville 1
KEYS, Noel 5
KEYSER, Cassius Jackson
KEYSER, Charles Shearer
KEYSER, Earl E. 4
KEYSER, Ephraim 1
KEYSER, Ernest Wise 4

KEYSER, Harriette A. 4
KEYSER, Leander Sylvester
KEYSER, R. Brent 1
KEYSTON, George Noel 5
KEYT, Alonzo Thrasher H
KEYWORTH, Maurice Reed 1
KEZER, Alvin 5
KHAMPAN, Tiao 4
KHARAS, Ralph Earle 4
KHARASCH, Morris Selig 3
KHOURI BEY, El Faris 4
KHRUSHCHEV, Nikita Sergeyevich 5
KIANG, Chiping H. C. 5
KIBBEY, Joseph H. 1
KIBLER, A. Franklin 3
KIBLER, Raymond Spier 5
KIBLER, Thomas L. 3
KICKING BIRD H
KIDD, Elizabeth 3
KIDD, Herbert A. 4
KIDD, Isaac Campbell 2
KIDD, Robert L(ouis) 5
KIDD, Samuel Elberts 5
KIDD, William H
KIDDE, Walter 2
KIDDER, Alfred Vincent 1
KIDDER, Benjamin Harrison
KIDDER, Bradley Paige 1
KIDDER, Daniel Parish H
KIDDER, Daniel Selvey 1
KIDDER, David 1
KIDDER, Frank Eugene 1
KIDDER, Fred Thomas 1
KIDDER, Frederic H
KIDDER, Jefferson Parish H
KIDDER, Kathryn 1
KIDDER, Nathaniel Thayer
KIDDER, Wellington Parker 1
KIDDLE, Henry 1
KIDWELL, Zedekiah H
KIEB, Raymond Frances Charles 3
KIECKHEFER, Ferdinand A. W.
KIEFER, Andrew R. 1
KIEFER, Carl J. 4
KIEFER, Daniel 1
KIEFER, Dixie 2
KIEFER, Edgar Weber 4
KIEFER, Emil 1
KIEFER, Guy Lincoln 1
KIEFER, Hermann 1
KIEFFER, George Linn 1
KIEFFER, Henry Martyn 1
KIEFFER, Joseph Spangler 1
KIEFFER, Paul 5
KIEFHOFER, William Henry 3
KIEFNER, Charles E. 5
KIEFT, Willem H
KIEHLE, David Litchard 4
KIEHNEL, Richard 2
KIEKHOEFER, H. J. 2
KIEL, Emil Charles 5
KIEL, Henry William 4
KIELY, John J. 2
KIENZLE, George Jacob 4
KIEPE, Edward John 4
KIEPURA, Jan 4
KIER, Samuel M. H
KIERAN, James Michael 1
KIERNAN, James George 1
KIERNAN, Loyd Julian 5
KIERNAN, Peter D. 3
KIERNAN, Thomas Joseph 4
KIERSTED, Andrew Jackson 1
KIERSTED, Wynkoop 1
KIES, William Samuel 2
KIESEL, Fred J. 1
KIESEL, Fred William 5
KIESLER, Frederick 4
KIESS, Edgar Raymond 1
KIESSELBACH, T. A. 4
KIEST, Edwin John 1
KIHN, W. Langdon 3
KILANDER, H(olger) Frederick 5
KILBORN, William T. 3
KILBOURN, Judson Giles 1
KILBOURNE, Charles Evans 1
KILBOURNE, Charles Evans 4
KILBOURNE, James H
KILBOURNE, James 1
KILBRETH, John William 3

KILBURN, Charles Lawrence 1
KILBY, Christopher H
KILBY, Clinton Maury 2
KILBY, Quincy 1
KILBY, Thomas Erby 2
KILDAHL, John Nathan 1
KILDARE, Owen Frawley 1
KILDAY, Paul Joseph 5
KILDOW, George Oliver 4
KILDUFF, Edward Jones 1
KILENYI, Julio 3
KILEY, John 3
KILEY, John Coleman 3
KILEY, Michael H. 1
KILEY, Moses E. 4
KILGALLEN, Dorothy 4
KILGEN, Eugene Robyn 5
KILGO, John Carlisle 1
KILGORE, Benjamin Wesley 2
KILGORE, Bernard 4
KILGORE, Constantine Buckley H
KILGORE, Daniel H
KILGORE, David H
KILGORE, Harley Martin 3
KILGORE, James H
KILHAM, Walter H. 2
KILIANI, Otto George Theobald 1
KILLAM, Charles Wilson 4
KILLE, Joseph H
KILLEBREW, Joseph Buckner 1
KILLEN, James Sinclair 5
KILLIAN, John Allen 3
KILLIAN, John Calvin 5
KILLIKELLY, Sarah Hutchins 1
KILLINGER, John Weinland H
KILLITS, John Milton 1
KILMAN, Leroy Noble 3
KILMER, Aline 1
KILMER, Chauncey 4
KILMER, Frederick Barnett 1
KILMER, Joyce 1
KILMER, Theron Wendell 2
KILMUIR, Earl 'of 1
KILNER, Walter Glenn 1
KILPATRICK, Armour Kemp 5
KILPATRICK, Harry Colman 3
KILPATRICK, Hugh Judson H
KILPATRICK, James Hines 1
KILPATRICK, John Reed 4
KILPATRICK, Thomas 1
KILPATRICK, Walter Kenneth 2
KILPATRICK, William D. 3
KILPATRICK, William Heard 4
KILTY, William H
KIMBALL, Alfred Redington 1
KIMBALL, Alfred Sanders 1
KIMBALL, Alonzo 1
KIMBALL, Amos Samuel 1
KIMBALL, Arthur Lalanne 1
KIMBALL, Arthur Reed 1
KIMBALL, Arthur Richmond 4
KIMBALL, Charles Dean 1
KIMBALL, Charles Nathaniel 1
KIMBALL, Clarence Oliver 1
KIMBALL, Comer Johnstone 4
KIMBALL, Curtis Nathaniel 1
KIMBALL, Dan A. 5
KIMBALL, David Pulsifer 1
KIMBALL, Dexter Simpson 3
KIMBALL, Edward Partridge 1
KIMBALL, Everett 2
KIMBALL, Fiske 3
KIMBALL, G. Cook 1
KIMBALL, George Albert 1
KIMBALL, George Elbert 4
KIMBALL, George Henry 1
KIMBALL, George Selwyn 1
KIMBALL, George Turner 3
KIMBALL, Gilman 1
KIMBALL, Gustavus Sylvester 1
KIMBALL, Hannah Parker 4

KIMBALL, Harriet McEwen 1
KIMBALL, Harry Swift 3
KIMBALL, Heber Chase H
KIMBALL, Henry Dox 5
KIMBALL, Herbert Harvey S
KIMBALL, Jacob Jr. H
KIMBALL, James Henry 2
KIMBALL, James Putnam 1
KIMBALL, John C. 1
KIMBALL, John White 1
KIMBALL, Joseph C. 4
KIMBALL, Justin Ford 1
KIMBALL, Kate Fisher 1
KIMBALL, Katharine 1
KIMBALL, LeRoy Elwood 4
KIMBALL, Marie Goebel 3
KIMBALL, Nathan H
KIMBALL, Philip Horatio 2
KIMBALL, Ralph Horace H
KIMBALL, Richard Burleigh H
KIMBALL, Robert Merriman 4
KIMBALL, Spofford Harris 4
KIMBALL, Stockton 3
KIMBALL, Sumner Increase H
KIMBALL, Thomas Rogers 1
KIMBALL, Walter Gardner 3
KIMBALL, Willard 1
KIMBALL, William Coggin 1
KIMBALL, William Preston 4
KIMBALL, William Wallace 1
KIMBALL, William Wirt 1
KIMBELL, Kay 4
KIMBER, Arthur Clifford 1
KIMBER, Harry Goldring 4
KIMBERLY, Lewis Ashfield 1
KIMBLE, John Haines 2
KIMBLE, Joseph Chanslor 5
KIMBROUGH, Bradley Thomas 1
KIMBROUGH, Herbert 5
KIMBROUGH, Robert Alexander 5
KIMBROUGH, Robert Alexander Jr. 4
KIMBROUGH, Thomas Charles 2
KIMES, Russell A. 4
KIMM, Neal Edwin 4
KIMMEL, Gustav Bernard 1
KIMMEL, Husband Edward 5
KIMMEL, Lester Franklin 4
KIMMEL, William H
KIMMELSTIEL, Paul 5
KINARD, F. Marion 4
KINARD, James Pinckney 3
KINCAID, Charles Euston 1
KINCAID, Elbert Alvis 3
KINCAID, John 1
KINCAID, Robert Lee 4
KINCAID, Trevor 1
KINCAID, William A. 1
KINCAID, William Wallace 2
KINCANNON, Andrew Armstrong 4
KINCER, Joseph Burton 5
KINCHELOE, David Hayes 3
KIND, John Louis 1
KINDEL, George John 1
KINDELBERGER, James Howard 4
KINDIG, James William 4
KINDLE, Edward Martin 1
KINDLEBERGER, David 1
KINDLEBERGER, Jacob 3
KINDLER, Hans 2
KINDRED, John Joseph 1
KINEALY, John Henry 1
KINEON, George Goodnow 2
KING, Adam H
KING, Aden J(ackson) 1
KING, Albert Freeman Africanus 1
KING, Albion Roy 5
KING, Alexander 4
KING, Alexander Campbell 1

KING, Alfred Rufus 1
KING, Alvin Olin 3
KING, Andrew H
KING, Arno Warren 4
KING, Arthur Dale 3
KING, Arthur S. H
KING, Austin Augustus H
KING, Basil 1
KING, Campbell 3
KING, Caroline Blanche 2
KING, Charles 5
KING, Charles 1
KING, Charles Banks 5
KING, Charles Bird H
KING, Charles Burton 5
KING, Charles D. B. 4
KING, Charles Francis 1
KING, Charles Kelley 3
KING, Charles William H
KING, Clarence 1
KING, Clark W. 4
KING, Clifford William 2
KING, Clyde Lyndon 1
KING, Cora Smith 1
KING, Cyrus H
KING, D. J. 3
KING, D. Ward H
KING, Dan H
KING, Daniel Putnam H
KING, David Bennett 4
KING, Dennis 5
KING, Dougall Macdougall 1
KING, Edgar 5
KING, Edmund Burritt 5
KING, Edna Elvira Swanson (Mrs. Edgar J. King)
KING, Edward 1
KING, Edward J. 1
KING, Edward Lacy 1
KING, Edward Leonard 1
KING, Edward Postell Jr. 3
KING, Edward S. 1
KING, Edward Smith H
KING, Edwin Burruss 5
KING, Eldon Paul 4
KING, Elisha Alonzo 5
KING, Ernest Joseph 3
KING, Everett Edgar 5
KING, Fain White 5
KING, Francis Scott 1
KING, Frank Lamar 5
KING, Frank O. 5
KING, Franklin Hiram 1
KING, Frederick Allen 1
KING, George Anderson 1
KING, George B. 4
KING, George Gordon H
KING, Grace Elizabeth 1
KING, Hamilton 1
KING, Harold Joseph 4
KING, Harold William 4
KING, Harry Andrews 1
KING, Helen Dean 4
KING, Henry H
KING, Henry 1
KING, Henry Churchill 1
KING, Henry Lord Page 3
KING, Henry Melville 1
KING, Henry Stouffer 2
KING, Herbert Hiram 5
KING, Homer C. 4
KING, Horace Williams 3
KING, Horatio 1
KING, Horatio Collins 1
KING, Howell Atwater 5
KING, Irving 5
KING, J. Cheston 1
KING, James A. 1
KING, James Aloysius 4
KING, James Gore H
KING, James H. 3
KING, James Harold 3
KING, James Joseph 1
KING, James Marcus 1
KING, James Moore 4
KING, James William 5
KING, James Wilson 4
KING, John * H
KING, John A. H
KING, John Alsop H
KING, John Crookshanks 2
KING, John Jefferson 1
KING, John Lord H
KING, John Pendleton H
KING, John Rigdon 1
KING, Jonas H
KING, Joseph Elijah 1
KING, Julie Rive 3
KING, LeRoy Albert 2
KING, Lida Shaw 1
KING, Lorenzo H. 2
KING, Louisa Yeomans (Mrs. Francis King) 5

KING, Martin Luther Jr. 4
KING, Mary Perry 5
KING, Maxwell Clark 5
KING, Melvin L. 2
KING, Merrill Jenks 1
KING, Oscar A. 1
KING, Paul H
KING, Paul Howard 2
KING, Preston H
KING, Putnam H
KING, Raymond Thomas 5
KING, Richard H
KING, Richard Hayne 2
KING, Robert Luther 5
KING, Roy Stevenson 3
KING, Rufus * H
KING, Rufus H. H
KING, Samuel H
KING, Samuel Archer H
KING, Samuel Archer 4
KING, Samuel Ward H
KING, Samuel Wilder 3
KING, Stanley 3
KING, Stanton Henry 3
KING, Steve M. 3
KING, Stoddard H
KING, Sylvan N. 4
KING, Theophilus 1
KING, Thomas Brown 4
KING, Thomas Butler H
KING, Thomas Luther 5
KING, Thomas Starr H
KING, Virginia Ann 4
KING, Wilburn Hill 1
KING, Wilford Isbell 5
KING, Will R. 1
KING, Willard Vinton 3
KING, William H
KING, William Albert 1
KING, William Fletcher 1
KING, William Frederick 1
KING, William Henry 2
KING, William Lyon Mackenzie 3
KING, William Perry 2
KING, William Peter 3
KING, William Reynolds 5
KING, William Robert 3
KING, William Rufus 4
KING, William Rufus Devane 3
KING, William Wirt 3
KING, Willis L. 1
KING, Willis Percival 4
KINGDON, Frank 5
KINGERY, Hugh Macmaster 1
KINGMAN, A(lice) Salome (Mrs. Wyatt Kingman) 5
KINGMAN, Eugene A. 4
KINGMAN, Henry Selden 2
KINGMAN, John J. 3
KINGMAN, Lewis 1
KINGMAN, Matthew Henry 2
KINGMAN, Russell Barclay 2
KING OF WILLIAM, James H
KINGSBURY, Albert 2
KINGSBURY, Benjamin Freeman 2
KINGSBURY, Frederick John 1
KINGSBURY, Jerome 2
KINGSBURY, John H
KINGSBURY, John A. 3
KINGSBURY, Joseph Thomas 1
KINGSBURY, Kenneth Raleigh 1
KINGSBURY, Nathan Corning 1
KINGSBURY, Seldon Bingham 1
KINGSBURY, Susan Myra 2
KINGSBURY, William Wallace H
KINGSCOTT, Louis Clifton 4
KINGSFORD, Howard Nelson 5
KINGSFORD, Joan Elizabeth 5
KINGSFORD, Thomas 5
KINGSLAND, Mrs. Burton 1
KINGSLEY, Bruce 1
KINGSLEY, Gordon 5
KINGSLEY, Calvin H
KINGSLEY, Chester Ward 1
KINGSLEY, Clarence Darwin
KINGSLEY, Darwin Pearl 1

KINGSLEY, Elbridge 1
KINGSLEY, Florence Morse 1
KINGSLEY, Hiram Webster 5
KINGSLEY, Howard L. 2
KINGSLEY, J. Sterling 1
KINGSLEY, James Luce H
KINGSLEY, John H. 4
KINGSLEY, Norman William 1
KINGSLEY, Sherman Colver 4
KINGSLEY, Willey Lyon 1
KINGSLEY, William H. 2
KINGSLEY, William Morgan 2
KINGSMILL, Harold 1
KINGSMILL, Hugh 2
KINGSTON, George Frederick 3
KINKADE, Reynolds Robert 1
KINKAID, Mary Holland 2
KINKAID, Moses Pierce 1
KINKAID, Thomas Cassin 5
KINKAID, Thomas Wright 1
KINKEAD, Cleves 1
KINKEAD, Edgar Benton 1
KINKEAD, Elizabeth Shelby 5
KINKEAD, Eugene F. 1
KINKELDEY, Otto 4
KINKHEAD, John Henry 1
KINLEY, David 1
KINLOCH, Cleland H
KINLOCH, Francis H
KINLOCH, Robert Alexander 1
KINNAN, Alexander Phoenix Waldron 1
KINNAN, William Asahel 3
KINNANE, Charles Herman 3
KINNANE, John E. 1
KINNARD, George L. 5
KINNARD, Leonard Hummel
KINNE, Edward DeWitt 1
KINNE, Helen 1
KINNE, La Vega G. 1
KINNEAR, James Wesley 1
KINNEAR, Wilson Sherman 1
KINNERSLEY, Ebenezer H
KINNETT, William Ennis 1
KINNEY, Abbot 1
KINNEY, Ansel McBryde 5
KINNEY, Antoinette Brown 2
KINNEY, Bruce 1
KINNEY, Clesson Selwyne 4
KINNEY, Coates 1
KINNEY, Elizabeth Clementine Dodge Stedman H
KINNEY, Gilbert 3
KINNEY, Henry Walsworth 5
KINNEY, Laurence Forman 4
KINNEY, Lucien Blair 5
KINNEY, Margaret West 5
KINNEY, O. S. H
KINNEY, Thomas Tallmadge 1
KINNEY, Timothy 4
KINNEY, Troy 1
KINNEY, William Burnet 1
KINNEY, William Morton 1
KINNICUT, Lincoln Newton 1
KINNICUTT, Francis Parker 1
KINNICUTT, Leonard Parker 1
KINNOCH, P. A. 3
KINO, Eusebio Francisco H
KINSELL, Laurance Wilkie 5
KINSELLA, Thomas H
KINSELLA, Thomas James 5
KINSEY, Alfred Charles 3
KINSEY, Charles H
KINSEY, E. Lee 4
KINSEY, James H
KINSEY, John H
KINSEY, John De Cou 5
KINSEY, Oliver P. 4
KINSLER, James C. 5
KINSLEY, Albert Thomas 2
KINSLEY, Carl 1
KINSLEY, Martin H
KINSLEY, Philip 1

KINSLEY, William Wirt 1
KINSMAN, David Nathaniel 1
KINSMAN, Delos Oscar 2
KINSMAN, Frederick Joseph 3
KINSMAN, J. Warren 4
KINSMAN, William A(bbot) 5
KINSOLVING, Arthur Barksdale 3
KINSOLVING, Arthur Barksdale Ii 4
KINSOLVING, George Herbert 1
KINSOLVING, Lucien Lee 1
KINSOLVING, Sally Bruce 4
KINSWORTHY, Edgar Burton
KINTER, William Lewis 1
KINTNER, Edwin G. 5
KINTNER, Samuel Montgomery 1
KINTPUASH H
KINTZING, Pearce 1
KINTZINGER, John W. 2
KINYOUN, Joseph James 1
KINZER, J. Roland 3
KINZIE, John H
KIOKEMEISTER, Fred Ludwig 5
KIP, Abraham Lincoln 1
KIP, Frederic Ellsworth 4
KIP, Leonard 1
KIP, William Ingraham H
KIPLINGER, Willard Monroe 4
KIPP, Charles John 1
KIPP, George Washington 1
KIPP, Orin Lansing 3
KIPPAX, John R. 1
KIRBY, Absalom 1
KIRBY, C. Valentine 2
KIRBY, Daniel Bartholomew 3
KIRBY, Daniel Noyes 2
KIRBY, Edmund Burgis 1
KIRBY, Ephraim H
KIRBY, Frank E. 1
KIRBY, Fred Morgan 1
KIRBY, George Hughes 4
KIRBY, Harold 3
KIRBY, J. Hudson H
KIRBY, John Jr. 1
KIRBY, John Henry 1
KIRBY, R. Harper 1
KIRBY, Robert J. 2
KIRBY, Rollin 3
KIRBY, William Fosgate 4
KIRBY, William Gerard 5
KIRBY, William Maurice 4
KIRBYE, J. Edward 1
KIRBY-SMITH, Edmund H
KIRCHHOFF, Charles 1
KIRCHNER, Arthur Adolph 4
KIRCHNER, George H. 1
KIRCHNER, Henry Paul 3
KIRCHNER, Otto 1
KIRCHWEY, George Washington 2
KIRCK, Charles Townsend
KIRK, Alan Goodrich 4
KIRK, Arthur Dale 2
KIRK, Charles Albert 5
KIRK, Dolly Williams 5
KIRK, Edward Cameron 1
KIRK, Edward Norris 1
KIRK, Ellen Olney 4
KIRK, Frank C. 4
KIRK, Harris C. 4
KIRK, Harris Elliott 3
KIRK, John Foster 1
KIRK, John Franklin 1
KIRK, John R. 1
KIRK, Lester King 5
KIRK, May 4
KIRK, Norman Thomas 4
KIRK, Raymond Eller 5
KIRK, Raymond V. 2
KIRK, Thomas Jefferson 4
KIRK, Waldorf Tilton 4
KIRK, William 1
KIRK, William Frederick
KIRKBRIDE, Franklin Butler 1
KIRKBRIDE, Thomas Story H
KIRKEBY, Arnold S. 4
KIRKHAM, Harold Laurens Dundas 2

KIRKHAM, John Henry 1
KIRKHAM, Stanton Davis 2
KIRKHAM, William Barri 5
KIRKLAND, Archie Howard 1
KIRKLAND, Caroline Matilda Stansbury 1
KIRKLAND, James Hampton 1
KIRKLAND, James Robert 3
KIRKLAND, John Thornton H
KIRKLAND, Joseph * H
KIRKLAND, Samuel H
KIRKLAND, Weymouth 4
KIRKLAND, Winifred Margaretta 2
KIRKLIN, Byrl Raymond 3
KIRKMAN, Marshall Monroe 1
KIRKPATRICK, Andrew H
KIRKPATRICK, Andrew 3
KIRKPATRICK, Blaine Evron
KIRKPATRICK, Carlos Stevens 3
KIRKPATRICK, Clifford 5
KIRKPATRICK, Edwin Asbury 1
KIRKPATRICK, Elbert W. 1
KIRKPATRICK, George Holland 5
KIRKPATRICK, Ivone Elliott 4
KIRKPATRICK, Leonard Henry 4
KIRKPATRICK, Sanford 4
KIRKPATRICK, Sidney Dale 5
KIRKPATRICK, Thomas Le Roy 2
KIRKPATRICK, William H
KIRKPATRICK, William Dawson 4
KIRKPATRICK, William Huntington 5
KIRKPATRICK, William James 1
KIRKPATRICK, William Sebring 1
KIRKUS, William 1
KIRKWOOD, Arthur Carter 5
KIRKWOOD, Daniel H
KIRKWOOD, Irwin 1
KIRKWOOD, John Gamble 3
KIRKWOOD, Joseph Edward 1
KIRKWOOD, Samuel Jordan H
KIRKWOOD, William Reeside 4
KIRN, George John 4
KIROACK, Howard 3
KIRSCH, John N. 4
KIRSCHBAUM, Arthur 4
KIRSHMAN, John Emmett 2
KIRSHNER, Charles Henry 2
KIRSTEIN, Arthur 4
KIRSTEIN, Louis Edward 2
KIRSTEIN, Max 5
KIRTLAND, Dorrance H
KIRTLAND, Fred Durrell 5
KIRTLAND, Jared Potter H
KIRTLAND, John Copeland 3
KIRTLAND, Lucian Swift 4
KIRTLEY, James Samuel 1
KIRWAN, Albert Dennis 5
KIRWAN, Michael Joseph 5
KIRWIN, Thomas Joseph 3
KISELEV, Evgeny Dmitrievich 4
KISER, Samuel Ellsworth 1
KISER, Samuel Ellsworth 2
KISSAM, Henry Snyder 1
KISSEL, John 1
KISSELL, Harry Seaman 2
KISTER, George Raphael 4
KISTLER, John Clinton 4
KISTLER, Raymon M. 4
KITCHEL, Lloyd 1
KITCHEL, William Lloyd 2
KITCHELL, Aaron 1
KITCHELL, Joseph Gray 2
KITCHEN, Bethuel H
KITCHENS, Wade Hampton 4
KITCHIN, Claude 1
KITCHIN, Thurman Delna 3

KITCHIN, William Copeman 1
KITCHIN, William Walton 1
KITSON, Harry Dexter 3
KITSON, Henry Hudson 2
KITSON, Samuel James 1
KITSON, Theo Alice Ruggles 1
KITTELL, Albert George 2
KITTELL, James Shepard 1
KITTELLE, Sumner Ely Wetmore 3
KITTERA, John Wilkes H
KITTERA, Thomas H
KITTINGER, Harold D. 2
KITTLE, Charles Morgan 1
KITTREDGE, Abbott Eliot 1
KITTREDGE, Alfred Beard 1
KITTREDGE, Frank Alvah 3
KITTREDGE, George Lyman H
KITTREDGE, George Washington 3
KITTREDGE, George Watson 2
KITTREDGE, Henry Grattan 1
KITTREDGE, Josiah Edwards 1
KITTREDGE, Mabel Hyde 3
KITTREDGE, Walter 1
KITTREDGE, Wheaton 1
KITTRELL, Norman Goree 1
KITTS, Joseph Arthur 2
KITTS, Willard Augustus 3'rd 4
KITTSON, Norman Wolfred H
KIVEL, John 1
KIVLIN, Vincent Earl 5
KIXMILLER, William 2
KJELLGREN, Bengt R. F. 5
KLABER, Eugene Henry 5
KLABUNDE, Earl Horace 4
KLAEBER, Frederick 4
KLAERNER, Richard Albert 4
KLAESTAD, Helge 4
KLAFFENBACH, Arthur O. 4
KLAIN, Zora 3
KLAMMER, Aloysius A. 3
KLAPP, William Henry 1
KLAPPER, Paul 3
KLARE, Robert Edward 4
KLATH, Thormood Oscar 4
KLAUBER, Adolph 1
KLAUBER, Edward 3
KLAUBER, Laurence Monroe 5
KLAUDER, Charles Zeller 4
KLAUS, Irving Goncer 5
KLAUSER, Karl 1
KLAUSMEYER, David Michael 5
KLAW, Marc 1
KLEBERG, Edward Robert 3
KLEBERG, Richard Miffin 3
KLEBERG, Rudolph 1
KLEBS, Arnold Carl 2
KLECKNER, Martin Seler 5
KLEEGMAN, Sophia Josephine,* 1
KLEEMAN, Arthur S. 4
KLEENE, Gustav Adolph 2
KLEIN, Arthur George 1
KLEIN, Bruno Oscar 1
KLEIN, Charles 1
KLEIN, Eugene S. 2
KLEIN, Francis Joseph 5
KLEIN, Frederick B. 3
KLEIN, Frederick Charles 1
KLEIN, Gerald Brown 5
KLEIN, Harry Martin John 5
KLEIN, Harry Thomas 4
KLEIN, Henry Weber 5
KLEIN, Herman William 3
KLEIN, Hermann 4
KLEIN, Horace C. 4
KLEIN, Jacob 4
KLEIN, John Warren 3
KLEIN, Joseph Frederic 1
KLEIN, Julius 5
KLEIN, Manuel 1
KLEIN, Melanie 5
KLEIN, Sandor Sidney 5

KLEIN, Simon Robert 4
KLEIN, William, Jr. 5
KLEIN, William M. 4
KLEINER, Hugo Gustav 5
KLEINER, Israel S. 4
KLEINPELL, William Darwin 3
KLEINSCHMIDT, Rudolph August 4
KLEINSMID, Rufus Bernard 'von 4
KLEISER, George William 1
KLEISER, Grenville 1
KLEISER, Lorentz 4
KLEIST, James Aloysius 3
KLEITZ, William L. 5
KLEMIN, Alexander 3
KLEMM, Louis Richard 1
KLEMME, Edward Julius 5
KLEMME, Roland M. 5
KLEMPERER, Otto 5
KLENKE, William Walter 4
KLEPETKO, Frank 1
KLEPPER, Frank B. 3
KLEPPER, Max Francis 1
KLETZKI, Paul 5
KLIBANOW, William J. 5
KLIEFORTH, Ralph George 4
KLIEN, Arthur Jay 1
KLIEWER, John Walter 1
KLIKA, Ervin Robert 5
KLIMM, Lester E. 4
KLINCK, Arthur William 5
KLINCK, Leonard Silvanus
KLINE, Allan Blair 5
KLINE, Ardolph L. 1
KLINE, C. Mahlon 1
KLINE, Charles H. 1
KLINE, Franz Josef 5
KLINE, George H
KLINE, George Milton 4
KLINE, George Washington
KLINE, I. Clinton 3
KLINE, Jacob 1
KLINE, John Robert 3
KLINE, Marcus C. L. 1
KLINE, Marion Justus 4
KLINE, Paul Robert 5
KLINE, Virgil Philip 1
KLINE, Whorten Albert 1
KLINE, William Fair 1
KLINE, William Jay 1
KLINEFELTER, Howard Emanuel 4
KLINGAMAN, Orie Erb 4
KLINGBIEL, Ray I. 5
KLINGE, Ernest F. 5
KLINGENSMITH, John Jr. H
KLINGLER, Harry J. 4
KLIPPART, John Hancock H
KLIPSTEIN, Ernest Carl 1
KLIPSTEIN, Louis Frederick H
KLOCK, Mabie Crouse 5
KLOEBER, Charles Edward 1
KLOPP, Edward Jonathan 1
KLOPP, Henry Irwin 1
KLOPSCH, Louis 1
KLOSS, Charles Luther 3
KLOSSNER, Howard Jacob 3
KLOTS, Allen Trafford 4
KLOTZ, Oskar 4
KLOTZ, Robert H
KLOTZBURGER, Edwin Carl 1
KLUBERTANZ, George Peter 5
KLUCKHOHN, Clyde Kay Maben 4
KLUCKHOLN, Frank Louis 4
KLUG, Norman R. 4
KLUGESCHEID, Richard Charles 5
KLUGHERZ, John Anthony 4
KLUSS, Charles LaVerne 4
KLUTTZ, Theodore Franklin 1
KLUYVER, Albert Jan 4
KLYCE, Scudder 1
KLYVER, Henry Peter 4
KNABE, Valentine Wilhelm Ludwig 1
KNABENSHUE, Paul 1
KNABENSHUE, Roy 5
KNABENSHUE, Samuel S. 3
KNAEBEL, Ernest 2

KNAPLUND, 4
  Paul Alexander
KNAPP, A(rthur) Blair 5
KNAPP, Adeline 6
KNAPP, Andrew Stephen 4
KNAPP, Anthony Lausett H
KNAPP, Arnold Herman 6
KNAPP, Arthur May 4
KNAPP, Bliss 3
KNAPP, Bradford 5
KNAPP, Charles H
KNAPP, Charles 1
KNAPP, Charles Luman 5
KNAPP, 1
  Charles Welbourne
KNAPP, H
  Chauncey Langdon
KNAPP, Cleon Talboys 3
KNAPP, 5
  Francis Atherton
KNAPP, Frank Averill 4
KNAPP, Fred Church 2
KNAPP, George 6
KNAPP, George Leonard 5
KNAPP, Grace Higley 6
KNAPP, Harold Everard 4
KNAPP, Harry Shepard 1
KNAPP, Henry Alonzo 1
KNAPP, Herman * 1
KNAPP, John Joseph 6
KNAPP, Joseph Palmer 3
KNAPP, Kemper K. 2
KNAPP, Lyman Enos 1
KNAPP, 1
  Martin Augustine
KNAPP, Philip Coombs 1
KNAPP, Robert Talbot 3
KNAPP, Samuel Lorenzo H
KNAPP, Seaman Asahel 1
KNAPP, Shepherd 2
KNAPP, Stanley Merrill 4
KNAPP, Thad Johnson 1
KNAPP, Thomas 4
  McCartan
KNAPP, Walter I(rving) 5
KNAPP, Willard A. 4
KNAPP, William Ireland 1
KNAPPEN, Loyal Edwin 1
KNAPPEN, 1
  Theodore Macfarlane
KNAPPENBERGER, 4
  J. William
KNAPPERTSBUSCH, 4
  Hans
KNATHS, (Otto) Karl 5
KNAUFFT, Ernest 4
KNAUSS, Harold Paul 4
KNAUTH, Arnold 4
  Whitman
KNAUTH, Oswald 4
  Whitman
KNEASS, George Bryan 5
KNEASS, H
  Samuel Honeyman
KNEASS, Strickland H
KNEASS, 1
  Strickland Landis
KNEASS, William H
KNECHT, Karl Kae 5
KNEEDLER, William L. 4
KNEELAND, Abner H
KNEELAND, 5
  George Jackson
KNEELAND, 5
  Robert Shepherd
KNEELAND, Samuel * H
KNEELAND, 1
  Stillman Foster
KNEELAND, Yale, Jr. 5
KNEIL, Robert Chipman 4
KNEIP, Herbert Joseph 4
KNEISEL, Franz 1
KNEISS, Gilbert Harold 4
KNEPPER, 4
  Edwin Garfield
KNEVELS, Gertrude 4
KNIBBS, Harry Herbert 2
KNICKERBOCKER, 3
  Fred Hugh
KNICKERBOCKER, H
  Harmen Jansen
KNICKERBOCKER, H
  Herman
KNICKERBOCKER, 2
  Hubert Renfro
KNICKERBOCKER, 5
  William E.
KNICKERBOCKER, 5
  William Skinkle
KNIFFIN, William Henry 3
KNIGHT, Adele Ferguson 4
KNIGHT, 1
  Albion Williamson
KNIGHT, Augustus Smith 2
KNIGHT, Austin Melvin 1
KNIGHT, Charles 5
KNIGHT, Charles Landon 1

KNIGHT, Charles Mellen 2
KNIGHT, Charles Robert 3
KNIGHT, Clarence A. 1
KNIGHT, Edgar Wallace 3
KNIGHT, H
  Edward Collings
KNIGHT, Edward Henry H
KNIGHT, Edward Hooker 2
KNIGHT, Edward Wallace 1
KNIGHT, Erastus Cole 1
KNIGHT, Eric 2
KNIGHT, Eugene Herbert 5
KNIGHT, 3
  Francis McMaster
KNIGHT, Frank A. 1
KNIGHT, Frank Hyneman 5
KNIGHT, 2
  Frederic Butterfield
KNIGHT, 1
  Frederic Harrison
KNIGHT, 1
  Frederic Irving
KNIGHT, 1
  George Alexander
KNIGHT, 2
  George Laurence
KNIGHT, George 1
  Thomson
KNIGHT, George Wells 1
KNIGHT, Goodwin (Jess) 5
KNIGHT, Grant Cochran 3
KNIGHT, Harold Audas 3
KNIGHT, Harry Clifford 5
KNIGHT, Harry Edward 2
KNIGHT, Harry S. 3
KNIGHT, Henry Cogswell H
KNIGHT, Henry Granger 2
KNIGHT, Howard Roscoe 4
KNIGHT, James Ernest 5
KNIGHT, Jesse 1
KNIGHT, Jesse William 3
KNIGHT, John 3
KNIGHT, 1
  John George David
KNIGHT, John Thornton 1
KNIGHT, Jonathan * H
KNIGHT, Leona Kaiser 4
KNIGHT, Louis Aston 4
KNIGHT, Lucian Lamar 1
KNIGHT, Milton 1
KNIGHT, Montgomery 2
KNIGHT, Nehemiah 1
KNIGHT, Nehemiah Rice H
KNIGHT, Nicholas 4
KNIGHT, Ora Willis 1
KNIGHT, Otis D. 4
KNIGHT, Peter Oliphant 2
KNIGHT, Ridgway 1
KNIGHT, Robert 1
KNIGHT, Robert Palmer 4
KNIGHT, Ryland 2
KNIGHT, Samuel 2
KNIGHT, Sarah Kemble H
KNIGHT, Stephen Albert 1
KNIGHT, Thomas 3
  Edmund
KNIGHT, 1
  Thomas Edmund Jr.
KNIGHT, Walter David 3
KNIGHT, Webster 1
KNIGHT, Wilbur Clinton 1
KNIGHT, William Allen 3
KNIGHT, William D. 4
KNIGHT, William Henry 4
KNIPE, Alden Arthur 2
KNIPE, Emilie Benson 3
KNIPP, Charles Tobias 2
KNISKERN, 4
  Leslie Albert
KNISKERN, 1
  Philip Wheeler
KNISKERN, Warren B. 1
KNOBLOCH, 5
  Henry F(rederick) J(acob)
KNODE, Oliver M. 4
KNODE, Ralph Howard 4
KNOLES, Tully Cleon 5
KNOLL, Hans G. 3
KNOLLYS, 4
  Edward George William
  Tyrwhitt
KNOOP, Frederic Barnes 5
KNOPF, Adolph 4
KNOPF, Blanche 5
KNOPF, Blanche (Wolf) 5
KNOPF, Carl Sumner 2
KNOPF, Philip 4
KNOPF, S. Adolphus 1
KNOPF, 5
  William Cleveland, Jr.
KNOPP, 1
  Herbert William Sr.
KNORR, Fred August 4
KNORTZ, Karl 1
KNOTT, A. Leo 1
KNOTT, David H. 5
KNOTT, Emmet Kennard 4

KNOTT, James E. 4
KNOTT, James Proctor 1
KNOTT, John Francis 4
KNOTT, Lester R. 4
KNOTT, Richard Wilson 1
KNOTT, Stuart R. 4
KNOTT, Thomas Albert 2
KNOTT, Van Buren 5
KNOTTS, Armanis F. 1
KNOTTS, Edward C. 1
KNOTTS, Howard Clayton 1
KNOTTS, Raymond 4
KNOUFF, Ralph Albert 4
KNOUS, William Lee 4
KNOWER, 1
  Henry McElderry
KNOWLAND, 4
  Joseph Russell
KNOWLES, 5
  Archibald Campbell
KNOWLES, Daniel Clark 1
KNOWLES, 5
  Edward Gillett
KNOWLES, 4
  Edward Randall
KNOWLES, 5
  Edwin Blackwell
KNOWLES, Ellin J. 1
KNOWLES, 1
  Frederic Lawrence
KNOWLES, 5
  Frederick Milton
KNOWLES, Hiram 1
KNOWLES, 1
  Horace Greeley
KNOWLES, Lucius James H
KNOWLES, Melita 5
KNOWLES, Morris 2
KNOWLES, Nathaniel 5
KNOWLES, Robert Bell 3
KNOWLSON, James S. 3
KNOWLTON, 3
  Ansel Alphonse
KNOWLTON, Charles H
KNOWLTON, 5
  Charles Osmond
KNOWLTON, 4
  Charles Osmond
KNOWLTON, 5
  Daniel Chauncey
KNOWLTON, Ebenezer H
KNOWLTON, Eliot A. 1
KNOWLTON, Frank Hall 1
KNOWLTON, 5
  Frank P(attengill)
KNOWLTON, 1
  George Willard
KNOWLTON, Helen 1
  Mary
KNOWLTON, 1
  Hosea Morrill
KNOWLTON, 1
  Marcus Perrin
KNOWLTON, P. Clarke 4
KNOWLTON, 3
  Philip Arnold
KNOWLTON, Robert 1
  Henry
KNOWLTON, Thomas H
KNOX, Adeline Trafton 4
KNOX, Dudley Wright 4
KNOX, Mrs. Frank 5
KNOX, George William 1
KNOX, Harry 1
KNOX, Henry H
KNOX, James H
KNOX, James E. 3
KNOX, 5
  Jessie Juliet (Daily)
KNOX, John Barnett 1
KNOX, John Clark 4
KNOX, John Jay H
KNOX, Louis 4
KNOX, Martin Van Buren 4
KNOX, Mary Alice 1
KNOX, Mrs. Charles B. 5
KNOX, Philander Chase 1
KNOX, Raymond Collyer 5
KNOX, Robert White 3
KNOX, Rush Hightower 3
KNOX, Samuel H
KNOX, 2
  Samuel Lippincott Griswold
KNOX, Thomas Wallace H
KNOX, William Elliott 4
KNOX, William Franklin 2
KNOX, William Shadrach 1
KNOX, William White 1
KNUBEL, 2
  Frederick Hermann
KNUBEL, 3
  Frederick Ritscher
KNUDSEN, 4
  Charles William
KNUDSEN, Thorkild R. 4
KNUDSEN, William S. 2

KNUDSON, 3
  Albert Cornelius
KNUDSON, Bennett Olin 4
KNUDSON, James K. 4
KNUDSON, John 3
  Immanuel
KNUTSON, Harold 3
KNUTSON, Kent Siguart 5
KOBAK, Edgar 4
KOBBE, Gustav 1
KOBBE, William August 1
KOBELT, Karl 4
KOBER, George Martin 1
KOBLER, Alfred 3
KOCH, H
  Charles Rudolph Edward
KOCH, Edward William 2
KOCH, Elers 3
KOCH, Felix John 1
KOCH, Fred Chase 5
KOCH, Fred Conrad 2
KOCH, Frederick Henry 2
KOCH, George Price 4
KOCH, Henry G. H
KOCH, Julius Arnold 3
KOCH, Otto 3
KOCH, Theodore Wesley 4
KOCHAN, Edward John 5
KOCHER, A. Lawrence 5
KOCHERSPERGER, 4
  Hiram Miller
KOCHERTHAL, Josua H
  'von
KOCHIN, Louis Mordecai 5
KOCHS, August 1
KOCIALKOWSKI, Leo 3
KOCKRITZ, Ewald 5
KOCOUREK, Albert 5
KODALY, Zoltan 5
KOEBEL, Ralph Francis 4
KOEHLER, Otto A. 5
KOEHLER, Robert 1
KOEHLER, 3
  Sylvester Rosa
KOEHLER, 3
  Wilhelm Reinhold Walter
KOEHRING, William J. 5
KOENIG, Adolph 1
KOENIG, 1
  George Augustus
KOENIG, Joseph Pierre 5
KOENIG, Louis F. 4
KOENIG, Myron L(aw) 5
KOENIGSBERG, Moses 2
KOEPEL, 4
  Norbert Francis
KOERNER, Andrew 1
KOERNER, Gustave H
KOERNER, Theodor 3
KOERNER, Theodor 5
KOERNER, William 1
KOERNER, 1
  William Henry Dethlep
KOESTER, Frank 1
KOFFKA, Kurt 3
KOHL, Edwin Phillips 4
KOHLBECK, Valentine 1
KOHLER, Elmer Peter 1
KOHLER, Fred 1
KOHLER, G. A. Edward 5
KOHLER, Herbert Calvin 5
KOHLER, 5
  Herbert Vollrath
KOHLER, Kaufmann 1
KOHLER, Max James 1
KOHLER, Ruth DeYoung 5
KOHLER, Walter Jodok 3
KOHLER, Wolfgang 4
KOHLER, Wolfgang 4
KOHLHEPP, Charles E. 5
KOHLMANN, Anthony H
KOHLMEIER, Albert L. 4
KOHLMER, Fred 5
KOHLSAAT, 1
  Christian Cecil
KOHLSAAT, Herman 1
  Henry
KOHLSTEDT, 5
  Donald Winston
KOHLSTEDT, 4
  Edward Delor
KOHN, August 1
KOHN, Henry H. 2
KOHN, Jacob 5
KOHN, Robert David 3
KOHNS, Lee 1
KOHNSTAMM, Frank R. 4
KOHUT, Alexander H
KOINER, C. Wellington 3
KOKATNUR, 3
  Vaman Ramachandra
KOKERITZ, K. A. Helge 4
KOKERNOT, Herbert Lee 5
KOLAR, Victor 5
KOLB, Charles August 4
KOLB, Dielman H

KOLB, 5
  Ellsworth Leonardson
KOLB, John Harrison 4
KOLB, Louis John 1
KOLBE, Parke Rexford 2
KOLE, Lessing Lawrence 5
KOLKER, Henry Joseph 2
KOLLE, 1
  Frederick Strange
KOLLEN, Gerrit John 1
KOLLER, Carl 2
KOLLER, Paul Warren 1
KOLLOCK, 1
  Charles Wilson
KOLLOCK, Mary 4
KOLLOCK, Shepard H
KOLLWITZ, 4
  Kathe Schmidt
KOLMAN, Burton A. 5
KOLMER, John Albert 4
KOLOWICH, George J. 3
KOLSETH, J. Harold 4
KOMAREWSKY, 3
  Vasili Ilyich
KOMAROV, Vladimir 4
KOMMERS, William John 5
KOMORA, Paul O. 3
KOMP, William H. Wood 3
KONE, Edward Reeves 4
KONENKOV, 5
  Sergei Timopheevitch
KONIG, George 1
KONINGS, Anthony H
KONJOVIC, Petar 5
KONKLE, Burton Alva 2
KONOP, Thomas Frank 4
KONTA, Alexander 1
KONTA, Annie Lemp 5
KONTA, Geoffrey 2
KONTI, Isidore 1
KONTZ, Ernest Charles 2
KOON, Martin B. 1
KOONS, Charles Alfred 5
KOONS, Charles Alfred 4
KOONS, John Cornelius 1
KOONS, 1
  Tilghman Benjamin
KOONTZ, Arthur Burke 4
KOONTZ, 3
  Frederick Bowers
KOONTZ, James R. 4
KOONTZ, Louis Knott 3
KOOP, William H. 1
KOOPMAN, Augustus 1
KOOPMAN, Harry 1
  Lyman
KOPALD, Louis Joseph 4
KOPETZKY, 3
  Samuel Joseph
KOPF, Carl Heath 3
KOPLAR, Sam 4
KOPLIK, Henry 1
KOPMAN, Benjamin 4
KOPP, Arthur William 5
KOPP, Arthur William 4
KOPP, George A(dams) 5
KOPP, Otto 4
KOPP, William F. 1
KOPPER, 3
  Samuel Keene Claggett
KOPPIUS, O. T. 4
KOPPLEMANN, 1
  Herman Paul
KORBEL, Mario 3
KORBLY, 1
  Charles Alexander
KORDA, Sir Alexander 3
KOREN, John 1
KOREN, Ulrik Vilhelm 1
KOREN, William Jr. 3
KORFF, 1
  Sergius Alexander
KORIN, 5
  Pavel Dmitrievich
KORN, Peter George 4
KORNEGAY, Wade 1
  Hampton
KORNER, Gustav Philipp H
KORNER, 5
  Jules Gilmer Jr.
KORNER, Theodor 5
KORNFELD, Albert 4
KORNFELD, Murray 5
KORNGOLD, 3
  Eric Wolfgang
KORNHAUSER, 3
  Sidney Isaac
KORSMEYER, 4
  Frederick August
KORSTIAN, 4
  Clarence Ferdinand
KORZYBSKI, 2
  Alfred Habdank
KOSA, Emil Jean, Jr. 5
KOSANOVITCH, Sava N. 4
KOSCINSKI, Arthur A. 3

KOSCIUSZKO, H
 Tadeusz Andrzej
 Bonawentura
KOSER, Ralph B. 5
KOSER, Stewart Arment 5
KOSMAK, George
 William 3
KOSSUTH, Lajos H
KOST, Frederick W. 1
KOST, John 1
KOSTALEK, John Anton 1
KOSTELLOW, 3
 Alexander Jusserand
KOSTER, 3
 Frederick Jacob
KOSZALKA, 5
 Michael Francis
KOTANY, Ludwig 1
KOTH, Arthur William 4
KOUDELKA, Joseph 1
 Maria
KOUES, Helen 4
KOUNTZ, John S. 1
KOUNTZE, 1
 Augustus Frederick
KOUNTZE, 5
 Charles Thomas
KOUNTZE, 'de Lancey 2
KOUNTZE, Harold 1
KOUSSEVITZKY, Sergei 3
KOUTZEN, Boris 4
KOVACH, George 4
 Stephen
KOVACS, Ernie 4
KOVACS, Richard 3
KOWAL, Chester * 4
KOWNATZKI, Hans 4
KOYL, Charles Herschel 1
KOYRE, Alexandre 5
KOZLOV, 4
 Frol Romanovich
KRACAUER, Siegfried 4
KRACKE, 3
 Frederick J. H.
KRACKE, Roy Rachford 3
KRAELING, Carl H. 4
KRAEMER, 3
 Casper John Jr.
KRAEMER, Henry 1
KRAETZER, 1
 Arthur Furman
KRAFFT, Carl R. 5
KRAFFT, Walter A. 3
KRAFFT, Walter E. 4
KRAFKA, Joseph Jr. 2
KRAFT, Edwin Arthur 4
KRAFT, James Lewis 3
KRAFT, John H. 5
KRAL, Josef Jiri 4
KRAMER, A. Walter 5
KRAMER, Albert Ludlow 2
KRAMER, Andrew 5
 Anthony
KRAMER, Edwin Weed 2
KRAMER, 2
 Frederick Ferdinand
KRAMER, 1
 George Washington
KRAMER, Hans 3
KRAMER, Harold Morton 1
KRAMER, 4
 Herman Frederick
KRAMER, John F. 5
KRAMER, 3
 Raymond Charles
KRAMER, Rudolph Jesse 3
KRAMER, Samuel 4
 Edmond
KRAMER, Simon Gad 5
KRAMER, 4
 Simon Pendleton
KRAMMES, Emma Ruess 3
KRANNERT, 5
 Herman C(harles)
KRANS, Horatio Sheafe 5
KRANS, Olaf H
KRANS, Olaf 4
KRANZ, Leon George 3
KRAPP, George Philip 1
KRASCHEL, 3
 Nelson George
KRASIK, Sidney 4
KRASS, Nathan 3
KRATHWOHL, 5
 William Charles
KRATT, Theodore 4
KRATZ, Alonzo Plumsted 5
KRATZ, Henry Elton 1
KRAUS, Adolf 4
KRAUS, Charles August 4
KRAUS, Edward Henry 5
KRAUS, John H
KRAUS, Milton 1
KRAUS, Rene Raoul 2
KRAUS, Walter Max 2
KRAUSE, Allen Kramer 4
KRAUSE, Carl Albert 1

KRAUSE, Chester T. 4
KRAUSE, Harry Theodore 5
KRAUSE, Louise B. 5
KRAUSE, 1
 Lyda Farrington
KRAUSE, Rudolph 4
KRAUSKOPF, Joseph 1
KRAUSS, 2
 Elmer Frederick
KRAUSS, William 1
KRAUSS, 1
 William Christopher
KRAUSS-BOELTE, Maria 4
KRAUTBAUER, H
 Franz Xaver
KRAUTH, Charles Philip 3
KRAUTH, H
 Charles Porterfield
KRAUTHOFF, 1
 Charles Rieseck
KRAUTHOFF, 1
 Louis Charles
KRAVCHENKO, Victor 4
 A.
KRAYBILL, Henry Reist 3
KREBS, Jacob 3
KREBS, Stanley LeFevre 5
KREBS, William Samuel 3
KRECH, Alvin William 1
KREFELD, William John 4
KREGER, Clarence W. 2
KREGER, Edward Albert 3
KREGER, 4
 Henry Ludwig Flood
KREHBIEL, Christian H
KREHBIEL, Christian 4
KREHBIEL, 2
 Christian Emanuel
KREHBIEL, Edward 3
KREHBIEL, Henry 4
 Edward
KREIDER, Aaron Shenk 3
KREIDER, 3
 Charles Daniel
KREINHEDER, Oscar 1
 Carl
KREIS, Henry 4
KREISER, 1
 Edward Franklin
KREISINGER, Henry 2
KREISLER, Fritz 4
KREISMANN, 5
 Frederick Herman
KREJCI, Milo William 4
KREMER, Charles 4
 Edward
KREMER, Charles S. 4
KREMER, George H
KREMER, J. Bruce 1
KREMER, Walter Wall 4
KREMERS, Edward 1
KREMERS, J. H. 4
KREMPEL, John P. 1
KRESEL, Isidor Jacob 3
KRESGE, Sebastian S. 3
KRESS, C. Adam 3
KRESS, 1
 Claude Washington
KRESS, Daniel H. 4
KRESS, George Henry 3
KRESS, John Alexander 1
KRESS, Rush Harrison 3
KRESS, Samuel Henry 3
KRESS, Walter Jay 5
KRESSMAN, 5
 Mabel A. Gridley (mrs.
 Frederick W. Kressman)
KRETSCHMER, 3
 Herman Louis
KRETZINGER, 1
 George Washington
KREUSCHER, 2
 Philip Heinrich
KREY, August Charles 4
KREYMBORG, Alfred 4
KREZ, Konrad H
KRIBBEN, Earl 3
KRICK, Charles Shalter 3
KRICK, Edwin Vernon 3
KRIDL, Manfred 3
KRIEBEL, Oscar Schultz 1
KRIEBEL, William F. 3
KRIEBLE, 4
 Vernon Kriebel
KRIEGE, Otto Edward 5
KRIEHN, George 4
KRILL, Alex Eugene 5
KRIMMEL, John Lewis H
KRISHNAN, 4
 Sir Kariamanikkam
 Srinivasa
KRISTOFFERSEN, 4
 Magnus K.
KRITZ, Karl 5
KROEBER, Alfred L. 5
KROECK, Louis Samuel 3
KROEGER, Adolph Ernst H

KROEGER, 1
 Ernest Richard
KROEGER, 2
 Frederick Charles
KROEH, 2
 Charles Frederick
KROEHLER, Peter 3
 Edward
KROEZE, Barend Herman 5
KROGER, Bernard Henry 1
KROHN, 1
 William Otterbein
KROL, Bastiaen Jansen H
KROLL, Jack 5
KROMER, Leon Benjamin 4
KRONBERG, Louis 4
KRONE, Max Thomas 5
KRONMILLER, John 4
KRONSHAGE, 5
 Theodore, Jr.
KRONWALL, Konstantin 4
KROOS, Oscar August 3
KROTEL, 1
 Gottlob Frederick
KROUT, Mary Hannah 1
KROYT, Boris 5
KRUCKMAN, Arnold 3
KRUEGER, 1
 Ernest Theodore
KRUEGER, 1
 John Frederick
KRUEGER, Otto 3
KRUEGER, Walter 4
KRUEGER, 4
 William Conrad
KRUELL, Gustav 1
KRUESI, Frank E. 2
KRUESI, John H
KRUESI, Paul John 4
KRUETGEN, Ernest J. 2
KRUG, Henry Jr. 4
KRUG, Julius Albert 5
KRUGER, 3
 Frederick Konrad
KRUM, Chester Harding 1
KRUM, Howard Lewis 4
KRUMB, Henry 4
KRUMBEIN, Paul Otto 2
KRUMBHAAR, E. B. 4
KRUMREIG, 4
 Edward Ludwig
KRUMWIEDE, Charles 1
KRUPP, 4
 Alfried 'von Bohlen 'und
 Halbach
KRUPSHAW, David Loeb 4
KRUSE, E. T. 3
KRUSE, 1
 Frederick William
KRUSEN, Wilmer 2
KRUTCH, Joseph Wood 5
KRUTTSCHNITT, 1
 Ernest Benjamin
KRUTTSCHNITT, Julius 1
KRYL, Bohumir 5
KUBAT, Jerald Richard 5
KUBEL, Stephen Joseph 4
KUBELIK, Jan 1
KUCERA, Louis Benedict 3
KUCZYNSKI, Robert 4
 Rene
KUDNER, Arthur Henry 2
KUEBLER, John R. 4
KUEHNE, Hugo Franz 4
KUERSTEINER, 1
 Albert Frederick
KUESTER, Clarence Otto 2
KUETHER, 3
 Frederick William
KUFOID, Charles Atwood 2
KUH, Sydney 1
KUH, Adam H
KUHN, Arthur K. 3
KUHN, C. John 4
KUHN, Ferd William 4
KUHN, Franz Christian 1
KUHN, Harry Waldo 4
KUHN, Joseph Ernst 1
KUHN, Oliver Owen 1
KUHN, Walt 3
KUHN, 1
 William Frederick
KUHNS, Austin 4
KUHNS, Harold Samuel 4
KUHNS, Joseph Henry H
KUHNS, 1
 Luther Melanchthon
KUHNS, Oscar 1
KUHNS, William Rodney 5
KUICHLING, Emil 4
KUIST, Howard Tillman 4
KUIZENGA, John E. 3
KULAS, Elroy John 3
KULER, Fritz 5
KULIKOWSKI, Adam 4
KULIKOWSKI, 5
 Adam (Hyppolit) H

KULP, Clarence Arthur 3
KULP, Victor Henry 4
KUMLER, Henry H
KUMLER, John A. 4
KUMM, Einar Axel 3
KUMM, H. Karl William 4
KUMMEL, Henry Barnard 2
KUMMER, 2
 Frederic Arnold
KUMP, Herman Guy 4
KUNESH, Joseph Francis 4
KUNG, H. H. 4
KUNHARDT, Kingsley 3
KUNIANSKY, Max 3
KUNITZER, Robert 1
KUNIYOSHI, Yasuo 3
KUNKEL, A. William 5
KUNKEL, Beverly Waugh 5
KUNKEL, Frank Henry 3
KUNKEL, Jacob Michael H
KUNKEL, John Christian H
KUNKEL, John Crain 5
KUNKEL, Louis Otto 5
KUNKEL, 2
 William Albert Jr.
KUNKLE, 3
 Bayard Dickenson
KUNO, Hisashi 5
KUNSTADTER, Albert 4
KUNSTADTER, Ralph
 Hess 4
KUNTZ, Albert 3
KUNWALD, Ernst 1
KUNZ, Adolf Henry 5
KUNZ, George Frederick 1
KUNZ, Jakob 1
KUNZ, Josef L(aurenz) 5
KUNZ, Stanley Henry 4
KUNZE, H
 John Christopher
KUNZE, Richard Ernest 1
KUNZE, 5
 William Frederick
KUNZEL, Fred 5
KUNZIG, Louis A. 3
KUNZMANN, 5
 Jacob Christoph
KUO, Ping Wen 5
KUPLIC, J. L. 5
KURCHATOV, Igor V. 3
KURN, James M. 2
KURRELMEYER,
 William 3
KURRIE, 1
 Harry Rushworth
KURT, Franklin Thomas 2
KURTH, Ernest Lynn 4
KURTH, Wilfred 3
KURTZ, Benjamin H
KURTZ, Benjamin Putnam 1
KURTZ, Charles Lindley 1
KURTZ, Charles M. 1
KURTZ, Ford 3
KURTZ, Jacob Banks 4
KURTZ, Louis Charles 5
KURTZ, Robert Merrill 4
KURTZ, 3
 Thomas Richardson
KURTZ, William Henry H
KURZ, Louis H
KURZ, Louis 4
KURZ, Louis Frederick 4
KURZ, Walter Charles 5
KURZMAN,
 Harold Phillip 5
KUSCHNER, 5
 Beatrice Barbara Katz
 (Mrs. Joseph P. Kuschner)
KUSKOV, H
 Ivan Aleksandrovich
KUSSY, Nathan 5
KUSTERMANN, Gustav 4
KUSWORM, Sidney
 Grover 5
KUTAK, Robert I. 3
KUTZ, Charles Willauer 5
KUTZ, George Fink 4
KUWATLY, Shukri Al 4
KUYKENDALL, H
 Andrew Jackson
KVALE, O. J. 1
KVALE, 5
 Walter Frederick
KYES, Preston 2
KYES, Roger M. 5
KYKER, 4
 Benjamin Franklin
KYLE, D. Braden 1
KYLE, Edwin Dewees 5
KYLE, Edwin Jackson 5
KYLE, Hugh Graham 1
KYLE, James Henderson 1
KYLE, John Johnson 1
KYLE, John Merrill 1
KYLE, John William 5
KYLE, Joseph 1
KYLE, Joseph Blair 1

KYLE, Laurence Harwood 5
KYLE, Melvin Grove 1
KYLE, Thomas Barton 4
KYLE, Willard Hugh 4
KYLE, William S. 4
KYLES, 5
 Lynwood Westinghouse
KYNE, Peter Bernard 1
KYNETT, Alpha Gilruth 1
KYNETT, H
 Alpha Jefferson
KYRK, Hazel 3
KYSER, William D. 1
KYSTER, 4
 Olaf Helgesen Jr.

L

LA BACH, James Oscar 1
LABAREE, Benjamin 1
LABAREE,
 Mary Schauffler
LA BARGE, Joseph H
LABBE, Antoine G. 3
LABBERTON, John M. 3
LABEAUME, Louis 3
LABELLE, J. Edouard 3
LA BORDE, Maximilian H
LA BRANCHE,
 Alcee Louis H
LABRUM, J. Harry 5
LA BUY, Walter J. 4
LACASSE, Gustave 3
LA CAUZA, Frank Emilio 4
LA CAVA, Gregory 3
LACEY, Edward Samuel 1
LACEY, James D. 1
LACEY, John 1
LACEY, John Fletcher 1
LACEY, John Wesley 1
LACEY, Raymond Henry 4
LACHAISE, Gaston 1
LACHAISE, Gaston 1
LA CHANCE, 5
 Leander Hanscom
LACHMAN, Arthur 4
LACKAYE, Wilton 1
LACKEY, Henry Ellis 3
LACKEY, John Newton 4
LACKLAND, Frank 2
 Dorwin
LACLEDE,
 Pierre Ligueste H
LACOCK, Abner 1
LACOMBE, Emile Henry 1
LACOSS, Louis 4
LA COSSITT, Henry 4
LACOUR-GAYET,
 Jacques 3
LA CROIX, 3
 Morris Felton
LACY, Ernest 1
LACY, George Carleton 3
LACY, James Horace 3
LACY, Paul B. 4
LACY, Thomas Norman 3
LACY, Walter Garner 3
LACY, William Henry 3
LACY, William Stokes 3
LADA-MOCARSKI, 4
 Valerian
LADD, Adoniram Judson 1
LADD, Alan Walbridge 4
LADD, Anna Coleman 2
LADD, Carl Edwin 2
LADD, Catherine H
LADD, Edwin Fremont 1
LADD, Eugene F. 1
LADD, George Edgar 3
LADD, George Tallman 1
LADD, George Trumbull 1
LADD,
 George Washington H
LADD, Herbert Warren 1
LADD, Horatio Oliver 1
LADD, Jesse A. 3
LADD, John W. 5
LADD, Joseph Brown H
LADD, Maynard 2
LADD, Niel Morrow 1
LADD, Sanford Burritt 4
LADD, Scott M. 1
LADD, William H
LADD, William Edwards 3
LADD, William Mead 1
LADD, William Palmer 1
LADD, William Sargeant 1
LADD, William Sargent 4
LADD-FRANKLIN,
 Christine 1
LADDS, Herbert Preston 4
LADENBURG, 3
 Rudolf Walter
LADEW, Edward R. 1
LADNER, Albert H. 1
LADNER, Grover C. 4

LANGE, Halvard Manthey 5
LANGE, Hans 4
LANGE, Louis H
LANGE, Oscar Richard 4
LANGE, Ray Loomis 4
LANGENBECK, Karl 4
LANGENBERG, Harry Hill 3
LANGENWALTER, Jacob Hermann 5
LANGER, Charles Heinrichs 3
LANGER, William 3
LANGERFELDT, Theodore Otto 1
LANGERMAN, Joseph 3
LANGFELD, Herbert Sidney 3
LANGFELD, Millard 2
LANGFITT, J. Porter 4
LANGFITT, Joseph Alonzo 4
LANGFORD, William Campbell
LANGFORD, George W. 3
LANGFORD, Laura Carter Holloway 4
LANGFORD, Malcolm Sparhawk 4
LANGFORD, Nathaniel Pitt
LANGHAM, Jonathan Nicholas 4
LANGHORNE, George Tayloe 4
LANGHORNE, Marshall 2
LANGLEY, Ernest Felix 3
LANGLEY, James McLellan 5
LANGLEY, John Wesley 1
LANGLEY, John Williams 4
LANGLEY, Katherine 2
LANGLEY, Samuel Pierpont
LANGLEY, Samuel Sorrels
LANGLEY, William C. 4
LANGLEY, Wilson D(avis) 5
LANGLIE, Arthur Bernard
LANGLOIS, Ubald 3
LANGMADE, Stephen Wallace 4
LANGMUIR, Dean 2
LANGMUIR, Irving 3
LANGMUIR, Peter Bulkeley
LANGNER, Lawrence 4
LANGRETH, George Lillingston
LANGSDORF, Alexander Suss 5
LANGSDORF, William Bell
LANGSHAW, Walter Hamer 4
LANGSTON, John Mercer H
LANGSTROTH, Lorenzo Lorraine H
LANGTON, Daniel Webster 1
LANGTON, James Ammon 2
LANGTRY, Albert Perkins 1
LANGTRY, Lillie 2
LANGTRY, Lillie 4
LANGWORTHY, Charles Ford 1
LANGWORTHY, Edward H
LANGWORTHY, Herman Moore 3
LANGWORTHY, James Lyon H
LANHAM, Fritz Garland 4
LANHAM, Henderson Lovelace 3
LANHAM, Samuel Willis Tucker 1
LANIER, Alexander Cartwright
LANIER, Charles
LANIER, Clifford Anderson H
LANIER, George Huguley 2
LANIER, James Franklin Doughty H
LANIER, Powless William
LANIER, Raphael O'Hara
LANIER, Sidney H
LANIGAN, George Thomas H
LANING, Harris 1
LANING, Jay Ford 3

LANING, Richard Henry 4
LANIUS, James Andrew 3
LANKERSHIM, James Boon 4
LANKES, Julius J. 4
LANKFORD, Menaicus 1
LANKFORD, William Chester 5
LANMAN, Charles H
LANMAN, Charles Rockwell
LANMAN, James H
LANMAN, Joseph H
LANNEAU, John Francis 4
LANNING, Robert Lee 5
LANNING, William Mershon 1
LANNON, James Patrick 3
LANPHEAR, Emory 4
LANSDALE, Maria Hornor 5
LANSDELL, Rinaldo Addison 3
LANSDEN, Dick Latta 1
LANSDON, William Clarence 4
LANSIL, Walter Franklin
LANSING, Ambrose 3
LANSING, Eleanor Foster (Mrs. Robert Lansing) 5
LANSING, Frederick H
LANSING, Gerit Yates H
LANSING, Gulian H
LANSING, John H
LANSING, John Belcher H
LANSING, John Ernest 3
LANSING, Robert 1
LANSING, William Esselstyne H
LANSINGH, Van Rensselaer 5
LANSTRUM, Oscar Monroe 1
LANTAFF, William C. (bill) 5
LANTER, Fred Merrill 4
LANTZ, David Ernest 4
LANZA, Anthony Joseph 4
LANZA, Gaetano 1
LANZA, Mario 3
LANZA, Marquise Clara 4
LANZETTA, James J. 3
LAPHAM, Elbridge Gerry H
LAPHAM, Increase Allen H
LAPHAM, J. H. 3
LAPHAM, John Raymond 1
LAPHAM, Oscar 1
LAPHAM, Roger Dearborn 4
LAPHAM, Samuel 5
LAPHAM, William Berry 4
LA PIANA, George 5
LAPLACE, Ernest 1
LAPORTE, Alphonse A. 4
LAPORTE, John H
LAPORTE, Otto 4
LAPORTE, Raymond 5
LA PORTE, William Ralph 3
LAPP, John A. 4
LA PRADE, Arthur Thornton 3
LAPRADE, Lloyd Stone 3
LAPSLEY, Robert Alberti 1
LARABEE, Frank Sheridan 1
LARAMIE, Jacques H
LARCO HERRERA, Rafael 5
LARCOM, Lucy H
LARD, Moses E. H
LARDNER, Henry Ackley 3
LARDNER, James Lawrence 5
LARDNER, James Lawrence H
LARDNER, John 3
LARDNER, John Joseph 2
LARDNER, Lena Bogardus 4
LARDNER, Ring W. 1
LARGE, John J. 1
LA RICHARDIE, Armand 'de
LARIMER, Edgar Brown 5
LARIMER, Loyal Herbert 5
LARIMORE, Joseph William 5
LARIMORE, Louise Doddridge 2
LARIMORE, N. Greene 1
LARK-HOROVITZ, Karl 3
LARKIN, Adrian Hoffman 2
LARKIN, Edgar Lucien 1

LARKIN, Francis Marion 1
LARKIN, Fred Viall 3
LARKIN, John H
LARKIN, John Adrian 2
LARKIN, Joseph Maurice 5
LARKIN, Oliver Waterman 5
LARKIN, Thomas B. 5
LARKIN, Thomas Oliver
LARKIN, William Harrison 5
LARMON, Russell Raymond
LARNED, Augusta 4
LARNED, Charles William 1
LARNED, Ellen Douglas 4
LARNED, John Insley Blair 3
LARNED, Joseph Gay Eaton H
LARNED, Josephus Nelson 1
LARNED, Linda Hull 1
LARNED, Simon H
LARNED, Trowbridge 1
LARNED, Walter Cranston
LARNER, Edward Atkins 5
LARNER, John Bell 1
LARNER, Robert Martin 1
LA ROCHE, Rene H
LA ROCHELLE, Philippe de
LAROCQUE, Joseph 1
LAROE, Wilbur Jr. 3
LAROQUE, George Paul 1
LA ROQUE, O. K. 3
LARPENTEUR, Charles H
LARRABEE, C. R. 4
LARRABEE, Charles Hathaway H
LARRABEE, Edward Allan 1
LARRABEE, William 1
LARRABEE, William Clark
LARRABEE, William Henry 1
LARRAZOLO, Octaviano Ambrosio 1
LARREMORE, Wilbur 1
LARRETA, Enrique 4
LARRICK, George P. 5
LARRINAGA, Tulio H
LARRINAGA, Tulio 4
LARSEN, Alfred 2
LARSEN, Christian 1
LARSEN, Ellouise Baker 4
LARSEN, Esper Signius Jr. 4
LARSEN, Finn Jacob 5
LARSEN, Hanna Astrup 2
LARSEN, Harold D. 4
LARSEN, Henning 5
LARSEN, Henry Louis 4
LARSEN, Lauritz 1
LARSEN, Lewis A. 3
LARSEN, Lewis P. 3
LARSEN, Merwin John 4
LARSEN, Peter Laurentius 1
LARSEN, William 5
LARSEN, William Washington 1
LARSON, Agnes M(athilda) 5
LARSON, Carl W. 3
LARSON, Christian Daa 1
LARSON, Cora Gunn 1
LARSON, George Victor 3
LARSON, Gustus Ludwig 4
LARSON, John Augustus 4
LARSON, Lars Moore 1
LARSON, Laurence Marcellus
LARSON, O. T. 4
LARSON, Randell 1
LARSON, Winford Porter 2
LARSSON, Gustaf 1
LA RUE, Carl Downey 5
LA RUE, Daniel Wolford 5
LA RUE, John W. 5
LA RUE, Mabel Guinnip 5
LA RUE, William Earl 5
LA SALLE, 'sieur 'de H
LASATER, Ed Cunningham 1
LASBY, William Frederick 5
LASCARI, Salvatore 4
LASELLE, Mary Augusta 4
LA SERE, Emile H
LASH, Israel George H
LASH, James Hamilton 5
LASHAR, Walter B. 3
LA SHELLE, Kirke 1

LASHER, George Starr 4
LASHER, George William 1
LASHLEY, K. S. 3
LASHLY, Arthur Valentine
LASHLY, Jacob Mark 4
LASKER, Albert Davis 3
LASKER, Bruno 5
LASKER, Loula Davis 4
LASKEY, John Ellsworth 2
LASKI, Harold Joseph 2
LASKOSKE, Aloysius William 5
LASKY, Jesse L. 3
LASKY, Wayne Edward 5
LA SPISA, Jake Anthony 5
LASSEN, Peter H
LASSER, Jacob Kay 3
LASSITER, Francis Rives
LASSITER, Herbert Carlyle 3
LASSITER, Newton Hance
LASSITER, Robert 5
LASSITER, William 5
LASTINGER, John Williams
LATANE, James Allen 5
LATANE, John Holladay 1
LATCH, Edward Biddle 1
LATCHAW, David Austin 2
LATCHAW, John Roland Harris 3
LATHAM, Carl Ray 4
LATHAM, Charles Louis 5
LATHAM, Harold Strong 5
LATHAM, Louis Charles H
LATHAM, Milton Slocum H
LATHAM, Orval Ray 1
LATHAM, Rex Knight 1
LATHAM, Vida A. 4
LATHAN, Robert 1
LATHBURY, Albert Augustus 4
LATHBURY, Clarence 1
LATHBURY, Mary Artemisia 1
LATHE, Herbert William 1
LATHEM, Abraham Lance 3
LATHERS, Richard 1
LATHROP, Alanson P. 1
LATHROP, Austin Eugene 3
LATHROP, Bryan 1
LATHROP, Charles Newton 1
LATHROP, Francis 1
LATHROP, Gardiner 1
LATHROP, George Parsons H
LATHROP, Henry Burrowes 1
LATHROP, John H
LATHROP, John 1
LATHROP, John Carroll 1
LATHROP, John Hiram 1
LATHROP, John Howland 4
LATHROP, Julia Clifford 1
LATHROP, Palmer Jadwin 3
LATHROP, Rose Hawthorne 1
LATHROP, Samuel H
LATHROP, William Langson 1
LATIL, Alexandre 1
LATIMER, Asbury Churchwell 1
LATIMER, Claiborne Green 4
LATIMER, Clyde Burney 3
LATIMER, Elizabeth Wormeley 1
LATIMER, Henry H
LATIMER, Julian Lane 1
LATIMER, Margery Bodine 1
LATIMER, Thomas Erwin 1
LATIMER, Thomas Sargent
LATIMER, Wendell Mitchell 3
LA TOUR, Le Blonde 'de H
LATOURETTE, Earl C. 3
LATOURETTE, Howard Fenton
LATROBE, Benjamin Henry * H
LATROBE, Charles Hazelhurst
LATROBE, Fredinand Claiborne 1
LATROBE, John Hazelhurst Boneval H
LATSHAW, David Gardner 5

LATTA, H
LATTA, Alexander Bonner
LATTA, James P. 1
LATTA, Robert Edward 3
LATTA, Samuel Whitehill 4
LATTA, Thomas Albert 1
LATTIG, Herbert Elmer 3
LATTIMER, George W. 1
LATTIMORE, John Aaron Cicero
LATTIMORE, John Compere
LATTIMORE, Offa Shivers
LATTIMORE, Samuel Allan 1
LATTIMORE, William H
LATTMAN, Walter 4
LATTRE 'DE TASSIGNY, Jean Joseph Marie Gabriel 'de 3
LATZER, John A. 3
LAU, Robert Frederick 2
LAUBACH, Charles 1
LAUBACH, Frank Charles 5
LAUBACH, Howard L. 5
LAUBENGAYER, Richard August 4
LAUBENGAYER, Robert J. 3
LAUBER, Joseph 2
LAUCHHEIMER, Charles Henry 1
LAUCK, William Jett 4
LAUD, Sam 4
LAUDER, Harry 4
LAUER, Conrad Newton 2
LAUER, Stewart Ellwood 4
LAUER, Walter Ernest 4
LAUFER, Berthold 1
LAUFER, Calvin Weiss 1
LAUGHINGHOUSE, Charles O'Hagan
LAUGHLIN, Clara Elizabeth 2
LAUGHLIN, Frank C. 2
LAUGHLIN, Gail 3
LAUGHLIN, George Ashton 1
LAUGHLIN, George McCully Jr.
LAUGHLIN, Harry Hamilton 2
LAUGHLIN, Irwin 1
LAUGHLIN, James Laurence
LAUGHLIN, John Edward, Jr. 5
LAUGHLIN, Julian 1
LAUGHLIN, Napoleon Bonaparte 4
LAUGHLIN, Samuel Ott Jr. 3
LAUGHLIN, Sceva Bright 2
LAUGHLIN, T. Cowden 5
LAUGHTON, Charles 4
LAUGHTON, George 1
LAUGHTON, Sarah Elizabeth 1
LAUNT, Francis Albemarle Delbretons
LAURANCE, John H
LAURENS, Henry H
LAURENS, John H
LAURENT, Robert 5
LAURENTI, Mario 1
LAURGAARD, Olaf 2
LAURIAT, Charles Emelius 1
LAURIE, James H
LAURIE, James Woodin 1
LAURIE, William 1
LAURIE, Charles Christian
LAURVIK, J(ohn) Nilsen 5
LAURYSSEN, Gaston 4
LAUT, Agnes C. 1
LAUTERBACH, Edward 1
LAUTERBACH, Jacob Zallel 2
LAUTERBACH, Richard E. 3
LAUTERPACHT, Hersch 4
LAUTMANN, Herbert Moses 5
LAUTZ, Henry B(itzel) 5
LAUX, August 1
LAVAL, Jean M. 1
LAVALLE, John 5
LAVALLEE, Calixa H
LAVEILLE, Joseph H
LAVELL, Cecil Fairfield 2

LAVELLE, Michael J. — 1
LAVELY, Henry Alexander — 4
LAVENDER, Harrison Morton — 3
LA VERENDRYE, Pierre Gaultier 'de Varennes — H
LAVERY, Urban A. — 3
LAVES, Kurt — 2
LAVIALLE, Peter Joseph — 2
LAVIDGE, A. W. — 4
LAVINDER, Claude Hervey — 5
LAVIS, Fred — 5
LAW, Andrew — H
LAW, Arthur Ayer — 1
LAW, Charles Blakeslee — 1
LAW, Evander McIver — 1
LAW, Francis Marion — 5
LAW, Fred Hayes — 2
LAW, Frederick Houk — 3
LAW, George — H
LAW, Herbert Edward — 5
LAW, James — 1
LAW, James Richard — 3
LAW, John — H
LAW, John Adger — 2
LAW, Jonathan — H
LAW, Lyman — H
LAW, Richard — H
LAW, Robert — 1
LAW, Robert Adger — 4
LAW, Russell — 2
LAW, Sallie Chapman Gordon
LAW, Thomas Hart — H
LAW, William Adger — 1
LAWALL, Charles Elmer — 5
LA WALL, Charles Herbert
LAWDER, Henry Miller — 4
LAWES, Lewis E. — 2
LAWLER, Frank — H
LAWLER, Joab — H
LAWLER, John J. — 2
LAWLER, Thomas Bonaventure
LAWLER, Thomas G. — 1
LAWLESS, John T. — 4
LAWLESS, Theodore Kenneth — 5
LAWLOR, Daniel J. — 3
LAWLOR, William F. — 3
LAWLOR, William Patrick — 1
LAWRANCE, Charles Lanier — 3
LAWRANCE, Marion — 1
LAWRANCE, William Irvin — 1
LAWRENCE, Abbott — H
LAWRENCE, Abraham Riker — 1
LAWRENCE, Albert Lathrop — 4
LAWRENCE, Amory Appleton — 1
LAWRENCE, Amos — H
LAWRENCE, Amos Adams — H
LAWRENCE, Andrew Middleton — 2
LAWRENCE, Armon Jay — 4
LAWRENCE, Benjamin Franklin — 4
LAWRENCE, Carl Gustavus — 3
LAWRENCE, Charles Kennedy — 2
LAWRENCE, Charles Solomon — 1
LAWRENCE, Cornelius Van Wyck — H
LAWRENCE, David — 5
LAWRENCE, David Leo — 4
LAWRENCE, Edwin Gordon — 3
LAWRENCE, Effingham — H
LAWRENCE, Egbert Charles — 1
LAWRENCE, Ellis Fuller — 2
LAWRENCE, Ernest Orlando — 3
LAWRENCE, Florus Fremont — 4
LAWRENCE, Frank Pell — 3
LAWRENCE, George Newbold — H
LAWRENCE, George Pelton — 1
LAWRENCE, George Warren — 1
LAWRENCE, Gertrude — 1
LAWRENCE, Henry F. — 4
LAWRENCE, Henry Wells — 1

LAWRENCE, Howard C. — 4
LAWRENCE, Isaac — 1
LAWRENCE, James — H
LAWRENCE, James Cooper — 1
LAWRENCE, James Earnest — 3
LAWRENCE, James Peyton Stuart — 4
LAWRENCE, John Strachan — 1
LAWRENCE, John Watson — H
LAWRENCE, John William — 5
LAWRENCE, Joseph — H
LAWRENCE, Joseph Stagg — 3
LAWRENCE, Margaret — 1
LAWRENCE, Newbold Trotter — 5
LAWRENCE, Ralph Restieaux — 5
LAWRENCE, Richard Smith — H
LAWRENCE, Richard Wesley — 2
LAWRENCE, Robert H, Jr. — 5
LAWRENCE, Robert H. Jr. — 4
LAWRENCE, Robert Means — 1
LAWRENCE, Samuel — H
LAWRENCE, Samuel Crocker — 1
LAWRENCE, Sidney — H
LAWRENCE, Thomas — 1
LAWRENCE, Victor H. — 3
LAWRENCE, William * — 1
LAWRENCE, William * — 5
LAWRENCE, William Appleton — 5
LAWRENCE, William Beach — H
LAWRENCE, William Henry — 3
LAWRENCE, William Hereford — 5
LAWRENCE, William Howard — 5
LAWRENCE, William Mangam — 1
LAWRENCE, William Thomas
LAWRENCE, William Van Duzer — 1
LAWRENCE, William Witherle — 3
LAWRIE, Lee — 4
LAWRIE, Ritchie Jr. — 1
LAWS, Annie — 1
LAWS, Bolitha James — 3
LAWS, Curtis Lee — 2
LAWS, Elijah — 1
LAWS, Frank Arthur — 1
LAWS, George William — 1
LAWS, George William — 1
LAWS, Samuel Spahr — 1
LAWSHE, Abraham Lincoln — H
LAWSON, Albert Gallatin — 1
LAWSON, Albert Thomas — 4
LAWSON, Alexander — H
LAWSON, Alfred William — 3
LAWSON, Andrew Cowper — 3
LAWSON, Claude Sims — 4
LAWSON, Douglas E. — 4
LAWSON, Edward Burnett — 4
LAWSON, Ernest — 1
LAWSON, Evald Benjamin — 4
LAWSON, George — 3
LAWSON, George Benedict — 4
LAWSON, Huron Willis — 5
LAWSON, James — H
LAWSON, James Gilchrist — 1
LAWSON, James Joseph — 4
LAWSON, John — H
LAWSON, John Daniel — H
LAWSON, John Davison — 1
LAWSON, Joseph Albert — 3
LAWSON, Laurin Leonard — 3
LAWSON, Leonidas Merion — H
LAWSON, Martin Emert — 3
LAWSON, Paul Bowen — 3
LAWSON, Publius Virgilius — 1
LAWSON, Robert — 1
LAWSON, Roberta Campbell

LAWSON, Thomas — H
LAWSON, Thomas Goodwin — 1
LAWSON, Thomas R. — 3
LAWSON, Thomas William — 1
LAWSON, Victor Fremont — 4
LAWSON, W. Elsworth — 4
LAWSON, Warner — 5
LAWSON, William C. — 1
LAWTHER, Harry Preston — 2
LAWTON, Alexander Robert — 5
LAWTON, Alexander Robert — H
LAWTON, Alexander Rudolf — 1
LAWTON, Ezra Mills — 1
LAWTON, Frederick — 1
LAWTON, Henry W. — 1
LAWTON, Louis Bowen — 5
LAWTON, Samuel Tilden — 4
LAWTON, Shailer Upton — 4
LAWTON, William Cranston — 4
LAWTON, William Henry — 4
LAWWILL, Stewart — 5
LAWYER, George — 1
LAWYER, Jay — 4
LAWYER, Thomas — 1
LAY, Alfred Morrison — H
LAY, Benjamin — 1
LAY, Charles Downing — 3
LAY, Frank Morrill — 3
LAY, George Washington — 1
LAY, George William — 4
LAY, Henry Champlin — 1
LAY, John Louis — H
LAY, Julius Gareche — 1
LAY, Robert Dwight — 1
LAY, Wilfrid — 5
LAYCOCK, Charles Wilbur — 1
LAYCOCK, Craven — 4
LAYLIN, Lewis Cass — 1
LAYMAN, Waldo Arnold — 3
LAYNE, J. Gregg — 1
LAYNG, James D. — 1
LAYTE, Ralph R. — 4
LAYTON, Caleb Rodney — 1
LAYTON, Frank Davis — 3
LAYTON, Frederick — 1
LAYTON, Joseph E. — 4
LAYTON, Walter Thomas — 4
LAZAN, Benjamin J. — 4
LAZAR, Benedict Joseph — 2
LAZARO, Ladislas — 1
LAZAROVICH-HREBELIANOVICH, Princess — 3
LAZARUS, Emma — H
LAZARUS, Reuben Avis — 5
LAZARUS, Robert — 5
LAZARUS, Simon — 2
LAZEAR, Jesse — H
LAZEAR, Jesse William — 3
LAZELLE, Henry Martyn — 1
LAZENBY, Albert — 4
LAZENBY, William Rane — 1
LAZO, Hector — 4
LAZRUS, S. Ralph — 3
LAZZARI, Carolina Antoinette — 2
LEA, Clarence Frederick — 4
LEA, Fanny Heaslip — 3
LEA, Henry Charles — 1
LEA, Homer — 1
LEA, Isaac — H
LEA, John McCormick — 3
LEA, Luke — H
LEA, Luke — 1
LEA, Mathew Carey — H
LEA, Mathew Carey — 1
LEA, Preston — 1
LEA, Pryor — H
LEA, Robert Wentworth — 4
LEACH, Abby — 1
LEACH, Albert Ernest — 1
LEACH, Arthur Burtis — 4
LEACH, Charles Nelson — 5
LEACH, Daniel Dyer — H
LEACH, Dewitt Clinton — 4
LEACH, Edmund C. — 1
LEACH, Edward Giles — 1
LEACH, Ellis — 5
LEACH, Eugene Walter — 1
LEACH, Frank Aleamon — 5
LEACH, Frank Aleamon, Jr. — 5
LEACH, George E. — 3
LEACH, Henry Goddard — 5
LEACH, Howard Seavoy — 5
LEACH, Hugh — 5
LEACH, J. Granville — 1
LEACH, James Madison — H
LEACH, John Sayles — 4

LEACH, MacEdward — 4
LEACH, Ralph Waldo Emerson — 5
LEACH, Raymond Hotchkiss — 2
LEACH, Shepherd — H
LEACH, W(alter) Barton — 5
LEACH, William Fillmore — 5
LEACH, William Herman — 4
LEACOCK, Arthur Gordner — 2
LEACOCK, Stephen Butler — 2
LEADBETTER, Caroline Pittock — 5
LEADBETTER, Daniel Parkhurst — H
LEADBETTER, Frederick William — 2
LEAHY, Edward L. — 3
LEAHY, Frank — 5
LEAHY, Lamar Richard — 3
LEAHY, Paul — 4
LEAHY, Timothy John — 1
LEAHY, William Augustine — 3
LEAHY, William D. — 3
LEAHY, William Edward — 3
LEAKE, Eugene W. — 3
LEAKE, Frank — 4
LEAKE, James Payton — 1
LEAKE, Joseph Bloomfield — 1
LEAKE, Shelton Farrar — H
LEAKE, Walter — H
LEAKEY, Louis Seymour Bazett — 5
LEALE, Charles Augustus — 1
LEALE, Medwin — 1
LEAMING, Edmund Bennett — 1
LEAMING, Jacob Spicer — 1
LEAMING, Jeremiah — H
LEAMING, Thomas — H
LEAMY, Frank Ashton — 4
LEAMY, Frederick Walter — 3
LEAMY, Hugh — 1
LEAMY, James Patrick — 3
LEANDER, Hugo Austin — 5
LEAR, Ben — 4
LEAR, Fred Roy — 3
LEAR, Harry Bonnell — 4
LEAR, Tobias — H
LEARNARD, George Edward — 5
LEARNARD, Henry Grant — 1
LEARNED, Amasa — H
LEARNED, Arthur Garfield — 3
LEARNED, Dwight Whitney — 4
LEARNED, Ebenezer — H
LEARNED, Ellin Craven — 1
LEARNED, Henry Barrett — 1
LEARNED, Marion Dexter — 1
LEARNED, Walter — 1
LEARNED, William Law — 1
LEARNED, William Setchel — 2
LEARSI, Rufus — 4
LEARY, Cornelius Lawrence Ludlow
LEARY, Daniel Bell — 2
LEARY, Francis Thomas — 5
LEARY, Frederick — 3
LEARY, Herbert Fairfax — 3
LEARY, John Joseph Jr. — 2
LEARY, Leo H. — 4
LEARY, Lewis Gaston — 3
LEARY, Montgomery Elihu — 5
LEARY, Peter Jr. — 1
LEARY, Richard Phillips — 1
LEARY, Timothy — 1
LEARY, William Henry — 3
LEASE, Emory Bair — 1
LEASE, Mary Elizabeth Mrs. — 1
LEATHERS, Waller Smith — 2
LEATHERS OF PURFLEET, Baron
LEATHERWOOD, Elmer O. — 1
LEAVELL, Frank Hartwell — 2
LEAVELL, James Berry — 1
LEAVELL, Landrum Pinson — 1
LEAVELL, Richard Marion — 3
LEAVELL, Ullin Whitney — 4

LEAVELL, William Hayne — 1
LEAVELLE, Arnaud Bruce — 3
LEAVELLE, Robert Bryan — 5
LEAVENWORTH, Elias Warner — H
LEAVENWORTH, Francis Preserved — 1
LEAVENWORTH, Henry — H
LEAVITT, Ashley Day — 3
LEAVITT, Burke Fay — 4
LEAVITT, Charles Welford — 1
LEAVITT, Dudley — H
LEAVITT, Erasmus Darwin — 1
LEAVITT, Frank McDowell — 1
LEAVITT, Halsey B. — 4
LEAVITT, Humphrey Howe — H
LEAVITT, John McDowell — H
LEAVITT, Joshua — H
LEAVITT, Julius Adelbert — 1
LEAVITT, Mary Greenleaf Clement — 1
LEAVITT, Roger — 3
LEAVITT, Scott — 4
LEAVITT, Sheldon — 1
LEAVY, Charles Henry — 3
LEAYCRAFT, J. Edgar — 1
LE BARON, John Francis — 1
LE BARON, John Kittredge — 4
LE BARON, William — 3
LEBER, Charles Tudor — 4
LEBHAR, Godfrey Montague
LE BLANC, Thomas John — 2
LE BLOND, Charles Hubert — 3
LE BLOND, Harold R. — 5
LEBO, Thomas Coverley — 1
LE BOEUF, Randall James — 1
LEBOLD, Foreman M. — 3
LEBOUTILLIER, George — 3
LE BRETON, Tomas Alberto — 5
LE BRUN, Napoleon Eugene Henry Charles — H
LEBRUN, Rico — 4
LECHE, Paul — 4
LECHE, Richard Webster — 4
LECHER, Louis Arthur — 2
LECHFORD, Thomas — H
LECHNER, Carl Bernard — 5
LECKIE, Adam Edward Lloyd — 1
LECKIE, Katherine — 1
LECKRONE, Walter — 4
LECLAIR, Edward E(mile, Jr. — 5
LECLAIR, Titus G. — 5
LE CLEAR, Thomas — H
LE CLERC, J. Arthur — 3
LECOMPTE, Irville Charles — 5
LECOMPTE, Joseph — H
LECOMPTE, Karl Miles — 5
LECONTE, John — H
LECONTE, John Lawrence — H
LE CONTE, Joseph — 1
LE CONTE, Joseph Nisbet — 2
LE CONTE, Robert Grier — 1
LE CORBUSIER, Charles-Edouard — 4
LECOUNT, Edwin Raymond — 1
LECUONA, Ernesto — 4
LEDBETTER, Allison Woodville — 4
LEDBETTER, Huddie — 4
LEDBETTER, Walter A. — 1
LEDDY, Bernard Joseph — 5
LEDERER, Charles — 3
LEDERER, Charles — 2
LEDERER, Erwin Reginald — 5
LEDERER, Francis Loeffler
LEDERER, George W. — 1
LEDERER, John — 1
LEDERER, Norbert Lewis — 3
LEDERER, Richard M. — 3
LEDERLE, Ernst Joseph — 1
LEDLIE, George — 1
LEDNICKI, Waclaw — 5
LEDNICKI, Waclaw — 5
LEDOUX, Albert Reid — 1
LEDOUX, John Walter — 1
LEDOUX, Louis Vernon — 2
LE DUC, William Gates — 1

LEDVINA, Emmanuel B. 5
LEDWITH, 1
  William Laurence
LEDYARD, Erwin 1
LEDYARD, Henry 1
LEDYARD, 1
  Henry Brockholst
LEDYARD, John H
LEDYARD, Joshua Heard 5
LEDYARD, Lewis Cass 1
LEDYARD, 1
  Lewis Cass Jr.
LEDYARD, William H
LEE, Agnes 1
LEE, Albert 2
LEE, Albert Lindley 1
LEE, Alfred H
LEE, Alfred Emory 1
LEE, Algernon 3
LEE, Alice Louise 4
LEE, Andrew Ericson 1
LEE, Ann H
LEE, Archie Laney 3
LEE, Arthur H
LEE, Arthur 4
LEE, Bee Virginia 4
LEE, Benjamin 1
LEE, Benjamin Fisler 1
LEE, Benjamin Franklin 1
LEE, Blair 2
LEE, Blewett 4
LEE, Bradner Wells 1
LEE, Burton James 1
LEE, Canada 3
LEE, Charles * H
LEE, Charles Alfred H
LEE, Charles Hamilton 4
LEE, David B. 5
LEE, David Russell 1
LEE, 5
  Delia Foreacre (Mrs. Blewett Lee)
LEE, E. Trumbull 1
LEE, Edward Edson 2
LEE, Edward Hervey 1
LEE, Edward Thomas 2
LEE, Edwin Augustus 4
LEE, Edwin F. 2
LEE, Elisha 1
LEE, Eliza Buckminster H
LEE, Elmer 4
LEE, Elmo Pearce 2
LEE, Fitzhugh 1
LEE, Francis Bazley 1
LEE, Francis D. 1
LEE, Francis Lightfoot H
LEE, Frank 1
LEE, Frank Augustus 4
LEE, Frank Hood 3
LEE, Frank Theodosius 2
LEE, Frederic Edward 1
LEE, Frederic Girard 1
LEE, Frederic Paddock 5
LEE, Frederic Schiller 1
LEE, Gentry 4
LEE, George Bolling 2
LEE, George Cabot 3
LEE, 1
  George Washington Curtis
LEE, George Winthrop 1
LEE, Gerald Stanley 2
LEE, Gertrude Adams 3
LEE, Gordon 1
LEE, Gordon Canfield 4
LEE, Graham 3
LEE, Guy Carleton 1
LEE, 5
  Gypsy Rose (Rose Louise Hovick)
LEE, Hannah Sawyer H
LEE, Harry 1
LEE, Harry Winfield 4
LEE, Henry * H
LEE, Henry 1
LEE, Henry Haworth 1
LEE, Henry Thomas 1
LEE, Hildegarde L. 1
LEE, Homer 1
LEE, Hugh Johnson 4
LEE, Ivy Ledbetter 1
LEE, James Beveridge 4
LEE, 1
  James Grafton Carleton
LEE, James J. 5
LEE, James Melvin 1
LEE, James P. 3
LEE, James Paris 1
LEE, James T. 1
LEE, James Wideman 1
LEE, Jason 1
LEE, Jennette 3
LEE, Jennette 4
LEE, Jesse 1
LEE, Jesse Matlock 1
LEE, John H
LEE, John Clarence 1

LEE, 3
  John Clifford Hodges
LEE, John Doyle H
LEE, John Mallory 1
LEE, John Penn 1
LEE, John Stebbins 1
LEE, Jordan G. Jr. 3
LEE, Joseph H
LEE, Joseph 4
LEE, 5
  Joseph Wilcox Jenkins
LEE, Joshua 1
LEE, Joshua Bryan 4
LEE, Lansing B. 2
LEE, 2
  Laurence Frederick
LEE, Leslie Alexander 1
LEE, Luther H
LEE, Luther James Jr. 1
LEE, Manfred B. 5
LEE, Margaret 1
LEE, Mary C. Skeel 4
LEE, 5
  Mary Catherine (Jenkins)
LEE, Melicent Humason 2
LEE, Moses Lindley 1
LEE, Muna 4
LEE, Oliver Justin 4
LEE, Oscar Grant 4
LEE, Otis 2
LEE, Paul Wayne 3
LEE, Peter Martinus 4
LEE, Porter Raymond 1
LEE, Ray Elmer 4
LEE, Raymond Eliot 3
LEE, Richard H
LEE, Richard Bland H
LEE, Richard Edwin 1
LEE, Richard Henry H
LEE, Robert C. 5
LEE, Robert Corwin 5
LEE, Robert E. 1
LEE, Robert Edward H
LEE, Robert Edward 1
LEE, Robert H. 3
LEE, Roger Irving 4
LEE, Rose Hum 4
LEE, Samuel Henry 1
LEE, Samuel Phillips H
LEE, Samuel Todd 3
LEE, Silas 1
LEE, Stephen Dill 1
LEE, T. G. 1
LEE, Thomas * H
LEE, Thomas Bailey 2
LEE, Thomas Fitzhugh 5
LEE, Thomas George 1
LEE, Thomas Sim H
LEE, Thomas Zanslaur 1
LEE, Umphrey 3
LEE, Wallace Howe 1
LEE, Warren Isbell 5
LEE, Wesley T(erence) 5
LEE, William H
LEE, William 1
LEE, William C. 2
LEE, William Erwin 1
LEE, William Granville 1
LEE, William H. 1
LEE, H
  William Henry Fitzhugh
LEE, William L. 4
LEE, William Little H
LEE, William States 1
LEE, 2
  Willis Augustus Jr.
LEE, Willis Thomas 1
LEECH, Edward Towner 2
LEECH, Harper 1
LEECH, J. Russell 3
LEECH, Paul Nicholas 1
LEEDOM, Boyd Stewart 5
LEEDOM, John Peter 4
LEEDS, 1
  Charles Tileston
LEEDS, Daniel H
LEEDS, John H
LEEDS, Jules C. 1
LEEDS, Morris Evans 3
LEEDS, Paul 1
LEEDS, Rudolph Gaar 5
LEEDS, Samuel Penniman 1
LEEDY, Charles Denoe 1
LEEDY, John W. 1
LEEK, John Halvor 5
LEEMAN, Paul James 1
LEEMING, Tom 5
LEERMAKERS, 5
  Peter Anthony
LEES, James Thomas 1
LEESER, Isaac H
LEESMAN, Elmer Martin 1
LEESON, 3
  Robert Ainsworth
LEET, Isaac H
LEETE, Charles Henry 1

LEETE, 3
  Frederick DeLand
LEETE, John Hopkin 1
LEETE, William H
LEETE, William White 1
LEFAVOUR, Heary 2
LEFEBVRE, Gordon 3
LEFEVER, Joseph H
LEFEVER, Peter Paul H
LEFEVRE, Albert 5
LEFEVRE, Arthur 1
LEFEVRE, Edwin 1
LEFEVRE, Edwin 2
LE FEVRE, Egbert 1
LEFEVRE, Frank Jacob 5
LEFEVRE, George 1
LEFEVRE, Jay 5
LEFFEL, James H
LEFFERTS, 1
  George Morewood
LEFFERTS, John 1
LEFFERTS, Marshall H
LEFFINGWELL, Albert 1
LEFFINGWELL, 1
  Charles Wesley
LEFFINGWELL, 5
  Forrest Emmett
LEFFINGWELL, 4
  Russell Cornell
LEFFINGWELL, 1
  William Elderkin
LEFFINGWELL, 1
  William Henry
LEFFLER, Charles Doyle 1
LEFFLER, Charles Doyle 4
LEFFLER, George Leland 3
LEFFLER, Isaac H
LEFFLER, Ray Victor 4
LEFFLER, Ross Lillie 4
LEFFLER, Shepherd 1
LEFFLER, 4
  William Skilling
LEFFMANN, Henry 1
LEFLORE, Greenwood H
LE FORGEE, 5
  Charles Chambers
LEFSCHETZ, Solomon 5
LEFTWICH, Jabez 1
LEFTWICH, John William H
LE GALLAIS, Hugues 4
LE GALLIENNE, Richard 2
LEGARDA, Benito 4
LEGARE, George S. 1
LEGARE, Hugh Swinton H
LEGARE, James H
  Mathewes
LEGER, Jacques Nicolas 4
LEGGE, Alexander 1
LEGGE, Barnwell R. 3
LEGGE, Lionel Kennedy 4
LEGGE, Robert Thomas 5
LEGGETT, 1
  Benjamin Franklin
LEGGETT, 1
  Eugene Sheldon
LEGGETT, H
  Mortimer Dormer
LEGGETT, William 1
LEGGETTE, Lubin Poe 5
LEGH-JONES, George 4
LEGIER, John 5
LEGLER, Henry Eduard 1
LE GRAND, Abraham 3
LE GRAS, Gustave 1
LEHLBACH, 1
  Frederick Reimold
LEHMAN, Albert Carl 1
LEHMAN, 5
  Alcuin Williams
LEHMAN, Allan S. 3
LEHMAN, Ambrose 1
  Edwin
LEHMAN, Arthur 1
LEHMAN, 2
  Clarence Oliver
LEHMAN, 3
  Edwin Partridge
LEHMAN, Eugene Heitler 5
LEHMAN, Ezra 1
LEHMAN, Frank Alfred 1
LEHMAN, George Mustin 5
LEHMAN, Herberth 4
LEHMAN, Irving 2
LEHMAN, Linwood 3
LEHMAN, Louis Oliver 3
LEHMAN, Philip 2
LEHMAN, Robert 5
LEHMAN, William Eckart H
LEHMANN, Emil 5
  Wilhelm
LEHMANN, 1
  Frederick William
LEHMANN, 4
  Frederick William Jr.
LEHMANN, Karl 4
LEHMANN, Katharine 4

LEHMER, Derrick 3
  Norman
LEHNERTS, Edward M. 3
LEHR, Arthur 4
LEHR, Henry Solomon 1
LEHR, John Camillus 3
LEHRBAS, Lloyd Allan 4
LEHRMAN, 5
  Daniel Sanford
LEHTINEN, 4
  Artturl August
LEHY, John Francis 1
LEIB, Michael H
LEIB, Owen D. H
LEIB, Samuel Franklin 1
LEIBERT, 1
  Morris William
LEIBOLD, Paul Francis 5
LEIBOWITZ, Rene 1
LEICHLITER, Gould A. 5
LEIDESDORF, 1
  Samuel David
LEIDING, 3
  Harriette Kershaw
LEIDY, Joseph H
LEIDY, Joseph II 1
LEIDY, Paul H
LEIGH, H
  Benjamin Watkins
LEIGH, Randolph 3
LEIGH, Richard Henry 2
LEIGH, Robert Devore 4
LEIGH, Southgate 1
LEIGH, Townes Randolph 2
LEIGH, Vivien 4
LEIGH, 3
  William Robinson
LEIGHTON, 1
  Benjamin Franklin
LEIGHTON, Delmar 4
LEIGHTON, 2
  Frank Thomson
LEIGHTON, George E. 1
LEIGHTON, 3
  Joseph Alexander
LEIGHTON, 3
  Kathryn Woodman
LEIGHTON, Marshall Ora 3
LEIGHTON, 5
  Morris Morgan
LEIGHTON, William H
LEIMBACH, Alfred T. 5
LEINBACH, Paul Seibert 1
LEINDECKER, 3
  John Philip
LEINEN, Raymond F. 1
LEIPER, George Gray H
LEIPER, Macon Anderson 4
LEIPER, Thomas H
LEIPZIGER, 1
  Henry Marcus
LEISEN, 5
  (James) Mitchell
LEISENRING, 5
  Edward B, Jr.
LEISENRING, 3
  Edward Barnes
LEISENRING, 4
  Luther Morris
LEISERSON, 3
  William Morris
LEISHMAN, John G. 1
LEISLER, Jacob H
LEIST, Henry Gottlieb 1
LEISY, Ernest Erwin 5
LEITCH, Joseph Dugald 1
LEITCH, Mary Sinton 3
LEITER, H
  Benjamin Franklin
LEITER, Joseph 1
LEITER, Levi Zeigler 1
LEITH, Charles Kenneth 3
LEITZELL, 3
  Charles Wilson
LE JAU, Francis H
LEJEUNE, John Archer 2
LELAND, Charles A. 1
LELAND, 1
  Charles Godfrey
LELAND, Cyrus Austin 2
LELAND, Frank Bruce 5
LELAND, 2
  George Adams Jr.
LELAND, Henry Martyn 1
LELAND, John H
LELAND, Joseph Daniels 1
LELAND, Lester 1
LELAND, Ora Miner 4
LELAND, Samuel Phelps 1
LELAND, Waldo Gifford 4
LELONG, Lucien 3
LELY, Nicholas George 3
LEMAN, Beaudry 5
LEMANN, Isaac Ivan 1
LEMANN, Monte M. 1
LEMARE, Edwin Henry 1
LEMASS, Sean Francis 5

LEMAY, Alan 4
LEMCKE, Gesine 1
LEMDEREUR, 4
  Glenn Nestor
LEMKE, Peter Henry H
LEMKE, William 3
LEMKIN, Raphael 3
LEMLEY, Harry Jacob 4
LEMLY, Henry Rowan 1
LEMLY, Samuel Conrad 1
LEMMEL, William Hugo 3
LEMMON, Dal Millington 3
LEMMON, John Gill 1
LEMMON, Reuben C. 1
LEMMON, Robert Stell 1
LEMMON, 5
  Sara Allen Plummer
LEMMON, Walter S. 1
LEMON, Allan Clark 2
LEMON, Frank Kyle 2
LEMON, Harvey B. 4
LEMON, Luther Orange 3
LEMON, Willis Storrs 3
LEMOND, James S. 4
LEMONNIER, Andre 4
LEMOYNE, H
  Francis Julius
LE MOYNE, H
  Jacques 'de Morgues
LE MOYNE, H
  Jean Baptiste
LE MOYNE, 5
  Louis Valcoulon
LE MOYNE, Pierre H
LE MOYNE, William J. 1
LENAHAN, 4
  James Lawrence
LENAHAN, John T. 4
LENEY, H
  William Satchwell
L'ENFANT, H
  Pierre Charles
LENFESTEY, 3
  Nathan Coggeshall
LENGEL, 5
  William C(harles)
LENGEL, William C. 4
LENGFELD, Felix 1
L'ENGLE, Claude 4
L'ENGLE, 4
  William Johnson
LENHER, Victor 1
LENIHAN, Bernard James 4
LENIHAN, 3
  Mathias Clement
LENIHAN, 3
  Michael Joseph
LENIHAN, 1
  Thomas Mathias
LENKER, John Luther 4
LENKER, John Nicholas 1
LENNEN, Philip Weiting 3
LENNON, John Brown 1
LENNON, Thomas J. 1
LENNOX, H
  Charlotte Ramsay
LENNOX, Edwin 3
LENNOX, Patrick Joseph 2
LENNOX, William 1
LENNOX, 4
  Gordon
LENOX, James 1
LENOX, John Powell 1
LENROOT, Irvine Luther 2
LENSKI, 1
  Richard Charles Henry
LENT, Frederick 2
LENT, James H
LENTELLI, Leo 4
LENTHALL, John H
LENTINE, Joseph 5
LENTZ, Bernard 4
LENTZ, John Jacob 1
LENTZ, 1
  Max Carl Guenther
LENYGON, Francis 1
  Henry
LENZ, Sidney S. 3
LEON, Harry Joshua 5
LEON, Maurice 3
LEONARD, Abiel 1
LEONARD, Adna B. 1
LEONARD, Adna Wright 1
LEONARD, Albert 1
LEONARD, 1
  Alexander Thomas
LEONARD, Alton 1
  William
LEONARD, Arthur Gray 1
LEONARD, Arthur 5
  Thomas
LEONARD, Charles Hall 1
LEONARD, Charles Henri 1
LEONARD, 4
  Charles Leslie

LEXOW, Clarence 1
LEY, 3
Frederick Theodore
LEY, Harold Alexander 3
LEY, Willy 5
LEYDON, John Koebig 5
LEYENDECKER, Frank 1
X.
LEYENDECKER, 3
Joseph Christian
LEYMAN, Harry Stoll 5
LEYPOLDT, Frederick H
LEYS, 1
James Farquharson
LEYS, 5
Wayne Albert Risser
LEYSEN, Ralph J. 3
LEYSHON, Hal Irwin 4
L'HALLE, H
Constantin 'de
L'HEUREUX, Camille 4
L'HEUREUX, 3
Herve Joseph
LHEVINNE, Josef 2
L'HOMMEDIEU, Ezra H
LHOTE, Andre 4
LI, Kuo-Ching 4
LIAUTAUD, Andre 3
LIBBEY, 1
Edward Drummond
LIBBEY, Jonas Marsh 1
LIBBEY, Laura Jean 1
LIBBEY, William 1
LIBBY, Arthur Stephen 5
LIBBY, Arthur Stephen 2
LIBBY, Charles Freeman 1
LIBBY, Edward Norton 1
LIBBY, 5
Frederick Joseph
LIBBY, 1
Melanchthon Fennessy
LIBBY, Orin Grant 3
LIBBY, Samuel Hammonds 5
LIBBY, Warren Edgar 3
LIBERMAN, 5
Samuel Halpern
LIBERTE, Jean 4
LIBMAN, Emanuel 1
LICHITER, 4
McIlyar Hamilton
LICHTENBERG, Bernard 2
LICHTENBERG, Leopold 5
LICHTENBERGER, 5
Arthur Carl
LICHTENBERGER, 3
James Pendleton
LICHTENSTEIN, Joy 5
LICHTENSTEIN, Walter 4
LICHTENTAG, Alexander 1
LICHTENWALTER, 5
Franklin H.
LICHTY, John Alden 1
LICHTY, 5
L(ester) (Clyde)
LICK, James H
LICK, Maxwell John 2
LIDDELL, Donald Macy 5
LIDDELL, Eva Louise 1
LIDDELL, Frank Austin 4
LIDDELL, Henry 4
LIDDELL, Howard Scott 1
LIDDELL, Mark Harvey 1
LIDDLE, Charles Allen 1
LIDDON, 1
Benjamin Sullivan
LIE, Jonas 1
LIEB, Charles 3
LIEB, 3
Charles Christian
LIEB, John William 1
LIEBEL, Michael, Jr. 5
LIEBEL, 4
Willard Koehler
LIEBER, B. Franklin 1
LIEBER, Eugene 4
LIEBER, Francis H
LIEBER, G. Norman 4
LIEBER, Hugh Gray 4
LIEBER, Richard 2
LIEBERMAN, Elias 1
LIEBERS, Otto Hugo 5
LIEBES, 5
Mrs. Dorothy Wright
LIEBLING, 4
Abbott Joseph
LIEBLING, Emil 1
LIEBLING, George 4
LIEBLING, Leonard 2
LIEBMAN, Joshua Loth 1
LIEBMAN, Julius 1
LIEBMANN, Philip 5
LIECTY, Austin N. 5
LIEDER, 3
Frederick William Charles
LIEDER, Paul Robert 3
LIEFELD, Albert 1
LIEN, Arnold Johnson

LIEN, Elias Johnson 4
LIENAU, Detlef H
LIES, Eugene Theodore 5
LIEURANCE, Thurlow 4
LIFE, Andrew Creamor 1
LIFE, Frank Mann 1
LIFSCHEY, Samuel 4
LIGGETT, Hunter 1
LIGGETT, Louis Kroh 2
LIGGETT, 1
Walter William
LIGGINS, John 1
LIGHT, 3
Charles Porterfield
LIGHT, Evelyn 1
LIGHT, Rudolph Alvin 5
LIGHTBURN, 4
George William
LIGHTBURN, 1
Joseph A. J.
LIGHTNER, 1
Clarence Ashley
LIGHTNER, 5
Ezra Wilberforce
LIGHTNER, Milton C. 5
LIGHTON, William 4
Rheem
LIGON, Thomas Watkins H
LIHME, C. Bai 2
LIKLY, William F. 4
LILE, William Minor 1
LILES, Luther Brooks 2
LILIENTHAL, Howard 1
LILIENTHAL, 1
Jesse Warren
LILIENTHAL, 3
Joseph Leo Jr.
LILIENTHAL, Max H
LILIENTHAL, Samuel 3
LILIUOKALANI H
LILIUOKALANI 4
LILJENCRANTZ, 1
Ottilie Adaline
LILJESTRAND, Goran 5
LILLARD, Benjamin 4
LILLARD, Walter Huston 5
LILLARD, Walter Huston 4
LILLEY, Charles Sumner 1
LILLEY, George 1
LILLEY, George Leavens 4
LILLEY, Mial E. 4
LILLEY, Robert 4
LILLIBRIDGE, 1
William Otis
LILLICK, Ira S. 4
LILLIE, 1
Abraham Bruyn Hasbrouck
LILLIE, Charles A. 4
LILLIE, Frank Rattray 2
LILLIE, Gordon William 1
LILLIE, Gordon William 4
LILLIE, Harold Irving 3
LILLIE, Howard Russell 4
LILLIE, Lucy Cecil 1
LILLIE, Ralph Stayner 3
LILLIE, Samuel Morris 1
LILLIS, Donald Chace 5
LILLIS, James F. 4
LILLIS, Thomas F. 1
LILLY, D. Clay 2
LILLY, Josiah Kirby 1
LILLY, Josiah Kirby 4
LILLY, Linus Augustine 2
LILLY, Richard C. 3
LILLY, Samuel H
LILLY, 3
Thomas Jefferson
LILLY, William H
LIMA, 1
Manoel 'de Oliveira
LIMBACH, 5
Russell Theodore
LIMBERT, Lee Middleton 4
LIMERICK, 2'd 'earl H
LIMON, Jose Arcadio 5
LIN, Piao 5
LINCECUM, Gideon H
LINCOLN, Abraham H
LINCOLN, Allen B. 1
LINCOLN, Arleigh Leon 4
LINCOLN, 3
Azariah Thomas
LINCOLN, Benjamin H
LINCOLN, Charles Clark 1
LINCOLN, 3
Charles Monroe
LINCOLN, Charles Perez 1
LINCOLN, 1
Charles Sherman
LINCOLN, 4
Charles Zebina
LINCOLN, Daniel Waldo 5
LINCOLN, David Francis 1
LINCOLN, Edmond E. 3
LINCOLN, Enoch H
LINCOLN, 5
Francis Church

LINCOLN, 3
Gatewood Sanders
LINCOLN, J. Freeman 4
LINCOLN, 1
James Claiborne
LINCOLN, James Finney 4
LINCOLN, James Rush 4
LINCOLN, H
James Sullivan
LINCOLN, Jeanie Gould 1
LINCOLN, John Cromwell 3
LINCOLN, John Larkin H
LINCOLN, 2
Jonathan Thayer
LINCOLN, Joseph Crosby 2
LINCOLN, Julius 3
LINCOLN, Leontine 1
LINCOLN, Leroy Alton 3
LINCOLN, Levi * 1
LINCOLN, Mary Johnson 1
LINCOLN, Mary Todd H
LINCOLN, 4
Murray Danforth
LINCOLN, 1
Natalie Sumner
LINCOLN, Paul Martyn 2
LINCOLN, Robert Todd 1
LINCOLN, Rufus Pratt H
LINCOLN, Solomon 1
LINCOLN, Sumner H. 1
LINCOLN, Waldo 1
LINCOLN, 4
William Ensign
LINCOLN, William Henry 1
LINCOLN, H
William Slosson
LIND, 5
Ethel C. (mrs. Walter C. Lind)
LIND, Jenny H
LIND, John 1
LIND, Samuel Colville 4
LINDABURY, 1
Richard Vliet
LINDAHL, Josua 1
LINDAHL, 3
Oscar Nathanael
LINDBECK, 5
John M(atthew) H(enry)
LINDBERG, Abram Frank 1
LINDBERG, Conrad Emil 1
LINDBERG, 4
David Oscar Nathaniel
LINDBERG, 3
Irving Augustus
LINDBERGH, 1
Charles August
LINDBLAD, Bertil H
LINDE, Christian H
LINDEBERG, 3
Harrie Thomas
LINDEGREN, Alina M. 5
LINDEMAN, 1
Charles Bernard
LINDEMAN, 3
Eduard Christian
LINDEMAN, Frank Jr. 4
LINDENKOHL, Adolph 1
LINDENTHAL, Gustav 1
LINDER, Frederick M. 3
LINDER, 1
Oliver Anderson
LINDERMAN, Frank Bird 3
LINDERMAN, H
Henry Richard
LINDERMAN, 1
Robert Packer
LINDERSTROM-LANG, 3
Kaj
LINDGREN, Waldemar 1
LINDHEIMER, H
Ferdinand Jacob
LINDLEY, Albert 4
LINDLEY, 1
Curtis Holbrook
LINDLEY, Daniel H
LINDLEY, 3
Erasmus Christopher
LINDLEY, Ernest Hiram 1
LINDLEY, Harlow 5
LINDLEY, Hervey 1
LINDLEY, Jacob H
LINDLEY, James Johnson H
LINDLEY, Paul Cameron 1
LINDLEY, Walter 1
LINDLEY, Walter C. 3
LINDNER, 3
Clarence Richard
LINDNER, Robert M. 4
LINDQUIST, Francis O. 1
LINDQUIST, Robert John 4
LINDQUIST, 2
Rudolph Daniel
LINDSAY, Alexander Jr. 1
LINDSAY, 1
Anna Robertson Brown
LINDSAY, Arthur Hawes 2

LINDSAY, Arthur Oliver 3
LINDSAY, D. Moore 4
LINDSAY, 5
F(rank) M(errill)
LINDSAY, George Henry 1
LINDSAY, George LeRoy 2
LINDSAY, 1
George Washington
LINDSAY, Hal 4
LINDSAY, Henry 1
Drennan
LINDSAY, Howard 1
LINDSAY, James Hubert 1
LINDSAY, John Douglas 1
LINDSAY, 1
John Summerfield
LINDSAY, John Wesley 1
LINDSAY, Lynn Grout 5
LINDSAY, Marrill Kirk 4
LINDSAY, Maud 1
McKnight
LINDSAY, Robert Burns 2
LINDSAY, Roy Wallace 4
LINDSAY, Samuel 1
McCune
LINDSAY, 5
The Rt. Hon. Sir Ronald
LINDSAY, Thomas Bond 1
LINDSAY, Thomas 1
Corwin
LINDSAY, Vachel 1
LINDSAY, William 1
LINDSAY, William Sharp 4
LINDSEY, Benjamin Barr 2
LINDSEY, 1
Daniel Weisiger
LINDSEY, Edward Allen 5
LINDSEY, 2
Edward Sherman
LINDSEY, Harry W. Jr. 3
LINDSEY, 1
Joseph Bridgeo
LINDSEY, Julian Robert 5
LINDSEY, 1
Kenneth Lovell
LINDSEY, Louis 5
LINDSEY, H
Stephen Decatur
LINDSEY, 3
Sterling Paul Jr.
LINDSEY, 5
Therese Kayser (Mrs. S. A. Lindsey)
LINDSEY, 1
Washington Ellsworth
LINDSEY, William 1
LINDSEY, William Henry 1
LINDSLEY, 1
Charles Augustus
LINDSLEY, 4
Charles Frederick
LINDSLEY, 1
Henry Dickinson
LINDSLEY, 3
Herbert Kitchel
LINDSLEY, John Berrien H
LINDSLEY, Philip 4
LINDSLEY, Smith M. 1
LINDSLEY, William Dell H
LINDSTROM, Carl E., 5
LINDSTROM, 2
Ernest Walter
LINEBARGER, 1
Charles Elijah
LINEBARGER, 4
Paul Myron Anthony
LINEBARGER, 1
Paul Myron Wentworth
LINEBAUGH, 1
Daniel Haden
LINEBERGER, 2
Walter Franklin
LINEHAN, John C. 1
LINEHAN, Neil J. 4
LINEN, James A. Jr. 3
LINES, Edwin Stevens 1
LINES, George 1
LINES, H. Wales 1
LINEWEAVER, 4
Goodrich Wilson
LINFIELD, 1
Frances Eleanor Ross
LINFIELD, 3
Frederick Bloomfield
LINFORD, James Henry 1
LINFORD, Leon Blood 3
LING, Charles Joseph 5
LING, David W. 4
LING, Reese M. 4
LINGARD, James W. H
LINGELBACH, Anna 1
Lane
LINGELBACH, William 1
E.
LINGENFELTER, 3
Mary Rebecca
LINGHAM, Fred J. 3

LINGLE, Bowman Church 3
LINGLE, David Judson 4
LINGLE, Thomas Wilson 4
LINGLE, Walter Lee 3
LINGLEY, 1
Charles Ramsdell
LINHART, Samuel Black 1
LINING, John 1
LINK, Henry Charles 3
LINK, John Ephraim 2
LINK, Samuel Albert 2
LINK, Theodore Carl 4
LINK, William W. 2
LINN, Alonzo 1
LINN, Alvin Frank 1
LINN, Archibald Ladley H
LINN, Henry W. 5
LINN, James 1
LINN, James Weber 2
LINN, John H
LINN, John Blair H
LINN, Lewis Fields H
LINN, Paul Hinkle 1
LINN, Robert A. 4
LINN, 3
William Alexander
LINN, 3
William Bomberger
LINNARD, 1
Joseph Hamilton
LINNELL, 4
William Shepherd
LINNEMAN, Herbert F. 5
LINNEN, Edward Bangs 1
LINNEY, Frank Armfield 1
LINNEY, Robert Joseph 5
LINSCHEID, Adolph 3
LINSCOTT, 5
Robert Newton
LINSLEY, 5
Duncan Robertson
LINSON, Corwin Knapp 5
LINTHICUM, 1
Charles Clarence
LINTHICUM, 1
George Milton
LINTHICUM, 1
John Charles
LINTHICUM, Richard 3
LINTNER, Joseph Albert H
LINTON, Edwin 1
LINTON, Frank B. A. 4
LINTON, Morris Albert 4
LINTON, Ralph 2
LINTON, Robert 2
LINTON, William James H
LINTON, William Seelye 1
LINTOTT, 2
Edward Barnard
LINVILLE, 2
Henry Richardson
LIONBERGER, Isaac H. 3
LIPCHITZ, Jacques 5
LIPMAN, 2
Charles Bernard
LIPMAN, Clara 3
LIPMAN, 3
Frederick Lockwood
LIPMAN, Jacob Goodale 1
LIPPARD, George H
LIPPHARD, 5
William Benjamin
LIPPINCOTT, 1
Charles Augustus
LIPPINCOTT, Craige 4
LIPPINCOTT, 4
Horace Mather
LIPPINCOTT, J. Bertram 1
LIPPINCOTT, James 1
LIPPINCOTT, 2
James Starr
LIPPINCOTT, Job H. 2
LIPPINCOTT, 1
Joseph Barlow
LIPPINCOTT, 1
Joshua Ballinger
LIPPINCOTT, H
Martha Shepard
LIPPINCOTT, Richard H. 1
LIPPINCOTT, Sara Jane 1
LIPPINCOTT, 1
William Adams
LIPPINCOTT, 1
William Henry
LIPPITT, 5
Charles Warren
LIPPITT, 1
Charles Warren
LIPPITT, Francis James 1
LIPPITT, Henry H
LIPPITT, 1
Henry Frederick
LIPPITT, 4
William Donald
LIPPMANN, 1
Julie Mathilde
LIPPMANN, Robert Korn 4

LIPPS, Oscar Hiram 5
LIPSCHULTZ, Samuel 4
LIPSCOMB, Abner Smith H
LIPSCOMB, H
  Andrew Adgate
LIPSCOMB, David 1
LIPSCOMB, Glenard P. 5
LIPSCOMB, William H. 3
LIPSEY, Plautus Iberus 5
LIPSEY, 5
  Plautus Iberus, Jr.
LIPSITZ, Louis 1
LIPSKY, Louis 4
LIPSKY, Louis 1
LIPTON, 3
  Sir Thomas Johnstone
LISA, Manuel H
LISCHER, Benno Edward 3
LISCUM, Emerson H. H
LISLE, Arthur Beymer 2
LISLE, H
  Marcus Claiborne
LISLE, Robert Patton 1
LISMAN, Frederick J. 1
LISSER, Louis 1
LISSNER, Meyer 1
LIST, Ambrose Shaw 1
LIST, Carl F. 5
LIST, Emanuel 4
LIST, Georg Friedrich 1
LIST, Kurt 5
LISTEMANN, Bernhard 1
LISTEMANN, Fritz 1
LISTER, 3
  Charles Baynard
LISTER, Ernest 1
LISTER, 4
  Walter Bartlett
LISTOE, Soren 4
LISTON, H. Sr. 3
LITCH, Ernest Wheeler 1
LITCHFIELD, 5
  Edward Harold
LITCHFIELD, H
  Electus Backus
LITCHFIELD, 3
  Electus Darwin
LITCHFIELD, Elisha 2
  Grace Denio
LITCHFIELD, Lawrence 1
LITCHFIELD, 4
  Lawrence Jr.
LITCHFIELD, 4
  Mary Elizabeth
LITCHFIELD, Paul Weeks 3
LITCHFIELD, 1
  William Elias
LITCHMAN, 1
  Charles Henry
LITMAN, Simon 5
LITSEY, Edwin Carlile 5
LITSINGER, 5
  Edward Robert;
LITT, Jacob 1
LITTAUER, 2
  Lucius Nathan
LITTEL, Emlyn T. H
LITTELL, Clair Francis 4
LITTELL, Clarence Guy H
LITTELL, Eliakim H
LITTELL, Frank Bowers 3
LITTELL, Isaac William 1
LITTELL, Philip 2
LITTELL, Robert 1
LITTELL, H
  Samuel Harrington
LITTELL, Squier H
LITTELL, William 1
LITTEN, 3
  Frederic Nelson
LITTICK, Orville Beck 3
LITTIG, 1
  Lawrence William
LITTLE, Alden Howe 4
LITTLE, 4
  Archibald Alexander
LITTLE, Arthur 1
LITTLE, Arthur D. 1
LITTLE, 5
  Arthur Mitchell
LITTLE, Arthur W. 2
LITTLE, Arthur Wilde 1
LITTLE, Bascom 1
LITTLE, Charles 1
LITTLE, Charles Coffin H
LITTLE, Charles Eugene 4
LITTLE, Charles Joseph 1
LITTLE, Charles Newton 1
LITTLE, Chauncey B. 3
LITTLE, 2
  Clarence Belden
LITTLE, 5
  Clarence C(ook)
LITTLE, David M. 3
LITTLE, 1
  Edward Campbell

LITTLE, Edward Preble H
LITTLE, Frances 4
LITTLE, George H
LITTLE, George 4
LITTLE, George Obadiah 4
LITTLE, George Thomas 4
LITTLE, 4
  Gilbert Francis
LITTLE, Harry Britton 2
LITTLE, 5
  Herbert Satterthwaite
LITTLE, Homer Payson 4
LITTLE, J. Wesley 4
LITTLE, James Lovell 2
LITTLE, John Dozier 1
LITTLE, John Sebastian 1
LITTLE, Joseph James 1
LITTLE, Kenneth Buxton 4
LITTLE, Louis McCarty 4
LITTLE, Lucius Freeman 5
LITTLE, 5
  Mitchell Stuart
LITTLE, Peter H
LITTLE, Philip 2
LITTLE, Richard Henry 2
LITTLE, Riley McMillan 1
LITTLE, Robbins 1
LITTLE, Robert Rice 2
LITTLE, Russell A. 1
LITTLE, Sidney Wahl 4
LITTLE, Tom 5
LITTLE, 3
  William Augustus
LITTLE, 1
  William Nelson II
LITTLE CROW V H
LITTLEDALE, 3
  Clara Savage
LITTLEFIELD, 1
  Charles Edgar
LITTLEFIELD, 4
  Charles William
LITTLEFIELD, 1
  Eben Northup
LITTLEFIELD, 1
  George Emery
LITTLEFIELD, George 4
  W.
LITTLEFIELD, 1
  Milton Smith
LITTLEFIELD, 1
  Nathan Whitman
LITTLEFIELD, H
  Nathaniel Swett
LITTLEFIELD, Walter 2
LITTLEHALES, 2
  George Washington
LITTLEJOHN, 1
  Abraham Newkirk
LITTLEJOHN, H
  De Witt Clinton
LITTLEJOHN, 1
  Elbridge Gerry
LITTLEJOHN, 4
  John Martin
LITTLEPAGE, Adam 4
  Brown
LITTLEPAGE, Lewis H
LITTLEPAGE, 2
  Thomas Price
LITTLETON, Benjamin H. 4
LITTLETON, 1
  Frank Leslie
LITTLETON, J. T. 4
LITTLETON, Jesse M. 1
LITTLETON, 1
  Jesse Talbot
LITTLETON, 1
  Martin Wiley
LITTLETON, 1
  William Graham
LITTLE TURTLE H
LITTLEWOOD, William 4
LITZENBERG, 1
  Homer Laurence
LITZENBERG, 2
  Jennings Crawford
LITZINGER, Marie 3
LIVELY, Charles Elson 5
LIVELY, 1
  Daniel O'Connell
LIVELY, Frank 1
LIVERIGHT, 1
  Horace Brisbin
LIVERMAN, Harry 4
LIVERMORE, Abiel H
  Abbot
LIVERMORE, Arthur H
LIVERMORE, H
  Edward St Loe
LIVERMORE, George H
LIVERMORE, 4
  George Robertson
LIVERMORE, Mary 1
  Ashton
LIVERMORE, 5
  Norman Banks

LIVERMORE, Russell B. 3
LIVERMORE, Samuel * H
LIVERMORE, 1
  Thomas Leonard
LIVERMORE, 1
  William Roscoe
LIVERNASH, 4
  Edward James
LIVERSIDGE, 3
  Horace Preston
LIVINGOOD, 5
  Charles Jacob;
LIVINGSTON, Arthur 2
LIVINGSTON, 2
  Burton Edward
LIVINGSTON, Crawford 1
LIVINGSTON, 5
  Douglas Clermont
LIVINGSTON, Edward H
LIVINGSTON, George 3
LIVINGSTON, Goodhue 3
LIVINGSTON, H
  Henry Walter
LIVINGSTON, Homer J. 1
LIVINGSTON, James 1
LIVINGSTON, 1
  James Duane
LIVINGSTON, 5
  Jesse Elsmer
LIVINGSTON, John H
  Henry
LIVINGSTON, H
  John William
LIVINGSTON, 1
  Leonidas Felix
LIVINGSTON, Paul 4
  Yount
LIVINGSTON, H
  Peter Van Brugh
LIVINGSTON, Philip 1
LIVINGSTON, Philip H
LIVINGSTON, Robert 4
LIVINGSTON, H
  Robert Irvin
LIVINGSTON, H
  Robert Le Roy
LIVINGSTON, H
  Robert R. *
LIVINGSTON, 4
  Robert Teviot
LIVINGSTON, Sigmund 2
LIVINGSTON, Walter H
LIVINGSTON, William H
LIVINGSTON, 4
  William Henry
LIVINGSTONE, 2
  Colin Hamilton
LIVINGSTONE, 1
  John Alexander
LIVINGSTONE, William 1
LIVINSTON, 1
  Henry Brockholst
LIZARS, Rawson Goodsir 5
LLEWELLYN, 5
  Frederick Britton
LLEWELLYN, 1
  Joseph Corson
LLEWELLYN, 4
  Karl Nickerson
LLEWELLYN, Silas James 1
LLEWELLYN, 3
  William H. H.
LLOYD, Alfred Henry 1
LLOYD, Alice Crocker 2
LLOYD, Arthur Selden 1
LLOYD, Bolivar Jones 3
LLOYD, Curtis Gates 1
LLOYD, David H
LLOYD, David Demarest 4
LLOYD, Demarest 1
LLOYD, E. Russell 3
LLOYD, 4
  Edmund Grindal Rawson
LLOYD, Edward *
LLOYD, Edward Lester 3
LLOYD, Edward Read 4
LLOYD, Edward VIII 3
LLOYD, Edward VIII 3
LLOYD, 5
  Ella Stryker Mapes
LLOYD, Francis Ernest 1
LLOYD, Frank S. 3
LLOYD, Frank T. 3
LLOYD, 1
  Frederic Ebenezer John
LLOYD, 5
  Harold (Clayton)
LLOYD, Henry 1
LLOYD, Henry Demarest 5
LLOYD, Henry Demarest 1
LLOYD, 1
  Hinton Summerfield
LLOYD, Horatio Gates 1
LLOYD, James * H
LLOYD, James Tighlman 2
LLOYD, John Uri 1

LLOYD, 5
  L(awrence) Duncan
LLOYD, Marshall Burns 1
LLOYD, Morton Githens 1
LLOYD, 1
  Nelson McAllister
LLOYD, Ralph Bramel 3
LLOYD, Ralph Irving 5
LLOYD, Samuel 1
LLOYD, Samuel 3
LLOYD, Stacy Barcroft 1
LLOYD, Stewart Joseph 3
LLOYD, Thomas H
LLOYD, 3
  Walter Hamilton Jr.
LLOYD, Wesley 1
LLOYD, William Allison 2
LLOYD, William Henry 1
LLOYD, Woodrow Stanley 5
LOAN, H
  Benjamin Franklin
LOAR, James Leazure 1
LOASBY, Arthur William 1
LOBDELL, Charles E. 2
LOBDELL, Effie L(eola) 5
LOBDELL, Harold E. 4
LOBECK, Armin Kohl 3
LOBECK, Charles O. 1
LOBENSTINE, 3
  Edwin Carlyle
LOBER, Georg John 4
LOBERG, Harry John 4
LOBINGIER, 1
  Andrew Stewart
LOBO, Fernando 4
LOBRANO, Gustave S. 3
LOCHER, Casper William 2
LOCHER, Cyrus 1
LOCHMAN, John George H
LOCHREN, William 1
LOCHRIDGE, P. D. 1
LOCKE, Alain LeRoy 3
LOCKE, Bessie 3
LOCKE, Charles E. 1
LOCKE, Charles Edward 1
LOCKE, David Ross H
LOCKE, Edward 2
LOCKE, Edwin 1
LOCKE, Eugene Murphy 5
LOCKE, Eugene Perry 2
LOCKE, Francis 1
LOCKE, Frank Lovering 1
LOCKE, Franklin Day 1
LOCKE, George Herbert 4
LOCKE, 1
  Harry Leslie Franklin
LOCKE, James 1
LOCKE, 1
  James Dewitt Clinton
LOCKE, James William 5
LOCKE, John * H
LOCKE, John Staples 1
LOCKE, M. Katherine 1
LOCKE, Matthew H
LOCKE, Richard Adams H
LOCKE, Robert Wynter 5
LOCKE, Robinson 1
LOCKE, 1
  Victor Murat, Jr.
LOCKE, Walter 3
LOCKERBY, 1
  Frank McCarthy
LOCKETT, Andrew M. 1
LOCKETT, James 4
LOCKEY, Joseph Byrne 1
LOCKEY, Mary Ishbel 1
LOCKHART, Arthur John 3
LOCKHART, 3
  Burton Wellesley
LOCKHART, Caroline 5
LOCKHART, Charles 4
LOCKHART, Clinton 1
LOCKHART, Ernest Ray 5
LOCKHART, Frank P. 2
LOCKHART, Gene 2
LOCKHART, Henry Jr. 2
LOCKHART, James H
LOCKHART, James 1
  Henry
LOCKHART, 1
  Malcolm Mabry
LOCKHART, 3
  Walter Samuel
LOCKHEED, Allan 5
  Haines
LOCKLEY, Fred 5
LOCKLEY, 1
  Lawrence Campbell
LOCKMAN, 3
  DeWitt McClellan
LOCKMAN, John Thomas 1
LOCKRIDGE, Frances 4
LOCKRIDGE, 3
  Ross Franklin
LOCKRIDGE, 2
  Ross Franklin Jr.
LOCKWOOD, Albert 1

LOCKWOOD, 5
  Alfred Collins
LOCKWOOD, 1
  Belva Ann Bennett
LOCKWOOD, 1
  Benjamin Curtis
LOCKWOOD, 4
  Charles Andrews Jr.
LOCKWOOD, 1
  Charles Clapp
LOCKWOOD, 1
  Charles Daniel
LOCKWOOD, 3
  Charles Davenport
LOCKWOOD, 1
  Daniel Newton
LOCKWOOD, 4
  Daniel Wright
LOCKWOOD, Edward T. 1
LOCKWOOD, 2
  Francis Cummins
LOCKWOOD, 1
  George Browning
LOCKWOOD, George 1
  Rae
LOCKWOOD, Harold J. 4
LOCKWOOD, Harold 1
  Paul 5
LOCKWOOD, 5
  Helen Drusilla
LOCKWOOD, Henry 1
LOCKWOOD, Henry 1
  Hayes
LOCKWOOD, 1
  Henry Roswell
LOCKWOOD, 1
  Homer Nichols
LOCKWOOD, Ingersoll 4
LOCKWOOD, Ira Hiram 3
LOCKWOOD, James
  Booth H
LOCKWOOD, 1
  John Alexander
LOCKWOOD, John Salem 1
LOCKWOOD, Laura
  Emma 4
LOCKWOOD, Luke 1
  Vincent 3
LOCKWOOD, Mary
  Smith 4
LOCKWOOD, Preston 1
LOCKWOOD, H
  Ralph Ingersoll
LOCKWOOD, Richard 1
  John 4
LOCKWOOD, Samuel
  Drake H
LOCKWOOD, 1
  Sara Elizabeth Husted
LOCKWOOD, 5
  Stephen Timothy
LOCKWOOD, Thomas B. 2
LOCKWOOD, Thomas
  Dixon 3
LOCKWOOD, Wilton 3
LOCRAFT, Thomas Hall 4
LOCY, William Albert 1
LODGE, Gonzalez 1
LODGE, Henry Cabot 1
LODGE, John Christian 1
LODGE, John Ellerton 2
LODGE, Lee Davis 1
LODIAN, L. 4
LODOR, Richard 1
LOEB, Arthur Joseph 5
LOEB, Benjamin M. 4
LOEB, Carl M. 3
LOEB, Hanau Wolf 1
LOEB, Howard A. 3
LOEB, Isidor 3
LOEB, Jacob Moritz 2
LOEB, Jacques 1
LOEB, James 1
LOEB, Leo 3
LOEB, Louis 1
LOEB, Milton B. 5
LOEB, Morris 1
LOEB, Sophie Irene 1
LOEB, William 1
LOEFFEL, William John 4
LOEFFLER, Carl August 5
LOEFFLER,
  Charles Martin Tornov
LOEHWING, 4
  Walter Ferdinand
LOESCH, Frank Joseph 2
LOETSCHER, 4
  Frederick William
LOEVENHART, 3
  Arthur Solomon
LOEW, Edward Victor 4
LOEW, Marcus 1
LOEWE, Dietrich Eduard 1
LOEWENTHAL, Isidor H
LOEWI, Otto 4
LOEWY, Edwin 3
LOEWY, Erwin 3

LOUGHRIDGE, H
  Robert McGill
LOUGHRIDGE, William H
LOUIS, Andrew 5
LOUIS, John Jeffry 3
LOUIS, Max C. 4
LOUNSBERRY, 4
  Frank Burton
LOUNSBURY, 3
  Charles Edwin
LOUNSBURY, 1
  George Edward
LOUNSBURY, 3
  George Fenner
LOUNSBURY, 1
  Phineas Chapman
LOUNSBURY, Ralph
  Reed
LOUNSBURY, 1
  Thomas Raynesford
LOURIE, Arthur 4
LOURIE, David A. 1
LOUTFI, Omar
LOUTHAN, Hattie Horner 5
LOUTHAN, 3
  Henry Thompson
LOUTHERBOURG, H
  Annibale Christian Henry
  'de
LOUTTIT, 3
  Chauncey McKinley
LOUTTIT, 4
  George William
LOUTTIT, 5
  William Easton, Jr.
LOUTZENHEISER, Joe
L. 2
LOUW, Eric Hendrik 5
LOVATT, 5
  George Ignatius
LOVE, Albert Gallatin 5
LOVE, Albert Irving 5
LOVE, Alfred Henry 1
LOVE, Andrew Leo 4
LOVE, Charles Everts 3
LOVE,
  Cornelius Ruxton, Jr.
LOVE, Don Lathrop 1
LOVE,
  Edward Bainbridge
LOVE, Emanuel King H
LOVE, Frank Samuel 1
LOVE, Harry Houser 4
LOVE, J. Mack 1
LOVE, James H
LOVE, James Jay 4
LOVE, James Lee 3
LOVE, 5
  James Sanford, Jr.
LOVE, James Spencer 4
LOVE, John H
LOVE, John W. 3
LOVE, Julian Price 5
LOVE, Peter Early H
LOVE, Robertus 1
LOVE, Smoloff Palace 1
LOVE, Stephen Hunter
LOVE, Thomas Bell 2
LOVE, Thomas Cutting H
LOVE, Thomas J. 3
LOVE, William Carter
LOVE, William De Loss
LOVEJOY, Arthur
  Oncken
LOVEJOY, Asa Lawrence
LOVEJOY, Elijah Parish
LOVEJOY, Esther Pohl 4
LOVEJOY,
  Francis Thomas Fletcher
LOVEJOY, Frank William 2
LOVEJOY,
  George Edwards
LOVEJOY, George Newell 4
LOVEJOY, Jesse Robert 2
LOVEJOY, John Meston
LOVEJOY, Owen H
LOVEJOY, Owen Reed
LOVEJOY, Philip 4
LOVEJOY, Thomas E.
LOVELACE, Curtis M. 4
LOVELACE,
  Delos Wheeler
LOVELACE, Francis H
LOVELACE, 4
  William Randolph II
LOVELAND, Albert J. 4
LOVELAND,
  Edward Rutherford
LOVELAND, 1
  Francis William
LOVELAND, Gilbert 4
LOVELAND,
  Hansell William
LOVELAND, Seymour
LOVELAND, H
  William Austin Hamilton
LOVELL, Alfred Henry 4

LOVELL, Earl B. 2
LOVELL, James
LOVELL, John H
LOVELL, John Epy 2
LOVELL, John Harvey 1
LOVELL, Joseph H
LOVELL, Mansfield H
LOVELL, 2
  Moses Richardson
LOVELL, Ralph L. 2
LOVELL, Walter Raleigh 5
LOVELY, John A. 1
LOVEMAN, Amy 3
LOVEMAN, Robert 1
LOVERIDGE, 5
  Blanche Grosbec
LOVERIDGE, Earl W. 3
LOVERING, Charles T. 4
LOVERING, Henry Bacon 1
LOVERING, Joseph H
LOVERING, William C. 4
LOVET-LORSKI, Boris 5
LOVETT, 2
  Archibald Battle
LOVETT, Edgar Odell 3
LOVETT, John H
LOVETT, Robert H. 1
LOVETT, Robert Morss 1
LOVETT, Robert Scott 1
LOVETT, 1
  Robert Williamson
LOVETT, William Cuyler 4
LOVETTE, Joyce Metz 5
LOVETTE, 5
  Leland Pearson
LOVETTE, 4
  Leland Pearson
LOVETTE, Oscar Byrd 1
LOVEWELL, John H
LOVEWELL,
  Joseph Taplin
LOVEWELL, 4
  Samuel Harrison
LOVING, Starling 1
LOVINS, William Thomas 4
LOVRE, Harold O. 5
LOW, A. Augustus 1
LOW, Abiel Abbot H
LOW, Abraham Adolph 3
LOW, Albert Howard 1
LOW,
  Benjamin Robbins Curtis
LOW, Berthe Julienne
LOW, David 4
LOW, Ethelbert Ide 2
LOW, Francis Stuart 4
LOW, H
  Frederick Ferdinand
LOW, Frederick Rollins 1
LOW, Isaac
LOW, Juliette Gordon H
LOW, Juliette Gordon 4
LOW, Marcus A. 1
LOW, Mary Fairchild 2
LOW, 3
  Mrs. Marie Dickson
LOW, Nicholas H
LOW, Seth
LOW, Sir A. Maurice 1
LOW, Will Hicok
LOW, William Gilman 1
LOWBER, James William
LOWDEN, Frank Orren 2
LOWDEN, Isabel 3
LOWDERMILK,
  Patricia Cannales
LOWE, Arthur Houghton 1
LOWE, Charles H
LOWE, Clarence George 4
LOWE, Clement Belton 4
LOWE, David Perley H
LOWE, Donald Vaughn 5
LOWE, Elias Avery 5
LOWE, Emily Lynch 4
LOWE, Ephraim Noble 1
LOWE, Frank E. 4
LOWE, George Hale 4
LOWE, Herman A. 4
LOWE, Joe
LOWE, John 1
LOWE, John Smith
LOWE, John William 2
LOWE, Louis Robert
LOWE, Louise 5
LOWE, Malcolm Branson 5
LOWE, Martha Perry 4
LOWE, Ralph Phillips H
LOWE, Richard Barrett 4
LOWE, Stanley 5
LOWE, Thaddeus S. C. 4
LOWE, Thomas Merritt 4
LOWE, Titus 3
LOWE, Walter Irenaeus 4
LOWE, William Baird 2
LOWE, William Webb 4
LOWELL,
  Abbott Lawrence

LOWELL, Amy 1
LOWELL, 1
  Daniel Ozro Smith
LOWELL, Delmar Rial 1
LOWELL, Edward
  Jackson
LOWELL, Francis Cabot H
LOWELL, Francis Cabot 1
LOWELL, Guy 1
LOWELL, James Arnold 1
LOWELL, James Harrison 2
LOWELL, James Russell 1
LOWELL, Joan 4
LOWELL, John * H
LOWELL, John 1
LOWELL, Josephine Shaw 1
LOWELL, Joshua Adams H
LOWELL, Orson 1
LOWELL, Percival 1
LOWELL, H
  Robert Traill Spence
LOWELL, Sherman James 1
LOWEN, 3
  Charles Jules Jr.
LOWENBERG, Bettie 4
LOWENSTEIN, Henry
  Polk
LOWENSTEIN, Lloyd L. 4
LOWENSTEIN, 5
  Melvyn Gordon
LOWENSTEIN, Solomon 1
LOWENSTINE, Mandel 1
LOWER, Christian H
LOWER, William Edgar 4
LOWEREE, F. Harold 4
LOWES, John Livingston 2
LOWETH, 1
  Charles Frederick
LOWIE, Robert Harry 3
LOWMAN, Harmon 5
LOWMAN, Seymour 1
LOWMAN, Webster B. 1
LOWNDES, Arthur 5
LOWNDES,
  Charles Henry Tilghman
LOWNDES, 4
  Charles Lucien Baker
LOWNDES, Lloyd 2
LOWNDES, 2
  Mary Elizabeth
LOWNDES, Rawlins H
LOWNDES, Thomas H
LOWNDES, William H
LOWNEY, Walter M. 1
LOWNSBERY, 5
  Charles Hatch
LOWREY, Bill G. 4
LOWREY, 4
  Frederick Jewett
LOWREY, Harvey H. 4
LOWREY, Lawson Gentry 3
LOWREY, Mark Perrin H
LOWRIE, James Walter 1
LOWRIE, John Cameron 1
LOWRIE, 1
  Samuel Thompson
LOWRIE, Walter H
LOWRIE, Walter 5
LOWRIE, Will Leonard 2
LOWRY, D. R. 2
LOWRY, Edith Belle 1
LOWRY, Edith C. 5
LOWRY, Edward George 2
LOWRY, 4
  Fesington Carlyle
LOWRY, Frank Clifford 5
LOWRY, Frank J. 3
LOWRY, H(omer) H(iram) 5
LOWRY, Hiram Harrison 2
LOWRY, Horace 1
LOWRY, Howard Foster 4
LOWRY, Howard James 5
LOWRY, John 4
LOWRY, Joseph E. 4
LOWRY, Malcolm 1
LOWRY, Robert * 1
LOWRY, Thomas 2
LOWRY, Thomas Claude 2
LOWSLEY, 3
  Oswald Swinney
LOWSTUTER, 3
  William Jackson *
LOWTH, Frank James 5
LOWTHER, Granville 1
LOWTHER, Hugh Sears 2
LOWY, Alexander 1
LOY, Matthias 3
LOY, Sylvester K. 3
LOYALL, George H
LOYALL, George Robert 1
LOZIER, H
  Clemence Sophia Harned
LOZIER, Ralph Fulton 2
LUBBOCK, H
  Francis Richard
LUBECK, Henry 1
LUBIN, David 1

LUBIN, Simon Julius 1
LUBITSCH, Ernst 2
LUBKE, Carl Heinrich 5
LUBOMIRSKI, 1
  Prince Casimir
LUBY, James 1
LUBY, Sylvester Daniel 4
LUCAS, Albert Pike 2
LUCAS, Anthony Francis 1
LUCAS, Arthur 4
LUCAS, Arthur Fletcher 5
LUCAS, Arthur Melville 2
LUCAS, Daniel Bedinger 1
LUCAS, Edward H
LUCAS, 4
  Francis Ferdinand
LUCAS, 1
  Frederic Augustus
LUCAS, James H. H
LUCAS, Jim Griffing 5
LUCAS, H
  John Baptiste Charles
LUCAS, John Henry 1
LUCAS, John Porter 2
LUCAS, Johnathan 1
LUCAS, Jonathan H
LUCAS, Leo Sherman 4
LUCAS, Noah 3
LUCAS, Oliver G. 3
LUCAS, Robert 1
LUCAS, Robert H. 2
LUCAS, Scott Wike 4
LUCAS, Thomas John 1
LUCAS, William 3
LUCAS, 3
  William Cardwell
LUCAS, William Palmer 4
LUCCOCK, Emory Wylie 4
LUCCOCK, 1
  George Naphtali
LUCCOCK, 2
  George Naphtall
LUCCOCK, 4
  Halford Edward
LUCCOCK, Naphtali 1
LUCE, Alice Hanson
LUCE, Cyrus Gray 1
LUCE, Edgar Augustine 1
LUCE, Harry James 1
LUCE, Harvey Gardner 4
LUCE, Henry Robinson 4
LUCE, Robert 2
LUCE, Stephen Bleecker 1
LUCEY, Dennis Benedict 1
LUCEY, Patrick Joseph 1
LUCEY, Patrick Joseph 4
LUCEY, Thomas Elmore 1
LUCIER, Phillip Joseph 5
LUCKE, Balduin 3
LUCKE, Charles Edward 2
LUCKENBACH,
  Edgar Frederick
LUCKENBACH, John
  Lewis
LUCKENBILL, 1
  Daniel David
LUCKEY, David Franklin 5
LUCKEY,
  George Washington Andrew
LUCKEY, Henry Carl 1
LUCKEY, James S. 1
LUCKHARDT, 3
  Arno Benedict
LUCKIESH, Matthew 4
LUCKING, Alfred 1
LUCKING, 4
  William Alfred
LUDDEN,
  Patrick Anthony
LUDDY, 5
  Michael G(abriel)
LUDELING, H
  John Theodore
LUDERS, Gustav Carl 1
LUDEWIG, Jos W. 2
LUDIN, Mohammed Kahir 4
LUDINGTON,
  Arthur Crosby
LUDINGTON, 1
  Charles Henry
LUDINGTON,
  Marshall Independence
LUDLAM, Reuben 1
LUDLOW, Arthur Clyde 1
LUDLOW, Daniel H
LUDLOW, Edwin 1
LUDLOW, F. Milton 3
LUDLOW, Fitz Hugh H
LUDLOW, Gabriel George 1
LUDLOW, George C. 1
LUDLOW, George
  Duncan H
LUDLOW, Henry Gilbert 1
LUDLOW, Henry Hunt 1
LUDLOW, Jacob Lott 1
LUDLOW, James Meeker 1
LUDLOW, Louis Leon 1

LUDLOW, Nicoll 1
LUDLOW, Noah Miller H
LUDLOW, Roger H
LUDLOW, 4
  Theodore Russell
LUDLOW, Thomas
  William H
LUDLOW, William H
LUDLOW, William Orr 3
LUDLUM, Clarence Allen 2
LUDLUM, Seymour
  DeWitt 3
LUDOVICI, Alice Emelie 5
LUDWELL, Philip H
LUDWICK, Christopher H
LUDWIG, 5
  Charles H(eyler)
LUDWIG, Emil 2
LUDWIG, 4
  Sylvester Theodore
LUDY, Llewellyn V. 3
LUECK, Martin Lawrence 1
LUECKE, John 3
LUECKE, Martin 1
LUEDDE, William Henry 3
LUEDEKING, Robert 1
LUEDER, Arthur Charles 3
LUEDKE, August J. 3
LUELLING, Henderson H
LUERS, John Henry H
LUETTE, 5
  Eleanor (Mrs. Paul Luette, Jr.)
LUFF, Ralph Gordon 4
LUFKIN, 1
  Elgood Chauncey
LUFKIN, Garland 3
LUFKIN, Wilfred W. 1
LUFKIN,
  Willfred Weymouth Jr.
LUGG, Charles Henry 4
LUGG, Thomas Bransford 5
LUHAN, Mabel Dodge 4
LUHN, Hans Peter 4
LUHRING, Oscar
  Raymond 2
LUHRS, Henry Ernest 4
LUHRSEN, Julius G. 3
LUKA, Milo 3
LUKAS, Paul 5
LUKE, Arthur Fuller 1
LUKE, Edmon G. 5
LUKE, Thomas
LUKEMAN, Augustus 1
LUKEN, Martin Girard 5
LUKENS, Herman Tyson 1
LUKENS, H
  Rebecca Webb Pennock
LUKIN, Charles James 4
LUKS, George Benjamin 1
LULEK, Ralph Norbert 5
LULL, Cabot 5
LULL, Edward Phelps H
LULL, Gerard Bramley 5
LULL, Henry Morris 2
LULL, Herbert Galen 5
LULL, Richard Swann 3
LUM, David Walker 4
LUM, Ralph Emerson 3
LUMBROZO, Jacob H
LUMLEY, 3
  Frederick Elmore
LUMMIS, 1
  Charles Fletcher
LUMMUS, Henry Tilton 4
LUMPKIN, Alva Moore 1
LUMPKIN, John Henry 5
LUMPKIN, Joseph Henry H
LUMPKIN, Joseph Henry 1
LUMPKIN, Samuel 1
LUMPKIN, Wilson H
LUMSDEN, Leslie Leon 2
LUMSDON, 1
  Christine Marie
LUNA, Solomon 1
LUNA, Tranquilino 1
LUNA Y H
  ARELLANO, Tristan 'de
LUND, Charles Carroll 5
LUND, Chester Benford 4
LUND, Emil 4
LUND, Fred Bates 5
LUND, Frederick Hansen 1
LUND, Lawrence Henry 3
LUND, Robert Leathan 4
LUNDAY, Charles G. 5
LUNDBECK, 2
  Gustaf Hilmer
LUNDBERG, Alfred J. 3
LUNDBERG, Charles J. 2
LUNDBERG, 5
  Clarence Harry
LUNDBERG, Frank A. 5
LUNDBORG, Florence 2
LUNDEBERG, Harry 3
LUNDEEN, Ernest 1

LUNDELL, 3
  Gustav Ernst Fredrick
LUNDIE, Edwin Hugh 5
LUNDIE, John 1
LUNDIN, 1
  Carl Axel Robert
LUNDIN, Frederick 4
LUND-QUIST, Carl E. 4
LUNDQUIST, 3
  Harold Leonard
LUNDSTRUM, 5
  Allan Winston
LUNDY, Ayres Derby 1
LUNDY, Benjamin H
LUNDY, Elmer Johnston 2
LUNDY, Wilson Thomas 4
LUNG, George Augustus 1
LUNGER, John B. 4
LUNGREN, 4
  Fernand Harvey
LUNKEN, Edmund H. 2
LUNKEN, Eshelby F. 3
LUNN, Arthur Constant 4
LUNN, George Richard 2
LUNSFORD, William 4
LUNT, George H
LUNT, Horace Gray 4
LUNT, Orrington H
LUNT, William Edward 3
LUPTON, Charles Thomas 1
LUPTON, John Thomas 1
LUQUER, Lea McIlvaine 1
LUQUIENS, 1
  Frederick Bliss
LURCAT, Jean-Marie 4
LURIE, Louis Robert 5
LURTON, 3
  Douglas Ellsworth
LURTON, Horace Harmon 1
LUSE, Claude Zeph 1
LUSK, Charles Keeler 1
LUSK, Clayton Riley 3
LUSK, Frank Stillman 1
LUSK, 5
  Georgia L. (mrs.)
LUSK, Graham 1
LUSK, James Loring 1
LUSK, James W. 1
LUSK, Willard Clayton 1
LUSK, William Foster 1
LUSK, William Thompson H
LUST, Adeline Cohnfeld 4
LUSTIG, Alvin 3
LUSTMAN, 5
  Seymour Leonard
LUSTRAT, Joseph 1
LUTEN, Daniel Benjamin 2
LUTERBRIDGE, 1
  Eugene Harvey
LUTES, Delia Thompson 2
LUTHER, 1
  Edwin Cornelius
LUTHER, Flavel Sweeten 1
LUTHER, Hans 5
LUTHER, John Carlyle 5
LUTHER, Mark Lee 5
LUTHER, Seth H
LUTHER, 4
  Willard Blackinton
LUTHRINGER, 3
  George Francis
LUTHULI, Albert John 4
LUTHY, Fred 4
LUTKIN, 1
  Peter Christian
LUTTRELL, John E. 5
LUTTRELL, John King H
LUTZ, Brenton Reid 4
LUTZ, Charles Abner 2
LUTZ, E. Russell 5
LUTZ, Edwin George 4
LUTZ, Frank Eugene 2
LUTZ, Frank J. 1
LUTZ, 4
  George Washington
LUTZ, Grace Livingston 2
LUTZ, Philip 2
LUTZ, Ralph Haswell 5
LUTZ, Samuel G. 3
LUTZ, William A. 4
LUXFORD, Ansel F(rank) 4
LUYTIES, Carl Johann 1
LYALL, James 1
LYALL, Toni Owen 5
LYBARGER, 4
  Donald Fisher
LYBARGER, Lee Francis 1
LYBRAND, Archibald 1
LYBYER, Albert Howe 2
LYDECKER, 1
  Charles Edward
LYDECKER, F. A. 4
LYDECKER, 4
  Garit Abraham
LYDECKER, Garrett J. 1
LYDENBERG, 3
  Harry Miller

LYDENBERG, 4
  Harry Miller
LYDER, Jay W. 5
LYDICK, Jesse Dean 2
LYDON, Eugene K. 4
LYDON, Richard Paul 2
LYDSTON, G. Frank 1
LYETH, 3
  J. M. Richardson
LYFORD, James Otis 1
LYFORD, Oliver Smith 3
LYFORD, Oliver Smith 3
LYFORD, Will Hartwell 1
LYKES, Joseph T. 4
LYLE, Aaron H
LYLE, 1
  Benjamin Franklin
LYLE, Clay 5
LYLE, Eugene P, Jr. 5
LYLE, 2
  Henry Hamilton Moore
LYLE, Hubert Samuel 4
LYLE, William Thomas 1
LYMAN, Albert Josiah 1
LYMAN, 1
  Alexander Steele
LYMAN, Amy Brown 4
LYMAN, Arthur Theodore 1
LYMAN, Benjamin Smith 1
LYMAN, Charles 1
LYMAN, Charles Baldwin 1
LYMAN, 1
  Charles Huntington
LYMAN, 5
  Charles Huntington, III
LYMAN, Chester Smith H
LYMAN, Chester Wolcott 1
LYMAN, David Brainerd 1
LYMAN, David Russell 1
LYMAN, Edward Branch 4
LYMAN, Edward Dean 4
LYMAN, Elias 1
LYMAN, Elmer Adelbert 1
LYMAN, Eugene William 1
LYMAN, Frank 1
LYMAN, Frank Hubbard 3
LYMAN, 1
  Frederick Wolcott
LYMAN, George Dunlap 3
LYMAN, George Richard 1
LYMAN, George Richards 1
LYMAN, Harry Webster 1
LYMAN, Hart 1
LYMAN, Henry Darius 1
LYMAN, Henry Munson 1
LYMAN, Homer Childs 4
LYMAN, James 1
LYMAN, Joseph H
LYMAN, Joseph 1
LYMAN, Joseph Bardwell 1
LYMAN, Joseph Stebbins 1
LYMAN, Lauren Dwight 5
LYMAN, Phineas 1
LYMAN, Richard Roswell 4
LYMAN, Robert Hunt 1
LYMAN, Rufus Ashley 3
LYMAN, Samuel H
LYMAN, Sarah E. 1
LYMAN, Theodore * H
LYMAN, Theodore 3
LYMAN, William H
LYMAN, William Denison 1
LYMER, Elmer E. 1
LYMER, William Barker 1
LYNCH, Anna 2
LYNCH, C. Arthur H
LYNCH, Charles H
LYNCH, Charles 4
LYNCH, Charles F. 4
LYNCH, Charles Wesley 1
LYNCH, Clyde Alvin 4
LYNCH, Daniel Joseph 3
LYNCH, Edward James 1
LYNCH, Ella Frances 2
LYNCH, Florence 2
LYNCH, 2
  Frank Worthington
LYNCH, Frederick 1
LYNCH, 4
  Frederick Bicknell
LYNCH, Frederick J. 3
LYNCH, George Arthur 4
LYNCH, James Daniel 4
LYNCH, James Kennedy 5
LYNCH, James Mathew 1
LYNCH, James William 1
LYNCH, Jeremiah 1
LYNCH, Jerome Morley 4
LYNCH, John H
LYNCH, John A. 1
LYNCH, John David 1
LYNCH, John Fairfield 2
LYNCH, John Joseph H
LYNCH, John Roy 1
LYNCH, Joseph Bertram 4
LYNCH, Joseph Patrick 3

LYNCH, 1
  Matthew Christoper
LYNCH, Patrick Neeson H
LYNCH, Raymond A. 5
LYNCH, Robert Newton 1
LYNCH, Thomas * H
LYNCH, Thomas Francis 5
LYNCH, Walter A. 1
LYNCH, Walton D. 4
LYNCH, Warren J. 1
LYNCH, Willard A. 3
LYNCH, William Francis H
LYNCH, William Orlando 3
LYND, Robert Staughton 5
LYNDE, Benjamin H
LYNDE, Carleton John 5
LYNDE, Francis 1
LYNDE, Samuel Adams 1
LYNDE, William Pitt H
LYNDON, Lamar 1
LYNDS, Elam H
LYNE, James Garnett 1
LYNE, 1
  Wickliffe Campbell
LYNETT, Edward James 2
LYNETT, Edward James 1
LYNETT, 3
  Elizabeth Ruddy
LYNN, Charles J. 3
LYNN, David 4
LYNN, Harry Hudson 1
LYNN, Robert Henry 3
LYNN, Robert Marshall 1
LYON, A. Maynard 1
LYON, Adrian 5
LYON, Alfred E. 4
LYON, 4
  Andrew Hutchinson
LYON, Anne Bozeman 1
LYON, Asa H
LYON, Caleb H
LYON, Cecil Andrew 1
LYON, David Gordon 1
LYON, Dorsey Alfred 2
LYON, Edmund 1
LYON, Edmund Daniel 2
LYON, Edwin Bowman 1
LYON, Eldridge Merick 1
LYON, Elias Potter 1
LYON, Ernest 2
LYON, Ernest Neal 1
LYON, Francis Strother H
LYON, Frank 3
LYON, Frank Emory 1
LYON, Frederick Saxton 2
LYON, George Armstrong 1
LYON, George F. 1
LYON, George Harry 5
LYON, Gideon Allen 1
LYON, Hastings 3
LYON, Henry Ware 1
LYON, Herb 5
LYON, J(ames) Adair 1
LYON, James H
LYON, James Alexander 3
LYON, John Denniston 4
LYON, John Stanley 4
LYON, Leonard Saxton 3
LYON, LeRoy Springs 1
LYON, Leverett Samuel 3
LYON, Lucius H
LYON, Marcus Ward Jr. 2
LYON, Mary 1
LYON, Matthew H
LYON, Milford Hall 5
LYON, Nathaniel H
LYON, Nelson Reed 4
LYON, Pritchett Alfred 5
LYON, Scott Cary 2
LYON, T. Lyttleton 4
LYON, Walter Jefferson 4
LYON, William Henry 1
LYON, William Penn 1
LYONS, Albert Brown 1
LYONS, Chalmers J. 1
LYONS, Champ 1
LYONS, Charles William 1
LYONS, Coleburn 5
LYONS, Dennis Francis 1
LYONS, Gerald Edward 2
LYONS, James J. 5
LYONS, John Sprole 2
LYONS, 1
  Judson Whitlocke
LYONS, Julius J. 1
LYONS, Katharine 1
LYONS, Lucile Manning 1
LYONS, Peter H
LYONS, Robert Edward 2
LYONS, Samuel Ross 4
LYONS, Thomas Richard 1
LYONS, 1
  Timothy Augustine
LYSTER, H
  Henry Francis Le Hunte
LYSTER, 1
  Theodore Charles

LYTE, E. Oram 1
LYTELL, Bert 3
LYTER, Jean Curtis 4
LYTLE, Almon Wheeler 4
LYTLE, J. Horace H
LYTLE, Robert Todd H
LYTLE, William Haines H
LYTTELTON, Oliver 4
LYTTLETON, H
  William Henry
LYTTON, Bart 5

M

MAAG, 5
  William Frederick, Jr.
MAAS, Anthony J. 1
MAAS, Carlos J. 5
MAAS, Melvin Joseph 4
MAASKE, Roben J. 3
MAASS, Herbert Halsey 3
MAASS, Otto 4
MABBOTT, Thomas 5
  Ollive
MABEE, George W. 2
MABERY, 1
  Charles Frederic
MABEY, Charles R. 5
MABIE, Edward Charles 3
MABIE, Hamilton Wright 1
MABIE, Henry Clay 1
MABIE, Louise Kennedy 3
MABON, Thomas 4
  McCance
MABRY, Milton Harvey 4
MABURY, Margaret Ellis 4
MAC ADAM, 4
  George Hartley
MAC AFEE, John Blair 1
MACALARNEY, 2
  Robert Emmet
MACALESTER, Charles * H
MAC ALISTER, James 3
MACALISTER, Sir Ian 3
MACALLISTER, 1
  Archibald Thomas Jr.
MAC ALPINE, 1
  Robert John
MACANALLY, James R. 5
MACARTHUR, Alfred 4
MAC ARTHUR, 1
  Archibald
MAC ARTHUR, Arthur * 1
MACARTHUR, 1
  Arthur Frederic
MACARTHUR, Charles 3
MACARTHUR, Douglas 4
MAC ARTHUR, James 1
MACARTHUR, John R. 1
MACARTHUR, John R. 3
MACARTHUR, 1
  Robert Helmer
MAC ARTHUR, 1
  Robert Stuart
MAC ARTHUR, Walter 4
MACARTNEY, 3
  Clarence Edward Noble
MACARTNEY, John W. 5
MACARTNEY, 1
  Thomas Benton Jr.
MACAULAY, 2
  Fannie Caldwell
MACAULAY, 4
  Fannie Caldwell
MACAULAY, 5
  Frederick Robertson
MACAULAY, 1
  Peter Stewart
MACAULEY, Alvan 3
MACAULEY, 5
  Charles Raymond
MACAULEY, 1
  Charles Raymond
MACAULEY, Edward 4
MACAULEY, Irving P. 4
MACBETH, 1
  Alexander Barksdale
MACBETH, Florence 4
MACBETH, 1
  George Alexander
MACBETH, George Duff 5
MACBETH, Henry 4
MACBRAYNE, Lewis E. 3
MACBRIDE, D. S. 4
MACBRIDE, 1
  Philip Douglas
MACBRIDE, 1
  Thomas Huston
MACCALLA, 1
  Clifford Sheron
MACCALLUM, 2
  John Archibald
MAC CALLUM, John 5
  Bruce
MACCALLUM, 2
  William George
MAC CAMERON, Robert 1

MACCARTY, 4
  William Carpenter
MACCAUD, 5
  Francis William
MACCAUGHEY, 3
  Vaughan
MAC CAULEY, Clay 1
MACCHESNEY, Chester 5
  M.
MACCHESNEY, 5
  Clara Taggart
MACCHESNEY, 3
  Nathan William
MACCLINTOCK, Paul 5
MACCLINTOCK, Samuel 5
MAC CLINTOCK, 1
  William Darnall
MACCLOSKEY, 5
  James Edward, Jr.
MACCOLL, Alexander 5
MAC COLL, 1
  James Roberton
MAC COLL, 1
  William Bogle
MACCOLL, 1
  William Hamilton
MAC CONNELL, 1
  Charles Jenkins
MACCONNELL, 3
  John Wilson
MAC CORD, 1
  Charles William
MACCORKLE, 1
  Emmett Wallace
MAC CORKLE, 1
  William Alexander
MACCORMACK, 1
  Daniel William
MACCORNACK, Walter 4
  Roy
MACCORRY, P. J. 4
MAC COUN, Townsend 4
MACCOY, William Logan 2
MAC CRACKEN, 1
  Henry Mitchell
MACCRACKEN, 5
  Henry Noble
MACCRACKEN, John 1
  Henry
MACCRACKEN, 2
  William Patterson, Jr.
MACCULLOUGH, 3
  Gleason Harvey
MACCURDY, George 2
  Grant
MACCUTCHEON, Aleck 3
MAC DANIEL, Frank 1
MACDANIEL, Robert D. 1
MAC DILL, David 1
MACDONALD, 1
  Alexander
MACDONALD, 2
  Alexander Black
MACDONALD, Angus 3
  Lewis
MACDONALD, Anna 5
  Addams
MACDONALD, 1
  Archibald Arnott
MAC DONALD, Arthur 1
MACDONALD, Arthur 5
  Jay
MACDONALD, 4
  Augustin Sylvester
MACDONALD, 3
  Bernard Callaghan
MACDONALD, Betty 3
MACDONALD, Byrnes 3
MACDONALD, 4
  Carlos Frederick
MACDONALD, Charles 1
MACDONALD, 2
  Duncan Black
MACDONALD, George 4
MACDONALD, 1
  George Alexander
MACDONALD, 3
  George Everett
MACDONALD, George 2
  Saxe
MACDONALD, Godfrey 4
MACDONALD, Gordon 1
MACDONALD, Henry 3
MACDONALD, Ian 4
  (Gibbs)
MACDONALD, James 1
  Allan
MACDONALD, James R. 4
MACDONALD, H
  James Wilson Alexander
MACDONALD, 4
  James Wilson Alexander
MACDONALD, Jeanette 4
MACDONALD, Jesse 5
  Juan
MACDONALD, 2
  John Alexander

MACDONALD, John H. 4
MACDONALD, John William 1
MACDONALD, Milton Tenney 4
MACDONALD, Moses H
MACDONALD, Neil Carnot 1
MACDONALD, Pirie 2
MACDONALD, Ranald H
MACDONALD, Robert 4
MACDONALD, Thomas Harris 3
MAC DONALD, William 1
MACDONALD, William Alexander 4
MACDONALD, William H.
MAC DONALD, William J. 5
MACDONALD, Willis Goss 1
MACDONALL, Angus 1
MACDONOUGH, Thomas H
MACDOUGAL, Daniel Trembly 3
MAC DOUGALD, Dan 3
MAC DOUGALL, Clinton Dugald 1
MACDOUGALL, Edward Archibald 3
MACDOUGALL, Hamilton Crawford 2
MACDOUGALL, Mrs. Alice Foote 4
MAC DOUGALL, Robert 1
MACDOUGALL, William Dugald 2
MACDOWELL, Charles Henry 3
MACDOWELL, Edward Alexander 1
MACDOWELL, Katherine Sherwood Bonner H
MACDOWELL, Mrs. Edward 3
MACDOWELL, Thain Wendell 4
MACDUFFEE, Cyrus Colton 4
MACDUFFIE, John 1
MACE, Daniel H
MACE, Frances Laughton 1
MACE, Frank William 4
MACE, Harold Loring 2
MACE, William Harrison 1
MACEACHERN, Malcolm T. 3
MACEDO SOARES, Jose Carlos 5
MAC ELREE, Wilmer W. 1
MACELROY, Andrew Jackson 5
MAC ELROY, Andrew Jackson 4
MACELWANE, James B. 3
MACELWANE, John Patrick 5
MACELWEE, Roy Samuel 2
MACEWEN, Ewen Murchison 2
MACEWEN, Walter 3
MACFADDEN, Bernarr 3
MACFADYEN, Alexander 1
MACFARLAN, William Charles 2
MACFARLAND, Charles Stedman 3
MACFARLAND, Finlay Leroy 1
MACFARLAND, Frank Mace 3
MACFARLAND, Henry Brown Floyd 1
MACFARLAND, Lanning 5
MACFARLAND, Robert Alfred 3
MACFARLANE, Alexander 4
MACFARLANE, Catharine 5
MACFARLANE, Charles William 5
MACFARLANE, David Laing 1
MACFARLANE, Howard Pettingill 5
MACFARLANE, John C. 1
MACFARLANE, John Muirhead 4
MACFARLANE, Joseph Arthur 4
MACFARLANE, Peter 3
MACFARLANE, Peter Clark 1
MACFARLANE, Robert H

MACFARLANE, W. E. 2
MACFEELY, Robert 1
MAC GAHAN, Barbara 1
MACGAHAN, Januarius Aloysius H
MAC GILLIVRAY, Alexander Dyer 1
MACGILLIVRAY, William H
MACGILVARY, Norwood 2
MAC GILVARY, Paton 2
MACGINLEY, John Bernard 5
MAC GINNISS, John 1
MAC GOWAN, Alice H
MACGOWAN, David Bell 5
MACGOWAN, Gault 5
MAC GOWAN, Granville 1
MAC GOWAN, John Encil 5
MACGOWAN, John Koe 5
MACGOWAN, Kenneth 4
MAC GRATH, Harold 5
MACGREGOR, Charles Peter 5
MACGREGOR, Clarence 3
MACGREGOR, David Hutchison 5
MACGREGOR, David Hutchison 3
MACGREGOR, Frank Silver 5
MAC GREGOR, Henry Frederick 1
MACHARG, John Brainerd 3
MACHARG, William 3
MACHEBEUF, Joseph Projectus H
MACHEN, Arthur Webster 3
MACHEN, J. Gresham H
MACHEN, Willis Benson H
MACHIR, James H
MACHLETT, Raymond R. 3
MACHMER, William Lawson 3
MACHOLD, Henry Edmund 5
MACHROWICZ, Thaddeus M(ichael) 4
MACIEJEWSKI, Anton Frank 3
MACINNES, Duncan Arthur 4
MAC INNIS, John Murdoch 1
MACINTOSH, Douglas Clyde 2
MAC INTOSH, John Alexander 1
MACINTYRE, Archibald James 5
MACISAAC, Fred 1
MACIVER, Robert Morrison 5
MACK, A. B. 3
MACK, Andrew 1
MACK, Augustus Frederick Jr. 4
MACK, Carl Theodore 1
MACK, Connie 3
MACK, Edgar M. 2
MACK, Edward 3
MACK, Edwin S. 1
MACK, George Herbert 5
MACK, Henry Whitcomb 4
MACK, Howard 3
MACK, Isaac Foster 1
MACK, J(ames) S(tephen) 5
MACK, John E. 3
MACK, John Givan Davis 1
MACK, John M. 1
MACK, John Sephus 4
MACK, Julian Ellis 4
MACK, Julian William 2
MACK, Norman Edward 1
MACK, Richard Alfred 4
MACK, Russell Vernon 3
MACK, Warren Bryan 3
MACK, William 5
MACKALL, Alexander) Lawton 1
MACKALL, Leonard Leopold 1
MACKALL, Louis 1
MACKALL, Paul 3
MACKAY, Clarence Hungerford 4
MACKAY, Constance D'Arcy 4
MACKAY, Donald Dundas 4
MACKAY, Donald Sage 1
MACKAY, Helen 4

MACKAY, 5
Helen (Mrs. Archibald Mackay)
MACKAY, 3
Henry Squarebriggs Jr.
MACKAY, James 1
MACKAY, John Keiller 5
MACKAY, John William 5
MACKAY, Margaret 5
MACKAY, Robert 5
MACKAY, Roland Parks 4
MACKAY, William Andrew 1
MACKAY, William Eshorne 5
MACKAYE, Arthur Loring 4
MACKAYE, Harold Steele 1
MACKAYE, James 1
MACKAYE, H
James Morrison Steele
MACKAYE, Percy 3
MACKAY-SMITH, Alexander 1
MACKEACHIE, Douglas Cornell 2
MACKECHNIE, Hugh Neil 4
MACKEE, George Miller 3
MACKEEVER, John C. 3
MACKELLAR, Patrick H
MACKELLAR, Thomas 5
MAC KELLAR, Thomas 4
MACKELLAR, 2
William Henry Howard
MACKEN, Walter 4
MACKENZIE, A. 1
Cameron
MACKENZIE, 5
Alastair St. Clair
MACKENZIE, Alexander H
Alexander Slidell
MACKENZIE, Arthur 5
MACKENZIE, 4
Arthur Stanley
MACKENZIE, Cameron 1
MACKENZIE, Donald H
MACKENZIE, Donald 2
MACKENZIE, 3
Donald Hector
MACKENZIE, 1
Frederick William
MACKENZIE, H
George Henry
MACKENZIE, J. Gazzam 5
MACKENZIE, 1
James Cameron
MACKENZIE, Jean 1
Kenyon
MACKENZIE, John 1
Noland
MACKENZIE, Kenneth H
MACKENZIE, 1
Kenneth Alexander J.
MACKENZIE, 5
Kenneth Gerard
MACKENZIE, 1
Morris Robinson Slidell
MACKENZIE, Murdo 1
MACKENZIE, 2
Philip Edward
MACKENZIE, H
Ranald Slidell
MACKENZIE, Robert 1
MACKENZIE, H
Robert Shelton
MACKENZIE, 1
Roderick Dempster
MACKENZIE, Tandy 4
MACKENZIE, 2
Thomas Hanna
MACKENZIE, William H
MACKENZIE, 2
William Adams
MACKENZIE, 1
William Douglas
MACKENZIE, 3
William Ross
MACKENZIE, William 3
Roy
MACKEOWN, 3
Samuel Stuart
MACKEY, H
Albert Gallatin
MACKEY, Charles Osborn 4
MACKEY, 1
Charles William
MACKEY, 1
Edmund William McGregor
MACKEY, Harry A. 1
MACKEY, Joseph T. 4
MACKEY, Levi Augustus H
MACKEY, 4
William Fleming
MACKIE, Alexander 4
MACKIE, David Ives 5

MACKIE, Ernest Lloyd 5
MACKIE, 2
Joseph Bolton Cooper
MACKIE, 5
Pauline Bradford (Mrs. Herbert M. Hopkins)
MACKIE, Thomas Turlay 3
MACKIN, Joseph Hoover 5
MACKINNEY, Loren Carey 4
MACKINNON, Allan P. 3
MACKINNON, Eugene 3
MACKINNON, George V. 1
MACKINNON, 5
Harold Alexander
MACKINNON, James Angus 3
MACKINNON, Lee Warner 1
MACKINTOSH, Alexander 2
MACKINTOSH, 1
George Lewis
MACKINTOSH, 4
Harold Vincent
MACKINTOSH, Kenneth 5
MACKINTOSH, 5
William Archibald
MACKLIN, James Edgar 1
MACKLIN, 4
Justin Wilford
MACKLIN, W. A. Stewart 5
MACKNIGHT, Dodge 3
MACKUBIN, Florence 1
MACKY, Eric Spencer 3
MACLACHAN, 1
David Cathcart
MACLACHLAN, Daniel A. 1
MACLACHLAN, James A. 4
MACLACHLAN, 3
John Miller
MAC LACHLAN, Lachlan 1
MACLACHLAN, 4
Margery Jean
MACLAFFERTY, 1
James Henry
MACLANE, 5
Gerald Robinson
MACLANE, M. Jean 4
MAC LANE, Mary 1
MACLANE, Mary 2
MAC LAREN, Archibald 1
MACLAREN, Malcolm 2
MACLAURIN, 1
Richard Cockburn
MACLAURIN, 3
William Rupert
MACLAY, Edgar Stanton 4
MACLAY, Isaac Walker 1
MACLAY, James 1
MACLAY, Otis Hardy 1
MACLAY, Robert Samuel 1
MACLAY, Samuel H
MACLAY, William * H
MACLAY, William Brown H
MACLAY, 1
William Plunkett
MACLAY, William Walter 3
MACLEAN, 3
Alexander Tweedie
MACLEAN, Angus Dhu 1
MACLEAN, Annie Marion 1
MACLEAN, 2
Arthur Winfield
MACLEAN, 4
Basil Clarendon
MACLEAN, 1
Charles Fraser
MACLEAN, 1
Charles Thomas Agnew
MACLEAN, Clara Dargan 4
MACLEAN, Daniel 4
MACLEAN, George 1
Edwin
MACLEAN, Henry Coit 1
MACLEAN, 2
James Alexander
MACLEAN, John H
MACLEAN, John H
MACLEAN, John Norman 2
MACLEAN, Munroe H
Deacon
MACLEAN, Paul Robert 5
MACLEAN, Ray Butts 2
MACLEAN, 1
Samuel Richter
MACLEAN, Stuart 5
MACLEAR, Anne Bush 1
MACLEISH, Andrew 1
MACLEISH, John E. 5
MACLELLAN, Kenneth F. 5
MACLELLAN, Robert J. 3

MACLELLAN, 5
Robert Llewellyn
MACLENNAN, Francis 1
MACLENNAN, 2
Francis William
MACLENNAN, Frank Pitts 1
MACLENNAN, 5
Simon Fraser
MACLEOD, 4
Bruce Hamilton
MACLEOD, Colln Munro 5
MACLEOD, 2
Donald Campbell
MACLEOD, 1
Frederick Joseph
MACLEOD, Iain Norman 5
MACLEOD, 1
John James Rickard
MACLEOD, Malcolm James 1
MACLEOD, Robert Brodie 5
MAC LEOD-THORP, L. E. G. 2
MACLOSKIE, George 1
MACLURE, William H
MACMANUS, Seumas 4
MACMANUS, Seumas 5
MACMILLAN, Cargill 5
MACMILLAN, Conway 2
MACMILLAN, Cyrus 3
MACMILLAN, 5
Sir Ernest Campbell
MACMILLAN, 1
George Whitfield
MACMILLAN, Hugh R. 3
MACMILLAN, Jason Leon 4
MACMILLAN, John Alwyn 3
MACMILLAN, 4
John Hugh Jr.
MACMILLAN, Kerr 1
MACMILLAN, Duncan 1
MACMILLAN, Lucy Hayes 4
MAC MILLAN, Thomas C. 1
MACMILLAN, 2
William Duncan
MACMONNIES, Frederick 4
MAC MULLAN, Ralph A. 5
MACMULLEN, Wallace 2
MACMURRAY, James E. 4
MACMURRAY, 4
John Van Antwerp
MACNAIR, 2
Florence Wheelock Ayscough
MACNAIR, 2
Harley Farnsworth
MACNAIR, James Duncan 4
MACNAMARA, 4
Arthur James
MACNAUGHTON, Edgar 5
MACNAUGHTON, 4
Ernest Boyd
MACNAUGHTON, James 2
MACNAUGHTON, 5
Lewis Winslow
MACNAUGHTON, 4
Moray Fraser
MACNEAL, Robert E. 4
MACNEAL, Ward J. 2
MACNEICE, Louis 4
MACNEILL, Carol Brooks 5
MACNEIL, Hermon Atkins 2
MACNEIL, Neil 5
MACNEIL, Sayre 4
MAC NEILL, 1
Charles Mather
MACNEISH, Noel Stones 4
MACNEVEN, William James H
MACNICOL, Roy Vincent 5
MACNIDER, Hanford 4
MACNIDER, Hanford 5
MACNIDER, 3
William 'de Berniere
MACNULTY, William K. 4
MACOMB, Alexander H
MACOMB, 4
Augustus Canfield
MACOMB, David Betton 1
MACOMB, 1
Montgomery Meigs
MACOMBER, Alexander 3
MACOMBER, John R. 3
MACOMBER, William 1
MACON, Nathaniel H
MACON, Robert Bruce 1
MACPHAIL, William

MAC PHERSON, Earle Steele 3
MACPHERSON, Walter Henry 3
MACPHIE, Elmore I. 3
MAC PHIE, John Peter 4
MAC QUEARY, Thomas Howard 1
MACQUEARY, Thomas Howard 2
MACQUEEN, Donald Bruce 5
MAC QUEEN, Peter 1
MACQUIGG, Charles Ellison 3
MACRAE, Elliott Beach
MACRAE, Elmer Livingston 3
MAC RAE, Floyd Willcox 4
MACRAE, George Wythe 4
MACRAE, Harry B. 3
MACRAE, Hugh 5
MAC RAE, James Cameron 1
MACRAE, John 2
MACRAE, William Alexander 1
MACSPARRAN, James H
MACTAVISH, William Caruth 5
MACVANE, Silas Marcus 3
MACVEAGH, Charles 1
MACVEAGH, Ewen Cameron 5)
MACVEAGH, Franklin 1
MACVEAGH, Lincoln 5
MAC VEAGH, Wayne 5
MAC VEY, William Pitt 5
MAC VICAR, John 4
MACVICAR, John George 2
MACVITTY, Karl 'de G. 3
MACWHORTER, Alexander H
MACY, 4
MACY, Anne Mansfield Sullivan
MACY, Arthur 4
MACY, C. Ward 4
MACY, Carleton 4
MACY, Edith Dewing 3
MACY, Edward Warren 3
MACY, George
MACY, Jesse 1
MACY, John
MACY, John B. H
MACY, Josiah 4
MACY, Josiah, Jr. 5
MACY, Nelson 3
MACY, Paul Griswold 4
MACY, V. Everit 1
MACY, Valentine E(verit, Jr. 5
MACY, W. Kingsland 4
MADDEN, Edwin Charles 4
MADDEN, Eva Anne
MADDEN, James Loomis 5
MADDEN, John 5
MADDEN, John Fitz 2
MADDEN, John Griffith 4
MADDEN, John Joseph
MADDEN, John Thomas 2
MADDEN, Joseph Warren 5
MADDEN, M. Lester
MADDEN, Martin Barnaby 1
MADDEN, Mrs. Maude Whitmore 4
MADDIN, Percy Downs 2
MADDOCK, Catharine Young Glen 5
MADDOCK, Walter Grierson 4
MADDOCK, William Eli 5
MADDON, John W. 3
MADDOX, Dwayne Depew
MADDOX, Fletcher 1
MADDOX, John J. 2
MADDOX, Louis Wilson 5
MADDOX, Robert Foster 5
MADDOX, Samuel T. 1
MADDOX, William Arthur 1
MADDOX, William Percy
MADDRY, Charles Edward 4
MADDUX, Jared 5
MADDUX, Parker Simmons 3
MADDY, John Edgar 4
MADEIRA, Jean Browning 5
MADEIRA, Louis Childs
MADEIRA, Percy Child 2
MADELEVA, Sister Mary 4
MADIGAN, LaVerne 4
MADILL, Grant Charles 2
MADISON, Charles C.

MADISON, Dorothea Payne Todd H
MADISON, Edmond H. 1
MADISON, Frank Dellno 2
MADISON, Harold Lester 3
MADISON, James * H
MADISON, Lucy Foster 1
MADSON, Norman Arthur 4
MAENNER, Theodore Henry 3
MAES, Camillus Paul 1
MAESTRE, Sidney 4
MAETERLINCK, Maurice 4
MAFFITT, David H
MAFFITTZ, John Newland H
MAGAN, Percy Tilson 2
MAGARY, Alvin Edwin 2
MAGAW, Charles Albert 5
MAGEE, Carlton Cole 3
MAGEE, Charles Lohr 5
MAGEE, Christopher Lyman 1
MAGEE, Clare 5
MAGEE, J(unius) Ralph 5
MAGEE, James Dysart 2
MAGEE, James M. 2
MAGEE, John H
MAGEE, John 2
MAGEE, John Benjamin 2
MAGEE, John Fackenthal 4
MAGEE, Walter Warren 1
MAGEE, William Addison 1
MAGEE, William Michael 2
MAGELLAN, Ferdinand H
MAGELSSEN, William Christian 3
MAGER, Charles Augustus 5
MAGEVNEY, Eugene A. 4
MAGGARD, Edward Harris 5
MAGGS, Douglas Blount 5
MAGIE, David 2
MAGIE, William Francis 2
MAGIE, William Jay 5
MAGIL, Mary Ellen Ryan (Mrs. Elias Magil)
MAGILL, Edmund Charles 1
MAGILL, Edward Hicks 1
MAGILL, Frank Stockton 2
MAGILL, George Paull 3
MAGILL, Hugh Stewart 4
MAGILL, Robert Edward 1
MAGILL, Roswell 4
MAGILL, Samuel Edward 5
MAGILL, William Seagrove 5
MAGILLIGAN, Donald James 5
MAGIN, Francis W. 4
MAGINNES, Albert Bristol 4
MAGINNIS, Charles Donagh 3
MAGINNIS, Martin 1
MAGINNIS, Samuel Abbot 1
MAGISTAD, Oscar Conrad 3
MAGLIN, William Henry 3
MAGNER, F. J. 2
MAGNER, James Joseph 5
MAGNER, John F. 1
MAGNER, Thomas Francis 2
MAGNES, Judah Leon 2
MAGNIER, Anthony Aloysius 3
MAGNUS, Joseph Emil 4
MAGNUSSON, Carl Edward 1
MAGNUSSON, Magnus Vignir 5
MAGNUSSON, Peter Magnus 4
MAGOFFIN, Beriah H
MAGOFFIN, James Wiley 4
MAGOFFIN, Ralph Van Deman 2
MAGONE, Daniel 5
MAGONIGLE, Edith Marion 1
MAGONIGLE, H. Van Buren 1
MAGOON, Charles E. 1
MAGOON, Henry Sterling H
MAGOR, S. F. 3
MAGOUN, George Frederic H
MAGOUN, Henry A. 1
MAGOUN, Herbert William

MAGOUN, Jeanne Bartholow (Mrs. Francis P.) 5
MAGOWAN, Sir John Hall 3
MAGRADY, Frederick W. 3
MAGRATH, Andrew Gordon H
MAGRATH, George Burgess 1
MAGRATH, William 3
MAGRAW, Lester Andrew 2
MAGRITTE, Rene 4
MAGRUDDER, Benjamin Drake 1
MAGRUDDER, David Lynn 1
MAGRUDER, Allan Bowie H
MAGRUDER, Bruce 3
MAGRUDER, Calvert 5
MAGRUDER, Frank Abbott 3
MAGRUDER, George Lloyd 1
MAGRUDER, John 3
MAGRUDER, John Bankhead H
MAGRUDER, John H. Jr. 4
MAGRUDER, Julia 1
MAGRUDER, Patrick H
MAGRUDER, Thomas Pickett 1
MAGRUDER, William Thomas 1
MAGSAYSAY, Ramon 3
MAGUIRE, Hamilton Ewing 5
MAGUIRE, James G. 4
MAGUIRE, Jeremiah De Smet
MAGUIRE, John Arthur 5
MAGUIRE, Matthew 4
MAGUIRE, Raymer Francis
MAGUIRE, Russell 4
MAGUIRE, Walter N. 4
MAGUIRE, William G. 5
MAHAFFEY, Jesse Lynn 2
MAHAFFEY, John Quincy 4
MAHAFFIE, Charles Delahunt 5
MAHAN, Alfred Thayer 1
MAHAN, Asa H
MAHAN, Bryan Francis 3
MAHAN, Dennis Hart H
MAHAN, Dennis Hart 1
MAHAN, Edgar Clyde 2
MAHAN, George Addison 1
MAHAN, Lawrence Elmer 2
MAHAN, Milo H
MAHAN, Patrick Joseph 1
MAHANA, George Shaw 5
MAHANY, Rowland Blennerhassett
MAHAR, Edward Albert 5
MAHENDRA, Bir Bikram Shah Deva
MAHER, Aldea 3
MAHER, Aly Pacha
MAHER, Chauncey Carter 5
MAHER, Dale Wilford 2
MAHER, George Washington
MAHER, James Denis 1
MAHER, James P. 4
MAHER, Stephen John 1
MAHESHWARI, Panchanan 4
MAHIN, Edward Garfield 5
MAHIN, Frank Cadle 2
MAHIN, Frank Webster 1
MAHIN, John Lee 1
MAHL, William 1
MAHLE, Arthur Edwin 4
MAHLER, Ernst 4
MAHLER, Gustav H
MAHLER, Gustav 4
MAHON, Russell C. 4
MAHON, Stephen Keith 5
MAHON, Thaddeus Maclay 4
MAHON, Wilfred John 1
MAHON, William D. 2
MAHONE, William H
MAHONEY, Bernard Joseph 5
MAHONEY, Caroline Smith 1
MAHONEY, Charles H. 4
MAHONEY, Daniel Joseph 4
MAHONEY, Edward R. 5
MAHONEY, George William 3

MAHONEY, Jeremiah T. 5
MAHONEY, John C. 2
MAHONEY, John Dennis 5
MAHONEY, John Friend 3
MAHONEY, John Joseph 4
MAHONEY, Joseph Nathaniel 2
MAHONEY, Peter Paul H
MAHONEY, Walter Butler 3
MAHONEY, William Frank 1
MAHONEY, William J. 2
MAHONY, Emon Ossian 1
MAHONY, Michael Joseph
MAHONY, Thomas Harrison 5
MAHOOD, J. W. 4
MAHOOL, John Barry 1
MAHURAN, Stuart Ansala
MAHY, George Gordon 4
MAIDEN, Robert King
MAIER, George 3
MAIER, Walter Arthur * 2
MAILHOUSE, Max 2
MAILLER, William Henry 1
MAILLIARD, John Ward Jr.
MAILLY, William
MAIN, Archibald M. 4
MAIN, Arthur Elwin 1
MAIN, Charles Thomas 2
MAIN, Hanford 1
MAIN, Herschel 1
MAIN, Hubert Platt 1
MAIN, John Fleming 1
MAIN, John Hanson Thomas
MAIN, William H
MAIN, William Holloway 1
MAINE, Mary Talulah
MAINS, George Preston 1
MAINS, Kathryn Pauline
MAINWARING, William Bernard 3
MAIR, William J. 4
MAIRS, Elwood Donald 5
MAIRS, Samuel 3
MAIRS, Thomas Isaiah 5
MAISCH, Henry Charles Christian 1
MAISCH, John Michael H
MAITLAND, George H. 4
MAITLAND, James Dreher 4
MAITLAND, Royal Lethington 2
MAJALI, Hazaa
MAJESKI, John F. 5
MAJOR, Alfred Job 4
MAJOR, Cedric A. 4
MAJOR, Charles
MAJOR, David R. 1
MAJOR, Duncan Kennedy Jr. 2
MAJOR, Elliott Woolfolk 2
MAJOR, J(ames) Earl 5
MAJOR, Samuel C. 1
MAJOR, William Warner
MAKEMIE, Francis H
MAKEPEACE, Charles D. 4
MAKEPEACE, Colin MacRae
MAKINSON, George Albert 1
MAKITA, Yolchiro 5
MAKUEN, G. Hudson
MALAKIS, Emile 4
MALAN, Clement Timothy 4
MALAN, Daniel Francois
MALBONE, Edward Greene H
MALBONE, Francis H
MALBURN, William Peabody 2
MALBY, George R. 1
MALCARNEY, Arthur Leno 5
MALCOLM, D. O. 4
MALCOLM, Daniel H
MALCOLM, George Arthur 4
MALCOLM, Gilbert 4
MALCOLM, James Peller H
MALCOLM, Roy 4
MALCOLM, Russell Laing 5
MALCOLM, William Lindsay
MALCOLM, X. 4
MALCOM, Howard H
MALCOMSON, Charles Tousley 1
MALCOMSON, James W. 1

MALDARELLI, Oronzio 4
MALIN, Patrick Murphy 4
MALINOVSKY, Rodion Yakovlevich 4
MALINOWSKI, Bronislaw Kasper 2
MALISOFF, William Marias 2
MALITZ, Lester M. 4
MALKIEL, Leon Andrew 4
MALKO, Nicolai 4
MALL, Franklin Paine 2
MALLALIEU, Wilbur Vincent
MALLALIEU, Willard Francis 1
MALLARY, R. De Witt 1
MALLARY, Rollin Carolas H
MALLERY, Earl Dean 3
MALLERY, Garrick H
MALLERY, Otto Tod 3
MALLET, John William 1
MALLET-PREVOST, Severo 2
MALLETT, Daniel Trowbridge 4
MALLETT, Donald Roger 5
MALLETT, Reginald 1
MALLETT, Wilbert Grant 1
MALLINCKRODT, Edward 1
MALLINCKRODT, Pauline H
MALLINCKROOT, Edward Jr. 4
MALLISON, Richard Speight 5
MALLOCH, Douglas 1
MALLON, Alfred Edward 2
MALLON, Guy Ward 4
MALLON, Paul 3
MALLON, Winifred 3
MALLORY, C. C. 3
MALLORY, Clifford Day 4
MALLORY, Francis H
MALLORY, Frank Burr 2
MALLORY, Hugh 2
MALLORY, Hugh Shepherd Darby
MALLORY, Meredith H
MALLORY, Robert 4
MALLORY, Rufus H
MALLORY, Stephen Russell H
MALLORY, Stephen Russell 1
MALLORY, Tracy Burr 3
MALLOY, John Anthony 2
MALLY, Frederick William
MALM, Gustav Nathanael 1
MALONE, Booth M. 4
MALONE, Clarence M. 4
MALONE, Clifton J. 4
MALONE, Dana
MALONE, Dudley Field 3
MALONE, George Wilson 4
MALONE, J. Walter
MALONE, J. Walter Jr. 1
MALONE, James C. 1
MALONE, James Thomas 1
MALONE, John Wesley 5
MALONE, Kemp 5
MALONE, Noel H. 4
MALONE, Paul Bernard 1
MALONE, Richard Harwell
MALONE, Thomas Henry 1
MALONE, Walter 1
MALONE, William Battle 1
MALONEY, Francis 2
MALONEY, John Philip 3
MALONEY, Joseph F. 4
MALONEY, Paul Herbert 5
MALONEY, Richard Lee 4
MALONEY, Walter H. 5
MALONEY, William J. M. A. 3
MALONY, Harry James 5
MALOTT, Clyde A. 3
MALSBARY, George Elmer 5
MALTBIE, Milo Roy 5
MALTBIE, William Henry 1
MALTBIE, William Mills 4
MALTBY, Margaret Eliza 1
MALTBY, Ralph B. 3
MALTER, Henry 1
MALTZ, George L. 4
MALTZAN, Adolf Georg Otto Freiherr Von
MALVERN, Viscount 5
MAN, Alrick Hubbell 1
MAN, Ernest A. 1

* Indicates More Than One Such Name Listed

MARKS, William Dennis 1
MARKS, 4
Wirt Peebles Jr.
MARKWARD, 1
Joseph Bradley
MARKWART, 1
Arthur Hermann
MARKWOOD, 3
Michael Edward
MARLAND, 2
Ernest Whitworth
MARLAND, William C. 4
MARLATT, Abby Lillian 5
MARLATT, 3
Charles Lester
MARLER, 1
Herbert Meredith
MARLEY, James Preston 3
MARLIN, Harry Halpine 1
MARLING, 1
Alfred Erskine
MARLING, James H. H
MARLING, John Leake 5
MARLOR, Henry S. 4
MARLOW, Frank William 2
MARLOW, Thomas A. 1
MARLOWE, Julia 3
MARMADUKE, H
John Sappington
MARMER, Harry Aaron 3
MARMER, Milton Jacob 5
MARMION, Keith Robert 5
MARMION,
Robert Augustine
MARMON, Howard C. 2
MARMON, Jeff Berry 1
MARMUR, Jacland 5
MARNELL, 1
Robert Overton
MARONEY, 3
Frederick William
MAROT, Helen 1
MAROT, Mary Louise 5
MARQUAND, Allan 1
MARQUAND, Henry
Gurdon 1
MARQUAND, 4
John Phillips
MARQUARDT, Carl
Eugene 5
MARQUART, Edward
John 3
MARQUAT, 4
William Frederic
MARQUESS, William
Hoge 1
MARQUETT, H
Turner Mastin
MARQUETTE, Jacques H
MARQUIS, Albert Nelson 2
MARQUIS, David
Calhoun 1
MARQUIS, Don 1
MARQUIS, Donald
George 5
MARQUIS, George 4
MARQUIS, George Paull 1
MARQUIS, John Abner 1
MARQUIS, 1
Robert Lincoln
MARQUIS, 1
Rollin Ruthwin
MARQUIS, 2
Samuel Simpson
MARQUIS, Vivienne 4
MARQUIS,
William Stevenson
MARQUIS, William Vance 1
MARR, Alem H
MARR, Carl 1
MARR, H
George Washington Lent
MARRIAGE, 3
E. Charles D.
MARRINER, Robie D. 3
MARRINER, Theodore 1
MARRIOTT, 1
Abraham Robert
MARRIOTT, Arthur C. 3
MARRIOTT, Crittenden 1
MARRIOTT, Ross W. 3
MARRIOTT, W. Mckim 1
MARRON, Adrian
Raphael 4
MARRONE, Joseph 4
MARRS, 1
Starlin Marion Newberry
MARRS, Wyatt 4
MARSCHALL, Nicola H
MARSCHALL, Nicola 1
MARSDEN, Raymond
Robb 2
MARSDEN, Robert
Samuel 4
MARSH, Arthur Merwin 2
MARSH, Ben R. 4
MARSH, Benjamin Clarke 5

MARSH, Benjamin F. 1
MARSH, C. Dwight 4
MARSH, Charles H
MARSH, Charles Edward 4
MARSH, Edward Clark 1
MARSH, Egbert 2
MARSH, Francis Hedley 2
MARSH, Frank Burr 1
MARSH, Frank Earl Jr. 4
MARSH, Frank Edward 4
MARSH, Fred Dana 2
MARSH, George Perkins H
MARSH, George T. 2
MARSH, Herbert Eugene 2
MARSH, James 1
MARSH, James A. 2
MARSH, James Prentiss 2
MARSH, John * H
MARSH, John Bigelow 4
MARSH, Joseph Franklin 3
MARSH, Joseph William 1
MARSH, Mae 4
MARSH, Myron Maurice 4
MARSH, Othniel Charles H
MARSH, 5
Raymond E(ugene)
MARSH, Reginald 3
MARSH, Robert McCurdy 3
MARSH, Spencer Scott 2
MARSH, 5
Susan Louise Cotton (Mrs. Eugene Marsh)
MARSH, Sylvester H
MARSH, Tamerlane Pliny 4
MARSH, Walter Randall 2
MARSHALL,
Albert Brainerd
MARSHALL, 3
Albert Edward
MARSHALL, Albert Ware 5
MARSHALL, H
Alexander Keith
MARSHALL, Alfred H
MARSHALL, Alfred 1
MARSHALL, Alfred C. 2
MARSHALL, 3
Arthur Lawrence
MARSHALL, Benjamin H
MARSHALL, 2
Benjamin Howard
MARSHALL,
Benjamin Tinkham
MARSHALL, Bernard
Gay 3
MARSHALL, 4
Caroline Louise
MARSHALL, 3
Carrington Tanner
MARSHALL, Charles 1
MARSHALL, 1
Charles Clinton
MARSHALL, 2
Charles Donnell
MARSHALL, 1
Charles Edward
MARSHALL, H
Charles Henry
MARSHALL, Christopher H
MARSHALL, Clara 5
MARSHALL, 1
Clarence James
MARSHALL, Daniel H
MARSHALL, 4
E. Kennerly Jr.
MARSHALL, Edison 1
MARSHALL, Edward 2
MARSHALL, Edward
Asaph 4
MARSHALL,
Edward Chauncey
MARSHALL, Edwin
Jessop 1
MARSHALL, Elder
Watson 5
MARSHALL, Elton Lewis 5
MARSHALL, 4
Francis Cutler
MARSHALL, Frank James 2
MARSHALL,
Frederick Rupert
MARSHALL, 3
George Anthony
MARSHALL,
George Catlett
MARSHALL, Harold 4
MARSHALL,
Harold Joseph
MARSHALL, 1
Henry Rutgers
MARSHALL, Henry
Wright 3
MARSHALL, Herbert 1
MARSHALL, Herbert
Camp 5
MARSHALL, Howard
Drake 5
MARSHALL, Humphrey * H

MARSHALL, James A. K. 3
MARSHALL, H
James Markham
MARSHALL, James Rush 1
MARSHALL, James
Wilson H
MARSHALL, John H
MARSHALL, John * 1
MARSHALL, John 1
MARSHALL, John Albert 2
MARSHALL, 4
John Augustine
MARSHALL, John Daniel 4
MARSHALL, John Noble 5
MARSHALL, John Patten 1
MARSHALL, 5
Lenore G. (mrs. James Marshall)
MARSHALL, Leon Carroll 4
MARSHALL, Louis H
MARSHALL, Louis 1
MARSHALL, M. Lee 3
MARSHALL, 4
Marguerite Mooers
MARSHALL, 4
Nira Lovering
MARSHALL, Peter 2
MARSHALL, Ray Gifford 2
MARSHALL,
Raymond Willett
MARSHALL, Rembert 3
MARSHALL, 4
Richard Coke Jr.
MARSHALL, 4
Robert Bradford
MARSHALL, 4
Robert Edward
MARSHALL, Robert Eliot 1
MARSHALL,
Rosamond Van 'der Zee
MARSHALL, Ross Smiley 4
MARSHALL, 1
Roujet De Lisle
MARSHALL, Roy E(dgar) 5
MARSHALL, Roy E. 1
MARSHALL, Samuel
Scott H
MARSHALL, Stewart M. 4
MARSHALL, Thomas H
MARSHALL, Thomas * 1
MARSHALL, H
Thomas Alexander
MARSHALL, 5
Thomas Alfred, Jr.
MARSHALL, 5
Thomas Chalmers
MARSHALL, H
Thomas Francis
MARSHALL, Thomas
Frank 1
MARSHALL, 5
Thomas Franklin
MARSHALL, Thomas L. 4
MARSHALL, 1
Thomas Maitland
MARSHALL, Thomas
Riley 1
MARSHALL, Thomas
Worth 3
MARSHALL, 2
Tully Phillips
MARSHALL, Verne 4
MARSHALL, Wade
Hampton 1
MARSHALL, Waldo H. 1
MARSHALL, 5
Walter P(eter)
MARSHALL, William A. 1
MARSHALL, 1
William Alexander
MARSHALL,
William Champe
MARSHALL, 3
William Gilbert
MARSHALL, 4
William Kennedy
MARSHALL, 5
William LeGramd
MARSHALL, 1
William Louis
MARSHALL, H
William Rainey
MARSHALL, 2
William Stanley
MARSHMAN, John
Tryon 4
MARSHUTZ, 4
Elmer Glenville
MARSHUTZ, Joseph H. 3
MARSIGLIA, Gherlando 4
MARSLAND, Cora 4
MARSTEN, 1
Francis Edward
MARSTON, Anson 3
MARSTON, Edgar Lewis 1
MARSTON, George W. 1
MARSTON, George White 2

MARSTON, Gilman H
MARSTON, 1
Percival Freeman
MARSTON, 2
Sylvanus Boardman
MARSTON, 2
William Moulton
MART, Leon T. 4
MARTEL, Charles 2
MARTEL, Romeo Raoul 4
MARTELL, Eldred Roland 3
MARTENS, 1
Frederick Herman
MARTENS, 5
Walter Frederic
MARTI-IBANEZ, Felix
MARTIN, A. C. H
MARTIN, Abe 1
MARTIN,
Albert Thompson
MARTIN, Alexander H
MARTIN, Alfred Wilhelm 1
MARTIN, Alvah Howard 1
MARTIN, Andrew
Bennett
MARTIN, Anne Henrietta 3
MARTIN, Artemas 1
MARTIN, Arthur T. 2
MARTIN, Asa Earl 4
MARTIN, Auguste Marie
MARTIN, Barclay H
MARTIN, Benjamin Ellis
MARTIN, H
Benjamin Franklin
MARTIN, Bradley 1
MARTIN, Bradley 4
MARTIN, Burton
McMahan 1
MARTIN, Carey 3
MARTIN, Carl Neidhard 5
MARTIN, Celora E. 1
MARTIN, Chalmers 1
MARTIN, Charles Cyril 1
MARTIN, 3
Charles Fletcher
MARTIN, Charles Henry 2
MARTIN, Charles Irving 1
MARTIN, Chester W. 4
MARTIN, Clarence 2
MARTIN,
Clarence Augustine
MARTIN, 3
Clarence Eugene
MARTIN, 5
Crawford Collins
MARTIN, Daniel J. 5
MARTIN, Daniel Strobel 1
MARTIN, David B. 1
MARTIN, David Herron 4
MARTIN, 1
Dempster Disbrow
MARTIN, Douglas
DeVeny 4
MARTIN, Earle 1
MARTIN, Earle D. 1
MARTIN, Eben Wever 1
MARTIN, Edgar 1
MARTIN, Edgar Stanley 1
MARTIN, Edward 4
MARTIN, Edward 1
MARTIN,
Edward Hamilton
MARTIN, H
Edward Livingston
MARTIN, 1
Edward Sandford
MARTIN, Edwin Manton 3
MARTIN, Edwin Moore 1
MARTIN, Elbert Sevier H
MARTIN, Ellis 4
MARTIN, Ernest Gale 1
MARTIN, Everett Dean 1
MARTIN, F. O. 1
MARTIN, Fernando Wood 1
MARTIN, 5
Florence Arminta DeLong (Minta Martin)
MARTIN, Floyd A. 3
MARTIN, H
Francois-Xavier
MARTIN, Frank 3
MARTIN, Frank Joseph 1
MARTIN, Frank Lee 1
MARTIN, Franklin H. 1
MARTIN,
Frederick LeRoy
MARTIN, Frederick Roy 3
MARTIN, H
Frederick Stanley
MARTIN, 1
Frederick Townsend
MARTIN, G. Forrest 1
MARTIN, George
Abraham 2
MARTIN, George Brown 2
MARTIN, George Curtis 5

MARTIN, George E. 2
MARTIN, 1
George Ellsworth
MARTIN, George Henry 1
MARTIN, George Madden 2
MARTIN, 4
George Marshall
MARTIN, George Riley 1
MARTIN,
George Washington
MARTIN, George
Whitney 3
MARTIN, George William 4
MARTIN, Gertrude Shorb 5
MARTIN, Gertrude Shorb 4
MARTIN, Glenn L. 3
MARTIN, Gustav Julius 1
MARTIN, Guy H. 1
MARTIN, 5
Harold Montgomery
MARTIN, Harry
Brownlow 3
MARTIN, Harry Leland 3
MARTIN,
Helen Reimensnyder
MARTIN, Henry Austin H
MARTIN, Henry Newell H
MARTIN,
Herbert Spencer
MARTIN, Homer Dodge H
MARTIN, Hugh 5
MARTIN, Isaac Jack 4
MARTIN, J. H. Thayer 3
MARTIN, James 1
MARTIN, James Green 4
MARTIN, James Lawrence 3
MARTIN, James Loren 1
MARTIN, 3
James MacDonald
MARTIN, James Sankey 4
MARTIN, John 1
MARTIN, John 3
MARTIN, John Alexander 1
MARTIN, John Andrew 1
MARTIN, H
John Blennerhasset
MARTIN, John C. 3
MARTIN, John Calvin 1
MARTIN, John Donelson 4
MARTIN, John Irwin 1
MARTIN, John James 1
MARTIN, John Preston H
MARTIN, John Wellborn 3
MARTIN, Joseph 2
MARTIN, Joseph I. 3
MARTIN,
Joseph William Jr.
MARTIN, Joshua Lanier H
MARTIN, Josiah H
MARTIN, 2
Julius Corpening
MARTIN,
Kingsley Leverich
MARTIN, Larkin Morris 1
MARTIN, 5
Lawrence Crawford
MARTIN, Leroy Albert 5
MARTIN, Lester 3
MARTIN, Lillien Jane 2
MARTIN,
Louis Adolphe Jr.
MARTIN, Luther H
MARTIN, Luther III 4
MARTIN, Mabel Wood 3
MARTIN, Martha Evans 1
MARTIN,
Mellen Chamberlain
MARTIN, Melvin Albert 1
MARTIN, Miles Macon 4
MARTIN, Morgan Lewis H
MARTIN, Motte 4
MARTIN, Patrick Minor 5
MARTIN, Paul Alexander 1
MARTIN, Paul Curtis 4
MARTIN, Paul Leo 1
MARTIN, Percy Alvin 3
MARTIN, Ralph Andrew 5
MARTIN,
Reginald Wesley
MARTIN, Renwick Harper 5
MARTIN, Riccardo 1
MARTIN, Robert Grant 1
MARTIN, Robert Hugh 1
MARTIN, Robert Nicols H
MARTIN, Roscoe
Coleman 5
MARTIN, Royce George 1
MARTIN, Samuel Albert 3
MARTIN, Santford 3
MARTIN, Selden Osgood 1
MARTIN,
Sylvester Mitchell
MARTIN, T. T. 1
MARTIN,
Thomas Commerford

MARTIN, 5
Thomas Ellsworth
MARTIN, Thomas Joseph 5
MARTIN, Thomas Paul 3
MARTIN, 4
Thomas Powderly
MARTIN, Thomas Staples 1
MARTIN, Thomas Wesley 4
MARTIN, V. G. 3
MARTIN,
Victoria Claflin Woodhull
MARTIN, Wallace Harold 5
MARTIN,
Walter Bramblette
MARTIN, Walton 3
MARTIN, Whitmell Pugh 1
MARTIN, William 1
MARTIN,
William Alexander Parsons
MARTIN, William Dobbin H
MARTIN, 5
William Elejius
MARTIN, 2
William Franklin
MARTIN, William Hope 4
MARTIN, William Joseph 5
MARTIN, William Joseph 2
MARTIN, William Leslie 4
MARTIN, William Logan 1
MARTIN, William Logan 4
MARTIN,
William McChesney
MARTIN, William 4
Thomas
MARTIN, 3
William Thompson
MARTIN, Winfred Robert 1
MARTINDALE, Earl 4
Henry
MARTINDALE, F. Carew H
MARTINDALE,
Henry Clinton
MARTINDALE, John H
Henry
MARTINDALE, Thomas
MARTIN DU GARD, 3
Roger
MARTINE, James Edgar 1
MARTINEAU, Harriet H
MARTINEAU, John Ellis 1
MARTINEK, 5
Frank V(ictor)
MARTINELLI, Giovanni 5
MARTINEZ, Felix 1
MARTINEZ, Xavier 2
MARTINI, Roland 4
MARTINO, Gaetano 4
MARTINOT, Sadie 4
MARTINS, Maria Alves 5
MARTINU, Bohuslav 3
MARTINY, Philip 1
MARTS, 5
Arnaud Cartwright
MARTS, Carroll Hartman 1
MARTWICK, 5
William Lorimer
MARTY, Martin H
MARTYN, Carlos 1
MARTYN, Chauncey
White 1
MARTYN, H
Sarah Towne Smith
MARTZ, Hyman Scher
MARVEL, Josiah 3
MARVEL, 'lk 1
MARVELL, George Ralph 2
MARVIN, 2
Charles Frederick
MARVIN, Cloyd Heck 5
MARVIN, Dudley H
MARVIN, Dwight 5
MARVIN, Dwight
Edwards 1
MARVIN, Enoch Mather H
MARVIN, Frank Olin 1
MARVIN, Fred Richard 1
MARVIN, 1
Frederic Rowland
MARVIN, George 3
MARVIN, Henry Howard 3
MARVIN, James Arthur 4
MARVIN, Joseph Benson 1
MARVIN, Langdon Parker 1
MARVIN, Richard Pratt H
MARVIN, Thomas O. 5
MARVIN, Walter S(ands) 5
MARVIN, Walter Taylor 2
MARVIN, William Glenn 1
MARVIN, 1
Winthrop Lippitt
MARWEDEL, H
Emma Jacobina Christiana
MARX, Alexander 3
MARX, Charles David 1
MARX, Guido Hugo 3
MARX, Harry S. 2
MARX, Karl H

MARX, Oscar B. 1
MARX, Otto 4
MARX, Robert S. 4
MARX, Samuel Abraham 4
MARYE, George Thomas 1
MARZALL, John Adams 3
MARZO, Eduardo
MASARYK, Jan 2
MASCHKE, Maurice 4
MASCUCH, John Thomas 3
MASE, Stanley Wilson 4
MASEFIELD, John 4
MASENG, Sigurd 3
MASHBURN, Arthur)
Gray 5
MASHBURN, Lloyd A. 5
MASLAND,
John W(esley), Jr.
MASLOW, Abraham
Harold 5
MASON, A. Lawrence 1
MASON, Abraham John H
MASON, Alfred Bishop 1
MASON, Alfred De Witt 1
MASON, Amelia Gere 1
MASON,
Armistead Thomson
MASON, Arthur Ellery 1
MASON, Augustus Lynch 1
MASON, 3
Bernard Sterling
MASON, C. Avery 5
MASON, 1
Caroline Atwater
MASON, Cassity E. 1
MASON, Charles H
MASON, 4
Charles Frederick
MASON, 4
Charles Harrison
MASON, Charles Noble 5
MASON, Claibourne Rice 4
MASON, Daniel Gregory 3
MASON, David Hastings 1
MASON, Edward
Campbell 1
MASON, 1
Edward Tuckerman
MASON, Edward Wilson 2
MASON, Emily Virginia H
MASON, Francis 1
MASON, Frank Holcomb 1
MASON, Frank Stuart 1
MASON, 5
G(eorge) Grant, Jr.
MASON, George * 1
MASON, George Allen 3
MASON, George
Champlin H
MASON, George Dewitt 5
MASON, George Grant 4
MASON, 4
George Jefferson
MASON, George W. 3
MASON, Guy 3
MASON, Harold Whitney 4
MASON, Harriet L. 4
MASON, Harry Howland 4
MASON, Henry H
MASON, Henry Freeman 4
MASON, Herbert Delavan 2
MASON, J. Alden 4
MASON, James Brown H
MASON, James Monroe 5
MASON, James Murray 4
MASON, James Orley 3
MASON, James Tate 1
MASON, James Weir 1
MASON, Jeremiah H
MASON, Jesse Henry 4
MASON, John H
MASON, John 1
MASON, John Calvin H
MASON, John Henry 1
MASON, John Mitchell H
MASON, John Thomson H
MASON, John William H
MASON, John Young H
MASON, Jonathan 1
MASON,
Joseph Warren Teets
MASON, 3
Julian Starkweather
MASON, L. Walter 4
MASON, Leslie Fenton 5
MASON, Lewis Duncan 1
MASON, Lowell H
MASON, Luther Whiting 1
MASON, 5
Madison Charles Butler
MASON, Mary Augusta 5
MASON,
Mary Knight Wood
MASON, Maud M. 3
MASON, Max 4
MASON, Michael L. 5
MASON, Moses Jr. H

MASON, 2
Newton Eliphalet
MASON, Noah Morgan 4
MASON, Otis Tufton 1
MASON, 5
Mortimer) Phillips
MASON, Richard Barnes H
MASON, Roy Martell 5
MASON, Rufus Osgood 1
MASON, Samson H
MASON, Samuel 1
MASON, Silas Boxley 1
MASON, Silas Cheever 1
MASON, H
Stevens Thomson *
MASON, Thomson 3
MASON, Victor Louis 1
MASON, Wallace Edward 2
MASON, Walt 1
MASON, Wilbur Nesbitt 5
MASON, William * 1
MASON, William 1
MASON, William Clarke 3
MASON, William Ernest 1
MASON, William Madison 5
MASON, William Pitt 1
MASON, William Sanford H
MASON, William Smith 4
MASON, William 3
Woodman
MASQUERAY, 1
Emmanuel Louis
MASQUERIER, Lewis H
MASSAGLIA, Joseph, Jr. 5
MASSASSOIT 3
MASSEE,
Edward Kingsley
MASSEE, 5
Jasper Cortenus
MASSEE, May 4
MASSEE, 2
William Wellington
MASSEY, George Betton 1
MASSEY, 1
George Valentine
MASSEY, John 4
MASSEY, 1
Lucius Saunders
MASSEY, Richard W. 3
MASSEY, Vincent 4
MASSEY, Wilbur Fisk 1
MASSEY, 1
William Alexander
MASSIE, David Meade 1
MASSIE, Eugene Carter 1
MASSIE, Robert Kinloch 1
MASSIE,
Robert Kinloch Jr.
MASSINGALE, 1
Sam Chapman
MASSLICH, 1
Chester Bentley
MASSMANN, Frederick
H. 5
MASSON, Robert Louis 5
MASSON, Thomas L. 1
MAST, Burdette Pond 4
MAST, Phineas Price H
MAST, Samuel Ottmar 2
MASTER, Henry Buck 2
MASTERS, Edgar Lee 2
MASTERS, Frank Merino 3
MASTERS, 5
Harris Kennedy
MASTERS, 3
Howard Russell
MASTERS, John Volney 3
MASTERS, Josiah H
MASTERS, Keith 2
MASTERS, Victor Irvine 3
MASTERSON, John 4
Joseph
MASTERSON, Kate 5
MASTERSON, Patrick J. 1
MASTERSON, H
William Barclay
MASTERSON, 4
William Barclay
MASTERSON, 5
William Edward
MASTERSON, 1
William Wesley
MASTICK, Seabury Cone 5
MASTIN, Claudius Henry H
MASTIN, 1
William McDowell
MASTON, Robert H. 3
MASUR, Jack H
MASURY, John Wesley 1
MATAS, Rudolph 3
MATCHETT, 1
Charles Horatio
MATCHETT, 2
David Fleming
MATEER, Calvin Wilson 1
MATELIGER, Jan Ernst H
MATHENY, Ezra Stacy 5

MATHER, Alonzo Clark 1
MATHER, Arthur 2
MATHER, Cotton H
MATHER, Elmer James 3
MATHER, 3
Frank Jewett Jr.
MATHER, Fred 1
MATHER, 1
Frederic Gregory
MATHER, 3
Gordon Macdonald
MATHER, Increase H
MATHER, 4
John Waterhouse
MATHER, 1
Margaret Morgan Herbert
MATHER, Richard 1
MATHER, Robert 1
MATHER, Rufus Graves 3
MATHER, S. Livingston 4
MATHER, Samuel H
MATHER, Samuel 1
MATHER, Samuel Holmes H
MATHER,
Samuel Livingston
MATHER, Stephen Tyng 1
MATHER, Thomas Ray 2
MATHER, William Allan 4
MATHER, William Gwinn 3
MATHER, William Tyler
MATHER, H
William Williams
MATHERLY, 3
Walter Jeffries
MATHERS, Frank C(urry) 5
MATHERS, Hugh
Thompson
MATHES, James Monroe 3
MATHES, William C. 4
MATHESIUS, 4
Walther Emil Ludwig
MATHESON, Alexander
E. 1
MATHESON, 3
George Wilson
MATHESON, 1
James Pleasant
MATHESON, John F. 4
MATHESON,
Kenneth Gordon
MATHESON, Martin 5
MATHESON, Robert 3
MATHESON, William
John 1
MATHEWS, Albert 1
MATHEWS, 3
Albert Prescott
MATHEWS, Alfred 1
MATHEWS, Alfred E. H
MATHEWS, Arthur Frank 2
MATHEWS, Basil Joseph 1
MATHEWS, 1
Charles Thomson
MATHEWS, 1
Clarence Wentworth
MATHEWS, Clifton 4
MATHEWS, Cornelius H
MATHEWS, 1
Delancey North
MATHEWS, 2
Edward Bennett
MATHEWS, F. Schuyler 1
MATHEWS, Frances
Aymar 2
MATHEWS, Frank A. Jr. 4
MATHEWS, Frank Stuart 1
MATHEWS, George 2
MATHEWS, George C. 2
MATHEWS, George
Martin 1
MATHEWS, Henry Mason H
MATHEWS, James 1
MATHEWS, James Abram 1
MATHEWS, James
Edward 1
MATHEWS, James 2
Thomas
MATHEWS, Joanna Hooe 1
MATHEWS, John H
MATHEWS, 1
John Alexander
MATHEWS, John Elie 3
MATHEWS, John Lathrop 1
MATHEWS, Joseph
Howard 5
MATHEWS, 4
Joseph McDowell
MATHEWS, S. Sherberne 1
MATHEWS, Samuel H
MATHEWS, Shailer 2
MATHEWS, Vincent 1
MATHEWS, William 1
MATHEWS, 3
William Burdette
MATHEWS, 3
William Hooker

MATHEWS, 5
William Rankin
MATHEWS, 1
William Smith Babcock
MATHEWS, William T. H
MATHEWSON, 1
Charles Frederick
MATHEWSON, H
Christopher
MATHEWSON, 4
Christopher
MATHEWSON, 5
Edward Payson
MATHEWSON, Elisha H
MATHEWSON, 2
Ozias Danforth
MATHEWSON, 2
Stanley Bernard
MATHEY, Dean 5
MATHIAS, Henry Edwin 4
MATHIAS, Robert David 3
MATHIES, Wharton 5
MATHIESON, 2
Samuel James
MATHIEU, Beltran 4
MATHIOT, Joshua 1
MATHIS, Harry R. 4
MATHISON, 1
Edward Thomson
MATIGNON, H
Francis Anthony
MATILE, Leon Albert 1
MATISSE, Henri 3
MATISSE, Henri 4
MATLACK, James H
MATLACK, Timothy 1
MATSON, Aaron H
MATSON, 2
Carlton Kingsbury
MATSON, Caroline Ruby 4
MATSON, Clarence Henry 2
MATSON, 1
Courtland Cushing
MATSON, Donald Darrow 5
MATSON,
Frederick Eugene
MATSON, 1
George Charlton
MATSON, Henry 1
MATSON, Leroy E. 4
MATSON, Max M. 5
MATSON, Ralph Charles 2
MATSON, Robert H. 3
MATSON,
Roderick Nathaniel
MATSON, Roy Lee 3
MATSON, Smith Corbin 1
MATSON, 3
Theodore Malvin
MATSON, William 1
MATSUDAIRA, Tsuneo 2
MATTEI, Albert Chester 5
MATTERN, David Earl 3
MATTERSON, Clarence
H. 4
MATTESON, Charles 1
MATTESON, 1
Frank Willington
MATTESON, 3
Herman Howard
MATTESON, Joel Aldrich H
MATTESON,
Leonard Jerome
MATTESON,
Orsamus Benajah
MATTESON, H
Tompkins Harrison
MATTESON, Victor
Andre 5
MATTFELD, Marie 5
MATTHAEI,
Frederick Carl
MATTHAI, 3
Joseph Fleming
MATTHAI, William Henry 4
MATTHES,
Francois Emile
MATTHES, 3
Gerard Hendrik
MATTHEW, Allan
Pomeroy
MATTHEW, 1
William Diller
MATTHEWMAN, 1
Lisle 'de Vaux
MATTHEWS, Albert * 2
MATTHEWS, Armstrong
R. 3
MATTHEWS, Arthur John 2
MATTHEWS, Brander 1
MATTHEWS, Burrows 3
MATTHEWS, 4
Charles Herbert
MATTHEWS, 5
Charles Samuel
MATTHEWS, Claude H

MCANDREW, James William 1
MCANDREW, William 1
MCANDREW, William Robert 5
MCANDREWS, James 2
MCANENY, William Joseph
MCANENY, George 3
MCANNEY, B. O. 4
MCARDLE, Joseph A. 4
MCARDLE, Montrose Pallen 4
MCARDLE, Thomas Eugene 4
MCARTHUR, Clifton Nesmith 1
MCARTHUR, Duncan H
MCARTHUR, John H
MCARTHUR, John 1
MCARTHUR, Lewis Linn 1
MCARTHUR, Lewis Linn Jr. 3
MCARTHUR, William Pope H
MCARTHUR, William Taylor 1
MCATEE, John Lind 1
MCAULEY, Thomas H
MCAULIFFE, Cornelius
MCAULIFFE, Daniel J. 3
MCAULIFFE, Eugene 3
MCAULIFFE, John 4
MCAULIFFE, Joseph John 2
MCAULIFFE, Maurice Francis 2
MCAVITY, Malcolm 2
MCAVOY, Charles D. 1
MCAVOY, John Vincent
MC AVOY, Thomas D. 4
MCAVOY, Thomas Timothy 5
MCBAIN, Howard Lee 1
MCBAIN, James William 3
MCBAINE, James Patterson 4
MCBEAN, Thomas H
MCBEATH, James Mark 4
MCBEE, Earl Thurston 5
MCBEE, Mary Vardrine 4
MCBEE, Silas 1
MCBRAYER, Louis Burgin
MCBRIDE, Allan Clay 2
MCBRIDE, Andrew Jay 4
MCBRIDE, F. Scott 3
MCBRIDE, George McCutchen 5
MCBRIDE, George Wickliffe 1
MCBRIDE, Harold Herkimer 4
MCBRIDE, Harry Alexander 4
MCBRIDE, Henry 1
MCBRIDE, James Harvey 1
MCBRIDE, Karl R. Sr. 1
MCBRIDE, Malcolm Lee 2
MCBRIDE, Robert Edwin 2
MCBRIDE, Robert W. 1
MCBRIDE, Thomas Allen 1
MCBRIDE, William Manley 3
MCBRIEN, Dean Depew 1
MCBRIEN, Jasper Leonidas
MCBROOM, Charles Emmett 4
MCBRYDE, Archibald H
MCBRYDE, Charles Neil 5
MCBRYDE, James Bolton 1
MCBRYDE, John McLaren 1
MCBRYDE, Warren Horton 5
MCBURNEY, Charles
MCBURNEY, John White 4
MCBURNEY, Ralph
MCBURNEY, Robert Ross H
MCCABE, Charles B. 5
MCCABE, Charles Cardwell 1
MCCABE, Charles Martin 5
MCCABE, Edward Raynsford Warner
MCCABE, Francis Xavier 5
MCCABE, Harriet Calista 1
MCCABE, James Dabney H
MCCABE, John Collins 1
MCCABE, Lida Rose 1
MCCABE, W. Gordon 1
MCCABE, William Hugh 4
MCCADDEN, John Edward 4

MCCAFFERTY, Thomas Bowles 3
MCCAFFERY, Richard Stanislaus 2
MCCAFFREY, John H
MCCAGG, Ezra Butler 1
MCCAHAN, David 1
MCCAIG, William Dougal 3
MCCAIN, Charles Curtice 2
MCCAIN, Charles Simonton 3
MCCAIN, Dewey Marven 4
MCCAIN, George Nox 1
MCCAIN, Henry Pinckney 1
MCCAIN, James Ross 4
MCCAIN, John Sidney 1
MCCAIN, Paul Pressly 2
MCCAIN, Samuel Adams 4
MCCAINE, Alexander H
MCCALEB, Ella 1
MCCALEB, John Bell 1
MCCALEB, Theodore Howard H
MCCALEB, Walter Flavius 5
MCCALL, Arthur G. 3
MCCALL, Edward Everett 1
MCCALL, Edward Rutledge H
MCCALL, Fred(erick) B(ays) 5
MCCALL, Harry 4
MCCALL, John A. 1
MCCALL, John Etheridge 1
MCCALL, Milton Lawrence 4
MCCALL, Oswald Walter Samuel 3
MCCALL, Peter H
MCCALL, Samuel Walker 1
MCCALL, Thomas 2
MCCALL, Thomas Montgomery 4
MCCALLA, Albert 1
MCCALLA, Bowman Henry 1
MCCALLA, Elizabeth Hazard Sargent 4
MCCALLA, William Latta H
MCCALLAM, James Alexander 5
MCCALLEY, Henry 1
MCCALLIE, Robert Lewis 4
MCCALLIE, Samuel Washington
MCCALLIE, Spencer Jarnagin 2
MCCALLIE, Thomas Spencer 1
MCCALLUM, Angus 5
MCCALLUM, Daniel Craig H
MCCALLUM, Francis Marion 2
MCCAMANT, Wallace 2
MCCAMBRIDGE, William J. 4
MCCAMEY, Harold Emerson
MCCAMIC, Charles 3
MCCAMMON, George Edward 4
MCCAMMON, Joseph Kay
MCCAMMON, Milo Franklin
MCCAMPBELL, Charles Wilbur 4
MCCAMPBELL, Eugene Franklin
MCCAMPBELL, Leavelle 2
MCCANCE, Pressly Hodge 4
MCCANDLESS, Bruce 5
MCCANDLESS, David Alexander
MCCANDLESS, James W. 4
MCCANDLESS, John Andrew
MCCANDLESS, Lincoln Loy 1
MCCANDLESS, Robert Buchanan 3
MCCANDLISS, Lester Chipman
MCCANN, Alfred W. 1
MCCANN, Charles Mallette 3
MCCANN, George 1
MCCANN, Harold Gilman 5
MCCANN, Harrison King 4
MCCANN, James J. 4
MCCANN, R. L. 5
MCCANN, Rebecca 1
MCCANN, Robert Caldwell 4

MCCANN, Thomas Addison 2
MCCANN, William Penn 1
MCCANN, William Sharp 5
MCCANTS, E. Crayton 3
MCCARDELL, Claire 3
MCCARDELL, Lee Adrian 4
MCCARDELL, Roy Larcom 5
MCCARDLE, Carl Wesley 5
MCCAREY, Thomas) Leo 5
MCCARL, John Raymond 1
MCCARRAN, Jeff 2
MCCARRAN, Patrick A. 3
MCCARREN, Patrick H. 1
MCCARRENS, John S. 2
MCCARROLL, Henry Relton 5
MCCARROLL, James H
MCCARROLL, Russell Hudson 2
MCCARROLL, William 1
MCCARTAN, Edward 2
MCCARTEE, Divie Bethune H
MCCARTER, Henry 2
MCCARTER, James W. 1
MCCARTER, Margaret Hill 1
MCCARTER, Robert Harris 1
MCCARTER, Thomas Nesbitt 3
MCCARTER, Thomas Nesbitt
MCCARTER, Thomas Nesbitt Jr.
MCCARTER, Uzal H. 1
MCCARTHY, Carlton 4
MCCARTHY, Charles 1
MCCARTHY, Charles Hallan 2
MCCARTHY, Charles James 1
MCCARTHY, Daniel Edward 1
MCCARTHY, Daniel J. 3
MCCARTHY, Denis Aloysius 1
MCCARTHY, Dennis H
MCCARTHY, Edward 4
MCCARTHY, Edward 5
MCCARTHY, Eugene 4
MCCARTHY, Eugene Ross 5
MCCARTHY, Frank Jeremiah 3
MCCARTHY, Henry Francis 4
MCCARTHY, James Anthony Joseph 1
MCCARTHY, James E. 3
MCCARTHY, James Frederick 1
MCCARTHY, John E. 4
MCCARTHY, John Ralph 4
MCCARTHY, Joseph Edward 1
MCCARTHY, Joseph Francis 4
MCCARTHY, Joseph R. 5
MCCARTHY, Justin Howard
MCCARTHY, Kathryn O'loughlin 3
MCCARTHY, Kenneth Cecil 4
MCCARTHY, Leighton Goldie 3
MCCARTHY, Louise Roblee (Mrs. Eugene Ross Mccarthy) 5
MCCARTHY, Michael Henry 1
MCCARTHY, P. H. 5
MCCARTHY, William Henry
MCCARTHY, Wilson 3
MCCARTNEY, Albert Joseph 4
MCCARTNEY, James Lincoln 5
MCCARTNEY, James S. 4
MCCARTNEY, Mary Elizabeth Maxwell H
MCCARTNEY, Washington H
MCCARTY, Andrew Zimmerman H
MCCARTY, C. Walter 4
MCCARTY, Dan 3
MCCARTY, E(dward) Prosper 5
MCCARTY, Johnathan H
MCCARTY, Milburn 4
MCCARTY, Orin Philip 1

MCCARTY, Richard H
MCCARTY, Richard Justin 3
MCCARTY, Sidney Louis 5
MCCARTY, Thomas J.
MCCARTY, William Mason H
MCCARTY, William Murdock 1
MCCARTY, William T. 5
MCCASH, Isaac Newton 5
MCCASKEY, Charles Irving 3
MCCASKEY, Hiram Dryer 1
MCCASKEY, John Piersol 3
MCCASKEY, William Spencer 1
MCCASKILL, Oliver LeRoy 3
MCCASKILL, Virgil Everett 1
MCCASLIN, Robert Horace 3
MCCAUGHAN, Russell Craig 3
MCCAUGHAN, William John 1
MCCAULEY, Calvin Hudson 1
MCCAULEY, Charles Adam Hoke 4
MCCAULEY, Charles Stewart H
MCCAULEY, Clayton M. 3
MCCAULEY, David Vincent 1
MCCAULEY, Edward Yorke H
MCCAULEY, James Wayne 3
MCCAULEY, Jeremiah 1
MCCAULEY, Lena May 1
MCCAULEY, Mary Ludwig Hays H
MCCAULEY, William Fletcher 1
MCCAUSLEN, William Cochran H
MCCAUSTLAND, Elmer James 5
MCCAW, Henry 3
MCCAW, Walter Drew 1
MCCAWLEY, Alfred L. 4
MCCAWLEY, Charles Grymes H
MCCAWLEY, Charles Laurie 1
MCCAY, Bruce Benjamin 4
MCCAY, Charles Francis H
MCCAY, Leroy Wiley 1
MCCELLAN, Bryon Charles 2
MCCHESNEY, Calvin Stewart 1
MCCHESNEY, Dora Greenwell 1
MCCHESNEY, Elizabeth Studdiford 1
MCCHESNEY, May Louise (Logan) 5
MCCHESNEY, Wilbert Renwick 2
MCCHORD, Charles Caldwell 1
MCCLAIN, Dayton Ernest 5
MCCLAIN, Edward Lee 1
MCCLAIN, Emlin 1
MCCLAIN, John Wilcox 4
MCCLAIN, Joseph A, Jr. 5
MCCLAIN, Josiah
MCCLAMMY, Charles Washington H
MCCLANAHAN, Ellis Joshua 4
MCCLANAHAN, Harry Monroe 1
MCCLARAN, John Walter 3
MCCLARY, Nelson Alvin 3
MCCLASKEY, Henry Morrison, Jr. 5
MCCLATCHY, Carlos Kelly 1
MCCLATCHY, Charles Kenny 1
MCCLATCHY, Valentine Stuart 1
MCCLAUGHRY, Robert Wilson 1
MCCLAVE, Charles Rowley
MCCLEAN, Harry J. 4
MCCLEAN, Moses H
MCCLEARY, James Thompson 1

MCCLEARY, Robert Altwig 5
MCCLEAVE, Robert 5
MCCLEERY, James H
MCCLELLAN, Abraham H
MCCLELLAN, Carswell H
MCCLELLAN, Elisabeth 1
MCCLELLAN, George H
MCCLELLAN, George Brinton H
MCCLELLAN, George Brinton 1
MCCLELLAN, Henry Brainerd 1
MCCLELLAN, John 1
MCCLELLAN, John Jasper 1
MCCLELLAN, Robert H
MCCLELLAN, Thomas Cowan
MCCLELLAN, Thomas Nicholas
MCCLELLAN, William 3
MCCLELLAND, Charles P. 2
MCCLELLAND, Charles Samuel 1
MCCLELLAND, George William
MCCLELLAND, Harold Mark 4
MCCLELLAND, Henry Thom 4
MCCLELLAND, James Farley 3
MCCLELLAND, James Henderson 4
MCCLELLAND, Robert H
MCCLELLAND, Ross St. John 5
MCCLELLAND, Silas Edward 3
MCCLELLAND, T. Calvin
MCCLELLAND, Thomas 1
MCCLELLAND, William H
MCCLELLAND, William 4
MCCLEMENT, William Craig
MCCLEMENT, John Hall 1
MCCLENACHAN, Blair H
MCCLENAGHAN, George Pinckney
MCCLENAHAN, David A. 4
MCCLENAHAN, Howard 1
MCCLENAHAN, Perry Eugene 5
MCCLENAHAN, Robert Stewart 5
MCCLENCH, William Wallace
MCCLENE, James H
MCCLENNEN, Edward Francis 2
MCCLENNY, George L. 2
MCCLERNAND, Edward John 1
MCCLERNAND, John A. 1
MCCLINTIC, George Warwick 2
MCCLINTIC, Guthrie 4
MCCLINTIC, Howard H. 2
MCCLINTIC, James V. 2
MCCLINTIC, Robert Hofferd 5
MCCLINTOCK, Andrew Hamilton 1
MCCLINTOCK, Earl Irving 4
MCCLINTOCK, Emory 1
MCCLINTOCK, Euphemia E. 5
MCCLINTOCK, Gilbert Stuart 1
MCCLINTOCK, Harry Winfred 5
MCCLINTOCK, J. O. 4
MCCLINTOCK, James Harvey 1
MCCLINTOCK, John Calvin 5
MCCLINTOCK, John Calvin
MCCLINTOCK, Mary Law 1
MCCLINTOCK, Miller 3
MCCLINTOCK, Norman 1
MCCLINTOCK, Oliver 1
MCCLINTOCK, Walter 2
MCCLISH, Eli
MCCLOSKEY, James Paul 2
MCCLOSKEY, John H
MCCLOSKEY, John Francis 3
MCCLOSKEY, Manus 5

MCCLOSKEY, Matthew H. 5
MCCLOSKEY, Robert Green 5
MCCLOSKEY, Thomas David 5
MCCLOSKEY, William George 1
MCCLOUD, Bentley Grimes 3
MCCLOUD, Charles A. 1
MCCLOUD, Earl 3
MCCLOW, Lloyd L. 5
MCCLOY, Charles Harold 3
MCCLUNG, Calvin Morgan 1
MCCLUNG, Clarence Erwin 2
MCCLUNG, George Harlan 3
MCCLUNG, Hugh Lawson 1
MCCLUNG, Lee 1
MCCLUNG, Reid Lage 4
MCCLUNG, Will Clinton 1
MCCLUNG, William H. 3
MCCLURE, Alexander Kelly 1
MCCLURE, Alexander Wilson H
MCCLURE, Alfred James Pollock 4
MCCLURE, Charles H
MCCLURE, Charles Freeman Williams 3
MCCLURE, Charles Wylie 4
MCCLURE, Daniel E. 4
MCCLURE, George H
MCCLURE, George Henry 4
MCCLURE, Howard (Orton) 5
MCCLURE, James Gore King 1
MCCLURE, James Gore King 3
MCCLURE, John Clarence 4
MCCLURE, Marjorie Barkley 4
MCCLURE, Martha 2
MCCLURE, Matthew Thompson Jr. 4
MCCLURE, Meade Lowrie 1
MCCLURE, Nathaniel Fish 2
MCCLURE, Norman Egbert 4
MCCLURE, Robert A. 3
MCCLURE, Robert Owen 3
MCCLURE, Roy Donaldson 3
MCCLURE, Samuel Grant 2
MCCLURE, Samuel Sidney 2
MCCLURE, W. Frank 3
MCCLURE, Walter Tennant 4
MCCLURE, William L. 3
MCCLURE, Worth 4
MCCLURG, Alexander Caldwell
MCCLURG, James H
MCCLURG, Joseph Washington H
MCCLURG, Walter Audubon 1
MCCLURKIN, John Knox
MCCLURKIN, Robert 3
MCCLURKIN, Robert J. G. 3
MCCLUSKEY, Edmund Roberts 4
MCCLUSKEY, Thomas Joseph 1
MCCOACH, David Jr. 3
MCCOBB, Paul (Winthrop) 5
MCCOLL, Jay Robert 1
MCCOLL, Robert Boyd 5
MCCOLLESTER, Lee Sullivan 2
MCCOLLESTER, Parker 3
MCCOLLESTER, Sullivan Holman 1
MCCOLLOCH, Frank Cleveland 5
MCCOLLOM, John Hildreth 1
MCCOLLOM, Vivian C. 4
MCCOLLUM, Earl 2
MCCOLLUM, Elmer Verner 4
MCCOMAS, Francis John 1
MCCOMAS, Henry Clay 5
MCCOMAS, Louis Emory 1
MCCOMAS, O. Parker 3
MCCOMAS, William H

MCCOMB, Arthur James 3
MCCOMB, Edgar 3
MCCOMB, Eleazer H
MCCOMB, John H
MCCOMB, Samuel 4
MCCOMB, William 4
MCCOMB, William Andrew 1
MCCOMB, William Randolph 3
MCCOMBS, Carl Esselstyn 2
MCCOMBS, Vernon Monroe 3
MCCOMBS, William Frank 4
MCCONACHIE, Harry Steele 5
MCCONACHIE, Lauros Grant
MCCONATHY, Osbourne 2
MCCONAUGHY, James 1
MCCONAUGHY, James Lukens 2
MCCONAUGHY, Robert 1
MCCONIHE, Malcolm Stuart 5
MCCONN, Charles Maxwell 3
MCCONNAUGHEY, George Carlton 4
MCCONNAUGHEY, Robert Kendall 4
MCCONNEL, John Ludlum H
MCCONNEL, Mervin Gilbert 3
MCCONNEL, Murray 4
MCCONNEL, Roger Harmon 5
MCCONNELL, Andrew M. 5
MCCONNELL, Charles Melvin 3
MCCONNELL, Felix Grundy H
MCCONNELL, Fernando Coello 1
MCCONNELL, Fowler Beery 4
MCCONNELL, Francis John 3
MCCONNELL, Franz Marshall 5
MCCONNELL, H. Hugh 3
MCCONNELL, H. S. 3
MCCONNELL, Herbert S(tevenson) 5
MCCONNELL, Ira Welch 1
MCCONNELL, James Eli 1
MCCONNELL, James Moore 3
MCCONNELL, John Preston 4
MCCONNELL, Joseph Moore 1
MCCONNELL, Lincoln 1
MCCONNELL, Luther Graham 4
MCCONNELL, Robert Darll 5
MCCONNELL, Robert Perche 5
MCCONNELL, Roy F. 4
MCCONNELL, Samuel David 1
MCCONNELL, Samuel Parsons 1
MCCONNELL, W. Joseph 3
MCCONNELL, Wallace Robert 4
MCCONNELL, William J. 1
MCCONNICO, Andrew Jackson 5
MCCONWAY, William 1
MCCOOK, Alexander McDowell 1
MCCOOK, Anson George 1
MCCOOK, Edward Moody 1
MCCOOK, Henry Christopher 1
MCCOOK, John James 1
MCCOOK, Willis Fisher 1
MCCORD, Alvin Carr 3
MCCORD, Andrew H
MCCORD, David James H
MCCORD, George Herbert 4
MCCORD, James Nance 5
MCCORD, Joseph 2
MCCORD, Joseph Alexander 4
MCCORD, Leon 4
MCCORD, Louisa Susanna Cheves H
MCCORD, Myron Hawley 1

MCCORD, Robert D. 4
MCCORD, William Clay 4
MCCORD, William H. 4
MCCORKLE, Graham K. 4
MCCORKLE, Joseph Walker H
MCCORKLE, Thomas Smith 3
MCCORMAC, Eugene Irving 2
MCCORMACK, Alfred 3
MCCORMACK, Arthur Thomas 3
MCCORMACK, Buren H. 5
MCCORMACK, Emmet J. 4
MCCORMACK, George Bryant 1
MCCORMACK, John 2
MCCORMACK, Joseph Nathaniel 1
MCCORMACK, M. Harriet Joyce (mrs. John W. Mccormack) 1
MCCORMACK, Thomas Joseph 1
MCCORMICK, Albert Edward 4
MCCORMICK, Albert M. D. 1
MCCORMICK, Alexander Agnew 5
MCCORMICK, Alexander Hugh 1
MCCORMICK, Andrew Phelps 1
MCCORMICK, Anne O'hare 3
MCCORMICK, Bradley Thomas 3
MCCORMICK, Charles Perry 5
MCCORMICK, Charles Tilford 4
MCCORMICK, Charles Wesley 1
MCCORMICK, Chauncey 3
MCCORMICK, Cyrus 5
MCCORMICK, Cyrus Hall H
MCCORMICK, Cyrus Hall 1
MCCORMICK, David 4
MCCORMICK, Donald 2
MCCORMICK, Edith Rockefeller 1
MCCORMICK, Edmund Burke 1
MCCORMICK, Ernest O. 5
MCCORMICK, Fowler 5
MCCORMICK, Frederick 3
MCCORMICK, George Chalmers 5
MCCORMICK, George Wellesley 3
MCCORMICK, Gertrude Howard (Mrs. Vance C. Mccormick) 5
MCCORMICK, Gertrude Howard 3
MCCORMICK, Harold Fowler 1
MCCORMICK, Harriet Hammond 1
MCCORMICK, Henry Buehler 1
MCCORMICK, Howard 2
MCCORMICK, James Robinson H
MCCORMICK, James Thomas 3
MCCORMICK, John Dale 4
MCCORMICK, John Francis 2
MCCORMICK, John Henry 5
MCCORMICK, John Newton 1
MCCORMICK, John Vincent 5
MCCORMICK, Langdon 3
MCCORMICK, Leander Hamilton 1
MCCORMICK, Leander J. 1
MCCORMICK, Lynde Dupuy 3
MCCORMICK, Marshall 1
MCCORMICK, Medill 1
MCCORMICK, Myron 4
MCCORMICK, Patrick Joseph 3
MCCORMICK, Paul 1
MCCORMICK, Paul John 4
MCCORMICK, R. Hall 1
MCCORMICK, Richard Cunnigham 1
MCCORMICK, Robert H
MCCORMICK, Robert Elliott 5

MCCORMICK, Robert Hall 4
MCCORMICK, Robert Laird 1
MCCORMICK, Robert Rutherford 3
MCCORMICK, Robert Sanderson 1
MCCORMICK, Samuel Black 1
MCCORMICK, Stephen H
MCCORMICK, Thomas Carson 3
MCCORMICK, Thomas Gerard 4
MCCORMICK, Vance Criswell 2
MCCORMICK, William 5
MCCORMICK, William Bernard 3
MCCORMICK, William Laird 1
MCCORMICK, Willoughby M. 1
MCCORNACK, John Knox 1
MCCORT, John J. 4
MCCORVEY, Gessner Tutwiler 1
MCCORVEY, Thomas Chalmers H
MCCOSH, Andrew J. 3
MCCOSH, James 4
MCCOSKER, Alfred Justin 2
MCCOTTER, Cyrus Rawson 3
MCCOURT, Walter Edward 5
MCCOWEN, Edward Oscar 3
MCCOWN, Albert 5
MCCOWN, Chester Charlton 2
MCCOWN, Edward C. 5
MCCOWN, Theodore Doney 5
MCCOY, Bernice 1
MCCOY, Daniel H
MCCOY, Elijah 4
MCCOY, Elijah 3
MCCOY, Frank Ross 1
MCCOY, George Walter H
MCCOY, Henry Bayard 2
MCCOY, Henry Kent H
MCCOY, Herbert Newby 1
MCCOY, Horace Lyman 3
MCCOY, Isaac 4
MCCOY, James Henry 5
MCCOY, John Hall 5
MCCOY, John Willard 4
MCCOY, Robert H
MCCOY, Samuel Duff 1
MCCOY, Walter Irving 5
MCCOY, Whitley Peterson 3
MCCOY, William H
MCCOY, William Daniel 3
MCCRACKEN, Charles Chester 4
MCCRACKEN, Harlan Linneus 5
MCCRACKEN, Robert James 5
MCCRACKEN, Robert McDowell 4
MCCRACKEN, Samuel 1
MCCRACKEN, Thomas Cooke 1
MCCRACKEN, William Denison 1
MCCRACKIN, Josephine Clifford 1
MCCRADY, Edward 5
MCCRADY, John 4
MCCRAE, Thomas 4
MCCRAKEN, Tracy Stephenson 4
MCCRARY, Alvin Jasper H
MCCRARY, George Washington 5
MCCRARY, John Alva 3
MCCRARY, John Raymond H
MCCRATE, John Dennis 3
MCCRAW, William 1
MCCRAY, Warren T. 1
MCCREA, Annette E. 3
MCCREA, Archie Elbert 1
MCCREA, Charles Harold 1
MCCREA, James 1
MCCREA, James Alexander 1
MCCREA, Nelson Glenn 3
MCCREA, Roswell Cheney 1
MCCREA, Tully

MCCREADY, Robert Thompson Miller 2
MCCREARY, George Boone 5
MCCREARY, George Deardorff 1
MCCREARY, James Bennett H
MCCREARY, John H
MCCREATH, Andrew S. 4
MCCREDIE, Marion Macmaster H
MCCREERY, Charles H
MCCREERY, Donald Chalmers
MCCREERY, Elbert L. 1
MCCREERY, Fenton Reuben 1
MCCREERY, James W. 1
MCCREERY, Thomas Clay H
MCCREERY, William H
MCCREIGHT, George Artemus 4
MCCROREY, Henry Lawrence 3
MCCRORY, Samuel Henry 5
MCCRORY, Wilton Wade 5
MCCROSKY, Theodore Tremain 4
MCCROSSIN, Edward Francis 4
MCCROSSIN, William Patrick Jr. 5
MCCRUM, Blanche Prichard 1
MCCUE, C. A. 4
MCCUE, Frank Love 4
MCCUISH, John B. 3
MCCULLAGH, George C 3
MCCULLAGH, John 4
MCCULLAGH, Joseph Burbridge H
MCCULLERS, Carson Smith 5
MCCULLEY, Bruce 3
MCCULLEY, Johnston H
MCCULLOCH, Ben 2
MCCULLOCH, Catharine Waugh 1
MCCULLOCH, Champe Carter Jr. 2
MCCULLOCH, Charles Alexander 1
MCCULLOCH, Duncan 2
MCCULLOCH, Edgar Allen 1
MCCULLOCH, Frank Hathorn H
MCCULLOCH, George 1
MCCULLOCH, Hugh 3
MCCULLOCH, James Edward H
MCCULLOCH, John 4
MCCULLOCH, John Wellington H
MCCULLOCH, Oscar Carleton 1
MCCULLOCH, Philip Doddridge 1
MCCULLOCH, Richard 3
MCCULLOCH, Robert 3
MCCULLOCH, Roscoe Conkling 3
MCCULLOCH, Walter Fraser 3
MCCULLOCH, William Alexander 3
MCCULLOCH, William Edward H
MCCULLOGH, Thomas Grubb 1
MCCULLOH, Allan H
MCCULLOH, Charles Sears 5
MCCULLOH, James Sears H
MCCULLOUGH, Campbell Rogers 1
MCCULLOUGH, Ernest 4
MCCULLOUGH, Hall Park H
MCCULLOUGH, Hiram R. 1
MCCULLOUGH, James E. 5
MCCULLOUGH, John H
MCCULLOUGH, John Griffith 1
MCCULLOUGH, Joseph Allen 1
MCCULLOUGH, Myrtle Reed 1

MCCULLOUGH, Myrtle Reed 2
MCCULLOUGH, Richard Philip 4
MCCULLOUGH, Theodore Wilson 1
MCCULLOUGH, Willis 2
MCCUMBER, Porter James 1
MCCUNE, Charles Nathaniel 4
MCCUNE, George Shannon
MCCUNE, Henry Long 2
MCCUNE, Samuel L. 1
MCCUNN, John Niven 4
MCCUNNIFF, William Barlow 5
MCCURDY, Arthur Williams 4
MCCURDY, Charles William
MCCURDY, Fleming Blanchard 3
MCCURDY, Irwin Pounds 1
MCCURDY, James Huff 1
MCCURDY, Laurence 4
MCCURDY, Merle M. 5
MCCURDY, Richard Aldrich 1
MCCURDY, Stewart LeRoy 1
MCCURDY, Thomas Alexander 1
MCCURDY, William Edward 4
MCCUSKER, Hubert Joseph 4
MCCUTCHAN, Robert Guy 5
MCCUTCHAN, Robert Guy 3
MCCUTCHEN, Edward Johnson 1
MCCUTCHEN, George 3
MCCUTCHEN, Samuel Proctor 4
MCCUTCHEON, John Tinney 2
MCCUTCHEON, Keith Barr 5
MCCUTCHEON, Malcolm Wallace 5
MCCUTCHEON, Otis Eddy 1
MCCUTCHEON, Roger Philip 4
MCCUTHCHEON, Ben Frederick 1
MCCUTHCHEON, George Barr 1
MCDANIEL, Arthur Bee 2
MCDANIEL, Edward Davies 4
MCDANIEL, George White 1
MCDANIEL, Henry Bonner 5
MCDANIEL, Henry Dickerson 1
MCDANIEL, Lodowick 4
MCDANIEL, Reuben E. 1
MCDANIEL, Sanders 5
MCDANIEL, Walton Brooks
MCDANIEL, William 1
MCDANIELS, Joseph Hetherington
MCDANNALD, Alexander H. 3
MCDANNALD, Clyde Elliott 2
MCDAVITT, Thomas 1
MCDEARMON, James Calvin H
MCDERMOTT, Allan Langdon 1
MCDERMOTT, Arthur Vincent 2
MCDERMOTT, Charles J. 1
MCDERMOTT, Edward John 1
MCDERMOTT, Frank 1
MCDERMOTT, George Robert
MCDERMOTT, George Thomas 1
MCDERMOTT, Jack Chipman 4
MCDERMOTT, James Thomas 5
MCDERMOTT, Michael James
MCDERMOTT, R. Thomas 5
MCDERMOTT, William F. 3

MCDEVITT, George Edwin 5
MCDEVITT, James Lawrence 4
MCDEVITT, Philip R. 1
MCDIARMID, Erret Weir H
MCDILL, Alexander Stuart
MCDILL, James Wilson 1
MCDILL, John Rich 1
MCDOEL, William Henry 4
MCDONALD, Alexander 1
MCDONALD, Alexander 4
MCDONALD, Alexander Roderick
MCDONALD, Allen Colfax 2
MCDONALD, Angus Daniel 2
MCDONALD, Bill 5
MCDONALD, Charles Henry
MCDONALD, Charles James H
MCDONALD, Charles Sanford 1
MCDONALD, Edward Francis H
MCDONALD, Edwin C. 5
MCDONALD, Ellice 3
MCDONALD, Etta Austin Blaisdell 5
MCDONALD, Eugene F. Jr. 3
MCDONALD, Florin Lee 4
MCDONALD, Frederick Honour 5
MCDONALD, Harl 1
MCDONALD, Harry A. 4
MCDONALD, Howard 1
MCDONALD, Hunter 1
MCDONALD, James Grover 3
MCDONALD, James 1
MCDONALD, James Richard
MCDONALD, James Walton 3
MCDONALD, Jesse Fuller 2
MCDONALD, Jessie Claire
MCDONALD, John B. 1
MCDONALD, John Bacon 1
MCDONALD, John Daniel 3
MCDONALD, John Samuel 1
MCDONALD, Joseph Albert 4
MCDONALD, Joseph Ewing H
MCDONALD, Joseph John 5
MCDONALD, Karola Jenny 5
MCDONALD, Lloyd Davison 3
MCDONALD, Margaret Puth (Mrs. Thomas H. Mcdonald, Jr.)
MCDONALD, Morris 1
MCDONALD, Roy William 5
MCDONALD, Samuel F. 5
MCDONALD, Stewart 3
MCDONALD, Thomas Edward 1
MCDONALD, W. Stewart 4
MCDONALD, William 2
MCDONALD, William C. 1
MCDONALD, William Douglas 4
MCDONALD, William James 2
MCDONALD, William Jesse
MCDONALD, Witten 1
MCDONNELL, Charles Edward 1
MCDONNELL, Donald N. 5
MCDONNELL, Edward Orrick 4
MCDONNELL, Thomas Francis Irving 1
MCDONNELL, Thomas John 4
MCDONNOUGH, James H
MCDONOGH, John H
MCDONOUGH, Frank Wheatley 2
MCDONOUGH, Gordon Leo 5
MCDONOUGH, James Buchanan 5

MCDONOUGH, John Henry 1
MCDONOUGH, John James 1
MCDONOUGH, John Justin 4
MCDONOUGH, John Thomas 4
MCDONOUGH, Roger Ignatius 4
MCDONOUGH, Thomas Francis 4
MCDOUGAL, David Stockton H
MCDOUGAL, Douglas Cassel 4
MCDOUGAL, James Barton 4
MCDOUGAL, Myrtle Archer (Mrs. Daniel Archibald Mcdougal) 5
MCDOUGALL, Alexander H
MCDOUGALL, Alexander 1
MCDOUGALL, Alexander Miller 3
MCDOUGALL, Edward George 5
MCDOUGALL, George Francis 3
MCDOUGALL, James Alexander H
MCDOUGALL, John Alexander 3
MCDOUGALL, Walter Hugh 4
MCDOUGALL, William 1
MCDOUGLE, Ernest Clifton 5
MCDOUGLE, Herbert Irwin 4
MCDOUGLE, Ivan Eugene 3
MCDOWALL, Robert Edward 5
MCDOWELL, Alexander 1
MCDOWELL, Alfred Henderson Jr. 1
MCDOWELL, Arthur Roscoe 1
MCDOWELL, Charles H
MCDOWELL, Charles Samuel Jr. 2
MCDOWELL, Clotilda Lyon 3
MCDOWELL, Edmund Wilson 4
MCDOWELL, Ephraim H
MCDOWELL, George Stanley
MCDOWELL, Henry Burden 1
MCDOWELL, Henry Clay H
MCDOWELL, Irvin H
MCDOWELL, James H
MCDOWELL, James Foster H
MCDOWELL, John 1
MCDOWELL, John 3
MCDOWELL, John Anderson
MCDOWELL, John Sherman 1
MCDOWELL, Joseph H
MCDOWELL, Joseph Jefferson
MCDOWELL, Louise Sherwood 4
MCDOWELL, Mary E. 1
MCDOWELL, Philetus H(arold) 2
MCDOWELL, Rachel Kollock
MCDOWELL, Ralph Walker 1
MCDOWELL, Tremaine 3
MCDOWELL, William Fraser 1
MCDOWELL, William George
MCDOWELL, William Osborne 4
MCDUFFIE, Duncan 3
MCDUFFIE, George H
MCDUFFIE, John 3
MCDUFFIE, John Van H
MCDUFFIE, William C. 4
MCEACHERN, Daniel Victor 5
MCEACHERN, John Newton 3
MCEACHRON, Duncan Lendrum 1
MCEACHRON, Karl Boyer 3
MCELDOWNEY, Charles Roy 3

MCELDOWNEY, Henry C. 1
MCELDUFF, John Vincent 3
MCELFRESH, William Edward 2
MCELHANY, J. L. 3
MCELHINNEY, John H. 3
MCELMELL, Jackson 5
MCELRATH, Thomas H
MCELREATH, Walter 3
MCELROY, Benjamin Lincoln 3
MCELROY, Clarence Underwood
MCELROY, George Wightman 1
MCELROY, Henry F. 1
MCELROY, James W. 5
MCELROY, John H
MCELROY, John 1
MCELROY, Mary Arthur 1
MCELROY, Neil H. 5
MCELROY, Robert 3
MCELROY, William H. 4
MCELROY, William Thomas
MCELVEEN, William Thomas 1
MCELVENNY, Robert Talbot 4
MCELWAIN, Charles Church 5
MCELWAIN, Edwin 4
MCELWAIN, Frank Arthur 3
MCELWAIN, Henry Ely Jr. 4
MCELWAIN, J. Franklin 3
MCELWAIN, William Henry 5
MCENARY, Dale Robert 2
MCENERNEY, Garrett William
MCENERY, Samuel Douglas 1
MCENTEE, Jervis H
MCENTEGART, Bryan J. 5
MCENTIRE, Richard Brooke 3
MCEVOY, James 1
MCEVOY, Joseph Patrick 3
MCEWAN, William Leonard 1
MCEWEN, James Henry 2
MCEWEN, Merrill Clyde 4
MCEWEN, Robert Ward 3
MCFADDEN, Effie Belle 5
MCFADDEN, George 1
MCFADDEN, George H. 1
MCFADDEN, James Augustine 3
MCFADDEN, John Francis 3
MCFADDEN, Louis T. 1
MCFADDEN, Manus H
MCFADDEN, Obadiah Benton
MCFADDEN, S. Willis 4
MCFADDEN, William Hartman 3
MCFADEN, Frank Talbot 1
MCFADYEN, Bernice Musgrove
MCFALL, John Monteith 3
MCFARLAN, Duncan H
MCFARLAND, Archie J. 3
MCFARLAND, David Ford 5
MCFARLAND, Earl 3
MCFARLAND, Eugene James
MCFARLAND, Francis Patrick H
MCFARLAND, Gary 5
MCFARLAND, George Austin 1
MCFARLAND, Greyble Lewis, Jr. 5
MCFARLAND, Jean Henderson 4
MCFARLAND, John Clemson 5
MCFARLAND, John Horace 2
MCFARLAND, John Thomas 1
MCFARLAND, Joseph 2
MCFARLAND, Kermit 5
MCFARLAND, Raymond 5
MCFARLAND, Robert White 1
MCFARLAND, Russell S(cott) 5
MCFARLAND, Samuel Gamble H

MCFARLAND, Silas Clark 1
MCFARLAND, Thomas Bard 1
MCFARLAND, Thomas C. 3
MCFARLAND, Walter Martin 1
MCFARLAND, Wilfred Myers 4
MCFARLANE, Arthur Emerson 2
MCFARLANE, Charles T. 5
MCFAUL, James Augustine 1
MCFAYDEN, Donald 5
MCFEE, Henry Lee 3
MCFEE, Lapsley Armstrong 1
MCFEE, William 4
MCFEELY, Richard Harding
MCFERRIN, John Berry H
MCFETRIDGE, William Lane 5
MCFIE, John Robert 1
MCGAFFEY, Ernest 1
MCGAFFIN, Alexander 1
MCGAHAN, Paul James 5
MCGANN, Marion Eudora Hotchkiss (Mrs. James Mcgann) 4
MCGANNON, Matthew Charles 4
MCGARRAH, Albert Franklin 4
MCGARRAH, Gates W. 1
MCGARRY, William James 1
MCGARRY, William Rutledge 5
MCGARVEY, John William 1
MCGARVEY, Robert Neill 3
MCGARVEY, William 1
MCGAUGH, Elmer Thomas
MCGAUGHEY, Edward Wilson H
MCGAUGHEY, William Ray 4
MCGAUGHY, James Ralph 3
MCGAURAN, John Baptist 5
MCGAVICK, Alexander Joseph 2
MCGAVIN, Charles 5
MCGAVRAN, Edward G(rafton) 5
MCGAW, Alex James 5
MCGAW, George Keen 1
MCGEACHY, Archibald Alexander 1
MCGEE, Anita Newcomb 4
MCGEE, Clifford W. 3
MCGEE, Cushman 4
MCGEE, Homer Edgar 4
MCGEE, James Ellington 1
MCGEE, John Bernard 1
MCGEE, John Franklin 1
MCGEE, Milton 1
MCGEE, Thomas D'Arcy H
MCGEE, W. J. 1
MCGEEHAN, William O. 1
MCGEEVER, John F. 5
MCGEHEE, Harvey 5
MCGEHEE, Harvey 5
MCGEHEE, Lucius Polk 4
MCGEHEE, Micijah C. Jr. 1
MCGEOCH, John Alexander 2
MCGEORGE, William Jr. 4
MCGHEE, James E. 4
MCGHEE, Paul Ansley 1
MCGIFFERT, Arthur Cushman 1
MCGIFFERT, James 2
MCGIFFERT, Julian Esselstyn 2
MCGIFFIN, Malcolm 1
MCGIFFIN, Philo Norton 5
MCGIFFIN, William J. 3
MCGILL, Andrew Ryan 1
MCGILL, C. H. 4
MCGILL, David Frazier 1
MCGILL, George 4
MCGILL, J. Nota 1
MCGILL, James Henry 2
MCGILL, John H
MCGILL, John Dale 1
MCGILL, John Thomas 2
MCGILL, Ralph Emerson 5
MCGILL, Stephenson Waters 5

MCGILL, Thomas Julian 1
MCGILL, William L. 3
MCGILLICUDDY, Daniel John 1
MCGILLIVRAY, Alexander H
MCGILLYCUDDY, Valentine Trant O'Connell 4
MCGILVARY, Evander Bradley 3
MCGILVREY, John Edward 3
MCGINLEY, Anna Mathilda Agnes 4
MCGINLEY, Charles Calvin
MCGINLEY, Daniel Eugene 1
MCGINNESS, John Randolph 1
MCGINNIES, Joseph A. 2
MCGINNIS, Alan Ross 4
MCGINNIS, Edwin 1
MCGINNIS, Felix Signoret 2
MCGINNIS, George 4
MCGINNIS, Patrick Benedict 5
MCGINNIS, William F. 1
MCGINNIS, William Hereford 1
MCGINTY, Francis Patrick 3
MCGINTY, George Banks 1
MCGIVERAN, Stanley J. 4
MCGIVNEY, Michael Joseph H
MCGLACHLIN, Edward Fenton 2
MCGLANNAN, Alexius 1
MCGLAUFLIN, William Henry 1
MCGLENNON, Cornelius A. 1
MCGLOTHLIN, William Joseph 1
MCGLYNN, Edward 1
MCGLYNN, Frank 3
MCGOHEY, John F. X. 5
MCGOLDRICK, Thomas Aloysius 3
MCGOLRICK, James 1
MCGONAGLE, William Albert 1
MCGOODWIN, Henry Kerr 1
MCGOORTY, John P. 3
MCGOVERN, Francis Edward 2
MCGOVERN, James Lawrence 3
MCGOVERN, John 1
MCGOVERN, John Terence 4
MCGOVERN, Patrick Alphonsus 3
MCGOVERN, William Montgomery 4
MCGOVERN, William Robbins 4
MCGOVNEY, Dudley Odell 2
MCGOWAN, Arthur C. 3
MCGOWAN, Edwin W. 4
MCGOWAN, James Jr. 4
MCGOWAN, John 1
MCGOWAN, Lord 4
MCGOWAN, Samuel H
MCGOWAN, Samuel 1
MCGOWEN, James Greer 2
MCGOWN, Chester Stowe 5
MCGRADY, Edward Francis 4
MCGRADY, Thomas 1
MCGRANAHAN, James 1
MCGRANAHAN, Ralph Wilson 1
MCGRANAHAN, Raymond DePue 5
MCGRANERY, James Patrick 1
MCGRATH, Benjamin R. 1
MCGRATH, J. Howard 4
MCGRATH, James H
MCGRATH, John Joseph 3
MCGRATH, Joseph F. 3
MCGRATH, Justin 1
MCGRATH, Sister Mary 1
MCGRATH, Raymond Dyer 5
MCGRATH, William H. 3
MCGRAW, Curtis Whittlesey 3
MCGRAW, James H, Jr. 5
MCGRAW, James H. 2
MCGRAW, James J. 1
MCGRAW, John Harte

MCGRAW, John Joseph H
MCGRAW, John Joseph 4
MCGRAW, John Thomas 4
MCGRAW, Max 4
MCGRAW, Robert Bush 4
MCGRAW, Theodore Andrews 1
MCGREADY, James H
MCGREGOR, Alexander Grant 3
MCGREGOR, Douglas 4
MCGREGOR, George Wilbur 4
MCGREGOR, Gordon Roy 5
MCGREGOR, J. Harry 3
MCGREGOR, James Clyde 1
MCGREGOR, James Howard 3
MCGREGOR, Robert Gardner 2
MCGREGOR, Stuart Malcolm 4
MCGREGOR, Thomas 1
MCGREGOR, Thomas Burnett 4
MCGREGOR, Tracy W. 1
MCGREGOR, William Morrell 5
MCGREGORY, Joseph Frank 1
MCGREW, Clarence Alan 5
MCGREW, Donald Cargill 4
MCGREW, George Harrison 1
MCGREW, Henry Edwin 5
MCGREW, John Gilbert 5
MCGRIGOR, Sir Rhoderick 3
MCGROARTY, John Steven 2
MCGROARTY, Susan H
MCGUFFEY, William Holmes H
MCGUGIN, Dan E. 1
MCGUGIN, Harold 3
MCGUIGAN, F. H. 3
MCGUIGAN, Hugh 5
MCGUIGAN, Hugh (Alister) 5
MCGUIGAN, Joseph J. 5
MCGUINNESS, Eugene Joseph 3
MCGUIRE, Bird Segle 4
MCGUIRE, Charles Bonaventure H
MCGUIRE, Edgar Robinson 1
MCGUIRE, George Alexander 1
MCGUIRE, Hunter Holmes 1
MCGUIRE, James Clark 1
MCGUIRE, James K. 4
MCGUIRE, John 4
MCGUIRE, John A. 2
MCGUIRE, Joseph Deakins 1
MCGUIRE, Joseph Hubert 2
MCGUIRE, Louis David 3
MCGUIRE, Martin Rawson Patrick 5
MCGUIRE, Michael Francis 3
MCGUIRE, Murray Mason 2
MCGUIRE, Ollie Roscoe 4
MCGUIRE, Stuart 2
MCGUIRE, Ulysses Melville 1
MCGUIRE, William Anthony 1
MCGUNNEGLE, George Kennedy 4
MCGURK, Joseph F. 4
MCHALE, Kathryn 3
MCHANEY, Edgar La Fayette 2
MCHANEY, Powell B. 3
MCHARG, Henry K. 5
MCHARG, Ormsby 5
MCHATTIE, William Alexander 5
MCHATTON, Robert Lytle H
MCHENDRIE, Andrew Watson 5
MCHENRY, Carl Holbrook 4
MCHENRY, Donald Edward 4
MCHENRY, Edwin Harrison 1
MCHENRY, Henry Davis H
MCHENRY, James H
MCHENRY, John Geiser 1

MCHENRY, John Hardin H
MCHUGH, Daniel Joseph 4
MCHUGH, James F. (jimmy) 5
MCHUGH, John 1
MCHUGH, William Douglas 1
MCILHENNEY, Charles Morgan 1
MCILHENNEY, Francis Salisbury 1
MCILHENNEY, John D. 1
MCILHENNY, Edward Avery 2
MCILHENNY, John Avery 4
MCILHINEY, Parker Cairns 1
MCILROY, Malcolm Strong 3
MCILVAIN, Robert Wallace 3
MCILVAINE, Abraham Robinson H
MCILVAINE, Charles 1
MCILVAINE, Charles Pettit H
MCILVAINE, Harold Ralph Clair 4
MCILVAINE, James Hall 1
MCILVAINE, John Wilson 4
MCILVAINE, Joseph 1
MCILVAINE, William H
MCILVAINE, William Brown 2
MCILWAINE, Henry Read 1
MCILWAINE, Richard 4
MCILWAINE, William Baird 1
MCINALLY, William Keith 1
MCINDOE, Walter Duncan H
MCINERNEY, Francis Xavier 3
MCINERNEY, James Lawrence 5
MCINERNY, John Joseph 4
MCINERNY, Timothy A. 4
MCINNERNEY, Thomas H. 3
MCINNIS, Charles Ballard 5
MCINTIRE, Albert Washington 1
MCINTIRE, Charles 1
MCINTIRE, Paul Goodloe 3
MCINTIRE, Ross T. 3
MCINTIRE, Samuel H
MCINTIRE, Walter Oscar 5
MCINTIRE, Warren Wallace 1
MCINTOSH, Alexander Angus 3
MCINTOSH, Alexander Ennis 4
MCINTOSH, Arthur Tuttle 3
MCINTOSH, Burr William 2
MCINTOSH, Charles Herbert 5
MCINTOSH, Charles Kenneth 3
MCINTOSH, Donald 3
MCINTOSH, Henry Payne 1
MCINTOSH, Henry Thomas 2
MCINTOSH, James Henry 1
MCINTOSH, John Baillie 1
MCINTOSH, Joseph Wallace 3
MCINTOSH, Lachian H
MCINTOSH, Walter Kenneth 2
MCINTOSH, William H
MCINTOSH, William M. 2
MCINTYRE, Alfred Robert 2
MCINTYRE, Augustine 3
MCINTYRE, Brouwer Davis 4
MCINTYRE, Frank 2
MCINTYRE, Frederick W. 1
MCINTYRE, Hugh Henry 1
MCINTYRE, John Francis 1
MCINTYRE, John T. 3
MCINTYRE, Marvin Hunter 2
MCINTYRE, Oscar Odd 1
MCINTYRE, Robert 5
MCINTYRE, Robson Duncan 5
MCINTYRE, Rufus H
MCINTYRE, William Davis 4

MCINTYRE, William H. 2
MCISAAC, Archibald MacDonald 3
MCIVER, Charles Duncan 1
MCIVER, George Willcox 3
MCIVER, Henry 1
MCIVER, Joseph 1
MCIVER, Milo Kenneth 4
MCIVOR, Nicholas Williams 1
MCIVOR-TYNDALL, Alexander James 1
MCKAMY, David Knox 3
MCKAY, Ambrose Noble 1
MCKAY, Claude 2
MCKAY, Claude 5
MCKAY, David O. 1
MCKAY, Donald H
MCKAY, Donald Cope 3
MCKAY, Douglas 3
MCKAY, Frederick Sumner 3
MCKAY, James Iver H
MCKAY, Kenneth Ivor 2
MCKAY, Neal H. 4
MCKAY, Neil S. 4
MCKAY, Oscar Reed 2
MCKAY, Paul Leonard 5
MCKAY, Seth Shepard 5
MCKAY, Stanley Albert 4
MCKAY, Thomas Clayton 5
MCKAY, William M. 2
MCKAY, William O. 3
MCKEAG, Anna Jane 2
MCKEAN, Frank Chalmers 1
MCKEAN, Horace Grant 1
MCKEAN, Hugh Kiefer 4
MCKEAN, James Bedell H
MCKEAN, Joseph Borden H
MCKEAN, Josiah Slutts, H
MCKEAN, Samuel H
MCKEAN, Thomas 1
MCKEAN, Thomas 2
MCKEAN, William Vincent 1
MCKEAN, William Wister H
MCKECHNIE, Neil Kenneth 5
MCKECHNIE, Robert Edward 2
MCKEE, Alexander Ellsworth 1
MCKEE, Arthur G. 5
MCKEE, David Harris 4
MCKEE, David Ritchie 5
MCKEE, Frederick Chadwick 4
MCKEE, George Colin H
MCKEE, Henry S. 3
MCKEE, John H
MCKEE, John Dempster 2
MCKEE, Joseph V. 3
MCKEE, Oliver Jr. 2
MCKEE, Paul Boole 4
MCKEE, Ralph Harper 5
MCKEE, Rose 5
MCKEE, Ruth Karr 3
MCKEE, Samuel H
MCKEE, Sol Reid 4
MCKEE, William James 1
MCKEE, William Parker 1
MCKEEHAN, Charles Louis 1
MCKEEHAN, Hobart Deitrich 3
MCKEEHAN, Joseph Parker 3
MCKEEL, Ben S. 2
MCKEEN, Benjamin 2
MCKEEN, James 1
MCKEEN, Joseph H
MCKEEN, Stanley Stewart 4
MCKEEN, William Riley 5
MCKEEVER, Chauncey 1
MCKEEVER, Duncan Clark 4
MCKEEVER, Emmet G. 5
MCKEEVER, Francis Michael 5
MCKEEVER, Franklin Garrett 1
MCKEEVER, William Arch 1
MCKEIGHAN, William Arthur H
MCKEITH, David Jr. 1
MCKELL, William E. 4
MCKELLAR, Kenneth Douglas 3
MCKELVEY, Graham Norton 5
MCKELVEY, John Jay 2
MCKELVEY, S. Willis 5

MCKELVIE, Samuel Roy 3
MCKELVY, Francis Graham 3
MCKELVY, J. D. 4
MCKELWAY, Alexander Jeffrey 1
MCKELWAY, St Clair 1
MCKENDREE, William H
MCKENDRICK, Edward John 5
MCKENNA, Charles Francis 1
MCKENNA, Edward William 1
MCKENNA, Joseph 1
MCKENNA, Norbert Augustine 4
MCKENNA, Philip M. 5
MCKENNA, Roy Carnegie 3
MCKENNAN, Thomas McKean Thompson H
MCKENNAN, Thomas McKean Thompson 1
MCKENNEY, A. Carlton 3
MCKENNEY, Frederic Duncan 2
MCKENNEY, James Hall 1
MCKENNEY, Robert Lee 2
MCKENNEY, Ruth 5
MCKENNEY, Thomas Loraine H
MCKENNY, Charles 1
MCKENNY, Francis Xavier 4
MCKENTY, Jacob Kerlin H
MCKENZIE, Alexander 1
MCKENZIE, Aline 2
MCKENZIE, Fayette Avery 3
MCKENZIE, George 1
MCKENZIE, Harry Carroll 1
MCKENZIE, James A. 1
MCKENZIE, John Charles 1
MCKENZIE, John Cummings 1
MCKENZIE, John Heyward 1
MCKENZIE, Kenneth 2
MCKENZIE, Lewis H
MCKENZIE, Robert Tait 1
MCKENZIE, Roderick Duncan 1
MCKENZIE, Vernon 4
MCKENZIE, William Dexter 5
MCKENZIE, William P. 5
MCKENZIE, William White 5
MCKEOGH, Arthur 1
MCKEON, John H
MCKEON, John J. 2
MCKEOWN, Tom D. 3
MCKERNAN, Maureen (Mrs. John Cooper Ross)
MCKERNON, Edward 2
MCKERR, George Joseph 4
MCKIBBEN, Frank Pape 4
MCKIBBEN, James A. 1
MCKIBBEN, Paul Stilwell 1
MCKIBBIN, Chambers 4
MCKIBBIN, George Baldwin 1
MCKIBBIN, John 4
MCKIBBIN, Joseph Chambers H
MCKIBBIN, William 1
MCKIM, Alexander H
MCKIM, Baltimore H
MCKIM, Charles Follen 1
MCKIM, Isaac H
MCKIM, James Miller H
MCKIM, John 1
MCKIM, Judson Jackson 1
MCKIM, Randolph Harrison 1
MCKIM, William Duncan 1
MCKIMMON, Jane Simpson (Mrs. Charles Mckimmon)
MCKINLAY, Arthur Patch 3
MCKINLAY, Chauncey Angus 5
MCKINLAY, Duncan E. 1
MCKINLAY, John 3
MCKINLEY, Abner 1
MCKINLEY, Albert Edward 1
MCKINLEY, Carlyle 1
MCKINLEY, Charles Ethelbert 1
MCKINLEY, Earl Baldwin 1
MCKINLEY, Ida Saxton 1

942

MCKINLEY, J. Charnley 3
MCKINLEY, James F. 1
MCKINLEY, James Wilfred 3
MCKINLEY, John H
MCKINLEY, Lloyd 4
MCKINLEY, William 5
MCKINLEY, William 1
MCKINLEY, William Brown 1
MCKINLOCK, George Alexander 1
MCKINLY, John H
MCKINNEY, Alexander Harris 1
MCKINNEY, Annie (Valentine) Booth 5
MCKINNEY, Arthur Wesley 4
MCKINNEY, Buckner Abernathy 1
MCKINNEY, Colin Pierson 2
MCKINNEY, David 1
MCKINNEY, Frank Cowen 3
MCKINNEY, Ida Scott Taylor 5
MCKINNEY, James 1
MCKINNEY, Kate Slaughter 4
MCKINNEY, Laurence 5
MCKINNEY, Luther Franklin 3
MCKINNEY, Madge M. 3
MCKINNEY, Philip Watkins 1
MCKINNEY, Robert C. 1
MCKINNEY, Theophilus Elisha 4
MCKINNEY, Thomas Emery 1
MCKINNEY, Walter H. 3
MCKINNEY, William Mark 3
MCKINNIE, James Renwick 4
MCKINNIS, George E. Sr. 3
MCKINSEY, Folger 5
MCKINSEY, J. C. C. 3
MCKINSEY, James O. 1
MCKINSTRY, Addis Emmett 1
MCKINSTRY, Alexander 4
MCKINSTRY, Charles Hedges
MCKINSTRY, Elisha Williams H
MCKINSTRY, Grace E. 1
MCKINSTRY, Helen May 2
MCKISICK, Lewis 1
MCKISSICK, Anthony Foster
MCKISSICK, James Rion 2
MCKISSOCK, Thomas H
MCKISSON, Robert Erastus 4
MCKITTRICK, Roy 5
MCKITTRICK, Thomas Harrington
MCKITTRICK, William James 1
MCKNIGHT, Alexander G. 3
MCKNIGHT, Alexander Hearne 1
MCKNIGHT, Anna Caulfield 2
MCKNIGHT, Charles 5
MCKNIGHT, George Harley 1
MCKNIGHT, Harvey Washington
MCKNIGHT, Henry Turney 5
MCKNIGHT, James Rankin 3
MCKNIGHT, Robert H
MCKNIGHT, Roy Jerome 4
MCKONE, Don Townsend 4
MCKOWEN, John Clay 4
MCKOWN, Harry Charles 4
MCKOWNE, Frank A. 2
MCKUSICK, Marshall Noah 3
MCLACHLAN, Archibald C. 4
MCLACHLAN, James 1
MCLACHLEN, Archibald Malcolm 4
MCLAGLEN, Victor 3
MCLAIN, Chester Alden 3
MCLAIN, Frank Alexander 4
MCLAIN, John Scudder 1
MCLAIN, John Speed 1

MCLAIN, Raymond S. 3
MCLALLEN, Walter Field 4
MCLANAHAN, Austin 2
MCLANAHAN, James Xavier H
MCLANE, A.V. 5
MCLANE, Allan 1
MCLANE, Charles Lourie 5
MCLANE, James Woods 1
MCLANE, John 1
MCLANE, John Roy 5
MCLANE, Louis H
MCLANE, Patrick 5
MCLANE, Robert Milligan H
MCLANE, William Ward 1
MCLAREN, Donald 1
MCLAREN, Walter Wallace 5
MCLAREN, William Edward
MCLAREN, William Gardner 5
MCLARTY, Norman Alexander 2
MCLAUGHLIN, Allan Joseph 5
MCLAUGHLIN, Andrew Cunningham
MCLAUGHLIN, Charles V(incent) 5
MCLAUGHLIN, Chester Bentline 1
MCLAUGHLIN, Chester Bond 3
MCLAUGHLIN, Dean Benjamin 4
MCLAUGHLIN, Dorsey Elmer 2
MCLAUGHLIN, Edward H. 4
MCLAUGHLIN, Emma Moffat (Mrs. Alfred Mclaughlin) 5
MCLAUGHLIN, George Asbury 1
MCLAUGHLIN, George Dunlap 2
MCLAUGHLIN, Harold Newell 5
MCLAUGHLIN, Henry Woods 3
MCLAUGHLIN, Hugh 1
MCLAUGHLIN, J. Frank 4
MCLAUGHLIN, James 1
MCLAUGHLIN, James Campbell
MCLAUGHLIN, James Matthew 4
MCLAUGHLIN, James W. 1
MCLAUGHLIN, Joseph 1
MCLAUGHLIN, Mary Louise
MCLAUGHLIN, Melvin Orlando
MCLAUGHLIN, Paul 5
MCLAUGHLIN, Robert Samuel 5
MCLAUGHLIN, Robert William
MCLAUGHLIN, Roland Rusk 5
MCLAUGHLIN, Stuart Watts 5
MCLAUGHLIN, Thomas H. 2
MCLAURIN, Anselm Joseph 1
MCLAURIN, John Lowndes 1
MCLAUTHLIN, Herbert Weston 1
MCLAWS, Lafayette H
MCLEAISH, Robert Burns 4
MCLEAN, A. Neil 4
MCLEAN, Alney H
MCLEAN, Andrew 1
MCLEAN, Angus 1
MCLEAN, Angus Wilton 4
MCLEAN, Archibald 1
MCLEAN, Arthur Edward 1
MCLEAN, Donald 1
MCLEAN, Edward Beale 5
MCLEAN, Edward Cochrane
MCLEAN, Emily Nelson Ritchie 1
MCLEAN, Finis Ewing H
MCLEAN, Franklin Chambers 5
MCLEAN, George Payne 1
MCLEAN, Heber Hampton 5
MCLEAN, James Henry H
MCLEAN, James Stanley 3
MCLEAN, John H

MCLEAN, John Emery 4
MCLEAN, John Knox 1
MCLEAN, John M(ilton) 5
MCLEAN, John Roll 1
MCLEAN, Milton Robbins 3
MCLEAN, Ridley 1
MCLEAN, Robert Norris 4
MCLEAN, Samuel H
MCLEAN, Simon James 3
MCLEAN, Thomas Chalmers 1
MCLEAN, Walter 1
MCLEAN, William H
MCLEAN, William L. 1
MCLEAN, William L. Jr. 3
MCLEAN, William Swan Jr. 1
MCLEARY, James Harvey 1
MCLEES, Archibald H
MCLELLAN, Archibald 1
MCLELLAN, Asahel Walker 2
MCLELLAN, Hugh Dean 5
MCLELLAN, Isaac 1
MCLELLAN, Thomas George 5
MCLEMORE, Albert Sydney 2
MCLEMORE, Jeff 5
MCLENDON, Lennox Polk 5
MCLENDON, Sol Brown 4
MCLENE, Jeremiah H
MCLENEGAN, Charles Edward 1
MCLENNAN, Donald Roderick 2
MCLENNAN, Grace Tytus 1
MCLENNAN, Peter Baillie 1
MCLEOD, Alexander H
MCLEOD, Clarence John 3
MCLEOD, Frank Hilton 2
MCLEOD, Hugh H
MCLEOD, Malcolm 4
MCLEOD, Martin H
MCLEOD, Mary Louise DeMarco 5
MCLEOD, Murdoch 3
MCLEOD, N.H.f. 5
MCLEOD, Nelson Wesley 4
MCLEOD, Scott 4
MCLEOD, Thomas Gordon 1
MCLEOD, Walter Herbert 4
MCLESKEY, Waymon B. 4
MCLESTER, James Somerville 3
MCLESTER, Judson Cole Jr. 4
MCLEVY, Jasper 4
MCLIN, Anna Eva 5
M'CLINTOCK, John H
MCLOUGHLIN, John H
MCLOUTH, Donald B. 3
MCLOUTH, Lawrence Amos 1
MCLUCAS, Walter Scott 3
MCLURE, Charles Derickson 4
MCMAHAN, Anna Benneson 1
MCMAHAN, George Thomas 5
MCMAHON, Alphonse 2
MCMAHON, Amos Philip 5
MCMAHON, Arthur Laurence
MCMAHON, Bernard H
MCMAHON, Brien 3
MCMAHON, Henry George 5
MCMAHON, James 1
MCMAHON, John A. 1
MCMAHON, John Eugene 1
MCMAHON, John Joseph 1
MCMAHON, John Robert 3
MCMAHON, John Van Lear H
MCMAHON, Joseph H. 1
MCMAHON, Lawrence Stephen H
MCMAHON, Martin Thomas 1
MCMAHON, Stephen John 3
MCMAHON, Thomas F. 2
MCMAHON, Thomas J. 3
MCMAIN, Eleanor Laura 2
MCMANAMAN, Edward Peter 4
MCMANAMON, James Emmett 3
MCMANAMY, Frank 2
MCMANES, James H

MCMANES, Kenmore Mathew 5
MCMANIS, John Thomas 4
MCMANUS, Charles Edward 2
MCMANUS, George 3
MCMANUS, George Henry 5
MCMANUS, John Joseph
MCMANUS, William H
MCMARTIN, Charles 3
MCMARTIN, William Joseph 5
MCMASTER, Fitz Hugh 5
MCMASTER, Guy Humphreys H
MCMASTER, James Alphonsus H
MCMASTER, John Bach 1
MCMASTER, John Stevenson 1
MCMASTER, LeRoy 2
MCMASTER, Philip Duryee 5
MCMASTER, Ross Huntington 5
MCMASTER, William Henry,* 5
MCMASTER, William Henry 1
MCMATH, Francis Charles 1
MCMATH, Robert Edwin 5
MCMATH, Robert Emmett 4
MCMATH, Robert R. 4
MCMEANS, George Beale 1
MCMECHAN, Francis Hoeffer 1
MCMEEN, Samuel Groenendyke 1
MCMEIN, Neysa 2
MCMENAMIN, Hugh L. 2
MCMENAMY, Francis Xavier 2
MCMENIMEN, William V. 4
MCMICHAEL, Clayton 1
MCMICHAEL, Morton H
MCMICHAEL, Thomas Hanna 1
MCMILLAN, Alexander H
MCMILLAN, Alexander 4
MCMILLAN, Alfred E. 5
MCMILLAN, Charles 1
MCMILLAN, Claude Richelieu 4
MCMILLAN, Daniel Hugh 4
MCMILLAN, Duncan J. 1
MCMILLAN, Edward John 4
MCMILLAN, Fred Orville 3
MCMILLAN, George Scholefield 5
MCMILLAN, Homer 3
MCMILLAN, James Thayer 1
MCMILLAN, James Winning 2
MCMILLAN, Neil Alexander 1
MCMILLAN, Philip Hamilton 1
MCMILLAN, Putnam Dana 4
MCMILLAN, Robert Johnston 2
MCMILLAN, Samuel 4
MCMILLAN, Samuel James Renwick H
MCMILLAN, Thomas Sanders 1
MCMILLAN, William H
MCMILLAN, William Charles 1
MCMILLAN, William H. 1
MCMILLAN, William Joshua 5
MCMILLAN, William Linn 1
MCMILLEN, Alonzo Bertram 1
MCMILLEN, Dale Wilmore 5
MCMILLEN, Fred Ewing 3
MCMILLEN, James Adelbert 1
MCMILLIN, Alvin Nugent 3
MCMILLIN, Benton 1
MCMILLIN, Emerson 1
MCMILLIN, Francis Briggs 1
MCMILLIN, Frederick Nelson 1

MCMILLIN, John Milton 3
MCMILLIN, Lucille Foster 2
MCMILLIN, Stewart Earl 3
MCMINN, Joseph H
MCMORRAN, Henry 3
MCMORRIS, Charles H. 3
MCMORROW, Francis Joseph 4
MCMORROW, Thomas 3
MCMULLAN, Harry 4
MCMULLAN, Oscar 3
MCMULLEN, Adam 5
MCMULLEN, Charles Bell 5
MCMULLEN, Chester Bartow 3
MCMULLEN, Clements 3
MCMULLEN, Fayette 1
MCMULLEN, Hugh Aloysius 1
MCMULLEN, John H
MCMULLEN, John Joseph 5
MCMULLEN, Lynn Banks 4
MCMULLEN, Richard Cann 2
MCMURDY, Robert 2
MCMURRAY, Charles Backman 1
MCMURRAY, DeWitt 4
MCMURRAY, Howard Johnstone 4
MCMURRAY, James Donald 5
MCMURRAY, James Henry 1
MCMURRAY, John 5
MCMURRAY, Orrin Kip 2
MCMURRAY, William Josiah 1
MCMURRICH, J. Playfair 3
MCMURRICH, James Playfair H
MCMURRICH, James Playfair 4
MCMURRY, Charles Alexander 1
MCMURRY, Frank Morton 1
MCMURRY, Lida Brown 2
MCMURRY, William Fletcher 1
MCMURTRIE, Douglas Crawford 2
MCMURTRIE, Uz 1
MCMURTRIE, William Gilmer 1
MCMURTRY, James Gilmer 3
MCMURTRY, John H
MCMURTRY, Lewis S. 1
MCMURTRY, William John 3
MCNAB, Alexander J. 3
MCNAB, Archibald Peter 2
MCNABB, Joe Hector 2
MCNABB, Samuel W. 1
MCNAGNY, Phil McClellan 5
MCNAIR, Alexander H
MCNAIR, Fred Walter 1
MCNAIR, Frederick Vallette 1
MCNAIR, James Birtley 5
MCNAIR, John 5
MCNAIR, John Babbitt 5
MCNAIR, Lesley James 2
MCNAIR, William Sharp 1
MCNALLY, Andrew 3
MCNALLY, Frederick George 1
MCNALLY, James Clifford
MCNALLY, Joseph Thomas 5
MCNALLY, Paul Aloysius 3
MCNALLY, William Duncan 4
MCNALLY, William J. 4
MCNAMARA, Harley Vincent
MCNAMARA, John M. 4
MCNAMARA, Joseph Augustine 5
MCNAMARA, Martin D. 4
MCNAMARA, Patrick Vincent 4
MCNAMARA, Robert Charles
MCNAMARA, Robert Charles 4
MCNAMEE, C. Declan 4
MCNAMEE, Charles Joseph 4
MCNAMEE, Graham 2
MCNAMEE, Luke 5

MCNAMEE, 2
  William John Jr.
MCNARNEY, Joseph T. 5
MCNARY, Charles Linza 5
MCNARY, 4
  Henrietta Williamson
MCNARY, James Graham 4
MCNARY, William S. 4
MCNAUGHER, John 2
MCNAUGHT, 1
  Francis Hector
MCNAUGHT, James 4
MCNAUGHT, James B. 3
MCNAUGHTON, 4
  Andrew George Latta
MCNAUGHTON, John
Hugh 1
MCNAUGHTON, 4
  John Theodore
MCNAUGHTON, 5
  William Francis
MCNAUGHTON, 4
  William Francis
MCNEAL, Alice 4
MCNEAL, Donald Hamlin 4
MCNEAL, Edgar Holmes 3
MCNEAL, Joshua Vansant 1
MCNEAL, Thomas Allen 2
MCNEALY, 3
  Raymond William
MCNEAR, 2
  George Plummer Jr.
MCNEELY, 5
  Harry G(regory)
MCNEELY, 5
  Robert Whitehead
MCNEES, Sterling G. 3
MCNEIL, Edwin Colyer 4
MCNEIL, Everett 1
MCNEIL, Hiram Colver 1
MCNEIL, Kenneth
Gordon 5
MCNEIL, 5
  Sister Mary Donald
MCNEIL, Robert Lincoln 5
MCNEILL, Archibald 1
MCNEILL, Daniel H
MCNEILL, Edwin
Ruthven 5
MCNEILL, George Edwin 1
MCNEILL, 1
  George Rockwell
MCNEILL, Hector H
MCNEILL, I. C. 4
MCNEILL, John Charles 1
MCNEILL, John Hanson
MCNEILL, Neal Edward 3
MCNEILL, Thomas W. 3
MCNEILL, William Gibbs H
MCNEIR, George
MCNEIR, William 4
MCNEIRNY, Francis H
MCNEW,
  John Thomas Lamar
MCNICHOL, Paul John 4
MCNICHOLAS, John T. 3
MCNICHOLS, 1
  John Patrick
MCNIECE, 5
  Harold Francis
MCNIECE, Robert Gibson 1
MCNINCH, Frank R. 3
MCNULTA, John 1
MCNULTA, John 4
MCNULTY, C. H. 5
MCNULTY, Frank J. 5
MCNULTY, George
Albert 4
MCNULTY, James 5
MCNULTY, John
Laurence 3
MCNULTY, 4
  Robert Wilkinson
MCNUTT, Alexander H
MCNUTT, Anna Mary 5
MCNUTT, Paul Vories 4
MCNUTT, 4
  William Fletcher
MCPEAK, 4
  William Wallace
MCPHEE, Julian A. 4
MCPHEETERS, 4
  Chester Amos
MCPHEETERS, 4
  William Emmett
MCPHEETERS, 1
  William Marcellus
MCPHERREN, 5
  Charles Elmo
MCPHERSON, H
  Aimee Semple
MCPHERSON, 2
  Aimee Semple
MCPHERSON, 4
  Aimee Semple
MCPHERSON, Charles 2
MCPHERSON, Edward H

MCPHERSON, 3
  Harry Wright
MCPHERSON, Hobart M. 3
MCPHERSON, Isaac V. 2
MCPHERSON, Isaac V. 4
MCPHERSON, H
  James Birdseye
MCPHERSON, John
Bayard 1
MCPHERSON, John
Edward 1
MCPHERSON, 3
  John Hanson Thomas
MCPHERSON, H
  John Rhoderic
MCPHERSON, Logan
Grant 1
MCPHERSON, Ross 1
MCPHERSON, Samuel
Dace 3
MCPHERSON, 4
  Sherman Tecumseh
MCPHERSON, Simon
John 1
MCPHERSON, Smith 4
MCPHERSON, William 3
MCPHERSON, 1
  William Lenhart
MCPIKE, Henry H. 4
MCQUADE, 5
  Vincent Augustine
MCQUAID, Bernard John 1
MCQUAID, 4
  William Ravenel
MCQUARRIE, Irvine 4
MCQUEEN, 4
  Frederick Emil
MCQUEEN, Henry Clay 1
MCQUEEN, John H
MCQUEEN, 5
  L(oren) A(ngus)
MCQUEEN, Stewart 1
MCQUIGG, John Rea 5
MCQUILKIN, 3
  Robert Crawford
MCQUILLEN, John Hugh H
MCQUILLIN, Eugene 1
MCRAE, Austin Lee 1
MCRAE, Bruce 1
MCRAE, Duncan Kirkland H
MCRAE, George W. 3
MCRAE, James Henry 1
MCRAE, James Wilson 3
MCRAE, John Jones H
MCRAE, Milton A. 1
MCRAE, Roderick 4
MCRAE, Thomas
Chipman 1
MCRCLOSKEY, 1
  George V. A.
MCREYNOLDS, 5
  Frederick Wilson
MCREYNOLDS, 3
  George Edgar
MCREYNOLDS, 2
  James Clark
MCREYNOLDS, 2
  John Oliver
MCREYNOLDS, 1
  Peter Wesley
MCREYNOLDS, 1
  Samuel Davis
MCREYNOLDS, 3
  William Henry
MCRILL, Albert Leroy 3
MCROBERTS, 2
  Harriet Pearl Skinner
MCROBERTS, Samuel H
MCSHANE, Andrew
James 1
MCSHERRY, James 3
MCSHERRY, Richard H
MCSKIMMON, 5
  William Bingham
MCSOLEY, 3
  Raymond Joseph
MCSORLEY, Edward 4
MCSORLEY, Joseph 4
MCSPADDEN,
  Joseph Walker
MCSPARRAN, John
Aldus 5
MCSURELY, 2
  William Harvey
MCSWAIN, John Jackson 1
MCSWEENEY, Henry 2
MCSWEENEY, John 1
MCSWEENEY,
  Miles Benjamin
MCTAGUE, 4
  Charles Patrick
MCTAMMANY, John H
MCTAMMANY, John 4
MCTARNAHAN, 3
  William Chamberlin
MCTYEIRE, H
  Holland Nimmons

MCVAY, 2
  Charles Butler Jr.
MCVEA, Emilie Watts 1
MCVEAN, Charles H
MCVEIGH, John
Newburn 3
MCVEY, Frank LeRond 3
MCVEY, William E. 1
MCVEY, William Estus 4
MCVICAR, Nelson 4
MCVICKAR, John H
MCVICKAR, 1
  William Neilson
MCVICKER, James
Hubert 4
MCVINNEY, Russell J. 5
MCWADE, Robert
Malachi 1
MCWANE, James Ransom 1
MCWHINNEY, 1
  Thomas Martin
MCWHIRTER, Felix T. 1
MCWHIRTER, 3
  Luella Frances Smith
MCWHIRTER, 4
  William Allan
MCWHORTER,
  Ashton Waugh
MCWHORTER, Ernest D. 2
MCWHORTER, Henry
Clay 1
MCWILLIAM, John R. 4
MCWILLIAMS, 1
  Clarence A.
MCWILLIAMS, 5
  John Probasco
MCWILLIAMS, 3
  Roland Fairbairn
MCWILLIAMS, 1
  Thomas Samuel
MCWILLIE, 1
  Thomas Anderson
MCWILLIE, William H
MEACHAM, James H
MEACHAM, 5
  W(illiam) Banks
MEAD, Albert Davis 2
MEAD, Albert Edward 1
MEAD, Arthur Emett 4
MEAD, Charles Larew 1
MEAD, Charles Marsh 1
MEAD, Cowles H
MEAD, D. Irving 3
MEAD, Daniel Webster 2
MEAD, Edward Campbell 1
MEAD, Edward Sherwood 5
MEAD, Edwin Doak 1
MEAD, Elizabeth Storrs 1
MEAD, Elwood 1
MEAD, Frederick Sumner 1
MEAD, George Herbert 5
MEAD, George Houk 4
MEAD, George Jackson 2
MEAD, 2
  George Whitefield
MEAD, George Wilson 4
MEAD, Gilbert Wilcox 2
MEAD, Harry L. 4
MEAD, James M. 4
MEAD, John Abner 1
MEAD, 1
  Kate Campbell Hurd
MEAD, Larkin Goldsmith 1
MEAD, Leon 1
MEAD, Leonard Charles 4
MEAD, Lucia True Ames 1
MEAD, Nelson Prentiss 4
MEAD, Solomon Cristy 5
MEAD, Sterling V. 1
MEAD, Theodore Hoe 4
MEAD, Warren Judson 4
MEAD, William Edward 5
MEAD, 1
  William Rutherford
MEAD, William Whitman 5
MEADE, Edwin Ruthven H
MEADE, Eleanore Hussey 5
MEADE, Francis Louis 3
MEADE, Frank B. 2
MEADE, George
MEADE, George Edward 5
MEADE, George Gordon H
MEADE, James J. 3
MEADE, Janifer Dewitt 4
MEADE, H
  Richard Kidder *
MEADE, Richard Kidder 1
MEADE, H
  Richard Worsam *
MEADE, Richard Worsam 1
MEADE, Robert Leamy 1
MEADE, William H
MEADOR, Chastain Clark 1
MEADOWCROFT, 1
  William Henry
MEADOWS, 4
  Clarence Watson

MEADOWS, James Allen 5
MEAGHER, James
Francis 1
MEAGHER, James Luke 1
MEAGHER, Raymond 3
MEAGHER, H
  Thomas Francis
MEAKIN, L. H. 4
MEALEY, Carroll Edward 4
MEANEY, Thomas
Francis 5
MEANS, David
MacGregor 1
MEANS, Earl A. 4
MEANS, Eldred Kurtz 3
MEANS, Emily Adams 1
MEANS, Frank Wilson 3
MEANS, Gaston Bullock H
MEANS, George Hamilton 4
MEANS, Haston Bullock 4
MEANS, James Howard 4
MEANS, 2
  Philip Ainsworth
MEANS, Rice William 2
MEANS, Stewart 2
MEANS, Thomas Herbert 5
MEANWELL, Walter E. 3
MEANY, Edmond
Stephen 1
MEANY, Edward P. 1
MEARA, Frank S. 1
MEARNS, Edgar A. H
MEARNS,
  Edgar Alexander
MEARNS, Hughes 4
MEARS, David Otis 1
MEARS, Eliot Grinnell 3
MEARS, Frederick 1
MEARS, 1
  Helen Farnsworth
MEARS, J. Ewing 4
MEARS, John William 1
MEARS, Leverett 1
MEARS, 3
  Louise Wilhelmina
MEARS, Mary 1
MEASE, James H
MEASON, Isaac 1
MEBANE, Alexander H
MEBANE, B. Frank 4
MEBANE, Daniel 5
MEBANE, 5
  Harry Bartlett, Jr.
MEBANE, Robert Sloan 1
MECH, Stephen John 5
MECHAU, Frank Jr. 4
MECHEM, Floyd Russell 1
MECHEM, Merritt
Cramer 2
MECHEM, Philip 5
MECHERLE, George
Jacob 3
MECHERLE, 3
  Raymond Perry
MECHLIN, Leila 1
MECKLIN, John Martin 5
MECKLIN, John Moffatt 3
MECOM, Benjamin H
MEDALIE, George Zerdin 3
MEDARY, Milton Bennett 1
MEDARY, Samuel H
MEDBURY, 1
  Charles Sanderson
MEDEARIS, 5
  T(homas) W(hittier)
MEDFORD, William 5
MEDHURST, 3
  Sir Charles E. H.
MEDILL, Joseph H
MEDILL, William H
MEDLEY, Mat 4
MEDSGER, Oliver Perry 5
MEE, William 1
MEECH, Ezra H
MEEHAN, M. Joseph 4
MEEHAN, Thomas 1
MEEHAN, Thomas A. 4
MEEK,
  Alexander Beaufort
MEEK,
  Benjamin Franklin
MEEK, Charles Simpson 3
MEEK, Edward Roscoe 5
MEEK,
  Fielding Bradford
MEEK, Howard Bagnall 5
MEEK, John Henry 1
MEEK, Joseph A(icinus) 3
MEEK, Joseph L. H
MEEK, Robert Abner 3
MEEK, Seth Eugene 1
MEEK, Sterner St Paul 5
MEEKER, Arthur 1
MEEKER, Arthur 4
MEEKER, Claude 1
MEEKER, Ezra 1
MEEKER, Frank Leroy 1

MEEKER, George Herbert 2
MEEKER, Jacob Edwin 1
MEEKER, James Rusling H
MEEKER, Jonathan Magie 1
MEEKER, Jotham H
MEEKER, Moses H
MEEKER, Nathan Cook H
MEEKER, Royal 3
MEEKINS, Isaac Melson 2
MEEKINS, Lynn Roby 1
MEEKISON, David 4
MEEKS, 4
  Carroll Louis Vanderslice
MEEKS, 3
  Clarence Gardner
MEEKS, Everett Victor 3
MEEKS, James A. 3
MEEM, Harry Grant 2
MEEMAN, Edward John 4
MEERSCHAERT, 1
  Theophile
MEES, Arthur 1
MEES, Carl Leo 1
MEES, 4
  Charles Edward Kenneth
MEES, Otto 3
MEES, Theophilus 1
MEESE, Alfred Hall 4
MEESE, William Henry 1
MEESER, Spenser Byron 1
MEESSEN, Hubert Joseph 4
MEFTAH, Davood Khan 5
MEGAN, Charles P. 2
MEGAN, Graydon 4
MEGAPOLENSIS,
  Johannes H
MEGARGEE, Edwin 3
MEGARO, Gaudens 3
MEGGERS, 4
  William Frederick
MEGGINSON, William 5
MEGOWEN, Carl Robert 4
MEGRAN, Herbert Brown 3
MEGRAW, Herbert
Ashton 3
MEGRUE, Roi Cooper 1
MEHAFFY, Tom Miller 2
MEHAN, John Dennis 5
MEHLBERG,
  Josephine Janina Bednarski
  Spinner (Mrs. Henry
MEHLER, John Sauter 4
MEHLIN, Theodore Grefe 5
MEHLING, Theodore
John 4
MEHORNAY, Robert Lee 3
MEHREN, Edward J. 4
MEIDELL, Harold M. 5
MEIER, Fabian Allan 4
MEIER, Fred Campbell 1
MEIER, Julius L. 1
MEIER, Norman Charles 4
MEIER, 1
  Walter Frederick
MEIERE, M. Hildreth 4
MEIGGS, Henry H
MEIGHAN, Thomas 3
MEIGHEN, Arthur 4
MEIGHEN, 3
  John Felix Dryden
MEIGS,
  Arthur Ingersoll
MEIGS, Arthur Vincent 1
MEIGS, H
  Charles Delucena
MEIGS, Henry H
MEIGS, James Aitken H
MEIGS, John 1
MEIGS, John Forsyth H
MEIGS, Josiah H
MEIGS, Merrill Church 4
MEIGS, Montgomery 1
MEIGS,
  Montgomery Cunningham
MEIGS, Return Jonathan H
MEIGS,
  Return Jonathan Jr. *
MEIGS, Robert Van 5
MEIGS, 1
  William Montgomery
MEIKLE, George Stanley 1
MEIKLEJOHN, Alexander 4
MEIKLEJOHN, 1
  George De Rue
MEIKS, Lyman Thompson 5
MEILINK, John Girard 3
MEIN, John Gordon 5
MEIN, William Wallace 5
MEINE, Franklin Julius 5
MEINECKE,
  Emilio Pepe Michael
MEINEL, William John 4
MEINHOLD, H. E. 5
MEINHOLTZ,
  Frederick E.
MEINRATH, Joseph 1
MEINS, Carroll Leach 3

* Indicates More Than One Such Name Listed

MESSENGER, 1
North Overton
MESSENGER, 4
Robert Pocock
MESSER, Alpha 1
MESSER, Asa H
MESSER, 1
Edmund Clarence
MESSER, L. Wilbur 1
MESSER, Samuel 4
MESSER, William Stuart 4
MESSERSMITH, George S. 3
MESSERSMITH, George S.
MESSINA, Angelina Rose 5
MESSING, 5
Abraham Joseph
MESSINGER, 1
Charles Raymond
MESSINGER, Edwin John 4
MESSITER, Arthur Henry 1
MESSLER,
Eugene Lawrence
MESSLER, H
Thomas Doremus
MESSMER, 1
Sebastian Gebhard
MESSNER, Julian
MESSNER, Kathryn G. 4
MESTA, Frank Albert 4
MESTA, L. W. 3
MESTERN, H. Edward 5
MESTREZAT, 1
Stephen Leslie
MESTROVIC, Ivan 4
METCALF, Arunah H
METCALF, Clell Lee 2
METCALF, Edward Potter 4
METCALF, Frank Arthur 1
METCALF, George P. 4
METCALF, 4
George Wallace
METCALF, Haven 2
METCALF, Henry Brewer 1
METCALF, 1
Henry Harrison
METCALF, Irving Wight 4
METCALF, 2
Jesse Houghton
METCALF, Joel Hastings 1
METCALF, John Calvin 2
METCALF, 4
John Milton Putnam
METCALF, Leonard 1
METCALF, 1
Lorettus Sutton
METCALF, Maynard
Mayo 1
METCALF, Ralph
Olney 3
METCALF, Stephen
Olney
METCALF, Theron H
METCALF, Victor
Howard 1
METCALF, 1
Wilder Stevens
METCALF, Willard Leroy 1
METCALF, William 4
METCALF, Zeno Payne 3
METCALFE, 1
George Richmond
METCALFE, Henry 4
METCALFE, H
Henry Bleecker
METCALFE, 1
James Stetson
METCALFE, Richard Lee 3
METCALFE, H
Samuel Lytler
METCALFE, Thomas H
METCALFE, 3
Tristram Walker
METEYARD, 1
Thomas Buford
METTAUER, John Peter H
METTEN, John Farrell 5
METTEN, William F. 4
METTLER, John Wyckoff 3
METTLER, L. Harrison 4
METTS, 5
John Van Bokkelen
METZ, Abraham Louis 4
METZ, Albert Frederick 4
METZ, Arthur Ray 4
METZ, Christian H
METZ, Herman A. 1
METZENBAUM, 2
Myron Firth
METZGAR, 4
Charles Watson
METZGER, 4
Delbert Everner
METZGER, Fraser 3
METZGER, 3
Frederick Elder
METZGER, Hutzel

METZGER, Irvin Dilling 2
METZGER, Ralph Alfred 5
METZLER, William Henry 4
METZMAN, Gustav 3
METZMAN, Gustav 4
MEUSER, Edwin Henry 2
MEY, H
Cornelius Jacobsen
MEYER, Adolf 3
MEYER, 1
Adolphus William
MEYER, Albert Gregory 4
MEYER, Alfred 3
MEYER, Alfred Henry 2
MEYER, Alfred Reuben 5
MEYER, Annie Nathan 3
MEYER, Arthur John 1
MEYER, Arthur Simon 3
MEYER, Arthur William 5
MEYER, B. G. 2
MEYER, Balthasar Henry 5
MEYER, Ben R. 3
MEYER, Charles F. 2
MEYER, 3
Charles Garrison
MEYER, 4
Charles Harrison
MEYER, Charles Zachary 5
MEYER, 1
Christian Frederick
Gottleib
MEYER, Clarence Earle 4
MEYER, Edward Barnard 1
MEYER, Ely 5
MEYER,
Estelle Reel (Mrs. Cort F.
Meyer)
MEYER, Eugene 3
MEYER, Frank Straus 5
MEYER, Frederick H. 5
MEYER, Frederick Henry 4
MEYER, Fredrik 5
MEYER, George Homer 1
MEYER,
George 'von Lengerke
MEYER, George W. 4
MEYER, George William 5
MEYER, H. Kenneth 4
MEYER, 3
Henry Coddington Jr.
MEYER, Henry Herman 3
MEYER, Herbert Alton 3
MEYER,
Herbert Alton, Jr.
MEYER, Herbert Willy 5
MEYER,
Herman Henry Bernard
MEYER, Hugo Richard 4
MEYER, John Franklin 2
MEYER, John Jacob 3
MEYER, Joseph F. 1
MEYER, Julius Eduard 5
MEYER, Julius Paul 2
MEYER, Karl Albert 5
MEYER, Lothar 5
MEYER, Lucy Rider 1
MEYER, Martin A. 2
MEYER, Max F(riedrich) 5
MEYER, 3
Maximilian Courtland
MEYER, Rudolph J. 5
MEYER,
Schuyler Merritt
MEYER,
Theodore Frederick
MEYER, Wallace 5
MEYER, William Briggs 4
MEYER, Willy 5
MEYERCORD,
George Rudolph
MEYERDING, 5
Henry William
MEYERHOF, Otto 3
MEYERHOLZ, 5
Charles Henry
MEYERS, Carl W. 3
MEYERS, Carlisle Paul 5
MEYERS, Erwin A. 5
MEYERS, George Julian 5
MEYERS, J. Edward 3
MEYERS, Joseph 3
MEYERS, Joseph Hugh 5
MEYERS, Robert C. V. 1
MEYERS, 5
Sidney Stuyvesant
MEYERS, William John 1
MEYLAN, George Louis 3
MEYLAN, Paul Julien 4
MEYNE, Gerhardt 5
MEYROWITZ, Emil B. 4
MEZES, Sidney Edward 1
MEZZROW, 5
Mezz, (Milton Mesirow)
MIANTONOMO H
MICH, Daniel D. 4
MICHAEL 3

MICHAEL, Arthur 1
MICHAEL, Arthur 2
MICHAEL, Elias 1
MICHAEL, Helen Abbott 1
MICHAEL, Jerome 1
MICHAEL, Max 3
MICHAEL, Moina Belle 1
MICHAEL, William Henry 1
MICHAELIDES, 4
George Peter
MICHAELIS, 5
George V. S.
MICHAELIS, Leonor 2
MICHAELIS, Richard C. 1
MICHAELIUS, Jonas H
MICHAELS, 2
Charles Frederick
MICHAELS, Ernest Edwin 5
MICHAELS, Henry 3
MICHAELS, Hunter 4
MICHAELSON, M. 2
Alfred
MICHAL, Aristotle D. 3
MICHALSON, Carl 4
MICHAUD, Gustave 4
MICHAUD, John Stephen 4
MICHAUD, Regis 5
MICHAUX, Andre H
MICHAUX, H
Francois Andre
MICHEL, 5
Charles E(ugene)
MICHEL, Ernest Adolph 5
MICHEL, 5
Lincoln Mattheus
MICHEL, Richard Fraser 1
MICHEL, Virgil George H
MICHEL, Virgil George 4
MICHEL, William 4
MICHEL, William C. 5
MICHEL,
William Middleton
MICHELFELDER, 3
Sylvester Clarence
MICHELS, 5
Nicholas Aloysius
MICHELSON, 1
Albert Abraham
MICHELSON, 1
Albert Heminway
MICHELSON, Arnold 5
MICHELSON, Charles 2
MICHELSON, 5
Henry E(rnest)
MICHELSON, Miriam 2
MICHELSON, Truman 5
MICHENER, Earl Cory 3
MICHENER, Ezra H
MICHENER, 1
Louis Theodore
MICHIE, A. Hewson 3
MICHIE, H(enry) Stuart 5
MICHIE, James Newton 1
MICHIE, Peter Smith 1
MICHIE,
Robert Edward Lee
MICHIE, Thomas Johnson 5
MICHI KINI KWA H
MICHINARD, Frank 4
MICHLER, Francis 3
MICHLER, Nathaniel H
MICKELSEN, Stanley R. 4
MICKELSON, 4
George Theodore
MICKEY, 5
Harold Chandler
MICKEY, John Hopwood 1
MICKLE, Joe J. 4
MICKLE, 1
William English
MICOU, Richard Wilde 1
MIDDELSCHULTE, 2
Wilhelm
MIDDLEBROOK, 1
Louis Francis
MIDDLEBROOKS, 4
Audy Jefferson
MIDDLEBUSH, 5
Frederick Arnold
MIDDLESWARTH, Ner H
MIDDLETON, Arthur * 1
MIDDLETON, Arthur D. 1
MIDDLETON, 3
Austin Ralph
MIDDLETON, 3
Charles Gibson
MIDDLETON, 4
Cornelius W.
MIDDLETON, George H
MIDDLETON, George 4
MIDDLETON, Henry * H
MIDDLETON, John Izard H
MIDDLETON, H
Nathaniel Russell
MIDDLETON, Peter H
MIDDLETON, 2
Stanley Grant

MIDDLETON, 4
Thomas Cooke
MIDDLETON, 4
William Vernon
MIDDOUR, Emory J. 3
MIDGLEY, John William 1
MIDGLEY, Thomas Jr. 2
MIEDEL, Robert Eugene 5
MIELATZ, 4
Charles Frederick William
MIELZINER, Leo 1
MIELZINER, Moses 1
MIERS, Earl Schenck 5
MIERS, Henry Virgil 5
MIERS, Robert Walter 1
MIERSCH, 4
Paul Frederic Theodore
MIES VAN DER ROHE, Ludwig 5
MIFFLIN, 1
George Harrison
MIFFLIN, Lloyd 1
MIFFLIN, Thomas H
MIGHELS, Ella Sterling 3
MIGHELS, Ella Sterling 4
MIGHELS,
Philip Verrill
MIGNONE, Albert 5
MIKELL, Henry Judah 4
MIKELL, 2
William Ephraim
MIKESELL, Doyle 3
MIKESELL, Jerome Byron 5
MIKESELL, 5
William Henry
MIKHALAPOV, 5
George Sergei
MILAM, Arthur Yeager 3
MILAM, Carl Hastings 4
MILAS, 5
Nicholas Althanasius
MILBANK, 2
Albert Goodsell
MILBANK, Dunlevy 3
MILBANK, Jeremiah 5
MILBERT, H
Jacques Gerard
MILBOURNE, Harvey
Lee 4
MILBURN, Arthur W. 1
MILBURN, 5
Edward Garland
MILBURN, George 4
MILBURN, 1
George Roszelle
MILBURN, John George 1
MILBURN, William Henry 1
MILDEN, Alfred William 2
MILEN, 4
Frederick Blumenthal
MILES, Basil 1
MILES, C. Edwin 4
MILES, Carlton Wright 3
MILES, Clarence Paul 1
MILES, Daniel Curtis 1
MILES, Dudley 3
MILES, Edson Russell 4
MILES, Ellen E. 4
MILES, Emma Bell 2
MILES, Evan 1
MILES, Frederick H
MILES, Hooper Steele 4
MILES, Joshua Weldon 1
MILES, Louis Wardlaw 1
MILES, Lovick Pierce 3
MILES, Milton Edward 1
MILES, Nelson Appleton 1
MILES, Perry Lester 1
MILES, Robert Parker 1
MILES, 3
Robert Whitfield
MILES, Vincent Morgan 2
MILES, Willard Wesbery 1
MILES, William Porcher 1
MILEY, Jess Wells 3
MILEY, John Henry 2
MILFORD, 1
Morton Marshall
MILHAM, 3
Willis Isbister
MILHOLLAND, John 1
Elmer
MILK, Arthur Leslie 4
MILKS, Howard Jay 3
MILLAR, 1
Alexander Copeland
MILLAR, 1
Edward Alexander
MILLAR, Preston Strong 2
MILLAR, Robert Cameron 5
MILLAR, Robert Wyness 3
MILLAR, Ronald 5
MILLAR, William Bell 1
MILLARD, Bailey 1
MILLARD, 2
Charles Dunsmore

MILLARD, 2
Charles Sterling
MILLARD, Clifford 4
MILLARD, Douglas 1
MILLARD, Earl 5
MILLARD, Everett Lee 1
MILLARD, Floyd Hays 2
MILLARD, Frank Ashley 4
MILLARD, Harrison H
MILLARD, 1
Joseph Hopkins
MILLARD, Paul Adsworth 2
MILLARD, 5
Thomas Franklin Fairfax
MILLARD, 5
Willard B(arrows, Jr.
MILLARD, 4
William Barrett
MILLAY, 3
Edna St Vincent
MILLAY, 2
Kathleen Kalloch
MILLBERRY, 5
Guy Stillman
MILLEDGE, John H
MILLEDOLER, Philip H
MILLEN, John 4
MILLENER, John A. 1
MILLER, A. Blanchard 1
MILLER, A. Blanchard 2
MILLER, A. K. 4
MILLER, Adolph Caspar 2
MILLER, Albert Edward 1
MILLER, Albert L. 3
MILLER, Alden Holmes 4
MILLER, 1
Alexander Macomb
MILLER, 1
Alfred Brashear
MILLER, Alfred Jacob H
MILLER, Alfred Parkin 1
MILLER, Alfred Stanley 1
MILLER, Alice Duer 2
MILLER, Amos Calvin 2
MILLER, Andrew 5
MILLER, 3
Andrew Jackson Jr.
MILLER, Andrew James 1
MILLER, Andrew Joyce 1
MILLER, Anna Jenness 5
MILLER, Arthur 4
MILLER, Arthur Lewis 4
MILLER,
Arthur McQuiston
MILLER, Arthur W. 1
MILLER,
Augustus Samuel
MILLER, Austin Vicente 3
MILLER, Barse 5
MILLER, Benjamin Kurtz 1
MILLER, Benjamin LeRoy 2
MILLER, Benjamin M. 4
MILLER,
Benjamin Orville
MILLER, Bert H. 2
MILLER, 5
Bertha Everett Mahony
MILLER, Bina West 3
MILLER,
Bloomfield Jackson
MILLER, Byron E. 1
MILLER, C. Jeff 1
MILLER, Carl A. 3
MILLER, Carroll 2
MILLER, Charles 1
MILLER, 2
Charles Addison
MILLER, Charles Armand 1
MILLER, Charles C. 1
MILLER, Charles Ervine 1
MILLER, 1
Charles Franklin
MILLER, Charles Henry 1
MILLER, Charles Lewis 4
MILLER, Charles R. 3
MILLER, Charles R. D. 4
MILLER, Charles Ransom 1
MILLER, Charles Russel 1
MILLER, Charles Wesley 1
MILLER, Charles Wilbur 3
MILLER, 1
Charles William Emil
MILLER, 3
Christian Otto Gerberding
MILLER, 1
Cincinnatus Heine
MILLER, Clarence A. 1
MILLER, Clarence B. 1
MILLER, 2
Clement Woodnutt
MILLER, Clyde Winwood 1
MILLER, Crosby Parke 1
MILLER, Daniel Fry H
MILLER, Daniel H. H
MILLER, Daniel Long 1
MILLER, Darius 1
MILLER, David Aaron 1

MILLER, David Lewis 5
MILLER, Dayton Clarence 1
MILLER, Dewitt 1
MILLER, Dick 5
MILLER, Dickinson Sergeant 4
MILLER, Don Clark 5
MILLER, Don Hugo 5
MILLER, Dudley Livingston 5
MILLER, E. P. Smith 1
MILLER, E(ugene) K(earfott) 5
MILLER, Edgar Calvin LeRoy 5
MILLER, Edgar Grim Jr. 3
MILLER, Edmund Howd 1
MILLER, Edmund Thornton 3
MILLER, Edmund W. 4
MILLER, Edward Alanson 4
MILLER, Edward Furber 1
MILLER, Edward Godfrey, Jr. 5
MILLER, Edward Terhune 1
MILLER, Edward Tylor 4
MILLER, Edward Waite 1
MILLER, Edwin Lee 2
MILLER, Edwin Lillie 1
MILLER, Elihu Spencer H
MILLER, Elizabeth Smith 1
MILLER, Emerson R. 1
MILLER, Emily Huntington 1
MILLER, Emma Guffey 5
MILLER, Ephraim 1
MILLER, Ernest B. 3
MILLER, Ernest Henry 1
MILLER, Ernest Ivan 5
MILLER, Ethel Hull 4
MILLER, Eugene Harper 1
MILLER, Eugene Walter 3
MILLER, Ezra H
MILLER, Francis Garner 1
MILLER, Francis Trevelyn 3
MILLER, Frank A. 4
MILLER, Frank Augustus 1
MILLER, Frank Ebenezer 1
MILLER, Frank Harvey 1
MILLER, Frank Justus 1
MILLER, Frank William 4
MILLER, Franklin Thomas 1
MILLER, Fred J. 1
MILLER, Fred W. 2
MILLER, Frederic Howell 4
MILLER, Frederic Magoun 3
MILLER, Frederick A. * 3
MILLER, Freeman Edwin 1
MILLER, Galen 5
MILLER, George 3
MILLER, George 4
MILLER, George Abram 5
MILLER, George Carter 1
MILLER, George E. 1
MILLER, George Frederick 4
MILLER, George Funston H
MILLER, George Henry 5
MILLER, George Lee 1
MILLER, George M. H
MILLER, George Macculloch 1
MILLER, George McAnelly 4
MILLER, George Morey 1
MILLER, George Noyes 1
MILLER, George Stewart 5
MILLER, Gerrit Smith 1
MILLER, Gerrit Smith Jr. 3
MILLER, Gilbert Heron 5
MILLER, Glenn 2
MILLER, Grace Moncrieff 1
MILLER, Gray 2
MILLER, Gustavus Hindman 1
MILLER, Harlan 5
MILLER, Harold C. 3
MILLER, Harriet Mann 1
MILLER, Harry (McKinley) 5
MILLER, Harry Edward 1
MILLER, Harry Irving 1
MILLER, Harvey H. 3
MILLER, Helen Richards Guthrie 2
MILLER, Helen Topping 5
MILLER, Helen Topping 4
MILLER, Henry * 1
MILLER, Henry 4

MILLER, Henry B. 1
MILLER, Henry Russell 3
MILLER, Henry Watkins 1
MILLER, Herbert Adolphus 5
MILLER, Hilliard Eve 2
MILLER, Homer Virgil Milton H
MILLER, Horace Alden 1
MILLER, Humphreys Henry Clay
MILLER, Irving Elgar 5
MILLER, Isaac Eugene 3
MILLER, J. Jay 1
MILLER, J. M. C. 4
MILLER, J. Martin 4
MILLER, J. Maxwell 1
MILLER, Jacob F. 1
MILLER, Jacob Welsh H.
MILLER, Jacob William 1
MILLER, James 1
MILLER, James Alexander 2
MILLER, James Collins 1
MILLER, James Conelese 3
MILLER, James Decatur, Jr. 5
MILLER, James Kenneth 5
MILLER, James Monroe 1
MILLER, James Russell 1
MILLER, Jesse H
MILLER, Jesse Isidor 2
MILLER, Joaquin 1
MILLER, John * H
MILLER, John 1
MILLER, John Anthony 5
MILLER, John Barnes 1
MILLER, John Bleecker 4
MILLER, John Briggs 4
MILLER, John Calvin 1
MILLER, John D. 2
MILLER, John Eschelman 1
MILLER, John Ford 1
MILLER, John Franklin H
MILLER, John Franklin * 1
MILLER, John Gaines H
MILLER, John Henderson 1
MILLER, John Henry 1
MILLER, John Krepps H
MILLER, John Maffit Jr. 2
MILLER, John Richardson 4
MILLER, John Rulon Jr. 1
MILLER, John S. 4
MILLER, John Stocker 1
MILLER, Jonathan Peckham H
MILLER, Joseph H
MILLER, Joseph Dana 1
MILLER, Joseph Henry 3
MILLER, Joseph Hillis 3
MILLER, Joseph Leggett 1
MILLER, Joseph Nelson 1
MILLER, Joseph Torrence 1
MILLER, Josiah H
MILLER, Julian Creighton 5
MILLER, Julian Howell 4
MILLER, Julian Sidney 2
MILLER, Justin 5
MILLER, Kelly 1
MILLER, Kempster Blanchard 1
MILLER, Kennth Hayes 3
MILLER, Knox Emerson 5
MILLER, Lawrence William
MILLER, Lee Graham 4
MILLER, Lee P. 1
MILLER, Leo Edward 3
MILLER, Leo L. 5
MILLER, Leslie Andrew 5
MILLER, Leslie Freeland 3
MILLER, Leslie William 1
MILLER, Leverett Saltonstall 1
MILLER, Lewis H
MILLER, Lewis Bennett 1
MILLER, Logan C. 3
MILLER, Loren 4
MILLER, Loren Barker 3
MILLER, Louise Klein 2
MILLER, Loye Holmes 1
MILLER, Lucius Hopkins 2
MILLER, Luther Deck 5
MILLER, M. V. 3
MILLER, Malcolm E. 4
MILLER, Marcus P. 1
MILLER, Marion Mills 4
MILLER, Mary Rogers 1
MILLER, Maude Murray 1
MILLER, Max 4
MILLER, Max 5

MILLER, Melville Winans 4
MILLER, Merrill 1
MILLER, Merritt Finley 5
MILLER, Michael A. 4
MILLER, Milton 5
MILLER, Milton A. 1
MILLER, Morris Smith H
MILLER, Nathan H
MILLER, Nathan L. 3
MILLER, Nellie Burget 3
MILLER, Newton 1
MILLER, Olive Thorne 1
MILLER, Oscar Phineas 1
MILLER, Otto 3
MILLER, Paul Duryea 4
MILLER, Paul E. 1
MILLER, Paul Gerard 1
MILLER, Perry 1
MILLER, Perry B. 1
MILLER, Pleasant Moorman H
MILLER, Pleasant Thomas 5
MILLER, R. Paul 4
MILLER, R. T. Jr. 1
MILLER, Ralph English 3
MILLER, Ransford Stevens 1
MILLER, Ray T. 4
MILLER, Reed 1
MILLER, Richard E. 1
MILLER, Richard E. 1
MILLER, Richard Henry 2
MILLER, Richard Thompson 4
MILLER, Robert Frederick 5
MILLER, Robert Johnson 1
MILLER, Robert Netherland
MILLER, Robert Rowland 5
MILLER, Robert Talbott 1
MILLER, Robert Talbott Jr. 4
MILLER, Robert Walter 3
MILLER, Robert Watt 5
MILLER, Roger 1
MILLER, Roswell 1
MILLER, Rufus Wilder 1
MILLER, Russell 4
MILLER, Russell Benjamin 1
MILLER, Russell King 1
MILLER, Rutger Bleecker H
MILLER, Samuel Charles 3
MILLER, Samuel Duncan 1
MILLER, Samuel Franklin H
MILLER, Samuel Freeman 1
MILLER, Samuel Haas 1
MILLER, Samuel Howard 5
MILLER, Samuel Warren 4
MILLER, Samuel William 4
MILLER, Shackelford 1
MILLER, Sidney Lincoln 3
MILLER, Sidney Trowbridge 1
MILLER, Smith H
MILLER, Spencer Sr. H
MILLER, Stephen Decatur
MILLER, Stephen Ivan 5
MILLER, Sydney Robotham 2
MILLER, Theodore Joseph 3
MILLER, Thomas Condit 4
MILLER, Thomas Marshall 1
MILLER, Thomas Root 4
MILLER, Troup 5
MILLER, Vaughn 1
MILLER, W. Leslie 2
MILLER, Walter 2
MILLER, Walter 3
MILLER, Walter McNab 4
MILLER, Warner 1
MILLER, Warren Hastings 4
MILLER, Watson B. 4
MILLER, Webb 1
MILLER, Wilhelm 5
MILLER, William H
MILLER, William 1
MILLER, William Davis 1
MILLER, William E. 2
MILLER, William Henry H
MILLER, William Henry Harrison 1
MILLER, William Jasper 4
MILLER, William Jennings 3
MILLER, William Morrison 4

MILLER, William Niswonger 4
MILLER, William Rickarby H
MILLER, William Snow 1
MILLER, William Starr H
MILLER, William Todd 4
MILLER, William Wilson 1
MILLER, Willis Dance 5
MILLES, Carl Wilhelm Emil 3
MILLET, Clarence 3
MILLET, Francis Davis 1
MILLETT, George Van 5
MILLETTE, John W. 2
MILLHAUSER, DeWitt 1
MILLIGAN, Alexander Reed 1
MILLIGAN, Edward 1
MILLIGAN, Ezra McLeod 1
MILLIGAN, Harold V. 3
MILLIGAN, Jacob L. 3
MILLIGAN, John Jones H
MILLIGAN, Melvin Lee 4
MILLIGAN, Orlando Howard 3
MILLIGAN, Robert Wiley 1
MILLIGAN, Samuel 4
MILLIGAN, William Edwin 1
MILLIKAN, Clark Blanchard 4
MILLIKAN, George Lee 3
MILLIKAN, Max Franklin 5
MILLIKAN, Robert Andrews 4
MILLIKEN, Arnold White 4
MILLIKEN, Carl Elias 4
MILLIKEN, Edwin C. 4
MILLIKEN, Gerrish H. 2
MILLIKEN, John David 4
MILLIKEN, Joseph K. 1
MILLIKEN, Joseph Knowles 1
MILLIKEN, Seth Llewellyn H
MILLIKEN, Seth Mellen 1
MILLIKIN, Benjamin L. 1
MILLIKIN, Eugene Donald 3
MILLIMAN, Elmer 2
MILLIN, Sarah Gertrude 4
MILLING, Robert Edward 2
MILLING, Robert Edward Jr. 4
MILLINGTON, Charles Stephen 1
MILLINGTON, Ernest John Oldknow 3
MILLION, John Wilson 1
MILLIS, Harry Alvin 2
MILLIS, Harry Lee 1
MILLIS, John 1
MILLIS, Wade 1
MILLIS, Walter 5
MILLIS, William Alfred 1
MILLMAN, Edward 4
MILLNER, Walker LeRoy 5
MILLOY, James S. 5
MILLS, Abbot Low 1
MILLS, Albert Leopold 1
MILLS, Alfred Elmer 1
MILLS, Anson 1
MILLS, Augustus K. Iii 3
MILLS, Benjamin Fay 1
MILLS, Blake David 4
MILLS, C. Wright 4
MILLS, Charles Burdick 4
MILLS, Charles Francis 1
MILLS, Charles Henry 1
MILLS, Charles Karsner 1
MILLS, Charles Smith 2
MILLS, Charles Wilson 5
MILLS, Clark H
MILLS, Clyde Marvin 1
MILLS, Cyrus Taggart H
MILLS, Darius Ogden 1
MILLS, Dwight M. 5
MILLS, Earl Cuthbert 2
MILLS, Earle Watkins 5
MILLS, Edmund Mead 1
MILLS, Edward Kirkpatrick Jr. 4
MILLS, Edwin Claude 3
MILLS, Elijah Hunt H
MILLS, Enos A. 1
MILLS, Frank Moody 4
MILLS, Frederick Cecil 4
MILLS, Harriet May 1
MILLS, Harriette Melissa 1
MILLS, Henry Edmund 1
MILLS, Herbert Elmer 3
MILLS, Herbert Hagerman 5

MILLS, Hillis 4
MILLS, Hiram Francis 1
MILLS, Isaac Newton 1
MILLS, J. Warner 1
MILLS, James Edward 3
MILLS, Jesse T. 4
MILLS, Job Smith 1
MILLS, John 2
MILLS, John Sedwick 1
MILLS, Joseph John 4
MILLS, Lennox A(lgernon) 5
MILLS, Luther Laflin 1
MILLS, Matthew 5
MILLS, Ogden 1
MILLS, Ogden Livingston 1
MILLS, Robert * H
MILLS, Roger Quarles 1
MILLS, Samuel John H
MILLS, Samuel Myers 1
MILLS, Sebastian Bach 1
MILLS, Stephen Crosby 1
MILLS, Susan Lincoln 1
MILLS, Thomas Brooks 1
MILLS, Thornton Allen 1
MILLS, Thornton Anthony 1
MILLS, Weymer Jay 2
MILLS, William C. 1
MILLS, William Fitz Randolph 2
MILLS, William Hayne 2
MILLS, William Howard 1
MILLS, William Joseph 1
MILLS, William McMaster 4
MILLS, William Merrill 4
MILLS, William Webster 1
MILLSAPS, Reuben Webster 1
MILLSON, John Singleton H
MILLSOP, Thomas E. 4
MILLSPAUGH, Arthur Chester 3
MILLSPAUGH, Charles Frederick 1
MILLSPAUGH, Frank Crenshaw 3
MILLSPAUGH, Frank Rosebrook 1
MILLSPAUGH, Jesse Fonda 1
MILLSPAUGH, William Hulse 3
MILLWARD, Russell Hastings 5
MILLWARD, William H
MILMORE, Martin H
MILNE, Alan Alexander 3
MILNE, Caleb Jones Jr. 1
MILNE, David 1
MILNE, Frances Margaret (Tener)
MILNE, J. Scott 3
MILNE, James M. 1
MILNE, John 3
MILNE, William James 4
MILNER, Duncan Chambers 1
MILNER, Henry Key 1
MILNER, John Turner H
MILNER, Moses Embree 1
MILNER, Robert Teague 5
MILNER, Willis Justus Jr. 4
MILNES, William Jr. H
MILNOR, George Sparks 3
MILNOR, James H
MILNOR, William 1
MILOFSKY, Allan Henry 5
MILROY, Charles Martin 1
MILROY, Robert Huston H
MILROY, William Forsyth 1
MILROY, William McCracken 4
MILTENBERGER, George Warner 1
MILTNER, Charles Christopher 4
MILTON, George Fort 1
MILTON, George Fort 3
MILTON, John H
MILTON, John Brown 1
MILTON, William Hall 1
MILTON, William Hall 2
MILTON, William Hall 4
MILTON, William Hammond 4
MILTOUN, Francis (Francis Miltoun Mansfield) 5
MIMS, Edwin 3
MIMS, Livingston 1
MIMS, Stewart Lea 4

MINAHAN, Daniel Francis — 5
MINAHAN, Victor Ivan — 3
MINARD, Archibald Ellsworth — 3
MINARY, Thomas Jay — 1
MINCHIN, George H. — 5
MINCHIN, Nina Mesirow — 5
MINCKLER, Robert Lee — 4
MINER, Ahiman Louis — H
MINER, Alonzo Ames — 1
MINER, Asher — 1
MINER, Charles — 5
MINER, Charles Wright — 4
MINER, Edward Griffith — 3
MINER, George Roberts — 1
MINER, H. C. — 3
MINER, Harlan Sherman — 1
MINER, Jack — 4
MINER, James A. — 1
MINER, James Burt — 2
MINER, Julius Howard — 4
MINER, Luella — 1
MINER, Myrtilla — H
MINER, Phineas — 1
MINER, Robert Bradford — 5
MINER, Roy Waldo — 3
MINER, William Harvey — 1
MINGENBACK, Eugene Carl — 5
MINGOS, Howard L. — 3
MINICH, Verne Elwood — 3
MINICK, James William — 2
MINIER, George Washington — 1
MINIFIE, William Charles — 5
MINIGER, Clement Orville — 2
MINITER, Edith (Dowe) — 5
MINIUT, Peter — 3
MINNAERT, Marcel Gilles Jozef — 5
MINNICH, Dwight Elmer — 4
MINNICH, Harvey C. — 3
MINNICK, John Harrison — 5
MINNIGERODE, C. Powell — 3
MINNIGERODE, Lucy — 1
MINNIGERODE, Meade — 4
MINOR, Anne Rogers — 1
MINOR, Benjamin Blake — 1
MINOR, Benjamin Saunders — 2
MINOR, Berkeley Jr. — 4
MINOR, Charles Launcelot — 1
MINOR, Clark Haynes — 4
MINOR, Edward S. — 1
MINOR, George Henry — 1
MINOR, H. Dent — 2
MINOR, John Barbee — 1
MINOR, Lucian — H
MINOR, Raleigh Colston — 1
MINOR, Robert — 3
MINOR, Robert Crannell — 1
MINOR, Thomas Chalmers — 1
MINOR, Virginia Louisa — H
MINOT, Charles Sedgwick — 1
MINOT, George Richards — H
MINOT, George Richards — 2
MINOT, John Clair — 2
MINOT, Joseph Grafton — 2
MINOT, William * — 1
MINSCH, William J. — 5
MINSHALL, Robert J. — 3
MINSHALL, Thaddeus A. — 4
MINTER, Mary Miles — 4
MINTER, William Ramseur — 2
MINTO, Walter — 1
MINTON, Henry Collin — 1
MINTON, Maurice Meyer — 4
MINTON, Melville — 3
MINTON, Sherman — 4
MINTURN, James Francis — 1
MINTURN, Robert Bowne — H
MIRANDA, Francisco 'de — 1
MIRICK, George Alonzo — 1
MIRISCH, Harold Joseph — 5
MIRKINE-GUETZEVITCH, Boris — 3
MIRO, Esteban Rodriquez — H
MIRRIELEES, Edith Ronald — 4
MIRZA, Iskander — 5
MIRZA, Youel Benjamin — 2
MISBACH, Lorenz — 3
MISER, Hugh Dinsmore — 5
MISHIMA, Yukio, (Kimitake Hiraoka) — 5
MISTRAL, Gabriela — 1
MITCHAM, Orin Burlingame — 1

MITCHEL, Charles Burton — H
MITCHEL, Edwin Kent — 5
MITCHEL, Frederick Augustus — 1
MITCHEL, John Purroy — 1
MITCHEL, Ormsby MacKnight — H
MITCHELL, Albert — 3
MITCHELL, Albert Graeme — 1
MITCHELL, Albert Roscoe — 1
MITCHELL, Alexander — H
MITCHELL, Alfred — 1
MITCHELL, Alfred Newton — 5
MITCHELL, Allan Charles Gray — 4
MITCHELL, Anderson — 1
MITCHELL, Arthur Evan — 3
MITCHELL, Arthur W. — 1
MITCHELL, Bruce — 4
MITCHELL, Charles Anderson — 3
MITCHELL, Charles Andrews — 1
MITCHELL, Charles Bayard — 2
MITCHELL, Charles Dennis — 1
MITCHELL, Charles Edward — 1
MITCHELL, Charles Edwin — 3
MITCHELL, Charles Elliott — 1
MITCHELL, Charles F. — H
MITCHELL, Charles Franklin — 5
MITCHELL, Charles Le Moyne — H
MITCHELL, Charles Scott — 5
MITCHELL, Charles Tennant — 2
MITCHELL, Clarence Blair — 5
MITCHELL, Clifford — 1
MITCHELL, Curtis — 4
MITCHELL, David — 3
MITCHELL, David Brydie — H
MITCHELL, David Dawson — 2
MITCHELL, David Ray — 5
MITCHELL, Donald Grant — 1
MITCHELL, Edmund — 1
MITCHELL, Edward Cushing — 1
MITCHELL, Edward Page — 1
MITCHELL, Edwin Knox — 1
MITCHELL, Edwin Thomas — 3
MITCHELL, Elisha — 5
MITCHELL, Emory Forrest — 5
MITCHELL, F. Edward — 5
MITCHELL, G. P. — 2
MITCHELL, George — 4
MITCHELL, George Edward — H
MITCHELL, George Franklin — 3
MITCHELL, George T. — 2
MITCHELL, George W. — 4
MITCHELL, Guy Elliott — 1
MITCHELL, Hal E. — 4
MITCHELL, Harold E. — 3
MITCHELL, Harry B. — 3
MITCHELL, Harry Dawson — 1
MITCHELL, Harry Luzerne — 2
MITCHELL, Harry Walter — 1
MITCHELL, Hazel Haynes — 5
MITCHELL, Helen Codman — 4
MITCHELL, Henry — 1
MITCHELL, Henry * — 1
MITCHELL, Henry Bedinger — 3
MITCHELL, Henry Sewall — 3
MITCHELL, Hinckley Gilbert — 1
MITCHELL, Homer Rawlins — 3
MITCHELL, Howard Hawks — 2
MITCHELL, Howard Walton — 2
MITCHELL, Hugh Chester — 3
MITCHELL, Hugh Gordon — 5
MITCHELL, Humphrey — 3

MITCHELL, Isaac — H
MITCHELL, James — 1
MITCHELL, James Alfred — 1
MITCHELL, James Coffield — H
MITCHELL, James Farnandis — 4
MITCHELL, James George — 4
MITCHELL, James Herbert — 4
MITCHELL, James McCormick — 2
MITCHELL, James P. — 4
MITCHELL, James S. — H
MITCHELL, James Tyndale — 1
MITCHELL, John * — H
MITCHELL, John — 1
MITCHELL, John Ames — 1
MITCHELL, John Blanton — 5
MITCHELL, John Doyle — 5
MITCHELL, John Fulton Berrien — 3
MITCHELL, John H. — 1
MITCHELL, John Inscho — 1
MITCHELL, John J. — 1
MITCHELL, John Joseph — 1
MITCHELL, John Kearsley — 1
MITCHELL, John Kearsley — 1
MITCHELL, John Lendrum — 3
MITCHELL, John Marvin — 5
MITCHELL, John McKenney — 5
MITCHELL, John Murray — 1
MITCHELL, John Nicholas — 4
MITCHELL, John R. — 1
MITCHELL, John Raymond — 5
MITCHELL, John William — 1
MITCHELL, Jonathan — H
MITCHELL, Julian — 5
MITCHELL, Langdon Elwyn — 1
MITCHELL, Leander Perry — 1
MITCHELL, Leeds — 3
MITCHELL, Lucy Myers Wright — H
MITCHELL, Maggie — 1
MITCHELL, Margaret — 2
MITCHELL, Margaret Johnes — 5
MITCHELL, Maria — H
MITCHELL, Mason — 1
MITCHELL, Nahum — H
MITCHELL, Nathaniel — H
MITCHELL, Nathaniel McDonald — 4
MITCHELL, O. W. H. — 3
MITCHELL, Oscar — 1
MITCHELL, Philip Henry — 3
MITCHELL, R. Verne — 5
MITCHELL, Ralph Clinton, Jr. — 5
MITCHELL, Richard Bland — 1
MITCHELL, Richard F(urlong) — 5
MITCHELL, Robert — H
MITCHELL, Robert — 1
MITCHELL, Robert Byington — 1
MITCHELL, Roscoe Lee — 5
MITCHELL, Ruth Comfort — 3
MITCHELL, S. Weir — 1
MITCHELL, Samuel Alfred — 3
MITCHELL, Samuel Alfred — 4
MITCHELL, Samuel Augustus — 1
MITCHELL, Samuel Chiles — 4
MITCHELL, Samuel Phillips — 1
MITCHELL, Samuel S. — 1
MITCHELL, Samuel Thomas — 1
MITCHELL, Sidney — 1
MITCHELL, Sidney Alexander — 4
MITCHELL, Sidney Zollicoffer — 2
MITCHELL, Steele — 2
MITCHELL, Stephen Mix — H
MITCHELL, Stewart — 1
MITCHELL, Sydney Bancroft — 2
MITCHELL, Sydney Bancroft — 1
MITCHELL, Sydney Knox — 5

MITCHELL, Thomas — 4
MITCHELL, Thomas A. — 5
MITCHELL, Thomas Dache — H
MITCHELL, Thomas Edward — 3
MITCHELL, Thomas Edward — 4
MITCHELL, Thomas Rothmaler — H
MITCHELL, Viola — 1
MITCHELL, Walter — 1
MITCHELL, Walter Jenifer — 3
MITCHELL, Walter Lee — 1
MITCHELL, Walter Scott — 1
MITCHELL, Wesley Clair — 2
MITCHELL, Willard A. — H
MITCHELL, William * — H
MITCHELL, William * — 1
MITCHELL, William Carl — 1
MITCHELL, William DeWitt — 4
MITCHELL, William Edward — 3
MITCHELL, William Henry — 1
MITCHELL, William John — 5
MITCHELL, William Ledyard — 5
MITCHELL, William Samuel — 1
MITCHELL, William Whittier — 1
MITCHELL, Wilmot Brookings — 5
MITCHILL, Samuel Latham — H
MITCHILL, Theodore Clarence — 4
MITKE, Charles A. — 5
MITRE, Don Luis — 3
MITROPOULOS, Dimitri — 4
MITSCHER, Marc Andrew — 2
MITTELMAN, Edward — 4
MITTEN, Thomas Eugene — 1
MITTON, George W. — 2
MITTY, John Joseph — 4
MIX, Arthur Jackson — 3
MIX, Charles Louis — 1
MIX, Edward Townsend — H
MIX, Melville Walter — 4
MIX, Tom — 3
MIX, William Winter — 1
MIXER, Albert Harrison — 1
MIXTER, Charles Whitney — 4
MIXTER, George — 5
MIXTER, Samuel Jason — 1
MIXTER, William Gilbert — 1
MIZE, Robert Herbert — 4
MIZE, Sidney Carr — 4
MIZNER, Henry Rutgeras — 4
MIZNER, Wilson — 3
MOALE, Edward — 4
MOBLEY, Mayor Dennis — 5
MOBLEY, Radford E. — 5
MOCK, Charles Adolphus — 4
MOCK, Fred McKinley — 4
MOCK, Harry Edgar — 3
MOCKMORE, Charles Arthur — 3
MOCKRIDGE, John Charles Hillier — 5
MODARELLI, Alfred E. — 4
MODDER, Montagu Frank — 3
MODEL, Jean — 5
MODELL, Clarion — 5
MODERWELL, Charles McClellan — 3
MODJESKA, Helena — 1
MODJESKI, Ralph — 1
MODZELEWSKI, Zymunt — 3
MOE, Alfred Kean — 5
MOEHLENPAH, Henry A. — 2
MOEHLMAN, Arthur B. — 3
MOEKLE, Herman Liveright — 5
MOELLER, Harold Frederick — 5
MOELLER, Henry — 1
MOELLER, Louis — 1
MOELLER, Philip — 3
MOELLMANN, Albert — 5
MOELLRING, George H. — 1
MOEN, Reuben O. — 4
MOENCH, Charles L. — 1
MOENKHAUS, William J. — 5
MOENKHAUS, William J. — 2
MOERDYKE, Peter — 1
MOERK, Frank Xavier — 2
MOEUR, Benjamin Baker — 4
MOFFAT, David Halliday — 1

MOFFAT, David William — 2
MOFFAT, Donald — 3
MOFFAT, Douglas Maxwell — 3
MOFFAT, Frederick G. — 1
MOFFAT, James Clement — H
MOFFAT, James David — 1
MOFFAT, James E. — 3
MOFFAT, Jay Pierrepont — 1
MOFFAT, John Little — 1
MOFFATT, Fred Cushing — 5
MOFFATT, James — 1
MOFFATT, James Hugh — 3
MOFFATT, James Strong — 4
MOFFATT, Lucius Gaston — 5
MOFFATT, Seth Crittenden — H
MOFFET, John — 3
MOFFETT, Charles Alexander — 3
MOFFETT, Cleveland — 1
MOFFETT, Donovan Clifford — 4
MOFFETT, Elwood Stewart — 5
MOFFETT, George Monroe — 3
MOFFETT, James Andrew — 3
MOFFETT, James William — 4
MOFFETT, Louis Burdelle — 5
MOFFETT, Samuel Austin — 1
MOFFETT, Samuel Erasmus — 1
MOFFETT, Thomas Clinton — 2
MOFFETT, William Adger — 1
MOFFETT, William Walter — 1
MOFFIT, Alexander — 5
MOFFIT, S. P. — 3
MOFFITT, Herbert Charles — 4
MOFFITT, Hosea — H
MOFFITT, James Kennedy — 3
MOFFITT, Walter Volentine — 2
MOFFLY, Charles K. — 4
MOGENSEN, Walter Alexander — 4
MOHAMMED, V. — 4
MOHLER, A. L. — 1
MOHLER, Daniel Nathan — 3
MOHLER, Henry Keller — 1
MOHLER, Jacob Christian — 3
MOHLER, John Frederick — 1
MOHLER, John Robbins — 5
MOHLER, Samuel Loomis — 1
MOHN, Thorbjorn Nilson — 1
MOHOLY-NAGY, Laszio George — 2
MOHR, Charles — 1
MOHR, Charles Adam — 5
MOHR, Charles Theodor — 1
MOHUN, Barry — 1
MOINET, Edward Julien — 3
MOIR, Henry — 1
MOIR, John Troup — 4
MOISE, Edwin Warren — 4
MOISE, Harold A. — 3
MOISE, Pennina — H
MOISEIWITSCH, Benno — 4
MOISSEIFF, Leon Solomon — 2
MOLDEHNKE, Edward Frederick — 1
MOLDENHAWER, Julius Valdemar — 2
MOLDENKE, Charles Edward — 1
MOLDENKE, Richard — 5
MOLDVEEN-GERONIMUS, Miriam Esther
MOLE, Harvey E. — 3
MOLEEN, George Arnold — 1
MOLINEUX, Edward Leslie
MOLINEUX, Marie Ada — 5
MOLINEUX, Roland Burnham — 4
MOLITOR, David Albert — 2
MOLITOR, Frederic Albert
MOLITOR, Hans — 3
MOLLENHAUER, Emil — 1
MOLLENHAUER, Henry — H
MOLLER, Mathias Peter — 1
MOLLER, Mathias Peter Jr.
MOLLIN, Fernand E. — 3
MOLLISON, Irvin Charles
MOLLISON, James Alexander

MOORE, John G. 4
MOORE, John Leverett 4
MOORE, John M. 1
MOORE, John Merrick 3
MOORE, John Milton 2
MOORE, John Monroe 2
MOORE, John Small 5
MOORE, John Trotwood 1
MOORE, John W. 2
MOORE, John Walker 3
MOORE, John Weeks 4
MOORE, John White 1
MOORE, John William 2
MOORE, Joseph 4
MOORE, Joseph Arthur 1
MOORE, Joseph B. 1
MOORE, Joseph Earle 3
MOORE, Joseph Haines 2
MOORE, Josiah John 1
MOORE, Josiah Staunton 4
MOORE, Julian H. 1
MOORE, Kenneth W. 5
MOORE, Laban Theodore H
MOORE, Lewis Baxter 4
MOORE, Lillian 1
MOORE, Lillian Russell 1
MOORE, Louis Herbert 1
MOORE, Lyle Stickley 3
MOORE, Lyman Sweet 2
MOORE, Marianne Craig 5
MOORE, Mark Egbert 5
MOORE, Mary 5
MOORE, Mary Norman 5
MOORE, Maurice H
MOORE, Maurice Malcolm 4
MOORE, Miles Conway 1
MOORE, Milton Harvey 5
MOORE, Mrs. John Trotwood 3
MOORE, Mrs. N. Hudson 1
MOORE, Nathan Grier 2
MOORE, Nathaniel Drummond 1
MOORE, Nathaniel Fish H
MOORE, Orren Cheney H
MOORE, Orval Floyd 3
MOORE, Oscar Fitzallen 5
MOORE, Paul 3
MOORE, Paul H. 4
MOORE, Paul J. 4
MOORE, Philip North 1
MOORE, Randle T. 5
MOORE, Ransom Asa 1
MOORE, Richard Bishop 1
MOORE, Richard Channing H
MOORE, Richard Curtis 4
MOORE, Robert H
MOORE, Robert Allan 5
MOORE, Robert Foster 4
MOORE, Robert H(arris) 5
MOORE, Robert Lee 5
MOORE, Robert Lee 4
MOORE, Robert Martin 3
MOORE, Robert McDonald 4
MOORE, Robert Murray 5
MOORE, Robert S. 1
MOORE, Robert Thomas 3
MOORE, Robert Walton 1
MOORE, Robert Webber 4
MOORE, Roberts Cosby 5
MOORE, Roy 3
MOORE, Roy W. 5
MOORE, Rupert Eastmer 5
MOORE, Samuel H
MOORE, Samuel 1
MOORE, Samuel McDowell H
MOORE, Samuel Preston H
MOORE, Samuel Wallace 1
MOORE, Sherwood 4
MOORE, Sir Henry 4
MOORE, Stephen 1
MOORE, Sydenham H
MOORE, Thomas 4
MOORE, Thomas Joseph 4
MOORE, Thomas Justin 4
MOORE, Thomas Love 1
MOORE, Thomas Morrell 4
MOORE, Thomas Overton H
MOORE, Thomas Verner 5
MOORE, Thomas Verner 4
MOORE, Thomas Waterman 5
MOORE, Veranus Alva 1
MOORE, Victor 5
MOORE, Victor F. 5
MOORE, Vida Frank 1
MOORE, Walter Bedford 2
MOORE, Walter William 1
MOORE, Walton Norwood 4
MOORE, Warren G. Sr. 4

MOORE, William * H
MOORE, William Charles 4
MOORE, William Emmet 1
MOORE, William Emmet 2
MOORE, William Eves 1
MOORE, William Garrett 2
MOORE, William George 5
MOORE, William Henry 1
MOORE, William Sturtevant
MOORE, William Sutton H
MOORE, William Thomas 4
MOORE, William Underhill 2
MOORE, Willis Luther 4
MOORE, Wilmer Lee 4
MOORE, Zephaniah Swift H
MOOREHEAD, Frederick Brown 2
MOOREHEAD, Singleton Peabody 4
MOOREHEAD, Warren King 1
MOOREHEAD, William Gallogly 1
MOORES, Charles Bruce 1
MOORES, Charles Washington
MOORES, J. Henry 1
MOORES, Merrill 1
MOORHEAD, Dudley Thomas 5
MOORHEAD, Frank Graham 3
MOORHEAD, Harley G. 2
MOORHEAD, James Kennedy H
MOORHEAD, Louis David 1
MOORHEAD, Louis David
MOORHEAD, Maxwell K. 5
MOORHEAD, Robert Lowry 5
MOORHEAD, William Singer 3
MOORHOUSE, Harold Roy 4
MOORMAN, Charles Harwood 1
MOOSER, William H
MOOSMULLER, Oswald William H
MOOT, Adelbert 1
MOQUE, Alice Lee 1
MORA, F. Luis 1
MORA, Joseph Jacinto 1
MORAIS, Sabato H
MORALES, Sanchez 1
MORA MIRANDA, Marcial 5
MORAN, Annette 1
MORAN, Benjamin H
MORAN, Daniel Edward 1
MORAN, Daniel James 2
MORAN, Edward H
MORAN, Edward Carleton Jr. 4
MORAN, Eugene Francis 4
MORAN, Francis Thomas 3
MORAN, Fred T. 1
MORAN, James Thomas 1
MORAN, John Henry 3
MORAN, John Joseph 5
MORAN, Leon 1
MORAN, Percy 1
MORAN, Peter 1
MORAN, Richard Bartholomew 5
MORAN, Robert 1
MORAN, Thomas H
MORAN, Thomas 1
MORAN, Thomas 4
MORAN, Thomas A. 1
MORAN, Thomas Francis 5
MORAN, William Edward, Jr.
MORAN, William Joseph 4
MORANDI, Giorgio 4
MORAWETZ, Albert Richard 4
MORAWETZ, Victor 3
MORCOM, Clifford Bawden
MORDE, Theodore A. 3
MORDECAI, Alfred H
MORDECAI, Alfred 1
MORDECAI, Moses Cohen
MORDECAI, Samuel Fox 4
MORDECAI, T. Moultrie 4
MORDEN, William J. 5
MORE, Brookes 2
MORE, Charles Church 4
MORE, E. Anson 1
MORE, Herman 5
MORE, John Herron 5

MORE, Louis Trenchard 2
MORE, Nicholas H
MORE, Paul Elmer 1
MOREAU, Arthur Edmond 3
MOREAU 'DE SAINT MERY, Mederic-Louis-Elie H
MOREAU-LISLET, Louis Casimir Elisabeth H
MOREAUX, Amable Oli 2
MOREHEAD, Albert Hodges 4
MOREHEAD, Charles Allen 3
MOREHEAD, Charles Slaughter H
MOREHEAD, French Hugh 3
MOREHEAD, James Turner * H
MOREHEAD, John Alfred 1
MOREHEAD, John Henry 2
MOREHEAD, John Lindsay 4
MOREHEAD, John Motley H
MOREHEAD, John Motley 1
MOREHEAD, John Motley 4
MOREHOUSE, Albert Kellogg 3
MOREHOUSE, Daniel Walter 1
MOREHOUSE, Frances Milton 2
MOREHOUSE, Frederic Cook 1
MOREHOUSE, George Pierson 4
MOREHOUSE, George Read 1
MOREHOUSE, Henry Lyman 1
MOREHOUSE, Julius Stanley 4
MOREHOUSE, Linden Husted 1
MOREHOUSE, Linden Husted 4
MOREHOUSE, Lyman Foote 5
MOREHOUSE, P. Gad Bryan 5
MOREHOUSE, Ward 4
MOREHOUSE, William Russell 1
MORELAND, Edward Leyburn 3
MORELAND, John Richard 2
MORELAND, William Hall 2
MORELAND, William Haywood 2
MORELL, George Webb H
MORELL, Parker 5
MORELL, William Nelson 5
MORELOCK, Horace Wilson 3
MORENO, Arthur Alphonse 3
MORESCHI, Joseph V. 5
MOREY, Arthur Thornton 4
MOREY, Charles Rufus 3
MOREY, Charles William 4
MOREY, Chester S. 1
MOREY, Frank 1
MOREY, Henry Martyn 3
MOREY, John William 3
MOREY, Lloyd 4
MOREY, Samuel H
MOREY, Victor Pinkerton 3
MOREY, William Carey 1
MORFA, Raymond J. 3
MORFIT, Campbell H
MORFORD, Henry 4
MORFORD, James Richard 4
MORGAN, Abel H
MORGAN, Alfred Powell 5
MORGAN, Angela 4
MORGAN, Ann Haven 4
MORGAN, Anna 1
MORGAN, Anne 3
MORGAN, Anne Eugenia Felicia 4
MORGAN, Appleton 1
MORGAN, Bayard Quincy 4
MORGAN, Brooks Sanderson 5
MORGAN, Carey E. 1
MORGAN, Caroline Starr 5

MORGAN, Casey Bruce 1
MORGAN, Charles H
MORGAN, Charles 3
MORGAN, Charles Carroll 1
MORGAN, Charles Eldridge 2
MORGAN, Charles Henry 1
MORGAN, Charles Herbert 1
MORGAN, Charles Hill 1
MORGAN, Christopher H
MORGAN, Clifford Veryl 3
MORGAN, Clinton Emory 3
MORGAN, Daniel 1
MORGAN, Daniel Edgar 2
MORGAN, Daniel Nash 1
MORGAN, David E. 1
MORGAN, DeWitt Schuyler 1
MORGAN, Dick Thompson 1
MORGAN, Edmund Morris Jr. 4
MORGAN, Edward Broadbent 1
MORGAN, Edward M. 1
MORGAN, Edwin Barber H
MORGAN, Edwin Denison 1
MORGAN, Edwin Franklin Abell 4
MORGAN, Edwin Lee 4
MORGAN, Edwin Vernon 1
MORGAN, Elford C(hapman) 5
MORGAN, Eliot S. N. H
MORGAN, Ephraim Franklin 2
MORGAN, Ezra Leonidas 1
MORGAN, F. Coelies 1
MORGAN, Forrest 4
MORGAN, Francis Patterson 1
MORGAN, Frank 3
MORGAN, Frank Millett 3
MORGAN, Fred Bogardus 3
MORGAN, Frederic Lindley 5
MORGAN, G. Campbell 4
MORGAN, Geoffrey Francis 3
MORGAN, George H
MORGAN, George 1
MORGAN, George Allen 5
MORGAN, George Hagar 1
MORGAN, George Horace 4
MORGAN, George O. 3
MORGAN, George Wagner 3
MORGAN, George Washbourne H
MORGAN, George Washington H
MORGAN, George Wilson 5
MORGAN, George Wilson 1
MORGAN, Harcourt Alexander 3
MORGAN, Harry Dale 1
MORGAN, Harry Hays 1
MORGAN, Henry A. 4
MORGAN, Henry William 1
MORGAN, Herbert Rollo 3
MORGAN, Hugh Jackson 5
MORGAN, Ike 5
MORGAN, Isaac B. 3
MORGAN, Jacob L. 5
MORGAN, James H
MORGAN, James 3
MORGAN, James Bright 1
MORGAN, James Dada H
MORGAN, James Dudley 1
MORGAN, James Henry 1
MORGAN, James Norris 1
MORGAN, James W. 3
MORGAN, Jerome J. 4
MORGAN, John 1
MORGAN, John Heath 5
MORGAN, John Hill 2
MORGAN, John Hunt H
MORGAN, John Jacob Brooke 2
MORGAN, John Jordan 1
MORGAN, John Livingston Rutgers 1
MORGAN, John Paul H
MORGAN, John Pierpont H
MORGAN, John Pierpont 2
MORGAN, John Thoburn 5
MORGAN, John Tyler 1
MORGAN, Junius Spencer H
MORGAN, Junius Spencer 4
MORGAN, Justin H
MORGAN, Justin Colfax 3
MORGAN, Lewis Henry 1

MORGAN, Lewis Lovering 5
MORGAN, Louis M. H
MORGAN, Matthew Somerville H
MORGAN, Maud 2
MORGAN, Michael Ryan 1
MORGAN, Minot Canfield 5
MORGAN, Monta B. Sr. 3
MORGAN, Morris Hicky 1
MORGAN, Octavius 1
MORGAN, Ora Sherman 4
MORGAN, Paul Beagary 3
MORGAN, Percy Tredegar 4
MORGAN, Peto Whittaker 4
MORGAN, Philip Hicky H
MORGAN, Philip M. 4
MORGAN, Ralph 4
MORGAN, Raymond A. 4
MORGAN, Robert Kenneth 4
MORGAN, Robert M. 3
MORGAN, Russell Van Dyke 3
MORGAN, Samuel Tate 4
MORGAN, Sister M. Sylvia 4
MORGAN, Stephen 4
MORGAN, Stokeley Williams 4
MORGAN, Tali Esen 5
MORGAN, Theophilous John H
MORGAN, Thomas Alfred 4
MORGAN, Thomas 5
MORGAN, Thomas Francis, Jr. 2
MORGAN, Thomas Hunt 2
MORGAN, Thomas J. 1
MORGAN, Thomas John 1
MORGAN, Thomas W. 1
MORGAN, Tom P. 2
MORGAN, Wallace 2
MORGAN, Walter Piety 3
MORGAN, Walter Sydney 3
MORGAN, William H
MORGAN, William 1
MORGAN, William Berry 4
MORGAN, William Conger 5
MORGAN, William 4
MORGAN, William Edgar 2'd 2
MORGAN, William Fellowes 1
MORGAN, William Forbes 1
MORGAN, William Gerry 1
MORGAN, William Henry * 1
MORGAN, William M. 1
MORGAN, William McKendree 2
MORGAN, William Sacheus 5
MORGAN, William Stephen H
MORGAN, William Thomas 2
MORGAN, William Yost 1
MORGENSTIERNE, Wilhelm Thorleif Munthe 4
MORGENTHAU, Henry 2
MORGENTHAU, Henry Jr. 4
MORGULIS, Sergius 5
MORIARITY, Patrick Eugene H
MORIARTY, Charles Patrick 4
MORIARTY, Eugene 5
MORIARTY, William Daniel 1
MORIN, John M. 2
MORINI, Erika 4
MORISON, George Abbot 1
MORISON, George Shattuck 1
MORISON, James Henderson Stuart 2
MORISSE, Richard Diehm 5
MORITZ, Adrianus Johannes Leonard 5
MORITZ, John A. 1
MORITZ, Richard Daniel 4
MORITZ, Robert Edouard 1
MORITZEN, Julius 5
MORK, P. Ralph 3
MORLAN, Webster Smith 1
MORLEY, Christopher 3
MORLEY, Clarence Joseph 5
MORLEY, Edward Williams

MORLEY, Frank 1
MORLEY, George Bidwell 1
MORLEY, John Henry 1
MORLEY, 1
  Margaret Warner
MORLEY, 2
  Sylvanus Griswold
MORLING, Edgar Alfred 1
MORMAN, James Bale 1
MORNINGSTAR, 4
  Thomas Wood
MORON, Alonzo 5
  Graseano
MORONEY, Carl J. 3
MORONEY, James 5
  McQueen
MOROSCO, Oliver 5
MOROSO, John Antonio 3
MORPHY, Paul Charles H
MORRELL, Benjamin H
MORRELL, H
  Daniel Johnson
MORRELL, 4
  Edward De Veaux
MORRELL, 1
  Imogene Robinson
MORREY, 3
  Charles Bradfield
MORRIL, David Lawrence H
MORRILL, Albert Henry 2
MORRILL, Albro David 2
MORRILL, Anson Peaslee 1
MORRILL, Charles Henry 1
MORRILL, Edmund N. 1
MORRILL, Henry Albert 4
MORRILL, John Adams 2
MORRILL, Justin H
MORRILL, Lot Myrick H
MORRILL, Mendon 4
MORRILL, H
  Samuel Plummer
MORRILL, Warren Pearl 2
MORRILL, William Kelso 1
MORRIS, 5
  Alice A. Parmelee
MORRIS, Anthony * H
MORRIS, 1
  Benjamin Wistar
MORRIS, 2
  Benjamin Wistar III
MORRIS, Cadwalader H
MORRIS, Calvary H
MORRIS, Caspar H
MORRIS, Charles H
MORRIS, Charles * 1
MORRIS, Charles Gould 4
MORRIS, 5
  Charles Harwood
MORRIS, 3
  Charles Shoemaker
MORRIS, Charles Wendel 4
MORRIS, Chester 5
MORRIS, Clara 1
MORRIS, Claude Frank 5
MORRIS, Clyde Tucker 5
MORRIS, Constance Lily 3
MORRIS, Daniel H
MORRIS, Dave Hennen 2
MORRIS, Don 4
MORRIS, 4
  Donald Florence
MORRIS, Douglas 1
MORRIS, Earl Halstead 3
MORRIS, Edgar Leslie 1
MORRIS, Edmund H
MORRIS, Edward 1
MORRIS, Edward Dafydd 1
MORRIS, Edward Joy H
MORRIS, 1
  Edward Parmelee
MORRIS, Edwin Bateman 5
MORRIS, 1
  Effingham Buckley
MORRIS, Elias Camp 1
MORRIS, 5
  Elisabeth Woodbridge (Mrs. Charles Gould Morris)
MORRIS, Elizabeth H
MORRIS, Ernest Melvin 3
MORRIS, 3
  Evangeline Hall
MORRIS, Felix James 1
MORRIS, Florance Ann 2
MORRIS, Frank Edward 4
MORRIS, Frank Hubbard 1
MORRIS, Frank R. 3
MORRIS, 4
  Frederick Kuhne
MORRIS, 5
  Frederick Wistar, III
MORRIS, George 2
MORRIS, George Davis 4
MORRIS, George Edward 1
MORRIS, George Ford 5
MORRIS, George Kenneth 5
MORRIS, George Maurice 1
MORRIS, George Perry 1

MORRIS, George Pope H
MORRIS, H
  George Sylvester
MORRIS, 1
  George Van Derveer
MORRIS, Gouverneur 2
MORRIS, Gouverneur 3
MORRIS, Harold Cecil 4
MORRIS, Harrison Smith 1
MORRIS, 2
  Henry Crittendon
MORRIS, Homer 1
  Lawrence
MORRIS, Howard 1
MORRIS, Hugh Martin 4
MORRIS, Ira Nelson 5
MORRIS, Isaac Newton H
MORRIS, J. Cheston 2
MORRIS, James Charlton 4
MORRIS, James Cralk 2
MORRIS, James Ward 4
MORRIS, John 3
MORRIS, John Baptist 4
MORRIS, John Gottlieb H
MORRIS, Jonathan David H
MORRIS, Joseph H
MORRIS, Joseph 5
  Joseph Chandler
MORRIS, Joseph E. 4
MORRIS, L. W. 3
MORRIS, 3
  Leland Burnette
MORRIS, Lewis * H
MORRIS, Lewis Coleman 1
MORRIS, Lewis Richard 1
MORRIS, Lewis Spencer 2
MORRIS, Lloyd 5
MORRIS, Luzon Burritt H
MORRIS, 1
  Martin Ferdinand
MORRIS, Mathias 1
MORRIS, Nelson 1
MORRIS, Newbold 1
MORRIS, Newbold 4
MORRIS, Oscar Matison 2
MORRIS, Page 1
MORRIS, Pat G. 4
MORRIS, Percy Amos 5
MORRIS, Richard H
MORRIS, Richard Lewis 3
MORRIS, 1
  Richard Valentine
MORRIS, Robert * H
MORRIS, Robert Clark 1
MORRIS, Robert Eugene 1
MORRIS, Robert Hugh 2
MORRIS, Robert Hunter 4
MORRIS, Robert Nelson 4
MORRIS, Robert Seymour 5
MORRIS, Robert Tuttle 2
MORRIS, Roger 1
MORRIS, 1
  Roger Sylvester
MORRIS, Roland Sletor 2
MORRIS, Samuel Brooks 4
MORRIS, Samuel Henry 4
MORRIS, Samuel Leslie 1
MORRIS, Samuel Wells 1
MORRIS, Thomas * 1
MORRIS, 1
  Thomas Armstrong
MORRIS, Thomas John 1
MORRIS, William 1
MORRIS, William Alfred 2
MORRIS, 1
  William Charles
MORRIS, 5
  William Henry Harrison
MORRIS, William Hicks 5
MORRIS, H
  William Hopkins
MORRIS, William Robert 4
MORRIS, 4
  William Shivers
MORRIS, 4
  William Sylvanus
MORRIS, William Thomas 2
MORRIS, William Torrey 5
MORRIS, William V. H
MORRISON, A. Cressy 4
MORRISON, 1
  Albert Alexander
MORRISON, 1
  Alexander Francis
MORRISON, Cameron 3
MORRISON, Charles B. 1
MORRISON, 4
  Charles Clayton
MORRISON, 5
  Charles Munro
MORRISON, 5
  Charles Samuel
MORRISON, 1
  Charles Walthall
MORRISON, Clinton 1
MORRISON, 4
  'deLesseps S.

MORRISON, 3
  Donald Harvard
MORRISON, 4
  Edward Lester
MORRISON, Edwin Rees 4
MORRISON, Frank 2
MORRISON, Frank 3
  Barron
MORRISON, 1
  Frederick Douglas
MORRISON, 1
  George Austin
MORRISON, H
  George Washington
MORRISON, 5
  Harry Winford
MORRISON, Henry Clay 1
MORRISON, Henry Clay 2
MORRISON, 2
  Henry Clinton
MORRISON, Ivan 3
MORRISON, Jack Harold 5
MORRISON, James 3
  Dalton
MORRISON, James Dow 1
MORRISON, James Frank 4
MORRISON, H
  James Lowery Donaldson
MORRISON, 1
  Jasper Newton
MORRISON, Jim 5
MORRISON, John Arch 4
MORRISON, John F. 1
MORRISON, John Irwin H
MORRISON, John Tracy 4
MORRISON, Joseph 2
MORRISON, 5
  Joseph L(ederman)
MORRISON, Joseph Peter 3
MORRISON, Levi 1
MORRISON, Lewis 1
MORRISON, 1
  Mary J. Whitney
MORRISON, 1
  Mrs. May Treat
MORRISON, 1
  Nathan Jackson
MORRISON, 5
  Ocie Butler, Jr.
MORRISON, Phoebe 5
MORRISON, Ralph 2
  Waldo
MORRISON, Robert Hugh 5
MORRISON, Robert John 2
MORRISON, 4
  Robert Stewart
MORRISON, Roger Leroy 5
MORRISON, 5
  Sarah Elizabeth
MORRISON, Stanley 4
MORRISON, 1
  Theodore Nevin
MORRISON, Thomas 2
MORRISON, 3
  Wayland Augustus
MORRISON, 4
  Willard Langdon
MORRISON, William H
MORRISON, 4
  William Barrett
MORRISON, 2
  William Brown
MORRISON, 1
  William Ralls
MORRISON, 4
  William Shepherd
MORRISON, 5
  Zaidee Lincoln
MORRISON, Zelma 5
  Reeves
MORRISS, H
  Elizabeth Cleveland (Mrs. John)
MORRISSEY, Andrew 1
MORRISSEY, 1
  Andrew Marcus
MORRISSEY, James Peter 5
MORRISSEY, John 4
MORRISSEY, Michael A. 4
MORRISSEY, 4
  Patrick Henry
MORRON, John Reynolds 3
MORROW, Albert Sydney 1
MORROW, 1
  Cornelius Wortendyke
MORROW, Dwight 1
  Whitney
MORROW, Edwin P. 1
MORROW, 3
  Frederick Keenan
MORROW, George 1
  Keenan
MORROW, 1
  George Washington
MORROW, Glenn R. 5
MORROW, Hubert T. 3
MORROW, Hugh 4

MORROW, James Binkley 1
MORROW, James E. 1
MORROW, Jay Johnson 1
MORROW, Jeremiah H
MORROW, John 3
MORROW, John 1
MORROW, John D. A. 5
MORROW, 2
  Lester William Wallace
MORROW, Marco 5
MORROW, 3
  Mrs. Dwight Whitney
MORROW, Mrs. Honore 1
MORROW, Prince Albert 1
MORROW, Theodore F. 4
MORROW, Thomas 1
MORROW, Thomas H
  Vaughan
MORROW, W. Carr 1
MORROW, W. K. 1
MORROW, 2
  Walter Alexander
MORROW, 1
  William Chambers
MORROW, William W. 1
MORROW, 5
  Winston Vaughan
MORROW, 5
  Wright Chalfant
MORSCH, Lucile M. 5
MORSCHAUSER, Joseph 2
MORSE, Albert Laverne 5
MORSE, H
  Alexander Porter
MORSE, Alpheus H
MORSE, Anson Daniel 1
MORSE, Anson Ely 4
MORSE, Arthur David 5
MORSE, Arthur Henry 2
MORSE, Benjamin Clarke 1
MORSE, 4
  Charles Adelbert
MORSE, Charles Henry 1
MORSE, Charles Hosmer 1
MORSE, Charles Hosmer 3
MORSE, Charles Wyman 2
MORSE, Charles Wyman 4
MORSE, Clark T. 3
MORSE, David Sherman 5
MORSE, E. Rollins 4
MORSE, 1
  Edward Leland Clark
MORSE, Edward Lind 1
MORSE, Edward Peck 4
MORSE, 1
  Edward Sylvester
MORSE, Edwin Kirtland 2
MORSE, Edwin Wilson 1
MORSE, Elmer Addison 5
MORSE, Frank Lincoln 1
MORSE, Freeman Harlow H
MORSE, Fremont 1
MORSE, Glenn Tilley 3
MORSE, Godfrey 1
MORSE, Harmon 1
  Northrop
MORSE, Harold M. 4
MORSE, Harry Wheeler 1
MORSE, Henry Dutton H
MORSE, Horace Taylor 4
MORSE, Hosea Ballou 1
MORSE, Ira Herbert 5
MORSE, Irving Haskell 5
MORSE, Isaac Edward H
MORSE, James Herbert 1
MORSE, Jedidiah H
MORSE, Jerome Edward 1
MORSE, John Lovett 1
MORSE, John Torrey Jr. 1
MORSE, Josiah 2
MORSE, Leon Jeremiah 3
MORSE, Leopold 1
MORSE, Lester Samuel 5
MORSE, Lucy Gibbons 1
MORSE, 5
  Margaret Fessenden
MORSE, 4
  Merrill Salisbury
MORSE, Oliver Andrew H
MORSE, Perley 2
MORSE, Richard Cary 1
MORSE, Richard Cary 4
MORSE, Robert Hosmer 1
MORSE, Robert McNeil 1
MORSE, Roy L. 2
MORSE, H
  Samuel Finley Breese
MORSE, 5
  Samuel Finley Brown
MORSE, Sidney 1
MORSE, Sidney Edwards H
MORSE, Waldo Grant 1
MORSE, Warner Jackson 1
MORSE, Wilbur Jr. 3
MORSE, Withrow 3

MORSS, Charles Anthony 1
MORSS, Everett 1
MORSS, Samuel E. 1
MORSTEIN MARX, Fritz 5
MORT, Paul R. 4
MORTENSEN, Martin 5
MORTENSON, 5
  Ernest Dawson
MORTENSON, Peter 1
  Alvin
MORTEZA 4
MORTIMER, 1
  Alfred Garnett
MORTIMER, 3
  Frank Cogswell
MORTIMER, James 3
  Daniel
MORTIMER, Lee 4
MORTIMER, Mary H
MORTON, Asa Henry 4
MORTON, Charles H
MORTON, Charles 1
MORTON, Charles Adams 1
MORTON, Charles Gould 1
MORTON, Charles W. 4
MORTON, Conrad 1
  Vernon
MORTON, David 3
MORTON, Eliza Happy 1
MORTON, H
  Ferdinand Joseph La Menthe
MORTON, 4
  Ferdinand Joseph La Menthe
MORTON, Frank Roy 1
MORTON, 1
  Frederick William
MORTON, George * H
MORTON, 1
  George Carpenter
MORTON, George Edwin 1
MORTON, Henry 1
MORTON, Henry H. 1
MORTON, 2
  Howard McIlvain
MORTON, Ira Abbott 3
MORTON, Jack A. 5
MORTON, Jackson 1
MORTON, 1
  James Ferdinand
MORTON, James Geary 5
MORTON, 1
  James Madison Jr.
MORTON, James Proctor 5
MORTON, James St Clair H
MORTON, Jennie Chinn 1
MORTON, Jeremiah 1
MORTON, 1
  Jeremiah Rogers
MORTON, John H
MORTON, John 2
MORTON, Joseph 2
MORTON, Joy 1
MORTON, 1
  Julius Sterling
MORTON, Levi Parsons 1
MORTON, Marcus * H
MORTON, Nathaniel H
MORTON, H
  Oliver Hazard Perry
MORTON, Oren Frederic 1
MORTON, Paul 1
MORTON, Perry William 4
MORTON, 3
  Richard Albert Dunlap
MORTON, 5
  Rosalie Slaughter
MORTON, Samuel George H
MORTON, Samuel Walker 1
MORTON, 1
  Sarah Wentworth Apthorpe
MORTON, Sterling 4
MORTON, Thomas 1
MORTON, Thomas 4
  George
MORTON, W. Brown 4
MORTON, 1
  William Henry Stephenson
MORTON, H
  William Thomas Green
MORWITZ, Edward 1
MOSBY, Charles Virgil 2
MOSBY, John Singleton 1
MOSCHCOWITZ, 1
  Alexis Victor
MOSCHCOWITZ, Paul 2
MOSCOSO 'DE H
  ALVARADO, Luis 'de
MOSCOWITZ, Grover M. 2
MOSELEY, 4
  Ben Perley Poore
MOSELEY, Charles West 3
MOSELEY, 1
  Edward Augustus
MOSELEY, 1
  Edward Buckland

MOSELEY, Frederick S, Jr. 5
MOSELEY, George Van Horn 4
MOSELEY, Hal Walters 2
MOSELEY, John Ohleyer 3
MOSELEY, Jonathan Ogden H
MOSELEY, Lonzo B. 4
MOSELEY, Mercer Pamplin 1
MOSELEY, William Abbott H
MOSELY, Philip Edward 5
MOSENTHAL, Herman 3
MOSENTHAL, Joseph H
MOSER, Alfred A. 5
MOSER, Charles Kroth 5
MOSER, Christopher Otto 1
MOSER, Clarence Patten 5
MOSER, Ellsworth
MOSER, Guy L. 4
MOSER, Henry S. 5
MOSER, Jefferson Franklin 1
MOSER, William 4
MOSES, Alfred Joseph 1
MOSES, Andrew 4
MOSES, Anna Mary Robertson 4
MOSES, Bernard 1
MOSES, C. A. 4
MOSES, Colter Hamilton 4
MOSES, Frederick Taft 3
MOSES, George Higgins 1
MOSES, Harry Morgan 3
MOSES, Henry L. 4
MOSES, Horace Augustus 1
MOSES, John 2
MOSES, Montrose Jonas 1
MOSES, Thomas 3
MOSES, Thomas Freeman 1
MOSESSOHN, David N. 1
MOSESSOHN, Moses Dayyan 1
MOSESSOHN, Nehemiah 1
MOSHER, Aaron Alexander Roland 3
MOSHER, Clelia Duel 1
MOSHER, Eliza Marla 1
MOSHER, Esek Ray 2
MOSHER, George Clark 1
MOSHER, George Frank 1
MOSHER, Gouverneur Frank 1
MOSHER, Harris Peyton 3
MOSHER, Howard Townsend 1
MOSHER, Ira 4
MOSHER, Raymond Mylar 3
MOSHER, Robert Brent 1
MOSHER, Samuel Barlow 5
MOSHER, Thomas Bird 1
MOSHER, William Allison 5
MOSHER, William Eugene 2
MOSIER, Harold Gerard 5
MOSIER, Jeremiah George 1
MOSIER, Orval McKinley 4
MOSIMAN, Samuel K. 1
MOSKOWITZ, Belle Israels 1
MOSLER, Edwin H. 3
MOSLER, Henry 1
MOSS, Albert Bartlett 1
MOSS, Charles McCord 1
MOSS, Charles Melville 4
MOSS, Emma Sadler 5
MOSS, Frank 1
MOSS, Frank J. 5
MOSS, Fred August 4
MOSS, Herbert James 3
MOSS, Hunter Holmes Jr. 1
MOSS, James Alfred 1
MOSS, John Calvin H
MOSS, Joseph 3
MOSS, Lemuel 1
MOSS, Leslie Bates 2
MOSS, Louis John 2
MOSS, Mary 1
MOSS, Maxmilian 4
MOSS, Ralph W. 4
MOSS, William Lorenzo 3
MOSS, William Washburn 1
MOSS, Woodson 1
MOSSADEGH, Mohammed 4
MOSSER, Charles Marcel 5
MOSSMAN, B. Paul 5
MOSSMAN, Frank E. 2
MOST, Johann Joseph H
MOST, Johann Joseph 4
MOSTELLER, L. Karlton 5

MOTE, Carl Henry 2
MOTE, Donald Roosevelt 5
MOTEN, Bennie 4
MOTEN, Roger Henwood 3
MOTHERWELL, Robert Burns II 2
MOTLEY, Emery Tyler 3
MOTLEY, John Lothrop H
MOTLEY, Warren 4
MOTLEY, Willard Francis 4
MOTON, Robert Russa 1
MOTRY, Hubert Louis 3
MOTT, Charles Stewart 5
MOTT, Frank Luther 4
MOTT, George Scudder 1
MOTT, Gershom 1
MOTT, Gordon Newell H
MOTT, James * 5
MOTT, James Wheaton 2
MOTT, John Griffin 2
MOTT, John R. 3
MOTT, Jordan Lawrence 1
MOTT, Lewis Freeman 1
MOTT, Lucretia Coffin H
MOTT, Luther Wright 4
MOTT, Omer Hillman 2
MOTT, Richard 5
MOTT, Rodney Loomer 5
MOTT, T. Bentley 3
MOTT, Valentine H
MOTT, Valentine 1
MOTT, William Elton 5
MOTTE, Isaac H
MOTTER, Orton B. 1
MOTTET, Henry 3
MOTTET, Jeanie Gallup (Mrs. Henry Mottet) 5
MOTTIER, David Myers 1
MOTZKIN, Theodore S. 5
MOUDY, Walter Frank 5
MOUHTAR BEY, Ahmed 4
MOULD, Elmer Wallace King 3
MOULD, Jacob Wray H
MOULTON, Arthur Wheelock 4
MOULTON, Charles Robert 2
MOULTON, Charles Wells 1
MOULTON, Charles William 1
MOULTON, Earl L. 3
MOULTON, Edwin F. 1
MOULTON, Forest Ray 3
MOULTON, Frank Prescott 4
MOULTON, George Mayhew 1
MOULTON, Harold Glen 4
MOULTON, Louise Chandler 1
MOULTON, Mace H
MOULTON, Richard Green 1
MOULTON, Sherman Roberts 2
MOULTON, Vern 3
MOULTON, Warren Joseph 1
MOULTON, William Horace 4
MOULTON, Willis Bryant 1
MOULTRIE, John H
MOULTRIE, William H
MOULTROP, Irving Edwin 1
MOUNGER, W. M. 4
MOUNT, Arnold John 2
MOUNT, Finley Pogue 1
MOUNT, James Atwell 1
MOUNT, Oliver Erskine 1
MOUNT, Wallace 1
MOUNT, William Sidney H
MOUNTCASTLE, George Williams 5
MOUNTCASTLE, Robert Edward Lee 1
MOUNTIN, Joseph W. 3
MOURSUND, Andrew Fleming, Jr. 5
MOURSUND, Walter Henrik 3
MOUSEL, Lloyd Harvey 5
MOUSER, Grant Earl Jr. 2
MOUTON, Alexander H
MOUZON, Edwin DuBose 1
MOWAT, Magnus 5
MOWATT, Anna Cora Ogden 5
MOWBRAY, Albert Henry 2
MOWBRAY, George Mordey H
MOWBRAY, H. Siddons 1

MOWBRAY-CLARKE, John 3
MOWER, Charles Drown 1
MOWER, Charles Drown 2
MOWER, Joseph Anthony H
MOWERY, William Byron 3
MOWRER, Frank Roger 5
MOWRER, Paul Scott 5
MOWRY, Daniel Jr. H
MOWRY, Harold 3
MOWRY, Ross Rutledge 3
MOWRY, William Augustus 1
MOXLEY, William J. 4
MOXOM, Philip Stafford 1
MOYER, Andrew Jackson 3
MOYER, Benton Leslie 4
MOYER, Burton Jones 5
MOYER, Charles H. 4
MOYER, David Gurstelle 5
MOYER, Gabriel Hocker 2
MOYER, Harold Nicholas 1
MOYER, Harvey Vernon 3
MOYER, James Ambrose 1
MOYER, Joseph Kearney 5
MOYER, William Henry 4
MOYLAN, Stephen H
MOYLE, Henry Dinwoodey 4
MOYLE, James Henry 2
MOYLE, Walter Gladstone 5
MOYNIHAN, James Humphrey 4
MOYNIHAN, P. H. 2
MOZEE, Phoebe Anne Oakley H
MOZEE, Phoebe Anne Oakley 4
MOZIER, Joseph H
MRAK, Ignatius 1
MUCKENFUSS, Anthony Moultrie 1
MUCKEY, Floyd Summer 1
MUCKLE, John Selser 1
MUCKLE, M. Richards 1
MUDD, Harvey Gilmer 1
MUDD, Harvey Seeley 3
MUDD, Mildred Esterbrook 3
MUDD, Seeley G. 4
MUDD, Seeley Wintersmith 1
MUDD, Sydney E. 3
MUDD, Sydney Emanuel 1
MUDD, William Swearingen 2
MUDGE, Alfred Eugene 2
MUDGE, Claire R. 4
MUDGE, Courtland Sawin 4
MUDGE, Edmund Webster 2
MUDGE, Enoch H
MUDGE, Henry U. 1
MUDGE, Isadore Gilbert 3
MUDGE, James 1
MUDGE, Lewis Seymour 2
MUDGE, Verne Donald 3
MUDGE, William Leroy 4
MUEHLBERGER, Clarence Weinert 1
MUEHLING, John Adam 2
MUELLER, Adolph 2
MUELLER, Alfred H
MUELLER, Arthur E. A. 4
MUELLER, Edward 3
MUELLER, Fred William 5
MUELLER, Hans 4
MUELLER, Hans Alexander 4
MUELLER, Hermann 1
MUELLER, John Henry 4
MUELLER, John Howard 4
MUELLER, John Victor 4
MUELLER, Karl Anton 5
MUELLER, Paul 5
MUELLER, Paul Albert 3
MUELLER, Paul Ferdinand 1
MUELLER, Paul John 4
MUELLER, Theodore Edward 3
MUELLER, Theodore Frederick 3
MUELLER, Theophil Herbert 4
MUELLER, Werner 4
MUENCH, Aloisius Joseph 4
MUENCH, Hugo, Jr. 5
MUENNICH, Ferenc 4
MUENSCHER, Walter C. 4
MUHLEMAN, George Washington 5
MUHLEMAN, Maurice Louis 1

MUHLENBERG, Francis Swaine H
MUHLENBERG, Frederick Augustus Conrad H
MUHLENBERG, Gotthilf Henry Ernest H
MUHLENBERG, Henry Augustus H
MUHLENBERG, Henry Augustus Philip H
MUHLENBERG, Henry Melchior H
MUHLENBERG, John Peter Gabriel H
MUHLENBERG, William Augustus H
MUHLFELD, George O. 2
MUHLMANN, Adolf 4
MUHSE, Albert Charles 4
MUIR, Andrew Forest 5
MUIR, Charles Henry 1
MUIR, Downie Davidson Jr. 1
MUIR, E. Stanton 4
MUIR, James 3
MUIR, James Irvin 4
MUIR, Jere T. 5
MUIR, John * 1
MUIR, Joseph Johnstone 1
MUIR, William 1
MUIRHEAD, James Fullarton 1
MUKERJI, Dhan Gopal 1
MULDER, John 3
MULDOON, Hugh Cornelius 3
MULDOON, Peter J. 1
MULDOON, William H
MULDOON, William 4
MULEY SOLIMAN H
MULFINGER, George Abraham 1
MULFORD, Clarence Edward 3
MULFORD, Elisha H
MULFORD, John Willett 4
MULFORD, Prentice 1
MULFORD, Raymon Howard 5
MULFORD, Roland Jessup 5
MULFORD, Walter 5
MULHAUPT, Frederick J. 1
MULHERIN, William Anthony 2
MULHERON, Anne Morton 2
MULHOLLAND, Frank L. 2
MULHOLLAND, Henry Bearden 4
MULHOLLAND, John 5
MULHOLLAND, William 1
MULKEY, Frederick William 1
MULL, George Fulmer 1
MULL, J. Harry 1
MULL, John Wesley 5
MULLALLY, Thornwell 2
MULLALY, Charles J. 2
MULLALY, John 1
MULLAN, George Vincent 2
MULLAN, James McElwane 1
MULLAN, W. G. Read 1
MULLANEY, James Vincent 4
MULLANEY, John Barry 5
MULLANPHY, John H
MULLANY, James Robert Madison H
MULLANY, John Francis 1
MULLANY, Patrick Francis H
MULLEN, Arthur Francis 2
MULLEN, James 1
MULLEN, James William 1
MULLEN, Ruth Ackerman (Mrs. Frank A. Mullen) 1
MULLEN, Thomas Richard 3
MULLEN, Tobias 1
MULLEN, William E. 5
MULLENBACH, James 1
MULLENIX, Charles A. 3
MULLENIX, Rollin Clarke 2
MULLER, Adolf Lancken 5
MULLER, Amelia A. 3
MULLER, Carl 4
MULLER, Carl Christian 1
MULLER, Edouard 2
MULLER, George P. 2
MULLER, Herman Edwin 4

MULLER, Hermann Joseph 4
MULLER, James Arthur 2
MULLER, Jonas Norman 5
MULLER, Margarethe 4
MULLER, Nichols 4
MULLER, Siegfried Hermann 4
MULLER, Siemon William 1
MULLER, W. Max 1
MULLER, Walter J. 4
MULLER-URY, Adolfo 2
MULLETT, Mary B. 1
MULLGARDT, Louis Christian 4
MULLIGAN, Catharine A(rcher) 5
MULLIGAN, Charles J. 1
MULLIGAN, Charles Wise 5
MULLIGAN, David B. 3
MULLIGAN, James Hilary 1
MULLIGAN, Richard Thomas 1
MULLIKEN, Alfred Henry 1
MULLIKEN, Otis E. 5
MULLIKEN, Samuel Parsons 1
MULLIKIN, Sidney Albert 1
MULLIN, Francis Anthony 2
MULLIN, Joseph H
MULLIN, Sam S. 5
MULLIN, William Valentine 1
MULLINNIX, Henry Maston 2
MULLINS, Edgar Young 1
MULLINS, George Walker 1
MULLINS, Isla May 1
MULLINS, James 5
MULLINS, Thomas C. H
MULLOWNEY, John James 3
MULLOY, William Theodore 3
MULROONEY, Edward Pierce 5
MULRY, Joseph Aloysius 1
MULTER, Smith Lewis 3
MULVANE, David Winfield 1
MULVIHILL, Michael Joseph 1
MUMFORD, Charles 4
MUMFORD, Charles Carney 1
MUMFORD, Ethel Watts 1
MUMFORD, Frederick Blackmar 3
MUMFORD, George H
MUMFORD, George Saltonstall 2
MUMFORD, Gurdon Saltonstall H
MUMFORD, Herbert Windsor 1
MUMFORD, James Gregory 1
MUMFORD, John Kimberly 1
MUMFORD, Mary Eno 1
MUMFORD, Philip G. 3
MUMFORD, Samuel Cranage 1
MUMMA, Harlan L. 5
MUMMA, James Hebron 5
MUMMA, Morton Claire, Jr. 1
MUMMA, Walter Mann 4
MUMMART, Clarence Allen 1
MUMPER, Norris McAllister 2
MUMPER, William Norris 4
MUNCH, Edvard 1
MUNCIE, Curtis Hamilton 1
MUNCIE, J. H. 3
MUNDE, Paul Fortunatus 1
MUNDELEIN, George William 1
MUNDHEIM, Samuel 1
MUNDIE, William Bryce 1
MUNDT, G. Henry 4
MUNDT, Walter J. 5
MUNDY, Ethel Frances 1
MUNDY, Ezekiel Wilson 1
MUNDY, Johnson Marchant H
MUNDY, Talbot 1
MUNDY, William Nelson 1
MUNFORD, Mary Cooke Branch 4

MUNFORD, Robert — H
MUNFORD, Walter F. — 3
MUNFORD, William — H
MUNGEN, William — H
MUNGER, Claude Worrell — 3
MUNGER, Dell H. — 4
MUNGER, Harold Henry — 5
MUNGER, Royal Freeman — 2
MUNGER, Theodore Thornton — 1
MUNGER, Thomas Charles — 1
MUNGER, William Henry — 1
MUNHALL, Leander Whitcomb — 1
MUNIZ, Joao Carlos — 4
MUNK, Joseph Amasa — 1
MUNKITTRICK, Richard Kendall — 1
MUNN, Charles Allen — 1
MUNN, Charles Clark — 1
MUNN, Hiram H. — 4
MUNN, James Buell — 4
MUNN, John Pixley — 1
MUNN, Orson Desaix — 1
MUNN, Orson Desaix — 3
MUNN, William Phipps — 1
MUNNIKHUYSEN, Walter Farnandis — 4
MUNNS, Mrs. Margaret Cairns — 3
MUNOZ, Jorge — 1
MUNOZ GRANDES, Agustin — 5
MUNRO, Annette Gardner — 3
MUNRO, Dana Carleton — 1
MUNRO, David Alexander — 1
MUNRO, Donald — 5
MUNRO, Emily Gardner — 1
MUNRO, George — H
MUNRO, H. G. — 3
MUNRO, Henry — H
MUNRO, James Alan — 5
MUNRO, John Cummings — 1
MUNRO, Robert Frater — 5
MUNRO, Walter J. — 3
MUNRO, Walter Lee — 1
MUNRO, Wilfred Harold — 1
MUNRO, William Bennett — 3
MUNROE, Charles Andrews — 3
MUNROE, Charles Edward — 1
MUNROE, Henry Smith — 1
MUNROE, Hersey — 1
MUNROE, James Phinney — 1
MUNROE, John Alexander — 5
MUNROE, Kirk — 1
MUNROE, Robert Clifford — 4
MUNROE, William Adams — 1
MUNROE, William Robert — 4
MUNSELL, Albert Henry — 1
MUNSELL, Charles Edward — 1
MUNSELL, Frank — 1
MUNSELL, Harry B. — 4
MUNSELL, Joel — H
MUNSEY, Frank Andrew — 1
MUNSN, John Maurice — 3
MUNSON, C. La Rue — 1
MUNSON, Edward Lyman — 1
MUNSON, Edwin Sterling — 5
MUNSON, Frank C. — 1
MUNSON, Gorham B. — 1
MUNSON, James Decker — 1
MUNSON, James Eugene — 1
MUNSON, John B. — 4
MUNSON, John G. — 3
MUNSON, John P. — 1
MUNSON, Lewis S, Jr. — 5
MUNSON, Loveland — 1
MUNSON, Myron Andrews — 1
MUNSON, Samuel Edgar — 5
MUNSON, Samuel Lyman — 1
MUNSON, Thomas Volney — 1
MUNSON, Welton Marks — 1
MUNSON, William Benjamin — 1
MUNSTER, August W. — 3
MUNSTERBERG, Hugo — 1
MUNTZ, Earl Edward — 4
MUNZ, Friedrich — 1
MUNZIG, George Chickering — 1
MURALT, Carl Leonard de — 5
MURANE, Cornelius Daniel — 4

MURAT, Achille Napoleon — H
MURATORE, Lucien — 3
MURCH, Chauncey — 1
MURCH, Maynard Hale — 4
MURCH, Thompson Henry — H
MURCH, Walter Tandy — 4
MURCHIE, Alexander — 3
MURCHIE, Harold Hale — 4
MURCHIE, Robert Charles — 2
MURCHISON, Carl — 4
MURCHISON, Claudius Temple — 1
MURCHISON, Clinton Williams — 5
MURCHISON, Kenneth Mackenzie — 1
MURDOCH, Frank Hitchcock — H
MURDOCH, James Edward — H
MURDOCH, James Y. — 4
MURDOCH, John — 1
MURDOCH, John Gormley — 1
MURDOCH, Thomas — 1
MURDOCK, Charles Albert — 1
MURDOCK, George John — 2
MURDOCK, Harold — 1
MURDOCK, Harris H. — 3
MURDOCK, Henry Taylor — 5
MURDOCK, James — H
MURDOCK, John Robert — 5
MURDOCK, John Samuel — 3
MURDOCK, Joseph Ballard — 1
MURDOCK, Marcellus Marion — 5
MURDOCK, Thomas Patrick — 3
MURDOCK, Victor — 2
MURFEE, Hopson Owen — 3
MURFEE, James Thomas — 1
MURFIN, James Orin — 1
MURFIN, Orin Gould — 1
MURFREE, Mary Noailles — 1
MURFREE, Walter Lee — 3
MURFREE, William Hardy — H
MURIE, Olaus Johan — 4
MURKLAND, Charles Sumner — 1
MURLIN, John Raymond — 5
MURLIN, Lemuel Herbert — 1
MURNANE, George — 5
MURPH, Daniel Shuford — 3
MURPHEY, Archibald De Bow — H
MURPHEY, Charles — H
MURPHEY, Robert Joseph — 5
MURPHREE, Albert Alexander — 1
MURPHREE, Eger V. — 4
MURPHREE, Thomas Alexander — 2
MURPHY, Albert S. — 4
MURPHY, Alfred J. — 1
MURPHY, Alice Harold — 4
MURPHY, Arthur Alban — 3
MURPHY, Arthur Edward — 4
MURPHY, Arthur M. — 4
MURPHY, Arthur Phillips — 1
MURPHY, Carl — 4
MURPHY, Charles F. — 1
MURPHY, Charles Joseph — 4
MURPHY, D. Hayes — 5
MURPHY, Daniel D. — 1
MURPHY, Daniel J. — 4
MURPHY, Daniel Joseph — 5
MURPHY, Dominic I. — 1
MURPHY, Edgar Gardner — 1
MURPHY, Edmond George — 1
MURPHY, Edmund Albert — 1
MURPHY, Edward Jr. — 1
MURPHY, Edward Francis — 1
MURPHY, Edward Thomas — 3
MURPHY, Ernest — 3
MURPHY, Eugene Edward — 4
MURPHY, Eva Morley — 4
MURPHY, Evert James — 1
MURPHY, Merle Farmer — 5
MURPHY, Francis — 1
MURPHY, Francis Daniel — 5
MURPHY, Francis Parnell — 3
MURPHY, Francis S. — 5
MURPHY, Frank — 2
MURPHY, Frank Morrill — 1

MURPHY, Franklin — 1
MURPHY, Franklin William — 1
MURPHY, Fred Towsley — 2
MURPHY, Frederick E. — 1
MURPHY, Frederick Vernon — 3
MURPHY, George H. — 1
MURPHY, Gerald — 4
MURPHY, Grayson M. P. — 1
MURPHY, Harry C. — 4
MURPHY, Henry Constant — 2
MURPHY, Henry Cruse — H
MURPHY, Henry Killam — 5
MURPHY, Herbert Francis — 4
MURPHY, Hermann Dudley — 2
MURPHY, Herschel Stratton — 4
MURPHY, Howard Ansley — 4
MURPHY, Isaac — H
MURPHY, J. Edwin — 1
MURPHY, J. Francis * — 1
MURPHY, J. Harvey — 1
MURPHY, James A. — 3
MURPHY, James B. — 3
MURPHY, James Cornelius * — 1
MURPHY, James R. — 4
MURPHY, James Shields — 5
MURPHY, James William — 3
MURPHY, Jeremiah Henry — H
MURPHY, Jimmy — 4
MURPHY, John * — 1
MURPHY, John Benjamin * — 1
MURPHY, John Donahoe — 2
MURPHY, John H. — 4
MURPHY, John Patrick — 5
MURPHY, John T. — 1
MURPHY, John Thomas — 2
MURPHY, John Vernon — 3
MURPHY, John W. — H
MURPHY, John W. — 4
MURPHY, Joseph Aloysius Charles — 1
MURPHY, Joseph B. — 3
MURPHY, Joseph Dudley — 5
MURPHY, Joseph Nathaniel — 1
MURPHY, Lambert — 3
MURPHY, Laurence A. — 4
MURPHY, Lawrence William — 5
MURPHY, Loren Edgar — 4
MURPHY, Mabel Ansley — 5
MURPHY, Marvin — 1
MURPHY, Michael Charles — H
MURPHY, Michael Charles — 1
MURPHY, Michael Thomas — 4
MURPHY, Morgan — 5
MURPHY, N. Barnard — 3
MURPHY, Nathan Oakes — 1
MURPHY, Nettie Seeley — 4
MURPHY, Ray Dickinson — 4
MURPHY, Richard Louis — 1
MURPHY, Robert Cushman — 5
MURPHY, Samuel Silenus — 1
MURPHY, Samuel Wilson — 2
MURPHY, Stanwood — 5
MURPHY, Starr Jocelyn — 1
MURPHY, Thomas — 1
MURPHY, Thomas Dowler — 4
MURPHY, Thomas Edward — 1
MURPHY, Thomas Francis — 4
MURPHY, Thomas Timothy Francis — 5
MURPHY, W. Leo — 5
MURPHY, Walter — 2
MURPHY, Walter J. — 3
MURPHY, Walter Patton — 2
MURPHY, William Charles Jr. — 1
MURPHY, William F. — 2
MURPHY, William Gordon — 3
MURPHY, William Larkin — 1
MURPHY, William Mansuetus — 2
MURPHY, William Robert — 1
MURPHY, William Sumter — H
MURPHY, William Walton — H
MURRAH, William Belton — 1
MURRAY, A. N. — 1
MURRAY, Alexander — H
MURRAY, Alfred Lefurgy — 4

MURRAY, Ambrose Spencer — H
MURRAY, Arthur — 1
MURRAY, Arthur T. — 3
MURRAY, Augustus Taber — 1
MURRAY, Benjamin Franklin — 4
MURRAY, Charles — 5
MURRAY, Charles Bernard — 1
MURRAY, Charles Burleigh — 1
MURRAY, Charles H. — 1
MURRAY, Charles Theodore — 4
MURRAY, David — 1
MURRAY, David Ambrose — 2
MURRAY, Earle — 3
MURRAY, Eugene — 2
MURRAY, George Dominic — 3
MURRAY, George Welwood — 2
MURRAY, Gilbert — 3
MURRAY, Grace Peckham — 4
MURRAY, Howell Worth — 1
MURRAY, James Edward — 4
MURRAY, James Ormsbee — H
MURRAY, James P. — 5
MURRAY, James T. — 5
MURRAY, Jennie Scudder (Mrs. C. Edward Murray) — 5
MURRAY, John * — H
MURRAY, John Courtney — 4
MURRAY, John Gardner — 1
MURRAY, John Gregory — 3
MURRAY, John Gwennap — 4
MURRAY, John L. — H
MURRAY, John O'Kane — H
MURRAY, John Scott — 1
MURRAY, John Tucker — 5
MURRAY, Joseph — 4
MURRAY, Joseph Wilson — 3
MURRAY, Judith Sargent Stevens — H
MURRAY, Lawrence N(ewbold) — 5
MURRAY, Lawrence O. — 1
MURRAY, Leo Tildon — 3
MURRAY, Lindley — H
MURRAY, Maxwell — 2
MURRAY, Nathaniel Carleton — 3
MURRAY, Nicholas — H
MURRAY, O. Willard — 5
MURRAY, Oscar G. — 1
MURRAY, Owen Meredith — 3
MURRAY, Peter — 3
MURRAY, Philip — 3
MURRAY, Reid Fred — 3
MURRAY, Robert — H
MURRAY, Robert — 5
MURRAY, Robert B(laine, Jr. — 1
MURRAY, Robert Drake — 1
MURRAY, Roy Irving — 3
MURRAY, Samuel — 1
MURRAY, Sidney Charles — 3
MURRAY, Sidney Eugene — 5
MURRAY, Sister M. Reparata — 3
MURRAY, Thomas Jr. — H
MURRAY, Thomas E. — 4
MURRAY, Thomas Hamilton — 1
MURRAY, Thomas Jefferson — 4
MURRAY, Tom — 5
MURRAY, Wallace — 5
MURRAY, Wiliam Spencer — 1
MURRAY, William — H
MURRAY, William D. — 1
MURRAY, William Francis — 1
MURRAY, William Henry — 3
MURRAY, William Henry Harrison — 1
MURRAY, William Hilary — 3
MURRAY, William Vans — H
MURRAY-AARON, Eugene — 4
MURRAY-JACOBY, H. — 4
MURRELL, John A. — H
MURRIE, William F. R. — 1
MURRIETA, Joaquin — H
MURRILL, William Alphonso — 3
MURROW, Edward R. — 4
MURRY, John Middleton — 3

MURTFELDT, Edward Warden — 4
MUSCHAMP, George Morris — 5
MUSCHENHEIM, Frederick Augustus — 3
MUSE, Vance — 3
MUSE, William Foster — 1
MUSE, William Sulivane — 1
MUSE, William Taylor — 5
MUSGRAVE, George Clarke — 1
MUSGRAVE, Harrison — 1
MUSGRAVE, Walter Emmett — 3
MUSGRAVE, William Everett — 1
MUSICK, Charles Elvon — 5
MUSICK, John Roy — 1
MUSIN, Ovide — 1
MUSMANNO, Michael Angelo — 5
MUSS-ARNOLT, William — 1
MUSSELMAN, Clarence Alfred — 2
MUSSELMAN, Fren — 4
MUSSELMAN, J(ohn) Rogers — 5
MUSSELWHITE, Harry Webster — 3
MUSSER, George Washington — 1
MUSSER, John — 2
MUSSER, John Herr — 1
MUSSER, John Herr — 5
MUSSER, Paul Howard — 3
MUSSEY, Ellen Spencer — 1
MUSSEY, Henry Raymond — 4
MUSSEY, Reuben Dimond — H
MUSSOLINI, Benito — 4
MUSTAPHA II — H
MUSTARD, Harry Stoll — 4
MUSTARD, Horace Ransom — 4
MUSTARD, Wilfred Pirt — 1
MUTCH, William James — 2
MUTCHLER, William — H
MUTER, Leslie Frederick — 1
MUTESA, Edward Frederick William Walugembe Mutebi Luwangula — 5
MUTO, Anthony — 4
MUYBRIDGE, Eadweard — H
MUZIO, Claudia — 1
MUZZALL, Ernest Linwood — 4
MUZZARELLI, Antoine — 1
MUZZEY, David Saville — 4
MUZZY, H(enry) Earle — 5
MYER, Albert James — H
MYER, Albert Lee — 1
MYER, Edmund John — 4
MYER, Henry — H
MYER, Isaac — 1
MYER, Jesse Shire — 1
MYER, John Walden — 5
MYER, Joseph Charles — 5
MYER, Sewall — 5
MYER, Walter Evert — 5
MYERS, Abraham Charles — H
MYERS, Albert Cook — 1
MYERS, Alonzo Franklin — 5
MYERS, Amos — H
MYERS, Barton — 1
MYERS, Burton Dorr — 3
MYERS, Charles Augustus — 3
MYERS, Charles Franklin — 3
MYERS, Clifford R. — 1
MYERS, Clyde Hadley — 2
MYERS, Cortland — 1
MYERS, Curtis Clark — 3
MYERS, David Albert — 3
MYERS, David Jackson Duke — 5
MYERS, David Moffat — 3
MYERS, Dean Wentworth — 3
MYERS, Diller S. — 2
MYERS, Edward DeLos — 5
MYERS, Elizabeth (Fetter) Lehman (Mrs. J. Upton Myers) — 5
MYERS, Francis John — 3
MYERS, Frank Clayton — 3
MYERS, Frank Kerchner — 1
MYERS, Garry Cleveland — 5
MYERS, George Edmund — 5
MYERS, George Hewitt — 5
MYERS, George Sylvester — 1
MYERS, George William — 1
MYERS, Gustavus — 2
MYERS, Harry White — 5

* Indicates More Than One Such Name Listed

MYERS, Henry Alonzo 3
MYERS, Henry Guy 4
MYERS, Henry L. 2
MYERS, Howard 2
MYERS, Howard Barton 3
MYERS, Jack Allen 5
MYERS, James 4
MYERS, James Jefferson 1
MYERS, Jefferson 2
MYERS, Jerome 1
MYERS, John Dashiell 2
MYERS, John J. H
MYERS, John Llewellyn 2
MYERS, John Platt 4
MYERS, John Quincy 2
MYERS, John Sherman 5
MYERS, John Twiggs 5
MYERS, Johnston 4
MYERS, Joseph Simmons 5
MYERS, Lewis Edward 1
MYERS, Louis Keller 5
MYERS, Louis Wescott 1
MYERS, M. Lorton 4
MYERS, Minnie Walter 4
MYERS, Paul Noxon 4
MYERS, Philip Van Ness 1
MYERS, Quincy Alden 4
MYERS, Robert Holthy 5
MYERS, Sumner B. 4
MYERS, Theodore Walter 1
MYERS, Victor Caryl 2
MYERS, Walter Jr. 1
MYERS, Will Martin 5
MYERS, William Heyward 4
MYERS, William Kurtz 3
MYERS, William Shields 2
MYERS, William Starr 3
MYERSON, Abraham 2
MYGATT, Gerald 1
MYHRMAN, Othelia 1
MYLER, Joseph James 1
MYLES, Beverly Russell 3
MYLES, John H
MYNDERS, Alfred D. 5
MYNDERSE, Wilhelmus 4
MYRDDIN-EVANS,
  Sir Guildhaume
MYRICK, 5
  Arthur Beckwith
MYRICK, Harry Pierce
MYRICK, Herbert 1
MYRICK, John Rencklin 1
MYRICK, 1
  Julian Southall
MYRICK, Shelby 4
MYRON, Paul

N

NABERS, Benjamin Duke H
NABORS, 4
  Eugene Augustus
NABOURS, 5
  Robert Kirkland
NABUCO, Joaquim 1
NACHTRIEB, 2
  Henry Francis
NACK, William H
NACY, Richard Robert 4
NADAL, Charles Coleman
NADAL, Ehrman Syme 1
NADAL, Thomas William 3
NADEAU, Ira Alfred
NADLER, Carl S. 3
NADLER, Marcus
NAECKEL, Erwin George 3
NAEGELE, 2
  Charles Frederick
NAFE, Cleon A.
NAFF, George Tipton 5
NAFFZIGER, 4
  Howard Christian
NAFZIGER, Ralph LeRoy 4
NAGEL, Charles
NAGEL, Conrad 5
NAGEL, Conrad F. Jr. 3
NAGEL, Joseph Darwin
NAGEL, 5
  Stina (Mrs. Leon Hill)
NAGER, Rudolf Felix 5
NAGLE, Charles Francis
NAGLE, Clarence Floyd 3
NAGLE, James C.
NAGLE, John Joseph 4
NAGLE, 1
  Patrick Sarsfield
NAGLE, Raymond
  Thomas
NAGLE, Urban 4
NAGLER, Floyd August
NAGLER, Forrest 1
NAGY, Imre 3
NAHL, H
  Charles Christian
NAHL, H
  Hugo Wilhelm Arthur
NAHM, Max Brunswick 3

NAIDEN, Earl L. 2
NAIL, James H. 1
NAIR, John Henry, Jr. 5
NAIRN, Sir Michael 3
NAIRNE, Thomas H
NAISMITH, James 1
NALDER, Frank Fielding 1
NALLY, Edward Julian 4
NAMIER,
  Sir Lewis Bernstein
NAMM, 5
  Benjamin Harrison
NAMMACK, 1
  Charles Edward
NANCE, Albinus 1
NANCE, Ellwood Cecil 4
NANCE, Walter Buckner 4
NANCE, Willis Dean 5
NANCREDE, 1
  C. B. Guerard 'de
NANCREDE, H
  Paul Joseph Guerard 'de
NANGLE, John Joseph 4
NANKIVELL, 5
  Frank Arthur
NANZ, Robert Hamilton 3
NAON, Romulo S. 1
NAPHEN, Henry Francis 1
NAPIER,
  George Moultrie
NAPIER, Thomas Hewell 4
NAPOLI, Alexander J. 5
NAPTON, H
  William Barclay
NARAYANAN, 4
  Teralandur Gopalacharya
NARDIN, 3
  William Thompson
NARVAEZ, Panfilo H
NASH, Abner H
NASH, Albert C. 2
NASH, Arthur 1
NASH, Bert Allen 2
NASH, 5
  C(arlton) Stewart
NASH, Charles Ellwood 1
NASH, Charles Sumner 2
NASH, Charles W. 2
NASH, Daniel H
NASH, Edgar Smiley 1
NASH, Edwin A. 1
NASH, Elliott E. 5
NASH, Francis 1
NASH, Francis Philip 1
NASH, Frank C. 2
NASH, Frederick H
NASH, George Kilbon 1
NASH, George Williston 2
NASH, Harriet A. 1
NASH, Henry Sylvester 1
NASH, Herbert Charles 1
NASH, Isaac H(enry) 5
NASH, J. Newton 4
NASH, Jay Bryan 4
NASH, John Henry 2
NASH, Leonidas Lydwell 1
NASH, Louis Rogers 5
NASH, Luther Roberts 5
NASH, Lyman Junius 1
NASH, Ogden 1
NASH, 1
  Paul Cleveland Bennett
NASH, Philip Curtis 2
NASH, Simeon H
NASH, Walter 1
NASH, 1
  William Alexander
NASH, William Holt 1
NASMYTH, George 1
NASON, Albert John 2
NASON, 2
  Arthur Huntington
NASON, Elias H
NASON, Frank Lewis 1
NASON, Henry Bradford H
NASON, 5
  Leonard Hastings (Steamer)
NASON, 5
  Thomas Willoughby
NASSAU, Jason John 4
NASSAU, Robert Hamill 1
NASSER, Gamal Abdel 5
NAST, Albert Julius 1
NAST, Conde 2
NAST, Thomas H
NAST, Thomas 1
NAST, William H
NATE, Joseph Cookman 1
NATELSON, Morris 5
NATHAN, Alfred 1
NATHAN, Edgar Joshua 1
NATHAN, George Jean 5
NATHAN, J(acob) Philip 1
NATHAN, Maud 2
NATHANSON, H
  Ira Theodore

NATION, H
  Carry Amelia Moore
NATION, 4
  Carry Amelia Moore
NATIONS, Gilbert Owen 5
NAUDAIN, Arnold H
NAUJOKS, Herbert Hugh 4
NAUMBURG, 5
  George Washington
NAUMBURG, Walter
  Wehle 3
NAUSS, Henry G. 5
NAVAGH, James
  Johnston
NAVARRO, Jose Antonio H
NAVE, 4
  Anna Eliza Semans
NAVE, 1
  Frederick Solomon
NAVE, Orville James 1
NAVIN,
  Robert B(ernard)
NAYLON, Edmund Barry 5
NAYLOR, Addison Wood 4
NAYLOR, Charles H
NAYLOR, E. E. 4
NAYLOR, Emmett Hay 1
NAYLOR, James Ball 1
NAYLOR, John Calvin 4
NAYLOR, John Lewis 4
NAYLOR, 2
  Joseph Randolph
NAYLOR, William Keith 2
NAYLOR, Wilson Samuel 4
NAZIMOVA, Alla 4
NAZIMUDDIN, 4
  Al-Haj Khwaja
NEAD, 1
  Benjamin Matthias
NEAGLE, John H
NEAGLE, Pickens 2
NEAL, Alva Otis 1
NEAL, David 1
NEAL, Ernest Eugene 5
NEAL, George Ira 1
NEAL, Herbert Vincent 1
NEAL, James Arthur 1
NEAL, James Henry 1
NEAL, John H
NEAL, John Randolph H
NEAL, John Randolph 3
NEAL, Joseph Clay 1
NEAL, 3
  Josephine Bicknell
NEAL, Lawrence Talbott 4
NEAL, Mills Ferrell 5
NEAL, Paul Ardeen 3
NEAL, Phil Hudson 2
NEAL, Robert Wilson 1
NEAL, Thomas 1
NEAL, Will E. 3
NEAL, William Joseph 2
NEAL, William M. 5
NEAL, William Watt 5
NEAL, William Weaver 5
NEALE, Laurance Irving 3
NEALE, Leonard H
NEALE, M. Gordon 4
NEALE, Raphael H
NEALE, Walter 4
NEAMAN, Pearson E. 4
NEARY, John Stuart 5
NEATH, Jasper Arthur 3
NEBEKER, 5
  Frank Knowlton
NEBEL, Berthold 4
NECKERE, H
  Leo Raymond De
NEDVED, 4
  Elizabeth Kimball (Mrs.
  Rudolph James Nedved)
NEE, Maurice Lyden 4
NEEDHAM, 1
  Charles Austin
NEEDHAM, 2
  Charles Willis
NEEDHAM, Claude Ervin 3
NEEDHAM, Daniel 5
NEEDHAM, Henry Beach 1
NEEDHAM, James H
NEEDHAM, James 2
  Carson
NEEDHAM, 4
  Maurice Henshaw
NEEDLES, Arthur Chase 1
NEEDLES, Enoch Ray H
NEEF, 1
  Francis Joseph Nicholas
NEEF, Frederick Emil 5
NEEL, William D. 5
NEELANDS, 4
  Thomas D., Jr.
NEELEY, George A. 1
NEELEY, John Lawton 5
NEELLEY, John Haven 4
NEELY, 3
  Charles Gracchus

NEELY, Henry Adams 1
NEELY, 5
  John Marshall, III
NEELY, Matthew M. 3
NEELY, Thomas Benjamin 4
NEET, George W. 3
NEF, John Ulric 5
NEFF, 3
  Charles Thompson Jr.
NEFF, Elizabeth Hyer 5
NEFF, Elmer Hartshorn 2
NEFF, Frank Chaffee 2
NEFF, Frank Howard 1
NEFF, George N. 5
NEFF, Grover Cleveland 5
NEFF, Harold Hopkins 5
NEFF, J. Louis 5
NEFF, Jay H. 4
NEFF, John Henry 5
NEFF, Joseph A. 5
NEFF, Joseph Seal 1
NEFF, Pat Morris 3
NEFF, Paul Joseph 3
NEFF, Silas S. 1
NEFF, Ward Andrew 3
NEFTEL, William B. 4
NEGLEY, Daniel H
NEGLEY, James Scott 1
NEGUS, Sidney Stevens 4
NEHER, Fred 1
NEHLIG, Victor 1
NEHRING, Millard J. 4
NEHRLING, Henry 1
NEHRU, Jawaharlal 4
NEIDEG, 1
  William Jonathan
NEIDHARD, Charles H
NEIDLINGER, 1
  William Harold
NEIFERT, Ira Edward 3
NEIGHBORS, H
  Robert Simpson
NEIL, Edward Wallace 1
NEIL, George M. 5
NEIL, Matt Marshall 1
NEILD, Edward Fairfax 3
NEILER, Samuel Graham 2
NEILL, Charles Patrick 2
NEILL, Edward Duffield 1
NEILL, James Maffett 4
NEILL, John H
NEILL, 1
  John Selby Martin
NEILL, 5
  Lelia Winslow Bray (Mrs.
  Charles R. Neill)
NEILL, Paul 2
NEILL, Richard Renshaw 1
NEILL, Thomas Hewson H
NEILL, William H
NEILSON, Charles Hugh 4
NEILSON, Francis 4
NEILSON, 2
  Harry Rosengarten
NEILSON, Jason Andrew 5
NEILSON, John H
NEILSON, Lewis 4
NEILSON, Nellie 2
NEILSON, Nevin Paul 5
NEILSON, 1
  Raymond Perry Rodgers
NEILSON, Thomas Hall 4
NEILSON, Thomas 1
  Rundle
NEILSON, William Allan 1
NEILSON, 3
  William George
NEILSON,
  William LaCoste
NEISWANGER, David 4
NEL, Louis Taylor 5
NELAN, Charles 4
NELL, Louis 1
NELL, William Cooper 4
NELLES, Percy W. 3
NELLIGAN, Howard Paul 4
NELMS, William Lewis 4
NELSON, Adolphus P. 1
NELSON, 5
  Alexander Lockhart
NELSON, 4
  Alfred Brierley
NELSON, Alfred L. 1
NELSON, Arthur E. 3
NELSON, Benjamin F. 1
NELSON, 5
  Bertram Griffith
NELSON, Burton Edsal 5
NELSON, C. Ferdinand 3
NELSON, Carl K. 1
NELSON, 1
  Charles Alexander
NELSON, Charles Donald 5
NELSON, 4
  Charles Pembroke
NELSON, 3
  Clara Albertine

NELSON, Clarence 5
NELSON, 1
  Cleland Kinloch
NELSON, Daniel Thurber 1
NELSON, David H
NELSON, Donald Marr 3
NELSON, Edgar Andrew 3
NELSON, Edward Beverly 4
NELSON, Edward William 1
NELSON, Elmer Martin 3
NELSON, 1
  Elnathan Kemper
NELSON, Frank 4
NELSON, Frank Howard 1
NELSON, George Bliss 2
NELSON, George Francis 1
NELSON, George Herbert 4
NELSON, 3
  Godfrey Nicholas
NELSON, Harold Hayden 3
NELSON, Henry Addison 1
NELSON, Henry Loomis 1
NELSON, Herbert Undeen 3
NELSON, Homer
  Augustus H
NELSON, Hugh H
NELSON, Jabez Curry 3
NELSON, James Boyd 3
NELSON, Jeremiah H
NELSON, John * H
NELSON, John Edward 3
NELSON, John Evon 3
NELSON, John Mandt 5
NELSON, 4
  John Marbury Jr.
NELSON, 4
  Joseph David Jr.
NELSON, Joseph E. 4
NELSON, Julia Bullard 1
NELSON, Julius 1
NELSON, Knute 1
NELSON, Mack Barnabas 5
NELSON, Martin 4
NELSON, Martin Johan 5
NELSON, Nels Christian 4
NELSON, Nelson O. 4
NELSON, Ole C. 3
NELSON, Orville Norman 5
NELSON, Oscar 5
NELSON, Perry Albert 4
NELSON, Peter Bering 4
NELSON, Ralph Thomas 5
NELSON,
  Rensselaer Russell
NELSON, Reuben H
NELSON,
  Reuben Emmanuel
NELSON, Richard Arthur 4
NELSON, Richard Henry 5
NELSON, Richard J. 4
NELSON,
  Robert Franklin
NELSON, Robert Oliver 4
NELSON, Robert W. 5
NELSON, Robert William 5
NELSON, Roger H
NELSON, Rufus Jerry 5
NELSON, Samuel H
NELSON, Samuel A. 4
NELSON,
  Sofus Bertelson
NELSON, Theodore 4
NELSON, Thomas * H
NELSON, Thomas 4
NELSON,
  Thomas Amos Rogers
NELSON, Thomas 1
  Kinloch
NELSON, Thomas Maduit H
NELSON, Thurlow C. 4
NELSON, Warren Otto 4
NELSON, William * H
NELSON, William * 1
NELSON, William 5
NELSON,
  William Hamilton
NELSON, William Lester 4
NELSON, 1
  William Rockhill
NELSON, Wolfred 1
NEMEROV, David 4
NEMEYER, 5
  S(idney) Lloyd
NEMMERS, Erwin Plein 1
NEPOMUK, H
  Felix Constatin Alexander
  Johann
NEPRASH, Jerry Alvin 3
NERAZ, John Claudius H
NERINCKX, Charles H
NERLOVE, Samuel Henry 5
NES, Henry 1
NESBIT,
  Charles Francis
NESBIT, Harrison 1
NESBIT, Otis Burgess 1

NESBIT, Valentine Jordan — 1
NESBIT, Wilbur D. — 1
NESBIT, William Marsiglia — 3
NESBITT, Frank Watterson — 2
NESBITT, John Maxwell — H
NESBITT, Wilson — H
NESLAGE, Oliver J. — 3
NESLEN, Clarence Cannon — 5
NESMITH, James Willis — H
NESMITH, John — H
NESS, Eliot — 3
NESTOR, Agnes — 2
NESTOS, Ragnvald Anderson — 2
NETERER, Jeremiah — 2
NETHERCUT, Edgar S. — 5
NETHERSOLE, Olga — 3
NETHERWOOD, Douglas Blakeshaw — 2
NETTLETON, Alvred Bayard — 1
NETTLETON, Asahel — H
NETTLETON, Edwin S. — H
NETTLETON, George Henry — 3
NETTLETON, Walter — 1
NEUBERG, Carl Alexander — 3
NEUBERG, Maurice Joseph — 2
NEUBERGER, Richard Lewis — 3
NEUBERGER, Richard Lewis — 4
NEUBURGER, Rudolf — 3
NEUENDORFF, Adolph Heinrich Anton Magnus — H
NEUHOFF, Charles Sidney — 5
NEUMAN, Abraham C. — 5
NEUMAN, Fred G. — 3
NEUMANN, Arnold John Robert — 2
NEUMANN, Edward Morsbach — H
NEUMANN, Ernest K. — 3
NEUMANN, F. Wight — 1
NEUMANN, Frank — 4
NEUMANN, Henry — 4
NEUMANN, John Nepomucene — H
NEUMANN, Sigmund — 4
NEUMANN, William Louis — 5
NEUMARK, Arthur Jay — 4
NEUMARK, David — 5
NEUMEYER, Albert Gustave — 5
NEUPERT, Carl Nicholas — 5
NEUPERT, Edmund — H
NEUTRA, Richard Joseph — 5
NEUWIRTH, Isaac — 5
NEVADA, Emma (Mrs. Raymond Palmer) — 5
NEVE, Juergen Ludwig — 2
NEVILLE, Donald Weston — 5
NEVILLE, Edwin Lowe — 2
NEVILLE, Glenn — 4
NEVILLE, John — 5
NEVILLE, Joseph — H
NEVILLE, Keith — 3
NEVILLE, Paul Edwin — 5
NEVILLE, Robert — 5
NEVILLE, Robert Henry — 2
NEVILLE, Wendell Cushing — 1
NEVILLE, William — 1
NEVILS, W. Coleman — 3
NEVIN, Alfred — H
NEVIN, Arthur Finley — 2
NEVIN, Edwin Henry — H
NEVIN, Ethelbert — 1
NEVIN, George Balch — 1
NEVIN, Gordon Balch — 2
NEVIN, James Banks — 1
NEVIN, John Williamson — H
NEVIN, Robert Jenkins — 1
NEVIN, Robert Murphy — 4
NEVIN, Robert Peebles — 1
NEVIN, Robert Reasoner — 1
NEVIN, Theodore Williamson — 1
NEVIN, William Channing — 4
NEVIN, William Latta — 5
NEVINS, Allan — 5
NEVINS, Bert — 4
NEVIUS, Henry M. — 1
NEVIUS, John Livingston — H
NEW, Anthony — H

NEW, Catherine McLaen — 5
NEW, Clarence Herbert — 1
NEW, George Edward — 1
NEW, Gordon Balgarnie — 3
NEW, Harry Stewart — 1
NEW, Jeptha Dudley — H
NEW, John Chalfant — 1
NEWBERNE, Robert Edward Lee — 1
NEWBERRY, Edgar A. — 4
NEWBERRY, Farrar — 5
NEWBERRY, John Josiah — 3
NEWBERRY, John Stoughton — H
NEWBERRY, John Strong — H
NEWBERRY, Mary Wheeler — 1
NEWBERRY, Oliver — H
NEWBERRY, Perry — 1
NEWBERRY, Roger Wolcott — 4
NEWBERRY, Truman Handy — 1
NEWBERRY, Walter Cass — 1
NEWBERRY, Walter Loomis — H
NEWBERRY, William Belknap — 4
NEWBILL, Willard Douglas — 3
NEWBOLD, Fleming — 2
NEWBOLD, Thomas — H
NEWBOLD, W. Romaine — 1
NEWBORG, Leonard David — 5
NEWBRANCH, Harvey Ellsworth — 3
NEWBROUGH, John Ballou — H
NEWBURGER, Joseph — 1
NEWBURGER, Joseph Emanuel — 1
NEWBURY, Frank Davies — 5
NEWBURY, Michael — 5
NEWBURY, Mollie Netcher — 3
NEWBY, Leonidas Perry — 4
NEWBY, Nathan — 3
NEWCOMB, Arthur Thurston — 1
NEWCOMB, Charles Benjamin — 1
NEWCOMB, Charles Leonard — 1
NEWCOMB, Ezra Butler — 1
NEWCOMB, Harry Turner — 2
NEWCOMB, Harvey — H
NEWCOMB, Horatio Victor — 1
NEWCOMB, James Edward — 4
NEWCOMB, James Farmer — 2
NEWCOMB, John Lloyd — H
NEWCOMB, Josephine Louise Le Monnier — H
NEWCOMB, Josiah Turner — 2
NEWCOMB, Kate Pelham — 3
NEWCOMB, Katharine Hinchman — 1
NEWCOMB, Simon — 5
NEWCOMB, Wyllys Stetson — H
NEWCOMBE, Frederick Charles — 1
NEWCOMER, Alphonso Gerald — 1
NEWCOMER, Christian — H
NEWCOMER, Henry Clay — 4
NEWCOMER, Stanley J. — 4
NEWCOMER, Waldo — 1
NEWCOMET, Horace Edgar — 1
NEWEL, Stanford — 1
NEWELL, Charles Herbert — 1
NEWELL, Cicero — 1
NEWELL, Clarence DeRocha — 1
NEWELL, Edward Jackson — 4
NEWELL, Edward Theodore — 1
NEWELL, Franklin Spilman — 2
NEWELL, Frederick Haynes — 1
NEWELL, George Edwards — 1
NEWELL, George Glenn — 2
NEWELL, Henry Clinton — 5
NEWELL, Herman Wilson — 3
NEWELL, Jake F. — 1
NEWELL, James W. — 5

NEWELL, Jessie Edna Whitehead — 5
NEWELL, Joseph Shipley — 3
NEWELL, Lyman Churchill — 1
NEWELL, Peter — 1
NEWELL, Quitman Underwood — 1
NEWELL, Robert — 1
NEWELL, Robert Brewer — 2
NEWELL, Robert Henry — 1
NEWELL, Robert Reid — 4
NEWELL, Wilbur Charles — 3
NEWELL, William Augustus — 1
NEWELL, William Henry — 1
NEWELL, William Reed — 5
NEWELL, William Stark — 3
NEWELL, William Wells — 1
NEWELL, William Whiting — 1
NEWELL, Wilmon — 2
NEWENS, Adrian M. — 5
NEWEY, Frederick John — 2
NEWFANG, Oscar — 2
NEWFIELD, Morris — 2
NEWGARDEN, Paul W. — 2
NEWHALL, Alfred Augustus — 1
NEWHALL, Arthur Brock — 3
NEWHALL, C. Stevenson — 3
NEWHALL, Charles Francis — 5
NEWHALL, Charles Francis — 4
NEWHALL, Charles Stedman — 4
NEWHALL, Charles Watson — 2
NEWHALL, Henry Whiting — 5
NEWHALL, J. Lincoln — 3
NEWHALL, John Bailey — H
NEWHALL, Parker — 4
NEWHALL, Thomas — 2
NEWHARD, Peter — H
NEWHART, Horace — 2
NEWHOUSE, Samuel — 4
NEWHOUSE, Walter Harry — 5
NEWKIRK, Clement Roy — 4
NEWKIRK, Garrett — 1
NEWKIRK, Matthew — 1
NEWKIRK, Newton — 1
NEWKIRK, Samuel Drake — 3
NEWLANDS, Francis Griffith — 1
NEWLEAN, John Walter — 1
NEWLIN, Gurney Elwood — 3
NEWLIN, Ora Allen — 2
NEWLIN, Thomas — 4
NEWLIN, William Jesse — 3
NEWLON, Jesse H. — 1
NEWMAN, Albert Broadus — 3
NEWMAN, Albert Henry — 1
NEWMAN, Alexander — H
NEWMAN, Alfred — 5
NEWMAN, Allen George — 1
NEWMAN, Angelia French Thurston — 1
NEWMAN, Barnett — 4
NEWMAN, Barnett — 5
NEWMAN, Bernard — 5
NEWMAN, Bernard J. — 1
NEWMAN, Carol Montgomery — 1
NEWMAN, Charles Morehead — 5
NEWMAN, Dora Lee — 5
NEWMAN, E. M. — 3
NEWMAN, Edgar Douglas — 4
NEWMAN, Edwin A. — 4
NEWMAN, Ernest — 3
NEWMAN, Erwin William — 5
NEWMAN, Frances — 1
NEWMAN, Helen Catherine — 1
NEWMAN, Henry — H
NEWMAN, Henry Parker — 1
NEWMAN, Herman — 5
NEWMAN, Horatio Hackett — 3
NEWMAN, J. Kiefer Jr. — 1
NEWMAN, Jacob — 1
NEWMAN, Jacob Kiefer — 1
NEWMAN, James Joseph — 5
NEWMAN, James R. — 4
NEWMAN, Jared Treman — 1
NEWMAN, John Grant — 3
NEWMAN, John Philip — H
NEWMAN, John Philip — 1
NEWMAN, John Urquhart — 5
NEWMAN, Louis Israel — 5
NEWMAN, Oliver Peck — 5
NEWMAN, Robert — 1

NEWMAN, Samuel Phillips — H
NEWMAN, Stephen Morrell — 1
NEWMAN, William H. — 1
NEWMAN, William Truslow — 1
NEWMAN, Willie Betty — 4
NEWMARK, Harris — 1
NEWMARK, Maurice Harris — 1
NEWMARK, Nathan — 4
NEWMYER, Arthur Grover — 1
NEWNAN, Daniel — H
NEWPORT, Christopher — H
NEWSAM, Albert — H
NEWSHAM, Joseph Parkinson — 3
NEWSOM, Curtis Bishop — 3
NEWSOM, Herschel D. — 5
NEWSOM, John Flesher — 1
NEWSOM, William Monypeny — 1
NEWSOM, William Monypeny — 2
NEWSOME, Albert Ray — 3
NEWSON, Henry Byron — 1
NEWTON, Alfred Edward — 1
NEWTON, Arthur William — 4
NEWTON, Byron R. — 5
NEWTON, Charles Bertram — 5
NEWTON, Charles Damon — 1
NEWTON, Clarence Lucian — 3
NEWTON, Cleveland Alexander — 2
NEWTON, Eben — H
NEWTON, Elbridge Ward — 4
NEWTON, Glenn D. — 5
NEWTON, Henry Jotham — 1
NEWTON, Homer Curtis — 3
NEWTON, Howard Chamberlian — 4
NEWTON, Hubert Anson — H
NEWTON, Isaac * — H
NEWTON, Isaac Burkett — 1
NEWTON, James Thornwell — 1
NEWTON, John — H
NEWTON, John Henry — 2
NEWTON, John Orville — 1
NEWTON, John Wharton — 5
NEWTON, Joseph Fort — 5
NEWTON, Maurice — 5
NEWTON, McGuire — 1
NEWTON, Oscar — 1
NEWTON, R. Heber — 1
NEWTON, Richard — H
NEWTON, Robert Safford — H
NEWTON, Thomas * — H
NEWTON, Thomas Willoughby — H
NEWTON, Walter Hughes — 1
NEWTON, Walter Russell — 4
NEWTON, Watson J. — 1
NEWTON, William Wilberforce — 1
NEWTON, Willoughby — H
NEYLAN, John Francis — 4
NEYLAND, Harry — 3
NEYLAND, Robert Reese Jr. — 4
NEYMANN, Clarence Adolph — 3
NEZ COUPE — H
NGO DINH DIEM — 4
NIAS, Henry — 1
NIBLACK, Albert Parker — 1
NIBLACK, Silas Leslie — 1
NIBLACK, William Ellis — H
NIBLEY, Charles Wilson — 1
NIBLO, Urban — 1
NIBLO, William — H
NICCOLLS, Samuel Jack — 1
NICE, Harry — 1
NICELY, Harold Elliott — 5
NICELY, James Mount — 4
NICHOL, Edward Sterling — 5
NICHOL, Francis David — 4
NICHOL, Frederick William — 4
NICHOLAS, Anna — 1
NICHOLAS, Edwin August — 3
NICHOLAS, George — H
NICHOLAS, John — H
NICHOLAS, John Spangler — 4
NICHOLAS, Philip Norborne — H
NICHOLAS, Richard Ulysses — 3

NICHOLAS, Robert Carter * — H
NICHOLAS, William Gardiner — 1
NICHOLAS, William Oliver — 5
NICHOLAS, Wilson Cary — H
NICHOLL, Horace Wadham — 1
NICHOLLS, C. W. 'delyon — 1
NICHOLLS, Francis Tillon — 1
NICHOLLS, George Heaton — 5
NICHOLLS, John Calhoun — H
NICHOLLS, Rhoda Holmes — 3
NICHOLLS, Richard — H
NICHOLLS, Samuel Jones — 1
NICHOLLS, Thomas David — 5
NICHOLS, William Durrett — 3
NICHOLS, Anne — 1
NICHOLS, Arthur Burr — 5
NICHOLS, Charles A. — 1
NICHOLS, Charles Gerry — 4
NICHOLS, Charles Henry — H
NICHOLS, Charles Henry — 1
NICHOLS, Charles Lemuel — 1
NICHOLS, Charles Walter — 5
NICHOLS, Clarina Irene Howard — H
NICHOLS, Clark Asahel — 5
NICHOLS, Edward Hall — 1
NICHOLS, Edward Leamington — 2
NICHOLS, Edward Tattnall — H
NICHOLS, Edward West — 1
NICHOLS, Egbert Ray — 3
NICHOLS, Ernest Fox — 1
NICHOLS, Francis Henry — 4
NICHOLS, Frank R. — 4
NICHOLS, Frederick Day — 5
NICHOLS, Frederick George — 3
NICHOLS, George Elwood — 1
NICHOLS, George Ward — H
NICHOLS, Harry Peirce — 1
NICHOLS, Henry Drew — 4
NICHOLS, Henry Sargent Prentiss — 1
NICHOLS, Henry Windsor — 4
NICHOLS, Herbert — 1
NICHOLS, Herbert L. — 4
NICHOLS, Hobart Jr. — 4
NICHOLS, Ichabod — H
NICHOLS, Isabel McIlhenny — 2
NICHOLS, Jack John Conover — H
NICHOLS, James — 1
NICHOLS, James Robinson — H
NICHOLS, Jesse Clyde — 2
NICHOLS, John Benjamin — 3
NICHOLS, John Francis — 5
NICHOLS, John Grayson — 2
NICHOLS, John Richard — 1
NICHOLS, Malcolm E. — 3
NICHOLS, Mark Lovel — 5
NICHOLS, Mary Sargeant Neal Gove — H
NICHOLS, Matthias H. — H
NICHOLS, Neil Ernest — 3
NICHOLS, Othniel Foster — 3
NICHOLS, Robert Hastings — 3
NICHOLS, Roy Franklin — 5
NICHOLS, Ruth Rowland — 4
NICHOLS, Spencer Baird — 3
NICHOLS, Spencer Van Bokkelen — 2
NICHOLS, Thomas Flint — 1
NICHOLS, Walter Edmond — 5
NICHOLS, Walter Franklin — 2
NICHOLS, Walter Hammond — 1
NICHOLS, William Ford — 1
NICHOLS, William Henry — 1
NICHOLS, William LeRoy — 3
NICHOLS, William Theophilus — 2
NICHOLS, William Wallace — 2
NICHOLSON, Alfred Osborn Pope — H

NICHOLSON, 5
Edward Everett
NICHOLSON, H
Eliza Jane Poitevent Holbrook
NICHOLSON, Francis H
NICHOLSON, Frank Lee 3
NICHOLSON, 4
Frank Walter
NICHOLSON, 1
George Edward
NICHOLSON, 5
George Mansel
NICHOLSON, 2
George Robert Henderson
NICHOLSON, George T. 1
NICHOLSON, 4
Hammond Burke
NICHOLSON, 5
Harold George
NICHOLSON, 1
Henry Hudson
NICHOLSON, Isaac Lea 4
NICHOLSON, J. Lee 4
NICHOLSON, James H
NICHOLSON, H
James Bartram
NICHOLSON, 4
James Bartram
NICHOLSON, 5
James Thomas
NICHOLSON, 1
James William
NICHOLSON, H
James William Augustus
NICHOLSON, John * H
NICHOLSON, John Page 1
NICHOLSON, John Reed 1
NICHOLSON, 4
John Rutherford
NICHOLSON, H
Joseph Hopper
NICHOLSON, 3
Leonard Kimball
NICHOLSON, Meredith 2
NICHOLSON, 5
Norman Edwin
NICHOLSON, Paul Coe 3
NICHOLSON, Ralph 5
NICHOLSON, 1
Reginald Fairfax
NICHOLSON, 5
Robert Harvey
NICHOLSON, Samuel H
NICHOLSON, Samuel D. 1
NICHOLSON, 1
Samuel Edgar
NICHOLSON, Samuel M. 1
NICHOLSON, 5
Samuel Thorne
NICHOLSON, Seth
Barnes 4
NICHOLSON, Somerville 1
NICHOLSON, Soterios 3
NICHOLSON, Thomas 4
NICHOLSON, Timothy 4
NICHOLSON, 2
Vincent DeWitt
NICHOLSON, 4
Walter Wicks
NICHOLSON, Watson 3
NICHOLSON, 1
William Jones
NICHOLSON, 1
William Rufus
NICHOLSON, H
William Thomas
NICKELS, 1
John Augustine Heard
NICKELS, 5
Mervyn Millard
NICKERSON, 4
Frank Stillman
NICKERSON, 1
Hiram Robert
NICKERSON, Hoffman 4
NICKERSON, John 3
NICKERSON, 4
Kingsbury S.
NICKEUS, Johnson 1
NICKLAS, 2
Charles Aubrey
NICKS, F. William 5
NICODEMUS, 3
Frank Courtney Jr.
NICOL, Alexander R. 4
NICOL, Charles Edgar 1
NICOL, Jacob 5
NICOLA, Lewis H
NICOLAI, Harry T. 4
NICOLASSEN, 5
George Frederick
NICOLAY, Helen 3
NICOLAY, John George 1
NICOLET, Jean H
NICOLL, De Lancey 1
NICOLL, Henry H

NICOLL, James Craig 1
NICOLL, Matthias Jr. 1
NICOLLET, H
Joseph Nicolas
NICOLLS, Matthias H
NICOLLS, Richard H
NICOLLS, William H
NICOLLS, 1
William Jasper
NICUM, John 1
NIEBUHR, H. Richard 4
NIEBUHR, Reinhold 5
NIEDERMEYER, 1
Frederick David
NIEDRINGHAUS, 1
Frederick G.
NIEDRINGHAUS, 2
George Hayward
NIEDRINGHAUS, 1
George W.
NIEDRINGHAUS, 1
Henry Frederick
NIEDRINGHAUS, 1
J. P. Erwin
NIEDRINGHAUS, 1
Thomas Key
NIEHAUS, Charles Henry 1
NIEHAUS, 5
Fredrich Wilhelm
NIELDS, John P. 2
NIELSEN, Alice 1
NIELSEN, Fred Kenelm 4
NIELSEN, 5
Harald Herborg
NIELSEN, 5
Johannes Maagaard
NIEMAN, Lucius W. 1
NIEMANN, Carl 1
NIEMEYER, John Henry 1
NIERENSEE, John R. H
NIERMAN, John L. 3
NIES, James Buchanan 1
NIESZ, Homer E. 1
NIETO 'DEL RIO, Felix 3
NIEUWLAND, 1
Julius Arthur
NIEZER, Charles M. 1
NIFONG, Frank Gosney 4
NIGHTINGALE, 1
Augustus Frederick
NIGHTINGALE, 4
William Thomas
NIHART, 3
Benjamin Franklin
NIJINSKY, Vaslav 4
NIKANDER, John Kustaa 1
NIKOLSKY, Alexander A. 1
NILAN, John Joseph 1
NILES, Alfred Salem 1
NILES, Alva Joseph 2
NILES, Blair 3
NILES, Edward Hulbert 1
NILES, George McCallum 1
NILES, Henry Carpenter 3
NILES, Henry Clay 1
NILES, Hezekiah H
NILES, Jason H
NILES, John Milton 1
NILES, Kossuth 1
NILES, Nathan Erie 1
NILES, Nathaniel * H
NILES, Nathaniel 1
NILES, Philip Bradford 3
NILES, Samuel H
NILES, Walter Lindsay 2
NILES, William Harmon 1
NILES, William Henry 4
NILES, William White 1
NILES, 1
William Woodruff
NILLES, Herbert George 4
NILSSON, Hjalmar 1
NILSSON, Victor 2
NIMITZ, 1
Chester William
NIMKOFF, Meyer F. 4
NIMMONS, George Croll 1
NIMS, Eugene Dutton 3
NIMS, Harry Dwight 4
NINDE, 1
Edward Summerfield
NINDE, William Xavier 1
NIPHER, Francis Eugene 1
NISBET, Charles H
NISBET, 2
Charles Richard
NISBET, H
Eugenius Aristides
NISBET, James Douglas 1
NISBET, Robert Hogg 4
NISBET, 1
Walter Olin, Jr.
NISLEY, Harold A. 4
NISONGER, 5
Herschel Ward
NISSEN, 3
Harry Archibald

NISSEN, Hartvig 4
NISSEN, Henry W. 1
NISSEN, Ludwig 1
NITSCHMANN, David H
NITZE, William Albert 1
NITZSCHE, Elsa Koenig 3
NITZSCHE, George E. 4
NIVEN, H
Archibald Campbell
NIVEN, John Ballantine 3
NIVEN, William 1
NIX, James Thomas 2
NIXON, Brevard 1
NIXON, Charles Elston 2
NIXON, Eugene White 5
NIXON, George Felton 3
NIXON, George Stuart 4
NIXON, Howard Kenneth 4
NIXON, John * H
NIXON, John Thompson 4
NIXON, Justin Wroe 1
NIXON, Lewis 1
NIXON, Oliver Woodson 1
NIXON, Pat Irland 4
NIXON, Paul 3
NIXON, Samuel F. 4
NIXON, Thomas Carlyle 5
NIXON, William C. 5
NIXON, William Penn 1
NIZA, Marcos 'de 5
NKRUMAH, Kwame 5
NOA, Ernestine 5
NOAH, Mordecai Manuel H
NOAILLES, Louis Marie H
NOAKES, Edward Bruce 3
NOAKES, Frank LeRoy 5
NOBACK, Gustave J. 3
NOBILI, John 4
NOBLE, 5
Charles C(asper)
NOBLE, 1
Charles Franklin
NOBLE, Charles Henry 1
NOBLE, Charles P. 1
NOBLE, David Addison H
NOBLE, Edmund 1
NOBLE, Edward John 3
NOBLE, Eugene Allen 2
NOBLE, 1
Frederick Alphonso
NOBLE, G. Kingsley 1
NOBLE, George Bernard 5
NOBLE, George Lawrence 4
NOBLE, Harold Joyce 4
NOBLE, Henry Smith 1
NOBLE, Howard Scott 4
NOBLE, James H
NOBLE, John 4
NOBLE, John 4
NOBLE, John Martin 5
NOBLE, John Willock 1
NOBLE, 2
Marcus Cicero Stephens
NOBLE, Merrill Emmett 5
NOBLE, Ralph Edward 5
NOBLE, Raymond 2
Goodman
NOBLE, Robert Ernest 1
NOBLE, Robert Houston 1
NOBLE, Robert Peckham 5
NOBLE, Samuel H
NOBLE, 3
Sir Percy Lockhart Harnam
NOBLE, H
Thomas Satterwhite
NOBLE, 4
Thomas Satterwhite
NOBLE, Thomas Tertius 3
NOBLE, 2
Urbane Alexander
NOBLE, W. Clark 1
NOBLE, William Brown 1
NOBLE, William Henry H
NOBLE, William Lincoln 1
NOBLES, Milton 1
NOBLITT, Quintin G. 1
NOBS, Ernest 3
NOCK, Albert Jay 2
NOCK, Arthur Darby 4
NOE, Adolf Carl 4
NOE, 4
James Thomas Cotton
NOEGGERATH, H
Emil Oscar Jacob Bruno
NOEL, Cleo Allen, Jr. 5
NOEL, Edmund Favor 1
NOEL, F. Regis 3
NOEL, James William 1
NOEL, Joseph Roberts 1
NOEL, Richard C. 1
NOELL, John William H
NOELL, Thomas Estes 1
NOELTE, Albert 2
NOEST, Jan Izaak 3

NOFER, Edward John 3
NOFFSINGER, 5
Hugh Godwin
NOFFSINGER, 4
John Samuel
NOGUCHI, Hideyo 1
NOLAN, Dennis Edward 3
NOLAN, Edward James 3
NOLAN, James Bennett 4
NOLAN, John Henry 4
NOLAN, John I. 1
NOLAN, John J. Jr. 3
NOLAN, Philip H
NOLAN, Preston M. 1
NOLAN, Thomas 1
NOLAN, Val 5
NOLAN, 5
William Ignatius
NOLAND, Edgar Smith 5
NOLAND, Lloyd 2
NOLAND, Lowell E(van) 1
NOLAND, Stephen Croan 4
NOLAND, 3
William Churchill
NOLDE, Emil 4
NOLDE, O. Frederick 5
NOLEN, John 1
NOLEN, William Whiting 1
NOLI, Fan Stylian 4
NOLL, Arthur Howard 1
NOLL, 3
Edward Angus August
NOLL, John Francis 3
NOLLEN, Gerard Scholte 4
NOLLEN, Henry Scholte 2
NOLLEN, John Scholte 3
NOLTE, Charles Beach 2
NOLTE, Fred Otto 1
NOLTE, Julius Mosher 1
NOLTE, Louis Gustavus 2
NOLTING, 1
William Greaner
NOMLAND, Ruben 3
NONES, Robert Hodgson 1
NOOJIN, Balpha Lonnie 3
NOON, Malik Firoz Khan 5
NOON, Paul A.T. 5
NOONAN, Edward J. 5
NOONAN, Edward T. 4
NOONAN, 4
Greogory Francis
NOONAN, Herbert C. 3
NOONAN, James Patrick H
NOONAN, James Patrick 1
NOONAN, John A. 3
NOONAN, Joseph 3
Michael
NOONAN, Thomas 3
Hazard
NOONAN, William T. 1
NORA, Joseph J. 5
NORBECK, Kermit 5
George
NORBECK, Peter 1
NORBERG, Carl F. 1
NORBERG, Rudolph Carl 3
NORBLAD, Walter 4
NORBURY, Frank Parson 1
NORBY, Joseph Gerhard 4
NORCROSS, Cleveland 5
NORCROSS, 5
Frank Herbert
NORCROSS, George 1
NORCROSS, 1
Grenville Howland
NORCROSS, 1
Orlando Whitney
NORCROSS, 1
Wilbur Harrington
NORD, James Garesche 3
NORD, Walter Godfrey 5
NORDBERG, Bruno 1
Victor
NORDBERG, 4
Harry Malcolm
NORDBY, Jorgen 1
NORDELL, 1
Philip Augustus
NORDEN, 5
Fred Washington
NORDEN, N. Lindsay 3
NORDENHAUG, Josef 5
NORDFELDT, 3
Bror Julius Olsson
NORDHOFF, Charles 2
NORDHOFF, 2
Charles Bernard
NORDHOFF, Heinrich 5
NORDHOFF-JUNG, 4
Sofie Amalie
NORDICA, Lillian 1
NORDSTROM, Sven 3
Johan
NORELIUS, Eric 5
NORELL, Norman 5
NORGREN, Carl August 5
NORHEIMER, Isaac H

NORLIE, Olaf Morgan 4
NORLIN, George 2
NORMAN, Anne 5
NORMAN, Bradford Jr. 3
NORMAN, Edward A. 3
NORMAN, Fred 2
NORMAN, John H
NORMAN, 3
Jonathan Van Dyke
NORMAN, Mark Wilber 3
NORMAN, Montagu
Collet 2
NORMAN, Robert Claude 1
NORMANDIN, 4
Fortunal Ernest
NORMAN-WILCOX, 5
Gregor
NORRELL, William F. 4
NORRIS, Benjamin White H
NORRIS, Charles 1
NORRIS, 5
Charles Camblos
NORRIS, Charles E. 1
NORRIS, Charles Gilman 2
NORRIS, Earle Bertram 5
NORRIS, Edgar Hughes 3
NORRIS, Edward H
NORRIS, Edwin Lee 1
NORRIS, Ernest Eden 3
NORRIS, Frank 1
NORRIS, Frank Callan 4
NORRIS, 2
George Washington
NORRIS, 2
George Washington
NORRIS, 2
George William *
NORRIS, Harry Waldo 2
NORRIS, Henry 1
NORRIS, 1
Henry Hutchinson
NORRIS, Henry McCoy 1
NORRIS, Herbert T. 3
NORRIS, Homer Albert 1
NORRIS, Isaac * H
NORRIS, Isaac 4
NORRIS, James 3
NORRIS, James D. 4
NORRIS, James Flack 1
NORRIS, James Lawson 1
NORRIS, John Franklyn 5
NORRIS, Kathleen 4
NORRIS, Kenneth True 5
NORRIS, Lester J. Jr. 4
NORRIS, Mary Harriott 1
NORRIS, Moses Jr. H
NORRIS, Philip Ashton 2
NORRIS, Richard Cooper 2
NORRIS, Scott A. 4
NORRIS, 1
True Livingston
NORRIS, William H
NORRIS, William 5
NORRIS, 5
William Arthur, Jr.
NORRIS, William Fisher 1
NORRIS, William Kibby 3
NORSWORTHY, Naomi 1
NORTH, Arthur A. 4
NORTH, Cecil Clare 4
NORTH, Charles Edward 4
NORTH, Charles H. 1
NORTH, Edward 1
NORTH, Elisha 1
NORTH, Emmett Pipkin 1
NORTH, Francis Reid 4
NORTH, Frank Joshua H
NORTH, Frank Mason 1
NORTH, Harry B. 5
NORTH, Henry Emerson 4
NORTH, Isaac Franklin 4
NORTH, James Mortimer 3
NORTH, John Alden 5
NORTH, Ludlow Frey
NORTH, Orlando H
NORTH, Simeon * 1
NORTH,
Simon Newton Dexter
NORTH, Solomon Taylor 4
NORTH, Walter Harper 3
NORTH, William H
NORTHCOTE, 5
Stafford Mantle
NORTHCOTT, Elliott 2
NORTHCOTT, John A. 3
Jr.
NORTHCOTT, 3
William Allen
NORTHCOTT, 3
William Newton
NORTHEN, Edwin Clyde 3
NORTHEN, William Ezra H
NORTHEN,
William Jonathan
NORTHEND, Charles H
NORTHEND, Mary
Harrod 1

NORTHEND, William Dummer — 1
NORTHINGTON, James Montgomery — 4
NORTHROP, Birdsey Grant — H
NORTHROP, Cyrus — 1
NORTHROP, David Ward — 1
NORTHROP, Eugene P(urdy) — 5
NORTHROP, George Norton — 4
NORTHROP, Harry Pinckney — 1
NORTHROP, Henry Davenport — 1
NORTHROP, Herbert L. — 1
NORTHROP, Lucius Bellinger — H
NORTHROP, Stephen Abbott — 1
NORTHRUP, Ansel Judd — 1
NORTHRUP, Edwin Fitch — 1
NORTHRUP, Elliott Judd — 3
NORTHRUP, Frederic B. — 4
NORTHRUP, George Washington — 1
NORTHRUP, William Perry — 1
NORTHRUP, Clark Sutherland — 4
NORTHUP, George Tyler — 4
NORTHUP, John Eldridge — 1
NORTHUP, William Guile — 1
NORTON, A(rthur) Warren — 5
NORTON, Alice Peloubet — 1
NORTON, Andrews — H
NORTON, Arthur Brigham — 1
NORTON, Arthur Henry — 1
NORTON, Charles Dyer — 1
NORTON, Charles Eliot — 1
NORTON, Charles Hotchkiss — 3
NORTON, Charles Ladd — 1
NORTON, Charles Ledyard — 1
NORTON, Charles Phelps — 1
NORTON, Charles Stuart — 1
NORTON, Daniel Field — 3
NORTON, Daniel Sheldon — H
NORTON, David Z. — 1
NORTON, E. Hope — 4
NORTON, Ebenezer Foote — H
NORTON, Edith Eliza Ames — 1
NORTON, Edward Lee — 4
NORTON, Edwin — 1
NORTON, Edwin Clarence — 2
NORTON, Eliot — 1
NORTON, Eugene Levering — 4
NORTON, Frederick Owen — 1
NORTON, George Lowell — 1
NORTON, George W. — 1
NORTON, George Washington — 1
NORTON, Grace — 1
NORTON, Grace Fallow — 5
NORTON, Harold Percival — 1
NORTON, Henry Kittredge — 4
NORTON, Howard Magruder — 4
NORTON, J. Pease — 3
NORTON, James — 1
NORTON, James Albert — 4
NORTON, Jesse Olds — H
NORTON, John — 1
NORTON, John Nicholas — H
NORTON, John Pitkin — H
NORTON, John Warner — 1
NORTON, Laurence Harper — 4
NORTON, Laurence J. — 3
NORTON, Mary Teresa — 1
NORTON, Miner Gibbs — 4
NORTON, Nelson Ira — H
NORTON, Patrick Daniel — 5
NORTON, Porter — 1
NORTON, Ralph Hubbard — 3
NORTON, Richard — 1
NORTON, Robert Castle — 3
NORTON, Roy — 2
NORTON, Sidney Augustus — 1
NORTON, Stephen Alison — 1
NORTON, Thomas Herbert — 2
NORTON, Wilbur H. — 1
NORTON, William Bernard — 1

NORTON, William Edward — 1
NORTON, William Harmon — 2
NORTON, William Warder — 2
NORTONI, Albert Dexter — 1
NORTONI, Albert Dexter — 2
NORVAL, Theophilus Lincoln — 2
NORVELL, John — H
NORVELL, Saunders — 5
NORWICH, Viscount — 3
NORWOOD, C. Augustus — 1
NORWOOD, Charles Joseph — 1
NORWOOD, Edwin P. — 1
NORWOOD, George — 1
NORWOOD, John Nelson — 4
NORWOOD, John Wilkins — 2
NORWOOD, Maxwell C. — 4
NORWOOD, Robert — 1
NORWOOD, Thomas Manson — 1
NOSS, Theodore Bland — 1
NOSTRAND, Peter Elbert — 4
NOSWORTHY, Thomas Arthur — 4
NOTESTEIN, Jonas O. — 1
NOTESTEIN, Wallace — 4
NOTESTEIN, William Lee — 4
NOTHSTEIN, Ira Oliver — 5
NOTMAN, Arthur — 2
NOTMAN, John — H
NOTNAGEL, Leland Hascall — 3
NOTOPOULOS, James A. — 4
NOTT, Abraham — H
NOTT, Charles Cooper — 1
NOTT, Eliphalet — 1
NOTT, Henry Junius — H
NOTT, Josiah Clark — H
NOTT, Otis Fessenden — H
NOTT, Samuel — H
NOTT, Stanley Charles — 3
NOTTER, Harley A. — 3
NOTTINGHAM, Wayne B. — 4
NOTTINGHAM, William — 1
NOTZ, Frederick William Augustus — 1
NOTZ, William Frederick — 1
NOURSE, Amos — H
NOURSE, Edward Everett — 1
NOURSE, Elizabeth — 1
NOURSE, Henry Stedman — 1
NOURSE, John Thomas Jr. — 3
NOURSE, Joseph Pomeroy — 3
NOVAK, Frank John Jr. — 2
NOVAK, Ralph B(ernard) — 5
NOVAK, Sonia — 5
NOVARRO, Ramon (real name Ramon Gil Samaniego) — 5
NOVELLO, Ivor — 4
NOVER, Barnet — 5
NOVOTNY, Charles K. — 4
NOVY, Frederick George — 3
NOVY, Robert Lev — 5
NOWELS, Trellyen Ernest — 2
NOWLAN, George Clyde — 4
NOWLIN, William Dudley — 1
NOXON, Frank Wright — 4
NOXON, Herbert Richards — 5
NOYAN, Pierre-Jacques Payende — H
NOYES, Alexander Dana — 2
NOYES, Alfred — 3
NOYES, Arthur Amos — 1
NOYES, Arthur P. — 4
NOYES, C. Reinold — 3
NOYES, Carleton — 3
NOYES, Charles Floyd — 5
NOYES, Charles Lothrop — 1
NOYES, Charles Phelps — 1
NOYES, Charles Rutherford — 4
NOYES, Clara D. — 1
NOYES, Crosby Stuart — 1
NOYES, Daniel Rogers — 1
NOYES, E. Louise — 5
NOYES, Edward Allen — 1
NOYES, Edward Follansbee — H
NOYES, Edward MacArthur — 1
NOYES, Frank Brett — 2
NOYES, Frank Eugene — 1
NOYES, George Henry — 1
NOYES, George Loftus — 5
NOYES, George Rapall — 5

NOYES, George Rapall — H
NOYES, Guy Lincoln — 1
NOYES, Harry Alfred — 4
NOYES, Henry Drury — 1
NOYES, Henry Erastus — 1
NOYES, Irving George — 4
NOYES, James Atkins — 3
NOYES, John — 1
NOYES, John Humphrey — H
NOYES, John Rutherford — 3
NOYES, Joseph Cobham — H
NOYES, La Verne W. — 1
NOYES, Linwood Irving — 4
NOYES, Marion Ingalls — 4
NOYES, Morgan Phelps — 5
NOYES, Newbold — 1
NOYES, Pierrepont Burt — 3
NOYES, Robert Gale — 4
NOYES, Theodore Richards — 1
NOYES, Theodore Williams — 5
NOYES, Walter Chadwick — 1
NOYES, William Albert — 2
NOYES, William Curtis — H
NUCKOLLS, Stephen Friel — H
NUELLE, Joseph Henry — 4
NUELSEN, John Louis — 2
NUESSLE, Francis E. — 5
NUESSLE, William L. — 4
NUFER, Albert F. — 3
NUFFER, Joseph Henry — 4
NUFFIELD, Viscount — 4
NUGEN, Robert Hunter — H
NUGENT, Daniel Cline — 4
NUGENT, Frank Stanley — 4
NUGENT, James Alexander — 2
NUGENT, John F. — 1
NUGENT, Paul Cook — 1
NUGENT, Robert Logan — 4
NUGENT, Thomas Joseph — 5
NUGENT, Walter Henry — 5
NUHN, Clifford Jeremiah — 1
NUHN, John Alfred — 4
NULSEN, Charles Kilbourne — 3
NULTON, Louis McCoy — 3
NUNEMAKER, John Horace — 3
NUNEZ, Alvar Cabeza 'de Vaca — H
NUNN, Clement Singleton — 5
NUNN, Harold Francis — 5
NUNN, Marshall — 3
NUNN, Paul N. — 1
NUNO, Jaime — H
NUNO, Jaime — 1
NURI AS-SAID — 3
NURKSE, Ragnar — 4
NURSE, Rebecca — H
NUSSBAUM, Arthur — 4
NUSSBAUM, Paul Joseph — 1
NUTE, Alonzo — H
NUTHEAD, William — 1
NUTT, Clifford Cameron — 3
NUTT, Hubert Wilbur — 5
NUTT, Joseph Randolph — 2
NUTT, Robert Lee — 2
NUTTALL, George Henry Falkiner — 2
NUTTALL, Leonard John Jr. — 1
NUTTALL, Thomas — H
NUTTALL, Zelia — 1
NUTTER, Donald Grant — 4
NUTTER, Edmondson John Masters — 4
NUTTER, Edward Hoit — 1
NUTTER, George Read — 1
NUTTING, Charles Cleveland — 1
NUTTING, George Edward — 4
NUTTING, Harold Judd — 4
NUTTING, Herbert Chester — 1
NUTTING, John Danforth — 1
NUTTING, Margaret Ogden — 5
NUTTING, Mary Adelaide — 2
NUTTING, Mary Olivia — 1
NUTTING, Newton Wright — H
NUTTING, Perley Gilman — 4
NUTTING, Wallace — 1
NUTTLE, Harry (Hopkins) — 5
NUTTMAN, Louis Meredith — 5
NUVEEN, John — 1
NUVEEN, John — 5
NUYTTENS, Pierre — 2

NYBURG, Sidney Lauer — 3
NYCE, Benjamin Markley — 3
NYDEGGER, James Archibald — 1
NYDEN, John Augustus — 4
NYE, Archibald — 4
NYE, Edgar Hewitt — 2
NYE, Edgar Wilson — H
NYE, Frank E. — 1
NYE, Frank Mellen — 4
NYE, Gerald P. — 5
NYE, Irene — 5
NYE, James Warren — H
NYE, John Hooper — 4
NYE, Reuben Lovell — 3
NYE, Wallace George — 4
NYE, Ward Higley — 5
NYGAARD, Harlan Kenneth — 4
NYGAARD, Hjalmar C. — 4
NYLANDER, Lennart — 3
NYQUIST, Carl — 5
NYQUIST, Edna Elvera — 5
NYSTROM, Paul Henry — 5
NYSTROM, Wendell Clarence — 5
NYSWANDER, Reuben Edson Jr. — 1

O

OAKES, Frederick Warren — 4
OAKES, George Washington Ochs — 1
OAKES, James — 4
OAKES, Thomas Fletcher * — 4
OAKES, Urian — H
OAKEY, P. Davis — 4
OAKLEAF, Joseph Benjamin — 1
OAKLEY, Amy — 4
OAKLEY, Annie — H
OAKLEY, Annie — 1
OAKLEY, Francis Clark — 4
OAKLEY, Henry Augustus — 4
OAKLEY, Horace Sweeney — 1
OAKLEY, Imogen Brashear — 1
OAKLEY, Seymour Adams — 1
OAKLEY, Thomas Jackson — H
OAKLEY, Thornton — 3
OAKLEY, Violet — 1
OAKMAN, Walter G. — 1
OAKSEY, Geoffrey Lawrence — 5
OARE, Robert Lenn — 4
OATES, James Franklin — 4
OATES, William Calvin — 1
OBALDIA, Jose Doming 'de — 4
OBEAR, Hugh Harris — 5
OBENAUER, Marie Louise — 2
OBENCHAIN, William Alexander — 1
OBENSHAIN, Wiley S(hackford) — 5
OBER, Frank Roberts — 4
OBER, Frederick Albion — 1
OBER, Henry Kulp — 1
OBER, Sarah Endicott — 4
OBERFELL, George Grover — 4
OBERG, Erik — 3
OBERHANSLEY, Henry Ernest — 2
OBERHARDT, William — 3
OBERHOFFER, Emil — 1
OBERHOLSER, Harry Church — 4
OBERHOLTZER, Ellis Paxson — 1
OBERHOLTZER, Sara Louisa — 4
OBERHOLTZER, Sara Louisa Vickers — H
OBERLAENDER, Gustav — 1
OBERLINK, Boyd Stevenson — 5
OBERLY, Henry Sherman — 4
OBERMANN, Julian J. — 3
OBERNDORF, Clarence Paul — 3
OBERNDORFER, Anne Shaw Faulkner (Mrs. Marx E. Oberndorfer) — 4
O'BERRY, John E. — 4
OBERTEUFFER, George — 3
OBERWORTMANN, Nugent Robert — 4
OBICI, Amedeo — 2

O'BOYLE, Francis Joseph — 2
O'BRIAN, John Lord — 5
O'BRIEN, Charles F. — 1
O'BRIEN, Denis — 3
O'BRIEN, Denis Augustine — 3
O'BRIEN, Dennis Francis — 2
O'BRIEN, Edgar David — 5
O'BRIEN, Edward Charles — 1
O'BRIEN, Edward Francis — 2
O'BRIEN, Edward James — 3
O'BRIEN, Edward Joseph Harrington — 1
O'BRIEN, Ernest Aloysius — 2
O'BRIEN, Fitz-James — H
O'BRIEN, Francis Patrick — 4
O'BRIEN, Frank A. — 1
O'BRIEN, Frank Cornelius — 5
O'BRIEN, Frank James — 4
O'BRIEN, Frank Michael — 2
O'BRIEN, Frederick — 1
O'BRIEN, Frederick William — 4
O'BRIEN, George D. — 3
O'BRIEN, Henry Rust — 5
O'BRIEN, Howard Vincent — 2
O'BRIEN, James H. — 4
O'BRIEN, James Patrick — 4
O'BRIEN, James Putnam — 1
O'BRIEN, Jeremiah — H
O'BRIEN, John — H
O'BRIEN, John — 1
O'BRIEN, John A. — 4
O'BRIEN, John Cornelius — 1
O'BRIEN, John F. — 1
O'BRIEN, John Joseph — 1
O'BRIEN, John P. — 3
O'BRIEN, Joseph John — 3
O'BRIEN, Justin McCortney — 5
O'BRIEN, Kenneth — 3
O'BRIEN, Leo Frederick — 5
O'BRIEN, Matthew Anthony — H
O'BRIEN, Miles — 4
O'BRIEN, Morgan Joseph — 1
O'BRIEN, Patrick Henry — 5
O'BRIEN, Richard — H
O'BRIEN, Robert Lincoln — 3
O'BRIEN, S. Weldon — 1
O'BRIEN, Sara Redempta — 5
O'BRIEN, Sister M. Raphael — 3
O'BRIEN, Thomas Charles — 3
O'BRIEN, Thomas Dillon — 1
O'BRIEN, Thomas George — 5
O'BRIEN, Thomas Henry — 2
O'BRIEN, Thomas J. — 4
O'BRIEN, Thomas James — 1
O'BRIEN, Vincent — 3
O'BRIEN, William Austin — 5
O'BRIEN, William Claire — 5
O'BRIEN, William David — 4
O'BRIEN, William James — 1
O'BRIEN, William Shoney — H
O'BRIEN, William Smith — 2
O'BRIEN, William V. O. — 1
O'BRINE, David — 4
O'BRYNE, Michael Edward, Jr. — 5
O'BYRNE, John J. — 5
O'CALLAGHAN, Edmund Bailey — H
O'CALLAGHAN, Jeremiah — 1
O'CALLAGHAN, Peter Joseph — H
OCAMPOS, Bernardo — 3
O'CASEY, Sean — 4
OCCOM, Samson — H
OCHS, Adolph S. — 1
OCHS, Arthur, Jr. — 5
OCHS, Clarence L. — 5
OCHS, Julius — H
OCHS, Milton Barlow — 3
OCHSNER, Albert John — 1
OCHSNER, Edward H. — 3
OCHTMAN, Dorothy — 1
OCHTMAN, Leonard — 1
OCKENDEN, Ina Marie Porter — 4
OCKERBLAD, Nelse Frederick — 3

OCKERSON, John Augustus — H
OCKERSON, John Augustus — 2
OCKERSON, John Augustus — 4
O'CONNELL, Ambrose — 4
O'CONNELL, C. Leonard — 3
O'CONNELL, Daniel Theodore — 4
O'CONNELL, David Joseph — 1
O'CONNELL, Dennis Joseph — 1
O'CONNELL, Desmond Henry — 5
O'CONNELL, Eugene — H
O'CONNELL, Harold J. — 4
O'CONNELL, James — 1
O'CONNELL, James Timothy — 4
O'CONNELL, John Henry — 5
O'CONNELL, John Joseph — 1
O'CONNELL, John Joseph — 1
O'CONNELL, John Matthew — 2
O'CONNELL, John Michael Jr. — 1
O'CONNELL, Joseph E. — 4
O'CONNELL, Joseph Francis — 2
O'CONNELL, Joseph Francis Jr. — 4
O'CONNELL, Mary — H
O'CONNELL, Maurice D. — 4
O'CONNELL, Michael John — 3
O'CONNELL, Patrick Augustin — 3
O'CONNELL, Percy Douglas — 4
O'CONNELL, William Henry — 1
O'CONNELL, William Henry — 2
O'CONNER, William Douglas — H
O'CONNOR, Andrew — 1
O'CONNOR, Basil — 4
O'CONNOR, Bernard Francis — 5
O'CONNOR, Denis S. — 5
O'CONNOR, Edwin — 5
O'CONNOR, Evangeline M. — 5
O'CONNOR, Flannery — 4
O'CONNOR, Frank — 3
O'CONNOR, Frank Aloysius
O'CONNOR, George Bligh — 3
O'CONNOR, George Henry
O'CONNOR, J. F. T. — 2
O'CONNOR, James — H
O'CONNOR, James — 1
O'CONNOR, James — 2
O'CONNOR, James Francis — 4
O'CONNOR, James Francis — 5
O'CONNOR, James Frederick
O'CONNOR, Jeremiah J. — 4
O'CONNOR, John B. — 4
O'CONNOR, John J. — 3
O'CONNOR, John J. — 4
O'CONNOR, John Joseph — 5
O'CONNOR, John Lawrence
O'CONNOR, Joseph — 1
O'CONNOR, Leslie Michael — 4
O'CONNOR, Michael — H
O'CONNOR, Michael Patrick — H
O'CONNOR, Robert Daniel — 5
O'CONNOR, T. V. — 1
O'CONNOR, William Van
O'CONOR, Charles — H
O'CONOR, Daniel Joseph — 5
O'CONOR, Herbert Romulus — 3
O'CONOR, John Francis Xavier — 4
O'CONOR, Norreys Jephson — 3
O'CONOR, Vincent John — H
OCONOSTOTA — H
O'DANIEL, W. Lee — 5
O'DAY, Caroline
O'DAY, Daniel — 1
ODDIE, Tasker Lowndes — 5
ODDIE, Walter M. — H
O'DEA, Edward John — 1

O'DEA, James — 1
ODEGARD, Peter H. — 4
ODELL, Albert Grove — 2
ODELL, Arthur Lee — 3
ODELL, Benjamin Barker — 1
ODELL, Daniel Ingalis — 4
O'DELL, De Forest — 3
ODELL, Frank Glenn — 4
ODELL, George Clinton Densmore — 2
O'DELL, George Edward — 4
ODELL, George Thomas — 4
ODELL, Jonathan — H
ODELL, Joseph Henry — 1
ODELL, Moses Fowler — H
ODELL, Paul Edwin — 5
ODELL, William R. — 5
ODELL, William Robert — 1
ODELL, Willis Patterson — 2
ODELL, Willmot Mitchell — 1
ODEM, Brian Sylvester — 4
ODEN, Robert — 4
ODENBACH, Frederick Louis — 1
ODENHEIMER, Cordelia Powell (Mrs. — 5
ODENHEIMER, Frank Gilliams — H
ODENHEIMER, William Henry — H
ODENWELLER, Charles J(oseph, Jr. — 5
ODETS, Clifford — 4
ODGERS, Joseph H. — 4
ODIN, John Mary — H
ODIORNE, Thomas — H
ODLAND, Martin Wendell — 5
ODLIN, Arthur Fuller — 1
ODLUM, Hortense McQuarrie — 5
ODOM, Frederick Marion — 5
ODOM, William — 1
O'DONAGHUE, Denis — 1
O'DONNELL, Charles Leo — 2
O'DONNELL, Emmett, Jr. — 5
O'DONNELL, George Anthony — 3
O'DONNELL, John Hugh — 4
O'DONNELL, John Parsons — 1
O'DONNELL, Mary Eleanor — 1
O'DONNELL, Thomas Jefferson — 4
O'DONOGHUE, Daniel W. — 5
O'DONOGHUE, John Brennan — 4
O'DONOVAN, Charles — 1
O'DONOVAN, William Rudolf — 1
ODUM, Howard Washington — 3
O'DWYER, Joseph — H
O'DWYER, William — 4
OEFELE, Felix 'von — 4
OEHLERT, Lewis H. — 5
OEHMLER, Leo — 1
OELRICHS, Hermann — 1
OEMLER, Arminus — 1
OEMLER, Marie Conway — 4
OENSLAGER, George — 3
OERTEL, Hanns — 4
OERTEL, Horst — 4
OERTEL, Johannes Adam — 1
OERTEL, John James Maximilian
OESCHGER, William — 4
OESTERLE, Joseph Francis — 2
OESTREICH, Otto Albert — 4
OESTREICHER, John C. — 3
O'FALLON, Benjamin — H
O'FALLON, James — H
O'FALLON, John — H
O'FARRELL, Michael Joseph — H
O'FARRELL, Patrick — H
O'FERRALL, Charles Triplett — H
OFFENHAUER, Roy Ernest — 4
OFFERMANN, Henry F. — 3
OFFIELD, Charles Kirkpatrick
OFFIELD, James R. — 4
OFFLEY, Cleland Nelson — 1
OFFLEY, David — H
OFFNER, Richard — 4
OFFUTT, Thiemann Scott — 5
O'FLAHERTY, Hal — 5
O'FLANAGAN, Dermot — 5
OFSTIE, Ralph Andrew — 3

O'GARA, Alfred — 5
O'GARA, Cuthbert Martin — 5
O'GARA, John Edward — 5
OGBURN, Charlton — 4
OGBURN, William Fielding — 4
OGDEN, Aaron — H
OGDEN, Charles Franklin — 1
OGDEN, David — H
OGDEN, David A. — H
OGDEN, David Bayard — H
OGDEN, Dunbar Hunt — 3
OGDEN, Edward William — 2
OGDEN, Francis Barber — H
OGDEN, George Dickie — 4
OGDEN, George Washington — 4
OGDEN, Henry Alexander — 1
OGDEN, Henry Neely — 2
OGDEN, Henry Warren — 1
OGDEN, Herbert Gouverneur — 1
OGDEN, Herschel Coombs — 2
OGDEN, James Matlock — 5
OGDEN, Jay Bergen — 2
OGDEN, Peter Skene — H
OGDEN, Robert Curtis — 1
OGDEN, Robert Morris — 1
OGDEN, Rollo — 1
OGDEN, Samuel — H
OGDEN, Thomas Ludlow — H
OGDEN, Uzal — H
OGDEN, William Butler — H
OGDON, Ina Duley — 5
OGDON, Ina Duley — 5
OGELSBY, Warwick Miller — 5
OGG, Frederic Austin — 3
OGILBY, Charles Fitz Randolph — 4
OGILBY, Frederick Darley — 5
OGILBY, Remsen Brinckerhoff — 2
OGILVIE, Clarence Cooper — 3
OGILVIE, Clinton — 1
OGILVIE, James — H
OGILVIE, John — 3
OGILVIE, Walter Ellsworth
OGLE, Alexander — H
OGLE, Andrew Jackson — H
OGLE, Arthur Hook — 5
OGLE, Charles — H
OGLE, Kenneth Neil — 5
OGLE, Samuel — H
OGLEBAY, Crispin — 5
OGLESBY, Nicholas Ewing — 3
OGLESBY, Richard — H
OGLESBY, William Thomas — 5
OGLESBY, Woodson Ratcliffe — 3
OGLETHORPE, James Edward — H
OGOOD, Henry Broadwell
O'GORMAN, James A. — 2
O'GORMAN, Thomas — 1
O'GRADY, John — 1
OGSBURY, Charles R(eid) — 5
O'HAGAN, Anne (Miss) — 5
O'HAGAN, Thomas — 5
O'HAIR, Frank Trimble — 1
O'HALLORAN, Cornelius Hawkins — 4
O'HANLON, Thomas — 1
O'HANRAHAN, Inka Irene (Mrs. Seamus O'hanrahan) — 5
O'HARA, Barratt — 5
O'HARA, Edward Arthur — 5
O'HARA, Edward H. — 1
O'HARA, Edwin Vincent — 3
O'HARA, Eliot — 5
O'HARA, Frank — 1
O'HARA, Frank — 1
O'HARA, Frank Hurburt — 4
O'HARA, Geoffrey — 4
O'HARA, Gerald Patrick — 4
O'HARA, James — H
O'HARA, John (Henry) — 4
O'HARA, John Bernard — 4
O'HARA, John Francis — 4
O'HARA, Joseph Alphonsus — 2
O'HARA, Neal — 5
O'HARA, Theodore — H
O'HARA, Thomas Andrew — 4
O'HARA, William L. — 5

O'HARA, William T. S. Sr. — 4
O'HARE, Thomas C. — 3
O'HARRA, Cleophas Cisney — 1
O'HARRA, Margaret Tustin — 2
O'HARROW, Dennis — 4
O'HEARN, James Ambrose — 4
O'HERN, Charles A. — 1
O'HERN, Jennie Margaret (Mrs. William P. O'hern) — 5
O'HERN, Lewis Jerome — 1
O'HIGGINS, Bernardo — H
O'HIGGINS, Harvey — 1
OHL, Henry Jr. — 1
OHL, Jeremiah Franklin — 1
OHL, Josiah Kingsley — 1
OHL, Robert Austin — 5
OHLIN, Roy Percival — 5
OHLINGER, Gustavus — 5
OHLMACHER, Albert Philip — 1
OHLMACHER, Joseph Christian — 5
OHLSON, Otto Frederick — 5
OHMANN-DUMESNIL, Amant Henry — 5
OHRBACH, Nathan M. — 5
OHRN, Arnold Theodore — 4
OHRSTROM, George Lewis — 3
OJEDA, Don Emilio de — 5
OKAKURA, Kakuzo — 4
O'KANE, Walter Collins — 5
O'KEEFE, Anna (Miss) — 4
O'KEEFE, Arthur Joseph — 2
O'KEEFE, Dennis (Edward James Flanagan) — 5
O'KEEFFE, Arthur — 2
O'KELLEY, Thomas Washington — 1
O'KELLY, James — H
O'KELLY, Sean Thomas — 4
OKEY, John Waterman — H
OKIE, R. Brognard — 2
OLANDER, Victor A. — 2
O'LAUGHLIN, John Callan — 2
OLAYA, Enrique — 1
OLBRICH, Michael D. — 1
OLCOTT, Ben Wilson — 5
OLCOTT, Charles Sumner — 1
OLCOTT, Chauncey — 1
OLCOTT, Eben Erskine — 1
OLCOTT, Frederic P. — 1
OLCOTT, George N. — 1
OLCOTT, Henry Steel — 1
OLCOTT, Jacob Van Vechten — 1
OLCOTT, Simeon — H
OLCOTT, William James — 4
OLCOTT, William Morrow Knox — 1
OLCOTT, William Tyler — 1
OLD, Francis Paxton — 4
OLD, Howard Norman — 3
OLD, William D. — 4
OLDBERG, Arne — 1
OLDBERG, Oscar — 1
OLDEN, Charles Smith — H
OLDER, Clifford — 2
OLDER, Cora (Miranda) — 5
OLDER, Fremont — 2
OLDFATHER, William Abbott — 2
OLDFIELD, William Allan — 1
OLDHAM, G. Ashton — 4
OLDHAM, John — H
OLDHAM, Lemuel E. — 5
OLDHAM, Robert Pollard — 5
OLDHAM, William Fitzjames — 1
OLDHAM, William K. — 1
OLDHAM, Williamson Simpson — H
OLDS, Edson Baldwin — H
OLDS, Edwin Glenn — 4
OLDS, George — 4
OLDS, George Daniel — 1
OLDS, Irving S. — 4
OLDS, Leland — 5
OLDS, Ransom Ell — 3
OLDS, Robert — 2
OLDS, Robert Edwin — 1
OLDS, Walter — 4
OLDSCHOOL, Oliver — H
O'LEARY, Cornelius M. — 1
O'LEARY, Daniel — 4
O'LEARY, Daniel — 4
O'LEARY, Denis — 4
O'LEARY, Edmund Bernard

O'LEARY, James A. — 2
O'LEARY, John William — 2
O'LEARY, Paul Arthur — 4
O'LEARY, Thomas M. — 2
O'LEARY, Wesley A. — 1
O'LEARY, William Doris — 3
OLEN, Walter A. — 1
OLER, Wesley Marion — 1
OLESHA, Yuri Karlovich — 4
OLESON, John Prince — 3
OLIN, Abram Baldwin — H
OLIN, Arvin Solomon — 1
OLIN, Franklin W. — 3
OLIN, Gideon — H
OLIN, Henry — H
OLIN, Hubert Leonard — 4
OLIN, John Myers — 1
OLIN, Richard M. — 1
OLIN, Stephen — H
OLIN, Stephen Henry — 1
OLIN, Walter Herbert — 1
OLIN, William Milo — 1
OLINGER, Henri Cesar — 4
OLINSKY, Ivan Gregorewitch — 5
OLIPHANT, A. Dayton — 4
OLIPHANT, Charles Lawrence — 5
OLIPHANT, Ernest Henry Clark — 4
OLIPHANT, Harold Duncan — 5
OLIPHANT, Herman — 1
OLITSKY, Peter Kosciusko — 4
OLIVARES, Jose de — 5
OLIVE, Edgar William — 5
OLIVE, George Scott — 4
OLIVER, Allen Laws — 5
OLIVER, Andrew * — H
OLIVER, Arthur L. — 1
OLIVER, Augustus Kountze
OLIVER, Charles Augustus — 1
OLIVER, Daniel Charles — 1
OLIVER, Edna May — 2
OLIVER, Edward Allen — 3
OLIVER, Edwin Austin — 1
OLIVER, Edwin Letts — 3
OLIVER, Edwin Letts — 1
OLIVER, Fitch Edward — H
OLIVER, George Sturges — 4
OLIVER, George Tener — 1
OLIVER, Grace Atkinson — 1
OLIVER, Henry Kemble — H
OLIVER, Henry Madison, Jr. — 5
OLIVER, Henry W. — 1
OLIVER, James — 1
OLIVER, James Harrison — 1
OLIVER, John Chadwick — 4
OLIVER, John Rathbone — 4
OLIVER, Joseph — H
OLIVER, Joseph — 1
OLIVER, Joseph Doty — 1
OLIVER, L. Stauffer — 4
OLIVER, Martha Capps — 1
OLIVER, Paul Ambrose — 1
OLIVER, Peter — H
OLIVER, Robert Shaw — 1
OLIVER, Thomas Edward — 2
OLIVER, Webster J. — 5
OLIVER, William Bacon — 4
OLIVER, William F(rederick) — 5
OLIVER, William Morrison — 1
OLIVETTI, Adriano — 4
OLLENHAUER, Erich — 4
OLLESHEIMER, Henry — 1
OLLMANN, Loyal Frank — 4
OLMSTEAD, Albert Ten Eyck — 2
OLMSTEAD, Frank Robert — 3
OLMSTED, Charles Sanford — 1
OLMSTED, Charles Tyler — 1
OLMSTED, Denison — H
OLMSTED, E. Stanley — 5
OLMSTED, Everett Ward — 2
OLMSTED, Frederick Law — 1
OLMSTED, Frederick Law — 3
OLMSTED, George Welch — 1
OLMSTED, Gideon — H
OLMSTED, James Frederic — 1
OLMSTED, James Greeley
OLMSTED, James Montrose Duncan — 3
OLMSTED, John Bartow — 4
OLMSTED, John Charles — 1
OLMSTED, Marlin Edgar — 1
OLMSTED, Millicent
OLMSTED, Victor Hugo

OLMSTED, William Beach 1
OLNEY, Albert J. 3
OLNEY, George W. 1
OLNEY, Jesse H
OLNEY, Louis Atwell 1
OLNEY, Peter Butler 1
OLNEY, Richard * 1
OLNEY, Warren 1
OLNEY, Warren Jr. 1
O'LOUGHLIN, John M(artin) 5
OLP, Ernest Everett 1
OLRICH, Ernest Louis 4
OLSEN, Clarence Edward 5
OLSEN, Herluf Vagn 1
OLSEN, Ingerval M. 2
OLSEN, John Charles 2
OLSEN, Julius 1
OLSEN, Leif Ericson 4
OLSEN, Nils Andreas 1
OLSEN, Thomas Siegfried 3
OLSON, Axel Ragnar 3
OLSON, Carl Walter 3
OLSON, Charles 5
OLSON, Culbert 4
OLSON, Edwin August 2
OLSON, Ernst William 1
OLSON, Floyd Bjerstjerne 1
OLSON, George Edgar 2
OLSON, Grant Franklin 3
OLSON, H. Edwin 1
OLSON, Harry 1
OLSON, Henry 1
OLSON, James Edward 5
OLSON, John Frederick 5
OLSON, Julius Emil 4
OLSON, Julius Johann 4
OLSON, Kenneth Eugene 5
OLSON, Oscar Ludvig 3
OLSON, Oscar Thomas 4
OLSON, Oscar William 3
OLSON, Ralph J. 5
OLSON, Ralph O. 3
OLSON, Raymond Ferdinand 4
OLSSEN, William Whittingham 4
OLSSON, Alexander 3
OLSSON, Elis 3
OLSSON, Olof 1
OLSTON, Albert B. 4
OLT, George Russell 3
OLYPHANT, David Washington Cincinnatus H
OLYPHANT, Robert 1
OLYPHANT, Robert Morrison 1
O'MAHONEY, Joseph Christopher 4
O'MAHONEY, Joseph Michael 4
O'MAHONY, John H
O'MALLEY, Austin 1
O'MALLEY, Charles P. 5
O'MALLEY, Frank Ward 1
O'MALLEY, Henry 1
O'MALLEY, John Francis 5
O'MALLEY, Thomas F. 5
OMAN, Charles Malden 1
OMAN, Joseph Wallace 2
OMAR H
O'MEALIA, E. Leo 4
O'MEARA, Mark 1
O'MEARA, Stephen 1
O'MELVENY, Henry William 1
OMWAKE, George L. 1
OMWAKE, Howard Rufus 2
OMWAKE, John H
ONAHAN, William James 1
ONAN, David Warren 3
ONATE, Juan 'de H
ONDERDONK, Adrian Holmes 5
ONDERDONK, Benjamin Tredwell
ONDERDONK, Frank Scovill 1
ONDERDONK, Gilbert 4
ONDERDONK, Henry H
ONDERDONK, Henry Ustick H
ONDRAK, Ambrose Leo 4
O'NEAL, Charles Thomas 1
O'NEAL, Claude E(dgar) 5
O'NEAL, Edward Asbury III 3
O'NEAL, Edward Ashbury H
O'NEAL, Emmet 1
O'NEAL, Emmet 4
O'NEAL, James 5
O'NEAL, Samuel Amos 1
O'NEAL, William Russell 2

O'NEALE, Margaret H
O'NEALL, John Belton H
O'NEIL, Charles 1
O'NEIL, Frank R. 1
O'NEIL, George F. 5
O'NEIL, Hugh Roe 5
O'NEIL, James 1
O'NEIL, John Francis 1
O'NEIL, Joseph Henry 1
O'NEIL, Patrick Henry 4
O'NEIL, Ralph Thomas 1
O'NEIL, William Francis 4
O'NEILL, Albert T. 3
O'NEILL, Burke 4
O'NEILL, Charles H
O'NEILL, Charles 2
O'NEILL, Charles Austin 3
O'NEILL, Edmond 1
O'NEILL, Edward Emerson 3
O'NEILL, Edward L. 3
O'NEILL, Eugene Gladstone 3
O'NEILL, Eugene M. 1
O'NEILL, Florence 4
O'NEILL, Frank J. 5
O'NEILL, Harry P. 3
O'NEILL, Hugh 1
O'NEILL, J. Henry 4
O'NEILL, J. Vincent 4
O'NEILL, James Lewis 3
O'NEILL, James Milton 5
O'NEILL, John H
O'NEILL, John Edward 4
O'NEILL, John J. 3
O'NEILL, Lewis Patrick 5
ONKEN, William Henry, Jr. 5
OOMS, Casper W. 4
OOSTERMEYER, Jan 4
OOSTING, Henry J. 5
OPDYCKE, John Baker 3
OPDYCKE, Leonard Eckstein 1
OPDYKE, George 1
OPDYKE, William Stryker 1
OPERTI, Albert 1
OPHEIM, Leonard Bertinius 5
OPHULS, William 1
OPIE, Eugene Lindsay 5
OPIE, Thomas 4
OPP, Julie 1
OPPENHEIM, Amy Schwartz 3
OPPENHEIM, Ansel 1
OPPENHEIM, Edward Phillips 2
OPPENHEIM, James 1
OPPENHEIM, Nathan 1
OPPENHEIM, Samuel 1
OPPENHEIMER, Fritz Ernest 5
OPPENHEIMER, Robert 4
OPPENHEIMER, Sir Ernest * 3
OPPER, Clarence Victor 4
OPPER, Frederick Burr 1
OPTIC, Oliver H
ORAHOOD, Harper M. 1
ORBISON, Thomas James 1
ORCHARD, John Ewing 4
ORCUTT, Calvin B. 1
ORCUTT, Hiram H
ORCUTT, William Dana 1
ORCUTT, William Warren 2
ORD, Edward Otho Cresap H
ORD, George 1
ORDAL, Ola Johannessen 1
ORDAL, Zakarias J. 3
ORDEAN, Albert Le Grand 1
ORDONEZ, Castor 1
ORDRONAUX, John 1
ORDWAY, Edward Warren 4
ORDWAY, J. G. 4
ORDWAY, John 1
ORDWAY, John Morse 1
ORDWAY, Samuel Hanson 5
ORDWAY, Samuel Hanson 1
ORDWAY, Thomas 3
ORE, Oystein 5
O'REAR, Edward Clay 5
O'REAR, John Davis 1
O'REGAN, Anthony H
O'REILLY, Alexander 1
O'REILLY, Andrew John Goldsmith 2
O'REILLY, Bernard H

O'REILLY, Bernard Patrick 1
O'REILLY, Charles J. 1
O'REILLY, Gabriel Ambrose 5
O'REILLY, Henry H
O'REILLY, James 1
O'REILLY, James Thomas 1
O'REILLY, John Boyle 1
O'REILLY, Mary Boyle 1
O'REILLY, Peter J. 1
O'REILLY, Robert Maitland 1
O'REILLY, Thomas Charles 1
ORENDORFF, Alfred 1
ORLADY, George Boal 1
ORMAN, James Bradley 1
ORME, John Pinckney 1
ORMOND, Alexander Thomas 1
ORMSBEE, Ebenezer Jolls 1
ORMSBEE, Thomas Hamilton 5
ORMSBY, Oliver Samuel 3
ORMSBY, Stephen H
ORMSBY, Waterman Lilly H
ORMSTON, Mark D. 4
ORNDOFF, Benjamin Harry 5
ORNDORFF, William Ridgely 1
ORNDUFF, William Wilmer 5
ORNE, Caroline Frances 1
ORNE, John 1
ORNER, Irvin Melvin 4
ORNITZ, Samuel 3
O'ROURKE, Charles Edward 2
O'ROURKE, Fidelis (Arthur J.) 1
O'ROURKE, John Thomas 4
O'ROURKE, Lawrence James 1
O'ROURKE, Patrick Ira 3
O'ROURKE, William Thomas 1
OROZCO, Jose Clemente 2
ORR, Alexander Dalrymple H
ORR, Alexander Ector 1
ORR, Benjamin H
ORR, Carey 4
ORR, Charles 1
ORR, Charles Prentiss 1
ORR, Douglas William 5
ORR, Flora Gracia 3
ORR, George 1
ORR, Gustavus John 1
ORR, H. Winnett 3
ORR, Hugh H
ORR, Isaac Henry 1
ORR, James Lawrence H
ORR, James Lawrence 1
ORR, James Washington 1
ORR, John Alvin 3
ORR, John Boyd (Lord Boyd of Brechin) 5
ORR, John William H
ORR, Joseph Kyle 1
ORR, Louis 4
ORR, Louis McDonald 4
ORR, Louis Thomas 5
ORR, Robert 1
ORR, Robert Jr. H
ORR, Robert Hall 5
ORR, Robert William 5
ORR, Robert Williamson 3
ORR, Thomas E. 3
ORR, Thomas Grover 1
ORR, Thomas L. 1
ORR, Walter Stuart 4
ORR, Warren Henry 4
ORR, William 1
ORR, William Anderson 3
ORRIS, S. Stanhope 1
ORROK, George Alexander 2
ORRY-KELLY 1
ORT, Samuel Alfred 1
ORTEGA 'Y GASSET, Jose 1
ORTEGA Y GASSET, Jose 1
ORTEIG, Raymond 1
ORTH, Bertrand 1
ORTH, Charles J. 1
ORTH, Godlove Stein 1
ORTH, John 1
ORTH, Lizette Emma 1
ORTH, O. Sidney 1
ORTH, Samuel Peter 1
ORTHWEIN, Charles F. H
ORTHWEIN, Percy James 3

ORTHWINE, Rudolf Adolf 5
ORTLOFF, Henry Stuart 5
ORTMANN, Arnold Edward 1
ORTON, Clayton Roberts 3
ORTON, Dwayne 5
ORTON, Edward 1
ORTON, Edward Jr. H
ORTON, Harlow South 4
ORTON, Helen Fuller 3
ORTON, James H
ORTON, Samuel Torrey 2
ORTON, William H
ORTON, William Allen 1
ORTON, William Aylott 3
ORVILLE, Howard T. 4
ORVIS, Ellis Lewis 4
ORWELL, George 4
ORY, Edward Kid 5
O'RYAN, John F. 4
O'RYAN, William Francis 4
OSBON, Bradley Sillick 1
OSBORN, Abraham Coles 1
OSBORN, Albert Dunbar 5
OSBORN, Albert Sherman 2
OSBORN, Alexander Faickney 4
OSBORN, Alexander Perry 3
OSBORN, Charles H
OSBORN, Chase Salmon 2
OSBORN, Cyrus Richard 5
OSBORN, Edwin Faxon 1
OSBORN, Erastus William 1
OSBORN, Frank Chittenden 2
OSBORN, Frederick Arthur 5
OSBORN, George Augustus 1
OSBORN, H. Fairfield 1
OSBORN, Henry Chisholm 4
OSBORN, Henry Leslie 1
OSBORN, Henry Stafford H
OSBORN, Herbert 1
OSBORN, Hervey James 4
OSBORN, Laughton H
OSBORN, Loran David 3
OSBORN, Luther W. 4
OSBORN, Marvin Griffing 3
OSBORN, Merritt J. 3
OSBORN, Monroe 2
OSBORN, Norris Galpin 1
OSBORN, Selleck H
OSBORN, Sidney Preston 4
OSBORN, Stewart Patrick 4
OSBORN, Thomas Andrew H
OSBORN, Thomas Ogden 1
OSBORN, William Church 3
OSBORN, William H. 1
OSBORN, William Henry H
OSBORNE, Antrim Edgar 4
OSBORNE, Arthur Dimon 1
OSBORNE, Charles Devens 4
OSBORNE, Duffield 1
OSBORNE, Earl Dorland 1
OSBORNE, Edward William 1
OSBORNE, Edwin Sylvanus 1
OSBORNE, Ernest G. 4
OSBORNE, George Abbott 1
OSBORNE, Henry Zenas 1
OSBORNE, James Insley 3
OSBORNE, James Van Wyck 1
OSBORNE, John H
OSBORNE, John Ball 5
OSBORNE, John E. 1
OSBORNE, John Stuart 4
OSBORNE, Loyall Allen 2
OSBORNE, Milton Smith 1
OSBORNE, Oliver 1
OSBORNE, Thomas 5
OSBORNE, Reginald Stanley
OSBORNE, Thomas Burr H
OSBORNE, Thomas Burr 1
OSBORNE, Thomas Mott 1
OSBORNE, William Hamilton 2
OSBORNE, William McKinley
OSBORN-HANNAH, Jane 3

OSBOURN, Samuel Edmund 5
OSBOURNE, Alfred Slack 4
OSBOURNE, Lloyd 2
OSBURN, Worth James 3
OSCAR, Stephen A. 3
OSCEOLA H
OSENBAUGH, Charles Merril 1
OSEROFF, Abraham 4
OSGOOD, Alfred Townsend 3
OSGOOD, Charles Grosvenor 4
OSGOOD, Edwin Eugene 5
OSGOOD, Ellis Carlton 5
OSGOOD, Etta Haley 1
OSGOOD, Farley 1
OSGOOD, Frances Sargent Locke H
OSGOOD, Gayton 3
OSGOOD, Pickman H
OSGOOD, George Laurie 4
OSGOOD, Henry Brown 1
OSGOOD, Henry Osborne 1
OSGOOD, Herbert Levi 1
OSGOOD, Howard 1
OSGOOD, Irene 1
OSGOOD, Jacob H
OSGOOD, John Cleveland 1
OSGOOD, Phillips Endecott 3
OSGOOD, Robert Bayley 3
OSGOOD, Roy Clifton 3
OSGOOD, Samuel H
OSGOOD, Samuel Stillman
OSGOOD, Samuel Walter 1
OSGOOD, Wilfred Hudson 2
OSGOOD, William Fogg 2
O'SHAUGHNESSY, Edith Coues 1
O'SHAUGHNESSY, Elim 4
O'SHAUGHNESSY, John K. 3
O'SHAUGHNESSY, M. M. 1
O'SHAUGHNESSY, Nelson 1
O'SHAUNESSY, George Francis 1
O'SHEA, Benjamin 3
O'SHEA, John Augustine 1
O'SHEA, John J. 3
O'SHEA, Michael Vincent 1
O'SHEA, William James 1
O'SHEA, William Joseph 3
OSK, Roselle H. 3
OSKISON, John Milton 5
OSLAND, Birger 4
OSLER, William 4
OSMENA, Sergio 4
OSMOND, I. Thornton 1
OSMUN, A. Vincent 3
OSMUN, Russell A. 3
OSMUN, Thomas Embley 1
OSORIO, Oscar 5
OSORIO LIZARAZO, Jose Antonio 4
OSTENACO H
OSTENSO, Martha 1
OSTER, Henry Richard 2
OSTERBERG, Max 1
OSTERHAUS, Hugo 1
OSTERHAUS, Hugo Wilson 5
OSTERHAUS, Peter Joseph 1
OSTERHOLM, Martin 1
OSTERHOUT, Winthrop John Vanleuven 4
OSTERTAG, Blanche 5
OSTHAUS, Carl Wilhelm Ferdinand 4
OSTHAUS, Edmund 1
OSTRAND, James Adolph 1
OSTRANDER, Dempster 1
OSTRANDER, Don Richard 5
OSTRANDER, Fannie Eliza 1
OSTRANDER, Isabel 1
OSTRANDER, John Edwin 1
OSTRANDER, Russell Cowles 1
OSTROLENK, Bernhard 2
OSTROM, Henry 1
OSTROM, Kurre Wilhelm 4
OSTROMISLENSKY-, Iwan Iwanowich H
OSTROMISLENSKY-, Iwan Iwanowich 4
O'SULLIVAN, Curtis D. 4
O'SULLIVAN, Frank 2

O'SULLIVAN, Jeremiah — H
O'SULLIVAN, John Louis — H
O'SULLIVAN, Vincent — 4
OSUNA, Juan Jose — 3
OSWALD, Felix Leopold — 1
OSWALD, John Clyde — 1
OTERMEN, Antonio 'de — H
OTERO, Miguel Antonio — H
OTERO, Miguel Antonio — 2
OTEY, Ernest Glenwood — 4
OTEY, James Hervey — H
OTEY, Peter Johnston — 1
OTHMAN, Frederick C. — 3
OTIS, Alphonse Elmer Spencer
OTIS, Arthur Sinton — 4
OTIS, Bass — H
OTIS, Charles — 2
OTIS, Edward Osgood — H
OTIS, Elisha Graves — H
OTIS, Elwell Stephen — 1
OTIS, George Alexander — H
OTIS, Harold — 3
OTIS, Harrison Gray — H
OTIS, Harrison Gray — 1
OTIS, James — H
OTIS, John — H
OTIS, Joseph Edward — 3
OTIS, Joseph Edward — 4
OTIS, Merrill E. — 2
OTIS, Norton P. — 1
OTIS, Philo Adams — 1
OTIS, Samuel Allyne — 4
OTIS, Spencer — 4
OTIS, William Augustus — 1
OTIS, William Kelly — 1
OTJEN, Theobald — 4
O'TOOLE, Donald Lawrence
O'TOOLE, William Joseph
OTSUKA, Raymond M. — 5
OTT, Edward Amherst — 4
OTT, Emil — 4
OTT, George — 1
OTT, Harvey Newton — 5
OTT, Isaac — 1
OTT, William Pinkerton — 2
OTTAWAY, Elmer James — 1
OTTE, Hugo Emil — 2
OTTE, Louis Edward — 3
OTTEMILLER, John H(enry) — 5
OTTENDORFER, Anna Behr Uhl — H
OTTENDORFER, Oswald — 1
OTTER, John M. — 4
OTTER, Thomas — H
OTTERBEIN, H. C. — 3
OTTERBEIN, Philip William — H
OTTERBOURG, Edwin M. — 4
OTTERSON, John Edward — 4
OTTING, Bernard John — 3
OTTING, Leonard Henry — 3
OTTINGER, Albert — 1
OTTINGER, Lawrence — 3
OTTLEY, John King — 2
OTTLEY, Passie Fenton — 1
OTTLEY, Roi — 4
OTTMAN, Ford Cyrinde — 1
OTTMANN, William — 2
OTTO, Benjamin — 4
OTTO, Bodo — H
OTTO, John Conrad — 1
OTTO, Max Carl — 5
OTTOERBOURG, Edwin M. — 5
OTTOFY, Ladialaus Michael — 2
OTTOFY, Louis — 5
OTTS, John Martin Philip — 1
OUCHTERLONEY, James Delgarens — 4
OUCHTERLONY, John Arvid — 1
OUDIN, Maurice Agnus — 1
OUGHTERSON, Ashley W. — 3
OULAHAN, Richard Victor — 1
OURAY — H
OURSLER, Fulton — 3
OURSLER, Grace Perkins — 3
OURY, Granville Henderson — H
OUSLEY, Clarence — 2
OUTACITY — H
OUTCAULT, Richard Felton — 1
OUTERBRIDGE, Albert Albouy — 1
OUTERBRIDGE, Alexander Ewing Jr.

OUTERBRIDGE, Eugene Harvey — 1
OUTHWAITE, Joseph H. — 1
OVENSHINE, Alexander Thompson — 5
OVENSHINE, Samuel — 1
OVERALL, John Wesley — 4
OVERBECK, Reynolds Covel — 5
OVERBY, Oscar Rudolph — 4
OVERESCH, Harvey E. — 5
OVERFIELD, Chauncey Percival — 1
OVERFIELD, Peter D. — 5
OVERHOLSER, Earle Long — 2
OVERHOLSER, Edward — 1
OVERHOLSER, Winfred — 4
OVERMAN, Frederick — H
OVERMAN, Lee Slater — 1
OVERS, Walter Henry — 1
OVERSTREET, Harry Allen — 5
OVERSTREET, James — H
OVERSTREET, James Whetstone — 4
OVERSTREET, Jesse — 1
OVERSTREET, Lee-Carl — 1
OVERTON, Daniel Hawkins — 1
OVERTON, Frank — 3
OVERTON, Grant — 1
OVERTON, Gwendolen — 5
OVERTON, James Bertram — 1
OVERTON, John — H
OVERTON, John Holmes — 2
OVERTON, Walter Hampden — H
OVERTON, Watkins — 3
OVERTON, Winston — 1
OVIATT, Delmar Thomas — 5
OVINGTON, Earle — 1
OVINGTON, Irene Helen — 1
OVINGTON, Mary White — 3
OWEN, Allen Ferdinand — 1
OWEN, Allison — 3
OWEN, Arthur David Kemp — 5
OWEN, Carl Maynard — 3
OWEN, Charles Archibald — 3
OWEN, Charles Sumner — 2
OWEN, D. T. — 1
OWEN, David Blair — 1
OWEN, David Dale — H
OWEN, David Edward — 5
OWEN, David Edward — 4
OWEN, Edward — 4
OWEN, Emmett Marshall — 1
OWEN, Fred K. — 1
OWEN, George Washington — H
OWEN, Griffith — H
OWEN, James — H
OWEN, James — 3
OWEN, John — H
OWEN, John Paul — 3
OWEN, John S. — 1
OWEN, John Wilson — 2
OWEN, Kenneth Marvin — 4
OWEN, L. F. — 3
OWEN, Mary Alicia — 1
OWEN, Robert — H
OWEN, Robert Dale — 1
OWEN, Robert Latham — 3
OWEN, Russell — 2
OWEN, Stephen Walker — 1
OWEN, Stewart Douglas — 5
OWEN, Thomas Henry — 4
OWEN, Thomas McAdory — 1
OWEN, Walter Cecil — 1
OWEN, Wesley M. — 1
OWEN, William Baxter — 1
OWEN, William Bishop — 1
OWEN, William Frazer — 2
OWEN, William Otway — 1
OWEN, William Russell — 1
OWENS, Frederick William — 4
OWENS, George Welshman — H
OWENS, Grover Thomas — 1
OWENS, Hamilton — 4
OWENS, James Francis — 2
OWENS, John Edmond — H
OWENS, John Edwin — 1
OWENS, John Whitefield — 5
OWENS, Madison Townsend — 1
OWENS, Michael Joseph — 1
OWENS, Ray L. — 3
OWENS, Robert Bowie — 1
OWENS, Thomas Leonard — 2
OWENS, Walter D. — 1
OWLETT, Gilbert Mason — 3
OWRE, Alfred — 1

OWSLEY, Alvin Mansfield — 4
OWSLEY, Bryan Young — H
OWSLEY, Frank Lawrence — 3
OWSLEY, William — H
OWST, Wilberfoss George — 1
OXNAM, G. Bromley — 4
OXNARD, Benjamin Alexander — 1
OXNARD, Henry Thomas — 1
OXNARD, Robert — 1
OXNARD, Thomas — 4
OXNER, George Dewey — 4
OXTOBY, Frederic Breading — 1
OXTOBY, Walter Ewing — 1
OXTOBY, William Henry — 1
OYEN, Henry — 1
OYEN, Valborg Hansine (Mrs. Arnt J. Oyen) — 5
OYSTER, James F. — 1
OZENFANT, Amedee-Jullen — 4
OZLIN, Thomas William — 2
OZMUN, Edward Henry — 1

P

PAASIKIVI, Juho Kusti — 3
PABST, Charles Frederick — 5
PABST, Fred — 3
PABST, Frederick — 1
PACA, William — H
PACE, Charles Nelson — 4
PACE, Edward Aloysius — 1
PACE, Frank — 5
PACE, Homer St Clair — 2
PACE, Jerome Grant — 1
PACE, Julian Harrison — 1
PACE, Leo L. — 4
PACE, Mary Anna — 1
PACE, Pearl Carter (Mrs. Stanley D. Pace) — 5
PACE, Thomas A(ndrew) — 5
PACENT, Louis Gerard — 3
PACH, Walter — 3
PACHELBEL, Carl Theodorus — H
PACHLER, William Joseph — 5
PACHMANN, Vladimir 'de — 1
PACK, Charles Lathrop — 1
PACK, Frederick James — 1
PACK, George Willis — 1
PACK, Randolph Greene — 3
PACK, Robert Francis — 4
PACK, Robert Wallace — 4
PACKARD, Alpheus Spring — H
PACKARD, Alpheus Spring — 1
PACKARD, Alton — 1
PACKARD, Arthur Worthington — 3
PACKARD, Bertram E. — 2
PACKARD, Burdett Aden — 1
PACKARD, Charles Stuart Wood — 1
PACKARD, Francis Randolph — 3
PACKARD, Frank Edward — 4
PACKARD, Frank Lucius — 2
PACKARD, Frederick Adolphus — H
PACKARD, George — 1
PACKARD, George Arthur — 1
PACKARD, George Byron — 1
PACKARD, George Randolph — 1
PACKARD, Horace — 1
PACKARD, James Ward — 1
PACKARD, Jasper — 1
PACKARD, John Hooker — 1
PACKARD, Joseph * — 1
PACKARD, Laurence Bradford — 3
PACKARD, Lewis Richard — H
PACKARD, Ralph Gooding — 4
PACKARD, Silas Sadler — H
PACKARD, Walter E. — 4
PACKARD, William Alfred — 1
PACKARD, Winthrop — 2
PACKER, Asa — H
PACKER, Francis Herman — 3
PACKER, Fred Little — 5
PACKER, Herbert Leslie — 5
PACKER, Horace Billings — 3

PACKER, John Black — H
PACKER, William Fisher — H
PACKMAN, James Joseph — 5
PADDLEFORD, Clementine Haskin — 4
PADDOCK, Algernon Sidney — H
PADDOCK, Benjamin Henry — H
PADDOCK, Buckley B. — 1
PADDOCK, Charles William — 2
PADDOCK, George Arthur — 4
PADDOCK, Hiram Lester — 2
PADDOCK, John Adams — H
PADDOCK, Lucius Carver — 1
PADDOCK, Miner Hamlin — 4
PADDOCK, R. B. — 3
PADDOCK, Robert Lewis — 1
PADDOCK, Wendell — 3
PADDOCK, Willard Dryden — 5
PADDOCK, Willard Dryden
PADELFORD, Frank William — 2
PADELFORD, Frederick Morgan
PADELFORD, Silas Catching — 5
PADEN, William Mitchel — 4
PADEREWSKI, Ignace Jan — 1
PADGETT, Earl C. — 2
PADGETT, Lemuel Phillips — 1
PADGETT, Lemuel Phillips Jr. — 4
PADILLA, Ezequiel — 5
PADILLA, Juan 'de — H
PADWAY, Joseph Arthur — 2
PAEPCKE, Walter Paul — 3
PAEPCKE, Walter Paul — 4
PAETOW, Louis John — 1
PAGAN, Bolivar — 4
PAGAN, Oliver Elwood — 5
PAGE, Alfred Rider — 1
PAGE, Arthur Clinton — 3
PAGE, Arthur Wilson — 4
PAGE, Bertrand A. — 1
PAGE, Calvin — 1
PAGE, Carroll Smalley — 1
PAGE, Charles * — 1
PAGE, Charles Grafton — H
PAGE, Curtis Hidden — 2
PAGE, David Perkins — H
PAGE, Earl Dexter — 4
PAGE, Edward Day — 1
PAGE, Elizabeth Fry — 5
PAGE, Elwin Lawrence — 5
PAGE, Frank Copeland — 3
PAGE, Frederick Harlan — 5
PAGE, George Bispham — 2
PAGE, George T. — 1
PAGE, Henry — 1
PAGE, Herman — 2
PAGE, Horace Francis — H
PAGE, James — 4
PAGE, James Morris — 1
PAGE, James Rathwell — 4
PAGE, John * — H
PAGE, John Chatfield — 3
PAGE, John Henry — 1
PAGE, John Randolph — 1
PAGE, Kirby — 3
PAGE, Leigh — 3
PAGE, Lewis Coues — 1
PAGE, Logan Waller — 1
PAGE, Mann * — H
PAGE, Marie Danforth — 1
PAGE, Nathaniel Clifford — 1
PAGE, Ralph Walter — 2
PAGE, Ralph Walter — 4
PAGE, Richard Gregory — 3
PAGE, Richard Lucian — 1
PAGE, Robert — H
PAGE, Robert G(uthrie) — 5
PAGE, Robert M. — 5
PAGE, Robert Newton — 1
PAGE, Robert Powel Jr. — 1
PAGE, Roger McKeene — 2
PAGE, S. Davis — 1
PAGE, Sherman — 1
PAGE, Thomas Jefferson — H
PAGE, Thomas Nelson — 1
PAGE, Thomas Walker — 1
PAGE, Walter Gilman — 1
PAGE, Walter Hines — 1
PAGE, William — H
PAGE, William Herbert — 3
PAGE, William Nelson — 1
PAGE, William Tyler — 2
PAGET, Lowell — 4
PAHLOW, Edwin William — H

PAHLOW, Gertrude Curtis Brown — 1
PAIGE, Calvin D. — 1
PAIGE, Clifford E. — 3
PAIGE, Del R. — 4
PAIGE, Hildegard Brooks — 1
PAIGE, Raymond North — 4
PAIGE, Robert Myron — 4
PAIN, Philip — H
PAINE, Albert Bigelow — 1
PAINE, Albert Ware — 1
PAINE, Bayard Henry — 3
PAINE, Bryon — H
PAINE, Charles — 1
PAINE, Charles — 1
PAINE, Charles Jackson — 1
PAINE, Charles Leslie — 4
PAINE, Clara Audrea (Mrs. Clarence Summer Paine) — 5
PAINE, Elijah — 1
PAINE, Ellery Burton — 5
PAINE, Ephraim — H
PAINE, Francis Brinley Hebard — 1
PAINE, Francis Ward — 1
PAINE, George Eustis — 3
PAINE, George H. — 3
PAINE, Gregory Lansing — 5
PAINE, Halbert Eleazer — 1
PAINE, Harlan Lloyd — 5
PAINE, Harriet Eliza — 1
PAINE, Henry Gallup — 1
PAINE, Henry Warren — 1
PAINE, Horace Marshfield — 1
PAINE, Howard Simmons — 3
PAINE, Hugh E. — 5
PAINE, James Lawrence — 2
PAINE, John Alsop — 1
PAINE, John Gregg — H
PAINE, John Knowles — 1
PAINE, Karl — H
PAINE, Martyn — 1
PAINE, Nathaniel — 1
PAINE, Nathaniel Emmons — 1
PAINE, Paul Mayo — 3
PAINE, Ralph Delahaye — 1
PAINE, Robert — H
PAINE, Robert Findlay — 1
PAINE, Robert Treat * — H
PAINE, Robert Treat — 1
PAINE, Robert Treat II — 2
PAINE, Roger W. — 4
PAINE, Roland D. — 5
PAINE, Thomas — H
PAINE, William Alfred — 1
PAINE, William Wiseham — 1
PAINE, Willis Seaver — 1
PAINTER, Carl Wesley — 5
PAINTER, Charles Fairbank — 2
PAINTER, Franklin Verzelius Newton — 1
PAINTER, Gamaliel — 1
PAINTER, George Alexander Stephen
PAINTER, Henry McMahan
PAINTER, Russell Floyd — 5
PAINTER, Sidney — 3
PAINTER, Theophilus Shickel
PAINTER, William — 1
PAINTER, William — 4
PALACHE, Charles — 3
PALAMAR, Michael — 4
PALEN, Frederick Pomeroy
PALEN, Rufus — H
PALEN, Rufus James — 1
PALEY, Samuel — 4
PALFREY, John Gorham — H
PALFREY, John Gorham — 1
PALFREY, Sara Hammond — 4
PALLEN, Conde Benoist — 1
PALLETTE, Edward Marshall — 2
PALLISER, Charles — 1
PALLISER, Melvin G. — 1
PALLOTTI, Francis A. — 2
PALMA, Tomas Estrada — 1
PALMARO, Marcel A. — 5
PALMA 'Y VELASQUEZ, Rafael — 1
PALMER, A. Emerson — 1
PALMER, A. Mitchell — H
PALMER, A. Mitchell — 1
PALMER, Abraham John — 1
PALMER, Agnes Lizzie — 1
PALMER, Albert 'de Forest

PALMER, 2
  Albert Kenny Craven
PALMER, 1
  Albert Marshman
PALMER, Albert Robert 2
PALMER, 3
  Albert Wentworth
PALMER, Alice Freeman 1
PALMER, H
  Alonzo Benjamin
PALMER, Andrew Henry 2
PALMER, Anna Campbell 1
PALMER, Arthur 3
PALMER, Arthur Hubbell 1
PALMER, Arthur William 4
PALMER, Aulick 1
PALMER, 4
  Bartlett Joshua
PALMER, 5
  Bell Elliott (Mrs. James
  Allerton Palmer)
PALMER, 1
  Benjamin Morgan
PALMER, Beriah H
PALMER, Bertha Honore 1
PALMER, Bertha Rachel 3
PALMER, 2
  Bradley Webster
PALMER, C. William 4
PALMER, Carleton H. 5
PALMER, 5
  Carroll (Edwards)
PALMER, Charles M. 2
PALMER, Charles Ray 1
PALMER, Charles Skeele 1
PALMER, Chase 1
PALMER, Chauncey D. 1
PALMER, Chesley Robert 5
PALMER, Claude Irwin 1
PALMER, Clyde Eber 3
PALMER, 1
  Cornelius Solomon
PALMER, Daniel David H
PALMER, Daniel David 1
PALMER, David J. 3
PALMER, Dean 1
PALMER, Edgar 2
PALMER, Edward L. Jr. 3
PALMER, Edwin R. 4
PALMER, 3
  Elbridge Woodman
PALMER, Elihu H
PALMER, Erastus Dow 1
PALMER, Everett Walter 5
PALMER, Fanny Purdy 4
PALMER, H
  Frances Flora Bond
PALMER, Francis Eber 5
PALMER,
  Francis Leseure
PALMER, Frank Herbert 1
PALMER, Frank Nelson 3
PALMER, Frank Wayland 1
PALMER, Fred Chester 5
PALMER, Frederic 1
PALMER, Frederic Jr. 4
PALMER, Frederick 3
PALMER, George Herbert 1
PALMER, George Louis 3
PALMER,
  George Washington
PALMER, Gordon Davis 1
PALMER, Harold Gilbert 3
PALMER, Henrietta Lee 1
PALMER, Henry E. 1
PALMER, Henry L. 1
PALMER, Henry
  Robinson 4
PALMER, Henry Wilber 1
PALMER,
  Horatio Richmond
PALMER, Howard 2
PALMER, Innis Newton H
PALMER, Irving Allston 5
PALMER, James Croxall H
PALMER, James Shedden 1
PALMER, Joel H
PALMER, John H
PALMER, John McAuley 1
PALMER, John McAuley 1
PALMER, John William 3
PALMER,
  John Williamson
PALMER, Joseph H
PALMER, 1
  Julius Auboineau
PALMER, Leigh Carlyle 3
PALMER, Leroy Sheldon 2
PALMER, Leslie Richard 1
PALMER, Loren 1
PALMER, Lynde 4
PALMER,
  Martin Franklin
PALMER, Mrs. Potter H
PALMER,
  Nathaniel Brown
PALMER, Pauline

PALMER, Philip Mason 3
PALMER, Potter 1
PALMER, Potter 2
PALMER, Ray H
PALMER, Ray 2
PALMER, Robert 3
PALMER, 1
  Samuel Sterling
PALMER, Silas H. 4
PALMER, Stephen S. 3
PALMER, Stuart 4
PALMER, 3
  Theodore Sherman
PALMER, Thomas
  Waverly 5
PALMER, Thomas
  Waverly 1
PALMER,
  Thomas Witherell
PALMER, Truman Garrett 1
PALMER, Walter Launt 1
PALMER, Walter Walker 3
PALMER, Warren
  Sherman 4
PALMER, William Adams 1
PALMER, William Beach 4
PALMER, William Henry 1
PALMER,
  William Jackson
PALMER, 1
  William Pendleton
PALMER, 5
  William Spencer
PALMERSTON, H
  3'd 'viscount
PALMORE, 1
  William Beverly
PALMQUIST, 5
  Elim Arthur Eugene
PALOU, Francisco H
PALTSITS, Victor Hugo 3
PAM, Max 1
PAMMEL, Louis Hermann 1
PANARETOFF, Stephen 4
PANBOURNE, Oliver 1
PANCOAST,
  Henry Khunrath
PANCOAST, 1
  Henry Spackman
PANCOAST, Joseph H
PANCOAST, Seth 1
PANCOAST,
  Thomas Jessup
PANCOST, E. Ellsworth 3
PANE-GASSER, John 4
PANETH, F. A. 3
PANGBORN, Earl Leroy 4
PANGBORN,
  Frederic Werden
PANGBORN, Georgia
  Wood 5
PANGBORN,
  Thomas Wesley
PANICO, Giovanni 1
PANNELL, Faye 5
PANNELL, Henry Clifton 2
PANNILL, 3
  Charles Jackson
PANOFSKY, Erwin 1
PANSY 1
PANTON, William 4
PANUNZIO,
  Constantine Maria
PAPAGOS, Alexander 3
PAPANICOLAOU, 4
  George Nicholas
PAPE, Eric 1
PAPE, William J. 4
PAPEZ, James Wenceslas 1
PAPI, Gennaro 1
PAPPENHEIMER, Alwin
  M. 4
PAQUET, Anthony C. H
PAQUETTE, 5
  Charles Alfred
PAQUIN, 4
  Albert Joseph Jr.
PAQUIN, Lawrence G. 4
PAQUIN, Paul 1
PAQUIN, Samuel Savil 2
PARADISE, Frank Ilsley 1
PARAMANANDA,
  Swami
PARDEE, Ario H
PARDEE, Don Albert 1
PARDEE, George Cooper 1
PARDEE, 5
  Harold Ensign Bennett
PARDEE, Israel Platt 1
PARDEE, James Thomas 1
PARDO, Felipe 1
PARDOW,
  William O'Brien
PARDUE, Louis A. 4
PARENT, Alphonse Marie 5
PARENTE, 5
  Pascal Prosper

PARET, J(ahial) Parmly 5
PARET, Thomas Dunkin 4
PARET, William 1
PARGELLIS, Stanley 4
PARHAM, 1
  Frederick William
PARIS, 3
  Auguste Jean Jr.
PARIS, W. Francklyn 3
PARIS, William Edward 3
PARISH, Elijah H
PARISH, John Carl 1
PARISH, Walter Alvis 3
PARISH, 4
  William Jackson
PARK, Charles Caldwell 1
PARK, Charles Edwards 4
PARK, Charles Francis 2
PARK, Edward Amasa 1
PARK, Edward Cahill 4
PARK, Edwards Albert,* 5
PARK, Frank 4
PARK, Franklin Atwood 1
PARK, Guy Brasfield 2
PARK, J. A. 3
PARK, J. Edgar 3
PARK, James H
PARK, John Alsey 3
PARK, Julian 4
PARK, Lawrence 1
PARK, Linton H
PARK, Marion Edwards 4
PARK, Maud Wood 3
PARK, Milton H
PARK, Orville Augustus 2
PARK, Robert Emory 2
PARK, Robert Ezra 2
PARK, Roswell H
PARK, Roswell 1
PARK, Royal Wheeler 1
PARK, Sam 1
PARK, Samuel Culver 1
PARK, Trenor William H
PARK, William 4
PARK, William Hallock 1
PARK, William Lee 4
PARKE, Benjamin H
PARKE, Francis Neal 3
PARKE, Henry Walter 5
PARKE, John H
PARKE, John Grubb 1
PARKE, John Shepard 3
PARKE, William More 4
PARKER, A. Warner 1
PARKER, 2
  Addison Bennett
PARKER, 3
  Albert George Jr.
PARKER, 5
  Alexander Wilson
PARKER, 1
  Alexis 'du Pont
PARKER, Alton Brooks 1
PARKER, Amasa Junius H
PARKER, Amasa Junius 1
PARKER, Amory 4
PARKER, Andrew 1
PARKER, Arthur Caswell 3
PARKER, Ben Hutchinson 5
PARKER, 1
  Benjamin Franklin
PARKER, Charles A. 1
PARKER, 4
  Charles Barnsdall
PARKER, H
  Charles Christopher
PARKER, 4
  Charles Christopher
PARKER, 1
  Charles Edward *
PARKER, Charles Morton 1
PARKER, 2
  Charles Wolcott
PARKER, Chauncey
  David 5
PARKER, 2
  Chauncey Goodrich
PARKER, 3
  Chauncey Goodrich Jr.
PARKER, Cola Godden 4
PARKER, Cortlandt 1
PARKER, Cortlandt 3
PARKER, Daingerfield 1
PARKER, Daniel Francis 1
PARKER, DeWitt Henry 2
PARKER, 4
  Dorothy Rothschild
PARKER, Edith Putnam 1
PARKER, 1
  Edmund Southard
PARKER, Edward Burns 3
PARKER, Edward Cary 1
PARKER, Edward Frost 1
PARKER, Edward J. 4
PARKER, 1
  Edward Melville

PARKER, 1
  Edward Sanders Jr.
PARKER, Edward
  Wheeler 4
PARKER, Edwin B. 1
PARKER, Edwin Pond 1
PARKER, Edwin Wallace H
PARKER, Ely Samuel H
PARKER, Emmett
  Newton 1
PARKER, Evan James 4
PARKER, 1
  Fitzgerald Sale
PARKER,
  Fletcher Douglas
PARKER, H
  Foxhall Alexander
PARKER, Frances 5
PARKER, Francis Hubert 1
PARKER, Francis LeJau 5
PARKER, Francis Warner 1
PARKER,
  Francis Wayland
PARKER, Frank 2
PARKER, Frank Wilson 1
PARKER, Franklin Eddy 1
PARKER, 5
  Franklin Eddy Jr.
PARKER,
  Franklin Nutting
PARKER, Frederic, Jr. 5
PARKER, 2
  Frederic Charles Wesby
PARKER, George Albert 1
PARKER, George Amos 1
PARKER, George B. 1
PARKER,
  George Frederick
PARKER, George Howard 3
PARKER, George Proctor 1
PARKER,
  George Swinnerton
PARKER, Glenn Lane 1
PARKER, Grady P. 5
PARKER, H. E. 3
PARKER, H. Wayne 5
PARKER, Harry Lee 3
PARKER, Henry Griffith 1
PARKER, Henry Taylor 1
PARKER, Herbert 4
PARKER,
  Herschel Clifford
PARKER, Hilon Adelbert 1
PARKER, Homer Cling 2
PARKER, Horatio Newton 1
PARKER,
  Horatio William
PARKER, 1
  Hosea Washington
PARKER, Isaac H
PARKER, Isaac Charles H
PARKER, J. Heber 3
PARKER, J. Roy 3
PARKER, James * H
PARKER, James 1
PARKER, 1
  James Cutler Dunn
PARKER, James Edmund 1
PARKER, James Henry 1
PARKER, James I. 4
PARKER,
  James Southworth
PARKER, James W. 3
PARKER, Jameson 5
PARKER, Jane Marsh 4
PARKER, Jo A. 5
PARKER, Joel * H
PARKER, John * H
PARKER, John 3
PARKER, John Adams 1
PARKER, John Bernard 3
PARKER, John D. 4
PARKER, John Gowans 3
PARKER, John Henry 2
PARKER, John Johnston 3
PARKER, John Mason H
PARKER, John Milliken 1
PARKER, Joseph Benson 1
PARKER, Josiah H
PARKER,
  Julia Evelina Smith
PARKER, 4
  Julius Frederick
PARKER, Junius 1
PARKER, 4
  Kenneth Colburn
PARKER, Laigh C. 3
PARKER, Lawton S. 3
PARKER, 1
  Leonard Fletcher
PARKER, Lewis Wardlwa 1
PARKER, Lottie Blair 1
PARKER, Lovell Hallet 1
PARKER, Marion W. 4
PARKER, Maude 3
PARKER, Millard
  Mayhew 4

PARKER, 1
  Moses Greeley
PARKER, Myron Melvin 4
PARKER, Nahum H
PARKER, Peter H
PARKER, R. Wayne 1
PARKER, Ralph Robinson 2
PARKER, Richard H
PARKER, Richard Elliot 1
PARKER, Richard Green H
PARKER, Robert 3
PARKER, Robert Hunt 5
PARKER, Robert Shumate 2
PARKER, Samuel 1
PARKER, Samuel Chester 1
PARKER, Samuel Wilson 1
PARKER, Severn Eyre 1
PARKER, Stanley V. 5
PARKER, Theodore H
PARKER, 2
  Theodore Bissell
PARKER, Thomas H
PARKER, 4
  Thomas Cleveland
PARKER, Torrance 2
PARKER, 3
  Valeria Hopkins
PARKER, 5
  Walter Huntington
PARKER, Walter Robert 3
PARKER,
  Walter Winfield
PARKER, Wesby Reed 4
PARKER, Willard H
PARKER, Willard 4
PARKER, 1
  William Belmont
PARKER, William Edward 2
PARKER, William Gordon 5
PARKER, William H. 1
PARKER, William Harwar H
PARKER, William Henry 5
PARKER, William M. 2
PARKER, William Riley 5
PARKER,
  William Stanley
PARKERSON, Jesse Jones 4
PARKES, 5
  Charles Herbert
PARKES, Henry Bamford 5
PARKES, William Ross 1
PARKHILL,
  Charles Breckinridge
PARKHILL, 4
  James William
PARKHURST, C. Francis 1
PARKHURST, Charles 1
PARKHURST,
  Charles Henry
PARKHURST, 5
  Frederic Augustus
PARKHURST, 1
  Frederic Hale
PARKHURST, Helen Huss 3
PARKHURST, 1
  Howard Elmore
PARKHURST,
  John Adelbert
PARKHURST, John
  Foster
PARKHURST, John
  Gibson
PARKHURST, Lewis 1
PARKINS, Almon Ernest 5
PARKINSON,
  Burney Lynch
PARKINSON,
  Daniel Baldwin
PARKINSON, 2
  Donald Berthold
PARKINSON, John
  Barber
PARKINSON,
  Robert Henry
PARKINSON, Thomas I. 3
PARKINSON, 4
  William Lynn
PARKINSON, 5
  William Nimon
PARKMAN, Francis H
PARKMAN, Henry 1
PARKMAN, Henry 1
PARKS, Addison Karrick 2
PARKS, Charles Wellman 1
PARKS, Clifford C. 1
PARKS, E. Taylor 4
PARKS, Edd Winfield 5
PARKS, Edward Lamay 1
PARKS, Ethel R. 4
PARKS, Floyd Lavinius 4
PARKS, Frank Thomas 4
PARKS, Gorham H
PARKS, Henry Martin 3
PARKS, James Lewis * 1
PARKS, John Louis 5
PARKS, John Shields 1
PARKS, Leighton 5
PARKS, Marvin McTyeire 1

PARKS, 3
Robert Lee McAllister
PARKS, Rufus
PARKS, Samuel Conant 2
PARKS, Tilman Bacon 3
PARKS, William H
PARKS, Wythe Marchant
PARKYNS, George Isham H
PARLANGE, Charles
PARLETTE, Ralph 1
PARLEY, Peter
PARLIN, Frank Edson 1
PARLIN, H. T. 3
PARLIN, William Henry
PARLOA, Maria 1
PARMELE, Harris
Barnum 4
PARMELE, Mary Platt 1
PARMELEE, 3
Cullen Warner
PARMELEE, 1
Henry Francis
PARMELEE, Howard
Coon 3
PARMELEE, Julius Hall 4
PARMELEE, Lewis
Dwight 3
PARMENTER, 2
Bertice Marvin
PARMENTER,
Charles Sylvester
PARMENTER, 4
Charles Winfield
PARMENTER, 3
Christine Whiting
PARMENTER, 3
George Freeman
PARMENTER, Roswell A. 4
PARMENTER, William H
PARMENTIER, Andrew H
PARMLEY, 1
Joseph William
PARMLEY, Walter Camp 1
PARMLY, Eleazar
PARNALL, Christopher 4
PARNELL, Harvey 1
PARPART, Arthur Kemble 4
PARR, Harry L. 4
PARR, Jerome Henry 3
PARR, Joseph Greer 3
PARR, Samuel Wilson 1
PARR, William David 1
PARRAN, Thomas * 4
PARRETT, Arthur N. 3
PARRETT, H
William Fletcher
PARRINGTON, 1
Vernon Louis
PARRIOTT, F. B. 3
PARRIOTT, 2
James Deforis
PARRIS, Albion Keith H
PARRIS, Alexander
PARRIS, Samuel H
PARRIS,
Virgil Delphini
PARRISH, 3
Albert Garrett
PARRISH, Anne
PARRISH, Anne 3
PARRISH, Carl 4
PARRISH, 1
Celestia Susannah
PARRISH, Charles H
PARRISH, Clara Weaver 1
PARRISH, Edward H
PARRISH, Isaac * H
PARRISH, John Bertrand 5
PARRISH, Joseph
PARRISH, Karl Calvin 1
PARRISH, Lucian Walton 1
PARRISH, Maxfield 4
PARRISH, Philip Hammon 3
PARRISH, Randall 1
PARRISH, Robert Lewis 1
PARRISH, Stephen 1
PARROTT, Claude Byron 4
PARROTT, H
Enoch Greenleafe
PARROTT, James Marion 1
PARROTT, John Fabyan 1
PARROTT, Marcus Junius 1
PARROTT, Percival John 3
PARROTT, Robert Parker H
PARROTT, Thomas Marc 3
PARRY, H
Charles Christopher
PARRY, Charles Thomas H
PARRY, David Maclean 1
PARRY, Emma Louise 3
PARRY, John Jay 3
PARRY, John Stubbs 1
PARRY, Sidney Loren 5
PARRY, Will H. 1
PARSELL, 1
Charles Victor
PARSHALL, De Witt 3

PARSHLEY, 3
Howard Madison
PARSON, 1
Hubert Templeton
PARSONS, H
Albert Richard
PARSONS, Albert Ross 1
PARSONS, 1
Albert Stevens
PARSONS, Alice Beal 4
PARSONS, Alice Knight 4
PARSONS, 3
Archibald Livingstone
PARSONS, 4
Arthur Barrette
PARSONS, 3
Arthur Hudson Jr.
PARSONS, 1
Azariah Worthington
PARSONS, Charles H
PARSONS, Charles * 4
PARSONS, Charles 1
PARSONS, Charles B. 4
PARSONS, 1
Charles Baldwin
PARSONS, 2
Charles Francis
PARSONS, 3
Charles Lathrop
PARSONS, Claude Van 1
PARSONS, 5
Donald Johnson
PARSONS, Eben Burt 1
PARSONS, Edmund Byrd 1
PARSONS, 4
Edward Alexander
PARSONS, Edward
Lambe 4
PARSONS, Edward Smith 2
PARSONS, Edward Young H
PARSONS, Elsie Clews 2
PARSONS, 5
Emma Follin (Mrs. Clifford
W. Parsons)
PARSONS, 5
Ernest William
PARSONS, Eugene 1
PARSONS, 1
Fannie Griscom
PARSONS, Floyd William 4
PARSONS,
Frances Theodora
PARSONS, Francis 1
PARSONS, Frank 1
PARSONS, Frank Alvah 1
PARSONS, Frank Nesmith 1
PARSONS, 3
Frederick Williams
PARSONS, Geoffrey 3
PARSONS, 1
Harry 'deBerkeley
PARSONS, Herbert 1
PARSONS, J. Lester 3
PARSONS, 5
J(ames) Russell
PARSONS, James Kelly 5
PARSONS, 1
James Russell Jr.
PARSONS, John B. 4
PARSONS, John Calvin 5
PARSONS, John Edward 1
PARSONS, 5
John Frederick
PARSONS, 4
Lester Shields
PARSONS, Lewis Baldwin 1
PARSONS, H
Lewis Eliphalet
PARSONS, Lewis Morgan 5
PARSONS, 5
Llewellyn B(radley)
PARSONS, Llewellyn B. 4
PARSONS, Louella O. 5
PARSONS, Mrs. Henry 1
PARSONS, Payn Bigelow 1
PARSONS, 2
Philip Archibald
PARSONS, 3
Reginald Hascall
PARSONS, Richard 1
PARSONS,
Robert Stevens
PARSONS, Samuel 1
PARSONS, Samuel
Holden H
PARSONS, Starr 2
PARSONS, Theophilus * H
PARSONS, Thomas Smith 1
PARSONS, H
Thomas William
PARSONS, Usher H
PARSONS, Wallace
Emery 3
PARSONS, Wilfrid 3
PARSONS, Willard H. 5
PARSONS, William 2

PARSONS, 5
William Barclay
PARSONS, 1
William Barclay
PARSONS, 1
William Edward
PARSONS, William Lewis 5
PARSONS, 3
William Sterling
PARSONS, William Wood 1
PARSONS, 4
Willis Edwards
PARTINGTON, 1
Frederick Eugene
PARTIPILO, 5
Anthony Victor
PARTLOW, Ira Judson 3
PARTLOW, 5
William Dempsey
PARTNER, Winnie Leroy 4
PARTON, Arthur 1
PARTON, Ernest 1
PARTON, 1
Henry Woodbridge
PARTON, James H
PARTON, 2
Lemuel Frederick
PARTON, H
Sara Payson Willis
PARTRIDGE, 3
Albert Gerry
PARTRIDGE, Alden H
PARTRIDGE, Bellamy 4
PARTRIDGE, 4
Charles Patrick
PARTRIDGE, 2
Donald Barrows
PARTRIDGE, 1
Edward Lasell
PARTRIDGE, 5
Everett P(ercy)
PARTRIDGE, 2
Frank Charles
PARTRIDGE, George H
PARTRIDGE, 3
George Everett
PARTRIDGE, H
James Rudolph
PARTRIDGE, John Slater 1
PARTRIDGE, Richard 1
PARTRIDGE, 1
Sidney Catlin
PARTRIDGE, 1
William Ordway
PARVIN,
Theodore Sutton
PARVIN, Theophilus 1
PASCALIS-
OUVRIERE, Felix H
PASCHAL, 2
Franklin Cressey
PASCHAL, H
George Washington
PASCHALL, John 3
PASCO, Samuel 1
PASHKOVSKY, 3
Theophilus Nicholas
PASKO, H
Wesly Washington
PASMA, Henry Kay 2
PASMORE, 2
Henry Bickford
PASQUIN, Anthony H
PASSANNATE, Charles 3
PASSANO, Edward B. 2
PASSARELLI, 3
Luigi Alfonso
PASSAVANT, H
William Alfred
PASSMORE, Ellis Pusey 1
PASSMORE, Lincoln K. 1
PASTERNAK, 4
Boris Leonidovitch
PASTORIUS, H
Francis Daniel
PASVOLSKY, Leo 3
PATCH, 2
Alexander McCarrell Jr.
PATCH, Edith Marion 3
PATCH, Frank Wallace 1
PATCH, Helen Elizabeth 3
PATCH, Kate Whiting 1
PATCH, 1
Nathaniel Jordan Knight
PATCH, Ralph Reginald 3
PATCH, Sam H
PATCHEN, Kenneth 5
PATCHIN, Frank Glines 1
PATCHIN, Philip Halsey 3
PATCHIN, Robert Halsey 3
PATE, Maurice 4
PATE, Randolph McC 4
PATE, Walter Romny 5
PATEK, Stanislaw 4
PATENAUDE, Esioff
Leon 5

PATENOTRE, 5
Eleanor Elverson
PATERSON, Albert Barnett 3
PATERSON, 4
Donald Gildersleeve
PATERSON, Isabel 4
PATERSON, James Venn 2
PATERSON, John H
PATERSON, 4
Robert Gildersleeve
PATERSON, 1
Van Rensselaer
PATERSON, William H
PATERSON, William Tait 5
PATIGIAN, Haig 3
PATILLO, Henry H
PATINO, Simon I. 2
PATON, James Morton 2
PATON, Lewis Bayles 1
PATON, Stewart 2
PATON, Thomas Bugard 1
PATON, William Agnew 1
PATON, William Kennell 3
PATRI, Angelo 4
PATRICK, David Lyall 5
PATRICK, Edwin Daviess 2
PATRICK, Fred Albert 1
PATRICK, George Edward 1
PATRICK, H
George Thomas White
PATRICK, Hugh Talbot 1
PATRICK, John Hayward 5
PATRICK, Joseph Cecil 4
PATRICK, Luther 2
PATRICK, H
Marsena Rudolph
PATRICK, Mary Mills 1
PATRICK, Mason
Mathews 1
PATRICK, 5
Ransom Rathbone
PATRICK, Robert F. 5
PATRICK, 1
Robert Goodlett
PATRICK, Roy Leonard 3
PATRICK, Ted 4
PATT, John Francis 5
PATTANGALL, 2
William Robinson
PATTEE, Ernest Noble 2
PATTEE, Fred Lewis 3
PATTEE, 1
William Sullivan
PATTEN, Amos Williams 1
PATTEN, 5
Bradley Merrill
PATTEN, 5
Charles Harreld
PATTEN, Everett Frank 4
PATTEN, George Yager 3
PATTEN, Gilbert 2
PATTEN, 4
Helen Philbrook
PATTEN, Henry 3
PATTEN, James A. 1
PATTEN, James Horace 4
PATTEN, John H
PATTEN, John A. 1
PATTEN, Simon Nelson 1
PATTEN, Thomas Gedney 1
PATTEN, William 1
PATTEN, Zeboim Charles 2
PATTERSON, A. L. 4
PATTERSON, 1
Adoniram Judson
PATTERSON, 2
Alexander Evans
PATTERSON, Alicia 4
PATTERSON, 1
Alvah Worrell
PATTERSON, 1
Andrew Henry
PATTERSON, 1
Antoinette De Courcey
PATTERSON, 4
Archibald Williams
PATTERSON, 3
Austin McDowell
PATTERSON, 1
Burd Shippen
PATTERSON, C. Stuart 1
PATTERSON, 2
Catherine Norris
PATTERSON, 1
Charles Brodie
PATTERSON, 1
Charles Edward
PATTERSON, 4
Charles Howard
PATTERSON, 1
Charles Loeser
PATTERSON, 4
Charles Lord
PATTERSON, Daniel
Todd H

PATTERSON, 5
David H, Jr.
PATTERSON, H
David Trotter
PATTERSON, 4
Edmund Booth
PATTERSON, Edward 1
PATTERSON, 5
Edward White
PATTERSON,
Edwin Wilhite
PATTERSON, 2
Eleanor Medill
PATTERSON, 5
Ernest Minor
PATTERSON, 5
Ernest Odell
PATTERSON, Everett M. 1
PATTERSON,
Flora Wambaugh
PATTERSON, Francis F. Jr. 1
PATTERSON, Frank
Allen 2
PATTERSON, Frank
Miner 1
PATTERSON, 5
Frederick Beck
PATTERSON, 1
Frederick William
PATTERSON,
Gaylard Hawkins
PATTERSON, 5
George Francis
PATTERSON,
George Robert
PATTERSON, 4
George Stuart
PATTERSON, H
George Washington
PATTERSON, 1
George Washington
PATTERSON, 2
Gerard Francis
PATTERSON, 4
Gilbert Brown
PATTERSON, Giles Jared 4
PATTERSON, 5
Graham Creighton
PATTERSON, Grove
Hiram 3
PATTERSON, Harold C. 4
PATTERSON, Harry
Jacob 2
PATTERSON, Harry
Jacob 3
PATTERSON, Isaac Lee 1
PATTERSON, James 5
PATTERSON, 3
James Albert
PATTERSON, 1
James Kennedy
PATTERSON,
James Lawson
PATTERSON, 1
James O'Hanlon
PATTERSON, H
James Willis
PATTERSON, 4
Jane Lippitt
PATTERSON, John H
Fulton
PATTERSON, 1
John Henry *
PATTERSON, 1
John Letcher
PATTERSON, 5
John Neville
PATTERSON, John
Thomas 4
PATTERSON, 1
Joseph McDowell
PATTERSON, 2
Joseph Medill
PATTERSON, Joseph T. 5
PATTERSON,
Lamar Gray 4
PATTERSON, Lemuel B. 1
PATTERSON,
Lillian Beatrice
PATTERSON, 5
Mrs. Lindsay (lucy
Bramlette Patterson)
PATTERSON, 1
Malcolm Rice
PATTERSON, Marion D. 2
PATTERSON, Morehead 4
PATTERSON, Morris H
PATTERSON, Otto 5
PATTERSON, Paul 3
PATTERSON, 3
Paul Chenery
PATTERSON, Paul L. 3
PATTERSON, 5
Ralph Morris

PATTERSON, Raymond Albert 1
PATTERSON, Richard Cunningham Jr. 4
PATTERSON, Robert * H
PATTERSON, Robert Foster 5
PATTERSON, Robert Franklin 1
PATTERSON, Robert Mayne 1
PATTERSON, Robert Porter 3
PATTERSON, Robert Urie 3
PATTERSON, Robert Wilson 1
PATTERSON, Roscoe Conkling 3
PATTERSON, Ross Vernet 1
PATTERSON, Rufus Lenoir II 2
PATTERSON, Samuel 4
PATTERSON, Shirley Gale 1
PATTERSON, Thomas H
PATTERSON, Thomas 1
PATTERSON, Thomas Edward H
PATTERSON, Thomas Harman H
PATTERSON, Thomas J. H
PATTERSON, Thomas Macdonald 1
PATTERSON, Virginia Sharpe 1
PATTERSON, Walter H
PATTERSON, Walter Kennedy 1
PATTERSON, William * H
PATTERSON, William Brown 1
PATTERSON, William Francis 4
PATTERSON, William J. 3
PATTERSON, William Leslie 5
PATTERSON, William R. 1
PATTERSON, Wright A. 3
PATTESON, S. Louise 4
PATTESON, Seargent Smith Prentiss 1
PATTI, Adelina 1
PATTIE, James Ohio H
PATTILLO, Nathan Allen 4
PATTISON, Everett Wilson
PATTISON, Granville Sharp H
PATTISON, Harold 5
PATTISON, Isaac Caldwell Jr. 4
PATTISON, James William
PATTISON, John 4
PATTISON, John M. 1
PATTISON, John R. 1
PATTISON, Martin 1
PATTISON, Robert Emory
PATTISON, Salem Griswold 4
PATTISON, Thomas H
PATTISON, Thomas Harwood 1
PATTISON, William J. 1
PATTON, Abigail Hutchinson H
PATTON, Albert F. 4
PATTON, Carl Safford 1
PATTON, Charles E. 4
PATTON, Cornelius Howard 1
PATTON, David Hubert 5
PATTON, Francis Landey 4
PATTON, Fred 3
PATTON, G. Farrar 1
PATTON, George Smith Jr. 2
PATTON, Haskell Riley 4
PATTON, Henry William 1
PATTON, Horace Bushnell
PATTON, Jacob Harris 1
PATTON, James McDowell 1
PATTON, John H
PATTON, John 1
PATTON, John Mercer 1
PATTON, John Shelton 1
PATTON, Joseph McIntyre 1
PATTON, Katharine 2
PATTON, Leroy Thompson 3
PATTON, Nat 3
PATTON, Normand Smith 1

PATTON, Odis Knight 5
PATTON, Raymond Stanton 1
PATTON, Robert Howard 1
PATTON, Robert Williams 2
PATTON, Walter Melville
PATTON, Willard 1
PATTON, William H
PATTON, William Augustus 1
PATTON, William Macfarland 1
PATTON, William Weston H
PATTY, Willard Walter 4
PATY, Raymond Ross 3
PAUGHER, Adrien 'de H
PAUKER, Ana
PAUL, A. J. Drexel 3
PAUL, Amasa Copp
PAUL, Charles Edward 5
PAUL, Charles Ferguson 4
PAUL, Charles Howard
PAUL, Charles Thomas 1
PAUL, Elliot Harold 3
PAUL, Gabriel H
PAUL, Harry Gilbert 2
PAUL, Henry Martyn 1
PAUL, J. Gilman D'arcy 5
PAUL, Jeremiah Jr. H
PAUL, John * 1
PAUL, John 4
PAUL, John Haywood 5
PAUL, John R. 1
PAUL, John Rodman 1
PAUL, Josephine Bay 4
PAUL, Joshua Hughes 1
PAUL, Maury Henry Biddle 2
PAUL, Nanette Baker 1
PAUL, Randolph Evernghim 3
PAUL, Ray Sherman 1
PAUL, Sarah Woodman 4
PAUL, Willard Augustus 1
PAUL, Willard Stewart 1
PAUL, William Brown 4
PAUL, William Glae 1
PAULDING, Charles Cook 1
PAULDING, Hiram H
PAULDING, James Kirke H
PAULDING, William Jr. H
PAULEN, Ben Sanford 5
PAULEN, Ben Sanford 5
PAULEY, Scott Samuel 5
PAULHAMUS, W. H. 1
PAUL I 4
PAULI, Hertha 5
PAULI, Wolfgang 5
PAULL, Lee Cunningham 5
PAULLIN, Charles Oscar 2
PAULLIN, James Edgar 3
PAULSEN, Howard C. 3
PAULSON, Frederick Holroyd 4
PAULSON, Richard Hulet 1
PAULUS, Francis Petrus 1
PAULY, Karl Bone 4
PAUMGARTNER, Bernhard 5
PAUNACK, August Oscar 3
PAUR, Emil 4
PAUST, Elnar Bernhardt 5
PAUSTOVSKY, Konstantin Georgievich 5
PAVLOSKA, Irene 4
PAVY, Octave H
PAWLING, Levi H
PAWLOWSKI, Felix Wladyslaw 3
PAWNEE BILL 1
PAX, Walter Thomas 4
PAXON, Frederic John 1
PAXSON, Edgar Samuel 5
PAXSON, Edward M. 1
PAXSON, Frederic Logan 2
PAXSON, W. A. 4
PAXTON, Edwin John 5
PAXTON, Edwin John 1
PAXTON, J. Hall 3
PAXTON, James Dunlop 3
PAXTON, John Gallatin 1
PAXTON, John Randolph 1
PAXTON, John Richard 5
PAXTON, Joseph Francis 1
PAXTON, Kenneth T. 5
PAXTON, Philip H
PAXTON, Thomas B. 1
PAXTON, William McGregor
PAXTON, William Miller 1
PAXTON, William Percy 3
PAYEN 'DE NOYLAN, Gilles-Augustin H
PAYERAS, Mariano H

PAYNE, Anthony Monck-Mason 5
PAYNE, Bruce Ryburn 1
PAYNE, Byron Samuel 5
PAYNE, Charles Albert 4
PAYNE, Charles Edward 2
PAYNE, Charles Henry 1
PAYNE, Charles Rockwell
PAYNE, Christopher H. 4
PAYNE, Christy 4
PAYNE, Daniel Alexander H
PAYNE, E. George 3
PAYNE, Edward Waldron 1
PAYNE, Elisabeth Stancy 2
PAYNE, Eugene Beauharnais 1
PAYNE, F(anny) Ursula 5
PAYNE, Franklin Storey 1
PAYNE, Frederick Huff 3
PAYNE, George Frederick
PAYNE, George Henry 2
PAYNE, Henry B. H
PAYNE, Henry C. 1
PAYNE, Jason 2
PAYNE, John A. 2
PAYNE, John Barton 1
PAYNE, John Carroll 4
PAYNE, John H. 1
PAYNE, John Howard 4
PAYNE, Kenneth Wilcox 4
PAYNE, Leon Mather 5
PAYNE, Leonidas Warren Jr. 2
PAYNE, Lewis Thornton Powell H
PAYNE, Montgomery Ashby 5
PAYNE, Oliver Hazard 1
PAYNE, Oliver Hiram 5
PAYNE, Philip 4
PAYNE, Robert Lee 1
PAYNE, Sereno Elisha 1
PAYNE, Will 3
PAYNE, William Harold 4
PAYNE, William Henry 1
PAYNE, William Kenneth 4
PAYNE, William Knapp 4
PAYNE, William Morton 1
PAYNE, William Wallace 1
PAYNE, William Winter 5
PAYNTER, Lemuel H
PAYNTER, Thomas H. 1
PAYSON, Edward H
PAYSON, Edward Saxton 4
PAYSON, Eliot Robertson 2
PAYSON, Franklin Conant 1
PAYSON, George Shipman 1
PAYSON, Laurence G. 4
PAYSON, Seth H
PAYSON, William Farquhar
PAYTON, Jacob Simpson 4
PAZ, Ezequiel P. 3
PEABODY, Andrew Preston
PEABODY, Arthur 2
PEABODY, Augustus Stephen
PEABODY, Cecil Hobart 1
PEABODY, Charles 1
PEABODY, Charles Augustus *
PEABODY, Dean Jr. 3
PEABODY, Elizabeth Palmer H
PEABODY, Endicott 2
PEABODY, Ernest H. 4
PEABODY, Francis 1
PEABODY, Francis Greenwood
PEABODY, Francis Stuyvesant 1
PEABODY, Francis Weld 1
PEABODY, Frederick Forrest
PEABODY, Frederick William
PEABODY, George H
PEABODY, George Foster 1
PEABODY, George Harman 5
PEABODY, George Livingston
PEABODY, Harry Ernest 1
PEABODY, Helen Sophia 4
PEABODY, Henry Clay 1
PEABODY, James Hamilton
PEABODY, Joseph H

PEABODY, Josephine Preston 1
PEABODY, Lucy Evelyn 4
PEABODY, Mrs. Henry Wayland 3
PEABODY, Nathaniel H
PEABODY, Oliver William Bourn H
PEABODY, Robert Swain 1
PEABODY, Selim Hobart 1
PEABODY, Stuyvesant 2
PEABODY, William Bourn Oliver H
PEABODY, William Rodman 1
PEACE, Bony Hampton 1
PEACE, Roger Craft 5
PEACH, Robert English 5
PEACH, Robert Wesfly 1
PEACOCK, Dred 1
PEACOCK, Joseph Leishman 3
PEACOCK, M. A. 3
PEACOCK, Thomas Brower 1
PEACOCK, Virginia Tatnall 5
PEACOCK, Wesley Sr. 1
PEAIRS, Hervey B. 1
PEAK, J. Elmer 4
PEAK, John Lee 1
PEAKE, Alonzo William 4
PEAKE, Elmore Elliott 5
PEAKS, Archibald Garfield
PEALE, Albert Charles 1
PEALE, Anna Claypoole H
PEALE, Charles Clifford 3
PEALE, Charles Willson H
PEALE, Franklin H
PEALE, James H
PEALE, Raphael H
PEALE, Rembrandt H
PEALE, Rembrandt 1
PEALE, Sarah Miriam H
PEALE, Titian Ramsay H
PEARCE, Charles A. 5
PEARCE, Charles Edward 1
PEARCE, Charles Sidney 5
PEARCE, Charles Sprague
PEARCE, Charles Sumner 4
PEARCE, Clinton Ellicott 4
PEARCE, Dutee Jerauld H
PEARCE, Eugene Hamer 1
PEARCE, Eva F. 5
PEARCE, Haywood Jefferson 2
PEARCE, J. Newton 1
PEARCE, James Alfred 1
PEARCE, James Alfred 1
PEARCE, John Elias 1
PEARCE, John Musser 3
PEARCE, Liston Houston 1
PEARCE, Louise 3
PEARCE, McLeod Milligan 2
PEARCE, Richard 4
PEARCE, Richard Mills Jr. 1
PEARCE, Stephen Austen H
PEARCE, Warren Frederick 4
PEARCE, Webster Houston
PEARCE, William 2
PEARCE, William Cliff 1
PEARCE, William Greene 4
PEARD, Frank Furnival 4
PEARE, Robert S. 3
PEARL, Mary Jeanette 5
PEARL, Raymond 1
PEARLSTONE, Hyman 4
PEARMAIN, Alice Whittemore Upton
PEARMAIN, Sumner Bass 1
PEARNE, Wesley Ulysses 1
PEARRE, George Alexander
PEARSALL, Benjamin Simon 1
PEARSALL, Charles H. C. 3
PEARSALL, James Welch 1
PEARSALL, Robert Ellis 1
PEARSE, Arthur Sperry 3
PEARSE, Carroll Gardner 4
PEARSE, John Barnard 1
PEARSE, Langdon 3
PEARSON, Alfred John 1
PEARSON, Alfred L. 5
PEARSON, Andrew C. 1
PEARSON, Arthur Emmons 1

PEARSON, Charles William 1
PEARSON, Drew (Andrew Russell) 5
PEARSON, Edmund Lester 1
PEARSON, Edward Jones 1
PEARSON, Eliphalet H
PEARSON, Frank Bail 4
PEARSON, Fred Stark 1
PEARSON, Gerald H(amilton) J(effrey) 5
PEARSON, Gustaf Adolph 2
PEARSON, Henry Carr 5
PEARSON, Henry Clemens 1
PEARSON, Henry Greenleaf
PEARSON, Herron Carney 3
PEARSON, Hesketh 4
PEARSON, James John 1
PEARSON, Jay Frederick Wesley 4
PEARSON, John James H
PEARSON, Joseph H
PEARSON, Joseph Thurman Jr. 3
PEARSON, Josephine Anderson 5
PEARSON, Leon Morris 4
PEARSON, Leonard 1
PEARSON, Lester Bowles 5
PEARSON, Lola Clark 3
PEARSON, Matthew Edgar 3
PEARSON, Oscar William 3
PEARSON, Paul Martin 3
PEARSON, Peter Henry 1
PEARSON, Ralph M. 5
PEARSON, Raymond Allen 1
PEARSON, Richard Metcalf 3
PEARSON, Richmond 1
PEARSON, Richmond Mumford H
PEARSON, Robert Logan 3
PEARSON, Samuel 4
PEARSON, Thomas 4
PEARSON, Thomas Gilbert 2
PEARSON, Walter Washington 4
PEARSON, William Alexander 3
PEARSON, William Lazarus 3
PEARSON, William Norman 5
PEARSONS, Daniel Kimball 1
PEARY, Josephine Diebitsch
PEARY, Robert Edwin 1
PEASE, Alan W. 3
PEASE, Alfred Humphreys H
PEASE, Arthur Stanley 4
PEASE, Calvin H
PEASE, Charles Giffin 1
PEASE, Charles Henry 1
PEASE, Elisha Marshall H
PEASE, Ernest Mondell 1
PEASE, Francis Gladheim
PEASE, Frederick Henry 1
PEASE, Joseph Ives H
PEASE, Kingsley Eugene 5
PEASE, Lucius Curtis (Lute Pease) 5
PEASE, Murray 4
PEASE, Robert Norton 4
PEASE, Theodore Calvin 4
PEASE, Zephaniah W. 1
PEASLEE, Amos Jenkins 5
PEASLEE, Charles Hazen 1
PEASLEE, Edmund Randolph H
PEASLEE, Horace Whittier 3
PEASLEE, John Bradley 1
PEASLEE, Robert James 1
PEAT, Wilbur David 4
PEATE, John 1
PEATTIE, Donald Culross 4
PEATTIE, Elia Wilkinson
PEATTIE, Louise Redfield
PEATTIE, Robert 1
PEATTIE, Roderick 3
PEAVEY, Frank Hutchinson H
PEAVEY, Leroy Deering 1

PERKINS, Albert Thompson 1
PERKINS, Angle Villette Warren 1
PERKINS, Bertram Lucius 5
PERKINS, Bishop H
PERKINS, Bishop Walden H
PERKINS, Carroll N. 3
PERKINS, Charles Albert 2
PERKINS, Charles Callahan H
PERKINS, Charles Edwin 5
PERKINS, Charles Elliott 1
PERKINS, Charles Elliott 2
PERKINS, Charles Enoch 1
PERKINS, Charles Harvey 4
PERKINS, Charles Plummer 1
PERKINS, Clarence 2
PERKINS, DeForest H. 1
PERKINS, Dwight Heald 1
PERKINS, E. Benson 4
PERKINS, Edmund Taylor 1
PERKINS, Edwin Ruthven Jr. 3
PERKINS, Elias H
PERKINS, Elisha H
PERKINS, Elisha Henry 1
PERKINS, Elizabeth Ward (Mrs. Charles Bruen Perkins) 5
PERKINS, Emily Swan 1
PERKINS, Frances 4
PERKINS, Francis Davenport 5
PERKINS, Frank Walley 1
PERKINS, Fred Bartlett 5
PERKINS, Frederic Beecher H
PERKINS, Frederic Williams 2
PERKINS, Frederick 1
PERKINS, George Clement 1
PERKINS, George Douglas 1
PERKINS, George Hamilton H
PERKINS, George Henry 1
PERKINS, George Walbridge 1
PERKINS, George Walbridge 3
PERKINS, Harold E. 3
PERKINS, Henry Augustus 3
PERKINS, Henry Farnham 5
PERKINS, Herbert Farrington 1
PERKINS, Jacob H
PERKINS, James Breck 1
PERKINS, James Handasyd H
PERKINS, James Handasyd 1
PERKINS, James McDaniel 4
PERKINS, Janet Russell 1
PERKINS, Jared H
PERKINS, John Jr. H
PERKINS, John Carroll 3
PERKINS, John Russell 1
PERKINS, Justin H
PERKINS, Lucy Fitch 1
PERKINS, Maurice 1
PERKINS, Maxwell Evarts 2
PERKINS, Milo Randolph 5
PERKINS, Nathaniel James 5
PERKINS, Ralph 4
PERKINS, Randolph 1
PERKINS, Reece Wilmer 1
PERKINS, Robert Patterson 1
PERKINS, Roger Griswold 1
PERKINS, S. Albert 3
PERKINS, Samuel Elliott H
PERKINS, Thomas Clark 5
PERKINS, Thomas Handasyd H
PERKINS, Thomas Jefferson 3
PERKINS, Thomas Nelson 1
PERKINS, Walter Eugene 5
PERKINS, Walton 1
PERKINS, William Allen 4
PERKINS, William Harvey 4
PERKINS, William Oscar 1
PERKINS, William R. 4
PERKINS, William Robertson 2
PERKY, Kirtland Irving 1
PERLEA, Ionel 5
PERLEY, Ira H
PERLEY, Sidney 1
PERLITZ, Charles Albert Jr. 4
PERLMAN, Jacob 5
PERLMAN, Nathan D. 3
PERLMAN, Philip B. 4
PERLMAN, Selig 3
PERLSTEIN, Meyer Aaron 5
PERLZWEIG, William A. 2
PERMAR, Robert 2
PERO, Giuseppe 4
PEROT, T. Morris Jr. 2
PEROT, Thomas Morris 1
PERRET, Auguste 3
PERRET, Frank Alvord 4
PERRIGO, James 3
PERRILL, Augustus Leonard H
PERRIN, Bernadotte 1
PERRIN, Dwight Stanley 3
PERRIN, Fleming Allen Clay 2
PERRIN, Frank L. 5
PERRIN, Herbert Towle 4
PERRIN, John 1
PERRIN, John William 1
PERRIN, Lee J. 2
PERRIN, Marshall Livingston 1
PERRIN, Porter Gale 4
PERRIN, Raymond St James 1
PERRIN, Willard Taylor 1
PERRINE, Charles Dillon 4
PERRINE, Enoch 1
PERRINE, Frederic Auten Combs 1
PERRINE, Henry H
PERRINE, Henry Pratt 3
PERRINE, Irving 4
PERRINE, Van Dearing 3
PERROT, Nicholas H
PERRY, Aaron Fyfe H
PERRY, Albertus 1
PERRY, Alexander James 1
PERRY, Alfred Tyler 1
PERRY, Andre James 4
PERRY, Antoinette 2
PERRY, Antonio 2
PERRY, Arthur 1
PERRY, Arthur Cecil 4
PERRY, Arthur F. 2
PERRY, Arthur Latham 1
PERRY, Barbour 4
PERRY, Ben Edwin 5
PERRY, Benjamin Franklin H
PERRY, Bertrand James 4
PERRY, Bliss 3
PERRY, Carroll 1
PERRY, Charles 1
PERRY, Charles Milton 2
PERRY, Christopher Raymond H
PERRY, Clarence Arthur 2
PERRY, Clay Lamont 5
PERRY, David 1
PERRY, David Brainerd 1
PERRY, Donald Putnam 4
PERRY, E. Wood 1
PERRY, Edward Aylesworth H
PERRY, Edward Baxter 1
PERRY, Edward Delavan 1
PERRY, Eli H
PERRY, Ernest Bert 4
PERRY, Ernest James 2
PERRY, Everett Robbins 1
PERRY, George Dorn 1
PERRY, George Hough 2
PERRY, George Sessions 3
PERRY, Hector H. 5
PERRY, Henry Eldredge 2
PERRY, Hoyt Ogden 4
PERRY, Isaac Newton 4
PERRY, James Clifford 1
PERRY, James De Wolf 1
PERRY, James DeWolf 2
PERRY, John 5
PERRY, John Holliday 3
PERRY, John Hoyt 1
PERRY, John Jasiel H
PERRY, John Lester 3
PERRY, John Morris 3
PERRY, John Richard 3
PERRY, Joseph Franklin 4
PERRY, Kenneth 4
PERRY, Lawrence 3
PERRY, Lewis 5
PERRY, Lewis Ebenezer 4
PERRY, Lilla Cabot 1
PERRY, Louis Clausiel 1
PERRY, Marsden Jasiel 1
PERRY, Matthew Calbraith H
PERRY, Middleton Lee 5
PERRY, Nehemiah H
PERRY, Nora H
PERRY, Oliver Hazard H
PERRY, Oscar Butler 2
PERRY, R. Ross 1
PERRY, Ralph Barton 3
PERRY, Richard Ross, Jr. 5
PERRY, Roland Hinton 1
PERRY, Roy Vincelle 4
PERRY, Rufus Lewis H
PERRY, Stella George Stern 3
PERRY, Stuart H
PERRY, Stuart Hoffman 3
PERRY, Thomas 1
PERRY, Thomas Johns H
PERRY, Thomas Sergeant 1
PERRY, Wallace 3
PERRY, Walter Scott 1
PERRY, William * H
PERRY, William Flake 1
PERRY, William Hayes 4
PERRY, William L. 5
PERRY, William Stevens H
PERRYMAN, Francis Spencer 4
PERRYMAN, Walter Lewis Jr. 4
PERSHING, Cyrus L. 1
PERSHING, Howell Terry 1
PERSHING, James Hammond 2
PERSHING, John Joseph 2
PERSICO, E. Luigi H
PERSINGER, Louis 4
PERSKIE, Joseph B. 3
PERSON, Harlow Stafford 3
PERSON, Hiram Grant 1
PERSON, John Elmer 4
PERSON, John L. 5
PERSON, Robert S. 4
PERSON, Seymour Howe 3
PERSON, Thomas H
PERSONS, Augustus Archilus 1
PERSONS, Frederick Torrel 2
PERSONS, Gordon 4
PERSONS, John Williams 5
PERSONS, Warren Milton 1
PERSONS, William Frank 3
PESCHAU, Ferdinand William Elias 1
PESCHGES, John Hubert 2
PETEET, Walton 5
PETEGORSKY, David W. 3
PETER, Alfred Meredith 4
PETER, Arthur 2
PETER, George H
PETER, Hugh H
PETER, John Frederick H
PETER, Luther Crouse 2
PETER, Marc 4
PETER, Marc 5
PETER, Philip Adam 4
PETER, Robert H
PETER, Sarah Worthington King H
PETER, William Frederick 3
PETERKIN, Daniel 1
PETERKIN, George William 1
PETERKIN, Mrs. Julia Mood 4
PETERKIN, William Gardner 2
PETERMAN, Mynie Gustav 5
PETERMANN, Albert E. 2
PETERS, Absalom H
PETERS, Albert Theodore 4
PETERS, Andrew James 1
PETERS, Charles Rollo 4
PETERS, Christian Henry Frederick H
PETERS, David Wilbur 3
PETERS, Edward Dyer 1
PETERS, Frederick Romer 1
PETERS, George Boddie 4
PETERS, George Henry 1
PETERS, Heber Wallace 5
PETERS, J. A. 1
PETERS, James 5
PETERS, James Arthur 5
PETERS, James L. 3
PETERS, John Andrew 1
PETERS, John Andrew 4
PETERS, John Charles H
PETERS, John Dwight 4
PETERS, John Punnett 1
PETERS, John Punnett 3
PETERS, John Russell 5
PETERS, Le Roy Samuel 2
PETERS, Lewis Edwin 4
PETERS, Lulu Hunt 1
PETERS, Madison Clinton 1
PETERS, Marian Phelps * 4
PETERS, R. Earl 3
PETERS, Ralph 4
PETERS, Ralph Jr. 3
PETERS, Raymond Elmer 5
PETERS, Richard * H
PETERS, Samuel Andrew H
PETERS, Samuel Ritter 1
PETERS, Thomas Pollock 1
PETERS, Thomas Willing 1
PETERS, Walter Harvest 3
PETERS, William Cumming H
PETERS, William E. 4
PETERS, William Henry 1
PETERS, William John 2
PETERSEN, Andrew N. 5
PETERSEN, Carl Edward 2
PETERSEN, Hjalmar 5
PETERSEN, Martin 3
PETERSEN, Martin 4
PETERSEN, Theodore Scarborough 4
PETERSEN, William Earl 5
PETERSEN, William Ferdinand 3
PETERSON, Alfred Emanuel 1
PETERSON, Alfred Walter 4
PETERSON, Arthur 1
PETERSON, Charles Jacobs H
PETERSON, Charles Simeon 2
PETERSON, Elmer George 3
PETERSON, Elmer Theodore 5
PETERSON, Frederick 1
PETERSON, Harry Claude 1
PETERSON, Henry H
PETERSON, Henry John 3
PETERSON, Herbert 2
PETERSON, J. Marvin 3
PETERSON, J. Whitney 3
PETERSON, James Earl Sr. 2
PETERSON, John B. 4
PETERSON, John Bertram 2
PETERSON, John Valdemar 5
PETERSON, Joseph 1
PETERSON, Lawrence Eugene 4
PETERSON, Lawrence John 3
PETERSON, May 3
PETERSON, Mell Andrew 5
PETERSON, Olof August 1
PETERSON, Peter 1
PETERSON, Reuben 1
PETERSON, Robert H
PETERSON, Virgil Lee 3
PETERSON, Virgilia 4
PETERSON, William H. 4
PETHICK, Harry H. 4
PETHICK-LAWRENCE, Frederick William 4
PETIGRU, James Louis H
PETRI, Carl Johan 4
PETRIE, George H
PETRIE, George 2
PETRIE, George Laurens 1
PETRIKIN, David H
PETRIKIN, William Lloyd 3
PETROFF, Strashimer Alburtus 2
PETRUNKEVITCH, Alexander 4
PETRY, Edward Jacob 1
PETTEE, Charles Holmes 3
PETTEE, George Daniel 4
PETTEE, James Horace 1
PETTEE, Lemuel Gardner 3
PETTEE, William Henry 1
PETTEE, William Jay 1
PETTEGREW, Marion Edgar 5
PETTENGILL, George 3
PETTENGILL, Herman Judson 1
PETTER, Rodolphe C. 2
PETTERSON, Leroy David 5
PETTET, Zellmer Roswell 4
PETTEYS, Alonzo 5
PETTIBONE, Augustus Herman 1
PETTIBONE, Frank G. 4
PETTIBONE, George A. 4
PETTIBONE, Holman Dean 4
PETTIBONE, Wilson Boyd 4
PETTIGREW, Charles H
PETTIGREW, Ebenezer H
PETTIGREW, George Atwood 1
PETTIGREW, James Johnston H
PETTIGREW, Richard Franklin 1
PETTIJOHN, Charles Clyde 2
PETTIJOHN, John J. 1
PETTINGELL, Frank Hervey 1
PETTINGILL, William LeRoy 3
PETTIS, Charles Emerson 5
PETTIS, Clifford Robert 1
PETTIS, Spencer Darwin H
PETTIT, Charles H
PETTIT, George Albert Joseph 1
PETTIT, Harvey P. 4
PETTIT, Henry 1
PETTIT, John H
PETTIT, John Upfold H
PETTIT, Thomas McKean H
PETTITT, Byron Buck 5
PETTUS, Edmund Winston 1
PETTUS, Erle 4
PETTUS, James Thomas 5
PETTUS, Maia 3
PETTUS, Willaim Bacon 3
PETTUS, William Jerdone 5
PETTY, A. Ray 1
PETTY, Alonzo McAllister 1
PETTY, C. Wallace 1
PETTY, James William 4
PETTY, Orlando Henderson 1
PETTY, Orville Anderson 2
PETTY, William H
PETZOLDT, William A. 4
PEURIFOY, John E. 3
PEVSNER, Antoine 4
PEW, Arthur E. Jr. 4
PEW, J(ohn) Howard 5
PEW, James Edgar 2
PEW, John Brooks 4
PEW, John G. 3
PEW, Joseph Newton Jr. 4
PEW, Marien Edwin 1
PEXTON, George Ellsworth 1
PEYNADO, Francisco J. 4
PEYRAUD, Frank Charles 2
PEYSER, Ethan Allen 3
PEYSER, Julius I. 3
PEYSER, Theodore A. 1
PEYTON, Balie H
PEYTON, Bernard Robertson 3
PEYTON, Bertha Menzier 2
PEYTON, Charles Dewey 4
PEYTON, Ephraim Goeffrey 3
PEYTON, Garland 5
PEYTON, Harlan Ide 3
PEYTON, John Howe 1
PEYTON, John Lewis H
PEYTON, Joseph Hopkins H
PEYTON, Samuel Oldham H
PEZET, Frederico Alfonso 4
PFAFF, Franz 1
PFAFF, Orange Garrett 1
PFAFF, William 1
PFAHLER, George Edward 3
PFAHLER, William H. 1
PFANSTIEHL, Carl 2
PFATTEICHER, Ernst Philip 2
PFEFFER, Edward Charles 3
PFEIFFENBERGER-, James Mather 4

*** Indicates More Than One Such Name Listed**

PFEIFFENSCHNEI- 4
DER, Justus
PFEIFFER, Annie Merner 2
PFEIFFER, Carl H
PFEIFFER, Edward 4
PFEIFFER, Jacob 2
PFEIFFER, Oscar Joseph 4
PFEIFFER, Robert Henry 3
PFEIFFER, 5
Timothy Newell
PFEIL, John Simon 5
PFEIL, Stephen 4
PFEILER, William Karl 5
PFINGST, Adolph O. 2
PFISTER, Jean Jacques 2
PFISTER, 5
Joseph Clement
PFISTERER, 5
Henry Albert
PFLAGER, Harry Miller 3
PFLAGER, Henry Barber 5
PFLUEGER, 4
John Seiberling
PFOHL, John Kenneth 4
PFORZHEIMER, 3
Carl Howard
PFOST, Gracie Bowers 4
PFOTENHAUER,
Frederick 1
PFUND, A. Herman 2
PHAIR, John J(oseph) 5
PHALEN, Harold
Romaine 3
PHALEN, James Matthew 3
PHALEN, Paul Stephens 5
PHANEUF, Louis Eusebe 3
PHARR, 5
Hurieosco Austill
PHELAN, Edward Joseph 4
PHELAN, James * H
PHELAN, James Duval 1
PHELAN, James J. 1
PHELAN, John 3
PHELAN, 1
Michael Francis
PHELAN, Richard 5
PHELAN, Sidney M. Jr. 3
PHELAN, Warren
Waverly 1
PHELPS, Albert Charles 1
PHELPS, H
Almira Hart Lincoln
PHELPS, Andrew Henry 4
PHELPS, Anson Greene H
PHELPS, Arthur Stevens 2
PHELPS, Ashton 1
PHELPS, Austin H
PHELPS, Charles 5
PHELPS, Charles Edward 1
PHELPS,
Charles Edward Jr.
PHELPS, 4
Charles Edward Davis
PHELPS, Charles Henry 1
PHELPS,
Clarence Lucien
PHELPS, Darwin H
PHELPS, Delos Porter 1
PHELPS, Earle Bernard 3
PHELPS, Edward Bunnell 1
PHELPS, Edward John 1
PHELPS, Edward Shethar 1
PHELPS, Elisha H
PHELPS, Erskine Mason 1
PHELPS, Esmond 3
PHELPS, 2
George Harrison
PHELPS, George Turner 1
PHELPS, Guy Fitch 1
PHELPS, Guy Merritt 2
PHELPS, Guy Rowland H
PHELPS, Harry 1
PHELPS, Helen Watson 5
PHELPS, Henry Willis 2
PHELPS, Isaac King 5
PHELPS, J(ames) Manley 5
PHELPS, James H
PHELPS, James Ivey 2
PHELPS, John Jay 2
PHELPS, John Noble 5
PHELPS, John Smith H
PHELPS, Lancelot H
PHELPS, Lawrence 4
PHELPS, Marian 4
PHELPS, Oliver H
PHELPS, Ruth Shepard 5
PHELPS, Samuel Shethar 2
PHELPS, Shelton Joseph 2
PHELPS, Stephen 4
PHELPS, Thomas Stowell 1
PHELPS,
Thomas Stowell Jr.
PHELPS, Timothy Guy H
PHELPS, 4
William Franklin
PHELPS, William Henry 1
PHELPS, William Lyon 2

PHELPS, H
William Wallace
PHELPS, William Walter H
PHELPS, 1
William Woodward
PHEMISTER, Dallas B. 3
PHENIX, George Perley 1
PHIFER, Fred Wood 1
PHILBIN, Eugene A. 1
PHILBIN, Philip J. 1
PHILBRICK, 4
Herbert Shaw
PHILBROOK, 1
Warren Coffin
PHILE, Philip H
PHILENIA H
PHILIP
PHILIP, Andre 5
PHILIP, George 2
PHILIP, Hoffman 3
PHILIP, John W. 1
PHILIPP, 1
Emanuel Lorenz
PHILIPP, Richard 3
PHILIPPE, Robert Rene 5
PHILIPPI, E. Martin 2
PHILIPS, Carlin 5
PHILIPS, George Morris 3
PHILIPS, Jesse Evans 4
PHILIPS, John F. 1
PHILIPS, Martin Wilson H
PHILIPS, William Pyle 3
PHILIPSE, Frederick H
PHILIPSON, David 2
PHILLER, George 1
PHILLIPPE, 5
Gerald Lloyd
PHILLIPPI, 1
Joseph Martin
PHILLIPPI, 5
Stanley Isaac
PHILLIPS, Albanus 2
PHILLIPS, Albanus, Jr. 5
PHILLIPS, 1
Alexander Hamilton
PHILLIPS,
Alexander Lacy
PHILLIPS,
Alexander Roy
PHILLIPS, 1
Alexander Van Cleve
PHILLIPS, 5
Alfred Edward
PHILLIPS,
Alfred Noroton
PHILLIPS, 1
Andrew Wheeler
PHILLIPS, Arthur L. 1
PHILLIPS, Asa Emory 1
PHILLIPS, Barnet 1
PHILLIPS, 5
Benjamin Dwight
PHILLIPS, Bert Geer 5
PHILLIPPE, 3
Carl Chrisler
PHILLIPS, Carl L. 4
PHILLIPS, 2
Catherine Coffin
PHILLIPS, Charles 1
PHILLIPS, 5
Charles Gordon
PHILLIPS, 3
Charles Henry
PHILLIPS, Charles L. 4
PHILLIPS,
Charles Leonard
PHILLIPS, 4
Chauncey Hatch
PHILLIPS, Coles 3
PHILLIPS, David Graham 1
PHILLIPS, Duane Seneca 1
PHILLIPS, Duncan 4
PHILLIPS, Edna M. 5
PHILLIPS, 3
Edward Charles
PHILLIPS, 4
Elliot Schuyler
PHILLIPS, 3
Ellis Laurimore
PHILLIPS, 2
Ethel Calvert
PHILLIPS, 5
Everett Franklin
PHILLIPS, 1
Francis Clifford
PHILLIPS, Frank 3
PHILLIPS, 5
Frank McGinley
PHILLIPS, Frank Reith 2
PHILLIPS, George H
PHILLIPS, 1
George Felter
PHILLIPS, 1
Glenn Randall
PHILLIPS, Harold Cooke 4

PHILLIPS, 5
Harry Hungerford Spooner,
Jr.
PHILLIPS, Harry Irving 4
PHILLIPS, Henry H
PHILLIPS, Henry A. 3
PHILLIPS, Henry Albert 3
PHILLIPS, 3
Henry Disbrow
PHILLIPS, Henry Myer H
PHILLIPS, 1
Henry Wallace
PHILLIPS, Herbert S. 4
PHILLIPS, James Andrew 1
PHILLIPS, James David 5
PHILLIPS, 5
James Frederick
PHILLIPS, Jay Campbell 2
PHILLIPS, Jesse J. 1
PHILLIPS, Jesse Snyder 3
PHILLIPS, John * H
PHILLIPS, John 1
John Bakewell
PHILLIPS, John Burton 1
PHILLIPS, John C. 2
PHILLIPS, John Charles 1
PHILLIPS, John George 4
PHILLIPS, John Herbert 1
PHILLIPS, 3
John Marshall
PHILLIPS, 3
John McFarlane
PHILLIPS, John Sanburn 2
PHILLIPS, 5
Kathryn Sisson (Mrs. Ellis
L. Phillips)
PHILLIPS, Lee Allen 1
PHILLIPS, Lee Eldas 2
PHILLIPS, Lena Madesin 4
PHILLIPS, Leon C. 3
PHILLIPS, LeRoy 5
PHILLIPS, 2
Levi Benjamin
PHILLIPS, Llewellyn 1
PHILLIPS, Louis 3
PHILLIPS, 2
Marie Tello (Mrs. Charles
J. Yaegle)
PHILLIPS, 4
Maude Gillette
PHILLIPS, Merton Ogden 5
PHILLIPS, 5
Michael James
PHILLIPS, Milton Eves 1
PHILLIPS, Morris 1
PHILLIPS, Nelson 4
PHILLIPS, 3
Norman Ethelbert
PHILLIPS, 1
Paul Chrisler
PHILLIPS, Percival 1
PHILLIPS, Percy Wilson 5
PHILLIPS, Philip * 1
PHILLIPS, Philip Lee 1
PHILLIPS, Ray Edmund 4
PHILLIPS, 1
Richard Harvey
PHILLIPS, 5
Richard Jones
PHILLIPS, Robert 2
PHILLIPS, 5
Roger Sherman
PHILLIPS, Samuel H
PHILLIPS, Samuel Edgar 3
PHILLIPS, H
Stephen Clarendon
PHILLIPS, T. D. 1
PHILLIPS, T. Redfield 3
PHILLIPS, 3
Thomas Ashley
PHILLIPS, Thomas I. 1
PHILLIPS, 3
Thomas Raphael
PHILLIPS, Thomas W. 1
PHILLIPS, 3
Thomas Wharton Jr.
PHILLIPS, 1
Ulrich Bonnell
PHILLIPS, Waite 4
PHILLIPS, 3
Wallace Banta
PHILLIPS, Watson Lyman 2
PHILLIPS, Wendell 1
PHILLIPS,
Wendell Christopher
PHILLIPS, Willard H
PHILLIPS, William * H
PHILLIPS, William H
PHILLIPS,
William Addison
PHILLIPS, 1
William Battle
PHILLIPS, William Eric 4
PHILLIPS, 1
William Fowke Ravenel

PHILLIPS, 4
William Irving
PHILLIPS, 2
Ze Barney Thorne
PHILLIPSON, 3
Irving Joseph
PHILLPOTTS, Eden 4
PHILP, John W. 2
PHILPOTT, Gordon M. 4
PHILPOTT, 4
Harvey Cloyd Sr.
PHILPOTT, Peter Willey 4
PHILPUTT, 1
Allan Bearden
PHILPUTT, James M. 1
PHILSON, Robert H
PHIN, John 1
PHINIZY, Bowdre 1
PHINIZY, Ferdinand H
PHINIZY, Hamilton 1
PHIPPS, Don Holcomb 5
PHIPPS, 1
Frank Huntington
PHIPPS, Henry 1
PHIPPS, John Shaffer 1
PHIPPS, Lawrence Cowle 3
PHIPPS, Michael Grace 5
PHIPS, Sir William H
PHISTER, Elijah Conner H
PHISTER, Montgomery 1
PHLEGAR, Archer A. 1
PHOENIX, Charles E. H
PHOENIX, 1
Jonas Phillips
PHOENIX, Lloyd 1
PHOLIEN, Joseph 4
PHRANER, Wilson 4
PHYFE, Duncan H
PHYFE, 1
William Henry Pinkney
PHYSICK, Philip Syng H
PHYTHIAN, Robert Lees 1
PIAAT, 4
Sarah Morgan Bryan
PIAF, Edith 4
PIASECKI, Peter F. 5
PIASTRO, Mishel 5
PIATT, Donn H
PIATT, John James 1
PIAZZA, Ferdinand 5
PIAZZONI, Gottardo 5
PIBUL SONGGRAM,
Luang
PICARD, Frank A. 4
PICARD, George Henry 1
PICARD, Ralph Alan 5
PICASSO, Pablo Ruiz 5
PICCARD, Jean Felix 4
PICCIRILLI, Attilio 2
PICCIRILLI, Furio 5
PICHEL, Irving 3
PICK, Albert 3
PICK, Bernhard 1
PICK, Lewis Andrew 3
PICKARD,
Florence Willingham
PICKARD, 3
Frederick William
PICKARD, 3
Greenleaf Whittier
PICKARD, John 1
PICKARD, Josiah Little 1
PICKARD, Samuel Nelson 5
PICKARD, Samuel
Thomas 1
PICKARD, Ward Wilson 2
PICKARD, 1
William Lowndes
PICKEL, Frank Welborn 1
PICKEL, 3
Margaret Barnard
PICKELL, Frank Gerald 1
PICKELLS, 5
Charles William
PICKEN, Lillian Hoxie 4
PICKENS, Andrew H
PICKENS, 2
Andrew Calhoun
PICKENS,
Francis Wilkinson
PICKENS, Israel H
PICKENS, James Madison 5
PICKENS, Samuel O. 1
PICKENS, William 3
PICKENS,
William Augustus
PICKERELL, 4
George Henry
PICKERING, Abner 4
PICKERING, Charles H
PICKERING, 1
Edward Charles
PICKERING, John * H
PICKERING, Loring 3
PICKERING, Timothy H
PICKERING, 1
William Alfred

PICKERING, 1
William Henry
PICKET, Albert H
PICKETT, Albert James H
PICKETT, Charles E. 4
PICKETT, Clarence Evan 4
PICKETT, Fermen Layton 1
PICKETT, George Edward H
PICKETT, Hugh Dale 3
PICKETT, H
James Chamberlayne
PICKETT, John Erasmus 3
PICKETT, 1
La Salle Corbell
PICKETT, Thomas
Edward 1
PICKETT, 3
Warren Wheeler
PICKETT, 1
William Clendenin
PICKHARDT, 1
William Paul
PICKING, Henry F. 1
PICKLE, George Wesley 4
PICKLESIMER, Hayes H
PICKMAN, Benjamin Jr. H
PICKNELL, William Lamb H
PICKREL, 4
William Gillespie
PICKRELL, Homer P. 5
PICOT, Louis Julien H
PICQUET, Francois H
PICTON, Thomas H
PIDDOCK, 1
Charles Albert
PIDGE, 4
John Bartholomew Gough
PIDGIN, Charles Felton 1
PIECK, Wilhelm 4
PIEPER, Emil G. 1
PIEPER, Ezra H. 3
PIEPER, 1
Franz August Otto
PIEPER, John Jacob 1
PIEPER, 4
William Charles
PIER, Arthur Stanwood H
PIER, 2
Garrett Chatfield
PIER, William Lauren 4
PIERCE, Alfred Mann 5
PIERCE, Anna Eloise 3
PIERCE, Arthur Henry 4
PIERCE,
Arthur Sylvanus
PIERCE, Benjamin H
PIERCE, Byron Root 1
PIERCE,
Carleton Custer
PIERCE,
Charles Franklin
PIERCE, Charles Sumner 3
PIERCE, Claude Connor 2
PIERCE, Clay Arthur 5
PIERCE, 5
Daniel Thompson
PIERCE, Dante Melville 3
PIERCE, Earle Vaydor 5
PIERCE, Edward Lillie H
PIERCE, Edward Lillie
PIERCE, Edward Peter 1
PIERCE,
Francis Marshal
PIERCE, Frank 3
PIERCE, Frank Reynolds 4
PIERCE, Frank W. 3
PIERCE, Franklin H
PIERCE, 1
Frederick Clifton
PIERCE, 4
Frederick Ernest
PIERCE, 1
Frederick Louis
PIERCE, George Edwin 3
PIERCE, George Foster H
PIERCE, George Warren 3
PIERCE,
George Washington
PIERCE, 1
Gilbert Ashville
PIERCE, Grace Adele 1
PIERCE, H. Clay 1
PIERCE, Henry Hill 1
PIERCE, Henry Lillie H
PIERCE, Henry Niles 1
PIERCE, Jason Noble 2
PIERCE, John Davis H
PIERCE, Joseph Hart 1
PIERCE, Josiah Jr. 1
PIERCE, Lawrence Blunt 4
PIERCE, Leonard A. 4
PIERCE, Lorne 1
PIERCE, Lyman L. 1
PIERCE, Marvin 5
PIERCE, Newton Barris 1
PIERCE, Norval Harvey 2
PIERCE, Oliver Willard 5

PIERCE, Palmer Eddy 1
PIERCE, Ray Vaughn 4
PIERCE, Rice A. 4
PIERCE,
  Robert Fletcher Young 4
PIERCE, Robert L. 4
PIERCE, Roger 4
PIERCE, Shelly 3
PIERCE, 2
  Ulysses Grant Baker
PIERCE, 1
  Wallace Lincoln
PIERCE, Walter Marcus 3
PIERCE, Walworth H
PIERCE, William H
PIERCE, William Kasson H
PIERCE, William Leigh H
PIERCE, Winslow Shelby 4
PIERI,
  Louis Arthur Raymond
PIERON, Henri 4
PIERPONT,
  Francis Harrison H
PIERPONT,
  Henry Edwards 5
PIERPONT, James H
PIERPONT, James 1
PIERPONT, John H
PIERREPONT, Edwards H
PIERREPONT, Robert
  Low 2
PIERSEL, Alba Chambers 1
PIERSOL, George Arthur 1
PIERSOL, George Morris 4
PIERSON, Abraham * 1
PIERSON, Arthur Tappan 1
PIERSON, 4
  Charles Ernest
PIERSON, 1
  Charles Wheeler
PIERSON, Coen Gallatin 5
PIERSON, 1
  Delavan Leonard
PIERSON, H
  Hamilton Wilcox
PIERSON, Isaac H
PIERSON, Isaac 1
PIERSON,
  Israel Coriell
PIERSON, J. Fred 1
PIERSON, H
  Jeremiah Halsey
PIERSON, Job H
PIERSON, Lewis Eugene 3
PIERSON, Romaine 1
PIERSON, Silas Gilbert 2
PIERSON, William * H
PIERZ, Franz H
PIETERS, Adrian John 1
PIETERS,
  Aleida Johanna 1
PIETRO,
  Cartaino 'di Sciarrine 1
PIETSCH, Karl 1
PIETSCH, 1
  Theodore Wells
PIEZ, Charles 1
PIFER, Drury Augustus 5
PIFFARD, Henry Granger 1
PIGEON, Richard 5
PIGFORD, Clarence E. 2
PIGGOT, James H
PIGGOT, Robert H
PIGMAN, George Wood 1
PIGOTT, James M. 5
PIGOTT, John Thomas 4
PIGOTT, Paul 5
PIGOTT, William Trigg 2
PIGUET, Leon A. 4
PIHLBLAD, 2
  Ernst Frederick
PIKE, Albert H
PIKE, Austin Franklin H
PIKE, Charles Burrall 4
PIKE, Clayton Warren 1
PIKE, F. H. 3
PIKE,
  Frederick Augustus H
PIKE, Granville Ross 4
PIKE, Harry Hale 5
PIKE, James H
PIKE, James Albert 5
PIKE, James Shepherd H
PIKE, Joseph Brown 4
PIKE, Nicolas H
PIKE, Percy M. 5
PIKE, Robert H
PIKE, Robert Gordon 1
PIKE, William John 1
PIKE, H
  Zebulon Montgomery
PILAT, Carl Francis 5
PILAT, Ignaz Anton 1
PILCHER, James Evelyn 1
PILCHER, James Taft 2
PILCHER, Joshua H

PILCHER, 1
  Lewis Frederick
PILCHER, Lewis Stephen 4
PILE, William Anderson H
PILES, Samuel Henry 4
PILGRIM, 1
  Charles Winfield
PILLARS, 1
  Charles Adrian
PILLEMER, Louis 3
PILLING, H
  James Constantine
PILLOW, Gideon Johnson 1
PILLSBURY, 1
  Albert Enoch
PILLSBURY, 3
  Alfred Fiske
PILLSBURY, 1
  Arthur Judson
PILLSBURY, 1
  Charles Alfred
PILLSBURY, 1
  Charles Alfred
PILLSBURY, 1
  Charles Stinson
PILLSBURY, Edwin S. 4
PILLSBURY, 5
  Eleanor Bellows (Mrs.
  Philip Winston Pillsbury)
PILLSBURY, 4
  Evans Searle
PILLSBURY, 5
  George Bigelow
PILLSBURY, 3
  Harriette Brown
PILLSBURY, Harry N. 1
PILLSBURY, 3
  Henry Church
PILLSBURY, 1
  Horace Davis
PILLSBURY, 1
  John Elliott
PILLSBURY, John Henry 1
PILLSBURY, 5
  John Sargent
PILLSBURY, 1
  John Sargent
PILLSBURY, Parker 1
PILLSBURY, 1
  Rosecrans W.
PILLSBURY, 5
  Walter Bowers
PILLSBURY, 4
  Walter Bowers
PILLSBURY, 3
  William Howard
PILMORE, Joseph H
PILSBRY, 3
  Henry Augustus
PILSBURY, Amos H
PILSBURY, Timothy H
PILSWORTH, 4
  Malcolm Nevil
PILZER, Maximilian 3
PIM, W. Paul 3
PINANSKI, 2
  Abraham Edward
PINANSKI, Samuel 5
PINCHBECK, 1
  Pinckney Benton Stewart
PINCHBECK, 3
  Raymond Bennett
PINCHOT, 2
  Amos Richard Eno
PINCHOT, 4
  Cornelia Bryce
PINCHOT, Gifford 5
PINCHOT, James W. 5
PINCKARD, 1
  Harold Recenus
PINCKNEY, Charles H
PINCKNEY, 1
  Charles Cotesworth
PINCKNEY, H
  Charles Cotesworth
PINCKNEY, H
  Elizabeth Lucas
PINCKNEY, H
  Henry Laurens
PINCKNEY, John Adams 5
PINCKNEY, 3
  Josephine Lyons Scott
PINCKNEY, 1
  Merritt Willis
PINCKNEY, Thomas H
PINCUS, Gregory 4
PINDALL, James H
PINDALL, 1
  Xenophon Overton
PINDELL, Henry Means 1
PINE, David Andrew 5
PINE, Frank Woodworth 1
PINE, James 3
PINE, John B. H
PINE, Robert Edge H
PINE, William Bliss 2
PINERO, Jesus T. 3

PINESS, George 5
PINGREE, Hazen S. 1
PINGREE, 1
  Samuel Everett
PINK, Louis Heaton 3
PINKERTON, Allan H
PINKERTON, Kathrene 4
PINKERTON, Lewis Letig H
PINKERTON, Lowell Call 3
PINKERTON, 1
  William Allan
PINKHAM, Lucile Deen 4
PINKHAM, Lucius 1
  Eugene
PINKHAM, Lydia Estes H
PINKNEY, Edward Coote H
PINKNEY, Ninian 1
PINKNEY, William H
PINNELL, Emmett Louis 5
PINNELL, LeRoy 5
  Kenneth
PINNEO, Dotha Stone 1
PINNER, Max H
PINNER, Max 2
PINNEY, E. Jay 4
PINNEY, 1
  George Miller Jr.
PINNEY, Harry Bowman 5
PINNEY, Norman H
PINSKI, David 5
PINSON, 1
  William Washington
PINTARD, John H
PINTARD, Lewis H
PINTEN, Joseph Gabriel 2
PINTNER, Rudolf 1
PINTO, Alva Sherman 2
PINTO, Isaac H
PINTO, Salvator 4
PINZA, Ezio 3
PIPER, Alexander Ross 3
PIPER, Arthur 1
PIPER, 1
  Charles Vancouver
PIPER, Edgar Bramwell 1
PIPER, Edwin Ford 1
PIPER, Fred LeRoy 3
PIPER, Horace L. 4
PIPER, James 1
PIPER, Raymond F. 4
PIPER, William H
PIPER, William Thomas 5
PIPES, Louis A(lbert) 5
PIPES, Martin Luther 1
PIPKIN, Charles Wooten 1
PIPPETT, Roger 1
PIQUENARD, Alfred H. 4
PIRANI, Eugenio 'di 1
PIRAZZINI, Agide 1
PIRCE, William Almy H
PIRE, 1
  Dominique Georges
PIRELLI, Alberto 5
PIRIE, Emma Elizabeth 3
PIRIE, Frederick W. 4
PIRIE, John Taylor 1
PIRIE, Samuel Carson 1
PIRKEY, 4
  Everett Leighton
PIRQUET, 1
  Clemens Freiherr von
PIRSSON, James W. H
PIRSSON, 1
  Louis Valentine
PIRTLE, James Speed 1
PISAR, Charles Juneau 3
PISCATOR, Erwin H
PISE, H
  Charles Constantine
PISHTEY, 5
  Joseph Josephson
PITAVAL, John Baptist 1
PITCAIRN, 4
  Harold Frederick
PITCAIRN, John 1
PITCAIRN, Norman 2
  Bruce
PITCAIRN, Raymond 4
PITCAIRN, Robert 5
PITCHER, 5
  Charles Sidney
PITCHER, Molly H
PITCHER, Nathaniel H
PITCHER, Zina H
PITCHFORD, John H. 1
PITCHLYNN, H
  Peter Perkins
PITFIELD, Robert Lucas 5
PITKIN, 1
  Francis Alexander
PITKIN, H
  Frederick Walker
PITKIN, Timothy H
PITKIN, 2
  Walter Boughton
PITKIN, William * H
PITKIN, Wolcott H. 3

PITMAN, Benn 1
PITMAN, Frank Wesley 2
PITMAN, J. Asbury 3
PITMAN, James Hall 4
PITMAN, John 1
PITMAN, 1
  Norman Hinsdale
PITNER, 1
  Thomas Jefferson
PITNEY, 1
  John Oliver Halsted
PITNEY, Mahlon 1
PITNEY, Shelton 2
PITOU, Augustus 1
PITT, David Alexander 3
PITT, Louis Wetherbee 1
PITT, Robert Healy 3
PITT, William H
PITTENGER, 3
  Lemuel Arthur
PITTENGER, William 1
PITTENGER, 3
  William Alvin
PITTMAN, Alfred 4
PITTMAN, H
  Charles Wesley
PITTMAN, 5
  Ernest Wetmore
PITTMAN, 4
  Hannah Daviess
PITTMAN, Hobson 5
PITTMAN, Key 1
PITTMAN, 3
  Marvin Summers
PITTMAN, 1
  Nathan Rowland
PITTMAN, 4
  Vail Montgomery
PITTMAN, 1
  William Buckner
PITTOCK, Henry Lewis 1
PITTS, 1
  Alexander Davidson
PITTS, Hiram Avery H
PITTS, 5
  Llewellyn William
PITTS, 4
  Llewellyn William
PITTS, 5
  Mary Helen McCrea Weaver
PITZER, 1
  Alexander White
PIUS XII 3
PIVER, 5
  Sara Elizabeth Early (Mrs.
  Sara Early Piver)
PIXLEY, Frank 1
PIXLEY, Henry David 1
PIZARRO, Francisco H
PIZITZ, Louis 3
PIZZETTI, Ildebrando H
PLACE, Ira Adelbert 1
PLACE, Perley Oakland 4
PLACE, Roland Percy 4
PLACE, Wilard Fiske 4
PLACHY, Fred Joseph 5
PLACIDE, Alexander H
PLACIDE, Henry H
PLACK, William L. 2
PLAGENS, 2
  Joseph Casimir
PLAISTED, 2
  Frederick William
PLAISTED, H
  Harris Merrill
PLAMONDON, 4
  Alfred Daniel Jr.
PLANCK, H
  Max Karl Ernst Ludwig
PLANK, 3
  William Bertolette
PLANT, David H
PLANT, Henry Bradley 1
PLANT, Marion Borchers 1
PLANT, Morton F. 1
PLANT, Oscar Henry 1
PLANTS, Tobias Avery H
PLANTZ, Myra Goodwin 4
PLANTZ, Samuel 1
PLASCHKE, Paul Albert 4
PLASSMANN, Ernst H
PLASSMANN, Thomas 3
PLASTER, Jerry Glen 3
PLASTIRAS, Nicholas 3
PLATE, Walter 4
PLATER, George H
PLATER, Thomas H
PLATH, Sylvia 4
PLATNER, John Winthrop 1
PLATNER, Samuel Ball 1
PLATOU, Ralph Victor 5
PLATT, Casper 4
PLATT, Charles 1
PLATT, Charles Adams 1
PLATT, 4
  Charles Alexander
PLATT, Edmund 1

PLATT, Franklin 1
PLATT, 3
  Frederick Joseph
PLATT, Harvey P. 4
PLATT, Henry Clay 1
PLATT, Henry Russell 1
PLATT, Howard V. 4
PLATT, Isaac Hull 1
PLATT, James Henry Jr. 1
PLATT, James Perry 1
PLATT, John 2
PLATT, John Osgood 2
PLATT, Jonas H
PLATT, Joseph Brereton 4
PLATT, Livingston 5
PLATT, 1
  Orville Hitchcock
PLATT, Robert Swanton 4
PLATT, Samuel 5
PLATT, Thomas Collier 1
PLATT, William Popham 1
PLATT, Zephaniah H
PLATTEN, John Wesley 3
PLATZEK, M. Warley 1
PLAUT, Edward 5
PLAYER, 3
  William Oscar Jr.
PLAYTER, Harold 5
PLEADWELL, 3
  Frank Lester
PLEASANT, 1
  Ruffin Golson
PLEASANTS, Henry Jr. 4
PLEASANTS, J. Hall 1
PLEASANTS, James H
PLEASANTS, 3
  James Jay Jr.
PLEASANTS, H
  John Hampden
PLEASONTON, Alfred H
PLEASONTON, H
  Augustus James
PLEHN, Carl Copping 2
PLESSNER, Theodore 1
PLIMPTON, 1
  George Arthur
PLIMPTON, 3
  George Lincoln
PLOCK, Richard Henry 3
PLONK, Emma Laura 4
PLOWMAN, George 1
  Taylor
PLUEMER, Adolph 4
PLUM, David Banks 2
PLUM, Harry Clarke 1
PLUM, Harry Grant 3
PLUMB, Albert Hale 1
PLUMB, Charles Sumner 1
PLUMB, Fayette Rumsey 4
PLUMB, Glenn Edward 1
PLUMB, Preston B. H
PLUMBE, George Edward 1
PLUMBE, John H
PLUME, Joseph Williams 1
PLUME, Stephen Kellogg 3
PLUMER, Arnold H
PLUMER, George H
PLUMER, William H
PLUMER, William Jr. H
PLUMER, William Swan H
PLUMLEY, 4
  Charles Albert
PLUMLEY, Frank 1
PLUMMER, 1
  Charles Griffin
PLUMMER, 3
  Daniel Clarence
PLUMMER, 1
  Edward Clarence
PLUMMER, 1
  Edward Hinkley
PLUMMER, Frank Everett 4
PLUMMER, Franklin E. H
PLUMMER, Henry H
PLUMMER, James Kemp 1
PLUMMER, John Watrous 5
PLUMMER, Jonathan H
PLUMMER, Mary Wright 1
PLUMMER, Ralph Walter 5
PLUMMER, Samuel C. 5
PLUMMER, Walter Percy 1
PLUMMER, 1
  William Alberto
PLUNKETT, 1
  Charles Peshall
PLUNKETT, Charles T. 1
PLUNKETT, 2
  Edward Milton
PLUNKETT, 1
  William Brown
PLYLER, 5
  Alva Washington
PLYLER, John Laney 4
PLYLER, Marion Timothy 5
PLYM, Francis John 1
PLYMIRE, 5
  Reginald Floyd

PLYMPTON, Eben 1
PLYMPTON, George Washington 1
POCAHONTAS H
PO-CHEDLEY, Donald Stephen 5
POCKMAN, Philetus Theodore 1
PODELL, David Louis 2
POE, Clarence 4
POE, Edgar Allan H
POE, Edgar Allan 4
POE, Elisabeth Ellicott 2
POE, Elizabeth Arnold H
POE, Floyd 5
POE, John Prentiss 4
POE, John William 1
POE, Orlando Metcalfe 4
POE, Pascal Eugene Jr. 4
POEBEL, Arno 3
POEHLER, W(illiam A(ugust) 5
POELS, Henry Andrew 4
POETKER, Albert H. 4
POFFENBARGER, George 4
POFFENBARGER, Livia Simpson 1
POGANY, Willi 3
POHLERS, Richard Camillo 3
POHLMAN, Augustus Grote 3
POHLMANN, Julius 1
POILLON, Howard Andrews 3
POILLON, William Clark 5
POINDEXTER, George H
POINDEXTER, Joseph Boyd 3
POINDEXTER, Miles 2
POINSETT, Joel Roberts H
POINT, Nicholas H
POINT DU SABLE, Jean Baptiste
POINTS, Arthur Jones 5
POLACCO, Giorgi 4
POLACHEK, Victor Henry
POLACK, William Gustave 3
POLAK, John Osborn 1
POLAND, Luke Potter
POLAND, William Carey 1
POLANYI, Karl
POLASEK, Albin 4
POLDERVAART, Arie 5
POLE, Elizabeth
POLE, John William 3
POLEMAN, Horace Irvin 4
POLERI, David Samuel
POLHAMUS, Jose Nelson 5
POLHEMUS, James H. 4
POLING, Daniel Alfred 5
POLING, Daniel V. 4
POLIVKA, Jaroslav Joseph 3
POLK, Albert Fawcett 5
POLK, Charles Peale H
POLK, Forrest Raymond 4
POLK, Frank Lyon 2
POLK, James G. 3
POLK, James Knox H
POLK, Leonidas H
POLK, Leonidas Lafayette
POLK, Lucius Eugene H
POLK, Ralph Lane 1
POLK, Rufus King 1
POLK, Sarah Childress
POLK, Thomas
POLK, Trusten
POLK, William
POLK, William Hawkins H
POLK, William Mecklenburg 1
POLLACK, Ervin Harold 5
POLLACK, Louis
POLLAK, Gustav
POLLAK, Robert 1
POLLAK, Virginia Morris 4
POLLAK, Walter Hellprin 1
POLLAN, Arthur Adair
POLLARD, Arthur Gayton
POLLARD, Cash Blair 2
POLLARD, Charles Louis
POLLARD, Claude 5
POLLARD, Edward Alfred
POLLARD, Edward Bagby 1
POLLARD, Ernest Mark
POLLARD, Harold Stanley

POLLARD, Harry Strange 5
POLLARD, Henry Douglas 2
POLLARD, Isaac 1
POLLARD, John Garland 1
POLLARD, John William Hobbs 5
POLLARD, Percival 1
POLLARD, Warren Randolph 4
POLLARD, William B. Sr. 3
POLLARD, William Jefferson 1
POLLEY, Samuel Cleland 2
POLLIA, Joseph P. 3
POLLITT, Levin Irving 5
POLLITZER, Sigmund 1
POLLMAN, William 1
POLLOCK, Benjamin Reathe 4
POLLOCK, Channing 2
POLLOCK, Charles Andrew 1
POLLOCK, Edwin Taylor 5
POLLOCK, Horatio Milo 3
POLLOCK, Jackson 4
POLLOCK, Jackson 4
POLLOCK, James H
POLLOCK, John C. 1
POLLOCK, Lewis John 4
POLLOCK, Oliver 1
POLLOCK, Pinckney Daniel 1
POLLOCK, Simon Oscar 4
POLLOCK, Thomas Cithcart 2
POLLOCK, Walter Briesler 1
POLLOCK, Wayne 4
POLSLEY, Daniel Haymond H
POLTORATZKY, Marianna A. 5
POLYAK, Stephen 3
POLYZOIDES, Adamantios Theophilus 5
POMAREDE, Leon 4
POMERAT, Charles Marc 4
POMERENE, Atlee 1
POMEROY, Allan 4
POMEROY, Charles 4
POMEROY, Daniel Eleazer 4
POMEROY, Elizabeth Ella 4
POMEROY, Eltweed 5
POMEROY, John Larrabee 1
POMEROY, John Norton H
POMEROY, John Norton 1
POMEROY, Marcus Mills H
POMEROY, Ralph Brouwer 1
POMEROY, Samuel Clarke
POMEROY, Seth H
POMEROY, Theodore Medad 1
PONCE 'DE LEON, Juan H
PONCHER, Henry George 3
POND, Allen Bartlit 1
POND, Alonzo Smith 3
POND, Anson Phelps 4
POND, Ashley 1
POND, Bremer Whidden 3
POND, Charles Fremont 1
POND, Dana 4
POND, Enoch 1
POND, Francis Jones 5
POND, Frederick Eugene 1
POND, George Edward 1
POND, George Gilbert 1
POND, Irving Kane 1
POND, James B. 4
POND, James Burton 1
POND, John Allan 5
POND, Peter 1
POND, Philip 2
POND, Robert Andrew 5
POND, Samuel William 1
POND, Silvanus Billings 4
POND, Theodore Hanford 1
POND, Wilf Pocklington 1
PONT-AU-SABLE, Jean Baptiste H
PONTIAC H
PONTIUS, Albert William 1
POOK, Samuel Hartt 1
POOL, David de Sola 1
POOL, Eugene Hillhouse 2
POOL, Joe 5
POOL, John 1
POOL, Leonidas Moore 1
POOL, Maria Louise H

POOL, Walter Freshwater H
POOLE, Abram 4
POOLE, Cecil Percy 1
POOLE, Charles Augustus 4
POOLE, Charles Hubbard 1
POOLE, DeWitt Clinton 3
POOLE, Ernest 1
POOLE, Eugene Alonzo 1
POOLE, Fanny Huntington Runnells 5
POOLE, Fenn E. 3
POOLE, Fitch H
POOLE, Franklin Osborne 2
POOLE, Frederic 1
POOLE, Herman 5
POOLE, John 5
POOLE, Lynn D. 5
POOLE, Murray Edward 1
POOLE, Robert Franklin 3
POOLE, Rufus Gilbert 5
POOLE, Sidman Parmelee 3
POOLE, William Frederick H
POOLER, Charles Alfred 5
POOLEY, Charles A. 1
POOLEY, Edward Murray 5
POOR, Agnes Blake 1
POOR, Charles Henry H
POOR, Charles Lane 1
POOR, Charles Marshall 5
POOR, Daniel H
POOR, Enoch 4
POOR, Frank A. 3
POOR, Fred Arthur 4
POOR, Henry Varnum, III 5
POOR, Henry William 1
POOR, John H
POOR, John Alfred 1
POOR, John Merrill 1
POOR, Ruel Whitcomb 1
POOR, Russell Spurgeon 5
POOR, Walter Everett 3
POORE, Benjamin Andrew 1
POORE, Benjamin Perley H
POORE, Charles Graydon 5
POORE, Henry Rankin 1
POORMAN, Alfred Peter 3
POPE, Albert Augustus 1
POPE, Alexander 1
POPE, Alfred Atmore 1
POPE, Allan Melvill 4
POPE, Amy Elizabeth 5
POPE, Arthur Upham 5
POPE, Bayard Foster 5
POPE, Carey Joseph 1
POPE, Curran 1
POPE, Edward Waldron 1
POPE, Francis Horton 5
POPE, Franklin Leonard 5
POPE, Frederick 5
POPE, George 1
POPE, Gustavus Debrille 3
POPE, Henry Francis 3
POPE, Herbert 3
POPE, James Worden 5
POPE, John * H
POPE, John Dudley 4
POPE, John Russell 1
POPE, Nathaniel H
POPE, Patrick Hamilton 1
POPE, Percival Clarence 1
POPE, Ralph Elton 3
POPE, Ralph Wainwright 1
POPE, Walter Lyndon 5
POPE, William Hayes 1
POPE, Young John 1
POPHAM, George H
POPMA, Gerritt Jacob 1
POPOFF, Stephen 1
POPOVIC, Vladimir 5
POPOV-VENIAMINOV, Joann H
POPPEN, Emmanuel Frederick 4
POPPENHEIM, Mary Barnett 1
POPPENHUSEN, Conrad Herman 2
POPPER, William 4
PORCHER, Francis Peyre H
PORMORT, Philemon H
PORRAS, Belisario 4
PORRITT, Edward 1
PORRO, Thomas J. 4
PORTAL, Baron Wyndham Raymond 2
PORTELA, Epifanio 4
PORTER, A. Kingsley 1
PORTER, A. W. Noel 4
PORTER, Albert 1

PORTER, Albert Gallatin H
PORTER, Alexander H
PORTER, Andrew H
PORTER, Arthur Le Moyne 5
PORTER, Augustus Seymour H
PORTER, Benjamin Curtis 1
PORTER, Bruce 5
PORTER, Charles Allen 1
PORTER, Charles Burnham
PORTER, Charles Howell H
PORTER, Charles Scott 5
PORTER, Charles Vernon 4
PORTER, Charley Lyman 4
PORTER, Charlotte Williams
PORTER, Claude R. 2
PORTER, Cole 4
PORTER, Dana 4
PORTER, David H
PORTER, David Dixon H
PORTER, David Dixon 2
PORTER, David Rittenhouse H
PORTER, Delia Lyman 1
PORTER, Dwight 1
PORTER, Earle S. 3
PORTER, Ebenezer H
PORTER, Eleanor Hodgman
PORTER, Ernest Warren 5
PORTER, Eugene Hoffman
PORTER, F. Addison 1
PORTER, Fitz-John 1
PORTER, Florence Collins
PORTER, Frank Chamberlin 2
PORTER, Frank M. 4
PORTER, Frank Monroe 5
PORTER, Fred Thomas 5
PORTER, Gene Stratton 1
PORTER, George French 1
PORTER, Gilbert Edwin 2
PORTER, Gilchrist H
PORTER, H. M. 1
PORTER, Harold Everett 1
PORTER, Henry (Harry) Alanson 5
PORTER, Henry Alford 2
PORTER, Henry Dwight 1
PORTER, Henry H. 1
PORTER, Henry Hobart 2
PORTER, Henry Kirke 1
PORTER, Holbrook Fitz-John 1
PORTER, Horace 1
PORTER, Hugh 1
PORTER, Hugh Omega 4
PORTER, J(ames) Sherman 1
PORTER, James H
PORTER, James A. 5
PORTER, James Davis 1
PORTER, James Dunlop 5
PORTER, James Hyde 2
PORTER, James Madison H
PORTER, James Madison III 4
PORTER, James Pertice 3
PORTER, James Temple 1
PORTER, James W. 3
PORTER, Jermain Gildersleeve 1
PORTER, Joe Frank 3
PORTER, John H
PORTER, John Addison 1
PORTER, John Addison 1
PORTER, John Clinton 3
PORTER, John Henry 1
PORTER, John Lincoln 1
PORTER, John Luke H
PORTER, John Lupher 1
PORTER, John William 1
PORTER, Joseph Franklin 2
PORTER, Joseph Yates 1
PORTER, Kirk Harold 5
PORTER, L(ester) G(ilbert) 5
PORTER, Linn Boyd 1
PORTER, Louis Hopkins 2
PORTER, Lucius Chapin 3
PORTER, Miles Fuller 1
PORTER, Newton Hazelton 2
PORTER, Noah H
PORTER, Peter Buell H
PORTER, Phil 4
PORTER, Quincy 4
PORTER, Robert Langley 4

PORTER, Robert Percival 1
PORTER, Roland Guyer 3
PORTER, Rose 1
PORTER, Royal A(rthur) 5
PORTER, Rufus H
PORTER, Russell Williams 2
PORTER, Samuel 1
PORTER, Sarah H
PORTER, Seton 3
PORTER, Silas Wright 1
PORTER, Stephen Geyer 1
PORTER, Sydney 1
PORTER, Theodoric 1
PORTER, Thomas Conrad 1
PORTER, Timothy H. 1
PORTER, Valentine Mott 1
PORTER, Washington Tullis
PORTER, Whitney Clair 5
PORTER, William Curren 4
PORTER, William David 1
PORTER, William Gove 1
PORTER, William Henry *
PORTER, William N(ichols) 5
PORTER, William Townsend 2
PORTER, William Trotter H
PORTER, William Wagener 1
PORTER, William Wallace
PORTERFIELD, Allen Wilson 3
PORTERFIELD, Lewis Broughton 2
PORTERFIELD, Robert Huffard 5
PORTERIE, Gaston Louis 1
PORTEVIN, Albert Marcel Germain Rene 4
PORTIER, Michael H
PORTINARI, Candido 4
PORTMAN, Eric 5
PORTMANN, Ursus Victor 4
PORTNOFF, Alexander 2
PORTOLA, Gaspar 'de H
PORTOR, Laura Spencer 3
PORY, John H
POSEGATE, Mabel 3
POSEY, Chester Alfred 5
POSEY, Thomas H
POSEY, William Campbell 1
POSNER, Edwin 5
POSNER, Harry 4
POSNER, Louis Samuel 5
POSNER, Stanley I. 4
POSSE, Rose (Baroness); also known as Rose Moore Strong.
POST, Alice Thacher 2
POST, Chandler Rathfon 1
POST, Charles Johnson 3
POST, Charles William 1
POST, Christian Frederick H
POST, Edwin 1
POST, Elwyn Donald 4
POST, Emily 1
POST, Frank Truman 1
POST, George Adams 1
POST, George Browne 1
POST, George Edward 1
POST, Herbert Wilson 4
POST, Hoyt Garrod 4
POST, Isaac H
POST, James D. 1
POST, James Howell 1
POST, James Otis 3
POST, Josephine Fowler H
POST, Jotham Jr. H
POST, Kenneth 3
POST, Lawrence T. 1
POST, Levi Arnold 1
POST, Louis Freeland 1
POST, Martin Hayward 1
POST, Melville Davisson 1
POST, Philip Sidney H
POST, Regis Henri 2
POST, Roswell Olcott 1
POST, Truman Marcellus H
POST, W. Merritt
POST, Waldron Kintzing H
POST, Wilber E.
POST, Wiley 1
POST, William Stone 1
POST, Wright H

POSTL, Karl Anton H
POSTLE, Wilbur Everett 1
POSTLETHWAITE, 4
  Robert Hodgshon
POSTLETHWAITE, 5
  William Wallace;
POSTNIKOV, 5
  Fedor Alexis (F. A. Post)
POSTON, H
  Charles Pebrille
POSTON, 1
  Elias McClellan
POTEAT, Edwin McNeill 1
POTEAT, Edwin McNeill 3
POTEAT, Hubert McNeill 3
POTEAT, James Douglass 2
POTEAT, William Louis 5
POTHIER, Aram J. 4
POTOCKI, Jerzy 4
POTT, 2
  Francis Lister Hawks
POTT, John H
POTT, 4
  William Sumner Appleton
POTTENGER, 4
  Francis Marion
POTTER, 4
  Albert Franklin
POTTER, Albert Knight 4
POTTER, 1
  Alfred Claghorn
POTTER, Alfred Knight 1
POTTER, Allen H
POTTER, Alonzo 4
POTTER, Burton Willis 5
POTTER, Charles 5
POTTER, 4
  Charles Francis
POTTER, Charles Lewis 1
POTTER, Charles Nelson 5
POTTER, Chester Magee 3
POTTER, Clarkson Nott 1
POTTER, Cora Urquhart 1
POTTER, David 5
POTTER, David Morris 5
POTTER, 5
  Delbert Maxwell
POTTER, Edward Clark 1
POTTER, Edward Eels 1
POTTER, Edwin Augustus 1
POTTER, Eliphalet Nott 1
POTTER, H
  Elisha Reynolds *
POTTER, Ellen Culver 3
POTTER, Emery Davis H
POTTER, Frank B(ell) 1
POTTER, Frank Maxson 2
POTTER, George Milton 5
POTTER, George W. 3
POTTER, Harry S. 5
POTTER, Henry Codman 5
POTTER, Henry Noel 5
POTTER, Henry Staples 1
POTTER, Homer Dexter 1
POTTER, Horatio H
POTTER, James H
POTTER, John Fox 1
POTTER, John Milton 2
POTTER, John Wesley 4
POTTER, Justin 1
POTTER, Louis 1
POTTER, 1
  Margaret Horton
POTTER, Marion E. 3
POTTER, Mark Winslow 1
POTTER, Mary Knight 1
POTTER, Mary Ross 5
POTTER, 1
  Mrs. James Brown
POTTER, Nathaniel H
POTTER, 5
  Nathaniel Bowditch
POTTER, 1
  Orlando Brunson
POTTER, Orrin W. 1
POTTER, Paul Meredith 1
POTTER, Platt H
POTTER, Robert H
POTTER, Robert Brown H
POTTER, 4
  Rockwell Harmon
POTTER, Roderick 4
POTTER, Samuel John 4
POTTER, 4
  Samuel Otway Lewis
POTTER, Stephen 5
POTTER, Thomas Albert 2
POTTER, Thomas Paine 5
POTTER, Wilfrid Carne 2
POTTER, William 1
POTTER, 1
  William Bancroft
POTTER, 1
  William Bleecker
POTTER, 3
  William Chapman
POTTER, William Henry 1

POTTER, William J. 4
POTTER, William James H
POTTER, William Parker 1
POTTER, William Plumer 1
POTTER, William W. 5
POTTER, William Warren 1
POTTER, William Wilson 1
POTTERTON, 1
  Thomas Edward
POTTHAST, Edward 1
  Henry
POTTLE, Emory Bemsley H
POTTS, Alfred Fremont 1
POTTS, 1
  Benjamin Franklin
POTTS, Charles Edwin 3
POTTS, Charles Sower 1
POTTS, David Jr. H
POTTS, James Henry 1
POTTS, James Henry 2
POTTS, Jonathan 1
POTTS, Louis Moses 1
POTTS, Richard 1
POTTS, Robert 1
POTTS, Robert Joseph 4
POTTS, Templin Morris 1
POTTS, William 1
POTTS, Willis John 5
POTTS, 5
  Wylodine Gabbert (Mrs. Thomas C. Potts)
POTZGER, John E. 3
POU, Edward William 1
POU, James Hinton 1
POUCH, William Henry 3
POUILLY, H
  Jacques Nicholas Bussiere 'de
POUILLY, Joseph 'de H
POULENC, Francis * 4
POULSON, Zachariah 1
POULSSON, Anne Emilie 1
POUND, Arthur 4
POUND, 1
  Cuthbert Winfred
POUND, Earl Clifford 2
POUND, Ezra 5
POUND, G(rellet) C. 5
POUND, Jere M. 1
POUND, Jere M. 4
POUND, Louise 3
POUND, Roscoe 4
POUND, Thomas H
POURTALES, H
  Louis Francois 'de
POUSETTE-DART, 4
  Nathaniel
POWDERLY, 1
  Terence Vincent
POWDERMAKER, 5
  Hortense
POWE, Thomas Erasmus 2
POWEL, Harford 1
POWEL, John Hare H
POWELL H
POWELL, Aaron Macy H
POWELL, 5
  Adam Clayton, Jr.
POWELL, Alden L. 3
POWELL, Alfred H. H
POWELL, Arthur Gray 1
POWELL, 3
  Arthur James Emery
POWELL, 4
  Benjamin Harrison
POWELL, 5
  Caroline Amelia
POWELL, 1
  Caroline Amelia
POWELL, Carroll A. 2
POWELL, Cecil Frank 5
POWELL, 1
  Charles Francis
POWELL, Charles L. 1
POWELL, Charles Stuart H
POWELL, 3
  Charles Underhill
POWELL, Cuthbert H
POWELL, David 1
POWELL, Dawn 4
POWELL, 1
  Desmond Stevens
POWELL, Dick 4
POWELL, Doane 1
POWELL, Donald Adams 5
POWELL, E. Alexander 3
POWELL, E. Harrison 1
POWELL, Earl 1
POWELL, 1
  Edward Alexander
POWELL, Edward Henry 4
POWELL, Edward 5
  Lindsay
POWELL, Edward Payson 1
POWELL, Edward 5
  Thomson

POWELL, 2
  Elmer Ellsworth
POWELL, 2
  Elmer Nathaniel
POWELL, Fred Wilbur 1
POWELL, Frederick 4
POWELL, G. Harold 1
POWELL, G. Thomas 4
POWELL, G. Thomas 5
POWELL, George May 1
POWELL, Hunter Holmes 1
POWELL, John 4
POWELL, John Benjamin 2
POWELL, John H. 1
POWELL, John Lee 4
POWELL, John Wesley 5
POWELL, Joseph Wright 3
POWELL, Joseph Yancey 4
POWELL, Junius L. 4
POWELL, H
  Lazarus Whitehead
POWELL, Levin H
POWELL, Lucien Whiting 1
POWELL, Lula E. 3
POWELL, Lyman Pierson 1
POWELL, Maud 1
POWELL, Nathan 5
POWELL, Noble Cilley 5
POWELL, Paul 5
POWELL, Paulus 5
POWELL, Paulus Prince 4
POWELL, Rachel Hopper 4
POWELL, Richard Holmes 2
POWELL, 5
  Richard Sterling
POWELL, Robert 1
POWELL, Samuel H
POWELL, Snelling H
POWELL, 1
  Talcott Williams
POWELL, Thomas H
POWELL, Thomas 1
POWELL, Thomas Carr 2
POWELL, Thomas 4
  Edward
POWELL, Thomas Reed 3
POWELL, Warren 3
  Thomson
POWELL, Weldon 4
POWELL, 1
  William Bramwell
POWELL, William Byrd H
POWELL, William Dan 1
POWELL, William David 1
POWELL, William Frank 1
POWELL, 4
  William Hamilton
POWELL, William Henry H
POWELL, William Henry 1
POWELL, William M. H
POWELL, Wilson Marcy 1
POWELSON, 5
  Wilfrid Van Nest
POWER, Charles Gavan 5
POWER, Frank W. 3
POWER, 1
  Frederick Belding
POWER, 1
  Frederick Dunglison
POWER, Howard 3
  Anderson
POWER, James Edward 5
POWER, John H
POWER, 5
  John Joseph, Jr.
POWER, Thomas Charles 1
POWER, Tyrone 3
POWERS, Caleb 1
POWERS, Carol Hoyt 1
POWERS, Charles Andrew 1
POWERS, Daniel William 2
POWERS, Delmar Thomas 2
POWERS, Edwin Booth 4
POWERS, Eugene Paul 5
POWERS, Franklin Brown 4
POWERS, 1
  Frederick Alton
POWERS, 1
  George McClellan
POWERS, Gershom 5
POWERS, Grover Francis 5
POWERS, H. Henry 4
POWERS, 4
  Harry Huntington
POWERS, Harry Joseph 1
POWERS, Harry Joseph 2
POWERS, Hiram 5
POWERS, Horatio Nelson H
POWERS, Hugh Winfield 1
POWERS, James Knox 1
POWERS, James T. 4
POWERS, John Craig 5
POWERS, Joseph Harrell 5
POWERS, Joseph Neely 1
POWERS, LeGrand 4
POWERS, Leland Todd 1
POWERS, Leon Walter 3

POWERS, Levi Moore 1
POWERS, Llewellyn 1
POWERS, Luther Milton 5
POWERS, 1
  Orlando Woodworth
POWERS, Pliny H. 4
POWERS, Ralph Averill 5
POWERS, Ridgely Ceylon 5
POWERS, 5
  Robert Davis, Jr.
POWERS, Samuel Leland 1
POWERS, Samuel Ralph 5
POWERS, Sidney 1
POWERS, 5
  Thomas Jefferson
POWERS, Tom 3
POWERS, William Dudley 4
POWERS, William L. 1
POWHATAN H
POWLEY, N. R. H
POWLISON, Charles Ford 2
POWNALL, Mrs. H
POWNALL, Thomas H
POWYS, John Cowper 4
POWYS, Llewelyn 2
POYDRAS, 1
  Julien 'de Lallande
POYNTER, 1
  Charles William McCorkle
POYNTER, Clara Martin 4
POYNTER, Henrietta 4
POYNTER, Paul 3
POYNTER, William A. 1
POYNTON, John Albert 1
POYNTZ, James M. 1
POZNANSKI, Gustavus H
PRADO 4
  UGARTECHE, Manuel
PRADT, Louis Augustus 4
PRAEGER, Otto 5
PRAHL, Augustus John 5
PRALL, Anning S. 1
PRALL, Charles Edward 1
PRALL, David Wight 1
PRALL, William 1
PRANG, Louis 1
PRANG, Mary Dana 1
  Hicks
PRANKARD, 1
  Harry Irving II
PRASAD, Rajendra 4
PRATHER, 1
  Perry Franklin
PRATHER, Thomas J. 4
PRATT, 5
  Agnes Edwards Rothery
PRATT, Arthur Peabody 5
PRATT, Auguste G. 5
PRATT, Bela Lyon 1
PRATT, Charles H
PRATT, Charles 3
PRATT, Charles C. 3
PRATT, Charles Dudley 1
PRATT, Charles Henry 3
PRATT, Charles Millard 1
PRATT, 5
  Charles Stebbings
PRATT, Charles Stuart 4
PRATT, Daniel * H
PRATT, Daniel 2
PRATT, Daniel Darwin H
PRATT, Don Forrester 2
PRATT, Dwight Mallory 1
PRATT, Edward Barton 4
PRATT, Edwin Hartley 1
PRATT, Ella Farman 1
PRATT, Enoch H
PRATT, Fletcher 3
PRATT, Florence Gibb 1
PRATT, Frank Randall 3
PRATT, Frederic Bayley 1
PRATT, Frederick Haven 3
PRATT, 5
  Frederick Sanford
PRATT, George Collins 5
PRATT, George Dupont 1
PRATT, George Dwight 1
PRATT, George K. 3
PRATT, Harcourt J. 1
PRATT, Harold Irving 5
PRATT, Harry Edward 1
PRATT, Harry Emerson 3
PRATT, Harry Hayt 1
PRATT, Harry Noyes 2
PRATT, Harry Rogers 3
PRATT, Henry Cheever 1
PRATT, Henry Conger 5
PRATT, Henry Sherring 1
PRATT, Herbert Lee 1
PRATT, James Alfred 5
PRATT, James Bissett 2
PRATT, James Timothy H
PRATT, John Francis 1
PRATT, John Lowell 5
PRATT, John Teele 1
PRATT, Joseph Hersey 2
PRATT, Joseph Hyde 1

PRATT, Joseph M. 2
PRATT, Le Gage 1
PRATT, Lewellyn 1
PRATT, Lucy 5
PRATT, Matthew H
PRATT, Orson H
PRATT, Orville Clyde 3
PRATT, Parley Parker H
PRATT, Pascal Paoli 1
PRATT, Richard Henry 1
PRATT, Richardson 3
PRATT, 4
  Ruth Sears Baker
PRATT, Samuel Wheeler 1
PRATT, Sedgwick 1
PRATT, Sereno S. 1
PRATT, Silas Gamaliel 1
PRATT, Stewart Camden 3
PRATT, Thomas George 1
PRATT, Thomas Willis H
PRATT, Waldo Selden 1
PRATT, Wallace 1
PRATT, William Veazie 1
PRATT, Zadock H
PRATTE, Bernard H
PRAY, Charles Nelson 4
PRAY, Isaac Clark 1
PRAY, James Sturgis 1
PRAY, Theron Brown 4
PREBLE, Edward 1
PREBLE, Edward A. 3
PREBLE, Fred Myron 1
PREBLE, George Henry H
PREBLE, Robert Bruce 2
PREBLE, William Pitt 1
PREBLE, 4
  William Pitt Jr.
PREETORIUS, Emil 1
PREGEANT, 5
  Victor Eugene, III
PRELLWITZ, 2
  Edith Mitchill
PRELLWITZ, Henry 1
PRENDERGAST, 1
  Albert Collins
PRENDERGAST, Charles 2
PRENDERGAST, 1
  Edmond Francis
PRENDERGAST, James 1
  M.
PRENDERGAST, 3
  Maurice Brazil
PRENDERGAST,
  William A.
PRENTICE,
  Bernon Sheldon
PRENTICE, E. Parmalee 3
PRENTICE, H
  George Dennison
PRENTICE, 1
  George Gordon
PRENTICE, James Stuart 5
PRENTICE, Samuel Oscar 1
PRENTICE, Sartell 1
PRENTICE, 4
  William Kelly
PRENTICE, 1
  William Packer
PRENTIS, 3
  Henning Webb Jr.
PRENTIS,
  Robert Riddick
PRENTISS,
  Benjamin Maybury
PRENTISS, 1
  Daniel Webster
PRENTISS, H
  Elizabeth Payson
PRENTISS,
  Francis Fleury
PRENTISS, George Lewis 1
PRENTISS, Henry James 1
PRENTISS, John Holmes H
PRENTISS, John Wing 1
PRENTISS, Samuel 1
PRENTISS, H
  Seargent Smith
PRENTISS, Theodore 3
PRESBREY, Eugene W. 1
PRESBREY, Frank 1
PRESBY, 5
  Charlotte Sulley
PRESCOTT,
  Albert Benjamin
PRESCOTT, Anson Ward 5
PRESCOTT,
  Arthur Taylor
PRESCOTT, 1
  Charles Henry
PRESCOTT, 5
  Daniel Alfred
PRESCOTT, Dorothy 1
PRESCOTT, 5
  Edward Purcell
PRESCOTT, Frank Clarke 1
PRESCOTT, 3
  Frederick Clarke

PRESCOTT, George Bartlett H
PRESCOTT, Henry Washington 2
PRESCOTT, John S. 3
PRESCOTT, Mary Newmarch H
PRESCOTT, Oliver H
PRESCOTT, Oliver 1
PRESCOTT, Samuel H
PRESCOTT, Samuel Cate 4
PRESCOTT, Stedman 5
PRESCOTT, William H
PRESCOTT, William Hickling H
PRESCOTT, William Ray 4
PRESS, Samuel David 5
PRESSER, Theodore 1
PRESSEY, Henry Albert 5
PRESSLY, Frank Young 4
PRESSLY, Mason Wylie 4
PRESSMAN, Joel J. 4
PREST, William Morton 5
PRESTON, Adelaide B. 5
PRESTON, Andrew W. 1
PRESTON, Ann H
PRESTON, Arthur Murray 5
PRESTON, Austin Roe 3
PRESTON, Byron Webster 1
PRESTON, Cecil Anthony 1
PRESTON, Charles Miller 2
PRESTON, Douglas A. 1
PRESTON, Elwyn Greeley 3
PRESTON, Erasmus Darwin 1
PRESTON, Frances Folsom 2
PRESTON, Francis H
PRESTON, George H. 5
PRESTON, George Junkin 1
PRESTON, Guy Henry 3
PRESTON, Harold 1
PRESTON, Harriet Waters 1
PRESTON, Herbert R. 1
PRESTON, Howard Hall 3
PRESTON, Howard Payne 4
PRESTON, Howard Willis 1
PRESTON, Hulon 4
PRESTON, Jacob Alexander H
PRESTON, James Harry 1
PRESTON, John Fisher 5
PRESTON, John Smith H
PRESTON, John White 5
PRESTON, Jonas H
PRESTON, Jonathan H
PRESTON, Josephine Corliss 3
PRESTON, Keith 1
PRESTON, Malcolm Greenhough 5
PRESTON, Margaret Junkin H
PRESTON, Ord 3
PRESTON, Paul H
PRESTON, Robert J. 5
PRESTON, Roger 3
PRESTON, Thomas Jex Jr. 4
PRESTON, Thomas L. 3
PRESTON, Thomas Ross 3
PRESTON, Thomas Scott H
PRESTON, William H
PRESTON, William Ballard H
PRESTON, William Campbell H
PRESTRIDGE, John Newton 1
PRETTYMAN, Cornelius William 2
PRETTYMAN, E(lijah) Barrett 5
PRETTYMAN, Forrest Johnston 2
PRETTYMAN, Virgil 5
PREUS, Jacob Aall Ottesen 4
PREUS, Ove J. H. 3
PREUSS, Arthur 1
PREUSS, Lawrence 3
PREVOST, Eugene-Prosper H
PREVOST, Francois Marie H
PREYER, Allan Talmage 4
PREYER, Carl Adolph 2
PREYER, William Yost 5
PRIBER, Christian H
PRIBRAM, Ernest August 1
PRICE, Abel Fitzwater 1
PRICE, Andrew 3
PRICE, Bertram John 2
PRICE, Bruce 1
PRICE, Burr 3
PRICE, Butler Delaplaine 1
PRICE, Carl Fowler 2
PRICE, Charles Browne 1
PRICE, Charles S. 4
PRICE, Charles Wilson 1
PRICE, Chester B. 4
PRICE, David James 3
PRICE, Edwin R. 4
PRICE, Eldridge Cowman 1
PRICE, Eli Kirk H
PRICE, Enoch Jones 2
PRICE, Francis 4
PRICE, Frank 1
PRICE, Frank J. 1
PRICE, Franklin Haines 3
PRICE, George Clinton 4
PRICE, George Edmund 1
PRICE, George Hunter 1
PRICE, George McCready 4
PRICE, George Merriman 3
PRICE, George Moses 2
PRICE, Hannibal 5
PRICE, Harrison Jackson 2
PRICE, Harvey Lee 3
PRICE, Henry Ferris 4
PRICE, Hickman 1
PRICE, Hiram 1
PRICE, Hobert 4
PRICE, Homer Charles 3
PRICE, Howard Campbell 3
PRICE, Ira Maurice 1
PRICE, Jacob Embury 1
PRICE, James Houston 4
PRICE, James Hubert 2
PRICE, James L. 1
PRICE, James Woods 3
PRICE, Jesse Dashiell 1
PRICE, John D. 3
PRICE, John G. 1
PRICE, Joseph Lindon 5
PRICE, Julian 2
PRICE, Lee 4
PRICE, Lucien 4
PRICE, Margaret (Mrs. Hickman Price, Jr.) 5
PRICE, Margaret Wright 5
PRICE, Marshall Langton 1
PRICE, Miles Oscar 5
PRICE, Milo B. 1
PRICE, Ore Lee 5
PRICE, Orlo Josiah 2
PRICE, Oscar Jay 1
PRICE, Overton Westfeldt 1
PRICE, P. Frank 3
PRICE, R. Holleman 3
PRICE, Raymond B. 5
PRICE, Richard Nye 1
PRICE, Richard Rees 5
PRICE, Robert Beverly 4
PRICE, Robert Henderson 4
PRICE, Robert Martin 1
PRICE, Rodman McCamley H
PRICE, Sadie F. 1
PRICE, Samuel H
PRICE, Samuel D. 1
PRICE, Samuel Woodson H
PRICE, Samuel Woodson 4
PRICE, Silas Eber 1
PRICE, Stephen H
PRICE, Sterling H
PRICE, Theodore Hazeltine 1
PRICE, Thomas Lawson H
PRICE, Thomas Randolph 1
PRICE, Walter L. 4
PRICE, Walter Winston 2
PRICE, Warren Elbridge 4
PRICE, Warwick James 1
PRICE, William Cecil H
PRICE, William Cecil 4
PRICE, William Gray, Jr. 5
PRICE, William Henry 4
PRICE, William Hundley, Jr. 5
PRICE, William Jennings 3
PRICE, William Pierce 1
PRICE, William Raleigh 1
PRICE, William Thompson H
PRICE, William Thompson 1
PRICE, William Wightman 5
PRICHARD, Augustus Bedlow 4
PRICHARD, Frank Perley 1
PRICHARD, Harold Adye 2
PRICHARD, Lev H. 2
PRICHARD, Sarah Johnson 1
PRICHARD, Vernon E. 2
PRICKETT, Joe Milroy 3
PRICKETT, William 4
PRICKITT, William Augustus 1
PRIDDY, Lawrence 2
PRIDE, Frederick W.R. 5
PRIDGEON, Charles Hamilton 1
PRIDMORE, John Edmund Oldaker 1
PRIEST, Alan 5
PRIEST, George Madison 2
PRIEST, Henry Samuel 1
PRIEST, Ira Allen 4
PRIEST, Irwin G. 1
PRIEST, James Percy 3
PRIEST, Walter Scott 1
PRIEST, Wells Blodgett 3
PRIESTLEY, George Colin 1
PRIESTLEY, Herbert Ingram 2
PRIESTLEY, James H
PRIESTLEY, Joseph H
PRIME, Benjamin Youngs H
PRIME, Ebenezer Scudder 1
PRIME, Edward Dorr Griffin H
PRIME, Frederick 1
PRIME, Frederick Edward 1
PRIME, Nathaniel Scudder H
PRIME, Ralph Earl 1
PRIME, Samuel Irenaeus H
PRIME, Samuel Thornton Kemeys 1
PRIME, William Cowper 1
PRIMER, Sylvester 1
PRIME-STEVESON, Edward Irenaeus 4
PRIMROSE, John 3
PRIMS, James Edwin 5
PRINCE, Arthur Warren 3
PRINCE, Benjamin F. 1
PRINCE, Eugene Mitchell 4
PRINCE, Frank Moody 1
PRINCE, Frederick Henry 3
PRINCE, George Harrison 1
PRINCE, George W. 1
PRINCE, Helen Choate 4
PRINCE, John Dyneley 2
PRINCE, John Tilden 1
PRINCE, John W. 4
PRINCE, L. Bradford 1
PRINCE, Leon Cushing 1
PRINCE, Leon Nathaniel 5
PRINCE, Morton 1
PRINCE, Nathan Dyer 2
PRINCE, Oliver Hillhouse H
PRINCE, Sydney Rhodes 2
PRINCE, Thomas H
PRINCE, Walter Franklin 1
PRINCE, William * H
PRINCE, William Loftin 2
PRINCE, William Robert H
PRINDLE, Edwin Jay 2
PRINDLE, Elizur H. H
PRINDLE, Frances Weston Carruth 4
PRINDLE, Franklin Cogswell 1
PRING, Martin H
PRINGEY, Joseph Colburn 3
PRINGLE, Benjamin H
PRINGLE, Coleman Roberson 1
PRINGLE, Cyrus Guernsey 1
PRINGLE, Ernest Henry 3
PRINGLE, Henry Fowles 3
PRINGLE, Henry Nelson 2
PRINGLE, James Nelson 2
PRINGLE, Joel Roberts Poinsett 1
PRINGLE, John Julius H
PRINGLE, Ralph 1
PRINGLE, Ralph W. 3
PRINGLE, Robert Smith 1
PRINGLE, William James 1
PRINGSHEIM, Neena Hamilton (Mrs.) 5
PRINOSCH, Francis J. 5
PRINTZ, Johan Bjornsson H
PRINZ, Hermann 3
PRINZMETAL, Isadore Harry 5
PRIOR, Herbert M. 3
PRIOR, William Matthew H
PRISK, Charles Henry 1
PRISK, William Frederick 4
PRITCHARD, Arthur John 1
PRITCHARD, Arthur Thomas 1
PRITCHARD, Harry N. 5
PRITCHARD, Harry Otis 1
PRITCHARD, Jeter Connelly 1
PRITCHARD, John F. 4
PRITCHARD, John Wagner 1
PRITCHARD, Myron Thomas 1
PRITCHARD, Richard E. 4
PRITCHARD, Richard Edward 4
PRITCHARD, Samuel Reynolds 1
PRITCHARD, Stuart 1
PRITCHARD, William Hobbs 1
PRITCHETT, Carr Waller 1
PRITCHETT, Clifton Augustine 3
PRITCHETT, Henry Smith 1
PRITCHETT, Joseph Johnston 5
PRITCHETT, Lafayette Bow 4
PRITCHETT, Norton 4
PRITZKER, Donald Nicholas 5
PRIZER, Edward 1
PROBASCO, Henry 1
PROBASCO, Scott Livingston 4
PROBERT, Frank Holman 1
PROBERT, Lionel Charles 1
PROBST, Charles Oliver 1
PROBST, Marvin 5
PROBST, Nathan 5
PROCHNIK, Edgar Leo Gustav 4
PROCOPE, Hjalmar Johan Fredrik 3
PROCTER, Addison Gilbert 1
PROCTER, Arthur Wyman 4
PROCTER, William 3
PROCTER, William Cooper 1
PROCTOR, A. Phimister 3
PROCTOR, Bernard Emerson 3
PROCTOR, Carroll Leigh 5
PROCTOR, Edna Dean 1
PROCTOR, Fletcher Dutton 1
PROCTOR, Frederick Cocke 1
PROCTOR, Henry Hugh 1
PROCTOR, James McPherson 3
PROCTOR, John Robert 1
PROCTOR, John Thomas 1
PROCTOR, Joseph H
PROCTOR, Lucien Brock H
PROCTOR, Mortimer Robinson 5
PROCTOR, Redfield 1
PROCTOR, Redfield 3
PROCTOR, Robert 5
PROCTOR, Thomas Redfield 1
PROCTOR, Thomas William 1
PROCTOR, William H
PROCTOR, William Martin 1
PROFFIT, George H. H
PROFFITT, Edward J. W. 4
PROFFITT, Henry Walton 5
PROHASKA, John Van 5
PROKOFIEFF, Serge 3
PROKOSCH, Eduard 1
PROPER, Datus DeWitt 4
PROPER, Datus Edwin 4
PROPPER DE CALLEJON, Don Eduardo 5
PROSCHOWSKI, Frantz James Edward 4
PROSKAUER, Joseph M. 5
PROSSER, Charles Allen 5
PROSSER, Charles Smith 1
PROSSER, Paul Pittman 1
PROSSER, Seward 2
PROTHERO, James Harrison 1
PROTHEROE, Daniel 1
PROTTENGEIER, Conrad Gettfried 2
PROUD, Robert H
PROUDFIT, David Law H
PROUT, Frank J. 4
PROUT, G. R. 3
PROUT, Henry Goslee 5
PROUT, William Christopher 1
PROUTY, Charles Azro 1
PROUTY, George Herbert 1
PROUTY, Solomon Francis 4
PROUTY, Winston Lewis 5
PROVENCE, Herbert Winston 5
PROVENCE, Samuel Moore 4
PROVINE, John William 2
PROVINE, Robert Calhoun 4
PROVINSE, John H. 4
PROVOOST, Samuel H
PROVOST, Etienne H
PROVOSTY, Olivier O. 1
PROWELL, George R. 1
PROWSE, Robert John 5
PRUDDEN, Russell Field 5
PRUDDEN, T. Mitchell 1
PRUDEN, Oscar L. 1
PRUD'HOMME, John Francis Eugene H
PRUGH, Byron Edgar Peart 1
PRUITT, Raymond S. 3
PRUNTY, Merle Charles 5
PRUSSING, Eugene Ernst 1
PRUTTON, Carl Frederick 5
PRUYN, H. Sewall 5
PRUYN, John Van Schaick Lansing H
PRUYN, Robert Clarence 4
PRUYN, Robert Hewson H
PRYOR, Arthur 2
PRYOR, Edward Bailey 1
PRYOR, Ike T. 1
PRYOR, James Chambers 2
PRYOR, Nathaniel H
PRYOR, Ralph H(untington) 5
PRYOR, Roger Atkinson 1
PRYOR, Samuel F. 1
PRYOR, Sara Agnes 1
PRYOR, Thomas Brady 3
PRYOR, William Rice 1
PUBLICKER, Harry 3
PUCHNER, Irving A. 5
PUCKETT, Charles Alexander 5
PUCKETT, Erastus Paul 3
PUCKETT, Newbell Niles 4
PUCKETT, William Olin 5
PUCKETTE, Charles McDonald 3
PUCKNER, William August 1
PUDDEFOOT, William George 1
PUELICHER, Albert Siefert 4
PUELICHER, John Huegin 1
PUENTE, Giuseppe Del H
PUFFER, J. Adams 3
PUGET, Peter Richings H
PUGH, Arthur Benton 1
PUGH, Charles E. 1
PUGH, Ellis H
PUGH, Evan H
PUGH, George Bernard 1
PUGH, George Ellis H
PUGH, Griffith Thompson 5
PUGH, James Lawrence 1
PUGH, John H
PUGH, John Jones 2
PUGH, Robert Chalfant 1
PUGH, Samuel J. 4
PUGH, William Barrow 3
PUGH, William Leonard 5
PUGH, William Samuel 3
PUGMIRE, Ernest Ivison 3
PUGSLEY, Charles William 1
PUGSLEY, Cornelius Amory 1
PUJO, Arsene Paulin 1
PULASKI, Casimir H
PULIDO, Augusto F. 5
PULITZER, Albert 1
PULITZER, Joseph 1
PULITZER, Joseph 3
PULITZER, Ralph 1
PULITZER, Walter 1
PULLEN, Elisabeth 5

PULLEN, Herbert Armitage — 1
PULLEN, Roscoe LeRoy — 3
PULLER, Edwin Seward — 2
PULLEY, Frederick — 5
PULLIAM, Roscoe — 2
PULLIAM, William Ellis — 1
PULLING, Arthur Clement — 4
PULLMAN, George Mortimer — H
PULLMAN, James Minton — 1
PULLMAN, John — 5
PULLMAN, John Stephenson — 2
PULLY, Bernard Shaw — 5
PULSIFER, Harold Trowbridge — 2
PULSIFER, Harry Bridgman — 2
PULSIFER, Nathan Trowbridge — 1
PULSIFER, William E. — 1
PULTE, Joseph Hippolyt — H
PULTZ, Leon M(erle) — 5
PULVER, Arthur Wadworth — 1
PULVERMACHER, Joseph — 4
PUMPELLY, Josiah Collins — 1
PUMPELLY, Raphael — 1
PUNDERFORD, John Keeler — 1
PUPIN, Michael Idvorsky — 1
PURCE, Charles Lee — 1
PURCELL, Charles Henry — 3
PURCELL, Francis Andrew — 5
PURCELL, Ganson — 4
PURCELL, George William — 3
PURCELL, Henry — 1
PURCELL, John Baptist — H
PURCELL, Richard J. — 3
PURCELL, Theodore Vincent — 3
PURCELL, William — 1
PURCELL, William E. — 1
PURCELL, William Henry — 2
PURDON, Alexander — H
PURDON, Charles 'de 'la Cherois — 4
PURDUE, Albert Homer — 1
PURDUE, John — H
PURDUM, Smith White — 2
PURDY, Corydon Tyler — 2
PURDY, Edward A. — 1
PURDY, George Flint — 5
PURDY, Ken William — 1
PURDY, Lawson — 3
PURDY, Milton Dwight — 1
PURDY, Richard Augustus — 1
PURDY, Richard Townsend — 5
PURDY, Ross Coffin — 3
PURDY, Smith Meade — H
PURDY, Thomas C. — 4
PURDY, Victor William — 1
PURDY, Warren Grafton — 1
PURIN, Charles Maltador — 5
PURINGTON, Florence — 3
PURINGTON, George Colby — 1
PURINTON, Daniel Boardman — 1
PURINTON, Edward Earle — 1
PURINTON, Herbert Ronelle — 3
PURKISS, Albert C. — 5
PURMORT, Charles Hiram — 4
PURMORT, LaDoyt Gilman — 1
PURNELL, Benjamin — H
PURNELL, Benjamin — 4
PURNELL, Frank — 1
PURNELL, Fred Sampson — 1
PURNELL, Oscar M. — 4
PURNELL, Thomas Richard — 1
PURNELL, William C(hilds) — 5
PURNELL, William Henry — H
PURNELL, William Reynolds — 3
PURPLE, Samuel Smith — 1
PURRINGTON, William Archer — 1
PURRY, Jean Pierre — H
PURSH, Frederick — H
PURUCKER, Gottfried 'de — 2

PURVES, Clifford Burrough — 4
PURVES, Dale Benson — 4
PURVES, Edmund Randolph — 4
PURVES, George T. — 1
PURVIANCE, David — H
PURVIANCE, Samuel Anderson — H
PURVIANCE, Samuel Dinsmore — H
PURVIS, Charles B. — 4
PURVIS, William Edmond — 1
PURYEAR, Charles — 3
PURYEAR, Richard Clauselle — H
PUSEY, Brown — 3
PUSEY, Caleb — H
PUSEY, Edwin Davis — 5
PUSEY, William Allen — 1
PUSHMAN, Hovsep — 4
PUSHMATAHAW — H
PUTERBAUGH, Jay G. — 4
PUTERBAUGH, Leslie D. — 1
PUTHUFF, Hanson Duvall — H
PUTNAM, Albert William — 3
PUTNAM, Alfred Porter — 1
PUTNAM, Arthur — 1
PUTNAM, Claude Adams — 4
PUTNAM, Eben — 1
PUTNAM, Eben Fiske Appleton — 3
PUTNAM, Edward Kirby — 1
PUTNAM, Edwin — 1
PUTNAM, Emily James — 2
PUTNAM, Francis J. — 4
PUTNAM, Frederic Ward — 1
PUTNAM, George — 3
PUTNAM, George — 1
PUTNAM, George Ellsworth — 1
PUTNAM, George Haven — 1
PUTNAM, George Jacob — 4
PUTNAM, George Martin — 1
PUTNAM, George Palmer — H
PUTNAM, George Palmer — 2
PUTNAM, George Rockwell — 1
PUTNAM, Gideon — H
PUTNAM, H. St Clair — 1
PUTNAM, Harrington — 1
PUTNAM, Harvey — H
PUTNAM, Helen Cordelia — 1
PUTNAM, Herbert — 3
PUTNAM, Israel — H
PUTNAM, James Jackson — 1
PUTNAM, James Osborne — 1
PUTNAM, James William — 1
PUTNAM, James Wright — 1
PUTNAM, John Bishop — 1
PUTNAM, John Pickering — 1
PUTNAM, John Risley — 2
PUTNAM, Mark Edson — 1
PUTNAM, Nina Wilcox — 4
PUTNAM, Rufus — H
PUTNAM, Russell Benjamin — 3
PUTNAM, Ruth — 1
PUTNAM, Stephen Greeley — 4
PUTNAM, Thomas Milton — 2
PUTNAM, Warren Edward — 1
PUTNAM, Warren Edward — 2
PUTNAM, William Hutchinson — 3
PUTNAM, William Le Baron — 1
PUTNAM, William Lowell — 1
PUTNAM, William Rowell — 3
PUTNEY, Albert Hutchinson
PUTNEY, Elmore M. — 3
PUZINAS, Paul Peter — 5
PYEATT, John Samuel — 1
PYKE, W. E. — 4
PYLE, Ernest Taylor — 2
PYLE, Helen Mary — 5
PYLE, Howard — 1
PYLE, John Sherman — 4
PYLE, Joseph Gilpin — 1
PYLE, Katharine — 1
PYLE, Robert — 3
PYLE, Walter Lytle — 1
PYLE, William H. — 2
PYNCHON, John — 1
PYNCHON, Thomas Ruggles
PYNCHON, William — H
PYNE, Frederick Glover — 4
PYNE, George Rovillo — 2
PYNE, M. Taylor — 1
PYNE, Percy Rivington II
PYNE, Percy Rivington II — 3

PYRE, George John — 5
PYRE, James Francis Augustin
PYRKE, Berne Ashley — 4
PYRON, Walter Braxton — 3
PYRTLE, E. Ruth — 5
PYUN, Yung-tai — 5

Q

QASSIM, Abdul Karim — 4
QUACKENBOS, John Duncan — 1
QUACKENBOSS, Alexander — 4
QUACKENBUSH, Larry — 4
QUACKENBUSH, Stephen Platt — H
QUADE, Maurice Northrop — 4
QUADE, Omar H. — 4
QUAIFE, Milo Milton — 3
QUAIL, Frank Adgate — 1
QUAILE, George Emerson — 1
QUAIN, Eric P. — 5
QUAINTANCE, Altus Lacy — 5
QUALTROUGH, Edward Francis — 1
QUANAH — H
QUANAH — 4
QUANTRELL, Ernest E. — 4
QUANTRILL, William Clarke — H
QUARLES, Charles — 1
QUARLES, Charles Bullen — 5
QUARLES, Donald A. — 3
QUARLES, Edwin Latham — 1
QUARLES, James — 3
QUARLES, James Addison — 1
QUARLES, James Thomas — 5
QUARLES, Joseph Very — 1
QUARLES, Joseph Very III — 2
QUARLES, Louis — 5
QUARLES, Ralph P. — 1
QUARLES, Tunstall — H
QUARLES, William Charles — 1
QUARTER, William — H
QUARTLEY, Arthur — H
QUASIMODO, Salvatore — 5
QUATTROCCHI, Edmondo — 4
QUAY, Arthur Hayes — 3
QUAY, Matthew Stanley — 1
QUAYLE, Henry Joseph — 5
QUAYLE, John Francis — 1
QUAYLE, John Harrison — 2
QUAYLE, Oliver A. Jr. — 1
QUAYLE, Osborne R. — 3
QUAYLE, William Alfred — 1
QUEALY, Patrick J. — 1
QUEALY, Susan Jane — 3
QUEEN, Walter — H
QUEENY, Edgar Monsanto — 1
QUEENY, John Francis — 5
QUELCH, John — H
QUERBES, Andrew — 1
QUEREAU, Edmund Chase
QUERY, Walter Graham — 5
QUESADA, Manuel Castro — 5
QUESNAY, Alexandre-Marie — H
QUESTA, Edward J. — 4
QUEZON 'Y MOLINA, Manuel Luis — 2
QUIAT, Ira L(ouis) — 1
QUICK, George W. — 4
QUICK, Herbert — 1
QUICK, Walter — 4
QUIDOR, John — H
QUIGG, James F. — 4
QUIGG, Lemuel E. — 4
QUIGGLE, Edmund Blanchard — 1
QUIGLEY, Harry Nelson — 1
QUIGLEY, James Cloyd — 3
QUIGLEY, James Edward — 1
QUIGLEY, John Paul — 4
QUIGLEY, Martin Joseph — 4
QUIGLEY, Samuel — 3
QUIGLEY, William Middleton — 3
QUILICI, George L. — 5
QUILL, Michael J. — 4
QUILLEN, I. James — 4
QUILLEN, Robert — 2
QUILLER-COUCH, Arthur Thomas — 1
QUILLIAN, Paul Whitfield — 2

QUIMBY, Frank) Brooks — 5
QUIMBY, Charles Elihu — 1
QUIMBY, Harriet — 1
QUIMBY, Neal Frederic — 4
QUIMBY, Phineas Parkhurst
QUIN, Charles Kennon — 5
QUIN, Clinton Simon — 3
QUIN, Huston — 1
QUIN, Percy Edwards — 1
QUINAN, John Russell — H
QUINBY, Frank Haviland — 1
QUINBY, Henry Brewer — 1
QUINBY, Isaac Ferdinand — H
QUINBY, William Carter — 5
QUINBY, William Emory — 1
QUINCEY, Josiah — H
QUINCY, Charles Frederick
QUINCY, Edmund — H
QUINCY, Josiah — H
QUINCY, Josiah — 1
QUINCY, Josiah Phillips
QUINE, William E. — 1
QUINLAN, John — H
QUINLAN, Joseph A. — 1
QUINLIVAN, Ray James — 4
QUINN, Arthur Hobson — 1
QUINN, Charles Henry — 5
QUINN, Daniel Hellenist — 1
QUINN, Daniel Joseph — 1
QUINN, Edmond — 1
QUINN, James Baird — 1
QUINN, James H. — 1
QUINN, James Leland — 1
QUINN, John — 1
QUINN, John Francis — 5
QUINN, John Joseph — 2
QUINN, Patrick Henry — 3
QUINN, Ralph Hughes — 1
QUINN, Terence John — 1
QUINN, Theodore Kinget — 4
QUINN, Thomas Charles — 4
QUINT, Wilder Dwight — 1
QUINTARD, Charles Todd — H
QUINTARD, Edward — 1
QUINTARD, George William — 1
QUINTERO, Lamar Charles
QUINTON, Cornelia Bentley Sage
QUINTON, Harold — 5
QUINTON, John Henry — 1
QUINTON, William — 1
QUIRINO, Elpidio — 3
QUIRK, James Robert — 1
QUIRK, James Thomas — 5
QUIRK, John F. — 4
QUIRKE, Terence Thomas — 1
QUISENBERRY, Anderson Chenault — 1
QUISENBERRY, Hiter Nelson
QUISENBERRY, Russell A. — 4
QUITMAN, John Anthony — H
QUONIAM 'DE SCHOMPRE, Guy Emile Marie Joseph — 3
QUYNN, Allen George — 5

R

RAAB, Julius — 4
RAAB, Wilhelm — 5
RAABE, Arthur Edward — 4
RABAUT, Louis Charles — 4
RABB, Kate Milner — 1
RABEL, Ernst — 5
RABENORT, William Louis — 1
RABER, Oran Lee — 1
RABIN, Michael — 5
RABINOFF, Max — 4
RABINOVITZ, Joseph — 4
RABOCH, Wenzel Albert — 2
RABOCH, Wenzel Albert — 2
RABY, James Joseph — 4
RACCA, Vittorio — 4
RACE, John H. — 1
RACHFORD, Benjamin Knox
RACHMANINOFF, Sergei
RACHMIEL, Jean — 5
RACKEMANN, Francis Minot
RACKLEY, John Ralph — 5
RADBILL, Samuel — 1
RADCLIFF, Jacob — H
RADCLIFFE, Amos H. — 3

RADCLIFFE, Harry Southwell — 4
RADCLIFFE, Wallace — 1
RADEMACHER, Hans — 5
RADEMACHER, Joseph — 1
RADER, Paul — 1
RADER, Perry Scott — 4
RADER, Robert Fort — 4
RADER, William — 1
RADFORD, Benjamin Johnson — 1
RADFORD, Cyrus S. — 3
RADFORD, Robert Somerville — 1
RADFORD, William * — H
RADFORD, William A. — 4
RADFORD, William H. — 4
RADIN, Edward David — 4
RADIN, Max — 3
RADIN, Paul — 3
RADINSKY, Ellis — 3
RADISSON, Pierre Esprit — H
RADNER, William — 3
RADO, Sandor — 5
RADO, Tibor — 4
RADOSAVLJEVICH-, Paul Rankov — 1
RADWAN, Edmund P. — 4
RAE, Bruce — 1
RAE, Charles Whiteside — 1
RAE, John — H
RAE, John — 4
RAE, William McLane — 4
RAEGENER, Louis Christian — 1
RAEMAEKERS, Louis — 3
RAEMER, Clifford M. — 5
RAFF, Richard Davis — 1
RAFFEINER, John Stephen — H
RAFFERTY, James A. — 3
RAFFERTY, William Carroll — 1
RAFFETY, W. Edward — 1
RAFINESQUE, Constantine Samuel — H
RAFTERY, John Henry — 4
RAFTERY, Oliver Tenry — 1
RAGAN, Frank Xavier — 5
RAGEN, Joseph Edward — 5
RAGIR, Benjamin A. — 3
RAGLAND, George — 3
RAGLAND, Samuel Evan — 3
RAGLAND, William T. — 5
RAGO, Henry Anthony — 5
RAGON, Heartsill — 1
RAGOZIN, Zenaide Alexeievna — 5
RAGSDALE, Bartow Davis — 2
RAGSDALE, Edward Tillottson — 5
RAGSDALE, J. Willard — 1
RAGSDALE, James W. — 4
RAGSDALE, Tallulah — 3
RAGSDALE, Van Hubert — 3
RAGUET, Condy — H
RAHMAN, Abdul — 1
RAHMAN, Tunku Abdul — 3
RAHMN, Elza Lothner — 5
RAHN, Otto — 2
RAIBLE, John R. — 2
RAIFORD, Lemuel Charles — 2
RAILEY, Fleming G. — 4
RAILEY, Thomas Tarlton — 1
RAINE, James Watt — 2
RAINE, William MacLeod — 1
RAINER, Joseph — 4
RAINES, George Neely — 3
RAINES, John — 1
RAINES, John Marlin — 5
RAINEY, Anson — 1
RAINEY, Henry Thomas — 1
RAINEY, John W. — 1
RAINEY, Joseph Hayne — H
RAINEY, Lilius Bratton — 5
RAINEY, Ma — 4
RAINEY, Ma — 4
RAINS, Claude — 4
RAINS, Gabriel James — H
RAINS, George Washington
RAINS, Leon — 3
RAINSFORD, William Stephen — 1
RAINWATER, Clarence Elmer — 1
RAIRDEN, Bradstreet Stinson — 2
RAISA, Rosa — 4
RAITT, Effie Isabel — 2
RAIZEN, Chales Sanford — 4
RAJAGOPALACHAR-YA, Chakravarti — 5
RAK, Mary Kidder — 3

RAVENEL, Mazyck Porcher 2
RAVENEL, St Julien H
RAVENEL, William 'de Chastignier 4
RAVENSCROFT, Edward Hawks 3
RAVENSCROFT, John Stark H
RAVLIN, Grace 3
RAVNDAL, Gabriel Bie 2
RAVOGLI, Augustus 4
RAWIDOWICZ, Simon 3
RAWL, Bernard Hazelius 1
RAWLE, Francis H
RAWLE, Francis 1
RAWLE, James 1
RAWLE, William H
RAWLE, William Henry 1
RAWLEIGH, William Thomas 5
RAWLES, Jacob Beekman 1
RAWLES, William A. 1
RAWLEY, Joseph Pearson 1
RAWLINGS, Eugene Hubbard 1
RAWLINGS, Majorie Kinnan 3
RAWLINGS, Norborne L. 5
RAWLINS, George Herndon 4
RAWLINS, John Aaron H
RAWLINS, Joseph Lafayette 1
RAWLINS, William Thomas 1
RAWLINSON, Frank Joseph 1
RAWN, Ira Griffith 1
RAWSON, Albert Leighton 1
RAWSON, Carl Wendell 5
RAWSON, Charles A. 4
RAWSON, Edward Kirk 4
RAWSON, Frederick Holbrook 1
RAY, Anna Chapin 2
RAY, Arthur Benning 3
RAY, Charles Andrew 1
RAY, Charles Bennett H
RAY, Charles Henry H
RAY, Charles Wayne 1
RAY, David Heydorn 4
RAY, E. Lansing 3
RAY, Edward Chittenden 4
RAY, Franklin Arnold 1
RAY, Frederick Augustus, Jr. 5
RAY, G. J. 1
RAY, George Washington 1
RAY, Guy W. 5
RAY, Herbert James 5
RAY, Isaac H
RAY, Jefferson Davis 1
RAY, John Edwin 1
RAY, Joseph H
RAY, Joseph R. Sr. 4
RAY, Louise Crenshaw 3
RAY, Marle Beynon 1
RAY, Milton S. 2
RAY, Ossian 1
RAY, P. Henry 1
RAY, P(erley) Orman 5
RAY, Philip Alexander 5
RAY, Randolph 5
RAY, S(ilvey) J(ackson) 5
RAY, T. Bronson * 1
RAY, William Henry H
RAYBOLD, Walter James 1
RAYBURN, Sam 4
RAYCORFT, Joseph Edward 3
RAYMER, Albert Reesor 1
RAYMOND, Alexander Gillespie 3
RAYMOND, Andrew Van Vranken 1
RAYMOND, Anna Almy 1
RAYMOND, Benjamin Wright H
RAYMOND, Bradford Paul 1
RAYMOND, C. Rexford 1
RAYMOND, Charles Beebe 1
RAYMOND, Charles Walker 2
RAYMOND, Clifford Samuel 3
RAYMOND, Daniel H
RAYMOND, Donat 4
RAYMOND, Dora Neill Mrs. 1
RAYMOND, Evelyn Hunt 1
RAYMOND, Fred Morton 2

RAYMOND, Frederick Wingate 5
RAYMOND, George Lansing 1
RAYMOND, Harry Howard 1
RAYMOND, Henry Ingle 4
RAYMOND, Henry Jarvis H
RAYMOND, Henry Warren 1
RAYMOND, Howard Monre 2
RAYMOND, Jerome Hall 1
RAYMOND, John Baldwin H
RAYMOND, John Howard H
RAYMOND, John T. 1
RAYMOND, Jonathan Stone 4
RAYMOND, Joseph Howard 1
RAYMOND, Josephine Hunt (Mrs. Jerome Hall Raymond) 5
RAYMOND, Mary Elizabeth 3
RAYMOND, Maud Mary Wotring 4
RAYMOND, Miner H
RAYMOND, Nell C. 4
RAYMOND, Robert Fulton 1
RAYMOND, Rossiter Worthington 1
RAYMOND, Thomas Lynch 1
RAYMOND, William Galt 1
RAYMOND, William Lee 2
RAYNER, Emma 1
RAYNER, Isidor 1
RAYNER, Kenneth H
RAYNOLDS, Herbert F. 5
RAYNOLDS, Joshua Saxton 1
RAYNOLDS, Robert 4
RAYNOR, Hayden 4
RAZMARA, Ali 3
REA, Gardner 4
REA, George Bronson 1
REA, Mrs. Henry R. 5
REA, John H
REA, John Andrew 1
REA, John Dougan 1
REA, John Patterson 1
REA, Paul Marshall 2
REA, Robert 1
REA, Samuel 1
READ, Albert Cushing 1
READ, Almon Heath H
READ, Benjamin Stalker 1
READ, Cecil Byron H
READ, Charles H
READ, Charles Francis 2
READ, Charles O. 1
READ, Charles William 1
READ, Conyers 3
READ, Daniel * H
READ, George H
READ, George Campbell H
READ, George Windle H
READ, Granville M. 4
READ, Harlan Eugene 4
READ, Harold D. 2
READ, Herbert 5
READ, Jacob H
READ, John * H
READ, John Elliot 1
READ, John Joseph 1
READ, John Meredith * H
READ, Maurice Gallison 4
READ, Melbourne Stuart 1
READ, Nathan 4
READ, Oliver Middleton 5
READ, Opie 1
READ, Thomas H
READ, Thomas 4
READ, Thomas Albert H
READ, Thomas Buchanan H
READ, Thomas Thornton 2
READ, William Augustus H
READ, William Brown 1
READ, William Lewis 1
READ, William Thackara 3
READE, Edwin Godwin 1
READE, John Moore 1
READE, Philip 1
READER, Francis Smith 4
READING, Earl 'of H
READING, John Roberts H
READING, Richard William 3
READIO, Wilfred Allen 4
READY, Charles H
READY, Frank A. 4
READY, Joseph Louis 3
READY, Lester Seward 2

READY, Michael Joseph 3
REAGAN, Frank J. 3
REAGAN, John Henninger 1
REAGAN, Lewis M. 4
REALF, Richard H
REALS, Willis H(oward) 5
REALS, Willis H. 1
REAM, Norman Bruce 1
REAMES, Alfred Evan 2
REAMS, Frazier 5
REAMY, Thaddeus Asbury 1
REANEY, George Humes 2
REARICK, Allan Chamberlain 1
REASER, Matthew Howell 4
REASER, Wilbur Aaron 1
REATH, Theodore Wood 4
REAVES, Samuel Watson 4
REAVIS, Charles Frank 1
REAVIS, James Bradly 1
REAVIS, James Overton 5
REAVIS, William Claude 3
REAVLEY, Lester S. 4
REBASZ, Eurith Trabue Pattison 4
REBEC, George 2
REBER, John 3
REBER, John U. 3
REBER, Louis Ehrhart 1
REBER, Samuel 1
REBER, Samuel 5
REBERT, Gordon Nevin 4
REBORI, Andrew Nicholas 4
REBSCHER, J. M. 4
RECCORD, Augustus Phineas 2
RECHT, Charles 4
RECK, Franklin Mering 4
RECKLING, William Joseph 4
RECKMEYER, Luella 4
RECKNAGEL, Arthur Bernard 4
RECORD, James Lucius 2
RECORD, Samuel James 2
RECORDS, Edward 4
RECORDS, Ralph LaFayette 1
RECTOR, Edward 1
RECTOR, Elbridge Lee 1
RECTOR, Frank 1
RECTOR, Henry Massey H
RECTOR, John B. 4
RECTOR, Lizzie E. 3
RECTOR, Thomas M. 3
RECTOR, Walter Whiting 1
RED CLOUD H
RED CLOUD 4
REDDALL, Frederic 4
REDDICK, Donald 3
REDDING, Charles Summerfield 1
REDDING, John Mac Lean 4
REDDING, Joseph Deighn 1
REDDING, Leo L. 1
REDDING, Otis 1
REDDING, Robert Jordan 1
REDDISH, George Fults 4
REDE, Wyllys 4
RED EAGLE H
REDEKE, Ernest William 4
REDER, Bernard 4
REDFEARN, Daniel Huntley 4
REDFERN, Donald Verne 4
REDFERN, Merrill F. 3
REDFIELD, Amasa Angell 1
REDFIELD, Casper Lavater 2
REDFIELD, Edward Willis 4
REDFIELD, Henry Stephen 1
REDFIELD, Isaac Fletcher H
REDFIELD, Justus Starr H
REDFIELD, Robert 3
REDFIELD, William C. H
REDFIELD, William C. 1
REDHEAD, Edwin Richard 1
REDIGER, Michel Jon 5
REDING, John Randall 1
REDINGTON, Paul Goodwin 1
REDINGTON, Paul Goodwin 2
RED JACKET H
REDMAN, Ben Ray 4
REDMAN, Harry Newton 5
REDMAN, John H

REDMAN, Joseph Reasor 5
REDMAN, Lawrence V. 2
REDMOND, Daniel George 3
REDMOND, Daniel Walter 1
REDMOND, Granville 1
REDPATH, James H
REDSTONE, Edward H. 3
REDWAY, Jacques Wardlaw 2
RED WING H
REDWOOD, Abraham H
REEB, James Joseph 4
REECE, B. Carroll 4
REECE, Mrs. Carroll (louise Goff) 5
REECE, Richard H. 3
REED, A. F. 4
REED, Albert Augustus 5
REED, Albert Granberry 1
REED, Alfred 1
REED, Alfred Zantzinger 4
REED, Allen Visscher 1
REED, Amy Louise 2
REED, Anna Yeomans (Mrs. Joseph Ambrose Reed) 5
REED, Boardman 1
REED, Carroll Roscoe 3
REED, Cass Arthur 3
REED, Charles Alfred Lee 1
REED, Charles Bert 1
REED, Charles Dana 2
REED, Charles John 4
REED, Charles Manning H
REED, Chauncey William 3
REED, Chester Allyn 4
REED, Clare Osborne (Mrs. Charles B. Reed) 5
REED, Clyde Martin 2
REED, Daniel Alden 3
REED, David H
REED, David Aiken 3
REED, Donald Ross 5
REED, Earl F. 4
REED, Earl Howell 1
REED, Earl Howell 1
REED, Edward Bliss 1
REED, Edward Cambridge H
REED, Edwin 1
REED, Edwin Clarence 5
REED, Elizabeth Armstrong 1
REED, Elmer Ellsworth 1
REED, Florence 4
REED, Frank Fremont 1
REED, Frank Hynes 3
REED, Frank LeFevre 1
REED, Frank Otis 1
REED, Franklin Hancock 4
REED, George Edward 1
REED, George Letchworth 5
REED, George William 3
REED, Guy Euclid 1
REED, Harlow John 5
REED, Harry Bertram 1
REED, Harry E. 4
REED, Harry James 1
REED, Harry Lathrop 5
REED, Helen Leah 1
REED, Henry Albert 1
REED, Henry Clay 1
REED, Henry Hope H
REED, Henry Morrison 1
REED, Henry Thomas 1
REED, Herbert 5
REED, Horace 1
REED, Howard Sprague 3
REED, Hugh Daniel 1
REED, Isaac H
REED, Ivy Kellerman,* 5
REED, James H
REED, James 4
REED, James A. 2
REED, James Byron 5
REED, James Calvin 1
REED, James Hay 1
REED, John * H
REED, John 1
REED, John 4
REED, John Alton 1
REED, John C. 2
REED, John Calvin 3
REED, John Oren 1
REED, Joseph H
REED, Joseph Rea 1
REED, Lowell Jacob 1
REED, Luman H
REED, Luther Dotterer 5
REED, Martin M. Jr. 1

REED, Mary Dean (Mrs. Verner Z. Reed) 5
REED, Mary Williams (Kate Carew) 5
REED, Milton 1
REED, Perley Isaac 5
REED, Philip H
REED, Philip Loring 4
REED, Ralph John 1
REED, Ralph Thomas 4
REED, Richard Clark 1
REED, Richard Forman 1
REED, Robert Bowman 2
REED, Robert Cameron 1
REED, Robert Rentoul H
REED, Robert Rentoul 2
REED, Rodman Smith Jr. 4
REED, Roland 1
REED, Sampson H
REED, Sarah A. 1
REED, Simeon Gannett H
REED, Stuart F. 1
REED, Stuart R. 4
REED, Sylvanus Albert 1
REED, Thomas Brackett 1
REED, Thomas Buck H
REED, Thomas Harrison 5
REED, Thomas Milburne 1
REED, Verner Zevola 1
REED, Victor Joseph 5
REED, Walter H
REED, Walter Lawrence 3
REED, Warren Augustus 1
REED, Washington 3
REED, Willard 2
REED, William H
REED, William Bradford H
REED, William Hale 3
REED, William M. 3
REED, William Reynolds 5
REED, William Thomas Jr. 5
REEDER, Andrew Horatio H
REEDER, Charles L. 4
REEDER, Charles Leonard 5
REEDER, Edwin Hewett 1
REEDER, Edwin Thorley 4
REEDER, Frank 1
REEDER, Glezen Asbury, Jr. 1
REEDER, Grace Amelia 1
REEDER, Ward Glen 4
REEDER, William Augustus 1
REEDER, William Herron 1
REEDY, J. Martin 3
REEDY, Rose Stroman (Mrs. F. C. Reedy) 5
REEDY, William Marion 1
REEMAN, Edmund Henry 3
REEP, Samuel Austen 5
REES, Albert William 1
REES, Alfred Cornelius 1
REES, Byron Johnson 1
REES, Corwin Pottenger 1
REES, Edward H. 5
REES, George E. 4
REES, James H
REES, John Krom 1
REES, Maurice Holmes 2
REES, Robert Irwin 4
REES, Rollin R. 1
REES, Thomas 1
REES, Thomas Henry 2
REES, William Henry 1
REESE, Albert Moore 4
REESE, Charles H. 5
REESE, Charles Lee 1
REESE, Curtis Williford 4
REESE, Dale F. 3
REESE, David Addison H
REESE, Frederick Focke 1
REESE, George Lee 5
REESE, Gilbert A. 1
REESE, Herbert Meredith 3
REESE, J. Allen 4
REESE, John James H
REESE, Joseph Hammond 5
REESE, Lizette Woodworth 1
REESE, Lizette Woodworth 2
REESE, Lowell Otus 3
REESE, Manoah Bostic 1
REESE, Millard 5
REESE, Scott Charles 5
REESE, T. T. 1
REESE, Theodore Irving 1
REESE, Wilbur Ford 5
REESER, Edwin B. 5
REESIDE, John Bernard Jr. 3

REESMAN, Budd Aaron 5
REEVE, Arthur Benjamin 1
REEVE, Charles McCormick 4
REEVE, Felix Alexander 1
REEVE, James Knapp 1
REEVE, Sidney Armor 1
REEVE, Tapping H
REEVE, William David 5
REEVE, William Foster, III 5
REEVES, Alec Harley 5
REEVES, Alfred Gandy 5
REEVES, Archie R. 5
REEVES, Arthur Middleton H
REEVES, Charles Francis 4
REEVES, Daniel F. 5
REEVES, Francis Brewster 1
REEVES, Frank Daniel 5
REEVES, George Curtis 5
REEVES, Herbert James 4
REEVES, Ira Louis 1
REEVES, Isaac Stockton Keith 1
REEVES, James Aloysius Wallace 2
REEVES, James Haynes 5
REEVES, Jeremiah Bascom 2
REEVES, Jesse Siddall 2
REEVES, John Dudley Jr. 4
REEVES, John Richard Thomas, Jr. 5
REEVES, John Ruel 3
REEVES, John Walter Jr. 4
REEVES, Joseph Mason 2
REEVES, Owen Thornton 2
REEVES, Perry Willard 2
REEVES, Robert James 4
REEVES, Ruth 3
REEVES, Thomas Rosser 1
REEVES, Walter 3
REEVES, Walter Perkins 5
REEVES, William Peters 5
REEVES, Winona Evans 5
REGAN, Ben
REGAN, Frank Stewart 2
REGAN, Frank W. 4
REGAN, James L. 1
REGAN, Louis John 3
REGAR, Robert Smith 3
REGENSBURGER, Richard William 3
REGER, David Bright 3
REGISTER, Edward Chauncey 1
REGISTER, Francis Henry 1
REGISTER, George Scott 5
REGISTER, Henry Bartol 4
REHAN, Ada 1
REHDER, Alfred
REHERD, Herbert Ware 3
REHN, Frank Knox Morton 1
REHSE, George Washington 4
REICH, Jacques 1
REICH, Johann Mathias H
REICH, Max Isaac 2
REICHARD, Gladys Amanda 3
REICHARD, John Davis
REICHEL, Charles Gotthold H
REICHEL, Frank Hartranft 4
REICHEL, William Cornelius H
REICHELDERFER, Luther Halsey
REICHERT, Edward Tyson 1
REICHERT, Irving Frederick 4
REICHERT, Mother Thomas 5
REICHERT, Rudolph Edward 4
REICHMANN, Carl 4
REICHMANN, Donald August 5
REICK, William Charles 1
REID, Albert Turner
REID, Alberta Bancroft (Mrs.) 5
REID, Charles Chester 4
REID, Charles Simpson 2
REID, Charles Wesley
REID, Daniel Gray 1
REID, David Boswell H
REID, David Settle H

REID, deLafayette 5
REID, E. C. 3
REID, Elliott Gray 5
REID, Ernest W. 4
REID, Fergus 2
REID, Frank R. 2
REID, Frederick Horman 2
REID, George Croghan 1
REID, George T. 5
REID, Gilbert 1
REID, Harry Fielding 2
REID, Helen Dwight 4
REID, Helen Rogers (Mrs. Ogden Mills Reid) 5
REID, Henry John Edward 5
REID, Ira De Augustine 5
REID, James L. H
REID, James L. 1
REID, James Randolph H
REID, John Morrison 4
REID, John Simpson 4
REID, John William H
REID, Kenneth 3
REID, Kenneth Alexander 3
REID, Loudon Corsan 5
REID, Mont Rogers 2
REID, O. L. 5
REID, Ogden Mills 2
REID, Philip Joseph 5
REID, Richard 4
REID, Robert 1
REID, Robert Haley 5
REID, Robert Raymond H
REID, Samuel Chester H
REID, Silas Hinkle 3
REID, Sydney 4
REID, T. Roy 5
REID, Thomas Mayne H
REID, Thorburn 3
REID, W. Max 1
REID, Walter Williamson
REID, Whitelaw 1
REID, Will J. 3
REID, William 4
REID, William Alfred 5
REID, William Clifford 2
REID, William Duncan 2
REID, William James 1
REID, William James Jr. 2
REID, William R. 3
REID, William Shields H
REID, William Thomas 4
REIDY, Daniel Joseph 4
REIDY, Peter J. 5
REIF, Edward C. 4
REIF, Herbert R. 5
REIFF, Cecil K. 4
REIFF, Evan Allard 4
REIFFEL, Charles 2
REIFSNIDER, Charles Shriver 3
REIFSNIDER, Lawrence Fairfax 3
REIGER, Siegfried Heinrich
REIGHARD, Jacob 2
REIK, Henry Ottridge 1
REIK, Theodor 5
REILAND, Karl 5
REILLEY, Mrs. J. Eugene 1
REILLY, Frank Joseph 4
REILLY, Frank Kennicott
REILLY, Henry Joseph 4
REILLY, James Aloysius 3
REILLY, James William 1
REILLY, John David 5
REILLY, John Liguori 2
REILLY, Joseph John 3
REILLY, Maurice T. 4
REILLY, Michael Kiernan
REILLY, Peter C. 3
REILLY, Thomas Lawrence
REILLY, Walter B. 4
REILLY, William John 5
REILLY, Wilson H
REILY, E. Mont 3
REILY, George W. 3
REILY, Luther H
REIMANN, Stanley P. 5
REIMER, Marie 4
REIMERS, Frederick W. 3
REIMERT, William Daniel 5
REIMOLD, Orlando Schairer 4
REINAGLE, Alexander H
REINDAHL, Knute 1
REINER, Fritz 4

REINER, Joseph 1
REINHARD, Adolph Earl 5
REINHARD, L. Andrew 4
REINHARDT, Ad 4
REINHARDT, Aurelia Henry 4
REINHARDT, Charles William 4
REINHARDT, Django 5
REINHARDT, Emil Fred 5
REINHARDT, G(eorge) Frederick
REINHARDT, George Frederick 5
REINHARDT, Guenther 5
REINHARDT, Max 2
REINHARDT, Ralph Homer 5
REINHART, Benjamin Franklin H
REINHART, Charles Stanley H
REINHART, Earl F. 3
REINHART, Joseph W. 1
REINHAUS, Stanley Marx 5
REINHEIMER, Bartel Hilen 2
REINHOLD, Eli Spayd 4
REINHOLD, James P. 4
REINHOLDT, Julius William 1
REINHOLDT, Julius William 4
REINICKE, Frederick George 5
REINKE, Edwin Eustace 2
REINKING, Otto August 4
REINSCH, Paul Samuel H
REIRSEN, Johan Reinhart
REIS, Arthur M. 2
REISER, Armand Edouard 5
REISINGER, Curt H. 4
REISINGER, Harold Carusi 2
REISINGER, Hugo 1
REISMAN, Morton 1
REISNER, Christian Fichthorne 1
REISNER, Edward Hartman 3
REISNER, George Andrew 2
REISS, Jacob L. 3
REISSNER, Albert 5
REIST, Henry Gerber 2
REITER, Bernard L. 2
REITER, George Cook 1
REITH, Francis C. 4
REITZ, Walter R. 4
REITZEL, Albert Emmet 4
REITZEL, Marques E. 4
REITZEL, Robert H
RELFE, James Hugh 4
RELLER, Charles J. 4
RELLSTAB, John 1
RELYEA, Charles M. 1
REMAK, Gustavus Jr. 2
REMANN, Frederick H
REMARQUE, Erich Maria 5
REMBAUGH, Bertha 4
REMBERT, Arthur Gaillard 1
REMENSNYDER, Junius Benjamin 1
REMENYI, Joseph 3
REMER, Charles Frederick 5
REMER, Helen 1
REMEY, George Collier 1
REMICK, Grace May 5
REMICK, J. Gould 4
REMICK, James Waldron 2
REMINGTON, Eliphalet H
REMINGTON, Franklin 3
REMINGTON, Frederic 1
REMINGTON, Harold 1
REMINGTON, Harvey Foote 2
REMINGTON, Joseph Price 1
REMINGTON, Philo H
REMINGTON, Preston 3
REMINGTON, William Procter 4
REMLEY, Milton 1
REMMEL, Arthur Kizer 5
REMMEL, Ellen Cates 4
REMMEL, Harmon Liveright 1
REMMEL, Valentine 4
REMON CANTERA, Jose Antonio 3
REMOND, Charles Lenox H
REMONDINO, Peter Charles 1

REMSBURG, John Eleazer 1
REMSEN, Daniel Smith 1
REMSEN, Ira 1
REMSTER, Charles 1
REMY, Alfred 1
REMY, Charles Frederick 5
REMY, Henri H
RENAUD, Ralph Edward 5
RENCHER, Abraham H
REND, William Patrick 1
RENDALL, John Ballard 1
RENFROW, William Cary 1
RENICK, Felix 1
RENIER, Joseph Emile 4
RENISON, Robert John 4
RENNEBOHM, Oscar 5
RENNER, George Thomas Jr. 3
RENNER, Karl 3
RENNER, Otto 4
RENNERT, Hugo Albert 1
RENNIE, Joseph 2
RENNIE, Sylvester Wilding 5
RENNIE, Thomas A. C. 3
RENO, Claude Trexler 4
RENO, Conrad 1
RENO, Doris Smith (Mrs. Paul Halvor Reno) 5
RENO, Guy Benjamin 5
RENO, Itti Kinney 4
RENO, Jesse Lee H
RENO, Jesse Wilford 4
RENOUF, Edward 1
RENSHAW, Alfred Howard 1
RENSHAW, Raemer Rex 1
RENTSCHLER, Frederick B. 3
RENTSCHLER, George Adam 5
RENTSCHLER, Gordon S. 2
RENTSCHLER, Harvey Clayton 2
RENWICK, Edward Sabine 1
RENWICK, Henry Brevoort H
RENWICK, James * H
RENWICK, William Whetten 1
RENYX, Guy Worden 3
REPASS, Joseph Wharton 1
REPASS, William Carlyle 2
REPLOGLE, Jacob Leonard 2
REPPLIER, Agnes 3
REPPY, Alison 3
REPPY, Roy Valentine 5
REQUA, Earl Francis 5
REQUA, Mark Lawrence 1
REQUIER, Augustus Julian H
RESE, Frederick H
RESNICK, Joseph Yale 5
RESOR, Stanley 4
RESSLER, Edwin DeVore 1
RESTARICK, Henry Bond 1
RETHERS, Harry Frederick 1
RETTGER, Leo Frederick 5
RETTIG, H. Earl 5
REU, Johann Michael 2
REUBEN, Odell Richardson 5
REUBEN, Robert Ervin 4
REULING, George 1
REUTER, Edward Byron 2
REUTER, Irving Jacob 5
REUTER, Rudolph Ernst 5
REUTERDAHL, Arvid 1
REUTERDAHL, Henry 1
REUTHER, Walter Philip 5
REUTLINGER, Harry F. 4
REVEL, Bernard 1
REVELL, Alexander Hamilton 1
REVELL, Fleming H, Jr. 5
REVELL, Fleming Hewitt 1
REVELLE, Thomas P. 1
REVELS, Hiram Rhoades H
REVERE, Clinton T. 4
REVERE, Edward H. R. 3
REVERE, Joseph Warren H
REVERE, Paul H
REVERMAN, Theodore Henry 1
REVILL, Milton Kirtley 3
REW, Irwin 1
REXDALE, Robert 1
REXFORD, Eben Eugene 1

REXFORD, Frank A. 1
REY, Anthony H
REYBOLD, Eugene 4
REYBURN, John Edgar 1
REYBURN, Laurens H. 4
REYBURN, Robert 1
REYBURN, Samuel Wallace
REYERSON, Lloyd Hilton 5
REYES, Alfonso 3
REYMERT, Martin 4
REYNAL, Eugene 5
REYNAL, Louis 4
REYNARD, Grant 5
REYNAUD, Paul 4
REYNDERS, John V. W. 2
REYNIERS, James A. 5
REYNOLDS, Alexander Welch H
REYNOLDS, Alfred 1
REYNOLDS, Allen Holbrook 1
REYNOLDS, Amesbury L. 4
REYNOLDS, Arthur 2
REYNOLDS, Bruce D. 3
REYNOLDS, Carl Vernon 5
REYNOLDS, Charles Alexander H
REYNOLDS, Charles Bingham 1
REYNOLDS, Charles Lee 5
REYNOLDS, Charles Ransom 5
REYNOLDS, Chester A. 3
REYNOLDS, Conger 5
REYNOLDS, Cuyler 1
REYNOLDS, Dudley Sharpe 1
REYNOLDS, Edwin 1
REYNOLDS, Elmer Lewis 4
REYNOLDS, Elmer Robert 1
REYNOLDS, Ernest Shaw 1
REYNOLDS, Frank Bernard 1
REYNOLDS, Frank James 3
REYNOLDS, Frank William 5
REYNOLDS, Frederick Jesse 1
REYNOLDS, George Delachaumette 1
REYNOLDS, George Greenwood 1
REYNOLDS, George McClelland 1
REYNOLDS, George William 2
REYNOLDS, Gideon H
REYNOLDS, Grace Morrison 3
REYNOLDS, Henry James 2
REYNOLDS, Herbert Byron 5
REYNOLDS, Igantius Aloysius H
REYNOLDS, Isham E. 2
REYNOLDS, Jackson Eli 5
REYNOLDS, James B. H
REYNOLDS, James Bronson 1
REYNOLDS, James Burton 2
REYNOLDS, John * 1
REYNOLDS, John Edwin 1
REYNOLDS, John Fulton H
REYNOLDS, John Gilliford 4
REYNOLDS, John Hazard 1
REYNOLDS, John Henry 5
REYNOLDS, John Hughes 4
REYNOLDS, John Lacey Jr. 1
REYNOLDS, John Merriman 1
REYNOLDS, John Parker 3
REYNOLDS, John Whitcome 1
REYNOLDS, Joseph H
REYNOLDS, Joseph B. 1
REYNOLDS, Joseph Jones H
REYNOLDS, Joseph Jones 1
REYNOLDS, Joseph Smith 1
REYNOLDS, Lawrence 4
REYNOLDS, Myra 1
REYNOLDS, Myron Herbert 1
REYNOLDS, Paul Revere 2
REYNOLDS, Powell Benton 1
REYNOLDS, Quentin 4
REYNOLDS, Richard J. 4
REYNOLDS, Richard Samuel 3

REYNOLDS, Robert J. 1
REYNOLDS, Robert Rice 4
REYNOLDS, Samuel Godfrey H
REYNOLDS, Samuel Guilford 4
REYNOLDS, Thomas Harvey 2
REYNOLDS, Virginia Mrs. 1
REYNOLDS, Walter Ford 4
REYNOLDS, Wellington Jarard 2
REYNOLDS, Wiley Richard 5
REYNOLDS, William H
REYNOLDS, William Howard 5
REYNOLDS, William Neal H
REZANOV, Nikolai Petrovich H
RHAESA, William A. 5
RHEA, Hortense 1
RHEA, John H
RHEA, John S. 4
RHEA, William Edward 2
RHEA, William Francis 1
RHEAD, Louis John 1
RHEAUME, Louis 4
RHEE, Syngman 5
RHEEM, Richard Scoffield H
RHEES, John Morgan H
RHEES, Rush 1
RHEES, William Jones 1
RHEINHARDT, Rudolph H. 1
RHEINSTROM, Henry 4
RHETT, Andrew Burnet 2
RHETT, Robert Barnwell H
RHETT, Robert Goodwyn 1
RHETTS, Charles Edward 5
RHIND, Alexander Colden H
RHIND, Charles 1
RHIND, J. Massey 1
RHINE, Abraham Benedict 1
RHINELANDER, Philip Mercer 1
RHINELANDER, T. J. Oakley 4
RHINOCK, Joseph Lafayette 1
RHOAD, Albert Oliver 4
RHOADES, Cornelia Harsen 1
RHOADES, Edward Henry Jr. 3
RHOADES, John Harsen 1
RHOADES, John Harsen 2
RHOADES, Lewis Addison 1
RHOADES, Lyman 4
RHOADES, Mabel Carter 5
RHOADES, Nelson Osgood 1
RHOADES, Ralph Omer 4
RHOADES, William Caldwell Plunkett 1
RHOADS, Charles James 3
RHOADS, Cornelius Packard 3
RHOADS, James H
RHOADS, Joseph J. 3
RHOADS, McHenry 2
RHOADS, Samuel H
RHOADS, Samuel Nicholson; 5
RHODE, Clarence J. 3
RHODE, Paul Peter 1
RHODES, Bradford 1
RHODES, Charles Dudley 1
RHODES, Edward Everett 3
RHODES, Elisha Hunt 4
RHODES, Eugene Manlove 1
RHODES, Foster Twichell 5
RHODES, Frederic Harrison 2
RHODES, Frederick Leland 1
RHODES, George Pearson 1
RHODES, Harrison 1
RHODES, Henry Abraham 3
RHODES, James Ford 1
RHODES, Jeremiah 1
RHODES, John Bower 4
RHODES, John Franklin 2
RHODES, Marion Edward 4
RHODES, Mosheim 1
RHODES, Robert Clinton 2
RHODES, Rufus Napoleon 1
RHODES, Stephen Holbrook

RHODES, Willard E. 5
RHONE, Rosamond Dodson 4
RHYNE, Brice Wilson 1
RIALE, Franklin Nelman 1
RIANO Y GAYANGOS, Don Juan 5
RIBAR, Ivan 2
RIBAUT, Jean H
RIBBLE, Frederick D. G. 5
RIBNER, Irving 5
RICARD, Jerome Sixtus 1
RICAUD, James Barroll H
RICCI, Ulysses Anthony 4
RICCIUS, Hermann Porter 4
RICE, Abigail Ruth Burton (Mrs. Carl V. Rice) 5
RICE, Albert E. 1
RICE, Albert White 4
RICE, Alexander Hamilton H
RICE, Alexander Hamilton 3
RICE, Alice Caldwell Hegan 1
RICE, Alonzo Leora 4
RICE, Arthur Louis 2
RICE, Arthur Wallace 1
RICE, Ben H. Jr. 1
RICE, Benjamin Franklin H
RICE, Cale Young 2
RICE, Calvin Winsor 1
RICE, Charles H
RICE, Charles A. 5
RICE, Charles Allen Thorndike H
RICE, Charles Edmund 1
RICE, Charles Francis 1
RICE, Charles M. 3
RICE, Claton Silas 5
RICE, Craig 3
RICE, Dan H
RICE, David H
RICE, Devereux Dunlap 1
RICE, Edmund H
RICE, Edmund 1
RICE, Edward Irving 1
RICE, Edward Loranus 3
RICE, Edward Young 1
RICE, Edwin Wilbur 1
RICE, Edwin Wilbur Jr. 1
RICE, Elmer 4
RICE, Ernest 1
RICE, Eugene 4
RICE, F. Willis H
RICE, Fenelon Bird 1
RICE, Frank James 1
RICE, Franklin Pierce 1
RICE, Frederick Adolph 3
RICE, George Brackett 2
RICE, George Samuel 1
RICE, George Staples 1
RICE, Grantland 3
RICE, Greek Lent 3
RICE, Harmon Howard 1
RICE, Harry Lee 3
RICE, Heber Holbrook 3
RICE, Henry H
RICE, Henry Mower 1
RICE, Herbert Ambrose 1
RICE, Herbert Howard 1
RICE, Herbert Leigh 1
RICE, Herbert Wayland 1
RICE, Howard Crosby 4
RICE, Isaac Leopold 1
RICE, Jack Horton 4
RICE, James Edward 1
RICE, James Henry Jr. 1
RICE, John H
RICE, John Andrew 5
RICE, John Andrew 1
RICE, John Birchard H
RICE, John Blake H
RICE, John Campbell 1
RICE, John Hodgen 1
RICE, John Holt 1
RICE, John Hovey 1
RICE, John McConnell 1
RICE, John Pierrepont 2
RICE, John Winter 5
RICE, Jonas Shearn 1
RICE, Joseph J. 1
RICE, Joseph Mayer 1
RICE, Kingsley Loring 4
RICE, Laban Lacy 5
RICE, Lewis Frederick 1
RICE, Lloyd Preston 3
RICE, Luther 1
RICE, M. Wilfred 5
RICE, Maurice Smythe 2
RICE, Merton Stacher 2
RICE, Nathan Lewis H
RICE, Paul Harper 3

RICE, Paul North 4
RICE, Philip Blair 3
RICE, Richard Ashley 3
RICE, Richard Austin 1
RICE, Richard Henry 1
RICE, Robert 5
RICE, Stephen Ewing 3
RICE, Stuart Arthur 5
RICE, Theron Hall 1
RICE, Theron Moses H
RICE, Thomas 1
RICE, Thomas Dartmouth H
RICE, Thomas Stevens 2
RICE, Thurman Brooks 3
RICE, Victor Moreau H
RICE, W. North 1
RICE, Wallace 1
RICE, Willard Martin 1
RICE, William 1
RICE, William Ball 1
RICE, William Gorham 4
RICE, William Marsh H
RICE, William Morton Jackson 1
RICE, William Whitney 1
RICH, Adelbert P. 1
RICH, Arnold Rice 5
RICH, Burdett Alberto 1
RICH, Carl W. 5
RICH, Charles H
RICH, Charles Alonzo 2
RICH, Edgar Judson 2
RICH, Ednah Anne 5
RICH, Edson Prosper 4
RICH, Edward P. 1
RICH, Elmer 4
RICH, Giles Willard 2
RICH, Isaac H
RICH, John A. 4
RICH, John Harrison 3
RICH, John Lyon 3
RICH, John T. 1
RICH, Obadiah H
RICH, Raymond Thomas 5
RICH, Robert Fleming 5
RICH, Ronald Emil 5
RICH, Samuel Heath 2
RICH, Sir Robert H
RICH, Thaddeus 5
RICH, Williston C. 3
RICHARD, Charles 1
RICHARD, Ernst D. 1
RICHARD, Gabriel H
RICHARD, Harold Charles 3
RICHARD, James William 1
RICHARD, John H. H
RICHARD, Matthias 2
RICHARDS, Alfred Ernest 1
RICHARDS, Alfred Newton 4
RICHARDS, Alice Haliburton 1
RICHARDS, Bernard Gerson 5
RICHARDS, Charles Brinckerhoff 1
RICHARDS, Charles Gorman 5
RICHARDS, Charles Herbert 1
RICHARDS, Charles Lenmore 5
RICHARDS, Charles Malone 5
RICHARDS, Charles Russ 1
RICHARDS, Charles Russell 1
RICHARDS, Charles Walter 1
RICHARDS, Cyril Fuller 3
RICHARDS, De Forest 1
RICHARDS, Dickinson W. 5
RICHARDS, Donald 3
RICHARDS, E. F. 4
RICHARDS, Eben 2
RICHARDS, Edgar 4
RICHARDS, Edward A. 1
RICHARDS, Ellen Henrietta 1
RICHARDS, Emerson Lewis 4
RICHARDS, Emily S. Tanner 1
RICHARDS, Erwin Hart 1
RICHARDS, Eugene Lamb 1
RICHARDS, Eugene Scott 4
RICHARDS, Frederick Thompson 1
RICHARDS, George * 1
RICHARDS, George 2
RICHARDS, George Franklin 3
RICHARDS, George Gill 3

RICHARDS, George Handyside 3
RICHARDS, George Huntington 5
RICHARDS, George Warren 3
RICHARDS, Harry Sanger 1
RICHARDS, Henry Melchior Muhlenberg 5
RICHARDS, Herbert Maule 5
RICHARDS, Herbert Montague 4
RICHARDS, Irving Trefethen H
RICHARDS, Jacob H
RICHARDS, James L. 3
RICHARDS, Janet E. Hosmer 2
RICHARDS, Jean Marie 5
RICHARDS, John * H
RICHARDS, John E. 1
RICHARDS, John Gardiner 1
RICHARDS, John Kelvey 1
RICHARDS, John Thomas 2
RICHARDS, Joseph H. 5
RICHARDS, Joseph Havens Cowles 1
RICHARDS, Joseph William 1
RICHARDS, Laura Elizabeth 2
RICHARDS, Lela Horn (pseudonym Lee Neville) 5
RICHARDS, Lewis Loomis 1
RICHARDS, Louise 5
RICHARDS, Mark H
RICHARDS, Mrs. Waldo 1
RICHARDS, Nathan Charles 2
RICHARDS, Paul Stanley 5
RICHARDS, Paul William 3
RICHARDS, Preston 3
RICHARDS, Ralph H(are) 5
RICHARDS, Ralph Strother 2
RICHARDS, Ray 3
RICHARDS, Rezin Howard 4
RICHARDS, Robert Hallowell 2
RICHARDS, Robert Haven 3
RICHARDS, Robert Watt 4
RICHARDS, Roger G. 5
RICHARDS, Rosalind (Miss) 5
RICHARDS, Samuel H. 3
RICHARDS, Stephen L. 3
RICHARDS, T. Addison 1
RICHARDS, Theodore William 1
RICHARDS, Thomas Cole 5
RICHARDS, William H
RICHARDS, William Alford 1
RICHARDS, William Henry 4
RICHARDS, William Joseph 4
RICHARDS, William Rogers 1
RICHARDS, William Trost 1
RICHARDS, Zalmon 1
RICHARDSON, Abby Sage 1
RICHARDSON, Albert Deane H
RICHARDSON, Alexander Henderson 5
RICHARDSON, Anna Euretta 2
RICHARDSON, Anna Steese 2
RICHARDSON, Basil 1
RICHARDSON, Charles 1
RICHARDSON, Charles Francis 1
RICHARDSON, Charles Freemont 1
RICHARDSON, Charles Henry 1
RICHARDSON, Charles Williamson 3
RICHARDSON, Clarence H. 1
RICHARDSON, Clifford 4
RICHARDSON, David Crockett 1
RICHARDSON, Donovan MacNeely 1
RICHARDSON, Dorothy 3
RICHARDSON, Edmund H

RICHARDSON, Edward Elliott 3
RICHARDSON, Edward H(enderson) 5
RICHARDSON, Edward Peirson 2
RICHARDSON, Edwin Sanders 3
RICHARDSON, Ellen A. 1
RICHARDSON, Elliott Verne 1
RICHARDSON, Ernest Cushing 1
RICHARDSON, Ernest Gladstone 1
RICHARDSON, Francis Asbury 1
RICHARDSON, Francis Henry 1
RICHARDSON, Frank Chase 1
R!CHARDSON, Frederick 1
RICHARDSON, Frederick Albert 5
RICHARDSON, Friend William 2
RICHARDSON, George Adams 3
RICHARDSON, George Burr 5
RICHARDSON, George Lynde 1
RICHARDSON, George Tilton 1
RICHARDSON, Guy A. 4
RICHARDSON, H. George 5
RICHARDSON, Harry Alden 1
RICHARDSON, Henry Brown 1
RICHARDSON, Henry Hobson H
RICHARDSON, Henry Smith 5
RICHARDSON, Hester Dorsey 1
RICHARDSON, Hilary Goode 5
RICHARDSON, Hugh 1
RICHARDSON, Ira 3
RICHARDSON, Israel Bush H
RICHARDSON, James Bailey 3
RICHARDSON, James Daniel 1
RICHARDSON, James Hugh 4
RICHARDSON, James Julius 1
RICHARDSON, James Montgomery 4
RICHARDSON, James Parmelee 2
RICHARDSON, John Peter H
RICHARDSON, John S(anford) 5
RICHARDSON, John Smythe H
RICHARDSON, Joseph * H
RICHARDSON, Katharine Berry 1
RICHARDSON, Leon Josiah 4
RICHARDSON, Lunsford 3
RICHARDSON, M. S. 5
RICHARDSON, Mark E(dwin) 5
RICHARDSON, Mark Wyman 4
RICHARDSON, Maurice Howe 1
RICHARDSON, Norman Egbert 2
RICHARDSON, Norval 1
RICHARDSON, Oliver Huntington 1
RICHARDSON, Philip 2
RICHARDSON, Robert H
RICHARDSON, Robert Charlwood Jr. 3
RICHARDSON, Robert Kimball 3
RICHARDSON, Robert Newton 3
RICHARDSON, Robert Price 5
RICHARDSON, Robert William 4
RICHARDSON, Roland George Dwight 2
RICHARDSON, Roy Mundy Davidson 5
RICHARDSON, Rufus Byam 1

RITTER, Edward Frederick 1
RITTER, Frederic Louis H
RITTER, Halsted Lockwood 3
RITTER, Howard L(ester) 5
RITTER, John H
RITTER, Joseph Elmer 4
RITTER, Louis E. 1
RITTER, Paul 1
RITTER, Thelma 5
RITTER, Verus Taggart 2
RITTER, William Emerson 2
RITTER, William Leonard 5
RITTMAN, Walter Frank 3
RITTMASTER, Alexander, III 5
RITZ, Harold A. 2
RITZMAN, Ernest George 3
RIVAS, Damaso de 5
RIVENBURG, Romeyn Henry 4
RIVERA, Diego 3
RIVERA, Jose Garibi 5
RIVERA, Luis Munoz 1
RIVERS, Eurith Dickinson 4
RIVERS, G. L. Buist 4
RIVERS, L. Mendel 5
RIVERS, Moultrie Rutledge 1
RIVERS, Thomas H
RIVERS, Thomas Milton 4
RIVERS, William Cannon 2
RIVERS, William Walter 4
RIVES, Alfred Landon 1
RIVES, Edwin Earle 3
RIVES, Francis Everod H
RIVES, George Lockhart 1
RIVES, John Cook H
RIVES, William Cabell H
RIVES, Zeno J. 5
RIVES-WHEELER, Hallie Ermine 1
RIVINGTON, James H
RIVINUS, Francis Markoe 3
RIVITZ, Hiram S. 3
RIVKIN, William Robert 4
RIX, Carl Barnett 4
RIX, Charles Northrup 1
RIX, Frank Reader 1
RIXEY, John Franklin 1
RIXEY, Presley Marion 1
RIXFORD, Elizabeth M. Leach 3
RIXFORD, Emmet 1
RIZER, Henry Clay 4
ROACH, Abby Meguire 5
ROACH, Alden G. 3
ROACH, David James 3
ROACH, John H
ROACH, John Millard 1
ROACH, Sidney C. 5
ROACH, Thomas Watson 1
ROADHOUSE, Chester Linwood 5
ROADS, Charles 4
ROADSTRUM, Victor N. 4
ROANE, Archibald H
ROANE, John H
ROANE, John Jones H
ROANE, John Selden H
ROANE, Spencer H
ROANE, William Henry H
ROARK, Ruric Nevel 1
ROBB, Charles Henry 1
ROBB, Clair E. 4
ROBB, Eccles Donald 2
ROBB, Edward 4
ROBB, Elise de la Fontaine (Mrs. Robert Cumming Robb) 5
ROBB, Eugene Spivey 5
ROBB, Hunter 1
ROBB, James H
ROBB, James Hampden 1
ROBB, Richard Alexander 5
ROBB, Russell 1
ROBB, Russell 3
ROBB, Seymour 4
ROBB, Thomas Bruce 4
ROBB, William Lispenard 1
ROBB, Willis Oscar 1
ROBBIE, Alexander Cumming 4
ROBBINS, Alexander Henry 1
ROBBINS, Arthur Graham 4
ROBBINS, Asher H
ROBBINS, Benjamin H. 4
ROBBINS, Burnett W. 3
ROBBINS, Chandler H
ROBBINS, Charles Burton 2
ROBBINS, Charles F. 3
ROBBINS, Charles Leonidas 1
ROBBINS, Edmund Yard 2
ROBBINS, Edward Denmore 1
ROBBINS, Edward Everett 1
ROBBINS, Edward Rutledge 5
ROBBINS, Edwin Clyde 2
ROBBINS, Francis LeBaron 1
ROBBINS, Franklin G. 5
ROBBINS, Frederick Wright 4
ROBBINS, Gaston A. 5
ROBBINS, George Ridgway 4
ROBBINS, George Robbins H
ROBBINS, Harry Clark 4
ROBBINS, Harry Pelham 2
ROBBINS, Harry Wolcott 3
ROBBINS, Hayes 1
ROBBINS, Henry Spencer 1
ROBBINS, Horace Wolcott 1
ROBBINS, Howard Chandler 3
ROBBINS, Irvin 1
ROBBINS, Jim 4
ROBBINS, John H
ROBBINS, John Williams 1
ROBBINS, Joseph Chandler 5
ROBBINS, Joseph Chandler 4
ROBBINS, Laurence Ballard 4
ROBBINS, Leonard H. 2
ROBBINS, Mary Caroline 1
ROBBINS, Merton Covey 1
ROBBINS, Milton Herbert 5
ROBBINS, Milton Holley, Jr. 5
ROBBINS, Reginald Chauncey 3
ROBBINS, Richard Whitfield 5
ROBBINS, Royal 1
ROBBINS, Samuel Dowse 5
ROBBINS, Thomas H
ROBBINS, Thomas Hinckley, Jr. 5
ROBBINS, Walter 3
ROBBINS, Warren Delano 1
ROBBINS, Wilford Lash 1
ROBBINS, Wilfred William 3
ROBE, Charles Franklin 1
ROBERDEAU, Daniel H
ROBERDEAU, Isaac H
ROBERDS, William Greene 4
ROBERSON, Frank Remont 1
ROBERT, Christopher Rhinelander H
ROBERT, Henry Martyn 1
ROBERT, James Marshall 4
ROBERT, Joseph Thomas 4
ROBERT, Sarah Emily Corbin 5
ROBERT, William Pierre 4
ROBERTS, Albert H. 2
ROBERTS, Anne Mason 5
ROBERTS, Anthony Ellmaker H
ROBERTS, Arthur Jeremiah 1
ROBERTS, Benjamin Franklin 3
ROBERTS, Benjamin H. 3
ROBERTS, Benjamin Kearney 1
ROBERTS, Benjamin Stone H
ROBERTS, Benjamin Titus H
ROBERTS, Benson Howard 1
ROBERTS, Brigham Henry 1
ROBERTS, Henry) Chalmes 5
ROBERTS, Charles Asaph 4
ROBERTS, Charles Burleson 3
ROBERTS, Charles DuVal 4
ROBERTS, Charles George Douglas 3
ROBERTS, Charles Humphrey 4
ROBERTS, Charles Wesley 2
ROBERTS, Charlotte Fitch 1
ROBERTS, Clarence 2
ROBERTS, Clarence J. 1
ROBERTS, Clifford 3
ROBERTS, Colette Jacqueline 5
ROBERTS, Cyrus Swan 1
ROBERTS, Delmar 4
ROBERTS, Donald F. 4
ROBERTS, Edmund H
ROBERTS, Edward Alexander 4
ROBERTS, Edward Dodson 5
ROBERTS, Edward Howell 3
ROBERTS, Edwin Ewing 1
ROBERTS, Elizabeth Madox 1
ROBERTS, Ellis Henry 1
ROBERTS, Ellsworth A. 4
ROBERTS, Elmer 1
ROBERTS, Elzey 4
ROBERTS, Ernest Porter 5
ROBERTS, Ernest William 1
ROBERTS, Florence 1
ROBERTS, Frank Calvin Jr. 4
ROBERTS, Frank Harold Hanna 4
ROBERTS, Frank Hubert 5
ROBERTS, Frank Hunt Hurd 1
ROBERTS, George 5
ROBERTS, George Brooke H
ROBERTS, George Edward Theodore 5
ROBERTS, George Evan 2
ROBERTS, George Litch 1
ROBERTS, George Lucas 1
ROBERTS, George Newman 1
ROBERTS, Harlan Page 1
ROBERTS, Harold DeWitt 3
ROBERTS, Harris Lee 1
ROBERTS, Henry 1
ROBERTS, Henry Lithgow 5
ROBERTS, Herbert Rufus 3
ROBERTS, Howard 1
ROBERTS, Ina Brevoort 5
ROBERTS, Isaac Phillips 1
ROBERTS, Issachar Jacob H
ROBERTS, James Arthur 1
ROBERTS, James Cole 1
ROBERTS, James Hudson 4
ROBERTS, Job H
ROBERTS, John Bingham 1
ROBERTS, John Emerson 4
ROBERTS, John S. 3
ROBERTS, Jonathan H
ROBERTS, Jonathan William 4
ROBERTS, Joseph Harry Newton 3
ROBERTS, Joseph Jenkins H
ROBERTS, Kate Louise 2
ROBERTS, Katharine Eggleston 4
ROBERTS, Kenneth 3
ROBERTS, Kingsley 2
ROBERTS, Lloyd Sherwood 5
ROBERTS, Lydia Jane 4
ROBERTS, Madison Hines 4
ROBERTS, Malcolm Ferguson 5
ROBERTS, Marshall Owen H
ROBERTS, Mary Fanton 3
ROBERTS, Mary M. 3
ROBERTS, Morton 4
ROBERTS, Nathan Smith H
ROBERTS, Odin 1
ROBERTS, Oran Milo H
ROBERTS, Owen Josephus 3
ROBERTS, Percival Jr. 2
ROBERTS, Peter 1
ROBERTS, Phill Tandy Jr. 4
ROBERTS, Robert 1
ROBERTS, Robert Richford H
ROBERTS, Robert Whyte H
ROBERTS, Roy Allison 4
ROBERTS, Samuel Jennings 5
ROBERTS, Samuel Judson 1
ROBERTS, Seldon L. 1
ROBERTS, Shelby Saufley 1
ROBERTS, Solomon White H
ROBERTS, Stanley Burroughs 1
ROBERTS, Stephen W(ilbur) 5
ROBERTS, Stewart Ralph 1
ROBERTS, T. Scott 3
ROBERTS, Tarlton Taylor 5
ROBERTS, Theodore 1
ROBERTS, Thomas Paschall 4
ROBERTS, Thomas Reaser 5
ROBERTS, Thomas Sadler 2
ROBERTS, Trevor V. 4
ROBERTS, Vasco Harold 1
ROBERTS, W. Frank 3
ROBERTS, Walter Adolphe 4
ROBERTS, Walter Nelson 4
ROBERTS, Warren Russell 2
ROBERTS, Wightman Durand 1
ROBERTS, Willa Mae 4
ROBERTS, William Allerton 5
ROBERTS, William Alva 3
ROBERTS, William Charles 1
ROBERTS, William Henry 1
ROBERTS, William Milnor H
ROBERTS, William Randall H
ROBERTSON, A. James 5
ROBERTSON, A. Willis 5
ROBERTSON, Abram Heaton 1
ROBERTSON, Alexander George Morison 2
ROBERTSON, Alexander Mitchell 1
ROBERTSON, Alice 1
ROBERTSON, Alice Mary 1
ROBERTSON, Andrew Wells 4
ROBERTSON, Archibald H
ROBERTSON, Archibald Thomas 1
ROBERTSON, Ashley Herman 1
ROBERTSON, Ben 2
ROBERTSON, Beverly Holcombe 1
ROBERTSON, Carl Trowbridge 1
ROBERTSON, Charles 4
ROBERTSON, Charles Barr 1
ROBERTSON, Charles M. 4
ROBERTSON, Charles Raymond 3
ROBERTSON, David Allan 4
ROBERTSON, David Brown 4
ROBERTSON, David Ritchie 4
ROBERTSON, Dennis Holme 4
ROBERTSON, Donald 1
ROBERTSON, Edward P. 1
ROBERTSON, Edward Vivian 4
ROBERTSON, Edward White H
ROBERTSON, Edwin Wales 1
ROBERTSON, Ella Broadus 2
ROBERTSON, Felix Huston 1
ROBERTSON, Fred 5
ROBERTSON, George H
ROBERTSON, George 1
ROBERTSON, George 4
ROBERTSON, George Lawrence 3
ROBERTSON, Harold Eugene 2
ROBERTSON, Harold Hansard 3
ROBERTSON, Harrison 1
ROBERTSON, Harrison M. 3
ROBERTSON, Holcombe McGavock 5
ROBERTSON, Howard Percy 4
ROBERTSON, J. B. A. 1
ROBERTSON, J. Breathitt 3
ROBERTSON, James * H
ROBERTSON, James Alexander 1
ROBERTSON, James Rood 1
ROBERTSON, Jerome Bonaparte H
ROBERTSON, John H
ROBERTSON, John Brunt 4
ROBERTSON, John Dill 1
ROBERTSON, John Stevenston 1
ROBERTSON, Joseph Andrew 1
ROBERTSON, Lawrence Vernon 5
ROBERTSON, Leroy J. 5
ROBERTSON, Louis Alexander 4
ROBERTSON, Lucy Henderson 4
ROBERTSON, Marion Clinton 3
ROBERTSON, Miles E. 5
ROBERTSON, Morgan 1
ROBERTSON, Norman A(lexander) 5
ROBERTSON, Oswald Hope 4
ROBERTSON, Peter 1
ROBERTSON, Ralph E. 4
ROBERTSON, Reuben B. Jr. 3
ROBERTSON, Reuben B. Jr. 4
ROBERTSON, Reuben Buck 5
ROBERTSON, Robert Crawford 5
ROBERTSON, Robert Henderson 4
ROBERTSON, Robert Spelman 5
ROBERTSON, Samuel Matthews 1
ROBERTSON, Stuart 1
ROBERTSON, Thomas Aaron 3
ROBERTSON, Thomas Austin H
ROBERTSON, Thomas Bolling H
ROBERTSON, Thomas Ernest 5
ROBERTSON, Thomas James H
ROBERTSON, Thomas M. 1
ROBERTSON, W. Spencer 3
ROBERTSON, Walter H
ROBERTSON, Walter Melville 3
ROBERTSON, Walter Spencer 5
ROBERTSON, Wilbur Wade 1
ROBERTSON, William Bryan 2
ROBERTSON, William Cornelius 1
ROBERTSON, William Gordon 1
ROBERTSON, William Henry H
ROBERTSON, William Henry 4
ROBERTSON, William Joseph H
ROBERTSON, William Joseph 3
ROBERTSON, William Schenck H
ROBERTSON, William Spence 3
ROBERTSON, Wishart McLea 4
ROBERTSON, Wyndham H
ROBESON, George Maxwell H
ROBESON, Henry Bellows 1
ROBEY, Louis W. 5
ROBEY, Ralph West 5
ROBEY, William Henry 3
ROBIDON, Antoine H
ROBIE, Edward Dunham 1
ROBIE, Frederick 1
ROBIE, Reuben H
ROBIE, Walter Franklin 1
ROBINEAU, Simon Pierre 3
ROBINETTE, Edward Burton 1
ROBINS, Augustine Warner 1
ROBINS, Charles A. 5
ROBINS, Charles Russell 2
ROBINS, Edward 2

*** Indicates More Than One Such Name Listed**

ROBINS, Elizabeth, (Mrs. George Richmond Parks) (pseud. C.E.) — 5
ROBINS, Henry Burke — 2
ROBINS, Henry Ephraim — 1
ROBINS, John Aloysius — 3
ROBINS, Margaret Dreier — 2
ROBINS, Raymond — 3
ROBINS, Reuben William — 4
ROBINS, Sally Nelson — 1
ROBINS, Thomas — 3
ROBINSON, A. L. — 3
ROBINSON, Albert Alonzo — 1
ROBINSON, Albert Gardner — 1
ROBINSON, Alexander Cochrane — 3
ROBINSON, Allan — 2
ROBINSON, Annie Douglas Green — 2
ROBINSON, Arthur Granville — 4
ROBINSON, Arthur R. — 4
ROBINSON, B(rittain) B(ragunler) — 5
ROBINSON, Barclay — 5
ROBINSON, Benjamin Lincoln — 1
ROBINSON, Benjamin Willard — 2
ROBINSON, Bernard Buckley — 4
ROBINSON, Beverley — 1
ROBINSON, Beverley Randolph — 3
ROBINSON, Beverly — H
ROBINSON, Bill — 2
ROBINSON, Boardman — 3
ROBINSON, Byron — 1
ROBINSON, Chalfant — 2
ROBINSON, Charles — H
ROBINSON, Charles Alexander — 5
ROBINSON, Charles Alexander Jr. — 4
ROBINSON, Charles Dorman — 1
ROBINSON, Charles Henry — 4
ROBINSON, Charles Kerchner — 1
ROBINSON, Charles Leonard Frost
ROBINSON, Charles Mulford — 4
ROBINSON, Charles Seymour — H
ROBINSON, Charles Snelling — 4
ROBINSON, Christopher — H
ROBINSON, Clarke — 4
ROBINSON, Claude Everett — 4
ROBINSON, Clement Franklin — 4
ROBINSON, Clifton Frederick — 4
ROBINSON, Clinton F. — 4
ROBINSON, Conway — H
ROBINSON, Corinne Roosevelt — 1
ROBINSON, Cyrus — 3
ROBINSON, David Moore — 3
ROBINSON, DeLorme Wilson — 3
ROBINSON, Doane — 1
ROBINSON, Douglas — 2
ROBINSON, Dwight Nelson — 3
ROBINSON, Dwight Parker — 4
ROBINSON, Edith — 4
ROBINSON, Edward * — H
ROBINSON, Edward G. — 5
ROBINSON, Edward Levi — 2
ROBINSON, Edward Mott — H
ROBINSON, Edward Stevens — 1
ROBINSON, Edward Van Dyke — 1
ROBINSON, Edwin Arlington — 2
ROBINSON, Edwin Meade — 3
ROBINSON, Erdis — 2
ROBINSON, Ernest Franklin — H
ROBINSON, Ezekial Gilman — 5
ROBINSON, Fannie Ruth — 1
ROBINSON, Florence Richardson

ROBINSON, Florence Vincent — 1
ROBINSON, Frank Upham — 1
ROBINSON, Frank Wisner — 2
ROBINSON, Franklin Clement — 1
ROBINSON, Fred J(ames) — 5
ROBINSON, Fred Norris — 4
ROBINSON, Frederick Bertrand — 1
ROBINSON, G. B. — 3
ROBINSON, G. Canby — 4
ROBINSON, George Dexter — H
ROBINSON, George Livingstone — 3
ROBINSON, George Thomas — 2
ROBINSON, George William — 2
ROBINSON, George Wilse — 3
ROBINSON, Gerold Tanquary — 5
ROBINSON, Gifford Simeon — 1
ROBINSON, Gustavus Hill — 5
ROBINSON, H. Perry — 1
ROBINSON, Harold McAfee — 1
ROBINSON, Harrison Sidney — 2
ROBINSON, Harry Charles — 2
ROBINSON, Helen Ring — 1
ROBINSON, Henry Cornelius — H
ROBINSON, Henry Douglas — 1
ROBINSON, Henry Mauris — 1
ROBINSON, Henry Morton — 1
ROBINSON, Henry Seymour — 5
ROBINSON, Howard Lee — 5
ROBINSON, Howard West — 3
ROBINSON, Ira Ellsworth — 5
ROBINSON, Jack Roosevelt — H
ROBINSON, James Carroll — 4
ROBINSON, James Dixon — 4
ROBINSON, James Dixon Jr.
ROBINSON, James E. — 1
ROBINSON, James Harvey — 1
ROBINSON, James Hathaway — 4
ROBINSON, James Lee — 1
ROBINSON, James M. — 4
ROBINSON, James Sidney — H
ROBINSON, Jane Bancroft — 3
ROBINSON, Jesse Mathews — H
ROBINSON, John * — H
ROBINSON, John — 1
ROBINSON, John Beverley
ROBINSON, John Cleveland — H
ROBINSON, John Edward — 1
ROBINSON, John Larne — H
ROBINSON, John M. — 4
ROBINSON, John Marshall
ROBINSON, John McCracken — H
ROBINSON, John Mitchell — H
ROBINSON, John S. — 3
ROBINSON, John Sherman — 3
ROBINSON, John Trumbull
ROBINSON, John W. — 2
ROBINSON, Jonathan — H
ROBINSON, Joseph — 2
ROBINSON, Joseph E. — 4
ROBINSON, Joseph Gibson
ROBINSON, Joseph Taylor — 1
ROBINSON, Julia Almira — 2
ROBINSON, Karl Frederic — 4
ROBINSON, Leland Rex — 4
ROBINSON, Lennox — 3
ROBINSON, Leonard George — 2

ROBINSON, Leonidas Dunlap — 4
ROBINSON, Lewis Wood — 1
ROBINSON, Louis Newton — 3
ROBINSON, Lucien Moore — 1
ROBINSON, Lucius Franklin — 1
ROBINSON, Lucius W. — 1
ROBINSON, Lucius Waterman — 1
ROBINSON, Luther Emerson — 3
ROBINSON, Lydia Gillingham — 5
ROBINSON, Mabel Louise — 1
ROBINSON, Mary Dummett Nauman — 4
ROBINSON, Mary Yandes — 4
ROBINSON, Maurice Henry — 2
ROBINSON, Millard Lyman — 2
ROBINSON, Milton Stapp — H
ROBINSON, Moncure — H
ROBINSON, Moses — 1
ROBINSON, Noel — 2
ROBINSON, Orin Pomeroy Jr. — 3
ROBINSON, Orville — H
ROBINSON, P. Gervais — 2
ROBINSON, Pat — 4
ROBINSON, Remus Grant — 1
ROBINSON, Richard Hallett Meredith — 3
ROBINSON, Richard Lee — 1
ROBINSON, Robert P. — 1
ROBINSON, Rodney Potter — 3
ROBINSON, Roscoe R. — 1
ROBINSON, Rowland Evans — 1
ROBINSON, Samuel — 2
ROBINSON, Samuel Murray — 5
ROBINSON, Samuel Sanford — 2
ROBINSON, Sara Tappan Doolittle — 4
ROBINSON, Silas Arnold — 5
ROBINSON, Solon — H
ROBINSON, Solon — 4
ROBINSON, Stephen Bernard — 4
ROBINSON, Stewart Mac Master — 4
ROBINSON, Stillman Williams — 1
ROBINSON, Stuart — H
ROBINSON, Theodore — H
ROBINSON, Theodore Douglas — 1
ROBINSON, Theodore Winthrop — 2
ROBINSON, Therese Albertine Louise 'von Jakob — H
ROBINSON, Thomas Jr. — H
ROBINSON, Thomas — 3
ROBINSON, Thomas John Bright
ROBINSON, Thomas Linton — 1
ROBINSON, Tracy — 4
ROBINSON, Victor — 2
ROBINSON, W. Courtland
ROBINSON, Waltour M. — 4
ROBINSON, Wilfred Henry — 3
ROBINSON, Wilfreid — 5
ROBINSON, William * — 1
ROBINSON, William — 4
ROBINSON, William Alexander
ROBINSON, William Alexander — 3
ROBINSON, William Callyhan — 1
ROBINSON, William Christopher — 4
ROBINSON, William Dean — 3
ROBINSON, William Duffield — 1
ROBINSON, William Edward — 5
ROBINSON, William Erigena — H
ROBINSON, William H. — 5
ROBINSON, William Henry — 1
ROBINSON, William Henry — 3
ROBINSON, William J. — 1
ROBINSON, William M. — 4

ROBINSON, William Morrison Jr. — 4
ROBINSON, William S. — 2
ROBINSON, William Stevens — 3
ROBINSON, William Theodore — 1
ROBINSON, William Wallace Jr. — 1
ROBINSON, Wirt — 1
ROBINSON, Wm Henry — 3
ROBISON, David Fullerton — H
ROBISON, Henry Barton — 3
ROBISON, Samuel Shelburn — 3
ROBISON, William Ferretti — 2
ROBNETT, Ronald Herbert — 3
ROBOT, Isidore — H
ROBSION, John Marshall — 2
ROBSON, Frank E. — 2
ROBSON, James A. — 1
ROBSON, Martin Cecil — 1
ROBSON, May — 2
ROBSON, May Waldron — 1
ROBSON, Stuart — 1
ROBUS, Hugo — 4
ROBYN, Alfred George — 1
ROBYN, Edward — H
ROCHAMBEAU, 'comte 'de — H
ROCHE, Ambrose Francis — 1
ROCHE, Arthur Somers — 1
ROCHE, Frederick W. — 5
ROCHE, James Jeffrey — 1
ROCHE, John A. — 1
ROCHE, John Joseph — 4
ROCHE, John Pierre — 3
ROCHE, Joseph T. — 4
ROCHE, Martin — 1
ROCHE, Michael Joseph — 4
ROCHE, William James — 1
ROCHESTER, Edward Sudler — 2
ROCHESTER, Nathaniel — H
ROCHESTER, William Beatty — H
ROCHESTER, William Beatty — 1
ROCHLEN, Ava Michael — 5
ROCK, George Frederick — 3
ROCK, George Henry — 2
ROCKEFELLER, John Davison — 1
ROCKEFELLER, John Davison Jr. — 4
ROCKEFELLER, Lewis Kirby — 5
ROCKEFELLER, Percy Avery — 1
ROCKEFELLER, William — 1
ROCKEFELLER, William Goodsell — 1
ROCKEFELLER, Winthrop — 5
ROCKENBACH, Samuel Dickerson — 3
ROCKETT, James Francis — 2
ROCKEY, Alpha Eugene — 1
ROCKEY, Howard — 1
ROCKEY, Keller E. — 5
ROCKHILL, William — H
ROCKHILL, William Woodville — 4
ROCKINGHAM, Charles Watson-Wentworth — 4
ROCKNE, Knute Kenneth — 1
ROCKWELL, Alfred Perkins — 1
ROCKWELL, Alphonso David — 1
ROCKWELL, Charles H. — 1
ROCKWELL, Charles Henry — 3
ROCKWELL, David Ladd — 5
ROCKWELL, Edward Henry — 2
ROCKWELL, Fletcher Webster — 5
ROCKWELL, Homer — 5
ROCKWELL, John Arnold — H
ROCKWELL, Joseph H. — 1
ROCKWELL, Julius — H
ROCKWELL, Julius Ensign — 1
ROCKWELL, Kiffin Yates — 1
ROCKWELL, Kiffin Yates — 4
ROCKWELL, Maryelda — 5
ROCKWELL, Robert Fay — 4
ROCKWELL, Samuel — 4
ROCKWELL, William Hayden — 1
ROCKWELL, William Walker — 3

ROCKWOOD, Charles Greene
ROCKWOOD, Elbert William — 1
ROCKWOOD, Frank Ernest — 1
ROCKWOOD, George Gardner — 1
ROCKWOOD, George I. — 5
ROCKWOOD, Robert Everett — 3
RODALE, Jerome Irving — 5
RODD, Thomas — 4
RODDA, F. C. — 4
RODDENBERY, Seaborn Anderson — 1
RODDEY, Philip Dale — H
RODDEY, William Joseph — 4
RODDIS, Hamilton — 3
RODDY, Gilbert Morgan — 5
RODDY, Harry Justin — 1
RODDY, Harry Justin — 2
RODDY, James E. — 4
RODDY, William Franklin — 1
RODE, Alfred — 5
RODE, Ralph Becker — 3
RODEBUSH, Worth Huff — 4
RODEFER, Charles Mayger
RODEHEAVER, Homer Alvan — 3
RODEN, Carl Bismarck — 3
RODEN, Henry Wisdom — 4
RODENBAUGH, Henry Nathan
RODENBECK, Adolph Julius — 3
RODENBERG, William A. — 1
RODENBOUGH, Theophilus Francis
RODER, Martin — H
RODES, Robert Emmett — 4
RODEY, Bernard Shandon — 2
RODEY, Pearce Coddington — 3
RODGER, James George — 4
RODGERS, Christopher Raymond Perry
RODGERS, Cleveland — 3
RODGERS, Cowan — 1
RODGERS, David John — 3
RODGERS, Frederick — 1
RODGERS, George Washington * — H
RODGERS, James Linn — 1
RODGERS, John * — H
RODGERS, John Augustus — 1
RODGERS, John Gilmour — 1
RODGERS, John Isaac — 1
RODGERS, Philip R. — 4
RODGERS, Raymond — 5
RODGERS, Raymond Perry — 1
RODGERS, Robert Lewis — 1
RODGERS, Ted V. — 4
RODGERS, Thomas Slidell
RODGERS, William — 1
RODGERS, William Blackstock — 1
RODGERS, William Cunningham
RODGERS, William Ledyard
RODGERS, William S. S. — 4
RODGERS, William Thomas
RODKEY, Robert Gordon — 1
RODMAN, Clarence James — 5
RODMAN, Hugh — 1
RODMAN, Isaac Peace — 1
RODMAN, John Croom — 3
RODMAN, John Stewart — 3
RODMAN, T. Clifford — 4
RODMAN, Thomas Jackson — H
RODMAN, Walter Sheldon — 2
RODMAN, Warren Anson — 4
RODMAN, William — 1
RODMAN, William Blount — 2
RODMAN, William Louis — 1
RODNEY, Caesar — H
RODNEY, Caesar Augustus — 1
RODNEY, Daniel — 1
RODNEY, George Brydges — H
RODNEY, George Brydges — 1

RODNEY, 4 Richard Seymour	ROGERS, 1 Edmund James Armstrong	ROGERS, Sherman S. 1	ROLLINS, 5 Clara Sherwood (Mrs.)	ROOSEVELT, 1 Henry Latrobe
RODNEY, Thomas H	ROGERS, Edward H	ROGERS, Sion Hart H	ROLLINS, Edward Henry H	ROOSEVELT, H Hilborne Lewis
RODRIGUEZ, 1 Jose Ignacio	ROGERS, Edward Sidney 2	ROGERS, Stephen 1	ROLLINS, Edward 1 Warren	ROOSEVELT, James I. 1
RODRIGUEZ- 5 SERRA, Manuel	ROGERS, H Edward Standiford	ROGERS, Thomas H	ROLLINS, Frank West 1	ROOSEVELT, Kermit 2
RODRIQUEZ, Abelardo 4	ROGERS, Ernest Albert 5	ROGERS, Thomas Jones H	ROLLINS, 1 George Sherman	ROOSEVELT, 4 Mrs. Theodore
RODZINSKI, Artur 3	ROGERS, Ernest Andrew 3	ROGERS, Tyler Stewart 4	ROLLINS, Hyder Edward 3	ROOSEVELT, Nicholas J. H
ROE, Arthur 2	ROGERS, Ernest Elias 2	ROGERS, Vance 4	ROLLINS, James Sidney 1	ROOSEVELT, 2 Philip James
ROE, Azel Stevens H	ROGERS, Eustace Barron 1	ROGERS, Waldo Henry 4	ROLLINS, James Wingate 1	ROOSEVELT, 1 Robert Barnwell
ROE, Charles Francis 1	ROGERS, Fairman 1	ROGERS, 4 Walter Alexander	ROLLINS, John Fox 4	ROOSEVELT, 1 S. Montgomery
ROE, Clifford Griffith 4	ROGERS, 4 Floyd Sterling Jr.	ROGERS, Walter Stowell 4	ROLLINS, Montgomery 1	ROOSEVELT, Theodore H
ROE, Edward Drake Jr. 1	ROGERS, Francis 3	ROGERS, Warren Lincoln 4	ROLLINS, Thornton 1	ROOSEVELT, Theodore 1
ROE, Edward Payson H	ROGERS, Frazier 3	ROGERS, Weaver Henry 1	ROLLINS, 3 Wallace Eugene	ROOSEVELT, Theodore 4
ROE, Francis Asbury 1	ROGERS, Fred A. 3	ROGERS, Will 4	ROLLINS, 1 Walter Huntington	ROOSEVELT, 2 Theodore Jr.
ROE, Frederick William 1	ROGERS, Fred S. 2	ROGERS, 5 Willard Benjamin	ROLLINSON, William H	ROOSEVELT, W. Emlen 1
ROE, George 4	ROGERS, 5 Frederick Morris	ROGERS, William Allen 1	ROLPH, James Jr. 1	ROOT, Amos Ives 1
ROE, Gilbert Ernstein 1	ROGERS, 4 Frederick Titsworth	ROGERS, William Arthur 2	ROLPH, John Gladwyn 3	ROOT, Azariah Smith 1
ROE, Herman 4	ROGERS, George Alfred 5	ROGERS, H William Augustus	ROLPH, Samuel Wyman 4	ROOT, Chapman Jay 4
ROE, James A. 4	ROGERS, 4 George Bartlett	ROGERS, William Banks 1	ROLSHOVEN, Julius 4	ROOT, Edward Clary 5
ROE, John Orlando 1	ROGERS, George Blake 4	ROGERS, William Barton H	ROLT-WHEELER, 4 Francis William	ROOT, Edward Tallmadge 2
ROE, Joseph Hyram 5	ROGERS, George F. 2	ROGERS, William Boddie 1	ROLVAAG, Ole Edvart 1	ROOT, Edwin Alvin 1
ROE, Joseph Wickham 4	ROGERS, 1 George McIntosh	ROGERS, 4 William Crowninshield	ROLZ-BENNETT, Jose 5	ROOT, Edwin Park 1
ROE, Nora Ardella 4	ROGERS, George Vernor 4	ROGERS, William F. 4	ROMA, Caro 4	ROOT, Elihu 1
ROE, Vingie Eve 3	ROGERS, Gordon B. 4	ROGERS, William Harlow 1	ROMAINS, Jules 5	ROOT, Elihu Jr. 4
ROE, William Edgar 1	ROGERS, Haratio 1	ROGERS, William King 1	ROMAN, Andre Bienvenu H	ROOT, Elisha King H
ROEBER, Eugene Franz 1	ROGERS, H Harriet Burbank	ROGERS, 5 William Loveland	ROMAN, 2 Frederick William	ROOT, Erastus H
ROEBLING, Ferdinand W. 1	ROGERS, 4 Harriet Burbank	ROGERS, 2 William Nathaniel	ROMAN, James Dixon H	ROOT, Ernest Rob 5
ROEBLING, 1 Ferdinand William Jr.	ROGERS, Harry Clayton 5	ROGERS, William Oscar 4	ROMAN, 3 Victor M. Reyes Y.	ROOT, Frank Albert 4
ROEBLING, H John Augustus	ROGERS, Harry H. 3	ROGERS, 1 William Pennock	ROMANOWITZ, Harry 5 Alex	ROOT, Frank Douglas 4
ROEBLING, 1 Washington Augustus	ROGERS, Harry Lovejoy 3	ROGERS, William Perry 1	ROMANS, Bernard H	ROOT, Frederic Woodman 1
ROEBUCK, John Ransom 5	ROGERS, Harry Stanley 3	ROGERS, Wynne Grey 1	ROMAYNE, Nicholas 4	ROOT, 1 Frederick Stanley
ROEBUCK, John Ransom 4	ROGERS, Henry Darwin H	ROGERSON, 1 Charles Edward	ROMBAUER, 4 Roderick Emile	ROOT, George Frederick H
ROEDDER, 2 Edwin Carl Lothar Clemens	ROGERS, Henry H. 1	ROGOSIN, I. 5	ROMBERG, Sigmund 3	ROOT, Howard Frank 4
ROEDER, Adolph 4	ROGERS, 1 Henry Huddleston	ROHBACH, 1 James Alexander	ROME, Charles A. 3	ROOT, Jesse H
ROEDER, 5 Bernard Franklin	ROGERS, Henry J. H	ROHDE, Ruth Bryan 3	ROMEIKE, Henry 1	ROOT, Jesse L. 3
ROEDER, Fred Vincent 5	ROGERS, Henry Munroe 1	ROHE, Charles Henry 4	ROMER, Arthur C. 4	ROOT, John Wellborn 1
ROEDER, 4 Geraldine Morgan	ROGERS, Henry Treat 1	ROHE, George Henry 1	ROMERA-NAVARRO, 4 Miguel	ROOT, John Wellborn 4
ROEHM, Alfred Isaac 2	ROGERS, Henry Wade 1	ROHLFING, 3 Charles Carroll	ROMIG, Edgar Franklin 1	ROOT, Joseph Cullen 5
ROEHR, Julius Edward 1	ROGERS, Herbert Wesley 1	ROHLFS, 4 Anna Katharine Green	ROMIG, John Samuel 1	ROOT, Joseph Edward 1
ROEHRIG, 1 Frederic Louis Otto	ROGERS, 2 Hopewell Lindenberger	ROHLFS, Charles 1	ROMINGER, Carl Ludwig 1	ROOT, Joseph Mosley 1
ROELKER, 1 Charles Rafael	ROGERS, Howard J. 3	ROHLMAN, Henry P. 3	ROMMEL, 2 George McCullough	ROOT, Joseph Pomeroy H
ROELKER, 3 William Greene	ROGERS, Howard Jason 5	ROHN, Oscar 1	ROMODA, Joseph J. 4	ROOT, Louis Carroll 1
ROEMER, Ferdinand H	ROGERS, Hubert E. 3	ROHNSTOCK, J. Henry 3	ROMUALDEZ, Norberto 5	ROOT, Lyman C. 1
ROEMER, Henry A. 5	ROGERS, Isaiah 1	ROHR, Elizabeth 3	RONAN, Daniel John 5	ROOT, Mary Pauline 4
ROEMER, John Lincoln 4	ROGERS, J. Harris 1	ROHR, Frederick Hilmer 5	RONAN, James Joseph 1	ROOT, Milo Adelbert 1
ROEMER, Joseph 3	ROGERS, J. Speed 3	ROHRBACH, 3 John Francis Deems	RONAYNE, Maurice 1	ROOT, Oren 1
ROEMERSHAUSER, 5 Alvin E(arl)	ROGERS, James H	ROHRBACH, John J. 3	RONDTHALER, Edward 3	ROOT, Oren 4
ROERICH, 2 Nicholas Konstantin	ROGERS, James Blythe 1	ROHRBOUGH, Edward 4 G.	RONDTHALER, 3 Howard Edward	ROOT, Robert Cromwell 4
ROESCH, Charles Edward 1	ROGERS, 4 James Frederick	ROHRBOUGH, 1 Ralph Virgil	RONGY, Abraham Jacob 2	ROOT, Robert Kilburn 3
ROESCH, Karl Alexander 5	ROGERS, James Gamble 2	ROHRER, 3 Albert Lawrence	RONNEBECK, Arnold 2	ROOT, Walter Harold 5
ROESCH, Walter Alfred 4	ROGERS, James Grafton 5	ROHRER, Karl 1	RONNEBERG, 5 Earl Fridthjov	ROOT, Walter Stanton 5
ROESSLER, John Edward 4	ROGERS, James Harvey 1	ROHWER, Henry 1	RONON, Gerald 4	ROOT, William Campbell 5
ROESSNER, 5 Elmer (Stirling)	ROGERS, 1 James Hotchkiss	ROIG, Antonio A. 4	ROOD, A. Edward 4	ROOT, William Thomas 2
ROETHKE, Theodore 4	ROGERS, James Sterling 5	ROIG, Harold Joseph 5	ROOD, Dorothy B. A. 4	ROOT, William Webster 1
ROETHKE, William A. C. 4	ROGERS, James Tracy 1	ROJANKOVSKY, Feodor 5 S.	ROOD, James Theron 1	ROOT, Winfred Trexler 2
ROETTER, Paulus 1	ROGERS, Jason 1	ROJAS, P. Ezequiel 1	ROOD, Ogden Nicholas 1	ROOTH, Ivar 5
ROEVER, William Henry 3	ROGERS, John * H	ROJTMAN, Marc B. 4	ROOD, Paul William 2	ROOTS, Logan Herbert 1
ROGAN, Fred Leon 3	ROGERS, John * 1	ROLAPP, Henry Hermann 1	ROOK, 4 Charles Alexander	ROOTS, Logan Holt H
ROGAN, James S. 3	ROGERS, John Edward 2	ROLER, 1 Edward Oscar Fitzalan	ROOK, Edward Francis 4	ROPER, Alvin Whitehead 1
ROGAN, Ralph Frederic 1	ROGERS, John Henry 1	ROLETTE, Jean Joseph H	ROOK, Gustav S. 1	ROPER, Daniel Calhoun 2
ROGERS, Alfred Moore 4	ROGERS, John I. 4	ROLFE, 2 Alfred Grosvenor	ROOKER, 5 Frederick Zadok	ROPER, Denney Warren 4
ROGERS, Alfred Thomas 2	ROGERS, John Jacob 1	ROLFE, Charles Wesley 1	ROOME, Kenneth Andrew 5	ROPER, John Caswell 3
ROGERS, Allan Buttrick 4	ROGERS, John Rankin 1	ROLFE, Daniel Thomas 5	ROONEY, John Jerome 1	ROPER, John Wesley 4
ROGERS, Allen 1	ROGERS, John Raphael 1	ROLFE, George William 2	ROONEY, Marie Collins 3	ROPER, Lewis Murphree 1
ROGERS, Allen Hastings 1	ROGERS, John William 4	ROLFE, 4 Henry Winchester	ROOP, Hervin Ulysses 5	ROPER, Robert Poore 4
ROGERS, Arthur 4	ROGERS, Joseph Egerton 3	ROLFE, John H	ROOP, James Clawson 5	ROPER, William Winston 1
ROGERS, Arthur Curtis 1	ROGERS, Joseph Morgan 1	ROLFE, John Carew 2	ROORBACH, George 1 Byron	ROPERS, Harold 5
ROGERS, Arthur Kenyon 1	ROGERS, Julia Ellen 4	ROLFE, John Furman 1	ROOS, 3 Charles Frederick	ROPES, 1 Charles Joseph Hardy
ROGERS, Arthur Small 4	ROGERS, 1 Lebbeus Harding	ROLFE, Stanley Herbert 5	ROOS, Delmar Gerle 5	ROPES, James Hardy 1
ROGERS, Austin Flint 3	ROGERS, Lester Burton 5	ROLFE, William James 1	ROOS, Edwin G. 5	ROPES, John Codman 1
ROGERS, Austin Leonard 1	ROGERS, Lester Cushing 5	ROLFS, Fred Maas 5	ROOS, Frank John Jr. 4	ROPES, Joseph H
ROGERS, B. Talbot 1	ROGERS, Lore Alford 5	ROLFS, Peter Henry 5	ROOS, Robert Achille 3	ROPES, William Ladd 1
ROGERS, Bernard 5	ROGERS, Louis William 4	ROLLAND, Romaine 2	ROOS, Walter L. 5	RORABACK, Alberto T. 1
ROGERS, Bruce 1	ROGERS, Malcolm Joseph 5	ROLLEFSON, 3 Gerhard Krohn	ROOSA, 1 Daniel Bennett St John	RORABACK, J. Henry 4
ROGERS, 1 Cephas Brainerd	ROGERS, Marvin Carson 5	ROLLER, Charles S. Jr. 4	ROOSEVELT, 4 Anna Eleanor	RORABAUGH, Guy 5 Oscar
ROGERS, Charles H	ROGERS, Mary Cochrane 1	ROLLER, 1 Robert Douglas Jr.	ROOSEVELT, 1 Edith Kermit Carow	RORER, David H
ROGERS, Charles Butler 1	ROGERS, Max 1	ROLLER, Thomas J. 3	ROOSEVELT, H Franklin Delano	RORER, James Birch 5
ROGERS, Charles Custis 1	ROGERS, May 4	ROLLERT, Edward 5 Dumas	ROOSEVELT, 2 Franklin Delano	RORER, Sarah Tyson 1
ROGERS, Charles Darius 1	ROGERS, McLain 3	ROLLINS, H Alice Marland Wellington	ROOSEVELT, 4 Franklin Delano	RORER, Virgil Eugene 2
ROGERS, Charles Edwin 2	ROGERS, Moses H	ROLLINS, 4 Carl Purington	ROOSEVELT, 4 George Emlen	RORICK, John C. 4
ROGERS, 1 Charles Gardner	ROGERS, Oscar H. 1	ROLLINS, 3 Charles E. Jr.	ROOSEVELT, 1 George Washington	RORIMER, James J. 4
ROGERS, Clara Kathleen 1	ROGERS, 1 Philip Fletcher	ROLLINS, 4 Charles Leonard		RORIMER, Louis 1
ROGERS, Daisy Fiske 3	ROGERS, Randolph H			RORTY, 1 Malcolm Churchill
ROGERS, David Banks 4	ROGERS, Robert H			ROSA, Edward Bennett 1
ROGERS, David Barss 4	ROGERS, 1 Robert Cameron			ROSANOFF, Martin 3 Andre
ROGERS, David Camp 1	ROGERS, Robert Emmons 5			ROSATI, Joseph H
ROGERS, Donald Aquilla 5	ROGERS, Robert Empie H			ROSBAUD, Hans 4
ROGERS, Donald G. 3	ROGERS, Robert Samuel 1			ROSE, 4 Albert Chatellier
ROGERS, Dwight L. 3	ROGERS, Robert William 1			ROSE, Aquila H
ROGERS, Edith Nourse 4	ROGERS, Sampson, Jr. 5			ROSE, Arnold M. 4
	ROGERS, Samuel H. 4			ROSE, Benjamin Morris 5
	ROGERS, Samuel Lyle 4			ROSE, Billy 4
				ROSE, Carlton Raymond 5
				ROSE, Charles Bedell 4
				ROSE, Chauncey H

ROSE, D. Kenneth 4
ROSE, Dana 5
ROSE, David S. 4
ROSE, Donald Frank 4
ROSE, Dwight Chappell 5
ROSE, E(rnest) H(erbert) 5
ROSE, Edward H
ROSE, Edward Everley H
ROSE, Ernestine Louise Silsmondi Potowski H
ROSE, Flora 3
ROSE, Floyd 3
ROSE, Forrest Hobart 5
ROSE, Frank Bramwell 1
ROSE, Frank Watson 5
ROSE, George B. 2
ROSE, Guy 1
ROSE, Heloise Durant (Mrs. C. H. M. Rose) 5
ROSE, Henry Howard 4
ROSE, Henry Martin 1
ROSE, Henry Reuben 3
ROSE, Herschel Hampton 2
ROSE, Hugh Edward Hon 2
ROSE, John Carter 1
ROSE, John Marshall 1
ROSE, Joseph Nelson 1
ROSE, Josiah Tryon 3
ROSE, Landon Cabell 1
ROSE, Lisle A. 5
ROSE, Marcus A. 4
ROSE, Martha Emily Parmelee 1
ROSE, Mary D. Swartz 5
ROSE, Maurice 2
ROSE, Philip Sheridan 4
ROSE, Ray Clarke 5
ROSE, Robert Forest 5
ROSE, Robert Hugh 5
ROSE, Robert Lawson H
ROSE, Robert Selden H
ROSE, Rufus Edwards 1
ROSE, S. Brandt 5
ROSE, Thomas Ellwood 1
ROSE, U. M. 1
ROSE, Wallace Dickinson 1
ROSE, Walter Malins 5
ROSE, Wickliffe 1
ROSE, William Brandon 2
ROSE, William Ganson 5
ROSE, William Hazael 4
ROSEBAULT, Charles Jerome 2
ROSEBUSH, Judson George 5
ROSECRANS, Egbert 2
ROSECRANS, Sylvester Horton H
ROSECRANS, William Starke; 5
ROSECRANS, William Starke H
ROSEKRANS, John Newton 4
ROSELAND, Harry 3
ROSELIUS, Christian H
ROSEN, Baron 2
ROSEN, Charles 3
ROSEN, Charles F. 5
ROSEN, Julius Jack 5
ROSEN, Max 3
ROSEN, Peter 3
ROSEN, Samuel 5
ROSEN, Victor Hugo 5
ROSENAU, Milton Joseph 3
ROSENBACH, Abraham S. Wolf 3
ROSENBACH, Joseph Bernhardt 3
ROSENBAUM, Edward Philip H
ROSENBAUM, Lewis Newman 3
ROSENBAUM, Otho Bane 5
ROSENBAUM, Samuel Rawlins 5
ROSENBAUM, Solomon Guedalia 1
ROSENBERG, Arthur 2
ROSENBERG, Henry H
ROSENBERG, Henry A. 3
ROSENBERG, Israel 3
ROSENBERG, James N. 5
ROSENBERG, S. L. Millard 1
ROSENBERG, Samuel 5
ROSENBERGER, Absalom 4
ROSENBERGER, Carl 3
ROSENBERGER, Gerald E. 4

ROSENBERRY, Lois Carter Kimball Mathews (Mrs. Marvin Bristol 5
ROSENBERRY, M. Claude 3
ROSENBERRY, Marvin Bristol 3
ROSENBLATT, Sol A(riah) 5
ROSENBLUETH, Arturo Stearns 5
ROSENBLUM, Frank 5
ROSENBLUM, Herman 5
ROSENBLUM, Jacob Joseph 5
ROSENBLUM, William Franklin 4
ROSENDALE, Simon Wolfe 1
ROSENFELD, Maurice 5
ROSENFELD, Paul 2
ROSENFELD, Sydney 1
ROSENFIELD, John 4
ROSENGARTEN, Adolph George 2
ROSENGARTEN, Frederic 3
ROSENGARTEN, George David 1
ROSENGARTEN, Joseph George 4
ROSENGRANT, E. Judson 4
ROSENHEIM, Alfred Faist 2
ROSENHOLTZ, Joseph Leon 4
ROSENKAMPFF, Arthur H. 3
ROSENMAN, Samuel Irving 5
ROSENMILLER, Joseph Lewis 4
ROSENSOHN, Etta Lasker 4
ROSENSON, Alexander Moses 5
ROSENSTEIN, David 4
ROSENSTENGEL, W. E. 5
ROSENSTOCK-HUESSY, Eugen 5
ROSENTHAL, Albert 1
ROSENTHAL, Benjamin 3
ROSENTHAL, David S. 3
ROSENTHAL, Doris 1
ROSENTHAL, Herman 1
ROSENTHAL, Ida 5
ROSENTHAL, Jean 5
ROSENTHAL, Lessing 2
ROSENTHAL, Louis S. 1
ROSENTHAL, Max 1
ROSENTHAL, Moritz 5
ROSENTHAL, Morris Sigmund 3
ROSENTHAL, Sarah G(ertrude) 5
ROSENTHAL, Toby E. 1
ROSENWALD, Julius 3
ROSER, Henry Harvoleau 4
ROSEWATER, Andrew 1
ROSEWATER, Charles Colman 2
ROSEWATER, Edward 3
ROSEWATER, Stanley Meinrath 3
ROSEWATER, Victor 1
ROSIER, Joseph 3
ROSING, Leonard August 4
ROSING, Vladimir 4
ROSLING, George 5
ROSS, Abel Hastings H
ROSS, Albert * 1
ROSS, Albert Randolph 4
ROSS, Alexander H
ROSS, Alexander Coffman 3
ROSS, Alfred Joseph 5
ROSS, Allan Charles 4
ROSS, Arthur Leonidas 4
ROSS, Arthur M(ax) 5
ROSS, Austin C. 3
ROSS, Bennett Battle 1
ROSS, Bernard Rogan H
ROSS, Betsy H
ROSS, Carmon 2
ROSS, Charles Ben 2
ROSS, Charles Griffith 5
ROSS, Clarence Frisbee 2
ROSS, Clay Campbell 2
ROSS, Clinton 1
ROSS, David H
ROSS, David E. 2
ROSS, Denman Waldo 1
ROSS, Donald 5
ROSS, Earle D(udley) 5
ROSS, Edmund Gibson H

ROSS, Edmund Gibson 4
ROSS, Edward Alsworth 5
ROSS, Emory 5
ROSS, Erskine Mayo 1
ROSS, Frank Alexander 5
ROSS, Frank Elmore 4
ROSS, Frank James 4
ROSS, Frank MacKenzie 5
ROSS, Frederick Jeffery 3
ROSS, G. A. Johnston 1
ROSS, George H
ROSS, George H. 4
ROSS, Harold Wallace 4
ROSS, Harry Seymour 2
ROSS, Henry Davis 1
ROSS, Henry Howard H
ROSS, Homer Lachlin 4
ROSS, J. Walker 1
ROSS, James 1
ROSS, James Delmage 1
ROSS, James Lycurgus 1
ROSS, John * H
ROSS, John Dawson 1
ROSS, John Elliot 2
ROSS, John Jacob 3
ROSS, John Mason 2
ROSS, John O. 4
ROSS, John Wesley 1
ROSS, John William 1
ROSS, John William * 4
ROSS, Jonathan 1
ROSS, Joseph 4
ROSS, Julian Lenhart 5
ROSS, Lawrence Sullivan H
ROSS, Leonard Fulton 1
ROSS, Leroy Williams 1
ROSS, Lester J. 5
ROSS, Letitia Roano Dowdell 3
ROSS, Lewis P. 1
ROSS, Lewis T. 3
ROSS, Lewis Winans 1
ROSS, Luther Sherman 4
ROSS, Malcolm 4
ROSS, Martin H
ROSS, Michael 4
ROSS, Ogden 5
ROSS, Patrick Hore Warriner 1
ROSS, Perley Ason 1
ROSS, Peter V. 2
ROSS, Philip James 3
ROSS, Robert Edwin 1
ROSS, Samuel Louis 5
ROSS, Sarah Gridley 4
ROSS, Sobieski H
ROSS, Thomas H
ROSS, Thomas Randolph 4
ROSS, Walter L. 1
ROSS, Wilbert Davidson 2
ROSS, William Bradford 1
ROSS, William Horace 5
ROSS, William McAllister 1
ROSS, Worth Gwynn 1
ROSSBACH, Edgar Hilary 3
ROSSBY, Carl-Gustaf Arvid 3
ROSSEAU, Lovell Harrison H
ROSSEAU, Percival Leonard 1
ROSSELL, John Settles 1
ROSSELL, William Trent 1
ROSSELLE, William Quay 5
ROSSEN, Robert 4
ROSSER, Luther Zeigler 1
ROSSER, Thomas Lafayette 1
ROSSETER, John Henry 5
ROSSETTER, George W. 3
ROSSETTI, Victor H. 4
ROSSEY, Chris C. 2
ROSSI, Angelo Joseph 2
ROSSI, Louis Mansfield 2
ROSSI, Luis Banchero 2
ROSSITER, Clinton 5
ROSSITER, Edward Van Wyck 1
ROSSITER, Ehrick Kensett 2
ROSSITER, Fred J. 4
ROSSITER, Frederick McGee 5
ROSSITER, Perceval Sherer 1
ROSSITER, Stealy Bales 1
ROSSITER, Thomas Prichard H
ROSSITER, William Sidney 1
ROSSLYN, John 4
ROSSMAN, George 4
ROSSMAN, Joseph 5
ROSSMAN, Samuel S. 5

ROSSO, Augusto 4
ROSTOCK, Frank Witte 4
ROSTOVTZEFF, Michael Ivanovich 3
ROSZEL, Brantz Mayer 1
ROTCH, A. Lawrence 1
ROTCH, Arthur H
ROTCH, Thomas Morgan 1
ROTCH, William 1
ROTCH, William 1
ROTCHFORD, Hugh Babb H
ROTH, Ben 3
ROTH, Feri 5
ROTH, Filibert 1
ROTH, Frederick George Richard 2
ROTH, Henry Warren 4
ROTH, John Ernest 4
ROTH, Paul Hoerlein 4
ROTH, William P. 4
ROTHAFEL, Samuel Lionel H
ROTHAFEL, Samuel Lionel 4
ROTHBERG, Sidney 5
ROTHENBERG, Milton 5
ROTHENBERG, Morris 3
ROTHENBURGER, William Frederic 5
ROTHERMEL, Amos Cornelius 2
ROTHERMEL, John Goodhart 1
ROTHERMEL, John H. 1
ROTHERMEL, Peter Frederick H
ROTHIER, Leon 5
ROTHKO, Mark 5
ROTHMAN, Stephen 4
ROTHROCK, Addison M(ay) 5
ROTHROCK, David Andrew 4
ROTHROCK, Edward Streicher 4
ROTHROCK, Joseph Trimble 1
ROTHSCHILD, Alonzo 1
ROTHSCHILD, Karl 5
ROTHSCHILD, Louis F. 3
ROTHSCHILD, Marcus A. 1
ROTHSCHILD, Maurice 2
ROTHSCHILD, Walter Nathan 4
ROTHSTEIN, Irma 5
ROTHWELL, Bernard Joseph 2
ROTHWELL, Gideon Frank H
ROTHWELL, Richard Pennefather 1
ROTHWELL, Will A. 1
ROTNEM, Ralph Arthur 5
ROTTGER, Curtis Hoopes 4
ROTZELL, Willett Enos 1
ROUAULT, Georges 3
ROUCOLLE, Adrienne (Miss) 5
ROUDEBUSH, Alfred Holt 2
ROULAND, Orlando 2
ROULHAC, Thomas Ruffin 4
ROULSTON, Marjorie Hillis 5
ROULSTONE, George H
ROUND, William Marshall Fitts 1
ROUNDS, Arthur Charles 1
ROUNDS, Leslie Raymond 4
ROUNDS, Ralph Stowell 2
ROUNTREE, George 1
ROUQUETTE, Adrien Emmanuel H
ROUQUETTE, Francois Dominique H
ROURKE, Constance Mayfield 1
ROURKE, Frank W. 2
ROUS, (Francis) Peyton 5
ROUSE, Adelaide Louise 1
ROUSE, Arthur B. 5
ROUSE, Henry Clark 1
ROUSE, John Delos 4
ROUSE, John Gould 4
ROUSH, Gar A. 3
ROUSH, Oliver Eugene 5
ROUSMANIERE, Edmund Swett 1
ROUSS, Charles Broadway 1
ROUSSE, Thomas Andrew 4
ROUSSEAU, Harry Harwood 5

ROUSSEVE, Ferdinand Lucien 4
ROUTH, Eugene Coke 5
ROUTLEY, Thomas Clarence 4
ROUTT, John Long 1
ROUTZAHN, Evart Grant 1
ROUTZOHN, Harry Nelson 3
ROUXEL, Gustave Augustin 1
ROVENSKY, Joseph Charles 3
ROVENSTINE, E. A. 4
ROVER, Leo Aloysius 4
ROVERSI, Louis 1
ROW, Robert Keable 1
ROW, William Hamilton 4
ROWAN, Andrew Summers 2
ROWAN, Charles A. 1
ROWAN, Charles Joseph 1
ROWAN, John H
ROWAN, Joseph 1
ROWAN, Richard Wilmer 5
ROWAN, Stephen Clegg H
ROWAN, Thomas Leslie 5
ROWAN, William A. 5
ROWBOTTOM, Harry E. 1
ROWCLIFF, Gilbert 5
ROWE, Albert Holmes 5
ROWE, Allan Winter 1
ROWE, Benjamin Ackley 1
ROWE, Clifford Paul 5
ROWE, Frederick William 2
ROWE, Gilbert Theodore 4
ROWE, Guy 5
ROWE, Hartley 1
ROWE, Henrietta Gould 5
ROWE, Henry Clarke 4
ROWE, Henry Kalloch 1
ROWE, Jesse Perry 5
ROWE, Joseph Eugene 5
ROWE, L. Earle 4
ROWE, Leo S. 2
ROWE, Peter H
ROWE, Peter Trimble 2
ROWE, Robert G. 5
ROWE, Stuart Henry 5
ROWE, Walter Ellsworth 3
ROWE, William Stanhope 1
ROWELL, Chester Harvey 2
ROWELL, George Presbury 1
ROWELL, George Smith 4
ROWELL, Hugh Grant 4
ROWELL, James G. 3
ROWELL, John W. 1
ROWELL, Jonathan Harvey 1
ROWELL, Joseph Cummings 1
ROWELL, Ross Erastus 5
ROWELL, Wilbur Everett 2
ROWELL, Wilfrid Asa 3
ROWLAND, Adoniram Judson 1
ROWLAND, Arthur John 1
ROWLAND, Benjamin, Jr. 5
ROWLAND, Charles H. 4
ROWLAND, Charles Leonard 1
ROWLAND, Clarence H. 5
ROWLAND, Dunbar 1
ROWLAND, Harry T. 3
ROWLAND, Henry Augustus 1
ROWLAND, Henry Cottrell 1
ROWLAND, James Marshall Hanna 3
ROWLAND, Joseph Medley 1
ROWLAND, Kate Mason 1
ROWLAND, Vernon Cecil 4
ROWLAND, William Samuel 1
ROWLANDS, William H
ROWLANDSON, Mary White H
ROWLEE, Willard Winfield 1
ROWLETT, Robert 1
ROWLEY, Francis Harold 1
ROWLEY, Frank S. 3
ROWLEY, George 4
ROWLEY, John 1
ROWLEY, William C. 4
ROWSE, Samuel Worcester H
ROWSON, Susanna Haswell H
ROXAS, Manuel 2
ROY, Arthur Jay 2
ROY, Francis Albert 1
ROY, Lillian Elizabeth 5

ROY, Percy Albert 2
ROY, Philip Seddon 4
ROY, Reuben Finnell 4
ROY, Sharat Kumar 4
ROY, Victor Leander, Sr. 5
ROYAL, Forrest 2
ROYAL, George 1
ROYAL, Ralph 1
ROYALL, Anne Newport H
ROYALL, Kenneth Claiborne 5
ROYALL, Ralph 3
ROYALL, Tucker 1
ROYALL, William Bailey 1
ROYALTY, Paul 4
ROYCE, Alexander Burgess
ROYCE, Asa Marshfield 4
ROYCE, Donald 5
ROYCE, Frederick Page 1
ROYCE, George Monroe 4
ROYCE, Homer Elihu H
ROYCE, Josiah 1
ROYCE, Luman Herbert 1
ROYCE, Robert Russel 5
ROYCE, Sarah Eleanor Bayliss H
ROYE, Edward James H
ROYER, Arnold Lennel 1
ROYER, J. E. E. 3
ROYLE, Edwin Milton 2
ROYSE, Samuel Durham 1
ROYSTER, Hubert Ashley 5
ROYSTER, James Finch 1
ROYSTER, Lawrence Thomas 5
RUARK, Robert Chester 4
RUBATTEL, Rodolphe 4
RUBEL, A. C. 4
RUBEN, Barney 3
RUBENDALL, Clarence 2
RUBENS, Harry 1
RUBENS, Horatio Seymour
RUBEY, Thomas Lewis 1
RUBIN, J. Robert 3
RUBIN, William Benjamin
RUBIN DE LA BORBOLLA, Daniel Fernando 5
RUBINKAM, Nathaniel Irwin 1
RUBINOVITZ, George 5
RUBINOW, Isaac Max 3
RUBINSTEIN, Beryl 4
RUBINSTEIN, Helena 1
RUBIO, Antonio 3
RUBIO, David 4
RUBLEE, George 3
RUBLEE, Horace H
RUBLEE, William Alvah 1
RUBY, Edward Ernest 5
RUBY, Lionel 5
RUCH, Giles Murrel 2
RUCKER, Allen Willis 4
RUCKER, Atterson Walden 2
RUCKER, Casper Bell 2
RUCKER, D. H. H
RUCKER, Daniel Henry 1
RUCKER, Elbert Marion 1
RUCKER, Louis H. 1
RUCKER, Marvin Pierce 4
RUCKER, William Colby 1
RUCKER, William Waller 1
RUCKMAN, John Wilson 4
RUCKMICK, Christian Alban
RUCKSTULL, Fred Wellington 2
RUDD, Judson Archer 5
RUDD, Stephan A. 1
RUDD, Thomas Brown 4
RUDD, William Platt 1
RUDDER, James Earl 5
RUDDIMAN, Edsel Alexander 5
RUDDIMAN, Edsel Alexander 3
RUDDOCK, John Carroll 4
RUDDOCK, Malcolm Irving 4
RUDDY, Edward Michael 5
RUDDY, Howard Shaw 1
RUDENBERG, Reinhold 4
RUDENKO, William Bernard 4
RUDER, William Ernst 4
RUDERSDORFF, Hermine H
RUDGE, William Edwin 1
RUDICK, Harry J. 5
RUDINGER, Ellen Eckstein (Mrs. George Rudinger)

RUDKIN, Frank H. 1
RUDKIN, Margaret Fogarty 4
RUDOLPH, Charles 4
RUDOLPH, Cuna H. 1
RUDOLPH, Herbert Blaine 3
RUDOLPH, Irving 4
RUDOLPH, Jacob H. 1
RUDOLPH, Robert Livingston 3
RUE, Lars 4
RUE, Levi Lingo 1
RUE, Milton 5
RUE, Ralph H. 4
RUEBUSH, James Hott 5
RUEDEMANN, Rudolf 3
RUEDIGER, Gustav F. 1
RUEDIGER, William Carl 1
RUEHE, Harrison August 3
RUETENIK, Herman Julius 4
RUFF, G. Elson 1
RUFF, Robert Hamric 2
RUFFIN, Edmund H
RUFFIN, Margaret Ellen Henry 5
RUFFIN, Sterling 2
RUFFIN, Thomas * H
RUFFINI, Elise Erna 5
RUFFNER, Charles Shumway 1
RUFFNER, Ernest Howard 4
RUFFNER, Henry 1
RUFFNER, William Henry 1
RUFUS, Will Carl 2
RUGER, Thomas Howard 4
RUGG, Arthur Prentice 1
RUGG, Charles Belcher 1
RUGG, Frederic Waldo 1
RUGG, Harold 4
RUGG, Henry Warren 1
RUGG, Herbert Dean 5
RUGG, Robert Billings 2
RUGGLES, Arthur Hiler 4
RUGGLES, Benjamin 1
RUGGLES, Carl 5
RUGGLES, Charles 5
RUGGLES, Charles Herman H
RUGGLES, Clyde Orval 3
RUGGLES, Colden L'Hommedieu 1
RUGGLES, E. Wood 2
RUGGLES, George David 1
RUGGLES, Henry Joseph 1
RUGGLES, John H
RUGGLES, Nathaniel H
RUGGLES, Oliver W. 1
RUGGLES, Samuel Bulkley H
RUGGLES, Timothy H
RUGGLES, William Burroughs 4
RUGH, Charles Edward 4
RUHE, Percy Bott 5
RUHL, Arthur Brown 5
RUHL, Christian H. 4
RUHL, James Brough 4
RUHL, Robert Waldo 4
RUHLENDER, Henry 1
RUHRAH, John 1
RUIZ, Jose Martinez 4
RUIZ GUINAZO, Enrique 4
RULAND, Lloyd Stanton 3
RULE, Arthur Richards 1
RULE, James Noble 1
RULE, William 1
RULON, Phillip Justin 5
RUMBOLD, Frank Meeker 1
RUMBOLD, Thomas Frazier 1
RUMELY, Edward A. 4
RUMELY, V. P. 4
RUMELY, William Nicholas 4
RUMFORD, Count H
RUML, Beardsley 3
RUMMEL, Joseph F. 4
RUMPF, Arthur Newell 5
RUMPLE, J. N. W. 1
RUMSEY, Benjamin 1
RUMSEY, Charles Cary 1
RUMSEY, David 4
RUMSEY, Dexter Phelps 4
RUMSEY, Israel Parsons 4
RUMSEY, James H
RUMSEY, Mary Harriman 4
RUMSEY, William 1
RUNCIE, Constance Fauntleroy 1
RUNDALL, Charles O. 3
RUNDELL, Oliver Samuel 3

RUNDLE, George Mortimer 4
RUNDQUIST, George E. 5
RUNGE, Edith Amelie 5
RUNGIUS, Carl 3
RUNK, John H
RUNKLE, Benjamin Platt 1
RUNKLE, Delmer 1
RUNKLE, Erwin William 1
RUNKLE, Harry Godley 4
RUNKLE, Harry Maize 4
RUNKLE, John Daniel 1
RUNKLE, Lucia Isabella 4
RUNNELLS, Clive 1
RUNNELLS, John Sumner 1
RUNNELS, Orange Scott 1
RUNNER, Harvey Evan 4
RUNNING, Theodore Rudolph 5
RUNYAN, Elmer Gardner 4
RUNYAN, William B. 3
RUNYON, Alfred Damon 2
RUNYON, John William 4
RUNYON, W. Parker 1
RUNYON, William Nelson 1
RUOFF, Henry Woldmar 1
RUOPP, Harold Washington 4
RUOTOLO, Onorio 4
RUPE, Dallas Gordon 5
RUPEL, I(saac) Walker 4
RUPERTUS, William Henry 2
RUPLEY, Arthur Ringwalt 4
RUPLEY, Joseph William 5
RUPP, Charles, Jr. 5
RUPP, Israel Daniel H
RUPP, Lawrence Henry 1
RUPP, Otto Burton 4
RUPP, Werner Andrew 4
RUPP, William 1
RUPPEL, Louis 3
RUPPENTHAL, Jacob Christian 4
RUPPERT, George E. 2
RUPPERT, Jacob Jr. 1
RUPPERT, Max King 4
RUPPRECHT, Frederick Kelsey 3
RUSBY, Henry Hurd 1
RUSH, Benjamin H
RUSH, Benjamin 2
RUSH, Charles Andrew 4
RUSH, Franklin Smithwick 1
RUSH, Guy Mansfield 4
RUSH, Jacob H
RUSH, James H
RUSH, John Andrew 2
RUSH, Olive 4
RUSH, Richard H
RUSH, Sylvester R. 1
RUSH, Thomas E. 1
RUSH, William H
RUSHING, James Andrew 5
RUSHMORE, David Barker 1
RUSHMORE, Edward 4
RUSHMORE, John Dikeman 4
RUSHMORE, Stephen 5
RUSHTON, Herbert J. 2
RUSHTON, Ray 1
RUSHTON, Richard Holt 4
RUSK, Henry Perly 3
RUSK, Jeremiah McLain 1
RUSK, John 1
RUSK, Ralph Leslie 4
RUSK, Thomas Jefferson H
RUSKIN, Jerrold Harold 5
RUSLING, James Fowler 1
RUSS, Hugh McMaster 5
RUSS, John H
RUSS, John Denison H
RUSS, John Megginson 4
RUSS, John T. 3
RUSSEL, Edgar 1
RUSSEL, George Howard 1
RUSSEL, Henry 1
RUSSEL, Walter S. 1
RUSSELL, Addison Peale 1
RUSSELL, Albert Hyatt 4
RUSSELL, Alexander 3
RUSSELL, Alexander Wilson
RUSSELL, Alfred 1
RUSSELL, Annie 1
RUSSELL, Arthur Joseph 4
RUSSELL, Arthur Perkins 2
RUSSELL, Benjamin * H
RUSSELL, Bertrand, Earl Russell
RUSSELL, Bruce Alexander 4

RUSSELL, Charles 3
RUSSELL, Charles Addison 1
RUSSELL, Charles Augustus 4
RUSSELL, Charles Edward 1
RUSSELL, Charles Howland 1
RUSSELL, Charles Marion 4
RUSSELL, Charles Partridge 4
RUSSELL, Charles Taze 1
RUSSELL, Charles Tier 3
RUSSELL, Charles Wells 1
RUSSELL, Clinton Warden 2
RUSSELL, Daniel 2
RUSSELL, Daniel Lindsay 1
RUSSELL, David Abel H
RUSSELL, David Allen H
RUSSELL, Doris Aurelia 4
RUSSELL, Edmund A. 4
RUSSELL, Edward Hutson 5
RUSSELL, Edward Lafayette 1
RUSSELL, Elbert 3
RUSSELL, Elias Harlow 1
RUSSELL, Ernest John 3
RUSSELL, Faris R. 5
RUSSELL, Francis Thayer 3
RUSSELL, Francis Wayland 5
RUSSELL, Frank 1
RUSSELL, Frank F. 5
RUSSELL, Frank Marion 1
RUSSELL, Frederick Fuller 4
RUSSELL, George 3
RUSSELL, George Edmond 3
RUSSELL, George Harvey 2
RUSSELL, George Louis Jr. 1
RUSSELL, Gordon 1
RUSSELL, H(arry) Earle 5
RUSSELL, Harry Luman 5
RUSSELL, Harry Newton 1
RUSSELL, Helen Crocker 4
RUSSELL, Helen Gertrude 5
RUSSELL, Henry 2
RUSSELL, Henry Benajah 1
RUSSELL, Henry Dozier 5
RUSSELL, Henry Moore 4
RUSSELL, Henry Norris 1
RUSSELL, Herbert Edwin 4
RUSSELL, Herman 1
RUSSELL, Horace 2
RUSSELL, Howard Hyde 2
RUSSELL, Irwin H
RUSSELL, Isaac Franklin 1
RUSSELL, Israel Cook 1
RUSSELL, J. Henry 1
RUSSELL, J. J. 3
RUSSELL, J. Stuart 4
RUSSELL, James Earl 2
RUSSELL, James McPherson H
RUSSELL, James Solomon 1
RUSSELL, Jane Anne 4
RUSSELL, Jeremiah H
RUSSELL, John 3
RUSSELL, John Andrew 1
RUSSELL, John Edward 1
RUSSELL, John Henry H
RUSSELL, John Henry 1
RUSSELL, Jonathan H
RUSSELL, Joseph * H
RUSSELL, Joseph Ballister 1
RUSSELL, Joseph Holt 4
RUSSELL, Joshua Edward 3
RUSSELL, L(ulu) Case 2
RUSSELL, Lee Maurice 2
RUSSELL, Lillian 1
RUSSELL, Louis Arthur 1
RUSSELL, Manley Holland 5
RUSSELL, Martin J. 1
RUSSELL, Mother Mary Baptist H
RUSSELL, Nelson Vance 4
RUSSELL, Norman Felt Shelton 3
RUSSELL, Osborne H
RUSSELL, Pastor 1
RUSSELL, Paul Snowden 2
RUSSELL, Richard Brevard 5
RUSSELL, Richard Brevard 1

RUSSELL, Richard Joel 5
RUSSELL, Robert 4
RUSSELL, Robert Lee 3
RUSSELL, Robert McWatty 1
RUSSELL, Robert Watrous 4
RUSSELL, Samuel, Jr. 5
RUSSELL, Samuel Lyon H
RUSSELL, Scott 3
RUSSELL, Sol Smith 1
RUSSELL, Stanley Addison 1
RUSSELL, Talcott Huntington 1
RUSSELL, Thomas Halbert 1
RUSSELL, Thomas Herbert 2
RUSSELL, Walter 4
RUSSELL, Walter C. 3
RUSSELL, Walter Earle 2
RUSSELL, William * H
RUSSELL, William Eustus H
RUSSELL, William Fiero 3
RUSSELL, William Fletcher H
RUSSELL, William Henry H
RUSSELL, William Hepburn H
RUSSELL, William Hepburn 5
RUSSELL, William Logie 3
RUSSELL, William Logie 4
RUSSELL, William Loughlin 1
RUSSELL, William T. 1
RUSSELL, William Worthington 3
RUSSUM, B. C. 5
RUSSUM, Sarah Elizabeth H
RUSSWURM, John Brown H
RUST, Albert 3
RUST, Charles Herbert 3
RUST, Henry Bedinger 3
RUST, John Daniel 3
RUST, Mack Donald 4
RUST, Walter L. 3
RUSTGARD, John 2
RUSTIN, Henry 4
RUSTON, John Edward 1
RUSTON, William Otis 1
RUTAN, Charles Hercules 3
RUTAN, Harold Duane 1
RUTGERS, Henry 2
RUTH, Carl Douglas 3
RUTH, George Herman 5
RUTH, Henry Swartley 1
RUTH, John A. 1
RUTH, John P(illing) 1
RUTHERFORD, Albert Greig 3
RUTHERFORD, Alexander H. 1
RUTHERFORD, Clarendon 4
RUTHERFORD, George H. 5
RUTHERFORD, Margaret 1
RUTHERFORD, Mildred Lewis H
RUTHERFORD, Robert 1
RUTHERFORD, S. Morton 4
RUTHERFORD, Samuel H
RUTHERFURD, John 1
RUTHERFURD, John H
RUTHERFURD, Lewis Morris 1
RUTHRAUFF, John Mosheim 5
RUTHVEN, Alexander G(rant) 2
RUTLAND, James Richard 4
RUTLEDGE, Ann
RUTLEDGE, Benjamin Huger 3
RUTLEDGE, Carl P. H
RUTLEDGE, Edward 2
RUTLEDGE, George Perry H
RUTLEDGE, John H
RUTLEDGE, John Jr. H
RUTLEDGE, Thomas G. 4
RUTLEDGE, Wiley Blount 1
RUTT, Christian Louis 1
RUTTENBER, Edward Manning 1
RUTTER, Frank Roy
RUTTER, Henley Chapman 1
RUTTER, Josiah Baldwin 3

RUTTER, Robert Lewis 4
RUUD, Martin Bronn 1
RUUTZ-REES, Caroline 3
RUYLE, John Bryan 3
RUZICKA, Charles 3
RYALL, Daniel Bailey H
RYALS, Thomas Edward 2
RYAN, Abram Joseph H
RYAN, Arthur 5
RYAN, Clement Daniel 2
RYAN, Clendenin J. 1
RYAN, Cornelius Edward 5
RYAN, Daniel Joseph 1
RYAN, Dennis H
RYAN, Edward Francis 3
RYAN, Edward George H
RYAN, Edward William 1
RYAN, Elmer James 3
RYAN, 3
  Evelyn Althea Murphy
RYAN, Francis Joseph 3
RYAN, Franklin Winton 3
RYAN, 3
  Frederick Behrens
RYAN, George Joseph 2
RYAN, Harris Joseph 1
RYAN, J. Harold 4
RYAN, James 3
RYAN, James Augustine 3
RYAN, James Hugh 2
RYAN, James W. 1
RYAN, John Augustine 2
RYAN, John D. 1
RYAN, John J. Jr. 4
RYAN, John William 5
RYAN, Lewis Cook 1
RYAN, Marah Ellis 1
RYAN, Marah Ellis 4
RYAN, Martin Francis 1
RYAN, Michael J. 2
RYAN, 1
  Michael Sylvester
RYAN, O'Neill 1
RYAN, Patrick John 1
RYAN, Patrick John 3
RYAN, Patrick L. 5
RYAN, Raymond Richard 1
RYAN, Robert 5
RYAN, Stanley Martin 3
RYAN, Stephen Vincent H
RYAN, Thomas 1
RYAN, Thomas Curran 1
RYAN, Thomas Fortune 1
RYAN, Timothy Edward 4
RYAN, Vincent J. 3
RYAN, Will Carson 5
RYAN, William 1
RYAN, William Fitts 5
RYAN, William Henry 1
RYAN, William Patrick 1
RYAN, William Thomas 3
RYBNER, 1
  Martin Cornelius
RYBURN, Frank M. 4
RYCKMAN, 4
  Charles Silcott
RYCKMANS, Pierre 3
RYDBERG, Per Axel 1
RYDEN, George Herbert 1
RYDER, Albert Pinkham 1
RYDER, Arthur Hilton 2
RYDER, Arthur William 1
RYDER, Charles Jackson 1
RYDER, Charles Wolcott 4
RYDER, Chauncey Foster 3
RYDER, 1
  Frederick Milliachip
RYDER, George Hope 2
RYDER, Harry Osborne 1
RYDER, Oscar Baxter 5
RYDER, Robert Oliver 1
RYDER, H
  Thomas Philander
RYDER, William Henry 1
RYERSON, Edward 5
  Larned
RYERSON, Edward 1
  Larned
RYERSON, Edwin Warner 4
RYERSON, Joseph Turner 2
RYERSON, 1
  Martin Antoine
RYERSON, 5
  William Newton
RYGEL, John 3
RYGG, Andrew Nilsen 3
RYGH, George Taylor 4
RYKEN, Theodore James H
RYKENS, Paul 5
RYLANCE, Joseph Hine 1
RYLAND, Joseph R. 4
RYLAND, Robert H
RYLAND, Robert Knight 3
RYLAND, William Semple 1
RYLEE, William Jackson 4
RYMAN, James H. T. 1

RYNEARSON, Edward 1
RYNNING, Ole H
RYON, Harrison 5
RYONS, Joseph Leslie 4
RYS, 2
  Carl Friedrich Wilheim
RYUS, Celeste Nellis 5

S

SAALFIELD, 5
  Ada Louise (Ada Louise
  Sutton)
SAALFIELD, 3
  Albert George
SAAR, 1
  Louis Victor Franz
SAARINEN, 5
  Aline Bernstein
SAARINEN, Eero 4
SAARINEN, Eliel 3
SABATH, Adolph J. 1
SABATINI, Rafael 2
SABEN, Mowry 3
SABIN, Alvah H
SABIN, Alvah Horton 1
SABIN, 3
  Charles Hamilton
SABIN, Dwight May 1
SABIN, Edwin Legrand 5
SABIN, Elbridge Hosmer 1
SABIN, Ellen Clara 2
SABIN, Florence Rena 3
SABIN, Frances Ellis 2
SABIN, Henry 1
SABIN, Joseph 1
SABIN, Louis Carlton 3
SABIN, Wallace Arthur 1
SABINE, George Holland 4
SABINE, Lorenzo H
SABINE, 1
  Wallace Clement
SABINE, 2
  Wallace Clement
SABINE, 1
  William Tufnell
SACAGAWEA H
SACCO, Nicola 3
SACHS, Bernard 2
SACHS, Curt 5
SACHS, Ernest 3
SACHS, Howard Joseph 5
SACHS, James Henry 5
SACHS, Joseph 2
SACHS, Julius 1
SACHS, Morris Bernard 3
SACHS, Nelly 5
SACHS, Paul Joseph 4
SACHS, Teviah 3
SACHSE, 2
  Helena V. (mrs. Sadtler)
SACHSE, 1
  Julius Friedrich
SACHSE, Richard 4
SACK, Alexander Naoum 3
SACK, Henri S(amuel) 5
SACK, Leo R. 5
SACKETT, Carl Leroy 5
SACKETT, Earl L. 5
SACKETT, 1
  Frederic Moseley Jr.
SACKETT, 1
  Henry Woodward
SACKETT, Robert Lemuel 2
SACKETT, 5
  Samuel Jefferson
SACKETT, 5
  Sheldon F(red)
SACKETT, H
  William August
SACKETT, William Edgar 5
SACKS, Emanuel 3
SACKVILLE, Lord H
SACKVILLE-WEST, H
  Lionel
SACKVILLE-WEST, 4
  Lionel
SACKVILLE- 3
  WEST, Victoria
SADACCA, Henri 5
SADD, Walter Allen 5
SADLAK, 5
  Antoni Nicholas
SADLEIR, Michael 3
SADLER, Everit Jay 3
SADLER, 1
  Herbert Charles
SADLER, Lena Kellogg 1
SADLER, McGruder Ellis 4
SADLER, Reinhold 5
SADLER, 1
  Sylvester Baker
SADLER, Thomas William H
SADLER, Wilbur Fisk 5
SADLIER, Denis H
SADOWSKI, George G. 4

SADTLER, H
  John Phillip Benjamin
SADTLER, Samuel Philip 1
SAENDERL, Simon H
SAENGER, Oscar 4
SAERCHINGER, 5
  Cesar (Victor Charles)
SAFANIE, Murray D. 4
SAFAY, Fred A. 3
SAFFIN, William 1
SAFFIN, William 4
SAFFOLD, 2
  William Berney
SAFFORD, Agnes Mabel 1
SAFFORD, 2
  Harry Robinson
SAFFORD, James Merrill 1
SAFFORD, Mary Augusta 4
SAFFORD, Truman Henry 1
SAFFORD, William Edwin 1
SAGE, Agnes Carolyn 4
SAGE, Bernard Janin H
SAGE, Charles Gurdon 4
SAGE, Dean 1
SAGE, Eben Charles 1
SAGE, Ebenezer 1
SAGE, Evan Taylor 1
SAGE, Henry Williams H
SAGE, John Charles 1
SAGE, John Davis 1
SAGE, John Hall 1
SAGE, Kay 4
SAGE, Mrs. Russell 1
SAGE, Russell 1
SAGE, William 4
SAGE, William Hampden 1
SAGEBEER, Joseph Evans 1
SAGENDORPH, Kent 3
SAGENDORPH, Robb 5
SAGER, Edward Anton 2
SAGUE, James E. 4
SAHA, Meghnad 4
SAHLER, Charles Oliver 1
SAHLER, Helen 3
SAHLGREN, G. F. Joran 4
SAIDLA, 4
  Leo Erval Alexander
SAILER, Joseph 1
SAILLY, Peter H
SAINSBURY, 3
  William Charles
SAINT, Lawrence 4
SAINT, Percy 5
SAINT-AULAIRE, H
  Felix Achille
SAINT-COSME, 5
  Jean Francois Buisson 'de
SAINT-DENIS, 5
  Michel Jacques
ST. Denis, Ruth 5
SAINT GAUDENS, 1
  Augustus
SAINT-GAUDENS, 3
  Homer Schiff
SAINT GAUDENS, Louis 1
ST. John, 5
  Charles Griffin
ST. John, Francis R. 5
ST. John, 1
  Thomas Raymond
ST. Laurent, 5
  Louis Stephen
ST. Lewis, Roy 5
SAINT-MEMIN, H
  Charles Bathazar Julien
  Fevret 'de
ST. Onge, William Leon 5
SAINT-PALAIS, H
  Jacques Maurice Landes 'de
SAIT, Edward McChesney 2
SAITO, Hirosi 1
SAJOUS, 1
  Charles Eucharistie 'de'
  Medici
SAKEL, Manfred Joshua 3
SAKOLSKI, Aaron M. 3
SALANT, William 2
SALAZAR, 5
  Ontonio de Oliveira
SALAZAR, Ruben 5
SALAZAR 5
  ARGUMEDO, Carlos
SALE, Charles Partlow 1
SALE, George 1
SALE, Samuel 1
SALEM, Hermann R. 4
SALERNO, George Fred 5
SALERNO, Vito Lorenzo 5
SALES, Murray W. 2
SALESKY, 4
  Bernard Leonard
SALIERS, Earl Adolphus 3
SALINAS, Pedro 3
SALINGER, Benjamin I. 1
SALINGER, Harry 3
SALISBURY, Albert 1

SALISBURY, H
  Edward Elbridge
SALISBURY, 4
  George Robert
SALISBURY, James Henry 1
SALISBURY, Morse 4
SALISBURY, Rollin D. 1
SALISBURY, Stanton W. 4
SALISBURY, 3
  Stuart McFarland
SALIT, Norman 4
SALLEY, 5
  Alexander Samuel, Jr.
SALLEY, Nathaniel Moss 5
SALLMON, William 2
  Henry
SALMANS, Levi Brimmer 1
SALMON, Alvah Glover 4
SALMON, Daniel Elmer 1
SALMON, Edwin Ashley 4
SALMON, Joshua S. 1
SALMON, Lucy Maynard 1
SALMON, Thomas 1
SALMON, Udall J. 4
SALMON, 1
  William Charles
SALMON, Wilmer Wesley 1
SALM-SALM, Prince H
SALM-SALM, Princess H
SALM-SALM, Princess 4
SALOMON, Erich 4
SALOMON, Fred Z. 1
SALOMON, Haym H
SALOMON, Herbert 3
SALPETER, Harry 5
SALPETER, High 5
SALPOINTE, H
  John Baptist
SALSBURG, Zevi Walter 5
SALSBURY, Lant King 1
SALSGIVER, Paul L. 3
SALSICH, LeRoy 3
SALT, Albert Lincoln 2
SALTEN, Felix 3
SALTER, Leslie Earnest 4
SALTER, Lewis Spencer 4
SALTER, Mary Turner 1
SALTER, 4
  Moses Buckingham
SALTER, Richard Gene 5
SALTER, 3
  Robert Mundhenk
SALTER, Sumner 2
SALTER, William 1
SALTER, 1
  William Mackintire
SALTER, William Thomas 3
SALTONSTALL, Dudley H
SALTONSTALL, Gurdon H
SALTONSTALL, Leverett H
SALTONSTALL, 5
  Nathaniel
SALTONSTALL, Richard H
SALTUS, Edgar 1
SALTZGABER, 1
  Gaylord Miller
SALTZMAN, 2
  Charles McKinley
SALTZMAN, Joel 4
SALVAGE, 2
  Sir Samuel Agar
SALVANT, Robert Milton 3
SALVATIERRA, H
  Juan Maria
SALVATORE, Victor 4
SALVEMINI, Gaetano 4
SALZEDO, Carlos 4
SALZMANN, Joseph H
SAMALMAN, Alexander 3
SAMAROFF, Olga 3
SAMES, Albert Morris 3
SAMFIELD, Max 1
SAMFORD, John A. 5
SAMFORD, Thomas 1
  Drake
SAMFORD, 1
  William Hodges
SAMINSKY, Lazare 3
SAMMARCO, G. Mario 5
SAMMET, G. Victor 5
SAMMIS, Arthur Maxwell 5
SAMMOND, Frederic 5
SAMMOND, 5
  Herbert Stavely
SAMMOND, 4
  Herbert Stavely
SAMMONS, F. Elmer 3
SAMMONS, Thomas H
SAMMONS, Thomas 1
SAMMONS, Wheeler 3
SAMMONS, William 2
  Henry
SAMPEY, John Richard 5
SAMPEY, 2
  John Richard, Jr.
SAMPLE, John Glen 5

SAMPLE, Paul Lindsay 3
SAMPLE, Robert Fleming 1
SAMPLE, H
  Samuel Caldwell
SAMPLE, 4
  Samuel Williamson
SAMPLE, William Dodge 2
SAMPLE, 2
  William Roderick
SAMPSELL, 5
  Marshall Emmett
SAMPSON, Alden 1
SAMPSON, Archibald J. 1
SAMPSON, Emma Speed 2
SAMPSON, Ezekiel Silas H
SAMPSON, Flemon Davis 4
SAMPSON, 1
  Francis Asbury
SAMPSON, Henry Ellis 2
SAMPSON, Henry 1
  Thomas 4
SAMPSON, 2
  John Albertson
SAMPSON, John Pattrson 4
SAMPSON, Martin Wright 1
SAMPSON, 1
  Thornton Rogers
SAMPSON, William 5
SAMPSON, 5
  William James, Jr.
SAMPSON, 1
  William Thomas
SAMPSON, Zabdiel H
SAMS, Earl Corder 3
SAMS, 5
  James Hagood, Jr.
SAMS, Oliver Newton 1
SAMS, Robert Shields 5
SAMSON, George 1
  Clement 1
SAMSON, H
  George Whitefield
SAMSON, 1
  William Holland
SAMUEL, Bernard 3
SAMUEL, Bunford 2
SAMUEL, Edmund 1
  William 1
SAMUEL, Henry Paul 4
SAMUEL, Herbert 4
SAMUEL, Maurice 5
SAMUEL, Ralph E. 4
SAMUELS, Arthur Hiram 1
SAMUELS, Benjamin 4
SAMUELS, 1
  Edward Augustus
SAMUELS, Green Berry H
SAMUELS, 2
  Maurice Victor
SAMUELS, Samuel 1
SAMUELSON, Agnes 4
SAMY, Mahmoud 5
SANBORN, Alvan Francis 4
SANBORN, Arthur 1
  Loomis
SANBORN, Benjamin H. 1
SANBORN, Charles 3
  Henry
SANBORN, Edwin David H
SANBORN, Elwin Roswell 1
SANBORN, 1
  Franklin Benjamin
SANBORN, 1
  Helen Josephine
SANBORN, Henry 4
  Nichols
SANBORN, 4
  Herbert Charles
SANBORN, J. Pitts 1
SANBORN, John Albert 4
SANBORN, John Bell 1
SANBORN, John 1
  Benjamin
SANBORN, John Carfield 5
SANBORN, Joseph Brown 1
SANBORN, 2
  Katherine Abbott
SANBORN, Mary Farley 1
SANBORN, Walter Henry 1
SANBORNE, 3
  Henry Kendall
SANCHEZ, Allan Juan 5
SANCHEZ, Jose Bernardo H
SANCHEZ, 1
  Nellie Van 'de Grift
SANCHEZ- 1
  LATOUR, Francisco
SANDALL, 5
  Charles Edward
SANDBURG, Carl 4
SANDEFER, 1
  Jefferson Davis
SANDELL, Perry James 4
SANDEMAN, Robert H
SANDER, John Ferdinand 5
SANDERS, Alvin Howard 4
SANDERS, Archie D. 1

SANDERS, H
Billington McCarter
SANDERS, 3
Charles Finley
SANDERS, H
Charles Walton
SANDERS, Daniel Clarke H
SANDERS, 1
Daniel Jackson
SANDERS, H
Elizabeth Elkins
SANDERS, Euclid 4
SANDERS, Everett 3
SANDERS, Frank Knight 1
SANDERS, 4
Frederic William
SANDERS, George 5
SANDERS, H
George Nicholas
SANDERS, 3
Harold Frederick
SANDERS, Henry Arthur 3
SANDERS, Henry Martin 1
SANDERS, Henry Nevill 5
SANDERS, James Harvey H
SANDERS, Jared Young 1
SANDERS, 2
Jared Young Jr.
SANDERS, 4
Jared Young Jr.
SANDERS, John Adams 4
SANDERS, Joseph M. 1
SANDERS, Lee Stanley 5
SANDERS, Louis Peck 1
SANDERS, Morgan
Gurley 3
SANDERS, Newell 1
SANDERS, Robert David 3
SANDERS, Samuel D. 4
SANDERS, Thomas Henry 3
SANDERS, 2
Thomas Jefferson
SANDERS, W. Burton 4
SANDERS, 5
Walter Benjamin
SANDERS, Wilbur Fisk 1
SANDERS, 1
William Brownell
SANDERSON, 3
Charles Rupert
SANDERSON, 5
Edward Frederick
SANDERSON, Edwin
Nash 1
SANDERSON, 4
Eugene Claremont
SANDERSON, Ezra
Dwight 2
SANDERSON, George 1
SANDERSON,
George Andrew
SANDERSON, 1
George Augustus
SANDERSON, Henry H
SANDERSON, Henry 1
SANDERSON, John H
SANDERSON, John 3
SANDERSON, Joseph 4
SANDERSON, Lewis R. 1
SANDERSON, Percy Sir 1
SANDERSON, Robert H
SANDERSON, 4
Robert Louis
SANDERSON, 5
Samuel Gilbert
SANDERSON, Sibyl
SANDERSON, Walter W. 5
SANDFORD, James T. H
SANDFORD, Thomas H
SANDIDGE, John Milton H
SANDIFER, 3
Joseph Randolph
SANDISON, George
Henry 4
SANDLIN, John Nicholas 5
SANDOR, Mathias 1
SANDOR, Pal 5
SANDOZ, Mari Susette 4
SANDROK, Edward
George 5
SANDS, 4
Alexander H. Jr.
SANDS, Benjamin Aymar 1
SANDS, H
Benjamin Franklin
SANDS, Comfort H
SANDS, David H
SANDS, Frank 3
SANDS, George Lincoln 1
SANDS, Herbert Stead 2
SANDS, James Hoban 1
SANDS, Joshua H
SANDS, Joshua Ratoon H
SANDS, Lawrence Eyster 1
SANDS, Merrill Burr 3
SANDS, Oliver Jackson 4
SANDS, Robert Charles H

SANDS, Thomas Edmund 5
SANDS, 2
William Franklin
SANDSTEN, Emil Peter 4
SANDSTROM, Emil 4
SANDT, 1
George Washington
SANDWEISS, David
Jacob 4
SANDY, William Charles 5
SANDYS, Edwyn William 1
SANDYS, George H
SANDZEN, Sven Birger 3
SANER, John Crawford 2
SANER, Robert E. Lee 1
SANFORD, Albert Hart 2
SANFORD, Alfred Fanton 3
SANFORD, Allan Douglas 2
SANFORD, Arthur
Hawley 3
SANFORD, Charles F. 2
SANFORD,
Chester Milton
SANFORD, Conley Hall 3
SANFORD, Daniel
Sammis 1
SANFORD, Edmund
Clark 1
SANFORD, 3
Edward Field Jr.
SANFORD, Edward Terry H
SANFORD, 1
Elias Benjamin
SANFORD, Fernando 2
SANFORD, 4
Fillmore Hargrave
SANFORD, Francis Baird 2
SANFORD, Frank
Goodwin 5
SANFORD, George Bliss 1
SANFORD, Giles H
SANFORD, Graham 2
SANFORD, 3
Harold Williams
SANFORD, Henry
Lindsay 1
SANFORD, Henry
Shelton H
SANFORD, Hugh Wheeler 4
SANFORD, James Clark 1
SANFORD, John H
SANFORD, John 1
SANFORD, John B. 5
SANFORD, John Edgar 4
SANFORD, John W. A. H
SANFORD, Jonah H
SANFORD, 3
Joseph William
SANFORD, Louis Childs 1
SANFORD, Maria L. 1
SANFORD, Myron Reed 1
SANFORD, Nathan H
SANFORD, Orin Grover 2
SANFORD, Rollin B. 5
SANFORD, Roscoe Frank 3
SANFORD, 2
Steadman Vincent
SANGER, Alexander 1
SANGER, Charles Robert 1
SANGER, H
George Partridge
SANGER, Henry H. 3
SANGER, John Pomeroy 3
SANGER,
Joseph Prentice
SANGER, Margaret 4
SANGER, Paul Weldon 5
SANGER, Ralph 1
SANGER, William Cary 1
SANGER,
Winnie Monroney (Mrs.
Fenton M. Sanger)
SANGREN, Paul Vivian 1
SANGSTER, 1
Margaret Elizabeth
SANIAL, Lucien 4
SANKEY, Ira Allan 1
SANKEY, Ira David 1
SANNER, Sydney 5
SANNO,
James Madison Johnston
SANSBURY, 4
Marvin Orville
SANSOM, Marion 1
SANSOM, Sir George 4
SAN SOUCI, Emery John 1
SANSUM, William David 1
SANTA ANNA, H
Antonio Lopez 'de
SANTAYANA, George 3
SANTE, 5
Christopher Alfred
SANTE, Hans Heinrich 5
SANTE, Le Roy 4
SANTEE, Ellis Monroe 1
SANTEE, Harris Ellett 1

SANTELMANN, 2
William Henry
SANTOS, 1
Epifanio 'de 'los
SAPHORE, Edwin Warren 2
SAPIR, Edward 1
SAPIRO, Aaron 3
SAPP, Arthur Henry 2
SAPP, William Fletcher H
SAPP, 1
William Frederick
SAPP, William Robinson H
SAPPINGTON, 2
Clarence Olds
SAPPINGTON, John . H
SAPPINGTON, 3
Samuel Watkins
SAR, Samuel Leib 4
SARBACHER, 5
George W(illam, Jr.
SARCHET, 5
Corbin Marquand
SARD, Grange 1
SARDEAU, 5
Helene (Mrs. George
Biddle)
SARDESON, 3
Frederick William
SARETT, Lew 3
SARG, Tony 2
SARGEANT, 5
Frank Wadleigh
SARGEANT, William H. 1
SARGENT, H
Aaron Augustus
SARGENT, Amor Hartley 5
SARGENT, 5
Archer Downing
SARGENT, 1
Charles Sprague
SARGENT, 4
Charles Wesley
SARGENT, 5
Christopher Gilbert
SARGENT, Dudley Allen 1
SARGENT, Edward 5
SARGENT, Epes H
SARGENT, Fitzwilliam H
SARGENT, Fitzwilliam 3
SARGENT, Frank Pierce 1
SARGENT, 1
Franklin Haven
SARGENT, Fred Wesley 1
SARGENT, Frederick 1
SARGENT, 1
Frederick Le Roy
SARGENT, George Henry 1
SARGENT, Henry H
SARGENT, Henry Barry 4
SARGENT,
Henry Bradford
SARGENT, H
Henry Winthrop
SARGENT,
Herbert Howland
SARGENT, James 2
SARGENT, James Clyde 3
SARGENT, 1
John Garibaldi
SARGENT, John Osborne H
SARGENT, John Singer 1
SARGENT, 1
Ledyard Worthington
SARGENT, H
Lucius Manlius
SARGENT, Nathan H
SARGENT, Nathan 1
SARGENT, Noel Gharrett 1
SARGENT, Paul Dudley 5
SARGENT, Porter 5
SARGENT, Porter E. 3
SARGENT, Walter 1
SARGENT, 1
William Durham
SARGENT, 4
William Edward
SARGENT, Winthrop * H
SARLES, Elmore Yocum 1
SARNOFF, David 5
SARONY, Napoleon H
SARPER, Selim 5
SARPY, Peter A. H
SARTAIN, Emily 1
SARTAIN, John H
SARTAIN, Paul Judd 2
SARTAIN, Samuel 1
SARTAIN, William 1
SARTHER, John M. 3
SARTON, George 2
SARTORI, 5
Joseph Francis
SARTORI, 1
Louis Constant
SARTORIUS, Irving A. 3
SARTWELL, Henry
Parker H

SARTZ, 1
Richard Sophus Nielsen
SASLAVSKY, Alexander 1
SASS, George Herbert 1
SASS, Herbert Ravenel 3
SASSACUS H
SASSCER, Lansdale G. 4
SASSOON,
Siegfried Loraine
SATENSTEIN, Edward 5
SATENSTEIN, Sidney 4
SATER, John Elbert 1
SATERLEE, 3
Gerald Britton
SATHRE, 1
Jacob Cornelius
SATTER, Gustav H
SATTER, Mark J. 5
SATTERFIELD, 2
Dave Edward Jr.
SATTERFIELD, 5
John Vines, Jr.
SATTERFIELD, M. H. 3
SATTERFIELD, 2
Robert Samuel
SATTERLEE, Eugene 1
SATTERLEE,
George Reese
SATTERLEE, Henry
Yates 1
SATTERLEE, 2
Herbert Livingston
SATTERLEE, Hugh 4
SATTERLEE, H
Richard Sherwood
SATTERLEE, Walter 3
SATTERTHWAITE,
Livingston
SATTERTHWAITE, 1
Thomas Edward
SATTGAST, 4
Charles Richard
SATTLER, Eric Ericson 1
SATTLER, Robert 1
SATTLER, 5
William Martin
SAUD III 3
SAUER, Emil 4
SAUER, LeRoy Dagobert 2
SAUER, William Emil 3
SAUERWEIN, Allan 1
SAUGRAIN DE H
VIGNI, Antoine Francois
SAUL, Charles Dudley 2
SAUL, Walter Biddle 4
SAULSBURY, Eli H
SAULSBURY, Gove H
SAULSBURY, Willard H
SAULSBURY, Willard 1
SAUND, Dalip S(ingh) 5
SAUNDERS, Alvin H
SAUNDERS, Arthur Percy 3
SAUNDERS, 1
Charles Francis
SAUNDERS,
Charles Gurley
SAUNDERS, Charles W. 5
SAUNDERS, DeAlton 5
SAUNDERS, Dudley
Dunn 1
SAUNDERS, Edward
Watts 1
SAUNDERS, Eugene
Davis 5
SAUNDERS, Eugene
Davis 1
SAUNDERS, Frederick 1
SAUNDERS, Frederick A. 4
SAUNDERS, 1
Harold Eugene
SAUNDERS, H
Henry Dmochowski
SAUNDERS, John Monk 1
SAUNDERS, John R. 1
SAUNDERS, Joseph H. 2
SAUNDERS, 2
Joseph Taylor
SAUNDERS, 1
Kenneth James
SAUNDERS, Lawrence 5
SAUNDERS, 3
Lowell Waller
SAUNDERS, Marshall 2
SAUNDERS, Paul Hill 2
SAUNDERS, Prince H
SAUNDERS, R. L. 4
SAUNDERS, 1
Ripley Dunlap
SAUNDERS,
Robert Chancellor
SAUNDERS,
Romulus Mitchell
SAUNDERS, Samuel
James 3
SAUNDERS, Walter Mills 4
SAUNDERS, William H

SAUNDERS, H
William Laurence
SAUNDERS, 1
William Lawrence
SAUNDERSON, 3
Henry Hallam
SAUREL, Paul 1
SAURET, Emile 4
SAUVE, Paul 3
SAUVEUR, Albert 1
SAVAGE, Albert Russell 1
SAVAGE, 1
Alexander Duncan
SAVAGE, Alfred Orville 5
SAVAGE, Arthur William 1
SAVAGE, Charles Albert 4
SAVAGE, 2
Charles Courtenay
SAVAGE, 5
Charles Winfred
SAVAGE, Edward H
SAVAGE, Elmer Seth 2
SAVAGE, Ezra Perin 1
SAVAGE, Francis Martin 1
SAVAGE, George Martin 1
SAVAGE, 4
George Slocum Folger
SAVAGE, 1
Giles Christopher
SAVAGE, Harlow Dow 1
SAVAGE, Henry Wilson 1
SAVAGE, Hiram Newton 1
SAVAGE, James H
SAVAGE, James Edwin 5
SAVAGE, John * H
SAVAGE, John Houston 1
SAVAGE, John Lucian 1
SAVAGE, John Marbacher 4
SAVAGE, John Simpson H
SAVAGE, Leonard Jimmie 5
SAVAGE, 2
Marion Alexander
SAVAGE, Maxwell 2
SAVAGE, Minot Judson 1
SAVAGE, Philip Henry 1
SAVAGE, Richard Henry 1
SAVAGE, Theodore Fiske 3
SAVAGE, Thomas
Edmund 4
SAVAGE, H
Thomas Staughton
SAVAGE, Toy Dixon 2
SAVAGE, Watson Lewis 1
SAVERY, William * H
SAVERY, William 2
SAVIDGE, Frank
Eugene Coleman
SAVIDGE, Frank
Raymond 1
SAVILLE, Bruce Wilder 1
SAVILLE, Caleb Mills 5
SAVILLE,
Marshall Howard
SAVILLE, Thorndike 5
SAVORD, Ruth 4
SAVORGNAN, 5
Alessandro
SAVORY, 4
George Washington
SAWADA, Kyoichi 5
SAWDERS, James Caleb 4
SAWIN,
Theophilus Parsons
SAWTELLE, 1
Charles Greene
SAWTELLE, Cullen H
SAWTELLE, George 1
SAWTELLE,
William Henry
SAWTELLE, 1
William Luther
SAWVEL, Franklin B. 4
SAWYER, Bonner Dupree 5
SAWYER, C. Adrian Jr. 3
SAWYER, Carl Walker 4
SAWYER,
Charles Baldwin
SAWYER, Charles E. 1
SAWYER, Charles Henry 1
SAWYER, Charles Pike 1
SAWYER, 4
Charles Winthrop
SAWYER, Donald
Hubbard 1
SAWYER,
Frederick Adolphus
SAWYER,
George Frederick
SAWYER, Harold Everett 5
SAWYER, Henry
Buckland 5
SAWYER, Hiram Arthur 2
SAWYER, J. Estcourt 1
SAWYER, John Pascal 2
SAWYER, John Talbott 1
SAWYER, 1
Joseph Dillaway

SCHMIDT, Adolph D. Jr.	4			
SCHMIDT,	5			
Alfred Francis William				
SCHMIDT,	5			
Arthur Alexander				
SCHMIDT, Austin G.	4			
SCHMIDT,	2			
Carl Louis August				

SCHMIDT, Adolph D. Jr. 4
SCHMIDT, 5
Alfred Francis William
SCHMIDT, 5
Arthur Alexander
SCHMIDT, Austin G. 4
SCHMIDT, 2
Carl Louis August
SCHMIDT, 2
Edward Charles
SCHMIDT, 4
Edward William
SCHMIDT, 3
Elmer Frederick Edward
SCHMIDT, Emil G. 3
SCHMIDT, 4
Erich Friedrich
SCHMIDT, Ernest R. 5
SCHMIDT, Erwin 4
Rudolph
SCHMIDT, 2
Francis Albert
SCHMIDT, Frank Henry 5
SCHMIDT,
Frederick Augustus
SCHMIDT, 2
Friedrich Georg Gottlob
SCHMIDT, George August 4
SCHMIDT, George Small 1
SCHMIDT, Harry 4
SCHMIDT,
Herbert William
SCHMIDT, Joseph Martin 1
SCHMIDT, Karl P. 3
SCHMIDT, Louis Ernst 3
SCHMIDT, Nathaniel 4
SCHMIDT, Orvis Adrian 5
SCHMIDT, Otto L. 5
SCHMIDT, Paul Gerhard 3
SCHMIDT, Peter Paul 5
SCHMIDT, 3
Petrus Johannes
SCHMIDT, Richard Ernst 5
SCHMIDT, Walter August 4
SCHMIDT, Walter Seton 3
SCHMIDT, William 1
SCHMIDT, William Jr. 3
SCHMIDT, 4
William Richard
SCHMITT, Arthur J. 5
SCHMITT, Cooper Davis 3
SCHMITT, Gladys 4
SCHMITT, Oscar C. 3
SCHMITT, Roland G. 4
SCHMITT, Rupert P. 3
SCHMITZ, Carl Ludwig 4
SCHMITZ, Dietrich 4
SCHMITZ, Henry 4
SCHMITZ, 3
Herbert Eugene
SCHMITZ, 4
Joseph William
SCHMON, Arthur Albert 4
SCHMUCK, 1
Elmer Nicholas
SCHMUCKER, H
Beale Melanchthon
SCHMUCKER, John
George H
SCHMUCKER, 5
Samuel Christian
SCHMUCKER, Samuel D. 1
SCHMUCKER, H
Samuel Simon
SCHMUS, Elmer Ezra 3
SCHNABEL, Artur 3
SCHNABEL, Charles J. 1
SCHNABEL, Truman
Gross 5
SCHNACKENBERG, 5
Elmer Jacob
SCHNADER, 5
William A(braham)
SCHNAKENBERG,
Henry 5
SCHNÄUFFER, H
Carl Heinrich
SCHNECKER,
Peter August
SCHNEDER, David
Bowman 4
SCHNEE, Verne H. 3
SCHNEEBELI, G. Adolph 3
SCHNEEBELI, G. Adolph 4
SCHNEIDER, 2
Adolph Benedict
SCHNEIDER, Albert 1
SCHNEIDER, Benjamin H
SCHNEIDER, Carl E. 5
SCHNEIDER,
Charles Conrad
SCHNEIDER, 5
Clement Joseph
SCHNEIDER, 5
Edward Alexander
SCHNEIDER, 3
Edward Christian

SCHNEIDER, Erich 5
SCHNEIDER, 2
Frederick William
SCHNEIDER, George 5
SCHNEIDER, George J. 1
SCHNEIDER, Herman 1
SCHNEIDER, Joseph 1
SCHNEIDER, 4
Oscar Albert
SCHNEIDER, 4
Ralph Edward
SCHNEIDER, 1
Samuel Hiram
SCHNEIDER, Theodore H
SCHNEIDER, 3
Walter Arthur
SCHNEIDER, William B. 4
SCHNEIDERS, 5
Alexander A(loysius)
SCHNEIDEWIND,
Richard 5
SCHNEIRLA,
Theodore Christian
SCHNELLER, 4
Frederic Andrew
SCHNELLER, George
Otto H
SCHNERING, Otto 3
SCHNITZLER,
John William
SCHNUR, 1
George Henry Jr.
SCHNURR, Martin K. 4
SCHOBECK,
Arthur Elmer
SCHOCH, Eugene Paul 5
SCHODDE, George Henry 1
SCHODER, 5
Ernest-William
SCHOELLKOPF, 2
Alfred Hugo
SCHOELLKOPF, 5
J. Fred, Iv
SCHOELLKOPF, Jacob F. 2
SCHOELLKOPF,
Paul Arthur
SCHOEMAKER, 3
Daniel Martin
SCHOEN, Charles T. 4
SCHOEN, John Edmund 5
SCHOENBERG, Arnold 3
SCHOENECK, Edward 4
SCHOENEFELD, Henry 4
SCHOENFELD, 3
H. F. Arthur
SCHOENFELD, Hermann 1
SCHOENFELD, 3
William Alfred
SCHOEPF, W. Kesley 1
SCHOEPFLE, Chester S. 3
SCHOEPPEL, Andrew F. 4
SCHOEPPERLE, Victor 4
SCHOETZ, Max 1
SCHOFF, Hannah Kent 4
SCHOFF, Stephen Alonzo 1
SCHOFF, Wilfred Harvey 1
SCHOFIELD, 5
Albert George
SCHOFIELD, 3
Charles Edwin
SCHOFIELD, 2
Frank Herman
SCHOFIELD, Frank Lee 1
SCHOFIELD, Harvey A. 1
SCHOFIELD, Henry 1
SCHOFIELD, 1
John McAllister
SCHOFIELD, 2
Mary Lyon Cheney
SCHOFIELD, William 1
SCHOFIELD,
William Henry
SCHOLER, Walter 5
SCHOLL, John William 5
SCHOLL, William M. 5
SCHOLLE, Hardinge 5
SCHOLTE,
Hendrick Peter H
SCHOLTZ, Joseph D. 5
SCHOLZ, Emil Maurice 2
SCHOLZ, 4
Karl William Henry
SCHOLZ, 1
Richard Frederick
SCHOMMER, John J. 4
SCHOMP, Albert L. 5
SCHONBERGER,
E(manuel) D(eo)
SCHONFELD, William A. 5
SCHONHARDT, Henri 3
SCHOOLCRAFT,
Arthur Allen
SCHOOLCRAFT,
Henry Rowe H
SCHOOLCRAFT,
John Lawrence H
SCHOOLER, Lewis 4

SCHOONHOVEN, 3
Helen Butterfield
SCHOONHOVEN, 1
John James
SCHOONMAKER, H
Cornelius Corneliusen
SCHOONMAKER,
Edwin Davies
SCHOONMAKER, 2
Frederic Palen
SCHOONMAKER, Nancy
M. 4
SCHOONOVER, 3
Draper Talman
SCHOONOVER, 5
Frank Earle
SCHOPF, Johann David H
SCHOPFLIN, Jack 4
SCHORGER, 5
Arlie William
SCHORLING, Raleigh 4
SCHORSCH, 3
Alexander Peter
SCHORTEMEIER, 4
Frederick Edward
SCHOTT, 1
Charles Anthony
SCHOTT, Henry 1
SCHOTT, 4
Lawrence Frederick
SCHOTT, Max 3
SCHOULER, James 1
SCHOULER, John 1
SCHOULER, William H
SCHOUR, Isaac 4
SCHOYER, Alfred McGill 4
SCHRADE, Leo Franz 5
SCHRADER, Charles E. 5
SCHRADER, 2
Frank Charles
SCHRADER, Franz 4
SCHRADER, Fred L. 4
SCHRADER, 2
Frederick Franklin
SCHRADER, George H. 5
SCHRADIECK, Henry 4
SCHRAKAMP, Josepha 4
SCHRAM, Jack Aron 4
SCHRAMM, E. Frank 4
SCHRATCHLEY, 1
Francis Arthur
SCHRECKENGAST, 1
Isaac Butler
SCHRECKER, Paul 4
SCHREIBER, 3
Carl Frederick
SCHREIBER, Walter 3
SCHREINER, George
Abel 5
SCHREINER, Oswald 5
SCHREMBS, Joseph 2
SCHRENK, Hermann 'von 3
SCHREYVOGEL, Charles 1
SCHRIBER, Louis 3
SCHRICKER, 4
Henry Frederick
SCHRIECK, H
Sister Louise Van 'der
SCHRIEVER, William 3
SCHRIVER, Edmund H
SCHRODER, 5
William Henry
SCHRODINGER, Erwin 4
SCHROEDER, 4
Albert William
SCHROEDER, Alwin 4
SCHROEDER, Bernard A. 3
SCHROEDER, Carl A. 4
SCHROEDER, 1
Ernest Charles
SCHROEDER, 1
Frederick A.
SCHROEDER, 3
John Charles
SCHROEDER, .H
John Frederick
SCHROEDER, 5
Joseph Edwin
SCHROEDER, Paul Louis 4
SCHROEDER, Reginald 4
SCHROEDER, 3
Rudolph William
SCHROEDER, Seaton 1
SCHROEDER, Walter 1
SCHROEDER, 4
Werner William
SCHROEDER, 1
William Edward
SCHROFF, Joseph 4
SCHUCHARDT, 1
Rudolph Frederick
SCHUCHARDT, 3
William Herbert
SCHUCHERT, Charles 2
SCHUCK, Arthur Aloys 1
SCHUCK, 5
Arthur Frederick

SCHUELEIN, Hermann 5
SCHUERMAN, 1
William Henry
SCHUETTE, 1
Conrad Herman Louis
SCHUETTE, Walter Erwin 3
SCHUETTE, 4
William Herman
SCHUETZ,
Leonard William
SCHUH, Henry Frederick 4
SCHUHMANN,
George William
SCHUIRMANN, 5
Roscoe Ernest
SCHULE, James Raymond 5
SCHULER, Anthony J. 2
SCHULER, Hans 4
SCHULER, Loring Ashley 5
SCHULGEN, 3
George Francis
SCHULHOFF, 5
Henry Bernard
SCHULL, Herman Walter 5
SCHULLINGER, 5
Rudolph Nicholas
SCHULMAIER, A.
Talmage 3
SCHULMAN, Jack Henry 4
SCHULMAN, Samuel 3
SCHULTE, David A. 2
SCHULTE, 1
Herman 'von Wechlinger
SCHULTE, William Henry 3
SCHULTHEISS, Carl Max 4
SCHULTZ,
Alfred Reginald
SCHULTZ, 3
Clifford Griffith
SCHULTZ, Clinton M. 4
SCHULTZ, Edward
Waters 5
SCHULTZ, Ernst William 1
SCHULTZ, George F. 5
SCHULTZ, Henry H
SCHULTZ, Henry 4
SCHULTZ, James Willard 2
SCHULTZ, John Richie 2
SCHULTZ, Louis 5
SCHULTZ, William Eben 4
SCHULTZE, Arthur 4
SCHULTZE, Augustus 1
SCHULTZE, Carl Emil 1
SCHULTZE, Leonard 3
SCHULZ, Carl Gustav 4
SCHULZ, Edward Hugh 5
SCHULZ, Leo 2
SCHULZE, Paul 2
SCHULZE, Paul Jr. 3
SCHUMACHER, 5
Anton Herbert
SCHUMACHER, 4
Ferdinand
SCHUMACHER, 5
Henry Cyril
SCHUMACHER, 4
Matthew Aloysius
SCHUMACHER, 2
Thomas Milton
SCHUMAN, Robert 4
SCHUMANN, Edward
Armin 5
SCHUMANN, 4
John Joseph Jr.
SCHUMANN-
HEINK, Ernestine 1
SCHUMM, Herman
Charles 3
SCHUMPETER, 2
Joseph Alois
SCHUNEMAN, H
Martin Gerretsen
SCHUNK, Arthur John 5
SCHUPP, Otto 4
SCHUPP, Robert William 2
SCHUREMAN, James H
SCHURICHT, Carl 4
SCHURMAN,
George Wellington
SCHURMAN, Jacob
Gould 2
SCHURZ, Carl 1
SCHURZ, Carl Lincoln 4
SCHURZ, William Lytle 4
SCHUSSELE, Christian H
SCHUSTER, George Lee 4
SCHUTT, Harold Smith 4
SCHUTTE, Louis Henry 3
SCHUTTLER, Peter H
SCHUTZE, Martin 1
SCHUTZER, Paul George 5
SCHUTZMAN, Julius 4
SCHUYLER, Aaron 1
SCHUYLER, Daniel J. 3
SCHUYLER, Eugene H
SCHUYLER,
George Washington H

SCHUYLER, Hamilton 1
SCHUYLER, James Dix 1
SCHUYLER, 1
Karl Cortlandt
SCHUYLER, 1
Livingston Rowe
SCHUYLER, Margurita H
SCHUYLER, Montgomery 1
SCHUYLER, Montgomery 3
SCHUYLER, Peter H
SCHUYLER, H
Philip Jeremiah
SCHUYLER, Philip John H
SCHUYLER, 4
Philippa Duke
SCHUYLER, 1
Walter Scribner
SCHUYLER, William 1
SCHWAB, Charles M. 1
SCHWAB, Francis Xavier 2
SCHWAB, Gustav Henry 1
SCHWAB, Harvey A. 3
SCHWAB, 1
John Christopher
SCHWAB, John George 2
SCHWAB, Martin Constan 2
SCHWAB, Paul Josiah 4
SCHWAB, Robert Sidney 5
SCHWAB, Roy Valentine 5
SCHWAB, Sidney Isaac 2
SCHWABACHER, Albert
E. 4
SCHWABACHER, 3
James Herbert
SCHWABE, George Blaine 3
SCHWABE, H. August 1
SCHWACKE, John Henry 2
SCHWAIN, Frank Robert 4
SCHWALM, Earl George 4
SCHWALM, 5
Vernon Franklin
SCHWAMB, Herbert H. 5
SCHWAMB, Peter 2
SCHWAMM, Harvey 3
SCHWAN, Theodore 4
SCHWARDT, 4
Herbert Henry
SCHWARTZ, A. Charles 4
SCHWARTZ, 2
Andrew Thomas
SCHWARTZ, B. Davis 5
SCHWARTZ, Charles 5
SCHWARTZ, Delmore 4
SCHWARTZ, Hans Jorgen 3
SCHWARTZ, 2
Harwood Muzzy
SCHWARTZ, Herbert J. 3
SCHWARTZ, 5
Isaac Hillson
SCHWARTZ, Jack William 5
SCHWARTZ, John H
SCHWARTZ,
Julia Augusta
SCHWARTZ, Karl 1
SCHWARTZ, Lew 5
SCHWARTZ, Louis 4
SCHWARTZ, Maurice 5
SCHWARTZ, Milton
Henry 5
SCHWARTZ, Samuel D. 5
SCHWARTZ,
Walter Marshall, Sr.
SCHWARTZ, 5
William Spencer
SCHWARZ, 5
Berthold Theodore Dominic
SCHWARZ, Edward R. 4
SCHWARZ, Frank Henry 3
SCHWARZ, 1
George Frederick
SCHWARZ, Helen Geneva 4
SCHWARZ, 5
Henry Frederick;
SCHWARZ, Otto Henry 3
SCHWARZ, William Tefft 4
SCHWARZBURGER, Carl 4
SCHWARZE, 2
William Nathaniel
SCHWARZENBACH, 5
Ernest Blackbrook
SCHWARZMANN,
Herman J. H
SCHWARZSCHILD, 3
William Harry
SCHWATKA, Frederick H
SCHWATT, Isaac Joachim 1
SCHWEBACH, James 1
SCHWEDTMAN, F.
Charles 3
SCHWEGLER, 3
Raymond Alfred
SCHWEIGARDT, 2
Frederick William
SCHWEIKERT,
Harry Christian
SCHWEINFURTH, 1
Charles Frederick

SCHWEINFURTH,	1	SCOTT, Emmett Jay	3	SCOTT, Thomas Morton	1	SCRUGGS,	3	SEAMANS,	1
Julius Adolph		SCOTT, Ernest	1	SCOTT, Tom	4	William Marvin		Clarence Walker	

SCHWEINFURTH, 1
Julius Adolph
SCHWEINHAUT, 5
Henry Albert
SCHWEINITZ, H
Edmund Alexander
SCHWEINITZ, 1
Emil Alexander 'de
SCHWEINITZ, 1
George Edmund 'de
SCHWEITER, Leo Henry 5
SCHWEITZER, Albert 4
SCHWEITZER, Paul
SCHWEIZER, 3
Albert Charles
SCHWEIZER, J. Otto 5
SCHWELLENBACH, 3
Edgar Ward
SCHWELLENBACH, 2
Lewis Baxter
SCHWENTKER, 3
Francis Frederic
SCHWEPPE, 5
Charles Hodgdon
SCHWERT, Pius Louis 1
SCHWERTNER, 1
August John
SCHWIDETZKY, H
Oscar O. R.
SCHWIETERT, 4
Arthur Henry
SCHWINGEL, 5
Vincent John
SCHWINN, 5
Frederick Sievers
SCHWINN, 4
Sidoine Jordon
SCHWITALLA, 4
Alphonse Mary
SCHWYZER, Arnold 2
SCIDMORE, 1
Eliza Ruhamah
SCIDMORE, 1
George Hawthorne
SCIPIO, Lynn A. 5
SCISM, Don 3
SCLATER, 3
John Robert Paterson
SCOFIELD, Carl Schurz 4
SCOFIELD, 1
Cyrus Ingerson
SCOFIELD, Edward 1
SCOFIELD, H
Glenni William
SCOFIELD, Louis A. 4
SCOFIELD,
Walter Keeler
SCOFIELD,
William Bacon
SCOGGINS, 3
Charles Elbert
SCOLLARD, Clinton 1
SCONCE, Harvey James 2
SCOON, Robert 5
SCOPES, John T. 5
SCORE, 2
John Nelson Russell
SCOTSON-CLARK, 1
George Frederick
SCOTT, Albert Lyon 2
SCOTT, 5
Albert Woodburn, Jr.
SCOTT, 4
Alexander Armstrong
SCOTT, 1
Alfred James Jr.
SCOTT, Angelo Cyrus 2
SCOTT, Arthur Carroll 1
SCOTT, Arthur Curtis 5
SCOTT, Austin 1
SCOTT, Bruce 1
SCOTT, 2
Carlyle MacRoberts
SCOTT, Carrie Emma 1
SCOTT, Charles H
SCOTT, Charles 1
SCOTT, Charles Felton 2
SCOTT, 1
Charles Frederick
SCOTT, 5
Charles Herrington
SCOTT, Charles L. 3
SCOTT, 4
Charles Payson Gurley
SCOTT, Charlotte Angas 1
SCOTT, Colin Alexander 1
SCOTT, D. R. 3
SCOTT, David H
SCOTT, Donald 4
SCOTT, Donnell Everett H
SCOTT, Dred 1
SCOTT, Earl Francis 1
SCOTT, Eben Greenough 4
SCOTT, Ellen C. 1
SCOTT, Elmer 3
SCOTT, Elmon 5
SCOTT, Emily M. 4

SCOTT, Emmett Jay 3
SCOTT, Ernest 1
SCOTT, Ernest Darius 5
SCOTT, Ernest Findlay 3
SCOTT, Eugene Crampton 5
SCOTT, Fitzhugh 3
SCOTT, Francis Markoe 1
SCOTT, Frank Augustus 2
SCOTT, Frank Hall 1
SCOTT, Frank Hamline 1
SCOTT, Frank Jesup 4
SCOTT, 2
Franklin William
SCOTT, Fred Newton 1
SCOTT, 1
Frederic William
SCOTT, 4
Frederick Andrew
SCOTT, 3
Frederick Hossack
SCOTT, Garfield 3
SCOTT, George 4
SCOTT, George Cromwell 2
SCOTT, George Eaton 3
SCOTT, George Gilmore 5
SCOTT, George Winfield 5
SCOTT, Gordon Hatler 5
SCOTT, Gustavus H
SCOTT, Guy Charles 1
SCOTT, Hamilton Gray 4
SCOTT, Harold Wilson 5
SCOTT, Harriet Maria 1
SCOTT, Harvey David 1
SCOTT, Harvey W. 1
SCOTT, Henri 2
SCOTT, Henry Dickerson 2
SCOTT, Henry Edwards 2
SCOTT, Henry Tiffany 2
SCOTT, Henry Wilson 2
SCOTT, Herbert 5
SCOTT, Hugh Briar 4
SCOTT, Hugh Lenox 1
SCOTT, Hugh McDonald 1
SCOTT, Irving Murray 1
SCOTT, Isaac MacBurney 2
SCOTT, Isaiah Benjamin 1
SCOTT, Jack Garrett 3
SCOTT, James Brown 2
SCOTT, James Edward 5
SCOTT, James Hutchison 4
SCOTT, James Wilmot 1
SCOTT, Jeannette 1
SCOTT, Job H
SCOTT, John * H
SCOTT, John 1
SCOTT, John Adams 2
SCOTT, John Addison 3
SCOTT, John Guier 4
SCOTT, John Hart 4
SCOTT, John Loughran 4
SCOTT, John Marcy 5
SCOTT, John Morin H
SCOTT, John Prindle 2
SCOTT, John R. K. 2
SCOTT, John Randolph 1
SCOTT, John Reed 5
SCOTT, John William 1
SCOTT, Jonathan French 2
SCOTT, Joseph 3
SCOTT, Julia Green 1
SCOTT, Julian 1
SCOTT, Leroy 1
SCOTT, Llewellyn Davis 1
SCOTT, Lon Allen 1
SCOTT, Lucy Jameson 1
SCOTT, Martin J. 3
SCOTT, Mary Augusta 1
SCOTT, Miriam Finn 2
SCOTT, Nathan Bay 1
SCOTT, Norman 3
SCOTT, Norman 5
SCOTT, Orange H
SCOTT, Oreon Earle 3
SCOTT, Paul Ryrie 4
SCOTT, Paul Whitten 3
SCOTT, Philip B. 4
SCOTT, Philip Drennen 4
SCOTT, Richard H. 1
SCOTT, Richard Hugh 3
SCOTT, 1
Richard John Ernst
SCOTT, Robert 4
SCOTT, Robert Kingston 1
SCOTT, Robert Lindsay 3
SCOTT, H
Robert Nicholson
SCOTT, Roger Burdette 5
SCOTT, Roy Wesley 3
SCOTT, 5
Russell B(urton)
SCOTT, S. Spencer 5
SCOTT, Samuel Parsons 1
SCOTT, Sutton Selwyn 1
SCOTT, Thomas H
SCOTT, H
Thomas Alexander
SCOTT, Thomas Fielding H

SCOTT, Thomas Morton 1
SCOTT, Tom 4
SCOTT, Tully 1
SCOTT, Walter H
SCOTT, Walter 1
SCOTT, Walter Canfield 3
SCOTT, Walter Dill 3
SCOTT, Walter E. Jr. 3
SCOTT, 5
Wendell G(arrison)
SCOTT, Wilfred Welday 1
SCOTT, Will 1
SCOTT, Willard 4
SCOTT, William H
SCOTT, William 1
SCOTT, William Amasa 2
SCOTT, H
William Anderson
SCOTT, 2
William Berryman
SCOTT, 1
William Earl Dodge
SCOTT, William Edouard 4
SCOTT, William Forse 4
SCOTT, William Henry 1
SCOTT, William Kerr 3
SCOTT, H
William Lawrence
SCOTT, William R. 1
SCOTT, William Sherley 1
SCOTT, William Wilson 1
SCOTT, Willis Howard 4
SCOTT, Winfield H
SCOTT, 5
Winfield Townley
SCOTTEN, 5
Robert McGregor
SCOTTEN,
Samuel Chatman
SCOTT-HUNTER, George 5
SCOTTI, Antonio 1
SCOULLER, James Brown 1
SCOULLER, 1
John Crawford
SCOVEL, Sylvester 1
SCOVEL,
Sylvester Fithian
SCOVELL, 1
Melville Amasa
SCOVIL, Samuel 3
SCOVILLE, 5
Annie Beecher
SCOVILLE, Jonathan H
SCOVILLE, H
Joseph Alfred
SCOVILLE, Robert 1
SCOVILLE, Samuel Jr. 3
SCOVILLE, 4
Wilbur Lincoln
SCRANTON, Cassius A. 5
SCRANTON, H
George Whitefield
SCRANTON, 4
Marion Margery Warren
SCRANTON, Worthington 3
SCREWS, 5
William Preston
SCREWS,
William Wallace
SCRIBNER,
Arthur Hawley
SCRIBNER, Charles H
SCRIBNER, Charles 1
SCRIBNER, Charles 3
SCRIBNER, Charles Ezra 1
SCRIBNER, Frank Jay 4
SCRIBNER,
Frank Kimball
SCRIBNER, George Kline 3
SCRIBNER,
Gilbert Hilton
SCRIBNER,
Gilbert Hilton
SCRIBNER,
Gilbert Hilton
SCRIBNER, Harvey 1
SCRIBNER,
Mrs. Lucy Skidmore
SCRIPPS, Edward Wyllis 1
SCRIPPS, James Edmund 1
SCRIPPS, John Locke H
SCRIPPS, Robert Paine 1
SCRIPPS,
William Edmund
SCRIPTURE, 4
Edward Wheeler
SCRIPTURE, 1
William Ellis
SCRIVEN, 1
George Percival
SCROGGS, 4
Joseph Whitefield
SCROGGS, William Oscar 3
SCRUGGS, Anderson M. 3
SCRUGGS, Loyd 5
SCRUGGS, 1
William Lindsay

SCRUGGS, 3
William Marvin
SCRUGHAM, James 2
Graves
SCRUGHAM, 2
William Warburton
SCRYMSER, 1
James Alexander
SCUDDER, Charles Locke 2
SCUDDER, Doremus 2
SCUDDER, 3
Edward Wallace
SCUDDER, Henry Joel H
SCUDDER, Horace Elisha 1
SCUDDER, Hubert B. 5
SCUDDER, H
Isaac Williamson
SCUDDER, Janet 1
SCUDDER, John H
SCUDDER, John 1
Anderson
SCUDDER, John Milton H
SCUDDER, Moses Lewis 1
SCUDDER, Myron Tracy 1
SCUDDER, Nathaniel H
SCUDDER, 1
Samuel Hubbard
SCUDDER, Townsend 3
SCUDDER, Tredwell 1
SCUDDER, Vida Dutton 3
SCUDDER, 1
Wallace McIlvaine
SCUDDER, Zeno H
SCULL, John H
SCULLEN, Anthony 5
James
SCULLY, C. Alison 3
SCULLY, Hugh Day 5
SCULLY, James Wall 1
SCULLY, Thomas J. 1
SCULLY, William A. 5
SCULLY, 1
William Augustine
SCUPHAM, 5
George William
SCUPIN, Carl Albert 5
SCURRY, Richardson H
SEABERRY, 4
Virgil Theodore
SEABROOK, C. F. 4
SEABROOK, 2
William Buehler
SEABROOKE, Thomas Q. 1
SEABURY, Charles Ward 1
SEABURY, David 3
SEABURY, David 1
SEABURY, 2
Francis William
SEABURY, George Tilley 1
SEABURY, Samuel * H
SEABURY, Samuel 3
SEABURY, William Jones 1
SEABURY,
William Marston
SEACHREST, Effie M. 3
SEACREST, 5
Frederick Snively
SEACREST, 2
Joseph Claggett
SEAGER, Allan 5
SEAGER, Charles Allen 2
SEAGER, Henry Rogers 1
SEAGER, Lawrence H. 1
SEAGLE, Oscar 2
SEAGO, Erwin 5
SEAGRAVE, Frank Evans 1
SEAGRAVE, 4
Gordon Stiffer
SEAGRAVE, Louis H. 4
SEAGROVE, Gordon Kay 1
SEAL, John Frederick 4
SEALOCK, William Elmer 1
SEALS, Carl H. 3
SEALS, John H. 5
SEALSFIELD, Charles H
SEALY, Frank L. 1
SEAMAN, Arthur 1
Edmund
SEAMAN, Augusta Huiell 1
SEAMAN, H
Elizabeth Cochrane
SEAMAN, 1
Elizabeth Cochrane
SEAMAN, Eugene Cecil 5
SEAMAN, George Milton 1
SEAMAN, Gilbert 1
Edmund
SEAMAN, Henry Bowman 1
SEAMAN, Henry John H
SEAMAN, John 3
Thompson
SEAMAN, 1
Louis Livingston
SEAMAN, William Grant 4
SEAMAN, 1
William Henry *

SEAMANS, 1
Clarence Walker
SEARBY, Edmund Wilson 2
SEARCH, Preston Willis 1
SEARCH, 1
Theodore Corson
SEARCY, Chesley Hunter 1
SEARCY, 5
Mrs. Earle Benjamin
SEARCY, Hubert Floyd 5
SEARCY, James Thomas 4
SEARER, Jay Charles 5
SEARING, Hudson Roy 3
SEARING, H
John Alexander
SEARING, 4
Laura Catherine Redden
SEARLE, Alonzo T. 4
SEARLE, Arthur 1
SEARLE, Augustus Leach 3
SEARLE, Charles James 1
SEARLE, Charles Putnam 1
SEARLE, George Mary 1
SEARLE,
Harriet Richardson (Mrs.
William D. Searle)
SEARLE, James H
SEARLE, John Preston 1
SEARLE, Robert Wyckoff 5
SEARLE, Robert Wycroff 4
SEARLES, Colbert 1
SEARLS, Carroll 5
SEARLS, David Thomas 5
SEARS, Barnas H
SEARS, Charles Brown 3
SEARS, Charles Hatch 2
SEARS, Clinton Brooks 1
SEARS, Edmund Hamilton H
SEARS, Edmund Hamilton 2
SEARS, Francis Philip 1
SEARS, Frank Irving 3
SEARS, Fred Coleman 1
SEARS, 1
Frederic William
SEARS, Frederick W. 1
SEARS, George Gray 1
SEARS, Herbert Mason 1
SEARS, Hess Thatcher 5
SEARS, Isaac 1
SEARS, James Hamilton 1
SEARS, Jesse Brundage 4
SEARS, 5
John Van Der Zee
SEARS, Joseph Hamblen 2
SEARS, Julian D(ucker) 5
SEARS, 1
Kenneth Craddock
SEARS, Laurence 4
SEARS, Lester Merriam 4
SEARS, Lorenzo 1
SEARS, Nathan Pratt 2
SEARS, 1
Nathaniel Clinton
SEARS, Philip S. 3
SEARS, Richard Warren 1
SEARS, Robert H
SEARS, Russell Adams 1
SEARS, Samuel Powers 1
SEARS, Sarah Choate 1
SEARS, Taber 1
SEARS, Walter Herbert 3
SEARS, Walter James 1
SEARS, Willard Thomas 1
SEARS, William Henry 1
SEARS, William Joseph 1
SEARS, Willis G. 5
SEARS, Zelda 1
SEARSON, James William 1
SEASHORE, 1
August Theodore
SEASHORE, Carl Emil 2
SEASHORE, 1
Robert Holmes
SEASTONE, 1
Charles Victor
SEATON, John Lawrence 5
SEATON, John Lawrence 4
SEATON, Roy Andrew 5
SEATON, 1
William Winston
SEATTLE H
SEAVER, Ebenezer H
SEAVER, Edwin Pliny 1
SEAVER, Frank Roger 4
SEAVER, Fred Jay 5
SEAVER, Kenneth 1
SEAVERNS, Joel Herbert 4
SEAVEY, Clyde Leroy 5
SEAVEY, Warren Abner 4
SEAWELL, 1
Aaron Ashley Flowers
SEAWELL, Emmet 5
SEAWELL, Herbert Floyd 5
SEAWELL, Molly Elliott 1

SEAY, Abraham Jefferson — 1
SEAY, Edward Tucker — 2
SEAY, Frank — 1
SEAY, George James — 3
SEAY, Harry Lauderdale — 3
SEAY, William Albert — 5
SEBALD, Weber William — 3
SEBAST, Frederick Martin — 3
SEBASTIAN, Benjamin — H
SEBASTIAN, Jerome D. — H
SEBASTIAN, John — 1
SEBASTIAN, William King — H
SEBELIUS, Sven Johan — 3
SEBENIUS, John Uno — 1
SEBREE, Edmund B. — 4
SEBREE, Uriel — 1
SEBRING, Harold Leon — 5
SECCOMB, John — 1
SECHER, Samuel — H
SECKENDORFF, Max Gebhard — 1
SECKLER-HUDSON, Catheryn — 4
SECOR, John Alstyne — 4
SECORD, Arthur Wellesley — 3
SECORD, Frederick — 4
SECRIST, Horace — 2
SEDDON, James — H
SEDDON, William Little — 1
SEDER, Arthur Raymond — 5
SEDGWICK, Allan E. — 2
SEDGWICK, Anne Douglas — 1
SEDGWICK, Arthur George — 1
SEDGWICK, Catharine Maria — H
SEDGWICK, Charles Baldwin — H
SEDGWICK, Francis Minturn — 5
SEDGWICK, Henry Dwight — H
SEDGWICK, Henry Dwight — 1
SEDGWICK, Henry Dwight — 3
SEDGWICK, John — H
SEDGWICK, Julius Parker — 1
SEDGWICK, Robert — 1
SEDGWICK, Samuel Hopkins — 1
SEDGWICK, Theodore * — H
SEDGWICK, Theodore 2'd — 1
SEDGWICK, William Thompson — 1
SEDLEY, Henry — 1
SEDWICK, Ellery — 4
SEE, Elliot M. — 5
SEE, Harold Philip — 5
SEE, Horace — 4
SEE, Thomas Jefferson Jackson — 4
SEEBIRT, Eli Fowler — 3
SEEDS, Russel M. — 4
SEEGAL, David — 5
SEEGER, Alan — 4
SEEGER, Charles Louis — 2
SEEGER, Edwin W. — 5
SEEGER, Eugene — 1
SEEGER, Stanley Joseph — 3
SEEGER, Walter G. — 5
SEEGERS, John Conrad — 1
SEEGMILLER, Wilhelmina — H
SEELBACH, Louis — 5
SEELER, Edgar Viguers — 1
SEELEY, Elias P. — H
SEELEY, Frank Barrows — 3
SEELEY, John Edward — 1
SEELEY, Levi — 1
SEELIG, M. G. — 5
SEELOS, Francis X. — H
SEELVE, Laurens Hickok — 4
SEELY, Fred Loring — 2
SEELY, Henry Martyn — 1
SEELY, Herman Gastrell — 3
SEELY, Walter Hoff — 1
SEELYE, Elizabeth Eggleston — 3
SEELYE, Julius Hawley — 1
SEELYE, L. Clark — 1
SEELYE, Theodore Edward — 4
SEEM, Ralph Berger — 1
SEERLEY, Frank Newell — 1
SEERLEY, Homer Horatio — 4
SEES, John Vincent — 2
SEESTED, August Frederick — H
SEEVER, William John — 2

SEEVERS, Charles Hamilton — 4
SEEVERS, William Henry — H
SEFERIADES, George — 1
SEFRIT, Frank Ira — 3
SEGAL, Paul Moses — 5
SEGAR, Joseph Eggleston — H
SEGEL, David — 5
SEGER, Charles Bronson — 1
SEGER, George N. — 1
SEGER, Gerhart Henry — 4
SEGHERS, Charles Jean — H
SEGNI, Antonio — 5
SEGUIN, Edouard — H
SEGUIN, Edward Constant — H
SEIBEL, Frederick Otto — 1
SEIBEL, George — 3
SEIBELS, Edwin Granville — 3
SEIBELS, George Goldthwaite — 5
SEIBERLING, Charles Willard — 2
SEIBERLING, Francis — 2
SEIBERLING, Frank A. — 3
SEIBERT, James Walter — 4
SEIBERT, John F. — 1
SEIBERT, Walter R. — 4
SEIBERT, William Adam — 1
SEIBOLD, Louis — 2
SEIBOLD, Myron James — 5
SEIDEL, Emil — 2
SEIDEL, Toscha — 4
SEIDEMANN, Henry Peter — 3
SEIDENBUSH, Rupert — H
SEIDENSTICKER, Oswald — H
SEIDERS, George Melville — 1
SEIDL, Anton — H
SEIDNER, Howard Mayo — 5
SEIF, William Henry — 1
SEIFERT, Mathias Joseph — 2
SEIFRIZ, William — 3
SEIGLE, John Sanders — 5
SEIGNOBOSC, Francoise — 4
SEINSHEIMER, J. Fellman — 3
SEIP, Theodore Lorenzo — 1
SEISS, Joseph Augustus — 1
SEITZ, Albert Blazier — 4
SEITZ, Charles Edward — 5
SEITZ, Don Carlos — 1
SEITZ, Frank Noah — H
SEITZ, George Albert — 2
SEITZ, Ira James — 5
SEIVER, George Otto — 4
SEIXAS, Gershom Mendes — H
SEJOUR, Victor — H
SEKERA, Zdenek — 5
SEKERS, Nicholas Thomas — 5
SELBY, Augustine Dawson — 1
SELBY, Charles Baxter — 1
SELBY, Howard Williams — 3
SELBY, Mark Webster — 5
SELBY, Thomas Jefferson — 5
SELBY, William — 1
SELDEN, Charles A(lbert) — 5
SELDEN, Dudley — H
SELDEN, George Baldwin — 4
SELDEN, Lynde — 5
SELDES, Gilbert (Vivian) — 5
SELDOMRIDGE, Harry Hunter — 4
SELECMAN, Charles Claude — 3
SELEKMAN, Benjamin Morris — 4
SELF, James C. — 3
SELFRIDGE, Harry Gordon — 2
SELFRIDGE, Thomas Oliver * — 1
SELIG, Lester North — 5
SELIG, William Nicholas — 2
SELIGER, Robert V. — 3
SELIGMAN, Albert Joseph — 1
SELIGMAN, Arthur — 1
SELIGMAN, Ben B(aruch) — 5
SELIGMAN, Edwin Robert Anderson — 1
SELIGMAN, Henry — 1
SELIGMAN, Isaac — 1
SELIGMAN, Newton — H
SELIGMAN, Jefferson — 1
SELIGMAN, Jesse — H

SELIGMAN, Joseph — H
SELIGMAN, Selig Jacob — 5
SELIGMANN, Kurt — 4
SELIJNS, Henricus — H
SELINGER, Jean Paul — 1
SELKE, George Albert — 5
SELKE, W(ilhelm) Erich (Christian) — 5
SELL, Edward Herman Miller — 1
SELL, Henry Thorne — 1
SELL, Lewis L. — 3
SELLAR, Robert F. — 1
SELLARDS, Elias Howard — 5
SELLECK, Willard Chamberlain — 2
SELLECK, William Alson — 2
SELLEN, Arthur Godfrey — 4
SELLERS, Coleman — 1
SELLERS, Coleman Jr. — 1
SELLERS, David Foote — 2
SELLERS, Edwin Jaquett — 1
SELLERS, Horace Wells — 1
SELLERS, Isaiah — H
SELLERS, James Freeman — 1
SELLERS, Kathryn — 1
SELLERS, Matthew Bacon — 1
SELLERS, Robert Daniel — 4
SELLERS, Robert Henry — 4
SELLERS, Sandford — 1
SELLERS, William — 1
SELLERY, George Clarke — 4
SELLEW, George Tucker — 4
SELLEW, Walter Ashbel — 4
SELLMAN, William Nelson — 4
SELLS, Cato — 5
SELLS, Elijah Watt — 1
SELLSTEDT, Lars Gustaf — 1
SELMER, Ernst Westerlund — 5
SELTZER, Charles Alden — 1
SELTZER, Theodore — 3
SELVAGE, Watson — 5
SELVIDGE, Robert Washington — 2
SELVIG, Conrad George — 2
SELWYN, Edgar — 2
SELYE, Lewis — H
SELZ, Lawrence Hochstadter — 4
SELZNICK, David Oliver — 4
SEMAN, Philip Louis — 3
SEMANS, Edwin Walker — 5
SEMANS, Harry Merrick — 5
SEMBOWER, Charles Jacob — 5
SEMBRICH, Marcella — 1
SEMELROTH, William James — 4
SEMLER, George Herbert — 3
SEMMANN, Liborius — 5
SEMMES, Alexander Jenkins — H
SEMMES, Benedict Joseph — H
SEMMES, John Edward — 4
SEMMES, Raphael — H
SEMMES, Thomas Jenkins — H
SEMNACHER, William M. — 4
SEMPLE, Ellen Churchill — 1
SEMPLE, Henry Churchill — 1
SEMPLE, James — 4
SEMPLE, William Tunstall — 4
SEMSCH, Otto Francis — 5
SENAN, Jose Francisco 'de Paula — H
SENANAYAKE, Don Stephen — 3
SENANAYAKE, Dudley Shelton — 5
SENCENBAUGH, Charles Wilber — 3
SENEAR, Francis Eugene — 3
SENEFF, Edward H. — 1
SENER, James Beverley — H
SENEY, George Ingraham — H
SENEY, Henry William — 4
SENEY, Joshua — H
SENGIER, Edgar — 4
SENGSTACK, John F(rederick) — 5
SENIOR, Clair Marcil — 4
SENIOR, Harold Dickinson — 1
SENIOR, John Lawson — 2
SENIOR, Joseph Howe — 4
SENIOR, Samuel Palmer — 4
SENN, Nicholas — 1
SENN, Thomas J. — 2
SENNER, Joseph Henry — 1
SENNET, George Burritt — H

SENNETT, Mack — H
SENNETT, Mack — 4
SENNING, John Peter — 3
SENSENBRENNER, Frank Jacob — 3
SENSENEY, George Eyster — 2
SENSENICH, Roscoe Lloyd — 4
SENSENIG, David Martin — 1
SENTELL, George Washington — 3
SENTELLE, Mark Edgar — 3
SENTER, John Henry — 1
SENTER, Leon B. — 4
SENTER, Ralph Townsend — 2
SENTER, William Tandy — H
SENTNER, Richard Faulkner — 5
SEQUOYAH — H
SERAFIN, Tullio — 4
SERAKOFF, Leonard — 4
SERESS, Raoul — 4
SERGEANT, Elizabeth Shepley — 1
SERGEANT, John * — H
SERGEANT, Jonathan Dickinson — H
SERGEANT, Thomas — H
SERGEL, Charles Hubbard — 1
SERLES, Earl R. — 3
SERLIN, Oscar — 5
SERPELL, Susan Watkins — 1
SERRA, Junipero — H
SERRELL, Edward Wellmann — 1
SERRILL, William Jones — 3
SERVEN, Abram Ralph — 2
SERVICE, Robert William — 3
SERVISS, Frederick LeVerne — 3
SERVISS, Garrett Putman — 1
SERVOSS, Thomas Lowery — H
SESKIS, I. J. — 3
SESSINGHAUS, Gustavus — H
SESSIONS, Charles H. — 2
SESSIONS, Clarence William — 1
SESSIONS, Kenosha — 2
SESSIONS, Walter Loomis — 1
SESSIONS, William Edwin — 1
SESSUMS, Davis — 1
SESTINI, Benedict — H
SETCHELL, William Albert — 2
SETH, Julien Orem — 4
SETON, Elizabeth Ann Bayley — H
SETON, Ernest Thompson — 2
SETON, Grace Thompson — 3
SETON, Julia — 4
SETON, Robert — 1
SETTERFIELD, Hugh E. — 5
SETTI, Giulio — 2
SETTLE, Evan E. — 1
SETTLE, George Thomas — 4
SETTLE, Thomas * — H
SETTLE, Warner Ellmore — 4
SETZE, Julius Adolphus — 4
SETZER, Richard Woodrow — 5
SEUBERT, Edward George — 2
SEVER, George Francis — 2
SEVERANCE, Caroline Maria Seymour — 1
SEVERANCE, Cordenio Arnold — 1
SEVERANCE, Frank Hayward — 1
SEVERANCE, Henry Ormal — 2
SEVERANCE, John Long — 1
SEVERANCE, Luther — H
SEVERANCE, Mark Sibley — 4
SEVERENS, Henry Franklin — 4
SEVERN, Edmund — 3
SEVERS, John Ward — 4
SEVERSON, Lewis Everett — 1
SEVERY, Melvin Linwood — 4
SEVEY, Robert — 3
SEVIER, Ambrose Hundley — H
SEVIER, Charles Edwin — 3
SEVIER, Henry Hulme — 1
SEVIER, Henry Hulme — 2
SEVIER, John — H
SEVIER, Joseph Ramsey — 5

SEVIER, Landers — 3
SEVIER, Randolph — 4
SEVIGNY, Albert — 1
SEVITZKY, Fabien — 4
SEWALL, Arthur — 1
SEWALL, Arthur Wollaston — 1
SEWALL, Charles S. — H
SEWALL, Edmund Devereux —
SEWALL, Frank — 1
SEWALL, Harold Marsh — 1
SEWALL, Harriet Winslow — H
SEWALL, Henry — 1
SEWALL, James Wingate — 2
SEWALL, John Smith — 1
SEWALL, Jonathan — H
SEWALL, Jonathan Mitchell —
SEWALL, Lee Goodrich — 5
SEWALL, May Wright — 1
SEWALL, Rufus King — 1
SEWALL, Samuel * — H
SEWALL, Stephen — H
SEWARD, Allin Carey, Jr. — 5
SEWARD, Coy Avon — 4
SEWARD, Frederick William —
SEWARD, George Frederick — 1
SEWARD, Herbert Lee — 4
SEWARD, James Lindsay — H
SEWARD, John Perry — 1
SEWARD, Samuel Swayze — 1
SEWARD, Samuel Swayze Jr. — 1
SEWARD, Theodore Frelinghuysen — 1
SEWARD, William — 1
SEWARD, William Henry — 1
SEWARD, William Henry — 1
SEWELL, Albert Henry — 1
SEWELL, Amanda Brewster — 1
SEWELL, Jesse Parker — 5
SEWELL, John Stephen — 1
SEWELL, Oscar Marion — 1
SEWELL, Robert 'van Vorst — 1
SEWELL, William Joyce — 1
SEXTON, George Samuel — 1
SEXTON, Harold Eustace — 1
SEXTON, John Chase — 1
SEXTON, John Moody — 1
SEXTON, Lawrence Eugene — 1
SEXTON, Leonidas — H
SEXTON, Lewis Albert — 1
SEXTON, Pliny Titus — 1
SEXTON, Sherman J. — 3
SEXTON, Thomas Lawrence — 4
SEXTON, Thomas Scott — 5
SEXTON, Walton Roswell — 2
SEXTON, William Henry — 1
SEXTON, William Thomas — 3
SEYBERT, Adam — H
SEYBERT, Henry — H
SEYBERT, John — H
SEYBOLT, Robert Francis — 3
SEYFERT, Carl Keenan — 4
SEYFFARTH, Gustavus — 1
SEYFFERT, Leopold — 3
SEYMORE, Truman — 3
SEYMOUR, Alexander Duncan Jr. —
SEYMOUR, Arthur Bliss — 1
SEYMOUR, Augustus Theodore — 4
SEYMOUR, Augustus Theodore —
SEYMOUR, Burge Miles — 4
SEYMOUR, Charles —
SEYMOUR, Charles Milne — 3
SEYMOUR, David Lowrey — H
SEYMOUR, Edward Woodruff — H
SEYMOUR, Flora Warren — 2
SEYMOUR, Frederick — 1
SEYMOUR, George Dudley — 2
SEYMOUR, George Franklin — 1
SEYMOUR, George Steele — 2
SEYMOUR, Gideon — 3
SEYMOUR, Harold J. — 5
SEYMOUR, Horatio * — H
SEYMOUR, Horatio Winslow — 1
SEYMOUR, James Alward — 2
SEYMOUR, John Sammis — 1
SEYMOUR, Mary Harrison — 3

SEYMOUR, Morris Woodruff 1
SEYMOUR, Origen Storrs H
SEYMOUR, Ralph Fletcher 4
SEYMOUR, Robert Gillin 1
SEYMOUR, Samuel H
SEYMOUR, Storrs Ozias 3
SEYMOUR, Thomas Day 1
SEYMOUR, Thomas Hart
SEYMOUR, William H
SEYMOUR, William 1
SEYMOUR, William Wolcott
SEYMOUR, William Wotkyns 1
SHAAD, George Carl
SHABONEE H
SHACK, Ferdinand 4
SHACKELFORD, Edward Madison 2
SHACKELFORD, James M. 1
SHACKELFORD, John Williams H
SHACKELFORD, Virginius Randolph 2
SHACKFORD, Martha Hale 5
SHACKLEFORD, Dorsey W. 4
SHACKLEFORD, Robert Wooten 4
SHACKLEFORD, Thomas Mitchell 1
SHACKLEFORD, Thomas Mitchell, Jr. 5
SHACKLETON, Robert 4
SHADID, Michael Abraham
SHAFER, George F. 2
SHAFER, George H. 2
SHAFER, Helen Almira
SHAFER, Jacob K. H
SHAFER, John Douglas 1
SHAFER, Morris Luther 5
SHAFER, Paul W. 3
SHAFER, Robert 3
SHAFER, Sara Andrew 1
SHAFFER, Charles Norman 4
SHAFFER, Cornelius Thadeus
SHAFFER, Edward H. 2
SHAFFER, Floyd Elmer 4
SHAFFER, John Charles 5
SHAFFER, John Charles 2
SHAFFER, Joseph Crockett 3
SHAFFER, Lewis 5
SHAFFER, Newton Melman 1
SHAFFER, Philip Anderson 4
SHAFFER, Ray Osborn 4
SHAFFER, William Frederick 4
SHAFFNER, Henry Fries 2
SHAFFNER, Taliaferro Preston H
SHAFROTH, John Franklin 1
SHAFROTH, John Franklin 4
SHAFTER, William Rufus 1
SHAFTESBURY, Archie D. 4
SHAHAN, Thomas Joseph 1
SHAHN, Ben 5
SHAINWALD, Richard Herman 3
SHAINWALD, Richard S. 3
SHAKESPEARE, William Jr. 3
SHALER, Alexander 1
SHALER, Charles 1
SHALER, Clarence Addison 2
SHALER, Nathaniel Southgate 1
SHALER, William H
SHALLBERG, Gustavus Adolphus 3
SHALLCROSS, Cecil Fleetwood 2
SHALLENBERGER, Ashton C. 1
SHALLENBERGER, Martin C. 3
SHALLENBERGER, William Shadrach 1
SHAMBAUGH, Benjamin Franklin 1
SHAMBAUGH, Bertha M. H. (mrs. Benjamin F. Shambaugh) 5

SHAMBAUGH, George Elmer 5
SHAMBURGER, Carl Shuford 5
SHANAFELT, Thomas M. 4
SHANAHAN, David Edward 1
SHANAHAN, Edmund Thomas
SHANAHAN, Foss 4
SHANAHAN, John Daniel 4
SHANAHAN, John W. 1
SHANAHAN, T. J. 4
SHANANAN, Jeremiah Francis H
SHAND, Robert Gordon 1
SHAND, S. James 3
SHANDS, Aurelius Rives 1
SHANDS, Courtney 5
SHANDS, Garvin Dugas 1
SHANE, George (Walker) 5
SHANK, Corwin Sheridan 5
SHANK, Donald J. 4
SHANK, Samuel Herbert 5
SHANKLAND, Edward Clapp
SHANKLAND, Sherwood Dodge 2
SHANKLIN, Arnold 4
SHANKLIN, George Sea H
SHANKLIN, John Gilbert 1
SHANKLIN, William Arnold 1
SHANKS, David Carey 1
SHANKS, Henry Thomas 3
SHANKS, Lewis Piaget 1
SHANKS, Royal E. 4
SHANKS, William Franklin Gore
SHANLEY, James Andrew 1
SHANLEY, John 1
SHANNAHAN, John Newton 1
SHANNON, Edgar Finley 1
SHANNON, Effie 5
SHANNON, Fred Albert 4
SHANNON, Frederick Franklin
SHANNON, George Pope 4
SHANNON, J. J. 3
SHANNON, Joseph B. 2
SHANNON, Nellie 1
SHANNON, Richard Cutts 1
SHANNON, Robert Thomas 1
SHANNON, Spencer Sweet 4
SHANNON, Thomas H
SHANNON, Thomas Bowles 3
SHANNON, Thomas Vincent H
SHANNON, Wilson H
SHANTZ, Homer LeRoy 3
SHAPIRO, Harry 4
SHAPIRO, Joseph 5
SHAPIRO, Joseph M. 5
SHAPLEIGH, Alfred Lee 4
SHAPLEIGH, Bertram 2
SHAPLEIGH, Frank Henry 1
SHAPLEIGH, Waldron 5
SHAPLEY, Harlow 5
SHAPLEY, Rufus Edmonds 4
SHAPORIN, Yuri 4
SHARETT, Moshe 4
SHARKEY, Joseph Edward 5
SHARKEY, William Lewis H
SHARMAN, Jackson Roger 3
SHARON, William H
SHARP, Benjamin 1
SHARP, Carl J. 5
SHARP, Clayton Halsey 3
SHARP, Dallas Lore 1
SHARP, Daniel H
SHARP, Eckley Grant 4
SHARP, Edgar A. 4
SHARP, Edward Raymond 4
SHARP, Edwin Rees 1
SHARP, Frank Chapman 4
SHARP, George Clough 5
SHARP, George Gillies 3
SHARP, George Matthews 4
SHARP, George Winters 3
SHARP, Henry Staats 5
SHARP, Hunter 1
SHARP, John H
SHARP, John Fletcher 1
SHARP, John H. 5
SHARP, Joseph C. 2
SHARP, Joseph Lessil 5
SHARP, Katharine Lucinda

SHARP, Marlay Albert 3
SHARP, Mrs. John C. 1
SHARP, Robert 1
SHARP, Robert Sherman 1
SHARP, Solomon P. H
SHARP, Thomas Enoch 3
SHARP, Waldo Z. 1
SHARP, Walter Bedford 4
SHARP, William H
SHARP, William F. 2
SHARP, William Graves 1
SHARP, William Wilson 4
SHARPE, Alfred Clarence 1
SHARPE, Francis Robert 2
SHARPE, Henry Augustus 1
SHARPE, Henry Dexter 3
SHARPE, Henry Granville 2
SHARPE, Horatio H
SHARPE, John C. 2
SHARPE, Merrell Quentin 4
SHARPE, Nelson 1
SHARPE, Peter 1
SHARPE, Philip Burdette 4
SHARPE, William H
SHARPLES, James H
SHARPLES, Philip M. 1
SHARPLES, Stephen Paschall 1
SHARPLESS, Frederic Cope 5
SHARPLESS, Frederick F. 3
SHARPLESS, Isaac 1
SHARSWOOD, George H
SHARTS, Joseph William 5
SHASTID, Thomas Hall 1
SHASTRI, Lal Bahadur 4
SHATTUC, William B. 1
SHATTUCK, Aaron Draper 1
SHATTUCK, Arthur 3
SHATTUCK, Charles Houston 1
SHATTUCK, Edward Stevens 4
SHATTUCK, Edwin Paul 4
SHATTUCK, Frederick Cheever 1
SHATTUCK, George Brune 1
SHATTUCK, George Burbank 1
SHATTUCK, George Cheever 5
SHATTUCK, George Cheyne * H
SHATTUCK, H. Morgan 4
SHATTUCK, Harriette Lucy Robinson 4
SHATTUCK, Henry Lee 5
SHATTUCK, Howard Francis 5
SHATTUCK, John Garrett 4
SHATTUCK, Lemuel H
SHATTUCK, Lemuel C. 1
SHATTUCK, Mayo Adams 3
SHATTUCK, Samuel Walker 1
SHATTUCK, William 3
SHATZER, Charles Gallatin 4
SHAUCK, John Allen 1
SHAUGHNESSY, Clark Daniel 5
SHAUGHNESSY, Gerald 3
SHAUGHNESSY, Sir Thomas George 1
SHAVER, Charles William 4
SHAVER, Clement Lawrence 3
SHAVER, Dorothy 3
SHAVER, George Frederick 4
SHAVER, Jesse Milton 1
SHAW, Aaron H
SHAW, Albert 2
SHAW, Albert Duane 1
SHAW, Anna Howard 1
SHAW, Arch Wilkinson 4
SHAW, Avery Albert 2
SHAW, Charles Bunsen 4
SHAW, Charles Frederick 1
SHAW, Charles Gray 4
SHAW, Clarence Reginald 3
SHAW, Earl 4
SHAW, Edgar Dwight 1
SHAW, Edward Richard 1
SHAW, Edwin Adams 3
SHAW, Edwin Coupland 2

SHAW, Elijah H
SHAW, Elwyn Riley 3
SHAW, Esmond 5
SHAW, Eugene Wesley 4
SHAW, Florence Sylvia Berlowitz
SHAW, Frances Wills 1
SHAW, Frank L. 3
SHAW, Frederick Benjamin 5
SHAW, Frederick William 2
SHAW, G. Bernard 4
SHAW, Gardiner Howland 4
SHAW, George Bullen H
SHAW, George Elmer 1
SHAW, George Hamlin 3
SHAW, Harriett McCreary Jackson 2
SHAW, Henry * H
SHAW, Henry Larned Keith 1
SHAW, Henry Marchmore H
SHAW, Henry Wheeler H
SHAW, Hobart Doane 4
SHAW, Howard Burton 2
SHAW, Howard Van Doren 1
SHAW, J. W. 1
SHAW, James Byrnie 2
SHAW, John * H
SHAW, John Balcom 1
SHAW, John Stewart 3
SHAW, John William 4
SHAW, Joseph Alden 1
SHAW, Joshua H
SHAW, Lemuel 1
SHAW, Leo Nelson 4
SHAW, Leslie Mortier 1
SHAW, Lloyd 3
SHAW, Lucien 1
SHAW, Mary 1
SHAW, Nathaniel H
SHAW, Oliver 1
SHAW, Oliver Abbott 2
SHAW, Phillips Bassett 5
SHAW, Quincy A. 5
SHAW, Quincy A. 2
SHAW, Ralph Martin 2
SHAW, Ralph Robert 5
SHAW, Reuben T. 3
SHAW, Richard 3
SHAW, Robert 2
SHAW, Robert Alfred 2
SHAW, Robert Anderson 1
SHAW, Robert Gould H
SHAW, Robert Kendall 5
SHAW, Robert Sidey 4
SHAW, Roger 3
SHAW, Samuel * H
SHAW, Samuel Gormley 4
SHAW, Sterling Price 5
SHAW, Thomas H
SHAW, Thomas 4
SHAW, Thomas Mott 4
SHAW, Tristram H
SHAW, Walter Adam 3
SHAW, Walter Keith 1
SHAW, William Bristol 2
SHAW, William Edward 5
SHAW, William Frederick 1
SHAW, William James 3
SHAW, William Smith 5
SHAWHAN, Narcissa Tayloe Maupin (Mrs. Charles S.) 1
SHAWKEY, Morris Purdy 1
SHAWN, Edwin M. (ted Shawn) 5
SHAY, Frank 2
SHAYLER, Ernest Vincent 4
SHAYS, Daniel H
SHEA, Andrew Bernard 5
SHEA, Daniel William 1
SHEA, Edmund Burke 5
SHEA, Edward Lane 4
SHEA, James R. 3
SHEA, John Dawson Gilmary H
SHEA, John J. 4
SHEA, John Joseph 1
SHEA, Joseph Bernard 1
SHEA, Joseph Hooker 5
SHEA, Lewis Anthony 5
SHEA, William Joseph 4
SHEAFE, James H
SHEAFER, Arthur Whitcomb 2
SHEAFFER, Craig Royer 4
SHEAFFER, Daniel Miller 4
SHEAFFER, Walter A. 2
SHEAN, Charles M. 1
SHEAR, Cornelius Lott 4
SHEAR, John Knox 3

SHEAR, Theodore Leslie 2
SHEARD, Titus 1
SHEARER, Andrew 1
SHEARER, Augustus Hunt 1
SHEARER, George Lewis 1
SHEARER, Henry 4
SHEARER, J. Harry 4
SHEARER, John Bunyan 1
SHEARER, John Louis 4
SHEARER, John Sanford 1
SHEARER, Tom Ellas 5
SHEARER, Tom Ellas 1
SHEARIN, Hubert Gibson 1
SHEARMAN, Thomas Gaskell 1
SHEARN, Clarence John 3
SHEATS, William Nicholas 1
SHEATSLEY, Clarence Valentine 1
SHEATSLEY, Jacob 4
SHECUT, John Linnaeus Edward Whitridge H
SHEDD, Fred Fuller 1
SHEDD, George Clifford 1
SHEDD, J. Herbert 1
SHEDD, John Cutler 1
SHEDD, John Graves 1
SHEDD, Solon 2
SHEDD, Thomas Clark 3
SHEDD, William Alfred 4
SHEDD, William Greenough Thayer 1
SHEDDEN, Lucian Love 1
SHEEAN, James B. 3
SHEEDY, Dennis 1
SHEEDY, Joseph Edward 3
SHEEDY, Morgan M. 1
SHEEHAN, Daniel Michael 4
SHEEHAN, Donal 3
SHEEHAN, J. Eastman 3
SHEEHAN, John Charles 1
SHEEHAN, Joseph Raymond 1
SHEEHAN, Perley Poore 5
SHEEHAN, Robert Francis Jr. 2
SHEEHAN, Robert John 4
SHEEHAN, Robert Wade 5
SHEEHAN, Timothy J. 1
SHEEHAN, William Francis 1
SHEEHAN, William Mark 4
SHEEHAN, Winfield R. 2
SHEEHY, Joe Warren 5
SHEEHY, Maurice S(tephen)
SHEELER, Charles 4
SHEELY, William Clarence 5
SHEEN, Daniel Robinson 1
SHEERIN, Charles Wilford 2
SHEERIN, James 1
SHEETS, Frank Thomas 3
SHEETS, Harold F. 5
SHEETS, Millard Owen 4
SHEFFER, Daniel 1
SHEFFER, Henry Maurice 4
SHEFFEY, Daniel H
SHEFFEY, Edward Fleming 1
SHEFFIELD, Alfred Dwight 4
SHEFFIELD, Develo Z. 1
SHEFFIELD, Frederick 5
SHEFFIELD, J. S. 4
SHEFFIELD, James Rockwell 1
SHEFFIELD, Joseph Earl H
SHEFFIELD, William Paine * 1
SHEIL, Bernard J(ames) 5
SHEININ, John J(acobi) 5
SHELBURNE, James M. 2
SHELBURNE, Lord H
SHELBY, David Davie 1
SHELBY, Evan H
SHELBY, Gertrude Singleton Mathews 5
SHELBY, Isaac H
SHELBY, John Todd 1
SHELBY, Joseph Orville H
SHELBY, Robert Evart 3
SHELBY, William Read 1
SHELDEN, Carlos Douglas 1
SHELDON, Addison Erwin 2
SHELDON, Arthur Frederick 1
SHELDON, Caroline M. 1
SHELDON, Charles 1
SHELDON, Charles Mills 1

SHELDON, Charles Monroe — 2
SHELDON, Charles Stuart — 1
SHELDON, David Newton — H
SHELDON, Edward Austin — H
SHELDON, Edward Brewster — 2
SHELDON, Edward Stevens — 1
SHELDON, Edward Wright — 1
SHELDON, Frederick Beaumont — 1
SHELDON, G. L. — 5
SHELDON, George Lawson — 3
SHELDON, George Preston — 1
SHELDON, George Rumsey — 1
SHELDON, George William — 1
SHELDON, Grace Carew — 5
SHELDON, Harold Horton — 4
SHELDON, Henry Clay — 1
SHELDON, Henry Davidson — 2
SHELDON, Henry Newton — 1
SHELDON, John Lewis — 3
SHELDON, John M. — 4
SHELDON, Joseph — 1
SHELDON, Lionel Allen — 1
SHELDON, Ralph Edward — 4
SHELDON, Rowland Caldwell — 1
SHELDON, Roy Horton — 5
SHELDON, Samuel — 1
SHELDON, Walter L. — 1
SHELDON, William Evarts — H
SHELDON, Wilmon Henry — 5
SHELDON, Winthrop Dudley — 4
SHELEKHOV, Grigorii Ivanovich — H
SHELEY, Basil LeRoy — 4
SHELFORD, Victor E(rnest) — 5
SHELLABARGER, Samuel — H
SHELLABARGER, Samuel — 3
SHELLEY, George Elgin — 4
SHELLEY, Harry Rowe — 2
SHELLEY, Henry Charles — 5
SHELLEY, Henry V. — 3
SHELLEY, Oliver Hazard Perry — 2
SHELLEY, Tully — 4
SHELMIRE, Horace Weeks — 4
SHELTON, Charles Eldred — 1
SHELTON, Don Odell — 1
SHELTON, E. Kost — 3
SHELTON, Frederick William — H
SHELTON, Jane de Forest — 5
SHELTON, Louise — 1
SHELTON, Orman Leroy — 3
SHELTON, Samuel A. — 4
SHELTON, Thomas Wall — 1
SHELTON, Whitford Huston — 4
SHELTON, Willard Ellington — 5
SHELTON, William Arthur — 5
SHELTON, William Henry — 4
SHENEHON, Francis Clinton — 1
SHENEMAN, Hester Mary Dickerson (Mrs. Mckinley Sheneman) — 5
SHENK, Hirmna Herr — 3
SHENK, John Wesley — 3
SHENTON, Herbert Newhard — 1
SHEPARD, Andrew N. — 1
SHEPARD, Bertram David — 4
SHEPARD, C. Sidney — 1
SHEPARD, Charles Biddle — H
SHEPARD, Charles Edward — 1
SHEPARD, Charles Henry — 1
SHEPARD, Charles Upham — H
SHEPARD, Earl Dorman — 5

SHEPARD, Edward Martin — 1
SHEPARD, Edward Morse — 1
SHEPARD, Edwin M. — 1
SHEPARD, Finley Johnson — 2
SHEPARD, Frank Edward — 4
SHEPARD, Frank Russell — 3
SHEPARD, Fred Douglas — 4
SHEPARD, Frederick Job — 1
SHEPARD, George Wanzor — 3
SHEPARD, Guy Conwell — 4
SHEPARD, Harriett Elma — 2
SHEPARD, Harvey Newton — 1
SHEPARD, Helen Miller — 1
SHEPARD, Horace B. — 2
SHEPARD, Irwin — 1
SHEPARD, James Edward — 2
SHEPARD, James Henry — 1
SHEPARD, John Jr. — 2
SHEPARD, John Frederick — 1
SHEPARD, Luther Dimmick — 1
SHEPARD, Odell — 1
SHEPARD, Seth — 1
SHEPARD, Stuart Gore — 1
SHEPARD, Theodore F. — 4
SHEPARD, Thomas — H
SHEPARD, Walter James — 1
SHEPARD, William — H
SHEPARD, William Biddle — 1
SHEPARD, William Orville — 1
SHEPARD, William Pierce — 1
SHEPARD, Woolsey Adams — 4
SHEPARDSON, Francis Wayland — 1
SHEPARDSON, Frank Lucius — 3
SHEPARDSON, George Defrees — 1
SHEPARDSON, Ruth Pearson Chandler — 2
SHEPARDSON, Whitney Hart — 4
SHEPERD, James Edward — 1
SHEPHERD, Alexander R. — 4
SHEPHERD, Arthur — 4
SHEPHERD, Charles Reginald — 1
SHEPHERD, Clifford John — 1
SHEPHERD, Ernest Stanley — 2
SHEPHERD, Grace M. — 5
SHEPHERD, Harold — 1
SHEPHERD, Henry Elliot — 4
SHEPHERD, James Leftwich — 4
SHEPHERD, Patricia Drake (Mrs. James Leftwich Shepherd Iii) — 5
SHEPHERD, Pearce — 5
SHEPHERD, Russell E. — 2
SHEPHERD, Theodosia Burr — 1
SHEPHERD, William Chauncey — 4
SHEPHERD, William Gunn — 1
SHEPHERD, William R. — 1
SHEPLER, Joseph McGuire —
SHEPLER, Matthias — H
SHEPLEY, Ether — H
SHEPLEY, George Foster — H
SHEPLEY, George Foster — 1
SHEPLEY, George Leander — 1
SHEPLEY, Henry Richardson — 4
SHEPPARD, Harry R. — 5
SHEPPARD, James Carroll — 4
SHEPPARD, James J. — 1
SHEPPARD, John Calhoun — 1
SHEPPARD, John Levi — 1
SHEPPARD, John Rutherford — 2
SHEPPARD, John Shoemaker — 2
SHEPPARD, Lawrence Baker — 5
SHEPPARD, Lucius Elmer — 1
SHEPPARD, Morris — 2
SHEPPARD, Robert Dickinson — 4
SHEPPARD, Samuel Edward — 2
SHEPPARD, Walter Wade — 1

SHEPPARD, Warren — 1
SHEPPARD, William Bostwick — 1
SHEPPARD, William Henry — 4
SHEPPERD, Augustine Henry — H
SHEPPERD, John Henry — 1
SHEPPERSON, Archibald Bolling — 4
SHEPPEY, Marshall — 2
SHERBAKOFF, Constantine Dmitriev — 4
SHERBON, Florence Brown — 2
SHERBURNE, Ernest C. — 3
SHERBURNE, John Henry — 4
SHERBURNE, John Samuel — H
SHERBY, Daniel — 3
SHERE, Lewis — 5
SHEREDINE, Upton — 4
SHERER, Dunham B. — 4
SHERER, Rex W. — 5
SHERER, William — 4
SHERIDAN, Ann — H
SHERIDAN, George Augustus —
SHERIDAN, Harold James — 4
SHERIDAN, John Lawrence —
SHERIDAN, Lawrence Vinnedge — 5
SHERIDAN, Michael Vincent — 1
SHERIDAN, Philip Henry — H
SHERIDAN, Sarah M. — 5
SHERIDAN, Thomas Francis — 4
SHERIDAN, Thomas Harold — 3
SHERIDAN, Wilbur Fletcher — 1
SHERILL, George Raymond — 4
SHERK, Kenneth Wayne — 5
SHERLEY, Swagar — 1
SHERLOCK, Charles Reginald —
SHERLOCK, Chesia C. — 1
SHERMAN, Althea Rosina — 2
SHERMAN, Andrew Magoun — 1
SHERMAN, Buren Robinson —
SHERMAN, Carl — 1
SHERMAN, Charles Colebrook — 1
SHERMAN, Charles Lawrence — 5
SHERMAN, Charles Lawton — 3
SHERMAN, Charles Pomeroy — 2
SHERMAN, Christopher Elias — 1
SHERMAN, Clifford Gould — 4
SHERMAN, Clifton Lucien — 2
SHERMAN, Edward Augustine — 1
SHERMAN, Elijah Bernis — 1
SHERMAN, Ellen Burns — 3
SHERMAN, Forrest Percival — 3
SHERMAN, Frank — 1
SHERMAN, Frank Asbury — 1
SHERMAN, Frank Dempster —
SHERMAN, Franklin — 2
SHERMAN, Frederick C. — 3
SHERMAN, Gordon Edward — 4
SHERMAN, H. M. Jr. — 4
SHERMAN, Harry Mitchell — 1
SHERMAN, Henry Clapp — 3
SHERMAN, Henry Stoddard — 3
SHERMAN, Homer Henkel — 2
SHERMAN, Hoyt — 1
SHERMAN, James Morgan — 2
SHERMAN, James Schoolcraft — 3
SHERMAN, John — H
SHERMAN, John — 1
SHERMAN, John Dickinson —
SHERMAN, John Francis — 1
SHERMAN, John K(urtz) — 5
SHERMAN, Judson W. — H

SHERMAN, Lawrence William, Jr. — 5
SHERMAN, Lawrence Y. — 1
SHERMAN, Louis Ralph — 3
SHERMAN, Lucius Adelno — 1
SHERMAN, Mary Belle King —
SHERMAN, Maurice Sinclair — 2
SHERMAN, Merritt Masters — 1
SHERMAN, Mildred P. — 4
SHERMAN, Moses Hazeltine —
SHERMAN, Philemon Tecumseh — 4
SHERMAN, Ray Eugene — 2
SHERMAN, Roger — H
SHERMAN, Roger — 4
SHERMAN, Socrates Norton — H
SHERMAN, Stuart Pratt — 1
SHERMAN, Thomas B. — 5
SHERMAN, Thomas Ewing — 4
SHERMAN, Thomas Townsend — 1
SHERMAN, Thomas West — H
SHERMAN, Wells Alvord — 3
SHERMAN, William Arthur — 3
SHERMAN, William Bowen — 5
SHERMAN, William O'neill — 3
SHERMAN, William Tecumseh — H
SHERMAN, William Winslow — 1
SHERO, Lucius Rogers — 1
SHERO, William Francis — 2
SHERPICK, Eugene Arthur — 4
SHERRARD, Charles Cornell — 4
SHERRARD, Glenwood John — 3
SHERRARD, Thomas Herrick — 1
SHERRERD, William D. — H
SHERRIFF, Andrew Rothwell — 1
SHERRILL, Alvan Foote — 4
SHERRILL, Charles Hitchcock — 1
SHERRILL, Clarence Osborne — 5
SHERRILL, Edwin Stanton — 4
SHERRILL, Eliakim — H
SHERRILL, Gibbs Wynkoop — 3
SHERRILL, James Winn — 3
SHERRILL, John Bascom — 1
SHERRILL, Lewis Joseph — 3
SHERRILL, Miles Osborne — 1
SHERRILL, Miles Standish — 4
SHERRILL, R. E. — 3
SHERRILL, Ruth Erwin — 1
SHERRILL, Samuel Wells — 5
SHERRILL, Stephen H. — 1
SHERRILL, William Lander — 5
SHERRY, George Gregory — 4
SHERWELL, G. Butler — 4
SHERWELL, Guillermo Antonio —
SHERWIN, Belle — 3
SHERWIN, Henry Alden — 1
SHERWIN, John Collins — 1
SHERWIN, Proctor Fenn — 1
SHERWIN, Ralph Sidney — 3
SHERWIN, Thomas — H
SHERWIN, Thomas — 1
SHERWOOD, Adiel — H
SHERWOOD, Andrew — 1
SHERWOOD, Arnold Cooper — 5
SHERWOOD, Carl G. — 1
SHERWOOD, Carlton Montgomery — 5
SHERWOOD, Emily Lee — 4
SHERWOOD, George Herbert —
SHERWOOD, Granville Hudson —
SHERWOOD, Henry — H
SHERWOOD, Herbert Francis — 1
SHERWOOD, Isaac R. — 1
SHERWOOD, Katharine Margaret Brownlee — 1

SHERWOOD, Margaret Pollock — 3
SHERWOOD, Mary Elizabeth Wilson — 1
SHERWOOD, Noble Pierce — 4
SHERWOOD, Robert Emmet — 3
SHERWOOD, Rosina Emmet — 3
SHERWOOD, Samuel — H
SHERWOOD, Samuel Burr — 1
SHERWOOD, Sidney — 1
SHERWOOD, Thomas Adiel — 4
SHERWOOD, William — 3
SHERWOOD, William Hall — 1
SHERWOOD-DUNN, Berkeley — 5
SHERZER, William Hittell — 1
SHETTER, Stella Cross — 1
SHEVELSON, S. Harris — 4
SHEWHART, Walter Andrew —
SHEWMAKE, Oscar Lane — 4
SHEWMAN, Eben B. — 3
SHIBER, Etta — 2
SHIBLEY, Alice Smith Patterson — 4
SHIDEHARA, Baron Kijuro — 5
SHIDELER, W. H. — 3
SHIDY, Leland Perry — 1
SHIEL, George Knox — H
SHIELD, Lansing P. — 3
SHIELD, Lansing P. — 1
SHIELDS, A. C. — 2
SHIELDS, Benjamin Glover — H
SHIELDS, Charles R. — 1
SHIELDS, Charles Woodruff — 1
SHIELDS, Ebenezer J. — H
SHIELDS, Edmund Claude — 2
SHIELDS, Emily L. — 4
SHIELDS, G. O. — 1
SHIELDS, George Howell — 1
SHIELDS, George Robert — 2
SHIELDS, James * — H
SHIELDS, John Franklin — 1
SHIELDS, John Knight — 1
SHIELDS, Paul Vincent — 4
SHIELDS, Roy Franklin — 4
SHIELDS, Thomas Edward — 1
SHIELDS, Thomas Todhunter — 3
SHIELDS, William S. — 1
SHIELS, Albert — 1
SHIELS, George Franklin — 2
SHIELS, James — 5
SHIENTAG, Bernard Lloyd — 3
SHIER, Calrton S. — 3
SHIGEMITSU, Mamoru — 3
SHIKELLAMY — H
SHILLABER, Benjamin Penhallow — H
SHILLADY, John R. — 5
SHILLING, Alexander — 1
SHILOAH, Reuven — 3
SHIMEK, Bohumil — 1
SHIMER, Hervey Woodburn — 4
SHIMER, Porter William — 1
SHIMP, Herbert Gilby — 2
SHINE, Francis Eppes — 4
SHINGLER, Don Gilmore — 4
SHINKLE, Edward Marsh — 4
SHINN, Asa — H
SHINN, Charles Howard — 1
SHINN, Everett — 3
SHINN, Florence Scovel — 1
SHINN, George Wolfe — 1
SHINN, Henry Arthur — 2
SHINN, Milicent Washburn — 1
SHINN, William Norton — H
SHIPHERD, John Jay — H
SHIPHERD, Zebulon Rudd — H
SHIPLE, George J. — 3
SHIPLEY, Charles Raymond — 4
SHIPLEY, Edward Ellis — 4
SHIPLEY, Frederick William —
SHIPLEY, George — 2
SHIPLEY, Maynard — 1
SHIPLEY, Richard Larkin — 2
SHIPLEY, Samuel R. — 1
SHIPLEY, Walter Penn — 2

SHIPLEY, 3
William Stewart
SHIPMAN, 1
Arthur Leffingwell
SHIPMAN, 4
Benjamin Jonson
SHIPMAN, Herbert 1
SHIPMAN, Louis Evan 1
SHIPMAN, Nathaniel 1
SHIPMAN, Samuel 1
SHIPMAN, 1
William Rollin
SHIPP, Albert Micajah H
SHIPP, Barnard 4
SHIPP, Cameron 4
SHIPP, Frederic B. 1
SHIPP, Scott 1
SHIPP, Thomas Roerty 3
SHIPPEE, 2
Lester Burrell
SHIPPEN, Edward * H
SHIPPEN, Edward 1
SHIPPEN, Eugene
Rodman 3
SHIPPEN, Joseph 1
SHIPPEN, Rush Rhees 1
SHIPPEN, William * H
SHIPPEY, Henry) Lee 5
SHIPSEY, Edward 1
SHIPSTEAD, Henrik 4
SHIPTON, A. W. 1
SHIPTON, James Ancil 1
SHIRAS, George Jr. 1
SHIRAS, George III 2
SHIRAS, Oliver Perry 1
SHIRLAW, Walter
SHIRLEY, Cassius Clay 4
SHIRLEY, Robert Kirby 3
SHIRLEY, William H
SHIVE, John W(esley) 5
SHIVELY, 1
Benjamin Franklin
SHIVELY, 3
Carlton Adamson
SHIVERICK, Asa 1
SHIVERS, R. Kevin 4
SHLENKER, Irvin Morris 5
SHOAFF, Fred B. 4
SHOALS, George 4
SHOBER, Francis E. 4
SHOBER, Francis Edwin H
SHOBER, John Bedford 4
SHOCK, Thomas Macy 4
SHOCK, William Henry 4
SHOCKLEY, 3
Frank William
SHOCKLEY, 5
M. Augustus Wroten
SHOEMAKER, 2
Charles Chalmers
SHOEMAKER, 1
Charles Frederick
SHOEMAKER, 5
Daniel Naylor
SHOEMAKER, Harlan 2
SHOEMAKER, 1
Henry Francis
SHOEMAKER, 3
Henry Wharton
SHOEMAKER, John
Vietch 1
SHOEMAKER, 5
Joseph Addison
SHOEMAKER, H
Lazarus Denison
SHOEMAKER, 1
Michael Myers
SHOEMAKER,
Rachel Hinkle
SHOEMAKER, Raymond
L. 4
SHOEMAKER,
Richard Heston
SHOEMAKER, Robert H
SHOEMAKER, Samuel
Moor
SHOEMAKER, Waite
Almon 1
SHOEMAKER,
William Rawle
SHOFFSTALL,
Arthur Scott
SHOHAT, 2
James Alexander
SHOHL, Walter Max 5
SHOLES, H
Christopher Latham
SHOLLEY, 4
Sidney Llewellyn
SHOLTZ, David 3
SHOMO, E. H. 5
SHONTS, Theodore Perry 1
SHONTZ, Vernon Lloyd 3
SHOOK, Alfred M. 1
SHOOK, Charles Francis 4
SHOOK, Edgar 5
SHOOK, Glenn Alfred 3

SHOONMAKER, Marius H
SHOOP, 4
Clarence Adelbert
SHOOP, Duke 3
SHOOP, John Daniel 1
SHOPE, Richard Edwin 4
SHOPE, Simeon P. 4
SHOR, George Gershon 5
SHORE, Clarence Albert 4
SHORE, Maurice J. 4
SHOREY, Clyde Everett 1
SHOREY, Paul 1
SHORIKI, Matsutaro 5
SHORT, Albert 4
SHORT, Charles H
SHORT, Charles Wilkins 1
SHORT, H
Francis Burgette
SHORT, Frank Hamilton 1
SHORT, Joseph 3
SHORT, 4
Joseph Hudson Jr.
SHORT, 1
Josephine Helena
SHORT, 4
Livingston Lyman
SHORT, Sidney Howe H
SHORT, Wallace Mertin 5
SHORT, Walter Campbell 2
SHORT, William H
SHORT, 1
William Harrison
SHORT, Zuber Nathaniel 5
SHORTALL, John G. 1
SHORTALL, 4
Thomas Francis
SHORTER, Eli Sims 1
SHORTER, John Gill H
SHORTLE, Abraham
Given 1
SHORTLIDGE, 1
Jonathan Chauncey
SHORTRIDGE, Charles
M. 4
SHORTRIDGE, N. Parker 3
SHORTRIDGE,
Samuel Morgan
SHORTS, Bruce Carman 2
SHORTT, Elster Clayton 4
SHOTT, Hugh Ike 3
SHOTWELL, Abel V. 4
SHOTWELL,
James Thomson
SHOUDY, Loyal Ambrose 3
SHOULDERS, Harrison
H.
SHOUP, 2
Arthur Glendinning
SHOUP, Earl Leon 3
SHOUP, Eldon Campbell 3
SHOUP, Francis Asbury 1
SHOUP, George Laird 1
SHOUP, Guy V. 5
SHOUP, Merrill Edgar 4
SHOUP, Oliver Henry 1
SHOUP, Paul 2
SHOUSE, James D. 4
SHOVE, Eugene Percy 1
SHOW, Arley Barthlow
SHOWALTER, 1
Anthony Johnson
SHOWALTER,
Jackson Whipps
SHOWALTER, 4
Joseph Baltzell
SHOWALTER, Noah
David 1
SHOWALTER,
William Joseph
SHOWER,
George Theodore
SHOWER, Jacob H
SHOWERMAN, Grant 1
SHOWERS, J. Balmer
SHOWMAN, Harry
Munson 2
SHRADY, 1
George Frederick
SHRADY, Henry Merwin 4
SHREVE, 5
Charles Everett
SHREVE, Forrest 3
SHREVE, Henry Miller H
SHREVE, Milton William 1
SHREVE, 2
Richmond Harold
SHREVE, Thomas
Hopkins H
SHREVE, 4
Wickliffe Winston
SHRINER, 3
Charles Anthony
SHRINER, Herb 5
SHRIVER, Alfred 1
SHRIVER,
Alfred Jenkins

SHRIVER, George
McLean 2
SHRIVER, John Shultz 1
SHRIVER, William Payne 3
SHRODER, William Jacob 3
SHROPSHIRE, 4
Courtney William
SHRUM, George Dixon 4
SHRYOCK, 5
Burnett Henry, Sr.
SHRYOCK, Gideon H
SHRYOCK, Henry
William 1
SHRYOCK, Joseph
Grundy 3
SHRYOCK, 5
Richard Harrison
SHUBERT, Jacob J. 4
SHUBERT, Lee 3
SHUBRICK, John Templer H
SHUBRICK,
William Branford
SHUCK, Jehu Lewis 1
SHUEY,
Edwin Longstreet
SHUEY, Lillian Hinman 4
SHUEY, William John 1
SHUFELDT, H
Robert Wilson
SHUFELDT, 1
Robert Wilson
SHUFF, John A. 5
SHUFORD, A. Alex, Jr. 5
SHUFORD, Alonzo Craig 1
SHUFORD, 3
Forrest Herman
SHUFORD, George A. 4
SHUGERMAN, Abe Louis 4
SHULER, Ellis W. 3
SHULL, A. Franklin 4
SHULL, Charles Graves 1
SHULL, Deloss Carlton 1
SHULL, Deloss P. 1
SHULL, Frank Leslie 5
SHULL, George Harrison 3
SHULL, James Marion 2
SHULL, Joseph H. 2
SHULMAN, Charles E. 5
SHULMAN, Harry 3
SHULTERS, Hoyt Volney 1
SHULTZ, William John 5
SHULZ, Adolph Robert 4
SHULZE, John Andrew 4
SHUMAKER, E. Ellsworth 4
SHUMAKER, Edward
Seitz 1
SHUMAKER, Ross W. 4
SHUMAN, Abraham 4
SHUMAN, Davis 4
SHUMAN, 1
Edwin Llewellyn
SHUMAN, John Franklin 4
SHUMATE, Roger V. 3
SHUMBERGER,
John Calvin
SHUMWAY, 1
Daniel Bussier
SHUMWAY, Edgar
Solomon 4
SHUMWAY, Edward D. 4
SHUMWAY, Sherman N. 1
SHUMWAY, Waldo 3
SHUMWAY, 1
Walter Bradley
SHUNK, Francis Rawn H
SHUNK, Joseph Lorain 1
SHUNK,
William Alexander
SHUNK, William Findlay 1
SHUPE, Henry Fox 1
SHUPING, 5
Clarence Leroy
SHURCLIFF, 3
Arthur Asahel
SHURLY, Burt Russell 5
SHURTER, Edwin DuBois 1
SHURTLEFF,
Charles Allerton
SHURTLEFF, 1
Ernest Warburton
SHURTLEFF, Eugene 3
SHURTLEFF, 1
Glen Kassimer
SHURTLEFF, H
Nathaniel Bradstreet
SHURTLEFF, 1
Roswell Morse
SHUSTER, W. Morgan 4
SHUTE, Abraham Lincoln 2
SHUTE, Daniel Kerfoot 1
SHUTE, Emmett R. 4
SHUTE, Henry Augustus 1
SHUTE, Nevil 3
SHUTE, Nevil 4
SHUTE, Samuel H
SHUTE, Samuel Moore 1
SHUTTER, Marion Daniel 1

SHUTTLEWORTH, 4
V. Craven
SHUTTS, Frank Barker 2
SHVERNIK, 5
Nikola (Mikhallvich)
SHY, George Milton 4
SIAS, Ernest J. 3
SIBELIUS, 3
Jean Julius Christian
SIBERELL, Lloyd E. 5
SIBERT, William Luther 4
SIBLEY, Bolling 5
SIBLEY, Clyde Lawson 5
SIBLEY, Edwin Henry 4
SIBLEY, Frank J. 4
SIBLEY, 1
Frederick Hubbard
SIBLEY, Frederick W. 5
SIBLEY,
George Champlain
SIBLEY, Harper 3
SIBLEY, Henry Hastings H
SIBLEY, Hiram H
SIBLEY, Hiram Luther 4
SIBLEY, John 5
SIBLEY, John Langdon 1
SIBLEY, Jonas 5
SIBLEY, Joseph Crocker 1
SIBLEY, Josiah 5
SIBLEY, Mark Hopkins H
SIBLEY, Robert 3
SIBLEY, Rufus Adams 4
SIBLEY, Samuel Hale 3
SIBLEY, Solomon H
SIBLEY,
William Giddings
SICARD, Montgomery 1
SICK, Emil George 4
SICKEL, William George 1
SICKELS, David Banks 1
SICKELS, H
Frederick Ellsworth
SICKELS, Ivin 2
SICKELS, Nicholas H
SICKLES, Daniel Edgar 1
SIDAROUSS, Pasha 3
SIDBURY, James Buren 3
SIDDALL, Hugh Wagstaff 2
SIDDALL, 1
John MacAlpine
SIDDONS, 1
Frederick Lincoln
SIDELL, William Henry H
SIDERS, Walter Raleigh 3
SIDGREAVES,
Sir Arthur F.
SIDI MUHAMMED H
SIDIS, Boris 1
SIDLEY, William Pratt 3
SIDLO, Thomas L. 3
SIDNEY, Margaret 1
SIDO, George Henry 3
SIDWELL, Thomas
Watson 1
SIEBECKER, 1
Robert George
SIEBEL, John Ewald 1
SIEBENTHAL, 1
Claude Ellsworth
SIEBERT, Wilbur Henry 4
SIECK, Louis John 3
SIEDENBURG, Frederic 1
SIEDER, Otto F. 5
SIEFERT, 4
Henry Otto Rudolf
SIEFF, Israel Moses 5
SIEFKIN, C. Gordon 4
SIEFKIN,
Forest De Witt
SIEFKIN, George 4
SIEG, Lee Paul 4
SIEGEL, David Porter 3
SIEGEL, David Tevel 3
SIEGEL, Irwin 2
SIEGEL, Isaac 1
SIEGEL, Lester 4
SIEGEL, Roy Richard 4
SIEGRIST, Mary 3
SIELAFF, Gustav Julius 4
SIEMON, Daniel William 4
SIEMONN, George 3
SIEMS, Allan Gleason 2
SIENI, Cyril H
SIES, Raymond William 1
SIEVERS, Fred John 3
SIEVERS, 4
Frederick William
SIEVERT, Leo Ellsworth 4
SIFTON, Harry Austin 1
SIFTON, Victor 4
SIGALL, Joseph 'de 1
SIGEL, Franz * 1
SIGERFOOS, 2
Charles Peter
SIGERIST, Henry Ernest 3
SIGLER, Thomas Amon 5

SIGMUND, 4
Frederick Lester
SIGMUND, Jay G. 1
SIGNER, Merton I. 3
SIGOURNEY, H
Lydia Howard Huntley
SIGSBEE, 1
Charles Dwight
SIHLER,
Ernest Gottlieb
SIKES, Clarence S. 5
SIKES, Enoch Walter 4
SIKES, George Cushing 1
SIKES, William Wirt H
SIKORSKY, Igor I. 5
SILBERBERG, Mendel B. 4
SILBERMAN, Alfred M. 2
SILBERMAN, M. J. 4
SILBERSACK,
Walter Frank
SILBERSTEIN, Ludwik 2
SILCOX, 1
Fredinand Augustus
SILCOX, John B. 4
SILER, Vinton Earnest 5
SILKETT, Albert Frank 5
SILKNITTER, G. F. 3
SILL, Anna Peck H
SILL, Edward Rowland H
SILL, 3
Frederick Herbert
SILL, 1
John Mahelm Berry
SILL, Louise Morgan
SILL, Thomas Hale H
SILLANPAA, Frans Emil 4
SILLEN, Lars Gunnar 5
SILLIMAN, Augustus Ely H
SILLIMAN, Benjamin H
SILLIMAN, Benjamin Jr. H
SILLIMAN,
Charles Augustus
SILLIMAN, Harry Inness 5
SILLIMAN,
Reuben Daniel
SILLOWAY, 1
Thomas William
SILLS, 3
Kenneth Charles Morton
SILLS, Milton 1
SILSBEE,
Arthur Boardman
SILSBEE, Nathaniel H
SILSBY, Wilson 3
SILVA, William Posey 2
SILVER, Abba Hillel 4
SILVER, Ernest Leroy 3
SILVER, Gray 1
SILVER, H. Percy 1
SILVER, Jesse Forrest 5
SILVER, Maxwell 4
SILVER, Thomas H
SILVERA, Frank Alvin 5
SILVERMAN, Alexander 4
SILVERMAN, Archibald 4
SILVERMAN, David 3
SILVERMAN, Irving 5
SILVERMAN, Joseph 1
SILVERMAN, Leslie 5
SILVERMAN, Morris 4
SILVERMAN, Sime H
SILVERMAN, Sime H
SILVERS, Earl Reed 2
SILVESTER, 5
Lindsay McDonald
SILVESTER, Peter H
SILVESTER, Peter Henry H
SILVESTER,
Richard William
SILVEUS, 5
William Arents
SILZER, George S. 1
SIM, John Robert 1
SIMIC, Stanoje 5
SIMKHOVITCH,
Mary Melinda Kingsbury
SIMKHOVITCH,
Vladimir Gregorievitch
SIMKINS, Eldred H
SIMKINS, Henry Walter 1
SIMKINS, 1
William Stewart
SIMLER, George Brenner 5
SIMLEY, Irvin T. 5
SIMMILL, Elvin Raymond 4
SIMMONDS,
Albert Carleton Jr.
SIMMONDS, 5
Frank William
SIMMONS,
Daniel Augustus
SIMMONS, David
Andrew 3
SIMMONS, Dayton
Cooper 5
SIMMONS, Dwight Lane 5
SIMMONS, Edward 1

SIMMONS, Edward Alfred — 1
SIMMONS, Edward Campbell — 1
SIMMONS, Edward Henry Harriman — 3
SIMMONS, Elizabeth Margret — 2
SIMMONS, Ernest J. — 5
SIMMONS, Franklin — 1
SIMMONS, Furnifold McLendell
SIMMONS, Geo Finlay — 3
SIMMONS, George Abel — H
SIMMONS, George E(vans) — 5
SIMMONS, George H. — 1
SIMMONS, George Welch — 1
SIMMONS, Henry Clay — 1
SIMMONS, Henry Martyn — 1
SIMMONS, J. Edward — 1
SIMMONS, J. P. — 4
SIMMONS, James Fowler — 1
SIMMONS, James Henry — 5
SIMMONS, James Stevens — 1
SIMMONS, James William — 5
SIMMONS, John F. — 4
SIMMONS, Leo Charles — 3
SIMMONS, Lessie Southgate — 1
SIMMONS, Robert Cantrell
SIMMONS, Thomas J. — 3
SIMMONS, Thomas Jackson — 2
SIMMONS, Thomas Jefferson — H
SIMMONS, Virgil M. — 3
SIMMONS, Wallace Delafield — 4
SIMMONS, Warren Seabury — 2
SIMMONS, Will — 2
SIMMONS, William Marvin — 1
SIMMS, Albert Gallatin — 4
SIMMS, Jeptha Root — H
SIMMS, John Field — 3
SIMMS, Joseph — 1
SIMMS, Lewis Wesley — 3
SIMMS, Paris Marion — 2
SIMMS, Ruth Hanna — 2
SIMMS, S. Chapman — 1
SIMMS, William Elliot — H
SIMMS, William Gilmore — H
SIMMS, William Philip — 3
SIMON, Abram — 1
SIMON, Andre Louis — 1
SIMON, Charles Edmund — 1
SIMON, Clarence Turkle — 1
SIMON, Edward Paul — 2
SIMON, Franklin — 1
SIMON, Frederick M. — 4
SIMON, Grant Miles — 5
SIMON, Henry William — 1
SIMON, Joseph — 1
SIMON, Julian Edwin — 4
SIMON, Leon Charles — 3
SIMON, Louis A. — 3
SIMON, Naif Louis — 5
SIMON, Richard Leo — 4
SIMON, Sir Francis — 3
SIMON, William — 1
SIMON, Yves R. — 5
SIMOND, Louis — H
SIMOND, Maynard Ewing — 4
SIMONDS, Alvan Tracy — 1
SIMONDS, Frank H. — 1
SIMONDS, Frederic William
SIMONDS, George Sherwin — 1
SIMONDS, Gifford Kingsbury — 1
SIMONDS, Godfrey Baldwin — 3
SIMONDS, James Persons — 4
SIMONDS, Ossian Cole — 1
SIMONDS, William — H
SIMONDS, William Adams — 4
SIMONDS, William Edgar — 1
SIMONDS, William Edward — 2
SIMONE, G. F. Edgardo — 2
SIMONS, Algie Martin — 3
SIMONS, Amory Coffin — 5
SIMONS, Charles Casper — 4
SIMONS, George Albert — 3
SIMONS, Hans — 1
SIMONS, Howard Perry — 5
SIMONS, James — 1
SIMONS, Kenneth W. — 2
SIMONS, May Wood — 2
SIMONS, Minot — 1
SIMONS, Samuel — H
SIMONS, Sarah Emma — 4

SIMONS, Wilford Collins — 3
SIMONSON, Gustave — 4
SIMONSON, Henry James Jr.
SIMONSON, Lee — 4
SIMONSON, William A. — 1
SIMONTON, Charles H. — 1
SIMONTON, Ida Vera — 1
SIMONTON, James William
SIMONTON, John Wiggins — 1
SIMONTON, William — H
SIMPICH, Frederick — 2
SIMPKINS, George W. — 4
SIMPSON, Albert B. — 1
SIMPSON, Alex Jr. — 1
SIMPSON, Alfred Dexter — 3
SIMPSON, Charles Torrey — 1
SIMPSON, Clarence L(orenzo) — 5
SIMPSON, Cuthbert Aikman — 5
SIMPSON, David Ferguson — 1
SIMPSON, Edmund — H
SIMPSON, Edward — 1
SIMPSON, Edward
SIMPSON, Frances — 4
SIMPSON, Frank Edward — 2
SIMPSON, Frank Farrow — 4
SIMPSON, Frank Leslie — 1
SIMPSON, Friench — 1
SIMPSON, Hartley — 5
SIMPSON, Herbert Downs — 4
SIMPSON, Herman — 5
SIMPSON, Howard Edwin — 4
SIMPSON, James — 1
SIMPSON, James Jr. — 1
SIMPSON, James Clarke — 2
SIMPSON, James Hervey — H
SIMPSON, James Inglis — 1
SIMPSON, Jerry — 1
SIMPSON, John — 1
SIMPSON, John A. — 1
SIMPSON, John Childs — 4
SIMPSON, John Dixon — 4
SIMPSON, John Nathan — 5
SIMPSON, John R. — 5
SIMPSON, John R. — 3
SIMPSON, John Woodruff — 4
SIMPSON, Joseph Warren — 2
SIMPSON, Josephine Sarles — 4
SIMPSON, Kemper — 1
SIMPSON, Kenneth Farrand
SIMPSON, Kenneth Miller — 3
SIMPSON, Kirke Larue — 5
SIMPSON, Marcus De Lafayette — 1
SIMPSON, Matthew — H
SIMPSON, Michael Hodge — H
SIMPSON, Richard Franklin
SIMPSON, Richard Lee — 5
SIMPSON, Richard Murray — 3
SIMPSON, Richard Murray — 4
SIMPSON, Robert — 1
SIMPSON, Robert Edward — 5
SIMPSON, Robert Tennent — 1
SIMPSON, Samuel — 1
SIMPSON, Sid — 3
SIMPSON, Sidney Post — 2
SIMPSON, Sloan — 5
SIMPSON, Stephen — H
SIMPSON, Sumner — 1
SIMPSON, Sutherland — 1
SIMPSON, Thomas McNider Jr. — 4
SIMPSON, Virgil Earl — 4
SIMPSON, William Augustus
SIMPSON, William B. — 2
SIMPSON, William Dunlap — H
SIMPSON, William James — 1
SIMPSON, William Kelly — 2
SIMRALL, Josephine Price
SIMRELL, William Le Grand — 1
SIMS, Alexander Dromgoole — H
SIMS, Alva Ray — 4
SIMS, Cecil — 2
SIMS, Charles Abercrombie — 2
SIMS, Charles N. — H
SIMS, Charles N. — 1
SIMS, Clifford Stanley — 1

SIMS, Edwin W. — 2
SIMS, Frederick Wilmer — 1
SIMS, Harry Marion — 4
SIMS, Henry Upson — 4
SIMS, James Marion — H
SIMS, John Francis — 1
SIMS, Leonard Henly — H
SIMS, Marian McCamy — 4
SIMS, Newell LeRoy — 4
SIMS, Richard Maury — 1
SIMS, Thetus Wilrette — 1
SIMS, W. Scott — 1
SIMS, William Sowden — 1
SINCERBEAUX, Frank H. — 5
SINCLAIR, Alexander Doull — 4
SINCLAIR, Alexander Grant — 1
SINCLAIR, Angus — 1
SINCLAIR, Earle Westwood — 2
SINCLAIR, Harold Augustus — 4
SINCLAIR, Harry Ford — 3
SINCLAIR, James Herbert — 2
SINCLAIR, John Elbridge — 1
SINCLAIR, John Franklin — 3
SINCLAIR, John Stephens — 5
SINCLAIR, Lee Wiley — 1
SINCLAIR, Peter Thomas — 5
SINCLAIR, Robert Soutter — 1
SINCLAIR, W. R. — 1
SINCLAIR, William — 4
SINCLAIR, William Albert — 5
SINDEBAND, Maurice Leonard
SINEK, William J. — 4
SINGER, Berthold — 5
SINGER, Edgar Arthur Jr. — 3
SINGER, Frederic — 1
SINGER, Frederick George — 5
SINGER, Harold Douglas — 1
SINGER, Harold Ralph — 2
SINGER, Isaac Merrit — H
SINGER, Isidore — 1
SINGER, Israel Joshua — 2
SINGER, Otto — 1
SINGER, Willard Edison — 5
SINGER, William H. Jr. — 3
SINGERLY, William Miskey — H
SINGLETARY, B. Henry — 4
SINGLETON, Albert Olin — 2
SINGLETON, Asa Leon — 2
SINGLETON, Esther — 1
SINGLETON, James Washington — H
SINGLETON, Marvin Edward — 1
SINGLETON, Otho Robards — H
SINGLETON, Thomas Day — H
SINGLETON, William Daniel — 5
SINGLEY, B. Lloyd — 1
SINGMASTER, Elsie — 3
SINGMASTER, James Arthur — 4
SINGMASTER, John Alden — 1
SINK, Charles Albert — 5
SINK, Robert Frederick — 4
SINKLER, John P. B. — 3
SINKLER, Wharton — 1
SINNICKSON, Thomas * — H
SINNOTT, Alfred Arthur — 3
SINNOTT, Arthur J. — 2
SINNOTT, Edmund Ware — 5
SINNOTT, Nicholas John — 1
SINSEL, Rupert Alston — 5
SINZ, Walter Alexander — 4
SIODMAK, Robert — 5
SIOUSSAT, St George Leakin
SIPLE, Paul Allman — 5
SIPPEL, Bettie Manroe — 5
SIPPLE, Chester Ellsworth — 4
SIPPY, Bertram Welton — 1
SIPPY, John Johnson — 3
SIQUELAND, Tryggve Albert — 1
SIRES, Ronald Vernon — 4
SIROIS, Edward D. — 5
SIROKY, Villem — 5
SIROVICH, William I. — 1
SIRRINE, Joseph Emory — 5

SISAVANG VONG — 3
SISCO, Frank Thayer — 4
SISCO, Gordon A. — 3
SISCOE, Frank Gotch — 5
SISE, Lincoln Fleetford — 2
SISE, Paul F. — 3
SISLEY, Lyman A.
SISSON, Charles Newton — 2
SISSON, Charles Peck — 2
SISSON, Edgar Grant — 2
SISSON, Edward Octavius
SISSON, Francis Hinckley — 1
SISSON, Fred James — 2
SISSON, Jean — 5
SISSON, Septimus — 1
SISSON, Thomas Upton — 1
SISTO, Louis Stanley — 5
SITES, Frank Crawford — 4
SITGREAVES, Charles — H
SITGREAVES, John — H
SITGREAVES, Samuel — H
SITJAR, Buenaventura — H
SITTERLY, Charles Fremont — 2
SITTING BULL — H
SITWELL, Dame Edith — 4
SITWELL, Sir) Osbert — 5
SIVITER, Anna Pierpont — 1
SIVITER, William Henry — 1
SIVRIGHT, Cal — 2
SIZER, Lawrence Bradford — 5
SIZER, Nelson — H
SIZER, Theodore — 4
SIZOO, Joseph Richard — 4
SJOLANDER, John Peter — 4
SKAGGS, William Henry — 2
SKANIADARIIO — H
SKAPSKI, Adam Stanislas — 5
SKARIATINA, Irina — 4
SKARSTEDT, Ernst Teofil — 2
SKEEL, Adelaide — 5
SKEEL, Franklin Deuel — 1
SKEEL, Roland Edward — 1
SKEELE, Walter Fisher — 1
SKEELS, Wines Harris — 5
SKEEN, John A. — 3
SKELLEY, William Charles — 3
SKELLEY, William Grove — 1
SKELTON, Charles — H
SKELTON, Henrietta — 1
SKELTON, Leslie James — 1
SKELTON, William B. — 4
SKENANDOA — H
SKENE, Alexander Johnston Chalmers — 1
SKERPAN, Alfred Andrew — 5
SKEVINGTON, Samuel John — 2
SKEWES, James Henry — 3
SKIDMORE, Charles H. — 5
SKIDMORE, Hubert Standish — 2
SKIDMORE, Lemuel — 4
SKIDMORE, Louis — 4
SKIDMORE, Louis — 1
SKIFF, Frederick James Volney
SKIFTER, Hector Randolph — 4
SKILES, Jonah William Durward — 4
SKILES, William Vernon — 2
SKILES, William Woodburn — 1
SKILLERN, Ross Hall — 1
SKILLIN, John — H
SKILLIN, Simeon — H
SKILLIN, Simeon Jr. — H
SKILLING, David Miller — 5
SKILLING, William Thompson — 5
SKILLMAN, Thomas Julien — 1
SKILTON, Charles Sanford
SKILTON, DeWitt Clinton — 1
SKILTON, John Davis — 3
SKINNER, Aaron Nichols — 1
SKINNER, Alburn Edward — 1
SKINNER, Avery Warner — 1
SKINNER, Belle — 1
SKINNER, Beverly Oden — 5
SKINNER, Charles Drake — 3
SKINNER, Charles Edward *

SKINNER, Charles Montgomery — 1
SKINNER, Charles Rufus — 1
SKINNER, Charles Wilbur — 2
SKINNER, Clarence Aurelius — 5
SKINNER, Clarence Edward — 4
SKINNER, Clarence Russell — 2
SKINNER, Constance Lindsay
SKINNER, David A. — 5
SKINNER, Edward Holman — 3
SKINNER, Eleanor Louise — 3
SKINNER, Ernest Brown — 1
SKINNER, Ernest M. — 5
SKINNER, Eugene William — 4
SKINNER, Frank Woodward — 4
SKINNER, Halcyon — H
SKINNER, Harold Stanfield — 4
SKINNER, Harry — 4
SKINNER, Henrietta Channing Dana — 1
SKINNER, Henry — 1
SKINNER, Howard K. — 5
SKINNER, Hubert Marshall — 1
SKINNER, James M. — 5
SKINNER, James W. — 3
SKINNER, John Harrison — 4
SKINNER, John Stuart — 2
SKINNER, Joseph Allen — H
SKINNER, Laurence Hervey — 2
SKINNER, Lewis Bailey — 5
SKINNER, Otis — 1
SKINNER, Paul Butler — 5
SKINNER, Richard — H
SKINNER, Robert P. — 4
SKINNER, Stella — 1
SKINNER, Thomas Clagett — 1
SKINNER, Thomas Harvey — H
SKINNER, Thomson Joseph — H
SKINNER, William — H
SKINNER, William — 2
SKINNER, William Converse — 4
SKINNER, William Woolford — 5
SKIPPER, Glenn Blount — 1
SKOG, Charles Arthur — 4
SKOGMO, Philip Waldo — 3
SKOOG, Andrew Leonard — 5
SKOOG, Karl Frederick — 1
SKOTTSBERG, Carl Johan F. — 4
SKOURAS, George P. — 4
SKOURAS, Spyros P. — 5
SKULNIK, Menasha — 5
SLABAUGH, Harold Watson — 5
SLACK, Charles Morse — 5
SLACK, Charles William — 2
SLACK, L(emuel) Ert(us) — 5
SLACK, Leighton P. — 1
SLACK, Munsey — 1
SLADE, Albert Arthur — 5
SLADE, Arthur Joseph — 5
SLADE, Caleb Arnold — 5
SLADE, Caroline McCormick — 3
SLADE, Charles — H
SLADE, Charles Blount — 2
SLADE, Emma Maleen Hardy — 4
SLADE, George Theron — 1
SLADE, John C. — 4
SLADE, Joseph Alfred — H
SLADE, William — H
SLADE, William Adams — 3
SLADEN, Fred Winchester — 2
SLAFTER, Edmund Farwell — 1
SLAGHT, William Ernest Andrew
SLAGLE, Dean — 4
SLAGLE, Robert Lincoln — 1
SLARROW, Malcolm G. — 3
SLATE, Frederick — 1
SLATEN, Arthur Wakefield — 2
SLATER, A. James — 4
SLATER, Denniston Lyon — 5
SLATER, Fred C. — 4
SLATER, Harry George — 5

* Indicates More Than One Such Name Listed

SMITH, Ethan Henry 1
SMITH, Ethan Henry 2
SMITH, Ethelbert Walton 3
SMITH, Eugene 1
SMITH, Eugene Allen 1
SMITH, Eugene Hanes 1
SMITH, Everett 4
SMITH, Everett William 4
SMITH, Ezekiel Ezra 3
SMITH, F. Berkeley 4
SMITH, F. Hopkinson 1
SMITH, F. Janney 5
SMITH, Ferdinand Conrad 3
SMITH, Ferris 3
SMITH, Fitz-Henry, Jr. 5
SMITH, Forrest 4
SMITH, Frances Stanton 5
SMITH, Francis Alward 4
SMITH, Francis Asbury 1
SMITH, Francis Edwin 5
SMITH, Francis Henney H
SMITH, Francis Henry 1
SMITH, Francis Marion 1
SMITH, Francis Ormand Jonathan 3
SMITH, Frank 1
SMITH, Frank Austin 2
SMITH, Frank Bulkeley 1
SMITH, Frank C. 5
SMITH, Frank Channing Jr. 3
SMITH, Frank Grigsby 3
SMITH, Frank Leslie 3
SMITH, Frank Marshall 1
SMITH, Frank O. 1
SMITH, Frank Sullivan 1
SMITH, Frank Webster 2
SMITH, Frank Whitney 2
SMITH, Franklin G. 1
SMITH, Franklin Guest 1
SMITH, Franklin Orion 1
SMITH, Fred Andrew 5
SMITH, Fred B. 1
SMITH, Fred Emory 4
SMITH, Fred M. 2
SMITH, Frederick Appleton 1
SMITH, Frederick Arthur 5
SMITH, Frederick Augustus 1
SMITH, Frederick C. 3
SMITH, Frederick H. 1
SMITH, Frederick Madison 2
SMITH, Frederick Miller 5
SMITH, G. Wallace 3
SMITH, G. Williamson 1
SMITH, George H
SMITH, George Albert 1
SMITH, George Albert 3
SMITH, George Albert, Jr. 5
SMITH, George Carson 1
SMITH, George D. 4
SMITH, George Edson Philip 5
SMITH, George Gilbert 4
SMITH, George Harris 2
SMITH, George Hathorn 4
SMITH, George Henry 1
SMITH, George Hunter 4
SMITH, George Jay 4
SMITH, George Joseph 4
SMITH, George L. 3
SMITH, George Luke H
SMITH, George M. 1
SMITH, George M. 4
SMITH, George Milton 3
SMITH, George Otis 2
SMITH, George P. F. 4
SMITH, George Rodney 4
SMITH, George Ross 4
SMITH, George Theodore 1
SMITH, George W. 1
SMITH, George Walter Vincent 1
SMITH, George Weissinger 1
SMITH, Gerald Birney 1
SMITH, Gerald Hewitt 3
SMITH, Gerrit H
SMITH, Gerrit 1
SMITH, Gertrude 1
SMITH, Gilbert Morgan 3
SMITH, Giles Alexander H
SMITH, Goldwin 1
SMITH, Gordon Arthur 2
SMITH, Grafton Adrian 5
SMITH, Green Clay 1
SMITH, Gregory L. 1
SMITH, Griffin H
SMITH, Gustavus Woodson H

SMITH, Guy Lincoln 5
SMITH, H. A. A. 1
SMITH, H. Alexander 4
SMITH, H. Augustine 3
SMITH, H. Lester 1
SMITH, H. M. Jr. 1
SMITH, Hal Horace 2
SMITH, Hal Horace, Jr. 5
SMITH, Hamilton H
SMITH, Hamilton Lamphere 1
SMITH, Hariette Knight 4
SMITH, Harlan Ingersoll 1
SMITH, Harmon 1
SMITH, Harold Babbitt 2
SMITH, Harold Dewey 1
SMITH, Harold Leonard 5
SMITH, Harold Stephen 1
SMITH, Harold Travis 3
SMITH, Harold Vincent 4
SMITH, Harold Wellington 3
SMITH, Harriet Lummis 2
SMITH, Harrison 5
SMITH, Harry Alexander * 1
SMITH, Harry Bache 5
SMITH, Harry de Forest 5
SMITH, Harry Eaton 1
SMITH, Harry James 1
SMITH, Harry Pearse 3
SMITH, Harry Worcester 3
SMITH, Haviland 5
SMITH, Hay Watson 5
SMITH, Helen Evertson 4
SMITH, Henry A. M. 1
SMITH, Henry Boynton H
SMITH, Henry Bradford 1
SMITH, Henry Cassorte 1
SMITH, Henry Cooper 4
SMITH, Henry Erskine 3
SMITH, Henry Gerrish 3
SMITH, Henry Justin 5
SMITH, Henry Leavitt 1
SMITH, Henry Lee, Jr. 5
SMITH, Henry Lester 1
SMITH, Henry Louis 3
SMITH, Henry Michelet 3
SMITH, Henry Monmouth 3
SMITH, Henry Preserved 1
SMITH, Henry Tomlinson 1
SMITH, Herbert Atwood 3
SMITH, Herbert Augustine 2
SMITH, Herbert Booth 4
SMITH, Herbert Edward 5
SMITH, Herbert Eugene 1
SMITH, Herbert Huntington 1
SMITH, Herbert Knox 1
SMITH, Herbert Wilson 5
SMITH, Herman Lyle 3
SMITH, Hezekiah H
SMITH, Hezekiah Bradley 1
SMITH, Hiram 1
SMITH, Hiram Moore 2
SMITH, Hiram Ypsilanti H
SMITH, Hoke 1
SMITH, Holland McTyeire 4
SMITH, Holmes 1
SMITH, Homer 1
SMITH, Homer William 4
SMITH, Horace H
SMITH, Horace Boardman H
SMITH, Horace Herbert 4
SMITH, Horatio Elwin 2
SMITH, Howard Anthony 4
SMITH, Howard Caswell 4
SMITH, Howard Dwight 1
SMITH, Howard Leslie 4
SMITH, Howard Remus 5
SMITH, Howard Wayne 5
SMITH, Hubert Winston 5
SMITH, Hugh Allison 5
SMITH, Hugh Carnes 2
SMITH, Hugh F. Jr. 1
SMITH, Hugh McCormick 1
SMITH, Huntington 4
SMITH, Hurlbut William 3
SMITH, Huron H. 1
SMITH, Ida B. Wise 5
SMITH, Ignatius 3
SMITH, Irving Gardner 4
SMITH, Isaac * H
SMITH, Isaac B. 1
SMITH, Isaac Townsend 4
SMITH, Isabel E. 1
SMITH, Isaiah Perley 4
SMITH, Israel 1
SMITH, Israel A. 3
SMITH, J. Allen 1
SMITH, J. Burritt 1
SMITH, J. Frank 1
SMITH, J. M. Powis 1

SMITH, J. Paul 3
SMITH, J. Ritchie 1
SMITH, J. Waldo 5
SMITH, J. Warren 1
SMITH, J. Emil 5
SMITH, J. Neil 5
SMITH, Jacob Getlar 3
SMITH, Jacob Hurd 1
SMITH, James * H
SMITH, James Jr. 1
SMITH, James Allwood 1
SMITH, James Argyle 1
SMITH, James D. 3
SMITH, James Dickinson 1
SMITH, James Ellwood 1
SMITH, James Francis 1
SMITH, James Gerald 2
SMITH, James Henry Oliver 1
SMITH, James Irwin 4
SMITH, James Kellum 4
SMITH, James McCune H
SMITH, James McLain 1
SMITH, James Perrin 1
SMITH, James Porter 1
SMITH, James Power 1
SMITH, James Sheppard 1
SMITH, James Strudwick 1
SMITH, James W. 3
SMITH, James Walter 2
SMITH, James Willison 1
SMITH, James Youngs H
SMITH, Jane Luella Dowd 4
SMITH, Jane Norman 1
SMITH, Jeanie Oliver Davidson 1
SMITH, Jedediah Kilburn H
SMITH, Jedediah Strong H
SMITH, Jeremiah H
SMITH, Jeremiah 1
SMITH, Jeremiah Jr. 1
SMITH, Jesse Merrick 1
SMITH, Jessie Willcox 1
SMITH, Jim Clifford 2
SMITH, Job Lewis H
SMITH, Joe Frazer 3
SMITH, Joe L. 4
SMITH, Joel West 1
SMITH, John * 1
SMITH, John Addison Baxter 1
SMITH, John Ambler H
SMITH, John Armstrong H
SMITH, John Augustine 4
SMITH, John Bernhardt 1
SMITH, John Blair H
SMITH, John Butler 1
SMITH, John Charles 4
SMITH, John Corson 1
SMITH, John Cotton * H
SMITH, John Day 1
SMITH, John Elijah 5
SMITH, John Eugene H
SMITH, John Frederick 3
SMITH, John Gregory H
SMITH, John Hammond 4
SMITH, John Henry Jr. 3
SMITH, John Hyatt H
SMITH, John Jay H
SMITH, John Joseph 5
SMITH, John Lawrence H
SMITH, John Lawrence 1
SMITH, John Lewis 3
SMITH, John M. C. 1
SMITH, John P. 2
SMITH, John Rowson H
SMITH, John Rubens 1
SMITH, John Sloan 5
SMITH, John Speed H
SMITH, John T. H
SMITH, John Talbot 1
SMITH, John Thomas 2
SMITH, John Walter 5
SMITH, John Walter 1
SMITH, John Wesley -1
SMITH, Jonathan Bayard 1
SMITH, Joseph * H
SMITH, Joseph * 1
SMITH, Joseph Adams 1
SMITH, Joseph Brodie 2
SMITH, Joseph Earl 1
SMITH, Joseph Fielding 5
SMITH, Joseph Fielding 1
SMITH, Joseph Fielding 4
SMITH, Joseph Francis 2
SMITH, Joseph Lindon 1
SMITH, Joseph Mather H
SMITH, Joseph Newton 1
SMITH, Joseph P. 4
SMITH, Joseph Rowe 1
SMITH, Joseph Showalter H
SMITH, Joseph Thomas 1
SMITH, Josephine Wernicke 3

SMITH, Josiah H
SMITH, Josiah Renick 1
SMITH, Judson H
SMITH, Julia Evelina H
SMITH, Julia Holmes 1
SMITH, Julius Clarence 5
SMITH, June C. 2
SMITH, Junius H
SMITH, Justin Harvey 1
SMITH, K. Wesley 4
SMITH, Kenneth Gladstone 2
SMITH, Kirby Flower 1
SMITH, Langdon 1
SMITH, Laura Rountree 1
SMITH, Lawrence 4
SMITH, Lawrence Henry 3
SMITH, Lee Thompson 4
SMITH, Lemuel Augustus Sr. 3
SMITH, Lemuel F. 3
SMITH, Leo R. 4
SMITH, Leon E. 4
SMITH, Leon Perdue 4
SMITH, Leon Perdue 4
SMITH, Leonidas D'Entrecasteaux 1
SMITH, Levi Pease 5
SMITH, Lewis Elden 4
SMITH, Lewis Martin 3
SMITH, Lewis Wilbur 3
SMITH, Lewis Worthington 2
SMITH, Lillian 4
SMITH, Livingston Waddell 3
SMITH, Lloyd DeWitt 1
SMITH, Lloyd Gaston 3
SMITH, Lloyd Pearsall H
SMITH, Lloyd Raymond 2
SMITH, Lloyd Waddell 5
SMITH, Lloyd Weir 3
SMITH, Logan Pearsall 2
SMITH, Lothrop 3
SMITH, Louie Henrie 5
SMITH, Lowell H. 4
SMITH, Lura Eugenie Brown 1
SMITH, Luther Ely 3
SMITH, Luther Wesley 5
SMITH, Lybrand Palmer 2
SMITH, Lyman Cornelius 1
SMITH, Lyndon Ambrose 1
SMITH, Lynwood H. 3
SMITH, M. Ellwood 2
SMITH, Mabell Shippie Clarke 1
SMITH, Madison Roswell 4
SMITH, Marcus H
SMITH, Marcus Aurelius 1
SMITH, Margaret Bayard H
SMITH, Margaret Vowell 1
SMITH, Marion 2
SMITH, Marion Couthouy 1
SMITH, Marion Gertrude 3
SMITH, Marjorie C. 5
SMITH, Mark H
SMITH, Mark A. 1
SMITH, Martha Rose Kapantaes (Mrs. Robert Clifford Smith) 5
SMITH, Martin F. 3
SMITH, Martin Luther H
SMITH, Marvin Boren 3
SMITH, Mary Elizabeth 1
SMITH, Mary Prudence Wells 1
SMITH, Mason 4
SMITH, Matthew 3
SMITH, Matthew F. 1
SMITH, Matthew Hale H
SMITH, Matthew John Wilfred 4
SMITH, (Thomas) Max 5
SMITH, May Riley 1
SMITH, McGregor 5
SMITH, Melancton H
SMITH, Meriwether H
SMITH, Merle Negley 5
SMITH, Merriman 1
SMITH, Milton H. 1
SMITH, Milton Truman 3
SMITH, Minna Caroline 1
SMITH, Morgan Lewis 1
SMITH, Moses 4
SMITH, Munroe 1
SMITH, Murray 3
SMITH, Myrtle Holm 3
SMITH, Nathan * 1
SMITH, Nathan Ryno H

SMITH, Nathaniel H
SMITH, Nathaniel Waite 5
SMITH, Newman 4
SMITH, Nicholas 1
SMITH, Nicol Hamilton 5
SMITH, Nora Archibald 1
SMITH, Norman Kemp 5
SMITH, Norman Murray 5
SMITH, O. Warren 1
SMITH, Oberlin H
SMITH, O'Brien H
SMITH, Oliver H
SMITH, Oliver Hampton H
SMITH, Oramandal 3
SMITH, Orlando Jay 1
SMITH, Orma Jacob 2
SMITH, Ormond Gerald 1
SMITH, Orson 1
SMITH, Otis David 1
SMITH, Otterbein Oscar 1
SMITH, Owen Lun West 4
SMITH, Paul Edward 5
SMITH, Paul Francis 4
SMITH, Paul Jordan 5
SMITH, Paul Kenneth 4
SMITH, Payson 1
SMITH, Percey Franklyn 3
SMITH, Percy William 4
SMITH, Perry 1
SMITH, Perry Dunlap 4
SMITH, Persifor Frazer 1
SMITH, Peter H
SMITH, Peter P. 3
SMITH, Philip E. 5
SMITH, Philip Sidney 3
SMITH, Phillips Waller 1
SMITH, Preserved 2
SMITH, Quintius Cincinnatus 1
SMITH, R. Waverley 1
SMITH, R(obert) Blackwell, Jr. 5
SMITH, Ralph Chester 4
SMITH, Ralph Eliot 5
SMITH, Ralph M. 5
SMITH, Ralph Tyler 5
SMITH, Ralph Winfield 5
SMITH, Randle Jasper 4
SMITH, Ray L. 3
SMITH, Raymond Abner 5
SMITH, Raymond Underwood 3
SMITH, Reed 2
SMITH, Reginald Heber 5
SMITH, Reuben Robert 5
SMITH, Rex 1
SMITH, Richard H
SMITH, Richard Hewlett 2
SMITH, Richard Paul 4
SMITH, Richard Penn H
SMITH, Richard R. 1
SMITH, Richard Root 1
SMITH, Richard Somers H
SMITH, Robert * 1
SMITH, Robert A. C. 1
SMITH, Robert Armstrong 4
SMITH, Robert Aura 3
SMITH, Robert Brandon 2
SMITH, Robert Burns 1
SMITH, Robert Chester 1
SMITH, Robert Edwin 3
SMITH, Robert Fitch 1
SMITH, Robert H. 4
SMITH, Robert Hardy 5
SMITH, Robert Hays 5
SMITH, Robert Keating 1
SMITH, Robert Lee 1
SMITH, Robert Metcalf 3
SMITH, Robert P. 1
SMITH, Robert Paterson 1
SMITH, Robert Seneca 4
SMITH, Robert Shufeldt 4
SMITH, Robert Sidney 5
SMITH, Robert Sidney 1
SMITH, Robert Sidney 3
SMITH, Robinson 5
SMITH, Rodney 1
SMITH, Roland Cotton 1
SMITH, Roland Kidder 1
SMITH, Roswell 1
SMITH, Roy Campbell 1
SMITH, Roy Harmon 1
SMITH, Roy Leon 1
SMITH, Ruel Perley 1
SMITH, Rufus D. 3
SMITH, Russell H
SMITH, Ruth Ann Cook 3
SMITH, S. Archibald 3
SMITH, S. Calvin 1
SMITH, S. Jennie 1
SMITH, S. Stephenson 4
SMITH, S(amuel) L(eonard) 5
SMITH, Sadie Adams 4
SMITH, Samray 5
SMITH, Samuel * H

* Indicates More Than One Such Name Listed

SMITH, Samuel 4
SMITH, Samuel A. H
SMITH, Samuel Axley H
SMITH, Samuel Edwin 1
SMITH, Samuel Francis H
SMITH, Samuel George 1
SMITH, Samuel Harrison H
SMITH, Samuel Stanhope 1
SMITH, Samuel William 1
SMITH, Seba 3
SMITH, H
   Soloman Franklin
SMITH, Solomon Albert 4
SMITH, Sophia H
SMITH, Stephen 1
SMITH, Stevenson 3
SMITH, 1
   Stuart Robertson
SMITH, Susan T. 1
SMITH, Sydney 2
SMITH, Sylvester Clark 1
SMITH, T. Guilford 1
SMITH, T. V. 4
SMITH, Theobald 1
SMITH, Theodore Clarke 4
SMITH, Thomas * H
SMITH, Thomas * 4
SMITH, Thomas Adams H
SMITH, Thomas Arthur 4
SMITH, Thomas Berry 1
SMITH, Thomas F. 1
SMITH, Thomas Franklin 1
SMITH, 5
   Thomas Jefferson
SMITH, Thomas Kilby H
SMITH, Thomas Newill H
SMITH, Thomas Octavius 1
SMITH, Thomas R. 2
SMITH, Thomas William 5
SMITH, 3
   Thurber Montgomery
SMITH, Truman H
SMITH, Ulysses Simpson 2
SMITH, Uriah 1
SMITH, Vincent E. 5
SMITH, Vincent Weaver 4
SMITH, Vine Harold 5
SMITH, Vivian Thomas 3
SMITH, W. A. 3
SMITH, W. H. B. 4
SMITH, Wade Cothran 4
SMITH, Walt Allen 5
SMITH, Walter Bedell 4
SMITH, Walter Byron 2
SMITH, Walter Driscoll 3
SMITH, Walter George 1
SMITH, 1
   Walter Inglewood
SMITH, Walter Lloyd 1
SMITH, Walter McMynn 1
SMITH, Walter Robinson 1
SMITH, Walter Tenney 1
SMITH, Walter Tenney 2
SMITH, Walter Winfred 2
SMITH, Warren Du Pre 1
SMITH, 5
   Warren Lounsbury
SMITH, Warren Robert 3
SMITH, Wayne Carleton 4
SMITH, Wendell 4
SMITH, Wilbert L. 1
SMITH, 3
   Wilbur Cleveland
SMITH, Wilbur Fisk 1
SMITH, 1
   Willard Adelbert
SMITH, William * H
SMITH, William 1
SMITH, William Alden 1
SMITH, H
   William Alexander
SMITH, 1
   William Alexander
SMITH, William Andrew H
SMITH, William Austin 1
SMITH, H
   William Benjamin
SMITH, William Clarke 1
SMITH, William Clarke 2
SMITH, 2
   William Cunningham
SMITH, William Eason 2
SMITH, William Edward 1
SMITH, William Ephraim H
SMITH, William Farrar 1
SMITH, William Francis 4

SMITH, 2
   William Griswold
SMITH, William Hall 4
SMITH, 4
   William Harrison
SMITH, William Hawley 1
SMITH, William Henry * H
SMITH, William Henry 1
SMITH, William Henry 1
SMITH, William Hinckle 2
SMITH, William Hopton 1
SMITH, H
   William Loughton
SMITH, William Mason 1
SMITH, H
   William Nathan Harrell
SMITH, William Oliver 1
SMITH, William Orlando 4
SMITH, William Owen 1
SMITH, William Owen 2
SMITH, William Robert 1
SMITH, William Roy 5
SMITH, William Russell H
SMITH, William Ruthven 1
SMITH, 3
   William Skeldon Adamson
SMITH, William Sooy 1
SMITH, H
   William Stephens
SMITH, 5
   William Stevenson
SMITH, 1
   William Strother
SMITH, William Thayer 1
SMITH, William Thomas 2
SMITH, William W. Ii 1
SMITH, William Walker 2
SMITH, William Walter 2
SMITH, William Ward 4
SMITH, William Waugh 1
SMITH, 2
   William Wilberforce
SMITH, Willis 3
SMITH, Willis, Jr. 5
SMITH, Wilmot M. 1
SMITH, Wilson George 1
SMITH, Winchell 1
SMITH, Winford Henry 4
SMITH, Winthrop Hiram 1
SMITH, Worthington H
SMITH, H
   Worthington Curtis
SMITH, Young Berryman 4
SMITH, 1
   Zachariah Frederick
SMITH, Zemro Augustus 1
SMITH, Zilpha Drew 1
SMITHEE, James Newton 1
SMITHER, 1
   Henry Carpenter
SMITHERS, H
   Ernest Leonard
SMITHERS, 1
   Nathaniel Barrett
SMITHERS, William West 2
SMITHEY, 1
   Louis Philippe
SMITHEY, Royall Bascom 1
SMITHEY, 5
   William Royall
SMITHIES, Frank 1
SMITH-PETERSEN, Marius 3
   Nygaard
SMITHSON, James H
SMITHSON, Noble 1
SMITHSON, 1
   William Walpole
SMITHWICK, John Harris 1
SMOCK, John Conover 1
SMOCK, P(eter) Monroe 5
SMOCK, Wendell Merritt 1
SMOHALLA H
SMOHALLA 4
SMOLEY, 3
   Constantine Kenneth
SMOOT, Charles Head 1
SMOOT, Reed 1
SMOOT, Thomas Arthur 1
SMULL, Jacob Barstow 4
SMULL, 4
   Thomas Jefferson Jr.
SMULSKI, John F. 1
SMUTS, Jan Christiaan 3
SMYKAL, Richard 3
SMYSER, Martin L. 1
SMYSER, William Emory 1
SMYTH, Albert Henry 1
SMYTH, Alexander H
SMYTH, 4
   Calvin Mason Jr.
SMYTH, 1
   Charles Henry Jr.
SMYTH, Clifford 4
SMYTH, 1
   Constantine Joseph

SMYTH, Egbert Coffin 1
SMYTH, Ellison Adger 1
SMYTH, Ellison Adger 2
SMYTH, Francis Scott 5
SMYTH, H
   George Washington
SMYTH, Henry Field 3
SMYTH, Henry Lloyd 2
SMYTH, 2
   Herbert Crommelin
SMYTH, Herbert Weir 1
SMYTH, James Adger 1
SMYTH, Julian Kennedy 1
SMYTH, 5
   Margarita Pumpelly
SMYTH, Newman 1
SMYTH, S. Gordon 3
SMYTH, Thomas 1
SMYTH, Timothy Clement H
SMYTH, William * H
SMYTH, William Henry 1
SMYTH, Wilma Louise 5
SMYTH, Winfield Scott 1
SMYTHE, 1
   Augustine Thomas
SMYTHE, 1
   George Franklin
SMYTHE, George Winfred 5
SMYTHE, J. Henry Jr. 1
SMYTHE, Sidney Thomas 3
SMYTHE, William E. 1
SNAPE, John 2
SNAPP, Henry H
SNAPP, Howard Malcolm 1
SNARE, Frederick 3
SNARR, Frederic Earle 4
SNARR, Otto Welton 4
SNAVELY, John Robert 4
SNEAD, Thomas Lowndes 1
SNEATH, E. Hershey 1
SNEATH, H
   Mrs. Samuel B. (laura S. Sneath)
SNEDDEN, David 5
SNEDECOR, James 1
   George
SNEDEKER, 3
   Caroline Dale
SNEDEKER, 1
   Charles Dippolt
SNEED, Albert Lee 4
SNEED, Frank Woolford 1
SNEED, 1
   John Louis Taylor
SNEED, William Henry H
SNEED, William Lent 2
SNELHAM, John Sydney 4
SNELL, Albert M. 3
SNELL, Bertrand H. 1
SNELL, Earl Wilcox 2
SNELL, George H
SNELL, Henry Bayley 2
SNELL, John Leslie 5
SNELLING, 1
   Charles Mercer
SNELLING, Henry Hunt H
SNELLING, Josiah H
SNELLING, Rodman Paul 1
SNELLING, 4
   Walter Otheman
SNELLING, H
   William Joseph
SNETHEN, Nicholas H
SNEVE, Haldor 1
SNEVILY, 3
   Henry Mansfield
SNIDER, Clyde Frank 5
SNIDER, Denton Jaques 1
SNIDER, Joseph Lyons 3
SNIDER, Luther Crocker 4
SNIDER, Samuel Prather 4
SNIFF, Littleton M. 1
SNIFFEN, 1
   Culver Channing
SNIVELY, Samuel Frisby 4
SNIVELY, 1
   William Andrew
SNOBERGER, Rantz 4
SNODDY, 1
   Elmer Ellsworth
SNODDY, Leland Bradley 3
SNODGRASS, 4
   Charles Edward
SNODGRASS, David E. 1
SNODGRASS, 1
   David La Fayette
SNODGRASS, 1
   George Merrill
SNODGRASS, John Fryall H
SNODGRASS, John 2
   Harold
SNODGRASS, Robert 1
SNODGRASS, 5
   Robert Evans
SNODGRASS, 5
   Robert Richard
SNOOK, Homer Clyde 2

SNOOK, John S. 5
SNOOK, John Wilson 5
SNOW, Albert Sydney 1
SNOW, Alpheus Henry 1
SNOW, Alva Edson 4
SNOW, Benjamin Warner 1
SNOW, Carmel 4
SNOW, Chalres Ernest 4
SNOW, 1
   Charles Armstrong
SNOW, Charles Henry 1
SNOW, Chauncey Depew 4
SNOW, Donald Francis 1
SNOW, Edgar Parks 5
SNOW, Elbert Clay 4
SNOW, Elbridge Gerry 1
SNOW, Eliza Roxey H
SNOW, Ernest Albert 1
SNOW, Francis 5
SNOW, 1
   Francis Huntington
SNOW, 2
   Franklin Augustus
SNOW, Frederic 1
SNOW, Henry Sanger 4
SNOW, J. Parker 3
SNOW, John Ben 5
SNOW, Leslie Perkins 1
SNOW, Leslie W. 3
SNOW, Lorenzo H
SNOW, Louis Franklin 1
SNOW, Marshall Solomon 1
SNOW, Sydney Bruce 2
SNOW, Walter Bradlee 4
SNOW, Warren Howland 1
SNOW, William Dunham 1
SNOW, William Freeman 1
SNOW, William Josiah 2
SNOW, William W. H
SNOWDEN, A. Loudon 1
SNOWDEN, James Henry 1
SNOWDEN, James Ross H
SNOWDEN, 5
   R(obert) Brinkley
SNOWDEN, 1
   Robert Bogardus
SNOWDEN, Thomas 1
SNOWDEN, Yates 1
SNURE, John 1
SNYDER, A. Cecil 3
SNYDER, Adam Wilson 1
SNYDER, Alban Goshorn 5
SNYDER, 1
   Albert Whitcomb
SNYDER, Arthur 4
SNYDER, Baird III 1
SNYDER, Carl 1
SNYDER, Carl J. 3
SNYDER, Charles B. J. 1
SNYDER, Charles Edward 3
SNYDER, Charles McCoy 1
SNYDER, Charles Philip 1
SNYDER, 1
   Edgar Callender
SNYDER, Edward 1
SNYDER, Eldredge 4
SNYDER, Franklyn Bliss 3
SNYDER, Fred Beal 3
SNYDER, 5
   Frederic Sylvester
SNYDER, Harry 1
SNYDER, Henry 1
SNYDER, Henry George 3
SNYDER, Henry Nelson 1
SNYDER, Henry Steinman 1
SNYDER, Homer P. 1
SNYDER, Howard McC. 3
SNYDER, J. Ralph 1
SNYDER, Jefferson H
SNYDER, John H
SNYDER, John Buell 2
SNYDER, John I. Jr. 4
SNYDER, John Otterbein 1
SNYDER, John Taylor 3
SNYDER, 1
   Jonathan Le Moyne
SNYDER, Leroy Edwin 2
SNYDER, 1
   Meredith Pinxton
SNYDER, Monroe B. 1
SNYDER, Murray 5
SNYDER, Nicholas R. 4
SNYDER, Oliver P. H
SNYDER, Oscar John 1
SNYDER, Reginald Clare 1
SNYDER, Robert McClure 1
SNYDER, Simon H
SNYDER, Simon 1
SNYDER, Valentine P. 1
SNYDER, Virgil 1
SNYDER, William Edward 3
SNYDER, 1
   William Lamartine
SNYDER, William P. Jr. 4
SNYDER, 1
   Zachariah Xenophon

SOARES, 5
   Theodore Gerald
SOBEL, Bernard 4
SOBIESKI, John 4
SOBILOFF, Hyman 5
   Jordan
SOBOL, Louis 2
SOBOLEV, Arkady A. 4
SOBOLEWSKI, H
   J. Friedrich Edvard
SOCKMAN, 3
   Ralph Washington
SODDY, Frederick 3
SODT, William George 3
SOERGEL, E. W. 3
SOGGE, Tillman M. 3
SOHN, Joseph 1
SOHON, Frederick Wyatt 5
SOILAND, Albert 2
SOKOLOFF, Nikolai 4
SOKOLOFF, 3
   Ruth H. Ottaway
SOKOLOW, 1
   Alexander Theodore
SOKOLSKY, 1
   George Ephraim
SOLBERG, Charles Orrin 2
SOLBERG, Thorvald 2
SOLBERT, 3
   Oscar Nathaniel
SOLETHER, Pliny Louis 3
SOLEY, James Russell 1
SOLEY, Mayo Hallton 3
SOLF Y MURO, Alfredo 5
SOLGER, H
   Reinhold Ernst Friedrich Karl
SOLHEIM, Arthur Oliver 5
SOLIDAY, David Shriver 5
SOLIDAY, Joseph Henry 2
SOLIS, Isaac Nathan 4
SOLIS-COREN, Solomon H
SOLLERS, 5
   Augustus Rhodes
SOLLITT, Sumner S. 4
SOLLMANN, 4
   Torald Hermann
SOLLOTT, Ralph Preston 3
SOLLY, Samuel Edwin 1
SOLOMON, Edward 1
   Davis
SOLOMON, Louis H. 4
SOLON, Faustin Johnson 4
SOLON, Harry 5
SOLON, Leon Victor 5
SOLOW, Herbert 4
SOLTES, Mordecai 3
SOMERDIKE, John 1
   Mason
SOMERS, Andrew L. 1
SOMERS, Orlando Allen 3
SOMERVELL, 5
   Brehon Burke
SOMERVILLE, 4
   Frederick Howland
SOMERVILLE, 1
   Harry Philip
SOMERVILLE, 2
   Henderson Middleton
SOMERVILLE, 3
   James Alexander
SOMERVILLE, Ormond 3
   James Fownes
SOMERVILLE, 4
   Pearl Cliffe
SOMERVILLE, Randolph 4
SOMERVILLE, H
   Thomas Hugh
SOMERVILLE, H
   William Clark
SOMES, Daniel Eton H
SOMMER, Alvin Emery 4
SOMMER, Charles G. 1
SOMMER, Daniel Philip 4
SOMMER, Ernst August 3
SOMMER, Frank Henry 3
SOMMER, Henry Getz 2
SOMMER, Luther Allen 3
SOMMER, Martin S. 5
SOMMER, Peter W. 4
SOMMER, Reuben E. 3
SOMMER, William H. 4
SOMMERICH, 5
   Otto Charles
SOMMERS, 5
   Charles Leissring
SOMMERS, Henry 4
   Cantine
SOMMERS, Martin 4
SOMMERS, Paul Bergen 3
SOMMERVILLE, 1
   Charles William
SOMMERVILLE, 1
   Maxwell
SOMMERVILLE, 1
   Walter Byers

SOMOZA, Anastasio 3
SOMOZA, Luis 4
SONDERN, 5
Frederic Ewald
SONDLEY, F. A. 3
SONES, 3
Warren Wesley David
SONFIELD, Robert Leon 5
SONIAT, Leonce Martin 1
SONNABEND, Abraham 4
M.
SONNAKOLB,
Franklin Schuyler
SONNE, Fred Theodore 4
SONNECK, 1
Oscar George Theodore
SONNEDECKER, 4
Thomas Harry
SONNENBERG, Henry L. 3
SONNENSCHEIN, Hugo 3
SONNETT, John Francis 5
SONNEYSYN, 5
H. O. (sonny)
SONNICHSEN, Albert 1
SONNICHSEN, Yngvar 1
SONNTAG, Marcus S. 1
SONNTAG, William Louis 1
SONSTEBY, John J. 5
SONTAG, Raymond
James 5
SOONG, T.V. 5
SOOYSMITH, Charles 1
SOPER, 1
Alexander Coburn
SOPER, Edmund Davison 4
SOPER, Erastus Burrows 1
SOPER, George Albert 2
SOPER, Henry Marlin 5
SOPER, Horace Wendell 5
SOPER, John Harris 4
SOPER, Morris Ames 4
SOPER, Pliny Leland 3
SOPHIAN, 3
Lawrence Henry
SOPHOCLES, H
Evangelinus Apostolides
SOPHOULIS, 3
Themistocles
SORDONI, 5
Andrew John, Jr.
SORDONI, 4
Andrew John Sr.
SORENSEN, Charles E. 5
SORENSEN, 5
John Hjelmhof
SORENSEN, Royal
Wasson 4
SORENSON, Roy 5
SORG, Paul John 1
SORG, Theodore 3
SORIANO, Andres 4
SORIN, H
Edward Frederick
SORLIE, Arthur Gustav 1
SOROKIN, 4
Pitrim Alexandrovitch
SORRELL, Lewis Carlyle 4
SORRELLS, John Harvey 2
SORSBY, William Brooks 4
SOSKIN, William 3
SOSMAN, Merrill C. 3
SOSMAN, 5
Robert Browning
SOTHERAN, 4
Alice Hyneman
SOTHERAN, Charles 1
SOTHERN, Edward
Askew H
SOTHERN, Edward Hugh 5
SOTTER, George William 3
SOTZIN, Heber Allen 4
SOUBY, A. Max 1
SOUCEK, Apollo 3
SOUCHON, Edmond 1
SOUDER, Edwin Mills 2
SOUERS, Loren Edmunds 4
SOUERS, Sidney William 5
SOULE, Andrew
MacNairn 1
SOULE, Asa Titus 4
SOULE, Caroline Gray 4
SOULE, Charles Carroll 1
SOULE, Edward Lee 5
SOULE, 5
Elizabeth Sterling
SOULE, George 1
SOULE, Henri Remy 4
SOULE, Joshua H
SOULE, Malcolm Herman 3
SOULE, Nathan 1
SOULE, Pierre H
SOULE, Robert Homer 3
SOULE, Winsor 3
SOURDIS, Evarista 4
SOUSA,
Carlos Martins Pereira
SOUSA, John Philip 1

SOUSER, Kenneth 5
SOUTH, Jerry C. 1
SOUTH, John Glover 1
SOUTHACK, Cyprian H
SOUTHALL, James Cocke H
SOUTHALL, 4
James Powell Cocke
SOUTHALL, Robert
Goode 3
SOUTHAM, H. S. 3
SOUTHAM, J. D. 3
SOUTHARD, Elmer
Ernest 1
SOUTHARD, 1
George Franklin
SOUTHARD, Harry
Green 4
SOUTHARD, Henry H
SOUTHARD, Isaac H
SOUTHARD, 1
James Harding
SOUTHARD, Louis
Carver 1
SOUTHARD, Lucien H
SOUTHARD, Samuel
Lewis H
SOUTHER, Henry 1
SOUTHERD, Lucien H. H
SOUTHERLAND, J.
Julien 3
SOUTHERLAND, 1
William Henry Hudson
SOUTHERN, 4
Allen Carriger
SOUTHERN, 3
William Neil Jr.
SOUTHGATE, 2
George Thompson
SOUTHGATE, Horatio 1
SOUTHGATE, 1
James Haywood
SOUTHGATE, Richard 2
SOUTHGATE, 1
Thomas Somerville
SOUTHGATE, H
William Wright
SOUTHWICK, 4
Albert Plympton
SOUTHWICK, George N. 1
SOUTHWICK, 1
George Rinaldo
SOUTHWICK, 1
Henry Lawrence
SOUTHWICK, 1
John Leonard
SOUTHWICK, Soloman H
SOUTHWORTH, 1
Emma Dorothy Eliza
Nevitte
SOUTHWORTH, 2
Franklin Chester
SOUTHWORTH, 4
George Champlin Shepard
SOUTHWORTH, 5
George Clark
SOUTHWORTH, 4
Melvin Deane
SOUTHWORTH, 1
Thomas Shepard
SOWDON, 1
Arthur John Clark
SOWELL, Ashley B. 2
SOWELL, Ellis Mast 3
SOWELL, Ingram Cecil 2
SOWELL, Paul Dibrell 5
SOWER, 1
Charles Gilbert Sr.
SOWER, Christopher * H
SOWERBY, Leo 4
SOWERS, Don Conger 2
SOWERS, Joseph Cullen 5
SPAAK, Paul Henri 5
SPACKMAN, 4
Cyril Saunders
SPACKMAN, 3
Harold Burton
SPAETH, Adolph 1
SPAETH, Bernard Anton 3
SPAETH, J. Duncan 3
SPAETH, Otto Lucien 3
SPAETH, 1
Reynold Albrecht
SPAETH, Sigmund 5
SPAFFORD, 2
Edward Elwell
SPAFFORD, 1
Frederick Angier
SPAFFORD, 2
George Catlin
SPAHR, Boyd Lee 5
SPAHR, 1
Charles Barzillai
SPAHR, George W. 1
SPAHR, Herman Louis 5
SPAHR, Walter Earl 5
SPAID, 4
Arthur Rusmiselle Miller

SPAID, William Wesley 5
SPAID, 3
William Winfield
SPAIGHT, Richard Dobbs H
SPAIGHT, H
Richard Dobbs Jr.
SPAIN, Charles Lyle 2
SPAIN, Charles R. 4
SPAIN, Gail Elliott 4
SPAIN, Will Cook 3
SPALDING, Albert 3
SPALDING, 1
Albert Goodwill
SPALDING, Alfred Baker 5
SPALDING, 5
Alice Huntington
SPALDING, 1
Burleigh Folsom
SPALDING, Catherine H
SPALDING, 4
Charles Hubbard
SPALDING, Eliza Hart H
SPALDING, 4
Elizabeth Hill
SPALDING, 3
Franklin Spencer
SPALDING, 1
Frederick Putnam
SPALDING, George 4
SPALDING, 1
George Burley
SPALDING, George R. 3
SPALDING, Henry
Harmon H
SPALDING, Hughes 5
SPALDING, J. Walter 1
SPALDING, Jack Johnson 1
SPALDING, James Alfred 1
SPALDING, James Field 1
SPALDING, Jesse 1
SPALDING, 1
John Franklin
SPALDING, 1
John Lancaster
SPALDING, Keith 4
SPALDING, Keith 5
SPALDING, Lyman H
SPALDING, Martin John 4
SPALDING, 1
Phebe Estelle
SPALDING, 1
Philip Leffingwell
SPALDING, Rufus Paine 1
SPALDING, Thomas H
SPALDING, 1
Volney Morgan
SPALDING, 4
Walter Raymond
SPALDING, 1
William Andrew
SPAMER, Richard 1
SPANG, 5
Joseph Peter, Jr.
SPANGENBERG, H
Augustus Gottlieb
SPANGLER, David H
SPANGLER, 4
Harrison Earl
SPANGLER, Henry
Thomas 4
SPANGLER, Henry
Wilson 1
SPANGLER, Jacob H
SPANGLER, 1
James Williams
SPANGLER, Timon John 1
SPANIER, 1
Francis Joseph
SPANN, Otis 5
SPARGO, John 1
SPARGO, John Webster 3
SPARHAWK, 1
Frances Campbell
SPARKES, Boyden 4
SPARKMAN, Stephen M. 4
SPARKS, Arthur Watson 1
SPARKS, Charles I. 1
SPARKS, Chauncey 5
SPARKS, Edwin Erle 1
SPARKS, Frank Hugh 4
SPARKS, Frank Melville 3
SPARKS, 1
George McIntosh
SPARKS, Jared H
SPARKS, John 1
SPARKS, Joseph 1
SPARKS, 5
N(orman) R(obert)
SPARKS, Sir T. Ashley 4
SPARKS, Thomas Ayres 1
SPARKS, Thomas J. 2
SPARKS, Will 1
SPARKS, Will Morris 2
SPARKS, William Henry 1
SPARLING, Samuel
Edwin 4
SPARROW, Carroll Mason 1

SPARROW, Ray F. 4
SPARROW, 3
Stanwood Willston
SPARROW, William H
SPARROW, 1
William Warburton Knox
SPATTA, George 5
SPAULDING,
Edward Gleason
SPAULDING, H
Elbridge Gerry
SPAULDING, 5
Eugene Ristine
SPAULDING, 4
Forrest Brisbin
SPAULDING, 3
Francis Trow
SPAULDING, 4
Frank Ellsworth
SPAULDING, 1
George Lawson
SPAULDING, Helim G. 2
SPAULDING, 4
Henry George
SPAULDING, 3
Huntley Nowell
SPAULDING, John Cecil 4
SPAULDING, Levi H
SPAULDING, 4
Major Franklin
SPAULDING, 1
Nathan Weston
SPAULDING, 1
Oliver Lyman
SPAULDING, 2
Oliver Lyman
SPAULDING, 2
Rolland Harty
SPAULDING, Sumner 3
SPAULDING, 1
William Stuart
SPAYD, Milferd Aaron 5
SPEAKMAN, Frank L. 5
SPEAKMAN, G. Dixon 3
SPEAKMAN, Harold 1
SPEAKS, John Charles 2
SPEAKS, Oley 2
SPEAR, Albert Moore 1
SPEAR, Arthur Prince 4
SPEAR, Charles H
SPEAR, Ellis 1
SPEAR, Ellwood Barker 5
SPEAR, John William 1
SPEAR, Lawrence York 3
SPEAR, Lewis Benson 4
SPEAR, Nathaniel 2
SPEAR, Samuel Thayer H
SPEAR, William Thomas 1
SPEARE, 4
Charles Frederic
SPEARE, Dorothy 3
SPEARE, Edward Ray 4
SPEARE, Frank Palmer 5
SPEARE, William Martin 5
SPEARING, J. Zach 2
SPEARING, Joseph Hall 4
SPEARL, George 2
SPEARMAN, 1
Frank Hamilton
SPEARS, John Randolph 1
SPEARS, Raymond Smiley 3
SPEARS, Samuel Tilden 1
SPEARS, William Oscar 4
SPEASE, Edward 2
SPECK,
Frank Gouldsmith
SPECTORSKY, Auguste 5
C.
SPEED, Horace 4
SPEED, James H
SPEED, 5
James Breckinridge
SPEED, John Gilmer 1
SPEED, Keats 3
SPEED, Kellogg 3
SPEED, Thomas H
SPEED, Thomas 5
SPEED, 5
Virginia Perrin (Mrs. W.
S. Speed)
SPEED, 3
William Shallcross
SPEER, Alfred Alten 1
SPEER, Emma Bailey 4
SPEER, Emory 1
SPEER, James Henry 3
SPEER, James Ramsey 2
SPEER, Peter Moore 1
SPEER, Robert Elliott 2
SPEER, Robert Kenneth 3
SPEER, Robert Milton H
SPEER, Robert Walter 1
SPEER, H
Thomas Jefferson
SPEER, William 1
SPEER, William H. 3

SPEER, 1
William McMurtrie
SPEERS, Chester Henry 4
SPEERS, James M. 1
SPEERS, 4
Theodore Cuyler
SPEERS, William Ewing 4
SPEICHER, 4
Eugene Edward
SPEIDEL, Edward 2
SPEIDEL, 3
Merritt Charles
SPEIDEL, Thomas D. 3
SPEIGHT, Jesse 1
SPEIR, Samuel Fleet H
SPEIS, August H
SPEISER, 4
Ephraim Avigdor
SPEKKE, Arnolds 5
SPELFOGEL, 5
Morris Richard
SPELLACY, Edmund
Frank 3
SPELLACY, 3
Thomas Joseph
SPELLMAN, 4
Francis Cardinal
SPELLMEYER, Henry 1
SPENCE, Brent 4
SPENCE, Clara B. 1
SPENCE, Frederick 2
SPENCE, John Fletcher 1
SPENCE, John Lee
SPENCE, John Selby 5
SPENCE, John Selby 1
SPENCE, Kenneth
Monroe 4
SPENCE, 4
Kenneth Wartinbee
SPENCE, Thomas Ara H
SPENCE, Walter 1
SPENCE, William H. 1
SPENCE, 4
William Kenneth
SPENCER, Alfred Jr. 1
SPENCER, Almon Edwin 4
SPENCER, Ambrose H
SPENCER, Anna Garlin 1
SPENCER, Arthur Coe 1
SPENCER, Bunyan 1
SPENCER, Byron 4
SPENCER, C. Luther 4
SPENCER, 3
Charles Eldridge Jr.
SPENCER, 1
Claudius Buchanan
SPENCER, Corwin H. 1
SPENCER, Edgar A. 1
SPENCER, 2
Edward Buckham Taylor
SPENCER, Elihu H
SPENCER, Elijah H
SPENCER, 4
Evelene Armstrong
SPENCER, 1
Francis Marion
SPENCER, Frank E. 3
SPENCER, Frank Robert 3
SPENCER, George Albert 5
SPENCER, 1
George Eliphaz
SPENCER, 1
George Mazelton
SPENCER, 1
Guilford Lawson
SPENCER, Hazelton 2
SPENCER, Henry Russell 1
SPENCER, Herbert H
SPENCER, 3
Herbert Lincoln
SPENCER, 1
Horatio Nelson
SPENCER, Ichabod Smith H
SPENCER, J. Brookes 3
SPENCER, J. W. 1
SPENCER, James Bradley 1
SPENCER, James Clark 1
SPENCER, James Harland 5
SPENCER, James Morton 4
SPENCER, Jesse Ames 3
SPENCER, John 3
SPENCER, John Canfield H
SPENCER, John Mitchell 1
SPENCER, John R. 1
SPENCER, John Wesley 1
SPENCER, Joseph H
SPENCER, Kenneth 3
SPENCER, 3
Kenneth Aldred
SPENCER, Lee Bowen 5
SPENCER, Lorillard * 1
SPENCER, Lyle Manly 5
SPENCER, 5
M(atthew) Lyle
SPENCER, 3
Mrs. Lilian White
SPENCER, Niles 3

* Indicates More Than One Such Name Listed

SPENCER, Oliver Martin 1
SPENCER, Paul 1
SPENCER, Percy Craig 5
SPENCER, Percy LeBaron 1
SPENCER, Pitman Clemens H
SPENCER, Platt Rogers H
SPENCER, Richard H
SPENCER, Richard 4
SPENCER, Robert 1
SPENCER, Robert Closson 5
SPENCER, Robert Lyle 2
SPENCER, Robert Nelson 5
SPENCER, Samuel 1
SPENCER, Samuel Riley 3
SPENCER, Sara Andrews 1
SPENCER, Selden Palmer 1
SPENCER, Theodore 2
SPENCER, Thomas H
SPENCER, Vernon 2
SPENCER, Walker Brainerd 1
SPENCER, William Brinerd H
SPENCER, William Homer
SPENCER, William L. 4
SPENCER, William Loring 5
SPENCER, William Vaughan 1
SPENCER, Willing 5
SPENCER-NAIRN, Sir Robert
SPENS, Conrad E. 1
SPENZER, John George 1
SPERANZA, Gino 1
SPERBER, Jacob 1
SPERR, Frederick William
SPERRY, Charles Stilman 1
SPERRY, Earl Evelyn 1
SPERRY, Elmer Ambrose 1
SPERRY, Leavenworth Porter 3
SPERRY, Lewis 4
SPERRY, Lyman Beecher 1
SPERRY, Marcy Leavenworth 2
SPERRY, Nehemiah Day 1
SPERRY, Watson Robertson 1
SPERRY, Willard Gardner 4
SPERRY, Willard Learoyd 3
SPEWACK, Samuel 5
SPEYER, James 1
SPEYER, Leonora 3
SPEYERS, Arthur Bayard 1
SPICER, Anne Higginson 1
SPICER, Clarence Winfred
SPICER, Clinton Elbert 5
SPICER, Henry Russell 5
SPICER, Robert Barclay 5
SPICER, William Ambrose 5
SPICER-SIMSON, Margaret 5
SPICER-SIMSON, Theodore 3
SPIEGEL, Edwin John 4
SPIEGEL, Frederick Siegfried 1
SPIEGEL, Modie Joseph 2
SPIEKER, Edward Henry 1
SPIEKER, George Frederick 1
SPIER, Leslie 4
SPIERING, Theodore 1
SPIES, Albert 1
SPIES, Tom Douglas 3
SPIESS, Carlos Augustus 4
SPIETH, Lawrence Caleb 4
SPIKE, Robert Warren 1
SPILLANE, Edward 4
SPILLANE, Richard 2
SPILLER, Harold Alfred 4
SPILLER, William Gibson 1
SPILLERS, Charles Lee 4
SPILLMAN, Ora Seldon 1
SPILLMAN, William Jasper 1
SPILMAN, Bernard Washington 5
SPILMAN, Edward Guthrie 1
SPILMAN, Lewis Hopkins 1
SPILMAN, Robert Scott 3
SPILMAN, Robert Scott, Jr. 5

SPILSBURY, Edmund Gybbon 1
SPINDEN, Herbert Joseph 4
SPINDLER, Garold Ralph 4
SPINGARN, Arthur B. 5
SPINGARN, J. E. 1
SPINGOLD, Nathan Breiter 3
SPINING, George Lawrence 1
SPINK, Cyrus H
SPINK, J. G. Taylor H
SPINK, Mary Angela 1
SPINK, Mary Angela 2
SPINK, Solomon Lewis H
SPINKA, Matthew 5
SPINKS, Lewis 2
SPINNER, Francis Elias 1
SPINNEY, George Wilbur 2
SPINNEY, Louis Bevier 3
SPINOLA, Francis Barretto
SPIRO, Charles David 1
SPIRO, Solon 4
SPITZ, Armand N(eustadter) 5
SPITZ, Leo 3
SPITZER, Ceilan Milo 1
SPITZKA, Edward Anthony
SPITZKA, Edward Charles 1
SPIVACK, Robert Gerald 5
SPIVAK, Charles David 1
SPIVEY, Ludd Myrl 4
SPIVEY, Thomas Sawyer 1
SPLINT, Sarah Field 3
SPOEHR, Herman Augustus
SPOFFORD, Ainsworth Rand 1
SPOFFORD, Harriet Prescott
SPOFFORD, W. E. 4
SPOHN, George Welda 2
SPONG, Harper W. 4
SPONSLER, Olenus Lee 3
SPOONER, Charles Horace 3
SPOONER, Edmund D. 4
SPOONER, Florence Garrettson 1
SPOONER, Henry Joshua 1
SPOONER, John Colt 1
SPOONER, Lysander H
SPOONER, Shearjashub 4
SPOONTS, Morris Augustus
SPOOR, John Alden 1
SPOTSWOOD, Alexander H
SPOTTED TAIL H
SPOTTS, William Bigler 3
SPRACHER, Dwight L. 5
SPRAGINS, Robert L. 4
SPRAGUE, Achsa W. 1
SPRAGUE, Albert Arnold 1
SPRAGUE, Albert Arnold 5
SPRAGUE, Albert Tilden, Jr.
SPRAGUE, Augustus Brown Reed 1
SPRAGUE, Austin Velorous Milton 4
SPRAGUE, Benjamin Oxnard 2
SPRAGUE, Carleton 1
SPRAGUE, Charles H
SPRAGUE, Charles Arthur 5
SPRAGUE, Charles Ezra 1
SPRAGUE, Charles Franklin 1
SPRAGUE, Charles James 1
SPRAGUE, Clifton Albert 3
SPRAGUE, Ezra Kimball 2
SPRAGUE, Frank Headley 4
SPRAGUE, Frank Julian 1
SPRAGUE, Franklin M. 1
SPRAGUE, George Clare 4
SPRAGUE, Henry Harrison
SPRAGUE, Homer Baxter 1
SPRAGUE, Howard B. 5
SPRAGUE, Hugh Almeron 4
SPRAGUE, Jesse Rainsford 2
SPRAGUE, John Titcomb H
SPRAGUE, Julian King 1
SPRAGUE, Kate Chase H
SPRAGUE, Kenneth Burdette 5
SPRAGUE, Kenneth Burdette 4
SPRAGUE, Leslie Willis 1
SPRAGUE, Levi L. 1

SPRAGUE, Lucian C. 4
SPRAGUE, M. D. 4
SPRAGUE, Mary Aplin 4
SPRAGUE, Oliver Mitchell Wentworth 3
SPRAGUE, Peleg * H
SPRAGUE, Robert James 1
SPRAGUE, Thomas Henry 2
SPRAGUE, Thomas Lamison 5
SPRAGUE, William * H
SPRAGUE, William 1
SPRAGUE, William Buell 1
SPRAGUE, William Cyrus 1
SPRAGUE, William Wallace 4
SPRAGUE-SMITH, Charles 1
SPRAGUE-SMITH, Isabelle Dwight 3
SPRATLING, William 4
SPRATLING, William Philip 4
SPRATT, Frederick 1
SPRAY, Chalres Cranston 4
SPRAY, Ruth Hinshaw 1
SPRECKELS, Adolph Bernard 1
SPRECKELS, Claus 1
SPRECKELS, John Diedrich 3
SPRECKELS, Rudolph 1
SPRENG, Samuel Peter 2
SPRENG, Theodore Frederick Henry
SPRENGLING, Martin 3
SPRIGG, James Cresap H
SPRIGG, John Thomas H
SPRIGG, Louis Rivers 4
SPRIGG, Michael Cresap H
SPRIGG, Richard Jr. H
SPRIGG, Thomas H
SPRIGLE, Ray 3
SPRING, Alfred H
SPRING, Gardiner H
SPRING, George E. 4
SPRING, Howard 4
SPRING, La Verne Ward 4
SPRING, Laurence Ellsworth 4
SPRING, Leverett Wilson 1
SPRING, Samuel H
SPRING, Samuel Newton 3
SPRINGER, Alfred 2
SPRINGER, Charles 1
SPRINGER, Durand William 4
SPRINGER, Edward Thomas 4
SPRINGER, Francis Edwin 1
SPRINGER, Frank 1
SPRINGER, Franklin Wesley 1
SPRINGER, George Peter 5
SPRINGER, John Franklin 2
SPRINGER, John McKendree 5
SPRINGER, John Wallace 4
SPRINGER, Raymond Smiley 1
SPRINGER, Rebecca Ruter 1
SPRINGER, Reuben Runyan H
SPRINGER, Thomas Grant 5
SPRINGER, William McKendree 1
SPRINGHORN, Carl 5
SPRING-RICE, Sir Cecil Arthur 1
SPRINGS, Elliott White 3
SPRINGS, Holmes Buck 3
SPRINGS, Lena Jones 2
SPRINGS, Leroy 1
SPRINGWEILER, Erwin Frederick 5
SPRONG, Severn D. 2
SPROSS, Charles Gilbert 5
SPROSS, Charles Gilbert 4
SPROTT, Jarl S. 2
SPROUL, Elliott Wilford
SPROUL, William Cameron
SPROUL, William H. 1
SPROULE, Charles H. 1
SPROULE, William 1
SPROULL, Thomas H
SPROULL, William Oliver 1

SPROUSE, Claude Willard 3
SPROUT, Will Carleton 4
SPROWL, James Allen 4
SPROWLS, Joseph Barnett, Jr. 5
SPRUANCE, Benton M. 4
SPRUANCE, Presley H
SPRUANCE, Raymond Ames 5
SPRUANCE, William Corbit 1
SPRUNT, Alexander 1
SPRUNT, Alexander, Jr. 5
SPRY, William 1
SPURGEON, William Porter 1
SPURGIN, William Fletcher 1
SPURR, Josiah Edward 2
SPURR, Josiah Edward 3
SPURZHEIM, Johann Kaspar H
SPYKMAN, Nicholas John 2
SQUANTO H
SQUIBB, Edward Robinson H
SQUIER, Carl B. 4
SQUIER, Ephraim George 1
SQUIER, George Owen 1
SQUIER, John Bentley 2
SQUIER, Lee Welling 4
SQUIER, Miles Powell H
SQUIERS, Arnon Lyon 1
SQUIERS, Herbert Goldsmith
SQUIRE, Amos Osborne 2
SQUIRE, Andrew 1
SQUIRE, Edward Jacob 4
SQUIRE, Frances 1
SQUIRE, Francis Hagar 3
SQUIRE, Watson Carvosso
SQUIRES, Charles William 2
SQUIRES, George Forbes 3
SQUIRES, Ralph Anthony 4
SQUIRES, Vernon Purinton 1
SQUIRES, Walter Albion 5
SQUIRES, William Henry Tappey 2
ST. Ange, Louis De Bellerive H
ST. Clair, Arthur H
ST. Clair, Leonard Pressley 4
ST. Clair-moss, Luella W.
ST. Cyr, John Alexander 4
ST. Denis, Louis Juchereau 'de
ST. George, William Sterne
ST. Husson, Sieur 'de
ST. John, Charles H
ST. John, Charles Edward 1
ST. John, Charles Elliott 1
ST. John, Charles J. 1
ST. John, Cynthia Morgan 1
ST. John, Daniel Bennett 1
ST. John, Edward Porter 4
ST. John, Everitte 1
ST. John, George Clair 4
ST. John, Henry H
ST. John, Isaac Munroe H
ST. John, J. Hector 1
ST. John, John Pierce 1
ST. John, John Price H
ST. John, John Price H
ST. John, Samuel Benedict 1
ST. John, Theodore Raymond 3
ST. Lausson, Simon Francois Daumont
ST. Leger, Barry H
ST. Martin, Louis H
ST. Sure, Adolphus Frederic 2
ST. Vrain, Ceran De Hault De Lassus 'de H
STAAF, Oscar 4
STAAKE, William Heaton 1
STABLER, Herman 2
STABLER, Howard Douglas
STABLER, James Pleasants
STABLER, John Gates 1

STABLER, Jordan Herbert 1
STABLER, Laird Joseph 1
STABLETON, John Kay 4
STACE, Arthur William 2
STACE, Walter Terence 5
STACEY, Alfred Edwin 1
STACEY, Anna Lee 2
STACEY, John Franklin 1
STACK, Edmund John 5
STACK, Frederic William 5
STACK, J. W. 3
STACK, John 5
STACK, Joseph Michael 3
STACKHOUSE, Eli Thomas H
STACKHOUSE, Perry James 2
STACKHOUSE, Wesley Thomas 4
STACKPOLE, Albert Hummel 5
STACKPOLE, Edward J. 4
STACKPOLE, Everett Schermerhorn
STACKPOLE, James Hall 4
STACKPOLE, Pierpont L. 5
STACY, Merrill E.
STACY, Thomas Hobbs 1
STACY, Walter Parker 3
STADDEN, Corry Montague
STADELMAN, William Francis 1
STADIE, William Christopher 3
STADLER, Charles A. 4
STADLER, Lewis John 3
STADLER, William Lewis 5
STADTFELD, Joseph 2
STAFFORD, Charles Lewis
STAFFORD, Cora Elder 4
STAFFORD, Geoffrey Wardle 3
STAFFORD, John Aloysius
STAFFORD, John Richard 1
STAFFORD, Maurice L. 3
STAFFORD, Orin Fletcher 2
STAFFORD, Thomas Polhill
STAFFORD, Wendell Phillips 5
STAFFORD, William Bascom 4
STAFSETH, H(enrik) J(oakim) 5
STAGE, Charles Willard 1
STAGER, Anson H
STAGG, Amos Alonzo 4
STAGG, Charles H
STAGG, Charles Tracey 1
STAGG, John Weldon 1
STAHEL, Julius 1
STAHL, John Meloy 2
STAHL, Karl Friedrich 1
STAHL, William Harris 5
STAHLMAN, Edward Bushrod
STAHLSCHMIDT, Arthur Edward 4
STAHR, Henry Irvin 4
STAHR, John Summers 1
STAINBACK, Ingram Macklin 4
STAIR, Edward Douglas 5
STAKELY, Charles A. 5
STAKELY, Charles Averett
STALBERG, Jonah 5
STALDER, Jackson R. 5
STALDER, Walter 5
STALEY, A. Rollin 1
STALEY, Allen Conklin 4
STALEY, Augustus Eugene
STALEY, Cady 4
STALEY, John Richard 4
STALEY, John Wilson 4
STALEY, R. C. 1
STALIN, Joseph Vissarionovich
STALIN, Joseph Vissarionovich
STALKER, Arthur William
STALL, Sylvanus 1
STALLINGS, Jesse F. 4
STALLINGS, Laurence 5
STALLO, John Bernard 4
STALLWORTH, James Adams H

STALLWORTH, Nicholas Eugene 1
STALNAKER, Frank D. 1
STALNAKER, Luther Winfield 3
STAM, Colin Ferguson 4
STAM, Jacob 5
STAMBAUGH, Armstrong Alexander 4
STAMBAUGH, John 1
STAMM, Earle Williams 4
STAMM, Edward P. 4
STAMM, Frederick Keller 4
STAMM, John Samuel 3
STAMM, Vincil R. 5
STAMPS, Thomas Dodson 4
STANARD, Edwin Obed 1
STANARD, Mary Newton 4
STANARD, William Glover 3
STANBERY, Henry H
STANBERY, William H
STANBURY, Walter Albert 3
STANCHFIELD, John Barry 1
STANCLIFF, Evert Lee 3
STANCLIFT, Henry Clay 2
STANDEN, William Thomas 4
STANDER, Henricus Johannes 2
STANDEVEN, Herbert Leslie 2
STANDEVEN, James Wylie 5
STANDIFER, James H
STANDIFORD, Elisha David H
STANDISH, John Van Ness 1
STANDISH, Myles H
STANDISH, Myles 1
STANDISH, S. H. 3
STANDLEY, William Harrison 4
STANFIELD, J. Fisher 3
STANFIELD, Robert Nelson 2
STANFIELD, Theodore H
STANFORD, Albert Clinton 3
STANFORD, Edward Valentine 4
STANFORD, Homer Reed 3
STANFORD, Jane Lathrop 1
STANFORD, John H
STANFORD, Leland 4
STANFORD, Rawghlie Clement 4
STANFORD, Richard H
STANFORD, Wesley M. 4
STANGE, Charles Henry 5
STANGELAND, Katharina Marie (Mrs. Charles E. Stangeland) 1
STANGLAND, Benjamin F. 4
STANISLAUS, I(gnatius) V(alerius) Stanley 5
STANLAWS, Penrhyn 3
STANLEY, A. Owsley 3
STANLEY, Albert Augustus 1
STANLEY, Carleton Wellesley 5
STANLEY, Caroline Abbot 1
STANLEY, Cassius Miller 4
STANLEY, Clarance 5
STANLEY, David Sloane 1
STANLEY, Edmund 1
STANLEY, Edwin James 1
STANLEY, Edwin M(onroe) 5
STANLEY, Emory Day 1
STANLEY, Francis Edgar H
STANLEY, Francis Edgar 4
STANLEY, Frank Arthur 4
STANLEY, Frederic Bartlett 2
STANLEY, Frederick Jonte 4
STANLEY, Freelan O. 1
STANLEY, George James 4
STANLEY, Harold 4
STANLEY, Helen 4
STANLEY, Hiram Alonzo 4
STANLEY, Hugh Wright 3
STANLEY, James G. 4
STANLEY, John Joseph 1
STANLEY, John Mix H
STANLEY, Louise 3

STANLEY, Maurice 4
STANLEY, Osso Willis 4
STANLEY, Philip B. 4
STANLEY, Robert Crooks 3
STANLEY, Sir Henry Morton G. C. B. 1
STANLEY, Thomas Bahnson 5
STANLEY, W. E. 4
STANLEY, Wendell M(eredith) 5
STANLEY, William 1
STANLEY, William 2
STANLEY, William Eugene 3
STANLEY, William Henry 4
STANLEY-BROWN, Joseph 1
STANLEY-BROWN, Joseph 2
STANLY, Edward H
STANLY, John H
STANLY, Walter Lawrence 2
STANNARD, E. Tappan 2
STANNARD, Mrs. Margaret J. 4
STANSBURY, Ele 4
STANSBURY, Howard H
STANSBURY, Joseph 4
STANSBURY, Karl E. 4
STANSBURY, Paul William 4
STANSELL, Robert Basil 5
STANTON, A. Glenn 5
STANTON, Benjamin 2
STANTON, Charles Spelman H
STANTON, Edwin McMasters H
STANTON, Elizabeth Cady 1
STANTON, Frank Lebby 1
STANTON, Frank M. 4
STANTON, Frank McMillan 3
STANTON, Frederick Perry H
STANTON, Harry Leavenworth 5
STANTON, Henry Brewster H
STANTON, Henry Francis 3
STANTON, Henry Thompson 3
STANTON, Horace Coffin 4
STANTON, John 1
STANTON, John Gilman 1
STANTON, Jonathan Young 1
STANTON, Joseph Jr. H
STANTON, Lucy M. 1
STANTON, Oscar Fitzalan 4
STANTON, Philip Ackley 4
STANTON, Richard Henry 4
STANTON, Robert Brewster 1
STANTON, Stephen Berrien 5
STANTON, Thaddeus H. 1
STANTON, Theodore 1
STANTON, Timothy William 3
STANTON, William 4
STANWICK, John H
STANWOOD, Edward 1
STAPLES, Abram Penn 4
STAPLES, Abram Penn 3
STAPLES, Arthur Gray 4
STAPLES, Charles Henry 3
STAPLES, Charles Jason 4
STAPLES, Henry Franklin 3
STAPLES, John Norman 2
STAPLES, Percy A. 3
STAPLES, Philip Clayton 2
STAPLES, Seth Stitt 4
STAPLES, Thomas S. 3
STAPLES, Waller Redd 4
STAPLES, William Read H
STAPLETON, Ammon 1
STAPLETON, Benjamin F. 3
STAPLETON, Luke D. 4
STAPLETON, William 4
STARBIRD, Alfred 3
STARBUCK, Edwin Diller 2
STARBUCK, Kathryn Helene 4
STARBUCK, Raymond Donald 4
STAREK, Fred 5
STAREN, John Edgar 4
STARIHA, John 1

STARIN, John Henry 1
STARK, Abe 5
STARK, Albert Philander 4
STARK, Clarence Oscar 5
STARK, Dudley Scott 5
STARK, Edwin Jackson 4
STARK, Edwin M. 4
STARK, Francis Raymond 4
STARK, George W. 5
STARK, Harold Raynsford 5
STARK, Harry Rodgers 4
STARK, Henry Ignatius 2
STARK, Henry Jacob Lutcher 5
STARK, John H
STARK, Lloyd Crow 5
STARK, Louis 5
STARK, Orton K(irkwood) 5
STARK, Otto 1
STARK, William Ledyard 4
STARKEY, Thomas Alfred 2
STARKLOFF, Max C(arl) 5
STARKS, William Henry Lord 4
STARKWEATHER, Chauncey Clark 1
STARKWEATHER, David Austin H
STARKWEATHER, George Anson H
STARKWEATHER, Henry Howard H
STARKWEATHER, John K. 5
STARKWEATHER, Louis Pomeroy 3
STARKWEATHER, William Edward Bloomfield 5
STARLING, William 1
STARNES, George Talmage 3
STARNES, Joe 4
STARR, Belle H
STARR, Cornelius V. 5
STARR, Eliza Allen 1
STARR, Frederick 1
STARR, Henry Frank 5
STARR, Ida May Hill 4
STARR, Lee Anna 5
STARR, Louis 1
STARR, Louis Edward 4
STARR, M. Allen 1
STARR, Merritt 1
STARR, Nathan 1
STARR, Oliver 4
STARR, Raymond Wesley 5
STARR, William G. 4
STARRETT, Helen Ekin 1
STARRETT, Henry Prince 1
STARRETT, Lewis Frederick 1
STARRETT, Milton Gerry 2
STARRETT, Paul 1
STARRETT, Theodore 1
STARRETT, William Aiken 1
STARRING, Frederick A. 1
STARRING, Mason Brayman 1
START, Charles Monroe 1
START, Edwin Augustus 1
START, Henry R. 1
STASON, E(dwin) Blythe 5
STASTNY, Olga Frances 3
STATE, Charles 5
STATHAS, Pericles Peter 5
STATHERS, Birk Smtih 2
STATLER, Alice Seidler (Mrs. Ellsworth Milton Statler) 5
STATLER, Ellsworth Milton 1
STATON, Adolphus 4
STATON, Harry 3
STATTER, Arthur Frederick 5
STATTON, Arthur Biggs 4
STAUB, Albert William 3
STAUB, Gordon James 4
STAUB, Walter Adolph 2
STAUBER, Leslie Alfred 4
STAUBLE, Wilbur Carl 5
STAUDINGER, Hermann 4
STAUFFACHER, Charles Henry 3
STAUFFACHER, Edward L. 4
STAUFFEN, Ernest Jr. 3
STAUFFER, Charles Albert 5
STAUFFER, Clinton Raymond 4

STAUFFER, David McNeely 1
STAUFFER, Donald Alfred 3
STAUFFER, Grant 2
STAUFFER, Herbert Milton 5
STAUFFER, Vernon 1
STAUGHTON, William H
STAUNTON, Sidney Augustus 1
STAUNTON, William H
STAUNTON, William Field 2
STAYTON, Edward M. 3
STAYTON, John William H
STAYTON, Joseph Markham 1
STAYTON, Robert Weldon 4
STAYTON, William H. 4
STEACIE, Edgar William Richard 4
STEAD, Robert 2
STEAD, William Henry 3
STEADMAN, Alva Edgar 4
STEADMAN, John Marcellus Jr. 2
STEADWELL, B. Samuel 2
STEAGALL, Henry Bascom 2
STEALEY, Orlando O. 1
STEALEY, Sydnor Lorenzo 5
STEARLEY, Ralph F. 5
STEARLY, Wilson Reiff 1
STEARNE, Allen Michener 3
STEARNES, Reaumur Coleman 2
STEARNS, Abel H
STEARNS, Albert Warren 1
STEARNS, Alfred Ernest 2
STEARNS, Arthur French 4
STEARNS, Asahel 1
STEARNS, Carl Leo 5
STEARNS, Charles Cummings 1
STEARNS, Charles Falconer 2
STEARNS, Eben Sperry H
STEARNS, Edith Shaffer 3
STEARNS, Foster 3
STEARNS, Frank Preston 4
STEARNS, Frank Waterman 1
STEARNS, Frederic Pike 1
STEARNS, Frederick William 1
STEARNS, George Luther H
STEARNS, Gustav 3
STEARNS, Harold Edmund 2
STEARNS, Henry Putnam 1
STEARNS, John Newton H
STEARNS, John William 4
STEARNS, Joyce Clennam 2
STEARNS, Junius Brutus 1
STEARNS, Lutie Eugenia 5
STEARNS, Marshall Winslow 4
STEARNS, Neele Edward 4
STEARNS, Oliver H
STEARNS, Osborne Putnam 4
STEARNS, Ozora Pierson H
STEARNS, Robert Edwards Carter 2
STEARNS, Sarah Burger 1
STEARNS, Shubal H
STEARNS, Theodore 1
STEARNS, Wallace Nelson 2
STEARNS, William Augustus H
STEARNS, William Guilford 3
STEARNS, William Marion 1
STEBBINS, Arthur D. 2
STEBBINS, Arthur D. 3
STEBBINS, Byron H. 4
STEBBINS, Edwin Allen 3
STEBBINS, Emma 1
STEBBINS, G(eorge) Waring 5
STEBBINS, George Coles 2
STEBBINS, Henry George H
STEBBINS, Henry Hamlin 1
STEBBINS, Homer Adolph 4
STEBBINS, Horatio H
STEBBINS, John W. 4
STEBBINS, Kathleen B. 4
STEBBINS, Rufus Phineas H
STEBLER, William John 4

STECHER, Henry William 1
STECHER, Robert Morgan 5
STECHSCHULTE, Victor Cyril 3
STECK, Charles Calvin 5
STECK, Daniel Frederic 3
STECK, George H
STECKEL, Abram Peters 3
STECKER, Robert Donald 4
STECKLER, Alfred 4
STEDDOM, Rice Price 5
STEDMAN, Charles Manly 1
STEDMAN, Edmund Clarence 1
STEDMAN, George Woolverton 3
STEDMAN, Giles Chester 4
STEDMAN, Henry Rust 1
STEDMAN, John Moore 1
STEDMAN, John Weiss 3
STEDMAN, Louise Adella 5
STEDMAN, Thomas Lathrop 4
STEDMAN, William H
STEED, J. Lyman 2
STEED, Robert Dennis 2
STEEDLY, Benjamin Broadus 1
STEEDMAN, Charles H
STEEDMAN, Edwin Harrison 4
STEEDMAN, James Blair H
STEEL, Alfred G. B. 2
STEEL, George Alexander 1
STEEL, Rowe Summerville 5
STEEL, Westbrook 5
STEELE, Albert Wilbur 1
STEELE, Alfred N. 3
STEELE, Charles 4
STEELE, Daniel 1
STEELE, Daniel Atkinson King 1
STEELE, David 2
STEELE, David McConnell 2
STEELE, Edgar Clarence 4
STEELE, Esther Baker 1
STEELE, Frank B. 5
STEELE, Frederic Dorr 2
STEELE, Frederick 1
STEELE, George W. H
STEELE, George Washington 1
STEELE, Harry Lee 5
STEELE, Heath McClung 3
STEELE, Henry J. 1
STEELE, Henry Maynadier 1
STEELE, Hiram Roswell 1
STEELE, James Dallas 1
STEELE, James King H
STEELE, Joel Dorman H
STEELE, John H
STEELE, John 1
STEELE, John Benedict H
STEELE, John Dutton 5
STEELE, John Murray 5
STEELE, John Nelson 5
STEELE, John Nevett H
STEELE, Joseph M. 5
STEELE, Leon Charles 2
STEELE, Leslie J. 1
STEELE, Robert Benson 5
STEELE, Robert Denham 5
STEELE, Robert Wilbur 5
STEELE, Robert Wilbur 1
STEELE, Rufus 1
STEELE, Sidney John 1
STEELE, Theodore Clement 1
STEELE, Thomas J. 1
STEELE, Thomas M. 1
STEELE, Thomas Sedgwick 1
STEELE, Walter Leak H
STEELE, Walter Simeon 3
STEELE, Wilbur Daniel 1
STEELE, Wilbur Fletcher 4
STEELE, William Gaston H
STEELE, William La Barthe 2
STEELL, Willis 1
STEELL, Willis 2
STEENBERG, Richard Wilbur 4
STEENBOCK, Harry 4
STEENDAM, Jacob H
STEENE, William 4
STEENERSON, Halvor 1
STEENROD, Lewis H
STEENROD, Norman Earl 5

STEENSTRA, Peter Henry 1
STEENWYCK, Cornelis H
STEEP, Thomas 2
STEERE, Joseph Beal 1
STEERE, Joseph Hall 1
STEERE, Kenneth David 4
STEERE, Lloyd Randol 4
STEERS, George H
STEESE, James Gordon 3
STEFAN, Karl 3
STEFANINI, 2
Francois Ange Antoine
STEFANSSON, Vilhjalmur 4
STEFFAN, Roger 3
STEFFENS, Cornelius M. 1
STEFFENS, Lincoln 1
STEFFENS, 3
Theodore Henry
STEFFENSEN, Vernal R. 4
STEGEMAN, Gebhard 2
STEGER, 3
Christian Talbot
STEGER, Julius 3
STEGER, Peyton 1
STEHLE, Aurelius 1
STEICHEN, Edward 5
STEIDTMANN, Waldo E. 3
STEIGER, Ernst 1
STEIGER, George 2
STEIGERS, 1
William Corbet
STEIGUER, 2
Louis Rudolph 'de
STEIL, 5
William Nicholas
STEIN, Albert Harvey 5
STEIN, Edward Thomas 4
STEIN, Evaleen 1
STEIN, Fred W, Sr. 5
STEIN, Gertrude 2
STEIN, Harold 4
STEIN, I. Melville 4
STEIN, James Rauch 5
STEIN, John Philip 1
STEIN, Louis P. 3
STEIN, Robert 1
STEINBACH, 5
Everett Mark
STEINBACH, Milton 5
STEINBECK, John Ernst 5
STEINBERG, Milton 3
STEINBERG, 4
Samuel Sidney
STEINBRINK, Meier 4
STEINDEL, Bruno 5
STEINDLER, Arthur 3
STEINDORFF, Georg 3
STEINEM, Pauline 4
STEINER, 1
Bernard Christian
STEINER, Celestin John 5
STEINER, Edward Alfred 3
STEINER, Leo K. 2
STEINER, Lewis Henry H
STEINER, Max 1
STEINER, Robert Eugene 3
STEINER, Walter Ralph 1
STEINER, 4
William Howard
STEINER, 2
Williams Kossuth
STEINERT, Alan 5
STEINETZ, Bernard G. 4
STEINFELD, Albert 1
STEINGRUBER-
WILDGANS, Ilona 5
STEINHARDT, 2
Laurence A.
STEINHART, Frank 1
STEINHART, Jesse H. 4
STEINHAUS, Arthur H. 5
STEINHAUS, 5
Edward A(rthur)
STEININGER, Fred H. 5
STEINITZ, William 1
STEINLE, Roland Joseph 5
STEINLE, Roland Joseph 4
STEINMAN, 1
Andrew Jackson
STEINMAN, 4
David Barnard
STEINMAN, James Hale 4
STEINMETZ, 1
Charles Proteus
STEINMETZ, 1
Joseph Allison
STEINMETZ, Maurice 5
STEINREICH, 4
Kenneth Pease
STEINSAPIR, Saul P. 5
STEINWAY, 1
Charles Herman
STEINWAY, H
Christian Friedrich
Theodore
STEINWAY, H
Henry Engelhard

STEINWAY, Theodore E. 3
STEINWAY, William H
STEINWAY, 4
William Richard
STEINWEG, 4
William Louis
STEIWER, Frederick 1
STEJNEGER, Leonhard 2
STELLA, Antonio 1
STELLA, Joseph 2
STELLE, 4
Charles Clarkson
STELLE, John 4
STELLHORN, 1
Frederick William
STELLWAGEN, 1
Edward James
STELLWAGEN, 2
Seitorde Michael
STELTER, Benjamin F. 3
STELWAGON, 1
Henry Weightman
STELZLE, Charles 1
STEMBEL, Roger Nelson 2
STEMLER, Otto Adolph 2
STEMPEL, Guido 1
Hermann 3
STEMPF, Victor Herman 2
STEMPLE, Frank 4
STENGEL, Alfred 1
STENGEL, 5
Frederick William
STENGLE, Charles Irwin 3
STENZEL, Lula Vinette 5
STEPELTON, 5
Norman Allen
STEPHAN, 3
Frank Lawrence
STEPHAN, 5
Frederick Franklin
STEPHAN, George 2
STEPHEN, George 3
STEPHENS, Abraham P. H
STEPHENS, 4
Albert Lee Sr.
STEPHENS, H
Alexander Hamilton
STEPHENS, Alice Barber 1
STEPHENS, 1
Ambrose E. B.
STEPHENS, Ann Sophia H
STEPHENS, 5
Benjamin Hugbl
STEPHENS, 1
Charles Asbury
STEPHENS, Claude P. 4
STEPHENS, 4
Clyde Harrison
STEPHENS, Dan
Voorhees 1
STEPHENS, 4
Daniel Mallory
STEPHENS, 1
David Stubert
STEPHENS, Edwin Lewis 1
STEPHENS, 1
Edwin William
STEPHENS, Ferris J. 5
STEPHENS, Frank 1
STEPHENS, George 2
STEPHENS, 2
George Asbury
STEPHENS, George Ware 1
STEPHENS, Guy Frederic 4
STEPHENS, H. Morse 1
STEPHENS, 5
Harley Clifford
STEPHENS, 3
Harold Montelle
STEPHENS, Harry T. 2
STEPHENS, 1
Herbert Taylor
STEPHENS, Howard V. 3
STEPHENS, 2
Hubert Durrett
STEPHENS, James 3
STEPHENS, 5
James C(ollins)
STEPHENS, John Hall 4
STEPHENS, John Leonard 1
STEPHENS, John Lloyd H
STEPHENS, John Vant 2
STEPHENS, Kate 1
STEPHENS, 1
Lawrence Vest
STEPHENS, Leroy 4
STEPHENS, Linton H
STEPHENS, Louis L. 4
STEPHENS, Martin Bates 1
STEPHENS, Oren Melson 5
STEPHENS, Percy Rector 4
STEPHENS, Philander H
STEPHENS, 5
Philip B(lanton)
STEPHENS, 1
Redmond Davis
STEPHENS, Robert Allan 2

STEPHENS, 1
Robert Neilson
STEPHENS, 3
Roswell Powell
STEPHENS, 4
Russell Stout
STEPHENS, 4
Theodore Pierson
STEPHENS, Uriah Smith H
STEPHENS, 5
W(illiam) Barclay
STEPHENS, Ward 1
STEPHENS, 2
William Dennison
STEPHENSON, Benjamin H
STEPHENSON, H
Benjamin Franklin
STEPHENSON, C. S. 4
STEPHENSON, Carl 3
STEPHENSON, 1
Edward Morris
STEPHENSON, 4
Franklin Bache
STEPHENSON, 3
George Malcolm
STEPHENSON, 5
Gilbert Thomas
STEPHENSON, Henry
Thew 5
STEPHENSON, Isaac 1
STEPHENSON, James H
STEPHENSON, James 2
STEPHENSON, 3
James Pomeroy
STEPHENSON, John 2
STEPHENSON, 1
Joseph Maxwell
STEPHENSON, 1
Nathaniel Wright
STEPHENSON, 4
Orlistus Bell
STEPHENSON, 1
Rome Charles
STEPHENSON, S. Town 2
STEPHENSON, Sam 5
STEPHENSON, 4
Wendell Holmes
STEPHENSON, William 3
STEPHENSON, 4
William B. Jr.
STEPHENSON, 4
William Benjamin
STEPHENSON, 5
William Lawrence
STEPHENSON, 1
William Prettyman
STEPHENSON, 4
William Worth
STEPPAT, Leo 2
STEPTOE, H
Philip Pendleton
STERETT, Andrew H
STERETT, Samuel H
STERIGERE, John Benton H
STERKI, Victor 4
STERLEY, William F. 5
STERLING, Ansel 3
STERLING, Bruce F. 1
STERLING, 3
Donald Justus
STERLING, 1
Edward Canfield
STERLING, 3
Frederick Augustine
STERLING, George 1
STERLING, 5
George Matheson
STERLING, Graham Lee 5
STERLING, Guy 1
STERLING, James H
STERLING, John A. 4
STERLING, John C. 1
STERLING, John Whalen H
STERLING, John William 1
STERLING, Micah H
STERLING, Ross Shaw 1
STERLING, Theodore 3
STERLING, Thomas 1
STERLING, W. T. 3
STERN, Alfred Whital 4
STERN, Bernhard Joseph 5
STERN, Bill 5
STERN, David Becker 4
STERN, Edgar Bloom 4
STERN, Elizabeth 3
STERN, Henry Root 5
STERN, Horace 5
STERN, Isaac Farber 1
STERN, Jo Lane 1
STERN, Joseph Smith 1
STERN, Joseph William H
STERN, Joseph William 1
STERN, Julius David 5
STERN, Kurt Guenter 3
STERN, Lawrence Fish 5
STERN, Louis 1
STERN, Louis 5

STERN, Nathan 2
STERN, Sigmund 3
STERN, Simon Adler 1
STERN, 5
William Bernhard
STERNBERG, 2
Charles Hazellus
STERNBERG, 1
George Miller
STERNBERG, Walter 4
STERNBERGER, 5
Mrs. Estelle Miller
STERNBURG, 1
Herman 'von Speck
STERNE, Albert Eugene 1
STERNE, Maurice 3
STERNE, Niel Paul 1
STERNE, Simon 1
STERNE, 5
Theodore Eugene
STERNER, Albert 2
STERNHAGEN, John 3
Meler
STERNHELL, Charles 5
Max
STERRETT, 2
Frances Roberta
STERRETT, 1
James Macbridge
STERRETT, 1
James Ralston
STERRETT, 1
John Robert Sitlington
STETEFELDT, H
Carl August
STETSON, Augusta E. 1
STETSON, 1
Caleb Rochford
STETSON, Charles H
STETSON, H
Charles Augustus
STETSON, 1
Charles Walter
STETSON, 3
Eugene William
STETSON, Harlan True 4
STETSON, Henry Crosby 4
STETSON, Herbert Lee 4
STETSON, Isaiah Kidder 1
STETSON, 1
John Batterson
STETSON, Lemuel H
STETSON, Paul Clifford 1
STETSON, 3
Raymond Herbert
STETSON, Thomas Drew 1
STETSON, 1
William Wallace
STETSON, 1
Willis Kimball
STETTEN, DeWitt 3
STETTINIUS, Edward R. 1
STETTINIUS, 2
Edward R. Jr.
STETTNER, 4
Ludwig Wilhelmin
STEUART, George Hume 1
STEUART, 3
James Aloysius
STEUBEN, H
friedrich Wilhelm Ludolf
Gerhard Augustin 'v
STEUER, Max David H
STEUER, Max David 1
STEUERMANN, Edward 4
STEVENOT, 5
Fred Gabriel;
STEVENS, H
Aaron Fletcher
STEVENS, Abel H
STEVENS, Adie Allan 3
STEVENS, Albert Clark 4
STEVENS, Alden 5
STEVENS, H
Alexander Hodgdon
STEVENS, 5
Alexander Raymond
STEVENS, 1
Alviso Burdett
STEVENS, 1
Anna C. Mann (mrs. Frank
Jay Stevens)
STEVENS, Arthur Albert 1
STEVENS, Ashton 3
STEVENS, Beatrice 2
STEVENS, 1
Benjamin Franklin
STEVENS, H
Bradford Newcomb
STEVENS, Charles A. 1
STEVENS, Charles Abbot H
STEVENS, 3
Charles Brooks
STEVENS, Charles Ellis 1
STEVENS, H
Clement Hoffman
STEVENS, Cyrus Lee 4

STEVENS, 3
Daisy McLaurin
STEVENS, Daniel Gurden 1
STEVENS, David 2
STEVENS, Don Albert 5
STEVENS, Doris 4
STEVENS, Durham White 1
STEVENS, E. Ray 1
STEVENS, Eben Sutton 4
STEVENS, 2
Edward Fletcher
STEVENS, 3
Edward Francis
STEVENS, 5
Edward Lawrence
STEVENS, H
Edwin Augustus
STEVENS, 1
Edwin Augustus
STEVENS, Elbert Marcus 1
STEVENS, Elisha H
STEVENS, Ellen Yale 5
STEVENS, Elmer T. 5
STEVENS, Ernest James 5
STEVENS, Eugene 2
Morgan
STEVENS, 1
Evarts Chapman 3
STEVENS, 5
Everett Duncan
STEVENS, 5
Francis Bowden
STEVENS, Frank Jay 5
STEVENS, Frank Lincoln 1
STEVENS, Frank Walker 1
STEVENS, 2
Frederic Bliss
STEVENS, 5
Frederic William
STEVENS, 5
Frederick Charles
STEVENS, 5
Frederick Clement
STEVENS, 5
Frederick Waeir
STEVENS, George Barker 1
STEVENS, George 1
Thomas
STEVENS, George Walter 1
STEVENS, 1
George Washington
STEVENS, 5
Gorham Phillips
STEVENS, Harry Clay 1
STEVENS, Hazard 1
STEVENS, Henry H
STEVENS, Henry Davis 4
STEVENS, 5
Henry Leonidas, Jr.
STEVENS, Henry M. 3
STEVENS, H
Hestor Lockhart
STEVENS, 1
Hiram Fairchild
STEVENS, Hiram Sanford H
STEVENS, Horace Jared 1
STEVENS, 5
Howard Eveleth
STEVENS, Inger 5
STEVENS, Isaac Ingalls H
STEVENS, Isaac Newton 1
STEVENS, J. Franklin 1
STEVENS, James H
STEVENS, James Floyd 5
STEVENS, 1
James Franklin
STEVENS, James Stacy 1
STEVENS, James William 1
STEVENS, John * H
STEVENS, John Amos 1
STEVENS, John Austin H
STEVENS, John Austin 1
STEVENS, John Calvin 1
STEVENS, John F. 4
STEVENS, John Leavitt 1
STEVENS, John Loomis 4
STEVENS, John Morgan 5
STEVENS, Lawrence M. 5
STEVENS, Leith 5
STEVENS, Leslie Clark 3
STEVENS, Lewis Miller 4
STEVENS, Lillian M. N. 1
STEVENS, Maltby 3
STEVENS, Milton J. 5
STEVENS, Nathaniel 2
STEVENS, Neil Everett 5
STEVENS, P. F. 1
STEVENS, Patricia 5
STEVENS, Ray Parker 4
STEVENS, 2
Raymond Bartlett
STEVENS, 1
Raymond William
STEVENS,
Robert Livingston
STEVENS, Robert Smith H

STEVENS, Robert Sproule 5
STEVENS, Rollin Howard 2
STEVENS, Roy George 2
STEVENS, S(tanley) Smith 5
STEVENS, Samuel Nowell 4
STEVENS, Sheppard 4
STEVENS, Solon Whithed 4
STEVENS, Terrill D. 4
STEVENS, Thaddeus H
STEVENS, Thomas Holdup * H
STEVENS, Thomas Holdup III 1
STEVENS, Thomas McCorvey 2
STEVENS, Thomas Wood 1
STEVENS, Thomas Wood 2
STEVENS, Truman S. 3
STEVENS, Wallace 3
STEVENS, Walter Barlow 1
STEVENS, Walter Husted H
STEVENS, Walter Le Conte 1
STEVENS, Wayne Edson 3
STEVENS, William Arnold 1
STEVENS, William Bacon H
STEVENS, William Bertrand 2
STEVENS, William Burnham 4
STEVENS, William Chase 3
STEVENS, William Dodge 2
STEVENS, William Harrison Spring 5
STEVENS, William Lester 5
STEVENS, William Oliver 3
STEVENSON, Adlai Ewing 1
STEVENSON, Adlai Ewing 4
STEVENSON, Alec Brock 5
STEVENSON, Alexander Russell Jr.
STEVENSON, Andrew H
STEVENSON, Andrew 1
STEVENSON, Archibald Ewing 4
STEVENSON, Archie Mac Nicol 4
STEVENSON, Beulah 4
STEVENSON, Burton 4
STEVENSON, C. Albert 5
STEVENSON, Carter Littlepage H
STEVENSON, Charles Hugh 2
STEVENSON, Edward Irenaeus 2
STEVENSON, Edward Irenaeus 4
STEVENSON, Edward Luther 2
STEVENSON, Eldon, Jr. 5
STEVENSON, Elliott Grasette 1
STEVENSON, Eugene 1
STEVENSON, Frank Herbert 1
STEVENSON, Frederic Augustus
STEVENSON, Frederick 2
STEVENSON, Frederick Alfred
STEVENSON, Frederick Boyd 1
STEVENSON, George 1
STEVENSON, Guy 4
STEVENSON, Holland Newton 3
STEVENSON, Howard A. 3
STEVENSON, J. Ross 1
STEVENSON, James H
STEVENSON, James Henry 1
STEVENSON, James S. H
STEVENSON, John Alford 2
STEVENSON, John James
STEVENSON, John White H
STEVENSON, Katharine Adelia Lent 1
STEVENSON, Lewis Green 1
STEVENSON, Marcia Jacobs 5
STEVENSON, Marion 5
STEVENSON, Mark Delimon 1
STEVENSON, Markley 4
STEVENSON, Matilda Coxe 1
STEVENSON, Paul Eve 1

STEVENSON, Richard Corwine 3
STEVENSON, Richard Taylor 1
STEVENSON, Robert Montgomery 4
STEVENSON, Sara Yorke 1
STEVENSON, Sarah Hackett
STEVENSON, Thomas Patton 4
STEVENSON, W. C. 3
STEVENSON, Wade 5
STEVENSON, Walter Anson 4
STEVENSON, Wilbert Everett 4
STEVENSON, William Francis 2
STEVENSON, William Henry 3
STEVENSON, William Holmes 1
STEVENSON, William Patton 3
STEVENSON, William Taylor 3
STEVICK, David William
STEWARD, Ira H
STEWARD, Joseph H
STEWARD, Julian H. 2
STEWARD, LeRoy T. 2
STEWARD, Lewis H
STEWARD, Thomas Gifford
STEWARDSON, Emlyn Lamar 1
STEWARDSON, John H
STEWARDSON, Langdon Cheves 4
STEWART, Adiel Fitzgerald 4
STEWART, Albert 4
STEWART, Alexander 1
STEWART, Alexander Mair 1
STEWART, Alexander P. H
STEWART, Alexander Turney
STEWART, Allison Vance 4
STEWART, Alpheus Lloyd 1
STEWART, Alphonso Chase 1
STEWART, Alvan H
STEWART, Andrew H
STEWART, Cecil Parker 2
STEWART, Charles * 1
STEWART, Charles Allan 5
STEWART, Charles D. 5
STEWART, Charles Seaforth
STEWART, Charles West 2
STEWART, Colin Campbell
STEWART, David H
STEWART, David 4
STEWART, David Denison 1
STEWART, De Lisle 2
STEWART, Donald Farquharson
STEWART, Douglas 1
STEWART, Douglas Hunt 5
STEWART, Duncan 1
STEWART, Edwin 1
STEWART, Eliza Daniel 5
STEWART, Ella Seass 5
STEWART, Ethelbert 1
STEWART, Ford 5
STEWART, Francis Robert 5
STEWART, Francis Torrens 1
STEWART, Frank Mann 4
STEWART, Frank R. 5
STEWART, Fred 5
STEWART, Fred Carlton 1
STEWART, Frederick William 5
STEWART, George 3
STEWART, George 5
STEWART, George Black 1
STEWART, George Craig 1
STEWART, George David 1
STEWART, George H. 1
STEWART, George James 3
STEWART, George Neil 1
STEWART, George Taylor 1
STEWART, George Walter 1
STEWART, Gideon Tabor 1
STEWART, Gilbert Henry 5
STEWART, Grace Bliss 1
STEWART, Graeme 1
STEWART, Harlon L. 1
STEWART, Humphrey John

STEWART, Isabel Maitland 4
STEWART, Ivey Withers 4
STEWART, J. D. 2
STEWART, Jacob Henry H
STEWART, James H
STEWART, James 3
STEWART, James Augustus H
STEWART, James Christian 2
STEWART, James Fleming 1
STEWART, James Garfield 3
STEWART, Jane Agnes 2
STEWART, John * H
STEWART, John 1
STEWART, John Aikman 1
STEWART, John Alexander 5
STEWART, John Appleton 1
STEWART, John David H
STEWART, John K. 4
STEWART, John Lammey 1
STEWART, John Leighton 1
STEWART, John Leslie 5
STEWART, John Minor 1
STEWART, John Quincy 5
STEWART, John Truesdale 1
STEWART, John Wolcott 1
STEWART, Joseph 1
STEWART, Joseph Spencer 2
STEWART, Joseph William Alexander
STEWART, Judd 2
STEWART, Julius L. 4
STEWART, Lispenard 1
STEWART, Malcolm Chilson 5
STEWART, Malcolm Montrose 1
STEWART, Merch Bradt 4
STEWART, Morris Albion 4
STEWART, Nathaniel Bacon 1
STEWART, Oline Johnson 5
STEWART, Oliver Wayne 2
STEWART, Oscar Milton 3
STEWART, Paul 3
STEWART, Paul Morton 3
STEWART, Paul William 3
STEWART, Percy Hamilton 5
STEWART, Philip Battell H
STEWART, Philo Penfield 4
STEWART, Randall 3
STEWART, Rex William 2
STEWART, Richard Siegfried 1
STEWART, Robert 3
STEWART, Robert Giffen 1
STEWART, Robert Laird H
STEWART, Robert Marcellus 2
STEWART, Robert Wright 1
STEWART, Rowe 1
STEWART, Russell C. 2
STEWART, Russell C.
STEWART, Samuel Vernon H
STEWART, Sir William Drummond 4
STEWART, T. Mccants 1
STEWART, Thomas Jamison
STEWART, Thomas Milton 2
STEWART, Tom 5
STEWART, Walter Allan 5
STEWART, Walter W. 4
STEWART, Wilbur Filson 3
STEWART, William 4
STEWART, William Alvah 1
STEWART, William Finney Bay 1
STEWART, William Henry 2
STEWART, William Kilborne 1
STEWART, William Lyman 4
STEWART, William Lyman Jr. 1
STEWART, William Morris 1
STEWART, William Rhinelander 1
STEWART, William Shaw
STEYNE, Alan Nathaniel 2
STIBITZ, George 2
STICKLE, John Wesley 5
STICKLES, Arndt Mathis 3
STICKLEY, Ezra Eugenius

STICKLEY, Gustav 4
STICKLEY, Albert 1
STICKNEY, Alpheus Beede 1
STICKNEY, Amos 1
STICKNEY, Herman Osman
STICKNEY, Joseph L. 1
STICKNEY, Julia Noyes 4
STICKNEY, Samuel Crosby 1
STIDGER, William Leroy 2
STIDLEY, Leonard Albert 3
STIEFFEL, Hermann H
STIEG, Max 5
STIEGEL, Henry William H
STIEGLITZ, Alfred 2
STIEGLITZ, Julius 1
STIFLER, James Madison 1
STIFLER, James Madison 3
STIGLER, William G. 1
STILES, Charles Wardell 1
STILES, Edward H. 4
STILES, Ezra H
STILES, Fred Bailey 5
STILES, George K(ean) 5
STILES, Hinson 5
STILES, James Esmond 4
STILES, James F. Jr. 4
STILES, John Dodson H
STILES, Meredith Newcomb 1
STILES, Percy Goldthwait 1
STILES, Theodore Lamme 1
STILES, William Curtis 5
STILES, William Henry H
STILL, Alfred 5
STILL, Andrew Taylor 1
STILL, Clyfford 4
STILL, William 1
STILLE, Alfred 1
STILLE, Charles Janeway 5
STILLINGS, Charles Arthur 1
STILLINGS, Ephraim Bailey 3
STILLMAN, Charles Clark 1
STILLMAN, James Alexander 5
STILLMAN, John Maxson H
STILLMAN, Paul Roscoe 2
STILLMAN, Samuel H
STILLMAN, Stanley 1
STILLMAN, Thomas Bliss 3
STILLMAN, Walter N.
STILLMAN, William James 1
STILLMAN, William Olin 1
STILLWELL, Homer Allison 4
STILLWELL, Lewis Buckley 1
STILLWELL, Thomas Neel H
STILLWELL, William Burney 5
STILSON, Oscar Reeves 1
STILWELL, Abner J. 3
STILWELL, Arthur Edward 1
STILWELL, Edmund William 2
STILWELL, Herbert Fenton 5
STILWELL, Joseph W. 4
STILWELL, Silas Moore H
STIMETS, Charles Calvin 5
STIMPSON, George William H
STIMPSON, Herbert Baird 1
STIMPSON, William 5
STIMPSON, William G. 1
STIMSON, Arthur Marston 1
STIMSON, Charles D. 2
STIMSON, Daniel MacMartin 2
STIMSON, Frederic Jesup 1
STIMSON, Henry Albert 3
STIMSON, Henry Lewis 1
STIMSON, John Ward 1
STIMSON, Julia Catherine
STIMSON, Lewis Atterbury

STIMSON, Philip Moen 5
STIMSON, Rufus Whittaker 4
STIMSON, Thomas Douglas 1
STINCHFIELD, Frederick Harold 2
STINCHFIELD, Roger Adams 5
STINE, Charles Milton Altland 3
STINE, John William Jr. 3
STINE, Milton Henry 1
STINE, Wilbur Morris 1
STINESS, John Henry 1
STINESS, Walter Russell 4
STINSON, John Turner 5
STIRES, Ernest Milmore 3
STIRLEN, Eugene Dare 4
STIRLING, J. Bowman 5
STIRLING, Yates 1
STIRLING, Yates Jr. 2
STIRTON, Ruben Arthur 1
STITES, Fletcher Wilbur 1
STITES, John 1
STITH, William H
STITH, Wilmer Curtis 4
STITT, Edward Rhodes 2
STITT, Edward Walmsley 1
STITT, William Britton 5
STIVEN, Frederic Benjamin 2
STIVERS, Edwin Jacob 4
STIVERS, Kazia Armington 4
STIVERS, Moses Dunning H
STIX, Ernest William 3
STIX, Sylvan L. 5
STOAKS, Charles E. 4
STOBBS, George Russell 4
STOBO, Robert H
STOCK, Chester 4
STOCK, Frederick A. 2
STOCK, Harry T. 3
STOCK, Joseph Whiting H
STOCKARD, Charles Rupert 1
STOCKARD, Henry Jerome 1
STOCKARD, Virginia Alice Cottey 1
STOCKBARGER, Donald C. 3
STOCKBERGER, Warner W. 2
STOCKBRIDGE, Francis Brown H
STOCKBRIDGE, Frank Parker 1
STOCKBRIDGE, Henry 1
STOCKBRIDGE, Henry Smith H
STOCKBRIDGE, Horace Edward 1
STOCKDALE, Allen Arthur 5
STOCKDALE, Grant 4
STOCKDALE, Paris B. 4
STOCKDALE, Thomas Ringland H
STOCKDER, Archibald Herbert 4
STOCKER, Harry Emilius 1
STOCKHAM, Alice Bunker 1
STOCKHAM, Edward Villeroy 1
STOCKHAM, William Henry 1
STOCKING, Charles Francis 5
STOCKING, Charles Howard 3
STOCKING, Jay Thomas 1
STOCKING, William Alonzo Jr. 1
STOCKMAN, Lowell 4
STOCKSLAGER, Charles O. 4
STOCKSTROM, Louis 2
STOCKTON, Charles G. 1
STOCKTON, Charles Herbert 1
STOCKTON, Edward A. Jr. 2
STOCKTON, Ernest 3
STOCKTON, Francis Richard 1
STOCKTON, Fred Everett 1
STOCKTON, George 1
STOCKTON, Howard 1
STOCKTON, J(ames) Roy 5
STOCKTON, John Potter H
STOCKTON, Joseph 1

STOCKTON,
 Joseph Denniston 4
STOCKTON, Kenneth E. 3
STOCKTON, Louise 5
STOCKTON, Richard * H
STOCKTON, Robert Field H
STOCKTON, Robert
 Henry 1
STOCKTON,
 Thomas Hewlings H
STOCKTON,
 William Tennent 1
STOCKWELL,
 Chester Twitchell
STOCKWELL, 5
 Eugene Lafayette
STOCKWELL, 2
 Frank Clifford
STOCKWELL, 1
 Frederick Emerson
STOCKWELL, 4
 Herbert Grant
STOCKWELL, John
 Nelson
STOCKWELL, 5
 John Wesley, Jr.
STOCKWELL, Samuel B. H
STOCKWELL, 1
 Thomas Blanchard
STOCKWELL, 3
 Walter Lincoln
STODDARD, 5
 A(rthur) E(lsworth)
STODDARD, 4
 Alexander Jerry
STODDARD, Amos H
STODDARD, 1
 Charles Augustus
STODDARD, 5
 Charles Coleman
STODDARD, 1
 Charles Warren
STODDARD, Cora 5
 Frances
STODDARD, David
 Tappan H
STODDARD, Ebenezer H
STODDARD, 1
 Elizabeth Drew Barstow
STODDARD, Enoch Vine 5
 Florence Jackson
STODDARD, 5
 Francis Hovey
STODDARD, 3
 Francis Russell
STODDARD, Harry G. 5
STODDARD, Henry
 Luther
STODDARD, Howard J. 5
STODDARD, 5
 James Alexander
STODDARD, John Fair H
STODDARD, John
 Lawson 1
STODDARD, John
 Tappan 1
STODDARD, Joshua C: H
STODDARD, Lothrop 3
STODDARD, 1
 Richard Henry
STODDARD, 5
 Robert Curtis
STODDARD, Sanford 3
STODDARD, Solomon H
STODDARD, Thomas A. 5
STODDARD, 3
 William Leavitt
STODDARD,
 William Osborn
STODDART, 5
 Charles William
STODDART, James Henry 1
STODDART,
 Joseph Marshall
STODDART, 5
 L(aurence) A.
STODDERT, Benjamin H
STODDERT, John
 Truman H
STOECKEL, Carl 1
STOECKEL, 1
 Gustave Jacob
STOECKEL, Robbins B. 4
STOEHR, Max W. 3
STOEK, Harry Harkness 1
STOEPLER, Ambrose M. 5
STOESSEL, Albert 2
STOETZER, 1
 Herman Goethe
STOEVER, Martin Luther 1
STOEVER, 4
 William Caspar
STOFFER, Bryan Sewall 4
STOKDYK, Ellis Adolph 2
STOKE, John M. 4

STOKELY, Jehu Thomas 3
STOKELY, Samuel H
STOKELY, 4
 William Burnett Jr.
STOKES, Andrew Jackson 3
STOKES, Anson Phelps 1
STOKES, Anson Phelps 3
STOKES, Arthur Charles 1
STOKES, 1
 Charles Francis
STOKES, 4
 Charles Senseney
STOKES, Edward Casper 2
STOKES, Edward Lowber 4
STOKES, Francis Joseph 3
STOKES, Frank Wilbert 3
STOKES, 1
 Frederick Abbot
STOKES, Harold Phelps 5
STOKES, Henry Bolter 4
STOKES, Henry Newlin 5
STOKES, 1
 Henry Warrington
STOKES, Horace Winston 2
STOKES, 2
 Isaac Newton Phelps
STOKES, J. G. Phelps 3
STOKES, James William 1
STOKES,
 John Harrison, Jr.
STOKES, John Patrick 1
STOKES, John Stogdell 2
STOKES, Joseph, Jr. 5
STOKES, Montfort 4
STOKES, Richard Leroy 3
STOKES, Rose Pastor 1
STOKES, 3
 Thomas Lunsford Jr.
STOKES, H
 William Brickly
STOKES, William Herman 3
STOLAND, Ole Olufson 3
STOLBERG, Benjamin 3
STOLEE, Michael J. 2
STOLL, 1
 Charles Augustus
STOLL, Harry 4
STOLL, Philip Henry 3
STOLL, Richard Charles 2
STOLLER, James Hough 4
STOLLER, Morton Joseph 4
STOLPER, Gustav 4
STOLTZ, Charles Edward 4
STOLTZ, Robert Bear 2
STOLZ, Benjamin 1
STOLZ, Joseph 1
STOLZ, Karl Ruf 2
STOLZ, Leon 5
STOMBERG, Andrew
 Adin 2
STONE, Abraham 3
STONE, Albert Jmes 3
STONE, Alfred 1
STONE, Alfred Holt 4
STONE, Alfred Parish H
STONE, Allison 1
STONE, Amasa H
STONE, Andrew Jackson 4
STONE, 2
 Arthur Fairbanks
STONE, Arthur John 1
STONE, Barton Warren H
STONE, Caleb 4
STONE, Calvin Perry 3
STONE,
 Carlos Huntington
STONE, Charles Arthur 2
STONE, 1
 Charles Augustus
STONE, Charles Edwin 3
STONE, Charles Francis 1
STONE, 5
 Charles Frederic
STONE, Charles Holmes 4
STONE, Charles Newhall 1
STONE, Charles Pomeroy H
STONE, Charles Warren 1
STONE,
 Charles Waterman
STONE,
 Charles Wellington
STONE, 3
 Claudius Ulysses
STONE, Cliff Winfield 5
STONE, Clyde Ernest 2
STONE, David H
STONE, David Lamme 5
STONE, David Marvin 1
STONE, Eben Francis H
STONE,
 Ebenezer Whittier
STONE, Ellen Maria 1
STONE, Emanuel Olson 1
STONE, Emerson Law 3
STONE, Fred Andrew 3
STONE, Fred Denton 1
STONE, Frederick 1

STONE, Frederick E. 5
STONE, George Edward 1
STONE, 1
 George Frederick
STONE, George Hapgood 1
STONE, H
 George Washington
STONE, 1
 George Whitefield
STONE, H(enry) Charles 5
STONE, H. Chase 5
STONE, Harlan Fiske 5
STONE, Harold 3
STONE, Harry Everette 4
STONE, Harry R. 4
STONE, Henry Lane 1
STONE, 3
 Herbert Lawrence
STONE, Herbert Stuart 5
STONE, Horace Greeley 1
STONE, Horace M. 2
STONE, Horatio 1
STONE, Hugh Lamar 4
STONE, Isaac Scott 4
STONE, Isabelle 5
STONE, Ivan McKinley 5
STONE, 5
 J(ohn) McWilliams
STONE, James Lauriston 5
STONE, James Samuel 1
STONE, James W. H
STONE, John Augustus H
STONE, John Charles 1
STONE, John Francis 1
STONE, John Holden 1
STONE, John Marshall 1
STONE, John Paul 5
STONE, John Pittman 1
STONE, John Seely H
STONE, John Stone 2
STONE, John Theodore 1
STONE, John Wesley 1
STONE, Joseph Cecil 2
STONE, Joseph E. 3
STONE, Judson F. 3
STONE, 2
 Julius Frederick
STONE, 3
 Kenneth Franklin
STONE, Kimbrough 3
STONE, L. A. 4
STONE, Lauson 3
STONE, Lewis 3
STONE, Livingston 1
STONE, Lucy H
STONE, 4
 Malcolm Bowditch
STONE, 5
 Margaret Manson Barbour
STONE, Mason Sereno 4
STONE, Melville Elijah 1
STONE, Michael Jenifer H
STONE, N. I. 4
STONE, Nat 1
STONE, Ormond 1
STONE, Patrick Thomas 4
STONE, Philip Carlton 5
STONE, Raleigh Webster 1
STONE, Ralph 3
STONE, Ralph Walter 4
STONE, Robert Elwin 5
STONE, Robert Franklin 1
STONE, Robert Spencer 5
STONE, Royal Augustus 2
STONE, Rufus Barrett 1
STONE, Samuel H
STONE, Samuel M. 3
STONE, 3
 Theodore Thaddeus
STONE, Thomas H
STONE, H
 Thomas Treadwell
STONE, Walker 5
STONE, Walter King 5
STONE, Walter Robinson 1
STONE, Warren 1
STONE, Wilbur Fisk 1
STONE, Willard John 2
STONE, William * H
STONE, William Alexis 1
STONE, William Alexis 1
STONE, William Alexis 4
STONE, William Joel 1
STONE, William Leete 1
STONE, William Leete 1
STONE, William Oliver H
STONE,
 William S(ebastian)
STONE, Wilson S(tuart) 1
STONE, 1
 Winthrop Ellsworth
STONE, Witmer 1
STONEHOUSE, 4
 Ned Bernard
STONEMAN, Frank B. 1
STONEMAN, George H

STONER, Dayton 2
STONER, Frank E. 4
STONER, George Hiram 1
STONER, 1
 Mrs. Winifred Sackville
STONER, William David 4
STONG, Philip Duffield 3
STONIER, Harold 3
STONOROV, Oskar 5
STOOKEY, Byron 4
STOOKEY, 1
 Lyman Brumbaugh
STOOKEY, 3
 Stephen Wharton
STOOKSBURY, 4
 William Lafayette
STOOTHOFF, Everett O. 5
STORCKMAN, 5
 Clem Franklin
STORER, Bellamy H
STORER, Bellamy H
STORER, Clement H
STORER,
 David Humphreys
STORER, 1
 Francis Humphreys
STORER,
 Horatio Robinson
STORER, John
 Humphreys 1
STORER, 1
 Maria Longworth
STORER, Norman Wilson 3
STORER,
 Robert Treat Paine
STOREY, Moorfield 1
STOREY, 4
 Robert Gerald Jr.
STOREY, Thomas Andrew 2
STOREY, Walter Rendell 5
STOREY, Wilbur Fisk H
STOREY, William Benson 1
STORING, James Alvin 4
STORKE, 2
 Arthur Ditchfield
STORKE, Thomas More 5
STORM, Hans Otto 2
STORM, John M. 3
STORM, 5
 Mildred Raum (Mrs.
 Edward
 D. Storm)
STORMS, Albert Boynton 1
STORROW, James
 Jackson H
STORROW, James
 Jackson 1
STORRS, Caryl B. 1
STORRS, Harry Asahel 5
STORRS, Henry Randolph H
STORRS, John 4
STORRS, Leonard Kip 1
STORRS, Lewis Austin 2
STORRS, Lucius Seymour 1
STORRS, Richard Salter H
STORRS, Richard Salter 5
STORRS,
 Robert Williamson, III
STORRS, William Lucius H
STORY, Douglas 5
STORY, Francis Quarles 4
STORY, George Henry 1
STORY, Isaac 1
STORY, John Patten 1
STORY, Joseph 1
STORY, Julian 1
STORY, Nelson Jr. 1
STORY, 2
 Russell McCulloch
STORY, Walter P. 5
STORY, Walter Scott 3
STORY, William Edward 1
STORY, William Wetmore H
STORZ, Todd 4
STOSE, George Willis 1
STOTESBURY,
 Edward Townsend
STOTESBURY, 2
 Louis William
STOTSENBURG, 1
 Evan Brown
STOTT, Henry Gordon 1
STOTT, Roscoe Gilmore 3
STOTZ, Edward Jr. 4
STOUDT, John Baer 2
STOUFFER, Gordon A. 3
STOUFFER, 4
 Samuel Andrew
STOUGH, 1
 Henry Wellington
STOUGHTON, Bradley 3
STOUGHTON,
 Charles William
STOUGHTON, H
 Edwin Wallace
STOUGHTON, William H

STOUGHTON, H
 William Lewis
STOUT, Aaron James 4
STOUT, Arlow Burdette 3
STOUT, Arthur Purdy 4
STOUT, Byron Gray H
STOUT, Charles Banks 5
STOUT, 5
 Charles Frederick Cloua
STOUT, Elmer William 4
STOUT, George Abeel 5
STOUT, George Clymer 5
STOUT, Henry Elbert 5
STOUT, Henry Rice 1
STOUT, Hiram Miller 5
STOUT, Howard A. 3
STOUT, James Coffin 1
STOUT, James Huff 1
STOUT, John Elbert 5
STOUT, Joseph Duerson 2
STOUT, Lansing H
STOUT, Lawrence Edward 5
STOUT, Oscar Van Pelt 1
STOUT, Ralph Emerson 1
STOUT, Selatie Edgar 5
STOUT, Tom 1
STOUT, Wesley Winans 5
STOUT, 3
 William Bushnell
STOVALL, 1
 Pleasant Alexander
STOVALL, 3
 Wallace Fisher
STOVALL, 4
 William Robert
STOVER, George Henry 1
STOVER, John Hubler H
STOVER, Martin Luther 1
STOVER, William Miller 4
STOW, Baron H
STOW, Charles Messer 3
STOW, Marcellus H. 3
STOW, Micollius Noel 4
STOW, Silas H
STOWE, 3
 Ansel Roy Monroe
STOWE, Calvin Ellis 4
STOWE, Charles Edward 1
STOWE,
 Frederick Arthur
STOWE, H
 Harriet Elizabeth Beecher
STOWE, Lyman Beecher 4
STOWE, Robert Lee 4
STOWELL,
 Calvin Llewellyn
STOWELL, 1
 Charles Frederick
STOWELL, Charles Henry 1
STOWELL, Ellery Cory 3
STOWELL, Frederick M. 1
STOWELL, Jay Samuel 5
STOWELL,
 Kenneth Kingsley
STOWELL, 4
 Louise Maria Reed
STOWELL, 1
 Thomas Blanchard
STOWELL, 1
 William Henry Harrison
STOWER, John G. H
STRABEL, Thelma 3
STRACHAN, Paul
 Ambrose 5
STRACHAN,
 Thomas Curr Jr.
STRACHAUER, Arthur C. 4
STRACHEY, John 4
STRACHEY, Lionel 1
STRACHEY, William 4
STRADER, Bernard Earl 2
STRADER, Peter Wilson H
STRADLEY, Bland Lloyd 3
STRADLEY, 3
 Leighton Paxton
STRADLING,
 George Flowers
STRAEHLEY, Erwin Sr. 2
STRAFER, Harriette R. 5
STRAGNELL, Gregory 2
STRAHAN,
 Charles Morton
STRAHAN, Hazel Blair 4
STRAHAN, Kay Cleaver 1
STRAHM, Victor H. 3
STRAHORN,
 Robert Edmund
STRAIGHT, 4
 Herbert Randall
STRAIGHT, 1
 Willard Dickerman
STRAIN, Isaac G. H
STRAIT,
 Thomas Jefferson
STRAKE, George William 5
STRAKOSCH, Maurice

Name	
STRANAHAN, Edgar Howard	2
STRANAHAN, James Samuel Thomas	H
STRANAHAN, Nevada Northrop	4
STRANAHAN, Robert Allen	4
STRANDJORD, Nels Magne	5
STRANG, Elmore Steele	4
STRANG, James Jesse	1
STRANG, Lewis Clinton	1
STRANG, S. Bartow	3
STRANGE, John	4
STRANGE, Michael	3
STRANGE, Robert	1
STRANGE, Robert	1
STRANGE, Robert	4
STRANSKY, Franklin J.	4
STRANSKY, Josef	1
STRASBURGER, Milton	3
STRASSBURGER, Ralph Beaver	4
STRATEMEYER, Edward	1
STRATEMEYER, George E.	5
STRATHALMOND, Lord	5
STRATHEARN, Harold	4
STRATON, John Roach	1
STRATTON, Charles Creighton	H
STRATTON, Charles Sherwood	H
STRATTON, Clarence	3
STRATTON, Clif (Clifton Jarius)	5
STRATTON, Clif Jr.	4
STRATTON, Don B.	3
STRATTON, Frederick Eugene	1
STRATTON, Frederick Smith	1
STRATTON, George Malcolm	3
STRATTON, Harold M.	4
STRATTON, John	H
STRATTON, Lloyd	4
STRATTON, Margaret Elizabeth	4
STRATTON, Melville Norcross	5
STRATTON, Nathan Taylor	H
STRATTON, Samuel Sommerville	5
STRATTON, Samuel Wesley	1
STRATTON, William B.	1
STRAUB, Christian Markle	H
STRAUB, Lorenz George	4
STRAUB, Oscar Itin	4
STRAUB, Walter F.	4
STRAUCH, John B.	2
STRAUGHN, James Henry	5
STRAUGHN, William Ringgold	1
STRAUP, Daniel Newton	1
STRAUS, Aaron	3
STRAUS, Adolph D.	1
STRAUS, Herbert Nathan	1
STRAUS, Isidor	1
STRAUS, Jesse Isidor	1
STRAUS, Martin L. Ii	3
STRAUS, Michael w(olf)	5
STRAUS, Nathan	1
STRAUS, Nathan	4
STRAUS, Oscar	3
STRAUS, Oscar Solomon	1
STRAUS, Percy Selden	1
STRAUS, Roger Williams	3
STRAUS, Samuel J. Tilden	5
STRAUS, Simon William	1
STRAUSS, Albert	1
STRAUSS, Charles	1
STRAUSS, Henry Harrison	3
STRAUSS, Herbert Donald	5
STRAUSS, Joseph	2
STRAUSS, Joseph Baermann	1
STRAUSS, Juliet V.	3
STRAUSS, Maurice J.	3
STRAUSS, Moses	1
STRAUSS, Nathan	1
STRAUSS, Richard	2
STRAVINSKY, Igor Fedorovich	5
STRAW, William Parker	1
STRAWBRIDGE, Frederic H(eap)	5
STRAWBRIDGE, James Dale	H
STRAWBRIDGE, Robert	H
STRAWBRIDGE, William Correy	1
STRAWN, Jacob	H
STRAWN, Julia Clark	4
STRAWN, Lester Herbert	4
STRAWN, Silas Hardy	2
STRAYER, George Drayton	4
STRAYER, Louis William	5
STRAYER, Paul Johnston	4
STRAYER, Paul Moore	4
STREAMER, A. Camp	3
STREAMER, Volney	3
STREAN, Maria Judson	1
STREAT, Hearn W.	2
STREB, Charles Alexis	3
STREBEL, Ralph Frederick	3
STREBLOW, Albert George	4
STRECKER, Edward Adam	3
STRECKER, Herman	1
STRECKER, John Kern	1
STREEPEY, George William	4
STREERUWITZ, William H. Ritter 'von	4
STREET, Alfred Billings	H
STREET, Augustus Russell	H
STREET, Ida Maria	4
STREET, J. Fletcher	2
STREET, Jacob Richard	3
STREET, James Howell	3
STREET, John Northcott	4
STREET, Joseph Montfort	H
STREET, Julian	2
STREET, Oliver Day	2
STREET, Randall S.	H
STREET, Robert	H
STREET, Robert Gould	1
STREET, Thomas Atkins	1
STREET, Webster	1
STREETER, Edward Clark	5
STREETER, Frank Sherwin	1
STREETER, George Linius	2
STREETER, George Wellington	4
STREETER, John Williams	1
STREETER, Thomas Winthrop	4
STREETT, David	1
STREETT, St. Clair	5
STREIGHTOFF, Frank Hatch	1
STRENG, J. Truman	3
STRETCH, David Albert	4
STRIBLING, Thomas Sigismund	4
STRICKER, Frederick David	5
STRICKER, Paul Frederick	4
STRICKLAND, Charles Hobart	4
STRICKLAND, Francis Lorette	3
STRICKLAND, Frederic Hastings	1
STRICKLAND, Frederick Guy	5
STRICKLAND, Lily	3
STRICKLAND, Randolph	H
STRICKLAND, Robert Marion	2
STRICKLAND, Silas A.	H
STRICKLAND, William	H
STRICKLER, Cyrus Warren, Sr.	5
STRICKLER, Givens Brown	1
STRICKLER, John	4
STRICKLER, Thomas Johnson	3
STRIDE, Joseph Burton	1
STRIEBY, William	1
STRIETMANN, A. P.	4
STRIJDOM, Johannes Gerhardus	3
STRIKE, Clifford John	3
STRINGER, Arthur	3
STRINGER, George Alfred	1
STRINGER, Lawrence Beaumont	2
STRINGFELLOW, Henry Martyn	1
STRINGFIELD, Lamar	3
STRINGHAM, Irving	1
STRINGHAM, Silas Horton	H
STRINGHAM, Warde Barlow	5
STRITCH, Samuel Alphonsus	3
STROBEL, Charles Louis	1
STROBEL, Edward Henry	1
STROBRIDGE, Idah Meacham	1
STROCK, Daniel	1
STRODACH, Paul Zeller	2
STRODE, George King	3
STROH, Donald Armpriester	3
STROHM, Adam Julius	1
STROHM, Gertrude	1
STROHM, John	H
STROM, Carl Walther	5
STROMBERG, Gustaf	5
STROMBERG, Hunt	5
STROMME, Peer	1
STRONG, Anna Louise	4
STRONG, Augustus Hopkins	1
STRONG, Austin	3
STRONG, Benjamin	1
STRONG, Caleb	1
STRONG, Charles Augustus	H
STRONG, Charles Hall	4
STRONG, Charles Henry	4
STRONG, Charles Howard	4
STRONG, Charles Lyman	H
STRONG, Charles Stanley	4
STRONG, Edward Kellogg Jr.	4
STRONG, Edward Trask	1
STRONG, Edwin Atson	4
STRONG, Elnathan Ellsworth	2
STRONG, Frank	1
STRONG, Frederick Finch	5
STRONG, Frederick Smith	1
STRONG, George Alexander	4
STRONG, George Crockett	H
STRONG, George Frederic	3
STRONG, George Veazey	2
STRONG, Harry Allen	3
STRONG, Harry Eugene	4
STRONG, Hattie Maria	3
STRONG, Henry A.	1
STRONG, James *	H
STRONG, James George	1
STRONG, James Hooker	1
STRONG, James Woodward	1
STRONG, Jedediah	H
STRONG, John Henry	4
STRONG, Josiah	1
STRONG, Julius Levi	H
STRONG, L. Corrin	1
STRONG, Lee A.	1
STRONG, Moses McCure	H
STRONG, Nathan L.	1
STRONG, Ormand Butler	1
STRONG, Reuben Myron	4
STRONG, Richard Pearson	2
STRONG, Robert Alexander	3
STRONG, Samuel M.	3
STRONG, Selah Brewster	5
STRONG, Selah Brewster	1
STRONG, Solomon	H
STRONG, Stephen	H
STRONG, Sterling Price	4
STRONG, Sydney Dix	1
STRONG, Sylvester Emory	1
STRONG, Theodore	H
STRONG, Theron George	1
STRONG, Theron Rudd	H
STRONG, Thomas Nelson	4
STRONG, Walter Ansel	1
STRONG, Wayne F.	3
STRONG, Wendell Melville	2
STRONG, William *	H
STRONG, William Barstow	1
STRONG, William Duncan	4
STRONG, William Ellsworth	2
STRONG, William L.	1
STRONG, William Walker	3
STROOCK, James E.	4
STROOCK, Solomon M.	4
STROSACKER, Charles John	4
STROTHER, Dan J(ames) F(rench)	5
STROTHER, David Hunter	H
STROTHER, French	1
STROTHER, George French	1
STROTHER, James French	H
STROTHER, James French	1
STROTHER, James H.	4
STROUD, Morris Wistar	1
STROUD, William Daniel	4
STROUP, Thomas Andrew	2
STROUSE, Myer	H
STROUT, Charles Henry	4
STROUT, Edwin Albert	3
STROUT, Sewall Cushing	1
STROVER, Carl Bernhard Wittekind	1
STROZIER, Fred Lewis	1
STROZIER, Robert Manning	3
STRUB, Paul	5
STRUBBERG, Friedrich Armand	H
STRUBE, Gustav	5
STRUBLE, George R.	4
STRUBLE, Mildred	2
STRUCK, Ferdinand Theodore	2
STRUDWICK, Edmund	H
STRUDWICK, Edmund Charles Fox	H
STRUDWICK, William Francis	H
STRUM, Justin	4
STRUM, Louie Willard	3
STRUNK, William	2
STRUNSKY, Simeon	2
STRUTHER, Jan	3
STRUTHERS, G. H.	1
STRUTHERS, Joseph	1
STRUTHERS, Robert	1
STRUVE, Gustav	H
STRUVE, Otto	4
STRYKER, Lloyd Paul	1
STRYKER, Melancthon Woolsey	1
STRYKER, Samuel Stanhope	1
STRYKER, William Scudder	1
STUART, Albert Rhett	5
STUART, Alexander Hugh Holmes	H
STUART, Alexander Tait	1
STUART, Ambrose Pascal Sevilon	H
STUART, Andrew	1
STUART, Archibald *	H
STUART, C. A.	4
STUART, Carl Kirk	4
STUART, Charles	H
STUART, Charles Beebe	1
STUART, Charles Duff	4
STUART, Charles Edward	5
STUART, Charles Edward	2
STUART, Charles Jenckes Barnes	1
STUART, Charles Macaulay	1
STUART, Charles T.	3
STUART, Charles W. T.	1
STUART, Daniel Delehanty Vincent	5
STUART, David	H
STUART, Della Tovrea (Mrs. William P. Stuart)	5
STUART, Donald Clive	3
STUART, Duane Reed	4
STUART, Edward	3
STUART, Edwin Roy	1
STUART, Edwin Sydney	1
STUART, Elbridge Amos	5
STUART, Elbridge Hadley	1
STUART, Eleanor	1
STUART, Francis Hart	1
STUART, Francis Lee	1
STUART, George	2
STUART, George Rutledge	1
STUART, Gilbert	H
STUART, Harold Leonard	4
STUART, Harry Allen	3
STUART, Henry Carter	1
STUART, Henry Waldgrave	5
STUART, Holloway Ithamer	3
STUART, Ian	5
STUART, Isaac William	H
STUART, James Austin	4
STUART, James Edward	1
STUART, James Edwin	5
STUART, James Everett	1
STUART, James Ewell Brown	H
STUART, James Lyall	4
STUART, James Reeve	1
STUART, James Reeve	1
STUART, John	H
STUART, John	5
STUART, John Todd	H
STUART, Milo H.	1
STUART, Moses	H
STUART, Philip	H
STUART, Robert	H
STUART, Robert C.	4
STUART, Robert Leighton	H
STUART, Robert Terry	3
STUART, Robert Young	1
STUART, Ruth McEnery	1
STUART, Theresa Crystal	4
STUART, William Hervey	5
STUART, William Plato	1
STUB, Hans Gerhard	1
STUB, Jacob Aall Ottesen	2
STUBBERT, J. Edward	4
STUBBINS, Allan Linder	4
STUBBLEFIELD, Frances Ogden	3
STUBBLEFIELD, William Higgason	4
STUBBS, Henry Elbert	1
STUBBS, John C.	1
STUBBS, John Osmon	5
STUBBS, Joseph Edward	1
STUBBS, Mattie Wilma	3
STUBBS, Merrill	5
STUBBS, Ralph Sprengle	5
STUBBS, Truett Tristian	5
STUBBS, Walter Roscoe	1
STUBBS, William Carter	1
STUBENRAUCH, Arnold Valentine	1
STUBER, William G.	3
STUCK, Hudson	1
STUCKENBERG, John Henry Wilburn	1
STUCKSLAGER, Willard Coldren	1
STUDEBAKER, Clement	1
STUDEBAKER, Clement Jr.	1
STUDEBAKER, Ellis M.	3
STUDEBAKER, John Mohler	1
STUDENSKI, Paul	4
STUDER, Jacob Henry	1
STUDLEY, Elmer E.	2
STUECK, Frederick	5
STUEMPFIG, Walter	5
STUHLMAN, Otto Jr.	4
STUKES, Taylor Hudnall	5
STULL, Charles Henry	5
STULL, Ray Thomas	5
STUMM, Erwin C(harles)	4
STUMM, Richard A.	4
STUMP, Felix Budwell	5
STUMP, John Sutton	1
STUMP, Joseph	1
STUNTZ, Arba L.	4
STUNTZ, Homer Clyde	1
STUNTZ, Stephen Conrad	1
STURANI, Giuseppe	1
STURDEVANT, Clarence L.	3
STURDEVANT, William Lommer	3
STURDIVANT, J(ames) Holmes	5
STURDY, Herbert Francis	5
STURGEON, Daniel	H
STURGEON, Guy	4
STURGES, Charles Mathews	3
STURGES, Donald George	5
STURGES, Dwight Case	1
STURGES, Jonathan	H
STURGES, Lewis Burr	H
STURGES, Preston	3
STURGES, Wesley A.	4
STURGES, William Spencer	4
STURGIS, Charles Inches	3
STURGIS, Clarence Eugene	1
STURGIS, Cyrus Cressey	4
STURGIS, Frank Knight	1
STURGIS, Frederic Russell	1
STURGIS, Guy Hayden	5
STURGIS, Henry Sprague	5
STURGIS, John Hubbard	H

* Indicates More Than One Such Name Listed

SWARTZ, 2
Charles Kephart
SWARTZ, Edward James 1
SWARTZ, Harry Raymond 2
SWARTZ, Herman Frank 5
SWARTZ, Joel 4
SWARTZ, Joshua W. 4
SWARTZ, Katherine H. 4
SWARTZ, Mifflin Wyatt 5
SWARTZ, Osman Ellis 5
SWARTZ, Philip Allen 4
SWARTZ, Samuel Jackson 1
SWARTZ, Willis George 4
SWARTZBAUGH, 4
William Lamson
SWASEY, Albert Loring 3
SWASEY, Ambrose 1
SWATLAND, 4
Donald Clinton
SWAVELY, Eli 5
SWAYNE, Alfred Harris 1
SWAYNE, Charles 1
SWAYNE, Noah Haynes H
SWAYNE, Wager 1
SWAYZE, Francis Joseph 1
SWAYZE, 1
George Banghart Henry
SWEARINGEN, Embry L. 1
SWEARINGEN, Henry H
SWEARINGEN, 1
Henry Chapman
SWEARINGEN, 5
John Eldred
SWEARINGEN, 5
Lloyd Edward
SWEARINGEN, 5
Mack Buckley
SWEARINGEN, Van
Cicero 5
SWEARINGEN, 5
Victor Clarence
SWEATT, William R. 1
SWEENEY, 3
Alvin Randolph
SWEENEY, Bo 1
SWEENEY, Edward C. 4
SWEENEY, George H
SWEENEY, 5
George Clinton
SWEENEY, James G. 1
SWEENEY, James J. 5
SWEENEY, James P. 4
SWEENEY, John William 5
SWEENEY, Martin L. 4
SWEENEY, 5
Mildred I. Mcneal
SWEENEY, 3
Orland Russell
SWEENEY, 3
Thomas Bell Sr.
SWEENEY, H
Thomas William
SWEENEY, 4
Walter Campbell
SWEENEY, H
William Northcut
SWEENEY, 1
Zachary Taylor
SWEENIE, Denis J. 1
SWEENY, Charles Amos 5
SWEENY, Peter Barr H
SWEENY, Peter Barr 4
SWEENY, 5
William Montgomery
SWEET, Ada Celeste 3
SWEET, Ada Celeste 1
SWEET, Alexander Edwin 1
SWEET, Alfred Henry 4
SWEET, Carroll Fuller 3
SWEET, Cyrus Bardeen 4
SWEET, Edwin Forrest 1
SWEET, Ellingham Tracy 2
SWEET, Elnathan 1
SWEET, Frank Herbert 1
SWEET, George Sullivan 4
SWEET, Harold Edward 5
SWEET, John Edson 1
SWEET, 3
John Henry Throop Jr.
SWEET, John Hyde 4
SWEET, Joshua Edwin 3
SWEET, Louis Dennison 1
SWEET, Louis Matthews 3
SWEET, 5
Marion Atwood (Mrs.
Hamilton Howard Sweet)
SWEET, Owen Jay 1
SWEET, Thaddeus C. 1
SWEET, Timothy Bailey 1
SWEET, William Ellery 2
SWEET, William Luther 4
SWEET, William Merrick 1
SWEET, William Warren 3
SWEETLAND, 1
Cornelius Sowle
SWEETLAND,
William Howard

SWEETS, David Matthis 1
SWEETS, Henry Hayes 3
SWEETSER, Arthur 4
SWEETSER, Charles H
SWEETSER, Delight 1
SWEETSER, Edwin
Chapin 1
SWEETSER, 2
John Anderson
SWEETSER, 1
Kate Dickinson
SWEITZER, Caesar 5
SWEM, Lee Allan 3
SWENEY, Joseph Henry 1
SWENGEL, Uriah Frantz 1
SWENK, Myron Harmon 1
SWENSON, 1
David Ferdinand
SWENSON, Eric P. 2
SWENSON, 2
Laurits Selmer
SWENSON, Lowell
Harvey 4
SWENSON, Merrill G. 4
SWENSSON, Carl Aaron 1
SWEPSTON, John E. 4
SWERDFEGER, 1
Elbert Byron
SWERTFAGER, 4
Walter Milton
SWETLAND, 1
Roger Williams
SWETT, Frank Tracy; 5
SWETT, John 1
SWETT, Louis William 1
SWETT, Sophia Miriam 1
SWETT, Susan Hartley 1
SWEZEY, Goodwin
Deloss 1
SWIFT, Archie Dean 4
SWIFT, Benjamin H
SWIFT, Carl Brown 1
SWIFT, Charles Henry 2
SWIFT, 1
Clarence Franklin
SWIFT, Douglas 2
SWIFT, Eben 1
SWIFT, Edgar James 1
SWIFT, Edward Foster 1
SWIFT, 4
Edward Wellington
SWIFT, Elijah Kent 3
SWIFT, Ernest Fremont 5
SWIFT, Ernest John 1
SWIFT, Fletcher Harper 1
SWIFT, George B. 4
SWIFT, George Wilkins 1
SWIFT, 1
Gustavus Franklin
SWIFT, 2
Gustavus Franklin
SWIFT, Harold Higgins 4
SWIFT, Harry Ladrew 3
SWIFT, Homer Fordyce 3
SWIFT, Innis Palmer 1
SWIFT, Ivan 2
SWIFT, James Carroll 1
SWIFT, James Marcus 2
SWIFT, Jireh Jr. 1
SWIFT, John Franklin H
SWIFT, John Trumbull 4
SWIFT, Joseph Gardner H
SWIFT, Josiah Otis 2
SWIFT, Lewis 1
SWIFT, Lindsay 1
SWIFT, Louis Franklin 1
SWIFT, Lucian 3
SWIFT, Nathan Butler 3
SWIFT, Oscar William 1
SWIFT, 1
Polemus Hamilton
SWIFT, Samuel 1
SWIFT, Willard Everett 2
SWIFT, William 1
SWIFT, William Henry H
SWIFT, Zephaniah H
SWIGART, Charles H. 4
SWIGART, 1
Edmund Kearsley
SWIGER, Wilbur Moore 1
SWIGGART, 4
William Harris
SWIGGETT, 2
Douglas Worthington
SWIGGETT, 3
Douglas Worthington
SWIGGETT, Glen Levin 4
SWIM, Chester Lawrence 5
SWIM, Dudley 5
SWINBURNE, John H
SWINBURNE, 1
William Thomas
SWINDALL, Charles 1
SWINDEREN, 4
Jonkheer Reneke 'de Marees
'van

SWINDLER, 4
Mary Hamilton
SWINEHART, Gerry 4
SWINERTON, Alfred B. 4
SWINEY, Daniel 4
SWING, Albert Temple 1
SWING, David H
SWING, Philip David 4
SWING, Raymond 5
SWINGLE, D. B. 5
SWINGLE, Frank Bell 5
SWINGLE, Walter T. 3
SWINGLER, 5
William S(herman)
SWINNEY, 2
Edward Fletcher
SWINT, John J. 4
SWINT, Samuel H. 4
SWINTON, John 1
SWINTON, William H
SWIRBUL, Leon A. 4
SWIREN, Max 5
SWISHER, 3
Benjamin Franklin
SWISHER, 1
Charles Clinton
SWISSHELM, H
Jane Grey Cannon
SWITZ, 5
Theodore MacLean
SWITZER, 1
George Washington
SWITZER, 5
Mary Elizabeth
SWITZER, Maurice 1
SWITZER, Robert Mauck 4
SWOOPE, Jacob 1
SWOOPE, William Irvin 4
SWOPE, Ammon 4
SWOPE, Charles Siegel 3
SWOPE, Gerard 3
SWOPE, Guy J. 5
SWOPE, Herbert Bayard 3
SWOPE, King 4
SWOPE, Samuel Franklin H
SWORD, James Brade 1
SWORDS, Henry Cotheal 1
SYDENSTRICKER, Edgar 1
SYDENSTRICKER,
Virgil Preston
SYDNESS, Joseph Truman 5
SYDNOR, 3
Charles Sackett
SYDNOR, 2
Giles Granville
SYKES, Charles Henry 2
SYKES, Edward 5
SYKES, Edward Turner 4
SYKES, Eugene Octave 2
SYKES, Frederick Henry 1
SYKES, George * H
SYKES, Howard Calvin 4
SYKES, James 1
SYKES, Jerome H. 1
SYKES, Mabel 1
SYKES, M'Cready 3
SYKES, Richard Eddy 2
SYKES, Wilfred 4
SYLE, Louis 'du Pont 1
SYLVA, Marguerita 1
SYLVESTER, Allie Lewis 4
SYLVESTER, Emma 5
SYLVESTER, 4
Evander Wallace
SYLVESTER, 1
Frederick Oakes
SYLVESTER, 4
Herbert Milton
SYLVESTER, H
James Joseph
SYLVIS, William H. H
SYME, Conrad Hunt 2
SYME, John P. 5
SYMES, George Gifford H
SYMES, J. Foster 3
SYMINGTON, Donald 2
SYMMERS, Douglas 3
SYMMES, Edwin Joseph 1
SYMMES, Frank Jameson 1
SYMMES, John Cleves H
SYMMONDS, 1
Charles Jacobs
SYMONDS, Brandreth 1
SYMONDS, 1
Frederick Martin
SYMONDS, Gardiner 5
SYMONDS, Joseph White 1
SYMONDS, 5
Nathaniel Millberry
SYMONDS, 4
Percival Mallon
SYMONDS, Walter Stout 3
SYMONS, Gardner 1
SYMONS, Noel S. 4
SYMONS, 5
Thomas Baddeley

SYMONS, Thomas
William 1
SYMS, Benjamin H
SYNG, Philip H
SYNNOTT, Joseph J. 1
SYNNOTT, 1
Thomas Whitney
SYPHER, 4
Josiah Rhinehart
SYPHERD, Wilbur Owen 5
SYVERTON, Jerome T. 4
SYVERTSEN, 4
Rolf Christian
SZE, Sao-Ke Alfred 3
SZEKELY, Ernest 3
SZIGETI, Joseph 5
SZILARD, Leo 4
SZINNYEY, Stephen Ivor 1
SZLUPAS, John 4
SZOLD, Henrietta 2
SZUMOWSKA, Antoinette 1
SZYK, Arthur 3

T

TABB, John Banister 1
TABELL, Edmund Weber 4
TABER, David Fairman 3
TABER, 2
Erroll James Livingstone
TABER,
George Hathaway Jr.
TABER, Harry Persons 4
TABER, Henry 1
TABER, John 4
TABER, Louis John 4
TABER,
Mary Jane Howland
TABER, Norman Stephen 3
TABER, Ralph Graham 4
TABER, Stephen H
TABER, Thomas 2'd H
TABER, William Ira 1
TABOR, Carl Henry 2
TABOR, Edward A. 4
TABOR,
Horace Austin Warner
TABORS, Robert Gustav 4
TACK, Augustus Vincent 2
TACKETT, John Robert 4
TACKETT, 3
William Clarence
TADD, J. Liberty 1
TAEUSCH, 4
Carl Frederick
TAFEL, Gustav 1
TAFF, Joseph Alexander 2
TAFFE, John H
TAFFINDER, 4
Sherwoode Ayerst
TAFT, Alphonso H
TAFT, Charles Phelps 1
TAFT, David Gibson 4
TAFT, Elihu Barber 4
TAFT, George Wheaton 4
TAFT, Harry Deward 3
TAFT, Henry Waters 2
TAFT, Horace Dutton 2
TAFT, Hulbert 3
TAFT, Kendall B(enard) 5
TAFT, Kingsley A. 5
TAFT, Levi Rawson 1
TAFT, Lorado 1
TAFT, Lorado 3
TAFT, Robert 3
TAFT, Robert Alphonso 3
TAFT, Robert Burbidge 3
TAFT, Robert Wendell 1
TAFT, Royal Chapin 1
TAFT, Russell Smith 1
TAFT, William Howard H
TAG, Casimir 1
TAGG, Francis Thomas 1
TAGGARD, Genevieve 2
TAGGARD, Arthur Fay 3
TAGGART, 2
David Alexander
TAGGART, David Arthur 1
TAGGART, 4
Elmore Findlay
TAGGART, 3
Eugene Francis
TAGGART, Frank Fulton 2
TAGGART, Joseph 4
TAGGART, Marion Ames 1
TAGGART, Ralph Enos 3
TAGGART, Rush 1
TAGGART, Samuel H
TAGGART, Thomas 1
TAGGART, 2
Thomas Douglas
TAGGART, Walter
Thomas
TAGLIABUE, Giuseppe H
TAGUE, Peter F. 1
TAINTER,
Charles Sumner

TAINTOR, Henry ?x 1
TAINTOR, Jesse F 1
TAIT, 1
Arthur Fitzwillian
TAIT, Charles H
TAIT, Frank Morris 4
TAIT, George 3
TAIT, John Robinso 1
TAITT, Francis Ma n 2
TAKACH, Basil 2
TAKAHIRA, Kogor 4
TAKAMINE, Jokich 1
TALBERT, Joseph ? itt 1
TALBERT, Samuel ? bbs 5
TALBERT, W. Jaspe 4
TALBOT, 2
Adolphus Robert
TALBOT, Arthur Ne ell 2
TALBOT, 5
Edith Armstrong
TALBOT, Ellen Bliss 4
TALBOT, Ethelbert 1
TALBOT, Eugene
Solomon
TALBOT, Francis Xa ier 1
TALBOT, 3
George Frederick
TALBOT, Guy Webs r 5
TALBOT, Henry Pau 1
TALBOT, Howard 1
TALBOT, Isham H
TALBOT, Israel Tisda e 1
TALBOT, John H
TALBOT, John Willia 1
TALBOT, 5
M(urrell) W(illiams)
TALBOT, Marion 2
TALBOT, Mary Whit 3
TALBOT, Silas 1
TALBOT, Walter LeM ar 2
TALBOT, 5
Winifred Luella Win er
(Mrs. John E. Talbo)
TALBOTT, H
Albert Gallatin
TALBOTT, Everett G y 2
TALBOTT, Harold E. 3
TALBOTT, Harold E 4
TALBOTT, Henry Ja nes 1
TALBOTT, J. Fred C 1
TALBOTT, Nelson S 3
TALBURT, Harold M. 4
TALCOTT, Andrew 1
TALCOTT, 1
Charles Andrew
TALCOTT, 1
Edward N. Kirk
TALCOTT, 2
James Frederick
TALCOTT, Joseph H
TALIAFERRO, Benjamin H
TALIAFERRO, 5
Harry Monroe
TALIAFERRO, 4
Henry Beckwith
TALIAFERRO, 2
James Piper
TALIAFERRO, John H
TALIAFERRO, Lawrence 4
TALIAFERRO,
Nicholas Lloyd
TALIAFERRO, 1
Thomas Hardy
TALIAFERRO, 1
Thomas Seddon Jr.
TALIAFERRO, H
William Booth
TALL, Lida Lee 2
TALLANT, Hugh 3
TALLE, Henry O(scar) 5
TALLERDAY, Howard G. 4
TALLEY, 5
Bascom Destrehan, Jr.
TALLEY, Dyer Findley 2
TALLEY, Lynn Porter 2
TALLEYRAND-
PERIGORD, Charles
Maurice
'de
TALLIAFERO, Richard H
TALLICHET, Jules Henri 1
TALLMADGE, Benjamin H
TALLMADGE,
Frederick Augustus
TALLMADGE, Guy
Kasten 4
TALLMADGE, James Jr. H
TALLMADGE,
Nathaniel Pitcher
TALLMADGE, Thomas
Eddy 1
TALLMAN, Clay 5
TALLMAN, Peleg H
TALLY, Robert Emmet 1
TALLY, William F. 4
TALMADGE, Eugene 2
TALMADGE, Norma 3

TALMAGE, James Edward 1
TALMAGE, John Van Nest H
TALMAGE, T. Dewitt 1
TALMAN, Charles Fitzhugh 1
TALMAN, E. Lee 4
TALON, Pierre H
TAMARKIN, Jacob David 2
TAMARON, Pedro H
TAMIRIS, Helen 4
TAMIROFF, Akim 5
TAMM, Igor Y. 5
TAMMANY H
TAMMEN, Agnes Reid 2
TAMMEN, Harry Heye H
TAMMEN, Harry Heye 4
TANEY, Roger Brooke H
TANG, K. Y. 4
TANGEMAN, Robert Stone 4
TANGEMAN, Walter W. 4
TANGUY, Yves 3
TANI, Masayuki 4
TANIZAKI, Junichiro 4
TANNAHILL, Samuel O. 1
TANNEBERGER, David H
TANNEHILL, Adamson H
TANNENBAUM, Samuel Aaron 2
TANNER, Adolphus Hitchcock H
TANNER, Benjamin H
TANNER, Benjamin Tucker 1
TANNER, Edwin Platt 1
TANNER, Eugene Simpson 5
TANNER, Fred Wilbur 3
TANNER, Frederick Chauncey 4
TANNER, George Clinton 4
TANNER, Harold Brooks 5
TANNER, Henry Ossawa 1
TANNER, Henry Schenck H
TANNER, Jacob 5
TANNER, James 1
TANNER, John Henry 1
TANNER, John Riley 1
TANNER, Kenneth Spencer 4
TANNER, Rollin Harvelle 5
TANNER, Sheldon C. 4
TANNER, Willard Brooks 4
TANNER, William Vaughn 3
TANNER, Zera Luther 1
TANNRATH, John Joseph 1
TANSIL, John Bell 3
TANSILL, Charles Callan 4
TANZER, Laurence Arnold 4
TAPLEY, Walter Moore, Jr. 5
TAPLIN, Frank E. 1
TAPLINGER, Richard Jacques 5
TAPP, Jesse W. 4
TAPP, Sidney C. 5
TAPPAN, Arthur H
TAPPAN, Benjamin H
TAPPAN, Benjamin 1
TAPPAN, David Stanton 1
TAPPAN, Eli Todd H
TAPPAN, Eva March 1
TAPPAN, Frank Girard 4
TAPPAN, Henry Philip H
TAPPAN, Lewis H
TAPPAN, Mason Weare H
TAPPAN, William Bingham H
TAPPEN, Frederick D. 1
TAPPEN, Paul W. 4
TAPPER, Bertha Feiring 1
TAPPER, Thomas 3
TAPPIN, John Lindsley 4
TAPSCOTT, Ralph Henry 4
TAQUINO, George James 3
TARACOUZIO, Timothy Andrew 3
TARBELL, Arthur Wilson 2
TARBELL, Edmund C. 1
TARBELL, Frank Bigelow 1
TARBELL, Gage E. 1
TARBELL, Horace Sumner 1
TARBELL, Ida Minerva 2
TARBELL, Joseph H
TARBELL, Martha 2
TARBELL, Thomas Freeman 3
TARBOUX, Joseph G. 3
TARBOX, Increase Niles H
TARBOX, John Kemble H
TARBUTTON, Ben James 4
TARCHER, Jack David 4
TARCHIANI, Alberto 4
TARKINGTON, Grayson Emery 1
TARKINGTON, John Stevenson 1
TARKINGTON, Newton Booth 2
TARLER, George Cornell 2
TARPEY, Michael Francis 1
TARR, Christian H
TARR, Frederick Courtney 3
TARR, Frederick Hamilton 2
TARR, Leslie Riley 5
TARR, Ralph Stockman 1
TARR, William Arthur 1
TARRANT, Warren Downes 1
TARRANT, William Theodore 5
TARSNEY, John C. 4
TARVER, Malcolm Connor 4
TARVER, William Allen 1
TASHLIN, Frank 5
TASKER, Cyril 3
TASKEY, Harry LeRoy 3
TASSIN, Algernon 'de Vivier 1
TASSIN, Wirt 1
TATE, Benjamin Ethan 4
TATE, Farish Carter 4
TATE, Fred N. 4
TATE, H. Theodore 4
TATE, H. Theodore 5
TATE, Hugh McCall 1
TATE, Jack Bernard 5
TATE, James Alexander 3
TATE, John Matthew, Jr. 5
TATE, John Torrence 3
TATE, Magnus H
TATE, Robert 4
TATE, Sam 1
TATE, William Knox 1
TATGENHORST, Charles 4
TATHAM, William H
TATLOCK, Henry 2
TATLOCK, John 1
TATLOCK, John S. P. 2
TATMAN, Charles Taylor 2
TATNALL, Henry 1
TATOM, Absalom H
TATSCH, J. Hugo 1
TATTNALL, Edward Fenwick H
TATTNALL, Josiah * H
TATUM, Arthur 4
TATUM, Arthur Lawrie 3
TAUB, Edward Allen 5
TAUB, Sam 3
TAUBE, Mortimer 4
TAUBENHAUS, Jacob Joseph 1
TAUBER, Richard 2
TAUBMAN, George Primrose 2
TAUBMAN, Tom 4
TAUL, Micah H
TAULBEE, William Preston H
TAUSSIG, Albert Ernst 2
TAUSSIG, Charles William 2
TAUSSIG, Edward David 1
TAUSSIG, Francis Brewster 5
TAUSSIG, Frank William 1
TAUSSIG, Frederick Joseph 2
TAUSSIG, James Edward 2
TAUSSIG, Joseph Knefler 2
TAUSSIG, Rudolph Julius 1
TAUSSIG, William 1
TAVENNER, Clyde Howard 1
TAVENNER, Clyde Howard 2
TAVENNER, Frank Stacy Jr. 4
TAVES, Brydon 2
TAWNEY, Guy Alan 2
TAWNEY, James A. 1
TAWRESEY, John Godwin 2
TAYLER, Benjamin Walter Rogers 1
TAYLER, Joseph Henry 3
TAYLER, Lewis H
TAYLER, Robert Walker 1
TAYLOR, Abner 4
TAYLOR, Albert Davis 3
TAYLOR, Albert Hoyt 4
TAYLOR, Albert Pierce 1
TAYLOR, Albert Reynolds 1
TAYLOR, Alexander Wilson H
TAYLOR, Alfred Alexander 1
TAYLOR, Alfred Simpson 2
TAYLOR, Alrutheus Ambush 3
TAYLOR, Alva Edwards 1
TAYLOR, Amos Elias 5
TAYLOR, Amos Leavitt 4
TAYLOR, Archibald Wellington 3
TAYLOR, Arthur Nelson 4
TAYLOR, Asher Clayton 1
TAYLOR, Aubrey E. 2
TAYLOR, Barnard Cook 1
TAYLOR, Bayard H
TAYLOR, Benjamin Franklin H
TAYLOR, Benjamin Irving 2
TAYLOR, Bert Leston 1
TAYLOR, Caleb Newbold H
TAYLOR, Carson Lee 4
TAYLOR, Charles Elisha 1
TAYLOR, Charles Fayette H
TAYLOR, Charles Fayette 1
TAYLOR, Charles Fremont 1
TAYLOR, Charles Gillies Jr. 3
TAYLOR, Charles Henry * 1
TAYLOR, Charles Jay 1
TAYLOR, Charles Lewis 1
TAYLOR, Charles Ralph 5
TAYLOR, Charles Vincent 2
TAYLOR, Charles William 2
TAYLOR, Charlotte De Bernier Scarbrough H
TAYLOR, Claude Ambrose 4
TAYLOR, Creed H
TAYLOR, David Watson 1
TAYLOR, Deems 4
TAYLOR, Donald Stephen 5
TAYLOR, E. Alexis 4
TAYLOR, E. Leland 2
TAYLOR, Earl Burt 2
TAYLOR, Edward H
TAYLOR, Edward Ballinger 1
TAYLOR, Edward Livingston 1
TAYLOR, Edward R. 5
TAYLOR, Edward Randolph 1
TAYLOR, Edward Robeson 1
TAYLOR, Edward Thomas 1
TAYLOR, Edward Thompson H
TAYLOR, Edwin 3
TAYLOR, Edwy Lycurgus 2
TAYLOR, Emerson Gifford 5
TAYLOR, Emily (Heyward) Drayton 5
TAYLOR, Eugene Hartwell 4
TAYLOR, Ezra B. 1
TAYLOR, F. Carroll 3
TAYLOR, F. W. Howard 2
TAYLOR, F. Walter 1
TAYLOR, Floyd 3
TAYLOR, Francis Henry 3
TAYLOR, Francis Matthew Sill 1
TAYLOR, Frank 1
TAYLOR, Frank Bursley 4
TAYLOR, Frank Flagg 3
TAYLOR, Frank J. 5
TAYLOR, Frank L. 4
TAYLOR, Frank Mansfield 1
TAYLOR, Fred Manville 4
TAYLOR, Frederic William 2
TAYLOR, Frederick Eugene 1
TAYLOR, Frederick R. 3
TAYLOR, Frederick William 1
TAYLOR, Frederick Winslow 1
TAYLOR, G. Mosser 4
TAYLOR, George * H
TAYLOR, George Jr. 4
TAYLOR, George Boardman 1
TAYLOR, George Braxton 2
TAYLOR, George Chadbourne 4
TAYLOR, George Washington 4
TAYLOR, George William 5
TAYLOR, Graham 1
TAYLOR, Graham Romeyn 2
TAYLOR, H. Birchard 3
TAYLOR, H. Genet 1
TAYLOR, Hannis 1
TAYLOR, Harden Franklin 4
TAYLOR, Harris 3
TAYLOR, Harry 1
TAYLOR, Harry G. 1
TAYLOR, Harry Gordon 5
TAYLOR, Harry Leonard 3
TAYLOR, Henry A. Colt 1
TAYLOR, Henry Clay 1
TAYLOR, Henry Fitch 1
TAYLOR, Henry Kirby 1
TAYLOR, Henry Lewis 4
TAYLOR, Henry Ling 1
TAYLOR, Henry Longstreet 1
TAYLOR, Henry Osborn 1
TAYLOR, Herbert Addison 2
TAYLOR, Herbert Worthington 1
TAYLOR, Hillsman 4
TAYLOR, Horace A. 4
TAYLOR, Howard 1
TAYLOR, Howard Canning 2
TAYLOR, Howard Emerson 1
TAYLOR, Howard Floyd 4
TAYLOR, Howard Rice 3
TAYLOR, Isaac Montrose 1
TAYLOR, Isaac Stockton 1
TAYLOR, J. Gurney 3
TAYLOR, J. Madison 1
TAYLOR, J. Will 1
TAYLOR, Jacob B. 4
TAYLOR, James Alfred 3
TAYLOR, James Anderson 1
TAYLOR, James Barnett H
TAYLOR, James Earl H
TAYLOR, James H. 5
TAYLOR, James Henry 5
TAYLOR, James Henry 3
TAYLOR, James Knox 4
TAYLOR, James Loockerman 4
TAYLOR, James Milburn 5
TAYLOR, James Monroe 1
TAYLOR, James Morford 1
TAYLOR, James W. 1
TAYLOR, James Wickes H
TAYLOR, John * H
TAYLOR, John Bellamy 4
TAYLOR, John Blyth 5
TAYLOR, John James H
TAYLOR, John Lampkin H
TAYLOR, John Louis H
TAYLOR, John Metcalf 1
TAYLOR, John Phelps 1
TAYLOR, John Thomas 4
TAYLOR, John W. H
TAYLOR, John Yeatman 1
TAYLOR, Jonathan H
TAYLOR, Joseph Fillmore 3
TAYLOR, Joseph Jackson 2
TAYLOR, Joseph Judson 1
TAYLOR, Joseph Richard 3
TAYLOR, Joseph Robert 5
TAYLOR, Joseph Russell 1
TAYLOR, Joseph S. 1
TAYLOR, Joseph Wright H
TAYLOR, Julian Daniel 1
TAYLOR, Katharine Haviland 1
TAYLOR, Laurette 2
TAYLOR, Leland Russell 4
TAYLOR, Lewis Harvie 1
TAYLOR, Lillian E. 5
TAYLOR, Lily Ross 5
TAYLOR, Lloyd William 2
TAYLOR, Lodusky J. 4
TAYLOR, Louis Sherman 4
TAYLOR, Marie Hansen 4
TAYLOR, Marion Sayle 1
TAYLOR, Maris 4
TAYLOR, Marshall William H
TAYLOR, Mary Imlay 1
TAYLOR, Maurice 3
TAYLOR, Merris 4
TAYLOR, Miles H
TAYLOR, Montgomery Meigs 3
TAYLOR, Moses H
TAYLOR, Moses 1
TAYLOR, Myron C. 3
TAYLOR, Nathaniel Green H
TAYLOR, Nathaniel William H
TAYLOR, Nelson H
TAYLOR, Nelson 1
TAYLOR, Norman 5
TAYLOR, Oliver Guy 3
TAYLOR, Ora Autumn 4
TAYLOR, Orville 5
TAYLOR, Oury Wilburn 3
TAYLOR, Paul Bennett 4
TAYLOR, R. Tunstall 1
TAYLOR, Raynor H
TAYLOR, Reese Hale 4
TAYLOR, Richard H
TAYLOR, Richard (Denlson) 5
TAYLOR, Richard Cowling H
TAYLOR, Richard V. 1
TAYLOR, Robert H
TAYLOR, Robert Fenwick 4
TAYLOR, Robert Howard 1
TAYLOR, Robert John 5
TAYLOR, Robert Lee 5
TAYLOR, Robert Longley 1
TAYLOR, Robert Love 1
TAYLOR, Robert Stewart 1
TAYLOR, Robert William 4
TAYLOR, S. Earl 5
TAYLOR, S(amuel) N(ewton) 5
TAYLOR, Samuel Alfred 3
TAYLOR, Samuel Harvey H
TAYLOR, Samuel Mac 1
TAYLOR, Samuel Mitchell 1
TAYLOR, Thomas 2
TAYLOR, Thomas Hendricks 4
TAYLOR, Thomas Nicholls 3
TAYLOR, Thomas Ulvan 4
TAYLOR, Vernon F. 5
TAYLOR, Victor V. 2
TAYLOR, Vincent George 3
TAYLOR, Waller H
TAYLOR, Walter Andrews 4
TAYLOR, Walter Herron 1
TAYLOR, Warner 3
TAYLOR, Wayne Chatfield 4
TAYLOR, Will Samuel 5
TAYLOR, William H
TAYLOR, William 1
TAYLOR, William Albert 2
TAYLOR, William Alexander 1
TAYLOR, William Alton 2
TAYLOR, William C. 3
TAYLOR, William Dana 1
TAYLOR, William George Langworthy 1
TAYLOR, William H. 1
TAYLOR, William Henry 1
TAYLOR, William James 2
TAYLOR, William Johnson 1
TAYLOR, William Ladd 1
TAYLOR, William Mackergo H
TAYLOR, William Mode 2
TAYLOR, William Osgood 3
TAYLOR, William Penn H
TAYLOR, William Rivers 1
TAYLOR, William Rogers H
TAYLOR, William Septimus 2
TAYLOR, William Sylvester 1
TAYLOR, William Vigneron H
TAYLOR, William Watts 1
TAYLOR, Willis Ratcliffe 2
TAYLOR, Zachary H
TAZEWELL, Henry H
TAZEWELL, Littleton Waller H
TEACH, Edward H
TEACHENOR, Frank Randall 3
TEAD, Edward Sampson 1
TEAGARDEN, Jack Weldon Leo 4
TEAGLE, Walter Clark 4
TEAGUE, Charles C. 3
TEAGUE, Walter Dorwin 4
TEAL, Joseph Nathan 1
TEALL, Edward Nelson 2

THOMPSON, Will
Scroggs 4
THOMPSON, 3
Willard Chandler
THOMPSON, Willard
Owen 3
THOMPSON, William * H
THOMPSON, 4
William Barlum
THOMPSON, William
Bess 1
THOMPSON, 5
William Blaine, Jr.
THOMPSON, 1
William Boyce
THOMPSON, 4
William Francis
THOMPSON, 1
William Gilman
THOMPSON, 1
William Goodrich
THOMPSON, William
Hale 2
THOMPSON,
William Henry
THOMPSON, 2
William Herbert
THOMPSON, 1
William Howard
THOMPSON, 2
William Joseph
THOMPSON, 3
William Leland
THOMPSON, 4
William McLean
THOMPSON, 2
William Ormonde
THOMPSON, 1
William Oxley
THOMPSON, H
William Tappan
THOMPSON, 3
William Thomas
THOMPSON, 1
William Townsend
THOMPSON, William W. 5
THOMPSON, Zadock H
THOMS, Craig Sharpe 2
THOMS, Herbert 5
THOMS, William Edward 4
THOMS, William M. 4
THOMSEN, Mark
Lawrence 1
THOMSEN, Rasmus 2
THOMSON, Alexander H
THOMSON, Alexander 1
THOMSON, 2
Arthur Conover
THOMSON, Charles H
THOMSON, 4
Charles Alexander
THOMSON, Charles Goff 1
THOMSON, Charles
Marsh 2
THOMSON, David Sidney 3
THOMSON, Edgar Steiner 4
THOMSON, Edward H
THOMSON, Edward 4
THOMSON, Edward H. 4
THOMSON, 4
Edward William
THOMSON, Elihu 1
THOMSON, Francis A. 3
THOMSON, Frank H
THOMSON, 1
Henry Czar Merwin
THOMSON, James E. M. 4
THOMSON, James Lewis 4
THOMSON, 3
James McIlhany
THOMSON, 5
James Sutherland
THOMSON, 1
James William *
THOMSON, John * H
THOMSON, John 1
THOMSON, John
Cameron
THOMSON, John Edgar H
THOMSON, John
Renshaw H
THOMSON, Keith 4
THOMSON, Logan G. 2
THOMSON, Mark H
THOMSON, Mortimer
Neal H
THOMSON, 2
Osmund Rhoads Howard
THOMSON, Peter Gibson 1
THOMSON, 5
Philip Livingston
THOMSON, 3
Reginald Heber
THOMSON, Roy B. 3
THOMSON, Samuel 1
THOMSON, H
Samuel Harrison

THOMSON, 3
Sir Godfrey Hilton
THOMSON, T. Kennard 3
THOMSON, 1
Thaddeus Austin
THOMSON, W. H.
Seward 1
THOMSON, William H
THOMSON, William 1
THOMSON, William H. 2
THOMSON, William
Hanna 1
THOMSON, William
Judah
THOMSON, H
William McClure
THORBORG, Kerstin 5
THORBURN, Grant 1
THORBURN, 4
Thomas Rankin
THOREAU, Henry David H
THOREK, Max 3
THOREZ, Maurice 4
THORFINN H
THORGRIMSON, 5
Oliver Bernhard
THORINGTON, James 2
THORINGTON, 1
William Sewell
THORKELSON, 5
Halsten Joseph
THORKELSON, Jacob 5
THORN, Frank Manly 4
THORN, James 3
THORNAL, 5
Benjamin Campbell
THORNBER, John James 5
THORNBURG,
Charles Lewis
THORNBURG, 1
Zenas Charles
THORNBURGH, George 1
THORNBURGH, H
Jacob Montgomery
THORNDIKE, 1
Ashley Horace
THORNDIKE, Augustus 4
THORNDIKE, Edward
Lee 2
THORNDIKE, Israel H
THORNDIKE, Lynn 4
THORNDIKE, Paul 1
THORNDIKE, 1
Townsend William
THORNDIKE, Willis Hale 5
THORNE, Charles Embree 2
THORNE,
Charles Hallett
THORNE, H
Charles Robert *
THORNE, Chester 1
THORNE, Clifford 1
THORNE, Edwin 1
THORNE, 5
Elisabeth Griffin
THORNE, 4
Frederick Wisner
THORNE, James Reynolds 5
THORNE, Landon K. 4
THORNE, Lansing S. 4
THORNE, Oakleigh 2
THORNE, Robert Julius 3
THORNE, Samuel 1
THORNE, William 4
THORNE, William Henry 4
THORNE, 1
William Van Schoonhoven
THORNHILL, Arthur H. 5
THORNLEY, Fant Hill 5
THORNTHWAITE, 4
Charles Warren
THORNTON, Edward
Quin 2
THORNTON, 3
Edwin William
THORNTON, 1
Gustavus Brown
THORNTON, Hamilton 3
THORNTON, 3
Harrison John
THORNTON, James
Brown 1
THORNTON, Jessy Quinn H
THORNTON, 1
John Randolph
THORNTON, John
Wingate H
THORNTON, 1
Leila Cameron Austell
THORNTON, Matthew H
THORNTON, Patrick M. 3
THORNTON, Robert Lee 4
THORNTON, H
Sir Henry Worth
THORNTON, T. Eugene 4
THORNTON, Walter
Edwin 4

THORNTON, 4
Walter Francis
THORNTON, William H
THORNTON, William D. 3
THORNTON, William
Mynn 1
THORNTON, 1
William Taylor
THORNTON, 1
William Wheeler
THORNWELL, H
James Henley
THORP, Charles Monroe 2
THORP, Clark Elwin 5
THORP, Frank 1
THORP, Frank Hall 4
THORP, George Gowen 4
THORP, Harry Walter 4
THORP, John H
THORP, Willard Brown 3
THORPE, Burton Lee 5
THORPE, Drew Maxwell 4
THORPE,
Ervin Llewellyn
THORPE, Francis Newton 1
THORPE, George Cyrus 1
THORPE, James Francis H
THORPE, James Francis 1
THORPE, Merle 3
THORPE, Rose Hartwick 4
THORPE, Spencer Roane 4
THORPE, Thomas Bangs 1
THORS, Olafur 4
THORS, Thor 4
THORSEN, David S. 5
THORSON, 5
Gunnar Axel Wright
THORSON, Nelson Thor 3
THORSON, Thomas 1
THORSON, Truman C. 4
THORVALDSON, Gunnar
S. 5
THORVALDSSON, Eric H
THRASHER, Allen
Benton 1
THRASHER, 4
Frederic Milton
THRASHER, John Sidney H
THRASHER, Max Bennett 1
THRASHER, Paul McNeel 2
THREADGILL, 5
Frances Falwell (Mrs. John
Threadgill)
THRELKELD, 4
Clyde Hollis
THROCKMORTON, 1
Archibald Hall
THROCKMORTON, 5
Charlotte Edgerton Alvord
("Charles
THROCKMORTON,
Cleon 4
THROCKMORTON, 3
George Kenneth
THROCKMORTON, H
James Webb
THROCKMORTON, 4
Tom Bentley
THROGMORTON, 1
William P.
THROOP, Enos Thompson H
THROOP, Frank Dwight 2
THROOP, George Reeves 2
THROOP, H
Montgomery Hunt
THROPP, 5
Joseph Earlston
THRUSTON, Buckner H
THRUSTON, 1
Gates Phillips
THRUSTON, Lucy
Meacham 4
THRUSTON, 2
Rogers Clark Ballard
THULSTRUP, Thure 'de 1
THUM, Ernest Edgar 4
THUM, Patty Prather 1
THUM, William 4
THUMAN, J. Herman 4
THUMB, Gen Tom H
THURBER, Caroline 3
THURBER, Charles H
THURBER, 1
Charles Herbert
THURBER,
Edward Gerrish
THURBER, 1
Francis Beatty
THURBER, George H
THURBER, Harry
Raymond 4
THURBER, Howard Ford 1
THURBER, James Grover 1
THURMAN, H
Allen Granberry
THURMAN, Allen
William 4

THURMAN, Hal C. 3
THURMAN, H
John Richardson
THURMAN, Samuel R. 4
THURMON, Francis M. 4
THURMOND, 5
Erasmus Khleber
THURMOND, John
William
THURNAUER, Gustav 2
THURSBY, Emma Cecelia 2
THURSTON, H
Benjamin Babcock
THURSTON, 1
Charles Rawson
THURSTON, 2
Edward Sampson
THURSTON, 3
Ernest Lawton
THURSTON, 2
Henry Winfred
THURSTON, Howard 1
THURSTON,
Ida Treadwell
THURSTON, John Mellen 1
THURSTON, Lee
Mohrmann 3
THURSTON, Lloyd 5
THURSTON,
Lorrin Andrews
THURSTON, Robert
Henry
THURSTON, H
Robert Lawton
THURSTON, Samuel
Royal H
THURSTON, 1
Theodore Payne
THURSTON, 4
William Ravenel
THURSTONE, Louis Leon 3
THWAITE,
Charles Edward Jr.
THWAITES, Reuben Gold 1
THWING, Charles Burton 4
THWING, 1
Charles Franklin
THWING, Edward Waite 4
THWING, Eugene 1
THYE, Edward John 5
TIBBALS, 2
Charles Austin Jr.
TIBBALS, 3
Seymour Selden
TIBBALS, 4
William Huntington
TIBBATTS, H
John Wooleston
TIBBETS, Addison S. 4
TIBBETT, 4
Lawrence Mervil
TIBBETTS, 1
Frederick Horace
TIBBITS, 1
Charles Edward Dudley
TIBBITS, George H
TIBBLES, Thomas Henry 1
TIBOLT, Robert P. 5
TIBOR, Lee Anthony 4
TICE, Frederick 3
TICHBORNE, 1
Josephine Caroline Sawyer
TICHENOR,
Alfred Benton
TICHENOR, Austin Kent 5
TICHENOR, Isaac H
TICHENOR, Isaac Taylor H
TICKNOR, Caroline 1
TICKNOR, Elisha 4
TICKNOR, Francis Orray H
TICKNOR, George H
TICKNOR, Howard
Malcom 1
TICKNOR, William Davis H
TIDBALL, John Caldwell 1
TIDBALL, Thomas Allen 4
TIDWELL, Josiah Blake 2
TIEBOUT, Cornelius 4
TIEBOUT, Harry Morgan 4
TIEDEMAN, 1
Christopher Gustavus
TIEDEMANN, Tudor H.
A. 3
TIEF, Francis Joseph 4
TIEKEN, Theodore 1
TIEMANN,
Daniel Fawcett 1
TIERNAN,
Charles Bernard 1
TIERNEY, Harry Austin 4
TIERNEY, John M. 4
TIERNEY, John Thomas 2
TIERNEY, Leo Francis 5
TIERNEY, Michael 1
TIERNEY, Richard Henry 1
TIERNEY, 3
William Laurence

TIERNON, John Luke 1
TIETJENS, Eunice 2
TIETJENS, Paul 5
TIETSORT, 5
Franics Judson
TIFFANY, H
Alexander Ralston
TIFFANY, 1
Charles Comfort
TIFFANY, Charles Lewis 1
TIFFANY, Charles Lewis 2
TIFFANY, 1
Flavel Benjamin
TIFFANY, Francis 1
TIFFANY, 3
Francis Buchanan
TIFFANY, Hanford 4
TIFFANY, 2
Herbert Thorndike
TIFFANY, J. Raymond 3
TIFFANY, Louis Comfort 1
TIFFANY, Louis McLane 1
TIFFANY, Nina Moore 3
TIFFANY, Orrin Edward 4
TIFFANY, Ross Kerr 1
TIFFANY, 4
Walter Checkley
TIFFIN, Edward H
TIFFT, Henry Neville 1
TIFT, Nelson H
TIGERT, John James 1
TIGERT, John James 2
TIGERT, John James 4
TIGH,
William Frederick
TIGHE, Ambrose 1
TIGHE, 3
Laurence Gotzian
TIGHE, Lawrence Giblin 2
TIGHT, William George 1
TIHEN, John Henry 1
TILDEN, Charles Joseph 3
TILDEN, Daniel Rose H
TILDEN, Douglas 1
TILDEN, Edward 1
TILDEN, Francis Calvin 4
TILDEN, George Thomas 1
TILDEN, John Henry 4
TILDEN, Joseph Mayo 1
TILDEN, 3
Josephine Elizabeth
TILDEN, Louis Edward 5
TILDEN, Samuel Jones H
TILDEN, William Tatem H
TILDEN, William Tatem 1
TILDEN, William Tatem 4
TILDSLEY, John Lee 2
TILDY, Zoltan 4
TILESTON, Mary Wilder 1
TILESTON, Thomas H
TILESTON, Wilder 5
TILFORD, Frank 1
TILFORD, Henry Johnson 5
TILFORD, Joseph Green 1
TILGHMAN, Edward H
TILGHMAN, Matthew H
TILGHMAN,
Richard Albert
TILGHMAN, Tench H
TILGHMAN, William H
TILGHMAN,
William Matthew H
TILGHMAN, 4
William Matthew
TILLER, Theodore Hance 3
TILLERY, Lee 4
TILLES, Roy E. 4
TILLETT, 1
Charles Walter
TILLETT, 3
Charles Walter
TILLETT, Wilbur Fisk 1
TILLEY, 1
Benjamin Franklin
TILLEY, Morris Palmer 2
TILLICH, Paul Johannes 4
TILLINGHAST,
Benjamin Franklin
TILLINGHAST,
Benjamin Franklin
TILLINGHAST,
Caleb Benjamin
TILLINGHAST, 4
Charles Carpenter
TILLINGHAST, 3
Harold Morton
TILLINGHAST, H
Joseph Leonard
TILLINGHAST, 1
Mary Elizabeth
TILLINGHAST, Pardon
E.
TILLINGHAST, Thomas H
TILLMAN, Abram Martin 2
TILLMAN, Benjamin
Ryan 1
TILLMAN, George N. 1

TILLMAN, James Davidson 4
TILLMAN, John Newton 1
TILLMAN, John Plummer 1
TILLMAN, Lewis H
TILLMAN, Nathaniel Patrick 4
TILLMAN, Samuel Escue 2
TILLOTSON, Edwin Ward 4
TILLOTSON, Loyal Garis 4
TILLOTSON, Thomas H
TILLSON, George William 1
TILLSON, John Charles Fremont 1
TILLSON, John Charles Fremont 2
TILLY, David L. 4
TILNEY, Albert Arthur 1
TILNEY, Frederick 1
TILROE, William Edwin 1
TILSON, Ann Coe (Mrs. Donald Heath Tilson) 5
TILSON, John Quillin 3
TILSON, William Josiah 2
TILT, Charles Arthur 3
TILTON, Dwight 1
TILTON, Edward Lippincott 1
TILTON, Elizabeth (Mrs. William Tilton) 5
TILTON, Frederic Arthur 2
TILTON, George Henry 1
TILTON, Howard Winslow 1
TILTON, James H
TILTON, John Philip 3
TILTON, John Rollin H
TILTON, McLane Jr. 1
TILTON, Ralph 1
TILTON, Theodore 1
TILY, Herbert James 2
TILYOU, George Cornelius H
TILYOU, George Cornelius 4
TIMBERLAKE, Charles B. 1
TIMBERLAKE, Gideon 3
TIMBERLAKE, Henry H
TIMBERMAN, Andrew 1
TIMBLIN, Louis M. 3
TIMBY, Theodore Ruggles 1
TIMKEN, Henry H
TIMKEN, Henry 1
TIMKEN, Henry H. Jr. 1
TIMLIN, William Henry 1
TIMLOW, Elizabeth Weston 1
TIMM, Henry Christian H
TIMM, John A(rrend) 5
TIMME, Ernst G. 1
TIMME, Walter 3
TIMMERMAN, Arthur Henry 1
TIMMERMAN, George Bell 5
TIMMERMAN, George Bell 4
TIMMINS, Jules Robert 5
TIMMONS, Dever 4
TIMMONS, Edward J. Finley 4
TIMMONS, Wofford Colquitt 3
TIMON, John H
TIMOSHENKO, Stephen 5
TIMOTHY, Lewis 1
TIMPY, Jack J. 3
TIMROD, Henry H
TIMS, John Chapel 1
TIMS, John Francis 5
TINCHER, J. N. 3
TINCKER, Mary Agnes 1
TINDALL, Glenn Means 1
TINGELSTAD, Oscar Adolf 3
TINGEY, Thomas H
TINGLE, John Bishop 3
TINGLE, Leonard 1
TINGLEY, Charles Love Scott 4
TINGLEY, Clyde 4
TINGLEY, Katherine 1
TINGLEY, Louisa Paine 3
TINGLEY, Richard Hoadley 1
TINKER, Chauncey Brewster 4
TINKER, Clarence L. 2
TINKER, Earl Warren 1
TINKER, Edward Larocque 5

TINKER, Edward Richmond 3
TINKER, Martin Buel 3
TINKHAM, Henry Crain 1
TINKHAM, Herbert Linwood 1
TINKHAM, Richard Parsons 5
TINKMAN, George Holden 3
TINLEY, Mathew Adrian 3
TINNEY, Frank 1
TINNON, Robert McCracken 1
TINSLEY, Gladney Jack 3
TINSLEY, John Francis 3
TINSLEY, Richard Parran 1
TINSMAN, Homer Ellsworth 2
TIPPET, Charles Frederick Basil 4
TIPPETS, Joseph Henderson 5
TIPPETTS, Charles Sanford 5
TIPPLE, Bertrand Martin 5
TIPPLE, Ezra Squier 1
TIPPY, Worth Marion 4
TIPTON, Ernest Moss 1
TIPTON, John * H
TIPTON, Laurence B. 1
TIPTON, Royce Jay 5
TIPTON, Royce Jay 4
TIREY, Ralph Noble 4
TIRINDELLI, Pier Adolfo 4
TIRRELL, Charles Quincy 1
TIRRELL, Frank A. Jr. 3
TIRRELL, Henry Archelaus 5
TISCH, Alfred Francis 5
TISDALL, Fitz Gerald 5
TISDEL, Frederick Monroe 5
TISELIUS, Arne (Wilhelm Kaurin) 5
TISINGER, Benjamin Louis 1
TISON, Alexander 1
TISQUANTUM H
TISSERANT, H. E. Cardinal Eugene 5
TITCHENER, Edward Bradford 1
TITCHENER, John Bradford 5
TITCOMB, Harvey Burgess 5
TITCOMB, John Wheelock 1
TITCOMB, Mary Lemist 1
TITCOMB, Virginia Chandler 5
TITHERINGTON, Richard Handfield 1
TITSWORTH, Alfred Alexander 1
TITSWORTH, Clarence E. 5
TITSWORTH, Grant 4
TITSWORTH, Judson 5
TITSWORTH, Paul Emerson 1
TITTERINGTON, Sophie Bronson 4
TITTLE, Elmer Anthony 5
TITTLE, Ernest Fremont 2
TITTLE, Walter 4
TITTMANN, Charles Trowbridge 4
TITTMANN, Otto Hilgard 1
TITUS, Andrew Phillips 5
TITUS, Bennett Eaton 5
TITUS, Edward Coddington 5
TITUS, Ellwood Valentine 2
TITUS, Louis 5
TITUS, Obadiah H
TITUS, Paul 3
TITUS, Paul 3
TITUS, Robert Cyrus 1
TIVNAN, Edward P. 1
TIYANOGA H
TJADER, Richard 1
TOASPERN, Otto 4
TOBENKIN, Elias 4
TOBEY, Charles William 3
TOBEY, Edward Silas H
TOBIAS, Channing Heggie 4
TOBIN, Charles Milton 5
TOBIN, Daniel Aloysius 4
TOBIN, Daniel J. 3
TOBIN, Edmund Paul 5

TOBIN, George Timothy 4
TOBIN, James Edward 5
TOBIN, John Charles 3
TOBIN, Maurice Joseph 3
TOBIN, Ralph C. 3
TOBIN, Richard Montgomery 3
TOBIN, Robert Gibson 3
TOBIN, Robert James 3
TOBITT, Edith 3
TOBOLSKY, Arthur Victor 5
TOBY, Edward 4
TOCH, Ernst 2
TOCH, Maximilian 2
TOCQUEVILLE, Alexis Henri Maurice Clerel 'de H
TOD, David H
TOD, George H
TOD, J. Kennedy 1
TOD, John H
TOD, John 3
TODD, Albert May 1
TODD, Albert W. 2
TODD, Ambrose Giddings 1
TODD, Arthur James 2
TODD, Casey 1
TODD, Chapman Coleman 1
TODD, Charles Burr 4
TODD, Charles Stewart H
TODD, Clare Chrisman 3
TODD, David 1
TODD, Earle Marion 1
TODD, Edward Howard 5
TODD, Eli H
TODD, Elmer Ely 1
TODD, Elmer Kenneth 5
TODD, Eugene, Jr. 5
TODD, Fannie Burgess (Mrs. Harold Arthur Todd) 5
TODD, Forde Anderson 5
TODD, Frank Chisholm 1
TODD, George Carroll 2
TODD, George Davidson 4
TODD, George Walter 1
TODD, H. Stanley 1
TODD, Harold Arthur 4
TODD, Harry L. 1
TODD, Henry Alfred 1
TODD, Henry Davis 1
TODD, Hiram Charles 4
TODD, Hiram Eugene 2
TODD, James Edward 1
TODD, John H
TODD, John Blair Smith H
TODD, John Reynard 2
TODD, Joseph Clinton 5
TODD, Jouett Ross 4
TODD, Laurence 3
TODD, Lawrie H
TODD, Lemuel 1
TODD, Luther Edward 1
TODD, M. Hampton 4
TODD, Mabel Loomis 1
TODD, Marion 1
TODD, Michael 3
TODD, Paul Harold 5
TODD, Percy R. 1
TODD, Robert Henry 4
TODD, Robert I. 1
TODD, Sereno Edwards H
TODD, T. Wingate 5
TODD, Thomas H
TODD, Thomas 3
TODD, Walter Edmond Clyde 5
TODD, Walter Ledyard 5
TODD, William Henry 1
TODD, William T. Jr. 3
TOEBBE, Augustus Marie H
TOFFENETTI, Dario Louis 4
TOFFTEEN, Olof Alfred 4
TOFTOY, Holger Nelson 4
TOGLIATTI, Palmiro 5
TOGNAZZINI, Roland 5
TOLAN, John Harvey 2
TOLAND, Clarence G(aines) 5
TOLAND, Edmund M. 2
TOLAND, Hugh Huger 1
TOLBERT, Benjamin Arthur 1
TOLBERT, Joseph W(arren) 5
TOLBERT, Raymond Augustine 4
TOLBERT, Ward Van 'der Hoof 2
TOLEDO-HERRARTE, Luis 5
TOLER, Fred W. 5
TOLFREE, James Edward 1
TOLIN, Ernest A. 4
TOLISCHUS, Otto David 4

TOLL, Roger Wolcott 1
TOLL, William Edward 1
TOLLEFSON, Martin 4
TOLLER, Ernst H
TOLLER, Ernst H
TOLLES, Marian Donahue (Mrs. N. Arnold Tolles) 5
TOLLES, Newman Arnold 5
TOLLES, Sheldon Hitchcock 1
TOLLESON, William N. 2
TOLLETT, Raymond Lee 5
TOLLEY, Harold Sumner 4
TOLLEY, Howard Ross 3
TOLLMIEN, Walter Gustav 5
TOLMAN, Albert Harris 1
TOLMAN, Albert Walter 5
TOLMAN, Charles Prescott 4
TOLMAN, Cyrus Fisher Jr. 2
TOLMAN, Edgar Bronson 2
TOLMAN, Edward Chase 4
TOLMAN, Frank Leland 4
TOLMAN, Herbert Cushing 1
TOLMAN, Judson Allen 2
TOLMAN, Richard Chace 2
TOLMAN, Ruth S. 3
TOLMAN, Warren W. 1
TOLMAN, William Howe 1
TOLMIE, William Fraser H
TOLSON, George Tolover 4
TOLSTOY, Count Alexei Nikolaevich H
TOLTZ, Max 1
TOM, Howard 4
TOMAJAN, John S. 5
TOMBER, Max L. 5
TOME, Jacob H
TOMEI, Peter Andrew 5
TOMKINS, Calvin 1
TOMKINS, Floyd Williams 1
TOMLIN, Bradley Walker 3
TOMLIN, James Harvey 4
TOMLINS, William Lawrence 4
TOMLINSON, Allen U. 1
TOMLINSON, Arthur Hibbs 1
TOMLINSON, Charles C. 5
TOMLINSON, Charles Fawcett 2
TOMLINSON, Everett Titsworth 1
TOMLINSON, George Ashley 1
TOMLINSON, Gideon H
TOMLINSON, H. M. 3
TOMLINSON, Homer Aubrey 5
TOMLINSON, Roy Everett 1
TOMLINSON, Thomas Ash 5
TOMLINSON, Vincent Eaton 1
TOMLINSON, William Gosnell 5
TOMOCHICHI H
TOMPERS, George Urban 1
TOMPERT, Russell Howard 1
TOMPKINS, Arnold 1
TOMPKINS, Arthur Sidney 1
TOMPKINS, Boylston Adams 5
TOMPKINS, Caleb H
TOMPKINS, Charles Henry 1
TOMPKINS, Charles Hook 3
TOMPKINS, Christopher H
TOMPKINS, Christopher H
TOMPKINS, Cydnor Bailey 3
TOMPKINS, Daniel A. 1
TOMPKINS, Daniel D. H
TOMPKINS, De Loss Monroe H
TOMPKINS, Elizabeth Knight 4
TOMPKINS, Frank Hector 1
TOMPKINS, H. D. 3
TOMPKINS, Juliet Wilbor 3
TOMPKINS, Leslie Jay 3
TOMPKINS, Lucius Douglas H
TOMPKINS, Nathaniel 5
TOMPKINS, Patrick Watson H
TOMPSON, Benjamin H

TOMS, Robert Morrell 3
TOMS, Zach 4
TONDORF, Francis Anthony 1
TONE, Franchot 5
TONE, Frank Jerome 2
TONER, Edward C. 1
TONER, James Vincent 3
TONER, Joseph Meredith 1
TONG, Hollington K. 5
TONGUE, Thomas H. 1
TONKS, Oliver Samuel 1
TONNER, John Andrew 4
TONTY, Henry 'de H
TOOHEY, John Peter 2
TOOKER, Lewis Frank 1
TOOKER, Norman Brown 4
TOOKER, Sterling Twiss 5
TOOKEY, Clarence H(all) 5
TOOLE, Joseph Kemp 1
TOOLE, S. Westcott 5
TOOLIN, John Martin 5
TOOMBS, Henry Johnston 5
TOOMBS, Percy Walthall 1
TOOMBS, Robert Augustus H
TOOMEY, De Lally Prescott 1
TOON, Thomas Fentress 1
TOOTELL, Robert Ballard 5
TOOTHAKER, Charles Robinson 3
TOOTLE, Milton Jr. 2
TOPAKYAN, Haigazoun Hohannes 1
TOPE, Homer W. 1
TOPLIFF, Samuel H
TOPLITZKY, Joe 1
TOPPAN, Charles H
TOPPAN, Robert Noxon 1
TOPPIN, Harry Pattinson 1
TOPPING, John Alexander 1
TORBERT, Alfred Thomas Archimedes H
TORBERT, John Bryant 1
TORBERT, William Sydenham 5
TORBETT, Joe Hall 3
TORCHIANA, Henry Albert 'van Coenen 1
TORCHIO, Philip 1
TORCHIO, Phillip Jr. 3
TOREK, Franz 1
TORGERSEN, Harold 4
TORGERSEN, Harold W. 4
TORIAN, Oscar Noel 5
TORKELSON, Martin Wilhelm 4
TORNEY, George Henry 1
TORNGREN, Ralf 4
TORO, Emilio 'del 4
TORRANCE, David 1
TORRANCE, Eli 1
TORRANCE, Francis J. 5
TORRANCE, Henry 5
TORRANCE, Stiles Albert 1
TORRE, Carlos de la 5
TORRENCE, George Paull 4
TORRENCE, Joseph Thatcher H
TORRENCE, Olivia Howard Dunbar 5
TORRENCE, Ridgely 5
TORRENS, D.T. 5
TORRENS, William Erskine 1
TORREY, Bradford 1
TORREY, Charles Cutler 5
TORREY, Charles Turner H
TORREY, Elbridge 1
TORREY, Elliot Bouton 1
TORREY, George Burroughs 2
TORREY, Herbert Gray 1
TORREY, John H
TORREY, Joseph 1
TORREY, Marian Marsh 5
TORREY, Raymond Hezekiah 1
TORREY, Reuben Archer 1
TORREYSON, Burr Walter 1
TORRISON, John William 4
TORRISON, Oscar M. 1
TORY, John Stewart Donald 4
TOSCANINI, Arturo 3
TOTH, William 1
TOTTEN, Charles Adiel Lewis 1
TOTTEN, George Muirson H

TOTTEN,
  George Oakley Jr. 1
TOTTEN, Joe Byron 2
TOTTEN, Joseph Gilbert H
TOTTEN, Ralph James 2
TOTTEN, Silas
TOTTON, Frank Mortimer 3
TOTTY, S. V. 4
TOUCEY, Isaac H
TOULMIN, Harry H
TOULMIN, 4
  Harry Aubrey Jr.
TOULMIN,
  Harry Theophilus
TOULMIN, John Edwin 5
TOUMEY, James William 1
TOUPS, Roland Leon 4
TOUR, Reuben S. 3
TOURET, Frank Hale 2
TOURGEE, 1
  Albion Winegar
TOURJEE, Eben H
TOURSCHER, 1
  Francis Edward
TOURTELLOT, 2
  George Platt
TOURTELLOTTE, 1
  Edward Everett
TOUSANT, Emma
  Sanborn 5
TOUSEY, Sinclair H
TOUSEY, William George 1
TOUSSAINT H
  L'OUVERTURE, Pierre
  Francois Dominique
TOUTON, Frank Charles 1
TOUVELLE, William E. 4
TOVEN, Joseph Richard 5
TOWAR, Albert Selah
TOWART, William G. 2
TOWER, Carl Vernon 5
TOWER, Charlemagne 1
TOWER, 3
  Edwin Briggs Hale Jr.
TOWER, George Edward 1
TOWER, 5
  George Warren Jr.
TOWER, James Eaton 2
TOWER, John H
TOWER, Olin Freeman 2
TOWER, Ralph Winfred 1
TOWER, Walter Sheldon 5
TOWER, 5
  William Lawrence
TOWERS, Albert Garey 1
TOWERS, John Alden 3
TOWERS, John Henry 3
TOWERS, Walter Kellogg 2
TOWL, Forrest Milton 2
TOWLE, Carroll S. 1
TOWLE, Charles Brother 3
TOWLE, Charlotte 4
TOWLE, H
  George Makepeace
TOWLE, J. Norman 3
TOWLE, Norman Lincoln 4
TOWLER, John H
TOWLER, Thomas Willard 5
TOWN, David Edward 4
TOWN, Ithiel H
TOWNE, 3
  Arthur Whittlesey
TOWNE, Benjamin H
TOWNE, Charles Arnette 1
TOWNE, Charles Hanson 2
TOWNE, Edward Owings 4
TOWNE, Elizabeth 4
TOWNE, Ezra Thayer 1
TOWNE, George Lewis 4
TOWNE, Henry Robinson 1
TOWNE, John Henry H
TOWNE, John Henry 2
TOWNE, Robert Duke 3
TOWNE, Salem B. 1
TOWNE, Walter James 1
TOWNE, William Elmer 5
TOWNER, Daniel Brink 1
TOWNER, Horace Mann 1
TOWNER, Neile Fassett 4
TOWNER, 2
  Rutherford Hamilton
TOWNER, Zealous Bates H
TOWNES, 4
  Edgar Eggleston
TOWNES, John Charles 1
TOWNLEY, Calvert
TOWNLEY, Sidney Dean 2
TOWNS, Charles B. 2
TOWNS, H
  George Washington
  Bonaparte
TOWNSEND, Amos H
TOWNSEND,
  Charles Elroy
TOWNSEND, H
  Charles Haskell

TOWNSEND, 1
  Charles Haskins
TOWNSEND, 2
  Charles Henry Tyler
TOWNSEND, 1
  Charles Orrin
TOWNSEND,
  Charles Wendell
TOWNSEND,
  Curtis McDonald
TOWNSEND, 4
  Dallas Selwyn
TOWNSEND, Edgar
  Jerome 3
TOWNSEND, Edward
  Davis H
TOWNSEND, 2
  Edward Waterman
TOWNSEND, 1
  Edwin Franklin
TOWNSEND, 2
  Ernest Nathaniel
TOWNSEND, 4
  Francis Everett
TOWNSEND, 4
  Frederic Martin
TOWNSEND, Frederick 2
TOWNSEND, George H
TOWNSEND, 1
  George Alfred
TOWNSEND, 2
  George Washington
TOWNSEND, Harvey
  Gates 1
TOWNSEND, Henry C. 1
TOWNSEND, Horace 1
TOWNSEND, Hosea 1
TOWNSEND, James Bliss 1
TOWNSEND, *
  James Mulford
TOWNSEND, John G. Jr. 4
TOWNSEND, John Kirk H
TOWNSEND, John
  Wilson 4
TOWNSEND, 1
  Joseph Hendley
TOWNSEND, 1
  Julius Curtis
TOWNSEND, Lawrence 3
TOWNSEND, Luther
  Tracy 1
TOWNSEND, M. Clifford 4
TOWNSEND, 1
  Marion Ernest
TOWNSEND, 1
  Martin Ingham
TOWNSEND, Mary
  Ashley 1
TOWNSEND, Mary
  Evelyn 3
TOWNSEND, H
  Mira Sharpless
TOWNSEND, Oliver
  Henry 5
TOWNSEND, Oscar 5
TOWNSEND, 4
  Prescott Winson
TOWNSEND, Randolph
  W.
TOWNSEND, Robert H
TOWNSEND, 1
  Robert Donaldson
TOWNSEND, 2
  Smith DeLancey
TOWNSEND, Sylvester
  D. 1
TOWNSEND, 2
  Theodore Irving
TOWNSEND, 4
  Virginia Frances
TOWNSEND, Washington H
TOWNSEND, 5
  Wayne LaSalle
TOWNSEND, 3
  Willard Saxby
TOWNSEND, William H. 4
TOWNSEND, William
  Hay 1
TOWNSEND, 1
  William Kneeland
TOWNSEND,
  William Warren
TOWNSEND, Wilson 4
TOWNSEND, 1
  Wisner Robinson
TOWNSHEND, Charles H
TOWNSHEND, H
  Norton Strange
TOWNSHEND, H
  Richard Wellington
TOWNSLEY, 1
  Clarence Page
TOWNSLEY, Louis 5
TOWSE, J. Ranken 1
TOY, Crawford Howell 1
TOY, Harry Stanley 3
TOY, Walter Dallam 4

TOZERE, Frederic 5
TOZIER, Josephine 4
TOZZER, Alfred Marston 3
TOZZER, 1
  Arthur Clarence
TRABERT, George Henry 4
TRABUE, Charles Clay 1
TRABUE, Edmund Francis 1
TRABUE, Isaac Hodgen 1
TRABUE, Marion Rex 5
TRACEWELL, Robert J. 1
TRACEY, Charles
TRACEY, James Frances 1
TRACY, Albert Haller H
TRACY, Andrew H
TRACY, 1
  Benjamin Franklin
TRACY, Charles Chapin 1
TRACY, Clarissa Tucker 1
TRACY, Daniel William 3
TRACY, Ernest B. 2
TRACY, Evarts 1
TRACY, Frank Basil 1
TRACY, Frank W. 1
TRACY, George Allison 5
TRACY, Henry Chester 2
TRACY, Henry Wells H
TRACY, 2
  Howard Van Sinderen
TRACY, James Grant 1
TRACY, James Madison 1
TRACY, John Clayton 3
TRACY, John Evarts 1
TRACY, Joseph H
TRACY, Joseph Powell 1
TRACY, William) Lee 5
TRACY, Leo James 4
TRACY, Lyall 1
TRACY, Martha 2
TRACY, Merle Elliott 1
TRACY, Nathaniel H
TRACY, Phineas Lyman 1
TRACY, Roger Sherman 1
TRACY, Roger Walker 4
TRACY, Russel Lord 1
TRACY, Samuel Mills 1
TRACY, Spencer 4
TRACY, Thomas Henry 4
TRACY, Uri H
TRACY, Uriah H
TRACY, William W. 5
TRAEGER, 1
  Cornelius Horace
TRAEGER, William Isham 1
TRAER, Charles Solberg 2
TRAFFORD, 2
  Bernard Walton
TRAFTON, Gilbert Haven 2
TRAFTON, Mark H
TRAFTON, William
  Henry 1
TRAIN, Arthur 2
TRAIN, Charles J. 1
TRAIN, Charles Russell H
TRAIN, Charles Russell 4
TRAIN, 1
  Elizabeth Phipps
TRAIN, Enoch H
TRAIN, Ethel Kissam 1
TRAIN, George Francis 1
TRAIN, Harold Cecil 5
TRAIN, John Lambert 3
TRAINER, 5
  David Woolsey Jr.
TRAINER, 5
  Maurice Newlin
TRAJETTA, Philip H
TRALLE, Henry Edward 2
TRAMBURG, John
  William 4
TRAMMEL, 1
  Leander Newton
TRAMMELL, Niles 5
TRAMMELL, Park 1
TRAMWELL, Paul
  Barclay 4
TRANE, Reuben Nicholas 3
TRANER, Fredrick W. 4
TRANER, Fredrick W. 4
TRANSEAU, Edgar
  Nelson 5
TRANT, James Buchanan 5
TRANTHAM, Henry 4
TRAP, William Martin 3
TRAPHAGEN, Frank
  Weiss 1
TRAPIER, Paul H
TRAPP, Martin Edwin 3
TRASK, 1
  John Ellingwood Donnell
TRASK, John William 3
TRASK, Kate Nichols 1
TRASK, Spencer 1
TRASK, William Blake 1
TRATMAN, 5
  Edward Ernest Russell

TRATTNER, 4
  Ernest Robert
TRAUB, Peter Edward 3
TRAUBEL, Helen 5
TRAUBEL, Horace 1
TRAUDT, Bernard G. 5
TRAUGOTT, Albert
  Maser 3
TRAUTMAN, George M. 4
TRAUTMANN, 1
  William Emil
TRAUTWINE, H
  John Cresson
TRAUTWINE, 1
  John Cresson Jr.
TRAVEN, B. 5
TRAVER, John Gideon 2
TRAVERS, 2
  Edward Schofield
TRAVIS, 2
  Charles Mabbett
TRAVIS, Homer Lee 4
TRAVIS, Ira Dudley 1
TRAVIS, Juluis Curtis 4
TRAVIS, Philip H. 4
TRAVIS, 3
  Robert Falligant
TRAVIS, Simeon Ezekiel 3
TRAVIS, Walter John H
TRAVIS, Walter John 1
TRAVIS, Wesley Elgin 5
TRAVIS, William Barret 1
TRAWICK, 5
  Arcadius McSwain
TRAWICK, Henry 1
TRAWICK, Leonard M. 4
TRAYLOR, John H. 4
TRAYLOR, Melvin Aivah 1
TRAYLOR, Robert Lee 4
TRAYNOR, Philip
  Andrew 4
TRAYNOR, 4
  William Bernard
TRAYNOR, 4
  William James Henry
TRAYSER, Lewis W. 4
TREACY, John P. 4
TREADWAY, Allen
  Towner 2
TREADWAY, 3
  Charles Terry
TREADWELL, Aaron
  Louis 2
TREADWELL, Daniel H
TREADWELL, 5
  Edward Francis
TREADWELL, George A. 5
TREADWELL, John H
TREADWELL, Nancy
  Claar 5
TREANOR, Arthur Ryan 3
TREANOR, 4
  James Aloysius Jr.
TREANOR, John 1
TREANOR, 1
  Joseph Holland
TREANOR, 1
  Walter Emanuel
TREAT, Charles Gould 1
TREAT, Charles Henry 1
TREAT, Charles Payson 1
TREAT, Charles Watson 4
TREAT, George Winfield 3
TREAT, Jay Porter 4
TREAT, John Harvey 1
TREAT, Joseph Bradford 1
TREAT, Mary 1
TREAT, Payson Jackson 1
TREAT, Robert H
TREAT, Robert Byron 1
TREAT, Samuel H
TREAT, Samuel Hubbel H
TRECKER, 2
  Joseph Leonard
TRECKER, Theodore 4
TREDER, Oscar F. R. 3
TREDWAY, H
  William Marshall
TREDWELL, Daniel M. 1
TREDWELL, Thomas H
TREE, Herbert Beerbohm 1
TREE, Lambert 1
TREECE, Elbert Lee 4
TREES, Clyde C. 4
TREES, Harry A. 4
TREES, Joe Clifton 2
TREES, Merle Jay 4
TREFZGER, Emil Anton 4
TREGOE, James Harry 1
TRELEASE, 4
  Richard Mitchell
TRELEASE, Sam F. 3
TRELEASE, Sam Farlow 4
TRELEASE, William 2
TREMAIN, Albert Wright 5
TREMAIN, 2
  Eloise Ruthven

TREMAIN, George Lee 5
TREMAIN, Henry Edwin 1
TREMAIN, Lyman H
TREMAINE, Burton Gad 2
TREMAINE, 5
  Charles Milton
TREMAINE, 3
  Frederick Orlin
TREMAINE, Henry
  Barnes 1
TREMAN, Charles
  Edward 1
TREMAN, Robert Henry 1
TREMBLAY, Rene 4
TRENARY, 4
  James Marshall
TRENCH, 3
  William Washington
TRENCHARD, Edward C. H
TRENCHARD, 3
  Hugh Montague
TRENCHARD, H
  Stephen Decatur
TRENCHARD, 1
  Thomas Whitaker
TRENDLE, 5
  George Washington
TRENERY, Matthew John 5
TRENHOLM, H
  George Alfred
TRENHOLM, William Lee 1
TRENHOLME, 1
  Norman Maclaren
TRENT, 1
  Richard Henderson
TRENT, William H
TRENT, William Johnson 4
TRENT, 1
  William Peterfield
TRESCOT, William Henry H
TRESIDDER, 2
  Donald Bertrand
TRESOLINI, Rocco John 5
TRESSLER, Irving Dart 2
TRESSLER, Jacob Cloyd 3
TRESSLER, 1
  Victor George Augustine
TRETTIEN, 1
  Augustus William
TREUDLEY, Frederick 4
TREVELLICK, Richard F. 4
TREVELYAN, 1
  George Macaulay
TREVER, 1
  Albert Augustus
TREVER, George Henry 1
TREVES, Norman 4
TREVISAN, Vittorio 3
TREVOR, John Bond 3
TREVOR, Joseph Ellis 1
TREVORROW, 2
  Robert Johns
TREVOY, William Vivian 1
TREWIN, James Henry 1
TREXLER, Frank M. 2
TREXLER, Harry C. 1
TREXLER, Samuel Geiss 2
TREZVANT, James H
TRIBBLE, Lewis Herndon 4
TRIBBLE, Samuel Joel 1
TRIBUS, Louis Lincoln 1
TRICKETT, William 1
TRIEBEL, 4
  Frederick Ernst
TRIEBER, Jacob 1
TRIGG, Abram H
TRIGG, Ernest T. 3
TRIGG, John Johns H
TRIGGS,
  Flloyd Willding
TRIGGS, Oscar Lovell 4
TRILLEY, Joseph 1
TRIM, Gordon Mariner 4
TRIMBLE, Allen H
TRIMBLE, Carey Allen H
TRIMBLE, David H
TRIMBLE, Ernest Greene 5
TRIMBLE, Harvey Marion 1
TRIMBLE, H
  Isaac Ridgeway
TRIMBLE, James W. 5
TRIMBLE, John H
TRIMBLE, Richard 1
TRIMBLE, Robert H
TRIMBLE, 4
  Robert Maurice
TRIMBLE, Selden Y. 4
TRIMBLE, South 2
TRIMBLE, William Allen H
TRIMBLE, William Pitt 2
TRINE, Charles Clarke 1
TRINE, Ralph Waldo 5
TRINKLE, Elbert Lee 3
TRINKS, Willibald 5
TRIPLER, Charles E. 1
TRIPLETT, 3
  Arthur Fairfax

TRIPLETT, Elijah Henry 4
TRIPLETT, John Edwin 2
TRIPLETT, Norman 1
TRIPLETT, Philip H
TRIPP, Bartlett 1
TRIPP, Frank Elihu 4
TRIPP, Guy Eastman 1
TRIPP, Louis H. 4
TRIPP, 5
  William Henry, Jr.
TRIPPE, Andrew Cross 1
TRIPPE, James McConky 1
TRIPPE, John 1
TRIPPET, Oscar A. 1
TRISCOTT, 1
  Samuel Peter Rolt
TRIST, Nicholas Philip H
TRITLE, John Stewart 2
TRIVELLI, Albert F. 4
TROBEC, James 4
TROCHE, Ernst Gunter 5
TROEGER, John
  Winthrop 1
TROLAND, 1
  Leonard Thompson
TROOP, J. G. Carter 1
TROOST, George Wilbur 3
TROOST, Gerard H
TROPER, Morris C. 4
TROTT, Benjamin H
TROTT, 5
  Clement Augustus
TROTT, Nicholas H
TROTT, Stanley B. 3
TROTTER, 1
  Alfred Williams
TROTTER, Frank Butler 1
TROTTER, James Fisher H
TROTTER, Melvin E. 1
TROTTER, Newbold
  Hough H
TROTTER, Spencer 1
TROTTI, Lamar 3
TROTTI, Samuel Wilds H
TROTTMAN, 4
  James Franklin
TROTZ, J. O. Emmanuel 1
TROUBETZKOY, 2
  Amelie Rives
TROUBETZKOY,
  Prince Pierre
TROUP, Alexander 1
TROUP, George Michael 1
TROUP, Robert H
TROUT, Clement E. 4
TROUT, David McCamel 3
TROUT, Ethel Wendell 1
TROUT, Grace Wilbur 4
TROUT, Hugh Henry Sr. 2
TROUT, Michael Carver 1
TROUYET, Carlos 5
TROW, John Fowler H
TROWBRIDGE, 4
  Alexander Buel
TROWBRIDGE, Alvah 1
TROWBRIDGE, 5
  Arthur Carleton
TROWBRIDGE, Augustus 1
TROWBRIDGE, Carl
  Hoyt 5
TROWBRIDGE, 1
  Charles Christopher
TROWBRIDGE, Edmund H
TROWBRIDGE, 1
  Edward Dwight
TROWBRIDGE, John 1
TROWBRIDGE,
  John Townsend
TROWBRIDGE,
  Mary Elizabeth Day
TROWBRIDGE, Perry
  Fox 1
TROWBRIDGE, H
  Rowland Ebenezer
TROWBRIDGE, 1
  S. Breck Parkman
TROWBRIDGE, Vaughan 5
TROWBRIDGE, H
  William Pettit
TROXELL, 5
  Edward Leffingwell
TROXELL, 4
  Millard Francis
TROXELL, 5
  Thomas Franklin
TROY, Alexander 1
TROY, George Francis 5
TROY, John Henry 3
TROY, John Weir 2
TROY, Peter Henry 3
TROY, Thomas Francis 4
TROYE, Edward
TRUAX, Arthur Harold 4
TRUAX, Charles Henry 1
TRUAX, Charles Vilas 5
TRUAX, 1
  Chauncey Shaffer

TRUBY, Albert Ernest 5
TRUCCO, Manuel 5
TRUDE, Alfred Samuel 1
TRUDEAU, 1
  Edward Livingston
TRUE, Alfred Charles 1
TRUE, Allen Tupper 3
TRUE, 5
  Frederick William
TRUE, Gordon Haines 1
TRUE, Hiram L. 4
TRUE, John Preston 1
TRUE, 5
  Lilian (Sarah) Crawford
TRUE, Rodney Howard 1
TRUE, Theodore Edmond 1
TRUEBLOOD, 1
  Benjamin Franklin
TRUEBLOOD, Dennis
  Lee 4
TRUEBLOOD, Ralph
  Waldo 3
TRUEBLOOD, 3
  Thomas Clarkson
TRUELL, Rohn 5
TRUELSEN, Henry 4
TRUEMAN, Walter
  Harley 5
TRUEMAN, William H. 1
TRUESDALE, Philemon
  E. 2
TRUESDALE, 1
  William Haynes
TRUESDELL, 1
  Hobart George
TRUESDELL, Karl 3
TRUETT, George W. 2
TRUETTE, 1
  Everett Ellsworth
TRUITT, James Steele 5
TRUITT, Max O'Rell 3
TRUITT, Ralph Purnell 5
TRUITT, Warren 1
TRUJILLO,
  MOLINA, Rafael Leonidas
TRULLINGER, R. W. 3
TRULY, Jefferson 4
TRUMAN,
  Benjamin Cummings
TRUMAN, Harry S. 5
TRUMAN, James
TRUMAN, Ralph Emerson 4
TRUMBAUER, Frank 4
TRUMBAUER, Horace 4
TRUMBAUER, Horace 4
TRUMBO, Andrew 3
TRUMBO, Arthur Cook 3
TRUMBULL, Annie Eliot 2
TRUMBULL, Benjamin 1
TRUMBULL,
  Charles Gallaudet
TRUMBULL, Frank 1
TRUMBULL, Gurdon 1
TRUMBULL, Henry Clay 1
TRUMBULL,
  James Hammond
TRUMBULL, John * H
TRUMBULL, John H. 4
TRUMBULL, Jonathan * H
TRUMBULL, Jonathan 1
TRUMBULL, Joseph * H
TRUMBULL, Levi R. 4
TRUMBULL, Lyman 4
TRUMP, Edward Needles 4
TRUMPLER, 3
  Robert Julius
TRUSCOTT,
  Frederick Wilson
TRUSCOTT, 4
  Lucian King Jr.
TRUSDELL,
  Charles Gregory
TRUSLOW, Francis
  Adams 5
TRUSSELL,
  C(harles) P(rescott)
TRUSTY, S(amuel) David 5
TRUTEAU, Jean Baptiste H
TRUXAL, Andrew Gehr 5
TRUXTUN, Thomas H
TRUXTUN,
  William Talbot
TRYON, Dwight William 1
TRYON, Frederick Gale 1
TRYON, H
  George Washington
TRYON, James Libby 3
TRYON, James Rufus 5
TRYON,
  Lillian (Wainwright) Hart
  (Mrs. Winthrop Pitt Tryon)
TRYON, Rolla Milton 3
TRYON, William 1
TRYON, Winthrop Pitt 5
TSALDARIS, Constantin 5
TSCHAPPAT, William H. 1
TSCHIRKY, Oscar 3

TSCHUDY, Arnold Nord 3
TSCHUDY, 2
  Herbert Bolivar
TSIANG, Tingfu F. 4
TSUKIYAMA, Wilfred C. 4
TUBBS, Arthur Lewis 2
TUBBS, Edward 3
TUBBS, Eston Valentine 2
TUBBS, Frank Dean 1
TUBBY, William Bunker 1
TUBERMAN, Walter H. 3
TUBMAN, Harriet 1
TUBMAN, Harriet 4
TUBMAN, 5
  William V(acanarat)
  S(hadrach)
TUCK, Amos H
TUCK, Edward 1
TUCK, Henry 1
TUCK, 1
  Somerville Pinkney
TUCK, 4
  Somerville Pinkney
TUCK, William Hallam 4
TUCKER, B. Fain 5
TUCKER, 5
  Benjamin Ferree
TUCKER, H
  Benjamin Ricketson
TUCKER, 4
  Benjamin Ricketson
TUCKER, Beverley H
TUCKER, 5
  Beverley Dandridge
TUCKER, 1
  Beverley Dandridge
TUCKER, 2
  Beverley Randolph
TUCKER, C. M. 3
TUCKER, 4
  Carlton Everett
TUCKER, Charles Cowles 1
TUCKER, Clarence R. 5
TUCKER, Ebenezer 1
TUCKER, Frank 2
TUCKER, 1
  Gardiner Chylson
TUCKER, George H
TUCKER, George Fox 1
TUCKER,
  Gilbert Milligan
TUCKER, Harry 2
TUCKER, Henry
  Holcombe H
TUCKER, H
  Henry St George
TUCKER, 1
  Henry St George
TUCKER, 3
  Henry St George
TUCKER, Hiram G. 4
TUCKER, Hugh Clarence 5
TUCKER, Irvin B. 2
TUCKER, John Francis 5
TUCKER, John Francis 1
TUCKER, H
  John Randolph *
TUCKER, 3
  Katharine Dickinson
TUCKER, Luther H
TUCKER, N. Beverley 4
TUCKER, H
  Nathaniel Beverley
TUCKER, Preston Thomas 3
TUCKER, 5
  Raymond R(oche)
TUCKER, 3
  Richard Blackburn
TUCKER, Richard Hawley 1
TUCKER, Samuel 3
TUCKER, Samuel Marion 4
TUCKER, Sophie 4
TUCKER, St George H
TUCKER, Starling 1
TUCKER, Thomas Tudor H
TUCKER, 1
  Tilghman Mayfield
TUCKER, W. Leon 1
TUCKER, 4
  William Clifford
TUCKER, 4
  William Conquest
TUCKER, William Jewett 1
TUCKER, Willis Gaylord 1
TUCKERMAN, Alfred 1
TUCKERMAN, Arthur 3
TUCKERMAN, Bayard 1
TUCKERMAN, Edward 1
TUCKERMAN, Frederick 1
TUCKERMAN, H
  Frederick Goddard
TUCKERMAN, H
  Henry Theodore
TUCKERMAN, Joseph H
TUCKERMAN, L. B. 4
TUCKERMAN,
  Samuel Parkman

TUCKEY, William H
TUDOR, Charles William 5
TUDOR, Frederic
TUDOR, Ralph Arnold 4
TUDOR, William H
TUECHTER, 2
  August Herman
TUFTS, Bowen 1
TUFTS, Charles H
TUFTS, Cotton H
TUFTS, Edgar 5
TUFTS, James Arthur 1
TUFTS, James Hayden 2
TUFTS, John H
TUFTY, Herbert Iver 5
TUGMAN, William
  Masten 4
TUHOLSKE, Herman 1
TUIGG, John
TUKEY, Harold Bradford 5
TULANE, Paul H
TULEY, Henry Enos 1
TULEY, Murray F.
TULEY, Philip Speed 2
TULLER, Edward Pratt 5
TULLER, John Jay 4
TULLIS, H. H. 3
TULLIS, Robert Lee 5
TULLOSS, Rees Edgar 3
TULLY, Jim 1
TULLY, Joseph Merit 4
TULLY, H
  Pleasant Britton
TULLY, Richard Walton 2
TULLY, William H
TULLY, William John 1
TUMILTY, 5
  Howard T(insley)
TUMULTY, 3
  Joseph Patrick
TUNISON, Abram Vorhis 5
TUNISON, 3
  George McGregor
TUNISON, 4
  Joseph Salathiel
TUNKS, Walter F. 3
TUNNELL, Ebe Walter 1
TUNSTALL, 3
  Robert Baylor
TUNSTALL, 1
  Robert Williamson
TUOHY, Edward Boyce 3
TUOHY, Walter Joseph 4
TUOMEY, Michael H
TUOMIOJA, 4
  Sakari Severi
TUPOLEV, 5
  Andrei Nikolaevich
TUPPER, Benjamin H
TUPPER, Claude A. 1
TUPPER, Frederick 1
TUPPER, Henry Allen * 1
TUPPER, James Waddell 1
TUPPER, Kerr Boyce 1
TURCHIN, John Basil 1
TURCK, Fenton Benedict 5
TURCK, Fenton Benedict 1
TURCOTTE, Edmond 4
TURINI, Giovanni 1
TURK, Milton Haight 2
TURK, Morris Howland 1
TURKEVICH, Leonty 4
TURKLE, Alonzo John 1
TURLEY, 5
  Clarence Milton
TURLEY, Henry Clay 4
TURLEY, Jay 1
TURLEY, Thomas Battle 1
TURLINGTON, Edgar 5
TURNAGE, Allen Hal 5
TURNBULL, Andrew H
TURNBULL, Andrew
  Blair 4
TURNBULL, 5
  Andrew Winchester
TURNBULL, Barton P. 1
TURNBULL, 1
  Charles Smith
TURNBULL, 1
  Edwin Litchfield
TURNBULL, 1
  Francese Hubbard
  Litchfield
TURNBULL, J. Gordon 3
TURNBULL, Laurence 1
TURNBULL, Margaret 2
TURNBULL,
  Martin Ryerson
TURNBULL, Robert H
TURNBULL, Robert 4
TURNBULL, Robert
  James H
TURNBULL, Walter 1
TURNBULL,
  Mason 1
TURNBULL, William H

TURNEAURE, 3
  Frederick Eugene
TURNER, Abe W. 2
TURNER, 1
  Archelaus Ewing
TURNER, Arthur Henry 1
TURNER, Asa H
TURNER, H
  Benjamin Sterling
TURNER, Charles Jr. H
TURNER, Charles Edward 1
TURNER, 1
  Charles Henry Black
TURNER, Charles Root 1
TURNER, 1
  Charles Willard
TURNER, 1
  Charles Yardley
TURNER, Clarence W. 3
TURNER,
  Claude Allen Porter
TURNER, Daniel * H
TURNER, 5
  Daniel Lawrence
TURNER, 5
  Daniel W(ebster)
TURNER, 1
  Douglas Kellogg
TURNER, Edward H
TURNER, 3
  Edward Crawford
TURNER, Edward Lewis 3
TURNER, Edward
  Raymond 1
TURNER, Farrant Lewis 3
TURNER, 1
  Fennell Parrish
TURNER, Fred J. 4
TURNER, 1
  Frederick Jackson
TURNER, Gardner Clyde 5
TURNER, George 1
TURNER, George Kibbe 5
TURNER, Harold 4
TURNER, Harold Rhoades 3
TURNER, Helen M. 3
TURNER, Henry
  Chandlee 3
TURNER, 5
  Henry Chandlee, Jr.
TURNER, Henry H. 5
TURNER, Henry McNeal 1
TURNER, Henry Ward 1
TURNER, Herbert Beach 1
TURNER, J. Walter 3
TURNER, James * H
TURNER, James 3
TURNER, James H. 1
TURNER, James Jewett 1
TURNER, James Patrick 1
TURNER, John Pickett 4
TURNER, John Roscoe 3
TURNER, John Wesley H
TURNER, H
  Jonathan Baldwin
TURNER, 1
  Joseph Augustine
TURNER, Josiah H
TURNER, Kenneth B. 3
TURNER, Laura Lemon 1
TURNER,
  Lawrence Emerson
TURNER, Lewis M. 1
TURNER, Martin Luther 1
TURNER, Maurice Clark 3
TURNER, Nat H
TURNER, Oscar H
TURNER, Oscar 4
TURNER, Ralph Edmund 4
TURNER, Richmond
  Kelly 4
TURNER, 4
  Rodolphus Kibbe
TURNER, Roscoe 5
TURNER, Ross Sterling 1
TURNER, Roy Joseph 5
TURNER,
  Samuel Gilbert Hathaway
TURNER,
  Samuel Hulbeart
TURNER, Scott 5
TURNER, H
  Thomas Johnston
TURNER, Walter Victor 1
TURNER, Wilfred Dent 1
TURNER, William
  William De Garmo
TURNER, William Henry
TURNER, William Jay 2
TURNER, William Wood 5
TURNEY, Daniel Braxton 1
TURNEY, Hopkins Lacy
TURNEY, Jacob
TURNEY, Peter
TURNEY, William Ward

TURNLEY, Parmenas Taylor 1
TURPIE, David 1
TURPIN, Ben H
TURPIN, Ben
TURPIN, C. Murray 2
TURPIN, Edna Henry Lee 3
TURPIN, Rees
TURQUETIL, Arsene 5
TURRELL, Charles Alfred
TURRELL, Edgar Abel 4
TURRELL, Jane H
TURRENTINE, Samuel Bryant 3
TURRILL, Charles Beebe 1
TURRILL, Joel H
TURTON, Franklin E. 3
TUSKA, Gustave Robisher
TUSTIN, Ernest Leigh 1
TUTEN, J(ames) Russell 5
TUTHILL, Alexander Mackenzie 5
TUTHILL, Joseph Hasbrouck H
TUTHILL, Richard Stanley 1
TUTHILL, Selah H
TUTHILL, Theodore Robinson 1
TUTHILL, William Burnet
TUTHILL, William Burnet 4
TUTT, Charles Leaming 4
TUTT, John Calhoun 1
TUTTLE, Albert Henry 1
TUTTLE, Alexander Harrison 1
TUTTLE, Arthur J. 2
TUTTLE, Arthur Lemuel 1
TUTTLE, Arthur Smith 2
TUTTLE, Bloodgood 1
TUTTLE, Charles Augustus
TUTTLE, Charles H(enry) 5
TUTTLE, Charles Wesley H
TUTTLE, Clarence Ewing 4
TUTTLE, Daniel Sylvester 1
TUTTLE, David Kitchell 1
TUTTLE, Edwin Frank 5
TUTTLE, Emma Rood 4
TUTTLE, George Albert 2
TUTTLE, George Marvine 1
TUTTLE, George Montgomery 1
TUTTLE, George Thomas 1
TUTTLE, Henry 3
TUTTLE, Henry Emerson 2
TUTTLE, Henry William 4
TUTTLE, Herbert H
TUTTLE, Hiram Americus 1
TUTTLE, Hudson 1
TUTTLE, James Patterson 1
TUTTLE, Joseph Farrand 1
TUTTLE, Julius Herbert 2
TUTTLE, Lucius 1
TUTTLE, Mary McArthur Thompson 1
TUTTLE, Morton Chase 3
TUTTLE, Thomas Dyer 5
TUTTLE, W(illiam) B(uckhout) 5
TUTTLE, William Edgar Jr. 1
TUTWILER, Henry H
TUTWILER, Julia Strudwick
TUTWILER, Temple Wilson 3
TUTWILER, Thomas Henry 1
TWEED, Charles Harrison 1
TWEED, George Peter 2
TWEED, Harrison 1
TWEED, William Marcy H
TWEEDELL, Edward David 1
TWEEDELL, James Collier 4
TWEEDY, Frank 1
TWEEDY, Henry Hallam 1
TWEEDY, John Hubbard H
TWEEDY, Samuel H

TWELLS, Robert 4
TWENHOFEL, William Henry 3
TWICHELL, Ginery 1
TWICHELL, Joseph Hopkins
TWIGGS, David Emanuel H
TWING, Martin Walter 4
TWINING, Alexander Catlin H
TWINING, Frank Barton 2
TWINING, Kinsley 1
TWINING, Nathan Crook 1
TWISS, George Ransom 1
TWITCHELL, Amos H
TWITCHELL, Hannah (Mrs. Milton C. Twitchell) 5
TWITCHELL, Herbert Kenaston 1
TWITCHELL, La Fayette 1
TWITCHELL, Pierrepont Edwards 4
TWITCHELL, Ralph Emerson
TWITMYER, Edwin Burket 1
TWITTY, Joseph Jones 4
TWITTY, Victor Chandler 4
TWOHY, Daniel W. 5
TWOMBLY, Alexander Stevenson 1
TWOMBLY, Clifford Gray 2
TWOMBLY, Edward Bancroft 5
TWOMBLY, Hamilton McKown 1
TWOMBLY, Henry Bancroft 3
TWOMEY, M. Joseph 2
TYDINGS, Millard E. 4
TYE, Hiram H. 2
TYE, John L. 1
TYLER, Alice Sarah 5
TYLER, Ansel Augustus 5
TYLER, Asher H
TYLER, Bayard Henry 1
TYLER, Benjamin Bushrod 4
TYLER, Bennet H
TYLER, Charles A. 3
TYLER, Charles Mellen 1
TYLER, Cornelius Boardman 3
TYLER, D. Gardiner 1
TYLER, Daniel H
TYLER, Frank Edwards 1
TYLER, George Crouse 2
TYLER, Harry Walter 1
TYLER, Henry Mather 1
TYLER, James Gale 1
TYLER, James Hoge 1
TYLER, James M. 1
TYLER, John * 1
TYLER, John Mason 1
TYLER, John Poyntz 1
TYLER, John W. 4
TYLER, Lyon Gardiner 1
TYLER, Mason Whiting 1
TYLER, Morris Franklin 1
TYLER, Moses Coit 1
TYLER, Odette 2
TYLER, Ransom Hubert H
TYLER, Robert 1
TYLER, Robert Ogden H
TYLER, Royall H
TYLER, Samuel H
TYLER, Stanley A. 4
TYLER, Stephen Leslie 4
TYLER, Wilfred Charles 4
TYLER, William H
TYLER, William Seymour 1
TYLER, William Trevor 1
TYNAN, Joseph James 1
TYNAN, Thomas J. 5
TYNDALE, Hector H
TYNDALL, Charles Herbert 1
TYNDALL, Henry Myron 2
TYNDALL, Robert H. 2
TYNDALL, William Thomas 4
TYNDELL, Charles Noyes 5
TYNE, Thomas James 1
TYNER, Charles L. 1
TYNER, George Parker 1
TYNER, James Noble 1
TYNG, Edward H
TYNG, Sewell Tappan 2
TYNG, Stephen Higginson H
TYNG, Theodosius Stevens 4
TYREE, Evans 4
TYREE, Lewis 3
TYRRELL, Frank G. 4

TYRRELL, Henry 1
TYRRELL, Henry Grattan 2
TYRRELL, W. Bradley 4
TYSEN, John Colquhoun 5
TYSON, Carroll Sargent 3
TYSON, Francis Doughton 4
TYSON, Jacob H
TYSON, James 1
TYSON, Job Roberts H
TYSON, John Ambrose 5
TYSON, John D. 4
TYSON, John Russell 1
TYSON, Lawrence Davis 1
TYSON, Levering 4
TYSON, Ralph Maguire 4
TYSON, Stuart Lawrence 1
TYSSOWSKI, John 4

U

UANNA, William Lewis 4
UBICO, Jorge 4
UCHIDA, Baron Yasuya 4
UDALL, Denny Hammond 3
UDALL, Levi Stewart 4
UDDEN, Johan August 1
UDELL, Alonzo E. 4
UDREE, Daniel H
UEBELACKER, David Adams 4
UEHLING, Edward A. 3
UELAND, Andreas 1
UFER, Walter 1
UFFORD, Walter Shepard 1
UGARTE, Manuel 4
UGARTE, Salvator 4
UGHETTA, Henry Leopold 4
UHDE, Hermann 4
UHL, Charles F. 4
UHL, Willis Lemon 1
UHLE, Bernhard 4
UHLE, Frederich Max 4
UHLER, Horace Scudder 3
UHLER, Jacob P. 1
UHLER, Joseph Michael 2
UHLER, Philip Reese 1
UHLMANN, Erich Myron 4
UHLMANN, Fred H
UIHLEIN, Edgar John 3
UIHLEIN, Erwin C(harles) 5
UIHLEIN, Robert A. 3
UIHLEIN, Robert August 3
UKERS, William Harrison
ULBRICHT, Walter 5
ULE, Guy Maxwell 5
ULIO, James Alexander 3
ULKE, Henry 1
ULLMAN, Berthold Louis 4
ULLMAN, Frederic Jr. 2
ULLMAN, James Ramsey 5
ULLMANN, Harry Maas 5
ULLMANN, Siegfried 4
ULLOA, Antonio H
ULLOA, Francisco 'de H
ULMAN, Joseph N. 2
ULMAN, William Alban 4
ULMANN, Albert 1
ULMANN, Doris 1
ULREY, Albert Brennus 1
ULRICH, Barry Stribling
ULRICH, Barry Stribling 2
ULRICH, Charles Frederic 1
ULRICH, Edward Oscar 2
ULRICH, Leslie Robert 4
UMBECK, Sharvy Greiner 5
UMBEL, Robert Emory 2
UMBERGER, Harry John Charles 3
UMBREIT, Samuel John 5
UMBSTAETTER, Herman Daniel 1
UMPHREY, Harry E. 4
UMPLEBY, Joseph B. 4
UMSTEAD, William Bradley 3
UNCAS H
UNCLE, Sam H
UNCLES, John Francis 4
UNDERHILL, Charles Lee 2
UNDERHILL, Charles Reginald 3
UNDERHILL, Edwin Stewart 1
UNDERHILL, Frank Pell 1
UNDERHILL, James 1
UNDERHILL, John H
UNDERHILL, John Garrett 2

UNDERHILL, John Quincy 1
UNDERHILL, Walter H
UNDERWOOD, Benjamin Franklin 1
UNDERWOOD, Bert Elias 2
UNDERWOOD, Clarence F. 1
UNDERWOOD, E. Marvin H
UNDERWOOD, Felix Joel 3
UNDERWOOD, Francis Henry H
UNDERWOOD, Frederick Douglass 2
UNDERWOOD, George Arthur 2
UNDERWOOD, Herbert Shapleigh 4
UNDERWOOD, Horace Grant 1
UNDERWOOD, Ira Julian 1
UNDERWOOD, John Cox 1
UNDERWOOD, John Curtiss H
UNDERWOOD, John Thomas 1
UNDERWOOD, John Thomas 4
UNDERWOOD, John William Henderson H
UNDERWOOD, Joseph Merritt 3
UNDERWOOD, Joseph Rogers 2
UNDERWOOD, Lillias Stirling Horton 4
UNDERWOOD, Lineas Dott 1
UNDERWOOD, Loring 1
UNDERWOOD, Lucien Marcus 1
UNDERWOOD, Mell G. 5
UNDERWOOD, Oscar W. 4
UNDERWOOD, Oscar Wilder Jr.
UNDERWOOD, Sara A. 1
UNDERWOOD, Thomas Ingle 3
UNDERWOOD, Thomas Rust 3
UNDERWOOD, Warner Lewis H
UNDERWOOD, William Jackson 1
UNDERWOOD, William Lyman 1
UNDSET, Sigrid 2
UNGAR, Arthur Arnold 4
UNGER, Frederic William 5
UNGERLEIDER, Samuel, Jr. 5
UNSELD, Benjamin Carl 1
UNTERMEYER, Jean Starr 5
UNTERMYER, Alvin 4
UNTERMYER, Samuel 1
UNTHANK, James Bryant 4
UNWIN, Sir Stanley 5
UPCHURCH, John Jordan H
UPDEGRAFF, Allan H
UPDEGRAFF, David Brainard
UPDEGRAFF, Harlan 3
UPDEGRAFF, Milton 1
UPDEGRAFF, Paul Walter 3
UPDEGRAFF, Thomas H
UPDIKE, Daniel H
UPDIKE, Daniel Berkeley 2
UPDIKE, Edward Lafayette 3
UPDIKE, Eugene Grover 1
UPDIKE, Godfrey Ernest 1
UPDIKE, Ralph E. Sr. 1
UPDYKE, Frank Arthur 1
UPHAM, Alfred Horatio 4
UPHAM, Charles Melville 3
UPHAM, Charles Wentworth H
UPHAM, Francis B. Jr. 4
UPHAM, Francis Bourne 1
UPHAM, Frank Brooks 1
UPHAM, Frederic William 1
UPHAM, George Baxter H
UPHAM, Jabez H
UPHAM, John Howell Janeway 5
UPHAM, Nathaniel 1
UPHAM, Roy 1
UPHAM, Samuel Foster 1

UPHAM, Thomas Cogswell H
UPHAM, Warren 1
UPHAM, William H
UPHAM, William H. 1
UPJOHN, Hobart Brown 2
UPJOHN, Richard H
UPJOHN, Richard Mitchell 1
UPLEGER, Arthur C(hristan) 5
UPP, Charles W. 4
UPPVALL, Axel Johan 4
UPSHAW, William David 3
UPSHUR, Abel Parker H
UPSHUR, John Henry 1
UPSHUR, John Nottingham 2
UPSHUR, William Peterkin
UPSON, Andrew Seth 1
UPSON, Anson Judd 1
UPSON, Arthur (Wheelock) 5
UPSON, Charles H
UPSON, Charles Ayrault 5
UPSON, Fred Wilbert 2
UPSON, Lent Dayton 1
UPSON, Maxwell Mayhew 5
UPSON, Ralph Hazlett 5
UPSON, Walter Lyman 5
UPSTON, John Edwin 3
UPTHEGROVE, Fay Roscoe
UPTON, Charles Horace H
UPTON, Clifford Brewster 3
UPTON, Clifford Brewster 4
UPTON, Daniel 1
UPTON, Emory H
UPTON, George Bruce H
UPTON, George Burr 2
UPTON, George Putnam 1
UPTON, Harriet Taylor 2
UPTON, Jacob Kendrick 1
UPTON, La Roy Sunderland 1
UPTON, Louis Cassius 3
UPTON, Robert H
UPTON, Robert W. 5
UPTON, William Treat 5
UPTON, Winslow 1
URANN, Marcus Libby 4
URBAN, Joseph 1
URBAN, Wilbur Marshall 5
URDANG, George 4
URELL, M. Emmet 4
UREN, Lester Charles 4
U'REN, William Simon 1
URETZ, Lester Robert 5
URICE, Jay Adams 3
URICH, Walter K. 5
URIELL, Frank (Francis) Harold
URION, Henry Kimball 4
URIS, Percy 5
URMY, Clarence 1
URNER, Hammond 2
URNER, Mabel Herbert 3
URQUHART, Leonard Church
URQUHART, Norman Currie 5
URSO, Camilla H
URY, Ralph Jay 5
USHER, Abbott Payson 4
USHER, Edward Preston 2
USHER, John Palmer 1
USHER, Nathaniel Reilly
USHER, Noble Luke H
USHER, Robert James 2
USINGER, Robert L(eslie) 5
USSHER, Brandram Boileau 1
UTASSY, George 'd' 3
UTERHART, Henry Ayres 2
UTLEY, George Burwell 1
UTLEY, Henry Munson 1
UTLEY, Joseph Simeon 1
UTLEY, Samuel 1
UTLEY, Stuart Wells 1
UTNE, John Arndt 5
UTT, James Boyd 5
UTTER, David 4
UTTER, George Benjamin 3
UTTER, George Herbert 1
UTTER, Rebecca Palfrey 1
UTTER, Robert Palfrey 1
UTTERBACK, Hubert 2
UTTERBACK, John Gregg 5
UTTLEY, Clinton B.

VACHON, Alexandre 3
VACHON, Joseph Peter 4
VACHON, Louis A, Jr. 5
VAGIS, Polygnotos G(eorge)
VAHEY, James Henry 2
VAIL, Aaron H
VAIL, Alfred Lewis
VAIL, Charles Davis 2
VAIL, Charles Delamater 1
VAIL, Charles Henry 1
VAIL, Curtis Churchill Doughty 3
VAIL, Derrick T. Sr. 1
VAIL, Derrick Tilton 5
VAIL, Eugene 4
VAIL, George H
VAIL, Henry 1
VAIL, Henry Hobart H
VAIL, Richard B. 3
VAIL, Robert William Glenrole 4
VAIL, Stephen Montfort H
VAIL, Theodore Newton H
VAIL, Thomas Hubbard H
VAILE, Anna Louise Wolcott
VAILE, Joel Frederick 1
VAILE, Rawson 3
VAILE, William Newell
VAILLANCOURT, Cyrille 5
VAILLANT, George Clapp 2
VAILLANT, Louis David 2
VAILLANT DE GUESLIS, Francois H
VAJNA, George 5
VALASEK, Otakar 3
VALE, Roy Ewing 3
VALENCIA, Guillermo Leon 5
VALENTA, Frank Louis 3
VALENTE, Frances Louis 4
VALENTIEN, Anna Marie
VALENTINE, Byron Warren 4
VALENTINE, Caro Syron 4
VALENTINE, David Thomas H
VALENTINE, Edward Abram Uffington
VALENTINE, Edward Robinson 5
VALENTINE, Edward Virginius 1
VALENTINE, John J. 1
VALENTINE, John W(adsworth) 5
VALENTINE, Lewis Joseph 2
VALENTINE, Lila Meade 1
VALENTINE, Milton 1
VALENTINE, Milton Henry 4
VALENTINE, Patrick Anderson 1
VALENTINE, Robert Grosvenor
VALENTINE, Willard Lee 2
VALENTINER, William Reinhold 3
VALENTINO, Rudolph
VALERY, Paul 4
VALEUR, Robert 5
VALK, Joseph Elihu 5
VALK, William Weightman H
VALLANCE, Harvard Forrest 3
VALLANCE, William Roy 4
VALLANDIGHAM, Clement Laird H
VALLEJO, Mariano Guadalupe H
VALLENTINE, Benjamin Bennaton 2
VALLENTINE, Benjamin Benton 1
VALLETTA, Vittorio 4
VALLIANT, Leroy Branch 1
VALUE, Beverly Reid 1
VAN, Billy B. 3
VAN AERNAM, Henry 1
VAN ALEN, James Isaac H
VAN ALEN, John Evert H
VAN ALEN, William 3
VAN ALEN, Daniel D. 1
VAN-ALLEN, John W. 4
VAN ALLEN, William Harman 5
VAN ALSTYNE, Eleanor Van Ness 2
VAN ALSTYNE, Henry Arthur 5

VAN ALSTYNE, J. H. 2
VAN ALSTYNE, Thomas Jefferson 1
VAN AMBURGH, Fred D.
VANAMEE, Grace Davis 2
VAN AMRINGE, John Howard 1
VAN ANDA, Carr V. 2
VAN ANTWERP, Eugene Ignatius 4
VAN ANTWERP, William Clarkson 1
VAN ARSDALE, Nathaniel H. 4
VAN ATTA, Robert S. 5
VAN ATTEN, William Teunis 5
VANAUKEN, Charles S. 5
VAN AUKEN, Wilbur Rice
VAN BARNEVELD, Charles Edwin 2
VAN BAUN, William Weed 1
VAN BEINUM, Eduard 3
VAN BENSCHOTEN, James Cooke 1
VAN BENSCHOTEN, William Henry 1
VAN BEUREN, Amedee J. 1
VAN BEUREN, Frederick Theodore Jr. 2
VAN BEUREN, Johannes H
VAN BOMEL, Leroy Allison 4
VAN BOSKERCK, Robert Ward 1
VAN BRUNT, Charles H. 1
VAN BRUNT, Henry 1
VAN BRUNT, Jeremiah Rutger 2
VAN BUREN, Albert Alexander 1
VAN BUREN, Alicia Keisker 1
VAN BUREN, James Heartt 1
VAN BUREN, John * H
VAN BUREN, John Dash 4
VAN BUREN, Martin 1
VAN BUREN, Maud 3
VAN BUREN, Robert 3
VAN BUREN, William Holme H
VAN BUSKIRK, Arthur B. 1
VANCE, Arthur Turner 1
VANCE, Burton 1
VANCE, Estil 3
VANCE, Harold Sines 3
VANCE, Harrell Taylor Jr. 4
VANCE, Henry T(homas) 5
VANCE, Hiram Albert 1
VANCE, James Isaac 1
VANCE, James Milton 1
VANCE, Jessica Smith 1
VANCE, John Thomas 2
VANCE, Johnstone 3
VANCE, Joseph 3
VANCE, Joseph Anderson 3
VANCE, Louis Joseph 1
VANCE, Robert Brank H
VANCE, Robert Cummings 1
VANCE, Selby Frame 1
VANCE, William Reynolds 1
VANCE, Wilson 1
VANCE, Zebulon Baird H
VAN CLEAVE, Harley Jones 3
VAN CLEAVE, James Wallace 1
VAN CLEEF, Mynderse 1
VAN CORTLANDT, Oloff Stevensen
VAN CORTLANDT, Philip H
VAN CORTLANDT, Pierre H
VAN CORTLANDT, Pierre Jr. H
VAN CORTLANDT, Stephanus H
VAN COTT, Cornelius 1
VAN COTT, Waldemar Quayle 3
VANCOUVER, George H
VAN CURLER, Arent H
VAN DAM, Rip H
VANDE BOGART, Guy Hudson 4

VAN DE CARR, Charles Rutherford Jr. 4
VAN DE GRAAFF, Robert Jemison 5
VAN 'DE GRAAFF, Robert Jemison 4
VANDEGRIFT, Margaret 1
VANDEGRIFT, Rolland A. 2
VANDEMAN, Esther Boise 1
VAN DEMAN, Henry Elias 1
VAN DEMAN, John D. 4
VAN DEMAN, Ralph Henry 5
VAN 'DE MARK, William Slau 4
'VAN 'DE MORTEL, J. B. V. M. J. 4
VANDENBERG, Arthur H. Jr. 4
VANDENBERG, Arthur Hendrick 3
VANDENBERG, Hoyt Sanford 3
'VAN 'DEN BERG, Lawrence Hoffman 2
VAN 'DEN BROEK, Jan A. 3
VAN DEN BROEK, Theodore A. H
VANDENHOFF, George H
VAN DEPOELE, Charles Joseph H
VANDERBILT, Aaron 4
VANDERBILT, Alfred Gwynne 1
VANDERBILT, Arthur T. 3
VANDERBILT, Cornelius H
VANDERBILT, Cornelius 1
VANDERBILT, Cornelius Iii 2
VANDERBILT, Frederick William 1
VANDERBILT, George Washington 1
VANDERBILT, Harold Stirling 5
VANDERBILT, Merritt David 5
VANDERBILT, Newell Fitzgerald; 5
VANDERBILT, O. Deg 3
VANDERBILT, Reginald Claypoole 1
VANDERBILT, William Henry H
VANDERBILT, William Kissam 1
VANDERBILT, William Kissam 2
VANDERBLUE, Homer Bews 3
VANDERBURGH, William Henry H
VANDERCOOK, John W. 4
'VAN 'DER DONCK, Adriaen
VAN DER GRACHT, W. A. J. M. Van Waterschoot 5
VANDERGRIFT, Jacob Jay H
VANDERGRIFT, John Jay 4
VANDERHOOF, Albert Whittier 5
VANDERHOOF, Douglas 4
'VAN 'DER KEMP, Francis Adrian H
VANDERKLEED, Charles Edwin 4
VANDERLIP, Frank Arthur 1
VANDERLIP, John Russell
VANDERLIP, Kelvin Cox 3
VANDERLIP, Mrs. Frank A.
VANDER LUGT, Gerrit T. 5
VANDERLYN, John H
VANDER MEULEN, John Marinus 1
VAN DER NAILLEN, Albert 4
VANDERPLOEG, Watson H. 3
VANDERPOEL, Aaron H
VANDERPOEL, Emily C. Noyes 1
VANDERPOEL, John Henry H
VANDERPOEL, Robert P. 3
VANDERPOOL, Frederick William 2

VANDERPOOL, Wynant Davis 2
VAN DER STUCKEN, Frank V. 1
VANDERVEER, Abraham H
VANDER VEER, Albert 1
VAN 'DER VEER, McClellan 4
VANDERVOORT, James W. 1
VAN DERVOORT, William H. 1
VANDER VRIES, John Nicholas
VANDERWARKER, Richard Dean 5
VANDER WEE, John Baptist H
VAN DER WEYDEN, Harry 4
'VANDERZEE, Abram 4
VAN DEUSEN, Edwin H. 4
VAN DEUSEN, George William
VAN DEUSEN, Henry Reed 5
VAN DEUSEN, Robert Hicks 5
VAN DEVANTER, Willis 1
VAN 'DE VELDE, James Oliver H
VAN DE VEN, Cornelius 1
VANDEVENTER, Braden 2
VAN DEVENTER, John Herbert
VAN DEVENTER, William Luther 3
VANDEVER, William H
VAN DE VYVER, Augustine 1
VAN DE WATER, Frederic F(ranklyn) 5
VANDEWATER, George Roe 1
VAN 'DE WATER, Virginia Terhune 2
'VAN DIEST, Edmond Cornelis 3
VAN DINE, S. S. 4
VAN DISSEL, E. F. Cartier 4
VANDIVER, Almuth Cunningham 1
VANDIVER, Harry Shultz 5
VANDIVER, J. S. 3
VANDIVER, Willard Duncan 1
VAN DOORN, William 2
VAN DOREN, Carl 3
VAN DOREN, Harold Livingston
VAN DOREN, Irita 4
VAN DOREN, Mark 5
VAN DOREN, Ray Newton 1
VAN DORN, Earl H
VAN DRESSER, Marcia 1
'VAN DRUTEN, John William 3
VAN DUSEN, Charles B. 3
VAN DUYN, Edward Seguin 5
VAN DUZER, Henry Sayre 1
VAN DUZER, Lewis Sayre 1
VAN DYCK, Cornelius Van Alen H
VAN DYCK, Ernest-Marie Hubert 3
VAN DYCK, Francis Cuyler 1
VAN DYCK, Vedder 4
VAN DYCK, Carl Chester 1
VAN DYKE, Edwin Cooper 5
VAN DYKE, Harry Benjamin 5
VAN DYKE, Henry H
VAN DYKE, Henry Jackson
VAN DYKE, J. W. 1
VAN DYKE, John H
VAN DYKE, John Charles 1
VAN DYKE, Joseph Smith 1
VAN DYKE, Karl Skillman 4
VAN DYKE, Nicholas * H
VAN DYKE, Paul 1
VAN DYKE, Tertius 3
VAN DYKE, Theodore Strong 4
VAN DYKE, Walter 1
VAN DYKE, William Duncan
VAN DYKE, William Duncan Jr. 3

VAN DYNE, Frederick
VANE, Sir Henry H
VAN ELTEN, Kruseman 1
VAN EPPS, Clarence 5
VAN EPPS, Eugene Francis 5
VAN EPPS, Percy Myers 4
VAN EPS, Frank Stanley 1
VAN ES, Leunis 3
VAN ETTEN, Edgar 4
VAN ETTEN, Nathan Bristol 3
VAN ETTISCH, Raymond Treder 3
VAN EVERA, Benjamin Douglass 5
VAN FLEET, Frederick Alvin 3
VAN FLEET, Vernon W. 1
VAN FLEET, Walter 3
VAN FLEET, William Cary 1
VAN GAASBECK, Peter H
'VAN GELDER, Robert 3
VAN GORDON, Cyrena 4
VAN HAGEN, Leslie Flanders 4
VAN HAGEN, Peter Albrecht H
VAN HAMM, Caleb Marsh 1
VANHANSWYK, Louis John 1
VAN HARLINGEN, Arthur 1
VAN HAZEL, Willard 4
VAN HECKE, Maurice Taylor 4
VAN HISE, Charles Richard 1
VAN HOESEN, Henry Bartlett 4
'VAN HOOGSTRATEN, Willem 4
VAN HOOK, La Rue 1
VAN HOOK, Weller 1
VAN HOOSE, Azor Warner 1
VAN HOOSEN, Bertha 3
VAN HORN, Burt H
VAN HORN, Charles William 1
VAN HORN, Francis Joseph 3
VAN HORN, Frank Robertson 1
VAN HORN, Peter Harry 1
VAN HORN, Robert Bowman 5
VAN HORN, Robert Osborn 1
VAN HORN, Robert Thompson 1
VAN HORNE, Archibald H
VAN HORNE, David H
VAN HORNE, Espy H
VAN HORNE, Isaac H
VAN HORNE, John 3
VAN HORNE, Sir William Cornelius 1
VAN HORNE, William Grant 4
VAN HORNE, William McCadden 1
VAN HOUTEN, Isaac B. H
'VAN HOUTEN, Jan 3
VAN IDERSTINE, Robert 1
VANIER, Georges Philias
VAN ILPENDAM, Jan Jansen H
VANIMAN, Roy Lawrence
VAN INGEN, Gilbert 3
VAN INGEN, Philip 1
VAN INGEN, W. B. 3
VAN KEUREN, Alexander Hamilton
VAN KIRK, Charles Clark 1
VAN KIRK, Jay Calvin 4
VAN KIRK, Lawrence E. 3
VAN KIRK, Walter William 3
VAN KLEECK, Edwin Robert 4
VAN KLEECK, Mary 5
VAN LAER, Alexander Theabald 1
VAN LAER, Arnold Johan Ferdinand
VAN LAHR, Leo J. 2
VAN LARE, Stanley Everett 5
VAN LEER, Blake Ragsdale
VAN LEER, Carlos Clark 5

VAN LENNEP, Henry John — H
VAN LENNEP, William Bird — 1
VAN LIEW, Charles Cecil — 4
VAN LOAN, Charles Emmet — 1
'VAN LOBEN SOLS, Ernst Diederick — 4
'VAN LOON, Hendrik Willem — 2
VAN MAANEN, Adriaan — 2
VAN MARTER, Martha — 4
VAN METER, John Blackford — 1
VANMETER, John Inskeep — H
VAN METER, Ralph Albert — 3
VAN METRE, Thurman William — 4
VANN, Irving Goodwin — 1
VANN, Richard Tilman — 2
VANNAH, Kate — 1
VANNAH, Kate — 4
VAN NAME, Addison — 1
VAN NAME, Elmer Garfield — 5
VANNAME, F. W. Jr. — 4
VAN NAMEE, George Rivet — 2
VAN NATTA, John Wilson — 4
VAN NESS, Isaac J. — 2
VAN NESS, John Peter — H
VAN NESS, Thomas — 1
VAN NESS, William Peter — H
VAN NEST, Abraham Rynier — H
VANNEST, Charles Garrett — 2
VAN NEST, G. Willett — 1
VAN NICE, Errett — 5
VAN NOPPEN, Leonard Charles — 1
VAN NORDEN, Charles — 1
VAN NORDEN, Rudolph Warner — 5
VAN NORDEN, Warner — 1
VAN NORDEN, Warner Montagnie — 3
VAN NORMAN, Amelie Veiller — 1
VAN NORMAN, Frederick Dewey — 5
VAN NORMAN, Hubert Everett — 1
VAN NORMAN, Louis Edwin — 3
VAN NORSTRAND, David — H
VAN NUYS, Ezra Allen — 2
VAN NUYS, Frederick — 2
VAN NUYS, James Benton — 4
VAN ORMAN, F. Harold — 3
VAN ORNUM, John Lane — 2
VAN ORSDEL, Josiah Alexander — 1
VAN OSDEL, John Mills — H
'VAN PAASSEN, Pierre — 4
VAN PATTEN, Nathan — 3
VAN PATTEN, William James — 1
VAN PELT, Clayton Forrest — 4
VAN PELT, John Robert — 1
VAN PELT, John Vredenburgh — 4
VAN PETTEN, Edward Cyrus — 5
VAN PETTEN, John B. — 1
VAN POOLE, Chalmer Melanchton — 3
VAN PRAAG, Henry L. — 2
VAN QUICKENBORNE, Charles Felix — H
'VAN RAALTE, Albertus Christiaan — H
VAN RENSSELAER, Cortland — H
VAN RENSSELAER, Henry Bell — H
VAN RENSSELAER, Howard — 1
VAN RENSSELAER, Jeremiah — H
VAN RENSSELAER, Killian Killian
VAN RENSSELAER, M. King — 1
VAN RENSSELAER, Mariana Griswold — 1
VAN RENSSELAER, Martha — 1
VAN RENSSELAER, Maunsell — H
VAN RENSSELAER, Nicholas — H
VAN RENSSELAER, Solomon Van Vechten — H
VAN RENSSELAER, Stephen — 1
VAN REYPEN, William Knickerbocker — 1
VAN RIPER, John Crowell — 1
VAN RIPER, Walter D. — 5
VAN ROOSBROECK, Gustave Leopold — 1
VAN ROYEN, Jan Herman — 1
VAN SANT, Joshua — H
VAN SANT, Samuel Rinnah — 1
VAN SANT, Wilbur — 5
VAN SANTVOORD, Alfred — 1
VAN SANTVOORD, George — H
VAN SANTVOORD, Seymour — 1
VAN SAUN, Walter — H
VAN SCHAACK, Henry Cruger — 1
VAN SCHAACK, Henry Cruger — 4
VAN SCHAACK, Peter — H
VAN SCHAICK, Clarence Llewellyn — 5
VAN SCHAICK, Gosen — H
VAN SCOY, Thomas — 1
VAN SCOYOC, Leland Stanford — 5
VAN SICKLE, Frederick Levi — 1
VAN SICKLE, James Hixon — 1
VAN SICKLE, Kenneth Ardean — 3
VAN SICKLE, Selah — H
VAN SICLEN, Matthew — 1
VAN SINDEREN, Adrian — 4
VAN SINDEREN, Henry Brinsmade — 4
VANSITTART, 1'st Baron 'of Denham Robert Gilbert — 3
VAN SLINGERLAND, Nellie Bingham — 4
VAN SLYKE, Clarence Allan — 1
VAN SLYKE, Donald D. — 5
VAN SLYKE, George Martin — 1
VAN SLYKE, Lucius Lincoln — 1
VAN SOELEN, Theodore — 4
VAN SPLUNTER, John Marcus — 3
VAN STEENDEREN, Frederick Cornelius Leonard — 1
'VAN STEENWYK, Elmer Arnold — 1
VANSTON, W. Justus K. — 3
VAN STONE, Nathan Edward — 5
VAN SWEARINGEN, Thomas — H
VAN SWERINGEN, Mantis James — H
VAN SWERINGEN, Oris Paxton — 1
VAN SYCKEL, Bennet — 1
VANT, Irving Artemus — 1
VAN TRUMP, Philadelph — H
VAN TUYL, George Casey Jr. — 1
VAN TWILLER, Wouter — H
VAN TYNE, Claude Halstead — 1
VANUXEM, Lardner — H
VAN VALKENBURG, Hermon L. — 4
VAN VALKENBURG, Hermon Leach — 5
VAN VALKENBURGH, Arba Seymour — 1
VAN VALKENBURGH, Charles M. — 1
VAN VALKENBURGH, Robert Bruce — H
VAN VALZAH, Robert — 2
VAN VECHTEN, Abraham — 1
VAN VECHTEN, Carl — 4
VAN VECHTEN, Ralph — 1
VAN VLECK, Edward Burr — 2
VAN VLECK, John Monroe — 1
VAN VLECK, Will George — 4
VAN VLECK, William Cabell — 3
VAN VLIET, Robert Campbell — 2
VAN VOAST, James — 1
VAN VOLKENBURG, Jack Lamont — 4
VAN VOORHIS, Daniel — 3
VAN VOORHIS, Henry Clay — 2
VAN VOORHIS, John — 1
VAN VOORHIS, Robert Henry — 4
VAN VORHES, Nelson Holmes — H
VAN VORHIS, Flavius Josephus — 1
VAN VORST, Bessie — 1
VAN VORST, Marie — 1
'VAN WAGENEN, Anthony — 1
VAN WAGENEN, James Hubert — 1
VAN WART, Walter Bright — 5
VAN WESEP, Alleda — 4
VAN WESTRUM, Adriaan Schade — 1
VAN WICKEL, Jesse Frederick — 3
VAN WINKLE, Edgar Beach — 1
VAN WINKLE, Isaac Homer — 2
VAN WINKLE, Marshall — 5
VAN WINKLE, Peter Godwin — H
VAN WINKLE, Walling Wallenson — 1
VAN WYCK, Augustus — 4
VAN WYCK, Charles Henry — H
VAN WYCK, Robert Anderson — 1
VAN WYCK, William — 4
VAN WYCK, William William — H
VAN WYK, William P. — 2
VAN ZANDT, Charles Collins — H
VAN ZANDT, Clarence Duncan — 1
VAN ZANDT, Clarence Elmer — 1
VAN ZANDT, Khleber Miller — 1
VAN ZANDT, Marie — 1
VAN ZANDT, Richard Lipscomb — 1
VANZETTI, Bartolomeo — 4
VAN ZILE, Edward Sims — 1
VAN ZILE, Philip Taylor — 1
VARDAMAN, James Kimble — 1
VARDELL, Charles Gildersleeve — 4
VARDELL, Charles Graves — 3
VARDEN, George — 3
VARDILL, John — H
VARE, William Scott — 1
VARELA, Jacobo — 5
VARELA Y MORALES, felix Francisco Jose Maria 'de 'la C — H
VARESE, Edgard — 4
VARGAS, Getulio — 5
VARIAN, Bertram Stetson — 1
VARIAN, Charles Stetson — 1
VARIAN, Donald Cord — 5
VARIAN, George Edmund — 1
VARIAN, Russell Harrison — 3
VARICK, James — 1
VARICK, Richard — H
VARIELL, Arthur Davis — 1
VARLEY, John Philip — 1
VARNEY, Charles Edward — 4
VARNEY, William Frederick — 1
VARNEY, William Henry — 4
VARNEY, William Wesley — 2
VARNUM, James M. — 1
VARNUM, James Mitchell — 1
VARNUM, John — 1
VARNUM, Joseph Bradley — H
VARNUM, William Harrison — 2
VARSER, Lycurgus Rayner — 4
VASCHE, Joseph Burton — 4
VASEY, Frank Thomas — 1
VASEY, George — H
VASILIEFF, Nicholas Loanovich — 5
VASILIEV, Alexander Alexandrovich — 5
VASQUEZ, Francisco Leonte — 1
VASS, Alonzo Frederick — 1
VASSALL, John — H
VASSAR, Matthew — H
VATTEMARE, Nicolas Marie Alexandre — H
VAUCLAIN, Samuel Matthews — 1
VAUDREUIL-CAVAGNAL, Pierre 'de Rigaud — H
VAUGHAN, Alfred Jefferson — 1
VAUGHAN, Arthur Winn — 2
VAUGHAN, Benjamin — H
VAUGHAN, Charles — H
VAUGHAN, Charles Parker — 1
VAUGHAN, Daniel — H
VAUGHAN, David Davies — 5
VAUGHAN, Elmer E. — 1
VAUGHAN, Floyd Lamar — 1
VAUGHAN, George — 2
VAUGHAN, George Tully — 2
VAUGHAN, George William — 4
VAUGHAN, Guy W. — 4
VAUGHAN, Harold Stearns — 5
VAUGHAN, Harry Briggs Jr. — 4
VAUGHAN, Herbert Hunter — 2
VAUGHAN, Horace Worth — 1
VAUGHAN, John Colin — 1
VAUGHAN, John Gaines — 1
VAUGHAN, John George — 2
VAUGHAN, John Henry — 1
VAUGHAN, John Russell — 3
VAUGHAN, John Samuel — 3
VAUGHAN, John Walter — 2
VAUGHAN, Lawrence J. — 1
VAUGHAN, Richard Miner — 3
VAUGHAN, T. Wayland — 1
VAUGHAN, Victor Clarence — 2
VAUGHAN, Warren Taylor — 2
VAUGHAN, Wayland Farries — 4
VAUGHAN, William Hutchinson — 5
VAUGHAN, William Wirt — H
VAUGHAN WILLIAMS, Ralph — 3
VAUGHN, Earnest Van Court — 5
VAUGHN, Francis Arthur — 1
VAUGHN, Robert Gallaway — 3
VAUGHN, Samuel Jesse — 5
VAUGHN, William James — 1
VAUGHT, Edgar Sullins — 3
VAUX, Calvert — H
VAUX, George Jr. — 1
VAUX, Richard — H
VAUX, Roberts — 1
VAWTER, Charles Erastus — 1
VAWTER, John William — 1
VAWTER, Keith — 1
VAYHINGER, Monroe — 1
VEACH, Robert Wells — 5
VEAL, Frank Richard — 5
VEASEY, Clarence Archibald — 3
VEATCH, Arthur Clifford — 1
VEATCH, Byron Elbert — 1
VEAZEY, I. Parker — 4
VEAZEY, Thomas Ward — 1
VEAZIE, George Augustus — 1
VEBLEN, Andrew Anderson — 1
VEBLEN, Oswald — 4
VEBLEN, Thorstein B. — 1
VECKI, Victor G. — 1
VEDDER, Beverly Blair — 3
VEDDER, Charles Stuart — 1
VEDDER, Commodore Perry — 1
VEDDER, Edward Bright — 3
VEDDER, Elihu — 1
VEDDER, Henry Clay — 1
VEDITZ, Charles William Augustus — 1
VEEDER, Albert Henry — 2
VEEDER, Curtis Hussey — 2
VEEDER, Henry — 2
VEEDER, Major Albert — 1
VEEDER, Van Vechten — 2
VEENEMAN, William H. — 5
VEITCH, Fletcher Pearre — 2
VEKSLER, Vladimir I. — 4
VELARDE, Hernan — 1
VELAZQUEZ, Hector — 1
VELTIN, Louise 'de Launay — 1
VELVIN, Ellen — 1
VENABLE, Abraham Bedford — H
VENABLE, Abraham Watkins — H
VENABLE, Charles Scott — 1
VENABLE, Francis Preston — 1
VENABLE, Joseph Glass — 1
VENABLE, Richard Morton — 1
VENABLE, William Henry — 1
VENABLE, William Mayo — 3
VENEMANN, H. Gerald — 3
VENING MEINISZ, Felix — 4
VENNEMA, Ame — 1
VENNEMA, John — 3
VENTH, Carl — 4
VENTING, Albert — 4
VENTRIS, Michael George Francis — 4
VERBECK, Guido Fridolin — 1
VERBECK, Guido Herman Fridolin — H
VER BECK, Hanna — 1
VERBECK, William — 1
VER BECK, William Francis — 1
VER BECK, William Francis — 4
VERBEEK, Gustave — 4
VERBEKE, Alexis O. — 1
VERBRUGGHEN, Henri — 1
VERDAGUER, Peter — 1
VERDELIN, Henry — 4
VERDI, William Francis — 5
VEREEN, William Jerome — 3
VERENDRYE, Sieur 'de 'la — H
VERGENNES, 'comte 'de — H
VERHAEGEN, Peter Joseph — H
VERHAGEN, Aloysius Alphonsus — 1
VERHOEFF, Frederick Herman — 5
VERITY, George Matthew — 2
VERKUYL, Gerrit — 5
VERMILION, Charles William — 1
VERMILYA, Charles E. — 5
VERMILYE, Mrs. Kate Jordan — 1
VERMILYE, William Moorhead — 2
VERMUELE, Cornelius Clarkson — 2
VERNER, Samuel Phillips — 5
VERNIER, Chester Garfield — 2
VERNON, Ambrose White — 5
VERNON, Clarence Clark — 1
VERNON, James William — 3
VERNON, Leroy Tudor — 1
VERNON, Samuel — H
VERNON, Samuel Milton — 1
VERNON, William — H
VERNON, William Tecumseh — 3
VERNOR, Richard Edward — 3
VERONDA, Maurice — 4
VEROT, Jean Marcel Pierre Auguste — H
VERPLANCK, Daniel Crommelin — 3
VERPLANCK, Gulian Crommelin — H

WADDELL, John Alexander Low — 1
WADDELL, John Newton — H
WADDELL, Joseph Addison — 1
WADDILL, Edmund Jr. — 1
WADDINGTON, Ralph Henry — 5
WADE, Benjamin Franklin — H
WADE, Cyrus U. — 4
WADE, Edward — 1
WADE, Festus John — 1
WADE, Frank Bertram — 3
WADE, Frank Edward — 1
WADE, George Garretson — 3
WADE, Herbert Treadwell — 3
WADE, James Francis — 1
WADE, James Franklin — 1
WADE, Jason Lloyd — 5
WADE, Jeptha Homer — H
WADE, John Donald — 4
WADE, John E. — 5
WADE, Joseph Sanford — 4
WADE, Lester A. — 4
WADE, Martin Joseph — 1
WADE, Mary Hazelton — 1
WADE, Mary L. Hill — 4
WADE, William Ligon — 5
WADHAMS, Albion Varette — 1
WADHAMS, Edgar Philip — H
WADHAMS, Frederick Eugene — 1
WADHAMS, Robert Pelton
WADHAMS, William Henderson — 5
WADLEIGH, Bainbridge — H
WADLEIGH, Francis Rawle — 4
WADLEIGH, George Henry — 1
WADLIN, Horace Greeley — 1
WADSWORTH, Alfred Powell — 3
WADSWORTH, Arthur Littleford — 5
WADSWORTH, Augustus Baldwin — 3
WADSWORTH, Charles Jr. — 1
WADSWORTH, Charles Curtiss — 5
WADSWORTH, Craig Wharton — 5
WADSWORTH, Craig Wharton — 4
WADSWORTH, Daniel — H
WADSWORTH, Eliot — 3
WADSWORTH, Frank Lawton Olcott — 1
WADSWORTH, George — 3
WADSWORTH, Guy Woodbridge — 4
WADSWORTH, Harrison Lowell — 4
WADSWORTH, Hiram Warren — 1
WADSWORTH, James * — H
WADSWORTH, James Wolcott — 1
WADSWORTH, James Wolcott — 4
WADSWORTH, Jeremiah — H
WADSWORTH, Marshman Edward — 1
WADSWORTH, Oliver Fairfield — 1
WADSWORTH, Peleg — 1
WADSWORTH, William Austin — 1
WADSWORTH, William Henry — H
WADY, Clifton Sanford — 3
WAESCHE, Russell Randolph — 2
WAFFLE, Albert Edward — 4
WAGENAAR, Bernard — 5
WAGENER, Anthony Pelzer — 5
WAGENER, David Douglas — H
WAGENHEIM, Michael Benjamin — 5
WAGER, Alan Turner — 4
WAGER, Charles Henry Adams — 1
WAGGAMAN, George Augustus — H
WAGGENER, Balie Payton — 1
WAGGENER, Leslie — 3
WAGGENER, William Peyton — 2
WAGGONER, Alvin — 1

WAGGONER, David E. — 2
WAGNALLS, Adam Willis — 1
WAGNER, Arthur Lockwood — 1
WAGNER, Charles Gray — 1
WAGNER, Charles L. — 5
WAGNER, Charles Philip — 4
WAGNER, Daniel — H
WAGNER, Frank Caspar — H
WAGNER, Frederick Runyon — 3
WAGNER, George — 4
WAGNER, Harr — 1
WAGNER, Henry Franklin — 2
WAGNER, Henry Raup — 3
WAGNER, Herbert Appleton — 2
WAGNER, Herman Alexander — 4
WAGNER, Hugh Kiernan — 1
WAGNER, James Elvin — 5
WAGNER, John Henry — H
WAGNER, John Henry — 4
WAGNER, Jonathan Howard — 5
WAGNER, Kenneth Hall — 4
WAGNER, Louis — 1
WAGNER, Martin — 3
WAGNER, Oscar — 1
WAGNER, Peter Joseph — H
WAGNER, Rob — 2
WAGNER, Robert Ferdinand
WAGNER, Russell Halderman — 3
WAGNER, Samuel — 1
WAGNER, Samuel Tobias — 1
WAGNER, Steward — 3
WAGNER, Webster — H
WAGNER, Wieland — 4
WAGNER, William — H
WAGNER, Wilmer Gouger — 1
WAGONER, Philip Dakin — 4
WAGONER, Winfred Ethestal — 2
WAGSTAFF, Alfred — 1
WAGSTAFF, Henry McGilbert — 5
WAHL, George Moritz — 1
WAHL, Lutz — 1
WAHL, William Henry — 1
WAHLSTROM, Matthias — 4
WAHRHAFTIG, Felix Solomon — 5
WAID, Dan Everett — 1
WAID, George S. — 4
WAIDNER, Charles William — 1
WAILES, Benjamin Leonard Covington — H
WAILES, Edward Thompson — 5
WAILES, George Handy — 5
WAILES, George Handy — 4
WAINDLE, Roger F(rancis) — 5
WAINWRIGHT, Dallas Bache — 4
WAINWRIGHT, Guy Alwyn — 3
WAINWRIGHT, John — 4
WAINWRIGHT, Jonathan Mayhew — H
WAINWRIGHT, Jonathan Mayhew — 2
WAINWRIGHT, Jonathan Mayhew
WAINWRIGHT, Marie — 1
WAINWRIGHT, Richard — H
WAINWRIGHT, Richard — 1
WAINWRIGHT, Samuel Hayman — 3
WAIT, Charles Edmund — 1
WAIT, Henry Heileman — 1
WAIT, Horatio Loomis — 1
WAIT, John Cassan — 1
WAIT, Lucien Augustus — 1
WAIT, Robert T. P. — H
WAIT, Samuel — 1
WAIT, William — 1
WAIT, William B. — 1
WAIT, William Cushing — 1
WAIT, William Henry — 1
WAITE, Alice Vinton — 2
WAITE, Byron Sylvester — 1
WAITE, Catharine Van Valkenburg — 4
WAITE, Charles Burlingame — 1
WAITE, Clark Francis — 3
WAITE, Davis Hanson — 1
WAITE, Edward Foote — 3

WAITE, Frederick Clayton — 3
WAITE, George Thomas — 1
WAITE, Harvey Rice — 5
WAITE, Henry Matson — 2
WAITE, Henry Randall — 1
WAITE, Herbert Harold — 1
WAITE, J. Herbert — 3
WAITE, John David — 4
WAITE, John Leman — 1
WAITE, Merton Benway — 2
WAITE, Morison Remich — 4
WAITE, Morrison Remick — H
WAITE, Sumner — 3
WAITE, Warren C. — 3
WAITS, Edward McShane — 1
WAITT, Ernest Linden — 5
WAKE, Charles Staniland — 1
WAKEFIELD, Arthur Paul — 2
WAKEFIELD, Cyrus — H
WAKEFIELD, Edmund Burritt — 1
WAKEFIELD, Ernest Alonzo — 4
WAKEFIELD, Eva Ingersoll — 5
WAKEFIELD, Lyman E. — 2
WAKEFIELD, Paul M. — 5
WAKEFIELD, Ralph — 5
WAKEFIELD, Ray Bruchman — 4
WAKEFIELD, Ray Cecil — 2
WAKEFIELD, Sherman Day — 3
WAKEHURST, Lord (John deVere Loder) — 5
WAKELAND, Charles Richard — 5
WAKELEE, Edmund Waring — 2
WAKELEY, Arthur Cooper — 1
WAKELEY, Joseph Burton — H
WAKELEY, Thompson Morris — 5
WAKEMAN, Abram — H
WAKEMAN, Antoinette 'van Hoesen — 4
WAKEMAN, Keith — 1
WAKEMAN, Seth — H
WAKEMAN, Seth — 5
WAKEMAN, Thaddeus Burr — 1
WAKEMAN, Wilbur Fisk — 1
WALBRIDGE, Cyrus Packard
WALBRIDGE, David Safford — H
WALBRIDGE, Earle F. — 4
WALBRIDGE, George Hicks
WALBRIDGE, Henry Sanford — H
WALBRIDGE, Hiram — H
WALBRIDGE, Nelson Lee — 5
WALCOT, Charles Melton — H
WALCOT, Charles Doolittle — 1
WALCOTT, Chester Howe — 2
WALCOTT, Earle Ashley — 1
WALCOTT, Frederic Collin — 3
WALCOTT, Gregory Dexter — 3
WALCOTT, Gregory Dexter — 4
WALCOTT, Harry Mills — 3
WALCOTT, Henry Pickering — 1
WALCOTT, Robert — 3
WALCUTT, Charles C. Jr. — 1
WALCUTT, William — H
WALD, Abraham — 3
WALD, Gustavus Henry — 1
WALD, Jerry — 4
WALD, Lillian D. — 1
WALDECK, Carl Gustav — 1
WALDECK, Herman — 4
WALDEN, Austin Thomas — 4
WALDEN, Freeman — 1
WALDEN, Hiram — H
WALDEN, John Morgan — 1
WALDEN, Lionel — 1
WALDEN, Madison Miner — H
WALDEN, Percy Talbot — 2
WALDEN, Treadwell — 1
WALDEN, Walter — 5
WALDER, Ernest George — 2
WALDERNE, Richard — H
WALDO, Charles Gilbert — 4

WALDO, Clarence Abiathar — 1
WALDO, David — H
WALDO, Dwight Bryant — 1
WALDO, Frank — 1
WALDO, Fullerton Leonard — 5
WALDO, George C. — 3
WALDO, George E. — 2
WALDO, Leonard — 1
WALDO, Lillian McLean — 5
WALDO, Loren Pinckney — 1
WALDO, Rhinelander — 1
WALDO, Richard H. — 2
WALDO, Samuel — H
WALDO, Samuel Lovett — 1
WALDO, Samuel Putnam — 1
WALDO, Selden Fennell — 3
WALDO, William Earl — 4
WALDON, Sidney Dunn — 2
WALDORF, Ernest Lynn — 2
WALDORF, Wilella Louise — 2
WALDOW, William F. — 1
WALDRIP, Marion Nelson — 5
WALDRON, Alfred M. — 4
WALDRON, Arthur Maxson — 3
WALDRON, Clare Bailey — 2
WALDRON, Henry — H
WALDRON, James Albert — 1
WALDRON, Jeremy Richard — 3
WALDRON, John J. — 5
WALDRON, John William — 1
WALDRON, Webb — 2
WALDRON, William Henry — 2
WALDROP, R. Walter — 2
WALDSEEMULLER, Martin — H
WALDSTEIN, Louis — 1
WALDSTEIN, Martin E. — 4
WALES, George C. — 1
WALES, George Edward — 1
WALES, George Russell — 1
WALES, Henry — 3
WALES, James Albert — 5
WALES, James Albert — H
WALES, John — H
WALES, Leonard Eugene — H
WALES, Philip Skinner — 1
WALES, Salem Howe — 1
WALES, Wellington — 5
WALET, Eugene Henry, Jr. — 5
WALGREEN, Charles Rudolph
WALK, Charles Edmonds — 5
WALK, George Everett — 4
WALK, James Wilson — 1
WALKE, Frank Hicks — 1
WALKE, Henry — H
WALKE, Willoughby — 1
WALKER, Abbie Phillips — 2
WALKER, Albert Henry — 1
WALKER, Albert Perry — 1
WALKER, Aldace F. — 1
WALKER, Alexander — H
WALKER, Alexander Edward — 4
WALKER, Alexander Stewart — 3
WALKER, Alfred — 2
WALKER, Alice Johnstone — 5
WALKER, Amasa — H
WALKER, Annie Kendrick — 5
WALKER, Arthur Lucian — 3
WALKER, Arthur Tappan — 1
WALKER, Asa — 1
WALKER, Benjamin — 2
WALKER, Bradford Hastings
WALKER, Bryant — 1
WALKER, Buz M. — 1
WALKER, C. Howard — 1
WALKER, C. Irvine — 4
WALKER, Charles Abbot — 1
WALKER, Charles Bertram — 5
WALKER, Charles Christopher Brainerd — H
WALKER, Charles Clement — 5
WALKER, Charles Jabez — 1
WALKER, Charles Swan — 4
WALKER, Charles Thomas — 1
WALKER, Charles Wellington — 5

WALKER, Charlotte Abell — 4
WALKER, Clifford Mitchell — 3
WALKER, Cornelius — 1
WALKER, Curtis Howe — 3
WALKER, Danton MacIntyre — 4
WALKER, David * — H
WALKER, David Harold — 4
WALKER, David Shelby — H
WALKER, Dougal Ormonde Beaconsfield — 3
WALKER, Dow Vernon — 2
WALKER, Dugald Stewart — 1
WALKER, Edward Dwight — H
WALKER, Edwin — 1
WALKER, Edwin Robert — 1
WALKER, Elisha — 1
WALKER, Emory Judson — 1
WALKER, Faye — H
WALKER, Felix — H
WALKER, Francis — 1
WALKER, Francis — 2
WALKER, Francis Amasa — H
WALKER, Frank Banghart — 1
WALKER, Frank Buckley — 4
WALKER, Frank Comerford — 3
WALKER, Frank Ray — 1
WALKER, Frank Robinson — 4
WALKER, Fred Allan — 4
WALKER, Fred Livingood — 5
WALKER, Frederick — 1
WALKER, Fredinand Graham — 1
WALKER, Freeman — H
WALKER, Gayle Courtney — 1
WALKER, George — H
WALKER, George — 2
WALKER, George Abram — 3
WALKER, George Henry — 5
WALKER, George Leon — 1
WALKER, George Levi — 4
WALKER, George Richard — 4
WALKER, George Winfield — 2
WALKER, Gilbert Carlton
WALKER, Guy Morrison — 5
WALKER, Harry — 5
WALKER, Harry Bruce — 3
WALKER, Harry Leslie — 1
WALKER, Harry Wilson — 1
WALKER, Harvey — 5
WALKER, Henry Clay Jr. — 4
WALKER, Henry Hammersley — 1
WALKER, Henry Lee — 4
WALKER, Henry Oliver — 1
WALKER, Henry Yonge — 3
WALKER, Herbert William — 4
WALKER, Hobart Alexander — 5
WALKER, Horatio — 1
WALKER, Hugh Kelso — 2
WALKER, Irving Miller — 5
WALKER, Isaac Pigeon — H
WALKER, Ivan N. — 1
WALKER, J(oseph) Frederic — 5
WALKER, J(ohn) Randall — 1
WALKER, Jacob Garrett — 1
WALKER, James * — H
WALKER, James Alexander
WALKER, James Barr — H
WALKER, James Baynes — 1
WALKER, James Everett — 4
WALKER, James Herbert — 1
WALKER, James J. — 2
WALKER, James Peter — H
WALKER, James V. — 4
WALKER, James Wilson Grimes — 3
WALKER, Jay P. — 4
WALKER, John — H
WALKER, John Baldwin — 2
WALKER, John Brisben — 1
WALKER, John Earl — 3
WALKER, John Grimes — 1
WALKER, John Leonard — 5
WALKER, John Moore — 1
WALKER, John Williams — H
WALKER, John Yates Gholson — 1
WALKER, Jonathan Hoge — H
WALKER, Joseph — 2
WALKER, Joseph Albert — 4
WALKER, Joseph Henry — 1
WALKER, Joseph Reddeford — H

WALKER, Kenneth N. 3
WALKER, Kenzie Wallace 3
WALKER, Lapsley Greene 1
WALKER, Leroy Pope H
WALKER, Lewis, 3d 5
WALKER, Lewis B. 4
WALKER, Lewis Carter 1
WALKER, Louis Carlisle 4
WALKER, Mary H
WALKER, Mary Adelaide 2
WALKER, Mary E. 1
WALKER, 2
  Meriwether Lewis
WALKER, Myron
  Hamilton 1
WALKER, Nat Gaillard 2
WALKER, Nathan Wilson 1
WALKER, Nellie Verne 5
WALKER, Nelson Macy 2
WALKER, Newton
  Farmer 1
WALKER, 4
  Norman McFarlane
WALKER, Paul Atlee 4
WALKER, Percy H
WALKER, Perley F. 1
WALKER, H
  Pinkney Houston
WALKER, 1
  Platt Dickinson
WALKER, Ralph Curry 4
WALKER, Ralph Thomas 5
WALKER, Ramsay M. 1
WALKER, Reuben Eugene 1
WALKER, Reuben
  Lindsay H
WALKER, Richard Wilde 1
WALKER, Robert 3
WALKER, Robert Barney 5
WALKER, Robert
  Coleman 3
WALKER, Robert E. 3
WALKER, 1
  Robert Franklin
WALKER, Robert James H
WALKER, Robert John H
WALKER, Roberts 1
WALKER, Roger A. P. 3
WALKER, Rollin Hough 5
WALKER, Ross H. 5
WALKER, Ruth Irene 4
WALKER, Ryan 1
WALKER, Samuel J. 4
WALKER, Scott Wells H
WALKER, Sears Cook H
WALKER, Stanley 5
WALKER, Stanton 5
WALKER, 4
  Stewart McCulloch
WALKER, Stuart 1
WALKER, Stuart Wilson 1
WALKER, Theodore C. 4
WALKER, 3
  Theodore Penfield
WALKER, Thomas H
WALKER, Thomas Barlow 1
WALKER, Thomas Joseph 2
WALKER, Timothy * H
WALKER, Tom P. 4
WALKER, Walter 3
WALKER, Walter 4
WALKER, Walton Harris 3
WALKER, William H
WALKER, William Adams H
WALKER, William David H
WALKER, William Henry 1
WALKER, H
  William Henry Talbot
WALKER, William Hultz 1
WALKER, H
  William Johnson
WALKER, William
  Kemble 1
WALKER, William S. 5
WALKER, Willis J. 2
WALKER, Williston 3
WALKINSHAW, 4
  Robert Boyd
WALKLEY, 4
  Raymond Lowery
WALKOWITZ, Abraham 4
WALL, Albert Chandler 2
WALL, Alexander James 2
WALL, Edward Clarence 1
WALL, Edward Everett 2
WALL, Edward John 4
WALL, Francis Lowry 4
WALL, Frank Jerome 4
WALL, Garret Dorset H
WALL, Garrett Buckner 1
WALL, George Willard 4
WALL, Hubert Stanley 5
WALL, James Walter 4
WALL, Stuart S. 4
WALL, William H
WALL, William Guy H
WALL, William Guy 1

WALLACE, 3
  Addison Alexander
WALLACE, 3
  Alexander Gilfillan
WALLACE, H
  Alexander Stuart
WALLACE, Austin 1
WALLACE, 2
  Benjamin Bruce
WALLACE, Bruce Hinds 4
WALLACE, 4
  Charles Frederick
WALLACE, Charles
  Hodge 2
WALLACE, 3
  Charles William
WALLACE, Charlton 2
WALLACE, Daniel 1
WALLACE, Daniel Alden 3
WALLACE, David H
WALLACE, David A. 5
WALLACE, David
  Duncan 3
WALLACE, David M. 5
WALLACE, Dillon 1
WALLACE, Donald H. 3
WALLACE, Edwin
  Sherman 4
WALLACE, Elizabeth 3
WALLACE, 2
  George Barclay
WALLACE, 3
  George Macdonald
WALLACE, Grant 1
WALLACE, Harold Ayer 3
WALLACE, 3
  Harry Brookings
WALLACE, Henry 1
WALLACE, Henry Agard 4
WALLACE, 1
  Henry Cantwell
WALLACE, Horace
  Binney H
WALLACE, Howard T. 4
WALLACE, Hugh
  Campbell H
WALLACE, Hugh D. 3
WALLACE, Ira 4
WALLACE, J. Sherman 1
WALLACE, James 1
WALLACE, James M. 5
WALLACE, John Findley 1
WALLACE, John J. 1
WALLACE, John William H
WALLACE, John Winfield H
WALLACE, H
  Jonathan Hasson
WALLACE, Joseph 1
WALLACE, Lewis 1
WALLACE, Lurleen Burns 5
WALLACE, 5
  Margaret Adair
WALLACE, H
  Nathaniel Dick
WALLACE, 2
  Oates Charles Symonds
WALLACE, R. James 4
WALLACE, 3
  Robert Charles
WALLACE, Robert
  Dwight 4
WALLACE, Robert Minor 1
WALLACE, Robert Moore 1
WALLACE, Rothvin 1
WALLACE, Rush Richard 1
WALLACE, 5
  Schuyler Crawford
WALLACE, Stuart Allen 4
WALLACE, Susan Elston 1
WALLACE, Thomas F. 5
WALLACE, Thomas Ross 4
WALLACE, Tom 4
WALLACE, William Jr. 1
WALLACE, H
  William Alexander Anderson
WALLACE, H
  William Andrew
WALLACE, 5
  William Charles
WALLACE, William
  Henry 1
WALLACE, William
  Henry 3
WALLACE, H
  William Henson
WALLACE, William
  James 1
WALLACE, 5
  William McLean
WALLACE, William Miller 1
WALLACE, 4
  William Robert
WALLACE, William Ross H
WALLACK, Henry John H

WALLACK, H
  James William *
WALLACK, H
  John Johnstone Lester
WALLAU, Herman L. 5
WALLEN, Saul 5
WALLEN, 1
  Theodore Clifford
WALLENBERG, 5
  Axel Fingal
WALLENBERG, Marc, Jr. 5
WALLENIUS, Carl
  Gideon 2
WALLENSTEIN, 5
  Merrill Bernard
WALLER, Allen George 4
WALLER, Cecile Howell 3
WALLER, Claude 1
WALLER, Curtis L. 3
WALLER, 1
  David Jewett Jr.
WALLER, Elwyn 1
WALLER, Emma H
WALLER, Frank 1
WALLER, George Platt 4
WALLER, 1
  Gilbert Johnson
WALLER, Helen Hiett 4
WALLER, Henry 4
WALLER, John Lightfoot H
WALLER, John Robert 1
WALLER, Lewis 1
WALLER, 4
  Littleton W. T.
WALLER, 1
  Littleton Waller Tazewell
WALLER, Mary Ella 1
WALLER, Osmar
  Lysander 1
WALLER, Peter August 1
WALLER, Rose 1
WALLER, Thomas 4
WALLER, 1
  Thomas McDonald
WALLER, Willard Walter 2
WALLER, Wilmer Joyce 5
WALLERSTEIN, Edward 5
WALLEY, Samuel Hurd H
WALLGREN, Monrad C. 4
WALLICHS, 5
  Glenn Everett
WALLIHAN, Allen Grant 4
WALLIN, Alfred 1
WALLIN, 5
  J(ohn) E(dward) Wallace
WALLIN, Samuel 4
WALLIN, Van Arthur 2
WALLIN, William John 4
WALLING, Anna
  Strunsky 5
WALLING, Ansel Tracy H
WALLING, Emory A. 1
WALLING, 1
  William English
WALLING, William
  Henry 5
WALLING, 1
  Willoughby George
WALLINGFORD, 1
  John Duvall
WALLINGTON, 4
  Nellie Urner
WALLIS, 1
  Everett Stanley
WALLIS, 3
  Frederick Alfred
WALLIS, George Edward 5
WALLIS, Jenny 1
WALLIS, Philip 1
WALLIS, Severn Teackle H
WALLIS, William Fisher 5
WALLS, David Crawford 3
WALLS, Frank Xavier 2
WALLS, William L. 1
WALMSLEY, 5
  Walter Newbold Jr.
WALN, Nicholas H
WALN, Nora 4
WALN, Robert * H
WALRATH, Florence
  Dahl 3
WALRATH, John Henry 4
WALSH, Allan B. 5
WALSH, Arthur 2
WALSH, Basil Sylvester 2
WALSH, Benjamin Dann H
WALSH, Blanche 1
WALSH, 2
  Catherine Shellew
WALSH, Charles Clinton 1
WALSH, Correa Moylan 4
WALSH, David Ignatius 3
WALSH, Edmund 3
WALSH, Edward J. 2
WALSH, Emmet M. 4
WALSH, 5
  Sister Frances Marie

WALSH, Frank P. 1
WALSH, 4
  Frederick Harper
WALSH, 3
  George Ethelbert
WALSH, Gerald Groveland 1
WALSH, Gerald Powers 4
WALSH, Henry Collins 1
WALSH, James A. 1
WALSH, James Anthony 1
WALSH, James Joseph 2
WALSH, James Lawrence 3
WALSH, John 1
WALSH, John Edward 5
WALSH, John Gaynor 3
WALSH, John Henry 1
WALSH, John Klaerr 4
WALSH, Joseph 1
WALSH, Joseph Patrick 5
WALSH, 1
  Julius Sylvester
WALSH, 5
  Lawrence Aloysius
WALSH, Louis Sebastian 1
WALSH, Matthew James 4
WALSH, Michael H
WALSH, Raycroft 3
WALSH, Raymond Arnold 1
WALSH, Raymond James 4
WALSH, Richard John 4
WALSH, Robert H
WALSH, Robert Douglas 1
WALSH, Roy Edward 5
WALSH, Theodore Edwin 5
WALSH, Thomas 1
WALSH, Thomas F. 1
WALSH, Thomas James 1
WALSH, Thomas Joseph 3
WALSH, Thomas W. 1
WALSH, Thomas Yates 4
WALSH, William H
WALSH, William Francis 2
WALSH, William Henry 1
WALSH, William Thomas 1
WALSON, Charles Moore 3
WALSTER, Harlow Leslie 4
WALSTON, Charles 1
WALSTON, Vernon C. 4
WALTER, A. Henry 4
WALTER, Albert G. H
WALTER, Alfred 1
WALTER, Allan Wylie 4
WALTER, Bruno 1
WALTER, Ellery 1
WALTER, Elliot Vincent 5
WALTER, Eugene 1
WALTER, Francis Eugene 4
WALTER, Frank J. 1
WALTER, Frank Keller 2
WALTER, George William 1
WALTER, Herbert Eugene 1
WALTER, Howard Arnold 1
WALTER, Luther Mason 2
WALTER, M. E. 4
WALTER, Raymond F. 1
WALTER, Robert 1
WALTER, Thomas H
WALTER, Thomas Ustick H
WALTER, William Emley 1
WALTER, William Henry H
WALTERS, Alexander 1
WALTERS, 3
  Anderson Howel
WALTERS, Carl 3
WALTERS, Charles S. 3
WALTERS, 3
  Francis Marion Jr.
WALTERS, Frank 4
WALTERS, 5
  George Alexander
WALTERS, 2
  Gus Washington
WALTERS, Henry 1
WALTERS, Henry C. 5
WALTERS, Jack Edward 4
WALTERS, Leon L. 1
WALTERS, R. G. 3
WALTERS, Raymond 3
WALTERS, Rolland J. D. 4
WALTERS, 1
  Theodore Augustus
WALTERS, William H. H
WALTERS, 5
  William Thompson
WALTHALL, Edward
  Cary H
WALTHER, 2
  Carl Ferdinand Wilhelm
WALTHER, 3
  Henry Wellman Emile
WALTMAN, 3
  Harry Franklin
WALTMAN, 3
  William DeWitt
WALTON, 3
  Albert Douglass

WALTON, Alfred Grant 5
WALTON, Arthur Calvin 5
WALTON, Arthur Keith 5
WALTON, Charles Edgar 1
WALTON, 1
  Charles M(ilton, Jr.
WALTON, 1
  Clifford Stevens
WALTON, Eleanor Going 5
WALTON, H
  Eliakim Persons
WALTON, Frank
  Richmond 3
WALTON, George H
WALTON, 1
  George Augustus
WALTON, George
  Lincoln 1
WALTON, Howard
  Charles 5
WALTON, Howard
  Charles 4
WALTON, James Henry 1
WALTON, Lee Barker 2
WALTON, Lester Aglar 5
WALTON, Lucius Leedom 1
WALTON, Mason
  Augustus 1
WALTON, Matthew H
WALTON, Norman
  Burdett 2
WALTON, Norton Hall 5
WALTON, Sydney Grant 4
WALTON, Thomas
  Cameron 1
WALTON, Thomas Otto 4
WALTON, William 1
WALTON, William Bell 1
WALTON, 3
  William Randolph
WALTZ, 5
  Elizabeth Cherry
WALTZ, 4
  Millard Fillmore
WALWORTH, 1
  Clarence Alphonsus
WALWORTH, Ellen
  Hardin 4
WALWORTH, 4
  Jeanette Ritchie Hadermnan
WALWORTH, H
  Mansfield Tracy
WALWORTH, Reuben
  Hyde H
WALZ, John Albrecht 3
WALZ, William Emanuel 4
WAMBAUGH, Eugene 1
WAMBAUGH, Sarah 3
WANAMAKER, 2
  Allison Temple
WANAMAKER, John 1
WANAMAKER, Rodman 1
WANAMAKER, Thomas
  B. 1
WANDELL, Samuel
  Henry 2
WANDLESS, 5
  Edgar Griffin
WANDS, Ernest Henry 5
WANGCHUK, 2
  Maharaja Jigme Dorji
WANGENHEIM, Julius 2
WANGER, Irving Price 4
WANK, Roland Anthony 5
WANLASS, Ralph Page 5
WANN, Frank B. 3
WANN, Louis 3
WANNAMAKER, 2
  John Skottowe
WANNAMAKER, 5
  Olin Dantzler
WANNAMAKER, 5
  William Hane
WANTLAND, 5
  Wayne W(arde)
WANTON, Joseph H
WANTY, George Proctor 1
WANTZ, Ray 3
WANVIG, Chester Odin 3
WANZER, H. Stanley 4
WAPLES, Rufus 1
WAPPAT, 1
  Blanche King Smith
WARBASSE, James Peter 5
WARBEKE, John Martyn 3
WARBOURG, Eugene 4
WARBURG, Felix M. 1
WARBURG, Gerald Felix 5
WARBURG, James Paul 5
WARBURG, Otto
  Heinrich 5
WARBURG, Paul Moritz 1
WARBURTON, 3
  Barclay Harding
WARBURTON, Stanton 3
WARD, Aaron H
WARD, Aaron 1

WARD, Aaron Montgomery — H
WARD, Aaron Montgomery — 4
WARD, Albert Norman — 1
WARD, Alger Luman — 5
WARD, Anna Lydia — 1
WARD, Arch — 3
WARD, Archibald Robinson — 5
WARD, Artemas — H
WARD, Artemas Jr. — H
WARD, Artemus — H
WARD, Arthur Sprague — 5
WARD, Cabot — 1
WARD, Catharine Weed Barnes — 1
WARD, Charles Allen — 3
WARD, Charles Augustus — 3
WARD, Charles Carroll — 3
WARD, Charles Howell — 2
WARD, Charles Sumner — 1
WARD, Christopher Longstreth — 2
WARD, Clarence Richard — 5
WARD, Clifford — 4
WARD, Cyrenus Osborne — H
WARD, David — 1
WARD, David J. — 4
WARD, Delancey Walton — 4
WARD, Duren J. H. — 4
WARD, E. G. — 4
WARD, Edgar Melville — 1
WARD, Edward Joshua — 2
WARD, Elijah — H
WARD, Elizabeth Stuart Phelps — 1
WARD, Evans — 4
WARD, Fannie — 3
WARD, Florence Elizabeth — 1
WARD, Florence Jeanette Baier
WARD, Florence Nightingale Ferguson — 1
WARD, Frank Edwin — 3
WARD, Frank Gibson — 1
WARD, Franklin Wilmer — 1
WARD, Frederick King — 1
WARD, Frederick Townsend — H
WARD, Freeman — 2
WARD, Genevieve — 1
WARD, George Clinton — 1
WARD, George Ehinger — 5
WARD, George Gray — 1
WARD, George Gray — 3
WARD, George Morgan — 1
WARD, Gilbert Oakley — 1
WARD, Grant Eben — 3
WARD, Hallett Sydney — 5
WARD, Hamilton — 1
WARD, Harry Edwin — 4
WARD, Harry Frederick — 4
WARD, Henry Augustus — 1
WARD, Henry Baldwin — 2
WARD, Henry Clay — 1
WARD, Henry Dana — H
WARD, Henry Galbraith — 1
WARD, Henry Heber — 5
WARD, Henry Levi — 2
WARD, Henry Tibbels — 4
WARD, Henry Winfield — 4
WARD, Henshaw — 1
WARD, Herbert Dickinson — 1
WARD, Herbert Shaeffer — 4
WARD, Herbert William — 4
WARD, J. H. — 3
WARD, Jacob C. — H
WARD, James Edward — H
WARD, James Harmon — H
WARD, James Warner — H
WARD, James William — 1
WARD, John Chamberlain — 1
WARD, John Chamberlain — 1
WARD, John Elliott — 2
WARD, John Henry Hobart — 5
WARD, John Quincy Adams
WARD, John Wesley — 1
WARD, John William George — 2
WARD, Jonathan — H
WARD, Joseph — H
WARD, Joshua — 5
WARD, Julia Elizabeth — 1
WARD, Kenneth William — 5
WARD, Leo L. — 3
WARD, Leslie Dodd — 1
WARD, Lester Frank — H
WARD, Lester Frank — 1
WARD, Lester Frank — 4
WARD, Lydia Avery Coonley

WARD, Lyman — 2
WARD, Marcus Lawrence — H
WARD, Marcus Llewellyn — 4
WARD, Matthias — H
WARD, May Alden — 4
WARD, Milan Lester — 4
WARD, Montgomery — 1
WARD, Nancy — H
WARD, Nathaniel — H
WARD, Orlando — H
WARD, Ossian Peay — 5
WARD, Peirce Colton — 5
WARD, Perley Erik — 4
WARD, Ralph Ansel — 3
WARD, Reginald Henshaw — 1
WARD, Richard — H
WARD, Richard Halsted — H
WARD, Robert De Courcy — 4
WARD, Robert W. — 5
WARD, Robert William — 4
WARD, Samuel * — H
WARD, Samuel — 4
WARD, Samuel Bladwin — 1
WARD, Samuel Ringgold — H
WARD, Seth — 4
WARD, Stevenson E. — 3
WARD, Susan Hayes — 4
WARD, Thomas * — H
WARD, Thomas — 4
WARD, Thomas Bayless — H
WARD, Thomas Johnson — 4
WARD, Thomas Wren — 4
WARD, Wilbert — 3
WARD, Wilbur — 5
WARD, Willard Parker — 1
WARD, William — H
WARD, William Allen — 4
WARD, William Breining — 1
WARD, William Edgar — 4
WARD, William Evans — 5
WARD, William G. — 1
WARD, William Hayes — 1
WARD, William Hilles — 2
WARD, William I. — 3
WARD, William Rankin — 3
WARD, William Thomas — H
WARDALL, Ruth Aimee — 1
WARDALL, William Jed — 5
WARDE, Frederick — 1
WARDE, Mary Francis Xavier — H
WARDELL, Justus S. — 2
WARDELL, Morris L. — 3
WARDEN, David Bailie — H
WARDEN, Oliver Sherman — 3
WARDEN, Robert Bruce — H
WARDENBURG, F. A. — 1
WARDER, George Woodward — 1
WARDER, John Aston — H
WARDER, John Haines — 1
WARDER, Robert Bowne — 1
WARDER, Walter — 2
WARDLAW, Joseph Coachman — 1
WARDLAW, Patterson — 2
WARDLE, Robert, Jr. — 5
WARDLEY, Russell George — 5
WARDMAN, Ervin — 1
WARDROP, Robert — 1
WARDWELL, Allen — 3
WARDWELL, Daniel — H
WARDWELL, Frank Carlton — 5
WARDWELL, Harold Fletcher — 4
WARDWELL, Sheldon Eaton — 1
WARDWELL, William Thomas
WARE, Arthur — 1
WARE, Ashur — H
WARE, Edmund Asa — H
WARE, Edward Twichell — 1
WARE, Eugene F. — 1
WARE, Franklin Backus — 2
WARE, Harriet — 4
WARE, Harry Hudnall, Jr. — 5
WARE, Helen — 1
WARE, Henry — H
WARE, Henry Jr. — H
WARE, Horace Everett — H
WARE, John — H
WARE, John Fothergill Waterhouse
WARE, Lewis Sharpe — 1
WARE, Mary S. — 3
WARE, Nathaniel A. — 4
WARE, Nicholas — H
WARE, Norman Joseph — 2
WARE, Paul — 5
WARE, Sedley Lynch — 5
WARE, Walter Ellsworth — 4
WARE, William — H

WARE, William Robert — 1
WAREHAM, Harry P. — 3
WAREING, Ernest Clyde — 2
WARFIELD, Augustus Bennett — 4
WARFIELD, Benjamin Breckinridge — 1
WARFIELD, C. Dorsey — 2
WARFIELD, Catherine Ann Ware — H
WARFIELD, David — 3
WARFIELD, Edwin — 1
WARFIELD, Ethelbert Dudley — 1
WARFIELD, George Alfred — 1
WARFIELD, Harry Ridgely, Jr. — 5
WARFIELD, Henry Mactier — 4
WARFIELD, Henry Ridgely — H
WARFIELD, R. Emory — 1
WARFIELD, Ridgeley Brown — 1
WARFIELD, S. Davies — 1
WARFIELD, William — 2
WARHEIT, Isarel Albert — 5
WARING, Clarence Henry — 3
WARING, George Edwin — 1
WARING, J. Waties — 2
WARING, James Howard — 3
WARING, James Johnston — 4
WARING, Malvina Sarah — 3
WARING, Roane — 3
WARING, Thomas Richard — 1
WARK, Homer Ethan — 5
WARLICK, Hulon Otis Jr. — 4
WARMAN, Cy — 1
WARMAN, Edward B. — 1
WARMAN, Philip Creveling — 1
WARMOTH, Henry Clay — 1
WARNE, Francis Wesley — 1
WARNE, Frank Julian — 2
WARNER, Adoniram Judson — 1
WARNER, Albert — 4
WARNER, Albert Lyman — 5
WARNER, Alton G. — 4
WARNER, Amos Griswold — 1
WARNER, Anna Bartlett — 1
WARNER, Anne — 1
WARNER, Beverley Ellison — 1
WARNER, Brainard Henry — 1
WARNER, C(harles) A(lbert) — 5
WARNER, Charles — 3
WARNER, Charles Dudley — 1
WARNER, Charles Mortimer — 1
WARNER, David Ashley — 4
WARNER, DeVer Howard — 1
WARNER, Donald Ticknor — 1
WARNER, Edward — 3
WARNER, Ellsworth Colonel — 2
WARNER, Eltinge Fowler — 4
WARNER, Ernest Noble — 4
WARNER, Everett Longley — 4
WARNER, Ezra Joseph * — 1
WARNER, Frank — 2
WARNER, Fred Maltby — 1
WARNER, Gertrude Bass — 1
WARNER, Glenn Scobey — 3
WARNER, Hannah — 4
WARNER, Harold — 2
WARNER, Harry Jackson — 3
WARNER, Harry Morris — 3
WARNER, Harry O. — 5
WARNER, Henry Byron — 5
WARNER, Henry Edward — 1
WARNER, Hiram — H
WARNER, Horace Emory — 1
WARNER, Horace Everett — 1
WARNER, Ira David — 4
WARNER, J. Foster — 1
WARNER, James Cartwright — H
WARNER, John DeWitt — 1
WARNER, John F. — 4
WARNER, Jonathan — 4
WARNER, Jonathan Trumbull — H
WARNER, Joseph Bangs — 1
WARNER, Joseph Everett — 3
WARNER, Langdon — 1
WARNER, Lucien Calvin — H

WARNER, Lucien Thompson — 3
WARNER, Milo Joseph — 4
WARNER, Milton Jones — 3
WARNER, Olin Levi — H
WARNER, Paul McC — 4
WARNER, Rawleigh — 5
WARNER, Richard Ambrose — 3
WARNER, Robert Wilberforce — 4
WARNER, Samuel Larkin — H
WARNER, Seth — H
WARNER, Southard Parker — 1
WARNER, Susan Bogert — H
WARNER, Thor — 3
WARNER, Vespasian — 1
WARNER, Willard — 1
WARNER, William — 1
WARNER, William Bishop — 2
WARNER, William Everett — 5
WARNER, Worcester ·Reed — 1
WARNICK, Spencer K(ellogg) — 5
WARNOCK, Arthur Ray — 1
WARNOCK, William Robert — 4
WARNOW, Mark — 2
WARNSHUIS, Abbe Livingston — 3
WARRELL, James — H
WARREN, Althea — 1
WARREN, Arthur — 1
WARREN, Arthur Fiske — 5
WARREN, Avra Milvin — 3
WARREN, Benjamin S. — 1
WARREN, Bentley Wirt — 1
WARREN, Charles — 3
WARREN, Charles Beecher — 1
WARREN, Charles Elliott — 2
WARREN, Charles Howard — 1
WARREN, Charles Hyde — 3
WARREN, Constance — 5
WARREN, Cornelia — 5
WARREN, Cornelius — 1
WARREN, Cyrus Moors — H
WARREN, Edward Allen — H
WARREN, Edward Henry — 1
WARREN, Edward K. — 1
WARREN, Edward Leroy — 1
WARREN, Edward Royal — 1
WARREN, Edwin Walpole — 1
WARREN, Fiske — 1
WARREN, Francis Emory — 1
WARREN, Frank Edward — 1
WARREN, Frank Furniss — 4
WARREN, Frank Lincoln — 1
WARREN, Fred D. — 3
WARREN, Frederick Andrew — 2
WARREN, Frederick Emory — 2
WARREN, Frederick Morris — 1
WARREN, George Frederick — 1
WARREN, George Washington — 1
WARREN, George William — 1
WARREN, Gouverneur Kemble — H
WARREN, Harold Broadfield — 1
WARREN, Harry Marsh — 1
WARREN, Henry Clarke — 1
WARREN, Henry Ellis — 3
WARREN, Henry Kimball — 4
WARREN, Henry Pitt — 1
WARREN, Henry White — 1
WARREN, Herbert Langford — 1
WARREN, Howard Crosby — 1
WARREN, Irene — 1
WARREN, Israel Perkins — H
WARREN, J. Collins — 1
WARREN, James — H
WARREN, James Carey — 3
WARREN, James E. — 1
WARREN, James Goold — 4
WARREN, James Thomas — 2
WARREN, John — H
WARREN, John Collins — 1
WARREN, Joseph — H
WARREN, Joseph — 2
WARREN, Joseph Mabbett — H
WARREN, Joseph Weatherhead — 1
WARREN, Josiah — H

WARREN, Julius Ernest — 4
WARREN, Leonard — 3
WARREN, Lillie Eginton — 4
WARREN, Lott — H
WARREN, Maude Lavinia — 1
WARREN, Mercy Otis — H
WARREN, Minton — 1
WARREN, Minton Machado — 2
WARREN, Percy Holmes — 4
WARREN, Richard Henry — 1
WARREN, Robert B. — 2
WARREN, Russell — H
WARREN, Samuel Dennis — 1
WARREN, Samuel Edward — 1
WARREN, Samuel Prowse — 1
WARREN, Sir Peter — H
WARREN, Speed — 5
WARREN, Stanley Perkins — 4
WARREN, Thomas Davis — 5
WARREN, Whitney — 2
WARREN, Willard Clinton
WARREN, William * — H
WARREN, William C. — 1
WARREN, William Fairfield
WARREN, William Homer — 4
WARREN, William Marshall — 3
WARREN, William Robinson — 2
WARREN, William Tilman — 4
WARREN, William Wirt — H
WARREN, Winslow — 1
WARRICK, Dupuy Goza — 4
WARRINER, Edward Augustus — 1
WARRINER, Eugene Clarente — 2
WARRINER, Lewis Legrand — 4
WARRINER, Reuel Edward — 5
WARRINER, Samuel Dexter — 2
WARRING, Charles Bartlett — 1
WARRINGTON, Albert Powell
WARRINGTON, George Howard
WARRINGTON, John W. — 1
WARRINGTON, Lewis — H
WARSHAW, Jacob — 2
WARSHAWSKY, Abel George — 4
WARTENBERG, Robert — 3
WARTHIN, Aldred Scott — 3
WARTON, Frank Riggs — 3
WARVELLE, George William — 4
WARWICK, C. Laurence — 3
WARWICK, Charles Franklin — 1
WARWICK, Herbert Sherwood, Jr. — 5
WARWICK, John George — H
WARWICK, Walter Winter — 1
WARWICK, William Edmund — 1
WASCHER, Howard George — 4
WASEY, L. — 4
WASH, Carlyle Hilton — 2
WASHABAUGH, Jacob Edgar
WASHAKIE — H
WASHBURN, Albert Henry — 1
WASHBURN, Alfred Hamlin — 5
WASHBURN, Benjamin Martin
WASHBURN, Cadwallader — 4
WASHBURN, Cadwallader Colden — H
WASHBURN, Charles Ames — H
WASHBURN, Charles Grenfill
WASHBURN, Claude Carlos — 1
WASHBURN, Edward Abiel — H
WASHBURN, Edward Roger — 5
WASHBURN, Edward Wight — 1
WASHBURN, Emory — H
WASHBURN, F. S. — 4
WASHBURN, Francis — 1

WASHBURN, Frank Sherman 1
WASHBURN, Frederic Augustus 2
WASHBURN, Frederic Baldwin 1
WASHBURN, Frederic Leonard
WASHBURN, George 1
WASHBURN, George Frederic 4
WASHBURN, George Hamlin 1
WASHBURN, Henry Bradford 4
WASHBURN, Henry Dana H
WASHBURN, Henry Stevenson 1
WASHBURN, Homer Charles
WASHBURN, Ichabod H
WASHBURN, Israel H
WASHBURN, Ives 2
WASHBURN, Jed L. 1
WASHBURN, John 1
WASHBURN, John Henry 1
WASHBURN, John Hosea 1
WASHBURN, Louis Cope 1
WASHBURN, Margaret Floy
WASHBURN, Peter Thacher H
WASHBURN, Reginald 3
WASHBURN, Robert 2
WASHBURN, Stanley 3
WASHBURN, Victor Duke 4
WASHBURN, William Barrett H
WASHBURN, William Drew 1
WASHBURN, William Ives 1
WASHBURN, William Sherman 1
WASHBURN, William Tucker 1
WASHBURNE, Elihu Benjamin H
WASHBURNE, George Adrian 2
WASHBURNE, Heluiz Chandler (Mrs. Carleton W. Washburne) 5
WASHINGER, William Henry 1
WASHINGTON, Booker Tallaferro 1
WASHINGTON, Bushrod H
WASHINGTON, George H
WASHINGTON, George Corbin H
WASHINGTON, George Thomas 5
WASHINGTON, Henry Stephens 1
WASHINGTON, Horace Lee 4
WASHINGTON, John Macrae H
WASHINGTON, Lawrence 1
WASHINGTON, Martha Dandridge Custis H
WASHINGTON, Thomas 3
WASHINGTON, W. Lanier
WASHINGTON, William Henry H
WASINGER, Gordon Bernard 5
WASKEY, Frank Hinman 1
WASKEY, Frank Hinman 4
WASLEY, Ruth Ellen 5
WASON, Charles William 1
WASON, Edward H. 1
WASON, Leonard Chase 1
WASON, Robert Alexander 3
WASON, Robert R. 3
WASON, William J. Jr. 3
WASSAM, Clarence Wyckliffe
WASSERMAN, Earl Reeves 5
WASSERMANN, Friedrich 5
WASSERVOGEL, Isidor 4
WASSON, Alfred Washington
WASSON, George Savary 3
WASSON, Theron 5
WASSON, Thomas Campbell 2
WASSON, William Walter 5

WASTE, William Harrison 1
WATCHORN, Robert 4
WATERBURY, Frank C. 1
WATERBURY, Frederick 4
WATERBURY, Henry S. 1
WATERBURY, John Isaac 1
WATERFALL, Harry William 2
WATERHOUSE, Alfred James 4
WATERHOUSE, Benjamin H
WATERHOUSE, Frank 1
WATERHOUSE, George Booker 3
WATERHOUSE, George Shadford 5
WATERHOUSE, John 2
WATERHOUSE, Joseph Raymond 1
WATERHOUSE, Richard Green 1
WATERHOUSE, Sylvester H
WATERLOO, Stanley 1
WATERMAN, Alan Tower 4
WATERMAN, Arba Nelson 1
WATERMAN, Charles Dana 4
WATERMAN, Charles M. 1
WATERMAN, Charles Winfield 1
WATERMAN, Charles Winfield 4
WATERMAN, Earle Lytton 3
WATERMAN, Frank Allan 5
WATERMAN, Herbert 2
WATERMAN, Julian Seesel
WATERMAN, Leroy 5
WATERMAN, Lewis Anthony 1
WATERMAN, Lewis Edson H
WATERMAN, Lucius 1
WATERMAN, Marcus 4
WATERMAN, Nixon 2
WATERMAN, Robert H. H
WATERMAN, Sigismund 4
WATERMAN, Thomas Whitney H
WATERMAN, Warren Gookin 3
WATERMAN, Willoughby Cyrus 4
WATERS, Campbell Easter 5
WATERS, Clara Erskine Clement
WATERS, Daniel 1
WATERS, Dudley E. 1
WATERS, Eugene A. 3
WATERS, Francis E. 1
WATERS, Henry Jackson 1
WATERS, James Stephen 4
WATERS, John H. 1
WATERS, Lewis William 2
WATERS, Moses H. 4
WATERS, N. Mcgee 1
WATERS, Robert 1
WATERS, Russell Judson 1
WATERS, Samuel M. 3
WATERS, Thomas Franklin 1
WATERS, William Everett 1
WATERS, William Laurence 3
WATERS, William Otis 1
WATERS, William P. 3
WATERSON, Karl William 4
WATHEN, John Roach
WATIE, Stand H
WATIES, James Rives 4
WATKEYS, Charles W. 5
WATKIN, William Ward 1
WATKINS, Aaron Sherman 1
WATKINS, Albert 1
WATKINS, Albert Galiton H
WATKINS, Alexander Farrar 1
WATKINS, Arthur Charles
WATKINS, Charles D. 1
WATKINS, Charles L. 4
WATKINS, Charles W. 1
WATKINS, Dale Baxter 1
WATKINS, David Ogden 1
WATKINS, Edgar 2
WATKINS, Elton Sr. 3
WATKINS, Everett C. 3

WATKINS, Ferre C. 4
WATKINS, Frank Thomas 3
WATKINS, Franklin Chenault 5
WATKINS, Frederick Mundell 5
WATKINS, G. Robert 5
WATKINS, George Claiborne H
WATKINS, Harry Evans 4
WATKINS, Henry Hitt 5
WATKINS, Henry Vaughan 2
WATKINS, J(ames) Stephen 5
WATKINS, Jabez Bunting 1
WATKINS, James (Keir) 5
WATKINS, John Elfreth 2
WATKINS, John Elfreth 1
WATKINS, John Thomas 1
WATKINS, Joseph Conrad 5
WATKINS, Raymond Edward 2
WATKINS, Robert Henry 4
WATKINS, Thomas H. 4
WATKINS, Thomas James 5
WATKINS, Vernon Phillips 5
WATKINS, Walter Kendall 4
WATKINS, William Turner 4
WATKINS, William Woodbury 1
WATLING, John Wright 3
WATMOUGH, James Horatio 1
WATMOUGH, John Goddard H
WATNER, Abraham 4
WATRES, Louis Arthur 1
WATROUS, Charles Leach 1
WATROUS, Elizabeth Snowden Nichols
WATROUS, George Ansel 1
WATROUS, George Dutton H
WATROUS, Harry Willson 1
WATROUS, Richard Benedict 3
WATSON, Adolphus Eugene 2
WATSON, Albert 3
WATSON, Alfred Augustin 1
WATSON, Alonzo
WATSON, Amelia Montague 1
WATSON, Andrew 1
WATSON, Archibald Robinson 3
WATSON, Benjamin Frank 1
WATSON, Bruce Mervellon 2
WATSON, Byron S. 1
WATSON, Charles G. 5
WATSON, Charles Henry 1
WATSON, Charles Roger 1
WATSON, Clarence Wayland 1
WATSON, Cooper Kinderdine H
WATSON, David Emmett 1
WATSON, David Kemper 4
WATSON, David Robert 5
WATSON, David Thompson 1
WATSON, Drake 1
WATSON, Dudley Crafts 5
WATSON, Earnest Charles 5
WATSON, Ebbie Julian 1
WATSON, Edith Sarah 3
WATSON, Edward Minor 1
WATSON, Edward Minor 2
WATSON, Edward Willard 1
WATSON, Edwin Martin 2
WATSON, Elizabeth Lowe 4
WATSON, Elkanah H
WATSON, Emile Emdon 3
WATSON, Emory Olin 1
WATSON, Ernest W(illiam) 1
WATSON, Eugene Payne 1
WATSON, Eugene Winslow 1
WATSON, F. B. 3
WATSON, Floyd Rowe 5
WATSON, Frank Dekker 3
WATSON, Frank Rushmore 1
WATSON, G. Clarke 4
WATSON, George D. 1
WATSON, George Henry 3

WATSON, H. Sumner 1
WATSON, Harry Legare 3
WATSON, Henry Chapman 1
WATSON, Henry Clay H
WATSON, Henry Cood 1
WATSON, Henry David 1
WATSON, Henry Winfield 1
WATSON, Hugh Hammond 2
WATSON, Irving Allison 1
WATSON, James H
WATSON, James 1
WATSON, James Craig H
WATSON, James D. 1
WATSON, James E. 2
WATSON, James Gray 3
WATSON, James Madison 1
WATSON, James Sibley 3
WATSON, James Webster 1
WATSON, John B. 3
WATSON, John Brown 2
WATSON, John Crittenden 1
WATSON, John Fanning H
WATSON, John Franklin 5
WATSON, John H. Jr. 4
WATSON, John Henry 1
WATSON, John Jay 1
WATSON, John Jordan Crittenden 1
WATSON, John Thomas 3
WATSON, John William Clark H
WATSON, Joseph Franklin 1
WATSON, Kenneth Nicoll 5
WATSON, Lewis Findlay H
WATSON, Mark Skinner 4
WATSON, Paul Barron 2
WATSON, Ralph Hopkins 4
WATSON, Robert 1
WATSON, Robert 2
WATSON, Robert Walker 1
WATSON, Russell Ellsworth 5
WATSON, Samuel Newell 1
WATSON, Sereno H
WATSON, Thomas Augustus 1
WATSON, Thomas E. 1
WATSON, Thomas John 3
WATSON, Thomas Leonard 1
WATSON, Walter Allen 1
WATSON, Willard Oliphint 5
WATSON, William 1
WATSON, William Franklin 3
WATSON, William Gorrell 4
WATSON, William Henry 1
WATSON, William Richard 2
WATT, Barbara Hall 5
WATT, Ben H. 1
WATT, David Alexander 4
WATT, Homer Andrew 1
WATT, James Robert 1
WATT, Richard Morgan 1
WATT, Robert J. 4
WATT, Robert McDowell 4
WATT, Rolla Vernon 1
WATTERS, Henry Eugene 1
WATTERS, Philip Melancthon 5
WATTERS, Rev. Philip Sidney 1
WATTERS, Thomas 1
WATTERS, William Henry 3
WATTERSON, Harvey Magee H
WATTERSON, Henry 1
WATTERSTON, George 1
WATTIS, Edmund Orson 1
WATTLES, Gurdon Wallace 3
WATTLES, Willard Austin 1
WATTS, Albert Edward 5
WATTS, Arthur S. 4
WATTS, Arthur Thomas 4
WATTS, Charles Henry 1
WATTS, Edward Seabrook 1
WATTS, Ethelbert 1
WATTS, Frank Overton 1
WATTS, Frederick H
WATTS, George Washington 1
WATTS, H. Bascom 3
WATTS, Harry Dorsey 4
WATTS, Harvey Maitland 4
WATTS, Herbert Charles 1
WATTS, John H
WATTS, John Clarence 1
WATTS, John Sebrie H

WATTS, Joseph Thomas 3
WATTS, Legh Richmond 1
WATTS, Lyle Ford 4
WATTS, Mary Stanbery 4
WATTS, Ralph L. 2
WATTS, Richard Cannon 1
WATTS, Ridley 1
WATTS, Roderick John 3
WATTS, Stanley Saul 5
WATTS, Thomas Hill H
WATTS, Thomas Joseph 3
WATTS, William Carleton 3
WATTS, William Lord 4
WAUCHOPE, George Armstrong 2
WAUGH, Alfred S. H
WAUGH, Beverly H
WAUGH, Evelyn Arthur St John
WAUGH, Frank Albert 2
WAUGH, Frederick Judd 1
WAUGH, Ida 1
WAUGH, John McMaster
WAUGH, Karl Tinsley 5
WAUGH, Samuel Bell H
WAUGH, Samuel Clark 4
WAUGH, Sidney 4
WAUGH, William Francis 1
WAUGH, William Hammond 5
WAUGH, William Jasper 5
WAUL, Thomas Neville 1
WAVELL, Archibald Percival 3
WAVERLEY, Viscount 3
WAXMAN, Franz 4
WAXMAN, Percy 2
WAY, Cassius 2
WAY, George Brevitt 4
WAY, John 1
WAY, Joseph Howell 1
WAY, Luther B. 1
WAY, Royal Brunson 2
WAY, Sylvester Bedell 1
WAY, Warren Wade 2
WAY, William 5
WAYBURN, Ned 2
WAYLAND, Francis H
WAYLAND, Francis 1
WAYLAND, Julius Augustus 1
WAYLAND-SMITH, Robert 4
WAYMACK, William Wesley 4
WAYMAN, Alexander Walker H
WAYMOUTH, George 1
WAYNE, Anthony H
WAYNE, Arthur Trezevant 4
WAYNE, Charles Stokes 4
WAYNE, Isaac H
WAYNE, James Moore H
WAYNE, Joseph Jr. 2
WEAD, Charles Kasson 1
WEADOCK, Bernard Francis 2
WEADOCK, Edward E. 4
WEADOCK, John C. 3
WEADOCK, Thomas Addis Emmet 1
WEAGANT, Roy Alexander 1
WEAGLY, Mrs. Roy C. F. 3
WEAKLEY, Charles Enright 5
WEAKLEY, Robert H
WEAKLEY, Samuel Davies 1
WEAR, D. Walker 4
WEAR, Frank Lucian 1
WEAR, Joseph W. 1
WEARE, Meshech 4
WEARING, Thomas 4
WEATHERBY, Charles Alfred 2
WEATHERBY, LeRoy Samuel
WEATHERFORD, William H
WEATHERFORD, Willis Duke 5
WEATHERHEAD, Albert J. Jr. 4
WEATHERLY, James Meriwether 4
WEATHERLY, Ulysses Grant 1
WEATHERLY, W(illiam) H. 5
WEATHERWAX, Preston Alonzo 5
WEATHERWAX, Hazelett Paul
WEAVER, Aaron Ward 1

WEAVER, Andrew Thomas 4
WEAVER, Archibald Jerard H
WEAVER, Arthur J. 2
WEAVER, Bennett 5
WEAVER, Charles Blanchard 4
WEAVER, Charles Clinton 2
WEAVER, Charles Parsons 4
WEAVER, Clarence Eugene 1
WEAVER, Claude 3
WEAVER, Edward Ebenezer 1
WEAVER, Erasmus Morgan 1
WEAVER, Fred(erick H(enry) 5
WEAVER, George Calvin 3
WEAVER, George Howitt 2
WEAVER, Gilbert Grimes 5
WEAVER, Harry Otis 1
WEAVER, Harry Sands 1
WEAVER, Henry Grady 2
WEAVER, James B. 1
WEAVER, James Bellamy 1
WEAVER, James Harvey 5
WEAVER, John 1
WEAVER, John Van Alstyn 1
WEAVER, Jonathan 1
WEAVER, Martha Collins 4
WEAVER, Myron McDonald 4
WEAVER, Paul John 2
WEAVER, Philip H
WEAVER, Philip Johnson 5
WEAVER, Powell 3
WEAVER, R.C. 5
WEAVER, Rudolph 2
WEAVER, Rufus B. 1
WEAVER, Rufus Washington 2
WEAVER, Samuel Pool 4
WEAVER, Silas Matteson 1
WEAVER, Walter L. 1
WEAVER, Walter Reed 2
WEAVER, William Dixon 1
WEAVER, Zebulon 2
WEBB, Alexander Stewart 1
WEBB, Alexander Stewart 2
WEBB, Atticus 5
WEBB, Carl N. 3
WEBB, Charles Aurelius 2
WEBB, Charles Henry 1
WEBB, Charles M. 5
WEBB, Charles Wallace 2
WEBB, Clifton 4
WEBB, Daniel H
WEBB, Daniel Clary 3
WEBB, Earle W. 4
WEBB, Edward Fleming 1
WEBB, Edwin Douglas 5
WEBB, Edwin Yates 3
WEBB, Ernest Clay 3
WEBB, Frank Elbridge 2
WEBB, Frank Rush 1
WEBB, George H. 1
WEBB, George James H
WEBB, George Thomas 4
WEBB, Gerald Bertram 2
WEBB, Hanor A. 4
WEBB, Henry Walter 1
WEBB, J. Burkitt 4
WEBB, James Avery 3
WEBB, James Duncan 4
WEBB, James Henry 1
WEBB, James Watson H
WEBB, John Maurice 1
WEBB, Joseph James 3
WEBB, Kenneth Seymour 4
WEBB, Nathan 1
WEBB, Richard L. 4
WEBB, Robert Alexander 1
WEBB, Robert H. 3
WEBB, Robert Thomas 1
WEBB, Robert Williams 2
WEBB, Sir Clifton 4
WEBB, Stuart Weston 5
WEBB, T(homas) Dwight. 5
WEBB, Thomas H
WEBB, Thomas Smith H
WEBB, Ulys Robert 3
WEBB, Ulysses Sigel 2
WEBB, Vanderbilt 3
WEBB, Vivian Howell (Mrs. Thompson Webb) 5
WEBB, Walter Loring 1
WEBB, Walter Prescott 4
WEBB, Willard Isaac, Jr. 5
WEBB, William Alexander 1
WEBB, William Alfred 2
WEBB, William Henry 1
WEBB, William Robert 1
WEBB, William Seward 1
WEBB, William Snyder 4
WEBB, William Walter 1
WEBBER, Amos Richard 2
WEBBER, Charles Wilkins H
WEBBER, George Harris 1
WEBBER, Henry William 1
WEBBER, Herbert John 2
WEBBER, James Benson Jr. 3
WEBBER, Le Roy 1
WEBBER, Oscar 4
WEBBER, Richard Hudson 4
WEBBER, Samuel H
WEBBER, Samuel Gilbert 4
WEBBINK, Paul 5
WEBER, Adna Ferrin 5
WEBER, Albert H
WEBER, Albert J. 4
WEBER, Alfred 3
WEBER, Arthur William 5
WEBER, Carl Jefferson 4
WEBER, Edouard 5
WEBER, Frederick Theodore 3
WEBER, Gustav C. E. 4
WEBER, Gustavus Adolphus 2
WEBER, Harry M. 3
WEBER, Henri Carleton 1
WEBER, Henry Adam 4
WEBER, Herman Carl 1
WEBER, Jessie Palmer 1
WEBER, Joe Nicholas 5
WEBER, John 4
WEBER, John B. 1
WEBER, John Langdon 1
WEBER, Joseph M. 2
WEBER, Lois 1
WEBER, Max 1
WEBER, Max 4
WEBER, Paul 3
WEBER, Randolph Henry 4
WEBER, Samuel Edwin 5
WEBER, William Lander 1
WEBERN, Anton 4
WEBNER, Frank Erastus 4
WEBSTER, Arthur Gordon 1
WEBSTER, Clyde Irvin 5
WEBSTER, Cornelius Crosby 2
WEBSTER, Daniel H
WEBSTER, David 1
WEBSTER, Edward Harlan 1
WEBSTER, Edwin Hanson H
WEBSTER, Edwin Harrison 5
WEBSTER, Edwin Sibley 3
WEBSTER, Edwin Sibley Jr. 3
WEBSTER, Eugene Carroll 1
WEBSTER, Francis Marion 1
WEBSTER, Frank Daniel 1
WEBSTER, Frank G. 1
WEBSTER, Frederic Smith 4
WEBSTER, George Sidney 1
WEBSTER, George Smedley 1
WEBSTER, George Van O'Linda 1
WEBSTER, George Washington 1
WEBSTER, Harold E. 4
WEBSTER, Harold Tucker 3
WEBSTER, Harrie 1
WEBSTER, Helen Livermore 1
WEBSTER, Henry Kitchell 1
WEBSTER, Hutton 3
WEBSTER, Hutton Jr. 3
WEBSTER, J. Stanley 4
WEBSTER, James R. 3
WEBSTER, Jean 1
WEBSTER, John Clarence 2
WEBSTER, John Hunter 1
WEBSTER, John Lee 1
WEBSTER, John White H
WEBSTER, Joseph Dana H
WEBSTER, Leslie Tillotson 2
WEBSTER, Lorin 1
WEBSTER, Margaret 5
WEBSTER, Marjorie Fraser 4
WEBSTER, Nathan Burnham 1
WEBSTER, Noah H
WEBSTER, Paul Kimball 3
WEBSTER, Pelatiah H
WEBSTER, Ralph Waldo 1
WEBSTER, Reginald H. 4
WEBSTER, Robert Morris 5
WEBSTER, Sidney 1
WEBSTER, Taylor H
WEBSTER, Warren 1
WEBSTER, William 5
WEBSTER, William Clarence 5
WEBSTER, William Franklin 4
WEBSTER, William Grant 4
WEBSTER, William Reuben 2
WECHSLER, Isreal Spanier 4
WECKLER, Herman L. 5
WECTER, Dixon 3
WEDDELL, Alexander Wilbourne 2
WEDDELL, Donald J. 3
WEDDERBURN, Joseph Henry Maclagan 2
WEDDERSPOON, William Rhind 1
WEDDINGTON, Frank Ruel 4
WEDEL, Paul John 5
WEDEL, Theodore Otto 5
WEDEMEYER, William Walter 1
WEE, Mons O. 2
WEED, Alonzo Rogers 1
WEED, Charles Frederick 1
WEED, Clarence Moores 2
WEED, Clive 1
WEED, Edwin Gardner 1
WEED, Frank Watkins 2
WEED, George Ludington 1
WEED, Hugh Hourston Craigie 3
WEED, J. Spencer 5
WEED, Jefferson 4
WEED, LeRoy Jefferson 4
WEED, Lewis Hill 3
WEED, Samuel Richards 1
WEED, Smith Mead 1
WEED, Theodore Linus 5
WEED, Thurlow H
WEED, Walter Harvey 2
WEEDEN, William Babcock 1
WEEDON, Leslie Washington 1
WEEKLEY, William Marion 1
WEEKS, Alanson 2
WEEKS, Andrew Jackson 1
WEEKS, Arland Deyett 1
WEEKS, Bartow Sumter 1
WEEKS, Benjamin D. 3
WEEKS, Carl 4
WEEKS, Charles Peter 1
WEEKS, David Fairchild 1
WEEKS, Edgar 1
WEEKS, Edwin Lord 1
WEEKS, Edwin Ruthven 1
WEEKS, Francis Darling 4
WEEKS, Frank Bentley 1
WEEKS, George H. 1
WEEKS, Grenville Mellen 1
WEEKS, H. Hobart 3
WEEKS, John A. 5
WEEKS, John Eliakim 2
WEEKS, John Elmer 2
WEEKS, John L. 3
WEEKS, John Wingate H
WEEKS, John Wingate 1
WEEKS, Joseph H
WEEKS, Joseph Dame H
WEEKS, Mary Harmon 1
WEEKS, Ralph Emerson 3
WEEKS, Raymond 3
WEEKS, Robert Kelley H
WEEKS, Rufus Wells 1
WEEKS, Sinclair 5
WEEKS, Stephen Beauregard 1
WEEKS, Stephen Holmes 1
WEEKS, Walter Scott 2
WEEKS, William Raymond 4
WEEMS, Capell Lain 4
WEEMS, John Crompton H
WEEMS, Julius Buel 1
WEEMS, Mason Locke H
WEEMS, Wharton Ewell 4
WEER, John Henry 2
WEESE, A. O. 3
WEET, Herbert Seeley 5
WEFALD, Knud 1
WEGENER, Theodore H. 3
WEGER, George Stephen 1
WEGG, David Spencer 1
WEGLEIN, David Emrich 5
WEGMANN, Edward 1
WEHE, Frank Rumrill 4
WEHLE, Louis Brandeis 3
WEHLER, Charles Emanuel 3
WEHMEYER, Lewis E(dgar) 5
WEHRLE, Vincent 2
WEHRLE, William Otto Joseph 3
WEHRMANN, Henry 5
WEHRWEIN, George Simon 2
WEIBLE, Rillmond Fernando 5
WEIBY, Maxwell Oliver 4
WEICHEL, Alvin F. 4
WEICHER, John 5
WEICHSEL, Christian C(arl) 5
WEICKER, Theodore 1
WEICKER, Theodore 5
WEIDENMANN, Jacob H
WEIDIG, Adolf 1
WEIDLER, Albert Greer 3
WEIDLER, Deleth Eber 4
WEIDLER, Victor Otterbein 3
WEIDMAN, Frederick Deforest 3
WEIDMAN, Samuel 2
WEIDNER, Carl A. 1
WEIDNER, Revere Franklin 1
WEIGEL, Albert Charles 4
WEIGEL, George Kibler 5
WEIGEL, William 1
WEIGHTMAN, Richard Coxe 1
WEIGHTMAN, Richard Hanson H
WEIK, Jesse William 3
WEIKEL, Anna Hamlin 5
WEIKEL, Charles Henry Harrison 5
WEIL, A. Leo 1
WEIL, Adolph Leopold 3
WEIL, Ann Yezner 5
WEIL, Carl 1
WEIL, Frank L. 3
WEIL, Fred Alban 1
WEIL, Irving 1
WEIL, Lee Herman 5
WEIL, Louis A. 3
WEIL, Oscar 4
WEIL, Richard Jr. 3
WEILAND, Christian Frederick 'van Leeuwen 3
WEILER, Royal William 2
WEILL, Kurt 3
WEIMAN, Rita 3
WEIMER, Albert Barnes 1
WEIMER, Bernal Robinson 5
WEIMER, Claud F. 3
WEINBERG, Benjamin Franklin 5
WEINBERG, Bernard 5
WEINBERG, Sidney James 5
WEINBERG, Tobias 5
WEINERMAN, Edwin Richard 5
WEINERT, Albert 2
WEINGARTEN, Joe 4
WEINIG, Arthur John 4
WEINMAN, Adolph Alexander 3
WEINMANN, Joseph Peter 4
WEINREICH, Uriel 4
WEINSTEIN, Alexander 2
WEINSTEIN, Joe 4
WEINSTOCK, Harris 1
WEINSTOCK, Herbert 5
WEINTAL, Edward 5
WEINZIRL, Adolph 4
WEIR, Ernest Tener 3
WEIR, F. Roney 1
WEIR, Hugh C. 1
WEIR, Irene 2
WEIR, J. Alden 1
WEIR, James Jr. 1
WEIR, John Ferguson 1
WEIR, John M. 2
WEIR, Levi Candee 1
WEIR, Paul 5
WEIR, Robert Fulton 1
WEIR, Robert Walter H
WEIR, Samuel 2
WEIR, W. Victor 4
WEIR, William Clarence 5
WEIR, William Figley 3
WEIS, Mrs. Charles William Jr. 4
WEISBERG, Harold Charles 5
WEISBERGER, David 4
WEISE, Arthur James 4
WEISENBURG, Theodore 1
WEISENBURGER, Walter Bertheau 2
WEISER, Emilius James 1
WEISER, Harry Boyer 3
WEISER, Johann Conrad H
WEISER, Walter R. 1
WEISGERBER, William Edwin 3
WEISL, Edwin Louis 5
WEISMAN, Russell 2
WEISMANN, Walter W. 5
WEISS, Adolph A. 5
WEISS, Albert Paul 1
WEISS, Anton Charles 1
WEISS, George 5
WEISS, John H
WEISS, John Morris 4
WEISS, Lewis Allen 3
WEISS, Louis Stix 3
WEISS, Samuel 3
WEISS, Samuel 4
WEISS, Seymour 5
WEISS, William 3
WEISS, William Casper 1
WEISS, William Erhard 2
WEISSE, Charles H. 1
WEISSE, Faneuil Dunkin 1
WEISSERT, Augustus Gordon 4
WEITZEL, George Thomas 1
WEITZEL, Godfrey H
WEITZMAN, Ellis 5
WEIZMANN, Chaim 4
WEIZMANN, Chalm 3
WELBORN, Curtis R. 5
WELBORN, Ira Clinton 5
WELBORN, Jesse Floyd 5
WELBY, Amelia Ball Coppuck H
WELCH, Adonijah Strong H
WELCH, Anthony Cummings 4
WELCH, Archibald Ashley 1
WELCH, Ashbel H
WELCH, Charles Edgar 1
WELCH, Charles Whitefield 2
WELCH, Deshler 4
WELCH, Douglas 5
WELCH, Edward Sohier 2
WELCH, Frank H
WELCH, George Martin 3
WELCH, Herbert 5
WELCH, Howard A. 3
WELCH, J. Leo 4
WELCH, John H
WELCH, John Collins 4
WELCH, John Edgar 5
WELCH, John R. 4
WELCH, Joseph N. 4
WELCH, Norman A. 4
WELCH, Paul M. 5
WELCH, Paul R. 3
WELCH, Philip Henry H
WELCH, Richard J. 2
WELCH, Roy Dickinson 3
WELCH, Samuel Wallace 1
WELCH, Stewart Henry 2
WELCH, Thomas Anthony 3
WELCH, Vincent S. 3
WELCH, W. S. 3
WELCH, William Addams 2
WELCH, William Henry * 1
WELCH, William McNair 5
WELCH, William Wickham H
WELD, Alfred Winsor 4
WELD, C. Minot 1
WELD, Francis Minot 2
WELD, Frank Augustine 4
WELD, J. Linzee 3
WELD, Laenas Gifford 1
WELD, Stephen Minot 1
WELD, Theodore Dwight H
WELD, Thomas 3
WELD, William Ernest 3
WELD, William Ernest 4
WELDIN, John Chilcote 5
WELDON, Charles Dater 1
WELDON, Lawrence 1
WELDON, R. Laurence 5
WELFLE, Frederick Edgar 3
WELFORD, Walter 5
WELKE, Edward Arthur 3
WELKER, Herman 3

*** Indicates More Than One Such Name Listed**

WELKER, Philip Albert 1
WELKER, William Henry 3
WELLBORN, H
  Marshall Johnson
WELLBORN, 4
  Maximilian Bethune
WELLBORN, Olin 1
WELLBORN, Olin III 4
WELLDON, Samuel A. 4
WELLER, Carl Vernon 3
WELLER, 4
  Charles Frederick
WELLER, Charles Heald 1
WELLER, Frank I. 3
WELLER, Fred Warren 4
WELLER, George Emery 1
WELLER, John B. H
WELLER, LeRoy 5
WELLER, 1
  Michael Ignatius
WELLER, Ovington E. 2
WELLER, Reginald Heber 1
WELLER, Royal H. 1
WELLER, Stuart 1
WELLES, Charles F. H
WELLES, Edgar Thaddeus 1
WELLES, Edward
  Kenneth 5
WELLES, George Denison 2
WELLES, Gideon H
WELLES, 2
  Henry Hunter Jr.
WELLES, 3
  Kenneth Brakeley
WELLES, Noah H
WELLES, Roger 1
WELLES, Sumner 4
WELLFORD, 3
  Edwin Taliaferro
WELLHOUSE, Frederick 1
WELLING, James Clarke H
WELLING, John C. 4
WELLING, Milton
  Holmes 5
WELLING, Richard 2
WELLINGTON, H
  Arthur Mellen
WELLINGTON, C. G. 3
WELLINGTON, Charles 1
WELLINGTON, 3
  Charles Oliver
WELLINGTON, 1
  George Brainerd
WELLINGTON, 1
  George Louis
WELLINGTON, 4
  Herbert Galbraith
WELLINGTON, William
  H. 1
WELLIVER, 2
  Judson Churchill
WELLMAN, 2
  Arthur Holbrook
WELLMAN, Beth Lucy 3
WELLMAN, Charles
  Aaron 5
WELLMAN, Creighton 5
WELLMAN, Francis L. 4
WELLMAN, Guy 1
WELLMAN, 3
  Hiller Crowell
WELLMAN, Mabel
  Thacher 5
WELLMAN, Paul Iselin 4
WELLMAN, Samuel
  Thomas 1
WELLMAN, 4
  Sargent Holbrook
WELLMAN, Walter 1
WELLONS, William Brock H
WELLS, Addison E. 1
WELLS, Agnes Ermina 3
WELLS, Alfred H
WELLS, Almond Brown 1
WELLS, Amos Russel 1
WELLS, Arthur George 1
WELLS, Arthur Register 3
WELLS, Benjamin Willis 1
WELLS, Brooks Hughes 1
WELLS, Bulkeley 1
WELLS, Calvin 1
WELLS, Carolyn 2
WELLS, Carveth 3
WELLS, Catherine Boott 1
WELLS, 5
  Channing McGregory
WELLS, Charles Edwin 1
WELLS, Charles Luke 1
WELLS, Charles Raymond 4
WELLS, Chester 2
WELLS, Daniel Halsey 1
WELLS, David Ames H
WELLS, David Collin 1
WELLS, David Dwight 1
WELLS, Donald A. 4
WELLS, Ebenezer Tracy 2
WELLS, Edgar Herbert

WELLS, 1
  Edgar Huidekoper
WELLS, Edward D. 4
WELLS, Edward Hubbard 4
WELLS, Edward L. 4
WELLS, Edward P. 1
WELLS, Erastus H
WELLS, Everett F. 5
WELLS, Frank Oren 1
WELLS, 1
  Frederic De Witt
WELLS, Frederic Lyman 4
WELLS, Frederick Brown 3
WELLS, George Burnham 1
WELLS, George Fitch 1
WELLS, George Miller 3
WELLS, 1
  George Washington
WELLS, Harry Edward 2
WELLS, Harry Gideon 2
WELLS, Heber Manning 1
WELLS, Henry H
WELLS, Henry Parkhurst 1
WELLS, Herbert George 2
WELLS, Herbert Johnson 1
WELLS, Hermon J. 3
WELLS, Horace H
WELLS, Horace Lemuel 1
WELLS, Ira Kent 1
WELLS, J. Brent 4
WELLS, James Earl 1
WELLS, James Madison 1
WELLS, 1
  James Simpson Chester
WELLS, Joel Cheney * 3
WELLS, Joel Reaves 5
WELLS, John * H
WELLS, John Barnes 1
WELLS, John Daniel 1
WELLS, John Edwin 2
WELLS, John Mason 5
WELLS, John Miller 1
WELLS, John Sullivan H
WELLS, John Walter 1
WELLS, Kenneth Robert 3
WELLS, Lemuel Henry 1
WELLS, 5
  Marguerite Jo Van Dalsem
  (Mrs. Thaddeus R. Wells)
WELLS, 4
  Marguerite Milton
WELLS, Newell Woolsey 4
WELLS, Newton Alonzo 1
WELLS, Orlando William 3
WELLS, Oscar 3
WELLS, 1
  Philip Patterson
WELLS, Ralph Olney 2
WELLS, Richard Harris 2
WELLS, Robert William H
WELLS, Roger Clark 4
WELLS, Rolla 1
WELLS, Samuel Calvin 4
WELLS, Samuel Roberts H
WELLS, Stuart Wilder 5
WELLS, 5
  Theodore D(onald)
WELLS, Thomas Bucklin 2
WELLS, Thomas Tileston 1
WELLS, 3
  Walter Farrington
WELLS, Webster 1
WELLS, William Calvin 3
WELLS, William Charles 1
WELLS, William Charles 1
WELLS, William Edwin 1
WELLS, William Harvey 1
WELLS, William Hill H
WELLS, William Hughes 1
WELLS, William Vincent H
WELLS, William Widney 5
WELLSTOOD, William 1
WELSH, Ashton Leroy 1
WELSH, Charles 1
WELSH, George A. 5
WELSH, Herbert 1
WELSH, John H
WELSH, Judson Perry 1
WELSH, Lilian 4
WELSH, Robert James 1
WELSH, Robert Kaye 2
WELSH, Vernon M. 5
WELSHIMER, Pearl H. 1
WELSHIMER, Sidney
  Helen Louise
WELTE, Carl Michael 3
WELTMER, Sidney
  Abram 1
WELTY, 5
  Benjamin Franklin
WEMPLE, William Lester 5
WEMPLE, William Yates 1
WEMYSS, H
  Francis Courtney
WEMYSS, William Hatch 5
WENCHEL, John Philip 4
WENCKEBACH, Carla 1

WENDE, Ernest 1
WENDEL, 2
  Hugo Christian Martin
WENDELL, Arthur
  Rindge 3
WENDELL, Barrett 1
WENDELL, 1
  Edith Greenough
WENDELL, 1
  George Vincent
WENDELL, James Isaac 1
WENDELL, 1
  Oliver Clinton
WENDEROTH, Oscar 5
WENDLING, 1
  George Reuben
WENDOVER, H
  Peter Hercules
WENDT, Edwin Frederick 3
WENDT, Henry W. 4
WENDT, Julia Bracken 1
WENDT, William 2
WENDTE, 1
  Charles William
WENE, Elmer H. 5
WENGER, Joseph Numa 5
WENGER, 3
  Oliver Clarence
WENGERT, 4
  Egbert Semmann
WENIGER, Willibald 3
WENKE, Adolph E. 4
WENLEY, 4
  Archibald Gibson
WENLEY, Robert Mark 1
WENNER, Frank 3
WENNER, George
  Unangst 1
WENNER, 5
  Howard Theodore
WENNER, William Ervin 4
WENNING, T. H. 2
WENNINGER, 1
  Francis Joseph
WENRICH, 5
  Calvin Naftzinger
WENSLEY, Robert Lytle 4
WENTE, Carl Frederick 5
WENTE, 1
  Edward Christopher
WENTWORTH, Benning H
WENTWORTH, 2
  Catherine Denkman
WENTWORTH, Cecile De 1
WENTWORTH, 3
  Edward Norris
WENTWORTH, 3
  Franklin Harcourt
WENTWORTH, Fred
  Wesley 1
WENTWORTH, 1
  George Albert
WENTWORTH, John * H
WENTWORTH, John 3
WENTWORTH, John Jr. 1
WENTWORTH, 5
  Marion Craig
WENTWORTH, Paul H
WENTWORTH, Tappan H
WENTWORTH, 5
  Waker Allerton
WENTWORTH, H
  William Pitt
WENTZ, 1
  Daniel Bertsch Jr.
WENTZ, George Elmore 4
WENTZ, Louis Haines 2
WENZEL, Caroline 3
WENZELL, Albert Beck 1
WENZELL, 4
  Henry Burleigh
WENZLAFF, 4
  Gustav Gottlieb
WEPPNER, Oliver A. 4
WERBE, 3
  Thomas Chandler Sr.
WERDEN, Reed H
WERDEN, Robert M. 5
WERDER, Xavier Oswald 1
WERFEL, Franz 4
WERKMAN, 4
  Chester Hamlin
WERLE, Edward C. 4
WERLEIN, 2
  Elizabeth Thomas
WERNAER, 5
  Robert Maximilian
WERNER, Adolph 1
WERNER, Heinz 4
WERNER, Henry Paul 3
WERNER, Henry Paul 4
WERNER, Max 1
WERNER, 3
  Oscar Emil Wade
WERNER, Victor Davis 5
WERNER, William E. 1
WERNER, William M. 3

WERNTZ, 4
  William Welling
WERNWAG, Lewis H
WERRENRATH, Reinald 3
WERT, James Edwin 1
WERTENBAKER, 3
  Charles Christian
WERTENBAKER, 1
  Charles Poindexter
WERTENBAKER, 4
  Thomas Jefferson
WERTH, Alexander 5
WERTHEIM, Maurice 3
WERTMAN, Floyd Rollan 2
WERTMAN, 4
  Kenneth Franklin
WERTMULLER, H
  Adolph Ulrich
WERTS, George Theodore 1
WERTZ, Edwin Slusser 2
WERTZ, George M. 1
WESBROOK, 1
  Frank Fairchild
WESCOAT, L. S. 5
WESCOTT, 2
  Cassius Douglas
WESCOTT, James Barney 3
WESCOTT, John Wesley 1
WESCOTT, 5
  Orville De Witt
WESEEN, Maurice Harley 1
WESLEY, Charles Sumner 1
WESLEY, 5
  Clarence Newton
WESSELHOEFT, Conrad 1
WESSELHOEFT, 1
  Lily Foster
WESSELHOFT, Walter 4
WESSELINK, John 1
WESSELLS, 1
  Henry Walton Jr.
WESSLINK, 4
  Gerritt William
WESSON, Charles Macon 3
WESSON, Daniel Baird 1
WESSON, David 1
WEST, Allen Brown 1
WEST, Andrew Fleming 2
WEST, Anson 1
WEST, Archa Kelly H
WEST, Arthur 5
WEST, Arthur Benjamin 5
WEST, Benjamin * H
WEST, Caleb Walton 1
WEST, Charles 5
WEST, Charles Cameron 1
WEST, Charles Edwin 1
WEST, Charles H. 1
WEST, Clifford Hardy 4
WEST, DuVal 3
WEST, E. Lovette 2
WEST, Edward Augustus 3
WEST, Egbert Watson 5
WEST, Elizabeth Howard 2
WEST, Erdman 4
WEST, Ernest Holley 5
WEST, Francis H
WEST, George H
WEST, George Henry 1
WEST, George N. 1
WEST, 1
  Hamilton Atchison
WEST, Helen Hunt H
WEST, Henry Litchfield 4
WEST, Henry Sergeant H
WEST, Henry Skinner 5
WEST, Howard H(iram) 5
WEST, James Edward 2
WEST, James Harcourt 1
WEST, James Hartwell 1
WEST, James Samuel 5
WEST, Jesse Felix 1
WEST, John Chester 4
WEST, Joseph H
WEST, Judson S. 3
WEST, Junius Edgar 2
WEST, Kenyon 4
WEST, Levon 5
WEST, 4
  Mary Brodie Crump
WEST, Max 1
WEST, Millard F. 1
WEST, Milton H. 2
WEST, Nathanael H
WEST, Nathanael 4
WEST, Olin 3
WEST, Oswald 1
WEST, Paul 1
WEST, Paul Brown 4
WEST, Preston C. 5
WEST, Raymond M. 2
WEST, Robert Rout 4
WEST, Roy Owen 3
WEST, Samuel H
WEST, Samuel H. 1
WEST, Samuel Wallens 5
WEST, Thomas H

WEST, Thomas Dyson 1
WEST, Thomas Franklin 1
WEST, Thomas Henry 1
WEST, Thomas Henry 4
WEST, Thomas Henry Jr. 1
WEST, Victor J. 1
WEST, William Edward H
WEST, William Henry 1
WEST, William Stanley 1
WEST, Willis Mason 1
WESTBROOK, Arthur E. 4
WESTBROOK, H
  Elroy Herman
WESTBROOK, John H
WESTBROOK, Lawrence 4
WESTBROOK, H
  Theodoric Romeyn
WESTCOTT, 3
  Allan Ferguson
WESTCOTT, 5
  Charles Drake
WESTCOTT, Edward
  Noyes H
WESTCOTT, Frank Nash 1
WESTCOTT, H
  James Diament Jr.
WESTCOTT, John Howell 2
WESTCOTT, Thompson H
WESTCOTT, 3
  Thompson Seiser
WESTENGARD, 1
  Jens Iverson
WESTENHAVER, David
  C. 1
WESTERFIELD, Ray Bert 4
WESTERFIELD, 5
  Samuel Zaza, Jr.
WESTERGAARD, 3
  Harald Malcolm
WESTERLO, Rensselaer H
WESTERMAN, Harry
  James 2
WESTERMANN, 3
  William Linn
WESTERN, Forrest 5
WESTERN, Lucille H
WESTERVELT, 4
  Emery Emmanuel
WESTERVELT, H
  Jacob Aaron
WESTERVELT, 1
  Marvin Zabriskie
WESTERVELT,
  William Irving
WESTERVELT, 3
  William Young
WESTFALL, Alfred R. 3
WESTFALL, Byron Lee 5
WESTFALL, 1
  Katherine Storey
WESTFALL, Othel D. 4
WESTFALL, W. D. A. 3
WESTGATE, John Minton 1
WESTGATE, 2
  Lewis Gardner
WESTHAFER, 2
  William Rader
WESTHUES, Henry J. 5
WESTINGHOUSE, 1
  George
WESTINGHOUSE, 1
  Henry Herman
WESTINGHOUSE,
  Marguerite Erskine Walker
WESTLAKE, Emory H. 4
WESTLAKE, J. Willis 1
WESTLEY,
  George Hembert
WESTON, Charles Sidney 2
WESTON, 1
  Charles Valentine
WESTON, 1
  Edmund Brownell
WESTON, Edward 1
WESTON, Edward 3
WESTON, Edward F. 5
WESTON, Edward Payson 1
WESTON, Eugene, Jr. 4
WESTON, 5
  Francis Hopkins
WESTON, Frank Morey 5
WESTON, George 4
WESTON, Harold 5
WESTON, Harry Elisha 5
WESTON, Henry Griggs 1
WESTON, James Augustus 1
WESTON, James Francis 3
WESTON, John Burns 1
WESTON, John Francis 1
WESTON, Karl Ephraim 1
WESTON, Nathan Austin 1
WESTON, Robert Spurr 2
WESTON, S. Burns 5
WESTON, Sidney Adams 5
WESTON, 1
  Stephen Francis
WESTON, Theodore

WESTON, Thomas H
WESTON, William H
WESTON, William 5
WESTOVER, Myron F. 1
WESTOVER, Oscar 4
WESTOVER, Russell Channing
WESTOVER, Wendell 4
WESTWOOD, Horace 3
WESTWOOD, Richard W. 4
WETHERALD, Charles E. 5
WETHERBEE, Frank Irving 5
WETHERBEE, George 4
WETHERED, John H
WETHERELL, Elizabeth H H
WETHERILL, Charles Mayer
WETHERILL, Horace Greeley 4
WETHERILL, Samuel * H
WETJEN, Albert Richard 2
WETMORE, Claude Hazeltine 4
WETMORE, Edmund 1
WETMORE, Edward Ditmars 2
WETMORE, Elizabeth Bisland 1
WETMORE, Frank O. 1
WETMORE, George Peabody
WETMORE, James Alphonso
WETMORE, Maude A. K. 3
WETMORE, Monroe Nichols 3
WETTACH, Robert Hasley 4
WETTEN, Albert Hayes 3
WETTEN, Emil C. 2
WETTERAU, Theodore Carl, Jr. 5
WETTLING, Louis Eugene
WETZEL, Harry H. 1
WETZEL, John Wesley 2
WETZEL, Lewis H
WETZLER, Joseph 1
WEXLER, Harry 4
WEXLER, Solomon
WEYANDT, Carl Stanley 4
WEYBURN, Lyon 4
WEYER, Edward Moffat 5
WEYERHAEUSER, 'Charles Augustus 1
WEYERHAEUSER, Frederick
WEYERHAEUSER, Frederick Edward 2
WEYERHAEUSER, John Philip
WEYERHAEUSER, John Philip Jr.
WEYERHAEUSER, Rudolph Michael 2
WEYGANDT, Carl Victor 4
WEYGANDT, Cornelius 3
WEYHE, Erhard 5
WEYL, Charles 5
WEYL, Hermann 3
WEYL, Max 1
WEYL, Walter Edward
WEYLER, George Lester 5
WEYMOUTH, Aubrey 1
WEYMOUTH, Clarence Raymond 2
WEYMOUTH, Frank Elwin 1
WEYMOUTH, George Warren 1
WEYMOUTH, Thomas Rote 3
WEYRAUCH, Martin Henry 3
WEYSSE, Arthur Wisswald 5
WHALEN, Grover A. 4
WHALEN, John 1
WHALEN, Robert E. 3
WHALEY, A. R. 4
WHALEY, George P. 2
WHALEY, James V. 4
WHALEY, Kellian Van Rensalear H
WHALEY, Percival Huntington
WHALEY, Richard Smith 1
WHALING, Thornton 4
WHALLEY, Edward H
WHALLON, Edward Payson 1
WHALLON, Reuben H
WHAM, Benjamin 5
WHAPLES, Meigs H. 1
WHAREY, James Blanton 2

WHARTON, Anne Hollingsworth 1
WHARTON, Arthur Orlando 5
WHARTON, Carol Forbes 3
WHARTON, Charles Henry H
WHARTON, Charles S. 5
WHARTON, Edith 1
WHARTON, Francis H
WHARTON, Henry Marvin 1
WHARTON, Henry Redwood 1
WHARTON, James E. 2
WHARTON, James Pearce 4
WHARTON, Jesse 1
WHARTON, Joseph H
WHARTON, Lang 2
WHARTON, Morton Bryan 1
WHARTON, Richard H
WHARTON, Robert H
WHARTON, Samuel H
WHARTON, Theodore Finley 2
WHARTON, Thomas H
WHARTON, Thomas Isaac H
WHARTON, Thomas Kelah H
WHARTON, Turner Ashby 1
WHARTON, Vernon Lane 4
WHARTON, William Fisher 1
WHARTON, William H. H
WHATCOAT, Richard H
WHATMOUGH, Joshua 4
WHEAT, Alfred Adams 2
WHEAT, Carl Irving 4
WHEAT, George Seay 2
WHEAT, Renville 5
WHEAT, William Howard 2
WHEATLAND, Marcus Fitzherbert 1
WHEATLEY, Phillis H
WHEATLEY, Richard 4
WHEATLEY, William 5
WHEATLEY, William Alonzo
WHEATON, Frank 1
WHEATON, Henry H
WHEATON, Horace 1
WHEATON, Laban 1
WHEATON, Loyd H
WHEATON, Nathaniel Sheldon
WHEDON, Daniel Denison H
WHEDON, John Fielding 5
WHEELAN, Fairfax Henry 1
WHEELAN, James Nicholas
WHEELER, Albert Gallatin 1
WHEELER, Albert Harry 5
WHEELER, Alvin Sawyer 1
WHEELER, Andrew Carpenter
WHEELER, Arthur Dana 1
WHEELER, Arthur Leslie 1
WHEELER, Arthur Martin 1
WHEELER, Benjamin Ide 1
WHEELER, Burr 4
WHEELER, C. Gilbert 1
WHEELER, Candace Thurber
WHEELER, Candace Thurber 1
WHEELER, Charles Barker
WHEELER, Charles Brewster
WHEELER, Charles Gardner 3
WHEELER, Charles Kennedy 4
WHEELER, Charles Stetson
WHEELER, Daniel Davis 1
WHEELER, David Hilton 1
WHEELER, Ebenezer Smith
WHEELER, Edward Jewitt 1
WHEELER, Edward Warren 4
WHEELER, Esther Willard
WHEELER, Everett Pepperrell
WHEELER, Ezra H
WHEELER, Franklin Carroll

WHEELER, Frederick Freeman 1
WHEELER, Frederick Seymour 1
WHEELER, George Bourne 2
WHEELER, George Carpenter 1
WHEELER, George Montague 4
WHEELER, George Wakeman 1
WHEELER, Grattan Henry H
WHEELER, Harold Francis 3
WHEELER, Harris Ansel 4
WHEELER, Harrison H. H 1
WHEELER, Harry A. 3
WHEELER, Henry 1
WHEELER, Henry Lord 1
WHEELER, Henry Nathan 1
WHEELER, Herbert Locke 1
WHEELER, Hiram C. 4
WHEELER, Hiram Nicholas 1
WHEELER, Homer Jay 2
WHEELER, Homer Webster 1
WHEELER, Howard Duryce 3
WHEELER, Howard V. 3
WHEELER, Hoyt Henry 1
WHEELER, James Cooper 1
WHEELER, James Everett 1
WHEELER, James Rignall 1
WHEELER, Janet 5
WHEELER, Jean Huleatt (Mrs. Joseph Coolidge Wheeler)
WHEELER, Jerome Byron 1
WHEELER, John Brooks 2
WHEELER, John DeBerry 5
WHEELER, John Egbert 2
WHEELER, John Hill 1
WHEELER, John Martin 1
WHEELER, John Samuel 5
WHEELER, John Taylor 3
WHEELER, John Wilson 1
WHEELER, Joseph 1
WHEELER, Joseph C. 5
WHEELER, Joseph Trank 1
WHEELER, Leslie Allen 5
WHEELER, Loren E. 1
WHEELER, Marianna 4
WHEELER, Mary Curtis 5
WHEELER, Mary Sparkes 1
WHEELER, Maxwell Stevenson 3
WHEELER, Nathaniel H
WHEELER, Nelson P. 1
WHEELER, Olin Dunbar 1
WHEELER, Post 3
WHEELER, Raymond Holder 4
WHEELER, Richard Smith 1
WHEELER, Rollo Clark 4
WHEELER, Royall Tyler 5
WHEELER, Ruth 2
WHEELER, Schuyler Skaats 1
WHEELER, Scott 5
WHEELER, Stephen Morse 4
WHEELER, Walton M. Jr. 1
WHEELER, Wayne Bidwell 1
WHEELER, William Adolphus H
WHEELER, William Alman 1
WHEELER, William Archie H
WHEELER, William Morton 5
WHEELER, William Reginald 1
WHEELER, William Riley 4
WHEELER, William Webb 1
WHEELER, Wilmot Fitch 4
WHEELOCK, Charles Delorma 4
WHEELOCK, Edward 1
WHEELOCK, Edwin Dwight 4
WHEELOCK, Eleazar H
WHEELOCK, Harry Bergen 1
WHEELOCK, Irene Grosvenor 1
WHEELOCK, John 1
WHEELOCK, Joseph Albert 1
WHEELOCK, Lucy 2

WHEELOCK, Ward 3
WHEELOCK, William Almy 1
WHEELOCK, William Hawxhurst 2
WHEELWRIGHT, Edmund March 1
WHEELWRIGHT, John H
WHEELWRIGHT, John Tyler 1
WHEELWRIGHT, Philip Ellis 5
WHEELWRIGHT, Robert 4
WHEELWRIGHT, Thomas Stewart 1
WHEELWRIGHT, William H
WHEELWRIGHT, William Dana 1
WHELAN, Charles A. 1
WHELAN, Charles Elbert 1
WHELAN, Edward J. 5
WHELAN, James H
WHELAN, Ralph 2
WHELAN, Richard Vincent H
WHELAND, Edward F. 3
WHELAND, Zenas Windsor 1
WHELCHEL, B. Frank 3
WHELEN, Townsend 4
WHELESS, Joseph 5
WHELPLEY, Benjamin Lincoln 4
WHELPLEY, Henry Milton 1
WHELPLEY, James Davenport 4
WHELPLEY, Medley Gordon Brittain 5
WHELPTON, Pascal Kidder 4
WHERRETT, Harry Scott 2
WHERRY, Arthur Cornelius 2
WHERRY, Elwood Morris 1
WHERRY, John 1
WHERRY, Kenneth S. 3
WHERRY, William Buchanan 1
WHERRY, William Mackey 1
WHERRY, William Mackey Jr. 4
WHETSTONE, Walter 1
WHETZEL, Herbert Hice 2
WHICHER, George Frisbie 3
WHICHER, George Meason 1
WHIDDEN, Bruce 5
WHIFFEN, Mrs. Thomas H
WHIFFEN, Mrs. Thomas 4
WHIGHAM, Henry James 4
WHILEY, Charles Whipple 1
WHINERY, Samuel 1
WHIPPLE, Abraham H
WHIPPLE, Allen Oldfather 4
WHIPPLE, Amiel Weeks 1
WHIPPLE, Charles Henry 1
WHIPPLE, Charles John 3
WHIPPLE, Edwin Percy 1
WHIPPLE, George Chandler
WHIPPLE, Guy Montrose 1
WHIPPLE, Harvey 4
WHIPPLE, Henry Benjamin 1
WHIPPLE, Leonidas Rutledge 4
WHIPPLE, Lucius Albert 3
WHIPPLE, Oliver Mayhew 1
WHIPPLE, Ralph W. 3
WHIPPLE, Sherman Leland 1
WHIPPLE, Squire H
WHIPPLE, Thomas Jr. H
WHIPPLE, Wayne 2
WHIPPLE, William 1
WHIPPLE, William Denison 1
WHIPPLE, William G. 5
WHISENAND, James Franklin 4
WHISTLER, George Washington H
WHISTLER, James Abbott McNeill 1
WHISTLER, Joseph Nelson Garland 1
WHISTON, Frank Michael 5
WHITACRE, Frank Edward 5
WHITACRE, Horace J. 2

WHITACRE, John J. 4
WHITAKER, Albert Conser 5
WHITAKER, Alexander H
WHITAKER, Alma 3
WHITAKER, Charles Harris 1
WHITAKER, Clem H
WHITAKER, Daniel Kimball 4
WHITAKER, Edward Gascoigne 1
WHITAKER, Edwards 4
WHITAKER, Epher 1
WHITAKER, Frank M. 1
WHITAKER, George 5
WHITAKER, Harriet Catherine Reed (Mrs. Charles Richard
WHITAKER, Harriet Reed 4
WHITAKER, Herbert Coleman 1
WHITAKER, Herman 1
WHITAKER, Hervey Williams H
WHITAKER, John Albert 3
WHITAKER, John Thompson 4
WHITAKER, Martin D. 4
WHITAKER, Mary Scrimzeour
WHITAKER, Milton C. 4
WHITAKER, Nathaniel H
WHITAKER, Nelson L. 3
WHITAKER, Nicholas Tillinghast 1
WHITAKER, Orvil R(obert) 5
WHITAKER, Ozi William 1
WHITAKER, Robert 2
WHITAKER, Samuel Estill 4
WHITAKER, Walter Claiborne 1
WHITAKER, William Force 1
WHITALL, Samuel Rucker 1
WHITBECK, R. H. H
WHITCHER, Frances Miriam Berry H
WHITCHER, Frank Weston 1
WHITCHER, Mary H
WHITCHURCH, Irl Goldwin 5
WHITCOMB, G. Henry 1
WHITCOMB, Ida Prentice 1
WHITCOMB, James H
WHITCOMB, Merrick 4
WHITCOMB, Selden Lincoln 1
WHITCOMB, William Arthur 2
WHITE, Aaron Pancoast 2
WHITE, Albert Beebe 3
WHITE, Albert Blakeslee 1
WHITE, Albert Easton 4
WHITE, Albert Smith 1
WHITE, Alexander * H
WHITE, Mrs. Alexander B. (rassie Hoskins)
WHITE, Alexander M. 5
WHITE, Alfred Holmes 3
WHITE, Alfred Ludlow 1
WHITE, Alfred Tredway 1
WHITE, Allison H
WHITE, Alma 2
WHITE, Alvan Newton 2
WHITE, Andrew H
WHITE, Andrew Dickson 1
WHITE, Andrew John, Jr. 5
WHITE, Arthur Cleveland 4
WHITE, Arthur Fairchild
WHITE, Aubrey Lee 3
WHITE, Austin John 2
WHITE, Bartow H
WHITE, (John) Beaver 5
WHITE, Benjamin H
WHITE, Benjamin Franklin 4
WHITE, Bessie Bruce 5
WHITE, Bouck 5
WHITE, Campbell Patrick H
WHITE, Canvass H
WHITE, Caroline Earle 1
WHITE, Charles Abiathar 1
WHITE, Charles Daniel 3
WHITE, Charles Edgar 4
WHITE, Charles Elmer Jr.

WHITE, 2
Charles Harrison
WHITE, Charles Henry 1
WHITE, Charles Henry 3
WHITE, H
Charles Ignatius
WHITE, Charles James 4
WHITE, Charles Joyce 1
WHITE, Charles Lincoln 1
WHITE, Charles Stanley 5
WHITE, Charles Thomas 3
WHITE, 4
Clarence Cameron
WHITE, Clarence H. 2
WHITE, Clarence Hudson 1
WHITE, 3
Compton Ignatius
WHITE, 1
Courtland Yardley Jr.
WHITE, David H
WHITE, David 1
WHITE, David Stuart 2
WHITE, Dudley Allen 3
WHITE, 5
E(dward) Laurence
WHITE, 3
Edmund Valentine
WHITE, Edward Albert 2
WHITE, Edward Brickell 1
WHITE, Edward Douglass H
WHITE, Edward Douglass 1
WHITE, Edward Franklin 1
WHITE, 4
Edward Higgins II
WHITE, Edward Joseph 1
WHITE, Edward Lucas 1
WHITE, Edwin 1
WHITE, Edwin 3
WHITE, Edwin Augustine 1
WHITE, Elijah B. 1
WHITE, Eliza Orne 2
WHITE, H
Ellen Gould Harmon
WHITE, 4
Ellen Gould Harmon
WHITE, 1
Emerson Elbridge
WHITE, 5
Emma Eaton (Mrs. Edward Franklin White)
WHITE, Erskine Norman 1
WHITE, 3
Florence Donnell
WHITE, Frances Hodges 4
WHITE, Francis 1
WHITE, Francis 4
WHITE, 5
Francis Johnstone
WHITE, Francis Samuel 1
WHITE, Francis W. 1
WHITE, Frank * 1
WHITE, Frank Edson 1
WHITE, Frank Marshall 4
WHITE, Frank Newhall 1
WHITE, Frank Russell 1
WHITE, Frank Shelley 1
WHITE, Frederick W. 1
WHITE, Gaylord Starin 1
WHITE, George H
WHITE, George 3
WHITE, George Ared 3
WHITE, George Avery 3
WHITE, George Edward 2
WHITE, George Frederic 1
WHITE, George Leonard H
WHITE, George Loring 5
WHITE, George Starr 4
WHITE, George W. 1
WHITE, H
George Washington
WHITE, George Whitney 1
WHITE, Georgia Laura 3
WHITE, Gilbert 1
WHITE, Greenough 1
WHITE, H. Lee 5
WHITE, Harold Tredway 4
WHITE, Harry 1
WHITE, Harry Dexter H
WHITE, Harry Dexter 2
WHITE, Harry Dexter 1
WHITE, Hays B. 1
WHITE, Helen Constance 4
WHITE, Henry * H
WHITE, Henry 1
WHITE, Henry Adelbert 3
WHITE, Henry Alexander 1
WHITE, Henry Clay * H
WHITE, Henry Dale 5
WHITE, Henry Ford 4
WHITE, Henry Middleton 3
WHITE, Henry Seely 1
WHITE, 1
Herbert Humphrey
WHITE, Herbert Judson 2
WHITE, Hervey 4
WHITE, Horace 1
WHITE, Horace 2

WHITE, Horace Greeley 1
WHITE, Horace Henry 2
WHITE, Horatio Stevens 1
WHITE, Howard Ganson 4
WHITE, Howard Judson 1
WHITE, Hugh H
WHITE, Hugh 1
WHITE, Hugh Lawson H
WHITE, Hugh Lawson 1
WHITE, Ike D. 5
WHITE, Isaac Deforest 1
WHITE, Israel C. 1
WHITE, J. Campbell 4
WHITE, J. Du Pratt 1
WHITE, J. Harrison 2
WHITE, J. Warren 4
WHITE, Jacob Lee 2
WHITE, James * H
WHITE, James A. 2
WHITE, James Andrew 4
WHITE, James Bain H
WHITE, James Barlow 4
WHITE, James Charles 5
WHITE, James Clarke 1
WHITE, James Dempsey 4
WHITE, James Gilbert 1
WHITE, James Halley 1
WHITE, James McLaren 1
WHITE, James Terry 1
WHITE, James Watson 1
WHITE, James William 1
WHITE, Jay 1
WHITE, Jesse Hayes 5
WHITE, John * H
WHITE, John Baker 4
WHITE, John Barber 1
WHITE, John Blake H
WHITE, John Blake 4
WHITE, John Campbell 1
WHITE, John Chanler 3
WHITE, John DeHaven 1
WHITE, John Ellington 1
WHITE, John Griswold 1
WHITE, John Hazen 1
WHITE, John P. 5
WHITE, John Phillip; 1
WHITE, John Roberts 4
WHITE, John Stuart 1
WHITE, John Turner 2
WHITE, John W. 3
WHITE, John Williams 1
WHITE, John Z. 4
WHITE, Joseph Augustus 4
WHITE, Joseph Hill 5
WHITE, H
Joseph Livingston
WHITE, Joseph M. H
WHITE, H
Joseph Worthington
WHITE, Josh 5
WHITE, Joshua Warren 3
WHITE, Kemble 5
WHITE, Lawrence Grant 3
WHITE, Lazarus 4
WHITE, Lee A. 5
WHITE, Leonard H
WHITE, Leonard Dupee 3
WHITE, 3
Llewellyn Brooke
WHITE, Luke Matthews 3
WHITE, Lynn Townsend 1
WHITE, Lynne Loraine 4
WHITE, Marcus 1
WHITE, 3
Marian Ainsworth
WHITE, Matthew Jr. 1
WHITE, 4
Michael Alfred Edwin
WHITE, Nehemiah 1
WHITE, Nelia Gardner 3
WHITE, Newman Ivey 2
WHITE, 1
Octavius Augustus
WHITE, Paul W. 3
WHITE, Pearl H
WHITE, Pearl 4
WHITE, Percival 5
WHITE, Peter 1
WHITE, Philip (Rodney) 5
WHITE, Phillips H
WHITE, Phineas H
WHITE, Ray Bridwell 2
WHITE, Richard Grant H
WHITE, Robe Carl 1
WHITE, Robert 1
WHITE, Robert Vose 4
WHITE, Rodney Douglas 4
WHITE, Rollin Henry 4
WHITE, Roy Barton 4
WHITE, Rufus Austin 1
WHITE, S. Marx 5
WHITE, Sallie Joy 1
WHITE, Samuel H
WHITE, Samuel Stockton H
WHITE, 2
Sebastian Harrison
WHITE, Stanford 1

WHITE, Stanley 1
WHITE, Stephen Mallory 1
WHITE, 1
Stephen Van Culen
WHITE, Stewart Edward 2
WHITE, Terence Hanbury 1
WHITE, Thomas Dresser 4
WHITE, Thomas Holden 3
WHITE, Thomas Justin 1
WHITE, Thomas Raeburn 3
WHITE, Thomas Willis 1
WHITE, Trentwell Mason 3
WHITE, Trueman Clark 1
WHITE, Trumbull 1
WHITE, Trumbull 2
WHITE, W. Wilson 4
WHITE, 3
Wallace Humphrey Jr.
WHITE, Walter 3
WHITE, Walter C. 1
WHITE, Walter Louis 4
WHITE, Walter Porter 2
WHITE, 5
Walter W(illiam)
WHITE, Weldon Bailey 4
WHITE, Wilbert Webster 2
WHITE, Wilbur Wallace 3
WHITE, William H
WHITE, William 4
WHITE, William Alanson 1
WHITE, William Alfred 5
WHITE, William Allen 1
WHITE, William Chapman 3
WHITE, William Charles 1
WHITE, 4
William Crawford
WHITE, William E. 1
WHITE, William Henry 1
WHITE, 5
William L(indsay)
WHITE, 3
William Lawrence
WHITE, William Mathews 4
WHITE, William Monroe 1
WHITE, H
William Nathaniel
WHITE, William Parker 2
WHITE, 1
William Pierrepont
WHITE, 4
William Prescott
WHITE, William Wallace 2
WHITE, William Wurts 5
WHITE, Windsor T. 3
WHITEAKER, Robert O. 4
WHITEBROOK, 4
Lloyd George
WHITE EYES H
WHITEFIELD, Edwin H
WHITEFIELD, George H
WHITEFORD, 2
Gilbert Hayes
WHITEFORD, Roger J. 4
WHITEFORD, 5
William Kepler
WHITEHAIR, 1
Charles Wesley
WHITEHEAD, 3
Alfred North
WHITEHEAD, Cabell 2
WHITEHEAD, 1
Charles Nelson
WHITEHEAD, Cortlandt 1
WHITEHEAD, 3
Donald Strehle
WHITEHEAD, Edwin 1
Kirby
WHITEHEAD, 4
Ennis Clement
WHITEHEAD, Henry C. 5
WHITEHEAD, 1
James Thomas
WHITEHEAD, John 1
WHITEHEAD, John 3
John Boswell
WHITEHEAD, John Meek 1
WHITEHEAD, Joseph 4
WHITEHEAD, 1
Ralph Radcliffe
WHITEHEAD, 1
Richard Henry
WHITEHEAD, 5
Robert Frederick
WHITEHEAD, 5
T(homas) North
WHITEHEAD, H
Wilbur Cherrier
WHITEHEAD, H
William Adee
WHITEHILL, Clarence 1
WHITEHILL, 4
Howard Joseph
WHITEHILL, James H
WHITEHILL, John H
WHITEHILL, Robert H

WHITEHORNE, Earl 1
WHITEHOUSE, Brooks 5
WHITEHOUSE, F. Cope 1
WHITEHOUSE, 5
Florence Brooks
WHITEHOUSE, 4
Henry Remsen
WHITEHOUSE, Horace 3
WHITEHOUSE, 1
James Horton
WHITEHOUSE, H
John Osborne
WHITEHOUSE, 5
Robert Treat
WHITEHOUSE, Sheldon 4
WHITEHOUSE, 5
Vira Boarman (Mrs. Norman de R. Whitehouse)
WHITEHOUSE, 1
William Fitz Hugh
WHITEHOUSE, 1
William Penn
WHITEHURST, Camelia 1
WHITEHURST, 4
John Leyburn
WHITEIS, 5
William Robert
WHITELAW, John 5
Bertram
WHITELEY, Emily Stone 1
WHITELEY, Isabel Nixon 5
WHITELEY, 5
James Gustavus
WHITELEY, H
Richard Henry
WHITELEY, H
William Gustavus
WHITELOCK, George 1
WHITELOCK, 1
Louis Clarkson
WHITELOCK, 4
Louise Clarkson
WHITELOCK, 1
William Wallace
WHITEMAN, Paul 4
WHITEMAN, 5
Samuel Dickey
WHITENER, Paul A. W. 3
WHITENTON, 1
William Maynard
WHITER, Edward Tait 4
WHITESELL, William M. 1
WHITESIDE, Arthur Dare 4
WHITESIDE, Frank Reed 1
WHITESIDE, 4
George Morris II
WHITESIDE, 4
George Walter
WHITESIDE, 3
Horace Eugene
WHITESIDE, 1
James Leonard
WHITESIDE, Jenkin H
WHITESIDE, John H
WHITESIDE, Walker 2
WHITFIELD, Albert Hall 4
WHITFIELD, Henry H
WHITFIELD, Henry 2
Lewis
WHITFIELD, J. Edward 1
WHITFIELD, James H
WHITFIELD, James Bryan 2
WHITFIELD, H
John Wilkins
WHITFIELD, Robert Parr 1
WHITFORD, 5
Alfred E(dward)
WHITFORD, 3
Edward Everett
WHITFORD, 1
Greeley Webster
WHITFORD, Oscar F. 1
WHITFORD, 3
Robert Naylor
WHITFORD, 1
William Calvin
WHITFORD, 1
William Clarke
WHITHORNE, Emerson 3
WHITIN, Ernest Stagg 2
WHITING, Arthur 1
WHITING, Borden Durfee 4
WHITING, 1
Charles Goodrich
WHITING, 1
Charles Sumner
WHITING, Edward Elwell 5
WHITING, Fred 1
WHITING, Fred T. 3
WHITING, 5
Frederic Allen
WHITING, 1
George Elbrige
WHITING, Gertrude 1
WHITING, Harry Hayes 1
WHITING, Henry H
WHITING, Henry Hyer 1

WHITING, John Talman 4
WHITING, Justin Rice 1
WHITING, Justin Rice 4
WHITING, Lilian 2
WHITING, Mary Gray 4
WHITING, Richard Henry H
WHITING, Robert Rudd 1
WHITING, Samuel H
WHITING, Sarah Frances 1
WHITING, Walter Rogers 5
WHITING, William H
WHITING, William 1
WHITING, 3
William Alonzo
WHITING, 1
William Fairfield
WHITING, William Henry 1
WHITING, 2
William Henry Jr.
WHITING, H
William Henry Chase
WHITLEY, Cora Call 1
WHITLEY, James Lucius 5
WHITLEY, 5
Johnson DeCosta
WHITLEY, Samuel Henry 2
WHITLOCK, Brand 1
WHITLOCK, Eliza H
Kemble
WHITLOCK, 5
Elliott Howland
WHITLOCK, 2
Herbert Percy
WHITLOCK, 1
William Francis
WHITMAN, 3
Alfred Freeman
WHITMAN, Armitage 4
WHITMAN, Arthur 3
Dudley
WHITMAN, 1
Benaiah Longley
WHITMAN, 1
Charles Huntington
WHITMAN, Charles Otis 1
WHITMAN, 2
Charles Seymour
WHITMAN, Edmund 5
Allen
WHITMAN, Edward A. 2
WHITMAN, 4
Eugene Winfield
WHITMAN, Ezekiel H
WHITMAN, Ezra Bailey 1
WHITMAN, Frank 1
Perkins
WHITMAN, Frank S. 1
WHITMAN, 3
Hendricks Hallett
WHITMAN, Henry 4
Harold
WHITMAN, John Lorin 1
WHITMAN, John Munro 1
WHITMAN, Lemuel H
WHITMAN, LeRoy 5
WHITMAN, 1
Malcolm Douglass
WHITMAN, Marcus H
WHITMAN, H
Narcissa Prentiss
WHITMAN, Ralph 2
WHITMAN, Roger B. 2
WHITMAN, 4
Roswell Hartson
WHITMAN, Royal 2
WHITMAN, Russell 2
WHITMAN, 1
Russell Ripley
WHITMAN, H
Sarah Helen Power
WHITMAN, Walter 1
WHITMAN, William 1
WHITMAN, 1
William Edward Seaver
WHITMARSH, 5
Francis Leggett
WHITMARSH, Henry 1
Allen
WHITMARSH, 4
Hubert Phelps
WHITMARSH, 1
Theodore Francis
WHITMER, David H
WHITMER, 4
Robert Forster
WHITMORE, 4
Annie Goodell
WHITMORE, Carl 3
WHITMORE, Elias H
WHITMORE, 5
Eugene R(andolph)
WHITMORE, 2
Frank Clifford
WHITMORE, H
George Washington
WHITMORE, 1
William Henry

Name	
WHITMYER, Edward Charles	1
WHITNALL, Harold Orville	2
WHITNER, Daniel Jay	4
WHITNEY, Adeline Dutton Train	1
WHITNEY, Alexander Fell	2
WHITNEY, Alfred Rutgers	2
WHITNEY, Allen Banks	1
WHITNEY, Allen Sisson	3
WHITNEY, Anne	1
WHITNEY, Asa *	H
WHITNEY, Carl Everett	1
WHITNEY, Carrie Westlake	5
WHITNEY, Caspar	1
WHITNEY, Charles Smith	3
WHITNEY, Courtney	5
WHITNEY, David Rice	1
WHITNEY, Edward Baldwin	1
WHITNEY, Edwin Morse	3
WHITNEY, Eli	H
WHITNEY, Eli	1
WHITNEY, Emily Henrietta	4
WHITNEY, Frank I.	5
WHITNEY, George	4
WHITNEY, Gertrude Capen	1
WHITNEY, Gertrude Vanderbilt	2
WHITNEY, Guilford Harrison	5
WHITNEY, Gwin Allison	1
WHITNEY, Harry	1
WHITNEY, Harry Edward	1
WHITNEY, Harry Payne	1
WHITNEY, Henry Clay	4
WHITNEY, Henry Howard	2
WHITNEY, Henry Melville	1
WHITNEY, Henry Mitchell	
WHITNEY, Herbert Baker	4
WHITNEY, James Amaziah	
WHITNEY, James Lyman	1
WHITNEY, John Dunning	4
WHITNEY, Joseph Lafeton	4
WHITNEY, Josiah Dwight	H
WHITNEY, Loren Harper	1
WHITNEY, Marian Parker	2
WHITNEY, Mary Watson	1
WHITNEY, Milton	1
WHITNEY, Myron W.	1
WHITNEY, Nathaniel Ruggles	4
WHITNEY, Nelson Oliver	1
WHITNEY, Paul Clinton	3
WHITNEY, Payne	1
WHITNEY, Robert Bacon	3
WHITNEY, Samuel Brenton	1
WHITNEY, Thomas Richard	H
WHITNEY, Wheelock	3
WHITNEY, William Channing	2
WHITNEY, William Collins	1
WHITNEY, William Dwight	H
WHITNEY, William Fiske	1
WHITNEY, William Locke	1
WHITNEY, Willis Rodney	3
WHITON, Herman Frasch	4
WHITON, James Morris	1
WHITRIDGE, Frederick Wallingford	
WHITRIDGE, Morris	1
WHITSETT, William Thornton	1
WHITSIDE, Samuel Marmaduke	1
WHITSITT, William Heth	
WHITSON, Andrew Robeson	5
WHITSON, Edward	
WHITSON, John Harvey	1
WHITT, Hugh	3
WHITTAKER, Edmund Boyd	
WHITTAKER, James	4
WHITTAKER, James Thomas	1
WHITTAKER, Miller F.	3
WHITTED, Elmer Ellsworth	4
WHITTEKER, John Edwin	1
WHITTELSEY, Abigail Goodrich	H
WHITTEMORE, Amos	H
WHITTEMORE, Arthur Easterbrook	5
WHITTEMORE, Benjamin Franklin	H
WHITTEMORE, Charles Otto	4
WHITTEMORE, Clark McKinley	3
WHITTEMORE, Don Juan	
WHITTEMORE, Edward Loder	1
WHITTEMORE, Eugene Beede	4
WHITTEMORE, Harris	1
WHITTEMORE, Henry	4
WHITTEMORE, Herbert Lucius	3
WHITTEMORE, James Madison	1
WHITTEMORE, John Weed	4
WHITTEMORE, Laurence Frederick	1
WHITTEMORE, Luther Denny	4
WHITTEMORE, Thomas	H
WHITTEMORE, Thomas	3
WHITTEMORE, William John	3
WHITTEMORE, Wyman	3
WHITTEN, John Charles	1
WHITTEN, Robert	1
WHITTHORNE, Washington Curran	
WHITTIER, Charles Comfort	5
WHITTIER, Charles Franklin	1
WHITTIER, Clarke Butler	
WHITTIER, John Greenleaf	H
WHITTIER, William Frank	1
WHITTINGHAM, William Rollinson	H
WHITTINGHILL, Dexter Gooch	5
WHITTINGTON, William Madison	4
WHITTLE, Francis McNeece	1
WHITTLE, Stafford Gorman	
WHITTLES, Thomas Davis	5
WHITTLESEY, Derwent	3
WHITTLESEY, Eliphalet	1
WHITTLESEY, Elisha	H
WHITTLESEY, Frederick	H
WHITTLESEY, Henry De Witt Sr.	4
WHITTLESEY, Thomas Tucker	H
WHITTLESEY, William Augustus	
WHITTREDGE, Worthington	
WHITTY, Dame May	2
WHITTY, James Howard	1
WHITWELL, Frederick Silsbee	
WHITWORTH, George Gillatt	1
WHITWORTH, Pegram	5
WHORF, John	3
WHORF, Richard	4
WHORTON, John Lacy	1
WHYBURN, Gordon Thomas	5
WHYBURN, William Marvin	5
WHYTE, Carl Barzellous	4
WHYTE, Frederick William Carrick	
WHYTE, James Primrose	1
WHYTE, Jessel Stuart	3
WHYTE, John	3
WHYTE, Malcolm K.	4
WHYTE, William Pinckney	1
WIBORG, Frank Bestow	1
WICHER, Edward Arthur	4
WICK, Charles J.	4
WICK, James L.	5
WICK, Samuel	5
WICK, William Watson	4
WICKARD, Claude Raymond	
WICKENDEN, Arthur Consaul	4
WICKENDEN, William Elgin	2
WICKER, Cassius Milton	1
WICKER, George Ray	1
WICKER, John Jordan	3
WICKERSHAM, Cornelius Wendell	4
WICKERSHAM, Cornelius Wendell Jr.	4
WICKERSHAM, Edward Dean	4
WICKERSHAM, George Woodward	
WICKERSHAM, James	1
WICKERSHAM, James Pyle	H
WICKES, Eliphalet	H
WICKES, Forsyth	4
WICKES, Lambert	H
WICKES, Stephen	1
WICKES, Thomas H.	1
WICKETT, Frederick Henry	
WICKHAM, Henry Frederick	1
WICKHAM, Henry Taylor	3
WICKHAM, John	H
WICKHEM, John Dunne	2
WICKLIFFE, Robert C.	1
WICKLIFFE, Robert Charles	H
WICKMAN, Carl Eric	3
WICKS, Frank Scott Corey	3
WICKS, Robert Russell	4
WICKSER, Philip John	2
WICKSON, Edward James	1
WICKWARE, Francis Graham	
WICOFF, John Van Buren	3
WIDDEMER, Mabel Cleland	4
WIDEMAN, Francis James	3
WIDENER, George D.	5
WIDENER, Joseph E.	2
WIDENER, Joseph Early	H
WIDENER, Joseph Early	4
WIDENER, Peter A. Brown	1
WIDGERY, William	5
WIDMANN, Bernard Pierre	
WIDTSOE, John Andreas	3
WIDTSOE, Leah Dunford	5
WIEAND, Albert Cassel	3
WIEBOLDT, Elmer F.	5
WIEBOLDT, Raymond Carl	5
WIECHMANN, Ferdinand Gerhard	1
WIECZOREK, Max	3
WIEGAND, Charles Dudley	5
WIEGAND, Gustave Adolph	3
WIEGAND, Karl McKay	2
WIEGMAN, Fred Conrad	3
WIEHE, Theodore Charles	5
WIELAND, Arthur J.	3
WIELAND, G. R.	3
WIELAND, Heinrich Otto	3
WIELBOLDT, William A.	1
WIEMAN, Elton Ewart	5
WIENER, Leo	1
WIENER, Meyer	5
WIENER, Norbert	1
WIENER, Paul Lester	4
WIENS, Henry Warkentin	5
WIER, Jeanne Elizabeth	3
WIER, John	
WIER, Robert Withrow	5
WIER, Roy W.	4
WIERS, Edgar Swan	1
WIESE, Otis L.	
WIESENBERGER, Arthur	5
WIESS, Harry Carothers	2
WIEST, Howard	2
WIGFALL, Louis Tresevant	H
WIGGAM, Albert Edward	4
WIGGANS, Cleo Claude	5
WIGGER, Winand Michael	1
WIGGERS, Carl John	4
WIGGIN, Albert Henry	3
WIGGIN, Frank H.	1
WIGGIN, Frederick Alonzo	
WIGGIN, Frederick Holme	
WIGGIN, Frederick Holme	
WIGGIN, Kate Douglas	1
WIGGIN, Twing Brooks	4
WIGGINS, Benjamin Lawton	1
WIGGINS, Carleton	1
WIGGINS, Charles II	2
WIGGINS, Frank	1
WIGGINS, Guy	1
WIGGINS, Horace Leland	1
WIGGINS, Sterling Pitts	2
WIGGINS, William D.	3
WIGGINTON, George Peter	
WIGGINTON, Peter Dinwiddie	
WIGGINTON, Thomas Albert	4
WIGGLESWORTH, Edward *	H
WIGGLESWORTH, Edward	2
WIGGLESWORTH, George	
WIGGLESWORTH, Michael	H
WIGGLESWORTH, Richard Bowditch	4
WIGHT, Charles Albert	5
WIGHT, E. Van Dyke	3
WIGHT, Francis Asa	2
WIGHT, Frank Clinton	1
WIGHT, John Fitch	5
WIGHT, John Green	1
WIGHT, Orlando Williams	H
WIGHT, Pearl	1
WIGHT, Peter Bonnett	5
WIGHT, Thomas	5
WIGHT, William Drewin	2
WIGHT, William Ward	4
WIGMORE, John Henry	2
WIGNELL, Thomas	H
WIHT, Thomas	3
WIKOFF, Frank J.	4
WIKOFF, Henry	H
WILBAR, Charles Luther, Jr.	5
WILBER, David	1
WILBER, David Forrest	1
WILBER, Edward Bacon	3
WILBER, Francis Allen	2
WILBER, George M.	1
WILBER, Herbert Wray	4
WILBOR, William Chambers	
WILBOUR, Isaac	H
WILBUR, Charles Edgar	1
WILBUR, Charles Toppan	1
WILBUR, Cressy Livingston	
WILBUR, Curtis Dwight	3
WILBUR, Elisha Packer	1
WILBUR, Henry W.	1
WILBUR, Hervey	H
WILBUR, Hervey Backus	1
WILBUR, James Benjamin	1
WILBUR, John	1
WILBUR, John Milnor	5
WILBUR, Ray Lyman	2
WILBUR, Rollin Henry	1
WILBUR, Samuel	H
WILBUR, Sibyl	1
WILBUR, William Allen	2
WILBY, Arthur Clyde	2
WILBY, Ernest	3
WILBY, Francis Bowditch	
WILCOX, Alexander Martin	1
WILCOX, Ansley	1
WILCOX, Armour David	1
WILCOX, Cadmus Marcellus	H
WILCOX, Charles Bowser	1
WILCOX, Clair	5
WILCOX, Clarence E.	3
WILCOX, Clarence Rothwell	4
WILCOX, Delos Franklin	1
WILCOX, DeWitt Gilbert	5
WILCOX, Edward Byers	1
WILCOX, Edwin Mead	1
WILCOX, Elias Bunn	5
WILCOX, Ella Wheeler	1
WILCOX, Elmer Almy	4
WILCOX, Frank Langdon	4
WILCOX, Frederick Bernon	
WILCOX, George Horace	1
WILCOX, George Milo	1
WILCOX, Henry Buckley	1
WILCOX, Herbert Budington	3
WILCOX, J. Mark	4
WILCOX, Jeduthun	H
WILCOX, Jerome K.	4
WILCOX, John A.	H
WILCOX, John C.	2
WILCOX, John Walter Jr.	2
WILCOX, Leonard	H
WILCOX, LeRoy T.	3
WILCOX, Lucius Merle	4
WILCOX, Marrion	1
WILCOX, Nelson James	2
WILCOX, Perley S.	1
WILCOX, Reynold Webb	1
WILCOX, Robert William	1
WILCOX, Roy Porter	2
WILCOX, Sheldon E.	4
WILCOX, Sidney Freeman	1
WILCOX, Stephen	H
WILCOX, Timothy Erastus	1
WILCOX, Walter Dwight	3
WILCOX, William Craig	1
WILCOX, William Walter	2
WILCZYNSKI, Ernest Julius	1
WILD, Fred	4
WILD, Harrison Major	1
WILD, Henry Daniel	4
WILD, John Caspar	H
WILD, John Daniel	5
WILD, Laura Hulda	5
WILDE, Arthur Herbert	2
WILDE, George Francis Faxon	
WILDE, Norman	1
WILDE, Percival	3
WILDE, Richard Henry	H
WILDENSTEIN, Lazare Georges	4
WILDENTHAL, Bryan	4
WILDER, Abel Carter	H
WILDER, Alexander	1
WILDER, Amos Parker	1
WILDER, Arthur Ashford	1
WILDER, Burt Green	1
WILDER, Charles Wesley	5
WILDER, Charlotte Frances	
WILDER, Daniel Webster	1
WILDER, George Warren	1
WILDER, Gerald Gardner	2
WILDER, Gerrit Parmile	1
WILDER, Harris Hawthorne	
WILDER, Herbert Augustus	
WILDER, Herbert Merrill	1
WILDER, Inez Whipple	1
WILDER, John Emery	1
WILDER, John Thomas	2
WILDER, Laura Ingalls	3
WILDER, Laurence Russell	1
WILDER, Marshall Pinckney	H
WILDER, Marshall Pinckney	1
WILDER, Mrs. Louise Beebe	1
WILDER, Ralph Everett	1
WILDER, Robert Parmelee	
WILDER, Russell Morse	1
WILDER, Salmon Willoughby	5
WILDER, Sampson Uryling Stoddard	H
WILDER, T. Edward	1
WILDER, Wilbur Elliott	3
WILDER, William Hamlin	1
WILDER, William Henry *	1
WILDERMUTH, Ora Leonard	4
WILDES, Frank	1
WILDMAN, Clyde Everett	1
WILDMAN, Edwin	3
WILDMAN, Marian Warner (Mrs. Jesse A. Fenner)	5
WILDMAN, Murray Shipley	
WILDMAN, Zalmon	H
WILDNER, Harry Charles	4
WILDRICK, Isaac	H
WILDS, George James Jr.	3
WILDS, William Naylor	1
WILE, Frederic William	1
WILE, Frederic William Jr.	
WILE, Ira Solomon	2
WILE, Udo Julius	1
WILE, William Conrad	1
WILES, Charles Peter	2
WILES, Irving Ramsay	2
WILES, John Henry	1
WILES, Kimball	5
WILES, Lemuel Maynard	1

WILEY, Alexander 4
WILEY, Andrew J. 1
WILEY, Ariosto Appling 1
WILEY, H
 Calvin Henderson
WILEY, David H
WILEY, Edwin 1
WILEY, Ephraim Emerson H
WILEY, 1
 Franklin Baldwin
WILEY, H(enry) Orton 5
WILEY, 1
 Harvey Washington
WILEY, Henry Ariosto 2
WILEY, Herbert V. 3
WILEY, Hugh 5
WILEY, Isaac William 1
WILEY, James Sullivan H
WILEY, John Alexander 1
WILEY, John Cooper 4
WILEY, Louis 1
WILEY, Robert Hopkins 3
WILEY, Samuel Ernest 5
WILEY, Walter H. 4
WILEY, William Foust 2
WILEY, William Halsted 1
WILEY, William Ogden 3
WILFLEY, 1
 Lebbeus Redman
WILFLEY, 1
 Xenophon Pierce
WILFORD, 5
 Loran Frederick
WILGRESS, L. Dana 5
WILGUS, 1
 Horace La Fayette
WILGUS, Sidney Dean 1
WILGUS, William John 2
WILHELM, Donald 2
WILHELM, 5
 Richard Herman
WILHELM, Stephen
 Roger 4
WILHELMINA,
 Helena Pauline Maria
WILHELMJ, 4
 Charles Martel
WILHELMSEN, Karl John 3
WILHOIT, Eugene Lovell 4
WILKE, Otto John 5
WILKER, Arthur V. 3
WILKERSON, 1
 Albert Wadsworth
WILKERSON, 2
 James Herbert
WILKERSON, 3
 Marcus Manley
WILKERSON, 4
 William Wesley Jr.
WILKES, Charles H
WILKES, Eliza Tupper 4
WILKES, George H
WILKES, Jack Stauffer 5
WILKES, 5
 James Claiborne, Sr.
WILKES, John 3
WILKES, 1
 John Summerfield
WILKESON, Frank H
WILKESON, Samuel H
WILKIE, Franc Bangs H
WILKIE, Harold McLean 3
WILKIE, John Elbert 1
WILKIN, Jacob W. 1
WILKIN, James Whitney H
WILKIN, Samuel Jones H
WILKINS, Beriah 1
WILKINS, Ernest Hatch 4
WILKINS, Frank Lemoyne 1
WILKINS, Harold Tom 4
WILKINS, Horace M. 3
WILKINS, J. Ernest 3
WILKINS, John A. 3
WILKINS, 2
 Lawrence Augustus
WILKINS, Lawson 4
WILKINS, Milan William 1
WILKINS, 5
 Raymond Sanger
WILKINS, Ross H
WILKINS, Sir Hubert 5
WILKINS, 1
 Thomas Russell
WILKINS, 2
 Thomas Russell
WILKINS, Vaughan 3
WILKINS, Walter 4
WILKINS, William H
WILKINS, William Glyde 1
WILKINS, William James 3
WILKINSON, 5
 Alfred Dickinson
WILKINSON, 1
 Alfred Ernest
WILKINSON, Andrew 1
WILKINSON, Cecil J. 4

WILKINSON, 3
 Charles Fore Jr.
WILKINSON, David H
WILKINSON, Ford L. Jr. 3
WILKINSON, 3
 George Lawrence
WILKINSON, 1
 Horace Simpson
WILKINSON, 2
 Howard Sargent
WILKINSON, 3
 Ignatius Martin
WILKINSON, James H
WILKINSON, 4
 Jasper Newton
WILKINSON, Jemima H
WILKINSON, Jeremiah H
WILKINSON, John H
WILKINSON, Joseph A. 3
WILKINSON, 4
 Joseph Biddle
WILKINSON, 1
 Joseph Green
WILKINSON,
 Marguerite Ogden Bigelow
WILKINSON, 1
 Melville Le Vaunt
WILKINSON, H
 Morton Smith
WILKINSON, 3
 Robert Johnson
WILKINSON, Robert
 Shaw
WILKINSON, Theodore S. 2
WILKINSON, Warring 1
WILKINSON, 5
 William Albert
WILKINSON, 1
 William Cleaver
WILKINSON, 1
 William Cook
WILKINSON, 5
 William Donald
WILKINSON, 3
 William John
WILKS, Samuel Stanley 4
WILL, Allen Sinclair 1
WILL, Arthur A. 2
WILL, Arthur Percival 3
WILL, Louis 1
WILL, 2
 Theodore St. Clair
WILL, Thomas Elmer 4
WILLARD, Archibald M. H
WILLARD, Archibald M. 4
WILLARD, Arthur Cutts 4
WILLARD, Arthur Lee 1
WILLARD,
 Ashton Rollins
WILLARD, 1
 Charles Andrew
WILLARD, H
 Charles Wesley
WILLARD, Chester Ezra 4
WILLARD, Daniel 2
WILLARD, 4
 Daniel Everett
WILLARD, DeForest
WILLARD, DeForest P. 3
WILLARD, Edward Smith 1
WILLARD, 4
 Eleanor Withey
WILLARD, Emma Hart H
WILLARD, 4
 Ernest Russell
WILLARD, H
 Frances Elizabeth Caroline
WILLARD, Frank H. 3
WILLARD, Frank Henry 4
WILLARD, 2
 Frederic Wilson
WILLARD, 1
 Henry Augustus
WILLARD, Horace Mann
WILLARD, Ira Farnum 4
WILLARD, James Field 1
WILLARD, John 4
WILLARD, John Artemas 4
WILLARD, Josch Edward 1
WILLARD, Joseph * H
WILLARD, 4
 Joseph Augustus
WILLARD, Josiah Flynt 1
WILLARD, 3
 Julius Terrass
WILLARD, Leigh 3
WILLARD, 5
 Lillian Winifred
WILLARD, 4
 Monroe Livingstone
WILLARD, Roy H(obson) 5
WILLARD, Samuel * H
WILLARD, Sidney H
WILLARD, Simon * H
WILLARD, Solomon H
WILLARD,
 Sylvester David H

WILLARD, Theodore A. 2
WILLARD, Thomas
 Rigney 1
WILLARD, 5
 William A(lbert)
WILLARD, 1
 William Charles
WILLAUER, Whiting 4
WILLCOX, 1
 Cornelis 'de Witt
WILLCOX, David 1
WILLCOX, James M. 1
WILLCOX, Julius Abner 1
WILLCOX, 1
 Louise Collier
WILLCOX, Mary Alice 3
WILLCOX, 1
 Orlando Bolivar
WILLCOX, 4
 Walter Francis
WILLCOX, 2
 Walter Ross Baumes
WILLCOX, Westmore 5
WILLCOX, William G. 1
WILLCOX, William Henry 1
WILLCOX, 1
 William Russell
WILLEBRANDT, 4
 Mabel Walker
WILLEN, 5
 Pearl Larner (Mrs. Joseph
 Willen)
WILLET, Anne Lee 2
WILLETS, David Gifford 5
WILLETS, Gilson 5
WILLETT, George F. 5
WILLETT, 2
 Herbert Lockwood
WILLETT, 4
 Howard Levansellaer Sr.
WILLETT, Marinus H
WILLETT, Oscar Louis 2
WILLETT, William, Jr. 5
WILLETTS, Herbert 5
WILLETTS, 4
 William Prentice
WILLEVER, John Calvin 5
WILLEY, Calvin H
WILLEY, 5
 Charles Herbert
WILLEY, D. Allen 1
WILLEY, Earle D. 2
WILLEY, Henry 1
WILLEY, John Heston 2
WILLEY, 4
 Norman Bushnell
WILLEY, Norman LeRoy 1
WILLEY, Samuel Hopkins 4
WILLFORD, 3
 Albert Clinton
WILLGING, Eugene P. 4
WILLGING, Joseph C. 3
WILLHITE, 2
 Frank Vanatta
WILLI, Albert B(ond) 5
WILLIAM III H
WILLIAMS, A. J. 3
WILLIAMS, 1
 Abraham Pease
WILLIAMS, Albert Frank 3
WILLIAMS, 4
 Albert Nathaniel
WILLIAMS, Albert Rhys 4
WILLIAMS, 3
 Alexander Elliot
WILLIAMS, 4
 Alexander Scott
WILLIAMS, 3
 Alford Joseph Jr.
WILLIAMS, 2
 Alfred Brockenbrough
WILLIAMS, Alfred Hicks 5
WILLIAMS, Alfred Mason H
WILLIAMS, 5
 Alfred Melvin
WILLIAMS, 5
 Alpheus Americus
WILLIAMS, H
 Alpheus Starkey
WILLIAMS, Anna Bolles 4
WILLIAMS, Anna Wessels 5
WILLIAMS, H
 Archibald Hunter Arrington
WILLIAMS, Arthur 1
WILLIAMS, Arthur B. 1
WILLIAMS, 5
 Arthur Llewellyn
WILLIAMS, 4
 Ashton Hilliard
WILLIAMS, 4
 Aubrey Willis
WILLIAMS, B. Y. 3
WILLIAMS, Barney H
WILLIAMS, Ben Ames 3
WILLIAMS, Ben J. 3
WILLIAMS, Benjamin
WILLIAMS, Berkeley 3

WILLIAMS, Bert 4
WILLIAMS, Bert C. 3
WILLIAMS, 2
 Blanche Colton
WILLIAMS, Bradford 4
WILLIAMS, C. Arthur 1
WILLIAMS, Carl 3
WILLIAMS, Carlos Grant 2
WILLIAMS, H
 Catharine Read Arnold
WILLIAMS, Cecil Brown
WILLIAMS, 1
 Channing Moore
WILLIAMS, Charles Bray 3
WILLIAMS, 2
 Charles Burgess
WILLIAMS, 1
 Charles David
WILLIAMS, Charles Finn 3
WILLIAMS, H
 Charles Grandison
WILLIAMS, 1
 Charles Luther
WILLIAMS, 3
 Charles Mallory
WILLIAMS, 4
 Charles McCay
WILLIAMS, Charles Page 3
WILLIAMS, 3
 Charles Parker
WILLIAMS, 1
 Charles Richard
WILLIAMS, 4
 Charles Sneed
WILLIAMS, 1
 Charles Sumner
WILLIAMS, 4
 Charles Thomas
WILLIAMS, 1
 Charles Turner
WILLIAMS, 4
 Charles Urquhart
WILLIAMS, 4
 Charles Wesley
WILLIAMS, 4
 Charles Weston
WILLIAMS, H
 Christopher Harris
WILLIAMS, 2
 Clarence Russell
WILLIAMS, 3
 Clarence Stewart
WILLIAMS, 1
 Clarissa Smith
WILLIAMS, Clark 4
WILLIAMS, Claude Allen
WILLIAMS, Clayton Epes 4
WILLIAMS, '5
 Clement Clarence
WILLIAMS, 5
 Clifford Leland
WILLIAMS, 5
 Clifton Curtis, Jr.
WILLIAMS, 4
 Clifton Curtis Jr.
WILLIAMS, Clyde 3
WILLIAMS, Constant 1
WILLIAMS, Cora Lenore 1
WILLIAMS, 4
 Curtis Chandler
WILLIAMS, Cyril 1
WILLIAMS, Cyrus Vance 2
WILLIAMS, D.B. 5
WILLIAMS, Dana Scott 1
WILLIAMS, 5
 Daniel Albert
WILLIAMS, Daniel H. 1
WILLIAMS, 5
 Daniel Roderick
WILLIAMS, David * 1
WILLIAMS, David Evans 1
WILLIAMS, David P, Jr. 5
WILLIAMS, 4
 David Reichard
WILLIAMS, H
 David Rogerson
WILLIAMS, Dean 3
WILLIAMS, Dion 5
WILLIAMS, Dwight 1
WILLIAMS, 3
 Edmund Randolph
WILLIAMS, Ednyfed H. 3
WILLIAMS, 1
 Edward Franklin
WILLIAMS, Edward Higginson Jr.
WILLIAMS, 2
 Edward Huntington
WILLIAMS, 2
 Edward Thomas
WILLIAMS, 4
 Edward Thomas Towson
WILLIAMS, Edwin H
WILLIAMS, 5
 Egerton Ryerson, Jr.
WILLIAMS, Eleazar H

WILLIAMS, 1
 Elihu Stephen
WILLIAMS, Elisha * H
WILLIAMS, 1
 Elizabeth Sprague
WILLIAMS, Elkanah H
WILLIAMS, 4
 Emerson Milton
WILLIAMS, 5
 Emma Elizabeth Thomas
WILLIAMS, Emmons Levi 3
WILLIAMS, 1
 Ennion Gifford
WILLIAMS, 4
 Ennion Skelton
WILLIAMS, Ephraim H
WILLIAMS, 4
 Erastus Appleman
WILLIAMS, Ernest 1
WILLIAMS, 5
 Ernest Bland, Jr.
WILLIAMS, Ernest S. 2
WILLIAMS, Espy 1
WILLIAMS, 5
 Eustace Leroy
WILLIAMS, Everard Mott 5
WILLIAMS, 1
 Francis Bennett
WILLIAMS, 2
 Francis Churchill
WILLIAMS, 1
 Francis Henry
WILLIAMS, 1
 Francis Howard
WILLIAMS, Frank Alvan 4
WILLIAMS, Frank B. 1
WILLIAMS, Frank Bacus 3
WILLIAMS, Frank Eugene 3
WILLIAMS, Frank French 1
WILLIAMS, Frank L. 2
WILLIAMS, Frank Martin 1
WILLIAMS, Franklin G. 4
WILLIAMS, 1
 Frankwood Earl
WILLIAMS, Fred Lincoln 3
WILLIAMS, H
 Frederic Arlington
WILLIAMS, Frederic M. 1
WILLIAMS, 5
 Frederick Ballard
WILLIAMS, 3
 Frederick Ballard
WILLIAMS, 3
 Frederick Crawford
WILLIAMS, 1
 Frederick Wells
WILLIAMS, Gardner Fred 1
WILLIAMS, 1
 Gardner Stewart
WILLIAMS, George 3
WILLIAMS, 1
 George Alfred
WILLIAMS, 2
 George Bassett
WILLIAMS, 1
 George Burchell
WILLIAMS, George C. 5
WILLIAMS, 1
 George Clinton Fairchild
WILLIAMS, 1
 George Forrester
WILLIAMS, George Fred 1
WILLIAMS, 1
 George Gilbert
WILLIAMS, George
 Henry 1
WILLIAMS, 5
 George Howard
WILLIAMS, H
 George Huntington
WILLIAMS, 3
 George Orchard
WILLIAMS, 1
 George Philip
WILLIAMS, George S. 3
WILLIAMS, 2
 George Van Siclen
WILLIAMS, 1
 George Walton
WILLIAMS, H
 George Washington
WILLIAMS, 1
 George Washington
WILLIAMS, Gershom
 Mott 1
WILLIAMS, Gladstone 5
WILLIAMS, Gorham
 Deane 1
WILLIAMS, Griff 3
WILLIAMS, Guinn 2
WILLIAMS, H. Evan 1
WILLIAMS, Harold 1
WILLIAMS, Harold E. 5
WILLIAMS, Harold E. 1
WILLIAMS, 4
 Harold Putnam
WILLIAMS, Harrison 3

WILLIAMS, 5
Helen Burton (Mrs. Edward J. Williams)
WILLIAMS, Henry
WILLIAMS, Henry A. H 3
WILLIAMS, 2
Henry Davison
WILLIAMS, Henry Edison 2
WILLIAMS, Henry
Eugene 1
WILLIAMS, 1
Henry Francis
WILLIAMS, Henry
Horace 1
WILLIAMS, 2
Henry Morland
WILLIAMS, Henry Robert 1
WILLIAMS, Henry Shaler 1
WILLIAMS, Henry Smith 2
WILLIAMS, H
Henry Willard
WILLIAMS, 1
Henry Winslow
WILLIAMS,
Herbert Oswald
WILLIAMS, Herbert
Owen 1
WILLIAMS, 5
Herbert Pelham
WILLIAMS, 1
Herbert Upham
WILLIAMS, Herschel 1
WILLIAMS, Hezekiah H
WILLIAMS, Homer B. 4
WILLIAMS, Homer D. 1
WILLIAMS, Horatio Burt 3
WILLIAMS, Hugh 2
WILLIAMS, Ira Jewell 5
WILLIAMS, Irving 3
WILLIAMS, Isaac Jr. H
WILLIAMS, Israel H
WILLIAMS, J. Nelson 4
WILLIAMS, J. Ross 4
WILLIAMS, J. Whitridge 1
WILLIAMS, Jack 3
WILLIAMS, James H
WILLIAMS, 1
James Cranston
WILLIAMS, H
James Douglas
WILLIAMS, James Leon 4
WILLIAMS, James
Monroe 1
WILLIAMS, 4
James Peter Jr.
WILLIAMS, James Robert 1
WILLIAMS, James Robert 3
WILLIAMS, 5
James Thomas, Jr.
WILLIAMS, James Wray H
WILLIAMS, Jared H
WILLIAMS, Jared Warner H
WILLIAMS, Jerome Oscar 3
WILLIAMS, 4
Jesse Feiring
WILLIAMS, Jesse Lynch H
WILLIAMS, Jesse Lynch 1
WILLIAMS, Job 1
WILLIAMS, John * H
WILLIAMS, John 4
WILLIAMS, John Alonzo 3
WILLIAMS, John Castree 3
WILLIAMS, John Clark 2
WILLIAMS, John Edward 2
WILLIAMS, John Elias 1
WILLIAMS,
John Fletcher
WILLIAMS, John Foster H
WILLIAMS, John H. 4
WILLIAMS, John Harvey 4
WILLIAMS, John Healy 1
WILLIAMS, John Howard 3
WILLIAMS, John Insco H
WILLIAMS, John Joseph 1
WILLIAMS, 5
John Joseph, Jr.
WILLIAMS, 1
John Langbourne
WILLIAMS, H
John McKeown Snow
WILLIAMS, John Paul 5
WILLIAMS, John Powell 3
WILLIAMS, John Ralston 1
WILLIAMS, John Sharp 1
WILLIAMS, John Skelton 1
WILLIAMS, John Taylor 5
WILLIAMS, 4
John Townsend
WILLIAMS, Jonathan H
WILLIAMS, Joseph John 1
WILLIAMS, 5
Joseph Judson, Jr.
WILLIAMS, H
Joseph Lanier
WILLIAMS, 2
Joseph Vincent
WILLIAMS, Joseph White 1

WILLIAMS, Judith Blow 3
WILLIAMS, Keith Shaw 3
WILLIAMS,
Kenneth Powers
WILLIAMS, L. Judson 1
WILLIAMS, Lacey Kirk 2
WILLIAMS, 1
Langbourne M.
WILLIAMS, Ledru A. 4
WILLIAMS, Lemuel H
WILLIAMS, 2
Leroy Blanchard
WILLIAMS, Lewis H
WILLIAMS, Lewis Blair 4
WILLIAMS, Lewis
Kemper 5
WILLIAMS, Linsly Rudd 3
WILLIAMS,
Louis Coleman
WILLIAMS, Louis Laval 3
WILLIAMS, 4
Louis Sheppard
WILLIAMS, Marmaduke H
WILLIAMS, Marshall Jay 1
WILLIAMS, 5
Martha McCulloch
WILLIAMS, 2
Mary Wilhelmine
WILLIAMS, Maynard
Owen 4
WILLIAMS, Michael 3
WILLIAMS, Miles Evans 4
WILLIAMS, 1
Milton Mathias
WILLIAMS, Mornay 1
WILLIAMS,
Moseley Hooker
WILLIAMS, Moses * 1
WILLIAMS, Nathan H
WILLIAMS, Nathan
Boone 5
WILLIAMS, 1
Nathan Winslow
WILLIAMS, Nathaniel H
WILLIAMS, Neil Hooker 3
WILLIAMS, O. B. 3
WILLIAMS, Ora 5
WILLIAMS, Orva Gilson 1
WILLIAMS,
Oscar Fitzalan
WILLIAMS, 3
Othneil Glanville
WILLIAMS, Otho Holland 1
WILLIAMS,
Pardon Clarence
WILLIAMS,
Parley Lycurgus
WILLIAMS, 5
Philip Francis
WILLIAMS, R. Lancaster 3
WILLIAMS, Ralph E. 1
WILLIAMS,
Ralph Olmsted
WILLIAMS, 5
Ransome Judson
WILLIAMS, Reuel H
WILLIAMS, 2
Richard Peters
WILLIAMS, 1
Richard Richardson
WILLIAMS, Robert * H
WILLIAMS, Robert * 1
WILLIAMS, Robert 2
WILLIAMS, Robert 3
WILLIAMS, Robert 4
WILLIAMS,
Robert Campbell
WILLIAMS, 3
Robert Carlton
WILLIAMS, Robert Day 1
WILLIAMS, Robert E. 3
WILLIAMS, 1
Robert Einion
WILLIAMS, Robert Gray 2
WILLIAMS, Robert Lee 2
WILLIAMS, 4
Robert Maurice
WILLIAMS, 5
Robert Parvin
WILLIAMS,
Robert Purcell Jr.
WILLIAMS, Robert R. 4
WILLIAMS, Robert White 2
WILLIAMS,
Robert Willoughby
WILLIAMS, Roger H
WILLIAMS, Roger 3
WILLIAMS, Roger 4
WILLIAMS, Roger Butler 4
WILLIAMS, Roger D. 1
WILLIAMS, Roger Henry 3
WILLIAMS, 5
Roswell Carter, Jr.
WILLIAMS, Roy Hughes 3
WILLIAMS, Roy T. 2
WILLIAMS, 1
Rufus Phillips

WILLIAMS, 4
Russell Raymond Jr.
WILLIAMS, Samuel Clay 2
WILLIAMS, Samuel Cole 1
WILLIAMS, 3
Samuel Hubbard
WILLIAMS, 5
Samuel Leonard
WILLIAMS, Samuel May H
WILLIAMS, Samuel Wells H
WILLIAMS, Sarah 1
WILLIAMS, Seth 4
WILLIAMS, Seward
Henry 5
WILLIAMS, Sherman 1
WILLIAMS, Sherrod 3
WILLIAMS, Sidney Clark 3
WILLIAMS, Sidney James 3
WILLIAMS, 3
Stanley Thomas
WILLIAMS, 5
Stephen Riggs
WILLIAMS, Stephen West H
WILLIAMS, Talcott 1
WILLIAMS,
Theodore Chickering
WILLIAMS, 2
Theresa Amelia
WILLIAMS, Thomas H
WILLIAMS, Thomas 1
WILLIAMS, 2
Thomas Frederick
WILLIAMS, H
Thomas Hickman
WILLIAMS, Thomas Hill H
WILLIAMS, 4
Thomas Jefferson
WILLIAMS, 1
Thomas Reynolds
WILLIAMS, Thomas Scott H
WILLIAMS, 1
Thomas Sutler
WILLIAMS, H
Thomas Wheeler
WILLIAMS, 1
Timothy Shaler
WILLIAMS, Travis 5
WILLIAMS, Tyrrell 2
WILLIAMS, Van Zandt 1
WILLIAMS, W. Erskine 1
WILLIAMS, Walter 1
WILLIAMS, Walter Long 2
WILLIAMS, 2
Wayland Wells
WILLIAMS, Wayne
Cullen 3
WILLIAMS, Wheeler 5
WILLIAMS, William * 1
WILLIAMS, William 2
WILLIAMS, 4
William Asbury
WILLIAMS, 4
William Carlos
WILLIAMS, 2
William Clayton Jr.
WILLIAMS, William Crow 5
WILLIAMS, William E. 4
WILLIAMS, William Elza 1
WILLIAMS, 1
William George
WILLIAMS, 1
William Henry
WILLIAMS, 3
William Horace
WILLIAMS, 1
William Martin
WILLIAMS, William Muir 1
WILLIAMS, William R. 5
WILLIAMS, William R. H
WILLIAMS, William Reid 1
WILLIAMS, 1
William Robert
WILLIAMS, H
William Sherley
WILLIAMS, 1
William Taylor Burwell
WILLIAMS, Wilson 3
WILLIAMS, Wynant
James 3
WILLIAMS, Wythe 3
WILLIAMS, 4
Yancey Sullivan
WILLIAMS,
Zachariah Mitchell
WILLIAMSON, Andrew 1
WILLIAMSON, Ben 1
WILLIAMSON, Charles H
WILLIAMSON, 4
Charles Clarence
WILLIAMSON,
Charles Spencer
WILLIAMSON, Clifton P. 5
WILLIAMSON, Francis T. 4
WILLIAMSON, 2
Frederick Ely
WILLIAMSON, 2
Frederick Warren

WILLIAMSON, George 2
WILLIAMSON, George 5
WILLIAMSON, 3
George Emery
WILLIAMSON, 4
Hiram Louis
WILLIAMSON, Hugh H
WILLIAMSON, H
Isaac Halstead
WILLIAMSON, 1
James Alexander
WILLIAMSON, 1
James De Long
WILLIAMSON, 1
James Nathaniel Jr.
WILLIAMSON, 4
James Preston
WILLIAMSON, Jessie 2
WILLIAMSON, 4
John Ernest
WILLIAMSON, 4
John Finley
WILLIAMSON, John I. 1
WILLIAMSON, 4
John Newton
WILLIAMSON, John
Pogue 1
WILLIAMSON, Joseph 1
WILLIAMSON, Julia May 1
WILLIAMSON, Mary
Lynn 3
WILLIAMSON, 5
Mrs. Mary Robinson
WILLIAMSON, 5
Oliver Robison
WILLIAMSON, Roy
Elisha 2
WILLIAMSON, Samuel E. 1
WILLIAMSON, 1
Sydney Bacon
WILLIAMSON, Thom 1
WILLIAMSON, Thomas 3
WILLIAMSON, William 5
WILLIAMSON, 1
William Collins
WILLIAMSON, H
William Durkee
WILLIAMSON, William
F. 4
WILLIAMSON, 1
William James
WILLIAMSON, 1
William Thomas
WILLIE, Asa Hoxie H
WILLIFORD, 3
Forrest Estey
WILLING, John Thomson 4
WILLING, Thomas H
WILLINGHAM, 5
Edward Bacon
WILLINGHAM, Henry J. 2
WILLINGHAM, 1
Robert Josiah
WILLINGHAM, William
A. 2
WILLINGS, George Carke 3
WILLIS, Albert Shelby 1
WILLIS, Alfred 4
WILLIS, Bailey 2
WILLIS, H
Benjamin Albertson
WILLIS, 5
Charles Francis
WILLIS, Clodius Harris 4
WILLIS, Edwin Caldwell 3
WILLIS, Edwin Edward 5
WILLIS, Francis H
WILLIS, 1
Frank Bartlette
WILLIS, George Francis 1
WILLIS, H. Parker 4
WILLIS, Harold Buckley 4
WILLIS, Henry 5
WILLIS, Herman Allen 5
WILLIS, Horace Harold 5
WILLIS, Jack Macy 4
WILLIS, Nathaniel H
WILLIS, 1
Nathaniel Parker
WILLIS, Olympia Brown 1
WILLIS, Park Weed 5
WILLIS, Paul 1
WILLIS, Raymond Eugene 3
WILLIS, Simeon S. 4
WILLIS, William H
WILLISON, 5
George F(indlay)
WILLISTON, 5
Arthur Lyman
WILLISTON, 1
Edward Bancroft
WILLISTON, Samuel H
WILLISTON, Samuel 4
WILLISTON, 1
Samuel Wendell
WILLISTON, Seth H

WILLITS, Edwin H
WILLITS, George Sidney 1
WILLITS, Oliver Gaston 5
WILLKIE, E. E. 3
WILLKIE, 3
Herman Frederick
WILLKIE, Wendell Lewis 2
WILLMAN, Leon Kurtz 5
WILLMARTH, 1
James Willard
WILLMERING, Henry 4
WILLNUS, Harry G. 5
WILLOUGHBY, Barrett 3
WILLOUGHBY, 1
Benjamin Milton
WILLOUGHBY, Charles
A. 5
WILLOUGHBY, 2
Charles Clark
WILLOUGHBY, 3
Charles Grant
WILLOUGHBY, 3
Edwin Eliott
WILLOUGHBY, 4
Harold Rideout
WILLOUGHBY, 4
Hugh Laussaf
WILLOUGHBY, 1
John Edmund
WILLOUGHBY, 2
Julius Edgar
WILLOUGHBY, Westel
Jr. H
WILLOUGHBY, 2
Westel Woodbury
WILLOUGHBY, 4
William Charles
WILLOUGHBY, 4
William Franklin
WILLOUGHBY,
Woodbury 4
WILLS, Albert Potter 1
WILLS, 1
Charles Tomlinson
WILLS, David 4
WILLS, David Crawford 1
WILLS, F. Reed 4
WILLS, George Stockton 3
WILLS, Royal Barry 4
WILLS, William Henry 2
WILLSON, 1
Augustus Everett
WILLSON,
Charles Albert
WILLSON, David Burt 1
WILLSON, Forceythe H
WILLSON, 1
Frederick Newton
WILLSON, 4
George Hayward
WILLSON, James William 1
WILLSON, John Owens 1
WILLSON,
Lester Sebastian
WILLSON, Marcius 1
WILLSON, Robert
Newton 1
WILLSON, 1
Robert Wheeler
WILLSON, Russell 2
WILLSON, Sidney Louis 2
WILLYS, John North 1
WILM, 5
Grace Gridley (Mrs. Emil Carl Wilm)
WILMARTH, 1
Lemuel Everett
WILMER, 3
Cary Breckinridge
WILMER, Frank J. 2
WILMER, James Jones H
WILMER, H
Joseph Pere Bell
WILMER, Richard Hooker H
WILMER, H
William Holland
WILMER, 1
William Holland
WILMERDING, 1
Lucius Kellogg
WILMETH, Frank Lincoln 1
WILMETH, James Lillard 3
WILMORE, 1
Augustus Cleland
WILMORE, John Jenkins 2
WILMOT, David H
WILMOT, Frank Moore 1
WILMOT,
George Washington
WILMOT, Nellie Maroa 4
WILMOT, R. J. 3
WILMS, John Henry 1
WILNER, 3
Robert Franklin
WILSHIRE, Gaylord 1
WILSHIRE, Joseph 3

* Indicates More Than One Such Name Listed

WILSHIRE, William Wallace H
WILSON, Adair 4
WILSON, Albert Dwight 3
WILSON, Albert Frederick 1
WILSON, Alexander * H
WILSON, Alexander 3
WILSON, Alexander Massey 2
WILSON, Mrs. Alfred Gaston (matilda Raush Wilson) 5
WILSON, Allen Benjamin H
WILSON, Alonzo Edes 2
WILSON, Alpheus Waters H
WILSON, Andrew 4
WILSON, Andrew Gordon 4
WILSON, Andrew Wilkins Jr. 1
WILSON, Arthur Orville 2
WILSON, Arthur Riehl 3
WILSON, Augusta Jane Evans 1
WILSON, Benjamin 3
WILSON, Benjamin Lee 1
WILSON, Bert 5
WILSON, Bird H
WILSON, Burwell L. 3
WILSON, Byron Henry 1
WILSON, Cairine Reay M. 4
WILSON, Calvin Dill 2
WILSON, Carey 1
WILSON, Carroll Atwood 2
WILSON, Carroll Louis 2
WILSON, Carroll Louis 3
WILSON, Charles H
WILSON, Charles 4
WILSON, Charles A. 5
WILSON, Charles Alfred 1
WILSON, Charles Branch 1
WILSON, Charles Bundy 1
WILSON, Charles Edward 4
WILSON, Charles Erwin 4
WILSON, Charles Gustavas 4
WILSON, Charles Henry 5
WILSON, Charles Irving 1
WILSON, Charles Scoon 3
WILSON, Clarence Hall 5
WILSON, Clarence Rich 1
WILSON, Clarence True 1
WILSON, Clifford Brittin 2
WILSON, Daniel Munro 4
WILSON, David Cooper 3
WILSON, David Gilbert Jr. 4
WILSON, David Mathias 4
WILSON, David Roger 2
WILSON, David Wright 4
WILSON, Dunning Steele 1
WILSON, E. Graham 4
WILSON, Edgar 1
WILSON, Edgar Bright 3
WILSON, Edgar Campbell H
WILSON, Edmund 4
WILSON, Edmund 5
WILSON, Edmund Beecher 1
WILSON, Edward Arthur 5
WILSON, Edward Clarkson 2
WILSON, Edward Harlan 3
WILSON, Edward Latimer 5
WILSON, Edward Livingston 1
WILSON, Edward Preble 4
WILSON, Edward Stansbury 1
WILSON, Edward Taylor 3
WILSON, Edward William 5
WILSON, Edwin Bidwell 4
WILSON, Edwin Carleton 5
WILSON, Edwin Mood 5
WILSON, Edwin Walter 1
WILSON, Ella Calista 4
WILSON, Ellen Axson 1
WILSON, Ephraim King * H
WILSON, Erasmus 3
WILSON, Ernest Dana 3
WILSON, Ernest Henry 1
WILSON, Eugene Benjamin 1
WILSON, Eugene McLanahan H
WILSON, Eugene Smith 1
WILSON, Felix Zollicoffer 4
WILSON, Fletcher Aloysius 1
WILSON, Floyd Baker 4
WILSON, Floyd M. 4
WILSON, Francis 1
WILSON, Francis Cushman 3

WILSON, Francis Mairs Huntington 2
WILSON, Francis Murray 1
WILSON, Francis Servis 3
WILSON, Frank Elmer 1
WILSON, Frank John 5
WILSON, Frank N. 1
WILSON, Franklin Augustus 1
WILSON, G. Lloyd 3
WILSON, George * 1
WILSON, George Allison 3
WILSON, George Arthur 5
WILSON, George Arthur 4
WILSON, George Barry 2
WILSON, George Francis H
WILSON, George Grafton 1
WILSON, George Henry 1
WILSON, George Henry 2
WILSON, George P(ickett) 5
WILSON, George Smith 1
WILSON, George W. * 2
WILSON, George West 1
WILSON, Gilbert 4
WILSON, Gill Robb 4
WILSON, Grafton Lee 5
WILSON, Grenville Dean H
WILSON, Grove 3
WILSON, Guy Mitchell 4
WILSON, H. Augustus 1
WILSON, Halsey William 3
WILSON, Harley Peyton 4
WILSON, Harold Albert 4
WILSON, Harold Edward 1
WILSON, Harold Kirby 3
WILSON, Harry Bruce 1
WILSON, Harry Langford 1
WILSON, Harry Leon 1
WILSON, Harry Robert 5
WILSON, Henry * H
WILSON, Henry Braid 3
WILSON, Henry H. 1
WILSON, Henry Harrison 1
WILSON, Henry Lane 1
WILSON, Henry Van Peters 4
WILSON, Henyr Parke Custis H
WILSON, Herbert Couper 1
WILSON, Herbert Michael 1
WILSON, Hiram Roy 5
WILSON, Howard E. 4
WILSON, Howard Stebbins 3
WILSON, Hugh Robert 2
WILSON, I. H. 3
WILSON, Ida Lewis 1
WILSON, Irving Livingstone 2
WILSON, Isaac H
WILSON, J. C. 4
WILSON, J. Edgar 1
WILSON, J. Frank 5
WILSON, Jackson Stitt 2
WILSON, James * H
WILSON, James * 1
WILSON, James A. 2
WILSON, James Cornelius 1
WILSON, James Cunningham 1
WILSON, James Falconer H
WILSON, James Grant 1
WILSON, James Harrison 1
WILSON, James Jefferson H
WILSON, James Knox H
WILSON, James Ormond 1
WILSON, James Walter 5
WILSON, James Wilbur 5
WILSON, Jesse Everett 4
WILSON, Joel 4
WILSON, John * H
WILSON, John 1
WILSON, John Arthur 2
WILSON, John David 5
WILSON, John Fleming 1
WILSON, John Franklin 4
WILSON, John Fry 1
WILSON, John G. 3
WILSON, John Gordon 2
WILSON, John Haden 5
WILSON, John Henry 1
WILSON, John L. 1
WILSON, John Leighton H
WILSON, John Madison 5
WILSON, John McCalmont 1
WILSON, John McMillan 4
WILSON, John Moulder 1
WILSON, John P. 1
WILSON, John P. 2
WILSON, John Reid 2
WILSON, John Thomas H
WILSON, John Timothy 1

WILSON, Joseph H
WILSON, Joseph C(hamberlain) 5
WILSON, Joseph Chamberlain 1
WILSON, Joseph Dawson 1
WILSON, Joseph G. 3
WILSON, Joseph Gardner 1
WILSON, Joseph Miller 1
WILSON, Joseph R. 4
WILSON, Joseph Robert 3
WILSON, Joseph Rogers 1
WILSON, Joshua Lacy H
WILSON, Julian Alexander 5
WILSON, Julian DuBois 3
WILSON, Julian Morris 1
WILSON, L. B. 3
WILSON, Lawrence Glass 1
WILSON, Leonard 5
WILSON, Leonard Seltzer 5
WILSON, Leroy A. 3
WILSON, Lester MacLean 1
WILSON, Lewis Albert 5
WILSON, Lewis Gilbert 4
WILSON, Lloyd Tilghman 1
WILSON, Lorenzo Arthur 1
WILSON, Louis Blanchard 2
WILSON, Louis N. 1
WILSON, Louis Round 1
WILSON, Lucius Edward 2
WILSON, Lucy Langdon Williams 1
WILSON, Luther Barton 1
WILSON, Lyle Campbell 4
WILSON, Lyman Perl 3
WILSON, Mardon Dewees 4
WILSON, Margaret Barclay 1
WILSON, Margaret Woodrow 2
WILSON, Mary Elizabeth 3
WILSON, Matthew H
WILSON, Maurice Emery 1
WILSON, Milburn Lincoln 5
WILSON, Millard Thomas 4
WILSON, Mira Bigelow 3
WILSON, Morris Watson 1
WILSON, Mortimer 1
WILSON, Moses Fleming 4
WILSON, Mrs. Woodrow 5
WILSON, Murray Alderson 5
WILSON, Myron Henry Jr. 4
WILSON, Nathan H
WILSON, Nathaniel 1
WILSON, Orlando Winfield 5
WILSON, Orme 4
WILSON, Otis Guy 5
WILSON, Paul Oran 5
WILSON, Percy 2
WILSON, Peter H
WILSON, Philip Duncan 5
WILSON, Philip Sheridan 1
WILSON, Philip St Julien 1
WILSON, Philip Whitwell 3
WILSON, Respess S. 3
WILSON, Richard Henry (Richard Fisguill) 5
WILSON, Richard Hulbert 4
WILSON, Riley Joseph 2
WILSON, Robert H
WILSON, Robert 1
WILSON, Robert Burns 1
WILSON, Robert Cade 3
WILSON, Robert Dick 1
WILSON, Robert Edward Lee 1
WILSON, Robert Erastus 4
WILSON, Robert Forrest 1
WILSON, Robert Lee 3
WILSON, Robert North 5
WILSON, Robert Perry 5
WILSON, Roy William 3
WILSON, Rufus Rockwell 2
WILSON, Rufus Rockwell 5
WILSON, Russell 2
WILSON, Russell H. 5
WILSON, S. Davis 1
WILSON, Samuel H
WILSON, Samuel Bailey 3
WILSON, Samuel Graham 1
WILSON, Samuel Knox 3
WILSON, Samuel Mackay 2
WILSON, Samuel Mountford 1
WILSON, Samuel Ramsay H

WILSON, Samuel Thomas H
WILSON, Samuel Tyndale 1
WILSON, Scott 1
WILSON, Stanley Calef 4
WILSON, Stanyarne 1
WILSON, Stephen 4
WILSON, Stephen Fowler H
WILSON, T. B. 3
WILSON, Theodore Delavan H
WILSON, Thomas * H
WILSON, Thomas * 1
WILSON, Thomas A. 5
WILSON, Thomas Bayne 4
WILSON, Thomas Edward 3
WILSON, Thomas Henry 4
WILSON, Thomas James 1
WILSON, Thomas Murray 4
WILSON, Thomas Webber 2
WILSON, Thomas William 2
WILSON, Val Haining 4
WILSON, Walter K. 3
WILSON, Walter Sibbald 4
WILSON, Warren Hugh 1
WILSON, Wilbur M. 5
WILSON, Wilford Murry 4
WILSON, William * H
WILSON, William 1
WILSON, William 3
WILSON, William B. 1
WILSON, William Bauchop 1
WILSON, William Earl 5
WILSON, William Edward 5
WILSON, William Edward 4
WILSON, William Hasell 1
WILSON, William Henry 1
WILSON, William Huntington 5
WILSON, William James 5
WILSON, William Lyne H
WILSON, William Oliver 1
WILSON, William Otis 2
WILSON, William Powell 1
WILSON, William Riley 5
WILSON, William Robert Anthony 1
WILSON, William Warfield 4
WILSON, Willian Lyne 2
WILSON, Wlmo C. 4
WILSON, Woodrow H
WILSON, Woodrow 1
WILSON, Woodrow 4
WILSTACH, Frank Jenners 1
WILSTACH, Paul 3
WILTBANK, William White 1
WILTSE, Sara Eliza 1
WILTSEE, William Pharo 3
WILTSIE, Charles Hastings 1
WILTZ, Louis Alfred H
WILWERDING, Walter Joseph 4
WIMAN, Charles Deere 3
WIMAN, Erastus 1
WIMAR, Carl H
WIMBERLY, Charles Franklin 2
WIMBERLY, Lowry Charles 3
WIMMER, Boniface H
WINANS, Charles Sumner 1
WINANS, Edwin Baruch 2
WINANS, Edwin Baruch 2
WINANS, Henry Morgan 4
WINANS, James Albert 5
WINANS, James January H
WINANS, James Merritt 4
WINANS, Ross H
WINANS, Samuel Ross 1
WINANS, Thomas DeKay 1
WINANS, William H
WINANT, John Gilbert 2
WINBIGLER, Charles Fremont 1
WINBORNE, John Wallace 5
WINBOURN, Robert Emmet 1
WINBURN, Hardy Lathan 1
WINCH, Horace Carlton 5
WINCHELL, Alexander H
WINCHELL, Alexander Newton 3
WINCHELL, Benjamin La Fon 2
WINCHELL, Horace Vaughn 1
WINCHELL, John H. 5
WINCHELL, Newton Horace 1
WINCHELL, Samuel Robertson 4
WINCHELL, Walter 5

WINCHESTER, Benjamin Severance 3
WINCHESTER, Caleb Thomas 1
WINCHESTER, Charles Wesley 1
WINCHESTER, Elhanan H
WINCHESTER, James H
WINCHESTER, James Price 2
WINCHESTER, James Ridout 1
WINCHESTER, Millard E. 4
WINCHESTER, Oliver Fisher H
WINCHESTER, William Eugene 2
WIND, Edgar 5
WINDELS, Paul 4
WINDELS, Paul 5
WINDER, Adam Heber 1
WINDER, G. Norman 4
WINDER, John Henry H
WINDER, Levin H
WINDER, William Henry H
WINDES, Thomas G. 1
WINDET, Victor 2
WINDHOLZ, Louis H. 2
WINDINGSTAD, Ole 3
WINDMULLER, Louis 1
WINDOM, William H
WINDRIM, James Hamilton 1
WINDRIM, John Torrey H
WINDRIM, John Torrey 4
WINDSOR, H. R. H. 5
WINDSOR, Henry Haven 1
WINDSOR, Henry Haven Jr. 4
WINDSOR, James H(arvey, II) 5
WINDSOR, Phineas Lawrence 5
WINDSOR, Wilbur Cunningham 3
WINDSOR, William Augustus 1
WINE, William E. 3
WINEBRENNER, John H
WINEMAN, Mode 1
WINES, Enoch Cobb H
WINES, Frederick Howard 1
WINFIELD, Arthur M. 1
WINFIELD, Charles Henry H
WINFIELD, George Freeman 2
WINFIELD, James Macfarlane 1
WINFIELD, James Macfarlane 4
WINFREY, Elisha William 1
WING, Asa Shove
WING, Austin Eli H
WING, Charles Benjamin 2
WING, Charles Hallet 1
WING, Daniel Gould 1
WING, Francis Joseph 1
WING, Frank (Francis Marion) 5
WING, Henry Hiram 1
WING, John Durham 3
WING, Leonard F. 2
WING, Mrs. Lucy Madeira 4
WING, Orion N. 3
WING, Russell Merritt 1
WING, Wilson Gordon 2
WING, Wilson Munford 5
WINGATE, Charles Edgar Lewis 2
WINGATE, Charles Frederick 1
WINGATE, George Wood 1
WINGATE, Joseph Ferdinand H
WINGATE, Paine H
WINGATE, Uranus Owen Brackett 1
WINGE, Ojvind 4
WINGER, Albert E. 5
WINGER, Maurice Homer 3
WINGER, Otho 2
WINGERT, Emmett Laurson 5
WINGET, Arthur Knox 5
WINGET, Benjamin H
WINGFIELD, Edward Maria
WINGFIELD, George 4
WINGFIELD, Marshall 4
WINGO, Otis Theodore 3
WINKELMAN, Nathaniel William 3

WINKELMANN, Christian H. 2
WINKING, Cyril H. 5
WINKLER, Edwin Theodore H
WINKLER, Ernest William 4
WINKLER, John K. 3
WINKLER, Max 1
WINKWORTH, Edwin David 3
WINLOCK, Herbert Eustis 2
WINLOCK, Joseph H
WINLOW, Clara Vostrovsky (Mrs. Albert E. Winlow) 5
WINN, Charles V. 2
WINN, Frank Long 1
WINN, James Herbert 4
WINN, Jane Frances 1
WINN, John F. 4
WINN, John Sheridan 1
WINN, Milton 4
WINN, Richard H
WINN, Robert Hiner 2
WINN, Thomas Clay 1
WINN, William Alma 5
WINNEMUCCA, Sarah H
WINNER, Clifford 4
WINNER, Septimus 1
WINSBOROUGH, Hallie Paxson 1
WINSER, Beatrice
WINSER, Henry Jacob H
WINSEY, A(lexander) Reid 5
WINSHIP, Albert Edward 1
WINSHIP, Blanton 2
WINSHIP, Walter Edwin 5
WINSLOW, Alfred Augustus 1
WINSLOW, Arthur 1
WINSLOW, Arthur Ellsworth 3
WINSLOW, Benjamin Emanuel 4
WINSLOW, Cameron McRae 1
WINSLOW, Carleton Monroe 2
WINSLOW, Carroll Dana 3
WINSLOW, Catherine Mary 1
WINSLOW, Charles-Edward Amory
WINSLOW, E. Eveleth
WINSLOW, Edward * H
WINSLOW, Edward Delbert 1
WINSLOW, Erving 1
WINSLOW, Francis Asbury 1
WINSLOW, Frederic I. 1
WINSLOW, George Frederick 1
WINSLOW, Guy Monroe 3
WINSLOW, Helen Maria 1
WINSLOW, Herbert 1
WINSLOW, Hubbard H
WINSLOW, John H
WINSLOW, John Ancrum H
WINSLOW, John Bradley 1
WINSLOW, John Flack H
WINSLOW, John Randolph 4
WINSLOW, Josiah H
WINSLOW, Kate Reignolds H
WINSLOW, Leon Loyal 4
WINSLOW, Miron H
WINSLOW, Randolph 4
WINSLOW, Rex (Shelton) 5
WINSLOW, Robert Lane, Jr. 5
WINSLOW, Samuel Ellsworth 4
WINSLOW, Sidney Wilmot 1
WINSLOW, Sidney Wilmot Jr. 4
WINSLOW, Thacher 3
WINSLOW, Thyra Samter 4
WINSLOW, Warren H
WINSLOW, William Copley 1
WINSOR, Frank Edward 1
WINSOR, Frederick 1
WINSOR, James Davis Jr. 3
WINSOR, Justin H
WINSOR, Mulford 3
WINSOR, Paul 4
WINSOR, Robert 1
WINSTEIN, S(aul) 5
WINSTON, Annie Steger 1
WINSTON, Charles Henry 4

WINSTON, Francis Donnell 2
WINSTON, Frederick Hampden 1
WINSTON, Frederick Seymour
WINSTON, Garrard Bigelow 3
WINSTON, George Taylor 4
WINSTON, Gilmer 2
WINSTON, Isaac 1
WINSTON, John Anthony H
WINSTON, John Clark 1
WINSTON, Joseph H
WINSTON, Robert Watson 2
WINSTON, Sanford Richard 5
WINT, Theodore Jonathan 1
WINTER, Alice Ames 1
WINTER, Alice Beach 5
WINTER, Andrew 3
WINTER, Charles Allan 2
WINTER, Charles Edwin 2
WINTER, Elisha I. H
WINTER, Elizabeth Campbell
WINTER, Emil 1
WINTER, Ezra Augustus 2
WINTER, Ferdinand 1
WINTER, Francis Anderson
WINTER, George H
WINTER, George Ben Wade 1
WINTER, Herman 3
WINTER, Irvah Lester 1
WINTER, John Garrett 3
WINTER, Nevin Otto 2
WINTER, Thomas Daniel 1
WINTER, Thomas Gerald
WINTER, William 1
WINTER, William D. 3
WINTERBOTHAM, Joseph 3
WINTERBURN, Florence (May) Hull
WINTERBURN, George William
WINTERHALTER, Albert Gustavus
WINTERNITZ, Milton Charles 3
WINTERS, Harry S(underland) 5
WINTERS, Robert (Henry) 5
WINTERS, Yvor 4
WINTERSTEINER, Oskar Paul
WINTHER, Oscar Osburn 5
WINTHROP, Beekman 1
WINTHROP, Bronson 2
WINTHROP, Henry Rogers 3
WINTHROP, James H
WINTHROP, John * H
WINTHROP, Robert Charles
WINTHROP, Theodore H
WINTNER, Aurel 3
WINTON, Alexander 1
WINTON, Andrew Lincoln 2
WINTON, George Beverly 1
WINZLER, Richard John 5
WIRE, G. E. 3
WIREBAUGH, Evelyn Burbank (Mrs. Harold W. Wirebaugh) 5
WIRJOPRANOTO, Sukardjo 4
WIRT, Loyal Lincoln 5
WIRT, William H
WIRT, William Albert 1
WIRTH, Fremont Philip 4
WIRTH, Louis 3
WIRTH, Russell D. L. 5
WIRTHLIN, Joseph L. 4
WIRTSCHAFTER, Zolton Tillson 4
WIRTZ, Alvin J. 3
WIRZ, Henry H
WISCOTT, William Joseph 5
WISE, Aaron H
WISE, Arthur Chamberlin 3
WISE, Boyd Ashby 5
WISE, Byrd Douglas 5
WISE, Claude Merton 4
WISE, Daniel H
WISE, Edmond E. 1
WISE, Edward 1
WISE, Harold A. 3
WISE, Harold Edward

WISE, Henry Alexander H
WISE, Henry Augustus H
WISE, Henry Morris 4
WISE, Isaac Mayer H
WISE, James 1
WISE, James Walter 1
WISE, John * H
WISE, John Sergeant 1
WISE, Jonah Bondi 3
WISE, Leo Henry 1
WISE, Louise Waterman 2
WISE, Marion Johnson 1
WISE, Otto Irving 1
WISE, Peter Manuel 1
WISE, Russell Vincent 5
WISE, Stephen Samuel 2
WISE, Thomas Alfred 2
WISE, William Clinton 1
WISE, William Frederic 3
WISEMAN, Bruce Kenneth 3
WISEMAN, Sir William 4
WISH, Harvey 5
WISHARD, John G. 1
WISHARD, Luther Deloraine 2
WISHARD, Samuel Ellis 1
WISHARD, William Niles 1
WISHART, Alfred Wesley 1
WISHART, Charles Frederick 3
WISHART, John Elliott 1
WISHART, William C. 4
WISHON, A. Emory 2
WISHON, Albert Graves 1
WISLIZENUS, Frederick Adolph H
WISLOCKI, George Bernays 3
WISMER, Harry 4
WISNER, Frank George 1
WISNER, George Monroe 1
WISNER, George Y. 1
WISNER, Henry H
WISNER, Oscar Francis 2
WISSER, John Philip 1
WISSLER, Clark 3
WISSLER, Jacques H
WIST, Benjamin Othello 3
WISTAR, Caspar * H
WISTAR, Isaac Jones 1
WISTER, Annis Lee 1
WISTER, Owen 1
WISTER, Sally H
WISWALL, Frank Lawrence 5
WISWALL, Richard H. 1
WISWELL, Andrew Peters 1
WISWELL, George Nelson 4
WITEBSKY, Ernest 5
WITHAM, Ernest C. 1
WITHERBEE, Frank Spencer 1
WITHERELL, James H
WITHEROW, William Porter 3
WITHERS, Frederick Clarke
WITHERS, Garrett Lee 3
WITHERS, Harry Clay 1
WITHERS, John Thomas 5
WITHERS, John William 2
WITHERS, Robert Edwin 3
WITHERS, Robert Enoch 1
WITHERS, William Alphonso 1
WITHERSPOON, Archibald William 3
WITHERSPOON, Herbert 1
WITHERSPOON, John 1
WITHERSPOON, John A. 1
WITHERSPOON, Robert H
WITHERSPOON, Samuel Andrew 1
WITHERSPOON, Thomas Casey 3
WITHERSPOON, William Wallace 5
WITHERSTINE, Christopher Sumner 1
WITHEY, Morton Owen 4
WITHINGTON, Charles Francis 1
WITHINGTON, David Little 1
WITHINGTON, Irving Platt 4
WITHINGTON, Leonard H
WITHINGTON, Robert 3
WITHINGTON, Winthrop 3
WITHROW, Gardner Robert
WITHROW, John Lindsay 1
WITHYCOMBE, James 1
WITMER, Charles B. 1
WITMER, Francis Potts 5
WITMER, Lightner 3

WITMER, R(obert) B(onner) 5
WITSCHEY, Robert E. 4
WITSCHI, Emil 5
WITSELL, Edward Fuller 5
WITSELL, William Postell 4
WITT, John Henry H
WITT, Joshua Chitwood 1
WITT, Max Siegfried 1
WITTE, Edwin Emil 5
WITTE, Fred(erick) C(hristopher)
WITTE, Max Ernest 1
WITTE, William Henry H
WITTEN, Harold Bryan 5
WITTENMYER, Edmund 1
WITTER, Dean 5
WITTER, Jean Carter 5
WITTGENSTEIN, Ludwig Josef Johann 4
WITTHAUS, Rudolph August 1
WITTICH, Fred William 4
WITTIG, Gustav Frederick 3
WITTKE, Carl Frederick 5
WITTKOWER, Rudolf 5
WITTMER, John L. 3
WITTNER, Fred 5
WITTWER, Eldon E. 4
WITTY, William Henry; 5
WITWER, Harry Charles 1
WITZEMANN, Edgar John 2
WIXSON, Franklin Galbraith 4
WIXSON, Helen Marsh 1
WOBBER, Herman 4
WOEHLKE, Walter Victor 3
WOELFKIN, Cornelius 1
WOELFLE, Arthur W. 1
WOELPER, Benjamin Franklin Jr.
WOERMANN, John William 2
WOERNER, William F. 1
WOERTENDYKE, James H. 5
WOFFORD, Kate Vixon 3
WOFFORD, William Tatum H
WOGAN, John B. 5
WOGLOM, William Henry 3
WOHL, David Philip 3
WOHLENBERG, Ernest T. F. 4
WOHLENBERG, Walter Jacob 3
WOHLLEBEN, William Joseph 4
WOHLSEN, Ralph J. 5
WOJDYLA, Henry Edward 5
WOLBACH, Edwin J. 3
WOLBACH, Simeon Burt 3
WOLBARST, Abraham Leo 2
WOLCOTT, Edward Oliver 1
WOLCOTT, Frank Bliss 4
WOLCOTT, Henry Roger 1
WOLCOTT, Jesse Paine 4
WOLCOTT, John Dorsey 2
WOLCOTT, Josiah Oliver 1
WOLCOTT, L. W. 5
WOLCOTT, Oliver H
WOLCOTT, Robert Henry 1
WOLCOTT, Roger 1
WOLCOTT, Roger 5
WOLCOTT, Roger Henry 2
WOLCOTT, Samuel Huntington 4
WOLD, Peter Irving 3
WOLD, Theodore 2
WOLDMAN, Albert Alexander 5
WOLF, Adolph Grant 2
WOLF, August Stephen 5
WOLF, Charles George Lewis 5
WOLF, Edmund Jacob 1
WOLF, Emma 2
WOLF, Frank 2
WOLF, George H
WOLF, George W. 4
WOLF, H. Carl 3
WOLF, H. D. 4
WOLF, Henry 1
WOLF, Henry Milton 3
WOLF, Irwin Damasius 4
WOLF, Isaac Jr. 4
WOLF, Joseph 1
WOLF, Leonard George 5
WOLF, Luther Benaiah 1
WOLF, Orrin E. 4

WOLF, Paul Alexander 3
WOLF, Rennold 1
WOLF, Robert Bunsen 3
WOLF, Simon 1
WOLF, William A. 4
WOLF, William Penn H
WOLFE, Albert Benedict 5
WOLFE, Arthur Lester 1
WOLFE, Catharine Lorillard H
WOLFE, Clayton A. 3
WOLFE, Edgar Thurston 3
WOLFE, Harry Kirke 1
WOLFE, Harry Preston 2
WOLFE, J. Theodore 4
WOLFE, James H
WOLFE, James Edward 5
WOLFE, James H. 3
WOLFE, James Jacob 1
WOLFE, John David H
WOLFE, Kenneth B. 5
WOLFE, Lawrence 3
WOLFE, Manson Horatio 4
WOLFE, Paul Austin 4
WOLFE, Richard Russell 5
WOLFE, Robert Frederick 1
WOLFE, S. Herbert 1
WOLFE, Simeon Kalfius H
WOLFE, Theodore Frelinghuysen 1
WOLFE, Thomas Clayton 1
WOLFE, Thomas Kennerly 5
WOLFEL, Paul Ludwig 4
WOLFENBARGER, Andrew G.
WOLFENDEN, James 2
WOLFER, John A. 3
WOLFERMAN, Fred 3
WOLFERS, Arnold Oscar 5
WOLFF, Frank Alfred 5
WOLFF, George Dering H
WOLFF, Harold G. 4
WOLFF, John Eliot 1
WOLFF, William Almon 1
WOLFIT, Donald 4
WOLFIT, Donald 5
WOLFORD, Frank Lane 4
WOLFORD, Leo Thorp 5
WOLFROM, Melville L(awrence) 5
WOLFSKILL, William H
WOLFSOHN, Joel David 4
WOLFSON, Erwin Service 4
WOLFSON, Howard E(dward)
WOLFSON, Kurt 5
WOLFSTEIN, David I. 2
WOLL, Fritz Wilhelm 1
WOLL, Matthew 3
WOLLE, John Frederick 1
WOLLENHAUPT, Hermann Adolf H
WOLLENWEBER, Ludwig August H
WOLMAN, Leo 4
WOLPE, Stefan 5
WOLSEY, Louis 3
WOLTERS, Larry (Lorenz Gerhard) 5
WOLTERSDORF, Arthur Fred 2
WOLTMAN, Frederick Enos 5
WOLTMAN, Henry 4
WOLVERTON, Charles A. 5
WOLVERTON, Charles Edwin 1
WOLVERTON, John Marshall 5
WOLVIN, Augustus B. 1
WOMACK, Joseph Pitts 5
WOMBLE, John Philip Jr. 3
WOMELDORPH, Stuart Early 4
WOMER, Parley Paul 3
WONSON, Roy Warren 2
WOOD, Abiel H
WOOD, Abraham 4
WOOD, Alexander C. 4
WOOD, Alexander Thomas 4
WOOD, Alice Holabird 1
WOOD, Amos Eastman H
WOOD, Andrew Hollister 1
WOOD, Arthur B. 3
WOOD, Arthur D. 3
WOOD, Arthur Julius 4
WOOD, Asa Butler 2
WOOD, Barry 5
WOOD, Benjamin H
WOOD, Benjamin 4
WOOD, Benson 1
WOOD, Bernard Augustine 4
WOOD, Bradford Ripley H

WOOD, Carl Bruce 4
WOOD, Carroll David 1
WOOD, Casey Albert 2
WOOD, Chandler Mason 1
WOOD, Charles 2
WOOD, 2
  Charles Erskine Scott
WOOD, Charles Milton 1
WOOD, Charles P. 5
WOOD, Charles Seely 1
WOOD, Clark Verner 1
WOOD, Clement 3
WOOD, Clinton Tyler 1
WOOD, Corydon L. 1
WOOD, David Duffie 1
WOOD, David Muir 3
WOOD, De Volson H
WOOD, Edgar Liberty 1
WOOD, Edith Elmer 2
WOOD, Edmund Palmer 5
WOOD, Edward Edgar 4
WOOD, Edward Jenner 1
WOOD, Edward Stickney 1
WOOD, Edwin Ellsworth 1
WOOD, Edwin Orin 1
WOOD, Eric Fisher 4
WOOD, Ernest Edward 1
WOOD, Eugene 1
WOOD, Fernando H
WOOD, Floyd Bernard 3
WOOD, 2
  Frances Gilchrist
WOOD, Francis Asbury 2
WOOD, Francis Carter 1
WOOD, Frank Hoyt 1
WOOD, Frederic Taylor 1
WOOD, Frederick Hill 2
WOOD, 2
  Frederick William
WOOD, George * H
WOOD, George 1
WOOD, George Arthur 1
WOOD, George Bacon 2
WOOD, George Henry 2
WOOD, George McLane 1
WOOD, George Willard 2
WOOD, Grant 1
WOOD, Guy Bussey 3
WOOD, Harold E. 4
WOOD, Harry Parker 1
WOOD, Hart 3
WOOD, Henry * 1
WOOD, Henry 2
WOOD, Henry A. Wise 1
WOOD, Henry Clay 1
WOOD, Horatio C. 1
WOOD, Horatio Charles 1
WOOD, 3
  Horatio Charles Jr.
WOOD, Horatio D. 1
WOOD, Howland 1
WOOD, Hudson A. 4
WOOD, Ira Wells 1
WOOD, Irving Francis 1
WOOD, Isaac Lemuel 4
WOOD, Isabel Warwick 5
WOOD, James H
WOOD, James 1
WOOD, James Anderson 2
WOOD, James Craven 2
WOOD, James Frederick H
WOOD, James J. 1
WOOD, James Madison 3
WOOD, James Perry 4
WOOD, James R. 1
WOOD, James Rushmore H
WOOD, Jethro H
WOOD, John * H
WOOD, John Anderson 1
WOOD, John C(lark) 5
WOOD, John Enos 4
WOOD, John Hepler 1
WOOD, John Jacob H
WOOD, John M. H
WOOD, John Quinby 4
WOOD, John S. 4
WOOD, John Scott 3
WOOD, John Seymour 1
WOOD, John Stephens 5
WOOD, John Travers 3
WOOD, John Walter 3
WOOD, John Wilson 2
WOOD, Joseph * H
WOOD, Joseph 1
WOOD, Kenneth Foster 1
WOOD, Ledger 5
WOOD, Leonard 1
WOOD, Lewis 3
WOOD, Lloyd Fuller 4
WOOD, Loren Newton 4
WOOD, Lydia Collins 1
WOOD, Marshall William 1
WOOD, Mary I. 3
WOOD, Matthew Laurence 1
WOOD, Montraville 1
WOOD, Moses Lindley 4

WOOD, Myron Ray 2
WOOD, Nathan Eusebius 1
WOOD, Nathan Robinson 5
WOOD, Oliver Ellsworth 1
WOOD, Palmer Gaylord 1
WOOD, Paul Meyer 4
WOOD, Paul Spencer 3
WOOD, 3
  Pierpont Jonathan Edwards
WOOD, Ralph 3
WOOD, Reuben H
WOOD, Reuben Terrell 3
WOOD, Richard 1
WOOD, Richard D. H
WOOD, Robert E. 1
WOOD, Robert Williams 3
WOOD, Samuel 1
WOOD, Samuel Grosvenor 2
WOOD, Samuel Newitt H
WOOD, 5
  Sarah Sayward Barrell Keating
WOOD, Silas H
WOOD, Spencer Shepard 1
WOOD, Stella Louise 3
WOOD, 1
  Sterling Alexander
WOOD, Stuart 1
WOOD, Theodore Thomas 4
WOOD, Thomas H
WOOD, Thomas Denison 4
WOOD, Thomas Edward 4
WOOD, Thomas John 1
WOOD, Thomas John 3
WOOD, Thomas Waterman 1
WOOD, Waddy Butler 1
WOOD, Walter 1
WOOD, Walter 4
WOOD, Walter Aaron 5
WOOD, Walter Abbott H
WOOD, Will Christopher 1
WOOD, William H
WOOD, William Allen 5
WOOD, 5
  William Barry, Jr.
WOOD, William Burke H
WOOD, William Elliott 3
WOOD, William H. S. 1
WOOD, William Hamilton 3
WOOD, William Madison 1
WOOD, William Robert 1
WOOD, William Roscoe 1
WOOD, William Thomas 4
WOOD, Willis Delano 5
WOOD, Word Harris 3
WOOD-ALLEN, Mary 1
WOODARD, 5
  Charles Augustus
WOODARD, 1
  Frederick Augustus
WOODARD, G. C. 4
WOODARD, James Edward 2
WOODBERRY, 1
  George Edward
WOODBERRY, Miriam L. 5
WOODBERRY, Rosa 1
WOODBINE, 3
  George Edward
WOODBRIDGE, 4
  Charles Kingsley
WOODBRIDGE, 5
  Dudley Warner
WOODBRIDGE, 2
  Dwight Edwards
WOODBRIDGE, H
  Frederick Enoch
WOODBRIDGE, 1
  Frederick James Eugene
WOODBRIDGE, 3
  Homer Edwards
WOODBRIDGE, John H
WOODBRIDGE, John Arven 5
WOODBRIDGE, Samuel Homer 1
WOODBRIDGE, Samuel Merrill 1
WOODBRIDGE, William H
WOODBRIDGE, William Channing H
WOODBURN, Ethelbert Cooke 4
WOODBURN, James Albert 2
WOODBURNE, Angus Stewart 1
WOODBURY, Charles Herbert 1
WOODBURY, Charles J. 4
WOODBURY, Charles Jeptha Hill 1
WOODBURY, Daniel Phineas H
WOODBURY, Ellen Carolina 'de Quincy 1

WOODBURY, Frank Porter 4
WOODBURY, Gordon 1
WOODBURY, Helen Sumner 1
WOODBURY, Ida Sumner Vose 1
WOODBURY, Malcolm Sumner 1
WOODBURY, Marcia Oakes 1
WOODBURY, Robert Morse 5
WOODBURY, Urban Andrain 1
WOODBURY, Walter E. 4
WOODCOCK, Amos Walter Wright 4
WOODCOCK, Charles Edward 1
WOODCOCK, David H
WOODDY, Claiborne Alphonso 1
WOODFORD, Arthur Burnham 1
WOODFORD, Frank B. 4
WOODFORD, M. Dewitt 4
WOODFORD, Stewart Lyndon 1
WOODFORD, William H
WOODHEAD, Harry 4
WOODHEAD, William 4
WOODHOUSE, Arthur Sutherland Pigott 4
WOODHOUSE, Charles Williamson 4
WOODHOUSE, James H
WOODHOUSE, Samuel W. H
WOODHULL, Alfred Alexander 1
WOODHULL, Daniel Ellis 5
WOODHULL, John Francis 1
WOODHULL, Maxwell Van Zandt 1
WOODHULL, Nathaniel H
WOODHULL, Victoria Claflin 1
WOODHULL, Victoria Claflin 4
WOODHULL, Zula Maud 5
WOODIN, William Hartman 1
WOODLEY, Oscar Israel 1
WOODLOCK, Thomas Francis 4
WOODMAN, Abby Johnson 4
WOODMAN, Albert Stanton 1
WOODMAN, Alpheus Grant 5
WOODMAN, Clarence Eugene 1
WOODMAN, Durand 1
WOODMAN, Frederic Thomas 3
WOODMAN, J. Edmund 1
WOODMAN, John H
WOODMAN, Lawrence Ewalt 5
WOODMAN, Raymond Huntington 2
WOODRING, Harry Hines 4
WOODROW, H. R. 1
WOODROW, James 1
WOODROW, Jay W. 3
WOODROW, Nancy Mann Waddel 1
WOODROW, Samuel Hetherington 2
WOODRUFF, Anne Helena 4
WOODRUFF, Carle Augustus 1
WOODRUFF, Caroline Salome 2
WOODRUFF, Charles Albert 1
WOODRUFF, Charles Edward 1
WOODRUFF, Clinton Rogers 2
WOODRUFF, Edwin Blanchard 5
WOODRUFF, Edwin Hamlin 1
WOODRUFF, Elmer Grant 3
WOODRUFF, Ernest 4
WOODRUFF, Francis Eben 1

WOODRUFF, Frank Edward 4
WOODRUFF, Frederick William 3
WOODRUFF, George 2
WOODRUFF, George Catlin H
WOODRUFF, George Hobart 2
WOODRUFF, George Washington 1
WOODRUFF, Harvey T. 1
WOODRUFF, Helen S. 1
WOODRUFF, Henry Mygatt 1
WOODRUFF, James Albert 5
WOODRUFF, John H
WOODRUFF, John T. 2
WOODRUFF, Joseph Talmage Battis 1
WOODRUFF, Julia Louisa Matilda 1
WOODRUFF, Lorande Loss 2
WOODRUFF, Nathan H. 4
WOODRUFF, Olive 4
WOODRUFF, Robert Eastman 1
WOODRUFF, Rollin Simmons 1
WOODRUFF, Roy Orchard 3
WOODRUFF, Theodore Tuttle H
WOODRUFF, Thomas Adams 4
WOODRUFF, Thomas M. H
WOODRUFF, Timothy Lester 1
WOODRUFF, Wilford H
WOODRUFF, William Edward H
WOODRUFF, William Wight 5
WOODRUM, Clifton Alexander 3
WOODS, Alan Churchill 4
WOODS, Albert Fred 2
WOODS, Alfred W. 3
WOODS, Alice (Miss) 1
WOODS, Alva H
WOODS, Andrew Henry 5
WOODS, Arthur 2
WOODS, Baldwin Munger 3
WOODS, Bertha Gerneaux 3
WOODS, Charles Albert 1
WOODS, Charles Carroll 1
WOODS, Charles Dayton 1
WOODS, Charles Robert H
WOODS, Cyrus E. 1
WOODS, David Walker Jr. 4
WOODS, Edgar Hall 3
WOODS, Edgar Lyons 4
WOODS, Edward Augustus 1
WOODS, Francis Marion 4
WOODS, Frank Henry 3
WOODS, Frank P. 4
WOODS, Frederick Adams 1
WOODS, Frederick Shenstone 3
WOODS, George Benjamin 3
WOODS, Harry Irwin 5
WOODS, Henry H
WOODS, Henry 1
WOODS, Henry Cochrane 5
WOODS, Henry Ernest 1
WOODS, Hiram 1
WOODS, Homer Boughner 2
WOODS, J. Albert 4
WOODS, James Haughton 1
WOODS, James Pleasant 2
WOODS, John * H
WOODS, John Carter Brown 1
WOODS, Kate Tannatt 1
WOODS, Katharine Pearson 1
WOODS, Leonard * H
WOODS, Littleton A. 4
WOODS, Louis Earnest 5
WOODS, Mark White 5
WOODS, Matthew 1
WOODS, Michael Leonard 4
WOODS, Neander Montgomery 1
WOODS, Robert Archey 1
WOODS, Robert Patterson 3
WOODS, Rufus 3
WOODS, Sam Edison 3
WOODS, Samuel Van Horn 1

WOODS, Thomas Cochrane 3
WOODS, Thomas Francis 2
WOODS, Thomas Hall 1
WOODS, Thomas Smith 4
WOODS, Virna 1
WOODS, 5
  Walter Leslie James
WOODS, Walter Orr 3
WOODS, William H
WOODS, William Allen H
WOODS, William Burnham H
WOODS, William George 4
WOODS, William Hervey 4
WOODS, William Seaver 4
WOODS, 5
  William Sharpless Derrick
WOODS, William Stone 1
WOODS, William Wells 1
WOODS, 1
  William Whitfield
WOOD-SEYS, Roland Alex 4
WOODSIDE, H
  John Archibald
WOODSIDE, John Thomas 2
WOODSIDE, John Thomas 3
WOODSIDE, John W. 3
WOODSIDE, Robert I. 3
WOODSMALL, Ruth Frances 4
WOODSON, Archelaus M. 1
WOODSON, Aytch P. 3
WOODSON, Carter Godwin 3
WOODSON, George Frederick 4
WOODSON, Mary Blake 1
WOODSON, Omer Lee 3
WOODSON, Robert Everard Jr. 4
WOODSON, Samuel Hughes * H
WOODSON, Urey 1
WOODSON, Walter Browne 2
WOODSON, Walter Worsham 1
WOODWARD, Allan Harvey 3
WOODWARD, Augustus Brevoort H
WOODWARD, Benjamin Duryea 2
WOODWARD, Calvin Milton 1
WOODWARD, Charles Edgar 2
WOODWARD, Chester 1
WOODWARD, Clark Howell 4
WOODWARD, Clifford Dewey 2
WOODWARD, Comer McDonald 5
WOODWARD, Edmund Lee 1
WOODWARD, Ellen Sullivan 5
WOODWARD, Ellsworth 1
WOODWARD, Ernest 5
WOODWARD, Fletcher D(rummond) 5
WOODWARD, Frank Lincoln 1
WOODWARD, Franklin Cowles 1
WOODWARD, Frederic 3
WOODWARD, George 3
WOODWARD, George A. 4
WOODWARD, George Washington 1
WOODWARD, Harold Christopher 1
WOODWARD, Henry H
WOODWARD, Hugh Beistle 5
WOODWARD, Hugh McCurdy 1
WOODWARD, J. B. 1
WOODWARD, James T. 1
WOODWARD, John 1
WOODWARD, John Charles 1
WOODWARD, Joseph Addison 1
WOODWARD, Joseph Hersey II 4
WOODWARD, Joseph Hooker 1
WOODWARD, Joseph Janvier H

WOODWARD, 1
Julius Hayden
WOODWARD, 5
Lester Armand
WOODWARD, 5
Ernest) Llewellyn, Sir
WOODWARD, Luther
Ellis 4
WOODWARD, P. Henry 1
WOODWARD, Robert B. 4
WOODWARD, 1
Robert Simpson
WOODWARD, 3
Robert Strong
WOODWARD, 3
Roland Beavan
WOODWARD, H
Samuel Bayard
WOODWARD, 3
Samuel Bayard
WOODWARD, 1
Samuel Lippincott
WOODWARD,
Samuel Walter
WOODWARD, Stanley 1
WOODWARD, Stanley 4
WOODWARD, 2
Walter Carleton
WOODWARD, William H
WOODWARD, William 1
WOODWARD, 2
William Creighton
WOODWARD, William E. 3
WOODWARD, 1
William Finch
WOODWORTH, 4
Clyde Melvin
WOODWORTH, 1
Edward Knowlton
WOODWORTH, 1
Frank Goodrich
WOODWORTH, 5
G(eorge) Wallace
WOODWORTH, 3
Herbert Grafton
WOODWORTH, James
Grant 4
WOODWORTH, H
James Hutchinson
WOODWORTH, Jay
Backus 1
WOODWORTH, Kennard 3
WOODWORTH, H
Laurin Dewey
WOODWORTH, Melvin J. 3
WOODWORTH, 1
Newell Bertram
WOODWORTH, Philip
Bell 1
WOODWORTH, 4
Robert Sessions
WOODWORTH, Samuel H
WOODWORTH, 4
Stewart Campbell
WOODWORTH, William
W. H
WOODY, Clifford 2
WOODY, Frank H. 4
WOODY, McIver 5
WOODY, Walter Thomas 4
WOODY, Walton L. 3
WOODYARD, 1
Harry Chapman
WOODYATT, 3
Rollin Turner
WOOFTER, 1
Thomas Jackson
WOOL, John Ellis H
WOOLARD, Warden 4
WOOLBERT, 1
Charles Henry
WOOLDRIDGE, 1
Charles William
WOOLDRIDGE, 5
Edmund Tyler
WOOLEVER, Harry Earl 1
WOOLF, Albert Edward 1
WOOLF, Benjamin
Edward H
WOOLF, Philip 1
WOOLF, Samuel Johnson 2
WOOLFOLK, 3
William Gordon
WOOLLARD, 1
William Edward
WOOLLCOTT, Alexander 2
WOOLLEN, Evans 2
WOOLLEN, Evans Jr. 3
WOOLLETT, William L. 4
WOOLLETT, William M. H
WOOLLEY, Alice Stone 2
WOOLLEY, Celia Parker 1
WOOLLEY, Charles H. 3
WOOLLEY, Clarence
Mott 5
WOOLLEY, D. Wayne 4
WOOLLEY, Edward Mott 2

WOOLLEY, 1
Edwin Campbell
WOOLLEY, 3
Helen Bradford Thompson
WOOLLEY, Herbert
Codey 3
WOOLLEY, 1
John Granville
WOOLLEY, 2
Mrs (Anna) Lazelle Thayer
WOOLLEY, Mary Emma 1
WOOLLEY, Monty 4
WOOLLEY, Paul
Gerhardt 1
WOOLLEY, 3
Robert Wickliffe
WOOLLEY, 2
Victor Baynard
WOOLMAN, C. E. 4
WOOLMAN, Henry
Newbold 3
WOOLMAN, John H
WOOLMAN, Mary
Schenck 4
WOOLNER, Adolph 2
WOOLRYCH,
Francis Humphry William
WOOLSEY, George 5
WOOLSEY, John Munro H
WOOLSEY, John Munro 4
WOOLSEY, John Munro 4
WOOLSEY, Lester Hood
WOOLSEY, H
Melancthon Taylor
WOOLSEY, 2
Ross Arlington
WOOLSEY, 1
Sarah Chauncey
WOOLSEY, H
Theodore Dwight
WOOLSEY, 1
Theodore Salisbury *
WOOLSON, 3
Abba Louisa Goold
WOOLSON, H
Constance Fenimore
WOOLSON, Harry
Thurber 5
WOOLSON, Ira Harvey 1
WOOLSON, L. Irving 4
WOOLSTON, Howard
Brown 1
WOOLWINE, Thomas Lee 4
WOOLWINE, 1
William David
WOOLWORTH, 2
Charles Sumner
WOOLWORTH, Frank W. 1
WOOLWORTH, James
Mills 1
WOOMER, Ephraim
Milton H
WOOSLEY, John Brooks 3
WOOSTER, H
Charles Whiting
WOOSTER, David H
WOOSTER, 5
Lorraine Elizabeth
WOOSTER, Lyman Child 4
WOOTAN, James Blythe 1
WOOTAN, James K. 5
WOOTEN, Benjamin
Allen 2
WOOTEN, 5
Benjamin Harrison
WOOTEN, Horace Oliver 2
WOOTEN, June Price 3
WOOTEN, Ralph H. 5
WOOTEN, 3
William Preston
WOOTON, Paul 4
WOOTTON, Bailey
Peyton 2
WOOTTON, Richens Lacy H
WORCESTER, Alfred 3
WORCESTER, 3
Charles Henry
WORCESTER, David 2
WORCESTER, Dean 1
WORCESTER,
Edward Strong
WORCESTER, Edwin
Dean 1
WORCESTER, Elwood 1
WORCESTER, Franklin 1
WORCESTER,
Harry Augustus
WORCESTER, Henry E. 5
WORCESTER, H
Joseph Emerson
WORCESTER, 2
Joseph Ruggles
WORCESTER, Noah H
WORCESTER, 5
P(hilip) G(eorge)
WORCESTER, Samuel H

WORCESTER, H
Samuel Austin
WORCESTER, H
Samuel Thomas
WORCESTER, Thomas H
WORCESTER, 1
William Loring
WORCESTER, 5
Willis George
WORD, Thomas Jefferson 1
WORDEN, Beverly Lyon 1
WORDEN, Charles Beatty 5
WORDEN, Charles
Howard 1
WORDEN, 1
Edward Chauncey I.
WORDEN, J. Perry 2
WORDEN, James Avery 1
WORDEN, John Lorimer H
WORDIN, 1
Nathaniel Eugene
WORK, Edgar Whitaker 1
WORK, Henry Clay H
WORK, Hubert 2
WORK, James Aiken 4
WORK, Jeremiah Boston 1
WORK, Milton C. 2
WORK, Monroe Nathan 2
WORK, William Roth 4
WORKING, 2
Daniel Webster
WORKMAN, Fanny
Bullock 1
WORKMAN, James Mims 4
WORKMAN, W. Hunter 4
WORKS, George A. 3
WORKS, John Downey 1
WORLEY, Clair L. 4
WORLEY, Henry William 1
WORLEY, John Stephen 3
WORMAN, Ben James 5
WORMAN, James Henry 1
WORMAN, Ludwig 2
WORMELEY, 1
Katharine Prescott
WORMLEY, James H
WORMLEY, H
Theodore George
WORMSER, I. Maurice 3
WORMSER, Leo F. 5
WORMWOOD, 5
Kenneth Mendum
WORNER, Jno 3
WORRALL, 1
Ambrose Alexander
WORRALL, 2
David Elbridge
WORRALL, Joseph
Howard 4
WORRELL, William Hoyt 3
WORSLEY, Abinus A. 1
WORST, John H. 3
WORTENDYKE, H
Jacob Reynier
WORTH, James Huntting 5
WORTH, Jonathan H
WORTH, William E. 3
WORTH, William Jenkins H
WORTH, William Scott 1
WORTHAM, James
Lemuel 3
WORTHEN, Amos Henry H
WORTHEN, Edmund
Louis 4
WORTHEN, George 3
WORTHEN,
Thomas Wilson Dorr
WORTHING, 2
Archie Garfield
WORTHINGTON, 1
Augustus Storrs
WORTHINGTON, 2
Charles Campbell
WORTHINGTON,
Edward William
WORTHINGTON, George 1
WORTHINGTON,
George Heber
WORTHINGTON, H
Henry Rossiter
WORTHINGTON, John 1
WORTHINGTON, John I. 1
WORTHINGTON, H
John Tolley Hood
WORTHINGTON,
Thomas
WORTHINGTON, H
Thomas Contee
WORTHINGTON, 1
Walter Fitzhugh
WORTHINGTON,
William 1
WORTHINGTON, 2
William Alfred
WORTHY, Edmund Henry 5
WORTMAN, Denys 3
WORTMAN, Doris Nash 4

WOTHERSPOON, 2
Marion Foster
WOTHERSPOON, 1
William Wallace
WOTTON, Grigsby Hart 4
WOTTRICH, Wilfred 4
WOULFE, Henry Francis 4
WOVOKA H
WOVOKA 4
WOYTINSKY, Wladimir
S. 4
WOZENCRAFT, 4
Frank Wilson
WRAGG, Samuel Holmes 3
WRAGG, William H
WRAITH, William 5
WRAPE, James Wyre 5
WRATHER, William
Embry 4
WRAXALL, Peter H
WRAY, 5
James Glendenning
WRAY, Newton 4
WREDEN, Nicholas 3
WREN, Christopher 1
WREN, Frank George 4
WREN, William Clinton 3
WRENCH, Jesse E. 4
WRENCH, Sir Evelyn 4
WRENN, Henry S. 3
WRENNE, Thomas
William 1
WRIGHT, Albert Allen 1
WRIGHT, Alfred 3
WRIGHT, Ammi Willard 1
WRIGHT, 5
Arnauld Leonard
WRIGHT, Arthur Davis 2
WRIGHT, Arthur Mullin 4
WRIGHT, Arthur Silas 1
WRIGHT, 1
Arthur Williams
WRIGHT, Ashley Bascom H
WRIGHT, 1
Augustine Washington
WRIGHT, H
Augustus Romaldus
WRIGHT, Austin Tappan 1
WRIGHT, Ben D. 4
WRIGHT, Ben F. 4
WRIGHT, Benjamin H
WRIGHT, Boykin Cabell 3
WRIGHT, Bruce Simpson 4
WRIGHT, Burton Henry 1
WRIGHT, Carrie Douglas 4
WRIGHT, Carroll 1
WRIGHT,
Carroll Davidson
WRIGHT, Cecil Augustus 5
WRIGHT, Cecil Augustus 4
WRIGHT, Charles 1
WRIGHT, Charles Jr. 4
WRIGHT, Charles Baker 2
WRIGHT,
Charles Barstow
WRIGHT, H
Charles Cushing
WRIGHT, Charles Edward 4
WRIGHT, 3
Charles Henry Conrad
WRIGHT, 4
Charles Herbert
WRIGHT, 1
Charles Jefferson
WRIGHT, Charles Lovel 5
WRIGHT, Chauncey H
WRIGHT, 4
Chester Whitney
WRIGHT, 4
Clifford Ramsey
WRIGHT, Cobina 5
WRIGHT, 1
Cyrus Mansfield
WRIGHT, Daniel Boone 1
WRIGHT, Daniel Thew 2
WRIGHT, David McCord 5
WRIGHT, Donald S. 4
WRIGHT, Donald Thomas 4
WRIGHT, Edward
Bingham 1
WRIGHT, Edward Everett 4
WRIGHT,
Edward Pulteney
WRIGHT, Edward R. 3
WRIGHT, Edward Richard 2
WRIGHT,
Edwin Ruthvin Vincent
WRIGHT, Eliphalet Nott 4
WRIGHT, 5
Elizabeth Washburne (Mrs.
Hamilton Wright)
WRIGHT, Elizur H
WRIGHT, Ernest Hunter 5
WRIGHT, Fielding Lewis 3
WRIGHT, Frances 1
WRIGHT, Francis Marion 1
WRIGHT, Frank Ayres 2

WRIGHT, Frank C. 2
WRIGHT, Frank James 3
WRIGHT, Frank Lee 3
WRIGHT, Frank Lloyd 3
WRIGHT, 3
Frederick Eugene
WRIGHT, George Bohan 1
WRIGHT, George E. 5
WRIGHT, George Francis 5
WRIGHT, George Francis 4
WRIGHT,
George Frederick
WRIGHT, 1
George Frederick
WRIGHT, George Grover H
WRIGHT, George Hand 3
WRIGHT, George Murray 5
WRIGHT, H
George Washington
WRIGHT, George William 4
WRIGHT, Gilbert G. 1
WRIGHT, Graham 3
WRIGHT, Grant 4
WRIGHT, Hamilton 1
WRIGHT, 3
Hamilton Mercer
WRIGHT, Harold Abbott 4
WRIGHT, Harold Bell 2
WRIGHT, Harry Noble 5
WRIGHT, Helen R. 5
WRIGHT, Helen Smith 5
WRIGHT, H
Hendrick Bradley
WRIGHT, Henry Burt 1
WRIGHT, Henry Clarke H
WRIGHT, Henry Collier 1
WRIGHT, Henry Harry H
WRIGHT, Henry John 1
WRIGHT, Henry Parks 1
WRIGHT, Herbert 2
WRIGHT, Herbert E. 2
WRIGHT, Herbert Perry 2
WRIGHT, 4
Horace Caldwell
WRIGHT, 3
Horace Melville
WRIGHT, H
Horatio Governeur
WRIGHT, Irene Aloha 5
WRIGHT, Isaac Miles 5
WRIGHT, J. Butler 1
WRIGHT, J. Montgomery 1
WRIGHT, James Franklin 1
WRIGHT, James Harris 1
WRIGHT, James Homer 1
WRIGHT, James Lendrew 4
WRIGHT, James Lloyd 3
WRIGHT, Jessie 5
WRIGHT, 4
Joanna Maynard Shaw
WRIGHT, John 1
WRIGHT, John Bittinger 1
WRIGHT, John Calvin 5
WRIGHT, John Crafts H
WRIGHT, John Henry 1
WRIGHT, John Kirtland 5
WRIGHT, John Lloyd 5
WRIGHT, John Pilling 2
WRIGHT, John Stephen H
WRIGHT, John Vines 1
WRIGHT, John Wells 1
WRIGHT, John Westley 1
WRIGHT, John Westley 5
WRIGHT, John Womack 3
WRIGHT, H
Jonathan Jasper
WRIGHT, Joseph 1
WRIGHT, Joseph Albert H
WRIGHT,
Joseph Alexander
WRIGHT, H
Joseph Jefferson Burr
WRIGHT, Joseph Purdon 5
WRIGHT, Julia MacNair 1
WRIGHT, Julian May 1
WRIGHT, Leroy A. 2
WRIGHT, Louis Tompkins 3
WRIGHT, 4
Louise Sophie Wigfall
WRIGHT, Luke E. 1
WRIGHT, 1
Luther Lamphear
WRIGHT, Mabel Osgood 1
WRIGHT, 4
Marcellus Eugene
WRIGHT, Marcus Joseph 1
WRIGHT, Marie Robinson 1
WRIGHT, 5
Mary Clabaugh (Mrs. Arthur
F. Wright)
WRIGHT, Mary Tappan 1
WRIGHT, 1
Maurice Lauchlin
WRIGHT, Merle St Croix 2
WRIGHT, Milton 1
WRIGHT, Milton 2
WRIGHT, Moorhead 2

WRIGHT, Myron Benjamin — H
WRIGHT, Nathaniel Curwin — 1
WRIGHT, Norris N. — 3
WRIGHT, Orville — 2
WRIGHT, Patience Lovell — H
WRIGHT, Paul — 4
WRIGHT, Peter Clark — 2
WRIGHT, Purd B. — 4
WRIGHT, Quincy — 5
WRIGHT, Richard — 4
WRIGHT, Richard Robert — 2
WRIGHT, Richard Robert Jr. — 4
WRIGHT, Richardson Little — 4
WRIGHT, Robert — H
WRIGHT, Robert Charlton — 2
WRIGHT, Robert Clinton — 1
WRIGHT, Robert Herring — 1
WRIGHT, Robert William — H
WRIGHT, Ross Pier — 4
WRIGHT, Roydon Vincent — 2
WRIGHT, Rufus — H
WRIGHT, Samuel Gardiner — H
WRIGHT, Selden Stuart Mrs. — 4
WRIGHT, Silas Jr. — H
WRIGHT, Stanley Willard — 5
WRIGHT, Stephen Mott — 1
WRIGHT, Sydney Longstreth — 5
WRIGHT, Theodore — 1
WRIGHT, Theodore Francis — 1
WRIGHT, Theodore Lyman — 1
WRIGHT, Theodore Paul — 5
WRIGHT, Thew — 5
WRIGHT, Thomas Roane Barnes — 4
WRIGHT, Turbutt — H
WRIGHT, Walter Henry — 1
WRIGHT, Walter King — 4
WRIGHT, Walter Livingston Jr. — 2
WRIGHT, Warren — 3
WRIGHT, Wilbur — 1
WRIGHT, Wilbur Seaman — 1
WRIGHT, Wilfred L. — 2
WRIGHT, Willard Huntington — 1
WRIGHT, William — H
WRIGHT, William Bleecker — 4
WRIGHT, William Bull — H
WRIGHT, William Burnet — 1
WRIGHT, William Carter — 1
WRIGHT, William Frederick — 4
WRIGHT, William Hammond — 3
WRIGHT, William Janes — 1
WRIGHT, William Kelley — 1
WRIGHT, William Mason — 2
WRIGHT, William Ryer — 1
WRIGHT, William Thomas Jr. — 3
WRIGHT, William Wood — 5
WRIGHTSMAN, Charles John — 3
WRIGHTSON, George D. — 4
WRIGLEY, Thomas — 5
WRIGLEY, William Jr. — 1
WRISLEY, George A. — 4
WROBLEWSKI, Wladyslaw — 5
WROCK, Arthur Henry — 1
WRONG, H. Hume — 3
WROTH, Edward Pinkney — 2
WU, Chao-Chu — 1
WUERPEL, Edmund Henry — 5
WULLING, Frederick John — 2
WULSIN, Frederick Roelker — 4
WULSIN, Lucien — 4
WULSIN, Lucien — 5
WUNDER, Charles Newman — 4
WUNDER, Clarence Edmond — 1
WUNDERLICH, Fritz — 4
WUNDHEILER, Alexander Wundt — 3
WUNSCH, Ernest Conrad — 4
WUORINEN, John H. — 5
WURDEMANN, Audrey May — 4
WURDEMANN, Harry Vanderbilt — 1

WURLITZER, Farny R. — 5
WURLITZER, Rudolph H. — 2
WURMAN, Harry P. — 4
WURTS, Alexander Jay — 1
WURTS, John — H
WURTS, John — 4
WURTS, John Halsey — 4
WURTSMITH, Paul Bernard — 2
WURTTEMBERG, Friedrich Paul Wilhelm — H
WURZ, John Francis — 4
WURZBACH, Harry McLeary — 1
WURZBURG, Francis Lewis — 3
WU TING-FANG — 2
WYANT, Adam Martin — 1
WYANT, Alexander Helwig — H
WYANT, Paul Byron — 3
WYATT, Bernard Langdon — 4
WYATT, Edith Franklin — 3
WYATT, J. B. Noel — 1
WYATT, Landon R. — 5
WYATT, Lee B. — 3
WYATT, Sir Francis — H
WYATT-BROWN, Hunter — 3
WYCHE, Charles Cecil — 4
WYCHE, Richard Thomas — 4
WYCKOFF, Albert Clarke — 5
WYCKOFF, Ambrose Barkley — 4
WYCKOFF, Arcalous Welling — 1
WYCKOFF, Cecelia G. — 5
WYCKOFF, Cecelia G. — 4
WYCKOFF, Charles Truman — 4
WYCKOFF, John — 1
WYCKOFF, Richard DeMille — 5
WYCKOFF, Walter Augustus — 1
WYER, James Ingersoll — 3
WYER, Malcolm Glenn — 4
WYER, Samuel S. — 4
WYETH, John — H
WYETH, John Allan — 1
WYETH, Nathan C. — 4
WYETH, Nathaniel Jarvis — H
WYETH, Newell Convers — 2
WYKOFF, Leward Cornelius — 2
WYLEGALLA, Victor Bernard — 4
WYLES, Tom Russell — 3
WYLIE, Andrew — H
WYLIE, Andrew — 1
WYLIE, David Gourley — 1
WYLIE, Douglas M. — 1
WYLIE, Dwight Witherspoon — 1
WYLIE, Edna Edwards — 1
WYLIE, Elinor Hoyt — 3
WYLIE, Herbert George — 4
WYLIE, Ida Alexa Ross — 3
WYLIE, Laura Johnson — 1
WYLIE, Philip Gordon — 5
WYLIE, Richard Cameron — 1
WYLIE, Robert — H
WYLIE, Robert Bradford — 3
WYLIE, Robert H. — 4
WYLIE, Samuel Brown — H
WYLIE, Walker Gill — 1
WYLLIE, John Cook — 5
WYLLIE, Robert (Edward) Evan — 5
WYLLYS, George — H
WYMAN, Alfred Lee — 3
WYMAN, Bruce — 1
WYMAN, Charles Alfred — 5
WYMAN, Eugene Lester — 5
WYMAN, Frank Theodore — 1
WYMAN, Hal C. — 1
WYMAN, Henry Augustus — 1
WYMAN, Herbert Gardner — 4
WYMAN, Jefferies — H
WYMAN, Levi Parker — 4
WYMAN, Lillie Buffum Chace — 1
WYMAN, Morrill — H
WYMAN, Phillips — 3
WYMAN, Robert Harris — H
WYMAN, Seth — H
WYMAN, Walter — 1
WYMAN, Walter Forestus — 1
WYMAN, Walter Scott — 2
WYMAN, Willard Gordon — 5
WYMAN, William D. — 1
WYMAN, William Frizzell — 4
WYMAN, William Stokes — 1
WYNEGAR, Howard LaVerne — 3

WYNKOOP, Asa — 2
WYNKOOP, Bernard Martell — 1
WYNKOOP, Henry — H
WYNN, Ed — 5
WYNN, William Joseph — 4
WYNN, William Thomas — 3
WYNNE, Cyril — 5
WYNNE, Madeline Yale — 4
WYNNE, Robert John — 1
WYNNE, Shirley Wilmott — 2
WYNNE, Thomas Neil — 4
WYNNS, Thomas — H
WYTHE, George — 1
WYUM, Obed Alonzo — 5
WYVELL, Manton M. — 1

X

XANTUS, Janos — H
XCERON, Jean — 4

Y

YAGER, Arthur — 4
YAGER, Joseph Arthur — 4
YAGER, Louis — 5
YAGER, Vincent — 5
YAGLOU, Constantin Prodromos — 4
YALE, Caroline Ardelia — 1
YALE, Elihu — H
YALE, Leroy Milton — 1
YALE, Linus — 1
YANCEY, Bartlett — H
YANCEY, Edward Burbridge — 2
YANCEY, James — 4
YANCEY, Joel — 1
YANCEY, Richard Hunter — 1
YANCEY, William Lowndes — H
YANDELL, David Wendel — H
YANDELL, Enid — 1
YANDELL, Lunsford Pitts — H
YANES, Francisco Javier — 1
YANGCO, Teodore R. — 4
YANNEY, Benjamin Franklin — 3
YANT, William Parks — 4
YANTIS, George Franklin — 2
YARBOROUGH, Warren Furman — 1
YARD, Robert Sterling — 2
YARDLEY, Farnham — 3
YARDLEY, Herbert O. — 3
YARGER, Henry Lee — 1
YARNALL, Alexander Coxe — 4
YARNALL, Stanley Rhoads — 4
YARNELL, Harry Ervin — 3
YARNELL, Ray — 4
YARROW, Harry Crecy — 4
YARROW, Philip — 3
YARYAN, Homer T. — 4
YATES, Abraham — H
YATES, Arthur Gould — 1
YATES, Arthur Wolcott — 4
YATES, Charles Colt — 2
YATES, Cullen — 1
YATES, Eugene Adams — 3
YATES, Henry A. — 1
YATES, Henry Whitefield — 1
YATES, Herbert John — 4
YATES, John Barentse — H
YATES, John Lawrence — 1
YATES, John Van Ness — H
YATES, Julian Emmet — 3
YATES, Katherine Merritte — 4
YATES, Lorenzo Gordin — 1
YATES, Matthew Tyson — H
YATES, Paul Clifford — 4
YATES, Peter Waldron — H
YATES, Raymond Francis — 4
YATES, Richard — 4
YATES, Richard — 1
YATES, Robert — H
YATES, Robert Carl — 4
YATES, Stephen — 5
YATES, Ted — 4
YATMAN, Marion Fay — 4
YAW, Ellen Beach — 2
YAWKEY, Cyrus Carpenter — 2
YEAGER, Albert Franklin — 4
YEAGER, Howard Austin — 4
YEAGER, Joseph — 1
YEAMAN, George Helm — 1
YEAMAN, Malcolm — 1
YEAMANS, Sir John — H

YEAPLE, Whitney S. K. — 4
YEARDLEY, Sir George — H
YEARDON, Richard — H
YEASTING, William Henry — 5
YEATER, Charles Emmett — 4
YEATES, Jasper — H
YEATES, Jesse Johnson — 1
YEATES, William Smith — 1
YEATMAN, James E. — H
YEATMAN, Pope — 3
YEATMAN, Richard Thompson
YEATON, Arthur Charles — 3
YECHTON, Barbara — 1
YEISER, John O. — 1
YEISLEY, George Conrad — 1
YELL, Archibald — 1
YELLIN, Samuel — 1
YELLOWLEY, Edward C. — 5
YENDES, Lucy A. — 4
YENS, Karl — 2
YEOMANS, Charles — 3
YEOMANS, Earl Raymond — 5
YEOMANS, Frank Clark — 5
YEOMANS, George Dallas — 1
YEOMANS, Henry Aaron — 5
YEOMANS, James D. — 1
YEOMANS, John William — H
YEOMANS, Robert DeWitte — 5
YEPSEN, Lloyd Nicoll — 3
YERBY, William James — 3
YERGER, William — H
YERGIN, Howard Vernon — 3
YERKES, Charles Tyson — 1
YERKES, John Watson — 1
YERKES, Leonard A. — 4
YERKES, Robert Mearns — 3
YERKES, Royden Keith — 5
YEUELL, Gladstone Horace — 4
YEWELL, George Henry — 1
YLVISAKER, Ivar Daniel — 1
YLVISAKER, Lauritz S. — 5
YNTEMA, Hessell Edward — 4
YOAKUM, Benjamin F. — 1
YOAKUM, Clarence Stone — 2
YOAKUM, Henderson — H
YOCUM, A. Duncan — 1
YOCUM, Seth Hartman — 2
YOCUM, Wilbur Fisk — 4
YODER, Albert Henry — 1
YODER, David Carl — 4
YODER, Jocelyn Paul — 3
YODER, Lloyd Edward — 5
YODER, Robert Anderson — 1
YODER, Robert McAyeal — 5
YODER, Worth Nicholas — 5
YOHN, Frederick Coffay — 1
YOKOYAMA, Taiwan — 1
YON, Pietro A. — 2
YONGE, Philip Keyes — 1
YORE, Clem — 1
YORK, Amos Chesley — 3
YORK, Edward Howard, Jr. — 5
YORK, Edward Palmer — 1
YORK, Francis Lodowick — 3
YORK, Frank — 4
YORK, Harlan Harvey — 5
YORK, Harry Clinton — 3
YORK, Samuel Albert — 1
YORKE, George Marshall — 1
YORKE, Peter Christopher
YORKE, Thomas Jones — H
YOSHIDA, Shigeru — 4
YOST, Bartley Francis — 5
YOST, Casper Salathiel — 1
YOST, Fielding Harris — 2
YOST, Gaylord — 3
YOST, Jacob
YOST, Jacob Senewell — H
YOST, Joseph Warren — 4
YOST, Mary
YOU, Dominique — H
YOUMANS, Edward Livingston
YOUMANS, Frank A. — 1
YOUMANS, William Jay — 1
YOUNG, Aaron — H
YOUNG, Abram Van Eps — 1
YOUNG, Alexander — H
YOUNG, Alfred — 4
YOUNG, Allyn Abbott — 1
YOUNG, Ammi Burnham — 4
YOUNG, Andrew Harvey — 1
YOUNG, Archer Everett — 5
YOUNG, Art — 4
YOUNG, Arthur Howland — 4
YOUNG, Arthur J. — 4
YOUNG, Augustus — H
YOUNG, Benjamin — 4
YOUNG, Benjamin E. — 3

YOUNG, Benjamin Loring — 4
YOUNG, Bennett Henderson — 1
YOUNG, Bert Edward
YOUNG, Bicknell — 1
YOUNG, Brigham — H
YOUNG, Bryan Rust — H
YOUNG, C. Griffith — 4
YOUNG, C. Jac — 1
YOUNG, Charles Augustus — 1
YOUNG, Charles Duncanson — 3
YOUNG, Charles Henry — 5
YOUNG, Charles Luther — 1
YOUNG, Charles Sommers; — 5
YOUNG, Charles Van Patten — 5
YOUNG, Chic (Murat Bernard Young) — 5
YOUNG, Claiborne Addison — 5
YOUNG, Clara Kimball — 4
YOUNG, Clarence Hoffman — 3
YOUNG, Clarence Marshall — 5
YOUNG, Clark Montgomery — 1
YOUNG, Clement Calhoun — 2
YOUNG, Courtland H. — 1
YOUNG, David — H
YOUNG, Denton True — H
YOUNG, Denton True — 4
YOUNG, Dwight Edwin — 4
YOUNG, Ebenezer — H
YOUNG, Edward Joseph — 5
YOUNG, Edward M. — 1
YOUNG, Edward T. — 5
YOUNG, Elizabeth Guion (Bab Sears)
YOUNG, Ella Flagg — 1
YOUNG, Ernest Charles — 5
YOUNG, Evan E. — 2
YOUNG, Ewing — H
YOUNG, Francis Brett — 3
YOUNG, Frank Herman — 4
YOUNG, Frank Mobley Jr.
YOUNG, Franklin Knowles — 4
YOUNG, Frederic George
YOUNG, George — 3
YOUNG, George Jr. — 3
YOUNG, George A.
YOUNG, George Brigham — 1
YOUNG, George Bright — 1
YOUNG, George Brooks — 1
YOUNG, George Gilray — 5
YOUNG, George Henry — 5
YOUNG, George Husband — 4
YOUNG, George Joseph — 1
YOUNG, George Morley — 1
YOUNG, George Rude — 1
YOUNG, George Ulysses — 4
YOUNG, George Washington
YOUNG, Gilbert Amos — 2
YOUNG, Gordon — 3
YOUNG, Gordon Elmo — 1
YOUNG, H. Olin — 1
YOUNG, Helen Louise — 2
YOUNG, Henry Lane — 4
YOUNG, Herbert A. — 4
YOUNG, Horace Gedney
YOUNG, Howard Isaac — 4
YOUNG, Hugh Hampton — 2
YOUNG, J. Addison — 4
YOUNG, J. H. — 4
YOUNG, Jacob William Albert
YOUNG, James Carleton — 1
YOUNG, James Henry — 1
YOUNG, James Kelly — 1
YOUNG, James Nicholas — 3
YOUNG, James Rankin — 1
YOUNG, James Scott — 1
YOUNG, James Thomas — 5
YOUNG, James Webb — 5
YOUNG, Jeremiah Simeon — 2
YOUNG, Jesse Bowman — 1
YOUNG, John — H
YOUNG, John Clarke — H
YOUNG, John Edwin — 4
YOUNG, John Philip — H
YOUNG, John Richardson — H
YOUNG, John Russell — H
YOUNG, John Russell — 4
YOUNG, John Wesley — 1
YOUNG, Joseph Hardie — 3
YOUNG, Josue Maria — H
YOUNG, Julia Evelyn
YOUNG, Karl

YOUNG, Kenneth Todd 5
YOUNG, Lafayette 1
YOUNG, Lafayette Jr. 1
YOUNG, Laurence W. 5
YOUNG, Leon Decatur 2
YOUNG, Leonard 5
YOUNG, 4
  Leonard Augustus
YOUNG, Lester Willis 5
YOUNG, Levi Edgar 5
YOUNG, Lewis Emanuel 3
YOUNG, Lucien 5
YOUNG, Mahonri 3
YOUNG, Margaret Rankin 1
YOUNG, Mary Vance 2
YOUNG, Morrison Waite 1
YOUNG, Newton 1
  Clarence
YOUNG, Odus Graham 1
YOUNG, Otto 1
YOUNG, Owen D. 4
YOUNG, Percy S. 3
YOUNG, Philip 3
YOUNG, Philip Endicott 3
YOUNG, H
  Pierce Manning Butler
YOUNG, Plummer
  Bernard 4
YOUNG, Richard 5
YOUNG, Richard Hale 5
YOUNG, H
  Richard Montgomery
YOUNG, 1
  Richard Whitehead
YOUNG, Rida Johnson 1
YOUNG, Robert Anderson 1
YOUNG, Robert Nicholas 4
YOUNG, Robert Ralph 5
YOUNG, Robert 3
  Thompson 5
YOUNG, Roland 3
YOUNG, Rose 5
YOUNG, Roy Archibald 4
YOUNG, Roy Odo 3
YOUNG, S. Edward 5
YOUNG, Sam Martin 1
YOUNG, H
  Samuel Baldwin Marks
YOUNG, Samuel Hall 4
YOUNG, Sanborn 5
YOUNG, Smith Greshem 4
YOUNG, Stark 4
YOUNG, 1
  Stewart Woodford
YOUNG, Thomas H
YOUNG, Thomas Crane 3
YOUNG, Thomas Gorsuch 4
YOUNG, Thomas Kay 5
YOUNG, Thomas Lowry H
YOUNG, Thomas Shields 1
YOUNG, Thomas White 4
YOUNG, Truman Post 2
YOUNG, Udell Charles 4
YOUNG, Victor 3
YOUNG, Wallace Jesse 1
YOUNG, H
  Walter Jorgensen
YOUNG, Walter Stevens 2
YOUNG, 5
  Whitney Moore, Jr.
YOUNG, William 1
YOUNG, William A. 4
YOUNG, William Brooks 5
YOUNG, William Foster 4
YOUNG, 5
  William Lesquereux
YOUNG, William Lindsay 3
YOUNG, H
  William Singleton
YOUNG, William Wesley 4
YOUNGBERG, 5
  Gilbert A(lbin)
YOUNGDAHL, 5
  Benjamin Emanuel
YOUNGDAHL, 2
  Oscar Ferdinand
YOUNGDAHL, 5
  Reuben Kenneth Nathaniel
YOUNGER, Jesse Arthur 1
YOUNGER, John 2
YOUNGER, John Elliott 5
YOUNGER, H
  Thomas Coleman
YOUNGER, 4
  Thomas Coleman
YOUNGERT, Sven Gustaf 1
YOUNGGREEN, 2
  Charles Clark
YOUNG-HUNTER, John 3
YOUNGKEN, 4
  Heber Wilkinson
YOUNGMAN, Frank
  Nourse 5
YOUNGQUIST, G. Aaron 3
YOUNGS, 5
  J(ohn) W(illiam)
  T(heodore)

YOUNGS, John H
YOUNGS, Merle L. 4
YOUNGS, William J. 1
YOUNGSON, 5
  William Wallace
YOUNT, Barton Kyle 2
YOUNT, H
  George Concepcion
YOUNT, Miles Frank 5
YOUNT, Norman Fleming 5
YOUTZ, Herbert Alden 4
YOUTZ, Lewis Addison 3
YOUTZ, Philip Newell 5
YOWELL, Everett Irving 1
YSAYE, Eugene 1
YUDAIN, Theodore 5
YUDKIN, Arthur M. 3
YUGOV, Anton 4
YUI, O. K. 4
YULEE, David Levy H
YUNCKER, Truman
  George 4
YUNG, Wing 1
YUNGBLUTH, 3
  Bernard Joseph
YUST, Walter 3
YUST, 2
  William Frederick
YUSUF KARAMANLI H
YUTZY, Henry Clay 5
YUTZY, Thomas Daniel 4

Z

ZABEL, Morton Dauwen 4
ZABRISKIE, 1
  Andrew Christian
ZABRISKIE, Edwin G. 3
ZABRISKIE, George 2
ZABRISKIE, 3
  George Albert
ZABRISKIE, 5
  Robert Lansing
ZACH, Leon 4
ZACH, Max Wilhelm 1
ZACHARIAS, Ellis Mark 4
ZACHER, Louis Edmund 2
ZACHOS, H
  John Celivergas
ZADEIKIS, Povilas 3
ZADKINE, Ossip 4
ZAENGLEIN, Paul Carl 5
ZAHARIAS, H
  Babe Didrikson
ZAHARIAS, 4
  Mildred Didrikson
ZAHEDI, Fazlollah 4
ZAHM, Albert Francis 3
ZAHM, John Augustine 1
ZAHN, Edward James Jr. 4
ZAHNISER,
  Arthur DeFrance
ZAHNISER, Charles Reed 5
ZAHNISER, Howard 4
ZAHORSKY, John 4
ZAKRZEWSKA, 1
  Marie Elizabeth
ZALDIVAR, Rafael 1
ZALINSKI, 1
  Edmund Louis Gray
ZALINSKI, Moses Gray 1
ZALVIDEA, H
  Jose Maria 'de
ZAMORANO, H
  Austin Juan Vincente
ZAND, Stephen Joseph 4
ZANDER, Henry George 1
ZANE, Abraham Vanhoy 1
ZANE, Charles S. 4
ZANE, Ebenezer H
ZANE, John Maxcy 1
ZANGERIE, John A. 5
ZANTZINGER, 3
  Clarence Clark
ZAPFFE, Frederick Carl 3
ZAPOTOCKY, Antonin 3
ZAPP, Carroll Francis 5
ZARING, 4
  Clarence Arthur
ZARING, E. Robb 4
ZAROUBIN, Georgi N. 3
ZARTMANN, 5
  Parley Emmett
ZAUGG, Walter Albert 4
ZAVITZ, Edwin Cornell 4
ZAWADZKI, Aleksander 4
ZDANOWICZ, 3
  Casimir Douglass
ZECH, Frederick Jr. 1
ZECHMEISTER, 5
  Laszlo Karoly Erno
ZECKWER, Richard 1
ZEDER, Fred Morrell 3
ZEDLER, John 5
ZEHNDER, Charles
  Henry 1
ZEHNER, J. Alexander 4

ZEHRING, Blanche 3
ZEHRUNG, 4
  Winfield Scott
ZEIDLER, 2
  Carl Frederick
ZEIGEN, Frederic 2
ZEIGLER, Lee Woodward 3
ZEILIN, Jacob H
ZEISBERGER, David H
ZEISLER, 1
  Fannie Bloomfield
ZEISLER, Joseph 1
ZEISLER, Sigmund 1
ZEIT, 1
  F. Robert Aenishaenslin
ZEITLER, 5
  Emerson Walter
ZEITLIN, Jacob 1
ZELENY, Anthony 2
ZELENY, Charles 1
ZELENY, John 3
ZELIE, John Sheridan 2
ZELLER, George Anthony 1
ZELLER, Joseph William 4
ZELLER, 1
  Julius Christian
ZELLER, Walter George 5
ZELLER, Walter Philip 3
ZELLERBACH, Isadore 2
ZELLERBACH, 4
  James David
ZEMLINSKY, 4
  Alexander Von
ZEMURRAY, Samuel 4
ZENDER, Austin R. 5
ZENGER, John Peter H
ZENNER, 4
  Philip McKnight
ZENOR, William T. 4
ZENOS, Andrew C. 1
ZENTMAYER, Joseph H
ZENTMAYER, William 5
ZERBAN, 3
  Frederick William
ZERBE, Alvin Sylvester 1
ZERBE, Farran 2
ZERBE, James Slough 4
ZERBE, Karl 5
ZERBEY, Joseph Henry 4
ZEREGA 4
  'DIZEREGA, Louis
  Augustus
ZERNIKE, Frits 4
ZETTERSTRAND, 1
  Ernst Adrian
ZETTLER, Emil Robert 2
ZEUCH, Herman J. 1
ZEUNER, Charles H
ZHDANOV, 2
  Andrei Alexandrovich
ZIEGEMEIER, 1
  Henry Joseph
ZIEGENFUSS, 1
  Samuel Addison
ZIEGENHEIN, William J. 4
ZIEGET, Julius 5
ZIEGFELD, Florenz * 5
ZIEGLER, 1
  Charles Edward
ZIEGLER, David H
ZIEGLER, Edward 2
ZIEGLER, Edwin Allen 4
ZIEGLER, Lloyd Hiram 2
ZIEGLER, 5
  Maxine Evelyn Hogue (Mrs.
  James R. Ziegler)
ZIEGLER, S. Lewis 1
ZIEGLER, William 1
ZIEGLER, William Jr. 3
ZIEGLER, William Jr. 4
ZIEGLER, 5
  Winfred Hamlin
ZIER, Merlin William 5
ZIESING, August 2
ZIESING, Richard Jr. 4
ZIETLOW, John L. W. 4
ZIFF, William Bernard 3
ZIGLER, David Howard 4
ZIGLER, John Darrel 4
ZIHLMAN, Frederick N. 1
ZILBOORG, Gregory 3
ZIMAND, Savel 4
ZIMBALIST, 5
  Mary Louise Curtis
ZIMM, Bruno Louis 2
ZIMMER, 5
  Bernard Nicolas
ZIMMER, H. Ward 3
ZIMMER, Henry Wenzell 4
ZIMMER, John Todd 5
ZIMMER, Verne A. 2
ZIMMER, William Homer 5
ZIMMERER, Charles John 5
ZIMMERLEY, 2
  Howard Henry
ZIMMERMAN, 5
  Charles Ballard

ZIMMERMAN, 3
  Charles Fishburn
ZIMMERMAN, 4
  Edward Americus
ZIMMERMAN, Eugene 1
ZIMMERMAN, Fred R. 3
ZIMMERMAN, Harvey J. 5
ZIMMERMAN, 3
  Henry Martin
ZIMMERMAN, 5
  Herbert John
ZIMMERMAN, 5
  Hyman Harold
ZIMMERMAN, 2
  James Fulton
ZIMMERMAN, Jeremiah 1
ZIMMERMAN, Leander
  M. 5
ZIMMERMAN, 4
  Louis Seymour
ZIMMERMAN, 5
  M(ax) M(andell)
ZIMMERMAN, Orville 2
ZIMMERMAN, Percy
  White 3
ZIMMERMAN, 3
  Rufus Eicher
ZIMMERMAN, Thomas
  C. 1
ZIMMERMAN, William 4
ZIMMERMAN, 1
  William Carbys
ZIMMERMAN, 4
  Erich Walter
ZIMMERMANN, 3
  Herbert George
ZIMMERMANN, Herbert
  P. 4
ZIMMERMANN, 2
  John Edward
ZIMMERN, Sir Alfred 3
ZINK, Harold 4
ZINKE, E. Gustav 1
ZINN, Aaron Stanton 1
ZINN, Alpha Alexander 2
ZINN, Charles James 5
ZINN, George A. 4
ZINN, James Alexander 5
ZINNECKER, 3
  Wesley Daniel
ZINSSER, August 2
ZINSSER, Hans 1
ZINSSER, Rudolph 3
ZINZENDORF, H
  Nicholaus Ludwig
ZIONCHECK, Marion A. 1
ZIRATO, Bruno 5
ZIRKLE, Conway 5
ZIROLI, Nicola Victor 5
ZISKIN, Daniel E. 3
ZITO, Frank J. 3
ZIWET, Alexander 1
ZNANIECKI, 3
  Florian Witold
ZOBEL, Alfred Jacob 3
ZOELLER, Henry Adolph 5
ZOELLNER, Joseph Sr. 2
ZOERNER, Carl Bernard 4
ZOFFMAN, George F. 3
ZOGBAUM, 1
  Rufus Fairchild
ZOLLARS, Ely Vaughan 1
ZOLLICOFFER, H
  Felix Kirk
ZOLLINGER, Gulielma 1
ZOLNAY, George Julian 2
ZON, Raphael 3
ZONDERVAN, B. D. 4
ZOOK, George Frederick 3
ZOPPI, Vittorio 4
ZORACH, William 4
ZORBAUGH, 2
  Charles Louis
ZORBAUGH, 4
  Harvey Warren
ZORLU, Fatin Rustu 4
ZORN, Edwin George 3
ZORN, Paul Manthey 5
ZOSHCHENKO, 4
  Mikhail Mikhailovich
ZOVICKIAN, Anthony 5
ZUBLY, John Joachim H
ZUCKER, Paul 5
ZUCKERMAN, Paul
  Stuart 4
ZUEBLIN, Charles 1
ZUGGER, Aloysius Henry 5
ZUKER, 4
  William Berdette
ZULAUF, Romeo Maxwell 3
ZULAUF, Romeo Maxwell 4
ZUNDEL, John H
ZUNTS, James Edwin 4
ZUPPKE, Robert Carl 3
ZURCHER, George 1
ZURLINDEN, Frank J. 2
ZURN, Melvin Ackerman 5

ZWEIFEL, Henry 5
ZWEIG, Stefan 2